California
1860
Census Index

Volume II
L - Z

Other Titles by Index Publishing

1860 Federal Census

Connecticut
District of Columbia
Florida
Oregon
Rhode Island
South Carolina

California
1860
Census Index

Volume II
L - Z

by Index Publishing

Heritage Quest
Bountiful, Utah
1999

Heritage Quest, A divison of AGLL, Inc., PO Box 329, Bountiful, Utah 84011-0329

©1999, AGLL Inc. All rights reserved

Printed in the United States of America
03 02 01 00 99   5 4 3 2

ISBN 0-945433-49-2

Contents

Foreword

The Census Act of 1790 provided a mandate for counting the United States population at ten-year intervals. The purpose of the census was to insure proper citizen representation at the national level of government, the House of Representatives. Early census data is sparse and shows only the names of heads of household. Statistics of other family members are given by age group, sex, and race (either white or Negro).[1]

The Census Act was amended frequently over the years, however, and by 1850 the schedules reveal much more about individuals within each household. They include each person's name, age, sex, race, place of birth, and for those over 15 years of age, occupation. From 1850 to 1870, the Bureau of the Census collected data according to two designated units, district and subdivision. Districts usually corresponded to a State or part of a State and subdivision to a county or part thereof. Descriptions of these units, delineating boundaries, are available in microfilm as "Descriptions of Census Enumeration Districts, 1830-1890, and, 1910-1950 in National Archives Series T1224, available in 146 rolls. National Archives Series T1210 contains 10 rolls for 1900.[2]

This index volume has been greatly anticipated and promises to fill in many genealogical gaps. As for the census itself, it is not entirely accurate. Each census taker took to the road the first day of June 1870 with the task of completing the count within the subsequent five month period. One notable feature of this particular census is that events were to be recorded as though the census takers had performed their duties on June 1, 1870 regardless of when they actually visited a home. Adherence to the rule made for some awkward notations. Generally, all those who normally lived under the same roof as of June 1st were to be counted as members of that household, even if they were not home on the actual day the census takers dropped by. If a family member had died after June 1st but before the day the census taker visited, that individual was listed as still living. Conversely, infants born after June 1, 1870 were omitted from the listing even if they crawled up to the census taker and bit his leg.[3]

Forms for recording the 1870 schedules contained 20 columns with the following headings (punctuation and capitalization as found in the original):

1. Dwelling houses numbered in the order of visitation.
2. Families numbered in the order of visitation.
3. The name of every person whose place of abode on the first day of June, 1870 was in the family.

Description

4. Age at last birthday. If under 1 year, give months in fractions, thus 3/12.
5. Sex - Males (M), Females (F).
6. Color - White (W), Black (B), Mulatto (M), Chinese (C), Indian (I).
7. Profession, Occupation, or Trade of each person, male or female.

Real Estate Owned

8. Value of Real Estate.
9. Personal Property.
10. Place of Birth, State or Territory of the U.S., Country if foreign born.

Parentage

11. Father of foreign birth.
12. Mother of foreign birth.
13. If born within the year, state month (Jan., Feb., etc.).
14. If married within the year, state month (Jan., etc.).
15. Attended school within the year.

Education

16. Cannot read.
17. Cannot write.
18. Whether deaf and dumb, blind, insane or idiotic.

Constitutional Relations

19. Male Citizen of the U.S. of 21 years of age and upwards.
20. Male Citizen of U.S. 21 years of age and upwards whose right to vote is denied or abridged on other grounds than rebellion or other crime.

When using this index to find your ancestors, keep the following caveat in mind:

1. **Misspellings.** Census enumerators were not necessarily well educated, spelling was not standardized, and there was a high rate of illiteracy among the population. Thus, names were typically spelled as they sounded to the enumerators. In short, the art of transcribing unfamiliar surnames could have been as challenging as transliterating German to Chinese.

2. **Name changes.** Through the years, many people anglicized their names. For example: Schwartz became Black; Weiss became White; Zimmerman became Carpenter; and Schneider became Taylor. The list goes on.

3. **Variant Spellings.** If you know an ancestor was in a specific township or county, don't be discouraged if the name doesn't appear in the census index. Instead search for him

page by page in the last or the next census. His name might appear as a variant spelling you may have missed in the index.

4. **County boundary changes.** As states developed, the boundaries of their various townships and counties changed quite often. Hence, though a family may have remained in the same location, they may have been enumerated in a different township or county from year to year. To determine the correct county in which to search, refer to the map on page xxi.[5]

5. **Errors!** Two copies of the 1870 schedules were made. The intent was to keep the original copy in the courthouse of the County. A copy, transcribed from the original, was to be sent to the Federal courthouse for that jurisdiction, and a second copy was to be sent to Washington, D.C. The generation of handwritten copies made for many errors. In addition to errors made in recopying, many microfilm copies are difficult to read, and handwriting varies ... some good, some bad. Even the best indexer may make an error[.]

6. **Enumeration mistakes.** The enumerator might not have read his instructions. He could have listed a child born after 1 June when he visited the house on 20 August, or not listed a person still alive on 1 June who died between 2 June and 20 August. Or, Dad might have been helping a neighbor build a barn and would have been enumerated in the neighbor's household.

Finally, use your imagination and common sense in census research! Those of us who know how painstaking it is to read census page after census page applaud the publication of this computer generated index.

Good Hunting!

Jane Adams Clarke

Introduction

Format of the Index

The index is alphabetized by surname, given name, middle name or initial, occupation or title, age, and county. All entries that cannot be alphabetized, for whatever reason, are put at the beginning of the index.

Only Heads-of-Household are extracted with the following exceptions:

1. Someone residing within the home who has a different surname, regardless of age.

2. Any male 50 years of age or older.

3. Any female 70 years of age or older.

4. Any color or race change (where the surname stays the same). In this case the oldest person listed is extracted.

5. All individuals living in an institution such as an orphanage, hospital, or poor house.

Special Symbols and Markings

* Interpretation of the name is in doubt.

\+ Spelling of the name while "unusual" is correct, as the census taker listed it.

? Portions of the name were illegible, due to a torn, smeared, or ink blotted page.

— The information was not given.

[ ] Brackets have been used to include additional information about the person listed. Such information might be occupation, title, malady, or miscellaneous information useful to the user.

Race Codes

W   White
B   Black
M   Mulatto
I   Indian
H   Hispanic
O   Oriental
C   Chinese
J   Japanese
X   Mixed
—   Not Given

In cities, the following designations are used to identify wards. A ward number precedes the designator -WD, for example:

1-WD   1st Ward
2-WD   2nd Ward
S-WD   South Ward
N-WD   North Ward

General Indexing Rules

When abbreviations appear in the entries on the microfilm they are spelled as-is. Since it is not always possible to tell exactly what an abbreviation stands for, they are normally not spelled out. For example:

Jas Brown would be entered as BROWN, Jas

One major exception to this rule occurs when the surname has been abbreviated. The name is extracted once, "as is," and then a second time "spelled out," if a highly probable name can be derived from the abbreviation. For example, if the census taker listed the name as Thadeus Wmwell it is extracted once as it is shown and then it is spelled out in a second (double) entry, Thadeus Williamwell, because it is unlikely that anyone would search for this individual under the abreviated spelling.

There is no space entered between compound names in the index. Apostrophes and hyphens are the only special punctuation marks used, and they are only used when the entry looks like a mistake without them. When the apostrophes are added it becomes clear that the D' is a contraction for De. When a surname has been hyphenated it is entered, as is, with the hyphen. For example:

SMITH-BARNEY, Juliet.

There are three special groups of names that do not neatly fit into any single category. They are: Nuns, Brothers (Ecclesiastical), and Indians.

After a woman has taken her final vows and begins her life as a nun, she is no longer addressed by her surname. She instead becomes Sister Mary, Sister Margaret, Sister Victoria, etc. Because of this, most nuns are listed simply as Sister "_____." In order to keep all the nuns who have not been listed with a surname in one area in the index, they are entered:

SISTER, Catherine
SISTER, Mary Beth
SISTER, Victoria

By entering them in this way, it is possible to make one quick search to see if any of the nuns is the person being sought. Should any of the nuns happen to be listed with a surname, they are entered as usual.

The same rules that apply to nuns apply to ecclesiastical brothers and to Indians, except that the word "BROTHER" or "INDIAN" is substituted for "SISTER." The terms "Brother" and "Indian" are used here as the surname and it is entered as above. If, however, they happen to be listed with a surname they are entered as usual.

There are some entries with no surname or given name listed on the census record. For entries with no name, three dashes have been used.

A bracketed area is used to include additional or miscellaneous information which might help conclusively identify the person. This includes, but is not limited to, occupations, titles, and maladies. They, however, are only entered when the given name is missing or when such information has been included in the name field on the microfilmed record. Examples are:

KILLAM, [Seamtress]
WOLSON, [Blacksmith]
FARNSWORTH, [Blind]
ADAMS, [Deceased-Estate]
BROOKS, [Insane-In Jail]
KONRAD, Wilhelm [Dr]
PATRIDGE, John [Barrister]
GRANT, U S [President]
PIPER, Jas [General]

In all cases, only important titles are placed in brackets. Brackets are not put around Mr., Ms., Mrs., Sir, Jr., or Sr.

Standard Abbreviations

Locality names such as Creek, River, Ward, etc. have been abbreviated. These abbreviations have been standardized and will be used consistently in all census indexes:

Ms	Miss	P O	Post Office
Mrs	Mistress	-WD	Ward
Mr	Mister	J-PCT	Justice Precinct
Jr	Junior	TWP	Township
Sr	Senior	CO	County
Wid	Widow	PAR	Parish
Rev	Reverend	DIST	District
Dr	Doctor	TERR	Territory
M D	Medical Doctor	BLVD	Boulevard
J P	Justice of the Peace	LN	Lane
Agt	Agent	RD	Road
BT	Beat	CRK	Creek
BORO	Borough	RVR	River

Occasionally, names have been entered twice. The reason for this is that if the name were extracted only as it is listed, it could be placed in a position in the index where most users would never think to look. In such cases, when appropriate, the name has been "double entered", once as it was listed and a second time as it should be listed. This is done only for "gross" errors in spelling or for highly likely different interpretations. For example, the census taker listed the name as Whosay Pelassquez when it should have been Jose Velassquez. It has been extracted this way:

> PELASSQUEZ, Whosay (First time)
> VELASSQUEZ, Jose   (Second time)

When the interpretation of an entry is in doubt, an asterisk (*) is used to show this. If more than one interpretation is highly possible, it will be double-entered.

If part of the name is illegible due to a smeared, torn, or ink-blotted page; question marks are used to show this. Although the number of question marks has been designed to "roughly" show the number of letters perceived to be missing, after three, the value of adding additional question marks is dubious at best. Questions marks, however, are not used for difficult interpretations and never more than three question marks are used per entry. Therefore, if it appears that this entry could be the person bei ng sought, a check of the original microfilm is recommended. In all cases, it is important to remember that the person extracting the information has been trained to do what would be deemed the most helpful.

Occasionally, entries have been encountered that were plainly written and spelled but, appear to be errors. In these cases, a plus sign (+) has been entered after the entry to show that while it looks like an error, it is spelled as the census taker listed it. The plus sign has been used sparingly and only for "really strange" looking names. Example:

ZBREWSKI, Stanislaus+
SQAKAWSKI, William+

Page Numbers

Although most pages of the original census records show several different page numbers, this index uses the National Archives' numbers which were hand stamped in the upper right corner of the page when the records were bound into volumes. There are quite a few page numbering errors. Because of this, it is not unusual to find several pages listed with identical numbers. In addition, pages may even be listed as 491, 491a, 491b, or 491c. When a letter is included on the end of a page number, that page number is listed minus that letter.

Another problem is page numbers which were omitted. For example, if the page numbers were listed on the microfilm as 491, 492, 493, no number, 496, 497, the number 494 is used after page 493. It has been done this way because 494 would be the most logical choice. Page 495 would be omitted and the numbering would then commence with page 496 and continue in its regular fashion.

Although great care has been taken in reading and editing this index, errors may have occurred. In a continuous effort to improve the index the editors would appreciate being informed should any be found. Please send all corrections to:

Heritage Quest
PO Box 329
Bountiful, UT 84011-0329

Table of Common Interpretations

The following table may be useful in looking for names in the census index. The letter the census taker intended to write is in the first column. The second column gives the most common alternative interpretations. These are given in a very rough order of probability. When unable to locate an entry as you expected to find it these other intrepretations should be routinely checked. For example, if you fail to find the name "Aaron," it might have been indexed as ADRAN, HARON, or even HOSAU. "Warren" might appear as WARNER or "Warner" as WARREN.

Letter	Possible Interpretation
A	H, C, O
a	o, u, ei
B	R, P, S
b	li, le, t, h, l
C	G, E, O, Ce
c	e, i, o, u
D	G, S, I, T
d	u, a, n, ie, ct, o
e	i, c
ee	u, n, ll, w
F	T, S, G
f	s, j, g, q, t
G	S, Q, Z, Ci
g	y, z, q
H	N, W, He, F
h	k, li, lc, le
I	J, L, S, T
i	e, c, l
ie	ei, u, ee, w
J	I, L, S
j	y, g, f
Jno	Mr, Mo
K	H, R, B
k	h, le lr, te
L	S, T, F
l	e, i, t
ll	tt, ee, u
M	W, H, N
m	w, rr, ni

Letter	Possible Interpretation
N	H, W, V, Ne
n	u, a, o, w, m
O	C, U, V, D
o	a, u, n, ei, tt
P	R, B, I
p	ss, g, js
Q	Z, D, I
q	g, y, z
R	Pi, B, S
r	e, s, i
S	L, I, J
s	r, i, e
sc	x
ss	fs, p, rr
T	F, S, L
t	l, f, ir, i
te	k
tt	ll
U	V, A, O
u	ee, a, o, n, w
V	N, W, li, Jr, B
v	u, n, b, rr
W	M, N, U
w	m, rr, ur
X	H, Z, N
x	sc, c, r
Y	F, Z, Q
y	g, q, j
Z	g, Q

Birthplace Codes

USA

AK	Alaska
AL	Alabama
AZ	Arizona
CA	California
CO	Colorado
CT	Connecticut
DC	District of Columbia
DE	Delaware
DTER	Dakota Territory
FL	Florida
GA	Georgia
HI	Hawaii
IA	Iowa
ID	Idaho
IL	Illinois
IN	Indiana
ITER	Indian Territory
KS	Kansas
KY	Kentucky
LA	Louisiana
MA	Massachusetts
MD	Maryland
ME	Maine
MI	Michigan
MN	Minnesota
MO	Missouri
MS	Mississippi
MT	Montana
NC	North Carolina
ND	North Dakota
NE	Nebraska
NH	New Hampshire
NJ	New Jersey
NM	New Mexico
NV	Nevada
NY	New York
OH	Ohio
OK	Oklahoma
OR	Oregon
PA	Pennsylvania
RI	Rhode Island
SC	South Carolina
SD	South Dakota
TN	Tennessee
TX	Texas
UNKN	Unknown
US	United States
UT	Utah
VA	Virginia
VT	Vermont
WA	Washington
WI	Wisconsin
WV	West Virginia
WY	Wyoming

FOREIGN

ABER	Anhalt Bernburg
ADES	Anhalt Dessau
AFRI	Africa
ALGE	Algeria
ALOR	Alsace Lorraine (Elsass Lothringen)
ALSA	Alsace
ANHA	Anhalt
ANTI	Antigua
ARAB	Arabia
ARGE	Argentina
ARME	Armenia
ASEA	At Sea
ASIA	Asia
AUSL	Australia
AUST	Austria
AZOR	Azores
BADE	Baden
BAHA	Bahamas
BARB	Barbados
BAVA	Bavaria (Bayern)
BELG	Belguim
BENG	Bengal
BERM	Bermuda
BOHE	Bohemia
BOSN	Bosnia
BRAN	Brandenburg
BRAZ	Brazil
BREM	Bremen
BRUN	Brunswick (Braunschweig)
BUCH	Buchau
BULG	Bulgaria
BURM	Burma
CAME	Central America
CANA	Canada
CAPE	Cape of Good Hope
CEYL	Ceylon
CHIL	Chile
CHIN	China
CISL	Canary Islands
COLO	Colombia
CROA	Croatia
CUBA	Cuba
CZEC	Czechoslovakia
DALM	Dalmatia
DENM	Denmark
ECUA	Ecuador
EGYP	Egypt
EIND	East Indies
ENGL	England
EPRU	Prussia (East) (Ostpreussen)
EURO	Europe
FINL	Finland
FLOW	Lower Franconia (Unterfranken
FMID	Middle Franconia (Mittelfranken)
FRAN	France
FRNC	Franconia
FRNH	Frankenhausen
FRNK	Frankfurt
FUPP	Upper Franconia
GALI	Galicia
GBRI	Great Britain
GENO	Genoa
GERM	Germany
GIBR	Gibraltar
GREE	Greece
GREN	Grenada
GUAD	Guadaloupe
GUAM	Guam
GUAT	Guatemala
GUYA	Guyana
HAIT	Haiti

HAMB	Hamburg	NETH	Netherlands	SCOT	Scotland
HANO	Hanover	NGRA	New Granada	SCRO	St. Croix
HCAS	Hesse Cassel (Kurhessen)	NICA	Nicaragua	SCRU	Santa Cruz
HDAR	Hesse Darmstadt	NISL	Nevis Island	SDOM	Santo Domingo
HESS	Hesse	NORW	Norway	SERB	Serbia
HHEC	Hohenzollern (Hechingen)	NZEA	New Zealand	SHAN	Shanghai, China
HHOM	Hesse Homberg	OEMP	Ottoman Empire	SHOL	Schleswig Holstein (Rudolstadt)
HOHE	Hohenzollern	OLDE	Oldenburg		
HOLD	Hesse Olddorf	PALA	Palatinate	SIAM	Siam
HOLL	Holland	PALE	Palestine	SICI	Sicily
HOND	Honduras	PARA	Paraguay	SILE	Silesia (Schlesien)
HSIG	Hohenzollern (Sigmaringen)	PERS	Persia	SKIT	St. Kitts
HUNG	Hungary	PERU	Peru	SMAR	St. Martins
ICEL	Iceland	PFAL	Pfalz	SMEI	Saxony, Meiningen
INDI	India	PHIL	Philippines	SPAI	Spain
IOFC	Isle of Corsica	PIED	Piedmont	SSON	Schwarzburg (Sondershausen)
IOFG	Isle of Guernsey	PLOW	Palatinate, Lower		
IOFM	Isle of Man	POLA	Poland	STHO	St. Thomas
IOFW	Isle of Wight	POME	Pomerania (Pommern)	STUT	Stuttgart
IREL	Ireland	PORT	Portugal	SURI	Surinam
ITAL	Italy	POSE	Posen	SVIN	St. Vincent
ITER	Indian Territory	PPFA	Palatinate, Pfalz	SWAB	Swabia
JAMA	Jamaica	PRHE	Palatinate, Rhenish	SWED	Sweden
JAPA	Japan	PRIC	Puerto Rico	SWEE	Saxony (Weimar Eisenach)
JERU	Jerusalem	PRUS	Prussia	SWIT	Switzerland
JUTL	Jutland	PSAX	Saxony-Province of	SYRI	Syria
LAUE	Lauenburg	PUPP	Palatinate, Upper	THUR	Thuringia
LDET	Lipp Detmold	RALL	Reuss Altere Linie	TRIN	Trinidad
LIEC	Liechtenstein	REUS	Reuss	TRIP	Tripoli
LITH	Lithuania	RGRE	Reuss Griez	TURK	Turkey
LOMB	Lombardy	RHIN	Rhineland (Rheinprovinz)	TUSC	Tuscany
LSCH	Lippe Schaumberg	RJUL	Reuss Jungere Linie	UKRA	Ukraine
LUEB	Luebeck	ROMA	Romania	UNKN	Unknown
LUXE	Luxemburg	ROST	Rostock	URUG	Uruguay
MADE	Madera	RSCG	Reuss Schleiz Gera	VENE	Venezuela
MALT	Malta	RSCH	Reuss Schleiz	VISL	Virgin Islands
MECK	Mecklenburg	RUSS	Russia	WALD	Waldeck Hesse (Nassau)
MEXI	Mexico	SALT	Saxony, Altenburg	WALE	Wales
MONT	Montenegro	SAME	South America	WEST	Westphalia (Westfalen)
MORA	Moravia	SARD	Sardinia	WIND	West Indies
MORO	Morrocco	SAXO	Saxony-Kingdom of	WPRU	Prussia (West) (Westpreussen)
MSCH	Mecklenburg (Schwerin)	SCAN	Scandinavia		
MSTR	Mecklenburg (Strelitz)	SCHW	Schwarzburg	WURT	Württemberg
NCOD	No Code	SCOG	Saxony (Coburg Gotha)	YUGO	Yugoslavia

Name	County Locale	Roll	Page
L CONG YAH			
---*	Yuba Long Bar	72	756
L CONG			
Yah*	Yuba Long Bar	72	756
L OW			
---	Sierra Downieville	661000	
L			
Ching	Nevada Nevada	61	299
Fong	Nevada Grass Valley	61	229
Kong*	El Dorado Mountain	581188	
Let	Sierra Twp 7	66	876
Moon	Mariposa Twp 3	60	613
Sing	Nevada Grass Valley	61	229
Wa	Nevada Nevada	61	300
L??			
---	Calaveras Twp 5	57	195
L???			
Margt*	San Francisco San Francisco 8	681254	
Yory	Calaveras Twp 5	57	193
L??RIAN			
Henry	Mariposa Twp 3	60	587
L??SMAN			
Henry*	Mariposa Twp 3	60	587
L??SNAN			
Henry*	Mariposa Twp 3	60	587
L'ANDRE			
Le More*	Tuolumne Twp 2	71	284
L'BRIEN			
Jas	Nevada Grass Valley	61	218
L'HAY			
Leon	San Francisco San Francisco 2	67	687
LA			
---	Calaveras Twp 8	57	50
---	El Dorado Diamond	58	801
---	Mariposa Twp 3	60	553
---	Mariposa Twp 3	60	608
---	Placer Ophirville	62	656
---	San Francisco San Francisco 4	681195	
---	San Joaquin Stockton	641092	
---	Sierra Downieville	661025	
---	Sierra Twp 5	66	927
---	Sierra Twp 5	66	932
---	Sierra Twp 5	66	944
---	Sierra Cox's Bar	66	950
---	Tuolumne Twp 5	71	514
---	Yuba New York	72	740
---	Yuba Fosters	72	842
---*	Yuba Fosters	72	843
Ah	Butte Cascade	56	699
Am	Nevada Bridgeport	61	460
Ang	Yuba Long Bar	72	766
Bang	Mariposa Twp 3	60	553
Bang	Mariposa Twp 3	60	607
Ching	Sacramento Ward 4	63	610
Cum	Mariposa Coulterville	60	681
Cum*	Mariposa Twp 3	60	588
Dam	Yuba New York	72	739
E*	San Francisco San Francisco 3	67	46
Ece	Yuba Long Bar	72	771
Ee	Yuba Long Bar	72	771
Foo	Sacramento Ward 3	63	489
Foon	Del Norte Happy Ca	58	664
Forque*	Sacramento Granite	63	249
Guike*	Butte Ophir	56	817
Han	San Francisco San Francisco 4	681204	
Hau	San Francisco San Francisco 4	681204	
Hoey	Sacramento Ward 4	63	609
Hong	Butte Bidwell	56	728
Hong	El Dorado Casumnes	581160	
How	Butte Cascade	56	698
How	Nevada Grass Valley	61	229
Hoy	Yuba Long Bar	72	760
Hoy	Yuba Fosters	72	830
Hue	Butte Cascade	56	692
Kee	Mariposa Twp 3	60	578
King	Mariposa Twp 3	60	569
Kon	Calaveras Twp 4	57	325
Kow	Mariposa Twp 3	60	569
Lee	Yuba Long Bar	72	749
Lin	El Dorado Georgetown	58	678
Lo Ching	San Francisco San Francisco 4	681209	
Lon	Tehama Red Bluff	70	934
Long	Tehama Red Bluff	70	934
Lou	Mariposa Twp 3	60	588
Loy	Yuba Fosters	72	843
Lu	Mariposa Twp 3	60	543
Mang	Yuba Long Bar	72	768
Mong	Yuba Long Bar	72	756
Moon	Mariposa Twp 3	60	588
Nam	Nevada Bridgeport	61	506
Qung	Placer Auburn	62	582
Sa	Nevada Rough &	61	397
See Lou	Mariposa Twp 3	60	607
See*	Nevada Rough &	61	397
Shong	Tehama Red Bluff	70	934
Sing	Mariposa Twp 3	60	578

Name	County Locale	Roll	Page
LA			
Sing	Sacramento Ward 3	63	490
Sing	San Joaquin Stockton	641038	
Su*	Nevada Rough &	61	397
Sue	Sierra Twp 5	66	927
Ting	Tehama Red Bluff	70	932
Tong	Tehama Red Bluff	70	934
Tonk	Sierra Downieville	661015	
Tuck	Sacramento Ward 1	63	68
Vang	Mariposa Twp 3	60	553
Wa	Mariposa Twp 3	60	553
Woo	El Dorado Salmon Falls	581042	
Yang	Placer Auburn	62	578
Yo	San Francisco San Francisco 4	681175	
Yoh	Alameda Oakland	55	57
LAAM			
---	Nevada Bridgeport	61	460
LAANDERS			
Andrew	Santa Clara Santa Clara	65	518
LAANG			
---*	Yuba Long Bar	72	766
LAARVELLES			
Jose	Napa Napa	61	115
LAARVELLIS			
Jose*	Napa Napa	61	115
LAAS			
Ramina*	San Francisco San Francisco 1	68	819
LABA			
Santiago	Los Angeles San Pedro	59	483
LABACA			
---*	Mendocino Big Rock	60	875
---*	Tulara Visalia	71	4
LABADEI			
Peter*	Yuba Fosters	72	821
LABADIC			
L	Tuolumne Twp 2	71	337
LABADIE			
L	Tuolumne Columbia	71	337
Louis*	Yuba Foster B	72	828
Peter*	Yuba Fosters	72	821
LABAERRE			
Victor	Tuolumne Twp 3	71	462
LABAHSTIS			
Americus*	Mendocino Big Rvr	60	850
LABAINE			
Victor	Tuolumne Twp 3	71	462
LABALISTER			
Americus*	Mendocino Big Rvr	60	850
Chas	Mendocino Big Rvr	60	850
Chas T	Mendocino Big Rvr	60	851
James E	Mendocino Big Rvr	60	851
Jno A	Mendocino Big Rvr	60	851
Jno S	Mendocino Big Rvr	60	851
LABAN			
H F	Santa Clara Alviso	65	411
LABANE			
Edward	Alameda Brooklyn	55	106
LABANET			
Jos	Sacramento Ward 1	63	109
LABAR			
Brigada	Colusa Monroeville	57	453
John*	Stanislaus Emory	70	751
LABARCA JOHN			
---*	Tulara Visalia	71	4
LABARCA			
John	Tulara Twp 2	71	4
LABARDO			
Pierre	Tuolumne Twp 3	71	464
Purre	Tuolumne Twp 3	71	464
LABARER			
Lyman	Sacramento Ward 4	63	519
LABARI			
Michael	Calaveras Twp 8	57	62
LABAT			
Fred	Placer Mountain	62	707
LABATARD			
Alfonzo	San Francisco San Francisco 3	67	20
LABATE			
Henry J	San Francisco San Francisco 2	67	642
LABATOUR			
G H	Tuolumne Jamestown	71	451
LABATT			
Henry J	San Francisco San Francisco 2	67	642
John	Los Angeles Los Angeles	59	392
Joseph J	San Francisco San Francisco 7	681356	
LABBA			
J C	Stanislaus Branch	70	698
LABBEN			
Meta*	San Francisco San Francisco 10	351	67
LABBI			
August*	Stanislaus Branch	70	701
LABBOTT			
Stephen	San Joaquin Castoria	64	885
LABBS			
O	Santa Clara Fremont	65	435

Name	County Locale	Roll	Page
LABE			
Joseph	Yuba Marysville	72	919
LABEAN			
Henry	Butte Chico	56	557
LABEAU			
Henry*	Butte Chico	56	557
LABEIREE			
John S*	Contra Costa Twp 2	57	572
LABEIRU			
John S*	Contra Costa Twp 2	57	572
LABEL			
Alex	San Francisco San Francisco 2	67	694
H	Santa Clara San Jose	65	291
Henry*	San Francisco San Francisco 1	68	854
Jacob	Santa Clara San Jose	65	287
LABELL			
G B	Mariposa Twp 1	60	654
LABELLE			
Henry	San Francisco San Francisco 7	681371	
LABEN			
Meta*	San Francisco San Francisco 10	67	351
LABENAS			
P	El Dorado Placerville	58	876
LABENAUGH			
Thos*	Sacramento San Joaquin	63	349
LABER			
Lorenzo*	Sacramento Granite	63	262
Saml	Sacramento Dry Crk	63	372
William	Calaveras Twp 6	57	153
LABERATOUR			
C	Tuolumne Twp 1	71	260
LABERATOUS			
C*	Tuolumne Twp 1	71	260
LABERNO			
Antonio*	Mariposa Coulterville	60	685
LABERRIO			
Antonio*	Mariposa Coulterville	60	685
LABERT			
John E	Solano Benecia	69	282
R H	San Francisco San Francisco 1	68	903
LABERTIO			
Antonio*	Mariposa Coulterville	60	685
LABET			
Pierre	San Francisco San Francisco 2	67	724
LABETONN			
P L*	Tuolumne Big Oak	71	132
LABETOR			
P S	Tuolumne Twp 4	71	175
LABETOUN			
P L*	Tuolumne Big Oak	71	132
LABETOWN			
P L	Tuolumne Twp 4	71	132
LABETOWNE			
Cassimer*	Tuolumne Twp 4	71	132
LABEYRO			
Isaaon*	Tuolumne Columbia	71	334
Isadore	Tuolumne Twp 2	71	334
Isason*	Tuolumne Columbia	71	334
LABI			
Peter	Los Angeles Santa Ana	59	447
LABIA			
Jose	Los Angeles Los Angeles	59	492
LABILL			
J B	Mariposa Twp 1	60	654
LABIN			
John	San Francisco San Francisco 10	67	310
LABINES			
Jas G	Butte Kimshaw	56	581
LABINTHE			
Franklin	San Luis Obispo San Luis Obispo	65	10
LABIR			
Joseph*	Yuba New York	72	732
LABISH			
Charles	Santa Cruz Santa Cruz	66	606
LABIT			
A J	El Dorado Placerville	58	925
LABLA			
Lem	Placer Rattle Snake	62	638
LABLOND			
John	Calaveras Twp 9	57	347
LABLOUD			
John	Calaveras Twp 9	57	347
LABNER			
Anthony	Sacramento Ward 1	63	76
LABNEY			
Charles	Siskiyou Shasta Rvr	69	116
LABOIT			
Fernando	Los Angeles Los Angeles	59	343
LABOM			
Felicita	San Francisco San Francisco 10	67	184
LABOMME			
Eli	Stanislaus Branch	70	700
LABON			
Jack	Sierra Twp 7	66	886

California 1860 Census Index

Name	County Locale	M653 RollPage
LABONI		
Manuel D*	San Francisco 1	68 831
	San Francisco	
LABONO		
Jarento	Tehama Red Bluff	70 914
LABONSSERE		
Chas	Sacramento Ward 1	63 38
LABOO		
Jno	Butte Chico	56 559
LABOR		
Jas C	Stanislaus Emory	70 756
Jerome*	Mariposa Twp 1	60 624
Joseph	Yuba New York	72 732
LABORDE		
John C	Yuba Marysville	72 880
Pien	Tulara Keyesville	71 54
LABORDS		
Pien	Tulara Twp 3	71 54
LABORE		
Manuel D*	San Francisco 1	68 831
	San Francisco	
LABORER		
John*	Calaveras Twp 10	57 273
LABORG		
Antoio	Los Angeles Shaffer	59 396
Antonio	Los Angeles Los Angeles	59 396
LABORIA		
Jose	Los Angeles Tejon	59 541
LABORN		
Felicita	San Francisco San Francisco 10	184
		67
LABOTA		
---	Tulara Twp 3	71 69
LABOUR		
John*	Calaveras Twp 10	57 273
LABOURDETTE		
M	Tuolumne Big Oak	71 129
LABOURREAR		
George*	Alameda Oakland	55 18
LABOURRIAR		
George*	Alameda Oakland	55 18
LABOUSDETTE		
M	Tuolumne Twp 4	71 129
LABOUSSCRE		
Chas*	Sacramento Ward 1	63 38
LABOUSSERE		
Chas*	Sacramento Ward 1	63 38
LABRA		
John	Amador Twp 3	55 390
LABRANA		
Jack*	Mariposa Twp 3	60 614
LABRENO		
Pascal*	San Francisco San Francisco 3	67 77
LABRIAC		
Joseph	Santa Cruz Santa Cruz	66 620
LABRIAE		
Joseph	Santa Cruz Santa Cruz	66 620
LABRIDIE		
Peter*	Yuba Foster B	72 821
LABRINO		
Pascal*	San Francisco San Francisco 3	67 77
LABRISKIE		
Albert J	Yuba Marysville	72 966
Wm M	San Francisco San Francisco 2	67 792
LABRNO		
Parcul	San Francisco San Francisco 3	67 77
LABRO		
Larato	Tuolumne Twp 2	71 337
Lasato	Tuolumne Columbia	71 337
LABRON		
Jas	Amador Twp 3	55 384
LABROS		
John	Yolo Slate Ra	72 687
John	Yuba Slate Ro	72 687
LABROT		
P	Yolo Slate Ra	72 686
P	Yuba North Ea	72 686
LABRUS		
J	San Francisco San Francisco 2	67 678
LABSTER		
J M	Tehama Antelope	70 888
LABSTOUN		
Cassimer*	Tuolumne Big Oak	71 132
LABSTOURE		
Cassimer*	Tuolumne Big Oak	71 132
LABUCE		
Marietta	San Joaquin Stockton	641070
LABUR		
J*	Stanislaus Emory	70 741
LABURC		
Edward*	San Francisco San Francisco 8	681294
LABURE		
Edmund	San Francisco San Francisco 8	681294
LABUSKEE		
Albert J	Yuba Marysville	72 966
LAC WALLING		
John*	Nevada Bridgeport	61 440

Name	County Locale	M653 RollPage
LAC		
Lee	San Francisco San Francisco 11	161
		67
LACA		
---	Placer Auburn	62 597
LACAL		
John	Alameda Oakland	55 36
LACAMAN		
A	El Dorado Diamond	58 808
LACAMD		
Ernest	San Francisco San Francisco 7	681426
LACAN		
Peter	Trinity East For	701027
LACARDE		
Prosper	Los Angeles Los Angeles	59 376
LACARIAH		
---	San Diego Agua Caliente	64 864
LACARRA		
Ardino	Los Angeles Los Angeles	59 511
LACARRO		
Bernardo*	Los Angeles Los Angeles	59 510
Birnardo*	Los Angeles Los Angeles	59 510
LACARSE		
John	Tuolumne Twp 2	71 321
LACASA		
John	Monterey Pajaro	601013
LACASTA		
Peter	Calaveras Twp 5	57 201
LACASTE		
John	Tuolumne Big Oak	71 137
LACAZE		
Victor	San Francisco San Francisco 10	358
		67
LACE		
Edwin*	Yuba Rose Bar	72 799
J S	Nevada Nevada	61 320
John	Marin Sauciteto	60 749
M	Yuba Fosters	72 829
Thomas	Sierra St Louis	66 805
LACER		
David*	Nevada Nevada	61 247
LACEROL		
Lpedro*	Los Angeles Los Angeles	59 383
Pedro	Los Angeles Los Angeles	59 383
LACERTA		
Francisco	Santa Clara San Jose	65 375
LACEVIS		
John	Sierra Downieville	661002
LACEY		
Artemes	Alameda Brooklyn	55 155
Chas	San Francisco San Francisco 9	681060
J C	Nevada Grass Valley	61 215
R P	Nevada Nevada	61 254
Robt J	San Francisco San Francisco 2	67 773
S	Nevada Grass Valley	61 215
Thomas	El Dorado White Oaks	581012
W	El Dorado Placerville	58 819
Wm	Nevada Washington	61 336
LACFORD		
Charles F*	Yuba Marysville	72 904
LACH		
---	Los Angeles Elmonte	59 266
James	Stanislaus Branch	70 709
John*	Plumas Quincy	62 959
L M	Mariposa Twp 3	60 574
Pack*	Mariposa Twp 3	60 614
Thomas	Calaveras Twp 7	57 21
Thos J	Sacramento Granite	63 259
LACHAMOIS		
Achille	Los Angeles Los Angeles	59 352
LACHAPPELE		
Louis	Calaveras Twp 7	57 2
LACHAPPELLE		
Louis	Calaveras Twp 7	57 2
Louis*	Calaveras Twp 8	57 53
LACHE		
William	Los Angeles Los Angeles	59 322
LACHEALAPT		
Givani	Mariposa Twp 3	60 547
LACHELLA		
John	Calaveras Twp 8	57 72
LACHENAIS		
Michael	Los Angeles Los Angeles	59 368
LACHLEY		
Lewis	San Joaquin Elkhorn	64 959
LACHMAN		
B	Nevada Nevada	61 257
D	Nevada Nevada	61 257
John	Siskiyou Scott Va	69 53
Lewis	San Francisco San Francisco 6	67 400
LACHMANN		
George	San Francisco San Francisco 7	681330
LACHMARON		
George*	San Francisco San Francisco 7	681330
LACHMAUN		
George*	San Francisco San Francisco 7	681330

Name	County Locale	M653 RollPage
LACHUM		
---	Mariposa Twp 3	60 607
LACIANER		
Francisco	Yuba Marysville	72 929
LACIDAS		
---	San Diego Agua Caliente	64 824
LACIE		
David*	Nevada Nevada	61 247
LACIRIX		
John*	Sierra Downieville	661002
LACISON		
Nancy J	Santa Clara San Jose	65 356
LACITER		
Ruben	Placer Virginia	62 667
LACIVIC		
John*	Sierra Downieville	661002
LACK		
---	El Dorado Salmon Falls	581045
---	Nevada Bridgeport	61 506
---	Placer Virginia	62 679
---	Stanislaus Branch	70 714
---	Yolo No E Twp	72 677
---	Yolo Slate Ra	72 715
---	Yuba North Ea	72 677
Berryman	Klamath Klamath	59 224
Demcus F	Siskiyou Shasta Rvr	69 115
Henry	Santa Clara Alviso	65 408
M M	Butte Ophir	56 767
Samuel	Yuba New York	72 735
LACKAMP		
John H	Placer Dutch Fl	62 720
LACKAN		
Michael	Yolo Washington	72 571
LACKEMEN		
---	Tulara Twp 2	71 37
LACKEN		
Thomas	Sierra Downieville	661002
LACKENS		
William	San Francisco San Francisco 2	67 557
LACKETT		
Byron	El Dorado Mountain	581184
D*	Yuba Rose Bar	72 797
Hanan S	El Dorado Mountain	581183
Mary	El Dorado Mountain	581186
LACKEY		
Anna	Yuba Marysville	72 871
John	Colusa Monroeville	57 450
John	Nevada Nevada	61 297
John	Siskiyou Yreka	69 187
John P	Colusa Colusi	57 419
Thos	Napa Napa	61 64
William	Calaveras Twp 7	57 23
LACKIN		
Michael	Butte Ophir	56 791
Thomas*	Sierra Downieville	661002
LACKLAN		
Wm*	Calaveras Twp 9	57 369
LACKLAND		
Wm	Calaveras Twp 9	57 368
LACKLAR		
Wm	Calaveras Twp 9	57 369
LACKMAN		
S	Nevada Nevada	61 275
LACKNEY		
H	Napa Napa	61 78
J W*	Napa Yount	61 36
Wm*	Sacramento Ward 3	63 427
LACKOR		
Ben	Tuolumne Columbia	71 294
LACKY		
William	Placer Iona Hills	62 890
LACLERE		
Jean	San Francisco San Francisco 2	67 735
LACLING		
John	Sierra La Porte	66 775
LACOBY		
John F*	Tulara Visalia	71 100
LACOM		
---	Trinity Weaverville	701075
LACOMBEE		
Louis*	Sacramento Ward 1	63 41
Louis*	Sacramento Ward 1	63 15
LACOMBER		
Louis	Sacramento Ward 1	63 15
LACOMBIE		
Louis*	Sacramento Ward 1	63 15
Louis*	Sacramento Ward 1	63 41
LACOMIE		
Andrew	Calaveras Twp 7	57 38
LACOMPH		
John*	Yuba Marysville	72 903
LACONCHA		
Carsen	Amador Twp 5	55 331
Carson	Amador Twp 5	55 331
LACONT		
Alex	Placer Secret R	62 617

California 1860 Census Index

Name	County Locale	M653 Roll Page
LACORE		
Isaac	Sierra Downieville	66 978
James	Sierra Downieville	66 978
LACORN		
Peter	Shasta Shasta	66 677
LACORTA		
Peter	Calaveras Twp 5	57 201
LACOST		
Leon	San Joaquin Stockton	641039
T	San Francisco San Francisco 5	67 477
LACOSTA		
Peter	Calaveras Twp 5	57 201
Pierre	Calaveras Twp 5	57 200
LACOSTER		
Thomas	Mariposa Twp 1	60 638
LACOT		
R	Amador Twp 1	55 459
LACOUER		
Peter*	Shasta Shasta	66 677
LACOUNT		
Edward	Contra Costa Twp 3	57 616
LACOUR		
L	San Francisco San Francisco 6	67 437
LACOVER		
Peter*	Shasta Shasta	66 677
LACRAMPE		
M	San Francisco San Francisco 2	67 710
LACROIS		
L	Stanislaus Branch	70 700
LACROUSE		
Francisco	Calaveras Twp 4	57 330
LACROUSI		
John D*	San Mateo Twp 1	65 61
LACROZE		
John	San Francisco San Francisco 7	681441
LACRUSE		
Edwldro*	Mariposa Twp 1	60 625
LACRUZ		
Dominge	San Francisco San Francisco 3	67 52
Domingo	San Francisco San Francisco 3	67 52
Fanlanda*	Santa Cruz Santa Cruz	66 607
Fanlauda*	Santa Cruz Santa Cruz	66 607
Faulanda*	Santa Cruz Santa Cruz	66 607
Yanlanda	Santa Cruz Santa Cruz	66 607
Youlanda	Santa Cruz Santa Cruz	66 607
LACTRICT		
Chas*	Santa Clara Santa Clara	65 497
LACU		
David*	Nevada Nevada	61 247
LACUCO		
Thomas*	Calaveras Twp 7	57 4
LACUMBO		
Augusto*	Calaveras Twp 7	57 13
LACURE		
Jesus	San Joaquin Stockton	641072
LACUSE		
Francisco	San Joaquin Stockton	641073
LACY		
---	Sacramento Ward 1	63 55
Albert	Calaveras Twp 7	57 26
Bridget	Tehama Red Bluff	70 922
Charles E	Yuba Marysville	72 967
E S	San Francisco San Francisco 6	67 421
George	Mariposa Coulterville	60 699
George	Tuolumne Twp 1	71 247
George*	Mariposa Coulterville	60 699
Isaac	Merced Monterey	60 942
Isaac	Monterey Monterey	60 942
Isaac	Yolo Cottonwood	72 557
James	Sacramento Ward 1	63 27
James	Shasta Shasta	66 671
James*	Shasta Shasta	66 663
Jno*	Sacramento Franklin	63 332
Joseph	Merced Monterey	60 941
Joseph	Monterey Monterey	60 941
L W	San Joaquin Stockton	641056
Lawrence	Sacramento Ward 4	63 554
Martha R	Alameda Brooklyn	55 86
Nicholas	Contra Costa Twp 3	57 607
Nicholas	San Francisco San Francisco 2	67 594
LADA		
Perfeto*	Napa Napa	61 115
LADAN		
Thomas	Tehama Lassen	70 864
LADBATTER		
Mary	Sacramento Ward 1	63 97
LADBATTES		
Mary*	Sacramento Ward 1	63 97
LADD		
A T	San Francisco San Francisco 10	175 67
Annie	Sacramento Ward 4	63 514
Arnold W P	Los Angeles Los Angeles	59 372
Carissa	Tuolumne Twp 2	71 324
Charles	San Francisco San Francisco 7	681426
G W	San Francisco San Francisco 6	67 449

Name	County Locale	M653 Roll Page
LADD		
Geo S	San Francisco San Francisco 5	67 480
George	San Francisco San Francisco 5	67 487
Harvey C	San Bernardino	64 666
	San Bernardino	
Horace	Placer Iona Hills	62 866
Hubert	Sacramento Ward 4	63 514
J L	San Francisco San Francisco 5	67 529
Jno A	Sacramento Ward 4	63 504
Jra	San Joaquin Stockton	641078
Lorenzo D	Siskiyou Yreka	69 155
M J	Sacramento Ward 4	63 545
P M	Nevada Rough &	61 400
Perfeto*	Napa Napa	61 115
Smith	Butte Kimshaw	56 581
Thomas	Plumas Quincy	62 987
W F	San Francisco San Francisco 4	681222
W H	Sierra Downieville	66 960
William	Del Norte Crescent	58 631
William	Del Norte Crescent	58 632
LADDICK		
G H	El Dorado Greenwood	58 716
LADDLUNEYER		
Wm	Butte Kimshaw	56 579
LADDO		
Alphonso*	Alameda Murray	55 228
Magues	San Joaquin Stockton	641068
LADDS		
Alphonso*	Alameda Murray	55 228
LADDY		
John	Yuba Rose Bar	72 814
Thomas	Tuolumne Twp 1	71 483
LADEN		
J	San Joaquin Stockton	641094
P	Siskiyou Scott Va	69 50
P	Siskiyou Scott Va	69 57
LADER		
Mary*	Sacramento Ward 4	63 595
LADERSDOFF		
William*	Sierra St Louis	66 809
LADEW		
Caroline	Yolo Cache	72 639
Michael	Santa Clara Almaden	65 265
LADIN		
Mary	Sacramento Ward 1	63 147
LADNE		
Mary*	Sacramento Ward 1	63 147
LADNER		
C*	Nevada Grass Valley	61 166
LADO		
Hose*	El Dorado Placerville	58 896
LADON		
Hulio	Mariposa Twp 1	60 654
John	Calaveras Twp 6	57 140
LADONIX		
N*	Stanislaus Branch	70 700
LADOO		
P	Sutter Nicolaus	70 827
LADORE		
John	Calaveras Twp 5	57 140
LADOW		
Stephen W	Sierra Scales D	66 802
LADRET		
Jean	Calaveras Twp 7	57 47
LADRILLO		
Pascual	Los Angeles Santa Ana	59 444
LADROVER		
Dary	Yolo Cache	72 639
LADRY		
George A*	Mariposa Twp 3	60 618
Isador	Tuolumne Twp 1	71 260
Jean	Tuolumne Twp 1	71 260
John*	Sierra La Porte	66 775
LADS		
Philip*	Nevada Red Dog	61 544
LADU		
Mary*	Sacramento Ward 4	63 595
LADUE		
Cary	Yolo Cache	72 642
J	Nevada Eureka	61 356
Joseph	Amador Twp 2	55 304
Mary*	Sacramento Ward 1	63 147
LADUSE		
Robert	Yolo Slate Ra	72 687
Robert	Yuba North Ea	72 687
LADWORTH		
Nicholas*	Marin Point Re	60 731
Nichols	Marin Point Re	60 731
LAE		
---	El Dorado Kelsey	581130
---	San Francisco San Francisco 11	146 67
---	Tuolumne Don Pedro	71 163
Ah	Tuolumne Twp 4	71 163
LAEE		
Pitew*	Calaveras Twp 9	57 371

Name	County Locale	M653 Roll Page
LAEER		
John*	Butte Oro	56 674
LAEN		
---	Mariposa Twp 3	60 551
LAENCO		
Thomas	Calaveras Twp 7	57 4
LAER		
---	Mariposa Twp 3	60 576
LAERABEE		
George B*	San Francisco 8	681285
	San Francisco	
LAERIDER		
C*	El Dorado Eldorado	58 941
LAEROE		
Manuella*	San Francisco 7	681387
	San Francisco	
LAERUSE		
Morea	El Dorado Mud Springs	58 999
Wm	El Dorado Mud Springs	58 999
LAETRY		
John*	Sierra La Porte	66 775
LAEY		
George*	Mariposa Coulterville	60 699
LAEYHLIN		
Miles*	San Francisco San Francisco 11	90 67
LAF		
Sum	Placer Illinois	62 752
LAFAIVER		
Wm	Butte Oregon	56 638
Wm*	Butte Oregon	56 638
LAFANTANIE		
Mary	Shasta French G	66 718
LAFARE		
Martin	Los Angeles San Gabriel	59 408
Wm	Alameda Brooklyn	55 98
LAFARGAE		
Charles*	Tuolumne Columbia	71 317
LAFARGAN		
Anton	Tuolumne Jamestown	71 469
LAFARGE		
Vincent	Santa Clara Alviso	65 412
LAFARGUE		
Charles*	Tuolumne Columbia	71 317
LAFARSEE		
R	El Dorado Placerville	58 849
LAFART		
John*	Nevada Eureka	61 388
LAFAVER		
Louis	Tuolumne Sonora	71 216
LAFAVRE		
Louis	Tuolumne Twp 1	71 216
LAFAY		
W*	Butte Oregon	56 630
Wm	Butte Oregon	56 630
LAFAYETTE		
---	Sierra Downieville	66 975
Ang*	Yolo Putah	72 545
Aug*	Yolo Putah	72 545
Hiram	Sonoma Mendocino	69 448
O	Sutter Bear Rvr	70 821
Theodor	Santa Clara Redwood	65 459
LAFBAGER		
Charles	Placer Iona Hills	62 891
LAFEE		
A	Solano Vacaville	69 322
LAFEHAM		
S S	Sacramento Ward 4	63 574
LAFEILL		
Saml	San Francisco San Francisco 12	365 67
LAFENS		
B L*	Calaveras Twp 9	57 392
LAFENTER		
L	Nevada Eureka	61 394
LAFERANA		
Jack	Mariposa Twp 3	60 614
LAFERTINN		
D*	Nevada Eureka	61 388
LAFERTUM		
D*	Nevada Eureka	61 388
LAFERTY		
Jas*	Butte Kimshaw	56 596
Michal	Nevada Bloomfield	61 516
Owen	Klamath Liberty	59 241
LAFERY		
Gertralle	Santa Clara Santa Clara	65 487
LAFEUER		
Cyrus*	Yolo Putah	72 545
LAFEVER		
Joseph	Marin Tomales	60 725
LAFEVRE		
A J	Mendocino Calpella	60 816
Andres	San Francisco San Francisco 2	67 657
LAFEY		
Charly*	Calaveras Twp 4	57 341

Name	County Locale	M653 Roll	Page
LAFFAN			
Nicholas*	Mendocino Big Rvr	60	850
Niclolas*	Mendocino Big Rvr	60	850
LAFFANNACK			
A	Nevada Nevada	61	296
LAFFARD			
Jose J	San Francisco San Francisco 2	67	581
L	El Dorado Diamond	58	786
LAFFAYETTE			
Aug*	Yolo Putah	72	545
LAFFER			
Geo	Nevada Grass Valley	61	144
LAFFERT			
Chas	San Francisco San Francisco 10	67	246
LAFFERTY			
Albert G	Humbolt Mattole	59	127
Barney	Solano Benecia	69	316
C	Nevada Eureka	61	390
Chas	San Francisco San Francisco 10	67	246
Daniel	Solano Suisan	69	232
Edmond	Sierra St Louis	66	817
Felix	San Francisco San Francisco 11	67	147
H B	San Joaquin Stockton	64	1046
James	Siskiyou Yreka	69	144
James	Siskiyou Cottonwood	69	97
James	Yuba Long Bar	72	742
Jas	San Francisco San Francisco 1	68	858
John	Placer Iona Hills	62	863
John	Sonoma Vallejo	69	616
Mary	Yuba Long Bar	72	742
Patrick	San Francisco San Francisco 1	68	901
LAFFETT			
Peter	Yolo Washington	72	572
LAFFLIN			
Mathew O	Sierra Twp 5	66	941
LAFFON			
Robert	Yuba Slate Ro	72	697
LAFFORD			
T J	El Dorado White Oaks	58	1029
LAFFORTH			
J	Nevada Washington	61	336
LAFFUATT			
P	Tuolumne Twp 4	71	157
LAFFYETTE			
Aug*	Yolo Putah	72	545
LAFINTER			
L*	Nevada Eureka	61	394
LAFLANNACK			
A	Nevada Nevada	61	296
LAFLECHE			
Alphonso	Sierra Port Win	66	794
LAFLER			
Geo	El Dorado Mountain	58	1184
John R	Sierra Poker Flats	66	841
LAFLICHE			
George T	Alameda Oakland	55	54
LAFLIN			
R G	Sacramento Franklin	63	308
LAFLOWER			
Joseph	El Dorado Gold Hill	58	1096
LAFOFIAR			
---	Mariposa Twp 1	60	627
LAFOG			
John	Los Angeles Los Angeles	59	389
LAFOGTAIN			
Ramon	San Bernardino Santa Barbara	64	156
LAFOLLET			
Antonie	Calaveras Twp 6	57	142
LAFOMBY			
John	Shasta Cottonwood	66	723
LAFOMY			
John	Shasta Cottonwoood	66	723
LAFON			
John	Los Angeles Los Angeles	59	389
LAFONDUED			
Jean*	Mariposa Twp 3	60	570
LAFONNTAIN			
E	El Dorado Placerville	58	835
LAFONSE			
---	Butte Chico	56	549
---*	Butte Chico	56	550
LAFONT			
J C	Nevada Grass Valley	61	147
John	Nevada Eureka	61	388
LAFONTAIN			
Alexandrena*	Placer Michigan	62	849
LAFONTAINE			
A J	San Francisco San Francisco 3	67	15
LAFONTE			
M	Placer Illinois	62	706
LAFONTUD			
Jeun M	Mariposa Twp 3	60	570
Juan*	Mariposa Twp 3	60	570
LAFONTUED			
Jim M*	Mariposa Twp 3	60	570
Lun M	Mariposa Twp 3	60	570
LAFOON			
James	Plumas Meadow Valley	62	933
LAFORCE			
William	Nevada Bloomfield	61	512
LAFORGE			
Ira	Sacramento San Joaquin	63	359
LAFORT			
J C	Nevada Grass Valley	61	147
Louis	Calaveras Twp 9	57	378
LAFORTA			
Mitchel	Calaveras Twp 6	57	167
LAFORTIUN			
D*	Nevada Eureka	61	388
LAFORTUM			
D*	Nevada Eureka	61	388
LAFORY			
Augle*	Mariposa Coulterville	60	675
LAFOURT			
Albert	San Francisco San Francisco 2	67	701
LAFOUSE			
--*	Butte Chico	56	550
LAFOUTUED			
Jim M*	Mariposa Twp 3	60	570
LAFRAITT			
Lazardo*	Sacramento Granite	63	253
LAFRANCE			
B	Sacramento Ward 4	63	558
Joseph	Placer Iona Hills	62	879
LAFRAND			
Joseph*	Calaveras Twp 4	57	340
LAFRANE			
Theidon	Sierra Twp 7	66	878
Theodore	Sierra Twp 7	66	878
Thodon*	Sierra Twp 7	66	878
LAFRANK			
Joseph*	Calaveras Twp 4	57	340
S	Trinity Rush Crk	70	965
LAFRIERE			
Jean	Santa Clara Santa Clara	65	502
LAFRUITT			
Lazardo*	Sacramento Granite	63	253
LAFSEN			
C*	Nevada Grass Valley	61	186
LAFTAW			
John	Placer Goods	62	694
LAFTERS			
John	El Dorado Kelsey	58	1132
LAFUENTE			
Jose De J	Los Angeles Santa Ana	59	455
LAFUJA			
---*	Mendocino Round Va	60	884
LAFURT			
John*	Nevada Eureka	61	388
LAFUST			
Louis	Calaveras Twp 9	57	378
LAG			
---	Amador Twp 1	55	496
---	Butte Bidwell	56	717
---	Placer Illinois	62	745
---*	El Dorado Casumnes	58	1177
---	Butte Bidwell	56	717
James E	San Francisco San Francisco 3	67	15
LAGACHE			
Jean	San Francisco San Francisco 2	67	781
LAGADO			
Phillip	Fresno Twp 1	59	81
LAGAIRE			
A	Tuolumne Twp 3	71	465
LAGAN			
Michael	Sierra St Louis	66	810
Patrick*	Sierra St Louis	66	807
Peter*	Yuba Linda	72	993
LAGANCHY			
B	El Dorado Greenwood	58	711
LAGANGE			
G*	Nevada Grass Valley	61	235
LAGANNA			
J	Sacramento Ward 1	63	13
LAGANT			
A	Nevada Grass Valley	61	224
LAGANY			
P F	Amador Twp 7	55	417
LAGARET			
Philip	Siskiyou Yreka	69	155
LAGARRA			
Juaquin	Los Angeles Los Angeles	59	348
LAGARY			
P F	Amador Twp 7	55	417
LAGAUGE			
G	Nevada Grass Valley	61	235
LAGDAM			
Mary Ann*	Yuba Marysville	72	911
LAGDIN			
Pierre H*	Yuba Long Bar	72	750
LAGE			
---	Sierra Twp 5	66	934
Micheal	El Dorado Coloma	58	1108
LAGELIN			
Pierre H*	Yuba Long Bar	72	750
LAGEM			
Louis	Mariposa Twp 3	60	600
LAGER			
A*	Nevada Bridgeport	61	498
John	Solano Montezuma	69	372
Judah*	Tuolumne Twp 1	71	206
Mary*	San Francisco San Francisco 2	67	653
Peter	Tuolumne Sonora	71	207
LAGERET			
Philip	Siskiyou Yreka	69	155
LAGERMINO			
Augustino	Calaveras Twp 7	57	12
LAGES			
C	Sacramento Ward 4	63	546
LAGET			
James	Tehama Cottonwoood	70	901
LAGGINS			
S W	Tehama Lassen	70	865
LAGHE			
John*	Calaveras Twp 6	57	161
LAGHUNOW			
Thos	Yolo Cache	72	613
LAGHUROM			
Thos*	Yolo Cache Crk	72	613
LAGIAR			
Julias	Calaveras Twp 6	57	147
LAGIN			
A	El Dorado Georgetown	58	679
LAGIR			
L	Yuba Foster B	72	834
LAGIS			
Peter*	Tuolumne Twp 1	71	207
LAGLE			
Wm*	Sacramento Brighton	63	193
LAGLIARDO			
Juan*	Calaveras Twp 9	57	373
LAGNA			
Franciscp	Calaveras Twp 7	57	45
LAGNAIT			
Louisa*	Calaveras Twp 9	57	351
LAGNERER			
Peter*	Siskiyou Yreka	69	171
LAGNEVER			
Peter	Siskiyou Yreka	69	171
LAGNEWAY			
Mr*	Sonoma Vallejo	69	622
LAGNUTT			
Edward	Mariposa Coulterville	60	694
LAGNVELL			
Janneth G	Siskiyou Yreka	69	171
Launeto G	Siskiyou Yreka	69	171
LAGO			
---	Tulara Twp 3	71	67
Juan	Los Angeles Santa Ana	59	459
Phillip	Calaveras Twp 7	57	45
LAGOMASINO			
B	San Joaquin Stockton	64	1073
LAGON			
Andrew	Sierra St Louis	66	810
Michael*	Sierra St Louis	66	810
LAGONIAGRA			
Lewis	Plumas Quincy	62	944
LAGOUGE			
G*	Nevada Grass Valley	61	235
LAGRAN			
Jas	Placer Dutch Fl	62	728
LAGRANGE			
J*	San Francisco San Francisco 2	67	802
Lafayette	Marin Bolinas	60	745
Lafeyetto	Marin Bolinas	60	745
Luther*	Yuba Bear Rvr	72	1012
M C	Alameda Brooklyn	55	106
LAGRI			
L	Yuba Fosters	72	834
LAGUAIT			
Louisa*	Calaveras Twp 9	57	351
LAGUAR			
Julius*	Calaveras Twp 6	57	147
LAGUE			
R	El Dorado Placerville	58	833
LAGUEO			
G*	Mariposa Twp 3	60	566
LAGUMAN			
Henry	Sierra Twp 7	66	897
LAGUNA			
---	Tulara Keyesville	71	67
---	Tulara Keyesville	71	70
A De Leo De	San Francisco 8	68	1284
Casemin	Los Angeles Los Angeles	59	307
Francisco	El Dorado Placerville	58	930

California 1860 Census Index

LAGUNA -
LAKE

Name	County Locale	M653 Roll	Page
LAGUNA			
Jesus	Los Angeles Los Angeles	59	307
LAGUOR			
Antonio	Calaveras Twp 9	57	358
LAGURE			
Hosea M*	Alameda Oakland	55	57
LAGURO			
G	Mariposa Twp 3	60	566
LAGURRIE			
J	Nevada Grass Valley	61	148
LAGY			
Henry	Contra Costa Twp 2	57	577
LAH			
Ho	Sierra La Porte	66	774
LAHADIE			
Louis	Yuba Fosters	72	828
LAHAFF			
Delia	San Francisco San Francisco 2	67	601
LAHAN			
---	Mendocino Calpella	60	824
LAHEN			
Jacob*	Placer Michigan	62	811
LAHENN			
Jacb*	Calaveras Twp 8	57	106
LAHERE			
John*	Sacramento Ward 1	63	85
LAHERTY			
Jas*	Butte Kimshaw	56	596
John	San Francisco San Francisco 12	67	384
LAHEVE			
John*	Sacramento Ward 1	63	85
LAHEY			
Daniel	Sierra Twp 7	66	894
Dennis	San Francisco San Francisco 11	67	162
Hannah*	San Francisco San Francisco 3	67	33
Jerry*	San Francisco San Francisco 11	67	108
Timothy	Alameda Oakland	55	57
Timothy	San Francisco San Francisco 9	68	1026
LAHEYAL			
M	Tuolumne Twp 2	71	335
LAHG			
Ticin	Sierra Twp 7	66	877
LAHICHES			
Marrion	Mariposa Coulterville	60	680
LAHIN			
Jim	Nevada Bloomfield	61	507
LAHMAN			
Hy	San Francisco San Francisco 2	67	630
LAHOFF			
Delia*	San Francisco San Francisco 2	67	601
LAHOM			
Jas	Butte Oregon	56	614
LAHONAN			
Robert	Siskiyou Yreka	69	186
LAHOR			
Jerome	Mariposa Twp 1	60	624
LAHORDE			
---*	Mariposa Twp 3	60	614
LAHORN			
Jas*	Butte Oregon	56	614
LAHORRE			
Jas*	Butte Oregon	56	614
LAHOY			
G	Nevada Grass Valley	61	184
Michael	San Francisco San Francisco 9	68	960
LAHR			
John	El Dorado White Oaks	58	1027
Mat	El Dorado White Oaks	58	1027
P	El Dorado White Oaks	58	1028
LAHRAM			
Wm	Stanislaus Branch	70	702
LAHSE			
Nicholas*	Placer Twp 2	62	660
LAHURTY			
Jas	Butte Kimshaw	56	596
LAHWAN			
Hy	San Francisco San Francisco 2	67	630
LAHY			
Jno	Sonoma Petaluma	69	550
Patrick*	Marin Tomales	60	717
LAHYE			
Ellen	San Francisco San Francisco 7	68	1430
LAI			
---	San Francisco San Francisco 9	68	1093
---	Sonoma Sonoma	69	639
A	Sonoma Sonoma	69	639
Ah	Yuba Bear Rvr	72	1000
LAID			
K*	Mariposa Twp 3	60	584
LAIDLEY			
W G	San Francisco San Francisco 5	67	543
LAIDLY			

Name	County Locale	M653 Roll	Page
LAIDLY			
Jas*	San Francisco San Francisco 10	67	306
Jos	San Francisco San Francisco 10	67	306
LAIE			
---	Mariposa Twp 3	60	620
Ah	Tuolumne Twp 4	71	163
Peterr*	Calaveras Twp 9	57	371
Piterr*	Calaveras Twp 9	57	371
Thomas*	Sierra St Louis	66	805
LAIG			
---	Yuba Marysville	72	896
LAIGE			
---	Sierra Twp 5	66	932
LAIGHE			
John	San Francisco San Francisco 12	67	386
Patk	San Francisco San Francisco 12	67	383
LAIGHTON			
Chas	San Francisco San Francisco 10	67	202
P W	Butte Ophir	56	791
LAIGS			
Lee	Mariposa Twp 3	60	608
LAIGSTAFF			
William	Placer Iona Hills	62	860
LAIKE			
Fum	Plumas Quincy	62	965
LAIKIN			
J	Nevada Eureka	61	376
LAIL			
John	Shasta Millvill	66	739
LAILLAND			
Aug	Del Norte Crescent	58	641
LAIM			
---	Nevada Bridgeport	61	492
Willet*	Tulara Twp 1	71	97
LAIME			
Louis	San Francisco San Francisco 2	67	717
LAIN			
Ah	Yuba Suida	72	991
Duncan M*	Solano Vacaville	69	341
Sing	Mariposa Twp 3	60	563
LAINBERT			
Frank*	Yuba Marysville	72	889
LAINE			
---	Siskiyou Callahan	69	10
Ed	Butte Cascade	56	692
H	San Francisco San Francisco 5	67	552
John	Nevada Bridgeport	61	499
Lein	Butte Ophir	56	824
M	Siskiyou Callahan	69	10
Mr	Siskiyou Callahan	69	10
LAINES			
Phillip	El Dorado Placerville	58	918
LAING			
---	Del Norte Crescent	58	660
---	Mariposa Twp 3	60	545
---	Plumas Quincy	62	949
C Ruth	Colusa Colusi	57	419
George	Trinity Eastman	70	960
Harriet	San Francisco San Francisco 4	68	1143
James B	Colusa Colusi	57	419
McKeith	Calaveras Twp 9	57	372
LAINHART			
B	Butte Ophir	56	745
LAINSBURY			
H G	Yuba Marysville	72	915
LAIO			
Juliam	Monterey San Juan	60	992
LAIR			
---	Mariposa Twp 3	60	576
---	Mariposa Twp 3	60	579
---*	Amador Twp 7	55	419
---*	Mariposa Twp 3	60	576
---*	Mariposa Twp 3	60	579
LAIRABEE			
George B*	San Francisco 8	68	1285
	San Francisco		
LAIRD			
C C	Marin Point Re	60	730
Daniel	Solano Benecia	69	288
Elizabeth	Santa Clara Gilroy	65	242
Elizer P	San Joaquin Elkhorn	64	959
Fanny	Santa Clara Redwood	65	451
Fielding	Santa Clara Santa Clara	65	483
G P	Marin Point Re	60	730
H S	Marin Point Re	60	731
J W	Santa Clara Redwood	65	450
James	Placer Secret R	62	623
James	Santa Clara Fremont	65	441
Jane	Yuba Marysville	72	900
John	Amador Twp 5	55	361
John W	Stanislaus Empire	70	732

Name	County Locale	M653 Roll	Page
LAIRD			
Joseph	El Dorado Mud Springs	58	988
M	Santa Clara Redwood	65	446
M S	Marin Point Re	60	731
Saml	Placer Horseshoe	62	650
Thomas	San Francisco San Francisco 3	67	9
William F	San Joaquin Douglass	64	914
LAIRIO			
Hosa	Mariposa Twp 1	60	653
LAIRY			
Anna*	Santa Clara Alviso	65	407
LAISTEN			
John*	Mariposa Twp 3	60	573
LAISTER			
John*	Mariposa Twp 3	60	573
LAISTON			
John*	Mariposa Twp 3	60	573
LAITARILLT			
M*	Nevada Grass Valley	61	154
LAITH			
Frank	Sonoma Vallejo	69	619
LAITHICUIM			
John F*	Yuba Marysville	72	905
LAIYHLIN			
Miles	San Francisco San Francisco 11	67	90
LAJAN			
Jose M	San Bernardino San Salvador	64	660
LAJCOCK			
Jacob*	Los Angeles Los Angeles	59	339
LAJEANE			
Mary	Sierra Downieville	66	971
LAJER			
Judah	Tuolumne Sonora	71	206
LAJNOLD			
John E*	Placer Dutch Fl	62	715
LAJOH			
Alagis	San Joaquin Stockton	64	1065
LAJOR			
Judah*	Tuolumne Twp 1	71	206
LAJUS			
Remy*	Tuolumne Twp 4	71	134
Reney*	Tuolumne Twp 4	71	134
Rensy	Tuolumne Big Oak	71	134
LAK			
---	El Dorado Georgetown	58	695
---	San Francisco San Francisco 4	68	1182
C W	Sutter Butte	70	788
LAKE			
---	Alameda Oakland	55	52
---	Amador Twp 7	55	415
---	Amador Twp 1	55	477
---	Amador Twp 1	55	495
---	Amador Twp 1	55	496
---	Amador Twp 1	55	497
---	Amador Twp 1	55	499
---	Amador Twp 1	55	500
---	Amador Twp 1	55	501
---	Calaveras Twp 4	57	300
---	El Dorado Diamond	58	807
---	El Dorado Placerville	58	904
---	El Dorado Mud Springs	58	964
---	Tuolumne Chinese	71	510
---	Tuolumne Twp 5	71	522
---	Tuolumne Chinese	71	524
---	Yuba Fosters	72	841
C	Nevada Eureka	61	352
Charles	Amador Twp 3	55	386
Charles	Santa Clara San Jose	65	381
D P	Butte Cascade	56	692
D P	El Dorado Georgetown	58	677
Daniel	Sierra La Porte	66	786
Danl B	Butte Kimshaw	56	572
Daul B	Butte Kimshaw	56	572
David	El Dorado Salmon Falls	58	1063
David	Nevada Red Dog	61	545
David	Placer Iona Hills	62	860
Delos	San Francisco San Francisco 5	67	483
Ed	Sacramento Ward 4	63	514
Eliza C	San Francisco San Francisco 5	67	476
G P	Merced Twp 1	60	895
George	San Francisco San Francisco 9	68	1099
H	Sacramento Sutter	63	307
H	Sacramento Ward 1	63	5
H W	Klamath Klamath	59	225
J	Siskiyou Klamath	69	97
Jacob	San Joaquin Douglass	64	921
Jefferson	Sacramento Sutter	63	301
John	El Dorado Kelsey	58	1149
John	Tehama Red Bluff	70	928
Jos S	San Mateo Twp 2	65	125
Joseph	Sacramento Ward 4	63	534
Laurence	Los Angeles Los Angeles	59	358
Louise	Sacramento Ward 1	63	139
M	Placer Dutch Fl	62	709
Myron	Plumas Quincy	62	983

Copyright 1999 by Heritage Quest, a division of AGLL, Inc., Bountiful, UT 84011. All rights reserved

California 1860 Census Index

Name	County Locale	M653 RollPage
LAKE		
Nelson P	Contra Costa Twp 2	57 541
O	Sacramento Franklin	63 307
Peter	Siskiyou Callahan	69 7
Richard	Placer Michigan	62 849
Robert	Yuba Long Bar	72 768
Roda	El Dorado Kelsey	581133
Sydia	Amador Twp 3	55 402
Syne	Butte Cascade	56 700
W	Nevada Grass Valley	61 184
William	Mendocino Calpella	60 809
Winston H	San Joaquin Douglass	64 921
Wm	Amador Twp 3	55 377
Wm M	Plumas Meadow Valley	62 906
LAKEBRINK		
Wm	Santa Clara Santa Clara	65 482
LAKEMAN		
C	Mendocino Big Rvr	60 851
Charles	Mendocino Ukiah	60 800
Charles	San Francisco San Francisco 2	67 560
Charles*	Mendocino Ukiah	60 800
H A	San Francisco San Francisco 2	67 586
LAKEMONE		
---	Tulara Twp 2	71 36
LAKENAN		
J M	Nevada Nevada	61 292
LAKENANCE		
Frank*	Yuba Marysville	72 936
LAKENAW		
J M	Nevada Nevada	61 292
LAKENBILL		
Hen	Amador Twp 7	55 412
LAKENOW		
---*	Tulara Visalia	71 39
LAKER		
Fredk	San Francisco San Francisco 2	67 635
Jno	Sacramento Ward 1	63 84
LAKERMAN		
W	San Francisco San Francisco 5	67 493
LAKET		
R	El Dorado Diamond	58 801
LAKIN		
Lemuel	Klamath Trinidad	59 221
LAKOMAN		
Charles*	Mendocino Ukiah	60 800
LAKOULEME		
---*	Tulara Visalia	71 38
LAKOWME		
---*	Tulara Visalia	71 36
LAKSE		
Nicholas*	Placer Twp 2	62 660
LAKUCK		
Manalra	San Francisco San Francisco 2	67 615
LAKY		
Thomas	El Dorado White Oaks	581006
LALA		
---	San Bernardino San Bernadino	64 669
LALACA		
---*	Mendocino Big Rock	60 875
LALADIE		
Louis*	Yuba Foster B	72 828
Thomas	Yuba Fosters	72 828
LALAND		
Pierre*	San Francisco San Francisco 11	137 67
LALARTAR		
Gaspard*	Calaveras Twp 4	57 300
Gaspord*	Calaveras Twp 4	57 300
LALAS		
Ramina*	San Francisco San Francisco 1	68 819
LALASA		
---*	Mendocino Round Va	60 884
LALASU		
---*	Mendocino Round Va	60 884
LALAUD		
Pierre*	San Francisco San Francisco 11	137 67
LALE		
John J	Tuolumne Big Oak	71 133
LALEE		
---	Yuba Long Bar	72 749
LALGADO		
Jose	San Luis Obispo San Luis Obispo	65 20
Juan	Monterey Monterey	60 955
LALISA		
Y	El Dorado Placerville	58 870
LALLA		
Elva	Mariposa Twp 3	60 553
Ena*	Mariposa Twp 3	60 553
Eva*	Mariposa Twp 3	60 553
LALLAMANT		
D	Sacramento Ward 1	63 3
LALLAN		
F	Nevada Nevada	61 262
LALLARILLE		
M*	Nevada Grass Valley	61 154

Name	County Locale	M653 RollPage
LALLE		
Pedro*	Los Angeles Los Angeles	59 324
LALLEAN		
Joseph	Tuolumne Twp 2	71 279
LALLEMAN		
J	San Francisco San Francisco 2	67 678
LALLEMAND		
Hery	San Francisco San Francisco 2	67 703
Hevy*	San Francisco San Francisco 2	67 703
LALLEY		
John	Tuolumne Columbia	71 333
Matthew	Tuolumne Twp 3	71 464
LALLIDAN		
Joseph	Tuolumne Twp 2	71 279
LALLIN		
Louis	Amador Twp 1	55 468
LALLMAUD		
Joseph	San Francisco San Francisco 3	67 16
S	Nevada Grass Valley	61 226
LALLONE		
Camelia	El Dorado Mud Springs	58 995
LALLS		
T	Nevada Grass Valley	61 226
LALLY		
B	Mariposa Twp 1	60 642
Jno	Klamath Dillins	59 214
John*	Amador Twp 2	55 268
M	San Francisco San Francisco 5	67 511
Mary	San Francisco San Francisco 6	67 415
Mary	San Francisco San Francisco 2	67 593
Pat*	Placer Sacramento	62 645
LALMENTO		
Tanjhea	Amador Twp 5	55 332
LALOHER		
Louise*	Sacramento Ward 1	63 78
LALONCE		
Edward*	Sierra Port Win	66 794
LALOND		
Edward*	Sierra Port Win	66 794
LALONDE		
J D*	Sacramento Ward 1	63 46
LALOR		
Jerome	Mariposa Twp 1	60 624
LALOROP		
Peter*	Shasta French G	66 718
LALOUDE		
J D*	Sacramento Ward 1	63 46
LALOUP		
Peter*	Shasta French G	66 718
LALRMAN		
L*	San Francisco San Francisco 3	67 73
LALSBURY		
D L*	El Dorado Diamond	58 768
LALTH		
Frank*	Sonoma Vallejo	69 619
LALTON		
James	Sierra Scales D	66 800
LALUZ		
Jose	San Diego Agua Caliente	64 823
LALY		
John*	Placer Ophirville	62 655
Michl	San Francisco San Francisco 9	681056
LAM TOO		
---	Butte Kimshaw	56 598
LAM		
---	Amador Twp 5	55 333
---	Amador Twp 5	55 334
---	Amador Twp 5	55 359
---	Amador Twp 7	55 415
---	Amador Twp 1	55 458
---	Amador Twp 1	55 477
---	Calaveras Twp 5	57 139
---	Calaveras Twp 6	57 151
---	Calaveras Twp 6	57 165
---	Calaveras Twp 4	57 342
---	El Dorado White Oaks	581031
---	El Dorado Salmon Hills	581064
---	El Dorado Coloma	581107
---	El Dorado Newtown	58 777
---	El Dorado Placerville	58 899
---	El Dorado Placerville	58 919
---	Mariposa Coulterville	60 693
---	Nevada Grass Valley	61 228
---	Nevada Bridgeport	61 493
---	Sacramento Ward 3	63 490
---	Sierra Downieville	661020
---	Sierra Twp 5	66 932
---	Siskiyou Scott Va	69 32
---	Tulara Twp 1	71 96
---	Tuolumne Twp 6	71 535
---*	Amador Twp 3	55 410
---*	Calaveras Twp 7	57 40
---*	El Dorado Salmon Falls	581064
---*	Sierra Twp 5	66 932
---*	Yuba Foster B	72 831

Name	County Locale	M653 RollPage
LAM		
Ah	Calaveras Twp 7	57 36
Ah	Tuolumne Twp 4	71 181
Ah*	Butte Oro	56 687
Ching	Butte Oro	56 675
Lee*	Plumas Quincy	62 925
Ling	Sierra Twp 5	66 947
M E	Placer Michigan	62 826
Manuel	Monterey San Juan	60 995
Tehu	San Francisco San Francisco 3	67 55
Yip	San Francisco San Francisco 10	356 67
LAMA		
Maria*	San Francisco San Francisco 2	67 707
LAMACH		
Octavus	Alameda Oakland	55 13
LAMACK		
C	Nevada Grass Valley	61 166
LAMAINS		
J*	Nevada Eureka	61 391
LAMALPHA		
Jos S A*	Sacramento Ward 4	63 587
LAMAN HA		
---	Mendocino Calpella	60 826
LAMAN		
H J	Butte Kimshaw	56 597
J	Nevada Nevada	61 283
Jno	Nevada Nevada	61 320
P*	Nevada Grass Valley	61 161
S	Nevada Grass Valley	61 157
LAMANCS		
Pascal*	Calaveras Twp 6	57 161
LAMANCY		
John	San Francisco San Francisco 2	67 662
LAMANES		
Paseal	Calaveras Twp 6	57 161
LAMANGO		
---	Fresno Twp 3	59 100
LAMANHU		
---	Mendocino Calpella	60 826
LAMANIS		
J*	Nevada Eureka	61 391
LAMANT		
Cell	Santa Clara Gilroy	65 240
LAMAR		
A L	Sacramento Georgian	63 341
Antoine	Butte Kimshaw	56 570
J B	Mendocino Ukiah	60 808
Joseph	Plumas Quincy	62 966
P	Nevada Grass Valley	61 161
LAMAREZ		
James	Yuba Marysville	72 962
LAMARGAE		
Alexander*	Sierra Twp 7	66 916
LAMARGAR		
Alexander	Sierra Twp 7	66 916
LAMARGUE		
Alexander*	Sierra Twp 7	66 916
LAMARIA		
F	Shasta Shasta	66 677
LAMARK		
J B	Butte Bidwell	56 722
LAMARQUE		
Alexander*	Sierra Twp 7	66 916
B L	Nevada Grass Valley	61 161
LAMARRE		
J	Sacramento Granite	63 234
LAMARTINE		
J	Tuolumne Columbia	71 333
Joseph	Los Angeles Azuza	59 276
Peter	Santa Clara Almaden	65 277
LAMASLIN		
Ellen	Sacramento Ward 3	63 449
LAMASNE		
I*	Mariposa Twp 1	60 630
LAMASTER		
Franyworth	Sierra Pine Grove	66 830
LAMASTINE		
J	Tuolumne Twp 2	71 333
LAMATAS		
---	Fresno Twp 2	59 74
LAMATTE		
Chas	Butte Kimshaw	56 590
LAMAUCS		
Pascal*	Calaveras Twp 6	57 161
LAMAY		
Mary	Marin San Rafael	60 760
LAMB		
A	Sutter Butte	70 779
A D	Sonoma Bodega	69 522
A K*	Yuba Rose Bar	72 811
Abrum*	Plumas Quincy	62 971
Adam	Nevada Bloomfield	61 527
Alex	Siskiyou Scott Va	69 42
B	Tuolumne Jacksonville	71 167
Caleb	Nevada Bloomfield	61 526

California 1860 Census Index

Name	County Locale	M653 Roll	Page
LAMB			
Charles	Santa Cruz Watsonville	66	536
Dana	Tulara Visalia	71	21
Daniel	Tuolumne Big Oak	71	142
Downing	Sonoma Washington	69	676
Edward	Alameda Brooklyn	55	98
Edward*	Alameda Murray	55	224
Eliza	Placer Virginia	62	689
F	El Dorado Placerville	58	867
F B	San Francisco San Francisco 5	67	521
Francis	San Francisco San Francisco 10	169 67	
Frank	Sacramento Dry Crk	63	376
Fred	Amador Twp 1	55	498
G	Nevada Eureka	61	389
Geo	San Francisco San Francisco 6	67	434
Geroge H	El Dorado Greenwood	58	730
H	Nevada Eureka	61	389
Hamilton	Yuba Parks Ba	72	778
Helen	San Francisco San Francisco 2	67	658
Henry	Contra Costa Twp 2	57	541
Horace	Sonoma Armally	69	513
Hugh	El Dorado Big Bar	58	743
J	Calaveras Twp 9	57	418
J C	San Mateo Twp 1	65	55
J M*	San Mateo Twp 3	65	79
J S	El Dorado Placerville	58	873
J S	Mendocino Twp 1	60	892
Jacob	Nevada Red Dog	61	550
James	Alameda Brooklyn	55	88
James	Mariposa Coulterville	60	695
James	Napa Hot Springs	61	3
James	Siskiyou Scott Va	69	42
Jams	Alameda Brooklyn	55	88
Jas	Butte Mountain	56	741
John	Butte Ophir	56	824
John	Calaveras Twp 8	57	85
John	El Dorado Union	58	1092
John	Sonoma Santa Rosa	69	412
John T	San Joaquin Castoria	64	879
Joseph	Siskiyou Yreka	69	146
Joshua	El Dorado Greenwood	58	726
Joshua E	Sonoma Washington	69	668
Larkin	Sacramento Cosumnes	63	388
Levi	Tulara Twp 1	71	109
M	El Dorado Placerville	58	867
M	Klamath Liberty	59	242
M	Sierra St Louis	66	816
M A	El Dorado Placerville	58	869
Martin B	San Francisco San Francisco 11	151 67	
Matilda	Sacramento Ward 1	63	23
Michael	Sierra St Louis	66	815
Moses	Yolo Cottonwood	72	658
Newton	Siskiyou Yreka	69	146
Patrick	Alameda Brooklyn	55	97
Patrick*	Yuba Linda	72	985
Peter	Tuolumne Columbia	71	352
Phillip	San Francisco San Francisco 9	68	988
S	Shasta Millvill	66	754
Sarah	San Francisco San Francisco 7	68	1335
Shadrack	Mendocino Ukiah	60	795
Thos	San Francisco San Francisco 2	67	745
W	El Dorado Placerville	58	867
W	San Francisco San Francisco 2	67	678
W B	Butte Ophir	56	792
W H	Tuolumne Twp 1	71	222
William	Napa Clear Lake	61	140
Wm	Placer Virginia	62	690
Z	San Mateo Twp 1	65	56
LAMBACH			
Chas	Sacramento Ward 4	63	532
LAMBARD			
O W	Sacramento Ward 1	63	8
LAMBART			
F	Tuolumne Twp 4	71	128
LAMBDEN			
George W	Yuba Marysville	72	904
LAMBECK			
S S	Sacramento Granite	63	244
LAMBEH			
Robt*	Santa Cruz Santa Cruz	66	625
LAMBEN			
Robt*	Santa Cruz Santa Cruz	66	625
LAMBERE			
Clarind*	Alameda Oakland	55	4
LAMBERI			
Clanna*	Alameda Oakland	55	4
Clarind*	Alameda Oakland	55	4
Clarma	Alameda Oakland	55	4
LAMBERRT			
Perrie	San Francisco San Francisco 10	357 67	
LAMBERT			
Adolphus	Contra Costa Twp 1	57	498
Albert	Plumas Quincy	62	994

Name	County Locale	M653 Roll	Page
LAMBERT			
Aners*	Sierra Twp 5	66	930
B	San Mateo Twp 3	65	74
Benj	Mariposa Twp 3	60	573
Benjm	Mendocino Little L	60	835
Benjn	Mendocino Little L	60	835
Casper	Amador Twp 2	55	290
Charles	San Francisco San Francisco 4	681	135
Charlotte	San Francisco San Francisco 10	182 67	
Chas L	Sonoma Mendocino	69	463
Conrad*	Napa Yount	61	30
Daniel	Mendocino Little L	60	832
Danl	Mendocino Little L	60	832
Do Ain*	Los Angeles Los Angeles	59	362
Dodoro*	Los Angeles Los Angeles	59	362
E	El Dorado Placerville	58	869
E	Sacramento Ward 1	63	30
Edwd A	San Francisco San Francisco 5	67	502
Elisha	San Joaquin Castoria	64	909
Frank	San Francisco San Francisco 3	67	80
Frank	Sonoma Mendocino	69	459
Frank	Yuba Marysville	72	889
Fred	Sacramento Ward 1	63	67
G B	Yolo Cache Crk	72	665
G E	Yolo Cache Crk	72	665
G P	Nevada Rough &	61	426
Geo G	San Francisco San Francisco 2	67	587
German	San Francisco San Francisco 2	67	800
Gilbert	San Francisco San Francisco 7	681	359
H	El Dorado Placerville	58	888
H	Merced Twp 1	60	905
H W	Tuolumne Columbia	71	309
Harris	San Francisco San Francisco 10	181 67	
Henry	Tuolumne Twp 4	71	129
J	El Dorado Placerville	58	890
J	Yolo No E Twp	72	679
J	Yuba North Ea	72	679
J S	Nevada Nevada	61	282
J W	Butte Bidwell	56	722
Jeremiah	Mendocino Little L	60	837
Jno	Butte Kimshaw	56	579
Jno	Mendocino Little L	60	838
Jno	San Francisco San Francisco 9	681	056
Jno H	Klamath Liberty	59	238
John	Tuolumne Twp 2	71	278
John R	Tuolumne Sonora	71	201
Jonathan	Tuolumne Jamestown	71	449
Joseph	Alameda Oakland	55	43
L	San Francisco San Francisco 5	67	542
L A	Tuolumne Twp 1	71	241
Margaritt	Sonoma Mendocino	69	463
Matilda	Tuolumne Columbia	71	335
Mr	Sonoma Salt Point	69	692
N G*	Tuolumne Twp 1	71	201
Nesley	Solano Suisan	69	215
Patrick	Tuolumne Twp 1	71	258
Perrie	San Francisco San Francisco 10	357 67	
Q	San Joaquin Elkhorn	64	994
Richd	Sonoma Petaluma	69	543
Richd	Sonoma Petaluma	69	544
Robt	Santa Cruz Santa Cruz	66	627
S	Nevada Grass Valley	61	193
S D	Shasta Millvill	66	748
S R	Sutter Yuba	70	762
Sarah J	Solano Suisan	69	223
Stephen	Santa Clara Almaden	65	268
Teodoro	Los Angeles Los Angeles	59	403
Thomas	El Dorado Mud Springs	58	994
Thomas	Humbolt Mattole	59	126
V D	Sonoma Vallejo	69	620
W	Yolo Cottonwoood	72	655
Wesley	Solano Suisan	69	215
Wm	San Francisco San Francisco 4	681	157
Wm	San Francisco San Francisco 10	211 67	
Wm	Sonoma Salt Point	69	692
LAMBERTAN			
C E	Sierra St Louis	66	806
LAMBERTON			
A	Shasta Shasta	66	759
Thos	Placer Dutch Fl	62	717
LAMBEST			
J W*	Butte Bidwell	56	722
S S	Sacramento Granite	63	244
LAMBET			
G	Nevada Grass Valley	61	166
LAMBETE			
Robt*	Santa Cruz Santa Cruz	66	625
LAMBETH			
A	Nevada Eureka	61	392
E P	Sonoma Santa Rosa	69	388
LAMBIE			
Alexander	Siskiyou Callahan	69	5

Name	County Locale	M653 Roll	Page
LAMBING			
F*	Shasta Millvill	66	754
LAMBIT			
A	Nevada Grass Valley	61	166
LAMBKIN			
Saml	San Francisco San Francisco 2	67	793
LAMBLACK			
Christn	San Francisco San Francisco 9	681	065
LAMBLEY			
Edward	Los Angeles Los Angeles	59	364
Mathew	Contra Costa Twp 3	57	598
LAMBO			
---	Fresno Twp 3	59	99
LAMBOCHTA			
Dominick*	Calaveras Twp 6	57	163
LAMBOCLITA			
Dominick*	Calaveras Twp 6	57	163
LAMBOHN			
George M*	Yuba Marysville	72	904
LAMBORN			
Stephen M	San Francisco 10	268 67	
LAMBORT			
V D	Sonoma Vallejo	69	620
LAMBOURNE			
Frederick	Los Angeles Elmonte	59	252
LAMBS			
Jonathan	Sonoma Petaluma	69	554
Thomas	Alameda Oakland	55	20
William*	Napa Clear Lake	61	140
LAMBURGH			
N P	Nevada Little Y	61	535
LAMBURN			
L*	Sutter Butte	70	786
LAMBURT			
Amos	Sierra Twp 5	66	930
J B	Nevada Eureka	61	366
S B	Nevada Eureka	61	366
LAMBURTH			
W F	Sierra Twp 7	66	883
LAMBUY			
Julia	San Luis Obispo San Luis Obispo	65	16
LAMBY			
John	San Francisco San Francisco 2	67	740
John*	San Francisco San Francisco 2	67	669
LAMCHAMP			
Henry	Tuolumne Twp 3	71	424
LAMCROUX			
Francis	Nevada Bloomfield	61	521
LAMDEN			
J F	Napa Napa	61	100
LAMDER			
H*	Shasta Shasta	66	734
LAMDRIA			
F*	Shasta Shasta	66	677
LAME			
---	Tuolumne Chinese	71	526
Bartolo*	Monterey San Juan	60	981
Maria	San Francisco San Francisco 7	681	400
Michael	Amador Twp 1	55	496
William K	San Joaquin Stockton	641	085
LAMED			
L	Tuolumne Big Oak	71	153
LAMEISTER			
Antene	Nevada Bloomfield	61	513
Antone	Nevada Bloomfield	61	513
LAMEKA			
---	Fresno Twp 2	59	115
LAMEM			
---*	Mariposa Twp 3	60	614
LAMEN			
John*	Mariposa Twp 3	60	604
LAMENT			
---	Sacramento Granite	63	249
Hellie N*	Alameda Brooklyn	55	85
Hettie N*	Alameda Brooklyn	55	85
Nellie N	Alameda Brooklyn	55	85
LAMENTO			
---	Butte Chico	56	566
Roface	Calaveras Twp 5	57	211
Rofue	Calaveras Twp 5	57	210
LAMER			
Jacob*	San Francisco San Francisco 1	68	924
John H	Placer Secret R	62	611
John*	Mariposa Twp 3	60	604
L B	Marin Point Re	60	730
S B*	Marin Point Re	60	730
LAMERAUX			
Francis	Nevada Bloomfield	61	521
LAMERCANX			
Geo	Sonoma Petaluma	69	590
LAMERMAN			
Henderick	Yuba Suida	72	994
Hendrick	Yuba Linda	72	994
LAMERS			
John	Solano Benecia	69	315

Name	County Locale	M653 Roll Page
LAMERTINE		
C	Nevada Nevada	61 270
LAMESTER		
William	Monterey San Juan	60 988
LAMETT		
Chas	Calaveras Twp 9	57 363
LAMEY		
Jno M*	Sacramento Ward 4	63 506
LAMG		
---*	Calaveras Twp 8	57 82
LAMGAN		
Edward	Humbolt Bucksport	59 159
LAMGARD		
J*	Sacramento Ward 1	63 17
LAMHART		
Conrad*	Napa Yount	61 30
LAMHIRT		
H W	Tuolumne Twp 2	71 309
LAMICE		
P	Yolo Cache Crk	72 624
LAMIER		
Paul	Calaveras Twp 9	57 347
LAMIN		
Martha A	Nevada Bridgeport	61 486
LAMINE		
A O	Solano Suisan	69 237
LAMING		
D F	Mendocino Big Rvr	60 846
LAMIR		
S B*	Marin Point Re	60 730
LAMIRE		
C M	El Dorado Placerville	58 932
Ulysses	San Francisco San Francisco 9	681052
LAMIS		
Filenda	Yolo Cache Crk	72 641
LAMIUT		
---	Sacramento Granite	63 249
LAMIY		
G*	Nevada Grass Valley	61 143
LAMKIN		
Chas H	Sonoma Healdsbu	69 475
LAMLING		
John*	Calaveras Twp 9	57 356
LAMLY		
Jonas	Tuolumne Twp 5	71 502
LAMM		
James	Tuolumne Twp 1	71 218
LAMMAN		
J M	Nevada Nevada	61 258
W J	Shasta Shasta	66 678
LAMMARD		
C	Butte Kimshaw	56 572
LAMMARS		
M	San Francisco San Francisco 1	68 830
LAMME		
L L*	Solano Vacaville	69 330
M J	Solano Vacaville	69 339
N	Solano Vacaville	69 321
LAMMEL		
M J	Yolo Putah	72 545
LAMMON		
H	Sonoma Petaluma	69 574
Martin	Yolo Slate Ra	72 716
Martin	Yuba Slate Ro	72 716
P J	Nevada Eureka	61 358
LAMMOND		
C	Butte Kimshaw	56 572
LAMMORREE		
C A*	Yuba Rose Par	72 796
LAMMURREE		
C A*	Yuba Rose Par	72 796
LAMNA		
Peter*	Yolo Cottonwood	72 657
LAMNARREE		
C A*	Yuba Rose Bar	72 796
LAMOLL		
B	Nevada Eureka	61 365
LAMOLT		
G H*	San Francisco San Francisco 5	67 543
LAMON		
---	Mendocino Twp 1	60 888
A	Yolo Cache	72 621
Martha A	Nevada Bridgeport	61 486
Pat*	Amador Twp 2	55 265
R E*	Sierra Downieville	66 978
LAMONA		
John	Siskiyou Shasta Rvr	69 116
LAMONANX		
Geo	Sonoma Petaluma	69 546
LAMOND		
---	Fresno Twp 2	59 66
LAMONE		
---*	Tulara Visalia	71 36
A O*	Solano Suisan	69 237
LAMONEY		
Seth	Placer Michigan	62 858

Name	County Locale	M653 Roll Page
LAMONG		
---	Yuba Long Bar	72 756
LAMONGER		
Francis	Plumas Quincy	62 967
LAMONIE		
Baptiste	San Francisco San Francisco 2	67 793
LAMONNS		
William	Marin Cortemad	60 782
LAMONSH		
M	Butte Bidwell	56 718
LAMONSHS		
M	Butte Bidwell	56 718
LAMONT		
Alexander	Solano Green Valley	69 242
Joel H*	Calaveras Twp 6	57 141
Lacius	Calaveras Twp 9	57 361
Louis	Calaveras Twp 9	57 361
LAMONTAIN		
Rosa	Santa Clara San Jose	65 287
LAMOR		
Jose	Tehama Red Bluff	70 916
LAMOREE		
J P	Yuba Rose Par	72 796
LAMOREL		
J P*	Yuba Rose Bar	72 796
LAMORIE		
A O*	Solano Suisan	69 237
LAMORY		
E	Santa Clara Santa Clara	65 469
LAMOSA		
---	Fresno Twp 2	59 90
LAMOTH		
Paul	San Francisco San Francisco 3	67 50
LAMOTT		
Alexis	Yolo Slate Ra	72 710
Alexis	Yuba Slate Ro	72 710
Chas	Calaveras Twp 9	57 363
G H*	San Francisco San Francisco 5	67 543
H G	Sonoma Armally	69 488
Manuel	Calaveras Twp 9	57 347
V	Nevada Nevada	61 291
Wm	Santa Clara Redwood	65 451
LAMOTTE		
Chas*	Butte Kimshaw	56 590
LAMOUCHE		
Meru	Santa Clara Almaden	65 270
LAMOUNE		
Louis*	Los Angeles Los Angeles	59 380
LAMOUNT		
William*	Marin Cortemad	60 782
LAMOURIE		
Louis	Los Angeles Los Angeles	59 380
LAMOURIR		
Louis*	Los Angeles Los Angeles	59 380
LAMOYNE		
John	Mariposa Twp 3	60 553
LAMP		
Anse	Contra Costa Twp 2	57 552
Gardner C	Butte Ophir	56 771
Oliver	Butte Ophir	56 771
Saml	Butte Eureka	56 651
LAMPDEN		
William	San Francisco San Francisco 7	681373
LAMPE		
C A	San Francisco San Francisco 6	67 469
E C	Butte Oregon	56 625
Ed	Sacramento Ward 1	63 57
George*	Solano Fremont	69 382
Henry	Calaveras Twp 6	57 133
LAMPEE		
Robert	Santa Cruz Santa Cruz	66 607
Thomas M	Santa Cruz Santa Cruz	66 607
LAMPERT		
John*	Sierra Poverty	66 799
Matilda	San Francisco San Francisco 2	67 639
LAMPERY		
Peter	Sierra Excelsior	661034
LAMPHER		
Aaron A*	Siskiyou Yreka	69 129
Charles A	San Francisco San Francisco 11	103
		67
Edson	Calaveras Twp 7	57 9
L	Butte Oregon	56 626
LAMPHERE		
Harry	Yuba Marysville	72 926
LAMPHERT		
Aaron A*	Siskiyou Yreka	69 129
LAMPHIER		
Enon	Sonoma Bodega	69 536
G	Siskiyou Scott Ri	69 72
H C	Tuolumne Twp 1	71 265
Jos*	Sacramento Ward 4	63 611
LAMPHIES		
H C	Tuolumne Twp 1	71 265
Jos*	Sacramento Ward 4	63 611
LAMPHIRE		
Harry*	Yuba Marysville	72 926

Name	County Locale	M653 Roll Page
LAMPHIRE		
R	San Francisco San Francisco 5	67 548
LAMPHY		
Philip	Mendocino Little L	60 832
LAMPINE		
W	El Dorado Mud Springs	581000
LAMPIRAN		
Henry*	San Francisco San Francisco 7	681401
LAMPKIN		
N J	Sierra Downieville	661021
Richard H	Sierra Scales D	66 800
W J	Sierra Downieville	661021
LAMPLE		
David	Yuba Slate Ro	72 688
Isreal*	Butte Oregon	56 611
Isreeal*	Butte Oregon	56 611
LAMPLES		
Asa	Los Angeles Elmonte	59 246
LAMPLEY		
Philip	Mendocino Little L	60 832
LAMPLUER		
Jos*	Sacramento Ward 4	63 611
LAMPLUES		
Jos*	Sacramento Ward 4	63 611
LAMPMAN		
H	San Francisco San Francisco 9	681070
John	Yuba Slate Ro	72 693
Randall	Siskiyou Shasta Rvr	69 114
W	Sutter Bear Rvr	70 825
William	San Mateo Twp 2	65 113
LAMPMANN		
Joseph	San Francisco San Francisco 8	681294
LAMPMAUN		
Joseph*	San Francisco San Francisco 8	681294
LAMPMON		
John	Yolo Slate Ra	72 693
LAMPOSON		
Royal M	Tuolumne Montezuma	71 511
LAMPREY		
Henry	San Francisco San Francisco 9	681048
John	San Joaquin Oneal	64 937
LAMPRICHT		
A	Stanislaus Empire	70 728
LAMPSON		
Alex	Butte Chico	56 534
George*	Calaveras Twp 9	57 364
Gorge	Calaveras Twp 9	57 364
R A*	Butte Oregon	56 629
S	Santa Cruz Shasta	66 653
LAMPTON		
Eugene	El Dorado Union	581091
LAMPTUR		
Aaron A	Siskiyou Yreka	69 129
LAMPURAN		
Charles*	Placer Michigan	62 845
LAMRECAUX		
---	Sierra Twp 7	66 891
LAMREN		
Garner	Mariposa Twp 1	60 640
LAMRINGER		
Jno*	Butte Chico	56 563
LAMRY		
G	Nevada Grass Valley	61 143
LAMS		
Patrick	Alameda Oakland	55 40
LAMSON		
David	Calaveras Twp 7	57 25
George F	Los Angeles Los Angeles	59 348
Horatio	Plumas Quincy	62 974
John	Monterey San Juan	60 988
Samuel	Los Angeles Los Angeles	59 367
William H	Los Angeles San Pedro	59 483
Wm	Calaveras Twp 9	57 380
LAMTY		
John*	San Francisco San Francisco 2	67 669
LAMU		
Louis*	Trinity W Weaver	701054
LAMURA		
---	Fresno Twp 1	59 51
LAMURE		
L L*	Solano Vacaville	69 330
LAMUS		
J	Nevada Eureka	61 372
LAMY		
T*	Nevada Grass Valley	61 165
LAN SA		
---*	Calaveras Twp 8	57 61
LAN		
---	Amador Twp 5	55 353
---	Butte Oregon	56 641
---	Calaveras Twp 4	57 332
---	Calaveras Twp 8	57 91
---	Del Norte Crescent	58 631
---	El Dorado White Oaks	581012
---	El Dorado White Oaks	581033
---	El Dorado Salmon Falls	581043

Name	County Locale	M653 Roll/Page
LAN		
---	El Dorado Salmon Falls	581052
---	El Dorado Salmon Falls	581067
---	El Dorado Coloma	581102
---	El Dorado Coloma	581116
---	El Dorado Coloma	581119
---	El Dorado Diamond	58 798
---	El Dorado Diamond	58 805
---	El Dorado Placerville	58 829
---	El Dorado Placerville	58 832
---	El Dorado Placerville	58 842
---	El Dorado Placerville	58 843
---	El Dorado Placerville	58 899
---	El Dorado Placerville	58 933
---	El Dorado Eldorado	58 942
---	El Dorado Mud Springs	58 955
---	El Dorado Mud Springs	58 973
---	El Dorado Mud Springs	58 981
---	El Dorado Mud Springs	58 991
---	El Dorado Mud Springs	58 998
---	Fresno Twp 1	59 25
---	Mariposa Twp 3	60 553
---	Mariposa Twp 3	60 564
---	Mariposa Twp 3	60 569
---	Mariposa Twp 3	60 575
---	Mariposa Twp 3	60 576
---	Mariposa Twp 3	60 580
---	Mariposa Twp 3	60 581
---	Mariposa Twp 3	60 582
---	Mariposa Twp 3	60 608
---	Mariposa Twp 3	60 619
---	Mariposa Coulterville	60 688
---	Nevada Grass Valley	61 227
---	Placer Secret R	62 621
---	San Francisco San Francisco 4	681174
---	San Francisco San Francisco 4	681207
---	Shasta Shasta	66 677
---	Shasta Horsetown	66 709
---	Sierra St Louis	66 813
---	Sierra Twp 7	66 875
---	Sierra Cox'S Bar	66 951
---	Sierra Downieville	66 995
---	Stanislaus Branch	70 714
---	Stanislaus Emory	70 747
---	Stanislaus Emory	70 748
---	Stanislaus Emory	70 752
---	Trinity Lewiston	70 956
---	Tuolumne Twp 3	71 460
---	Tuolumne Twp 6	71 535
---	Yuba Rose Bar	72 800
---*	Amador Twp 4	55 332
---*	Mariposa Twp 3	60 576
---*	Mariposa Twp 3	60 580
---*	Mariposa Twp 3	60 581
---*	Mariposa Twp 3	60 582
---*	Sacramento Cosumnes	63 390
---*	Shasta Shasta	66 671
---*	Tuolumne Jacksonville	71 167
---*	Tuolumne Big Oak	71 178
---*	Tuolumne Big Oak	71 181
Adolph*	San Francisco San Francisco 3	67 274
Ah	Tuolumne Twp 4	71 181
An	Del Norte Crescent	58 631
At	Mariposa Twp 3	60 619
At Pon	San Francisco San Francisco 4	681186
Choy	El Dorado Eldorado	58 942
Chun	Tehama Red Bluff	70 932
Dee	El Dorado Big Bar	58 738
E	Mariposa Twp 3	60 569
Fear	Mariposa Twp 3	60 620
Foo	Placer Illinois	62 752
G*	Nevada Washington	61 335
Hay	El Dorado Eldorado	58 942
Hee	San Francisco San Francisco 5	671206
Ho	San Francisco San Francisco 4	681186
Hoy	San Francisco San Francisco 4	681186
Hoy	San Francisco San Francisco 5	671206
Hu	San Francisco San Francisco 5	671206
Kela*	San Francisco San Francisco 4	681187
Ko	San Francisco San Francisco 4	681181
Lee	San Francisco San Francisco 4	681207
Leon*	Calaveras Twp 9	57 361
Lu	San Francisco San Francisco 4	681207
M B*	Shasta Cottonwoood	66 737
Moo	San Francisco San Francisco 4	681210
Pah	Stanislaus Emory	70 748
See	Placer Illinois	62 745
Sgn*	El Dorado Georgetown	58 703
Shee	San Francisco San Francisco 4	681181
Shu	San Francisco San Francisco 4	681181
Syn	El Dorado Georgetown	58 703
Tou	San Francisco San Francisco 4	681190
LANA		
---	Tulara Keyesville	71 65
J M*	San Mateo Twp 3	65 79
P P*	Calaveras Twp 9	57 348
LANACIE		
Lucian	El Dorado Coloma	581104
LANAGAN		
Daniel	Placer Rattle Snake	62 625
Rebecca	Sonoma Santa Rosa	69 395
LANAGAR		
J E	Siskiyou Scott Ri	69 70
LANAGE		
Chas	Napa Napa	61 70
LANAGHAN		
Jas	San Francisco San Francisco 9	681069
Jno	San Francisco San Francisco 9	681069
LANAGIN		
Wm	Butte Ophir	56 751
LANAM		
Jackson	Yuba Marysville	72 970
LANAN		
Jackson	Yuba Marysville	72 970
John	Sierra Twp 7	66 908
LANANE		
Thos	Butte Cascade	56 689
LANARA		
John	Calaveras Twp 9	57 362
LANARD		
F E	Santa Clara Santa Clara	65 489
LANARILLE		
M*	Nevada Grass Valley	61 154
LANAS		
Andres	Monterey Alisal	601035
Antonio	Monterey San Juan	60 994
Dana*	Monterey San Juan	601000
Dema*	Monterey San Juan	601000
Richd	San Francisco San Francisco 9	681069
LANATA		
Joseph*	Yuba Marysville	72 919
LANATTA		
B	Klamath S Fork	59 203
Peter	Sierra Downieville	66 968
LANB		
Henry	Butte Hamilton	56 519
Henry R	Butte Hamilton	56 519
LANBERT		
Eugene	San Bernardino S Buenav	64 221
LANBERTON		
C E	Sierra St Louis	66 806
LANBHEIM		
Samson	Los Angeles Los Angeles	59 339
LANBI		
Charles	Los Angeles San Gabriel	59 422
LANBOR		
Byrchard	Tulara Twp 1	71 89
Edward*	Yuba Rose Bar	72 793
LANBORN		
L D	Solano Benecia	69 282
LANBURN		
William	Siskiyou Scott Va	69 56
LANBURY		
J A W	El Dorado Placerville	58 853
LANCASTE		
Freak	San Francisco San Francisco 1	68 905
LANCASTER		
Americas V*	Sierra Pine Grove	66 829
Americus V	Sierra Pine Grove	66 829
Chas	San Francisco San Francisco 2	67 737
Chas	Sonoma Salt Point	69 693
Frangworth	Sierra Pine Grove	66 830
Franzworth*	Sierra Pine Grove	66 830
G P	Placer Forest H	62 766
Geo E	Butte Kimshaw	56 576
H	Butte Eureka	56 654
H B	Amador Twp 2	55 324
I C	Amador Twp 2	55 307
J	Sutter Butte	70 799
J A	Nevada Nevada	61 326
John	Sonoma Salt Point	69 694
Joseph	Nevada Bloomfield	61 515
M	San Francisco San Francisco 5	67 523
M	Sonoma Petaluma	69 576
Preston	Tuolumne Twp 2	71 392
R	San Francisco San Francisco 4	681230
Richard	Shasta Shasta	66 732
Starlin	Calaveras Twp 5	57 139
Strlin	Calaveras Twp 6	57 139
T C	Amador Twp 2	55 307
W	Sonoma Petaluma	69 589
W B	Placer Auburn	62 566
W W	Tuolumne Sonora	71 482
Wm	San Francisco San Francisco 10	166 67
Wm	Tuolumne Twp 1	71 482
LANCE		
Andrew	Butte Kimshaw	56 581
G W	Trinity Weaverville	701078
Geo	El Dorado Casumnes	581166
Geo	Tuolumne Columbia	71 328
H	Nevada Nevada	61 265
Jacob	Del Norte Crescent	58 649
Jonah S	Yuba Long Bar	72 754
L	San Mateo Twp 2	65 120
Ora	Del Norte Crescent	58 649
W*	San Francisco San Francisco 5	67 521
Wm*	Placer Secret R	62 617
LANCEFORD		
Wm	San Bernardino San Salvador	64 647
Wm	San Bernardino San Salvador	64 648
LANCELOT		
Joseph*	Siskiyou Yreka	69 150
LANCEN		
Thomas*	Siskiyou Scott Va	69 41
LANCENTS		
Jane	Calaveras Twp 5	57 206
LANCER		
Jean	San Francisco San Francisco 1	68 879
LANCESTRO		
---	Tulara Twp 3	71 68
---	Tulara Twp 3	71 71
LANCEY		
James	Sierra Downieville	661007
Sarah	San Francisco San Francisco 11	112 67
Thomas	Placer Forest H	62 771
Thos C	San Francisco San Francisco 2	67 587
LANCH		
J	Nevada Grass Valley	61 150
J	Sutter Yuba	70 760
LANCHALY		
John	Placer Virginia	62 662
LANCHAN		
Jeremiah	Sonoma Sonoma	69 659
LANCHART		
Conrad*	Napa Yount	61 30
LANCHES		
Hosa	Los Angeles Azuza	59 279
LANCHEY		
Lesi	San Luis Obispo San Luis Obispo	65 6
LANCHEZ		
Juan M	Los Angeles Elmonte	59 259
LANCISCO		
---	Sacramento Cosumnes	63 408
---	Sacramento Franklin	63 333
LANCK		
J B*	Siskiyou Scott Va	69 37
LANCOE		
Perry	Yuba Marysville	72 942
LANCRAFT		
William*	Nevada Red Dog	61 543
LANCTOL		
B	San Francisco San Francisco 6	67 437
LANCY		
John*	Nevada Eureka	61 389
Margaret	Yuba Marysville	72 897
LANCYELE		
W J	Calaveras Twp 9	57 374
LAND		
---	El Dorado Mountain	581187
---	El Dorado Mud Springs	58 966
---	Mariposa Twp 1	60 657
---	San Joaquin Stockton	641087
A	Sierra Twp 5	66 928
Asial D	Sierra Pine Grove	66 830
C	El Dorado Placerville	58 851
C B	San Francisco San Francisco 4	681132
I	Amador Twp 7	55 420
J E	Napa Napa	61 98
John	Nevada Little Y	61 531
Jose E	San Francisco San Francisco 2	67 670
Lance	Mariposa Twp 3	60 557
P P	Calaveras Twp 9	57 348
Smith	Butte Kimshaw	56 581
Tanse	Mariposa Twp 3	60 557
William C	San Joaquin Tulare	64 870
LANDA		
John	San Francisco San Francisco 3	67 74
LANDABA		
Phillip*	Calaveras Twp 9	57 354
LANDAKER		
Lazare	San Francisco San Francisco 8	681287
LANDAM		
Henry*	Placer Secret R	62 613
LANDAMAR		
John	Nevada Little Y	61 536
LANDAN		
Henry*	Placer Secret R	62 613
LANDAU		
Henry*	Placer Secret R	62 613
LANDCRAFT		
W H	Butte Kimshaw	56 576
LANDE		
Stephen	San Francisco San Francisco 3	67 60

Name	County Locale	M653 Roll/Page
LANDE		
Stephen D	San Francisco 3	67 60
	San Francisco	
LANDECKEN		
Henry	Sierra Twp 5	66 928
LANDEEKER		
L	El Dorado Placerville	58 819
LANDEN		
L C	El Dorado Mud Springs	58 999
William B	Tuolumne Twp 6	71 539
LANDER		
A	Mariposa Twp 1	60 642
Aaron	San Francisco San Francisco 7	681366
B D	Siskiyou Scott Va	69 58
Cyrus	Tuolumne Columbia	71 316
Edward	San Francisco San Francisco 7	681441
Eli	Tuolumne Twp 1	71 264
Frank*	Santa Cruz Pescadero	66 645
Geo	El Dorado Diamond	58 771
H	El Dorado Diamond	58 807
Henry	Sierra Downieville	661019
J P	El Dorado Placerville	58 932
James	Alameda Oakland	55 21
James	Santa Cruz Pescadero	66 645
James H	Los Angeles Los Angeles	59 334
John*	Mariposa Coulterville	60 677
John*	San Francisco San Francisco 3	67 74
M B	Calaveras Twp 9	57 370
O W	Santa Clara San Jose	65 314
P C	San Francisco San Francisco 6	67 428
P P	El Dorado Big Bar	58 738
W	Calaveras Twp 9	57 401
W E*	Shasta Millvill	66 756
Waren	Trinity Lewiston	70 957
Warren	Trinity Lewiston	70 957
LANDEREWAE		
Jacob N*	Yuba Marysville	72 943
LANDERGEN		
Bridget*	Napa Napa	61 104
LANDERJEN		
Bridget*	Napa Napa	61 104
LANDERMAN		
Jacob N	Yuba Marysville	72 943
LANDERS		
Charles	Placer Michigan	62 830
E	Calaveras Twp 9	57 400
F E L	Sierra Twp 7	66 882
J	Butte Bidwell	56 716
Jas	Sacramento Granite	63 252
Jason*	Sierra Poker Flats	66 842
Jerry	San Francisco San Francisco 1	68 904
Joseph	Mariposa Twp 3	60 571
Joshua	San Francisco San Francisco 7	681364
L B	Tuolumne Twp 1	71 187
Larry	Sacramento Natonia	63 281
Martha	San Francisco San Francisco 2	67 687
Simon	San Mateo Twp 3	65 96
William	Tulara Visalia	71 9
Willshire	Sierra Gibsonville	66 857
Wm	Humbolt Mattole	59 125
LANDERSDOFF		
William	Sierra St Louis	66 809
LANDERZ		
F	Tuolumne Sonora	71 209
LANDES		
J	San Francisco San Francisco 6	67 454
Mrs	Sierra Twp 7	66 880
Ners*	Sierra Twp 7	66 880
W H*	Butte Chico	56 541
LANDESBERGER		
J	San Francisco San Francisco 6	67 453
LANDESON		
Jose D	San Francisco San Francisco 3	67 63
LANDEY		
Geo	El Dorado Mud Springs	58 965
L B	Tuolumne Sonora	71 187
LANDEZ		
W H	Butte Chico	56 541
LANDFORD		
H H*	Tuolumne Sonora	71 222
John	El Dorado White Oaks	581018
LANDGRIST		
E*	Butte Ophir	56 765
LANDGROF		
Frederick	San Diego Colorado	64 808
LANDICKEN		
Henry	Sierra Twp 5	66 928
LANDIGAN		
J	Napa Napa	61 75
James	Tuolumne Springfield	71 370
LANDIN		
Mary	Sacramento Ward 1	63 147
LANDINI		
Antonio	San Bernardino Santa Barbara	64 150
LANDIS		
Benjamin	Yuba Suida	72 983

Name	County Locale	M653 Roll/Page
LANDIS		
David	Sonoma Bodega	69 537
Samuel	Yuba Suida	72 982
Samuel	Yuba Linda Twp	72 984
LANDISBERGER		
J	San Francisco San Francisco 6	67 453
LANDISON		
Jose D	San Francisco San Francisco 3	67 63
LANDISTER		
Thomas J	San Luis Obispo	65 40
	San Luis Obispo	
LANDLESS		
T	El Dorado Kelsey	581153
LANDMAN		
John	Siskiyou Yreka	69 158
John	Siskiyou Yreka	69 165
LANDMM		
Reuben*	Tulara Visalia	71 84
LANDNUM		
Joseph*	Stanislaus Buena Village	70 724
LANDOIS		
F	San Francisco San Francisco 2	67 795
LANDOLT		
Francis	Yuba Marysville	72 875
LANDON		
C G	Butte Ophir	56 763
Edward	Santa Clara Gilroy	65 232
G A*	Mariposa Twp 1	60 666
George	Sonoma Bodega	69 537
James H*	Sierra Pine Grove	66 834
L*	Napa Hot Springs	61 11
Margaret	Contra Costa Twp 3	57 617
William	El Dorado Salmon Hills	581055
LANDOTT		
Francis*	Yuba Marysville	72 875
LANDRAIN		
James	Santa Clara San Jose	65 348
LANDRAS		
Carl*	San Francisco San Francisco 9	681034
Petre	Alameda Oakland	55 7
LANDREAN		
M	Tuolumne Big Oak	71 135
LANDRIGAN		
Jno	Fresno Twp 1	59 82
LANDRIOAN		
---	Tulara Twp 2	71 27
LANDRO		
LANDRUM		
J S	Shasta Shasta	66 669
J T	Shasta Shasta	66 669
LANDRY		
Norbert	San Francisco San Francisco 3	67 25
LANDRYNS		
J*	San Francisco San Francisco 9	681057
LANDS		
Patrick F*	Sacramento Ward 1	63 96
William	Marin Point Re	60 732
LANDSBERGER		
H	San Francisco San Francisco 3	67 72
T	San Francisco San Francisco 3	67 82
LANDSBURGER		
H	San Francisco San Francisco 4	681226
L	El Dorado Placerville	58 864
LANDSIRE		
Mary M	San Francisco San Francisco 2	67 636
LANDSWAY		
H*	Nevada Eureka	61 392
LANDSWING		
H	Nevada Eureka	61 392
LANDSWUIZ		
H*	Nevada Eureka	61 392
LANDT		
Benjamin	Yuba Marysville	72 963
Henry*	Plumas Quincy	62 936
LANDUM		
James*	Stanislaus Emory	70 746
LANDUNN		
Reuben*	Tulara Visalia	71 84
LANDUS		
Larry	Sacramento Natonia	63 281
LANDWICH		
Salvadore	Tuolumne Twp 2	71 282
LANDY		
Jno	San Francisco San Francisco 9	681070
Michael*	Sierra Twp 7	66 866
LANDYARF		
Jacob*	San Francisco San Francisco 7	681429
LANDYCORK		
John	Napa Yount	61 55
LANE		
---	Calaveras Twp 4	57 299
---	El Dorado Salmon Falls	581043
---	El Dorado Salmon Falls	581064
---	El Dorado Salmon Falls	581067
---	El Dorado Union	581094
---	El Dorado Coloma	581105

Name	County Locale	M653 Roll/Page
LANE		
---	El Dorado Coloma	581109
---	El Dorado Coloma	581115
---	El Dorado Kelsey	581130
---	El Dorado Kelsey	581143
---	El Dorado Mountain	581188
---	El Dorado Greenwood	58 727
---	Fresno Twp 1	59 25
---	Mariposa Twp 3	60 551
---	Mariposa Twp 3	60 553
---	Mariposa Twp 3	60 612
---	San Francisco San Francisco 7	681342
---	Sierra St Louis	66 813
---*	Tuolumne Big Oak	71 182
A	San Francisco San Francisco 2	67 726
A M	El Dorado Georgetown	58 705
Ah	Tuolumne Twp 4	71 182
Allen G	San Bernardino S Timate	64 689
Amos	Calaveras Twp 6	57 172
Andrew	San Francisco San Francisco 10	202 67
Ann	Alameda Oakland	55 73
Anna	Amador Twp 6	55 432
Anthony W	Calaveras Twp 6	57 152
Arial D	Sierra Pine Grove	66 830
Benjamin	Yuba Bear Rvr	721004
Benjn F	Del Norte Crescent	58 648
C H	El Dorado Big Bar	58 739
C O	Sacramento Ward 1	63 9
Charles	Del Norte Ferry P O	58 666
Charles	Placer Iona Hills	62 891
Charles	San Francisco San Francisco 11	152 67
Charley*	Amador Twp 2	55 270
Chas	Butte Cascade	56 692
Chas	Butte Bidwell	56 732
Chas	San Francisco San Francisco 9	681040
Cornelius	San Francisco San Francisco 9	681032
Daniel	Tulara Keeneysburg	71 47
Danl S*	Calaveras Twp 10	57 288
David*	Solano Vacaville	69 366
E	Sierra La Porte	66 777
E C	Calaveras Twp 9	57 374
E C	Yolo Cottonwoood	72 661
E W	Stanislaus Emory	70 751
Edward	Yuba Marysville	72 887
Eliha P	San Bernardino San Bernadino	64 672
Eliza	Nevada Bridgeport	61 450
Ellen	Amador Twp 2	55 271
Ellen	San Francisco San Francisco 10	242 67
Emily	San Francisco San Francisco 8	681311
Fred	El Dorado Kelsey	581147
Frederick	Solano Suisan	69 239
George	Calaveras Twp 9	57 357
George	Tehama Antelope	70 894
H B	Siskiyou Scott Ri	69 75
Hannah	El Dorado Coloma	581071
He	Mariposa Twp 3	60 618
Henry	Siskiyou Yreka	69 150
Heven*	Sierra Chappare	661040
Isaac	Siskiyou Scott Va	69 43
J	Sutter Butte	70 788
J	Tehama Cottonwood	70 898
J	Tuolumne Springfield	71 371
J A	Alameda Brooklyn	55 101
J B	Nevada Bridgeport	61 488
J J	San Francisco San Francisco 9	681086
J M	Sonoma Bodega	69 540
J N	Alameda Brooklyn	55 101
J P	Shasta Shasta	66 678
J R	Butte Oregon	56 633
J S	Calaveras Twp 9	57 373
J W	Colusa Spring Valley	57 434
James	Alameda Brooklyn	55 106
James	Colusa Grand Island	57 471
James	San Francisco San Francisco 7	681431
Jas R*	Butte Kimshaw	56 583
Jas S	Napa Napa	61 92
Jeremiah	Del Norte Happy Ca	58 664
Jo J	Sonoma Santa Rosa	69 412
John	Napa Yount	61 31
John	Nevada Bridgeport	61 480
John	San Francisco San Francisco 1	68 830
John	Sierra La Porte	66 765
John	Sierra St Louis	66 813
John	Sierra St Louis	66 818
John	Solano Suisan	69 225
John	Solano Vallejo	69 255
John	Tehama Lassen	70 884
John	Tuolumne Sonora	71 236
John*	Napa Yount	61 31
John*	San Francisco San Francisco 9	681097
Jos R*	Butte Chico	56 561
Joseph	Santa Clara Redwood	65 458
Joseph	Santa Cruz Soguel	66 582

Name	County Locale	Roll	Page
LANE			
Josk*	Butte Chico	56	561
Jule	San Francisco San Francisco 8	68	1234
Julius	Nevada Bridgeport	61	475
Kwm	Nevada Eureka	61	360
Louis	Santa Clara San Jose	65	325
M	Placer Dutch Fl	62	731
M	San Francisco San Francisco 9	68	1060
M	San Francisco San Francisco 5	67	493
Martha O	Santa Clara Gilroy	65	246
Mary	Alameda Oakland	55	28
Matea	San Bernardino San Bernadino	64	672
Menry	Siskiyou Yreka	69	150
Michael	San Francisco San Francisco 2	67	598
Michael	San Francisco San Francisco 1	68	920
Mickerson	S Timate	64	690
	San Bernardino		
N C	San Francisco San Francisco 8	68	1265
Nathaniel	San Francisco San Francisco 7	68	1328
Nichols	San Bernardino San Bernadino	64	672
Patrick	San Francisco San Francisco 10		263
		67	
Perry	Amador Twp 6	55	448
Peten*	Calaveras Twp 9	57	371
Peter	San Francisco San Francisco 1	68	909
Petew*	Calaveras Twp 9	57	371
R B	San Joaquin Stockton	64	1202
R D	Yolo Slate Ra	72	699
R F*	Napa Yount	61	32
R S	Napa Yount	61	32
Richd	Sacramento Cosumnes	63	401
Robert	San Francisco San Francisco 9	68	1047
Robert L	San Francisco San Francisco 7	68	1335
S	Calaveras Twp 9	57	407
Saml	Santa Clara Gilroy	65	247
Saml B	San Bernardino S Timate	64	688
Samluel	Santa Cruz Santa Cruz	66	634
Samuel	Santa Cruz Santa Cruz	66	634
Sarah	Alameda Oakland	55	14
Sawrance	Alameda Brooklyn	55	101
Stephen	Trinity Douglas	70	979
T	Nevada Eureka	61	360
T G	Butte Oregon	56	613
T S	Tehama Red Bluff	70	912
T*	Nevada Eureka	61	360
Thomas	Sierra Twp 5	66	935
Thomas	Sierra Twp 5	66	939
Thos	Sacramento Ward 1	63	129
Thos A	San Francisco San Francisco 2	67	731
Thos H	Santa Clara Santa Clara	65	512
Thos P	Butte Hamilton	56	521
Thos*	Sacramento Brighton	63	191
Timothy	Monterey Monterey	60	964
Tom	Sacramento Ward 1	63	57
W	Sacramento Alabama	63	412
W H	Tehama Lassen	70	873
W W	Butte Kimshaw	56	600
William	Marin Point Re	60	731
William	Solano Suisan	69	204
William R	Mendocino Arrana	60	856
Wm	Nevada Eureka	61	360
Wm	Yolo No E Twp	72	678
Wm	Yuba North Ea	72	678
Wm	Yuba Rose Bar	72	801
Wm R	Sonoma Santa Rosa	69	413
Y*	Nevada Eureka	61	360
LANEDON			
Wm	Alameda Brooklyn	55	103
LANEGAN			
Patrick	Solano Vallejo	69	271
LANEHART			
Conrad*	Napa Yount	61	30
LANELER			
Frank*	Santa Cruz Pescadero	66	645
LANELING			
John*	Calaveras Twp 9	57	356
LANELL			
L	El Dorado Placerville	58	867
LANELOT			
Joseph*	Siskiyou Yreka	69	150
LANENFELDT			
Wm	Placer Rattle Snake	62	600
LANENSTENI			
Lewis*	San Francisco San Francisco 2	67	617
LANENSTINE			
Lewis	San Francisco San Francisco 2	67	617
LANEPE			
George*	Solano Fremont	69	382
LANER			
---	Mariposa Twp 3	60	569
Anthony*	San Francisco San Francisco 2	67	795
Chas*	El Dorado Georgetown	58	694
Chas*	Nevada Bloomfield	61	507
Conrad*	El Dorado Casumnes	58	1174
Geo S	Tuolumne Twp 2	71	328
LANERN			
Charles*	Placer Michigan	62	854

Name	County Locale	Roll	Page
LANERY			
---	El Dorado Mud Springs	58	985
Geo	San Francisco San Francisco 9	68	1068
LANES			
---	Mariposa Twp 3	60	569
Anthony	San Francisco San Francisco 2	67	795
Conrad	El Dorado Casumnes	58	1174
Desire	Mariposa Twp 1	60	668
Geo	El Dorado Salmon Hills	58	1052
John C	Mariposa Coulterville	60	700
Nicholasa	Los Angeles Los Angeles	59	385
LANESTON			
Alexr	Sonoma Petaluma	69	556
LANESUM			
James*	Stanislaus Emory	70	746
LANEVE			
Perry*	Yuba Marysville	72	942
LANEW			
J D*	Calaveras Twp 9	57	405
LANEY			
Ann	Nevada Bridgeport	61	457
Geo	Nevada Grass Valley	61	146
J S	Calaveras Twp 9	57	373
John	Nevada Bridgeport	61	389
R	Sacramento Ward 4	63	517
Richard E D	San Joaquin Castoria	64	878
LANFENBURY			
Louisa	Sonoma Petaluma	69	547
LANFISH			
Joseph	Sierra Excelsior	66	1034
LANFKETTER			
J A*	Sacramento Ward 4	63	589
LANFKETTES			
J A*	Sacramento Ward 4	63	589
LANFORD			
A	Tehama Red Bluff	70	903
Berkley*	San Joaquin O'Neal	64	1001
Charles*	Yuba Marysville	72	910
LANFRANCO			
John T	Los Angeles Los Angeles	59	343
LANFRIED			
L W	El Dorado Placerville	58	867
LANFRUG			
Peter	Alameda Oakland	55	7
LANG			
---	Amador Twp 1	55	496
---	Calaveras Twp 5	57	176
---	Calaveras Twp 7	57	41
---	Calaveras Twp 8	57	59
---	Calaveras Twp 8	57	63
---	Calaveras Twp 8	57	68
---	Calaveras Twp 8	57	71
---	Calaveras Twp 8	57	74
---	Calaveras Twp 8	57	76
---	Calaveras Twp 8	57	91
---	El Dorado Salmon Falls	58	1043
---	El Dorado Salmon Falls	58	1046
---	El Dorado Salmon Falls	58	1048
---	El Dorado Salmon Falls	58	1051
---	El Dorado Salmon Falls	58	1053
---	El Dorado Coloma	58	1085
---	El Dorado Cold Spring	58	1101
---	El Dorado Coloma	58	1108
---	El Dorado Coloma	58	1109
---	El Dorado Coloma	58	1110
---	El Dorado Coloma	58	1116
---	El Dorado Casumnes	58	1161
---	El Dorado Casumnes	58	1174
---	El Dorado Casumnes	58	1176
---	El Dorado Mountain	58	1178
---	El Dorado Mountain	58	1187
---	El Dorado Mountain	58	1188
---	El Dorado Georgetown	58	700
---	El Dorado Diamond	58	794
---	El Dorado Diamond	58	803
---	El Dorado Placerville	58	925
---	El Dorado Mud Springs	58	952
---	El Dorado Mud Springs	58	962
---	El Dorado Mud Springs	58	973
---	El Dorado Mud Springs	58	981
---	Mariposa Twp 3	60	544
---	Mariposa Twp 3	60	546
---	Mariposa Twp 3	60	550
---	Mariposa Twp 3	60	551
---	Mariposa Twp 3	60	552
---	Mariposa Twp 3	60	553
---	Mariposa Twp 3	60	563
---	Mariposa Twp 3	60	564
---	Mariposa Twp 3	60	572
---	Mariposa Twp 3	60	578
---	Mariposa Twp 3	60	580
---	Mariposa Twp 1	60	641
---	Mariposa Twp 1	60	659
---	Mariposa Twp 1	60	661
---	Mariposa Coulterville	60	681
---	Mariposa Coulterville	60	687

Name	County Locale	Roll	Page
LANG			
---	Mariposa Coulterville	60	692
---	Nevada Grass Valley	61	229
---	Nevada Grass Valley	61	230
---	Nevada Grass Valley	61	231
---	Nevada Grass Valley	61	234
---	Nevada Eureka	61	385
---	Nevada Bridgeport	61	439
---	Placer Auburn	62	572
---	Placer Rattle Snake	62	629
---	Placer Virginia	62	679
---	Placer Virginia	62	681
---	Placer Virginia	62	687
---	Placer Dutch Fl	62	737
---	Plumas Quincy	62	946
---	Sacramento Granite	63	250
---	Sacramento Ward 1	63	54
---	Sacramento Ward 4	63	610
---	Sacramento Ward 1	63	66
---	Sacramento Ward 1	63	71
---	San Francisco San Francisco 9	68	1088
---	San Francisco San Francisco 4	68	1182
---	San Francisco San Francisco 4	68	1188
---	San Francisco San Francisco 11		145
		67	
---	San Francisco San Francisco 2	67	697
---	Shasta Shasta	66	669
---	Shasta Shasta	66	677
---	Sierra Downieville	66	1009
---	Sierra Downieville	66	1024
---	Sierra St Louis	66	806
---	Sierra Pine Grove	66	827
---	Sierra Twp 7	66	877
---	Sierra Downieville	66	985
---	Tuolumne Twp 3	71	433
---	Tuolumne Twp 3	71	440
---	Tuolumne Twp 1	71	478
---	Tuolumne Knights	71	530
---	Tuolumne Don Pedro	71	537
---	Yolo No E Twp	72	668
---	Yuba Long Bar	72	759
---	Yuba Long Bar	72	765
---	Yuba Parks Ba	72	779
---	Yuba Fosters	72	826
---	Yuba Fosters	72	842
---	Yuba Linda	72	993
---*	Alameda Oakland	55	63
---*	El Dorado Casumnes	58	1176
---*	El Dorado Georgetown	58	700
---*	El Dorado Georgetown	58	705
---*	Mariposa Twp 1	60	659
---*	Nevada Bridgeport	61	458
---*	Siskiyou Klamath	69	90
---*	Yuba Long Bar	72	759
---*	Yuba Long Bar	72	765
---*	Yuba Fosters	72	842
A	Sierra Twp 5	66	931
A M	Tuolumne Twp 1	71	257
Aaron	Butte Chico	56	567
Ah	Butte Eureka	56	649
Ah	Calaveras Twp 7	57	8
Ah	Tuolumne Twp 4	71	160
Ah	Yuba Suida	72	990
Ah	Yuba Suida	72	993
Albert	Santa Cruz Pescadero	66	649
C	El Dorado Casumnes	58	1161
Charles E	Yuba Marysville	72	967
Chas	Alameda Brooklyn	55	153
Chas E	San Francisco San Francisco 2	67	621
David	Placer Goods	62	694
Dustin	Placer Dutch Fl	62	725
Edward	Alameda Brooklyn	55	199
Eliza	San Francisco San Francisco 10		322
		67	
Ellen	Sacramento Granite	63	269
F	San Francisco San Francisco 2	67	663
Fan	Nevada Grass Valley	61	234
Foo Choo	Yuba Long Bar	72	760
Frank	Sierra Twp 7	66	896
G	Nevada Grass Valley	61	217
G T	Butte Eureka	56	652
George	Sacramento San Joaquin	63	351
George	Sacramento Ward 4	63	545
George	Santa Cruz Pajaro	66	563
H	Sacramento Granite	63	250
H G	Nevada Grass Valley	61	235
Hat	Mariposa Twp 3	60	579
He	Mariposa Twp 3	60	550
Henry	Santa Clara Gilroy	65	234
Hiram	Calaveras Twp 7	57	42
Hugh*	Placer Virginia	62	690
J L	San Francisco San Francisco 2	67	636
J L	Yolo Cache Crk	72	666
Jacob	Tuolumne Jamestown	71	452
Jacob	Tuolumne Chinese	71	491

Name	County Locale	M653 Roll Page
LANG		
James	San Francisco San Francisco 10	290 67
James	San Mateo Twp 1	65 68
James	Solano Suisan	69 228
Jim	Siskiyou Klamath	69 94
John	Tehama Cottonwood	70 901
John A	Butte Cascade	56 701
John*	Amador Twp 2	55 318
Kow	Mariposa Twp 3	60 546
L	Butte Eureka	56 652
Le	Mariposa Twp 1	60 665
Lee	Tuolumne Big Oak	71 181
Lewis	San Francisco San Francisco 3	67 46
Lewis*	Yuba Marysville	72 870
Lu	Tuolumne Twp 4	71 181
M	Trinity Weaverville	701063
Mag*	Calaveras Twp 9	57 354
Maj*	Calaveras Twp 1	57 354
Maxwell	El Dorado Salmon Falls	581048
May*	Calaveras Twp 9	57 354
Moy Lei*	San Francisco San Francisco 3	67 26
Patrick	Solano Suisan	69 227
R V	Nevada Grass Valley	61 235
S T	Nevada Eureka	61 361
Sag	El Dorado Georgetown	58 747
Saml W	San Francisco San Francisco 10	197 67
See	Plumas Quincy	62 945
Soon	El Dorado Mud Springs	58 955
T*	Nevada Grass Valley	61 165
Thomas*	Amador Twp 4	55 234
Thos	Sacramento Ward 1	63 62
William	Santa Cruz Pajaro	66 563
Wm T	Tehama Lassen	70 874
Y	Sierra St Louis	66 806
Yoy*	Tuolumne Twp 5	71 523
Zet*	Yuba Bear Rvr	721000
LANGAMATI		
Lantela*	Calaveras Twp 4	57 340
LANGARD		
J*	Sacramento Ward 1	63 17
LANGBEIN		
Ludolph	Sierra Twp 7	66 889
LANGBEUR		
Ludolph	Sierra Twp 7	66 889
LANGDEN		
L H	Sacramento Franklin	63 326
Richd*	Napa Clear Lake	61 134
LANGDON		
C	Trinity Lewiston	70 963
C W	Napa Napa	61 104
Conors	San Mateo Twp 3	65 75
David	San Francisco San Francisco 1	68 908
F	Siskiyou Scott Ri	69 78
George*	Placer Michigan	62 835
Henry	El Dorado Coloma	581073
James A	Humbolt Mattole	59 122
John	Plumas Quincy	62 987
John	Stanislaus Branch	70 707
Jos	Placer Auburn	62 567
Joseph	Placer Auburn	62 565
L	Sonoma Bodega	69 540
Levi	Calaveras Twp 10	57 287
Martin	Trinity E Weaver	701059
Minor K	Humbolt Mattole	59 124
Nye	Sacramento Ward 3	63 488
Porter	Humbolt Eel Rvr	59 150
Richd*	Napa Clear Lake	61 134
Samuel	San Joaquin Stockton	641036
William	San Mateo Twp 3	65 80
LANGE		
---	Placer Folsom	62 647
Charles	Tuolumne Sonora	71 209
De	San Francisco San Francisco 10	206 67
F	San Francisco San Francisco 2	67 795
Frederick	San Joaquin Stockton	641031
G*	Nevada Grass Valley	61 144
George	San Francisco San Francisco 7	681444
John	Tuolumne Columbia	71 338
Peter	Sierra Twp 5	66 922
Wm	Humbolt Eel Rvr	59 145
LANGEL		
Fred	San Francisco San Francisco 2	67 770
LANGELEL		
And	Trinity Indian C	70 987
LANGEN		
Mary	Alameda Brooklyn	55 96
LANGENBACH		
Chas	Sacramento Ward 1	63 47
LANGENETTI		
J	Tuolumne Twp 4	71 153
LANGER		
Antonio*	San Francisco San Francisco 3	67 83
Frederick*	Sacramento Sutter	63 309

Name	County Locale	M653 Roll Page
LANGER		
Nelson	San Joaquin Stockton	641019
P	Nevada Grass Valley	61 155
LANGERBURGOR		
F	Los Angeles Tejon	59 526
LANGERMANN		
Wm	San Francisco San Francisco 2	67 776
LANGFIELD		
Lewis	San Francisco San Francisco 2	67 711
LANGFOR		
Dfrances	Sierra Gibsonville	66 855
LANGFORD		
A J	Butte Hamilton	56 526
Edward	Nevada Rough &	61 403
Edward	Sierra Twp 7	66 914
Henry	Butte Bidwell	56 716
Henry	Calaveras Twp 10	57 280
Henry	Yuba Marysville	72 979
I J	Merced Twp 1	60 908
John	Los Angeles Elmonte	59 247
P S	Santa Clara Redwood	65 448
Thos	San Francisco San Francisco 1	68 895
Wm	Placer Virginia	62 683
LANGFRED		
William	El Dorado Georgetown	58 702
LANGHER		
Robert	Tuolumne Twp 5	71 511
LANGHLIN		
John	Shasta French G	66 718
Mary	San Francisco San Francisco 10	234 67
Miles	San Francisco San Francisco 11	90 67
Onin	Solano Fairfield	69 198
Patrick M	Sierra Port Win	66 795
LANGHORN		
Daniel	Yuba New York	72 737
John W	Santa Clara Gilroy	65 249
LANGHORNE		
A	Santa Clara San Jose	65 305
LANGHTAN		
William*	El Dorado Placerville	58 908
LANGHTON		
F H	Sonoma Vallejo	69 631
Saml B	Tuolumne Twp 3	71 441
LANGIS		
Henry	El Dorado Mud Springs	581000
LANGISTER		
W	Calaveras Twp 9	57 412
LANGKEIN		
Elij	Yolo Cache	72 640
LANGLAENR		
John D*	Colusa Monroeville	57 456
LANGLAUS		
---	Stanislaus Emory	70 753
LANGLEY		
Danl	Butte Bidwell	56 712
Danl	Butte Bidwell	56 729
David	San Francisco San Francisco 9	68 975
F M	San Mateo Twp 2	65 126
Henry	San Joaquin Stockton	641009
Henry G	San Francisco San Francisco 3	67 17
J M	Sonoma Petaluma	69 595
Jas	Butte Wyandotte	56 661
Jas	Placer Mountain	62 707
Jno	San Francisco San Francisco 9	68 977
John	El Dorado Eldorado	58 935
John O	Humbolt Table Bl	59 142
Joseph	San Joaquin O'Neal	641005
Keil	Calaveras Twp 6	57 160
L P	Butte Ophir	56 755
L*	El Dorado Placerville	58 931
Michael	Sierra Scales D	66 803
Milles	Sierra Scales D	66 803
Moses D	Solano Montezuma	69 369
P	Butte Kimshaw	56 595
Pierre*	Plumas Meadow Valley	62 928
R G	Sonoma Bodega	69 537
S*	El Dorado Placerville	58 931
W	Sutter Yuba	70 764
William	San Francisco San Francisco 8	681254
William A	San Francisco San Francisco 8	681254
William G	San Joaquin Stockton	641085
Wm	Plumas Quincy	62 917
Wm	Sonoma Vallejo	69 614
LANGLIN		
D M	Sonoma Santa Rosa	69 400
LANGLOIS		
J	San Francisco San Francisco 5	67 527
LANGLON		
H*	Nevada Nevada	61 318
LANGLOT		
A G	Yolo Cache	72 636
LANGLOW		
J	San Francisco San Francisco 5	67 527
LANGMAID		
Owen	Tuolumne Jamestown	71 449

Name	County Locale	M653 Roll Page
LANGMAID		
S G	Tuolumne Jamestown	71 449
LANGMAN		
Jhon	San Francisco San Francisco 3	67 79
John	San Francisco San Francisco 3	67 79
Joseph	Sacramento Ward 4	63 534
LANGMASTER		
Benjn	Calaveras Twp 4	57 340
LANGNALD		
Chas*	San Francisco San Francisco 1	68 855
LANGNESA		
Jose	Tuolumne Montezuma	71 506
LANGO		
---	Sierra Downieville	66 985
John	Tuolumne Twp 5	71 513
LANGOUT		
L Joseph	Yuba Foster B	72 833
LANGRETTO		
S*	Mariposa Twp 3	60 614
LANGRIDGE		
George	Yuba Rose Bar	72 813
Henry	San Francisco San Francisco 9	681071
LANGSTADTER		
S	San Francisco San Francisco 10	179 67
LANGSTER		
J	Marin Point Re	60 729
LANGSTON		
Lewis	Tulara Visalia	71 109
Richd	San Francisco San Francisco 12	387 67
S	Sacramento Cosummes	63 394
Wm	Yolo Slate Ra	72 704
Wm	Yuba Slate Ro	72 704
LANGTHY		
James*	El Dorado Georgetown	58 754
LANGTIEY		
Lewis	Klamath Salmon	59 208
LANGTON		
A T	San Francisco San Francisco 3	67 25
Aaron	Yuba Marysville	72 909
Akron	Yuba Marysville	72 909
H T	Butte Hamilton	56 527
H*	Nevada Nevada	61 318
J G	Butte Chico	56 541
Joel	Yuba Fosters	72 821
John C	Sierra Twp 7	66 905
Richd	Tuolumne Sonora	71 236
Saml W	Sierra Downieville	66 959
LANGTREE		
W	Calaveras Twp 9	57 388
LANGUALD		
Chas*	San Francisco San Francisco 1	68 855
LANGUENETTA		
J	San Joaquin Stockton	641090
LANGUESA		
Jose	Tuolumne Twp 5	71 506
LANGUINATTA		
Joseph*	Calaveras Twp 7	57 45
LANGUINATTI		
John	Calaveras Twp 8	57 62
LANGUS		
Rosario	Contra Costa Twp 1	57 509
LANGVILLE		
G W	Sacramento Ward 1	63 83
LANGWORTHY		
G B	Santa Clara San Jose	65 343
LANGZEPPO		
Gustaves	Calaveras Twp 8	57 107
LANHOLM		
Frederick	Alameda Brooklyn	55 102
LANI		
Inle	San Francisco San Francisco 8	681234
LANIAN		
J	Nevada Nevada	61 283
LANIE		
---	El Dorado Kelsey	581134
Francis	Yuba Foster B	72 835
LANIENELL		
W J*	Calaveras Twp 9	57 374
LANIFE		
E C	Butte Oregon	56 625
LANIG		
Robert	Sacramento San Joaquin	63 351
LANIGONIA		
---	San Bernardino San Bernadino	64 684
LANILING		
John	Calaveras Twp 9	57 356
LANILLA		
Maryketa*	Tuolumne Twp 1	71 220
LANINEL		
C B	El Dorado Mud Springs	58 994
LANINER		
Thos	Nevada Bridgeport	61 472
LANING		
G*	Nevada Grass Valley	61 143

California 1860 Census Index

Name	County Locale	M653 Roll	Page
LANISA			
Inarin	San Bernardino San Bernadino	64	677
LANJ			
---*	Mariposa Twp 3	60	564
LANJDON			
William	San Joaquin Elkhorn	64	996
LANK			
---	Amador Twp 2	55	312
---	Mariposa Twp 1	60	659
Carrie	San Francisco San Francisco 9	68	1003
John A	Tuolumne Twp 2	71	380
S M	Nevada Grass Valley	61	161
LANKANAM			
Henry*	Calaveras Twp 4	57	312
LANKANIM			
Henry*	Calaveras Twp 4	57	312
LANKANUM			
Henry*	Calaveras Twp 4	57	312
LANKANUN			
Henry*	Calaveras Twp 4	57	312
LANKARIN			
Frederick	San Francisco San Francisco 7	68	1337
LANKE			
Siles	Amador Twp 2	55	277
LANKENSHIRE			
Isaac*	Solano Vallejo	69	245
LANKER			
Sam*	Nevada Bridgeport	61	506
LANKERSHENN			
Isaac	San Francisco San Francisco 12	67	371
LANKERSHIN			
Isaac*	Solano Vallejo	69	245
LANKERSHIRE			
Isaac*	Solano Vallejo	69	245
LANKFON			
Henry	Amador Twp 2	55	299
LANKFORD			
Benj	Contra Costa Twp 1	57	516
John	Santa Clara Fremont	65	421
LANKIN			
Wm	Nevada Grass Valley	61	158
LANKMAN			
Joel*	Los Angeles Tejon	59	528
LANKTRE			
Joseph	Nevada Rough &	61	424
LANKTREE			
Joseph	Nevada Rough &	61	424
LANLABA			
Phillip*	Calaveras Twp 9	57	354
LANLASS			
W	Shasta Millvill	66	749
LANLEN			
Lillburn	Yolo Slate Ra	72	704
LANLERWAPER			
Christian*	San Francisco San Francisco 10	67	319
LANLES			
A*	Mariposa Twp 3	60	597
LANLIS			
Frank	Sonoma Vallejo	69	630
Maria	San Francisco San Francisco 2	67	763
LANLISS			
Lillburn*	Yuba Slate Ro	72	704
LANLOR			
Eduard*	Yuba Rose Bar	72	793
Edward*	Yuba Rose Bar	72	793
LANLORN			
Henry	Yuba Parks Ba	72	774
LANMAN			
J	San Joaquin Stockton	64	1033
W J	Shasta Shasta	66	678
LANMANN			
J N	El Dorado Kelsey	58	1143
LANMARTINE			
H*	El Dorado Diamond	58	796
LANMERMAN			
Martin	Calaveras Twp 5	57	190
LANN			
---	Marin Cortemad	60	786
Chas	Tuolumne Twp 4	71	138
Edward*	Alameda Murray	55	224
LANNA			
Peter	Yolo Cottonwoood	72	657
LANNAN			
Thomas*	San Diego San Diego	64	766
LANNAY			
Peter	San Francisco San Francisco 9	68	994
LANNCHILL			
J*	Tuolumne Garrote	71	175
LANNDERS			
Ricordo	Calaveras Twp 7	57	24
LANNECK			
B	Amador Twp 1	55	500
LANNEGAN			
J	Sacramento Cosumnes	63	404

Name	County Locale	M653 Roll	Page
LANNEGAN			
P	Sacramento Sutter	63	293
Wm*	San Francisco San Francisco 1	68	857
LANNEN			
E	San Francisco San Francisco 5	67	533
Garner*	Mariposa Twp 1	60	640
LANNER			
Thomas*	Nevada Bridgeport	61	446
Thomus*	Nevada Bridgeport	61	446
LANNES			
A P	Siskiyou Scott Ri	69	72
LANNEVIY			
Martin*	Calaveras Twp 4	57	329
LANNEY			
Barney	San Francisco San Francisco 3	67	58
Henry	El Dorado Georgetown	58	746
LANNGED			
L*	Nevada Grass Valley	61	162
LANNGER			
L*	Nevada Grass Valley	61	162
LANNING			
J N	Sonoma Armally	69	498
Thomas*	Mendocino Anderson	60	865
LANNINGER			
Jno	Butte Chico	56	563
LANNIS			
Lewis	Plumas Quincy	62	1003
Patrick	Alameda Oakland	55	5
LANNOX			
John*	Sierra Twp 5	66	943
LANNUDY			
P P*	Yuba North Ea	72	673
LANNY			
C	Solano Vallejo	69	272
James	San Francisco San Francisco 9	68	954
LANO			
---	Calaveras Twp 10	57	284
---	Fresno Twp 2	59	103
Y	San Francisco San Francisco 12	67	395
LANONIS			
Joseph	Calaveras Twp 5	57	216
LANOS			
Jose	San Diego Agua Caliente	64	821
M F*	Sacramento Ward 1	63	18
LANOTA			
Joseph*	Yuba Marysville	72	919
LANOTO			
---	Fresno Twp 2	59	113
Joseph*	Yuba Marysville	72	919
LANOVER			
G C	Colusa Grand Island	57	470
LANPHER			
Aaron A	Siskiyou Yreka	69	151
Charles A	San Francisco San Francisco 11	67	103
S T	Marin Bolinas	60	728
LANPRASNCO			
Mathew	Los Angeles Los Angeles	59	343
LANRAY			
V E	San Francisco San Francisco 2	67	698
LANREE			
Jas R	Santa Clara Santa Clara	65	482
LANREN			
Joseph	Trinity Lewiston	70	963
LANREW			
Jean*	Los Angeles Los Angeles	59	376
LANREY			
Christopher*	Marin Cortemad	60	782
LANROLL			
B*	Nevada Eureka	61	365
LANROTEE			
William*	Yuba New York	72	732
LANRSDELL			
L*	Sonoma Bodega	69	521
LANS			
---	Mariposa Twp 3	60	544
LANSAKA			
Phillip*	Calaveras Twp 9	57	354
LANSALPHA			
Jos S A*	Sacramento Ward 4	63	587
LANSBERGER			
A	San Francisco San Francisco 3	67	26
LANSBURG			
C	San Francisco San Francisco 1	68	878
LANSCASTER			
H	San Francisco San Francisco 5	67	487
LANSDALE			
Alfred	Monterey Alisal	60	1044
Flescher T	Humbolt Union	59	186
J W	San Francisco San Francisco 12	67	372
R R	Shasta Horsetown	66	693
Susan	Shasta Horsetown	66	697
W	Shasta Shasta	66	684
Wm	Calaveras Twp 9	57	373

Name	County Locale	M653 Roll	Page
LANSE			
Isaac	Yolo Putah	72	551
LANSEGEUR			
Felix	San Francisco San Francisco 10	67	318
LANSEN			
Mary	San Francisco San Francisco 10	67	201
Thomas	Siskiyou Scott Va	69	41
LANSENA			
John*	Calaveras Twp 9	57	351
LANSENCE			
J H*	Mariposa Twp 3	60	575
William*	Siskiyou Yreka	69	137
LANSENCON			
L*	Tuolumne Twp 3	71	465
LANSER			
William*	Siskiyou Yreka	69	137
LANSERVAINN			
Meguel*	San Francisco San Francisco 10	67	320
LANSETT			
John	Butte Ophir	56	776
LANSEVAINE			
Po*	San Francisco San Francisco 10	67	320
LANSEY			
A K	Napa Napa	61	81
LANSEZEUR			
Felix*	San Francisco San Francisco 10	67	318
LANSFIELD			
Patrick	Solano Vallejo	69	250
LANSING			
Abram	Sacramento Sutter	63	298
Frank	Tuolumne Twp 2	71	281
G J	Nevada Eureka	61	381
Garret	Marin Bolinas	60	745
Garrik	Marin Bolinas	60	745
J	Sacramento Ward 1	63	122
J V	Nevada Eureka	61	379
James	Alameda Oakland	55	15
James	Sacramento Ward 1	63	11
Jas R	Butte Oregon	56	634
Wm	Nevada Grass Valley	61	200
LANSMAN			
John*	Tuolumne Big Oak	71	178
M	Nevada Eureka	61	392
R	San Francisco San Francisco 5	67	487
Wm*	Sacramento Ward 4	63	609
LANSNIG			
Jas R	Butte Oregon	56	634
LANSON			
Ali*	Sierra Twp 5	66	947
G A	Mariposa Twp 1	60	666
G W	Yuba Rose Bar	72	793
Hans	Klamath Orleans	59	215
Henry	Butte Chico	56	532
Henry*	Placer Todds Va	62	783
J D	Yolo Cache Crk	72	631
J W	Mariposa Twp 3	60	556
James	Amador Twp 2	55	309
L	Calaveras Twp 9	57	396
Pather	Amador Twp 6	55	426
Thomas*	Siskiyou Scott Va	69	41
LANSTENTH			
H A *	Stanislaus Emory	70	739
LANT			
Amos*	Calaveras Twp 5	57	172
Chas	Butte Mountain	56	739
James P*	Tuolumne Twp 3	71	438
LANTA			
Maria	San Diego Agua Caliente	64	850
LANTENA			
James*	Yuba Fosters	72	837
LANTER			
Henry	San Francisco San Francisco 8	68	1247
LANTERS			
Master	Alameda Brooklyn	55	101
LANTHAUME			
Louis*	San Francisco San Francisco 3	67	6
LANTHAUMO			
Louis	San Francisco San Francisco 3	67	6
LANTHWICK			
W*	Calaveras Twp 9	57	393
LANTLER			
J H	Tehama Moons	70	853
LANTO			
Mary	Mariposa Twp 3	60	554
LANTON			
George	Tuolumne Twp 2	71	351
Stephen	Yuba Bear Rvr	72	1005
T G	Solano Suisan	69	208
LANTOS			
Jose	Monterey Monterey	60	925
LANTOT			
H	Tuolumne Jacksonville	71	170

California 1860 Census Index

Name	County Locale	M653 Roll	Page
LANTSKY			
Vincent	Amador Twp 2	55	275
LANTUS			
---	San Luis Obispo San Luis Obispo	65	9
LANTY			
John*	Butte Ophir	56	754
LANTZ			
Wash	Butte Chico	56	531
LANUKA			
---	Fresno Twp 2	59	48
LANUN			
Charles*	Placer Michigan	62	854
LANUNELL			
W J*	Calaveras Twp 9	57	374
LANUV			
J D*	Calaveras Twp 9	57	405
LANVER			
S	Butte Cascade	56	697
LANVOLT			
G H*	San Francisco San Francisco 5	67	543
LANVOTT			
G H*	San Francisco San Francisco 5	67	543
LANY			
---	Sacramento Granite	63	250
---*	Mariposa Twp 3	60	580
---*	Yuba Long Bar	72	765
Jenry*	Sierra Twp 5	66	940
John	Amador Twp 2	55	318
M	Nevada Grass Valley	61	224
Se	Mariposa Twp 1	60	665
LANYDON			
Levi*	Calaveras Twp 10	57	287
LANYON			
James	Sierra Twp 7	66	900
LANZ			
Chas*	Sacramento Brighton	63	199
John*	Tuolumne Twp 1	71	236
LANZE			
Peter	Sierra Twp 5	66	922
LANZZALE			
John	Sierra Downieville	66	1010
LAO			
---*	Mariposa Twp 3	60	562
Kao*	San Francisco San Francisco 9	68	1096
LAOC			
---	Trinity Mouth Ca	70	1017
LAOG			
Lewis	Yuba Marysville	72	870
LAOHLAR			
Wm*	Calaveras Twp 9	57	369
LAOLE			
---	Sacramento Ward 1	63	51
LAON			
Ah	Tuolumne Twp 4	71	160
LAONAN			
James*	Sierra Downieville	66	977
LAONEY			
---	El Dorado Salmon Falls	58	1045
LAONG			
---	El Dorado Salmon Falls	58	1041
---	El Dorado Salmon Falls	58	1044
---	El Dorado Salmon Falls	58	1066
---	El Dorado Coloma	58	1107
---	El Dorado Mud Springs	58	958
LAP SING			
---	San Francisco San Francisco 8	68	1286
LAP			
---	Amador Twp 6	55	431
---	Mariposa Twp 1	60	664
---	Mariposa Twp 1	60	669
---	Placer Illinois	62	745
A	Siskiyou Scott Va	69	54
Caslas	Siskiyou Scott Va	69	55
Flinn	Butte Ophir	56	787
Kee	Butte Ophir	56	787
Lum	Placer Illinois	62	742
Sing	Butte Kimshaw	56	576
Sing	Butte Ophir	56	815
LAPA			
L	Nevada Nevada	61	260
LAPALE			
Francis	Tuolumne Twp 1	71	247
LAPAND			
Joseph*	Calaveras Twp 4	57	340
LAPANK			
Joseph	Calaveras Twp 4	57	340
LAPARGAE			
Charles	Tuolumne Twp 2	71	317
LAPARGUR			
J	Tuolumne Twp 3	71	469
LAPAT			
---	Sacramento Ward 1	63	52
LAPATCH			
John	Marin San Rafael	60	767
LAPATY			
J*	Nevada Grass Valley	61	184

Name	County Locale	M653 Roll	Page
LAPAZ			
Jose	San Diego Agua Caliente	64	817
LAPBAR			
J P	Alameda Brooklyn	55	83
LAPE			
Antonia	Calaveras Twp 8	57	86
John	El Dorado White Oaks	58	1015
John	El Dorado Salmon Falls	58	1038
LAPEL			
B	El Dorado Diamond	58	798
Franklin	Yolo Washington	72	574
LAPELTON			
Patrick	San Joaquin Stockton	64	1059
LAPENEN			
Louis De*San Francisco San Francisco 2		67	631
LAPENS			
B F*	Calaveras Twp 9	57	392
LAPEO			
Antonio	El Dorado Casumnes	58	1176
LAPER			
F	San Francisco San Francisco 5	67	549
Jacob*	Amador Twp 4	55	237
L	Placer Sacramento	62	642
LAPERCY			
A	San Francisco San Francisco 2	67	555
LAPERE			
Jno	Sacramento Ward 1	63	84
John	Sacramento Ward 1	63	85
LAPERS			
B F	Calaveras Twp 9	57	393
Jas	Stanislaus Buena Village	70	723
Jno*	Sacramento Ward 1	63	84
LAPES			
Antonio	El Dorado Casumnes	58	1176
Manuell	Amador Twp 3	55	395
LAPEY			
Alrapeona*	Calaveras Twp 7	57	11
John	Calaveras Twp 7	57	35
Jose	Calaveras Twp 8	57	86
S	El Dorado Placerville	58	870
LAPEYRE			
Frank	Yuba Parke Ba	72	781
LAPEZ			
Antonio	Amador Twp 2	55	288
LAPFGER			
Wm A*	San Francisco San Francisco 10	67	221
LAPH			
---	Tuolumne Twp 6	71	531
Edwd*	Santa Clara San Jose	65	307
Edwo*	Santa Clara San Jose	65	307
LAPHAM			
Amos F	Solano Green Valley	69	241
Charles	San Francisco San Francisco 7	68	1343
Orson	Solano Suisan	69	220
V	Solano Suisan	69	207
W W	El Dorado Kelsey	58	1149
W W*	Sacramento Ward 1	63	79
LAPHAN			
Amos F	Solano Green Valley	69	241
Orson	Solano Suisan	69	220
LAPHARN			
Charles	San Francisco San Francisco 7	68	1343
W W	Sacramento Ward 1	63	79
LAPI			
---	Nevada Bridgeport	61	493
LAPIA			
Luisia	Monterey S Antoni	60	971
LAPIDGE			
W F	San Francisco San Francisco 9	68	1073
LAPIER			
Felix	Yuba Slate Ro	72	706
Mary A	San Francisco San Francisco 2	67	579
Wm	San Francisco San Francisco 2	67	584
LAPIERE			
Geo	Santa Clara Fremont	65	430
LAPIN			
Alice	Alameda Oakland	55	62
LAPINCOTT			
E	Yolo Putah	72	551
LAPINER			
B	San Francisco San Francisco 2	67	789
LAPING			
Hugh	Mariposa Coulterville	60	675
John*	Sacramento Ward 1	63	85
LAPITZ			
---*	Tulara Visalia	71	4
LAPLACE			
Constant	Yuba Foster B	72	835
Constant	Yuba Fosters	72	835
LAPLANT			
Cassima	San Joaquin Oneal	64	939
Peter	Sonoma Bodega	69	521
LAPLANTE			
Dennis	Sierra La Porte	66	768

Name	County Locale	M653 Roll	Page
LAPLATT			
William	San Mateo Twp 2	65	121
LAPLEY			
N	El Dorado White Oaks	58	1022
LAPLIN			
H	Shasta French G	66	719
LAPLLEY			
Thomas	Tuolumne Twp 1	71	254
LAPNES			
Cyrus	Yolo Putah	72	545
LAPOINT			
L*	Sacramento Granite	63	237
LAPOLE			
Francis	Tuolumne Twp 1	71	247
LAPONIS			
A	Nevada Nevada	61	278
LAPONIT			
A	Nevada Nevada	61	278
LAPOO SA			
---	Plumas Quincy	62	969
LAPORT			
A	Tuolumne Twp 1	71	235
John	Sierra Downieville	66	1001
LAPORTE			
Wm	Merced Monterey	60	937
Wm	Monterey Monterey	60	937
LAPORY			
Angle	Mariposa Coulterville	60	675
LAPPAM			
W W*	Sacramento Ward 1	63	79
LAPPAN			
P K*	Trinity McGillev	70	1021
LAPPEN			
Wm	San Francisco San Francisco 1	68	892
LAPPERTY			
Barney	San Bernardino San Bernadino	64	670
LAPPIMAXOR			
J L	Sutter Vernon	70	845
LAPPING			
Benjamin*	Yuba Bear Rvr	72	1004
LAPRAIK			
Wm	Sierra Twp 7	66	894
LAPREAN			
August	Los Angeles Los Angeles	59	344
LAPRIEL			
Emma	San Francisco San Francisco 4	68	1216
LAPRY			
Hugh	Mariposa Coulterville	60	675
LAPSLEY			
Jas B	San Francisco San Francisco 1	68	898
Thomas	Tuolumne Twp 1	71	254
LAPUET			
John*	Los Angeles Los Angeles	59	360
LAPURLD			
D*	Butte Ophir	56	769
LAPWELL			
D	Butte Ophir	56	769
LAPY			
Francisco	Calaveras Twp 8	57	86
LAPYA			
---*	Mendocino Round Va	60	884
LAQUAIT			
Louise*	Calaveras Twp 9	57	351
LAQUAR			
Julius*	Calaveras Twp 6	57	147
L	El Dorado White Oaks	58	1007
LAQUARA			
Sylvester	San Joaquin Castoria	64	878
LAQUEO			
G*	Mariposa Twp 3	60	566
LAQUOR			
Antonio	Calaveras Twp 9	57	358
LAR WALLING			
John*	Nevada Bridgeport	61	440
LAR			
---	Mariposa Twp 3	60	553
---	Mariposa Twp 3	60	608
---	Mariposa Twp 3	60	609
---	Mariposa Twp 1	60	665
---	San Francisco San Francisco 9	68	1094
Hing	Yuba Fosters	72	830
Kao	San Francisco San Francisco 9	68	1096
Lee	Mariposa Coulterville	60	682
LAR'K E			
---*	Mariposa Twp 3	60	607
LARA			
Andres	Santa Clara Santa Clara	65	478
Berna*	Alameda Oakland	55	45
Bicente	Los Angeles Los Nieto	59	436
Gregoria	Tuolumne Chinese	71	490
James	Sierra Downieville	66	965
John	Tuolumne Twp 5	71	499
Juan	Marin Sauciteto	60	751
Leon	Calaveras Twp 7	57	3
Manuel	Marin Bolinas	60	728

California 1860 Census Index

Name	County Locale	M653 Roll	Page
LARA			
Miguel	San Francisco San Francisco	10	188
		67	
Paidad	Tuolumne Twp 1	71	235
Pilar	Los Angeles Los Nieto	59	437
Victoria	Plumas Quincy	62	938
LARABON			
Ellen	Tuolumne Chinese	71	499
LARABORO			
Ellen	Tuolumne Twp 5	71	499
LARACO			
Thos	Amador Twp 3	55	374
LARACY			
Moses*	Santa Clara Fremont	65	440
LARADO			
Louis	Calaveras Twp 5	57	209
LARAGO			
---	San Diego Agua Caliente	64	859
LARAJINA			
---	San Bernardino San Bernadino	64	685
LARALE			
Edward	San Francisco San Francisco 2	67	617
LARALER			
Catharin	Sonoma Sonoma	69	649
LARAM			
Antonia	San Francisco San Francisco 1	68	812
Antonio	San Francisco San Francisco 1	68	812
LARAMA			
N	Siskiyou Klamath	69	92
LARAMAD			
Pierre**	Plumas Quincy	62	990
LARAMAT			
Pierre*	Plumas Quincy	62	990
LARAMEE			
Jas	San Francisco San Francisco	10	308
		67	
LARANCHE			
Antoine	Sacramento Ward 1	63	34
LARANO			
Gertrude	Contra Costa Twp 1	57	490
LARARAN			
Jas	Sacramento Granite	63	251
LARARO			
Carsamela	San Joaquin Stockton	64	1072
LARAS			
Feliciana	Merced Monterey	60	928
Feliciana	Monterey Monterey	60	928
Mercedes	Sacramento Ward 1	63	104
LARASE			
S D	Calaveras Twp 9	57	363
T D	Calaveras Twp 9	57	363
Wm	Santa Clara San Jose	65	293
LARASON			
J	Yuba New York	72	725
L	Yuba New York	72	725
Mary	Santa Clara Gilroy	65	232
LARAUCHE			
Antoine*	Sacramento Ward 1	63	34
LARAVASSUER			
Dominick*	San Francisco	11	133
	San Francisco	67	
LARAVY			
Cassima*	Tuolumne Twp 3	71	454
LARAY			
Cassim	Tuolumne Jamestown	71	454
LARAZOLA			
B	San Francisco San Francisco 2	67	570
LARBUSH			
P F	Shasta Horsetown	66	690
LARCAMS			
Amos	San Francisco San Francisco 7	68	1338
LARCARDE			
G	Tuolumne Twp 1	71	260
LARCARSE			
G	Tuolumne Twp 1	71	260
LARCE			
Ludnig	San Francisco San Francisco 2	67	710
Ludwig	San Francisco San Francisco 2	67	710
Wm*	Placer Secret R	62	617
LARCEN			
Charles	Tuolumne Twp 3	71	437
Charley	Tuolumne Jamestown	71	437
LARCH			
H	Sutter Yuba	70	759
Washington	Colusa Colusi	57	424
LARCIA			
Espitacio	San Luis Obispo	65	23
	San Luis Obispo		
LARCK			
S A	Calaveras Twp 9	57	418
LARCO			
Bathes*	Santa Cruz Soguel	66	586
Bathis	Santa Cruz Soguel	66	586
N	San Francisco San Francisco 1	68	821
LARCOIX			
P*	Stanislaus Branch	70	700

Name	County Locale	M653 Roll	Page
LARCON			
N B	Tuolumne Twp 2	71	279
Thomas H	Tuolumne Twp 1	71	260
LARCUS			
Martin	San Francisco San Francisco 9	68	1100
LARD			
Geo	Santa Clara Santa Clara	65	499
James	Tulara Yule Rvr	71	25
John	El Dorado White Oaks	58	1026
John*	Siskiyou Klamath	69	86
Pablo	Fresno Twp 1	59	84
Porter	Tulara Visalia	71	27
R	Mariposa Twp 3	60	584
LARDARAS			
Jose	El Dorado Georgetown	58	684
LARDER			
Aunlaco*	Placer Auburn	62	583
Auntaco*	Placer Auburn	62	583
John	Santa Cruz Soguel	66	585
LARDERS			
Manuel	Tuolumne Twp 2	71	389
LARDIS			
Manuel	Tuolumne Shawsfla	71	389
LARDLY			
Jas*	San Francisco San Francisco	10	306
		67	
LARDNER			
Francis S	Sacramento Ward 1	63	42
Wm	San Francisco San Francisco 3	67	27
LARDOSA			
---	Fresno Twp 2	59	68
LARE			
---	Mariposa Twp 3	60	620
LAREAS			
Andres*	Monterey Alisal	60	1035
LAREGLE			
Catharine	San Francisco San Francisco	11	141
		67	
LAREIDER			
M*	Mariposa Twp 3	60	622
LAREIMEE			
Mary*	Yuba Marysville	72	849
LAREINCE			
Mary	Yuba Marysville	72	849
LAREN			
Cardelia	El Dorado Mud Springs	58	994
J	Sacramento Sutter	63	300
John M*	Sacramento Ward 4	63	550
LARENCE			
Antonio	Mariposa Twp 3	60	617
LAREND			
Antonio*	Mariposa Twp 3	60	604
LARENET			
Louis	Alameda Oakland	55	20
LARENNY			
M	El Dorado Diamond	58	806
LARENO			
J D*	Calaveras Twp 9	57	405
LARENZ			
Thos	San Francisco San Francisco 1	68	931
LARENZO			
---	Monterey S Antoni	60	970
LARER			
Caroline*	San Francisco San Francisco 4	68	1228
LARERAU			
Jos	Sacramento Granite	63	251
LARERDE			
M	Mariposa Twp 3	60	622
LARERDER			
E*	Nevada Grass Valley	61	168
LARERDES			
M*	Mariposa Twp 3	60	622
LARERENCON			
S	Tuolumne Twp 3	71	465
LARES			
Peter	San Mateo Twp 1	65	61
LARESE			
S D	Calaveras Twp 9	57	363
LARETO			
Vincento*	Sacramento Ward 1	63	105
LARETTO			
Francisco	Calaveras Twp 9	57	377
LAREUX			
Lewis	Alameda Brooklyn	55	78
LAREY			
Moses*	Santa Clara Fremont	65	440
LAREZ			
Jean	Tuolumne Twp 2	71	321
LAREZO			
Phileppi	Fresno Twp 1	59	82
LARG			
W	San Francisco San Francisco 9	68	1081
LARGADAR			
---	Mariposa Twp 3	60	548
LARGAS			
Kassuth	Calaveras Twp 7	57	47

Name	County Locale	M653 Roll	Page
LARGE			
---	Mendocino Calpella	60	823
G*	Nevada Grass Valley	61	144
Henry	San Francisco San Francisco 3	67	26
James	El Dorado Mud Springs	58	990
Jas W	Placer Goods	62	697
Juliana	San Francisco San Francisco	10	185
		67	
Margaret	Santa Clara San Jose	65	349
Peter	Yuba Marysville	72	855
Peter	Yuba Marysville	72	860
Samuel	Tuolumne Big Oak	71	177
Tomas	San Francisco San Francisco 9	68	1025
LARGEN			
Rev J	El Dorado Placerville	58	837
LARGENT			
Eldrige	Calaveras Twp 7	57	19
John	Plumas Quincy	62	960
LARGER			
Phillip	Calaveras Twp 8	57	68
LARGHLIN			
Wm	Napa Yount	61	36
LARGIER			
John	Yuba Foster B	72	836
LARGIN			
John	Yuba Fosters	72	836
LARGMORSINO			
P	Calaveras Twp 8	57	82
LARGMORSINU			
P	Calaveras Twp 8	57	82
LARGO			
---	Mendocino Calpella	60	823
---	Tulara Keyesville	71	67
---	Tulara Twp 3	71	68
---	Tulara Twp 3	71	70
---	Tulara Twp 3	71	71
Jose	San Diego Agua Caliente	64	859
Jose	San Diego Agua Caliente	64	864
Juan	San Bernardino San Bernadino	64	680
Juan	San Bernardino S Timate	64	715
Juan	San Bernardino S Timate	64	717
Manuel	San Bernardino San Bernadino	64	679
S	Solano Montezuma	69	375
LARGOMARCIN			
Francis	Calaveras Twp 6	57	164
LARGOMARCUS			
Francis*	Calaveras Twp 6	57	164
LARGOMARSIMO			
George	Calaveras Twp 7	57	12
LARGOMENCIA			
Lenn*	Calaveras Twp 7	57	13
LARGON			
J	El Dorado Placerville	58	857
LARGORNENCIA			
Lean*	Calaveras Twp 7	57	13
LARGRENOT			
P	Calaveras Twp 9	57	378
LARGSTAFF			
William*	Placer Iona Hills	62	860
LARGUNOT			
J	Calaveras Twp 9	57	378
LARGUS			
Lenard	Placer Secret R	62	608
LARHAWK			
Stephen*	Sierra Downieville	66	1006
LARHO			
---	Mendocino Twp 1	60	890
LARIA			
Jose	Merced Twp 1	60	906
LARIACO			
---	San Diego Agua Caliente	64	839
LARIANCE			
Yguacia	San Diego Temecula	64	787
LARIAS			
Andres*	Monterey Alisal	60	1035
Dema	Monterey San Juan	60	1000
Gabriel	Santa Clara Almaden	65	276
Gracia	Monterey San Juan	60	984
Pelar	Monterey San Juan	60	979
LARIBEE			
John R	Yuba Bear Rvr	72	1005
LARICA			
Antonae	Santa Cruz Santa Cruz	66	610
Antonal*	Santa Cruz Santa Cruz	66	610
Antonio	Santa Cruz Santa Cruz	66	610
Antorral*	Santa Cruz Santa Cruz	66	610
Autorrae*	Santa Cruz Santa Cruz	66	610
Autorral*	Santa Cruz Santa Cruz	66	610
LARID			
J	Amador Twp 7	55	420
LARIDY			
Jno*	San Francisco San Francisco 9	68	1070
LARIEDES			
M	Mariposa Twp 3	60	622
LARIERS			
Jose M	Monterey San Juan	60	1009

California 1860 Census Index

Name	County Locale	M653 Roll	Page
LARIGAN			
M	Sacramento Granite	63	242
Mike*	Sacramento Mississipi	63	184
LARILLA			
V	Calaveras Twp 8	57	108
LARIMER			
J	Nevada Grass Valley	61	208
Thos	Nevada Bridgeport	61	472
LARIMIE			
Santiago	Yuba Marysville	72	947
LARIMIX			
Santiago	Yuba Marysville	72	947
LARIN			
---	Nevada Bridgeport	61	492
Bernard	Solano Vallejo	69	262
James*	Alameda Brooklyn	55	80
L	Nevada Nevada	61	252
LARINDO			
Jenette	Calaveras Twp 9	57	352
Jinette*	Calaveras Twp 9	57	352
LARINER			
John	Amador Twp 6	55	441
LARING			
Petro	Calaveras Twp 7	57	37
LARINO			
J D*	Calaveras Twp 9	57	405
LARINS			
Manuel	Monterey San Juan	60	1008
LARIO			
---	San Bernardino S Timate	64	750
LARIOS			
Antonio	Santa Clara Fremont	65	441
Clemente	Santa Clara Gilroy	65	253
Jose	Los Angeles San Gabriel	59	423
Justo	Santa Clara Gilroy	65	252
Pedro	Santa Clara Santa Clara	65	521
LARISMAN			
Wm*	Sacramento Ward 4	63	609
LARISON			
Samuel	Sonoma Cloverdale	69	685
LARITA			
Viconti	San Luis Obispo San Luis Obispo	65	11
LARITO			
Vincento*	Sacramento Ward 1	63	105
LARITRO			
Vincento	Sacramento Ward 1	63	105
LARIUS			
Jose M	Monterey San Juan	60	1009
Manuel	Monterey San Juan	60	1008
LARIVE			
Maynre*	Alameda Oakland	55	43
Mayure*	Alameda Oakland	55	43
LARIWEE			
Mary*	Yuba Marysville	72	849
LARK			
Harrison*	Mariposa Twp 3	60	605
LARKAN			
Michael	Yolo Washington	72	571
LARKAND			
J Q	Calaveras Twp 9	57	371
LARKEN			
Francis	Santa Cruz Pajaro	66	570
Malcom	Tulara Visalia	71	30
Michael	Sierra Downieville	66	1030
LARKES			
Chas	Mariposa Twp 3	60	558
LARKEY			
James	San Francisco San Francisco 2	67	755
John	Contra Costa Twp 3	57	589
LARKIN			
---*	Mendocino Calpella	60	821
A D	Butte Chico	56	537
Ann	San Francisco San Francisco 2	67	658
C H	San Francisco San Francisco 6	67	439
Catherine	San Francisco San Francisco 3	67	61
Dennis	San Francisco San Francisco 1	68	816
Francis*	Santa Cruz Pajaro	66	570
George M	Plumas Quincy	62	962
H	El Dorado Diamond	58	785
Henry	Santa Clara Santa Clara	65	497
J	Nevada Grass Valley	61	153
James H	Sierra Forest Grove	66	822
Jas	Butte Wyandotte	56	659
Jas	San Francisco San Francisco 1	68	917
Jno	San Francisco San Francisco 10	244 67	
John	El Dorado Placerville	58	934
John	Placer Illinois	62	738
John	Shasta Millvill	66	740
John M	Placer Secret R	62	608
Lawrence	San Joaquin Douglass	64	927
Mary	San Francisco San Francisco 6	67	455
Mathew	San Joaquin Oneal	64	938
Mike	Sonoma Petaluma	69	573
Peter	Shasta Horsetown	66	705
Rachel	San Francisco San Francisco 4	68	1160
LARKIN			
Randolph	San Mateo Twp 1	65	63
S O	Santa Clara Santa Clara	65	520
Seth	Marin Tomales	60	721
Thomas*	Sierra Downieville	66	1002
Thos	Sacramento Natonia	63	280
Thos	San Francisco San Francisco 10	293 67	
Thos	San Mateo Twp 1	65	63
Thos	Santa Clara Santa Clara	65	503
Thos	Shasta Horsetown	66	708
Thos J	San Francisco San Francisco 3	67	62
Thos N	San Bernardino San Bernardino	64	666
Thos W	Butte Kimshaw	56	587
W H	Sacramento Ward 1	63	103
Wm	Sacramento Granite	63	222
Wm	Solano Benecia	69	308
LARKING			
G L	El Dorado Diamond	58	793
LARKINS			
Francis*	Santa Cruz Pajaro	66	570
G A	Tuolumne Shawsfla	71	377
John	Placer Iona Hills	62	890
Thos	Sonoma Russian	69	437
W M	El Dorado Kelsey	58	1151
Wm	San Francisco San Francisco 10	201 67	
LARKOMOSO			
C	Amador Twp 1	55	481
LARKS			
Orlando	San Francisco San Francisco 10	236 67	
LARKY			
Henry*	Sacramento San Joaquin	63	353
M*	El Dorado Eldorado	58	937
LARMAMER			
A*	San Francisco San Francisco 9	68	1105
LARMER			
Jos	San Francisco San Francisco 10	308 67	
Thomas*	Nevada Bridgeport	61	446
LARMIE			
I N	Napa Napa	61	63
J N	Napa Napa	61	63
LARMIN			
Mich*	Butte Oregon	56	620
LARMME			
Mich	Butte Oregon	56	620
LARMNE			
L L*	Solano Vacaville	69	330
LARMON			
William	Fresno Twp 2	59	49
LARMOND			
Oscar E*	San Francisco San Francisco 7	68	1431
LARMONE			
Robert M*	Yuba Parke Ba	72	782
LARMOUR			
Robert M*	Yuba Parks Ba	72	782
LARMSKY			
John	San Joaquin Elkhorn	64	976
LARMUR			
A	Tehama Tehama	70	949
LARN			
Caroline*	San Francisco San Francisco 4	68	1228
Manuel	Monterey San Juan	60	995
LARNAN			
James*	Sierra Downieville	66	977
LARNARD			
Aurther	Calaveras Twp 8	57	90
LARNARGAN			
Mary	San Francisco San Francisco 10	296 67	
LARNDER			
H*	Shasta Shasta	66	734
LARNE			
James*	Alameda Brooklyn	55	80
Patrick M	San Luis Obispo	65	15
	San Luis Obispo		
LARNED			
L	Tuolumne Twp 4	71	153
LARNEN			
Ptk	San Francisco San Francisco 10	274 67	
LARNER			
S B*	Marin Point Re	60	730
LARNERTINE			
C*	Nevada Nevada	61	270
LARNEY			
Jno M*	Sacramento Ward 4	63	506
LARNINE			
Mich*	Butte Oregon	56	620
LARNING			
D W	Sierra Downieville	66	1000
LARNIS			
Jose	Los Angeles Los Angeles	59	497
LARNORD			
Jasiah*	Calaveras Twp 8	57	90
LARNURGAN			
Mary	San Francisco San Francisco 10	296 67	
LARNUS			
J*	Nevada Eureka	61	372
LARO			
Dolaris	Calaveras Twp 9	57	390
J F*	Mendocino Ukiah	60	798
Julian	Monterey San Juan	60	992
LAROBIE			
William	Contra Costa Twp 3	57	598
LAROBY			
J	Sutter Nicolaus	70	830
LAROCHE			
Abel	San Francisco San Francisco 3	67	82
Alexander	Los Angeles Los Angeles	59	374
LAROCK			
Manaira	San Francisco San Francisco 2	67	615
LARONA			
Lerene*	Calaveras Twp 7	57	1
Lirene	Calaveras Twp 7	57	1
Sirene*	Calaveras Twp 7	57	1
LAROND			
George*	Yuba New York	72	732
LARONDO			
Francis	Tuolumne Columbia	71	313
LARONED			
George*	Yuba New York	72	732
LARONET			
George	Yuba New York	72	732
LARONX			
M	Nevada Eureka	61	388
LARONY			
Augustus	El Dorado White Oaks	58	1022
LARORHO			
Abil	San Francisco San Francisco 3	67	82
LARORINE			
G	Merced Twp 1	60	902
LAROSA			
Matilda	Yuba Marysville	72	932
Wahtda	Yuba Marysville	72	932
LAROSE			
Francis	Colusa Grand Island	57	473
Jennet	San Francisco San Francisco 8	68	1304
S S	Butte Kimshaw	56	589
S S*	Butte Kimshaw	56	589
LAROSENA			
W W	Santa Clara San Jose	65	286
LAROUS			
Jesus	Tuolumne Twp 3	71	437
Ramon	Tuolumne Jamestown	71	437
LAROUX			
J*	Nevada Eureka	61	372
Jalm*	Calaveras Twp 7	57	38
LARPY			
O	Alameda Brooklyn	55	169
LARR			
G*	Nevada Washington	61	335
J H	Butte Hamilton	56	525
LARRA			
Juan	San Bernardino Santa Barbara	64	197
LARRALL			
Catharine	San Francisco San Francisco 2	67	598
LARRAM			
Chas	San Francisco San Francisco 2	67	704
LARRANCE			
W	Shasta Millvill	66	741
LARRAWAY			
Lino	Sacramento Ward 4	63	524
LARRELL			
Gustar	San Francisco San Francisco 2	67	795
Gustav	San Francisco San Francisco 2	67	795
LARREN			
William	Yuba Bear Rvr	72	1012
LARRENCE			
W	Shasta Millvill	66	741
LARRENO			
Lorenzo	Tuolumne Twp 5	71	499
LARRI			
V	San Francisco San Francisco 2	67	634
LARRIBEE			
Henry	Santa Clara Santa Clara	65	505
Henry P	Humbolt Eel Rvr	59	145
LARRIMORE			
R	San Francisco San Francisco 2	67	657
LARRIN			
Alice	Sonoma Vallejo	69	620
LARRING			
Peter*	Tuolumne Big Oak	71	143
LARRIS			
C	Calaveras Twp 9	57	387
Phillippe	Los Angeles San Jose	59	291
LARRISON			
James H	Plumas Quincy	62	921
Nancy J	Contra Costa Twp 3	57	590
Wilson	Plumas Quincy	62	921

California 1860 Census Index

Name	County Locale	M653 Roll Page
LARROBBY		
Robert	Sierra Twp 7	66 868
LARROBLEY		
Robert*	Sierra Twp 7	66 868
LARROCK		
Eugine	Contra Costa Twp 3	57 584
LARROE		
Manuella*	San Francisco 7	681387
	San Francisco	
LARRONT		
Louis*	Calaveras Twp 9	57 361
LARROTEE		
William*	Yuba New York	72 732
LARRSON		
J D	Yolo Cache	72 631
Ssusan	San Francisco San Francisco 9	681105
LARRUMENDO		
Padro*	Contra Costa Twp 3	57 600
LARRUMINDO		
Padro*	Contra Costa Twp 3	57 600
LARRY		
---*	Mariposa Twp 3	60 580
Bridget	Solano Vallejo	69 250
James	Shasta Horsetown	66 688
James	Sierra Twp 5	66 940
Jeramiah	Shasta French G	66 716
Jeramiah	Shasta French G	66 716
Jerry*	Sierra Twp 5	66 940
S T*	Nevada Eureka	61 361
T	Nevada Eureka	61 365
W	Nevada Grass Valley	61 212
Wm	Sonoma Bodega	69 524
LARRYE		
G	Nevada Grass Valley	61 144
LARS		
James*	Sacramento Ward 1	63 84
LARSBACH		
A	El Dorado Spanish	581124
J	El Dorado Spanish	581124
LARSEN		
Antine	Siskiyou Yreka	69 146
Antone	Siskiyou Yreka	69 146
Antonio	Mariposa Twp 3	60 604
C	Siskiyou Klamath	69 89
LARSON		
A	Yolo Cache Crk	72 621
Elias J	Sierra Pine Grove	66 820
Hans	San Francisco San Francisco 7	681426
J	Sacramento Ward 1	63 67
J W	Siskiyou Klamath	69 89
L	Calaveras Twp 9	57 396
O C	Sonoma Sonoma	69 658
Ralem C	Yolo Cache Crk	72 631
William*	Napa Yount	61 31
LARSTON		
John*	Mariposa Twp 3	60 573
LARTHIS		
J L	Yolo Cache	72 624
LARTIGNE		
V	Stanislaus Branch	70 699
LARTMAN		
Ernest*	Stanislaus Emory	70 741
LARTON		
Joseph*	Calaveras Twp 4	57 330
LARTWELL		
Fredrick*	Sierra Poker Flats	66 837
LARTY		
Moore K	Calaveras Twp 4	57 340
Moore R*	Calaveras Twp 4	57 340
Moose K	Calaveras Twp 4	57 340
LARUAN		
James*	Sierra Downieville	66 977
LARUE		
Abraham	Humbolt Mattole	59 125
Bridget	Los Angeles Los Angeles	59 387
Edward W	San Joaquin Douglass	64 917
James D	San Joaquin Stockton	641027
Jas	Sacramento Franklin	63 328
Jos	Butte Oregon	56 619
LARUN		
Jean	San Francisco San Francisco 7	681396
LARURDER		
E*	Nevada Grass Valley	61 168
LARUW		
J D*	Calaveras Twp 9	57 405
LARVALL		
Catharine*	San Francisco 2	67 598
	San Francisco	
LARVES		
Antonio	San Luis Obispo San Luis Obispo 65	38
Henry*	El Dorado Georgetown	58 704
LARVILLE		
Wm*	Napa Yount	61 33
LARVIN		
Alice	Sonoma Vallejo	69 620
Jas	Sonoma Vallejo	69 619

Name	County Locale	M653 Roll Page
LARVINE		
Sylvania B	Yuba Marysville	72 931
LARVLEN		
George	El Dorado Georgetown	58 705
LARVSON		
Lawrence	Marin Point Re	60 729
LARWA		
Maria	San Francisco San Francisco 2	67 707
LARWERS		
Solida	Fresno Twp 1	59 83
LARY		
---	Amador Twp 6	55 430
---	Mariposa Coulterville	60 687
---	Mariposa Coulterville	60 691
---	Nevada Grass Valley	61 231
D O	San Mateo Twp 3	65 101
David	Yuba Marysville	72 867
Francis	Santa Clara Almaden	65 276
Jno*	Butte Eureka	56 650
John*	Amador Twp 2	55 318
Kate	San Francisco San Francisco 10	183
		67
L	Nevada Grass Valley	61 156
Nicholas	Amador Twp 2	55 322
Nicholas	Amador Twp 2	55 322
Sarey N*	Sierra Twp 5	66 923
Stephen	Nevada Bloomfield	61 511
T	Nevada Grass Valley	61 156
LARYDEN		
C C	Shasta Shasta	66 734
LARYE		
G*	Nevada Grass Valley	61 144
L H D*	Tehama Red Bluff	70 923
LARYOMAISIN		
Jeromis	Calaveras Twp 8	57 89
LARYOMORCEN		
John*	Calaveras Twp 5	57 228
LARYOVIN		
Manuel*	Calaveras Twp 5	57 203
LARZ		
James*	Shasta Shasta	66 671
LARZI		
Samuel	Tuolumne Twp 4	71 177
LAS		
---	Mariposa Twp 3	60 598
---	San Bernardino S Timate	64 693
LASA		
Pedro	San Bernardino San Bernadino	64 677
LASABEE		
Pierse*	El Dorado Big Bar	58 737
LASADO		
Angustine	San Joaquin Stockton	641065
Louis	Calaveras Twp 5	57 209
LASAELLY		
Mme*	San Francisco San Francisco 10	261
		67
Mone*	San Francisco San Francisco 10	261
		67
LASAHEE		
Pierse*	El Dorado Big Bar	58 737
LASAHER		
Pierse*	El Dorado Big Bar	58 737
LASALLE		
Isabella	Placer Todds Va	62 764
Joseph	Santa Clara Santa Clara	65 469
LASAMA		
Pabsano	Mariposa Twp 1	60 625
LASANA		
---*	Stanislaus Oatvale	70 720
LASANO		
Frank	Tuolumne Chinese	71 490
LASARE		
Mr	Sonoma Sonoma	69 636
LASARGO		
August	San Joaquin Stockton	641070
LASARO		
Mr	Sonoma Sonoma	69 636
LASATER		
Mathew	Napa Yount	61 35
LASBRY		
Henry	Klamath Dillins	59 214
LASCELLE		
Augustus	Tuolumne Chinese	71 501
LASCHANSKA		
John	Shasta Shasta	66 655
LASCHANTKA		
John	Shasta Shasta	66 655
LASCHARE		
Louise	San Francisco San Francisco 7	681366
LASCHON		
John	Tuolumne Montezuma	71 508
LASCHOW		
John	Tuolumne Twp 5	71 508
LASCI		
---	San Francisco San Francisco 2	67 798
Domingo	San Francisco San Francisco 2	67 798

Name	County Locale	M653 Roll Page
LASCUS		
Marea A	Los Angeles San Jose	59 285
LASEELLE		
Augustus	Tuolumne Twp 5	71 501
LASELL		
Robt	Tehama Tehama	70 949
LASELLE		
Jos*	Nevada Bridgeport	61 441
LASENSKA		
F	Yolo Putah	72 587
LASES		
I	Amador Twp 5	55 329
J	Amador Twp 5	55 329
LASEY		
G T	Butte Eureka	56 652
Louis	Alameda Brooklyn	55 131
LASFERICE		
Henry*	Mariposa Twp 3	60 571
LASH		
William	Contra Costa Twp 2	57 571
LASHA		
Gilbert	Placer Dutch Fl	62 732
LASHALLS		
H	Sacramento Ward 1	63 90
LASHANCE		
Andrew*	Butte Ophir	56 747
LASHAPEL		
N	Amador Twp 1	55 491
LASHAUCE		
Andrew	Butte Ophir	56 747
LASHER		
Gilbert	Placer Mountain	62 708
Henry*	Mariposa Twp 3	60 605
LASHIER		
Francis H	Colusa Spring Valley	57 432
LASHLEY		
Z	Butte Chico	56 551
LASHPEL		
Louis	Amador Twp 1	55 491
LASILLE		
Jos	Nevada Bridgeport	61 441
LASIN		
L	Nevada Nevada	61 252
LASITER		
Mathew*	Napa Yount	61 35
LASK		
---	Yolo No E Twp	72 685
Harrison*	Mariposa Twp 3	60 605
John*	San Francisco San Francisco 3	67 33
Louis	Yuba Marysville	72 900
LASKE		
J	Siskiyou Cottonwoood	69 97
LASKENANN		
Frank*	Yuba Marysville	72 936
LASKY		
Bernard	Sacramento Ward 4	63 556
Henry*	Sacramento San Joaquin	63 353
Levy	Los Angeles Los Angeles	59 341
M	El Dorado Eldorado	58 937
T*	San Francisco San Francisco 1	68 850
LASLARCO		
P	San Joaquin Stockton	641085
LASLEY		
A J	Napa Yount	61 31
J	Butte Ophir	56 786
LASMER		
Herman	San Francisco San Francisco 4	681151
LASNETT		
John J*	San Bernardino San Bernadino	64 619
LASOCN		
Thomas A	Tuolumne Twp 1	71 260
LASOIGNE		
Lament	Yuba Marysville	72 873
LASON		
Alman W	Plumas Quincy	62 992
Wm R	Plumas Meadow Valley	62 929
LASONDE		
J D	Sacramento Ward 1	63 46
LASPERE		
J	Butte Oro	56 683
LASPERICE		
Henry*	Mariposa Twp 3	60 571
LASPERILL		
Henry*	Mariposa Twp 3	60 571
LASPIRIER		
Henry	Mariposa Twp 3	60 571
LASQUARTTE		
Francisco	Calaveras Twp 6	57 116
LASQUERRE		
Agustine	Yuba Parks Ba	72 778
Jacques	Yuba Parks Ba	72 778
LASQUIT		
Joshua C	Yuba Bear Rvr	721013
LASRIETT		
John J*	San Bernardino San Bernadino	64 619
LASS		
---*	Nevada Rough &	61 437

Name	County Locale	M653 Roll	Page
LASS			
J H	Tuolumne Twp 4	71	172
J W	Tuolumne Jacksonville	71	172
LASSA			
M	Tuolumne Twp 1	71	146
R	Nevada Grass Valley	61	201
LASSAIE			
Adolph	Plumas Meadow Valley	62	928
LASSAN			
Leopold	Contra Costa Twp 1	57	536
LASSANO			
Espirido	Calaveras Twp 7	57	19
LASSAR			
J	Mariposa Twp 1	60	654
LASSELL			
H	Tuolumne Twp 4	71	173
L H	Sierra Downieville	66	1020
LASSEN			
C*	Nevada Grass Valley	61	186
Fred	San Francisco San Francisco 9	68	1055
G C	Tehama Red Bluff	70	913
Henry	Santa Clara Freemont	65	416
Lary N	Sierra Twp 5	66	923
Las	El Dorado White Oaks	58	1026
Peter	Plumas Quincy	62	955
Peter	San Francisco San Francisco 9	68	1084
LASSER			
John	Placer Secret R	62	615
LASSERCY			
A*	San Francisco San Francisco 2	67	555
LASSET			
Henry	San Francisco San Francisco 2	67	692
LASSEW			
Peter*	San Francisco San Francisco 9	68	1084
LASSIA			
Joseph	Alameda Oakland	55	19
LASSIDGE			
W F*	San Francisco San Francisco 9	68	1073
LASSIE			
R	Nevada Grass Valley	61	150
LASSIN			
Ann	San Francisco San Francisco 4	68	1219
David	El Dorado Mud Springs	58	999
LASSING			
John	Contra Costa Twp 2	57	577
LASSITER			
James H	Yuba Marysville	72	900
LASSITOR			
James	San Diego Agua Caliente	64	855
LASSLIN			
Wm	Sacramento Franklin	63	324
LASSO			
Bell	Tuolumne Big Oak	71	182
Bill	Tuolumne Twp 4	71	182
Francisco	Calaveras Twp 9	57	372
LASSON			
H C	El Dorado Salmon Falls	58	1047
Lary N*	Sierra Twp 5	66	923
LASSWELL			
Isaac	Yuba Suida	72	988
Isac	Yuba Linda	72	988
Mary	Sonoma Cloverdale	69	685
Thomas	Yuba Suida	72	988
William	Yuba Bear Rvr	72	996
LAST			
A H	Amador Twp 3	55	387
LASTER			
John	Trinity Taylor'S	70	1036
LASTHY			
Mary	San Francisco San Francisco 10	67	247
LASTIC			
Edward	San Francisco San Francisco 4	68	1153
LASTIE			
Edward	San Francisco San Francisco 4	68	1153
LASTRE			
Felipe	Los Angeles Los Angeles	59	299
Trinidad Valled	Los Angeles Los Angeles	59	300
LASTRETO			
L	San Francisco San Francisco 1	68	821
N	San Francisco San Francisco 3	67	5
LASTRITO			
N	San Francisco San Francisco 3	67	5
LASTRO			
Angelira	San Francisco San Francisco 3	67	55
Angelvia*	San Francisco San Francisco 3	67	55
LASUE			
---	Sierra Twp 5	66	927
LASUNE			
Den Raphel	Amador Twp 2	55	301
LASVIGSUE			
Lamuel	Yuba Marysville	72	873
LASWELL			
James	Sierra Gibsonville	66	860
William	San Mateo Twp 3	65	100
LASWETTA			
Francisco J	Los Angeles Los Angeles	59	361
LASY			
August*	Placer Rattle Snake	62	603
LAT			
---	Amador Twp 2	55	293
---	Amador Twp 2	55	318
---	El Dorado Salmon Falls	58	1045
---	El Dorado Georgetown	58	701
---	El Dorado Mud Springs	58	958
---	San Francisco San Francisco 9	68	1087
---	San Francisco San Francisco 4	68	1197
---	Siskiyou Klamath	69	80
A	Sacramento Granite	63	245
LATALIE			
V	San Francisco San Francisco 2	67	797
LATAN			
---	Nevada Red Dog	61	556
LATANG			
Elwado	Tuolumne Shawsfla	71	375
LATAPIE			
Sophie	Sonoma Sonoma	69	645
LATARO			
Frank	Tuolumne Twp 3	71	422
Manuel	Tuolumne Twp 3	71	422
LATAS			
Maria	San Francisco San Francisco 1	68	819
LATCH			
Joseph	Siskiyou Yreka	69	183
LATCHAM			
Danl	Butte Chico	56	560
LATCHER			
---	San Francisco San Francisco 3	67	39
John	San Joaquin Oneal	64	931
Louise*	Sacramento Ward 1	63	78
Nicholas	Alameda Brooklyn	55	94
LATCHLEY			
S	Nevada Grass Valley	61	153
LATE			
---	El Dorado Kelsey	58	1129
Chun	Sacramento Granite	63	251
Dajara*	Yuba Rose Bar	72	812
George	Calaveras Twp 4	57	342
Irwing	Sacramento Ward 3	63	432
Jann	Mariposa Twp 1	60	547
Pajara	Yuba Rose Bar	72	812
LATEN			
Jack	Sierra Twp 7	66	886
LATER			
Domingo	Mariposa Twp 3	60	547
George	San Joaquin Oneal	64	938
Peter*	Sierra St Louis	66	811
Throthus	Mariposa Twp 1	60	646
LATERTY			
Pepter	Sierra Downieville	66	970
LATES			
G B	Butte Oregon	56	629
G V*	Butte Oregon	56	629
LATGRIEGER			
Jacob	Yuba Marysville	72	967
LATHAM			
Charles	Santa Clara Gilroy	65	236
Geo	Placer Virginia	62	668
George	Plumas Quincy	62	987
Gurtrude	Placer Folsom	62	647
J P	Santa Clara San Jose	65	302
James	Klamath Klamath	59	225
James	San Francisco San Francisco 2	67	577
James	Sonoma Russian	69	441
John	Fresno Twp 3	59	10
John	Santa Cruz Pescadero	66	641
M S	Sacramento Ward 4	63	549
Melton S	Alameda Oakland	55	8
Robert	San Joaquin Douglass	64	924
Russell	Alameda Oakland	55	33
Sarah W	Yolo Cottonwoood	72	650
W W	El Dorado Grizzly	58	1181
W W*	Sacramento Mississipi	63	185
William B	Yuba Marysville	72	878
LATHAN			
W W*	El Dorado Grizzly	58	1181
W W*	Sacramento Mississipi	63	185
LATHARN			
Milton	Sacramento Ward 4	63	608
LATHERBACK			
D	Mariposa Twp 1	60	666
LATHERHACK			
D	Mariposa Twp 1	60	666
LATHERIS			
Latheris	San Mateo Twp 2	65	128
LATHEROP			
Ray	Sierra Twp 5	66	919
LATHERTY			
Peter	Sierra Downieville	66	970
LATHLAR			
Jame	Yuba New York	72	726
LATHORP			
J D	El Dorado Georgetown	58	752
John	Butte Ophir	56	793
LATHROP			
Asahel	San Bernardino San Bernardino	64	683
B G	San Mateo Twp 3	65	87
Benjn	Sierra Twp 5	66	919
Bridget	San Mateo Twp 3	65	87
Charles	Tuolumne Jamestown	71	426
D	Sacramento Ward 4	63	611
E J	Solano Vallejo	69	249
F	Solano Vacaville	69	325
H	Butte Hamilton	56	523
H	Butte Ophir	56	794
H B Jr	Butte Kimshaw	56	573
James	Plumas Quincy	62	952
James	Plumas Quincy	62	996
Jas	Butte Kimshaw	56	599
Jas	Butte Eureka	56	654
Jas*	Butte Kimshaw	56	599
Jnos	Butte Eureka	56	654
John	Sacramento Cosumnes	63	409
John J	San Francisco San Francisco 7	68	1340
L B	Santa Clara San Jose	65	392
Lydia	Alameda Oakland	55	52
Maria	Solano Vacaville	69	357
Marion	Solano Vacaville	69	357
Mrs	Placer Dutch Fl	62	721
O C	Tehama Red Bluff	70	919
Saml	Nevada Nevada	61	240
Wm	Santa Clara Redwood	65	454
LATHROPE			
George	Plumas Quincy	62	980
LATHUELE			
Philebor*	Alameda Brooklyn	55	98
LATHUTTE			
Philebor*	Alameda Brooklyn	55	98
LATHWELL			
Philebor	Alameda Brooklyn	55	98
LATHZE			
N	San Francisco San Francisco 9	68	1064
LATIAS			
Francisco	Yuba Marysville	72	920
LATIBER			
P	El Dorado Mud Springs	58	983
LATILA			
---	Mendocino Calpella	60	825
LATIM			
Henry	Stanislaus Branch	70	700
LATIMER			
B G	San Francisco San Francisco 10	67	338
Daniel	Calaveras Twp 5	57	243
F B	Tuolumne Twp 3	71	449
James B*	Tuolumne Twp 3	71	464
John	San Francisco San Francisco 3	67	61
John	San Francisco San Francisco 3	67	75
Mary	Sacramento Ward 4	63	501
LATIMERE			
James B	Tuolumne Twp 3	71	464
LATIMORE			
James	Tuolumne Twp 1	71	245
Lorenza	Placer Goods	62	695
Mary	Yuba Marysville	72	923
LATINOIS			
Arsenino	Calaveras Twp 4	57	313
LATIPIE			
Jas W*	Butte Kimshaw	56	597
LATIRO			
Manuel*	Tuolumne Twp 2	71	287
LATIVO			
Manuel	Tuolumne Twp 2	71	287
LATIVUR			
James B	Tuolumne Twp 3	71	464
LATKINSON			
H	Nevada Grass Valley	61	176
LATMELL			
---	Mendocino Calpella	60	825
LATMILL			
---	Mendocino Calpella	60	825
LATO			
At	Napa Clear Lake	61	125
P	Stanislaus Emory	70	737
LATON			
A J	Mariposa Twp 3	60	609
A P*	Mariposa Twp 3	60	609
C	Butte Chico	56	541
C A	Nevada Grass Valley	61	173
J	Yuba Rose Bar	72	797
Jo	Tehama Red Bluff	70	905
Josiah	Butte Eureka	56	647
Miles	Sonoma Armally	69	492
Wash C	Amador Twp 1	55	481
LATONE			
Edward	Sierra Port Win	66	794
LATONI			
Augustiv	Calaveras Twp 8	57	92

Name	County Locale	M653 Roll	Page
LATONI			
Augustus*	Calaveras Twp 8	57	92
LATONO			
E	San Francisco San Francisco 3	67	40
LATORE			
Cruz	Yuba Marysville	72	920
LATOU			
Chang	Calaveras Twp 5	57	175
LATOUR			
Chelix	Nevada Bloomfield	61	522
Francis	Calaveras Twp 8	57	93
Gustane	Calaveras Twp 7	57	43
Jean	Calaveras Twp 7	57	38
Louis	Calaveras Twp 7	57	90
Peter	Calaveras Twp 7	57	6
Phelix	Nevada Bloomfield	61	522
LATRE			
Leonata	Calaveras Twp 7	57	46
LATRICK			
H S	El Dorado Big Bar	58	743
LATROADER			
Lewis	Stanislaus Branch	70	699
LATROADIC			
Louis*	Stanislaus Branch	70	698
LATROP			
A	Colusa Spring Valley	57	435
LATRUTLE			
N	Sierra Downieville	66	968
LATSAGNE			
John	Stanislaus Emory	70	754
LATSCHAN			
Jno	Fresno Millerto	59	2
LATSHEE			
Louise	Sacramento Ward 1	63	78
LATSHLEY			
L	Nevada Grass Valley	61	153
LATSON			
A C	Napa Napa	61	69
LATSUTTE			
W*	Sierra Downieville	66	968
LATT			
---	Del Norte Happy Ca	58	664
---	Yolo Slate Ra	72	711
---	Yuba Slate Ro	72	711
John	Yolo No E Twp	72	677
LATTA			
R W	Napa Napa	61	89
Robert	Siskiyou Yreka	69	126
LATTALLARDE			
Cesario San Bernardino	Santa Barbara	64	149
Maria Anta	Santa Barbara	64	149
	San Bernardino		
LATTE			
Pedro*	Los Angeles Los Angeles	59	324
LATTEE			
Jas	Sonoma Sonoma	69	641
LATTEN			
J	Nevada Eureka	61	378
LATTERY			
John	Sacramento San Joaquin	63	363
LATTES			
Henry	El Dorado Indian D	58	1158
LATTH			
Frank*	Sonoma Vallejo	69	619
LATTIE			
A	Sacramento Ward 1	63	4
E C	Sonoma Sonoma	69	657
LATTIMER			
Jas R	Butte Hamilton	56	519
Lorenzo	Sonoma Santa Rosa	69	391
Lorenzo D	Sonoma Santa Rosa	69	391
William	Contra Costa Twp 3	57	605
LATTIN			
Ambrose	Yuba Marysville	72	960
Andrew	Yuba Marysville	72	960
J	Butte Ophir	56	795
LATTURE			
Francis	Contra Costa Twp 3	57	601
LATTY			
---	Mendocino Calpella	60	828
S*	Nevada Red Dog	61	547
LATVO			
Manuel	Tuolumne Twp 2	71	287
LATWICK			
George	Siskiyou Yreka	69	148
LATY			
R*	Calaveras Twp 9	57	400
LATYEN			
Henry*	El Dorado Cold Spring	58	1099
LATZ			
Herman	San Francisco San Francisco 3	67	22
J	San Francisco San Francisco 5	67	498
R	Calaveras Twp 9	57	400
S W	San Francisco San Francisco 5	67	498
LATZEN			
Henry	El Dorado Cold Spring	58	1099

Name	County Locale	M653 Roll	Page
LAU			
---	Mariposa Twp 3	60	569
---	Mariposa Twp 3	60	582
---	Mariposa Twp 3	60	608
---	Mariposa Twp 3	60	609
---	San Francisco San Francisco 4	68	1195
---	San Francisco San Francisco 4	68	1200
---	Sierra Twp 7	66	875
---	Stanislaus Emory	70	743
---*	Mariposa Twp 3	60	576
---*	Mariposa Twp 3	60	580
---*	Mariposa Twp 3	60	581
---*	Mariposa Twp 3	60	582
---*	Shasta Shasta	66	671
Adolph*	San Francisco San Francisco 3	67	22
Co	San Francisco San Francisco 4	68	1196
James*	Mariposa Twp 3	60	567
Kela	San Francisco San Francisco 4	68	1187
Ko	San Francisco San Francisco 4	68	1191
Leon*	Calaveras Twp 9	57	361
Mong	San Francisco San Francisco 4	68	1191
Su	San Francisco San Francisco 4	68	1191
LAUAGIN			
W	Butte Ophir	56	751
LAUARILLE			
M*	Nevada Grass Valley	61	154
LAUBE			
Rodolph*	Placer Auburn	62	561
LAUBES			
Frank*	Sonoma Vallejo	69	630
LAUBI			
Charles	Los Angeles San Gabriel	59	422
LAUCASTEN			
H	Butte Eureka	56	654
LAUCE			
W*	San Francisco San Francisco 5	67	521
LAUCHE			
Josemay*	Placer Auburn	62	584
LAUCK			
J B	Siskiyou Scott Va	69	37
LAUCY			
Margaret	Yuba Marysville	72	897
LAUD			
John P	San Joaquin Oneal	64	930
LAUDA			
Angelo	Tuolumne Sonora	71	241
John*	San Francisco San Francisco 3	67	74
LAUDER			
D R	Colusa Butte Crk	57	465
LAUDGRIST			
E*	Butte Ophir	56	765
LAUDIMAN			
Andrew J	San Joaquin Oneal	64	934
LAUDON			
L*	Napa Hot Springs	61	11
LAUDRAS			
Carl*	San Francisco San Francisco 9	68	1034
LAUDRIZAN			
M	Tuolumne Twp 4	71	135
LAUDRUM			
William	San Joaquin Castoria	64	882
LAUDRYNS			
J*	San Francisco San Francisco 9	68	1057
LAUDSBERGER			
T*	San Francisco San Francisco 3	67	82
LAUDT			
Henry*	Plumas Quincy	62	936
LAUDY			
Michael*	Sierra Twp 7	66	866
LAUELLA			
Maryketa	Tuolumne Sonora	71	220
LAUEN			
Thomas	Yuba Marysville	72	924
LAUER			
Chas	Nevada Bloomfield	61	507
E	Siskiyou Yreka	69	188
LAUERY			
Geo*	San Francisco San Francisco 9	68	1068
LAUFKETTER			
J A*	Sacramento Ward 4	63	589
LAUFKETTES			
J A*	Sacramento Ward 4	63	589
LAUFRAN			
Ljoseph*	San Mateo Twp 1	65	71
LAUG			
Chang	Alameda Brooklyn	55	80
LAUGDON			
Wm	Alameda Brooklyn	55	103
LAUGENBACH			
Chas*	Sacramento Ward 1	63	47
LAUGER			
Antonio*	San Francisco San Francisco 3	67	83
LAUGFORD			
I J	Merced Twp 1	60	908
LAUGH			
P	Nevada Grass Valley	61	155

Name	County Locale	M653 Roll	Page
LAUGHAN			
James M	Sonoma Mendocino	69	454
Thos	Sonoma Mendocino	69	447
LAUGHEAD			
Joseph	Los Angeles Elmonte	59	254
LAUGHER			
George*	Placer Michigan	62	855
Robert	Tuolumne Montezuma	71	511
LAUGHERTY			
Jno	Nevada Eureka	61	372
LAUGHERY			
John	Amador Twp 2	55	278
LAUGHEY			
John	Placer Nicolaus	62	692
LAUGHHORN			
Thos*	San Mateo Twp 3	65	78
LAUGHIN			
Mike*	Napa Napa	61	85
LAUGHLAN			
Dennis	San Francisco San Francisco 11	67	128
Jno F	Sacramento Ward 1	63	63
LAUGHLEN			
James	Tuolumne Shawsfla	71	398
LAUGHLER			
Ellen	Alameda Oakland	55	26
Michael	Alameda Brooklyn	55	155
LAUGHLIN			
B M	El Dorado Placerville	58	928
Bridget	San Francisco San Francisco 8	68	1287
Catharine	Del Norte Crescent	58	648
Catharine	San Francisco San Francisco 12	67	381
Dennis	Solano Fremont	69	384
Edward	Calaveras Twp 8	57	77
Edward	Sierra Morristown	66	1053
Edwd	Santa Clara Gilroy	65	224
Elizabeth	Sonoma Santa Rosa	69	404
George K*	San Francisco 8	68	1317
H C	San Francisco		
H C	Siskiyou Klamath	69	91
I M	El Dorado Placerville	58	932
J	San Francisco San Francisco 5	67	543
J M	San Francisco San Francisco 5	67	539
J P M	Monterey San Juan	60	989
James	Siskiyou Callahan	69	7
James	Sonoma Russian	69	434
James	Tuolumne Twp 2	71	398
James	Tuolumne Twp 3	71	458
Jas E	Sacramento Ward 1	63	107
John	Shasta French G	66	718
John	Tuolumne Twp 1	71	190
John H*	Solano Benecia	69	285
John M	Sonoma Russian	69	431
John O	Del Norte Crescent	58	647
John O	Sierra La Porte	66	766
John*	Solano Benecia	69	285
Lemidas	Sonoma Russian	69	439
Leonidas	Sonoma Russian	69	439
M	Nevada Eureka	61	367
Margaret M*	Twp 1	57	536
	Contra Costa		
Marshall	Sonoma Russian	69	446
Mary	San Francisco San Francisco 10	67	234
Michael	Calaveras Twp 5	57	196
Owin	Solano Fairfield	69	198
Stephen O	Butte Oregon	56	630
Thos	Nevada Eureka	61	374
William M*	Yuba Marysville	72	943
William*	Yuba Marysville	72	943
Wm	Napa Yount	61	36
Wm	Tuolumne Sonora	71	193
LAUGHLUN			
Michael	Calaveras Twp 5	57	196
LAUGHORNE			
Thos	Santa Clara San Jose	65	308
LAUGHRAN			
Mary A	San Francisco San Francisco 2	67	628
LAUGHREY			
John	Siskiyou Callahan	69	12
LAUGHRIN			
Terence	San Francisco San Francisco 11	67	118
LAUGHRY			
John*	Placer Nicolaus	62	692
LAUGHSEY			
John	Siskiyou Callahan	69	12
LAUGHTAN			
William*	El Dorado Placerville	58	908
LAUGHTERS			
James	Sierra La Porte	66	779
LAUGHTON			
Saml B	Tuolumne Jamestown	71	441
LAUGLEY			
Danl*	Butte Bidwell	56	729

Name	County Locale	M653 Roll	Page
LAUGLEY			
David	San Francisco San Francisco 9	68	975
Jno	San Francisco San Francisco 9	68	977
L P*	Butte Ophir	56	755
Pierre*	Plumas Meadow Valley	62	928
LAUGLIN			
Elizabeth	Sonoma Santa Rosa	69	404
H M	San Francisco San Francisco 5	67	513
Mike M	Napa Napa	61	85
LAUGLON			
Joseph M	San Diego San Diego	64	767
LAUGRIDGE			
Henry*	San Francisco San Francisco 9	68	1071
LAUGTON			
John C*	Sierra Twp 7	66	905
Richd	Tuolumne Twp 1	71	236
LAUILLA			
Maryketa*	Tuolumne Twp 1	71	220
LAUIZER			
---	Mariposa Twp 1	60	632
LAUK			
---	Yuba Long Bar	72	760
John A*	Tuolumne Shawsfla	71	380
LAUKFORD			
Thomas	Tuolumne Shawsfla	71	385
LAULES			
A*	Mariposa Twp 3	60	597
Frank*	Sonoma Vallejo	69	630
LAULIS			
Maria*	San Francisco San Francisco 2	67	763
LAUM			
Joel*	Santa Clara Fremont	65	428
LAUMER			
George*	Siskiyou Yreka	69	136
LAUMIE			
A T	Nevada Nevada	61	294
LAUN			
---	Mariposa Twp 3	60	572
---*	Shasta Shasta	66	670
Hiy	Mariposa Coulterville	60	682
LAUNAY			
Peter*	San Francisco San Francisco 9	68	994
LAUNDS			
J	Calaveras Twp 9	57	400
LAUNG			
I C	Tuolumne Big Oak	71	139
LAUNING			
Thomas*	Mendocino Anderson	60	865
LAUNIVIY			
Martin*	Calaveras Twp 4	57	329
LAUNM			
George*	Siskiyou Yreka	69	136
LAUNNCE			
Louisa	Butte Bidwell	56	710
LAUNNEI			
W	Calaveras Twp 9	57	416
LAUNOX			
John	Sierra Twp 5	66	943
LAUNS			
Henry C*	Placer Virginia	62	690
LAUNSBURY			
Chas	Monterey San Juan	60	995
LAUPE			
L H D*	Tehama Red Bluff	70	923
LAUPHER			
George*	Yuba Marysville	72	896
S T*	Marin Bolinas	60	728
LAUPHIER			
Dennis	Sonoma Healdsbu	69	473
LAUR			
---	Amador Twp 3	55	410
---	Siskiyou Scott Va	69	32
Anthony W	Calaveras Twp 6	57	152
Caroline	San Francisco San Francisco 4	68	1228
John	Butte Oro	56	674
LAURA			
---	Yuba Bear Rvr	72	1014
---	Yuba Bear Rvr	72	1015
A G	Santa Clara San Jose	65	321
Cornelia	Tuolumne Shawsfla	71	402
John	Tuolumne Columbia	71	338
Pedro	Fresno Twp 1	59	82
LAURABEE			
George B	San Francisco San Francisco 8	68	1285
LAURAIN			
Adolph	Tuolumne Shawsfla	71	402
LAURANA			
A G	Sutter Sutter	70	811
LAURANCE			
H	Santa Clara Almaden	65	270
McH*	Alameda Murray	55	218
Nich*	Alameda Murray	55	218
Richad*	Sacramento Granite	63	266
Richard*	Sacramento Granite	63	266
Richard*	Sacramento Granite	63	266
LAURASAN			
C	Trinity Grass Valley	70	962

Name	County Locale	M653 Roll	Page
LAUREEN			
Theodore	San Mateo Twp 1	65	72
LAUREN			
Garner	Mariposa Twp 1	60	640
Mark A	Yuba Suida	72	992
Pauline	Santa Clara Santa Clara	65	464
LAURENC			
Henry	Santa Cruz Pescadero	66	644
LAURENCE			
---	San Mateo Twp 3	65	108
Antonio	Mariposa Twp 3	60	617
C	Siskiyou Scott Ri	69	65
Charles	Plumas Quincy	62	972
Charles	Sierra Twp 5	66	943
Charles*	Los Angeles Santa Ana	59	443
Chas	Calaveras Twp 10	57	263
Danl	San Francisco San Francisco 1	68	838
George W	Monterey San Juan	60	995
Harry	Tuolumne Twp 1	71	138
Henry	Los Angeles Los Angeles	59	366
Henry	Los Angeles Los Angeles	59	36
Henry	Santa Clara Alviso	65	412
Henry	Santa Cruz Pescadero	66	644
J	Nevada Nevada	61	330
J B	San Francisco San Francisco 2	67	797
J H	Mariposa Twp 3	60	575
J*	Nevada Nevada	61	330
Jacob*	Butte Chico	56	559
John	El Dorado Kelsey	58	1153
Jose	Santa Cruz Santa Cruz	66	610
Joseph	Napa Napa	61	93
Lemret*	Yuba Fosters	72	835
Lemreta	Yuba Foster B	72	835
Leniret*	Yuba Fosters	72	835
Pat	Amador Twp 6	55	424
R H	Napa Clear Lake	61	131
Saml M	Calaveras Twp 6	57	155
Sister	Santa Clara San Jose	65	373
T	El Dorado Kelsey	58	1151
T	Nevada Nevada	61	374
T	Trinity Dead Wood	70	958
William	Calaveras Twp 5	57	146
Wm B	San Francisco San Francisco 3	67	49
LAURENSAIN			
Jose	Santa Cruz Santa Cruz	66	610
LAURENT			
Sastine	San Francisco San Francisco 7	68	1397
Y	Tuolumne Sonora	71	216
LAURER			
William	Siskiyou Yreka	69	137
LAURERE			
Jean*	Los Angeles Los Angeles	59	376
LAUREU			
Jean*	Los Angeles Los Angeles	59	376
LAUREW			
Jean*	Los Angeles Los Angeles	59	376
LAURIA			
Kate*	San Francisco San Francisco 2	67	603
LAURID			
Kate*	San Francisco San Francisco 2	67	603
Blair	San Francisco San Francisco 2	67	755
LAURIN			
Charles*	Calaveras Twp 5	57	240
LAURINER			
Wm B	San Francisco San Francisco 3	67	48
LAURING			
D F*	Mendocino Big Rvr	60	846
LAURINS			
Joseph	Calaveras Twp 7	57	8
LAUROBE			
William	Yuba New York	72	732
LAURON			
R E*	Sierra Downieville	66	978
LAURRAY			
Peter*	San Francisco San Francisco 9	68	994
LAURSDELL			
L*	Sonoma Bodega	69	521
LAURVY			
J	El Dorado Kelsey	58	1151
LAURY			
David	Humbolt Eureka	59	167
J C	Tuolumne Twp 4	71	139
LAUS			
Antonio	Contra Costa Twp 3	57	588
Rifugio	Contra Costa Twp 3	57	587
LAUSA			
John	Tuolumne Twp 2	71	338
LAUSE			
O	El Dorado Placerville	58	870
LAUSENA			
John*	Calaveras Twp 9	57	351
LAUSENCE			
William	Siskiyou Yreka	69	138
William*	Siskiyou Yreka	69	137
LAUSENCON			
L*	Tuolumne Twp 3	71	465

Name	County Locale	M653 Roll	Page
LAUSEND			
John*	Calaveras Twp 9	57	351
LAUSETT			
John*	Butte Ophir	56	776
LAUSEZEUR			
Felix*	San Francisco San Francisco 10	67	318
LAUSMAN			
John	Tuolumne Twp 4	71	178
Wm*	Sacramento Ward 4	63	609
LAUSON			
G A	Mariposa Twp 1	60	666
Henry	Solano Suisan	69	225
Henry*	Placer Todds Va	62	783
J C	San Francisco San Francisco 5	67	520
James	Plumas Quincy	62	973
L	San Francisco San Francisco 1	68	923
Oli*	Sierra Twp 5	66	947
R E	Sierra Downieville	66	978
William*	Napa Yount	61	31
LAUSTON			
J	El Dorado Kelsey	58	1151
LAUSWAIZ			
H*	Nevada Eureka	61	392
LAUT			
Buery	Santa Clara San Jose	65	333
LAUTEINISAR			
John B*	Calaveras Twp 6	57	178
LAUTEN			
William	San Francisco San Francisco 9	68	1032
LAUTENA			
James*	Yuba Fosters	72	837
LAUTENCE			
James*	Yuba Fosters	72	837
LAUTER			
Henry*	San Francisco San Francisco 8	68	1247
LAUTERNISAR			
John B*	Calaveras Twp 6	57	178
LAUTERWAPER			
Christian	San Francisco San Francisco 10	67	319
Christian *	San Francisco San Francisco 10	67	319
LAUTHAUMI			
Louis*	San Francisco San Francisco 3	67	6
LAUTHER			
Benj	Plumas Quincy	62	951
LAUTHICUIN			
John F*	Yuba Marysville	72	905
LAUTHY			
Mary	San Francisco San Francisco 10	67	247
LAUTINSHOLAGER			
Theado*	Placer Auburn	62	559
LAUTY			
John*	Butte Ophir	56	754
LAUTZ			
P M	Amador Twp 1	55	474
Wash*	Butte Chico	56	531
LAUVAN			
James	Sierra Downieville	66	977
LAUX			
Augustus	Colusa Butte Crk	57	464
Nicholas	Colusa Butte Crk	57	464
LAUY			
---	Mariposa Twp 3	60	619
LAUYDON			
Levi*	Calaveras Twp 10	57	287
LAUZ			
John*	Tuolumne Twp 1	71	236
LAUZZOLE			
John	Sierra Downieville	66	1010
LAV			
---*	El Dorado Casumnes	58	1160
LAVAGH			
Wm F*	Tuolumne Twp 2	71	274
LAVAHAN			
J D	Shasta Shasta	66	735
LAVALA			
Balantin	Sierra Downieville	66	965
LAVALE			
Edward	San Francisco San Francisco 2	67	617
LAVALLOIS			
Francois	Sacramento Ward 1	63	146
LAVALLORS			
Francois	Sacramento Ward 1	63	146
LAVALY			
Edward	Yuba Bear Rvr	72	1013
LAVAN			
John	San Francisco San Francisco 7	68	1443
John	Sierra Twp 7	66	908
LAVANS			
Cambro	Mariposa Twp 1	60	625
LAVAOTY			
Edward*	Yuba Bear Rvr	72	1013
LAVAR			
Casalo	Calaveras Twp 7	57	9

Name	County Locale	M653 Roll	Page
LAVARASSIER			
Dominick*	San Francisco 11		133
	San Francisco	67	
LAVARETTA			
Juan	Sacramento Ward 1	63	93
LAVARK			
Jose	Calaveras Twp 6	57	128
LAVARSORO			
Antonio*	Tuolumne Big Oak	71	140
LAVARTY			
Edward*	Yuba Bear Rvr	72	1013
LAVAS			
Joseph	Mariposa Twp 1	60	640
LAVASO			
Paul	Calaveras Twp 7	57	10
LAVASTY			
Edward*	Yuba Bear Rvr	72	1013
LAVAUS			
Cambro*	Mariposa Twp 1	60	625
LAVAZOLA			
B*	San Francisco San Francisco 2	67	570
LAVEJOY			
S G	Tuolumne Twp 1	71	258
LAVELING			
John*	Calaveras Twp 9	57	356
LAVELL			
Peater	Amador Twp 5	55	329
LAVELLE			
Ed	Mariposa Twp 3	60	571
LAVELLO			
Ed	Mariposa Twp 3	60	571
LAVEN			
J	Santa Clara Fremont	65	434
John	Alameda Brooklyn	55	118
Thos	Sacramento Ward 4	63	524
LAVEND			
Antonio*	Mariposa Twp 3	60	604
LAVENDER			
Rosana	Napa Napa	61	57
LAVENIMER			
A*	San Francisco San Francisco 9	681	105
LAVENNA			
Francis*	Calaveras Twp 5	57	258
LAVENS			
Cambro	Mariposa Twp 1	60	625
LAVENSON			
D	Sacramento Ward 4	63	544
M	Sacramento Ward 4	63	499
LAVENTHAL			
John	San Francisco San Francisco 2	67	796
LAVENUA			
Francis*	Calaveras Twp 5	57	258
LAVERA			
Frank	Alameda Brooklyn	55	125
LAVERS			
A R	Nevada Grass Valley	61	147
William*	Tulara Twp 3	71	48
LAVERT			
Enoch	Tuolumne Twp 1	71	194
LAVERTY			
Isaac	Colusa Spring Valley	57	429
J	San Joaquin Stockton	64	1100
M	El Dorado Kelsey	581	146
LAVERY			
Margaret	San Francisco San Francisco 10		177
		67	
Mayard	San Francisco San Francisco 10		177
		67	
LAVES			
Manuel	Santa Clara San Jose	65	293
LAVESON			
F	Napa Napa	61	103
LAVEZALE			
Mc Caley	Sierra Downieville	66	954
McCaley	Sierra Downieville	66	954
LAVEZZO			
Frances	Amador Twp 3	55	400
LAVIAGO			
Pabla	Tuolumne Sonora	71	232
LAVIAS			
Lucien	Santa Clara San Jose	65	327
LAVIASA			
Jose	San Francisco San Francisco 3	67	6
LAVIGA			
Paul	Tuolumne Sonora	71	224
LAVIGIN			
Victor	Stanislaus Branch	70	700
LAVIGNE			
Louis	Calaveras Twp 7	57	47
LAVILLA			
Frances*	San Francisco San Francisco 8	681	302
LAVILLA?			
Frances	San Francisco San Francisco 8	681	302
LAVILLO			
Frances	San Francisco San Francisco 8	681	302
LAVINEMER			
A*	San Francisco San Francisco 9	681	105

Name	County Locale	M653 Roll	Page
LAVING			
Peter*	Tuolumne Big Oak	71	143
LAVINGTON			
Saml	Sacramento Ward 1	63	45
LAVINIMER			
A*	San Francisco San Francisco 9	681	105
LAVIRES			
Ephraim	Calaveras Twp 10	57	287
LAVIS			
Carnull	El Dorado Gold Hill	581	096
John	El Dorado Gold Hill	581	096
Otto	Santa Cruz Santa Cruz	66	636
William	El Dorado Union	581	093
William J	San Francisco San Francisco 7	681	332
LAVISA			
Andrea*	Calaveras Twp 7	57	13
LAVISCE			
Andrea*	Calaveras Twp 7	57	13
LAVISH			
Albertina	Santa Cruz Soguel	66	597
Charles	Santa Cruz Santa Cruz	66	606
LAVISON			
F*	Napa Napa	61	103
LAVMOUR			
Robert M*	Yuba Parks Ba	72	782
LAVORDIS			
Francisco	Calaveras Twp 4	57	330
LAVORIA			
Angel	Amador Twp 1	55	507
LAVRALL			
Catharine*	San Francisco 2	67	598
	San Francisco		
LAVREEN			
Pedro*	Contra Costa Twp 1	57	497
LAVROBBY			
Robert*	Sierra Twp 7	66	868
LAVTON			
John*	Shasta Shasta	66	675
LAVVALL			
Catharine*	San Francisco 2	67	598
	San Francisco		
LAVVEBBY			
Robert*	Sierra Twp 7	66	868
LAW			
---	Amador Twp 2	55	280
---	Amador Twp 2	55	326
---	Amador Twp 5	55	360
---	Amador Twp 7	55	419
---	Calaveras Twp 6	57	151
---	El Dorado Casumnes	581	160
---	Mariposa Twp 3	60	544
---	Mariposa Twp 3	60	553
---	Mariposa Twp 3	60	564
---	Mariposa Twp 3	60	569
---	Mariposa Twp 3	60	572
---	Mariposa Coulterville	60	674
---	Placer Secret R	62	622
---	Placer Horseshoe	62	650
---	Placer Virginia	62	679
---	Placer Virginia	62	684
---	Placer Virginia	62	701
---	San Francisco San Francisco 4	681	195
---	Shasta Shasta	66	668
---	Sierra Downieville	661	009
---	Sierra Downieville	661	010
---	Sierra Downieville	661	015
---	Sierra Downieville	661	025
---	Sierra Twp 7	66	876
---	Sierra Twp 7	66	884
---	Sierra Cox'S Bar	66	951
---	Sierra Downieville	66	983
---	Sierra Downieville	66	989
---	Sierra Downieville	66	995
---	Siskiyou Scott Va	69	32
---	Stanislaus Emory	70	745
---	Yuba North Ea	72	681
---	Yuba Slate Ro	72	712
---	Yuba Linda	72	993
A	Shasta Horsetown	66	702
Adolph*	San Francisco San Francisco 3	67	22
Ah	Yuba Suida	72	993
Ah*	Butte Oregon	56	627
Ah*	Sacramento Cosumnes	63	382
Chas	San Francisco San Francisco 9	681	075
Co	San Francisco San Francisco 4	681	196
E*	Mariposa Twp 3	60	569
Frederick	Tuolumne Twp 3	71	461
Fredrick	Tuolumne Twp 3	71	461
G*	Nevada Washington	61	335
Henry	San Bernardino San Bernardino	64	636
Henry	San Francisco San Francisco 6	67	413
Ho	San Francisco San Francisco 4	681	186
J	Sutter Bear Rvr	70	818
J B	Nevada Bridgeport	61	470
James J	Yuba Marysville	72	906
Joseph M	Yuba Parks Ba	72	775

Name	County Locale	M653 Roll	Page
LAW			
Jra Green*	Alameda Brooklyn	55	146
Lan	Tuolumne Twp 4	71	167
Leon	Calaveras Twp 9	57	361
Ling	Butte Bidwell	56	720
Mat	Tulara Twp 3	71	46
Mong	San Francisco San Francisco 4	681	191
More	Mariposa Twp 3	60	551
Owen	Tehama Antelope	70	885
Pee	Sierra Cox'S Bar	66	951
Riley R	Yuba Suida	72	986
See	San Francisco San Francisco 4	681	191
Tow	San Francisco San Francisco 4	681	190
Tung*	Sacramento Cosumnes	63	388
William	Calaveras Twp 8	57	64
Yung*	Sacramento Cosumnes	63	388
LAWAINCE			
J*	Siskiyou Scott Ri	69	72
LAWAINEE			
J*	Siskiyou Scott Ri	69	72
LAWANA			
Clara G	Yuba Marysville	72	936
LAWANOS			
Clara G	Yuba Marysville	72	936
LAWARGUE			
Alexander*	Sierra Twp 7	66	916
LAWARNCE			
J	Siskiyou Scott Ri	69	72
LAWBERT			
David	San Joaquin Castoria	64	889
LAWBURTH			
H F	Sierra Twp 7	66	883
LAWCETT			
Baty	Sierra St Louis	66	806
LAWDAMEN			
John	Nevada Little Y	61	536
LAWDER			
E*	Nevada Grass Valley	61	168
LAWE			
---	El Dorado Kelsey	581	134
John	San Francisco San Francisco 9	681	097
LAWEN			
Martin	Sierra Twp 7	66	874
LAWENBERG			
J	Sierra La Porte	66	772
LAWER			
C W	Marin Novato	60	738
LAWERENCE			
B F	El Dorado Casumnes	581	169
Henry*	San Francisco San Francisco 1	68	921
Jay B	San Francisco San Francisco 7	681	401
John	El Dorado Casumnes	581	170
Srain	San Joaquin Douglass	64	919
LAWERNCE			
Helden	San Francisco San Francisco 7	681	426
John M	San Francisco San Francisco 1	68	903
Patrick	San Francisco San Francisco 1	68	809
LAWERS			
John*	Solano Benecia	69	315
LAWERY			
A	Nevada Eureka	61	380
Wm	Sacramento Ward 1	63	145
LAWHANSEN			
Henry*	San Francisco San Francisco 8	681	295
LAWHANSON			
Henry	San Francisco San Francisco 8	681	295
LAWHAUSEN			
Henry*	San Francisco San Francisco 8	681	295
LAWHEAD			
Benj	Tuolumne Montezuma	71	509
LAWHIDER			
Lewis	El Dorado Grizzly	581	182
LAWIN			
Barny	Sonoma Vallejo	69	621
Reuben	Santa Cruz Santa Cruz	66	601
LAWING			
Peter	Tuolumne Twp 4	71	143
LAWINGTON			
Saml	Sacramento Ward 1	63	45
LAWKEE			
Thomas M	Santa Cruz Santa Cruz	66	607
LAWLEN			
George	El Dorado Georgetown	58	705
LAWLEP			
Jno	Sonoma Mendocino	69	457
John	San Francisco San Francisco 7	681	330
Mariah	Solano Fairfield	69	199
Thomas	San Francisco San Francisco 8	681	317
LAWLER			
A P	San Francisco San Francisco 2	67	744
Catharin	Sonoma Sonoma	69	649
Cathatharine	Tuolumne Twp 2	71	383
Catherine	San Francisco San Francisco 4	681	119
Charles	Sierra Twp 7	66	874
Francis P	San Francisco San Francisco 9	681	099
Hannah	Sacramento Ward 1	63	95

California 1860 Census Index

Name	County Locale	M653 Roll	Page
LAWLER			
Henry	Sierra Gibsonville	66	851
Herney	Sierra Gibsonville	66	851
James	Humbolt Bucksport	59	161
James	Sierra Twp 7	66	893
James	Solano Benecia	69	287
Jerry	Siskiyou Yreka	69	152
John	San Francisco San Francisco 8	681	284
Joseph	San Francisco San Francisco 11	119 67	
Josheia	San Francisco San Francisco 10	306 67	
Joshua	San Francisco San Francisco 10	306 67	
L D	Nevada Eureka	61	381
Mary	San Francisco San Francisco 1	68	850
Mary	Yolo Washington	72	567
Michael	Placer Auburn	62	581
Michael	Sierra Twp 7	66	914
Pat	Sonoma Vallejo	69	615
Patrick	San Mateo Twp 3	65	107
Peter	San Francisco San Francisco 10	171 67	
R C	San Francisco San Francisco 2	67	743
Thomas	Tuolumne Twp 1	71	187
William B	Yuba Marysville	72	878
William M	Tuolumne Twp 2	71	383
LAWLERS			
Martin	Alameda Brooklyn	55	101
LAWLES			
John	San Francisco San Francisco 3	67	38
Maria	San Francisco San Francisco 2	67	763
Thomas	Tuolumne Sonora	71	187
William B*	Yuba Marysville	72	878
LAWLESS			
Benj	Sacramento Ward 1	63	64
Bird	Tulara Visalia	71	13
Burchard	Tulara Visalia	71	89
Eliza	Sacramento Ward 4	63	591
Jas	San Francisco San Francisco 6	67	416
Jno	Sonoma Mendocino	69	457
John	San Francisco San Francisco 7	681	330
John	San Francisco San Francisco 2	67	655
Lawrence	San Francisco San Francisco 10	278 67	
Mariah	Solano Fairfield	69	199
Michael	Contra Costa Twp 1	57	531
Patrick	Humbolt Eureka	59	165
Patrick	Sonoma Bodega	69	537
Thomas	San Francisco San Francisco 8	681	317
W	Butte Hamilton	56	523
W	Shasta Millvill	66	749
Walter	San Francisco San Francisco 7	681	425
LAWLEY			
Edward	Los Angeles San Pedro	59	481
Jno	Sacramento Granite	63	247
John*	Napa Napa	61	94
L M	Butte Oregon	56	630
Timothy	Napa Napa	61	67
LAWLIFS			
W F	Del Norte Crescent	58	640
LAWLIN			
Henry	Santa Clara Almaden	65	278
LAWLISS			
Charles	San Joaquin Elliott	64	944
LAWLON			
C	El Dorado Casumnes	581	174
Chas	San Francisco San Francisco 10	173 67	
John*	Sacramento Mississipi	63	185
LAWLOR			
Eduard*	Yuba Rose Bar	72	793
Edward	Klamath Orleans	59	215
James	El Dorado Kelsey	581	128
James	Klamath Liberty	59	233
John H	San Francisco San Francisco 7	681	439
LAWLY			
Kora	San Francisco San Francisco 10	243 67	
Nora	San Francisco San Francisco 10	243 67	
LAWMALTER			
Eva*	Placer Auburn	62	580
LAWMAN			
J M	Nevada Nevada	61	258
Saml	Santa Clara Santa Clara	65	486
LAWMASTER			
Adam	Placer Auburn	62	561
Rictria*	Placer Auburn	62	562
Rictrid*	Placer Auburn	62	562
LAWMATTER			
Eva*	Placer Auburn	62	580
LAWN			
Allen	Nevada Eureka	61	388
Chas	Tuolumne Big Oak	71	138
James H	Monterey San Juan	601	009

Name	County Locale	M653 Roll	Page
LAWN			
Joseph H	Monterey Pajaro	601	024
LAWNCHE			
Charles	Alameda Oakland	55	7
LAWNE			
S	Sutter Butte	70	798
LAWNER			
George*	Siskiyou Yreka	69	136
LAWNESS			
John	San Francisco San Francisco 1	68	903
LAWOR			
W B	El Dorado Casumnes	581	164
LAWPHER			
George	Yuba Marysville	72	896
LAWRANA			
E	Sutter Sutter	70	811
LAWRANCE			
D P	Shasta French G	66	712
Danl B	Alameda Brooklyn	55	171
David B	Alameda Washington	55	171
G H	Tuolumne Twp 1	71	275
J	Calaveras Twp 9	57	405
J	Sutter Butte	70	783
John	Alameda Brooklyn	55	146
McH*	Alameda Murray	55	218
Nis	Alameda Brooklyn	55	146
T	Sutter Vernon	70	845
LAWRANSON			
E	Tuolumne Shawsfla	71	415
Robt	Tuolumne Twp 2	71	415
LAWRCEMER			
A*	San Francisco San Francisco 9	681	105
LAWRECAUX			
Joseph	Sierra Twp 7	66	891
LAWRENC			
Wm H	San Francisco San Francisco 10	262 67	
LAWRENCE			
A	Nevada Eureka	61	381
Adam	Yuba Marysville	72	950
Albert C	Santa Clara Fremont	65	420
Albert M	Placer Auburn	62	595
Alexander	Yuba New York	72	719
Alxander	Yolo Slate Ra	72	719
C	Siskiyou Scott Ri	69	65
C A	Nevada Eureka	61	364
Charles	Los Angeles Santa Ana	59	443
Charles	Tuolumne Big Oak	71	129
Charles*	Los Angeles Santa Ana	59	443
Chas	Calaveras Twp 10	57	263
Chas	Mendocino Big Rvr	60	845
Cyrus	Plumas Quincy	62	990
D P	Shasta French G	66	712
D W	Siskiyou Scott Va	69	24
Danl B	Alameda Brooklyn	55	168
David	Sierra Port Win	66	797
E A	San Francisco San Francisco 5	67	484
E J	Marin San Rafael	60	767
Elijah	Butte Kimshaw	56	572
Emanuel	Sonoma Santa Rosa	69	401
Ephraim	Placer Auburn	62	595
Ereline A*	Monterey Pajaro	601	018
Eveline	Monterey Pajaro	601	018
Frances	Yuba Marysville	72	898
Francis	Yuba Marysville	72	898
Frank	El Dorado White Oaks	581	017
Frank	Shasta Horsetown	66	699
Fred	San Francisco San Francisco 3	67	70
Geo	Santa Clara Santa Clara	65	513
Geo	Tuolumne Twp 3	71	447
Geo S	San Francisco San Francisco 9	68	983
George	Sierra Port Win	66	791
George A	Contra Costa Twp 1	57	533
George W	Monterey San Juan	60	995
George*	Sierra Port Wie	66	791
H	San Francisco San Francisco 9	681	097
Harry	Tuolumne Big Oak	71	138
Henry	Marin Tomales	60	721
Henry	Sacramento Ward 4	63	567
Henry	San Francisco San Francisco 6	67	417
Henry*	Marin Tomales	60	721
Henry*	San Francisco San Francisco 1	68	921
Horatio	Santa Clara San Jose	65	286
Hy	San Francisco San Francisco 2	67	785
J	Nevada Nevada	61	291
J	Sonoma Cloverdale	69	684
J B	San Francisco San Francisco 2	67	797
J C	Amador Twp 2	55	273
J H	Tuolumne Twp 2	71	293
J J	San Francisco San Francisco 6	67	471
J*	Yolo Putah	72	549
Jacob	Butte Chico	56	559
James	Humbolt Mattole	59	126
James	Nevada Bridgeport	61	448
James	San Francisco San Francisco 9	681	100
James	Sierra Downieville	661	023

Name	County Locale	M653 Roll	Page
LAWRENCE			
James	Yuba Fosters	72	837
James A	Sonoma Armally	69	480
James R	San Francisco San Francisco 8	681	307
Jno	Butte Kimshaw	56	580
John	El Dorado Kelsey	581	153
John	El Dorado Casumnes	581	170
John	Nevada Bloomfield	61	519
John	Placer Ophir	62	652
John	Placer Iona Hills	62	897
John	Sierra Twp 7	66	896
John	Siskiyou Shasta Valley	69	117
John E	Tuolumne Twp 3	71	447
Jos A	Del Norte Crescent	58	624
Joseph	Marin Cortemad	60	756
Joseph	Napa Napa	61	93
K	San Francisco San Francisco 9	681	070
L L	San Francisco San Francisco 1	68	829
Leonard	Butte Kimshaw	56	580
Louis	Contra Costa Twp 1	57	537
Louisa	Butte Bidwell	56	710
M	El Dorado Placerville	58	865
M	San Francisco San Francisco 9	681	070
M	San Francisco San Francisco 5	681	097
M	San Francisco San Francisco 4	681	162
M	San Francisco San Francisco 6	67	454
M T	Sacramento San Joaquin	63	367
Manuel*	San Francisco San Francisco 1	68	850
Manuel*	Del Norte Crescent	58	624
Marim*	Calaveras Twp 8	57	95
Mary	San Bernardino San Salvador	64	658
Nelson	Napa Napa	61	100
Paul	San Francisco San Francisco 1	68	920
Peter	Contra Costa Twp 2	57	548
Philip	Tuolumne Shawsfla	71	400
R H	Napa Clear Lake	61	131
Richard	Sacramento Granite	63	266
S C	Sonoma Petaluma	69	583
Steven	Sonoma Vallejo	69	612
Thomas	Marin Cortemad	60	782
Thos	Santa Clara Santa Clara	65	488
W	San Francisco San Francisco 9	681	059
W	Tuolumne Twp 3	71	450
W D	Sacramento Ward 3	63	443
W H	Tuolumne Twp 3	71	445
Warren	Mariposa Twp 1	60	638
William	Placer Iona Hills	62	884
William D	San Francisco San Francisco 7	681	347
William H	San Joaquin Oneal	64	933
William L	Yuba Marysville	72	909
William S	Yuba Marysville	72	909
Wm	Mariposa Twp 1	60	647
Wm	Placer Secret R	62	615
Wm	Tehama Lassen	70	870
Wm	Tuolumne Shawsfla	71	389
Wm B	San Francisco San Francisco 3	67	48
Wm H	San Francisco San Francisco 10	262 67	
LAWRENCIA			
Goachim	Tuolumne Visalia	71	91
Goachun	Tulara Twp 1	71	91
LAWRENS			
Charles	Sierra Downieville	661	029
LAWRENSON			
Patrick	San Francisco San Francisco 7	681	334
LAWREO			
Joseph	Trinity Lewiston	70	963
LAWRER			
William*	Siskiyou Yreka	69	137
LAWREY			
Christopher	Marin Cortemad	60	782
George	Solano Fremont	69	382
T	El Dorado Placerville	58	873
LAWRIA			
Kate*	San Francisco San Francisco 2	67	603
LAWRICE			
P	Yolo Cache	72	624
LAWRIE			
Chas	Sacramento Franklin	63	315
Jas R	Santa Clara Santa Clara	65	467
LAWRINCE			
George*	Sierra Port Win	66	791
LAWRL			
Lupus	Tuolumne Twp 2	71	370
LAWRNCE			
Jno	Butte Kimshaw	56	580
LAWROX			
J	Nevada Eureka	61	372
LAWRY			
Walter	Sierra Twp 7	66	900
LAWS			
Eliza	Sacramento Granite	63	252
George	Trinity Prices B	701	019
George	Yuba Marysville	72	901
Jas	San Francisco San Francisco 2	67	794

Name	County Locale	M653 Roll	Page
LAWS			
John	San Francisco San Francisco 10	194	
		67	
Jos	San Francisco San Francisco 2	67	794
R C	Nevada Washington	61	337
Wm	El Dorado Georgetown	58	691
LAWSAN			
Geo N	Sacramento Natonia	63	278
LAWSDALE			
W*	Shasta Shasta	66	684
LAWSEN			
Andrew	San Francisco San Francisco 7	681443	
C	Mariposa Twp 1	60	671
Geo N	Sacramento Natonia	63	278
James	Sierra Downieville	661017	
James*	Amador Twp 2	55	309
LAWSENCER			
Ezekiel	San Joaquin Elkhorn	64	980
LAWSMON			
Squire	Sierra Twp 7	66	899
LAWSON			
A	Butte Bidwell	56	712
A	Placer Mountain	62	708
A	San Francisco San Francisco 9	681069	
Albert	San Francisco San Francisco 6	67	420
Andrew	Calaveras Twp 8	57	96
Andrew	Marin Novato	60	739
Benjamin	San Joaquin Tulare	64	870
C	Mariposa Twp 1	60	671
Charles	Tuolumne Twp 3	71	438
Chas	San Francisco San Francisco 9	681072	
Chas	San Francisco San Francisco 2	67	704
Christian	San Francisco San Francisco 7	681444	
Danl	Tuolumne Jamestown	71	445
F	Sacramento Georgian	63	344
F	San Francisco San Francisco 5	67	544
G W	Yuba Rose Bar	72	793
Geo T	Siskiyou Klamath	69	84
Gilbert A	Yuba Linda	72	983
H C	El Dorado Salmon Hills	581060	
H M	Nevada Nevada	61	321
Henry	Sacramento Ward 1	63	34
Henry	Solano Suisan	69	225
J	Sutter Nicolaus	70	827
J S	Sacramento San Joaquin	63	360
James	Yuba Linda	72	994
James F	Yuba Suida	72	994
Jane*	Plumas Quincy	62	978
Jno	Butte Chico	56	560
Jno	Mendocino Round Va	60	879
John	Calaveras Twp 9	57	356
John	Calaveras Twp 9	57	371
John	El Dorado Mountain	581189	
John	Marin Bolinas	60	745
John	Sacramento Georgian	63	344
John	Sierra Twp 7	66	913
John	Tuolumne Twp 2	71	287
John*	Calaveras Twp 5	57	240
Joshua	Yolo Cache Crk	72	632
L	Mendocino Anderson	60	869
Lawrence	Marin Point Re	60	729
Nelson	San Joaquin Stockton	641050	
Norman	Sacramento Ward 4	63	599
O	Marin Cortemad	60	781
P	Amador Twp 6	55	427
P	Sutter Sutter	70	811
P	Trinity Trinity	70	971
P S	Sacramento Ward 3	63	423
Peter	Mariposa Twp 1	60	671
Peter	Tuolumne Twp 1	71	214
Ralim C	Yolo Cache	72	631
Robert	Calaveras Twp 9	57	348
S H	Mendocino Anderson	60	870
Saml	Stanislaus Emory	70	751
Samuel	El Dorado Kelsey	581127	
Samuel	Mendocino Anderson	60	867
Susan	San Francisco San Francisco 9	681105	
Thomas	Del Norte Crescent	58	641
Thomas L	Calaveras Twp 7	57	13
Thos	San Francisco San Francisco 6	67	462
William	Napa Yount	61	31
William	Tulara Twp 3	71	53
Wm	Calaveras Twp 9	57	380
LAWSOR			
Robert*	Calaveras Twp 9	57	348
LAWTELL			
Alfred	El Dorado Mud Springs	581000	
LAWTER			
Charles	Sierra Twp 7	66	874
LAWTHER			
Wm*	Del Norte Crescent	58	650
LAWTHIR			
Wm*	Del Norte Crescent	58	650
LAWTON			
A S C	Amador Twp 2	55	266
C	El Dorado Casumnes	581174	

Name	County Locale	M653 Roll	Page
LAWTON			
Charles	Santa Cruz Santa Cruz	66	619
David	Siskiyou Yreka	69	166
Dennis	Nevada Bridgeport	61	501
F	San Francisco San Francisco 10	250	
		67	
Frank	Yuba Marysville	72	979
George	Tuolumne Columbia	71	351
George	Tuolumne Jamestown	71	451
H	San Francisco San Francisco 5	67	537
H D	Sacramento Ward 4	63	520
H W	El Dorado Mountain	581186	
Harriet	Solano Benecia	69	304
J G Jr	Solano Suisan	69	208
Jno	Sacramento Ward 4	63	536
John H	San Francisco San Francisco 8	681257	
John W	San Francisco San Francisco 12	378	
		67	
John*	Sacramento Mississipi	63	185
S G	Butte Hamilton	56	528
Stephen	Yuba Bear Rvr	721005	
Theodore	San Francisco San Francisco 10	230	
		67	
W	San Francisco San Francisco 5	67	540
W W	San Francisco San Francisco 10	250	
		67	
William	San Francisco San Francisco 11	154	
		67	
LAWUX			
J*	Nevada Eureka	61	372
LAWVER			
S	Butte Cascade	56	697
LAWYER			
A J	El Dorado Kelsey	581140	
Abbey	Sacramento Ward 4	63	498
Augustus	Sacramento Ward 4	63	528
Elbridgo*	Tulara Twp 3	71	45
Eugene	Monterey San Juan	60	995
Francisco*	Santa Cruz Santa Cruz	66	632
Frank	Amador Twp 5	55	348
Geo	Stanislaus Empire	70	735
J M	Tuolumne Twp 3	71	453
LAWYOR			
Thomas	El Dorado Mud Springs	58	999
LAX			
Frank	El Dorado Eldorado	58	947
Moses	El Dorado Coloma	581113	
Stephen	Nevada Nevada	61	287
William	El Dorado Salmon Hills	581054	
LAXTON			
R	El Dorado Placerville	58	934
W W	Amador Twp 3	55	405
LAY			
---	Amador Twp 3	55	379
---	Amador Twp 1	55	502
---	Amador Twp 1	55	503
---	Calaveras Twp 5	57	212
---	Calaveras Twp 10	57	276
---	Del Norte Crescent	58	633
---	El Dorado White Oaks	581011	
---	El Dorado White Oaks	581032	
---	El Dorado Salmon Falls	581046	
---	El Dorado Salmon Falls	581050	
---	El Dorado Salmon Falls	581053	
---	El Dorado Salmon Falls	581054	
---	El Dorado Salmon Falls	581063	
---	El Dorado Coloma	581121	
---	El Dorado Kelsey	581133	
---	El Dorado Mountain	581190	
---	El Dorado Diamond	58	788
---	El Dorado Diamond	58	803
---	El Dorado Diamond	58	816
---	El Dorado Placerville	58	830
---	El Dorado Placerville	58	842
---	El Dorado Placerville	58	929
---	El Dorado Eldorado	58	941
---	El Dorado Eldorado	58	942
---	El Dorado Mud Springs	58	961
---	El Dorado Mud Springs	58	985
---	El Dorado Mud Springs	58	986
---	El Dorado Mud Springs	58	992
---	Mariposa Twp 3	60	608
---	Mariposa Twp 3	60	619
---	Mariposa Twp 3	60	620
---	Mariposa Coulterville	60	683
---	Mariposa Coulterville	60	685
---	Nevada Grass Valley	61	228
---	Nevada Grass Valley	61	229
---	Nevada Grass Valley	61	230
---	Nevada Grass Valley	61	231
---	Nevada Grass Valley	61	234
---	Nevada Nevada	61	299
---	Nevada Rough &	61	396
---	Nevada Rough &	61	399
---	Nevada Rough &	61	431
---	Nevada Bridgeport	61	460

Name	County Locale	M653 Roll	Page
LAY			
---	Nevada Bridgeport	61	461
---	Nevada Bridgeport	61	463
---	Nevada Bridgeport	61	492
---	Nevada Bridgeport	61	506
---	Nevada Bloomfield	61	521
---	Placer Auburn	62	576
---	Placer Auburn	62	581
---	Placer Folsom	62	649
---	Plumas Quincy	62	949
---	Shasta Horsetown	66	698
---	Shasta Horsetown	66	706
---	Sierra Downieville	661029	
---	Stanislaus Emory	70	743
---	Yolo No E Twp	72	681
---	Yolo Slate Ra	72	715
---	Yuba Long Bar	72	758
---*	Amador Twp 2	55	289
---*	Calaveras Twp 5	57	212
---*	El Dorado Salmon Falls	581064	
---*	Mariposa Twp 3	60	581
Ah	Tuolumne Twp 4	71	181
At	Mariposa Twp 3	60	620
Daniel	El Dorado Mud Springs	58	998
E A*	Amador Twp 2	55	288
Frank	Sonoma Sonoma	69	655
James	Nevada Bridgeport	61	450
James	Plumas Meadow Valley	62	905
James	Solano Vallejo	69	244
James*	Nevada Bridgeport	61	450
John	Solano Vallejo	69	251
Me	El Dorado Coloma	581086	
Peter	Siskiyou Yreka	69	186
Sam*	Nevada Washington	61	342
Say	Mariposa Twp 3	60	562
Sing	Placer Auburn	62	582
T H	Stanislaus Emory	70	742
Yay	Mariposa Twp 3	60	544
Young	Mariposa Twp 3	60	544
LAYAL			
Lawriana	Fresno Twp 1	59	83
LAYARD			
Simon	San Francisco San Francisco 5	67	479
LAYAS			
O	El Dorado Placerville	58	859
LAYAWAY			
Mr	Sonoma Vallejo	69	622
LAYBRAND			
Jas	San Francisco San Francisco 10	260	
		67	
LAYCOCK			
---	Mendocino Round Va	60	884
Diyden*	Mendocino Round Va	60	877
Dujden*	Mendocino Round Va	60	877
Jacob*	Los Angeles Los Angeles	59	339
Joseph	Solano Vacaville	69	319
Mary*	Napa Napa	61	96
Sarah*	Solano Vacaville	69	319
LAYCORK			
Mary	Napa Napa	61	96
LAYDON			
Charles	Santa Clara Gilroy	65	244
LAYEE			
Chew*	Yuba Foster B	72	830
LAYER			
Hunting	San Francisco San Francisco 8	681268	
Mary*	San Francisco San Francisco 2	67	653
Reuben L*	San Francisco 10	188	
	San Francisco	67	
LAYERS			
H	Mariposa Twp 3	60	554
LAYET			
Paul	Humbolt Eureka	59	163
LAYFAETTE			
Martin	Yolo No E Twp	72	683
Martin	Yuba Slate Ro	72	683
LAYFIELD			
Geo	San Francisco San Francisco 9	681004	
Jas	Sacramento Natonia	63	278
LAYHAY			
Thomas	Nevada Bridgeport	61	442
LAYHRE			
Joh	Calaveras Twp 6	57	148
John*	Calaveras Twp 6	57	148
LAYJOEL			
R B	Nevada Grass Valley	61	144
LAYJOES			
R B	Nevada Grass Valley	61	144
LAYLAU			
John	Del Norte Klamath	58	653
LAYLEY			
Charles*	Placer Todds Va	62	764
Daniel*	Placer Todds Va	62	764
LAYM			
F H*	Nevada Nevada	61	323
LAYMAN			
---	Mendocino Round Va	60	882

California 1860 Census Index

Name	County Locale	M653 Roll	Page
LAYMAN			
Jno	Mendocino Anderson	60	871
LAYMANCE			
Isaac C	Sonoma Mendocino	69	465
J W	Sutter Nicolaus	70	835
LAYNAN			
Julius*	Stanislaus Branch	70	699
LAYNE			
F H*	Nevada Nevada	61	323
Jno A*	Butte Chico	56	535
Marshall	El Dorado Salmon Falls	58	1037
LAYNEWAY			
Mr*	Sonoma Vallejo	69	622
LAYNSTON			
William*	Contra Costa Twp 3	57	605
LAYNX			
F H*	Nevada Nevada	61	323
LAYON			
---	Nevada Grass Valley	61	229
LAYORAN			
Jane W	San Francisco San Francisco 9	68	1056
LAYRAS			
A	Sacramento Ward 1	63	45
LAYRETTE			
S	Mariposa Twp 3	60	614
LAYRIX			
F H*	Nevada Nevada	61	323
LAYS			
William	Contra Costa Twp 1	57	493
LAYTIN			
Wh*	Butte Oro	56	687
LAYTON			
A	El Dorado Coloma	58	1071
Augustus	Placer Iona Hills	62	885
Charles L	Monterey Monterey	60	957
David	Calaveras Twp 10	57	265
Edward	Santa Cruz Pescadero	66	647
Elbridge	Siskiyou Scott Ri	69	70
Eliza	Placer Secret R	62	609
Frank D	San Francisco San Francisco 2	67	638
G F	Nevada Grass Valley	61	177
Garret	Placer Secret R	62	609
Geo	Placer Dutch Fl	62	709
H	Nevada Nevada	61	269
H F	San Francisco San Francisco 1	68	887
Hannah	El Dorado Georgetown	58	707
Horace	Colusa Mansville	57	437
J S	Placer Todds Va	62	784
James	Calaveras Twp 10	57	280
Jas	San Francisco San Francisco 1	68	896
John	Solano Green Valley	69	242
John*	Mariposa Twp 1	60	663
Jon	Solano Green Valley	69	242
Lenard	Placer Secret R	62	609
N	Colusa Monroeville	57	443
N	Nevada Nevada	61	269
Richard	Placer Secret R	62	609
Richard	Sierra Downieville	66	1016
Robt C	Plumas Quincy	62	980
Sarah	Santa Clara Fremont	65	426
W H	Butte Oro	56	687
Wm	Amador Twp 5	55	367
Wm H	Tuolumne Big Oak	71	134
LAYTOYNI			
A	Stanislaus Branch	70	700
LAYTTAKINN			
Roland Y	Sierra Eureka	66	1047
LAYUES			
P*	El Dorado Placerville	58	833
LAYUSTON			
William*	Contra Costa Twp 3	57	605
LAYWER			
A W	Marin Novato	60	738
LAZ			
---	Trinity Lewiston	70	956
---	Yuba Slate Ro	72	715
LAZALEE			
Mary	Yolo Washington	72	567
LAZAR			
David*	Nevada Nevada	61	328
LAZARA			
Maria	Los Angeles Los Angeles	59	370
LAZARD			
Simon	San Francisco San Francisco 5	67	479
Solomon	Los Angeles Los Angeles	59	339
LAZARNS			
Saml	Del Norte Crescent	58	621
LAZARO			
Jose	Santa Cruz Pajaro	66	530
Olvina*	Yuba Marysville	72	925
LAZAROOICH			
John	Los Angeles Los Angeles	59	357
LAZAROVICH			
John	Los Angeles Los Angeles	59	357
LAZARUS			
Leobose	Solano Vallejo	69	259

Name	County Locale	M653 Roll	Page
LAZERODY			
John	Sierra Eureka	66	1046
LAZEWILL			
Thomas	Yuba Marysville	72	909
LAZIE			
Robert	Plumas Meadow Valley	62	913
LAZIER			
Antone	Mendocino Round Va	60	878
David*	Nevada Nevada	61	328
LAZUR			
David*	Nevada Nevada	61	328
LAZZIE			
E	Nevada Nevada	61	262
LAZZO			
Garmon	Tuolumne Twp 3	71	425
LBSOR			
E F*	Calaveras Twp 9	57	370
LCHOLY			
Luis*	Calaveras Twp 4	57	332
LCURY			
Frank*	Sonoma Sonoma	69	660
LDOSA			
Ventosa	Tulara Keyesville	71	55
LE ANG			
---	Nevada Rough &	61	433
---	Nevada Rough &	61	434
LE BAENF			
Thelesphoer*	Sierra La Porte	66	772
LE BAEUF			
Thelesphoer*	Sierra La Porte	66	772
LE BARR			
John	Placer Forest H	62	773
LE BEAN			
Charles	Siskiyou Yreka	69	186
LE BLANCE			
Adelle	San Francisco San Francisco 2	67	698
LE BLAUC			
Yis	Sierra Twp 7	66	864
LE BOYD			
John*	Amador Twp 2	55	261
LE CHEE			
---	Nevada Red Dog	61	539
LE CHUG			
---*	Nevada Bridgeport	61	460
LE CLANG			
---*	Nevada Bridgeport	61	458
LE CLEVE			
Eugene	Tuolumne Twp 4	71	139
LE CONNT			
A*	Sacramento Ward 1	63	28
LE COUNT			
A*	Sacramento Ward 1	63	28
M	Sacramento Franklin	63	315
LE CRAW			
Felix	San Bernardino San Bernadino	64	640
LE CROG			
Emile*	Los Angeles Santa Ana	59	448
Fredk	San Francisco San Francisco 2	67	626
LE CROY			
Emile*	Los Angeles Santa Ana	59	448
LE CUM			
Ah*	Sacramento Ward 1	63	152
LE DAM			
---	Yuba New York	72	739
LE DUE			
M C	Amador Twp 2	55	306
LE DUKE			
Fanny	San Francisco San Francisco 6	67	449
LE FOE			
---*	Tuolumne Knights	71	528
LE GALLE			
J	Sacramento Ward 1	63	24
LE GATE			
W H	Amador Twp 2	55	295
LE GOFF			
Pierre	Tuolumne Twp 4	71	140
LE GROW			
Asa	Plumas Quincy	62	992
LE HAN			
Mert*	Yuba Rose Bar	72	803
LE HARDY			
Charles*	Yuba Parke Ba	72	785
LE HE ANG			
---	Yuba Long Bar	72	756
LE KING			
---	Nevada Red Dog	61	549
LE LING			
---	Mariposa Twp 3	60	613
LE LONG			
John	San Bernardino San Bernadino	64	640
LE LOO			
---	Yuba Long Bar	72	759
LE MAIN			
John*	Humbolt Pacific	59	138
LE MAN			
---	Nevada Bridgeport	61	460

Name	County Locale	M653 Roll	Page
LE NIAPONE			
---*	Mariposa Twp 3	60	614
LE NIREY			
---*	Nevada Red Dog	61	539
LE NIVEY			
---*	Nevada Red Dog	61	539
LE OC			
---	Nevada Red Dog	61	549
LE ON			
---	Nevada Rough &	61	436
LE ONG			
---	Nevada Rough &	61	438
---	Nevada Bridgeport	61	439
---	Nevada Bridgeport	61	460
---	Nevada Red Dog	61	549
---	Tuolumne Chinese	71	522
LE PAGE			
Alexander*	Placer Damascus	62	846
LE PAUL			
Jean*	Sacramento Ward 1	63	149
LE PLU			
Henri	Plumas Quincy	62	1001
LE QUE			
---	Mariposa Twp 3	60	608
LE RAY			
J	Amador Twp 2	55	287
LE ROY			
Jesse	San Joaquin Elliott	64	1104
LE SANG			
---	Mariposa Twp 3	60	608
LE SELT			
---*	Nevada Bridgeport	61	459
LE SEVER			
Henry	Sacramento Ward 1	63	39
LE SING			
---	Nevada Bridgeport	61	458
LE SONG			
---*	Alameda Oakland	55	33
LE SOU			
---	Nevada Bridgeport	61	459
LE STRADE			
---*	Mariposa Twp 3	60	600
LE VALLE			
J	Sacramento Ward 1	63	24
LE VANT			
---	Mariposa Twp 3	60	614
LE WAH			
Kep*	Sacramento Ward 1	63	59
LE WAY			
---	Nevada Rough &	61	437
LE WO			
---	Nevada Rough &	61	434
LE YEE			
Pong	Yuba Long Bar	72	766
LE			
---	Calaveras Twp 4	57	334
---	El Dorado Georgetown	58	701
---	Mariposa Twp 3	60	546
---	Mariposa Twp 3	60	563
---	Mariposa Twp 3	60	612
---	Mariposa Coulterville	60	681
---	Mariposa Coulterville	60	687
---	San Francisco San Francisco 9	68	1056
---	San Francisco San Francisco 3	67	7
---	Sierra La Porte	66	774
---	Sierra Twp 7	66	877
---	Sierra Downieville	66	982
---	Tuolumne Twp 3	71	439
---	Yuba Long Bar	72	759
A	Yolo Putah	72	551
An*	Mariposa Twp 3	60	576
Ang	Nevada Rough &	61	434
Ang	Nevada Bridgeport	61	460
Au*	Mariposa Twp 3	60	576
Aug	Nevada Rough &	61	433
Cam	Calaveras Twp 4	57	334
Camp	Sacramento Granite	63	249
Chang	El Dorado Mud Springs	58	992
Ching	Nevada Bridgeport	61	491
Chon	Nevada Grass Valley	61	228
Chow	Nevada Grass Valley	61	228
Chug	Nevada Bridgeport	61	460
Chung	Alameda Oakland	55	34
Chung	Calaveras Twp 4	57	341
Clay	Nevada Bridgeport	61	458
Cong	Butte Wyandotte	56	665
Cong	El Dorado Placerville	58	842
Cum	Calaveras Twp 4	57	334
Cum	Placer Illinois	62	753
Du	Mariposa Twp 3	60	590
Fae	Tuolumne Big Oak	71	149
Foe*	Tuolumne Knights	71	528
Fong	El Dorado Placerville	58	886
Fong*	Placer Auburn	62	576
Foo	Tuolumne Twp 6	71	528
Foy	Calaveras Twp 4	57	320

Name	County Locale	M653 RollPage
LE		
Gue	Sierra Downieville	66 984
Hep	Sacramento Granite	63 268
Hi	Nevada Rough &	61 396
Hite	Yuba Long Bar	72 762
Hon	Tuolumne Big Oak	71 147
Hong	Alameda Oakland	55 34
Hong	Yuba Long Bar	72 764
How	Calaveras Twp 4	57 334
Kong	El Dorado Mud Springs	58 992
Kou*	Mariposa Twp 3	60 576
Kow	Mariposa Twp 3	60 578
Lan	Stanislaus Emory	70 752
Lang	El Dorado Placerville	58 831
Lary	Amador Twp 6	55 432
Leavis	Stanislaus Emory	70 744
Leo*	Butte Oregon	56 632
Li	El Dorado Georgetown	58 756
Ling	Nevada Rough &	61 434
Long	Nevada Rough &	61 396
Long	Nevada Rough &	61 434
Lou	Yuba Long Bar	72 759
Low	Butte Oregon	56 643
Man	Nevada Rough &	61 397
Man	Nevada Bridgeport	61 460
Mang	Calaveras Twp 6	57 182
Mans	Mariposa Twp 3	60 620
Mow	Calaveras Twp 4	57 334
Mung	Calaveras Twp 6	57 182
Nah	Sacramento Ward 1	63 145
Nim	Nevada Rough &	61 409
Niny	Calaveras Twp 5	57 193
On	Nevada Rough &	61 436
One	Nevada Bloomfield	61 522
Ong	Nevada Rough &	61 396
Ong	Nevada Rough &	61 423
Ong	Nevada Rough &	61 425
Ong	Nevada Rough &	61 426
Ong	Nevada Rough &	61 438
Ong	Nevada Bridgeport	61 439
Ong	Tuolumne Twp 5	71 522
Ong	Yuba Long Bar	72 759
Ony	Calaveras Twp 5	57 219
Ony	Calaveras Twp 4	57 314
Ory	Sierra La Porte	66 780
Oue	Nevada Bloomfield	61 522
Peng	Yuba Long Bar	72 764
Pur	Amador Twp 5	55 330
Qua	Mariposa Twp 3	60 575
San	Nevada Rough &	61 409
Sary	Amador Twp 6	55 432
See	Mariposa Twp 3	60 613
Selt	Nevada Bridgeport	61 459
Sing	Nevada Bridgeport	61 458
Sing	Sacramento Granite	63 249
Son	Nevada Bridgeport	61 459
Song	Alameda Oakland	55 34
Song*	Alameda Oakland	55 33
Sung	Nevada Rough &	61 395
Te	Calaveras Twp 10	57 283
Ti	Calaveras Twp 10	57 283
To	Sierra Downieville	66 999
Ton	Stanislaus Emory	70 753
Tong	Alameda Oakland	55 33
Tong*	Placer Auburn	62 576
Uing	Calaveras Twp 6	57 134
Ung	Calaveras Twp 5	57 255
Uny	Calaveras Twp 5	57 255
Wa	Nevada Bloomfield	61 521
Way	Nevada Rough &	61 437
Wee	Nevada Rough &	61 399
Wing	Calaveras Twp 5	57 193
Wo	Nevada Rough &	61 434
Wo	Nevada Bloomfield	61 521
Won	Placer Iona Hills	62 896
Wu	Calaveras Twp 5	57 252
Wu	Nevada Rough &	61 399
Ya	Yuba Long Bar	72 766
Ya Pong	Yuba Long Bar	72 766
Yah	Tuolumne Big Oak	71 179
Young	Mariposa Twp 3	60 544
Young*	Calaveras Twp 4	57 337
Yow	Calaveras Twp 5	57 203
Yow	Stanislaus Emory	70 752
Yuang	Calaveras Twp 4	57 337
LE?ARO		
Antonio*	San Francisco San Francisco 3	67 83
LE?GLES		
Jacob	Tuolumne Twp 1	71 239
LEA KING		
---	Placer Stewart	62 606
LEA		
---	Calaveras Twp 4	57 334
---	Calaveras Twp 8	57 50
---	El Dorado Indian D	581159
---	El Dorado Georgetown	58 705

Name	County Locale	M653 RollPage
LEA		
---	El Dorado Mud Springs	58 956
---	Mariposa Twp 3	60 545
---	Mariposa Twp 1	60 651
---	Placer Rattle Snake	62 626
---	Placer Rattle Snake	62 627
---	Placer Rattle Snake	62 631
---	Placer Ophirville	62 654
---	Placer Virginia	62 665
---	Placer Virginia	62 672
---	San Francisco San Francisco 4	681195
---	Sierra Twp 5	66 945
---*	Mariposa Coulterville	60 684
F	Solano Vacaville	69 331
Geo	Amador Twp 2	55 318
Gone	El Dorado Placerville	58 831
Henry	El Dorado Mud Springs	58 952
John	Tehama Pasakent	70 858
John	Yolo No E Twp	72 676
King	Mariposa Twp 3	60 569
Lerke*	Tuolumne Twp 2	71 415
Leven	Tuolumne Twp 1	71 269
Luke	Tuolumne Shawsfla	71 415
R	Sacramento Brighton	63 208
Thomas M	Tuolumne Twp 4	71 136
Thos	Sacramento San Joaquin	63 358
Thos	Tuolumne Twp 4	71 125
LEABAUGH		
A*	Sacramento Franklin	63 328
LEABERT		
Antonia	Mariposa Coulterville	60 685
LEACH WM		
Curtis	Del Norte Crescent	58 645
LEACH		
A W	Amador Twp 2	55 271
Antone	Butte Chico	56 539
Arch	Stanislaus Emory	70 748
Cassander	Solano Vacaville	69 359
Cassandir	Solano Vacaville	69 359
Charles G	Tuolumne Big Oak	71 131
Charles S	San Joaquin Elkhorn	64 964
Charles W	San Joaquin Douglass	64 914
Chas	San Francisco San Francisco 9	681055
Chas	San Francisco San Francisco 9	681060
E W	Napa Napa	61 98
Frances	San Bernardino San Bernadino	64 623
G G	El Dorado White Oaks	581017
Henry	Trinity Minersville	70 969
Henry W	Tuolumne Big Oak	71 131
Isaac B	Placer Auburn	62 569
J C	San Francisco San Francisco 5	67 484
J F	Shasta Horsetown	66 702
James	Los Angeles Los Angeles	59 403
James C	Tuolumne Twp 2	71 284
Jas	Monterey Alisal	601035
John	Amador Twp 5	55 358
John	Humbolt Union	59 189
John	Placer Rattle Snake	62 599
John A	Solano Vacaville	69 359
Joseph*	Amador Twp 4	55 254
Julius	Fresno Twp 1	59 33
L M	Mariposa Twp 3	60 574
L P	El Dorado Newtown	58 781
Lewis	Fresno Twp 1	59 33
Robt	San Francisco San Francisco 10	223 67
Stephen W	San Francisco San Francisco 7	681350
Thomas	Tuolumne Twp 2	71 401
W	El Dorado Eldorado	58 948
Warren*	Sacramento Ward 3	63 610
William	Del Norte Crescent	58 633
William	Del Norte Crescent	58 634
Z C	Nevada Bridgeport	61 487
LEACHMAN		
A T	El Dorado Salmon Falls	581038
John	Siskiyou Scott Va	69 53
L E	Nevada Red Dog	61 542
LEACHY		
---	Mendocino Calpella	60 827
LEACK		
Warren*	Sacramento Ward 4	63 610
LEAD FACE		
---	Fresno Twp 1	59 119
LEADAIN		
Henry*	Butte Ophir	56 751
LEADAM		
Henry	Butte Ophir	56 751
LEADER		
D*	Nevada Eureka	61 390
Wm	Tuolumne Twp 2	71 297
LEADLING		
John*	Alameda Brooklyn	55 133
LEADNER		
S W	San Francisco San Francisco 6	67 403

Name	County Locale	M653 RollPage
LEAF		
Chas	Butte Kimshaw	56 581
LEAG		
---	Placer Virginia	62 680
---	Trinity Mouth Ca	701014
LEAGERWOOD		
Wm	Solano Suisan	69 222
LEAGO		
Timon	Fresno Twp 1	59 82
LEAGRA		
---	Yuba Bear Rvr	721015
LEAGUE		
Charles*	Amador Twp 6	55 244
Wm	Alameda Brooklyn	55 103
LEAGUESAN		
Mariano	San Francisco San Francisco 6	67 439
LEAH		
---	Calaveras Twp 4	57 320
---	Yuba Long Bar	72 752
LEAHAM		
Elizabeth	San Francisco San Francisco 2	67 724
LEAHAMS		
James	San Francisco San Francisco 2	67 723
LEAHEY		
Hannah*	San Francisco San Francisco 3	67 33
Jerry	San Francisco San Francisco 11	108 67
LEAHROOK		
Geo	Sacramento Granite	63 252
LEAHY		
Danl	San Francisco San Francisco 2	67 677
Eduard	Yuba Rose Bar	72 803
Edward	Yuba Rose Bar	72 803
Mathew	Los Angeles Los Angeles	59 335
Thomas	Los Angeles Los Angeles	59 338
Timothy	Colusa Grand Island	57 469
Timothy	Tuolumne Twp 3	71 461
LEAJO		
L	Mariposa Twp 3	60 594
LEAK		
---	Sierra Twp 5	66 932
---	Sierra Twp 5	66 933
---*	Trinity Weaverville	701072
A	Amador Twp 1	55 451
Care W	Calaveras Twp 9	57 360
Carr W	Calaveras Twp 9	57 360
R R	Merced Twp 1	60 895
LEAKE		
---	Placer Stewart	62 606
LEAKS		
Chas A*	Calaveras Twp 6	57 119
LEAL		
Nim	Butte Bidwell	56 708
LEALEY		
J H	Napa Clear Lake	61 132
Wm	El Dorado Kelsey	581154
LEALS		
J*	Mariposa Twp 3	60 583
LEAM		
---*	Placer Illinois	62 754
W M	San Francisco San Francisco 5	67 529
LEAMAN		
J	Amador Twp 1	55 495
John	Mariposa Twp 3	60 617
O	Shasta Shasta	66 728
W W	Calaveras Twp 8	57 89
LEAMORE		
F	Tuolumne Twp 2	71 403
John*	Napa Napa	61 100
LEAN		
---	Amador Twp 7	55 414
---	Amador Twp 5	55 425
---	Butte Ophir	56 781
---	El Dorado Salmon Falls	581043
---	Placer Virginia	62 676
---	Placer Illinois	62 704
---	Placer Dutch Fl	62 714
---	Sierra Twp 7	66 886
---	Sierra Twp 5	66 934
Cornelius	San Francisco San Francisco 12	375 67
Fin	Butte Ophir	56 820
Fot	Butte Ophir	56 819
Fur	Butte Ophir	56 787
Fur	Butte Ophir	56 804
Hop	Butte Ophir	56 801
Hop	Butte Ophir	56 813
Hops	Butte Ophir	56 818
J	Nevada Grass Valley	61 171
M B	Shasta Cottonwood	66 737
Stephen	Shasta Shasta	66 735
W M	El Dorado Casumnes	581172
William	Shasta Cottonwood	66 736
Wm	Calaveras Twp 9	57 374
LEANART		
D	Mariposa Coulterville	60 678

California 1860 Census Index

Name	County Locale	M653 Roll	Page
LEANDER			
J	Siskiyou Scott Va	69	60
LEANDO			
Jospeh	Calaveras Twp 5	57	203
LEANDRA			
---	San Bernardino Santa Ba	64	219
---	San Bernardino S Buenav	64	220
LEANDRE			
R	Siskiyou Scott Ri	69	62
LEANDRO			
---	San Bernardino San Bernadino	64	669
---	San Diego Temecula	64	784
Miguil	San Bernardino Santa Barbara	64	202
LEANE			
---	Sierra Twp 7	66	886
---	Sierra Twp 7	66	898
LEANG			
---	Placer Secret R	62	622
---	Placer Secret R	62	623
LEANMAIRE			
W	Mariposa Twp 1	60	636
LEANORT			
D	Mariposa Coulterville	60	678
LEANS			
John H	San Mateo Twp 3	65	81
LEANSE			
Isaac	Yolo Putah	72	551
LEANSMAN			
Henry*	Mariposa Twp 3	60	587
LEANY			
Ed	Sacramento Natonia	63	285
LEAO			
---	Mariposa Twp 3	60	562
---	Placer Rattle Snake	62	625
LEAP			
---	Tuolumne Twp 6	71	536
Carlas*	Siskiyou Scott Va	69	55
Carlos*	Siskiyou Scott Va	69	55
Corlos	Siskiyou Scott Va	69	55
Tom	Placer Illinois	62	751
Z	El Dorado Diamond	58	804
LEAPALD			
P	Santa Clara San Jose	65	335
LEAPER			
W G	Siskiyou Scott Va	69	56
LEAPP			
Jas	Placer Dutch Fl	62	714
LEAR			
---	Mariposa Twp 3	60	609
Crozir	Mariposa Twp 1	60	647
H F	El Dorado Diamond	58	768
Henry	Solano Vacaville	69	338
N	El Dorado Placerville	58	870
Richard	Santa Cruz Santa Cruz	66	630
Thomas	San Francisco San Francisco 9	681002	
Thomas	San Francisco San Francisco 11	67	142
LEARDIS			
John	Mariposa Coulterville	60	677
LEARETTA			
John	Calaveras Twp 7	57	43
LEAREY			
James*	Siskiyou Scott Va	69	22
LEARGER			
Daniel	Calaveras Twp 9	57	370
LEARGOR			
Daniel	Calaveras Twp 9	57	370
LEARING			
H	San Francisco San Francisco 4	681231	
LEARITT			
Holland	Amador Twp 1	55	474
LEARL			
Geo*	Tuolumne Big Oak	71	128
LEARMOND			
Oscar E*	San Francisco San Francisco 7	681431	
LEARNARD			
C E	Calaveras Twp 7	57	17
LEARNED			
Andw M	San Francisco San Francisco 10	67	331
LEARNEY			
Philip	Napa Yount	61	42
LEARNORD			
Jasiah*	Calaveras Twp 8	57	90
LEARNY			
T	San Francisco San Francisco 5	67	533
LEARONGOOD			
Jno	Tehama Pasakent	70	860
LEARRY			
T	San Francisco San Francisco 5	67	533
LEARS			
W J	Shasta Horsetown	66	702
LEARY			
Anderson*	Yuba Marysville	72	907
Anna	Yuba Marysville	72	908
Barney	El Dorado Mud Springs	58	995
C E	Tuolumne Twp 2	71	322
Catharine	San Francisco San Francisco 7	681443	
Catherine	Santa Clara San Jose	65	340
Daniel	Napa Yount	61	42
Danl	San Francisco San Francisco 1	68	835
Dennis	Trinity Weaverville	701064	
Dennis O*	San Francisco San Francisco 8	681275	
E*	Trinity Sturdiva	701007	
Ed*	Sacramento Natonia	63	285
Frank	Sonoma Sonoma	69	660
G	Nevada Grass Valley	61	225
J	Sacramento Franklin	63	329
J	Sutter Nicolaus	70	834
James	Sonoma Petaluma	69	604
Jas	Sacramento Sutter	63	289
Jas	Sacramento Ward 3	63	475
Jno	Butte Oregon	56	610
Jno	Butte Eureka	56	650
Jno*	Butte Oregon	56	610
Jno*	Butte Eureka	56	650
John	Calaveras Twp 7	57	48
John	El Dorado Mud Springs	58	998
John	San Francisco San Francisco 12	67	370
John	Yuba Long Bar	72	755
John C	El Dorado Coloma	581078	
John O*	El Dorado Coloma	581078	
John O*	El Dorado Diamond	58	765
L	El Dorado White Oaks	581004	
M	El Dorado Placerville	58	870
M O	San Francisco San Francisco 10	67	313
Mathew	Amador Twp 2	55	322
Michael*	Butte Kimshaw	56	607
Michl*	Sacramento Ward 1	63	94
P	Sutter Bear Rvr	70	825
Patrick	Amador Twp 3	55	371
Robt*	Sacramento Ward 4	63	544
Sam	Klamath Liberty	59	240
T	Nevada Grass Valley	61	203
T E	Sacramento Ward 4	63	497
W	San Francisco San Francisco 9	681073	
W*	San Francisco San Francisco 9	681074	
Wm	Sonoma Bodega	69	534
LEASE			
Conrad	Alameda Brooklyn	55	81
H A	Butte Chico	56	533
O B	El Dorado Gold Hill	581097	
LEASHER			
William	Plumas Quincy	62	939
LEASNAN			
Henry*	Mariposa Twp 3	60	587
LEASON			
M	Calaveras Twp 9	57	417
LEASS			
---	Nevada Rough &	61	437
LEATCH			
Geo W	Sacramento Ward 1	63	73
Joseph	Siskiyou Yreka	69	183
W H	Mendocino Anderson	60	867
LEATHERER			
Charles	Humbolt Union	59	180
LEATHERS			
Valias	Yolo Cache	72	624
LEATHUS			
John	Yolo Cache Crk	72	624
Valers	Yolo Cache Crk	72	624
LEATO			
Leon	Calaveras Twp 7	57	9
LEATRY			
Thos	Sacramento Ward 1	63	109
LEAU			
---	Mariposa Twp 3	60	569
LEAVAR			
Frank	El Dorado Salmon Falls	581050	
LEAVARA			
S	Amador Township	55	466
LEAVE			
---	Sierra Twp 7	66	898
LEAVECK			
Simon*	Tuolumne Big Oak	71	135
LEAVENWORTH			
Mark	Santa Clara San Jose	65	280
Rafael	Santa Clara San Jose	65	312
LEAVER			
George	Contra Costa Twp 2	57	550
Margaret	Marin Bolinas	60	740
Rudolph	Sierra Twp 5	66	935
LEAVERITE			
J L*	San Francisco San Francisco 9	681102	
LEAVERITT			
J L	San Francisco San Francisco 9	681102	
LEAVERS			
C M*	Sacramento Granite	63	242
LEAVETT			
Edward	San Francisco San Francisco 3	67	52
J	San Francisco San Francisco 5	67	536
LEAVEY			
Elisha P*	Yuba Rose Bar	72	803
Oliver*	Humbolt Table Bl	59	141
LEAVICK			
Simon	Tuolumne Twp 4	71	135
LEAVIG			
Elisha P*	Yuba Rose Bar	72	803
LEAVIT			
Joseph	Contra Costa Twp 2	57	551
LEAVITT			
Alonzo E	Plumas Quincy	62	967
Ann P	San Francisco San Francisco 7	681361	
Benjamin	Yolo New York	72	720
Benjamin	Yuba New York	72	720
Chas H	Placer Sacramento	62	646
David C	Placer Folsom	62	640
E M	San Francisco San Francisco 9	681075	
Edward	San Francisco San Francisco 3	67	52
George	Calaveras Twp 6	57	155
J S	San Francisco San Francisco 6	67	459
John	Sacramento Ward 1	63	98
Moses	Yuba Parks Ba	72	782
S B	El Dorado Grizzly	581179	
S C	Nevada Grass Valley	61	161
S D	Nevada Grass Valley	61	161
S R	El Dorado Grizzly	581179	
William H	Calaveras Twp 6	57	118
Wm R	Contra Costa Twp 1	57	536
LEAVY			
A D	Tuolumne Springfield	71	374
Anna	Yuba Marysville	72	908
George*	Amador Twp 4	55	254
Mary B	Yuba Marysville	72	908
Robt*	Sacramento Ward 4	63	544
LEAW			
---	Mariposa Twp 3	60	544
LEAWARD			
James B*	Yuba Marysville	72	847
John	Yuba Bear Rvr	721005	
LEAWELL			
W A	Napa Napa	61	68
W M	Tuolumne Big Oak	71	153
LEAWERD			
H	El Dorado Diamond	58	814
LEAWOOD			
Owen	Calaveras Twp 9	57	384
LEAY			
Chas	Sonoma Salt Point	69	692
LEBA			
Anistaria	Tuolumne Chinese	71	491
Anistasia	Tuolumne Twp 5	71	491
LEBAKE			
Carl	Sacramento Ward 4	63	499
LEBAN			
Adolph*	Yuba New York	72	725
John	Amador Twp 2	55	318
LEBARON			
W	Sutter Bear Rvr	70	824
LEBARRON			
Erastus	El Dorado Kelsey	581136	
LEBART			
Fred	Siskiyou Cottonwoood	69	102
LEBASSE			
Amond	Siskiyou Callahan	69	3
Amond*	Siskiyou Callahan	69	4
LEBASTAPOOL			
Geo	Mariposa Twp 3	60	549
LEBASTIN			
Dennis	Siskiyou Yreka	69	147
Denniz	Siskiyou Yreka	69	147
LEBAU			
John	Amador Twp 2	55	318
LEBBERRY			
H	Mariposa Twp 3	60	610
LEBBETS			
M C*	Napa Hot Springs	61	5
LEBBEY			
W H	Nevada Eureka	61	376
LEBBIE			
C	Nevada Grass Valley	61	158
LEBBITS			
M C*	Napa Hot Springs	61	5
LEBEAN			
B	Amador Twp 1	55	491
LEBEAVE			
Jeremiah*	Yuba Bear Rvr	721006	
LEBENBERG			
Chs*	San Francisco San Francisco 3	67	26
LEBENDELFER			
D S	Placer Dutch Fl	62	730
LEBERER			
Lorenzo	Alameda Brooklyn	55	82
LEBERON			
W	San Mateo Twp 2	65	120

Name	County Locale	M653 Roll	Page
LEBETRFIELD			
W D	San Francisco San Francisco 3	67	80
LEBKISHER			
H Y*	Marin Cortemad	60	786
LEBLANCE			
E F	Siskiyou Klamath	69	92
LEBLIS			
Eugene	Sierra Poker Flats	66	840
LEBLOND			
Amader*	Alameda Oakland	55	5
Amadie*	Alameda Oakland	55	5
LEBO			
Joel	Napa Clear Lake	61	121
LEBOEAF			
Francis	Yuba Marysville	72	906
LEBOLD			
Thoms*	El Dorado Georgetown	58	706
LEBONE			
Felix	San Francisco San Francisco 2	67	684
LEBONER			
W J*	Calaveras Twp 9	57	389
LEBOREER			
W J*	Calaveras Twp 9	57	389
LEBOURCH			
G	San Francisco San Francisco 2	67	682
LEBOY			
Joseph	Calaveras Twp 7	57	5
LEBRA			
Elaria	Tuolumne Twp 1	71	256
Samuel	Amador Twp 3	55	390
LEBRAN			
Adolph*	Yuba New York	72	725
LEBRAU			
Adolph*	Yuba New York	72	725
LEBREF			
F J*	Mariposa Twp 1	60	669
LEBRIAS			
Leon	Butte Oregon	56	619
LEBROE			
Jeremiah	Yuba Bear Rvr	721006	
LEBRY			
F J	Mariposa Twp 1	60	669
LEBUCK			
S L	Nevada Grass Valley	61	147
LEBUMDAH			
---	Mendocino Round Va	60	881
LEBY			
---	San Francisco San Francisco 4	681	177
Lewis	San Bernardino San Bernadino	64	627
S	Tuolumne Twp 2	71	326
LECADMAN			
---	Mendocino Twp 1	60	890
LECARO			
Antonio*	San Francisco San Francisco 3	67	83
LECATA			
R	El Dorado Diamond	58	804
LECAUF			
---	Sacramento Granite	63	249
LECEA			
Pepa	San Francisco San Francisco 10	327 67	
LECEN			
Gobenone	Siskiyou Callahan	69	7
Goberoene*	Siskiyou Callahan	69	7
Jobening	Siskiyou Callahan	69	7
LECERE			
Francois	Yuba Marysville	72	965
LECH			
Ah	Butte Oregon	56	641
LECHLER			
Peter B	Yuba Linda Twp	72	982
LECHNAR			
George	Sierra Eureka	661047	
LECHTENSTEIN			
Richard*	San Francisco San Francisco 4	681	123
LECIERC			
Louis S	Calaveras Twp 4	57	339
LECIND			
Husevia*	Mariposa Twp 1	60	630
LECK			
---	Butte Oregon	56	617
---	El Dorado Coloma	581123	
---*	Yuba Fosters	72	841
Sing*	Mariposa Twp 3	60	579
LECKENHOSS			
Chas	Amador Twp 7	55	412
LECKIE			
John	San Francisco San Francisco 10	328 67	
LECKMAN			
M	Sacramento Sutter	63	303
LECKREMO			
---	Fresno Twp 2	59	46
LECLAIR			
Peter	Calaveras Twp 8	57	99
LECLAU			
John Baptist*	Alameda Murray	55	228

Name	County Locale	M653 Roll	Page
LECLEIC			
Louis S*	Calaveras Twp 4	57	339
LECLERC			
Louis S*	Calaveras Twp 4	57	339
LECLERK			
Theo	Stanislaus Buena Village	70	723
LECOCQ			
Alfred	Tuolumne Twp 5	71	492
LECOHAN			
Edward*	Calaveras Twp 5	57	210
LECOKE			
Mich	Sacramento Granite	63	266
LECOMBELA			
William	Sierra Scales D	66	801
LECOMPH			
M*	El Dorado Georgetown	58	689
LECOMPLE			
John*	Yuba Marysville	72	903
LECOMPT			
Lewis	Santa Cruz Pajaro	66	531
Pierre	San Francisco San Francisco 7	681	394
LECOMPTE			
Anna	San Francisco San Francisco 7	681	349
LECONEY			
J	San Francisco San Francisco 6	67	472
LECONG			
---	El Dorado Mountain	581186	
LECONVRIER			
Frank	Los Angeles Los Angeles	59	353
LECOR			
A J	Yolo Washington	72	563
Carlos	Los Angeles San Pedro	59	484
LECORDER			
Desin	San Francisco San Francisco 4	681	162
LECORE			
Peter	Butte Bidwell	56	725
LECOSTA			
John	Alameda Murray	55	228
LECOT			
R	Amador Twp 1	55	459
LECOUNG			
---	El Dorado Mud Springs	58	966
LECOUNT			
J J	San Francisco San Francisco 5	67	478
LECOURER			
Frank	Los Angeles Los Angeles	59	365
LECOURRIER			
Wank	Los Angeles Los Angeles	59	353
LECOUVER			
Frank	Los Angeles Los Angeles	59	365
LECRAFT			
Saml H*	Calaveras Twp 6	57	139
LECRIEJ			
Robert*	Siskiyou Scott Ri	69	62
LECRIEV			
Henry	Sierra Eureka	661050	
LECRIG			
Robert*	Siskiyou Scott Ri	69	62
LECRIY			
Robert	Siskiyou Scott Ri	69	62
LECROFT			
Saml H	Calaveras Twp 5	57	139
LECROG			
Emile*	Los Angeles Santa Ana	59	448
J	San Francisco San Francisco 2	67	788
LECROQ			
Emile*	Los Angeles Santa Ana	59	448
LECROX			
Juan	Los Angeles Los Angeles	59	504
LECROY			
Felix	Los Angeles Los Angeles	59	316
LECRTE			
Stephen*	Calaveras Twp 5	57	225
LECRTO			
Stephen*	Calaveras Twp 5	57	225
LECRUZ			
John	San Francisco San Francisco 11	137 67	
LECTERC			
Louis S*	Calaveras Twp 4	57	339
LECTERE			
Louis S*	Calaveras Twp 4	57	339
LECTORO			
---	Fresno Twp 2	59	101
LECTOVALD			
Jacob	San Francisco San Francisco 11	115 67	
LECTRO			
Antonio*	San Francisco San Francisco 11	124 67	
LECUME			
---	Mendocino Round Va	60	881
LECURE			
---*	Tulara Visalia	71	4
LECUSS			
Mary J	Solano Vacaville	69	341

Name	County Locale	M653 Roll	Page
LEDA			
Ramone	Los Angeles Elmonte	59	254
Saml R	Alameda Brooklyn	55	78
LEDAN			
Francis*	Placer Dutch Fl	62	712
LEDAU			
John Baptist*	Alameda Murray	55	228
LEDAY			
Soni	San Francisco San Francisco 10	179 67	
Soui*	San Francisco San Francisco 10	179 67	
LEDBETTER			
Henry	Butte Hamilton	56	519
LEDBURROW			
Mk	Nevada Eureka	61	363
LEDBURROWS			
M	Nevada Eureka	61	363
LEDCOAT			
T	Nevada Grass Valley	61	201
LEDDELL			
George	Santa Cruz Santa Cruz	66	603
LEDDICK			
S B	Nevada Red Dog	61	543
LEDDIN			
James	San Francisco San Francisco 9	681010	
LEDDY			
James	San Francisco San Francisco 7	681	331
James	Yuba Marysville	72	864
John	Placer Michigan	62	815
Jos	Amador Twp 6	55	441
Pat	Sonoma Santa Rosa	69	418
Thomas	Colusa Muion	57	459
Thos*	Mariposa Twp 3	60	563
LEDEAC			
Chas*	Placer Auburn	62	582
LEDEAE			
Chas*	Placer Auburn	62	582
LEDEILLAN			
Victorine	San Francisco San Francisco 10	249 67	
LEDEN			
Leon*	Yuba Fosters	72	832
LEDERMAN			
Henry	Amador Twp 4	55	246
LEDESMA			
Rafaeld	San Francisco San Francisco 2	67	656
LEDETIA			
Charles	Siskiyou Yreka	69	134
LEDFORD			
A S	Amador Twp 3	55	383
Charles	Colusa Grand Island	57	473
T	San Francisco San Francisco 5	67	497
Van C	Tuolumne Sonora	71	212
W R	Yolo Cache Crk	72	664
LEDGER			
A	Nevada Bridgeport	61	498
LEDGERWOOD			
Wm	Solano Suisan	69	222
LEDIKAR			
Thos F*	Stanislaus Oatvale	70	718
LEDLER			
J C	Sacramento Ward 1	63	80
LEDLEY			
Geo	El Dorado White Oaks	581020	
LEDLIA			
Ledlia	Siskiyou Yreka	69	134
LEDLIE			
J C*	Sacramento Ward 1	63	80
LEDLIR			
J C*	Sacramento Ward 1	63	80
LEDON			
Francis*	Placer Dutch Fl	62	712
Julion	Mariposa Twp 1	60	625
Tulion	Mariposa Twp 1	60	625
LEDONE			
Chas	El Dorado Greenwood	58	724
LEDRE			
Jose*	Santa Cruz Santa Cruz	66	623
LEDRER			
Leon*	Yuba Fosters	72	832
LEDRO			
Jose*	Santa Cruz Santa Cruz	66	623
LEDRU			
Leon*	Yuba Fosters	72	832
LEDUC			
J B*	Siskiyou Scott Ri	69	65
LEDUE			
J B	Siskiyou Scott Ri	69	65
LEDUKE			
Isidor	Santa Clara San Jose	65	295
LEDWETH			
A F	San Francisco San Francisco 6	67	463
LEDWIDGE			
John	Sonoma Santa Rosa	69	400
LEDWITH			
? F*	San Francisco San Francisco 6	67	463

Name	County Locale	M653 Roll	Page
LEDWITH			
A F*	San Francisco San Francisco	6 67	463
LEDYARD			
G C	Butte Hamilton	56	523
Samuel*	San Joaquin O'Neal	64	1004
LEE CHUNG			
---	San Joaquin Stockton	64	1087
LEE DUE			
M C	Amador Twp 2	55	306
LEE HI			
---	Solano Vallejo	69	248
LEE HOU			
---	Mariposa Twp 3	60	613
LEE KA			
---	Mariposa Twp 3	60	609
LEE LON			
---*	Yuba Fosters	72	842
LEE ME			
---	Mariposa Twp 3	60	607
LEE			
---	Alameda Oakland	55	35
---	Alameda Oakland	55	53
---	Alameda Oakland	55	63
---	Alameda Oakland	55	64
---	Alameda Oakland	55	71
---	Amador Twp 4	55	247
---	Amador Twp 4	55	251
---	Amador Twp 4	55	252
---	Amador Twp 2	55	280
---	Amador Twp 2	55	288
---	Amador Twp 2	55	291
---	Amador Twp 2	55	292
---	Amador Twp 2	55	294
---	Amador Twp 2	55	310
---	Amador Twp 2	55	311
---	Amador Twp 2	55	312
---	Amador Twp 2	55	315
---	Amador Twp 2	55	319
---	Amador Twp 2	55	327
---	Amador Twp 4	55	332
---	Amador Twp 5	55	333
---	Amador Twp 5	55	335
---	Amador Twp 5	55	341
---	Amador Twp 5	55	348
---	Amador Twp 5	55	355
---	Amador Twp 5	55	365
---	Amador Twp 3	55	386
---	Amador Twp 3	55	394
---	Amador Twp 3	55	402
---	Amador Twp 3	55	403
---	Amador Twp 3	55	408
---	Amador Twp 3	55	410
---	Amador Twp 7	55	413
---	Amador Twp 7	55	414
---	Amador Twp 7	55	415
---	Amador Twp 7	55	418
---	Amador Twp 7	55	419
---	Amador Twp 6	55	422
---	Amador Twp 6	55	423
---	Amador Twp 6	55	424
---	Amador Twp 6	55	428
---	Amador Twp 6	55	430
---	Amador Twp 6	55	431
---	Amador Twp 6	55	446
---	Amador Twp 6	55	447
---	Amador Twp 6	55	449
---	Amador Twp 6	55	450
---	Amador Twp 1	55	458
---	Amador Twp 1	55	477
---	Amador Twp 1	55	478
---	Amador Twp 1	55	497
---	Amador Twp 1	55	501
---	Butte Hamilton	56	530
---	Butte Kimshaw	56	577
---	Butte Kimshaw	56	578
---	Butte Kimshaw	56	589
---	Butte Kimshaw	56	598
---	Butte Kimshaw	56	600
---	Butte Kimshaw	56	605
---	Butte Oregon	56	613
---	Butte Oregon	56	615
---	Butte Oregon	56	618
---	Butte Oregon	56	638
---	Butte Wyandotte	56	672
---	Butte Oro	56	677
---	Butte Cascade	56	700
---	Butte Cascade	56	701
---	Butte Bidwell	56	709
---	Butte Bidwell	56	720
---	Butte Bidwell	56	726
---	Butte Mountain	56	735
---	Butte Ophir	56	801
---	Butte Ophir	56	806
---	Butte Ophir	56	811
---	Butte Ophir	56	818

Name	County Locale	M653 Roll	Page
LEE			
---	Calaveras Twp 8	57	107
---	Calaveras Twp 5	57	141
---	Calaveras Twp 5	57	149
---	Calaveras Twp 6	57	159
---	Calaveras Twp 5	57	204
---	Calaveras Twp 10	57	259
---	Calaveras Twp 10	57	280
---	Calaveras Twp 4	57	316
---	Calaveras Twp 4	57	328
---	Calaveras Twp 9	57	362
---	Calaveras Twp 7	57	42
---	Calaveras Twp 7	57	44
---	Calaveras Twp 8	57	49
---	Calaveras Twp 8	57	60
---	Calaveras Twp 8	57	63
---	El Dorado Salmon Falls	58	1040
---	El Dorado Salmon Falls	58	1043
---	El Dorado Salmon Falls	58	1045
---	El Dorado Salmon Falls	58	1046
---	El Dorado Coloma	58	1077
---	El Dorado Union	58	1089
---	El Dorado Coloma	58	1103
---	El Dorado Coloma	58	1109
---	El Dorado Casumnes	58	1160
---	El Dorado Georgetown	58	700
---	El Dorado Georgetown	58	756
---	El Dorado Diamond	58	784
---	El Dorado Diamond	58	796
---	El Dorado Diamond	58	798
---	El Dorado Diamond	58	803
---	El Dorado Diamond	58	808
---	El Dorado Placerville	58	840
---	El Dorado Placerville	58	906
---	El Dorado Placerville	58	923
---	El Dorado Placerville	58	924
---	El Dorado Placerville	58	931
---	El Dorado Placerville	58	934
---	El Dorado Mud Springs	58	991
---	Fresno Twp 1	59	26
---	Fresno Twp 1	59	27
---	Fresno Twp 3	59	32
---	Fresno Twp 2	59	49
---	Klamath Liberty	59	235
---	Mariposa Twp 3	60	546
---	Mariposa Twp 3	60	550
---	Mariposa Twp 3	60	551
---	Mariposa Twp 3	60	560
---	Mariposa Twp 3	60	562
---	Mariposa Twp 3	60	563
---	Mariposa Twp 3	60	564
---	Mariposa Twp 3	60	572
---	Mariposa Twp 3	60	576
---	Mariposa Twp 3	60	578
---	Mariposa Twp 3	60	580
---	Mariposa Twp 3	60	582
---	Mariposa Twp 3	60	586
---	Mariposa Twp 3	60	588
---	Mariposa Twp 3	60	608
---	Mariposa Twp 3	60	612
---	Mariposa Twp 3	60	613
---	Mariposa Twp 3	60	618
---	Mariposa Twp 3	60	619
---	Mariposa Twp 3	60	620
---	Mariposa Twp 1	60	650
---	Mariposa Twp 1	60	666
---	Mariposa Coulterville	60	683
---	Mariposa Coulterville	60	685
---	Mariposa Coulterville	60	687
---	Mariposa Coulterville	60	691
---	Mariposa Coulterville	60	692
---	Nevada Grass Valley	61	228
---	Nevada Grass Valley	61	232
---	Nevada Nevada	61	306
---	Nevada Rough &	61	423
---	Nevada Rough &	61	432
---	Nevada Bridgeport	61	461
---	Nevada Bridgeport	61	493
---	Placer Rattle Snake	62	637
---	Placer Michigan	62	819
---	Plumas Meadow Valley	62	909
---	Plumas Quincy	62	947
---	Sacramento Mississipi	63	188
---	Sacramento Granite	63	251
---	Sacramento Granite	63	259
---	Sacramento Natonia	63	280
---	Sacramento Natonia	63	283
---	Sacramento Sutter	63	307
---	Sacramento Sutter	63	308
---	Sacramento Cosumnes	63	384
---	Sacramento Cosumnes	63	388
---	Sacramento Cosumnes	63	392
---	Sacramento Cosumnes	63	400
---	Sacramento Ward 3	63	490
---	Sacramento Ward 1	63	52
---	Sacramento Ward 1	63	53

Name	County Locale	M653 Roll	Page
LEE			
---	Sacramento Ward 1	63	54
---	Sacramento Ward 1	63	56
---	Sacramento Ward 4	63	613
---	Sacramento Ward 1	63	61
---	San Francisco San Francisco 9	68	1094
---	San Francisco San Francisco 9	68	1095
---	San Francisco San Francisco 4	68	1184
---	San Francisco San Francisco 4	68	1185
---	San Francisco San Francisco 4	68	1190
---	San Francisco San Francisco 4	68	1191
---	San Francisco San Francisco 4	68	1192
---	San Francisco San Francisco 4	68	1195
---	San Francisco San Francisco 4	68	1196
---	San Francisco San Francisco 4	68	1199
---	San Francisco San Francisco 4	68	1203
---	San Francisco San Francisco 5	67	1206
---	San Francisco San Francisco 4	68	1209
---	San Francisco San Francisco 11	67	145
---	San Francisco San Francisco 6	67	470
---	San Francisco San Francisco 2	67	676
---	San Joaquin Stockton	64	1088
---	Shasta Horsetown	66	701
---	Sierra Downieville	66	1003
---	Sierra Downieville	66	1004
---	Sierra Downieville	66	1005
---	Sierra Downieville	66	1009
---	Sierra Downieville	66	1014
---	Sierra Downieville	66	1027
---	Sierra Downieville	66	1029
---	Sierra Morristown	66	1055
---	Sierra La Porte	66	774
---	Sierra St Louis	66	805
---	Sierra St Louis	66	813
---	Sierra St Louis	66	815
---	Sierra St Louis	66	816
---	Sierra St Louis	66	817
---	Sierra Pine Grove	66	832
---	Sierra Whiskey	66	843
---	Sierra St Louis	66	861
---	Sierra Twp 7	66	876
---	Sierra Twp 7	66	877
---	Sierra Twp 5	66	924
---	Sierra Twp 5	66	932
---	Sierra Twp 5	66	933
---	Sierra Twp 5	66	935
---	Sierra Twp 5	66	942
---	Sierra Twp 5	66	945
---	Sierra Twp 5	66	947
---	Sierra Cox'S Bar	66	949
---	Sierra Cox'S Bar	66	951
---	Sierra Downieville	66	953
---	Sierra Downieville	66	981
---	Sierra Downieville	66	985
---	Siskiyou Callahan	69	8
---	Stanislaus Emory	70	743
---	Tehama Red Bluff	70	932
---	Trinity Mouth Ca	70	1018
---	Trinity Price'S	70	1019
---	Trinity Taylor'S	70	1035
---	Trinity Lewiston	70	956
---	Trinity Dead Wood	70	958
---	Trinity China Bar	70	959
---	Tuolumne Big Oak	71	149
---	Tuolumne Jacksonville	71	167
---	Tuolumne Columbia	71	307
---	Tuolumne Shawsfla	71	394
---	Tuolumne Twp 3	71	433
---	Tuolumne Jamestown	71	434
---	Tuolumne Jamestown	71	436
---	Tuolumne Twp 3	71	438
---	Tuolumne Jamestown	71	439
---	Tuolumne Twp 3	71	452
---	Tuolumne Jamestown	71	455
---	Tuolumne Jamestown	71	456
---	Tuolumne Twp 3	71	457
---	Tuolumne Twp 3	71	458
---	Tuolumne Twp 3	71	467
---	Tuolumne Columbia	71	474
---	Tuolumne Twp 1	71	478
---	Tuolumne Sonora	71	485
---	Tuolumne Twp 5	71	513
---	Tuolumne Jacksonville	71	514
---	Tuolumne Chinese	71	525
---	Tuolumne Chinese	71	526
---	Tuolumne Twp 6	71	528
---	Tuolumne Green Springs	71	531
---	Tuolumne Don Pedro	71	535
---	Tuolumne Twp 6	71	536
---	Tuolumne Twp 6	71	540
---	Yolo No E Twp	72	677
---	Yolo No E Twp	72	681
---	Yolo No E Twp	72	685
---	Yolo Slate Ra	72	708

California 1860 Census Index

Name	County Locale	M653 Roll	Page
LEE			
---	Yolo Slate Ra	72	710
---	Yolo Slate Ra	72	711
---	Yolo Slate Ra	72	712
---	Yolo Slate Ra	72	713
---	Yolo Slate Ra	72	715
---	Yolo Slate Ra	72	716
---	Yolo Slate Ra	72	717
---	Yuba North Ea	72	677
---	Yuba North Ea	72	681
---	Yuba North Ea	72	682
---	Yuba North Ea	72	685
---	Yuba Slate Ro	72	708
---	Yuba Slate Ro	72	711
---	Yuba Slate Ro	72	713
---	Yuba Slate Ro	72	715
---	Yuba Slate Ro	72	716
---	Yuba New York	72	740
---	Yuba Long Bar	72	757
---	Yuba Long Bar	72	760
---	Yuba Long Bar	72	762
---	Yuba Long Bar	72	763
---	Yuba Rose Bar	72	800
---	Yuba Fosters	72	827
---	Yuba Fosters	72	836
---	Yuba Fosters	72	841
---	Yuba Fosters	72	842
---	Yuba Fosters	72	843
---	Yuba Marysville	72	895
---	Yuba Marysville	72	921
---	Yuba Marysville	72	927
---	Yuba Marysville	72	928
---	Yuba Linda	72	992
---*	Amador Twp 4	55	233
---*	Amador Twp 4	55	252
---*	Butte Eureka	56	651
---*	Calaveras Twp 4	57	339
---*	El Dorado Coloma	58	1078
---*	El Dorado Georgetown	58	700
---*	Mariposa Twp 3	60	586
---*	Sacramento Centre	63	181
---*	Sacramento Centre	63	182
---*	Sacramento Ward 1	63	54
---*	San Francisco San Francisco 1	68	858
---*	Tuolumne Big Oak	71	179
---*	Yuba Slate Ro	72	717
---*	Yuba Long Bar	72	753
---*	Yuba Rose Bar	72	800
---*	Yuba Foster B	72	827
---*	Yuba Foster B	72	836
---*	Yuba Fosters	72	841
---*	Yuba Fosters	72	842
---*	Yuba Fosters	72	843
A	El Dorado Placerville	58	862
A	Sacramento Granite	63	221
A	Sacramento Granite	63	251
A	Sacramento Granite	63	259
A	Sacramento Natonia	63	283
A	Sutter Sutter	70	816
A	Yolo Putah	72	551
A T	El Dorado Casumnes	58	1173
A W*	Mariposa Twp 3	60	577
Aaron	San Francisco San Francisco 4	68	1146
Abram	Sacramento San Joaquin	63	348
Ack	Yuba North Ea	72	676
Adam*	Yolo Cottonwoood	72	556
Af	Butte Oregon	56	626
Agustus	El Dorado Casumnes	58	1165
Ah	Butte Oregon	56	618
Ah	Butte Oregon	56	638
Ah	Butte Eureka	56	651
Ah	Butte Cascade	56	700
Ah	Butte Cascade	56	701
Ah	Butte Bidwell	56	709
Ah	Butte Bidwell	56	720
Ah	Butte Bidwell	56	726
Ah	Calaveras Twp 7	57	231
Ah	Sacramento Granite	63	231
Ah	Sacramento Dry Crk	63	373
Ah	Trinity Point Ba	70	976
Ah	Tuolumne Twp 4	71	147
Ah	Tuolumne Twp 4	71	149
Ah	Tuolumne Twp 4	71	159
Ah	Tuolumne Twp 4	71	167
Ah	Tuolumne Twp 2	71	307
Ah	Tuolumne Twp 2	71	394
Ah	Yuba Suida	72	992
Albert	San Francisco San Francisco 2	67	785
Ale*	Sierra Twp 7	66	916
Alex	El Dorado Kelsey	58	1150
Alex	Siskiyou Scott Va	69	57
Alfred	Yuba Marysville	72	880
Allen	Humbolt Table Bl	59	140
Almara M	Alameda Oakland	55	69
Alonzo	Sierra La Porte	66	789
Ambrose	San Francisco San Francisco 9	68	1081
LEE			
Andrew	El Dorado Casumnes	58	1175
Andrew	Nevada Bridgeport	61	478
Ang	Yuba Parks Ba	72	780
Ann	Sacramento Ward 4	63	554
Ann*	San Francisco San Francisco 1	68	892
Antonio	San Francisco San Francisco 11	67	116
Ar	Sierra Cox'S Bar	66	951
Ar	Trinity Indian C	70	989
Ark	Yuba Long Bar	72	767
Arthur*	San Mateo Twp 1	65	48
As*	Tuolumne Jacksonville	71	169
At	Mariposa Twp 3	60	620
Austin	Solano Fremont	69	380
B F	Solano Montezuma	69	370
Bang	Mariposa Twp 3	60	553
Bee	Butte Ophir	56	809
Bell F	San Francisco San Francisco 7	68	1331
Ben	Butte Cascade	56	699
Bernard	Solano Vallejo	69	269
C C	Tehama Antelope	70	891
C J	Sierra Twp 7	66	904
C R T*	San Bernardino Santa Barbara	64	170
C R V*	San Bernardino Santa Barbara	64	170
C*	Siskiyou Callahan	69	3
Caroline	Sierra La Porte	66	773
Carrie	Sonoma Washington	69	671
Cha	Yolo No E Twp	72	675
Chag	Sacramento Natonia	63	281
Chang	Sacramento Ward 1	63	156
Chang	Sacramento Ward 3	63	492
Charles	Amador Twp 1	55	487
Charles	Placer Iona Hills		
Charles	San Francisco San Francisco 8	68	1235
Charles	Sonoma Santa Rosa	69	392
Chas	El Dorado Georgetown	58	694
Chas	Sacramento San Joaquin	63	357
Chas	Tehama Lassen	70	866
Chem	Plumas Meadow Valley	62	909
Chin	Butte Ophir	56	816
Ching	Alameda Brooklyn	55	78
Ching	Fresno Twp 1	59	27
Ching	Sierra La Porte	66	767
Ching*	Alameda Oakland	55	14
Chong*	Alameda Brooklyn	55	78
Chow	San Francisco San Francisco 4	68	1209
Chow	Yuba Parks Ba	72	780
Choy	San Francisco San Francisco 4	68	1200
Chun	Mariposa Twp 3	60	572
Clement	Sacramento Ward 1	63	46
Clement	Sacramento Ward 4	63	567
Clotilda	San Francisco San Francisco 2	67	794
Come	Tuolumne Don Pedro	71	534
Con	Butte Ophir	56	770
Cong	Butte Bidwell	56	707
Cong	Butte Bidwell	56	727
Cordon	Butte Wyandotte	56	659
Cow*	Butte Oro	56	687
Cum	Mariposa Twp 3	60	588
Daniel	Sacramento Franklin	63	313
Daniel	Tuolumne Twp 3	71	463
David	Amador Twp 1	55	489
David	Shasta Cottonwood	66	724
E	Klamath Liberty	59	242
E	San Joaquin Stockton	64	1098
E E	El Dorado Placerville	58	866
E P	Butte Ophir	56	783
E W	Sutter Nicolaus	70	839
Edward	Yolo Cache Crk	72	594
Eli	Sonoma Petaluma	69	593
Elisebeth	Sacramento Ward 4	63	595
Fa Coha*	Yuba Long Bar	72	757
Fat	Yuba Fosters	72	830
Fin	Butte Cascade	56	690
Fing	Butte Bidwell	56	709
Fong	San Francisco San Francisco 5	67	1206
Foo	Butte Cascade	56	699
Foo	Butte Bidwell	56	723
Fou*	Yuba Marysville	72	965
Fow	Calaveras Twp 10	57	278
Foy	San Francisco San Francisco 5	67	1206
Francis	Contra Costa Twp 3	57	599
Frank D	San Francisco San Francisco 4	68	1128
Fung	San Francisco San Francisco 4	68	1193
G	San Francisco San Francisco 4	68	1230
G W	Mariposa Twp 3	60	583
G W	Sutter Nicolaus	70	840
Gabriel	San Joaquin Stockton	64	1082
Geo	Sacramento Granite	63	250
Geo	Sacramento Natonia	63	280
Geo	San Francisco San Francisco 1	68	901
Geo M	Amador Twp 2	55	321
Geo W	Amador Twp 2	55	321
Geo W	Yolo Cache	72	635
George	Marin Cortemad	60	788
LEE			
George	Nevada Little Y	61	535
George	Yuba Marysville	72	898
George A	Plumas Quincy	62	943
George Thos	San Mateo Twp 1	65	69
George*	Nevada Little Y	61	535
Gin	Butte Cascade	56	690
Goergia	Sierra Twp 7	66	890
Gordon	Butte Wyandotte	56	659
Gos W*	Placer Virginia	62	683
Graham	Humbolt Eureka	59	166
H	El Dorado Placerville	58	849
H	Sierra Downieville	66	997
H	Sutter Sutter	70	813
H C	El Dorado Mud Springs	58	959
Han	Mariposa Twp 3	60	613
Han	Yolo No E Twp	72	680
Han*	Mariposa Twp 3	60	581
Hannah*	Napa Napa	61	104
Harriet	Napa Yount	61	51
Harry	Sacramento Sutter	63	295
Harvey	Sacramento Ward 1	63	36
Henry	El Dorado Mountain	58	1183
Henry	Santa Clara Santa Clara	65	496
Henry	Siskiyou Klamath	69	90
Henry	Solano Vallejo	69	280
Henry	Tuolumne Don Pedro	71	541
Henry C	San Francisco San Francisco 10	67	234
Henry G	Sacramento Ward 3	63	474
Henry H	Yuba Marysville	72	930
Hi	Amador Twp 2	55	312
Hi	Solano Vallejo	69	248
Hike	Yuba Parke Ba	72	783
Hilt	Yuba Fosters	72	836
Hin	Butte Ophir	56	806
Hing	Butte Cascade	56	699
Hing	Butte Bidwell	56	716
Hing	Yuba Long Bar	72	767
Hing	Yuba Fosters	72	831
Hite	Yuba Long Bar	72	762
Hite	Yuba Fosters	72	834
Hiti*	Yuba Fosters	72	834
Ho	San Francisco San Francisco 5	67	1206
Ho	Yuba Bear Rvr	72	1000
Ho	Yuba Long Bar	72	766
Ho*	Yuba Bear Rvr	72	1000
Hob	Santa Clara Santa Clara	65	514
Hong	Butte Oregon	56	625
Hong	Butte Oregon	56	643
Hong	Butte Eureka	56	649
Hong	Butte Bidwell	56	719
Hong	Yuba Slate Ro	72	708
Hong	Yuba Fosters	72	831
Hony	Sonoma Petaluma	69	574
Hoop	Mariposa Twp 3	60	543
Hoop	Tuolumne Twp 2	71	347
Hop	San Francisco San Francisco 4	68	1191
Hop	San Francisco San Francisco 4	68	1201
Hop*	Tuolumne Twp 2	71	416
Hoto*	Butte Ophir	56	809
Hou	Butte Ophir	56	807
Hou	Butte Ophir	56	810
Hou	Mariposa Twp 3	60	564
How	Mariposa Twp 3	60	550
How	Mariposa Twp 3	60	599
Hoy	Butte Bidwell	56	724
Hoy	Butte Ophir	56	788
Hugh	Santa Cruz Pajaro	66	531
In*	Mariposa Twp 3	60	578
Isaac	Alameda Oakland	55	62
Iva	Mariposa Twp 3	60	553
J	Shasta Shasta	66	665
J H	Shasta Shasta	66	665
J H	Tehama Red Bluff	70	917
J R	Solano Vallejo	69	249
J T	Sutter Nicolaus	70	840
J W	Nevada Bridgeport	61	445
Jake	Mariposa Twp 1	60	672
James	Amador Twp 6	55	436
James	Marin Cortemad	60	780
James	Plumas Quincy	62	943
James	Plumas Quincy	62	959
James	Sacramento Cosummes	63	398
James	San Francisco San Francisco 9	68	1065
James	Santa Clara San Jose	65	356
James	Santa Cruz Pajaro	66	575
James	Sierra Whiskey	66	847
James D	San Mateo Twp 1	65	47
James N	Sutter Nicolaus	70	840
Jane	Nevada Bridgeport	61	475
Jas	San Francisco San Francisco 9	68	1060
Jas	San Francisco San Francisco 2	67	798
Jas W	San Francisco San Francisco 10	67	357
Jim	Plumas Quincy	62	970

Name	County Locale	Roll	Page
LEE			
Jim	Sacramento Ward 3	63	443
Jing	Del Norte Crescent	58	641
Jno	Sonoma Sonoma	69	658
Jno D	Sacramento Ward 1	63	31
John	Calaveras Twp 9	57	358
John	Mariposa Twp 3	60	610
John	Plumas Quincy	62	1001
John	Sacramento Sutter	63	308
John	Sacramento Ward 1	63	35
John	Sacramento Ward 1	63	64
John	San Francisco San Francisco 4	68	1135
John	Sierra Cold Can	66	836
John	Solano Vallejo	69	272
John	Yolo Cache Crk	72	635
John	Yuba Marysville	72	927
John A	Sonoma Russian	69	439
John B	Sierra Twp 7	66	882
John C	Alameda Oakland	55	69
John C	Santa Clara San Jose	65	356
John C*	Napa Napa	61	107
John E	Sacramento Ward 4	63	533
John H	San Bernardino San Bernadino	64	638
John S	Sacramento Ward 3	63	424
John S	Siskiyou Callahan	69	12
John*	Sacramento Centre	63	173
Joke	Butte Ophir	56	810
Jon	Tulara Visalia	71	106
Jon	Tulara Twp 1	71	96
Jos	San Francisco San Francisco 2	67	798
Joseph	Plumas Quincy	62	992
Joseph	San Luis Obispo San Luis Obispo	65	15
Joseph	Santa Clara San Jose	65	340
Joseph	Tuolumne Twp 1	71	246
Joseph R	Yuba Marysville	72	905
Julins	Monterey Monterey	60	926
Ka	Mariposa Twp 3	60	553
Kam	Mariposa Twp 3	60	572
Kan	El Dorado Placerville	58	825
Kan	San Francisco San Francisco 4	68	1201
Karn	Mariposa Twp 3	60	572
Kee	Mariposa Twp 3	60	588
Ki	Del Norte Crescent	58	641
Kim	Yuba Long Bar	72	770
Kin	El Dorado Georgetown	58	686
Kin	Yuba Long Bar	72	770
King	Butte Bidwell	56	727
King	Mariposa Twp 3	60	543
King	Mariposa Twp 3	60	544
King	Mariposa Twp 3	60	560
King	Mariposa Twp 3	60	563
King	Mariposa Twp 3	60	569
King*	El Dorado Georgetown	58	701
Kip Ti	San Francisco San Francisco 4	68	1203
Kong	Sacramento Granite	63	232
Kou	Mariposa Twp 3	60	569
Kou	Mariposa Twp 3	60	572
Kou	Mariposa Twp 3	60	582
Kou*	Mariposa Twp 3	60	569
Kou*	Mariposa Twp 3	60	580
Kow	Mariposa Twp 3	60	544
Kow	Mariposa Twp 3	60	546
Kow	Mariposa Twp 3	60	553
Kow	Mariposa Twp 3	60	564
Kow	Mariposa Twp 3	60	569
Kow	Mariposa Twp 3	60	572
Kow	Sacramento Ward 1	63	71
Kow	San Francisco San Francisco 9	68	1095
Kow	San Francisco San Francisco 4	68	1183
Kow	San Francisco San Francisco 4	68	1203
Kow*	Mariposa Twp 3	60	569
Kum Fah*	Plumas Quincy	62	970
Kung	San Francisco San Francisco 4	68	1201
Ky	El Dorado Greenwood	58	729
Lang	Mariposa Twp 3	60	552
Lang	Mariposa Twp 3	60	564
Lary	Mariposa Twp 3	60	564
Law	Mariposa Twp 3	60	544
Lay*	Yuba Long Bar	72	764
Le	Mariposa Twp 3	60	562
Lee	Amador Twp 5	55	365
Lee	Mariposa Twp 3	60	544
Lee	Mariposa Twp 3	60	546
Lee	Mariposa Twp 3	60	569
Lee	Yuba Foster B	72	827
Lee Tap	Yuba Fosters	72	827
Leuy	Mariposa Twp 3	60	546
Levin	Tuolumne Twp 1	71	269
Like	Yuba Foster B	72	830
Ling	Butte Bidwell	56	725
Ling	Sacramento Granite	63	269
Ling*	Butte Oro	56	687
Ling*	Calaveras Twp 6	57	118
Lo	San Francisco San Francisco 9	68	1093
Log	Yuba Fosters	72	827
Lon	Butte Cascade	56	698
LEE			
Lon	Mariposa Twp 3	60	569
Lon	Yuba Fosters	72	842
Long	Mariposa Twp 3	60	564
Loo	Mariposa Twp 3	60	560
Loo	Yuba Long Bar	72	770
Lou	Mariposa Twp 3	60	564
Lou	San Francisco San Francisco 4	68	1183
Lou	San Francisco San Francisco 4	68	1185
Louisa	Fresno Twp 3	59	14
Low	Mariposa Twp 3	60	569
Low	Mariposa Twp 3	60	572
Loy	San Francisco San Francisco 4	68	1174
Lucinda	Sonoma Armally	69	482
Lui	Butte Ophir	56	814
Lui*	Mariposa Twp 3	60	551
Lum	Mariposa Twp 3	60	575
Lum*	Mariposa Twp 3	60	576
Lung*	Mariposa Twp 3	60	552
Luy	Mariposa Twp 3	60	545
Luy	Mariposa Twp 3	60	551
M	San Francisco San Francisco 2	67	775
M	San Mateo Twp 3	65	95
M G	Sutter Nicolaus	70	840
M J	San Francisco San Francisco 5	67	501
Ma No*	Yuba Fosters	72	843
Mall	Yuba Foster B	72	830
Man	Mariposa Twp 3	60	588
Man*	Mariposa Twp 3	60	580
Mang	Yuba Long Bar	72	768
Margaret	San Francisco San Francisco 10	67	188
Mark	Butte Bidwell	56	710
Mary	Alameda Brooklyn	55	195
Mary A	Yolo Cottonwoood	72	557
Mary*	Mariposa Twp 3	60	576
May	Mariposa Twp 3	60	544
Me	Yuba Fosters	72	843
Mee	San Francisco San Francisco 4	68	1198
Mew	Butte Ophir	56	806
Michael	Amador Twp 2	55	304
Michael	San Francisco San Francisco 11	67	96
Michael	Tuolumne Big Oak	71	138
Ming	Yuba Fosters	72	830
Mitchell	Tuolumne Twp 1	71	210
Moke	Butte Bidwell	56	715
Mong	Mariposa Twp 3	60	576
Moo	San Francisco San Francisco 4	68	1193
Mory	San Francisco San Francisco 4	68	1179
Mouy*	Mariposa Twp 3	60	576
Mowy*	Sacramento Mississipi	63	190
Moy	San Francisco San Francisco 9	68	1096
Moy	San Francisco San Francisco 4	68	1191
Mr	Siskiyou Callahan	69	8
Mur	San Francisco San Francisco 4	68	1176
My	Mariposa Twp 3	60	563
N	Sonoma Santa Rosa	69	400
Nancy A*	Sacramento Centre	63	178
Nay	Mariposa Twp 3	60	550
Nelson H	Sacramento Ward 1	63	23
Non	Mariposa Twp 3	60	564
Non	Sacramento Cosummes	63	384
Non*	Mariposa Twp 3	60	576
Norman	Santa Clara Santa Clara	65	509
Nou*	Mariposa Twp 3	60	576
Now	Mariposa Twp 3	60	546
O	Yuba Long Bar	72	765
Oa	Yuba Marysville	72	947
Oh	Del Norte Crescent	58	640
Ole*	Sierra Twp 7	66	916
On	Yuba Marysville	72	947
Ong	Butte Oregon	56	612
Ong	Yuba Long Bar	72	770
Ong	Yuba Fosters	72	830
Onk	Yuba North Ea	72	676
P	San Francisco San Francisco 4	68	1230
P	Siskiyou Klamath	69	90
P H	Sacramento Ward 3	63	444
Partrich G	Alameda Brooklyn	55	172
Patrick	Alameda Brooklyn	55	140
Patrick	Placer Virginia	62	677
Patrick	Placer Michigan	62	838
Patrick	San Francisco San Francisco 7	68	1412
Patrick	San Francisco San Francisco 10	67	305
Patrick G	Alameda Washington	55	172
Peter	Calaveras Twp 8	57	51
Peter	Sacramento Ward 1	63	49
Peter	Sierra Twp 7	66	883
Peu	Butte Bidwell	56	720
Pin	Butte Bidwell	56	728
Po	El Dorado Placerville	58	831
Pon*	Butte Ophir	56	808
Poner	Butte Bidwell	56	720
Poo Fah*	Plumas Quincy	62	970
LEE			
Pow	Butte Ophir	56	805
Pow*	Butte Ophir	56	807
Poy	Butte Bidwell	56	709
Prosper	Alameda Brooklyn	55	163
Puing	Tuolumne Don Pedro	71	540
Qua	Mariposa Twp 3	60	569
Qua*	Mariposa Twp 3	60	575
Qui	Mariposa Twp 3	60	545
Qui	Mariposa Twp 3	60	546
Qui	Mariposa Twp 3	60	563
Qui	Mariposa Twp 3	60	564
Qui	Mariposa Twp 3	60	566
Qui	Mariposa Twp 3	60	571
Qui	Mariposa Twp 3	60	572
Qui*	Mariposa Twp 3	60	551
Qui*	Mariposa Twp 3	60	564
Quou	Mariposa Twp 3	60	563
Qur	Sacramento Natonia	63	281
Quy	Mariposa Twp 3	60	546
R	Sierra Downieville	66	992
R H*	Sacramento Centre	63	177
R M	El Dorado Greenwood	58	712
R P	Sacramento Ward 1	63	87
Reuben	Yuba Bear Rvr	72	1008
Robert	San Francisco San Francisco 6	67	447
Robert F	Santa Cruz Watsonville	66	535
Robt	Butte Chico	56	549
Rong	San Francisco San Francisco 5	67	1205
Rose	San Francisco San Francisco 10	67	182
Row	Butte Ophir	56	810
S	Alameda Brooklyn	55	108
S E	Yuba New York	72	736
S H	Siskiyou Scott Ri	69	63
S W*	Mariposa Twp 3	60	577
Sam	Butte Eureka	56	649
Sam	Butte Mountain	56	735
Sam*	San Francisco San Francisco 9	68	1094
Sam*	Yuba Long Bar	72	756
Saml W	Napa Yount	61	31
Samuel	Alameda Oakland	55	51
San	Mariposa Twp 3	60	608
San	Mariposa Twp 3	60	613
San	San Francisco San Francisco 5	67	1205
Sarah	El Dorado Casumnes	58	1169
Say	Mariposa Twp 3	60	564
See	Mariposa Twp 3	60	544
See W*	Nevada Bridgeport	61	445
See*	Mariposa Twp 3	60	544
Sils	San Mateo Twp 3	65	92
Sim	Butte Cascade	56	692
Sin	Butte Cascade	56	704
Sing	Butte Bidwell	56	726
Sing	Butte Ophir	56	809
Sing	Butte Ophir	56	810
Sing	Butte Ophir	56	815
Sing	Mariposa Twp 3	60	572
Sing	Plumas Meadow Valley	62	909
Siny	Sacramento Granite	63	250
Siry	Amador Twp 5	55	365
So	San Francisco San Francisco 5	67	1205
Solomon	Siskiyou Klamath	69	90
Son	Mariposa Twp 3	60	580
Song	Alameda Oakland	55	35
Soy	San Francisco San Francisco 5	67	1205
Spee	Mariposa Coulterville	60	682
Squire	Sacramento Granite	63	249
Sucka*	Plumas Quincy	62	970
Sue	Del Norte Crescent	58	641
Sung	Plumas Quincy	62	1008
Sy	El Dorado Greenwood	58	719
T	Shasta Shasta	66	671
T A H	Sonoma Santa Rosa	69	415
T J	Amador Twp 5	55	369
Theodore	San Joaquin Elkhorn	64	985
Theodore	Yuba Rose Bar	72	788
Thom	El Dorado Georgetown	58	707
Thomas	Alameda Oakland	55	8
Thomas	Sierra Cox'S Bar	66	949
Thomas	Solano Benecia	69	289
Thomas	Sutter Nicolaus	70	840
Thomas	Tuolumne Twp 2	71	342
Thomas M	Santa Cruz Pajaro	66	575
Thos	Nevada Bloomfield	61	511
Thos	San Francisco San Francisco 1	68	919
Thti*	Yuba Fosters	72	834
Ti	San Francisco San Francisco 4	68	1201
Tom	Nevada Eureka	61	373
Tong	Amador Twp 2	55	327
Tong	Tuolumne Twp 1	71	476
Tory	Amador Twp 2	55	327
Tou*	Yuba Marysville	72	965
Tuck*	Sacramento Ward 1	63	70
Tup*	Nevada Nevada	61	304
Ua	Mariposa Twp 3	60	569

Name	County Locale	M653 RollPage
LEE		
Ung	Calaveras Twp 4	57 317
Unp	Yuba Long Bar	72 769
Uny	Calaveras Twp 4	57 317
W	Butte Chico	56 562
W	El Dorado Kelsey	581149
W	Shasta Millvill	66 749
W	Sonoma Santa Rosa	69 400
W C	Sutter Sutter	70 816
W G	Sonoma Armally	69 485
W H	Amador Twp 3	55 379
W H H	Sacramento Ward 1	63 19
W L	Placer Dutch Fl	62 720
W L	Sacramento Lee	63 211
W S	Mariposa Twp 3	60 575
W W	San Joaquin Stockton	641045
Wa	Mariposa Twp 3	60 569
Wah	Tuolumne Don Pedro	71 535
Wan	Sacramento Ward 1	63 68
Wang	Placer Iona Hills	62 896
Wann*	San Francisco San Francisco 1	68 892
Was	Mariposa Twp 3	60 569
Wat*	Merced Twp 1	60 914
Way	Mariposa Twp 3	60 544
Way	Mariposa Twp 3	60 564
We	Butte Bidwell	56 711
Weea	Butte Cascade	56 699
Wg	Butte Cascade	56 692
Whan	Calaveras Twp 9	57 362
Whar	Calaveras Twp 9	57 362
William	Marin San Rafael	60 773
William	Placer Michigan	62 823
William	San Francisco San Francisco 11	106 67
William	San Francisco San Francisco 7	681431
William	San Mateo Twp 3	65 91
William	Shasta Millvill	66 745
William	Siskiyou Cottonwood	69 102
William	Tulara Twp 2	71 6
Wim	Butte Bidwell	56 723
Wing	Butte Cascade	56 700
Wing	Fresno Twp 3	59 31
Wing	San Francisco San Francisco 9	681086
Wm	San Francisco San Francisco 10	281 67
Wm	Santa Clara San Jose	65 338
Wm B	Los Angeles Elmonte	59 251
Wm F	Tuolumne Twp 3	71 455
Wm H H	Sacramento Ward 1	63 109
Wm M	Solano Benecia	69 288
Wm S	Alameda Oakland	55 70
Wo	Nevada Rough &	61 434
Wo	San Francisco San Francisco 4	681177
Wo	San Francisco San Francisco 5	671206
Wong	El Dorado Greenwood	58 728
Woy	Mariposa Twp 3	60 576
Yap	Mariposa Twp 3	60 543
Yin	Del Norte Happy Ca	58 664
Yinke*	Butte Ophir	56 812
Yon	San Francisco San Francisco 9	681095
You	San Francisco San Francisco 4	681182
Young	Mariposa Twp 3	60 544
Young	Mariposa Twp 3	60 553
Yuke	Butte Ophir	56 803
Yup	Nevada Nevada	61 300
Yup	Nevada Nevada	61 302
Yup	Placer Iona Hills	62 897
Zon	Mariposa Twp 3	60 544
LEEACHI		
A	Sierra Downieville	66 968
LEEAMAN		
J*	Amador Twp 1	55 495
LEECE		
J*	Nevada Eureka	61 348
LEECH		
A	Trinity Bates	70 967
Fredk	Trinity Minersville	70 969
James	Trinity Indian C	70 987
John	Santa Clara San Jose	65 311
L	Trinity Bates	70 967
M C	Trinity Ferry	70 977
Maria	Monterey Monterey	60 950
Robert	Yolo Slate Ra	72 695
S H	Trinity Bates	70 967
W S	Trinity McGillev	701021
LEECHMAN		
M J	Tuolumne Big Oak	71 137
LEED		
Harvey W*	Yuba Marysville	72 867
W	Tuolumne Twp 4	71 163
LEEDER		
Franklin	Santa Cruz Santa Cruz	66 635
LEEDING		
F	Sonoma Sonoma	69 658
LEEDON		
Wm	Yolo New York	72 720

Name	County Locale	M653 RollPage
LEEDS		
Ebenezer	Yuba Marysville	72 851
Ebenzer	Yuba Marysville	72 851
John	Yuba Marysville	72 865
L D	Sacramento Granite	63 228
Philip*	Nevada Red Dog	61 544
Phillip*	Nevada Red Dog	61 555
LEEDWICH		
John*	Yuba Marysville	72 926
LEEDY		
Adam*	Amador Twp 5	55 339
LEEFHIN		
Charley E*	Alameda Oakland	55 33
LEEFHIOR		
Charley E*	Alameda Oakland	55 33
LEEFUS		
Joshua*	San Francisco San Francisco 1	68 916
LEEGEAS		
H*	San Francisco San Francisco 3	67 64
LEEGELKEN		
John D*	San Francisco San Francisco 12	376 67
LEEGEN		
Frederick	Marin San Rafael	60 766
LEEGIAS		
H	San Francisco San Francisco 3	67 64
LEEHA		
---	San Francisco San Francisco 9	68 964
LEEHAMED		
Jacob	San Francisco San Francisco 8	681319
LEEHAMID		
Jacob*	San Francisco San Francisco 8	681319
LEEHAUND		
Jacob*	San Francisco San Francisco 8	681319
LEEHE		
---*	San Francisco San Francisco 9	68 964
LEEHORN		
Joseph	Contra Costa Twp 2	57 580
LEEING		
---*	Mariposa Twp 3	60 569
LEEK		
---	Butte Oregon	56 617
August	Klamath Liberty	59 231
Chas	Klamath Liberty	59 231
Leock	San Francisco San Francisco 6	67 470
LEEKAMN		
Henry	Calaveras Twp 10	57 299
LEEKER		
Henry	Alameda Brooklyn	55 123
LEEL		
L M	Yolo Merritt	72 579
LEELAND		
John	Nevada Little Y	61 532
LEELEY		
---	Sierra Twp 5	66 942
John*	Yuba Rose Bar	72 793
LEELY		
John	Santa Cruz Santa Cruz	66 619
John	Yuba Rose Bar	72 793
John*	Santa Cruz Santa Cruz	66 619
Orrene	Yuba Slate Ro	72 695
LEEMAN		
Benj	Alameda Brooklyn	55 123
Carl	Yolo No E Twp	72 672
H S	Butte Eureka	56 650
J H	Sacramento Sutter	63 304
John	Yuba North Ea	72 672
Joshua	Yolo Washington	72 599
Kate	Sacramento Sutter	63 304
P G*	Nevada Grass Valley	61 153
Saml	Butte Eureka	56 651
LEEMOIER		
Charles	Amador Twp 1	55 507
LEEN		
---	Butte Kimshaw	56 600
---	Shasta French G	66 712
---	Tuolumne Twp 5	71 507
Farr	Butte Ophir	56 813
Hop	San Francisco San Francisco 4	681186
Hung	Amador Twp 7	55 412
J B	Yolo Merritt	72 580
LEENARD		
Jno	Sacramento Granite	63 254
LEENCELLE		
Balthazar	Calaveras Twp 5	57 194
LEENDUIS		
Jas*	Sacramento Granite	63 252
LEENG		
---	El Dorado Eldorado	58 940
LEENOPYTOCKS		
---	Fresno Twp 3	59 8
LEEONG		
---	El Dorado Mud Springs	58 962
---	El Dorado Mud Springs	58 981
LEEP		
---	Amador Twp 7	55 414

Name	County Locale	M653 RollPage
LEEP		
---	Amador Twp 6	55 422
LEEPER		
A P	Butte Chico	56 539
C	San Francisco San Francisco 5	67 519
LEEPP		
---	Yolo Slate Ra	72 715
LEEPS		
Henry	Yuba Marysville	72 934
LEER		
Henry	San Francisco San Francisco 3	67 86
Oerastus	Contra Costa Twp 1	57 489
Richard	Santa Cruz Santa Cruz	66 628
LEERA		
Berna*	Alameda Oakland	55 45
Francisco	Mariposa Twp 3	60 547
LEERGO		
John	Sierra Twp 7	66 874
LEERNAY		
Louis	Yuba Fosters	72 835
LEERNEY		
J*	Tuolumne Big Oak	71 179
James	Yuba Rose Bar	72 805
LEEROG		
J	San Francisco San Francisco 2	67 788
LEERY		
John*	Yuba Rose Bar	72 793
LEES		
Eugene	San Francisco San Francisco 8	681311
Ezaiah M	San Francisco San Francisco 2	67 643
Isaiah M	San Francisco San Francisco 2	67 643
James*	Sierra Downieville	66 961
Saml*	Butte Oregon	56 626
LEESBER		
Jas	San Francisco San Francisco 2	67 676
LEESBUTTLE		
Daniel	El Dorado Diamond	58 766
LEESE		
Edward	Alameda Oakland	55 38
LEESEN		
L	San Francisco San Francisco 5	67 517
LEESMRING		
J P*	Merced Twp 1	60 895
LEESON		
George E	Sierra Downieville	661016
R	Yuba Fosters	72 824
LEESTER		
Jas*	San Francisco San Francisco 2	67 676
LEET		
---	Sacramento Ward 3	63 487
---	San Francisco San Francisco 11	146 67
---	Yolo No E Twp	72 681
Benj F	Placer Virginia	62 685
Freeman G*	Sacramento American	63 160
J A	Sierra Twp 7	66 901
J A	Sierra Forest C	66 910
LEETE		
Ah	Yuba Suida	72 991
LEETMAN		
L E	Tehama Red Bluff	70 903
LEETRE		
M	San Francisco San Francisco 5	67 538
LEETYER		
W	San Francisco San Francisco 6	67 453
LEETZ		
J	Siskiyou Scott Ri	69 74
John	Santa Cruz Santa Cruz	66 666
L	Siskiyou Scott Ri	69 74
LEETZY		
John	San Francisco San Francisco 1	68 807
LEEVE		
Francisco	Mariposa Twp 3	60 547
LEEVY		
---	El Dorado Mountain	581178
LEEWARD		
John	San Diego Colorado	64 807
LEFAUNT		
Peter	Siskiyou Cottonwoood	69 97
LEFE URE		
Antoine*	Calaveras Twp 6	57 179
LEFEBER		
A	Tuolumne Jacksonville	71 172
LEFEBRE		
Antoine*	Calaveras Twp 6	57 179
Leon*	Calaveras Twp 10	57 296
LEFEICOIR		
B*	San Francisco San Francisco 4	681165
LEFEICON		
B*	San Francisco San Francisco 4	681165
LEFEICVIR		
B*	San Francisco San Francisco 4	681165
LEFEON		
John*	Calaveras Twp 6	57 140
LEFEORE		
John	Calaveras Twp 5	57 140

California 1860 Census Index

Name	County Locale	M653 Roll Page	Name	County Locale	M653 Roll Page	Name	County Locale	M653 Roll Page
LEFER			**LEFVERE**			**LEGGETT**		
Antonio	Mariposa Twp 1	60 665	Mack	Sierra Scales D	66 801	Phillipe	Santa Cruz Santa Cruz	66 617
Antonio*	Mariposa Twp 3	60 604	**LEG**			Thomas*	El Dorado Casumnes	581169
LEFERGE			---	El Dorado Georgetown	58 693	Thos W	Sacramento Ward 1	63 26
Soloman	Alameda Brooklyn	55 189	---	El Dorado Georgetown	58 762	Wm M	Sonoma Mendocino	69 457
LEFEROE			Cen	Butte Ophir	56 808	**LEGGOT**		
Pascal	San Francisco San Francisco 2	67 631	John	El Dorado Coloma	581115	Phillip	Marin Cortemad	60 789
LEFERRE			Mu	Butte Ophir	56 807	**LEGGOTT**		
Alima	San Francisco San Francisco 2	67 717	**LEGACY**			Phillip	Marin Cortemad	60 789
Cyrus	Placer Forest H	62 803	Dolfet	El Dorado Salmon Hills	581064	**LEGHTNOR**		
LEFERVE			Dolfit	El Dorado Salmon Falls	581064	Jno*	Sonoma Petaluma	69 602
Pascal	San Francisco San Francisco 2	67 631	**LEGAFF**			**LEGIES**		
LEFEUNTIAN			John*	Calaveras Twp 4	57 339	Eladia	Calaveras Twp 7	57 24
A	Siskiyou Klamath	69 91	**LEGAGE**			**LEGIN**		
LEFEUNTOAN			S	Nevada Grass Valley	61 187	John	Trinity Taylor'S	701036
A	Siskiyou Klamath	69 91	**LEGAIRE**			**LEGINA**		
LEFEURE			A	Tuolumne Twp 3	71 465	Natioidi*	Alameda Oakland	55 19
Antoine*	Calaveras Twp 6	57 179	**LEGAIS**			**LEGITAN**		
LEFEVER			Thos	Mariposa Twp 3	60 617	Hiram*	Yuba Marysville	72 915
A	Tuolumne Twp 4	71 172	**LEGALA**			**LEGNARDO**		
E	Tuolumne Jacksonville	71 170	Paul	Calaveras Twp 9	57 359	---	San Bernardino S Timate	64 697
Josiah	Sierra Twp 7	66 885	**LEGALL**			**LEGNIA**		
O M	Sonoma Armally	69 515	Thos A*	Stanislaus Branch	70 703	Naturdi*	Alameda Oakland	55 19
LEFEVRE			**LEGAN**			**LEGOE**		
Alima*	San Francisco San Francisco 2	67 717	John*	El Dorado Eldorado	58 937	William	Plumas Quincy	62 938
B R	Shasta Shasta	66 675	**LEGANBE**			**LEGONA**		
John*	Calaveras Twp 6	57 140	Paul	Amador Twp 1	55 459	Natioido*	Alameda Oakland	55 19
LEFEVRN			**LEGAR**			**LEGONE**		
G*	Del Norte Crescent	58 642	Antonio	Calaveras Twp 8	57 50	Frank	Mariposa Twp 3	60 555
LEFF			Frank	Calaveras Twp 7	57 6	**LEGORA**		
Barbara	San Luis Obispo San Luis Obispo	65 41	**LEGARA**			Den	Mariposa Twp 3	60 594
LEFFENFELT			Den*	Mariposa Twp 3	60 594	Sabastine*	Alameda Brooklyn	55 146
Wm	Sacramento Ward 1	63 81	Francisco	Alameda Brooklyn	55 189	**LEGOTT**		
LEFFEREFELT			Sosa	Alameda Brooklyn	55 173	John	Siskiyou Yreka	69 186
Wm*	Sacramento Ward 1	63 81	**LEGARD**			**LEGOUBE**		
LEFFERLS			Jos	San Francisco San Francisco 2	67 670	Alphonso	San Francisco San Francisco 8	681234
E W	Calaveras Twp 6	57 120	**LEGARDE**			**LEGOUNG**		
LEFFERTY			John	Del Norte Crescent	58 642	---	Calaveras Twp 5	57 203
Jas	Napa Napa	61 100	**LEGARE**			**LEGOUNY**		
LEFFIN			Alvin	Alameda Brooklyn	55 173	---	Calaveras Twp 5	57 203
John	San Bernardino San Salvador	64 646	Chas	Alameda Oakland	55 7	**LEGRAN**		
LEFFINGNELL			James	Alameda Brooklyn	55 199	Joseph	Los Angeles Los Nieto	59 426
W	San Francisco San Francisco 5	67 505	**LEGAS**			**LEGRAND**		
LEFFINGWELL			David	Colusa Grand Island	57 477	A	Siskiyou Scott Va	69 49
Joseph	Marin Tomales	60 726	**LEGATA**			A*	Tuolumne Twp 1	71 212
Wm	Sierra Twp 7	66 891	Andrew	Calaveras Twp 7	57 38	A*	Siskiyou Scott Va	69 49
LEFFINWELL			**LEGATE**			Chas	Mariposa Twp 1	60 648
H L	San Francisco San Francisco 6	67 443	Frank	Amador Twp 5	55 362	Edward	Contra Costa Twp 3	57 611
LEFFLER			**LEGATHE**			**LEGRANE**		
Margaret	San Joaquin Elkhorn	64 954	W M*	San Joaquin Elliott	64 944	Emory	Amador Twp 1	55 459
LEFFT			**LEGATO**			**LEGRAS**		
Wilkins	Yuba Bear Rvr	72 997	Joseph	Calaveras Twp 7	57 44	H*	San Francisco San Francisco 3	67 64
LEFIE			**LEGATT**			**LEGRAVE**		
---*	Mendocino Calpella	60 822	H R	Nevada Grass Valley	61 238	C A	Amador Twp 1	55 454
LEFIEVRE			**LEGAY**			**LEGRE**		
F	San Francisco San Francisco 10	267 67	J B	San Francisco San Francisco 5	67 485	Peter*	Mariposa Twp 3	60 618
LEFIL			**LEGECEY**			**LEGRENDE**		
---*	Mendocino Calpella	60 822	Peter	Sierra Port Win	66 795	E	Amador Twp 1	55 461
LEFING			**LEGEND**			**LEGRET**		
---	Sierra Twp 5	66 925	John	Los Angeles Los Angeles	59 396	H	Tuolumne Sonora	71 221
LEFINGNELL			**LEGENDER**			Peter	Mariposa Twp 3	60 618
S	El Dorado Placerville	58 931	A	Amador Twp 6	55 443	**LEGRN**		
LEFIO			N	Amador Twp 6	55 443	George*	Calaveras Twp 6	57 114
---*	Mendocino Calpella	60 822	**LEGENT**			**LEGROP**		
LEFLER			Hammon	Klamath Dillins	59 214	Frank	Sacramento Ward 1	63 111
Charles J	San Joaquin Elkhorn	64 973	**LEGER**			**LEGROSS**		
Providence	San Joaquin Stockton	641030	August	Alameda Oakland	55 13	Antone	Yolo Cache Crk	72 606
LEFLES			**LEGERHOLM**			Frank	Sacramento Ward 1	63 111
Isaac V*	San Joaquin Stockton	641030	John*	Santa Cruz Santa Cruz	66 632	**LEGS**		
LEFO			**LEGERO**			---	Fresno Twp 3	59 21
---	Mendocino Calpella	60 822	Manuel	Fresno Twp 1	59 83	---	Tulara Twp 2	71 37
LEFONT			**LEGEUD**			**LEGUAY**		
Cosia	Calaveras Twp 6	57 125	John	Los Angeles Los Angeles	59 396	Iramon*	Stanislaus Branch	70 700
LEFORD			**LEGG**			**LEGUERA**		
J L	Mariposa Twp 1	60 636	---	Yolo No E Twp	72 682	Juan	Santa Cruz Watsonville	66 540
LEFORT			Frank W	Humbolt Table Bl	59 140	**LEGUFF**		
Edward	Amador Twp 3	55 379	Joseph	Siskiyou Cottonwood	69 109	John*	Calaveras Twp 4	57 339
LEFOUNTAN			Robt	Nevada Nevada	61 296	**LEGUN**		
Nelson	Siskiyou Klamath	69 96	Sam*	Nevada Washington	61 342	George*	Calaveras Twp 6	57 114
LEFOY			T	Nevada Eureka	61 380	**LEGUNE**		
Joseph	Calaveras Twp 7	57 5	**LEGGE**			Jeson*	Alameda Brooklyn	55 100
LEFRANS			William	Yuba New York	72 744	Jesor*	Alameda Brooklyn	55 100
Chas	Santa Clara San Jose	65 366	**LEGGET**			**LEGUR**		
LEFREE			James	Sonoma Bodega	69 535	John*	Sacramento Ward 1	63 75
Louis*	San Francisco San Francisco 7	681390	Phillipe	Santa Cruz Santa Cruz	66 617	**LEGURE**		
LEFTARP			**LEGGETT**			George*	Contra Costa Twp 3	57 613
Joseph	Santa Clara Santa Clara	65 511	J	Nevada Eureka	61 391	**LEGWETT**		
LEFTON			J	Sacramento Cosumnes	63 410	John*	Nevada Red Dog	61 553
Stephen*	Solano Montezuma	69 371	J K	San Francisco San Francisco 5	67 527	**LEH**		
Wm*	Sacramento Ward 3	63 459	James	Yuba Marysville	72 941	---	Sierra St Louis	66 805
LEFTURICH			James M	Yuba Marysville	72 941	**LEHAKA**		
James	Santa Cruz Soguel	66 595	Jno	Sacramento Ward 1	63 26	Henry	Siskiyou Klamath	69 85
LEFTWICH			Joseph	Solano Benecia	69 312	**LEHAN**		
James	Santa Cruz Soguel	66 595	Joshua	Solano Benecia	69 298	Adolph*	Yuba New York	72 725
LEFURI			M H	Nevada Grass Valley	61 176	Mert*	Yuba Rose Bar	72 803
John*	Calaveras Twp 6	57 140	Mary	Sacramento Ward 4	63 611	**LEHATZLEIN**		
						George*	Los Angeles San Pedro	59 485

California 1860 Census Index

Name	County Locale	M653 Roll	Page
LEHEIZKEN			
Jacob	San Francisco San Francisco 1	68	811
LEHENTU			
Paul	Tuolumne Twp 3	71	465
LEHER			
Daniel	Marin Cortemad	60	780
George	Santa Clara San Jose	65	307
LEHERICY			
Pierre J	San Francisco San Francisco 2	67	686
LEHEWTER			
Andrew	Calaveras Twp 6	57	127
LEHI			
---	Calaveras Twp 5	57	222
LEHIGH			
Geo	Sacramento Granite	63	263
Jerry	Sierra Twp 5	66	946
John	Solano Vallejo	69	255
Lucy	Sierra Twp 5	66	946
Margaret	San Francisco San Francisco 3	67	11
Nellie	Sierra Downieville	66	967
LEHINAN			
John	Marin Cortemad	60	791
LEHMAN			
Adam	Yolo Cache	72	631
Andrew	Los Angeles Los Angeles	59	328
Antonie	Los Angeles Los Angeles	59	349
Benj	Siskiyou Scott Ri	69	62
C A	Sacramento Ward 1	63	24
Casper	Sacramento Ward 1	63	48
George	Los Angeles Los Angeles	59	366
George	Los Angeles Los Angeles	59	36
J D	San Joaquin Stockton	64	1053
J S	Trinity Trinity	70	970
J W	Sacramento Ward 1	63	24
John	Marin Cortemad	60	791
L	Sacramento Ward 1	63	144
LEHMANS			
Benj*	Siskiyou Scott Ri	69	62
LEHMEN			
Chas	Sacramento Ward 3	63	456
LEHOLY			
Luis*	Calaveras Twp 4	57	332
LEHRAM			
Jacob*	Napa Napa	61	108
LEHRKA			
Henry*	Siskiyou Klamath	69	85
LEHUZAY			
Samul	San Francisco San Francisco 7	68	1396
LEHY			
Lawrence	Tuolumne Twp 1	71	247
Thomas	San Francisco San Francisco 12	394 67	
LEI ONG			
---	Butte Oregon	56	612
LEI			
---	Butte Kimshaw	56	605
---	Calaveras Twp 8	57	105
---	Calaveras Twp 5	57	204
---	El Dorado Georgetown	58	701
---	El Dorado Greenwood	58	731
---	El Dorado Mud Springs	58	971
---	San Francisco San Francisco 4	68	1184
---	San Francisco San Francisco 4	68	1212
---	Tuolumne Twp 5	71	523
---	Yuba Slate Ro	72	710
---*	Butte Kimshaw	56	589
---*	Yuba Slate Ro	72	717
Ach*	Yuba Long Bar	72	767
Chas	El Dorado Georgetown	58	694
Lay*	Yuba Long Bar	72	764
O*	Yuba Long Bar	72	765
LEIAH			
Timothy	Sierra Downieville	66	1018
LEIB			
Adam	Plumas Quincy	62	991
LEIBER			
Chas	Sacramento Sutter	63	289
Hodes F*	Calaveras Twp 5	57	187
LEIBERT			
N	Nevada Grass Valley	61	169
LEIBIR			
Hodes F*	Calaveras Twp 5	57	187
LEIBY			
Saml	Amador Twp 7	55	413
LEICHAN			
H P	Sonoma Petaluma	69	571
LEICHMAN			
M A	Sacramento Ward 4	63	534
LEID			
---	Tulara Twp 1	71	117
LEIDER			
Franklin*	Santa Cruz Santa Cruz	66	635
LEIDERMAN			
Herman	San Francisco San Francisco 8	68	1295
LEIDERSDOFF			
William*	Sierra St Louis	66	809
LEIDINTATH			
William	Calaveras Twp 8	57	88
LEIDS			
Philip*	Nevada Red Dog	61	544
LEIESORA			
Joseph*	Mariposa Twp 3	60	548
LEIETTE			
O A	Shasta Shasta	66	734
LEIFELT			
Morris	San Joaquin Stockton	64	1034
LEIFHOLDT			
F	Siskiyou Cottonwood	69	97
LEIFUS			
Joshua*	San Francisco San Francisco 1	68	916
LEIG			
F*	El Dorado Placerville	58	874
LEIGAR			
David	El Dorado Coloma	58	1080
LEIGH			
Cornelius*	Sacramento Granite	63	247
Hugh	Tuolumne Jamestown	71	443
J J	San Francisco San Francisco 2	67	671
W T	Sacramento San Joaquin	63	368
LEIGHMAN			
Geo	Napa Napa	61	60
LEIGHT			
Henry	Butte Ophir	56	786
LEIGHTER			
A	San Francisco San Francisco 5	67	494
Antone	El Dorado Gold Hill	58	1098
LEIGHTNER			
Thomas	Alameda Brooklyn	55	202
LEIGHTON			
A V	Tuolumne Twp 2	71	316
David	Tuolumne Sonora	71	194
J H	El Dorado Placerville	58	826
Joseph*	Calaveras Twp 6	57	154
S P	Trinity Trinity	70	973
Stephen	San Luis Obispo San Luis Obispo	65	6
William M	Los Angeles Los Angeles	59	294
LEIGLE			
Arsenne	Los Angeles Los Angeles	59	373
LEIGLEISE			
John*	Siskiyou Callahan	69	3
LEIGLER			
Lewis	Calaveras Twp 4	57	329
LEIGLINGER			
Henry	San Joaquin Stockton	64	1054
LEILER			
John	Yuba Long Bar	72	755
LEILL			
Lauis*	Calaveras Twp 9	57	399
Louis*	Calaveras Twp 9	57	399
LEILSON			
A	San Joaquin Stockton	64	1090
LEIMAN			
Ann	San Francisco San Francisco 9	68	985
P G	Nevada Grass Valley	61	153
P*	Nevada Grass Valley	61	153
LEIMBACK			
Herman*	Sacramento San Joaquin	63	348
LEIMPACH			
Fred*	San Francisco San Francisco 9	68	1054
LEIMPO			
---*	Fresno Twp 2	59	18
LEIN			
---	Nevada Rough &	61	434
---	Placer Illinois	62	753
---	Shasta Horsetown	66	708
---	Tuolumne Jacksonville	71	167
---*	Nevada Rough &	61	434
---*	Tuolumne Big Oak	71	181
Ah	Tuolumne Twp 4	71	181
Fred	Placer Rattle Snake	62	638
Won	Fresno Twp 1	59	26
LEINA			
Jean	Calaveras Twp 8	57	65
LEINBURGHER			
H	Sacramento Ward 1	63	116
LEING			
---	Mariposa Twp 3	60	569
LEINHART			
Joseph	Plumas Meadow Valley	62	932
LEINMYER			
Joseph*	Alameda Brooklyn	55	144
LEINNYER			
Joseph*	Alameda Brooklyn	55	144
LEINP			
Paul	San Francisco San Francisco 11	92 67	
LEINS			
J	San Francisco San Francisco 1	68	915
Wash	San Francisco San Francisco 1	68	918
LEINTO			
Sacreta	Alameda Brooklyn	55	202
LEIP			
---	Placer Illinois	62	746
Yom	Placer Illinois	62	746
LEIPINTZ			
G	San Francisco San Francisco 7	68	1434
LEIPP			
John	Los Angeles Santa Ana	59	443
LEIPRIC			
Lyon	San Francisco San Francisco 2	67	792
LEIPSEY			
---	Mendocino Calpella	60	824
LEIPSIC			
Lyon	San Francisco San Francisco 2	67	792
LEIR			
Mary	Sacramento Ward 1	63	131
LEIRA			
Concepcion	Santa Barbara San Bernardino	64	197
Jesus	San Bernardino Santa Barbara	64	170
LEIRQUIR			
J*	Alameda Brooklyn	55	79
LEIRRER			
S	Calaveras Twp 9	57	392
LEIRSON			
M	El Dorado Placerville	58	863
LEIS			
James	Sierra Downieville	66	961
Pedro	Mariposa Twp 3	60	547
Saml	Butte Oregon	56	626
LEISA			
Goudaloup	Santa Ba San Bernardino	64	218
Goudaloup	S Buenav San Bernardino	64	219
LEISBUTTLE			
A	El Dorado Diamond	58	766
LEISE			
Jacob P	Merced Monterey	60	929
Jacob P	Monterey Monterey	60	929
LEISENFELD			
P*	San Francisco San Francisco 3	67	31
LEISER			
Eliza	San Francisco San Francisco 6	67	439
John	El Dorado Placerville	58	914
John A*	San Francisco San Francisco 2	67	680
LEISEWRING			
J P*	Merced Twp 1	60	895
LEISH			
James	San Joaquin Castoria	64	902
LEISKE			
Chas*	San Francisco San Francisco 1	68	854
LEISLEY			
Robt	Sacramento Franklin	63	334
LEISMAN			
Henry	Trinity East For	70	1025
LEISNET			
Nicholas	San Francisco San Francisco 8	68	1305
LEISNGSTOR			
M*	El Dorado Placerville	58	854
LEISSENWETZ			
H	San Francisco San Francisco 7	67	527
LEISTE			
Chas*	San Francisco San Francisco 1	68	854
LEISURDEGERS			
John*	Placer Illinois	62	741
LEISURRING			
J P*	Merced Twp 1	60	895
LEIT			
---	El Dorado Diamond	58	790
---	Yuba North Ea	72	681
Antonio*	San Francisco San Francisco 8	68	1246
LEITCH			
Edward	Sierra Pine Grove	66	833
Isaac H	Placer Auburn	62	593
LEITCHFIELD			
Ansel	San Joaquin Castoria	64	872
LEITH			
Lewis*	Plumas Quincy	62	924
Louisa	San Francisco San Francisco 2	67	658
Wm	Plumas Meadow Valley	62	906
LEITHERN			
H	El Dorado Placerville	58	852
LEITZER			
W	San Francisco San Francisco 6	67	453
LEIVA			
Antonio	Los Angeles Santa Ana	59	451
Cruz	Los Angeles Santa Ana	59	445
Estaban	Monterey San Juan	60	997
Francisco	Santa Barbara San Bernardino	64	178
Luciano	Los Angeles Los Angeles	59	330
Santiago	Los Angeles Los Angeles	59	311
LEIVITIN			
John	El Dorado White Oaks	58	1011
LEIVRAN			

California 1860 Census Index

Name	County Locale	M653 Roll	Page
LEIVRAN			
Mary	San Francisco San Francisco 10	320	67
LEIVRE			
Fanny	San Francisco San Francisco 10	351	67
LEIW			
---*	Nevada Rough &	61	434
LEIWY			
John	Solano Suisan	69	215
LEIX			
Wm	San Francisco San Francisco 2 67	799	
LEJBA			
Agnacio	Santa Clara Almaden	65	268
LEJO			
---*	Mendocino Calpella	60	822
LEJUNE			
---	San Francisco San Francisco 7 681	400	
LEK			
---	San Francisco San Francisco 10	355	67
Fu	San Francisco San Francisco 11	158	67
Tong	San Francisco San Francisco 10	356	67
LEKO			
---	Tulara Twp 2	71	36
LEKROGOAT			
Louis*	San Joaquin Castoria	64	875
LELAN			
Lewis*	Yuba New York	72	723
Louis	Yuba New York	72	723
LELAND			
Alescander	Tuolumne Twp 3	71	448
Alexancer	Tuolumne Jamestown	71	448
Amos S	Alameda Brooklyn	55	194
C M	Mariposa Twp 1	60	670
Delphina	Placer Ophirville	62	659
E Estelle	Butte Kimshaw	56	608
Ellen	San Francisco San Francisco 2 67	584	
G A	Tuolumne Twp 3	71	429
George	Alameda Brooklyn	55	204
H M	Yolo Washington	72	567
Henry	Yuba Marysville	72	874
Johnson	Sonoma Healdsbu	69	477
Lemuel	Butte Ophir	56	772
Mary H	Del Norte Crescent	58	649
N M	Yolo Washington	72	567
Richard	Santa Cruz Pajaro	66	551
S A	San Francisco San Francisco 6 67	468	
W H	Butte Bidwell	56	713
W P	Butte Kimshaw	56	608
Wm	Alameda Brooklyn	55	204
LELANTHAL			
John	San Francisco San Francisco 2 67	632	
LELAVANIG			
E	Calaveras Twp 9	57	378
LELECHEAN			
Numa*	Plumas Meadow Valley	62	900
LELECHEAU			
Numa*	Plumas Meadow Valley	62	900
LELF			
R M	El Dorado Diamond	58	793
LELH			
James*	Alameda Brooklyn	55	100
LELIAVE			
Jeremiah*	Yuba Bear Rvr	721006	
LELINE			
C	Amador Twp 3	55	376
LELING			
Joseph	San Francisco San Francisco 3 67	42	
LELL			
James*	Alameda Brooklyn	55	100
LELLAND			
G W	Alameda Brooklyn	55	120
LELLE			
James*	Alameda Brooklyn	55	100
LELLHORN			
T J*	Napa Napa	61	57
LELLI			
Domingo	San Francisco San Francisco 2 67	798	
LELLIE			
W H*	Napa Napa	61	114
LELLIS			
Isaac	Siskiyou Cottonwooood	69	102
LELLS			
S	Calaveras Twp 9	57	393
LELLY			
David	Yolo Washington	72	605
LELONG			
---	Nevada Bloomfield	61	521
Bernabe	Los Angeles Los Angeles	59	396
Joseph	San Francisco San Francisco 3 67	42	
Martin	Los Angeles Los Angeles	59	395
Martin	San Bernardino S Timate	64	687
LELOSIPE			
Dloupe*	Mariposa Coulterville	60	675

Name	County Locale	M653 Roll	Page
LELOSIPE			
Loris*	Mariposa Coulterville	60	675
Lous*	Mariposa Coulterville	60	675
LELOUPE			
Louis*	Mariposa Coulterville	60	675
LELSBY			
Henry	Sacramento Granite	63	242
LELSIE			
Alonzo	Calaveras Twp 7	57	3
LELSRUVE			
C A	Amador Twp 1	55	454
LELTAY			
---*	Butte Chico	56	551
LELVELLIS			
Enasen*	Calaveras Twp 6	57	136
LELVER			
James L	Mariposa Twp 3	60	546
LELVI			
Wm	San Francisco San Francisco 2 67	801	
LEM			
---	Butte Oregon	56	613
---	Calaveras Twp 7	57	39
---	Del Norte Happy Ca	58	667
---	El Dorado Salmon Hills	581058	
---	El Dorado Placerville	58	924
---	Mariposa Twp 3	60	607
---	Mariposa Twp 1	60	662
---	Mariposa Twp 1	60	667
---	Placer Auburn	62	568
---	Placer Virginia	62	671
---	Plumas Meadow Valley	62	910
---	Plumas Quincy	62	920
---	Plumas Quincy	62	946
---	Plumas Quincy	62	948
---	Shasta Horsetown	66	698
---	Sierra Twp 5	66	928
---	Trinity Dead Wood	70	958
---	Yuba Long Bar	72	757
---*	Butte Kimshaw	56	600
---*	Butte Oregon	56	613
---*	Mariposa Twp 3	60	607
Fie	Plumas Meadow Valley	62	913
Foo	Plumas Quincy	62	945
Luck	Plumas Quincy	621009	
Pah	Yuba New York	72	739
See	Plumas Meadow Valley	62	909
Sing	Butte Kimshaw	56	580
Sing	Butte Kimshaw	56	587
Sing*	Plumas Quincy	62	950
Sle	Placer Illinois	62	753
Soo	Tuolumne Big Oak	71	150
Sung	Placer Virginia	62	671
LEMA			
Enos*	Yuba Marysville	72	946
Major	Mariposa Twp 3	60	594
Smith	Monterey San Juan	60	990
LEMAIN			
H	Amador Twp 3	55	385
LEMAINE			
Henry	Sierra Twp 7	66	871
LEMAIR			
Joseph	San Francisco San Francisco 11	135	67
LEMAITRE			
William	San Francisco San Francisco 11	113	67
LEMAM			
William*	Calaveras Twp 9	57	352
LEMAME			
Henry	Sierra Twp 7	66	871
LEMAN			
---	Mendocino Twp 1	60	889
Angrisk	Sacramento Ward 1	63	24
C	Calaveras Twp 9	57	404
C A	Nevada Rough &	61	420
Daniel	Siskiyou Scott Va	69	32
David	Sacramento Alabama	63	412
Frederick	Calaveras Twp 8	57	57
J	San Francisco San Francisco 3 67	20	
Jams A	Shasta Shasta	66	678
Jos	Butte Kimshaw	56	581
L	Sonoma Petaluma	69	580
Louis	Placer Michigan	62	840
Martin	Shasta Shasta	66	676
W J	Nevada Rough &	61	418
Walter N	San Francisco San Francisco 7 681	360	
William	San Francisco San Francisco 7 681	393	
LEMAR			
Themper*	Mariposa Twp 1	60	639
Thernper*	Mariposa Twp 1	60	639
Thompir*	Mariposa Twp 1	60	639
Thumper*	Mariposa Twp 1	60	639
Tim	Mariposa Twp 3	60	588
LEMAS			
---*	Mariposa Twp 3	60	602
Abert	Mariposa Twp 3	60	548

Name	County Locale	M653 Roll	Page
LEMASNE			
J	Mariposa Twp 1	60	630
LEMASS			
Antonio	San Luis Obispo San Luis Obispo 65	39	
Manuel	San Luis Obispo San Luis Obispo 65	19	
LEMAY			
P D	Santa Clara Gilroy	65	231
LEMBECK			
Charles	Los Angeles Santa Ana	59	443
LEMBINE			
E	San Francisco San Francisco 4 681	134	
LEMCUS			
John	Placer Forest H	62	766
LEMDERLEN			
Isaac*	Calaveras Twp 6	57	143
LEMDERTEN			
Isaac	Calaveras Twp 6	57	143
LEMDESLER			
Isaac*	Calaveras Twp 5	57	143
LEME			
Daniel C	Tuolumne Don Pedro	71	539
Daniel O*	Tuolumne Twp 6	71	539
LEMECHON			
Louis	San Francisco San Francisco 2 67	687	
LEMEMPA			
---	Fresno Twp 2	59	113
LEMENWORTH			
Thos*	Sonoma Sonoma	69	650
LEMERE			
James*	Alameda Oakland	55	4
LEMEREX			
A	Sutter Vernon	70	847
M	Sutter Vernon	70	847
LEMERO			
---	Fresno Twp 2	59	50
James*	Alameda Oakland	55	4
LEMERS			
Andrew	Sacramento Granite	63	251
LEMESNEY			
Thos	Shasta Horsetown	66	688
LEMESUEY			
Thos*	Shasta Horsetown	66	688
LEMETEYER			
Henry	San Francisco San Francisco 8 681	306	
LEMEUX			
Henry	Sacramento Ward 4	63	589
LEMIA			
Wm T*	Alameda Brooklyn	55	117
LEMIDT			
F	Sacramento Sutter	63	290
LEMIN			
Wm T*	Alameda Brooklyn	55	117
LEMINO			
---	Butte Chico	56	550
LEMION			
Jesse	Alameda Brooklyn	55	105
LEMKAN			
---	Tuolumne Shawsfla	71	417
John	Tuolumne Twp 2	71	417
LEMKE			
Henry	Klamath Liberty	59	242
LEMLESLEN			
Isaac*	Calaveras Twp 5	57	143
LEMLLING			
Henry*	Alameda Brooklyn	55	92
LEMM			
---	Plumas Meadow Valley	62	909
---*	Plumas Quincy	62	926
Christopher	Plumas Quincy	62	943
See	Plumas Meadow Valley	62	909
LEMMAY			
F D*	Siskiyou Klamath	69	91
T D	Siskiyou Klamath	69	91
LEMMING			
Alfred*	Mariposa Coulterville	60	677
LEMMON			
Alexander	Yuba New York	72	726
Amy V	Calaveras Twp 9	57	367
Jno	Alameda Brooklyn	55	193
Robert	Los Angeles Shaffer	59	396
Wm	Yuba New York	72	724
LEMMONEZ			
Morand	Tuolumne Columbia	71	304
LEMMONS			
Joseph	Humbolt Union	59	186
N C	Sutter Sutter	70	811
LEMN			
John*	Butte Ophir	56	749
LEMNAN			
William*	San Francisco San Francisco 9 681	042	
LEMNEX			
A	Butte Wyandotte	56	664
LEMNOX			
A*	Butte Wyandotte	56	664
LEMOANG			
Peter	Calaveras Twp 9	57	363

California 1860 Census Index

Name	County Locale	M653 Roll Page
LEMOANGE		
Peter*	Calaveras Twp 9	57 363
LEMOANGO		
Peter*	Calaveras Twp 9	57 363
LEMOINE		
---	San Francisco San Francisco 10	328 67
L	Sacramento Georgian	63 335
L D	Sierra Twp 7	66 868
LEMON		
Bernard	San Francisco San Francisco 2	67 662
Calvin	El Dorado Placerville	58 906
David	El Dorado White Oaks	581014
Frank	Calaveras Twp 5	57 223
Frank	Plumas Quincy	62 992
H H	Butte Oregon	56 624
James	Shasta Horsetown	66 695
James M	Solano Suisan	69 235
Jas	Sacramento Ward 1	63 141
John B	Solano Fairfield	69 197
Joseph	San Bernardino San Bernadino	64 673
Joseph	Sierra Forest C	66 909
Joseph*	Alameda Brooklyn	55 91
Mary Ann	San Francisco San Francisco 2	67 661
Pelonco	Tuolumne Twp 1	71 186
Piloco	Tuolumne Sonora	71 186
S B	Sacramento Ward 4	63 517
Samuel	Colusa Monroeville	57 452
LEMONDS		
L	San Francisco San Francisco 10	307 67
LEMONIE		
Baptiste	San Francisco San Francisco 2	67 793
LEMONS		
G H	Sacramento San Joaquin	63 355
George	Sacramento San Joaquin	63 355
John	Placer Michigan	62 821
John T	Tuolumne Sonora	71 480
Josiah	San Francisco San Francisco 2	67 658
Sidney	San Francisco San Francisco 3	67 38
Thos	Sacramento Ward 3	63 432
Thos	Sacramento Ward 3	63 456
LEMONT		
Herriet*	San Francisco San Francisco 8	681249
Isaac*	Placer Michigan	62 836
John	Butte Cascade	56 692
R	Solano Vacaville	69 335
LEMONWORTH		
Thos	Sonoma Sonoma	69 650
LEMORA		
Ed	Nevada Bloomfield	61 522
LEMORALLO		
Joseph*	San Francisco San Francisco 3	67 16
LEMORE		
Joseph*	Alameda Brooklyn	55 91
LEMORIE		
A	Mariposa Twp 1	60 635
LEMP		
---	Placer Illinois	62 753
Paul	San Francisco San Francisco 11	92 67
LEMPKAN		
A H	Tuolumne Twp 2	71 417
LEMS		
Daniel C*	Tuolumne Twp 6	71 539
LEMSHAN		
---	Mendocino Big Rvr	60 854
LEMSLEMAR		
John*	Calaveras Twp 9	57 372
LEMSLEWAR		
John*	Calaveras Twp 9	57 372
LEMSON		
Hardy	Butte Kimshaw	56 588
John	Monterey San Juan	60 988
LEMTEYER		
H	San Francisco San Francisco 10	298 67
LEMUOX		
A*	Butte Wyandotte	56 664
LEMUP		
Christian*	Mariposa Coulterville	60 698
LEMY		
---	Sacramento Granite	63 249
A*	Sacramento Granite	63 249
LEN CHOY		
---	Tuolumne Montezuma	71 504
LEN		
---	Amador Twp 5	55 366
---	Amador Twp 6	55 431
---	Calaveras Twp 5	57 166
---	Calaveras Twp 7	57 44
---	El Dorado Coloma	581106
---	El Dorado Diamond	58 815
---	Fresno Twp 2	59 41
---	Mariposa Twp 3	60 551
---	Mariposa Twp 3	60 564

Name	County Locale	M653 Roll Page
LEN		
---	Mariposa Twp 1	60 651
---	Mariposa Twp 1	60 657
---	Mariposa Twp 1	60 667
---	San Francisco San Francisco 4	681184
---	San Francisco San Francisco 4	681185
---	San Francisco San Francisco 2	67 624
---	Shasta Horsetown	66 706
---	Shasta French G	66 712
---	Sierra La Porte	66 780
---	Sierra Twp 5	66 932
---	Sierra Twp 5	66 933
---	Sierra Downieville	66 984
---	Trinity Taylor'S	701035
---	Trinity E Weaver	701059
---	Tuolumne Twp 6	71 535
---	Yolo No E Twp	72 679
---	Yolo No E Twp	72 681
---	Yolo No E Twp	72 684
---	Yolo No E Twp	72 685
---	Yuba Bear Rvr	721000
---	Yuba North Ea	72 675
---	Yuba North Ea	72 679
---	Yuba North Ea	72 681
---	Yuba Slate Ro	72 684
---	Yuba Slate Ro	72 685
---	Yuba Long Bar	72 759
---	Yuba Fosters	72 841
---*	Sacramento Cosumnes	63 397
---*	San Francisco San Francisco 3	67 73
---*	Sierra Twp 5	66 933
---*	Yuba Fosters	72 841
Choy	Tuolumne Twp 5	71 504
Feat	San Francisco San Francisco 4	681202
Henry	Sacramento Granite	63 242
Hew	Yuba Marysville	72 921
How	Butte Ophir	56 788
Hoy	Yuba Fosters	72 836
John*	Sierra Port Win	66 798
Jue	El Dorado Georgetown	58 692
King	Yuba Long Bar	72 759
Low	Calaveras Twp 5	57 194
Shaom*	El Dorado Georgetown	58 700
Sing	Sacramento Natonia	63 281
Song	San Francisco San Francisco 4	681186
Tom	Yuba Long Bar	72 759
Ung	Yuba Long Bar	72 767
Wee	Yuba Marysville	72 925
Wo To	San Francisco San Francisco 4	681202
Yong*	San Francisco San Francisco 3	67 73
LEN'S		
Son*	Mariposa Twp 3	60 609
LENA		
---	Siskiyou Klamath	69 78
China	Siskiyou Callahan	69 2
Jos*	Butte Kimshaw	56 605
William	Yuba Long Bar	72 752
LENAHAN		
C	Tuolumne Twp 2	71 367
Hannah	Solano Benecia	69 306
John	Tuolumne Springfield	71 367
Michael	Solano Benecia	69 306
LENAHON		
Ann	San Francisco San Francisco 10	244 67
LENARD		
Chas	Amador Twp 2	55 266
J	Nevada Nevada	61 280
J*	Nevada Nevada	61 316
James	Mariposa Coulterville	60 676
James	San Francisco San Francisco 8	681294
John	Amador Twp 2	55 282
John	Mariposa Twp 3	60 571
Owen	Humbolt Bucksport	59 161
Philomeria	Santa Clara San Jose	65 305
Pratt	Placer Secret R	62 617
Saml	Placer Secret R	62 610
Thomas	El Dorado Placerville	58 878
V M	Placer Sacramento	62 643
W	El Dorado Placerville	58 878
Wm S	Calaveras Twp 6	57 173
LENARDES		
Joseph	El Dorado Placerville	58 919
Leon	El Dorado Placerville	58 919
LENARDS		
James	Mariposa Coulterville	60 676
N	El Dorado Casumnes	581176
LENAREZ		
Pedro	Monterey Pajaro	601015
LENARIAS		
Jacinta	Monterey San Juan	601007
LENARIUS		
Chilco	Los Angeles San Jose	59 284
LENARR		
Natividad*	Mariposa Twp 3	60 586
LENARRI		
Angelli	Mariposa Twp 3	60 600

Name	County Locale	M653 Roll Page
LENARS		
Natívida G	Mariposa Twp 3	60 586
LENASS		
Natividad G*	Mariposa Twp 3	60 586
LENBBEN		
Theadore	Humbolt Eureka	59 164
LENBERG		
W*	San Joaquin Stockton	641098
LENCE		
H B	Siskiyou Klamath	69 80
Wm*	Nevada Eureka	61 363
LENCEN		
Michael	Yuba Marysville	72 904
LENCEY		
John	El Dorado Coloma	581121
LENCH		
E W	Sacramento Ward 1	63 30
James*	San Francisco San Francisco 9	681032
LENCHALL		
Lewis	Butte Bidwell	56 728
LENCHO		
Mr	Marin San Rafael	60 768
LENCHY		
---	Mendocino Calpella	60 827
LENCINGER		
R	Amador Twp 1	55 497
LEND		
Frank*	San Francisco San Francisco 3	67 69
Jno	San Francisco San Francisco 10	194 67
LENDEE		
---*	Sierra Twp 5	66 934
LENDENAN		
Isaac S	Placer Secret R	62 624
LENDENBOUN		
Isaac*	San Francisco San Francisco 9	681051
LENDENBURGER		
August	Los Angeles Santa Ana	59 440
LENDER		
D*	Nevada Eureka	61 390
J	San Francisco San Francisco 5	67 513
LENDERMAN		
F L	San Francisco San Francisco 6	67 425
LENDERMOST		
C	San Joaquin Stockton	641038
LENDERS		
Joseph*	Mariposa Twp 3	60 571
LENDINS		
Jas*	Sacramento Granite	63 252
LENDLEY		
Charles	Yuba Marysville	72 912
LENDNER		
L	San Francisco San Francisco 5	67 475
LENDRAGAN		
Larry	Fresno Twp 1	59 82
LENDSOY		
James	Tuolumne Jamestown	71 452
LENE		
---	Plumas Meadow Valley	62 913
---	Sierra Twp 7	66 876
LENEAE		
Susariah*	Mariposa Twp 3	60 566
LENEAM		
Felipe*	San Francisco San Francisco 1	68 844
LENEAUX		
Montraulle	San Francisco 3	67 7
	San Francisco	
LENEERY		
T A E*	Siskiyou Scott Va	69 41
LENEHAN		
Pat	San Francisco San Francisco 9	681025
LENER		
Jos	Butte Kimshaw	56 605
LENERT		
E	Calaveras Twp 9	57 369
LENERY		
T A E*	Siskiyou Scott Va	69 41
LENETT		
Hose	Butte Bidwell	56 709
LENEWKAMP		
John	Klamath Klamath	59 227
LENEX		
John*	Siskiyou Shasta Rvr	69 115
LENEY		
W	El Dorado Placerville	58 848
LENFESS		
Nancy E*	San Francisco San Francisco 10	288 67
LENFEST		
Nancy E*	San Francisco San Francisco 10	288 67
LENG		
---	Amador Twp 2	55 310
---	Amador Twp 2	55 311
---	Amador Twp 2	55 326
---	Calaveras Twp 4	57 341

California 1860 Census Index

Name	County Locale	M653 Roll	Page
LENG			
---	El Dorado Coloma	58	1109
---	San Francisco San Francisco 9	68	1095
---	San Francisco San Francisco 4	68	1195
---	Shasta Horsetown	66	709
---	Siskiyou Scott Ri	69	82
---	Trinity Mouth Ca	70	1018
---	Trinity Taylor'S	70	1033
---	Trinity Taylor'S	70	1035
---	Trinity Trinindad Rvr	70	1046
---	Trinity Trinindad Rvr	70	1047
---	Trinity Trinindad Rvr	70	1048
---	Trinity Weaverville	70	1075
---	Tuolumne Twp 3	71	446
---	Yolo Slate Ra	72	715
---*	Siskiyou Scott Ri	69	82
---*	Trinity Trinindad Rvr	70	1048
H*	Mariposa Twp 3	60	622
John	Siskiyou Scott Ri	69	67
Le	Mariposa Twp 3	60	613
LENGALD			
Jules	Los Angeles Los Nieto	59	437
LENGERFETTER			
Rufus*	Calaveras Twp 4	57	341
LENGO			
John*	Sierra Twp 7	66	874
LENGTHY			
---	Tulara Twp 1	71	122
LENGUE			
---	Sierra Downieville	66	979
LENGWORTH			
Wm J	Alameda Brooklyn	55	86
LENHARD			
Ed	San Francisco San Francisco 9	68	1084
J	El Dorado Newtown	58	776
LENHARDT			
A*	San Francisco San Francisco 2	67	678
Joseph	Calaveras Twp 7	57	29
LENHART			
G W	Nevada Nevada	61	255
Wm	Tehama Tehama	70	945
LENI			
---	El Dorado Salmon Hills	58	1053
LENICK			
Wm R	San Bernardino S Timate	64	689
LENIG			
H*	Mariposa Twp 3	60	622
LENIGER			
Chas	San Francisco San Francisco 10	67	355
LENING			
---	Calaveras Twp 4	57	327
LENIRE			
Iarois*	San Francisco San Francisco 2	67	723
Janis*	San Francisco San Francisco 2	67	723
Jarois*	San Francisco San Francisco 2	67	723
Jarris*	San Francisco San Francisco 2	67	723
Jarvis*	San Francisco San Francisco 2	67	723
LENIS			
Manuel	Placer Rattle Snake	62	636
P	Siskiyou Scott Ri	69	74
LENIX			
Robt	Sonoma Sonoma	69	640
LENJALD			
Jules*	Los Angeles Los Nieto	59	437
LENJREY			
A P*	Placer Michigan	62	845
LENLERSDOFF			
William*	Sierra St Louis	66	809
LENLIN			
W	Shasta Horsetown	66	696
LENLY			
S S	Nevada Nevada	61	242
LENMAN			
August	Sacramento Ward 1	63	34
LENMON			
James	Merced Twp 1	60	901
LENMONS			
Wm*	Amador Twp 3	55	409
LENMORE			
Eunis*	Tulara Visalia	71	95
LENN			
---	Mariposa Twp 3	60	608
---	Mariposa Twp 3	60	613
---	Mariposa Twp 1	60	665
---	Tuolumne Twp 4	71	163
---*	Mariposa Twp 3	60	582
Francis*	Plumas Quincy	62	1004
LENNA			
---	Mendocino Calpella	60	826
LENNAN			
H S*	Butte Eureka	56	650
Joseph	San Francisco San Francisco 11	67	115
Mary	Sacramento Ward 3	63	454
Michael	Calaveras Twp 5	57	175

Name	County Locale	M653 Roll	Page
LENNARD			
Robt*	San Francisco San Francisco 9	68	1046
LENNATE			
Patrick*	Sierra Monte Crk	66	1035
LENNE			
Pedro	Alameda Brooklyn	55	100
LENNEGAN			
Patrick	Yuba Rose Par	72	794
LENNEKEN			
W H	Nevada Grass Valley	61	210
LENNEN			
Margt	San Francisco San Francisco 9	68	983
LENNER			
Chas	El Dorado Georgetown	58	694
LENNEY			
Edwin L	Yuba Bear Rvr	72	1004
M G*	Shasta Horsetown	66	690
LENNEYAN			
Patrick*	Yuba Rose Bar	72	794
LENNI			
Duvemi*	San Francisco San Francisco 2	67	697
LENNIGER			
C	Amador Twp 2	55	269
LENNIHAN			
Patrick	Calaveras Twp 4	57	312
LENNON			
James	San Francisco San Francisco 11	67	131
Jesse	Alameda Brooklyn	55	105
Thomas	San Francisco San Francisco 11	67	151
LENNOR			
Lennon	San Joaquin O'Neal	64	1001
LENNOTO			
Mathew*	Sacramento Granite	63	245
LENNOX			
Adam	Calaveras Twp 5	57	251
Charles A	Yuba Rose Bar	72	797
Henry C	Yuba Marysville	72	864
Robt	Los Angeles Tejon	59	536
LENNRAN			
William*	San Francisco San Francisco 9	68	1042
LENNS			
Wm P*	Calaveras Twp 9	57	367
LENNY			
---	Butte Ophir	56	806
Chin	Butte Ophir	56	808
J W*	Butte Oro	56	688
Thos	San Francisco San Francisco 1	68	918
LENO			
---	San Diego Temecula	64	797
---	San Diego Agua Caliente	64	833
LENODON			
---*	San Diego San Diego	64	771
LENOH			
John	Siskiyou Scott Va	69	32
LENON			
---	Fresno Twp 1	59	87
John	El Dorado White Oaks	58	1018
LENORD			
Alex	Humbolt Table Bl	59	141
George	Calaveras Twp 9	57	386
Jaseph	Calaveras Twp 9	57	370
John	Calaveras Twp 9	57	356
John	Calaveras Twp 9	57	369
Joseph	Calaveras Twp 9	57	370
Maria	Calaveras Twp 6	57	129
Nancy J	Calaveras Twp 9	57	379
Peter	Calaveras Twp 9	57	361
LENOREBACKER			
John	Mariposa Twp 1	60	629
LENORES			
Minguel	San Bernardino San Bernadino	64	639
LENORMANT			
M	Nevada Eureka	61	391
LENORY			
Edward	San Luis Obispo San Luis Obispo	65	24
LENOUR			
Chas	Sacramento Ward 4	63	578
LENOX			
Edward H	Contra Costa Twp 2	57	558
John	Siskiyou Scott Rvr	69	115
John	Siskiyou Scott Va	69	32
John*	Siskiyou Shasta Rvr	69	115
Mathew	Yolo Washington	72	573
Theodore	Calaveras Twp 8	57	81
LENOYN			
Casamie	Alameda Brooklyn	55	208
LENP			
---	Placer Illinois	62	754
LENQUE			
---*	Sierra Downieville	66	979
LENRA			
J	San Francisco San Francisco 9	68	1101
LENRATER			
James	Calaveras Twp 8	57	103

Name	County Locale	M653 Roll	Page
LENRISON			
Leon	Calaveras Twp 5	57	201
LENRUGAN			
Patrick*	Yuba Rose Bar	72	794
LENRY			
M*	Placer Michigan	62	839
LENSIN			
Barnt*	Nevada Bridgeport	61	473
LENSON			
L F*	Yolo Putah	72	560
LENSTON			
William*	Solano Benecia	69	317
LENT			
Abraham	Alameda Oakland	55	36
Chas	Santa Clara San Jose	65	338
Christopher*	Plumas Quincy	62	942
Georgeana	San Francisco San Francisco 6	67	448
Georgene	San Francisco San Francisco 4	68	1228
Georgiana	San Francisco San Francisco 6	67	448
Georgine	San Francisco San Francisco 4	68	1228
H G	Yolo Slate Ra	72	700
H G	Yuba Slate Ro	72	700
John	Alameda Oakland	55	37
John	Calaveras Twp 7	57	23
John	Tuolumne Columbia	71	290
John A	Alameda Brooklyn	55	123
John Jr	Calaveras Twp 7	57	23
John*	Tuolumne Twp 2	71	290
Schreyles	Yuba Fosters	72	839
Schriyler	Yuba Fosters	72	839
Siles	Marin Cortemad	60	755
William	San Francisco San Francisco 7	68	1438
LENTA			
Juan M	Monterey San Juan	60	1002
LENTAN			
Juan*	Alameda Brooklyn	55	155
LENTELL			
John	Sacramento Ward 1	63	137
LENTETT			
John*	Sacramento Ward 1	63	137
LENTI			
Juan	Yuba New York	72	729
LENTNER			
Fred	San Francisco San Francisco 7	68	1396
LENTON			
Giobatta	Calaveras Twp 8	57	102
LENTRAIT			
G W	Nevada Nevada	61	255
LENTRY			
Josiah	Placer Secret R	62	615
LENTSIZEN			
Andreas P*	Alameda Brooklyn	55	145
LENTY			
I	El Dorado Placerville	58	877
LENTZ			
Catharine*	San Francisco	7	681411
Herman	Tuolumne Twp 2	71	282
Louis H*	San Francisco San Francisco 7	68	1411
S V	Yuba Parks Ba	72	777
LENU			
Francis*	Plumas Quincy	62	1004
LENURHARD			
G*	El Dorado Placerville	58	825
LENUS			
Wm P*	Calaveras Twp 9	57	367
LENUSHARD			
G*	El Dorado Placerville	58	825
LENVARASSA			
Susan	San Francisco San Francisco 2	67	607
LENVAVASSA			
Susan	San Francisco San Francisco 2	67	607
LENWATE			
Patrick*	Sierra Monte Crk	66	1035
LENWELL			
W M	Tuolumne Twp 4	71	153
LENY			
---	Amador Twp 2	55	281
---	Sacramento Granite	63	250
A	Sacramento Granite	63	249
C	Calaveras Twp 9	57	401
LENYERFETTER			
Rufus*	Calaveras Twp 4	57	341
LENZ			
Jerome C	Siskiyou Yreka	69	171
LENZAR			
Geo E	Siskiyou Callahan	69	6
LEO CHUE			
---	San Joaquin Stockton	64	1056
LEO			
---	Butte Eureka	56	655
---	Calaveras Twp 8	57	60
---	El Dorado Salmon Hills	58	1062
---	Fresno Twp 2	59	106
---	Fresno Twp 2	59	4

California 1860 Census Index

Name	County Locale	M653 RollPage
LEO		
---	Placer Auburn	62 597
---	Placer Rattle Snake	62 601
---	Placer Ophirville	62 654
---	Placer Virginia	62 676
---	Sierra Downieville	661005
---	Sierra St Louis	66 805
---	Sierra Twp 7	66 876
---	Sierra Twp 5	66 933
---	Sierra Downieville	66 999
---	Trinity China Bar	70 959
---	Yuba Long Bar	72 753
---*	Butte Eureka	56 651
---*	San Francisco San Francisco 1	68 858
Ah	Butte Oregon	56 632
Charles	San Francisco San Francisco 8	681235
Choy	Calaveras Twp 4	57 300
H	Napa Napa	61 82
Hannah	Napa Napa	61 104
Henry	Colusa Monroeville	57 456
Henry	Solano Vallejo	69 280
Lin	Sierra Downieville	66 979
Pabblo	San Mateo Twp 1	65 62
Thos	San Francisco San Francisco 12	385 67
Tri	Sacramento Ward 3	63 494
Wm M	Solano Benecia	69 288
LEOALLEN		
Apgh*	Yuba Marysville	72 846
LEOBON		
Alfonse	Monterey Pajaro	601011
LEOCH		
---	El Dorado Diamond	58 797
LEOCORN		
Francisco	Mariposa Coulterville	60 698
LEOD		
Jno M*	Fresno Millerto	59 1
Robt	Sonoma Washington	69 677
T M*	San Francisco San Francisco 5	67 503
LEODENA		
---	Marin Novato	60 734
LEOERATA		
---	Monterey San Juan	60 992
LEOG		
---	Amador Twp 2	55 327
---	Trinity Mouth Ca	701017
Herman	Yuba Marysville	72 873
Jacob	Yuba Marysville	72 873
LEOHR		
John	Nevada Eureka	61 379
LEOKAMER		
---	Fresno Twp 2	59 52
LEOKE		
---	El Dorado Placerville	58 898
LEOL		
Sanl	Nevada Grass Valley	61 153
LEOMANS		
Leo	Sacramento Ward 4	63 523
LEON D CIMA		
Virginia	San Francisco San Francisco 3	67 6
LEON DE		
Petra	San Francisco San Francisco 2	67 718
LEON		
---	Butte Ophir	56 812
---	Calaveras Twp 9	57 375
---	El Dorado Salmon Falls	581042
---	El Dorado Salmon Hills	581066
---	El Dorado Mountain	581189
---	Shasta Horsetown	66 708
---	Sierra Downieville	66 993
---	Sierra Downieville	66 996
---	Trinity Lewiston	70 957
---	Tulara Keyesville	71 68
---	Tulara Keyesville	71 71
---*	El Dorado Salmon Falls	581066
A J	Yolo Washington	72 563
Ahi	Fresno Twp 1	59 28
Angela	Los Angeles Los Angeles	59 294
Anlon	El Dorado Placerville	58 918
Antonia	Mariposa Twp 4	60 654
Antonie	Alameda Brooklyn	55 169
Ascencion	San Francisco	4 681157
Bartola	Los Angeles Los Angeles	59 510
Casimero	Tuolumne Sonora	71 227
Casimiro	Tuolumne Twp 1	71 227
Catharine	San Francisco San Francisco 9	68 984
Catherine*	San Francisco	9 68 984
Chow	Butte Ophir	56 804
Duan De D	Los Angeles Santa Ana	59 453
Francis*	Amador Twp 4	55 240
Francisco	Los Angeles Los Nieto	59 428
Francisco D	San Francisco	3 67 6
Franciss	Amador Twp 4	55 240

Name	County Locale	M653 RollPage
LEON		
Geo D	San Francisco San Francisco 9	68 984
Guliana	Monterey S Antoni	60 969
Gulrana	Monterey S Antoni	60 969
Gustavis	El Dorado Placerville	58 931
Ignacio	Los Angeles Los Angeles	59 518
J	Sacramento Ward 1	63 5
J W	Sacramento San Joaquin	63 368
Jacob	Calaveras Twp 10	57 261
James	Amador Twp 4	55 241
James*	Amador Twp 4	55 233
Jesus	Yuba Marysville	72 965
John	Placer Virginia	62 672
Jose	San Diego Agua Caliente	64 853
Joseph	Calaveras Twp 5	57 206
Josephine	Tuolumne Sonora	71 224
Juan	Sacramento Ward 1	63 58
Juan De D*	Los Angeles Santa Ana	59 453
Julia	San Francisco San Francisco 2	67 642
Julian	Los Angeles Los Angeles	59 387
Louis	Plumas Quincy	62 988
M	San Francisco San Francisco 4	681223
Manuel	Yuba Suida	72 982
Manuel	Yuba Linda Twp	72 983
P	San Joaquin Stockton	641098
P	Tuolumne Twp 4	71 157
Padro	Tuolumne Twp 1	71 227 67
Patrick	San Francisco San Francisco 10	242 67
Petra De*	San Francisco San Francisco 2	67 718
Philip*	Trinity North Fo	701026
Ponfset	Siskiyou Callahan	69 9
Poufset*	Siskiyou Callahan	69 9
R	Butte Bidwell	56 713
Ramon*	Sacramento Ward 1	63 152
S	Tuolumne Twp 2	71 328
Sam	Fresno Twp 2	59 19
Santos	San Bernardino S Buenav	64 212
Stephen	Sacramento Ward 1	63 57
Sye	Butte Ophir	56 803
Vecenta	Plumas Quincy	62 988
W M	Tuolumne Twp 4	71 154
Yaw*	Calaveras Twp 9	57 361
Yot	San Francisco San Francisco 4	681178
LEONA		
Matilda*	Calaveras Twp 6	57 179
LEONAN		
Edward	San Francisco San Francisco 7	681381
LEONAR		
Matilda*	Calaveras Twp 6	57 179
Ranah	Santa Cruz Santa Cruz	66 624
Rauah*	Santa Cruz Santa Cruz	66 624
LEONARD		
A V	Nevada Eureka	61 352
Abraham S	San Francisco San Francisco 7	681435
Albert	Sacramento Sutter	63 296
Andrew	Santa Cruz Pescadero	66 647
Bemond*	Trinity Weaverville	701055
Benjamin	Tulara Twp 3	71 51
Bernard	Sonoma Petaluma	69 562
Bernard*	Trinity Weaverville	701055
Beryer	Sierra Twp 5	66 918
Biryer	Sierra Twp 5	66 918
Bridget	San Francisco San Francisco 6	67 401
C	Shasta Millvill	66 726
C V	Klamath S Fork	59 203
Cathe	San Francisco San Francisco 9	681049
Catherine	San Francisco San Francisco 3	67 42
Charles	Mendocino Anderson	60 869
Charles	San Francisco San Francisco 7	681432
D	Trinity Indian C	70 983
D A	Siskiyou Scott Ri	69 73
Danl	San Francisco San Francisco 10	177 67
E W	San Francisco San Francisco 5	67 502
Edward	Sierra Whiskey	66 845
Edward	Sierra Downieville	66 978
Edward	Solano Benecia	69 281
Edward	Tuolumne Sonora	71 196
Edward A	San Francisco San Francisco 8	681315
Eliza	Shasta French G	66 713
Frances S	Alameda Brooklyn	55 126
Francis	San Francisco San Francisco 8	681279
G	Calaveras Twp 9	57 397
G	San Francisco San Francisco 5	67 490
G W	El Dorado Georgetown	58 694
Geo	Napa Napa	61 59
George	San Francisco San Francisco 3	67 7
George F	Los Angeles Los Angeles	59 326
Gilbert	Marin Bolinas	60 747
Godfrey	Mendocino Round Va	60 879
H N	Santa Clara Santa Clara	65 485
Harvey	San Francisco San Francisco 1	68 824
Hate*	San Francisco San Francisco 1	68 917
Hatt*	San Francisco San Francisco 1	68 917

Name	County Locale	M653 RollPage
LEONARD		
Henry	San Francisco San Francisco 3	67 61
Henry	Solano Benecia	69 317
Hiram	San Francisco San Francisco 7	681346
J	Nevada Nevada	61 316
J B	Sierra Downieville	661021
J G	Alameda Brooklyn	55 135
Jacob	Marin S Antoni	60 706
James	Alameda Oakland	55 54
James	Amador Twp 1	55 487
James A	Shasta Shasta	66 678
James O	Tuolumne Twp 3	71 422
Jas	Sacramento Ward 1	63 149
Jas	San Bernardino San Bernadino	64 627
Jas	San Francisco San Francisco 1	68 858
Jas	Yolo Washington	72 600
Jj B	Sierra Downieville	661021
Jno	Nevada Nevada	61 288
Jno	Sacramento Granite	63 254
John	Calaveras Twp 5	57 195
John	Sacramento Ward 1	63 92
John	San Mateo Twp 3	65 85
John	Solano Suisan	69 234
Johnson	Sierra Twp 7	66 874
Jos	Trinity Raabs Ba	701020
Joseph B	San Francisco San Francisco 11	152 67
Julia	Yuba Marysville	72 846
L	Amador Twp 1	55 467
L	Tehama Lassen	70 866
L G*	Tuolumne Columbia	71 290
Louis	San Francisco San Francisco 11	117 67
Louisa	Calaveras Twp 5	57 188
M D	San Francisco San Francisco 10	242 67
M D	Siskiyou Klamath	69 85
Michael	Santa Cruz Santa Cruz	66 611
Michael	Siskiyou Callahan	69 2
Michl	San Bernardino S Timate	64 687
Mrs	Siskiyou Yreka	69 166
N	Klamath S Fork	59 203
Owen	Tuolumne Twp 3	71 462
P	Napa Napa	61 103
P	Napa Napa	61 104
Pat	Butte Oregon	56 617
Pat	Sacramento Ward 1	63 83
Patrick	Contra Costa Twp 1	57 499
Patrick	San Francisco San Francisco 3	67 25
Patrick	San Francisco San Francisco 1	68 835
Patrick	Sierra Forest C	66 909
Patrick	Yuba Rose Bar	72 801
Peter	Plumas Quincy	621002
Phillip	Colusa Monroeville	57 444
R H	San Mateo Twp 3	65 107
S W	Siskiyou Klamath	69 87
Simpson	Tulara Twp 2	71 6
T G	Tuolumne Twp 2	71 290
T J	Siskiyou Klamath	69 87
Tho	Siskiyou Scott Va	69 44
Thomas	Siskiyou Callahan	69 2
Thomas	Solano Suisan	69 232
Thos	Nevada Rough &	61 430
Thos C	San Francisco San Francisco 10	303 67
W	Butte Hamilton	56 519
W	Siskiyou Scott Ri	69 73
W H	Amador Twp 2	55 281
W H	Trinity Trinity	70 972
Willard	Alameda Oakland	55 17
William	Los Angeles Los Angeles	59 340
William	Los Angeles Los Angeles	59 346
William	San Francisco San Francisco 7	681351
Wm	Sacramento Ward 1	63 36
Z G*	Tuolumne Columbia	71 290
LEONARDO		
F	San Francisco San Francisco 2	67 785
LEONARDSON		
Olaf*	Yuba Marysville	72 900
Olarf*	Yuba Marysville	72 900
Olorf*	Yuba Marysville	72 900
LEONARE		
Conception	Alameda Brooklyn	55 172
LEONATA		
Ancutio*	Calaveras Twp 9	57 364
LEONATO		
Ancutio*	Calaveras Twp 9	57 364
LEONDRO		
---	San Bernardino San Bernadino	64 669
LEONE		
Besanta	Sierra La Porte	66 773
Besanto	Sierra La Porte	66 773
Jose	Tuolumne Chinese	71 499
Pancho	Marin Novato	60 734
Ramon*	Sacramento Ward 1	63 152
Zenobia	San Joaquin Stockton	641074

California 1860 Census Index

Name	County Locale	M653 Roll	Page
LEONG			
---	Alameda Oakland	55	22
---	Amador Twp 6	55	435
---	Calaveras Twp 4	57	327
---	Calaveras Twp 9	57	358
---	El Dorado White Oaks	58	1031
---	El Dorado Salmon Falls	58	1041
---	El Dorado Salmon Falls	58	1045
---	El Dorado Salmon Hills	58	1060
---	El Dorado Salmon Hills	58	1064
---	El Dorado Salmon Falls	58	1066
---	El Dorado Salmon Falls	58	1067
---	El Dorado Coloma	58	1077
---	El Dorado Coloma	58	1102
---	El Dorado Coloma	58	1114
---	El Dorado Mountain	58	1178
---	El Dorado Mountain	58	1188
---	El Dorado Diamond	58	797
---	El Dorado Placerville	58	831
---	El Dorado Placerville	58	834
---	El Dorado Placerville	58	842
---	El Dorado Placerville	58	886
---	El Dorado Mud Springs	58	957
---	Fresno Twp 2	59	18
---	Placer Rattle Snake	62	602
---	Placer Rattle Snake	62	627
---	Placer Rattle Snake	62	629
---	Placer Folsom	62	640
---	Sacramento Ward 3	63	493
---	San Francisco San Francisco 9	68	1092
---	San Francisco San Francisco 4	68	1178
---	San Francisco San Francisco 4	68	1208
---	San Francisco San Francisco 4	68	1212
---	Trinity Mouth Ca	70	1016
---	Yuba Long Bar	72	759
---	Yuba Long Bar	72	761
---*	Calaveras Twp 5	57	245
---*	El Dorado Salmon Falls	58	1064
---*	Placer Auburn	62	572
Fou	San Francisco San Francisco 4	68	1190
Ha	San Francisco San Francisco 1	68	925
Hing	San Francisco San Francisco 5	67	508
Kei	San Francisco San Francisco 5	67	507
Ko	San Francisco San Francisco 4	68	1208
Thoy	San Francisco San Francisco 4	68	1190
Tow	San Francisco San Francisco 4	68	1190
Wo Ku	San Francisco San Francisco 5	67	509
Yk	San Francisco San Francisco 10	67	356
You*	San Francisco San Francisco 4	68	1185
Yuk	San Francisco San Francisco 10	67	356
LEONHART			
A*	Trinity E Weaver	70	1061
LEONIFTE			
Edwin F*	Del Norte Happy Ca	58	670
LEONIO			
A	El Dorado Placerville	58	870
LEONIPTE			
Edwin F*	Del Norte Happy Ca	58	670
LEONIS			
W L	Calaveras Twp 9	57	387
LEONN			
Joseph H	Calaveras Twp 9	57	356
LEONOR			
---	Los Angeles San Pedro	59	478
Juana	Los Angeles Los Nieto	59	439
LEONORA			
Carla	San Francisco San Francisco 2	67	791
LEONTEIN			
L	San Francisco San Francisco 2	67	655
LEONTINE			
Bapeny	San Francisco San Francisco 8	68	1302
Bapery*	San Francisco San Francisco 8	68	1302
Bassery*	San Francisco San Francisco 8	68	1302
LEONY			
---	Amador Twp 6	55	435
---	Calaveras Twp 10	57	273
---	San Francisco San Francisco 9	68	1092
LEOO			
---	Placer Virginia	62	681
---	Placer Illinois	62	742
LEOP			
---	Placer Illinois	62	746
LEOPALD			
L	Calaveras Twp 7	57	24
LEOPARD			
Sam	Tuolumne Sonora	71	479
LEOPO			
---	Fresno Twp 2	59	105
LEOPOLD			
---	Monterey San Juan	60	979
George	Plumas Meadow Valley	62	928
Saml	Tuolumne Twp 1	71	479
LEORE			
Jesus*	Yuba Marysville	72	965
LEORGER			
Antonio	Calaveras Twp 9	57	402
Antonio*	Calaveras Twp 9	57	402
LEORGIN			
Antonio*	Calaveras Twp 9	57	402
LEORIOR			
Juana	Los Angeles Santa Ana	59	439
LEORY			
---	Sierra La Porte	66	780
LEOTE			
Secile	Sierra Downieville	66	970
LEOTO			
Secilo	Sierra Downieville	66	970
LEOW			
---	Calaveras Twp 4	57	310
---	Del Norte Crescent	58	632
---	El Dorado Placerville	58	923
Catharine*	San Francisco 9	68	984
Geo D	San Francisco San Francisco 9	68	984
LEOWILL			
W	Stanislaus Oatvale	70	716
LEOY			
---	San Francisco San Francisco 9	68	1095
---	San Francisco San Francisco 4	68	1189
---	San Francisco San Francisco 4	68	1195
---	San Francisco San Francisco 4	68	1199
---	Trinity China Bar	70	959
---*	San Francisco San Francisco 4	68	1189
Elians*	Amador Twp 1	55	452
Elinns*	Amador Twp 1	55	452
Elwin*	Amador Twp 1	55	452
Jacob*	Yuba Marysville	72	873
Ken	San Francisco San Francisco 4	68	1199
Ko	San Francisco San Francisco 4	68	1208
Mi	San Francisco San Francisco 4	68	1190
We	San Francisco San Francisco 4	68	1190
LEOYD			
E	Sonoma Salt Point	69	691
LEP			
---	Amador Twp 5	55	366
---	Shasta Horsetown	66	697
LEPALSEDA			
Catanna	San Bernardino Santa Ba	64	216
Catanna	San Bernardino S Buenav	64	217
LEPANC			
Charles	San Francisco San Francisco 4	68	1165
LEPAON			
Honorine	Los Angeles Los Angeles	59	376
LEPARR			
Cyrus*	Yolo Putah	72	545
LEPE			
Pedro	Tuolumne Twp 1	71	227
LEPEON			
John*	Napa Napa	61	99
LEPER			
Antoine	Mariposa Twp 3	60	617
Antonio	Mariposa Twp 3	60	604
Hanson	Santa Clara San Jose	65	311
Henry	Santa Clara Santa Clara	65	504
Robert	Calaveras Twp 8	57	62
Jalise*	San Luis Obispo San Luis Obispo	65	29
LEPERRIER			
Frank	San Francisco San Francisco 7	68	1379
LEPET			
J	El Dorado Diamond	58	801
LEPHANER			
Joseph	El Dorado Greenwood	58	721
LEPIENTA			
Rocudia	Alameda Oakland	55	55
LEPINFELT			
J	El Dorado Placerville	58	870
LEPITT			
L	El Dorado Diamond	58	770
LEPKA			
Godlep	El Dorado White Oaks	58	1030
LEPLA			
Henry*	Sacramento Granite	63	223
LEPLANT			
P L	Marin S Antoni	60	709
LEPOINES			
Edward	Sierra Port Win	66	798
LEPOLD			
Jas M	Butte Ophir	56	785
Joseph*	Amador Twp 2	55	325
LEPON			
Charlie	San Joaquin Stockton	64	1062
LEPONES			
Edward	Sierra Port Win	66	798
LEPORLE			
Alemore	Alameda Oakland	55	54
LEPORTE			
John	Butte Ophir	56	802
LEPPEEN			
Fredk	San Francisco San Francisco 12	67	375
LEPPER			
Geo P	Placer Virginia	62	684
LEPPLEMAN			
E H	Nevada Grass Valley	61	159
LEPRACH			
Barnard	San Francisco San Francisco 4	68	1172
LEPSETTS			
Bridget	San Francisco San Francisco 2	67	611
LEPSKY			
Fredk	San Francisco San Francisco 2	67	640
LEPTROTH			
John F	Sierra Twp 7	66	875
LEPU			
Louis*	San Francisco San Francisco 7	68	1390
LEPULEODA			
Mauricis*	Monterey Monterey	60	936
LEPULVEDA			
Maria	San Diego S Luis R	64	779
Mauricis*	Monterey Monterey	60	936
LEQUERA			
Juan	Santa Cruz Watsonville	66	540
LER			
---	Amador Twp 2	55	308
---	Butte Kimshaw	56	577
---	Butte Kimshaw	56	584
---	Butte Kimshaw	56	589
---	Sacramento Natonia	63	280
---	Sierra Twp 7	66	876
Jasper N	Santa Clara San Jose	65	306
Ling*	Calaveras Twp 6	57	118
Mary	Santa Clara Santa Clara	65	487
LERABREW			
B	Sutter Bear Rvr	70	824
LERAISKY			
Louis*	Amador Twp 1	55	453
LERAN			
Antonia	Amador Twp 1	55	452
Antonio	Amador Twp 1	55	452
Ignacio	Mariposa Twp 3	60	614
LERANE			
V*	Sacramento Dry Crk	63	369
LERARES			
Benereta O*	San Francisco 4	68	1155
Benerita O*	San Francisco 4	68	1155
Benerita O*	San Francisco 4	68	1155
LERARINO			
Gregory*	Sacramento Ward 1	63	104
LERAUS			
Ellen	San Francisco San Francisco 9	68	1040
LERBEL			
L	Butte Bidwell	56	722
S	Butte Bidwell	56	722
LERBERT			
John G	San Francisco San Francisco 2	67	584
LERBS			
Henry	San Francisco San Francisco 1	68	810
LERCAS			
C T	Calaveras Twp 9	57	415
LERCE			
J W	Merced Twp 2	60	924
Jirah*	Marin S Antoni	60	706
LERCH			
Catharine S	San Francisco 7	68	1344
LERDDICERT			
Ellen*	San Francisco San Francisco 4	68	1115
LERDDICUT			
Ellen*	San Francisco San Francisco 4	68	1115
LERE			
Placide	Tuolumne Twp 1	71	233
LEREAM			
Felipe*	San Francisco San Francisco 1	68	844
LERELL			
L*	Napa Hot Springs	61	4
LEREN			
Selvester W	Yolo Merritt	72	580
T W	Nevada Eureka	61	392
LERENT			
Iacomo*	Mariposa Twp 3	60	615
Ignacio	Mariposa Twp 3	60	615
LEREY			
John	San Joaquin Stockton	64	1045
LERGISIVISLEG			
Fredk*	San Francisco San Francisco 3	67	66
LERGLEISE			
John	Siskiyou Callahan	69	3
LERGUESAN			
Mariano	San Francisco San Francisco 6	67	439
LERIBNEE			
J C*	Calaveras Twp 8	57	55
LERIBNER			
P M	Calaveras Twp 8	57	55
LERIG			
C*	Calaveras Twp 9	57	401

Name	County Locale	M653 Roll	Page
LERIGUNE			
Francois*	San Francisco San Francisco 2	67	795
LERIL			
Eugene	Yuba New York	72	725
LERIMONS			
Wm*	Amador Twp 3	55	409
LERINDE			
Peter*	Tuolumne Twp 2	71	291
LERINENS			
Frank*	Placer Rattle Snake	62	635
LERINSON			
A	Solano Vallejo	69	252
LERIRE			
Austine	El Dorado Coloma	581	102
LERIS			
Antone	El Dorado Salmon Falls	581	051
LERISTON			
George	Solano Benecia	69	283
LERKANS			
Thelesphori	Sierra La Porte	66	772
LERMA			
Jose	Los Angeles San Gabriel	59	409
LERMAN			
Stephen	Mariposa Coulterville	60	689
LERMEN			
Donald M	Napa Yount	61	55
LERMETTE			
M*	San Francisco San Francisco 3	67	20
LERMOND			
George	Placer Iona Hills	62	871
John*	Placer Iona Hills	62	880
LERMSKY			
Louis*	Amador Twp 1	55	453
LERN			
Ah	Tuolumne Twp 4	71	167
LERNANDEZ			
R	San Joaquin Stockton	641	096
LERNAR			
Raugh	Santa Cruz Santa Cruz	66	626
LERNBINE			
E*	San Francisco San Francisco 4	681	134
LERNER			
Anthony	San Francisco San Francisco 7	681	358
John	Yuba Marysville	72	882
LERNGNE			
Wm*	Mariposa Twp 3	60	600
LERNGUE			
Wm	Mariposa Twp 3	60	600
LERNLLING			
Alfred*	Alameda Brooklyn	55	92
Henry*	Alameda Brooklyn	55	92
LERNONT			
Harriet*	San Francisco San Francisco 8	681	249
LERNPACH			
Fred*	San Francisco San Francisco 9	681	054
LERNQUE			
Wm	Mariposa Twp 3	60	600
LEROID			
A	Santa Clara Redwood	65	453
LEROIS			
J	Nevada Grass Valley	61	166
LEROMIRA			
Angel	Calaveras Twp 9	57	371
LERONITTE			
Victoria	San Francisco San Francisco 2	67	644
LERONS			
Pierre	Yuba Slate Ro	72	688
LEROT			
Josephine	San Francisco San Francisco 10	67	182
LEROUX			
B	San Francisco San Francisco 6	67	441
C	San Francisco San Francisco 2	67	701
P	San Francisco San Francisco 6	67	441
Pierre	San Francisco San Francisco 11	67	134
LEROY			
A	El Dorado Placerville	58	828
Albert	Plumas Meadow Valley	62	931
Anne	San Francisco San Francisco 10	67	170
Chas	San Francisco San Francisco 2	67	755
E*	San Francisco San Francisco 2	67	695
Henry	Santa Clara Redwood	65	454
Henry	Yuba Marysville	72	902
Joseph	San Francisco San Francisco 9	68	975
Louis	Sacramento Ward 1	63	15
Saml	Sacramento Ward 1	63	16
T R	San Francisco San Francisco 6	67	454
LERR			
J	San Joaquin Stockton	641	090
Milon*	Calaveras Twp 9	57	371
LERRANO			
Jose Anto	San Diego San Diego	64	762
LERRE			
Emma	San Francisco San Francisco 6	67	473

Name	County Locale	M653 Roll	Page
LERREL			
John*	Yuba Rose Bar	72	808
LERRELL			
David*	San Francisco San Francisco 2	67	683
LERRICH			
M	Calaveras Twp 9	57	413
LERRIMAN			
---	San Francisco San Francisco 7	681	413
LERRY			
---	Amador Twp 5	55	366
A Z	Siskiyou Scott Va	69	51
Milan	Calaveras Twp 9	57	371
LERSAS			
Susanah*	Mariposa Twp 3	60	566
LERSCOMB			
Benjamine	Tuolumne Chinese	71	497
Chas	San Francisco San Francisco 3	67	86
LERSY			
Milan*	Calaveras Twp 9	57	371
LERT			
Jno	Sacramento Ward 1	63	85
LERTE			
Christian	San Francisco San Francisco 7	681	384
LERTORA			
G L	Mariposa Twp 1	60	671
LERTRAI			
Peter*	Calaveras Twp 6	57	167
LERTRAN			
H L	Sonoma Sonoma	69	657
LERTRO			
Antonio*	San Francisco San Francisco 11	67	124
LERUER			
John*	Yuba Marysville	72	882
LERUISKY			
Louis*	Amador Twp 1	55	453
LERUNAN			
August*	Sacramento Ward 1	63	34
LERUSKY			
Jouis	Amador Twp 1	55	453
LERUTH			
Michael*	Alameda Oakland	55	72
LERVA			
Rafail	San Bernardino Santa Barbara	64	171
LERVELLING			
Alfred	Alameda Brooklyn	55	92
Henry*	Alameda Brooklyn	55	92
LERVEY			
---	El Dorado Kelsey	581	136
LERY			
---	Amador Twp 2	55	310
---	Amador Twp 2	55	311
---	Amador Twp 2	55	312
---	Amador Twp 2	55	326
---*	Amador Twp 2 San Francisco 9	68	949
Elizabeth*	San Francisco		
Gen*	Amador Twp 2	55	302
Jas	Sacramento Ward 1	63	79
John*	San Francisco San Francisco 9	68	948
Louis*	San Francisco San Francisco 9	68	951
Milan	Calaveras Twp 9	57	371
LERZ			
Isac	Calaveras Twp 9	57	388
Sam	Calaveras Twp 9	57	388
LERZI			
Sam	Calaveras Twp 9	57	388
LERZYNSKY			
M	San Francisco San Francisco 10	67	214
LESA			
Eugene	Alameda Oakland	55	25
LESALDES			
Maria F	San Bernardino San Bernadino	64	683
LESALDO			
Pedro	Monterey San Juan	60	999
Petro	Monterey San Juan	60	999
LESARA			
Ohanio	Los Angeles Elmonte	59	258
LESAS			
Phillip	San Francisco San Francisco 2	67	689
LESATORE			
Pablo	Tulara Twp 1	71	99
LESBRAS			
Leon	Butte Oregon	56	619
LESCO			
Alice	San Francisco San Francisco 2	67	744
LESEBER			
Pierse*	El Dorado Big Bar	58	737
LESGISIVISLEG			
Fredk*	San Francisco San Francisco 3	67	66
LESGYINSKY			
A	San Francisco San Francisco 7	681	370
LESHANS			
John	Sonoma Bodega	69	538
LESHE			
David	Mendocino Big Rvr	60	840

Name	County Locale	M653 Roll	Page
LESHER			
F	Siskiyou Scott Ri	69	78
J	Siskiyou Scott Ri	69	78
Tho	Siskiyou Scott Va	69	51
LESHIE			
James*	Santa Cruz Santa Cruz	66	609
LESINET			
Nicholas	San Francisco San Francisco 8	681	305
LESING			
Bonevoco	Mariposa Twp 3	60	570
Romoe*	Mariposa Twp 3	60	570
Ronevoco*	Mariposa Twp 3	60	570
LESK			
August	Mendocino Arrana	60	859
LESKER			
Tho	Siskiyou Scott Va	69	51
LESLIA			
James*	Santa Cruz Santa Cruz	66	609
LESLIE			
A	El Dorado Placerville	58	893
Albert	Sacramento Natonia	63	275
Alonzo	Calaveras Twp 7	57	3
Bram	Siskiyou Scott Va	69	38
David	Mendocino Big Rvr	60	840
George	San Bernardino Santa Barbara	64	190
George	Tuolumne Sonora	71	187
Hector	Butte Chico	56	546
Hiram	Siskiyou Scott Va	69	38
J	El Dorado Placerville	58	893
J	Nevada Nevada	61	240
James	El Dorado Placerville	58	916
John	Amador Twp 7	55	411
Lyman	Tuolumne Shawsfla	71	398
Nelson	Placer Rattle Snake	62	632
Norman	Sacramento Ward 3	63	449
Robt	Placer Rattle Snake	62	632
Robt	San Francisco San Francisco 10	67	315
W	Calaveras Twp 9	57	418
William	El Dorado Kelsey	581	127
LESLIEG			
George*	Placer Auburn	62	568
LESLING			
George*	Placer Auburn	62	568
LESNER			
Olivia	Yuba Marysville	72	902
LESNEY			
Richd	San Francisco San Francisco 9	681	077
LESOG			
Henry	Yuba Marysville	72	902
LESONG			
Ronenoco*	Mariposa Twp 3	60	570
LESPICA			
Mateo	Stanislaus Branch	70	701
LESPIE			
Frank	Butte Wyandotte	56	664
LESPIR			
Frank	Butte Wyandotte	56	664
LESSAY			
Armand*	Calaveras Twp 6	57	173
LESSCHANDKY			
A*	Shasta Shasta	66	655
LESSCHANSKY			
A	Shasta Shasta	66	655
LESSER			
Antonio*	Mariposa Twp 3	60	604
LESSNER			
J A	Sacramento Ward 1	63	62
S A	Sacramento Ward 1	63	62
Yetler	San Francisco San Francisco 5	67	519
LESSO			
John	Siskiyou Klamath	69	97
LESSUY			
Armand*	Calaveras Twp 6	57	173
LESTER			
Albert	Sacramento Natonia	63	275
Andrew	San Joaquin Stockton	641	035
Bob	Marin Novato	60	737
C	San Francisco San Francisco 5	67	551
Eli	Sierra La Porte	66	786
Eli	Sonoma Cloverdale	69	685
Eli	Yuba Long Bar	72	741
Eli L	Sierra La Porte	66	766
Eli S	Sierra La Porte	66	766
Eli S	Sierra La Porte	66	786
Frank	Sierra La Porte	66	769
Geo	Sacramento Ward 4	63	517
Geo	San Francisco San Francisco 9	681	079
George W	Siskiyou Yreka	69	123
Henry	San Francisco San Francisco 5	67	494
Henry	San Joaquin Stockton	641	038
J B	Siskiyou Scott Va	69	52
Jesse	Sierra La Porte	66	769
Johathan	Sonoma Santa Rosa	69	421
John	Butte Ophir	56	759
John	San Francisco San Francisco 6	67	462

Name	County Locale	M653 Roll	Page
LESTER			
Lawrance	Alameda Murray	55	224
Oliver	Sacramento Ward 4	63	611
Sarah	Alameda Murray	55	225
Theo	Sacramento Ward 1	63	87
Thos	Sacramento Ward 1	63	87
Thos J	Placer Virginia	62	668
William	San Francisco San Francisco 9	681	100
Wm	Amador Twp 1	55	482
Wm	San Francisco San Francisco 10	194 67	
LESTOR			
Eli	Yuba New York	72	741
LESTR			
George W	Siskiyou Yreka	69	123
LESTRAN			
H L	Sonoma Sonoma	69	657
LESTRANGE			
John	Alameda Oakland	55	56
Margaret	San Francisco San Francisco 8	681	251
Margerat	San Francisco San Francisco 8	681	251
LESTRE			
Johnathan	Sonoma Santa Rosa	69	421
LESUER			
Olivar	Yuba Marysville	72	902
LESURE			
L	Nevada Washington	61	337
LESWELL			
A R	Sierra Downieville	661	018
LESWOOD			
Owen	Calaveras Twp 9	57	384
LESZEYNSKY			
Samuel	San Francisco San Francisco 7	681	356
LESZYNSKY			
Lerrer	San Francisco San Francisco 7	681	360
LET ARRIT			
---*	Mariposa Twp 3	60	614
LET			
---	Butte Kimshaw	56	603
---	El Dorado White Oaks	581	021
---	El Dorado Salmon Falls	581	045
---	El Dorado Salmon Falls	581	046
---	El Dorado Coloma	581	120
---	El Dorado Georgetown	58	693
---	El Dorado Greenwood	58	729
---	El Dorado Diamond	58	785
---	Napa Napa	61	89
---	Placer Folsom	62	647
---	Sacramento Ward 1	63	61
---	San Francisco San Francisco 9	681	096
---	Sierra St Louis	66	805
---	Yuba Bear Rvr	721	000
A L	Sierra Twp 7	66	876
Ah	Yuba Bear Rvr	721	000
Kou*	Mariposa Twp 3	60	579
To	San Francisco San Francisco 4	681	193
LETALIA			
Jose	Tuolumne Montezuma	71	508
LETANDS			
C M	Mariposa Twp 1	60	670
LETBERRY			
H*	Mariposa Twp 3	60	610
LETCHER			
Charles	San Francisco San Francisco 8	681	276
Foretine F	San Luis Obispo	65	2
	San Luis Obispo		
Jas W	Sacramento Ward 4	63	510
LETEHFIELD			
W D*	San Francisco San Francisco 3	67	80
LETENNANA			
John*	Yuba Marysville	72	902
LETENNANU			
John*	Yuba Marysville	72	902
LETENS			
C	San Francisco San Francisco 5	67	535
LETER			
Antoine	Calaveras Twp 5	57	224
LETERER			
L	Amador Twp 1	55	494
LETERRIEN			
L	Sacramento Sutter	63	297
LETERRIERE			
Pierre	San Francisco San Francisco 11	115 67	
LETFORD			
John	Fresno Twp 3	59	7
LETH			
---	Plumas Quincy	62	949
James*	Alameda Brooklyn	55	100
Wm	Tehama Pasakent	70	859
LETHGAN			
John	San Mateo Twp 1	65	58
W H	San Mateo Twp 1	65	58
LETHOROW			
Fernand*	San Mateo Twp 2	65	112
LETILIA			
Jose	Tuolumne Twp 5	71	508
LETING			
---	Nevada Bridgeport	61	460
LETLELLUR			
A*	Tuolumne Columbia	71	328
LETLILLUR			
A	Tuolumne Twp 2	71	328
LETOURNAN			
Jno M	San Francisco San Francisco 9	68	961
LETOURUAN			
Jno M*	San Francisco San Francisco 9	68	961
LETRENOWX			
Desire	Sierra La Porte	66	768
LETRINONT			
Desire	Sierra La Porte	66	768
LETRUMS			
Francis	Calaveras Twp 5	57	137
LETSON			
Thos	Sacramento Ward 1	63	98
LETT			
---	Del Norte Happy Ca	58	669
---	Yolo Slate Ra	72	710
---	Yuba Slate Ro	72	710
Thomas	Marin Novato	60	739
LETTELL			
Gilbert	Sacramento Natonia	63	277
LETTER			
Jacob*	Los Angeles Los Angeles	59	321
John	San Joaquin Elkhorn	64	990
LETTERETT			
A	El Dorado Diamond	58	814
LETTIBOND			
C*	Stanislaus Branch	70	711
LETTILLUR			
A*	Tuolumne Columbia	71	328
LETTIMER			
Henry	El Dorado Big Bar	58	738
William	Contra Costa Twp 3	57	607
LETTINGTON			
M	Yolo Putah	72	550
LETTON			
Thomas	San Francisco San Francisco 4	681	120
LETTS			
M E	Yolo Slate Ra	72	689
M E	Yuba Slate Ro	72	689
LETTUER			
Harer	Sierra Twp 5	66	943
LETTWRIGHN			
M*	Yolo Putah	72	550
LEU			
---	Calaveras Twp 10	57	283
---	El Dorado Placerville	58	842
---	Mariposa Twp 3	60	545
---	Placer Ophirville	62	654
---	Placer Virginia	62	684
---	Yuba North Ea	72	681
A	Sacramento Natonia	63	283
How	Butte Ophir	56	788
John	Yuba North Ea	72	676
Low	Calaveras Twp 5	57	194
LEUASS			
Natividad	Mariposa Twp 3	60	586
Natividad G*	Mariposa Twp 3	60	586
LEUCH			
James*	San Francisco San Francisco 9	681	032
LEUCK			
K*	Amador Twp 4	55	239
LEUDENBOUN			
Isaac*	San Francisco San Francisco 9	681	051
LEUER			
Marga	Amador Twp 1	55	491
LEUGO			
John*	Sierra Twp 7	66	874
LEUHARD			
Ed*	San Francisco San Francisco 9	681	084
LEUIS			
David	Nevada Bridgeport	61	470
John	Nevada Bridgeport	61	453
John	Yuba Fosters	72	837
Joseph*	Nevada Rough &	61	424
Nicholas	San Francisco San Francisco 2	67	773
LEUIUS			
S	Sacramento Granite	63	242
LEUIVINE			
L D*	Sierra Twp 7	66	868
LEUKOR			
Chas A*	Calaveras Twp 6	57	119
LEUKSEN			
Chas A*	Calaveras Twp 6	57	119
LEUL			
---	Mariposa Twp 3	60	544
LEUMAN			
William*	San Francisco San Francisco 9	681	042
LEUMANS			
Wm	Amador Twp 3	55	409
LEUMNEY			
Mary Cath*	San Francisco 2	67	661
	San Francisco		
LEUMONS			
Wm*	Amador Twp 3	55	409
LEUN			
---	El Dorado Placerville	58	923
---	Mariposa Twp 1	60	665
Hey	Mariposa Coulterville	60	682
LEUNAN			
Michael*	Calaveras Twp 6	57	175
LEUNDO			
Joseph	Calaveras Twp 5	57	203
LEUNEN			
Margt*	San Francisco San Francisco 9	68	983
LEUNG			
---	El Dorado Diamond	58	784
---	Placer Rattle Snake	62	636
---	Plumas Quincy	62	949
---	Shasta Horsetown	66	701
---	Trinity Mouth Ca	701	018
---	Trinity Taylor'S	701	035
---	Trinity Trinindad Rvr	701	048
---	Trinity Trinindad Rvr	701	050
Ah	Tuolumne Twp 4	71	182
Gang	Mariposa Twp 3	60	544
LEUNN			
---	Calaveras Twp 10	57	284
LEUNPACH			
Fred*	San Francisco San Francisco 9	681	054
LEUNY			
---	Calaveras Twp 5	57	145
---	Calaveras Twp 10	57	273
LEUORMANT			
M*	Nevada Eureka	61	391
LEUP			
---	Amador Twp 5	55	333
---	Placer Illinois	62	754
LEUR			
---	Shasta Horsetown	66	706
Min	El Dorado Big Bar	58	733
Richard*	El Dorado Eldorado	58	942
See	El Dorado Georgetown	58	686
LEURAM			
Mary*	San Francisco San Francisco 9	681	037
LEURGEL			
H	San Francisco San Francisco 3	67	68
LEURIK			
Andrew	El Dorado Kelsey	581	130
LEURON			
J	Shasta Shasta	66	668
LEURONE			
Jose	San Joaquin Castoria	64	900
LEURONER			
L*	El Dorado Diamond	58	802
LEURS			
Theodore	Calaveras Twp 5	57	207
LEUS			
Wong	Sacramento Granite	63	259
LEUSK			
John*	San Francisco San Francisco 3	67	33
LEUSTON			
William*	Solano Benecia	69	317
LEUT			
---	Calaveras Twp 4	57	320
John*	Tuolumne Twp 2	71	290
LEUTAN			
Juan*	Alameda Brooklyn	55	155
LEUTE			
Juan	Yuba New York	72	729
LEUTHBY			
N*	Yolo Putah	72	551
LEUTRIZEN			
Andreas P*	Alameda Brooklyn	55	145
LEUTZ			
Catharine*	San Francisco 7	681	411
	San Francisco		
Louis H*	San Francisco San Francisco 7	681	411
S V	Yuba Parks Ba	72	777
LEUY			
---	Stanislaus Branch	70	713
Fong*	San Francisco San Francisco 5	67	508
LEV			
Sue	Shasta Horsetown	66	701
LEVADO			
Thomas*	Alameda Murray	55	221
LEVAIA			
Antonio	Alameda Brooklyn	55	118
LEVAL			
George	Stanislaus Branch	70	698
LEVALL			
Alexander	Santa Cruz Pajaro	66	554
LEVALLEN			
Apgh	Yuba Marysville	72	846
LEVALLEY			
Henry	Sonoma Cloverdale	69	686

California 1860 Census Index

Name	County Locale	M653 Roll	Page
LEVAN			
D W	El Dorado Placerville	58	821
LEVAND			
Charles	Santa Cruz Pajaro	66	564
LEVANS*			
Charles*	Santa Cruz Pajaro	66	564
Henry	El Dorado Georgetown	58	691
LEVANT			
Samuel	Santa Cruz Santa Cruz	66	631
LEVANTARE			
Henry	Sonoma Bodega	69	523
LEVANTD			
Samuel*	Santa Cruz Santa Cruz	66	631
LEVANTO			
Samuel*	Santa Cruz Santa Cruz	66	631
LEVAR			
Manuela	San Francisco San Francisco 2	67	768
LEVARA			
S	Amador Twp 1	55	466
LEVARES			
Calistro	Los Angeles San Juan	59	471
LEVARIA			
Arrinto	Amador Twp 1	55	487
LEVARINO			
Nicolas	Mariposa Twp 3	60	614
LEVARO			
Antonio*	San Francisco San Francisco 3	67	83
Moris	Calaveras Twp 6	57	129
LEVEGNE			
Louis	Siskiyou Yreka	69	177
LEVEILLE			
A	Sacramento Granite	63	229
Francis	San Francisco San Francisco 12	67	384
LEVELL			
M	San Francisco San Francisco 6	67	464
S	Napa Hot Springs	61	4
LEVELLIN			
L S	El Dorado White Oaks	58	1027
LEVELT			
Jos H*	Sacramento Ward 1	63	87
LEVEN			
Qu	San Francisco San Francisco 4	68	1175
LEVENBERG			
E	San Francisco San Francisco 5	67	532
LEVENGE			
Joseph*	Calaveras Twp 6	57	172
LEVENIA			
Louiser	Mariposa Twp 1	60	635
LEVENS			
Sylvider	Sierra Twp 7	66	901
LEVENSHEN			
M	Tehama Red Bluff	70	916
LEVENSON			
Louis	San Francisco San Francisco 2	67	801
LEVENSTEIN			
Charlotte	San Francisco San Francisco 10	67	276
LEVENTHRALL			
Wolfe	Sonoma Healdsbu	69	472
LEVEQUE			
A N	San Francisco San Francisco 2	67	696
Adolph	San Francisco San Francisco 10	67	341
Louis	Siskiyou Yreka	69	177
LEVER			
Fredk	San Francisco San Francisco 9	68	1041
Hesmer	Calaveras Twp 5	57	252
LEVERE			
W D*	Sacramento Franklin	63	328
LEVERETT			
Edward J	San Francisco San Francisco 4	68	1213
LEVERICH			
S	Amador Twp 3	55	386
LEVERLEY			
Benj	Tuolumne Twp 1	71	261
LEVERMON			
Albert*	San Francisco San Francisco 4	68	1132
LEVERMORE			
Albert	San Francisco San Francisco 4	68	1132
Daniel*	Alameda Murray	55	217
Hosefa*	Alameda Murray	55	220
Joseph*	Alameda Murray	55	221
LEVERONES			
Estaven	Contra Costa Twp 1	57	493
LEVERONI			
Angelo	Tuolumne Big Oak	71	141
LEVERS			
Jos	Mariposa Twp 3	60	555
LEVERTLIS			
Layarus*	Calaveras Twp 7	57	6
LEVERTON			
John J*	Del Norte Crescent	58	647
Mary*	Del Norte Crescent	58	649
LEVERTY			
John	Sonoma Sonoma	69	633

Name	County Locale	M653 Roll	Page
LEVERY			
Moses	San Joaquin Stockton	64	1020
LEVET			
John B	San Francisco San Francisco 8	68	1320
LEVETT			
Abel H	Solano Benecia	69	314
J B	San Francisco San Francisco 3	67	83
LEVETTE			
J	Butte Oregon	56	641
LEVEXTON			
John J*	Del Norte Crescent	58	647
LEVEY			
Alexander*	San Francisco San Francisco 7	68	1436
	San Francisco		
Charles	San Francisco San Francisco 7	68	1435
Emiel	San Francisco San Francisco 7	68	1355
Gillman	Sierra St Louis	66	807
H L	San Francisco San Francisco 5	67	517
S*	Nevada Grass Valley	61	201
LEVG			
James	San Francisco San Francisco 2	67	714
LEVI			
A	San Francisco San Francisco 5	67	518
A	San Joaquin Stockton	64	1027
A	Trinity Rush Crk	70	965
A	Tuolumne Jamestown	71	426
A N	San Francisco San Francisco 4	68	1166
Albert	San Francisco San Francisco 2	67	660
Benjn	San Francisco San Francisco 9	68	1065
Bernard	San Francisco San Francisco 2	67	655
E	Marin Bolinas	60	727
E	San Francisco San Francisco 2	67	682
Elizabeth	San Francisco San Francisco 9	68	949
Francis	San Francisco San Francisco 2	67	695
H	Nevada Nevada	61	259
H	Nevada Nevada	61	260
H	San Francisco San Francisco 5	67	535
H*	Nevada Bridgeport	61	499
Henry	Calaveras Twp 6	57	174
Henry	San Francisco San Francisco 9	68	979
Hulda	San Francisco San Francisco 8	68	1289
Isaac	San Bernardino San Bernardino	64	624
J C	Nevada Eureka	61	369
Jacob	Trinity Weaverville	70	1070
Jacob	Tuolumne Twp 3	71	427
Jacob	Yuba Marysville	72	902
Joel	Tuolumne Columbia	71	328
John	San Francisco San Francisco 9	68	1070
John	San Francisco San Francisco 2	67	801
M	Nevada Nevada	61	259
M	San Francisco San Francisco 4	68	1153
M	San Francisco San Francisco 1	68	911
M B	San Francisco San Francisco 5	67	535
Margt	San Francisco San Francisco 9	68	966
Marquis	Yuba Marysville	72	899
Mary	San Francisco San Francisco 5	67	504
Nathan	Tuolumne Twp 3	71	427
P	San Francisco San Francisco 3	67	73
P L	San Francisco San Francisco 4	68	1163
Richard	Nevada Bridgeport	61	469
S	San Francisco San Francisco 4	68	1161
S W	Tehama Red Bluff	70	899
Saleigaman	Nevada Bloomfield	61	520
Samuel	San Francisco San Francisco 2	67	634
LEVIA			
John	Amador Twp 4	55	249
LEVICE			
A	San Francisco San Francisco 5	67	529
LEVIE			
Leonidas	San Francisco San Francisco 1	68	874
LEVIEP			
Gordon	Butte Bidwell	56	705
LEVIER			
Abner D	Humbolt Eureka	59	166
J	Calaveras Twp 9	57	391
LEVIGUNE			
Francois*	San Francisco San Francisco 2	67	795
LEVILL			
H L	Tuolumne Sonora	71	188
M	San Francisco San Francisco 6	67	464
LEVILLEIN			
Jules	Yuba Marysville	72	958
LEVIN			
Alenzo	Sacramento Natonia	63	278
Alonzo	Sacramento Natonia	63	278
Danl F	San Francisco San Francisco 2	67	708
James	Calaveras Twp 5	57	207
Joseph	Calaveras Twp 6	57	111
LEVINE			
A	San Francisco San Francisco 5	67	529
Jno	Sacramento Ward 4	63	527
LEVINGER			
Simon	San Francisco San Francisco 2	67	656
LEVINGS			
Wash	Butte Kimshaw	56	601
Washn	Butte Kimshaw	56	601

Name	County Locale	M653 Roll	Page
LEVINGSTON			
Chaning	San Francisco San Francisco 1	68	918
LEVINGTON			
J M	Amador Twp 6	55	425
LEVINS			
A K*	Placer Iona Hills	62	881
James	Calaveras Twp 5	57	207
LEVINSER			
H	San Francisco San Francisco 2	67	649
LEVINSKY			
H	San Francisco San Francisco 9	68	1063
Louis*	Amador Twp 1	55	453
Mark	Amador Twp 1	55	453
LEVINSON			
A	Solano Vallejo	69	252
Fredk	San Francisco San Francisco 9	68	967
Joseph	San Francisco San Francisco 2	67	652
Joseph	Tehama Tehama	70	947
Louis	San Francisco San Francisco 2	67	801
Sevin	Calaveras Twp 5	57	240
LEVINTHALE			
A*	San Francisco San Francisco 4	68	1162
LEVINTHALL			
A*	San Francisco San Francisco 4	68	1162
LEVIRE			
Morssy*	Alameda Oakland	55	61
LEVIS			
John	Calaveras Twp 5	57	140
Mitchell M*	San Francisco San Francisco 7	68	1407
	San Francisco		
Nicholas	San Francisco San Francisco 2	67	773
LEVISANA			
William W	Calaveras Twp 6	57	157
LEVISON			
Bamt*	Nevada Bridgeport	61	473
Bannt*	Nevada Bridgeport	61	473
Brant*	Nevada Bridgeport	61	473
J A	San Francisco San Francisco 2	67	644
Marcus	Marin Cortemad	60	792
T A	Yolo Washington	72	568
William	Calaveras Twp 5	57	188
LEVISTON			
George	Solano Benecia	69	283
LEVIT			
Daniel	Placer Mealsburg	62	702
G	Santa Clara Santa Clara	65	491
Moses	San Mateo Twp 3	65	103
LEVITGKY			
Davis	San Francisco San Francisco 10	67	205
LEVITH			
J	Butte Oregon	56	641
LEVITT			
H L	Tuolumne Twp 1	71	188
J	San Mateo Twp 3	65	103
Joseph	Tuolumne Columbia	71	308
Walter	Yuba New York	72	723
LEVITZKY			
Herman	San Francisco San Francisco 10	67	165
LEVONS			
Pierre	Tuolumne Twp 2	71	341
Purre	Tuolumne Columbia	71	341
LEVOY			
E*	San Francisco San Francisco 2	67	695
T R	San Francisco San Francisco 6	67	454
LEVOYN			
Charles	Yuba Marysville	72	934
LEVRITT			
G	Tuolumne Twp 3	71	452
LEVY			
---	Amador Twp 2	55	302
---	San Francisco San Francisco 4	68	1173
---	San Francisco San Francisco 4	68	1177
---*	Amador Twp 2	55	302
A	San Joaquin Stockton	64	1090
A	Shasta French G	66	716
A	Sierra Downieville	66	968
Aaron	San Francisco San Francisco 7	68	1425
Abraham	San Francisco San Francisco 7	68	1414
Adolph	Sacramento Ward 1	63	38
Adolphus	San Francisco San Francisco 3	67	29
Alexander	San Francisco San Francisco 3	67	38
Alexander*	San Francisco San Francisco 7	68	1436
	San Francisco		
B	El Dorado Diamond	58	768
B	Siskiyou Yreka	69	180
Barbet	Alameda Brooklyn	55	79
Benjamin	San Francisco San Francisco 8	68	1292
Benjamin	San Francisco San Francisco 9	68	938
Bonhant*	Placer Auburn	62	570
Bonhaut*	Placer Auburn	62	570
Bonnan	San Francisco San Francisco 7	68	1368
Catharine	San Francisco San Francisco 10	67	223
Charles	San Francisco San Francisco 7	68	1355

California 1860 Census Index

Name	County Locale	M653 Roll	Page
LEVY			
Chas	San Francisco San Francisco	9 68	973
Danl	San Francisco San Francisco	2 67	618
David	Sacramento Granite	63	227
David	San Francisco San Francisco	10	217 67
David	Siskiyou Yreka	69	173
Davis	Siskiyou Yreka	69	173
E	San Francisco San Francisco	5 67	499
Edward	San Francisco San Francisco	7 68	1393
Edward	San Francisco San Francisco	7 68	1396
Edward*	Napa Hot Springs	61	4
Elias	San Francisco San Francisco	7 68	1428
Elvans	Amador Twp 1	55	452
Flora	San Francisco San Francisco	9 68	937
Fo	San Francisco San Francisco	4 68	1175
Frances	San Francisco San Francisco	7 68	1367
G N*	Sacramento Ward 4	63	522
Geu*	Amador Twp 2	55	302
H	El Dorado Diamond	58	763
H	El Dorado Newtown	58	781
H	Shasta Shasta	66	658
Harison	Tuolumne Twp 2	71	331
Isaac	El Dorado Eldorado	58	935
Isaac	San Francisco San Francisco	2 67	618
J	El Dorado Coloma	58	1068
J	El Dorado Placerville	58	860
Jacob*	Yuba Marysville	72	873
James	Mariposa Twp 1	60	638
James	San Francisco San Francisco	2 67	714
Jas	Sacramento Ward 1	63	79
John	San Francisco San Francisco	10	222 67
John	San Francisco San Francisco	9 68	948
John	Tuolumne Big Oak	71	182
John*	San Francisco San Francisco	9 68	948
Jona	San Francisco San Francisco	2 67	622
Jonas	San Francisco San Francisco	2 67	622
Joseph	Nevada Bridgeport	61	474
Julia	San Francisco San Francisco	9 68	937
Julius	San Francisco San Francisco	8 68	1287
Julius	Tulara Twp 1	71	111
Justof	Nevada Bridgeport	61	474
Kaufman	Sacramento Ward 3	63	421
Ken	San Francisco San Francisco	4 68	1199
L	El Dorado Newtown	58	781
L	El Dorado Placerville	58	850
L	Sacramento Ward 1	63	47
L	San Francisco San Francisco	6 67	464
L	Santa Clara San Jose	65	281
Leon	San Bernardino Santa Barbara	64	155
Leuis*	San Francisco San Francisco	5 67	519
Lewis	San Bernardino San Bernadino	64	627
Lewis	San Francisco San Francisco	1 68	929
Lizzette	San Francisco San Francisco	4 68	1221
Lizzitte	San Francisco San Francisco	4 68	1221
Louis	Los Angeles Los Angeles	59	320
Louis	Sacramento Ward 3	63	426
Louis*	San Francisco San Francisco	9 68	951
M	El Dorado Indian D	58	1158
M	Sonoma Cloverdale	69	682
Mary	San Francisco San Francisco	4 68	1160
Mayer	Santa Clara San Jose	65	289
Michael	Sacramento Ward 1	63	25
Michael	Sacramento Ward 4	63	510
Michael	San Francisco San Francisco	4 68	1157
Morris	Los Angeles Los Angeles	59	359
Morris	Sacramento Ward 1	63	117
Morris	Sacramento Granite	63	224
Moses	Tulara Twp 1	71	102
Myer	San Francisco San Francisco	2 67	771
N*	El Dorado Diamond	58	765
Papey	San Francisco San Francisco	1 68	843
Po	San Francisco San Francisco	4 68	1175
R	Sacramento Ward 1	63	31
Richard	San Francisco San Francisco	2 67	693
Richard	Shasta Millvill	66	752
S	El Dorado Placerville	58	853
S	Sacramento Ward 1	63	47
S	Santa Clara San Jose	65	322
S A	Sacramento Ward 1	63	19
Saml	Sacramento Ward 1	63	16
Saml	San Francisco San Francisco	5 67	476
Saml W	Alameda Brooklyn	55	79
Saml*	Nevada Nevada	61	275
Samuel	Alameda Brooklyn	55	122
Samuel	Los Angeles Los Angeles	59	320
Samuel	San Francisco San Francisco	9 68	937
Sarah	San Francisco San Francisco	4 68	1220
Saul	Nevada Nevada	61	275
Simon	San Francisco San Francisco	8 68	1291
Simon	San Francisco San Francisco	2 67	797
Solomon	San Francisco San Francisco	3 67	40
T	El Dorado Placerville	58	859
Teller*	Contra Costa Twp 3	57	612
Theresa	Yuba Marysville	72	894
LEVY			
Thos	San Francisco San Francisco	1 68	931
Thos S	Placer Virginia	62	685
William	Placer Michigan	62	834
LEW			
---	Amador Twp 6	55	446
---	Calaveras Twp 5	57	247
---	Del Norte Crescent	58	631
---	Del Norte Crescent	58	641
---	Del Norte Crescent	58	660
---	El Dorado White Oaks	58	1025
---	El Dorado Salmon Falls	58	1048
---	El Dorado Salmon Falls	58	1055
---	El Dorado Union	58	1090
---	El Dorado Coloma	58	1122
---	El Dorado Diamond	58	784
---	El Dorado Diamond	58	816
---	El Dorado Placerville	58	899
---	El Dorado Placerville	58	904
---	El Dorado Placerville	58	932
---	El Dorado Eldorado	58	939
---	Napa Napa	61	98
---	Nevada Bridgeport	61	464
---	Placer Christia	62	736
---	San Francisco San Francisco	4 68	1211
---	Sierra Downieville	66	1008
---	Sierra Downieville	66	1009
---	Sierra Downieville	66	1015
---	Sierra Morristown	66	1055
---	Sierra Twp 5	66	927
---	Sierra Twp 5	66	942
---	Sierra Twp 5	66	945
---	Sierra Cox'S Bar	66	949
---	Sierra Downieville	66	973
---	Sierra Downieville	66	980
---	Sierra Downieville	66	981
---	Sierra Downieville	66	983
---	Tehama Red Bluff	70	934
---	Tuolumne Twp 5	71	525
---	Tuolumne Twp 6	71	531
---	Yolo No E Twp	72	677
---	Yuba North Ea	72	677
---	Yuba Slate Ro	72	706
---	Yuba Long Bar	72	759
---*	Calaveras Twp 5	57	247
---*	El Dorado Casumnes	58	1160
---*	Mariposa Twp 3	60	582
---*	Sierra Twp 5	66	933
---*	Sierra Twp 5	66	942
---*	Tuolumne Don Pedro	71	540
Ar	Sierra Downieville	66	984
Chey	Calaveras Twp 4	57	299
George	Sierra Downieville	66	955
Ger*	El Dorado Georgetown	58	684
John	Sierra Port Win	66	798
Kong	El Dorado Mud Springs	58	952
Kong	Yuba Long Bar	72	759
Moses*	Sierra Twp 7	66	905
So	Sierra Downieville	66	1005
Tow	Calaveras Twp 5	57	247
Tow	Sierra Downieville	66	1005
Yah	Plumas Meadow Valley	62	914
You	Sacramento Granite	63	269
LEWA			
---	El Dorado Coloma	58	1108
---	El Dorado Coloma	58	1109
LEWAH			
Lon	San Francisco San Francisco	10	356 67
LEWALD			
George	Tulara Visalia	71	103
LEWART			
Chas	Butte Bidwell	56	723
LEWARTSON			
R R*	El Dorado Placerville	58	862
LEWDEN			
T S	Butte Hamilton	56	527
T T	Butte Hamilton	56	527
LEWE			
---	Shasta Horsetown	66	703
LEWEL			
Chuton P	San Francisco San Francisco	2 67	643
John	Marin Cortemad	60	752
LEWELL			
Andrew J	Sierra St Louis	66	807
Charles	Santa Cruz Pescadero	66	649
David*	San Francisco San Francisco	2 67	643
Geo G	Placer Virginia	62	689
Moses	Sacramento Granite	63	254
Thomas	El Dorado Salmon Hills	58	1059
LEWELLEN			
D	Butte Chico	56	565
LEWELLIN			
J B	El Dorado Salmon Falls	58	1034
John B*	San Francisco San Francisco	1 68	904
LEWELLING			
John P	San Luis Obispo San Luis Obispo	65	34
LEWELLING			
John*	Alameda Brooklyn	55	133
Seth	Calaveras Twp 9	57	400
LEWELLYN			
Robert	San Francisco San Francisco	2 67	597
LEWEN			
---	Napa Napa	61	89
LEWERELL			
John	San Francisco San Francisco	1 68	844
LEWERO			
David	Solano Vallejo	69	274
LEWERS			
Jno	Sacramento Ward 1	63	31
LEWERTA			
---	Tulara Twp 2	71	32
LEWERY			
T A E*	Siskiyou Scott Va	69	41
LEWES			
William	Calaveras Twp 5	57	209
LEWETT			
J	Nevada Eureka	61	382
LEWEY			
---	El Dorado Kelsey	58	1136
---	Nevada Bridgeport	61	464
---	Sacramento Cosummes	63	409
James*	Sonoma Petaluma	69	604
W	Nevada Eureka	61	378
LEWIE			
Thos P*	Butte Hamilton	56	521
LEWIES			
J A*	San Francisco San Francisco	4 68	1130
LEWIG			
Wm A	Tuolumne Sonora	71	203
LEWIK			
George	Sierra Pine Grove	66	821
LEWIN			
E	Shasta Shasta	66	656
LEWING			
---	Placer Virginia	62	671
---	Trinity Weaverville	70	1075
LEWINS			
E	Sacramento Alabama	63	416
LEWIR			
Wm*	Sierra Twp 7	66	884
LEWIS C			
---	Siskiyou Callahan	69	9
LEWIS			
---	Amador Twp 2	55	300
---	Mariposa Twp 1	60	631
---	Mendocino Calpella	60	819
---	San Francisco San Francisco	7 68	1415
---	Yuba Linda Twp	72	983
A	Butte Oro	56	679
A	San Joaquin Stockton	64	1015
A	Santa Clara Gilroy	65	250
A	Sutter Butte	70	788
A G	Yolo Slate Ra	72	716
A G	Yuba Slate Ro	72	716
A K*	Placer Iona Hills	62	881
A R	Tuolumne Jamestown	71	444
A W	Nevada Nevada	61	289
A W	Sonoma Armally	69	507
Adolph	Calaveras Twp 5	57	175
Adolph*	Yuba Marysville	72	894
Agustus	Yolo Slate Ra	72	698
Almon	Nevada Bloomfield	61	517
An	Sacramento Natonia	63	284
Andrew	San Francisco San Francisco	2 67	642
Andrew J	San Joaquin Castoria	64	890
Ann	Sacramento Ward 4	63	586
Ann	Siskiyou Scott Va	69	29
Antonio	Alameda Brooklyn	55	100
Arant	Alameda Brooklyn	55	146
Augustus	San Francisco San Francisco	7 68	1436
Augustus	Yuba Slate Ro	72	698
Aurora	Marin Cortemad	60	753
Awrora	Marin Cortemad	60	753
B F	Trinity Grass Valley	70	962
Beanchamp*	Sierra Twp 5	66	936
Beauchamp*	Sierra Twp 5	66	936
Benj	Butte Oregon	56	643
Benj	Nevada Bloomfield	61	521
Benj	Plumas Quincy	62	945
Benj H	Calaveras Twp 9	57	374
Benjamin	Sierra Port Win	66	793
Benjamin F	San Francisco San Francisco	4 68	1129
Bey H*	Calaveras Twp 9	57	374
Biy H*	Calaveras Twp 9	57	374
Bnj H*	Calaveras Twp 9	57	374
Bony	Calaveras Twp 6	57	161
Bryan	Sonoma Santa Rosa	69	405
Byran	Sonoma Santa Rosa	69	405
C	Nevada Eureka	61	363
C	Sacramento Sutter	63	297
C	San Francisco San Francisco	5 67	532

California 1860 Census Index

LEWIS

Name	County Locale	M653 Roll	Page
C	Sutter Butte	70	799
C W	Sonoma Petaluma	69	599
C W	Yolo Cache	72	590
Caroline	San Francisco San Francisco 2	67	566
Catharin	Sonoma Sonoma	69	655
Cathrine	San Francisco San Francisco 1	68	834
Ceyrus	Calaveras Twp 6	57	155
Chares*	Monterey Alisal	60	1040
Charles	Monterey Alisal	60	1031
Charles	San Francisco San Francisco 11	67	120
Charles	San Joaquin Stockton	64	1042
Charles	Sonoma Armally	69	492
Charles E	Tuolumne Twp 6	71	530
Charles F	San Francisco San Francisco 6	67	401
Charls	Monterey Alisal	60	1040
Chas R	Fresno Twp 3	59	15
Christopher	Colusa Butte Crk	57	465
Colombus	Alameda Brooklyn	55	107
Columbus	Alameda Brooklyn	55	107
D	San Francisco San Francisco 7	68	1420
D B	Butte Kimshaw	56	604
D E	Merced Twp 1	60	902
D J	Sierra Eureka	66	1043
D W	Sacramento Centre	63	174
Daniel	Sacramento San Joaquin	63	351
Daniel	San Francisco San Francisco 7	68	1438
Daniel	Sierra Monte Crk	66	1036
Daniel	Sierra Gibsonville	66	857
Daniel	Sierra Downieville	66	960
Daniel G*	Tuolumne Twp 6	71	539
David	Alameda Brooklyn	55	186
David	Butte Wyandotte	56	669
David	Butte Ophir	56	795
David	Contra Costa Twp 3	57	617
David	Los Angeles Elmonte	59	263
David	Nevada Bridgeport	61	441
David	Nevada Bridgeport	61	445
David	Nevada Bridgeport	61	470
David	Placer Michigan	62	829
David	San Francisco San Francisco 3	67	57
David	San Francisco San Francisco 9	68	950
David	San Joaquin Douglass	64	922
David	Sierra Port Win	66	792
David C	Del Norte Crescent	58	660
David J	Sierra Twp 5	66	924
David L	Mariposa Coulterville	60	684
E	Calaveras Twp 9	57	403
E	San Joaquin Stockton	64	1042
E G	Tuolumne Twp 3	71	448
E J	Tehama Tehama	70	940
E Warren	San Francisco San Francisco 12	67	375
Ed	Sacramento Ward 1	63	86
Edmond	Sacramento San Joaquin	63	365
Ednicher	Sierra Whiskey	66	850
Edward	Sacramento Sutter	63	290
Edward J	Mendocino Round Va	60	877
Edward N	Calaveras Twp 6	57	155
Edward W	Calaveras Twp 6	57	155
Edwin	San Francisco San Francisco 8	68	1251
Eli	Nevada Eureka	61	357
Elizabeth	Colusa Muion	57	462
Elvira	San Joaquin Stockton	64	1024
Emanuel	San Joaquin Elkhorn	64	999
Emanuel	Trinity Rush Crk	70	965
Emily F	Alameda Oakland	55	47
Eran	Nevada Red Dog	61	556
Evan	Nevada Bridgeport	61	478
Even	Yolo Slate Ra	72	701
Even	Yuba Slate Ro	72	701
F	Santa Clara Alviso	65	401
F	Siskiyou Callahan	69	6
F A	San Francisco San Francisco 2	67	707
F B	San Francisco San Francisco 9	68	998
Fennimore*	Butte Cascade	56	693
Fermimore*	Butte Cascade	56	693
Fernimore	Butte Cascade	56	693
Ferris	Sierra Downieville	66	1023
Foulk	Siskiyou Yreka	69	192
Francis	Plumas Quincy	62	989
Francis W	Alameda Oakland	55	47
Francisco	Alameda Oakland	55	46
Frank	Alameda Brooklyn	55	150
Frank	Butte Cascade	56	697
Frank	San Joaquin Castoria	64	885
Frank	San Joaquin Castoria	64	900
Frank	Santa Clara San Jose	65	341
Frank	Santa Cruz Santa Cruz	66	612
Frank	Tehama Red Bluff	70	899
Frank M	Yuba Marysville	72	908
Fred	San Francisco San Francisco 2	67	740
Fred R	Napa Napa	61	95
G L	Calaveras Twp 8	57	66
G M	Tuolumne Columbia	71	312
Gaylard	Klamath Klamath	59	227
Geo	El Dorado White Oaks	58	1019
Geo	San Francisco San Francisco 10	67	326
Geo	Sonoma Sonoma	69	656
Geo M	Butte Hamilton	56	520
Geoge	Shasta Shasta	66	684
George	Placer Iona Hills	62	860
George	San Francisco San Francisco 2	67	692
George	San Mateo Twp 2	65	131
George	Shasta Shasta	66	684
George	Sierra Twp 7	66	893
George B	Colusa Spring Valley	57	433
George E	San Francisco San Francisco 5	67	535
George L	San Joaquin Douglass	64	917
H	Amador Twp 5	55	334
H	Amador Twp 6	55	429
H	Sacramento Ward 1	63	35
H M	San Francisco San Francisco 5	67	483
Henrietta	Colusa Muion	57	462
Henry	El Dorado Georgetown	58	704
Henry	Napa Napa	61	56
Henry	Sacramento Ward 4	63	582
Henry	San Francisco San Francisco 10	67	187
Henry	San Francisco San Francisco 2	67	565
Henry	San Joaquin Stockton	64	1025
Henry	San Joaquin Stockton	64	1041
Henry	Santa Clara Santa Clara	65	509
Henry	Tulara Visalia	71	104
Henry E	Los Angeles Los Angeles	59	294
Henry M	San Mateo Twp 2	65	119
Herman	Placer Iona Hills	62	872
Hesmer*	Calaveras Twp 5	57	252
Hiram	Sonoma Mendocino	69	453
Hiram	Sonoma Armally	69	509
Hon	San Francisco San Francisco 7	68	1389
Hugh	El Dorado Placerville	58	914
Isaac W	Tulara Visalia	71	105
Isac	Mariposa Twp 3	60	588
J	Butte Cascade	56	701
J	El Dorado Georgetown	58	683
J	El Dorado Placerville	58	875
J	Mariposa Twp 1	60	671
J	Nevada Grass Valley	61	162
J	Nevada Nevada	61	242
J	Nevada Nevada	61	294
J	Stanislaus Branch	70	706
J A	Calaveras Twp 9	57	414
J A*	San Francisco San Francisco 4	68	1130
J B	Nevada Little Y	61	535
J H	Sonoma Petaluma	69	571
J M	Placer Dutch Fl	62	722
J M	Sonoma Santa Rosa	69	416
J M	Tuolumne Twp 2	71	310
J Nich	Sacramento Ward 4	63	523
J P	Yuba Long Bar	72	753
J V	Yolo Cache	72	591
J W	Siskiyou Scott Va	69	40
Jack	Yuba Rose Bar	72	802
Jackson	Santa Clara San Jose	65	318
Jacob	Mariposa Twp 3	60	616
Jacob	Plumas Meadow Valley	62	899
Jacob	Sierra Twp 7	66	899
Jacob	Yolo Washington	72	599
James	Alameda Brooklyn	55	181
James	Calaveras Twp 8	57	70
James	Shasta Shasta	66	732
James	Siskiyou Scott Va	69	39
James	Siskiyou Scott Va	69	55
James	Tuolumne Twp 5	71	519
James	Yolo Slate Ra	72	698
James	Yolo Slate Ra	72	709
James	Yuba Slate Ro	72	698
James	Yuba Slate Ro	72	709
James	Yuba New York	72	734
James	Yuba Suida	72	982
James	Yuba Linda Twp	72	983
James C	Calaveras Twp 5	57	209
James H	Fresno Twp 2	59	17
James M	Solano Vacaville	69	339
James M	Stanislaus Empire	70	734
James W	Plumas Quincy	62	937
James*	Sonoma Petaluma	69	604
Jas	Sacramento Granite	63	255
Jas	San Francisco San Francisco 2	67	691
Jas	Tehama Lassen	70	869
Jas	Trinity Hay Fork	70	991
Jas H	Fresno Twp 3	59	15
Jasper	San Joaquin Douglass	64	926
Jasper N	Sonoma Mendocino	69	461
Jere	San Joaquin Elkhorn	64	984
Jesse	Tulara Twp 2	71	26
Jesse G	San Joaquin O'Neal	64	1006
Jessee	San Bernardino San Bernadino	64	621
Jessee	Tulara Visalia	71	26
Jessee B	Los Angeles San Gabriel	59	422
Jno	Butte Oregon	56	614
Jno	Sacramento Ward 4	63	500
Jno	Sonoma Petaluma	69	558
Jno C	Plumas Quincy	62	917
Jno M	Mendocino Arrana	60	861
Jno R	Sacramento Ward 1	63	77
Jno R	San Francisco San Francisco 6	67	401
Joel	Mendocino Round Va	60	879
Johanna	Yolo Washington	72	600
John	Butte Oro	56	680
John	Calaveras Twp 6	57	140
John	Del Norte Happy Ca	58	664
John	Mariposa Twp 3	60	590
John	Mariposa Twp 1	60	671
John	Mariposa Coulterville	60	689
John	Nevada Bridgeport	61	453
John	Placer Ophirville	62	659
John	Placer Virginia	62	666
John	Placer Virginia	62	667
John	Placer Yankee J	62	780
John	Sacramento San Joaquin	63	351
John	Sacramento San Joaquin	63	364
John	San Francisco San Francisco 7	68	1444
John	San Francisco San Francisco 1	68	838
John	San Francisco San Francisco 1	68	841
John	San Joaquin Castoria	64	911
John	San Joaquin Oneal	64	929
John	Sierra Twp 7	66	911
John	Siskiyou Klamath	69	91
John	Sonoma Armally	69	487
John	Sonoma Vallejo	69	628
John	Tuolumne Twp 1	71	187
John	Tuolumne Sonora	71	189
John	Tuolumne Don Pedro	71	534
John	Yolo Putah	72	560
John	Yuba Fosters	72	837
John B	Sonoma Vallejo	69	628
John C	Mariposa Twp 1	60	669
John C	Plumas Meadow Valley	62	912
John C	San Francisco San Francisco 2	67	588
John H*	Tuolumne Twp 2	71	473
John W	Calaveras Twp 4	57	326
Johnson	Yolo Washington	72	600
Jonah	Sierra Downieville	66	1020
Jos	Butte Ophir	56	787
Jos E	San Francisco San Francisco 9	68	1070
Jos E N	Butte Ophir	56	761
Joseph	Calaveras Twp 8	57	65
Joseph	Nevada Rough &	61	424
Joseph	San Joaquin Stockton	64	1047
Joseph	San Joaquin Douglass	64	919
Joseph	Solano Benecia	69	304
Joseph	Tulara Twp 2	71	25
Joseph A	Santa Clara Gilroy	65	223
Joseph*	Nevada Rough &	61	424
Joshua F	Tulara Visalia	71	89
Joshua H	Plumas Quincy	62	979
Joshua T*	Tulara Twp 1	71	89
Josph	Nevada Rough &	61	424
L	Sutter Butte	70	779
L P	El Dorado Placerville	58	863
Lamand*	Solano Vacaville	69	343
Landres	Nevada Bloomfield	61	510
Leon	San Francisco San Francisco 2	67	693
Leona	Yuba Foster B	72	824
Leonard	Plumas Quincy	62	961
Leonidas L	Sacramento Ward 4	63	495
Levy	Tulara Visalia	71	15
Lewis	Butte Bidwell	56	728
Lewis	Yuba Marysville	72	894
Lewis C	Sonoma Petaluma	69	554
Lindsey	Santa Clara Alviso	65	401
Linzey	Alameda Brooklyn	55	141
Louchiel	Butte Bidwell	56	715
Louis	Los Angeles Los Angeles	59	333
Louis	Yuba Marysville	72	894
Louisa	San Francisco San Francisco 6	67	408
Lucy Ann	Sonoma Mendocino	69	461
Lyon	San Francisco San Francisco 2	67	613
M	Nevada Washington	61	334
M	San Francisco San Francisco 5	67	532
M A	Tuolumne Columbia	71	299
M B	Sacramento Ward 4	63	501
M B	Sacramento Ward 4	63	528
M G	Calaveras Twp 9	57	367
M S	Calaveras Twp 9	57	367
M*	Calaveras Twp 9	57	405
Mafer A*	Calaveras Twp 5	57	185
Magor A	Calaveras Twp 5	57	185
Maj	Santa Clara Fremont	65	432
Major A	Calaveras Twp 6	57	185
Manuel	Mariposa Coulterville	60	690
Manwill	Mariposa Coulterville	60	690

Name	County Locale	M653 Roll	Page
LEWIS			
Marian	Sonoma Petaluma	69	561
Martin	Placer Goods	62	699
Martin	Plumas Quincy	62	937
Martin	Sonoma Petaluma	69	555
Martin B	Fresno Twp 1	59	34
Mary	San Francisco San Francisco 2	67	729
Mary	Tuolumne Twp 4	71	165
McGuire*	Sierra Cold Can	66	836
Mitchell M*	San Francisco 7	68	1407
	San Francisco		
Morris	San Francisco San Francisco 9	68	953
N	San Mateo Twp 3	65	93
Nancy	Solano Vacaville	69	346
Nancy J	Sonoma Mendocino	69	467
Nathal	Nevada Bridgeport	61	443
Nathen	Sacramento Natonia	63	284
Nathnl*	Nevada Bridgeport	61	443
Nathul*	Nevada Bridgeport	61	443
Nicholas	San Francisco San Francisco 1	68	841
O C	Sacramento Granite	63	262
Octavus W	Alameda Oakland	55	17
Ole	Yolo Washington	72	599
Oscar	San Francisco San Francisco 3	67	11
Oscar	San Francisco San Francisco 10	67	327
Owen	Sierra Pine Grove	66	835
P	Calaveras Twp 7	57	17
P	Siskiyou Scott Ri	69	74
P W	Sacramento Ward 4	63	531
Peter	Placer Michigan	62	832
Phillip	San Francisco San Francisco 2	67	653
R	San Francisco San Francisco 5	67	548
R	Sutter Yuba	70	768
R	Sutter Yuba	70	774
R B	San Joaquin Stockton	64	1096
R H	Marin Cortemad	60	752
R W	Sierra Cox'S Bar	66	952
Rachael	San Francisco San Francisco 2	67	643
Rachael S	Sonoma Mendocino	69	467
Reanchamp	Sierra Twp 5	66	936
Rebeca	Solano Vacaville	69	341
Rich	Butte Ophir	56	823
Richard	Klamath Trinidad	59	221
Richard	Sierra Monte Crk	66	1036
Richard	Sierra Port Win	66	798
Richd	Butte Ophir	56	776
Richd E	Sonoma Mendocino	69	467
Richmond	Mariposa Twp 1	60	649
Robert	Contra Costa Twp 1	57	484
Robert	Contra Costa Twp 3	57	605
Robert	Placer Michigan	62	851
Robert	Yuba Rose Bar	72	801
Robert W	Sierra Excelsior	66	1033
Rodman	San Francisco San Francisco 3	67	48
Rodman P	San Francisco San Francisco 3	67	48
Rolenson	Sierra Gibsonville	66	854
S	Amador Twp 5	55	329
S	El Dorado Diamond	58	808
S G*	Placer Sacramento	62	644
S J*	Placer Sacramento	62	644
S S	Nevada Bridgeport	61	485
Saben F	San Francisco San Francisco 7	68	1365
Sam	San Francisco San Francisco 9	68	1069
Samand	Solano Vacaville	69	343
Saml	Butte Oregon	56	627
Saml	Nevada Bridgeport	61	498
Saml	Placer Dutch Fl	62	719
Saml	Shasta Horsetown	66	710
Saml H	Fresno Twp 3	59	21
Samuel	Marin S Antoni	60	706
Samuel	San Francisco San Francisco 10	67	212
Samuel	Sierra Eureka	66	1043
Samuel	Sierra Forest C	66	909
Samuel	Siskiyou Scott Va	69	44
Samuel	Tulara Twp 2	71	22
Samuel J	Yuba Bear Rvr	72	1000
Sarah	Sonoma Mendocino	69	453
Sarah E	San Joaquin Elkhorn	64	999
Sethy	Sierra Eureka	66	1043
Sheppard	Sierra Downieville	66	1017
Solomon	San Francisco San Francisco 9	68	951
Stephen	Tehama Red Bluff	70	904
Sylvester	San Joaquin Elkhorn	64	978
T W	Solano Vacaville	69	339
Thomas	Calaveras Twp 5	57	203
Thomas	Calaveras Twp 9	57	357
Thomas	Plumas Meadow Valley	62	933
Thomas	San Joaquin Stockton	64	1070
Thomas	San Joaquin Elkhorn	64	998
Thomas	Solano Vallejo	69	245
Thomas	Yolo Slate Ra	72	701
Thomas	Yuba Slate Ro	72	701
Thomas	Yuba Marysville	72	911
Thomas A	Calaveras Twp 9	57	352
LEWIS			
Thomas F	El Dorado Greenwood	58	725
Thomas H	Fresno Twp 1	59	34
Thos	Shasta Horsetown	66	710
Thos	Tehama Lassen	70	880
Timothy	Butte Kimshaw	56	602
Timothy	Tuolumne Columbia	71	332
W	El Dorado Kelsey	58	1080
W	El Dorado Placerville	58	886
W	Santa Cruz Pescadero	66	653
W	Shasta Shasta	66	653
W A	Nevada Little Y	61	534
W H	El Dorado Placerville	58	919
W J	San Francisco San Francisco 3	67	74
W K	Sierra Downieville	66	1021
W L	Alameda Washington	55	174
W M	Tuolumne Twp 1	71	479
W W	Yolo Washington	72	605
Walter	Plumas Meadow Valley	62	929
William	Calaveras Twp 6	57	154
William	Nevada Bridgeport	61	455
William	San Francisco San Francisco 3	67	68
William	Sierra La Porte	66	781
William	Sierra Port Win	66	794
William	Sierra Port Win	66	798
William	Sierra Pine Grove	66	835
William	Siskiyou Yreka	69	137
William	Siskiyou Yreka	69	138
William	Siskiyou Klamath	69	90
William A	Calaveras Twp 5	57	209
William B	Calaveras Twp 5	57	146
William J	San Joaquin Elkhorn	64	965
William L	Calaveras Twp 8	57	82
William R	Siskiyou Yreka	69	124
William W	Calaveras Twp 8	57	55
William*	Stanislaus Emory	70	756
Wilson	Sacramento San Joaquin	63	365
Wm	Butte Oro	56	677
Wm	Butte Ophir	56	791
Wm	Napa Napa	61	99
Wm	Sacramento Cosummes	63	409
Wm	Sacramento Ward 4	63	586
Wm	San Francisco San Francisco 9	68	1057
Wm A	Santa Clara San Jose	65	295
Wm A	Tuolumne Twp 1	71	203
Wm O	Santa Clara Gilroy	65	223
Wm P*	Calaveras Twp 9	57	367
Wm R	Yolo Slate Ra	72	701
Wm R	Yuba Slate Ro	72	701
Zack*	Yuba Rose Bar	72	802
Zjack*	Yuba Rose Bar	72	802
LEWISON			
L F	Yolo Putah	72	560
M	Sutter Sutter	70	813
LEWISSON			
L	San Francisco San Francisco 5	67	486
LEWKIRK			
Eldridge*	Amador Twp 4	55	244
LEWMAN			
Henry	Sierra Cox'S Bar	66	950
LEWNENSOU			
E*	Tuolumne Twp 2	71	415
LEWNG			
---	El Dorado Coloma	58	1114
LEWO			
---	Placer Auburn	62	571
LEWON			
---	Napa Napa	61	89
LEWRY			
G W	Sacramento Granite	63	261
M M	Sierra La Porte	66	772
LEWS			
Wm	El Dorado Georgetown	58	691
LEWTHART			
Wm	Marin Bolinas	60	740
LEWTON			
William	Santa Cruz Pajaro	66	532
LEWUS			
Pierre	Yolo Slate Ra	72	688
LEWY			
---	Sacramento Mississipi	63	190
---	Shasta Horsetown	66	710
A A	Sutter Sutter	70	801
Francis	Sacramento Granite	63	261
LEWYER			
Charles*	El Dorado White Oaks	58	1032
Ed	Sacramento Ward 4	63	498
LEX			
John	San Luis Obispo San Luis Obispo	65	5
William	San Luis Obispo San Luis Obispo	65	4
LEXAN			
N	Sacramento Natonia	63	278
LEXAR			
M	Sacramento Natonia	63	278
LEXEY			
Charles E	Yuba New York	72	748
LEXINGER			
James*	San Francisco San Francisco 9	68	1021
LEXITY			
Amy*	Yuba Marysville	72	899
LEXTON			
Daniel	Marin Tomales	60	726
Geo W	El Dorado Coloma	58	1080
Joseph	San Joaquin Oneal	64	913
W	El Dorado Grizzly	58	1182
LEY			
---	Calaveras Twp 5	57	195
---	Del Norte Crescent	58	633
---	Mariposa Coulterville	60	683
---	Mariposa Coulterville	60	685
---	Nevada Bridgeport	61	460
---	Plumas Meadow Valley	62	914
---	Plumas Quincy	62	926
---	Plumas Quincy	62	947
---	Yuba Long Bar	72	759
A	Sacramento Granite	63	250
Cow	Butte Ophir	56	804
H D*	Napa Hot Springs	61	4
Henry D	Humbolt Union	59	183
Henry D Jr	Sonoma Healdsbu	69	477
How	Butte Ophir	56	802
John*	El Dorado Coloma	58	1115
Min	Butte Ophir	56	808
Mon	El Dorado Georgetown	58	700
LEYAN S			
L	Sierra Downieville	66	957
LEYANLT			
Frank	Yuba Long Bar	72	751
LEYAR			
John G*	Calaveras Twp 10	57	281
LEYARD			
John	Mariposa Twp 3	60	571
LEYAULT			
Frank	Yuba Long Bar	72	751
LEYDEN			
Henry	Amador Twp 2	55	303
William	Tuolumne Shawsfla	71	420
LEYDIN			
John	Calaveras Twp 7	57	27
LEYELKEN			
John D*	San Francisco San Francisco 12	67	376
LEYG			
---	Yuba North Ea	72	682
LEYGILL			
Thos A*	Stanislaus Branch	70	703
LEYHTNER			
Jas T	Sonoma Petaluma	69	602
LEYHTNOR			
Jno*	Sonoma Petaluma	69	602
LEYID			
G	Calaveras Twp 9	57	412
LEYLON			
G H	Nevada Grass Valley	61	217
LEYMAN			
Margaret	San Francisco San Francisco 4	68	1128
LEYMANS			
Mary	Mariposa Twp 3	60	587
LEYMOUR			
Emmery P	San Francisco San Francisco 4	68	1220
J S*	Sacramento Ward 4	63	515
Jas	Sacramento Granite	63	251
LEYNETZ			
Joseph*	Calaveras Twp 10	57	278
LEYON			
Hyram	Siskiyou Callahan	69	1
Hysam	Siskiyou Callahan	69	1
LEYOND			
Julle	Sierra Port Win	66	798
LEYONSS			
R	San Joaquin Stockton	64	1096
LEYREN			
L W	Nevada Eureka	61	392
LEYRGAN			
Mary*	San Francisco San Francisco 8	68	1254
LEYROY			
Catheine	Santa Clara San Jose	65	383
LEYRU			
William	Solano Fremont	69	386
LEYSON			
David	Butte Oregon	56	624
Jno	Butte Oregon	56	624
John W	Sierra Port Win	66	793
LEYTHNER			
Jno*	Sonoma Petaluma	69	602
LEYTON			
G H	Nevada Grass Valley	61	217
J	Nevada Grass Valley	61	217
John*	Yuba New York	72	728
LEYTOR			
George E	Tulara Twp 1	71	102
LEYUFF			
John	Calaveras Twp 4	57	339

California 1860 Census Index

Name	County Locale	M653 Roll Page
LEZAR		
Paul	Monterey Pajaro	601021
LEZIER		
Samuel	San Francisco San Francisco 11	126 67
LG		
---	El Dorado Georgetown	58 693
Kim*	El Dorado Georgetown	58 703
LGAMAN		
James B	Yuba Marysville	72 847
LGNACIO		
Jose*	San Diego Agua Caliente	64 814
LHAN		
Thr	San Francisco San Francisco 10	356 67
LHENG		
---*	Calaveras Twp 4	57 305
LHERRIN		
W*	Mariposa Twp 3	60 556
LHINY		
---	Tuolumne Twp 6	71 533
LHO		
---	Calaveras Twp 8	57 51
LHON		
---	Siskiyou Scott Va	69 46
LHOTWELL		
H	Tehama Pasakent	70 860
LHRW		
---	Calaveras Twp 6	57 150
LHVEN		
Chas*	Mariposa Twp 3	60 596
LHY		
Lin	Butte Ophir	56 805
LI JAVO		
---*	Nevada Red Dog	61 539
LI SING		
---	Nevada Rough &	61 435
LI		
---	Calaveras Twp 5	57 136
---	Del Norte Crescent	58 651
---	El Dorado Diamond	58 807
---	El Dorado Mud Springs	58 972
---	Mariposa Coulterville	60 681
---	Mariposa Coulterville	60 683
---	Mendocino Big Rvr	60 851
---	Sacramento Granite	63 247
---	Sacramento Ward 1	63 52
---	San Francisco San Francisco 3	67 7
---	Sierra Twp 5	66 942
---	Stanislaus Emory	70 743
---	Tuolumne Twp 6	71 533
---	Tuolumne Twp 6	71 537
---	Yuba Long Bar	72 766
---	Yuba Marysville	72 916
---*	Calaveras Twp 6	57 176
---*	Yuba Marysville	72 916
Chang	El Dorado Georgetown	58 700
Chung	Nevada Bridgeport	61 492
Chung Ti	Stanislaus Emory	70 743
Hi Ang	Yuba Long Bar	72 756
Ho	Yuba Marysville	72 921
Hown	Calaveras Twp 4	57 334
La	Calaveras Twp 5	57 250
Li	Stanislaus Emory	70 752
Luck	Placer Iona Hills	62 898
Mee	San Francisco San Francisco 9	681095
Sing	Nevada Rough &	61 435
LIA		
---	El Dorado Georgetown	58 703
---	Tuolumne Twp 5	71 524
---	Yolo No E Twp	72 685
LIADI		
Michael	Tuolumne Twp 4	71 137
LIANSMAN		
Henry*	Mariposa Twp 3	60 587
LIAS		
A	Colusa Spring Valley	57 433
James	Yuba Slate Ro	72 688
Juan	Monterey San Juan	601002
LIASI		
Michael	Tuolumne Big Oak	71 137
LIATT		
Edwin	Calaveras Twp 9	57 362
LIAVA		
Juan Antonio*	Los Nieto Los Angeles	59 436
LIBANCE		
Seth*	Placer Michigan	62 820
LIBASE		
Clermont	Placer Michigan	62 811
LIBBA		
J	San Francisco San Francisco 9	68 982
LIBBE		
Fred	Placer Secret R	62 608
Pierre	San Francisco San Francisco 8	681240
LIBBEE		
Michael	Siskiyou Yreka	69 174
LIBBER		
Cebria	Sierra Downieville	661018
Celirie*	Sierra Downieville	661018
LIBBERT		
John	El Dorado Salmon Falls	581041
LIBBETTS		
G	Nevada Grass Valley	61 153
LIBBEY		
Erastus S	Tuolumne Twp 3	71 449
Ivory	Napa Yount	61 46
Wm A	Tuolumne Jamestown	71 449
LIBBIE		
Cehrier*	Sierra Downieville	661018
Celria*	Sierra Downieville	661018
Oliver	Tuolumne Shawsfla	71 379
LIBBIN		
Oliver	Tuolumne Twp 2	71 379
LIBBIR		
C	Nevada Grass Valley	61 158
LIBBITS		
Allen	Amador Twp 4	55 233
M C*	Napa Hot Springs	61 5
LIBBO		
Pierre	San Francisco San Francisco 8	681240
LIBBY		
A E	Tuolumne Twp 4	71 173
Albert	San Francisco San Francisco 3	67 25
Charles	San Joaquin Castoria	64 911
Daniel	San Francisco San Francisco 7	681420
E S	Tuolumne Columbia	71 312
El	San Mateo Twp 1	65 55
Ella A	Alameda Oakland	55 20
G M	Placer Michigan	62 848
George A	Sierra Twp 5	66 923
John	Butte Mountain	56 740
John	Klamath Salmon	59 208
Mary	San Francisco San Francisco 8	681280
R W	Butte Wyandotte	56 658
Rudolph	Sacramento Ward 4	63 603
Sam	Mariposa Coulterville	60 696
Solomon	San Francisco San Francisco 10	171 67
William	San Francisco San Francisco 7	681399
William H	Plumas Meadow Valley	62 907
LIBEAU		
A	Sacramento Sutter	63 300
LIBENBERG		
Chs*	San Francisco San Francisco 3	67 26
LIBERATA		
---	Monterey San Juan	601010
LIBERSKI		
Roclek*	Yuba Marysville	72 878
Roclik*	Yuba Marysville	72 878
LIBERT		
Geo	Butte Bidwell	56 721
Henry	Amador Twp 3	55 405
LIBERTY		
Vincent	Marin San Rafael	60 770
LIBEST		
Geo	Butte Bidwell	56 721
LIBEY		
J B*	Calaveras Twp 9	57 407
LIBEZ		
J B*	Calaveras Twp 9	57 407
LIBIA		
Frannie	San Luis Obispo San Luis Obispo 65	4
LIBIANO		
---	San Diego Temecula	64 784
LIBIZ		
J B	Calaveras Twp 9	57 407
LIBKISHER		
H Y	Marin Cortemad	60 786
LIBLEY		
Peter	Amador Twp 3	55 375
LIBLY		
G H*	Yuba Slate Ro	72 713
LIBO		
Joel*	Napa Clear Lake	61 121
LIBOLD		
Felix	Yolo Cottonwood	72 654
LIBONER		
W J*	Calaveras Twp 9	57 389
LIBOT		
John F	Tuolumne Twp 1	71 240
LIBOVER		
W J*	Calaveras Twp 9	57 389
LIBRA		
Elaria	Tuolumne Twp 1	71 256
LIBRARY		
Robt	Butte Hamilton	56 525
LIBRICHT		
William	Plumas Meadow Valley	62 907
LIBS		
John*	Placer Auburn	62 574
LIBSON		
Wm*	Napa Napa	61 77
LIBSOW		
Wm*	Napa Napa	61 77
LIBURN		
R	El Dorado Diamond	58 765
LICA		
---	Fresno Twp 2	59 20
LICALPOLAS		
Nicholas	Placer Michigan	62 829
LICARDY		
Bertrand	Plumas Meadow Valley	62 934
LICCKO		
---	Tulara Twp 2	71 38
LICE		
Alanson*	San Francisco San Francisco 4	681160
Juan	Los Angeles Los Angeles	59 325
LICH		
J*	Calaveras Twp 9	57 398
Lewis*	Plumas Quincy	62 924
LICHAN		
Henry	Sonoma Petaluma	69 573
LICHEL		
Solomon	San Francisco San Francisco 10	203 67
LICHFIELD		
William	Solano Fremont	69 381
LICHFIER		
Andrew	El Dorado Georgetown	58 677
LICHINOR		
A	Tuolumne Twp 4	71 152
LICHLOR		
George	Los Angeles Tejon	59 521
LICHPIN		
Andrew*	El Dorado Georgetown	58 677
LICHTENBERG		
Moses	Solano Benecia	69 283
LICHTENFETTS		
G	San Francisco San Francisco 3	67 58
LICHTENSTEIN		
Richard	San Francisco San Francisco 4	681123
LICHTHALL		
W	El Dorado Diamond	58 772
LICK WAY		
---	Nevada Bridgeport	61 460
LICK		
---	Calaveras Twp 8	57 60
---	Nevada Bridgeport	61 464
---	Plumas Quincy	62 920
---	Sierra Twp 5	66 944
---	Tuolumne Twp 5	71 516
---*	Nevada Bridgeport	61 464
James	Santa Clara Santa Clara	65 509
James	Sierra Eureka	661048
John	Plumas Quincy	62 924
John H	Santa Clara Santa Clara	65 509
Way	Nevada Bridgeport	61 460
LICKER		
Henrich	San Francisco San Francisco 3	67 72
LICKHOFF		
---	San Francisco San Francisco 10	341 67
LICKNEY		
Fred	El Dorado Coloma	581105
LICKSON		
Henry	Plumas Meadow Valley	62 901
LICKSOW		
---	Tulara Twp 2	71 36
LICKY		
Cornelias	San Mateo Twp 3	65 88
LICLES		
Lewis J*	Calaveras Twp 4	57 326
LICLETTE		
Ersen	Alameda Oakland	55 13
LICNH		
J*	Calaveras Twp 9	57 398
LICOHAN		
Edward	Calaveras Twp 5	57 210
LICOMPH		
M*	El Dorado Georgetown	58 689
LICONDINA		
Antonio	Los Angeles Los Angeles	59 493
LIDAY		
George A*	Mariposa Twp 3	60 618
LIDBETTER		
Jonathan W	Calaveras Twp 10	57 281
LIDBROOK		
W*	Sacramento Ward 4	63 607
LIDDE		
Jacob*	Placer Forest H	62 800
LIDDEA		
William*	Santa Cruz Santa Cruz	66 630
LIDDELE		
William*	Santa Cruz Santa Cruz	66 630
LIDDELL		
George	Santa Cruz Santa Cruz	66 603
Mary K	San Francisco San Francisco 11	131 67

Name	County Locale	M653 Roll	Page
LIDDINGTON			
Daniel*	Marin Cortemad	60	787
LIDDLE			
Andrew	Sierra Downieville	66	1023
Henry	San Francisco San Francisco 7	68	1337
Jas W	Del Norte Happy Ca	58	662
Robert	San Francisco San Francisco 2	67	726
William	Placer Iona Hills	62	884
LIDDY			
Danl A	Santa Clara San Jose	65	289
Jacob	Yuba Slate Ro	72	698
James	San Francisco San Francisco 7	68	1331
Mary	San Francisco San Francisco 10	229	67
Samuel	San Francisco San Francisco 9	68	1037
Wm	Yolo Slate Ra	72	698
LIDELINGER			
George*	Yuba Fosters	72	840
LIDELINYER			
George	Yuba Fosters	72	840
LIDELL			
Agnes M	San Luis Obispo San Luis Obispo	65	15
LIDEO			
---	San Bernardino S Timate	64	701
LIDERMANN			
George	San Francisco San Francisco 7	68	1424
LIDESTONE			
Hans C*	Yuba Marysville	72	924
LIDING			
George A*	Mariposa Twp 3	60	618
LIDLE			
Robt	Butte Mountain	56	736
Thomas	Calaveras Twp 5	57	195
LIDLSTE			
E C*	Placer Dutch Fl	62	719
LIDNY			
George A*	Mariposa Twp 3	60	618
LIDON			
Jas	Sacramento Natonia	63	283
LIDRO			
Lethro*	Plumas Meadow Valley	62	908
LIDRY			
George A*	Mariposa Twp 3	60	618
LIDSY			
George A*	Mariposa Twp 3	60	618
LIDY			
J D*	Shasta Horsetown	66	692
LIDZ			
J D	Shasta Horsetown	66	692
LIE			
---	Amador Twp 6	55	422
---	Calaveras Twp 6	57	151
---	Calaveras Twp 7	57	46
---	El Dorado White Oaks	58	1021
---	El Dorado Salmon Falls	58	1034
---	El Dorado Salmon Falls	58	1047
---	El Dorado Salmon Falls	58	1058
---	El Dorado Kelsey	58	1136
---	El Dorado Placerville	58	831
---	El Dorado Mud Springs	58	958
---	Mariposa Twp 3	60	562
---	Mariposa Twp 1	60	643
---	Placer Rattle Snake	62	638
---	Sacramento Ward 3	63	492
---	Sacramento Ward 1	63	54
---	San Francisco San Francisco 4	68	1189
---	San Francisco San Francisco 4	68	1210
---	Sierra Downieville	66	1014
---	Sierra La Porte	66	790
---*	Calaveras Twp 4	57	339
Cung	Sacramento Ward 3	63	489
Fo	San Francisco San Francisco 5	67	1205
Hop	San Francisco San Francisco 4	68	1187
J H*	Sonoma Armally	69	496
Kin	El Dorado Georgetown	58	686
Ko	San Francisco San Francisco 4	68	1193
Ko	San Francisco San Francisco 5	67	1205
Kow	San Francisco San Francisco 5	67	1205
Moe	San Francisco San Francisco 5	67	1205
Tim	Sacramento Ward 3	63	491
LIEB			
Jos*	Amador Twp 2	55	265
LIEBER			
Henry	Sacramento Ward 3	63	449
John	Contra Costa Twp 3	57	588
LIEBERSMEYER			
Conrad	Los Angeles Los Angeles	59	390
LIEBHOUSER			
Antony	Yuba New York	72	727
LIEBLING			
Frank	Sacramento Ward 4	63	532
LIEBRIR			
Gustav*	Alameda Oakland	55	16
LIEFYRAN			
John	Tuolumne Montezuma	71	509
LIEGE			
Joseph	Tuolumne Twp 2	71	405
LIEHGRAN			
John*	Tuolumne Twp 5	71	509
LIEHTENFETTS			
G*	San Francisco San Francisco 3	67	58
LIEILD			
J*	Calaveras Twp 9	57	392
LIEL			
Wm	Sierra Downieville	66	967
LIEM			
Reuben	El Dorado Kelsey	58	1135
LIEMM			
Alex S*	San Francisco San Francisco 2	67	736
LIEN			
---	Butte Kimshaw	56	603
---*	Mariposa Twp 3	60	563
LIENEN			
Frank*	San Francisco San Francisco 3	67	72
LIENON			
Francisco	Tehama Tehama	70	941
LIENS			
John	Tuolumne Big Oak	71	128
LIEOHAN			
Edward	Calaveras Twp 5	57	210
LIEOMPTH			
M*	El Dorado Georgetown	58	689
LIEPEAN			
Henry	Calaveras Twp 8	57	62
LIER			
F	Merced Twp 1	60	902
Phillip	El Dorado Mud Springs	58	982
LIERA			
Francisco	Santa Barbara San Bernardino	64	169
LIERES			
Antonio*	Marin Bolinas	60	733
LIERGE			
Leopold*	Monterey Alisal	60	1028
LIERNAN			
R*	San Francisco San Francisco 7	68	1420
LIERNEY			
J	Tuolumne Twp 4	71	179
LIERREN			
Frank*	San Francisco San Francisco 3	67	72
LIES			
Ann	Yuba Fosters	72	837
Eugene	San Francisco San Francisco 8	68	1311
LIESENFELD			
P*	San Francisco San Francisco 3	67	31
LIESHNES			
Harriet*	Santa Cruz Santa Cruz	66	636
LIESMRING			
J P*	Merced Twp 1	60	895
LIET			
Antonio*	San Francisco San Francisco 8	68	1246
LIETHUES			
Harriet*	Santa Cruz Santa Cruz	66	636
LIETRIER			
Gustav*	Alameda Oakland	55	16
LIETT			
N S*	Calaveras Twp 9	57	393
LIETZ			
L*	Sacramento Ward 4	63	586
Mary	Sacramento Granite	63	234
LIEUXNICE			
A*	Del Norte Crescent	58	645
LIEVE			
H	Santa Clara Santa Clara	65	470
LIEVELLI			
Enasen	Calaveras Twp 5	57	136
LIEVELLIS			
Enasea*	Calaveras Twp 6	57	136
LIEVES			
Antonio	Marin Bolinas	60	733
LIEVILLI			
Erasei*	Calaveras Twp 6	57	136
LIEVIR			
Wm*	Sierra Twp 7	66	884
LIEW			
---	Sierra Morristown	66	1055
LIEWING			
John H	Colusa Colusi	57	422
LIEY			
S H*	Mariposa Twp 3	60	621
LIF			
Yan	Yuba Long Bar	72	763
LIFFENSTIEN			
Wm	Nevada Eureka	61	374
LIFFINGWELL			
Joseph	Marin Tomales	60	726
LIFFRINN			
L*	Mariposa Twp 3	60	586
LIFIELD			
John*	Sacramento Dry Crk	63	372
LIFLER			
Henry	Siskiyou Klamath	69	78
LIFT			
Samuel	Yuba Marysville	72	979
LIG			
---	Butte Ophir	56	808
---	Calaveras Twp 8	57	50
Let	El Dorado Big Bar	58	740
LIGALA			
Paul	Calaveras Twp 9	57	359
LIGARST			
John*	Humbolt Mattole	59	126
LIGE			
---	Placer Folsom	62	649
LIGER			
Geo	El Dorado Placerville	58	907
LIGERET			
Maria	Sacramento Ward 1	63	43
LIGEROR			
S	San Francisco San Francisco 4	68	1228
LIGESIBE			
Anton	El Dorado Greenwood	58	716
LIGGE			
A C	Calaveras Twp 9	57	416
LIGGELT			
Thomas*	El Dorado Casumnes	58	1169
LIGGETT			
A S	Sierra Twp 7	66	908
Benjamin	Placer Michigan	62	854
James	Colusa Grand Island	57	470
Robert	San Joaquin Oneal	64	935
Thomas	El Dorado Casumnes	58	1169
LIGGETTS			
A S	Sierra Twp 7	66	908
LIGGITT			
Daniel	Nevada Bridgeport	61	504
LIGH			
---*	Tuolumne Big Oak	71	182
Senett	Butte Bidwell	56	719
William*	Contra Costa Twp 1	57	489
LIGHLHOLDE			
Joseph*	Calaveras Twp 5	57	241
LIGHLNER			
Jno*	Sonoma Petaluma	69	599
LIGHT			
A B	Butte Wyandotte	56	665
Adam	Plumas Quincy	62	971
Amos C	Plumas Quincy	62	973
C H	Butte Cascade	56	693
Clun	Sacramento Granite	63	232
E A	El Dorado Diamond	58	788
E H	Butte Cascade	56	693
Elisha	Marin S Antoni	60	709
Elysha	Marin S Antoni	60	709
Emanuel	Sonoma Santa Rosa	69	399
Enoch	Butte Hamilton	56	513
Geo	El Dorado Casumnes	58	1164
H	Butte Ophir	56	769
H	San Joaquin Stockton	64	1094
Harvey	Stanislaus Branch	70	697
James	Humbolt Union	59	185
Jas	Butte Ophir	56	795
John	San Francisco San Francisco 9	68	1053
John	San Francisco San Francisco 1	68	913
Martin	Sacramento Ward 4	63	517
N	San Joaquin Stockton	64	1090
Philip	San Joaquin Stockton	64	1042
Samuel	El Dorado White Oaks	58	1007
W H	Butte Bidwell	56	729
W W	Sacramento Ward 3	63	468
Woolf	San Francisco San Francisco 8	68	1247
LIGHTCAP			
William	San Joaquin Oneal	64	938
LIGHTENBURG			
A	Sacramento Ward 1	63	119
LIGHTEUR			
Mary E*	Yuba Marysville	72	898
LIGHTFOOT			
Andw	Butte Chico	56	561
Jacob	San Joaquin Elkhorn	64	972
Martin	Placer Todds Va	62	785
Mortinson	Placer Forest H	62	803
Sophia	Tuolumne Twp 2	71	319
LIGHTFROST			
Sophia	Tuolumne Columbia	71	319
LIGHTHALL			
Abram	Tuolumne Twp 2	71	306
G E	Tuolumne Twp 2	71	306
LIGHTHOLDE			
Joseph	Calaveras Twp 5	57	241
LIGHTHOLDER			
Joseph*	Calaveras Twp 5	57	241
LIGHTNER			
Abia	Tulara Keyesville	71	57
Alria*	Tulara Twp 3	71	57
H L	Calaveras Twp 8	57	52
Isaac	Santa Clara Redwood	65	452
Jno	Sonoma Petaluma	69	599

Name	County Locale	M653 Roll	Page
LIGHTNER			
Joel	San Francisco San Francisco 2	67	564
Joel F	San Francisco San Francisco 2	67	564
Lizzie	San Francisco San Francisco 10	67	228
Mary E	Yuba Marysville	72	899
Robt	Sacramento Georgian	63	342
LIGHTNOR			
Jas T	Sonoma Petaluma	69	602
Jno*	Sonoma Petaluma	69	602
LIGHTON			
David	Tuolumne Twp 1	71	194
LIGHTSHOE			
John	Napa Napa	61	75
LIGHTSTAN			
Frank	Santa Clara San Jose	65	288
LIGIER			
John	Sierra Port Win	66	795
Z B	Siskiyou Scott Ri	69	74
LIGIMORA			
Joaquin	Tuolumne Twp 2	71	375
LIGINORA			
Joaquin	Tuolumne Shawsfla	71	375
LIGIS			
E	Calaveras Twp 9	57	375
O	Calaveras Twp 9	57	375
LIGISON			
Fred	El Dorado Kelsey	58	1139
LIGLITER			
George	Alameda Brooklyn	55	102
LIGMERONX			
M	Yuba New York	72	725
LIGNAC			
Peter	Calaveras Twp 7	57	17
LIGNADE			
H	Santa Clara San Jose	65	292
LIGNANDON			
R C	Santa Clara Redwood	65	455
LIGNEROUX			
M	Yuba New York	72	725
LIGNOLD			
John E*	Placer Dutch Fl	62	715
LIGNORE			
Theodore*	Sacramento Franklin	63	311
LIGO			
---	Mendocino Twp 1	60	889
Domez	Los Angeles San Jose	59	286
LIGONANO			
Chris	San Francisco San Francisco 5	67	481
LIGORORO			
Miteo	Tuolumne Twp 2	71	283
LIGPTROTH			
John F	Sierra Twp 7	66	875
LIGRIERO			
Francisco	San Luis Obispo San Luis Obispo	65	27
LIGUERAQ			
Juan	Santa Cruz Watsonville	66	540
LIH			
---	El Dorado Mountain	58	1178
LIHATCH			
John F	Sierra Twp 7	66	884
LIHEUTRE			
Paul*	Tuolumne Twp 3	71	465
LIHI			
Ying	Calaveras Twp 5	57	193
LIHIGH			
Nellie	Sierra Downieville	66	967
LIHMKIEPT			
H	San Francisco San Francisco 10	67	261
LIHO			
---	Shasta Shasta	66	671
LIK			
---	Del Norte Crescent	58	660
---	San Francisco San Francisco 4	68	1183
---	Yuba Long Bar	72	758
Tu	El Dorado Georgetown	58	761
LIKE			
---	Butte Oro	56	675
---	Tuolumne Twp 6	71	539
---*	Calaveras Twp 9	57	305
Gerno L	San Bernardino San Bernardino	64	670
Lee	Yuba Fosters	72	830
LIKENS			
Jno S	Klamath Liberty	59	238
LIKES			
J A	Solano Fremont	69	376
LIKIN			
---	El Dorado Kelsey	58	1132
LIKINS			
Joseph L	Solano Vallejo	69	268
Wm	Solano Vallejo	69	272
LIKKLE			
Henry	San Francisco San Francisco 7	68	1337
LIKONLME			
---*	Tulara Visalia	71	40
LILAERSTEIN			
Isaac*	Yuba Marysville	72	903
LILAS			
Manuel*	Mariposa Twp 3	60	617
LILAVANIG			
E	Calaveras Twp 9	57	378
LILB			
J W*	Calaveras Twp 9	57	382
LILBEY			
J W	El Dorado Placerville	58	857
LILCHA			
---	Mendocino Round Va	60	883
LILCOCH			
Robert	San Francisco San Francisco 3	67	43
LILE			
A	Calaveras Twp 9	57	411
S N	Tehama Red Bluff	70	899
LILEBRAN			
H	Amador Twp 5	55	367
LILEMONDER			
Pascal	Humbolt Pacific	59	131
LILER			
Robt	Plumas Quincy	62	924
LILES			
Tho*	Siskiyou Scott Ri	69	81
LILEY			
John	Amador Twp 1	55	495
L G*	Napa Hot Springs	61	1
LILGARO			
Alvin*	Alameda Washington	55	173
LILI			
A	Calaveras Twp 9	57	411
LILKELA			
---	Mendocino Round Va	60	882
LILL			
---	Del Norte Crescent	58	631
---	Sierra Twp 5	66	934
LILLARD			
C C	Sierra Twp 7	66	889
D B	Santa Clara Gilroy	65	235
G	Siskiyou Scott Ri	69	66
Jas I	Yolo Putah	72	560
Jas T	Yolo Putah	72	560
John J	Santa Clara Gilroy	65	235
LILLARDS			
C C	Sierra Twp 7	66	889
LILLBRAT			
Hartman*	San Joaquin Stockton	64	1047
LILLEAID			
John	Monterey San Juan	60	976
LILLERBEE			
John	Sierra Downieville	66	1001
LILLESPIE			
David	El Dorado Georgetown	58	691
LILLEY			
Grundy	Tuolumne Twp 3	71	448
John	Yolo Cache	72	595
Louis*	El Dorado Coloma	58	1079
Maria*	San Joaquin Stockton	64	1012
Oneiing*	Calaveras Twp 4	57	344
LILLIA			
R	San Mateo Twp 3	65	95
LILLIBRICHT			
D*	Stanislaus Emory	70	744
LILLICROP			
T H	Sierra Twp 7	66	872
LILLIE			
D R	Butte Cascade	56	693
W H	Napa Napa	61	114
LILLIES			
W H*	Napa Napa	61	114
LILLIN			
---	Merced Twp 2	60	922
LILLIS			
A*	Nevada Washington	61	333
O*	Nevada Washington	61	333
Owen	Nevada Little Y	61	531
William	San Francisco San Francisco 3	67	26
LILLMAN			
Frank	San Francisco San Francisco 2	67	588
LILLS			
David*	Sacramento Cosumnes	63	403
LILLY			
---	Mendocino Twp 1	60	886
B*	Butte Kimshaw	56	598
Catherine	San Francisco San Francisco 3	67	23
David	Yolo Fremont	72	605
G H	Yolo Slate Ra	72	713
George B	Calaveras Twp 4	57	344
H A*	Yuba Slate Ro	72	712
Isac H	Mariposa Coulterville	60	676
James	Tulara Keeneysburg	71	49
John C	Nevada Red Dog	61	547
Maggie	Santa Clara Santa Clara	65	461
Samuel	San Mateo Twp 3	65	100
LILSA			
Angie D	Mariposa Twp 1	60	666
LILSVES			
Antone*	Mariposa Coulterville	60	691
LILVA			
Francis*	Sacramento Granite	63	246
James*	Sacramento Granite	63	243
John*	Sacramento Granite	63	246
LILVERTHORN			
J	El Dorado Placerville	58	855
LILVESTER			
Jno	Butte Oregon	56	636
LILWES			
Antone*	Mariposa Coulterville	60	691
LIM HOP			
---	Butte Kimshaw	56	589
LIM			
---	Amador Twp 2	55	293
---	Amador Twp 6	55	432
---	Amador Twp 6	55	445
---	Butte Kimshaw	56	588
---	Butte Wyandotte	56	672
---	Calaveras Twp 9	57	358
---	El Dorado White Oaks	58	1023
---	El Dorado Salmon Falls	58	1059
---	El Dorado Mountain	58	1189
---	El Dorado Georgetown	58	691
---	El Dorado Georgetown	58	746
---	El Dorado Georgetown	58	748
---	El Dorado Diamond	58	790
---	El Dorado Diamond	58	806
---	El Dorado Placerville	58	884
---	Mariposa Twp 3	60	607
---	Mariposa Coulterville	60	682
---	Nevada Rough &	61	396
---	Nevada Rough &	61	432
---	Nevada Rough &	61	437
---	Placer Auburn	62	581
---	Placer Virginia	62	670
---	Placer Virginia	62	678
---	Placer Virginia	62	687
---	Placer Illinois	62	746
---	Placer Illinois	62	751
---	Placer Illinois	62	752
---	Placer Illinois	62	753
---	Placer Illinois	62	754
---	Placer Iona Hills	62	894
---	Plumas Meadow Valley	62	909
---	Plumas Quincy	62	926
---	Sierra Downieville	66	1000
---	Sierra St Louis	66	861
---	Sierra Twp 5	66	944
---	Sierra Downieville	66	980
---	Yuba North Ea	72	682
---	Yuba Long Bar	72	757
---	Yuba Long Bar	72	768
---*	Mariposa Twp 3	60	581
---*	Mariposa Coulterville	60	683
Ah	Tuolumne Twp 4	71	179
Choy	El Dorado Eldorado	58	944
Choy	Placer Auburn	62	577
Fun	Placer Illinois	62	751
Iru	El Dorado Georgetown	58	695
Nim	Butte Bidwell	56	711
Sham	El Dorado Georgetown	58	700
LIMA			
J	San Francisco San Francisco 9	68	1101
Major*	Mariposa Twp 3	60	594
LIMACY			
A R	Napa Clear Lake	61	125
LIMAM			
William*	Calaveras Twp 9	57	352
LIMANS			
Frank	Santa Clara Gilroy	65	247
LIMAR			
Jose*	Los Angeles Tejon	59	528
LIMB			
L	El Dorado Diamond	58	772
Patrick*	Yuba Linda	72	985
LIMBARD			
W	Shasta French G	66	717
LIMBECK			
Lewis	Nevada Bridgeport	61	483
LIMBER			
William	Napa Yount	61	52
LIMBERG			
Louis	Tuolumne Sonora	71	208
LIMBERGER			
Frederic	Los Angeles Los Angeles	59	391
LIMBO			
H H	Sacramento Georgian	63	341
LIME			
---	El Dorado White Oaks	58	1032
LIMEBURNER			
Jno H	Fresno Twp 3	59	13
LIMERY			
Chas	Plumas Meadow Valley	62	904
LIMES			
Henry	Placer Dutch Fl	62	717

California 1860 Census Index

Name	County Locale	M653 RollPage
LIMG		
---	El Dorado Coloma	581122
---	El Dorado Georgetown	58 686
---*	Placer Virginia	62 687
LIMH		
---	El Dorado Greenwood	58 714
LIMHOFF		
Augustus*	Placer Iona Hills	62 870
LIMKINS		
Chas	Sacramento Granite	63 265
LIML		
---	El Dorado Big Bar	58 738
LIMM		
---	Tuolumne Twp 5	71 507
---	Yuba Long Bar	72 759
Dora T*	San Francisco San Francisco 8	681294
LIMMER		
John S	Yuba Marysville	72 867
LIMMERMAN		
G L	Tuolumne Twp 4	71 176
LIMMS		
A	Nevada Grass Valley	61 146
LIMMUX		
---	Tulara Twp 2	71 40
LIMON		
S B	Sierra Twp 7	66 899
LIMONEZ		
Morand	Tuolumne Twp 2	71 304
LIMONS		
James	Santa Clara San Jose	65 347
Stephen	Sacramento Sutter	63 295
LIMONTON		
Robert G*	Humbolt Bucksport	59 159
LIMORALLO		
Joseph*	San Francisco San Francisco 3	67 16
LIMPACK		
Theodore	El Dorado White Oaks	581017
LIMPAL		
C W	San Francisco San Francisco 5	67 494
LIMPENSCOTT		
W P	San Francisco San Francisco 9	68 942
LIMPKINS		
Charles H*	Yuba Marysville	72 859
LIMPLETON		
L*	Calaveras Twp 9	57 391
LIMPLETOR		
T	Calaveras Twp 9	57 391
LIMPSON		
J	Monterey Monterey	60 963
LIMPTAN		
Jacob*	El Dorado White Oaks	581027
LIMPTTAN		
Jacob*	El Dorado White Oaks	581027
LIMTA		
---	Mendocino Calpella	60 825
LIN G		
---	Calaveras Twp 9	57 358
LIN KAY		
---*	Marin Cortemad	60 784
LIN SIN		
---	San Francisco San Francisco 2	67 798
LIN SO		
---	Sierra Morristown	661055
LIN TOY		
---	Calaveras Twp 8	57 60
LIN		
---	Alameda Oakland	55 52
---	Amador Twp 5	55 333
---	Amador Twp 7	55 417
---	Amador Twp 6	55 424
---	Amador Twp 1	55 502
---	Amador Twp 1	55 508
---	Butte Kimshaw	56 587
---	Butte Wyandotte	56 672
---	Calaveras Twp 6	57 134
---	Calaveras Twp 6	57 136
---	Calaveras Twp 6	57 151
---	Calaveras Twp 6	57 173
---	Calaveras Twp 5	57 205
---	Calaveras Twp 5	57 213
---	Calaveras Twp 5	57 234
---	Calaveras Twp 4	57 334
---	Calaveras Twp 4	57 339
---	Calaveras Twp 7	57 44
---	El Dorado White Oaks	581022
---	El Dorado White Oaks	581023
---	El Dorado White Oaks	581025
---	El Dorado Salmon Falls	581044
---	El Dorado Salmon Falls	581046
---	El Dorado Salmon Falls	581050
---	El Dorado Salmon Falls	581053
---	El Dorado Salmon Falls	581056
---	El Dorado Salmon Falls	581059
---	El Dorado Salmon Falls	581061
---	El Dorado Salmon Falls	581067
---	El Dorado Coloma	581076
LIN		
---	El Dorado Coloma	581078
---	El Dorado Coloma	581079
---	El Dorado Coloma	581085
---	El Dorado Coloma	581107
---	El Dorado Coloma	581109
---	El Dorado Coloma	581120
---	El Dorado Kelsey	581135
---	El Dorado Kelsey	581139
---	El Dorado Mountain	581178
---	El Dorado Georgetown	58 677
---	El Dorado Greenwood	58 710
---	El Dorado Greenwood	58 727
---	El Dorado Greenwood	58 729
---	El Dorado Greenwood	58 731
---	El Dorado Big Bar	58 737
---	El Dorado Diamond	58 783
---	El Dorado Diamond	58 784
---	El Dorado Diamond	58 796
---	El Dorado Diamond	58 803
---	El Dorado Placerville	58 830
---	El Dorado Placerville	58 832
---	El Dorado Placerville	58 843
---	El Dorado Placerville	58 897
---	El Dorado Placerville	58 919
---	El Dorado Placerville	58 933
---	El Dorado Eldorado	58 939
---	El Dorado Eldorado	58 941
---	El Dorado Eldorado	58 942
---	El Dorado Eldorado	58 944
---	Mariposa Twp 3	60 550
---	Mariposa Twp 1	60 648
---	Mariposa Twp 1	60 665
---	Mariposa Coulterville	60 682
---	Mariposa Coulterville	60 683
---	Mariposa Coulterville	60 688
---	Mendocino Big Rvr	60 852
---	Nevada Bridgeport	61 439
---	Placer Auburn	62 575
---	Placer Auburn	62 579
---	Placer Secret R	62 624
---	Placer Rattle Snake	62 626
---	Placer Rattle Snake	62 633
---	Placer Rattle Snake	62 637
---	Placer Virginia	62 671
---	Placer Virginia	62 679
---	Placer Virginia	62 684
---	Placer Illinois	62 741
---	Placer Illinois	62 745
---	Placer Illinois	62 746
---	Sacramento Granite	63 250
---	Sacramento Granite	63 268
---	Sacramento Granite	63 269
---	Sacramento Natonia	63 286
---	San Francisco San Francisco 4	681196
---	San Francisco San Francisco 1	68 885
---	San Joaquin Stockton	641088
---	Shasta Horsetown	66 704
---	Shasta Horsetown	66 710
---	Shasta French G	66 712
---	Sierra Downieville	661003
---	Sierra Downieville	661003
---	Sierra Downieville	661004
---	Sierra Downieville	661007
---	Sierra Downieville	661008
---	Sierra Downieville	661009
---	Sierra Downieville	661015
---	Sierra Downieville	661024
---	Sierra Downieville	661025
---	Sierra Downieville	661026
---	Sierra Downieville	661027
---	Sierra Morristown	661056
---	Sierra St Louis	66 861
---	Sierra Twp 5	66 927
---	Sierra Twp 5	66 933
---	Sierra Twp 5	66 944
---	Sierra Downieville	66 953
---	Sierra Downieville	66 973
---	Sierra Downieville	66 997
---	Sierra Downieville	66 999
---	Trinity Browns C	70 984
---	Tuolumne Twp 5	71 524
---	Tuolumne Twp 6	71 535
---	Yuba Bear Rvr	721000
---	Yuba North Ea	72 681
---	Yuba Long Bar	72 756
---	Yuba Fosters	72 827
---*	Amador Twp 2	55 302
---*	Calaveras Twp 6	57 182
---*	Calaveras Twp 4	57 342
---*	El Dorado Casumnes	581160
---*	El Dorado Georgetown	58 700
---*	Sacramento Cosumnes	63 392
---*	Sacramento Ward 4	63 613
---*	Tuolumne Jacksonville	71 169
---*	Yuba Foster B	72 827
LIN		
A	Sacramento Granite	63 268
A	Sacramento Granite	63 269
Ah	Butte Bidwell	56 708
Ah	Tuolumne Twp 4	71 163
Alec	Sierra Downieville	66 979
Chee	Placer Illinois	62 742
Chen	Butte Ophir	56 809
Cheo	Placer Illinois	62 741
Chow	Calaveras Twp 4	57 334
Choy	Butte Ophir	56 814
Choy*	Butte Ophir	56 818
Chu	Placer Illinois	62 740
Chu	Sacramento Granite	63 250
Chung	Sacramento Ward 1	63 156
Com	El Dorado Coloma	581084
Fan	Butte Ophir	56 814
Foke	Tuolumne Green Springs	71 531
Fong	Placer Illinois	62 741
Foo Law	Yuba Long Bar	72 763
Foy	Trinity Weaverville	701075
Fung	Yuba Marysville	72 916
Goon	Shasta Horsetown	66 704
Heck	Sierra Twp 5	66 933
Hew	Butte Ophir	56 815
Ho	Sacramento Ward 4	63 612
Hop	Butte Ophir	56 788
How	Calaveras Twp 4	57 334
Hoy	Calaveras Twp 4	57 334
Ju	El Dorado Georgetown	58 747
Ker	Calaveras Twp 4	57 337
Kin	Calaveras Twp 4	57 337
Koy	Marin Cortemad	60 784
Ku	Calaveras Twp 4	57 337
Lau	Stanislaus Emory	70 753
Lean	Butte Ophir	56 809
Lee	Butte Ophir	56 816
Lee	El Dorado Big Bar	58 737
Leu	Butte Ophir	56 787
Lipo*	Butte Ophir	56 810
Lung*	Sacramento Ward 1	63 52
Lung*	Sacramento Ward 1	63 70
Maqu	Butte Ophir	56 812
Nee	Butte Oro	56 675
Nu	Butte Oro	56 675
Quoy	Sacramento Ward 1	63 52
Samuel	Yuba Slate Ro	72 702
See	El Dorado Georgetown	58 761
Sewe	Butte Ophir	56 814
Shin	El Dorado Big Bar	58 737
Sim	Butte Kimshaw	56 582
Sin	Butte Bidwell	56 709
Sin	Butte Ophir	56 807
Sin	San Francisco San Francisco 2	67 798
Tee	Amador Twp 5	55 333
Ti	Calaveras Twp 4	57 307
Tong	El Dorado Greenwood	58 714
Wah	Calaveras Twp 4	57 307
Yak	Yuba Long Bar	72 766
Yett	Butte Ophir	56 806
Yong	Plumas Meadow Valley	62 914
Yup	Sacramento Granite	63 269
Zue*	El Dorado Greenwood	58 730
LIN'G		
Lin'G	Mariposa Twp 3	60 613
San*	Mariposa Twp 3	60 613
Sang	Mariposa Twp 3	60 613
Sin'G	Mariposa Twp 3	60 613
LINA		
---	Los Angeles Los Angeles	59 515
Michael	Santa Clara Santa Clara	65 520
William*	Yuba Long Bar	72 752
LINAHAN		
C	Tuolumne Springfield	71 373
LINAHIN		
J	Tuolumne Twp 2	71 309
LINAN		
T E	Stanislaus Empire	70 731
LINARD		
Athony	Santa Clara San Jose	65 305
J	Nevada Nevada	61 280
LINAREZ		
Ingacio	San Luis Obispo San Luis Obispo	65 43
LINARIAS		
Jacinta*	Monterey San Juan	601007
LINARIS		
Pedro*	Monterey Pajaro	601015
LINBAUGH		
John	Sonoma Armally	69 516
LINBELL		
Willie*	Yuba Marysville	72 879
LINBERGER		
David	Siskiyou Yreka	69 143
LINBILL		
Willie*	Yuba Marysville	72 879
LINCENTS		
Jane	Calaveras Twp 5	57 206

California 1860 Census Index

Name	County Locale	M653 Roll	Page
LINCH			
Bernard C	Humbolt Pacific	59	131
C E	El Dorado Newtown	58	777
Chas	Sonoma Armally	69	509
D	El Dorado Georgetown	58	700
D	Siskiyou Scott Ri	69	69
David	Sierra Monte Crk	66	1038
F	Tuolumne Jacksonville	71	166
J	Calaveras Twp 9	57	376
J	Calaveras Twp 9	57	389
J	San Francisco San Francisco 5	67	503
J	Tehama Cottonwoood	70	900
J*	Calaveras Twp 9	57	398
Jame	Sierra Grizzly	66	1057
James	Sierra Twp 5	66	937
Jeremiah	Sierra Twp 5	66	867
John	Sierra Downieville	66	1024
John	Sierra La Porte	66	777
John	Sierra Downieville	66	995
L	Calaveras Twp 9	57	389
L	Calaveras Twp 9	57	398
L L	Sacramento Ward 3	63	431
M A	San Joaquin Stockton	64	1094
Margaret	Tehama Tehama	70	941
P	Calaveras Twp 9	57	413
Patk	Klamath Liberty	59	233
Thos	Yolo Cottonwoood	72	647
LINCHAM			
Michael	Santa Clara Santa Clara	65	482
LINCHFIELD			
Frank	Sierra Twp 5	66	919
LINCHOCK			
L*	Sutter Bear Rvr	70	826
LINCHOUME			
---*	Tulara Visalia	71	35
LINCILT			
Paul	Los Angeles Los Angeles	59	515
LINCK			
Geo	Placer Folsom	62	641
LINCLAIR			
Jas*	Sacramento Granite	63	248
Wm H*	Sacramento Ward 1	63	34
LINCLAN			
Jas*	Sacramento Granite	63	248
LINCLON			
I	El Dorado Mud Springs	58	984
LINCO			
---*	Siskiyou Klamath	69	85
LINCOLB			
A K	Mariposa Coulterville	60	680
LINCOLES			
Lewis	Butte Oregon	56	623
LINCOLLN			
Benjamin	Tuolumne Twp 5	71	523
LINCOLM			
Elisha	Yuba Long Bar	72	751
LINCOLN			
A	Tuolumne Twp 2	71	376
A R	Mariposa Coulterville	60	680
Abe	San Francisco San Francisco 4	68	1109
Alfred P	Yuba Marysville	72	876
Augustus	Santa Cruz Santa Cruz	66	626
Aujvertus*	Santa Cruz Santa Cruz	66	626
Barney B	San Francisco San Francisco 7	68	1414
Benjamin	Tuolumne Chinese	71	523
C G	Butte Ophir	56	762
Elisha	Yuba Long Bar	72	751
G W	San Francisco San Francisco 5	67	502
George	Tuolumne Shawsfla	71	392
H C	San Francisco San Francisco 5	67	511
Harriet A	San Francisco San Francisco 8	68	1292
Henry	San Diego San Diego	64	767
Henry	Santa Cruz Santa Cruz	66	633
Ira B	Tuolumne Twp 2	71	350
J M	Sierra Downieville	66	975
Jno	Sacramento Lee	63	215
L H	San Francisco San Francisco 6	67	471
L M	Sacramento Sutter	63	289
Lemuel	Tuolumne Shawsfla	71	376
Lewis	Butte Oregon	56	623
Lucy	Yuba Marysville	72	945
Matilda H	Solano Suisan	69	220
Moses	San Joaquin Oneal	64	912
N	San Joaquin Stockton	64	1090
N	Tuolumne Springfield	71	372
N M	Solano Suisan	69	220
Nathan	Tuolumne Shawsfla	71	376
Wm	San Francisco San Francisco 2	67	567
LINCOLNE			
N	Tuolumne Twp 2	71	372
LINCOLNS			
N C	Tuolumne Columbia	71	363
LINCOMB			
Harriet	Sacramento Granite	63	265
J	Tehama Antelope	70	891
LINCON			
---	El Dorado Kelsey	58	1130

Name	County Locale	M653 Roll	Page
LINCON			
H M	Solano Vacaville	69	333
LINCUROSA			
Maria	Santa Cruz Pajaro	66	530
LIND			
---	Butte Kimshaw	56	588
A L*	Sierra Twp 5	66	943
C	Nevada Eureka	61	377
C J	Santa Clara San Jose	65	393
Charles	Yuba Marysville	72	913
Charles E	San Francisco San Francisco 3	67	56
Frank	San Francisco San Francisco 3	67	69
H	San Francisco San Francisco 5	67	541
Jacob	Sierra Chappare	66	1041
Jane	Yuba Marysville	72	914
Jno	San Francisco San Francisco 10	194	67
John	San Diego Agua Caliente	64	856
John G	San Francisco San Francisco 9	68	1057
John*	San Francisco San Francisco 9	68	1004
Lewis	Tuolumne Twp 2	71	360
M	El Dorado Diamond	58	772
Moses*	Sierra Twp 5	66	928
Na	Mariposa Twp 7	60	553
Wm	Del Norte Happy Ca	58	663
Wm	Santa Clara San Jose	65	385
LINDA			
A T	Yuba Rose Bar	72	791
LINDALL			
S	Butte Hamilton	56	524
W*	Shasta Cottonwoood	66	723
LINDAMANN			
Aaron	Tuolumne Sonora	71	209
LINDAN			
Arnold	San Francisco San Francisco 3	67	42
LINDAY			
A	Amador Twp 2	55	322
Thomas L	Calaveras Twp 8	57	57
LINDDLE			
Robt	El Dorado Kelsey	58	1138
LINDEMAN			
Ben	Amador Twp 7	55	412
Charles	San Francisco San Francisco 11	136 67
J H	Stanislaus Emory	70	739
M	San Francisco San Francisco 2	67	633
Tobias M	San Francisco San Francisco 7	68	1386
LINDEMAR			
Chs	San Francisco San Francisco 6	67	439
LINDEN			
Harry	Alameda Oakland	55	52
N D*	Calaveras Twp 9	57	395
LINDENBERGER			
V	San Francisco San Francisco 6	67	448
LINDER			
---	Sierra Twp 5	66	934
Danl	Santa Clara Redwood	65	450
F E	Marin Tomales	60	715
L B	Yuba North Ea	72	674
Louis	San Francisco San Francisco 7	68	1419
Moses	El Dorado Placerville	58	907
Robert	Klamath Liberty	59	239
Thomas	Calaveras Twp 6	57	135
LINDERHEIM			
Peter	San Francisco San Francisco 2	67	733
LINDERMAN			
---	San Francisco San Francisco 7	68	1374
F L	San Francisco San Francisco 6	67	425
Heinrich	Solano Vallejo	69	276
Heinrick	Solano Vallejo	69	276
John	San Francisco San Francisco 4	68	1217
LINDERS			
Joseph*	Mariposa Twp 3	60	571
LINDEY			
F H	Siskiyou Scott Ri	69	61
Jacob*	Placer Secret R	62	610
LINDFIL			
W	Calaveras Twp 9	57	394
LINDHEIMER			
Meyer	San Francisco San Francisco 2	67	708
LINDIMAR			
Chs*	San Francisco San Francisco 6	67	439
LINDIRNAR			
Chs*	San Francisco San Francisco 6	67	439
LINDLAY			
J H*	Butte Oregon	56	628
LINDLE			
Ennoch	Contra Costa Twp 2	57	580
LINDLER			
William	Los Angeles Los Angeles	59	366
William	Los Angeles Los Angeles	59	36
LINDLEY			
Charles	Yuba Marysville	72	912
Chas	Butte Ophir	56	755
David	San Francisco San Francisco 7	68	1340
J H	Butte Oregon	56	628

Name	County Locale	M653 Roll	Page
LINDLEY			
James	Yuba Marysville	72	909
L	Sacramento Ward 4	63	505
M J	San Francisco San Francisco 5	67	550
Martha J	San Francisco San Francisco 2	67	774
Wm	Butte Kimshaw	56	599
LINDLY			
D N	Siskiyou Scott Va	69	37
LINDMAN			
William	San Francisco San Francisco 9	68	1077
LINDMEN			
Christian	Sierra Twp 5	66	938
LINDMIN			
Christian	Sierra Twp 5	66	938
LINDNER			
J D	Sonoma Armally	69	510
L	San Francisco San Francisco 5	67	475
LINDOLL			
W*	Shasta Cottonwoood	66	723
LINDOLT			
W	Shasta Cottonwoood	66	723
LINDON			
John W	Santa Clara Redwood	65	457
L	Calaveras Twp 9	57	394
LINDOP			
William*	San Francisco San Francisco 9	68	1057
LINDOR			
L	Calaveras Twp 9	57	394
LINDORF			
E	Santa Clara Santa Clara	65	479
LINDROOS			
Gustavus*	Mendocino Arrana	60	863
LINDSAY			
Cornelius	Los Angeles San Gabriel	59	412
Cornelius A	Los Angeles San Gabriel	59	412
E C	Sacramento Sutter	63	299
E P	Colusa Colusi	57	421
James	Tuolumne Twp 3	71	452
John	Alameda Brooklyn	55	83
John J*	Tulara Visalia	71	81
John L	Yuba New York	72	720
John L	Tulara Twp 1	71	81
John M	San Francisco San Francisco 11	98 67
John R	San Francisco San Francisco 11	98 67
Joseph	Placer Secret R	62	610
N	Sutter Nicolaus	70	832
R	Sacramento Ward 1	63	19
Robt	Butte Kimshaw	56	592
Sarah	Placer Secret R	62	610
Wm	Sacramento Cosummes	63	405
Wm	Trinity Trinity	70	973
LINDSEY			
Aese*	Amador Twp 2	55	320
Aise*	Amador Twp 2	55	320
Aisr*	Amador Twp 2	55	320
Alton	Calaveras Twp 5	57	141
Behrem	Shasta Shasta	66	679
C A	Los Angeles Elmonte	59	247
Dugal	San Francisco San Francisco 6	67	685
E W	San Francisco San Francisco 6	67	438
Elizabeth	Sacramento Ward 4	63	509
Finley	Humbolt Union	59	186
Fulton	Santa Clara Alviso	65	415
G	San Francisco San Francisco 5	67	554
Ira	Siskiyou Shasta Rvr	69	115
Isa	Siskiyou Shasta Rvr	69	115
J H	Siskiyou Scott Ri	69	74
J N	Butte Chico	56	546
Jas	Placer Virginia	62	683
Jno	Butte Chico	56	560
John	Alameda Brooklyn	55	213
John L	Yolo New York	72	720
L B	Siskiyou Yreka	69	193
Martha J	San Francisco San Francisco 2	67	774
Mathew	San Francisco San Francisco 10	307 67
Oliver	Santa Clara Redwood	65	452
R	Nevada Eureka	61	349
R S	Nevada Nevada	61	291
Robt	Tuolumne Twp 2	71	281
Susannah	Sonoma Armally	69	501
Thomas	Calaveras Twp 9	57	373
Thos	Butte Chico	56	567
Thos	San Francisco San Francisco 10	263 67
Thos	Sonoma Petaluma	69	579
Tipton	Santa Clara Gilroy	65	244
W K	Sacramento Lee	63	212
LINDSHEY			
L*	Stanislaus Oatvale	70	717
LINDSLEY			
James	Tuolumne Twp 3	71	466
LINDSLY			
Robert	San Francisco San Francisco 3	67	67

Name	County Locale	M653 RollPage
LINDU		
---*	Sierra Twp 5	66 934
LINDUNAR		
Chs*	San Francisco San Francisco 6	67 439
LINDVILD		
R S	San Francisco San Francisco 5	67 525
LINDY		
Charles	Sierra Downieville	661016
Ernest	Mendocino Big Rvr	60 840
Swair*	Sierra Excelsior	661034
Thomas	Yuba Marysville	72 858
Thomas	Yuba Marysville	72 860
LINE		
---	Calaveras Twp 8	57 69
---	El Dorado Salmon Falls	581040
---	El Dorado Coloma	581122
---	Shasta Shasta	66 669
---	Sierra Morristown	661055
Ah	Yolo Merritt	72 580
Julia A	San Francisco San Francisco 7	681430
Thos	San Francisco San Francisco 10	248 67
Yop*	Sacramento Granite	63 258
Yun	El Dorado Greenwood	58 729
LINEAUX		
Montrauth	San Francisco 3	67 7
	San Francisco	
LINEBAUGH		
A	Sonoma Armally	69 517
LINEBERG		
Louis	Tuolumne Twp 1	71 208
LINEGAR		
John	Placer Ophir	62 652
LINEHAN		
John	Solano Fairfield	69 200
LINEM		
Dora T	San Francisco San Francisco 8	681294
LINEN		
James	San Francisco San Francisco 7	681366
Jane	San Francisco San Francisco 4	681117
Joseph	San Bernardino San Bernadino	64 670
Joseph	Solano Benecia	69 316
M	Calaveras Twp 9	57 389
M	Calaveras Twp 9	57 398
LINERLIN		
Augustu S	Santa Cruz Santa Cruz	66 628
LINES		
Elias	El Dorado Georgetown	58 674
Florenza	Monterey Alisal	601038
Michael	Sierra La Porte	66 783
LINET		
Autro P*	Calaveras Twp 9	57 353
LINEVA		
---	San Francisco San Francisco 10	248 67
LINEY		
Peter	Plumas Quincy	62 937
LINEYANA		
Antone	Alameda Brooklyn	55 189
LINF		
---	Calaveras Twp 8	57 106
LINFER		
Frances	El Dorado Mud Springs	58 984
LINFOOTH		
James	San Francisco San Francisco 11	110 67
LINFOROSA		
---	San Bernardino Santa Ba	64 219
LINFORTH		
Alfred	San Francisco San Francisco 7	681409
James	San Francisco San Francisco 8	681248
LING LEE		
---	Mariposa Coulterville	60 697
---	San Joaquin Stockton	641063
LING		
---	Amador Twp 2	55 286
---	Amador Twp 2	55 311
---	Amador Twp 2	55 328
---	Amador Twp 3	55 409
---	Amador Twp 6	55 425
---	Amador Twp 1	55 492
---	Amador Twp 1	55 511
---	Butte Kimshaw	56 569
---	Butte Kimshaw	56 576
---	Butte Eureka	56 653
---	Butte Ophir	56 806
---	Butte Ophir	56 808
---	Butte Ophir	56 809
---	Butte Ophir	56 813
---	Butte Ophir	56 818
---	Calaveras Twp 8	57 106
---	Calaveras Twp 8	57 108
---	Calaveras Twp 8	57 109
---	Calaveras Twp 6	57 149
---	Calaveras Twp 5	57 202
---	Calaveras Twp 5	57 211

Name	County Locale	M653 RollPage
LING		
---	Calaveras Twp 5	57 225
---	Calaveras Twp 4	57 334
---	Calaveras Twp 9	57 358
---	Calaveras Twp 7	57 37
---	Calaveras Twp 7	57 40
---	Calaveras Twp 7	57 41
---	Calaveras Twp 7	57 42
---	Calaveras Twp 7	57 44
---	Calaveras Twp 7	57 45
---	Calaveras Twp 7	57 46
---	Calaveras Twp 8	57 59
---	Calaveras Twp 8	57 60
---	Calaveras Twp 8	57 66
---	Calaveras Twp 8	57 74
---	Calaveras Twp 8	57 75
---	Calaveras Twp 8	57 76
---	Calaveras Twp 8	57 82
---	Calaveras Twp 8	57 87
---	Del Norte Crescent	58 633
---	Del Norte Happy Ca	58 663
---	Del Norte Happy Ca	58 669
---	El Dorado White Oaks	581025
---	El Dorado White Oaks	581032
---	El Dorado White Oaks	581033
---	El Dorado Salmon Falls	581046
---	El Dorado Salmon Falls	581047
---	El Dorado Salmon Falls	581055
---	El Dorado Salmon Falls	581060
---	El Dorado Coloma	581075
---	El Dorado Cold Spring	581101
---	El Dorado Coloma	581105
---	El Dorado Coloma	581107
---	El Dorado Coloma	581111
---	El Dorado Coloma	581120
---	El Dorado Coloma	581122
---	El Dorado Kelsey	581134
---	El Dorado Kelsey	581143
---	El Dorado Kelsey	581144
---	El Dorado Kelsey	581155
---	El Dorado Casumnes	581160
---	El Dorado Casumnes	581161
---	El Dorado Casumnes	581173
---	El Dorado Casumnes	581174
---	El Dorado Casumnes	581176
---	El Dorado Mountain	581178
---	El Dorado Mountain	581187
---	El Dorado Mountain	581188
---	El Dorado Mountain	581189
---	El Dorado Georgetown	58 684
---	El Dorado Georgetown	58 686
---	El Dorado Georgetown	58 691
---	El Dorado Georgetown	58 692
---	El Dorado Greenwood	58 731
---	El Dorado Greenwood	58 732
---	El Dorado Greenwood	58 755
---	El Dorado Diamond	58 774
---	El Dorado Diamond	58 785
---	El Dorado Diamond	58 801
---	El Dorado Diamond	58 806
---	El Dorado Diamond	58 812
---	El Dorado Diamond	58 815
---	El Dorado Diamond	58 816
---	El Dorado Placerville	58 834
---	El Dorado Placerville	58 899
---	El Dorado Placerville	58 905
---	El Dorado Eldorado	58 941
---	El Dorado Eldorado	58 942
---	El Dorado Mud Springs	58 956
---	El Dorado Mud Springs	58 963
---	El Dorado Mud Springs	58 969
---	El Dorado Mud Springs	58 973
---	El Dorado Mud Springs	58 990
---	El Dorado Mud Springs	58 991
---	Fresno Twp 3	59 31
---	Mariposa Twp 3	60 543
---	Mariposa Twp 3	60 545
---	Mariposa Twp 3	60 550
---	Mariposa Twp 3	60 551
---	Mariposa Twp 3	60 561
---	Mariposa Twp 3	60 564
---	Mariposa Twp 3	60 572
---	Mariposa Twp 3	60 588
---	Mariposa Twp 3	60 590
---	Mariposa Twp 3	60 612
---	Mariposa Twp 3	60 621
---	Mariposa Twp 1	60 627
---	Mariposa Twp 1	60 641
---	Mariposa Twp 1	60 653
---	Mariposa Twp 1	60 665
---	Mariposa Coulterville	60 681
---	Mariposa Coulterville	60 684
---	Mariposa Coulterville	60 685
---	Mariposa Coulterville	60 691
---	Mariposa Coulterville	60 698
---	Monterey Monterey	60 959

Name	County Locale	M653 RollPage
LING		
---	Nevada Grass Valley	61 227
---	Nevada Grass Valley	61 228
---	Nevada Grass Valley	61 229
---	Nevada Grass Valley	61 230
---	Nevada Grass Valley	61 232
---	Nevada Grass Valley	61 233
---	Nevada Nevada	61 300
---	Nevada Washington	61 341
---	Nevada Rough &	61 398
---	Nevada Bridgeport	61 460
---	Nevada Bridgeport	61 463
---	Nevada Bridgeport	61 486
---	Nevada Bloomfield	61 521
---	Nevada Bloomfield	61 530
---	Nevada Red Dog	61 541
---	Placer Auburn	62 577
---	Placer Rattle Snake	62 631
---	Placer Rattle Snake	62 635
---	Placer Folsom	62 647
---	Placer Virginia	62 670
---	Placer Virginia	62 671
---	Placer Virginia	62 674
---	Placer Virginia	62 675
---	Placer Virginia	62 678
---	Placer Virginia	62 680
---	Placer Virginia	62 681
---	Placer Virginia	62 686
---	Placer Virginia	62 687
---	Placer Virginia	62 701
---	Placer Illinois	62 739
---	Placer Illinois	62 740
---	Placer Illinois	62 741
---	Placer Illinois	62 749
---	Placer Illinois	62 751
---	Placer Iona Hills	62 893
---	Placer Iona Hills	62 898
---	Sacramento Granite	63 250
---	Sacramento Granite	63 259
---	Sacramento Sutter	63 301
---	Sacramento Sutter	63 307
---	Sacramento Ward 3	63 489
---	Sacramento Ward 1	63 51
---	Sacramento Ward 1	63 53
---	Sacramento Ward 1	63 60
---	Sacramento Ward 1	63 68
---	San Francisco San Francisco 9	681088
---	San Francisco San Francisco 9	681094
---	San Francisco San Francisco 4	681195
---	San Francisco San Francisco 4	681196
---	San Francisco San Francisco 4	681212
---	San Francisco San Francisco 10	314 67
---	San Francisco San Francisco 6	67 470
---	San Joaquin Stockton	641038
---	San Joaquin Stockton	641053
---	Shasta Horsetown	66 704
---	Shasta Horsetown	66 705
---	Shasta Horsetown	66 709
---	Sierra Downieville	661000
---	Sierra Downieville	661003
---	Sierra Downieville	661015
---	Sierra Downieville	661020
---	Sierra Downieville	661024
---	Sierra Morristown	661056
---	Sierra La Porte	66 780
---	Sierra La Porte	66 782
---	Sierra St Louis	66 806
---	Sierra St Louis	66 813
---	Sierra St Louis	66 861
---	Sierra St Louis	66 862
---	Sierra Twp 5	66 926
---	Sierra Twp 5	66 930
---	Sierra Twp 5	66 945
---	Sierra Twp 5	66 948
---	Sierra Cox'S Bar	66 950
---	Sierra Downieville	66 971
---	Sierra Downieville	66 982
---	Sierra Downieville	66 986
---	Sierra Downieville	66 999
---	Stanislaus Buena Village	70 721
---	Stanislaus Emory	70 752
---	Tuolumne Sonora	71 478
---	Tuolumne Sonora	71 485
---	Tuolumne Twp 5	71 503
---	Tuolumne Montezuma	71 507
---	Tuolumne Montezuma	71 509
---	Tuolumne Twp 5	71 514
---	Yolo No E Twp	72 675
---	Yolo No E Twp	72 676
---	Yolo No E Twp	72 677
---	Yolo No E Twp	72 681
---	Yolo No E Twp	72 682
---	Yolo No E Twp	72 684
---	Yolo No E Twp	72 685
---	Yolo Slate Ra	72 707

California 1860 Census Index

Name	County Locale	M653 Roll	Page
LING			
---	Yolo Slate Ra	72	708
---	Yolo Slate Ra	72	710
---	Yolo Slate Ra	72	712
---	Yolo Slate Ra	72	718
---	Yuba Bear Rvr	72	1005
---	Yuba North Ea	72	675
---	Yuba North Ea	72	676
---	Yuba North Ea	72	677
---	Yuba North Ea	72	681
---	Yuba North Ea	72	684
---	Yuba Slate Ro	72	685
---	Yuba North Ea	72	708
---	Yuba Slate Ro	72	710
---	Yuba Slate Ro	72	712
---	Yuba Slate Ro	72	715
---	Yuba New York	72	718
---	Yuba New York	72	719
---	Yuba New York	72	740
---	Yuba Long Bar	72	756
---	Yuba Long Bar	72	757
---	Yuba Long Bar	72	760
---	Yuba Long Bar	72	763
---	Yuba Rose Bar	72	800
---	Yuba Fosters	72	827
---	Yuba Fosters	72	834
---	Yuba Fosters	72	842
---	Yuba Marysville	72	921
---	Yuba Linda	72	990
---*	Calaveras Twp 10	57	235
---*	El Dorado Salmon Falls	58	1064
---*	Fresno Twp 1	59	28
---*	Nevada Nevada	61	300
---*	Nevada Washington	61	341
---*	Placer Auburn	62	570
---*	Sacramento Cosumnes	63	388
---*	Sacramento Cosumnes	63	392
---*	Trinity Trinindad Rvr	70	1048
---*	Yuba Foster B	72	827
---*	Yuba Foster B	72	830
---*	Yuba Foster B	72	834
---*	Yuba Fosters	72	841
---*	Yuba Fosters	72	842
---*	Yuba Fosters	72	843
A	Yuba Slate Ro	72	707
Ah	Amador Twp 4	55	332
Ah	Butte Eureka	56	653
Ah	Butte Cascade	56	692
Ah	Calaveras Twp 7	57	11
Ah	Calaveras Twp 7	57	30
Ah	Calaveras Twp 7	57	32
Ah	Calaveras Twp 7	57	33
Ah	Calaveras Twp 7	57	35
Ah	Tuolumne Twp 4	71	181
Ah*	Butte Oro	56	687
Can	Mariposa Coulterville	60	681
Charles	Siskiyou Callahan	69	9
Chee	Yuba Foster B	72	827
Chee	Yuba Foster B	72	834
Chew	Nevada Little Y	61	533
Chew*	Butte Ophir	56	806
Chey	Butte Ophir	56	807
Ching	Placer Illinois	62	742
Choi	Calaveras Twp 5	57	193
Chom	Yuba Long Bar	72	764
Choon	El Dorado Mud Springs	58	955
Chow	Yuba Long Bar	72	756
Chow*	Sacramento Ward 1	63	52
Choy	Butte Ophir	56	810
Choy	Butte Ophir	56	818
Chum	Placer Dutch Fl	62	737
Due	Yuba Long Bar	72	770
Fey	Butte Ophir	56	810
Fong	San Francisco San Francisco 5	67	509
Foo	Butte Ophir	56	810
Foo	Placer Illinois	62	751
Foo	Yuba Long Bar	72	765
Foy	Butte Ophir	56	808
Fun*	Butte Ophir	56	810
Fup	Nevada Grass Valley	61	231
Gay	Butte Mountain	56	742
Gee	Mariposa Coulterville	60	682
George W*	Plumas Quincy	62	936
Gon	Nevada Grass Valley	61	230
H	Mariposa Twp 3	60	622
He	Mariposa Coulterville	60	681
Heck	Sierra Twp 5	66	932
Hee	Yuba Foster B	72	827
Henry S	Butte Ophir	56	754
Hing	San Francisco San Francisco 5	67	508
Hong	Mariposa Twp 3	60	543
Hong	Yuba Fosters	72	830
Hop	Butte Bidwell	56	719
Hop	Butte Ophir	56	787
Hop	Butte Ophir	56	809
Hy	El Dorado Greenwood	58	730
LING			
I	Mariposa Twp 3	60	551
John	Placer Iona Hills	62	890
John*	Sacramento Cosumnes	63	396
John*	Yuba Slate Ro	72	707
John*	Yuba Slate Ro	72	708
Ke	Mariposa Coulterville	60	681
Kee	Butte Ophir	56	803
King	Yuba Long Bar	72	755
Kye	Butte Ophir	56	813
Lan*	Mariposa Twp 3	60	608
Lee	Butte Bidwell	56	725
Lee	Butte Ophir	56	772
Lee	Mariposa Coulterville	60	697
Lew	Butte Ophir	56	808
Ley	Butte Ophir	56	806
Ling	Yuba Long Bar	72	756
Lip	Butte Ophir	56	811
Loo	Yuba Long Bar	72	757
Loo	Yuba Parks Ba	72	775
Louie	Calaveras Twp 4	57	308
Lu	Sacramento Granite	63	259
Lui	Tuolumne Twp 4	71	181
Ly	El Dorado Greenwood	58	714
Mong	El Dorado Mud Springs	58	962
Nye	El Dorado Diamond	58	784
Pang	Yuba Long Bar	72	758
Peng	Yuba Long Bar	72	763
Pong	Yuba Long Bar	72	763
Sam	Butte Oregon	56	625
Sam	Butte Oregon	56	642
Sam*	Nevada Washington	61	341
Sam*	Yuba Long Bar	72	755
San*	Mariposa Twp 3	60	613
Sang	Nevada Nevada	61	303
Saum	Butte Bidwell	56	720
Sigh	Butte Ophir	56	814
Sighs	Butte Ophir	56	810
Sing	Butte Ophir	56	750
Sing	Butte Ophir	56	814
Sing	Sacramento Ward 1	63	37
Soo	Amador Twp 2	55	294
Sow	Butte Ophir	56	779
Sun*	Mariposa Twp 3	60	607
Sye	Butte Mountain	56	741
T W	Butte Chico	56	564
Tam	Yuba Long Bar	72	760
Tim	Butte Bidwell	56	725
Titen	Shasta Millvill	66	742
Titin	Shasta Millvill	66	742
Tom*	Yuba Long Bar	72	753
Ton	El Dorado Mud Springs	58	974
Ton	Yuba Long Bar	72	756
Ton Chu	Yuba Long Bar	72	764
Tong	El Dorado Big Bar	58	738
Tong	Sacramento Cosumnes	63	384
Tow	Yuba Long Bar	72	764
Towe	El Dorado Mud Springs	58	950
Tye	Butte Ophir	56	808
Tyr*	Butte Ophir	56	809
Wa	Sacramento Ward 1	63	66
Waw	Placer Auburn	62	581
Ye	El Dorado Mud Springs	58	961
Yong	Yuba Long Bar	72	756
Yong	Yuba Parks Ba	72	775
LINGAFELT			
J P	Del Norte Happy Ca	58	669
LINGANE			
Hannah	San Francisco San Francisco 10		222
		67	
LINGDON			
Joseph	Yuba New York	72	741
LINGEE			
	Fresno Twp 2	59	17
LINGERFETTER			
Rufus	Calaveras Twp 4	57	341
LINGES			
Andrew	Mariposa Twp 3	60	560
LINGHAMER			
Geo*	Sacramento Ward 4	63	604
LINGHARNER			
Geo*	Sacramento Ward 4	63	604
LINGHSY			
Jesse*	Siskiyou Scott Va	69	55
LINGHUEST			
Peter*	Mariposa Coulterville	60	694
LINGHURST			
Peter*	Mariposa Coulterville	60	694
LINGINBETTER			
John	Sierra Downieville	66	1030
LINGLEY			
Geo H*	Humbolt Table Bl	59	140
J	Siskiyou Scott Ri	69	81
Nicholas*	Humbolt Pacific	59	129
LINGMAN			
Jno*	Sacramento Ward 3	63	443
LINGO			
Geo W*	Sacramento Alabama	63	411
LINGON			
Margaret	Santa Clara San Jose	65	296
LINGSLEY			
J	Siskiyou Scott Ri	69	81
LINGSTON			
Francis	San Francisco San Francisco 1	68	910
LINGTEY			
Mychael*	Mariposa Twp 3	60	563
LINGTON			
Antonia	Mariposa Twp 3	60	556
John	Placer Goods	62	693
LINGUM			
Francois	San Francisco San Francisco 2	67	795
LINGUNE			
A*	San Francisco San Francisco 2	67	678
LINHARDT			
Michael	Yuba Marysville	72	926
LINHILL			
Willie	Yuba Marysville	72	879
LINHOFF			
Augustus*	Placer Iona Hills	62	870
LINHOLN			
Frederick	Alameda Brooklyn	55	102
LINHOLT			
Nes	Alameda Brooklyn	55	140
LINICH			
John	El Dorado White Oaks	58	1019
LINIDON			
Joseph*	Calaveras Twp 9	57	399
LINIDOR			
Joseph*	Calaveras Twp 9	57	399
LINIELL			
William	El Dorado Mud Springs	58	989
LINIEY			
David	Nevada Bridgeport	61	495
LINIKEN			
Ira W	San Francisco San Francisco 8	68	1298
LININGSTON			
Frank	San Francisco San Francisco 1	68	909
LINIS			
W A	Placer Forest H	62	802
LINISER			
Joseph*	Calaveras Twp 9	57	399
LINISOR			
Joseph*	Calaveras Twp 9	57	399
LINITH			
L*	El Dorado Newtown	58	779
LINIWICK			
George	Placer Iona Hills	62	867
LINK			
---	Sierra Downieville	66	1015
---*	Tulara Twp 2	71	4
Abram	Sacramento Granite	63	265
Alevan	Sacramento Granite	63	265
Chris	San Francisco San Francisco 10		299
		67	
Henry	Placer Michigan	62	852
Jacob	San Francisco San Francisco 2	67	571
Joseph N	Tuolumne Twp 5	71	518
Paul	Marin Cortemad	60	792
T	Calaveras Twp 9	57	418
T D	Yolo Cache	72	625
Valentine	San Francisco San Francisco 7	68	1407
LINKA			
Harmon*	Santa Clara San Jose	65	288
LINKAY			
---*	Tulara Visalia	71	4
LINKE			
---*	Tulara Visalia	71	4
LINKIN			
Wm F	Monterey Pajaro	60	1025
Wm L	Monterey Pajaro	60	1025
LINKINS			
Martha	Santa Clara San Jose	65	346
LINKLEY			
Patrick	Placer Rattle Snake	62	604
LINKS			
Daniel A	Siskiyou Yreka	69	144
LINL			
Eugent*	Yuba New York	72	725
LINLD			
J*	Calaveras Twp 9	57	392
LINLEY			
Eli H*	Humbolt Eel Rvr	59	147
Geo	San Joaquin O'Neal	64	1001
Levi*	Humbolt Eel Rvr	59	153
LINN			
---	Butte Kimshaw	56	588
---	Butte Eureka	56	651
---	Butte Cascade	56	692
---	Butte Ophir	56	812
---	Calaveras Twp 6	57	136
---	Calaveras Twp 4	57	328

Name	County Locale	M653 Roll	Page
LINN			
---	Calaveras Twp 9	57	352
---	Fresno Twp 2	59	18
---	Mariposa Twp 3	60	621
---	Sacramento Ward 4	63	563
---	Sierra St Louis	66	816
---	Sierra Cox'S Bar	66	951
---	Tuolumne Montezuma	71	507
---	Yolo No E Twp	72	677
---	Yolo No E Twp	72	682
---	Yuba North Ea	72	677
---	Yuba Long Bar	72	757
---	Yuba Long Bar	72	759
---*	Mariposa Twp 3	60	614
Ah	Butte Cascade	56	692
Bery	Butte Ophir	56	774
Ca*	Calaveras Twp 9	57	368
D R	Sacramento Ward 1	63	103
Frank	Sacramento Ward 1	63	146
Franklin	San Francisco San Francisco 9	68	1097
Hoh	Butte Ophir	56	806
J	Marin San Rafael	60	770
J	San Francisco San Francisco 1	68	923
J B	Amador Twp 1	55	488
J S	Nevada Nevada	61	261
Jacob	Sacramento Ward 1	63	88
James	Placer Todds Va	62	790
James	Sierra Pine Grove	66	820
John	Butte Ophir	56	749
John	San Francisco San Francisco 3	67	70
John	Yuba Rose Bar	72	802
Lee	Butte Ophir	56	815
Lewis	El Dorado Mountain	58	1186
O H	Placer Dutch Fl	62	719
Peter M*	San Francisco San Francisco 9	68	1084
Sing	Mariposa Twp 3	60	607
Tong	Yuba Long Bar	72	759
Walter C*	Fresno Twp 3	59	8
Yon	Fresno Twp 1	59	27
LINNARD			
Robt*	San Francisco San Francisco 9	68	1046
LINNBURG			
A R	Placer Yankee J	62	757
LINNCHAN			
Patrick	Calaveras Twp 4	57	312
LINNE			
Bob	Nevada Nevada	61	240
LINNEN			
Ann*	San Francisco San Francisco 9	68	985
Edward	Tuolumne Shawsfla	71	419
LINNET			
John*	Calaveras Twp 5	57	172
LINNEY			
Edwin S	Yuba Bear Rvr	72	1004
M G	Shasta Horsetown	66	690
LINNI			
Duvemi*	San Francisco San Francisco 2	67	697
LINNS			
Jno	Sonoma Petaluma	69	598
LINNY			
Anthony	Placer Secret R	62	619
LINNZ			
Jno	Sonoma Petaluma	69	598
LINO			
---	Sierra Downieville	66	1005
---*	Los Angeles Los Angeles	59	392
Pedro	Santa Clara San Jose	65	288
LINOLN			
A F	Tuolumne Twp 1	71	223
LINOT			
Antro P*	Calaveras Twp 9	57	353
LINRISON			
Leon	Calaveras Twp 5	57	201
LINRLGER			
---	El Dorado Greenwood	58	729
LINRY			
John*	Sierra Downieville	66	977
LINS			
Edward*	Nevada Bridgeport	61	490
Gabriel	Yuba Marysville	72	900
LINSAN			
Luce	Sonoma Sonoma	69	649
LINSAY			
Robt	Klamath S Fork	59	202
LINSCOLT			
John*	Plumas Quincy	62	953
LINSCOTT			
John*	Plumas Quincy	62	953
Thos S	Del Norte Happy Ca	58	661
LINSDER			
Jacob	Yolo Putah	72	545
LINSEY			
C B	Butte Ophir	56	800
David	Nevada Bridgeport	61	495
E	Marin Tomales	60	776
E	Tuolumne Twp 4	71	162
LINSEY			
J	El Dorado Kelsey	58	1148
Jacob*	Placer Secret R	62	610
Jas	Butte Ophir	56	823
William	Placer Forest H	62	802
LINSIDER			
Jacob*	Yolo Putah	72	546
LINSLEY			
Chas	Nevada Bridgeport	61	496
E C	Tehama Red Bluff	70	916
John	Butte Ophir	56	785
LINSMAN			
Dan	Klamath Liberty	59	237
LINSOTT			
Willard	Nevada Bloomfield	61	512
William	Nevada Bloomfield	61	512
LINSTALL			
P F	Tuolumne Columbia	71	289
LINSTED			
Fredk	San Francisco San Francisco 2	67	717
LINSTON			
William	Solano Benecia	69	317
LINSY			
Henry M	San Bernardino San Bernadino	64	684
Wm	San Bernardino S Timate	64	689
LINT			
Linner	San Francisco San Francisco 4	68	1121
Richard*	Mendocino Round Va	60	879
LINTALA			
Antone*	Nevada Rough &	61	436
LINTELL			
John	Yolo Putah	72	598
LINTEN			
John	Siskiyou Yreka	69	125
Robert	Siskiyou Yreka	69	125
LINTHAL			
Henry	San Francisco San Francisco 7	68	1420
LINTJNENS			
John D*	El Dorado Coloma	58	1112
LINTOCK			
George M*	Sierra Scales D	66	803
LINTON			
C B*	Sacramento American	63	172
Edmund	Plumas Quincy	62	924
Jno P	Sacramento Ward 3	63	434
M	Sacramento Franklin	63	323
P L	Trinity Mouth Ca	70	1016
Robert	El Dorado Placerville	58	912
Robert	Siskiyou Yreka	69	125
W J	Sacramento Franklin	63	323
Z S	Trinity Mouth Ca	70	1016
LINTONS			
J	Tuolumne Twp 4	71	174
LINTOOD			
Charles	Yuba Rose Bar	72	814
LINTRAD			
Hiram	Butte Cascade	56	703
LINTROP			
Chas	San Francisco San Francisco 1	68	829
LINTUAR			
James	Calaveras Twp 8	57	102
LINTY			
---	Shasta Shasta	66	670
Daniel	Tuolumne Twp 2	71	407
LINTYNENS			
John D*	El Dorado Coloma	58	1112
LINTZ			
Daniel	Tuolumne Shawsfla	71	407
Felise	Tuolumne Twp 2	71	330
Felix	Tuolumne Columbia	71	330
LINUAS			
Boiknill*	El Dorado Georgetown	58	751
LINULE			
Sylicie	Calaveras Twp 6	57	123
LINUS			
J	Tuolumne Twp 4	71	174
LINVILLE			
Abram H	Sonoma Santa Rosa	69	407
Allen	Del Norte Crescent	58	635
Bysom	Sonoma Santa Rosa	69	395
Josephine	Sonoma Santa Rosa	69	408
Sylvester H	Siskiyou Yreka	69	126
LINX			
Jose*	Tulara Twp 3	71	68
LINY			
---	Calaveras Twp 5	57	211
---	Yuba North Ea	72	682
---*	Yuba Foster B	72	834
Choi	Calaveras Twp 5	57	193
H	Mariposa Twp 3	60	622
LINYON			
William	Tuolumne Twp 2	71	281
LINZERMAN			
Christian	Humbolt Bucksport	59	161
LINZEY			
Thos	Alameda Brooklyn	55	150
LIO			
---	El Dorado Salmon Falls	58	1062
---	El Dorado Placerville	58	842
---	Sierra Downieville	66	999
LIOMLIN			
W*	Yolo Putah	72	553
LION			
---	Calaveras Twp 9	57	375
---	Fresno Twp 1	59	26
---	Sierra Downieville	66	993
Antonia	Mariposa Twp 1	60	654
Antonio	Mariposa Twp 1	60	654
Ascincion	San Francisco San Francisco 4	68	1157
C	Butte Eureka	56	646
H	Trinity Weaverville	70	1080
Jose	Contra Costa Twp 1	57	513
Juano	Monterey Alisal	60	1029
Nicolas	Santa Clara Almaden	65	277
S	Tuolumne Columbia	71	328
Santos	San Bernardino Santa Ba	64	212
W F	El Dorado Kelsey	58	1147
Wy	El Dorado Greenwood	58	714
LIONA			
J	El Dorado Diamond	58	801
LIONARD			
Thos	San Francisco San Francisco 10	67	303
LIONBERGER			
David	Siskiyou Yreka	69	143
LIONIS			
Juan	San Bernardino S Buenav	64	221
LIONS			
A	Sonoma Cloverdale	69	682
Wm	Sierra Twp 5	66	948
LIOR			
A Cirs*	Calaveras Twp 9	57	394
LIOY			
---	San Francisco San Francisco 4	68	1189
Ko	San Francisco San Francisco 4	68	1208
LIP			
---	Butte Oregon	56	614
---	Calaveras Twp 4	57	305
---	El Dorado Diamond	58	801
---	Placer Auburn	62	582
---	Sacramento Mississipi	63	190
---	San Francisco San Francisco 4	68	1173
---*	Sacramento Mississipi	63	190
Cen	Butte Ophir	56	809
Con	Butte Ophir	56	810
Kin	El Dorado Placerville	58	829
Mir	Calaveras Twp 4	57	313
Nim	Calaveras Twp 4	57	313
Paw	Sacramento Mississipi	63	190
Yan	Yuba Long Bar	72	763
Yea	Placer Auburn	62	581
LIPATINE			
Isaac*	Marin Cortemad	60	792
LIPE			
---	Sierra Downieville	66	1008
Antonio	Santa Clara Santa Clara	65	516
LIPENCOTT			
J	Yolo Cache Crk	72	610
W	Yolo Cache Crk	72	618
LIPERRVIA			
B*	San Francisco San Francisco 4	68	1222
LIPHMAR			
L	Mariposa Twp 3	60	586
LIPINAN			
Solomon*	Sacramento Ward 1	63	119
LIPINCOTT			
W	Yolo Cache	72	618
LIPKAN			
---	Shasta Shasta	66	669
LIPKERMAN			
Richard	Calaveras Twp 4	57	308
LIPLUYZER			
Augustus	San Francisco San Francisco 8	68	1286
LIPLUYZU			
Augustus	San Francisco San Francisco 8	68	1286
LIPMAN			
---	San Francisco San Francisco 2	67	639
H	San Francisco San Francisco 2	67	707
Isaac	San Francisco San Francisco 8	68	1269
Solomon	Sacramento Ward 1	63	119
LIPMANN			
Philip	San Francisco San Francisco 10	67	168
LIPPENAR			
L*	Mariposa Twp 3	60	586
LIPPENARD			
Joseph	San Francisco San Francisco 4	68	1134
LIPPENCOTT			
Benjo	Calaveras Twp 6	57	127
LIPPERT			
Geo	Santa Clara Santa Clara	65	485
Wm	Colusa Butte Crk	57	464

California 1860 Census Index

Name	County Locale	M653 RollPage
LIPPINCOTT		
B R	San Joaquin Stockton	641032
LIPPIT		
Caroline	San Francisco San Francisco 8	681249
Geo	Butte Bidwell	56 719
LIPPMAN		
L	Mariposa Twp 3	60 586
LIPPMAR		
L*	Mariposa Twp 3	60 586
LIPPTRAP		
Thos*	Sacramento Ward 3	63 468
LIPPTRASS		
Thos*	Sacramento Ward 3	63 468
LIPROCH		
Barnard	San Francisco San Francisco 4	681172
LIPSANNAN		
Richard*	Calaveras Twp 4	57 308
LIPSCOMB		
A	Calaveras Twp 9	57 389
A	Calaveras Twp 9	57 398
LIPSCOMBE		
John	Plumas Quincy	62 974
LIPSETT		
Alexander*	Placer Auburn	62 560
LIPSITT		
Alexander*	Placer Auburn	62 560
LIPSKY		
Fredk*	San Francisco San Francisco 2 67	640
M	Amador Twp 2	55 302
LIPSTINE		
Isaac	Marin Cortemad	60 792
LIPURVIA		
B	San Francisco San Francisco 4	681222
LIQUIRS		
Geronimo*	Los Angeles Los Angeles	59 500
LIQUOR		
S	San Francisco San Francisco 4	681228
LIR		
---	Butte Kimshaw	56 584
---	Mariposa Twp 1	60 650
---	Sacramento Granite	63 250
LIRAS		
Jose	San Bernardino Santa Ba	64 212
LIRBY		
Benjamin	San Joaquin Elkhorn	64 968
LIRCE		
Jirah*	Marin S Antoni	60 706
Wm*	Nevada Eureka	61 363
LIRE		
Richard	Solano Suisan	69 230
LIREVA		
---	San Francisco San Francisco 10	248 67
LIRGESIVESLIG		
Fredk	San Francisco San Francisco 3 67	66
LIRGHTON		
Geo W	Merced Twp 1	60 907
LIRLES		
Lewis J	Calaveras Twp 4	57 326
LIRMETTE		
M*	San Francisco San Francisco 3 67	20
LIRNEBY		
Chas	Butte Bidwell	56 721
LIRNILY		
Chas	Butte Bidwell	56 721
LIRON		
John*	Yuba Rose Bar	72 802
LIRONA		
Itaren*	Shasta Shasta	66 682
LIRSTOOD		
Charles*	Yuba Rose Bar	72 814
LIRTALA		
Antone*	Nevada Rough &	61 436
LIRTSAN		
James*	El Dorado Georgetown	58 760
LIRULO		
---*	Napa Napa	61 85
LIRY		
---	Amador Twp 2	55 302
Mi	Amador Twp 5	55 366
LIS		
---	Butte Cascade	56 701
---	Calaveras Twp 4	57 307
---	Sierra Twp 5	66 945
Ah	Butte Cascade	56 701
Lomes	Yolo Slate Ra	72 688
LISALDA		
Francisco	Santa Barbara San Bernardino	64 197
Maria	San Bernardino Santa Barbara	64 166
LISALDRO		
Inariano	San Bernardino San Bernadino	64 685
LISBON		
F	San Francisco San Francisco 6 67	433
LISCH		
M	Calaveras Twp 9	57 411

Name	County Locale	M653 RollPage
LISCOMB		
Charles	Humbolt Union	59 186
Chas*	San Francisco San Francisco 3 67	86
LISCUBERG		
S	Tehama Red Bluff	70 924
LISDAL		
James V	Santa Clara San Jose	65 331
Thos R	Calaveras Twp 9	57 353
LISDALE		
Isaac	San Joaquin Stockton	641079
Wm	Tuolumne Twp 4	71 135
LISDORE		
Johm	Santa Cruz Soguel	66 595
LISENA		
Napaleon*	Calaveras Twp 6	57 160
LISENER		
Napaleon*	Calaveras Twp 6	57 160
LISER		
Jacob	Amador Twp 1	55 461
LISEWA		
Napaleon*	Calaveras Twp 6	57 160
LISGENS		
M L	San Joaquin Stockton	641095
LISH		
Everett	Santa Cruz Pajaro	66 562
He	El Dorado Mud Springs	58 955
Wm H	San Francisco San Francisco 7	681330
LISHOUR		
Geo	Sacramento Ward 4	63 511
LISINBERG		
P	El Dorado Diamond	58 764
LISK		
Emelin	Tuolumne Sonora	71 231
Emilie	Tuolumne Twp 1	71 231
L A	Butte Chico	56 536
Mary	Monterey Alisal	601030
Myron	Monterey Alisal	601030
LISKE		
E E	Sacramento Ward 1	63 81
W H*	Yolo Cache	72 633
LISLE		
J G	Yolo Cottonwoood	72 652
Michael	Humbolt Eel Rvr	59 147
LISLES		
H H	Trinity Lewiston	70 957
LISLIE		
Henry	Placer Michigan	62 855
William	El Dorado Kelsey	581127
LISLIN		
Joseph*	Yuba Slate Ro	72 698
LISNER		
M	Yolo Slate Ra	72 702
LISON		
Albert W	Placer Secret R	62 620
Nicholas	Tuolumne Columbia	71 364
LISONE		
Stephen	Siskiyou Scott Va	69 22
LISROG		
J	San Francisco San Francisco 2 67	788
LISS		
Nim	Calaveras Twp 4	57 313
William F*	El Dorado Placerville	58 910
LISSAK		
Adolphus	San Francisco San Francisco 10	240 67
LISSAKPE		
A H	Santa Clara San Jose	65 283
LISSEN		
Joseph	Nevada Bloomfield	61 509
LISSKAN		
---	Shasta Shasta	66 669
LISSMAN		
---	San Francisco San Francisco 2 67	639
H	San Francisco San Francisco 2 67	707
LISSNER		
Louis*	San Francisco San Francisco 7	681356
M	Yuba Slate Ro	72 702
LIST		
Geo	Santa Clara Redwood	65 454
Myron	Monterey Alisal	601030
LISTER		
Martin	Placer Yankee J	62 756
W	San Francisco San Francisco 10	194 67
LISTON		
John T	San Mateo Twp 1	65 69
LISTONE		
David	Sierra Eureka	661043
LISTRADE		
Paul	San Francisco San Francisco 2 67	796
LISUM		
M B	Butte Ophir	56 746
LISVIN		
John	Tuolumne Sonora	71 187
LIT		
---	Calaveras Twp 4	57 307

Name	County Locale	M653 RollPage
LIT		
---	El Dorado White Oaks	581024
---	El Dorado White Oaks	581032
---	El Dorado White Oaks	581033
---	El Dorado Union	581089
---	El Dorado Casumnes	581160
---	El Dorado Georgetown	58 693
---	El Dorado Diamond	58 795
---	El Dorado Eldorado	58 939
---	El Dorado Eldorado	58 944
---	San Francisco San Francisco 9	681088
---	San Francisco San Francisco 4	681174
John	Tuolumne Twp 2	71 373
LITA		
Ah	Butte Oregon	56 636
LITARNER		
---	Mariposa Twp 1	60 655
LITCH		
C	Shasta Shasta	66 657
Frank	Shasta Shasta	66 657
James*	Monterey San Juan	601009
Mary	Sacramento Ward 4	63 529
LITCHENBERGER		
Geo	Amador Twp 7	55 412
LITCHER		
W L	Santa Clara San Jose	65 334
LITCHFIELD		
C A	Solano Montezuma	69 373
H	Butte Kimshaw	56 589
H	Nevada Eureka	61 387
James	Contra Costa Twp 2	57 560
M	Nevada Eureka	61 387
Miles	Shasta Horsetown	66 709
O A	Solano Montezuma	69 373
W D	San Francisco San Francisco 3 67	80
LITDER		
B	El Dorado Diamond	58 786
LITE		
---	Butte Oregon	56 631
---	Butte Oregon	56 636
Ah	Butte Oregon	56 631
Eli	Siskiyou Klamath	69 86
LITEDTNER		
Hans C	Yuba Marysville	72 924
LITEHOLD		
Michl	Butte Oregon	56 634
LITEKUTTER		
William*	Siskiyou Yreka	69 140
LITERMANIA		
David	Santa Clara Fremont	65 431
LITHGOW		
E	Amador Twp 2	55 277
LITHUS		
Silas W	Tehama Lassen	70 863
LITKER		
Jacob	Siskiyou Klamath	69 85
LITKES		
Jacob	Siskiyou Klamath	69 85
LITKUTTER		
William	Siskiyou Yreka	69 140
LITLE SAM		
---	Tulara Twp 2	71 31
LITMAN		
E H	San Francisco San Francisco 3 67	84
LITNER		
S N	Yolo Putah	72 552
LITNES		
Jas	Amador Twp 3	55 387
LITOCK		
August*	Placer Iona Hills	62 894
LITON		
Jose	Tuolumne Shawsfla	71 375
LITORT		
Constant	Tuolumne Sonora	71 241
Coustant	Tuolumne Twp 1	71 241
LITRONE		
Felix	Tuolumne Twp 2	71 336
LITRONS		
Felix*	Tuolumne Columbia	71 336
LITRY		
Fred*	Mariposa Twp 3	60 611
LITT		
Thomas	Marin Novato	60 739
LITTAKER		
P P	Butte Mountain	56 739
LITTDSAY		
Thomas	San Joaquin Castoria	64 903
LITTEL ANDRES		
---	Tulara Twp 1	71 119
LITTEL		
Ernst*	San Francisco San Francisco 7	681396
LITTEN		
Arthur	El Dorado White Oaks	581018
T B*	Siskiyou Scott Ri	69 63
LITTER		
H	Santa Clara Redwood	65 450

Name	County Locale	M653 Roll	Page
LITTERAL			
E G	Shasta Millvill	66	752
LITTICK			
John	Sierra Pine Grove	66	822
LITTLE ANDRES			
---	Tulara Twp 1	71	119
LITTLE BLACK			
---	Tulara Twp 1	71	120
LITTLE CHARLEY			
---	Tulara Twp 1	71	116
LITTLE EYE			
---	Tulara Twp 2	71	34
LITTLE FINNEY			
---	Tulara Twp 2	71	38
LITTLE JACK			
---	Tulara Twp 2	71	38
LITTLE JAKE			
---	Tulara Twp 2	71	36
LITTLE JIMMY			
---*	Tulara Visalia	71	38
LITTLE JOE			
---	Tulara Twp 1	71	115
---	Tulara Twp 2	71	31
LITTLE JOHN			
---	Tulara Twp 2	71	35
David	Santa Cruz Soguel	66	589
LITTLE SAM			
---	Tulara Twp 2	71	34
---*	Tulara Yule Rvr	71	31
---*	Tulara Visalia	71	34
LITTLE TOOTH			
---	Tulara Twp 2	71	40
LITTLE			
A	El Dorado Placerville	58	931
A	Sacramento Ward 1	63	18
A*	San Joaquin Stockton	641091	
Allen T	San Joaquin Oneal	64	930
Archibald	San Francisco San Francisco 9	681037	
B	Napa Napa	61	56
C	El Dorado Diamond	58	813
Chester	Sierra Twp 5	66	928
Clara	Sacramento Ward 1	63	67
D	San Mateo Twp 2	65	123
D M	Nevada Grass Valley	61	211
D Mrs	San Francisco San Francisco 2	67	775
Daniel	Santa Cruz Pajaro	66	559
David*	Mariposa Coulterville	60	686
E	Nevada Grass Valley	61	165
E M	Yolo Washington	72	568
Eye*	Tulara Visalia	71	34
Francis	San Francisco San Francisco 10	333 67	
Francis	Sierra St Louis	66	816
Francis W	San Francisco San Francisco 11	148 67	
G	Nevada Grass Valley	61	214
Geo	Amador Twp 2	55	266
Geo	Nevada Grass Valley	61	170
H	El Dorado Diamond	58	792
H	Santa Clara San Jose	65	351
H G	Sacramento Natonia	63	279
H O	Monterey Monterey	60	964
H S	Shasta Millvill	66	754
Hartwell	Sonoma Armally	69	516
Henry	Santa Clara Santa Clara	65	520
J	Nevada Grass Valley	61	173
J	Siskiyou Scott Va	69	46
Jackson	El Dorado Grizzly	581179	
James	Alameda Oakland	55	48
James	Calaveras Twp 7	57	40
James	Yolo Slate Ra	72	706
James	Yuba Slate Ro	72	706
Jas	San Francisco San Francisco 12	388 67	
Jas H	Amador Twp 2	55	261
Jas O	Santa Clara Redwood	65	445
John	Calaveras Twp 8	57	108
John	Calaveras Twp 7	57	29
John	El Dorado Kelsey	581145	
John	El Dorado Kelsey	581151	
John	Placer Sacramento	62	646
John	Sacramento Ward 1	63	111
John	San Francisco San Francisco 10	312 67	
John	San Francisco San Francisco 1	68	901
John	San Mateo Twp 3	65	101
John	San Mateo Twp 3	65	109
John	Solano Fremont	69	383
John P	Nevada Rough &	61	404
Jone	Mariposa Twp 3	60	566
Katy	Butte Cascade	56	689
Kema*	Mendocino Round Va	60	883
L H	Yuba New York	72	743
Lewis	Merced Monterey	60	944
Lewis	Monterey Monterey	60	944
Lorenzo	Tuolumne Twp 5	71	497

Name	County Locale	M653 Roll	Page
LITTLE			
Lydia F*	Trinity Weaverville	701071	
M	Sacramento Sutter	63	304
M J	Amador Twp 1	55	493
M J	Tehama Lassen	70	876
M K	El Dorado Big Bar	58	739
Milton	Monterey Monterey	60	927
Mrs	Sacramento Ward 3	63	483
N S	Shasta Millvill	66	754
P	Shasta Shasta	66	728
R A	Marin Novato	60	738
Robert	Solano Vacaville	69	326
Robert McDow	Solano Fremont	69	384
Robt E	San Francisco San Francisco 1	68	902
Saml	Amador Twp 2	55	282
Samuel	Los Angeles Elmonte	59	268
Sanford	Calaveras Twp 6	57	182
Stephen	Solano Fremont	69	382
Thos	Amador Twp 2	55	276
Thos C	San Francisco San Francisco 1	68	862
W A	El Dorado Mud Springs	58	980
William	Nevada Little Y	61	533
William	Siskiyou Shasta Rvr	69	117
William J	Contra Costa Twp 2	57	556
Wm	Trinity Weaverville	701071	
Wm B	San Francisco San Francisco 10	314 67	
LITTLEFIELD			
? B	Butte Oregon	56	628
A	El Dorado Greenwood	58	725
A F	Sierra Twp 5	66	929
Abbot	El Dorado Greenwood	58	726
Avery	Tuolumne Columbia	71	341
Bench	Nevada Bridgeport	61	469
Charles	Sierra Twp 7	66	892
Chas	San Francisco San Francisco 1	68	837
Chas	Santa Clara San Jose	65	343
Dan C	Yuba Marysville	72	908
David L*	Calaveras Twp 6	57	159
David S	Calaveras Twp 6	57	159
Frank O	San Francisco San Francisco 1	68	838
J	Butte Eureka	56	653
J	El Dorado Placerville	58	855
James	Solano Benecia	69	292
Jno	Sacramento Ward 4	63	524
Jno W	San Francisco San Francisco 10	237 67	
John	Tuolumne Columbia	71	327
John M	Santa Clara San Jose	65	320
Joshua A	Contra Costa Twp 3	57	611
Lambert	Amador Twp 4	55	246
Lange	Sierra Downieville	66	956
M L	Butte Oro	56	688
M S	Butte Oro	56	688
N B*	Butte Oregon	56	628
Robeert C*	San Joaquin Elkhorn	64	999
Rufus	Calaveras Twp 6	57	159
Rufus Jr	Calaveras Twp 6	57	159
Saml	Sierra Downieville	66	956
Samuel	Siskiyou Yreka	69	129
Samul	Siskiyou Yreka	69	129
Sheldon	Sierra Twp 5	66	920
Stephen	Amador Twp 1	55	475
Thos P	Sacramento Ward 3	63	451
W B	Butte Oregon	56	628
W B	Butte Bidwell	56	715
Wm	Sierra Morristown	661052	
LITTLEFORD			
John F	San Francisco San Francisco 7	681386	
LITTLEHALE			
Jams	San Joaquin Stockton	641037	
LITTLEJOHN			
Abram	Calaveras Twp 4	57	302
David	Santa Cruz Soguel	66	589
J	Sutter Yuba	70	768
James	Yuba Marysville	72	965
William	San Mateo Twp 3	65	89
LITTLEJOHNS			
John	San Mateo Twp 1	65	57
John	Siskiyou Yreka	69	124
LITTLEKEMA			
---*	Mendocino Round Va	60	883
LITTLEPEEDO			
Avery	Tuolumne Twp 2	71	341
LITTLEPRELD			
John	Tuolumne Twp 2	71	327
LITTLER			
Chas	Sonoma Petaluma	69	582
LITTLETON			
A J	Santa Clara Gilroy	65	240
Amelia	San Francisco San Francisco 10	173 67	
M	Sacramento Ward 3	63	453
M	Sacramento Ward 1	63	67
LITTLLETON			
M	Sacramento Ward 1	63	67

Name	County Locale	M653 Roll	Page
LITTNER			
J F	Sierra Twp 7	66	874
LITTON			
G W	Yuba Rose Bar	72	817
L	Sonoma Washington	69	669
Thomas*	San Francisco San Francisco 4	681120	
W H	Sonoma Washington	69	669
William	San Francisco San Francisco 4	681131	
William C	San Francisco San Francisco 4	681131	
LITUS			
D	Shasta Horsetown	66	693
LITZ			
Fred	Mariposa Twp 3	60	611
R*	Sacramento Brighton	63	204
LITZENBERGER			
J	Nevada Eureka	61	387
W	Nevada Eureka	61	387
LITZENBUGER			
J	Nevada Eureka	61	387
LITZENBURGH			
E A	San Mateo Twp 3	65	94
LITZINGER			
M	Sacramento Ward 1	63	20
LIU			
---	Amador Twp 4	55	247
---	Calaveras Twp 6	57	126
---	El Dorado Salmon Falls	581045	
---	El Dorado Placerville	58	843
---	El Dorado Placerville	58	870
---	San Francisco San Francisco 4	681196	
---	San Francisco San Francisco 2	67	688
LIUNG			
---	El Dorado Mountain	581188	
LIURE			
Austine	El Dorado Coloma	581102	
LIUS			
Edward*	Nevada Bridgeport	61	490
LIUT			
Richard*	Mendocino Round Va	60	879
LIVARK			
Jose	Calaveras Twp 6	57	128
LIVAS			
Domingo	San Luis Obispo 65	42	
	San Luis Obispo		
LIVAZ			
Jose	San Bernardino S Buenav	64	212
LIVE			
Jerome	Santa Cruz Pajaro	66	563
Leon	San Francisco San Francisco 1	68	918
Morris	Sonoma Vallejo	69	620
LIVEBY			
Joseph*	Monterey Pajaro	601014	
LIVEJ			
S H*	Mariposa Twp 3	60	621
LIVELEY			
David	Butte Cascade	56	704
LIVELY			
Jos	Placer Auburn	62	593
Joseph	Monterey Pajaro	601014	
LIVENIA			
Louiser	Mariposa Twp 1	60	635
LIVENS			
W	Santa Clara San Jose	65	391
LIVENSTINE			
Chaqrles	El Dorado Placerville	58	924
Charles	El Dorado Placerville	58	924
LIVENSTON			
A	El Dorado Placerville	58	869
Thomas	Santa Cruz Santa Cruz	66	611
LIVER			
Austin	Santa Clara Santa Clara	65	506
John*	Alameda Brooklyn	55	138
LIVEREAN			
Joseph	Sonoma Washington	69	679
LIVERMORE			
Daniel*	Alameda Murray	55	217
Hosefa*	Alameda Murray	55	220
Joseph*	Alameda Murray	55	221
O	San Francisco San Francisco 2	67	727
LIVERS			
William	Calaveras Twp 5	57	215
LIVERSAGE			
Sarah	Amador Twp 3	55	377
LIVERSEE			
R H	Tuolumne Twp 1	71	266
LIVERTON			
Mary*	Del Norte Crescent	58	649
LIVES			
Florenza*	Monterey Alisal	601038	
LIVETTE			
Petr	Tuolumne Twp 2	71	283
LIVEY			
S H*	Mariposa Twp 3	60	621
LIVEZERY			
John	Butte Ophir	56	794
LIVIDON			
Joseph*	Calaveras Twp 9	57	399

California 1860 Census Index

Name	County Locale	M653 Roll	Page
LIVIN			
James	Calaveras Twp 5	57	207
Louis	Placer Michigan	62	857
Qu	San Francisco San Francisco 4	681	175
LIVINE			
David K*	Calaveras Twp 5	57	207
LIVING			
Henry	San Francisco San Francisco 1	68	924
LIVINGBERGER			
James M*	Siskiyou Yreka	69	151
LIVINGBOGER			
James M*	Siskiyou Yreka	69	151
LIVINGE			
Joseph*	Calaveras Twp 6	57	172
LIVINGETON			
C	San Francisco San Francisco 2	67	721
LIVINGS			
George	San Francisco San Francisco 3	67	24
LIVINGSGOOD			
Jacob	Plumas Quincy	62	947
LIVINGSTON			
---	Mariposa Twp 3	60	612
A F	Butte Chico	56	533
Adolph	Tuolumne Sonora	71	214
Annie	San Francisco San Francisco 4	681	228
B J	Sacramento Ward 4	63	511
C	San Francisco San Francisco 2	67	721
Cath	Sacramento Ward 4	63	556
Chancey	San Francisco San Francisco 1	68	932
Charles	San Mateo Twp 3	65	89
Chas	Butte Bidwell	56	705
David M G	Sacramento Ward 4	63	531
E	Sierra Twp 7	66	901
Elija	Yuba Marysville	72	960
Eliza	Butte Bidwell	56	705
Frank	San Francisco San Francisco 2	67	622
H	San Francisco San Francisco 2	67	804
Helena	Sacramento Ward 1	63	117
Henry	Alameda Brooklyn	55	212
Henry	Sonoma Bodega	69	523
Jacob	San Francisco San Francisco 7	681	414
L	Siskiyou Yreka	69	188
M	San Francisco San Francisco 2	67	803
Mary	San Francisco San Francisco 8	681	249
Miles	Sonoma Armally	69	515
P	Monterey Monterey	60	925
P F	Tuolumne Twp 3	71	464
Pat	Tuolumne Twp 3	71	464
Richard	Plumas Quincy	62	921
Robert	San Francisco San Francisco 8	681	259
S	San Francisco San Francisco 4	681	221
Sho*	Napa Yount	61	39
Thomas	Alameda Brooklyn	55	149
Thos	Napa Yount	61	39
Thos	Stanislaus Empire	70	734
W S	El Dorado Georgetown	58	752
Wm	Butte Eureka	56	647
Wm	Los Angeles Los Angeles	59	491
Wm*	Stanislaus Oatvale	70	718
LIVINGSTONE			
Eliza	Yuba Marysville	72	960
Peter W	Yuba Marysville	72	921
S	San Francisco San Francisco 4	681	221
LIVINGSWAY			
James	San Francisco San Francisco 3	67	48
James	San Francisco San Francisco 3	67	49
LIVINGTON			
Richard	Solano Benecia	69	299
Robs	Klamath S Fork	59	197
LIVINSTON			
Thomas*	Santa Cruz Santa Cruz	66	611
LIVINTHALE			
A	San Francisco San Francisco 4	681	162
LIVINTSTON			
L	San Francisco San Francisco 10	204	67
LIVIY			
Isaac*	Tuolumne Columbia	71	326
LIVN			
Leopold	Calaveras Twp 8	57	55
LIVSTED			
Fredk	San Francisco San Francisco 2	67	717
LIVY			
Fo	San Francisco San Francisco 4	681	175
Isaac	Tuolumne Twp 2	71	326
John	Tuolumne Twp 4	71	182
S H*	Mariposa Twp 3	60	621
LIW			
---	Calaveras Twp 6	57	121
---	Del Norte Happy Ca	58	663
---	El Dorado Diamond	58	816
Ti	Calaveras Twp 4	57	307
LIWELL			
James	Colusa Spring Valley	57	434
LIWERY			
T A*	Siskiyou Scott Va	69	41

Name	County Locale	M653 Roll	Page
LIXINGER			
James*	San Francisco San Francisco 9	681	021
LIXN			
H??*	Calaveras Twp 5	57	193
LIXON			
Elinor	Sacramento Ward 4	63	531
LIXURGER			
James*	San Francisco San Francisco 9	681	021
LIY			
---	Sacramento Granite	63	250
---	Sacramento Granite	63	259
Yong	Placer Dutch Fl	62	737
LIYACT			
John S*	Placer Auburn	62	590
LIYAET			
John S*	Placer Auburn	62	590
LIYER			
G	El Dorado Diamond	58	797
LIYHLNER			
Jno*	Sonoma Petaluma	69	599
LIYNE			
Ah	Butte Bidwell	56	709
LIYROMD			
Chas*	Mariposa Twp 1	60	648
LIYSON			
John W	Sierra Port Win	66	793
LIZA			
Mall M*	Sacramento Granite	63	244
LIZARRAGA			
C V	San Francisco San Francisco 2	67	593
LIZRIMD			
Chas*	Mariposa Twp 1	60	648
LIZRUND			
Chas*	Mariposa Twp 1	60	648
LIZTTNER			
Jno	Sonoma Petaluma	69	545
LIZZA			
---*	Trinity S Fork	701	032
LIZZIE			
---	San Francisco San Francisco 10	290	67
---	Siskiyou Shasta Rvr	69	111
---*	Trinity S Fork	701	032
LIZZY			
---	Mendocino Round Va	60	878
LKIRM			
Joseph	Santa Cruz Santa Cruz	66	600
LLAMMORREE			
C A*	Yuba Rose Bar	72	796
LLAN			
Chas F*	Mariposa Twp 3	60	548
LLANES			
Angel*	Los Angeles Santa Ana	59	446
Antonio	Los Angeles Los Angeles	59	396
Antonio	Los Angeles San Juan	59	461
LLANLY			
S K*	Mariposa Twp 3	60	575
LLATSUTLE			
W*	Sierra Downieville	66	968
LLEFGRAN			
John*	Tuolumne Twp 5	71	509
LLEOM			
---	Amador Twp 1	55	504
LLEPHENS			
S C*	Sacramento Granite	63	242
LLOAN			
T	Nevada Grass Valley	61	158
LLOAT			
Lewis*	El Dorado Kelsey	581	152
LLOW			
---	Mariposa Twp 3	60	553
LLOYD			
E	Sonoma Salt Point	69	691
Edward	Placer Michigan	62	819
F S	Nevada Grass Valley	61	163
Geo	San Francisco San Francisco 2	67	674
George	Sacramento Ward 1	63	26
Griffith	Placer Forest H	62	799
H	Sacramento Ward 1	63	6
Isaac W	Sierra Monte Crk	661	038
J	Siskiyou Klamath	69	88
J W	Nevada Grass Valley	61	235
James	Nevada Bridgeport	61	475
James	San Diego Colorado	64	812
Jno	San Francisco San Francisco 9	681	077
John	Los Angeles Los Angeles	59	350
John	Nevada Eureka	61	344
John	Placer Michigan	62	810
John	Placer Michigan	62	816
John	San Diego Colorado	64	806
John	Sierra Excelsior	661	035
John	Trinity Weaverville	701	077
Kgeorge	Sacramento Ward 1	63	26
Mathias	Nevada Rough &	61	400
Moses	Nevada Bridgeport	61	470
Samuel	Sierra Port Win	66	793

Name	County Locale	M653 Roll	Page
LLOYD			
Thomas	Marin Cortemad	60	792
Thomas	Placer Michigan	62	819
Wm	Sonoma Petaluma	69	543
Wm	Trinity Weaverville	701	065
LLU			
Hop	Sacramento Granite	63	243
LLUE			
---*	Butte Ophir	56	811
LLUNG			
---	Sierra Downieville	66	989
LNAG			
---	Sierra St Louis	66	806
LNAGFORD			
Thos	Santa Clara San Jose	65	346
LNANILT			
E*	El Dorado Diamond	58	790
LNEERINGER			
John	Amador Twp 3	55	376
LNERES			
Manuel*	Contra Costa Twp 1	57	515
LNG			
---	Sierra Downieville	66	981
LNGH			
---	Tuolumne Twp 3	71	468
LNIDER			
Wm	Nevada Nevada	61	280
LNREAT			
Victorine	San Francisco San Francisco 4	681	151
LO CO POO SA			
---	Plumas Quincy	62	969
LO FEBER			
John*	Calaveras Twp 10	57	288
LO FOR			
---*	Nevada Rough &	61	436
LO FU			
---	Mariposa Coulterville	60	687
LO HOP			
---	Butte Hamilton	56	530
---	Butte Oregon	56	613
LO SEE			
---	Butte Hamilton	56	530
LO SING			
---	Butte Kimshaw	56	587
LO TAN			
---	Nevada Bridgeport	61	464
LO TAW			
---	Nevada Bridgeport	61	458
LO TOR			
---*	Nevada Rough &	61	436
LO TWO			
---	Nevada Rough &	61	436
LO TY			
---	Butte Kimshaw	56	608
LO YAP			
---	Butte Kimshaw	56	587
LO YRI			
---	Sacramento Ward 3	63	489
LO YU			
---	Sacramento Ward 1	63	60
---*	Sacramento Ward 3	63	489
LO			
---	Butte Kimshaw	56	582
---	Calaveras Twp 5	57	149
---	Mariposa Twp 1	60	661
---	Mariposa Coulterville	60	681
---	Sierra Downieville	66	982
---*	El Dorado Georgetown	58	693
Cha	Calaveras Twp 10	57	275
Chee	El Dorado Union	581	089
Chon	El Dorado Union	581	090
Chow	Butte Kimshaw	56	584
Fu	Mariposa Coulterville	60	687
Gin	El Dorado Georgetown	58	748
Gue	Sierra Downieville	66	984
He	Sacramento Granite	63	268
Hop	Butte Hamilton	56	530
Hop	Butte Oregon	56	613
K	Placer Iona Hills	62	897
Kee	San Francisco San Francisco 4	681	196
Kei*	Placer Michigan	62	844
Ku	San Francisco San Francisco 4	681	196
La	Yuba Long Bar	72	762
Lee*	Mariposa Twp 3	60	608
Lega	Placer Illinois	62	704
Lin	El Dorado Georgetown	58	678
Lin	El Dorado Eldorado	58	942
Low	Butte Hamilton	56	529
Mong	Butte Kimshaw	56	606
Mung	Butte Oregon	56	644
Mung	Butte Eureka	56	652
Mung*	Butte Oregon	56	587
Nee	San Francisco San Francisco 4	681	156
Ony	Calaveras Twp 5	57	219
Quo	Mariposa Coulterville	60	682
Quong	Yuba Long Bar	72	763

Name	County Locale	M653 Roll	Page
LO			
See *	Butte Hamilton	56	530
See *	Mariposa Twp 3	60	608
Sin	Alameda Oakland	55	24
Sing	Butte Kimshaw	56	587
Snoy	Sacramento Ward 3	63	52
Taw	Nevada Bridgeport	61	458
Taw	Nevada Bridgeport	61	485
Tie	Butte Kimshaw	56	606
Tom	San Francisco San Francisco 1	68	857
Ton	El Dorado Georgetown	58	704
Too	Mariposa Coulterville	60	682
Tor	Nevada Rough &	61	436
Tow	Butte Hamilton	56	529
Tow	Sacramento Ward 1	63	55
Toz	San Francisco San Francisco 2	67	673
Two	Nevada Rough &	61	436
Ty	Butte Kimshaw	56	608
Ty	Butte Oregon	56	613
Wy *	Sacramento Ward 1	63	60
Yap	Butte Kimshaw	56	587
Yen	Butte Hamilton	56	530
Yew *	Butte Hamilton	56	530
Yu *	Sacramento Ward 3	63	489
Yz *	Sacramento Ward 1	63	60
LO?BER			
H	Butte Oregon	56	641
LOA			
---	Yuba Marysville	72	921
Ah	Yuba Suida	72	991
LOACOM			
---	Shasta Shasta	66	670
LOAD			
--- *	Mariposa Twp 3	60	562
LOADERBACK			
H *	Napa Hot Springs	61	4
LOAG			
---	Calaveras Twp 7	57	42
---	Trinity Mouth Ca	70	1012
---	Trinity Taylor'S	70	1033
---	Trinity Taylor'S	70	1035
---	Trinity Big Flat	70	1041
---	Trinity Trinidad Rvr	70	1044
---	Trinity Trinidad Rvr	70	1047
---	Trinity Trinidad Rvr	70	1048
---	Trinity Trinidad Rvr	70	1049
---	Trinity Lewiston	70	957
--- *	Trinity Taylor'S	70	1033
James *	Shasta Shasta	66	654
John	Siskiyou Yreka	69	175
Joseph *	Yuba Linda Twp	72	982
William	Shasta Horsetown	66	703
LOAGUNA			
---	Mariposa Twp 1	60	629
LOAK			
---	Tuolumne Twp 5	71	510
LOAN			
---	El Dorado Placerville	58	899
---	Plumas Quincy	62	950
J P	Tehama Lassen	70	867
LOANE			
Henry S	Solano Vallejo	69	263
LOANER			
P L	Calaveras Twp 9	57	383
LOAR			
Jacob *	Placer Forest H	62	800
LOAREY			
Wm	Sonoma Bodega	69	525
LOAS			
William	Sierra Whiskey	66	849
LOAY			
William *	Shasta Horsetown	66	703
LOB			
Henry	San Francisco San Francisco 2	67	707
Rafael	Yuba Marysville	72	933
Simon	San Francisco San Francisco 2	67	706
Soo	Calaveras Twp 5	57	253
Sou	Calaveras Twp 5	57	253
LOBA			
Carlos	Santa Cruz Soguel	66	592
LOBALENISKE			
Paul	San Francisco San Francisco 9	68	1103
LOBALEWISKE			
Paul	San Francisco San Francisco 9	68	1103
LOBAUGH			
Ephraim	Humbolt Bucksport	59	159
LOBB			
C D	Yuba Marysville	72	959
Jas	Butte Kimshaw	56	596
Richard	Yuba Foster B	72	833
William	San Francisco San Francisco 3	67	46
LOBBS			
Alfred	Yolo Putah	72	548
LOBDELL			
Ebbon	Humbolt Eel Rvr	59	147
James	Calaveras Twp 6	57	159

Name	County Locale	M653 Roll	Page
LOBELIA			
Mary	Sutter Butte	70	797
LOBENSTIN			
Edward *	Calaveras Twp 6	57	180
LOBENSTINE			
Edward *	Calaveras Twp 6	57	180
LOBER			
Antonie	Nevada Eureka	61	348
Herman	Yolo Putah	72	560
Newman	Yolo Putah	72	560
LOBERLEY			
C *	Nevada Grass Valley	61	194
LOBERO			
Jose	San Bernardino Santa Barbara	64	151
LOBERT			
C	Calaveras Twp 9	57	393
LOBETT			
Virginia	Sonoma Sonoma	69	642
LOBIAS			
S	Calaveras Twp 9	57	393
LOBIN			
J H	Alameda Brooklyn	55	186
Philip	Napa Napa	61	61
LOBIS			
James *	El Dorado Georgetown	58	745
LOBNER			
Leopold	Placer Rattle Snake	62	600
LOBO			
Dolorus	Los Angeles Elmonte	59	255
Francisco	San Diego Agua Caliente	64	848
Lettenena	Los Angeles Elmonte	59	254
Manuel	San Diego Temecula	64	792
LOBON			
Alfonso *	Monterey Pajaro	60	1011
LOBREE			
Abram	San Francisco San Francisco 3	67	35
LOBRELL			
James	Calaveras Twp 6	57	159
LOBRERO			
John	Santa Cruz Santa Cruz	66	599
LOBRU			
Isaac *	San Francisco San Francisco 3	67	58
LOBRUSTIM			
Edward *	Calaveras Twp 6	57	180
LOBRUSTIN			
Edward *	Calaveras Twp 6	57	180
Isaac	San Francisco San Francisco 3	67	58
LOBURE			
Edward *	San Francisco San Francisco 8	68	1294
LOBY			
Jesse	Merced Twp 1	60	906
LOC			
---	Mariposa Twp 3	60	618
LOCAN			
Frank	San Francisco San Francisco 2	67	740
LOCB			
A *	Santa Clara San Jose	65	296
LOCH			
---	Butte Oregon	56	641
Jack *	Mariposa Twp 3	60	614
John *	Plumas Quincy	62	959
Thos *	Butte Oregon	56	633
LOCHE			
Peter	Sierra Twp 5	66	943
Thos H	Amador Twp 1	55	462
LOCHEDON			
Henry	Butte Ophir	56	795
LOCHEME			
---	Tulara Twp 2	71	36
LOCHER			
Conrad	Butte Ophir	56	790
Jas *	Butte Oregon	56	613
T	Butte Ophir	56	790
LOCHERDNO			
August *	Sierra Downieville	66	977
LOCHNIR			
Joseph	Tuolumne Columbia	71	342
LOCHR			
Chs C	San Francisco San Francisco 6	67	464
F	San Francisco San Francisco 6	67	472
LOCHRA			
Rosilia *	Los Angeles Los Angeles	59	496
LOCHRAN			
Edward	Solano Vallejo	69	276
P	Solano Benecia	69	308
LOCHROUGH			
Andrew	Calaveras Twp 7	57	14
LOCHVOW			
Chas	Alameda Brooklyn	55	144
LOCK CHOW			
--- *	Placer Auburn	62	560

Name	County Locale	M653 Roll	Page
LOCK			
---	Amador Twp 1	55	501
---	Butte Hamilton	56	530
---	Butte Kimshaw	56	607
---	Butte Kimshaw	56	608
---	Butte Oregon	56	625
---	Butte Oregon	56	640
---	El Dorado Coloma	58	1110
---	El Dorado Indian D	58	1159
---	El Dorado Diamond	58	786
---	El Dorado Placerville	58	886
---	El Dorado Placerville	58	900
---	El Dorado Placerville	58	903
---	El Dorado Mud Springs	58	955
---	Nevada Rough &	61	398
---	Nevada Rough &	61	434
---	Nevada Bridgeport	61	458
---	Nevada Bridgeport	61	505
---	Nevada Bridgeport	61	506
---	Placer Auburn	62	575
---	Placer Rattle Snake	62	636
---	Placer Virginia	62	666
---	Shasta Horsetown	66	704
---	Sierra Twp 5	66	933
---	Sierra Downieville	66	984
---	Stanislaus Branch	70	714
---	Tuolumne Twp 4	71	161
---	Tuolumne Don Pedro	71	535
---	Yuba Bear Rvr	72	1000
---	Yuba Long Bar	72	752
---	Yuba Long Bar	72	757
--- *	Amador Twp 4	55	233
--- *	Butte Oregon	56	625
--- *	Placer Auburn	62	571
Ah	Butte Oregon	56	640
Ah	Sacramento Granite	63	234
Ah	Yuba Bear Rvr	72	1000
Chong *	El Dorado Indian D	58	1159
Chow *	Placer Auburn	62	560
David	Yolo Slate Ra	72	707
David	Yuba Slate Ro	72	707
Ebenezer	Sierra Downieville	66	1023
Geo	Siskiyou Scott Va	69	50
George A	Amador Twp 1	55	470
Hoy	Yuba Long Bar	72	763
Hy	Yuba Long Bar	72	763
J R	San Francisco San Francisco 5	67	491
J S	San Joaquin Stockton	64	1059
Jack *	Mariposa Twp 3	60	614
John	Alameda Brooklyn	55	129
John	San Mateo Twp 2	65	128
Jonah *	Sacramento Mississipi	63	183
Jonathan	Napa Clear Lake	61	124
Kee	Placer Forest H	62	792
Lee	Placer Folsom	62	648
Louis	Placer Iona Hills	62	876
Mill	Yuba Fosters	72	827
R	Trinity Weaverville	70	1064
Thos	Butte Oregon	56	633
William	Yuba Fosters	72	837
Wm	Placer Virginia	62	688
LOCKARD			
Edward A	Calaveras Twp 5	57	231
James	El Dorado Placerville	58	920
T W	Sutter Sutter	70	812
LOCKART			
Gabriel	Tulara Keyesville	71	54
Yobuil	Tulara Twp 3	71	54
LOCKCOTTER			
Clous *	Calaveras Twp 4	57	313
LOCKE			
---	Placer Virginia	62	662
B S	Sacramento Ward 1	63	33
Charles	Tuolumne Twp 1	71	189
D M	Stanislaus Buena Village	70	723
Dean J	San Joaquin Elkhorn	64	988
Elisha	San Francisco San Francisco 7	68	1335
G W	Sacramento Ward 3	63	461
George	Colusa Grand Island	57	476
George L	San Joaquin Elkhorn	64	987
J S	El Dorado Indian D	58	1158
Jackson	Sacramento Dry Crk	63	373
Joseph	Stanislaus Buena Village	70	724
Josiah H	Stanislaus Buena Village	70	723
Lee	Amador Twp 1	55	475
Milton	Stanislaus Oatvale	70	718
Royal	San Francisco San Francisco 3	67	75
Royal P	San Francisco San Francisco 3	67	75
Ruth A	Placer Rattle Snake	62	628
Wm	Santa Clara Redwood	65	446
LOCKEMAN			
B	El Dorado Newtown	58	781
LOCKER			
H	Butte Oregon	56	641
H *	Butte Oregon	56	642
Jas	Butte Oregon	56	613

California 1860 Census Index

Name	County Locale	M653 Roll	Page
LOCKER			
John	Sacramento Ward 3	63	424
Levi W	Colusa Grand Island	57	481
Robert	Nevada Little Y	61	533
William	Napa Yount	61	45
LOCKERS			
J P	Sacramento Sutter	63	305
LOCKET			
George	Plumas Meadow Valley	62	907
LOCKETT			
E F M	Sacramento Brighton	63	206
J B	Sierra Morristown	66	1052
J L	Sacramento Brighton	63	206
LOCKEY			
Daniel*	Calaveras Twp 6	57	166
J P	Sacramento Sutter	63	305
LOCKFORT			
Mary	Yolo No E Twp	72	671
LOCKHART			
A C	Yolo Putah	72	615
Geo	El Dorado Mud Springs	58	960
H	Sacramento Cosumnes	63	390
H E	Siskiyou Scott Va	69	25
Jefferson	Placer Forest H	62	803
John	Solano Green Valley	69	242
Mary	Yuba North Ea	72	671
R C	Trinity Douglas	70	978
R W	Sacramento Centre	63	175
S R	Shasta Millvill	66	749
Saml	Sacramento Ward 3	63	429
LOCKHEAD			
John	San Francisco San Francisco 4	681	126
LOCKHEART			
Wm*	Nevada Nevada	61	271
LOCKHEATH			
Wm*	Nevada Nevada	61	271
LOCKHORS			
S R	Shasta Millvill	66	749
LOCKLAN			
Mary	Tehama Red Bluff	70	921
LOCKLAND			
Wm*	Calaveras Twp 9	57	368
LOCKLEY			
Edward	Tulara Twp 2	71	5
LOCKMAN			
C L	San Francisco San Francisco 7	681	393
James	Butte Kimshaw	56	608
Samuel	Yuba Marysville	72	868
LOCKNER			
Joseph	Tuolumne Twp 2	71	342
LOCKNEY			
T	Nevada Eureka	61	374
LOCKRIDGE			
Danl	Klamath S Fork	59	207
LOCKSHUE			
---	Shasta Horsetown	66	701
LOCKSLEY			
J O	Butte Kimshaw	56	572
LOCKSTAND			
Robert	San Joaquin Elkhorn	64	965
LOCKWOOD			
A J	Amador Twp 1	55	474
A J	El Dorado Cold Spring	581	099
Albert	San Francisco San Francisco 3	67	15
Alexd*	San Francisco San Francisco 8	681	288
Alexr*	San Francisco San Francisco 8	681	288
Bernard	Los Angeles Tejon	59	536
C Anne	San Francisco San Francisco 2	67	665
C L	Butte Kimshaw	56	572
Catharine J	San Joaquin Stockton	641	057
Charles	Sierra Twp 7	66	866
Edwin	Sierra Downieville	661	019
F D	Trinity Hay Fork	70	995
F W	Nevada Eureka	61	368
Gee	San Francisco San Francisco 5	67	479
Geo	San Francisco San Francisco 10	169 67	
Geo	San Francisco San Francisco 5	67	479
Geo A	Tuolumne Columbia	71	349
Geo E	Del Norte Crescent	58	650
H	Sacramento Sutter	63	303
H	Tehama Red Bluff	70	909
H*	Trinity Weaverville	701	066
Harden	Tehama Red Bluff	70	911
I D	San Francisco San Francisco 5	67	542
Isaac	Klamath S Fork	59	207
J W	Nevada Grass Valley	61	156
James	Solano Benecia	69	284
James L	Yuba Foster B	72	824
Jas	Sacramento Ward 1	63	106
Jas	San Mateo Twp 1	65	56
John	San Luis Obispo San Luis Obispo	65	2
John R	Plumas Meadow Valley	62	931
John W	Plumas Quincy	62	996
Joseph W	San Joaquin Tulare	64	869
Marlow	Sierra Twp 5	66	922

Name	County Locale	M653 Roll	Page
LOCKWOOD			
Martin	Sierra Twp 5	66	922
Pecket*	Calaveras Twp 4	57	319
Picker	Calaveras Twp 4	57	319
S C	Calaveras Twp 9	57	374
S D	San Francisco San Francisco 5	67	542
Seth	Placer Auburn	62	590
T W	Nevada Eureka	61	368
Thos	Sonoma Petaluma	69	600
Thos B	Alameda Oakland	55	73
W R	Butte Ophir	56	785
Wm R	El Dorado White Oaks	581	024
LOCO			
Chico	Merced Twp 1	60	896
Elijah*	Yuba Linda Twp	72	980
LOCOAH			
Juanah	Los Angeles Elmonte	59	259
LOCODEA			
Thomas*	Yuba Marysville	72	924
LOCODEN			
Thomas*	Yuba Marysville	72	924
LOCOM			
Francisco*	Mariposa Coulterville	60	698
LOCOSA			
Joseph	San Joaquin Stockton	641	070
LOCOY			
---	Fresno Twp 2	59	18
LOCRUSE			
Edwldro	Mariposa Twp 1	60	625
Eldwedro	Mariposa Twp 1	60	625
LOCRUZ			
Juan S	Alameda Oakland	55	47
LOCTOM			
---	Shasta Shasta	66	669
LOCUS			
George	Tuolumne Twp 1	71	242
LOCY			
---*	Yuba Linda	72	992
LODA			
Peter	Marin Novato	60	736
LODD			
C	Nevada Grass Valley	61	164
J J	San Francisco San Francisco 4	681	143
S*	Nevada Grass Valley	61	165
LODEGA			
Hannah	Alameda Oakland	55	36
LODELL			
Adalaid	Calaveras Twp 9	57	365
LODER			
Benj	Sacramento Ward 3	63	487
Frank	San Francisco San Francisco 11	112 67	
LODERER			
J N	Tuolumne Columbia	71	314
LODFREY			
G	Calaveras Twp 9	57	400
LODGE			
E	Butte Ophir	56	794
Michael	Santa Cruz Pescadero	66	651
Richard	Solano Benecia	69	286
Thomas	Placer Iona Hills	62	887
LODI			
Jerry	Sacramento Granite	63	261
Jery	Sacramento Granite	63	261
LODIGUES			
Julius	Placer Forest H	62	800
LODMAM			
Dennis	Amador Twp 1	55	451
LODMAN			
J A	Sierra Grizzly	661	058
LODMAND			
Dennis*	Amador Twp 1	55	451
LODMANO			
Dennis*	Amador Twp 1	55	451
LODMON			
G	Sutter Yuba	70	771
LODOTE NE			
---	Butte Chico	56	551
LODRICK			
Nicholas	Santa Cruz Soguel	66	588
LODS			
C F*	Sacramento Ward 3	63	460
LODU			
Peter	Marin Novato	60	736
LOE			
---	Calaveras Twp 4	57	326
---	Calaveras Twp 4	57	334
---	El Dorado White Oaks	581	021
---	Mariposa Twp 3	60	598
---	Mariposa Twp 1	60	664
---	San Francisco San Francisco 4	681	184
---	Sierra Twp 5	66	935
---	Tuolumne Big Oak	71	147
---*	Sacramento Cosumnes	63	390
Heoy*	San Francisco San Francisco 10	355 67	

Name	County Locale	M653 Roll	Page
LOE			
Hoy*	San Francisco San Francisco 10	355 67	
William*	Placer Michigan	62	820
LOEBER			
H	Butte Oregon	56	641
H*	Butte Oregon	56	642
LOEHR			
Chs C	San Francisco San Francisco 6	67	464
F	San Francisco San Francisco 6	67	472
Francis	San Francisco San Francisco 7	681	355
G W	Amador Twp 1	55	482
Thos H	Amador Twp 1	55	462
LOEK			
---	El Dorado Coloma	581	110
---	El Dorado Mud Springs	58	964
LOEKWOOD			
Alexa	San Francisco San Francisco 8	681	288
LOELER			
H*	Butte Oregon	56	642
LOEMORE			
Chas	Amador Twp 2	55	266
LOEN			
---*	Shasta Shasta	66	678
LOENTARD			
Hezekiah*	Yuba Marysville	72	893
LOENZANA			
Jose	San Bernardino S Buenav	64	212
LOER			
---	Calaveras Twp 5	57	211
LOERGOMARSINO			
Nichol	Calaveras Twp 7	57	33
LOET			
---*	El Dorado Salmon Falls	581	053
LOEWE			
Louis H	Calaveras Twp 8	57	51
Morris	Calaveras Twp 8	57	51
LOEY			
---	Sacramento Ward 1	63	156
---	San Francisco San Francisco 4	681	187
---	San Francisco San Francisco 4	681	188
---	San Francisco San Francisco 4	681	190
---	San Francisco San Francisco 10	356 67	
---	San Francisco San Francisco 1	68	925
A	San Francisco San Francisco 10	356 67	
Ah	Yuba Suida	72	992
Moey	San Francisco San Francisco 10	355 67	
LOEZ			
Ronaldsen	Tehama Red Bluff	70	931
LOF			
---	El Dorado Coloma	581	075
LOFA			
J*	San Joaquin Stockton	641	098
LOFENIA			
M*	Yolo Cottonwoood	72	649
LOFEY			
Charly	Calaveras Twp 4	57	341
LOFFELL			
J	Sutter Butte	70	798
LOFFERTY			
Barney	Solano Benecia	69	316
Fountain	Shasta Cottonwoood	66	723
P	Nevada Nevada	61	330
LOFFIN			
Martin	Sierra Twp 5	66	941
LOFFMAN			
S	Trinity Weaverville	701	069
LOFIANCE			
John	Siskiyou Cottonwoood	69	105
LOFIENCOT			
E	Yolo Putah	72	551
LOFLAND			
W L	El Dorado Eldorado	58	937
LOFLY			
Mary*	Sacramento Ward 1	63	76
LOFNITH			
Lazarde	Sacramento Granite	63	253
LOFO			
Joseph	Mariposa Twp 3	60	622
LOFONTAINE			
Mary*	Shasta French G	66	718
LOFS			
Peter	Calaveras Twp 6	57	157
LOFT			
Thomas	Sierra Pine Grove	66	819
LOFTES			
John	Solano Vallejo	69	276
LOFTIN			
John	Butte Cascade	56	701
LOFTIS			
John	Solano Vallejo	69	276
Jos	San Mateo Twp 3	65	105
LOFTON			
Francis R	Yuba Bear Rvr	72	997

California 1860 Census Index

Name	County Locale	M653 Roll	Page
LOFTON			
G	Napa Yount	61	51
LOFTUS			
Cathe	San Francisco San Francisco 9	68	1017
James C	Solano Benecia	69	286
James P	Solano Benecia	69	286
John	San Francisco San Francisco 3	67	27
Mary	Sacramento Ward 1	63	83
Michael	Solano Benecia	69	286
Owen	Yuba Marysville	72	907
Sarah	Solano Benecia	69	297
Thomas	Siskiyou Callahan	69	6
LOFTY			
George	Alameda Oakland	55	63
Mary	Sacramento Ward 1	63	76
LOG			
---	Calaveras Twp 8	57	69
---	El Dorado Georgetown	58	693
---	El Dorado Big Bar	58	738
---	El Dorado Big Bar	58	740
---	Nevada Rough &	61	425
---	Yuba Marysville	72	894
Ar	Trinity Lewiston	70	955
Tail	Del Norte Crescent	58	640
Tow	Tuolumne Twp 5	71	504
LOGA			
James	Santa Clara Alviso	65	397
LOGAL			
Benafacio	Yuba Marysville	72	919
Bonofacio*	Yuba Marysville	72	919
LOGAN			
---	Tulara Keeneysburg	71	49
---*	Tulara Keeneysburg	71	47
A	El Dorado Georgetown	58	679
A	Nevada Grass Valley	61	224
A D	Colusa Mansville	57	437
A J	Tehama Lassen	70	869
A L	Nevada Nevada	61	286
A S	Nevada Nevada	61	286
Alexander	Sierra St Louis	66	805
Alexr	Sierra Eureka	66	1046
Andy	Calaveras Twp 8	57	80
Archy	Placer Rattle Snake	62	632
C	Nevada Grass Valley	61	195
C	Nevada Grass Valley	61	198
Daniel	Siskiyou Scott Va	69	43
Dougal*	Plumas Quincy	62	1007
E	Butte Ophir	56	795
Edward H	Placer Secret R	62	609
George	Colusa Mansville	57	437
George	Shasta Shasta	66	757
Henry	San Francisco San Francisco 12	67	371
Hiram	Santa Clara Fremont	65	430
Hugh	Colusa Mansville	57	437
Hugh	Yolo Slate Ra	72	688
Hugh	Yuba Slate Ro	72	688
J	Nevada Grass Valley	61	220
J	Nevada Nevada	61	240
J	Sacramento Ward 1	63	20
J	Sutter Yuba	70	776
J	Tehama Red Bluff	70	925
J M	Butte Bidwell	56	710
J O	Tehama Antelope	70	889
Jack	Colusa Mansville	57	437
James	Alameda Brooklyn	55	199
James	El Dorado Cold Spring	58	1101
James	San Francisco San Francisco 7	68	1374
James	Shasta Millvill	66	726
James	Sierra Downieville	66	975
James	Solano Vallejo	69	269
James	Stanislaus Emory	70	750
James	Tehama Lassen	70	876
James	Tulara Twp 1	71	82
James	Yuba Marysville	72	928
John	Calaveras Twp 7	57	42
John	Nevada Bridgeport	61	501
John	Tulara Visalia	71	28
John R	Nevada Bloomfield	61	514
John*	El Dorado Eldorado	58	937
Jonathan	Tehama Lassen	70	869
Joseph	Santa Clara Redwood	65	444
L	El Dorado Placerville	58	870
L	Nevada Grass Valley	61	144
L	Nevada Grass Valley	61	147
L	Nevada Grass Valley	61	195
Lorenzo	Santa Cruz Santa Cruz	66	634
Lorenzo	Santa Cruz Santa Cruz	66	637
Lorern	Santa Cruz Santa Cruz	66	634
M	Nevada Grass Valley	61	118
Mary	Alameda Brooklyn	55	194
Mary	San Francisco San Francisco 10	67	243
O	Nevada Grass Valley	61	224
Oscar	Sacramento Franklin	63	313
Patrick	Sierra St Louis	66	807

Name	County Locale	M653 Roll	Page
LOGAN			
R	Nevada Grass Valley	61	186
Robert	Del Norte Klamath	58	654
Robert C	Sierra La Porte	66	776
Robt	Sacramento Natonia	63	279
Robt	Sacramento Ward 4	63	501
S	Nevada Grass Valley	61	147
S	Nevada Grass Valley	61	183
S	Sutter Nicolaus	70	830
S C	Tehama Cottonwoood	70	901
S H	Mendocino Ukiah	60	800
S*	Nevada Grass Valley	61	206
Saml	Santa Clara Alviso	65	403
Saml	Santa Clara Redwood	65	458
Samuel	Santa Cruz Pescadero	66	647
Samuel	Tuolumne Twp 5	71	520
Sarah	San Francisco San Francisco 2	67	635
Sarah	San Francisco San Francisco 2	67	730
Sarah	Stanislaus Emory	70	750
Thos	Placer Virginia	62	661
Thos	Sacramento Ward 4	63	533
Thos	Tehama Lassen	70	868
Thos M	Sacramento Ward 1	63	40
W	Sutter Bear Rvr	70	819
Walter	Napa Yount	61	53
Warden F	San Diego Colorado	64	808
William	Calaveras Twp 8	57	88
William	Klamath Liberty	59	241
William	San Francisco San Francisco 7	68	1386
William	Tuolumne Columbia	71	365
Wm	Napa Napa	61	74
Wm	Sacramento Georgian	63	337
Wm	Sonoma Mendocino	69	456
Wm	Tehama Lassen	70	874
Wm K	Plumas Quincy	62	916
Wm R	Tuolumne Twp 1	71	264
LOGANN			
James	Tulara Visalia	71	82
LOGANS			
Leobose	Solano Vallejo	69	259
LOGAR			
A*	Nevada Grass Valley	61	156
LOGARD			
L	El Dorado Placerville	58	876
LOGAVAR			
A	Nevada Nevada	61	297
LOGDEN			
Zebuel	Placer Virginia	62	675
LOGE			
Catharine	San Francisco San Francisco 7	68	1408
John	El Dorado Kelsey	58	1139
LOGEM			
Joseph	Alameda Brooklyn	55	162
LOGENNA			
J	Nevada Grass Valley	61	156
LOGGIN			
Alex	San Joaquin Elkhorn	64	978
LOGGINS			
Alexander	Sonoma Santa Rosa	69	395
Wm	Sonoma Santa Rosa	69	390
LOGH			
---	Mariposa Twp 3	60	543
LOGHRE			
John	Calaveras Twp 5	57	148
LOGITE			
A	Nevada Grass Valley	61	149
LOGITT			
A	Nevada Grass Valley	61	149
LOGLE			
Geo	Napa Napa	61	88
L B	Nevada Grass Valley	61	196
LOGLIARDO			
John*	Calaveras Twp 9	57	372
LOGNE			
Harrison	Yuba New York	72	739
LOGNOZ			
August	Sierra Downieville	66	968
LOGOG			
---	El Dorado Big Bar	58	740
LOGOIN			
Stephen	Calaveras Twp 5	57	197
LOGOINI			
Stephen*	Calaveras Twp 5	57	197
LOGOIREI			
Stephen*	Calaveras Twp 5	57	197
LOGOISE			
Stephen	Calaveras Twp 5	57	197
LOGOL			
Bonafacio*	Yuba Marysville	72	919
Bonofacio*	Yuba Marysville	72	919
LOGON			
---	Sierra Morristown	66	1056
D	San Francisco San Francisco 4	68	1320
S*	Nevada Grass Valley	61	206
LOGONG			
---	Sierra Twp 5	66	925

Name	County Locale	M653 Roll	Page
LOGREOR			
Manuel*	Calaveras Twp 9	57	402
LOGRIOR			
Manuel*	Calaveras Twp 9	57	402
LOGSDIN			
Mary Escolasti	Los Angeles Los Angeles	59	314
LOGSDON			
Joseph	Sierra Excelsior	66	1034
Tho	Siskiyou Scott Ri	69	81
LOGUAR			
Julius	Calaveras Twp 5	57	147
LOGUE			
James	Alameda Brooklyn	55	96
James	San Francisco San Francisco 6	67	438
LOGUR			
A	Nevada Grass Valley	61	156
LOGUS			
Antione*	San Francisco San Francisco 11	67	109
LOGWOOD			
Charles P	Monterey Alisal	60	1032
Thomas Y	Monterey Alisal	60	1032
Thos	Fresno Twp 3	59	15
LOH			
---	Sacramento Ward 1	63	50
Bernardino	San Luis Obispo San Luis Obispo	65	5
Hop	San Francisco San Francisco 9	68	1093
Rafael*	Yuba Marysville	72	933
LOHAN			
Dideo	Calaveras Twp 5	57	140
Didio	Calaveras Twp 6	57	140
J	Nevada Grass Valley	61	224
P	Nevada Grass Valley	61	224
T	Nevada Grass Valley	61	224
LOHANSE			
August	San Francisco San Francisco 3	67	63
LOHAUSE			
August*	San Francisco San Francisco 3	67	63
LOHER			
E H	San Francisco San Francisco 10	67	353
LOHIN			
Jim	Nevada Bloomfield	61	507
LOHINAN			
Hannah*	Sacramento Ward 1	63	117
LOHLCOTTER			
Clous*	Calaveras Twp 4	57	313
LOHMAN			
G C	Siskiyou Klamath	69	90
Hannah	Sacramento Ward 1	63	117
Henry	San Francisco San Francisco 10	67	297
J	Sacramento Ward 3	63	424
J B	Siskiyou Scott Va	69	27
John	Placer Forest H	62	766
John	San Francisco San Francisco 1	68	894
John H	Los Angeles Los Angeles	59	373
L*	San Francisco San Francisco 3	67	73
Peter	Sierra Twp 7	66	905
LOHMERER			
William	San Francisco San Francisco 7	68	1354
LOHN			
Emma E	San Francisco San Francisco 2	67	584
Peter	Contra Costa Twp 2	57	564
LOHNIAN			
Hannah*	Sacramento Ward 1	63	117
LOHOUSE			
August*	San Francisco San Francisco 3	67	63
LOHRY			
A	El Dorado Union	58	1087
LOHSE			
Charles	Contra Costa Twp 3	57	589
Herman*	Placer Auburn	62	589
Hermean*	Placer Auburn	62	589
John F	San Francisco San Francisco 2	67	583
LOHSENLIER			
John	Placer Illinois	62	705
LOHTCOTTEN			
Clous*	Calaveras Twp 4	57	313
LOHY			
Patrick*	Marin Tomales	60	717
LOHYDER			
F W	Sacramento Ward 3	63	433
LOI			
---	Calaveras Twp 6	57	149
---	Calaveras Twp 8	57	76
---	Calaveras Twp 8	57	82
---	El Dorado Mud Springs	58	972
---	Mariposa Twp 3	60	613
---	San Francisco San Francisco 4	68	1184
---	San Francisco San Francisco 11	67	146
---	Sierra La Porte	66	785
---	Yuba Bear Rvr	72	1000

California 1860 Census Index

Name	County Locale	M653 Roll	Page
LOI			
Ah	Calaveras Twp 7	57	16
Ah	Yuba Bear Rvr	72	1000
Kam	San Francisco San Francisco 11	160	67
LOID			
---	Sierra La Porte	66	782
LOIE			
---	Mariposa Twp 3	60	607
LOIGE			
---	Placer Rattle Snake	62	627
LOIGRE			
---	Placer Rattle Snake	62	627
LOIN			
---	El Dorado Placerville	58	902
---	Fresno Rvr	59	28
---	San Francisco San Francisco 4	681	174
Tun	El Dorado Greenwood	58	729
LOINY			
---	Shasta French G	66	713
LOIR			
Chil	El Dorado Greenwood	58	729
LOIREZ			
Miquel*	Santa Cruz Santa Cruz	66	632
LOIS			
---	Calaveras Twp 5	57	149
---	El Dorado Greenwood	58	714
LOISE			
E P	Amador Twp 2	55	302
Edmund	Calaveras Twp 4	57	335
Wm	Amador Twp 1	55	486
LOISIAI			
Adolph	San Francisco San Francisco 4	681	156
LOISRAI			
Adolph	San Francisco San Francisco 4	681	156
LOIUSA			
Mary	San Francisco San Francisco 11	107	67
LOJA			
Chas*	San Francisco San Francisco 1	68	900
LOJAS			
Francisco	Yuba Marysville	72	946
LOJON			
---*	Sierra Morristown	661	056
LOK			
---	El Dorado Georgetown	58	695
---	El Dorado Greenwood	58	714
---	El Dorado Diamond	58	784
---	El Dorado Eldorado	58	941
---	Mariposa Twp 1	60	651
---	Sacramento Granite	63	250
---	Sacramento Ward 1	63	70
---	San Francisco San Francisco 9	681	095
---	San Francisco San Francisco 4	681	212
LOKE			
---	Butte Oro	56	675
---	Calaveras Twp 4	57	334
---	El Dorado White Oaks	581	009
---	El Dorado Salmon Falls	581	041
---	El Dorado Salmon Falls	581	043
---	El Dorado Coloma	581	107
---	El Dorado Coloma	581	121
---	El Dorado Kelsey	581	133
---	El Dorado Diamond	58	790
---	El Dorado Placerville	58	830
---	El Dorado Placerville	58	832
---	El Dorado Placerville	58	900
---	El Dorado Mud Springs	58	970
---	El Dorado Mud Springs	58	971
---	El Dorado Mud Springs	58	972
---	El Dorado Mud Springs	58	973
---	Placer Virginia	62	679
---	Placer Virginia	62	687
---	Placer Illinois	62	739
---	Tuolumne Twp 5	71	510
---	Tuolumne Twp 5	71	524
---	Tuolumne Chinese	71	526
---	Tuolumne Knights	71	528
---	Tuolumne Don Pedro	71	535
---	Tuolumne Don Pedro	71	538
M M	Butte Ophir	56	797
Mee	Butte Bidwell	56	708
W F	El Dorado Diamond	58	791
LOKER			
---	Calaveras Twp 10	57	284
LOKERSEMUM			
---	Plumas Quincy	62	965
LOKING			
Antone	Alameda Brooklyn	55	78
Antonio	Alameda Brooklyn	55	78
LOKMAN			
L*	San Francisco San Francisco 3	67	73
LOLA			
---	Butte Oregon	56	637
---	San Bernardino S Timate	64	741
A*	Nevada Grass Valley	61	144
M	Sacramento Ward 1	63	5
LOLAMONSON			
G*	Napa Napa	61	106
LOLAN			
J	Yolo Washington	72	561
LOLB			
Richard	Yuba Fosters	72	833
LOLBEXTER			
John*	El Dorado Casumnes	581	161
LOLEN			
Tormin	San Bernardino Santa Barbara	64	170
LOLER			
M K	Calaveras Twp 9	57	382
LOLETT			
Virginia	Sonoma Sonoma	69	642
LOLEZ			
Timothy*	Yuba New York	72	722
LOLIS			
H	San Francisco San Francisco 4	681	155
LOLISS			
D B	El Dorado Casumnes	581	161
Thomas*	Calaveras Twp 5	57	171
LOLKS			
Chas	Placer Virginia	62	665
LOLL			
James*	Alameda Brooklyn	55	100
Richard	Yuba Fosters	72	838
LOLLA			
Catherine	San Francisco San Francisco 3	67	43
LOLLE			
James*	Alameda Brooklyn	55	100
LOLLER			
Leopold	Sacramento Ward 4	63	548
Pat	Sacramento Natonia	63	276
LOLLES			
Jas R*	Sacramento Ward 4	63	506
LOLLIS			
John*	Napa Napa	61	85
LOLLNER			
Haver*	Sierra Twp 5	66	943
LOLLOYD			
G	Calaveras Twp 9	57	395
LOLLS			
S*	Calaveras Twp 9	57	393
LOLLUER			
Haver*	Sierra Twp 5	66	943
LOLLY			
Anderson*	Calaveras Twp 9	57	351
LOLO			
Samuel	Sierra Twp 7	66	913
LOLOLI			
L*	El Dorado Georgetown	58	678
LOLONA			
---	Mendocino Twp 1	60	887
LOLOY			
---	Mendocino Twp 1	60	887
Patrick	Sierra Twp 7	66	911
LOLRUITINS			
Edward*	Calaveras Twp 5	57	180
LOLT			
Chas F	Butte Ophir	56	761
LOLUS			
James*	El Dorado Georgetown	58	745
LOM			
---	Calaveras Twp 6	57	166
---	Calaveras Twp 7	57	36
---	El Dorado Salmon Falls	581	063
---	El Dorado Coloma	581	102
---	El Dorado Kelsey	581	141
---	El Dorado Casumnes	581	160
---	El Dorado Diamond	58	784
---	El Dorado Diamond	58	794
---	El Dorado Diamond	58	797
---	El Dorado Diamond	58	798
---	El Dorado Placerville	58	923
---	El Dorado Mud Springs	58	972
---	Placer Virginia	62	679
---	Sierra Downieville	661	014
---	Sierra Cox'S Bar	66	950
---	Tuolumne Chinese	71	526
---*	El Dorado Salmon Falls	581	054
---*	El Dorado Coloma	581	122
Ke*	San Francisco San Francisco 4	681	192
Pah	Yuba New York	72	739
LOMA			
---	Mendocino Round Va	60	881
LOMAN			
Frederick	San Francisco San Francisco 7	681	412
Geo*	Nevada Nevada	61	268
H	Nevada Grass Valley	61	186
J C	El Dorado Placerville	58	835
John	Placer Forest H	62	766
Nathan	Sacramento Ward 4	63	505
S	Nevada Grass Valley	61	161
LOMAR			
---	Mendocino Round Va	60	882
J*	San Francisco San Francisco 6	67	473
LOMAS			
Saml	Sacramento Franklin	63	332
LOMAX			
George	Calaveras Twp 8	57	50
J	San Francisco San Francisco 6	67	473
James	Sacramento Ward 4	63	495
Jas	Sacramento Ward 4	63	569
William	Tulara Visalia	71	26
LOMBARD			
Henry	Yolo No E Twp	72	667
Hezikiah	Yuba Marysville	72	893
Ist*	Placer Michigan	62	847
Jst*	Placer Michigan	62	847
Lavinia	Yuba Marysville	72	875
O W*	Sacramento Ward 1	63	8
Sevonia W	Butte Ophir	56	766
LOMBARDO			
L	Tuolumne Twp 4	71	153
Louis	Tuolumne Big Oak	71	143
LOMBARDY			
Ambrose	Plumas Quincy	62	936
LOMBER			
Wm	San Francisco San Francisco 2	67	780
LOMBERDO			
Louis	Tuolumne Twp 4	71	143
LOMBERE			
Ginllame*	Alameda Oakland	55	7
Giullame*	Alameda Oakland	55	7
LOMBOON			
P	Nevada Grass Valley	61	166
LOMBORD			
John	Calaveras Twp 4	57	325
LOMBROCHT			
Fred	Sacramento Ward 4	63	554
LOMDDBERG			
A*	Sacramento Ward 1	63	12
LOME			
---	Shasta Horsetown	66	703
LOMEANGE			
Peter*	Calaveras Twp 9	57	363
LOMEDRY			
Chas*	Butte Ophir	56	777
LOMEKA			
---	Fresno Twp 3	59	98
LOMER			
Walter A	Alameda Brooklyn	55	119
LOMERE			
James	Alameda Oakland	55	4
LOMERS			
Daniel	San Francisco San Francisco 3	67	56
LOMERVILLE			
Robt	Stanislaus Buena Village	70	721
LOMERY			
L	Nevada Grass Valley	61	155
LOMET			
Joseph	Alameda Brooklyn	55	169
LOMEYER			
William	San Francisco San Francisco 7	681	344
LOMG			
---	Butte Eureka	56	649
---	Placer Virginia	62	679
LOMGARD			
J*	Sacramento Ward 1	63	17
LOMI			
---*	Trinity Trininad Rvr	701	048
LOMIG			
J*	Nevada Grass Valley	61	147
LOMIN			
Jas	Sacramento Natonia	63	272
LOMIS			
J	Nevada Grass Valley	61	147
Lucinda	Santa Clara Gilroy	65	238
LOMLARD			
Henry	Yolo No E Twp	72	667
LOMLET			
Charles	San Francisco San Francisco 7	681	418
LOMOANG			
Peter*	Calaveras Twp 9	57	363
LOMOANGE			
Peter*	Calaveras Twp 9	57	363
LOMOANGO			
Peter*	Calaveras Twp 9	57	363
LOMODI			
Romana	Calaveras Twp 6	57	150
LOMOLL			
John	Nevada Eureka	61	365
LOMOND			
Peter	Siskiyou Callahan	69	7
LOMP			
---	Placer Illinois	62	752
LOMR			
---*	Trinity Trininad Rvr	701	048
LOMSER			
---*	Mendocino Round Va	60	883

California 1860 Census Index

Name	County Locale	Roll	Page
LOMSIR			
---*	Mendocino Round Va	60	883
LON EY			
---	El Dorado Salmon Hills	58	1066
LON SY			
---	El Dorado Georgetown	58	693
LON			
---	Amador Twp 5	55	366
---	Butte Ophir	56	815
---	Calaveras Twp 5	57	202
---	Calaveras Twp 8	57	60
---	El Dorado White Oaks	58	1002
---	El Dorado White Oaks	58	1019
---	El Dorado Salmon Falls	58	1040
---	El Dorado Salmon Falls	58	1061
---	El Dorado Coloma	58	1107
---	El Dorado Coloma	58	1121
---	El Dorado Georgetown	58	680
---	El Dorado Georgetown	58	693
---	El Dorado Georgetown	58	697
---	El Dorado Greenwood	58	731
---	El Dorado Greenwood	58	732
---	El Dorado Diamond	58	787
---	El Dorado Diamond	58	812
---	El Dorado Placerville	58	834
---	Mariposa Twp 3	60	553
---	Mariposa Twp 3	60	564
---	Mariposa Twp 3	60	575
---	Mariposa Twp 3	60	579
---	Mariposa Twp 3	60	608
---	Mariposa Coulterville	60	700
---	Nevada Grass Valley	61	232
---	Nevada Rough &	61	432
---	Placer Rattle Snake	62	629
---	Placer Rattle Snake	62	638
---	Sacramento Cosumnes	63	397
---	San Francisco San Francisco 9	68	1093
---	San Francisco San Francisco 9	68	1094
---	San Francisco San Francisco 9	68	1095
---	San Francisco San Francisco 4	68	1175
---	San Francisco San Francisco 4	68	1176
---	San Francisco San Francisco 4	68	1177
---	San Francisco San Francisco 2	67	624
---	San Francisco San Francisco 3	67	9
---	Shasta Shasta	66	671
---	Shasta Shasta	66	677
---	Sierra Morristown	66	1055
---	Sierra La Porte	66	767
---	Sierra St Louis	66	813
---	Sierra St Louis	66	861
---	Sierra Twp 5	66	927
---	Sierra Twp 5	66	932
---	Sierra Cox'S Bar	66	951
---	Sierra Downieville	66	974
---	Sierra Downieville	66	979
---	Sierra Downieville	66	985
---	Stanislaus Emory	70	743
---	Tuolumne Twp 5	71	517
---	Tuolumne Twp 6	71	535
---	Yolo No E Twp	72	680
---	Yolo No E Twp	72	681
---	Yolo No E Twp	72	685
---	Yolo Slate Ra	72	711
---	Yuba North Ea	72	680
---	Yuba North Ea	72	681
---	Yuba North Ea	72	682
---	Yuba Slate Ro	72	711
---	Yuba Long Bar	72	761
---*	Amador Twp 4	55	332
---*	El Dorado Salmon Falls	58	1061
---*	El Dorado Salmon Falls	58	1066
---*	El Dorado Casumnes	58	1162
---*	Mariposa Twp 3	60	579
---*	Mariposa Twp 3	60	608
---*	San Francisco San Francisco 9	68	1094
---*	Sierra Downieville	66	1008
---*	Sierra Twp 5	66	931
---*	Yuba Linda	72	991
Ack	Del Norte Crescent	58	631
Ah	Butte Eureka	56	655
Ah	Tehama Tehama	70	950
Caw	Yuba Long Bar	72	763
Chon	El Dorado Salmon Falls	58	1047
Fu	Yuba Long Bar	72	762
Gei	El Dorado Coloma	58	1076
Hang	El Dorado Mud Springs	58	973
Hee	Calaveras Twp 5	57	193
Hee	Yuba Long Bar	72	767
Hei	Calaveras Twp 5	57	193
Hy	El Dorado Big Bar	58	737
Jose Maria*	San Mateo Twp 2	65	112
King	San Francisco San Francisco 4	68	1176
Lee	Butte Cascade	56	698
Lee*	Yuba Fosters	72	842
Loo	Mariposa Twp 3	60	612
Pe	San Francisco San Francisco 4	68	1177

Name	County Locale	Roll	Page
LON			
See	El Dorado Georgetown	58	702
Sei	El Dorado Georgetown	58	702
Song*	Mariposa Twp 1	60	627
Sun	Siskiyou Yreka	69	195
Tou	Yuba Long Bar	72	761
Yak	Yuba Long Bar	72	766
Ying	Placer Illinois	62	753
LONA			
---	El Dorado White Oaks	58	1022
---	El Dorado Union	58	1089
---	El Dorado Coloma	58	1112
---	El Dorado Mountain	58	1188
---	El Dorado Diamond	58	787
---*	El Dorado Salmon Falls	58	1064
LONACRI			
Thompson	Calaveras Twp 9	57	347
LONAGERA			
---	San Francisco San Francisco 4	68	1139
LONAHIN			
J	Tuolumne Columbia	71	309
LONARD			
Edward	Sierra Whiskey	66	845
LONAREL			
James*	Placer Yankee J	62	757
LONASULIGER			
Dora*	San Francisco San Francisco 7	68	1405
LONBERG			
Jos*	San Francisco San Francisco 6	67	429
LONBG			
---	Sierra Downieville	66	1009
LONBRECK			
George	Yuba Marysville	72	926
LONCHALL			
Louis	Butte Bidwell	56	728
LONCKS			
J R*	Sonoma Petaluma	69	591
LONCY			
Peter P*	Tuolumne Twp 3	71	458
LOND			
Moses*	Sierra Twp 5	66	928
LONDAN			
Thomas*	Santa Cruz Pescadero	66	649
LONDAR			
Thomas*	Placer Forest H	62	770
LONDBERY			
A	Sacramento Ward 1	63	12
LONDEN			
Frank M	Trinity Rearings	70	990
J	Monterey Monterey	60	956
Robert*	Yuba Rose Bar	72	806
Thomas*	Placer Forest H	62	770
LONDENBURG			
T*	San Francisco San Francisco 1	68	870
LONDENSLIGER			
Thomas*	San Francisco San Francisco 7	68	1406
LONDER			
Jake*	Mariposa Coulterville	60	677
LONDERBACK			
Andrew	San Francisco San Francisco 8	68	1238
LONDERBOM			
Nathl*	San Francisco San Francisco 9	68	1052
LONDERS			
Thomas*	Calaveras Twp 6	57	135
LONDIEN			
Gustavus	Yuba Marysville	72	882
LONDO			
J B	Marin Novato	60	735
LONDON			
Alexar	San Francisco San Francisco 7	68	1423
Emma*	Yuba Slate Ro	72	693
John	Nevada Bridgeport	61	476
John	Siskiyou Yreka	69	177
John*	Nevada Bridgeport	61	476
Joseh	Yolo Slate Ra	72	693
Joseph*	Yuba Slate Ro	72	693
Myers	San Francisco San Francisco 11	148	
		67	
Wm	San Francisco San Francisco 12	390	
		67	
LONDRAGEN			
Wm	Yuba Rose Bar	72	792
LONDRO			
R	El Dorado Diamond	58	783
LONE			
---	Butte Ophir	56	771
---	El Dorado Mountain	58	1188
---	El Dorado Placerville	58	831
---	El Dorado Placerville	58	906
---	El Dorado Mud Springs	58	992
---	Fresno Twp 1	59	26
---	Mariposa Twp 3	60	618
---	Nevada Rough &	61	409
---	Nevada Rough &	61	434
---	Nevada Bridgeport	61	506
---	Placer Virginia	62	665

Name	County Locale	Roll	Page
LONE			
---	Shasta Horsetown	66	708
---	Sierra Downieville	66	1010
---	Sierra Twp 7	66	886
---	Sierra Downieville	66	979
---	Yolo Merritt	72	580
---*	El Dorado Salmon Falls	58	1063
A	Sierra Morristown	66	1055
B K	Yolo Washington	72	565
Francis*	Yuba Rose Bar	72	816
Franics*	Yuba Rose Bar	72	816
Gideon	Yuba Long Bar	72	753
Ke	San Francisco San Francisco 4	68	1192
L O*	El Dorado Placerville	58	897
Louis R	Yolo No E Twp	72	671
Louis R	Yuba North Ea	72	671
Mary A	Yolo Cache Crk	72	632
Richard	Yuba Long Bar	72	750
Samuel	Yuba Slate Ro	72	696
LONEANS			
Frank*	Tuolumne Twp 2	71	391
LONENO			
Mozion	San Joaquin Stockton	64	1065
LONENTINA			
---	San Bernardino S Timate	64	712
---*	San Bernardino S Timate	64	741
LONER			
Hose	Mariposa Coulterville	60	691
John E*	San Francisco San Francisco 7	68	1416
Phillip	Mariposa Twp 1	60	625
Wesley	San Bernardino San Bernadino	64	671
LONES			
Francisco*	Mariposa Twp 3	60	603
H A	Nevada Nevada	61	275
Hugh	Calaveras Twp 9	57	371
LONESAVER			
Caroline	San Francisco San Francisco 4	68	1124
LONET			
Samuel	Alameda Brooklyn	55	104
LONETTA			
---	San Bernardino San Bernadino	64	677
LONEY			
---	El Dorado White Oaks	58	1022
---	El Dorado Salmon Falls	58	1061
---	El Dorado Mud Springs	58	961
---*	Butte Ophir	56	818
Geo	El Dorado Placerville	58	849
Giffroneh	El Dorado Salmon Falls	58	1035
H	El Dorado Placerville	58	834
James	Tuolumne Columbia	71	293
M*	Nevada Grass Valley	61	165
Patrick	Tuolumne Columbia	71	299
Peter	El Dorado Coloma	58	1121
Peter P	Tuolumne Twp 3	71	458
Robert	Alameda Brooklyn	55	113
S S	El Dorado Placerville	58	855
Sg*	El Dorado Georgetown	58	693
LONF			
---	Sierra Downieville	66	1026
J M	San Joaquin Stockton	64	1052
LONFFER			
Jacob	Mendocino Big Rvr	60	842
LONFFOR			
Jacob*	Mendocino Big Rvr	60	842
LONG BILL			
---	Tulara Twp 1	71	117
LONG BOW			
---	Fresno Twp 2	59	63
LONG HEAD			
---	Tulara Twp 2	71	38
LONG HORN			
---	Humbolt Eureka	59	173
LONG HUNG			
---	Sacramento Ward 1	63	69
LONG IVE			
---	Tulara Twp 1	71	119
LONG JANE			
---	Fresno Twp 3	59	22
LONG LEGS			
---	Tulara Twp 2	71	35
---	Tulara Twp 2	71	39
---*	Tulara Visalia	71	35
---*	Tulara Visalia	71	39
LONG NOSE			
---	Fresno Twp 2	59	94
LONG PAW			
---	Nevada Red Dog	61	549
LONG QUE			
---*	Placer Auburn	62	564
LONG TOM			
---*	Tulara Twp 1	71	114
---*	Tulara Visalia	71	34
LONG TOME			
---	Tulara Twp 2	71	34
LONG			
---	Alameda Oakland	55	14

California 1860 Census Index

LONG

Name	County Locale	M653 Roll	Page
---	Alameda Oakland	55	34
---	Alameda Oakland	55	38
---	Amador Twp 2	55	302
---	Amador Twp 2	55	310
---	Amador Twp 7	55	414
---	Amador Twp 6	55	423
---	Amador Twp 1	55	497
---	Amador Twp 1	55	504
---	Amador Twp 1	55	507
---	Butte Kimshaw	56	579
---	Butte Oregon	56	631
---	Butte Bidwell	56	723
---	Butte Ophir	56	801
---	Calaveras Twp 8	57	108
---	Calaveras Twp 6	57	149
---	Calaveras Twp 6	57	151
---	Calaveras Twp 4	57	339
---	Calaveras Twp 9	57	358
---	Calaveras Twp 7	57	36
---	Calaveras Twp 7	57	41
---	Calaveras Twp 7	57	44
---	Calaveras Twp 8	57	59
---	Calaveras Twp 8	57	63
---	Calaveras Twp 8	57	68
---	Calaveras Twp 8	57	71
---	Calaveras Twp 8	57	83
---	Calaveras Twp 8	57	94
---	Colusa Muion	57	458
---	El Dorado Salmon Falls	58	1040
---	El Dorado Salmon Hills	58	1059
---	El Dorado Salmon Falls	58	1061
---	El Dorado Coloma	58	1109
---	El Dorado Coloma	58	1110
---	El Dorado Coloma	58	1114
---	El Dorado Coloma	58	1122
---	El Dorado Indian D	58	1159
---	El Dorado Mountain	58	1188
---	El Dorado Mountain	58	1189
---	El Dorado Georgetown	58	677
---	El Dorado Georgetown	58	688
---	El Dorado Georgetown	58	693
---	El Dorado Georgetown	58	696
---	El Dorado Georgetown	58	700
---	El Dorado Greenwood	58	711
---	El Dorado Diamond	58	794
---	El Dorado Diamond	58	806
---	El Dorado Diamond	58	816
---	El Dorado Placerville	58	829
---	El Dorado Placerville	58	839
---	El Dorado Placerville	58	912
---	El Dorado Placerville	58	917
---	El Dorado Placerville	58	919
---	El Dorado Placerville	58	923
---	El Dorado Placerville	58	929
---	El Dorado Eldorado	58	948
---	El Dorado Mud Springs	58	949
---	El Dorado Mud Springs	58	956
---	El Dorado Mud Springs	58	990
---	Fresno Twp 1	59	25
---	Mariposa Twp 3	60	543
---	Mariposa Twp 3	60	544
---	Mariposa Twp 3	60	550
---	Mariposa Twp 3	60	564
---	Mariposa Twp 3	60	572
---	Mariposa Twp 3	60	578
---	Mariposa Twp 3	60	581
---	Mariposa Twp 1	60	626
---	Mariposa Twp 1	60	643
---	Mariposa Twp 1	60	655
---	Mariposa Twp 1	60	657
---	Mariposa Twp 1	60	658
---	Mariposa Twp 1	60	661
---	Mariposa Twp 1	60	673
---	Mariposa Coulterville	60	681
---	Mariposa Coulterville	60	700
---	Monterey Monterey	60	959
---	Nevada Nevada	61	299
---	Nevada Nevada	61	301
---	Nevada Nevada	61	302
---	Nevada Rough &	61	398
---	Nevada Rough &	61	426
---	Nevada Rough &	61	432
---	Nevada Bridgeport	61	458
---	Nevada Bridgeport	61	459
---	Nevada Bridgeport	61	460
---	Nevada Bridgeport	61	466
---	Placer Auburn	62	571
---	Placer Auburn	62	572
---	Placer Auburn	62	591
---	Placer Horseshoe	62	650
---	Placer Virginia	62	671
---	Placer Virginia	62	684
---	Placer Illinois	62	704
---	Placer Mountain	62	707
---	Placer Illinois	62	746
---	Placer Illinois	62	747
---	Placer Illinois	62	752
---	Placer Illinois	62	754
---	Plumas Quincy	62	926
---	Sacramento Granite	63	231
---	Sacramento Granite	63	245
---	Sacramento Sutter	63	307
---	Sacramento Sutter	63	308
---	Sacramento Cosumnes	63	388
---	Sacramento Ward 3	63	490
---	Sacramento Ward 4	63	613
---	Sacramento Ward 1	63	66
---	Sacramento Ward 1	63	69
---	Sacramento Ward 1	63	70
---	Sacramento Ward 1	63	71
---	San Francisco San Francisco 9	68	1054
---	San Francisco San Francisco 9	68	1088
---	San Francisco San Francisco 4	68	1173
---	San Francisco San Francisco 4	68	1174
---	San Francisco San Francisco 4	68	1181
---	San Francisco San Francisco 4	68	1187
---	San Francisco San Francisco 4	68	1193
---	San Francisco San Francisco 4	68	1194
---	San Francisco San Francisco 4	68	1195
---	San Francisco San Francisco 4	68	1196
---	San Francisco San Francisco 4	68	1198
---	San Francisco San Francisco 4	68	1199
---	San Francisco San Francisco 4	68	1200
---	San Francisco San Francisco 4	68	1203
---	San Francisco San Francisco 11		158
		67	
---	San Francisco San Francisco 5	67	506
---	San Francisco San Francisco 5	67	526
---	San Francisco San Francisco 1	68	857
---	San Francisco San Francisco 1	68	926
---	San Joaquin Stockton	64	1037
---	San Joaquin Stockton	64	1039
---	Shasta Shasta	66	684
---	Shasta Horsetown	66	701
---	Shasta Horsetown	66	705
---	Shasta Horsetown	66	710
---	Shasta French G	66	720
---	Sierra Downieville	66	1008
---	Sierra Downieville	66	1009
---	Sierra Morristown	66	1056
---	Sierra St Louis	66	816
---	Sierra Pine Grove	66	827
---	Sierra Twp 5	66	931
---	Sierra Downieville	66	953
---	Sierra Downieville	66	974
---	Sierra Downieville	66	990
---	Sierra Downieville	66	999
---	Siskiyou Cottonwoood	69	102
---	Stanislaus Branch	70	713
---	Stanislaus Branch	70	714
---	Trinity Mouth Ca	70	1015
---	Trinity Trinindad Rvr	70	1047
---	Trinity China Bar	70	959
---	Tuolumne Montezuma	71	507
---	Tuolumne Montezuma	71	509
---	Tuolumne Twp 5	71	516
---	Tuolumne Don Pedro	71	535
---	Tuolumne Don Pedro	71	538
---	Tuolumne Twp 6	71	539
---	Yolo No E Twp	72	677
---	Yolo No E Twp	72	683
---	Yolo No E Twp	72	684
---	Yuba North Ea	72	677
---	Yuba North Ea	72	681
---	Yuba Slate Ro	72	683
---	Yuba Slate Ro	72	684
---	Yuba Slate Ro	72	715
---	Yuba Long Bar	72	756
---	Yuba Long Bar	72	761
---	Yuba Long Bar	72	762
---	Yuba Fosters	72	827
---	Yuba Fosters	72	830
---	Yuba Fosters	72	842
---*	Amador Twp 2	55	302
---*	Amador Twp 5	55	366
---*	Calaveras Twp 5	57	247
---*	Calaveras Twp 4	57	339
---*	Mariposa Coulterville	60	687
---*	Nevada Bridgeport	61	458
---*	Sacramento Ward 1	63	60
---*	Siskiyou Scott Ri	69	82
---*	Tuolumne Big Oak	71	181
---*	Yuba Foster B	72	830
---*	Yuba Foster B	72	834
---*	Yuba Fosters	72	841
---*	Yuba Fosters	72	842
---*	Yuba Fosters	72	843
---*	Yuba Linda	72	992
A	El Dorado Placerville	58	888
A	El Dorado Mud Springs	58	990
A J	Merced Twp 1	60	898
A M*	Tuolumne Twp 1	71	257
A P	Calaveras Twp 7	57	14
A R	Solano Vacaville	69	328
A S	Sutter Yuba	70	772
Ah	Butte Oregon	56	631
Ah	Butte Bidwell	56	723
Ah	Calaveras Twp 7	57	37
Ah	Sacramento Cosumnes	63	386
Ah	Sacramento Cosumnes	63	396
Ah	Tuolumne Twp 4	71	181
Ah	Yuba Bear Rvr	72	1000
Ah	Yuba Suida	72	990
Ah	Yuba Suida	72	991
Ah	Yuba Suida	72	992
Albert*	Mariposa Twp 3	60	598
Albt	Butte Chico	56	557
Andrew	Humbolt Mattole	59	121
Andrew J	Yuba Marysville	72	887
Ann L	Placer Auburn	62	571
At	Mariposa Twp 3	60	620
Ba	Butte Oro	56	686
Bill	Tulara Visalia	71	117
Bosh	Butte Cascade	56	700
Bridget	Sacramento Ward 1	63	155
C	San Francisco San Francisco 5	67	543
C C	San Joaquin Stockton	64	1012
C E	San Francisco San Francisco 4	68	1151
Catharine	San Francisco San Francisco 2	67	681
Charles	San Francisco San Francisco 4	68	1137
Charles	Siskiyou Callahan	69	9
Charles	Yuba Slate Ro	72	706
Charles F	San Diego Colorado	64	807
Charles W	Humbolt Eureka	59	166
Chest	Butte Cascade	56	699
Chew	Butte Ophir	56	787
Chew	Butte Ophir	56	802
Chew	Butte Ophir	56	804
Chew	Butte Ophir	56	806
Chow	Butte Ophir	56	809
Chow	Tehama Red Bluff	70	934
Choy*	Butte Ophir	56	805
Cong	Butte Bidwell	56	717
Cox	Butte Cascade	56	699
Cub	Butte Ophir	56	788
D	San Francisco San Francisco 6	67	444
David	San Francisco San Francisco 1	68	930
Denis	Nevada Bridgeport	61	453
E D	San Joaquin Stockton	64	1094
E P	Calaveras Twp 7	57	3
E R	Calaveras Twp 7	57	3
Edward	El Dorado Georgetown	58	694
Edwd	San Joaquin Stockton	64	1043
Ein	Tuolumne Twp 4	71	181
Elizabeth	San Francisco San Francisco 9	68	1048
Elizabeth	San Francisco San Francisco 6	67	412
Ellan	Sacramento Granite	63	269
Ep	Sacramento Ward 3	63	492
Eric	El Dorado Mud Springs	58	975
F	Butte Kimshaw	56	606
F	Nevada Eureka	61	363
F D	El Dorado White Oaks	58	1002
F E	Tehama Antelope	70	892
Fa	Yuba Fosters	72	831
Faw	Placer Illinois	62	742
Feilding	Plumas Quincy	62	976
Foo	Butte Bidwell	56	716
Fook	Butte Bidwell	56	728
Frances	Humbolt Eureka	59	176
Frank	Sonoma Sonoma	69	655
Franklin	San Francisco San Francisco 11		132
		67	
Fung	Butte Wyandotte	56	665
G	Nevada Grass Valley	61	217
G	Nevada Grass Valley	61	220
Gaw	Shasta Horsetown	66	704
Gay	Butte Mountain	56	742
Gei	Amador Twp 2	55	302
Geo	Sacramento Granite	63	251
Geo W	Siskiyou Cottonwoood	69	101
Geo*	Sacramento Granite	63	251
George	Calaveras Twp 8	57	56
George	San Luis Obispo San Luis Obispo	65	16
George E	Tulara Visalia	71	107
George W*	Plumas Quincy	62	936
Gin	Butte Mountain	56	735
Gowie	Shasta Horsetown	66	701
H M	Butte Chico	56	556
Hay	Butte Cascade	56	704
Henry	Placer Michigan	62	831
Henry	Plumas Quincy	62	992
Henry	Sacramento Granite	63	227
Henry	Yuba New York	72	745
Henry S	Alameda Brooklyn	55	171
Henry S	Butte Ophir	56	754

LONG -
LONGHNS

California 1860 Census Index

Name	County Locale	M653 Roll Page
LONG		
Hi	Butte Bidwell	56 709
Hi	San Francisco San Francisco 5	671205
Hi*	Yuba Bear Rvr	721000
High	Butte Bidwell	56 723
Himg	San Francisco San Francisco 1	68 926
Hin	Butte Ophir	56 815
Hing	San Francisco San Francisco 7	681392
Hop	Butte Ophir	56 809
How	Butte Ophir	56 804
Hun*	Sacramento Ward 1	63 69
Hung	Sacramento Ward 1	63 69
Hup	Butte Ophir	56 811
Isaac	Butte Chico	56 561
Ism	Butte Cascade	56 700
Ive	Tulara Visalia	71 119
J	Nevada Eureka	61 363
J	Nevada Eureka	61 372
J	Nevada Eureka	61 373
J	Sacramento Ward 3	63 423
J	Siskiyou Scott Ri	69 71
J	Tuolumne Twp 4	71 165
J	Yolo Cache	72 641
J B	Marin Novato	60 739
J H	Nevada Bridgeport	61 472
J H	San Francisco San Francisco 5	67 538
J J	Sonoma Bodega	69 523
J L	Sacramento Sutter	63 289
J L	Yolo Cache Crk	72 666
J P	Tuolumne Twp 2	71 339
Jackson	Santa Clara Santa Clara	65 461
Jacob	Colusa Spring Valley	57 435
James	Calaveras Twp 7	57 38
James	Calaveras Twp 8	57 54
James	Shasta Shasta	66 654
James	Solano Benecia	69 307
James	Tuolumne Twp 5	71 500
James W	Butte Ophir	56 755
James*	Shasta Shasta	66 654
Jas	Sacramento Ward 3	63 421
Jas*	Placer Secret R	62 619
Jeramiah	Marin Cortemad	60 791
Jeremiah	Amador Twp 1	55 471
Jeremiah*	Trinity Weaverville	701077
Jerry	El Dorado White Oaks	581008
Jim	Butte Bidwell	56 719
Jno	Butte Chico	56 561
Jno	Nevada Nevada	61 249
John	El Dorado Placerville	58 921
John	Nevada Bridgeport	61 471
John	Placer Forest H	62 800
John	Sacramento Georgian	63 343
John	Sacramento Cosumnes	63 395
John	Sacramento Ward 1	63 67
John	San Francisco San Francisco 9	681043
John	San Francisco San Francisco 3	67 12
John	San Joaquin Elkhorn	64 950
John	Siskiyou Scott Va	69 56
John	Siskiyou Klamath	69 96
John	Tehama Lassen	70 874
John	Yolo Cache	72 636
John	Yuba North Ea	72 675
John	Yuba Slate Ro	72 706
John D	Calaveras Twp 9	57 381
John H	Placer Auburn	62 574
Jon D	Calaveras Twp 9	57 381
Jos*	Sacramento Ward 1	63 154
Joseph	Nevada Rough &	61 407
Joseph	Santa Clara Santa Clara	65 465
Joseph	Siskiyou Klamath	69 96
Joseph	Yuba Suida	72 982
Josiah	El Dorado Big Bar	58 737
Kee	Alameda Oakland	55 6
Kee	Butte Ophir	56 812
Kee	San Francisco San Francisco 4	681202
Kee	San Francisco San Francisco 5	671205
Kip	Butte Mountain	56 742
Kip	Sierra Downieville	66 985
Ku	San Francisco San Francisco 4	681202
Ku	San Francisco San Francisco 5	671205
L	Tuolumne Twp 1	71 257
L A	El Dorado Newtown	58 779
Lau	San Francisco San Francisco 4	681202
Lee	Butte Oro	56 687
Lee	Butte Oro	56 688
Lee	San Joaquin Stockton	641039
Lee	Yolo Slate Ra	72 708
Lem	Mariposa Twp 1	60 654
Leuis	Yuba Fosters	72 825
Lewis	Yuba Foster B	72 825
Lie	Butte Ophir	56 814
Ligh	Butte Ophir	56 812
Lim	Mariposa Twp 1	60 654
Ling*	Calaveras Twp 6	57 181
Lohn	Santa Clara Alviso	65 416
Loo	Yuba Long Bar	72 760

Name	County Locale	M653 Roll Page
LONG		
Louis	Placer Michigan	62 843
Louis H	Solano Vallejo	69 243
Louis H	Solano Vallejo	69 272
M	Tuolumne Twp 4	71 147
M A	Sonoma Russian	69 434
M D	Nevada Eureka	61 343
Manest*	San Francisco San Francisco 4	681172
Marnest*	San Francisco San Francisco 4	681172
Mary	San Francisco San Francisco 4	681151
Mary	Santa Cruz Santa Cruz	66 619
Mary	Solano Vallejo	69 247
Mary	Sonoma Bodega	69 541
Mathew	San Francisco San Francisco 2	67 628
Mathew	San Francisco San Francisco 1	68 918
Me	Butte Cascade	56 690
Mee	Butte Cascade	56 701
Mee	Butte Bidwell	56 713
Mee	Butte Ophir	56 816
Morris	Calaveras Twp 9	57 389
Moses	San Joaquin O'Neal	641006
Munfred	Yuba Marysville	72 961
N	Butte Eureka	56 654
Na	Butte Cascade	56 700
Nancy	San Francisco San Francisco 10	67 165
Ni	Butte Bidwell	56 708
Nicholas	Sonoma Sonoma	69 655
Note*	El Dorado Georgetown	58 708
Now	Butte Bidwell	56 720
Patrick	Sacramento Ward 1	63 9
Patrick	Tuolumne Twp 1	71 186
Peter	San Francisco San Francisco 2	67 743
Peter	Sierra Pine Grove	66 833
Pong*	Marin Cortemad	60 780
Que*	Placer Auburn	62 564
R A	Calaveras Twp 9	57 358
Reuben	Sacramento Georgian	63 337
Richad	Siskiyou Yreka	69 130
Richard	Shasta Millvill	66 752
Richard	Siskiyou Yreka	69 130
Richard	Solano Vacaville	69 328
Roe	Butte Bidwell	56 709
Rye	Butte Mountain	56 736
S	Nevada Grass Valley	61 146
S	San Francisco San Francisco 2	67 610
S	Siskiyou Scott Ri	69 71
S C	Tuolumne Columbia	71 317
S E	San Francisco San Francisco 5	67 524
S E	Sonoma Russian	69 434
S O	El Dorado Placerville	58 897
S T	Nevada Eureka	61 361
S W	Solano Vacaville	69 325
Salmon	Yuba Marysville	72 908
Sam	Butte Cascade	56 700
Sam	Butte Bidwell	56 708
Samuel	El Dorado White Oaks	581030
Samuel	San Joaquin Elkhorn	64 955
San	San Francisco San Francisco 4	681202
See*	El Dorado Georgetown	58 701
Shwu	Tehama Red Bluff	70 934
Si	Butte Bidwell	56 708
Sigh	Butte Cascade	56 702
Sigh	Butte Bidwell	56 711
Sigh	Butte Bidwell	56 731
Sigh	Butte Mountain	56 735
Sigh	Butte Ophir	56 760
Sigh	Butte Ophir	56 808
Sim	Butte Bidwell	56 723
Sin	Butte Cascade	56 704
Sinett	Butte Oro	56 675
Sing	Butte Bidwell	56 717
Sing	Butte Ophir	56 750
Snefs	Butte Bidwell	56 708
Stephen	Placer Forest H	62 801
Sye	Butte Mountain	56 741
Sye	Butte Ophir	56 813
Sye	Butte Ophir	56 814
Syh*	Butte Ophir	56 809
Syi*	Butte Ophir	56 809
T A	Mariposa Twp 1	60 660
T N	Butte Chico	56 564
Tem	Mariposa Twp 1	60 654
Thiy	Butte Ophir	56 803
Thomas	Calaveras Twp 9	57 367
Thomas	El Dorado Kelsey	581127
Thomas P	Solano Vacaville	69 356
Thos	Alameda Oakland	55 6
Thos	Sacramento Ward 4	63 505
Thos W	Mariposa Coulterville	60 683
Tie	Sacramento Ward 1	63 69
To	San Francisco San Francisco 5	671205
Tom	Tulara Visalia	71 114
Tuck	Sacramento Ward 1	63 69
Tung	Yuba Parks Ba	72 775
Tye	Butte Ophir	56 813

Name	County Locale	M653 Roll Page
LONG		
Victor	San Francisco San Francisco 4	681171
W	Butte Eureka	56 654
W	El Dorado Diamond	58 801
W	Nevada Eureka	61 357
W D	Tuolumne Twp 2	71 410
W H	Tehama Lassen	70 876
W R	Sacramento Brighton	63 204
W*	Nevada Eureka	61 357
Wah	Butte Bidwell	56 723
Wash	Sonoma Petaluma	69 569
Westley	San Joaquin Elliott	64 942
Wi	San Francisco San Francisco 11	67 147
Wilder	Sacramento Ward 1	63 154
William	El Dorado Georgetown	58 748
William	Plumas Quincy	62 952
William	Plumas Quincy	62 987
William	San Francisco San Francisco 8	681242
William	Solano Vacaville	69 342
William	Sonoma Washington	69 665
William B	Plumas Quincy	62 942
William F	Sierra Gibsonville	66 852
William H	Tuolumne Twp 6	71 532
Wm	Colusa Monroeville	57 445
Wm	Plumas Quincy	62 958
Wm	Sacramento American	63 168
Wm	San Bernardino San Salvador	64 656
Wm G	Sierra St Louis	66 805
Wm S	Humbolt Eureka	59 178
Wo	San Francisco San Francisco 4	681202
Yon	Amador Twp 1	55 481
You	San Francisco San Francisco 4	681185
Yow	Placer Auburn	62 573
LONGACRE		
E S	Calaveras Twp 9	57 364
Richard	Santa Clara Alviso	65 410
Thompson	Calaveras Twp 9	57 347
LONGAIN		
Louis	Alameda Brooklyn	55 187
LONGAN		
Edward	Solano Vallejo	69 263
LONGBUN		
Henry	Sierra Twp 7	66 865
Henry G	Sierra Twp 7	66 865
LONGCORS		
John	Yuba Long Bar	72 768
LONGDON		
Joseph	Yuba Long Bar	72 741
Peter	Santa Clara Alviso	65 410
LONGE		
Joseph	Yuba New York	72 730
M*	Nevada Grass Valley	61 150
R A*	Nevada Grass Valley	61 164
LONGEE		
F W*	Sonoma Petaluma	69 579
LONGENETTA		
C	Amador Twp 3	55 408
G B	Amador Twp 3	55 385
LONGENETTI		
A	Amador Twp 1	55 485
LONGENHAFER		
Chas	San Joaquin Stockton	641019
LONGER		
L	El Dorado Mud Springs	58 968
LONGEREVILLE		
Jean*	Tuolumne Chinese	71 495
LONGEWAY		
Danl	Tuolumne Sonora	71 187
LONGFELLOW		
D F	Mariposa Coulterville	60 698
E N	Tuolumne Twp 4	71 128
Henry	Nevada Rough &	61 423
J	Shasta Shasta	66 664
P*	Sacramento Lee	63 216
LONGFELLOWS		
P*	Sacramento Lee	63 216
LONGFUBURY		
Mike	Sonoma Petaluma	69 550
LONGHBOROUGH		
A H	San Francisco San Francisco 10	67 223
LONGHEAD		
Robt	Sacramento Ward 1	63 18
LONGHINA		
---	San Francisco San Francisco 2	67 623
LONGHLIN		
Dennis*	Sacramento Ward 1	63 145
John	San Francisco San Francisco 2	67 570
John	Sierra Poker Flats	66 838
John O*	Sierra Poker Flats	66 838
John*	San Francisco San Francisco 2	67 570
LONGHMAN		
J	San Francisco San Francisco 5	67 548
LONGHNS		
J W	Siskiyou Scott Ri	69 61

California 1860 Census Index

Name	County Locale	M653 Roll	Page
LONGHRAN			
Thos	Sacramento Dry Crk	63	377
LONGHURST			
Peter	Mariposa Coulterville	60	694
LONGHUS			
J W	Siskiyou Scott Ri	69	61
LONGIN			
Henry	Tuolumne Twp 3	71	437
LONGINETTA			
C	Amador Twp 3	55	408
John	Amador Twp 7	55	420
M A	Amador Twp 3	55	383
LONGKNIFE			
William	San Francisco San Francisco 7	68	1359
LONGLEY			
A	Butte Oro	56	684
A J	Butte Wyandotte	56	668
A R	Butte Oro	56	685
Charles	Marin Bolinas	60	733
F H	Siskiyou Scott Ri	69	61
G S	Calaveras Twp 8	57	73
Garrett	Butte Ophir	56	785
H	El Dorado Diamond	58	800
H C	Butte Ophir	56	791
Henry	El Dorado Placerville	58	906
Jas	Sacramento Natonia	63	286
John D	Butte Ophir	56	800
S A	Butte Ophir	56	754
T L	Butte Ophir	56	751
Thomas	Alameda Brooklyn	55	198
W J	Butte Kimshaw	56	596
William	Marin Point Re	60	732
LONGLINS			
Teforl*	Alameda Oakland	55	43
LONGLIUS			
Teforl*	Alameda Oakland	55	43
LONGLOSS			
Wm	Yolo No E Twp	72	678
Wm	Yuba North Ea	72	678
LONGMIRE			
Charles	Solano Vacaville	69	346
Daniel	Solano Vacaville	69	362
Joseph	Solano Vacaville	69	366
Lenord	Humbolt Eel Rvr	59	144
LONGMORE			
Joseph	Solano Vacaville	69	366
LONGNETTA			
John	Amador Twp 7	55	420
LONGNEVILLE			
Jean	Tuolumne Twp 5	71	495
LONGPOINT			
Rudolph	Sierra Twp 7	66	889
LONGREAN			
---*	San Diego San Diego	64	772
LONGREEN			
George	Calaveras Twp 7	57	23
LONGSHIRE			
James	Siskiyou Yreka	69	193
LONGSHORE			
James	Calaveras Twp 6	57	113
LONGSTAFF			
Jon	Placer Iona Hills	62	870
Mathew	Placer Iona Hills	62	878
LONGTON			
Henry	Sacramento Ward 4	63	592
LONGTREE			
James	Sacramento Ward 1	63	114
W*	Calaveras Twp 9	57	388
LONGWAY			
Danl	Tuolumne Twp 1	71	187
LONGWELL			
David*	San Mateo Twp 2	65	119
John C	Sonoma Russian	69	436
LONGWILE			
John C	Sonoma Russian	69	444
LONGWILL			
David*	San Mateo Twp 2	65	119
John C*	Sonoma Russian	69	444
LONGWORTH			
A	Nevada Nevada	61	315
Jack	Nevada Red Dog	61	552
Peter	Alameda Oakland	55	62
William*	Placer Iona Hills	62	895
Wm J	Alameda Brooklyn	55	86
LONGWORTHY			
H*	Stanislaus Buena Village	70	725
LONI			
Ke*	San Francisco San Francisco 4	68	1192
LONIE			
Thos P*	Butte Hamilton	56	521
LONIEGO			
Hario	San Diego Colorado	64	811
LONIERD			
Edward	Sierra Whiskey	66	845
LONIFE			
M*	Nevada Grass Valley	61	150

Name	County Locale	M653 Roll	Page
LONING			
J*	Nevada Grass Valley	61	147
LONINING			
Geo*	Yolo Cottonwood	72	658
LONION			
John	San Francisco San Francisco 8	68	1314
LONIS			
---	Mendocino Calpella	60	826
Sagerert	Alameda Brooklyn	55	180
LONIZELLA			
C	Placer Todds Va	62	764
LONJOY			
John	San Joaquin Stockton	64	1058
W	Tuolumne Twp 4	71	174
LONK			
Lee	Del Norte Crescent	58	633
LONLEP			
P J	El Dorado Mud Springs	58	967
LONMAN			
Jos*	Nevada Nevada	61	289
LONN			
---	Sierra Downieville	66	991
LONNDS			
F	Calaveras Twp 9	57	412
LONNEY			
John	Sonoma Bodega	69	536
LONNSMAN			
Christian	Yuba Suida	72	994
LONO			
---	El Dorado Eldorado	58	940
LONPEE			
Fred	Trinity China Bar	70	959
LONRAUS			
Frank*	Tuolumne Twp 2	71	391
LONREAT			
Victorine*	San Francisco 4	68	1151
	San Francisco		
LONS			
---*	Placer Auburn	62	577
LONSALA			
B N	Tuolumne Twp 4	71	156
LONSANILLE			
Estephen	San Francisco San Francisco 1	68	864
LONSO			
Frank	San Joaquin Stockton	64	1055
LONSTALET			
Louis	San Joaquin Stockton	64	1041
LONT			
Cetta*	Calaveras Twp 8	57	62
LONTHER			
E G	Sierra St Louis	66	813
LONTHEY			
J*	Sacramento Ward 3	63	428
LONTLE			
Martin M	El Dorado Greenwood	58	717
LONTMAN			
Justus*	San Joaquin O'Neal	64	1005
LONTMEYER			
Ernst*	Stanislaus Emory	70	741
LONUG			
Daniel*	Placer Forest H	62	805
LONVIERG			
---	Siskiyou Scott Va	69	48
LONVILLE			
William	San Bernardino Santa Barbara	64	204
LONY			
---	Amador Twp 5	55	366
---	Mariposa Coulterville	60	684
---	Placer Secret R	62	623
---	Sacramento Granite	63	250
---	Shasta French G	66	720
---	Yuba Fosters	72	842
Andrew R	Contra Costa Twp 2	57	568
G*	Nevada Grass Valley	61	220
Geo*	Sacramento Granite	63	251
Jas*	Placer Secret R	62	619
R	Nevada Grass Valley	61	149
LONYE			
M*	Nevada Grass Valley	61	150
LONYLEY			
Jas	Sacramento Natonia	63	286
LONZE			
Gherring	Calaveras Twp 7	57	31
LONZEY			
Andrew	Alameda Brooklyn	55	202
LONZPUY			
Achille	San Francisco San Francisco 10	358 67	
LONZPUZ			
Achille*	San Francisco San Francisco 10	358 67	
LOO CHONG			
---	Butte Oregon	56	613
LOO CHOW			
---	Butte Oregon	56	613
LOO QAH			
T*	Tuolumne Chinese	71	526

Name	County Locale	M653 Roll	Page
LOO SEE			
---	Tuolumne Jacksonville	71	514
LOO TUFO			
---*	Butte Kimshaw	56	598
LOO YOU			
---	Nevada Bridgeport	61	462
LOO			
---	Alameda Oakland	55	64
---	Amador Twp 4	55	235
---	Amador Twp 2	55	308
---	Amador Twp 2	55	311
---	Amador Twp 2	55	312
---	Amador Twp 6	55	430
---	Amador Twp 6	55	442
---	Amador Twp 1	55	502
---	Butte Kimshaw	56	586
---	Butte Kimshaw	56	587
---	Butte Oregon	56	613
---	Butte Oregon	56	615
---	Butte Oregon	56	623
---	Butte Oregon	56	644
---	Calaveras Twp 5	57	141
---	Calaveras Twp 5	57	147
---	Calaveras Twp 6	57	149
---	Calaveras Twp 5	57	201
---	Calaveras Twp 5	57	202
---	Calaveras Twp 5	57	232
---	Calaveras Twp 5	57	249
---	Calaveras Twp 7	57	44
---	Calaveras Twp 7	57	47
---	Calaveras Twp 8	57	68
---	Calaveras Twp 5	57	75
---	Del Norte Crescent	58	640
---	El Dorado White Oaks	58	1033
---	El Dorado Salmon Falls	58	1046
---	El Dorado Salmon Falls	58	1064
---	El Dorado Coloma	58	1115
---	El Dorado Casumnes	58	1161
---	El Dorado Georgetown	58	697
---	El Dorado Diamond	58	795
---	El Dorado Diamond	58	796
---	El Dorado Diamond	58	816
---	El Dorado Placerville	58	840
---	El Dorado Placerville	58	841
---	El Dorado Mud Springs	58	954
---	Fresno Twp 1	59	26
---	Mariposa Twp 3	60	562
---	Mariposa Twp 3	60	563
---	Mariposa Twp 3	60	569
---	Mariposa Twp 3	60	578
---	Mariposa Twp 3	60	607
---	Mariposa Twp 3	60	613
---	Mariposa Twp 3	60	618
---	Mariposa Twp 3	60	619
---	Mariposa Coulterville	60	692
---	Nevada Rough &	61	399
---	Nevada Bridgeport	61	463
---	Placer Auburn	62	562
---	Placer Auburn	62	568
---	Placer Stewart	62	606
---	Placer Horseshoe	62	650
---	Placer Illinois	62	748
---	Sacramento Ward 1	63	53
---	San Francisco San Francisco 4	68	1174
---	San Francisco San Francisco 4	68	1196
---	San Francisco San Francisco 4	68	1200
---	San Francisco San Francisco 4	68	1210
---	San Francisco San Francisco 7	68	1343
---	San Joaquin Stockton	64	1056
---	Sierra Downieville	66	1009
---	Sierra La Porte	66	774
---	Sierra St Louis	66	805
---	Sierra Whiskey	66	843
---	Tuolumne Twp 2	71	398
---	Tuolumne Twp 3	71	453
---	Tuolumne Twp 3	71	455
---	Tuolumne Twp 3	71	460
---	Tuolumne Twp 5	71	517
---	Yolo No E Twp	72	676
---	Yolo No E Twp	72	677
---	Yolo Slate Ra	72	717
---	Yuba North Ea	72	676
---	Yuba North Ea	72	677
---	Yuba Slate Ro	72	717
---	Yuba New York	72	740
---	Yuba Long Bar	72	760
---	Yuba Long Bar	72	761
---	Yuba Fosters	72	841
---*	Amador Twp 2	55	311
---*	Calaveras Twp 10	57	232
---*	Mariposa Twp 3	60	579
---*	Placer Auburn	62	562
---*	Tulara Visalia	71	37
Ach	Yuba Long Bar	72	756
Ack	Yuba Long Bar	72	756
Ado	Mariposa Twp 3	60	613

California 1860 Census Index

Name	County Locale	M653 RollPage
LOO		
Ah	Butte Oregon	56 644
Ah	Yuba Suida	72 990
Aw	Yuba Long Bar	72 763
Bow	Tuolumne Twp 5	71 516
Ching	Yuba Foster B	72 826
Chong	Butte Oregon	56 613
Chong	Yuba Fosters	72 830
Chow	Butte Oregon	56 613
Chow	Butte Mountain	56 736
Chow	Yuba Slate Ro	72 708
Choy	Yuba Fosters	72 827
Chute	Yuba Long Bar	72 770
Chuti	Yuba Long Bar	72 770
Fang	Yuba Long Bar	72 756
Fay	Yuba Long Bar	72 759
Fow	Tuolumne Don Pedro	71 535
Fung	Yuba Parks Ba	72 775
Hik	Yuba Long Bar	72 764
Hong	Yuba Fosters	72 834
How	Yuba Marysville	72 917
Hoy	Yuba Long Bar	72 764
Koe	San Francisco San Francisco 10	355 67
Kon	San Francisco San Francisco 4	681178
Kou	San Francisco San Francisco 4	681178
Ky	Mariposa Twp 3	60 562
Look	San Francisco San Francisco 4	681179
Luck	Butte Kimshaw	56 576
Man	Napa Napa	61 75
Mang	Yuba Long Bar	72 764
Meck	Yuba Fosters	72 831
Mee	San Francisco San Francisco 4	681179
Mei	San Francisco San Francisco 4	681179
Min	Yuba Long Bar	72 767
Mon	Yuba Long Bar	72 767
Quong	Yuba Parke Ba	72 782
Sam	Yolo Slate Ra	72 718
See	Mariposa Twp 3	60 620
Sh	Yuba Fosters	72 827
Sing	Butte Kimshaw	56 577
Song	Yuba Bear Rvr	721000
Sue	Shasta Horsetown	66 701
Tap	Butte Kimshaw	56 598
Tong	San Francisco San Francisco 5	67 493
Tong	Tuolumne Columbia	71 347
Tuck	Butte Kimshaw	56 576
Ufi	Butte Kimshaw	56 577
You	Nevada Bridgeport	61 462
Zu	San Francisco San Francisco 5	67 508
LOOA		
---	El Dorado Salmon Hills	581065
---	El Dorado Coloma	581109
---	El Dorado Mountain	581188
---	Placer Rattle Snake	62 627
LOOCK		
P	Tuolumne Twp 4	71 156
LOOD		
---	El Dorado Mountain	581188
A N	Sacramento Ward 1	63 44
Thos	Calaveras Twp 9	57 391
LOODE		
James	Sonoma Santa Rosa	69 405
LOODESS		
J	Sutter Bear Rvr	70 823
LOODJOY		
R B*	San Francisco San Francisco 3	67 48
LOODS		
Charles W	Tuolumne Twp 1	71 261
LOODY		
Charly W	Tuolumne Twp 1	71 261
LOOE		
Mary*	Yuba Marysville	72 923
LOOELL		
T	Nevada Grass Valley	61 224
LOOERT		
Enoch	Tuolumne Sonora	71 194
LOOF		
---	Placer Illinois	62 745
LOOFBURROW		
D T	El Dorado Gold Hill	581095
LOOH		
---*	Tuolumne Chinese	71 526
LOOHY		
James*	Solano Benecia	69 299
LOOK CHUNDK		
---	Tuolumne Green Springs	71 517
LOOK		
---	Alameda Oakland	55 53
---	Amador Twp 4	55 332
---	Amador Twp 5	55 342
---	Amador Twp 5	55 366
---	Amador Twp 6	55 422
---	Amador Twp 6	55 431
---	Amador Twp 1	55 499
---	Butte Hamilton	56 530
LOOK		
---	Butte Oregon	56 629
---	Butte Oregon	56 644
---	Butte Eureka	56 651
---	Calaveras Twp 5	57 192
---	Calaveras Twp 4	57 300
---	Calaveras Twp 4	57 327
---	El Dorado Georgetown	58 745
---	Mariposa Twp 3	60 580
---	Nevada Rough &	61 431
---	Nevada Rough &	61 436
---	Nevada Rough &	61 438
---	Nevada Bridgeport	61 461
---	Nevada Bridgeport	61 462
---	Sacramento Ward 1	63 51
---	Sacramento Ward 1	63 52
---	Sacramento Ward 1	63 59
---	San Francisco San Francisco 4	681211
---	San Francisco San Francisco 11	146 67
---	San Francisco San Francisco 1	68 926
---	Tuolumne Chinese	71 510
---	Tuolumne Twp 6	71 537
---*	Tuolumne Big Oak	71 179
---*	Tuolumne Chinese	71 526
A	Butte Eureka	56 651
Ah	Butte Oregon	56 629
Ah	Butte Oregon	56 644
Ah	Tuolumne Twp 4	71 179
Chuck	Tuolumne Twp 5	71 517
Fit	San Francisco San Francisco 4	681212
Fu	San Francisco San Francisco 4	681212
Gong	Tuolumne Twp 5	71 517
John	Contra Costa Twp 1	57 513
Sen	Shasta French G	66 712
Sew	Shasta French G	66 712
LOOKE GONG		
---	Tuolumne Green Springs	71 517
LOOKE		
---	Butte Kimshaw	56 603
---	Placer Illinois	62 742
Peter	Siskiyou Callahan	69 7
Saml*	Placer Secret R	62 620
LOOKEN		
Wm*	Plumas Quincy	62 965
LOOKER		
C	Sierra Downieville	661007
Fredk	San Francisco San Francisco 2	67 772
LOOKFAE		
Henry	Calaveras Twp 7	57 25
John	Calaveras Twp 7	57 25
LOOKSHINE		
---*	Shasta Horsetown	66 701
LOOKSHUE		
---*	Shasta Horsetown	66 701
LOOLS		
Isial*	Calaveras Twp 9	57 356
LOOM		
David	Nevada Bridgeport	61 445
LOOMAS		
L D	Mariposa Twp 1	60 642
S D	Mariposa Twp 1	60 642
S H	Mariposa Twp 1	60 642
Wm E	San Francisco San Francisco 3	67 74
LOOMAY		
J	Placer Secret R	62 613
LOOMBLY		
H M	Nevada Eureka	61 394
LOOMBS		
C J	Nevada Grass Valley	61 163
LOOMCEICE		
Wm	Colusa Muion	57 460
LOOME		
Hugh M*	Sacramento American	63 172
LOOMER		
Fred	Klamath S Fork	59 203
LOOMIER		
Sarah	Tuolumne Sonora	71 188
LOOMIS		
---	San Francisco San Francisco 3	67 74
A W	San Francisco San Francisco 6	67 437
Bardabus	Calaveras Twp 10	57 275
Barnabus	Calaveras Twp 10	57 275
Charles	Solano Suisan	69 207
Dudley J	San Francisco San Francisco 7	681327
E	Tuolumne Sonora	71 187
E J	Sacramento Ward 3	63 430
E W	Tehama Antelope	70 889
Filanda	Yolo Cache	72 641
G	Nevada Grass Valley	61 153
G A	El Dorado Cold Spring	581100
H W	Shasta Millvill	66 726
Harriet	Calaveras Twp 6	57 130
Hiram	Placer Iona Hills	62 875
J	El Dorado Placerville	58 817
J	Nevada Grass Valley	61 144
LOOMIS		
James	Calaveras Twp 6	57 130
James O	Solano Suisan	69 223
Josiah	El Dorado Placerville	58 903
L V	Tehama Lassen	70 879
Minerva	Trinity Weaverville	701065
Mr	Marin Bolinas	60 741
O A	Trinity North Fo	701024
Orrin	Trinity Minersville	70 968
Oscar	Stanislaus Oatvale	70 719
Pascal	San Francisco San Francisco 6	67 404
Ralph	Los Angeles San Pedro	59 481
Riley	San Francisco San Francisco 8	681322
Roland	San Francisco San Francisco 10	354 67
S	San Bernardino Santa Barbara	64 150
Samuel	Los Angeles San Pedro	59 481
Sarah L	Tuolumne Twp 1	71 188
T*	Nevada Grass Valley	61 166
LOOMY		
A	Shasta Millvill	66 748
J	Nevada Grass Valley	61 219
LOON		
---	Amador Twp 6	55 430
---	El Dorado Salmon Hills	581053
---	El Dorado Union	581089
---	Klamath Liberty	59 232
---	Trinity Lewiston	70 956
A	Calaveras Twp 9	57 417
Ann	Yuba Long Bar	72 760
F T*	Calaveras Twp 9	57 403
LOONE		
M	Nevada Eureka	61 346
Mr*	Nevada Eureka	61 346
LOONEY		
Dennis	Sierra Twp 5	66 920
H	Santa Cruz Shasta	66 653
J	Nevada Grass Valley	61 219
J B	Nevada Grass Valley	61 149
Jno M	Butte Hamilton	56 522
M	Nevada Grass Valley	61 161
Mary	Santa Clara Santa Clara	65 515
P	Nevada Grass Valley	61 156
Patrick	Sierra Downieville	661012
S	Nevada Grass Valley	61 212
Stephen	Marin Cortemad	60 784
T	Nevada Grass Valley	61 212
Wm	Butte Hamilton	56 521
LOONG		
---	Del Norte Happy Ca	58 664
---	San Francisco San Francisco 5	671205
---	San Francisco San Francisco 7	681417
---	San Francisco San Francisco 10	356 67
---	San Francisco San Francisco 5	67 532
---	Yolo Washington	72 562
A	San Francisco San Francisco 5	67 532
Cum*	Shasta Shasta	66 680
LOONGCUM		
---*	Shasta Shasta	66 680
LOONING		
J	Tehama Red Bluff	70 914
LOONT		
Daniel*	Colusa Grand Island	57 469
LOONY		
W	San Joaquin Stockton	641093
LOOOL		
---*	Mariposa Twp 3	60 562
LOOP		
---	Butte Kimshaw	56 600
---	Butte Oregon	56 640
---	Calaveras Twp 5	57 215
---	Placer Illinois	62 751
Ashel	Napa Clear Lake	61 135
Highs	Butte Ophir	56 816
S J	San Francisco San Francisco 10	329 67
Sa	Butte Eureka	56 652
Sye	Butte Ophir	56 816
LOOPOO		
---	Butte Bidwell	56 709
LOOPS		
Fe	San Francisco San Francisco 5	67 509
LOOR		
---	Mariposa Twp 3	60 569
---*	Mariposa Twp 3	60 579
LOORER		
Josea	Placer Auburn	62 585
LOORYCUM		
---*	Shasta Shasta	66 680
LOOS		
Philip*	Plumas Quincy	62 940
LOOSIN		
Joseph*	Mariposa Coulterville	60 676
LOOT		
---	Butte Kimshaw	56 588

Name	County Locale	M653 RollPage
LOOT		
---	Del Norte Crescent	58 633
---	Del Norte Crescent	58 643
---	El Dorado Salmon Falls	581046
---	El Dorado Salmon Hills	581053
---	Nevada Rough &	61 436
---*	El Dorado Salmon Falls	581053
LOOTE		
Saml*	Placer Secret R	62 620
LOOTENS		
Louis	Marin San Rafael	60 763
LOOTH		
---	Calaveras Twp 8	57 74
LOOTOON		
---	Shasta Shasta	66 669
LOOTS		
I*	Trinity Weaverville	701063
LOOTY		
J	Stanislaus Buena Village	70 722
LOOU		
---	El Dorado Mud Springs	58 992
LOOVE		
---	Mariposa Twp 3	60 562
LOOVL		
---*	Mariposa Twp 3	60 562
LOOVY		
Mary	Merced Monterey	60 930
Mary	Monterey Monterey	60 930
LOOW		
Ann*	Yuba Long Bar	72 760
Aun*	Yuba Long Bar	72 760
LOOY		
---	Plumas Quincy	62 950
---*	Plumas Quincy	62 969
---*	Yuba North Ea	72 676
---*	Yuba Foster B	72 830
---*	Yuba Marysville	72 908
Fong	San Francisco San Francisco 4	681203
LOP LIN		
---*	San Francisco San Francisco 4	681173
LOP		
---	Amador Twp 5	55 366
---	Butte Kimshaw	56 582
---	Butte Kimshaw	56 584
---	Butte Kimshaw	56 587
---	El Dorado Greenwood	58 723
---	El Dorado Placerville	58 906
---	Sierra Downieville	661008
Bot	Calaveras Twp 5	57 253
He	Sacramento Granite	63 269
Hill	Butte Ophir	56 783
Hon	Butte Ophir	56 815
Hye	Butte Ophir	56 802
John S P	Shasta Shasta	66 733
Ken	Butte Ophir	56 806
Ken	Butte Ophir	56 807
Keow	Calaveras Twp 5	57 253
Kin	Butte Ophir	56 803
Kow	Butte Ophir	56 804
Kye	Butte Ophir	56 807
Kye	Butte Ophir	56 808
Lee	San Francisco San Francisco 9	681087
Lee	San Francisco San Francisco 4	681176
Lin	Butte Ophir	56 808
Lin	San Francisco San Francisco 4	681173
Lou	Butte Ophir	56 807
Po	Calaveras Twp 5	57 253
Sing	Butte Ophir	56 788
Sing	Butte Ophir	56 806
Tut	Calaveras Twp 5	57 253
Tye	Butte Ophir	56 796
Yon	Butte Ophir	56 802
LOPA		
Jno	Nevada Nevada	61 262
LOPAS		
Ablena	Siskiyou Yreka	69 140
M	Solano Vacaville	69 334
LOPATA		
---	Fresno Twp 2	59 90
LOPATH		
Edward	Calaveras Twp 9	57 371
LOPAZ		
Cruz	Tuolumne Twp 1	71 225
Pedro	Tuolumne Twp 3	71 469
Pinrotho	Tuolumne Jamestown	71 443
Tule	Tuolumne Twp 3	71 456
Tulo	Tuolumne Jamestown	71 456
LOPCHOKE		
---*	Tulara Visalia	71 37
LOPE		
---	Nevada Rough &	61 426
Francesca	Alameda Brooklyn	55 215
Jno	Alameda Brooklyn	55 104
Pen*	Alameda Brooklyn	55 215
Peu	Alameda Brooklyn	55 215
Wm	Sonoma Petaluma	69 563

Name	County Locale	M653 RollPage
LOPELIN		
Joseph	Sacramento Ward 4	63 525
LOPEN PINTSEAD		
---*	Tulara Yule Rvr	71 31
LOPER		
Alfred*	Mariposa Twp 3	60 561
Alorgen*	Amador Twp 5	55 332
F	San Francisco San Francisco 5	67 549
George*	Mariposa Coulterville	60 688
Jno	Nevada Nevada	61 262
John	Humbolt Pacific	59 135
John E	Mariposa Coulterville	60 678
John*	Santa Cruz Santa Cruz	66 618
P O	El Dorado Diamond	58 782
William L	Calaveras Twp 8	57 72
LOPERES		
Jesiah	Sierra Twp 7	66 885
LOPES		
Alex	Amador Twp 1	55 486
Alonzen*	Amador Twp 5	55 332
Alorgen*	Amador Twp 5	55 332
Antone	El Dorado Salmon Falls	581050
Antone	Placer Dutch Fl	62 715
Antonio	El Dorado Diamond	58 766
Catronio	Los Angeles Los Angeles	59 516
Cyro*	Los Angeles Los Angeles	59 498
Filipi*	Los Angeles Los Angeles	59 492
Francis	Calaveras Twp 7	57 35
Francisco	Los Angeles Los Angeles	59 500
Francisco	Merced Twp 2	60 921
Gronancio	Los Angeles Los Angeles	59 516
Guiatan	Los Angeles Tejon	59 521
James	Placer Auburn	62 580
Jaun*	Placer Auburn	62 583
Jesus	Siskiyou Yreka	69 175
John E	Mariposa Coulterville	60 678
Jose	Solano Vacaville	69 337
Jose C*	Los Angeles Los Angeles	59 508
Jose D*	Los Angeles Los Angeles	59 503
Joseph	Nevada Rough &	61 425
Juan	Los Angeles Tejon	59 528
Juan*	Placer Auburn	62 583
L	El Dorado Diamond	58 808
Margarett	Tuolumne Big Oak	71 137
Maria A	Los Angeles Los Angeles	59 516
Patrocineo*	Monterey Alisal	601036
LOPETI		
Theodore	Fresno Twp 1	59 82
LOPEY		
Thomas	San Francisco San Francisco 6	67 449
Walter*	Butte Kimshaw	56 593
LOPEZ		
---	Tulara Twp 2	71 38
---*	Solano Benecia	69 315
---*	Tulara Visalia	71 38
A	Merced Twp 1	60 902
A	Nevada Grass Valley	61 180
Alvera	Butte Oregon	56 619
Alveso	Santa Clara San Jose	65 365
Anna	San Francisco San Francisco 2	67 767
Antone	Mariposa Twp 1	60 645
Antonia	Los Angeles Los Angeles	59 323
Antonia	Napa Napa	61 114
Antonie	Alameda Brooklyn	55 94
Antonie	Alameda Brooklyn	55 94
Antonio	Los Angeles San Jose	59 283
Antonio	Los Angeles Los Nieto	59 433
Antonio	Mariposa Twp 1	60 665
Antonio	Tuolumne Twp 2	71 389
Antonio	Tuolumne Twp 1	71 479
Antonio	Yuba Marysville	72 971
Antonio*	Plumas Quincy	62 988
Augustin	San Diego San Diego	64 765
Augustin	Santa Clara San Jose	65 358
B	Calaveras Twp 9	57 376
Bernadina	San Mateo Twp 2	65 133
Bernardino	Los Angeles Los Nieto	59 430
Bernedino	San Bernardino Santa Barbara	64 198
Bernidino	San Bernardino Santa Barbara	64 166
Blas	San Bernardino Santa Barbara	64 162
Bruno	Monterey San Juan	601007
Caraman	Mariposa Twp 1	60 628
Carlos	Los Angeles Los Angeles	59 400
Carlos	San Francisco San Francisco 2	67 768
Chino	Monterey San Juan	601002
Chris	Monterey San Juan	601002
Ciledonio	San Bernardino Santa Ba	64 218
Ciledonio	San Bernardino S Buenav	64 219
Clero	Contra Costa Twp 1	57 537
Cruz	Tuolumne Sonora	71 225
Cypriana*	San Mateo Twp 2	65 133
Damasio	Tehama Red Bluff	70 926

Name	County Locale	M653 RollPage
LOPEZ		
Diego	Los Angeles Los Angeles	59 322
Dieja	Santa Clara Almaden	65 271
Dolores	Los Angeles Los Nieto	59 426
Dolores	San Luis Obispo San Luis Obispo	65 44
Dolores	Santa Clara Gilroy	65 229
E	Calaveras Twp 9	57 375
E	Nevada Grass Valley	61 198
Fecundo	Los Angeles Santa Ana	59 446
Feliciano	Los Angeles Santa Ana	59 450
Felicidad	Monterey San Juan	60 999
Felipe	San Bernardino Santa Barbara	64 193
Fernando	San Diego Temecula	64 785
Fernando	San Diego Agua Caliente	64 861
Flunano	Calaveras Twp 9	57 354
Flunaris*	Calaveras Twp 9	57 354
Frances	Sonoma Sonoma	69 641
Francesca M	San Diego San Diego	64 769
Francis	Sonoma Sonoma	69 641
Francisca	Monterey Alisal	601043
Francisco	Calaveras Twp 10	57 260
Francisco	Contra Costa Twp 1	57 495
Francisco	Contra Costa Twp 3	57 599
Francisco	Los Angeles Los Angeles	59 393
Francisco	Los Angeles Los Nieto	59 432
Francisco	Mariposa Twp 1	60 646
Francisco	Monterey Alisal	601043
Francisco	San Bernardino Santa Barbara	64 165
Francisco	Tuolumne Shawsfla	71 389
Franco	Mariposa Twp 1	60 646
Gaeramenti*	Calaveras Twp 5	57 248
Georg	San Mateo Twp 1	65 58
George	Santa Clara Almaden	65 266
George	Santa Clara Almaden	65 270
Getrides	San Francisco San Francisco 2	67 768
Getrudes	San Francisco San Francisco 2	67 768
Gonihere*	San Francisco San Francisco 11	126
Gouthere*	San Francisco San Francisco 11	126
Gregorio	San Bernardino Santa Barbara	64 179
H	Merced Twp 1	60 898
Hasamo	Mariposa Twp 1	60 627
Hemisio	Santa Clara Almaden	65 269
Hosea	Alameda Brooklyn	55 190
Hosea	Alameda Oakland	55 46
Ignacio	Calaveras Twp 5	57 206
Ignacio	San Diego San Diego	64 769
Ignacio	Santa Clara Almaden	65 267
Ignacio	Santa Clara San Jose	65 289
Ignacio	Santa Clara San Jose	65 304
Isidro	Los Angeles Los Angeles	59 383
J L	Merced Twp 1	60 900
Jarin	Mariposa Coulterville	60 699
Jaun	Mariposa Coulterville	60 699
Jessie	San Luis Obispo San Luis Obispo	65 5
Jesus	Calaveras Twp 4	57 331
Jesus	Los Angeles Los Angeles	59 337
Jesus	Mariposa Twp 1	60 628
Jesus	San Diego Agua Caliente	64 861
Jesus	San Luis Obispo San Luis Obispo	65 31
Jesus	Santa Clara Almaden	65 274
Jesus	Santa Clara Almaden	65 277
Jesus	Santa Clara San Jose	65 331
Jesus	Tehama Red Bluff	70 930
Jesus	Yuba Marysville	72 922
Jgnacio*	Calaveras Twp 5	57 206
Jno	Butte Eureka	56 649
Joaquin	Los Angeles Santa Ana	59 456
John	Calaveras Twp 6	57 130
John	Tuolumne Sonora	71 225
John	Yuba Suida	72 982
John	Yuba Linda Twp	72 983
Joiaquin*	Calaveras Twp 9	57 362
Jose	Los Angeles Los Angeles	59 406
Jose	Los Angeles Los Nieto	59 427
Jose	San Bernardino Santa Barbara	64 182
Jose	San Diego S Buenav	64 210
Jose	San Francisco San Francisco 2	67 672
Jose	San Joaquin Stockton	641072
Jose	Santa Clara Almaden	65 271
Jose	Santa Clara San Jose	65 309
Jose And	San Bernardino S Buenav	64 211
Jose An	San Bernardino Santa Ba	64 211
Jose I	San Mateo Twp 2	65 133
Jose J	Los Angeles Santa Ana	59 458
Jose M	Del Norte Crescent	58 626
Jose M	El Dorado Georgetown	58 688
Jose M	Los Angeles Los Angeles	59 355
Jose M	Los Angeles Los Nieto	59 434
Jose M	Monterey Alisal	601043
Jose M	Monterey San Juan	60 999
Jose M	San Bernardino Santa Barbara	64 168
Jose M	San Bernardino Santa Barbara	64 175

California 1860 Census Index

Name	County Locale	M653 Roll	Page
LOPEZ			
Jose Maria	San Mateo Twp 2	65	111
Joseffa	San Bernardino S Buenav	64	208
Josep Maria	San Mateo Twp 2	65	111
Juagiun*	Calaveras Twp 9	57	362
Juaguin*	Calaveras Twp 9	57	362
Juan	Contra Costa Twp 1	57	495
Juan	Fresno Twp 1	59	82
Juan	Fresno Twp 1	59	84
Juan	Los Angeles Los Angeles	59	311
Juan	Los Angeles Los Angeles	59	373
Juan	Monterey San Juan	60	986
Juan	San Bernardino Santa Barbara	64	198
Juan	San Bernardino San Bernadino	64	639
Juan	Santa Clara San Jose	65	350
Juana	San Diego San Diego	64	757
Juaquin	Calaveras Twp 9	57	362
Julin	San Bernardino Santa Barbara	64	173
L	Nevada Washington	61	332
Labino	Santa Clara Almaden	65	269
Leandro	Los Angeles Los Angeles	59	399
Leme*	San Mateo Twp 2	65	133
Lena	Alameda Brooklyn	55	155
Leno	San Diego San Diego	64	757
Leonardo	San Luis Obispo San Luis Obispo	65	34
Loreta	Los Angeles Los Angeles	59	314
Loreto	Santa Clara Almaden	65	269
Lucus	Calaveras Twp 5	57	206
Luis	Los Angeles Los Angeles	59	384
Luis	Marin Cortemad	60	782
M	Nevada Nevada	61	258
Magill	Los Angeles San Jose	59	291
Maguil	Napa Napa	61	115
Manedi L	Alameda Brooklyn	55	87
Manuel	Alameda Brooklyn	55	155
Manuel	Calaveras Twp 9	57	402
Manuel	Contra Costa Twp 3	57	614
Manuel	Fresno Twp 1	59	82
Manuel	Los Angeles San Jose	59	282
Manuel	San Joaquin Stockton	641053	
Manuel A	Los Angeles San Jose	59	286
Manuela	Santa Clara San Jose	65	327
Manuell	Mariposa Twp 1	60	628
Manwell	Mariposa Twp 1	60	628
Maraito L*	Alameda Brooklyn	55	87
Marcedio	Alameda Oakland	55	55
Marcus	Los Angeles Santa Ana	59	455
Margareta	Tuolumne Twp 1	71	215
Margarta	Tuolumne Sonora	71	215
Maria	Calaveras Twp 6	57	161
Maria	Contra Costa Twp 1	57	496
Maria	San Bernardino Santa Barbara	64	193
Maria A	Los Angeles Los Angeles	59	309
Maria De Los A	San Gabriel Los Angeles	59	418
Mariano	San Bernardino Santa Barbara	64	167
Marin*	Calaveras Twp 6	57	161
Marrerto L*	Alameda Brooklyn	55	87
Martin	San Francisco San Francisco 2	67	695
Masamo*	Mariposa Twp 1	60	627
Maximo*	San Bernardino Santa Barbara	64	184
Miguel	San Bernardino San Bernadino	64	676
N	Sacramento Ward 1	63	4
Nasario	Marin Cortemad	60	784
Nicolas	Monterey Alisal	601043	
Nolverto	Mariposa Twp 1	60	656
Pasqual	Yuba Marysville	72	868
Patrocineo	Monterey Alisal	601036	
Pedro	Los Angeles Santa Ana	59	455
Pedro	San Bernardino Santa Barbara	64	193
Perfect	San Mateo Twp 2	65	111
Petra	Santa Clara San Jose	65	299
Philip	Mariposa Twp 1	60	645
Policenfra	Santa Ba San Bernardino	64	211
Pormmano	San Salvador San Bernardino	64	661
Qiburcio*	Los Angeles Los Nieto	59	439
Rafael	Monterey San Juan	601002	
Rafael	San Bernardino S Buenav	64	214
Rafail	San Bernardino Santa Ba	64	214
Ramon	San Francisco San Francisco 2	67	768
Ramon	Santa Clara San Jose	65	332
Refugio	Los Angeles Los Angeles	59	322
Refugio	Los Angeles Los Angeles	59	398
Refugio	Los Angeles Los Angeles	59	399
Romaldo	Los Angeles Los Nieto	59	430
Romeldo	Los Angeles Los Nieto	59	430
Romone	Mariposa Twp 1	60	636
S	San Francisco San Francisco 5	67	488
Sabino	Santa Clara San Jose	65	291
Salvador	Los Angeles San Juan	59	470
Samara	Tehama Tehama	70	942
Santiago	Los Angeles San Jose	59	289
Santiago	Tulara Visalia	71	30
LOPEZ			
Simon	Santa Clara Gilroy	65	233
Simona	Los Angeles Los Angeles	59	298
T	Nevada Eureka	61	366
Tabateo	Los Angeles Tejon To	59	535
Theodore	Los Angeles Azuza	59	272
Theodore	Tuolumne Twp 1	71	207
Thomas	San Francisco San Francisco 6	67	449
Thos	Mariposa Twp 1	60	647
Tiadoro	San Bernardino Santa Ba	64	207
Tiburcia	Trinity Weaverville	701070	
Tiburcio	Los Angeles Santa Ana	59	439
Tomas	Contra Costa Twp 1	57	491
Vicente	Los Angeles San Juan	59	467
Walter	Butte Kimshaw	56	593
LOPHA			
S	El Dorado Placerville	58	837
LOPINER			
B	San Francisco San Francisco 2	67	789
LOPIS			
Cronancio	Los Angeles Los Angeles	59	516
Cyro*	Los Angeles Los Angeles	59	498
Filipi*	Los Angeles Los Angeles	59	492
Jose C*	Los Angeles Los Angeles	59	508
Jose D*	Los Angeles Los Angeles	59	503
Luterio*	Los Angeles Los Angeles	59	489
Maria A	Los Angeles Los Angeles	59	516
LOPOR			
George*	Mariposa Coulterville	60	688
LOPOY			
Antone	Mariposa Twp 1	60	645
Antoni*	Mariposa Twp 1	60	645
LOPOZ			
Antoni	Mariposa Twp 1	60	645
LOPPAH			
---	Tulara Twp 2	71	39
LOPPED			
Alice	Alameda Oakland	55	8
LOPPENSTEIN			
L	Tehama Red Bluff	70	923
LOPS			
---	Nevada Rough &	61	426
LOPSHOKE			
---	Tulara Twp 2	71	37
LOPSOW			
---	Tulara Twp 2	71	39
LOPTON			
Charles	Yuba Marysville	72	936
LOPUS			
Apordina	Los Angeles Los Angeles	59	511
Guiatan	Los Angeles Tejon	59	521
Thomas*	Nevada Red Dog	61	552
LOQUO			
Antione*	San Francisco San Francisco 11	67	109
LOQUOR			
Manuel	Calaveras Twp 9	57	402
LOR			
---	Calaveras Twp 4	57	326
---	Nevada Bridgeport	61	463
---	Sierra St Louis	66	861
---*	Sierra Twp 7	66	876
---*	Nevada Bridgeport	61	463
LORA			
James	Tehama Cottonwoood	70	900
Na	Tehama Red Bluff	70	931
LORAIN			
---*	Mariposa Twp 3	60	614
Christian	El Dorado Mud Springs	58	995
Thomas	Los Angeles Los Angeles	59	512
LORAINE			
John	San Joaquin Stockton	641085	
John L	Yuba Marysville	72	919
Luis	Los Angeles Tejon	59	538
LORAISS			
Manuel*	Los Angeles Los Angeles	59	496
LORALO			
Jesus	Santa Clara San Jose	65	297
LORAN			
Casa	Calaveras Twp 8	57	90
Jaconio*	Mariposa Twp 3	60	614
Jaconio*	Mariposa Twp 3	60	615
LORANA			
Staran*	Shasta Shasta	66	682
Staven*	Shasta Shasta	66	682
LORANCE			
Celestine	San Francisco San Francisco 7	681418	
Joshua*	Humbolt Eel Rvr	59	147
LORANCHENDLE			
John	Marin Bolinas	60	749
LORANCHENDLER			
John	Marin Bolinas	60	749
LORANDO			
F	Merced Twp 1	60	906
LORANGER			
Isadore	Sacramento Ward 4	63	520
LORANSEN			
L	Amador Twp 2	55	309
S*	Amador Twp 2	55	309
LORANSON			
Rob*	Amador Twp 2	55	309
Rot	Amador Twp 2	55	309
Thos	Trinity Turner'S	70	997
LORATER			
Antonio*	Amador Twp 2	55	288
LORBER			
Joseph	San Diego Agua Caliente	64	816
Joseph	San Francisco San Francisco 3	67	10
LORBIR			
Joseph*	San Francisco San Francisco 3	67	10
LORBY			
Mary	San Francisco San Francisco 4	681109	
LORCH			
Fredrick	Tuolumne Twp 5	71	513
LORCHER			
John	Sierra Downieville	661016	
LORCHYNSCKY			
J*	Shasta Horsetown	66	707
LORCUTZ			
George	Sacramento Ward 3	63	457
LORD			
A W B	Yolo Putah	72	552
Arthur	Yuba New York	72	730
Berhand D*	Yuba Marysville	72	860
Birhand D*	Yuba Marysville	72	860
Chas S	San Francisco San Francisco 9	68	997
D S	San Francisco San Francisco 2	67	804
Daniel	San Joaquin Stockton	641079	
Daniel	San Joaquin Stockton	641085	
E H	Sacramento Brighton	63	203
Ed	Calaveras Twp 7	57	3
Edward	Solano Suisan	69	208
Edwin	Yuba New York	72	724
F T	Amador Twp 3	55	405
Frances D	Solano Fremont	69	377
Franklin	Solano Fremont	69	377
Geo H	Trinity Weaverville	701063	
Geo*	El Dorado Casumnes	581176	
George	San Bernardino San Bernadino	64	637
H	Nevada Nevada	61	284
Harlow	Butte Bidwell	56	718
Haslow*	Butte Bidwell	56	718
Hiram*	Colusa Butte Crk	57	467
Hisani*	Colusa Butte Crk	57	467
Hosea	Stanislaus Branch	70	698
Ira H	San Francisco San Francisco 3	67	83
J C	Nevada Eureka	61	376
J D	Sacramento Ward 3	63	438
J H	Yuba Rose Bar	72	813
James	San Mateo Twp 3	65	101
Jeo H	San Francisco San Francisco 3	67	83
Jonathan	Siskiyou Scott Va	69	53
Jos H	Stanislaus Empire	70	732
Joseph A	Del Norte Crescent	58	635
Joseph M	Los Angeles Los Angeles	59	380
L	Mariposa Twp 3	60	558
M	Nevada Grass Valley	61	151
Moses J	Yuba Marysville	72	897
R	San Joaquin Stockton	641095	
Richard	San Mateo Twp 3	65	105
Robt	Klamath Klamath	59	224
Samuel	Mariposa Twp 3	60	568
Thomas	Mendocino Big Rvr	60	840
Thomas	Placer Forest H	62	770
Thomas	San Francisco San Francisco 11	67	152
Thomas D	Calaveras Twp 6	57	132
Thos	Butte Ophir	56	750
W	El Dorado Diamond	58	796
W C	San Joaquin Stockton	641059	
W R	Shasta Shasta	66	680
William	Klamath Orleans	59	217
William	San Joaquin Stockton	641034	
William	San Joaquin Stockton	641041	
William	San Mateo Twp 3	65	80
Wm	Butte Wyandotte	56	666
LORDAL			
John P*	Yuba Marysville	72	872
LORDAT			
John P	Yuba Marysville	72	872
LORDE			
John	San Francisco San Francisco 9	681078	
LORDEN			
Daniel	San Francisco San Francisco 9	68	946
David	San Francisco San Francisco 9	68	946
LORDER			
H M	Calaveras Twp 9	57	369
LORDON			
Humphry	Calaveras Twp 9	57	381
Jas M	Calaveras Twp 9	57	381
LORDS			
Joseph	San Mateo Twp 3	65	109

California 1860 Census Index

Name	County Locale	M653 Roll	Page
LORDS			
W	Sacramento Alabama	63	415
LORE			
---	Tuolumne Twp 6	71	535
Alexander	Calaveras Twp 8	57	56
David*	Mariposa Twp 1	60	639
Frank*	Calaveras Twp 8	57	63
John*	Solano Benecia	69	315
William	Calaveras Twp 8	57	93
LOREALL			
Abraham	Mendocino Ukiah	60	803
Kraham*	Mendocino Ukiah	60	803
LOREDIAS			
Manuel	Yuba Suida	72	980
LOREDRAS			
Manuel	Yuba Linda Twp	72	980
LOREE			
---	Amador Twp 2	55	312
Saml	Amador Twp 7	55	413
LOREGE			
L M*	Nevada Nevada	61	327
LOREICK			
Werhtio*	Santa Cruz Santa Cruz	66	616
LOREIN			
John	San Bernardino San Bernadino	64	634
LOREL			
H C*	Tehama Red Bluff	70	905
LORELAND			
Louis	Solano Suisan	69	240
LOREMANS			
Facunda	Monterey Alisal	60	1036
LOREN			
Jerry	Tuolumne Sonora	71	191
Louis	Yuba Marysville	72	966
Timothy	Yuba Long Bar	72	771
LORENA			
M	San Francisco San Francisco 3	67	50
Staren*	Shasta Shasta	66	682
LORENCE			
Alfred	Santa Clara Gilroy	65	254
M	San Francisco San Francisco 3	67	50
Samuel	Siskiyou Yreka	69	145
LORENE			
Peter	Tuolumne Columbia	71	291
LORENGBURG			
J	San Francisco San Francisco 5	67	512
LORENGEN			
D J	San Francisco San Francisco 5	67	478
LORENIE			
Joseph W	Sierra Pine Grove	66	820
LORENSO			
Marlhio*	Santa Cruz Santa Cruz	66	616
Marthio*	Santa Cruz Santa Cruz	66	616
Merthio*	Santa Cruz Santa Cruz	66	616
Murlhio*	Santa Cruz Santa Cruz	66	616
Murthio*	Santa Cruz Santa Cruz	66	616
LORENSTEIN			
Jacob*	San Francisco San Francisco 4	681	120
LORENT			
Condo	San Francisco San Francisco 8	681	265
J O*	Calaveras Twp 9	57	392
LORENTINA			
---	San Bernardino S Timate	64	716
---	San Bernardino S Timate	64	722
---	San Bernardino S Timate	64	730
---	San Bernardino S Timate	64	731
---	San Bernardino S Timate	64	739
---	San Bernardino S Timate	64	743
---	San Bernardino S Timate	64	751
---	San Bernardino S Timate	64	754
---	San Bernardino S Timate	64	755
LORENTINO			
---	San Bernardino S Timate	64	754
LORENZ			
Henry	Trinity Raabs Ba	701	020
Nicholas	Trinity McGillev	701	021
LORENZA			
---	Los Angeles San Pedro	59	486
---	San Bernardino Santa Inez	64	137
Juana M	Monterey Pajaro	601	036
Loern	Alameda Brooklyn	55	153
LORENZANA			
Francisco	Santa Ba	64	212
	San Bernardino		
Getrades	San Bernardino Santa Ba	64	212
Getrades	San Bernardino S Buenav	64	212
Jose	San Bernardino Santa Ba	64	212
Mariana	Los Angeles Los Nieto	59	429
LORENZANNA			
Jess	San Bernardino S Buenav	64	215
Jesus	San Bernardino Santa Ba	64	215
Maria	San Bernardino Santa Barbara	64	174
LORENZANNO			
Dolores	San Bernardino Santa Barbara	64	170
Felipe	San Bernardino Santa Ba	64	216
Felipe	San Bernardino S Buenav	64	217

Name	County Locale	M653 Roll	Page
LORENZANNO			
Jose	San Bernardino Santa Barbara	64	153
Manuel	San Bernardino Santa Ba	64	216
Manuel	San Bernardino S Buenav	64	217
Maria	San Bernardino Santa Barbara	64	169
LORENZANO			
Facunda*	Monterey Alisal	601	036
Jose	Santa Cruz Santa Cruz	66	627
Manul	Santa Cruz Santa Cruz	66	628
Richard	Santa Cruz Santa Cruz	66	601
LORENZO			
---	Los Angeles Los Angeles	59	401
---	Monterey S Antoni	60	972
---	San Bernardino Santa Inez	64	138
---	San Bernardino S Buenav	64	221
---	San Bernardino S Timate	64	700
---	San Bernardino S Timate	64	707
---	San Bernardino S Timate	64	708
---	San Bernardino S Timate	64	719
---	San Bernardino S Timate	64	731
---	San Bernardino S Timate	64	736
---	San Bernardino S Timate	64	748
---	San Diego Agua Caliente	64	819
---	San Diego Agua Caliente	64	844
Fernando	San Francisco San Francisco 2	67	649
Geo W	Tuolumne Shawsfla	71	410
John	Alameda Brooklyn	55	159
Jose	Santa Cruz Pajaro	66	571
Jose	Santa Cruz Santa Cruz	66	629
N	San Francisco San Francisco 3	67	83
Phil	Butte Kimshaw	56	571
Sam	Sierra La Porte	66	767
LORER			
J H	El Dorado Coloma	581	082
LORERANDO			
Jose	Placer Forest H	62	801
LORERETTE			
F	San Francisco San Francisco 9	681	058
LORERIDGE			
O M*	Yuba Rose Bar	72	811
LORERN			
John	San Bernardino San Bernadino	64	634
LORERTTAR			
---*	Mariposa Twp 1	60	627
LORERZANO			
Richard*	Santa Cruz Santa Cruz	66	601
LORESTTAR			
---*	Mariposa Twp 1	60	627
LORETA LONOSA			
---	San Diego San Diego	64	772
LORETE			
---	San Bernardino San Bernadino	64	680
LORETT			
John	Monterey Alisal	601	043
LORETTA			
---	San Bernardino San Bernadino	64	680
---	San Bernardino S Timate	64	714
---	San Bernardino S Timate	64	717
---	San Bernardino S Timate	64	742
---	San Bernardino S Timate	64	746
LORETTAR			
---	Mariposa Twp 1	60	627
LORETTE			
---	San Bernardino S Timate	64	739
LORETTO			
Martinez*	San Francisco San Francisco 11	127 67	
LOREY			
---	El Dorado Salmon Falls	581	066
Albert*	Mariposa Twp 3	60	598
J M*	Nevada Grass Valley	61	189
John	San Francisco San Francisco 9	681	065
Thomas D	Sierra Pine Grove	66	830
LOREYEA			
Jos	Sacramento Ward 3	63	425
LOREZ			
Albert*	Mariposa Twp 3	60	598
Jean*	Tuolumne Columbia	71	321
LOREZZO			
Joseph	Solano Benecia	69	300
LORFIELD			
F	Butte Bidwell	56	716
LORG			
---	Calaveras Twp 9	57	358
---	El Dorado Eldorado	58	943
LORGA			
John*	Shasta Millvill	66	756
LORGAND			
J	Nevada Grass Valley	61	156
LORGANS			
Martin	El Dorado Coloma	581	111
LORGERO			
Jewalsi	Calaveras Twp 5	57	204
Jewolsio	Calaveras Twp 5	57	204
LORGIAN			
M	Tuolumne Jacksonville	71	166

Name	County Locale	M653 Roll	Page
LORGOMARCIN			
Joseph*	Calaveras Twp 6	57	164
LORGUIN			
M	San Francisco San Francisco 6	67	468
LORHLEN			
Cynthia	San Luis Obispo San Luis Obispo	65	13
LORIA			
Lucia	San Bernardino Santa Barbara	64	156
LORIAN			
---	San Diego Temecula	64	793
LORICH			
Charles	San Francisco San Francisco 9	68	957
LORID			
F*	Nevada Eureka	61	382
LORIEDICK			
Peter*	Calaveras Twp 5	57	230
LORIENG			
Charles O	Yuba Marysville	72	972
LORIET			
Peter	Mariposa Coulterville	60	679
LORIFF			
Samuel	Calaveras Twp 7	57	40
LORIG			
Andrew*	Yuba Marysville	72	887
LORIGAN			
M	Tuolumne Twp 4	71	166
LORIL			
---	Sierra La Porte	66	782
LORIMER			
Henry	Solano Benecia	69	316
LORIMUY			
Geo*	Yolo Cottonwoood	72	658
LORINA			
---	Placer Folsom	62	648
LORINCIA			
Polinario*	Santa Cruz Watsonville	66	540
LORINE			
Isadore B	Placer Dutch Fl	62	715
LORINEIA			
Polinario	Santa Cruz Watsonville	66	540
LORING			
Anne T	San Francisco San Francisco 12	392 67	
C	Amador Twp 4	55	254
C	San Joaquin Stockton	641	092
Charles	Calaveras Twp 7	57	18
Charles O	Yuba Marysville	72	972
Edward B*	San Francisco	681	251
	San Francisco 8		
G H	Nevada Nevada	61	254
Harriet	San Francisco San Francisco 4	681	143
Henry	San Joaquin Stockton	641	026
J H	Nevada Nevada	61	254
James	Tuolumne Twp 5	71	505
Jas	Trinity Trinity	70	975
John	Plumas Quincy	62	938
John M	Tuolumne Shawsfla	71	385
Lydia	Sacramento Ward 3	63	464
Marcus	Placer Michigan	62	821
Nich?	Sacramento Ward 1	63	48
Nichls	Sacramento Ward 1	63	48
Patrick	Contra Costa Twp 1	57	493
Simon W	San Francisco San Francisco 7	681	118
Thomas	Solano Benecia	69	314
Timothy	Yuba Long Bar	72	770
Wm A*	Amador Twp 4	55	237
LORINNA			
---	Los Angeles Tejon	59	529
LORK			
---	Nevada Rough &	61	431
---	Nevada Bridgeport	61	461
LORKINS			
C H	San Francisco San Francisco 3	67	83
LORLEN			
N D*	Calaveras Twp 9	57	395
LORLER			
W D*	Calaveras Twp 9	57	395
LORLING			
J	Calaveras Twp 9	57	392
J	Calaveras Twp 9	57	393
LORME			
Hugh M*	Sacramento American	63	172
LORMIG			
M*	Nevada Grass Valley	61	149
LORMON			
---	Sierra Twp 5	66	934
LORMY			
A	Shasta Millvill	66	748
M	Nevada Grass Valley	61	149
LORN			
---*	Shasta Shasta	66	678
LORNAR			
Mercedes*	Sacramento Ward 1	63	104
LORNDICK			
Peter*	Calaveras Twp 5	57	230
LORNEY			
Mary J	Sacramento Ward 4	63	599

California 1860 Census Index

Name	County Locale	M653 Roll	Page
LORNG			
---*	Shasta French G	66	713
LORNISS			
Manuel*	Los Angeles Los Angeles	59	496
LORO			
---	Sacramento Casumnes	63	381
David	Mariposa Twp 1	60	639
J	Tuolumne Twp 4	71	150
Jose M	Santa Cruz Watsonville	66	536
LOROE			
Thomas*	Siskiyou Callahan	69	11
LOROINE			
G	Merced Twp 1	60	902
R	Merced Twp 1	60	902
LORONA			
Francisco	Los Angeles Santa Ana	59	454
LORONDES			
Samuel*	San Francisco San Francisco 8	681	252
LORQUIN			
M	San Francisco San Francisco 6	67	468
LORR			
---	Tuolumne Twp 5	71	515
James	Monterey S Antoni	60	973
LORRAGERA			
---	San Francisco San Francisco 4	681	139
LORRAIN			
Wm	Tuolumne Twp 1	71	218
LORRAINE			
Wm	Tuolumne Sonora	71	218
LORRANO			
Ign Acio	San Diego San Diego	64	770
LORRANS			
Frank	Tuolumne Shawsfla	71	391
LORRDEN			
Spencer*	Trinity Lewiston	70	961
LORRER			
John E*	San Francisco San Francisco 7	681	416
LORRETTA			
Perfet*	Calaveras Twp 6	57	161
LORRETTO			
John	Calaveras Twp 6	57	161
LORREY			
Harmon	Santa Clara San Jose	65	296
M*	Nevada Grass Valley	61	165
LORRIE			
Joseph*	Siskiyou Callahan	69	6
LORRNERA			
Polinario	Santa Cruz Watsonville	66	540
LORRQUER			
J*	Alameda Brooklyn	55	79
LORRY			
---	Amador Twp 5	55	365
LORRYCUM			
---	Shasta Shasta	66	680
LORTER			
W D*	Calaveras Twp 9	57	395
LORTON			
J F	Butte Chico	56	540
J T*	Butte Chico	56	540
LORY			
---	Amador Twp 5	55	333
---	Amador Twp 5	55	335
---	Amador Twp 5	55	341
---	Amador Twp 5	55	345
---	Sacramento Cosumnes	63	384
---*	Amador Twp 5	55	366
G*	Nevada Grass Valley	61	220
Hay	Mariposa Twp 3	60	562
John P*	Yuba North Ea	72	676
LORYAN			
S*	Nevada Grass Valley	61	226
LORYAORTA			
William*	Placer Iona Hills	62	895
LORYAR			
S*	Nevada Grass Valley	61	226
LORYDON			
James*	El Dorado Georgetown	58	758
LORYEA			
Alfonso	Yolo No E Twp	72	669
Alfonso	Yuba North Ea	72	669
LORYOMORDN			
John*	Calaveras Twp 5	57	228
LOS ANGELOS			
M	San Joaquin Stockton	641	094
LOS ANGLES			
Marie	Amador Twp 2	55	288
LOS SANTOS			
Jose*	Contra Costa Twp 1	57	495
LOS			
---	El Dorado Coloma	581	084
---	Mariposa Twp 3	60	607
LOSA			
Camillo	San Diego Temecula	64	793
Inarsa	San Bernardino San Bernadino	64	685
Jose M	Los Angeles Los Angeles	59	370
Merced	San Diego San Diego	64	760

Name	County Locale	M653 Roll	Page
LOSA			
Ramon	San Diego Agua Caliente	64	847
LOSANA			
Valentina	San Francisco San Francisco 2	67	762
LOSANGELOS			
Thomas	Mariposa Twp 1	60	654
LOSANGILOS			
Thomas	Mariposa Twp 1	60	654
LOSANGILOUS			
Marianar	Mariposa Twp 1	60	654
LOSCE			
Harvey	Tuolumne Twp 2	71	368
LOSCHYNSCTY			
J*	Shasta Horsetown	66	707
LOSCHZNSCTY			
J*	Shasta Horsetown	66	707
LOSEAN			
Flor*	Placer Illinois	62	705
Tlor*	Placer Illinois	62	705
LOSEE			
Harvey	Tuolumne Springfield	71	368
LOSELLO			
Pedro	Solano Benecia	69	309
LOSER			
Albert	Sacramento Ward 4	63	572
Anthony*	Amador Twp 4	55	255
LOSEY			
John*	San Francisco San Francisco 9	681	065
LOSH			
---	El Dorado Eldorado	58	942
LOSIA			
Louis*	Calaveras Twp 6	57	178
LOSIER			
J	Yolo Slate Ra	72	716
J*	Yuba Slate Ro	72	716
LOSIN			
Joseph	Mariposa Coulterville	60	676
LOSIU			
Louis	Calaveras Twp 5	57	178
LOSKOTA			
---	Fresno Twp 2	59	67
LOSKROO			
Nicholas	Klamath S Fork	59	202
LOSKY			
John*	Amador Twp 2	55	278
T*	San Francisco San Francisco 1	68	850
LOSNEI			
Edward*	Solano Vallejo	69	277
LOSNK			
A F	Yuba Rose Bar	72	811
LOSONZA			
Jann*	Placer Illinois	62	706
LOSS			
---	Butte Wyandotte	56	672
---	Mariposa Coulterville	60	683
Andrew	San Francisco San Francisco 9	681	084
Peter	Calaveras Twp 6	57	157
LOSSE			
John	Sacramento Ward 3	63	445
LOSSEN			
John	Alameda Brooklyn	55	117
LOSSIER			
C	Sacramento Granite	63	227
Noisine*	Yuba Parke Ba	72	783
LOSSIMORE			
P	Yuba North Ea	72	686
LOSSING			
Peter	Calaveras Twp 6	57	168
LOSSON			
P G*	San Francisco San Francisco 9	681	066
R G*	San Francisco San Francisco 9	681	066
LOSTER			
John	Trinity Taylor'S	701	036
LOSTERO			
Agustin	Amador Twp 2	55	288
LOSUI			
Edward*	Solano Vallejo	69	277
LOSWELL			
A R	Sierra Downieville	661	018
LOSYED			
M*Jenkins	San Mateo Twp 3	65	103
LOT FONG			
---	Nevada Bridgeport	61	461
LOT			
---	Butte Kimshaw	56	603
---	Calaveras Twp 9	57	358
---	El Dorado Georgetown	58	701
---	El Dorado Georgetown	58	702
---	El Dorado Greenwood	58	730
---	El Dorado Big Bar	58	738
---	Sacramento Ward 1	63	59
---	San Francisco San Francisco 9	681	095
---*	El Dorado Georgetown	58	702
Fong	Nevada Bridgeport	61	461
Low	Butte Ophir	56	810
LOTA			
A	Nevada Grass Valley	61	144

Name	County Locale	M653 Roll	Page
LOTA			
Andress	Monterey Alisal	601	027
Esmal	San Bernardino Santa Ba	64	221
Isedera	Santa Clara Fremont	65	437
J	San Joaquin Stockton	641	098
Juan	Monterey San Juan	60	976
Loratte	San Bernardino Santa Inez	64	141
Miguil*	San Bernardino Santa Inez	64	141
LOTAN			
---	Nevada Bridgeport	61	466
LOTDO			
Frank*	El Dorado Georgetown	58	699
LOTE			
---	Trinity Lewiston	70	956
Jann	Mariposa Twp 3	60	547
Marko	Tuolumne Shawsfla	71	414
LOTEAS			
Francisco*	Yuba Marysville	72	920
LOTENS			
Francisco*	Yuba Marysville	72	920
LOTER			
Antoine	Calaveras Twp 5	57	224
LOTERI			
Louis*	Placer Michigan	62	855
LOTH			
John	Sacramento Granite	63	246
LOTHAM			
H M*	Sacramento Cosumnes	63	387
LOTHER			
Goss	Mariposa Twp 1	60	651
LOTHIAN			
Alex	Klamath Trinidad	59	222
Peter	Humbolt Union	59	189
LOTHINN			
J	Calaveras Twp 9	57	398
J*	Calaveras Twp 9	57	389
LOTHIUM			
J*	Calaveras Twp 9	57	389
LOTHROP			
Adelia	San Francisco San Francisco 7	681	400
Edward C	Yuba Marysville	72	870
George W	Yuba Marysville	72	881
LOTIE			
John*	Sacramento Granite	63	246
LOTIFIS			
Edwd	Sonoma Petaluma	69	588
LOTILEY			
C	Nevada Grass Valley	61	223
LOTISE			
Theodore	Sierra St Louis	66	807
LOTITO			
Frank*	El Dorado Georgetown	58	699
LOTMAN			
Andw	Napa Napa	61	69
LOTMORE			
S	Sutter Nicolaus	70	830
LOTNY			
Jacob	Yuba Marysville	72	935
LOTO			
---	San Diego Temecula	64	786
??Idera*	Santa Clara Fremont	65	437
Antonio	Sacramento Ward 1	63	57
Estevan	San Diego S Luis R	64	780
Jama*	Mariposa Twp 3	60	543
James	Tuolumne Twp 3	71	460
Jarm	Mariposa Twp 3	60	545
Jaun*	Mariposa Twp 3	60	545
Joaquin	San Diego S Luis R	64	781
Lorenso	San Diego S Luis R	64	779
Manuel*	Tuolumne Columbia	71	306
Marko	Tuolumne Twp 2	71	414
Miguel	Calaveras Twp 9	57	364
Ramis*	Santa Cruz Pescadero	66	645
Z Sidera*	Santa Clara Fremont	65	437
LOTORI			
Louis*	Placer Michigan	62	855
LOTOW			
---	Trinity Trinindad Rvr	701	048
LOTRY			
Jacob*	Yuba Marysville	72	935
LOTS			
Antonio*	Sacramento Ward 1	63	57
Bantisto	Monterey Monterey	60	948
Geo	El Dorado Union	581	092
LOTSMAN			
L	San Francisco San Francisco 3	67	73
LOTT			
Chas F	Butte Ophir	56	761
Chas F	San Francisco San Francisco 2	67	733
Edward	San Francisco San Francisco 2	67	705
J S	Nevada Grass Valley	61	222
Jno	Sacramento Ward 1	63	9
John	Sacramento Cosumnes	63	389
Miles*	Yuba Bear Rvr	721	008
Niles	Yuba Bear Rvr	721	008
Pino	Tuolumne Sonora	71	243

Name	County Locale	M653 Roll	Page
LOTT			
Richard*	Yuba Fosters	72	837
LOTTE			
Francis	Sacramento Ward 1	63	148
John*	Sacramento Granite	63	246
LOTTEE			
Jas	Sonoma Sonoma	69	641
LOTTERICK			
John	San Francisco San Francisco 3 67		2
LOTTHAMER			
Louis*	Sacramento Ward 4	63	549
LOTTIE			
E C	Sonoma Sonoma	69	657
LOTTIRCK			
John*	San Francisco San Francisco 3 67		2
LOTTMAN			
Wm*	Tuolumne Twp 3	71	428
LOTTO			
Aug	San Francisco San Francisco 2 67		784
LOTTRICK			
John*	San Francisco San Francisco 3 67		2
LOTTS			
Andrew	San Francisco San Francisco 3 67		85
Ludwig	Plumas Quincy	62	974
LOTTY			
---	Mendocino Calpella	60	828
S*	Nevada Red Dog	61	547
LOTUN			
---	Nevada Bridgeport	61	466
LOU AN			
---	Yuba New York	72	740
LOU CHOU			
---	Mariposa Twp 3	60	608
LOU KEE			
---	Mariposa Twp 3	60	608
LOU			
---	Calaveras Twp 5	57	202
---	Calaveras Twp 8	57	60
---	Contra Costa Twp 2	57	559
---	Mariposa Twp 3	60	546
---	Mariposa Twp 3	60	549
---	Mariposa Twp 3	60	575
---	Mariposa Twp 3	60	609
---	Mariposa Twp 3	60	620
---	Mariposa Twp 1	60	668
---	Nevada Grass Valley	61	227
---	Nevada Grass Valley	61	230
---	Nevada Grass Valley	61	232
---	Nevada Rough &	61	399
---	Placer Illinois	62	748
---	Sacramento Cosumnes	63	407
---	San Francisco San Francisco 4 68		1175
---	San Francisco San Francisco 4 68		1176
---	San Francisco San Francisco 4 68		1179
---	San Francisco San Francisco 4 68		1187
---	San Francisco San Francisco 4 68		1190
---	San Francisco San Francisco 4 68		1196
---	San Francisco San Francisco 4 68		1197
---	San Francisco San Francisco 4 68		1209
---	San Francisco San Francisco 4 68		1210
---	San Francisco San Francisco 4 68		1212
---	San Francisco San Francisco 11		161
		67	
---	Siskiyou Scott Va	69	32
---	Stanislaus Buena Village	70	724
---	Stanislaus Emory	70	752
---	Tuolumne Don Pedro	71	535
---	Yuba North Ea	72	681
---	Yuba New York	72	740
---*	Mariposa Twp 3	60	579
---*	Yuba Linda	72	991
A	Sacramento Granite	63	268
A T	San Francisco San Francisco 6 67		469
Ah	Calaveras Twp 7	57	14
Ah	Calaveras Twp 7	57	32
Ah	Calaveras Twp 7	57	33
Ah	Calaveras Twp 7	57	35
Ah	Calaveras Twp 7	57	37
Ah	Tuolumne Twp 4	71	149
Ah	Tuolumne Twp 4	71	159
An	Yuba New York	72	740
Diva	San Francisco San Francisco 4 68		1181
Eten	Tehama Lassen	70	882
Foi	San Francisco San Francisco 4 68		1186
Fu	San Francisco San Francisco 4 68		1180
Hou*	San Francisco San Francisco 11		146
		67	
Hung	San Francisco San Francisco 4 68		1180
Ing*	San Francisco San Francisco 3 67		2
Jose Maria*	San Mateo Twp 2	65	112
Ki	Yuba Long Bar	72	758
King	San Francisco San Francisco 4 68		1176
Kung	San Francisco San Francisco 4 68		1180
Mo	San Francisco San Francisco 4 68		1190
Mouy	San Francisco San Francisco 4 68		1190
Moy	San Francisco San Francisco 4 68		1190

Name	County Locale	M653 Roll	Page
LOU			
Nua	Placer Auburn	62	581
Ri	Yuba Long Bar	72	758
Tay	Yuba Long Bar	72	759
Tong	San Francisco San Francisco 11		160
		67	
Tow	Calaveras Twp 6	57	121
Tu	San Francisco San Francisco 4 68		1190
Wong	San Francisco San Francisco 6 67		453
Wox	San Francisco San Francisco 4 68		1181
LOUAY			
---	Butte Ophir	56	805
LOUBRIE			
Jerome	San Francisco San Francisco 3 67		16
LOUCHROUGH			
George	Calaveras Twp 7	57	14
LOUCI			
Joseph	San Joaquin O'Neal	64	1004
LOUCIS			
Lorenzo	Calaveras Twp 9	57	378
LOUCK			
---	Sierra Downieville	66	1027
LOUCKS			
George	Contra Costa Twp 3	57	587
J R*	Sonoma Petaluma	69	591
LOUD			
C H	Tuolumne Twp 2	71	327
Elihn	San Francisco San Francisco 7 68		1436
F*	Nevada Eureka	61	382
Harriet P	San Francisco San Francisco 6 67		407
Henry	Tehama Red Bluff	70	920
John B	Napa Napa	61	83
Michael	Butte Ophir	56	793
S D	Tuolumne Columbia	71	327
T	Nevada Eureka	61	382
LOUDAN			
Thomas*	Santa Cruz Pescadero	66	649
LOUDEN			
R H	San Francisco San Francisco 6 67		446
Robert*	Yuba Rose Bar	72	806
LOUDENATER			
F P*	San Francisco San Francisco 3 67		50
LOUDENBURG			
T*	San Francisco San Francisco 1 68		870
LOUDENSLAGER			
Conrad*	Alameda Brooklyn	55	147
LOUDENSLIGER			
Thomas*	San Francisco San Francisco 7 68		1406
LOUDERBACH			
H*	Napa Hot Springs	61	4
LOUDERBACK			
Andrew	San Francisco San Francisco 8 68		1238
Charles	San Francisco San Francisco 7 68		1437
D	Napa Hot Springs	61	4
David L	San Francisco San Francisco 4 68		1216
Sophia M	San Francisco San Francisco 9 68		1007
LOUDERBOM			
Nathl*	San Francisco San Francisco 9 68		1052
LOUDERS			
Thomas*	Calaveras Twp 6	57	135
LOUDIN			
R H	San Francisco San Francisco 6 67		446
LOUDMATER			
F P*	San Francisco San Francisco 3 67		50
LOUDON			
Clour	Calaveras Twp 10	57	277
Henry	Calaveras Twp 10	57	277
John	Siskiyou Yreka	69	177
John*	Nevada Bridgeport	61	476
LOUDSULIGER			
Dora*	San Francisco San Francisco 7 68		1405
LOUDWATER			
F P	San Francisco San Francisco 3 67		50
LOUE			
W*	El Dorado Placerville	58	851
LOUEL			
L	Mariposa Twp 3	60	559
LOUERANCE			
Antonio	Mariposa Coulterville	60	691
LOUG			
---	El Dorado Mud Springs	58	952
---	Yuba Bear Rvr	72	1000
LOUGA			
Belagren*	Placer Michigan	62	840
LOUGE			
G*	Nevada Grass Valley	61	167
L M*	Nevada Nevada	61	327
M	Nevada Nevada	61	270
LOUGEE			
Chas	Nevada Nevada	61	277
LOUGER			
Chas	Nevada Nevada	61	277
LOUGH			
Mary Jane	Mariposa Twp 3	60	543
LOUGHERTY			
Ellen	Sacramento Ward 3	63	451

Name	County Locale	M653 Roll	Page
LOUGHERTY			
Wm*	Plumas Quincy	62	960
LOUGHERY			
Jas	Butte Ophir	56	784
LOUGHLAN			
Denis	Solano Fremont	69	381
Michael	Calaveras Twp 5	57	195
LOUGHLIN			
Dennis	Sacramento Ward 1	63	145
George K	San Francisco San Francisco 8 68		1317
George*	San Francisco San Francisco 8 68		1317
Hugh	San Francisco San Francisco 12		368
		67	
Jno	Sacramento Ward 4	63	498
John O	Sierra Poker Flats	66	838
John*	San Francisco San Francisco 2 67		570
LOUGHRAN			
Peter	Solano Benecia	69	285
LOUGHRY			
Jesse*	Siskiyou Scott Va	69	55
LOUGHUS			
J W	Siskiyou Scott Ri	69	61
LOUGLEY			
William*	Marin Point Re	60	732
LOUI			
---	Calaveras Twp 5	57	247
LOUIDICK			
Peter*	Calaveras Twp 5	57	230
LOUIE			
---	Trinity Weaverville	70	1076
Jonah L	Yuba Long Bar	72	754
LOUIKER			
Louis*	Tuolumne Twp 3	71	455
LOUILIS			
Thomas	Calaveras Twp 5	57	135
LOUION			
John	San Francisco San Francisco 8 68		1314
LOUIS SZOLLOSY			
J B*	Sacramento Ward 1	63	46
LOUIS			
---	Amador Twp 2	55	301
---	Calaveras Twp 8	57	70
---	Mendocino Calpella	60	826
---	Mendocino Round Va	60	882
---	San Bernardino Santa Inez	64	137
---	San Bernardino Santa Inez	64	138
---	San Bernardino Santa Ba	64	216
---	San Bernardino San Bernadino	64	680
---	San Bernardino S Timate	64	704
---	San Bernardino S Timate	64	714
---	San Bernardino S Timate	64	733
---	San Bernardino S Timate	64	737
---	San Bernardino S Timate	64	738
---	San Bernardino S Timate	64	754
---	San Bernardino S Timate	64	755
---	San Francisco San Francisco 3 67		44
---	San Mateo Twp 3	65	108
---	San Mateo Twp 2	65	126
---	Sierra Scales D	66	804
---	Siskiyou Callahan	69	9
---	Tulara Twp 2	71	32
---	Yuba Linda Twp	72	983
---	Tulara Visalia	71	32
---*	Yuba Linda Twp	72	982
Alfred	Yuba Linda Twp	72	982
Amayo	Santa Cruz Santa Cruz	66	610
Andrew	Calaveras Twp 7	57	7
Ann	Contra Costa Twp 1	57	525
Antone	Siskiyou Yreka	69	139
Avarea	Los Angeles Azuza	59	276
Beatrise	San Francisco San Francisco 2 67		699
Benjamin	Contra Costa Twp 3	57	591
Benjamin	Contra Costa Twp 3	57	606
Bernard	El Dorado White Oaks	58	1016
Carolina	San Francisco San Francisco 9 68		951
Caroline	San Francisco San Francisco 9 68		951
Christian	Klamath S Fork	59	203
D A	Yolo Merritt	72	577
E G	Mariposa Twp 3	60	557
E J	Mariposa Twp 3	60	557
E W	San Francisco San Francisco 6 67		446
Edward	Contra Costa Twp 2	57	565
Edward	El Dorado Placerville	58	891
F	Butte Oregon	56	636
Ferdinando	Calaveras Twp 8	57	69
Ferris	Sierra Downieville	66	1023
Flores	Tuolumne Twp 3	71	463
Francois	Amador Twp 2	55	323
Frank	Contra Costa Twp 1	57	501
Frank	Siskiyou Yreka	69	142
Frank	Yuba New York	72	740
Geo	El Dorado Coloma	58	1117
George	Placer Michigan	62	829
George*	Yuba Marysville	72	901
Ghirabetti	Calaveras Twp 7	57	38
Henry	Placer Michigan	62	821
Henry	Siskiyou Yreka	69	147

Name	County Locale	M653 Roll	Page
LOUIS			
Hiram	Yolo Cottonwoood	72	650
Isaac G	Sierra Twp 7	66	897
J M	Tuolumne Columbia	71	310
J S	El Dorado Georgetown	58	691
James	Contra Costa Twp 1	57	529
Jean	San Francisco San Francisco 2	67	761
John	El Dorado White Oaks	58	1033
John	San Francisco San Francisco 10	67	194
John E*	San Francisco San Francisco 7	68	1416
Jose	Contra Costa Twp 1	57	509
Jose	San Bernardino San Bernadino	64	682
Joseph	Tuolumne Shawsfla	71	389
Joseph	Tuolumne Jamestown	71	456
L P	San Francisco San Francisco 6	67	407
Leona	Yuba Fosters	72	824
M	Klamath S Fork	59	202
M	Nevada Nevada	61	283
M*	Calaveras Twp 9	57	405
M*	San Francisco San Francisco 5	67	500
Magil	Los Angeles Los Angeles	59	513
Manuel	Tuolumne Twp 2	71	284
Manuel	Tuolumne Twp 2	71	284
Manuel	Tuolumne Twp 2	71	389
McCireg	San Francisco San Francisco 4	68	1170
Mellon	Placer Virginia	62	673
Merion	Siskiyou Yreka	69	175
Michon	Los Angeles Los Angeles	59	339
Oder*	Amador Twp 5	55	333
Robert	Contra Costa Twp 2	57	542
Rossa*	Placer Michigan	62	832
Saml	Nevada Nevada	61	242
Stephen	Contra Costa Twp 3	57	584
Victor	El Dorado White Oaks	58	1033
W	Sacramento Ward 4	63	606
William C	Contra Costa Twp 2	57	565
Wm	Mariposa Twp 1	60	642
Yawgon	San Francisco San Francisco 4	68	1124
LOUISA			
---	Mendocino Calpella	60	826
---	San Bernardino San Bernadino	64	669
---	San Bernardino San Bernadino	64	677
---	San Bernardino San Bernadino	64	682
---	San Bernardino S Timate	64	690
---	San Bernardino S Timate	64	695
---	San Bernardino S Timate	64	701
---	San Bernardino S Timate	64	704
---	San Bernardino S Timate	64	706
---	San Bernardino S Timate	64	710
---	San Bernardino S Timate	64	712
---	San Bernardino S Timate	64	713
---	San Bernardino S Timate	64	715
---	San Bernardino S Timate	64	717
---	San Bernardino S Timate	64	718
---	San Bernardino S Timate	64	719
---	San Bernardino S Timate	64	721
---	San Bernardino S Timate	64	724
---	San Bernardino S Timate	64	725
---	San Bernardino S Timate	64	726
---	San Bernardino S Timate	64	727
---	San Bernardino S Timate	64	728
---	San Bernardino S Timate	64	729
---	San Bernardino S Timate	64	730
---	San Bernardino S Timate	64	732
---	San Bernardino S Timate	64	735
---	San Bernardino S Timate	64	737
---	San Bernardino S Timate	64	739
---	San Bernardino S Timate	64	740
---	San Bernardino S Timate	64	741
---	San Bernardino S Timate	64	742
---	San Bernardino S Timate	64	743
---	San Bernardino S Timate	64	744
---	San Bernardino S Timate	64	745
---	San Bernardino S Timate	64	747
---	San Bernardino S Timate	64	748
---	San Bernardino S Timate	64	750
---	San Bernardino S Timate	64	752
---	San Bernardino S Timate	64	753
---	San Diego San Diego	64	771
---	San Diego Temecula	64	791
---	San Diego Temecula	64	805
Ellen*	Yuba Fosters	72	829
Ellin*	Yuba Fosters	72	829
Marcus	Butte Ophir	56	792
Maria	San Diego Temecula	64	805
Mary	San Francisco San Francisco 11	67	107
Mary Sister	Santa Clara San Jose	65	373
LOUISAVER			
Caroline*	San Francisco San Francisco 4	68	1124
LOUISE			
---	San Bernardino S Timate	64	695
John	San Francisco San Francisco 2	67	690
Maria	Sierra Downieville	66	962
LOUISER			
---	Mariposa Twp 1	60	655

Name	County Locale	M653 Roll	Page
LOUISIAN			
Charles	Calaveras Twp 7	57	18
LOUISSON			
M	San Francisco San Francisco 10	67	199
LOUIZA			
John	Calaveras Twp 4	57	325
LOUIZET			
Margaret	Napa Napa	61	114
LOUK			
---	Del Norte Crescent	58	633
---	Del Norte Happy Ca	58	667
---	Del Norte Happy Ca	58	668
LOUKES			
Geo	Santa Clara Redwood	65	453
LOUL			
B*	El Dorado Casumnes	58	1177
LOULE			
Bertram	Tuolumne Twp 3	71	469
G W	Napa Napa	61	100
Hiram	Butte Oregon	56	638
Wm	Yuba New York	72	735
LOULSBY			
Edw	Amador Twp 6	55	447
Thomas	Tuolumne Twp 1	71	261
LOULTIS			
Thos L	Calaveras Twp 6	57	115
LOUM			
John*	Butte Ophir	56	749
LOUMAN			
J B	Nevada Nevada	61	258
Jos*	Nevada Nevada	61	289
LOUME			
---	Tulara Twp 2	71	37
---*	Tulara Visalia	71	39
LOUMIS			
H W	Shasta Millvill	66	726
LOUMNE			
---	Tulara Twp 2	71	36
LOUN			
---	El Dorado Mud Springs	58	955
---	Nevada Bridgeport	61	485
Cho*	Butte Ophir	56	814
Yong	Placer Auburn	62	572
LOUNDER			
James	Tuolumne Twp 2	71	378
LOUNDRY			
Chas	Butte Ophir	56	777
LOUNDY			
James	Tuolumne Shawsfla	71	378
LOUNG			
---	Amador Twp 4	55	233
---	Shasta Horsetown	66	701
---	Trinity Lewiston	70	964
Ah	Yolo Washington	72	562
Joseph	Plumas Meadow Valley	62	927
LOUNGE			
Wm H	Mariposa Twp 1	60	635
LOUNSMAN			
Christian*	Yuba Linda	72	994
LOUNT			
D S	San Francisco San Francisco 6	67	437
George	Tehama Lassen	70	875
LOUNYGER			
John	San Francisco San Francisco 1	68	809
LOUP			
---	Placer Auburn	62	582
LOUPEE			
Fred	Trinity China Bar	70	959
LOUR			
---	Sierra Twp 5	66	932
LOURD			
Elizh	Tehama Pasakent	70	856
LOUREANO			
---	Monterey Monterey	60	953
LOURENA			
Fernando	San Mateo Twp 3	65	99
LOURETTE			
Auguste	Tuolumne Shawsfla	71	410
Louis	Tuolumne Shawsfla	71	410
LOUREZZO			
Bartolomew	Amador Twp 3	55	369
LOURG			
---*	Shasta French G	66	713
LOURI			
Stanislaus	Los Angeles Los Angeles	59	322
LOURIA			
Kate	San Francisco San Francisco 2	67	603
LOURIANO			
---	Monterey Monterey	60	953
LOURNE			
Ah	Calaveras Twp 7	57	14
LOURNEY			
Alice E	Napa Napa	61	104
LOURS			
Wm*	Mariposa Twp 1	60	642

Name	County Locale	M653 Roll	Page
LOURY			
A J	El Dorado Indian D	58	1159
Alex A	Yuba North Ea	72	674
David	Yolo No E Twp	72	674
Leon	Tuolumne Twp 1	71	247
LOUS			
---*	Placer Auburn	62	577
LOUSA			
Lady	Tehama Lassen	70	865
LOUSE			
M	San Francisco San Francisco 1	68	934
LOUSIANE			
Francisco	Los Angeles Tejon	59	521
LOUSIANO			
Francisco	Los Angeles Tejon	59	521
LOUSON			
R*	Yuba Foster B	72	824
LOUT			
G	Nevada Grass Valley	61	153
Jacob*	Yuba Marysville	72	898
LOUTE			
O P	El Dorado Georgetown	58	684
LOUTERA			
William	San Luis Obispo San Luis Obispo	65	15
LOUTH			
J	Nevada Grass Valley	61	157
LOUTHEY			
J*	Sacramento Ward 3	63	428
LOUTHURICK			
E M	Nevada Nevada	61	269
LOUTZENHEISER			
W	Nevada Grass Valley	61	174
LOUVY			
Leon*	Tuolumne Twp 1	71	247
LOUY			
---	Mariposa Twp 1	60	673
---	Mariposa Coulterville	60	684
---	San Francisco San Francisco 4	68	1173
---	San Francisco San Francisco 4	68	1190
Chi	San Francisco San Francisco 4	68	1191
Ci	San Francisco San Francisco 4	68	1191
Eugene	Mariposa Twp 1	60	636
LOUZ			
Manuel*	Placer Michigan	62	850
LOUZA			
John	Calaveras Twp 4	57	325
LOV			
---	San Francisco San Francisco 4	68	1174
---	Tuolumne Twp 3	71	468
Hat	Yuba Long Bar	72	764
Kon*	San Francisco San Francisco 4	68	1178
La	Yuba Long Bar	72	762
LOVA			
---	El Dorado Mountain	58	1178
Louis	Yuba Suida	72	982
Louis	Yuba Linda Twp	72	983
Phillippe	Los Angeles San Jose	59	281
LOVAN			
James	Plumas Meadow Valley	62	912
James R	Plumas Meadow Valley	62	931
LOVE			
---	Mariposa Twp 3	60	618
---	Placer Illinois	62	704
---	Sierra Twp 7	66	876
A B	Calaveras Twp 9	57	402
A W B	Yolo Putah	72	552
Alex	Tehama Antelope	70	896
Alfred	Sonoma Russian	69	442
Allen	Calaveras Twp 6	57	174
Benjamin	Tuolumne Big Oak	71	135
Bot*	Tuolumne Columbia	71	324
Charles	Placer Iona Hills	62	866
Chas	Santa Clara Alviso	65	411
Chas*	San Francisco San Francisco 1	68	902
D	Sierra La Porte	66	787
David	Mariposa Twp 1	60	639
Francis*	Yuba Rose Bar	72	816
Frank*	Calaveras Twp 8	57	63
G J	Trinity Weaverville	70	1062
Geo	El Dorado Coloma	58	1075
George	San Joaquin Castoria	64	911
H H	Amador Twp 1	55	489
H H	Napa Clear Lake	61	128
Harry	Santa Clara Santa Clara	65	465
Harry	Santa Clara Santa Cruz	66	629
Henry H	Del Norte Happy Ca	58	663
Jacob	Yuba Marysville	72	902
James	Santa Clara Alviso	65	411
James	Siskiyou Cottonwood	69	99
James	Tehama Lassen	70	866
James	Tehama Antelope	70	896
James H	San Francisco San Francisco 7	68	1442
Jas	Tehama Lassen	70	867
Jerome	Santa Cruz Pajaro	66	563
John	Napa Napa	61	108
John	Solano Benecia	69	315

California 1860 Census Index

LOVE -
LOW

Name	County Locale	Roll	Page
LOVE			
John	Tehama Antelope	70	889
John	Yolo Washington	72	568
John R	Napa Napa	61	81
John S	Yuba Marysville	72	845
John*	Solano Benecia	69	315
Marj	San Francisco San Francisco 2	67	723
Marquis	Yuba Marysville	72	899
Marshall	Shasta Millvill	66	749
Mary	San Francisco San Francisco 2	67	723
Mary	Yuba Marysville	72	923
Mary	Yuba Marysville	72	928
Mary*	Yuba Marysville	72	923
Millon P H	Placer Auburn	62	580
N S	San Francisco San Francisco 9	68	999
R K	Sacramento Ward 3	63	458
R K	Sacramento Ward 4	63	512
Rat	Tuolumne Twp 2	71	324
Robert	Plumas Meadow Valley	62	934
Robert	Tuolumne Columbia	71	312
Robert B	Contra Costa Twp 2	57	567
Robr	Yolo Washington	72	571
Robt	Yolo Washington	72	571
Rot*	Tuolumne Columbia	71	324
Rufus R	Tuolumne Chinese	71	499
Saml	Amador Twp 2	55	267
Saml	Santa Clara Alviso	65	409
Saml E	Shasta Horsetown	66	700
Samuel	Sierra La Porte	66	787
Thomas	Butte Ophir	56	776
William	San Mateo Twp 3	65	76
William	Solano Vacaville	69	344
Wm	Marin Cortemad	60	780
Wm	Napa Yount	61	54
Wm F	San Francisco San Francisco 3	67	19
Wm H	Tuolumne Jamestown	71	422
LOVEAND			
D D*	Napa Hot Springs	61	14
LOVEFOY			
D B*	Tuolumne Twp 3	71	427
LOVEGON			
Howard B	San Francisco San Francisco 10	67	300
LOVEGOY			
E M	Siskiyou Callahan	69	10
LOVEGROVE			
Charles	Sonoma Russian	69	440
James	Sonoma Washington	69	669
LOVEING			
Laura E	Placer Auburn	62	584
LOVEJOY			
A H	Marin Bolinas	60	741
A J	San Francisco San Francisco 6	67	414
D B	Tuolumne Jamestown	71	427
E M	Siskiyou Callahan	69	10
Ed	Yolo Cache	72	617
Edwin	Sonoma Mendocino	69	464
Henry C	Humbolt Union	59	191
Howard B	San Francisco San Francisco 10	67	300
J C	Mariposa Twp 3	60	574
John	Sonoma Petaluma	69	599
John K	Plumas Quincy	62	918
M	Nevada Eureka	61	391
R B	San Francisco San Francisco 3	67	48
R N	El Dorado Mud Springs	58	960
S G	Tuolumne Twp 1	71	258
Sam	Merced Twp 1	60	910
W	Tuolumne Garrote	71	174
LOVEL			
I*	Nevada Red Dog	61	542
J	Sacramento Cosummes	63	399
J*	Nevada Red Dog	61	542
W H	Marin Bolinas	60	732
William	Plumas Quincy	62	997
LOVELACE			
E B	Siskiyou Klamath	69	92
LOVELADY			
Jessee	Tulara Yule Rvr	71	23
Louisa	Tulara Twp 2	71	23
LOVELAND			
Cyrus C	Santa Clara Fremont	65	418
David H	San Joaquin Douglass	64	919
H	Yolo Putah	72	545
H	Yolo Putah	72	546
H S	San Mateo Twp 2	65	122
John E	San Joaquin O'Neal	64	1004
L F	San Francisco San Francisco 12	67	379
Lorenzo F	Alameda Oakland	55	7
Simeon	Napa Napa	61	66
T	San Joaquin Elkhorn	64	984
Vanis	Solano Suisan	69	240
LOVELANS			
Lorenzo F*	Alameda Oakland	55	7
LOVELESS			
Abner	Santa Clara Alviso	65	410

Name	County Locale	Roll	Page
LOVELESS			
D F	Calaveras Twp 9	57	355
Seth	El Dorado Indian D	58	1159
Thomas	Calaveras Twp 6	57	135
LOVELING			
John*	Calaveras Twp 9	57	356
LOVELL			
Aaron	Tuolumne Shawsfla	71	415
Auarou*	Tuolumne Twp 2	71	415
C B	San Francisco San Francisco 10	67	352
C L*	Sacramento Brighton	63	207
C S*	Sacramento Brighton	63	207
Charles L*	Humbolt Bucksport	59	160
Charles S*	Humbolt Bucksport	59	160
Edward C	San Francisco San Francisco 4	68	1139
G M	Nevada Eureka	61	361
George	Tehama Antelope	70	891
H L	Sonoma Vallejo	69	611
Hiram	Tuolumne Twp 2	71	288
Horatio	Sacramento Ward 1	63	11
J G	San Joaquin Oneal	64	935
J J	Santa Clara Santa Clara	65	494
James	Sonoma Santa Rosa	69	405
James G	Yuba Linda Twp	72	984
Jas	Butte Oregon	56	643
John	San Francisco San Francisco 1	68	906
Louis E	San Francisco San Francisco 3	67	15
Matilda	San Francisco San Francisco 7	68	1374
P H	El Dorado Placerville	58	850
Patrick	Calaveras Twp 5	57	240
Richard	San Joaquin Elkhorn	64	964
Richd	Sacramento Ward 4	63	522
Samuel W	Placer Auburn	62	592
Sarah	Contra Costa Twp 2	57	544
Stephen	Tuolumne Sonora	71	479
W	Butte Ophir	56	778
Wm	Sierra Twp 5	66	936
Wm M	Santa Clara Santa Clara	65	491
LOVELOCK			
Edwd	San Francisco San Francisco 1	68	862
Geo	Butte Kimshaw	56	601
LOVELY			
Francis	Siskiyou Callahan	69	5
Horace	San Francisco San Francisco 8	68	1319
James	Nevada Bloomfield	61	511
W R	Sacramento Georgian	63	340
LOVENSTEIN			
Jacob*	San Francisco San Francisco 4	68	1120
LOVENSTIEN			
Jacob*	San Francisco San Francisco 4	68	1120
LOVEPY			
Henry	Alameda Brooklyn	55	94
LOVER			
And J	Butte Kimshaw	56	594
C M	Nevada Grass Valley	61	144
Hose*	Mariposa Coulterville	60	691
J*	Nevada Grass Valley	61	216
LOVERAGE			
Owen J	Nevada Bridgeport	61	451
LOVERAW			
Philip	San Luis Obispo San Luis Obispo	65	42
LOVERIDGE			
A C	Amador Twp 1	55	473
H L	Amador Twp 1	55	489
J A	Amador Twp 1	55	473
O M	Yuba Rose Bar	72	811
O P	Yuba Rose Bar	72	810
LOVERING			
Reuben	San Francisco San Francisco 7	68	1426
LOVERT			
S O	Calaveras Twp 9	57	392
LOVES			
Hose*	Mariposa Coulterville	60	691
LOVETT			
C	Tehama Antelope	70	889
Charles	San Francisco San Francisco 9	68	1098
Chas	San Francisco San Francisco 1	68	847
E S	Sutter Butte	70	792
Geo T	Butte Chico	56	557
Hannah	San Francisco San Francisco 4	68	1151

Name	County Locale	Roll	Page
LOVELY			
James	Nevada Bloomfield	61	511
W R	Sacramento Georgian	63	340
LOVENSTEIN			
Jacob*	San Francisco San Francisco 4	68	1120
LOVENSTIEN			
Jacob*	San Francisco San Francisco 4	68	1120
LOVEPY			
Henry	Alameda Brooklyn	55	94
LOVER			
And J	Butte Kimshaw	56	594
C M	Nevada Grass Valley	61	144
Hose*	Mariposa Coulterville	60	691
J*	Nevada Grass Valley	61	216
LOVERAGE			
Owen J	Nevada Bridgeport	61	451

Name	County Locale	Roll	Page
LOVERAW			
Philip	San Luis Obispo San Luis Obispo	65	42
LOVERIDGE			
A C	Amador Twp 1	55	473
H L	Amador Twp 1	55	489
J A	Amador Twp 1	55	473
O M	Yuba Rose Bar	72	811
O P	Yuba Rose Bar	72	810
LOVERING			
Reuben	San Francisco San Francisco 7	68	1426
LOVERT			
S O	Calaveras Twp 9	57	392
LOVES			
Hose*	Mariposa Coulterville	60	691
LOVETT			
C	Tehama Antelope	70	889
Charles	San Francisco San Francisco 9	68	1098
Chas	San Francisco San Francisco 1	68	847
E S	Sutter Butte	70	792
Geo T	Butte Chico	56	557
Hannah	San Francisco San Francisco 4	68	1151
Horace	San Francisco San Francisco 2	67	630
Horace F	San Francisco San Francisco 2	67	630
Jas	Sacramento Ward 4	63	524
L H	Nevada Grass Valley	61	216
Michael	San Francisco San Francisco 3	67	85
Michael	San Mateo Twp 1	65	50
Mike	Amador Twp 1	55	454
O H	Sonoma Petaluma	69	573
Ramone	Monterey San Juan	60	1007
Saml C	Sacramento Ward 4	63	524
LOVEY			
Mary	Yuba Marysville	72	928
Samuel	Nevada Eureka	61	347
LOVEYNEW			
Joseph*	Calaveras Twp 5	57	226
LOVEYNIN			
Joseph*	Calaveras Twp 5	57	226
LOVGA			
John*	Shasta Millvill	66	756
LOVICH			
Charles	San Francisco San Francisco 9	68	957
LOVIE			
---	Trinity Lewiston	70	957
LOVIG			
W*	Nevada Eureka	61	357
LOVIGNIA			
Joseph*	Calaveras Twp 5	57	226
LOVIGNIO			
Joseph	Calaveras Twp 5	57	226
LOVILL			
O	San Francisco San Francisco 3	67	81
LOVILLA			
P	Calaveras Twp 8	57	69
LOVIN			
H R	Nevada Grass Valley	61	222
LOVINER			
Fred	Klamath S Fork	59	203
LOVING			
A	Sonoma Santa Rosa	69	425
A G	San Francisco San Francisco 5	67	537
Benjamin	Plumas Quincy	62	974
LOVRIN			
G W	Butte Ophir	56	769
LOVT			
---	El Dorado Salmon Falls	58	1044
LOVY			
---	San Francisco San Francisco 4	68	1173
Fong	San Francisco San Francisco 4	68	1203
Richard	Amador Twp 1	55	485
LOVZA			
John	Calaveras Twp 4	57	325
LOW KING			
---	Sacramento Ward 1	63	66
LOW WALLING			
John*	Nevada Bridgeport	61	440
LOW WULLING			
John*	Nevada Bridgeport	61	440
LOW			
---	Amador Twp 4	55	242
---	Amador Twp 7	55	414
---	Amador Twp 5	55	423
---	Amador Twp 1	55	497
---	Butte Oregon	56	626
---	Butte Oregon	56	627
---	Butte Eureka	56	655
---	Butte Oro	56	686
---	Butte Bidwell	56	711
---	Calaveras Twp 6	57	164
---	Calaveras Twp 6	57	165
---	Calaveras Twp 6	57	176
---	Calaveras Twp 5	57	202
---	Calaveras Twp 5	57	234
---	Calaveras Twp 5	57	235
---	Calaveras Twp 5	57	247
---	Calaveras Twp 5	57	251

California 1860 Census Index

Name	County Locale	M653 Roll	Page
LOW			
---	Calaveras Twp 10	57	275
---	Calaveras Twp 10	57	295
---	Calaveras Twp 4	57	326
---	Calaveras Twp 4	57	337
---	Calaveras Twp 7	57	40
---	Calaveras Twp 7	57	44
---	Calaveras Twp 8	57	62
---	Del Norte Crescent	58	631
---	El Dorado Salmon Falls	58	1043
---	El Dorado Salmon Hills	58	1063
---	El Dorado Salmon Falls	58	1066
---	El Dorado Casumnes	58	1177
---	El Dorado Georgetown	58	695
---	El Dorado Mud Springs	58	985
---	Klamath S Fork	59	206
---	Mariposa Twp 3	60	552
---	Mariposa Twp 3	60	564
---	Mariposa Twp 3	60	572
---	Mariposa Twp 1	60	640
---	Mariposa Coulterville	60	701
---	Nevada Nevada	61	302
---	Nevada Rough &	61	398
---	Placer Auburn	62	563
---	Placer Auburn	62	575
---	Placer Auburn	62	577
---	Placer Auburn	62	581
---	Placer Auburn	62	583
---	Placer Auburn	62	596
---	Placer Auburn	62	597
---	Placer Rattle Snake	62	598
---	Placer Rattle Snake	62	600
---	Placer Rattle Snake	62	602
---	Placer Rattle Snake	62	629
---	Placer Rattle Snake	62	633
---	Placer Rattle Snake	62	634
---	Placer Folsom	62	640
---	Placer Virginia	62	665
---	Placer Virginia	62	671
---	Placer Virginia	62	675
---	Placer Virginia	62	678
---	Placer Virginia	62	681
---	Placer Virginia	62	682
---	Placer Virginia	62	701
---	Placer Illinois	62	741
---	Placer Illinois	62	745
---	Placer Illinois	62	746
---	Placer Illinois	62	747
---	Placer Illinois	62	748
---	Placer Illinois	62	749
---	Placer Illinois	62	750
---	Placer Illinois	62	753
---	Sacramento Granite	63	268
---	Sacramento Cosumnes	63	384
---	Sacramento Cosumnes	63	386
---	Sacramento Cosumnes	63	392
---	Sacramento Cosumnes	63	395
---	Sacramento Cosumnes	63	400
---	Sacramento Ward 1	63	52
---	Sacramento Ward 1	63	55
---	Sacramento Ward 4	63	609
---	San Francisco San Francisco 9	68	1086
---	San Francisco San Francisco 9	68	1088
---	San Francisco San Francisco 9	68	1095
---	San Francisco San Francisco 9	68	1096
---	San Francisco San Francisco 4	68	1176
---	San Francisco San Francisco 4	68	1177
---	San Francisco San Francisco 4	68	1190
---	San Francisco San Francisco 4	68	1196
---	San Francisco San Francisco 4	68	1197
---	San Francisco San Francisco 4	68	1199
---	San Francisco San Francisco 4	68	1209
---	San Francisco San Francisco 4	68	1210
---	San Francisco San Francisco 4	68	1212
---	San Francisco San Francisco 11	160 67	
---	San Francisco San Francisco 11	161 67	
---	San Francisco San Francisco 1	68	924
---	San Francisco San Francisco 3	67	9
---	San Joaquin Stockton	64	1056
---	Shasta Shasta	66	678
---	Sierra Downieville	66	1003
---	Sierra Downieville	66	1004
---	Sierra Downieville	66	1005
---	Sierra Downieville	66	1007
---	Sierra Downieville	66	1008
---	Sierra Downieville	66	1014
---	Sierra Downieville	66	1015
---	Sierra Downieville	66	1020
---	Sierra Downieville	66	1026
---	Sierra Downieville	66	1029
---	Sierra Downieville	66	1031
---	Sierra Morristown	66	1056
---	Sierra La Porte	66	767
---	Sierra Twp 5	66	927
LOW			
---	Sierra Twp 5	66	931
---	Sierra Twp 5	66	932
---	Sierra Twp 5	66	945
---	Sierra Cox'S Bar	66	949
---	Sierra Downieville	66	973
---	Sierra Downieville	66	974
---	Sierra Downieville	66	983
---	Sierra Downieville	66	984
---	Sierra Downieville	66	985
---	Sierra Downieville	66	990
---	Sierra Downieville	66	991
---	Sierra Downieville	66	993
---	Sierra Downieville	66	996
---	Siskiyou Scott Va	69	32
---	Siskiyou Scott Va	69	46
---	Trinity Weaverville	70	1079
---	Trinity Lewiston	70	956
---	Tuolumne Montezuma	71	507
---	Tuolumne Twp 6	71	529
---	Tuolumne Twp 6	71	537
---	Yolo No E Twp	72	681
---	Yolo No E Twp	72	684
---	Yolo Slate Ra	72	711
---	Yuba North Ea	72	681
---	Yuba Slate Ro	72	684
---	Yuba North Ea	72	685
---	Yuba Long Bar	72	759
---	Yuba Long Bar	72	761
---	Yuba Fosters	72	831
---	Yuba Fosters	72	843
---*	Amador Twp 4	55	233
---*	Calaveras Twp 5	57	237
---*	Calaveras Twp 4	57	337
---*	Calaveras Twp 4	57	343
---*	El Dorado Salmon Falls	58	1063
---*	Mariposa Twp 3	60	582
---*	Mariposa Coulterville	60	681
---*	San Francisco San Francisco 9	68	1094
---*	Sierra Twp 5	66	931
---*	Sierra Twp 5	66	945
---*	Tuolumne Big Oak	71	181
---*	Yuba Foster B	72	831
---*	Yuba Fosters	72	843
A	Shasta Horsetown	66	702
A	Sierra Downieville	66	980
A	Tuolumne Twp 4	71	159
A T	San Francisco San Francisco 6	67	469
Ah	Butte Oregon	56	626
Ah	Butte Oregon	56	641
Ah	Butte Bidwell	56	711
Ah	Calaveras Twp 7	57	31
Ah	Sacramento Cosumnes	63	380
Ah	Sacramento Cosumnes	63	381
Ah	Sacramento Ward 3	63	492
Ah	Siskiyou Scott Va	69	32
Ah	Tuolumne Twp 4	71	181
Ah*	Butte Oregon	56	627
Ai	Calaveras Twp 6	57	135
Ar	Sierra Downieville	66	1014
B	Calaveras Twp 9	57	409
Ben	Sacramento Natonia	63	272
Byron N	Sierra Whiskey	66	850
C	Shasta Shasta	66	759
C Adolphe	San Francisco San Francisco 8	68	1286
C F	Butte Bidwell	56	706
C G	Butte Bidwell	56	706
Caw	Yuba Long Bar	72	763
Charles L	Yuba Marysville	72	863
Chas	Butte Cascade	56	695
Chew	Butte Mountain	56	742
Ching	Butte Bidwell	56	717
Ching	Butte Bidwell	56	728
Chong	Calaveras Twp 6	57	179
Chow	Butte Ophir	56	810
D*	Butte Oregon	56	631
David	Humbolt Eel Rvr	59	146
E R	Sutter Nicolaus	70	832
Edward	Sierra Twp 7	66	911
Elijah*	Yuba Linda Twp	72	980
Elijah	Yuba Suida	72	980
Fee	San Francisco San Francisco 4	68	1198
Foe	San Francisco San Francisco 4	68	1186
Fong	Tehama Red Bluff	70	934
Foo	Calaveras Twp 10	57	278
Francis	Sierra Twp 7	66	908
Fred	Nevada Rough &	61	411
Fred F	Yuba Marysville	72	863
Fred R	Sacramento Ward 4	63	526
Frederick	San Francisco San Francisco 10	229 67	
Frederick G	San Joaquin Elkhorn	64	961
Harry*	Sacramento Granite	63	242
Hee*	Yuba New York	72	740
Henry*	Sacramento Granite	63	242
LOW			
How	Calaveras Twp 4	57	334
Ing	San Francisco San Francisco 3	67	2
James	Mariposa Twp 3	60	567
John	Butte Ophir	56	754
John	Butte Ophir	56	789
John	Sacramento Ward 1	63	154
Ki	Yuba Long Bar	72	758
King	Sacramento Ward 1	63	66
Lamuel	Yolo Slate Ra	72	696
Le	Butte Oregon	56	643
Lee	Butte Ophir	56	803
Low	Mariposa Twp 3	60	553
Mark	Nevada Red Dog	61	555
Me	Yuba Slate Ro	72	708
Mo	San Francisco San Francisco 4	68	1190
Moses	Sierra Twp 7	66	905
Moses	Sierra Twp 7	66	908
Moses*	Sierra Twp 7	66	905
Mouy	San Francisco San Francisco 4	68	1190
Moy	San Francisco San Francisco 4	68	1190
Neing	San Francisco San Francisco 11	160 67	
On	Yuba Long Bar	72	763
P	Sutter Bear Rvr	70	825
Pah	Yuba Long Bar	72	759
Parh	Yuba Long Bar	72	759
Polley	Butte Mountain	56	735
Py	El Dorado Big Bar	58	737
R G	Sacramento Ward 1	63	1
S J	Sacramento Ward 4	63	610
Sam	Butte Eureka	56	652
Sam*	Yuba New York	72	740
Samuel	Yolo Slate Ra	72	702
Sh*	Yuba Long Bar	72	763
Sing	Butte Cascade	56	700
Sing	Butte Bidwell	56	713
Sing	Butte Bidwell	56	716
Sing	Butte Bidwell	56	720
Sing	Butte Bidwell	56	726
Sing	Butte Bidwell	56	731
Sing	Butte Ophir	56	801
Sing	Butte Bidwell	56	708
Sinitt	Butte Bidwell	56	708
Sow	San Francisco San Francisco 11	160	
Su	El Dorado Greenwood	58	732
Sznill	Butte Bidwell	56	708
Ti	San Francisco San Francisco 11	160 67	
Tie	San Francisco San Francisco 4	68	1190
Tin	Shasta Horsetown	66	711
Tom	Sierra Downieville	66	1005
Ton	Yuba Long Bar	72	759
Ton	Sierra Downieville	66	1005
Tow	Calaveras Twp 6	57	150
Tow	Yuba Long Bar	72	761
V	Sonoma Bodega	69	534
William	Calaveras Twp 7	57	16
William*	Placer Michigan	62	820
Wing	Butte Bidwell	56	709
Wing	Butte Ophir	56	808
Wong	San Francisco San Francisco 6	67	453
LOWARD			
W	Siskiyou Scott Ri	69	73
LOWAY			
---	Sierra Downieville	66	1025
LOWBIN			
W*	Yolo Putah	72	553
LOWBRIDGE			
Aaron	Placer Nicolaus	62	692
LOWD			
Mary	Sonoma Armally	69	503
LOWDEN			
J	Butte Hamilton	56	514
John	Monterey Alisal	60	1029
Robert	Yuba Rose Bar	72	806
Spencer	Tehama Lewiston	70	961
Spencer*	Trinity Lewiston	70	961
W S	Trinity Trinity	70	975
LOWDER			
Jno	Mendocino Calpella	60	814
LOWDERS			
William	San Diego San Diego	64	765
LOWDGE			
O A	Sierra Twp 7	66	886
LOWE			
---	El Dorado Coloma	58	1084
---	El Dorado Eldorado	58	948
---	El Dorado Mud Springs	58	961
---	Sierra Twp 7	66	876
---	Siskiyou Scott Ri	69	82
A	Nevada Bridgeport	61	465
A	Tuolumne Twp 4	71	156
Archibald	Santa Clara Santa Clara	65	522
B	Sonoma Washington	69	675
B K	Yolo Washington	72	565

California 1860 Census Index

Name	County Locale	M653 RollPage
LOWE		
Charle	El Dorado Coloma	58 1104
Chas	Santa Clara San Jose	65 349
Conrad	San Francisco San Francisco 2	67 680
Dan K	Marin San Rafael	60 760
Dank	Marin San Rafael	60 760
Edward	Solano Vallejo	69 277
Egbert	Sacramento Natonia	63 276
Ellen	Yolo Cache	72 607
F	Nevada Grass Valley	61 169
Francis*	Yuba Rose Bar	72 816
George	Placer Michigan	62 830
J P	El Dorado Mud Springs	58 982
James	San Francisco San Francisco 11	150
		67
Jane	Solano Benecia	69 296
Jane E	Solano Benecia	69 296
Jas B	Santa Clara San Jose	65 337
John	Marin Bolinas	60 746
John	Marin Cortemad	60 786
John	Placer Folsom	62 640
John	Placer Michigan	62 827
John	Placer Michigan	62 830
John	Yolo Putah	72 551
John R	Solano Vacaville	69 334
John*	San Francisco San Francisco 9	68 1097
L	Tehama Pasakent	70 859
L J	Tuolumne Big Oak	71 125
L J	Tuolumne Twp 4	71 127
Robert	Siskiyou Callahan	69 8
Robt	Sacramento Cosumnes	63 391
Thomas	Siskiyou Callahan	69 11
Thos	Merced Twp 1	60 915
W W	Sonoma Washington	69 675
William L	San Francisco San Francisco 9	68 990
Wm	Tuolumne Twp 4	71 143
LOWEE		
---	Shasta Horsetown	66 711
LOWEER		
Londer	Sonoma Mendocino	69 462
LOWEL		
L*	Mariposa Twp 3	60 559
Lufus	Tuolumne Springfield	71 370
O	Tuolumne Twp 4	71 152
LOWELL		
Anas	Sacramento Franklin	63 322
Andrew J*	Sierra St Louis	66 807
C	Nevada Grass Valley	61 146
Charles	Sierra Downieville	66 1016
David	Humbolt Eureka	59 170
Elisha*	Tuolumne Twp 1	71 212
Elishan	Tuolumne Sonora	71 212
Elishar*	Tuolumne Twp 1	71 212
Elishas*	Tuolumne Twp 1	71 212
Geo	Mendocino Big Rvr	60 848
Geo	Sacramento Ward 1	63 123
Horatio	Sacramento Ward 1	63 31
J	Nevada Grass Valley	61 216
James M	Sierra Gibsonville	66 858
Jas	Butte Oregon	56 643
Jno N	Alameda Brooklyn	55 157
John	Tehama Moons	70 851
M	Sacramento Franklin	63 322
Marshall	Solano Fremont	69 381
Nathan R	San Francisco San Francisco 9	68 991
The D	Sonoma Petaluma	69 593
Wm H	Nevada Nevada	61 250
LOWEN		
U L	Tehama Pasakent	70 855
LOWENBERG		
Sampson	San Francisco San Francisco 2	67 607
LOWENHEIM		
L	San Francisco San Francisco 2	67 639
LOWENSTEIN		
I	San Francisco San Francisco 2	67 677
LOWER		
Daniel	Tuolumne Don Pedro	71 539
G	Tehama Red Bluff	70 933
J	El Dorado Diamond	58 808
John	San Joaquin Elkhorn	64 957
L H	Shasta Horsetown	66 711
Leander	Sonoma Mendocino	69 462
Martin	Sierra Twp 7	66 874
Peter	Calaveras Twp 7	57 18
Wm	Los Angeles Tejon	59 526
LOWERS		
Emma*	Sacramento Ward 3	63 452
LOWERY		
---	Monterey San Juan	60 974
A	Nevada Eureka	61 380
D H	Siskiyou Callahan	69 16
Dennis	Siskiyou Callahan	69 6
G W	Nevada Bloomfield	61 510
J	Sacramento Cosumnes	63 393
J F	Siskiyou Callahan	69 16
James	Amador Twp 3	55 409

Name	County Locale	M653 RollPage
LOWERY		
James	Sacramento Georgian	63 336
Jas	Butte Bidwell	56 706
Jas	Butte Ophir	56 790
Jas	Sacramento Ward 1	63 101
John	Sacramento Ward 1	63 29
N	Tehama Red Bluff	70 933
P	Tuolumne Twp 4	71 157
Phebe	Sacramento Dry Crk	63 378
Valentine	San Francisco San Francisco 10	300
		67
William	Fresno Twp 1	59 82
LOWGEE		
F W*	Sonoma Petaluma	69 579
LOWGLEY		
Jas	Sonoma Petaluma	69 595
LOWGRASS		
Henry	Sierra Downieville	66 977
LOWHEURER		
Augustus	San Francisco San Francisco 7	68 1373
LOWINRY		
Geo	Yolo Cottonwoood	72 658
LOWLIN		
W*	Yolo Putah	72 553
LOWMAN		
D	Sierra Twp 7	66 878
Henry	Sierra Cox'S Bar	66 950
J B	Nevada Nevada	61 258
Jos	Nevada Nevada	61 289
Lawrence	Solano Vacaville	69 352
Margarete	Solano Vacaville	69 354
Margarett	Solano Vacaville	69 354
LOWN		
---	Sierra Downieville	66 1014
Ar	Sierra Downieville	66 1014
LOWNDES		
Samuel	San Francisco San Francisco 8	68 1252
LOWNES		
Caleb P	Solano Vacaville	69 343
LOWNESENCE		
L	Nevada Grass Valley	61 144
LOWNIE		
Joseph W*	Sierra Pine Grove	66 820
LOWNSBURY		
Geo	San Francisco San Francisco 12	390
		67
LOWNSEND		
Emiry	Napa Clear Lake	61 129
LOWNYGER		
John	San Francisco San Francisco 1	68 809
LOWORENCA		
Victor*	Monterey Monterey	60 962
LOWREY		
Geo W	Butte Chico	56 568
George	Solano Fremont	69 382
Jas	Butte Chico	56 533
Jas	Butte Chico	56 562
Jas E	Butte Chico	56 533
Jerome	Napa Napa	61 65
John	Contra Costa Twp 3	57 602
Joseph	San Francisco San Francisco 1	68 856
Susan	Butte Chico	56 536
Thomas H	Sierra Whiskey	66 846
LOWRIE		
Russell	Fresno Twp 3	59 12
LOWRING		
---	Siskiyou Scott Va	69 48
Geo	Mendocino Big Rvr	60 844
LOWRNEY		
Alice E*	Napa Napa	61 104
LOWRUEY		
Alice E*	Napa Napa	61 104
LOWRY		
A J	El Dorado Indian D	58 1159
Anthony	Tulara Twp 2	71 31
B R	San Joaquin Oneal	64 940
D B	Sierra Twp 7	66 866
David	Alameda Brooklyn	55 202
E S	San Bernardino Santa Barbara	64 190
Elizabeth	Sonoma Vallejo	69 625
Elyan	Sonoma Vallejo	69 625
F	San Francisco San Francisco 1	68 926
G N	Sacramento Granite	63 261
Geo W	Mendocino Calpella	60 809
Geoproctor	San Joaquin Stockton	64 1034
George	Alameda Brooklyn	55 199
George	Trinity Eastman	70 960
Green B	San Joaquin Castoria	64 907
H	Shasta Shasta	66 653
Harriet	Tehama Red Bluff	70 927
J	Sierra Twp 7	66 886
J D	Sonoma Vallejo	69 624
James	San Francisco San Francisco 6	67 438
James F	San Bernardino Santa Inez	64 141
John	Alameda Brooklyn	55 201
John	Sierra Downieville	66 977

Name	County Locale	M653 RollPage
LOWRY		
John*	Yuba Marysville	72 884
John*	Sierra Downieville	66 977
Leroy	Sonoma Vallejo	69 625
Levy	Shasta Shasta	66 672
Micolas M	Mendocino Calpella	60 811
Nicolas M	Mendocino Calpella	60 811
R	Amador Twp 1	55 485
Richard	San Francisco San Francisco 2	67 570
Robert	Tuolumne Twp 1	71 189
S	San Francisco San Francisco 5	67 481
W	El Dorado Diamond	58 790
W J	San Joaquin Stockton	64 1034
William	San Francisco San Francisco 11	90
		67
Wm	Sonoma Bodega	69 522
LOWS		
J G	El Dorado Georgetown	58 691
William	Sierra Whiskey	66 849
Wm*	Mariposa Twp 1	60 642
LOWSON		
Joseph	Sierra Twp 5	66 947
LOWTHER		
Frank	Sacramento Ward 4	63 505
Frank	Sacramento Ward 4	63 517
LOWWALLING		
John*	Nevada Bridgeport	61 440
LOWY		
---	Calaveras Twp 5	57 149
---	Nevada Bridgeport	61 460
Francis	Sacramento Granite	63 261
LOWZ		
J	Siskiyou Scott Ri	69 71
LOXTIN		
Chas	Butte Cascade	56 695
LOY		
---	Amador Twp 3	55 402
---	Amador Twp 6	55 430
---	Amador Twp 1	55 503
---	Calaveras Twp 8	57 100
---	Calaveras Twp 5	57 255
---	Calaveras Twp 10	57 268
---	Calaveras Twp 4	57 341
---	Calaveras Twp 8	57 49
---	Calaveras Twp 8	57 95
---	El Dorado White Oaks	58 1022
---	El Dorado Salmon Falls	58 1065
---	El Dorado Salmon Falls	58 1066
---	El Dorado Coloma	58 1085
---	El Dorado Kelsey	58 1132
---	El Dorado Kelsey	58 1136
---	El Dorado Georgetown	58 691
---	El Dorado Diamond	58 788
---	El Dorado Diamond	58 789
---	El Dorado Diamond	58 796
---	El Dorado Diamond	58 800
---	El Dorado Diamond	58 807
---	El Dorado Diamond	58 808
---	El Dorado Placerville	58 829
---	El Dorado Placerville	58 834
---	El Dorado Placerville	58 842
---	El Dorado Placerville	58 899
---	El Dorado Eldorado	58 948
---	El Dorado Mud Springs	58 961
---	Mariposa Twp 3	60 576
---	Mariposa Twp 3	60 581
---	Mariposa Twp 3	60 582
---	Mariposa Twp 3	60 586
---	Mariposa Twp 1	60 648
---	Mariposa Twp 1	60 673
---	Mariposa Coulterville	60 683
---	Mariposa Coulterville	60 685
---	Nevada Grass Valley	61 228
---	Nevada Nevada	61 299
---	Nevada Nevada	61 302
---	Nevada Bridgeport	61 439
---	Nevada Bridgeport	61 466
---	Placer Folsom	62 647
---	Placer Ophirville	62 656
---	Placer Virginia	62 675
---	Plumas Quincy	62 947
---	Sacramento Ward 1	63 59
---	Sacramento Ward 4	63 609
---	San Francisco San Francisco 4	68 1173
---	San Francisco San Francisco 4	68 1174
---	San Francisco San Francisco 4	68 1193
---	San Francisco San Francisco 4	68 1196
---	San Francisco San Francisco 4	68 1203
---	San Francisco San Francisco 5	67 1205
---	San Francisco San Francisco 7	68 1203
---	Shasta Horsetown	66 698
---	Shasta Horsetown	66 704
---	Shasta Horsetown	66 706
---	Sierra La Porte	66 785
---	Sierra Twp 5	66 932
---	Sierra Twp 5	66 933

California 1860 Census Index

Name	County Locale	M653 Roll Page
LOY		
---	Sierra Downieville	66 954
---	Trinity Big Flat	70 1041
---	Tuolumne Columbia	71 346
---	Tuolumne Montezuma	71 507
---	Tuolumne Chinese	71 510
---	Yolo No E Twp	72 676
---	Yolo No E Twp	72 682
---	Yolo No E Twp	72 683
---	Yolo Slate Ra	72 708
---	Yolo Slate Ra	72 712
---	Yuba North Ea	72 676
---	Yuba North Ea	72 681
---	Yuba North Ea	72 682
---	Yuba Slate Ro	72 683
---	Yuba Slate Ro	72 708
---	Yuba Slate Ro	72 712
---	Yuba Slate Ro	72 715
---	Yuba New York	72 739
---	Yuba Long Bar	72 759
---	Yuba Long Bar	72 764
---	Yuba Fosters	72 830
---	Yuba Fosters	72 836
---	Yuba Fosters	72 843
---*	Calaveras Twp 5	57 212
---*	Calaveras Twp 4	57 341
---*	Fresno Twp 1	59 30
---*	Mariposa Twp 3	60 581
---*	Mariposa Twp 3	60 586
---*	Nevada Nevada	61 302
---*	San Francisco San Francisco 9	681087
---*	San Francisco San Francisco 4	681189
---*	Trinity Taylor'S	701033
---*	Tuolumne Big Oak	71 181
---*	Yuba Foster B	72 830
---*	Yuba Foster B	72 836
---*	Yuba Fosters	72 843
Ah	Tuolumne Twp 2	71 346
Cene*	Butte Ophir	56 805
Chow	Butte Ophir	56 805
Chow	San Francisco San Francisco 4	681174
Choy	San Francisco San Francisco 9	681093
Fatt	Tuolumne Twp 4	71 158
Frederick D	Sierra Whiskey	66 845
Fredrick D	Sierra Whiskey	66 845
Hee	San Francisco San Francisco 4	681202
Hu	San Francisco San Francisco 4	681202
John	Yolo Slate Ra	72 710
John*	Yuba Slate Ro	72 710
John*	Yuba Slate Ro	72 711
Kim	Butte Bidwell	56 726
Ko	San Francisco San Francisco 4	681200
L	Yuba Long Bar	72 755
La	Yuba Fosters	72 843
Lin	Butte Ophir	56 813
M	Nevada Nevada	61 313
M V	Yuba Long Bar	72 755
M V	Yuba Long Bar	72 755
May	Yuba Foster B	72 830
Moy	San Francisco San Francisco 4	681203
Moy	San Francisco San Francisco 5	671207
Sam	Amador Twp 7	55 413
Thomas D	Mariposa Twp 1	60 654
To	San Francisco San Francisco 5	671205
Toy	Amador Twp 1	55 501
W W M	Solano Vacaville	69 326
Yee	San Francisco San Francisco 4	681192
Yu	San Francisco San Francisco 4	681192
LOYA		
Denes	Santa Clara Alviso	65 405
LOYALL		
P	San Francisco San Francisco 7	681438
LOYAS		
Juan	San Mateo Twp 2	65 134
LOYAT		
---	Siskiyou Klamath	69 79
Ah*	Siskiyou Klamath	69 79
LOYD		
Alice	San Francisco San Francisco 10	338 67
Bridget	Alameda Oakland	55 76
Charles*	El Dorado Salmon Falls	581047
Cherles*	El Dorado Salmon Falls	581047
David	Sonoma Santa Rosa	69 402
Dixon	Yolo Cache Crk	72 636
E	Sacramento Granite	63 221
Edward	Solano Suisan	69 222
Elijah*	Mendocino Arrana	60 859
G	Calaveras Twp 9	57 404
Jas B	Sonoma Santa Rosa	69 398
John	Napa Napa	61 68
John	San Francisco San Francisco 3	67 11
John W	Napa Hot Springs	61 15
R C R	Yolo Merritt	72 584
Richard	San Francisco San Francisco 3	67 68
Rob R	Yolo Merritt	72 584
LOYD		
Robt	El Dorado Gold Hill	581096
S H	San Francisco San Francisco 4	681222
Thom B	El Dorado Georgetown	58 683
Thom R	El Dorado Georgetown	58 683
Thomas	Mariposa Twp 1	60 654
Thomas	Solano Benecia	69 308
Thos	Sacramento Ward 3	63 430
Turner	Colusa Butte Crk	57 466
W S	San Joaquin Stockton	641100
William	San Francisco San Francisco 9	68 984
William	San Mateo Twp 2	65 120
Wm	Marin Bolinas	60 742
Wm L	Sonoma Armally	69 491
LOYDE		
Ralph	Plumas Quincy	62 943
LOYE		
---	Amador Twp 1	55 458
---	Sacramento Ward 1	63 50
---	Sacramento Ward 1	63 60
---	Sacramento Ward 1	63 61
---	Sierra Twp 5	66 931
LOYED		
Robt	Sierra Monte Crk	661035
LOYER		
Antonia	Santa Cruz Soguel	66 597
Antonio	Santa Cruz Soguel	66 597
Theodore	Calaveras Twp 5	57 228
LOYILO		
Aguata*	Alameda Brooklyn	55 131
LOYLE		
J	El Dorado Diamond	58 813
L B*	Nevada Grass Valley	61 196
P*	San Francisco San Francisco 5	67 501
LOYN		
Julius	Sacramento San Joaquin	63 351
LOYTERS		
George*	Alameda Oakland	55 63
LOYTUS		
George*	Alameda Oakland	55 63
LOYZ MERE		
---*	Sierra Downieville	661014
LOZ		
---	Fresno Twp 2	59 19
---*	Trinity Taylor'S	701033
Sing	San Francisco San Francisco 5	67 508
LOZA		
Guillermo	San Mateo Twp 2	65 132
Pedro*	Yuba Marysville	72 947
LOZANNO		
Conssa*	Yuba Marysville	72 923
LOZANYO		
Antonlo*	Alameda Brooklyn	55 139
LOZARO		
Nicholas	Tuolumne Shawsfla	71 408
LOZE		
Benjamin*	Placer Michigan	62 811
LOZENSTEIN		
Joseph	San Francisco San Francisco 4	681139
LOZIER		
A*	Nevada Grass Valley	61 156
Geo*	Sacramento Cosumnes	63 405
LOZINKI		
Paul	El Dorado Georgetown	58 676
LOZINSKI		
Augustine*	El Dorado Georgetown	58 676
Pant*	El Dorado Georgetown	58 676
Paul*	El Dorado Georgetown	58 676
LOZO		
Benjamin*	Placer Michigan	62 811
Pedro*	Yuba Marysville	72 947
LOZUIS		
Peter	Santa Clara San Jose	65 283
LPEDRO		
---	Los Angeles Los Angeles	59 392
LPERO		
Ohidoch	Calaveras Twp 5	57 187
LPINK		
Ezeikal*	Calaveras Twp 5	57 210
LPON		
---	Sierra Morristown	661055
LQUACIO		
Jose*	San Diego Agua Caliente	64 814
LRETTA		
Jalapa	Mariposa Twp 3	60 556
LRICKER		
Refoell*	El Dorado Placerville	58 896
LRINMKY		
Geo*	Sacramento San Joaquin	63 364
LROPATH		
Edward*	Calaveras Twp 9	57 371
LROTENS		
Louis*	Marin San Rafael	60 763
LRUSSELL		
Joseph	Del Norte Crescent	58 637
LSEE		
---	Calaveras Twp 4	57 307
LSEE		
Up	Nevada Washington	61 340
LSING		
Bonevoco*	Mariposa Twp 3	60 570
LSPENSER		
David	San Francisco San Francisco 9	681081
LT		
---*	Mariposa Coulterville	60 681
LTOLZ		
Eliza*	Sacramento Granite	63 252
LU		
---	Butte Kimshaw	56 580
---	Butte Cascade	56 699
---	Calaveras Twp 5	57 213
---	Calaveras Twp 10	57 273
---	Calaveras Twp 10	57 283
---	El Dorado Georgetown	58 703
---	El Dorado Georgetown	58 755
---	El Dorado Georgetown	58 761
---	Fresno Twp 2	59 20
---	Mariposa Twp 3	60 543
---	Nevada Bridgeport	61 463
---	Sacramento Natonia	63 283
---	Sacramento Sutter	63 308
---	San Francisco San Francisco 4	681176
---	San Francisco San Francisco 4	681185
---	San Francisco San Francisco 4	681186
---	San Francisco San Francisco 4	681187
---	San Francisco San Francisco 4	681189
---	San Francisco San Francisco 4	681190
---	San Francisco San Francisco 4	681191
---	San Francisco San Francisco 4	681192
---	San Francisco San Francisco 4	681193
---	San Francisco San Francisco 4	681195
---	San Francisco San Francisco 4	681196
---	San Francisco San Francisco 4	681199
---	San Francisco San Francisco 4	681203
---	San Francisco San Francisco 5	671206
---	San Francisco San Francisco 4	681209
---	San Francisco San Francisco 4	681210
---	San Francisco San Francisco 4	681212
---	Shasta Horsetown	66 701
---	Tuolumne Shawsfla	71 408
---	Tuolumne Twp 3	71 436
---	Tuolumne Jamestown	71 438
---	Tuolumne Jamestown	71 452
---	Tuolumne Twp 3	71 458
---	Tuolumne Twp 2	71 474
---	Tuolumne Twp 6	71 531
---*	Butte Kimshaw	56 589
---*	Calaveras Twp 10	57 233
---*	Calaveras Twp 4	57 326
---*	Calaveras Twp 4	57 339
---*	Mariposa Coulterville	60 681
A	Sacramento Granite	63 268
Ah	Calaveras Twp 7	57 32
An	Sacramento Granite	63 268
Bang	Placer Michigan	62 844
Bung	San Francisco San Francisco 4	681183
Chen	Yuba Long Bar	72 760
Chew	Yuba Long Bar	72 760
Chin	El Dorado Diamond	58 816
Chin	Placer Michigan	62 858
Ching	Butte Oro	56 675
Chong	Butte Oro	56 675
Chou	San Francisco San Francisco 4	681209
Chou	San Francisco San Francisco 4	681210
Choy	San Francisco San Francisco 4	681200
Cow	El Dorado Greenwood	58 714
Cum	Tuolumne Twp 1	71 476
Fong Ah	San Francisco San Francisco 5	671206
Fou	Stanislaus Emory	70 753
Foy	San Francisco San Francisco 5	671205
Foy	San Francisco San Francisco 5	671206
Fung	San Francisco San Francisco 4	681193
George*	Nevada Little Y	61 535
Ger	Sacramento Granite	63 250
Guing	Tuolumne Twp 6	71 540
Hang	Calaveras Twp 5	57 193
He	Tuolumne Twp 5	71 524
Ho	San Francisco San Francisco 5	671206
Ho	Yuba Long Bar	72 766
Hong	Sacramento Ward 1	63 35
Hong	Yuba Parks Ba	72 782
Hop	San Francisco San Francisco 4	681187
Hop	San Francisco San Francisco 4	681191
Hop	San Francisco San Francisco 4	681201
Hop*	Tuolumne Twp 2	71 416
Hung	Tehama Red Bluff	70 926
Jas W*	San Francisco San Francisco 10	357 67
Kan	San Francisco San Francisco 4	681201
Kih Qi	San Francisco San Francisco 4	681203
Ko	San Francisco San Francisco 4	681193
Ko	San Francisco San Francisco 5	671205
Kong	San Francisco San Francisco 5	671205

California 1860 Census Index

Name	County Locale	M653 Roll	Page
LU			
Koo	San Francisco San Francisco	10	356 67
Kou	San Francisco San Francisco	4	681183
Kou	San Francisco San Francisco	4	681203
Kou	San Francisco San Francisco	5	671205
Kung	San Francisco San Francisco	4	681201
Ling	Sierra Downieville	66	959
Lou	San Francisco San Francisco	4	681183
Lou	San Francisco San Francisco	4	681185
Mee	Placer Auburn	62	581
Moi	San Francisco San Francisco	5	671205
Mony	Sacramento Natonia	63	286
Moo	San Francisco San Francisco	4	681193
Mooy*	San Francisco San Francisco	4	681179
Moy	San Francisco San Francisco	4	681191
Mu	San Francisco San Francisco	4	681198
Muck	Calaveras Twp 6	57	121
Mur	San Francisco San Francisco	4	681212
Ong	Calaveras Twp 5	57	219
Quong	Placer Michigan	62	844
Sam	Fresno Twp 2	59	4
San	San Francisco San Francisco	5	671205
Sim	Butte Ophir	56	811
Sin	El Dorado Georgetown	58	747
So	San Francisco San Francisco	5	671205
Soy	San Francisco San Francisco	5	671205
Sun	Sacramento Granite	63	268
Suy	Sacramento Granite	63	259
Ti	San Francisco San Francisco	4	681201
To	San Francisco San Francisco	5	671205
Ton Jo	San Francisco San Francisco	4	681190
Wah	Tuolumne Twp 6	71	535
Wan	Sacramento Natonia	63	283
Wo	San Francisco San Francisco	4	681183
Wo	San Francisco San Francisco	5	671206
Wong	El Dorado Big Bar	58	737
Wool	El Dorado Georgetown	58	747
You	San Francisco San Francisco	4	681182
Yu	Sacramento Granite	63	269
Yu	Sacramento Natonia	63	283
Yun	Calaveras Twp 10	57	274
LUA			
---	Mariposa Twp 3	60	550
---	Mariposa Twp 3	60	553
---	Mariposa Twp 3	60	609
---	San Joaquin Stockton	64	1096
---*	Mariposa Twp 3	60	607
Goo	Sacramento Granite	63	243
Ky	Shasta Horsetown	66	704
Sy	Shasta Horsetown	66	704
LUAAS			
John	Marin Novato	60	734
LUABY			
Wm	Sacramento Ward 3	63	467
LUAHA HO			
---	Mendocino Calpella	60	823
LUALLEN			
John	Nevada Bloomfield	61	516
LUALLLYN			
Edward	Tuolumne Twp 3	71	441
LUALLYN			
Edward	Tuolumne Jamestown	71	441
LUALTEAT			
Jacob*	Tuolumne Twp 2	71	419
LUAN			
---	Shasta Horsetown	66	711
LUANE			
V*	Sacramento Dry Crk	63	369
LUANICK			
Peter	Tuolumne Jamestown	71	454
LUANN			
Joseph*	Yuba Fosters	72	837
LUANS			
Pedro*	Monterey San Juan	60	1002
LUAR			
---	Mariposa Twp 1	60	626
---	Placer Auburn	62	575
LUARIS			
Pedro	Monterey San Juan	60	1002
LUARSAN			
Jo*	Mariposa Coulterville	60	703
LUAS			
Jos Venita*	Mariposa Twp 3	60	548
LUASEY			
Charlott*	San Francisco San Francisco	2	67605
LUBAN			
Edward	El Dorado Union	58	1092
LUBBATE			
H*	San Francisco San Francisco	9	681101
LUBBATT			
H*	San Francisco San Francisco	9	681101
LUBBEN			
Meta*	San Francisco San Francisco	10	351 67

Name	County Locale	M653 Roll	Page
LUBBEN			
Mita*	San Francisco San Francisco	10	351 67
LUBBERMEYER			
L	San Francisco San Francisco	10	354 67
LUBBERT			
H	San Francisco San Francisco	5	67 532
LUBBINOR			
M	Santa Clara San Jose	65	290
LUBECK			
A	San Francisco San Francisco	6	67 419
D W*	Placer Auburn	62	565
John	Alameda Brooklyn	55	146
S	Nevada Nevada	61	278
LUBEE			
C W	San Francisco San Francisco	2	67 804
LUBER			
William*	Calaveras Twp 6	57	153
LUBERT			
James	San Francisco San Francisco	7	681399
Leander	Yuba Rose Bar	72	791
LUBIC			
C W	San Francisco San Francisco	2	67 804
Catharine	San Francisco San Francisco	2	67 795
LUBIN			
---	Santa Clara Fremont	65	438
LUBKEN			
Lewis	Nevada Rough &	61	425
LUBLET			
Wm	Tehama Moons	70	852
LUBNER			
Leopold	San Francisco San Francisco	8	681299
LUBOHANO			
Louisiana	Calaveras Twp 4	57	331
LUBOHRAM			
Lousianna	Calaveras Twp 4	57	331
LUBOLRAM			
Louisana*	Calaveras Twp 4	57	331
LUBOLRANO			
Louisiana*	Calaveras Twp 4	57	331
Louisiana*	Calaveras Twp 4	57	331
LUBUC			
Felix	San Francisco San Francisco	2	67 798
LUBY			
Johanna	San Francisco San Francisco	4	681109
Mary A	San Francisco San Francisco	4	681109
William	San Francisco San Francisco	4	681109
LUC			
Ah	Tuolumne Twp 4	71	168
Hun	Placer Rattle Snake	62	602
LUCA			
William	San Joaquin Castoria	64	901
LUCACIO			
Lucne*	Calaveras Twp 5	57	147
Lucrie*	Calaveras Twp 5	57	147
LUCACUA			
---	San Diego Agua Caliente	64	859
LUCAIN			
Luzin*	Shasta Shasta	66	672
LUCAN			
Lazen*	Shasta Shasta	66	672
Luzan*	Shasta Shasta	66	672
LUCANBELL			
Martin	Siskiyou Scott Va	69	50
LUCANBRELL			
Martin	Siskiyou Scott Va	69	50
LUCAS JUNR			
---	San Bernardino S Timate	64	741
LUCAS			
---	Los Angeles Los Angeles	59	398
---	Los Angeles San Juan	59	464
---	Los Angeles San Juan	59	473
---	San Bernardino San Bernadino	64	682
---	San Bernardino S Timate	64	716
---	San Bernardino S Timate	64	722
---	San Bernardino S Timate	64	727
---	San Bernardino S Timate	64	729
---	San Bernardino S Timate	64	740
---	San Bernardino S Timate	64	741
---	San Bernardino S Timate	64	742
---	San Bernardino S Timate	64	744
---	San Bernardino S Timate	64	746
---	San Bernardino S Timate	64	751
---	San Bernardino S Timate	64	753
---	San Bernardino S Timate	64	754
---	San Bernardino S Timate	64	755
Andrew J	Yuba Marysville	72	893
Benj W	Sonoma Santa Rosa	69	400
C L	Marin Cortemad	60	756
Charles F	Yuba Marysville	72	899
Charles J	Yuba Marysville	72	899
Charles M	San Joaquin Douglass	64	925
E	Nevada Eureka	61	377
Edward	Alameda Brooklyn	55	155
Frank	Marin Point Re	60	731

Name	County Locale	M653 Roll	Page
LUCAS			
Frederick	Placer Michigan	62	849
Fredk W	Monterey Alisal	60	1035
Geo	Sonoma Salt Point	69	693
J	San Francisco San Francisco	5	67 518
J	San Francisco San Francisco	5	67 533
Jacob	Santa Clara Santa Clara	65	469
James	Nevada Washington	61	332
James	Yolo Cache Crk	72	665
John	El Dorado Mountain	58	1183
John	Marin Novato	60	734
John	Mariposa Twp 1	60	640
John	San Francisco San Francisco	1	68 822
John	Siskiyou Yreka	69	174
John	Sonoma Santa Rosa	69	399
John L*	Sierra Pine Grove	66	823
John*	Mariposa Twp 1	60	640
Joseph	Del Norte Crescent	58	640
Lafaco	Calaveras Twp 6	57	151
Levi	Sierra Pine Grove	66	823
Lofoer	Calaveras Twp 6	57	151
Mand	Calaveras Twp 6	57	142
Manel*	Calaveras Twp 5	57	142
Margaret	Sierra Morristown	66	1051
Marid*	Calaveras Twp 5	57	142
Martin	Alameda Brooklyn	55	162
Maud*	Calaveras Twp 5	57	142
Moses	Humbolt Eureka	59	176
Ralfe	Amador Twp 2	55	326
Robert	Santa Clara San Jose	65	318
Robt K	San Francisco San Francisco	8	681309
Rolfe	Amador Twp 2	55	326
Susanah*	Mariposa Twp 3	60	566
Thomas	San Joaquin Stockton	64	1058
Thomas	San Joaquin Stockton	64	1062
Thomas H	Siskiyou Yreka	69	166
Thos J	Sonoma Santa Rosa	69	402
William	Siskiyou Yreka	69	193
Wm B	Los Angeles Elmonte	59	264
LUCAST			
Edward*	San Joaquin O'Neal	64	1001
LUCAT			
N	Amador Twp 3	55	375
LUCAUS			
A J	Amador Twp 7	55	419
LUCAY			
Mary E	San Francisco San Francisco	10	241 67
LUCAYER			
Barbaria	Tuolumne Sonora	71	239
LUCE			
---	Mariposa Twp 1	60	628
---	Monterey San Juan	60	977
---	Yuba North Ea	72	685
Abram	Placer Michigan	62	821
Albert	Placer Secret R	62	612
Allen	Santa Clara Gilroy	65	246
Ann	San Francisco San Francisco	9	681016
C	Sutter Bear Rvr	70	826
Chas	Santa Clara Santa Clara	65	488
Cheney	Sacramento Ward 3	63	465
Cinika	Nevada Rough &	61	423
D M	Siskiyou Klamath	69	80
E	Merced Twp 1	60	913
E	Yuba Rose Par	72	796
Edwin*	Yuba Rose Bar	72	799
F	San Francisco San Francisco	4	681230
G W	Placer Iona Hills	62	862
Geo	Placer Goods	62	696
George	Placer Michigan	62	834
H M	Yuba Long Bar	72	752
Henry	Calaveras Twp 4	57	339
Henry	Sonoma Armally	69	481
Henry*	Calaveras Twp 4	57	339
Heny*	Calaveras Twp 4	57	339
Israel	Sacramento Ward 4	63	537
J A	Tuolumne Twp 4	71	138
J L	Tehama Red Bluff	70	928
J W	Merced Twp 2	60	924
J*	Nevada Eureka	61	348
James J	Calaveras Twp 5	57	189
Jirah	Marin S Antoni	60	706
John	El Dorado Placerville	58	896
John	Marin Sauciteto	60	749
John	San Francisco San Francisco	1	68 854
John	Sonoma Russian	69	444
Joshua	Fresno Twp 3	59	15
Luther J*	Calaveras Twp 4	57	339
Luther S*	Calaveras Twp 4	57	339
Nilfan*	Sacramento Natonia	63	284
Nilfare*	Sacramento Natonia	63	284
Oliver	Placer Todds Va	62	763
Simon	Humbolt Mattole	59	123
V	Klamath Liberty	59	237
W	Calaveras Twp 9	57	414
W	Siskiyou Klamath	69	80

California 1860 Census Index

Name	County Locale	M653 Roll Page
LUCE		
Wilfan*	Sacramento Natonia	63 284
Wm	Nevada Eureka	61 363
Y Y	Tehama Cottonwood	70 900
LUCEANA		
Jose*	Monterey Pajaro	60 1018
LUCEN		
A*	Stanislaus Buena Village	70 721
Jose M*	Los Angeles Los Nieto	59 436
Jse M	Los Angeles Los Nieto	59 436
LUCENTO		
W	El Dorado Placerville	58 860
LUCERA		
Guadalupa	San Salvador San Bernardino	64 661
LUCERO		
Antonio	Monterey Monterey	60 963
Jose A	Los Angeles Los Nieto	59 427
Manuel	Los Angeles Santa Ana	59 444
Pedro	Monterey San Juan	60 974
LUCH		
---	Mariposa Twp 3	60 562
---	Mariposa Twp 1	60 664
C B	Tuolumne Twp 1	71 211
Robt	San Francisco San Francisco 10	344 67
Thomas	Tuolumne Sonora	71 196
LUCHERT		
Peter	Santa Clara San Jose	65 295
LUCHESI		
Pedro	San Bernardino Santa Barbara	64 169
LUCHI		
---*	Tulara Visalia	71 39
LUCHINE		
A*	Sierra Downieville	66 968
LUCHTEAD		
R A*	Nevada Bridgeport	61 475
LUCHTENSTEIN		
Richard	San Francisco San Francisco 4	681 123
LUCHTFUN		
A	El Dorado Georgetown	58 676
LUCI		
---	Shasta Shasta	66 670
LUCIA		
---	Fresno Twp 1	59 85
---	San Bernardino San Bernadino	64 684
---	Tulara Twp 3	71 69
Joseph	Amador Twp 4	55 244
Juan	San Luis Obispo San Luis Obispo	65 21
LUCIAN		
L B	Tehama Moons	70 854
LUCIANA		
---	San Bernardino San Bernardino	64 678
Jose	Monterey Pajaro	60 1018
LUCIDLY		
Nicholas	Fresno Twp 1	59 75
LUCIERO		
Jose	Santa Clara Gilroy	65 228
LUCILTES		
B*	Amador Twp 2	55 302
LUCINBURG		
Mr	Sonoma Sonoma	69 644
LUCINSEN		
James*	Sacramento Granite	63 258
LUCINY		
John J*	San Francisco San Francisco 9	68 954
LUCITLER		
B*	Amador Twp 2	55 302
LUCIUSEN		
James*	Sacramento Granite	63 258
LUCK		
---	Butte Kimshaw	56 582
---	Butte Kimshaw	56 608
---	Butte Oregon	56 617
---	Butte Oregon	56 620
---	Calaveras Twp 8	57 105
---	Del Norte Crescent	58 633
---	El Dorado Salmon Falls	581 066
---	Mariposa Twp 1	60 664
---	Placer Rattle Snake	62 601
---	Placer Virginia	62 671
---	Placer Illinois	62 740
---	Placer Illinois	62 747
---	Placer Illinois	62 748
---	Sacramento Granite	63 232
---	Sacramento Cosummes	63 392
---	Sierra Downieville	661 015
---	Sierra Downieville	661 027
---	Yuba Slate Ro	72 685
---	Yuba Slate Ro	72 715
---	Yuba Marysville	72 895
---*	Amador Twp 4	55 332
---*	Butte Oregon	56 625
---*	Calaveras Twp 5	57 232
---*	Calaveras Twp 10	57 234
---*	Nevada Bridgeport	61 464

Name	County Locale	M653 Roll Page
LUCK		
A	Sierra Downieville	66 974
C B	Tuolumne Sonora	71 211
F E	El Dorado Kelsey	581 152
Ferdinand	Solano Benecia	69 317
Fong	Placer Michigan	62 847
Fung	Sacramento Mississipi	63 190
Hew	Butte Hamilton	56 520
Hon*	Butte Hamilton	56 520
How*	Butte Hamilton	56 520
Ninn	Placer Iona Hills	62 897
Phillip	Colusa Mansville	57 437
Robert	Yuba Slate Ro	72 695
Solomon	Sonoma Vallejo	69 615
Wan	Placer Iona Hills	62 897
Wong	Sacramento Ward 4	63 612
LUCKAN		
Charles	Solano Benecia	69 285
LUCKE		
Conrad	El Dorado White Oaks	581 022
Henry	San Francisco San Francisco 3	67 8
LUCKEE		
---*	Tulara Visalia	71 37
LUCKENBACH		
A	Butte Eureka	56 649
LUCKENBACK		
Marcus	Monterey San Juan	60 987
LUCKENTACH		
J S*	Trinity Weaverville	701 069
LUCKER		
Robert	Nevada Little Y	61 533
LUCKERSBURY		
Ampuste	Butte Eureka	56 654
LUCKETT		
A W	Calaveras Twp 9	57 410
A W	Tuolumne Sonora	71 204
Jos A	Klamath Liberty	59 235
Thomas	Tuolumne Shawsfla	71 413
LUCKEY		
Chas	Santa Clara Fremont	65 421
J	Sacramento Ward 4	63 607
LUCKHANT		
Charles A	Los Angeles Los Angeles	59 335
LUCKHART		
Samuel	Plumas Meadow Valley	62 907
LUCKHEE		
---	Tulara Twp 2	71 35
LUCKINBURG		
Auguste	Butte Eureka	56 654
LUCKINGER		
Fred	Placer Ophirville	62 658
LUCKIR		
Stippin	Napa Clear Lake	61 121
LUCKIT		
M	Santa Clara Santa Clara	65 483
LUCKITT		
John	Yuba New York	72 723
LUCKLE		
A	Calaveras Twp 9	57 391
H	Calaveras Twp 9	57 391
LUCKLINSON		
Antony	Yuba New York	72 727
LUCKLOW		
---	Tulara Twp 2	71 36
LUCKLY		
A	Calaveras Twp 9	57 391
LUCKMAN		
W	El Dorado Mud Springs	581 000
LUCKO		
---	Tulara Twp 2	71 37
LUCKOT		
Wm L	Santa Clara Santa Clara	65 464
LUCKOYAMA		
---*	Mendocino Big Rvr	60 854
LUCKS		
Henry	San Francisco San Francisco 3	67 8
Richd	San Francisco San Francisco 9	681 021
LUCKSLEY		
J O	Butte Kimshaw	56 572
LUCKY BILL		
---	Fresno Twp 3	59 96
LUCKY		
---	Del Norte Klamath	58 657
Frank	Monterey Alisal	60 1026
LUCLIO		
Jesus*	Monterey San Juan	60 1001
LUCO		
Juan In	Solano Suisan	69 228
Juan M	Solano Suisan	69 228
LUCOCK		
Joseph	Sacramento Ward 4	63 612
LUCOMB		
Harriet	Sacramento Granite	63 265
LUCOME		
---	Tulara Twp 2	71 39
LUCOSO		
John	Calaveras Twp 7	57 22

Name	County Locale	M653 Roll Page
LUCRANISNO		
---	Tulara Twp 3	71 64
LUCRAZIER		
Francisco	Yuba Marysville	72 929
LUCRONIN		
Frederick*	Calaveras Twp 8	57 107
LUCROUSI		
Francisco	Calaveras Twp 4	57 330
LUCTHERS		
Henry	El Dorado Coloma	581 116
LUCTSEN		
James*	Yuba New York	72 733
LUCUS		
---	San Bernardino S Timate	64 714
Charles H	Sierra La Porte	66 771
Geo C	Tuolumne Shawsfla	71 380
H S	Nevada Bloomfield	61 509
J A	Tuolumne Columbia	71 323
Jesus	Monterey San Juan	60 1001
John	El Dorado Mountain	581 183
John L	Sierra Pine Grove	66 823
John S	Sierra Pine Grove	66 823
Mark M	Sierra Twp 7	66 863
Mark W	Sierra St Louis	66 863
Obidiah	Sacramento Granite	63 249
Obrdiah	Sacramento Granite	63 249
Pedro	Monterey San Juan	60 974
S M	Tuolumne Twp 2	71 380
Sylvester	Sierra Twp 7	66 901
Thodore	Colusa Colusi	57 427
Wm	El Dorado Mud Springs	58 979
LUCY		
---	Mendocino Calpella	60 821
---	Mendocino Calpella	60 827
---	Mendocino Round Va	60 879
---	Mendocino Round Va	60 881
---	Mendocino Round Va	60 882
---	Mendocino Twp 1	60 890
---	Mendocino Twp 1	60 891
---	San Francisco San Francisco 2	67 673
---	Shasta Horsetown	66 711
---	Tulara Twp 1	71 117
D J	San Francisco San Francisco 1	68 893
George	Solano Vallejo	69 264
Jas	Sacramento Granite	63 264
Mary E	San Francisco San Francisco 10	344 67
Thomas	San Francisco San Francisco 2	67 729
Tim	Tuolumne Twp 2	71 271
LUD		
E*	Yuba Rose Bar	72 796
LUDBENS		
Loulsa	Placer Rattle Snake	62 627
LUDBROOK		
W*	Sacramento Ward 4	63 607
LUDD		
Alexander	Calaveras Twp 8	57 52
C H	San Mateo Twp 1	65 47
LUDDEN		
L	Yolo Putah	72 545
LUDDERS		
L*	Yolo Putah	72 545
LUDDICERT		
Ellen*	San Francisco San Francisco 4	681 115
LUDDICUT		
Ellen*	San Francisco San Francisco 4	681 115
LUDDIN		
L*	Yolo Putah	72 545
LUDDINGHANS		
F	Sacramento Ward 3	63 431
LUDDINGTON		
David	Marin Cortemad	60 787
LUDDIRERT		
Ellen	San Francisco San Francisco 4	681 115
LUDDVEIRT		
Ellen*	San Francisco San Francisco 4	681 115
LUDDY		
M	Siskiyou Callahan	69 11
Mary	San Francisco San Francisco 9	681 024
T	San Francisco San Francisco 5	67 539
Thos	Klamath Liberty	59 233
W	Klamath Liberty	59 239
William	Tuolumne Twp 2	71 335
Wm	San Francisco San Francisco 12	383 67
LUDE		
---	Yuba North Ea	72 685
LUDEMAN		
M	San Francisco San Francisco 2	67 633
Wm	San Francisco San Francisco 3	67 50
LUDEN		
C M	Siskiyou Cottonwoood	69 99
P	Siskiyou Scott Va	69 50
LUDER		
M	San Francisco San Francisco 5	67 552
LUDERS		
Charles	El Dorado White Oaks	581 030

Name	County Locale	Roll	Page
LUDERS			
Harry*	Amador Twp 2	55	309
Lerne*	Alameda Brooklyn	55	143
Wm A	Alameda Oakland	55	52
LUDERSDOFF			
William*	Sierra St Louis	66	809
LUDGE			
Michael	Santa Cruz Pescadero	66	651
LUDIN			
Ann	Nevada Eureka	61	390
LUDING			
Bahram*	Shasta Shasta	66	679
Bohram*	Shasta Shasta	66	679
Paris	Yolo No E Twp	72	675
Paris	Yuba North Ea	72	675
Peter	Yolo No E Twp	72	667
LUDINIDGE			
Eliza	San Francisco San Francisco 1	68	861
LUDIO			
Jesus*	Monterey San Juan	60	1001
LUDLAM			
Anthony	San Francisco San Francisco 10	67	218
Fetch R*	San Francisco San Francisco 10	67	258
LUDLERR			
James	San Francisco San Francisco 6	67	421
LUDLEY			
James	Yuba Marysville	72	909
John	Sacramento Granite	63	263
LUDLIN			
Anna	Nevada Eureka	61	390
LUDLON			
James	San Francisco San Francisco 9	68	977
LUDLOW			
James	San Francisco San Francisco 6	67	421
James	San Francisco San Francisco 9	68	977
W	San Francisco San Francisco 9	68	1069
William B	El Dorado White Oaks	58	1001
LUDLUM			
James	Alameda Oakland	55	18
LUDMON			
Cornelius	San Francisco San Francisco 9	68	937
LUDNEN			
Henry*	Mariposa Twp 3	60	587
LUDOFF			
H	Sonoma Bodega	69	535
LUDOLF			
Rengolph*	San Francisco San Francisco 7	68	1328
LUDOLPH			
Chas	Butte Oregon	56	633
Julius	San Francisco San Francisco 7	68	1328
LUDOM			
Wm	Yuba New York	72	720
LUDON			
Andrew*	Sonoma Petaluma	69	597
Andw*	Sonoma Petaluma	69	597
LUDOW			
Stephen W*	Sierra Scales D	66	802
LUDRES			
Eugene	Siskiyou Yreka	69	186
LUDROW			
Wesley	Yuba Marysville	72	966
LUDS			
Philip*	Nevada Red Dog	61	544
Phillip*	Nevada Red Dog	61	555
LUDSON			
J C	Sonoma Petaluma	69	595
LUDSTRAM			
J	El Dorado Mud Springs	58	973
LUDUS			
Edward	San Francisco San Francisco 6	67	468
LUDWICK			
Charles	Humbolt Eureka	59	175
E K	El Dorado Diamond	58	808
Jno	Mendocino Big Rvr	60	848
John	San Francisco San Francisco 3	67	19
John	Yuba Marysville	72	926
Wm	Tehama Red Bluff	70	899
LUDWIEG			
Henry	Sacramento Sutter	63	293
LUDWIG			
---	San Francisco San Francisco 4	68	1221
Andrew	Placer Rattle Snake	62	635
Daml D	Butte Oregon	56	626
E B	Placer Michigan	62	852
Ebner	San Francisco San Francisco 8	68	1305
G H*	El Dorado Diamond	58	775
Henry	Sacramento Sutter	63	293
Henry	Sacramento Ward 4	63	512
John	San Francisco San Francisco 1	68	905
John*	San Francisco San Francisco 7	68	1419
L	Shasta Horsetown	66	695
Peter	Yolo No E Twp	72	667
Saml D	Butte Oregon	56	626

Name	County Locale	Roll	Page
LUDY			
Adam*	Amador Twp 5	55	339
Ernesita	Sierra Twp 7	66	865
LUE			
---	Calaveras Twp 9	57	388
---	Del Norte Crescent	58	630
---	El Dorado Diamond	58	816
---	Fresno Twp 1	59	27
---	Mariposa Twp 3	60	544
---	Mariposa Twp 1	60	664
---	Placer Folsom	62	649
---	Sacramento Cosumnes	63	392
---	Sacramento Cosumnes	63	408
---	Shasta Shasta	66	678
---	Sierra Morristown	66	1056
---	Sierra Pine Grove	66	827
---	Sierra Downieville	66	993
---*	Tuolumne Jacksonville	71	168
---*	Butte Ophir	56	809
A Quin	Sierra Downieville	66	985
Fee	Butte Wyandotte	56	666
Sam	Fresno Twp 1	59	28
Wo To	San Francisco San Francisco 4	68	1202
LUEARD			
Francisco	Calaveras Twp 4	57	333
LUEAS			
John*	El Dorado Placerville	58	925
Susanah	Mariposa Twp 3	60	566
LUEDKE			
R	San Francisco San Francisco 6	67	462
LUEF			
Adolph	Calaveras Twp 6	57	111
LUEIRO			
Jacirito	Santa Clara Gilroy	65	228
LUEK			
Fook	Placer Illinois	62	740
LUEKIS			
F M	Calaveras Twp 9	57	373
LUEL			
---	Placer Virginia	62	675
LUEMORE			
Joseph F	Alameda Oakland	55	4
Joseph*	Alameda Oakland	55	4
LUER			
Charles	El Dorado Casumnes	58	1175
Jacob	Amador Twp 1	55	461
Wilferd	Sacramento Natonia	63	284
LUERDE			
Balbanedo	Los Angeles San Gabriel	59	423
LUERES			
Riatano*	Napa Napa	61	71
LUERS			
John*	El Dorado Placerville	58	925
LUERTE			
Manrico	San Francisco San Francisco 2	67	568
Maruico	San Francisco San Francisco 2	67	568
P Bansh*	San Francisco San Francisco 2	67	568
LUERTER			
Coseah	Mariposa Twp 3	60	545
LUERZARIO			
Richard	Santa Cruz Santa Cruz	66	601
LUESMAN			
Earnest*	San Francisco San Francisco 11	67	136
LUEU			
---	San Francisco San Francisco 11	67	161
---*	San Francisco San Francisco 11	67	160
LUEUM			
F	El Dorado Placerville	58	838
LUEY			
---	Trinity Grass Valley	70	962
---*	Mariposa Coulterville	60	689
Fong*	San Francisco San Francisco 5	67	508
LUEZ			
---	Los Angeles San Juan	59	477
LUFALLET			
Antoine	Calaveras Twp 6	57	142
LUFELER			
William*	Siskiyou Yreka	69	192
LUFESEN			
William*	Siskiyou Yreka	69	192
LUFF			
Charles	Marin Bolinas	60	728
Charles W	Yuba Linda	72	989
Henry	Yuba Suida	72	989
J S	Butte Kimshaw	56	573
London	Sacramento Ward 1	63	34
Sondon	Sacramento Ward 1	63	34
LUFFEREL			
Wm	Yuba Fosters	72	839
LUFFERTY			
Caleb	Nevada Bloomfield	61	529
Calib	Nevada Bloomfield	61	529
LUFFEY			
Jno	Sacramento Ward 4	63	501

Name	County Locale	Roll	Page
LUFFICHE			
Aophonso	Sierra Port Win	66	794
LUFHIN			
Charley	Alameda Oakland	55	33
LUFKIN			
D T	Sacramento Franklin	63	327
James	San Francisco San Francisco 3	67	63
LUFOLLET			
Antoine	Calaveras Twp 5	57	142
LUFOY			
Catherine	Calaveras Twp 6	57	124
LUFS			
Henry	Sacramento Ward 1	63	32
Joseph	Mariposa Twp 3	60	622
LUFSEN			
William*	Siskiyou Yreka	69	192
LUFT			
Henry	Sacramento Ward 1	63	32
LUFTINS			
A	Butte Oro	56	684
LUFUS			
Joseph E	Nevada Rough &	61	425
LUG			
---	Mariposa Twp 3	60	551
---	Mariposa Coulterville	60	680
LUEY			
Fong*	San Francisco San Francisco 5	67	508
LUEZ			
---	Los Angeles San Juan	59	477
LUFALLET			
Antoine	Calaveras Twp 6	57	142
LUFELER			
William*	Siskiyou Yreka	69	192
LUFESEN			
William*	Siskiyou Yreka	69	192
LUFF			
Charles	Marin Bolinas	60	728
Charles W	Yuba Linda	72	989
Henry	Yuba Suida	72	989
J S	Butte Kimshaw	56	573
London	Sacramento Ward 1	63	34
Sondon	Sacramento Ward 1	63	34
LUFFEREL			
Wm	Yuba Fosters	72	839
LUFFERTY			
Caleb	Nevada Bloomfield	61	529
Calib	Nevada Bloomfield	61	529
LUFFEY			
Jno	Sacramento Ward 4	63	501
LUFFICHE			
Aophonso	Sierra Port Win	66	794
LUFHIN			
Charley	Alameda Oakland	55	33
LUFKIN			
D T	Sacramento Franklin	63	327
James	San Francisco San Francisco 3	67	63
LUFOLLET			
Antoine	Calaveras Twp 5	57	142
LUFOY			
Catherine	Calaveras Twp 6	57	124
LUFS			
Henry	Sacramento Ward 1	63	32
Joseph	Mariposa Twp 3	60	622
LUFSEN			
William*	Siskiyou Yreka	69	192
LUFT			
Henry	Sacramento Ward 1	63	32
LUFTINS			
A	Butte Oro	56	684
LUFUS			
Joseph E	Nevada Rough &	61	425
LUG			
---	Mariposa Twp 3	60	551
---	Mariposa Coulterville	60	681
---	Nevada Rough &	61	425
---	Nevada Bridgeport	61	460
---	Sierra Downieville	66	981
Ho	Mariposa Coulterville	60	681
LUGADA			
---	San Bernardino Santa Inez	64	138
---	San Bernardino Santa Inez	64	143
LUGAN			
Patrick*	Sierra St Louis	66	807
LUGARDA			
---	San Diego Agua Caliente	64	836
---	Santa Clara Santa Clara	65	505
LUGARDEN			
Eli	Yuba Marysville	72	952
LUGARMACAN			
I	El Dorado Diamond	58	804
LUGARO			
---	Santa Clara Santa Clara	65	505
LUGATI			
Joseph	Calaveras Twp 7	57	48
LUGAY			
Dennis	Santa Clara San Jose	65	354

Name	County Locale	M653 Roll	Page
LUGERO			
Falice* San Luis Obispo San Luis Obispo		65	29
LUGGS			
James	Los Angeles Azuza	59	278
John	Yolo Putah	72	545
LUGH??AD			
R A*	Nevada Bridgeport	61	475
LUGHE			
John*	Calaveras Twp 6	57	161
LUGHHEAD			
R A*	Nevada Bridgeport	61	475
LUGHKEAD			
R A*	Nevada Bridgeport	61	475
LUGLEISE			
John*	Siskiyou Callahan	69	3
LUGLIO			
Preano San Bernardino Santa Barbara		64	191
LUGNA			
John	Tuolumne Twp 4	71	178
LUGNERER			
Peter*	Siskiyou Yreka	69	171
LUGNIO			
---	Fresno Twp 2	59	19
LUGO			
---	Tulara Twp 3	71	64
Maria*	Los Angeles Los Angeles	59	496
Maria*	Los Angeles Los Angeles	59	498
Morcedes	Santa Barbara San Bernardino	64	203
Oristina	Monterey Alisal	60	1041
Pedro	Los Angeles San Pedro	59	478
Pilar	Los Angeles Los Angeles	59	367
Ramon San Bernardino Santa Barbara		64	177
Saturnino	Santa Barbara San Bernardino	64	149
Trinidad San Bernardino Santa Barbara		64	183
Wancisca Dlos Angeles Los Angeles		59	304
Ygnacio Los Angeles Los Angeles		59	306
Ygnacio San Bernardino Santa Barbara		64	167
LUGODON			
Tho*	Siskiyou Scott Ri	69	81
LUGON			
---	Calaveras Twp 5	57	226
LUGUE			
Simon*	Mariposa Twp 1	60	625
LUGUEZ			
Pedro*	Los Angeles Los Angeles	59	374
LUGUIENES			
Juana	Los Angeles Los Angeles	59	323
LUHDEN			
Louis San Francisco San Francisco		10 67	180
LUHER			
Lage	Mariposa Twp 3	60	565
LUHL			
Christian*	Tuolumne Springfield	71	369
LUHLING			
Henry San Francisco San Francisco		10 67	299
LUHMAN			
J	Siskiyou Klamath	69	94
LUHN			
Gerard L	Solano Benecia	69	315
LUHRS			
C F San Francisco San Francisco		6 67	434
Christopher	San Francisco San Francisco	3 67	48
Claus	Colusa Spring Valley	57	431
E F San Francisco San Francisco		6 67	434
H W San Francisco San Francisco		10 67	288
LUHRSINGER			
John San Francisco San Francisco		7 681	437
LUI			
---	Amador Twp 4	55	247
---	Butte Ophir	56	812
---	Butte Ophir	56	818
---	Calaveras Twp 5	57	149
---	Calaveras Twp 5	57	240
---	Calaveras Twp 4	57	334
---	Stanislaus Branch	70	714
---	Yuba Linda	72	991
Ah	Yuba Bear Rvr	72	1000
Ah	Yuba Suida	72	991
David L	Mariposa Coulterville	60	684
E	Sacramento Natonia	63	286
Sing	Butte Kimshaw	56	584
LUICE			
M	Sonoma Washington	69	675
LUICUS			
---	San Bernardino San Bernadino	64	677
LUID			
A L	Sierra Twp 5	66	943
LUIDLITTER			
Jonathan W	Calaveras Twp 10	57	281
LUIDO			
Moses	Sierra Twp 5	66	928

Name	County Locale	M653 Roll	Page
LUIDOP			
William* San Francisco San Francisco		9 681	057
LUIE			
Cam*	Sierra Port Win	66	798
LUIG			
---	Mariposa Coulterville	60	692
LUIGNE			
Simon	Mariposa Twp 1	60	625
LUIHSINGER			
Nicholas	Sierra Scales D	66	802
LUIK			
--- San Francisco San Francisco		5 67	507
LUIMBO			
M E	Sacramento Franklin	63	317
LUIMBURG			
Mr	Sonoma Sonoma	69	644
LUIMNEY			
Mary Cath*	San Francisco	2 67	661
LUIN			
---	Placer Virginia	62	671
---	San Joaquin Stockton	64	1084
---	Sierra Downieville	66	981
Cho*	Butte Ophir	56	814
John*	Santa Cruz Santa Cruz	66	633
Wao	Sacramento Natonia	63	280
LUING			
---	El Dorado Mountain	58	1188
LUINGROVE			
Geo*	Sacramento Natonia	63	281
LUINGSTON			
Wm*	Stanislaus Oatvale	70	718
LUIS			
---	Los Angeles San Gabriel	59	414
---	Los Angeles Los Nieto	59	431
---	Los Angeles Santa Ana	59	456
---	Los Angeles San Juan	59	470
---	Los Angeles San Juan	59	474
---	Monterey Monterey	60	958
---	San Diego San Diego	64	772
---	San Diego Agua Caliente	64	828
---	San Diego Agua Caliente	64	831
---	Santa Clara Santa Clara	65	462
Berliand*	Sierra Scales D	66	804
Berlrand*	Sierra Scales D	66	804
Bonificio Los Angeles Los Angeles		59	511
David L	Mariposa Coulterville	60	684
Edward*	Nevada Bridgeport	61	490
John	Mariposa Coulterville	60	689
Jose Los Angeles San Juan		59	465
Joseph	Calaveras Twp 10	57	268
Manuel	Yuba Parks Ba	72	783
Manuel	Yuba Foster B	72	823
P San Francisco San Francisco		3 67	78
Rerland	Sierra Scales D	66	804
Rerlrand*	Sierra Scales D	66	804
Rirlrand*	Sierra Scales D	66	804
LUISA			
---	Monterey San Juan	60	983
---	Monterey San Juan	60	991
Maria Los Angeles Los Angeles		59	326
LUISEY			
Kaffayette	Siskiyou Yreka	69	143
Laffayette	Siskiyou Yreka	69	143
LUISTON			
Andrew	San Mateo Twp 3	65	92
LUIT			
Richard*	Mendocino Round Va	60	879
LUITJNENS			
John D	El Dorado Coloma	58	1112
LUITY			
Emerita	Sierra Twp 7	66	865
LUIU			
--- San Francisco San Francisco		11 67	144
LUIY			
---	Mariposa Coulterville	60	691
Len	Sacramento Natonia	63	281
LUJAIN			
Louis*	El Dorado Georgetown	58	705
Swing*	El Dorado Georgetown	58	705
LUJAN			
Manuel*	San Mateo Twp 2	65	132
LUJO			
Elifanio	Santa Clara Almaden	65	269
Francisco*	Santa Barbara San Bernardino	64	190
LUK			
---	El Dorado Georgetown	58	692
---	El Dorado Greenwood	58	730
---	El Dorado Big Bar	58	740
---	Placer Illinois	62	749
---	Placer Illinois	62	750
--- San Francisco San Francisco		9 681	087
--- San Francisco San Francisco		9 681	088
--- San Francisco San Francisco		4 681	177

Name	County Locale	M653 Roll	Page
LUK			
---	San Francisco San Francisco	4 681	181
---	San Francisco San Francisco	4 681	187
---	San Francisco San Francisco	4 681	188
---	San Francisco San Francisco	4 681	198
---	San Francisco San Francisco	4 681	211
---	San Francisco San Francisco	10	356
---		67	
---	San Francisco San Francisco	1 68	926
---	Sierra Downieville	66	983
C	Sutter Yuba	70	763
Fredrich	Tuolumne Montezuma	71	511
Juan	Sacramento Ward 3	63	492
Leock San Francisco San Francisco		6 67	470
Lou San Francisco San Francisco		4 681	198
Low San Francisco San Francisco		4 681	198
See	El Dorado Georgetown	58	751
Sin	El Dorado Greenwood	58	730
Su	El Dorado Georgetown	58	748
LUKA			
Andrew	Placer Virginia	62	678
LUKE			
---	Butte Hamilton	56	529
---	Calaveras Twp 5	57	245
---	Calaveras Twp 5	57	254
---	Calaveras Twp 5	57	256
---	Mendocino Round Va	60	880
---	Mendocino Twp 1	60	891
---	Nevada Bloomfield	61	528
---	Nevada Red Dog	61	541
---	Placer Illinois	62	749
---	Sierra Morristown	66	1056
---	Tulara Twp 2	71	33
---	Tulara Twp 2	71	36
---	Yolo Slate Ra	72	715
---	Yuba Slate Ro	72	715
---*	Tulara Visalia	71	36
Ali	San Joaquin Douglass	64	919
Charles	Sierra Gibsonville	66	856
Charles A	Siskiyou Yreka	69	148
Edwin F*	Calaveras Twp 5	57	236
He Fam	Yuba Long Bar	72	770
Hoy	Yuba Fosters	72	827
J San Francisco San Francisco		5 67	552
John	Alameda Oakland	55	23
M	Sutter Nicolaus	70	830
Robert	Yuba Long Bar	72	768
Ti	Yuba Fosters	72	830
W	Sierra Twp 7	66	896
Warren E	Yuba Marysville	72	950
William	Calaveras Twp 8	57	64
Wm San Francisco San Francisco		5 67	554
Wm	Sierra Twp 7	66	896
LUKEN			
B D	El Dorado Kelsey	58	1137
Jos F*	Sacramento Ward 4	63	554
LUKENBILL			
Hen	Amador Twp 7	55	412
LUKENE			
Cacinto	Trinity Weaverville	70	1073
LUKER			
William	Tuolumne Twp 1	71	265
LUKERING			
J H	San Joaquin Stockton	64	1089
LUKES			
A	Trinity Trinity	70	974
Caroline San Francisco San Francisco		6 67	447
Lafe	Mariposa Twp 3	60	565
LUKI			
---	Nevada Bloomfield	61	528
LUKINS			
L	Butte Kimshaw	56	575
LUKMAN			
J*	Siskiyou Klamath	69	94
LUKO			
---*	Tulara Visalia	71	33
LUKOLOWSKI			
Isudoni	Calaveras Twp 6	57	125
LUKON			
---*	Tulara Visalia	71	34
LULAGHER			
Thos	Santa Clara Redwood	65	449
LULASTAN			
Gasparda*	Calaveras Twp 4	57	299
LULE			
---	El Dorado Georgetown	58	686
A B*	Sacramento Granite	63	234
LULERT			
Leander*	Yuba Rose Bar	72	791
LULES			
Wm*	Sacramento Natonia	63	275
LULEY			
Phila	Stanislaus Emory	70	752
LULHLO			
William	Klamath S Fork	59	197
LULIA			
---	Sierra Downieville	66	979

Name	County Locale	M653 Roll Page
LULIO		
Josephine*	Calaveras Twp 4	57 330
LULISAN		
John*	Placer Folsom	62 640
LULL		
---	Stanislaus Emory	70 744
A	Colusa Muion	57 461
Daniel	Alameda Brooklyn	55 158
Ellen	Alameda Oakland	55 2
H H	Butte Oregon	56 612
H H	Yuba Long Bar	72 752
Laurs	Calaveras Twp 9	57 399
Louis R	San Francisco San Francisco 8	681320
LULLERY		
M	Yolo Cottonwoood	72 555
LULLIS		
---	Sierra Downieville	66 989
LULLMAN		
Henry	Yuba Parke Ba	72 785
LULLY		
Wm B	Colusa Colusi	57 420
LULNMOKISH		
---	Tulara Twp 1	71 121
LULOFF		
B	San Francisco San Francisco 5	67 512
LULOUP		
Peter	Shasta French G	66 718
LULRADO		
Francisco	Santa Inez	64 143
	San Bernardino	
LULTYE		
C	San Francisco San Francisco 5	67 529
LULTZ		
Anthony	Yuba Linda	72 988
LULY		
P*	Sacramento Brighton	63 194
LUM LA		
---*	Calaveras Twp 8	57 60
LUM TOU		
---	Butte Kimshaw	56 588
LUM		
---	Amador Twp 6	55 428
---	Amador Twp 6	55 429
---	Amador Twp 6	55 447
---	Amador Twp 1	55 507
---	Amador Twp 1	55 511
---	Butte Kimshaw	56 589
---	Butte Ophir	56 779
---	Calaveras Twp 8	57 107
---	Calaveras Twp 5	57 136
---	Calaveras Twp 6	57 181
---	Calaveras Twp 5	57 214
---	Calaveras Twp 5	57 215
---	Calaveras Twp 5	57 218
---	Calaveras Twp 5	57 225
---	Calaveras Twp 5	57 226
---	Calaveras Twp 5	57 233
---	Calaveras Twp 4	57 315
---	Calaveras Twp 4	57 332
---	Calaveras Twp 8	57 59
---	El Dorado Salmon Hills	581059
---	El Dorado Salmon Falls	581060
---	El Dorado Coloma	581074
---	El Dorado Union	581091
---	El Dorado Kelsey	581135
---	El Dorado Kelsey	581144
---	El Dorado Casumnes	581160
---	El Dorado Georgetown	58 703
---	Fresno Twp 2	59 4
---	Mariposa Twp 3	60 572
---	Mariposa Twp 3	60 576
---	Mariposa Twp 3	60 580
---	Mariposa Twp 3	60 581
---	Mariposa Twp 3	60 582
---	Mariposa Twp 3	60 592
---	Mariposa Twp 3	60 607
---	Mariposa Twp 3	60 608
---	Mariposa Twp 3	60 613
---	Mariposa Twp 3	60 614
---	Mariposa Coulterville	60 683
---	Mariposa Coulterville	60 694
---	Mariposa Coulterville	60 700
---	Placer Auburn	62 571
---	Placer Auburn	62 572
---	Placer Auburn	62 573
---	Placer Folsom	62 640
---	Placer Horseshoe	62 650
---	Placer Virginia	62 670
---	Placer Virginia	62 671
---	Placer Virginia	62 684
---	Placer Virginia	62 685
---	Placer Virginia	62 701
---	Placer Dutch Fl	62 722
---	Placer Illinois	62 742
---	Placer Illinois	62 745
---	Placer Illinois	62 746
LUM		
---	Placer Illinois	62 751
---	Placer Illinois	62 752
---	Placer Iona Hills	62 893
---	Sacramento Ward 3	63 487
---	Sacramento Ward 1	63 54
---	Sacramento Ward 4	63 613
---	San Francisco San Francisco 8	681308
---	San Francisco San Francisco 1	68 925
---	Sierra Downieville	661020
---	Sierra Cox'S Bar	66 951
---	Sierra Downieville	66 981
---	Sierra Downieville	66 997
---	Siskiyou Callahan	69 12
---	Siskiyou Scott Va	69 46
---	Trinity Mouth Ca	701011
---	Trinity Raabs Ba	701020
---	Tuolumne Columbia	71 346
---	Tuolumne Twp 1	71 485
---	Tuolumne Twp 5	71 516
---	Tuolumne Twp 5	71 523
---	Tuolumne Don Pedro	71 540
---	Yuba Fosters	72 831
---*	Fresno Twp 2	59 26
---*	Marin Cortemad	60 785
---*	Mariposa Twp 3	60 572
---*	Mariposa Twp 3	60 580
---*	Mariposa Twp 3	60 614
---*	Sacramento Cosummes	63 390
---*	Tuolumne Big Oak	71 181
---*	Yuba Foster B	72 831
Ah	Tuolumne Twp 4	71 181
Ah	Tuolumne Twp 2	71 346
An	Yuba Long Bar	72 766
Aw	Yuba Long Bar	72 766
Choi	Calaveras Twp 6	57 179
Choo	Butte Kimshaw	56 582
Hop	Butte Kimshaw	56 589
J G	San Francisco San Francisco 5	67 511
Jas	Mariposa Twp 3	60 591
Jim	Tuolumne Twp 3	71 441
John*	Napa Yount	61 31
Joiny	Shasta Horsetown	66 701
Kie	Sacramento Ward 4	63 613
Lat	Butte Kimshaw	56 588
Loong	Shasta Horsetown	66 701
Lu*	Sacramento Granite	63 268
See	Tuolumne Twp 6	71 537
Sigh	El Dorado Big Bar	58 740
Sing*	Placer Auburn	62 572
Son	Mariposa Twp 3	60 619
Yorp	Placer Illinois	62 745
LUMAN		
John*	Placer Michigan	62 823
LUMAND		
Daniel	San Francisco San Francisco 4	681167
LUMARD		
Pierre*	Yuba Slate Ro	72 710
LUMAS		
Boiknill*	El Dorado Georgetown	58 751
LUMBACK		
B	San Joaquin Stockton	641098
LUMBARD		
C C	Butte Oro	56 682
Charles	Calaveras Twp 6	57 111
Peter	Sierra Downieville	66 957
Wm	Tuolumne Twp 3	71 449
LUMBARDO		
Castino	Tuolumne Twp 1	71 257
LUMBECK		
Wm	Siskiyou Callahan	69 12
LUMBER		
C	Sutter Butte	70 795
William	Napa Yount	61 52
LUMBERGER		
James	Alameda Oakland	55 44
LUMBERT		
J R	Butte Wyandotte	56 661
Joseph	Yuba Foster B	72 823
Wm	Calaveras Twp 9	57 395
LUMBEST		
J R	Butte Wyandotte	56 661
LUMBI		
J	San Francisco San Francisco 12	395 67
LUMBIRT		
Wm	Calaveras Twp 9	57 395
LUMBIT		
Joseph	Yuba Fosters	72 823
LUMBRE		
Juan	Los Angeles Azuza	59 273
LUMBURG		
M	Sacramento Brighton	63 206
LUME		
---	Fresno Twp 1	59 25
J	Nevada Grass Valley	61 219
LUMEN		
Ann*	San Francisco San Francisco 9	68 985
LUMENTO		
Rufuce	Calaveras Twp 5	57 211
LUMERY		
D	Sacramento Franklin	63 308
Robt	Nevada Bridgeport	61 454
LUMG		
---*	Calaveras Twp 8	57 82
LUMGROVE		
Geo*	Sacramento Natonia	63 281
LUMI		
---	Calaveras Twp 5	57 214
LUMING		
A	San Mateo Twp 3	65 103
LUMIS		
D S	Yolo Cache Crk	72 611
Lewis	Plumas Quincy	62 951
LUMKI		
---	Fresno Twp 2	59 113
LUMLEY		
Isabella	Butte Ophir	56 774
LUMLY		
Geo	San Francisco San Francisco 1	68 891
LUMM		
Alex S	San Francisco San Francisco 2	67 736
LUMME		
M J*	Solano Vacaville	69 339
LUMMERVILLE		
Wm	Mariposa Twp 3	60 565
LUMMIX		
---	Fresno Twp 2	59 36
LUMMONS		
Cordelin	El Dorado Kelsey	581140
LUMONT		
Harriet*	San Francisco San Francisco 8	681249
Joel H	Calaveras Twp 5	57 141
LUMORE		
Eunis	Tuolumne Visalia	71 95
Eunis*	Tulara Twp 1	71 95
LUMORTIN		
Stephen	Calaveras Twp 5	57 230
LUMOS		
Charles	Mariposa Twp 1	60 671
Charles T	Mariposa Twp 1	60 671
LUMP		
Christian	Mariposa Coulterville	60 698
LUMPKIN		
---	Fresno Twp 2	59 92
LUMPLE		
John	Stanislaus Empire	70 733
LUMPLETON		
L*	Calaveras Twp 9	57 391
LUMRI		
Julius	Stanislaus Branch	70 701
LUMRO		
---*	Tulara Visalia	71 39
LUMSDEN		
James	Tuolumne Chinese	71 494
Jams	Tuolumne Twp 5	71 494
N	San Francisco San Francisco 5	67 498
LUMSTON		
Wm R	San Joaquin Elkhorn	64 989
LUMT		
---	Placer Auburn	62 577
LUMUS		
A M	Tuolumne Twp 1	71 271
LUMUX		
Lucy	Tehama Lassen	70 861
LUN G		
Ah	Tuolumne Twp 4	71 182
Oh	Tuolumne Twp 4	71 181
LUN SING		
---*	Butte Kimshaw	56 587
LUN		
---	Amador Twp 4	55 332
---	Calaveras Twp 5	57 136
---	Calaveras Twp 5	57 183
---	Calaveras Twp 5	57 233
---	Calaveras Twp 8	57 87
---	Del Norte Crescent	58 631
---	Del Norte Crescent	58 633
---	Del Norte Crescent	58 651
---	El Dorado Salmon Falls	581064
---	El Dorado Georgetown	58 695
---	El Dorado Georgetown	58 747
---	El Dorado Georgetown	58 751
---	El Dorado Mud Springs	58 976
---	Fresno Twp 2	59 20
---	Mariposa Twp 3	60 592
---	Mariposa Twp 3	60 596
---	Mariposa Twp 3	60 607
---	Mariposa Twp 1	60 661
---	Mariposa Coulterville	60 682
---	Mariposa Coulterville	60 688
---	Mariposa Coulterville	60 699

Name	County Locale	M653 Roll	Page
LUN			
---	Mariposa Coulterville	60	701
---	Nevada Bridgeport	61	462
---	Nevada Bridgeport	61	485
---	Placer Auburn	62	579
---	Placer Rattle Snake	62	629
---	Placer Ophirville	62	659
---	Placer Virginia	62	678
---	Placer Illinois	62	745
---	Sacramento Ward 4	63	612
---	Sacramento Ward 4	63	65
---	San Francisco San Francisco 4	681	176
---	San Francisco San Francisco 4	681	177
---	San Francisco San Francisco 4	681	184
---	Sierra Downieville	661	009
---	Sierra Downieville	661	015
---	Sierra Downieville	661	027
---	Sierra Morristown	661	056
---	Sierra St Louis	66	816
---	Sierra Twp 5	66	926
---	Sierra Twp 5	66	948
---	Sierra Downieville	66	981
---	Tuolumne Twp 5	71	517
---*	Mariposa Twp 3	60	572
---*	Mariposa Twp 1	60	661
---*	Nevada Rough &	61	434
---*	Sacramento Cosumnes	63	396
---*	Sacramento Cosumnes	63	398
---*	Sacramento Ward 4	63	613
---*	Yuba Marysville	72	895
Geo	Sacramento Granite	63	268
Hop	San Francisco San Francisco 4	681	186
How*	Butte Ophir	56	803
Kerr*	Butte Ophir	56	788
Ko	San Francisco San Francisco 4	681	176
Lee Ke	San Francisco San Francisco 4	681	179
Luke	San Francisco San Francisco 4	681	179
Pow	San Francisco San Francisco 4	681	201
Se*	Mariposa Twp 3	60	612
Sing	Butte Kimshaw	56	584
Toon	Shasta Horsetown	66	711
Tou	San Francisco San Francisco 4	681	201
Tow	San Francisco San Francisco 4	681	201
LUNA			
---	Tulara Twp 3	71	65
---	Tulara Keyesville	71	67
---	Tulara Keyesville	71	69
Antonio	Santa Clara Burnett	65	261
Anuel	Yuba Marysville	72	946
Bensalada	Monterey San Juan	60	985
Domingo	Santa Clara San Jose	65	364
Enas*	Yuba Marysville	72	946
Francisco	Monterey San Juan	60	999
Hannah	Sacramento Ward 4	63	577
Hexacinth Sr	Solano Benecia	69	300
Heyacinth Sr	Solano Benecia	69	300
Jesus	Monterey San Juan	60	983
Manuela	Yuba Marysville	72	946
Marg	Sacramento Ward 4	63	577
Miguela	Yuba Marysville	72	954
Nerberto	Monterey Pajaro	601	013
Pedro*	Monterey San Juan	601	001
Thos	Monterey San Juan	60	982
LUNAM			
Mary*	San Francisco San Francisco 9	681	037
LUNAS			
---	Los Angeles San Pedro	59	486
Richd	San Francisco San Francisco 9	681	069
LUNATA			
Ancutio*	Calaveras Twp 9	57	364
LUNATU			
Arcitio	Calaveras Twp 9	57	364
LUNBARK			
Fred	El Dorado White Oaks	581	026
LUNBECK			
Lewis	Nevada Bridgeport	61	483
LUNBERG			
W*	San Joaquin Stockton	641	098
LUNBERGER			
Frederic	Los Angeles Los Angeles	59	391
LUNCELLO			
Balthazor*	Calaveras Twp 5	57	194
Balthozar	Calaveras Twp 5	57	194
LUNCERN			
Pasgunl	Calaveras Twp 5	57	221
Pasqual	Calaveras Twp 5	57	221
LUNCRAFT			
William*	Nevada Red Dog	61	543
LUNCY			
Ann*	Nevada Bridgeport	61	457
M*	San Francisco San Francisco 5	67	498
LUND HONG			
---*	Butte Kimshaw	56	588
LUND			
C	San Francisco San Francisco 5	67	538
C	Shasta Horsetown	66	697

Name	County Locale	M653 Roll	Page
LUND			
C N	El Dorado Diamond	58	814
Edward*	Placer Michigan	62	851
Henry	San Francisco San Francisco 3	67	22
Hong	Butte Kimshaw	56	588
Moses	Nevada Bloomfield	61	520
P	El Dorado Diamond	58	770
Peter	Tuolumne Big Oak	71	126
Peter	Tuolumne Twp 4	71	128
Peter	Tuolumne Twp 3	71	451
LUNDAY			
David	Santa Clara San Jose	65	385
LUNDBERG			
A*	Sacramento Ward 1	63	12
LUNDBERGER			
Geo	Sacramento Granite	63	260
LUNDBERT			
Peter T	San Francisco San Francisco 12	373	
		67	
LUNDBUGER			
Geo	Sacramento Granite	63	260
LUNDERLAND			
Thomas E*	Yuba Fosters	72	837
LUNDGUIRT			
Fred	Sacramento Ward 1	63	33
LUNDINGTON			
Geo C	Sonoma Petaluma	69	580
LUNDIRS			
Joseph	Mariposa Twp 3	60	571
LUNDQUIST			
Fred	Sacramento Ward 1	63	33
LUNDREGAN			
John	San Francisco San Francisco 2	67	719
LUNDRITH			
P H	Sacramento Ward 4	63	528
LUNDSAY			
John J*	Tulara Visalia	71	81
LUNDY			
Danl	Santa Clara San Jose	65	381
George	Amador Twp 5	55	331
Nathan	Tulara Visalia	71	108
Otho J	San Joaquin Elkhorn	64	974
R	Santa Clara San Jose	65	378
R	Siskiyou Scott Ri	69	83
Wm	Sonoma Vallejo	69	624
LUNE			
---	Placer Secret R	62	622
---	Sierra Downieville	661	027
---	Sierra Twp 7	66	898
---	Sierra Twp 5	66	944
---	Sierra Downieville	66	984
---	Tuolumne Montezuma	71	508
Danl S*	Calaveras Twp 10	57	288
E	Sierra La Porte	66	777
Farrell	Placer Virginia	62	685
LUNEBECK			
Wm	Siskiyou Callahan	69	12
LUNEFORD			
Emaline	El Dorado Mud Springs	58	993
LUNER			
Chas*	El Dorado Georgetown	58	694
LUNEY			
Ann*	Nevada Bridgeport	61	457
M*	San Francisco San Francisco 5	67	498
LUNG CHUNG			
---	Tuolumne Green Springs	71	517
LUNG MAM			
---	Mariposa Twp 3	60	609
LUNG SOO			
---	Butte Kimshaw	56	588
LUNG			
---	Amador Twp 1	55	503
---	Amador Twp 1	55	511
---	Calaveras Twp 6	57	122
---	Calaveras Twp 10	57	283
---	Calaveras Twp 7	57	46
---	Calaveras Twp 8	57	65
---	Calaveras Twp 8	57	71
---	Calaveras Twp 8	57	74
---	Calaveras Twp 8	57	76
---	Calaveras Twp 8	57	82
---	Del Norte Crescent	58	633
---	El Dorado White Oaks	581	024
---	El Dorado White Oaks	581	025
---	El Dorado Salmon Falls	581	045
---	El Dorado Salmon Falls	581	058
---	El Dorado Salmon Falls	581	063
---	El Dorado Coloma	581	085
---	El Dorado Union	581	091
---	El Dorado Kelsey	581	136
---	El Dorado Georgetown	58	686
---	El Dorado Greenwood	58	730
---	El Dorado Diamond	58	789
---	El Dorado Diamond	58	806
---	El Dorado Diamond	58	812
---	El Dorado Placerville	58	830

Name	County Locale	M653 Roll	Page
LUNG			
---	El Dorado Mud Springs	58	998
---	Fresno Twp 1	59	26
---	Fresno Twp 1	59	30
---	Los Angeles San Pedro	59	481
---	Mariposa Twp 3	60	551
---	Mariposa Twp 1	60	641
---	Mariposa Twp 1	60	644
---	Mariposa Twp 1	60	665
---	Mariposa Coulterville	60	691
---	Mariposa Coulterville	60	692
---	Mariposa Coulterville	60	700
---	Nevada Rough &	61	434
---	Nevada Bridgeport	61	439
---	Nevada Bridgeport	61	464
---	Nevada Bridgeport	61	485
---	Placer Auburn	62	575
---	Placer Auburn	62	582
---	Placer Rattle Snake	62	601
---	Placer Secret R	62	622
---	Placer Sacramento	62	646
---	Placer Folsom	62	647
---	Placer Folsom	62	648
---	Placer Folsom	62	649
---	Placer Ophirville	62	658
---	Placer Virginia	62	669
---	Placer Virginia	62	678
---	Placer Virginia	62	681
---	Placer Virginia	62	686
---	Placer Virginia	62	701
---	Placer Illinois	62	748
---	Placer Illinois	62	749
---	Placer Illinois	62	750
---	Placer Yankee J	62	781
---	Placer Iona Hills	62	869
---	Placer Iona Hills	62	893
---	Plumas Meadow Valley	62	913
---	Plumas Quincy	62	926
---	Plumas Quincy	62	949
---	Sacramento Mississipi	63	188
---	Sacramento Granite	63	232
---	Sacramento Granite	63	245
---	Sacramento Cosumnes	63	397
---	Sacramento Ward 3	63	491
---	Sacramento Ward 3	63	494
---	Sacramento Ward 1	63	53
---	Sacramento Ward 1	63	67
---	Sacramento Ward 1	63	68
---	San Francisco San Francisco 9	681	087
---	San Francisco San Francisco 9	681	093
---	San Francisco San Francisco 4	681	182
---	San Francisco San Francisco 4	681	183
---	San Francisco San Francisco 4	681	188
---	San Francisco San Francisco 4	681	196
---	San Francisco San Francisco 4	681	203
---	San Francisco San Francisco 2	67	687
---	Sierra Downieville	661	005
---	Sierra Morristown	661	055
---	Sierra La Porte	66	785
---	Sierra St Louis	66	809
---	Sierra Twp 7	66	899
---	Sierra Twp 5	66	927
---	Sierra Twp 5	66	928
---	Sierra Downieville	66	982
---	Sierra Downieville	66	985
---	Sierra Downieville	66	989
---	Trinity Taylor'S	701	033
---	Trinity Taylor'S	701	034
---	Trinity Taylor'S	701	035
---	Trinity Trinindad Rvr	701	046
---	Tuolumne Columbia	71	307
---	Tuolumne Twp 2	71	409
---	Tuolumne Jamestown	71	433
---	Tuolumne Jamestown	71	439
---	Tuolumne Jamestown	71	440
---	Tuolumne Jamestown	71	446
---	Tuolumne Jamestown	71	453
---	Tuolumne Twp 3	71	457
---	Tuolumne Twp 3	71	460
---	Tuolumne Twp 3	71	467
---	Tuolumne Twp 3	71	468
---	Tuolumne Twp 3	71	469
---	Tuolumne Twp 6	71	540
---	Yolo No E Twp	72	668
---	Yolo Slate Ra	72	715
---	Yuba Slate Ro	72	715
---	Yuba New York	72	739
---	Yuba Long Bar	72	758
---	Yuba Long Bar	72	761
---	Yuba Long Bar	72	765
---	Yuba Fosters	72	831
---	Yuba Fosters	72	834
---	Yuba Fosters	72	841
---	Yuba Marysville	72	874
---*	Butte Eureka	56	649
---*	Nevada Washington	61	340

California 1860 Census Index

Name	County Locale	M653 Roll	Page
LUNG			
---*	Placer Auburn	62	570
---*	Placer Auburn	62	571
---*	Placer Virginia	62	687
---*	Sacramento Cosumnes	63	392
---*	Sacramento Cosumnes	63	397
---*	Sacramento Ward 1	63	69
---*	Stanislaus Buena Village	70	724
---*	Trinity Taylor'S	70	1033
---*	Tuolumne Garrote	71	174
---*	Tuolumne Big Oak	71	181
---*	Tuolumne Big Oak	71	182
---*	Yuba Foster B	72	831
---*	Yuba Foster B	72	834
---*	Yuba Fosters	72	841
A*	Tuolumne Twp 2	71	386
Ah	Calaveras Twp 7	57	11
Ah	Calaveras Twp 7	57	32
Ah	Calaveras Twp 7	57	36
Ah	Sacramento Ward 1	63	152
Ah	Tuolumne Twp 2	71	307
Ah	Yuba Bear Rvr	72	1005
An	Del Norte Crescent	58	631
C H	Trinity Weaverville	70	1078
Choh	Sacramento Ward 1	63	152
Chow	Placer Illinois	62	740
Chow	Tehama Tehama	70	947
Chung	Tuolumne Twp 5	71	517
Cow	Tehama Red Bluff	70	925
Die	Butte Ophir	56	813
E	Calaveras Twp 9	57	389
Gang	Mariposa Twp 3	60	544
Gray	Shasta Shasta	66	684
Ko	San Francisco San Francisco 4	68	1175
Lie	Sacramento Ward 3	63	491
Moy Lei*	San Francisco San Francisco 3	67	26
Sam	Yolo Slate Ra	72	718
Sew	Tehama Red Bluff	70	932
Sing*	Calaveras Twp 6	57	181
Soo	Butte Kimshaw	56	588
Tong	Sacramento Cosumnes	63	395
Too	Tehama Red Bluff	70	932
Tuck	Sacramento Ward 1	63	68
Wi	Calaveras Twp 5	57	192
Wy	Tuolumne Twp 4	71	178
Ye	Sacramento Natonia	63	283
LUNGAMATI			
Luntela*	Calaveras Twp 4	57	340
LUNGAN			
Margt*	San Francisco San Francisco 8	68	1254
LUNGAS			
C	El Dorado Diamond	58	814
LUNGE			
---	Sacramento Ward 1	63	68
LUNGER			
L	Tuolumne Twp 4	71	168
T	Tuolumne Jacksonville	71	168
LUNGFORD			
Henry	Calaveras Twp 10	57	280
LUNGLET			
E G*	Napa Clear Lake	61	121
LUNGLIT			
E G*	Napa Clear Lake	61	121
LUNGU			
---*	Calaveras Twp 8	57	105
LUNI			
---	Sierra Twp 5	66	944
LUNIAS			
Hasel	El Dorado Casumnes	58	1175
LUNING			
John J*	San Francisco San Francisco 9	68	954
Nicholas	San Francisco San Francisco 8	68	1283
LUNIS			
H G	Sacramento Dry Crk	63	370
Jose	San Francisco San Francisco 9	68	1074
LUNK			
---	Sierra Downieville	66	983
LUNN			
---	Mariposa Twp 3	60	572
---	Sierra Morristown	66	1055
En	Tuolumne Twp 2	71	347
LUNNEUIG			
Martin	Calaveras Twp 4	57	329
LUNNEZ			
John	Solano Benecia	69	314
LUNNS			
William*	Stanislaus Emory	70	756
LUNNY			
C	Solano Vallejo	69	272
John J*	San Francisco San Francisco 9	68	954
LUNO			
---	Tulara Twp 3	71	66
---	Tulara Keyesville	71	67
---	Tulara Keyesville	71	70
---	Tulara Keyesville	71	72
John	Napa Napa	61	85

Name	County Locale	M653 Roll	Page
LUNO			
Lino	San Francisco San Francisco 6	67	442
Lu*	Sacramento Granite	63	268
LUNOL			
Antonio	Santa Clara San Jose	65	375
LUNONT			
Harriet*	San Francisco San Francisco 8	68	1249
LUNORE			
J W M	El Dorado Placerville	58	840
LUNSFORD			
Ruben	Napa Napa	61	70
LUNSORD			
S W	Amador Twp 1	55	483
LUNT			
Amos	Tuolumne Twp 1	71	270
Aos	Tuolumne Twp 1	71	270
Chas	Butte Mountain	56	739
Danl	San Francisco San Francisco 6	67	401
David	Sierra La Porte	66	777
David S	Sierra La Porte	66	777
Elmira	San Francisco San Francisco 6	67	401
J C	Tehama Antelope	70	893
James	Tuolumne Sonora	71	207
James P	Tuolumne Jamestown	71	438
Jas R	San Francisco San Francisco 6	67	406
Moses H*	Amador Twp 4	55	258
Richard	Sierra La Porte	66	789
W H	Calaveras Twp 7	57	22
LUNTA			
---	Mendocino Calpella	60	825
LUNTES			
Jose M*	Santa Cruz Soguel	66	593
LUNTIS			
Jose M	Santa Cruz Soguel	66	593
LUNTTEDT			
Jacob	Tuolumne Shawsfla	71	419
LUNXUCE			
A*	Del Norte Crescent	58	645
LUNY			
---	Calaveras Twp 6	57	134
---	Mariposa Coulterville	60	692
---	Sacramento Granite	63	245
---	Sacramento Natonia	63	284
---	Tuolumne Shawsfla	71	386
Wis	Calaveras Twp 5	57	192
LUNYA			
Polonio	San Bernardino Santa Barbara	64	193
Rafaila	San Bernardino Santa Barbara	64	193
LUNZ			
Preston	Siskiyou Scott Ri	69	78
LUO			
---	El Dorado Coloma	58	1123
---	Sierra Downieville	66	1008
Thi	San Francisco San Francisco 4	68	1181
Tlu*	San Francisco San Francisco 4	68	1181
LUOIS			
Timtohty	Tuolumne Twp 2	71	332
LUON			
---	El Dorado Coloma	58	1108
LUONG			
---	El Dorado Placerville	58	841
---*	Sacramento Ward 1	63	61
LUOY			
---	El Dorado Georgetown	58	680
---	San Francisco San Francisco 4	68	1178
LUP HOOP			
---	Butte Kimshaw	56	602
LUP TOO			
---	Butte Kimshaw	56	598
LUP			
---	Amador Twp 5	55	366
---	Butte Kimshaw	56	588
---	Butte Kimshaw	56	599
---	Butte Kimshaw	56	600
---	Placer Virginia	62	680
---	Placer Virginia	62	701
---	Placer Illinois	62	746
---	Sacramento Ward 1	63	51
---	Stanislaus Emory	70	748
---	Yuba Marysville	72	895
---*	Butte Ophir	56	818
Ah	Tuolumne Twp 4	71	163
Hoop	Butte Kimshaw	56	602
Kun	San Francisco San Francisco 2	67	754
Too	Butte Kimshaw	56	598
Yett	Butte Ophir	56	818
Yett	Butte Ophir	56	820
LUPE			
---	Butte Oregon	56	642
---	Placer Auburn	62	582
---	Placer Virginia	62	671
---*	Butte Kimshaw	56	605
J*	San Francisco San Francisco 3	67	26
LUPESENO			
---	Monterey S Antoni	60	969
LUPH			
Clara	San Francisco San Francisco 4	68	1155

Name	County Locale	M653 Roll	Page
LUPHO			
We	San Francisco San Francisco 10	67	276
LUPI			
---	Sacramento Granite	63	268
Ah	Butte Oregon	56	642
J*	San Francisco San Francisco 3	67	26
LUPIIITA			
Philip	Tuolumne Sonora	71	240
LUPITA			
Philip	Tuolumne Twp 1	71	240
LUPLEY			
Cuvrndih*	Calaveras Twp 6	57	152
Euvendich J*	Calaveras Twp 6	57	152
LUPP			
---	Yuba Slate Ro	72	715
Charles W	Yuba Suida	72	989
Russel B	Monterey Pajaro	60	1020
LUPPAH			
---	Tulara Twp 2	71	38
---*	Tulara Visalia	71	37
---*	Tulara Visalia	71	38
---*	Tulara Visalia	71	39
LUPPAHEMEMS			
---*	Tulara Visalia	71	37
LUPPAHEMENO			
---	Tulara Twp 2	71	37
LUPPAHO			
---	Tulara Twp 2	71	37
LUPPLE			
Jas	Sacramento Natonia	63	284
LUPRER			
William	Solano Fremont	69	386
LUPSHU			
---	Shasta Shasta	66	669
LUPSIC			
Isaac	San Francisco San Francisco 2	67	792
LUPSIE			
Isaac	San Francisco San Francisco 2	67	792
LUPSITA			
---	Tulara Twp 2	71	37
LUPSKIE			
August*	Sierra Twp 5	66	943
LUPSKIR			
August	Sierra Twp 5	66	943
LUPTON			
Edward	Contra Costa Twp 2	57	548
Joseph	El Dorado Casumnes	58	1174
R	Nevada Red Dog	61	551
S L	San Francisco San Francisco 6	67	460
LUPUS			
Joseph E	Nevada Rough &	61	425
LUQUE			
Simon*	Mariposa Twp 1	60	625
LUQUEZ			
Pedro	Los Angeles Los Angeles	59	374
LUQUIL			
Louis	Placer Iona Hills	62	867
LUR			
---	Calaveras Twp 5	57	205
---	El Dorado Georgetown	58	690
---	San Francisco San Francisco 4	68	1174
---	Sierra Downieville	66	1004
---	Sierra Downieville	66	1009
---	Sierra Downieville	66	981
LURA			
Berna*	Alameda Oakland	55	45
Goo*	Sacramento Granite	63	243
Jjuan	San Bernardino Santa Barbara	64	148
Juan*	Amador Twp 2	55	288
LURARD			
James	San Francisco San Francisco 8	68	1294
LURBER			
J B	Tehama Red Bluff	70	909
LURCH			
Charles	Sierra La Porte	66	772
John	Contra Costa Twp 3	57	596
John	Sierra Downieville	66	995
Jos	Calaveras Twp 6	57	119
LURCHAN			
Patrick	San Francisco San Francisco 9	68	959
LURCHARD			
Patrick	San Francisco San Francisco 9	68	959
LURCOULT			
L*	Sacramento Brighton	63	210
LURD			
Edward*	Placer Michigan	62	851
John*	San Francisco San Francisco 9	68	1004
LURDY			
J B	San Francisco San Francisco 5	67	503
LURE			
Cam	Sierra Port Win	66	798
LUREN			
Francisco	Calaveras Twp 4	57	331
LURENDI			
Peter	Calaveras Twp 10	57	287

California 1860 Census Index

Name	County Locale	M653 Roll/Page
LURENEY		
Bridget*	Calaveras Twp 6	57 160
LURFERLTON		
Henry	Sacramento Sutter	63 299
LURGENS		
B	El Dorado Mud Springs	58 993
LURGTON		
Antonia	Mariposa Twp 3	60 556
LURHAM		
E	Sierra Twp 7	66 903
LURI		
---*	Nevada Rough &	61 434
LURIA		
Marcellina	Contra Costa Twp 1	57 493
LURIAS		
---	Los Angeles San Juan	59 470
LURICE		
Isac D*	Mariposa Twp 1	60 624
LURIMER		
Adolphus	San Francisco San Francisco 9	681051
LURIN		
Fong	San Francisco San Francisco 5	67 509
LURIS		
T	Stanislaus Emory	70 737
LURK		
Benj*	Sacramento Ward 3	63 427
G	Tehama Lassen	70 868
LURKEN		
Thos L	Sacramento Natonia	63 280
LURN		
---*	Marin Cortemad	60 785
---*	Mariposa Twp 3	60 580
Jas*	Mariposa Twp 3	60 591
LURNER		
William H	San Francisco San Francisco 7	681364
LUROIS		
Louis	Tuolumne Twp 1	71 243
LURREN		
Frank*	San Francisco San Francisco 3	67 72
LURRNEY		
Bridget*	Calaveras Twp 6	57 160
LURRO		
Mitchel	Calaveras Twp 4	57 340
LURRY		
---	San Francisco San Francisco 8	681308
John*	Solano Suisan	69 215
LURVETCH		
Marie	Butte Ophir	56 766
LURY		
---	Amador Twp 5	55 366
---	Butte Ophir	56 813
Siry	Amador Twp 3	55 387
LUS		
Thomas	Calaveras Twp 8	57 79
Yon	Shasta Horsetown	66 711
LUSAC		
---	Fresno Twp 2	59 103
LUSARA		
Mannuel	Santa Cruz Santa Cruz	66 602
Manuel	Santa Cruz Santa Cruz	66 602
LUSARE		
Jaun	Santa Cruz Pajaro	66 571
Juan	Santa Cruz Pajaro	66 571
LUSAS		
---	San Bernardino S Timate	64 739
Susanah*	Mariposa Twp 3	60 566
LUSCO		
P	San Mateo Twp 1	65 63
LUSCOMB		
Chas*	San Francisco San Francisco 3	67 86
LUSDLRE		
Louis*	San Francisco San Francisco 2	67 687
LUSE		
George*	Placer Iona Hills	62 865
LUSER		
John A*	San Francisco San Francisco 2	67 680
LUSEY		
Elizabeth	Siskiyou Yreka	69 144
Thomas P*	San Francisco 7	681387
	San Francisco	
LUSH		
Isaac	Butte Kimshaw	56 571
Thomas	San Diego Agua Caliente	64 861
LUSI		
George*	Placer Iona Hills	62 865
LUSINGHER		
Henry*	San Joaquin O'Neal	641005
LUSIURE		
Odelon*	Del Norte Happy Ca	58 661
LUSIVER		
George	San Joaquin Castoria	64 886
LUSJI		
---*	El Dorado Georgetown	58 745
LUSK		
---	Amador Twp 1	55 463
Albert	San Francisco San Francisco 2	67 786

Name	County Locale	M653 Roll/Page
LUSK		
C D	San Francisco San Francisco 3	67 7
Chaes W*	El Dorado Georgetown	58 698
Ellen	San Francisco San Francisco 6	67 474
Henri M	Tuolumne Columbia	71 343
Henry	Shasta Horsetown	66 690
John	Yolo Cache Crk	72 644
John*	San Francisco San Francisco 3	67 33
Joseph	Alameda Oakland	55 23
Joseph*	San Francisco San Francisco 3	67 72
Mike	Yolo Cache Crk	72 633
Soloman	Sonoma Petaluma	69 615
LUSKE		
Henri M	Tuolumne Twp 2	71 343
W H*	Yolo Cache	72 633
LUSKELL		
Warren	Sacramento Granite	63 246
LUSKIN		
Charles	Yolo Putah	72 585
LUSKINE		
Charles	Yolo Putah	72 585
LUSKY		
George	Sacramento Georgian	63 339
LUSMRING		
J P*	Merced Twp 1	60 895
LUSOIS		
Louis	Tuolumne Sonora	71 243
LUSOUX		
John*	Calaveras Twp 4	57 326
LUSRA		
Carlos*	San Bernardino Santa Inez	64 145
LUSS		
Abram*	Yuba Marysville	72 871
Joseph	Mariposa Twp 3	60 622
LUSSAC		
---	Butte Chico	56 566
LUSSARO		
Juan	Santa Cruz Pajaro	66 566
LUSSKIE		
August*	Sierra Twp 5	66 943
LUSSURE		
Odelon*	Del Norte Happy Ca	58 661
LUST		
S	San Francisco San Francisco 5	67 518
LUSTAGE		
And*	Nevada Eureka	61 372
Aud*	Nevada Eureka	61 372
LUSTAR		
John*	Calaveras Twp 6	57 187
LUSTENBERGER		
Herbert	San Francisco San Francisco 11	145
		67
LUSTER		
Jas*	San Francisco San Francisco 2	67 676
LUSTIG		
Isaac	San Francisco San Francisco 3	67 29
LUSTIN		
W*	Sacramento Alabama	63 412
LUSY		
John	San Joaquin Castoria	64 884
LUT		
---	El Dorado White Oaks	581021
---	San Francisco San Francisco 9	681088
---	Tuolumne Twp 6	71 540
Antonio*	San Francisco San Francisco 8	681246
Charles	San Mateo Twp 1	65 61
Freeman G*	Sacramento American	63 160
M W	San Mateo Twp 1	65 62
LUTA		
---	El Dorado Georgetown	58 680
---	Nevada Bloomfield	61 509
Plulal	San Francisco San Francisco 2	67 791
LUTALA		
Antone	Nevada Rough &	61 436
LUTALER		
Antone	Nevada Rough &	61 436
LUTAN		
Chas	Sonoma Salt Point	69 691
LUTCH		
James*	Monterey San Juan	601009
LUTCHENFALS		
Gottlitch	San Mateo Twp 1	65 48
LUTCHER		
W	Shasta Shasta	66 675
LUTCLIFFE		
James*	Plumas Quincy	62 961
LUTE		
---	El Dorado Georgetown	58 680
---	Nevada Bloomfield	61 522
---	Yolo No E Twp	72 676
---	Yolo No E Twp	72 685
---	Yuba North Ea	72 676
---	Yuba Slate Ro	72 685
---	Yuba Long Bar	72 760
---	Yuba Long Bar	72 761
---*	Nevada Red Dog	61 556

Name	County Locale	M653 Roll/Page
LUTE		
A B*	Sacramento Granite	63 234
Aw	Yuba Long Bar	72 770
G W	Nevada Bloomfield	61 509
M	Sierra Twp 7	66 898
Nickolas	Plumas Quincy	62 987
LUTEKY		
George	Tuolumne Twp 2	71 276
Geroge	Tuolumne Twp 1	71 276
LUTEN		
W O	Amador Twp 7	55 412
LUTER		
C	San Joaquin Stockton	641092
Peter*	Sierra St Louis	66 811
LUTERIO		
James	Monterey S Antoni	60 970
LUTES		
Francis	Nevada Bridgeport	61 501
LUTGENS		
John	San Francisco San Francisco 7	681344
LUTH		
Andrew	Tuolumne Sonora	71 194
John	Alameda Brooklyn	55 82
LUTHAIN		
Christian	Tuolumne Twp 2	71 344
LUTHAN		
Christian	Tuolumne Columbia	71 344
LUTHENFAL		
Gottlitch	San Mateo Twp 1	65 48
LUTHER		
---	Amador Twp 5	55 367
---	San Francisco San Francisco 3	67 56
Alfred	Amador Twp 2	55 287
Anthony	Placer Virginia	62 690
Charles	Siskiyou Yreka	69 150
Christopher	Humbolt Mattole	59 128
D B	Yolo Cache	72 612
E J	San Francisco San Francisco 6	67 442
Frank	Santa Clara San Jose	65 284
George	Contra Costa Twp 3	57 586
Hale	Napa Napa	61 75
Higekich	El Dorado Greenwood	58 724
John	Sacramento Ward 3	63 483
John B	San Francisco San Francisco 7	681340
Preston	Sacramento Ward 4	63 527
R B	Sutter Sutter	70 812
Richard	Napa Yount	61 39
T M	Amador Twp 2	55 287
W B	Sutter Bear Rvr	70 819
Wm	Placer Goods	62 696
Wm H	Amador Twp 2	55 287
LUTHERFORD		
W	Sacramento Cosumnes	63 400
LUTHEROT		
Baptist	Trinity Lewiston	70 964
LUTHOR		
Jacob	Santa Clara Santa Clara	65 463
LUTI		
---	Nevada Bridgeport	61 485
---*	Nevada Red Dog	61 556
LUTICAMS		
Louis	Amador Twp 3	55 391
LUTINOIS		
Amae*	Calaveras Twp 4	57 313
LUTIUS		
Letrus*	Nevada Little Y	61 532
LUTMAN		
David	Trinity Rush Crk	70 965
Henry	Tehama Tehama	70 940
John R	Trinity Rush Crk	70 965
Paul	San Francisco San Francisco 3	67 71
Paul E	San Francisco San Francisco 3	67 71
LUTON		
---	Trinity Weaverville	701075
LUTRELL		
James L*	Alameda Brooklyn	55 90
LUTRID		
James L*	Alameda Brooklyn	55 90
LUTT		
---	Yolo No E Twp	72 677
---	Yuba North Ea	72 677
N S	Calaveras Twp 9	57 393
LUTTAGE		
M C	Nevada Eureka	61 372
LUTTATE		
M	San Francisco San Francisco 9	681101
LUTTEN		
Robert D	Tuolumne Twp 5	71 521
LUTTER		
Lewis*	Sacramento Sutter	63 309
Samuel	El Dorado Casumnes	581176
T	Butte Hamilton	56 527
LUTTGHER		
Gustavus	Sierra Port Win	66 795
LUTTGHES		
Gustavus*	Sierra Port Win	66 795

California 1860 Census Index

Name	County Locale	M653 Roll	Page
LUTTIER			
Martin	San Luis Obispo San Luis Obispo	65	32
LUTTLE			
G S	Siskiyou Scott Va	69	51
J W	Siskiyou Scott Va	69	29
W A	Siskiyou Klamath	69	86
W H	Siskiyou Klamath	69	86
LUTTLER			
Cephas*	Plumas Quincy	62	974
LUTTON			
R	San Francisco San Francisco 6	67	450
LUTTRALE			
J D	Amador Twp 3	55	401
J L*	Amador Twp 3	55	401
LUTTRELL			
J R	Siskiyou Scott Va	69	28
James	Siskiyou Scott Va	69	24
LUTTSELL			
James	Siskiyou Scott Va	69	24
LUTTYE			
C	San Francisco San Francisco 5	67	529
LUTULL			
John*	Alameda Brooklyn	55	91
LUTWIG			
John A	San Francisco San Francisco 7	68	1419
John*	San Francisco San Francisco 7	68	1419
LUTY			
Henry	San Joaquin Oneal	64	932
LUTZ			
A	San Francisco San Francisco 1	68	926
Adam	San Joaquin Stockton	64	1028
Anthony	Yuba Suida	72	988
B	Shasta Millvill	66	727
Geo	San Joaquin Stockton	64	1042
Geo	Siskiyou Klamath	69	85
George	San Francisco San Francisco 7	68	1379
Jacob	San Francisco San Francisco 1	68	892
Jacob	Sierra Whiskey	66	844
James	Sacramento Granite	63	260
Jams*	Sacramento Granite	63	260
John	Santa Cruz Santa Cruz	66	606
Jomes*	Sacramento Granite	63	260
Josiah	Butte Hamilton	56	520
Mark	Placer Forest H	62	794
P B	El Dorado Placerville	58	844
LUTZE			
Matthew	Plumas Meadow Valley	62	934
Ottis	Nevada Nevada	61	252
LUTZEN			
John	San Francisco San Francisco 7	68	1353
LUTZENAER			
Herman*	Santa Cruz Soquel	66	587
LUTZEUAN			
Herman*	Santa Cruz Soquel	66	587
LUTZINGER			
Jacob	Yuba Marysville	72	967
LUTZMAN			
Herman	Santa Cruz Soquel	66	587
LUU			
---	El Dorado Diamond	58	787
---	San Francisco San Francisco 4	68	1176
LUV			
---	Sierra Twp 5	66	934
---*	Sierra Twp 5	66	942
LUVA			
Clara	Los Angeles Los Angeles	59	515
Enas*	Yuba Marysville	72	946
Henry	San Francisco San Francisco 3	67	9
LUVELA			
Charles	Amador Twp 1	55	472
LUVER			
Wm	Sierra Twp 7	66	884
LUVERICH			
Jno	Tuolumne Big Oak	71	140
LUVERY			
T A E*	Siskiyou Scott Va	69	41
LUVY			
---*	San Francisco San Francisco 4	68	1178
LUW			
---	Calaveras Twp 4	57	315
---	Sierra Downieville	66	1009
LUWELAN			
Archibald*	San Francisco 3 San Francisco	67	86
LUX			
Fredrick	Tuolumne Twp 5	71	511
Henry	Nevada Bridgeport	61	473
Henry	San Francisco San Francisco 4	68	1130
Mary	Santa Clara Fremont	65	425
Sam	Placer Michigan	62	836
W	Shasta Horsetown	66	698
LUXARD			
John	Calaveras Twp 4	57	329
LUXARDE			
Francisco*	Calaveras Twp 4	57	333
LUXARDO			
E B	San Francisco San Francisco 2	67	801

Name	County Locale	M653 Roll	Page
LUXARDO			
Francisco	Calaveras Twp 4	57	333
LUXCOM			
Wm	San Francisco San Francisco 1	68	855
LUXEMO			
---	Tulara Twp 2	71	36
LUXMINO			
---*	Tulara Visalia	71	38
LUXMUNO			
---	Tulara Twp 2	71	38
LUXO			
---*	Tulara Visalia	71	39
LUXSOW			
---	Tulara Twp 2	71	40
LUXTIN			
N*	Sacramento Alabama	63	412
LUXZO			
---	Tulara Twp 2	71	39
LUY			
---	Placer Illinois	62	739
---*	Calaveras Twp 5	57	212
Cum	Tuolumne Twp 5	71	525
Hi	Sacramento Granite	63	268
LUYDAM			
Geo	Sacramento Ward 1	63	35
LUYDER			
Jno	Sacramento Natonia	63	272
LUYDIE			
Jno	Sacramento Natonia	63	272
LUYER			
Bernardino	San Luis Obispo	65	10
	San Luis Obispo		
LUYHRE			
John*	Calaveras Twp 6	57	148
LUYO			
Bicenta*	Los Angeles Los Angeles	59	496
Jose Mn*	Los Angeles Los Angeles	59	494
Vincent	Los Angeles Los Angeles	59	496
LUYON			
Honyo	El Dorado Mud Springs	58	994
LUYOR			
---	Calaveras Twp 5	57	226
LUZ			
---	San Diego San Diego	64	771
---	San Diego Agua Caliente	64	836
---	San Diego Agua Caliente	64	841
Maria	Santa Clara San Jose	65	328
Rufus*	Santa Clara San Jose	65	390
LUZANNO			
Conosa	Yuba Marysville	72	923
LUZARO			
Olivia*	Yuba Marysville	72	925
LUZERA			
Casimero	Los Angeles Tejon	59	541
LUZERO			
Dolores	San Diego San Diego	64	762
LUZLE			
Christopher	Yolo Merritt	72	580
LUZO			
Isabel*	San Bernardino Santa Barbara	64	203
Juan	San Bernardino Santa Inez	64	143
Xavier	Alameda Brooklyn	55	97
LVAG			
John*	Siskiyou Yreka	69	175
LVERSON			
Inger*	Alameda Brooklyn	55	113
LVITTE			
Peter	Tuolumne Twp 2	71	283
LVMODI			
Romana	Calaveras Twp 6	57	150
LVYTHRE			
John	Calaveras Twp 6	57	148
LW			
---	Mariposa Twp 3	60	563
---	Sierra Downieville	66	980
LWALLEN			
Apgh*	Yuba Marysville	72	846
LWANSTARRON			
T	El Dorado Diamond	58	800
LWASEY			
B	Shasta Shasta	66	674
LWENS			
D	El Dorado Diamond	58	814
LWEY			
---	Nevada Bridgeport	61	466
LWO			
---	Sierra Downieville	66	993
LWUG			
---	El Dorado Georgetown	58	755
LWW			
---	Mariposa Coulterville	60	687
Quow	Mariposa Twp 3	60	563
Tou	Mariposa Twp 3	60	564
War	Mariposa Twp 3	60	569
LY CHING			
---	El Dorado Greenwood	58	714

Name	County Locale	M653 Roll	Page
LY			
---	Amador Twp 1	55	496
---	Amador Twp 1	55	508
---	Butte Hamilton	56	529
---	Del Norte Crescent	58	630
---	El Dorado Georgetown	58	690
---	El Dorado Georgetown	58	701
---	El Dorado Georgetown	58	745
Gin	Del Norte Crescent	58	631
Hee	Del Norte Crescent	58	631
Ing	El Dorado Georgetown	58	703
Kim	El Dorado Georgetown	58	703
King	El Dorado Georgetown	58	701
Luay	Mariposa Twp 3	60	545
Rim*	El Dorado Georgetown	58	702
Sin	El Dorado Georgetown	58	747
Syng	El Dorado Greenwood	58	713
Wing	El Dorado Georgetown	58	702
Youpe	Placer Auburn	62	582
LYAL			
Lemuel	Sacramento Ward 3	63	477
LYAN			
---	San Francisco San Francisco 4	68	1193
John C	El Dorado Greenwood	58	725
LYANS			
John	El Dorado Big Bar	58	735
John	Tuolumne Twp 2	71	355
P K	El Dorado Big Bar	58	734
Samuel	Nevada Eureka	61	346
LYATT			
Andrew	Fresno Twp 3	59	15
LYBIA			
Antonio	Alameda Oakland	55	46
LYBRO			
Fran	Nevada Little Y	61	533
LYD			
---	Sonoma Sonoma	69	640
A	Sonoma Sonoma	69	640
LYDALL			
Joseph	Santa Clara Santa Clara	65	467
LYDDAS			
Gilbert*	Alameda Oakland	55	62
LYDE			
James*	Contra Costa Twp 3	57	617
M A	Alameda Oakland	55	66
LYDEH			
Robert	Santa Cruz Santa Cruz	66	628
LYDEN			
P*	Nevada Grass Valley	61	186
LYDER			
Agust*	Los Angeles Tejon	59	528
LYDIA			
---	Mendocino Round Va	60	880
LYDN			
P*	Nevada Grass Valley	61	186
LYDSTON			
G N	Tuolumne Jacksonville	71	166
James	Tuolumne Big Oak	71	134
LYDY			
James	Plumas Quincy	62	961
LYE			
---	Sacramento Ward 1	63	61
---	San Joaquin Stockton	64	1087
And	Sacramento Ward 4	63	588
Hugh	San Joaquin Stockton	64	1078
Peter	Stanislaus Branch	70	698
LYEN			
E D	San Francisco San Francisco 10	67	313
LYEPHN			
A	Butte Cascade	56	696
LYER			
Mau M	Sacramento Granite	63	244
LYERACIO			
John	Calaveras Twp 5	57	227
LYERS			
Andrew	Butte Bidwell	56	729
LYETER			
W S	San Francisco San Francisco 3	67	86
LYFORD			
I	Tuolumne Big Oak	71	141
John F	Fresno Twp 1	59	82
LYINS			
B*	Calaveras Twp 9	57	403
LYKINS			
J N	San Francisco San Francisco 5	67	511
LYLE			
A	Nevada Grass Valley	61	212
D	Nevada Grass Valley	61	212
G W	San Mateo Twp 1	65	60
J B	San Francisco San Francisco 10	67	221
J P	Colusa Monroeville	57	445
James*	Contra Costa Twp 3	57	617
R	Sacramento Lee	63	211
T W	San Francisco San Francisco 5	67	499

Name	County Locale	M653 Roll	Page
LYLES			
George W	Del Norte Crescent	58	628
LYLOAR			
Jas*	Sacramento Natonia	63	281
LYLOAS			
Jas*	Sacramento Natonia	63	281
LYLVA			
Jesus	Tuolumne Twp 3	71	463
LYM			
---	Del Norte Happy Ca	58	668
Rafasla	San Francisco San Francisco 2	67	643
Sin	Butte Ophir	56	802
LYMAN			
Albert	Sierra Downieville	66	1020
C	Nevada Grass Valley	61	150
C C	Placer Todds Va	62	783
Charles	Mendocino Big Rvr	60	846
Edward	San Francisco San Francisco 11	67	153
G J	Nevada Nevada	61	258
George	Sierra Twp 7	66	902
Henry	Tuolumne Columbia	71	303
James	Siskiyou Scott Va	69	52
James	Tuolumne Twp 2	71	303
John	Placer Forest H	62	796
Martin	San Francisco San Francisco 7	68	1327
O	Santa Clara San Jose	65	293
P	El Dorado White Oaks	58	1015
Pat	El Dorado Big Bar	58	733
R	Sierra Twp 7	66	902
S	Santa Clara Redwood	65	451
T J	Nevada Little Y	61	537
Wm	Stanislaus Empire	70	731
LYMAW			
James	Siskiyou Scott Va	69	52
LYME			
Charles	Tuolumne Twp 3	71	468
John C*	Calaveras Twp 4	57	336
LYMERS			
Sidney	Sierra St Louis	66	818
LYMIS			
D S	Yolo Cache	72	611
LYMM			
Patrick	San Francisco San Francisco 3	67	35
LYMON			
Dean B	Yolo Slate Ra	72	688
Dean B	Yuba Slate Ro	72	688
J	Nevada Grass Valley	61	223
LYMOR			
J	Nevada Grass Valley	61	223
LYMOTT			
C	Nevada Grass Valley	61	225
LYMS			
B*	Calaveras Twp 9	57	403
LYN			
Charles	Alameda Oakland	55	29
Gett	Butte Ophir	56	809
LYNA			
Kate*	Alameda Oakland	55	54
LYNAM			
Wm	Trinity Mouth Ca	70	1011
LYNCE			
John	Sacramento Brighton	63	201
LYNCG			
Jno	Butte Oregon	56	639
LYNCH			
A	Napa Napa	61	98
Alex	Butte Oregon	56	621
Alex	El Dorado Mud Springs	58	995
Alex	Plumas Quincy	62	960
B	Tuolumne Twp 4	71	134
Barney	Sacramento Sutter	63	306
Barney	Sacramento Sutter	63	307
Bridget	San Francisco San Francisco 7	68	1357
Bridget	San Francisco San Francisco 2	67	736
Bridjet*	San Francisco San Francisco 2	67	736
C	Napa Napa	61	97
C	Tuolumne Big Oak	71	154
C C	Sacramento Granite	63	236
C P	Napa Hot Springs	61	28
Catharine	San Francisco San Francisco 10	67	321
Catherine	San Joaquin Elkhorn	64	984
Charles	Placer Forest H	62	804
Charles	Placer Michigan	62	829
Charles	Tuolumne Twp 1	71	272
Charles	Tuolumne Twp 2	71	363
Christopher	Nevada Bridgeport	61	440
Cyrus S	Stanislaus Oatvale	70	717
D	Nevada Grass Valley	61	159
D	Shasta Millvill	66	752
D S	Tuolumne Twp 3	71	464
Daniel	San Francisco San Francisco 12	67	372
Danl	San Francisco San Francisco 12	67	363

Name	County Locale	M653 Roll	Page
LYNCH			
Danl	San Francisco San Francisco 6	67	456
David	San Mateo Twp 3	65	91
Delia	San Francisco San Francisco 1	68	893
Edward	Solano Vallejo	69	251
Ellen	San Francisco San Francisco 4	68	1110
Frank E	Monterey San Juan	60	984
G H	Butte Hamilton	56	515
Garret	Plumas Quincy	62	987
George	Napa Clear Lake	61	123
George	Santa Cruz Santa Cruz	66	612
George	Yuba Rose Bar	72	818
H	Sutter Butte	70	799
Henry	San Francisco San Francisco 3	67	21
Henry J	San Francisco San Francisco 7	68	1392
Hugh	Yuba Marysville	72	957
J	Nevada Eureka	61	347
J	Shasta Millvill	66	752
J	Siskiyou Scott Ri	69	68
J A	Tuolumne Columbia	71	329
J H	El Dorado Placerville	58	849
J M	Butte Hamilton	56	524
J W	Solano Suisan	69	205
James	Butte Oro	56	673
James	El Dorado Georgetown	58	746
James	Monterey S Antoni	60	968
James	Nevada Rough &	61	411
James	Placer Iona Hills	62	897
James	San Francisco San Francisco 11	67	150
James	San Francisco San Francisco 6	67	457
James	San Francisco San Francisco 6	67	460
James	Santa Cruz Santa Cruz	66	631
James	Shasta Shasta	66	761
James	Sonoma Bodega	69	539
James	Trinity Ferry	70	977
James	Yolo Slate Ra	72	698
James	Yuba Slate Ro	72	698
Jane	San Francisco San Francisco 10	67	334
Jas	Placer Secret R	62	620
Jas	Sacramento Ward 4	63	588
Jas	Sacramento Ward 4	63	603
Jedwick	Santa Cruz Soguel	66	597
Jere A	Sacramento Ward 1	63	64
Jeremiah	Shasta Shasta	66	660
Jno	Alameda Brooklyn	55	111
Jno	Butte Oregon	56	639
Jno*	Sacramento Ward 4	63	561
John	Butte Bidwell	56	714
John	Calaveras Twp 5	57	183
John	Del Norte Crescent	58	631
John	Del Norte Crescent	58	632
John	El Dorado Greenwood	58	720
John	El Dorado Mud Springs	58	976
John	Los Angeles San Pedro	59	485
John	Marin Cortemad	60	784
John	Monterey Alisal	60	1034
John	Napa Napa	61	109
John	Napa Clear Lake	61	127
John	Napa Napa	61	59
John	Nevada Red Dog	61	551
John	Placer Folsom	62	641
John	Plumas Quincy	62	962
John	Sacramento Ward 1	63	83
John	San Francisco San Francisco 11	67	119
John	San Francisco San Francisco 7	68	1419
John	San Francisco San Francisco 10	67	261
John	San Francisco San Francisco 12	67	363
John	San Francisco San Francisco 3	67	56
John	San Francisco San Francisco 2	67	780
John	San Joaquin Stockton	64	1041
John	San Mateo Twp 3	65	74
John	Sierra La Porte	66	713
John	Sonoma Vallejo	69	617
John	Tulara Twp 2	71	29
John C	Solano Vallejo	69	268
John G*	Marin Cortemad	60	784
John W	Napa Clear Lake	61	138
Jos	San Mateo Twp 1	65	69
Joseph	Plumas Quincy	62	976
Julia	Sacramento Ward 4	63	584
Julia	San Francisco San Francisco 8	68	1243
Kate	Butte Ophir	56	792
Lidywich*	Santa Cruz Soguel	66	597
Lizzie	San Francisco San Francisco 10	67	185
Luois J	San Joaquin Stockton	64	1029
M	Butte Ophir	56	758
M B	Calaveras Twp 8	57	54
Man	San Francisco San Francisco 8	68	1315
Margaret	San Francisco San Francisco 2	67	740
Mariab	Solano Fairfield	69	200

Name	County Locale	M653 Roll	Page
LYNCH			
Mariah	Solano Fairfield	69	200
Mary	Calaveras Twp 6	57	184
Mary	San Francisco San Francisco 8	68	1315
Mary	San Francisco San Francisco 10	67	181
Mat	Plumas Quincy	62	916
Mich	Sacramento Ward 1	63	82
Michael	Calaveras Twp 4	57	327
Michael	San Francisco San Francisco 11	67	119
Michael	San Francisco San Francisco 11	67	131
Michael	San Francisco San Francisco 7	68	1387
Michael	San Francisco San Francisco 10	67	213
Michael	Solano Benecia	69	285
Michael	Solano Benecia	69	303
Michael	Yuba Rose Bar	72	818
Michael	Yuba Suida	72	986
Morris	Tuolumne Sonora	71	241
Nancy A	Monterey San Juan	60	993
Nillean*	Monterey S Antoni	60	972
Oliver	Alameda Brooklyn	55	186
Orven	Tuolumne Twp 2	71	363
Owen	San Francisco San Francisco 1	68	873
Owen	Tuolumne Twp 2	71	272
Owen	Tuolumne Twp 2	71	363
P	El Dorado Placerville	58	850
P	Mariposa Twp 1	60	663
P	Nevada Grass Valley	61	156
P	Nevada Eureka	61	376
P B	San Francisco San Francisco 10	67	347
P S	Sacramento Georgian	63	341
Pat	San Francisco San Francisco 9	68	956
Pat	Sierra Downieville	66	978
Patk	Butte Wyandotte	56	672
Patrick	Calaveras Twp 7	57	38
Patrick	Contra Costa Twp 2	57	542
Patrick	Sacramento Granite	63	249
Patrick	Sacramento Ward 1	63	83
Patrick	San Francisco San Francisco 1	68	843
Patrick	Solano Vallejo	69	244
Patrick	Solano Vallejo	69	245
Patrick	Yolo No E Twp	72	679
Patrick	Yuba North Ea	72	679
Peter	San Francisco San Francisco 10	67	303
Peter	Yolo Slate Ra	72	718
Peter	Yuba New York	72	718
Peter*	Contra Costa Twp 1	57	503
Philip	Shasta Horsetown	66	707
Rebecca	Tuolumne Don Pedro	71	538
Robt	Sacramento Ward 4	63	529
Sedywick	Santa Cruz Soguel	66	597
Sidywich*	Santa Cruz Soguel	66	597
Sidywick	Santa Cruz Soguel	66	597
Susan	Monterey San Juan	60	993
T	Sacramento Ward 4	63	584
T	Tuolumne Twp 4	71	156
T J	Nevada Eureka	61	376
Therese	Sacramento Ward 4	63	500
Thomas	Alameda Oakland	55	28
Thomas	Calaveras Twp 4	57	330
Thomas	Marin Bolinas	60	748
Thomas	Marin San Rafael	60	764
Thomas	San Francisco San Francisco 7	68	1355
Thomas	San Francisco San Francisco 10	67	167
Thomas	Solano Suisan	69	222
Thomas	Yuba New York	72	740
Thos	Amador Twp 1	55	480
Thos	Napa Napa	61	89
Thos	Sacramento Ward 1	63	75
Thos	San Mateo Twp 3	65	84
Timo	Butte Ophir	56	773
Timothy	Nevada Bridgeport	61	499
Timothy	Placer Michigan	62	845
Timothy	San Francisco San Francisco 8	68	1243
Timothy	Sonoma Armally	69	484
Toby	Trinity Sturdiva	70	1006
William	Calaveras Twp 10	57	281
William	Monterey S Antoni	60	972
William	Plumas Quincy	62	987
Wm	Butte Ophir	56	783
Wm H	Sacramento Ward 4	63	498
LYND			
Jenny	Sonoma Washington	69	678
John	San Francisco San Francisco 6	67	419
John	San Francisco San Francisco 3	67	71
Kate*	Alameda Oakland	55	54
Wm M	San Francisco San Francisco 3	67	65
LYNDE			
C J	Calaveras Twp 8	57	77
Danl	Tuolumne Sonora	71	220

Name	County Locale	M653 Roll Page
LYNDE		
Edward M	Tuolumne Sonora	71 218
J B	San Francisco San Francisco 3	67 81
M D C	San Francisco San Francisco 10	214 67
Nathan	Tuolumne Twp 3	71 459
W C	Sacramento Ward 1	63 84
LYNDO		
J B	San Francisco San Francisco 3	67 81
LYNDON		
James H	Yuba Marysville	72 963
LYNDS		
John	Amador Twp 6	55 446
LYNDSAY		
James	El Dorado Big Bar	58 738
LYNE		
John	Tuolumne Twp 2	71 283
Laka	Butte Cascade	56 700
William	San Francisco San Francisco 3	67 53
LYNES		
Henry	Santa Cruz Pajaro	66 573
Mark	Alameda Washington	55 214
Thos	Mariposa Twp 3	60 617
LYNESS		
Jno*	Sacramento Ward 4	63 561
LYNET		
John	Los Angeles Los Angeles	59 360
T*	Nevada Grass Valley	61 165
LYNETO		
John G*	Marin Cortemad	60 784
LYNG		
---	Tuolumne Twp 1	71 478
See*	El Dorado Georgetown	58 701
LYNGAN		
Mary*	San Francisco San Francisco 8	681 254
LYNH		
Dane*	San Francisco San Francisco 12	363 67
LYNHAM		
Thos	San Francisco San Francisco 1	68 894
LYNI		
John	Tuolumne Twp 2	71 283
LYNICK		
Michael*	Calaveras Twp 8	57 96
LYNIH		
Thos	Napa Napa	61 89
LYNIX		
---	Tulara Twp 3	71 71
LYNN		
A	Nevada Nevada	61 271
Adolph	San Francisco San Francisco 9	681 008
Bradly	Alameda Brooklyn	55 132
E	Shasta Horsetown	66 706
Geo	Napa Yount	61 32
George W	Sierra Cold Can	66 836
Henry	Santa Cruz Pajaro	66 573
Henry	Stanislaus Emory	70 739
Homer J	Del Norte Crescent	58 650
Jacob	San Francisco San Francisco 8	681 275
James	Nevada Rough &	61 421
James	Santa Clara Santa Clara	65 505
James J	San Joaquin Castoria	64 883
Jas A	Santa Clara Santa Clara	65 505
Jas N	Santa Clara Fremont	65 425
John	Alameda Brooklyn	55 142
John J	Placer Nicolaus	62 692
Moses	San Francisco San Francisco 2	67 750
Peter	San Francisco San Francisco 9	681 064
Rosa L	Calaveras Twp 9	57 356
William	Placer Michigan	62 811
LYNOT		
D	Nevada Grass Valley	61 159
LYNOTT		
John	San Francisco San Francisco 7	681 375
LYO		
---	Amador Twp 4	55 233
LYOD		
Morris	Amador Twp 1	55 455
Wm	Sacramento Granite	63 267
LYOINS		
Charles	San Joaquin Stockton	641 061
LYON HEART		
---	Fresno Twp 2	59 45
LYON		
A B	Nevada Nevada	61 330
A J	Siskiyou Scott Ri	69 71
Albt G	Sonoma Sonoma	69 634
B	Nevada Nevada	61 294
B J	San Francisco San Francisco 5	67 543
Benj	Sacramento Sutter	63 300
Burnett H*	Calaveras Twp 6	57 120
C	Sacramento Brighton	63 200
C C	Tuolumne Twp 2	71 286
Catharine	San Francisco San Francisco 7	681 383
Christian	Sonoma Bodega	69 523
Cyans*	Los Angeles Los Angeles	59 492

Name	County Locale	M653 Roll Page
LYON		
Cyrus A	Stanislaus Emory	70 756
Cyrus*	Los Angeles Los Angeles	59 492
D B	Tehama Red Bluff	70 913
Dennis	San Francisco San Francisco 9	681 021
E D	San Francisco San Francisco 10	313 67
G A	Napa Clear Lake	61 129
Geo	San Francisco San Francisco 10	355 67
Isadore	San Francisco San Francisco 4	681 155
Isadow	San Francisco San Francisco 4	681 155
Israel W	San Francisco San Francisco 7	681 344
J	Nevada Grass Valley	61 191
J	San Francisco San Francisco 5	67 490
J	San Francisco San Francisco 5	67 518
J H	San Francisco San Francisco 7	681 439
J J	Sonoma Sonoma	69 660
J K	Marin Point Re	60 729
Jacob	El Dorado Salmon Falls	581 037
Jas	Napa Clear Lake	61 138
Jas	San Francisco San Francisco 10	335 67
Jasper	Santa Cruz Pescadero	66 645
Jno	Sacramento Ward 4	63 580
Jno	Sonoma Sonoma	69 655
Jno H	Sacramento Ward 4	63 510
John	Sacramento Ward 3	63 461
John	Solano Vacaville	69 344
John	Tuolumne Twp 1	71 214
John A	Calaveras Twp 4	57 309
L	Calaveras Twp 8	57 52
L B	Yuba Fosters	72 836
L R	Yuba Fosters	72 836
Lazaar*	San Francisco San Francisco 8	681 316
Lazaax*	San Francisco San Francisco 8	681 316
Lazam	San Francisco San Francisco 8	681 316
M	Calaveras Twp 7	57 24
M	San Francisco San Francisco 2	67 682
Margaret	San Francisco San Francisco 4	681 156
Mosely	Marin San Rafael	60 769
N	Tehama Antelope	70 889
O P	Siskiyou Scott Ri	69 71
Orson	Santa Clara San Jose	65 379
Pat	Tehama Red Bluff	70 923
R B	Sonoma Sonoma	69 637
Rafasla*	San Francisco San Francisco 2	67 643
Rafasta*	San Francisco San Francisco 2	67 643
Sampson	San Francisco San Francisco 7	681 383
Sanford	Los Angeles Los Angeles	59 492
Sarah A	Sonoma Sonoma	69 634
Seely	Placer Auburn	62 594
T	Merced Twp 1	60 897
T	Merced Twp 2	60 921
T	Nevada Grass Valley	61 196
Thos	Butte Oregon	56 627
Thos	San Francisco San Francisco 10	355 67
W H	San Francisco San Francisco 5	67 516
W M	Sonoma Petaluma	69 579
W S	San Francisco San Francisco 6	67 447
W S	San Francisco San Francisco 5	67 505
W V	Placer Iona Hills	62 859
Wm	Sacramento Ward 1	63 125
Wm A	Solano Suisan	69 204
LYONE		
S H*	El Dorado Mountain	581 186
LYONEL		
S H*	El Dorado Mountain	581 186
LYONS		
A B	Nevada Nevada	61 330
A E	San Francisco San Francisco 2	67 704
Aaron E	Monterey Monterey	60 948
Afa	San Joaquin Elkhorn	64 976
Alex	San Francisco San Francisco 1	68 817
Anne M	San Francisco San Francisco 2	67 572
Arthur	San Joaquin Douglass	64 921
B	Calaveras Twp 9	57 403
B S	San Francisco San Francisco 1	68 903
Burnett H*	Calaveras Twp 6	57 120
C	Sacramento Brighton	63 201
C	San Francisco San Francisco 9	681 082
C	San Francisco San Francisco 5	67 503
Casius	Placer Rattle Snake	62 598
Chas	Placer Illinois	62 706
Conrad	Butte Hamilton	56 526
Cornelius	San Francisco San Francisco 2	67 785
D H	Trinity Indian C	70 987
D P	Mariposa Twp 3	60 586
Daniel	Siskiyou Yreka	69 184
Danl	Sacramento Ward 3	63 468
Dennis	San Francisco San Francisco 4	681 112
Dennis	San Francisco San Francisco 11	152 67
Earley	Los Angeles Azuza	59 279
Edwd	Sacramento Mississipi	63 188

Name	County Locale	M653 Roll Page
LYONS		
Elizabeth	Mariposa Twp 3	60 601
Elizebeth	Mariposa Twp 3	60 601
Ellen	San Francisco San Francisco 6	67 421
Ellen	Yuba Marysville	72 974
Fks	Calaveras Twp 9	57 405
Fredrick	Tuolumne Twp 5	71 523
G	Nevada Grass Valley	61 164
G T	Nevada Eureka	61 347
Geo	Sacramento Lee	63 216
Geo	San Francisco San Francisco 2	67 755
George	San Diego San Diego	64 759
Henry	Calaveras Twp 8	57 55
Henry	El Dorado Georgetown	58 691
Henry	Mariposa Twp 1	60 629
Henry	Plumas Meadow Valley	62 900
Herman	Sacramento Ward 1	63 17
Hiram	Humbolt Mattole	59 125
Hiram	Sacramento Ward 1	63 17
Horaa	Yuba Fosters	72 836
Horace H	Yuba Fosters	72 836
Hughes	Tuolumne Twp 1	71 206
Isaac	Mariposa Twp 3	60 596
Isaden	San Francisco San Francisco 6	67 446
Isadore	San Francisco San Francisco 6	67 446
J	Nevada Washington	61 337
J	Nevada Eureka	61 346
J	San Francisco San Francisco 12	394 67
J H	El Dorado Grizzly	581 180
J W	El Dorado Diamond	58 768
James	El Dorado Coloma	581 074
James	Placer Michigan	62 835
James	Placer Damascus	62 846
James	San Francisco San Francisco 4	681 110
James	Santa Clara San Jose	65 382
James	Trinity Ferry	70 977
James	Yuba Bear Rvr	721 011
James	Yuba Marysville	72 906
James L	San Francisco San Francisco 7	681 399
James R	San Francisco San Francisco 7	681 337
Jane M	Sacramento Ward 1	63 127
Jas	Butte Chico	56 552
Jeremah	Yuba Rose Bar	72 816
Jeremiah*	Yuba Rose Bar	72 816
Jerimiah	Nevada Rough &	61 408
Jermiah	Nevada Rough &	61 408
Jesse	Yuba Rose Bar	72 788
Jno	Butte Eureka	56 653
John	Amador Twp 1	55 485
John	Butte Oro	56 683
John	Placer Virginia	62 678
John	San Francisco San Francisco 11	108 67
John	San Francisco San Francisco 7	681 333
John	San Francisco San Francisco 7	681 416
John	San Francisco San Francisco 10	199 67
John	San Francisco San Francisco 2	67 778
John	San Francisco San Francisco 1	68 904
John	Santa Clara Burnett	65 256
John	Tuolumne Twp 1	71 234
John	Tuolumne Columbia	71 355
John	Yuba Rose Bar	72 814
Jonathan	Klamath S Fork	59 203
Josep	Mariposa Twp 1	60 636
Joseph	Sierra Twp 5	66 918
Joseph V	Yuba Marysville	72 870
Julia	San Francisco San Francisco 1	68 829
L	San Joaquin Stockton	641 023
L P	Mariposa Twp 3	60 586
Luson	Yuba North Ea	72 669
M	Nevada Eureka	61 378
Marcy	Yuba Marysville	72 883
Margaret	Alameda Oakland	55 26
Margaret	San Francisco San Francisco 4	681 142
Margaret	San Francisco San Francisco 4	67 445
Maria	San Francisco San Francisco 4	681 119
Mary	Yuba Marysville	72 850
Mary A	Contra Costa Twp 3	57 584
Mary*	Yuba Marysville	72 883
Michael	Placer Forest H	62 800
Michael	San Francisco San Francisco 1	68 879
Michael	Yuba Marysville	72 868
Michael	Yuba Marysville	72 943
Morris	Solano Fairfield	69 198
Noah	Siskiyou Yreka	69 130
Patrick	El Dorado Coloma	581 123
Patrick	San Francisco San Francisco 9	68 952
Patrick	Sierra La Porte	66 789
Pierre	Tuolumne Sonora	71 479
R	El Dorado Placerville	58 859
R W	Placer Virginia	62 668
Ramond	El Dorado Big Bar	58 733
Robb	San Francisco San Francisco 4	681 220
Robt	San Francisco San Francisco 4	681 220

Name	County Locale	M653 Roll Page
LYONS		
S	Calaveras Twp 9	57 405
S	Nevada Eureka	61 350
S	Sierra Eureka	661043
S H	El Dorado Mountain	581186
Saml	Sacramento Granite	63 239
Saml	Sacramento Ward 4	63 517
Samuel*	Nevada Eureka	61 346
Selia	Placer Mealsburg	62 702
Susan	Yolo No E Twp	72 669
Tho'S	Mariposa Twp 3	60 604
Thos	Mariposa Twp 3	60 604
W	Merced Twp 1	60 902
W	San Francisco San Francisco 9	681082
W H	El Dorado Kelsey	581150
W P	San Francisco San Francisco 1	68 846
Walter*	San Francisco San Francisco 7	681338
Watter W*	San Francisco	681338
Wawter W	San Francisco	681338
William	Colusa Grand Island	57 472
William	El Dorado Coloma	581112
William	Marin Point Re	60 732
William	San Francisco San Francisco 4	681137
William	San Mateo Twp 3	65 108
Wm	Colusa Grand Island	57 472
Wm	El Dorado Mud Springs	58 991
Wm	Plumas Meadow Valley	62 908
Wm	San Francisco San Francisco 9	681060
Wm	San Francisco San Francisco 1	68 871
Wm	San Francisco San Francisco 1	68 932
Wm C	Placer Rattle Snake	62 635
Wm H	San Joaquin Stockton	641010
LYOUT		
John	Tuolumne Sonora	71 234
LYPER		
Henry	Butte Bidwell	56 714
LYPHEA		
F*	El Dorado Diamond	58 768
LYPHU		
H*	El Dorado Diamond	58 768
LYPSE		
Henry	Butte Bidwell	56 714
LYPSEY		
Robert	San Mateo Twp 1	65 68
LYRS		
H W*	San Joaquin Stockton	641025
LYRUS		
Mark	Alameda Brooklyn	55 93
LYSAAHT		
J	San Francisco San Francisco 5	67 537
LYSAUHT		
J	San Francisco San Francisco 5	67 537
LYSAULT		
William	San Francisco San Francisco 7	681427
LYSEDER		
Agust*	Los Angeles Tejon	59 528
LYSETT		
Michl	Sacramento Ward 1	63 155
LYSIN		
Jacob	San Mateo Twp 1	65 48
LYSLE		
David	Yuba Marysville	72 979
LYSLER		
Alexander	Yuba Marysville	72 963
LYSON		
R	Nevada Grass Valley	61 145
LYSPIS		
Antonio	Butte Bidwell	56 731
LYSTER		
W S*	San Francisco San Francisco 3	67 86
LYTAKER		
F E	Sonoma Petaluma	69 580
Margaret	Sonoma Petaluma	69 551
LYTHE		
James A	Siskiyou Yreka	69 170
LYTLE		
Andrew*	Shasta Shasta	66 760
Franas	Sacramento Dry Crk	63 371
G I	Sacramento Ward 1	63 132
G J*	Sacramento Ward 1	63 132
Gabriel	Tulara Visalia	71 75
J A	Tuolumne Twp 4	71 158
James A	Siskiyou Yreka	69 170
Jno F	Butte Chico	56 541
John	Yolo Putah	72 598
Merit T	Siskiyou Yreka	69 149
Mesit T	Siskiyou Yreka	69 149
Robt	Butte Oregon	56 614
Saml	Yolo Putah	72 598
T J	Sacramento Georgian	63 339
Theodore	Siskiyou Scott Va	69 59
Thos	Butte Ophir	56 794
Wm A	Tuolumne Shawsfla	71 389
Wm H	Tuolumne Twp 2	71 389

Name	County Locale	M653 Roll Page
LYTLO		
John F*	Butte Chico	56 541
Wm H*	San Francisco San Francisco 1	68 873
LYTTE		
Theodore	Siskiyou Scott Va	69 59
LYTTAM		
LYTTLE		
Benjamin	Humbolt Table Bl	59 140
Elijah	Siskiyou Yreka	69 156
Gabriel	Tulara Twp 1	71 75
Jasper	San Joaquin O'Neal	641008
John	El Dorado Big Bar	58 742
LYTTLEFIELD		
J	Butte Eureka	56 653
LYTZ		
Michael	Sacramento Ward 4	63 504
LYWICKER		
Henry*	Sacramento Ward 1	63 33
John*	Sacramento Ward 1	63 33
LZ		
---*	El Dorado Georgetown	58 693
M YOU		
---*	Nevada Nevada	61 301
M ZUP		
---	Nevada Nevada	61 303
M		
---	Sierra Downieville	661014
Dui	Nevada Nevada	61 299
Hon*	San Francisco San Francisco 4	681197
Lou	San Francisco San Francisco 4	681199
Sup	Nevada Nevada	61 303
M???HOLLAND		
Frank J*	Yuba Marysville	72 906
M???KIN		
H L*	Napa Napa	61 58
M??AN		
Giacerner*	Mariposa Twp 3	60 594
Giageme*	Mariposa Twp 3	60 594
MA SE MAW		
---	Yuba Long Bar	72 755
MA TU LIEF		
---	Mendocino Calpella	60 822
MA		
---	Butte Wyandotte	56 666
---	Calaveras Twp 5	57 193
---	Calaveras Twp 10	57 275
---	Mariposa Twp 1	60 666
---	San Francisco San Francisco 4	681199
Ah	Sierra Pine Grove	66 825
Chow	Nevada Grass Valley	61 229
Chow	Nevada Grass Valley	61 230
Choy	San Francisco San Francisco 4	681175
Con	Yuba New York	72 731
Fau	Nevada Grass Valley	61 232
He	Sacramento Granite	63 269
Hop	Sacramento Granite	63 269
How	Sacramento Ward 1	63 51
Luck*	Calaveras Twp 5	57 192
Maw S	Yuba Long Bar	72 755
No Lee	Yuba Fosters	72 843
Re	Yuba Slate Ro	72 715
Se Maw*	Yuba Long Bar	72 755
Soo	Sacramento Granite	63 269
Teh*	Alameda Oakland	55 57
Then	Yuba Long Bar	72 763
Ton	Nevada Grass Valley	61 229
Tou	Nevada Grass Valley	61 232
Tou	Nevada Grass Valley	61 233
Tow	Nevada Nevada	61 301
Tuck*	Calaveras Twp 5	57 192
Wa	Nevada Eureka	61 385
Way	Mariposa Twp 3	60 613
Yuck	Calaveras Twp 5	57 192
Yup	Nevada Grass Valley	61 227
MA???E		
Joseph*	Calaveras Twp 5	57 205
MA???ER		
Charles	Marin Tomales	60 724
MA???OND		
Thomas	Marin Tomales	60 724
MAABILA		
Jose*	Los Angeles Los Angeles	59 499
MAAG		
C	El Dorado Placerville	58 820
MAAHON		
Chas	San Francisco San Francisco 2	67 761
MAALER		
Hoanio	Mariposa Twp 1	60 654
MAANIEL		
M J	Santa Clara San Jose	65 354
MAAR		
---	Sacramento Cosummes	63 406
Robert	San Francisco San Francisco 11	149 67
MAARE		
Pat	Sonoma Petaluma	69 577

Name	County Locale	M653 Roll Page
MAARION		
Chas H	Sacramento Ward 4	63 510
MAASS		
H F	San Francisco San Francisco 2	67 572
MABBELT		
Ira	Sacramento Casumnes	63 381
MABBETT		
Ira	Sacramento Cosumnes	63 381
MABEL		
Jacob	El Dorado Casumnes	581162
S	Sacramento Granite	63 265
MABERRY		
Geo*	Sacramento Granite	63 258
MABIE		
A M	Sierra Twp 7	66 913
MABIER		
A W	Sierra Twp 7	66 913
MABIL		
H	Trinity Weaverville	701081
MABINE		
Rachel	Yolo Putah	72 554
MABITT		
Chas*	San Francisco San Francisco 9	681071
MABLE		
Charles	Yuba Marysville	72 932
MABLOCK		
Silas K	Tuolumne Twp 6	71 541
MABOON		
W*	Amador Twp 2	55 304
MABRY		
R M	Tuolumne Twp 1	71 185
R W	Tuolumne Sonora	71 185
MABY		
J	Nevada Grass Valley	61 151
MAC		
---	Nevada Rough &	61 399
---	Nevada Rough &	61 434
---	Tulara Twp 2	71 35
---*	Nevada Rough &	61 399
---*	Tulara Visalia	71 35
Kum	San Francisco San Francisco 1	68 872
Myron*	Sacramento Alabama	63 415
W*	Alameda Brooklyn	55 186
Wm	Sacramento Ward 4	63 560
MACABELLO		
Manuel	San Francisco San Francisco 3	67 64
MACADAMS		
Allen	Yuba Rose Bar	72 802
MACAFFEE		
A A	Yolo Slate Ra	72 710
MACAFFERTY		
Hugh	Yolo Slate Ra	72 709
Hugh	Yuba Slate Ro	72 709
James	Yuba Rose Bar	72 805
James	Yuba Rose Bar	72 806
MACALIVISA		
Jose*	Los Angeles Los Angeles	59 517
MACALL		
Daniel	Tulara Twp 2	71 30
MACALLIS		
John	Yuba Rose Bar	72 791
MACALUTO		
---	Fresno Twp 2	59 113
MACAM		
M	El Dorado Placerville	58 890
MACAMPLEY		
John*	Shasta Horsetown	66 698
MACARAS		
Rhalus	Los Angeles Elmonte	59 261
MACARDY		
John	Calaveras Twp 5	57 201
MACARIA		
---	Monterey S Antoni	60 970
---	San Bernardino Santa Barbara	64 202
MACARIO		
---	Monterey S Antoni	60 970
MACARKY		
Edward	Yuba Rose Bar	72 803
MACARO		
Joseph	Alameda Brooklyn	55 204
MACAROY		
Nicholas*	Yuba Rose Bar	72 793
MACARTHUR		
Alvin	Yuba New York	72 724
Hrin*	Yuba New York	72 724
MACARTNEY		
Thomas*	Yuba Rose Bar	72 801
MACARTY		
John	Yuba New York	72 734
Patrick	Yolo Slate Ra	72 712
Patrick	Yuba Slate Ro	72 712
MACARVY		
Nicholas*	Yuba Rose Bar	72 793
MACASLIN		
F	Yuba New York	72 734
MACAVOY		
Nicholas*	Yuba Rose Bar	72 793

Name	County Locale	M653 Roll Page
MACBAIRE		
Wm*	Yuba Rose Bar	72 813
MACBARRE		
Wm	Yuba Rose Bar	72 813
MACBETH		
Sarah R	San Francisco San Francisco	10 281
		67
MACBRIDE		
James	Yolo Slate Ra	72 693
James	Yolo Slate Ra	72 694
James	Yuba Slate Ro	72 693
James	Yuba Slate Ro	72 694
MACCAFFERY		
Elizabeth	Yuba Long Bar	72 746
MACCAFFEY		
Elisabeth	Yuba New York	72 746
MACCALL		
John	Yuba Fosters	72 837
John	Yuba Fosters	72 838
MACCALLY		
John	San Mateo Twp 1	65 61
MACCANLEY		
Wm C	Tuolumne Twp 3	71 438
MACCARTY		
Andrea	Yuba Rose Bar	72 793
James	Yuba Parks Ba	72 775
Joseph	Yuba Slate Ro	72 689
MACCAULEY		
Wm C	Tuolumne Jamestown	71 438
MACCHESNEY		
J B	Yuba New York	72 728
J B*	Yuba New York	72 728
MACCHINTY		
Thomas	Yuba Long Bar	72 744
MACCHOSNEY		
J B*	Yuba New York	72 728
MACCLARE		
W H	Yolo Slate Ra	72 705
MACCLEEN		
David	Yuba Rose Bar	72 815
MACCLELLAND		
Julius	Yuba Parks Ba	72 774
MACCLEM		
David	Yuba Rose Bar	72 815
MACCLOSKEY		
Calvin	Yuba Rose Bar	72 799
J	Yuba Rose Bar	72 788
MACCLOSKY		
Charles	Yuba Rose Bar	72 807
MACCLUNE		
Patrick	Calaveras Twp 5	57 238
MACCOLBUM		
Michael	Yuba Rose Bar	72 811
MACCOLE		
Thomas	Yuba New York	72 735
MACCOLLAM		
Michael*	Yuba Rose Bar	72 811
Ronald*	Yuba Rose Bar	72 800
MACCOLLUM		
Michael*	Yuba Rose Bar	72 811
Ronald	Yuba Rose Bar	72 800
MACCONI		
---*	Tulara Visalia	71 35
MACCONN		
Edward	Yuba New York	72 727
MACCONNELL		
John	Yuba Rose Bar	72 808
John	Yuba Rose Bar	72 813
MACCONRILL		
Henry	Yolo Slate Ra	72 686
MACCONVILLE		
Henry	Yuba North Ea	72 686
MACCORMACK		
Thomas	Yuba Fosters	72 832
MACCORMICK		
Noah M	Yolo Slate Ra	72 716
Noah M	Yuba Slate Ro	72 716
MACCORT		
Charles	Yuba Timbucto	72 787
MACCOW		
---	Tulara Twp 2	71 35
MACCRELLISH		
F	San Francisco San Francisco 5	67 481
MACCUE		
Timothy	Yuba Rose Bar	72 815
MACCUMMINS		
Wm	Yuba Rose Bar	72 817
MACDADE		
John	Yuba Long Bar	72 755
MACDILLON		
John G	Yolo Slate Ra	72 699
MACDON		
Christian	Yuba New York	72 721
MACDONALD		
H	Yolo Slate Ra	72 709
H	Yuba Slate Ro	72 709

Name	County Locale	M653 Roll Page
MACDONALD		
J W	Yolo Slate Ra	72 697
J W	Yuba Slate Ro	72 697
James	Yuba Rose Bar	72 790
John	Yolo Slate Ra	72 700
John	Yuba Slate Ro	72 700
L	Yuba Fosters	72 822
Mary	Yuba Rose Bar	72 816
Nelson	Yuba Fosters	72 825
MACDONOUGH		
Frank	Yuba Long Bar	72 755
MACDOON		
W J	Nevada Bridgeport	61 465
MACE		
Alfred J	Yuba Marysville	72 872
Alvin D	San Bernardino San Salvador	64 654
B F	Nevada Rough &	61 414
Elizth A	Fresno Twp 2	59 4
F	Amador Twp 3	55 410
J	Yuba Bear Rvr	72 1011
Jackson	San Bernardino San Bernadino	64 675
Jas Scott	Sacramento Sutter	63 299
Lizzie	Sacramento Ward 1	63 111
Russell P	Fresno Twp 2	59 4
Thomas	Santa Cruz Santa Cruz	66 640
Wm	Calaveras Twp 10	57 294
Wm	Sacramento Sutter	63 299
MACELLIA		
Joseph	Calaveras Twp 9	57 347
MACENCIA		
---*	San Bernardino S Timate	64 742
MACENTIRE		
Hugh	El Dorado Cold Spring	58 1101
MACER		
F	Mariposa Twp 1	60 639
J	Mariposa Twp 1	60 639
P	Mariposa Twp 1	60 639
MACERONIN		
---	Tulara Twp 2	71 34
MACESSENCIEN		
George	Yuba Marysville	72 888
MACESSESSICA		
George*	Yuba Marysville	72 888
MACESSESSING		
George*	Yuba Marysville	72 888
MACETTIA		
Joseph	Calaveras Twp 9	57 347
MACEY		
A F	Amador Twp 2	55 304
A H	Amador Twp 2	55 304
Hiram	Solano Suisan	69 213
Jacob	Calaveras Twp 10	57 266
James	Calaveras Twp 10	57 266
John A	Del Norte Crescent	58 625
MACFADDEN		
Thomas	Yuba Rose Bar	72 789
Thomas	Yuba Rose Bar	72 800
MACFARLAND		
P	Yuba Foster B	72 822
William	Yuba Foster B	72 832
MACFIELD		
David*	San Francisco San Francisco 2	67 738
MACGILL		
R R	San Francisco San Francisco 7	68 1440
Wm	Yuba Rose Bar	72 820
MACGRATH		
Patrick	Yuba Long Bar	72 750
MACH		
---*	Yuba Fosters	72 843
Chas	San Bernardino S Timate	64 689
Joseph*	Yuba Parke Ba	72 784
V	Butte Eureka	56 646
MACHADA		
Jose	San Bernardino Santa Barbara	64 197
Maria R	Los Angeles Los Angeles	59 295
MACHADO		
Agustin	Los Angeles Los Angeles	59 505
Andres	Los Angeles Los Angeles	59 506
Andris	Los Angeles Los Angeles	59 506
Cipriana	Yuba Marysville	72 949
Cipuano	Yuba Marysville	72 949
Dolores	Los Angeles San Pedro	59 484
Dolores	Los Angeles Los Angeles	59 505
Doloris	Los Angeles Los Angeles	59 505
Ignacio	Los Angeles Los Angeles	59 505
Jesus*	San Diego S Luis R	64 781
Joaquin	San Diego San Diego	64 767
Jose A	Los Angeles San Pedro	59 484
Juan	San Diego Temecula	64 792
M	Tuolumne Twp 2	71 310
Magil	Los Angeles Los Angeles	59 505
Maria A	San Diego San Diego	64 758
Maria L	San Diego San Diego	64 757
Maria S	San Diego San Diego	64 763
Rafael	San Diego Agua Caliente	64 861
MACHAERLLI		
Baptista*	Calaveras Twp 5	57 249

Name	County Locale	M653 Roll Page
MACHAERLLI		
David*	Calaveras Twp 5	57 249
MACHAFERY		
John	Yuba New York	72 736
MACHAHER		
W	El Dorado Placerville	58 895
MACHAM		
J*	Nevada Grass Valley	61 167
MACHARDS		
Cassar*	Calaveras Twp 6	57 151
MACHARRELI		
Muin	Calaveras Twp 5	57 249
Phillip*	Calaveras Twp 5	57 225
MACHAVELLI		
Phillip*	Calaveras Twp 5	57 225
MACHE		
---	Siskiyou Yreka	69 139
Patrick	San Francisco San Francisco 7	68 1396
MACHEAVELLO		
G B	San Francisco San Francisco 3	67 21
MACHELLA		
---	Butte Ophir	56 812
Ruceo	Butte Ophir	56 777
MACHELSON		
Anne*	San Francisco San Francisco 2	67 762
MACHEN		
F N	Tuolumne Sonora	71 218
MACHER		
Augustus*	Placer Michigan	62 845
MACHERLLI		
David	Calaveras Twp 5	57 249
MACHERTY		
Mordecai*	Yuba Slate Ra	72 706
MACHERY		
J	San Joaquin Stockton	64 1099
MACHES		
John*	San Francisco San Francisco 9	68 1031
MACHETTI		
Anyelo	Calaveras Twp 10	57 261
MACHEUMENE		
---*	Tulara Visalia	71 35
MACHI		
R D	San Francisco San Francisco 9	68 975
MACHIEL		
Jas	Calaveras Twp 9	57 400
MACHIN		
Ellen	Yuba Marysville	72 915
MACHINTZ		
Thomas*	Yuba New York	72 744
MACHITO		
Bartalo	Santa Clara Alviso	65 404
MACHLAN		
Thomas	Sierra Downieville	66 977
MACHO		
---	Fresno Twp 2	59 89
Andrews	Amador Twp 2	55 288
MACHOCHIN		
---	Mendocino Big Rock	60 875
MACHOE		
Manuell	Napa Yount	61 52
MACHOERLLI		
Baptiste*	Calaveras Twp 5	57 249
David*	Calaveras Twp 5	57 249
MACHOES		
Manuell*	Napa Yount	61 52
MACHOL		
Jacob	Yuba Marysville	72 876
MACHON		
T N	Tuolumne Twp 1	71 218
MACHRACHEN		
M	San Joaquin Stockton	64 1099
MACHT		
Alex	San Francisco San Francisco 6	67 461
Alix	San Francisco San Francisco 6	67 461
MACHTRIB		
Fredk	San Francisco San Francisco 10	254
		67
MACHTRICB		
Fredk*	San Francisco San Francisco 10	254
		67
MACHTRIEB		
Fredk*	San Francisco San Francisco 10	254
		67
MACHUCA		
Magdalena	San Francisco 2	67 695
	San Francisco	
MACHUM		
J*	Nevada Grass Valley	61 167
MACHUT		
Jas	Calaveras Twp 9	57 400
MACIA		
Antonia*	Santa Cruz Santa Cruz	66 611
Antonin*	Santa Cruz Santa Cruz	66 611
Antonio*	Santa Cruz Santa Cruz	66 611
MACID		
Antonuo*	Santa Cruz Santa Cruz	66 611

Name	County Locale	M653 RollPage
MACIEL		
Antionio	Santa Cruz Santa Cruz	66 611
Antonia*	Santa Cruz Santa Cruz	66 611
Antonuo*	Santa Cruz Santa Cruz	66 611
MACILLAS		
Nachelas	Mariposa Twp 1	60 669
Nicholas	Mariposa Twp 1	60 669
MACINCIA		
---	San Bernardino S Timate	64 715
MACINO		
---	San Diego Agua Caliente	64 836
MACINTYRE		
Albert	Yuba New York	72 723
George	Yuba Rose Bar	72 806
MACIO		
Juan	Santa Clara San Jose	65 373
MACJUIGGAN		
John*	Yuba Rose Bar	72 794
MACJUIGGIM		
John*	Yuba Rose Bar	72 794
MACK		
---	Amador Twp 5	55 352
---	Mariposa Twp 1	60 668
---	Mariposa Coulterville	60 688
---	San Mateo Twp 2	65 126
---	Yuba Fosters	72 843
A	Calaveras Twp 9	57 376
Albert	Tuolumne Twp 4	71 130
Alfred	San Luis Obispo San Luis Obispo	65 44
Andrew	Napa Clear Lake	61 134
Andrew J	Placer Rattle Snake	62 598
Anna	Sacramento Ward 4	63 540
August*	Stanislaus Buena Village	70 725
Augustus	Tuolumne Big Oak	71 130
Charles	Yolo Cottonwoood	72 656
Chas E	Sacramento Ward 4	63 560
Cornelius	Nevada Bridgeport	61 456
Daniel	San Francisco San Francisco 9	68 986
Edward	Sacramento Ward 4	63 515
Edward	Stanislaus Oatvale	70 716
F	Siskiyou Scott Va	69 51
G W	Sutter Sutter	70 801
Geo H	San Francisco San Francisco 1	68 904
George	Amador Twp 2	55 284
George	Los Angeles Azuza	59 276
H B	Nevada Grass Valley	61 216
J	Nevada Grass Valley	61 216
J	Nevada Grass Valley	61 226
J L	Sutter Sutter	70 817
J S	Sierra Twp 7	66 903
James	Colusa Spring Valley	57 429
James	Placer Secret R	62 617
James	San Francisco San Francisco 5	67 490
John	Sonoma Mendocino	69 455
John	Tulara Visalia	71 17
John	Yuba Rose Bar	72 794
Joseph	San Francisco San Francisco 3	67 59
Joseph	Yuba Parks Ba	72 784
Josias	Solano Vacaville	69 354
Mary	Sacramento Ward 1	63 109
Mary	Sacramento Ward 3	63 483
Miley	Colusa Spring Valley	57 429
Myron*	Sacramento Dry Crk	63 378
R	Sierra Downieville	661 007
Richd	Sonoma Santa Rosa	69 402
Robert	Los Angeles Los Angeles	59 339
Squire	Sierra Twp 5	66 948
Terry	Sacramento Ward 1	63 75
Thos	Santa Clara Alviso	65 402
W J	San Francisco San Francisco 5	67 522
William	Alameda Oakland	55 61
Wm	Tuolumne Twp 4	71 129
Wm H	Alameda Brooklyn	55 187
MACKANY		
W P	Sonoma Petaluma	69 589
MACKAY		
A W	Colusa Monroeville	57 440
James	Del Norte Crescent	58 628
Patrick	Colusa Monroeville	57 441
Walter	San Francisco San Francisco 7	681 436
MACKBEE		
William	Siskiyou Yreka	69 143
MACKE		
Chas	Sacramento Ward 4	63 592
MACKEE		
Frederick	Yuba Long Bar	72 769
MACKEEL		
Harvey	Yuba Rose Bar	72 806
MACKEGNE		
Robert*	Yuba Rose Bar	72 819
MACKEGUE		
Robert	Yuba Rose Bar	72 819
Robert*	Yuba Rose Bar	72 819
MACKELROY		
S T*	Nevada Grass Valley	61 197
MACKELTY		
Petrucius	Yuba Slate Ro	72 699

Name	County Locale	M653 RollPage
MACKEN		
James	San Francisco San Francisco 9	681 028
Lawrence	Tulara Twp 2	71 22
MACKENEN		
Henry C*	Yuba Rose Bar	72 791
James F	Yolo Slate Ra	72 698
James F	Yuba Slate Ro	72 698
MACKENIN		
Henry C*	Yuba Rose Bar	72 791
MACKENON		
Henry C*	Yuba Rose Bar	72 791
MACKENROY		
G	San Francisco San Francisco 4	681 153
Robt	San Francisco San Francisco 9	681 011
MACKENSPIE		
James*	Yuba Rose Bar	72 811
MACKENSYIE		
James*	Yuba Rose Bar	72 811
MACKENTYRE		
Jas B	San Francisco San Francisco 9	68 959
Jos	San Francisco San Francisco 9	68 959
MACKENZIE		
James	Yuba Rose Bar	72 811
Wm	Yolo Slate Ra	72 694
Wm	Yuba Slate Ro	72 694
MACKER		
Phillip	Calaveras Twp 5	57 146
T W*	Nevada Nevada	61 319
MACKEREL		
---	Tulara Twp 2	71 34
MACKERTY		
Merdean	Yolo Slate Ra	72 706
Mordelin*	Yuba Slate Ro	72 706
MACKES		
John*	San Francisco San Francisco 9	681 031
MACKESEL		
---*	Tulara Visalia	71 34
MACKEVELL		
Nicholas	San Francisco San Francisco 4	681 164
MACKEY		
Dennis	Trinity Raabs Ba	701 020
E	Nevada Grass Valley	61 226
Jas	San Francisco San Francisco 1	68 869
John	Humbolt Pacific	59 137
John	Trinity Hay Fork	70 992
John	Yolo No E Twp	72 679
John	Yuba North Ea	72 679
Kate	Sonoma Sonoma	69 659
Lewis	Placer Ophirville	62 654
P	Nevada Grass Valley	61 219
T	Nevada Grass Valley	61 203
T	Sutter Yuba	70 777
Thomas	Yolo No E Twp	72 672
Thomas	Yuba North Ea	72 672
W	Yolo Cottonwoood	72 646
MACKIE		
Geo	Nevada Eureka	61 374
James	Sonoma Russian	69 438
Jas	Placer Secret R	62 613
T W	Nevada Nevada	61 319
MACKIN		
A	Sacramento American	63 167
Ellen	Yuba Marysville	72 915
Henry	El Dorado Georgetown	58 755
John	San Francisco San Francisco 11	156
		67
Mary	San Francisco San Francisco 6	67 445
MACKING		
Fred	Sonoma Armally	69 482
MACKINS		
Jas	Calaveras Twp 9	57 384
MACKITE		
Jared S*	Calaveras Twp 5	57 187
MACKLAN		
Thomas	Sierra Downieville	66 977
MACKLE		
Peter	San Francisco San Francisco 2	67 560
MACKLIN		
Anthony	Tuolumne Twp 2	71 276
James*	El Dorado Georgetown	58 755
John	Sacramento Ward 1	63 92
MACKLOUN		
---	Tulara Twp 2	71 36
MACKLOWN		
---*	Tulara Visalia	71 36
MACKLU		
---*	Tulara Visalia	71 36
MACKNE		
Jared S*	Calaveras Twp 5	57 187
MACKNEY		
Charles	Yolo Cache Crk	72 590
Mrs	Sonoma Vallejo	69 624
W	Yolo Cache Crk	72 589
MACKS		
Chas W	San Francisco San Francisco 1	68 905
MACKSAUME		
---	Tulara Twp 2	71 35

Name	County Locale	M653 RollPage
MACKTTE		
Jared S*	Calaveras Twp 6	57 187
MACKUR		
Jared S*	Calaveras Twp 5	57 187
MACKWELL		
Nicholas	San Francisco San Francisco 4	681 164
MACKY		
E	Nevada Grass Valley	61 226
Thomas	Contra Costa Twp 3	57 586
MACLAIN		
John	Yuba Fosters	72 838
MACLANE		
Wm	Yuba Rose Bar	72 806
MACLASAR		
Cora	San Francisco San Francisco 6	67 464
MACLAUGHLIN		
Hiram	Yuba New York	72 747
James	Yuba Rose Bar	72 815
James	Yuba Rose Bar	72 819
John	Yuba New York	72 728
M	Yuba Rose Bar	72 811
Michael	Yuba Rose Bar	72 814
Pat	Yolo Slate Ra	72 718
Pat	Yuba New York	72 718
Patrick	Yuba Parks Ba	72 774
Peter	Yuba Rose Bar	72 805
Peter	Yuba Rose Bar	72 807
Peter*	Yuba Rose Bar	72 805
MACLAY		
Wallace J	Yuba Marysville	72 848
William J	Yuba Marysville	72 848
MACLEAS		
Stewart	Amador Twp 4	55 243
MACLELLAN		
John G	Yuba Slate Ro	72 699
MACLES		
Mayal*	El Dorado Coloma	581 118
MACLETTE		
Jared S*	Calaveras Twp 6	57 187
MACLINNS		
Anthony*	Calaveras Twp 6	57 161
MACLISON		
Henry	El Dorado Greenwood	58 710
MACLOUIS		
John	Yuba Fosters	72 837
MACLURE		
W H	Yuba Slate Ro	72 705
MACMAHON		
Edward	Yolo No E Twp	72 679
Edward	Yuba North Ea	72 679
Henry H	Los Angeles Los Angeles	59 336
Hugh	Yuba Long Bar	72 754
John	Yuba Long Bar	72 755
Thomas	Yuba Long Bar	72 755
Thomas	Yuba Long Bar	72 756
MACMAHORN		
John	Yuba Long Bar	72 755
MACMANNS		
Ann	Yolo New York	72 720
MACMASTER		
Samuel A	Yuba New York	72 720
Samuel N	Yolo New York	72 720
MACMELLAN		
James	Yolo No E Twp	72 673
James	Yuba North Ea	72 673
John	Yolo Slate Ra	72 691
MACMELLON		
A	Yuba New York	72 735
MACMILLOM		
John	Yuba Slate Ro	72 691
MACMILTY		
Petrucius	Yolo Slate Ra	72 699
MACMORRINS		
Ann*	Yuba New York	72 720
MACMURRAY		
V C	Yolo Slate Ra	72 705
V C	Yuba Slate Ro	72 705
MACNAHORA		
Thomas	Yuba Long Bar	72 755
MACNALE		
Theodore	Yuba Fosters	72 825
MACNALLY		
James	Yuba New York	72 737
MACNAMAM		
Thomas	Yuba Rose Bar	72 801
MACNAMARN		
Thomas*	Yuba Rose Bar	72 801
MACNAMARU		
Thomas*	Yuba Rose Bar	72 801
MACNANNY		
Patrick	Yuba Long Bar	72 750
MACNEIL		
Samuel	Yuba Foster B	72 836
Samuel	Yuba Fosters	72 836
MACNENOMEY		
Roger*	Yuba Foster B	72 829

Name	County Locale	M653 RollPage
MACNENOMY		
Roger*	Yuba Fosters	72 829
MACNONOMY		
Roger*	Yuba Foster B	72 829
MACNONONNY		
Roger*	Yuba Fosters	72 829
MACNUTT		
John F	Yuba Rose Bar	72 814
MACO		
D	Amador Twp 2	55 295
MACOHNER		
Jas*	Sacramento Ward 1	63 40
MACOHUER		
Jas*	Sacramento Ward 1	63 40
MACOLMER		
Jas	Sacramento Ward 1	63 40
MACOMB		
B F	Tuolumne Twp 3	71 437
MACOMBER		
J B*	Placer Iona Hills	62 874
Jos	San Francisco San Francisco 9	681003
Wm	San Francisco San Francisco 3	67 36
Wm E	El Dorado Greenwood	58 712
MACOMLIN		
J B*	Placer Iona Hills	62 874
MACON		
Henry	Amador Twp 2	55 285
William	Shasta Millvill	66 741
MACONDRY		
F M	San Francisco San Francisco 4	681141
MACONOLOGUE		
Catherine*	Yolo No E Twp	72 667
MACONOVICH		
Mitchell	San Francisco San Francisco 3	67 42
MACONTRERAS		
Jose	San Diego Agua Caliente	64 835
MACOOL		
Patrick	Tuolumne Jamestown	71 436
MACORBETE		
George	Yuba Marysville	72 926
MACORMICK		
James*	Yolo No E Twp	72 667
MACOTEE		
John F*	Alameda Oakland	55 73
MACOTER		
John F*	Alameda Oakland	55 73
MACOVICH		
C	Sacramento Ward 1	63 11
MACPHERSON		
Jno	Klamath Liberty	59 235
S G	San Francisco San Francisco 6	67 411
MACQUAID		
Henry	Yuba Rose Bar	72 789
J E	Yuba Slate Ba	72 700
James	Yuba Parke Ba	72 781
John	Yuba Rose Bar	72 807
John	Yuba Rose Bar	72 814
Thomas	Yuba Rose Bar	72 807
MACQUEEN		
Pat	Yolo Slate Ra	72 691
Pat	Yuba Slate Ro	72 691
Robert	Yuba Parks Ba	72 777
MACQUERICT		
J E	Yolo Slate Ra	72 700
MACQUINN		
William	San Francisco San Francisco 11	122 67
MACR		
Wm*	Calaveras Twp 10	57 294
MACRAE		
C L	Trinity China Bar	70 959
MACREARD		
Rob	Siskiyou Scott Ri	69 68
MACREASE		
Rob	Siskiyou Scott Ri	69 68
MACRUFF		
Leopold	San Francisco San Francisco 11	137 67
MACSHAFERY		
John	Yuba New York	72 736
MACSHANE		
---*	El Dorado Georgetown	58 703
MACSTEESTOSH		
Milo*	Yuba Marysville	72 940
MACTIC		
E B*	San Francisco San Francisco 1	68 875
MACULINO		
---	Los Angeles Los Angeles	59 495
MACUMBER		
H	Amador Twp 3	55 396
P Y	El Dorado Placerville	58 884
Zehdee	Alameda Oakland	55 56
MACUME		
Charles	El Dorado Placerville	58 929
MACUMPY		
Thomas	Tuolumne Jamestown	71 425

Name	County Locale	M653 RollPage
MACUPO		
---	Fresno Twp 2	59 116
MACURY		
Edward	Sierra Twp 7	66 904
MACWELL		
Abbert*	Mendocino Big Rvr	60 851
James	Sierra La Porte	66 788
MACWILLIAMS		
John	Yuba Rose Bar	72 799
MACY		
---	Yuba Bear Rvr	721015
Albert	San Francisco San Francisco 6	67 418
Alexander	Calaveras Twp 8	57 93
Arnold	Sierra Pine Grove	66 828
C C	Marin Novato	60 736
Chas F	San Francisco San Francisco 3	67 72
F B	Sacramento Ward 4	63 514
George	Amador Twp 6	55 426
George	Sierra Pine Grove	66 828
Lizzie	San Francisco San Francisco 2	67 556
Lucinda	Los Angeles Los Angeles	59 293
Robt B	San Francisco San Francisco 10	256 67
Vesta S	Sonoma Healdsbu	69 475
Wm M	Sonoma Healdsbu	69 475
MADACENDA		
---	San Luis Obispo San Luis Obispo	65 9
MADALENA		
---	Los Angeles San Juan	59 467
---	Los Angeles San Juan	59 470
MADALINA		
---	San Bernardino S Timate	64 716
---	San Bernardino S Timate	64 722
---	San Bernardino S Timate	64 723
---	San Bernardino S Timate	64 745
---	San Bernardino S Timate	64 751
---	San Bernardino S Timate	64 754
MADALINE		
---	San Bernardino S Timate	64 716
---	San Bernardino S Timate	64 723
MADALLANES		
Juana	Santa Clara Almaden	65 268
MADARA		
D*	Sonoma Washington	69 674
MADARIAGA		
Jose M	Monterey Monterey	60 948
MADARIAGO		
Jose M	Monterey Monterey	60 948
MADARIGA		
Juan	Monterey Monterey	60 948
MADARU		
D*	Sonoma Washington	69 674
MADCOM		
Martin	Amador Twp 2	55 293
MADDAN		
John	Placer Michigan	62 817
S	Nevada Eureka	61 369
MADDEN		
A J	Butte Chico	56 537
Antonie	Yuba Foster B	72 835
Bet	El Dorado Georgetown	58 693
C	Nevada Grass Valley	61 164
C	San Francisco San Francisco 5	67 495
C	Siskiyou Scott Va	69 38
Chas	Tehama Lewiston	70 961
Chas	Trinity Lewiston	70 961
D W	Sacramento Granite	63 236
Edward	Sierra Gibsonville	66 853
F L	El Dorado Georgetown	58 689
Francis	Santa Clara Alviso	65 409
J	Calaveras Twp 9	57 412
J	San Francisco San Francisco 5	67 548
James	San Francisco San Francisco 11	114 67
James	Siskiyou Scott Va	69 45
Jerome	Sacramento Ward 1	63 126
Jerry	Placer Forest H	62 774
Jno	San Francisco San Francisco 10	197 67
Jno*	Sacramento Ward 3	63 435
John	Mariposa Twp 1	60 665
John	San Francisco San Francisco 1	68 861
John	San Joaquin Stockton	641019
John	Sierra Gibsonville	66 852
John	Sierra Twp 7	66 863
John	Siskiyou Callahan	69 15
John	Yuba Linda	72 986
John C	El Dorado Placerville	58 896
Mabia	Contra Costa Twp 2	57 549
Marthias	Sacramento Ward 4	63 500
Martin	San Francisco San Francisco 11	141 67
Mary	Plumas Quincy	62 973
Michael	Humbolt Eureka	59 168
Michael	Solano Benecia	69 298
Michl	Sacramento Georgian	63 342

Name	County Locale	M653 RollPage
MADDEN		
Osborn	Plumas Quincy	62 924
P B	Placer Auburn	62 592
Patk	San Francisco San Francisco 10	340 67
Patrick	San Joaquin Stockton	641020
Peter	San Francisco San Francisco 11	128 67
Phillip	Butte Kimshaw	56 592
Richard	El Dorado Georgetown	58 749
Susan	Placer Rattle Snake	62 625
T	Nevada Grass Valley	61 162
Theresa	San Francisco San Francisco 1	68 812
Thomas	Sierra Twp 7	66 890
Thos	Calaveras Twp 9	57 380
Thos	Sierra Downieville	66 967
Thos P	San Francisco San Francisco 6	67 447
W	Sacramento Granite	63 221
Wash	Placer Dutch Fl	62 731
Washington	Placer Dutch Fl	62 709
MADDER		
E	El Dorado Diamond	58 764
Frank*	Placer Iona Hills	62 864
Samuel	El Dorado Placerville	58 919
Sarah	Alameda Brooklyn	55 211
MADDIGAN		
John	Santa Clara Santa Clara	65 475
MADDIN		
L	Calaveras Twp 9	57 369
Thomas	Shasta French G	66 715
MADDING		
M	Tuolumne Twp 4	71 151
MADDISEN		
John*	Shasta Shasta	66 657
MADDISON		
George	Placer Michigan	62 825
John	Shasta Shasta	66 657
Robert	Santa Cruz Soguel	66 579
MADDOCK		
H	San Joaquin Stockton	641090
Saml	Santa Clara San Jose	65 360
MADDOCKS		
Caleb	Yuba Rose Bar	72 797
E	Yuba Rose Bar	72 797
MADDON		
Antoine	Yuba Fosters	72 835
John	Siskiyou Callahan	69 9
R A	El Dorado Georgetown	58 693
S	Nevada Eureka	61 369
MADDONA		
Phil	Sonoma Petaluma	69 569
MADDOX		
David	Butte Bidwell	56 732
Ezra	Santa Clara Santa Clara	65 521
Frank*	Placer Iona Hills	62 864
H S	Butte Oro	56 680
Henry	Amador Twp 1	55 486
J P	Sonoma Santa Rosa	69 427
James F	El Dorado Eldorado	58 943
Jhn T	Yuba Bear Rvr	721005
John	Yuba Marysville	72 897
John T	Yuba Bear Rvr	721005
L D	Sonoma Santa Rosa	69 423
Phineas	Sonoma Russian	69 439
S	Yolo Putah	72 587
Sarah Ann	Sonoma Healdsbu	69 475
Wesley	Yolo Cache Crk	72 622
Winthrop	Sonoma Armally	69 500
Wm	Sonoma Russian	69 435
MADDRILL		
J	Nevada Grass Valley	61 160
MADDSON		
F L	El Dorado Georgetown	58 689
John	Santa Cruz Soguel	66 589
MADDUX		
David	Sacramento Ward 1	63 138
James	Sacramento Ward 1	63 138
Jos	Sacramento Ward 1	63 40
MADDY		
Frank	Placer Iona Hills	62 864
MADEJAN		
G	Santa Clara Fremont	65 436
MADELANA		
---	San Diego Agua Caliente	64 863
Maria	Monterey Pajaro	601017
MADELAOSO		
Antonio	Los Angeles Los Angeles	59 512
MADELAS		
R	Merced Twp 1	60 909
MADELINA		
---	San Bernardino San Bernadino	64 680
---	San Bernardino S Timate	64 692
---	San Bernardino S Timate	64 715
MADELINE		
---*	Mendocino Big Rock	60 876
Andrew	Marin S Antoni	60 710

California 1860 Census Index

Name	County Locale	M653 Roll	Page
MADELL			
N	Tuolumne Twp 4	71	155
MADELMI			
---*	Mendocino Big Rock	60	876
MADEN			
J	Sutter Yuba	70	760
Thomas B	Sierra Pine Grove	66	830
Thomas*	Napa Hot Springs	61	23
MADENA			
Geo*	Amador Twp 3	55	369
MADENE			
Jared S*	Calaveras Twp 5	57	187
MADENGER			
Fred	Trinity Weaverville	70	1069
MADENIS			
Antonio	Calaveras Twp 7	57	24
MADENO			
Igmatia	Calaveras Twp 7	57	27
Ignatius	Calaveras Twp 7	57	27
MADENS			
Andrew*	Mariposa Coulterville	60	698
MADEO			
---	Sacramento Granite	63	269
MADER			
Alex	San Francisco San Francisco 1	68	818
Charles*	Placer Forest H	62	803
Decatur	San Francisco San Francisco 9	68	953
H	Nevada Grass Valley	61	212
H	San Francisco San Francisco 5	67	513
Saml B	San Francisco San Francisco 9	68	1044
MADERIA			
Geo*	Amador Twp 3	55	269
MADERIAGO			
Francisco	Monterey Alisal	60	1040
MADERO			
Antonio	Los Angeles Los Angeles	59	306
MADERSO			
Caystane	San Luis Obispo San Luis Obispo	65	4
MADERSON			
Charles	Calaveras Twp 5	57	139
MADFIELD			
George P	Yuba Fosters	72	831
MADGDEN			
N	Yolo Washington	72	565
MADGE			
---	Sacramento Cosumnes	63	408
Fred	Placer Dutch Fl	62	725
Wm	Sacramento Georgian	63	340
MADGHN			
James S*	El Dorado Georgetown	58	691
MADGLIN			
James S*	El Dorado Georgetown	58	691
MADHY			
E A	Yolo Cottonwoood	72	648
MADICK			
Jonathan	El Dorado Mountain	58	1183
MADID			
John*	Calaveras Twp 5	57	207
MADIER			
Thomas*	Napa Hot Springs	61	23
MADIGAN			
Mary	Los Angeles Los Angeles	59	374
Robert	Santa Cruz Pescadero	66	651
Thomas	Santa Clara Fremont	65	436
Wm	Alameda Brooklyn	55	199
MADILAS			
R	Merced Twp 1	60	909
MADILL			
John	San Francisco San Francisco 2	67	626
Nelson	Tuolumne Twp 4	71	178
MADILON			
George	Tuolumne Twp 2	71	404
MADIN			
John Marie*	San Mateo Twp 1	65	47
Luther B	Alameda Brooklyn	55	175
Shoka	San Francisco San Francisco 4	68	1224
Thomas	Napa Hot Springs	61	23
MADINA			
Fourtin*	Calaveras Twp 6	57	138
Foustin	Calaveras Twp 6	57	138
Huntam*	Alameda Brooklyn	55	152
Theodore	Contra Costa Twp 1	57	494
MADINAS			
Fondin*	Calaveras Twp 5	57	138
Fourtin*	Calaveras Twp 5	57	138
MADIRA			
Emanuel	Los Angeles Azuza	59	273
MADIRD			
John Maria*	San Mateo Twp 1	65	47
MADIS			
James	San Francisco San Francisco 11	67	131
MADISEN			
James	Amador Twp 2	55	309
MADISON			
C	Sutter Butte	70	785

Name	County Locale	M653 Roll	Page
MADISON			
Charles	Contra Costa Twp 1	57	486
F	Sutter Vernon	70	846
Francis	Contra Costa Twp 2	57	575
G W	Tehama Red Bluff	70	913
George	Tuolumne Shawsfla	71	404
Gust???*	Tuolumne Sonora	71	215
Gustavus	Tuolumne Twp 1	71	215
H	El Dorado Coloma	58	1080
Henry	Nevada Bridgeport	61	502
Hiram	Nevada Bridgeport	61	475
James	San Francisco San Francisco 9	68	1098
James	Solano Fremont	69	386
James	Yuba Bear Rvr	72	997
Jas	San Francisco San Francisco 9	68	1064
John	Plumas Meadow Valley	62	906
John	San Francisco San Francisco 8	68	1309
John	San Francisco San Francisco 1	68	910
John Maria	San Mateo Twp 1	65	47
John*	Calaveras Twp 5	57	207
Joseph	Plumas Quincy	62	1002
Joseph	Plumas Quincy	62	955
Joshua	San Francisco San Francisco 8	68	1283
Maratt*	Nevada Red Dog	61	538
Meriett*	Nevada Red Dog	61	538
Oliver	Siskiyou Scott Ri	69	77
P	Yolo Washington	72	600
Robert	Yuba Marysville	72	868
Samuel	El Dorado Greenwood	58	724
Samuel	San Joaquin Elkhorn	64	972
MADISTA			
---	Los Angeles Los Angeles	59	515
MADLED			
John	Tuolumne Montezuma	71	504
Joseph	Tuolumne Twp 5	71	504
MADLEIGH			
W E	Butte Eureka	56	655
MADLEY			
B S	Yolo Putah	72	598
S	Sutter Bear Rvr	70	820
MADLIN			
John	Butte Ophir	56	762
MADLIR			
Steven	Sonoma Petaluma	69	595
MADNIA			
Hautane*	Alameda Brooklyn	55	152
MADON			
Antonio	Alameda Washington	55	173
MADONA			
Jean	Calaveras Twp 7	57	3
Joseph	Calaveras Twp 7	57	46
MADOR			
Thas	Napa Clear Lake	61	123
MADOW			
---	Nevada Nevada	61	301
Oliver	Placer Auburn	62	595
MADOX			
Harry	Nevada Bridgeport	61	444
John	El Dorado Mud Springs	58	993
MADRAND			
Jose	San Luis Obispo San Luis Obispo	65	4
MADREDO			
Falisanio*	Mariposa Twp 1	60	646
MADREDS			
Faliseaver*	Mariposa Twp 1	60	646
MADREGATES			
Luz*	San Francisco San Francisco 3	67	6
MADREGATIS			
Luz*	San Francisco San Francisco 3	67	6
MADRID			
Casimiro	Los Angeles Santa Ana	59	442
Dadorn	Mariposa Twp 1	60	647
Dolores	Los Angeles San Juan	59	466
Dudern	Mariposa Twp 1	60	647
Dudorn	Mariposa Twp 1	60	647
MADRIDE			
Falisane*	Mariposa Twp 1	60	646
MADRIDO			
Fahseimer*	Mariposa Twp 1	60	646
Falisani	Mariposa Twp 1	60	646
MADRIDS			
Fahsane*	Mariposa Twp 1	60	646
Falisan*	Mariposa Twp 1	60	646
Falisiam*	Mariposa Twp 1	60	646
MADRIGAL			
Pacual	San Francisco San Francisco 2	67	581
MADRIGALIS			
Luz	San Francisco San Francisco 3	67	6
MADRIGUERS			
Marciana	San Francisco San Francisco 2	67	702
MADRIL			
Dolores	Los Angeles San Juan	59	466
Matres	Santa Clara Almaden	65	267
MADRILE			
F	Merced Twp 1	60	900
L	Merced Twp 1	60	900

Name	County Locale	M653 Roll	Page
MADRILLE			
C	Merced Twp 1	60	905
S	Merced Twp 1	60	909
MADRION			
James	Sierra Chappare	66	1040
MADRO			
---	Sacramento Granite	63	269
MADRULLA			
Jose	Los Angeles Los Angeles	59	379
MADSLIN			
James S*	El Dorado Georgetown	58	691
MADUINS			
Anthony*	Calaveras Twp 6	57	161
MADUNA			
Juan	Del Norte Crescent	58	629
MADURN			
D	Sonoma Washington	69	674
F	Sonoma Washington	69	674
MAE			
---	Sierra Twp 7	66	876
---*	Nevada Rough &	61	399
Myron*	Sacramento Alabama	63	415
W*	Alameda Brooklyn	55	186
MAEA GAGROW			
Jose*	Mariposa Twp 1	60	625
MAECH			
Fras	San Francisco San Francisco 10	67	348
MAELLON			
Aug	San Francisco San Francisco 2	67	781
MAELSHI			
Samuel G	El Dorado Georgetown	58	691
MAER			
B F	Nevada Rough &	61	414
MAERAE			
C L	Trinity China Bar	70	959
MAES			
A	Santa Clara San Jose	65	335
Pedro F	Los Angeles Los Angeles	59	343
MAESFIELD			
Geo	El Dorado Placerville	58	837
MAESON			
Thomas B	El Dorado Greenwood	58	723
MAESONA			
Loveyis	Calaveras Twp 5	57	217
MAESTRI			
P D*	San Francisco San Francisco 10	67	308
P De*	San Francisco San Francisco 10	67	308
MAESTRON			
Alex	Sierra La Porte	66	772
MAEUR			
Henry	San Francisco San Francisco 10	67	323
MAEY			
Chas F	San Francisco San Francisco 3	67	72
MAFF			
C	Siskiyou Scott Ri	69	63
MAFFAT			
N	San Francisco San Francisco 3	67	74
MAFFATO			
Jane	San Francisco San Francisco 7	68	1337
MAFFER			
Higt	Santa Clara San Jose	65	299
MAFFET			
John	Santa Clara Santa Clara	65	507
MAFFETT			
Louis	Placer Michigan	62	828
MAFFORD			
Henry	Sonoma Santa Rosa	69	417
MAFLAS			
Rogoe	Santa Clara Gilroy	65	246
MAFOR			
L	Nevada Grass Valley	61	148
Vicente Soto	San Francisco San Francisco 1	68	814
MAFSETT			
M	Butte Bidwell	56	707
MAFSINGILL			
Philena	Sonoma Russian	69	430
MAG			
---	El Dorado Eldorado	58	946
---	Sacramento Cosumnes	63	406
Eugene*	El Dorado Georgetown	58	748
Jim	Butte Bidwell	56	717
MAGAFNY			
M	San Joaquin Stockton	64	1024
MAGAIO			
Batista	Trinity Indian C	70	988
MAGAIRE			
Bridges	San Francisco San Francisco 10	67	181
MAGAMEY			
Daniel*	Yuba Rose Bar	72	805
MAGAN			
Jane*	Nevada Grass Valley	61	194

Name	County Locale	M653 RollPage
MAGAN		
S	Nevada Grass Valley	61 168
Thomas R	San Francisco San Francisco 4	681219
MAGANITO		
---*	San Bernardino S Timate	64 736
MAGANNY		
Daniel	Yuba Rose Bar	72 805
MAGANTA		
---	Fresno Twp 1	59 117
MAGAR		
J	El Dorado Kelsey	581153
MAGARATO		
---	Marin San Rafael	60 772
MAGARD		
J H*	Los Angeles Tejon	59 527
MAGARETTA		
---	San Joaquin Stockton	641099
MAGARITY		
J	San Francisco San Francisco 1	68 918
MAGARY		
Amanda	San Francisco San Francisco 8	681300
Celias	Amador Twp 6	55 446
Chas	Amador Twp 6	55 446
MAGASCO		
---	Del Norte Klamath	58 656
MAGBURY		
John	Butte Cascade	56 698
MAGBY		
Robert*	Trinity Big Flat	701039
MAGDELEAW		
M	Tehama Red Bluff	70 921
MAGE		
B	Sutter Butte	70 789
L	Sutter Butte	70 789
MAGEAN		
Edward	San Francisco San Francisco 3	67 65
MAGEE		
Ann	San Diego Colorado	64 807
Colwill*	Amador Twp 3	55 369
Con	San Francisco San Francisco 11	124
		67
David W	Butte Oregon	56 626
H	Solano Vacaville	69 331
Henry	San Diego Temecula	64 792
James	Sacramento Ward 4	63 496
Jas	Napa Hot Springs	61 2
John	San Diego Temecula	64 792
John	Yuba Rose Bar	72 818
John*	Nevada Red Dog	61 537
Sylvester D	Yuba Marysville	72 863
Thomas	Shasta Horsetown	66 691
W H	San Francisco San Francisco 9	681097
William	Shasta Shasta	66 657
MAGEL		
---	El Dorado Placerville	58 821
MAGELLAN		
T	Yolo Slate Ra	72 692
T	Yuba Slate Ro	72 692
MAGELLENAS		
Eseqerio*	Marin Cortemad	60 791
Esequis	Marin Cortemad	60 791
MAGENIS		
Jno	Klamath Trinidad	59 223
MAGENITIC		
L*	Nevada Grass Valley	61 144
MAGENITIE		
L*	Nevada Grass Valley	61 144
MAGENNIS		
Jno	Klamath Klamath	59 228
MAGER		
James	Shasta Shasta	66 732
Jno*	San Francisco San Francisco 9	681070
John	Nevada Little Y	61 537
Simon	Stanislaus Branch	70 708
MAGERD		
J H*	Los Angeles Tejon	59 527
MAGEROSKE		
Charles	Marin Cortemad	60 792
MAGERS		
A A	Sierra Downieville	66 978
James	Shasta Shasta	66 732
W	Sierra Twp 7	66 905
MAGETTA		
Petrus	San Francisco San Francisco 11	156
		67
MAGFIELD		
Wayne	El Dorado Georgetown	58 691
MAGFIELS		
Robert	El Dorado Greenwood	58 710
MAGFOL		
John	San Francisco San Francisco 3	67 85
MAGGIE		
---	Trinity McGillev	701021
William	Amador Twp 4	55 245
MAGGLE		
Peter	El Dorado Placerville	58 919

Name	County Locale	M653 RollPage
MAGGNOOTTE		
Peter	San Francisco San Francisco 2	67 707
MAGGOT		
Chas	El Dorado Georgetown	58 678
MAGGOTT		
Jarvis	Sonoma Sonoma	69 637
MAGHAR		
M H*	Sacramento Ward 3	63 481
MAGHARD		
Daniel	Amador Twp 1	55 509
MAGHEN		
H H	Marin Tomales	60 721
O G*	Sonoma Petaluma	69 580
MAGHER		
James	San Francisco San Francisco 6	67 427
John	Tuolumne Columbia	71 364
Mary	San Francisco San Francisco 5	67 486
MAGHEW		
O G*	Sonoma Petaluma	69 580
MAGHIN		
John	Tuolumne Twp 2	71 364
MAGIA		
Hosea*	Mariposa Twp 3	60 574
MAGIL		
---	Los Angeles Los Angeles	59 497
MAGILL		
---	San Mateo Twp 2	65 116
Barn T	Tuolumne Sonora	71 233
Barnet*	Tuolumne Twp 1	71 233
Gracio	Tuolumne Twp 1	71 233
Michael	Yuba New York	72 740
Peter	San Mateo Twp 3	65 84
William	Tuolumne Twp 1	71 210
MAGIN		
Mary	Yolo Fremont	72 605
MAGINHUIMAN		
Ludwig	Santa Clara San Jose	65 295
MAGINITER		
L	Nevada Grass Valley	61 144
MAGINLY		
Patrick*	Yuba Long Bar	72 773
MAGINN		
Patk J	San Francisco San Francisco 10	289
		67
MAGINNIS		
Alice	San Francisco San Francisco 10	181
		67
Alice Miss	San Francisco San Francisco 10	181
	San Francisco	67
Alice Sister*	San Francisco San Francisco 10	181
	San Francisco	67
Anne	San Francisco San Francisco 10	182
		67
Bridget	San Francisco San Francisco 10	166
		67
Christopher	San Francisco San Francisco 10	166
	San Francisco	67
Hugh	Yolo Slate Ra	72 691
John	San Francisco San Francisco 10	166
		67
Mary	San Francisco San Francisco 10	184
		67
P*	San Francisco San Francisco 7	681437
Sister Alice*	San Francisco San Francisco 10	181
	San Francisco	67
MAGINTY		
A	Tuolumne Twp 3	71 423
Patrick	Yuba Long Bar	72 773
William	Yuba Parks Ba	72 774
Wlliam	Yuba Parks Ba	72 774
MAGLER		
Abram	San Francisco San Francisco 2	67 598
Peter	Placer Virginia	62 668
MAGLEY		
L	Nevada Grass Valley	61 157
MAGLIAVACA		
Jack	Mariposa Twp 1	60 630
MAGLIN		
Hannah	Shasta French G	66 715
MAGMRI		
Pat*	Nevada Bloomfield	61 527
MAGNANAT		
George	Siskiyou Callahan	69 5
MAGNARD		
Chas	Santa Clara Redwood	65 451
MAGNEER		
Francis*	San Francisco San Francisco 11	126
		67
MAGNER		
Dennis	San Francisco San Francisco 2	67 565
John*	San Francisco San Francisco 3	67 83
M	Mariposa Twp 1	60 623
Thos	San Francisco San Francisco 2	67 600
MAGNERS		
R F*	San Francisco San Francisco 4	681111
MAGNES		
A	San Francisco San Francisco 10	165
		67

Name	County Locale	M653 RollPage
MAGNES		
Frank	Butte Ophir	56 784
Robert*	Santa Clara San Jose	65 306
MAGNESS		
Walte	Sierra Twp 7	66 899
Walter	Sierra Twp 7	66 899
MAGNIDER		
Wm	San Francisco San Francisco 3	67 66
MAGNIS		
Elizabeth	Napa Hot Springs	61 13
T H	Napa Hot Springs	61 12
MAGNON		
Jno	Butte Oregon	56 636
MAGNORS		
R F*	San Francisco San Francisco 4	681111
MAGNUS		
Elizabeth	San Francisco San Francisco 10	186
		67
Jacob	Napa Yount	61 54
Robert*	Santa Clara San Jose	65 306
MAGO		
Joseph F	Mariposa Coulterville	60 697
MAGOEW		
Pat*	Nevada Red Dog	61 539
MAGOFFIN		
John	Amador Twp 6	55 426
MAGOM		
H K	Mariposa Twp 3	60 621
MAGOME		
B*	Sutter Butte	70 783
MAGOMEZ		
Jose	Marin Cortemad	60 783
MAGON		
W A*	Yuba Rose Bar	72 788
MAGONDA		
Dulesga*	Amador Twp 4	55 245
MAGONIGAL		
Jame	Yuba Rose Bar	72 804
Wm	Yuba Rose Bar	72 818
MAGOON		
H K	Mariposa Twp 3	60 621
Joseph	Humbolt Union	59 190
K H	Sonoma Armally	69 510
Lamule	Sonoma Armally	69 512
MAGOONE		
B*	Sutter Butte	70 783
MAGORD		
J H	Los Angeles Tejon	59 527
MAGORITY		
W	San Francisco San Francisco 6	67 422
MAGORK		
Patrick	San Francisco San Francisco 2	67 625
MAGORY		
H	San Joaquin Stockton	641089
MAGOUM		
James	Yuba Parks Ba	72 780
MAGOURN		
James	Yuba Parks Ba	72 780
John*	Yuba Rose Bar	72 804
MAGOVERN		
John*	Yuba Long Bar	72 748
John*	Yuba Rose Bar	72 804
MAGOWAN		
J	Yuba Long Bar	72 753
MAGOWON		
John*	Yuba Rose Bar	72 804
MAGPITE		
Wegni*	El Dorado Georgetown	58 691
MAGRADY		
J	San Francisco San Francisco 5	67 548
MAGRAFF		
D	Sutter Nicolaus	70 841
MAGRAN		
M*	Yolo Putah	72 545
MAGRATH		
Barth	Alameda Oakland	55 53
James	San Francisco San Francisco 5	67 513
John	San Francisco San Francisco 2	67 787
Margt E	San Francisco San Francisco 2	67 788
Michel	Amador Twp 2	55 319
Morris	San Francisco San Francisco 11	131
		67
Patrick	Sierra La Porte	66 765
Patrick K	Sierra La Porte	66 765
MAGRAW		
M	Yolo Putah	72 545
Pat*	Nevada Red Dog	61 539
Thos	Los Angeles Tejon	59 540
MAGREW		
Pat*	Nevada Red Dog	61 539
MAGRINE		
Andrew*	Calaveras Twp 8	57 101
MAGRUDER		
Danl	San Francisco San Francisco 1	68 834
Lloyd	Yuba Marysville	72 845
Theo	Del Norte Crescent	58 636

Name	County Locale	M653 RollPage
MAGRUDER		
Wm	San Francisco San Francisco	3 67 66
MAGS		
Spencer	Santa Clara Gilroy	65 225
MAGSAFINISH		
Antone	San Bernardino San Bernadino	64 670
MAGSDALE		
Jesse	Mariposa Twp 1	60 636
MAGTILL		
J*	Nevada Grass Valley	61 150
MAGTISS		
J*	Nevada Grass Valley	61 150
MAGTY		
Robert*	Trinity Big Flat	701039
MAGUE		
Leon*	Calaveras Twp 6	57 157
MAGUEDER		
Lloyd	Yuba Marysville	72 845
MAGUEER		
Francis*	San Francisco San Francisco	11 126 67
MAGUER		
M	Mariposa Twp 1	60 623
Thos*	San Francisco San Francisco	2 67 600
MAGUIGGAN		
John*	Yuba Rose Par	72 794
MAGUIL		
---	Mariposa Twp 1	60 630
---	Napa Napa	61 111
---	Napa Napa	61 78
---	Tulara Twp 3	71 44
---	Tulara Twp 3	71 47
---	Tulara Keyesville	71 63
---*	Tulara Keeneysburg	71 44
---*	Tulara Keeneysburg	71 47
Pablo	Tulara Twp 3	71 60
MAGUINA		
---	San Bernardino San Bernadino	64 678
MAGUIRE		
Ann	San Francisco San Francisco	10 166 67
Ann	San Francisco San Francisco	12 388 67
Antone	Sonoma Sonoma	69 645
Bridget	San Francisco San Francisco	10 181 67
Dennis	San Francisco San Francisco	11 91 67
Ellen	San Francisco San Francisco	12 379 67
Francis	San Bernardino Santa Barbara	64 148
Frank	Nevada Little Y	61 531
Geo	Siskiyou Scott Ri	69 64
H	Nevada Grass Valley	61 148
Jno	Sonoma Sonoma	69 645
John	Yuba Rose Par	72 797
Joseph*	Calaveras Twp 5	57 205
Kate A	San Francisco San Francisco	10 346 67
Katie	Sacramento Ward 1	63 128
M	Nevada Nevada	61 315
M	Siskiyou Callahan	69 6
Margaret	San Francisco San Francisco	10 344 67
Matt	Yuba Fosters	72 832
Pat	Nevada Bloomfield	61 527
Philip	Yuba Marysville	72 852
Philip	Yuba Marysville	72 857
Stephen	San Francisco San Francisco	6 67 433
Thomas	San Francisco San Francisco	3 67 9
Thos	Nevada Bridgeport	61 474
Thos	San Francisco San Francisco	9 681020
Thos	Tuolumne Big Oak	71 137
W D	Trinity East For	701025
MAGUIRI		
Andrew	Calaveras Twp 8	57 51
MAGUIRN		
Danl*	Amador Twp 6	55 438
MAGUIRSE		
Danl	Amador Twp 6	55 438
MAGUISE		
Geo	Sacramento Ward 4	63 512
Matt	Yuba Foster B	72 832
Thomas	San Francisco San Francisco	3 67 9
MAGUMGLIN		
Eli	Colusa Monroeville	57 452
MAGUNE		
Andrew*	Calaveras Twp 8	57 101
Jno	Nevada Nevada	61 282
MAGUNN		
Danl*	Amador Twp 6	55 438
MAGURDER		
Wm*	San Francisco San Francisco	3 67 66
MAGUS		
A A*	Sierra Downieville	66 978
MAGYER		
Jas*	Napa Napa	61 103

Name	County Locale	M653 RollPage
MAGZER		
Jas	Napa Napa	61 103
MAH TANG		
---	Nevada Nevada	61 301
MAH		
---	Amador Twp 6	55 447
---	Calaveras Twp 4	57 303
---	Del Norte Crescent	58 651
---	Placer Iona Hills	62 893
---	Plumas Meadow Valley	62 910
---	Plumas Quincy	62 950
Cun	Sacramento Ward 1	63 56
Cun	Siskiyou Yreka	69 195
Qung	Siskiyou Yreka	69 195
Tang	Nevada Nevada	61 301
MAHADY		
John	Calaveras Twp 5	57 198
MAHAM		
C	El Dorado Placerville	58 883
MAHAN		
---	El Dorado Georgetown	58 749
---	Mendocino Calpella	60 822
David P	Contra Costa Twp 3	57 597
Dennis	San Joaquin Stockton	641051
Edward	Tuolumne Jamestown	71 426
Eliza	Sacramento Ward 3	63 454
J	Sutter Sutter	70 812
J B	El Dorado Greenwood	58 712
James	Sonoma Cloverdale	69 680
Jas	Calaveras Twp 9	57 383
John	Sacramento Franklin	63 325
John	Shasta Shasta	66 732
John	Sonoma Mendocino	69 458
John*	Yuba Rose Bar	72 807
Martin	San Francisco San Francisco	10 284 67
Martin	Sierra St Louis	66 805
Mary	San Francisco San Francisco	10 270 67
Michael	Calaveras Twp 8	57 69
Owen	Sierra Poker Flats	66 838
Peter	Placer Michigan	62 814
Priscilla	El Dorado Georgetown	58 749
Rebecca E	Sonoma Mendocino	69 458
Thos	Sacramento San Joaquin	63 360
Timothy	Yuba Marysville	72 954
V	Sonoma Cloverdale	69 680
Wm	San Francisco San Francisco	10 167 67
MAHANY		
---	Mendocino Calpella	60 822
Cath*	Sacramento Ward 4	63 568
Pat	Sacramento Ward 4	63 606
MAHAR		
Jas	Calaveras Twp 9	57 383
John	Yuba Rose Bar	72 807
M	San Francisco San Francisco	5 67 529
Michael	Sierra Gibsonville	66 858
Thos	San Francisco San Francisco	9 681090
Wm	San Francisco San Francisco	10 285 67
MAHAS		
M	San Francisco San Francisco	5 67 529
MAHAW		
---	Mendocino Calpella	60 822
MAHAYE		
---	San Diego Agua Caliente	64 815
MAHAYLA		
---	Mendocino Big Rock	60 875
MAHBE		
Frederick*	Yuba Long Bar	72 742
MAHDEL		
Henry	San Francisco San Francisco	7 681422
MAHDUNALDO		
Manuel	Calaveras Twp 5	57 170
MAHE		
Gustav*	San Francisco San Francisco	10 327 67
MAHEFFERY		
John*	Amador Twp 2	55 301
MAHEFFONY		
John*	Amador Twp 2	55 301
MAHEFFORY		
John*	Amador Twp 2	55 301
MAHEN		
Francis	Plumas Meadow Valley	62 931
James	El Dorado Georgetown	58 705
N	Shasta Shasta	66 661
P S	Sierra Twp 7	66 891
Peter	Tuolumne Sonora	71 202
Summers	Tuolumne Twp 2	71 279
Summery	Tuolumne Twp 2	71 279
Timothy	Plumas Quincy	62 990
William D*	Solano Vacaville	69 339
MAHER		

Name	County Locale	M653 RollPage
MAHER		
Alice	San Francisco San Francisco	10 310 67
Anastacia	San Francisco San Francisco	2 67 663
Ann	San Francisco San Francisco	10 304 67
Dennis	Nevada Bridgeport	61 440
Dennis*	Shasta Horsetown	66 691
E	Trinity Big Flat	701039
Edward	San Francisco San Francisco	12 387
Henry	San Francisco San Francisco	2 67 801
James	San Joaquin Elkhorn	64 971
Jas	Calaveras Twp 9	57 356
Jas	San Francisco San Francisco	10 239 67
Jas*	San Francisco San Francisco	1 68 818
Jesus	Alameda Brooklyn	55 190
John	San Francisco San Francisco	2 67 650
John	Siskiyou Scott Va	69 50
John	Solano Suisan	69 231
Jos	San Francisco San Francisco	10 239 67
Julia	San Francisco San Francisco	10 239 67
Lawrance	Alameda Brooklyn	55 210
M	Shasta Shasta	66 687
Mary	San Francisco San Francisco	11 128 67
N	Shasta Shasta	66 661
Patrick	San Francisco San Francisco	2 67 610
Peter	Placer Rattle Snake	62 600
Thomas	Santa Cruz Watsonville	66 535
MAHERIE		
John	Sacramento Ward 1	63 57
MAHERS		
Antonia	Mariposa Twp 1	60 660
MAHEUSE		
Edward	Tuolumne Twp 3	71 426
MAHEW		
William D	Solano Vacaville	69 339
MAHIA		
Jesus	San Joaquin Castoria	64 900
Oreole	San Joaquin Castoria	64 900
MAHIN		
Michael	El Dorado Greenwood	58 729
Virginia M	San Luis Obispo San Luis Obispo	65 23
MAHINEY		
D	Nevada Eureka	61 352
P*	Nevada Eureka	61 348
MAHINNIS		
Alice Miss	San Francisco	10 181 67
MAHITT		
Chas	San Francisco San Francisco	9 681071
MAHL		
Gustav*	San Francisco San Francisco	10 327 67
MAHLAN		
P	Nevada Eureka	61 374
MAHLAND		
Wm	San Francisco San Francisco	10 215 67
MAHLE		
Frederick*	Yuba Long Bar	72 742
MAHLEE		
---	Tuolumne Montezuma	71 504
MAHLEISON		
Mike	Tuolumne Sonora	71 197
MAHLER		
Henry	El Dorado Coloma	581074
Henry	San Francisco San Francisco	7 681385
Henry*	El Dorado Coloma	581074
Phil	Sonoma Sonoma	69 651
W	El Dorado Newtown	58 778
MAHLEY		
Irom*	Stanislaus Emory	70 746
MAHLKE		
A L	San Francisco San Francisco	3 67 15
MAHLMAN		
Doretti	San Francisco San Francisco	10 322 67
MAHLON		
P*	Nevada Eureka	61 374
MAHMAH		
---	Mendocino Twp 1	60 889
MAHME		
K	San Francisco San Francisco	12 395 67
MAHN		
Arnold	Tuolumne Twp 2	71 373
Marry	Sacramento Ward 1	63 97
MAHO		
A K P*	Placer Folsom	62 639
MAHOKA		
Edward*	El Dorado Kelsey	581133

California 1860 Census Index

Name	County Locale	M653 RollPage
MAHOKE		
Edward*	El Dorado Kelsey	581133
MAHON		
Ann	San Francisco San Francisco 2	67 750
Edward	Marin Cortemad	60 792
Frank	San Francisco San Francisco 1	68 913
G T	Sierra Twp 7	66 886
J	San Francisco San Francisco 6	67 467
James	Marin Bolinas	60 740
John	San Francisco San Francisco 2	67 742
John	Yuba Long Bar	72 755
John E	San Francisco San Francisco 2	67 742
John F	San Francisco San Francisco 9	681019
Mary	Sacramento Ward 1	63 97
Mich	Butte Hamilton	56 515
Michael	San Francisco San Francisco 2	67 558
Michael	Yuba Foster B	72 832
Micheal	San Francisco San Francisco 2	67 558
P M	Butte Kimshaw	56 590
P S	Sierra Twp 7	66 891
T	Marin San Rafael	60 761
T	San Francisco San Francisco 5	67 514
MAHONA		
John	El Dorado Kelsey	581146
MAHONE		
Frank	Tehama Red Bluff	70 927
Geo	El Dorado Kelsey	581155
Wm	Tehama Antelope	70 887
MAHONEY		
Conaley	Amador Twp 4	55 239
Conoley*	Amador Twp 4	55 239
Cornelius	Amador Twp 4	55 239
Cunaley	Amador Twp 4	55 239
D	Nevada Eureka	61 352
Daniel	Amador Twp 1	55 509
Daniel	San Francisco San Francisco 9	68 987
David	San Francisco San Francisco 12	369 67
Dennis	Sacramento Ward 1	63 18
Dennis	San Francisco San Francisco 7	681375
Dennis	San Francisco San Francisco 7	681388
Dennis	San Francisco San Francisco 12	370 67
Dennis	Santa Cruz Santa Cruz	66 640
Edward	San Francisco San Francisco 1	68 908
Edwd	San Francisco San Francisco 9	681044
Elizabeth	Contra Costa Twp 2	57 553
Frank	Mariposa Twp 1	60 644
Fred	Tuolumne Columbia	71 362
George	San Francisco San Francisco 4	681166
H	San Francisco San Francisco 5	67 493
H	San Francisco San Francisco 5	67 522
Hannah	Alameda Brooklyn	55 89
J F	Placer Iona Hills	62 894
J W	Butte Chico	56 559
James	Contra Costa Twp 2	57 553
James	Placer Iona Hills	62 888
James	San Francisco San Francisco 3	67 18
Jas	San Francisco San Francisco 1	68 857
Jeremiah	San Francisco San Francisco 1	68 840
Joama*	Sacramento Ward 1	63 22
Joanna	Sacramento Ward 1	63 22
John	Sacramento Ward 4	63 514
John	San Francisco San Francisco 9	681069
John	San Francisco San Francisco 9	681102
John	San Francisco San Francisco 12	375 67
John	San Francisco San Francisco 6	67 403
John	Sierra Pine Grove	66 830
John	Stanislaus Empire	70 735
Joseph	Placer Grizzly	62 755
Kane	Sierra Poverty	66 799
Lewis	Marin Cortemad	60 792
Lewis	Santa Clara Alviso	65 413
Margaret	San Francisco San Francisco 10	349 67
Margaret	San Francisco San Francisco 2	67 664
Margret	Santa Cruz Pajaro	66 531
Margt	San Francisco San Francisco 8	681234
Maria	San Joaquin Stockton	641081
Martin	Santa Cruz Pajaro	66 575
Michael	Klamath Liberty	59 230
Morris	Sacramento Sutter	63 297
P	Nevada Nevada	61 245
P	Nevada Eureka	61 348
Patt	Klamath Liberty	59 230
Rose	Yuba Marysville	72 853
Rose	Yuba Marysville	72 858
Sarah	San Francisco San Francisco 2	67 649
Thomas	Alameda Oakland	55 61
Thomas	Tulara Twp 1	71 92
Thomas	Tuolumne Visalia	71 92
Thos	Nevada Bridgeport	61 454
Tilenun	Placer Iona Hills	62 882
Tim	Sacramento Ward 4	63 522
Timothy	San Francisco San Francisco 7	681376

Name	County Locale	M653 RollPage
MAHONEY		
Timothy	San Francisco San Francisco 7	681424
Timothy	San Francisco San Francisco 3	67 76
William	San Francisco San Francisco 8	681300
Wm	San Francisco San Francisco 12	369 67
Wm	Trinity Indian C	70 989
MAHONING		
Tim	San Francisco San Francisco 11	119 67
MAHONY		
A B	Yolo No E Twp	72 669
C B*	Yolo No E Twp	72 669
Cath*	Sacramento Ward 4	63 568
D	Sutter Nicolaus	70 840
Daniel	Placer Virginia	62 660
Frank	Mariposa Twp 1	60 644
Honora	Mendocino Big Rvr	60 842
Jno	Sacramento Ward 4	63 555
John	Calaveras Twp 7	57 38
John	Del Norte Crescent	58 660
John	El Dorado Placerville	58 934
John	Placer Rattle Snake	62 625
Keen	Shasta French G	66 722
L	Shasta Shasta	66 759
Maria	Alameda Oakland	55 25
Michiel	Nevada Little Y	61 534
Morris	Sacramento Ward 4	63 602
P	Shasta Horsetown	66 688
Thomas	Mendocino Big Rvr	60 842
Thomas	Placer Virginia	62 660
Thos	Nevada Bridgeport	61 454
Timothy	Alameda Oakland	55 73
Tom	Sacramento Ward 1	63 79
William	Contra Costa Twp 3	57 587
MAHOON		
Phia	Santa Cruz Santa Cruz	66 628
Price	Santa Cruz Santa Cruz	66 626
Thos	San Mateo Twp 1	65 68
MAHOONEY		
Jhn	Calaveras Twp 9	57 402
John	Calaveras Twp 9	57 349
MAHORTER		
Hugh	Trinity Indian C	70 987
MAHOTA		
Irwin	El Dorado Kelsey	581132
MAHOY		
John*	Nevada Red Dog	61 543
MAHTER		
---	Nevada Eureka	61 347
MAHUE		
Aldin	Santa Clara San Jose	65 288
MAHUN		
Martin*	Sierra St Louis	66 805
Robert G*	Sierra La Porte	66 770
MAHURIN		
Thomas	Tulara Twp 1	71 76
MAI-KEE		
---*	Mariposa Twp 3	60 580
MAI		
---	Calaveras Twp 8	57 68
---	Calaveras Twp 8	57 82
---	Calaveras Twp 8	57 92
---	Calaveras Twp 8	57 93
Ah	Calaveras Twp 7	57 34
MAI?R		
Wm*	Sacramento Ward 1	63 82
MAIA		
Nicholas	Los Angeles Los Angeles	59 490
MAIAN		
Giacoma*	Mariposa Twp 3	60 594
MAIART		
John*	Tuolumne Twp 2	71 405
MAICHEL		
Sansurs*	San Francisco San Francisco 7	681396
MAIDAIRD		
Wm*	Mariposa Twp 1	60 665
MAIDEN		
Henry	San Francisco San Francisco 1	68 891
MAIDGES		
Wm	Butte Bidwell	56 716
MAIDULDO		
---*	Monterey San Juan	60 999
MAIE		
John*	Sierra Downieville	66 968
MAIENNE		
Mary*	San Francisco San Francisco 11	129 67
MAIER		
Wm	Sacramento Ward 1	63 82
MAIEUNE		
Mary*	San Francisco San Francisco 11	129 67
MAIFIELD		
John	Siskiyou Scott Ri	69 65
MAIFNINGS		
William	Sierra Whiskey	66 849

Name	County Locale	M653 RollPage
MAIFTIN		
James	Tuolumne Sonora	71 190
MAIGE		
Francois N	San Francisco 8	681281
	San Francisco	
MAIGHAUE		
J*	Nevada Eureka	61 372
MAIGIPO		
B*	Tehama Red Bluff	70 932
MAIHELSON		
Anne	San Francisco San Francisco 2	67 762
MAIHES		
J D*	Tuolumne Twp 2	71 278
MAIIES		
William	San Francisco San Francisco 7	681432
MAIJEN		
B*	San Francisco San Francisco 3	67 78
MAIJIN		
B	San Francisco San Francisco 3	67 78
MAIKIS		
Jose M*	Monterey San Juan	60 996
MAIKS		
Henerietta*	San Francisco 7	681412
	San Francisco	
MAIL		
J C	Nevada Nevada	61 259
L G	Mariposa Twp 3	60 605
L J	Mariposa Twp 3	60 605
MAILEN		
David	San Bernardino S Timate	64 687
MAILER		
G S	Amador Twp 4	55 251
William*	El Dorado White Oaks	581002
MAILIN		
E	Butte Wyandotte	56 667
MAILINY		
Alonzo	Monterey Monterey	60 966
MAILLARD		
P J	Tuolumne Twp 1	71 232
MAILLAY		
R	Nevada Grass Valley	61 223
MAILLET		
L R	Butte Chico	56 540
MAILS		
Isaac	San Francisco San Francisco 8	681298
MAIMAN		
P	Siskiyou Cottonwoood	69 106
MAIN BUAH		
	Placer Auburn	62 560
MAIN		
---	Colusa Monroeville	57 455
---	Yuba Long Bar	72 767
Buah*	Placer Auburn	62 560
Hannah W	San Francisco 11	89 67
	San Francisco	
James	San Francisco San Francisco 2	67 676
John L*	Humbolt Pacific	59 138
Jonathan	Placer Virginia	62 663
Noble	Nevada Eureka	61 375
Stephen P	Yuba New York	72 724
Thomas D	Tulara Twp 3	71 49
Thos	San Francisco San Francisco 2	67 690
W W	Sonoma Petaluma	69 584
MAINE		
---	Mendocino Twp 1	60 892
Adoph	Placer Dutch Fl	62 718
C*	Nevada Grass Valley	61 169
Charles	San Francisco San Francisco 6	67 445
David	Butte Eureka	56 654
Henry	Marin Point Re	60 732
Jno	Butte Hamilton	56 518
John	Alameda Brooklyn	55 141
John	Sierra Poker Flats	66 838
MAINER		
Charles	San Francisco San Francisco 4	681120
Jane	Marin San Rafael	60 760
MAINES		
J D	Tuolumne Twp 1	71 278
MAININS		
C*	El Dorado Kelsey	581129
MAINNINGS		
William	Sierra Whiskey	66 849
MAINNIS		
C*	El Dorado Kelsey	581129
MAINS		
J R*	Sacramento Ward 1	63 22
MAINY		
M W	El Dorado Georgetown	58 758
MAINZ		
Antonie	Los Angeles Los Angeles	59 358
MAIOBRY		
John*	Shasta Cottonwoood	66 736
MAIPLE		
J H*	Butte Ophir	56 753
MAIR		
B*	Nevada Nevada	61 324

Name	County Locale	M653 Roll	Page
MAIR			
Dice	Placer Auburn	62	573
John	Sierra Downieville	66	968
MAIRCES			
John*	San Francisco San Francisco 9	681	060
MAIRE			
Wellwood*	Napa Yount	61	46
MAIRON			
Yeneineis*	Contra Costa Twp 1	57	532
Yireineis*	Contra Costa Twp 1	57	532
MAIS			
Antomi	Calaveras Twp 8	57	105
Christian	Plumas Meadow Valley	62	933
MAISE			
E N	Yolo Cache	72	593
Wellwood	Napa Yount	61	46
MAISELEY			
Aswin	Colusa Butte Crk	57	465
MAISELLUS			
E	Nevada Nevada	61	266
MAISHAL			
Henry	Plumas Meadow Valley	62	932
MAISS			
Charles	Siskiyou Yreka	69	144
MAISTEN			
Francis*	Plumas Quincy	62	936
MAISTER			
Christopher	Calaveras Twp 8	57	77
John	San Francisco San Francisco 3	67	71
MAISTU			
Christopher*	Calaveras Twp 8	57	77
MAITIN			
Charles	Yuba Bear Rvr	721	013
MAITIRENA			
Josefa	San Francisco San Francisco 2	67	698
MAITREGEAN			
Z B	Tuolumne Sonora	71	216
MAITRIGEAN			
Z B	Tuolumne Twp 1	71	216
MAITRO			
C	Nevada Grass Valley	61	196
MAIXES			
John*	San Francisco San Francisco 9	681	060
MAJ			
N*	Sutter Yuba	70	772
MAJAR			
Henry	Calaveras Twp 5	57	203
MAJE			
Dedrick	Tuolumne Shawsfla	71	413
Jesus	San Joaquin Stockton	641	071
MAJEOQUE			
Narcessus*	Contra Costa Twp 1	57	496
MAJER			
Charles	San Francisco San Francisco 3	67	44
F	Calaveras Twp 9	57	396
William	Shasta Shasta	66	657
Wm	Santa Clara Fremont	65	424
MAJERINE			
C	Nevada Washington	61	332
MAJESINE			
C*	Nevada Washington	61	332
MAJETINE			
C*	Nevada Washington	61	332
MAJHER			
Coher	Santa Clara Almaden	65	267
MAJI			
Dedrick	Tuolumne Twp 2	71	413
MAJIA			
Franco	Marin Cortemad	60	782
MAJINN			
Patk J	San Francisco San Francisco 10	67	289
MAJINNIS			
Anna	San Francisco San Francisco 10	67	182
Mary*	San Francisco San Francisco 10	67	184
MAJINS			
Joseph	Santa Cruz Santa Cruz	66	625
MAJIOLA			
Loreta	Santa Clara Almaden	65	267
MAJMADA			
J B	San Joaquin Stockton	641	074
MAJOO			
S*	Nevada Grass Valley	61	148
MAJOR			
---	Mendocino Round Va	60	884
---	Tulara Twp 2	71	34
F	Shasta Millvill	66	756
Geo A	Butte Hamilton	56	515
J W	Tuolumne Sonora	71	481
Jas C	Butte Hamilton	56	515
John C	Calaveras Twp 9	57	348
Joseph	Calaveras Twp 9	57	357
L C	Butte Kimshaw	56	570
MAJOR			
S C	Tuolumne Sonora	71	480
S*	Nevada Grass Valley	61	148
Saml	Tuolumne Twp 1	71	266
Vicente Soto*	San Francisco 1	68	814
	San Francisco		
W A*	Yuba Rose Bar	72	788
MAJORA			
Levi	Santa Clara Redwood	65	453
MAJORES			
Joseph	Santa Cruz Santa Cruz	66	627
MAJORITY			
Robert	Plumas Quincy	62	973
MAJORS			
---	Amador Twp 3	55	405
Adams	Calaveras Twp 9	57	385
C	Trinity Weaverville	701	051
Chas	Calaveras Twp 9	57	379
Columbus	Tulara Visalia	71	88
Daniel F	Contra Costa Twp 3	57	585
E	Yolo Cottonwoood	72	555
Henry	Calaveras Twp 5	57	203
J G	Butte Oregon	56	627
James P	Tulara Visalia	71	111
Joseph	Santa Cruz Santa Cruz	66	625
William	Santa Cruz Santa Cruz	66	611
MAJOU			
A	Nevada Grass Valley	61	202
MAJRANDO			
Rafhael	Santa Cruz Pajaro	66	541
MAJSTINE			
C*	Nevada Washington	61	332
MAJULL			
J	El Dorado Placerville	58	840
MAK			
---	Mariposa Twp 3	60	618
---	San Francisco San Francisco 9	681	093
---	San Francisco San Francisco 9	681	094
Le	San Francisco San Francisco 9	681	094
MAKADO			
---	Fresno Twp 2	59	102
MAKATAP			
---	Fresno Twp 2	59	103
MAKAY			
Charles P	Alameda Oakland	55	29
MAKE			
---	Amador Twp 7	55	415
---	Yolo Slate Ra	72	715
Lee*	El Dorado Georgetown	58	700
MAKELEUM			
---	Tulara Twp 2	71	36
MAKELHAW			
John	Santa Clara Santa Clara	65	464
MAKELY			
Wm	Yuba Fosters	72	831
MAKEN			
C M	El Dorado Diamond	58	766
Franklin	Sierra Port Win	66	794
James	El Dorado Georgetown	58	705
Peter	Tuolumne Twp 1	71	202
MAKENSON			
James*	Napa Yount	61	31
MAKENZIE			
A	San Francisco San Francisco 4	681	172
Wm W	Alameda Oakland	55	30
MAKER			
A K P*	Placer Folsom	62	639
D	Tuolumne Twp 4	71	161
Dennis	Shasta Horsetown	66	691
George S	Marin Cortemad	60	788
Jas	San Francisco San Francisco 1	68	818
John	Del Norte Happy Ca	58	661
O*	Nevada Washington	61	334
Patrick	Trinity Whites Crk	701	028
Thomas*	Sierra Pine Grove	66	834
William Von*	Nevada Rough &	61	426
MAKES			
G	El Dorado Diamond	58	796
MAKI			
See*	El Dorado Georgetown	58	700
MAKIAS			
Wm	Calaveras Twp 9	57	360
MAKIERS			
Louis	Calaveras Twp 9	57	390
MAKIN			
Catharine	San Francisco San Francisco 11	67	98
George	Plumas Meadow Valley	62	900
Jas	San Francisco San Francisco 2	67	600
Jos	San Francisco San Francisco 2	67	600
Thomas	Sierra Poker Flats	66	839
MAKINS			
Jas*	Calaveras Twp 9	57	384
M N	Placer Iona Hills	62	878
Wm H	Placer Sacramento	62	645
MAKINSON			
James*	Napa Yount	61	31
MAKINSON			
Kjames*	Napa Yount	61	31
MAKINTZ			
---	Tulara Twp 1	71	113
MAKLE			
Frederick*	Yuba Long Bar	72	742
MAKLEN			
---*	Tulara Visalia	71	36
MAKLER			
Henry*	El Dorado Coloma	581	074
MAKLEW			
---	Tulara Twp 2	71	36
MAKONEY			
John	El Dorado Mud Springs	58	984
P M	Amador Twp 3	55	393
MAKUKO			
---	Fresno Twp 2	59	50
MAKURGIE			
A*	San Francisco San Francisco 4	681	172
MAKYER			
Mayer	El Dorado Georgetown	58	675
MAL DON			
Christian*	Yuba New York	72	721
MAL			
---	Tulara Twp 1	71	121
MALA			
---	Sacramento Cosumnes	63	408
MALACHI			
---	San Diego Agua Caliente	64	860
Francis	Yuba Fosters	72	839
MALACKY			
Wm	San Francisco San Francisco 10	67	167
MALAE			
Tyri	Tuolumne Twp 1	71	225
MALAGAN			
O	Nevada Nevada	61	287
MALAGIN			
Jno	Nevada Nevada	61	328
John	Nevada Nevada	61	328
MALAGUERO			
Carlo	El Dorado Kelsey	581	135
MALAHAN			
Daniel	Tuolumne Shawsfla	71	378
MALAIN			
J	Solano Vacaville	69	331
MALALESTA			
L	San Francisco San Francisco 2	67	657
MALALY			
James*	Yuba Bear Rvr	721	013
S M*	Nevada Grass Valley	61	163
MALAND			
J S	Tehama Red Bluff	70	911
P*	Nevada Eureka	61	391
MALANE			
James	Trinity New Rvr	701	031
MALANEY			
Patrick	Solano Benecia	69	284
Thos	San Francisco San Francisco 9	681	078
MALANPHY			
John	Shasta Horsetown	66	698
MALANPLEY			
John*	Shasta Horsetown	66	698
MALANY			
M	El Dorado Placerville	58	828
MALAPHER			
John*	Mariposa Coulterville	60	679
MALAPLATA			
---	Santa Cruz Santa Cruz	66	608
MALAR			
John	San Francisco San Francisco 8	681	249
MALARIN			
Mariano	Monterey Monterey	60	948
Marians	Monterey Monterey	60	948
MALARINO			
Josefa	Monterey Alisal	601	040
MALARKY			
Eduard*	Yuba Rose Bar	72	803
Edward*	Yuba Rose Bar	72	803
John	Shasta Shasta	66	731
William*	Nevada Red Dog	61	540
MALARTY			
John	Shasta Shasta	66	731
MALARY			
C*	Shasta Shasta	66	687
MALASIA			
Jacob	Calaveras Twp 8	57	87
MALATESTS			
D	Tuolumne Jacksonville	71	171
MALATISTO			
D	Tuolumne Twp 4	71	171
MALATOSTO			
S	Solano Montezuma	69	375
MALATOTO			
S	Solano Montezuma	69	375
MALATOWICH			
S	San Francisco San Francisco 5	67	493

Name	County Locale	M653 Roll	Page
MALATTE			
John	San Francisco San Francisco	5 67	477
MALAY			
B	Nevada Grass Valley	61	213
Charles	Yuba Marysville	72	918
Charless	Yuba Marysville	72	918
Jno	Mendocino Anderson	60	871
MALBY			
---	San Francisco San Francisco	8	681320
I	Calaveras Twp 9	57	407
J	Calaveras Twp 9	57	407
W	Nevada Eureka	61	356
MALCALTHEN			
---*	Mariposa Twp 1	60	630
MALCALTHERS			
---*	Mariposa Twp 1	60	630
MALCH			
Abby	San Francisco San Francisco	10 67	241
MALCHI			
Felix	El Dorado Placerville	58	878
MALCHNITALON			
J*	Sacramento Ward 1	63	125
MALCHY			
Michael	Sierra St Louis	66	864
MALCINO			
D T	Amador Twp 3	55	380
MALCOLF			
J	Nevada Eureka	61	372
MALCOLM			
Alexander	Placer Iona Hills	62	879
Hugh	Solano Suisan	69	226
James	Placer Iona Hills	62	890
Mary	Santa Clara San Jose	65	316
Robt	San Francisco San Francisco	1 68	891
Walter	Calaveras Twp 4	57	315
MALCOLT			
J*	Nevada Eureka	61	372
MALCOM			
T	Yolo No E Twp	72	667
MALCOMB			
David	Butte Oro	56	673
Joseph	Tulara Twp 2	71	16
Saml	Placer Dutch Fl	62	724
MALCUDORF			
Adolf	Yuba Marysville	72	909
MALCULIN			
Walter	Calaveras Twp 4	57	315
MALCUN			
P*	El Dorado Placerville	58	892
MALDANADO			
E M	Humbolt Union	59	181
Louis	Calaveras Twp 9	57	347
MALDEMER			
Francisco	Alameda Brooklyn	55	94
MALDENON			
Jas	San Bernardino San Bernadino	64	684
MALDES			
---	Tulara Keyesville	71	65
MALDESO			
---	Tulara Twp 3	71	69
MALDETES			
---	Tulara Keyesville	71	66
---	Tulara Keyesville	71	72
MALDINE			
Sant Anne	Alameda Brooklyn	55	172
Santa Anna	Alameda Washington	55	172
MALDIRE			
Antone	Sierra Whiskey	66	843
MALDIVES			
Madalena	San Diego Colorado	64	809
MALDNEGRO			
Pablo	Napa Napa	61	115
MALDOM			
Peter	Nevada Red Dog	61	551
W J	Nevada Bridgeport	61	465
MALDON			
Christian*	Yuba New York	72	721
MALDONA			
Gal	San Francisco San Francisco	2 67	791
MALDONADE			
Louis*	Calaveras Twp 9	57	347
MALDONADO			
Fidel	Plumas Quincy	62	995
Jose	Contra Costa Twp 1	57	514
Louis	Calaveras Twp 9	57	347
Maria Y	Los Angeles Los Angeles	59	294
MALDOON			
Peter	Tuolumne Twp 2	71	308
MALDUMURK			
---	Fresno Twp 2	59	67
MALE			
John	Tuolumne Twp 1	71	277
John	Tuolumne Twp 2	71	388
MALEA			
Michael	Klamath Liberty	59	242

Name	County Locale	M653 Roll	Page
MALECK			
G H	San Francisco San Francisco	5 67	498
MALEDEW			
John	Sierra Downieville	66	972
MALEDON			
John	Sierra Downieville	66	972
MALEECHEY			
Michael	Calaveras Twp 5	57	229
MALEICHRY			
Michael*	Calaveras Twp 5	57	229
MALENA			
---	San Bernardino San Bernadino	64	681
Manuel	El Dorado Kelsey	58	1139
MALENCE			
Manuel	Los Angeles Santa Ana	59	441
MALENDIS			
Juan	Plumas Quincy	62	937
MALENDORF			
Adolp	Yuba Marysville	72	909
MALENDREZ			
M	Tuolumne Sonora	71	227
MALENS			
George	Sierra Whiskey	66	845
MALEONIS			
Francisco	Calaveras Twp 6	57	134
MALERELLAR			
Juan	Mariposa Twp 1	60	624
MALERY			
R	Nevada Red Dog	61	555
Rich O*	El Dorado White Oaks	58	1019
Sarah	Contra Costa Twp 2	57	547
MALESA			
---	Tulara Twp 3	71	44
MALESS			
---*	Tulara Sinks Te	71	44
MALET			
Henry	San Francisco San Francisco	2 67	555
MALETO			
Juan	Alameda Murray	55	217
MALETT			
J	San Francisco San Francisco	3 67	78
MALEY			
J*	Nevada Grass Valley	61	151
P	Yuba Bear Rvr	72	1007
R	Yuba Bear Rvr	72	1007
MALEZE???KI			
Adam*	Tulara Sinks Te	71	43
MALGATE			
John F	Butte Bidwell	56	728
MALGRAM			
H	Tuolumne Twp 4	71	149
John	San Francisco San Francisco	8	681287
MALGREW			
Francis	Calaveras Twp 4	57	315
MALHARM			
Andrew	Amador Twp 2	55	310
Andrew	Amador Twp 2	55	312
MALHERBE			
C	Alameda Brooklyn	55	98
MALIA			
---	San Bernardino S Timate	64	695
MALIADE			
Pere*	Alameda Brooklyn	55	97
MALIAGH			
David P	San Luis Obispo San Luis Obispo	65	37
MALIAS			
John	Yuba Long Bar	72	751
MALIBICK			
Nicholas*	Sonoma Petaluma	69	587
MALIBRICK			
Nicholas*	Sonoma Petaluma	69	587
MALICK			
Samuel	Sierra Twp 7	66	883
MALIDA			
Francisco	Contra Costa Twp 1	57	533
MALIM			
Concelota*	Alameda Brooklyn	55	215
MALIN			
Isaac	Tulara Twp 3	71	43
MALINA			
---	San Bernardino San Bernardino	64	679
J	Amador Twp 3	55	394
MALINADO			
Joseph	Calaveras Twp 5	57	224
MALINAR			
John	Santa Clara San Jose	65	291
MALINDA			
---*	Nevada Rough &	61	407
Marcos	Santa Clara San Jose	65	326
MALINDAS			
Vicenta	Los Angeles Elmonte	59	254
MALINDE			
Pere	Alameda Brooklyn	55	97
MALINDREZ			
M	Tuolumne Twp 1	71	227
MALINE			
A*	Nevada Washington	61	338

Name	County Locale	M653 Roll	Page
MALINE			
Concelotin*	Alameda Brooklyn	55	215
Jas	Butte Oregon	56	623
Wm	Nevada Eureka	61	347
MALINEO			
Joquin	Alameda Oakland	55	55
MALINEY			
A H	Nevada Nevada	61	275
Thomas*	Nevada Washington	61	335
MALINGHER			
Chas*	San Francisco San Francisco	1 68	834
MALINILLI			
P	San Francisco San Francisco	3 67	16
MALINO			
Zed D	Santa Clara San Jose	65	322
MALIO			
Joseph	Tuolumne Twp 2	71	415
William	Tuolumne Twp 2	71	415
MALIZE			
C	Nevada Grass Valley	61	153
Wm B*	Placer Sacramento	62	642
MALKMAN			
C S	Nevada Nevada	61	290
MALL			
Adam	San Francisco San Francisco	7	681369
Charlie	Yolo Slate Ra	72	686
Charlie	Yuba North Ea	72	686
Chas H	Napa Clear Lake	61	126
Lee	Yuba Fosters	72	830
MALLACARTE			
---	San Diego Agua Caliente	64	824
MALLAGH			
Millis	San Luis Obispo San Luis Obispo	65	45
MALLAHAN			
M	Siskiyou Scott Ri	69	73
MALLANEY			
John	Nevada Rough &	61	423
MALLANY			
Michl	Sacramento Ward 1	63	135
MALLARD			
A	Sacramento Ward 1	63	86
Geo H	Sacramento Ward 1	63	24
Joseph S	Los Angeles Los Angeles	59	340
P J	Tuolumne Sonora	71	232
MALLARY			
A	Sacramento Dry Crk	63	374
MALLATE			
A	Tuolumne Twp 4	71	170
MALLAY			
A*	Nevada Nevada	61	294
Juan	San Luis Obispo San Luis Obispo	65	23
R*	Nevada Grass Valley	61	223
MALLCO			
---*	Mariposa Twp 3	60	579
MALLDEN			
Thos	Santa Clara Redwood	65	448
MALLEL			
V	San Francisco San Francisco	2 67	748
MALLEN			
C R	Nevada Grass Valley	61	176
C*	Nevada Grass Valley	61	166
H*	San Joaquin Stockton	64	1099
J	El Dorado White Oaks	58	1017
James	San Joaquin Elkhorn	64	995
John	Calaveras Twp 7	57	1
John	San Francisco San Francisco	2 67	595
Robert	Sierra Twp 7	66	909
MALLENCE			
A L	Amador Twp 5	55	331
Al	Amador Twp 5	55	331
MALLENROD			
Geo	El Dorado Kelsey	58	1149
MALLEO			
---	Mariposa Twp 3	60	579
MALLER			
C W	Tehama Red Bluff	70	913
H*	San Joaquin Stockton	64	1099
P C*	San Francisco San Francisco	9	681099
William*	El Dorado White Oaks	58	1002
MALLERY			
Maitland	Plumas Quincy	62	989
MALLET			
Alex	Sacramento Ward 4	63	544
Baptiste	Los Angeles Los Angeles	59	355
John	San Francisco San Francisco	2 67	749
Joseph	Siskiyou Callahan	69	3
Joseph	Siskiyou Callahan	69	4
Louis	Placer Forest H	62	804
Patrick	Siskiyou Callahan	69	8
Peter	Tuolumne Twp 1	71	255
Wm	Sierra Twp 7	66	872
MALLETT			
Alford	San Francisco San Francisco	4	681171
Ellen	Contra Costa Twp 1	57	529
J	San Francisco San Francisco	9	681080

Name	County Locale	M653 Roll	Page
MALLETT			
J J	El Dorado Salmon Falls	58	1034
Phillip	Solano Benecia	69	285
MALLEY			
Charles	Marin Novato	60	739
James	Yuba New York	72	730
Margaret	San Francisco San Francisco 10	67	224
Peter	Placer Auburn	62	580
Richard	Yuba Marysville	72	943
MALLIGAN			
Michael	Tuolumne Twp 4	71	135
Owen	Tuolumne Columbia	71	295
P	Nevada Nevada	61	298
MALLIN			
C	Nevada Nevada	61	297
John	Tuolumne Twp 1	71	237
MALLINGLY			
J	Nevada Nevada	61	316
MALLINS			
Edward	Placer Forest H	62	799
MALLISE			
W	Siskiyou Callahan	69	7
MALLIT			
John	San Francisco San Francisco 2	67	749
MALLMAN			
F	Mendocino Big Rvr	60	840
MALLO			
---	Tulara Twp 3	71	65
MALLOCH			
Silas R	Tuolumne Don Pedro	71	541
MALLOCK			
Wm	Colusa Colusi	57	423
MALLOM			
Edward	Yuba New York	72	727
Jno	Sacramento Ward 1	63	9
MALLON			
Francis	Sonoma Armally	69	480
James	Calaveras Twp 7	57	4
James	Yuba Rose Bar	72	800
Jas	San Francisco San Francisco 1	68	860
Jeramiah	Mariposa Twp 3	60	606
John	Mariposa Twp 1	60	630
John	San Francisco San Francisco 2	67	595
John	San Francisco San Francisco 3	67	60
John	San Francisco San Francisco 2	67	764
John A	Mariposa Twp 1	60	630
M	Yolo Cache	72	596
Patrick	San Francisco San Francisco 10	67	288
Peter	Sacramento Ward 4	63	506
Robert	Sierra Forest C	66	909
MALLONE			
Thomas	San Joaquin Stockton	64	1036
MALLONY			
Ellias M	Mendocino Little L	60	833
MALLORY			
A R	Nevada Nevada	61	326
Andw	Sonoma Petaluma	69	584
C	Nevada Grass Valley	61	183
Elizabeth	Mendocino Little L	60	833
Ellias M	Mendocino Little L	60	833
George	San Francisco San Francisco 7	68	1406
Henry	San Joaquin Stockton	64	1024
Henry	Yolo No E Twp	72	672
Henry	Yuba North Ea	72	672
Jno	Sacramento Ward 1	63	9
Job	San Francisco San Francisco 3	67	73
John F	Tuolumne Twp 1	71	196
John H	Calaveras Twp 5	57	218
John P	Tuolumne Sonora	71	196
Margret	Calaveras Twp 9	57	386
Neplion B	Humbolt Eel Rvr	59	153
W S	Tuolumne Sonora	71	481
Wm D	Tuolumne Twp 1	71	278
MALLOS			
Emile*	Tuolumne Twp 2	71	287
MALLOSSIRA			
Anton	Mariposa Twp 1	60	672
MALLOSSIRO			
Anton*	Mariposa Twp 1	60	672
MALLOT			
Fred	Yuba Fosters	72	835
S	Nevada Nevada	61	249
V A	Nevada Nevada	61	249
MALLOWAY			
Wm	Colusa Colusi	57	427
MALLOWELL			
John	Mariposa Coulterville	60	699
MALLOX			
T	Yolo Cache	72	595
MALLOY			
A	Nevada Nevada	61	294
Edward	Yolo Slate Ra	72	694
Edward	Yuba Slate Ro	72	694
J C	Solano Vallejo	69	243
MALLOY			
James	Yuba New York	72	730
John	Yolo Slate Ra	72	694
John	Yuba Slate Ro	72	694
P	San Francisco San Francisco 9	68	1058
MALLUCK			
Henry	Sonoma Vallejo	69	626
MALLVOY			
Joseph	Calaveras Twp 7	57	22
MALLY			
Jno O*	Sonoma Petaluma	69	600
MALMAUX			
George*	Placer Michigan	62	855
MALME			
Ann*	San Francisco San Francisco 2	67	655
Arm*	San Francisco San Francisco 2	67	655
MALMEY			
John	Siskiyou Yreka	69	150
MALNEY			
John	Sierra Downieville	66	1018
MALNLARD			
Emanul	Plumas Meadow Valley	62	903
MALO			
Ramond	San Bernardino Santa Barbara	64	205
MALOAN			
E	Sutter Butte	70	799
MALOCK			
Joe	Yuba Bear Rvr	72	1016
MALOCOGER			
Daniel*	Yuba Marysville	72	892
MALOE			
Tyre	Tuolumne Sonora	71	225
MALOLY			
James*	Yuba Bear Rvr	72	1013
MALOM			
Benj*	Alameda Oakland	55	22
Edward	Yolo Cache Crk	72	647
John	Del Norte Crescent	58	625
MALON			
Antonio	Amador Twp 1	55	471
J	Nevada Grass Valley	61	219
MALONA			
J	Calaveras Twp 7	57	1
John	El Dorado Coloma	58	1078
MALONE			
A	Nevada Washington	61	338
A J	Nevada Nevada	61	322
A*	Nevada Washington	61	338
Ann	San Francisco San Francisco 10	67	202
C*	Nevada Grass Valley	61	195
Edward	Yolo Cottonwoood	72	647
Elizabeth	Solano Vacaville	69	362
F S	Sacramento Ward 1	63	44
G	Nevada Grass Valley	61	182
G	Nevada Grass Valley	61	195
H*	Nevada Grass Valley	61	195
Hugh	Yuba Rose Bar	72	793
J	Nevada Grass Valley	61	185
J	Nevada Nevada	61	246
J	Nevada Nevada	61	274
J	San Francisco San Francisco 3	67	67
J R T	Sacramento Lee	63	215
J W	Butte Ophir	56	774
James	Calaveras Twp 5	57	139
James	San Francisco San Francisco 9	68	941
James	Tuolumne Big Oak	71	134
James	Tuolumne Twp 1	71	208
James*	Calaveras Twp 6	57	139
Jas M	Placer Goods	62	698
Jno	Butte Hamilton	56	524
John	San Francisco San Francisco 1	68	902
John	Sierra Downieville	66	957
John	Tehama Red Bluff	70	917
M	Shasta Shasta	66	675
Margt	San Francisco San Francisco 7	68	1332
Mary	Yuba Marysville	72	890
Michael	Placer Secret R	62	624
Michael	San Francisco San Francisco 11	67	150
Michael	Trinity Weaverville	70	1077
P	Yolo Putah	72	553
Patrick	Nevada Eureka	61	355
Patrick	Trinity Taylor'S	70	1036
Patrick S	San Francisco San Francisco 7	68	1424
Perry	Los Angeles Elmonte	59	251
Porter	Solano Vacaville	69	361
R C	Sierra Twp 7	66	875
Therese	Sacramento Ward 1	63	88
Thomas	Sacramento Ward 1	63	140
Thos	Amador Twp 7	55	412
Thos	Placer Rattle Snake	62	637
W	Butte Oregon	56	610
William	Solano Vacaville	69	355
Wm	Butte Oregon	56	610
Wm	Nevada Eureka	61	347
MALONE			
Wm	Tehama Lassen	70	870
Wm	Tuolumne Big Oak	71	149
Wm J	Humbolt Bucksport	59	155
Wm*	Nevada Eureka	61	347
MALONEY			
A	Nevada Grass Valley	61	182
A	Nevada Eureka	61	364
A H	Nevada Nevada	61	275
Aaron	Contra Costa Twp 2	57	539
Aaron	Contra Costa Twp 2	57	544
Angenett	Contra Costa Twp 2	57	541
Ann	San Francisco San Francisco 3	67	41
D	San Francisco San Francisco 12	67	391
Daniel	San Francisco San Francisco 7	68	1423
Danl	Klamath Salmon	59	208
Delia	Calaveras Twp 5	57	196
H H	Nevada Washington	61	335
H W	Nevada Washington	61	335
J	San Francisco San Francisco 7	68	1076
J	San Francisco San Francisco 5	67	530
J	San Joaquin Stockton	64	1096
James	Marin Cortemad	60	786
Jno	Nevada Washington	61	332
John	El Dorado Coloma	58	1086
John	San Francisco San Francisco 1	68	862
John	Siskiyou Yreka	69	150
John	Solano Benecia	69	284
John	Trinity E Weaver	70	1060
John H	Tuolumne Twp 2	71	395
Jos E	Sacramento Ward 1	63	141
Kate	San Francisco San Francisco 4	68	1135
Lucy	Contra Costa Twp 2	57	544
M	San Joaquin Stockton	64	1100
Margt	San Francisco San Francisco 7	68	1331
Martin	Santa Cruz Soguel	66	584
Michael	Yuba New York	72	744
Michael	Yuba Long Bar	72	755
Michael	Yuba Long Bar	72	755
Michiel	Nevada Rough &	61	429
P*	Nevada Eureka	61	348
Patrick	San Francisco San Francisco 7	68	1381
Patrick	Yuba Bear Rvr	72	1006
Peter	Tuolumne Twp 2	71	284
R	Nevada Grass Valley	61	165
R	Nevada Grass Valley	61	178
Richard	San Francisco San Francisco 2	67	597
S W	Nevada Nevada	61	327
Stephen	Tuolumne Chinese	71	489
Tephen	Tuolumne Twp 5	71	489
Tho	Siskiyou Scott Va	69	60
Thomas	Contra Costa Twp 1	57	526
Thomas	Nevada Washington	61	335
Thomas	San Francisco San Francisco 3	67	75
Thomas	Trinity E Weaver	70	1059
Thomas*	Nevada Washington	61	335
W J	Nevada Nevada	61	324
Wm	Trinity Weaverville	70	1066
MALONEZ			
James	Siskiyou Yreka	69	148
MALONG			
Jakes	Siskiyou Yreka	69	148
MALONI			
Thos	Amador Twp 7	55	412
MALONNEY			
Tho*	Butte Oregon	56	636
MALONS			
James	Calaveras Twp 6	57	139
MALONY			
Bridget	San Joaquin Castoria	64	878
C H	El Dorado Diamond	58	763
J	Butte Ophir	56	781
J	Nevada Grass Valley	61	191
J	Nevada Grass Valley	61	213
J	Nevada Eureka	61	373
James	Sacramento Mississipi	63	185
John	Butte Ophir	56	773
Martin	Calaveras Twp 6	57	145
Michael	Yuba Marysville	72	876
Patrick	Yuba Bear Rvr	72	1006
Patrick	Yuba Marysville	72	864
Peter	Calaveras Twp 10	57	276
Thomas	Placer Iona Hills	62	895
Thos	Placer Secret R	62	612
Tim	Placer Iona Hills	62	867
Wm	Calaveras Twp 6	57	118
MALOON			
B	San Francisco San Francisco 2	67	793
John	San Mateo Twp 3	65	92
MALOONEY			
Michael	San Mateo Twp 3	65	80
MALORN			
Benj*	Alameda Oakland	55	22
MALORO			
---	Mendocino Calpella	60	823

Name	County Locale	M653 Roll	Page
MALORY			
A P	Sacramento Centre	63	178
C	Shasta Shasta	66	687
H	Nevada Grass Valley	61	157
J	Nevada Grass Valley	61	219
Marcella	Calaveras Twp 6	57	137
Marcelli	Calaveras Twp 6	57	137
MALOTH			
Herman	Plumas Quincy	62	937
MALOTRA			
Andrea	San Francisco San Francisco 11		124 67
MALOTT			
Benjamin F	Yuba Marysville	72	862
Joseph	Yuba Suida	72	980
MALOUN			
P*	El Dorado Placerville	58	892
MALOUNY			
Delia*	Calaveras Twp 5	57	196
MALOWAY			
Delia*	Calaveras Twp 5	57	196
MALOWNEY			
Tho	Butte Oregon	56	636
MALOWNY			
Delia*	Calaveras Twp 5	57	196
MALOX			
Milton	Mariposa Twp 1	60	631
MALOY			
C	Calaveras Twp 9	57	412
D	Nevada Grass Valley	61	196
D	Nevada Nevada	61	245
Dennis	Tehama Tehama	70	947
Ellen	Nevada Rough &	61	407
J	Nevada Grass Valley	61	155
J	Nevada Grass Valley	61	181
J	Nevada Grass Valley	61	206
J	Nevada Grass Valley	61	226
J	San Francisco San Francisco 5	67	503
J D	Nevada Grass Valley	61	162
James	Calaveras Twp 5	57	136
James	Placer Forest H	62	772
James	Yuba Bear Rvr	72	1013
John	Butte Ophir	56	791
John	Calaveras Twp 6	57	187
John	Nevada Eureka	61	392
John	Nevada Rough &	61	407
John	Placer Forest H	62	772
John	Tuolumne Sonora	71	234
L	Nevada Grass Valley	61	206
M	Trinity Trinity	70	974
Mary	San Francisco San Francisco 2	67	716
Miel	Sierra Eureka	66	1044
Neil	Sierra Eureka	66	1044
Pat	Nevada Rough &	61	421
R M	Nevada Nevada	61	286
W	Nevada Nevada	61	356
William	San Francisco San Francisco 3	67	21
MALREINE			
David	San Francisco San Francisco 6	67	449
MALRINO			
Pablo	Mariposa Twp 3	60	611
MALRON			
B M	Nevada Nevada	61	254
MALSAMA			
Jacob	Calaveras Twp 7	57	39
MALSEN			
John	Butte Ophir	56	763
MALSO			
James*	Yuba New York	72	724
MALSON			
Chas	Butte Ophir	56	771
Isaac	Sacramento Granite	63	239
John	Butte Ophir	56	763
William J	Sierra Whiskey	66	846
William T	Sierra Whiskey	66	846
MALSONI			
Jocklo	Calaveras Twp 7	57	43
MALT			
Peter*	El Dorado Placerville	58	915
MALTBEE			
Armstrong	San Francisco 3 San Francisco	67	32
MALTBY			
Albert	Tulara Visalia	71	106
Henry	Santa Clara San Jose	65	291
MALTE			
Manuel*	Alameda Brooklyn	55	125
MALTER			
Jacob	Placer Dutch Fl	62	716
MALTETT			
Harrison*	Mariposa Coulterville	60	693
MALTHER			
Thos*	San Francisco San Francisco 1	68	841
MALTMAN			
William W	Calaveras Twp 8	57	101
MALTON			
W	Santa Clara San Jose	65	391

Name	County Locale	M653 Roll	Page
MALTOON			
John*	San Francisco San Francisco 12		391 67
MALTRE			
B*	San Francisco San Francisco 2	67	584
MALTRI			
B*	San Francisco San Francisco 2	67	584
MALTZAR			
Conrad	San Francisco San Francisco 10		227 67
MALUMPY			
Thomas	Tuolumne Twp 3	71	425
MALUNEY			
P*	Nevada Eureka	61	348
MALUNPY			
Michael	Tuolumne Columbia	71	292
MALUS			
Bann	Placer Auburn	62	597
MALVANEY			
Ed	Tuolumne Columbia	71	353
MALVERGER			
Daniel*	Yuba Marysville	72	892
MALVILLE			
Michael	San Francisco San Francisco 2	67	580
MALVIN			
James	Yuba New York	72	724
William	Placer Michigan	62	838
MALWHAN			
W R*	El Dorado Placerville	58	893
MALWHEN			
W R*	El Dorado Placerville	58	893
MALWON			
A	El Dorado Placerville	58	844
MALY			
Eugene L	Siskiyou Scott Ri	69	70
Hugh	Mendocino Little L	60	832
MALYREW			
Francis	Calaveras Twp 4	57	315
MAM SAM PURTA			
---	Mendocino Big Rvr	60	854
MAM			
---	Amador Twp 2	55	326
---	El Dorado Georgetown	58	751
---	Placer Virginia	62	701
---	Yuba North Ea	72	675
---*	Mariposa Twp 3	60	620
MAMAL			
H	Nevada Grass Valley	61	160
MAMAN			
H	Nevada Grass Valley	61	154
Henry	San Francisco San Francisco 4	68	1155
MAMAR			
C*	Nevada Grass Valley	61	175
MAMDISON			
James	San Francisco San Francisco 9	68	1098
MAME			
S T*	Yolo Slate Ra	72	701
MAMEDA			
Juan*	Marin Cortemad	60	787
MAMELIA			
---	San Bernardino S Timate	64	694
MAMER			
Nancy	El Dorado Greenwood	58	725
MAMERON			
J	Calaveras Twp 9	57	409
MAMES			
R	Nevada Eureka	61	388
MAMI			
Geo S	San Francisco San Francisco 10		281 67
Michael*	Alameda Brooklyn	55	126
MAMIE			
D*	Nevada Eureka	61	389
MAMIEGAN			
William*	San Francisco San Francisco 7	68	1354
MAMIELL			
---*	Mariposa Twp 1	60	631
MAMING			
A L*	Nevada Nevada	61	284
MAMIR			
Charles*	San Francisco San Francisco 4	68	1120
MAMIS			
R*	Nevada Eureka	61	388
MAMLIN			
Peter	Butte Bidwell	56	707
MAMLOCK			
Simon	Sierra La Porte	66	771
MAMLUMPATE			
---	Mendocino Big Rvr	60	854
MAMMELL			
---	Yolo Washington	72	574
MAMMOX			
John*	Placer Michigan	62	835
MAMMS			
C*	El Dorado Kelsey	58	1129
MAMNOX			
John*	Placer Michigan	62	835

Name	County Locale	M653 Roll	Page
MAMON			
John	Calaveras Twp 8	57	85
Patrick	Sierra Downieville	66	994
MAMORE			
Daniel	Placer Auburn	62	595
MAMOY			
Ellen	San Francisco San Francisco 4	68	1132
MAMROO			
C T	San Francisco San Francisco 3	67	81
MAMROU			
E T*	San Francisco San Francisco 3	67	81
MAMS			
R A*	Nevada Grass Valley	61	174
MAMSELS			
Louis*	Calaveras Twp 9	57	354
MAMVEGAN			
William*	San Francisco San Francisco 7	68	1354
MAN CHU			
---	Sacramento Ward 1	63	70
MAN CON			
---*	Nevada Nevada	61	304
MAN COW			
---*	Nevada Nevada	61	304
MAN JOSE			
---	San Bernardino S Timate	64	718
MAN LEE			
---	Tuolumne Chinese	71	525
MAN OY			
---	Sacramento Ward 1	63	70
MAN SANG			
---	Nevada Rough &	61	432
MAN SEAUX			
A	Shasta Shasta	66	661
MAN YOU			
---	Nevada Nevada	61	304
MAN ZET			
---	Sacramento Ward 1	63	56
MAN			
---	Amador Twp 2	55	292
---	Amador Twp 2	55	294
---	Amador Twp 2	55	326
---	Amador Twp 2	55	327
---	Amador Twp 5	55	331
---	Amador Twp 5	55	335
---	Amador Twp 5	55	343
---	Amador Twp 5	55	345
---	Amador Twp 5	55	349
---	Amador Twp 5	55	356
---	Amador Twp 5	55	360
---	Amador Twp 5	55	365
---	Amador Twp 3	55	402
---	Amador Twp 7	55	414
---	Amador Twp 6	55	428
---	Amador Twp 6	55	450
---	Amador Twp 1	55	478
---	Amador Twp 1	55	479
---	Amador Twp 1	55	497
---	Amador Twp 1	55	503
---	Amador Twp 1	55	507
---	Amador Twp 1	55	508
---	Butte Ophir	56	809
---	Calaveras Twp 6	57	166
---	Calaveras Twp 5	57	205
---	Calaveras Twp 5	57	230
---	Calaveras Twp 5	57	244
---	Calaveras Twp 5	57	250
---	Calaveras Twp 5	57	254
---	Calaveras Twp 5	57	255
---	Calaveras Twp 5	57	256
---	Calaveras Twp 10	57	260
---	Calaveras Twp 10	57	261
---	Calaveras Twp 10	57	269
---	Calaveras Twp 10	57	271
---	Calaveras Twp 10	57	272
---	Calaveras Twp 10	57	274
---	Calaveras Twp 10	57	284
---	Calaveras Twp 4	57	299
---	Calaveras Twp 4	57	300
---	Calaveras Twp 4	57	307
---	Calaveras Twp 4	57	322
---	Calaveras Twp 4	57	330
---	Calaveras Twp 4	57	332
---	Calaveras Twp 9	57	371
---	Calaveras Twp 8	57	56
---	Del Norte Crescent	58	651
---	El Dorado Union	58	1091
---	El Dorado Georgetown	58	745
---	El Dorado Mud Springs	58	950
---	Klamath Liberty	59	239
---	Mariposa Twp 3	60	553
---	Mariposa Twp 3	60	563
---	Mariposa Twp 3	60	564
---	Mariposa Twp 3	60	569
---	Mariposa Twp 3	60	582
---	Mariposa Twp 3	60	588
---	Mariposa Twp 3	60	608

Name	County Locale	M653 Roll	Page
MAN			
---	Mariposa Twp 3	60	609
---	Mariposa Twp 3	60	618
---	Mariposa Twp 3	60	619
---	Mariposa Twp 1	60	626
---	Mariposa Twp 1	60	648
---	Mariposa Twp 1	60	650
---	Mariposa Twp 1	60	653
---	Mariposa Twp 1	60	655
---	Mariposa Twp 1	60	656
---	Mariposa Twp 1	60	673
---	Mariposa Coulterville	60	683
---	Monterey Monterey	60	965
---	Nevada Grass Valley	61	228
---	Nevada Grass Valley	61	233
---	Nevada Nevada	61	302
---	Nevada Nevada	61	303
---	Nevada Nevada	61	304
---	Nevada Nevada	61	309
---	Nevada Rough &	61	424
---	Nevada Rough &	61	431
---	Placer Auburn	62	575
---	Placer Auburn	62	596
---	Placer Rattle Snake	62	601
---	Placer Virginia	62	665
---	Placer Illinois	62	754
---	Plumas Quincy	62	1008
---	Sacramento Ward 3	63	490
---	San Francisco San Francisco 2	67	785
---	San Francisco San Francisco 2	67	790
---	Sierra Downieville	66	984
---	Sierra Downieville	66	998
---	Stanislaus Emory	70	745
---	Tuolumne Twp 2	71	409
---	Tuolumne Twp 3	71	433
---	Tuolumne Twp 3	71	440
---	Tuolumne Twp 3	71	442
---	Tuolumne Twp 3	71	446
---	Tuolumne Twp 3	71	457
---	Tuolumne Twp 1	71	477
---	Tuolumne Jacksonville	71	515
---	Tuolumne Twp 6	71	536
---	Tuolumne Don Pedro	71	540
---	Yolo No E Twp	72	675
---	Yolo No E Twp	72	681
---*	Mariposa Twp 3	60	608
---*	Nevada Nevada	61	302
---*	Sacramento Granite	63	250
---*	Shasta Shasta	66	669
---*	Stanislaus Emory	70	743
---*	Tuolumne Big Oak	71	181
A	Calaveras Twp 9	57	404
Ah	Tuolumne Twp 4	71	181
B*	Nevada Nevada	61	324
Can	Sierra Cox'S Bar	66	951
Charles	Marin Cortemad	60	754
Chay	Amador Twp 5	55	335
Che	Yuba Foster B	72	834
Chi	Calaveras Twp 10	57	295
Chow	Nevada Grass Valley	61	229
Chow	Nevada Nevada	61	303
Chow	Nevada Nevada	61	306
Choy	Calaveras Twp 4	57	334
Christ	Sierra Twp 5	66	942
Chu	Sacramento Ward 1	63	70
Cow	Nevada Nevada	61	304
Cum	Stanislaus Emory	70	744
F	Sutter Butte	70	791
Fon	Del Norte Crescent	58	631
Fred	Yolo Merritt	72	580
Hanah	Santa Clara San Jose	65	343
He	Yuba Fosters	72	843
Hoo	Calaveras Twp 10	57	274
Israel	Sierra Twp 7	66	896
J	Sutter Sutter	70	812
John	Sierra Twp 5	66	930
Julius	Placer Dutch Fl	62	715
Kee	San Francisco San Francisco 4	68	1211
Kie	Mariposa Twp 3	60	618
Kim	El Dorado Georgetown	58	703
Ku	San Francisco San Francisco 4	68	1211
L G	Nevada Grass Valley	61	217
Lee	San Francisco San Francisco 5	67	510
Lee	Tuolumne Twp 5	71	525
Loo	Napa Napa	61	75
Lung	Mariposa Twp 3	60	609
Nu	San Francisco San Francisco 2	67	697
Oy	Sacramento Ward 1	63	70
Robt*	Shasta Shasta	66	677
S L	Amador Twp 5	55	344
Sang	Nevada Rough &	61	432
Sing	Yuba Long Bar	72	767
Suy	El Dorado Georgetown	58	756
Tek*	San Francisco San Francisco 11	67	160
Wee	Calaveras Twp 5	57	220

Name	County Locale	M653 Roll	Page
MAN			
Wu	Calaveras Twp 5	57	220
You	Nevada Nevada	61	304
Young	Mariposa Twp 3	60	553
Zet	Sacramento Ward 1	63	56
MANA			
---	San Bernardino San Bernadino	64	669
Gregorio*	S Buenav	64	221
	San Bernardino		
Jose	Contra Costa Twp 1	57	489
Jose	Monterey San Juan	60	986
Junn*	Monterey Monterey	60	961
Paro	El Dorado Placerville	58	930
Voluntino	Stanislaus Emory	70	739
MANACK			
L*	Sacramento Granite	63	244
S*	Sacramento Granite	63	244
MANACO			
Frances	Amador Twp 5	55	360
MANADEL CARMEL			
---	San Bernardino Santa Inez	64	138
MANAFIELD			
George W	Marin Cortemad	60	784
MANAGAN			
Kate	Tuolumne Twp 1	71	200
Mary	Los Angeles Los Angeles	59	390
MANAGE			
Henry	Sierra Downieville	66	1028
MANAGHEN			
C	San Francisco San Francisco 3	67	65
MANAGHERR			
C	San Francisco San Francisco 3	67	65
MANAGINE			
Z*	Nevada Nevada	61	282
MANAHAN			
Edward	Contra Costa Twp 1	57	489
Francis P	San Francisco San Francisco 7	68	1390
John	Amador Twp 2	55	321
John	San Francisco San Francisco 9	68	1082
John B	Calaveras Twp 8	57	88
M	Shasta Shasta	66	687
Mary	San Francisco San Francisco 9	68	1082
Michael	Sierra Downieville	66	1011
Pat	Sonoma Sonoma	69	635
MANAIX			
John*	Solano Benecia	69	287
Mary A	Solano Benecia	69	287
MANAIY			
John*	Solano Benecia	69	287
MANAK			
Leopold	Sacramento Granite	63	244
MANAMAN			
Hugh	Calaveras Twp 5	57	216
MANAN			
Jiacome*	Mariposa Twp 3	60	594
MANANA			
---*	Los Angeles Los Angeles	59	497
MANANAY			
John	Yolo Cache Crk	72	589
MANANE			
Manuel	Monterey Monterey	60	925
MANANO			
Manuel	Monterey Monterey	60	925
MANAR			
Alex	El Dorado Coloma	58	1114
MANARAS			
P	Nevada Little Y	61	535
MANARD			
Epedie*	El Dorado Coloma	58	1079
Eprdic*	El Dorado Coloma	58	1079
MANARIA			
---*	Los Angeles Los Angeles	59	497
MANARRAS			
P	Nevada Little Y	61	535
MANASSA			
C W	Nevada Rough &	61	406
MANASSE			
J M	San Francisco San Francisco 5	67	515
MANASTIE			
R A	Nevada Nevada	61	290
MANATHA			
Dolores	Amador Twp 1	55	503
MANATORO			
John	San Francisco San Francisco 5	67	499
MANAWAY			
John	Yolo Cache	72	589
MANAYINE			
Z*	Nevada Nevada	61	282
MANAYUN			
Z	Nevada Nevada	61	282
MANBEE			
Peter	San Francisco San Francisco 2	67	802
MANBIC			
Bernard	San Francisco San Francisco 10	67	249
MANBU			
J W	Yolo Cache Crk	72	641

Name	County Locale	M653 Roll	Page
MANCA			
Feming	Yuba Marysville	72	936
MANCAREY			
Jonas H	Yuba Bear Rvr	72	1003
MANCE			
Geo	El Dorado Kelsey	58	1132
James M	Sierra Twp 7	66	863
Robert W*	Yuba Marysville	72	882
MANCEL			
William	Shasta Millvill	66	739
MANCER			
Frances*	Sacramento Ward 3	63	484
MANCESTIE			
R A*	Nevada Nevada	61	290
MANCH			
Elias*	San Francisco San Francisco 3	67	38
T	Sonoma Petaluma	69	605
MANCHALL			
Fg W	Del Norte Happy Ca	58	664
MANCHANT			
Samuel*	Santa Cruz Watsonville	66	537
MANCHESTER			
B W	Solano Suisan	69	214
C	Nevada Grass Valley	61	168
Geo W	San Francisco San Francisco 2	67	666
J	Nevada Grass Valley	61	150
J	Tuolumne Twp 2	71	471
J B	San Francisco San Francisco 5	67	482
L	Nevada Grass Valley	61	191
Leenean*	San Joaquin Castoria	64	874
Lyman	San Francisco San Francisco 10	67	287
R M	Nevada Nevada	61	279
S J	Nevada Eureka	61	370
T J	Nevada Eureka	61	370
T W	Nevada Bridgeport	61	487
MANCHEY			
Boniface	San Luis Obispo	65	19
	San Luis Obispo		
MANCHRIST			
C	Yolo Washington	72	600
MANCHUA			
Manuel*	Calaveras Twp 10	57	281
MANCHUCE			
Manuel	Calaveras Twp 10	57	281
MANCHUN			
Manuel*	Calaveras Twp 10	57	281
MANCINA			
Cristobal	Los Angeles Elmonte	59	253
MANCK			
J W	San Francisco San Francisco 1	68	928
MANCLAY			
Jeremiah	Tulara Visalia	71	106
MANCLEN			
M*	Sacramento Brighton	63	198
MANCLER			
M*	Sacramento Brighton	63	198
MANCOM			
Henry	El Dorado Salmon Falls	58	1050
MANCUSH			
---	Sacramento Cosummes	63	406
MANCY			
Jno	Klamath S Fork	59	203
MANDA			
Phelippe	Mariposa Twp 3	60	571
MANDALE			
A L	Nevada Nevada	61	287
MANDARK			
Raee	El Dorado Diamond	58	813
MANDEAW			
Victor	Colusa Spring Valley	57	433
MANDEGAN			
Albino	Tuolumne Twp 1	71	257
MANDEL			
E	Alameda Brooklyn	55	82
MANDELBAUM			
Frank	Sacramento Ward 3	63	480
MANDELL			
C F	El Dorado White Oaks	58	1002
Eugene	Solano Benecia	69	286
Frank*	Yuba Parke Ba	72	784
H M	Yolo Slate Ra	72	707
MANDELSON			
S	Amador Twp 3	55	384
MANDENO			
Joseph	Calaveras Twp 6	57	129
MANDERIS			
Jacinto	Santa Cruz Pajaro	66	546
MANDERMAN			
John	Butte Mountain	56	736
MANDERRAGA			
Manuel	Los Angeles Los Angeles	59	378
MANDERS			
Eligah H	Sierra Gibsonville	66	856
John	Tuolumne Twp 1	71	209
MANDES			
B	El Dorado Diamond	58	813

California 1860 Census Index

Name	County Locale	M653 Roll	Page
MANDES			
John	Calaveras Twp 6	57	118
Joseph	Placer Rattle Snake	62	635
Phelippe*	Mariposa Twp 3	60	571
MANDEVILLE			
H*	Butte Chico	56	542
J C	Butte Chico	56	542
J R	Siskiyou Scott Va	69	59
James	San Francisco San Francisco 4	681	112
James W	San Francisco San Francisco 4	681	112
Mary	Sacramento Franklin	63	312
Mary G	San Francisco San Francisco 8	681	288
MANDGE			
Lyman	Tehama Tehama	70	944
MANDIBLES			
Miquel	Los Angeles Los Nieto	59	432
MANDICK			
Peter	Sacramento Ward 1	63	10
MANDIES			
Sononia	Los Angeles Los Angeles	59	305
MANDIGA			
Stephen	Santa Clara Santa Clara	65	499
MANDIGAN			
Albino	Tuolumne Twp 1	71	257
MANDILLES			
Ramon	San Bernardino S Timate	64	687
MANDIN			
John*	Calaveras Twp 6	57	127
MANDITCH			
A	Nevada Nevada	61	244
MANDITT			
H M	Yuba Slate Ro	72	707
MANDLEBAUM			
Jos	Amador Twp 3	55	369
MANDLEY			
Wm	Sacramento Ward 4	63	522
MANDLI			
Gaoff*	San Francisco San Francisco 7	681	371
MANDMYLER			
Frederick*	San Francisco San Francisco 7	681	390
	San Francisco		
MANDO			
Louis	Tuolumne Twp 2	71	415
MANDONA			
Miguel	Monterey San Juan	601	001
Sircaco*	Monterey San Juan	601	001
MANDONADO			
Xavier	Los Angeles Los Nieto	59	433
MANDONE			
Emanuel*	Trinity Indian C	70	983
MANDOR			
Joseph	Calaveras Twp 5	57	200
MANDORF			
E	Nevada Nevada	61	244
S A	Nevada Nevada	61	244
S H	Nevada Nevada	61	244
MANDOZA			
Manuel*	Shasta Shasta	66	683
MANDOZE			
Manuel*	Shasta Shasta	66	683
MANDOZO			
Manuel	Shasta Shasta	66	683
MANDRADA			
F	Merced Twp 1	60	898
J	Merced Twp 1	60	898
MANDUS			
Abby	San Francisco San Francisco 4	681	224
MANDY			
Jno	Butte Hamilton	56	517
MANE			
Fredk	San Francisco San Francisco 10	67	324
Geo	Alameda Washington	55	170
Jnocencia*	Monterey Monterey	60	956
John	Butte Ophir	56	745
Le	Mariposa Twp 3	60	620
Thos	Tehama Pasakent	70	860
MANE?			
Manuel*	Mariposa Twp 3	60	598
MANEAR			
Francois	San Francisco San Francisco 2	67	769
MANEARY			
Jonas H*	Yuba Bear Rvr	721	003
MANEFICKA			
Wm	Tuolumne Twp 2	71	308
MANEGAN			
A C	Nevada Nevada	61	264
Martin*	San Francisco San Francisco 9	681	031
MANEH			
---	Mendocino Round Va	60	881
MANEI			
John M	San Francisco San Francisco 3	67	66
MANEK			
Manuel*	Mariposa Twp 3	60	598
MANEL			
Alexander	Solano Vallejo	69	268

Name	County Locale	M653 Roll	Page
MANEL			
Hosea*	Alameda Brooklyn	55	151
MANELA			
---	San Bernardino S Timate	64	745
MANELL			
Hisam P	El Dorado Georgetown	58	705
MANELLA			
Aggurtta*	Sierra La Porte	66	785
Aygurtter*	Sierra La Porte	66	785
MANELS			
Joseph*	Mendocino Big Rvr	60	846
MANER			
Henrice*	Alameda Murray	55	218
Louis	Butte Kimshaw	56	604
Pastian	Siskiyou Yreka	69	168
Pastrian*	Siskiyou Yreka	69	168
R	Nevada Grass Valley	61	196
MANERS			
P M*	San Francisco San Francisco 6	67	432
MANES			
Kinney	Yuba Marysville	72	937
Manuel	Yuba Marysville	72	910
MANEWELL			
Lavilan	Sierra Downieville	66	954
Sarilan*	Sierra Downieville	66	954
Savilan*	Sierra Downieville	66	954
MANEY			
Pilia*	Los Angeles Los Angeles	59	492
MANFIELD			
David	Marin Cortemad	60	786
H	Sierra St Louis	66	816
J J	Sierra Downieville	661	016
Thos	Amador Twp 2	55	324
MANFORD			
J	Sutter Vernon	70	842
MANG			
---	Amador Twp 2	55	315
---	Amador No 6	55	449
---	Amador Twp 1	55	507
---	Amador Twp 1	55	511
---	Calaveras Twp 6	57	149
---	Calaveras Twp 5	57	171
---	Calaveras Twp 5	57	192
---	Calaveras Twp 5	57	254
---	Calaveras Twp 5	57	256
---	Calaveras Twp 8	57	59
---	Calaveras Twp 8	57	60
---	Calaveras Twp 8	57	65
---	Calaveras Twp 8	57	82
---	Calaveras Twp 8	57	84
---	El Dorado Georgetown	58	702
---	Mariposa Twp 3	60	546
---	Mariposa Twp 3	60	552
---	Mariposa Twp 3	60	562
---	Mariposa Twp 3	60	576
---	Placer Virginia	62	687
---	Placer Mountain	62	707
---	Placer Illinois	62	747
---	Placer Iona Hills	62	898
---	Sacramento Ward 1	63	58
---	San Francisco San Francisco 4	681	197
---	Tuolumne Big Oak	71	147
---	Tuolumne Sonora	71	477
---	Tuolumne Montezuma	71	504
---	Tuolumne Montezuma	71	509
---	Yolo Slate Ra	72	713
---	Yuba Fosters	72	842
---*	Los Angeles Los Angeles	59	321
Ah	Calaveras Twp 7	57	33
Ah	Calaveras Twp 7	57	34
Ah	Tuolumne Twp 4	71	147
Chew	Mariposa Coulterville	60	682
En*	Merced Twp 1	60	914
Le	Mariposa Twp 3	60	552
Ran	Yuba Long Bar	72	753
Ron	Yuba Long Bar	72	753
Sie	El Dorado Georgetown	58	703
You	Mariposa Twp 3	60	544
Zon	Mariposa Twp 3	60	544
MANGAIES			
Jose	Monterey Monterey	60	955
MANGAMIN			
Victoria	Tuolumne Twp 4	71	137
MANGAN			
Angeli*	San Francisco San Francisco 3	67	16
Fredrick	Tuolumne Chinese	71	493
John	San Francisco San Francisco 1	68	930
John	Santa Clara Fremont	65	440
Michael	San Francisco San Francisco 11	67	108
MANGANE			
---	Fresno Twp 1	59	28
MANGARES			
Victoria	Tuolumne Chinese	71	490
MANGARIS			
Miguel	Monterey S Antoni	60	971

Name	County Locale	M653 Roll	Page
MANGEA			
Manuell	Amador Twp 5	55	336
MANGEL			
Charles	Yuba Marysville	72	928
MANGELS			
Catharine	San Francisco San Francisco 10 67		272
Chaus	San Francisco San Francisco 10 67		300
Clous	San Francisco San Francisco 10 67		300
Peter	San Francisco San Francisco 7	681	342
MANGEO			
Charles*	San Francisco San Francisco 3 67		24
MANGER			
C L	Nevada Grass Valley	61	186
Mar Jenis	Amador Twp 2	55	305
Peter	Los Angeles Los Angeles	59	353
R	Nevada Grass Valley	61	192
MANGERMAR			
Lewis*	Amador Twp 2	55	305
MANGERMAS			
Lewis*	Amador Twp 2	55	305
MANGERS			
M	San Francisco San Francisco 10 67		173
P W	San Francisco San Francisco 6	67	464
S B	Nevada Grass Valley	61	174
MANGHEM			
Mathew	Sierra Gibsonville	66	856
MANGIN			
Anna*	Sacramento Ward 4	63	565
Jeane Beluse	Nevada Bridgeport	61	454
John	Solano Suisan	69	229
P F	Sacramento Ward 4	63	526
MANGON			
Amos	Placer Forest H	62	798
MANGOR			
Thomas	San Francisco San Francisco 4	681	158
MANGRATIA			
Peter	Santa Clara Burnett	65	257
MANGUEL			
M	El Dorado Diamond	58	814
MANGUITO			
J*	Butte Kimshaw	56	600
MANGULL			
Nicholas	Santa Clara Santa Clara	65	463
MANGUS			
P A	San Francisco San Francisco 6	67	464
MANGUT			
---	Nevada Rough &	61	409
MANHAL			
John P	Placer Auburn	62	589
MANHALL			
L	Sierra Downieville	661	011
Manuel	Monterey Monterey	60	925
MANHALLEIN			
Manuel*	Sierra Downieville	66	977
MANHAN			
George	Calaveras Twp 6	57	144
Jas*	Placer Auburn	62	586
MANHAR			
---	Mendocino Big Rvr	60	853
MANHART			
J B	Amador Twp 1	55	467
MANHEIM			
C	Tuolumne Shawsfla	71	405
Isaac	San Francisco San Francisco 8	681	321
Saml	Klamath Orleans	59	216
MANHEN			
Francis*	Calaveras Twp 5	57	228
MANHIERN			
Henry	Humbolt Union	59	179
MANHOFFERS			
Joseph	Del Norte Crescent	58	620
MANIA			
Hosea*	Stanislaus Branch	70	701
Peter	San Francisco San Francisco 3	67	14
MANIANA			
---	San Bernardino S Timate	64	730
MANIANO			
---	San Bernardino San Bernadino	64	681
---	San Bernardino S Timate	64	723
---	San Bernardino S Timate	64	728
MANIBO			
---	Mendocino Twp 1	60	886
MANICK			
Thomas	Placer Forest H	62	801
MANICT			
R J*	Nevada Nevada	61	284
MANIE			
David	Butte Eureka	56	654
MANIEL			
S	Nevada Nevada	61	271
MANIER			
Charles*	San Francisco San Francisco 4	681	120

Name	County Locale	M653 RollPage
MANIER		
John A	Tuolumne Sonora	71 196
MANIES		
R*	Nevada Eureka	61 388
MANIFIELD		
G J*	Mariposa Twp 1	60 660
MANIGAN		
A C	Nevada Nevada	61 264
MANIGIN		
John	Tuolumne Twp 2	71 382
MANIHAN		
Bregit	Santa Clara Santa Clara	65 513
MANILL		
T	Nevada Eureka	61 375
MANILLA		
Joseph	San Mateo Twp 2	65 118
Pallolla*	San Mateo Twp 2	65 111
Pollolla	San Mateo Twp 2	65 111
MANILLIO		
Joco	Calaveras Twp 7	57 42
MANILLIS		
William	Klamath Liberty	59 231
MANILTON		
Z	Santa Clara Santa Clara	65 498
MANIN		
Abel	Santa Cruz Soguel	66 597
Charles	Tuolumne Green Springs	71 527
J V	Siskiyou Scott Va	69 55
Jose	San Bernardino San Bernardino	64 682
Juana	San Bernardino San Bernardino	64 682
MANINA		
Joanna*	San Francisco San Francisco 9	68 986
MANING		
Abraham	Placer Yankee J	62 775
Danl	Tuolumne Twp 2	71 277
MANIOHOFER		
M	Siskiyou Scott Ri	69 61
MANION		
C J*	Nevada Eureka	61 376
Curry*	Sierra Twp 7	66 913
F	Sutter Nicolaus	70 838
Sara	Placer Yankee J	62 760
Wm	Sonoma Santa Rosa	69 409
MANIORE		
Cuny	Sierra Twp 7	66 913
MANIOTT		
Thomas*	Sierra Twp 7	66 864
MANIOU		
Curry*	Sierra Twp 7	66 913
MANIR		
Pallo	Amador Twp 1	55 469
MANIRE		
D*	Nevada Eureka	61 389
MANIS		
J R*	Sacramento Ward 1	63 22
M	Nevada Nevada	61 247
MANITHER		
John	Sierra Twp 7	66 865
MANIX		
B	Nevada Washington	61 332
B	Nevada Eureka	61 378
J	Nevada Eureka	61 388
MANJAH		
---	Mendocino Big Rock	60 876
MANJARES		
Jose	Monterey Monterey	60 952
Jose G*	Monterey Monterey	60 952
MANJAUS		
Jose G*	Monterey Monterey	60 952
Miguel	Monterey S Antoni	60 971
MANJON		
M	Nevada Grass Valley	61 170
MANJOS		
Domiaga	Yuba Marysville	72 920
MANK		
---	Mariposa Twp 3	60 590
---*	El Dorado Georgetown	58 756
Franklin*	Marin Point Re	60 732
Henry*	San Francisco San Francisco 1	68 891
Robt	Sonoma Vallejo	69 630
MANKA		
C	Solano Suisan	69 206
Julia	San Francisco San Francisco 10	183 67
MANKART		
J B	Amador Twp 1	55 467
MANKELL		
Samuel*	Santa Cruz Pajaro	66 575
MANKEY		
John	Santa Cruz Santa Cruz	66 604
MANKIN		
Benj F	Sacramento Ward 4	63 546
John A	Tulara Visalia	71 100
Jose	Santa Cruz Santa Cruz	66 620
Thos*	Mariposa Twp 3	60 612
Wm	Mariposa Twp 3	60 615
MANKINS		
H	San Francisco San Francisco 1	68 894
James	Monterey San Juan	601007
John	Calaveras Twp 10	57 281
P P	Monterey San Juan	60 993
Walsa	Santa Cruz Pajaro	66 545
Walter	Santa Cruz Pajaro	66 545
MANKOPEA		
---	Fresno Twp 2	59 60
MANKOWAH		
---	Fresno Twp 3	59 40
MANKS		
F M	Amador Twp 6	55 426
MANL		
Chas*	Merced Twp 1	60 908
MANLA		
Anton	Tuolumne Twp 1	71 189
MANLBOROUGH		
H	Tuolumne Twp 2	71 390
MANLDIN		
B F*	Sacramento American	63 164
MANLE		
J	Tuolumne Twp 4	71 162
Joseph*	Calaveras Twp 9	57 354
MANLES		
John	Sacramento Sutter	63 299
MANLEY		
A G	Tuolumne Twp 2	71 309
Anthony	Alameda Brooklyn	55 104
Christopher	San Francisco 11	100
	San Francisco	67
David	El Dorado Placerville	58 878
Edward	Napa Hot Springs	61 14
Ellen	Napa Napa	61 104
F	Yolo Merritt	72 579
Geo	San Francisco San Francisco 9	681003
J	El Dorado Diamond	58 788
James H	Fresno Twp 2	59 5
M	San Francisco San Francisco 5	67 500
Solimon	San Francisco San Francisco 3	67 43
Solomon	San Francisco San Francisco 3	67 43
Thomas	Calaveras Twp 4	57 310
MANLIAS		
Juanita	Placer Iona Hills	62 868
MANLIVE		
William	Napa Clear Lake	61 140
MANLOCK		
Hannah	San Francisco San Francisco 9	68 962
W	San Francisco San Francisco 9	68 962
MANLONEY		
W	Nevada Washington	61 332
MANLORE		
David*	Plumas Quincy	621005
MANLOVE		
David*	Plumas Quincy	621005
W L*	Sacramento Brighton	63 193
W S*	Sacramento Brighton	63 193
William	Napa Clear Lake	61 140
MANLTMAN		
E S*	Sacramento Georgian	63 339
MANLY		
A C	Tuolumne Twp 2	71 273
A C	Tuolumne Twp 2	71 276
Cornelius*	Placer Auburn	62 585
James	Calaveras Twp 4	57 316
James	Solano Fremont	69 380
Joseph*	Calaveras Twp 9	57 354
Moses	Placer Yankee J	62 758
Thomas	El Dorado Georgetown	58 755
Thos	Alameda Brooklyn	55 130
Thos	Placer Dutch Fl	62 715
W S	Santa Clara San Jose	65 360
MANM		
Abel*	Santa Cruz Soguel	66 597
MANMEI		
M	El Dorado Greenwood	58 721
MANMOS		
Bernardo	Los Angeles Los Angeles	59 380
MANMY		
P	San Francisco San Francisco 4	681156
MANN		
---	Mariposa Twp 3	60 620
---	Tuolumne Don Pedro	71 163
A	Nevada Nevada	61 245
A	Sacramento Granite	63 227
A L	Nevada Grass Valley	61 186
A M	Amador Twp 1	55 504
Abel	Santa Cruz Soguel	66 597
Adison	Tulara Keyesville	71 61
Ah	Tuolumne Twp 4	71 163
Alexdr	San Francisco San Francisco 8	681322
Asa O*	Mendocino Little L	60 830
Augustus	Tuolumne Big Oak	71 139
Charles	Tulara Keeneysburg	71 46
Charles	Tuolumne Twp 5	71 527
Christian	Tuolumne Chinese	71 492
MANN		
Christopher	Santa Cruz Pajaro	66 545
Clara N	San Francisco San Francisco 6	67 460
David	Butte Chico	56 563
Dorwin D*	Alameda Brooklyn	55 127
Edward	Contra Costa Twp 3	57 604
Elbridge	Calaveras Twp 6	57 156
Feliciana	San Francisco San Francisco 2	67 790
Frank	Nevada Rough &	61 427
G A	Nevada Grass Valley	61 146
Geo S	San Francisco San Francisco 10	281 67
George	Sacramento Sutter	63 300
George	Solano Vallejo	69 250
George*	Plumas Quincy	62 975
H	San Francisco San Francisco 12	394 67
Henry	Plumas Quincy	62 951
Henry	Plumas Quincy	62 961
Henry	Siskiyou Klamath	69 90
Henry	Tuolumne Twp 5	71 492
Henry P	Yuba Marysville	72 962
Hermann	Tuolumne Twp 4	71 139
Ichael	Yuba Slate Ro	72 695
J	El Dorado Georgetown	58 673
J*	Tuolumne Big Oak	71 156
Jackson	Monterey Pajaro	601012
James	Siskiyou Klamath	69 96
James	Solano Vallejo	69 273
Jane	San Francisco San Francisco 8	681307
Jno	Butte Chico	56 549
Joel F	Yolo No E Twp	72 671
Joel F	Yuba North Ea	72 671
John	Butte Bidwell	56 712
John	Humbolt Mattole	59 127
John	Santa Clara Burnett	65 257
John	Tuolumne Twp 2	71 474
John C	Tuolumne Twp 5	71 492
John L	Sonoma Santa Rosa	69 422
John S	Amador Twp 4	55 236
John S	Sonoma Santa Rosa	69 422
Katy	Tuolumne Sonora	71 188
L	Nevada Grass Valley	61 195
Levi	Yuba Marysville	72 872
Lewis	Yuba Rose Bar	72 792
M	Calaveras Twp 9	57 397
M	Nevada Grass Valley	61 198
M	Solano Vacaville	69 323
M K	San Francisco San Francisco 9	681070
Mary E	Alameda Oakland	55 5
Michael	Yolo Slate Ra	72 695
Mike	San Francisco San Francisco 9	681070
P J	Del Norte Crescent	58 626
Peter	Sierra Twp 5	66 917
Peter J	Colusa Grand Island	57 478
Philip*	Mendocino Big Rvr	60 847
R A*	Nevada Grass Valley	61 174
S M	Nevada Nevada	61 260
Sarah A	Tuolumne Twp 3	71 449
Stephen	San Joaquin Elkhorn	64 971
Thos	Santa Clara San Jose	65 338
Thos H	Merced Twp 1	60 898
Valentine	Calaveras Twp 5	57 239
Warren	Yuba Long Bar	72 773
Washington	Tulara Twp 1	71 74
Wm	San Francisco San Francisco 1	68 917
Wm	Santa Clara San Jose	65 367
Wm D	Fresno Twp 3	59 13
Wm O	Sonoma Sonoma	69 639
MANNA		
---	San Francisco San Francisco 5	67 543
Manuel	Calaveras Twp 7	57 11
P H*	Nevada Grass Valley	61 238
MANNACH		
J*	San Francisco San Francisco 2	67 684
MANNAHAN		
W F	Calaveras Twp 9	57 412
MANNASSE		
Heyman*	San Diego San Diego	64 758
Joseph S	San Diego San Diego	64 762
MANNE		
Abel*	Santa Cruz Soguel	66 597
D*	Nevada Eureka	61 389
MANNEE		
P H	Nevada Grass Valley	61 238
MANNEL		
M	Butte Kimshaw	56 585
MANNELL		
---	Sacramento Granite	63 233
John	El Dorado Salmon Falls	581045
MANNELLA		
John	Calaveras Twp 5	57 227
MANNEN		
B W*	Siskiyou Scott Va	69 50
MANNER		
Alexander	San Francisco San Francisco 4	681146

California 1860 Census Index

Name	County Locale	M653 Roll	Page
MANNER			
Edward	Nevada Bloomfield	61	526
John	Sonoma Vallejo	69	609
John	Sonoma Sonoma	69	661
P H*	Nevada Grass Valley	61	238
W H	San Francisco San Francisco 9	68	1080
MANNERY			
Cath	Sacramento Ward 1	63	43
George	Calaveras Twp 4	57	336
Hugh	Calaveras Twp 6	57	151
MANNETT			
Joseph C	Calaveras Twp 10	57	265
MANNEY			
A	Nevada Nevada	61	287
Charles H	Tuolumne Sonora	71	212
M	Nevada Grass Valley	61	203
P*	San Francisco San Francisco 4	68	1156
S	Tuolumne Twp 4	71	162
MANNGAN			
---	San Francisco San Francisco 7	68	1341
MANNIA			
Joanna*	San Francisco San Francisco 9	68	986
MANNIE			
T W	Nevada Nevada	61	325
MANNIG			
D*	Nevada Eureka	61	388
MANNIN			
Bemard*	Yuba Long Bar	72	755
Bernard*	Yuba Long Bar	72	755
George	San Francisco San Francisco 7	68	1444
MANNING			
A	El Dorado White Oaks	58	1005
A	Nevada Nevada	61	275
A L	Nevada Nevada	61	284
Alfred	San Francisco San Francisco 7	68	1436
Andrew	Marin Tomales	60	725
B	El Dorado Kelsey	58	1136
B	Siskiyou Cottonwood	69	99
C	Tehama Lassen	70	877
Charles	Tuolumne Jamestown	71	455
D	Nevada Eureka	61	388
D	San Joaquin Stockton	64	1023
D*	Nevada Eureka	61	388
Daniel	Santa Cruz Pajaro	66	553
Danl	Tuolumne Twp 1	71	277
David*	El Dorado Greenwood	58	720
E	Calaveras Twp 9	57	389
E	Calaveras Twp 9	57	398
E	Sutter Nicolaus	70	835
Ed	Sacramento Ward 3	63	487
Edward	San Mateo Twp 3	65	82
Elias J	Sacramento Ward 4	63	572
Francis	San Francisco San Francisco 7	68	1384
Franklin	Yuba Marysville	72	945
George	Tuolumne Twp 1	71	211
Hugh	Calaveras Twp 6	57	151
J H	Tuolumne Twp 2	71	391
J M	San Francisco San Francisco 2	67	675
James	Mariposa Coulterville	60	674
James	San Francisco San Francisco 3	67	24
James	Santa Cruz Pajaro	66	553
James	Siskiyou Scott Va	69	40
James	Tuolumne Don Pedro	71	534
Jas	San Francisco San Francisco 1	68	835
Jas	San Francisco San Francisco 3	67	87
John	San Mateo Twp 2	65	120
John	Sonoma Armally	69	481
John M	San Francisco San Francisco 11	67	151
Kate	San Francisco San Francisco 10	67	223
L	Butte Cascade	56	700
Luke	El Dorado Greenwood	58	720
M	El Dorado Georgetown	58	695
M	Sacramento Cosummes	63	394
M	Solano Vacaville	69	329
M P	San Francisco San Francisco 6	67	461
Martin	Tuolumne Twp 1	71	264
Mathias	Calaveras Twp 9	57	373
Mathias	El Dorado Georgetown	58	676
Matilda	San Francisco San Francisco 1	68	860
Methias	El Dorado Georgetown	58	676
Michael	San Francisco San Francisco 4	68	1159
Michael	Tuolumne Twp 4	71	138
P	San Joaquin Stockton	64	1023
Pat	Nevada Rough &	61	421
Patrick	Calaveras Twp 5	57	195
Patrick	Solano Vallejo	69	246
Peter	San Francisco San Francisco 1	68	860
Peter	Trinity Taylor'S	70	1034
Phylander	San Mateo Twp 1	65	55
R	Napa Napa	61	112
Rose	San Francisco San Francisco 10	67	324
S M	Yolo Cache Crk	72	623
S*	Nevada Nevada	61	271

Name	County Locale	M653 Roll	Page
MANNING			
Saml	Santa Clara Fremont	65	419
Samuel	Santa Cruz Pajaro	66	553
Samuel	Tehama Antelope	70	893
Teresa	San Diego San Diego	64	767
W B D	Tuolumne Twp 1	71	257
William H	Los Angeles Los Angeles	59	333
William S	Los Angeles Los Angeles	59	345
Wm	Stanislaus Emory	70	739
Wm H*	Alameda Oakland	55	25
Wm W*	Alameda Oakland	55	25
MANNINS			
F	Calaveras Twp 9	57	414
MANNION			
James	Sonoma Mendocino	69	458
MANNIRY			
Jos*	San Francisco San Francisco 3	67	87
MANNIS			
John M	Sierra Morristown	66	1053
MANNIX			
L	Nevada Grass Valley	61	196
MANNON			
B W	Siskiyou Scott Va	69	50
Patrick	Sacramento Ward 3	63	455
MANNOR			
John	Sonoma Sonoma	69	661
MANNS			
A Johunnes	Tuolumne Sonora	71	192
Henry	Yuba Marysville	72	849
P M	San Francisco San Francisco 6	67	432
MANNUFSE			
Moses	San Diego Agua Caliente	64	861
MANNVILLE			
E	Siskiyou Scott Va	69	42
MANNY			
Hurschel	Alameda Brooklyn	55	84
J J	Klamath S Fork	59	207
James	Solano Benecia	69	285
Julia	San Francisco San Francisco 10	67	249
Patrick	Humbolt Eureka	59	172
S	Amador Twp 6	55	435
Saml	Amador Twp 2	55	266
T*	Nevada Grass Valley	61	205
MANO			
Andres	Los Angeles Los Angeles	59	323
MANOEL			
---	Tulara Twp 3	71	47
MANOHAN			
Edward	Contra Costa Twp 1	57	489
MANOID			
Geo	Sonoma Petaluma	69	579
MANOLIK			
---	Tulara Twp 1	71	120
MANOM			
M*	Nevada Eureka	61	389
MANON			
Jean	Butte Eureka	56	650
MANOO			
L D	Yolo Cache	72	626
MANOR			
A	Nevada Grass Valley	61	174
L D	Yolo Cache Crk	72	626
Pastian*	Siskiyou Yreka	69	168
Robt	Placer Stewart	62	606
MANOS			
Francisco	Calaveras Twp 5	57	227
Pedro	Monterey S Antoni	60	969
MANOY			
Peter D*	San Francisco San Francisco 2	67	650
MANPEN			
D	Shasta Horsetown	66	704
MANPIN			
D S	Colusa Grand Island	57	472
D*	Shasta Horsetown	66	704
W E	Solano Vacaville	69	330
MANQUITA			
Jose*	Butte Kimshaw	56	603
MANQUITTO			
J*	Butte Kimshaw	56	600
MANRACH			
J*	San Francisco San Francisco 2	67	684
MANRAR			
S*	Nevada Grass Valley	61	164
MANRATTA			
John*	Calaveras Twp 5	57	227
MANRAY			
M*	San Francisco San Francisco 10	67	313
Nathan B	San Francisco San Francisco 7	68	1336
MANRESE			
Joseph*	Yuba Parke Ba	72	782
MANREY			
F S*	Yuba Parks Ba	72	776
MANRIE			
D*	Nevada Eureka	61	389

Name	County Locale	M653 Roll	Page
MANRIGUES			
Brigida	Los Angeles San Juan	59	469
Francisca	Los Angeles Los Angeles	59	382
MANRING			
D N*	Butte Oregon	56	625
D W	Butte Oregon	56	625
MANRIQUES			
Brigida	Los Angeles San Juan	59	469
Juan	Los Angeles Santa Ana	59	459
Juan	Los Angeles San Juan	59	476
Manuel	Los Angeles San Juan	59	469
Maria	Los Angeles Los Angeles	59	312
MANRIYAN			
---	San Francisco San Francisco 7	68	1341
MANRO			
Michael	San Francisco San Francisco 2	67	784
MANROE			
J*	Nevada Grass Valley	61	224
William*	Placer Forest H	62	805
MANROL			
J L*	Nevada Grass Valley	61	186
MANROTT			
Thomas*	Sierra Twp 7	66	864
MANROW			
D A*	Sacramento Ward 3	63	460
J P	San Francisco San Francisco 12	67	368
MANRY			
Abraham*	Sierra Pine Grove	66	835
H	El Dorado Diamond	58	791
Jos*	Sacramento Ward 1	63	108
Richard	San Francisco San Francisco 2	67	734
MANS			
Adeline	Yuba Bear Rvr	72	1000
Chas*	Placer Auburn	62	585
Chas*	Placer Dutch Fl	62	728
Christopher	Santa Cruz Pajaro	66	545
James	Nevada Bloomfield	61	508
Josiah	Calaveras Twp 7	57	40
Le	Mariposa Twp 3	60	620
Mary E*	Nevada Bloomfield	61	508
MANSA			
Eldridge	Calaveras Twp 6	57	156
Maria C	Los Angeles Los Angeles	59	338
MANSAL			
---	San Mateo Twp 3	65	98
MANSANARIS			
J	Merced Twp 1	60	898
MANSANARY			
J	Merced Twp 1	60	898
MANSANOTE			
Aloysius	Santa Clara Santa Clara	65	481
MANSAULDO			
Bicenta	San Bernardino San Bernadino	64	667
MANSAW			
L*	Nevada Grass Valley	61	190
MANSDORFF			
Wm	San Francisco San Francisco 2	67	671
MANSEAUX			
A*	Shasta Shasta	66	661
MANSEBRO			
Jose*	Placer Michigan	62	850
MANSEL			
R	Nevada Grass Valley	61	146
R J	Nevada Nevada	61	284
MANSELL			
A	Colusa Monroeville	57	451
A J	Nevada Nevada	61	286
A L	Nevada Grass Valley	61	179
F	Nevada Nevada	61	248
H J	Nevada Nevada	61	286
J	Nevada Eureka	61	347
M	Nevada Grass Valley	61	169
R A	Nevada Nevada	61	273
Wm	Nevada Eureka	61	361
MANSER			
Henry	Nevada Bloomfield	61	512
R M	Amador Twp 3	55	396
MANSES			
James	Marin Bolinas	60	747
MANSFALL			
A	Nevada Grass Valley	61	149
MANSFIELD			
Amos	Santa Cruz Watsonville	66	539
Chas H	Sacramento Ward 3	63	488
David	Marin Cortemad	60	786
E W	Sacramento American	63	168
G	Nevada Grass Valley	61	166
G J*	Mariposa Twp 1	60	660
G L	Mariposa Twp 1	60	660
G T	Mariposa Twp 1	60	660
Geo	El Dorado Casumnes	58	1166
George	El Dorado Georgetown	58	697
George	Tuolumne Twp 4	71	134
George W	Marin Cortemad	60	784
Harry	Monterey S Antoni	60	973

Name	County Locale	M653 Roll	Page
MANSFIELD			
I M	Napa Napa	61	78
Isaac	Amador Twp 2	55	308
J	Amador Twp 2	55	320
J M	Napa Napa	61	78
J S	Marin Cortemad	60	789
J S	Shasta Shasta	66	659
James	Plumas Meadow Valley	62	904
James M	Mariposa Twp 1	60	660
James*	Nevada Rough &	61	433
John T	Calaveras Twp 6	57	147
Jos*	Amador Twp 2	55	316
Jro	Amador Twp 2	55	316
Jrs*	Amador Twp 2	55	316
L	Sonoma Mendocino	69	460
L E	Mariposa Twp 1	60	586
M	El Dorado Kelsey	58	1131
M	Nevada Grass Valley	61	206
Mary	Placer Rattle Snake	62	634
Michael	Placer Rattle Snake	62	634
R	El Dorado Coloma	58	1081
Rich	Sacramento Ward 4	63	526
T	Amador Twp 2	55	320
V M	San Francisco San Francisco 10	67	358
W	Nevada Grass Valley	61	191
William	Placer Michigan	62	850
William	Yuba Bear Rvr	72	1011
Wm	Tuolumne Columbia	71	308
Wm	Yuba New York	72	737
MANSGROVE			
J D*	Shasta Shasta	66	681
MANSI			
---	Mariposa Twp 3	60	585
MANSILL			
J*	Nevada Eureka	61	347
MANSIN			
---	Mariposa Twp 3	60	585
MANSINO			
Barto	Calaveras Twp 7	57	45
MANSIR			
Charles G	Los Angeles Los Angeles	59	344
MANSLY			
Robert	Placer Forest H	62	798
MANSO			
Charles	Marin Bolinas	60	744
Panlo	Tuolumne Chinese	71	520
Paulo	Tuolumne Twp 5	71	520
MANSON			
---	Mariposa Twp 3	60	585
Andrea	Calaveras Twp 8	57	50
John	Calaveras Twp 7	57	14
John	Plumas Quincy	62	994
John D	Calaveras Twp 7	57	14
John S	San Francisco San Francisco 2	67	635
L	Nevada Washington	61	331
L	Nevada Washington	61	341
L*	Nevada Grass Valley	61	190
Mathen	Marin S Antoni	60	708
Mathew	Marin S Antoni	60	708
Nancy H	Nevada Bridgeport	61	443
Patrick	Sierra Downieville	66	994
W L	Nevada Red Dog	61	547
MANSONEY			
T*	Nevada Washington	61	337
MANSONS			
Petromille	San Francisco San Francisco 2	67	703
Petrooonille*	San Francisco	67	703
	San Francisco		
Petroorille	San Francisco San Francisco 2	67	703
MANSOVETO			
Tvynazgine*	Sierra Poker Flats	66	839
MANSPILD			
Isaac	Amador Twp 2	55	308
MANSS			
Pauline	San Francisco San Francisco 2	67	712
MANSSAN			
R	Tuolumne Sonora	71	216
MANSTER			
Eliza	Nevada Bridgeport	61	470
MANSU			
William*	Placer Michigan	62	844
MANSUR			
Horrace*	Placer Rattle Snake	62	626
MANT			
Albert	Placer Virginia	62	664
MANTAC			
---	San Diego Agua Caliente	64	865
MANTAGUE			
Geo	Sacramento Ward 3	63	479
MANTE			
M	Shasta Horsetown	66	702
MANTEE			
Peter	San Francisco San Francisco 2	67	802
MANTEI			
J A*	Butte Ophir	56	824
MANTEL			
C	San Francisco San Francisco 2	67	658
W*	San Francisco San Francisco 2	67	696
MANTEN			
Sarah Miss	Calaveras Twp 6	57	127
MANTENS			
Mary*	San Francisco San Francisco 2	67	658
MANTER			
D D	El Dorado Coloma	58	1076
Fordyar*	Calaveras Twp 10	57	263
Fosdyarn*	Calaveras Twp 10	57	263
John	Placer Goods	62	696
Kordyar*	Calaveras Twp 10	57	263
MANTETH			
Alexander	Siskiyou Yreka	69	137
Alexander	Siskiyou Yreka	69	138
MANTHAN			
Jacob	El Dorado Greenwood	58	722
MANTIGE			
Josa	El Dorado Georgetown	58	694
MANTIN			
Stephen	Nevada Nevada	61	260
MANTINE			
P	Siskiyou Callahan	69	6
MANTINEZ			
Tomas	Monterey San Juan	60	1002
MANTINO			
Jose	Calaveras Twp 7	57	47
MANTINS			
Dennis*	San Francisco San Francisco 7	68	1352
MANTIUS			
Dennis	San Francisco San Francisco 7	68	1352
MANTLEBAUM			
C	San Francisco San Francisco 5	67	522
MANTO			
---	Butte Chico	56	550
---	Fresno Twp 2	59	108
MANTON			
L	Nevada Grass Valley	61	191
Pat	Nevada Bridgeport	61	465
S	Nevada Grass Valley	61	168
MANTONIO			
---	Marin Tomales	60	776
MANTORN			
James	San Joaquin Tulare	64	871
MANTS			
M*	Shasta Horsetown	66	702
MANTUA			
L	Los Angeles Azuza	59	277
MANTY			
Christopher	Colusa Grand Island	57	481
MANTZ			
William H*	Yuba Marysville	72	879
MANUCALA			
Anrelmi	Calaveras Twp 4	57	333
MANUE			
E	Nevada Bloomfield	61	512
MANUEL JIM			
---	Tulara Twp 3	71	47
MANUEL JOSE			
---*	Monterey Pajaro	60	1017
MANUEL TOM			
---	Tulara Twp 3	71	47
MANUEL			
---	Los Angeles Los Angeles	59	375
---	Los Angeles San Gabriel	59	414
---	Los Angeles Santa Ana	59	442
---	Los Angeles San Pedro	59	486
---	Los Angeles Tejon	59	529
---	Mariposa Twp 3	60	587
---	Mariposa Twp 1	60	640
---	Mariposa Twp 1	60	644
---	Mendocino Twp 1	60	889
---	Mendocino Twp 1	60	890
---	Merced Monterey	60	941
---	Monterey Alisal	60	1028
---	Monterey San Juan	60	992
---	Nevada Bloomfield	61	512
---	Placer Rattle Snake	62	632
---	Placer Rattle Snake	62	635
---	San Bernardino Santa Inez	64	135
---	San Bernardino Santa Inez	64	136
---	San Bernardino Santa Inez	64	137
---	San Bernardino Santa Barbara	64	157
---	San Bernardino Santa Barbara	64	200
---	San Bernardino San Bernadino	64	679
---	San Bernardino S Timate	64	692
---	San Bernardino S Timate	64	693
---	San Bernardino S Timate	64	697
---	San Bernardino S Timate	64	700
---	San Bernardino S Timate	64	703
---	San Bernardino S Timate	64	708
---	San Bernardino S Timate	64	710
---	San Bernardino S Timate	64	713
---	San Bernardino S Timate	64	715
---	San Bernardino S Timate	64	719
MANUEL (cont.)			
---	San Bernardino S Timate	64	720
---	San Bernardino S Timate	64	721
---	San Bernardino S Timate	64	724
---	San Bernardino S Timate	64	725
---	San Bernardino S Timate	64	730
---	San Bernardino S Timate	64	733
---	San Bernardino S Timate	64	734
---	San Bernardino S Timate	64	735
---	San Bernardino S Timate	64	737
---	San Bernardino S Timate	64	750
---	San Diego San Diego	64	771
---	San Diego San Diego	64	772
---	San Diego Temecula	64	786
---	San Diego Temecula	64	797
---	San Diego Temecula	64	800
---	San Diego Temecula	64	802
---	San Diego Agua Caliente	64	828
---	San Diego Agua Caliente	64	837
---	San Diego Agua Caliente	64	863
---	San Diego Agua Caliente	64	864
---	San Mateo Twp 2	65	134
---	Santa Clara Fremont	65	421
---	Tulara Keyesville	71	62
---	Tulara Keyesville	71	63
---	Yuba Marysville	72	946
---*	Mariposa Twp 1	60	644
---*	Tulara Keeneysburg	71	47
Alexander	Solano Vallejo	69	268
Anrodo	San Diego Agua Caliente	64	848
B F	Sierra Downieville	66	958
B J	Sierra Downieville	66	958
Frances	Alameda Brooklyn	55	116
Geo W	Napa Napa	61	101
J J	Siskiyou Yreka	69	193
Jose	Calaveras Twp 7	57	42
Jose	Los Angeles Los Angeles	59	375
Jose	Los Angeles Los Angeles	59	402
Jose	Los Angeles Los Angeles	59	405
Jose	Los Angeles San Pedro	59	480
Jose	Merced Monterey	60	942
Jose	Monterey Monterey	60	942
Jose	San Diego Temecula	64	787
Jose	San Diego Agua Caliente	64	817
Jose	Santa Cruz Soguel	66	587
Jose	Tuolumne Twp 3	71	468
Joseph	El Dorado Georgetown	58	708
Joseph	Marin Saucileto	60	749
Joseph	Sierra La Porte	66	773
Lewis	Placer Ophir	62	651
Luhan	Monterey San Juan	60	1001
M	Butte Kimshaw	56	585
Manuela	Santa Clara Alviso	65	414
Pachisco	San Mateo Twp 1	65	51
Petro	Alameda Brooklyn	55	147
Richard	Amador Twp 4	55	233
S	Nevada Grass Valley	61	209
William	Shasta Millvill	66	739
MANUELA			
---	Los Angeles Los Angeles	59	404
---	Los Angeles Tejon	59	529
---	Los Angeles Tejon	59	529
---	Monterey Monterey	60	937
---	San Bernardino Santa Inez	64	145
---	San Bernardino Santa Barbara	64	202
---	San Bernardino S Timate	64	696
---	San Bernardino S Timate	64	706
---	San Bernardino S Timate	64	727
---	San Bernardino S Timate	64	729
---	San Bernardino S Timate	64	732
---	San Bernardino S Timate	64	741
---	San Bernardino S Timate	64	742
---	San Bernardino S Timate	64	746
---	San Bernardino S Timate	64	748
---	San Bernardino S Timate	64	751
---	San Bernardino S Timate	64	753
---	San Bernardino S Timate	64	754
---	San Diego San Diego	64	772
MANUELITO			
---*	San Bernardino S Timate	64	703
MANUELL			
---	Mariposa Twp 1	60	631
Munill	Amador Twp 5	55	332
MANUELLA			
John*	Calaveras Twp 5	57	227
MANUELLEN			
Anguell	Mariposa Twp 1	60	632
Anquell	Mariposa Twp 1	60	632
MANUELLO			
John*	Calaveras Twp 5	57	227
MANUELS			
Jesus	San Joaquin Stockton	64	1064
Louis	Calaveras Twp 9	57	354
Mathew	Placer Iona Hills	62	882
Philip	Placer Iona Hills	62	882
MANUER			
Edward	Nevada Bloomfield	61	526

Name	County Locale	M653 RollPage
MANUL		
---	Los Angeles Tejon	59 529
Jose	Tuolumne Twp 3	71 468
S	Nevada Nevada	61 271
MANULES		
Joseph	Calaveras Twp 10	57 262
MANULIA		
Manuel	Calaveras Twp 10	57 260
MANUNCIA		
---	San Bernardino Santa Ba	64 221
MANUS		
John A	Tuolumne Twp 1	71 196
Julia	Alameda Oakland	55 27
P M*	San Francisco San Francisco 6 67 432	
MANUSS		
J M	Nevada Nevada	61 269
Peter	Shasta Shasta	66 686
MANVILL		
Peter	Tehama Antelope	70 893
MANVY		
Peter D*	San Francisco San Francisco 2 67 650	
MANWELL		
---	Mariposa Twp 1	60 629
---	Mariposa Twp 1	60 654
Bell Ville*	Amador Twp 4	55 241
Bellville*	Amador Twp 4	55 241
Lewis	Sierra Twp 7	66 913
Marker	Mariposa Twp 1	60 654
Parso	Mariposa Twp 1	60 654
MANWELLE		
Solino	Tuolumne Shawsfla	71 395
MANWELLEN		
Anguell	Mariposa Twp 1	60 632
MANWELLER		
---	Mariposa Twp 1	60 630
MANWELLO		
Solino	Tuolumne Twp 2	71 395
MANWIN		
John*	San Francisco San Francisco 2 67 796	
MANWLIK		
---	Tulara Twp 1	71 120
MANWOLIK		
---*	Tulara Visalia	71 120
MANX		
Henrietta	Solano Benecia	69 291
MANY ANA		
---	Fresno Twp 2	59 47
MANY		
---	Amador Twp 6	55 449
---	Calaveras Twp 6	57 121
---	Calaveras Twp 5	57 149
---	Calaveras Twp 6	57 171
---	Calaveras Twp 5	57 254
---	Calaveras Twp 5	57 256
---	Calaveras Twp 10	57 285
---	El Dorado Georgetown	58 701
Henry C	San Francisco San Francisco 2 67 617	
How	Calaveras Twp 4	57 304
Pan	Calaveras Twp 5	57 220
Thomas*	Shasta Shasta	66 687
Thos	Santa Clara San Jose	65 380
MANYAM		
---	Mendocino Twp 1	60 892
MANYARRES		
Jesus	Amador Twp 1	55 486
MANYN		
Emory	Alameda Brooklyn	55 190
MANZA		
Librada	Los Angeles Los Angeles	59 386
MANZANEH		
Maria A	Monterey Monterey	60 947
MANZANELE		
Maria A*	Monterey Monterey	60 947
MANZANELI		
Maria A	Monterey Monterey	60 947
MANZO		
Bernardo	Los Angeles Santa Ana	59 449
Savino	Los Angeles Los Angeles	59 295
MAO		
---	San Francisco San Francisco 4 681175	
---	Sierra Twp 7	66 876
MAOER		
E	Sutter Butte	70 795
MAONI		
---	Placer Secret R	62 623
MAONIO		
Samuel	Yuba Marysville	72 952
MAORAN		
---	Fresno Twp 3	59 31
MAORQUIS		
Jose*	Los Angeles Los Angeles	59 519
MAORTY		
John*	Del Norte Crescent	58 644
MAOSTES		
L	Calaveras Twp 9	57 374
MAP		
---	Amador Twp 2	55 293

Name	County Locale	M653 RollPage
MAPAKO		
Jose	Los Angeles Los Angeles	59 519
MAPELETA		
Fracoma	Mariposa Twp 3	60 549
MAPELS		
H	Sutter Bear Rvr	70 818
MAPES		
Geo	Sonoma Salt Point	69 690
Ira	Sonoma Salt Point	69 691
Sarah	Tulara Visalia	71 106
MAPET		
August*	Trinity North Fo	701026
MAPEY		
Francis	Sonoma Santa Rosa	69 391
MAPLE		
Mary	San Francisco San Francisco 1 68 876	
MAPLES		
Edward L	Plumas Quincy	62 989
John	Sonoma Bodega	69 530
Wm	Butte Mountain	56 737
MAPLETON		
B F	Siskiyou Scott Ri	69 81
MAPOL		
F A*	Sacramento Ward 4	63 577
MAPONE		
L	Mariposa Twp 3	60 614
MAPOPURT		
Anton*	Solano Benecia	69 316
Haton*	Solano Benecia	69 316
MAPPER		
Phillip	Mariposa Twp 1	60 653
MAPPIN		
F M	Tuolumne Twp 2	71 398
MAPREL		
George*	Nevada Red Dog	61 554
MAPSTEAD		
John	San Bernardino San Bernadino	64 685
MAPTSON		
Edward	San Joaquin Douglass	64 918
MAQRCH		
Ava	Shasta Horsetown	66 692
MAQUEER		
Francis*	San Francisco San Francisco 11 126 67	
MAQUIER		
Vincent*	Tuolumne Big Oak	71 142
MAQUIN		
---	San Bernardino S Timate	64 703
MAQUIRE		
Thos	Nevada Bridgeport	61 474
Thos	Tuolumne Twp 4	71 137
MAQUIS		
Ramona	Los Angeles Los Angeles	59 301
MAR		
---	Calaveras Twp 10	57 275
---	Calaveras Twp 5	57 339
---	El Dorado Salmon Hills	581064
---	El Dorado Union	581089
---	Mariposa Twp 3	60 619
---	Placer Ophirville	62 655
---	Sierra Twp 7	66 898
---*	Mariposa Twp 3	60 582
Amedia*	Plumas Meadow Valley	62 928
Fook	Placer Ophirville	62 658
Free*	Mariposa Twp 3	60 582
J M B	Nevada Bridgeport	61 473
John	Santa Clara San Jose	65 342
Joseph	Merced Monterey	60 944
Joseph	Monterey Monterey	60 944
MARA		
---	Shasta Shasta	66 670
Augustus*	Tuolumne Twp 3	71 463
Frank	Tuolumne Twp 3	71 459
Jacoba	San Bernardino San Salvador	64 661
Joseph	Amador Twp 1	55 463
Mate*	Tehama Red Bluff	70 930
Wm	Sacramento Ward 3	63 425
MARABELLO		
Manuel	San Francisco San Francisco 3 67 64	
MARABLA		
John*	El Dorado Mud Springs	58 949
MARABOUT		
Andra*	San Francisco San Francisco 11 125 67	
Audra*	San Francisco San Francisco 11 125 67	
MARAGA		
Verhipa*	Alameda Oakland	55 56
MARAGER		
Janna	Mariposa Twp 1	60 632
Jauna	Mariposa Twp 1	60 632
MARAI		
John*	Amador Twp 4	55 245
MARAJA		
Verhipa*	Alameda Oakland	55 56
MARAJILDA		
---	San Bernardino San Bernadino	64 669

Name	County Locale	M653 RollPage
MARALEANO		
Lugo*	San Francisco San Francisco 3 67 64	
MARALELA		
John*	El Dorado Mud Springs	58 949
MARALES		
Maguil	Napa Napa	61 115
MARALIANO		
Lergo*	San Francisco San Francisco 3 67 64	
Lirgo*	San Francisco San Francisco 3 67 64	
MARALL		
John*	Shasta French G	66 718
MARALY		
Maguel	Napa Napa	61 115
MARANDA		
Jose	Amador Twp 6	55 441
L	Nevada Eureka	61 392
Noche	Calaveras Twp 7	57 14
MARANDEZ		
---	Los Angeles Santa Ana	59 445
MARANGO		
J M	Tuolumne Twp 1	71 225
MARANO		
Albino*	Santa Clara San Jose	65 324
Alvino*	Santa Clara San Jose	65 324
Manuel	Marin Cortemad	60 779
Manuel	Tuolumne Twp 3	71 435
MARAOS		
Juan H	Tuolumne Twp 5	71 495
MARAR		
---	Mariposa Twp 1	60 630
MARARIA		
---	San Bernardino Santa Inez	64 137
MARAS		
A	Tuolumne Twp 4	71 160
MARASCHI		
Anton*	El Dorado Georgetown	58 703
Revd A	San Francisco San Francisco 10 317 67	
MARASEFER		
---	Mendocino Twp 1	60 889
MARASHI		
Antonio	Santa Clara Santa Clara	65 481
MARASKY		
Bernhard	Contra Costa Twp 1	57 486
Mina	San Francisco San Francisco 10 310 67	
MARAT		
Julens	San Francisco San Francisco 4 681153	
Julius	San Francisco San Francisco 4 681153	
MARATELLI		
N	El Dorado Georgetown	58 702
MARATTA		
Hona*	Alameda Brooklyn	55 165
MARAUGO		
J M	Tuolumne Sonora	71 225
MARAVETO		
---	Amador Twp 2	55 282
MARAVIS		
Jose	Los Angeles Elmonte	59 264
MARAY		
Jas*	Los Angeles Tejon	59 539
L H*	Napa Hot Springs	61 3
MARBALT		
E*	Sacramento San Joaquin	63 360
MARBATT		
E*	Sacramento San Joaquin	63 360
MARBELTON		
W	Sutter Butte	70 788
MARBER		
Joseph	Tuolumne Twp 4	71 133
MARBLE		
A	Nevada Washington	61 338
C M	San Francisco San Francisco 2 67 693	
David	Sierra Pine Grove	66 829
David B	Sierra Pine Grove	66 829
Elijah	Amador Twp 4	55 245
Elijah	Siskiyou Shasta Rvr	69 114
Elijzh	Siskiyou Shasta Rvr	69 114
F	San Francisco San Francisco 5 67 531	
F	San Francisco San Francisco 5 67 547	
Francis	Sierra Pine Grove	66 829
James	Shasta Cottonwood	66 724
John	Napa Clear Lake	61 139
L F*	Butte Cascade	56 689
Lloyd T	San Francisco San Francisco 5 67 545	
Nelson	San Francisco San Francisco 10 274 67	
Oliver	Sierra Pine Grove	66 829
P	San Francisco San Francisco 2 67 729	
P J	Butte Oregon	56 626
Richard	Nevada Bloomfield	61 525
S F	Butte Cascade	56 689
Solomon M	Sierra Pine Grove	66 829
Theodore	Mendocino Big Rock	60 872
Wilson	San Francisco San Francisco 10 274 67	

Name	County Locale	M653 Roll	Page
MARBLE			
Wm	Santa Clara Alviso	65	409
MARBOHO			
Henry	Tuolumne Twp 6	71	539
MARBORE			
---	Mendocino Round Va	60	881
MARCA			
Hese	El Dorado Coloma	581	115
MARCAL			
---	Fresno Twp 1	59	118
Janveal	Yuba Suida	72	982
MARCALS			
Benita	San Joaquin Stockton	641	073
MARCARD			
Frank	San Francisco San Francisco 7	681	346
MARCAS			
Won	El Dorado Mud Springs	58	966
MARCASY			
Jacob	Amador Twp 2	55	271
MARCE			
---	Mendocino Twp 1	60	886
Antone	Solano Benecia	69	282
Tunidos	Tehama Tehama	70	942
MARCEIS			
A W	El Dorado Placerville	58	911
MARCEL			
August	Amador Twp 1	55	451
Janveal	Yuba Linda Twp	72	983
Julian	Trinity Big Flat	701	039
MARCELENO			
J	El Dorado Placerville	58	868
MARCELINA			
---	San Bernardino S Timate	64	755
A	Mariposa Coulterville	60	690
S*	Mariposa Coulterville	60	690
MARCELINO			
Lugo	San Bernardino Santa Barbara	64	165
MARCELLA			
---	San Bernardino Santa Barbara	64	164
Ramon	San Diego Colorado	64	812
MARCELLANO			
Felipe	San Diego S Luis R	64	779
MARCELLENO			
---	San Diego Agua Caliente	64	853
---	San Diego Agua Caliente	64	857
MARCELLINA			
---	San Bernardino Santa Ba	64	219
---	San Bernardino S Buenav	64	220
---	San Mateo Twp 2	65	132
MARCELLINO			
---	San Mateo Twp 2	65	134
Peter	Sacramento Ward 1	63	57
MARCELLITA			
Carlotta	Sacramento Ward 3	63	439
MARCELLO			
Jos	San Francisco San Francisco 12	67	392
Pablo	Tuolumne Shawsfla	71	408
MARCELLONS			
H*	San Francisco San Francisco 3	67	73
MARCELLUS			
---	Marin San Rafael	60	768
H	San Francisco San Francisco 3	67	73
MARCELO			
---	Santa Clara Santa Clara	65	508
Jose Ma	Santa Clara Alviso	65	415
MARCEMINA			
---	San Bernardino S Timate	64	730
MARCEN			
Nicholas	San Francisco San Francisco 1	68	814
MARCENO			
Tracy*	San Mateo Twp 3	65	84
MARCENTI			
F	Calaveras Twp 9	57	406
MARCER			
Trinidad	Santa Cruz Pajaro	66	556
MARCES			
Whan	Mariposa Twp 1	60	653
MARCETTINA			
---	San Bernardino Santa Inez	64	137
MARCEY			
Chas	Napa Hot Springs	61	17
Timothy*	Sierra Twp 5	66	920
MARCH			
Ada	San Francisco San Francisco 6	67	469
Anderson J*	Napa Yount	61	30
Andirson J	Napa Yount	61	30
Ava	Shasta Horsetown	66	692
B	Sacramento Granite	63	234
D P	Napa Yount	61	30
Edmond	Sonoma Mendocino	69	451
Edward	Sonoma Mendocino	69	451
Edwin	Calaveras Twp 6	57	154
F	Sierra Twp 7	66	876
F S	Yolo Merritt	72	577
F*	Sierra Twp 7	66	876

Name	County Locale	M653 Roll	Page
MARCH			
Harry	San Mateo Twp 3	65	110
Ignatius	Sierra Twp 7	66	871
Israel	El Dorado Union	581	093
Israel	El Dorado Gold Hill	581	098
J J	Napa Yount	61	29
James A	Shasta Millvill	66	742
James O	Shasta Millvill	66	742
Johnothan B	Napa Yount	61	40
Jos	Klamath S Fork	59	205
L	Shasta Horsetown	66	710
P H	Sierra Downieville	66	968
R B	Napa Yount	61	29
Rhoda	Sierra Twp 7	66	900
Robert	Tulara Twp 1	71	86
Rosa	Yolo Merritt	72	578
Silas	Merced Twp 1	60	904
Thos	San Francisco San Francisco 1	68	866
Valentine	Shasta Horsetown	66	692
Wm J	Sonoma Mendocino	69	451
Wm S	Trinity Douglas	70	979
MARCHADO			
Jose	Los Angeles Azuza	59	274
MARCHAL			
Joseph	San Mateo Twp 1	65	53
MARCHALL			
Jn*	El Dorado Georgetown	58	754
R	El Dorado Gold Hill	581	098
Victor	Santa Clara San Jose	65	383
MARCHAM			
John*	Calaveras Twp 5	57	223
MARCHAN			
Damion	Los Angeles Santa Ana	59	446
MARCHAND			
Desire C	Yuba Marysville	72	848
Desire*	Yuba Marysville	72	848
Desiw*	Yuba Marysville	72	848
MARCHANT			
Jno	Sacramento Ward 1	63	90
John	Amador Twp 2	55	317
Samuel	Santa Cruz Watsonville	66	537
MARCHANTO			
Francolo	San Francisco San Francisco 1	68	845
MARCHARD			
Mr	Marin Novato	60	739
MARCHARN			
John*	Calaveras Twp 5	57	223
MARCHBANK			
Louisa	San Francisco San Francisco 10	67	181
MARCHBANKS			
Halford	Siskiyou Yreka	69	130
MARCHBUNKS			
Wm	Placer Folsom	62	641
MARCHE			
Andrew	Calaveras Twp 10	57	273
M	Yuba Parks Ba	72	786
MARCHEBONT			
August*	San Francisco San Francisco 2	67	684
MARCHELLA			
Roceo	Butte Ophir	56	777
Wm*	Butte Ophir	56	819
MARCHEN			
Francis	Calaveras Twp 5	57	228
MARCHER			
Andrew*	Calaveras Twp 10	57	273
J J	Trinity Indian C	70	986
MARCHERE			
Francis*	Calaveras Twp 5	57	228
MARCHERSAN			
John	Placer Iona Hills	62	872
MARCHESSAUTT			
Damien	Los Angeles Los Angeles	59	332
MARCHESSEAN			
S	El Dorado Mud Springs	58	994
MARCHETONT			
August*	San Francisco San Francisco 2	67	684
MARCHETTA			
Wm*	Butte Ophir	56	819
MARCHILDO			
---	Monterey San Juan	60	999
MARCHINO			
Manel	Tuolumne Shawsfla	71	375
MARCHINS			
Manuel	Tuolumne Twp 2	71	375
MARCHO			
---	Mendocino Round Va	60	885
MARCHURN			
John*	Calaveras Twp 5	57	223
MARCHUS			
Leopold	Contra Costa Twp 1	57	494
MARCIA			
A L	Merced Twp 1	60	909
A S	Merced Twp 1	60	909
Charles	Contra Costa Twp 1	57	526
J	San Francisco San Francisco 2	67	789

Name	County Locale	M653 Roll	Page
MARCIAR			
Jose M	Santa Cruz Pajaro	66	565
MARCIAS			
Jose M	Santa Cruz Pajaro	66	565
Lucas	Santa Clara Almaden	65	270
MARCIBA			
---	Monterey S Antoni	60	972
MARCIE			
Jose	Calaveras Twp 6	57	151
MARCIER			
Charles	San Francisco San Francisco 4	681	132
MARCIFUS			
---	San Diego Agua Caliente	64	828
MARCINTI			
F	Calaveras Twp 9	57	406
MARCIR			
Trindidad*	Santa Cruz Pajaro	66	556
Trinidad	Santa Cruz Pajaro	66	556
MARCISTER			
Geo	El Dorado Coloma	581	083
MARCK			
E A	Alameda Brooklyn	55	81
E N	Alameda Brooklyn	55	81
MARCKAM			
W	Sacramento Granite	63	236
MARCKER			
Mangus	Plumas Quincy	62	981
MARCKEY			
Julius*	San Mateo Twp 1	65	57
MARCKRIE			
Jose*	Santa Cruz Santa Cruz	66	620
MARCKS			
A	San Francisco San Francisco 2	67	651
MARCLAY			
Jeremiah*	Tulara Visalia	71	106
MARCLE			
John	Butte Ophir	56	769
MARCLIS			
Frances	Amador Twp 5	55	355
MARCO			
Antonio	Calaveras Twp 7	57	27
Artuse	Solano Benecia	69	282
Camilo	Calaveras Twp 8	57	92
Carnela	Calaveras Twp 7	57	36
H	Nevada Bridgeport	61	472
Joaquin	Santa Cruz Pajaro	66	546
Jose	Los Angeles Los Angeles	59	492
Jose	Mariposa Twp 1	60	650
Juan	San Joaquin Stockton	641	076
Juaquin	Santa Cruz Pajaro	66	546
MARCOLD			
Jacob	Tuolumne Chinese	71	522
MARCOLETTI			
Wm	San Francisco San Francisco 1	68	845
MARCOM			
Thos	Trinity E Weaver	701	057
W C	Trinity E Weaver	701	057
MARCONE			
Louis	Tuolumne Twp 1	71	254
MARCONI			
Louis	Tuolumne Twp 1	71	254
MARCORHFITE			
George	Yuba Marysville	72	926
MARCORRTZH			
Aug	Sacramento Ward 4	63	555
MARCOS			
Ignacia	Tuolumne Twp 1	71	225
Juan H*	Tuolumne Twp 5	71	495
Victoriana	Tuolumne Twp 1	71	225
MARCOSO			
H	El Dorado Eldorado	58	937
J	El Dorado Eldorado	58	937
MARCOVICH			
Aug	Sacramento Ward 1	63	29
John	Tuolumne Twp 4	71	133
MARCOVITCH			
Jno	Sacramento Ward 4	63	508
MARCOWLB			
D*	San Francisco San Francisco 2	67	612
MARCOWLT			
D	San Francisco San Francisco 2	67	612
MARCUAS			
Veveanna*	Yuba Marysville	72	922
MARCUD			
Girraled*	Monterey San Juan	601	001
MARCULL			
Marcus A*	Yuba Marysville	72	871
MARCULLO			
---	San Diego Agua Caliente	64	819
MARCUM			
J	Sacramento Alabama	63	413
Joseph	Sierra Pine Grove	66	823
M	Sacramento Alabama	63	411
MARCUS			
---	Marin Cortemad	60	788
---	San Bernardino San Bernadino	64	680

California 1860 Census Index

Name	County Locale	M653 Roll	Page
MARCUS			
---	San Diego Temecula	64	803
---	San Diego Agua Caliente	64	826
---	Santa Clara Santa Clara	65	508
---*	Marin Cortemad	60	788
Abram	San Francisco San Francisco 3	67	34
Charles	Humbolt Bucksport	59	159
Dolores	Yuba Marysville	72	944
Doming*	San Francisco San Francisco 9	681036	
Guraled	Monterey San Juan	601001	
Harris	Placer Michigan	62	810
Henry	Sacramento Ward 1	63	43
Jack	El Dorado Kelsey	581168	
John	Plumas Quincy	62	961
John	Solano Suisan	69	207
Jose T	San Luis Obispo San Luis Obispo	65	33
M	Sierra Twp 7	66	880
Manuel	Plumas Meadow Valley	62	932
Mary	Plumas Quincy	62	989
Watson	Sierra Twp 7	66	878
MARCUSE			
Himon	Tuolumne Twp 1	71	209
J	El Dorado Eldorado	58	946
Marcus A	Yuba Marysville	72	871
MARCUSO			
Hirmon	Tuolumne Sonora	71	209
MARCY			
Album*	San Francisco San Francisco 7	681444	
Albunn*	San Francisco San Francisco 7	681444	
Benjamin	Tulara Twp 2	71	33
Chas	Napa Hot Springs	61	17
Chas	Sacramento Alabama	63	411
Geo G	Colusa Spring Valley	57	430
Geo W	Colusa Spring Valley	57	429
Joseph	Calaveras Twp 4	57	303
MARD			
Thos	Mariposa Twp 3	60	605
MARDA			
James*	Placer Iona Hills	62	868
MARDAND			
Wm	Mariposa Twp 1	60	665
MARDE			
J L*	Mariposa Twp 3	60	603
MARDELL			
John*	Placer Rattle Snake	62	634
MARDEN			
Henry	Siskiyou Klamath	69	91
Ira	San Francisco San Francisco 2	67	616
W U*	Yolo Putah	72	550
MARDERY			
Patrick*	Siskiyou Scott Va	69	31
MARDGLAW			
William	San Joaquin Castoria	64	882
MARDGRAGF			
Sophia	San Francisco San Francisco 3	67	12
MARDIN			
A S	Amador Twp 4	55	253
Henry	Siskiyou Klamath	69	91
Ira*	San Francisco San Francisco 2	67	616
J W	Yolo Cache Crk	72	621
James	Yolo Washington	72	571
MARDINO			
Manuel	Tuolumne Shawsfla	71	389
MARDIS			
A	Yolo Cottonwood	72	653
B A	Tuolumne Sonora	71	201
H L	Yolo Cottonwoood	72	650
MARDLEY			
Jas	Yolo Cache	72	609
MARDO			
Martin	Tuolumne Twp 2	71	406
MARDOCK			
C	Calaveras Twp 9	57	391
Harrison	Calaveras Twp 6	57	147
MARDON			
Henry	Sonoma Russian	69	440
Wm	Sierra Morristown	661054	
MARDRILDO			
---*	Monterey San Juan	60	999
MARDUC			
Pedro	Monterey San Juan	60	980
MARDWELL			
Charles F	San Francisco San Francisco 7	681399	
MARE			
Cyril*	Calaveras Twp 6	57	155
F H*	Sierra Twp 7	66	908
John*	Sierra Downieville	66	968
T J*	Butte Hamilton	56	522
MAREA			
---	Los Angeles Elmonte	59	267
Hese	El Dorado Coloma	581115	
Hosa	Los Angeles San Jose	59	290
Manwell	Mariposa Twp 1	60	651
Vanet	Marin Cortemad	60	754
Vanete	Marin Cortemad	60	754
MAREAGAQROW			
Jose*	Mariposa Twp 1	60	625
MAREAR			
Hosa	Mariposa Twp 1	60	628
MAREARN			
George D	Calaveras Twp 4	57	329
MAREBRY			
John*	Shasta Cottonwood	66	736
MARECILLUS			
Antonio*	San Francisco San Francisco 3	67	14
MAREE			
Roza	Klamath Liberty	59	234
MAREGAN			
Martin*	San Francisco San Francisco 9	681031	
MAREHERE			
Francis*	Calaveras Twp 5	57	228
MAREHINE			
Gaeteno*	Sierra Poker Flats	66	839
MARELE			
John	Butte Ophir	56	769
MARELL			
Michael	Calaveras Twp 9	57	367
Micheal	Calaveras Twp 9	57	367
MAREN			
Thomas	El Dorado Placerville	58	924
MARENA			
Juan	Monterey San Juan	601001	
MARENAS			
K	El Dorado Placerville	58	840
MARENGO			
Margerita*	San Francisco 1	68	848
MARENLA			
C	El Dorado Casumnes	581176	
MARENO			
Hosa*	Siskiyou Yreka	69	172
Josa	Mariposa Twp 1	60	625
Jose*	Mariposa Twp 1	60	625
Juan	Napa Napa	61	115
Particio	San Francisco San Francisco 2	67	679
MARENS			
Augustus	Sierra La Porte	66	775
Jose*	Mariposa Twp 1	60	625
MARENTI			
Pedro	Monterey Pajaro	601017	
MAREQUITTO			
J*	Butte Kimshaw	56	600
MARER			
Alanwell	Mariposa Twp 1	60	651
Heser	Mariposa Coulterville	60	702
Hosea	Mariposa Coulterville	60	688
Jose	Mariposa Twp 1	60	647
Juaquin	Calaveras Twp 9	57	402
Manwell	Mariposa Twp 1	60	651
MARES			
Dolores	Los Angeles Los Angeles	59	371
Hosea	Mariposa Coulterville	60	688
Marcus	El Dorado Salmon Falls	581044	
T H	Sacramento Granite	63	236
W H	El Dorado Casumnes	581169	
MARET			
Jaques	Napa Napa	61	102
Jaquez	Napa Napa	61	102
MARETOLE			
Lawrence	Trinity East For	701027	
MAREUM			
Joseph	Sierra Pine Grove	66	823
MAREVEDE			
C*	San Francisco San Francisco 6	67	417
MARFEAL			
Theadson	Amador Twp 6	55	439
MARFET			
Eliza	San Francisco San Francisco 9	681078	
MARFORD			
J	Tehama Cottonwood	70	898
MARG			
A*	El Dorado Placerville	58	861
Keng*	Mariposa Twp 1	60	626
MARGAL			
Maria	Alameda Oakland	55	36
MARGALON			
Jose	Alameda Brooklyn	55	180
MARGAN			
E D*	Sierra Downieville	661023	
L B	Nevada Grass Valley	61	223
MARGANITI			
---	San Bernardino San Bernadino	64	680
MARGANTO			
---	San Bernardino San Bernadino	64	669
MARGARATINO			
Giacomo	San Francisco San Francisco 11	67	110
MARGARELLE			
Jose*	San Francisco San Francisco 3	67	8
MARGARET			
---	Sacramento Cosumnes	63	406
---	San Mateo Twp 2	65	119
---	Solano Benecia	69	289
MARGARET			
Smith	San Mateo Twp 1	65	51
MARGARETA			
---	San Bernardino S Timate	64	707
---	San Bernardino S Timate	64	735
MARGARETE			
Jose	Monterey San Juan	601002	
MARGARILE			
M*	Nevada Grass Valley	61	174
MARGARILLE			
Jose M	San Francisco San Francisco 3	67	8
Jose*	San Francisco San Francisco 3	67	8
MARGARINA			
---	Mendocino Calpella	60	826
MARGARITA			
---	Los Angeles Los Angeles	59	376
---	Los Angeles Los Angeles	59	401
---	Mendocino Calpella	60	826
---	Mendocino Round Va	60	882
---	San Bernardino Santa Inez	64	138
---	San Bernardino S Timate	64	719
---	San Bernardino S Timate	64	726
---	San Bernardino S Timate	64	727
---	San Bernardino S Timate	64	729
---	San Bernardino S Timate	64	738
---	San Bernardino S Timate	64	739
---	San Bernardino S Timate	64	741
---	San Bernardino S Timate	64	744
---	San Bernardino S Timate	64	745
---	San Bernardino S Timate	64	749
---	San Bernardino S Timate	64	750
---	San Bernardino S Timate	64	751
MARGARITE			
Mary	Sonoma Russian	69	429
MARGARITO			
---	San Bernardino San Bernadino	64	669
MARGATE			
John F	Butte Bidwell	56	715
MARGATEL			
R	Nevada Grass Valley	61	148
MARGATIL			
R	Nevada Grass Valley	61	148
MARGAUX			
Pierre*	Sacramento Ward 1	63	13
MARGAVATA			
---	San Bernardino S Timate	64	701
MARGE			
Alexander	Tuolumne Shawsfla	71	393
L	San Francisco San Francisco 2	67	798
Peter	San Francisco San Francisco 4	681167	
MARGEAUX			
Joseph	Yuba Long Bar	72	751
MARGEL			
F	Yolo Putah	72	554
MARGELL			
Marcus A*	Yuba Marysville	72	871
MARGEN			
Maria	San Bernardino Santa Barbara	64	181
MARGENA			
---	Mendocino Calpella	60	823
MARGENLA			
Oscar	Amador Twp 2	55	299
MARGEREZ			
Jose	Santa Clara Almaden	65	276
MARGERS			
Geo	Solano Benecia	69	309
MARGERY			
Frank	San Luis Obispo San Luis Obispo	65	1
MARGESON			
A	Nevada Grass Valley	61	185
MARGIA			
Antonia*	San Francisco San Francisco 2	67	738
Antonie*	San Francisco San Francisco 2	67	738
Antonio*	San Francisco San Francisco 2	67	738
Antonire*	San Francisco San Francisco 2	67	738
MARGIE			
Peter	Alameda Brooklyn	55	139
MARGIRTZ			
L	Siskiyou Klamath	69	97
MARGNED			
James	Los Angeles Los Angeles	59	344
MARGNETTE			
Geo*	Sacramento American	63	171
MARGNEUX			
Joseph	Yuba Long Bar	72	751
MARGO			
Alexander	Tuolumne Twp 2	71	393
Charles	Calaveras Twp 7	57	22
MARGON			
John*	Shasta Shasta	66	677
MARGONS			
William	San Francisco San Francisco 7	681440	
MARGOUX			
Alex	San Bernardino S Buenav	64	221
Frank	Stanislaus Branch	70	702
MARGRAN			
Mary	San Francisco San Francisco 2	67	694

Name	County Locale	M653 RollPage
MARGRANE		
E A	Mariposa Twp 3	60 549
MARGRAVE		
E A	Mariposa Twp 3	60 549
MARGROFF		
Joseph*	San Francisco San Francisco 7	681419
MARGUARD		
Geo	El Dorado Gold Hill	581095
MARGUELINE		
M*	Nevada Eureka	61 366
MARGUERITA		
---	San Diego San Diego	64 771
	San Diego Agua Caliente	64 863
MARGUES		
Altagaacia*	Los Angeles Los Angeles	59 507
Francisco	Los Angeles Los Angeles	59 358
Jose A*	Los Angeles Los Angeles	59 506
Rogue	Los Angeles Los Angeles	59 383
MARGUETTE		
Geo*	Sacramento American	63 171
MARGUIA		
Ceoza*	Calaveras Twp 5	57 199
MARGUIRE		
G	San Francisco San Francisco 5	67 488
MARGUIS		
Reuben	Santa Cruz Soguel	66 583
MARGUISS		
Geo	Butte Oregon	56 617
MARGURETE		
Jose	Monterey San Juan	601002
MARGUS		
Geo	Solano Benecia	69 309
MARGUTZ		
L	Siskiyou Klamath	69 97
MARHCUS		
John	Solano Suisan	69 236
MARHLE		
Jno	Sacramento Brighton	63 198
MARI		
---	Amador Twp 5	55 354
MARIA ANNA		
---	San Bernardino San Bernadino	64 678
MARIA ANTA		
---	San Bernardino Santa Inez	64 138
MARIA ANTO		
---	San Bernardino Santa Inez	64 141
MARIA ANTONIA		
---*	Los Angeles San Pedro	59 483
King	Santa Cruz Santa Cruz	66 634
MARIA D		
---	Monterey San Juan	60 992
MARIA DE JESUS		
---	San Bernardino S Timate	64 732
---	San Bernardino S Timate	64 741
---	San Bernardino S Timate	64 749
---	San Bernardino S Timate	64 751
MARIA DE LOS AN		
---	San Diego San Diego	64 772
MARIA G		
---	San Bernardino San Bernadino	64 678
MARIA GRACIO		
---	San Bernardino S Timate	64 734
MARIA IGNACIA		
---	San Diego San Diego	64 771
MARIA IGNACIO		
---	San Bernardino S Timate	64 755
MARIA JESUS		
---	San Diego San Diego	64 772
---*	Los Angeles San Juan	59 462
---*	Los Angeles Tejon	59 529
MARIA JOSEFA		
---	San Bernardino S Timate	64 718
MARIA PAULA		
---	San Bernardino Santa Inez	64 137
MARIA Y		
---	San Bernardino Santa Barbara	64 202
MARIA		
---	Fresno Twp 1	59 55
---	Los Angeles Los Angeles	59 371
---	Los Angeles Los Angeles	59 372
---	Los Angeles Los Angeles	59 376
---	Los Angeles Los Angeles	59 392
---	Los Angeles Los Angeles	59 402
---	Los Angeles Los Angeles	59 404
---	Los Angeles Los Nieto	59 435
---	Los Angeles San Juan	59 460
---	Los Angeles San Juan	59 469
---	Los Angeles San Juan	59 477
---	Los Angeles Los Angeles	59 517
---	Los Angeles Tejon	59 529
---	Los Angeles Tejon	59 529
---	Mendocino Calpella	60 822
---	Mendocino Calpella	60 825
---	Mendocino Calpella	60 826
---	Mendocino Calpella	60 827
---	Mendocino Calpella	60 828

Name	County Locale	M653 RollPage
MARIA		
---	Mendocino Round Va	60 880
---	Mendocino Twp 1	60 888
---	Mendocino Twp 1	60 889
---	Mendocino Twp 1	60 890
---	Monterey San Juan	601000
---	Monterey Monterey	60 937
---	Monterey S Antoni	60 972
---	Monterey San Juan	60 992
---	San Bernardino Santa Inez	64 136
---	San Bernardino Santa Inez	64 137
---	San Bernardino Santa Inez	64 138
---	San Bernardino Santa Inez	64 142
---	San Bernardino Santa Inez	64 143
---	San Bernardino Santa Barbara	64 147
---	San Bernardino Santa Barbara	64 197
---	San Bernardino Santa Ba	64 219
---	San Bernardino S Buenav	64 221
---	San Bernardino San Bernadino	64 667
---	San Bernardino San Bernadino	64 669
---	San Bernardino San Bernadino	64 677
---	San Bernardino San Bernadino	64 678
---	San Bernardino San Bernadino	64 679
---	San Bernardino San Bernadino	64 681
---	San Bernardino San Bernadino	64 682
---	San Bernardino San Bernadino	64 683
---	San Bernardino S Timate	64 690
---	San Bernardino S Timate	64 691
---	San Bernardino S Timate	64 692
---	San Bernardino S Timate	64 693
---	San Bernardino S Timate	64 694
---	San Bernardino S Timate	64 695
---	San Bernardino S Timate	64 696
---	San Bernardino S Timate	64 697
---	San Bernardino S Timate	64 698
---	San Bernardino S Timate	64 699
---	San Bernardino S Timate	64 701
---	San Bernardino S Timate	64 702
---	San Bernardino S Timate	64 703
---	San Bernardino S Timate	64 704
---	San Bernardino S Timate	64 705
---	San Bernardino S Timate	64 706
---	San Bernardino S Timate	64 707
---	San Bernardino S Timate	64 708
---	San Bernardino S Timate	64 709
---	San Bernardino S Timate	64 710
---	San Bernardino S Timate	64 713
---	San Bernardino S Timate	64 714
---	San Bernardino S Timate	64 715
---	San Bernardino S Timate	64 716
---	San Bernardino S Timate	64 720
---	San Bernardino S Timate	64 721
---	San Bernardino S Timate	64 722
---	San Bernardino S Timate	64 723
---	San Bernardino S Timate	64 725
---	San Bernardino S Timate	64 727
---	San Bernardino S Timate	64 732
---	San Bernardino S Timate	64 734
---	San Bernardino S Timate	64 736
---	San Bernardino S Timate	64 737
---	San Bernardino S Timate	64 738
---	San Bernardino S Timate	64 742
---	San Bernardino S Timate	64 743
---	San Bernardino S Timate	64 745
---	San Bernardino S Timate	64 746
---	San Bernardino S Timate	64 747
---	San Bernardino S Timate	64 753
---	San Diego San Diego	64 770
---	San Diego San Diego	64 771
---	San Diego San Diego	64 773
---	San Diego Temecula	64 790
---	San Diego Agua Caliente	64 837
---	San Diego Agua Caliente	64 844
---	San Diego Agua Caliente	64 851
---	San Diego Agua Caliente	64 852
---	San Diego Agua Caliente	64 863
---	San Mateo Twp 2	65 112
---	San Mateo Twp 2	65 133
---	Siskiyou Yreka	69 131
---	Tulara Twp 1	71 116
---	Tulara Twp 1	71 117
---	Tulara Twp 3	71 44
---	Tulara Keyesville	71 65
---	Tulara Keyesville	71 66
---*	Tulara Sinks Te	71 44
Ann	Sierra Twp 7	66 887
Anna	Yuba Long Bar	72 744
Anne	San Diego Agua Caliente	64 842
Antonia	San Diego Temecula	64 798
Antonio	Los Angeles Santa Ana	59 457
Antonio	San Diego S Luis R	64 777
Antonio	San Diego Temecula	64 802
Antonio	San Diego Agua Caliente	64 825
Antonio	San Diego Agua Caliente	64 830
Antonio*	Los Angeles Santa Ana	59 457
B	Nevada Washington	61 335

Name	County Locale	M653 RollPage
MARIA		
Bartolo	San Diego Temecula	64 786
Bassila	Santa Cruz Pajaro	66 567
Carmila	Santa Cruz Pajaro	66 565
Cesar*	Mariposa Twp 1	60 645
Crepencio	San Diego Temecula	64 803
David	Santa Clara Gilroy	65 248
De Los Angeles	San Gabriel	59 420
	Los Angeles	
Florentina	Los Angeles Los Angeles	59 326
Francis	El Dorado Greenwood	58 717
Francisco	Los Angeles Tejon	59 528
Francisco	San Diego San Diego	64 774
Francisco	San Diego S Luis R	64 779
G S*	Nevada Washington	61 335
Gregorio*	S Buenav	64 221
	San Bernardino	
Hesea*	Mariposa Twp 3	60 574
Hosea	Alameda Brooklyn	55 142
Hosea	Mariposa Twp 3	60 574
Hosia*	Stanislaus Branch	70 701
Inez	San Luis Obispo San Luis Obispo	65 45
Inocencia	Monterey Monterey	60 956
J	Merced Twp 1	60 900
Jesus	Calaveras Twp 7	57 25
Jesus	Monterey S Antoni	60 972
Jesus	San Bernardino Santa Ba	64 220
Jesus	San Bernardino San Bernadino	64 677
Jesus	Santa Cruz Santa Cruz	66 628
Jesus*	San Bernardino S Buenav	64 220
Josa	Amador Twp 5	55 339
Jose	Calaveras Twp 5	57 135
Jose	Calaveras Twp 5	57 147
Jose	Calaveras Twp 6	57 151
Jose	Calaveras Twp 7	57 26
Jose	Colusa Monroeville	57 453
Jose	Contra Costa Twp 1	57 489
Jose	Contra Costa Twp 1	57 508
Jose	Contra Costa Twp 1	57 514
Jose	Los Angeles Los Angeles	59 316
Jose	Los Angeles Los Angeles	59 404
Jose	Los Angeles San Gabriel	59 413
Jose	Los Angeles San Gabriel	59 415
Jose	Los Angeles Los Nieto	59 435
Jose	Los Angeles Santa Ana	59 442
Jose	Los Angeles San Pedro	59 480
Jose	Los Angeles San Pedro	59 487
Jose	Mariposa Twp 1	60 645
Jose	Mariposa Twp 1	60 646
Jose	Mendocino Little L	60 839
Jose	Monterey San Juan	601004
Jose	Monterey Alisal	601039
Jose	Monterey Monterey	60 961
Jose	Monterey San Juan	60 974
Jose	San Bernardino S Buenav	64 216
Jose	San Bernardino San Bernadino	64 682
Jose	San Bernardino S Timate	64 692
Jose	San Diego San Diego	64 776
Jose	San Diego Temecula	64 786
Jose	San Diego Temecula	64 787
Jose	San Diego Temecula	64 794
Jose	San Diego Temecula	64 801
Jose	San Diego Temecula	64 802
Jose	San Diego Temecula	64 803
Jose	San Diego Colorado	64 812
Jose	San Diego Agua Caliente	64 817
Jose	San Diego Agua Caliente	64 818
Jose	San Diego Agua Caliente	64 832
Jose	San Diego Agua Caliente	64 833
Jose	San Diego Agua Caliente	64 844
Jose	San Diego Agua Caliente	64 849
Jose	San Diego Agua Caliente	64 852
Jose	San Diego Agua Caliente	64 862
Jose	San Luis Obispo San Luis Obispo	65 22
Jose	Santa Cruz Pajaro	66 565
Jose	Santa Cruz Soguel	66 580
Jose	Sierra La Porte	66 777
Jose	Tuolumne Big Oak	71 135
Jose Jr	Calaveras Twp 6	57 135
Jose*	Calaveras Twp 6	57 135
Jose*	Calaveras Twp 6	57 147
Jose*	Los Angeles San Pedro	59 480
Jose*	Los Angeles San Pedro	59 487
Jose*	Mendocino Little L	60 839
Jose*	Santa Cruz Pajaro	66 565
Joseph	Calaveras Twp 7	57 34
Joseph	Monterey Monterey	60 925
Joseph	Placer Michigan	62 841
Juan	San Diego San Diego	64 774
Juan	San Diego San Diego	64 775
Juan	San Diego S Luis R	64 779
Juan	San Diego Temecula	64 792
Juan	San Diego Temecula	64 794
Juan	San Diego Agua Caliente	64 853
Juan	Santa Cruz Santa Cruz	66 623
Juana	Los Angeles San Gabriel	59 408

California 1860 Census Index

Name	County Locale	M653 Roll	Page
MARIA			
Juanna	San Bernardino S Buenav	64	222
Junn	Monterey Monterey	60	961
Marcissa	Placer Forest H	62	795
N	Amador Twp 1	55	481
Pedro	San Luis Obispo San Luis Obispo	65	21
Refugio	Los Angeles Los Angeles	59	368
Sacramento	Tehama Red Bluff	70	931
MARIADELAOSO			
Antonio	Los Angeles Los Angeles	59	512
MARIAH			
Casuse	Mariposa Twp 1	60	672
Josph	Mariposa Twp 1	60	653
MARIAHAN			
John	Amador Twp 3	55	379
MARIALLI			
Charles	Tuolumne Twp 1	71	269
MARIAM			
Barrows	Los Angeles Los Angeles	59	392
J S	Tuolumne Twp 1	71	239
MARIAN			
---	San Bernardino S Timate	64	708
---	San Bernardino S Timate	64	740
Diacame*	Mariposa Twp 3	60	594
MARIANA			
---	Los Angeles Los Angeles	59	497
---	Los Angeles Tejon	59	529
---	Mendocino Round Va	60	882
---	Mendocino Round Va	60	884
---	San Bernardino Santa Inez	64	138
---	San Bernardino Santa Barbara	64	186
---	San Bernardino S Timate	64	748
Frances	Amador Twp 3	55	387
Vincente	Tuolumne Twp 2	71	282
MARIANN			
---	San Bernardino S Timate	64	729
MARIANNA			
---	Mariposa Twp 1	60	653
MARIANO			
---	Los Angeles Los Angeles	59	370
---	Los Angeles Santa Ana	59	447
---	Marin Cortemad	60	787
---	San Bernardino S Timate	64	720
---	San Bernardino S Timate	64	727
---	San Bernardino S Timate	64	731
---	San Bernardino S Timate	64	735
---	San Bernardino S Timate	64	738
---	San Bernardino S Timate	64	739
---	San Bernardino S Timate	64	745
---	San Bernardino S Timate	64	749
---	San Bernardino S Timate	64	751
---	San Bernardino S Timate	64	753
---	San Bernardino S Timate	64	754
---	San Bernardino S Timate	64	755
---	San Diego Temecula	64	784
---	San Diego Agua Caliente	64	832
---	San Diego Agua Caliente	64	863
Celestina	Stanislaus Branch	70	701
MARIANT			
Joseph	Alameda Brooklyn	55	103
Rosa	Alameda Brooklyn	55	104
Rosae	Alameda Brooklyn	55	104
MARIAS			
Joseph	Sonoma Mendocino	69	462
MARIBBA			
Dennis*	San Francisco San Francisco 9	68	1078
MARIBEAU			
Joseph	San Francisco San Francisco 11	67	131
MARICELLUS			
Antonio*	San Francisco San Francisco 3	67	14
MARICH			
Elias*	San Francisco San Francisco 3	67	38
MARID			
---	Del Norte Klamath	58	654
MARIE A			
---	Monterey San Juan	60	991
MARIE			
---	Monterey Monterey	60	957
Borcher M	San Francisco San Francisco 8	68	1236
J B	San Francisco Tuolumne Jamestown	71	432
Jacques	Tuolumne Jamestown	71	432
Jesus	Sacramento Granite	63	253
John	Butte Ophir	56	745
Jose	Amador Twp 4	55	242
Jose	Butte Chico	56	532
Jose	Tuolumne Jamestown	71	432
Joseph	Tuolumne Twp 2	71	394
Louis A	Siskiyou Callahan	69	3
Manual	Tehama Red Bluff	70	931
Morcher M*	San Francisco San Francisco 8	68	1236
Moscher M*	San Francisco San Francisco 8	68	1236
Peter	San Francisco Tuolumne Twp 3	71	432
MARIEA			
---*	Monterey San Juan	60	991
MARIEDHOFER			
M*	Siskiyou Scott Ri	69	61
MARIELEVO			
Jose	Fresno Twp 1	59	82
MARIEN			
Joseph	Calaveras Twp 5	57	214
MARIEOHOFER			
M	Siskiyou Scott Ri	69	61
MARIET			
E	Mariposa Twp 3	60	556
Jose	Placer Michigan	62	819
MARIEY			
Laka	Mariposa Twp 3	60	545
Sapa*	Mariposa Twp 3	60	545
MARIEZ			
Sapa*	Mariposa Twp 3	60	545
MARIFIELD			
P	Tuolumne Jacksonville	71	164
MARIGNITO			
J*	Butte Kimshaw	56	600
MARIGOT			
Lydia	San Francisco San Francisco 10	67	182
MARIGUITA			
Jose	Butte Kimshaw	56	603
MARIHO			
C	Tuolumne Twp 2	71	290
MARIL			
---	Monterey Monterey	60	954
Frank	Sonoma Sonoma	69	636
MARILES			
L	Tuolumne Sonora	71	228
MARILEY			
Thos	Santa Clara San Jose	65	337
MARILIS			
S	Tuolumne Twp 1	71	228
MARILL			
Warren P	Sacramento Ward 1	63	135
Warren*	Sacramento Ward 1	63	135
MARILLA			
Joseph	San Mateo Twp 2	65	118
MARIM			
Gabriel*	Siskiyou Yreka	69	149
MARIMA			
Joanna*	San Francisco San Francisco 9	68	986
MARIME			
Gabriel	Siskiyou Yreka	69	149
MARIN			
Anson	Sierra Downieville	66	1030
B F	Alameda Oakland	55	5
George	Solano Fremont	69	380
J	Tuolumne Twp 4	71	156
Jacob	Placer Iona Hills	62	883
John	Santa Clara San Jose	65	296
John	Tuolumne Twp 2	71	311
Jose	Mariposa Twp 1	60	645
Jose	Tuolumne Twp 3	71	432
Joseph	Tuolumne Jamestown	71	432
Juan*	Alameda Oakland	55	55
Juaquin	Calaveras Twp 9	57	402
Michael*	Alameda Brooklyn	55	126
Navor	Calaveras Twp 4	57	332
Nobor	Calaveras Twp 4	57	332
Novor	Calaveras Twp 4	57	332
MARINA			
Alta	Sacramento Georgian	63	340
Hosea	Yuba Marysville	72	933
Joseph	Calaveras Twp 5	57	227
Repacio	Tuolumne Sonora	71	220
Repacir	Tuolumne Sonora	71	220
Santa	San Francisco San Francisco 8	68	1236
MARINAL			
Jacenta*	Tehama Red Bluff	70	931
MARINAS			
Jesus	Marin Cortemad	60	788
MARIND			
Frank	Calaveras Twp 5	57	200
MARINDA			
Augusta	Marin San Rafael	60	759
MARINE			
A	Amador Twp 7	55	417
Cecelia*	Amador Twp 4	55	240
Kofsuth	Los Angeles San Jose	59	292
MARINER			
E	San Francisco San Francisco 3	67	46
Henry E	San Francisco San Francisco 9	68	1039
Jane	Marin San Rafael	60	760
Pire	San Francisco San Francisco 7	68	1408
MARINES			
Jesus	Los Angeles Los Angeles	59	386
MARINEZ			
Juan	Merced Monterey	60	941
Ramon	Contra Costa Twp 1	57	515
MARING			
S	Amador Twp 6	55	435
MARINGO			
Marquita*	San Francisco San Francisco 1	68	848
MARINIR			
E	San Francisco San Francisco 3	67	46
MARINO			
Ferdinand*	Tuolumne Twp 1	71	225
Frank	Calaveras Twp 5	57	200
Hosea*	Alameda Brooklyn	55	124
Joseph	Calaveras Twp 5	57	227
Louis	Tuolumne Twp 1	71	255
Pio	Los Angeles Los Angeles	59	516
MARINRE			
Gabriel*	Siskiyou Yreka	69	149
MARINS			
C	Tuolumne Columbia	71	290
MARINU			
Joseph	Calaveras Twp 5	57	227
MARINVOCH			
F	San Francisco San Francisco 5	67	543
MARINY			
James*	Solano Benecia	69	285
John*	Placer Secret R	62	610
MARIO ANITA			
---	San Bernardino Santa Inez	64	143
MARIO JESUS			
---	San Bernardino Santa Inez	64	143
MARIO			
---	San Diego Agua Caliente	64	851
---	Tulara Twp 3	71	68
---	Tulara Keyesville	71	69
---	Tulara Twp 3	71	71
Amarily	Tuolumne Twp 2	71	295
Andrew*	Tuolumne Columbia	71	295
Andrias*	Tuolumne Columbia	71	295
Antonio	Los Angeles Santa Ana	59	441
Enacio	Tuolumne Twp 2	71	408
Garris	Amador Twp 3	55	369
Hasa	Siskiyou Yreka	69	136
J H	Butte Ophir	56	768
John	Calaveras Twp 10	57	261
Jose	Mariposa Twp 1	60	645
Jose	Mariposa Twp 1	60	646
Jose	Mariposa Twp 1	60	650
Jose	San Bernardino San Bernadino	64	640
Jose	Santa Cruz Pajaro	66	545
Jose	Tuolumne Columbia	71	290
Jose	Tuolumne Shawsfla	71	408
Jose	Tuolumne Shawsfla	71	413
Jose*	Calaveras Twp 6	57	147
Jose*	Mariposa Twp 1	60	650
Jude	Mariposa Twp 1	60	645
MARION			
David	Sierra La Porte	66	776
E P	Butte Hamilton	56	519
Frances	Amador Twp 3	55	344
G	San Francisco San Francisco 5	67	535
J V	Siskiyou Scott Va	69	55
James	Sierra Monte Crk	66	1036
Jean*	Butte Eureka	56	650
John	Nevada Bloomfield	61	520
John*	Calaveras Twp 8	57	85
M	San Francisco San Francisco 5	67	535
Martin	Sonoma Sonoma	69	653
Matrin	Sonoma Sonoma	69	653
Miles	San Francisco San Francisco 2	67	611
S	San Francisco San Francisco 5	67	535
Wm L	San Francisco San Francisco 3	67	10
MARIONA			
Vincente*	Tuolumne Twp 2	71	282
MARIOTT			
James	Nevada Bloomfield	61	524
MARIQUITO			
J*	Butte Kimshaw	56	600
MARIR			
Jose	Mariposa Twp 1	60	647
MARIRCO			
Fredinand*	Tuolumne Twp 1	71	225
MARIS			
J R*	Sacramento Ward 1	63	22
Juan	Santa Cruz Santa Cruz	66	625
William	San Bernardino Santa Barbara	64	170
Wm	Amador Twp 5	55	357
MARISAR			
J S	Mariposa Twp 3	60	561
MARISCO			
Ferdinand	Tuolumne Sonora	71	225
MARISE			
M	San Francisco San Francisco 4	68	1147
MARISO			
Charles*	Marin Bolinas	60	744
MARISS			
Pauline	San Francisco San Francisco 2	67	712
MARITA			
Wan	El Dorado Placerville	58	901
MARITE			
---	Tulara Keyesville	71	71

Name	County Locale	M653 RollPage
MARITN		
Ametri	El Dorado Greenwood	58 730
Edward	El Dorado Greenwood	58 726
Harris	Calaveras Twp 7	57 18
MARITTA		
Dennis	San Francisco San Francisco 9	681078
MARIUR		
Charles*	San Francisco San Francisco 4	681120
MARIVACO		
---	San Diego Agua Caliente	64 857
MARJA		
Joepha	San Joaquin Stockton	641058
MARJAN		
Andrew	Tuolumne Jamestown	71 441
MARJARK		
Hugh*	Nevada Bridgeport	61 449
MARK		
---	Stanislaus Emory	70 754
---	Tulara Twp 1	71 121
---*	Sierra Downieville	661007
A	Tuolumne Twp 4	71 157
Adolphe	Mariposa Twp 3	60 605
Arnold	San Francisco San Francisco 7	681433
C H	El Dorado Casumnes	581166
Chris	Mariposa Twp 3	60 600
Christian	Tuolumne Twp 1	71 241
Domingo	Calaveras Twp 8	57 90
E	Mariposa Twp 3	60 569
E	San Francisco San Francisco 5	67 518
E*	Mariposa Twp 3	60 569
Elise	Sacramento Ward 1	63 100
Eliss	Sacramento Ward 1	63 100
Eliza*	Placer Iona Hills	62 884
Henry	Santa Cruz Pajaro	66 550
Henry*	San Francisco San Francisco 1	68 891
J G	Tehama Red Bluff	70 933
Jacob	San Francisco San Francisco 9	68 990
Jas*	Sacramento Brighton	63 196
Kan*	Mariposa Twp 3	60 569
Kare*	Mariposa Twp 3	60 569
Keri	Mariposa Twp 3	60 569
Kon	Mariposa Twp 3	60 569
L	San Francisco San Francisco 2	67 799
Lydia	Sacramento Ward 1	63 147
M T	Humbolt Union	59 185
Nancy J	Sacramento Ward 3	63 457
S	Tehama Red Bluff	70 916
S J	Santa Clara Fremont	65 430
Wm	Butte Hamilton	56 518
MARKA		
Francisca*	Calaveras Twp 6	57 135
Francisco	Calaveras Twp 5	57 135
MARKAM		
Henry	Solano Fairfield	69 203
MARKANS		
Geo	El Dorado Kelsey	581134
MARKARO		
Jose	San Mateo Twp 1	65 68
MARKE		
---*	Mariposa Twp 3	60 569
H B	San Francisco San Francisco 6	67 472
MARKEL		
Michael	Placer Auburn	62 595
R V	Sonoma Petaluma	69 593
MARKELL		
David	Sonoma Armally	69 515
MARKEN		
Hannah	Sacramento Ward 4	63 534
MARKER		
Ada	Sacramento Granite	63 236
Benjm F	San Francisco San Francisco 7	681337
F T	Nevada Washington	61 337
Henry B	Yuba Marysville	72 927
John	Plumas Quincy	62 987
John	San Francisco San Francisco 4	681169
John	Sierra Forest C	66 910
Johnn	Sierra Twp 7	66 910
Peter N	Yuba Suida	72 982
William	Yuba Bear Rvr	721008
Wm	Butte Hamilton	56 518
MARKERT		
H	Sacramento Ward 4	63 513
MARKES		
Ace	Yuba Marysville	72 968
D W	El Dorado Mud Springs	58 978
Doc	Yuba Marysville	72 968
Donan	Contra Costa Twp 1	57 508
G	San Joaquin Stockton	641097
Isaac	Los Angeles San Juan	59 477
MARKET		
Jose	Monterey San Juan	60 974
R	Amador Twp 1	55 459
MARKETTI		
Angelo	Calaveras Twp 10	57 261
MARKEWITZ		
J	San Francisco San Francisco 10	266 67
MARKEY		
J	San Francisco San Francisco 5	67 549
John	Siskiyou Scott Va	69 49
Kate*	Sonoma Sonoma	69 659
Patrick	Siskiyou Scott Va	69 31
MARKHAM		
Columbia	San Francisco San Francisco 9	681104
David	Tehama Pasakent	70 855
Denetis	Tulara Visalia	71 79
Denitr*	Tulara Twp 1	71 79
L	San Joaquin Stockton	641100
Milton	Humbolt Eel Rvr	59 151
Warren	Sacramento American	63 157
William	Tulara Twp 2	71 26
Wm	Sonoma Petaluma	69 564
Wm	Tehama Pasakent	70 855
MARKIM		
Elisobeth	Solano Vacaville	69 336
Elizabeth	Solano Vacaville	69 336
MARKIN		
T G	Sacramento Granite	63 222
Thos*	Mariposa Twp 3	60 612
MARKINS		
Jas*	Calaveras Twp 9	57 384
MARKIS		
A	Sacramento Ward 3	63 428
Jose M	Monterey San Juan	60 996
MARKLAND		
Joseph E*	San Francisco 8	681291
	San Francisco	
MARKLAY		
John	Yolo Putah	72 554
MARKLEE		
John A	El Dorado Kelsey	581138
MARKLEGS		
F	Yolo Merritt	72 579
MARKLEND		
Joseph E*	San Francisco 8	681291
	San Francisco	
MARKLER		
John A	El Dorado Kelsey	581138
MARKLEY		
Andrew J	Contra Costa Twp 3	57 595
David	Amador Twp 1	55 459
David	Placer Virginia	62 667
David	Tuolumne Twp 2	71 392
David	Tuolumne Shawsfla	71 395
G W	Tuolumne Shawsfla	71 382
Gee	El Dorado Eldorado	58 945
Henry	Nevada Bloomfield	61 523
Joseph	Los Angeles Los Angeles	59 492
Josiah	Sierra Whiskey	66 843
Levi	San Francisco San Francisco 8	681252
M	Yolo Putah	72 552
W J	Tuolumne Shawsfla	71 392
MARKLEYER		
N J	Tuolumne Twp 2	71 392
MARKLOUD		
Joseph E*	San Francisco 8	681291
	San Francisco	
MARKLOW		
Joseph E	San Francisco San Francisco 8	681291
MARKLY		
Jerry	Mariposa Twp 3	60 577
Patrick	Calaveras Twp 9	57 385
MARKON		
Saml J*	Alameda Brooklyn	55 182
MARKONA		
A	Sutter Butte	70 791
MARKOS		
Felix	San Mateo Twp 1	65 60
MARKRICH		
A	Tuolumne Twp 1	71 269
M	Tuolumne Twp 1	71 269
MARKRY		
Patrick*	Siskiyou Scott Va	69 31
MARKS		
---	San Francisco San Francisco 4	681224
---	San Joaquin Stockton	641040
B	Butte Ophir	56 765
B	San Francisco San Francisco 10	191 67
B	Tuolumne Columbia	71 325
Barrow	Los Angeles Los Angeles	59 327
Berry	Sonoma Santa Rosa	69 388
Charles	San Francisco San Francisco 4	681169
Chas	Napa Napa	61 107
Chas	Sacramento Ward 1	63 28
Chas A	Trinity Redding	70 985
Daniel	Yuba Marysville	72 866
Daniel*	Yuba Slate Ro	72 694
Edmund	San Francisco San Francisco 10	250 67
MARKS		
Geo	El Dorado Union	581093
Geo	Siskiyou Callahan	69 18
George B	Tuolumne Springfield	71 373
George W	Sierra Scales D	66 801
H B	San Francisco San Francisco 6	67 472
Hannah	San Francisco San Francisco 5	67 476
Henerietta*	San Francisco San Francisco 7	681412
	San Francisco	
Henry	San Francisco San Francisco 9	681051
Henry	Trinity Whites Crk	701028
Isaac	Los Angeles San Juan	59 477
J A	Nevada Grass Valley	61 185
J A	San Joaquin Stockton	641044
J C	Nevada Grass Valley	61 188
J G	Tehama Red Bluff	70 916
J M	Tuolumne Twp 1	71 480
Jacob	Placer Auburn	62 574
James	Calaveras Twp 8	57 100
James	Tuolumne Columbia	71 290
Jas	Butte Bidwell	56 729
Jno	Butte Oregon	56 615
John	Plumas Quincy	621003
John	Siskiyou Callahan	69 18
John J	San Francisco San Francisco 3	67 61
Jos	San Francisco San Francisco 2	67 804
Jos	Trinity New Rvr	701030
Joseph	San Joaquin Stockton	641044
Joshua	Placer Auburn	62 568
Julis	Sacramento Ward 4	63 569
L	San Francisco San Francisco 2	67 799
Leno*	Tehama Red Bluff	70 915
Lens*	Tehama Red Bluff	70 915
Lewis	Amador Twp 4	55 237
Lewis	Butte Oregon	56 614
Lewis	Butte Bidwell	56 712
M	Nevada Grass Valley	61 202
M	Placer Auburn	62 574
M	San Francisco San Francisco 6	67 468
M	San Joaquin Stockton	641044
M	Santa Clara San Jose	65 296
M E	El Dorado Placerville	58 820
M S	Trinity North Fo	701024
M*	Sacramento Ward 4	63 507
Manuel	Los Angeles San Pedro	59 483
Miles	Fresno Twp 3	59 16
Morris	Sacramento Ward 1	63 119
Moses	San Joaquin Stockton	641044
Robert L	Siskiyou Shasta Rvr	69 111
Robt	Amador Twp 2	55 303
S D	Amador Twp 4	55 254
Saml	Butte Kimshaw	56 575
Samuel	Placer Auburn	62 564
Samuel	San Francisco San Francisco 4	681156
Samuel	San Francisco San Francisco 9	68 981
Samuel	San Joaquin Stockton	641044
Simon	San Francisco San Francisco 4	681166
Simon	San Francisco San Francisco 2	67 599
Solomon	San Francisco San Francisco 7	681376
Thomas E	San Francisco San Francisco 3	67 61
Thos	San Francisco San Francisco 10	288 67
W	Sacramento Brighton	63 205
William	Tulara Keyesville	71 60
MARKSON		
Mathew	Butte Bidwell	56 730
MARKSTED		
T	Butte Oro	56 684
MARKSWITZ		
M	Santa Clara San Jose	65 296
MARKUM		
F	Amador Twp 1	55 488
MARKUS		
Roman	Siskiyou Yreka	69 140
MARKWALD		
A	San Francisco San Francisco 5	67 487
MARKWELL		
A J	Sonoma Armally	69 486
MARKWOOD		
George	Calaveras Twp 6	57 134
William	Napa Yount	61 47
MARKY		
Richd	San Francisco San Francisco 1	68 844
MARLA		
P	Amador Twp 3	55 385
MARLAN		
Richard	Siskiyou Scott Va	69 32
MARLAR		
William	Tulara Twp 1	71 86
MARLE		
J	El Dorado Coloma	581107
Joseph*	Calaveras Twp 9	57 354
MARLEN		
Saml	Placer Mountain	62 707
MARLENO		
J	El Dorado Placerville	58 868

Name	County Locale	M653 RollPage
MARLEO		
Antonia	Amador Twp 5	55 362
Peter*	El Dorado Coloma	581079
MARLER		
Joseph	San Francisco San Francisco 1	68 849
MARLES		
Peter	El Dorado Coloma	581079
MARLETT		
C W	Nevada Red Dog	61 552
James	Sonoma Salt Point	69 691
John B	Amador Twp 1	55 495
MARLETTE		
Elisha	Sacramento Franklin	63 316
Peter*	Sacramento Franklin	63 316
MARLEY		
Anthony	Alameda Brooklyn	55 104
Anthony	Alameda Brooklyn	55 135
David	Napa Napa	61 66
E	Nevada Grass Valley	61 157
Francis	Sacramento Ward 3	63 484
Henry	Tuolumne Twp 1	71 268
L H	Butte Oro	56 676
Lewis	Amador Twp 2	55 313
Louis	Amador Twp 2	55 313
MARLIN		
E	Butte Wyandotte	56 667
Elizabeth	El Dorado Eldorado	58 947
John	Alameda Brooklyn	55 117
M C	Sacramento Ward 1	63 16
S E	San Francisco San Francisco 2	67 643
Samuel	Monterey Pajaro	601019
W H*	Yolo Putah	72 550
MARLINO		
Jos*	Sacramento Ward 1	63 28
MARLLINTO		
Aruator	San Joaquin Oneal	64 933
MARLON		
Chas*	Sacramento Dry Crk	63 368
E C*	Sonoma Petaluma	69 589
John	Napa Napa	61 115
MARLOW		
Chas*	Sacramento Dry Crk	63 368
Frank	Amador Twp 2	55 285
G R	Yuba New York	72 744
James C	Nevada Bridgeport	61 442
John	Sacramento Ward 4	63 554
John	Yuba Rose Bar	72 793
N L	Sonoma Armally	69 490
Owen	Nevada Bloomfield	61 524
P C	Merced Twp 1	60 913
Peater	Amador Twp 2	55 285
William	Sierra Gibsonville	66 851
MARLY		
John	San Francisco San Francisco 3	67 53
Joseph*	Calaveras Twp 9	57 354
MARM		
Juan*	Alameda Oakland	55 55
MARMALITA		
Jon	Tuolumne Twp 3	71 437
Jose	Tuolumne Jamestown	71 437
MARMAN		
H	Nevada Nevada	61 291
MARMAS		
Veveanna*	Yuba Marysville	72 922
MARMASHEAS		
---	Mendocino Calpella	60 828
MARMASHENS		
---	Mendocino Calpella	60 828
MARMESSE		
Leon	Siskiyou Yreka	69 186
MARMION		
P	Shasta Horsetown	66 690
MARMODAS		
Jesus	Calaveras Twp 4	57 331
MARMOLEJO		
Maria Y	Los Angeles Los Nieto	59 437
MARMON		
Henry	Amador Twp 1	55 498
MARMOSA		
Jose	Tuolumne Chinese	71 497
Maestro	Tuolumne Chinese	71 497
MARMOTES		
Anastacio	San Francisco San Francisco 2	67 673
MARMY		
Mary*	Alameda Oakland	55 72
MARN		
---	Amador Twp 2	55 326
---*	Mariposa Twp 3	60 620
MARNACH		
J*	San Francisco San Francisco 2	67 684
MARNE		
James H*	San Luis Obispo	65 9
	San Luis Obispo	
MARNELL		
Michael	Sierra Twp 7	66 869
Tho	Siskiyou Cottonwoood	69 100

Name	County Locale	M653 RollPage
MARNEY		
Lewis	Tehama Lassen	70 869
MARNI		
Hosa	Nevada Rough &	61 397
MARNIA		
Hona	Yuba Marysville	72 933
MARNING		
John	Sonoma Armally	69 481
MARNINS		
C	El Dorado Kelsey	581129
MARNS		
J R*	Sacramento Ward 1	63 22
MARNUS		
Jesus*	Marin Cortemad	60 788
MARO COLA		
Anselmo*	Calaveras Twp 4	57 333
MARO		
Jose	San Diego San Diego	64 759
MAROCALA		
Anrelimo*	Calaveras Twp 4	57 333
Aurelino*	Calaveras Twp 4	57 333
MAROI		
John*	Amador Twp 4	55 245
MAROKEY		
John*	Siskiyou Scott Va	69 49
MAROLALA		
Anrelino*	Calaveras Twp 4	57 333
Anrelmo*	Calaveras Twp 4	57 333
MARON		
C H*	Sonoma Petaluma	69 601
H S	Alameda Brooklyn	55 213
Joseph R*	Alameda Brooklyn	55 121
Moto*	San Francisco San Francisco 9	681062
MARONA		
J	Calaveras Twp 9	57 387
Martin	Sonoma Bodega	69 537
MARONDA		
Augusta	Marin San Rafael	60 759
MARONDY		
F M	San Francisco San Francisco 4	681141
MARONE		
Augustus	Alameda Brooklyn	55 150
MARONEY		
Dennis	Sacramento Dry Crk	63 379
Martha	San Francisco San Francisco 7	681403
Mathew	Yuba Suida	72 994
Matthew	Yuba Linda	72 994
MARONI		
A	San Francisco San Francisco 5	67 539
MARONO		
Juan	Los Angeles San Jose	59 281
MARONY		
M	Nevada Grass Valley	61 226
Mary*	Alameda Oakland	55 72
MAROON		
W*	Amador Twp 2	55 304
MAROONEY		
Thomas*	San Francisco San Francisco 7	681418
MAROROVOCH		
F	San Francisco San Francisco 5	67 543
MAROTTI		
Julius	Nevada Rough &	61 436
MAROW		
C	El Dorado Placerville	58 840
MAROY		
Charles	El Dorado Mud Springs	58 980
MARPE		
W F*	San Joaquin Stockton	641045
MARPHINO		
A	Amador Twp 1	55 490
MARPHY		
Hugh*	Calaveras Twp 4	57 328
J*	San Francisco San Francisco 5	67 538
John H	Monterey San Juan	60 989
Patrick	Calaveras Twp 5	57 215
MARPILD		
David*	San Francisco San Francisco 2	67 738
MARPLE		
J H	Butte Ophir	56 753
S W	El Dorado Placerville	58 863
W	Yuba Rose Bar	72 795
W L	El Dorado Placerville	58 863
MARPN		
C S	Yolo Putah	72 549
MARQAUX		
Pierre	Sacramento Ward 1	63 13
MARQENA		
---	Mendocino Calpella	60 823
MARQUARD		
Geo	El Dorado Gold Hill	581095
MARQUELINE		
M	Nevada Eureka	61 366
MARQUES		
Francisco	Humbolt Eel Rvr	59 145
Francisco	Los Angeles Los Angeles	59 358
Manuela	Santa Clara Almaden	65 271

Name	County Locale	M653 RollPage
MARQUES		
Peralta	Santa Clara Alviso	65 415
MARQUEZ		
Alvino	Santa Clara Almaden	65 273
Francesco	San Francisco San Francisco 11	156 67
Jesus	Santa Clara Santa Clara	65 479
MARQUILLO		
---	San Diego Agua Caliente	64 853
MARQUIS		
Altagaacia	Los Angeles Los Angeles	59 507
Francisco	Los Angeles Los Angeles	59 508
Franicsco	Los Angeles Los Angeles	59 508
Jesus	San Bernardino Santa Barbara	64 199
John	Yuba Long Bar	72 741
Jose A	Los Angeles Los Angeles	59 506
Jose R	Los Angeles Santa Ana	59 448
Mary	San Francisco San Francisco 2	67 799
Reuben	Santa Cruz Soguel	66 583
MARQUISS		
Geo*	Butte Oregon	56 617
MARR		
B*	Nevada Nevada	61 324
C	Nevada Grass Valley	61 175
Catharine	San Francisco San Francisco 2	67 658
Charly	Nevada Bloomfield	61 526
Christ*	Sierra Twp 5	66 942
Cyril	Calaveras Twp 6	57 155
F K	Amador Twp 4	55 258
Frank	Colusa Monroeville	57 457
George	Yuba Parks Ba	72 782
Gouten Louis	Calaveras Twp 10	57 275
Gouten Sonis	Calaveras Twp 10	57 275
Jas	San Francisco San Francisco 1	68 855
John*	Sierra Twp 5	66 930
Matten	San Francisco San Francisco 9	681104
Thomas	Sacramento American	63 162
MARRA		
---	Mendocino Calpella	60 827
Jose	Monterey Monterey	60 961
Jose	Tuolumne Twp 5	71 504
MARRACH		
J*	San Francisco San Francisco 2	67 684
MARRAIS		
Jacques	Yuba New York	72 723
MARRALAS		
A	Calaveras Twp 9	57 378
J	Calaveras Twp 9	57 378
MARRAN		
Alexander	Calaveras Twp 8	57 81
H	Nevada Grass Valley	61 160
John	Tehama Red Bluff	70 923
MARRAY		
Thomas	Marin Cortemad	60 784
MARREA		
G	El Dorado Casumnes	581175
MARREL		
Hosea*	Alameda Brooklyn	55 151
MARRELL		
Hiram P*	El Dorado Georgetown	58 705
John	El Dorado Kelsey	581129
Jos	San Francisco San Francisco 2	67 662
Phillip	Sierra Downieville	661031
MARREN		
James*	San Francisco San Francisco 3	67 21
MARREY		
Jos*	Sacramento Ward 1	63 108
MARRHEIM		
Isaac*	San Francisco San Francisco 8	681321
MARRIA		
Hosa	El Dorado Placerville	58 896
Jose	Calaveras Twp 7	57 39
MARRIANI		
Baptiste	Calaveras Twp 7	57 24
MARRICK		
Richard*	Placer Goods	62 693
MARRIEA		
Joseph	Calaveras Twp 7	57 12
MARRIEN		
C J	Nevada Eureka	61 376
MARRIET		
Mary	Sacramento Ward 1	63 101
MARRIKAS		
Carasi	Placer Forest H	62 802
MARRIL		
Fernando	Los Angeles Santa Ana	59 443
MARRILL		
Charles	El Dorado Placerville	58 904
MARRINA		
Joanna*	San Francisco San Francisco 9	68 986
MARRINIA		
Pabolina	Tulara Keyesville	71 55
MARRIO		
Angel	Yuba Marysville	72 974
MARRION		
C J	Nevada Eureka	61 376

California 1860 Census Index

Name	County Locale	M653 RollPage
MARRION		
Danl	San Francisco San Francisco 1	68 906
Joseph	El Dorado Coloma	581082
Jospeh	El Dorado Coloma	581082
MARRIOT		
Thomas	Sierra St Louis	66 864
MARRIOTT		
Thomas*	Sierra Twp 7	66 864
Thos T	Trinity New Rvr	701031
MARRIS		
J	Nevada Grass Valley	61 199
J H	Sonoma Santa Rosa	69 406
MARRISE		
M	San Francisco San Francisco 4	681147
MARRISON		
Charles	Yuba Fosters	72 833
John	San Joaquin Stockton	641070
P	Tuolumne Twp 3	71 423
Wm	Amador Twp 6	55 450
MARRISY		
Chrie*	Sacramento Natonia	63 277
Chris*	Sacramento Natonia	63 277
MARRITT		
Jacob	Amador Twp 4	55 242
MARRIW		
Juan*	Calaveras Twp 8	57 92
MARRIX		
B*	Nevada Eureka	61 378
MARRJEON		
V*	San Francisco San Francisco 5	67 527
MARRNA		
Juan*	Monterey San Juan	601001
MARRNY		
Mary*	Alameda Oakland	55 72
MARRON		
Avino*	San Diego San Diego	64 761
Felipa	San Diego San Diego	64 761
Frank	San Francisco San Francisco 2	67 617
James*	Sonoma Armally	69 508
Jas	San Francisco San Francisco 2	67 616
Jesus	San Diego San Diego	64 761
John	San Francisco San Francisco 2	67 571
Jos	San Francisco San Francisco 2	67 616
Juan	Los Angeles Los Angeles	59 400
Juan	San Diego San Diego	64 761
Nicholas	Amador Twp 1	55 490
Sylvestre	San Diego S Luis R	64 777
MARRONA		
G	Calaveras Twp 9	57 387
MARRONETT		
John	San Mateo Twp 3	65 104
MARROT		
Jean	San Francisco San Francisco 2	67 804
MARROTT		
Louis	El Dorado Eldorado	58 937
MARROTTE		
A	El Dorado Casumnes	581175
MARROW		
A S	San Mateo Twp 3	65 94
J	Sacramento Ward 4	63 576
Jose	Los Angeles Los Angeles	59 315
MARROWS		
Otis	Yolo Slate Ra	72 696
MARROY		
John	Yolo Putah	72 560
MARRUN		
Jose	Calaveras Twp 8	57 86
MARRY		
Dennis	Sonoma Vallejo	69 631
Pat*	Sonoma Petaluma	69 604
MARRYMAN		
Joseph	Del Norte Crescent	58 633
MARRZO		
A*	San Francisco San Francisco 5	67 539
MARS		
Alex	Amador Twp 1	55 462
Alex	Amador Twp 1	55 463
Jas A	San Francisco San Francisco 2	67 703
John	Plumas Quincy	62 944
John	San Mateo Twp 3	65 97
John	Sonoma Bodega	69 533
Peter	Nevada Bridgeport	61 505
Wm	Amador Twp 5	55 344
MARSA		
Michael	Tuolumne Twp 5	71 504
MARSAILLE		
F	Siskiyou Scott Ri	69 81
MARSALE		
Chas*	Sacramento Cosumnes	63 387
MARSALL		
Chas*	Sacramento Cosumnes	63 387
MARSDEN		
Leanard	Mariposa Coulterville	60 674
M	Yolo Cache	72 612
MARSDIN		
H	Yolo Cache Crk	72 612

Name	County Locale	M653 RollPage
MARSE		
A*	Nevada Nevada	61 288
MARSELLA		
Lewis	Amador Twp 4	55 249
MARSELLAS		
G W	Sacramento Ward 1	63 141
MARSELLUS		
E	Nevada Nevada	61 266
MARSEN		
James*	San Francisco San Francisco 3	67 21
MARSERIA		
Rafucio	Los Angeles San Jose	59 284
MARSFIELD		
Robt	Placer Secret R	62 624
MARSH		
A	El Dorado Casumnes	581173
A	Trinity Indian C	70 989
A D	Sutter Bear Rvr	70 824
Alfred	Tuolumne Twp 5	71 519
Alice	Contra Costa Twp 1	57 530
Allen	Calaveras Twp 10	57 278
Alx	Nevada Eureka	61 360
Bennett	Yuba Long Bar	72 750
Bernett	Yuba Long Bar	72 750
C	El Dorado Placerville	58 925
C	Nevada Grass Valley	61 178
C F	El Dorado Casumnes	581166
C W	Siskiyou Scott Va	69 56
Charles	Contra Costa Twp 3	57 600
D	Nevada Eureka	61 367
Erastus	Mendocino Big Rvr	60 843
Frank	Mariposa Coulterville	60 690
Franklin	Trinity Redding	70 985
G	Nevada Nevada	61 278
Geo D	Placer Auburn	62 571
Geo H	Amador Twp 5	55 363
Henry	Santa Clara Gilroy	65 244
Hery	Plumas Quincy	62 959
Ira	Amador Twp 1	55 462
J	El Dorado Georgetown	58 759
J	Nevada Grass Valley	61 206
J	Siskiyou Scott Va	69 50
J B	Mariposa Twp 3	60 546
J C	El Dorado Placerville	58 901
J F	El Dorado Salmon Falls	581066
J H	Placer Dutch Fl	62 734
J P	Mariposa Twp 3	60 575
J S	Yuba Bear Rvr	72 997
J W	Solano Suisan	69 210
James	Merced Twp 1	60 896
James	San Joaquin Castoria	64 901
James	Tuolumne Twp 5	71 519
Jeb	Trinity Indian C	70 989
John	Placer Forest H	62 797
John	Sacramento Natonia	63 272
John	Siskiyou Callahan	69 12
John	Sonoma Petaluma	69 561
John F	Yolo Slate Ra	72 692
John F	Yuba Slate Ro	72 682
Joshua	Contra Costa Twp 3	57 603
L W	Solano Suisan	69 210
Mary Jane	Yuba Parks Ba	72 779
Moses	San Francisco San Francisco 11	102 67
R C	Nevada Nevada	61 269
R G	Nevada Nevada	61 278
Richd C	Sacramento Ward 4	63 549
Robert	Tulara Keyesville	71 54
Samuel	Mendocino Ukiah	60 794
Samuel	Tuolumne Green Springs	71 519
Sylvester	Solano Vallejo	69 253
T	Merced Twp 1	60 909
T	Nevada Bridgeport	61 472
T	Sutter Bear Rvr	70 823
T P	Mariposa Twp 3	60 575
Thomas	Plumas Meadow Valley	62 913
Thomas	Tuolumne Columbia	71 326
Timothy	Plumas Quincy	62 952
W	Sacramento Sutter	63 305
William	Tulara Twp 3	71 51
William P	Calaveras Twp 6	57 149
Wm C	Sacramento Ward 3	63 486
MARSHA		
Margt	San Francisco San Francisco 9	68 991
MARSHAL		
A	San Mateo Twp 3	65 87
A S	Marin Tomales	60 718
Alfred	Calaveras Twp 4	57 303
Andrew F	Colusa Monroeville	57 453
Charles	Marin Point Re	60 732
Doctor	Klamath Klamath	59 224
Doctor*	Klamath Klamath	59 224
Edward	San Francisco San Francisco 4	681153
Enoch G	Calaveras Twp 6	57 124
Fanny	Marin Tomales	60 719
Henry	San Joaquin Elkhorn	64 964

Name	County Locale	M653 RollPage
MARSHAL		
Humprey*	San Francisco	2 67 769
Jms	Klamath Klamath	59 225
Jno	Mariposa Twp 3	60 567
Jno	San Francisco San Francisco 4	68 977
Johannah	San Francisco San Francisco 4	681228
John	Calaveras Twp 5	57 232
John	Humbolt Eel Rvr	59 147
John	San Francisco San Francisco 4	681167
John M	Calaveras Twp 9	57 357
Joseph	Calaveras Twp 5	57 187
Jus	Mariposa Twp 3	60 567
L A	Butte Wyandotte	56 660
Madison	Tulara Visalia	71 98
Michael	Santa Clara San Jose	65 351
Mohn	Calaveras Twp 5	57 232
Peter	San Francisco San Francisco 4	681169
S A	Butte Wyandotte	56 660
S A	Marin Tomales	60 713
Sylvester	Sacramento Ward 3	63 472
Thomas	Calaveras Twp 4	57 341
Thos W	Mariposa Twp 3	60 565
William	Calaveras Twp 6	57 134
William	Calaveras Twp 4	57 327
Wm	Mariposa Twp 3	60 567
MARSHALL		
A	Santa Clara Santa Clara	65 468
A	Santa Clara Santa Clara	65 483
A	Sonoma Santa Rosa	69 414
A D	San Francisco San Francisco 5	67 517
Alex	El Dorado Mountain	581183
Ann	Sonoma Armally	69 496
Aranah	Alameda Brooklyn	55 211
Asa	Yuba Bear Rvr	721003
Aus*	Mariposa Twp 3	60 565
B F	Calaveras Twp 9	57 386
Benjamin	Contra Costa Twp 3	57 596
Burrel	Sierra Cox'S Bar	66 949
C	Nevada Nevada	61 243
C L*	Yuba New York	72 719
C R	Placer Iona Hills	62 886
C S	Yolo Slate Ra	72 719
Caroline	San Francisco San Francisco 7	681400
Carroll	San Francisco San Francisco 12	384 67
Charles	Alameda Oakland	55 18
Cypria	San Francisco San Francisco 8	681241
Cyrus	San Bernardino Santa Barbara	64 150
Cyrus	Siskiyou Klamath	69 85
David	Placer Forest H	62 798
E B	Nevada Nevada	61 274
Earl	Alameda Brooklyn	55 204
Edward	Solano Vacaville	69 339
Elizabeth A	Solano Benecia	69 292
Elner	El Dorado Mud Springs	58 959
Frank	Calaveras Twp 8	57 81
Frank	El Dorado Georgetown	58 694
Frank	El Dorado Eldorado	58 947
Frank	Tuolumne Twp 2	71 473
Geo	Sacramento San Joaquin	63 367
Geo	Sonoma Salt Point	69 691
Geo W	Sacramento Ward 1	63 104
George	Yuba Marysville	72 952
Gerold	Sacramento Ward 1	63 104
H	Sacramento Brighton	63 209
H S	Trinity E Weaver	701057
Hannah	Alameda Brooklyn	55 125
Henry	Alameda Oakland	55 31
Henry	Sonoma Armally	69 496
Henry H	San Francisco San Francisco 2	67 579
Herman*	San Francisco San Francisco 1	68 929
Hugh	Sonoma Bodega	69 529
Humphey*	San Francisco	2 67 769
Humprey	San Francisco San Francisco 2	67 769
Isaac M	Sonoma Petaluma	69 599
Israel	Sacramento Ward 4	63 501
J D	Calaveras Twp 8	57 67
J G	Del Norte Crescent	58 642
J H	Nevada Eureka	61 362
J M	El Dorado Coloma	581072
J M	Santa Clara Almaden	65 268
J M	Tuolumne Columbia	71 346
J R	Sacramento Ward 1	63 85
J W	Nevada Eureka	61 362
Jacob	Sacramento San Joaquin	63 366
Jam W*	Sacramento Ward 1	63 105
James	El Dorado Casumnes	581168
James	Marin Tomales	60 778
James	Sacramento Georgian	63 344
James	San Francisco San Francisco 3	67 67
James	Sierra Twp 5	66 921
James	Tuolumne Columbia	71 293
James	Yuba Rose Bar	72 797
James	Yuba Rose Bar	72 801

California 1860 Census Index

Name	County Locale	M653 RollPage
MARSHALL		
James	Yuba Rose Bar	72 814
Jarn W*	Sacramento Ward 1	63 105
Jas	Sacramento Granite	63 261
Jas	San Francisco San Francisco 9	681081
Jas	San Francisco San Francisco 2	67 666
Jeremiah	Santa Cruz Santa Cruz	66 601
Jn*	El Dorado Georgetown	58 754
Jno	Tehama Antelope	70 889
Johathen*	Mariposa Twp 3	60 570
Johathon	Mariposa Twp 3	60 570
John	Alameda Brooklyn	55 104
John	Calaveras Twp 5	57 229
John	El Dorado Georgetown	58 754
John	Plumas Meadow Valley	62 928
John	San Joaquin Stockton	641081
John	Solano Benecia	69 314
John	Solano Montezuma	69 370
John	Stanislaus Emory	70 746
John	Tulara Visalia	71 16
John	Tulara Visalia	71 30
John R	Calaveras Twp 5	57 229
John W	Marin Cortemad	60 789
Johnthen*	Mariposa Twp 3	60 570
Jos	Klamath Liberty	59 234
Jos	Klamath Liberty	59 236
Joseph	Alameda Brooklyn	55 124
Joseph	Mendocino Big Rvr	60 852
Joseph	San Francisco San Francisco 9	681104
Joseph	Shasta Shasta	66 682
Joseph	Sierra Downieville	66 976
Joseph A	Nevada Bridgeport	61 452
Joseph W	Los Angeles Elmonte	59 265
Jus*	Mariposa Twp 3	60 565
Klippe	Alameda Murray	55 223
L	Sierra Downieville	661011
L H	Butte Oregon	56 618
L P	Solano Montezuma	69 370
Laughlin	Sonoma Russian	69 446
Leon C	San Francisco San Francisco 7	681340
Louis	Yuba Fosters	72 835
M H	Tuolumne Twp 2	71 471
M O	Nevada Grass Valley	61 192
M T	Nevada Grass Valley	61 171
Manuel	Klamath Liberty	59 236
Manuel	San Diego San Diego	64 769
Mary	San Francisco San Francisco 12	67 386
Melvina C	Santa Clara San Jose	65 392
Miran	Shasta Shasta	66 682
N	Santa Clara Fremont	65 427
O	Calaveras Twp 9	57 416
P	Marin Cortemad	60 783
R	El Dorado Diamond	58 789
R	Mariposa Twp 3	60 595
R	Trinity Douglas	70 974
R A	El Dorado Diamond	58 793
R C	Solano Vacaville	69 319
Ralph	San Joaquin Elliott	64 948
Reg	Santa Clara San Jose	65 295
Richard	Sierra Downieville	661024
Richs	Sonoma Petaluma	69 558
Robt	Mendocino Big Rvr	60 851
Robt	San Francisco San Francisco 10	67 351
Robt	Tuolumne Twp 1	71 256
S	El Dorado Diamond	58 815
S H	Klamath Liberty	59 238
Sallie	Solano Montezuma	69 370
Sam W	Sacramento Ward 1	63 105
Saml	Sonoma Petaluma	69 566
Saml E	Tuolumne Columbia	71 345
Samuel	Sierra Twp 5	66 921
Sus	Mariposa Twp 3	60 565
T R	Tuolumne Twp 2	71 346
T S	San Francisco San Francisco 3	67 84
Thoas	Mariposa Twp 3	60 565
Thomas	Contra Costa Twp 1	57 510
Thomas	El Dorado Eldorado	58 936
Thomas	San Joaquin Stockton	641079
Thomas	Tuolumne Columbia	71 297
Thomas F	Tuolumne Twp 2	71 297
Thos	Mariposa Twp 3	60 563
W B	Amador Twp 3	55 409
W M	Trinity Rush Crk	70 965
W R	Trinity Trinity	70 973
W W	Colusa Monroeville	57 440
William	Amador Twp 4	55 243
William	Calaveras Twp 4	57 327
William	Sierra Whiskey	66 845
Wm	Butte Mountain	56 737
Wm	Klamath Liberty	59 240
Wm	Napa Clear Lake	61 129
Wm	Sacramento Ward 3	63 456
MARSHALLEIN		
Manuel	Sierra Downieville	66 977
MARSHANN		
D B	Mendocino Big Rvr	60 847
MARSHAT		
Geo	Santa Clara San Jose	65 359
MARSHAW		
H	Sierra La Porte	66 772
MARSHEL		
Elias	Mariposa Coulterville	60 677
MARSHELL		
Paul	Yuba Bear Rvr	721007
MARSHFIELD		
John	San Joaquin Stockton	641042
MARSHULL		
William	Sierra Whiskey	66 845
MARSHUM		
Henry	Sonoma Bodega	69 529
MARSITO		
J	Calaveras Twp 9	57 378
MARSLAINE		
Edwd	San Francisco San Francisco 1	68 811
MARSLAND		
Elizabeth	San Francisco San Francisco 1	68 931
Mathew H	San Francisco 1	68 931
	San Francisco	
MARSLOW		
J R	Tuolumne Twp 2	71 401
MARSNA		
Juan*	Monterey San Juan	601001
MARSOE		
Fred	Calaveras Twp 9	57 373
MARSOLINA		
Louis	Tuolumne Big Oak	71 130
MARSON		
Cadwell	El Dorado Union	581090
Frederick*	Placer Iona Hills	62 897
Lewis	Alameda Oakland	55 43
Marce H	Tuolumne Twp 2	71 394
Marie H	Tuolumne Shawsfla	71 394
MARSOS		
Fred	Calaveras Twp 9	57 373
MARSSON		
Robert	Marin Tomales	60 724
MARSTAN		
Ann	San Francisco San Francisco 9	68 961
MARSTEN		
John	Mariposa Twp 3	60 600
MARSTERS		
E J	Tuolumne Shawsfla	71 387
MARSTIN		
Jno D	San Francisco San Francisco 9	681045
MARSTON		
Benj*	Alameda Brooklyn	55 182
C A	Sacramento Ward 1	63 37
C A*	Nevada Red Dog	61 540
E W	Tuolumne Columbia	71 345
E W*	Tuolumne Twp 2	71 234
F T	San Francisco San Francisco 9	681023
George	Alameda Brooklyn	55 151
J A	Mendocino Big Rvr	60 851
J H	Solano Suisan	69 211
J M	Calaveras Twp 7	57 9
J R	Tuolumne Shawsfla	71 401
John	Plumas Quincy	62 958
Jotham S*	Alameda Brooklyn	55 182
Robert	Marin Tomales	60 724
Saml J*	Alameda Brooklyn	55 182
Wm H	San Francisco San Francisco 6	67 401
MARSTOW		
Onen	Butte Ophir	56 762
Owen	Butte Ophir	56 762
MARSTRATTI		
Anyclo	Calaveras Twp 6	57 123
MARSY		
Thomas*	Shasta Shasta	66 687
MART		
B*	El Dorado Georgetown	58 759
Frank	Amador Twp 4	55 471
Leopold	Los Angeles Los Angeles	59 297
Samuel	Los Angeles Los Angeles	59 355
Stephen	Humbolt Eel Rvr	59 153
MARTA		
---	Los Angeles San Pedro	59 486
---	San Diego Agua Caliente	64 831
Francisco*	Calaveras Twp 6	57 135
MARTAELLE		
A	Amador Twp 3	55 375
MARTAL		
Doff	Yuba New York	72 737
MARTARY		
J*	Nevada Eureka	61 388
MARTASH		
---	Mendocino Calpella	60 822
MARTAYER		
---	Mendocino Twp 1	60 892
MARTE		
Jose	Alameda Brooklyn	55 128
MARTEL		
J	Nevada Grass Valley	61 149
Joseph	San Francisco San Francisco 8	681247
W*	San Francisco San Francisco 2	67 696
MARTELL		
C T	Nevada Grass Valley	61 198
Francis	Amador Twp 4	55 245
J	San Francisco San Francisco 5	67 512
J B	Yolo Slate Ra	72 689
John	San Francisco San Francisco 10	67 268
Joseph De*	San Francisco 2	67 748
	San Francisco	
Louis	Amador Township	55 464
MARTELLI		
Lagani	Calaveras Twp 7	57 46
MARTELLS		
Henry	El Dorado Georgetown	58 745
MARTEN		
A B*	Siskiyou Scott Ri	69 67
Catharine	San Francisco San Francisco 10	67 290
Charles*	Siskiyou Callahan	69 13
Jas	Sonoma Sonoma	69 652
Jens	Yuba Marysville	72 924
Prentis*	Mariposa Coulterville	60 674
MARTENA		
John D	Tuolumne Twp 5	71 488
MARTENAS		
Carus	Mariposa Twp 1	60 654
Casus	Mariposa Twp 1	60 654
Manuel	Tuolumne Twp 5	71 498
Nicolas	Tuolumne Chinese	71 497
MARTENE		
Antonio De*	Calaveras Twp 9	57 362
MARTENER		
Simon	Mariposa Twp 3	60 573
MARTENES		
Jose	Tulara Sinks Te	71 42
W	El Dorado Placerville	58 875
MARTENEZ		
Alonzo	Monterey Monterey	60 966
Pedro	Monterey San Juan	60 991
MARTENIS		
Tudes	Tulara Sinks Te	71 43
MARTENSTEIN		
Jacob	San Francisco San Francisco 8	681309
MARTENUS		
Delores	Mariposa Twp 1	60 629
MARTER		
Richard	San Francisco San Francisco 7	681329
MARTERAS		
Julius	Amador Twp 4	55 246
MARTERTON		
Patrick*	Calaveras Twp 6	57 182
MARTES		
N	Sacramento Ward 3	63 475
MARTESSON		
Charles*	Calaveras Twp 6	57 139
MARTETT		
Charles	Los Angeles Santa Ana	59 440
MARTFELD		
Wm	Sacramento Ward 1	63 113
MARTFIELD		
Wm	Sacramento Ward 1	63 77
MARTFILD		
Wm	Sacramento Ward 1	63 77
MARTH		
A	El Dorado Indian D	581159
Frank	San Mateo Twp 3	65 74
MARTHA		
---	Mendocino Calpella	60 817
---	Mendocino Calpella	60 821
---	Mendocino Twp 1	60 889
---	Shasta Shasta	66 684
Marg	San Francisco San Francisco 2	67 569
MARTHE		
John	Amador Twp 5	55 343
MARTHEN		
C F*	Sacramento Granite	63 246
MARTHER		
John	San Francisco San Francisco 11	67 141
MARTHEWS		
Edward	San Francisco San Francisco 4	681113
MARTHEWSON		
E*	El Dorado Coloma	581118
MARTHOE		
Manuel*	San Mateo Twp 1	65 59
MARTI		
---	Del Norte Happy Ca	58 663
MARTIARD		
Manuel*	Shasta Shasta	66 683
MARTIAS		
---	San Bernardino S Timate	64 692
MARTIC		
E B*	San Francisco San Francisco 1	68 875

Name	County Locale	M653 RollPage
MARTICA		
D S*	San Francisco San Francisco 1	68 810
MARTICE		
John*	Amador Twp 6	55 433
MARTIE		
John*	Calaveras Twp 7	57 23
MARTILL		
G	Tuolumne Twp 3	71 421
J B	Yuba Slate Ro	72 689
MARTIM		
John*	Calaveras Twp 8	57 81
MARTIMERS		
A*	Nevada Grass Valley	61 180
MARTIMS		
Coe*	Mariposa Twp 1	60 648
MARTIN JUNR		
---	San Bernardino S Timate	64 722
MARTIN		
---	Los Angeles Los Angeles	59 389
---	Los Angeles Los Angeles	59 404
---	Los Angeles San Gabriel	59 413
---	Mariposa Twp 1	60 643
---	Monterey S Antoni	60 969
---	Placer Dutch Fl	62 721
---	San Bernardino Santa Barbara	64 202
---	San Bernardino S Timate	64 693
---	San Bernardino S Timate	64 694
---	San Bernardino S Timate	64 706
---	San Bernardino S Timate	64 710
---	San Bernardino S Timate	64 712
---	San Bernardino S Timate	64 722
---	San Bernardino S Timate	64 723
---	San Bernardino S Timate	64 725
---	San Bernardino S Timate	64 728
---	San Bernardino S Timate	64 731
---	San Bernardino S Timate	64 732
---	San Bernardino S Timate	64 733
---	San Bernardino S Timate	64 739
---	San Bernardino S Timate	64 745
---	San Bernardino S Timate	64 747
---	San Bernardino S Timate	64 748
---	San Bernardino S Timate	64 753
---	San Bernardino S Timate	64 755
---	San Diego S Luis R	64 783
---	San Diego Agua Caliente	64 827
---	Sonoma Salt Point	69 692
A	Nevada Nevada	61 243
A	San Francisco San Francisco 5	67 515
A	Shasta Horsetown	66 703
A	Tuolumne Twp 1	71 253
A B	Nevada Nevada	61 284
A B	Siskiyou Scott Ri	69 67
A H	El Dorado Georgetown	58 700
A J	Butte Hamilton	56 517
A W	Tuolumne Columbia	71 364
Ab	Shasta Millvill	66 739
Abraham	San Francisco San Francisco 9	68 974
Addison	Sacramento Ward 3	63 461
Aguilar	Los Angeles Los Angeles	59 370
Albert	Amador Twp 4	55 245
Alex	San Francisco San Francisco 9	68 999
Alexander	Los Angeles San Juan	59 462
Alexander J	Yuba Marysville	72 940
Alfred	Tuolumne Twp 2	71 363
Ambrose	San Joaquin Stockton	641046
Amy	Tuolumne Columbia	71 329
Andrew	El Dorado Coloma	581107
Andrew	San Mateo Twp 2	65 124
Ann	San Francisco San Francisco 4	681123
Ann	San Francisco San Francisco 7	681342
Ann	Yuba Marysville	72 864
Ann E	San Francisco San Francisco 2	67 742
Antoine	Calaveras Twp 10	57 292
Antonio	San Bernardino San Salvador	64 661
Antonio*	Placer Auburn	62 583
Arid	Sonoma Mendocino	69 465
Arthur	Alameda Brooklyn	55 97
August	Yolo Slate Ra	72 686
August	Yuba North Ea	72 686
Azariah	Sonoma Healdsbu	69 477
B	El Dorado Coloma	581085
B	Nevada Grass Valley	61 175
B	Nevada Eureka	61 363
B	Tehama Tehama	70 935
B O	Tuolumne Twp 4	71 135
Barney	Yuba Rose Bar	72 814
Benj	San Bernardino San Salvador	64 656
Benjamin	Placer Yankee J	62 782
Bernard	Tuolumne Twp 1	71 215
Brown	Placer Yankee J	62 759
C	Nevada Nevada	61 253
C	Santa Clara San Jose	65 293
C	Siskiyou Cottonwood	69 106
C B	Nevada Grass Valley	61 182
C C	Klamath Trinidad	59 220
C T	Sacramento Ward 1	63 47

Name	County Locale	M653 RollPage
MARTIN		
Calib	El Dorado Casumnes	581163
Calvin H	Sierra Twp 7	66 910
Camille	San Joaquin Stockton	641066
Catharine	San Francisco San Francisco 10	230 67
Catharine	San Francisco San Francisco 10	290 67
Catharine	San Francisco San Francisco 2	67 564
Cathrine	San Mateo Twp 1	65 68
Charlay	Nevada Bridgeport	61 504
Charles	Marin S Antoni	60 710
Charles	Sacramento Ward 1	63 57
Charles	San Francisco San Francisco 8	681316
Charles	San Francisco San Francisco 7	681440
Charles	Siskiyou Callahan	69 13
Charles	Yuba Bear Rvr	721013
Charles A	Calaveras Twp 4	57 338
Charles A	Calaveras Twp 4	57 339
Charles W	San Joaquin Douglass	64 921
Charles*	Siskiyou Callahan	69 13
Charlotte	San Francisco San Francisco 6	67 408
Chas	Sacramento Ward 1	63 122
Chas	Sacramento Ward 1	63 14
Chas	San Francisco San Francisco 8	681001
Chas G	Alameda Brooklyn	55 154
Chas S	Calaveras Twp 10	57 279
Christopher	San Francisco San Francisco 3	67 30
Chs	San Francisco	
Chs	San Francisco San Francisco 5	67 512
Clifton	San Joaquin Oneal	64 938
Cornelius	Sonoma Mendocino	69 466
Cornelus	Sonoma Mendocino	69 466
Crosby G	Amador Twp 4	55 239
D	Butte Chico	56 534
D	Sacramento Ward 4	63 607
D	Sierra St Louis	66 818
D C	Merced Monterey	60 929
D C	Monterey Monterey	60 929
D M	Tuolumne Twp 1	71 480
Daniel	Calaveras Twp 4	57 316
Daniel	Los Angeles Los Angeles	59 371
Daniel	Plumas Quincy	62 998
Daniel	San Francisco San Francisco 7	681356
Daniel	Siskiyou Scott Va	69 60
Daniel	Yolo Slate Ra	72 694
Danl	Butte Ophir	56 800
Danl	San Francisco San Francisco 1	68 854
Danl E	San Francisco San Francisco 2	67 618
David	Butte Wyandotte	56 667
David	El Dorado Kelsey	581140
David G	Butte Bidwell	56 715
David J	San Joaquin Tulare	64 869
Delary S*	Yuba Bear Rvr	721010
Delary T*	Yuba Bear Rvr	721010
Domissco	Calaveras Twp 8	57 82
Dumes	San Mateo Twp 3	65 96
E	Nevada Nevada	61 260
E	San Joaquin Stockton	641066
E P	Mendocino Ukiah	60 793
Edward	El Dorado Greenwood	58 713
Edward	Klamath Klamath	59 226
Edward	Placer Todds Va	62 784
Edward	San Francisco San Francisco 9	681097
Edward	San Francisco San Francisco 2	67 568
Edward	Santa Cruz Watsonville	66 538
Edward	Tuolumne Twp 3	71 442
Edward	Tuolumne Jamestown	71 450
Edwd	San Francisco San Francisco 1	68 879
Edwd	San Francisco San Francisco 1	68 889
Elenor	San Francisco San Francisco 2	67 726
Elenora	San Francisco San Francisco 2	67 726
Eli	Colusa Monroeville	57 142
Eli	Colusa Monroeville	57 147
Eliza	San Francisco San Francisco 10	255 67
Eliza	San Francisco San Francisco 9	68 953
Eliza	Santa Clara San Jose	65 362
Eliza*	Napa Hot Springs	61 20
Elizabeth	Sonoma Mendocino	69 466
Ellen	Santa Clara San Jose	65 390
Elliott L	Yuba Rose Bar	72 801
Elliottl	Yuba Rose Bar	72 801
Elza	Napa Hot Springs	61 20
Emille	Yuba Foster B	72 835
Emma	Plumas Quincy	62 923
Esporola	Calaveras Twp 5	57 221
Espowla	Calaveras Twp 5	57 221
Espowlu	Calaveras Twp 5	57 221
F	Butte Kimshaw	56 585
F	Nevada Eureka	61 364
F De	Tuolumne Twp 4	71 126
F H M	Sierra La Porte	66 768
F P	Stanislaus Branch	70 702
Ferdinand	San Francisco San Francisco 2	67 646
Flerry	Yolo Slate Ra	72 686

Name	County Locale	M653 RollPage
MARTIN		
Flury	Yuba North Ea	72 686
Frances	Napa Napa	61 112
Frances	Sonoma Healdsbu	69 477
Francis	Napa Napa	61 112
Francis	Nevada Bridgeport	61 493
Francis	Sierra La Porte	66 768
Francis	Sonoma Santa Rosa	69 414
Francisco	Marin San Rafael	60 770
Francisco	San Francisco San Francisco 5	67 488
Francisco T	Twp 1	57 497
Frank	Contra Costa	
Frank	Sacramento Granite	63 255
Frank	San Joaquin Elliott	64 944
Frank	San Joaquin Elkhorn	64 954
Frank	Trinity Mouth Ca	701017
Frank	Tuolumne Columbia	71 357
Franks	Alameda Brooklyn	55 113
Fred	Amador Twp 5	55 343
Fred	Santa Clara Gilroy	65 248
Fredr	San Francisco San Francisco 1	68 930
G	Nevada Grass Valley	61 186
G	Nevada Eureka	61 365
G	San Francisco San Francisco 5	67 503
G W	Sacramento San Joaquin	63 365
G W	San Francisco San Francisco 6	67 422
Geo	Amador Twp 2	55 316
Geo	Butte Kimshaw	56 605
Geo	San Francisco San Francisco 9	681045
Geo D	Stanislaus Branch	70 708
Geo R	Sacramento Ward 4	63 566
George	Amador Twp 2	55 295
George	El Dorado Greenwood	58 715
George	Placer Michigan	62 858
George	Plumas Quincy	62 994
George	Shasta Millvill	66 755
George	Solano Fremont	69 384
George	Yuba Parks Ba	72 778
George H	Siskiyou Shasta Rvr	69 116
George*	Calaveras Twp 5	57 240
Gerret	San Francisco San Francisco 3	67 63
Gerrit	San Francisco San Francisco 3	67 63
Green	Santa Cruz Pajaro	66 562
Green T	Tuolumne Sonora	71 214
Green*	Santa Cruz Pajaro	66 562
H	Amador Twp 5	55 329
H	Stanislaus Oatvale	70 718
H	Tuolumne Twp 4	71 176
H B	Sonoma Santa Rosa	69 393
H D	Tuolumne Twp 1	71 480
H Q	El Dorado Diamond	58 764
H S	Trinity Sturdiva	701006
H S	Trinity Price'S	701019
Harvy	Santa Clara Gilroy	65 237
Helary T	Yuba Bear Rvr	721010
Henry	El Dorado Eldorado	58 947
Henry	Los Angeles Los Angeles	59 334
Henry	Plumas Quincy	62 937
Henry	Plumas Quincy	62 993
Henry	Sacramento Centre	63 176
Henry	San Bernardino San Bernadino	64 686
Henry	San Francisco San Francisco 9	681010
Henry	San Francisco San Francisco 7	681350
Henry	Santa Cruz Pajaro	66 577
Henry	Sierra Gibsonville	66 855
Henry	Sierra Twp 7	66 891
Henry	Trinity Weaverville	701068
Henry	Yolo No E Twp	72 672
Henry	Yuba North Ea	72 672
Hiram	Placer Rattle Snake	62 598
Hosea	Alameda Brooklyn	55 199
Hugh	Amador Twp 3	55 392
Hugh	Butte Chico	56 567
Isaac	Contra Costa Twp 1	57 510
Isaac	Tehama Moons	70 852
J	Amador Twp 3	55 395
J	Butte Oregon	56 620
J	El Dorado Kelsey	581156
J	Nevada Eureka	61 377
J	San Francisco San Francisco 5	67 541
J	Santa Clara Almaden	65 278
J	Shasta Millvill	66 741
J	Tuolumne Twp 4	71 153
J	Tuolumne Twp 4	71 160
J	Tuolumne Garrote	71 175
J	Yolo Slate Ra	72 698
J A	Sierra Twp 7	66 887
J A	Yuba Fosters	72 829
J B	Mariposa Coulterville	60 693
J D	Marin Tomales	60 713
J F	Tehama Lassen	70 874
J G	Butte Chico	56 552
J H	San Francisco San Francisco 6	67 435
J H	Yolo Washington	72 568
J J	Sutter Bear Rvr	70 822
J L*	Sacramento Cosumnes	63 398

California 1860 Census Index

M653

Name	County Locale	Roll	Page
MARTIN			
J N	El Dorado Coloma	58	1074
J N	Sonoma Salt Point	69	689
J N	Yolo Washington	72	568
J P	Santa Clara San Jose	65	305
J P*	Yuba Marysville	72	924
J S*	Sacramento Cosumnes	63	398
J W	Sacramento Franklin	63	314
J*	Yuba New York	72	733
Ja	Yuba Slate Ro	72	698
Jack	Sonoma Sonoma	69	654
Jackson H	San Bernadino San Bernardino	64	686
Jacob	El Dorado Greenwood	58	711
Jacob	Plumas Meadow Valley	62	927
Jacob	Siskiyou Yreka	69	170
Jacob M F	Sierra Downieville	66	1028
James	Alameda Brooklyn	55	199
James	Amador Twp 3	55	391
James	Colusa Spring Valley	57	433
James	Contra Costa Twp 1	57	524
James	Nevada Rough &	61	432
James	Placer Rattle Snake	62	637
James	Plumas Quincy	62	958
James	San Francisco San Francisco 11	139 67	
James	San Francisco San Francisco 11	140 67	
James	Santa Clara Gilroy	65	250
James	Santa Clara Fremont	65	430
James	Santa Cruz Soquel	66	599
James	Santa Cruz Santa Cruz	66	600
James	Sierra St Louis	66	863
James	Siskiyou Klamath	69	96
James	Tuolumne Twp 1	71	190
James	Yolo Washington	72	571
James	Yuba Linda	72	989
James A	Los Angeles San Jose	59	283
James B	Calaveras Twp 4	57	312
James H	Yuba Marysville	72	912
James M	Sonoma Healdsbu	69	473
James P	Amador Twp 2	55	267
James T	El Dorado Georgetown	58	693
James V	Calaveras Twp 6	57	152
Jas	Amador Twp 2	55	306
Jas	Butte Hamilton	56	517
Jas	Calaveras Twp 9	57	385
Jas	San Francisco San Francisco 9	68	1090
Jas	San Francisco San Francisco 1	68	909
Jas	Sonoma Sonoma	69	652
Jas M	Butte Cascade	56	704
Jas M	Butte Ophir	56	784
Jasbitan	El Dorado Greenwood	58	714
Jennie	San Francisco San Francisco 6	67	445
Jesus	Calaveras Twp 5	57	206
Jno	Mendocino Calpella	60	823
Jno	Sacramento Ward 1	63	20
Jno	Sacramento Natonia	63	281
Jno	San Francisco San Francisco 9	68	1082
Jno	San Francisco San Francisco 10	248 67	
Jno F	Klamath Klamath	59	226
Jno G	Butte Kimshaw	56	594
Jno W	Alameda Murray	55	220
Jno*	Alameda Brooklyn	55	134
Joel C	Yuba Marysville	72	861
Joel D	Yuba Marysville	72	856
Joel E	Tuolumne Twp 3	71	457
John	Alameda Murray	55	225
John	Alameda Murray	55	226
John	Amador Twp 6	55	433
John	Calaveras Twp 7	57	10
John	Calaveras Twp 5	57	198
John	Calaveras Twp 5	57	226
John	Calaveras Twp 10	57	299
John	Calaveras Twp 7	57	29
John	Calaveras Twp 8	57	73
John	Contra Costa Twp 2	57	542
John	Del Norte Crescent	58	646
John	Del Norte Ferry P O	58	665
John	El Dorado Salmon Falls	58	1048
John	El Dorado Georgetown	58	690
John	Fresno Twp 1	59	76
John	Humbolt Bucksport	59	158
John	Mariposa Twp 3	60	572
John	Mariposa Twp 1	60	666
John	Mariposa Coulterville	60	694
John	Mendocino Ukiah	60	803
John	Nevada Nevada	61	284
John	Sacramento Granite	63	251
John	Sacramento Sutter	63	300
John	Sacramento San Joaquin	63	360
John	San Francisco San Francisco 11	137 67	
John	San Francisco San Francisco 7	68	1389

Name	County Locale	Roll	Page
MARTIN			
John	San Francisco San Francisco 10	263 67	
John	San Francisco San Francisco 10	268 67	
John	San Francisco San Francisco 3	67	63
John	San Francisco San Francisco 3	67	77
John	San Francisco San Francisco 1	68	855
John	San Francisco San Francisco 1	68	901
John	San Joaquin Tulare	64	870
John	San Joaquin Elkhorn	64	964
John	San Mateo Twp 3	65	85
John	Santa Clara San Jose	65	353
John	Santa Clara San Jose	65	380
John	Shasta French G	66	716
John	Sierra Pine Grove	66	832
John	Tehama Pasakent	70	857
John	Tehama Red Bluff	70	899
John	Tehama Tehama	70	935
John	Trinity State Ba	70	1001
John	Trinity East For	70	1027
John	Trinity Weaverville	70	1072
John	Tuolumne Twp 4	71	142
John	Tuolumne Twp 1	71	262
John	Tuolumne Twp 2	71	291
John	Tuolumne Shawsfla	71	415
John	Yolo Cottonwoood	72	557
John	Yolo Putah	72	598
John	Yolo Cache Crk	72	606
John	Yolo Cache Crk	72	631
John	Yolo Cache Crk	72	643
John	Yuba Long Bar	72	755
John	Yuba Long Bar	72	755
John	Yuba Marysville	72	877
John	Yuba Marysville	72	940
John A	Butte Ophir	56	761
John A	Contra Costa Twp 1	57	535
John C	Alameda Oakland	55	48
John H	Tuolumne Twp 3	71	442
John H	Tuolumne Jamestown	71	453
John L	Santa Cruz Pajaro	66	533
John M	San Francisco San Francisco 9	68	1023
John*	Calaveras Twp 7	57	23
John*	Calaveras Twp 8	57	81
Jos	Amador Twp 2	55	305
Jos	San Francisco San Francisco 9	68	1090
Jos B	Alameda Brooklyn	55	139
Jose	Monterey San Juan	60	1001
Jose	San Bernardino Santa Inez	64	139
Jose Miguel	San Salvador	64	660
Jose*	Monterey San Juan	60	1001
Joseh	Calaveras Twp 9	57	372
Joseh	Shasta Horsetown	66	692
Joseph	Calaveras Twp 6	57	162
Joseph	Calaveras Twp 7	57	34
Joseph	Calaveras Twp 9	57	372
Joseph	Contra Costa Twp 1	57	518
Joseph	El Dorado Coloma	58	1081
Joseph	El Dorado Georgetown	58	706
Joseph	Humbolt Pacific	59	130
Joseph	Los Angeles Los Nieto	59	426
Joseph	Shasta Horsetown	66	692
Joseph	Sierra Poker Flats	66	841
Joseph	Sierra Twp 5	66	917
Joseph	Sonoma Petaluma	69	572
Joseph	Tulara Visalia	71	96
Joseph	Tuolumne Twp 3	71	442
Joseph	Tuolumne Twp 5	71	452
Joseph	Yolo Merritt	72	583
Joseph	Yolo Cottonwoood	72	654
Joseph	Yuba Bear Rvr	72	1012
Joseph	Yuba New York	72	726
Josiah	El Dorado Georgetown	58	695
Juan R	Monterey San Juan	60	1001
Juaquin	San Bernardino S Timate	64	687
Judah	San Francisco San Francisco 10	195 67	
Julius	Yuba Marysville	72	968
Jus*	Alameda Brooklyn	55	134
L	Siskiyou Yreka	69	190
L D	Tuolumne Twp 1	71	239
Landalaria	San Salvador	64	660
	San Bernardino		
Lawrence	San Joaquin Douglass	64	922
Lee	Sacramento Granite	63	230
Leo	San Francisco San Francisco 2	67	676
Leonard	Los Angeles San Jose	59	283
Leonard	Sierra Eureka	66	1043
Leroy	Alameda Brooklyn	55	126
Lizzie	San Francisco San Francisco 10	183 67	
Louis	Amador Twp 1	55	507
Louis	Calaveras Twp 6	57	147
Louis	Calaveras Twp 9	57	363
Louis	Calaveras Twp 8	57	91

Name	County Locale	Roll	Page
MARTIN			
Louis	San Francisco San Francisco 3	67	5
M	Calaveras Twp 9	57	417
M	El Dorado Coloma	58	1078
M	El Dorado Kelsey	58	1132
M	El Dorado Grizzly	58	1179
M	Trinity Taylor'S	70	1036
M C	Sacramento Ward 1	63	16
M C	Tehama Red Bluff	70	916
M C M	El Dorado Georgetown	58	676
M D	Yolo Cache	72	625
M S	San Francisco San Francisco 6	67	435
M W	Nevada Bridgeport	61	502
Margaret	San Francisco San Francisco 10	232 67	
Margaret	San Francisco San Francisco 6	67	438
Maria J	San Francisco San Francisco 2	67	637
Marid J	San Francisco San Francisco 2	67	637
Marie	San Francisco San Francisco 8	68	1281
Mary	Amador Twp 2	55	296
Mary	El Dorado Coloma	58	1085
Mary	San Francisco San Francisco 8	68	1302
Mary	San Francisco San Francisco 10	182 67	
Mary	San Francisco San Francisco 6	67	446
Mary Ann	Sonoma Mendocino	69	464
Mary J	Yuba Bear Rvr	72	1011
Mary K	San Francisco San Francisco 3	67	37
Mary O	San Francisco San Francisco 9	68	1015
Michael	Calaveras Twp 5	57	232
Michael	Los Angeles Los Angeles	59	361
Michael	San Francisco San Francisco 11	122 67	
Michael	San Francisco San Francisco 11	150 67	
Michael	San Francisco San Francisco 12	362 67	
Michael	Santa Cruz Pajaro	66	526
Michael	Sierra Twp 7	66	912
Michael	Yuba New York	72	736
Mick	San Francisco San Francisco 11	104 67	
Milton	El Dorado Georgetown	58	676
Moses	San Bernardino San Bernadino	64	634
Moses	Shasta Millvill	66	747
Mr	Sonoma Salt Point	69	692
Mrgaret	San Francisco San Francisco 10	232 67	
Mtthew	Plumas Meadow Valley	62	906
N	El Dorado Georgetown	58	679
N H	Tuolumne Sonora	71	208
Nathan	El Dorado Georgetown	58	703
Nicholas G	Yuba Parks Ba	72	782
Nicholas J	Yuba Parke Ba	72	782
Nina	Santa Clara San Jose	65	307
Noble	Nevada Red Dog	61	547
Ortega	Los Angeles Los Nieto	59	428
P	San Francisco San Francisco 2	67	656
P A	Amador Twp 1	55	480
P J	Nevada Red Dog	61	540
P P	Shasta Horsetown	66	702
Pat	Nevada Bridgeport	61	476
Patrick	Calaveras Twp 6	57	185
Patrick	Contra Costa Twp 1	57	502
Patrick	San Mateo Twp 3	65	96
Patrick	Santa Clara San Jose	65	359
Patrick	Sierra St Louis	66	805
Patrick	Trinity State Ba	70	1001
Peirre	Calaveras Twp 5	57	200
Peter	Calaveras Twp 4	57	311
Peter	Sacramento Sutter	63	300
Peter	Tuolumne Don Pedro	71	538
Petr	Nevada Bridgeport	61	451
Philip	Trinity East For	70	1027
Phillip	Klamath Liberty	59	241
Phillip	San Francisco San Francisco 8	68	1293
Pirre	Calaveras Twp 5	57	200
Prentis	Mariposa Coulterville	60	674
R B	Trinity Taylor'S	70	1034
R F	Shasta Millvill	66	739
R J	Solano Vacaville	69	339
R M	Sonoma Santa Rosa	69	392
R P	Tuolumne Twp 2	71	374
Rachael	San Francisco San Francisco 10	195 67	
Raymond	Calaveras Twp 7	57	16
Richd	San Francisco San Francisco 2	67	672
Richd	Trinity Weaverville	70	1056
Robert	Placer Rattle Snake	62	599
Robert	San Francisco San Francisco 8	68	1291
Robert	San Francisco San Francisco 7	68	1405
Robert M	Siskiyou Yreka	69	130
Robert S*	San Francisco San Francisco 2	67	741
Robt	Butte Cascade	56	694
Robt	Sacramento Ward 4	63	582
Robt	Trinity Weaverville	70	1068

California 1860 Census Index

Name	County Locale	M653 Roll	Page
MARTIN			
Robt L*	San Francisco San Francisco 2	67	741
Robt S	San Francisco San Francisco 2	67	741
Rosetta	Sacramento Ward 4	63	509
S	Sonoma Salt Point	69	692
S H	Yolo Cottonwoood	72	653
Salidad	Santa Clara Santa Clara	65	507
Sally	San Francisco San Francisco 10	67	320
Sam	Tulara Visalia	71	96
Saml	Butte Ophir	56	765
Saml G	Sacramento Ward 1	63	33
Samuel	El Dorado Eldorado	58	945
Samuel	Placer Iona Hills	62	884
Samuel	San Joaquin Elkhorn	64	963
Samuel	Solano Suisan	69	237
Samuel	Sonoma Armally	69	498
Samuel B	Alameda Brooklyn	55	161
Sarah	Yuba Long Bar	72	755
Sarah*	Yuba Long Bar	72	756
Seth	Nevada Red Dog	61	549
Silas	Colusa Spring Valley	57	430
Silas	Sonoma Petaluma	69	553
Simon B	Sonoma Mendocino	69	464
Stephen	San Francisco San Francisco 1	68	854
Steven	Sonoma Petaluma	69	595
Storer	Amador Twp 7	55	418
T	Nevada Grass Valley	61	193
T	Sacramento Granite	63	230
T	Shasta Millvill	66	741
T	Shasta Millvill	66	751
T G	Siskiyou Scott Ri	69	76
Thomas	Calaveras Twp 5	57	143
Thomas	Calaveras Twp 5	57	186
Thomas	Los Angeles San Jose	59	281
Thomas	Marin S Antoni	60	707
Thomas	Placer Rattle Snake	62	599
Thomas	Placer Michigan	62	829
Thomas	Sacramento Granite	63	267
Thomas	San Francisco San Francisco 4	68	1219
Thomas	San Francisco San Francisco 6	67	440
Thomas	Sierra Cox'S Bar	66	950
Thomas	Yuba Marysville	72	901
Thomas S	San Bernardino Santa Barbara	64	171
Thos	Amador Twp 2	55	325
Thos	Calaveras Twp 9	57	359
Thos	Klamath Klamath	59	226
Thos	Merced Twp 1	60	903
Thos	Nevada Bridgeport	61	467
Thos	Santa Cruz Santa Cruz	66	633
Thos	Trinity E Weaver	70	1057
Thos	Yolo Putah	72	549
Thos S	Calaveras Twp 10	57	279
Uriah	San Joaquin Castoria	64	876
Victor	San Francisco San Francisco 7	68	1450
W	Tehama Red Bluff	70	910
W	Yolo Cache	72	630
W G	Calaveras Twp 9	57	403
W H*	San Francisco San Francisco 6	67	427
W H*	Yolo Putah	72	550
W J	Nevada Grass Valley	61	201
W S	Sierra Twp 7	66	864
W U*	Yolo Putah	72	550
Walter	El Dorado Georgetown	58	703
Wheeler	San Francisco San Francisco 9	68	982
William	Contra Costa Twp 1	57	518
William	Contra Costa Twp 2	57	559
William	Fresno Twp 2	59	4
William	Monterey Monterey	60	958
William	Monterey S Antoni	60	973
William	Nevada Bloomfield	61	514
William	San Francisco San Francisco 9	68	1012
William	San Francisco San Francisco 11	67	99
William	San Mateo Twp 3	65	93
William	Sierra La Porte	66	769
William	Siskiyou Klamath	69	85
William	Solano Vacaville	69	345
William	Tuolumne Twp 1	71	252
William	Tuolumne Chinese	71	496
William M	Nevada Rough &	61	421
Wilmot	Tehama Lassen	70	863
Wm	Marin Cortemad	60	784
Wm	Placer Dutch Fl	62	718
Wm	Sacramento Granite	63	246
Wm	Santa Clara Gilroy	65	239
Wm	Tuolumne Twp 4	71	132
Wm A	Sacramento Ward 4	63	555
Wm C	Humbolt Union	59	179
Wm C	Los Angeles Elmonte	59	250
Wm D	Butte Kimshaw	56	569
Wm G	Alameda Oakland	55	20
Wm H	Alameda Murray	55	225
Wm H	San Francisco San Francisco 10	67	299

Name	County Locale	M653 Roll	Page
MARTIN			
Wm H	Santa Clara Gilroy	65	250
Wm L	Tuolumne Twp 1	71	480
Wm M	Placer Virginia	62	675
Wm P	Tuolumne Twp 1	71	260
Wm Pp	Tuolumne Twp 1	71	260
Wm*	Sacramento Granite	63	246
Wyman	Sacramento Granite	63	251
Wymund	Sacramento Granite	63	251
Ygnacio	Los Angeles Santa Ana	59	441
Ygnacio	Monterey San Juan	60	1001
Ygnacio*	Los Angeles Santa Ana	59	441
Ygnacio*	Monterey San Juan	60	1001
MARTINA			
---	Los Angeles Los Angeles	59	369
---	Monterey S Antoni	60	972
A	El Dorado Diamond	58	801
Davida	Calaveras Twp 7	57	34
Joseph	Calaveras Twp 7	57	43
Louis	Alameda Washington	55	170
P	Calaveras Twp 9	57	387
MARTINALE			
J*	El Dorado Placerville	58	875
MARTINALL			
John	San Mateo Twp 1	65	48
MARTINAS ROSA			
Hosea*	Calaveras Twp 9	57	353
MARTINAS			
Anthony	Calaveras Twp 6	57	161
Antonia	San Mateo Twp 3	65	77
C	El Dorado Placerville	58	825
Dolores M	Los Angeles Los Angeles	59	508
Doloris M	Los Angeles Los Angeles	59	508
Francisco	Marin Cortemad	60	792
Jose	Placer Forest H	62	791
Joseph	Calaveras Twp 10	57	283
Massimon*	San Mateo Twp 3	65	97
MARTINAZ			
Juan	Yuba Marysville	72	937
MARTINCLE			
J*	El Dorado Placerville	58	875
MARTINDALE			
N	Siskiyou Callahan	69	19
W W	Nevada Red Dog	61	543
MARTINDOUGH			
Lewis	Butte Bidwell	56	713
MARTINE			
---	Marin Novato	60	734
---	Marin Tomales	60	776
---*	Mariposa Twp 1	60	643
James*	Calaveras Twp 5	57	220
Jared S*	Calaveras Twp 5	57	187
Jesus	Sacramento Ward 1	63	105
John	Tuolumne Sonora	71	238
Maria D	Calaveras Twp 9	57	359
Stephans	Calaveras Twp 5	57	217
MARTINEAN			
Walter	San Francisco San Francisco 10	67	240
MARTINEANT			
Francis	San Francisco San Francisco 4	68	1150
MARTINEBY			
Jas C	Placer Ophirville	62	659
MARTINELL			
Bonaventura	Santa Cruz Pajaro	66	527
MARTINELLE			
Jefferson	San Francisco San Francisco 3	67	86
MARTINELLI			
Luis	Santa Cruz Pajaro	66	528
M	Stanislaus Emory	70	737
Stephen	Santa Cruz Pajaro	66	528
MARTINER			
Dominico*	Calaveras Twp 8	57	82
John	Santa Cruz Soguel	66	583
Simon	Mariposa Twp 3	60	573
MARTINES			
A	San Mateo Twp 3	65	98
Antonia	Amador Twp 5	55	339
Aukie*	San Mateo Twp 1	65	50
Cayetano	San Diego S Luis R	64	778
Coe*	Mariposa Twp 1	60	648
Concepcion	Los Angeles Azuza	59	272
Encamacior	Los Angeles Los Angeles	59	318
Eoe*	Mariposa Twp 1	60	648
Francisca	Monterey Monterey	60	945
Francisco	Los Angeles San Jose	59	288
Francisco	Marin Cortemad	60	785
Francisco D	Calaveras Twp 9	57	359
Grancisco	Marin Cortemad	60	792
Hosea	Alameda Brooklyn	55	199
Ignacio	Mariposa Twp 3	60	614
Jesus	Los Angeles Los Angeles	59	302
Jesus	Los Angeles Los Angeles	59	386
John	Santa Cruz Soguel	66	583
John D	Calaveras Twp 9	57	359
Jose	Los Angeles San Jose	59	281

Name	County Locale	M653 Roll	Page
MARTINES			
Jose	Tulara Twp 3	71	42
Jose M	Calaveras Twp 5	57	250
Joseph D	Calaveras Twp 9	57	359
Juan	Los Angeles San Jose	59	281
Juan	Los Angeles Los Angeles	59	314
Luis	Los Angeles Los Angeles	59	401
Marcinus*	Los Angeles San Jose	59	292
Maria D*	Calaveras Twp 9	57	359
Phillippe	Los Angeles San Jose	59	281
Santiago	Los Angeles San Jose	59	282
Santiago	Los Angeles San Pedro	59	482
Sarah	Los Angeles San Jose	59	285
Seraphini	Los Angeles San Jose	59	285
Siestro	Los Angeles San Jose	59	283
V	Merced Twp 1	60	900
MARTINESS			
Marcinies*	Los Angeles San Jose	59	292
MARTINET			
Jeffn	San Francisco San Francisco 10	67	287
Jeffr	San Francisco San Francisco 10	67	287
MARTINETEIN			
Peter	Tuolumne Twp 1	71	216
MARTINEY			
J	Tuolumne Twp 1	71	261
Thos*	Mariposa Twp 1	60	645
MARTINEZ			
---	Mariposa Twp 1	60	644
---	Mendocino Twp 1	60	889
A	Monterey Monterey	60	952
Agapite	Monterey Alisal	60	1041
Alberto	Monterey San Juan	60	1000
Alex	Contra Costa Twp 1	57	498
Andres	Santa Clara San Jose	65	365
Angel*	Monterey Alisal	60	1041
Antoine	Tuolumne Twp 3	71	456
Antonio	Los Angeles Los Angeles	59	335
Antonio	Santa Clara Fremont	65	442
Antonio	Tuolumne Jamestown	71	456
Anttria	San Bernardino Santa Barbara	64	196
Bantista*	Los Angeles Santa Ana	59	449
Bautista*	Los Angeles Santa Ana	59	449
Benancia	Los Angeles Santa Ana	59	454
Cecilia	Los Angeles Los Angeles	59	349
Chris	Sacramento Ward 1	63	81
Concepcion	Los Angeles Santa Ana	59	448
Concepein	Los Angeles San Jose	59	285
Dimicio	Los Angeles Los Angeles	59	346
Dionicio	Los Angeles Santa Ana	59	449
Dolores	Santa Cruz Pajaro	66	576
Emanuel	Los Angeles Elmonte	59	255
Eugenio	Monterey Monterey	60	949
Euginia	Santa Clara Almaden	65	274
Farncisca G	Los Angeles San Juan	59	460
Felipe	Los Angeles Los Angeles	59	403
Francisca	Los Angeles Los Angeles	59	296
Francisca	Merced Monterey	60	945
Francisca G	Los Angeles San Juan	59	460
Francisco	San Bernardino S Buenav	64	213
Francisco	Sonoma Healdsbu	69	475
Gerteres	Monterey Pajaro	60	1018
Gertrudes	Monterey Pajaro	60	1018
Gracio*	Monterey Alisal	60	1034
Guadalupe	Los Angeles Los Nieto	59	434
Hosea Paine	Mariposa Twp 3	60	545
Ignacio	San Luis Obispo San Luis Obispo	65	27
Ignacio*	Mariposa Twp 3	60	614
Izadora	Alameda Murray	55	227
J	Nevada Eureka	61	388
J	Tuolumne Twp 1	71	261
Jess	Los Angeles Los Nieto	59	430
Jesuf	Fresno Twp 1	59	76
Jesus	Los Angeles Los Nieto	59	430
Jesus	Los Angeles Santa Ana	59	448
Jesus	San Bernardino Santa Barbara	64	185
Jesus	Santa Clara Burnett	65	259
Jno	Butte Kimshaw	56	573
John	Tuolumne Twp 3	71	445
Jose	Mendocino Ukiah	60	795
Jose	Tuolumne Twp 2	71	375
Jose	Tuolumne Twp 2	71	410
Jose	Tuolumne Twp 3	71	443
Jose	Tuolumne Twp 3	71	445
Jose J	Contra Costa Twp 1	57	495
Jose Teodora	Contra Costa Twp 1	57	494
Joseph	Calaveras Twp 6	57	162
Josepha	Calaveras Twp 10	57	289
Juan	Monterey Monterey	60	941
Juan	Monterey Monterey	60	952
Juan	Napa Napa	61	116
Juan	Plumas Quincy	62	938
Juan	San Bernardino Santa Barbara	64	182

Name	County Locale	M653 Roll	Page
MARTINEZ			
Juan	San Bernardino S Buenav	64	213
Juan	Santa Clara San Jose	65	365
Juan Jose	Contra Costa Twp 1	57	490
Julian	Santa Clara Gilroy	65	228
Justo	Tuolumne Twp 1	71	227
Leandro	San Bernardino Santa Inez	64	143
Leonada	Alameda Brooklyn	55	208
Loretto*	San Francisco San Francisco 11		127
		67	
Manuel	Tuolumne Sonora	71	479
Marciline	Santa Clara San Jose	65	301
Maria	Los Angeles San Juan	59	463
Maria A	Monterey Alisal	601	034
Maria B	Los Angeles Santa Ana	59	452
Martina	Contra Costa Twp 1	57	498
Mnguel*	San Francisco San Francisco 2	67	688
Monica	Los Angeles Los Angeles	59	303
Mosea Painone	Twp 3	60	545
	Mariposa		
Nicholas	Los Angeles Los Nieto	59	428
Nicolas	Los Angeles Los Angeles	59	293
Nieves	Los Angeles Los Angeles	59	302
Norberto	Santa Clara Gilroy	65	234
P*	San Francisco San Francisco 9	681	101
Pablo	Contra Costa Twp 1	57	490
Padro	Tuolumne Sonora	71	228
Pedro	Monterey San Juan	60	991
Philip	Monterey Monterey	60	956
Pio	Santa Clara San Jose	65	302
Rafael	Los Angeles Los Nieto	59	431
Ramon	Tuolumne Twp 2	71	420
Romaro	Mariposa Twp 1	60	647
S	Tuolumne Twp 3	71	432
Serefino	San Diego Agua Caliente	64	820
Spastine	San Luis Obispo	65	19
	San Luis Obispo		
Susan	San Francisco San Francisco 11		128
		67	
T	Tuolumne Twp 2	71	408
Theo*	Mariposa Twp 1	60	645
Thos	Mariposa Twp 1	60	645
Tomas	Monterey San Juan	601	002
Trinedad	Monterey Pajaro	601	018
Ulojio	Monterey Alisal	601	030
Ulojro*	Monterey Alisal	601	030
Vic	Sacramento Ward 1	63	124
Vicente	Contra Costa Twp 1	57	497
Vicinte	Contra Costa Twp 1	57	498
Vicolas	Los Angeles Los Nieto	59	428
Victoria	Mariposa Twp 3	60	558
Victoria	San Joaquin Stockton	641	093
Voctoriano	Santa Clara Gilroy	65	227
Y Quaria	Sierra Downieville	661	031
MARTING			
Romaro	Mariposa Twp 1	60	647
MARTINI			
J F	Colusa Monroeville	57	445
James	Calaveras Twp 5	57	220
James	Calaveras Twp 8	57	81
James*	Calaveras Twp 5	57	220
John	Calaveras Twp 5	57	40
Joseph	Calaveras Twp 5	57	221
Joseph	Calaveras Twp 5	57	225
Lewis J	Colusa Monroeville	57	455
Santiago	Los Angeles Azuza	59	279
Stephane	Calaveras Twp 5	57	217
Stephen	Calaveras Twp 5	57	217
MARTINIO			
Eoe*	Mariposa Twp 1	60	648
MARTINIQUE			
Jose	Placer Forest H	62	772
MARTINIS			
Antoine	Calaveras Twp 5	57	248
MARTINIZ			
Dolores	Tuolumne Sonora	71	219
MARTINN			
Dominico*	Calaveras Twp 8	57	82
Mark	Calaveras Twp 6	57	130
MARTINO			
Asuza	Los Angeles Elmonte	59	260
Francisco	San Francisco San Francisco 11		111
		67	
Jesus	Sacramento Ward 1	63	105
Jos	Sacramento Ward 1	63	28
P	Calaveras Twp 9	57	387
MARTINON			
August	San Francisco San Francisco 10		249
		67	
Juan	San Francisco San Francisco 10		249
		67	
MARTINONE			
P*	Siskiyou Cottonwoood	69	103
MARTINOS			
Jose M	Calaveras Twp 5	57	250
Rosa	Calaveras Twp 5	57	248

Name	County Locale	M653 Roll	Page
MARTINOY			
Theo	Mariposa Twp 1	60	645
MARTINS			
---	Merced Twp 1	60	902
Angil	Monterey Alisal	601	041
C	Nevada Grass Valley	61	180
Ceo*	Mariposa Twp 1	60	648
Dnl M	Butte Oregon	56	625
Eoe*	Mariposa Twp 1	60	648
Eou*	Mariposa Twp 1	60	648
Felomina	Santa Clara Almaden	65	268
Fred	San Francisco San Francisco 2	67	623
Gandlanpi*	Los Angeles Los Angeles	59	490
Gaudloupe	Los Angeles Los Angeles	59	490
Gracio	Monterey Alisal	601	034
J	Butte Oregon	56	620
John	Calaveras Twp 5	57	226
John B	San Francisco San Francisco 2	67	719
John*	Mariposa Coulterville	60	694
Manuel	Yuba Parke Ba	72	785
Maria D*	Calaveras Twp 9	57	359
Pachisco	San Mateo Twp 1	65	51
T	San Mateo Twp 3	65	98
Tihurcio	San Bernardino S Timate	64	687
V	Merced Twp 1	60	900
MARTINSON			
Neles	Calaveras Twp 5	57	239
MARTINSTEIN			
Peter	Tuolumne Sonora	71	216
MARTINUS			
Ambrose*	Calaveras Twp 10	57	259
Rosa	Calaveras Twp 5	57	248
MARTINY			
J*	Nevada Eureka	61	388
MARTINZ			
Angel*	Monterey Alisal	601	041
Gracio*	Monterey Alisal	601	034
P	San Francisco San Francisco 9	681	101
MARTINZE			
Ambrose	Amador Twp 3	55	395
MARTIO			
Joseph	Calaveras Twp 7	57	35
MARTIONA			
Jose	Calaveras Twp 7	57	45
MARTIS			
Antonio*	Placer Auburn	62	583
Daniel*	Yuba Slate Ro	72	694
Jose	Merced Twp 2	60	916
MARTIST			
Joe	Mariposa Twp 3	60	600
MARTIUS			
---	San Bernardino San Bernadino	64	680
Gaudloupi*	Los Angeles Los Angeles	59	490
MARTLE			
Jael	Amador Twp 2	55	319
Tael	Amador Twp 2	55	319
MARTLYOFF			
A*	San Francisco San Francisco 2	67	670
MARTMAN			
Isaac	Los Angeles Los Angeles	59	351
Julius	Los Angeles Santa Ana	59	442
MARTN			
Jas M	Butte Cascade	56	704
MARTNELLE			
S*	Napa Napa	61	84
MARTON			
Denis	Amador Twp 5	55	342
Frank	Trinity Mouth Ca	701	017
Jack	Sonoma Sonoma	69	654
Jno	Mendocino Calpella	60	823
W H*	Yolo Putah	72	550
MARTONS			
Bg	El Dorado Diamond	58	801
MARTOREZ			
Ricardo	Alameda Brooklyn	55	208
MARTOSX			
Jose M	Los Angeles Los Angeles	59	310
MARTRITTA			
L	Amador Twp 3	55	376
MARTRO			
---	Monterey S Antoni	60	969
MARTS			
Jacob	San Joaquin Oneal	64	938
MARTSE			
William	Monterey Monterey	60	958
MARTSEN			
Christian	San Francisco San Francisco 11		156
		67	
MARTSIN			
Charley	Nevada Bridgeport	61	504
John	Alameda Brooklyn	55	146
MARTUELLE			
S	Napa Napa	61	84
MARTULO			
---	San Diego San Diego	64	775
MARTUMBAROS			
W	El Dorado Mud Springs	58	983

Name	County Locale	M653 Roll	Page
MARTUNS			
Coe*	Mariposa Twp 1	60	648
MARTURAN			
Isaac	Los Angeles Los Angeles	59	351
MARTURIS			
Eve	Mariposa Twp 1	60	648
MARTUROS			
R S	Monterey San Juan	60	994
MARTUS			
M	Calaveras Twp 9	57	406
MARTWELLE			
S*	Napa Napa	61	84
MARTY			
George*	Calaveras Twp 9	57	383
MARTYN			
John	Del Norte Crescent	58	620
MARTZ			
B W	Sacramento Ward 1	63	85
George	Calaveras Twp 9	57	383
MARTZER			
J B	Siskiyou Scott Va	69	37
Peter	Siskiyou Scott Va	69	37
MARUCAS			
Veveana	Yuba Marysville	72	922
MARUGALE			
B	Tuolumne Sonora	71	232
MARUGULES			
B	Tuolumne Twp 1	71	232
MARUIA			
R*	El Dorado Placerville	58	867
MARUL			
Hosea*	Alameda Brooklyn	55	151
MARURY			
Edward	Sierra Twp 7	66	904
MARVEL			
Peter	Sacramento Natonia	63	279
MARVEN			
John H	San Francisco San Francisco 7	681	339
MARVEY			
Jos	Sacramento Ward 1	63	108
Thomas J	Los Angeles Los Angeles	59	354
Walter M	Los Angeles Los Angeles	59	350
MARVIN			
C W	Santa Clara Redwood	65	444
David	San Mateo Twp 1	65	63
E S	Stanislaus Empire	70	731
Francis	Sacramento Ward 1	63	114
John H	San Francisco San Francisco 7	681	339
Joseph	San Joaquin Oneal	64	912
W W	Sacramento Ward 4	63	571
MARVIS			
Kasia M	Los Angeles San Jose	59	292
MARVONEY			
Thomas*	San Francisco San Francisco 7	681	418
MARVY			
Jas*	Los Angeles Tejon	59	539
MARWEDE			
C*	San Francisco San Francisco 6	67	417
MARWELL			
Jose	Tuolumne Columbia	71	306
MARX			
Chas J	Sacramento Ward 3	63	433
F F	Klamath Trinidad	59	222
H	San Francisco San Francisco 2	67	572
Henrietta	Solano Benecia	69	291
Isaac	San Francisco San Francisco 8	681	269
J M	El Dorado Casumnes	581	162
Jim	Klamath Trinidad	59	222
Mary T	Klamath Trinidad	59	222
Matter	San Francisco San Francisco 9	681	104
Nathl	Klamath Dillins	59	214
Sam	Humbolt Union	59	180
Sam	Sacramento Natonia	63	275
Samuel	San Francisco San Francisco 8	681	269
Simon	San Francisco San Francisco 8	681	268
MARXLEY			
James*	Siskiyou Scott Va	69	21
MARXON			
Benj*	Alameda Brooklyn	55	182
Jotham S*	Alameda Brooklyn	55	182
Saml J*	Alameda Brooklyn	55	182
MARY A			
Dallon	Sierra Downieville	66	972
MARY ANN			
---	Mendocino Calpella	60	827
---	Mendocino Big Rvr	60	855
MARY ANNA			
---	San Joaquin Stockton	641	099
MARY ELIZABETH			
Sister	Santa Clara San Jose	65	373
MARY J			
Mary J*	Sacramento Ward 1	63	152
MARY JANE			
---	Mendocino Calpella	60	828
Heinz	Sierra Downieville	66	972
Lieurcruce	Del Norte Crescent	58	645

MARY

Name	County Locale	Roll	Page
---	Amador Twp 2	55	315
---	Amador Twp 2	55	328
---	Amador Twp 5	55	331
---	Amador Twp 5	55	340
---	Amador Twp 5	55	347
---	Amador Twp 5	55	351
---	Amador Twp 5	55	356
---	Calaveras Twp 5	57	192
---	Mariposa Twp 3	60	550
---	Mariposa Twp 3	60	554
---	Mariposa Twp 3	60	576
---	Mariposa Twp 1	60	626
---	Mariposa Twp 1	60	631
---	Mendocino Calpella	60	820
---	Mendocino Calpella	60	824
---	Mendocino Calpella	60	826
---	Mendocino Calpella	60	827
---	Mendocino Big Rock	60	876
---	Mendocino Round Va	60	879
---	Mendocino Round Va	60	880
---	Mendocino Round Va	60	882
---	Mendocino Round Va	60	883
---	Mendocino Round Va	60	884
---	Mendocino Twp 1	60	888
---	Mendocino Twp 1	60	889
---	Mendocino Twp 1	60	890
---	Mendocino Twp 1	60	891
---	Mendocino Twp 1	60	892
---	Sacramento Cosumnes	63	407
---	San Bernardino S Timate	64	690
---	San Francisco San Francisco 10	67	277
---	San Mateo Twp 2	65	112
---	San Mateo Twp 1	65	65
---	Trinity E Weaver	70	1059
---	Tulara Twp 1	71	113
---	Tulara Twp 1	71	115
---	Tulara Twp 1	71	116
---*	Mariposa Twp 3	60	576
August	Tulara Visalia	71	106
Chea	Mariposa Coulterville	60	682
Hamilton	Sacramento Ward 1	63	45
He	Mariposa Twp 3	60	544
James	Yolo Washington	72	570
John	Calaveras Twp 7	57	38
John	Yuba Linda	72	983
John B	Calaveras Twp 7	57	4
Joseph	Calaveras Twp 7	57	45
Josh	El Dorado Georgetown	58	691
Kee	Mariposa Twp 3	60	544
Linus	Sierra Whiskey	66	847
R	San Francisco San Francisco 5	67	525
Saml	San Francisco San Francisco 1	68	927
Simon	San Francisco San Francisco 8	68	1268
Sims	Sierra Whiskey	66	847
Thomas*	Shasta Shasta	66	687
W	San Francisco San Francisco 5	67	534

MARYANIN

Victorae*	Tuolumne Big Oak	71	137

MARYANIR

Victorac*	Tuolumne Big Oak	71	137

MARYANN

---	Mendocino Twp 1	60	890

MARYE

W*	Siskiyou Scott Ri	69	76

MARYEEIA

Ceoza*	Calaveras Twp 5	57	199

MARYEON

V	San Francisco San Francisco 5	67	527

MARYEOU

V*	San Francisco San Francisco 5	67	527

MARYETTA

---	Mendocino Round Va	60	886

MARYFIELD

Amos	Marin Point Re	60	730

MARYHAM

J	Nevada Eureka	61	372

MARYHANE

J*	Nevada Eureka	61	372

MARYHAVE

J*	Nevada Eureka	61	372

MARYHEN

Levi*	Tulara Visalia	71	97

MARYLAND

J*	Nevada Eureka	61	372

MARYMAN

---	Tulara Visalia	71	119

MARYNAND

Wm	Sacramento Ward 1	63	21

MARYNAUD

Wm*	Sacramento Ward 1	63	21

MARYNIA

Ceozer*	Calaveras Twp 5	57	199

MARYO

A*	San Francisco San Francisco 5	67	539

MARYOR

Miguel	San Luis Obispo San Luis Obispo	65	12

MARYOW

A	San Francisco San Francisco 6	67	454

MARYUIA

Ceoza	Calaveras Twp 5	57	199

MARZ

Frank	Tuolumne Columbia	71	333

MARZE

W*	Siskiyou Scott Ri	69	76

MARZEARIX

Rachel	Sacramento Ward 4	63	579

MARZEN

Jos	Sacramento Ward 1	63	21

MARZIGER

Henry	Santa Cruz Pajaro	66	532

MARZIN

Antonia	Sacramento Ward 1	63	11
Antonso	Sacramento Ward 1	63	11

MARZION

John	El Dorado Kelsey	58	1129

MARZO

A	San Francisco San Francisco 5	67	539

MARZON

A	San Francisco San Francisco 6	67	454
John*	Shasta Shasta	66	677

MAS

Amedia*	Plumas Meadow Valley	62	928
J M B*	Nevada Bridgeport	61	473

MASA

Antonie	Alameda Murray	55	218
Armanda	San Francisco San Francisco 2	67	655
Florenteena	San Mateo Twp 2	65	127
Francisco	Los Angeles San Jose	59	284
Francisco	Mariposa Twp 1	60	624
Fransisco	Mariposa Twp 1	60	624
George*	Placer Iona Hills	62	873
Jacob	Calaveras Twp 9	57	361
Jefferson	Monterey Alisal	60	1033
Juan	Alameda Brooklyn	55	199
Luciana	San Mateo Twp 2	65	127
Mary	San Mateo Twp 2	65	127
Mate*	Tehama Red Bluff	70	930
Neives	Los Angeles San Gabriel	59	417
Nieves	Los Angeles San Gabriel	59	417
Romer	Sonoma Petaluma	69	559

MASAER

Pedro	Mariposa Twp 1	60	660

MASAMO

Lopez*	Mariposa Twp 1	60	627

MASAN

Csiaceme*	Mariposa Twp 3	60	594

MASAR

Oliver P	Alameda Brooklyn	55	87

MASARIO

---	Tulara Twp 3	71	72

MASCALINE

Riley	San Francisco San Francisco 2	67	714

MASCAR

John	San Francisco San Francisco 1	68	836

MASCAREL

Jose	Los Angeles Los Angeles	59	298

MASCARINA

Francisca	San Francisco San Francisco 2	67	758

MASCE

C	San Francisco San Francisco 9	68	1058

MASCEY

Lewis	Sierra Twp 7	66	868

MASCH

Johnothan B*	Napa Yount	61	40

MASCHARDO

Cosens*	Calaveras Twp 6	57	151

MASCHE

Wm	San Francisco San Francisco 9	68	1063

MASCHO

A	Merced Twp 1	60	902

MASCIMELIAN

M	Tuolumne Shawsfla	71	407

MASCIMILIAN

M	Tuolumne Twp 2	71	407

MASCON

Frank	Tuolumne Twp 1	71	253
Marykita	Tuolumne Twp 2	71	320

MASCOSO

Marykita*	Tuolumne Columbia	71	320

MASCWEL

Wm	Tuolumne Twp 1	71	266

MASCWELL

H W*	Tuolumne Columbia	71	289

MASDEN

Geo	San Francisco San Francisco 10	67	169
John	Placer Damascus	62	846
L	Santa Clara Redwood	65	444

MASE

James	Siskiyou Scott Va	69	29

MASE

Josiah*	Yuba Marysville	72	972
Robt*	Shasta Shasta	66	677
Thomas*	Santa Cruz Santa Cruz	66	640
Trinidad	Contra Costa Twp 2	57	577

MASEER

---*	Mendocino Round Va	60	885

MASEL

J G	Nevada Grass Valley	61	224
Tront*	Nevada Grass Valley	61	224

MASEMBRIANO

Jose	Marin Cortemad	60	783

MASEMO

---	San Diego Temecula	64	795

MASEN

Ferdinand*	Tuolumne Twp 6	71	540
Harris	Amador Twp 2	55	281
J D	Amador Twp 2	55	298
Loyal M	Sacramento Natonia	63	274
Victor	Amador Twp 2	55	297
Wm	Colusa Muion	57	461
Wm	Colusa Muion	57	462

MASENBURG

Henry	San Francisco San Francisco 9	68	960

MASENER

Felip Taco	Mariposa Twp 1	60	625

MASENO

Hasa*	Siskiyou Yreka	69	172

MASEPULVIDA

Juan*	Los Angeles Los Angeles	59	508

MASER

George*	Placer Iona Hills	62	873
Manuel	Tuolumne Sonora	71	235
Manwil*	Tuolumne Twp 1	71	235
Thomas	Plumas Meadow Valley	62	908

MASERLOA

Anneo	Placer Rattle Snake	62	630

MASES

Adalaid W*	Siskiyou Yreka	69	167
Gus	Calaveras Twp 8	57	77

MASESEHN

Antoni	El Dorado Georgetown	58	703

MASETILLI

N	El Dorado Georgetown	58	702

MASEWELL

H W*	Tuolumne Columbia	71	289

MASEWILL

H W	Tuolumne Twp 2	71	289

MASEY

Elizabeth	Sacramento Franklin	63	331
Geo	El Dorado Salmon Falls	58	1041
Henry C	San Francisco San Francisco 2	67	617
J B*	El Dorado Union	58	1094
Olevia*	El Dorado Union	58	1094

MASGORA

Daniel*	Calaveras Twp 8	57	80
Danil*	Calaveras Twp 8	57	80

MASGRAVE

Samuel	Siskiyou Yreka	69	125

MASGROVE

J D*	Shasta Shasta	66	681

MASH

Daniel	El Dorado White Oaks	58	1019
Jas	Placer Ophirville	62	656

MASHA

---	Mendocino Calpella	60	822

MASHAMSLE

---*	Mendocino Big Rvr	60	854

MASHAN

Jeremiah	Santa Cruz Santa Cruz	66	601

MASHARD

Manuel	Shasta Shasta	66	683

MASHELLY

Fredrick*	Sierra Poker Flats	66	839

MASHER

N	El Dorado Placerville	58	863
S C	Santa Clara Gilroy	65	226

MASHON

Herman	Butte Mountain	56	741

MASHVUCHA

---	Mendocino Twp 1	60	888

MASI

Robot	Shasta Shasta	66	677

MASIE

John	Siskiyou Callahan	69	3

MASIER

W M	Tuolumne Twp 1	71	247

MASIM

Louis	Tuolumne Twp 1	71	255

MASINEY

Charles	Yolo Cache	72	590

MASINIA

Salomon	Calaveras Twp 6	57	139

MASIS

Gus*	Calaveras Twp 8	57	77

MASK

Jas*	Sacramento Brighton	63	196

California 1860 Census Index

Name	County Locale	M653 RollPage
MASK		
Lee	Butte Bidwell	56 710
MASKARD		
Manuel	Shasta Shasta	66 683
MASKAWA		
---	Fresno Twp 3	59 39
MASKELINE		
Wm	Tehama Red Bluff	70 929
MASKELL		
A W	Santa Clara Santa Clara	65 510
R H	Sacramento Lee	63 213
MASKER		
Phillip	Calaveras Twp 6	57 146
MASKERNELL		
Seth*	San Francisco San Francisco 1	68 907
MASKERWELL		
Seth	San Francisco San Francisco 1	68 907
MASKEY		
Jacob	Butte Ophir	56 755
MASKIL		
Ellen	El Dorado Coloma	581073
MASKLAY		
David	Tuolumne Twp 2	71 395
MASKLEY		
G N	Tuolumne Twp 2	71 382
MASKS		
Robert L*	Siskiyou Shasta Rvr	69 111
MASKUS		
Roman*	Siskiyou Yreka	69 140
MASKWOOD		
William*	Napa Yount	61 47
MASLALA		
---	Mendocino Calpella	60 823
MASLAN		
Richard	Siskiyou Scott Va	69 32
MASLATA		
---	Mendocino Calpella	60 823
MASLEN		
Madison	San Joaquin Oneal	64 929
Wm*	Sacramento Granite	63 223
MASLER		
Joseph	Calaveras Twp 8	57 56
MASLETTE		
Peter*	Sacramento Franklin	63 316
MASLIN		
E H	Nevada Nevada	61 239
E W	Nevada Nevada	61 239
Thos	Merced Twp 1	60 903
MASLON		
E C*	Sonoma Petaluma	69 589
Tims*	Sacramento Mississipi	63 185
MASMER		
Louis	Los Angeles Los Angeles	59 358
MASN		
William	San Francisco San Francisco 7	681428
MASNE		
J L	Mariposa Twp 1	60 630
MASNODAS		
Jesus	Calaveras Twp 4	57 331
MASO NAN		
---	Mendocino Calpella	60 825
MASOCOLA		
Anrelino*	Calaveras Twp 4	57 333
MASON		
A	Sacramento Granite	63 236
A	Sacramento Ward 3	63 428
A	Tuolumne Twp 4	71 145
A J	Nevada Rough &	61 401
A S	Nevada Washington	61 336
A S	Sierra Pine Grove	66 832
A T	Butte Cascade	56 693
Alva	Nevada Bloomfield	61 529
Andrew	Sacramento Ward 1	63 63
Andrew J	Yuba Marysville	72 846
Ann	Santa Clara Fremont	65 437
Asa	Mariposa Twp 3	60 603
Augusta	San Francisco San Francisco 11	109 67
Augusto*	San Francisco San Francisco 11	109 67
B D	El Dorado White Oaks	581020
B D	El Dorado Cold Spring	581100
B H	Calaveras Twp 9	57 380
Benanardo	Butte Oregon	56 628
Beng*	Siskiyou Scott Va	69 40
Benimardo*	Butte Oregon	56 628
Benimasdo*	Butte Oregon	56 628
Benj	Siskiyou Scott Va	69 40
C H	Sonoma Petaluma	69 601
Charles	Tuolumne Columbia	71 291
Chas G	Monterey Monterey	60 963
Chas M	Sacramento Ward 4	63 527
Chester	Placer Michigan	62 822
Chs G	Monterey Monterey	60 963
D B	Siskiyou Scott Ri	69 81
David N	Yuba Marysville	72 893

Name	County Locale	M653 RollPage
MASON		
David W	Yuba Marysville	72 893
Dillin V*	Placer Ophirville	62 659
E G	Siskiyou Scott Ri	69 67
E H	Yolo Cache Crk	72 663
E Y	Siskiyou Scott Ri	69 67
Edgar	Del Norte Crescent	58 619
Edward	Tulara Keeneysburg	71 46
Edward	Tulara Keeneysburg	71 49
Edward F	Calaveras Twp 5	57 248
Elizabeth	Sacramento Ward 1	63 19
Ethan	Contra Costa Twp 1	57 534
F S	Shasta Millvill	66 749
Fernando	Los Angeles Los Angeles	59 387
Frederick	Tulara Twp 3	71 41
G A	Butte Hamilton	56 523
G L	Nevada Grass Valley	61 176
G P	Sacramento Ward 1	63 32
Geo	Butte Ophir	56 778
Geo	San Francisco San Francisco 1	68 896
Geo D	Napa Napa	61 104
Georg	Alameda Oakland	55 73
George	Plumas Quincy	62 981
George	Solano Benecia	69 283
George W	Yuba Marysville	72 905
George*	El Dorado Georgetown	58 702
Gerald	Alameda Oakland	55 42
Gilbert	Sierra St Louis	66 817
Grace	Placer Dutch Fl	62 716
H	Sierra St Louis	66 818
H E	Butte Oregon	56 626
H G	Stanislaus Branch	70 712
H S	Shasta Millvill	66 749
Harriet	Los Angeles Los Angeles	59 364
Hendrick	Placer Iona Hills	62 872
Henry	El Dorado Eldorado	58 945
Henry	Klamath Dillins	59 214
Henry	Sierra La Porte	66 784
Henry H	Sierra La Porte	66 784
Ira	Placer Forest H	62 772
Isaac F	Sierra Gibsonville	66 851
Ivory F	Mendocino Calpella	60 816
J	Nevada Nevada	61 280
J	Tehama Tehama	70 949
J A	Sacramento Ward 1	63 19
J D	Calaveras Twp 9	57 382
J H	Sacramento Ward 3	63 462
J P	Sacramento Ward 1	63 32
J R	San Francisco San Francisco 5	67 490
J W	Butte Oro	56 682
Jack	San Francisco San Francisco 11	126 67
Jacob	El Dorado Placerville	58 878
James	Mariposa Twp 3	60 612
James	San Diego San Diego	64 761
James	Sierra La Porte	66 788
James	Sierra La Porte	66 789
James	Solano Benecia	69 317
James	Tuolumne Twp 2	71 295
James L	Yuba Marysville	72 894
James W	Alameda Brooklyn	55 87
James*	Placer Michigan	62 824
Jas	Napa Napa	61 105
Jerem	Sonoma Armally	69 482
Jerome	Sonoma Armally	69 482
Jhn	El Dorado Georgetown	58 674
Jn	El Dorado Big Bar	58 744
Jno J	Klamath S Fork	59 199
Jno L	Nevada Nevada	61 285
Joanah	Solano Fairfield	69 201
Job*	Sacramento Alabama	63 417
John	Alameda Brooklyn	55 140
John	Butte Ophir	56 778
John	El Dorado Georgetown	58 674
John	Napa Napa	61 65
John	Placer Todds Va	62 784
John	San Francisco San Francisco 2	67 723
John	Tehama Pasakent	70 856
John	Tehama Red Bluff	70 899
John C	Trinity E Weaver	701059
John F	Santa Clara Redwood	65 451
John I	Plumas Meadow Valley	62 931
John L	Humbolt Eureka	59 175
John R	Yuba Marysville	72 951
Jos	Amador Twp 1	55 474
Jos	Sacramento Ward 1	63 19
Joseph	Contra Costa Twp 1	57 524
Joseph	El Dorado Placerville	58 917
Joseph	Tuolumne Twp 3	71 464
Joseph R*	Alameda Brooklyn	55 121
Juan*	Alameda Oakland	55 55
L	Nevada Grass Valley	61 177
L	Nevada Grass Valley	61 187
L S*	Placer Michigan	62 809
Llyman	Tuolumne Twp 3	71 450
Louis	Contra Costa Twp 2	57 556

Name	County Locale	M653 RollPage
MASON		
Louisa	San Francisco San Francisco 2	67 681
Loyal M	Sacramento Natonia	63 274
Lyman	Tuolumne Jamestown	71 450
Mary	Santa Clara San Jose	65 392
Mathew	Yuba Bear Rvr	72 996
Men	Tehama Lassen	70 867
N B	Nevada Nevada	61 285
Oliver P	Alameda Brooklyn	55 87
Otes*	Siskiyou Shasta Rvr	69 114
Otis*	Siskiyou Shasta Rvr	69 114
P	Siskiyou Cottonwoood	69 97
Patricia S	Colusa Monroeville	57 455
Patrick	Sierra Port Win	66 792
Paynes*	Mariposa Twp 3	60 612
Petrick	Sierra Port Win	66 792
R	Nevada Grass Valley	61 177
R T	Butte Oregon	56 614
Richard	Placer Forest H	62 802
Richard	Yolo Washington	72 602
Robert T	Los Angeles Los Angeles	59 359
Robt T	San Bernardino San Bernadino	64 668
Rufus	El Dorado Big Bar	58 742
S L	Placer Michigan	62 809
S*	Nevada Grass Valley	61 177
Saml	Stanislaus Emory	70 750
Samuel D	Sierra St Louis	66 817
Sylvester	San Luis Obispo	65 9
T W	El Dorado Greenwood	58 721
Thad W	Sacramento Ward 4	63 554
Theodore	Plumas Meadow Valley	62 928
Tho	Siskiyou Scott Va	69 52
Thomas	Placer Todds Va	62 784
Thomas	San Francisco San Francisco 2	67 697
Thomas	Yuba Marysville	72 867
Thos	Butte Oregon	56 610
Thos	San Mateo Twp 3	65 77
Thos J	Butte Kimshaw	56 594
W B	Nevada Nevada	61 285
Wallace	Nevada Bloomfield	61 509
Wallice	Nevada Bloomfield	61 509
William	El Dorado Kelsey	581140
William	Santa Cruz Santa Cruz	66 620
William	Sierra La Porte	66 788
Wm	Sonoma Vallejo	69 628
Wm	Trinity Mouth Ca	701013
Wm	Yolo Slate Ra	72 693
Wm	Yuba Slate Ro	72 693
Wm B	Del Norte Crescent	58 619
Wm C	Sonoma Russian	69 443
Wm D	Plumas Quincy	62 918
MASONG		
Luding	San Francisco San Francisco 1	68 930
MASONHOLDA		
F	El Dorado Diamond	58 814
MASONIA		
Maguina	San Luis Obispo	65 34
MASONS		
Katharaine	San Mateo Twp 2	65 120
MASOR		
Manwil*	Tuolumne Twp 1	71 235
MASOS		
Manwil*	Tuolumne Twp 1	71 235
MASOW		
Edward	Mendocino Calpella	60 816
Ivory F	Mendocino Calpella	60 816
MASQUET		
Eugene	Yuba Marysville	72 897
MASQUIEN		
Vincent	Tuolumne Twp 4	71 142
MASQUIER		
Vincent*	Tuolumne Big Oak	71 142
MASS		
C	San Francisco San Francisco 5	67 542
Edward	Sierra Twp 7	66 891
Henry	San Francisco San Francisco 1	68 856
J T	Colusa Colusi	57 424
Placedo	Alameda Brooklyn	55 196
R	San Francisco San Francisco 5	67 517
Wm T	Colusa Colusi	57 424
MASSA		
A	El Dorado Diamond	58 802
Antonia	Amador Twp 5	55 361
Nicholas	Amador Twp 3	55 399
MASSABE		
Joseph	Plumas Meadow Valley	62 899
MASSACAN		
Dominique	San Francisco 2	67 679
MASSAI		
Antonio	San Bernardino Santa Barbara	64 151
MASSAMO		
Thomas	Napa Napa	61 79
MASSAR		
John	Stanislaus Branch	70 699

California 1860 Census Index

Name	County Locale	M653 Roll Page
MASSE		
Hohn	Sierra Downieville	66 968
Joseph	Amador Twp 5	55 361
MASSEELY		
Fredrick*	Sierra Poker Flats	66 839
MASSEL		
August*	Trinity North Fo	701026
Benoish	Amador Twp 1	55 482
MASSEOTHO		
Frank*	San Francisco San Francisco 1	68 904
MASSEOTTE		
Frank*	San Francisco San Francisco 1	68 904
MASSEOTTO		
Frank*	San Francisco San Francisco 1	68 904
MASSERS		
J D	El Dorado Diamond	58 805
MASSES		
L*	Sacramento Granite	63 242
S*	Sacramento Granite	63 242
MASSETT		
Jos	San Francisco San Francisco 9	681045
M*	Butte Bidwell	56 707
MASSEY		
Atkins	San Francisco San Francisco 8	681268
B F	El Dorado White Oaks	581003
Francis	Sonoma Santa Rosa	69 391
H P	Butte Bidwell	56 716
J D M	El Dorado Grizzly	581179
J G	Tuolumne Twp 1	71 243
J N	Siskiyou Cottonwoood	69 99
J T	Calaveras Twp 9	57 394
Jhn	El Dorado Georgetown	58 703
John	El Dorado Georgetown	58 703
Louis	Nevada Bridgeport	61 497
Martin	San Francisco San Francisco 2	67 718
Peter	San Mateo Twp 1	65 48
Saml	Tuolumne Twp 2	71 284
Samuel	San Joaquin Stockton	641052
MASSIE		
Annie	San Francisco San Francisco 10	185
		67
M*	Nevada Grass Valley	61 169
Thomas D	El Dorado Georgetown	58 699
MASSILLER		
---	Mendocino Round Va	60 886
MASSIMA		
Adelaida	San Francisco San Francisco 7	681425
MASSIMON		
---	San Mateo Twp 3	65 77
MASSING		
Antony*	Sierra St Louis	66 817
MASSINGILL		
Philena	Sonoma Russian	69 430
MASSO		
John*	Sierra Downieville	66 968
MASSOL		
F A*	Sacramento Ward 4	63 577
MASSON		
Amelia	Tuolumne Twp 1	71 200
G S	Tuolumne Twp 2	71 284
G S	Tuolumne Twp 2	71 284
James*	Sonoma Armally	69 508
John	San Bernardino San Salvador	64 649
Jose C	San Diego S Luis R	64 777
L	Shasta Millvill	66 751
Louis	Tuolumne Columbia	71 348
T	Calaveras Twp 9	57 395
MASSONA		
Loveyis	Calaveras Twp 5	57 217
Lovigis	Calaveras Twp 5	57 217
MASSOPURT		
Anton*	Solano Benecia	69 316
MASSRIN		
John	Napa Yount	61 43
MASSTEN		
John	Mariposa Twp 3	60 600
MASSTON		
A*	Nevada Grass Valley	61 176
E W*	Tuolumne Twp 2	71 345
MASSTRALL		
T S	San Francisco San Francisco 3	67 84
MASSUM		
Jacob	El Dorado Eldorado	58 943
MASSUS		
Itile*	San Francisco San Francisco 5	67 516
MASSY		
Peter	San Mateo Twp 1	65 48
R L	Sacramento Ward 1	63 115
W J	El Dorado Kelsey	581148
William	Nevada Rough &	61 402
MAST		
Alexander	Humbolt Eel Rvr	59 150
Frank	Sonoma Sonoma	69 656
Herman	San Francisco San Francisco 10	341
		67
Lirsy*	Mariposa Coulterville	60 703

Name	County Locale	M653 Roll Page
MAST		
Lusy*	Mariposa Coulterville	60 703
MASTARREY		
Pedro	San Luis Obispo San Luis Obispo	65 42
MASTEELLY		
Fredrick*	Sierra Poker Flats	66 839
MASTEELY		
Fredrick*	Sierra Poker Flats	66 839
MASTEL		
Peter	El Dorado White Oaks	581031
MASTEN		
G W	Yolo Cache Crk	72 626
Gabe	Tehama Lassen	70 869
M C	San Francisco San Francisco 5	67 526
N K	San Francisco San Francisco 10	243
		67
Wm*	Sacramento Granite	63 223
MASTER		
---	Mendocino Round Va	60 884
Camile	San Francisco San Francisco 3	67 17
Henry	Sacramento Dry Crk	63 368
Richard	San Francisco San Francisco 7	681329
Sara	San Francisco San Francisco 1	68 877
Wm	Sacramento Ward 3	63 457
MASTERER		
Simon	Mariposa Twp 3	60 573
MASTERMAN		
E	Calaveras Twp 9	57 395
MASTERS		
Augustus*	Placer Michigan	62 845
B L*	Sacramento Brighton	63 193
B S*	Sacramento Brighton	63 193
Carl	El Dorado Georgetown	58 746
D	El Dorado Newtown	58 778
D	El Dorado Diamond	58 804
David	San Diego Agua Caliente	64 855
E	Sutter Sutter	70 807
Frank	Placer Michigan	62 839
Geo	Sacramento Granite	63 253
Herman	Fresno Twp 3	59 9
Jno B	Sacramento Mississipi	63 187
John D	Tulara Twp 2	71 33
M	Sutter Nicolaus	70 839
R M	San Francisco San Francisco 5	67 533
Thomas	San Francisco San Francisco 9	681101
W	Nevada Grass Valley	61 158
MASTERSON		
Charles	Calaveras Twp 6	57 139
E	Sacramento Alabama	63 411
Elizabeth	San Francisco San Francisco 10	187
		67
Frances	Nevada Bridgeport	61 468
H	Amador Twp 1	55 471
Hugh	San Joaquin Elliott	64 942
J	Siskiyou Scott Ri	69 75
Jas	Tehama Lassen	70 870
Peter	San Francisco San Francisco 11	134
		67
T	Amador Twp 1	55 454
Thos	Siskiyou Callahan	69 2
Trances*	Nevada Bridgeport	61 468
William	San Francisco San Francisco 7	681337
MASTERTON		
Jno	San Francisco San Francisco 10	254
		67
Patrick*	Calaveras Twp 6	57 182
Stephen	Calaveras Twp 5	57 217
MASTERTRON		
Stephen	Calaveras Twp 5	57 217
MASTESTON		
Patrick*	Calaveras Twp 5	57 182
MASTHERSON		
E	El Dorado Coloma	581118
MASTIC		
E B*	San Francisco San Francisco 1	68 875
S*	Calaveras Twp 9	57 400
MASTICK		
D	Tuolumne Twp 2	71 310
F M	Tuolumne Twp 1	71 258
MASTIE		
Levi	San Francisco San Francisco 1	68 863
S	Calaveras Twp 9	57 400
MASTIN		
David	Los Angeles Elmonte	59 267
N	El Dorado Georgetown	58 679
Reuben	Plumas Quincy	62 917
S G	Sacramento Ward 4	63 548
Wm	San Francisco San Francisco 2	67 750
MASTINA		
John*	Mariposa Coulterville	60 694
MASTINER		
Victoria	Mariposa Twp 3	60 558
MASTIR		
S*	Calaveras Twp 9	57 400
MASTOFF		
A	San Mateo Twp 1	65 47

Name	County Locale	M653 Roll Page
MASTON		
A C	Santa Clara Santa Clara	65 485
D H	Santa Clara Santa Clara	65 515
David	Humbolt Union	59 179
E N	Tuolumne Twp 2	71 331
E W	Tuolumne Columbia	71 331
H	El Dorado Placerville	58 866
Levi	San Francisco San Francisco 9	68 961
Levi H	San Francisco San Francisco 9	68 961
Tims*	Sacramento Mississipi	63 185
MASTONDIA		
Louis	Sacramento Ward 1	63 38
MASTRAL		
Levy	San Francisco San Francisco 3	67 39
MASTRETTI		
John	Calaveras Twp 7	57 29
MASTRO		
John	Calaveras Twp 7	57 20
Petro	Calaveras Twp 7	57 20
MASTRUDIA		
Louis	Sacramento Ward 1	63 38
MASTULLY		
Fredrick*	Sierra Poker Flats	66 839
MASTUS		
John	Contra Costa Twp 2	57 541
MASUGO		
Jase*	Los Angeles Los Angeles	59 494
MASULE		
Pauline	Monterey San Juan	60 977
MASUNAN		
---	Mendocino Calpella	60 825
MASUR		
---*	Mendocino Round Va	60 885
MASUTHERLAND		
Anna*	San Francisco San Francisco 1	68 874
MASYNIA		
Ceozer*	Calaveras Twp 5	57 199
MAT		
---	Amador Twp 5	55 343
---	Calaveras Twp 8	57 75
---	Fresno Twp 2	59 41
---	Placer Rattle Snake	62 633
Wendell	Placer Rattle Snake	62 632
MATA		
---	Del Norte Klamath	58 658
Feliciana	San Francisco San Francisco 2	67 702
Jorge	Los Angeles Santa Ana	59 451
Juan D	Los Angeles Azuza	59 273
MATALISTA		
Joseph	San Francisco San Francisco 2	67 720
MATALOT		
---	Fresno Twp 3	59 99
MATALZA		
Augustus	El Dorado Kelsey	581135
MATAMOROS		
Santa Ana	Los Angeles Los Angeles	59 317
MATARY		
J	Sacramento Franklin	63 308
MATASH		
---	Mendocino Calpella	60 822
MATATESLA		
Joseph*	San Francisco San Francisco 2	67 720
MATATESTA		
Joseph*	San Francisco San Francisco 2	67 720
MATBRADY		
Athony	Marin San Rafael	60 763
MATBUDY		
Athony*	Marin San Rafael	60 763
MATCHENS		
Caston*	San Francisco San Francisco 4	681218
MATCHET		
B	Sutter Nicolaus	70 831
MATCHIE		
Jas	Placer Virginia	62 685
MATCHINS		
Caston	San Francisco San Francisco 4	681218
MATCHINTALON		
---	Sacramento Ward 1	63 125
MATCHINTATON		
J*	Sacramento Ward 1	63 125
MATE		
Geo	El Dorado Salmon Falls	581047
R S	Tehama Antelope	70 894
MATEA		
Jorge*	Los Angeles Santa Ana	59 451
MATEAS		
---	Monterey San Juan	60 994
MATEER		
Henry	Alameda Brooklyn	55 202
MATEN		
J M	Solano Vacaville	69 330
Phillip	Siskiyou Yreka	69 148
Phillip C	Siskiyou Yreka	69 148
MATENUS		
Dolorus	Mariposa Twp 1	60 630
MATEO		
---	San Diego Agua Caliente	64 829

California 1860 Census Index

Name	County Locale	M653 RollPage
MATEO		
---	San Diego Agua Caliente	64 836
James	Tuolumne Sonora	71 242
Jorge*	Los Angeles Santa Ana	59 451
MATEOALVISO		
Jose A	Santa Clara Alviso	65 415
MATER		
E W*	Butte Oregon	56 638
James	Tulara Twp 3	71 43
Quanda	San Bernardino San Bernadino	64 682
MATERAS		
Phalas	Los Angeles Elmonte	59 262
MATERE		
B	Siskiyou Klamath	69 93
MATERIA		
---	San Bernardino S Timate	64 692
MATES		
August	Calaveras Twp 4	57 334
MATESIA		
---	Monterey Monterey	60 957
MATEZUSIKI		
Adam	Tulara Twp 3	71 43
MATFIELD		
Henry	San Francisco San Francisco 10	342 67
MATHAM		
Chas	San Francisco San Francisco 1	68 854
MATHAWAY		
Jacob	Los Angeles Los Angeles	59 365
MATHEAS		
L	San Francisco San Francisco 2	67 722
MATHEE		
W W*	Nevada Eureka	61 347
MATHEN		
James	Placer Michigan	62 816
MATHENEG		
Edlez	Yolo Washington	72 569
MATHENEY		
Edley	Yolo Washington	72 569
W D	El Dorado Placerville	58 852
MATHENS		
John	Yolo Cache Crk	72 616
Theodore	Shasta Horsetown	66 705
Thos*	San Francisco San Francisco 1	68 923
W H C	Nevada Bridgeport	61 501
MATHENSON		
Chas	San Francisco San Francisco 9	681072
MATHEO		
Jonas*	Nevada Eureka	61 392
W W*	Nevada Eureka	61 347
MATHER		
Archibal	El Dorado Greenwood	58 719
C	Nevada Grass Valley	61 186
C	Nevada Nevada	61 258
John	El Dorado Greenwood	58 719
Jonas	Nevada Eureka	61 392
Phillip	Calaveras Twp 6	57 146
Raymond	Plumas Quincy	62 942
Robert	San Francisco San Francisco 10	177 67
Solon H	Plumas Quincy	62 919
W W	Nevada Eureka	61 347
MATHERLY		
H H	El Dorado Coloma	581108
MATHERNIGTON		
J	El Dorado Mud Springs	58 997
MATHERONEI		
Berreon	Sierra Downieville	661001
MATHEROSON		
Samuel W	Alameda Brooklyn	55 198
MATHERS		
Cleveland	San Luis Obispo San Luis Obispo	65 3
Edward	San Luis Obispo San Luis Obispo	65 3
MATHERSON		
Alexr	Sonoma Vallejo	69 628
John*	San Francisco San Francisco 1	68 870
Neil	Mendocino Ukiah	60 804
MATHESER		
Asa*	Mariposa Twp 3	60 565
MATHESON		
Asa	Mariposa Twp 3	60 565
H	Sonoma Salt Point	69 693
John	San Francisco San Francisco 1	68 853
Maria A	Sonoma Mendocino	69 466
Rodrk	Sonoma Mendocino	69 466
Thos	Sonoma Mendocino	69 466
MATHESOSIN		
A W	Santa Clara San Jose	65 347
MATHEUS		
John	Mariposa Twp 1	60 665
Peter*	Alameda Oakland	55 44
MATHEW W		
Allen	Sierra Whiskey	66 850
MATHEW		
Ann	Alameda Oakland	55 25
MATHEW		
E	San Francisco San Francisco 5	67 532
Emery	Sierra Twp 7	66 900
Emery	Sierra Twp 7	66 908
Jacob	Yuba Marysville	72 894
Jas	Alameda Brooklyn	55 105
John	Calaveras Twp 8	57 90
Jules	Calaveras Twp 8	57 96
Julian	Napa Napa	61 110
Lawrence	Sacramento Ward 4	63 582
M C	San Francisco San Francisco 6	67 441
Richard	San Francisco San Francisco 4	681140
Thim	Sierra Twp 7	66 884
Thin	Sierra Twp 7	66 884
Thomas	Sierra Twp 7	66 883
Thos	Sacramento Georgian	63 344
MATHEWELL		
Susan	Los Angeles Los Angeles	59 336
MATHEWRIN		
---*	Calaveras Twp 8	57 96
MATHEWS		
A	El Dorado Placerville	58 865
A	San Mateo Twp 3	65 73
Abigail	Merced Monterey	60 942
Abigail	Monterey Monterey	60 942
Allen	Mariposa Twp 3	60 589
Amos	Yolo Washington	72 563
Ann	Alameda Oakland	55 29
Ann	San Francisco San Francisco 6	67 447
Arren S	Tulara Twp 1	71 108
B S	Calaveras Twp 8	57 80
Benj	San Bernardino San Salvador	64 651
Bridget	San Francisco San Francisco 4	681222
C W	San Francisco San Francisco 5	67 550
Charles	Butte Eureka	56 655
Charles	El Dorado Eldorado	58 944
Charles	Yuba New York	72 723
Chas	Butte Cascade	56 703
Chas	Butte Bidwell	56 730
Chas	Butte Ophir	56 791
Chas	Butte Ophir	56 800
Chas	Santa Clara San Jose	65 347
D	Sacramento Dry Crk	63 378
Daniel	San Joaquin Elkhorn	64 994
David	Sierra Monte Crk	661035
David	Sierra Port Win	66 792
E G	San Francisco San Francisco 2	67 665
Edward	El Dorado Georgetown	58 746
Edward	San Francisco San Francisco 4	681113
Edward	San Joaquin Stockton	641096
Edward	Sierra Downieville	66 986
Edward	Solano Suisan	69 232
Edward	Yuba Marysville	72 963
F	Sierra La Porte	66 790
F A	Butte Ophir	56 761
F H	San Francisco San Francisco 5	67 484
Felix	Contra Costa Twp 1	57 530
Fountain	San Mateo Twp 3	65 79
Francis	Placer Forest H	62 768
G M	Amador Twp 5	55 329
Geo	Santa Clara San Jose	65 353
Geo	Sonoma Petaluma	69 576
George	Alameda Brooklyn	55 99
Georgiana	San Francisco San Francisco 6	67 446
Henry	Alameda Brooklyn	55 155
Henry	Calaveras Twp 8	57 55
Henry	Contra Costa Twp 3	57 604
Henry	El Dorado Indian D	581158
J	Sutter Butte	70 796
J	Tuolumne Big Oak	71 145
J D	Nevada Grass Valley	61 236
J F	Nevada Bloomfield	61 509
J N	Nevada Bloomfield	61 518
J S	Siskiyou Scott Va	69 23
J T	Nevada Bloomfield	61 509
J W	Calaveras Twp 7	57 28
James	Amador Twp 4	55 235
James	El Dorado Cold Spring	581101
James	El Dorado Eldorado	58 936
James	El Dorado Eldorado	58 947
James	San Mateo Twp 3	65 79
Jas	Placer Rattle Snake	62 602
Jas	Sacramento Natonia	63 285
John	Alameda Brooklyn	55 103
John	Calaveras Twp 8	57 72
John	El Dorado Mud Springs	58 977
John	Mariposa Twp 1	60 665
John	Napa Napa	61 76
John	Placer Dutch Fl	62 731
John	Plumas Quincy	62 989
John	Sacramento Dry Crk	63 369
John	Sierra Port Win	66 793
John	Sierra Downieville	66 978
John	Solano Suisan	69 236
John	Yuba Marysville	72 963
John	Yuba Marysville	72 977
MATHEWS		
John L	Yolo Slate Ra	72 690
John L	Yuba Slate Ro	72 690
John M	Santa Clara Gilroy	65 231
John P	El Dorado White Oaks	581027
Jos V	Monterey Pajaro	601019
Joseph	Nevada Bridgeport	61 445
Jospeh	Sierra Scales D	66 801
Josua	Amador Twp 5	55 348
Justice	Butte Bidwell	56 706
L	Butte Hamilton	56 528
L	Calaveras Twp 7	57 5
Lee	Sierra La Porte	66 771
Lee	Sierra La Porte	66 774
Lieren	Calaveras Twp 7	57 18
Louise	El Dorado Greenwood	58 710
Luben M*	Fresno Twp 7	59 48
M	Amador Twp 7	55 420
Maroleste	Placer Dutch Fl	62 722
Martin	San Francisco San Francisco 1	68 919
Moses H	Yuba Fosters	72 839
Oscar S	Tulara Visalia	71 89
Overton	Sonoma Petaluma	69 568
P	San Joaquin Stockton	641098
Peter	San Luis Obispo San Luis Obispo	65 2
Peter*	Alameda Oakland	55 44
R L	Monterey San Juan	60 994
Rene	Sierra Scales D	66 801
Reuben	Tulara Visalia	71 89
Richd	San Bernardino San Bernadino	64 633
Suben M*	Fresno Twp 2	59 48
T	Nevada Grass Valley	61 218
T	Sutter Butte	70 781
Thomas	San Joaquin Stockton	641085
Thomas	Santa Clara Gilroy	65 249
Thomas	Solano Suisan	69 210
Thomas	Solano Vallejo	69 248
Thos	Sacramento San Joaquin	63 366
Thos	San Francisco San Francisco 1	68 914
Thos*	San Francisco San Francisco 1	68 923
U S	Santa Clara Santa Clara	65 488
W F	Sierra Downieville	66 975
W H C*	Nevada Bridgeport	61 501
W T	El Dorado Diamond	58 768
Warren S	Tulara Visalia	71 108
William	San Joaquin Stockton	641085
William*	Siskiyou Yreka	69 141
Wm	Amador Twp 2	55 262
Wm	Amador Twp 5	55 367
Wm	Butte Wyandotte	56 670
Wm	Butte Bidwell	56 726
Wm	Santa Clara San Jose	65 287
Wm	Santa Clara San Jose	65 342
Wm	Santa Clara Santa Clara	65 465
Wm R	Napa Yount	61 33
MATHEWSON		
C F	San Francisco San Francisco 5	67 525
D	Siskiyou Scott Va	69 57
E F	Siskiyou Scott Va	69 57
Henry	Contra Costa Twp 1	57 511
J	El Dorado Placerville	58 868
Jas S	Placer Dutch Fl	62 711
Jeremiah	Solano Vacaville	69 358
Luise	Santa Clara San Jose	65 342
V B	Siskiyou Scott Va	69 57
William	El Dorado Kelsey	581139
MATHEY		
Ed	El Dorado Mud Springs	58 995
MATHIAS		
---	Sacramento Granite	63 249
Joseph	Nevada Bridgeport	61 445
L	San Francisco San Francisco 2	67 722
MATHIEW		
A	San Francisco San Francisco 5	67 488
Joseph	Sierra Scales D	66 801
Rene	Sierra Scales D	66 801
MATHINS		
John	Yolo Cache	72 616
MATHIS		
Joseph	Tehama Tehama	70 945
N	Amador Twp 1	55 455
William	Contra Costa Twp 2	57 580
MATHISEN		
M	San Francisco San Francisco 9	681084
MATHISON		
A S	Trinity Weaverville	701070
John	El Dorado Big Bar	58 740
R	Calaveras Twp 9	57 401
Zeb	Alameda Brooklyn	55 155
MATHTON		
A*	Nevada Grass Valley	61 176
MATHU		
Wm	Nevada Nevada	61 290
MATHURHIAD		
George*	Placer Todds Va	62 786
MATHY		
J	Nevada Grass Valley	61 223

Name	County Locale	M653 Roll/Page
MATHY		
Jno W	Amador Twp 5	55 357
John	San Francisco San Francisco 4	681164
P	Nevada Grass Valley	61 223
MATIA		
---	San Bernardino S Timate	64 703
MATIAS		
---	San Diego Agua Caliente	64 823
MATIDE		
Lino*	Alameda Brooklyn	55 156
MATIDO		
Luno*	Alameda Brooklyn	55 156
MATIER		
John	Siskiyou Yreka	69 141
MATIES		
John*	Siskiyou Yreka	69 141
MATIGAN		
Mike*	Sonoma Sonoma	69 636
MATILDA		
---	Mendocino Calpella	60 824
---	Monterey San Juan	60 992
---	San Bernardino San Bernadino	64 678
---	San Bernardino S Timate	64 692
---	San Bernardino S Timate	64 696
---	San Bernardino S Timate	64 700
---	San Bernardino S Timate	64 701
---	San Bernardino S Timate	64 702
---	San Bernardino S Timate	64 703
---	San Bernardino S Timate	64 704
---	San Bernardino S Timate	64 705
---	San Bernardino S Timate	64 706
---	San Bernardino S Timate	64 707
---	San Bernardino S Timate	64 710
---	San Bernardino S Timate	64 711
---	San Bernardino S Timate	64 712
---	San Bernardino S Timate	64 713
---	San Bernardino S Timate	64 714
---	San Bernardino S Timate	64 715
---	San Bernardino S Timate	64 716
---	San Bernardino S Timate	64 717
---	San Bernardino S Timate	64 718
---	San Bernardino S Timate	64 720
---	San Bernardino S Timate	64 724
---	San Bernardino S Timate	64 725
---	San Bernardino S Timate	64 727
---	San Bernardino S Timate	64 728
---	San Bernardino S Timate	64 729
---	San Bernardino S Timate	64 730
---	San Bernardino S Timate	64 731
---	San Bernardino S Timate	64 732
---	San Bernardino S Timate	64 734
---	San Bernardino S Timate	64 736
---	San Bernardino S Timate	64 737
---	San Bernardino S Timate	64 739
---	San Bernardino S Timate	64 740
---	San Bernardino S Timate	64 741
---	San Bernardino S Timate	64 742
---	San Bernardino S Timate	64 743
---	San Bernardino S Timate	64 744
---	San Bernardino S Timate	64 748
---	San Bernardino S Timate	64 749
---	San Bernardino S Timate	64 750
---	San Bernardino S Timate	64 752
---	San Bernardino S Timate	64 753
---	San Bernardino S Timate	64 756
---	San Diego Agua Caliente	64 864
MATILDE		
---	San Bernardino Santa Inez	64 137
MATIN		
J San	San Francisco San Francisco 2	67 788
Jacob	Sonoma Petaluma	69 549
Rueben	Sierra Port Win	66 797
Ruebin	Sierra Port Win	66 797
MATINEZ		
Doloris	Tuolumne Twp 1	71 219
MATINS		
---	San Bernardino S Timate	64 691
MATIO		
---	Los Angeles Los Angeles	59 495
James	Tuolumne Twp 1	71 242
MATION		
G R	Sierra Twp 7	66 886
MATIREDAR		
---	San Bernardino S Timate	64 701
MATIS		
R	Tuolumne Garrote	71 173
Thos	Mariposa Twp 1	60 664
MATISON		
Henry	Tuolumne Twp 5	71 497
MATISS		
Edward	San Joaquin Elkhorn	64 983
MATIYAN		
Mike	Sonoma Sonoma	69 636
MATLAK		
Thomas	Yuba New York	72 735
MATLIS		
John	Tuolumne Twp 5	71 522
MATLOCK		
David	Stanislaus Branch	70 704
E	Calaveras Twp 9	57 386
E	San Joaquin Elkhorn	64 991
Edward	Yuba Fosters	72 836
William	Los Angeles San Pedro	59 480
MATLUE		
Wm*	Nevada Nevada	61 290
MATMAN		
Manuel	Monterey Alisal	601043
MATMERS		
A*	Nevada Grass Valley	61 180
MATNE		
---	Yolo Slate Ra	72 712
MATNER		
Peter	El Dorado Union	581092
MATNEY		
Thos	Napa Hot Springs	61 27
MATOCK		
F	Siskiyou Scott Va	69 60
MATOIR		
Matilda*	Sonoma Sonoma	69 651
MATON		
Matilda	Sonoma Sonoma	69 651
MATONE		
Patrick	Nevada Eureka	61 355
MATONEY		
Richard	San Francisco San Francisco 2	67 597
MATOON		
E	Butte Ophir	56 756
MATORS		
L*	Nevada Grass Valley	61 196
MATORY		
J	Sacramento Sutter	63 308
Mary*	Sacramento Brighton	63 200
MATOUSKI		
L	Yuba North Ea	72 687
MATOVICH		
M	San Francisco San Francisco 5	67 479
MATOWSKI		
L	Yolo Slate Ra	72 687
MATOX		
Milton	Mariposa Twp 1	60 631
MATOY		
Mary*	Sacramento Brighton	63 200
MATQUINB		
Abba Alla*	San Francisco 4	681224
---	San Francisco	
MATR		
---	Yuba Slate Ro	72 712
MATRA		
Manuel	Placer Rattle Snake	62 633
MATRON		
W	Amador Twp 2	55 304
MATSON		
C	Nevada Nevada	61 253
D D	Sierra Forest C	66 910
James	Calaveras Twp 8	57 51
James	Marin Cortemad	60 756
John	Calaveras Twp 8	57 101
John*	Butte Ophir	56 763
William	Calaveras Twp 4	57 311
Yentz*	Alameda Brooklyn	55 145
Yertz*	Alameda Brooklyn	55 145
MATT		
---	Shasta Horsetown	66 697
Barney	Siskiyou Cottonwood	69 98
John	Placer Iona Hills	62 882
John	Santa Clara San Jose	65 279
Mathias	El Dorado Placerville	58 913
Nathias	Placer Iona Hills	62 887
Peter*	El Dorado Placerville	58 915
MATTACK		
E*	Calaveras Twp 9	57 386
MATTAL		
Geirgo	San Francisco San Francisco 3	67 85
George	San Francisco San Francisco 3	67 85
M	San Francisco San Francisco 4	681171
MATTAMATO		
---	Mendocino Little L	60 839
MATTANEATO		
---	Mendocino Little L	60 839
MATTANIATO		
---	Mendocino Little L	60 839
MATTASIO		
---	San Diego Agua Caliente	64 830
MATTE		
Henry	San Francisco San Francisco 7	681421
MATTEIR		
Levenia	Mariposa Twp 1	60 635
MATTEMSEY		
H J*	Napa Hot Springs	61 25
MATTEN		
John	Sonoma Sonoma	69 636
MATTENEREY		
H J*	Napa Hot Springs	61 25
MATTENSON		
M J	San Francisco San Francisco 9	681081
MATTER		
Chas	Alameda Brooklyn	55 94
E W*	Mariposa Twp 3	60 585
Enoch*	Sacramento San Joaquin	63 352
Enock*	Sacramento San Joaquin	63 352
Robert	San Francisco San Francisco 10	177
		67
MATTERN		
Edwin	Placer Dutch Fl	62 722
MATTERS		
C	Tuolumne Sonora	71 480
D*	Tuolumne Twp 1	71 480
John	El Dorado Mountain	581183
MATTERSEY		
Fernando	San Luis Obispo	65 39
	San Luis Obispo	
MATTERSON		
John	El Dorado Greenwood	58 727
MATTERY		
John	Sonoma Santa Rosa	69 391
MATTESON		
C C	San Joaquin Oneal	64 939
D C	San Joaquin Stockton	641050
E E	Nevada Eureka	61 379
H	Nevada Eureka	61 379
MATTEWS		
M	Amador Twp 7	55 420
W	Siskiyou Scott Va	69 37
MATTHENSON		
Jeremiah*	San Francisco 8	681310
	San Francisco	
MATTHEW		
C	Sonoma Armally	69 482
John	Placer Michigan	62 826
Sal	Siskiyou Yreka	69 143
MATTHEWS		
Ann	San Francisco San Francisco 7	681351
C	Sonoma Armally	69 482
Charles	Calaveras Twp 5	57 206
Charles	Yuba New York	72 723
Chuck	Calaveras Twp 5	57 206
Daniel	San Joaquin Castoria	64 883
David	Sierra Monte Crk	661035
Edward	Yuba Marysville	72 963
Ehin*	Sonoma Petaluma	69 595
Elias	Sonoma Petaluma	69 595
Elim*	Sonoma Petaluma	69 595
Elisha	Butte Chico	56 536
F	Butte Kimshaw	56 592
Geo	Mendocino Calpella	60 816
Geo W	Sonoma Santa Rosa	69 393
George	Plumas Quincy	62 923
H	Nevada Nevada	61 318
H O	San Joaquin Stockton	641053
Henry	San Francisco San Francisco 10	228
		67
Ifory	Tuolumne Twp 1	71 278
Ivory	Tuolumne Twp 2	71 278
J H	Trinity Lewiston	70 961
J S	Siskiyou Scott Va	69 23
J W	Trinity Lewiston	70 961
James	Klamath S Fork	59 204
James	Trinity W Weaver	701054
James	Trinity E Weaver	701060
Jas	San Francisco San Francisco 10	344
		67
Jno	San Francisco San Francisco 9	681069
John	Sierra Downieville	66 978
John	Tuolumne Twp 1	71 236
John	Yuba Marysville	72 963
John	Yuba Marysville	72 977
John M	Yuba Marysville	72 908
Jos	Klamath Salmon	59 208
Joseph	San Francisco San Francisco 7	681417
Len	San Francisco San Francisco 1	68 822
Louisa	Siskiyou Yreka	69 168
Mc Kenie	Sonoma Santa Rosa	69 414
McKenie	Sonoma Santa Rosa	69 414
Nath	Sonoma Armally	69 505
Robert	Sacramento Ward 4	63 505
Robert	San Bernardino San Salvador	64 651
Robt	Sacramento Ward 4	63 536
Samuel	Placer Iona Hills	62 863
Sarah	San Francisco San Francisco 10	338
		67
T B	Sierra Downieville	66 978
Theodore	Shasta Horsetown	66 705
Thos	San Francisco San Francisco 9	681060
V	Trinity Mouth Ca	701014
W	San Francisco San Francisco 9	68 965
W	Siskiyou Scott Va	69 37
W B	Sonoma Vallejo	69 622
W F	Sierra Downieville	66 975
William	Siskiyou Yreka	69 141

Name	County Locale	M653 Roll	Page
MATTHEWS			
William	Siskiyou Klamath	69	89
William*	Siskiyou Yreka	69	141
Wm	Merced Monterey	60	933
Wm	Monterey Monterey	60	933
Wm M	Sonoma Santa Rosa	69	414
MATTHEWSON			
Chas*	San Francisco San Francisco 9	68	1072
E*	El Dorado Coloma	58	1118
James	San Francisco San Francisco 8	68	1299
Jeremiah	San Francisco San Francisco 8	68	1310
John	Solano Benecia	69	303
M J	San Francisco San Francisco 9	68	1081
R C	San Francisco San Francisco 2	67	734
Thomas D	San Francisco San Francisco 8	68	1263
MATTHEWY			
John	Tuolumne Sonora	71	236
MATTIAS			
---	San Diego Temecula	64	797
MATTICE			
S	Amador Twp 3	55	371
MATTIE			
Chas	Alameda Brooklyn	55	94
S	Nevada Grass Valley	61	148
MATTIER			
Geo	Butte Hamilton	56	515
Levenia	Mariposa Twp 1	60	635
Levinia	Mariposa Twp 1	60	635
MATTIGAN			
C D	Santa Clara San Jose	65	368
MATTIN			
John	Sonoma Sonoma	69	636
MATTINGLEY			
Richard L	Tuolumne Twp 4	71	178
MATTINGLY			
Benj	Sonoma Armally	69	508
J	Nevada Nevada	61	316
Richard L	Tuolumne Big Oak	71	178
Samson	San Francisco San Francisco 9	68	992
MATTINNEY			
H J	Napa Hot Springs	61	25
MATTIS			
John	Tuolumne Chinese	71	522
MATTISEN			
J	Nevada Nevada	61	266
M	San Francisco San Francisco 9	68	1084
MATTISON			
A	Calaveras Twp 9	57	401
J	Nevada Nevada	61	266
J E	Calaveras Twp 9	57	390
Jas	Tehama Lassen	70	869
Jas E	Calaveras Twp 9	57	369
Mary	San Joaquin Stockton	64	1013
T J	Calaveras Twp 9	57	383
MATTIST			
Joe*	Mariposa Twp 3	60	600
MATTIUGH			
Neal	Alameda Murray	55	223
MATTLER			
Henry	Tuolumne Twp 2	71	284
MATTLOCK			
Joseph	Placer Michigan	62	815
MATTMAN			
F	Mendocino Big Rvr	60	840
MATTOC			
Frank E	Alameda Oakland	55	31
MATTOCK			
E*	Calaveras Twp 9	57	386
James	El Dorado Mud Springs	58	996
John	Amador Twp 1	55	487
MATTOM			
Frank	Butte Ophir	56	768
MATTOON			
John*	San Francisco San Francisco 12	67	391
Price	Santa Cruz Santa Cruz	66	626
MATTOSA			
Maneoel	Mariposa Twp 1	60	672
MATTOW			
---	Yuba Bear Rvr	72	1014
---	Yuba Bear Rvr	72	1015
MATTOX			
J	Sutter Butte	70	799
L G	Nevada Nevada	61	283
Morris	Alameda Brooklyn	55	94
Saml	Del Norte Ferry P O	58	666
William	Alameda Brooklyn	55	149
MATTRE			
B	San Francisco San Francisco 2	67	584
MATTRI			
B*	San Francisco San Francisco 2	67	584
MATTRY			
John	San Francisco San Francisco 4	68	1164
MATTS			
Joseph	Mendocino Little L	60	834

Name	County Locale	M653 Roll	Page
MATTSOA			
Otto	Sierra Downieville	66	1016
MATTSON			
J A	Placer Michigan	62	828
Louis	Placer Iona Hills	62	871
MATTUCK			
Henry	Sonoma Vallejo	69	626
MATTUN			
William	Calaveras Twp 8	57	82
MATTUROUES			
Berrera	Sierra Downieville	66	1001
MATTY			
Jno O*	Sonoma Petaluma	69	600
Myers	San Francisco San Francisco 2	67	689
MATUR			
J M*	Solano Vacaville	69	330
MATZ			
John	San Francisco San Francisco 1	68	929
MATZEN			
C	Trinity Readings	70	996
Mary	Trinity Readings	70	996
MATZKER			
John	Santa Clara Redwood	65	457
MATZLER			
N	Sutter Nicolaus	70	832
MATZNUS			
Stanislow	Mariposa Twp 1	60	625
MATZOFF			
Maxx*	Del Norte Klamath	58	653
MATZUNS			
Stanislow*	Mariposa Twp 1	60	625
MAU			
---	Calaveras Twp 5	57	191
---	Calaveras Twp 5	57	205
---	Calaveras Twp 5	57	244
---	Calaveras Twp 5	57	250
---	Calaveras Twp 5	57	255
---	Calaveras Twp 5	57	256
---	Calaveras Twp 10	57	271
---	Calaveras Twp 10	57	272
---	Calaveras Twp 10	57	274
---	Plumas Quincy	62	950
---	San Francisco San Francisco 11	67	146
---	Tuolumne Twp 6	71	540
---*	Mariposa Twp 3	60	608
---*	Nevada Nevada	61	302
Fook	San Francisco San Francisco 11	67	161
Hung	San Francisco San Francisco 11	67	161
Tan	Siskiyou Yreka	69	194
Tek*	San Francisco San Francisco 11	67	160
MAUANO			
---	Los Angeles Tejon	59	529
MAUBIC			
Bernard	San Francisco San Francisco 10	67	249
MAUCE			
James M*	Sierra St Louis	66	863
Robert W*	Yuba Marysville	72	882
MAUCER			
Frances*	Sacramento Ward 3	63	484
MAUDICK			
Peter*	Sacramento Ward 1	63	10
MAUDLI			
Gaoff*	San Francisco San Francisco 7	68	1371
MAUDNI			
John C*	Yuba Foster B	72	829
MAUENEUME			
---*	Tulara Visalia	71	34
MAUGIN			
Anna*	Sacramento Ward 4	63	565
MAUGON			
James	Placer Forest H	62	774
MAUHAN			
George*	Calaveras Twp 6	57	144
Jas*	Placer Auburn	62	586
MAUHEIM			
Isaac*	San Francisco San Francisco 8	68	1321
MAUIR			
S M	Nevada Nevada	61	260
MAUK			
Franklin	Marin Point Re	60	732
Robt*	Sonoma Vallejo	69	630
MAUKIN			
Louis	Calaveras Twp 6	57	129
Thos*	Mariposa Twp 3	60	612
MAUKINS			
James	Monterey San Juan	60	1007
MAUKIRE			
Jose*	Santa Cruz Santa Cruz	66	620
MAUKRIE			
Jose*	Santa Cruz Santa Cruz	66	620
MAUKS			
F M	Amador No 6	55	426

Name	County Locale	M653 Roll	Page
MAUL			
Chas	Merced Twp 1	60	908
J	El Dorado Kelsey	58	1154
MAULA			
Anton	Tuolumne Sonora	71	189
MAULBERY			
W P	Butte Ophir	56	792
MAULBOROUGH			
H	Tuolumne Shawsfla	71	390
MAULD			
G*	Nevada Grass Valley	61	188
MAULDIN			
B F*	Sacramento American	63	164
Thos	San Francisco San Francisco 1	68	890
MAULE			
G	Tuolumne Twp 4	71	162
MAULETTI			
G B	San Francisco San Francisco 3	67	25
MAULEY			
A G*	Tuolumne Columbia	71	309
Christopher*	San Francisco San Francisco 11	67	100
MAULL			
J	Nevada Nevada	61	283
Micheal*	Calaveras Twp 9	57	367
MAULREK			
Hannah	San Francisco San Francisco 9	68	962
MAULTMAN			
E S*	Sacramento Georgian	63	339
MAULY			
Cornelius*	Placer Auburn	62	585
MAUM			
Abel*	Santa Cruz Soguel	66	597
MAUN			
---	Calaveras Twp 8	57	76
MAUNAN			
H*	Nevada Nevada	61	291
MAUNDER			
Edward	Sierra Twp 7	66	874
MAUNELLA			
John	Calaveras Twp 5	57	227
MAUNETTA			
John*	Calaveras Twp 5	57	227
MAUNGO			
Peter	El Dorado White Oaks	58	1008
MAUNIE			
T W*	Nevada Nevada	61	325
MAUNING			
A	Nevada Nevada	61	275
S*	Nevada Nevada	61	271
MAUNORTESE			
Josi*	Calaveras Twp 6	57	162
MAUNY			
Julia	San Francisco San Francisco 10	67	249
MAUOM			
M*	Nevada Eureka	61	389
MAUPIN			
D*	Shasta Horsetown	66	704
Sidney	Contra Costa Twp 2	57	576
Th E	Solano Vacaville	69	330
MAUR			
P	Sacramento Ward 1	63	29
MAURA			
Casper*	Plumas Quincy	62	924
MAURAN			
Janes	Amador Twp 5	55	367
MAURDAS			
Jose A	Contra Costa Twp 2	57	578
MAUREN			
Louis	Santa Clara Santa Clara	65	500
MAURER			
Edward	San Joaquin Stockton	64	1036
John	San Francisco San Francisco 7	68	1418
Jose Mauric	Fresno Twp 1	59	76
MAURICE			
Amasa	Butte Ophir	56	797
Asuasa	Butte Ophir	56	797
James	San Joaquin Stockton	64	1066
M N	San Francisco San Francisco 2	67	689
Patck	Butte Hamilton	56	527
Patric	San Francisco San Francisco 1	68	808
MAURICO			
Patine*	San Francisco San Francisco 1	68	808
MAURIL			
M	Santa Clara Almaden	65	263
MAURINA			
Joanna*	San Francisco San Francisco 9	68	986
MAURIO			
Hosea*	Alameda Brooklyn	55	124
MAURIQUES			
Manuel	Los Angeles San Juan	59	469
MAURNI			
M*	Nevada Eureka	61	389
MAUROW			
D A*	Sacramento Ward 3	63	460

Name	County Locale	M653 Roll Page
MAURY		
Abraham	Sierra Pine Grove	66 835
Mary	San Francisco San Francisco 1	68 873
Nerei B*	Plumas Meadow Valley	62 932
P Jnr	San Francisco San Francisco 3	67 22
Richard*	San Francisco San Francisco 2	67 734
MAUS		
Chas*	Placer Auburn	62 585
Chas*	Placer Dutch Fl	62 728
James*	Nevada Bloomfield	61 508
Mary E*	Nevada Bloomfield	61 508
MAUSEAW		
A*	Shasta Shasta	66 661
MAUSEN		
Jacob	Calaveras Twp 8	57 73
MAUSER		
Henry*	Nevada Bloomfield	61 512
Wm*	San Francisco San Francisco 3	67 18
MAUSRAY		
M	San Francisco San Francisco 10	313 67
MAUSSAN		
R*	Tuolumne Twp 1	71 216
MAUSUR		
Horrace*	Placer Rattle Snake	62 626
MAUTENS		
Mary*	San Francisco San Francisco 2	67 658
MAUTZ		
William H*	Yuba Marysville	72 879
MAUUA		
Elijah	San Joaquin Castoria	64 882
MAUVY		
Peter D*	San Francisco San Francisco 2	67 650
MAUZ		
Henry	Tehama Tehama	70 943
MAUZEE		
Nicholas	San Francisco San Francisco 11	157 67
MAVADRANO		
Antonio	San Francisco San Francisco 7	681 405
MAVALENSUALA		
Jose*	San Bernardino S Buenav	64 219
MAVALENZUELA		
Jase	Marin Cortemad	60 786
MAVALL		
John*	Shasta French G	66 718
MAVAN		
Diacame*	Mariposa Twp 3	60 594
MAVANO		
Manuel	Marin Cortemad	60 779
MAVARATTA		
Manuel	Contra Costa Twp 1	57 496
MAVER		
A R	Colusa Colusi	57 422
MAVERS		
Geo	Trinity Big Flat	701 040
MAVERT		
---	Sonoma Sonoma	69 640
A	Sonoma Sonoma	69 640
MAVIL		
Frank	Sonoma Sonoma	69 636
MAVIN		
George	Solano Fremont	69 380
MAVIR		
Jose*	Mariposa Twp 1	60 647
MAVISCE		
Llenovio*	Napa Napa	61 115
Llenovis*	Napa Napa	61 115
Stenovio*	Napa Napa	61 115
MAVISCO		
Llenovio*	Napa Napa	61 115
Llenovis*	Napa Napa	61 115
MAVITY		
John*	Del Norte Crescent	58 643
MAVNELL		
Michael*	Sierra Twp 7	66 869
MAVOON		
W*	Amador Twp 2	55 304
MAW WICKE		
---	Butte Kimshaw	56 592
MAW		
---	Calaveras Twp 9	57 371
---	El Dorado Casumnes	581 176
---	Nevada Nevada	61 303
---	Placer Illinois	62 705
---	Placer Illinois	62 749
---	Sacramento Cosumnes	63 409
---	San Francisco San Francisco 9	681 087
---	Tuolumne Twp 3	71 468
---	Tuolumne Twp 5	71 515
---*	San Francisco San Francisco 9	681 087
Ah	Sacramento Mississipi	63 190
Christ*	Sierra Twp 5	66 942
L G*	Nevada Grass Valley	61 217
Wicke	Butte Kimshaw	56 592
MAWAY		
---	Mariposa Twp 3	60 613

Name	County Locale	M653 Roll Page
MAWBRY		
John	Shasta Cottonwoood	66 736
MAWCALA		
Anrelino*	Calaveras Twp 4	57 333
MAWE		
---	Nevada Rough &	61 437
MAWELL		
C A	Nevada Grass Valley	61 177
MAWIHCK		
John*	El Dorado Coloma	581 113
MAWIHOK		
John*	El Dorado Coloma	581 113
MAWKER		
H	San Francisco San Francisco 4	681 160
MAWMES		
Gahert B*	Placer Auburn	62 589
MAWRAY		
M*	San Francisco San Francisco 10	313 67
Nathan B	San Francisco San Francisco 7	681 336
MAWREY		
F S	Yuba Parks Ba	72 776
MAWRY		
Jos*	Sacramento Ward 1	63 108
MAX		
---	Nevada Nevada	61 301
---	Tulara Twp 2	71 40
John	San Joaquin Douglass	64 926
MAXAM		
George D	Calaveras Twp 4	57 329
MAXCY		
Warren W	Los Angeles Elmonte	59 269
MAXELL		
John	Siskiyou Yreka	69 141
MAXEMENAH		
---*	Tulara Visalia	71 37
MAXEY		
Ashur E	San Diego Agua Caliente	64 864
Dan	Merced Twp 2	60 920
Daniel	Butte Oregon	56 639
J B	El Dorado Union	581 094
James W*	Contra Costa Twp 2	57 563
Jas M	Butte Chico	56 568
L	Tuolumne Twp 4	71 173
Levi A	Contra Costa Twp 2	57 575
N R	Nevada Little Y	61 531
Olevia	El Dorado Union	581 094
T	Tuolumne Garrote	71 173
Wm	Los Angeles Los Angeles	59 512
MAXFIELD		
Ann	San Francisco San Francisco 4	681 153
Benjamin	Yuba Foster B	72 833
David	Butte Bidwell	56 710
David	San Francisco San Francisco 2	67 738
Ezra F	San Francisco San Francisco 10	247 67
George P	Yuba Foster B	72 831
Levy	Alameda Brooklyn	55 147
MAXFIELDS		
David	Butte Bidwell	56 710
MAXHARDO		
Cosms*	Calaveras Twp 6	57 151
MAXHERENA		
Powell	Sonoma Mendocino	69 462
MAXHIN		
B	Sutter Yuba	70 762
MAXIM		
David	Santa Cruz Pajaro	66 559
John	Santa Cruz Pajaro	66 577
MAXIND		
Morin	Siskiyou Callahan	69 3
MAXINE		
David	Santa Cruz Pajaro	66 559
Monin*	Siskiyou Callahan	69 3
MAXIOME		
---	Tulara Twp 2	71 39
MAXIRN		
G M*	Tehama Pasakent	70 855
MAXIT		
Jos	San Francisco San Francisco 3	67 78
MAXIVEL		
Michael*	Marin San Rafael	60 763
MAXLEY		
James*	Siskiyou Scott Va	69 21
John	Siskiyou Scott Va	69 20
Joseph	Placer Iona Hills	62 873
MAXMEL		
John*	Calaveras Twp 4	57 338
MAXOAHE		
---*	Tulara Twp 2	71 39
MAXON		
B H	Calaveras Twp 9	57 380
Chas H	Del Norte Crescent	58 627
Jno	Butte Kimshaw	56 584
Jno P	Butte Chico	56 546
Sarah	Placer Dutch Fl	62 726

Name	County Locale	M653 Roll Page
MAXON		
W B	Butte Hamilton	56 527
MAXOW		
Jno	Butte Kimshaw	56 584
MAXSON		
Frank	Calaveras Twp 8	57 58
Juliet	Calaveras Twp 8	57 58
MAXTON		
J H	Solano Suisan	69 211
W	Nevada Grass Valley	61 163
Wm	Nevada Grass Valley	61 145
MAXUM		
Wm	Tehama Pasakent	70 858
MAXWEL		
---	Tulara Twp 2	71 40
G W	Tehama Antelope	70 886
MAXWELL		
---*	Tulara Visalia	71 40
A M	Placer Todds Va	62 763
A S	Nevada Grass Valley	61 217
A T	Nevada Grass Valley	61 217
Abbert*	Mendocino Big Rvr	60 851
Alexander	Tuolumne Twp 2	71 294
And	Yolo Washington	72 574
C	Sutter Bear Rvr	70 826
Cecelia S B	Sonoma Healdsbu	69 478
David	Sacramento Franklin	63 328
Dennis	Santa Clara Fremont	65 439
Elizabeth	San Francisco San Francisco 10	210 67
Geo	Nevada Eureka	61 392
Geo	San Francisco San Francisco 10	315 67
George N	Alameda Oakland	55 44
Gilbert	Fresno Twp 2	59 4
H	Nevada Washington	61 338
H	San Francisco San Francisco 4	681 154
Henry	San Francisco San Francisco 11	152 67
Hugh	San Francisco San Francisco 9	681 100
Isabella	Yolo Washington	72 575
J	Shasta Shasta	66 686
J J	Sonoma Cloverdale	69 686
J W	Klamath Klamath	59 224
J W	Trinity New Rvr	701 031
J W*	Napa Clear Lake	61 134
James	El Dorado Georgetown	58 706
James	Shasta Millvill	66 751
James	Sierra La Porte	66 788
James A	Siskiyou Shasta Rvr	69 113
James G	Sonoma Santa Rosa	69 390
Jas	San Francisco San Francisco 9	681 057
Jno L	Sonoma Healdsbu	69 478
John	Calaveras Twp 4	57 338
John	Sacramento Ward 4	63 553
John	Siskiyou Scott Va	69 39
John	Trinity Trinity	70 972
John	Yuba Marysville	72 975
John M	Sonoma Sonoma	69 649
John W C	Fresno Twp 1	59 82
John*	Calaveras Twp 4	57 338
Joss	Tuolumne Twp 2	71 306
L	Colusa Butte Crk	57 464
Linford	Alameda Brooklyn	55 161
Michael	Marin San Rafael	60 763
Michael	Tuolumne Columbia	71 349
Micheal	El Dorado Placerville	58 916
N	Yolo Cottonwoood	72 661
N B	Tuolumne Big Oak	71 139
Patrick	San Francisco San Francisco 11	147 67
Rich	Calaveras Twp 9	57 401
Richard	San Francisco San Francisco 4	681 159
Robt	Stanislaus Emory	70 739
Samuel	Monterey Pajaro	601 019
Stephen	Calaveras Twp 8	57 98
Stephen	Humbolt Eureka	59 176
T J	Yolo Cottonwoood	72 557
Thos	Stanislaus Oatvale	70 717
Thos	Trinity Sturdiva	701 007
Thos P	Stanislaus Empire	70 735
Tim	Sacramento Ward 1	63 138
W	Siskiyou Scott Ri	69 65
W	Yolo Washington	72 573
W Jr*	Yolo Cottonwoood	72 661
Walter	Alameda Brooklyn	55 86
Walter	San Francisco San Francisco 8	681 316
William	Placer Michigan	62 831
Wm	Tuolumne Twp 1	71 266
Wyman	Colusa Monroeville	57 441
MAXWILL		
George	San Bernardino Santa Barbara	64 170
Samuel*	Monterey Pajaro	601 019
MAXWINE		
---	Tulara Visalia	71 39
MAY HOW		
---*	Nevada Nevada	61 301

Name	County Locale	M653 Roll	Page
MAY LEI LUNG			
---*	San Francisco San Francisco 3	67	26
MAY			
---	Amador Twp 2	55	289
---	Amador Twp 2	55	292
---	Amador Twp 5	55	344
---	Amador Twp 3	55	408
---	Amador Twp 6	55	431
---	Amador Twp 1	55	502
---	Butte Oregon	56	625
---	Calaveras Twp 4	57	300
---	Calaveras Twp 4	57	300
---	El Dorado Salmon Falls	581046	
---	El Dorado Salmon Hills	581060	
---	Mariposa Twp 3	60	564
---	Mariposa Twp 3	60	613
---	Mariposa Twp 3	60	619
---	Nevada Nevada	61	301
---	Nevada Bridgeport	61	493
---	Nevada Bloomfield	61	528
---	Placer Rattle Snake	62	636
---	Placer Virginia	62	666
---	Sacramento Cosumnes	63	407
---	Sierra La Porte	66	785
---	Sierra Twp 5	66	932
---	Sierra Twp 5	66	945
---*	San Francisco San Francisco 4	681193	
A	El Dorado Newtown	58	777
A	Tuolumne Twp 4	71	131
A W	Sierra Monte Crk	661039	
Ah	Butte Cascade	56	700
Alfred	Placer Michigan	62	814
Alfred	Placer Michigan	62	825
Alfred	Yuba Marysville	72	941
August	Alameda Brooklyn	55	215
August	Tulara Visalia	71	106
Benjn F	San Francisco San Francisco 7	681363	
Cam	Tuolumne Twp 4	71	181
Charles	Sierra Scales D	66	802
Chas	Klamath Liberty	59	236
Chee*	San Francisco San Francisco 9	681094	
E	Mariposa Twp 3	60	552
Edgar	Placer Auburn	62	560
Edward	Solano Vallejo	69	277
Edwd	San Francisco San Francisco 1	68	855
Eugene	Placer Michigan	62	838
Eugene	San Francisco San Francisco 7	681374	
Eva*	San Francisco San Francisco 6	67	409
Ezra	Placer Dutch Fl	62	734
F W	Nevada Nevada	61	257
Fraklin	San Francisco San Francisco 7	681401	
Francis	Sierra Twp 7	66	873
Frank	Sacramento Ward 1	63	101
Franklin	San Francisco San Francisco 9	681076	
Fredrick	Nevada Little Y	61	535
Garlen	Sierra Twp 5	66	925
Garlin	Sierra Twp 5	66	925
Geo	El Dorado Kelsey	581142	
George	Alameda Brooklyn	55	114
George	Alameda Brooklyn	55	94
H	Sutter Vernon	70	846
H S	San Francisco San Francisco 1	68	915
H W	San Francisco San Francisco 5	67	500
Henry	El Dorado Big Bar	58	742
Henry	Shasta Shasta	66	732
Henry	Sierra Twp 7	66	913
Henry	Siskiyou Yreka	69	156
Henry	Sonoma Bodega	69	540
Henry A	Siskiyou Yreka	69	127
Hiram	Butte Hamilton	56	528
Hiram	El Dorado Placerville	58	914
Hop	Mariposa Twp 3	60	544
Hugh	Los Angeles Tejon	59	527
Hugh	Sonoma Petaluma	69	563
J	El Dorado Diamond	58	794
J	Nevada Nevada	61	325
J A	Nevada Grass Valley	61	145
J H	San Francisco San Francisco 5	67	492
J J	San Francisco San Francisco 2	67	648
J S*	Placer Michigan	62	884
J W*	Calaveras Twp 9	57	360
James D	Trinity Weaverville	701062	
Jessee	Sacramento Natonia	63	283
Jessu	Sacramento Natonia	63	283
Jno S	Alameda Oakland	55	24
Jocob	El Dorado Casumnes	581164	
John	El Dorado Georgetown	58	759
John	Placer Iona Hills	62	882
John	Siskiyou Shasta Valley	69	118
John	Siskiyou Yreka	69	147
John A	San Francisco San Francisco 2	67	734
John B	Trinity Weaverville	701080	
John B*	Calaveras Twp 7	57	4
Joseph	Placer Auburn	62	584
Julia	San Francisco San Francisco 10	214	
		67	

Name	County Locale	M653 Roll	Page
MAY			
Kee	Mariposa Twp 3	60	544
Kee	Mariposa Twp 3	60	580
Kh G	El Dorado Placerville	58	912
King	Mariposa Twp 3	60	543
Kuel	Mariposa Twp 3	60	546
Kyt	Mariposa Twp 3	60	618
Levi	San Francisco San Francisco 2	67	615
Louis	Sacramento Ward 1	63	144
Loy	Yuba Fosters	72	830
Lun	Placer Auburn	62	577
Martha	Contra Costa Twp 1	57	505
Mary	Sacramento Ward 1	63	101
Noah	Sacramento Granite	63	261
O N	Placer Dutch Fl	62	734
Penfield	Placer Michigan	62	821
Phillip	San Francisco San Francisco 7	681350	
Pugene*	El Dorado Georgetown	58	748
Richard	Yuba Marysville	72	944
Ruth A	Placer Virginia	62	689
S C	Sonoma Armally	69	508
Saml	Sacramento Granite	63	261
Samuel R	Siskiyou Yreka	69	139
Sidney	Sacramento Ward 4	63	537
Solomon	San Francisco San Francisco 2	67	606
Thomas	Placer Iona Hills	62	891
Thos	Sacramento Ward 1	63	139
W	San Francisco San Francisco 5	67	503
W L	Sacramento Ward 1	63	80
W T	Sacramento Ward 1	63	80
William	Contra Costa Twp 1	57	504
William	Contra Costa Twp 3	57	617
William	Tulara Twp 2	71	8
William B	Tuolumne Twp 3	71	454
Wm	Placer Lisbon	62	733
Wm	San Francisco San Francisco 3	67	83
Wm B	Napa Napa	61	93
MAYA			
---	Yuba Bear Rvr	721015	
MAYAHEW			
Michael	Solano Fremont	69	384
William	Solano Fremont	69	384
MAYAINE			
Eugene	Calaveras Twp 4	57	317
MAYAL			
John	Placer Michigan	62	823
MAYAN			
C*	Nevada Grass Valley	61	189
Jane*	Nevada Grass Valley	61	194
MAYAR			
C*	Nevada Grass Valley	61	189
Charles	Sierra Poker Flats	66	841
MAYARK			
Hugh	Nevada Bridgeport	61	449
MAYAS			
Charles*	Sierra Poker Flats	66	841
MAYATT			
H	El Dorado Mud Springs	58	991
MAYBANK			
C	Calaveras Twp 9	57	389
C	Calaveras Twp 9	57	398
MAYBERN			
Saml S*	Napa Clear Lake	61	125
MAYBERRY			
Chas	Sacramento Dry Crk	63	374
Geo	Mendocino Little L	60	833
Isaac	Los Angeles Los Angeles	59	321
J B	Nevada Nevada	61	239
William	Siskiyou Yreka	69	148
MAYBES			
Isabel	Santa Clara Santa Clara	65	508
MAYBLUM			
M	San Francisco San Francisco 2	67	615
MAYBORN			
Charles	Contra Costa Twp 1	57	522
MAYBUN			
Saml	Napa Clear Lake	61	125
Saml S	Napa Clear Lake	61	125
MAYBURY			
John	Butte Cascade	56	698
MAYD			
Eli	Sacramento Ward 4	63	518
MAYDENLUO			
Laura	Nevada Nevada	61	277
MAYDENLUS			
Lama	Nevada Nevada	61	277
MAYDOLE			
J	El Dorado Kelsey	581151	
MAYE			
Anna	Placer Forest H	62	770
George*	Placer Forest H	62	769
Martin	Placer Forest H	62	770
MAYEN			
Antonia	San Bernardino Santa Ba	64	209
Sarah	San Francisco San Francisco 4	681111	
MAYENBAUEN			
Henry	El Dorado Spanish	581124	

Name	County Locale	M653 Roll	Page
MAYENBAUREN			
Henry	El Dorado Spanish	581124	
MAYER			
A	Sacramento Ward 4	63	549
A F	Sacramento Ward 1	63	81
Antoinette	Sacramento Ward 1	63	45
B	San Francisco San Francisco 2	67	786
Carmine	Calaveras Twp 6	57	128
Chas R	Del Norte Happy Ca	58	670
Cornelia	Sacramento Ward 1	63	34
D C	Trinity China Bar	70	959
Fred	Nevada Rough &	61	430
George	Tuolumne Twp 1	71	257
Hellen	Nevada Red Dog	61	540
Henry	Sierra Twp 7	66	891
Hing	Sierra Twp 7	66	891
J A R	San Francisco San Francisco 4	681139	
James A	Sacramento Ward 1	63	34
Jas	San Francisco San Francisco 10	299	
		67	
John	San Francisco San Francisco 5	67	500
Jos	San Francisco San Francisco 10	299	
		67	
Joseph	San Francisco San Francisco 6	67	460
Joseph*	Placer Auburn	62	580
L	San Francisco San Francisco 4	681219	
M	San Francisco San Francisco 5	67	475
Margarett	Shasta French G	66	718
N	San Francisco San Francisco 5	67	523
Nathan	San Francisco San Francisco 2	67	620
Peter	San Francisco San Francisco 10	340	
		67	
Peter	Tuolumne Chinese	71	494
Phillip	San Francisco San Francisco 9	681050	
W	Nevada Grass Valley	61	201
Wm	Sacramento Granite	63	243
MAYERRISH			
Ernest	San Francisco San Francisco 7	681378	
MAYERS			
A A*	Sierra Downieville	66	978
B S	Nevada Bridgeport	61	487
C	Yolo Putah	72	552
C B	Nevada Nevada	61	298
C F	Nevada Bridgeport	61	456
Ephram	Nevada Rough &	61	438
Ephrum	Nevada Rough &	61	438
Frank	Tuolumne Jamestown	71	454
Henry	Sacramento Franklin	63	314
J	San Francisco San Francisco 10	256	
		67	
J*	Nevada Eureka	61	346
Jacob*	Yuba Rose Bar	72	794
Jno H	Klamath Klamath	59	228
Joseph R	Monterey S Antoni	60	967
L	Nevada Grass Valley	61	193
Levi	Nevada Rough &	61	413
Mary	San Francisco San Francisco 9	68	992
Philip	San Francisco San Francisco 11	156	
		67	
Robert	San Francisco San Francisco 2	67	777
Roberts	San Francisco San Francisco 2	67	668
S	Nevada Nevada	61	257
Simon	Nevada Nevada	61	257
MAYES			
A	Nevada Grass Valley	61	219
J R	Sonoma Armally	69	508
Phillip*	Klamath S Fork	59	198
Richd	Sonoma Santa Rosa	69	416
Robert H	Los Angeles San Jose	59	281
Thomas A	Los Angeles Liberty	59	245
W C	Tuolumne Jamestown	71	426
W G*	Santa Clara Fremont	65	428
MAYFIELD			
A	El Dorado Mud Springs	58	965
A	Placer Todds Va	62	790
Ann	San Francisco San Francisco 4	681153	
Arthur	Santa Clara Santa Clara	65	499
B F	Sonoma Armally	69	501
C S	Santa Clara Gilroy	65	248
F	Yolo Cache Crk	72	641
J J	Sutter Yuba	70	773
James	El Dorado Georgetown	58	673
James	Placer Michigan	62	821
Jas M	Napa Napa	61	71
Jno	Tehama Red Bluff	70	903
John	San Bernardino San Salvador	64	658
N M	Tehama Antelope	70	891
Saml	Santa Clara Gilroy	65	232
T	Sutter Yuba	70	773
W	Calaveras Twp 9	57	404
Wm	Sacramento Ward 4	63	603
MAYFLEN			
Wilson	Sacramento Granite	63	252
MAYFOL			
John*	San Francisco San Francisco 3	67	85
MAYFORD			
Saml	Sacramento Natonia	63	273

California 1860 Census Index

Name	County Locale	M653 RollPage
MAYGNS		
Isaac	San Francisco San Francisco	7 681337
MAYGOTT		
James	Sonoma Sonoma	69 637
MAYGUS		
Isaac	San Francisco San Francisco	7 681337
MAYHAR		
M H*	Sacramento Ward 3	63 481
MAYHART		
John	Napa Napa	61 104
MAYHEE		
Thomas	Contra Costa Twp 1	57 491
MAYHEM		
W G	Amador Twp 6	55 439
MAYHEN		
Charles	Tuolumne Twp 5	71 493
Jno A*	Alameda Brooklyn	55 111
N C	Siskiyou Yreka	69 181
MAYHER		
Jno	Alameda Brooklyn	55 190
Joseph	Mendocino Round Va	60 881
Oliver	Alameda Brooklyn	55 105
MAYHEW		
David W	Siskiyou Yreka	69 131
Eunice C	Sonoma Mendocino	69 465
F	Butte Oregon	56 626
Harrison L	San Francisco San Francisco	8 681302
Hetrow B	Calaveras Twp 6	57 132
Jessee	Sonoma Mendocino	69 465
Jno A*	Alameda Brooklyn	55 111
L Francis	San Francisco San Francisco	10 294 67
Levi*	Tulara Visalia	71 97
Mathew	Calaveras Twp 8	57 91
N C	Siskiyou Yreka	69 181
O G*	Sonoma Petaluma	69 580
Seth	San Francisco San Francisco	10 293 67
T	El Dorado Diamond	58 801
Thomas	Los Angeles Elmonte	59 268
Wm P	Tehama Lassen	70 880
MAYHIE		
Oliver	Alameda Brooklyn	55 105
MAYHU		
Thomas	Contra Costa Twp 1	57 491
MAYIOLI		
Dom*	San Francisco San Francisco	6 67 403
Don*	San Francisco San Francisco	6 67 403
Doni*	San Francisco San Francisco	6 67 403
MAYKNI		
Wm H	Sacramento Ward 4	63 526
MAYLAM		
---	Mendocino Twp 1	60 891
MAYLAND		
Edward	Alameda Brooklyn	55 147
H	Nevada Washington	61 335
Thomas	San Mateo Twp 3	65 73
MAYLE		
John	Calaveras Twp 9	57 363
Wm	Calaveras Twp 9	57 364
MAYLES		
M*	Sacramento Ward 4	63 507
MAYLONE		
G W	El Dorado Indian D	581158
MAYLOTT		
C A	Solano Suisan	69 211
S A	Solano Suisan	69 211
MAYMAN		
Frank	San Francisco San Francisco	8 681285
Frank S	San Francisco San Francisco	8 681285
N	Shasta Millvill	66 738
MAYMARD		
N	Shasta Millvill	66 738
MAYN		
Jno	Sacramento Natonia	63 278
MAYNARA		
Joseph	Sierra Gibsonville	66 860
MAYNARCE		
Joseph*	Sierra Whiskey	66 844
MAYNARD		
Andy	Nevada Eureka	61 345
C	El Dorado Diamond	58 794
Chas	Trinity Hay Fork	70 995
Duncan D	Calaveras Twp 5	57 218
E F	Sacramento Ward 3	63 498
F T	Tuolumne Twp 4	71 177
G	El Dorado Kelsey	581151
George	Yuba Slate Ro	72 693
Geroge	Yolo Slate Ra	72 693
H	Butte Kimshaw	56 587
H G	El Dorado Diamond	58 764
H*	Butte Kimshaw	56 587
Harlan P	Sierra La Porte	66 790
J R	Alameda Brooklyn	55 150
John C	San Mateo Twp 3	65 83
Joseph	Sierra Whiskey	66 844

Name	County Locale	M653 RollPage
MAYNARD		
Joseph*	Sierra Gibsonville	66 860
Joseph*	Sierra Whiskey	66 844
Lafayette	San Francisco San Francisco	7 681443
Levi P	Plumas Meadow Valley	62 932
P	Nevada Grass Valley	61 175
R	Nevada Grass Valley	61 204
R A	Nevada Grass Valley	61 174
R S	Santa Clara Redwood	65 457
Richard	El Dorado Diamond	58 794
Samuel	Sierra Whiskey	66 844
W H	El Dorado Diamond	58 794
MAYNARE		
P S	Santa Clara San Jose	65 354
MAYNE		
C	San Francisco San Francisco	5 67 500
James	Tuolumne Twp 1	71 264
William H	San Francisco San Francisco	9 681085
A L*	Nevada Grass Valley	61 202
MAYNEED		
A L*	Nevada Grass Valley	61 202
MAYNER		
John*	San Francisco San Francisco	3 67 83
MAYNERD		
A L*	Nevada Grass Valley	61 202
MAYNERS		
R F*	San Francisco San Francisco	4 681111
MAYNES		
Frank	Butte Ophir	56 784
Patrick	San Francisco San Francisco	7 681414
Smyth	San Francisco San Francisco	1 68 843
MAYNEWS		
Charles	Tuolumne Chinese	71 493
MAYNIN		
H	Nevada Eureka	61 368
MAYNIRE		
Nancy*	Siskiyou Yreka	69 148
MAYNNS		
R F	San Francisco San Francisco	4 681111
MAYNON		
H	Nevada Eureka	61 368
MAYNOR		
J	El Dorado Placerville	58 892
MAYNORS		
R F*	San Francisco San Francisco	4 681111
MAYO		
A J	Amador Twp 3	55 369
Ale	Stanislaus Empire	70 735
Elizabeth	Santa Clara Fremont	65 423
John	Los Angeles Tejon	59 522
John	Placer Michigan	62 817
John	Stanislaus Empire	70 734
Jose	Santa Clara San Jose	65 297
Joseph	San Joaquin Elkhorn	64 970
L*	Sacramento Brighton	63 201
Landes*	Yuba Marysville	72 960
Leandro	Yuba Marysville	72 960
Mariano	Tuolumne Twp 1	71 225
Mary A	San Francisco San Francisco	12 394 67
Nuas*	Placer Virginia	62 676
Ossian	San Francisco San Francisco	11 145 67
Pera Gordo*	San Francisco	5 67 481
	San Francisco	
S*	Sacramento Brighton	63 201
MAYON		
A	Nevada Eureka	61 388
T H	Yuba Timbucto	72 787
W A*	Yuba Rose Bar	72 788
MAYOR		
---	Fresno Twp 2	59 42
David	San Francisco San Francisco	3 67 77
Frederick	San Mateo Twp 1	65 55
John Jos*	Placer Dutch Fl	62 709
John*	Placer Dutch Fl	62 709
Louis	El Dorado Coloma	581117
Manuel	Tuolumne Twp 2	71 473
MAYORS		
James P	Tulara Twp 1	71 111
John	Tehama Lassen	70 876
MAYOUX		
Antone	Nevada Bloomfield	61 524
Jon	Calaveras Twp 4	57 317
S	Nevada Grass Valley	61 215
MAYOWAN		
J	Nevada Grass Valley	61 190
MAYRAMO		
Matthews	Sonoma Sonoma	69 641
MAYRAND		
Matthews*	Sonoma Sonoma	69 641
MAYRANE		
Matthews*	Sonoma Sonoma	69 641
MAYRER		
Joseph*	Placer Auburn	62 580
Michael*	Alameda Brooklyn	55 121
MAYRES		
John	Marin S Antoni	60 712

Name	County Locale	M653 RollPage
MAYRES		
Robert	Marin San Rafael	60 766
MAYRISCH		
Adolph	San Francisco San Francisco	10 277 67
MAYS		
Antonio	Monterey Monterey	60 947
Benjamin	Los Angeles Los Angeles	59 335
D	Yolo Cache	72 617
Geo	San Francisco San Francisco	3 67 80
George	San Francisco San Francisco	7 681404
George*	Mariposa Twp 1	60 668
George*	Placer Forest H	62 769
John	Mariposa Twp 3	60 594
John S	Solano Vacaville	69 355
John*	Mariposa Twp 3	60 594
Richd	Sonoma Santa Rosa	69 416
MAYSON		
Wm	San Francisco San Francisco	9 681079
MAYTISS		
J*	Nevada Grass Valley	61 150
MAYTITT		
J*	Nevada Grass Valley	61 150
MAYUR		
Leon	Calaveras Twp 6	57 157
MAYURK		
Hugh*	Nevada Bridgeport	61 449
MAYUS		
A A*	Sierra Downieville	66 978
MAYUTREW		
William*	Solano Fremont	69 384
MAYWARD		
Albert B	Los Angeles Los Angeles	59 351
Duncan D	Calaveras Twp 5	57 218
MAYWOOD		
Joh	Solano Vallejo	69 251
John	Solano Vallejo	69 251
MAZE		
Barton	Sacramento Franklin	63 320
MAZEANX		
Wm	Sacramento Ward 4	63 548
MAZENO		
Antonia	Tuolumne Sonora	71 229
MAZGIA		
Louis	Amador Twp 3	55 394
MAZINO		
Antonio	Tuolumne Twp 1	71 229
MAZNOR		
John	San Francisco San Francisco	3 67 83
Marian	San Bernardino S Timate	64 688
MAZON		
John*	Shasta Shasta	66 677
MAZONDA		
Dulesga*	Amador Twp 4	55 245
MAZONE		
Louis	Los Angeles Los Angeles	59 347
MAZRA		
Brewly	Solano Montezuma	69 370
MAZZENI		
Antonio	San Bernardino Santa Barbara	64 151
MAZZINNI		
Pedro	San Bernardino Santa Barbara	64 191
MAZZY		
Jos*	Klamath Orleans	59 216
MBAUGH		
John M	Placer Iona Hills	62 893
MBBER		
Martin*	San Francisco San Francisco	11 98 67
MC		
Peter* Jrehl	Butte Eureka	56 649
MCAARONS		
Charles	Contra Costa Twp 2	57 544
MCABEE		
M	Nevada Nevada	61 280
MCABER		
M	Nevada Nevada	61 280
MCABY		
P	Nevada Eureka	61 367
MCADAM		
John	Sacramento Dry Crk	63 369
Samuel	Santa Cruz Pajaro	66 568
MCADAMS		
Angus	Yuba Rose Bar	72 802
Archy	Amador Twp 4	55 234
D W	Napa Clear Lake	61 135
Edwd	Sonoma Petaluma	69 551
Ellen	San Francisco San Francisco	10 257 67
Ellen	Solano Vallejo	69 249
Henry	El Dorado Mud Springs	58 967
Jas	Trinity Trinity	70 975
Jos	Butte Kimshaw	56 571
Michael	Yuba Marysville	72 964
Patrick	Solano Benecia	69 284

California 1860 Census Index

Name	County Locale	M653 RollPage
MCADAMS		
Patrick	Solano Benecia	69 296
Peter	Solano Vallejo	69 249
T	Tuolumne Chinese	71 495
T	Tuolumne Twp 5	71 495
MCADAWS		
Jos	Butte Kimshaw	56 571
MCADDLE		
John	Monterey Pajaro	601021
MCADELE		
Zodok W San Francisco San Francisco 3		67 87
MCADOO		
David	Napa Napa	61 74
John	Solano Benecia	69 307
Martha	Solano Benecia	69 307
Thomas	Sonoma Armally	69 513
MCAEE		
Sarah*	San Francisco San Francisco 9	68 942
MCAFA		
Jas*	Sonoma Vallejo	69 612
MCAFEE		
A F	Sonoma Bodega	69 538
Alex	El Dorado Grizzly	581181
H B	El Dorado Casumnes	581175
James	Sonoma Petaluma	69 556
Jas*	Sonoma Vallejo	69 612
Joseph	Solano Benecia	69 281
William	Nevada Red Dog	61 544
William C	San Joaquin Elkhorn	64 974
Wm	Tuolumne Shawsfla	71 381
MCAFEI		
Jas*	Sonoma Vallejo	69 612
MCAFER		
Jas	Sonoma Vallejo	69 612
MCAFEY		
Lewis	Tuolumne Twp 1	71 268
MCAFFEE		
David	Sonoma Bodega	69 537
Robt	Tuolumne Big Oak	71 144
Thos	Amador Twp 3	55 387
MCAFFERY		
Nathan	Yolo Slate Ra	72 691
Rosanna San Francisco San Francisco 2		67 582
MCAFFEY		
Bullard	Tuolumne Twp 1	71 268
George	Tuolumne Twp 2	71 277
MCAFFREY		
George	Tuolumne Columbia	71 364
MCAFU		
Joseph	Solano Benecia	69 281
MCAHEES		
Jno M	Mendocino Anderson	60 871
MCALAVY		
Mary*	San Francisco San Francisco 10	165 67
MCALCUSE		
Pat*	Sacramento Ward 3	63 456
MCALE		
S*	Nevada Grass Valley	61 174
MCALFRY		
A D	Shasta Shasta	66 657
MCALHAWNEY		
J	Sutter Butte	70 798
MCALISTER		
A	Sierra Twp 5	66 929
A	Tuolumne Shawsfla	71 418
A Y	Tehama Tehama	70 941
C	San Francisco San Francisco 6	67 473
C S	Tuolumne Sonora	71 232
D A	Tehama Red Bluff	70 930
G	Nevada Grass Valley	61 211
G	Tuolumne Twp 1	71 262
Ira	Tuolumne Twp 1	71 262
Ira C	Tuolumne Twp 1	71 263
James	Plumas Quincy	62 923
James	Siskiyou Yreka	69 142
James	Tehama Tehama	70 936
John	Tuolumne Sonora	71 187
Pat	Nevada Bridgeport	61 453
Patrick	Monterey Pajaro	601020
Richard	Siskiyou Yreka	69 130
Thomas	Plumas Quincy	62 944
Wm	Calaveras Twp 10	57 294
MCALL		
William	San Francisco San Francisco 9	681041
William W	San Francisco San Francisco 9	681017
	San Francisco	
MCALLEN		
H	Mariposa Twp 3	60 565
H*	Mariposa Twp 3	60 565
J	Shasta Shasta	66 679
J C	Sonoma Armally	69 482
Thos M San Francisco San Francisco 1		68 876
MCALLERTTE		
John	San Francisco San Francisco 2	67 564
MCALLISTER		
A	San Francisco San Francisco 3	67 33

Name	County Locale	M653 RollPage
MCALLISTER		
Andrew	San Francisco San Francisco 9	681002
C	San Francisco San Francisco 6	67 473
Charles	Humbolt Pacific	59 133
D	Tehama Red Bluff	70 922
Geo	San Francisco San Francisco 9	681000
Hall*	San Francisco San Francisco 4	681231
J	Nevada Nevada	61 311
J M	Nevada Nevada	61 311
James	San Francisco San Francisco 8	681294
James	Siskiyou Yreka	69 142
Jas H	Sacramento Ward 3	63 421
Jno	Sacramento Ward 3	63 459
John	San Francisco San Francisco 11	121 67
Jones	San Joaquin Castoria	64 886
Mary	San Francisco San Francisco 9	68 956
McHall*	San Francisco San Francisco 4	681231
Richard	San Francisco San Francisco 9	68 942
W Hall*	San Francisco San Francisco 4	681231
W L	Calaveras Twp 8	57 107
Wm	San Francisco San Francisco 1	68 841
Wm F	San Francisco San Francisco 3	67 35
MCALLUSE		
Pat*	Sacramento Ward 3	63 456
MCALPEY		
A D	Trinity Weaverville	701063
MCALPIN		
Frank	San Francisco San Francisco 11	107 67
Robert	Mariposa Coulterville	60 693
Thos	Mariposa Coulterville	60 691
Thos	San Francisco San Francisco 10	236 67
Wm	Mariposa Coulterville	60 694
MCALROY		
James	San Francisco San Francisco 9	68 992
MCALTER		
W H	Sutter Nicolaus	70 837
MCAM		
Thos*	Sacramento Granite	63 258
MCAMBRIDGE		
C	Tuolumne Columbia	71 352
MCAMBRIGDE		
C	Tuolumne Twp 2	71 352
MCAMITTY		
Clint*	Siskiyou Yreka	69 191
MCAMNAW		
Daniel	Sierra Twp 5	66 918
MCANALLY		
John T	Solano Benecia	69 316
MCANAN		
Mary*	San Francisco San Francisco 10	332 67
MCANANAY		
McArthur	Yolo Cottonwoood	72 652
MCANAY		
W	El Dorado Kelsey	581153
MCANDELE		
Zedock W San Francisco San Francisco 8		681324
MCANDELL		
Zedock W*	San Francisco 8	681324
	San Francisco	
MCANDERSON		
---	Siskiyou Scott Va	69 30
William	Nevada Bloomfield	61 509
MCANDLE		
Patk	San Francisco San Francisco 2	67 794
MCANDREW		
J	Nevada Grass Valley	61 154
John	Tuolumne Columbia	71 472
Thos	San Francisco San Francisco 10	301 67
MCANDREWS		
J	Nevada Grass Valley	61 154
Pat	Tuolumne Twp 2	71 388
MCANE		
Thos*	Sacramento Granite	63 258
MCANLIES		
Norah*	Santa Cruz Pajaro	66 550
MCANLISSI		
Michael	San Joaquin Castoria	64 902
MCANN		
Wm*	San Francisco San Francisco 3	67 29
MCANNALLY		
John F San Bernardino San Bernadino		64 670
MCANSLAND		
Henry	Colusa Monroeville	57 447
MCANSLIN		
John*	Placer Rattle Snake	62 626
MCANUTTY		
Clint*	Siskiyou Yreka	69 191
MCAPEE		
Wm	Tuolumne Twp 2	71 381
MCAPIN		
James	Mendocino Arrana	60 859

Name	County Locale	M653 RollPage
MCAPPERY		
Lewis	Tuolumne Twp 1	71 268
MCAPPEY		
Bullard	Tuolumne Twp 1	71 268
MCAPPREY		
George	Tuolumne Twp 2	71 364
MCARAY		
William* San Francisco San Francisco 4		681145
MCARDEL		
Mary	Sonoma Petaluma	69 593
Zodok W San Francisco San Francisco 3		67 87
MCARDLE		
James	Fresno Twp 2	59 17
John	Santa Cruz Santa Cruz	66 628
Patk	San Francisco San Francisco 2	67 794
Thos	San Francisco San Francisco 1	68 872
Thos	San Francisco San Francisco 1	68 894
MCARDY		
G W	Nevada Bridgeport	61 484
MCARM		
Anne	Placer Virginia	62 667
MCARMSTRONG		
John	Plumas Quincy	62 951
MCARON		
John	Yolo Slate Ra	72 703
John	Yuba Slate Ro	72 703
MCAROY		
William	San Francisco San Francisco 4	681145
William*	San Francisco San Francisco 4	681145
MCARRAN		
Mary*	San Francisco San Francisco 10	332 67
P	San Francisco San Francisco 5	67 530
P*	San Francisco San Francisco 5	67 530
MCARRI		
Wm	Tuolumne Shawsfla	71 417
MCARTHERN		
Jane	Nevada Nevada	61 295
MCARTHUR		
Archibald	Siskiyou Shasta Valley	69 118
Caleb	Nevada Bloomfield	61 528
David	Nevada Nevada	61 295
F P	Calaveras Twp 8	57 53
I	San Francisco San Francisco 5	67 496
J	El Dorado Placerville	58 818
J M	Sonoma Santa Rosa	69 412
Julia	San Francisco San Francisco 10	232 67
W	Tuolumne Twp 4	71 173
MCARTHUS		
J	Nevada Nevada	61 294
MCARTNEY		
James	San Francisco San Francisco 9	68 945
MCARTY		
John	Nevada Bridgeport	61 502
MCARUN		
P	Placer Goods	62 697
MCASGALL		
A	San Francisco San Francisco 4	681230
MCATAVY		
Mary*	San Francisco San Francisco 10	165 67
MCATEE		
H	Siskiyou Yreka	69 156
J B	Sierra Whiskey	66 847
Pat	Nevada Bridgeport	61 498
William	Contra Costa Twp 1	57 500
MCATER		
James	Humbolt Eel Rvr	59 144
MCATES		
Pat	Nevada Bridgeport	61 498
MCATWITHER		
F P	Calaveras Twp 8	57 53
MCAULEY		
Arthur	Amador Twp 5	55 362
Mary	San Francisco San Francisco 11	131 67
MCAULIES		
Norah	Santa Cruz Pajaro	66 550
MCAULIF		
Dane	Trinity Big Flat	701039
MCAULIFF		
Daniel	Marin San Rafael	60 764
Florence San Francisco San Francisco 7		681350
MCAULISS		
Norah*	Santa Cruz Pajaro	66 550
MCAUSLAN		
P*	Sutter Yuba	70 763
MCAUSLIN		
John*	Placer Rattle Snake	62 626
MCAVERY		
Henry	Sonoma Petaluma	69 584
MCAVIN		
John	Sierra Twp 7	66 915
MCAVOY		
Anne	San Francisco San Francisco 2	67 574

California 1860 Census Index

Name	County Locale	M653 Roll	Page
MCAVOY			
Cath?*	Sacramento Ward 1	63	48
Cathe	Sacramento Ward 1	63	48
Cathr*	Sacramento Ward 1	63	48
Francis	San Francisco San Francisco 7	681	335
Margaret	Placer Forest H	62	769
O	Siskiyou Cottonwood	69	99
Rose	Sacramento Ward 1	63	49
William*	Siskiyou Yreka	69	151
MCAVRY			
William*	Siskiyou Yreka	69	151
MCAWEN			
A	Sacramento Sutter	63	297
MCAWY			
Michael	San Francisco San Francisco 1	68	903
MCBAIN			
Jno	Nevada Washington	61	334
MCBARNY			
Jno	Alameda Brooklyn	55	189
MCBARTY			
Edward	Calaveras Twp 5	57	216
MCBATH			
James	Plumas Quincy	62	945
MCBAYNE			
R	Shasta Shasta	66	678
MCBEAN			
Frank	Yuba Bear Rvr	721	011
I*	Nevada Washington	61	337
J	Nevada Washington	61	337
Norman	Sierra St Louis	66	805
Sparron	Mendocino Big Rvr	60	847
Sparrow	Mendocino Big Rvr	60	847
MCBEE			
B	San Francisco San Francisco 5	67	550
John G	Calaveras Twp 5	57	252
MCBEIGH			
E*	San Francisco San Francisco 9	68	945
MCBEIM			
Patrick	San Francisco San Francisco 4	681	169
MCBEINN			
Patrick*	San Francisco San Francisco 4	681	169
MCBEIRM			
Patrick*	San Francisco San Francisco 4	681	169
MCBELL			
H*	Mariposa Coulterville	60	678
MCBERRY			
Jas	Sonoma Sonoma	69	649
MCBETH			
Dan	Nevada Bridgeport	61	442
David	Sierra Twp 7	66	895
J	El Dorado Placerville	58	857
James	El Dorado White Oaks	581	020
James	Plumas Quincy	62	944
Jno	Butte Eureka	56	653
John	Plumas Quincy	62	936
R S	San Francisco San Francisco 10	166 67	
MCBEY			
Robert	Los Angeles Tejon	59	527
MCBILLIGAS			
Jose	Marin Cortemad	60	781
Jose*	Marin Cortemad	60	781
MCBILLIGIGSLEY			
H M*	Marin Cortemad	60	792
MCBILLIGRGSLEY			
H M*	Marin Cortemad	60	792
MCBILLINGSLEY			
H M*	Marin Cortemad	'60	792
MCBILLIYRGSLEY			
H M*	Marin Cortemad	60	792
MCBIRDSALE			
Jonathan	San Francisco San Francisco 11	99 67	
MCBIRNEY			
Jas	San Francisco San Francisco 10	315 67	
Jos	San Francisco San Francisco 10	315 67	
Wm	Sacramento Ward 3	63	469
MCBLAIN			
---*	Placer Auburn	62	567
MCBLAIR			
Robert	San Luis Obispo San Luis Obispo	65	23
MCBODDEN			
David	Sierra Pine Grove	66	822
Mathew*	Sierra Pine Grove	66	829
MCBOND			
R R	Sierra Downieville	66	976
MCBORDAN			
W*	Yolo Cache Crk	72	593
MCBRADLEY			
Henry	Santa Clara Alviso	65	410
MCBRALEY			
Sarah	San Francisco San Francisco 2	67	763
MCBRANNON			
Michael	Sierra Monte Crk	661	036

Name	County Locale	M653 Roll	Page
MCBRAYMAN			
Wm	San Francisco San Francisco 9	681	036
MCBRE			
Robert H	Calaveras Twp 6	57	158
MCBREAVY			
Geo B	San Francisco San Francisco 12	67	366
MCBREEN			
T	Amador Twp 1	55	498
MCBRIAN			
W	El Dorado Placerville	58	864
MCBRIDE			
---	Placer Goods	62	698
Alex	Santa Clara Redwood	65	453
Alexn	Butte Ophir	56	797
Archibald	Sierra Eureka	661	050
Barney	El Dorado Coloma	581	068
Barney	Mendocino Big Rvr	60	842
Bernard	Klamath Klamath	59	228
Cath	Sacramento Ward 4	63	562
Chas	Napa Napa	61	96
Daniel	San Mateo Twp 3	65	76
David	Santa Clara Freemont	65	416
Dennis	Tuolumne Twp 2	71	396
Edward	San Joaquin O'Neal	641	007
Francis	Klamath S Fork	59	202
Franklin	Amador Twp 3	55	390
Frederick	San Diego Colorado	64	812
Geo	Butte Bidwell	56	706
Henry	Mariposa Twp 3	60	603
Henry	Tuolumne Twp 3	71	445
Henry	Yuba Linda	72	988
Henry	Yuba Suida	72	988
Henry C	Siskiyou Yreka	69	127
Isaac B	San Joaquin Elliott	64	947
Isabella	San Francisco San Francisco 1	68	911
J	Calaveras Twp 9	57	389
J	Calaveras Twp 9	57	398
J	Stanislaus Emory	70	746
James	Calaveras Twp 4	57	326
James	El Dorado White Oaks	581	019
James	El Dorado Coloma	581	083
James	Placer Michigan	62	820
James	San Francisco San Francisco 5	67	537
Jas	San Mateo Twp 3	65	100
Jno	Butte Kimshaw	56	580
John	Calaveras Twp 8	57	108
John	Placer Auburn	62	597
John	Placer Michigan	62	855
John	Sierra Pine Grove	66	828
John	Siskiyou Callahan	69	12
Joseph	Calaveras Twp 7	57	40
Joseph	Solano Vacaville	69	358
Michael	Tuolumne Shawsfla	71	378
P	El Dorado Coloma	581	113
Patrick	Yuba Marysville	72	861
R B	El Dorado Placerville	58	862
Robert	Solano Benecia	69	296
Samuel	Solano Vacaville	69	348
Terruci	San Joaquin Douglass	64	918
Thomas	Calaveras Twp 5	57	174
Thomas	Calaveras Twp 6	57	174
Thomas	Tuolumne Sonora	71	243
Thos	Santa Clara San Jose	65	282
Thos	Sonoma Petaluma	69	617
Thos	Sonoma Vallejo	69	617
W	Stanislaus Branch	70	699
William	San Francisco San Francisco 3	67	70
MCBRIDES			
James	Calaveras Twp 4	57	326
MCBRIER			
E W	San Francisco San Francisco 2	67	579
MCBRIGHT			
Sarah	San Francisco San Francisco 1	68	893
MCBRINLY			
P	Tuolumne Twp 3	71	444
MCBROPHY			
Pat	Butte Bidwell	56	729
MCBROWN			
Aurelia C	Nevada Bloomfield	61	508
Ella	Nevada Bloomfield	61	508
John	Nevada Bloomfield	61	508
Louiza	Nevada Bloomfield	61	508
Samuel	Nevada Bloomfield	61	508
MCBRYAN			
Earls*	Alameda Oakland	55	25
MCBRYNE			
Francis	Calaveras Twp 6	57	150
Francis*	Calaveras Twp 6	57	150
MCBRYNS			
Francis*	Calaveras Twp 6	57	150
MCBURNEY			
Hamilton	Placer Todds Va	62	788
Jas	Placer Auburn	62	566
W H	Sacramento Ward 4	63	509
MCBUTH			
John	Calaveras Twp 8	57	69

Name	County Locale	M653 Roll	Page
MCCAASLAND			
Catherine*	Yuba Marysville	72	954
MCCAB			
Ellen	San Francisco San Francisco 9	681	017
MCCABA			
Barney	Sierra Twp 5	66	923
MCCABB			
Hamilton	Santa Clara San Jose	65	385
James	El Dorado Greenwood	58	724
MCCABBIN			
Thomas	Yuba Marysville	72	866
MCCABE			
---	Amador Twp 2	55	285
? T*	Napa Clear Lake	61	121
A	Santa Clara Santa Clara	65	484
A M	Nevada Eureka	61	355
Alphns B*	Napa Clear Lake	61	122
Alphus B*	Napa Clear Lake	61	122
Andrew J	San Francisco San Francisco 3	67	11
Ann	Sacramento Ward 1	63	119
Anne	Sacramento Ward 1	63	119
Chas	Sacramento Ward 1	63	34
Dennis	Tuolumne Columbia	71	304
Edward	El Dorado Eldorado	58	943
Eugene	San Francisco San Francisco 1	68	847
Henry	San Bernardino Santa Barbara	64	202
J	Nevada Eureka	61	355
J	San Francisco San Francisco 5	67	526
J	Tuolumne Twp 4	71	161
J L	Nevada Grass Valley	61	179
James	Los Angeles Los Angeles	59	369
James	Tuolumne Twp 2	71	358
James	Yuba Marysville	72	914
Jas	Sacramento Ward 4	63	562
Jas	San Francisco San Francisco 1	68	906
John	Contra Costa Twp 3	57	603
John	Nevada Bloomfield	61	507
John	San Francisco San Francisco 7	681	388
John	San Francisco San Francisco 2	67	670
John	San Joaquin Elkhorn	64	970
John	Santa Cruz Santa Cruz	66	602
John	Tuolumne Twp 1	71	241
John H	San Francisco San Francisco 3	67	17
John P	Tuolumne Sonora	71	204
M A	San Joaquin Stockton	641	093
Maria	Alameda Oakland	55	57
Mary	Sacramento Ward 1	63	115
Mary	San Francisco San Francisco 10	237 67	
Mary	Tuolumne Twp 2	71	302
Mory E	Tuolumne Columbia	71	302
Owen	Yuba Marysville	72	858
Owen	Yuba Marysvllle	72	860
P	Butte Oro	56	677
P	Napa Clear Lake	61	121
P T*	Napa Clear Lake	61	121
Patrick	Placer Michigan	62	856
Patrick	Yuba Marysville	72	968
Patrick Wm	San Francisco 2	67	611
	San Francisco		
Peter M	Shasta Shasta	66	730
Philip	Sacramento Ward 4	63	527
Richard	San Francisco San Francisco 11	95 67	
Robert	Sierra La Porte	66	788
T	Nevada Grass Valley	61	179
Thomas	Del Norte Crescent	58	643
Thomas	San Francisco San Francisco 11	149 67	
Thomas	Solano Benecia	69	295
Thomas	Yuba New York	72	736
Thomas*	Placer Michigan	62	840
MCCABLE			
Patrick	San Francisco San Francisco 2	67	612
MCCABR			
P	Butte Oro	56	677
MCCACAR			
Chas	Mariposa Twp 3	60	586
MCCACHISON			
A	Tuolumne Shawsfla	71	377
MCCADDEN			
James	Solano Vallejo	69	251
MCCADE			
Charles	Calaveras Twp 5	57	201
Dennis	Tuolumne Columbia	71	301
Edward	Tuolumne Columbia	71	301
James	Tuolumne Columbia	71	295
MCCAE			
Michael*	Calaveras Twp 6	57	183
MCCAEL			
James*	Sacramento Ward 1	63	138
MCCAETY			
D*	Nevada Eureka	61	346
MCCAFFARTY			
Pat	Nevada Bridgeport	61	496
MCCAFFEE			
J	Yolo Putah	72	560

Name	County Locale	M653 Roll	Page
MCCAFFERNAY			
Mathew*	Butte Ophir	56	781
MCCAFFERNEY			
Mathew	Butte Ophir	56	781
MCCAFFERTY			
Franklin	Humbolt Union	59	191
James	Sierra Pine Grove	66	829
John	Solano Vallejo	69	270
MCCAFFERY			
James	El Dorado Kelsey	58	1126
MCCAFFEY			
Margt	San Francisco San Francisco 2	67	716
N	Klamath Liberty	59	230
MCCAFFN			
Hugh	San Francisco San Francisco 2	67	765
MCCAFFREY			
Ed	Sacramento Ward 4	63	603
F	San Francisco San Francisco 12	67	394
H	Solano Vacaville	69	343
Hugh	San Bernardino Santa Barbara	64	154
James	San Bernardino Santa Barbara	64	177
James	Sierra La Porte	66	767
John	Solano Vallejo	69	266
Peter	Sierra Pine Grove	66	835
Th	Solano Vacaville	69	343
MCCAFFRY			
Bernard	Los Angeles Azuza	59	272
Hugh	San Francisco San Francisco 2	67	765
MCCAFFY			
Thomas	San Francisco San Francisco 7	68	1334
MCCAFPEY			
Michael	Nevada Bridgeport	61	495
MCCAFPREY			
John*	Solano Vallejo	69	266
MCCAFRAY			
Frank	Sierra Pine Grove	66	835
Peter	Sierra Pine Grove	66	835
MCCAFREY			
Michael	Nevada Bridgeport	61	495
MCCAGIN			
James	Nevada Bloomfield	61	513
MCCAGNE			
Robert*	Placer Auburn	62	561
MCCAGUE			
Robert*	Placer Auburn	62	561
MCCAHILL			
Anthony	San Francisco San Francisco 11	67	89
T	Nevada Eureka	61	387
Taaffe	Siskiyou Scott Va	69	42
Tarffe	Siskiyou Scott Va	69	42
MCCAID			
James	Yuba Marysville	72	901
John*	Mariposa Twp 3	60	617
MCCAIE			
James S*	Nevada Bridgeport	61	493
James*	Nevada Bridgeport	61	484
MCCAIF			
George	Sierra Pine Grove	66	834
William G	Sierra Pine Grove	66	834
MCCAIG			
James	San Joaquin Elliott	64	942
John*	Mariposa Twp 3	60	617
MCCAIL			
James	Sacramento Ward 1	63	138
James*	Sacramento Ward 1	63	138
MCCAIN			
Geo	Mendocino Big Rock	60	874
Geo W	Mendocino Big Rock	60	874
J	Shasta Millvill	66	756
J S	Trinity E Weaver	70	1061
James	San Joaquin Stockton	64	1079
Jas	San Francisco San Francisco 9	68	1071
John	Nevada Washington	61	331
John	Nevada Washington	61	341
John	Placer Forest H	62	769
John	Tehama Tehama	70	935
Jos	Sacramento Natonia	63	273
Jos	San Francisco San Francisco 9	68	1071
Timothy	Nevada Bridgeport	61	504
William	Nevada Red Dog	61	539
William G	Sierra Pine Grove	66	834
William G*	Sierra Pine Grove	66	834
MCCAINE			
Anna*	Sacramento Ward 1	63	140
Birdsall	Placer Sacramento	62	642
MCCAINEN			
John	Sierra Downieville	66	1030
MCCAINIS			
Martin*	Yuba New York	72	731
MCCAINLEY			
S	El Dorado Placerville	58	843
MCCAINSLAND			
H O	Tuolumne Twp 2	71	368
MCCAIRN			
Pat*	Mariposa Twp 3	60	593

Name	County Locale	M653 Roll	Page
MCCAISH			
James	Santa Cruz Pajaro	66	542
MCCAITY			
D	Nevada Eureka	61	372
John	Butte Bidwell	56	714
MCCAL			
James*	Mariposa Twp 3	60	609
MCCALA			
J	Nevada Grass Valley	61	154
MCCALAHAN			
John	Yuba Bear Rvr	72	1011
MCCALANCH			
Thos*	Nevada Red Dog	61	544
MCCALAND			
Robert*	Sierra Twp 7	66	879
MCCALARD			
Robert	Sierra Twp 7	66	879
MCCALASH			
S	Calaveras Twp 9	57	403
MCCALAUD			
Robert*	Sierra Twp 7	66	879
MCCALDWELL			
J	Tuolumne Twp 1	71	482
MCCALE			
John	Yolo Cache	72	642
John*	Santa Cruz Santa Cruz	66	602
John*	Santa Cruz Santa Cruz	66	635
Peer	Solano Benecia	69	304
Peter	Solano Benecia	69	304
Thomas*	Yuba New York	72	736
MCCALEC			
P T*	Napa Clear Lake	61	121
MCCALER			
? T*	Napa Clear Lake	61	121
Alphus B*	Napa Clear Lake	61	122
L T*	Napa Clear Lake	61	121
P	Butte Oro	56	677
MCCALEY			
Jno A	Sacramento Sutter	63	294
MCCALIC			
Alphus B*	Napa Clear Lake	61	122
P T*	Napa Clear Lake	61	121
MCCALIVIRA			
Jose	Los Angeles Los Angeles	59	517
MCCALL			
A	Santa Clara Redwood	65	450
Edward	San Mateo Twp 3	65	73
F	Yolo Cache Crk	72	612
F G	Shasta Horsetown	66	700
George	Yolo Cache	72	613
J	Nevada Nevada	61	290
J	Tehama Antelope	70	890
J I	El Dorado Placerville	58	888
J W	El Dorado Placerville	58	889
Jno	Mendocino Calpella	60	810
John	El Dorado Big Bar	58	735
John	Nevada Rough &	61	404
John	Santa Cruz Santa Cruz	66	602
John	Santa Cruz Santa Cruz	66	635
John	Yuba Bear Rvr	72	1000
John	Yuba Bear Rvr	72	1012
John*	Santa Cruz Santa Cruz	66	602
John*	Santa Cruz Santa Cruz	66	635
Mary	San Francisco San Francisco 4	68	1114
Michael	San Francisco San Francisco 2	67	650
P	Shasta Shasta	66	685
Patrick	Placer Iona Hills	62	866
Phillip M	El Dorado Big Bar	58	735
Robert	San Joaquin Elkhorn	64	962
S E S	Yolo Cache	72	597
Soloman	El Dorado White Oaks	58	1018
Thomas	El Dorado Big Bar	58	735
Thomas*	Yuba New York	72	736
W R	San Francisco San Francisco 3	67	74
MCCALLA			
John	Solano Vallejo	69	245
MCCALLAHAN			
A	Butte Chico	56	561
A K	Nevada Nevada	61	324
A R	Nevada Nevada	61	324
MCCALLAHAW			
A	Butte Chico	56	561
MCCALLAIN			
Robert	Placer Forest H	62	792
MCCALLAM			
Jesse*	Yuba Marysville	72	947
MCCALLAN			
Daniel	Plumas Quincy	62	995
Edwd	San Francisco San Francisco 10	67	219
Nathan*	Placer Michigan	62	852
MCCALLAND			
Robert	Tulara Twp 3	71	45
MCCALLASTER			
John	Calaveras Twp 8	57	88
MCCALLAUGH			
T D	Tuolumne Twp 1	71	251

Name	County Locale	M653 Roll	Page
MCCALLEEM			
Jesse*	Yuba Marysville	72	947
MCCALLEN			
D W	Alameda Brooklyn	55	128
John	Calaveras Twp 5	57	186
Patk	Butte Ophir	56	789
MCCALLER			
Wm	Tehama Pasakent	70	860
MCCALLESTER			
Bridget	Alameda Oakland	55	9
MCCALLIER			
Jas	Placer Rattle Snake	62	631
MCCALLIFF			
M	Nevada Nevada	61	246
MCCALLIFFE			
John	Plumas Quincy	62	1000
MCCALLIN			
L C	Siskiyou Callahan	69	9
MCCALLISH			
Geo	Amador Twp 5	55	338
MCCALLISTER			
E	Shasta Shasta	66	678
J	Nevada Nevada	61	258
John	Marin San Rafael	60	759
John	Siskiyou Yreka	69	169
Robert	Sierra Twp 7	66	913
Robert*	Sierra Twp 7	66	913
MCCALLOCH			
Jno	San Francisco San Francisco 10	67	248
MCCALLOM			
Geo N	Calaveras Twp 6	57	160
Geo W	Calaveras Twp 6	57	160
Mily	Tehama Red Bluff	70	918
MCCALLON			
L C*	Siskiyou Callahan	69	9
MCCALLOUGH			
Calvin	Tuolumne Twp 1	71	187
William	Yuba Marysville	72	971
MCCALLUM			
Daniel	Mariposa Twp 1	60	652
David M	Solano Fairfield	69	199
David*	Solano Fairfield	69	199
J	Calaveras Twp 9	57	400
James	Placer Michigan	62	856
Jesse	Yuba Marysville	72	947
MCCALLY			
Jno	San Francisco San Francisco 10	67	200
Michael	San Mateo Twp 3	65	76
MCCALMENT			
O P	Sacramento Ward 3	63	460
MCCALNY			
J J	Yolo Cache Crk	72	624
MCCALOUGH			
Elen A*	Siskiyou Yreka	69	139
MCCALU			
George*	Placer Yankee J	62	760
MCCALVOY			
J J	Yolo Cache	72	624
MCCALVRY			
Jno S	Sacramento Georgian	63	335
MCCALVY			
G W	Yolo Cache Crk	72	639
MCCAM			
Born*	Placer Ophirville	62	658
Jas*	Placer Secret R	62	612
MCCAMA			
Major*	Mendocino Little L	60	839
MCCAMACK			
A	Nevada Eureka	61	387
MCCAMBLIN			
W	Sacramento Granite	63	230
MCCAMBRIDGE			
J*	Nevada Eureka	61	380
MCCAMCE			
Major*	Mendocino Little L	60	839
MCCAME			
Anna*	Sacramento Ward 1	63	140
W S*	Mariposa Twp 1	60	650
MCCAMEE			
Major	Mendocino Little L	60	839
MCCAMELL			
William	Siskiyou Yreka	69	184
MCCAMISH			
James	Santa Cruz Pajaro	66	542
MCCAMLEY			
George	Contra Costa Twp 2	57	573
MCCAMMON			
John	Trinity S Fork	70	1032
MCCAMON			
Robert	Plumas Quincy	62	990
MCCAMP			
M	El Dorado Coloma	58	1071
MCCAMPBELL			
Jas H	Trinity Red Bar	70	998

California 1860 Census Index

Name	County Locale	M653 Roll Page		Name	County Locale	M653 Roll Page		Name	County Locale	M653 Roll Page
MCCAMPBELL				**MCCANN**				**MCCANSLAND**		
Wm	Sonoma Armally	69 487		Born*	Placer Ophirville	62 658		James	Marin Tomales	60 716
MCCAMR				Charles	San Francisco San Francisco 4	681172		Robert	Solano Fremont	69 376
W S	Mariposa Twp 1	60 650		Con	Plumas Quincy	621002		**MCCANSLOW**		
MCCAMTY				E D	San Francisco San Francisco 10	331		Frank	Yuba Marysville	72 864
H	Sacramento Granite	63 227				67		**MCCANTEY**		
MCCAN				E T	El Dorado Placerville	58 914		Jas	Yolo Cache	72 620
---	Amador Twp 5	55 346		E*	Nevada Grass Valley	61 145		Margaret*	Nevada Red Dog	61 542
Barney	Sierra Port Win	66 795		Edward	Placer Forest H	62 798		Peter	Santa Clara Santa Clara	65 507
F	Placer Dutch Fl	62 714		Eliza	San Francisco San Francisco 4	681172		**MCCANTHY**		
H	Shasta Horsetown	66 703		Ends*	Tuolumne Big Oak	71 139		Timothy	San Joaquin Oneal	64 938
James	Tuolumne Twp 4	71 129		Erid	Tuolumne Twp 4	71 139		**MCCANTRY**		
James*	Tuolumne Big Oak	71 129		Eud*	Tuolumne Big Oak	71 139		John	Marin Cortemad	60 752
Jas	Yolo Cache	72 606		Frances	Solano Benecia	69 291		**MCCANTS**		
Margrette	Amador Twp 2	55 285		Francis	Solano Benecia	69 291		Thos*	Sacramento Ward 4	63 586
William	Solano Fremont	69 379		Fredk	San Francisco San Francisco 10	259		**MCCANTY**		
Wm*	Calaveras Twp 9	57 369				67		Danl*	Calaveras Twp 10	57 283
MCCANADY				George	Alameda Brooklyn	55 92		**MCCAPIN**		
John	Tuolumne Columbia	71 472		Harrison	Colusa Grand Island	57 481		James	Sonoma Salt Point	69 690
John	Tuolumne Twp 2	71 472		Henry	Sacramento Ward 3	63 429		**MCCAR**		
MCCANAGHER				Henry	Sacramento Ward 3	63 430		M	Shasta French G	66 714
John*	Sacramento Ward 1	63 92		J	San Francisco San Francisco 9	681061		Michael*	Calaveras Twp 6	57 183
MCCANAHO				J	Siskiyou Klamath	69 90		**MCCARA**		
M	Amador Twp 6	55 422		James	Placer Forest H	62 792		Janet	Sacramento Ward 3	63 442
MCCANANT				James	Stanislaus Buena Village	70 724		**MCCARAGAN**		
Lewis*	Solano Vacaville	69 366		James	Tuolumne Twp 3	71 444		Wm	Plumas Quincy	621007
MCCANBS				James	Yuba Marysville	72 907		**MCCARAGHER**		
A M*	Shasta Millvill	66 754		James	Yuba Marysville	72 960		John	Sacramento Ward 1	63 92
MCCANDLE				Jams	Yuba Marysville	72 907		John*	Sacramento Ward 1	63 92
Avon	Sacramento Natonia	63 286		Jas	San Francisco San Francisco 9	681079		**MCCARBE**		
MCCANE				Jno	Nevada Nevada	61 282		J	Nevada Eureka	61 355
J A C*	Solano Montezuma	69 375		John	Alameda Oakland	55 13		**MCCARBY**		
James	Marin Cortemad	60 779		John	Calaveras Twp 5	57 228		Wm*	San Francisco San Francisco 3	67 85
James M*	Yuba Marysville	72 847		John	Del Norte Klamath	58 655		**MCCARD**		
Levi	Tehama Antelope	70 887		John	Placer Secret R	62 620		S	Nevada Eureka	61 381
Mike	Butte Cascade	56 690		John	Santa Clara Alviso	65 396		**MCCARDEL**		
Philip	Yuba Marysville	72 862		John	Tuolumne Twp 2	71 334		Denis	Nevada Rough &	61 433
Phillip	Yuba Marysville	72 862		John B	Tuolumne Twp 3	71 443		**MCCARDELL**		
MCCANEE				John F	Solano Benecia	69 291		Michael	Stanislaus Empire	70 732
Stephen	Yuba Marysville	72 965		John*	Calaveras Twp 5	57 228		**MCCARDELLI**		
MCCANHUR				Jos	Sacramento Natonia	63 273		B M	Nevada Grass Valley	61 193
J A	San Francisco San Francisco 1	68 929		Julius	Tuolumne Twp 3	71 443		**MCCARDIE**		
MCCANIHAY				M	Nevada Eureka	61 373		Benj F	Sonoma Mendocino	69 451
S W	Placer Goods	62 694		M	Tuolumne Shawsfla	71 411		**MCCARDLE**		
MCCANLEY				Michael	San Francisco San Francisco 12	394		Annie	San Francisco San Francisco 10	185
Alexander	Yuba Suida	72 982				67				67
Alexander	Yuba Linda Twp	72 983		P	Sacramento Ward 1	63 144		Jno	Klamath Liberty	59 240
C A*	Siskiyou Callahan	69 10		P M	Sacramento Ward 1	63 144		Michael	Tuolumne Columbia	71 352
C H*	Siskiyou Callahan	69 10		Pat	Mariposa Twp 3	60 593		Oron*	Sacramento Natonia	63 286
Caroline	San Francisco San Francisco 10	233		Pat	Mendocino Big Rvr	60 843		Ower*	Sacramento Natonia	63 286
		67		Pat	Mendocino Round Va	60 879		Phillip	San Francisco San Francisco 2	67 805
Charles	Marin Bolinas	60 728		Pat*	Mariposa Twp 3	60 593		**MCCARDY**		
D	Nevada Nevada	61 316		Patrick	Tuolumne Columbla	71 353		Elesha	Yuba Marysville	72 892
H H	Butte Kimshaw	56 575		Patrick	Tuolumne Columbia	71 357		Elisha	Nevada Little Y	61 536
James	Alameda Brooklyn	55 108		Peter	San Francisco San Francisco 11	139		Elisha	Yuba Marysville	72 892
James	Nevada Rough &	61 419				67		J F	Nevada Bridgeport	61 447
James	San Francisco San Francisco 7	681333		Phillip	Solano Benecia	69 294		J F*	Nevada Bridgeport	61 447
James*	Nevada Rough &	61 419		Robert	Solano Vallejo	69 247		**MCCARE**		
Jas	Yolo Cache Crk	72 620		Stephen	Yuba Marysville	72 965		James S*	Nevada Bridgeport	61 493
John F	Marin Cortemad	60 752		Tho	Siskiyou Klamath	69 90		James*	Nevada Bridgeport	61 484
M M	Stanislaus Emory	70 741		Thomas	Placer Michigan	62 841		John*	San Francisco San Francisco 5	67 546
Margaret	Yuba Marysville	72 953		Thomas	San Francisco San Francisco 5	67 494		**MCCAREN**		
Margaret*	Nevada Red Dog	61 542		Thomas	Sierra Downieville	66 962		Mary	San Francisco San Francisco 10	331
Mary*	Sacramento Ward 1	63 117		Thomas*	Siskiyou Yreka	69 152				67
R R*	Butte Oregon	56 632		W S	Mariposa Twp 1	60 650		**MCCARESLAND**		
Samuel	Yuba Marysville	72 976		W S*	Mariposa Twp 1	60 650		H O*	Tuolumne Columbia	71 357
T J	San Francisco San Francisco 10	206		Wm	Calaveras Twp 5	57 227		**MCCARGO**		
		67		Wm	Tuolumne Twp 1	71 185		Jno	Butte Kimshaw	56 589
W	Yuba Bear Rvr	721009		Wm L	Tuolumne Sonora	71 185		**MCCARIS**		
MCCANLIF				Wm R	Colusa Grand Island	57 471		Jno	Tehama Antelope	70 886
John	Trinity Oregon G	701008		**MCCANNA**				**MCCARITY**		
MCCANLIFF				John	Shasta French G	66 720		Danl*	Calaveras Twp 10	57 283
M	Nevada Eureka	61 364		Major*	Mendocino Little L	60 839		**MCCARL**		
R*	Nevada Eureka	61 364		Mary	Sacramento Ward 4	63 568		James*	Sacramento Ward 1	63 138
MCCANLIFFE				**MCCANNAHA**				M	Sacramento Brighton	63 194
P B	Santa Clara Santa Clara	65 514		J B	El Dorado Casumnes	581165		**MCCARLE**		
MCCANLLEY				**MCCANNEL**				Charles	Calaveras Twp 5	57 201
Ca*	Sacramento Dry Crk	63 369		F*	Butte Chico	56 534		Terance	Tuolumne Shawsfla	71 404
Geo*	Sacramento Dry Crk	63 369		**MCCANNELL**				**MCCARLEY**		
H*	Nevada Eureka	61 370		William	Siskiyou Yreka	69 184		John	Shasta Shasta	66 759
MCCANLLY				**MCCANNON**				**MCCARLIN**		
Joseph	Sonoma Bodega	69 524		John M	Trinity S Fork	701032		John	Alameda Oakland	55 48
MCCANLY				**MCCANNY**				**MCCARLIST**		
Cath*	San Francisco San Francisco 6	67 423		Francis	San Francisco San Francisco 2	67 621		T	Sutter Sutter	70 810
Daniel*	Tuolumne Twp 6	71 531		**MCCANOL**				**MCCARLS**		
John	San Francisco San Francisco 1	68 913		D O	Butte Kimshaw	56 571		Edward	San Francisco San Francisco 3	67 21
Margaret*	Yuba Marysville	72 953		**MCCANORA**				**MCCARLY**		
Thomas	Marin Cortemad	60 781		John*	Shasta French G	66 720		Mary	Alameda Brooklyn	55 89
Thomas*	Marin Cortemad	60 781		**MCCANSELAND**				**MCCARM**		
MCCANN				W P*	Butte Kimshaw	56 591		Jno	Nevada Nevada	61 282
---	San Francisco San Francisco 7	681357		**MCCANSLAN**				Pat*	Mariposa Twp 3	60 593
A	Tuolumne Twp 4	71 170		Peter	Yuba Marysville	72 861		**MCCARMEL**		
Ann	San Francisco San Francisco 10	339		William	Yuba Marysville	72 861		F*	Butte Chico	56 534
		67		**MCCANSLAND**				**MCCARMMACK**		
Ann E	Sonoma Mendocino	69 455		Catherine	Yuba Marysville	72 954		Joseph	Nevada Bloomfield	61 513
B	San Joaquin Stockton	641028		D*	El Dorado Gold Hill	581095		**MCCARN**		
								E	Nevada Grass Valley	61 145

California 1860 Census Index

Name	County Locale	M653 Roll	Page
MCCARN			
Jas*	Placer Secret R	62	612
Timothy	Nevada Bridgeport	61	504
MCCARNA			
Major*	Mendocino Little L	60	839
MCCARNE			
Anna*	Sacramento Ward 1	63	140
MCCAROL			
James	Marin San Rafael	60	763
MCCARR			
---	San Francisco San Francisco 3	67	13
Barney	Sierra Port Win	66	793
Dennis	San Francisco San Francisco 4	681	167
James*	Tuolumne Big Oak	71	129
Samuel	Contra Costa Twp 3	57	586
Wm	Calaveras Twp 9	57	369
MCCARRAH			
Wm	Sacramento Ward 1	63	83
MCCARRANT			
Lewis*	Solano Vacaville	69	366
MCCARRE			
E*	Nevada Grass Valley	61	145
MCCARRI			
Robt	Tuolumne Twp 2	71	417
Thomas	Tuolumne Twp 2	71	417
Wm	Tuolumne Twp 2	71	417
MCCARRICK			
Bridget	San Francisco San Francisco 10	67	204
P	San Francisco San Francisco 5	67	476
P M	San Francisco San Francisco 5	67	476
MCCARROL			
D O*	Butte Kimshaw	56	571
Henry	Calaveras Twp 4	57	328
MCCARROLL			
Bernard	San Francisco San Francisco 10	67	168
Francis	Sacramento Ward 1	63	27
James	Yuba Marysville	72	904
Jas H	Sacramento Ward 3	63	459
MCCARRON			
R*	Nevada Eureka	61	390
MCCARRTY			
Chal	Calaveras Twp 10	57	283
MCCARRY			
M A*	Tuolumne Columbia	71	304
Nelson	Placer Rattle Snake	62	630
MCCARSON			
James	El Dorado Georgetown	58	706
Thos	Sacramento Ward 1	63	118
MCCART			
Joseph	Sacramento Dry Crk	63	370
Perry	Placer Michigan	62	854
MCCARTEN			
A B*	Siskiyou Scott Va	69	44
MCCARTER			
J L	Calaveras Twp 9	57	366
John	San Francisco San Francisco 2	67	675
Joseph	Sierra Twp 7	66	867
Jsoeph	Sierra Twp 7	66	867
Mike	Sonoma Petaluma	69	599
P L	Calaveras Twp 9	57	366
MCCARTEY			
C	Trinity Oregon G	701	008
Dennis	Trinity State Ba	701	001
Gellis	Trinity Mouth Ca	701	013
Gillis	Trinity Mouth Ca	701	013
J C	Trinity State Ba	701	001
Jas	Napa Napa	61	109
Margaret*	Nevada Red Dog	61	542
William	San Francisco San Francisco 11	67	143
MCCARTH			
Danl	San Francisco San Francisco 1	68	893
MCCARTHA			
John	San Francisco San Francisco 10	67	291
MCCARTHER			
Joseph	Contra Costa Twp 3	57	588
MCCARTHEY			
Daniel	Los Angeles Los Angeles	59	511
John	Santa Cruz Soguel	66	584
John	Siskiyou Callahan	69	10
Thos	Amador Twp 6	55	425
MCCARTHY			
Anges	San Francisco San Francisco 1	68	910
Anne	Humbolt Eureka	59	171
Cath	Sacramento Ward 4	63	530
Charles	Sierra Cox'S Bar	66	952
Charley	Sierra Twp 7	66	864
D	San Francisco San Francisco 3	67	48
D	San Francisco San Francisco 3	67	49
D	Santa Clara Gilroy	65	239
D D	Tuolumne Sonora	71	222
D O	Tuolumne Twp 1	71	222
Daniel	Yuba Marysville	72	928
MCCARTHY			
David	Calaveras Twp 7	57	15
David	Calaveras Twp 5	57	171
David	Calaveras Twp 6	57	171
Dennis	Sacramento Georgian	63	336
E	Tuolumne Twp 4	71	148
Egune	San Francisco San Francisco 7	681	424
Elizabeth	Sierra Twp 7	66	910
Ellen	San Francisco San Francisco 2	67	681
Eugene	San Francisco San Francisco 2	67	641
Eugene	San Francisco San Francisco 2	67	715
H M	Solano Vacaville	69	342
J	Santa Clara San Jose	65	290
James	Tuolumne Twp 3	71	465
Jeremiah	Solano Vacaville	69	342
Jerry	San Francisco San Francisco 2	67	660
Jno	Sacramento Ward 4	63	508
John	Calaveras Twp 5	57	201
John	San Joaquin O'Neal	641	005
John	Santa Cruz Soguel	66	584
John	Tuolumne Montezuma	71	509
Joseph	Santa Clara Redwood	65	460
Juana	Monterey Alisal	601	036
Kate	San Francisco San Francisco 7	67	716
M	San Francisco San Francisco 5	67	491
M	San Francisco San Francisco 5	67	502
M	Tuolumne Big Oak	71	148
Martha	Sacramento Ward 4	63	571
Nelly	San Francisco San Francisco 3	67	57
Nicholas	Santa Cruz Pajaro	66	570
Nicolas	Santa Cruz Pajaro	66	570
Owen	Sacramento Georgian	63	347
P M	San Francisco San Francisco 10	67	181
P M Sister	San Francisco 10	67	181
	San Francisco		
P M Sister	San Francisco 10	67	181
	San Francisco		
Patrick	San Francisco San Francisco 3	67	31
Peter	Fresno Twp 1	59	83
Robt D	Sacramento Ward 4	63	513
Rosa	San Francisco San Francisco 4	681	129
Samuel	San Francisco San Francisco 3	67	61
Sister P M*	San Francisco 10	67	181
	San Francisco		
Thomas	Fresno Twp 1	59	76
Timothy	Santa Clara San Jose	65	383
William	Marin Cortemad	60	781
Winnie W	Alameda Brooklyn	55	211
Wm	San Francisco San Francisco 5	67	479
MCCARTIN			
A B*	Siskiyou Scott Va	69	44
James	Solano Suisan	69	213
MCCARTLY			
Michael*	San Francisco San Francisco 1	68	920
MCCARTNEY			
A M	Butte Chico	56	532
And	Klamath Liberty	59	242
B F	Sacramento Cosumnes	63	382
Bernard	Calaveras Twp 5	57	172
Bernard	Calaveras Twp 6	57	172
Cyrus	San Francisco San Francisco 8	681	300
Cyrus*	San Francisco San Francisco 8	681	300
D J	Siskiyou Scott Ri	69	76
Daniel	Siskiyou Scott Ri	69	65
Edward	Placer Stewart	62	605
Edward	Yuba Marysville	72	869
Geo F	Butte Chico	56	534
James	Plumas Meadow Valley	62	912
James	Santa Clara Alviso	65	401
James	Santa Clara Alviso	65	410
James	Santa Clara Santa Clara	65	497
Jas	Butte Chico	56	561
John	San Francisco San Francisco 9	681	098
John	Yuba Marysville	72	901
Mary	San Francisco San Francisco 3	67	66
Mary M	San Francisco San Francisco 1	68	893
Samuel	Sierra Downieville	66	995
Thomas*	Yuba Rose Bar	72	801
Thos	Sacramento Cosumnes	63	402
William	San Francisco San Francisco 9	68	952
William J	Yuba Marysville	72	934
Wm	Sierra Downieville	66	953
MCCARTON			
A B*	Siskiyou Scott Va	69	44
MCCARTWRIGHT			
Hiram*	Yuba Bear Rvr	721	001
MCCARTY			
---	San Francisco San Francisco 7	681	336
---	Yolo Cottonwood	72	668
A	Amador Twp 1	55	488
A P	Yolo Cottonwoood	72	652
Alex	Amador Twp 2	55	301
Alexander	Placer Iona Hills	62	894
Alexander	San Joaquin Elkhorn	64	952
Alfred	El Dorado Coloma	581	104
MCCARTY			
Andrew	Yolo Slate Ra	72	689
Ann	Shasta French G	66	715
Anna	San Francisco San Francisco 5	67	543
Anne	Solano Suisan	69	218
Barnard	Sierra Port Win	66	794
Bridge	San Francisco San Francisco 8	681	306
Bridget	San Francisco San Francisco 8	681	306
C	El Dorado White Oaks	581	027
C	Mariposa Twp 3	60	549
Charles	Calaveras Twp 4	57	304
Charles	San Francisco San Francisco 7	681	363
Charles	Tuolumne Big Oak	71	132
Charles	Tuolumne Twp 3	71	445
Chas	Placer Dutch Fl	62	734
Chas	San Francisco San Francisco 1	68	830
Chas	Sonoma Sonoma	69	642
Cornelia	San Francisco San Francisco 10	67	340
Cornelius	San Francisco San Francisco 8	681	239
D	Nevada Grass Valley	61	155
D	Nevada Grass Valley	61	170
D	Nevada Nevada	61	264
D	Nevada Eureka	61	346
D	Nevada Eureka	61	372
D	Nevada Rough &	61	427
D	Sacramento Ward 1	63	2
D	Tuolumne Twp 4	71	137
D*	Nevada Eureka	61	346
Daniel	Los Angeles Los Angeles	59	354
Daniel	San Joaquin Elkhorn	64	996
Danl	San Francisco San Francisco 9	681	086
Danl J	San Francisco San Francisco 10	67	254
David	Calaveras Twp 6	57	111
David	San Francisco San Francisco 7	681	394
Denis	Nevada Bridgeport	61	489
Denis	Nevada Little Y	61	531
Denis	Placer Secret R	62	624
Dennis	Contra Costa Twp 1	57	527
Dennis	Klamath Liberty	59	240
Dennis	Placer Auburn	62	565
Dennis	Sacramento Ward 3	63	432
Dennis	San Francisco San Francisco 3	67	48
Dennis	San Francisco San Francisco 1	68	851
Dennis	Solano Suisan	69	210
Dennis	Solano Benecia	69	285
Dennis	Tuolumne Jamestown	71	469
E	Calaveras Twp 9	57	400
E	Nevada Grass Valley	61	204
E	San Francisco San Francisco 6	67	453
Ed	Sacramento Ward 4	63	573
Edward	Los Angeles Los Angeles	59	339
Edward D	Yuba Marysville	72	931
Eliza	Solano Benecia	69	293
Eliza	Sonoma Petaluma	69	586
Ellen	San Francisco San Francisco 2	67	776
Ellen	Solano Benecia	69	295
Eugene	El Dorado White Oaks	581	020
F	Nevada Eureka	61	343
F	Nevada Eureka	61	344
F	Tuolumne Twp 4	71	158
Felix	Nevada Eureka	61	360
Florance	Tuolumne Columbia	71	362
Florence	San Francisco San Francisco 10	67	247
Frank	Mariposa Twp 1	60	638
Frank	San Francisco San Francisco 2	67	785
H	Nevada Nevada	61	292
Hannah	San Francisco San Francisco 9	68	960
Henry	Sonoma Sonoma	69	635
Honora	Alameda Brooklyn	55	177
Honora	Contra Costa Twp 1	57	534
Huey	Solano Green Valley	69	242
J	Butte Oregon	56	618
J	Nevada Grass Valley	61	203
J	Nevada Grass Valley	61	225
J	Nevada Eureka	61	361
J	Nevada Eureka	61	391
J	Sacramento Cosumnes	63	399
J	San Francisco San Francisco 2	67	766
J	Tuolumne Jacksonville	71	164
J	Tuolumne Twp 4	71	164
J C	Solano Benecia	69	315
J D	Sacramento Brighton	63	194
James	Nevada Rough &	61	421
James	San Francisco San Francisco 11	67	149
James	San Francisco San Francisco 9	68	938
James	Santa Clara Santa Clara	65	495
Jas	Butte Mountain	56	733
Jas	Sacramento Ward 1	63	79
Jas	San Francisco San Francisco 12	67	385
Jason	Placer Secret R	62	619
Jeramah*	Sonoma Petaluma	69	600

California 1860 Census Index

Name	County Locale	M653 Roll	Page
MCCARTY			
Jeremiah	Calaveras Twp 4	57	304
Jeremiah	Klamath Orleans	59	216
Jeremiah	San Francisco San Francisco 8	681	248
Jeremiah	San Francisco San Francisco 8	681	303
Jeremiah	San Francisco San Francisco 1	68	861
Jeremiah	Sonoma Petaluma	69	600
Jerimiah*	Sonoma Petaluma	69	600
Jerre	Trinity Whites Crk	701	028
Jerry	Sacramento Ward 4	63	603
Jerry	San Francisco San Francisco 9	681	031
Jerry	San Francisco San Francisco 2	67	662
Jerry	San Francisco San Francisco 9	68	960
Jerry	Tuolumne Columbia	71	359
Jerry	Tuolumne Shawsfla	71	377
Jerry	Tuolumne Twp 3	71	460
Jim	Tehama Tehama	70	937
Jno	Alameda Brooklyn	55	98
Jno	San Francisco San Francisco 10	209 67	
Jno	Tehama Antelope	70	886
Joana	San Francisco San Francisco 2	67	673
Johl	Siskiyou Yreka	69	148
John	Butte Bidwell	56	714
John	Marin Bolinas	60	741
John	Mariposa Twp 3	60	604
John	Napa Napa	61	113
John	Napa Hot Springs	61	3
John	Placer Dutch Fl	62	724
John	Placer Michigan	62	824
John	Placer Michigan	62	836
John	San Francisco San Francisco 9	681	033
John	San Francisco San Francisco 4	681	169
John	San Francisco San Francisco 8	681	253
John	San Francisco San Francisco 8	681	258
John	San Francisco San Francisco 7	681	394
John	San Francisco San Francisco 7	681	421
John	San Francisco San Francisco 7	681	424
John	San Francisco San Francisco 10	172 67	
John	San Francisco San Francisco 10	291 67	
John	San Francisco San Francisco 2	67	621
John	San Francisco San Francisco 2	67	650
John	San Francisco San Francisco 3	67	84
John	San Francisco San Francisco 1	68	895
John	Sierra Downieville	66	971
John	Siskiyou Yreka	69	148
John	Solano Vallejo	69	255
John	Trinity Oregon G	701	008
John	Tuolumne Twp 1	71	247
John	Tuolumne Columbia	71	308
John	Yuba Marysville	72	896
John*	San Francisco San Francisco 10	291 67	
Jonothan	Sacramento Ward 4	63	547
Jos	Sacramento Ward 1	63	78
Julia	Alameda Brooklyn	55	210
Julia	San Francisco San Francisco 10	350 67	
Kate	Sacramento Ward 1	63	111
Kate	Sacramento Ward 3	63	456
Luke	San Francisco San Francisco 11	148 67	
M	San Francisco San Francisco 6	67	464
M	San Francisco San Francisco 5	67	524
M	Shasta French G	66	718
Margt	San Francisco San Francisco 9	681	014
Martin	Santa Clara Redwood	65	446
Mary	Solano Vallejo	69	278
Mary Ann	Alameda Brooklyn	55	89
Mary E	Yolo Cottonwood	72	653
Mary E	Yuba Marysville	72	888
Mathew	Placer Auburn	62	588
Michael	Sacramento Ward 4	63	500
Michael	San Francisco San Francisco 7	681	363
Michael	Solano Suisan	69	204
Michael	Tuolumne Montezuma	71	509
Mike	Sonoma Petaluma	69	599
Morgan	Tuolumne Columbia	71	295
Morgan B	Los Angeles Los Angeles	59	356
O F	Alameda Oakland	55	75
P	El Dorado Placerville	58	856
P	San Joaquin Stockton	641	094
P*	Nevada Grass Valley	61	151
Pat	Nevada Little Y	61	537
Pat	Nevada Red Dog	61	537
Pat	Tehama Red Bluff	70	926
Pat	Tehama Tehama	70	939
Patrick	San Francisco San Francisco 10	179 67	
Patrick	Tuolumne Twp 2	71	308
Peter	Contra Costa Twp 3	57	602
Peter	Solano Vallejo	69	273
Redmond	San Francisco San Francisco 10	319 67	
MCCARTY			
Richard	Solano Suisan	69	219
Robert	Solano Suisan	69	227
Robt	Sonoma Vallejo	69	624
Sarah	Solano Suisan	69	212
T	Nevada Eureka	61	391
T S	Marin Bolinas	60	744
Tho	Sonoma Petaluma	69	600
Thomas	Calaveras Twp 8	57	65
Thomas	San Joaquin Douglass	64	916
Thomas	San Joaquin Douglass	64	922
Thos	Calaveras Twp 8	57	88
Thos	Nevada Eureka	61	349
Thos	Nevada Bridgeport	61	486
Thos	Sacramento Ward 4	63	553
Timothy	Alameda Brooklyn	55	118
Timothy	El Dorado Mud Springs	58	996
Timothy	Nevada Bridgeport	61	455
Timothy	San Francisco San Francisco 11	94 67	
Timothy	San Francisco San Francisco 9	68	956
W	Butte Ophir	56	747
William	Calaveras Twp 7	57	39
Wm	Alameda Brooklyn	55	183
Wm	Amador Twp 2	55	325
Wm	Placer Secret R	62	619
Wm	Sacramento Ward 4	63	583
Wm	San Francisco San Francisco 12	385 67	
Wm	San Francisco San Francisco 2	67	596
Wm	San Francisco San Francisco 3	67	85
Wm	Sierra Downieville	66	995
Wm	Sonoma Petaluma	69	602
Wm	Trinity Weaverville	701	067
Wm	Tuolumne Columbia	71	297
Wm*	San Francisco San Francisco 3	67	85
MCCARTZ			
James*	Placer Michigan	62	847
MCCARVER			
J	Sutter Sutter	70	806
Joseph	Sierra Twp 5	66	935
Josiah	Sierra Twp 5	66	939
MCCARY			
David W	Sierra St Louis	66	805
Jno	Butte Oregon	56	635
MCCARZ			
James*	Placer Michigan	62	847
MCCASHILL			
J R	Mariposa Twp 1	60	664
MCCASKELL			
Colon	Amador Twp 7	55	413
Hugh	Alameda Brooklyn	55	82
MCCASKER			
C E*	Tuolumne Columbia	71	330
MCCASKETE			
Hugh	Alameda Brooklyn	55	82
MCCASKEY			
Annie	Alameda Brooklyn	55	83
MCCASLEY			
Moser	Colusa Butte Crk	57	467
MCCASLIN			
C	San Joaquin Stockton	641	100
James	Tuolumne Columbia	71	360
MCCASSON			
Jno	Klamath Liberty	59	240
MCCASTER			
Margaret*	El Dorado Eldorado	58	939
MCCASTEY			
Wm*	Trinity Weaverville	701	067
MCCASTIN			
James	Tuolumne Twp 2	71	360
MCCASTON			
R M	Amador Twp 7	55	417
MCCASTU			
Margaret*	El Dorado Eldorado	58	939
MCCASTY			
Wm	San Francisco San Francisco 1	68	910
MCCATCHER			
William	San Luis Obispo San Luis Obispo	65	6
MCCATE			
Jas	Sacramento Brighton	63	194
MCCATENEY			
Thos	Solano Benecia	69	296
MCCATHSTER			
Robert*	Sierra Twp 7	66	913
MCCATHY			
C	El Dorado Eldorado	58	946
MCCATTEN			
John	Calaveras Twp 6	57	186
MCCAUGEN			
John	Nevada Bloomfield	61	524
MCCAUGHTRY			
Alx	Amador Twp 1	55	505
MCCAULAY			
Thos	San Francisco San Francisco 2	67	620
MCCAULEY			
C A	Siskiyou Callahan	69	10
MCCAULEY			
C A*	Siskiyou Callahan	69	10
C H*	Siskiyou Callahan	69	10
Caroline	San Francisco San Francisco 10	233 67	
Charles	Marin Bolinas	60	728
D	Nevada Nevada	61	316
Geo	Santa Clara Fremont	65	441
H H	Butte Kimshaw	56	575
James	Alameda Brooklyn	55	165
James	Nevada Rough &	61	419
James	San Francisco San Francisco 7	681	333
John	Nevada Bloomfield	61	530
John*	Calaveras Twp 6	57	160
Margaret*	Yuba Marysville	72	953
Mary	Sacramento Ward 1	63	117
Michael	Plumas Quincy	62	990
R R*	Butte Oregon	56	632
Saml	Butte Ophir	56	793
T J*	San Francisco San Francisco 10	206 67	
Thos	Butte Ophir	56	794
Wm	Butte Ophir	56	793
MCCAULIFF			
M*	Nevada Eureka	61	364
R*	Nevada Eureka	61	364
MCCAULL			
Peter	Sacramento Ward 1	63	41
MCCAULLEY			
Ca*	Sacramento Dry Crk	63	369
Geo*	Sacramento Dry Crk	63	369
H	Nevada Eureka	61	370
MCCAULLY			
Thos	Placer Rattle Snake	62	630
MCCAULY			
Cath	San Francisco San Francisco 6	67	423
Daniel	Tuolumne Green Springs	71	531
Daniel	Tuolumne Twp 6	71	531
Isaac	Sierra Downieville	66	957
Thomas*	Marin Cortemad	60	781
MCCAUN			
John	Calaveras Twp 5	57	228
Thomas*	Siskiyou Yreka	69	152
Wm	Calaveras Twp 5	57	227
MCCAUSELAND			
W P*	Butte Kimshaw	56	591
MCCAUSLAN			
Frank	Yuba Marysville	72	864
Peter	Yuba Marysville	72	856
William	Yuba Marysville	72	856
MCCAUSLAND			
Benj	Trinity Readings	70	996
D*	El Dorado Gold Hill	581	095
H D	Tuolumne Twp 2	71	357
H O	Tuolumne Springfield	71	368
H O*	Tuolumne Columbia	71	357
Robert	Solano Fremont	69	376
T	Trinity Weaverville	701	080
MCCAUSLEN			
E T*	Trinity Steiner	701	000
MCCAUSLIN			
E T*	Trinity Steiner	701	000
MCCAUTS			
Thos*	Sacramento Ward 4	63	586
MCCAVIN			
James	El Dorado White Oaks	581	004
John	Sierra Twp 7	66	915
MCCAVISLAND			
John	San Joaquin Stockton	641	073
MCCAVLEY			
R R	Butte Oregon	56	632
MCCAW			
John	Mariposa Twp 3	60	617
MCCAWBRIDGE			
J	Nevada Eureka	61	380
MCCAWLEY			
Alex	El Dorado White Oaks	581	019
Esther	Nevada Red Dog	61	542
John	Yolo Cache Crk	72	630
Thos*	Nevada Red Dog	61	542
W	Yuba Bear Rvr	721	009
MCCAWON			
R*	Nevada Eureka	61	390
MCCAWORA			
John*	Shasta French G	66	720
MCCAY			
Alex	Sonoma Vallejo	69	620
Alexander*	Sonoma Mendocino	69	455
Andrew	Alameda Brooklyn	55	187
Andw	Sonoma Petaluma	69	584
Dan	Siskiyou Yreka	69	185
F	Nevada Grass Valley	61	235
Jno	Butte Oregon	56	635
Jno	Sonoma Healdsbu	69	474
Jno*	Sonoma Healdsbu	69	474
John	Nevada Bridgeport	61	490

California 1860 Census Index

Name	County Locale	M653 Roll	Page
MCCAY			
John	Shasta Shasta	66	730
Mathen	Alameda Oakland	55	28
Robert	Mariposa Twp 1	60	669
Robt	Sacramento Ward 4	63	547
Robt	San Bernardino San Bernadino	64	668
Stephen	Calaveras Twp 10	57	263
Wm	Nevada Grass Valley	61	143
Wm	Sacramento Granite	63	266
MCCDONALD			
T A	Tuolumne Twp 3	71	425
MCCEAK			
Anthony	Sonoma Santa Rosa	69	410
MCCEAN			
Danl	Tuolumne Sonora	71	202
MCCEIREN			
M*	Sacramento Georgian	63	342
MCCEIVEN			
M*	Sacramento Georgian	63	342
MCCELVY			
Ann	San Joaquin Douglass	64	928
MCCEMAE			
James	Sierra Twp 7	66	878
MCCEMBS			
A M*	Shasta Millvill	66	754
MCCEMIN			
W L	El Dorado White Oaks	58	1013
MCCENGHT			
Phillip	Butte Cascade	56	692
MCCENTOCK			
Jemehiah*	Napa Clear Lake	61	125
Jememah*	Napa Clear Lake	61	125
Jemimah	Napa Clear Lake	61	125
MCCENTRICKS			
J L	Napa Clear Lake	61	124
J T	Napa Clear Lake	61	124
MCCEORTY			
James	Solano Vallejo	69	269
MCCEREVY			
Peter	San Mateo Twp 3	65	95
MCCERFY			
George	Nevada Rough &	61	436
MCCERMACK			
H*	Butte Chico	56	560
MCCERMICK			
Hugh	Placer Secret R	62	614
MCCERRON			
Margaret	Yuba Marysville	72	892
MCCERRY			
Robert T	San Francisco San Francisco 3	67	71
MCCEVLOUGH			
John	Tehama Tehama	70	935
MCCEWIN			
John	Tuolumne Sonora	71	483
John	Tuolumne Twp 1	71	483
MCCEY			
Andrew	Calaveras Twp 5	57	205
Henry	Tuolumne Twp 4	71	137
MCCGUIRE			
Joseph	Sierra Twp 7	66	887
MCCHA?OGA			
Maria	Monterey Alisal	60	1030
MCCHA?OGO			
Maria*	Monterey Alisal	60	1030
MCCHAFNEY			
Michael	Sacramento Franklin	63	334
MCCHAGHLAND			
Michael	Sierra Twp 7	66	893
MCCHALLEY			
A J	Sierra Twp 7	66	907
MCCHANDLER			
Harriet*	Shasta Shasta	66	659
MCCHANGE			
Donald*	Nevada Bridgeport	61	442
MCCHAREN			
Danl*	Tuolumne Sonora	71	236
MCCHARGE			
Donald*	Nevada Bridgeport	61	442
MCCHARLES			
Harrison	Nevada Rough &	61	419
MCCHARTY			
Ann	San Francisco San Francisco 8	68	1294
Ann*	San Francisco San Francisco 8	68	1294
MCCHEERY			
Peter	Tulara Visalia	71	81
MCCHERE			
Henry	San Joaquin Oneal	64	935
MCCHERNEY			
J C	Butte Oro	56	686
MCCHERY			
John	El Dorado Kelsey	58	1129
MCCHESHY			
J H	El Dorado White Oaks	58	1022
MCCHESLEY			
A H	Calaveras Twp 9	57	394
MCCHESNEY			
James	El Dorado White Oaks	58	1016
MCCHESNY			
James	Tuolumne Columbia	71	330
MCCHESTER			
M	El Dorado Salmon Hills	58	1057
MCCHISLEY			
A H	Calaveras Twp 9	57	394
MCCHISNY			
James	Tuolumne Twp 2	71	330
MCCHISTER			
M	El Dorado Salmon Falls	58	1057
MCCHISTOCK			
D	Tehama Red Bluff	70	914
MCCHLLEY			
M*	El Dorado Kelsey	58	1130
MCCHRISSY			
William	Calaveras Twp 8	57	54
MCCHRIST			
Sylves	Sonoma Santa Rosa	69	401
MCCHRISTIAN			
Charles	Sonoma Russian	69	439
J	Shasta Millvill	66	740
Louisa	Yuba Marysville	72	959
Mariah	Sonoma Armally	69	496
Mary A	Sonoma Russian	69	441
Patrick	Sonoma Armally	69	496
MCCHUR			
J M	Tehama Tehama	70	948
MCCHURGE			
Donald	Nevada Bridgeport	61	442
Donald*	Nevada Bridgeport	61	442
MCCHURY			
Peter	Tulara Twp 1	71	81
MCCHUSTIAN			
Louisa*	Yuba Marysville	72	959
MCCIAY			
James	Napa Yount	61	46
MCCIN			
Jas	Sacramento Granite	63	254
MCCIND			
C*	Nevada Grass Valley	61	179
MCCINNEY			
Ann*	Sierra Downieville	66	967
Peter	Placer Virginia	62	662
MCCINTOCK			
Jememah*	Napa Clear Lake	61	125
MCCIREG			
Catherine	San Francisco San Francisco 4	68	1170
MCCIRMACK			
H*	Butte Chico	56	560
MCCIVE			
James S	Nevada Bridgeport	61	493
James*	Nevada Red Dog	61	550
MCCLAGHAN			
Henry	San Diego Agua Caliente	64	814
MCCLAHAN			
M	Nevada Grass Valley	61	184
MCCLAID			
T*	Nevada Grass Valley	61	180
MCCLAIGHLIN			
H*	Shasta Shasta	66	731
MCCLAIN			
A	Nevada Nevada	61	325
A M*	Nevada Nevada	61	325
B F	Sutter Bear Rvr	70	825
Donnel	Tuolumne Twp 1	71	223
H	Sutter Sutter	70	816
Hugh	Humbolt Bucksport	59	160
J M	Tuolumne Twp 1	71	250
James	Tuolumne Columbia	71	324
James	Tuolumne Columbia	71	340
Jas	Sacramento Ward 4	63	512
John	Amador Twp 3	55	386
John	Tuolumne Twp 2	71	298
John	Yolo Putah	72	550
Joseph	Tuolumne Twp 2	71	333
L	Amador Twp 3	55	384
Mary	Tuolumne Columbia	71	331
Peter	Tuolumne Twp 1	71	221
Phillip*	Calaveras Twp 6	57	139
R*	Nevada Nevada	61	329
Robert	Nevada Bloomfield	61	516
Roderick	Tuolumne Columbia	71	338
Saml S	Tuolumne Twp 1	71	479
T*	Nevada Grass Valley	61	180
Wm	Mariposa Coulterville	60	686
MCCLAINE			
B G	Nevada Nevada	61	322
Patrick	Marin Bolinas	60	747
S M	Siskiyou Scott Va	69	44
Saml S	Tuolumne Sonora	71	479
MCCLAIR			
H	San Francisco San Francisco 5	67	543
J M	Tuolumne Twp 1	71	250
T*	Nevada Grass Valley	61	180
MCCLAIRE			
A M*	Nevada Nevada	61	325
R*	Nevada Nevada	61	329
MCCLALACK			
J	Siskiyou Klamath	69	87
MCCLAM			
A G*	El Dorado Coloma	58	1118
A L*	El Dorado Coloma	58	1118
MCCLAME			
Peter*	Placer Virginia	62	666
MCCLAMN			
Richd M*	Tehama Red Bluff	70	929
MCCLAN			
Charles	Shasta Shasta	66	728
Thomas	Placer Michigan	62	854
MCCLANA			
Malcom*	Tuolumne Twp 1	71	253
MCCLANAHAN			
D A	Del Norte Crescent	58	651
J B	Tuolumne Twp 2	71	408
J M	Colusa Monroeville	57	456
John	San Joaquin Oneal	64	938
L M	Shasta French G	66	722
Ruben	Amador Twp 4	55	246
Wash	Placer Forest H	62	796
MCCLANAN			
Alexander	Siskiyou Yreka	69	147
MCCLANCY			
James M	San Joaquin Elkhorn	64	995
MCCLANE			
A J	Shasta Shasta	66	683
A P	Shasta Shasta	66	683
Anna	Butte Ophir	56	766
C	El Dorado Newtown	58	776
D	El Dorado Placerville	58	882
Daniel	Yolo Washington	72	570
Duncan	El Dorado Placerville	58	912
James	El Dorado Kelsey	58	1153
Jas	Yolo Cache Crk	72	632
John	Butte Bidwell	56	711
John	Yolo Putah	72	550
Joseph	El Dorado Kelsey	58	1155
M	Marin Cortemad	60	752
Senica	Yolo Cache	72	632
Serice	Yolo Cache Crk	72	632
W	Yolo Putah	72	614
MCCLANG			
Jos	Placer Ophir	62	651
MCCLANHAN			
J L	Sutter Bear Rvr	70	825
MCCLANLY			
Daniel*	Placer Michigan	62	841
MCCLANMAKANE			
Jno*	Sacramento Georgian	63	338
MCCLANNAKANE			
Jno*	Sacramento Georgian	63	338
MCCLANNIN			
J K	Sierra Twp 5	66	946
MCCLARA			
Malcom*	Tuolumne Twp 1	71	253
MCCLARE			
H C	Shasta Millvill	66	741
James	San Francisco San Francisco 1	68	884
James	Trinity Cox'S Bar	70	1038
James*	Tuolumne Columbia	71	303
Jno	Trinity Cox'S Bar	70	1038
P M	Trinity E Weaver	70	1061
MCCLAREY			
T B	El Dorado Placerville	58	922
William	El Dorado Kelsey	58	1133
MCCLARK			
H C	Shasta Millvill	66	741
MCCLARKIFNG			
John	Sonoma Bodega	69	537
MCCLARR			
Barney	Sierra Port Win	66	793
MCCLARTTE			
John	San Luis Obispo San Luis Obispo	65	28
MCCLARY			
Carr	Placer Forest H	62	794
S	Butte Kimshaw	56	606
Troy	Tuolumne Jamestown	71	430
MCCLARYHLIN			
H*	Shasta Shasta	66	731
MCCLASKEY			
John H	Siskiyou Yreka	69	178
MCCLASKY			
Matthew*	San Francisco San Francisco 10	67	219
Patrick*	San Francisco San Francisco 2	67	762
Wm	Sierra Twp 7	66	879
MCCLASSEN			
J	Nevada Nevada	61	289
MCCLATCHEY			
Saml	Mariposa Twp 1	60	629
MCCLATCHY			
James	Sacramento Ward 1	63	124

Name	County Locale	M653 RollPage
MCCLATCHY		
Saml	Mariposa Twp 1	60 629
V	Sacramento American	63 169
MCCLAUD		
M	Placer Dutch Fl	62 730
MCCLAUGHEA		
Owen	San Joaquin Stockton	641082
MCCLAUGHLIN		
H	Shasta Shasta	66 731
R N	Sutter Sutter	70 810
MCCLAULL		
Peter	Sacramento Ward 1	63 41
MCCLAURE		
Peter*	Placer Virginia	62 666
MCCLAY		
Alexander	Amador Twp 4	55 242
Ann	Santa Clara Fremont	65 430
Chas	Santa Clara Santa Clara	65 468
Harvy	Santa Clara Gilroy	65 237
Jane	Sacramento Ward 4	63 590
Wm	Santa Clara San Jose	65 345
MCCLEAN		
Allen	Klamath Liberty	59 233
Hugh	Nevada Bridgeport	61 467
John	Plumas Quincy	62 995
Nathaniel	Sierra Whiskey	66 845
Wm	Mariposa Twp 1	60 646
MCCLEANY		
Isaac	Amador Twp 6	55 442
MCCLEAR		
Benj	San Francisco San Francisco 9	681055
MCCLEAREN		
James	Klamath S Fork	59 205
MCCLEARY		
Augustus	Sacramento Ward 1	63 34
Geo	Amador Twp 3	55 397
Isaac	Amador Twp 6	55 442
James	Sacramento Ward 4	63 537
John	Yuba Marysville	72 943
Robt	Sacramento Ward 1	63 34
MCCLEAU		
John	Calaveras Twp 6	57 118
MCCLEAVE		
Henry	Marin Tomales	60 718
MCCLEBLOSE		
Thos	Yolo Putah	72 549
MCCLEGGINS		
Thomas	El Dorado Georgetown	58 752
MCCLEGHOM		
Peter	Butte Kimshaw	56 586
MCCLEISTOCK		
William F	Yuba Marysville	72 859
William F	Yuba Marysville	72 860
MCCLELAND		
A	Yolo Cache Crk	72 616
Daniel	Santa Cruz Pajaro	66 545
E	Sutter Yuba	70 774
George	San Joaquin Elkhorn	64 967
MCCLELLAN		
Alice	San Francisco San Francisco 2	67 567
Chas	San Francisco San Francisco 2	67 629
Cyremius B	Yuba Marysville	72 876
David	San Francisco San Francisco 4	681135
David	San Mateo Twp 1	65 65
Edwd	Butte Chico	56 563
James W	Contra Costa Twp 3	57 610
John A	San Francisco San Francisco 12	366 67
M J	Napa Napa	61 58
M T*	Napa Napa	61 58
Maria	San Joaquin Stockton	641048
William	Solano Vacaville	69 344
MCCLELLAND		
A M	Yolo Cache	72 616
Alex	Amador Twp 2	55 298
Alexander	Yuba Marysville	72 870
E	San Francisco San Francisco 5	67 539
H	Los Angeles Tejon	59 524
I F	El Dorado Placerville	58 918
Jane	Sacramento Ward 1	63 82
Jas	Sacramento Granite	63 223
Jas	Sacramento Ward 1	63 76
Jas	San Francisco San Francisco 2	67 670
John J	Sonoma Santa Rosa	69 407
John N	San Mateo Twp 3	65 87
Loisa	Napa Hot Springs	61 21
Mary	Yuba Marysville	72 870
Wm	Butte Kimshaw	56 607
MCCLELLANE		
Cyrenins B	Yuba Marysville	72 876
MCCLELLEN		
T J	Nevada Bloomfield	61 517
MCCLELLM		
David	San Francisco San Francisco 4	681135
MCCLELLWELL		
J	Sacramento Granite	63 240

Name	County Locale	M653 RollPage
MCCLEMAN		
John	San Joaquin Oneal	64 939
MCCLEMENS		
Wm	Butte Oregon	56 638
MCCLEMENT		
Andrew	San Francisco San Francisco 1	68 889
MCCLEMSAN		
Joseph*	Tuolumne Twp 3	71 455
MCCLENAHAN		
A	Butte Ophir	56 759
Baily	Monterey Pajaro	601019
MCCLENAN		
Albert	Sierra Downieville	66 975
Albert M	Sierra Downieville	66 975
Joseph	Tuolumne Jamestown	71 455
MCCLENCHY		
P*	San Francisco San Francisco 9	681057
MCCLENDER		
Saml	Butte Wyandotte	56 657
MCCLENDIE		
Saml*	Butte Wyandotte	56 657
MCCLENDN		
Saml*	Butte Wyandotte	56 657
MCCLENDOM		
Louis	San Joaquin Castoria	64 907
MCCLENEHAN		
Michael	Monterey Pajaro	601018
MCCLENEN		
Alx	Napa Napa	61 77
MCCLENNAN		
A D	Mariposa Twp 1	60 629
Alex	Santa Clara Fremont	65 421
Amanda	Napa Hot Springs	61 15
Jhn P*	Napa Hot Springs	61 14
Joseph*	Tuolumne Twp 3	71 455
MCCLENNAR		
John P*	Napa Hot Springs	61 14
MCCLENNON		
Edward	Yuba Marysville	72 953
William	Yuba Marysville	72 962
MCCLENNORE		
Edward*	Yuba Marysville	72 953
MCCLENNY		
R T	Merced Twp 1	60 912
MCCLENON		
L F	Sutter Nicolaus	70 832
MCCLEOD		
Thos	Santa Clara Gilroy	65 247
MCCLERAND		
Thos	Santa Clara Santa Clara	65 465
MCCLERLAHAN		
Martin	San Joaquin Castoria	64 889
MCCLERMEN		
John	Humbolt Eel Rvr	59 144
MCCLERVER		
James	El Dorado White Oaks	581001
MCCLERY		
Sarah	Amador Twp 4	55 237
William	Amador Twp 4	55 258
MCCLESKEY		
Mary A	San Francisco San Francisco 11	100 67
MCCLEUCHY		
P*	San Francisco San Francisco 9	681057
MCCLEUNY		
R T	Merced Twp 1	60 912
MCCLEVIE		
Jas*	Sacramento Ward 1	63 39
MCCLICIHAM		
John	Santa Clara San Jose	65 385
MCCLIIIISTER		
Alexander	Yuba Marysville	72 953
MCCLILLAND		
H	Los Angeles Tejon	59 524
MCCLILLEY		
M*	El Dorado Kelsey	581130
MCCLIMMETS		
James	Calaveras Twp 8	57 70
MCCLINE		
John	Sacramento Cosummes	63 391
John	Yolo Putah	72 585
Pat	Nevada Nevada	61 319
MCCLING		
Daniel	San Francisco San Francisco 4	681147
Jerdah	Yolo Cache	72 616
MCCLINK		
Wm	Tehama Antelope	70 887
MCCLINNAN		
Robert	Stanislaus Emory	70 755
MCCLINON		
M C	Sutter Yuba	70 770
Mary	San Francisco San Francisco 3	67 73
MCCLINTECK		
Joseph	Alameda Brooklyn	55 86
MCCLINTER		
---	Amador Twp 2	55 277

Name	County Locale	M653 RollPage
MCCLINTIC		
Samuel	Marin Cortemad	60 779
Samuel*	Marin Cortemad	60 779
MCCLINTOCK		
F J	Shasta Shasta	66 675
F T	Shasta Shasta	66 675
J	Nevada Grass Valley	61 185
J	Nevada Eureka	61 374
J	Yolo Cache Crk	72 607
J	Yolo Cache	72 608
J S	Tuolumne Jamestown	71 441
Jno	Sacramento Ward 4	63 581
John	San Diego Agua Caliente	64 814
Joseph	Alameda Brooklyn	55 86
S W	Nevada Grass Valley	61 237
Sylvester	Mendocino Big Rock	60 872
William F*	Yuba Marysville	72 859
Wm	Alameda Oakland	55 53
Wm	Mendocino Ukiah	60 797
MCCLINTOE		
C F	Sacramento Brighton	63 201
MCCLINTON		
S	Amador Twp 2	55 262
MCCLINTOOK		
S W	Nevada Grass Valley	61 237
MCCLISH		
Thos	Sonoma Mendocino	69 450
MCCLISTER		
Alexander	Yuba Marysville	72 953
MCCLIVIE		
Jas	Sacramento Ward 1	63 39
Jas*	Sacramento Ward 1	63 39
MCCLLAND		
James*	Plumas Meadow Valley	62 905
MCCLLINS		
A R	Shasta Millvill	66 754
MCCLOCK		
Phillip	Calaveras Twp 10	57 282
MCCLOCKY		
Phillip	Calaveras Twp 10	57 282
MCCLOFLIN		
Jas	Yolo Putah	72 586
MCCLOGAN		
Bridget	San Francisco San Francisco 10	285 67
MCCLOND		
Roberrt*	Placer Michigan	62 817
Samuel	Placer Forest H	62 803
MCCLONP		
Anna	San Joaquin Castoria	64 904
MCCLORA		
Charles	Contra Costa Twp 3	57 591
MCCLORY		
And	Yolo Putah	72 554
Andr	Yolo Putah	72 554
Jno	Sacramento Ward 1	63 8
MCCLOSHY		
Collins*	Sierra Morristown	661053
MCCLOSKEY		
Mary A	San Francisco San Francisco 11	100 67
MCCLOSKY		
C C	Tuolumne Twp 2	71 324
Catharine	Sacramento Ward 1	63 1
J W	Del Norte Happy Ca	58 670
Matthew	San Francisco San Francisco 10	219 67
Thos	Santa Clara Santa Clara	65 513
W G	Sacramento San Joaquin	63 350
Wm	Santa Clara Santa Clara	65 509
MCCLOSTRY		
Collins*	Sierra Morristown	661053
MCCLOUD		
---	Mariposa Twp 3	60 555
A	Sacramento Sutter	63 306
Alonzo	San Joaquin Stockton	641016
Anna	San Francisco San Francisco 8	681321
C E	San Francisco San Francisco 10	319 67
Canada	Yuba Bear Rvr	721010
Charles A	San Joaquin Castoria	64 904
D	Nevada Nevada	61 264
D	Siskiyou Scott Ri	69 64
Dan	San Francisco San Francisco 9	681065
F	Nevada Nevada	61 281
Isaac	San Francisco San Francisco 2	67 676
J	El Dorado Casumnes	581172
J	Nevada Eureka	61 365
J A	Del Norte Happy Ca	58 669
J G	El Dorado Diamond	58 791
J M	Calaveras Twp 8	57 82
James	Plumas Quincy	621002
James	Santa Cruz Pajaro	66 574
James W	Mendocino Calpella	60 814
John	Contra Costa Twp 3	57 603
John	El Dorado Mountain	581185

Name	County Locale	M653 RollPage
MCCLOUD		
John	Nevada Nevada	61 327
John	Placer Auburn	62 566
Joseph	San Francisco San Francisco 2	67 578
Joseph R	San Joaquin Castoria	64 873
Joshua	San Francisco San Francisco 4	681213
R	El Dorado Salmon Hills	581058
Ross	Siskiyou Shasta Rvr	69 112
S	Nevada Eureka	61 354
W P	Nevada Rough &	61 403
William	Contra Costa Twp 1	57 535
Wm	Nevada Nevada	61 327
Wm	Nevada Eureka	61 354
Wm	Nevada Eureka	61 355
Wm	Placer Virginia	62 666
Wm	Sonoma Vallejo	69 631
Wm J	Nevada Nevada	61 327
MCCLOUDS		
D	Siskiyou Scott Ri	69 64
MCCLOUGH		
David	Monterey Pajaro	601025
Hugh V	San Francisco San Francisco 4	681168
MCCLOUR		
Dan	San Francisco San Francisco 9	681065
MCCLOVER		
Samuel	El Dorado Mud Springs	58 967
MCCLOWD		
John	San Mateo Twp 3	65 89
MCCLOY		
Jno A	Sacramento Ward 4	63 559
Robert	Calaveras Twp 8	57 53
W	Amador Twp 3	55 391
MCCLOYTS		
H T	Contra Costa Twp 1	57 528
MCCLROY		
James	Shasta French G	66 714
MCCLUCE		
A	Santa Clara Santa Clara	65 488
MCCLUCKEY		
Bridge*	Nevada Nevada	61 246
MCCLUE		
T*	San Francisco San Francisco 5	67 550
Wm	Mariposa Coulterville	60 686
MCCLUER		
E P*	Yolo Washington	72 565
MCCLUM		
A L	El Dorado Coloma	581118
MCCLUN		
J	Sutter Yuba	70 768
S	Sutter Yuba	70 763
MCCLUNE		
John	Shasta Millvill	66 740
L B	Sacramento Franklin	63 317
MCCLUNG		
B R	Trinity Trinity	70 970
John*	Placer Sacramento	62 644
MCCLUNN		
---	Placer Dutch Fl	62 729
MCCLUNNIN		
J K	Sierra Twp 5	66 946
MCCLUNY		
John*	Placer Sacramento	62 644
MCCLURE		
A	Amador Twp 5	55 345
A	San Mateo Twp 3	65 91
A J	Amador Twp 6	55 421
Albert	Del Norte Crescent	58 627
Aledxander	Marin Cortemad	60 784
Alexander	Marin Cortemad	60 784
Amanda	Tuolumne Columbia	71 303
B F	Napa Napa	61 76
Benj	Sacramento Georgian	63 344
C	Amador Twp 6	55 426
Daniel	San Diego Agua Caliente	64 816
Daniel	San Mateo Twp 1	65 52
David	Contra Costa Twp 2	57 566
G	Sutter Bear Rvr	70 819
H E	Merced Twp 2	60 923
Henry	San Joaquin Tulare	64 870
J	Sacramento Lee	63 216
J W	Sacramento Ward 1	63 86
James	Tuolumne Twp 2	71 303
Jas*	Sacramento Ward 1	63 39
Jno	San Francisco San Francisco 9	68 970
Jno	Tehama Lassen	70 884
John	Santa Cruz Pajaro	66 528
John	Shasta Millvill	66 740
John	Tehama Cottonwood	70 902
John	Yolo Putah	72 585
John R	Siskiyou Yreka	69 149
John R*	Siskiyou Yreka	69 149
L B	Napa Napa	61 77
L M	Tehama Antelope	70 888
Martin	Placer Secret R	62 614
R	Napa Hot Springs	61 15
Richd A	Alameda Brooklyn	55 178

Name	County Locale	M653 RollPage
MCCLURE		
S W	Trinity North Fo	701024
Samuel	Sierra La Porte	66 786
Samuel	Siskiyou Cottonwood	69 99
Silas	Alameda Brooklyn	55 162
T B	Napa Napa	61 77
W	Yolo Putah	72 585
William	Placer Yankee J	62 756
William	San Joaquin Elliott	64 945
William	San Mateo Twp 1	65 52
William	Sierra Poker Flats	66 841
Wm*	Mariposa Coulterville	60 686
MCCLURES		
C	San Francisco San Francisco 6	67 468
E	San Francisco San Francisco 6	67 468
MCCLURKEY		
M	El Dorado Placerville	58 835
MCCLURN		
Wm*	Mariposa Coulterville	60 686
MCCLURR		
E P	Yolo Washington	72 565
MCCLURY		
Henry	Tuolumne Columbia	71 305
Jerdah	Yolo Cache Crk	72 616
MCCLUSE		
John R*	Siskiyou Yreka	69 149
Samuel	Siskiyou Cottonwoood	69 99
MCCLUSKEY		
A M	Solano Vacaville	69 322
Bridge*	Nevada Nevada	61 246
Bridget	Nevada Nevada	61 246
James	San Joaquin Douglass	64 914
James	Tuolumne Twp 2	71 315
Jas	San Francisco San Francisco 1	68 837
John H	Siskiyou Yreka	69 178
T	Butte Ophir	56 768
MCCLUSKIE		
Jno	Sonoma Healdsbu	69 473
MCCLUSKY		
A	Yolo Fremont	72 604
Henry	San Francisco San Francisco 1	68 914
J A	Butte Oro	56 677
James*	Tuolumne Columbia	71 315
Jas	San Francisco San Francisco 10	330 67
John	Tuolumne Columbia	71 294
Jos	San Francisco San Francisco 12	361 67
M	Nevada Bridgeport	61 448
Margaret	San Francisco San Francisco 10	244 67
Michl	Sierra Downieville	66 975
P	Tuolumne Columbia	71 295
Patrick	San Francisco San Francisco 2	67 762
Thos	San Francisco San Francisco 2	67 631
W J	San Francisco San Francisco 10	300 67
Wm	Butte Ophir	56 799
Wm	Sierra Twp 7	66 879
Wm J	San Francisco San Francisco 10	300 67
MCCLUVER		
W	El Dorado Diamond	58 803
MCCMILLAN		
David	Santa Cruz Pescadero	66 645
MCCMILLIN		
J P	Shasta French G	66 721
MCCOACH		
W	Trinity Texas Ba	70 982
MCCOAD		
James*	Yuba Bear Rvr	721009
James*	Yuba Bear Rvr	721009
MCCOASHING		
John H	Yuba Bear Rvr	721000
MCCOAT		
Charles*	San Mateo Twp 1	65 56
MCCOBB		
David	Mendocino Big Rvr	60 851
John	San Joaquin Elkhorn	64 988
M D	Santa Clara Santa Clara	65 482
MCCOBE		
John	Calaveras Twp 4	57 319
MCCOCKIN		
Ellen	Sonoma Healdsbu	69 471
MCCOFFEE		
A A	Yuba Slate Ro	72 710
MCCOFFERTY		
Jonn	Solano Vallejo	69 270
MCCOFFRY		
P	El Dorado Coloma	581104
MCCOG		
Catharine	San Francisco San Francisco 2	67 697
MCCOHILL		
Philip	San Joaquin Stockton	641064
MCCOIS		
H W*	Nevada Rough &	61 423

Name	County Locale	M653 RollPage
MCCOL		
James*	Mariposa Twp 3	60 609
MCCOLAUGH		
Eben A*	Siskiyou Yreka	69 139
MCCOLBORN		
Ann	San Francisco San Francisco 1	68 852
MCCOLE		
John	Yolo Cache Crk	72 642
M	Nevada Grass Valley	61 158
Wm	Alameda Brooklyn	55 187
MCCOLF		
John*	San Francisco San Francisco 11	131 67
MCCOLFY		
Mary	Sacramento Ward 3	63 452
MCCOLGAN		
Francis	San Francisco San Francisco 11	133 67
Michael	San Francisco San Francisco 3	67 47
Michael M	San Francisco San Francisco 3	67 47
	San Francisco	
MCCOLGIN		
Eugene	San Mateo Twp 3	65 86
MCCOLIGAN		
D	Butte Bidwell	56 722
MCCOLL		
Hugh	Santa Cruz Soguel	66 589
M*	Nevada Grass Valley	61 158
MCCOLLAGH		
Mike	Alameda Brooklyn	55 105
MCCOLLAR		
L C	Siskiyou Callahan	69 9
MCCOLLAUGH		
John	Tuolumne Twp 2	71 354
M	Tuolumne Twp 2	71 305
T D	Tuolumne Twp 1	71 188
T D	Tuolumne Twp 1	71 251
MCCOLLEAN		
James	Sierra Twp 7	66 867
MCCOLLEN		
James	Yolo Cache	72 590
MCCOLLEY		
Herdin	Yolo Putah	72 546
Hiram	Yolo Putah	72 545
MCCOLLIAN		
James	Sierra Twp 7	66 867
MCCOLLIF		
John	Stanislaus Emory	70 745
MCCOLLIFF		
F	Nevada Nevada	61 258
Margaret	San Francisco San Francisco 2	67 594
MCCOLLIMOR		
A R*	Shasta Millvill	66 754
MCCOLLINS		
Amelia*	San Francisco San Francisco 7	681422
Joseph	Santa Cruz Pajaro	66 550
Marshal	Santa Cruz Pajaro	66 550
MCCOLLISNOR		
A R*	Shasta Millvill	66 754
MCCOLLISON		
A R*	Shasta Millvill	66 754
MCCOLLISTER		
A C	Marin San Rafael	60 766
MCCOLLIUN		
T W*	San Francisco San Francisco 8	681238
MCCOLLOCK		
J N	Sacramento Lee	63 213
MCCOLLORY		
Edward	Santa Cruz Pajaro	66 529
MCCOLLOUGH		
A	Sutter Yuba	70 770
B*	Mariposa Twp 3	60 595
Calom	Tuolumne Twp 1	71 483
Calvin	Tuolumne Sonora	71 187
Calvin	Tuolumne Sonora	71 483
E M	Tuolumne Twp 1	71 186
I G	Mariposa Twp 3	60 591
I N	Tuolumne Sonora	71 185
J	Sutter Yuba	70 771
J G	Mariposa Twp 3	60 591
J N	Tuolumne Twp 1	71 185
John*	Tuolumne Columbia	71 354
Joseph	Tuolumne Twp 1	71 204
M	Tuolumne Columbia	71 305
R	Mariposa Twp 3	60 595
Robert	Tulara Keeneysburg	71 45
T	San Francisco San Francisco 5	67 557
T D	Tuolumne Sonora	71 188
W D	Tuolumne Twp 2	71 351
William	Tulara Keyesville	71 55
Wm	San Francisco San Francisco 9	681073
Wm	San Francisco San Francisco 1	68 854
MCCOLLUM		
Daniel	Mariposa Twp 1	60 652
J N	Sacramento Cosumnes	63 406
James	Yolo Cache Crk	72 590

California 1860 Census Index

Name	County Locale	M653 RollPage
MCCOLLUM		
Joseph	Santa Cruz Pajaro	66 550
Marshal	Santa Cruz Pajaro	66 550
Robt*	Alameda Brooklyn	55 146
T W	San Francisco San Francisco 8	681238
W	Trinity Taylor'S	701034
MCCOLLUN		
W	Trinity Taylor'S	701034
MCCOLLUNS		
Robt*	Alameda Brooklyn	55 146
MCCOLMGH		
Eben A*	Siskiyou Yreka	69 139
MCCOLOGIN		
Danl	Butte Ophir	56 756
MCCOLOUGH		
Eben A*	Siskiyou Yreka	69 139
MCCOLRY		
A*	Nevada Grass Valley	61 221
MCCOLSKY		
A	Yolo Washington	72 604
MCCOLURGH		
Eben A*	Siskiyou Yreka	69 139
MCCOLVY		
A*	Nevada Grass Valley	61 221
J M	Nevada Grass Valley	61 221
MCCOMARS		
Wm	Butte Cascade	56 704
MCCOMAS		
Isaac	Yuba Marysville	72 890
MCCOMB		
A	Sacramento Sutter	63 306
E C	Solano Suisan	69 211
Ellen	San Francisco San Francisco 2 67 637
Geo	Placer Auburn	62 586
Hanah	Napa Napa	61 66
James	El Dorado Mud Springs	58 985
John	San Francisco San Francisco 9	681018
John	San Francisco San Francisco 7	681398
R	San Francisco San Francisco 9	681029
S D	El Dorado Mud Springs	58 986
William	El Dorado Salmon Falls	581054
William	El Dorado Salmon Hills	581054
William	Placer Forest H	62 767
MCCOMBE		
D W	Klamath Trinidad	59 222
Jno	Sacramento Natonia	63 270
MCCOMBER		
W	Yolo Cottonwoood	72 556
MCCOMBES		
J	Sutter Sutter	70 805
W P M	Trinity Steiner	701000
MCCOMBS		
A M	Shasta Millvill	66 754
Benj F	Contra Costa Twp 3	57 604
Isaac	Solano Vacaville	69 353
Jacob R	Contra Costa Twp 3	57 585
James	Sacramento Georgian	63 339
N	Sacramento Granite	63 239
MCCOMBY		
J*	Nevada Grass Valley	61 211
MCCOMET		
D	San Francisco San Francisco 9	681052
MCCOMICE		
Thomas C	Tuolumne Sonora	71 190
MCCOMILL		
B*	Shasta Horsetown	66 688
MCCOMLEY		
J*	Nevada Grass Valley	61 211
MCCOMMACK		
Joseph	Nevada Bloomfield	61 513
MCCOMT		
P	Nevada Nevada	61 274
MCCOMWELL		
Phillip*	Calaveras Twp 6	57 180
MCCONACHY		
Reid	Alameda Murray	55 223
MCCONAGHEY		
Peter*	San Francisco San Francisco 5 67 545
MCCONAGHY		
Jno	Klamath Trinidad	59 222
MCCONAHAN		
M	El Dorado Mud Springs	58 964
MCCONALLY		
Geo	Sonoma Sonoma	69 639
MCCONALY		
M	Sierra Eureka	661042
MCCONARS		
Wm	Butte Cascade	56 704
MCCONATHY		
J	Sonoma Bodega	69 531
Thos	Amador Twp 1	55 509
MCCONAUGHEY		
H C	Siskiyou Callahan	69 3
H C*	Siskiyou Callahan	69 3
William	Siskiyou Callahan	69 3
MCCONAUGHY		
H C*	Siskiyou Callahan	69 3

Name	County Locale	M653 RollPage
MCCONAUGHY		
Wiliam	Siskiyou Callahan	69 3
MCCONBE		
Benj*	El Dorado Cold Spring	581100
MCCONBOY		
AlexandeSan Francisco San Francisco 9	681099
MCCOND		
A	Sutter Butte	70 785
J*	Nevada Eureka	61 365
William T	San Francisco San Francisco 11	155
		67
MCCONDA		
M	Tuolumne Columbia	71 303
MCCONE		
Samuel	Marin Bolinas	60 745
Thos	San Mateo Twp 3	65 95
MCCONEE		
Andrew J	San Bernadino	64 676
MCCONELL	San Bernardino	
J T	Nevada Rough &	61 430
Jno	San Francisco San Francisco 10	206
		67
R A	Placer Michigan	62 856
MCCONET		
B*	Nevada Eureka	61 357
MCCONIGAL		
Joseph	El Dorado Union	581087
MCCONIHAY		
S W*	Placer Goods	62 694
MCCONKE		
Benj	El Dorado Cold Spring	581100
MCCONKEY		
Caroline	El Dorado Eldorado	58 943
John	El Dorado Eldorado	58 947
MCCONLE		
James*	Yuba Rose Bar	72 792
MCCONLEY		
Adam	Sonoma Petaluma	69 585
B	San Francisco San Francisco 9	681049
John	Calaveras Twp 6	57 160
John M*	Calaveras Twp 6	57 160
MCCONLIE		
Benj*	El Dorado Cold Spring	581100
MCCONLOGHE		
Catherine*	Yolo No E Twp	72 667
MCCONLOY		
AlexanderSan Francisco San Francisco 9	681099
MCCONLY		
J	Siskiyou Scott Ri	69 68
MCCONN		
Emily*	Nevada Rough &	61 414
J	Nevada Nevada	61 283
James	Mendocino Arrana	60 861
MCCONNAHA		
Burr P	Humbolt Union	59 181
MCCONNAL		
Ann	Sierra Twp 7	66 915
MCCONNAUGHEY		
John	Siskiyou Callahan	69 11
John*	Siskiyou Callahan	69 11
MCCONNAY		
Francis	Yuba Long Bar	72 755
MCCONNEL		
Alex	Plumas Meadow Valley	62 906
Christopher	Sierra Cox'S Bar	66 952
David A	Sierra Pine Grove	66 835
F	Butte Chico	56 534
F*	Butte Chico	56 534
J	Butte Chico	56 537
J C	Solano Vacaville	69 327
J*	Butte Chico	56 537
Jas	Butte Hamilton	56 524
John	San Joaquin Elkhorn	64 984
Thos*	Sacramento San Joaquin	63 351
W P	Solano Vacaville	69 329
MCCONNELL		
Hugh	San Francisco San Francisco 4	681221
J	Siskiyou Scott Ri	69 69
J C	Butte Ophir	56 800
J R	Nevada Nevada	61 329
Jackson	Nevada Red Dog	61 551
James	Nevada Rough &	61 411
James	San Diego Colorado	64 807
Jas	Sacramento Ward 1	63 7
Jno	San Francisco San Francisco 10	206
		67
John	San Francisco San Francisco 11	124
		67
John	San Francisco San Francisco 7	681386
John	San Francisco San Francisco 10	169
		67
John	Solano Benecia	69 308
Joseph	Colusa Butte Crk	57 466
M	Nevada Eureka	61 382
Mary	San Francisco San Francisco 2 67 573

Name	County Locale	M653 RollPage
MCCONNELL		
O H	El Dorado Placerville	58 903
Saml	Del Norte Happy Ca	58 668
William	Siskiyou Yreka	69 189
Wm	El Dorado Georgetown	58 676
Wm	San Francisco San Francisco 10	195
		67
Wm	Solano Suisan	69 227
MCCONNILL		
M	Nevada Eureka	61 382
Mathew	El Dorado White Oaks	581016
MCCONNOK		
W*	Nevada Grass Valley	61 219
MCCONNOR		
Samuel	El Dorado Georgetown	58 696
MCCONOHA		
Jack	Del Norte Klamath	58 652
MCCONOLGNE		
Chas	Sierra Port Win	66 797
MCCONOLGUE		
Chas*	Sierra Port Win	66 797
MCCONOLOGUE		
Catharine	Yolo No E Twp	72 667
Chas*	Sierra Port Win	66 797
MCCONOLQUE		
Chas*	Sierra Port Win	66 797
MCCONOLY		
Patrick	Sierra Downieville	66 957
MCCONOTHEY		
Andrew	Calaveras Twp 4	57 310
MCCONOTHY		
Andrew	Calaveras Twp 4	57 310
MCCONVELLE		
Jas	San Francisco San Francisco 6 67 448
MCCONVILL		
B*	Shasta Horsetown	66 688
MCCONVILLE		
Jno	Sacramento Ward 4	63 498
Jos	San Francisco San Francisco 6 67 448
MCCONVOY		
James	Sierra Pine Grove	66 828
MCCONWAUGHEY		
John*	Siskiyou Callahan	69 11
MCCONWAY		
J	El Dorado Salmon Falls	581057
T	El Dorado Salmon Hills	581057
MCCOOD		
James*	Yuba Bear Rvr	721009
MCCOOKY		
James	Tuolumne Green Springs	71 519
MCCOOMBS		
Joseph	Yuba Bear Rvr	72 999
MCCOON		
C	El Dorado Salmon Falls	581065
MCCOOSKY		
Jo*	Mariposa Twp 1	60 672
MCCOOTY		
Owen	El Dorado Mud Springs	58 983
MCCORAHOUSE		
Adaline	Tehama Antelope	70 893
MCCORCLE		
J*	Nevada Grass Valley	61 206
MCCORD		
A	Siskiyou Scott Va	69 51
F M	El Dorado Eldorado	58 935
Geo	Sacramento Ward 1	63 9
Isaac	Sacramento Casumnes	63 381
Isaac	Sacramento Cosumnes	63 381
J C	El Dorado Mud Springs	58 964
J H	Napa Hot Springs	61 2
Jas	Placer Virginia	62 673
Sylvester	San Francisco San Francisco 10	311
		67
Thos	San Francisco San Francisco 10	299
		67
William	Solano Suisan	69 211
MCCORDE		
J*	Nevada Grass Valley	61 206
Susana	Sacramento Granite	63 253
MCCORDEL		
Catherine J	Calaveras Twp 6	57 183
MCCORDER		
Susana	Sacramento Granite	63 253
MCCORE		
John	Tehama Pasakent	70 857
MCCORINEL		
Wm M	Sierra Twp 7	66 877
MCCORKLE		
A W	Butte Chico	56 545
Henry	Mariposa Twp 3	60 615
John	Plumas Meadow Valley	62 930
John P	Napa Yount	61 42
M K	Napa Napa	61 58
S A	Shasta Millvill	66 752
MCCORLEY		
And	Stanislaus Emory	70 743
MCCORMAC		
CatharineSan Francisco San Francisco 11	111
		67

California 1860 Census Index

Name	County Locale	M653 Roll	Page
MCCORMAC			
M	Siskiyou Scott Ri	69	69
MCCORMACK			
A J	El Dorado Georgetown	58	705
Ann	Tuolumne Sonora	71	223
C	Nevada Eureka	61	353
Edward	Yuba Marysville	72	852
Edward	Yuba Marysville	72	857
H	Butte Chico	56	560
J	El Dorado Placerville	58	880
J	El Dorado Placerville	58	933
J	Nevada Eureka	61	346
J	Siskiyou Klamath	69	86
J	Tuolumne Big Oak	71	179
James	El Dorado Eldorado	58	938
James	Sierra Downieville	66	1019
James	Yuba Bear Rvr	72	1009
James	Yuba Marysville	72	943
Jefferson	Fresno Twp 1	59	33
Jno E	Butte Kimshaw	56	579
John	Santa Cruz Santa Cruz	66	634
Joseph	Yuba Marysville	72	898
M	Butte Oregon	56	622
M*	Butte Oregon	56	622
Mark	Napa Napa	61	69
Perry	El Dorado Kelsey	58	1150
R	Nevada Eureka	61	387
Skolomon	Yuba Marysville	72	878
Solomon	Yuba Marysville	72	878
W	El Dorado Kelsey	58	1150
William	Yuba Marysville	72	886
Wm	Amador Twp 3	55	384
MCCORMACKE			
J	Sutter Nicolaus	70	830
MCCORMAE			
James	Sierra Twp 7	66	878
MCCORMEL			
Wm	Sierra Twp 7	66	877
MCCORMIC			
Geo	Butte Cascade	56	700
Henry	San Mateo Twp 3	65	103
Patrick	Tuolumne Columbia	71	314
Peter*	Alameda Brooklyn	55	93
MCCORMICH			
Goerge	San Francisco San Francisco 3	67	59
L M	Nevada Grass Valley	61	219
Wm	Alameda Brooklyn	55	177
MCCORMICK			
A C	Yolo Fremont	72	605
A G	Yolo Fremont	72	605
A J	El Dorado Georgetown	58	705
Alex	Tuolumne Twp 4	71	126
Alice	San Francisco San Francisco 8	681	266
Bridget	San Francisco San Francisco 10	222 67	
C	Amador Twp 3	55	372
C	Solano Vacaville	69	322
C G	Yolo Cache Crk	72	610
Catharine	San Francisco San Francisco 1	68	830
Charles	San Francisco San Francisco 7	681	439
Charles	Tulara Visalia	71	15
Chas	Nevada Nevada	61	246
Cornelius	San Francisco San Francisco 1	68	885
Daniel	Tuolumne Sonora	71	192
Ed	Fresno Twp 3	59	15
George	San Francisco San Francisco 3	67	59
H	Santa Clara Santa Clara	65	487
Henry B	Los Angeles Los Angeles	59	347
Hugh	San Francisco San Francisco 8	681	264
J	San Francisco San Francisco 5	67	537
J C	Nevada Eureka	61	354
J F	Tuolumne Twp 1	71	249
J H	Trinity Rattle Snake	701	029
J M	Shasta Millvill	66	752
J R	Tuolumne Twp 1	71	249
J W	Shasta Millvill	66	752
James	Placer Iona Hills	62	872
James	San Francisco San Francisco 4	681	169
James	Siskiyou Scott Va	69	32
James	Yolo No E Twp	72	667
James*	Yolo No E Twp	72	667
Jas	Butte Bidwell	56	713
Jas	Butte Ophir	56	782
Jas	Sacramento Granite	63	258
Jno	Sacramento Ward 1	63	41
Jno	Sacramento Ward 4	63	605
John	Alameda Brooklyn	55	200
John	Calaveras Twp 6	57	164
John	Calaveras Twp 8	57	90
John	Marin Bolinas	60	744
John	Placer Folsom	62	641
John	Sacramento Natonia	63	284
John	San Francisco San Francisco 8	681	233
John	San Francisco San Francisco 12	369 67	
John	San Francisco San Francisco 3	67	9
MCCORMICK			
John	Santa Clara San Jose	65	305
John	Santa Cruz Watsonville	66	539
John	Tuolumne Twp 1	71	260
John M	El Dorado Georgetown	58	705
John M	San Francisco San Francisco 3	67	9
John W	San Francisco San Francisco 3	67	31
Joseph	Mendocino Ukiah	60	802
Joseph	Placer Todds Va	62	790
Joseph	Shasta Millvill	66	745
Lorella	Placer Nicolaus	62	691
M	Amador Twp 2	55	308
M	Amador Twp 7	55	420
M	San Francisco San Francisco 5	67	495
M H	Sacramento Ward 1	63	86
M*	Butte Oregon	56	622
Mark	Calaveras Twp 10	57	266
Martha	Tuolumne Twp 1	71	229
Mary	San Francisco San Francisco 7	681	242
Mary	San Francisco San Francisco 10	255 67	
Owen	Stanislaus Branch	70	702
P H	Tuolumne Columbia	71	363
Patrick	Sierra Pine Grove	66	825
Peter	Santa Cruz Santa Cruz	66	601
Robert	Sierra Twp 7	66	887
S	Nevada Eureka	61	344
S M	El Dorado Placerville	58	846
S M	El Dorado Placerville	58	848
Stewart	El Dorado Mud Springs	58	954
T	San Francisco San Francisco 5	67	523
Thomas	Humbolt Eel Rvr	59	149
Thomas	Tulara Twp 3	71	61
Thos	Butte Hamilton	56	530
Thos	Sacramento Ward 1	63	128
Thos*	Butte Hamilton	56	530
Timothy	San Francisco San Francisco 1	68	835
W	El Dorado Placerville	58	856
W	Nevada Grass Valley	61	219
W	San Francisco San Francisco 5	67	490
W	Sutter Bear Rvr	70	819
W*	Nevada Grass Valley	61	219
William	Tuolumne Twp 1	71	191
Wm	Placer Goods	62	695
Wm L	Sacramento Ward 1	63	18
Wm M	Del Norte Crescent	58	624
Wm R	Amador Twp 1	55	494
MCCORMICKS			
C G	Yolo Cache	72	610
MCCORMIE			
Geo*	Butte Cascade	56	700
Peter	Alameda Brooklyn	55	93
MCCORMIK			
Thos	Plumas Meadow Valley	62	927
MCCORMIT			
Allexander	Calaveras Twp 9	57	353
MCCORMOK			
W*	Nevada Grass Valley	61	219
MCCORN			
James*	Placer Michigan	62	808
MCCORNEACK			
M E	Butte Kimshaw	56	579
MCCORNEL			
Thos*	Sacramento San Joaquin	63	351
MCCORNELL			
Jas	Stanislaus Buena Village	70	722
MCCORNICK			
Thomas	Tulara Keyesville	71	61
W*	Nevada Grass Valley	61	219
MCCORNWELL			
Phillip*	Calaveras Twp 6	57	180
MCCORRD			
J*	Nevada Eureka	61	365
MCCORRET			
B*	Nevada Eureka	61	357
MCCORRIT			
Patrick*	San Francisco San Francisco 3	67	56
MCCORRTSEY			
Wm	Butte Oregon	56	641
MCCORTH			
Ellen	San Francisco San Francisco 4	681	160
MCCORTHY			
Saml*	San Francisco San Francisco 1	68	851
MCCORTNEY			
J M	Sacramento Granite	63	258
MCCORTY			
Jeremiah	Contra Costa Twp 1	57	486
John	Sierra Downieville	66	971
Margt	San Francisco San Francisco 9	68	971
MCCORVAGHEY			
Peter*	San Francisco San Francisco 5	67	545
MCCORY			
Robert	San Mateo Twp 2	65	121
William	San Francisco San Francisco 3	67	81
Wm	Sonoma Bodega	69	537
MCCOSKY			
James	Tuolumne Twp 5	71	519
MCCOSLIN			
Saml	Nevada Bloomfield	61	522
MCCOSTA			
William	Placer Forest H	62	766
MCCOSTEA			
Wm	Alameda Oakland	55	25
MCCOT			
James	Mariposa Twp 3	60	609
MCCOTTER			
Margaret	Sonoma Petaluma	69	577
MCCOUGHLE			
Phillip	Butte Cascade	56	692
MCCOUGHLIN			
John	Sierra Twp 7	66	912
MCCOULD			
Catherine	Calaveras Twp 5	57	183
MCCOULE			
James	Yuba Rose Bar	72	792
James*	Yuba Rose Bar	72	792
MCCOUN			
Emily	Nevada Rough &	61	414
J*	Nevada Nevada	61	283
R B	Tuolumne Twp 4	71	169
Robert	Tuolumne Big Oak	71	180
Robert H	Tuolumne Big Oak	71	180
Wm	Calaveras Twp 5	57	227
MCCOUNICT			
Do M*	Nevada Grass Valley	61	175
MCCOUNT			
P	San Francisco San Francisco 2	67	663
MCCOURBE			
Jno*	Sacramento Granite	63	270
MCCOURNRICT			
Do M*	Nevada Grass Valley	61	175
MCCOURT			
B	Nevada Eureka	61	357
Henry F	San Francisco San Francisco 10	177 67	
Jno	Klamath Liberty	59	239
Jno	Sacramento Ward 3	63	435
Michael	San Francisco San Francisco 10	177 67	
P	Nevada Nevada	61	274
Patrick	San Francisco San Francisco 3	67	56
Sallie	San Francisco San Francisco 10	184 67	
Wm	San Francisco San Francisco 10	310 67	
MCCOURTING			
John H	Yuba Bear Rvr	72	1000
MCCOURTNEY			
John	Marin Cortemad	60	784
Wm	Butte Oregon	56	641
MCCOUZY			
Gabriel*	Yuba Marysville	72	911
MCCOVER			
Bridget	San Francisco San Francisco 10	231 67	
MCCOWAGHEY			
Peter	San Francisco San Francisco 5	67	545
MCCOWAN			
Edward	San Francisco San Francisco 3	67	22
Jesse	Yuba Marysville	72	848
Thomas	Mendocino Calpella	60	811
MCCOWBE			
Jno*	Sacramento Natonia	63	270
MCCOWEN			
Isaac	Yuba Marysville	72	890
Jas	Napa Napa	61	79
MCCOWN			
Emily*	Nevada Rough &	61	414
Guadalupe	Contra Costa Twp 1	57	494
Mike	Sonoma Sonoma	69	635
MCCOX			
Jno	Butte Oregon	56	640
Jon	Butte Oregon	56	640
MCCOXMACK			
Ann	Tuolumne Twp 1	71	223
MCCOY			
---	Napa Napa	61	57
A	Nevada Grass Valley	61	221
A G	Butte Ophir	56	746
A H D	Butte Oregon	56	633
A L	Trinity Lewiston	70	953
A W	El Dorado Big Bar	58	741
Alex	Calaveras Twp 5	57	228
Alex Hall	San Francisco San Francisco 4	681	152
Alexander	Placer Michigan	62	856
Alexander	Sonoma Mendocino	69	455
Alexander*	Sonoma Mendocino	69	455
Alfred	Santa Clara Santa Clara	65	492
Alonzo	Butte Oregon	56	616
Andy	Sierra Downieville	66	976
Ann S	Nevada Grass Valley	61	143
Annie	San Francisco San Francisco 4	681	142
Ayle S	Butte Oregon	56	633

Name	County Locale	M653 RollPage
MCCOY		
Betsy	El Dorado Big Bar	58 741
Buckuer	San Joaquin Oneal	64 913
Charles	Colusa Spring Valley	57 436
Cornilius	Santa Clara San Jose	65 340
D	Siskiyou Cottonwood	69 101
Daniel	Siskiyou Callahan	69 13
Daniel D	San Luis Obispo	65 1
	San Luis Obispo	
Danl	Napa Napa	61 113
David B	Santa Clara San Jose	65 352
F	El Dorado Diamond	58 770
G	Nevada Grass Valley	61 221
G H	Siskiyou Cottonwood	69 103
G S	Marin Tomales	60 774
George	Contra Costa Twp 3	57 597
George	Mariposa Twp 3	60 616
George	San Francisco San Francisco 11	150 67
H S*	Yolo Washington	72 603
H S*	Marin Tomales	60 774
H W	Nevada Rough &	61 423
Harvey	Contra Costa Twp 3	57 596
Harvey	Santa Clara Gilroy	65 242
Henry	Yuba Marysville	72 927
Henson	Los Angeles Elmonte	59 257
Hurin	Placer Secret R	62 617
Isaac	Solano Fremont	69 381
J	Nevada Grass Valley	61 192
J	San Joaquin Stockton	641100
J	Siskiyou Cottonwoood	69 104
J M	Sutter Butte	70 798
J P	El Dorado Placerville	58 860
Jack	Sacramento Ward 1	63 110
James	El Dorado Georgetown	58 674
James	Plumas Quincy	62 954
James	San Diego San Diego	64 770
James	San Francisco San Francisco 2	67 727
James	Solano Suisan	69 216
James	Solano Benecia	69 310
James T	Contra Costa Twp 3	57 601
Jane	Placer Rattle Snake	62 603
Jas	San Francisco San Francisco 1	68 870
Jno	Sacramento Ward 1	63 149
Jno*	Sonoma Healdsbu	69 474
John	Butte Bidwell	56 724
John	Del Norte Crescent	58 647
John	El Dorado Georgetown	58 677
John	Los Angeles Los Angeles	59 387
John	Santa Clara Santa Clara	65 494
John	Shasta Cottonwood	66 723
John	Shasta Millvill	66 745
John	Sierra Downieville	661017
John	Siskiyou Yreka	69 172
John	Tulara Petersburg	71 52
John	Tuolumne Twp 3	71 464
Joseph B	Tulara Twp 1	71 111
Joseph B	Tulara Visalia	71 111
Luther	Sonoma Bodega	69 528
Mary	San Francisco San Francisco 6	67 422
Mary A	San Francisco San Francisco 10	166 67
Mason	Sonoma Armally	69 489
Mennio	San Francisco San Francisco 6	67 473
Minnie	San Francisco San Francisco 6	67 473
Mr	Sonoma Petaluma	69 604
N N	Mariposa Coulterville	60 697
P K	San Mateo Twp 2	65 121
Pascal	Siskiyou Cottonwoood	69 103
Patrick	Santa Cruz Pajaro	66 525
R	Amador Twp 3	55 402
R	Santa Clara Santa Clara	65 493
Redman	Santa Clara San Jose	65 389
Robert	Solano Vacaville	69 323
Robt	El Dorado Big Bar	58 741
S C	Nevada Grass Valley	61 221
T	Nevada Grass Valley	61 235
Thos*	Butte Bidwell	56 719
W C	Mariposa Twp 3	60 587
W R	Shasta Millvill	66 725
W W	Mariposa Coulterville	60 697
W W	Santa Clara San Jose	65 389
W W	Siskiyou Scott Va	69 25
Weedin	Del Norte Crescent	58 645
Wiliam L	Yuba Marysville	72 940
William	Los Angeles Los Angeles	59 338
William	San Francisco San Francisco 3	67 81
William L	Yuba Marysville	72 940
Wm	Sacramento Granite	63 266
Wm	San Francisco San Francisco 1	68 811
Wm	Tehama Lassen	70 881
Wm L	Nevada Grass Valley	61 143
Wm N	Los Angeles Elmonte	59 257
MCCOYL		
W W	Siskiyou Scott Va	69 25
MCCRABY		
Wm E	Sierra St Louis	66 805

Name	County Locale	M653 RollPage
MCCRACHIN		
John	Alameda Brooklyn	55 111
MCCRACKAN		
Robert	San Joaquin Elkhorn	64 956
MCCRACKEN		
Arthur	San Francisco San Francisco 1	68 822
Chas	Sacramento Ward 1	63 10
Henry	San Francisco San Francisco 1	68 888
J C	Tehama Red Bluff	70 907
Jasper	Sonoma Santa Rosa	69 412
Jno C	Sonoma Sonoma	69 659
John	Alameda Brooklyn	55 111
John	El Dorado Kelsey	581129
John	Sonoma Sonoma	69 661
S H	Klamath Klamath	59 225
William	Yuba Marysville	72 905
MCCRACKER		
John	El Dorado Kelsey	581129
MCCRACKIN		
Geo	Santa Clara San Jose	65 347
MCCRACKING		
O	Tuolumne Twp 4	71 164
MCCRACKNEY		
Jno	Sonoma Vallejo	69 609
MCCRADY		
John	Humbolt Eureka	59 176
S J*	Mariposa Twp 3	60 585
Thomas	Yuba Marysville	72 892
MCCRAE		
Jno	Alameda Brooklyn	55 176
MCCRAFFREY		
A*	Calaveras Twp 9	57 396
MCCRAIG		
Hugh	Sacramento Ward 4	63 512
MCCRAITH		
Francis	San Francisco San Francisco 12	364 67
MCCRAKEN		
William D*	San Joaquin Douglass	64 924
MCCRANELL		
Wm R	Alameda Oakland	55 24
MCCRANEY		
J	Nevada Nevada	61 278
William	Contra Costa Twp 1	57 537
MCCRANSLAW		
James	Marin Tomales	60 716
MCCRANY		
Peter	Shasta Shasta	66 733
MCCRAPAN		
James	Santa Clara Almaden	65 277
MCCRARY		
---	San Francisco San Francisco 4	681138
Abner	San Bernardino San Salvador	64 648
B*	Siskiyou Scott Ri	69 76
Charles	Yolo Cottonwood	72 658
Charles*	Yolo Cottonwood	72 658
David W	Sierra St Louis	66 805
Drucilla	San Bernardino San Salvador	64 649
John	San Bernardino San Salvador	64 648
Peter	Shasta Shasta	66 733
Sidney H	Mendocino Calpella	60 815
Sidney J*	Mendocino Calpella	60 815
MCCRASKY		
John A	Santa Clara San Jose	65 346
MCCRASSEN		
E	San Joaquin Stockton	641096
Jas	Santa Clara San Jose	65 367
MCCRAUGH		
W	Yolo Cottonwoood	72 557
MCCRAVEN		
Awen*	Sierra Twp 7	66 910
MCCRAY		
Hughs	Calaveras Twp 7	57 10
Ira	Fresno Twp 2	59 48
James	Napa Yount	61 46
Jno	Fresno Twp 3	59 16
Saml S	Placer Virginia	62 663
Thos	Fresno Millerto	59 1
William	Fresno Twp 1	59 34
MCCREA		
Bridg	Sacramento Ward 1	63 49
Charles	Mendocino Arrana	60 858
Danl	Santa Clara San Jose	65 344
Fredk	San Francisco San Francisco 1	68 879
Jas	San Mateo Twp 2	65 86
John	San Joaquin Castoria	64 898
K	Nevada Eureka	61 379
M	San Francisco San Francisco 5	67 551
Thomas	Monterey Monterey	60 965
William*	Nevada Rough &	61 422
MCCREADY		
Ben	Tuolumne Big Oak	71 151
Ben	Tuolumne Twp 4	71 151
C	San Francisco San Francisco 9	681067
George W	Placer Auburn	62 563
Hannah*	Yuba Marysville	72 892

Name	County Locale	M653 RollPage
MCCREADY		
J B*	Mariposa Twp 3	60 585
J R	Mariposa Twp 3	60 585
Jas	Sacramento Ward 3	63 488
Manuel??	Mariposa Twp 3	60 586
Peter	Plumas Quincy	62 920
Robt	Mariposa Twp 3	60 591
Robt	Plumas Meadow Valley	62 907
S J*	Mariposa Twp 3	60 585
Wm	Calaveras Twp 5	57 195
MCCREAR		
Chas	Mariposa Twp 3	60 586
MCCREARY		
I N*	Nevada Bridgeport	61 483
J	Yuba Bear Rvr	721007
J H	Nevada Bridgeport	61 483
J N*	Nevada Bridgeport	61 483
Thos	Solano Vallejo	69 250
W H	Sacramento Ward 1	63 36
W P	Sacramento Ward 3	63 438
Wh	Sacramento Ward 1	63 36
MCCREAS		
Chas	Mariposa Twp 3	60 586
MCCREE		
Daniel	Placer Yankee J	62 756
John*	San Francisco San Francisco 5	67 546
MCCREENY		
Thos	Amador Twp 7	55 416
MCCREERE		
L W*	San Francisco San Francisco 1	68 878
MCCREERY		
Thos	Amador Twp 7	55 416
MCCREN		
J*	Nevada Grass Valley	61 199
William*	Nevada Rough &	61 422
MCCRENDY		
Wm*	Calaveras Twp 5	57 195
MCCREODY		
Wm*	Calaveras Twp 5	57 195
MCCRERY		
Jeo	Alameda Brooklyn	55 206
Michael	Alameda Brooklyn	55 160
MCCREUDY		
Wm*	Calaveras Twp 5	57 195
MCCREW		
M*	San Francisco San Francisco 5	67 551
William	Nevada Rough &	61 422
MCCREY		
D	Solano Vacaville	69 329
MCCRIA		
Thomas	Monterey Monterey	60 965
MCCRIGHT		
Jos	Trinity Soldiers	701005
MCCRILDLE		
James	Sierra Twp 7	66 872
MCCRILLIS		
Allen	Sierra Twp 7	66 892
H P	Tuolumne Twp 2	71 309
MCCRINDLE		
A B	Sierra Downieville	66 954
MCCRINK		
Peter	San Francisco San Francisco 3	67 51
Peter	San Francisco San Francisco 3	67 75
MCCRISTY		
Saml	Santa Clara Alviso	65 402
MCCROFF		
Michael	Sierra Downieville	661018
MCCROFLIN		
Patrick	San Francisco San Francisco 1	68 858
MCCROLAND		
Awen	Sierra Twp 7	66 893
MCCROLANDO		
Owen	Sierra Twp 7	66 893
MCCRONY		
Alex	El Dorado Grizzly	581181
MCCROOM		
Hugh*	Sierra Pine Grove	66 834
MCCROPEN		
William	San Francisco San Francisco 7	681442
MCCRORON		
Owen	Sierra Twp 7	66 910
MCCRORY		
D W	Sierra Morristown	661055
James	Solano Suisan	69 217
John	Sierra Twp 5	66 918
S M	Sierra Morristown	661055
MCCROSAN		
Edward*	San Francisco San Francisco 2	67 662
MCCROSKEY		
D C	Merced Twp 1	60 895
MCCROSKY		
Jo	Mariposa Twp 1	60 672
MCCROSSEN		
George	Los Angeles Los Angeles	59 366
George	Los Angeles Los Angeles	59 36
MCCROWEN		
Owen	Sierra Forest C	66 910

California 1860 Census Index

Name	County Locale	M653 Roll	Page
MCCROWN			
J	Nevada Nevada	61	278
MCCROY			
S	Mendocino Big Rvr	60	840
MCCROZ			
---	Fresno Twp 2	59	44
MCCRUDY			
Mariah*	Sonoma Sonoma	69	656
MCCRUE			
Genevive	San Francisco San Francisco 2	67	661
M	Nevada Grass Valley	61	144
MCCRUGHT			
James	Santa Clara San Jose	65	288
MCCRUM			
Hugh	Sierra Pine Grove	66	834
Hugh*	Sierra Pine Grove	66	834
James*	Mariposa Twp 3	60	595
Robert	Sierra Poker Flats	66	842
MCCRUMLIN			
John*	Calaveras Twp 5	57	218
MCCRUMLUS			
John	Calaveras Twp 5	57	218
MCCRURY			
A J*	Sierra Twp 7	66	886
Andrew	San Francisco San Francisco 10	67	335
MCCRUSAN			
Edward*	San Francisco San Francisco 2	67	662
MCCRUSHAN			
Noah	Mendocino Little L	60	836
MCCRUSTIAN			
Noah	Mendocino Little L	60	836
O	Amador Twp 7	55	418
MCCRUTCHY			
William	Placer Todds Va	62	762
MCCRUVEN			
Aiven*	Sierra Twp 7	66	910
MCCSHILL			
J R	Mariposa Twp 1	60	664
MCCU RCE			
Nathaniel	Sierra Twp 5	66	941
MCCUBBIN			
Thomas	Yuba Marysville	72	866
MCCUBBINS			
Alexander	Tulara Twp 2	71	22
F	Sutter Yuba	70	776
MCCUCE			
E P*	Yolo Washington	72	565
MCCUCHEN			
Alex	Tuolumne Twp 2	71	280
MCCUCHEON			
Jesse	Tehama Tehama	70	948
John	Monterey S Antoni	60	972
MCCUDDEN			
Anne	San Francisco San Francisco 2	67	662
James	Solano Vallejo	69	251
MCCUE			
Agatha	Sacramento Ward 4	63	571
J	Sonoma Bodega	69	530
Jas	Napa Napa	61	74
John	San Francisco San Francisco 5	67	546
Patrick	Sonoma Bodega	69	530
Thos	Sacramento Granite	63	258
MCCUEN			
H	Nevada Grass Valley	61	152
J	Nevada Grass Valley	61	219
J H*	Nevada Grass Valley	61	185
J*	Nevada Grass Valley	61	199
James M*	Yuba Marysville	72	847
L H	Nevada Grass Valley	61	219
Thomas	Placer Iona Hills	62	891
MCCUFFREY			
James	Sierra La Porte	66	767
MCCUIDY			
Mariah*	Sonoma Sonoma	69	656
MCCUIE			
James	Nevada Bridgeport	61	484
MCCUINE			
L	Butte Wyandotte	56	664
MCCUIRY			
A J*	Sierra Twp 7	66	886
MCCULANCH			
Thos*	Nevada Red Dog	61	544
MCCULDA			
Jerry	Sierra Eureka	66	1042
MCCULEEN			
Dan	El Dorado Georgetown	58	758
MCCULLAFF			
Dennis	Humbolt Mattole	59	124
MCCULLAGH			
James	Monterey San Juan	60	992
MCCULLAM			
James*	Calaveras Twp 5	57	200
Thomas	Placer Michigan	62	830
MCCULLAN			
James	Calaveras Twp 5	57	200
MCCULLANAN			
J	Merced Monterey	60	940
J	Monterey Monterey	60	940
MCCULLANE			
James*	Calaveras Twp 5	57	200
MCCULLEF			
J M	Solano Vacaville	69	329
MCCULLEN			
Marrion	Calaveras Twp 8	57	65
Philip	Sacramento Ward 4	63	525
William	Santa Cruz Santa Cruz	66	633
Wm	Placer Illinois	62	703
MCCULLEY			
C	El Dorado Newtown	58	778
J M	Solano Vacaville	69	329
M	El Dorado Kelsey	58	1130
MCCULLIAGH			
Mich*	Sacramento Natonia	63	285
MCCULLIGH			
Mich	Sacramento Natonia	63	285
MCCULLIN			
Robert	Fresno Twp 2	59	50
MCCULLOCH			
Elizabeth	Placer Dutch Fl	62	721
James	Mendocino Calpella	60	812
Jno*	San Francisco San Francisco 10	67	248
Robert	Tuolumne Chinese	71	521
S	Mendocino Calpella	60	812
S*	Mendocino Calpella	60	812
Wm	San Francisco San Francisco 9	68	1075
MCCULLOCK			
Andrew	Placer Mealsburg	62	702
Andrew	Santa Clara Almaden	65	268
Geo	Placer Dutch Fl	62	713
George	Fresno Twp 1	59	30
James	Mendocino Calpella	60	812
John	Santa Clara Almaden	65	268
John W	San Joaquin Castoria	64	907
Margaret	Placer Illinois	62	704
Robers M*	Tuolumne Twp 5	71	521
S*	Mendocino Calpella	60	812
Wm	Sacramento American	63	159
MCCULLOGH			
Amos	Sacramento Ward 1	63	41
John	Plumas Meadow Valley	62	934
MCCULLON			
Robt	Sonoma Petaluma	69	547
MCCULLOSH			
Wm	San Francisco San Francisco 9	68	1075
MCCULLOUGH			
Cynthia	Shasta Shasta	66	666
Danl	Tuolumne Twp 1	71	235
Edwd	Monterey Pajaro	60	1020
Eliza	Mariposa Twp 1	60	639
Geo	Placer Virginia	62	662
Henry	Solano Vallejo	69	262
Henry	Tulara Twp 2	71	5
John	Placer Todds Va	62	784
John	Sacramento San Joaquin	63	360
John	Tulara Twp 2	71	6
John	Tulara Twp 2	71	7
John D	Sonoma Santa Rosa	69	396
Joseph	Humbolt Eureka	59	170
L G	Sonoma Santa Rosa	69	397
M	Sutter Butte	70	782
Mike	Alameda Brooklyn	55	105
Morris	Alameda Brooklyn	55	105
Peter	Sierra La Porte	66	778
Robert	Sierra Downieville	66	1000
Robert	Tulara Yule Rvr	71	8
Saml	Del Norte Happy Ca	58	661
Thos	Mariposa Twp 1	60	639
William	Placer Iona Hills	62	872
William*	Yuba Marysville	72	971
MCCULLOW			
Enooc	Calaveras Twp 6	57	131
MCCULLUGH			
Mich*	Sacramento Natonia	63	285
MCCULLUM			
J	Calaveras Twp 9	57	400
J G	El Dorado Placerville	58	837
James*	San Francisco San Francisco 7	68	1440
O S	Placer Dutch Fl	62	719
MCCULLY			
E H	Shasta Shasta	66	664
Fanny	Sacramento Ward 4	63	511
George	San Bernardino S Timate	64	687
James	Tuolumne Twp 5	71	503
Jno	Butte Kimshaw	56	607
Thomas	Sierra Twp 5	66	918
MCCULOCK			
Jana	Santa Clara Almaden	65	272
MCCULTOM			
R H	Santa Clara San Jose	65	279
MCCUMBER			
Fred	Amador Twp 3	55	396
G W	Shasta Millvill	66	746
J E	El Dorado Placerville	58	887
MCCUME			
Thomas	Marin Tomales	60	720
MCCUMEY			
Ann*	Sierra Downieville	66	967
Ann*	Sierra Downieville	66	967
MCCUNBS			
A M*	Shasta Millvill	66	754
MCCUNE			
Alex	Sonoma Petaluma	69	546
Henry	Solano Vacaville	69	350
J	Nevada Eureka	61	358
J A A*	Solano Montezuma	69	375
J A C	Solano Montezuma	69	375
J M	Solano Vacaville	69	325
James C	Yuba Marysville	72	847
Jas	Placer Virginia	62	677
Jas	Sonoma Petaluma	69	602
John	Butte Ophir	56	758
John	Nevada Bridgeport	61	497
John W	Placer Auburn	62	594
Mathew	Nevada Rough &	61	398
Wm	Butte Oro	56	677
MCCUNEY			
A D	Siskiyou Scott Va	69	59
J D	Siskiyou Scott Va	69	59
MCCUNG			
Jas*	Placer Ophirville	62	659
MCCUNN			
Henry	Solano Benecia	69	313
MCCUNNY			
Jas*	Placer Ophirville	62	659
MCCUPS			
M	Santa Clara San Jose	65	349
MCCUR			
Con	Calaveras Twp 4	57	310
MCCURAY			
Saml	Klamath Trinidad	59	223
MCCURCE			
Nathaniel	Sierra Twp 5	66	941
MCCURDEY			
James*	Calaveras Twp 8	57	109
MCCURDY			
Elisha	Plumas Quincy	62	985
J	Nevada Grass Valley	61	144
J F	Nevada Bridgeport	61	447
Jas	Alameda Brooklyn	55	149
John	Placer Ophir	62	652
John	Sierra Downieville	66	1016
Mariah	Sonoma Sonoma	69	656
Owen	El Dorado Coloma	58	1107
Samule	Calaveras Twp 7	57	15
Sharlott	Sonoma Petaluma	69	566
Thos	Mariposa Coulterville	60	696
MCCURE			
James S*	Nevada Bridgeport	61	493
James*	Nevada Bridgeport	61	484
James*	Nevada Red Dog	61	550
Lewis	Tehama Pasakent	70	858
Wm	Santa Clara San Jose	65	372
MCCURIE			
John	Nevada Bridgeport	61	497
MCCURLEY			
Anthony	San Joaquin Douglass	64	915
J	Nevada Grass Valley	61	147
MCCURLY			
J	Nevada Grass Valley	61	147
MCCURMAS			
T J	El Dorado Casumnes	58	1162
T J*	El Dorado Casumnes	58	1162
MCCURMES			
T J*	El Dorado Casumnes	58	1162
MCCURNEY			
Ann*	Sierra Downieville	66	967
MCCURR			
Con*	Calaveras Twp 4	57	310
MCCURRY			
A J*	Sierra Twp 7	66	886
Alex	El Dorado Grizzly	58	1181
J	El Dorado Indian D	58	1159
M A	Tuolumne Twp 2	71	304
MCCURTIS			
P*	Nevada Grass Valley	61	151
MCCURTY			
Andrew	Yuba Slate Ro	72	689
P	Nevada Grass Valley	61	151
MCCURY			
A J	Sierra Twp 7	66	886
MCCUSDY			
Thos	Mariposa Coulterville	60	696
MCCUSETIN			
Thomas	El Dorado Mud Springs	58	995
MCCUSH			
John*	Napa Yount	61	54

California 1860 Census Index

Name	County Locale	M653 RollPage
MCCUSING		
William	El Dorado Placerville	58 891
MCCUSKER		
C E	Tuolumne Twp 2	71 330
MCCUSKY		
John	Mariposa Twp 3	60 563
MCCUSPEY		
S L	Butte Chico	56 534
MCCUSSEY		
S L*	Butte Chico	56 534
MCCUSTER		
James	El Dorado Mud Springs	58 972
M	El Dorado Placerville	58 845
MCCUSTHY		
Elisabeth	Sierra Forest C	66 910
Elizabeth	Sierra Twp 7	66 910
MCCUSTLE		
Peter	Santa Clara San Jose	65 355
MCCUSTON		
R M	Amador Twp 7	55 417
MCCUSTY		
John	Mariposa Twp 3	60 563
MCCUSUE		
Thomas	Marin Tomales	60 720
MCCUTCHAN		
Edward	Santa Clara San Jose	65 338
MCCUTCHEN		
J	Shasta Shasta	66 673
J T	Trinity Soldiers	701005
Jas	Santa Clara San Jose	65 356
John	Placer Auburn	62 568
Levi	Calaveras Twp 4	57 310
M E	Santa Clara Gilroy	65 240
MCCUTCHEON		
Ellen	San Francisco San Francisco 8	681246
MCCUTCHUR		
Alex	Placer Iona Hills	62 888
MCCUTLOUGH		
Robert*	Sierra Downieville	661000
MCCUTTOUGH		
Robert*	Sierra Downieville	661000
MCCUUE		
James M*	Yuba Marysville	72 847
MCCWE		
James*	Nevada Red Dog	61 550
MCDADE		
James	Tuolumne Twp 1	71 266
John	Siskiyou Klamath	69 92
MCDAESTEIN		
John*	Yuba Marysville	72 914
MCDAFFEE		
Martha A	Trinity Indian C	70 988
MCDAFFY		
R J	Tuolumne Jamestown	71 469
MCDALE		
Martin	Sierra Pine Grove	66 831
MCDAMALS		
Wm*	Sacramento Ward 1	63 83
MCDANELL		
Charles*	San Francisco San Francisco 4	681213
John M	Shasta French G	66 715
MCDANIAL		
Ben G	Humbolt Eureka	59 174
Franklin	Humbolt Bucksport	59 157
Wm	Humbolt Bucksport	59 157
MCDANIALS		
Wm*	Sacramento Ward 1	63 83
MCDANIEL		
Abner B	Los Angeles Elmonte	59 256
Andrew	El Dorado Gold Hill	581097
C	Calaveras Twp 9	57 391
Catharine	San Francisco San Francisco 8	681269
Charles	Plumas Quincy	62 959
Charles	San Francisco San Francisco 4	681213
Charles	Tuolumne Twp 2	71 342
Charles*	San Francisco San Francisco 4	681213
D G	Trinity Douglas	70 979
David	San Francisco San Francisco 7	681346
Dempsey	Yuba Marysville	72 852
Dempsey	Yuba Marysville	72 857
Douglas*	San Bernadino	64 615
	San Bernardino	
E W*	Mariposa Twp 3	60 587
Edward	Yuba Marysville	72 887
Elijah	Colusa Muion	57 460
F M	Placer Iona Hills	62 860
F M	Placer Iona Hills	62 867
Frances E*	Yolo Washington	72 561
Francis	Placer Virginia	62 670
George L	Yuba Marysville	72 879
Jackson	Santa Clara San Jose	65 351
Jas	San Francisco San Francisco 10	300
		67
Jessie J	Solano Benecia	69 281
Jno	Butte Hamilton	56 525
Jno M	Butte Hamilton	56 525

Name	County Locale	M653 RollPage
MCDANIEL		
Jno*	Butte Chico	56 558
John	Contra Costa Twp 2	57 573
John	Santa Cruz Pescadero	66 643
John	Sierra Twp 7	66 889
John	Yuba Marysville	72 878
Jos	San Francisco San Francisco 9	681052
L E	Stanislaus Emory	70 746
Margaret	Tulara Twp 1	71 98
O	Sonoma Washington	69 673
Patrick	San Francisco San Francisco 8	681259
R	Sutter Butte	70 787
R P	Nevada Rough &	61 405
Richard A	Yuba Marysville	72 886
S	Sutter Nicolaus	70 838
Thos	Butte Oregon	56 623
W R	Shasta Shasta	66 656
William	Monterey Alisal	601039
William D	Tulara Visalia	71 105
William H	San Joaquin Douglass	64 924
Wm	Colusa Monroeville	57 448
Wm	Placer Auburn	62 571
MCDANIELS		
W H	Del Norte Crescent	58 649
MCDANILE		
John	Sierra Twp 7	66 889
MCDANNENYH		
James*	Calaveras Twp 6	57 157
MCDANT		
Patrick	San Francisco San Francisco 1	68 840
MCDARAK		
E W*	Mariposa Twp 3	60 587
MCDARCK		
E W*	Mariposa Twp 3	60 587
MCDARRITT		
Michl*	San Francisco San Francisco 1	68 839
MCDAUGAL		
J T	Calaveras Twp 9	57 400
MCDAVID		
A Jackson	Alameda Brooklyn	55 175
Dennis	San Francisco San Francisco 8	681299
E W*	Mariposa Twp 3	60 587
Patrick	Sierra Whiskey	66 847
Randolph	Alameda Brooklyn	55 175
MCDAVIT		
D	San Joaquin Stockton	641092
James	Tuolumne Shawsfla	71 376
MCDAVITT		
Chas	San Francisco San Francisco 1	68 858
John	San Francisco San Francisco 2	67 601
Michl*	San Francisco San Francisco 1	68 839
MCDAWL		
Allex	Nevada Bridgeport	61 487
MCDAWLD		
Thomas	Calaveras Twp 10	57 282
MCDCDONNOUGH		
P	Tuolumne Twp 2	71 349
MCDE DONNOUGH		
P	Tuolumne Columbia	71 349
MCDEAK		
Anthony	Sonoma Santa Rosa	69 410
MCDEAMID		
C H	Tuolumne Twp 2	71 352
MCDEAN		
Archibold	San Francisco San Francisco 3	67 59
MCDECKER		
William*	Tuolumne Don Pedro	71 539
MCDEDA		
Edwd	San Francisco San Francisco 9	681002
MCDELANEY		
Chas	San Francisco San Francisco 2	67 729
MCDEMITT		
John	Placer Sacramento	62 645
MCDEMOTT		
Franklin	San Joaquin Elkhorn	64 952
James	San Joaquin Elkhorn	64 971
William F	San Joaquin Douglass	64 915
MCDENALD		
Alex	Sacramento Granite	63 256
James	Mariposa Twp 3	60 593
R*	Butte Bidwell	56 715
MCDENNIT		
James	Siskiyou Callahan	69 14
MCDENOUGH		
T	Sacramento Granite	63 264
MCDENZIE		
Alex	Calaveras Twp 4	57 318
MCDERERELL		
A S*	Sacramento Granite	63 264
MCDERMAN		
Bernard	Tuolumne Twp 2	71 352
MCDERMAT		
Jas	Sonoma Sonoma	69 654
MCDERMATT		
George	El Dorado Greenwood	58 721
John	Tuolumne Twp 3	71 455

Name	County Locale	M653 RollPage
MCDERMATT		
Thomas	San Francisco San Francisco 9	68 944
MCDERMER		
George	Santa Clara San Jose	65 321
MCDERMET		
Charles	Siskiyou Scott Va	69 26
Patk	San Francisco San Francisco 9	681024
MCDERMID		
Wm	Tuolumne Columbia	71 352
MCDERMILL		
W F	San Luis Obispo San Luis Obispo	65 29
MCDERMIT		
C F	Mariposa Twp 3	60 585
Charles	Siskiyou Scott Va	69 26
Frank	Sacramento Dry Crk	63 374
Geo*	Sacramento Ward 4	63 555
J	Calaveras Twp 9	57 355
James A	Siskiyou Callahan	69 14
P	Mariposa Twp 3	60 585
Pat	San Francisco San Francisco 9	68 994
Peter	Placer Auburn	62 567
MCDERMITT		
A	Amador Twp 3	55 395
Agnes	San Francisco San Francisco 1	68 822
H*	Nevada Eureka	61 371
John	Contra Costa Twp 3	57 617
Mary	San Francisco San Francisco 10	170
		67
Patk*	San Francisco San Francisco 10	168
		67
Sarah	San Francisco San Francisco 1	68 845
Thos	San Francisco San Francisco 10	340
		67
MCDERMOD		
John*	San Mateo Twp 1	65 67
MCDERMOT		
C A S	San Francisco San Francisco 9	68 973
C C	San Bernardino Santa Barbara	64 150
C F	Mariposa Twp 3	60 585
Celia	Sacramento Ward 1	63 97
Chas	Calaveras Twp 6	57 168
Chs	Sonoma Petaluma	69 591
F	Tuolumne Chinese	71 522
Geo*	Sacramento Ward 4	63 555
Hannah	San Francisco San Francisco 9	68 969
James	Calaveras Twp 5	57 216
Jas	Sonoma Sonoma	69 654
John	Tuolumne Jamestown	71 429
Jos	San Francisco San Francisco 10	274
		67
Michael	Tuolumne Twp 1	71 196
Patrick	San Francisco San Francisco 10	213
		67
William	Plumas Quincy	62 989
Wm	Sonoma Petaluma	69 564
MCDERMOTH		
Edward	Yuba Marysville	72 908
William	Calaveras Twp 5	57 210
William	Tuolumne Twp 6	71 532
William*	Calaveras Twp 5	57 210
MCDERMOTT		
A	Butte Ophir	56 764
Abram	Tuolumne Columbia	71 343
Andrew	San Francisco San Francisco 1	68 858
B	San Francisco San Francisco 6	67 458
B	San Francisco San Francisco 5	67 489
B	San Francisco San Francisco 5	67 492
B*	San Francisco San Francisco 6	67 458
Bill	San Francisco San Francisco 4	681229
Bridget	San Francisco San Francisco 7	681 653
Cath*	Alameda Brooklyn	55 114
Celia	Sacramento Ward 1	63 97
Chas	San Francisco San Francisco 2	67 595
Edward*	Yuba Marysville	72 908
F	Tuolumne Twp 5	71 522
Geo	Tuolumne Shawsfla	71 386
George	Solano Suisan	69 229
Hugh	Placer Forest H	62 806
J	Nevada Eureka	61 357
J	Tuolumne Big Oak	71 156
J	Tuolumne Twp 4	71 156
James	Calaveras Twp 5	57 216
James	Siskiyou Yreka	69 145
James	Siskiyou Scott Va	69 56
James	Solano Benecia	69 312
John	Tuolumne Jamestown	71 455
Jos	Sacramento Ward 3	63 441
Jos	San Francisco San Francisco 2	67 595
Joseph	Alameda Brooklyn	55 135
M	San Francisco San Francisco 5	67 518
Mary	San Francisco San Francisco 4	681115
Mary	San Francisco San Francisco 7	681414
Mary	Tuolumne Twp 1	71 260
Michael	San Francisco San Francisco 12	389
		67
P	Santa Clara San Jose	65 339

Name	County Locale	M653 Roll	Page
MCDERMOTT			
P	Santa Clara Alviso	65	408
T	San Francisco San Francisco 12	67	394
Thomas	San Francisco San Francisco 2	67	698
Thomas	San Francisco San Francisco 9	68	944
Thomas	Yuba Marysville	72	865
Thomas A	Solano Benecia	69	286
Thos	San Francisco San Francisco 10	67	274
Timothy	Alameda Brooklyn	55	95
W	San Francisco San Francisco 5	67	490
William	Calaveras Twp 5	57	210
William	Tuolumne Green Springs	71	532
William*	Calaveras Twp 5	57	210
Wm	Tuolumne Columbia	71	310
MCDERMUNT			
J	Sutter Yuba	70	766
MCDERNAN			
Hugh	Calaveras Twp 4	57	318
MCDERNOT			
Jas*	San Francisco San Francisco 9	681	072
Jos	San Francisco San Francisco 9	681	072
MCDERRIOT			
John*	Tuolumne Twp 3	71	429
MCDERRITT			
Jas	Plumas Quincy	62	960
MCDERVIT			
Saml	Calaveras Twp 6	57	184
MCDERVOT			
Jas*	San Francisco San Francisco 9	681	072
MCDEULT			
Jas*	San Francisco San Francisco 1	68	901
MCDEUTT			
Jas	San Francisco San Francisco 1	68	901
MCDEVIT			
Hugh	Placer Rattle Snake	62	626
MCDEVITT			
Bernard	San Francisco San Francisco 11	67	129
Elizabeth	San Francisco San Francisco 10	67	203
Mary A	Alameda Brooklyn	55	204
Mary Dalamati	Solano Benecia	69	300
Mary Dolamati	Solano Benecia	69	300
Patrick	Tuolumne Shawsfla	71	376
MCDEWELL			
A	Sacramento Granite	63	240
MCDEWIT			
Saml	Calaveras Twp 5	57	184
MCDEYNONS			
Andrw	Sierra Downieville	661	002
MCDIN			
David	Tuolumne Sonora	71	214
MCDINLEY			
J A*	Siskiyou Scott Va	69	26
MCDINNEL			
Ann*	San Francisco San Francisco 9	68	983
MCDIREGGE			
Edward	Sierra Eureka	661	046
MCDIRMOTT			
B*	San Francisco San Francisco 6	67	458
Peter W	Sacramento Ward 3	63	459
MCDIVELL			
A S*	Sacramento Granite	63	264
MCDIVRELL			
A S	Sacramento Granite	63	264
MCDOC			
Patrick	Tuolumne Twp 2	71	352
MCDOE			
Louis	Placer Michigan	62	831
MCDOINALD			
George	Yuba Linda	72	986
MCDOLARD			
Jas	Calaveras Twp 9	57	352
MCDOLE			
John	Mariposa Twp 1	60	634
MCDOLTON			
Catharine	San Joaquin Elkhorn	64	972
MCDOMALD			
A*	Nevada Nevada	61	245
MCDON			
M	San Francisco San Francisco 3	67	54
MCDONA			
Saml	Sonoma Petaluma	69	616
Saml	Sonoma Vallejo	69	616
MCDONAEA			
W	Napa Hot Springs	61	16
MCDONAH			
E W*	Mariposa Twp 3	60	587
MCDONAL			
Barney	San Francisco San Francisco 10	67	328
Fred	El Dorado Mud Springs	58	963
Richd	San Francisco San Francisco 9	681	078
MCDONALD			
---	San Francisco San Francisco 10	67	217

Name	County Locale	M653 Roll	Page
MCDONALD			
---	Sonoma Salt Point	69	690
---	Stanislaus Emory	70	756
A	Klamath S Fork	59	200
A	Mariposa Twp 1	60	663
A	Sacramento Ward 1	63	32
A	Sacramento Cosumnes	63	405
A	Sacramento Ward 4	63	544
A	Siskiyou Callahan	69	7
A	Sonoma Sonoma	69	659
A C	Mendocino Big Rock	60	872
A D	San Francisco San Francisco 10	67	200
A M	Santa Clara Alviso	65	406
Agnes	San Francisco San Francisco 9	681	055
Alex	Amador Twp 2	55	266
Alex	San Francisco San Francisco 1	68	892
Alex	San Francisco San Francisco 1	68	908
Alex	Siskiyou Scott Va	69	36
Alexander	Santa Cruz Santa Cruz	66	633
Alexander	Sierra Twp 7	66	880
Andrew	Mariposa Twp 3	60	561
Angus*	Placer Secret R	62	615
Ann	Alameda Oakland	55	4
Ann	Stanislaus Branch	70	697
Anna	Sierra Pine Grove	66	830
Annie	Sierra Pine Grove	66	830
Arch	Solano Benecia	69	288
Archer	Tuolumne Columbia	71	334
Augus*	Placer Secret R	62	615
Austin	San Joaquin O'Neal	641	004
Bridget	Siskiyou Yreka	69	184
Bridjet*	San Francisco San Francisco 1	68	931
C	Shasta Horsetown	66	690
C P	El Dorado Kelsey	581	155
C???	Tuolumne Twp 1	71	185
Calvin B	Sierra Downieville	66	963
Cane*	Nevada Bridgeport	61	502
Canl*	Nevada Bridgeport	61	502
Catharine	El Dorado Coloma	581	117
Caul	Nevada Bridgeport	61	502
Charles	Calaveras Twp 10	57	266
Charles	Del Norte Ferry P O	58	666
Chas	Butte Ophir	56	793
Christopher	Yuba Marysville	72	858
Christopher	Yuba Marysville	72	859
D	Del Norte Crescent	58	642
D	El Dorado Kelsey	581	157
D	San Francisco San Francisco 5	67	549
D L	Sacramento Ward 4	63	561
Daniel	San Francisco San Francisco 8	681	238
Daniel	Sierra Downieville	661	002
Danl	Amador Twp 1	55	488
Danl	Butte Oregon	56	618
Danl	Calaveras Twp 10	57	266
Danl	Napa Napa	61	91
Danl*	Napa Napa	61	91
Daul	Plumas Quincy	621	000
Daul*	Calaveras Twp 10	57	267
David	San Joaquin Stockton	641	025
David B	Calaveras Twp 4	57	331
Donald	Calaveras Twp 10	57	291
Donald	Sonoma Santa Rosa	69	396
Downey	Santa Cruz Santa Cruz	66	599
Duncan	San Francisco San Francisco 4	681	148
E M	Shasta French G	66	715
Ed	Sacramento Natonia	63	284
Edward	Placer Michigan	62	809
Edward N	Los Angeles San Pedro	59	480
Edwin	Placer Forest H	62	765
Elizabeth	Los Angeles Los Angeles	59	363
Elizabeth	Placer Goods	62	695
Enos	Solano Vallejo	69	275
F G	Calaveras Twp 9	57	384
Felix	San Francisco San Francisco 12	67	364
Frank	Napa Napa	61	67
Fred	Stanislaus Emory	70	747
G	Tuolumne Twp 1	71	185
G R	El Dorado Placerville	58	822
Geo	El Dorado Indian D	581	159
Geo	Mendocino Round Va	60	880
Geo	Stanislaus Empire	70	732
Geo	Tehama Lassen	70	868
Geo W	Santa Clara San Jose	65	377
George	Placer Damascus	62	846
George	Plumas Meadow Valley	62	906
George	Yuba Suida	72	986
George W	Yuba Marysville	72	929
Gidion	Nevada Bloomfield	61	529
H	Amador Twp 6	55	439
Hannah	Marin Novato	60	738
Henry	San Francisco San Francisco 2	67	757
Hiram	San Joaquin Elkhorn	64	972
Hiram C	Fresno Twp 2	59	48
Hy W	San Francisco San Francisco 1	68	907

Name	County Locale	M653 Roll	Page
MCDONALD			
Isaac	Tehama Antelope	70	893
Iwe J R*	Calaveras Twp 4	57	322
J	Nevada Grass Valley	61	225
J	Nevada Nevada	61	295
J	Nevada Eureka	61	370
J	Nevada Bridgeport	61	447
J	Sacramento Ward 1	63	82
J	San Francisco San Francisco 4	681	230
J	San Francisco San Francisco 7	681	443
J	San Francisco San Francisco 5	67	517
J H	Sacramento Granite	63	234
J J	Butte Mountain	56	736
J J	El Dorado Mud Springs	58	995
J J	Tuolumne Twp 2	71	298
J M	Sierra Eureka	661	046
J P	Sacramento Ward 4	63	527
Jack	Santa Clara Almaden	65	267
James	Contra Costa Twp 2	57	552
James	Marin Bolinas	60	744
James	Mariposa Twp 3	60	593
James	Placer Iona Hills	62	879
James	Plumas Quincy	621	001
James	Sacramento Centre	63	176
James	San Bernardino Santa Barbara	64	199
James	San Francisco San Francisco 9	681	101
James	San Francisco San Francisco 7	681	421
James	San Joaquin Stockton	641	070
James	Santa Clara San Jose	65	378
James	Santa Cruz Pajaro	66	544
James	Santa Cruz Santa Cruz	66	639
James	Siskiyou Scott Va	69	36
James A	Solano Benecia	69	288
James B	Siskiyou Shasta Rvr	69	115
James B	Yuba Marysville	72	876
James G	Los Angeles Los Angeles	59	358
James L	Yuba Bear Rvr	721	000
Jane	Yuba Marysville	72	912
Jas	Placer Secret R	62	621
Jas	Placer Folsom	62	641
Jas	Sacramento Sutter	63	291
Jas	Sacramento Ward 4	63	562
Jas	San Francisco San Francisco 2	67	672
Jas	San Francisco San Francisco 2	67	773
Jas	San Francisco San Francisco 1	68	855
Jas	Santa Clara San Jose	65	377
Jas	Stanislaus Buena Village	70	721
Jas J R	Calaveras Twp 4	57	322
Jas M	San Francisco San Francisco 12	67	387
Jas S	San Francisco San Francisco 12	67	373
Jeanette	Sacramento Ward 4	63	554
Jno	Sacramento Centre	63	176
Jno	Sacramento Ward 4	63	595
Jno	San Francisco San Francisco 9	68	984
John	Butte Oro	56	687
John	Calaveras Twp 9	57	380
John	Calaveras Twp 7	57	7
John	El Dorado Coloma	581	083
John	Los Angeles Tejon	59	524
John	Marin Tomales	60	722
John	Monterey S Antoni	60	973
John	Placer Forest H	62	765
John	Placer Iona Hills	62	877
John	Placer Iona Hills	62	887
John	Plumas Quincy	62	920
John	San Francisco San Francisco 11	67	123
John	San Francisco San Francisco 10	67	167
John	San Francisco San Francisco 1	68	909
John	Santa Clara San Jose	65	375
John	Santa Clara San Jose	65	376
John	Santa Cruz Watsonville	66	536
John	Sierra Pine Grove	66	831
John	Sierra Twp 7	66	882
John	Solano Green Valley	69	242
John	Sonoma Armally	69	493
John	Tehama Tehama	70	949
John A	Calaveras Twp 7	57	19
John C	Sierra Pine Grove	66	831
John T	Santa Cruz Watsonville	66	536
Jos	San Francisco San Francisco 2	67	773
Joseph	Amador Twp 4	55	244
Joseph	Placer Illinois	62	706
Joseph	San Diego Colorado	64	808
Jws J R*	Calaveras Twp 4	57	322
Kate	San Francisco San Francisco 2	67	652
Kincth	Sierra Eureka	661	042
L	El Dorado Coloma	581	069
L W	Placer Dutch Fl	62	710
M	Butte Kimshaw	56	592
M	Del Norte Crescent	58	623
M	Placer Dutch Fl	62	728

Name	County Locale	M653 RollPage
MCDONALD		
M	Sacramento Granite	63 258
M	Sacramento Ward 4	63 591
M	San Francisco San Francisco 1	68 812
M	Sonoma Cloverdale	69 681
M	Yolo Merritt	72 577
M N	Yolo Washington	72 562
M W	Yolo Washington	72 562
M*	Sacramento Granite	63 258
Maritas*	Santa Cruz Santa Cruz	66 600
Maritus*	Santa Cruz Santa Cruz	66 600
Martin	San Francisco San Francisco 3	67 43
Martin	Siskiyou Callahan	69 5
Mary	Sacramento Ward 1	63 40
Mary	Solano Benecia	69 297
Mary	Sonoma Petaluma	69 593
Mary A	San Francisco San Francisco 10	333 67
Mary J	San Francisco San Francisco 10	183 67
Mich	Sacramento Natonia	63 285
Milekiah	Contra Costa Twp 2	57 568
N	Amador Twp 4	55 254
N	Sacramento Alabama	63 411
N	Sutter Nicolaus	70 837
O C	Placer Christia	62 736
Oliver G	Plumas Meadow Valley	62 929
Owen	Sierra Port Win	66 795
Owen	Sierra Forest C	66 909
P	Nevada Grass Valley	61 205
P	Nevada Grass Valley	61 225
P	Nevada Eureka	61 370
P	Sacramento Ward 1	63 104
P	Sacramento Ward 1	63 134
Patrick	Alameda Brooklyn	55 156
Patrick	San Francisco San Francisco 2	67 666
Paul*	Calaveras Twp 10	57 266
Peter	San Mateo Twp 3	65 106
Peter	Sierra St Louis	66 811
R	Butte Bidwell	56 715
R	Nevada Nevada	61 292
R	Nevada Eureka	61 360
R	Stanislaus Emory	70 754
R A	Placer Michigan	62 819
R H	Calaveras Twp 9	57 374
R*	Butte Bidwell	56 715
Richard	Placer Michigan	62 849
Richd J	San Francisco San Francisco 12	373 67
Robert	Alameda Brooklyn	55 212
Ronald	San Francisco San Francisco 7	681362
Runald	San Joaquin Oneal	64 930
S	San Joaquin Stockton	641044
S	Tuolumne Shawsfla	71 391
Sam	Yuba Marysville	72 912
T A	Tuolumne Jamestown	71 425
T J	Solano Benecia	69 297
Terry	Yolo Slate Ra	72 710
Terry	Yuba Slate Ro	72 710
Thomas	Calaveras Twp 10	57 282
Thomas	Placer Michigan	62 838
Thomas	San Francisco San Francisco 7	681340
Thos	Butte Bidwell	56 711
Thos	Merced Twp 1	60 895
Thos	Santa Cruz Santa Cruz	66 599
Thos	Shasta Horsetown	66 698
Timothy	San Francisco San Francisco 8	681243
W	Napa Hot Springs	61 16
W	Solano Benecia	69 284
W	Solano Benecia	69 291
W M	Solano Benecia	69 284
William	Monterey Monterey	60 959
William	Plumas Meadow Valley	62 911
William P	Yuba Marysville	72 882
Winfred	Alameda Brooklyn	55 100
Wm	Humbolt Table Bl	59 141
Wm	Sacramento Ward 3	63 449
Wm	San Francisco San Francisco 10	171 67
Wm	San Francisco San Francisco 10	303 67
Wm	San Francisco San Francisco 2	67 575
Wm	San Francisco San Francisco 1	68 914
Wm B	Sonoma Mendocino	69 457
Wm C	Placer Rattle Snake	62 600
Wm R	Calaveras Twp 6	57 141
MCDONALDS		
Daniel	Sierra Downieville	661002
MCDONALE		
W	Sacramento Ward 3	63 468
MCDONALL		
Geo	El Dorado Mud Springs	58 999
John	El Dorado Casumnes	581104
John	El Dorado Mud Springs	58 999
Mary	San Francisco San Francisco 10	274 67

Name	County Locale	M653 RollPage
MCDONAUGH		
M	Nevada Nevada	61 264
Wm	Placer Virginia	62 673
MCDONEL		
Elizabeth	San Francisco San Francisco 9	68 973
Francis	San Francisco San Francisco 9	68 953
Jane V	San Francisco San Francisco 4	681151
MCDONELL		
D	El Dorado Placerville	58 890
Edward	El Dorado Coloma	581082
Geo	Sacramento Ward 1	63 140
Jas	Butte Cascade	56 690
John	El Dorado Mud Springs	58 972
Jos	Butte Cascade	56 690
Peter	Tuolumne Don Pedro	71 539
Thomas	Alameda Brooklyn	55 117
Thos	Alameda Brooklyn	55 157
MCDONEUL		
Ann*	San Francisco San Francisco 9	68 983
MCDONGAL		
Wm*	San Francisco San Francisco 2	67 694
MCDONGALL		
Chas	Sacramento Ward 1	63 42
William	Sierra Whiskey	66 844
MCDONIEL		
Joseph	San Joaquin Douglass	64 918
MCDONLEY		
J A	Siskiyou Scott Va	69 26
MCDONNAL		
Ann	Sierra Twp 7	66 915
MCDONNALD		
A	Butte Oregon	56 621
A	Nevada Nevada	61 245
A	Yolo Washington	72 562
A R	San Francisco San Francisco 6	67 418
Alex	Butte Kimshaw	56 579
D	El Dorado Kelsey	581157
D A	San Francisco San Francisco 6	67 420
E	Nevada Nevada	61 246
Ed	Alameda Brooklyn	55 89
Francis	San Francisco San Francisco 6	67 472
G W B	San Francisco San Francisco 6	67 418
J H	Sonoma Bodega	69 537
L	San Francisco San Francisco 6	67 469
M	Butte Kimshaw	56 592
M	Nevada Nevada	61 272
M	Nevada Nevada	61 282
M	San Francisco San Francisco 6	67 437
M	San Francisco San Francisco 6	67 454
Michael	Contra Costa Twp 1	57 485
Peter	Mariposa Coulterville	60 702
S	San Francisco San Francisco 6	67 469
William	San Francisco San Francisco 3	67 60
MCDONNALL		
M J	Nevada Nevada	61 272
MCDONNALS		
John	Contra Costa Twp 2	57 548
MCDONNEL		
Ann	San Francisco San Francisco 9	68 983
Edward	Alameda Oakland	55 48
Hugh	Tuolumne Twp 2	71 334
James	San Francisco San Francisco 11	157 67
Patrick	San Francisco San Francisco 9	68 950
Peter	Tuolumne Twp 6	71 539
Robert	San Francisco San Francisco 9	681040
William	Alameda Brooklyn	55 165
MCDONNELD		
A	Yolo Washington	72 562
MCDONNELE		
Phillip*	Calaveras Twp 8	57 58
MCDONNELL		
A	Tuolumne Twp 1	71 267
A	Tuolumne Columbia	71 354
A	Tuolumne Twp 2	71 354
Angus	San Francisco San Francisco 6	67 448
Augus*	San Francisco San Francisco 6	67 448
Bridget	San Francisco San Francisco 2	67 661
E A	Tuolumne Sonora	71 234
Ed	Alameda Brooklyn	55 89
Edd	San Francisco San Francisco 6	67 458
Edward	Alameda Oakland	55 62
J	Yolo Putah	72 588
James	Alameda Brooklyn	55 90
Jas	San Francisco San Francisco 2	67 655
Jas	Yolo Fremont	72 604
John	Calaveras Twp 5	57 201
John	Plumas Quincy	62 944
John	Solano Suisan	69 228
John	Tuolumne Montezuma	71 506
John	Tuolumne Twp 1	71 506
Jos M	San Francisco San Francisco 9	681044
Kate	Alameda Brooklyn	55 169
Michael	San Diego Colorado	64 807
Neal	Calaveras Twp 8	57 66
Powell	Alameda Oakland	55 69

Name	County Locale	M653 RollPage
MCDONNELL		
Randale	Calaveras Twp 8	57 64
Robert M	Alameda Brooklyn	55 212
S	Yolo Cache Crk	72 623
S R	El Dorado Placerville	58 914
W	San Francisco San Francisco 5	67 542
MCDONNET		
Catherine	San Francisco San Francisco 4	681214
MCDONNOLD		
William	San Francisco San Francisco 3	67 60
MCDONNOTT		
James*	Siskiyou Yreka	69 145
MCDONNOUGH		
J	El Dorado Placerville	58 850
J C	Yolo Washington	72 563
James	Calaveras Twp 6	57 157
MCDONOLD		
Harmah	Marin Novato	60 738
James	Marin Tomales	60 722
John	Marin Tomales	60 722
MCDONONGH		
M*	Sacramento Ward 1	63 119
MCDONOUGH		
Anna Eliza	Trinity Weaverville	701073
Cath	Sacramento Ward 4	63 521
Chas	Sierra Pine Grove	66 825
F M	Sacramento Granite	63 241
Henry	San Bernardino Santa Barbara	64 189
J C	Sacramento Ward 1	63 80
James	Yuba Marysville	72 876
Jas	Placer Folsom	62 641
Jas	San Francisco San Francisco 1	68 896
Jas	Santa Clara Almaden	65 271
Jno	San Francisco San Francisco 10	207 67
John	San Francisco San Francisco 2	67 575
John	Sierra St Louis	66 805
John	Solano Vallejo	69 257
Jos	Sacramento Ward 1	63 101
M	Nevada Nevada	61 264
M	Sacramento Ward 1	63 119
Philip	Solano Vacaville	69 351
Richd	San Francisco San Francisco 10	167 67
Richd	San Francisco San Francisco 10	309 67
Robert	San Francisco San Francisco 3	67 24
T	Sacramento Granite	63 264
Thomas	San Francisco San Francisco 11	134 67
Thomas	Tuolumne Jamestown	71 448
MCDORMICK		
Jas	San Francisco San Francisco 1	68 919
MCDORNALD		
A*	Nevada Nevada	61 245
MCDORSEY		
Bridget	Solano Vallejo	69 277
MCDOUELL		
William	Tulara Twp 1	71 80
MCDOUGAL		
B	San Francisco San Francisco 6	67 438
B C	Santa Clara San Jose	65 370
Chas	Placer Auburn	62 596
Chas	Sacramento Ward 4	63 562
E	San Francisco San Francisco 10	332 67
J A	El Dorado Placerville	58 818
J A	San Francisco San Francisco 10	245 67
J M	San Francisco San Francisco 3	67 46
James	Colusa Muion	57 459
James	Monterey Monterey	60 960
Jas	Butte Ophir	56 798
John	Butte Mountain	56 740
Lilly	San Francisco San Francisco 5	67 504
M H	Butte Cascade	56 700
W M C	Los Angeles Los Angeles	59 492
William C	Los Angeles Los Angeles	59 333
Wm	Butte Ophir	56 786
Wm	San Francisco San Francisco 2	67 694
MCDOUGALE		
John M	Calaveras Twp 8	57 68
MCDOUGALL		
Alex	Placer Yankee J	62 780
Chas	Sacramento Ward 1	63 42
D	Butte Ophir	56 791
D	Mariposa Twp 1	60 642
D	Nevada Eureka	61 357
David	Placer Forest H	62 774
David	Solano Vallejo	69 257
F A	Monterey San Juan	60 997
F D	San Francisco San Francisco 5	67 518
George	Placer Todds Va	62 785
George	Tulara Twp 3	71 59
J	San Francisco San Francisco 4	681225
James	Monterey Monterey	60 940

California 1860 Census Index

Name	County Locale	M653 RollPage
MCDOUGALL		
John	San Francisco San Francisco 5	67 504
T A	Monterey San Juan	60 997
Thomas	Tulara Twp 2	71 30
William	Sierra Whiskey	66 844
Wm	Sierra Twp 5	66 937
MCDOUGHES		
Duncan	Sierra Downieville	661029
MCDOUGLE		
Robt	El Dorado White Oaks	581020
MCDOUGLL		
James	Merced Monterey	60 940
MCDOVAL		
Richd	San Francisco San Francisco 9	681078
MCDOW		
E B*	Sutter Yuba	70 764
John	San Joaquin O'Neal	641006
MCDOWALD		
A	Mariposa Twp 1	60 663
MCDOWD		
Frances E	Yolo Washington	72 561
MCDOWEL		
Albert	Tuolumne Twp 2	71 276
Eliza	Sacramento Ward 3	63 443
Frances E*	Yolo Washington	72 561
James	Tuolumne Columbia	71 306
James	Tuolumne Twp 2	71 306
Logan	Tuolumne Twp 3	71 425
S	Sutter Bear Rvr	70 824
MCDOWELL		
A	San Francisco San Francisco 6	67 452
Eliza	San Francisco San Francisco 11	132 67
Geo	Sacramento Ward 1	63 140
Geo	San Francisco San Francisco 2	67 783
J	Sacramento Franklin	63 328
J W	Placer Todds Va	62 783
James	Sierra Scales D	66 800
James D	Plumas Quincy	62 958
Jane	San Francisco San Francisco 2	67 563
Jas	San Francisco San Francisco 10	335 67
Jesse	San Joaquin Elkhorn	64 959
John	San Joaquin Elkhorn	64 960
John	Sierra Twp 7	66 867
John A	Sierra Twp 7	66 867
Mortimore	Butte Oregon	56 632
Peter	Butte Kimshaw	56 588
Richard	San Joaquin Elkhorn	64 998
Samul	Plumas Quincy	62 962
Thos	San Francisco San Francisco 10	238 67
William	Tulara Visalia	71 80
Wm	Amador Twp 1	55 459
MCDOWL		
Alex	Nevada Bridgeport	61 487
MCDRUYITT		
H*	Nevada Eureka	61 371
MCDUFF		
A	Marin San Rafael	60 757
Andrew	San Francisco San Francisco 7	681430
Jno	Butte Oregon	56 639
M	Trinity Mouth Ca	701014
MCDUFFEE		
D B	Trinity Indian C	70 988
MCDUFFEY		
P*	El Dorado Placerville	58 881
Wm	Mariposa Twp 1	60 634
MCDUFFIC		
Charles	El Dorado Placerville	58 905
MCDUFFIE		
James	Santa Cruz Santa Cruz	66 635
Jas Y	San Francisco San Francisco 6	67 448
Jos Y	San Francisco San Francisco 6	67 448
MCDUFFIN		
Martha	Shasta French G	66 715
Martha M	Shasta French G	66 715
MCDUFFY		
Chris	Sacramento Ward 4	63 555
Henry	Monterey Alisal	601026
R J	Tuolumne Twp 3	71 469
MCDUGAL		
Danl	Klamath Orleans	59 216
MCDUMAN		
Bernard*	Tuolumne Columbia	71 352
MCDUMITT		
H*	Nevada Eureka	61 371
MCDUN		
M	Sutter Bear Rvr	70 818
MCDUNCAN		
Saml	Sonoma Bodega	69 530
MCDUNUTT		
H*	Nevada Eureka	61 371
MCDURIYIBT		
H*	Nevada Eureka	61 371
MCDURNAW		
Daniel	Sierra Twp 5	66 918
MCDUWELL		
Mortimore	Butte Oregon	56 632
MCDUYRE		
Pat	Sacramento Georgian	63 339
MCDYE		
Mary	San Francisco San Francisco 2	67 643
MCEACHEN		
Hugh*	Calaveras Twp 6	57 148
MCECHANEY		
James	Tuolumne Sonora	71 236
MCEDOY		
R Q	Nevada Nevada	61 290
MCEINEN		
Strenssa*	Mariposa Coulterville	60 677
Strinssa*	Mariposa Coulterville	60 677
MCELANY		
Edwd	San Francisco San Francisco 10	257 67
Mary	Sacramento Ward 4	63 501
MCELDOWNEY		
J	San Francisco San Francisco 5	67 547
MCELDRY		
Thaddeus	Los Angeles Los Angeles	59 322
Thos	Amador Twp 6	55 424
MCELDUFF		
Dan	Trinity Mouth Ca	701013
Danl	Trinity Mouth Ca	701013
E	Trinity Taylor'S	701036
MCELEESE		
Henry	Trinity Lewiston	70 953
MCELEN		
Wm	Napa Napa	61 75
MCELHAMY		
Fander P	Napa Clear Lake	61 140
Wm H*	Napa Clear Lake	61 139
MCELHANER		
Richard C	Calaveras Twp 5	57 212
MCELHANOY		
James*	Tuolumne Twp 1	71 236
MCELHANY		
Fander P	Napa Clear Lake	61 140
John	San Francisco San Francisco 12	372 67
William	Tulara Visalia	71 105
William*	Tulara Visalia	71 105
Wm H	Napa Clear Lake	61 139
MCELHAREN		
Danl	Tuolumne Twp 1	71 236
MCELHARRY		
Will	Yolo Putah	72 548
MCELHAWOY		
James*	Tuolumne Twp 1	71 236
MCELHENNY		
Will	Yolo Putah	72 548
MCELHERAN		
M C	San Francisco San Francisco 10	193 67
Mc	San Francisco San Francisco 10	193 67
MCELHUNA		
Richard	Calaveras Twp 5	57 212
MCELHUNO		
Richard C	Calaveras Twp 5	57 212
MCELINHNATT		
Elizabeth	San Francisco San Francisco 10	217 67
MCELIOY		
John	Plumas Meadow Valley	62 930
MCELIVEE		
John	San Francisco San Francisco 6	67 427
MCELLAN		
Edward	Calaveras Twp 5	57 205
MCELLEN		
Edward	Calaveras Twp 5	57 205
Michael	Calaveras Twp 5	57 184
Michael	Calaveras Twp 6	57 184
MCELLENEY		
Ann	Sacramento Ward 3	63 450
MCELLENO		
Edward	Calaveras Twp 5	57 205
MCELMON		
William*	Calaveras Twp 5	57 243
MCELMORE		
William	Calaveras Twp 10	57 243
MCELNENY		
J	El Dorado Coloma	581107
MCELNERY		
J	El Dorado Coloma	581107
MCELONG		
Maryann	Shasta Millvill	66 743
MCELOOY		
Moses	Colusa Mansville	57 439
MCELRANEN		
A N	Trinity E Weaver	701059
MCELRAY		
James	Mariposa Twp 3	60 568
MCELRAY		
Patrick*	Calaveras Twp 5	57 171
Patrick*	Calaveras Twp 6	57 171
MCELROY		
A	Mariposa Twp 1	60 644
A	Sacramento Ward 1	63 35
Ellen	Tuolumne Columbia	71 324
Hugh	San Francisco San Francisco 8	681250
James	Alameda Oakland	55 53
James	Mariposa Twp 3	60 568
James	San Francisco San Francisco 7	681389
James	Shasta French G	66 714
James	Trinity Mouth Ca	701014
Jno	Mendocino Arrana	60 859
John	Calaveras Twp 5	57 177
John	Calaveras Twp 6	57 177
John	San Francisco San Francisco 1	68 910
John	Santa Cruz Santa Cruz	66 603
Jos	San Francisco San Francisco 12	384 67
Joseph	Santa Cruz Pajaro	66 532
Maryan	Shasta Millvill	66 743
P	Solano Vallejo	69 270
Patrick	Calaveras Twp 5	57 141
Patrick*	Calaveras Twp 6	57 171
R H	Santa Clara Burnett	65 256
R Q	Nevada Nevada	61 290
Robt	Sacramento Ward 1	63 10
Robt	Sacramento Ward 1	63 14
S C	Butte Ophir	56 746
Susan	Mariposa Twp 1	60 644
Thomas	Tuolumne Twp 2	71 352
W R	San Francisco San Francisco 7	681409
William	Sierra La Porte	66 778
Willis	San Francisco San Francisco 9	681097
Wilson	San Francisco San Francisco 9	681071
Wm	Sonoma Salt Point	69 691
Wm C	San Francisco San Francisco 2	67 623
Wm L	Tuolumne Columbia	71 341
MCELSTER		
---	Amador Twp 2	55 299
MCELVAIN		
John	Shasta Millvill	66 743
MCELVAN		
James	Calaveras Twp 4	57 342
MCELVANE		
Jerry	San Bernardino San Bernadino	64 628
MCELVANEN		
A N*	Trinity E Weaver	701059
MCELVANY		
Wm	Trinity Big Flat	701040
MCELVAY		
James	Los Angeles Los Angeles	59 322
John	Tulara Twp 2	71 13
MCELVEY		
Frank*	Siskiyou Yreka	69 147
MCELVOY		
Joseph	Placer Forest H	62 771
MCELWAINE		
Edward	Plumas Quincy	62 915
MCELWANE		
John*	San Francisco San Francisco 1	68 836
MCELWEE		
Dan	Klamath Trinidad	59 221
John	Sacramento Ward 4	63 555
John	San Francisco San Francisco 6	67 427
MCELWRATH		
A	Tuolumne Columbia	71 293
A	Tuolumne Twp 2	71 293
MCEMANY		
William*	Tulara Visalia	71 105
MCEMENY		
Michael F*	Calaveras Twp 4	57 312
MCEMERRY		
Michael F*	Calaveras Twp 4	57 312
MCENAMG		
Wm*	Sacramento Ward 1	63 14
MCENARY		
Hannah	Tuolumne Twp 2	71 277
MCENCHAN		
Hugh*	Calaveras Twp 5	57 148
MCENCHEN		
Danl*	Calaveras Twp 5	57 148
Hugh*	Calaveras Twp 6	57 148
MCENCHER		
Danl*	Calaveras Twp 5	57 148
MCENCURE		
F D	Amador Twp 3	55 369
MCENEANY		
Catharine	San Francisco San Francisco 10	252 67
MCENEN		
Chas*	Butte Eureka	56 652
MCENHIE		
John	Contra Costa Twp 1	57 501
MCENIS		
Sister Francis	San Francisco San Francisco 10	181 67

Name	County Locale	M653 Roll	Page
MCENNENY			
Eliza*	San Francisco San Francisco 2	67	743
MCENNIS			
Francis Siste	San Francisco	10	181
	San Francisco	67	
Francis Sister	San Francisco	10	181
	San Francisco	67	
Liste Francis	San Francisco	10	181
	San Francisco	67	
MCENNORY			
Eliza	San Francisco San Francisco 2	67	743
MCENTEE			
John	San Francisco San Francisco 8	681	250
Margt	San Francisco San Francisco 8	681	252
Mary	San Francisco San Francisco 7	681	385
MCENTIRE			
Danl	Tuolumne Twp 2	71	393
MCENTOSH			
Columbus	Placer Rattle Snake	62	604
F W	Yolo Putah	72	549
J W	Yolo Putah	72	549
MCENTYRE			
---	Napa Napa	61	103
Chas	Napa Napa	61	58
H J	Napa Napa	61	106
Nancy	Napa Yount	61	49
P	Napa Napa	61	75
MCENY			
J C*	San Francisco San Francisco 5	67	505
MCERAING			
Wm*	Sacramento Ward 1	63	14
MCERAMG			
Wm*	Sacramento Ward 1	63	14
MCERAMY			
Wm	Sacramento Ward 1	63	14
MCERANIG			
Wm*	Sacramento Ward 1	63	14
MCERAWIG			
Wm*	Sacramento Ward 1	63	14
MCERETY			
Barney	Yolo Slate Ra	72	688
MCERITY			
Barney	Yuba Slate Ro	72	688
MCERLAIN			
Danl	Placer Secret R	62	610
MCERLANE			
John*	San Francisco San Francisco 1	68	835
MCERNESSY			
Michael F	Calaveras Twp 4	57	312
MCERRY			
J C*	San Francisco San Francisco 5	67	505
MCERVING			
M*	Merced Twp 2	60	915
MCEUCHEN			
Danl	Calaveras Twp 6	57	148
Danl*	Calaveras Twp 6	57	148
Hrejh*	Calaveras Twp 6	57	148
Hugh*	Calaveras Twp 6	57	148
MCEUEN			
Chas	Butte Eureka	56	652
Chas*	Butte Eureka	56	652
Sterissa*	Mariposa Coulterville	60	677
MCEURIENY			
Eliza*	San Francisco San Francisco 2	67	743
MCEURN			
Chas*	Butte Eureka	56	652
MCEUTYRE			
---	Napa Napa	61	103
MCEVAN			
E	Siskiyou Scott Va	69	24
Geo	Siskiyou Scott Va	69	32
John	Siskiyou Scott Ri	69	65
Mary A	Siskiyou Scott Va	69	27
MCEVANS			
D	El Dorado Diamond	58	815
MCEVAY			
Margaret	San Francisco San Francisco	10	206
		67	
MCEVOY			
Bernard	Contra Costa Twp 1	57	526
James	Sierra Port Win	66	795
John	San Mateo Twp 3	65	94
Ollvinn*	San Mateo Twp 3	65	95
T	San Mateo Twp 3	65	101
MCEVVY			
Jas	San Francisco San Francisco 2	67	671
MCEWAN			
E	Siskiyou Scott Va	69	24
Geo	Sacramento Ward 4	63	554
Geo	Siskiyou Scott Va	69	32
John	Siskiyou Scott Ri	69	65
John O	Siskiyou Yreka	69	128
Mary A	Siskiyou Scott Va	69	27
Robert S	Siskiyou Yreka	69	128
Tho	Siskiyou Scott Va	69	32
MCEWARD			
Tho	Siskiyou Scott Va	69	32

Name	County Locale	M653 Roll	Page
MCEWEN			
D	Trinity Steiner	701	000
Geo	San Francisco San Francisco 2	67	671
George W	Mariposa Twp 1	60	629
Hugh	Butte Oregon	56	642
Jas	San Francisco San Francisco 2	67	609
Jos	San Francisco San Francisco 2	67	609
Joseph	Siskiyou Yreka	69	145
Wm	Del Norte Happy Ca	58	667
MCEWIN			
Walter	Tuolumne Twp 2	71	363
MCEWING			
M	Merced Twp 1	60	915
MCFADDEN			
Bernard	Calaveras Twp 6	57	139
C	Santa Clara Gilroy	65	245
Charles W	Del Norte Crescent	58	624
Chas	Sacramento Ward 4	63	506
Dennis	Calaveras Twp 5	57	231
Fanny	Yuba Marysville	72	860
Fanny	Yuba Marysville	72	860
Geo	Sonoma Petaluma	69	582
George	Calaveras Twp 5	57	174
George	Calaveras Twp 5	57	174
H	Nevada Rough &	61	412
Hugh	Sacramento Ward 4	63	529
Hugh	Yolo Putah	72	549
J	Tuolumne Twp 4	71	159
Jas	Butte Chico	56	565
Jas	San Francisco San Francisco 1	68	812
Jessy	Monterey Alisal	601	039
Jno	Butte Hamilton	56	515
Jno	San Francisco San Francisco 10	270	
		67	
John	San Diego Colorado	64	807
Jos	San Francisco San Francisco 1	68	812
Joseph	Calaveras Twp 6	57	166
M	Trinity Weaverville	701	080
M H	Tuolumne Big Oak	71	142
Margh*	Yolo Putah	72	549
Mary	San Francisco San Francisco 10	351	
		67	
Nancy	San Francisco San Francisco 10	270	
		67	
Oliver	San Luis Obispo San Luis Obispo 65	12	
Patrick S	Los Angeles Los Angeles	59	302
Peter	Calaveras Twp 5	57	139
Peter	San Francisco San Francisco 1	68	919
S	Butte Bidwell	56	712
Sophia	San Francisco San Francisco 6	67	406
T H	Amador Twp 3	55	383
Thos	Butte Kimshaw	56	586
W C	Nevada Grass Valley	61	169
W S	Tuolumne Twp 4	71	126
William	Calaveras Twp 6	57	119
Wm	Nevada Nevada	61	255
MCFADDIN			
J	Sonoma Russian	69	435
Peter	Del Norte Crescent	58	631
Peter	Del Norte Crescent	58	632
S	Butte Bidwell	56	712
MCFADDON			
Patrick	Sierra Eureka	661	050
MCFADEN			
A	El Dorado Coloma	581	113
John	El Dorado Coloma	581	122
MCFADGEN			
Jno	Sacramento Ward 3	63	435
MCFADON			
Saml B	Butte Ophir	56	787
MCFAGAN			
Wm	Butte Cascade	56	698
MCFAGGER			
G W	San Francisco San Francisco 5	67	549
MCFAILAN			
Geo	Nevada Nevada	61	287
MCFAILAND			
Alice	Monterey San Juan	60	981
MCFALEN			
Thomas	San Francisco San Francisco 4	681	213
MCFALL			
A	Shasta Millvill	66	755
Ange	Sacramento Ward 4	63	561
J	Butte Cascade	56	700
James	Trinity Mouth Ca	701	014
John	Calaveras Twp 5	57	186
John	San Francisco San Francisco 3	67	62
Michael	San Francisco San Francisco 4	681	164
Mr	Marin Bolinas	60	740
Robert	El Dorado Coloma	581	123
Thomas	Placer Virginia	62	668
Wm	Marin Bolinas	60	740
MCFALLAN			
James E	Alameda Brooklyn	55	140
MCFALLEN			
John	Trinity Honest B	701	043

Name	County Locale	M653 Roll	Page
MCFARDDEN			
Pat	San Francisco San Francisco 9	681	103
MCFARDEN			
Dennis	San Francisco San Francisco 9	681	020
MCFARLAN			
---	Placer Virginia	62	670
A R	Placer Todds Va	62	789
Geo	Nevada Nevada	61	287
John	Plumas Quincy	62	956
John	San Francisco San Francisco 7	681	333
John	Shasta Shasta	66	674
Maggie	Alameda Brooklyn	55	85
Saml	San Joaquin Elkhorn	64	977
W*	Yolo Cottonwood	72	661
MCFARLAND			
A R	El Dorado Diamond	58	771
Abel	Sierra Gibsonville	66	853
Alex	Sierra Twp 5	66	918
Alexr	Sierra Twp 5	66	918
Alice	Monterey San Juan	60	981
B	Napa Hot Springs	61	1
B F	Placer Virginia	62	690
C D	San Joaquin Elkhorn	64	985
David	Napa Napa	61	63
David A	Sierra Pine Grove	66	820
Duncan	Sierra Eureka	661	043
E	Sacramento Granite	63	237
E	San Francisco San Francisco 6	67	468
E A	Tuolumne Twp 2	71	369
Elizabeth	Yuba Marysville	72	976
F	Nevada Nevada	61	313
F*	Nevada Nevada	61	313
Frank	Butte Ophir	56	757
G P	El Dorado Placerville	58	824
Hezchiah	San Francisco San Francisco 8	681	302
Hezekiah	San Francisco San Francisco 8	681	302
J	Calaveras Twp 9	57	407
J	San Francisco San Francisco 5	67	513
J	Tuolumne Garrote	71	174
J A	Sierra Pine Grove	66	820
J B	Tehama Lassen	70	880
J C	Amador Twp 6	55	449
J F	Placer Virginia	62	675
J H	Mendocino Ukiah	60	801
J H	Tuolumne Twp 1	71	236
J M	Tuolumne Columbia	71	340
J R	Sierra Eureka	661	043
James	Klamath S Fork	59	207
James	Napa Hot Springs	61	16
James	Plumas Meadow Valley	62	907
James	Sierra Pine Grove	66	830
James	Siskiyou Cottonwood	69	109
Jas	Butte Ophir	56	771
John	Calaveras Twp 8	57	77
John	El Dorado White Oaks	581	014
John	Nevada Rough &	61	426
John	Sacramento Dry Crk	63	371
John*	Calaveras Twp 8	57	77
M	Sierra Twp 7	66	884
M	Tuolumne Twp 1	71	259
Manuela	San Francisco San Francisco 2	67	760
Owen	San Francisco San Francisco 8	681	299
Robert	Humbolt Mattole	59	121
Robert	Marin Tomales	60	720
Robert	Solano Vallejo	69	272
S L	El Dorado Placerville	58	852
T B	Nevada Nevada	61	249
Thos	Napa Yount	61	55
W D	Stanislaus Branch	70	707
W H	Nevada Eureka	61	373
W*	Yolo Cottonwood	72	661
Wm	San Francisco San Francisco 10	265	
		67	
MCFARLANE			
A A*	El Dorado Big Bar	58	736
Andrew	Tulara Keyesville	71	59
David	Sierra Pine Grove	66	820
George	Tehama Tehama	70	938
J F	Tuolumne Twp 1	71	204
James	Tuolumne Twp 5	71	516
James C	Sierra Pine Grove	66	825
W	Stanislaus Branch	70	705
W*	Yolo Cottonwood	72	661
MCFARLAW			
J S	Merced Twp 2	60	917
MCFARLEN			
H	San Francisco San Francisco 5	67	480
MCFARLEND			
John	Santa Clara Santa Clara	65	483
MCFARLIN			
A	Amador Twp 5	55	362
A B	Sierra Excelsior	661	033
Duncan	Humbolt Eureka	59	174
E	Sonoma Cloverdale	69	685
Edward	Alameda Brooklyn	55	141
Frederic	Humbolt Eureka	59	165

Name	County Locale	M653 RollPage
MCFARLIN		
G W	Alameda Brooklyn	55 167
George	Humbolt Eureka	59 173
J F	Sonoma Bodega	69 533
John	Sonoma Cloverdale	69 685
Joseph	El Dorado Kelsey	581155
R	San Francisco San Francisco 6	67 454
Z	Amador Twp 5	55 342
MCFARLON		
John	Sonoma Cloverdale	69 685
MCFARLY		
Geo	El Dorado Coloma	581113
MCFARNEHAN		
Robt M*	El Dorado Placerville	58 878
MCFARRIN		
Andrew	Sierra Excelsior	661033
William*	Shasta Cottonwoood	66 724
MCFATE		
John*	Nevada Red Dog	61 541
T	Nevada Grass Valley	61 213
MCFATTON		
John	El Dorado White Oaks	581002
MCFAY		
Wilson	Placer Lisbon	62 733
MCFEE		
A	El Dorado Mud Springs	58 974
A D	El Dorado Coloma	581120
Angus	Shasta Shasta	66 760
Augus	Shasta Shasta	66 760
Benj	San Francisco San Francisco 2	67 762
D A	El Dorado Coloma	581123
John	Sierra Twp 7	66 889
John	Sonoma Sonoma	69 658
S	Nevada Nevada	61 263
Wm	San Francisco San Francisco 9	68 997
MCFEELEY		
Henry	Napa Napa	61 67
MCFEELY		
Barry	Tuolumne Twp 2	71 300
MCFENN		
Theod C*	San Francisco San Francisco 7	681422
MCFERN		
Robert	Humbolt Mattole	59 125
MCFERRIN		
William	Shasta Cottonwoood	66 724
MCFERRON		
---	San Francisco San Francisco 7	681407
MCFERSON		
George	Nevada Bridgeport	61 451
J L	Sacramento Franklin	63 323
James	Tuolumne Twp 1	71 249
MCFESSELL		
Fred	Sacramento Ward 4	63 591
MCFETERAGE		
J H*	Sutter Butte	70 803
MCFFORD		
James	Solano Suisan	69 229
MCFITERAGE		
J H*	Sutter Sutter	70 803
MCFITISH		
J W	Colusa Monroeville	57 456
L H	Colusa Monroeville	57 456
MCFLINN		
John	Placer Secret R	62 620
MCFOLEY		
S*	Nevada Eureka	61 357
MCFOLSOM		
A A*	El Dorado Big Bar	58 736
MCFOMIN		
J	San Joaquin Elkhorn	64 989
MCFORLAND		
John*	Calaveras Twp 8	57 77
MCFORRIN		
William*	Shasta Cottonwoood	66 724
MCFRAHIN		
B	Yolo Cache Crk	72 596
MCFRATH		
John*	Marin Cortemad	60 791
MCFREELEY		
John	Napa Napa	61 79
MCFULEY		
Henry	Napa Napa	61 67
MCFULL		
John	San Francisco San Francisco 3	67 62
MCFURNER		
J	Sutter Butte	70 780
MCFUTISH		
John	Colusa Monroeville	57 450
MCGADDEN		
Peter	Calaveras Twp 6	57 139
MCGAEN		
Edward*	Mariposa Coulterville	60 683
MCGAFFER		
G W	San Francisco San Francisco 5	67 549
MCGAFFICK		
Wm*	Solano Benecia	69 305

Name	County Locale	M653 RollPage
MCGAGEN		
Jas*	San Francisco San Francisco 12	376 67
MCGAH		
Thos	Sacramento Ward 3	63 448
MCGAHAN		
Patrick	Sacramento Ward 3	63 436
MCGAHEY		
J O	Merced Twp 1	60 895
James	Tulara Twp 1	71 96
James	Tulara Visalia	71 96
MCGAIN		
Barney	Tuolumne Twp 2	71 304
John	Yuba Marysville	72 959
Phillip	Calaveras Twp 5	57 139
MCGAIRE		
Phillip*	Calaveras Twp 6	57 139
MCGAIREY		
Edw	Napa Napa	61 95
MCGAIRK		
Charles	Tuolumne Twp 2	71 295
MCGALLY		
Geo	San Francisco San Francisco 2	67 794
MCGAMES		
Louis Marian*	San Bernadino	64 631
	San Bernardino	
MCGAMGAL		
Joseph	El Dorado Coloma	581113
MCGAMGEL		
Joseph	El Dorado Coloma	581113
MCGAN		
Jas*	Butte Kimshaw	56 583
Michael	Calaveras Twp 5	57 187
MCGANE		
Mary*	San Francisco San Francisco 2	67 758
MCGANEY		
F J	Solano Suisan	69 206
MCGANLEY		
A	San Francisco San Francisco 9	681069
MCGANLY		
Thos	San Francisco San Francisco 2	67 584
MCGANN		
George	Mendocino Ukiah	60 803
I H	Yuba Marysville	72 972
J H	Yuba Marysville	72 972
P	San Francisco San Francisco 5	67 533
Patrick*	Contra Costa Twp 1	57 522
Thomas	San Francisco San Francisco 3	67 48
MCGANNIS		
W	Nevada Grass Valley	61 212
MCGANZ		
Elizabeth	San Francisco San Francisco 4	681118
MCGAR		
Ellen	Sacramento Ward 3	63 450
Thos	Sacramento Ward 4	63 603
MCGARBEY		
Wm	Sacramento Ward 1	63 23
MCGARERN		
Jas	Calaveras Twp 9	57 384
MCGAREY		
Barney*	San Francisco San Francisco 3	67 30
John	Santa Clara San Jose	65 354
MCGARGLE		
John	San Francisco San Francisco 9	68 964
MCGARICK		
Menda	Tuolumne Twp 6	71 539
MCGARIGLE		
M	San Francisco San Francisco 10	332 67
MCGARIM		
Jno*	Nevada Nevada	61 280
MCGARLAND		
James	Siskiyou Cottonwoood	69 109
MCGARNY		
Wm	Sierra Twp 5	66 938
MCGARR		
Barney	San Joaquin Elkhorn	64 963
James	Calaveras Twp 8	57 74
Jas	Merced Twp 1	60 902
Jas*	Butte Kimshaw	56 583
Michael	Calaveras Twp 6	57 187
MCGARRAGAN		
John	Shasta Shasta	66 729
MCGARRAH		
Minda	Tuolumne Don Pedro	71 539
MCGARRANNA		
Gillingham	San Joaquin Stockton	641025
MCGARREN		
Ann*	Alameda Murray	55 227
MCGARREY		
Jas	Butte Ophir	56 794
Jas	Napa Napa	61 82
Wm*	Sierra Twp 5	66 938
MCGARRILL		
Patrick	Plumas Quincy	62 999
MCGARTH		
Winney	Santa Clara San Jose	65 334

Name	County Locale	M653 RollPage
MCGARVEY		
Alexander	Nevada Bloomfield	61 511
George	San Mateo Twp 3	65 105
Jas	Napa Napa	61 104
John	Butte Ophir	56 780
Mary	Butte Ophir	56 780
Owen	San Mateo Twp 3	65 101
Patrick	Sierra Twp 7	66 869
Robt	Stanislaus Branch	70 703
Wm	Del Norte Crescent	58 635
Wm	Sacramento Ward 1	63 23
Wm*	Sierra Twp 5	66 938
MCGARVIN		
F	Sutter Butte	70 793
John	Contra Costa Twp 2	57 576
MCGARY		
Edward	Solano Suisan	69 234
Elizabeth	San Francisco San Francisco 4	681118
Mary	San Joaquin O'Neal	641003
Wm J	Solano Fairfield	69 201
MCGATFIN		
Thomas	El Dorado Coloma	581123
MCGATH		
Jesse	San Joaquin Castoria	64 873
MCGATTS		
H	Sonoma Bodega	69 541
MCGAU		
Jas	Butte Kimshaw	56 583
MCGAUCHLAND		
Thomas J	Sierra Downieville	66 989
MCGAUIN		
Jno	Nevada Nevada	61 280
MCGAULLY		
Henry*	Santa Clara Santa Clara	65 511
MCGAULY		
Thos*	San Francisco San Francisco 2	67 584
MCGAUM		
Jno*	Nevada Nevada	61 280
MCGAVERY		
Jas	Sonoma Bodega	69 540
MCGAVNEY		
G	El Dorado Coloma	581113
MCGAWAN		
John	Calaveras Twp 9	57 388
MCGAWEN		
W V	Monterey San Juan	60 989
MCGAWEY		
Jas*	Napa Napa	61 82
Patrick	Sierra Twp 7	66 869
MCGEARY		
Albert	Tulara Visalia	71 106
Jas	Santa Cruz Santa Cruz	66 600
John	Yuba Marysville	72 958
Ned	Placer Rattle Snake	62 627
Patrick	Santa Cruz Pajaro	66 573
Robt*	San Francisco San Francisco 1	68 871
Thos	Butte Kimshaw	56 606
MCGEATH		
Ann	San Francisco San Francisco 4	681112
MCGEAVER		
C	El Dorado Coloma	581112
MCGEAVY		
Robt*	San Francisco San Francisco 1	68 871
MCGEE		
A	Colusa Monroeville	57 445
A	Tehama Tehama	70 935
Adam	San Francisco San Francisco 10	346 67
Alexander	Tulara Yule Rvr	71 8
Alfred	Tulara Visalia	71 9
Ann	Santa Cruz Soguel	66 596
Arthur	Klamath S Fork	59 199
B J	Solano Benecia	69 282
Bridget	Alameda Brooklyn	55 92
C L F	Sierra Twp 7	66 898
Carrie	Tehama Tehama	70 945
Charles J	Yuba Marysville	72 888
D	Nevada Grass Valley	61 186
D	Nevada Grass Valley	61 204
D A	El Dorado Coloma	581123
D*	Nevada Grass Valley	61 205
Daniel	Nevada Bloomfield	61 518
Danl	Sacramento Ward 1	63 8
David	Napa Napa	61 94
Edward	El Dorado Coloma	581082
Edward	Tehama Tehama	70 947
Eliza	San Francisco San Francisco 10	259 67
Ellen	San Francisco San Francisco 4	681131
Ellen	Tehama Tehama	70 944
Ephraim	Calaveras Twp 8	57 81
Geo	San Francisco San Francisco 1	68 824
Geo	Tuolumne Sonora	71 186
George	Sierra Twp 7	66 868
H A	Mendocino Calpella	60 809
Henry	Humbolt Bucksport	59 161

Name	County Locale	M653 Roll	Page
MCGEE			
Henry	Nevada Rough &	61	428
Hiram H	Siskiyou Callahan	69	18
Hugh	Los Angeles Los Angeles	59	347
Hugh	Santa Clara San Jose	65	318
J	Tuolumne Big Oak	71	149
J	Tuolumne Twp 4	71	149
James	Alameda Oakland	55	55
James	Contra Costa Twp 2	57	553
James	El Dorado Spanish	581	125
James	Tuolumne Twp 1	71	247
Jane	San Francisco San Francisco 4	681	113
Jno	Alameda Brooklyn	55	83
Jno	San Francisco San Francisco 9	681	068
John	Calaveras Twp 6	57	114
John	San Francisco San Francisco 3	67	31
John	San Francisco San Francisco 1	68	854
John	Sierra St Louis	66	809
John	Sonoma Santa Rosa	69	407
John B	Plumas Quincy	62	958
John F	Placer Folsom	62	639
Jon	San Francisco San Francisco 9	681	068
Joseph	Sacramento Ward 1	63	7
Joseph	Yuba Marysville	72	960
Joseph W	Yuba Marysville	72	960
K K	Sierra Twp 7	66	868
Lewis	Los Angeles Azuza	59	273
M	El Dorado Casumnes	581	176
Margaret	San Francisco San Francisco 2	67	733
Martin	Santa Cruz Santa Cruz	66	639
Mary	Sacramento Ward 4	63	604
Mary	Sierra St Louis	66	815
Mary A	Trinity Weaverville	701	076
Nelson	Placer Iona Hills	62	883
Noah	Shasta Shasta	66	730
Patrick	El Dorado Coloma	581	121
Patrick	San Francisco San Francisco 4	681	117
Robert	Tulara Twp 2	71	8
Robt	Sonoma Armally	69	492
S	El Dorado Placerville	58	860
S	Nevada Nevada	61	263
Thomas	Nevada Eureka	61	391
Thomas	Sacramento Granite	63	248
Thomas	San Francisco San Francisco 3	67	66
Thomas	Tuolumne Twp 3	71	464
Thos	Butte Eureka	56	654
Thos	Calaveras Twp 6	57	118
Thos	Nevada Rough &	61	429
Thos	San Francisco San Francisco 10	67	346
Truman M	San Joaquin Elliott	641	104
William	San Francisco San Francisco 9	681	045
William	Tulara Yule Rvr	71	25
Wm	Amador Twp 2	55	324
Wm	San Francisco San Francisco 1	68	845
Wm	Santa Clara Gilroy	65	245
MCGEEKER			
M	Tehama Lassen	70	881
MCGEELAN			
W	El Dorado Coloma	581	122
MCGEEN			
Frank	Sierra Twp 7	66	870
MCGEENY			
James	Trinity Minersville	70	968
MCGEHEE			
John	Sierra St Louis	66	812
M	Tuolumne Big Oak	71	130
MCGEHN			
John	Sierra St Louis	66	812
MCGELL			
Charles	San Joaquin Oneal	64	938
Edward*	Sierra Pine Grove	66	828
MCGELLIN			
Ewd	Santa Clara Fremont	65	434
MCGELORNY			
John	Calaveras Twp 4	57	314
MCGELVERY			
James B*	Calaveras Twp 4	57	337
John	Calaveras Twp 4	57	314
MCGEMAGEN			
Sarah	Monterey San Juan	60	976
MCGENALD			
M*	Sacramento Granite	63	258
MCGENDLY			
Cornelius	Tuolumne Chinese	71	500
MCGENDZ			
Cornelius*	Tuolumne Twp 5	71	500
MCGENEGAL			
D	Nevada Eureka	61	376
MCGENELY			
Cornelius*	Tuolumne Twp 5	71	500
MCGENEN			
Anna	San Francisco San Francisco 7	681	366
MCGENEY			
Patrick	Tuolumne Shawsfla	71	395
MCGENITY			
John	Shasta French G	66	714

Name	County Locale	M653 Roll	Page
MCGENJEU			
Joseph*	Calaveras Twp 8	57	100
MCGENJIO			
Joseph*	Calaveras Twp 8	57	100
MCGENN			
Jas	San Francisco San Francisco 12	67	370
MCGENNA			
Thos	Santa Cruz Santa Cruz	66	602
MCGENNIS			
B	Trinity E Weaver	701	058
Barney	Sierra Twp 5	66	929
Wm*	Nevada Nevada	61	313
MCGENNIZ			
Barney	Sierra Twp 5	66	929
MCGENSAS			
James	San Joaquin Stockton	641	094
MCGENTRY			
Niel	Sierra Gibsonville	66	859
MCGENTY			
Niel	Sierra Gibsonville	66	859
MCGEOGAN			
Maigler	Yuba Marysville	72	897
MCGEORGE			
H D	San Francisco San Francisco 3	67	86
James	San Francisco San Francisco 7	681	359
Louisa	Humbolt Eureka	59	170
R	Sonoma Santa Rosa	69	391
MCGER			
James	Mariposa Twp 3	60	549
MCGERANY			
James*	Sierra Twp 7	66	889
MCGERNES			
James	Amador Twp 6	55	435
MCGERVEY			
Richard H	San Francisco San Francisco 7	681	353
MCGERY			
James	Shasta Shasta	66	676
MCGETH			
Thomas	Sierra Downieville	661	010
MCGETHRICK			
Thos	Tehama Moons	70	854
MCGETRICK			
Thos	Sacramento Ward 4	63	611
MCGETTIGAN			
E J*	Nevada Nevada	61	258
MCGETTIGARE			
E J*	Nevada Nevada	61	258
MCGEUNA			
Thos*	Santa Cruz Santa Cruz	66	602
MCGEW			
John*	Sierra Eureka	661	045
MCGEWAN			
W H	Siskiyou Scott Ri	69	78
W H*	Siskiyou Scott Ri	69	78
MCGHEE			
George	Marin San Rafael	60	757
Michael	Marin Cortemad	60	784
Richard	Marin San Rafael	60	773
Wm	Sierra Morristown	661	052
MCGHERK			
Patrick H	Calaveras Twp 5	57	216
MCGIA			
Michael*	Sierra Twp 5	66	929
MCGIBBENS			
John W	Nevada Bridgeport	61	479
MCGIBBON			
A	Tuolumne Columbia	71	358
A	Yolo Washington	72	575
A	Yolo Putah	72	586
MCGIBBOY			
A	Yolo Putah	72	586
MCGIBLENS			
John W*	Nevada Bridgeport	61	479
MCGIBLEUS			
John W*	Nevada Bridgeport	61	479
MCGIBLEY			
James*	Placer Auburn	62	561
MCGIBNEY			
Edwd	San Francisco San Francisco 10	67	348
Mary	San Francisco San Francisco 10	67	241
MCGIENE			
Mary*	San Francisco San Francisco 2	67	758
MCGIER			
Michael*	Sierra Twp 5	66	929
MCGIL			
Jose	Monterey Monterey	60	938
MCGILBERY			
A	Stanislaus Emory	70	737
MCGILDE			
John	Calaveras Twp 5	57	176
MCGILDES			
John	Calaveras Twp 6	57	176
MCGILERY			
John	Sierra Downieville	661	021

Name	County Locale	M653 Roll	Page
MCGILINY			
John*	Sierra Downieville	661	021
MCGILL			
C	Shasta Shasta	66	673
Charles	Marin Novato	60	735
Danl	Calaveras Twp 4	57	326
E	Sierra St Louis	66	863
E M	Sierra Twp 7	66	863
Edward	Sierra Pine Grove	66	828
George	Sierra Downieville	661	002
H	San Francisco San Francisco 5	67	547
Hugh	Nevada Bloomfield	61	517
J	El Dorado Georgetown	58	693
J	Nevada Grass Valley	61	213
James	El Dorado Kelsey	581	139
Jas	Napa Napa	61	75
John	San Francisco San Francisco 7	681	372
John	Shasta Shasta	66	673
John	Siskiyou Yreka	69	147
John	Sonoma Mendocino	69	456
Jos	San Francisco San Francisco 10	67	273
Joseph	San Mateo Twp 1	65	49
Neil	Calaveras Twp 4	57	327
P	El Dorado Mud Springs	581	000
Patrick	Calaveras Twp 4	57	326
Patrick	San Diego Colorado	64	807
Patrick	Sonoma Mendocino	69	456
R	Sacramento Ward 4	63	518
R M	San Francisco San Francisco 5	67	476
Robert	Alameda Brooklyn	55	202
Robt	Plumas Quincy	62	920
Saml	Santa Clara Gilroy	65	223
Timothy	San Francisco San Francisco 3	67	57
Wm	El Dorado Georgetown	58	692
Wm	Nevada Nevada	61	278
MCGILLEN			
Francis	San Francisco San Francisco 1	68	849
MCGILLERRAY			
Jos	Trinity McGillev	701	021
MCGILLET			
Kate	San Francisco San Francisco 1	68	877
MCGILLEY			
Patrick	San Francisco San Francisco 10	67	208
MCGILLIRRAY			
Jos	Trinity McGillev	701	021
MCGILNY			
John*	Sierra Downieville	661	021
MCGILREY			
P	Amador Twp 3	55	387
MCGILTON			
Wm	Colusa Colusi	57	423
MCGILVENY			
James B	Calaveras Twp 4	57	337
MCGILVERY			
James B*	Calaveras Twp 4	57	337
MCGILVING			
James B	Calaveras Twp 4	57	337
MCGIMELY			
John	Humbolt Pacific	59	137
MCGIMES			
Thomas	El Dorado Mud Springs	58	982
MCGIMIS			
C	Siskiyou Scott Va	69	54
Patrick*	San Francisco San Francisco 2	67	763
MCGIMMIGAL			
M*	Nevada Eureka	61	376
MCGIMMIS			
John	El Dorado Coloma	581	123
MCGIMMS			
Wm	Butte Oregon	56	623
MCGIMPSEY			
J M	Mendocino Anderson	60	870
Jno	Mendocino Big Rvr	60	847
Jno*	Mendocino Big Rvr	60	847
MCGIN			
Michael	San Francisco San Francisco 1	68	902
Michael	Sierra Twp 5	66	929
Walker	Mariposa Coulterville	60	675
MCGINARTY			
Ben	Nevada Bloomfield	61	525
MCGINCEY			
John	Tuolumne Twp 1	71	207
MCGINDAR			
C	Siskiyou Cottonwood	69	108
MCGINE			
Jerry M	Placer Ophirville	62	657
Mary*	San Francisco San Francisco 2	67	758
MCGINEGAL			
D	Nevada Eureka	61	376
MCGINES			
Pat*	Placer Rattle Snake	62	636
MCGINEY			
Patrick	Tuolumne Twp 2	71	395
MCGINIS			
Abraham	Placer Virginia	62	667

California 1860 Census Index

Name	County Locale	M653 RollPage
MCGINIS		
Josh	Placer Goods	62 698
Lawrence	Placer Auburn	62 559
Pat*	Placer Rattle Snake	62 636
Thos H	Placer Rattle Snake	62 636
MCGINITY		
John	Shasta French G	66 714
MCGINIUS		
J*	Mariposa Coulterville	60 679
MCGINLAY		
Jno	Sacramento Ward 1	63 146
Jno*	Sacramento Ward 1	63 146
MCGINLEY		
John	Placer Folsom	62 640
John	Tuolumne Twp 1	71 207
MCGINLY		
Timothy	San Francisco San Francisco 1	68 879
MCGINN		
John*	Plumas Quincy	621007
Michael	Placer Folsom	62 641
Michael	Tuolumne Twp 2	71 295
Patrick	Sierra Monte Crk	661038
Wm	Placer Virginia	62 669
MCGINNAS		
Wm	Amador Twp 3	55 408
MCGINNES		
C	Sacramento San Joaquin	63 358
Louis Marian*	San Bernadino	64 631
	San Bernardino	
MCGINNESS		
John	Santa Cruz Pajaro	66 558
Peter	Sacramento Ward 4	63 542
MCGINNIF		
P H	Sacramento Ward 1	63 85
MCGINNINGAL		
M	Nevada Eureka	61 376
MCGINNIS		
---	Tuolumne Twp 2	71 324
Allen	Santa Clara San Jose	65 340
Ann	Sacramento Ward 4	63 558
B	Sacramento Sutter	63 295
E	San Francisco San Francisco 2	67 577
Edward	Calaveras Twp 10	57 280
Geo	San Joaquin Stockton	641047
George	Solano Suisan	69 215
Henry	Siskiyou Scott Va	69 39
Hugh	Yuba Slate Ro	72 691
J	Mariposa Coulterville	60 679
J	Nevada Grass Valley	61 203
J	San Francisco San Francisco 9	681057
J*	Mariposa Coulterville	60 679
James*	Amador Twp 4	55 254
Jas	Sacramento Natonia	63 280
Jas	Sacramento Ward 1	63 50
John	Humbolt Mattole	59 124
John	San Francisco San Francisco 1	68 879
John	Trinity Weaverville	701065
John	Tuolumne Columbia	71 324
John	Tuolumne Twp 2	71 371
Joseph	Yuba Marysville	72 863
L W	Nevada Grass Valley	61 160
Lerry*	San Francisco San Francisco 7	681431
Margt	San Francisco San Francisco 2	67 715
Mary	Santa Clara San Jose	65 332
P H	Sacramento Ward 1	63 85
Pat	San Francisco San Francisco 9	68 963
Patrick	Solano Suisan	69 226
Thos M	Trinity Mouth Ca	701013
W	Nevada Grass Valley	61 212
W	Nevada Grass Valley	61 235
W	Nevada Washington	61 335
W H	Nevada Grass Valley	61 235
Wm	Butte Oregon	56 623
Wm*	Nevada Nevada	61 313
MCGINNISS		
C	Sacramento Ward 4	63 598
MCGINNIT		
John	El Dorado Coloma	581123
MCGINNN		
Eleza	Yuba Marysville	72 886
MCGINNS		
Patrick*	San Francisco San Francisco 2	67 763
MCGINPSEY		
Jno*	Mendocino Big Rvr	60 847
MCGINSEN		
J	Siskiyou Scott Ri	69 76
MCGINSEY		
Patrick	Plumas Quincy	62 958
MCGINSON		
J	Siskiyou Scott Ri	69 76
MCGINTY		
---	Amador Twp 2	55 283
A	Stanislaus Emory	70 755
Eliza	Marin Tomales	60 720
Grace	Marin Novato	60 739
James	Marin Novato	60 738

Name	County Locale	M653 RollPage
MCGINTY		
James	Sierra Downieville	66 995
Mary A	Tuolumne Twp 2	71 314
Patrick	Tuolumne Twp 4	71 177
MCGIR		
Wheddon	Calaveras Twp 5	57 230
Whiddon*	Calaveras Twp 5	57 230
MCGIRK		
Jno	Sacramento Granite	63 256
MCGITTIGAN		
E	Solano Vallejo	69 255
E J	Nevada Nevada	61 258
MCGIUTY		
Mary	Colusa Colusi	57 422
MCGIVARN		
Patk	San Francisco San Francisco 10	202 67
MCGIVEAN		
Matilda	San Francisco San Francisco 2	67 565
MCGIVEE		
W	El Dorado Mountain	581185
MCGIVERE		
W*	El Dorado Mountain	581185
MCGIVERS		
Jas	Sacramento Natonia	63 280
MCGLADE		
Edwd	Del Norte Crescent	58 620
MCGLAEGHLIN		
E B*	Shasta Shasta	66 661
MCGLAIGHLIN		
E B*	Shasta Shasta	66 661
MCGLANGHEL		
John*	Calaveras Twp 8	57 52
MCGLANGHLIN		
Ann	Marin San Rafael	60 759
D M*	Shasta Shasta	66 684
MCGLANSKLIN		
Dennis	San Francisco San Francisco 4	681126
MCGLARY		
Margaret	Santa Clara San Jose	65 340
MCGLASHEN		
Ann	Sacramento Lee	63 213
John	Mendocino Ukiah	60 798
L	Sacramento Lee	63 213
MCGLASHEW		
John	Mendocino Ukiah	60 798
MCGLATEN		
John	El Dorado Coloma	581113
MCGLATHEN		
Patrick	El Dorado Coloma	581123
MCGLATHLIN		
John	Tuolumne Twp 1	71 238
MCGLATIN		
John	El Dorado Coloma	581113
MCGLAUFLIN		
Jno	Sonoma Sonoma	69 651
MCGLAUGHLIN		
Ann	Marin San Rafael	60 759
C	Siskiyou Cottonwood	69 100
D	Shasta Shasta	66 684
D M*	Shasta Shasta	66 684
Dennis	San Francisco San Francisco 4	681126
E B	Shasta Shasta	66 661
J	Siskiyou Scott Ri	69 76
J	Sutter Sutter	70 815
John	Shasta Shasta	66 662
Katy	Nevada Nevada	61 251
Thomas	Humbolt Bucksport	59 161
Tixby*	Nevada Nevada	61 251
Wm	Nevada Nevada	61 242
MCGLAUGLAN		
John	Amador Twp 5	55 362
MCGLEN		
H N	Sutter Nicolaus	70 840
J	Sutter Nicolaus	70 840
Jos	Placer Dutch Fl	62 729
Mary	Alameda Brooklyn	55 133
MCGLENER		
J S	El Dorado Grizzly	581181
MCGLENES		
J S	El Dorado Grizzly	581181
MCGLENN		
John	Tuolumne Columbia	71 349
Peter	Calaveras Twp 4	57 328
MCGLENSEY		
Mary	San Francisco San Francisco 9	68 983
Mary*	San Francisco San Francisco 9	68 983
MCGLENY		
Harry*	Sacramento Georgian	63 339
MCGLEUSEY		
Mary*	San Francisco San Francisco 9	68 983
MCGLEW		
Thomas	Los Angeles Los Angeles	59 349
MCGLINCHEY		
A	Butte Oro	56 684

Name	County Locale	M653 RollPage
MCGLINCHEY		
C	San Francisco San Francisco 10	337 67
MCGLINE		
James	Solano Benecia	69 308
MCGLINN		
Andrew	Calaveras Twp 7	57 17
Daniel	Placer Forest H	62 801
John	Calaveras Twp 7	57 48
John	Tuolumne Twp 2	71 349
Patrick	Placer Iona Hills	62 882
William	Yuba Marysville	72 907
MCGLINSAY		
Catharine	San Francisco San Francisco 8	681302
MCGLIUSAY		
Catharine	San Francisco San Francisco 8	681302
MCGLOFFINS		
Frank	Sonoma Vallejo	69 617
MCGLOFLIN		
Frank	Sonoma Petaluma	69 617
J	Yolo Putah	72 552
Jas	Yolo Putah	72 586
John	Yolo Putah	72 586
MCGLONE		
James	Solano Benecia	69 285
James	Solano Benecia	69 308
Mary	San Joaquin Castoria	64 878
T	Butte Mountain	56 738
MCGLONY		
Harry*	Sacramento Georgian	63 339
MCGLOOME		
Mary	San Joaquin Stockton	641082
MCGLOON		
P	Nevada Washington	61 337
MCGLOTHLIN		
Charles	Tuolumne Twp 1	71 238
James	San Francisco San Francisco 3	67 52
Neil	Tuolumne Sonora	71 229
Neill	Tuolumne Columbia	71 353
Null	Tuolumne Twp 2	71 353
Thomas	San Francisco San Francisco 9	68 956
MCGLOTHTIN		
Thomas	San Francisco San Francisco 9	68 956
MCGLOUGHAN		
Patrick*	San Mateo Twp 3	65 75
W	Sacramento Granite	63 237
MCGLOUGHLIN		
J	Sutter Sutter	70 808
Mary	San Francisco San Francisco 9	681017
MCGLU		
D*	Nevada Grass Valley	61 205
MCGLUE		
T	San Francisco San Francisco 5	67 550
MCGLUNE		
P	San Francisco San Francisco 5	67 511
MCGLUNFLIN		
Jno	Sonoma Sonoma	69 651
MCGLURK		
Patrick H	Calaveras Twp 5	57 216
MCGLYER		
Thomas*	Calaveras Twp 6	57 177
MCGLYN		
Thomas	Calaveras Twp 5	57 177
Thomas*	Calaveras Twp 6	57 177
MCGLYNN		
Andrew	San Francisco San Francisco 10	317 67
Catharine	San Francisco San Francisco 10	326 67
Daniel C	San Francisco San Francisco 8	681298
Danl C	Alameda Oakland	55 72
Francis	San Francisco San Francisco 3	67 32
Isabel	San Francisco San Francisco 2	67 629
John	Sacramento Georgian	63 340
John A	San Francisco San Francisco 8	681310
Mary	Placer Dutch Fl	62 730
MCGNEW		
W G*	Sutter Yuba	70 774
MCGNIRR		
John	San Francisco San Francisco 4	681115
MCGNOEN		
Henry	Siskiyou Scott Va	69 39
MCGO??AN		
Matilda E*	San Francisco 2	67 565
	San Francisco	
MCGOARTH		
Thos*	San Mateo Twp 3	65 94
MCGOCHLAN		
Michael	Sierra Downieville	66 956
MCGOFF		
Hugh	Shasta Shasta	66 760
Owen	Placer Iona Hills	62 866
MCGOH		
Patrick	Sacramento Franklin	63 326
MCGOHEN		
Thos	Nevada Rough &	61 435

California 1860 Census Index

Name	County Locale	M653 RollPage
MCGOLDRICK		
Thomas	San Francisco San Francisco 8	681239
MCGOMEN		
A B	San Francisco San Francisco 6	67 422
Edwin	Santa Clara San Jose	65 342
MCGOMGAL		
D M*	Tuolumne Big Oak	71 153
MCGOMN		
O*	Nevada Eureka	61 348
MCGONAGH		
John	Placer Iona Hills	62 878
MCGONAGHEY		
Peter*	San Francisco San Francisco 5	67 545
MCGONAHL		
Hannah*	San Francisco San Francisco 2	67 673
MCGONEAN		
Matilda E*	San Francisco 2	67 565
	San Francisco	
MCGONEGAL		
Felix	Klamath S Fork	59 199
Michael	Tuolumne Big Oak	71 136
MCGONER		
Joseph	San Joaquin Douglass	64 925
MCGONERN		
Peter**	Calaveras Twp 9	57 368
MCGONERR		
Peter*	Calaveras Twp 9	57 368
MCGONGEN		
P*	Trinity Lewiston	70 957
MCGONHEIN		
Mich*	Sacramento Natonia	63 285
MCGONHKIN		
Mich	Sacramento Natonia	63 285
MCGONHRIN		
Mich*	Sacramento Natonia	63 285
MCGONIGAL		
John	Siskiyou Shasta Valley	69 118
Michael	Placer Auburn	62 588
Robert	Tuolumne Twp 5	71 502
MCGONIN		
A*	Nevada Eureka	61 348
MCGONIS		
Catharine	Butte Bidwell	56 722
MCGONLEY		
J*	San Francisco San Francisco 5	67 506
MCGONNEGAL		
Robert E*	Calaveras Twp 9	57 348
MCGONOEGAL		
Robert E	Calaveras Twp 9	57 348
MCGONREGAL		
Robert E*	Calaveras Twp 9	57 348
MCGOON		
W	Yolo Cache Crk	72 595
MCGOONER		
Peter	San Francisco San Francisco 9	681077
MCGOREN		
Edward*	Mariposa Coulterville	60 683
MCGOREY		
Barney*	San Francisco San Francisco 3	67 30
MCGORK		
Jas	Butte Chico	56 544
Jas*	Butte Chico	56 544
MCGORMAN		
George	Sierra Pine Grove	66 829
MCGORNN		
A*	Nevada Eureka	61 348
MCGORVAGHEY		
Peter*	San Francisco San Francisco 5	67 545
MCGORVAN		
S C	Sonoma Bodega	69 521
MCGORY		
James	Shasta Shasta	66 676
MCGOUGAL		
D	Tuolumne Big Oak	71 153
D	Tuolumne Twp 4	71 153
MCGOUGEN		
P	Trinity Lewiston	70 957
MCGOUGH		
Daniel	Yuba Marysville	72 977
Jas	San Francisco San Francisco 1	68 875
S	Siskiyou Scott Ri	69 74
MCGOUGHE		
S	Siskiyou Scott Ri	69 74
MCGOUGLE		
Daniel	Yuba Marysville	72 977
MCGOURAISE		
William*	Yuba Marysville	72 943
MCGOURWISE		
William	Yuba Marysville	72 943
MCGOVARN		
Patk	San Francisco San Francisco 10	202
		67
MCGOVEN		
John	Nevada Rough &	61 433
Sila	Yolo Cache	72 589
MCGOVERN		
Ellen	San Francisco San Francisco 2	67 596

Name	County Locale	M653 RollPage
MCGOVERN		
Isabella	Calaveras Twp 9	57 368
J	San Francisco San Francisco 6	67 465
Jno	San Francisco San Francisco 12	381
		67
John	San Francisco San Francisco 7	681357
John	Stanislaus Empire	70 727
John	Yuba Long Bar	72 748
John M	Calaveras Twp 9	57 371
John*	Yuba Long Bar	72 748
M	Trinity Evans Ba	701003
Mary	San Francisco San Francisco 7	681365
Patrick	Calaveras Twp 9	57 350
Patrick	Calaveras Twp 9	57 370
Peter	Calaveras Twp 9	57 368
Peter*	Calaveras Twp 9	57 368
Phillip	Calaveras Twp 7	57 33
Phillip	Calaveras Twp 9	57 356
Phillip	San Francisco San Francisco 7	681425
Stephen	Marin Bolinas	60 745
Thomas	Placer Todds Va	62 762
Thos	Trinity Evans Ba	701002
MCGOVES		
Edward*	Mariposa Coulterville	60 683
MCGOVIRN		
J M	San Francisco San Francisco 6	67 465
MCGOVOM		
Phillip*	Calaveras Twp 9	57 356
MCGOVORN		
Phllip*	Calaveras Twp 9	57 356
MCGOW		
James	Calaveras Twp 6	57 153
MCGOWAN		
A	San Francisco San Francisco 5	67 541
A J	Sacramento Ward 1	63 67
Augustus J	Calaveras Twp 6	57 139
Charles	Placer Iona Hills	62 874
Chas	Sacramento Ward 1	63 63
Dar	Sacramento Ward 1	63 42
Dar*	Sacramento Ward 1	63 42
Dav*	Sacramento Ward 1	63 42
Ellen	Calaveras Twp 5	57 139
H	Sacramento Sutter	63 302
Henry	Santa Cruz Pajaro	66 542
J	Sacramento Ward 1	63 18
J	Siskiyou Cottonwoood	69 100
J	Yuba Long Bar	72 753
James	Tuolumne Twp 2	71 340
James B	Calaveras Twp 6	57 139
Jas	Santa Cruz Santa Cruz	66 625
Jas	Santa Cruz Santa Cruz	66 627
Jesse	Yuba Marysville	72 848
John	Alameda Oakland	55 59
John	San Francisco San Francisco 8	681243
John	San Francisco San Francisco 5	67 489
John	San Francisco San Francisco 11	90
		67
Kate	San Francisco San Francisco 10	198
		67
L	Siskiyou Cottonwoood	69 100
Mary	San Francisco San Francisco 10	246
		67
Mary	San Francisco San Francisco 9	68 955
Mathew	San Francisco San Francisco 3	67 47
Matilda E*	San Francisco 2	67 565
	San Francisco	
Patrick	Sacramento Ward 4	63 508
Peter	Sacramento Ward 1	63 27
Peter	San Francisco San Francisco 1	68 920
W H*	Siskiyou Scott Ri	69 78
William	Placer Iona Hills	62 864
MCGOWEN		
A	San Francisco San Francisco 6	67 422
A*	Nevada Eureka	61 348
Abram	Tuolumne Twp 2	71 357
C	Trinity Weaverville	701065
Henry	Siskiyou Scott Va	69 39
J	El Dorado Placerville	58 891
J	Nevada Nevada	61 244
James	El Dorado Mud Springs	58 970
James	Trinity Weaverville	701065
John	Yuba Marysville	72 941
Josiah L	Siskiyou Shasta Rvr	69 113
Lucinda	Yuba Marysville	72 910
O*	Nevada Eureka	61 348
R	El Dorado Placerville	58 893
Robt	Nevada Red Dog	61 546
Silas	Yolo Cache Crk	72 589
W C	Nevada Nevada	61 244
MCGOWIN		
A*	Nevada Eureka	61 348
O*	Nevada Eureka	61 348
MCGOWM		
W C*	Nevada Nevada	61 244
MCGOWN		
Leonidas	Yuba Marysville	72 910

Name	County Locale	M653 RollPage
MCGOWN		
Marg A	Sacramento Ward 3	63 443
Margt	San Francisco San Francisco 8	681268
MCGOWNN		
Mathew	San Francisco San Francisco 3	67 47
MCGOWRAISE		
William*	Yuba Marysville	72 943
MCGRACHIN		
Mary*	Placer Forest H	62 769
MCGRADE		
James	Yuba Bear Rvr	721000
MCGRADEE		
S	Nevada Grass Valley	61 181
MCGRADO		
James*	San Francisco San Francisco 7	681362
MCGRADY		
Hugh	Placer Michigan	62 851
MCGRAFF		
Michael	Sierra Downieville	661017
P	San Joaquin Stockton	641095
Thos	Placer Virginia	62 673
MCGRAFT		
Mathew	Contra Costa Twp 2	57 547
Peter	Contra Costa Twp 1	57 505
MCGRAGER		
Thomas	Shasta Millvill	66 750
MCGRAH		
Danl	Alameda Murray	55 223
Danl*	Alameda Murray	55 223
MCGRAIN		
James	Tuolumne Twp 2	71 358
MCGRAITH		
John	San Francisco San Francisco 12	364
		67
MCGRAM		
James	Tuolumne Columbia	71 322
MCGRAN		
Catharine	Tuolumne Green Springs	71 532
Dennis	Placer Yankee J	62 757
John	Mariposa Twp 3	60 587
MCGRANAHAN		
Ann	Sacramento Ward 1	63 26
G B	Butte Hamilton	56 527
MCGRANE		
Hugh	Solano Vallejo	69 271
James	Tuolumne Twp 2	71 322
Thomas	Solano Vallejo	69 267
MCGRANLY		
J W	Nevada Nevada	61 287
MCGRARY		
John	Yuba Marysville	72 958
Thos	Napa Hot Springs	61 22
MCGRASH		
Jas	Sacramento Ward 1	63 40
MCGRATH		
Alice	San Francisco San Francisco 7	681349
Ann	San Francisco San Francisco 4	681112
B	Nevada Grass Valley	61 159
Bridget	San Francisco San Francisco 2	67 744
Budget	San Francisco San Francisco 2	67 744
Cathne	San Francisco San Francisco 7	681383
Danl	San Francisco San Francisco 2	67 621
Dennis	San Francisco San Francisco 9	68 962
Edward	Butte Ophir	56 750
Edward	Tuolumne Jamestown	71 451
Ellen	Santa Clara San Jose	65 280
Frances	Amador Twp 3	55 378
Geo	San Francisco San Francisco 1	68 874
George	Siskiyou Shasta Valley	69 119
Henry	Placer Secret R	62 614
Hugh	Humbolt Eureka	59 163
Hugh	Trinity New Rvr	701030
J	San Francisco San Francisco 5	67 535
J R	San Francisco San Francisco 10	273
		67
James	Alameda Oakland	55 74
James	Humbolt Table Bl	59 143
James	Los Angeles San Gabriel	59 422
James	San Francisco San Francisco 7	681441
James	San Francisco San Francisco 9	68 943
James	Sierra St Louis	66 814
Jas	Sacramento Ward 4	63 542
Jeremiah	Yuba Marysville	72 882
John	Calaveras Twp 8	57 71
John	Contra Costa Twp 1	57 531
John	Del Norte Klamath	58 653
John	Marin Cortemad	60 791
John	San Francisco San Francisco 1	68 883
John	San Francisco San Francisco 9	68 941
John	Sierra Twp 7	66 889
John B	San Francisco San Francisco 7	681383
L	Nevada Grass Valley	61 187
L	Sacramento Ward 3	63 428
M	San Francisco San Francisco 5	67 552
M	Yolo Cache Crk	72 595
Margaret	San Francisco San Francisco 9	68 941

Name	County Locale	M653 Roll	Page
MCGRATH			
Martin	Calaveras Twp 6	57	178
Mary	Placer Virginia	62	660
Michael	Klamath Liberty	59	234
Michael	Tuolumne Columbia	71	363
P	San Francisco San Francisco	9	681 101
P	Trinity Evans Ba		701 002
Patrick	Tuolumne Twp 1	71	271
Peter	Calaveras Twp 6	57	153
Peter	Tuolumne Don Pedro	71	541
Peter M	Calaveras Twp 7	57	41
R	Nevada Grass Valley	61	218
R N	Nevada Grass Valley	61	218
Thomas	Placer Michigan	62	818
William	San Francisco San Francisco	11	153 67
William	Siskiyou Shasta Valley	69	119
Wm	Marin Cortemad	60	782
Wm	Sierra Downieville	66	961
MCGRATHS			
Edward	Butte Ophir	56	750
MCGRATTE			
Michael	Tuolumne Twp 2	71	363
MCGRAUGH			
M	Yolo Cottonwoood	72	557
MCGRAVA			
John*	San Francisco San Francisco	1	68 868
MCGRAVES			
Wm*	Butte Kimshaw	56	593
MCGRAW			
Danl*	Alameda Murray	55	223
E	Tuolumne Big Oak	71	150
E	Tuolumne Twp 4	71	150
Edward	Yuba Bear Rvr	72	999
Frances	Amador Twp 3	55	399
Jackson	Sacramento Ward 4	63	519
Jas	Sacramento Ward 3	63	478
Jno	Butte Oregon	56	639
John	El Dorado Casumnes		581 166
John	Nevada Bridgeport	61	498
John	Placer Todds Va	62	762
Martin	Calaveras Twp 5	57	198
Thomas	Sierra St Louis	66	809
MCGRAWLEY			
James	Amador Twp 4	55	235
MCGRAWLY			
J W	Nevada Nevada	61	287
MCGRAY			
J	Nevada Grass Valley	61	209
James G	Fresno Twp 3	59	10
Jerry	Amador Twp 2	55	320
Joh	Sonoma Bodega	69	525
John	Placer Virginia	62	664
John	San Francisco San Francisco	5	67 489
Terry	Amador Twp 2	55	320
MCGREA			
William*	Nevada Rough &	61	422
MCGREAL			
Thos	Alameda Brooklyn	55	94
MCGREAN			
John*	San Mateo Twp 2	65	120
MCGREAR			
John	El Dorado Kelsey		581 127
M	San Joaquin Stockton		641 063
MCGREAVY			
Geo B	San Francisco San Francisco	12	366 67
Peter	San Francisco San Francisco	1	68 824
Thos	San Francisco San Francisco	1	68 859
MCGREED			
David	San Joaquin Elkhorn	64	976
MCGREEN			
H*	Nevada Washington	61	336
MCGREER			
John	Mariposa Twp 3	60	595
MCGREEVY			
Edward	Placer Rattle Snake	62	630
MCGREGER			
David*	Plumas Quincy	62	995
Geo	San Francisco San Francisco	10	228 67
J	Sutter Nicolaus	70	835
P	Tuolumne Twp 4	71	158
MCGREGGER			
William	Calaveras Twp 8	57	72
MCGREGIN			
Charles	Colusa Grand Island	57	473
MCGREGOR			
A	Klamath Salmon	59	208
Alex	Calaveras Twp 5	57	172
Alex	Calaveras Twp 6	57	172
Alex	Nevada Bridgeport	61	452
Alexander	Placer Christia	62	756
Alexander	Tulara Twp 3	71	48
Alfred	Nevada Bridgeport	61	452
Alfred*	Nevada Bridgeport	61	449
MCGREGOR			
C	Tuolumne Twp 1	71	257
Geo	San Francisco San Francisco	10	228 67
George	Alameda Brooklyn	55	126
George	Tuolumne Twp 1	71	262
George	Tuolumne Twp 5	71	517
Geroge	Tuolumne Twp 1	71	262
Geroge	Tuolumne Green Springs	71	517
Hamilton	Solano Vacaville	69	335
Hamilton M	Solano Vacaville	69	335
Harry	Plumas Quincy	62	958
James	Trinity Big Bar		701 040
James	Tuolumne Columbia	71	354
Jas	Sacramento Ward 1	63	116
Jas	San Francisco San Francisco	2	67 685
Jas	San Francisco San Francisco	9	68 983
John	Humbolt Pacific	59	129
John	Placer Iona Hills	62	892
John	San Francisco San Francisco	10	330 67
John	Sierra Downieville	66	1010
John	Tuolumne Twp 2	71	354
John	Tuolumne Twp 3	71	461
Jos	San Francisco San Francisco	9	68 983
Kate	San Francisco San Francisco	4	681 226
P	Yolo Washington	72	570
Peter	Solano Vacaville	69	366
R	Butte Kimshaw	56	592
S	El Dorado Georgetown	58	690
S M	El Dorado Georgetown	58	690
MCGREGORY			
Albert	Butte Oregon	56	635
F	Solano Suisan	69	211
MCGREN			
William*	Nevada Rough &	61	422
MCGRENRY			
Carrie	San Francisco San Francisco	10	184 67
MCGREU			
William*	Nevada Rough &	61	422
MCGREVY			
Patrick	Marin Tomales	60	725
William	Marin Tomales	60	725
MCGREW			
H	El Dorado Newtown	58	781
H F	Siskiyou Klamath	69	85
J*	Sutter Yuba	70	777
John	El Dorado Kelsey		581 127
John	Shasta Shasta	66	731
MCGRIDER			
T H	Nevada Eureka	61	344
MCGRIER			
Jas	San Francisco San Francisco	2	67 627
Jos	San Francisco San Francisco	2	67 627
Owen	Placer Virginia	62	668
MCGRIERY			
Mary	Alameda Oakland	55	44
MCGRIFF			
M	Nevada Nevada	61	291
W	Yolo Cache	72	620
MCGRIGG			
James*	Sierra Twp 5	66	938
MCGRIGOR			
Alfred	Nevada Bridgeport	61	449
Wm	El Dorado Placerville	58	915
MCGRILLY			
Brian	Placer Secret R	62	624
MCGRIMES			
Hugh	Alameda Oakland	55	54
J	Nevada Eureka	61	358
MCGRIMIS			
Pat	San Francisco San Francisco	9	68 963
MCGRIMMIS			
Wm	Nevada Nevada	61	313
MCGRINIS			
Edward	Calaveras Twp 10	57	280
Patrick	San Francisco San Francisco	2	67 763
MCGRINNELL			
Michael	Placer Virginia	62	673
MCGRIRSE			
Arthur	Santa Cruz Pajaro	66	564
MCGRIUYON			
John*	Calaveras Twp 4	57	315
MCGROFF			
Michael	Sierra Downieville		661 018
MCGROGER			
Thomas	Shasta Millvill	66	750
MCGROGH			
John	Sonoma Petaluma	69	589
MCGROGOR			
Alfred*	Nevada Bridgeport	61	449
MCGRONRY			
Carrie	San Francisco San Francisco	10	184 67
MCGROTH			
John	Sierra Twp 7	66	889
MCGROTH			
P	San Francisco San Francisco	9	681 101
MCGROUR			
Jno*	San Francisco San Francisco	9	68 976
MCGROUS			
Jno*	San Francisco San Francisco	9	68 976
MCGROW			
Dennis	Sierra Downieville	66	995
Fredonia	San Francisco San Francisco	10	181 67
Fredonia Siste	San Francisco San Francisco	10	181 67
Fredonia Sister	San Francisco San Francisco	10	181 67
Fredoria Sister	San Francisco San Francisco	10	181 67
Martin	Calaveras Twp 5	57	198
Sister Fredoni	San Francisco San Francisco	10	181 67
MCGROWR			
Jno	San Francisco San Francisco	9	68 976
MCGRTH			
B	Nevada Grass Valley	61	159
MCGRUDER			
A	Nevada Nevada	61	298
Catharine	San Francisco San Francisco	10	349 67
George	Shasta Shasta	66	761
J	Nevada Nevada	61	290
Jt	Nevada Eureka	61	361
L	Nevada Grass Valley	61	211
P	Nevada Nevada	61	264
Richard W	Humbolt Union	59	180
T	Nevada Eureka	61	361
T H	Nevada Eureka	61	344
T M	Nevada Eureka	61	361
MCGRUE			
James*	Contra Costa Twp 3	57	609
Saml	Sonoma Petaluma	69	548
MCGRUEL			
Bridget	Alameda Oakland	55	62
MCGRUFF			
W	Sutter Vernon	70	846
MCGRUIGAL			
A*	Nevada Eureka	61	376
D*	Nevada Eureka	61	376
MCGRUIRE			
Edward	San Luis Obispo San Luis Obispo	65	7
MCGRURE			
Felix	Santa Cruz Pajaro	66	545
MCGRUYRE			
Wm H	Sacramento Franklin	63	325
MCGU			
Wheddon*	Calaveras Twp 5	57	230
MCGUAGON			
John	Calaveras Twp 4	57	315
MCGUANY			
James	Sierra Twp 7	66	889
MCGUCKIEN			
Rose	San Francisco San Francisco	10	260 67
MCGUE			
P	Nevada Grass Valley	61	152
R K	Sierra Twp 7	66	868
MCGUFFEE			
J	Siskiyou Scott Ri	69	72
MCGUFFIN			
R	Siskiyou Scott Ri	69	67
MCGUGEN			
Jas*	San Francisco San Francisco	12	376 67
MCGUI			
Jersey*	Placer Mountain	62	708
MCGUICK			
John*	Sacramento Granite	63	257
MCGUIE			
Mary N*	Solano Benecia	69	318
MCGUIER			
John	Sierra Downieville	66	964
MCGUIGAN			
Barney	San Francisco San Francisco	10	264 67
Pat	Tuolumne Twp 2	71	339
MCGUIGGAN			
John*	Yuba Rose Par	72	794
MCGUILAY			
Jno*	Sacramento Ward 1	63	146
MCGUIN			
E	Solano Vallejo	69	251
J	Nevada Grass Valley	61	224
Michael	Tuolumne Sonora	71	484
Phillip*	Calaveras Twp 6	57	139
Roger	Solano Vallejo	69	279
Walker*	Mariposa Coulterville	60	675
MCGUINCY			
John*	Tuolumne Sonora	71	207

Name	County Locale	M653 Roll	Page
MCGUINE			
J*	Nevada Grass Valley	61	224
MCGUINIS			
James*	Amador Twp 4	55	254
Joseph	Sierra Eureka	66	1047
Michael J	Yuba Marysville	72	939
Wm	Calaveras Twp 10	57	290
MCGUINN			
Ellen	San Francisco San Francisco 2	67	727
MCGUINNIS			
Henry	Siskiyou Scott Va	69	39
MCGUIR			
Andrew	Trinity Mouth Ca	70	1012
MCGUIRE			
A	San Francisco San Francisco 6	67	450
A	San Francisco San Francisco 2	67	686
A J	Mariposa Coulterville	60	691
And	Sacramento Ward 4	63	559
Andrew J	Sierra Cold Can	66	836
Ann	San Francisco San Francisco 10	67	337
Ann	San Francisco San Francisco 1	68	864
Anna	Yuba Marysville	72	845
Arthur*	Santa Cruz Pajaro	66	564
Barney	Tuolumne Columbia	71	295
Barney	Tuolumne Columbia	71	304
Benj F	Santa Clara Gilroy	65	253
Bridget	Contra Costa Twp 1	57	529
Broin*	Santa Clara Santa Clara	65	487
Brom*	Santa Clara Santa Clara	65	487
Broni*	Santa Clara Santa Clara	65	487
C	Nevada Eureka	61	365
Catharine	San Francisco San Francisco 7	68	1330
Catherine	San Francisco San Francisco 7	68	1330
Catherine	Santa Clara Santa Clara	65	509
Cornelius	Sonoma Armally	69	504
Danl	Tuolumne Big Oak	71	126
Davis E	Contra Costa Twp 2	57	550
Delia	San Francisco San Francisco 8	68	1301
E	Solano Vallejo	69	251
Eliza	Yuba Marysville	72	886
Ellen	San Francisco San Francisco 9	68	972
Ellie	Sierra Twp 7	66	910
Ellis	Sierra Forest C	66	910
F	El Dorado Diamond	58	799
Felix	Santa Cruz Pajaro	66	545
Francis	Contra Costa Twp 1	57	492
Francis	Contra Costa Twp 3	57	614
G P	Shasta French G	66	714
Geo	Sacramento Ward 3	63	469
H	Nevada Grass Valley	61	163
Hugh	Del Norte Klamath	58	653
Hugh	Placer Forest H	62	800
Hugh	San Francisco San Francisco 3	67	57
Hugh	San Joaquin Stockton	64	1027
J	Calaveras Twp 9	57	404
J	Nevada Grass Valley	61	160
J	Nevada Grass Valley	61	164
J	Nevada Grass Valley	61	167
J	Nevada Grass Valley	61	220
J	Nevada Grass Valley	61	224
J F	Santa Clara Burnett	65	258
J M	Nevada Grass Valley	61	224
J M	Nevada Rough &	61	416
J N	Sonoma Bodega	69	534
J W	Tuolumne Jamestown	71	444
J*	Nevada Grass Valley	61	224
James	Calaveras Twp 8	57	90
James	Mariposa Twp 5	60	577
James	Monterey San Juan	60	1003
James	Nevada Rough &	61	425
James	San Francisco San Francisco 7	68	1371
James	Santa Clara Gilroy	65	231
James	Sierra Twp 7	66	868
James	Solano Benecia	69	317
James	Tulara Visalia	71	91
James	Tuolumne Twp 1	71	236
James	Tuolumne Twp 1	71	238
James	Tuolumne Twp 2	71	305
James C	Plumas Quincy	62	984
Jane	Alameda Oakland	55	9
Jane	San Francisco San Francisco 3	67	58
Jas	Sacramento Ward 4	63	584
Jno	Nevada Eureka	61	393
Jno	Sacramento Ward 1	63	64
Jno P	San Francisco San Francisco 10	67	273
John	Amador Twp 7	55	419
John	Calaveras Twp 9	57	357
John	Contra Costa Twp 1	57	485
John	Contra Costa Twp 3	57	590
John	San Francisco San Francisco 4	68	1115
John	San Francisco San Francisco 10	67	335
John	San Francisco San Francisco 5	67	500
John	San Joaquin O'Neal	64	1005
John	Sierra Downieville	66	964
John	Tehama Antelope	70	892
John	Yuba Marysville	72	904
John	Yuba Marysville	72	959
John P	Sierra Twp 7	66	913
John*	Plumas Quincy	62	1007
Jos	San Francisco San Francisco 6	67	423
Joseph	Nevada Rough &	61	403
Joseph	Placer Auburn	62	559
Joseph	Sierra Twp 7	66	887
Kate	San Joaquin Stockton	64	1018
L	Santa Clara Redwood	65	459
L	Trinity Dead Wood	70	958
L M	Nevada Grass Valley	61	187
Lucius	Nevada Bridgeport	61	468
Lucuis	Nevada Bridgeport	61	468
M	El Dorado Kelsey	58	1126
M	Nevada Grass Valley	61	146
M	Sacramento Ward 1	63	73
M	Trinity Lewiston	70	957
M A	San Francisco San Francisco 6	67	467
M H	Nevada Nevada	61	327
M J	Nevada Nevada	61	327
M M	Solano Benecia	69	284
Ma A	San Francisco San Francisco 6	67	467
Martin	Solano Suisan	69	214
Mary	Sacramento Ward 3	63	97
Mary	San Francisco San Francisco 8	68	1315
Mary	San Francisco San Francisco 10	67	224
Mary	Santa Cruz Pajaro	66	564
Mary A	Napa Napa	61	58
Mary N*	Solano Benecia	69	318
Mathew	Solano Benecia	69	297
Michaek	Tuolumne Twp 1	71	484
Michael	San Francisco San Francisco 10	67	262
Michael	Sierra Poker Flats	66	838
Morgoni	Santa Clara Santa Clara	65	521
Nicholas	San Francisco San Francisco 3	67	24
Owen	Tuolumne Sonora	71	485
P	Calaveras Twp 9	57	411
P	Shasta French G	66	719
P	Trinity Lewiston	70	957
P B	Sonoma Armally	69	505
P M	Nevada Grass Valley	61	224
Parney	Alameda Brooklyn	55	156
Pat	Butte Bidwell	56	706
Pat	Sonoma Santa Rosa	69	408
Patk	Butte Cascade	56	693
Patrick	Plumas Quincy	62	1001
Patrick	Plumas Quincy	62	1002
Patrick	Plumas Quincy	62	978
Peter	San Francisco San Francisco 10	67	284
Peter	Santa Cruz Pajaro	66	545
Philip	San Francisco San Francisco 3	67	22
Philip	San Francisco San Francisco 1	68	884
Phillip	Alameda Oakland	55	42
Rose	San Francisco San Francisco 10	67	226
S	Shasta French G	66	719
Sarah	Napa Napa	61	92
T	Nevada Grass Valley	61	167
Thomas	San Diego Colorado	64	808
Thomas	Sierra Twp 5	66	938
Thos	Alameda Brooklyn	55	185
Thos	Nevada Rough &	61	438
Thos	Placer Auburn	62	589
Thos	San Francisco San Francisco 1	68	894
Urthur*	Santa Cruz Pajaro	66	564
W	Sacramento Lee	63	212
W B	Placer Michigan	62	809
W C	Sonoma Bodega	69	533
Walker*	Mariposa Coulterville	60	675
William	Calaveras Twp 5	57	180
William	Calaveras Twp 6	57	180
William	Calaveras Twp 9	57	347
William	El Dorado Mud Springs	58	960
Wm	San Francisco San Francisco 1	68	883
MCGUIRK			
Andrew	Tulara Twp 1	71	93
Andrew	Tuolumne Visalia	71	93
Charles	Tuolumne Columbia	71	295
MCGUIRS			
William	Calaveras Twp 9	57	347
MCGULPEN			
D*	Sacramento Granite	63	228
MCGULPIN			
D*	Sacramento Granite	63	228
MCGUMERY			
James	El Dorado Kelsey	58	1133
MCGUMGLE			
J E	Butte Ophir	56	769
MCGUN			
Thos	Sacramento Ward 4	63	521
Thos*	Calaveras Twp 9	57	358
MCGUNE			
James	Trinity Honest B	70	1043
Thomas	Colusa Spring Valley	57	435
MCGUNEGAL			
A	Nevada Eureka	61	376
J	Nevada Eureka	61	376
N	Nevada Eureka	61	376
MCGUNIGAL			
M	Siskiyou Callahan	69	7
N*	Nevada Eureka	61	376
MCGUNIGALL			
M	Siskiyou Callahan	69	7
M C	Siskiyou Callahan	69	7
MCGUNLEY			
Hugh	Sierra Downieville	66	977
MCGUNNESS			
John	Alameda Oakland	55	22
MCGUNNIGAL			
M*	Nevada Eureka	61	376
MCGUNNINGAM			
Wm	Colusa Spring Valley	57	432
MCGUNNIS			
Wm*	Nevada Nevada	61	313
MCGUO			
John*	Sierra Eureka	66	1045
MCGURCK			
Mich	Sacramento Granite	63	258
MCGURK			
James	Sacramento Ward 4	63	532
MCGURLEY			
Hugh	Sierra Downieville	66	977
MCGURR			
Thos*	Calaveras Twp 9	57	358
MCGURREN			
H	San Francisco San Francisco 5	67	493
MCGURREY			
Peter	San Francisco San Francisco 1	68	919
MCGURTH			
Thos	Sacramento Dry Crk	63	377
MCGURTY			
Timothy	San Joaquin Douglass	64	915
MCGUYRE			
F M	Sacramento Alabama	63	416
MCGWEN			
Joseph	Siskiyou Yreka	69	145
MCGWEON			
Jas	Calaveras Twp 9	57	384
MCHAFFEL			
Jno	San Francisco San Francisco 10	67	283
MCHAFFIE			
Jno	San Francisco San Francisco 10	67	283
MCHAFFIN			
W*	Tuolumne Twp 1	71	253
MCHALE			
J	Calaveras Twp 9	57	379
P	Sacramento Ward 1	63	49
Patrick	Sacramento Ward 4	63	582
Thos	Sacramento Ward 1	63	85
MCHALL			
D	Amador Twp 3	55	409
J	Calaveras Twp 9	57	379
James	Sierra Twp 7	66	865
Thomas C	Sierra Twp 7	66	865
Wm	Sonoma Armally	69	482
MCHAM			
Thos H*	Butte Bidwell	56	725
MCHAMON			
Jas	Sonoma Petaluma	69	568
MCHAN			
Peitrvet C*	San Francisco 4 San Francisco	68	1165
MCHANEY			
Chas	Sonoma Sonoma	69	650
Chas*	Sonoma Sonoma	69	650
MCHAR			
Aleseander*	Tuolumne Twp 2	71	402
Patrick*	Tuolumne Columbia	71	362
MCHARDY			
George	Nevada Bridgeport	61	471
MCHARRIGAN			
Edward	Yuba Marysville	72	868
MCHARRIS			
J*	Yolo Cache Crk	72	596
MCHARRY			
---	El Dorado Coloma	58	1118
Ann	Contra Costa Twp 1	57	492
James	Contra Costa Twp 1	57	492
Nathan	El Dorado Coloma	58	1118
MCHART			
Chas	Sacramento Dry Crk	63	372
Joedell*	Siskiyou Yreka	69	131
MCHAS			
Patrick	Tuolumne Twp 2	71	362

Name	County Locale	M653 RollPage
MCHATTON		
J J	El Dorado Diamond	58 764
John G	Sierra Morristown	661054
MCHAWEY		
Chas*	Sonoma Sonoma	69 650
MCHAY		
John*	San Francisco San Francisco 10	283
		67
MCHAYS		
---*	Mendocino Big Rvr	60 842
MCHEE		
Alexander	Sierra Pine Grove	66 826
MCHEENNY		
Marion*	Marin Tomales	60 724
MCHEL		
Engim*	Tuolumne Columbia	71 301
Engin*	Tuolumne Columbia	71 301
Eugene*	Tuolumne Columbia	71 301
MCHEM		
Thos H*	Butte Bidwell	56 725
MCHEMRY		
J P*	Amador Twp 2	55 324
MCHENNY		
Marion	Marin Tomales	60 724
MCHENRY		
Arthur	Nevada Bridgeport	61 481
C	San Joaquin Stockton	641095
Chas	San Francisco San Francisco 10	234
		67
D	Nevada Nevada	61 282
I P	Amador Twp 2	55 324
J	Monterey Monterey	60 964
J	Nevada Nevada	61 282
J	San Francisco San Francisco 5	67 523
J	Tehama Tehama	70 939
J D P	San Francisco San Francisco 5	67 484
J M	Nevada Nevada	61 282
J P*	Amador Twp 2	55 324
James	Santa Clara Santa Clara	65 474
James	Sonoma Armally	69 481
Jas	San Francisco San Francisco 2	67 626
John	San Francisco San Francisco 1	68 877
John	Tuolumne Twp 3	71 458
Jos	San Francisco San Francisco 2	67 626
M	Nevada Nevada	61 240
Marion	Marin Tomales	60 724
P	Nevada Eureka	61 349
Perring C	Calaveras Twp 4	57 335
Pineny C*	Calaveras Twp 4	57 335
Piurny C*	Calaveras Twp 4	57 335
Pureny C*	Calaveras Twp 4	57 335
Purrny C*	Calaveras Twp 4	57 335
R	Stanislaus Empire	70 726
Royce	Amador Twp 4	55 233
W	Nevada Nevada	61 240
William	San Joaquin Castoria	64 896
Wm	Amador Twp 2	55 307
MCHERING		
Peneny	Calaveras Twp 4	57 335
MCHERSON		
Daniel	Tuolumne Twp 1	71 268
MCHERTON		
L M	Tehama Red Bluff	70 916
MCHESSER		
A A	Sacramento San Joaquin	63 350
MCHIEL		
James*	Sacramento Ward 4	63 543
MCHIGH		
Mary	Sacramento Ward 1	63 31
MCHIKE		
Hugh	Mariposa Twp 3	60 617
MCHILDUTH		
Thomas	Yuba Marysville	72 978
MCHILLON		
Byon	El Dorado Mud Springs	58 996
MCHINE		
A	Tehama Tehama	70 942
T	Butte Mountain	56 738
MCHOLLAND		
Hugh	Placer Secret R	62 614
MCHOM		
Thos H	Butte Bidwell	56 725
MCHON		
---*	San Francisco San Francisco 4	681197
Thomas	Sierra Twp 7	66 866
MCHONEY		
Hannah	Alameda Brooklyn	55 89
Kane	Sierra Poverty	66 799
MCHORN		
Anna	Butte Bidwell	56 725
Thos H*	Butte Bidwell	56 725
MCHORTAN		
J*	Calaveras Twp 9	57 405
MCHOU		
---	San Francisco San Francisco 4	681197
MCHOW LITTLE		
Robert	Solano Fremont	69 384

Name	County Locale	M653 RollPage
MCHUDDLESON		
J	Stanislaus Empire	70 736
MCHUE		
Alexander	Tuolumne Shawsfla	71 402
Frank	Amador Twp 4	55 258
John	Tuolumne Twp 2	71 361
Michael	Tuolumne Twp 2	71 361
Micheal	Amador Twp 4	55 237
MCHUGH		
Andrew	Santa Cruz Watsonville	66 536
Barny	Mariposa Twp 3	60 599
Condy	San Joaquin Castoria	64 875
Cornelius	Tuolumne Twp 6	71 531
H T	San Francisco San Francisco 5	67 554
Hugh	San Francisco San Francisco 2	67 645
J M	Tuolumne Twp 2	71 366
James	Marin Tomales	60 726
James	Tuolumne Twp 5	71 496
Jno	Sacramento Ward 1	63 149
Jno	Sacramento Granite	63 235
John	Sacramento Ward 1	63 109
John	San Francisco San Francisco 8	681253
John	San Francisco San Francisco 10	342
		67
John	Sierra Pine Grove	66 830
John	Tuolumne Green Springs	71 532
John	Tuolumne Twp 6	71 532
M	Amador Twp 4	55 254
Mary	Sacramento Ward 1	63 134
Mary*	Sacramento Ward 1	63 73
P	San Joaquin Stockton	641094
Patrick	San Francisco San Francisco 8	681317
Patrick	San Mateo Twp 2	65 122
Patrick	Tuolumne Columbia	71 363
Peter	Sierra Twp 5	66 917
Roger	Tuolumne Montezuma	71 507
Rogers	Tuolumne Twp 5	71 507
T	Tuolumne Columbia	71 360
Thos	Sacramento American	63 167
William	Plumas Quincy	621006
MCHUGHES		
P	Trinity Taylor'S	701036
MCHULE		
Alick	Calaveras Twp 5	57 196
Ulick	Calaveras Twp 5	57 196
MCHULES		
Luke	Calaveras Twp 5	57 213
MCHULL		
Wm	Sonoma Armally	69 482
MCHUNTER		
John	Sacramento Cosumnes	63 384
MCHUR		
Patrick*	Tuolumne Columbia	71 362
MCHUTCHINS		
James	Tuolumne Twp 2	71 361
MCIDE		
G	Calaveras Twp 9	57 408
MCILHENEY		
Bridget	San Francisco San Francisco 11	118
		67
MCILIAM		
Lydia*	Nevada Rough &	61 430
MCILIANE		
Lydia*	Nevada Rough &	61 430
MCILKAVY		
John	Siskiyou Cottonwoood	69 98
MCILLEAVY		
John*	Siskiyou Cottonwoood	69 98
MCILLONEY		
Mary	Santa Clara Santa Clara	65 478
MCILROY		
M A	San Francisco San Francisco 5	67 497
MCILVAIN		
A	Nevada Nevada	61 288
A J	Nevada Nevada	61 288
MCILVANE		
Lydia	Nevada Rough &	61 430
Lydia*	Nevada Rough &	61 430
MCILVANI		
Lydia*	Nevada Rough &	61 430
MCINARNY		
Mary*	San Francisco San Francisco 10	198
		67
MCINEMAY		
John*	Marin S Antoni	60 712
MCINERNEY		
Thos	San Francisco San Francisco 1	68 837
MCINES		
Angus*	Solano Benecia	69 302
S	Calaveras Twp 9	57 391
MCINIS		
Angus	Solano Benecia	69 302
MCINNES		
Joseph*	Los Angeles Los Angeles	59 369
MCINNESS		
Joseph H	Los Angeles San Gabriel	59 422

Name	County Locale	M653 RollPage
MCINNUS		
Wm*	Mariposa Twp 3	60 610
MCINTASH		
R	San Francisco San Francisco 5	67 505
MCINTEE		
Sands	San Francisco San Francisco 11	113
		67
MCINTEN		
E C	Amador Twp 2	55 308
E C*	Amador Twp 2	55 308
MCINTER		
Ellen*	Sacramento Ward 3	63 449
MCINTERE		
E C*	Amador Twp 2	55 308
Jas	Butte Wyandotte	56 663
MCINTEST		
Geo	Mariposa Twp 3	60 593
Geo*	Mariposa Twp 3	60 593
MCINTIRE		
A	Trinity Point Ba	70 976
Alexander	San Luis Obispo	65 9
Andrew	Tuolumne Twp 5	71 503
C	San Francisco San Francisco 5	67 537
D	San Francisco San Francisco 5	67 535
Danial	Humbolt Eureka	59 170
Edward B	Amador Twp 4	55 239
Ellen*	Sacramento Ward 3	63 449
Geo	Sacramento Granite	63 238
George A	San Luis Obispo	65 15
I	Nevada Nevada	61 318
J	Nevada Nevada	61 318
J J	Napa Yount	61 31
J S	Solano Vallejo	69 270
James	Amador Twp 4	55 236
James	Shasta Horsetown	66 688
Jas	Butte Wyandotte	56 663
Jas	Butte Bidwell	56 729
Jas	Butte Ophir	56 792
Jas	Butte Ophir	56 797
John	Calaveras Twp 7	57 10
John	Solano Suisan	69 214
John L	San Diego Agua Caliente	64 846
Mary A	Tehama Tehama	70 948
R G	El Dorado Placerville	58 925
Robt N	Napa Yount	61 31
Tho	Tehama Tehama	70 944
MCINTOCH		
Wm	Butte Kimshaw	56 586
MCINTOSH		
A	Trinity Trinity	70 970
C	Nevada Eureka	61 361
Dan*	El Dorado Georgetown	58 752
Danl	Stanislaus Empire	70 731
David	Nevada Bridgeport	61 476
E	Nevada Nevada	61 267
E	Sierra Downieville	66 987
E J	San Joaquin Elkhorn	64 977
E M	Sierra Downieville	66 987
Edward	Marin Bolinas	60 733
Edward M	Marin Bolinas	60 733
Edwd	San Francisco San Francisco 1	68 899
Eli	Nevada Red Dog	61 544
George	El Dorado Georgetown	58 695
George A	El Dorado Georgetown	58 695
Henry	El Dorado Georgetown	58 707
Isaac	San Francisco San Francisco 6	67 456
Issac	San Francisco San Francisco 6	67 456
J E	Sonoma Armally	69 502
J M	Nevada Grass Valley	61 169
James	Nevada Bridgeport	61 493
James	Placer Michigan	62 853
James	Siskiyou Yreka	69 149
Jhn	Nevada Red Dog	61 547
Jno	Sacramento Brighton	63 194
John	Sierra Downieville	661024
John	Sierra Twp 7	66 910
Joseph	Placer Yankee J	62 780
R	Yuba Bear Rvr	721007
Robert	Solano Fremont	69 380
S G	Nevada Grass Valley	61 217
Saml	Fresno Twp 2	59 49
W	San Francisco San Francisco 2	67 775
William	Siskiyou Yreka	69 149
William	Siskiyou Yreka	69 150
Wm	Butte Kimshaw	56 586
Wm	Sacramento Ward 1	63 8
Wm	Sierra Downieville	661021
Z	San Joaquin Elkhorn	64 991
MCINTRYE		
Daniel	San Joaquin Elliott	641103
MCINTURF		
Wm*	Mendocino Arrana	60 861
MCINTURP		
Wm*	Mendocino Arrana	60 861

Name	County Locale	M653 Roll	Page
MCINTY			
Delia	San Francisco San Francisco	2 67	788
MCINTYER			
Hugh	Sierra Downieville	66	1030
MCINTYERE			
James	Mariposa Twp 3	60	557
MCINTYN			
James	Calaveras Twp 6	57	162
MCINTYRE			
A H	Sacramento Ward 1	63	96
Anna	Sacramento Ward 3	63	455
Bridget	San Francisco San Francisco	8 68	1268
Bry'*	Placer Michigan	62	834
C	Shasta Millvill	66	750
Chas	Santa Cruz Santa Cruz	66	632
Dan	San Francisco San Francisco	9 68	961
Duncan	San Bernardino San Bernadino	64	643
Ed G	Calaveras Twp 10	57	279
Ed J	Sacramento Ward 1	63	130
Ed J	Sacramento Ward 1	63	131
Edd	Sacramento Ward 1	63	79
Geo W	Sierra Twp 7	66	905
Horatio	Sonoma Russian	69	435
J B	Sacramento Sutter	63	290
James	Calaveras Twp 6	57	162
James	Calaveras Twp 4	57	313
Jas	Tehama Lassen	70	871
Jno	Sacramento Dry Crk	63	370
Jno	Sacramento Ward 4	63	554
John	Calaveras Twp 4	57	320
John	Los Angeles Azuza	59	278
John	San Francisco San Francisco	1 68	852
John	San Joaquin Castoria	64	893
John	San Joaquin Douglass	64	921
Jonas	San Joaquin Castoria	64	886
M	San Francisco San Francisco	12 67	363
Mary	Sacramento Ward 4	63	530
P	Sacramento Ward 1	63	86
Patrick	San Francisco San Francisco	11 67	152
Peter	Sierra Twp 7	66	904
R	San Francisco San Francisco	5 67	545
Robert	San Francisco San Francisco	7 68	1385
Thomas	San Joaquin Elkhorn	64	978
W	Butte Kimshaw	56	572
W	Sacramento Sutter	63	289
W P	Shasta Shasta	66	732
William	Placer Michigan	62	838
Wm	Butte Chico	56	551
Wm	Butte Chico	56	554
Wm	Butte Kimshaw	56	572
Wm	San Francisco San Francisco	2 67	620
Wm L	Sacramento Dry Crk	63	373
MCISAAC			
Charles	Humbolt Eureka	59	172
John	Sacramento Ward 1	63	130
John	Sacramento Ward 1	63	131
MCISLINN			
Bartly*	Placer Yankee J	62	757
MCIVER			
John	Sierra St Louis	66	810
John*	Amador Twp 1	55	473
MCIVES			
S	Calaveras Twp 9	57	391
MCIVEY			
Hector	Santa Clara Gilroy	65	245
MCJAMAR			
John*	Nevada Bridgeport	61	447
MCJANUARY			
Thomas	Tuolumne Shawsfla	71	378
MCJENKINS			
A J	El Dorado Greenwood	58	724
MCJEWETT			
H*	El Dorado Diamond	58	764
MCJLIANE			
Lydia*	Nevada Rough &	61	430
MCJNARNY			
Mary	San Francisco San Francisco	10 67	198
MCJOE			
Bob*	Santa Clara Santa Clara	65	511
MCJOHL			
Peter	Butte Eureka	56	649
MCJOVEN			
Edward	Mariposa Coulterville	60	683
MCJUHL			
Peter*	Butte Eureka	56	649
MCJUNDE			
Patrick*	Calaveras Twp 5	57	218
MCJVER			
John*	Amador Twp 1	55	473
MCKABE			
Edward	Alameda Brooklyn	55	80
John	Sacramento Cosumnes	63	402
MCKADER			
Michael	Butte Ophir	56	783

Name	County Locale	M653 Roll	Page
MCKAE			
Daniel	Tuolumne Twp 1	71	267
John	San Francisco San Francisco	1 68	809
MCKAERY			
David	San Francisco San Francisco	10 67	221
MCKAEY			
David	San Francisco San Francisco	10 67	221
MCKAHAN			
James	Tuolumne Twp 2	71	283
MCKAIAN			
Geo W	Sonoma Santa Rosa	69	394
MCKAIN			
Daniel	Tuolumne Twp 1	71	267
James	Mariposa Coulterville	60	697
James*	Mariposa Coulterville	60	697
MCKAINN			
Geo W	Sonoma Santa Rosa	69	394
MCKAIR			
C V	Calaveras Twp 7	57	48
MCKALE			
John	Tuolumne Twp 3	71	443
MCKALEY			
Arthur	Sierra Downieville	66	1022
MCKAM			
Peter	Amador Twp 3	55	405
MCKAN			
Cathe	San Francisco San Francisco	9 68	1085
Cathe*	San Francisco San Francisco	9 68	1085
Cathl*	San Francisco San Francisco	9 68	1085
Robt*	Sacramento Ward 4	63	508
MCKANE			
Frank	El Dorado Grizzly	58	1180
J H*	Sacramento Ward 3	63	470
Jacob*	Tulara Keyesville	71	60
Jas	Sacramento Brighton	63	198
John	Santa Clara San Jose	65	315
Joseph	El Dorado Grizzly	58	1180
L W*	Sacramento Brighton	63	209
Michael	Butte Ophir	56	775
Michael	Solano Benecia	69	284
R A	Stanislaus Empire	70	533
S W*	Sacramento Brighton	63	209
William	El Dorado Grizzly	58	1180
Wm*	Sacramento Ward 3	63	424
MCKANEY			
John M*	San Joaquin Castoria	64	897
MCKANNAH			
---	San Francisco San Francisco	1 68	859
MCKANRY			
J W	Sonoma Armally	69	493
MCKANSAY			
W	El Dorado Kelsey	58	1152
MCKARA			
Peter	Amador Twp 3	55	405
MCKARD			
Ellen*	Alameda Oakland	55	5
MCKAREE			
Michael	Butte Ophir	56	775
MCKARGANY			
Robert	Tuolumne Twp 2	71	379
MCKARGNEY			
Robert	Tuolumne Shawsfla	71	379
MCKARNERY			
Jos M	San Francisco San Francisco	10 67	192
MCKARNEY			
Jos	San Francisco San Francisco	10 67	192
MCKASKER			
Mary	San Francisco San Francisco	10 67	255
MCKAU			
Robt*	Sacramento Ward 4	63	508
MCKAW			
Ellen*	Alameda Oakland	55	5
MCKAWY			
John M*	San Joaquin Castoria	64	897
MCKAY			
A	Sacramento Franklin	63	317
Alex	Sonoma Armally	69	483
Allen	Humbolt Eureka	59	165
Angus	Sonoma Petaluma	69	596
Awgor*	Sonoma Petaluma	69	596
Awjm*	Sonoma Petaluma	69	596
Awym*	Sonoma Petaluma	69	596
B*	Trinity Honest B	70	1043
Burton	San Francisco San Francisco	11 67	104
C	Nevada Nevada	61	296
C H	Nevada Grass Valley	61	167
Chas	El Dorado Georgetown	58	702
Christopher	Butte Kimshaw	56	577
Corsina	Los Angeles Los Angeles	59	314
D	Placer Illinois	62	705

Name	County Locale	M653 Roll	Page
MCKAY			
Dancan	San Francisco San Francisco	2 67	569
David	San Francisco San Francisco	3 67	41
David	Yuba Marysville	72	968
Duncan	Trinity Weaverville	70	1051
E	Yolo Cache	72	593
Finly	Nevada Rough &	61	400
Henry	Butte Wyandotte	56	671
Henry	Humbolt Eureka	59	164
Isabella	San Francisco San Francisco	2 67	790
J	El Dorado Placerville	58	863
J	El Dorado Placerville	58	872
James	Sacramento Ward 1	63	93
James	San Francisco San Francisco	7 68	1398
James	San Francisco San Francisco	2 67	604
James	Solano Vallejo	69	251
Jas	San Francisco San Francisco	1 68	907
Jno	Alameda Brooklyn	55	183
Jno	Butte Oregon	56	622
John	Amador Twp 7	55	411
John	El Dorado Coloma	58	1123
John	Humbolt Mattole	59	126
John	San Joaquin Stockton	64	1085
John	Sierra Chappare	66	1040
John	Tulara Twp 1	71	93
John	Tuolumne Twp 2	71	345
John	Tuolumne Visalia	71	93
John G	Calaveras Twp 4	57	338
Jospeh	San Luis Obispo San Luis Obispo	65	16
M	Nevada Nevada	61	243
M	Sacramento Lee	63	218
M	Yolo Cache Crk	72	595
M*	Nevada Nevada	61	243
Margaret	San Francisco San Francisco	6 67	425
Mary A	San Francisco San Francisco	10 67	185
Michael*	Tuolumne Twp 1	71	241
P W	Mariposa Twp 3	60	552
Patrick	Calaveras Twp 4	57	328
Peter	San Francisco San Francisco	9 68	1064
R C	El Dorado Coloma	58	1074
R H	San Francisco San Francisco	5 67	502
Seth	Mendocino Arrana	60	861
Tavener	Sacramento Ward 4	63	583
Thomas	Marin Cortemad	60	752
Thos	Amador Twp 7	55	412
W	El Dorado Casumnes	58	1176
W H	Colusa Mansville	57	437
W Irvin	San Francisco San Francisco	7 68	1361
W R I	Solano Benecia	69	293
W R J	Solano Benecia	69	293
W T	Amador Twp 2	55	302
Wilkans*	Yuba Marysville	72	926
William	Nevada Red Dog	61	551
William	Yuba Marysville	72	926
Wm	Butte Chico	56	548
Wm	Nevada Nevada	61	243
Wm	Sacramento American	63	169
MCKEADNOY			
Patrick	San Francisco San Francisco	7 68	1335
MCKEAG			
Wm	Shasta French G	66	721
MCKEAN			
Alexr	San Francisco San Francisco	10 67	236
Chas	Santa Cruz Santa Cruz	66	631
Ira H	Solano Suisan	69	240
J	Nevada Grass Valley	61	145
James	Amador Twp 7	55	418
James	Sierra Twp 7	66	877
Mrs	Sacramento Ward 3	63	485
Robert	Sierra Scales D	66	800
William	San Mateo Twp 3	65	93
William	Solano Fremont	69	383
MCKEAND			
Eliza	Colusa Colusi	57	426
John	Colusa Colusi	57	426
MCKEANN			
B*	Mariposa Twp 3	60	598
MCKEANTY			
Danl*	Calaveras Twp 10	57	283
MCKEANY			
Patrick	San Francisco San Francisco	2 67	757
MCKEARN			
John	San Francisco San Francisco	7 68	1362
MCKEARNY			
P J	San Francisco San Francisco	3 67	64
MCKEARRTY			
Danl*	Calaveras Twp 10	57	283
MCKEBBEN			
Wm	San Francisco San Francisco	5 67	478
MCKEBBIN			
Wm	San Francisco San Francisco	5 67	478
MCKEBLEN			
George*	Yuba Marysville	72	871
MCKEBLER			
Gbeorge*	Yuba Marysville	72	871

Name	County Locale	M653 RollPage
MCKECKNIE		
Andrew	Amador Twp 4	55 253
MCKEDDNEY		
Patrick	San Francisco San Francisco 7	681335
MCKEE		
A H	San Mateo Twp 3	65 101
Aandrew	Placer Iona Hills	62 873
Albert	Colusa Colusi	57 424
Albert	Santa Clara San Jose	65 334
Alexande	Sierra La Porte	66 769
Alexander	Sierra La Porte	66 769
Alexander	Sierra Pine Grove	66 826
Alexander	Sierra Poker Flats	66 839
Allan	Plumas Quincy	62 966
B	Nevada Washington	61 334
B	Nevada Eureka	61 355
Cass	Siskiyou Cottonwood	69 101
Chas	San Francisco San Francisco 9	68 941
Collins	Sierra Morristown	661053
David	San Francisco San Francisco 2	67 675
David	Tuolumne Twp 1	71 187
Emma*	San Francisco San Francisco 9	681066
Ernna	San Francisco San Francisco 9	681066
F F	Nevada Eureka	61 355
F G	Merced Twp 1	60 910
Frank	Nevada Eureka	61 362
G N	Sacramento Alabama	63 415
Geo	Nevada Eureka	61 355
Geo	Nevada Eureka	61 362
George	Sacramento Ward 1	63 135
George	Sierra Twp 7	66 884
H	Nevada Nevada	61 266
H	Nevada Washington	61 336
Hugh	Sierra Morristown	661054
Isabella	Santa Clara San Jose	65 280
J	Siskiyou Scott Va	69 46
J B	Napa Napa	61 67
J M	Sierra Twp 7	66 874
James	Contra Costa Twp 3	57 584
James	San Joaquin Elliott	64 942
James R	Calaveras Twp 6	57 184
John	San Francisco San Francisco 2	67 565
John	Santa Cruz Pajaro	66 531
John	Sierra Downieville	661017
John M T	Yuba Marysville	72 940
Joseph	Santa Clara San Jose	65 377
K	Mariposa Twp 3	60 586
Lewis	Plumas Quincy	62 967
Maxwell	Contra Costa Twp 1	57 499
Melinda	Santa Clara San Jose	65 374
P	Merced Twp 1	60 911
R	Mariposa Twp 3	60 586
R	San Francisco San Francisco 9	681079
R*	Mariposa Twp 3	60 586
Robert	Tulara Sinks Te	71 42
Robinson	Santa Cruz Pajaro	66 558
Robt T	San Francisco San Francisco 3	67 75
S	Nevada Grass Valley	61 161
S B	Alameda Oakland	55 38
Samuel	Santa Cruz Pajaro	66 552
Samuel	Siskiyou Scott Ri	69 73
Samuel	Solano Montezuma	69 375
Samuel*	Siskiyou Scott Ri	69 73
T	Sutter Yuba	70 776
Terance	Tuolumne Columbia	71 336
William	Los Angeles San Gabriel	59 412
William F	San Joaquin Stockton	641060
Wm	Monterey Alisal	601038
Wm	Monterey Monterey	60 946
Wm	Nevada Nevada	61 323
Wm	Santa Clara San Jose	65 282
Wm H	Calaveras Twp 5	57 241
Wm H	Monterey Monterey	60 946
MCKEEDRY		
Samuel	San Mateo Twp 1	65 55
MCKEEFER		
David	Colusa Colusi	57 422
MCKEEHAN		
A F	El Dorado Mud Springs	58 961
Dennis	Nevada Nevada	61 251
W A	Solano Vacaville	69 352
MCKEEIN		
James*	Mariposa Coulterville	60 697
MCKEEIRR		
James*	Mariposa Coulterville	60 697
MCKEEN		
Ann	San Bernardino San Bernadino	64 616
J	Nevada Nevada	61 241
James	Santa Clara San Jose	65 350
Jas*	Sacramento Granite	63 261
L	Siskiyou Callahan	69 13
Patrick	Sierra St Louis	66 864
Patrick T	Sierra Twp 7	66 864
William	Amador Twp 4	55 257
Wm	Mariposa Twp 3	60 567
MCKEENE		
John	Tuolumne Twp 1	71 247

Name	County Locale	M653 RollPage
MCKEENE		
W S	Solano Suisan	69 220
MCKEENNY		
Marion*	Marin Tomales	60 724
MCKEES		
J W	Tuolumne Columbia	71 290
Samuel	Santa Cruz Pajaro	66 552
MCKEEVER		
Chas	San Francisco San Francisco 9	681026
MCKEGGO		
Alex*	Sacramento Ward 3	63 440
MCKEGGS		
Alex*	Sacramento Ward 3	63 440
MCKEIBER		
Chas	San Francisco San Francisco 9	681071
MCKEIBRY		
L C*	Nevada Bridgeport	61 489
MCKEIHAN		
John	Colusa Grand Island	57 475
MCKEIN		
Hugh	Plumas Quincy	62 958
John	Calaveras Twp 7	57 1
Mary*	San Francisco San Francisco 2	67 626
MCKEIRES		
Joseph*	Mariposa Twp 3	60 583
MCKEIRGIE		
A*	San Francisco San Francisco 4	681172
MCKEIVER		
Geo	Nevada Little Y	61 535
MCKELLIS		
Jack	Del Norte Klamath	58 652
MCKELREY		
Alex*	Alameda Brooklyn	55 128
MCKELSEY		
Alex*	Alameda Brooklyn	55 128
MCKELUP		
A	Napa Napa	61 74
MCKELUSS		
A*	Napa Napa	61 74
MCKELVER		
Patrick	Alameda Brooklyn	55 130
MCKELVEY		
Chas*	Napa Yount	61 51
J	San Francisco San Francisco 6	67 442
J	Sierra La Porte	66 766
MCKELVIE		
Samuel	San Francisco San Francisco 11	156 67
MCKEMAN		
Wallace*	San Joaquin Castoria	64 881
MCKEMOR		
J J*	San Francisco San Francisco 7	681409
MCKEN		
Adam	Tuolumne Columbia	71 307
Sarah*	San Francisco San Francisco 1	68 827
MCKENDRICK		
I	Nevada Nevada	61 317
J	Nevada Grass Valley	61 152
J	Nevada Nevada	61 317
MCKENDY		
John*	Mariposa Coulterville	60 678
MCKENEN		
James	Solano Suisan	69 224
Michael	Butte Ophir	56 781
Peter	Yolo Slate Ra	72 687
Peter	Yuba North Ea	72 687
MCKENER		
L	Butte Ophir	56 755
MCKENEY		
Francis	Calaveras Twp 8	57 71
MCKENGEE		
James	Nevada Bloomfield	61 516
Wm	Sierra La Porte	66 787
MCKENICE		
John A*	Solano Benecia	69 312
MCKENLAY		
Uriah	Amador Twp 7	55 415
MCKENLEY		
A	Amador Twp 7	55 420
Benj	El Dorado White Oaks	581003
D A	El Dorado White Oaks	581019
MCKENN		
Edward*	Sacramento Granite	63 257
MCKENNA		
A	Butte Chico	56 549
Alexander	Yuba Marysville	72 849
Charles	Tuolumne Twp 2	71 303
Danl	San Francisco San Francisco 9	68 994
Dennis	Klamath Klamath	59 227
F	Nevada Nevada	61 249
F	San Francisco San Francisco 5	67 489
F	Tuolumne Twp 2	71 308
Francis	San Francisco San Francisco 7	681413
Geo	Tuolumne Columbia	71 308
Hugh	Trinity North Fo	701026
Jas	Sacramento Ward 4	63 570

Name	County Locale	M653 RollPage
MCKENNA		
Jas P	San Francisco San Francisco 10	179 67
John	Santa Cruz Soguel	66 585
John C*	Placer Illinois	62 741
Jos P	San Francisco San Francisco 10	179 67
Joseph J	Placer Secret R	62 621
M	Sacramento Ward 3	63 460
Mary	Solano Benecia	69 288
Michael	Los Angeles Los Angeles	59 343
P	Sacramento Ward 4	63 524
Patrick	Los Angeles San Gabriel	59 422
Phillip	Nevada Bridgeport	61 485
T	San Francisco San Francisco 5	67 547
William	Solano Benecia	69 298
Wm	Humbolt Eel Rvr	59 147
MCKENNAN		
K	Marin Bolinas	60 749
MCKENNERY		
James M*	San Mateo Twp 3	65 109
John H	Fresno Twp 3	59 37
MCKENNEY		
B	Alameda Brooklyn	55 154
David	Plumas Meadow Valley	62 902
Dennis	Alameda Oakland	55 20
Eliz	Sacramento Ward 1	63 101
F	El Dorado Placerville	58 892
James	Yuba Marysville	72 858
Lucy	Santa Clara San Jose	65 342
Mark	San Francisco San Francisco 1	68 909
Michael	San Francisco San Francisco 10	212 67
Nelson*	Fresno Twp 3	59 10
Samul	Plumas Quincy	62 945
Thos	Sacramento Ward 1	63 106
Wm	Mariposa Twp 1	60 643
MCKENNI		
James	Yuba Slate Ro	72 693
MCKENNIE		
Thomas	San Francisco San Francisco 3	67 59
MCKENNON		
Alexander	Yuba Marysville	72 849
John	Placer Iona Hills	62 874
MCKENNY		
A	Nevada Grass Valley	61 236
Andrew	Fresno Twp 1	59 34
D	Tehama Red Bluff	70 916
Daniel*	San Francisco San Francisco 3	67 84
David	San Francisco San Francisco 3	67 84
Henry	San Francisco San Francisco 1	68 851
J	Calaveras Twp 9	57 411
James	Nevada Little Y	61 534
John	San Francisco San Francisco 7	681419
John	Yuba Marysville	72 896
Marion*	Marin Tomales	60 724
Michael	Sacramento Ward 3	63 484
Patrick	San Francisco San Francisco 2	67 757
R F	Nevada Rough &	61 414
Thomas	Marin Cortemad	60 792
Thomas	Sierra Twp 7	66 912
MCKENON		
George	Placer Michigan	62 817
MCKENRIE		
D	San Francisco San Francisco 5	67 551
John A*	Solano Benecia	69 312
MCKENRY		
Daniel*	San Francisco San Francisco 3	67 84
MCKENSEY		
Chas*	San Francisco San Francisco 9	681081
J R	Butte Oregon	56 628
J R*	Butte Oregon	56 628
Mary A	Nevada Rough &	61 418
Owen	Butte Ophir	56 783
MCKENSIE		
D*	San Francisco San Francisco 5	67 551
David*	Siskiyou Yreka	69 150
James	Yolo Slate Ra	72 693
MCKENSY		
John	Mariposa Coulterville	60 678
MCKENTY		
Catharine	San Francisco San Francisco 10	223 67
John*	Mariposa Coulterville	60 678
MCKENTZ		
Catharine*	San Francisco 10	223 67
	San Francisco	
MCKENZER		
James	Yuba Marysville	72 902
MCKENZIE		
A	Nevada Grass Valley	61 178
A	San Francisco San Francisco 4	681230
A	Santa Clara Santa Clara	65 511
A M	San Francisco San Francisco 5	67 542
Adam	Plumas Quincy	621007
Adam	Plumas Quincy	62 962

California 1860 Census Index

Name	County Locale	M653 Roll	Page
MCKENZIE			
Albert	San Francisco San Francisco 8	681	302
Alex	Placer Todds Va	62	790
Alexander	Tulara Twp 2	71	32
Ann L	Placer Auburn	62	586
C R	Siskiyou Klamath	69	91
Chas	San Francisco San Francisco 9	68	971
Constantine	Placer Iona Hills	62	872
Danl	Santa Clara San Jose	65	306
David	Sierra Chappare	66	1041
David	Tuolumne Montezuma	71	509
Elizabeth	San Francisco San Francisco 9	681	036
H H	Shasta Shasta	66	730
Hugh	San Francisco San Francisco 1	68	894
J	Napa Napa	61	105
James	Nevada Bloomfield	61	516
James	Yuba Marysville	72	902
Jas	Fresno Millerto	59	2
Jas	San Francisco San Francisco 1	68	854
Jno	Alameda Brooklyn	55	181
Jno	Sacramento Ward 1	63	88
Jno F	San Francisco San Francisco 10	67	228
Jno T	San Francisco San Francisco 10	67	228
John	Calaveras Twp 7	57	19
John	Placer Michigan	62	810
John	San Francisco San Francisco 10	67	353
John	Sierra Eureka	66	1049
John	Sierra Pine Grove	66	828
John	Solano Suisan	69	216
John	Solano Vallejo	69	267
John A	Solano Benecia	69	312
John Q	Sonoma Sonoma	69	650
Jos	San Francisco San Francisco 9	681	070
Joseph	Santa Clara Gilroy	65	244
Louis	San Francisco San Francisco 4	681	124
M S	Sacramento Granite	63	239
Micaco*	San Francisco San Francisco 1	68	853
Micad*	San Francisco San Francisco 1	68	853
Micael*	San Francisco San Francisco 1	68	853
Nellie	San Francisco San Francisco 10	67	243
Raleigh	Los Angeles Azuza	59	271
Roderick J	Sierra Downieville	66	960
W M	San Francisco San Francisco 10	67	268
William	Calaveras Twp 7	57	17
Wm	Del Norte Crescent	58	650
Wm	San Francisco San Francisco 10	67	268
Wm	Sierra La Porte	66	787
Wm N	Santa Clara Santa Clara	65	487
MCKENZIN			
Alex	Calaveras Twp 4	57	318
MCKENZIO			
Albert	San Francisco San Francisco 8	681	302
MCKEON			
A B	Solano Montezuma	69	374
Adam	Solano Montezuma	69	372
John	Calaveras Twp 7	57	1
L*	Siskiyou Callahan	69	13
Lawrence	San Francisco San Francisco 9	681	071
Mary	San Francisco San Francisco 2	67	626
Thomas	San Bernardino Santa Barbara	64	181
MCKEONN			
B	Mariposa Twp 3	60	598
MCKER			
Francis*	Los Angeles Los Angeles	59	491
James R	Calaveras Twp 5	57	184
Robt T*	San Francisco San Francisco 3	67	75
MCKERA			
Hugh	Sacramento Granite	63	260
MCKERBEY			
L C*	Nevada Bridgeport	61	489
MCKERBY			
L C*	Nevada Bridgeport	61	489
MCKERGREN			
Frank L	San Bernardino San Bernardino	64	634
MCKERM			
David*	Calaveras Twp 8	57	57
MCKERN			
Edward	Sacramento Granite	63	257
Hugh	Sacramento Granite	63	260
Jas	Sacramento Granite	63	257
MCKERNAN			
Hugh	Calaveras Twp 4	57	318
Wallace*	San Joaquin Castoria	64	881
MCKERNAR			
John*	Shasta Millvill	66	727
MCKERNE			
Chas	Sacramento Granite	63	257
MCKERNEY			
Michael	San Mateo Twp 1	65	47
MCKERNIR			
John*	Shasta Millvill	66	727

Name	County Locale	M653 Roll	Page
MCKERNON			
John	Shasta Millvill	66	727
MCKERONA			
Phillip	Nevada Bridgeport	61	485
MCKERREN			
Peter	San Francisco San Francisco 1	68	863
MCKERSEY			
Chas	San Francisco San Francisco 9	681	081
Chas*	San Francisco San Francisco 9	681	081
MCKERSON			
Benj	Calaveras Twp 9	57	400
MCKERTY			
John*	Mariposa Coulterville	60	695
MCKERVER			
J	Siskiyou Scott Ri	69	69
MCKERVOR			
J	Siskiyou Scott Ri	69	69
MCKERZEY			
A	Amador Twp 3	55	393
MCKES			
J M	Tuolumne Twp 2	71	290
MCKEU			
Sarah*	San Francisco San Francisco 1	68	827
MCKEUN			
Edward*	Sacramento Granite	63	257
MCKEURIE			
John A*	Solano Benecia	69	312
MCKEVIRE			
Hiram	Marin Bolinas	60	746
MCKEWAN			
James	El Dorado Mud Springs	58	970
MCKEWEN			
F	Butte Oregon	56	624
MCKEY			
J	Calaveras Twp 9	57	404
J	Tuolumne Big Oak	71	179
Jas	Butte Kimshaw	56	605
John	El Dorado Greenwood	58	724
Michael	Tuolumne Sonora	71	241
T	Calaveras Twp 9	57	416
MCKEYNILER			
D M*	Shasta Shasta	66	662
MCKEYNILES			
D M*	Shasta Shasta	66	662
MCKEZNILER			
D M*	Shasta Shasta	66	662
MCKEZNILES			
B M*	Shasta Shasta	66	662
MCKFIN			
Sarah*	Santa Clara Gilroy	65	237
MCKIBBEN			
Wm	San Francisco San Francisco 10	67	191
MCKIBBIN			
Thos	San Francisco San Francisco 6	67	462
MCKIBLEN			
George	Yuba Marysville	72	871
MCKIE			
Emma*	San Francisco San Francisco 9	681	066
Humphry	Sonoma Santa Rosa	69	418
Jmphry	Sonoma Santa Rosa	69	418
R	Tuolumne Twp 1	71	256
MCKIEKIEK			
J	El Dorado Mud Springs	58	968
MCKIEL			
James*	Sacramento Ward 4	63	543
MCKIES			
Samuel	Santa Cruz Pajaro	66	552
MCKIG			
Alin	El Dorado Georgetown	58	692
MCKIGNEY			
W H	Tuolumne Twp 1	71	220
MCKILAY			
Finfay	Monterey S Antoni	60	971
MCKILLER			
Jas	Sonoma Petaluma	69	566
MCKILLIN			
Alexander	Tulara Twp 1	71	110
Alexander	Tulara Visalia	71	110
MCKILLIP			
Chas	Sacramento Ward 4	63	526
MCKIM			
G W	El Dorado Salmon Falls	581	050
James	Plumas Quincy	62	966
Patrick H	Alameda Brooklyn	55	82
W L	Amador Twp 1	55	504
MCKIMIP			
Isabella	San Francisco San Francisco 7	681	328
MCKIMM			
F	Yolo Washington	72	599
MCKIMMON			
Mark*	Yuba Marysville	72	874
MCKIMOR			
J J*	San Francisco San Francisco 7	681	409
MCKINE			
Jas	Sacramento Granite	63	261

Name	County Locale	M653 Roll	Page
MCKINE			
Thos J	Sacramento Ward 4	63	543
MCKINELL			
W H G	Alameda Brooklyn	55	158
MCKINEN			
F	Yolo Washington	72	599
Peter	Siskiyou Callahan	69	16
MCKINEY			
Jeremiah	Plumas Quincy	62	963
MCKING			
C	Calaveras Twp 9	57	417
Donnald*	Nevada Red Dog	61	554
Wm	Santa Clara San Jose	65	386
MCKINGA			
Donald	Nevada Little Y	61	531
MCKINGEE			
Donnald*	Nevada Red Dog	61	554
Robert	Mariposa Coulterville	60	698
MCKINGER			
J P	Mariposa Twp 1	60	663
Robert*	Mariposa Coulterville	60	698
MCKINGIR			
J P	Mariposa Twp 1	60	663
MCKINGU			
Donnald*	Nevada Red Dog	61	554
MCKINLAY			
Finlay	Monterey S Antoni	60	971
James	Merced Monterey	60	936
James*	Monterey Monterey	60	936
MCKINLEY			
A	Nevada Grass Valley	61	158
Elliott	Placer Iona Hills	62	892
George	San Joaquin Elkhorn	64	964
James	San Luis Obispo San Luis Obispo	65	19
James	Shasta Shasta	66	663
James	Solano Benecia	69	307
Jas	San Francisco San Francisco 12	67	384
Joseph	El Dorado Casumnes	581	173
M R	Sacramento Lee	63	210
O B	Trinity Lewiston	70	961
R W	Marin San Rafael	60	767
Richard	Marin Cortemad	60	756
Thos C	Del Norte Happy Ca	58	662
William B	Solano Vacaville	69	355
William H	Calaveras Twp 5	57	220
MCKINLOY			
James*	Monterey Monterey	60	936
MCKINLY			
Geo	Napa Clear Lake	61	140
James	Calaveras Twp 5	57	195
James	Shasta Shasta	66	663
William B	Solano Vacaville	69	355
MCKINMAN			
James	San Francisco San Francisco 9	68	949
MCKINMON			
Mark	Yuba Marysville	72	874
MCKINN			
Jas	Sonoma Santa Rosa	69	391
John	Sacramento Dry Crk	63	379
Joseph	Sonoma Santa Rosa	69	417
MCKINNA			
Alex	Humbolt Bucksport	59	162
Eliza	Humbolt Eel Rvr	59	147
James	Humbolt Union	59	184
Patrick	Sierra Twp 7	66	891
Pete	Sonoma Petaluma	69	603
MCKINNAN			
John	Trinity Indian C	70	989
MCKINNAY			
A	Sutter Butte	70	792
E T	Sutter Sutter	70	804
MCKINNEN			
Robert	San Joaquin Castoria	64	879
MCKINNEY			
A	Amador Twp 1	55	495
Alexander	Nevada Bloomfield	61	511
Alexdander	Nevada Bloomfield	61	511
Charles	Shasta Shasta	66	758
Chas W	Placer Secret R	62	609
David	Sacramento Ward 1	63	58
E	Butte Kimshaw	56	578
Francis	San Francisco San Francisco 11	67	153
Frank	San Bernardino San Bernardino	64	673
H J	Nevada Bloomfield	61	526
H M	Nevada Bloomfield	61	526
J	Sacramento Ward 4	63	502
J H	Marin Cortemad	60	786
James	Santa Cruz Pajaro	66	558
Jams	Alameda Brooklyn	55	206
Jas	Del Norte Crescent	58	637
Jas	Sacramento American	63	159
Jefferson	Contra Costa Twp 2	57	566
Jno	Butte Kimshaw	56	584
John	Yuba Marysville	72	896

California 1860 Census Index

Name	County Locale	M653 Roll	Page
MCKINNEY			
Jos	Trinity Prices B	70	1019
Jos M	Trinity Price'S	70	1019
Joseph	San Joaquin Castoria	64	872
M	Butte Kimshaw	56	584
M B	Stanislaus Empire	70	726
Michael	San Francisco San Francisco 10	67	212
Michael	San Mateo Twp 1	65	47
Mortimer	San Joaquin Castoria	64	872
Murrdock	San Salvador San Bernardino	64	653
Nass B	Sacramento Ward 4	63	553
Nelson*	Fresno Twp 3	59	10
P	Butte Kimshaw	56	592
P	El Dorado Diamond	58	802
Pat	Sacramento Ward 1	63	107
Patrick	San Francisco San Francisco 7	68	1339
Peter	Trinity Weaverville	70	1068
Ptk	San Francisco San Francisco 10	67	206
S P	Siskiyou Scott Ri	69	81
T	San Francisco San Francisco 3	67	64
Thomas	Los Angeles Azuza	59	276
Thomas	Marin Cortemad	60	792
Thomas	Solano Suisan	69	226
W E	Sacramento Ward 4	63	496
Willis	Placer Dutch Fl	62	724
Wm	Mariposa Twp 1	60	643
MCKINNIN			
Danl	Nevada Bridgeport	61	452
Danl*	Nevada Bridgeport	61	452
MCKINNIP			
Isabella*	San Francisco San Francisco 7	68	1328
MCKINNIS			
Patrick	Calaveras Twp 6	57	124
Patrick	San Francisco San Francisco 2	67	675
Peter	Sacramento Franklin	63	331
MCKINNISS			
Isabella*	San Francisco San Francisco 7	68	1328
MCKINNON			
C	San Francisco San Francisco 5	67	554
Collin	Del Norte Crescent	58	649
H	San Francisco San Francisco 5	67	498
J	San Francisco San Francisco 4	68	1231
MCKINNY			
Charles*	Shasta Shasta	66	758
Frank	Sacramento Dry Crk	63	379
Ivory	Plumas Quincy	62	940
J	Calaveras Twp 9	57	411
James	Calaveras Twp 6	57	152
James	Placer Yankee J	62	776
S P	Siskiyou Scott Ri	69	81
Wiliam	Placer Todds Va	62	790
MCKINO			
M A	Mendocino Big Rvr	60	844
MCKINON			
Michael	Butte Ophir	56	781
MCKINSEE			
R	Tuolumne Twp 1	71	212
MCKINSEY			
A	El Dorado Gold Hill	58	1096
Alex	Yolo Merritt	72	581
Aliva*	Sierra Chappare	66	1040
Andrew J	Sierra Downieville	66	955
Duncan	Placer Secret R	62	618
Isaac	Marin Tomales	60	722
J R*	Butte Oregon	56	628
James	Tulara Keeneysburg	71	41
John	Marin Cortemad	60	752
John E	San Joaquin Stockton	64	1062
N	El Dorado Gold Hill	58	1096
W R	Butte Bidwell	56	730
MCKINSLEY			
A J	Tehama Cottonwood	70	902
W	Tehama Cottonwoood	70	901
MCKINSMON			
Mark*	Yuba Marysville	72	874
MCKINSONG			
Alex	Yolo Merritt	72	581
MCKINSTRY SMIT			
J*	Butte Eureka	56	653
MCKINSTRY			
George	San Diego Agua Caliente	64	843
John	San Francisco San Francisco 2	67	568
L	El Dorado Placerville	58	852
Levi	Tuolumne Shawsfla	71	404
MCKINZEE			
R	Tuolumne Sonora	71	212
MCKINZIE			
A	Nevada Nevada	61	246
David	Los Angeles Tejon	59	522
Emily	Santa Clara San Jose	65	352
Geo	Amador Twp 3	55	403
J	Napa Napa	61	105
J P	Mariposa Twp 1	60	663

Name	County Locale	M653 Roll	Page
MCKINZIE			
Kiderick J	Sierra Downieville	66	960
MCKINZY			
Thos	Amador Twp 1	55	480
MCKIPACK			
J P	Solano Suisan	69	213
MCKIRLAY			
H	San Francisco San Francisco 9	68	1075
MCKIRRY			
Jno	San Francisco San Francisco 9	68	1081
MCKIRSIE			
Jooeph*	Mariposa Twp 3	60	583
MCKIRSLE			
Joseph*	Mariposa Twp 3	60	583
MCKIRSON			
Benj	Calaveras Twp 9	57	400
MCKISKER			
Danl	Monterey Pajaro	60	1020
MCKISNY			
Charles*	Shasta Shasta	66	758
MCKISSACK			
J P	Solano Suisan	69	213
MCKISSICK			
Thomas M	Santa Clara Gilroy	65	244
MCKISSON			
Isiah J	Calaveras Twp 6	57	155
MCKITTRICK			
J	Nevada Eureka	61	377
MCKIVELL			
Michael	Plumas Quincy	62	955
MCKIVELT			
Bernard	Plumas Quincy	62	957
MCKIVER			
George	Nevada Little Y	61	532
MCKIVRY			
Jno	San Francisco San Francisco 9	68	1081
MCKIXER			
George	Nevada Little Y	61	532
MCKLINTICK			
Jno	San Francisco San Francisco 9	68	1034
MCKLISH			
Robert	San Luis Obispo San Luis Obispo	65	7
MCKLUSKLY			
Thomas	Tuolumne Sonora	71	484
MCKLUSKY			
Thomas	Tuolumne Twp 1	71	484
MCKNEIF			
Hugh	Plumas Quincy	62	961
MCKNIEL			
Wm	Humbolt Eel Rvr	59	148
MCKNIES			
Joseph*	Mariposa Twp 3	60	583
MCKNIGHT			
Abel	Siskiyou Yreka	69	129
Andw	San Francisco San Francisco 10	67	279
Ellen	San Francisco San Francisco 3	67	7
Hugh	Calaveras Twp 5	57	170
Hugh	Calaveras Twp 6	57	170
James	El Dorado Placerville	58	903
Jas	Sacramento Dry Crk	63	373
Jno	Sacramento Ward 4	63	521
John	Tuolumne Columbia	71	311
John	Yolo Cache Crk	72	594
Thos	Monterey San Juan	60	982
Thos	Napa Napa	61	113
Thos	Placer Virginia	62	663
Thos	Sacramento Franklin	63	319
Wm	El Dorado Greenwood	58	719
MCKNIGHTANDW			
Meyer	San Francisco San Francisco 10	67	279
MCKNNE			
John J	Contra Costa Twp 2	57	575
MCKNOWEN			
N	Sutter Bear Rvr	70	825
MCKNSSEK			
N M*	El Dorado Big Bar	58	740
MCKNU DSON			
Andrew	El Dorado Georgetown	58	679
MCKNZIE			
John*	San Francisco San Francisco 2	67	664
MCKOE			
Moise	Amador Twp 2	55	295
Patrick	Tuolumne Columbia	71	352
MCKONKEY			
William*	Yuba Linda	72	984
MCKOOK			
James	El Dorado Greenwood	58	713
MCKOOM			
Adelia	San Francisco San Francisco 10	67	221
MCKORN			
Adelia*	San Francisco San Francisco 10	67	221
MCKOUKEY			
William	Yuba Suida	72	984

Name	County Locale	M653 Roll	Page
MCKOUKEY			
William*	Yuba Linda	72	984
MCKRAIN			
E*	Tehama Red Bluff	70	923
MCKRANE			
J*	San Joaquin Stockton	64	1093
MCKREE			
John	San Francisco San Francisco 1	68	809
MCKRISA			
Joseph	Mariposa Twp 3	60	583
MCKRISTE			
Joseph*	Mariposa Twp 3	60	583
MCKRISTING SMIT			
J	Butte Eureka	56	653
MCKRUNAN			
James	San Francisco San Francisco 9	68	949
MCKUCHORY			
Thomas	Solano Benecia	69	298
MCKUCHRY			
Thomas	Solano Benecia	69	298
MCKUE			
Patrick	Solano Vallejo	69	269
MCKUHAN			
Dennis*	Nevada Nevada	61	251
MCKUMICE			
John*	Sierra Gibsonville	66	852
MCKUN			
Jas*	Sacramento Granite	63	261
MCKUNE			
B L	Mendocino Big Rock	60	875
Henry	Sacramento Ward 1	63	132
J H*	Sacramento Ward 3	63	470
Jacob	Tulara Twp 3	71	60
Mary	Sacramento Ward 1	63	132
Wm*	Sacramento Ward 3	63	424
MCKUNNER			
John	Sierra Gibsonville	66	852
MCKUNUCE			
John*	Sierra Gibsonville	66	852
MCKUONE			
Samuel*	San Bernardino Santa Barbara	64	153
MCKURIE			
Joseph	Alameda Brooklyn	55	195
MCKURLAY			
H	San Francisco San Francisco 9	68	1075
MCKURTOSH			
Dan*	El Dorado Georgetown	58	752
MCKUSKER			
Mary	San Francisco San Francisco 10	67	255
MCKUSLE			
Joseph*	Mariposa Twp 3	60	583
MCLABE			
P T	Santa Clara San Jose	65	338
MCLADE			
Ann	Nevada Bridgeport	61	485
MCLAEYBLIN			
Owen	Yuba Marysville	72	914
MCLAGHLIN			
Edward	Colusa Grand Island	57	471
MCLAGHLIR			
James	Mariposa Twp 3	60	566
MCLAIN			
Andrew	Calaveras Twp 7	57	48
Andrew	San Francisco San Francisco 3	67	55
Andrew*	Nevada Bridgeport	61	491
Catharine	San Francisco San Francisco 3	67	56
Duncan	Solano Vacaville	69	341
G D*	Nevada Grass Valley	61	171
J L	Tehama Red Bluff	70	912
J P	Sierra Twp 7	66	873
Joseh	Alameda Brooklyn	55	81
Michael	Contra Costa Twp 1	57	504
MCLAIPHLIN			
James	Mariposa Twp 3	60	566
MCLAIR			
G D*	Nevada Grass Valley	61	171
MCLALIE			
B	Amador Twp 3	55	380
MCLALLONGH			
Robt	Sonoma Vallejo	69	615
MCLALLOUGH			
Robt	Sonoma Petaluma	69	615
MCLAM			
Danill	El Dorado Georgetown	58	752
John	Placer Folsom	62	639
MCLAMAR			
John	Nevada Bridgeport	61	447
John*	Nevada Bridgeport	61	447
MCLAN			
Barney*	Sierra Port Win	66	795
G D*	Nevada Grass Valley	61	171
Jas	Yolo Cache Crk	72	606
MCLANE			
A	Amador Twp 3	55	377
A	San Francisco San Francisco 9	68	1060

Name	County	Locale	M653 Roll	Page
MCLANE				
A*	El Dorado	Georgetown	58	705
Amelia	San Francisco	San Francisco 2	67	752
Amos	El Dorado	Georgetown	58	745
Andrew*	Nevada	Bridgeport	61	491
Ann	San Francisco	San Francisco 2	67	626
David	Nevada	Bridgeport	61	494
David	Solano	Vacaville	69	366
David*	Solano	Vacaville	69	366
Duncan	San Francisco	San Francisco 7	68	1441
Duncan	Solano	Vacaville	69	342
Edwd	San Francisco	San Francisco 9	68	1022
Elizabeth	San Francisco	San Francisco 2	67	752
G H	Trinity	W Weaver	70	1054
Henry G	Tulara	Twp 1	71	96
James	Marin	Cortemad	60	779
James	San Francisco	San Francisco 7	68	1428
Jas	Butte	Cascade	56	690
John	Amador	Twp 7	55	414
Jos	Butte	Cascade	56	690
Kate	San Francisco	San Francisco 2	67	786
L	Amador	Twp 3	55	369
L	San Francisco	San Francisco 9	68	1033
L B	El Dorado	Georgetown	58	693
Lockwood*	Plumas	Quincy	62	992
Louis	San Francisco	San Francisco 10	67	324
Michael	Solano	Suisan	69	227
P	San Francisco	San Francisco 9	68	1059
Robert	Nevada	Bridgeport	61	494
W	Amador	Twp 3	55	378
MCLANGHLIN				
Hugh*	Placer	Michigan	62	849
James	El Dorado	Indian D	58	1157
John	El Dorado	Casumnes	58	1176
John	Trinity	Mouth Ca	70	1014
M O	El Dorado	Spanish	58	1124
Patrick	Solano	Vallejo	69	256
MCLANGHTON				
Charles	El Dorado	Coloma	58	1082
MCLANGLIN				
Ellen	Sonoma	Santa Rosa	69	392
John	Sierra	La Porte	66	769
Michael*	San Francisco	San Francisco 10	67	306
Mike*	Napa	Napa	61	85
MCLANI				
David	Nevada	Bridgeport	61	494
Robert	Nevada	Bridgeport	61	494
MCLANIS				
Andrew	Nevada	Bridgeport	61	491
MCLANLEY				
John	Calaveras	Twp 7	57	28
Michael	San Joaquin	Stockton	64	1077
MCLANLY				
John	San Francisco	San Francisco 2	67	779
MCLARD				
John	Yolo	Merritt	72	578
MCLARDY				
John	San Francisco	San Francisco 2	67	779
MCLAREN				
David	San Francisco	San Francisco 10	67	325
J	Sacramento	Ward 1	63	18
John*	Sacramento	Ward 4	63	550
Phillip	Calaveras	Twp 5	57	206
Phillips	Calaveras	Twp 5	57	206
MCLAREW				
Daniel	Los Angeles	Los Angeles	59	328
Willie	Los Angeles	Los Angeles	59	328
MCLARNIN				
Thos	Amador	Twp 1	55	489
MCLARREN				
P	San Francisco	San Francisco 5	67	489
MCLARTY				
William	Tuolumne	Montezuma	71	503
MCLAUGHIN				
Margt*	San Francisco	San Francisco 1	68	869
Mike*	Napa	Napa	61	85
MCLAUGHIR				
Thos	Calaveras	Twp 9	57	381
MCLAUGHLAN				
James	San Francisco	San Francisco 11	67	91
Mary	Sacramento	Ward 4	63	598
MCLAUGHLEN				
William	Sierra	La Porte	66	785
MCLAUGHLER				
James*	San Francisco	San Francisco 11	67	125
M A	Butte	Hamilton	56	522
William	Tuolumne	Twp 6	71	532
MCLAUGHLIN				
A	Nevada	Grass Valley	61	200
A	Sacramento	Ward 1	63	19
A J	Placer	Iona Hills	62	885
Alexander	San Diego	Agua Caliente	64	834
Amos M	Los Angeles	Los Angeles	59	491
Anna	San Francisco	San Francisco 8	68	1262
Arch	Nevada	Rough &	61	429
Barny	Placer	Michigan	62	851
Benjamin	Tulara	Visalia	71	30
Bridget	San Francisco	San Francisco 10	67	223
C	Siskiyou	Callahan	69	2
C	Tuolumne	Garrote	71	176
Catharine	San Francisco	San Francisco 8	68	1264
Charles	Humbolt	Union	59	185
Charles	Sierra	Morristown	66	1053
Chas	Sierra	Port Win	66	795
D	Sacramento	Granite	63	238
D	Sierra	Port Win	66	797
Dan	Sacramento	Ward 1	63	87
Daniel	San Francisco	San Francisco 7	68	1357
Donald	San Joaquin	Castoria	64	886
Duncan	San Francisco	San Francisco 6	67	453
Duncan	San Francisco	San Francisco 1	68	852
E	Nevada	Grass Valley	61	200
E	Nevada	Eureka	61	391
Edwar	Placer	Yankee J	62	760
Eliz	Sacramento	Ward 1	63	96
Ellen	San Francisco	San Francisco 10	67	185
Ellen	Sonoma	Petaluma	69	590
Francis	Yuba	Bear Rvr	72	999
Frank	San Francisco	San Francisco 2	67	662
Geo	San Francisco	San Francisco 1	68	891
Henry	Contra Costa	Twp 1	57	492
Hiram	Los Angeles	Los Angeles	59	293
Hugh	Sonoma	Healdsbu	69	475
Hugh*	Placer	Michigan	62	849
J	Butte	Cascade	56	701
J	Nevada	Grass Valley	61	156
J	San Francisco	San Francisco 5	67	539
J	Siskiyou	Klamath	69	89
J B	Siskiyou	Scott Ri	69	74
J P	Monterey	San Juan	60	989
Jack	Placer	Forest H	62	801
James	El Dorado	Indian D	58	1157
James	El Dorado	Georgetown	58	675
James	Mariposa	Twp 3	60	566
James	Placer	Todds Va	62	789
James	Placer	Todds Va	62	790
James	Sierra	Downieville	66	1007
James	Yolo	New York	72	720
James	Yuba	New York	72	720
James*	San Francisco	San Francisco 11	67	125
Jas	Sacramento	Ward 4	63	592
Jas	San Francisco	San Francisco 1	68	930
Jno	Butte	Chico	56	555
Jno	Sacramento	Ward 1	63	79
Jno A	Alameda	Brooklyn	55	164
Johanna*	San Francisco	San Francisco 1	68	903
John	Humbolt	Table Bl	59	143
John	Los Angeles	Azuza	59	277
John	Placer	Rattle Snake	62	625
John	Placer	Forest H	62	766
John	Sacramento	Franklin	63	316
John	Sacramento	San Joaquin	63	359
John	San Francisco	San Francisco 1	68	817
John	Santa Clara	Alviso	65	400
John	Sierra	La Porte	66	769
John	Siskiyou	Yreka	69	152
John	Siskiyou	Callahan	69	7
John	Solano	Benecia	69	285
John	Sonoma	Russian	69	431
John	Trinity	Mouth Ca	70	1014
John*	El Dorado	Casumnes	58	1176
Kate C	Yuba	Marysville	72	887
L	Sacramento	Ward 1	63	31
L	Sierra	Port Win	66	797
Louis	Stanislaus	Emory	70	738
Lugarda	Los Angeles	Shaffer	59	398
M	San Francisco	San Francisco 1	68	843
M A	Butte	Hamilton	56	522
M J	El Dorado	Spanish	58	1124
Machl	Sierra	Twp 7	66	911
Malachi A	San Francisco	San Francisco 8	68	1240
Malchia	San Francisco	San Francisco 8	68	1240
Many J	San Francisco	San Francisco 2	67	644
Margaret*	Contra Costa	Twp 1	57	536
Margt	San Francisco	San Francisco 2	67	661
Mary	Sacramento	Ward 1	63	108
Mary	Sacramento	Ward 1	63	114
Mary	Sacramento	Ward 1	63	116
Mary	Sacramento	Ward 4	63	550
Mary	Sacramento	Ward 4	63	608
Mary	San Francisco	San Francisco 10	67	219
Mary	San Francisco	San Francisco 10	67	243
Mary	San Francisco	San Francisco 1	68	843
Mary	Sonoma	Armally	69	482
Mary J	San Francisco	San Francisco 2	67	644
Michael	San Francisco	San Francisco 10	67	306
Michael	San Francisco	San Francisco 12	67	378
Michl	Sierra	Twp 7	66	911
Neal	San Francisco	San Francisco 7	68	1417
Owen	Alameda	Murray	55	225
Owen	Yuba	Marysville	72	914
P	Sacramento	Granite	63	234
Patrick	San Francisco	San Francisco 11	67	95
Patrick	Sierra	Twp 5	66	946
Patrick	Solano	Vallejo	69	256
Peter	Alameda	Brooklyn	55	97
Peter	Napa	Napa	61	78
Peter	Nevada	Rough &	61	427
Peter	San Francisco	San Francisco 8	68	1239
Peter	San Francisco	San Francisco 1	68	915
Phillip	Butte	Ophir	56	824
S	Sacramento	Ward 1	63	31
Saml	Calaveras	Twp 6	57	162
Saml*	Calaveras	Twp 6	57	162
Sarah	Sacramento	Ward 4	63	563
Susan	Sacramento	Ward 3	63	448
Thomas	San Joaquin	Tulare	64	871
Thomas	Tuolumne	Montezuma	71	503
Thos	Calaveras	Twp 9	57	381
Thos	Sacramento	Cosummes	63	397
Walte B	Solano	Vallejo	69	260
Walter B	Solano	Vallejo	69	260
Wash	Humbolt	Eureka	59	172
William	Contra Costa	Twp 2	57	575
William	Los Angeles	Los Angeles	59	370
William	San Francisco	San Francisco 7	68	1347
William	Tuolumne	Green Springs	71	532
William*	Yuba	Marysville	72	943
Wm A	Calaveras	Twp 9	57	356
Wm A	Sierra	Twp 5	66	929
Wm M	San Francisco	San Francisco 12	67	363
MCLAUGHLIND				
Duncan	San Francisco	San Francisco 6	67	453
MCLAUGHLIR				
Johanna*	San Francisco	San Francisco 1	68	903
MCLAUGHLOWEN				
Johnson	Santa Clara	Alviso	65	406
MCLAUGHTER				
James W	Fresno	Twp 3	59	10
MCLAUGHTON				
John*	El Dorado	Casumnes	58	1176
MCLAUGLIN				
D	Sonoma	Santa Rosa	69	400
Ellen	Sonoma	Santa Rosa	69	392
H*	San Francisco	San Francisco 5	67	513
Jas	San Francisco	San Francisco 2	67	676
John	San Francisco	San Francisco 1	68	849
M	San Francisco	San Francisco 1	68	918
Michael	San Francisco	San Francisco 1	68	849
Michael*	San Francisco	San Francisco 10	67	306
Mike*	Napa	Napa	61	85
Thomas	Tuolumne	Twp 5	71	503
Wm A	Calaveras	Twp 9	57	356
MCLAUGLIR				
Thos	Calaveras	Twp 9	57	381
MCLAUTHLIN				
Jaup*	Placer	Ophirville	62	655
MCLAUTIN				
Katarina	San Francisco	San Francisco 11	67	124
MCLAUTY				
A	Stanislaus	Emory	70	742
MCLAVIN				
John	Santa Clara	Almaden	65	263
MCLAWAN				
John	Calaveras	Twp 9	57	388
MCLAWLESS				
M	San Joaquin	Stockton	64	1096
MCLAWN				
Geo	San Francisco	San Francisco 9	68	1072
MCLAYHLAN				
James	San Francisco	San Francisco 11	67	91
MCLEA				
D*	San Francisco	San Francisco 5	67	490
MCLEAD				
K	El Dorado	Casumnes	58	1176
MCLEAN				
A	Napa	Clear Lake	61	131
Adam	Sierra	Whiskey	66	847

California 1860 Census Index

Name	County Locale	M653 RollPage
MCLEAN		
Alex	Placer Michigan	62 839
Andrew	Tuolumne Montezuma	71 512
Anthony	Placer Yankee J	62 759
Benjamin	Yuba Marysville	72 877
Charles	Mendocino Round Va	60 879
Charles	San Francisco San Francisco 7	681437
Edward	San Francisco San Francisco 2	67 557
Ellen	Yuba Marysville	72 905
Francis L	San Joaquin Oneal	64 937
G	San Joaquin Stockton	641093
Hugh A	Tulara Visalia	71 102
J G	Butte Kimshaw	56 589
Jas	Merced Twp 1	60 914
John	Fresno Twp 2	59 114
John	San Joaquin Stockton	641039
John	Yuba Bear Rvr	721006
John A	Colusa Monroeville	57 452
John T	Yuba Marysville	72 887
Michael	Colusa Colusi	57 426
Neil	Yuba Marysville	72 957
Pat	Mariposa Twp 3	60 603
Patrick	Mariposa Twp 3	60 617
Peter	San Francisco San Francisco 6	67 407
Peter	Trinity Weaverville	701073
W*	El Dorado Casumnes	581172
William	Placer Michigan	62 842
William	San Francisco San Francisco 11	162 67
Wm	Mariposa Twp 1	60 653
MCLEANY		
Jas	Butte Oregon	56 624
MCLEAOD		
Andrew J*	Alameda Brooklyn	55 181
MCLEAR		
George S	Plumas Quincy	62 996
Michael	Calaveras Twp 5	57 183
Patrick	Mariposa Twp 3	60 617
Thos	San Francisco San Francisco 9	681003
MCLEARD		
John	Yolo Merritt	72 578
MCLEARR		
Jas*	Merced Twp 1	60 914
MCLEARY		
Jas*	Butte Oregon	56 624
Levi	Sonoma Bodega	69 538
P	El Dorado Diamond	58 789
Robin	Fresno Twp 1	59 76
MCLEASY		
Jas*	Butte Oregon	56 624
MCLEE		
John	Sierra Twp 7	66 889
P	Sacramento San Joaquin	63 365
MCLEEN		
Ellen	Yuba Marysville	72 905
MCLEES		
James	Humbolt Eel Rvr	59 146
MCLEHEN		
Charles	San Joaquin Castoria	64 907
MCLELLAN		
Chas	Nevada Bridgeport	61 451
David	Contra Costa Twp 2	57 547
H W	Del Norte Crescent	58 631
Jno	Tuolumne Twp 4	71 140
John	Tulara Keyesville	71 61
M T*	Napa Napa	61 58
Newton	San Joaquin Castoria	64 874
R A	Placer Michigan	62 845
R S	Del Norte Crescent	58 631
R S	Del Norte Crescent	58 632
MCLELLAND		
Danl	San Francisco San Francisco 9	681031
Hugh	Solano Vallejo	69 259
J S	San Francisco San Francisco 3	67 46
Joseph	Santa Clara Santa Clara	65 468
R	San Francisco San Francisco 6	67 468
Wm L	Santa Clara Thomas	65 443
MCLELLON		
David	San Joaquin Stockton	641068
MCLELLUM		
John*	San Francisco San Francisco 3	67 41
MCLELLUND		
J S	San Francisco San Francisco 3	67 46
MCLELORE		
E	Nevada Grass Valley	61 151
MCLELOSE		
E*	Nevada Grass Valley	61 151
MCLEMENS		
Wm	Butte Oregon	56 638
MCLENEN		
Allen	Napa Napa	61 113
Allen*	Napa Napa	61 113
MCLENNAN		
A D	Mariposa Twp 1	60 629
Anna	San Francisco San Francisco 10	344 67

Name	County Locale	M653 RollPage
MCLENNEN		
A	Tuolumne Twp 2	71 354
MCLENNIN		
A	Tuolumne Columbia	71 354
MCLEOD		
Andrew J*	Alameda Brooklyn	55 181
Angus	Solano Montezuma	69 370
Ann	Santa Clara San Jose	65 283
Anus	Solano Montezuma	69 370
C C	Alameda Brooklyn	55 130
Daniel	Sonoma Armally	69 479
Ed	Solano Benecia	69 304
Hugh	Solano Vacaville	69 343
James	Plumas Quincy	62 962
Jno*	Fresno Millerto	59 1
Neil	Solano Vallejo	69 256
Neil	Solano Vallejo	69 261
Robert	Mendocino Arrana	60 858
Robert	Tuolumne Twp 5	71 491
T*	San Francisco San Francisco 5	67 503
W K	Tuolumne Columbia	71 298
W K	Tuolumne Twp 2	71 298
Wm	Sacramento Ward 4	63 597
Wm	Sierra Twp 5	66 918
Wm	Sonoma Mendocino	69 462
Wm	Tuolumne Jacksonville	71 164
Wm	Tuolumne Twp 4	71 164
MCLEON		
William	Yuba Marysville	72 968
MCLERD		
Margaret	Nevada Little Y	61 536
MCLERSON		
John	El Dorado Georgetown	58 680
MCLESSON		
John	El Dorado Georgetown	58 680
MCLESTRY		
C	San Francisco San Francisco 5	67 498
MCLEVIN		
Thomas	Tulara Visalia	71 101
MCLEVIS		
Margaret*	Nevada Little Y	61 536
MCLHAST		
Martin*	Calaveras Twp 5	57 178
MCLIGHT		
James	Amador Twp 3	55 380
MCLILLAN		
James C	Contra Costa Twp 2	57 545
John	Tulara Twp 3	71 61
MCLILLAND		
Mas	Santa Clara San Jose	65 360
MCLILLEN		
R L	Merced Twp 2	60 922
MCLILLUM		
John*	San Francisco San Francisco 3	67 41
MCLIM		
Thos*	Calaveras Twp 9	57 358
MCLIN		
C J*	Amador Twp 4	55 248
W	Solano Vacaville	69 331
MCLIND		
L	Santa Clara San Jose	65 353
MCLINN		
Peter	San Francisco San Francisco 9	681084
Thomas	Tulara Twp 1	71 101
MCLINNIN		
R S	Merced Twp 2	60 922
MCLINTOCK		
George	Sierra Scales D	66 803
MCLIROW		
Michael	Calaveras Twp 6	57 132
MCLIRTOSH		
Dan*	El Dorado Georgetown	58 752
MCLISTER		
John	Nevada Rough &	61 407
MCLLURE		
A J	Amador Twp 6	55 421
MCLOAG		
C	Calaveras Twp 9	57 405
MCLOD		
Malcom	Nevada Little Y	61 536
MCLOFLIN		
Ed	Sonoma Petaluma	69 566
Pat	Sonoma Petaluma	69 566
MCLONE		
Arthur	El Dorado Coloma	581112
MCLONERY		
Edward	Yuba Bear Rvr	721000
MCLONILY		
Michael*	Tuolumne Twp 2	71 276
MCLONKY		
E D	El Dorado Georgetown	58 689
MCLONNEY		
Francis*	Mendocino Ukiah	60 806
MCLORD		
R	Tehama Tehama	70 935
MCLOUD		
A	Sacramento Sutter	63 306

Name	County Locale	M653 RollPage
MCLOUD		
Agnes	Tuolumne Twp 1	71 262
F	San Joaquin Stockton	641068
N	Sutter Sutter	70 815
MCLOUERN		
Patrick*	Calaveras Twp 9	57 370
MCLOUERR		
Patrick*	Calaveras Twp 9	57 370
MCLOUGHLAN		
Patk	Trinity Big Flat	701040
MCLOUGHLIN		
Danl	Butte Ophir	56 769
Ellen	Sacramento Ward 4	63 580
Johnathan	Sacramento Ward 4	63 514
Wm	Sacramento Ward 4	63 514
MCLOUIRN		
John M*	Calaveras Twp 9	57 371
MCLOUIRR		
John M*	Calaveras Twp 9	57 371
MCLOVERN		
Patrick*	Calaveras Twp 9	57 370
MCLOWELL		
James	Sierra Gibsonville	66 858
MCLOWREY		
Edward*	Yuba Bear Rvr	721000
MCLOWRY		
Edward*	Yuba Bear Rvr	721000
MCLOY		
Thos*	Butte Bidwell	56 719
W W	Solano Vacaville	69 326
MCLUCHLEN		
Donald M	Sierra Whiskey	66 850
MCLUDEN		
C	Siskiyou Cottonwoood	69 99
MCLUIRE		
John*	Calaveras Twp 9	57 357
MCLUMBER		
H	Sonoma Bodega	69 520
MCLUN		
Thos*	Calaveras Twp 9	57 358
MCLUNESS		
Joseph H	Los Angeles San Gabriel	59 422
MCLUNG		
William	Tuolumne Twp 5	71 502
MCLURE		
Mary	Contra Costa Twp 1	57 506
Wm	Colusa Muion	57 459
MCLURNER		
Francis	Mendocino Ukiah	60 806
MCLURRE		
John*	Calaveras Twp 9	57 357
MCLURTY		
Barnard	Sierra Port Win	66 794
MCM??ISS		
Michael*	San Francisco San Francisco 7	681427
MCMAHAN		
Ann	Sacramento Ward 3	63 467
Ann	Tuolumne Columbia	71 311
Bridget*	Alameda Oakland	55 4
Danl	Calaveras Twp 5	57 178
Danl	Calaveras Twp 6	57 178
E H	Sierra Eureka	661049
Frank	Sierra Pine Grove	66 819
Henry	Siskiyou Shasta Valley	69 120
Heny	Siskiyou Shasta Valley	69 120
Hugh	Nevada Bridgeport	61 480
J	Nevada Nevada	61 244
J D	Solano Vacaville	69 361
J Shanna	Sierra La Porte	66 781
Jas	Sacramento Ward 4	63 524
Johanna	Sierra La Porte	66 781
John	Calaveras Twp 6	57 163
John	Sacramento Ward 4	63 521
John*	Mendocino Ukiah	60 800
Joseph	Sierra Pine Grove	66 820
M	Trinity Douglas	70 978
Mary	Sacramento Ward 3	63 475
Mary J	Yuba Suida	72 982
Mary J	Yuba Linda Twp	72 984
Mathew	San Francisco San Francisco 3	67 16
Michael	San Francisco San Francisco 3	67 62
Monar*	Calaveras Twp 5	57 228
P J	Sacramento Ward 1	63 76
Robt	Nevada Eureka	61 374
Saml	Santa Clara Almaden	65 275
T M	Sutter Nicolaus	70 838
Thomas	Calaveras Twp 5	57 228
Thomas*	Calaveras Twp 5	57 228
Thos	Napa Hot Springs	61 27
Timothy	Sierra La Porte	66 786
W B*	Mariposa Coulterville	60 675
MCMAHAR		
John	Mendocino Ukiah	60 800
John*	Mendocino Ukiah	60 800
MCMAHEN		
Ann	San Francisco San Francisco 2	67 595

California 1860 Census Index

Name	County Locale	M653 Roll	Page
MCMAHEN			
J E M	Sacramento Ward 1	63	27
Michael J	San Francisco San Francisco 2	67	773
Pat	Sacramento Granite	63	260
Philip*	Contra Costa Twp 3	57	600
MCMAHER			
Mary	Nevada Bridgeport	61	504
W B	Mariposa Coulterville	60	675
MCMAHILL			
George	Placer Todds Va	62	783
MCMAHN			
Bridget*	Alameda Oakland	55	4
Philip*	Contra Costa Twp 3	57	600
William	Contra Costa Twp 3	57	587
MCMAHON			
A	Sacramento Ward 1	63	14
Ann	San Francisco San Francisco 2	67	595
Anna	Merced Monterey	60	944
Anna	Monterey Monterey	60	944
Annie	San Mateo Twp 1	65	71
Arthur	Yuba Marysville	72	941
B	Del Norte Klamath	58	653
B	Nevada Nevada	61	254
Barney	Stanislaus Branch	70	711
Bernard E	San Francisco San Francisco 1	68	842
Bridget	Alameda Oakland	55	4
Catharine	San Francisco San Francisco 11		155
		67	
Catharine	San Francisco San Francisco 2	67	579
G	Nevada Grass Valley	61	226
H	Santa Clara Santa Clara	65	512
H J	Solano Vacaville	69	361
Hugh	Sierra Downieville	66	1016
J	Nevada Nevada	61	244
J E M	Sacramento Ward 1	63	27
J T	Trinity Weaverville	70	1066
James	Amador Twp 1	55	489
James	Monterey San Juan	60	980
James	Placer Michigan	62	845
James	Solano Benecia	69	298
James	Tuolumne Chinese	71	495
James	Tuolumne Twp 5	71	495
Jas	Butte Ophir	56	774
Jas	San Francisco San Francisco 2	67	593
Jas	Yolo Cottonwood	72	649
Jesse	Sacramento Dry Crk	63	370
Jno	Butte Hamilton	56	515
John	Placer Christia	62	736
John	Sierra La Porte	66	787
John	Stanislaus Emory	70	748
John	Tulara Twp 3	71	59
John	Tuolumne Twp 2	71	361
Jonathan	San Francisco San Francisco 11		123
		67	
Jos	San Francisco San Francisco 2	67	593
L	Butte Kimshaw	56	598
Lawrence	Humbolt Pacific	59	131
Mary	Nevada Bridgeport	61	504
Mary	San Francisco San Francisco 2	67	636
Michael	Sierra Downieville	66	1032
Michael J	San Francisco San Francisco 2	67	773
O	Sacramento Ward 1	63	83
Owen	Sacramento Ward 1	63	99
Owen	San Francisco San Francisco 1	68	831
P	Butte Kimshaw	56	590
P	Sacramento Cosummes	63	398
Patrick	Humbolt Eureka	59	166
Patrick	San Mateo Twp 1	65	59
Phillip	Los Angeles Azuza	59	277
Robt	Nevada Eureka	61	374
Thomas	Calaveras Twp 5	57	228
Thos	Tehama Red Bluff	70	926
William	Siskiyou Callahan	69	6
Wm	Placer Virginia	62	663
Wm	Solano Vacaville	69	361
MCMAIN			
Hannah	San Francisco San Francisco 11		89
		67	
Wm	Tehama Antelope	70	886
Wm C*	Sierra Downieville	66	994
MCMAINE			
Chandler	Placer Goods	62	695
MCMAINES			
Patrick	Santa Clara San Jose	65	282
MCMAINNIER			
John*	Solano Benecia	69	317
MCMAINS			
Martin	Yuba New York	72	731
MCMAINUS			
Patrick	Sacramento Ward 3	63	439
MCMAIRE			
Wm C*	Sierra Downieville	66	994
MCMAITSN			
J*	Monterey Monterey	60	956
MCMAKIN			
John	Sierra Downieville	66	962

Name	County Locale	M653 Roll	Page
MCMAKIN			
Pat	Sacramento Ward 3	63	488
MCMALAN			
Dennis M	San Joaquin Elkhorn	64	969
MCMALAS			
J*	Nevada Grass Valley	61	199
MCMALLAN			
M	Calaveras Twp 9	57	412
MCMALLY			
John	Tuolumne Twp 2	71	333
MCMALOE			
Bridget	Sonoma Armally	69	512
MCMALTERS			
Thos*	Nevada Rough &	61	405
MCMALTY			
Sarah J*	Tuolumne Twp 2	71	345
MCMAMAS			
L*	Stanislaus Buena Village	70	722
MCMAMIS			
W H*	Nevada Grass Valley	61	238
MCMAMMA			
John	Solano Benecia	69	317
MCMAMMOR			
John*	Solano Benecia	69	317
MCMAMNES			
Sarah*	San Francisco San Francisco 7	68	1331
MCMAMRIS			
E	Tuolumne Big Oak	71	147
MCMAN			
John	Sierra Downieville	66	955
John P	Calaveras Twp 4	57	340
Patrick	Tuolumne Twp 2	71	295
T L*	Nevada Nevada	61	268
T S	Nevada Nevada	61	268
MCMANAFEE			
Drucilla	Sonoma Bodega	69	536
MCMANAMY			
Wm C	Humbolt Bucksport	59	158
MCMANAS			
Phillip	Sierra Chappare	66	1041
MCMANAWAY			
W	Yolo Cache	72	594
MCMANEARA			
David	Sierra Twp 7	66	869
MCMANENS			
Jos	San Francisco San Francisco 9	68	1067
MCMANERS			
Jas*	San Francisco San Francisco 9	68	1067
MCMANES			
Bernard	San Francisco San Francisco 10		288
		67	
C	Shasta Horsetown	66	693
MCMANESS			
Elija*	Solano Benecia	69	318
Eliza*	Solano Benecia	69	318
MCMANET			
Bernard	San Francisco San Francisco 10		288
		67	
MCMANIHIE			
Daniel	Calaveras Twp 5	57	214
MCMANIHIR			
Daniel	Calaveras Twp 5	57	214
MCMANIN			
J*	Shasta Shasta	66	663
MCMANIS			
An	El Dorado Diamond	58	774
C	Nevada Nevada	61	326
James	El Dorado Kelsey	58	1144
Miruas*	El Dorado Kelsey	58	1126
Monias*	El Dorado Kelsey	58	1126
Murucus	El Dorado Kelsey	58	1126
Pat	Nevada Eureka	61	364
Patrick	El Dorado White Oaks	58	1008
Thomas	El Dorado Kelsey	58	1129
Wm P	Nevada Eureka	61	364
MCMANISS			
Michael	San Francisco San Francisco 7	68	1427
MCMANN			
A	Sacramento Ward 1	63	48
Alex	Sierra Poverty	66	799
Charles	San Francisco San Francisco 3	67	13
Hugh	San Francisco San Francisco 9	68	1036
J	Nevada Eureka	61	360
J P	Nevada Nevada	61	282
John	Contra Costa Twp 1	57	503
John	San Francisco San Francisco 7	68	1342
John	San Francisco San Francisco 7	68	1442
John	Yuba Marysville	72	906
M	Sonoma Sonoma	69	636
Mary E*	Mendocino Big Rvr	60	853
Michael	Tuolumne Chinese	71	497
Owen	Tuolumne Columbia	71	358
R	Nevada Eureka	61	371
R A	Nevada Nevada	61	284
R B	Nevada Nevada	61	283
Thomas	Contra Costa Twp 1	57	534

Name	County Locale	M653 Roll	Page
MCMANN			
Thos	Butte Bidwell	56	724
Wm	Del Norte Ferry P O	58	665
Wm	Tehama Tehama	70	947
MCMANNA			
Wm	Mariposa Twp 3	60	610
MCMANNAME			
J	San Francisco San Francisco 5	67	489
MCMANNARD			
William	Yuba Bear Rvr	72	1009
MCMANNAY			
Peter*	Tuolumne Twp 2	71	345
MCMANNEMAN			
Js	Sonoma Armally	69	496
MCMANNERS			
M	Nevada Grass Valley	61	226
MCMANNEY			
A	El Dorado Mud Springs	58	969
Mary	Tuolumne Twp 1	71	212
MCMANNING			
Hugh	Yuba Marysville	72	883
John	Calaveras Twp 5	57	191
MCMANNIS			
E	Tuolumne Twp 4	71	147
J C	El Dorado White Oaks	58	1017
Mich	Sacramento Ward 3	63	424
MCMANNO			
M*	Yolo Putah	72	551
MCMANNS			
Ann	San Francisco San Francisco 3	67	57
Barthomew*	Mendocino Big Rvr	60	852
C*	Nevada Nevada	61	326
C*	Shasta Horsetown	66	693
E	Nevada Rough &	61	431
E*	Nevada Rough &	61	431
J	Nevada Grass Valley	61	202
John*	Yuba Marysville	72	906
Mary E*	Mendocino Big Rvr	60	853
Patric	Mariposa Twp 1	60	623
Peter*	Shasta Shasta	66	686
R B	Nevada Nevada	61	286
S C	Nevada Grass Valley	61	145
W H	Nevada Grass Valley	61	238
MCMANNUS			
J	Amador Twp 3	55	369
J	San Joaquin Stockton	64	1092
Sarah*	San Francisco San Francisco 7	68	1331
MCMANNY			
Pat	Butte Bidwell	56	727
MCMANS			
C G*	Nevada Grass Valley	61	182
R A	Nevada Nevada	61	284
MCMANUES			
Patrick	San Francisco San Francisco 10		201
		67	
MCMANUS			
Ann	San Francisco San Francisco 3	67	57
Barthomew*	Mendocino Big Rvr	60	852
Bernard	Plumas Quincy	62	961
C	Sacramento Ward 1	63	147
C*	Shasta Horsetown	66	693
Cath	Sacramento Ward 3	63	440
Charles	Plumas Quincy	62	961
E	Nevada Rough &	61	431
Eliza J	Sonoma Mendocino	69	453
Ellen	San Francisco San Francisco 10		332
		67	
J	Nevada Nevada	61	269
J	Shasta Shasta	66	663
James	Los Angeles Elmonte	59	245
Jno G	Sonoma Mendocino	69	453
John	Solano Vallejo	69	268
L C	Nevada Grass Valley	61	145
Mary	San Francisco San Francisco 7	68	1355
Mary E*	Mendocino Big Rvr	60	853
Michael	Sacramento Ward 3	63	440
P	Mariposa Twp 1	60	661
Patric	Mariposa Twp 1	60	623
Patrick	Placer Auburn	62	589
Patrick	Sacramento Ward 3	63	439
Patrick	Solano Benecia	69	285
R B	Nevada Nevada	61	286
Wm	Tehama Lassen	70	883
MCMANUSS			
Peter*	Shasta Shasta	66	686
MCMANY			
E	San Francisco San Francisco 9	68	1069
E*	San Francisco San Francisco 9	68	1069
MCMAPER			
W B*	Mariposa Coulterville	60	675
MCMARA			
Ellen	Santa Clara San Jose	65	281
MCMARGHLIN			
Daniel	Sierra Port Win	66	795
MCMARI			
C D	El Dorado Kelsey	58	1147

California 1860 Census Index

Name	County Locale	M653 RollPage
MCMARIN		
M	Sonoma Sonoma	69 636
MCMARNNIS		
Sarah	San Francisco San Francisco 7	681331
MCMARR		
T L*	Nevada Nevada	61 268
MCMARRIN		
Frank	Santa Clara Fremont	65 430
MCMARROW		
John	Amador Twp 1	55 487
MCMARRY		
E*	San Francisco San Francisco 9	681069
J D	Nevada Bridgeport	61 447
MCMARRYMAN		
Peter	Humbolt Bucksport	59 161
MCMARSTER		
W*	El Dorado Kelsey	581149
MCMART		
Alexr	Sierra Twp 7	66 895
Alexs	Sierra Twp 7	66 895
MCMARTERS		
Jas*	Butte Oregon	56 625
MCMARTIN		
J	Monterey Monterey	60 956
James	Sonoma Armally	69 513
John	Placer Virginia	62 661
MCMARTUS		
Jas*	Butte Oregon	56 625
MCMARUNEA		
John*	Solano Benecia	69 317
MCMASTER		
John	Sierra Pine Grove	66 823
John	Yolo No E Twp	72 672
John	Yuba North Ea	72 672
W*	El Dorado Kelsey	581149
Wm	Alameda Brooklyn	55 108
MCMASTERS		
F	San Francisco San Francisco 5	67 501
Jas	Butte Oregon	56 625
Jobe C	Contra Costa Twp 3	57 596
Levi	Contra Costa Twp 3	57 596
Thos*	Nevada Rough &	61 405
MCMASTRIE		
J W	Siskiyou Cottonwood	69 98
MCMASTRY		
F M	Alameda Brooklyn	55 133
Lars*	Alameda Brooklyn	55 133
MCMATH		
Archy	Yuba Marysville	72 964
Em*	Sierra Downieville	66 961
MCMATTERS		
Thos	Nevada Rough &	61 405
MCMAUERS		
Jas*	San Francisco San Francisco 9	681067
MCMAUESS		
Elija*	Solano Benecia	69 318
MCMAUGHAN		
Daniel*	Sierra Port Win	66 795
MCMAUGHLIN		
Daniel*	Sierra Port Win	66 795
MCMCCONNEL		
John	Butte Ophir	56 771
MCMEAN		
W	Shasta French G	66 719
MCMEANS		
Jas	Sacramento Franklin	63 315
Jos	Tehama Red Bluff	70 927
L A*	Solano Suisan	69 213
R C	Merced Twp 1	60 911
S A*	Solano Suisan	69 213
MCMEARA		
Anna	San Francisco San Francisco 8	681252
MCMECHAN		
J M*	San Francisco San Francisco 5	67 484
MCMEHAN		
Rosana	Napa Napa	61 113
Wm	Napa Napa	61 68
MCMEIGHAN		
Peter	Siskiyou Yreka	69 130
MCMEIGHTON		
L S	El Dorado Casumnes	581161
MCMELLAN		
Hugh	San Francisco San Francisco 9	68 948
MCMELLEN		
James	Nevada Bridgeport	61 494
Mary*	Nevada Bridgeport	61 474
MCMELLON		
Jas	Butte Bidwell	56 711
Jas	Placer Goods	62 694
Wm	Butte Oro	56 687
MCMELLY		
A M	Tuolumne Columbia	71 331
MCMENAMY		
Wm	San Francisco San Francisco 10	251 67
MCMENDER		
Saml*	Butte Wyandotte	56 657

Name	County Locale	M653 RollPage
MCMENENSEN		
James*	Del Norte Klamath	58 653
MCMENEY		
Jose	San Francisco San Francisco 2	67 759
MCMERRY		
Robert	Nevada Bloomfield	61 515
MCMETLY		
C A*	San Francisco San Francisco 2	67 677
MCMEWEN		
Anna	San Joaquin Castoria	64 875
MCMICAN		
Thomas*	San Joaquin Oneal	64 936
MCMICHAEL		
C	San Francisco San Francisco 5	67 530
D	Tuolumne Twp 2	71 337
E	Monterey San Juan	60 990
E	San Francisco San Francisco 5	67 531
H S	Nevada Bridgeport	61 497
J	San Joaquin Stockton	641092
John	El Dorado Greenwood	58 721
Saml	Sierra Eureka	661047
MCMICHAL		
Robert	Siskiyou Klamath	69 88
MCMICHELS		
Barney	Nevada Rough &	61 414
MCMICKLE		
Stephen	San Francisco San Francisco 1	68 810
MCMIHON		
F	San Francisco San Francisco 9	68 956
MCMILEN		
Robt	Napa Napa	61 69
MCMILL		
M	San Francisco San Francisco 4	681167
MCMILLAN		
A	Stanislaus Oatvale	70 716
A	Stanislaus Emory	70 737
A G	Stanislaus Buena Village	70 720
Charles	San Francisco San Francisco 3	67 29
D J	El Dorado Placerville	58 934
Danl	San Francisco San Francisco 10	314 67
David	Santa Cruz Pescadero	66 645
F A	Amador Twp 6	55 448
G	Butte Kimshaw	56 592
G M	Butte Kimshaw	56 592
George	San Francisco San Francisco 7	681341
Hugh	San Francisco San Francisco 9	68 948
J B	Calaveras Twp 9	57 412
James	Amador Twp 3	55 374
James	El Dorado Greenwood	58 724
Jas	Sacramento Centre	63 174
Joel	San Joaquin Castoria	64 889
M	Stanislaus Emory	70 741
Peter D	San Francisco San Francisco 10	315 67
Robert	Alameda Brooklyn	55 122
Thomas	Solano Suisan	69 239
Thos	Stanislaus Oatvale	70 716
MCMILLEN		
A R	Amador Twp 4	55 251
D	San Francisco San Francisco 1	68 924
G W	Yolo Cottonwoood	72 556
J R	Shasta French G	66 721
James	Nevada Bridgeport	61 494
Jas	Yolo Putah	72 588
Jno	San Francisco San Francisco 9	68 950
John	Amador Twp 3	55 408
M F	Siskiyou Scott Ri	69 62
Mary	Nevada Bridgeport	61 474
Mary*	Nevada Bridgeport	61 474
R B	Yolo Putah	72 560
T D	Yolo Cottonwoood	72 556
Thomas	El Dorado Kelsey	581132
W F	Siskiyou Scott Ri	69 62
MCMILLER		
A B	Sacramento Granite	63 257
John	El Dorado Casumnes	581162
MCMILLEY		
A M A	Tuolumne Twp 2	71 331
MCMILLIM		
F A	Amador Twp 6	55 448
MCMILLON		
John	Sierra Gibsonville	66 860
Wm	Butte Oro	56 687
MCMILTY		
Jas	Tehama Antelope	70 885
MCMIN		
J	Shasta Horsetown	66 702
W C	Sutter Yuba	70 767
MCMINAMY		
Wm	San Francisco San Francisco 10	251 67
MCMINDS		
Ira	Amador Twp 1	55 479
MCMINECK		
Henry*	Sierra St Louis	66 811

Name	County Locale	M653 RollPage
MCMINER		
J C	Amador Twp 4	55 237
MCMINICK		
Henry	Sierra St Louis	66 811
MCMINN		
S	Yolo Putah	72 548
Saml C	San Francisco San Francisco 10	320 67
MCMINNS		
W	Yolo Putah	72 551
MCMISLAND		
J*	Calaveras Twp 9	57 412
MCMISTLE		
Thirair*	Calaveras Twp 7	57 48
MCMITCHELL		
J W	Butte Oregon	56 641
W	Sacramento Ward 1	63 133
MCMIVERAY		
F	Sacramento Ward 1	63 41
MCMLERY		
J*	Nevada Eureka	61 373
MCMLORY		
J*	Nevada Eureka	61 373
MCMLURE		
C	Amador Twp 6	55 426
MCMOHN		
W B*	Mariposa Coulterville	60 675
MCMONRAGE		
John*	Marin S Antoni	60 712
MCMOPER		
W B	Mariposa Coulterville	60 675
MCMORRIS		
Frank*	Yuba Marysville	72 904
MCMORRRAGE		
John*	Marin S Antoni	60 712
MCMUHAN		
John	Calaveras Twp 6	57 163
MCMULAND		
Danl	Sierra Twp 5	66 925
MCMULIGAN		
Michael	Calaveras Twp 4	57 332
MCMULIYAN		
Michal	Calaveras Twp 4	57 332
MCMULLAN		
John	San Francisco San Francisco 11	118 67
John	Solano Benecia	69 317
MCMULLE		
Arch	Solano Vallejo	69 277
MCMULLEN		
---	Mariposa Twp 3	60 605
---*	El Dorado Georgetown	58 699
Adam	El Dorado Big Bar	58 738
Alexander	Sierra Pine Grove	66 827
Alfred	Nevada Bloomfield	61 507
Andrew	Yuba Suida	72 981
Arch	Solano Vallejo	69 277
Charles	El Dorado Kelsey	581132
David	Marin Bolinas	60 744
David	Trinity Taylor'S	701036
Eliza	San Francisco San Francisco 10	357 67
F	El Dorado Georgetown	58 699
Frank	Santa Cruz Santa Cruz	66 631
H	Solano Suisan	69 232
Hugh	Tuolumne Big Oak	71 178
James	El Dorado Kelsey	581133
Jno	San Francisco San Francisco 9	68 950
Joh	Solano Suisan	69 224
John	Alameda Brooklyn	55 88
John	Calaveras Twp 6	57 154
John	San Francisco San Francisco 7	681428
John	San Joaquin Castoria	64 878
John	Solano Suisan	69 224
Jon	Amador Twp 2	55 299
Joseph	Sierra Pine Grove	66 827
M M	Mariposa Twp 3	60 618
Maria	San Joaquin Douglass	64 917
Michael	Mendocino Arrana	60 863
P	Amador Twp 2	55 273
Peter	Solano Benecia	69 301
Rankin	Placer Dutch Fl	62 714
Samuel	Mendocino Arrana	60 857
Thomas	El Dorado Kelsey	581132
Thos	Nevada Rough &	61 405
William	Santa Cruz Santa Cruz	66 633
Wm	Amador Twp 2	55 306
MCMULLER		
John	Calaveras Twp 6	57 154
MCMULLIN		
Alexander*	Tuolumne Twp 3	71 459
Danl	Santa Clara Fremont	65 427
H	Shasta Millvill	66 740
J	Nevada Nevada	61 246
James	Shasta Millvill	66 725
Jano	Amador Twp 5	55 367

Name	County Locale	M653 Roll	Page
MCMULLIN			
John	San Francisco San Francisco 1	68	909
John	San Francisco San Francisco 1	68	910
John	Santa Clara Fremont	65	427
N	Amador Twp 1	55	475
Peter	Solano Benecia	69	301
Thos	Santa Clara Fremont	65	427
MCMULTY			
M C	Sacramento Ward 1	63	26
Sarah J*	Tuolumne Twp 2	71	345
MCMUNAY			
A R	Nevada Nevada	61	289
MCMUNERS			
P*	San Francisco San Francisco 6	67	432
MCMUNIS			
Julia	Sonoma Sonoma	69	658
MCMUNORY			
W*	Sutter Butte	70	786
MCMUNOY			
P*	Yolo Putah	72	552
MCMURPHEY			
T	El Dorado Mud Springs	58	969
MCMURPHY			
A	El Dorado Eldorado	58	942
Ellen	San Francisco San Francisco 9	68	1080
Jos	San Francisco San Francisco 9	68	1080
MCMURRAY			
A R	Nevada Nevada	61	289
Amanda	Sonoma Petaluma	69	576
C	Merced Twp 2	60	918
F	Sacramento Ward 1	63	41
Hugh J	Yuba Marysville	72	873
J	Yolo Putah	72	552
J R	Nevada Nevada	61	268
J R	Nevada Nevada	61	272
James	Sonoma Washington	69	675
Jno	Trinity Red Bar	70	998
L	Amador Twp 2	55	313
Martha	Yolo Cottonwoood	72	652
Nancy	San Francisco San Francisco 2	67	694
Peter*	Tuolumne Twp 2	71	345
Thos	Alameda Brooklyn	55	189
MCMURREN			
John	Amador Twp 7	55	419
William	Siskiyou Yreka	69	130
MCMURREW			
William	Siskiyou Yreka	69	130
MCMURRY			
J	Sutter Nicolaus	70	841
J D	Nevada Bridgeport	61	447
L	Amador Twp 2	55	313
R L	Nevada Grass Valley	61	193
R S	Amador Twp 2	55	296
Sarah	San Francisco San Francisco 9	68	945
MCMURTER			
John	Tuolumne Twp 4	71	158
MCMURTEY			
G W	Solano Suisan	69	217
MCMURTIRE			
J W	Siskiyou Cottonwoood	69	98
MCMURTRY			
G W	Solano Suisan	69	217
J H	Nevada Grass Valley	61	147
Leslee B	Marin Bolinas	60	733
Thos	Plumas Quincy	62	983
W S*	Nevada Grass Valley	61	192
MCMURTY			
M V*	Sutter Butte	70	786
MCMUSTER			
James	El Dorado Coloma	58	1108
Paines	El Dorado Coloma	58	1108
MCMUVAY			
Pauline V	Contra Costa Twp 2	57	550
MCNAB			
Alexander	Calaveras Twp 4	57	332
Alexander	Calaveras Twp 4	57	337
Harry	Sonoma Petaluma	69	577
Henry	San Francisco San Francisco 3	67	18
MCNABB			
Bridget	San Francisco San Francisco 1	68	828
J	San Francisco San Francisco 2	67	725
J L	Calaveras Twp 7	57	4
James	Plumas Quincy	62	918
Michael	Calaveras Twp 6	57	157
R	Nevada Eureka	61	387
MCNABE			
Edward	Alameda Brooklyn	55	80
J	El Dorado Placerville	58	860
MCNABL			
Thos	San Francisco San Francisco 1	68	809
MCNAHAN			
Margt*	San Francisco San Francisco 1	68	841
MCNAIN			
Wm	Sierra Downieville	66	994
Wm C*	Sierra Downieville	66	994
MCNAIR			
Alexander	Yuba New York	72	744
MCNAIR			
Benj F	Yuba Marysville	72	866
Benjn F	Yuba Marysville	72	866
Chas	Sacramento American	63	159
David	Siskiyou Shasta Rvr	69	111
David*	Siskiyou Shasta Rvr	69	111
J D	Butte Ophir	56	771
James	Contra Costa Twp 3	57	609
Jas	Butte Chico	56	559
Joseph*	Solano Vacaville	69	327
Mathew*	San Francisco San Francisco 3	67	29
N	Nevada Eureka	61	354
N B	Nevada Eureka	61	354
Nat	Sacramento Ward 1	63	149
Thos	Butte Kimshaw	56	572
Wiley	Los Angeles Elmonte	59	248
MCNAIRE			
D	Butte Bidwell	56	711
Wm C*	Sierra Downieville	66	994
MCNAIS			
David*	Siskiyou Shasta Rvr	69	111
P	Calaveras Twp 9	57	417
MCNALLEY			
John	Tuolumne Twp 2	71	344
Michael	San Francisco San Francisco 7	68	1391
MCNALLY			
A J	Sierra Twp 7	66	907
C	Butte Bidwell	56	710
Charlotte	Calaveras Twp 4	57	345
Daniel	Alameda Brooklyn	55	98
Danill*	Alameda Brooklyn	55	98
Elizabeth	San Francisco San Francisco 10	67	186
Francis	Placer Todds Va	62	786
Frank	Sonoma Petaluma	69	589
George	Placer Forest H	62	774
Hugh	Alameda Brooklyn	55	130
J	Nevada Eureka	61	392
James	Nevada Red Dog	61	540
Jas	Butte Ophir	56	797
Jas	Sonoma Petaluma	69	589
Jno	San Francisco San Francisco 10	67	296
John	Plumas Quincy	62	944
John	San Francisco San Francisco 3	67	84
John	Tuolumne Columbia	71	333
John*	Nevada Red Dog	61	540
Mary	San Francisco San Francisco 7	68	1382
Mary E	San Francisco San Francisco 10	67	338
N	Butte Bidwell	56	707
P	Butte Bidwell	56	712
Pat	Butte Ophir	56	775
Pat	Butte Ophir	56	795
Pat	Tuolumne Twp 2	71	379
Patrick	Placer Virginia	62	673
Patrick	Solano Benecia	69	298
R	Tehama Red Bluff	70	916
Roger	San Francisco San Francisco 5	67	478
T	San Mateo Twp 2	65	121
Tally*	Nevada Rough &	61	419
Thos	Placer Dutch Fl	62	726
Tully*	Nevada Rough &	61	419
William	San Francisco San Francisco 7	68	1438
Wm	Mariposa Twp 1	60	663
MCNALTY			
James	San Francisco San Francisco 4	68	1139
MCNALU			
Thomas	Placer Forest H	62	771
MCNALY			
Milton	El Dorado Mud Springs	58	965
MCNAMAA			
J T*	Mariposa Twp 3	60	584
MCNAMAN			
Margaret	San Francisco San Francisco 2	67	584
Margaret	Yuba Marysville	72	979
MCNAMARA			
---	San Francisco San Francisco 10	67	349
A	Sutter Yuba	70	759
Amy	San Francisco San Francisco 2	67	730
Anne	San Francisco San Francisco 2	67	730
B M	San Mateo Twp 1	65	47
David*	Sierra Twp 7	66	869
Dorithy	San Francisco San Francisco 4	68	1135
Ellen	San Francisco San Francisco 10	67	312
F	Sacramento Granite	63	223
G S	Siskiyou Scott Ri	69	63
J G	Trinity Cox'S Bar	70	1038
J T	Mariposa Twp 3	60	584
James	Del Norte Crescent	58	628
James	San Francisco San Francisco 7	68	1332
James	Siskiyou Klamath	69	89
Jno	Mendocino Big Rvr	60	845
John	Alameda Brooklyn	55	125
MCNAMARA			
John	Amador Twp 1	55	475
John	Amador Twp 1	55	482
John	Monterey S Antoni	60	968
John*	Calaveras Twp 4	57	327
L T*	Mariposa Twp 3	60	584
M	Sacramento Granite	63	241
M	Siskiyou Scott Ri	69	73
M J	Del Norte Crescent	58	626
M*	Siskiyou Scott Ri	69	73
Margaret	Yuba Marysville	72	867
Margaret	Yuba Marysville	72	979
Mary	Sacramento Ward 1	63	91
Michael	San Francisco San Francisco 3	67	40
Patk	San Francisco San Francisco 10	67	172
Robert	San Francisco San Francisco 1	68	851
Thos	Klamath Liberty	59	230
William	Yuba Bear Rvr	72	1009
MCNAMARIA			
Michael*	San Francisco San Francisco 1	68	914
MCNAMARRA			
B M	San Mateo Twp 1	65	47
B M M	San Mateo Twp 1	65	47
Mathew	Calaveras Twp 8	57	96
Richard	Calaveras Twp 7	57	43
MCNAMARY			
Wm	Humbolt Eel Rvr	59	146
Wm J	Humbolt Eel Rvr	59	149
MCNAMAVA			
Michael*	San Francisco San Francisco 1	68	914
MCNAME			
Peter	El Dorado Mud Springs	58	970
MCNAMEE			
John	San Francisco San Francisco 11	67	96
Morris	San Francisco San Francisco 3	67	30
Patrick J	San Francisco San Francisco 3	67	30
Patrick*	San Francisco San Francisco 3	67	81
MCNAMENN			
John	Calaveras Twp 4	57	327
MCNAMER			
John	San Francisco San Francisco 3	67	66
John	San Francisco San Francisco 3	67	7
John	San Francisco San Francisco 3	67	85
John M	San Francisco San Francisco 3	67	7
Patrick*	San Francisco San Francisco 3	67	81
MCNAMERA			
John	Monterey S Antoni	60	968
MCNAMMA			
John*	Calaveras Twp 4	57	327
MCNAMMS			
Patrick	Calaveras Twp 5	57	215
MCNAMONA			
Michael*	Marin San Rafael	60	772
MCNAMONE			
Michael*	Marin San Rafael	60	772
MCNAMONER			
Michael*	Marin San Rafael	60	772
MCNAMORA			
Ellen	San Francisco San Francisco 10	67	312
J T	Mariposa Twp 3	60	584
MCNAMSUN			
John	Calaveras Twp 4	57	327
MCNAN			
William*	Mendocino Ukiah	60	797
MCNANEARA			
David*	Sierra Twp 7	66	869
MCNANNARY			
M	Sonoma Bodega	69	522
MCNANRE			
Maggie	Sacramento Ward 4	63	528
MCNANY			
Owen*	Del Norte Crescent	58	623
MCNAR			
Jas	Sacramento Brighton	63	194
MCNARA			
James	San Francisco San Francisco 9	68	977
MCNARMARY			
Mich	Sacramento Franklin	63	313
MCNARR			
Mathew*	San Francisco San Francisco 3	67	29
MCNARROUGH			
P	Tuolumne Sonora	71	217
MCNARRY			
Owen*	Del Norte Crescent	58	623
MCNARS			
John	Mariposa Twp 3	60	599
John*	Mariposa Twp 3	60	599
MCNASTY			
P	Amador Twp 1	55	484
MCNATTY			
James	Tuolumne Twp 2	71	285
MCNAUGHTEN			
James	Colusa Butte Crk	57	464

Name	County Locale	M653 RollPage
MCNAUGHTON		
A W	San Francisco San Francisco	9 681071
Danl	Tuolumne Twp 2	71 354
MCNEAL		
---	San Francisco San Francisco	2 67 583
Alva	El Dorado Kelsey	581137
Carre	San Francisco San Francisco	2 67 569
Carrie	San Francisco San Francisco	2 67 569
David	San Joaquin Elkhorn	64 978
Dennis	San Francisco San Francisco	9 681040
E F	El Dorado Mud Springs	58 997
F	Nevada Washington	61 331
F	Nevada Washington	61 341
Geo	Klamath S Fork	59 207
George	Sierra Morristown	661051
George A	San Joaquin Douglass	64 915
H	Sutter Yuba	70 773
Hamilton	Alameda Oakland	55 23
J	Sutter Sutter	70 807
Jas	San Francisco San Francisco	9 681089
John	Calaveras Twp 6	57 159
Lyman	Trinity Weaverville	701065
M	San Francisco San Francisco	5 67 553
Mary	San Francisco San Francisco	2 67 568
Michael	Solano Fremont	69 385
Neal	Butte Ophir	56 748
P	El Dorado Placerville	58 824
Robert	Marin Bolinas	60 740
S	Sutter Butte	70 784
S H	Tehama Red Bluff	70 919
Thomas	El Dorado Kelsey	581133
William	Amador Twp 4	55 251
William	Nevada Rough &	61 424
MCNEALS		
And	Mariposa Twp 3	60 598
MCNEALY		
A	El Dorado Placerville	58 883
MCNEAR		
Jno	Sonoma Petaluma	69 584
MCNEARY		
Jno	Klamath Liberty	59 238
MCNEEF		
Patrick*	Calaveras Twp 9	57 390
MCNEEL		
D	San Francisco San Francisco	9 681073
MCNEELEY		
James	San Joaquin Douglass	64 925
James J*	Tuolumne Twp 2	71 298
Timothy	Tehama Red Bluff	70 926
MCNEELLIE		
An	Sacramento Natonia	63 284
MCNEELY		
A	San Joaquin Stockton	641032
Adam	Trinity Big Flat	701040
And	Trinity Big Flat	701040
Andrew	Santa Cruz Pajaro	66 529
C L	Amador Twp 2	55 279
Elizabeth	San Joaquin Stockton	641032
Hugh	San Francisco San Francisco	2 67 728
J	Los Angeles Elmonte	59 256
J C	Amador Twp 2	55 278
Wm	Trinity Big Flat	701040
MCNEER		
Isaac	Mariposa Twp 3	60 591
MCNEES		
James	Yuba Marysville	72 897
MCNEFF		
Jno	Trinity Oregon G	701008
MCNEIF		
Patrick*	Calaveras Twp 9	57 390
MCNEIGHTON		
S S	El Dorado Casumnes	581161
MCNEIL		
Augustus	Calaveras Twp 4	57 333
D	San Francisco San Francisco	9 681073
Daniel	Placer Secret R	62 619
H*	Butte Cascade	56 692
Henry	Calaveras Twp 6	57 150
Henry	Calaveras Twp 5	57 242
J A	San Francisco San Francisco	3 67 73
James W	Calaveras Twp 10	57 278
Jno	Sacramento Ward 3	63 447
John	Contra Costa Twp 1	57 535
John	Placer Ophirville	62 654
Joseph	Contra Costa Twp 2	57 544
M H*	Napa Napa	61 101
Mary	San Francisco San Francisco	9 681104
Mary A	San Mateo Twp 3	65 74
Michael	Calaveras Twp 9	57 367
Michael	Placer Auburn	62 590
Micheal	Calaveras Twp 9	57 367
Neil	Nevada Red Dog	61 543
Patrick	Sierra St Louis	66 817
W H	Napa Napa	61 101
William	Contra Costa Twp 2	57 545
William	Contra Costa Twp 3	57 603

Name	County Locale	M653 RollPage
MCNEILE		
S	Sutter Sutter	70 807
MCNEILL		
B	Tuolumne Jacksonville	71 172
James*	Mendocino Calpella	60 810
Jas	San Joaquin Stockton	641100
John	Trinity Trinity	70 970
W I	Amador Twp 2	55 308
W J	Amador Twp 2	55 308
MCNEILLE		
Alonzo	Plumas Meadow Valley	62 905
Charles	Plumas Quincy	62 942
MCNEILLEY		
J	Nevada Eureka	61 368
MCNEIMARA		
Jeremiah	Santa Clara San Jose	65 333
MCNEISS		
James R	Plumas Meadow Valley	62 907
MCNELE		
Wm	Sierra Twp 7	66 911
MCNELLAND		
John	Calaveras Twp 4	57 331
MCNELLER		
An	Sacramento Natonia	63 284
Sarah	El Dorado Salmon Falls	581049
MCNELLIS		
Thomas	Placer Yankee J	62 777
MCNELLY		
Charles	Humbolt Eureka	59 176
James	Tuolumne Twp 1	71 248
P	Sacramento Cosummes	63 384
MCNELSON		
Geo	Butte Kimshaw	56 590
MCNELTEY		
Wm F*	Calaveras Twp 6	57 177
MCNENT		
Mr*	Sonoma Sonoma	69 635
MCNERNY		
Michael	Placer Rattle Snake	62 625
P*	Nevada Grass Valley	61 203
Thos	Placer Rattle Snake	62 625
MCNERRY		
P*	Nevada Grass Valley	61 203
MCNESS		
Andrew	San Joaquin Oneal	64 935
Henry	Butte Ophir	56 758
James*	Yuba Marysville	72 897
MCNESSEN		
---	San Francisco San Francisco	9 681084
MCNESTOR		
Michael	Tulara Visalia	71 98
MCNETT		
Andrew	Fresno Twp 3	59 14
MCNETTEY		
Wm F*	Calaveras Twp 6	57 177
MCNEUL		
John*	Calaveras Twp 6	57 159
Mr	Sonoma Sonoma	69 635
MCNEUT		
Mr*	Sonoma Sonoma	69 635
MCNEWE		
James	El Dorado Coloma	581112
MCNEWL		
John	Calaveras Twp 6	57 159
MCNICAR		
Chas	Tuolumne Twp 1	71 198
MCNICHELS		
Barney*	Nevada Rough &	61 414
MCNICHOLS		
Barney	Nevada Rough &	61 414
Mark	Calaveras Twp 5	57 196
Mork	Calaveras Twp 5	57 196
MCNIDER		
Mathew	Butte Mountain	56 739
MCNIEL		
A	Sacramento Ward 4	63 563
H	Butte Cascade	56 692
H B	Tuolumne Sonora	71 235
H*	Butte Cascade	56 692
J E	Sutter Vernon	70 845
M	Sacramento Ward 1	63 7
W B	Sacramento Mississipi	63 188
MCNIELL		
Loclan*	Santa Clara Alviso	65 411
MCNIER		
Francis*	Los Angeles Los Angeles	59 491
MCNIFFE		
Mary	San Francisco San Francisco	9 681030
MCNIGHT		
John	Sierra Downieville	661001
MCNILES		
Hugh	Mariposa Twp 3	60 617
MCNILLAS		
Joh	Solano Suisan	69 226
John	Solano Suisan	69 226
MCNILORY		
J*	Nevada Eureka	61 373

Name	County Locale	M653 RollPage
MCNINCH		
David	Sonoma Petaluma	69 604
MCNISH		
Jackson	Mariposa Twp 3	60 599
Jackson*	Mariposa Twp 3	60 599
Jas	Butte Kimshaw	56 581
Thomas	Tuolumne Twp 2	71 386
MCNITTEN		
Wm F*	Calaveras Twp 5	57 177
MCNOB		
Alexander	Calaveras Twp 4	57 332
MCNOBLE		
Michael	Calaveras Twp 6	57 163
MCNOMA		
Andw	Sonoma Petaluma	69 556
MCNORTON		
C D	El Dorado Mud Springs	58 956
L L*	El Dorado Coloma	581104
S L	El Dorado Coloma	581104
S L*	El Dorado Coloma	581104
MCNOUGHTON		
S	El Dorado Gold Hill	581096
S A	El Dorado Gold Hill	581096
MCNUF		
Patrick*	Calaveras Twp 9	57 390
MCNULBY		
E	Sutter Yuba	70 765
MCNULE		
J	Sutter Sutter	70 802
MCNULLEN		
Alexander	Sierra Pine Grove	66 827
MCNULLEY		
---	Nevada Bridgeport	61 444
J	Nevada Eureka	61 368
James	San Francisco San Francisco	9 68 952
MCNULLY		
Bridget	San Francisco San Francisco	2 67 663
J	Tuolumne Twp 4	71 170
James	San Francisco San Francisco	9 68 952
Jno	Tehama Red Bluff	70 922
John**	Nevada Red Dog	61 540
Michael	Placer Forest H	62 800
S	San Mateo Twp 3	65 109
Tully	Nevada Rough &	61 419
MCNULTEY		
John	Santa Clara Santa Clara	65 487
MCNULTY		
Bridget	Sacramento Ward 1	63 115
C A*	San Francisco San Francisco	2 67 677
Charles	Sierra Twp 7	66 870
Henry	Sierra Twp 7	66 869
J	Tuolumne Jacksonville	71 170
James	San Francisco San Francisco	4 681139
James	Solano Suisan	69 223
James	Solano Suisan	69 224
Jas	Sacramento Ward 4	63 581
Jno	Sacramento Ward 1	63 14
John	El Dorado Big Bar	58 735
John	Sacramento Ward 4	63 543
John	San Diego Agua Caliente	64 861
John	Sierra Twp 7	66 875
M C	Sacramento Ward 1	63 26
M C	San Francisco San Francisco	9 681080
Martin	San Joaquin Douglass	64 917
Mary	San Francisco San Francisco	10 182 67
Michael	Placer Auburn	62 560
Owen	Humbolt Table Bl	59 143
Sarah J	Tuolumne Columbia	71 345
T	Calaveras Twp 9	57 409
T	Santa Clara San Jose	65 310
Thos	Butte Oro	56 677
Thos	San Mateo Twp 3	65 75
William	San Mateo Twp 3	65 105
MCNULTZ		
John	Tehama Lassen	70 879
MCNULY		
Hugh	San Francisco San Francisco	2 67 728
MCNUTAN		
Wm F*	Calaveras Twp 5	57 177
MCNUTCHELL		
W	Sacramento Ward 1	63 133
MCNUTLY		
C A*	San Francisco San Francisco	2 67 677
James J*	Tuolumne Twp 2	71 298
MCNUTT		
David	Del Norte Crescent	58 641
Frederick	San Francisco San Francisco	11 156 67
Geo	San Francisco San Francisco	12 385 67
Jacob	San Joaquin Stockton	641011
MCNUTTY		
James	Tuolumne Twp 2	71 285
James J	Tuolumne Columbia	71 298
John	Tuolumne Twp 2	71 288

Name	County Locale	M653 Roll Page
MCNUTTY		
Mary	San Francisco San Francisco	10 182 67
T	Calaveras Twp 9	57 409
MCOCHERY		
Robert	Placer Virginia	62 670
MCOHARTY		
Ann*	San Francisco San Francisco	8 681294
MCOLGAN		
Margaret*	San Francisco	10 167 67
MCOLLEY		
J	Nevada Nevada	61 296
MCOLPAN		
Margaret*	San Francisco	10 167 67
MCOMB		
Hanah*	Napa Napa	61 66
MCOMCHALL		
H S*	Nevada Bridgeport	61 497
MCONARY		
Thos	Solano Vallejo	69 250
MCONERS		
William	San Mateo Twp 3	65 105
MCONICHAEL		
H S*	Nevada Bridgeport	61 497
MCONLEY		
Frank*	San Francisco San Francisco	9 68 957
MCONNEL		
John*	Yuba New York	72 746
MCONNNELL		
Jas	Yolo Washington	72 604
MCONWAY		
James*	San Francisco San Francisco	9 68 957
MCOREORON		
John	Mariposa Twp 1	60 634
MCORKLE		
M K*	Napa Napa	61 58
MCORTAGA		
Jose*	San Bernardino S Buenav	64 207
MCORTAGO		
Jose*	San Bernardino S Buenav	64 207
MCOTEER		
Bridget	San Francisco San Francisco	2 67 673
MCOTTERSON		
Elizabeth	Siskiyou Yreka	69 182
MCOWEN		
Walter	Tuolumne Columbia	71 363
MCOWENS		
James*	Napa Yount	61 48
MCOY		
---*	Napa Napa	61 57
A B	Napa Yount	61 48
Alex	Calaveras Twp 5	57 228
J*	Nevada Grass Valley	61 206
Stephen	Calaveras Twp 10	57 263
MCPACK		
Patrick	Tuolumne Twp 2	71 398
MCPARLAN		
Michael	San Francisco San Francisco	2 67 753
MCPARLANE		
James	Tuolumne Jacksonville	71 516
MCPARLEN		
B	San Francisco San Francisco	2 67 728
MCPARNEHAN		
Robt*	El Dorado Placerville	58 878
MCPARSON		
Maggie	Alameda Brooklyn	55 85
MCPARTEN		
B	San Francisco San Francisco	2 67 728
MCPARTLAND		
Ann	San Francisco San Francisco	10 318 67
MCPATRICK		
Wm	Napa Napa	61 60
Wm*	Napa Napa	61 60
MCPEAK		
Eugene	Sonoma Santa Rosa	69 419
Eugene	Sonoma Armally	69 507
J H	Sonoma Santa Rosa	69 419
Nathan	Sonoma Santa Rosa	69 419
MCPECK		
Sallie*	San Francisco San Francisco	10 185 67
MCPEEK		
James	Contra Costa Twp 1	57 525
MCPEIRSON		
Mathew	Butte Mountain	56 736
MCPENDY		
Joseph*	El Dorado Salmon Falls	581056
MCPHARL		
Andrew	Sonoma Petaluma	69 596
Andw	Sonoma Petaluma	69 596
MCPHATRIDGE		
J M	Yolo Cache Crk	72 633
MCPHATRIDGER		
J H	Yolo Cache	72 633
MCPHEARON		
W B*	Sonoma Washington	69 675
MCPHEARSON		
J	El Dorado Mud Springs	58 969
W B	Sonoma Washington	69 675
W B*	Sonoma Washington	69 675
MCPHEE		
D W	El Dorado Coloma	581116
Daniel	Mendocino Big Rvr	60 847
Daniel	Mendocino Big Rvr	60 850
Daviel	Mendocino Big Rvr	60 847
MCPHERDON		
Charles	Sonoma Washington	69 673
MCPHERSEN		
Conneth	Nevada Bridgeport	61 476
Connett	Nevada Bridgeport	61 476
MCPHERSON		
---	Santa Cruz Santa Cruz	66 637
A	Nevada Eureka	61 360
A	Nevada Eureka	61 361
A A	Butte Kimshaw	56 595
Alex	Mendocino Big Rvr	60 840
Alex	San Francisco San Francisco 1	68 850
Alexander	San Francisco San Francisco 3	67 53
Alexander M	San Francisco 3 / San Francisco	67 53
Alexr	Mendocino Big Rvr	60 840
C D	Tuolumne Twp 1	71 267
Cameron	Mendocino Big Rvr	60 849
Charles P	Sonoma Washington	69 673
Conneth	Nevada Bridgeport	61 476
Daniel	Tuolumne Twp 1	71 268
Danl	Stanislaus Buena Village	70 723
Danl R	Contra Costa Twp 2	57 571
Druscun*	Santa Cruz Santa Cruz	66 637
Duncan*	Santa Cruz Santa Cruz	66 637
E	Tuolumne Twp 1	71 276
Emily	San Francisco San Francisco	9 681047
Farbs	Tuolumne Twp 1	71 274
Forles	Tuolumne Twp 2	71 274
H	Placer Todds Va	62 785
Ivakson*	Calaveras Twp 4	57 312
Jackson	Calaveras Twp 4	57 312
James	Tulara Twp 2	71 3
Jas	Sacramento Ward 1	63 48
Jas	Sacramento Ward 4	63 505
Jno	Klamath Liberty	59 240
John	Placer Michigan	62 830
John	Tuolumne Twp 1	71 264
Jon	Tuolumne Twp 1	71 264
K	Tuolumne Sonora	71 483
M	Santa Clara San Jose	65 292
M T	Mariposa Coulterville	60 702
Martin	Santa Cruz Santa Cruz	66 638
P D	Amador Twp 1	55 482
R	Tuolumne Twp 1	71 265
R	Tuolumne Twp 1	71 483
S	El Dorado White Oaks	581030
Thomas	Santa Cruz Santa Cruz	66 638
Wm	Colusa Monroeville	57 457
Wm	Placer Dutch Fl	62 730
MCPHILIPS		
E	Tuolumne Jamestown	71 424
Margaret	San Joaquin Stockton	641039
MCPHINNEY		
Uriah B	Los Angeles San Pedro	59 480
MCPHLIPS		
E	Tuolumne Twp 3	71 424
MCPHOUR		
Elizabeth	San Francisco San Francisco	9 681002
MCPIES		
Antonio	Santa Clara San Jose	65 373
MCPIKE		
John	Stanislaus Empire	70 734
Mary	Sacramento Ward 1	63 106
MCPINDY		
Joseph*	El Dorado Salmon Falls	581056
MCPULLIAN		
William*	Placer Michigan	62 854
MCPURDY		
Joseph	El Dorado Salmon Hills	581056
MCQEANCEY		
Allen*	Plumas Quincy	621002
MCQENAIN		
Wm*	Stanislaus Branch	70 711
MCQIAMEY		
Allen*	Plumas Quincy	621002
MCQINNES		
Thos	Trinity Mouth Ca	701013
MCQOODE		
Bernard*	Calaveras Twp 6	57 151
MCQUADE		
A	Siskiyou Scott Ri	69 72
Bernard	Calaveras Twp 6	57 151
Bridget	San Francisco San Francisco	10 197 67
MCQUADE		
C L	San Francisco San Francisco	12 394 67
Catharine	Monterey Monterey	60 926
Ellen	San Francisco San Francisco	12 394 67
George	Tuolumne Sonora	71 232
H	Calaveras Twp 9	57 411
J	Mariposa Twp 3	60 600
J C	Sutter Yuba	70 771
J*	Mariposa Twp 3	60 600
Jas	San Francisco San Francisco	10 197 67
John	Alameda Brooklyn	55 103
John	Marin Cortemad	60 790
John	Nevada Bridgeport	61 502
John	San Francisco San Francisco	11 147 67
Jos	San Francisco San Francisco	10 197 67
Julia	Butte Ophir	56 785
Mary	San Francisco San Francisco	12 394 67
N	San Francisco San Francisco	12 394 67
O J	Butte Ophir	56 795
Patrick	Calaveras Twp 5	57 218
Peter	Plumas Meadow Valley	62 934
Peter	San Francisco San Francisco	10 197 67
W	Amador Twp 5	55 346
W	Sierra Downieville	66 976
MCQUAID		
John A	Yuba Marysville	72 872
Pat	San Francisco San Francisco	9 68 988
Veronica	San Francisco San Francisco	2 67 661
MCQUAIDE		
D D	Butte Oregon	56 631
David	Butte Oregon	56 618
MCQUAREY		
John	El Dorado White Oaks	581009
MCQUARTER		
Bnj F*	Calaveras Twp 9	57 359
MCQUAY		
Alexander	Placer Michigan	62 852
James	Placer Forest H	62 801
MCQUDE		
John	Calaveras Twp 9	57 372
MCQUEEN		
Anges	San Joaquin Elkhorn	64 982
James	San Joaquin Elkhorn	64 954
Margret	Sacramento San Joaquin	63 349
Peter	San Joaquin Douglass	64 918
Peter	Siskiyou Scott Ri	69 71
Robert	San Francisco San Francisco	8 681279
Thomas*	El Dorado Salmon Hills	581056
W	Yolo Merritt	72 584
MCQUERRY		
John	El Dorado Salmon Falls	581065
Joseph	El Dorado Salmon Hills	581065
MCQUESTIVA		
John	Yuba Marysville	72 914
MCQUESTON		
Chas C	Sierra Gibsonville	66 857
MCQUHUE		
Robert	San Joaquin Elkhorn	64 993
MCQUIAN		
Thomas	El Dorado Salmon Falls	581056
MCQUICK		
John	Sacramento Granite	63 257
MCQUIDE		
John	Calaveras Twp 9	57 372
MCQUIG		
M J	Sonoma Bodega	69 534
MCQUIGG		
John	Sierra Poker Flats	66 842
MCQUIGIN		
Arthur	Nevada Bloomfield	61 512
MCQUILEN		
James	Placer Illinois	62 739
MCQUILKIN		
Patrick	Placer Secret R	62 621
MCQUILL IAN		
Owen M	Placer Iona Hills	62 882
MCQUILLAN		
Henry	Shasta Horsetown	66 703
J B	San Francisco San Francisco	5 67 502
Onan*	Placer Iona Hills	62 877
Orran*	Placer Iona Hills	62 877
MCQUILLEN		
Jas	Sacramento Ward 1	63 10
Margl	San Francisco San Francisco	2 67 706
Margt	San Francisco San Francisco	2 67 706
MCQUILLER		
Mary M	San Francisco San Francisco	7 681400
MCQUILLIAN		
Edward	Marin Cortemad	60 787

California 1860 Census Index

Name	County Locale	M653 Roll	Page
MCQUILLIAN			
Edward*	Marin Cortemad	60	787
Joseph	San Francisco San Francisco 1	68	849
MCQUILLON			
James	Sierra Gibsonville	66	853
MCQUILTIN			
Stephen	Tuolumne Twp 1	71	254
MCQUIN			
John	Amador Twp 7	55	419
John Q	San Joaquin Elkhorn	64	965
Mathew	San Francisco San Francisco 7	681	408
Robert	San Francisco San Francisco 8	681	279
Walker	Mariposa Coulterville	60	675
Wm	Amador Twp 5	55	357
MCQUINCY			
John*	Tuolumne Sonora	71	207
MCQUINE			
Parick	San Francisco San Francisco 1	68	860
MCQUINLLEN			
Jas	Sacramento Ward 1	63	10
MCQUINN			
Ellen	San Francisco San Francisco 2	67	727
Jas	San Mateo Twp 1	65	57
John	Yuba Marysville	72	871
Margaret	San Francisco San Francisco 4	681	228
Robert	Alameda Brooklyn	55	92
T	San Francisco San Francisco 8	681	239
Thomas	San Francisco San Francisco 9	68	952
MCQUINNE			
Patrick	Plumas Quincy	621	002
MCQUIRCK			
Mich	Sacramento Granite	63	258
MCQUIRE			
A	Trinity Trinity	70	972
A J	Mariposa Coulterville	60	691
Andrew M	Trinity Mouth Ca	701	012
C	Nevada Eureka	61	365
Danl	Tuolumne Twp 4	71	128
James	Solano Benecia	69	317
James	Tuolumne Sonora	71	238
L	Trinity Dead Wood	70	958
P	Trinity Lewiston	70	957
Patk	Butte Cascade	56	693
Roger	Solano Vallejo	69	279
Thomas	Yuba Marysville	72	901
Thos	Butte Ophir	56	796
MCQUIRK			
John	Tuolumne Columbia	71	301
MCQUIRKE			
Francis	San Luis Obispo San Luis Obispo	65	28
MCQUIRO			
Mary	San Francisco San Francisco 8	681	315
MCQUISTER			
John	Tuolumne Twp 1	71	482
MCQUISTON			
Charles O	Sierra Whiskey	66	846
David	Amador Twp 2	55	304
T	El Dorado Diamond	58	806
MCQUMBY			
H C	Butte Hamilton	56	523
MCQUNNY			
J	Butte Hamilton	56	517
J*	Butte Hamilton	56	517
MCQUORTER			
Benj F*	Calaveras Twp 9	57	359
MCQURIE			
John	Tehama Tehama	70	941
MCQUTIN			
Wm	Amador Twp 3	55	388
MCRADY			
Sylvester	Calaveras Twp 9	57	373
MCRAE			
C J	Sierra Port Win	66	794
Christopher	Sierra Pine Grove	66	826
Christopher J	Sierra Pine Grove	66	826
Wm C	Butte Oregon	56	632
MCRAITH			
James	Placer Forest H	62	772
MCRANEY			
George	Tuolumne Twp 3	71	461
MCRAREY			
Jno	Monterey Alisal	601	028
Jno*	Monterey Alisal	601	028
MCRAW			
William	Mendocino Ukiah	60	797
MCRAY			
James	San Francisco San Francisco 2	67	604
M*	Nevada Nevada	61	243
William*	Yuba Marysville	72	926
Wm	Nevada Nevada	61	243
MCREA			
Eliza	Butte Mountain	56	739
Fredk	San Francisco San Francisco 1	68	901
George	Placer Todds Va	62	790
James	Santa Clara San Jose	65	287
MCREAC			
P A	Butte Ophir	56	823
MCREAE			
P A*	Butte Ophir	56	823
MCREAH			
John	Placer Rattle Snake	62	600
MCREAN			
I*	San Mateo Twp 3	65	106
MCREDE			
Joseph	San Francisco San Francisco 1	68	860
MCREDMAN			
Wm*	Napa Napa	61	86
MCREERY			
Sarah	Yuba Marysville	72	860
Sarah*	Yuba Marysville	72	860
MCREIGH			
E	San Francisco San Francisco 9	68	945
E*	San Francisco San Francisco 9	68	945
MCREYNOLDS			
J	Nevada Nevada	61	275
J	Nevada Nevada	61	313
Jacob	Sonoma Armally	69	492
Jacob	Sonoma Armally	69	516
James	Sonoma Armally	69	493
John	Sonoma Armally	69	504
Rob	Sonoma Armally	69	485
Stephen	Sonoma Armally	69	492
Wm	Sonoma Armally	69	492
MCRIAE			
P A*	Butte Ophir	56	823
MCRICKER			
J*	El Dorado Diamond	58	770
MCRINK			
Peter	San Francisco San Francisco 3	67	51
MCRISSIE			
David	Contra Costa Twp 2	57	571
MCROBERTS			
H	Butte Chico	56	554
W S	Nevada Nevada	61	239
MCRODDEN			
David*	Sierra Pine Grove	66	822
Mathew	Sierra Pine Grove	66	829
MCROTH			
Jas	Placer Christia	62	736
MCROY			
J	Trinity Rattle Snake	701	029
MCRUDDER			
Andrew*	El Dorado Georgetown	58	679
MCRUDDIN			
Andrew*	El Dorado Georgetown	58	679
MCRUICH			
Jno	Butte Kimshaw	56	577
MCRURY			
Sarah*	Yuba Marysville	72	860
Sarah*	Yuba Marysville	72	860
MCRUSSEK			
H J	El Dorado Big Bar	58	739
MCSACHLAN			
Jas	Placer Rattle Snake	62	598
MCSAFFICK			
Wm*	Solano Benecia	69	305
MCSALEN			
Robert	Amador Twp 4	55	237
MCSAM			
Joseph	Alameda Brooklyn	55	81
MCSAMAD			
M*	Nevada Nevada	61	292
MCSAMAR			
John*	Nevada Bridgeport	61	447
M*	Nevada Nevada	61	292
MCSANGHLIN			
Chas	Sierra Port Win	66	795
MCSANGLIN			
Michael*	San Francisco San Francisco 10	67	306
MCSAUGHTIN			
Mary	San Francisco San Francisco 10	67	243
MCSCHULTZ			
Joseph*	Fresno Twp 3	59	12
MCSEAN			
Alexander E	San Joaquin Castoria	64	899
J G *	Butte Kimshaw	56	589
MCSEEVER			
J	Siskiyou Scott Ri	69	69
MCSELLAN			
James	Contra Costa Twp 1	57	492
MCSELVEY			
William*	Tuolumne Columbia	71	353
MCSELVOY			
William*	Tuolumne Columbia	71	353
MCSEMBRIANO			
Jose	Marin Cortemad	60	783
MCSENEN			
Allen*	Napa Napa	61	113
MCSHADIN			
James	El Dorado Casumnes	581	176
MCSHANE			
Andrew	Santa Clara Santa Clara	65	523
Andrew	Tuolumne Twp 2	71	365
Edward	Monterey San Juan	60	987
P	Calaveras Twp 9	57	392
P	Calaveras Twp 9	57	393
Patrick	San Francisco San Francisco 7	681	345
Wm	Sacramento Franklin	63	313
MCSHAW			
Andrew	Tuolumne Twp 5	71	512
Andrew*	Tuolumne Columbia	71	365
MCSHEA			
Bernard	Plumas Quincy	621	002
MCSHEAN			
Joshua	Plumas Meadow Valley	62	928
William	San Joaquin Oneal	64	932
MCSHEARY			
A	Butte Ophir	56	779
MCSHEE			
W	Sutter Butte	70	799
MCSHELBY			
Grace	San Francisco San Francisco 7	681	330
MCSHELTY			
Frace	San Francisco San Francisco 7	681	330
MCSHERRY			
Hugh	San Francisco San Francisco 12	67	379
MCSILVOY			
William	Tuolumne Twp 2	71	353
MCSIN			
C J*	Amador Twp 4	55	248
MCSINTOCK			
George	Sierra Scales D	66	803
MCSKIMMER			
James*	Tuolumne Twp 6	71	532
MCSKIMMONS			
James	Tuolumne Green Springs	71	532
MCSLYNN			
Partrick	Alameda Brooklyn	55	169
MCSMITH			
---*	Mendocino Big Rvr	60	842
MCSMITTE			
M M	Mariposa Twp 3	60	618
MCSNEE			
Michael	Los Angeles Los Angeles	59	325
MCSNEGER			
William*	San Joaquin Stockton	641	011
MCSON			
---*	Nevada Nevada	61	305
MCSORLEY			
Ed	Nevada Rough &	61	419
William*	San Francisco San Francisco 11	67	90
MCSOUELY			
Michael	Tuolumne Twp 1	71	276
MCSPEAR			
Danl	Tuolumne Twp 1	71	270
MCSPERREN			
A	Napa Napa	61	106
A*	Napa Napa	61	106
MCSTANE			
Jeremiah	San Luis Obispo San Luis Obispo	65	24
MCSTEAL			
H	Butte Bidwell	56	720
MCSTEE			
John	Alameda Oakland	55	10
Michael	Santa Clara Alviso	65	397
MCSTELFREY			
Ed	Nevada Bridgeport	61	505
MCSTELL			
Henry*	Calaveras Twp 8	57	96
MCSTELPREY			
Ed	Nevada Bridgeport	61	505
MCSUADA			
Frank*	El Dorado Georgetown	58	699
MCSUFFICK			
Wm	Solano Benecia	69	305
MCSULLIVAN			
Jas	Sacramento Ward 1	63	78
MCSUTHERLAND			
---*	El Dorado Georgetown	58	706
MCSUVESS			
Joseph	Los Angeles Los Angeles	59	369
MCSWAGER			
Frank	Sierra Grizzly	661	057
MCSWAIN			
A C	Merced Twp 1	60	904
D	Merced Twp 1	60	904
MCSWARENGER			
John*	Placer Todds Va	62	785
MCSWEENEY			
P	Amador Twp 3	55	378
Pat	Nevada Red Dog	61	539
MCSWEENY			
Morgan	San Francisco San Francisco 1	68	902

California 1860 Census Index

Name	County Locale	M653 Roll	Page
MCSWEGAN			
J*	San Francisco San Francisco 9	68	945
J*	San Francisco San Francisco 9	68	945
MCTAGUE			
Henry	Butte Chico	56	567
Jno	Butte Kimshaw	56	592
MCTAMINEY			
P	San Francisco San Francisco 6	67	463
MCTANAHAN			
J C	El Dorado Cold Spring	581	101
MCTANIENEY			
P M	San Francisco San Francisco 6	67	463
MCTANNER			
Augustus	Sierra Chappare	661	040
MCTARNAHAN			
Farncis*	El Dorado Cold Spring	581	099
MCTARNEHAN			
Robt*	El Dorado Placerville	58	878
MCTARUMHAN			
Francis	El Dorado Cold Spring	581	099
MCTEASH			
John	San Francisco San Francisco 9	681	032
MCTEE			
Saml	Alameda Brooklyn	55	176
MCTENNLEY			
H C	Butte Hamilton	56	523
MCTERMAN			
Bridget	Butte Ophir	56	761
MCTEYSON			
Robt	Butte Ophir	56	786
MCTHAYER			
Joseph*	Sacramento Cosumnes	63	397
MCTHY			
M W	Tehama Red Bluff	70	914
MCTICKER			
Denas	Tuolumne Twp 6	71	532
MCTIERNAN			
Mich	Sacramento Ward 1	63	36
MCTIGUA			
Michael*	San Francisco San Francisco 3 67		28
MCTIGUER			
Michael*	San Francisco San Francisco 3 67		28
MCTIRETT			
Eliza*	San Francisco San Francisco 9	68	985
MCTIVETT			
Eliza*	San Francisco San Francisco 9	68	985
Eliza*	San Francisco San Francisco 9	68	985
MCTORLEY			
William*	San Francisco San Francisco 11 67		90
MCTRATH			
John	Marin Cortemad	60	791
MCTRAYER			
Joseph*	Sacramento Cosumnes	63	397
MCTRECHON			
B	Yolo Cache	72	596
MCTRERNAN			
Mich	Sacramento Ward 1	63	36
MCTUILLEN			
A	Trinity Big Flat	701	040
MCTUNY			
J M*	El Dorado Georgetown	58	750
MCTURCENT			
Wm	Sierra Downieville	661	030
MCTURCK			
W	Santa Cruz Shasta	66	653
MCTUSK			
John	San Diego Colorado	64	806
MCTUTTLE			
Henry	Sacramento Natonia	63	280
MCTYRE			
Patrick	San Francisco San Francisco 9	68	949
MCUBO			
Frederick*	Santa Cruz Pescadero	66	643
MCUCKIN			
John	Sierra Downieville	66	962
MCULLOUGH			
Thos	Mariposa Twp 1	60	639
MCUSH			
John*	Napa Yount	61	54
MCVAIR			
Joseph*	Solano Vacaville	69	327
MCVAIS			
Joseph M	Solano Vacaville	69	327
MCVANER			
Daniel	Marin San Rafael	60	759
MCVANIE			
Anna	Yuba Marysville	72	879
MCVARRY			
Thos	San Francisco San Francisco 1	68	863
MCVAUGHIN			
James*	Calaveras Twp 8	57	108
MCVAUGHTON			
A*	Napa Napa	61	56
MCVAY			
Daniel	El Dorado Coloma	581	123

Name	County Locale	M653 Roll	Page
MCVAY			
Henry	Butte Wyandotte	56	671
Henry	Butte Ophir	56	800
J	San Francisco San Francisco 5	67	506
James	San Francisco San Francisco 4	681	144
Joseph	Colusa Muion	57	462
T	Sutter Sutter	70	809
T C	Colusa Muion	57	462
Thomas	El Dorado White Oaks	581	012
W T	Butte Ophir	56	774
MCVEIGH			
Charles	Tulara Twp 1	71	101
W H	Shasta Horsetown	66	707
W N	Shasta Horsetown	66	707
MCVEIL			
M H *	Napa Napa	61	101
MCVESS			
Henry	Butte Ophir	56	758
MCVEY			
Henry	Tuolumne Big Oak	71	137
Samuel	Solano Vacaville	69	365
Thos	Trinity Lewiston	70	966
Wm	Mendocino Ukiah	60	796
Wm*	Mendocino Ukiah	60	796
MCVEZ			
Thos	Trinity Lewiston	70	966
MCVICAR			
Chas	Tuolumne Sonora	71	198
Dennas	Amador Twp 2	55	305
Dennis	Amador Twp 2	55	318
James*	Mendocino Big Rock	60	873
Saml	Fresno Twp 3	59	37
MCVICER			
H	Shasta French G	66	717
MCVICKER			
Denas	Tuolumne Green Springs	71	532
John	San Joaquin Stockton	641	043
MCVICOR			
Edward	Mendocino Big Rock	60	873
MCVIL			
James W*	Calaveras Twp 10	57	278
MCVOY			
Benjamin	San Joaquin Douglass	64	928
Samuel	Solano Vacaville	69	365
MCVRAY			
Jas	San Francisco San Francisco 1	68	868
MCWAINE			
Robert	Sierra Twp 7	66	912
MCWALES			
Chas	Alameda Brooklyn	55	155
MCWALTER			
---*	Mendocino Big Rvr	60	842
MCWAMARA			
H*	Siskiyou Scott Ri	69	73
M*	Siskiyou Scott Ri	69	73
MCWANRARY			
Michael*	Alameda Brooklyn	55	195
MCWARD			
Thos	Trinity W Weaver	701	054
MCWATHY			
J C	Nevada Nevada	61	296
MCWAY			
Louis	Tulara Visalia	71	3
MCWELLS			
John*	Sacramento Cosumnes	63	380
MCWELTEY			
Wm F*	Calaveras Twp 6	57	177
MCWELTY			
Wm F*	Calaveras Twp 6	57	177
MCWERNEY			
Lilley	Sierra Eureka	661	042
MCWHERTER			
J A	Tuolumne Twp 2	71	325
MCWHESTER			
J A	Tuolumne Columbia	71	325
MCWHINNEY			
Hugh	Mendocino Calpella	60	810
John	Mendocino Calpella	60	810
Saml	Mendocino Calpella	60	810
MCWHINNY			
Thomas	Plumas Quincy	62	992
MCWHITAKER			
Wm	Amador Twp 3	55	379
MCWHORTER			
A S	Trinity North Fo	701	026
MCWILHAMS			
Thomas	San Diego Agua Caliente	64	814
MCWILL			
Jas	Sacramento Alabama	63	412
MCWILLIAMS			
A S	Colusa Mansville	57	439
B A	Yolo Cottonwood	72	559
Barnard	Yuba Rose Par	72	796
Berden	Nevada Red Dog	61	541
Chas M	Butte Ophir	56	786
D	Tuolumne Twp 2	71	364

Name	County Locale	M653 Roll	Page
MCWILLIAMS			
David	Placer Grizzly	62	755
David ?*	Placer Secret R	62	615
Geo	Tuolumne Big Oak	71	143
Geo	Tuolumne Twp 4	71	143
George	Amador Twp 4	55	238
Green	Solano Suisan	69	223
I*	Calaveras Twp 9	57	410
J	Calaveras Twp 9	57	410
J	Nevada Eureka	61	366
James	Trinity Weaverville	701	080
James	Trinity Browns C	70	984
James	Yuba Marysville	72	862
John	El Dorado Mud Springs	58	953
John	Sierra Gibsonville	66	855
John	Yuba Marysville	72	862
John H	Plumas Quincy	62	919
M G	Colusa Monroeville	57	440
R A	Yolo Cottonwood	72	559
R J F	Klamath Liberty	59	238
Richard	Yuba Marysville	72	903
Robert	Colusa Mansville	57	439
S	Butte Oregon	56	626
S M	Butte Oregon	56	642
Wm A	Sacramento Ward 1	63	80
MCWILLIN			
Jas*	Yolo Putah	72	588
MCWILTEY			
Wm F*	Calaveras Twp 6	57	177
MCWINN			
Joseph	Sonoma Santa Rosa	69	417
S	Yolo Putah	72	548
MCWITTEY			
Wm F*	Calaveras Twp 6	57	177
MCWORTHY			
F J	San Francisco San Francisco 2	67	791
MCWORTLEY			
J C	Nevada Nevada	61	296
MCYALE			
W F	Sacramento Brighton	63	199
MCYARVEY			
Alexander	Nevada Bloomfield	61	511
MCYEMES			
James	Amador Twp 6	55	435
MDANIEL			
C	Calaveras Twp 9	57	391
MDONALD			
D*	San Francisco San Francisco 4	681	231
ME			
---	El Dorado Coloma	581	110
---	Mariposa Twp 3	60	551
---	Mariposa Twp 3	60	569
---	Mariposa Twp 3	60	581
---	Mariposa Twp 3	60	582
---	Mariposa Twp 3	60	613
---	Mariposa Twp 1	60	627
---	Mariposa Twp 1	60	661
---	Nevada Bridgeport	61	457
---	Sacramento Natonia	63	286
---	Sierra Twp 5	66	930
---	Trinity Weaverville	701	074
---	Tuolumne Columbia	71	346
---	Tuolumne Twp 3	71	421
---	Tuolumne Jamestown	71	436
---	Yuba Fosters	72	843
---*	Mariposa Twp 3	60	569
---*	Yuba Fosters	72	843
Ah	Tuolumne Twp 2	71	346
Choi	San Francisco San Francisco 4	681	190
Chon	San Francisco San Francisco 4	681	199
Chou	San Francisco San Francisco 4	681	199
Cow	Nevada Nevada	61	299
Geu	Calaveras Twp 5	57	254
Hoo	Sacramento Granite	63	251
Jake	Yuba Fosters	72	826
Kou*	San Francisco San Francisco 4	681	199
Lang	Nevada Grass Valley	61	234
Lay	El Dorado Coloma	581	086
Lee	Mariposa Twp 3	60	607
Lee	Yuba Fosters	72	843
Long	Butte Cascade	56	690
Mox	San Francisco San Francisco 4	681	211
Quin	Sierra Twp 7	66	876
Thomas	Mariposa Twp 1	60	653
Yene	Calaveras Twp 5	57	193
Yeno	Calaveras Twp 5	57	193
Yoke	Mariposa Coulterville	60	681
Yone	El Dorado Placerville	58	825
Yook	Yuba Marysville	72	921
ME???ER			
Charles	Marin Tomales	60	724
MEA			
---	Amador Twp 4	55	246
---	Placer Virginia	62	670
MEABURN			
John Q	Colusa Spring Valley	57	435

California 1860 Census Index

Name	County Locale	M653 RollPage
MEACE		
Elisha B*	Sierra Whiskey	66 850
MEACHAM		
A D	Siskiyou Yreka	69 185
A D	Siskiyou Scott Va	69 53
Alfred	Solano Suisan	69 229
Alonzo	Sonoma Santa Rosa	69 425
Benj	El Dorado Placerville	58 932
C F	Siskiyou Scott Va	69 55
David	Sonoma Santa Rosa	69 425
Henry	Yuba Long Bar	72 742
Jas B	San Mateo Twp 3	65 84
R	San Francisco San Francisco 6	67 442
MEACHAND		
C F	Siskiyou Scott Va	69 55
MEACHEM		
A D	Siskiyou Scott Va	69 53
F	El Dorado Kelsey	581145
MEACHEN		
John	San Francisco San Francisco 9	681035
MEACHUM		
J R	San Joaquin Stockton	641028
MEACK		
Charles	Yolo Cottonwoood	72 656
MEAD		
A	San Francisco San Francisco 6	67 470
Alfred	Colusa Butte Crk	57 464
Alfred	Sacramento Ward 4	63 550
Allen	Plumas Quincy	62 977
Andrew	Nevada Rough &	61 415
Andrew	Sierra Cox'S Bar	66 951
B	Nevada Grass Valley	61 145
Benj	San Francisco San Francisco 9	68 969
Benjamin B	Sierra St Louis	66 805
Benjn	San Francisco San Francisco 7	681423
Benjn	San Francisco San Francisco 7	681423
C H	Nevada Nevada	61 255
Caleb	Mariposa Twp 3	60 621
Chas	Sacramento Ward 1	63 125
Chas A	Calaveras Twp 6	57 163
Chas H	San Francisco San Francisco 3	67 40
Daniel	Plumas Quincy	62 964
Elisha B*	Sierra Whiskey	66 850
Eliza A	San Francisco San Francisco 10	222 67
Frances	Alameda Brooklyn	55 201
G M W	Siskiyou Yreka	69 193
Geo	El Dorado Casumnes	581160
George	Los Angeles Los Angeles	59 365
Harrison*	Los Angeles Los Angeles	59 364
Henry	Placer Dutch Fl	62 731
Homar J	Calaveras Twp 5	57 231
Horace J	Calaveras Twp 5	57 231
Irenus S	Sacramento Ward 3	63 487
J B Ash	Siskiyou Yreka	69 139
J H	El Dorado Placerville	58 819
J K	Amador Twp 2	55 298
James	Amador Twp 3	55 397
Jas	Sonoma Petaluma	69 591
John	Humbolt Bucksport	59 161
John	Los Angeles Los Angeles	59 364
John	San Francisco San Francisco 7	681412
John	Trinity North Fo	701023
Joseph	Sierra Pine Grove	66 821
L A G	Nevada Grass Valley	61 183
L C	Tehama Lassen	70 882
L G	Sacramento Ward 1	63 75
L J	Sacramento Ward 1	63 31
Lawnis*	El Dorado Georgetown	58 758
M	San Francisco San Francisco 9	681016
Mr	Sonoma Petaluma	69 573
O M	Shasta Horsetown	66 707
Patrick*	Placer Rattle Snake	62 603
Ralph	San Francisco San Francisco 9	681016
Richard	Los Angeles Los Angeles	59 364
Richard	Los Angeles San Pedro	59 481
Stephen	Calaveras Twp 2	57 20
T W	Nevada Grass Valley	61 192
Victoria	San Luis Obispo San Luis Obispo	65 15
W	Shasta Horsetown	66 642
W B	Shasta Shasta	66 729
W C	San Francisco San Francisco 5	67 522
W L	San Francisco San Francisco 5	67 527
W S	Nevada Bridgeport	61 497
William H	San Francisco San Francisco 4	681111
Wm	Sonoma Santa Rosa	69 389
MEADAN		
J H	San Francisco San Francisco 4	681161
MEADCROFT		
Wm	Santa Clara San Jose	65 391
MEADDS		
S C	Nevada Little Y	61 535
MEADE		
Andrew	Sierra Cox'S Bar	66 951
Hiram	Tulara Petersburg	71 51
J	San Francisco San Francisco 9	681061
MEADE		
J L	Mariposa Twp 3	60 603
J R	San Francisco San Francisco 1	68 904
John	San Francisco San Francisco 1	68 902
Phillip	Sierra Eureka	661043
Stephen	Napa Yount	61 40
Wm G	Sierra Chappare	661040
MEADEN		
Charles T	San Joaquin Stockton	641077
Reuben	Alameda Oakland	55 8
MEADER		
Charles	Calaveras Twp 7	57 5
Chas A*	Placer Dutch Fl	62 715
Henry	Monterey Monterey	60 953
J S	Merced Twp 2	60 921
MEADES		
Petra*	Yuba Marysville	72 946
MEADOR		
Daniel*	San Joaquin Stockton	641032
E M	Sonoma Santa Rosa	69 422
Thos*	Napa Clear Lake	61 123
William	Tulara Visalia	71 79
MEADOW		
Daniel*	San Joaquin Stockton	641032
J C	Sacramento Ward 3	63 460
M	Tehama Antelope	70 892
T J	Tuolumne Twp 1	71 211
MEADOWS		
F M	Merced Twp 1	60 910
James	Monterey Monterey	60 960
James	Monterey Monterey	60 961
James	Shasta Cottonwood	66 736
Peter	Tuolumne Shawsfla	71 398
R H	Calaveras Twp 8	57 70
T	Yuba New York	72 738
MEADS		
Hamilton	Siskiyou Yreka	69 178
J G	Nevada Bridgeport	61 469
S J	Sacramento Ward 1	63 31
MEADY		
A P	Sierra Downieville	66 961
MEAEL		
Harrison*	Los Angeles Los Angeles	59 364
MEAGAN		
Dennis	San Francisco San Francisco 11	105 67
MEAGER		
Richard	Calaveras Twp 7	57 21
MEAGHER		
Gilbert	Sierra La Porte	66 766
MEAHL		
Charles	Yuba Marysville	72 932
MEAL		
---	Tulara Twp 1	71 117
J H*	Nevada Grass Valley	61 180
MEALDUADE		
Phillip*	Sierra Eureka	661043
MEALEE		
John	Marin Tomales	60 726
MEALLON		
Aug	San Francisco San Francisco 2	67 781
MEALLY		
Edward	Sierra Port Win	66 794
MEALY		
Hugh	Mendocino Little L	60 832
MEAMBER		
A	Siskiyou Scott Va	69 30
MEAN		
---	Butte Ophir	56 808
---	Butte Ophir	56 813
---	Tuolumne Don Pedro	71 162
---*	San Francisco San Francisco 9	681087
---*	San Francisco San Francisco 11	161 67
Ah	Tuolumne Twp 4	71 162
Berling	San Francisco San Francisco 3	67 68
Burling	San Francisco San Francisco 3	67 68
Robert	Solano Montezuma	69 368
MEANA		
Ll	El Dorado Placerville	58 906
MEANAY		
James	Sacramento Dry Crk	63 376
MEANBER		
A*	Siskiyou Scott Va	69 30
MEANBES		
Lewis	Solano Benecia	69 316
MEANDERS		
Elijah H	Sierra Gibsonville	66 856
MEANDONER		
Emanuel	Trinity Indian C	70 983
MEANEBER		
A*	Siskiyou Scott Va	69 30
MEANER		
J E	Yolo Merritt	72 579
MEANES		
Thomas	El Dorado Cold Spring	581101
MEANING		
William	El Dorado Georgetown	58 760
MEANS		
A J	Stanislaus Oatvale	70 719
David	Placer Michigan	62 838
Elizabeth	Sonoma Russian	69 446
Elizabeth Mrs	Sonoma Russian	69 446
H H	San Joaquin Stockton	641037
J	El Dorado Placerville	58 837
J W	Sonoma Russian	69 437
Jas	Tehama Red Bluff	70 906
John	Amador Twp 2	55 295
John	Los Angeles Elmonte	59 268
Lycurgus	Sonoma Santa Rosa	69 422
N M	Sonoma Russian	69 439
Robert	Placer Michigan	62 835
Thos C	Klamath Liberty	59 230
W L	Merced Twp 1	60 902
William	Calaveras Twp 8	57 78
Wm	Tehama Pasakent	70 859
Wm	Tehama Antelope	70 891
Wm C	Placer Auburn	62 584
MEANTIS		
Lewis	San Bernardino San Bernadino	64 670
MEANY		
N H	Sierra Twp 7	66 899
W H	Sierra Twp 7	66 899
MEAPLE		
Richard E*	Yuba Marysville	72 959
MEAR		
Joseph	Siskiyou Yreka	69 125
W*	Stanislaus Branch	70 709
MEARA		
Jas A	Butte Kimshaw	56 602
MEARAS		
Theodore	Tuolumne Twp 5	71 520
MEARER		
H C*	Shasta Millvill	66 755
MEARES		
J R	Amador Twp 2	55 267
MEARL		
Harrison	Los Angeles Los Angeles	59 364
John	Los Angeles Los Angeles	59 364
MEARS		
Calvin	Mendocino Big Rvr	60 848
Elijah	Sierra Twp 7	66 865
Eliza	San Francisco San Francisco 2	67 691
J	Yolo Slate Ra	72 707
J	Yuba Slate Ro	72 707
James	Mendocino Ukiah	60 793
Jas	San Francisco San Francisco 2	67 725
Wm J	Sierra Downieville	661020
MEARTAS		
Louisa	Calaveras Twp 9	57 360
MEARTIM		
Barolilma	Calaveras Twp 7	57 39
MEARTIN		
Wm*	Sacramento Granite	63 246
MEARTUS		
Lauisa	Calaveras Twp 9	57 360
Laursa*	Calaveras Twp 9	57 360
MEARZ		
Wm	Sierra Downieville	661020
MEAS		
Joseph	Siskiyou Yreka	69 125
MEASAN		
Peter	Tuolumne Twp 4	71 178
MEASE		
John J	Placer Virginia	62 678
MEASER		
Peater	Amador Twp 5	55 332
MEASHER		
Fred*	Calaveras Twp 9	57 399
MEAT		
Casper	El Dorado Placerville	58 895
MEATCHER		
Henry	Calaveras Twp 7	57 17
MEATER		
A	Sutter Sutter	70 806
MEATHEN		
C F*	Sacramento Granite	63 246
MEATING		
N J	Placer Dutch Fl	62 734
MEATONO		
---	Fresno Twp 2	59 92
MEAU		
---*	San Francisco San Francisco 11	161 67
MEAUBES		
Lewis	Solano Benecia	69 316
MEAVER		
H C*	Shasta Millvill	66 755
MEAW		
---*	San Francisco San Francisco 9	681087
MEAYER		
Christian	Sierra Excelsior	661033

Name	County Locale	M653 Roll	Page
MEAYER			
S	San Francisco San Francisco 6	67	464
MEAYIS			
Elizabeth*	San Francisco 2 San Francisco	67	763
MEBALD			
P J*	Mariposa Twp 3	60	585
MEBER			
Samuel	Solano Benecia	69	294
MEBINS			
C F	San Francisco San Francisco 10	67	359
L	San Francisco San Francisco 10	67	359
MEBIUS			
C F	San Francisco San Francisco 10	67	359
L	San Francisco San Francisco 10	67	359
MEBLES			
Francisco	Mariposa Twp 3	60	549
MEC KLENBURG			
Josep*	Napa Hot Springs	61	10
MECALA			
Marina	Alameda Brooklyn	55	191
MECALIFF			
S	San Francisco San Francisco 5	67	504
MECATHNEY			
A	San Francisco San Francisco 5	67	512
MECCA			
Thomas	Yuba Marysville	72	943
MECHA			
---	Mendocino Round Va	60	883
MECHAHE			
---*	Tulara Visalia	71	40
MECHAILANG			
Wm*	Calaveras Twp 6	57	178
MECHAILANY			
Wm*	Calaveras Twp 6	57	178
MECHALIS			
Frederick*	San Francisco 7 San Francisco	68	1390
MECHAM			
George W	Contra Costa Twp 2	57	552
Petrick	San Mateo Twp 3	65	107
MECHAN			
P	San Francisco San Francisco 6	67	463
MECHEIR			
Eugene	Calaveras Twp 5	57	198
MECHEL			
---	Tulara Twp 2	71	34
MECHELLANTS			
J*	San Francisco San Francisco 5	67	491
MECHEN			
Edward	San Francisco San Francisco 2	67	706
MECHENER			
John G	El Dorado Greenwood	58	723
MECHLING			
Micheal*	El Dorado Coloma	58	1080
MECHOIR			
J P	Sacramento Ward 4	63	579
MECHUM			
Luther F	Humbolt Union	59	186
MECIO			
Antonio*	El Dorado Casumnes	58	1176
MECIR			
Jules Levi*	Yuba Marysville	72	958
MECK			
---	Calaveras Twp 10	57	260
A*	Calaveras Twp 9	57	400
Edward E	Tuolumne Twp 3	71	460
J	Nevada Grass Valley	61	181
Loo	Yuba Foster B	72	831
Wm*	San Francisco San Francisco 2	67	751
MECKACHO			
---	Tulara Twp 2	71	37
MECKBE			
James W	San Joaquin Elliott	64	1102
MECKEL			
C	Trinity North Fo	70	1023
John	Trinity East For	70	1025
MECKER			
Catherine	San Francisco San Francisco 3	67	6
MECKHAM			
John	Humbolt Union	59	191
MECKIMENSENI			
Lewis	San Francisco San Francisco 2	67	748
MECKLAND			
R	Nevada Grass Valley	61	158
MECKLAR			
John*	Shasta Horsetown	66	689
Michael	El Dorado Coloma	58	1068
Micheal	El Dorado Coloma	58	1068
MECKLER			
John*	Shasta Horsetown	66	689
MECKLIN			
Francis	Plumas Quincy	62	935
MECKLIN			
James	Placer Michigan	62	823
MECKLIS			
Frederick*	San Francisco 7 San Francisco	68	1391
MECKLOR			
John	Shasta Horsetown	66	689
MECKLY			
Isaac	Tulara Keeneysburg	71	47
MECKSHA			
Joseph	Siskiyou Callahan	69	12
MECLNADO			
Whano	Amador Twp 5	55	360
MECTUR			
Marshal L	San Francisco San Francisco 8	68	1276
MECUM			
J D	Trinity New Rvr	70	1031
MED???NER			
Charles	Marin Tomales	60	724
MEDANDO			
Adele	Sacramento Ward 1	63	13
MEDANTA			
Hosea	Alameda Brooklyn	55	189
MEDASES			
G	San Francisco San Francisco 3	67	83
MEDAY			
Jacob*	Sierra Cox'S Bar	66	950
MEDBERRY			
Christopher	Marin Point Re	60	730
E R	San Francisco San Francisco 6	67	437
MEDBURY			
Arnold	Calaveras Twp 8	57	79
MEDD			
Patrick*	Placer Rattle Snake	62	603
Sawnis*	El Dorado Georgetown	58	758
MEDDEN			
Mary	San Francisco San Francisco 9	68	1016
MEDDER			
Chas A*	Placer Dutch Fl	62	715
MEDDICK			
Hella M*	Placer Auburn	62	569
MEDDIGNER			
Charles*	Marin Tomales	60	724
MEDDISS			
Henry*	San Joaquin Stockton	64	1012
MEDDOWS			
Sidney	Sonoma Armally	69	494
Wm	El Dorado Placerville	58	931
MEDE			
Jeremiah	Santa Clara Freemont	65	416
MEDEA			
Manuel	Alameda Brooklyn	55	97
MEDEC			
Petre*	Alameda Brooklyn	55	79
MEDECINE CALF			
---	Fresno Twp 2	59	41
MEDEE			
Petre*	Alameda Brooklyn	55	79
MEDELHTON			
Wm	Sonoma Petaluma	69	614
MEDENEZ			
Dionicio	Butte Oregon	56	614
MEDERA			
Jesus	Santa Clara San Jose	65	304
MEDERTA			
---*	San Bernardino Santa Barbara	64	147
MEDERVA			
Jacob*	Sierra Cox'S Bar	66	951
MEDES			
John	Santa Clara Alviso	65	414
MEDGE			
Jack	Alameda Brooklyn	55	169
MEDHARDT			
Wm	Sacramento Ward 4	63	544
MEDICINE CALF			
---	Fresno Twp 2	59	69
MEDICINE			
---	Fresno Twp 1	59	78
MEDIN			
M	San Francisco San Francisco 6	67	470
MEDINA			
Andreas	San Diego Agua Caliente	64	862
Francisci Jr	Calaveras Twp 5	57	170
Francisci*	Calaveras Twp 5	57	170
Francisco P	Calaveras Twp 6	57	170
Francisco*	Calaveras Twp 5	57	170
Jacob	Sierra Cox'S Bar	66	951
Juan	San Bernardino Santa Inez	64	139
Juan	San Bernardino Santa Inez	64	140
Julian	San Diego San Diego	64	765
MEDINAS			
Andreas	San Diego San Diego	64	760
MEDINCE			
Frank	Sierra La Porte	66	773
MEDINGER			
George	Tuolumne Twp 5	71	496
MEDINGER			
Geroge	Tuolumne Chinese	71	496
MEDIUNA			
Charly*	Mariposa Twp 3	60	602
MEDLE			
Petre	Alameda Brooklyn	55	79
MEDLEY			
Jas	Fresno Twp 2	59	4
Marian	Tulara Visalia	71	19
S G	Colusa Spring Valley	57	435
MEDLIN			
Geo	Butte Hamilton	56	514
Hall	San Bernardino San Bernardino	64	617
Isaac	Los Angeles Azuza	59	278
Marion	Los Angeles Azuza	59	278
MEDLY			
Jno	Sacramento Ward 4	63	576
MEDONA			
Frank	Sierra La Porte	66	773
MEDOW			
John	Tulara Twp 2	71	17
MEDRIX			
Geo W*	Placer Virginia	62	701
MEDUR			
Joseph	San Francisco San Francisco 3	67	57
MEE			
---	Amador Twp 2	55	310
---	Amador Twp 2	55	312
---	Amador Twp 2	55	320
---	Amador Twp 1	55	503
---	Butte Cascade	56	692
---	Butte Cascade	56	698
---	Calaveras Twp 5	57	224
---	Calaveras Twp 5	57	258
---	Mariposa Twp 1	60	640
---	Mariposa Twp 1	60	641
---	Nevada Rough &	61	432
---	Plumas Meadow Valley	62	910
---	Sacramento Ward 1	63	52
---	Sacramento Ward 1	63	54
---	Tuolumne Sonora	71	485
---*	Nevada Rough &	61	432
Ah	Butte Cascade	56	692
Ah	Butte Cascade	56	698
Chu	San Francisco San Francisco 4	68	1176
Hee	San Francisco San Francisco 4	68	1201
James	San Mateo Twp 1	65	49
John*	San Francisco San Francisco 7	68	1393
Kunk	San Francisco San Francisco 4	68	1189
Lee*	San Francisco San Francisco 9	68	1096
Ling	Butte Ophir	56	806
Loke	Butte Bidwell	56	708
Long	Butte Cascade	56	701
Long	Butte Bidwell	56	713
Low	Yolo Slate Ra	72	708
Sing	Butte Ophir	56	803
Sydney*	San Bernardino San Bernardino	64	644
Tee	San Francisco San Francisco 9	68	1096
Thoy	San Francisco San Francisco 4	68	1201
MEECH			
James	Santa Cruz Santa Cruz	66	598
MEECHAM			
Fred*	Calaveras Twp 9	57	399
J J	Nevada Nevada	61	241
L	Nevada Grass Valley	61	166
Lafayette	Los Angeles Los Angeles	59	390
R R	Nevada Grass Valley	61	221
MEECHANO			
Lafayette	Los Angeles Los Angeles	59	390
MEECHER			
Fred*	Calaveras Twp 9	57	399
MEECHIM			
---	Nevada Nevada	61	299
MEECHOM			
---	Nevada Nevada	61	299
MEECHUM			
Manah	Marin S Antoni	60	711
Mariah	Marin S Antoni	60	711
MEECUM			
Isaac R	Butte Hamilton	56	526
R R	Butte Hamilton	56	526
MEED			
A	Sacramento Franklin	63	315
E A	El Dorado Placerville	58	843
Elijah	Sacramento Franklin	63	315
Ellen*	El Dorado Salmon Falls	58	1056
Harvey	Sacramento Franklin	63	315
J A	Sonoma Washington	69	666
J V	Siskiyou Scott Va	69	54
William	San Mateo Twp 3	65	100
William	Yuba Marysville	72	878
MEEDER			
Moses	Santa Cruz Santa Cruz	66	625
Moses	Santa Cruz Santa Cruz	66	627
MEEDMAN			
J	Tuolumne Jacksonville	71	164

Name	County Locale	M653 Roll	Page
MEEDON			
John	Santa Cruz Santa Cruz	66	630
Thos	Santa Cruz Santa Cruz	66	630
MEEFER			
Jno B	Sacramento Mississipi	63	188
MEEGLE			
G A*	Butte Mountain	56	739
MEEHAN			
James	Amador Twp 3	55	380
James*	Fresno Twp 1	59	82
M*	Solano Suisan	69	204
P	San Francisco San Francisco 6	67	463
Patrick	Solano Suisan	69	217
MEEK			
---	San Francisco San Francisco 5	67	510
A*	Calaveras Twp 9	57	400
Christian	Yuba Marysville	72	939
E G	Nevada Nevada	61	257
Edward E	Tuolumne Twp 3	71	460
H C	Amador Twp 1	55	457
Isaac	Tehama Tehama	70	935
J*	Nevada Grass Valley	61	181
Joe	Contra Costa Twp 2	57	582
John	Yuba Slate Ro	72	688
Nathan	San Bernardino San Salvador	64	657
S C	Nevada Nevada	61	250
S L	Amador Twp 3	55	372
S O	Nevada Nevada	61	250
Saml	Trinity Hay Fork	70	995
Thomas	El Dorado Placerville	58	878
William	Contra Costa Twp 2	57	579
William H	Yuba Marysville	72	893
Wm*	San Francisco San Francisco 2	67	751
MEEKEL			
Daniel	Sierra Pine Grove	66	834
MEEKER			
Aaron	Butte Hamilton	56	526
D E	Butte Kimshaw	56	605
David	Sacramento Ward 1	63	103
Elizabeth E	Sacramento Ward 3	63	434
Ephiram	San Joaquin Elkhorn	64	979
Frank	Sacramento Ward 1	63	146
Geo*	Nevada Nevada	61	264
John	Solano Benecia	69	315
John	Solano Vacaville	69	347
L R	Trinity Trinity	70	971
Pheby	Amador Twp 2	55	317
Thomas	Sierra Pine Grove	66	834
MEEKES			
A D	San Joaquin Elkhorn	64	992
W H*	Mariposa Twp 3	60	557
Westley Y	San Joaquin Elkhorn	64	992
MEEKHAM			
Danl F	San Bernardino San Salvador	64	647
MEEKI			
M	Nevada Grass Valley	61	167
MEEKIN			
A G	Tuolumne Big Oak	71	125
A G	Tuolumne Twp 4	71	127
MEEKIS			
W H*	Mariposa Twp 3	60	557
MEEKLEY			
Thomas	Yuba Marysville	72	958
MEEKS			
A J	Tuolumne Twp 1	71	480
Abram	Placer Dutch Fl	62	719
Calvin	San Luis Obispo San Luis Obispo	65	45
Charles	Calaveras Twp 7	57	14
Heanan	Amador Twp 5	55	331
Hiram	Calaveras Twp 8	57	77
John	San Francisco San Francisco 3	67	13
John	Yuba New York	72	734
Joseph	Nevada Rough &	61	415
Sophrona	Sonoma Armally	69	499
W H	Butte Ophir		
Wm	San Francisco San Francisco 1	68	906
MEELAND			
Daniel	Tuolumne Twp 4	71	137
MEELES			
Wm	Sacramento Natonia	63	280
MEELEY			
C	Yolo Cache	72	621
MEELHALL			
John*	San Francisco San Francisco 3	67	46
MEELL			
Emerson E*	Yuba Marysville	72	891
MEELLEN			
David S*	Yuba Marysville	72	931
MEELLS			
Edgar*	Sacramento Ward 4	63	613
John W	Santa Clara San Jose	65	389
MEELOY			
James*	Nevada Bridgeport	61	465
MEELSPANGH			
L	Yolo Putah	72	598
MEELSPRANGH			
L	Yolo Putah	72	598

Name	County Locale	M653 Roll	Page
MEELTON			
L	Butte Kimshaw	56	586
MEELY			
James	El Dorado Big Bar	58	743
MEEN			
---	Calaveras Twp 8	57	62
---	Sierra Twp 5	66	944
---	Tuolumne Montezuma	71	508
P	Santa Clara San Jose	65	287
MEEOVONDER			
J L*	Calaveras Twp 9	57	383
MEEP			
Andrew C*	Yuba Marysville	72	958
MEER			
Christopher	Alameda Oakland	55	54
MEERS			
John	Sacramento San Joaquin	63	352
O	Solano Vacaville	69	323
William	Placer Iona Hills	62	895
MEERSCHANN			
A*	Nevada Eureka	61	374
MEERSCHAUN			
A	Nevada Eureka	61	374
MEESCH			
J*	Tuolumne Big Oak	71	153
MEESE			
Samuel	Tuolumne Twp 4	71	141
William	Contra Costa Twp 2	57	574
MEESSNOR			
C*	El Dorado Georgetown	58	677
MEET			
Peter*	El Dorado Kelsey	58	1132
MEETEER			
Marshal L*	San Francisco 8	68	1276
	San Francisco		
MEETUR			
Marshal L*	San Francisco 8	68	1276
	San Francisco		
MEFFERT			
C B	Siskiyou Scott Va	69	46
MEFFORD			
James	Solano Suisan	69	229
MEFRES			
Lucinda H	Marin San Rafael	60	758
MEFSER			
H S*	Mariposa Twp 3	60	621
MEFSNER			
John*	Siskiyou Callahan	69	7
MEG			
Cyrus	Siskiyou Scott Va	69	27
Eugene*	El Dorado Georgetown	58	748
MEGALL			
S	Nevada Grass Valley	61	168
MEGAN			
Carrie	San Francisco San Francisco 1	68	884
Lauernce	San Francisco San Francisco 7	68	1387
Peter	Sacramento Ward 4	63	553
Thomas	Siskiyou Yreka	69	147
Wm	Colusa Monroeville	57	440
MEGANT			
Thomas	Marin Bolinas	60	740
MEGARIGLE			
James R	Plumas Quincy	62	956
MEGENS			
M J	El Dorado Georgetown	58	701
MEGENT			
Thomas	Marin Bolinas	60	740
MEGER			
Casper	El Dorado Greenwood	58	723
Fred	Shasta Shasta	66	757
James	Yuba Rose Bar	72	788
Joseph*	Calaveras Twp 6	57	180
R	Trinity Ferry	70	977
MEGERLE			
Christian	San Joaquin Elliott	64	1104
Henry	Sacramento Ward 4	63	511
MEGESLE			
Louis	Sacramento Ward 1	63	129
MEGHEN			
H H	Marin Tomales	60	721
MEGHER			
Daniel*	Sierra La Porte	66	765
MEGHES			
Tim	Mariposa Twp 1	60	666
MEGIAH			
Olean	Amador Twp 4	55	233
MEGINIGLE			
James	Colusa Spring Valley	57	432
MEGINNESS			
Louis Marian	San Bernadino San Bernardino	64	631
MEGINNISS			
Benj	San Bernardino San Bernadino	64	630
MEGINO			
Sam*	El Dorado Georgetown	58	706
MEGINUP			
James L	Plumas Meadow Valley	62	931

Name	County Locale	M653 Roll	Page
MEGKIS			
Tun*	Mariposa Twp 1	60	666
MEGLI			
Peter	Tuolumne Chinese	71	500
MEGLIN			
Hannah	Shasta French G	66	715
MEGNER			
Frank	Tuolumne Big Oak	71	138
MEGONA			
Peter	Alameda Oakland	55	20
MEGONEN			
David*	Yolo Washington	72	570
R M	Yolo Washington	72	570
MEGONEW			
David	Yolo Washington	72	570
MEGOWEN			
David*	Yolo Washington	72	570
R M	Yolo Washington	72	570
MEGREEGE			
J*	Nevada Grass Valley	61	148
MEGRETA			
Antonio	Santa Clara Santa Clara	65	478
MEGRIGE			
T*	Nevada Grass Valley	61	148
MEGRUGE			
J	Nevada Grass Valley	61	148
MEGSON			
James M	Tuolumne Twp 5	71	501
MEGUIRE			
Nathan	Yuba Marysville	72	882
MEGUS			
Stephen*	San Francisco San Francisco 1	68	862
MEHAM			
Anne	San Francisco San Francisco 2	67	569
MEHAN			
Pat	Sonoma Petaluma	69	607
Patrick	San Francisco San Francisco 4	68	1165
William	Yuba Marysville	72	961
MEHATHS			
Emanuel	Trinity Indian C	70	989
MEHCARD			
Victor*	Sacramento Ward 4	63	550
MEHCARE			
Victor*	Sacramento Ward 4	63	550
MEHEAS			
Sandeago*	Napa Hot Springs	61	27
Santiago*	Napa Hot Springs	61	27
MEHEIN			
Eugene	Calaveras Twp 5	57	198
MEHEL			
Eugim*	Tuolumne Twp 2	71	301
MEHEN			
Edwd	San Francisco San Francisco 9	68	1089
Ellen	San Francisco San Francisco 7	68	1334
James*	Sierra St Louis	66	810
John*	Napa Napa	61	83
MEHER			
Belty*	Alameda Brooklyn	55	139
Joseph*	Trinity Weaverville	70	1052
T S	Los Angeles Tejon	59	524
MEHERN			
Parick*	Solano Benecia	69	300
MEHERRO			
Patrick*	Solano Benecia	69	300
MEHEW			
Edwd	San Francisco San Francisco 9	68	1089
John*	Napa Napa	61	83
MEHIN			
John*	Napa Napa	61	83
MEHL			
Christian	San Francisco San Francisco 3	67	14
MEHLEN			
Otto	Mendocino Big Rvr	60	847
MEHLIVITZ			
Anton	San Francisco San Francisco 9	68	1043
MEHLON			
Otto	Mendocino Big Rvr	60	847
MEHNER			
Wm	Yolo Slate Ra	72	686
Wm	Yuba North Ea	72	686
MEHOR			
A*	Los Angeles Tejon	59	526
MEHOTENS			
Anna*	San Francisco San Francisco 10	67	331
MEHR			
Dennis	Solano Vallejo	69	278
MEHRBACH			
S	Trinity Weaverville	70	1063
MEHREN			
Jacob	Placer Iona Hills	62	859
MEHRSO			
Patrick	Solano Benecia	69	300
MEHRTENS			
Henry	San Francisco San Francisco 10	67	346

California 1860 Census Index

Name	County Locale	Roll	Page
MEHRTENS		M653	
Ida	San Francisco San Francisco	10 67	250
Martin H	San Francisco San Francisco	1 68	899
MEHUL			
---	Mendocino Round Va	60	881
MEHUNDER			
Sarah*	Calaveras Twp 5	57	241
MEI			
---*	Mariposa Twp 1	60	641
MEIBOHN			
Henry	Tuolumne Don Pedro	71	539
MEICE			
Mary Ann	Mendocino Ukiah	60	807
MEICERE			
Frank*	Calaveras Twp 6	57	142
MEICHAM			
David K	Contra Costa Twp 2	57	544
MEIDELL			
Frank A	Calaveras Twp 6	57	168
MEIER			
Jacob	Tuolumne Sonora	71	194
Julius A	San Diego San Diego	64	760
MEIF			
John	San Francisco San Francisco	7 68	1430
MEIFS			
J	El Dorado Diamond	58	799
MEIGAS			
J*	Nevada Grass Valley	61	149
MEIGGS			
Benj	San Francisco San Francisco	1 68	895
J*	Nevada Grass Valley	61	149
R	Nevada Grass Valley	61	193
R*	Nevada Grass Valley	61	166
MEIGH			
W H	El Dorado Placerville	58	844
MEIGHAN			
P J*	El Dorado Diamond	58	771
MEIGHANA			
John	El Dorado Kelsey	58	1132
MEIGHEN			
F	Tuolumne Twp 2	71	321
MEIGHER			
John	Sierra St Louis	66	806
William	Sierra St Louis	66	806
MEIGLE			
G A	Butte Mountain	56	739
John	Calaveras Twp 8	57	85
MEIGS			
Chas	Butte Wyandotte	56	666
MEIHAN			
John	San Francisco San Francisco	11 67	90
MEIKER			
D E*	Butte Kimshaw	56	605
John	Solano Benecia	69	315
MEIKLE			
George	Calaveras Twp 6	57	114
MEILBURGH			
Charles	Humbolt Eel Rvr	59	149
MEILE			
S J*	El Dorado Georgetown	58	676
MEILES			
Armster	Sierra Downieville	66	1017
MEILL			
Mallad S*	Monterey Alisal	60	1035
MEILLER			
Thomas*	Monterey San Juan	60	1003
MEILSEN			
H*	San Francisco San Francisco	2 67	674
MEIM			
G M*	San Francisco San Francisco	8 68	1297
MEIN			
---	Calaveras Twp 4	57	332
---	Plumas Quincy	62	926
Jules Levi*	Yuba Marysville	72	958
Marco	Sacramento Ward 1	63	34
Peter*	San Francisco San Francisco	11 67	100
MEINE			
---	Calaveras Twp 6	57	176
MEINECKE			
Chas	San Francisco San Francisco	2 67	591
MEINFER			
Fred*	Calaveras Twp 9	57	399
MEINGER			
William	Yuba Marysville	72	924
William P	Yuba Marysville	72	924
MEINHAW			
Z	San Francisco San Francisco	2 67	796
MEINIG			
Saml	Yolo Cache Crk	72	636
MEINK			
D	Siskiyou Scott Ri	69	67
MEINTRUM			
John*	Sacramento Alabama	63	417
MEINTRUM			
M*	Sacramento Alabama	63	416
MEIORE			
A*	Siskiyou Scott Ri	69	72
MEIR			
John	San Diego Agua Caliente	64	814
John*	Placer Dutch Fl	62	713
Lazarus	Sacramento Ward 3	63	457
Pat	Sacramento Ward 1	63	83
Wiliam*	Tulara Twp 3	71	51
Wm	Sacramento Ward 3	63	423
MEIRCHAUN			
A*	Nevada Eureka	61	374
MEIRDIFROID			
Po	Tuolumne Twp 3	71	465
MEIRORE			
A	Siskiyou Scott Ri	69	72
MEIRSCHAUN			
A*	Nevada Eureka	61	374
MEIRSON			
A	El Dorado Placerville	58	862
MEIS			
Mary A*	Sierra Eureka	66	1042
MEISS			
H	San Francisco San Francisco	2 67	801
MEISSNER			
H	San Francisco San Francisco	5 67	513
MEISSON			
Conrad	Calaveras Twp 8	57	74
MEISTEN			
Henry	Calaveras Twp 5	57	248
MEISTER			
August	Sacramento Ward 1	63	19
Frances	Solano Suisan	69	236
Henry*	Calaveras Twp 5	57	248
Paulina	Sacramento Ward 3	63	488
MEISTES			
James	El Dorado Georgetown	58	703
MEISTRATT			
Franklin*	San Joaquin Stockton	64	1037
MEITCHELL			
Alfred*	Placer Michigan	62	807
MEITSCHLER			
William F	Solano Benecia	69	316
MEIU			
Peter*	San Francisco San Francisco	11 67	100
MEIVRE			
A	Siskiyou Scott Ri	69	72
MEIYIS			
Elizabeth*	San Francisco	2 67	763
---	San Francisco		
MEJERS			
Christian	Santa Clara Fremont	65	421
Michael	Santa Clara Alviso	65	408
MEJES			
A	El Dorado Greenwood	58	709
MEJIA			
Ciclelo*	Calaveras Twp 5	57	241
Cidelo*	Calaveras Twp 5	57	241
Franco	Marin Cortemad	60	782
MEJILLA			
Encarnarcion	Los Angeles Los Angeles	59	316
MEJIO			
Agustin	Los Angeles San Gabriel	59	423
Agustio	Los Angeles San Gabriel	59	423
Cidelo	Calaveras Twp 5	57	241
MEK			
Tak	San Francisco San Francisco	11 67	159
MEKA			
---	Fresno Twp 3	59	100
MEKCARD			
Victor*	Sacramento Ward 4	63	550
MEKCARE			
Victor*	Sacramento Ward 4	63	550
MEKE			
George	San Bernardino San Bernadino	64	626
MEKEE			
Alexander	Sierra Poker Flats	66	839
MEKER			
Joseph*	Trinity Weaverville	70	1052
MEKERSON			
B R	El Dorado Placerville	58	859
MEKINS			
Louise	Calaveras Twp 6	57	114
MEKKELSON			
S P	Siskiyou Klamath	69	90
MEKO			
---	Fresno Twp 2	59	102
MEKS			
Simon	Calaveras Twp 5	57	241
MEL			
---	Tuolumne Twp 3	71	463
John	San Francisco San Francisco	8 68	1266
MELACOR			
---	Mendocino Twp 1	60	886
MELAN			
John H	Alameda Brooklyn	55	90
MELANCHE			
Pietro	San Francisco San Francisco	11 67	154
MELANEY			
Martha	Sacramento Granite	63	256
MELARKEY			
David	Colusa Colusi	57	421
MELATINIETO			
Andrew*	Yuba Marysville	72	919
MELBOAM			
Robert*	Yuba Suida	72	992
MELBOREN			
H B	San Francisco San Francisco	4 68	1165
MELBORN			
H B	San Francisco San Francisco	4 68	1165
MELBORNE			
A W	Nevada Nevada	61	321
MELBOURN			
James	Sacramento Sutter	63	301
Robert	Yuba Linda	72	992
MELBOURNE			
E L	Nevada Rough &	61	431
H C*	Yuba Timbucto	72	787
James	Sacramento Sutter	63	301
Joseph	Nevada Bridgeport	61	474
Susan	Solano Suisan	69	211
Thomas	Solano Suisan	69	226
MELBOWONE			
Susan*	Solano Suisan	69	211
MELBUM			
Isabel*	Nevada Bridgeport	61	450
MELBURE			
John*	Mariposa Twp 3	60	572
MELBURN			
Isabel	Nevada Bridgeport	61	450
John*	Mariposa Twp 3	60	572
MELBURR			
John H*	Mariposa Twp 3	60	572
MELCALY			
W	Shasta Millvill	66	752
MELCARES			
---	San Bernardino S Buenav	64	220
MELCHER			
Chester	Napa Napa	61	82
F G*	Los Angeles Los Angeles	59	491
John	Tuolumne Chinese	71	487
MELCHIOR			
Adam	El Dorado Kelsey	58	1138
MELCHOR			
---	Monterey S Antoni	60	972
MELDRUM			
B F G	Solano Benecia	69	312
MELDS			
Maria*	Placer Iona Hills	62	860
MELDWALER			
George	Marin Saucileto	60	751
MELEC			
John	Shasta Shasta	66	671
MELEE			
John	Shasta Shasta	66	671
MELEN			
William	Calaveras Twp 5	57	179
MELENDEZ			
Domingo	Los Angeles Santa Ana	59	452
MELENDRES			
Antonio	Los Angeles Los Angeles	59	355
MELENDREZ			
Maria F	Los Angeles Los Angeles	59	357
Miguela	Los Angeles Shaffer	59	398
MELENDROZ			
Maria F	Los Angeles Los Angeles	59	357
MELENGER			
Washington	El Dorado Mud Springs	58	965
MELERS			
P	Sacramento San Joaquin	63	353
MELEY			
Andrew	Yuba Bear Rvr	72	1014
Jane*	San Francisco San Francisco	2 67	656
William*	San Francisco San Francisco	7 68	1393
MELFIELD			
J W L	Tuolumne Shawsfla	71	397
MELFORD			
John*	Placer Michigan	62	853
MELGATE			
Wm*	Sacramento Natonia	63	276
MELGUEEN			
Ellen	San Francisco San Francisco	8 68	1285
MELGUIS			
Henry*	San Francisco San Francisco	11 67	97
MELHAM			
Robert	Yuba Long Bar	72	765
MELHEM			
Isabel*	Nevada Bridgeport	61	450

California 1860 Census Index

Name	County Locale	M653 Roll	Page
MELHUN			
Isabel*	Nevada Bridgeport	61	450
MELICECA			
Natonia*	Yuba Marysville	72	920
MELICIA			
Antonia	Yuba Marysville	72	920
MELICK			
Andrew	Plumas Quincy	62	935
Chester	San Francisco San Francisco 9	68	975
MELIN			
Charles	San Francisco San Francisco 9	68	1024
MELINA			
Henry	Nevada Rough &	61	430
J P*	Shasta Shasta	66	675
MELINDUZ			
Juan	Monterey Monterey	60	954
MELINE			
Edward	Sierra Monte Crk	66	1039
MELINER			
Henry*	Nevada Rough &	61	430
MELINEU			
J P*	Shasta Shasta	66	675
MELINU			
Henry*	Nevada Rough &	61	430
MELIS			
Louis	El Dorado Mud Springs	58	984
MELISH			
Walter	Santa Cruz Santa Cruz	66	611
MELITEIN			
Louis	Calaveras Twp 6	57	127
MELITH			
Walter*	Santa Cruz Santa Cruz	66	611
MELKSIN			
A F	El Dorado Placerville	58	819
MELL			
F	El Dorado Placerville	58	853
Sock	Yuba Foster B	72	827
Wm H	Alameda Brooklyn	55	127
MELLA			
John	San Francisco San Francisco 3 67		76
Pedro	Santa Cruz Pajaro	66	548
MELLACE			
Danl	Amador Twp 3	55	373
MELLADO			
G A	Nevada Red Dog	61	552
MELLAN			
C G	Yuba Long Bar	72	753
James	Yuba Rose Bar	72	804
Stephen G	Yuba Parks Ba	72	775
MELLAS			
George*	Calaveras Twp 5	57	240
MELLBRILL			
John*	El Dorado Coloma	58	1121
MELLE			
Jacob	San Francisco San Francisco 7	68	1437
MELLEGAN			
John	Sierra Pine Grove	66	819
MELLEN			
Jeromie*	Yuba Marysville	72	850
Joonie*	Yuba Marysville	72	850
MELLENVRONS			
C	Yolo Merritt	72	581
MELLER			
Annis	Santa Clara San Jose	65	288
Augusta	Alameda Brooklyn	55	175
H Y*	Sacramento Brighton	63	197
John*	San Francisco San Francisco 3 67		76
R H	El Dorado Georgetown	58	682
S K*	Calaveras Twp 9	57	375
MELLERS			
Antoine	Plumas Quincy	62	1001
George*	Calaveras Twp 5	57	240
MELLEY			
---	San Francisco San Francisco 10 67		350
MELLGE			
Augsut*	Sierra Downieville	66	1002
MELLIET			
Alenis*	San Francisco San Francisco 3 67		80
MELLIMAN			
Frederick*	San Francisco 3 67		15
	San Francisco		
MELLINA			
O	Stanislaus Emory	70	737
MELLINER			
J J	San Francisco San Francisco 5 67		478
MELLINGTON			
Jefferson	Amador Twp 2	55	289
MELLINTOCK			
J S	Tuolumne Twp 3	71	441
MELLIR			
George H*	Sierra Pine Grove	66	826
MELLISON			
Saml	Yolo Fremont	72	604
MELLIX			
George H*	Sierra Pine Grove	66	826
MELLMAN			
Herman W	Los Angeles San Pedro	59	480
MELLO SAARO			
John*	Calaveras Twp 5	57	187
Pedro*	Calaveras Twp 5	57	187
MELLO SUARO			
Pedro*	Calaveras Twp 6	57	187
MELLO			
G L	Mariposa Twp 3	60	584
MELLODY			
Jas	Sacramento Ward 4	63	524
MELLON			
Frank	Sacramento Ward 4	63	526
John	El Dorado Mud Springs	58	959
Joseph	Sacramento Ward 4	63	515
Mary	Sacramento Ward 1	63	130
Mary	Sacramento Ward 1	63	131
Moses J	Yuba Bear Rvr	72	999
Olindo	San Francisco San Francisco 2	67	683
Robt	Sacramento Ward 3	63	435
Robt	Sacramento Ward 4	63	569
W	San Francisco San Francisco 9	68	1079
MELLONEY			
Patrick	Santa Clara San Jose	65	333
Rosa	Santa Clara Fremont	65	430
MELLONEZ			
Patrick	Santa Clara San Jose	65	280
MELLONS			
Paul N	Siskiyou Callahan	69	3
MELLOS			
George	Calaveras Twp 5	57	240
MELLOT			
Frank	Alameda Brooklyn	55	98
MELLOURNE			
H C	Yuba Timbucto	72	787
MELLOW			
Francis	El Dorado Salmon Falls	58	1049
James	El Dorado Salmon Falls	58	1049
MELLOY			
Augustus	Amador Twp 4	55	258
MELLRILL			
John*	El Dorado Coloma	58	1121
MELLROSE			
William	Solano Benecia	69	299
Wm	Solano Benecia	69	284
MELLUM			
Isabel*	Nevada Bridgeport	61	450
MELLUS			
Daniel	Amador Twp 3	55	390
Harvey*	Placer Michigan	62	817
Henry	Los Angeles Los Angeles	59	336
Henry*	Placer Michigan	62	817
James	Santa Cruz Soguel	66	599
Wancis	Los Angeles Los Angeles	59	338
MELLVILE			
Moses	San Diego San Diego	64	767
MELLVILLE			
Henry	Mariposa Coulterville	60	678
MELLYE			
Augsut*	Sierra Downieville	66	1002
August	Sierra Downieville	66	1002
MELMER			
George	Sonoma Armally	69	515
MELNE			
Jas	San Francisco San Francisco 9	68	1060
MELODY			
Patrick	Amador Twp 4	55	258
MELON			
Dones*	Siskiyou Yreka	69	152
Fanny	Sacramento Ward 1	63	112
John	San Francisco San Francisco 10 67		305
John	Sierra Downieville	66	961
Jones	Siskiyou Yreka	69	152
MELONE			
H	Santa Clara San Jose	65	393
John	Sierra Twp 7	66	911
Mary*	San Francisco San Francisco 12 67		380
Patrick	Santa Clara Alviso	65	396
MELONEY			
Anna	Yuba Marysville	72	870
Margt	Sacramento Ward 4	63	536
MELONG			
Michael J	San Francisco San Francisco 10 67		209
MELONN			
Dennis*	San Francisco San Francisco 9	68	1000
MELONY			
John	Sacramento Natonia	63	276
Mary	Solano Benecia	69	314
Michael J	San Francisco San Francisco 10 67		209
Morris	Sierra Twp 7	66	873
MELOON			
Sarah	San Francisco San Francisco 10 67		228
MELOST			
M	Nevada Grass Valley	61	154
MELOWAY			
John*	Sacramento Natonia	63	276
MELOWEY			
John*	Sacramento Natonia	63	276
MELQUEEN			
Ellen	San Francisco San Francisco 8	68	1285
MELQUIS			
Henry*	San Francisco San Francisco 11 67		97
MELRE			
W F*	San Francisco San Francisco 6 67		471
MELRO			
W F	San Francisco San Francisco 6 67		471
MELROSE			
Andrew	Santa Clara Santa Clara	65	485
MELRRO			
John	San Francisco San Francisco 2 67		576
MELSON			
H C*	San Francisco San Francisco 1	68	888
MELTE			
C A	El Dorado Placerville	58	865
MELTER			
Joseph	Tehama Lassen	70	879
MELTON			
L	Butte Kimshaw	56	586
Wiliam	Placer Forest H	62	766
MELTY			
Jesse	Placer Rattle Snake	62	625
MELVAY			
Mary	San Francisco San Francisco 4	68	1116
MELVER			
John	Sierra Downieville	66	961
MELVERTS			
Henry	Marin Cortemad	60	756
MELVEY			
John	Siskiyou Scott Va	69	57
MELVILL			
Frank	Tehama Cottonwoood	70	898
MELVILLA			
P P	El Dorado Georgetown	58	704
MELVILLE			
A	Sacramento Ward 1	63	34
Edward	Solano Benecia	69	281
Ellen	Placer Dutch Fl	62	720
G M	Butte Cascade	56	690
George F	Yuba Marysville	72	871
George P	Sacramento Ward 4	63	553
James	Tuolumne Twp 2	71	345
John	San Francisco San Francisco 2	67	729
P P	El Dorado Georgetown	58	704
MELVIN			
Augustus	Placer Iona Hills	62	874
Det	El Dorado Big Bar	58	739
Ellen	Sacramento Ward 1	63	104
James	Tuolumne Columbia	71	354
Jas E	Placer Dutch Fl	62	734
John	Plumas Quincy	62	1000
John	Sierra Twp 5	66	943
Mary E	Del Norte Crescent	58	622
Nicholas	Del Norte Crescent	58	623
O D	El Dorado Diamond	58	810
Thompkins	Del Norte Crescent	58	647
W H	Del Norte Crescent	58	640
William*	El Dorado Cold Spring	58	1101
Wm	Sacramento Ward 1	63	9
MELVRO			
John	San Francisco San Francisco 2	67	576
MELZUIADES			
Jose	Monterey San Juan	60	986
MEM			
---	Plumas Meadow Valley	62	913
MEMACK			
L*	Sacramento Granite	63	244
S*	Sacramento Granite	63	244
MEMAM			
Josiph	Nevada Rough &	61	420
MEMDETH			
W J	Nevada Rough &	61	410
MEMDO			
M P	Colusa Monroeville	57	457
MEMENT			
---	San Francisco San Francisco 10 67		248
MEMER			
Joaquin*	Calaveras Twp 10	57	276
Loayuin*	Calaveras Twp 10	57	276
MEMFEE			
Richard*	Plumas Quincy	62	985
MEMFREY			
William*	San Francisco San Francisco 8	68	1318
MEMG			
---	Yuba Slate Ro	72	708

Name	County Locale	M653 Roll	Page
MEMG			
---	Yuba Slate Ro	72	713
MEMGAN			
E	Trinity Weaverville	70	1053
MEMIA			
James*	Mariposa Twp 1	60	624
MEMIFIELD			
James	Nevada Rough &	61	433
MEMIG			
Sam	Yolo Cache	72	636
MEMILLY			
S*	Yolo Cache	72	610
MEMPHY			
W	Sacramento Brighton	63	194
MEMSFIELD			
James*	Nevada Rough &	61	433
MEN			
---	Amador Twp 2	55	310
---	Amador Twp 6	55	433
---	Calaveras Twp 10	57	261
---	El Dorado Placerville	58	841
---	Nevada Bridgeport	61	459
---	Nevada Bridgeport	61	492
---*	Plumas Meadow Valley	62	914
Fred	Yolo Merritt	72	580
Fred*	Sacramento Ward 3	63	422
Lee	Butte Oro	56	677
Shee	San Francisco San Francisco 11	67	160
MENA			
---	Los Angeles Los Angeles	59	386
MENAFEE			
Nimrod	Sonoma Petaluma	69	552
MENAGUS			
John*	Calaveras Twp 9	57	370
MENAN			
Jno P*	Klamath S Fork	59	207
MENANDER			
Frederick	Placer Michigan	62	841
MENANDEZ			
Joseph	Tuolumne Sonora	71	211
MENANT			
Lambert	Los Angeles Los Angeles	59	390
MENARDI			
Wancisco	Los Angeles Los Angeles	59	314
MENASCO			
Coleman	Santa Cruz Pajaro	66	568
Milton	Santa Cruz Pajaro	66	552
MENASING			
---	El Dorado Georgetown	58	696
MENBE			
J W	Yolo Cache	72	641
MENCER			
Henry	Monterey San Juan	60	1004
Heron*	Monterey San Juan	60	1004
MENCH			
Abram	Klamath Orleans	59	216
Andrew	Santa Clara Fremont	65	435
Louisa	San Francisco San Francisco 10	67	344
Martin	Solano Benecia	69	311
MENCHACA			
Francisco	S Buenav San Bernardino	64	208
MENCHAN			
Jacob E	Calaveras Twp 10	57	263
MENCHARCA			
Francises	Santa Ba San Bernardino	64	208
MENCHARRINNI			
D*	San Francisco San Francisco 3	67	51
MENCHINI			
George*	Calaveras Twp 6	57	166
MENCHINIS			
George*	Calaveras Twp 6	57	166
Joseph	Calaveras Twp 6	57	166
MENCHUR			
---	Trinity Weaverville	70	1072
MENCKE			
Fred	Sacramento Ward 4	63	586
MENCO			
William	San Francisco San Francisco 8	68	1300
MENCOMTH			
M*	San Francisco San Francisco 1	68	912
MENCOMTT			
M*	San Francisco San Francisco 1	68	912
MENCRIEF			
W P	Butte Oregon	56	616
MENDAREZ			
Jose M	Mendocino Round Va	60	880
MENDAS			
Hosa	Mariposa Twp 1	60	628
MENDCHEIM			
M	San Francisco San Francisco 2	67	639
MENDEA			
Asencio	Merced Monterey	60	936
MENDEHUM			
M	San Francisco San Francisco 2	67	639
MENDEL?OHN			
S C	Sacramento Ward 1	63	42
MENDELDOHN			
S C*	Sacramento Ward 1	63	42
MENDELGOHN			
S C*	Sacramento Ward 1	63	42
MENDELL			
Charles	Nevada Little Y	61	532
Frank	Yuba Parks Ba	72	784
Frenk*	Yuba Parke Ba	72	784
MENDELLS			
E S	San Francisco San Francisco 6	67	444
MENDELSOHN			
S C	Sacramento Ward 1	63	42
MENDELSON			
E	San Francisco San Francisco 3	67	34
MENDENHALL			
Absolem	Alameda Brooklyn	55	159
D D	Colusa Monroeville	57	445
E T	Placer Lisbon	62	733
Wm	Contra Costa Twp 2	57	572
MENDENHILL			
J N	Yolo Cache	72	640
MENDENIA			
Antonio*	Yuba Marysville	72	946
MENDER			
R*	San Francisco San Francisco 5	67	543
MENDEROSO			
Estevan	Los Angeles Los Angeles	59	392
MENDERSON			
Andrew J	Los Angeles Los Angeles	59	357
John	Los Angeles Los Angeles	59	354
M M	Yolo Putah	72	551
MENDES			
D	San Francisco San Francisco 5	67	519
Francisco	Sacramento Ward 1	63	100
Ramond	Calaveras Twp 4	57	333
MENDEVIA			
Antonio*	Yuba Marysville	72	946
MENDEY			
Antonio*	Monterey Monterey	60	927
MENDEZ			
Anna	San Francisco San Francisco 11	67	141
Antonio	Merced Monterey	60	927
Antonio*	Monterey Monterey	60	927
Jose*	Santa Clara San Jose	65	390
Juan B	Los Angeles Los Angeles	59	301
Pedro	Los Angeles Los Angeles	59	311
Refugio	Los Angeles San Gabriel	59	414
Silberio	Los Angeles San Gabriel	59	411
MENDIA			
Ascension	Santa Cruz Watsonville	66	540
Asencio	Monterey Monterey	60	936
MENDIBLES			
Gabriela	Los Angeles Los Angeles	59	318
Jesus	Los Angeles Los Angeles	59	305
Jesus	Los Angeles Los Nieto	59	434
Miguel	Los Angeles Los Nieto	59	432
Trinidad	Los Angeles San Gabriel	59	423
Wancisco	Los Angeles Los Angeles	59	304
Wancisco	Los Angeles Los Angeles	59	313
MENDING			
Chas*	Mariposa Twp 3	60	560
MENDINHALL			
Martin	Contra Costa Twp 2	57	571
Wm M	Contra Costa Twp 2	57	566
MENDINO			
Rios	Yuba Marysville	72	946
MENDIS			
Kakon	Calaveras Twp 5	57	202
Kamon	Calaveras Twp 5	57	202
Peter	El Dorado White Oaks	58	1017
Ramon	Calaveras Twp 5	57	202
MENDITH			
B F	Sacramento Ward 1	63	105
MENDIVES			
Francisco*	Santa Clara Santa Clara	65	494
MENDIVIL			
Jesus	San Bernardino Santa Barbara	64	197
MENDLUTH			
A*	Calaveras Twp 9	57	391
MENDOCINO			
Geo	Sacramento American	63	172
MENDON			
G A*	San Francisco San Francisco 6	67	436
MENDONA			
Incogni	Los Angeles Elmonte	59	261
MENDOSA			
Bennett	Los Angeles Azuza	59	272
Blas	Santa Clara Almaden	65	270
Brigido	Tuolumne Twp 1	71	225
Eliza	San Francisco San Francisco 2	67	694
Jesus M	San Diego Colorado	64	812
MENDOSA			
Ramon*	Alameda Brooklyn	55	180
Ramore*	Alameda Brooklyn	55	180
MENDOSO			
Karens	Los Angeles Elmonte	59	268
MENDOSOTA			
Hosea	Alameda Brooklyn	55	190
MENDOYA			
Jose F	San Francisco San Francisco 3	67	83
Joso*	San Francisco San Francisco 3	67	83
MENDOZA			
Antone	Sierra Eureka	66	1043
Elira	San Francisco San Francisco 2	67	694
Feliz	San Bernardino Santa Inez	64	140
Graville	Mendocino Round Va	60	877
Jesus	San Bernardino Santa Barbara	64	178
Juan	Mariposa Twp 1	60	641
Mainuel	San Francisco San Francisco 2	67	698
Manuel	San Bernardino Santa Barbara	64	177
Martin	Los Angeles San Gabriel	59	417
P	Tuolumne Twp 4	71	156
Ramon	Monterey Monterey	60	929
Roque	Alameda Oakland	55	7
MENDROSO			
Estevan	Los Angeles Los Angeles	59	392
MENDUNE			
George*	Calaveras Twp 6	57	166
MENDURAS			
Gabriel	Monterey San Juan	60	986
MENE			
---	Plumas Meadow Valley	62	914
L E	Butte Ophir	56	766
MENEARS			
Peter*	Nevada Red Dog	61	552
MENEFEE			
James W	Sierra La Porte	66	786
MENEGALA			
Peter	Tuolumne Big Oak	71	180
MENELLS			
Joseph*	Mendocino Big Rvr	60	846
MENENDEZ			
Jose	San Bernardino Santa Ba	64	216
Jose	San Bernardino S Buenav	64	217
MENER			
A	Santa Clara Redwood	65	459
MENEROLE			
W	San Francisco San Francisco 6	67	406
MENESES			
Dolores	Yuba Marysville	72	944
MENEURS			
Peter*	Nevada Red Dog	61	552
MENEY			
Jose M*	San Francisco San Francisco 2	67	759
Jose Mx*	San Francisco San Francisco 2	67	759
MENEZ			
Jose*	Yuba Marysville	72	948
MENFELDER			
Louis	San Joaquin Stockton	64	1028
MENFIELD			
Marks	San Francisco San Francisco 2	67	767
MENG			
---	Placer Virginia	62	684
---	Sacramento Ward 1	63	51
---	Sacramento Ward 1	63	60
---	Trinity Mouth Ca	70	1018
---	Trinity McGilley	70	1021
---	Trinity Taylor'S	70	1033
---	Trinity Taylor'S	70	1034
---	Trinity Taylor'S	70	1035
---	Trinity Taylor'S	70	1036
---	Trinity Big Flat	70	1041
---	Trinity Big Flat	70	1042
---	Yuba Long Bar	72	761
---*	Trinity Big Flat	70	1041
Jacob*	San Francisco San Francisco 7	68	1325
MENGAL			
John	Sierra Cold Can	66	836
MENGARINI			
Gregorio	Santa Clara Santa Clara	65	481
MENGIS			
Agustin*	Los Angeles Tejon	59	539
Elizabeth*	San Francisco San Francisco 2	67	763
MENGL			
P	San Joaquin Stockton	64	1039
MENGNONG			
---	Trinity McGilley	70	1021
MENHART			
John	Siskiyou Callahan	69	9
MENHAST			
John*	Siskiyou Callahan	69	9
MENI			
Prosper	San Francisco San Francisco 2	67	694
MENICH			
Anthony*	Yuba Marysville	72	967
MENICIR			
Paul E	San Francisco San Francisco 7	68	1396

California 1860 Census Index

Name	County Locale	M653 Roll	Page
MENIES			
Anestacia*	Yuba Marysville	72	948
MENIFEE			
Richard*	Plumas Quincy	62	985
MENILLA			
Rogregrious*	San Mateo Twp 2	65	113
Thos	San Mateo Twp 2	65	113
MENILS			
Randolph*	San Francisco 9 San Francisco	68	944
MENIN			
Carmina*	Calaveras Twp 5	57	208
MENINS			
Joseph	Calaveras Twp 8	57	90
MENIOS			
Jose	Monterey San Juan	60	985
MENIS			
Bemala	San Joaquin Castoria	64	891
Edwin S	Calaveras Twp 5	57	239
MENISOLL			
B	El Dorado White Oaks	58	1003
MENISON			
Danial	Humbolt Eureka	59	171
MENITT			
Robt	Butte Kimshaw	56	595
MENIYMOM			
J	Yuba Slate Ro	72	712
MENK			
Eliza*	Placer Iona Hills	62	884
MENKA			
---	Shasta French G	66	713
MENKAY			
Henry	Calaveras Twp 5	57	187
MENKE			
A	Sacramento American	63	168
Chas	Sacramento Ward 4	63	511
MENKER			
Mary	San Francisco San Francisco 9	68	978
MENKLER			
Harres*	Sacramento Mississipi	63	187
Harris*	Sacramento Mississipi	63	187
MENKLEY			
Henry	Calaveras Twp 5	57	187
MENKOPAS			
---	Fresno Twp 2	59	59
MENLAND			
Robert*	Placer Michigan	62	843
MENLBRIGNER			
J*	Yolo Cache	72	596
MENLBY			
Calib C	Butte Ophir	56	800
MENLE			
Jacob	San Francisco San Francisco 9	68	1105
MENLICK			
L	Sacramento Granite	63	244
MENLLIA			
Thomas	Sierra Eureka	66	1043
MENLLY			
Michael*	Calaveras Twp 5	57	242
MENLOVE			
Fredrick	Calaveras Twp 6	57	135
MENLOZI			
Manuel	Placer Forest H	62	791
MENLTON			
J	Butte Wyandotte	56	660
Toron	Sierra La Porte	66	787
MENMER			
Julian*	Calaveras Twp 4	57	339
MENN			
A*	Sacramento Granite	63	250
G M	San Francisco San Francisco 8	68	1297
Siles B	El Dorado Big Bar	58	739
MENNADA			
Ramona*	Placer Auburn	62	585
MENNARD			
A	San Francisco San Francisco 1	68	930
MENNELLY			
S	Yolo Cache Crk	72	610
MENNIDOO			
Pablo	El Dorado Greenwood	58	718
MENNIMA			
Henry*	Contra Costa Twp 1	57	511
MENNING			
M	El Dorado Georgetown	58	695
Mathias*	El Dorado Georgetown	58	676
MENNIRN			
Jean S*	Calaveras Twp 6	57	115
MENNKERBECK			
Jacob*	San Francisco San Francisco 7	68	1329
MENNON			
C A	El Dorado Georgetown	58	759
MENNOS			
Jesus	Contra Costa Twp 1	57	489
MENNSON			
E	Butte Oregon	56	634
MENNY			
Clemment*	San Francisco 5 San Francisco	67	495
MENO			
Jacob	Tulara Twp 2	71	28
MENOIN			
E F*	Nevada Bridgeport	61	486
MENOLO			
T*	Tehama Red Bluff	70	926
MENON			
C	Nevada Eureka	61	368
MENONY			
E T	San Francisco San Francisco 6	67	411
MENOR			
Alex	Yolo Cache	72	612
Ernst*	San Francisco San Francisco 1	68	825
MENORH			
E F*	Nevada Bridgeport	61	486
MENOS			
Henry	Placer Michigan	62	820
MENOT			
---	Del Norte Klamath	58	654
MENOW			
C*	Nevada Eureka	61	368
MENRAL			
A*	San Francisco San Francisco 2	67	684
Louis*	Mariposa Twp 3	60	616
MENRAM			
Josiph*	Nevada Rough &	61	420
MENRICK			
Hamlin*	Napa Clear Lake	61	138
MENRIO			
Emily	Amador Twp 1	55	487
MENROE			
Henry	Colusa Monroeville	57	457
MENRON			
Augusta*	San Francisco San Francisco 9	68	1061
MENSAL			
Louis*	Mariposa Twp 3	60	616
MENSATILO			
---	Mendocino Twp 1	60	889
MENSDORFFER			
Konrad	Yuba Marysville	72	845
MENSE			
Hermon*	Humbolt Union	59	183
MENSEAN			
M	Siskiyou Klamath	69	91
MENSEL			
Otto	Calaveras Twp 7	57	25
MENSEN			
William	Nevada Bridgeport	61	444
MENSER			
Henry*	San Francisco San Francisco 9	68	1051
William*	Nevada Bridgeport	61	444
MENSHOUSE			
M*	San Francisco San Francisco 5	67	518
MENSHROP			
R*	Sacramento Brighton	63	198
MENSHROSS			
R*	Sacramento Brighton	63	198
MENSHUTH			
A	Calaveras Twp 9	57	391
MENSICE			
Hess	El Dorado Georgetown	58	689
Hira*	El Dorado Georgetown	58	689
Hirr*	El Dorado Georgetown	58	689
MENSIN			
Hirr*	El Dorado Georgetown	58	689
MENSING			
A	Nevada Nevada	61	260
Chas	Mariposa Twp 3	60	560
Rebecca	San Francisco San Francisco 10	67	359
MENSON			
Augusta*	San Francisco San Francisco 9	68	1061
MENSTEAD			
James	Tehama Pasakent	70	856
MENTAS			
Raphael	Santa Cruz Pajaro	66	566
MENTEAN			
Victor	Siskiyou Callahan	69	5
MENTEAU			
Victor*	Siskiyou Callahan	69	5
MENTEL			
Manuel	Alameda Brooklyn	55	87
Marmel*	Alameda Brooklyn	55	87
MENTER			
Chester	Siskiyou Yreka	69	140
James*	Contra Costa Twp 2	57	557
MENTERN			
W*	San Francisco San Francisco 5	67	544
MENTHEN			
C F*	Sacramento Granite	63	246
R S*	San Francisco San Francisco 1	68	915
Wm*	Butte Kimshaw	56	601
MENTHEW			
Wm*	Butte Kimshaw	56	601
MENTHEY			
Chas	Mariposa Twp 1	60	624
MENTHIA			
C F*	Sacramento Granite	63	246
MENTINARO			
Jose	Placer Yankee J	62	758
MENTLO			
Monroe	Contra Costa Twp 2	57	547
MENTO			
---	Fresno Twp 2	59	105
Owen	Yuba Long Bar	72	755
Rrin	Yuba Long Bar	72	755
MENTONE			
Fredrico	Calaveras Twp 5	57	135
MENTOU			
Calistra	Los Angeles Los Angeles	59	518
MENTRUM			
John*	Sacramento Alabama	63	417
MENTS			
Antone	Mariposa Twp 1	60	672
MENTSGER			
Frederick	San Francisco San Francisco 11	67	108
MENTURN			
Chas*	San Francisco San Francisco 1	68	873
MENTUS			
Raphael	Santa Cruz Pajaro	66	566
MENTZ			
J	San Francisco San Francisco 5	67	519
MENTZE			
Ernest	Los Angeles Los Angeles	59	367
MENTZGER			
Frederick	San Francisco San Francisco 11	67	108
MENUADA			
Ramona*	Placer Auburn	62	585
MENUELA			
---	San Bernardino S Timate	64	747
MENUR			
Carmina*	Calaveras Twp 5	57	208
MENUS			
Carmian	Calaveras Twp 5	57	208
MENVAL			
A*	San Francisco San Francisco 2	67	684
MENYON			
Patrick	San Francisco San Francisco 9	68	1029
MENZEIS			
Ann	San Francisco San Francisco 2	67	743
MENZEISS			
S	San Francisco San Francisco 2	67	742
MENZER			
P B	Tuolumne Twp 1	71	248
Wm	Tuolumne Twp 1	71	248
MEO			
---	Calaveras Twp 6	57	176
---	Placer Rattle Snake	62	633
---	Sierra Twp 7	66	889
MEOELYET			
William T*	Calaveras Twp 6	57	152
MEOGAN			
Dennis*	San Francisco San Francisco 11	67	105
MEOHAILANY			
Wm*	Calaveras Twp 5	57	178
MEOKE			
---	Trinity Lewiston	70	955
MEOLOVI			
F*	San Francisco San Francisco 5	67	503
MEOMACK			
Valentine*	Solano Benecia	69	317
MEON			
---	San Francisco San Francisco 4	68	1182
---	San Francisco San Francisco 9	68	1087
MEONA			
Jose	Los Angeles Elmonte	59	256
MEONETTA			
---	Fresno Twp 1	59	75
MEONEY			
Wm	Colusa Monroeville	57	448
MEONHER			
Fred*	Calaveras Twp 9	57	399
MEOORE			
A*	Siskiyou Scott Ri	69	72
MEORHBERGER			
Christian	San Francisco San Francisco 7	68	1325
MEOSHBERGER			
Christian*	San Francisco San Francisco 7	68	1325
MEOSTUNER			
H	Butte Kimshaw	56	585
MEOTO			
Pasqual*	Monterey S Antoni	60	968
MEOW			
---*	San Francisco San Francisco 9	68	1087
MEOY			
Chee*	San Francisco San Francisco 9	68	1094
MEPER			
A	Trinity Trinity	70	972
Eliza*	San Francisco San Francisco 7	68	1353

Name	County Locale	M653 RollPage
MEPERMOTH		
G H	Tehama Tehama	70 946
MEPICK		
James W	Solano Suisan	69 240
MEPING		
Benj*	San Francisco San Francisco 3	67 7
MEPMOTH		
B F	Sierra Downieville	661001
MEQUES		
M	Tuolumne Twp 2	71 338
MER KELBACH		
Catharine*	San Francisco	681316
	San Francisco	
MER SEE		
---	Fresno Twp 1	59 29
MER		
---	Butte Bidwell	56 711
---	Mariposa Twp 1	60 640
---*	Mariposa Twp 1	60 641
Ah	Butte Bidwell	56 711
Lin	Placer Virginia	62 671
T*	El Dorado Placerville	58 851
MERA		
---	San Bernardino S Timate	64 701
MERAAS		
T	El Dorado Placerville	58 860
MERAER		
Carmina*	Calaveras Twp 5	57 208
MERAIR		
Carmina*	Calaveras Twp 5	57 208
MERAIS		
Carmina*	Calaveras Twp 5	57 208
MERAN		
Christ*	Alameda Brooklyn	55 141
David*	San Francisco San Francisco 3	67 81
Jamez	Sierra Downieville	661002
MERANDA		
Cruz	Monterey Monterey	60 965
Fanfrancisco*	Alameda Brooklyn	55 152
Gill	Yuba Marysville	72 948
Gruz	Monterey Monterey	60 965
Josi	Calaveras Twp 5	57 182
MERANDI		
Stephen	Marin Bolinas	60 733
MERANDO		
Cardani*	Alameda Oakland	55 4
Caretane*	Alameda Oakland	55 4
Caretani*	Alameda Oakland	55 4
Caretaue*	Alameda Oakland	55 4
Caretaui*	Alameda Oakland	55 4
Domingo	Calaveras Twp 5	57 198
MERANO		
Maria J	Los Angeles Los Angeles	59 306
MERAR		
Peter*	Sierra Downieville	66 977
MERAS		
Henry	Plumas Quincy	62 991
MERATHECA		
J C	San Francisco San Francisco 2	67 628
MERATHUA		
J C	San Francisco San Francisco 2	67 628
MERBAC		
Nicholas*	San Francisco San Francisco 2	67 700
MERBANE		
G	Sonoma Washington	69 668
G M	Sonoma Washington	69 668
MERBECK		
Henry*	San Francisco San Francisco 8	681302
MERC		
Loyz	Sierra Downieville	661014
MERCA		
Jesus	San Joaquin Stockton	641069
MERCADO		
Jesus	Santa Clara Almaden	65 266
Jose	Santa Clara Almaden	65 268
Juan B	San Francisco San Francisco 2	67 683
MERCAR		
Camel*	Amador Twp 5	55 337
Canul*	Amador Twp 5	55 337
Carnel	Amador Twp 5	55 337
MERCE		
Achno*	Placer Virginia	62 667
MERCEALI		
Juan	Los Angeles San Jose	59 288
MERCEAR		
Julin	San Francisco San Francisco 2	67 797
MERCED		
---	Los Angeles Santa Ana	59 451
---	San Bernardino S Timate	64 697
---	San Bernardino S Timate	64 699
---	San Bernardino S Timate	64 700
---	San Bernardino S Timate	64 703
---	San Bernardino S Timate	64 705
---	San Bernardino S Timate	64 707
---	San Bernardino S Timate	64 722
---	San Bernardino S Timate	64 724

Name	County Locale	M653 RollPage
MERCED		
---	San Bernardino S Timate	64 728
---	San Bernardino S Timate	64 736
---	San Bernardino S Timate	64 738
---	San Bernardino S Timate	64 739
---	San Bernardino S Timate	64 746
---	San Bernardino S Timate	64 748
---	San Bernardino S Timate	64 749
---	San Bernardino S Timate	64 750
---	San Bernardino S Timate	64 753
Jose	Plumas Meadow Valley	62 933
Lorenzo	San Bernardino S Timate	64 720
MERCEDE		
John	Tuolumne Shawsfla	71 388
Tuboso	Tuolumne Shawsfla	71 376
MERCEDES		
---	Mariposa Twp 1	60 629
---	Sacramento Ward 1	63 81
MERCEED		
---	San Bernardino S Timate	64 709
MERCEIR		
Catharine	Yuba Rose Bar	72 797
MERCEN		
Christ*	Alameda Brooklyn	55 141
Mercides*	Marin Cortemad	60 784
MERCER		
Charles	Solano Suisan	69 231
Charles P	San Francisco San Francisco 11	114
		67
Edward	Sierra Twp 7	66 893
H	Shasta Horsetown	66 696
J J	Shasta Millvill	66 750
J L	Calaveras Twp 9	57 402
J T	Calaveras Twp 9	57 402
J T	Shasta Millvill	66 750
John	Del Norte Crescent	58 649
John B	San Diego Colorado	64 807
Joseph	Placer Iona Hills	62 867
Joseph	Placer Iona Hills	62 873
Mercides*	Marin Cortemad	60 784
Percir*	Placer Iona Hills	62 897
Perier*	Placer Iona Hills	62 897
Robert	Calaveras Twp 6	57 160
Robert	San Francisco San Francisco 1	68 932
William	Plumas Quincy	62 960
Wm E	Plumas Meadow Valley	62 905
MERCHAIN		
John*	Calaveras Twp 5	57 223
MERCHAN		
Francis*	Sacramento Ward 1	63 30
Jacob E	Calaveras Twp 10	57 263
MERCHANT		
---	Del Norte Klamath	58 654
Aaron	Sacramento Ward 4	63 559
Abram	Plumas Quincy	62 922
Albion R	Sierra Pine Grove	66 830
Albion R P	Sierra Pine Grove	66 830
Albron R	Sierra Pine Grove	66 830
Elcher	Solano Suisan	69 211
Elsher	Solano Suisan	69 211
F	San Francisco San Francisco 2	67 628
Geo	Sacramento Ward 3	63 485
J	Solano Vacaville	69 329
J B	San Francisco San Francisco 5	67 516
James	San Francisco San Francisco 4	681224
Jno	Sacramento Ward 3	63 488
Joel	Sonoma Petaluma	69 557
John	Sonoma Petaluma	69 582
Julius	Sierra Poker Flats	66 838
Martha	Sacramento Ward 4	63 559
Mary	Calaveras Twp 8	57 51
N E	El Dorado Georgetown	58 683
Samuel	Santa Cruz Watsonville	66 537
Thomas	Sonoma Armally	69 479
Thos	San Francisco San Francisco 2	67 733
MERCHARD		
Francis*	Sacramento Ward 1	63 30
MERCHARN		
John*	Calaveras Twp 5	57 223
MERCHAU		
Francis*	Sacramento Ward 1	63 30
MERCHAW		
Francis*	Sacramento Ward 1	63 30
MERCHISON		
James	San Joaquin Oneal	64 960
MERCIA		
Augustus	Tuolumne Twp 4	71 140
Francis	Calaveras Twp 6	57 167
MERCIEN		
Jules*	San Francisco San Francisco 7	681444
Louis	Sacramento Ward 1	63 63
MERCIER		
Baptiste	Yuba Parks Ba	72 783
Bicedo	Calaveras Twp 5	57 205
Catharine*	Yuba Rose Bar	72 797
Cloud	Siskiyou Yreka	69 168

Name	County Locale	M653 RollPage
MERCIER		
John	Tuolumne Twp 1	71 269
Joseph	Tuolumne Twp 1	71 479
Leopold	Yuba Foster B	72 835
MERCIEU		
Louis	Sacramento Ward 1	63 63
MERCIN		
Catharine	Yuba Rose Bar	72 797
Frank	Calaveras Twp 5	57 142
MERCION		
Bicedo*	Calaveras Twp 5	57 205
MERCIRE		
Frank*	Calaveras Twp 6	57 142
MERCIRR		
Joseph	Tuolumne Sonora	71 479
MERCISE		
Mariana	San Joaquin Stockton	641085
MERCISO		
Bicedo	Calaveras Twp 5	57 205
MERCITO		
J	Calaveras Twp 9	57 378
MERCO		
Caleo	Alameda Oakland	55 31
MERCURE		
F	El Dorado Indian D	581158
H	El Dorado Indian D	581158
MERCY		
Adelia	Placer Forest H	62 792
Alice	Calaveras Twp 7	57 20
Frank	Yuba New York	72 747
Heny	Calaveras Twp 7	57 20
James	Calaveras Twp 7	57 30
Margaret	Calaveras Twp 7	57 20
William	Calaveras Twp 7	57 20
MERDELL		
Charles	Nevada Little Y	61 532
MERDES		
Louisa	Alameda Brooklyn	55 77
MERDGET		
William T*	Calaveras Twp 6	57 152
MERDITH		
Mary	Sutter Nicolaus	70 836
MERDOZA		
Juan	Mariposa Twp 1	60 641
MERE		
Loyz*	Sierra Downieville	661014
MEREDES		
James	Monterey San Juan	601003
MEREDITH		
B F	Sacramento Ward 1	63 105
Catharine	San Francisco San Francisco 9	681016
Charles	El Dorado Eldorado	58 947
Chas H	Sacramento Centre	63 180
D W	Solano Vacaville	69 319
Elihn	Sonoma Mendocino	69 459
Elihu	Sonoma Mendocino	69 459
Griffith	Sierra Poker Flats	66 840
Henry	Sierra La Porte	66 767
J J	Butte Kimshaw	56 605
Jas S	Sacramento Granite	63 265
John	Fresno Twp 2	59 17
Mary	Sonoma Mendocino	69 459
Mary Ann	Sierra La Porte	66 767
Peter	San Francisco San Francisco 1	68 915
Sarah	San Francisco San Francisco 9	681016
T	Yuba New York	72 722
W C	Tuolumne Twp 1	71 480
William J	Yuba Rose Bar	72 814
Wm	Nevada Eureka	61 370
MEREEN		
Mercedes*	Marin Cortemad	60 784
MEREHANT		
Joseph	Sierra La Porte	66 769
MEREHINE		
Gaeteno	Sierra Poker Flats	66 839
MEREHOUSE		
Edward	San Luis Obispo San Luis Obispo	65 19
MEREIER		
Carmina*	Calaveras Twp 5	57 208
MEREITO		
J	Calaveras Twp 9	57 378
MERELL		
Frank	Santa Clara San Jose	65 385
MERELON		
Pierre	Yuba Rose Bar	72 800
MEREMIC		
Theodore*	Calaveras Twp 8	57 103
MERENCIANA		
---	San Bernardino Santa Inez	64 142
Maria	Los Angeles San Gabriel	59 420
MERENDEN		
Amanda	Yolo Putah	72 551
MERENO		
Jose	Plumas Quincy	62 995
MERENREAN		
P*	Tuolumne Sonora	71 482

Name	County Locale	M653 RollPage
MERERS		
John	El Dorado Newtown	58 780
MERES		
Annie	Tehama Antelope	70 891
N Ap Dill	Tehama Antelope	70 888
MERESELES		
A	Siskiyou Scott Va	69 46
MERET		
Geisbert	Placer Secret R	62 613
MERETHEN		
J C*	Solano Fremont	69 381
MERETTE		
G P	Shasta Shasta	66 675
MEREYNON		
Stephen	Sonoma Washington	69 677
MERGAN		
John	Shasta Shasta	66 662
M E	Sacramento Granite	63 259
MERGAR		
William	Placer Forest H	62 774
MERGE		
P	Yolo Washington	72 561
MERGENT		
A*	Nevada Grass Valley	61 196
MERGENTE		
Anna M	San Luis Obispo San Luis Obispo	65 39
MERGER		
Adolphus*	San Francisco 8 681289 San Francisco	
George	San Francisco San Francisco 4 681110	
MERGMERM		
J*	Calaveras Twp 9	57 397
MERGMUM		
J*	Calaveras Twp 9	57 397
MERGREW		
George*	Placer Michigan	62 824
MERHEL		
S*	Sacramento Granite	63 265
MERI		
Philip	Sacramento Ward 3	63 457
MERIA		
Baptista*	Mariposa Twp 3	60 594
MERIAAN		
Augustus	Tuolumne Big Oak	71 140
MERIAN		
H	Nevada Grass Valley	61 160
Marco	Marin Cortemad	60 792
MERIANO		
---	San Bernardino S Timate	64 703
MERICAN		
D W	Amador Twp 2	55 325
MERICK		
Emily	Mariposa Twp 1	60 624
MERIDES		
James	Monterey San Juan	601003
MERIDETH		
D W	Napa Clear Lake	61 129
MERIDITH		
E H	El Dorado Placerville	58 909
Henry	Sierra La Porte	66 767
Jas S	Sacramento Granite	63 265
John	Sierra Twp 7	66 864
M	Calaveras Twp 9	57 377
Mary Ann	Sierra La Porte	66 767
MERIDON		
G A	San Francisco San Francisco 6 67 436	
MERIER		
August*	Tuolumne Twp 2	71 282
MERIFIELD		
Peter	Tuolumne Twp 3	71 466
MERIGOT		
A	San Francisco San Francisco 6 67 470	
MERIHEW		
Wm	Sonoma Armally	69 486
MERIL		
James	Amador Twp 2	55 313
MERILL		
Nathan	Sonoma Sonoma	69 653
MERILLAT		
Lewis D	Tulara Visalia	71 103
Lewis O	Tulara Visalia	71 103
MERILLO		
F	Tuolumne Twp 4	71 161
MERIMAN		
James	Calaveras Twp 4	57 313
MERIMONTE		
John	San Mateo Twp 2	65 114
MERIMONTES		
A*	San Mateo Twp 2	65 116
Besmiths	San Mateo Twp 2	65 116
S	San Mateo Twp 2	65 116
Silso*	San Mateo Twp 2	65 114
MERIMONTIS		
A*	San Mateo Twp 2	65 116
MERIMONTY		
Ramunda	San Mateo Twp 2	65 117

Name	County Locale	M653 RollPage
MERIMONTY		
Silso*	San Mateo Twp 2	65 114
MERIMONTZ		
Enacis*	San Mateo Twp 3	65 98
MERINETT		
George	Sierra Twp 7	66 903
MERINIEN		
James*	Calaveras Twp 4	57 313
MERIS		
Henry	San Diego Colorado	64 808
MERIT		
Alvis	Napa Yount	61 47
Asa	Calaveras Twp 5	57 142
M B	San Francisco San Francisco 9 681077	
MERITHERO		
J C	Solano Fremont	69 381
MERITT		
James A	Napa Yount	61 38
P G	San Francisco San Francisco 9 68 959	
Richard	Mariposa Twp 1	60 638
William	Placer Iona Hills	62 895
MERIWETHER		
David	Alameda Brooklyn	55 168
MERJINO		
Sam*	El Dorado Georgetown	58 706
MERK		
A	Calaveras Twp 9	57 400
Chas	Mariposa Twp 1	60 624
MERKELBACH		
Catharine	San Francisco San Francisco 8 681316	
MERKER		
Chas*	San Francisco San Francisco 2 67 691	
Jno	Sacramento Ward 3	63 457
Wm F	Sacramento Ward 4	63 516
MERKINDOLLOR		
Geo	El Dorado Casumnes	581166
MERKINS		
H	San Francisco San Francisco 3 67 73	
MERKLE		
C	San Francisco San Francisco 9 68 948	
E	Amador Twp 2	55 297
Francis	Amador Twp 2	55 298
Peter	Los Angeles Santa Ana	59 440
MERKSE		
A*	Nevada Nevada	61 288
MERLE		
Adrian	San Francisco San Francisco 1 68 826	
Benoit V	Contra Costa Twp 1	57 528
Jales*	Yuba Parks Ba	72 786
Jules	Yuba Parke Ba	72 786
P V	San Francisco San Francisco 2 67 684	
Uganio**	Contra Costa Twp 1	57 528
MERLENO		
Jesus	San Francisco San Francisco 2 67 718	
MERLET		
John	Calaveras Twp 5	57 207
MERLEY		
Benj	Alameda Oakland	55 6
MERLIN		
John	Los Angeles Azuza	59 276
Martin*	San Francisco San Francisco 9 68 947	
MERLTORD		
Victor*	Contra Costa Twp 1	57 511
MERMAIN		
Charles	Yuba Parks Ba	72 784
MERMAN		
E	Shasta Shasta	66 686
MERMANTA		
Ylaria	Los Angeles Los Angeles	59 323
MERMON		
Alfred	Sierra Twp 5	66 947
MERMOND		
Louis	San Francisco San Francisco 10 358 67	
Louise	San Francisco San Francisco 10 358 67	
MERMOUGER		
Levi H*	San Joaquin Castoria	64 886
MERN		
Charles	San Francisco San Francisco 8 681274	
MERNAM		
Josiph*	Nevada Rough &	61 420
MERNAN		
E	Shasta Shasta	66 686
MERNANDEZ		
Adolph*	Yuba Marysville	72 919
Juana	Los Angeles Los Angeles	59 407
MERNDETH		
W J*	Nevada Rough &	61 410
MERNIA		
Geo E	Placer Mountain	62 708
James	Mariposa Twp 1	60 624
MERNNET		
C N*	Mariposa Twp 3	60 609
MERNSIL		
John*	Santa Clara Santa Clara	65 481

Name	County Locale	M653 RollPage
MERNSON		
G R	San Francisco San Francisco 3 67 79	
MERNSTER		
John	Trinity Soldiers	701005
MERODETH		
W W*	Napa Clear Lake	61 131
MERODITH		
W W	Napa Clear Lake	61 131
MEROIAM		
Abraham	San Francisco San Francisco 7 681353	
MEROLET		
Jon*	San Francisco San Francisco 2 67 662	
MEROMICH		
Thos	Yolo Cache	72 611
MEROW		
G M*	Sierra Twp 5	66 940
MERRALE		
Eliz	Sacramento Ward 3	63 470
MERRATZ		
James	Sacramento Ward 1	63 19
MERRDON		
G A*	San Francisco San Francisco 6 67 436	
MERREAME		
Edward*	Sierra Pine Grove	66 823
MERREAMI		
Edward*	Sierra Pine Grove	66 823
MERREL		
Ephraim	Sierra Scales D	66 800
George*	Placer Michigan	62 844
MERRELL		
C H	San Francisco San Francisco 5 67 494	
Chas	Sacramento Ward 4	63 499
Edward	San Francisco San Francisco 9 681097	
F C	San Francisco San Francisco 6 67 436	
George	San Joaquin Elliott	641102
Henry A	Tuolumne Twp 2	71 326
Peter	Los Angeles Elmonte	59 245
T C	San Francisco San Francisco 6 67 436	
MERRENGER		
Wm S*	Sacramento Ward 1	63 88
MERRERA		
Maria	Los Angeles Los Angeles	59 293
MERRETT		
A	Sacramento Ward 1	63 2
A W	Butte Kimshaw	56 595
George	Yuba Marysville	72 904
James	Nevada Bloomfield	61 525
Philip	Amador Twp 4	55 241
MERRIAH		
John	Sonoma Vallejo	69 626
MERRIAM		
E	Trinity Weaverville	701051
George	San Francisco San Francisco 3 67 51	
John	Butte Oro	56 673
O	Sacramento Ward 4	63 502
MERRIAME		
Edward	Sierra Pine Grove	66 823
MERRIAMI		
Edward	Sierra Pine Grove	66 823
MERRIAN		
Wm P	San Francisco San Francisco 2 67 803	
MERRICH		
John	Plumas Quincy	621001
MERRICK		
Alonz	Trinity S Fork	701032
Chas	Sacramento Mississipi	63 187
Eugene	Plumas Quincy	62 995
Hiram	Tulara Twp 1	71 101
Richard	Sierra Port Win	66 798
Richard*	Placer Goods	62 693
S D	Placer Virginia	62 662
W J*	Trinity Weaverville	701077
MERRIDAY		
Samuel	San Francisco San Francisco 2 67 652	
MERRIDETH		
D	San Mateo Twp 3	65 78
MERRIEK		
Hiram*	Tulara Visalia	71 101
MERRIFIELD		
Daniel	Mendocino Little L	60 839
James	Nevada Rough &	61 433
MERRIJOY		
J	San Joaquin Stockton	641100
MERRIL		
A D	Klamath Orleans	59 215
Frank*	Yuba Rose Bar	72 819
German	Humbolt Eel Rvr	59 151
Marcus H	San Joaquin Stockton	641070
MERRILL		
A	Santa Clara Santa Clara	65 463
A H	Placer Mealsburg	62 702
A H	Sacramento Ward 1	63 90
Albion E	San Joaquin Elkhorn	64 964
Annis	San Francisco San Francisco 2 67 600	
B F	San Francisco San Francisco 2 67 720	
B F	Tuolumne Twp 1	71 269

California 1860 Census Index

Name	County Locale	M653 Roll	Page
MERRILL			
Bigler	Placer Illinois	62	705
C	Nevada Grass Valley	61	165
C	Placer Virginia	62	668
C S	Solano Benecia	69	284
C S Jr	Solano Benecia	69	299
Charles	Yolo Slate Ra	72	705
Charles	Yuba Slate Ro	72	705
Daniel	Calaveras Twp 6	57	150
Derius	Plumas Quincy	62	1004
E	Trinity Rearings	70	990
Emma	San Francisco San Francisco 10		251
		67	
Frank	Sacramento Sutter	63	296
Geo H	Placer Rattle Snake	62	600
Giles	Mariposa Twp 3	60	584
H	Butte Eureka	56	656
H	Nevada Nevada	61	282
H	Trinity Weaverville	70	1077
Henry A	Tuolumne Columbia	71	326
Hirer	Yuba North Ea	72	673
Isaac	Sacramento Franklin	63	331
J	Butte Ophir	56	795
J	Nevada Eureka	61	375
J	Sacramento Granite	63	240
J D*	Sacramento Brighton	63	209
J N	Trinity Douglas	70	978
J P	Sonoma Washington	69	671
J T	Placer Michigan	62	845
J T	San Francisco San Francisco 7 681		439
Jesse	Siskiyou Cottonwooood	69	99
Jno R	San Francisco San Francisco 10		313
		67	
John	Contra Costa Twp 2	57	557
John	Siskiyou Scott Ri	69	62
John A	Solano Vallejo	69	251
Joseph	Contra Costa Twp 3	57	606
Joseph	San Francisco San Francisco 4 681		139
L L	San Francisco San Francisco 10		293
		67	
Lowell G	Calaveras Twp 8	57	100
Lyman	San Joaquin Castoria	64	903
M L*	Sacramento American	63	166
M S*	Sacramento American	63	166
Marshall	Nevada Rough &	61	399
Milton	Tulara Twp 3	71	44
Nat	Tehama Moons	70	852
Oliver B	Yolo No E Twp	72	673
Parker	San Francisco San Francisco 8 681		241
Richard*	Yuba Slate Ro	72	705
Robert	San Francisco San Francisco 7 681		438
Robt	Stanislaus Buena Village	70	721
Rufus R*	Yuba Marysville	72	880
S D*	Sacramento Brighton	63	209
S S	San Francisco San Francisco 10		293
		67	
Saml	Tuolumne Twp 1	71	266
Seth W	Del Norte Crescent	58	631
Seth W	Del Norte Crescent	58	632
Stephen	Sierra St Louis	66	814
Sylva	Sacramento Sutter	63	296
Sylvia	Sacramento Sutter	63	296
T	Nevada Eureka	61	375
Thomas	San Francisco San Francisco 5 67		477
Wm	Sacramento Cosummes	63	409
Wm	Sacramento Ward 4	63	553
MERRILLS			
Joseph*	Mendocino Big Rvr	60	846
MERRILS			
Randolph*	San Francisco 9 68		944
	San Francisco		
MERRIMAN			
Ira B	Sierra Gibsonville	66	851
J E	Placer Michigan	62	852
Jannis*	Sacramento Ward 1	63	128
Jimuis*	Sacramento Ward 1	63	128
Jomins	Sacramento Ward 1	63	128
Junnis*	Sacramento Ward 1	63	128
Lyman T	San Francisco San Francisco 10		194
		67	
Rich	San Francisco San Francisco 10		193
		67	
MERRIN			
C	Nevada Eureka	61	368
John	Los Angeles San Jose	59	284
MERRIOTT			
Paul	Stanislaus Emory	70	737
MERRIS			
Merhengton*	Calaveras Twp 10	57	276
MERRISAN			
John*	Placer Virginia	62	690
MERRISON			
D*	San Francisco San Francisco 4 681		231
John*	Placer Virginia	62	690
R B	Nevada Eureka	61	369
MERRIST			
O	Sonoma Salt Point	69	694

Name	County Locale	M653 Roll	Page
MERRIT			
Edwin S	Calaveras Twp 5	57	239
James H	San Francisco San Francisco 4 681		148
Robert	Tulara Visalia	71	103
Thos C	San Mateo Twp 2	65	116
Washington	Calaveras Twp 10	57	276
Wm	Napa Napa	61	71
MERRITHEW			
Barry*	Butte Oregon	56	627
Benj*	Butte Oregon	56	627
Berry*	Butte Oregon	56	627
MERRITHING			
Richd*	Sonoma Petaluma	69	563
MERRITHINS			
Richd*	Sonoma Petaluma	69	563
MERRITHUR			
Benj*	Butte Oregon	56	627
MERRITT			
A	Sacramento Ward 1	63	2
Enos W	Alameda Brooklyn	55	202
F	San Francisco San Francisco 9 681		072
F W	Siskiyou Cottonwoood	69	104
G L	Solano Vacaville	69	341
G M	Santa Clara San Jose	65	279
H J	Butte Kimshaw	56	596
H P	Yolo Putah	72	547
H W	El Dorado Eldorado	58	937
J D	San Bernardino San Bernadino	64	636
J P	Yolo Putah	72	547
James H	San Francisco San Francisco 4 681		148
John	Siskiyou Scott Ri	69	62
John*	Mariposa Twp 3	60	575
Joseph	Calaveras Twp 8	57	81
Josiah	Monterey Monterey	60	934
R D	Tuolmne Twp 2	71	395
Richard*	Yuba Slate Ro	72	705
Robt*	Butte Kimshaw	56	595
S A	Mariposa Twp 3	60	577
Samuel	Sonoma Salt Point	69	693
Stpen S	Sierra St Louis	66	814
Uhn*	Mariposa Twp 3	60	575
William	El Dorado Placerville	58	905
Win*	Mariposa Twp 3	60	575
Wlm*	Mariposa Twp 3	60	575
Wm	Mariposa Twp 3	60	575
Z L	El Dorado Kelsey	581	154
Z L	Sacramento Franklin	63	316
MERRL			
---	San Mateo Twp 3	65	106
MERRMAN			
Myer	Sierra La Porte	66	765
MERROT			
W J	Calaveras Twp 8	57	89
MERROUL			
Jhn	Calaveras Twp 6	57	113
MERRY			
Frances	Sacramento Ward 4	63	583
S	Calaveras Twp 9	57	392
Thomas	Contra Costa Twp 3	57	607
Thos B	San Francisco San Francisco 10		350
		67	
MERRYFIELD			
A D	San Francisco San Francisco 1 68		876
J C	Solano Vacaville	69	363
MERRYMAN			
A	Nevada Eureka	61	362
J	Yolo Slate Ra	72	712
John	Tuolumne Twp 1	71	233
Joseph	Del Norte Crescent	58	633
Richard	Yolo Slate Ra	72	711
Samuel	San Joaquin Castoria	64	911
T	Nevada Eureka	61	362
MERSAY			
John	Napa Yount	61	44
MERSEAS			
K	El Dorado Placerville	58	866
MERSELES			
A	Siskiyou Scott Va	69	46
MERSER			
Lorenzo	Humbolt Mattole	59	126
MERSERVE			
Wm J*	Sacramento Ward 1	63	45
MERSFELDER			
Charles	Calaveras Twp 8	57	56
Philopona	San Joaquin Castoria	64	900
MERSHER			
Christia	Trinity Dead Wood	70	958
MERSHITH			
A*	Calaveras Twp 9	57	391
MERSHONG			
Cornelius	Sonoma Mendocino	69	456
MERSHUTH			
A*	Calaveras Twp 9	57	391
MERSIPH			
Patrick*	Mariposa Twp 3	60	585
MERSTHEN			
J C*	Solano Fremont	69	381

Name	County Locale	M653 Roll	Page
MERTHAN			
Richard	San Francisco San Francisco 4 681		140
MERTIN			
William	Placer Iona Hills	62	895
MERTINIS			
Antonio*	Calaveras Twp 5	57	248
MERTINONE			
P*	Siskiyou Cottonwood	69	103
MERTIS			
Canrad*	Sierra Twp 5	66	917
Conrad	Sierra Twp 5	66	917
Edward	Sierra Twp 5	66	917
MERTOLER			
---	Mariposa Twp 1	60	628
MERTON			
A	Sacramento Sutter	63	304
MERTS			
Thos	Mariposa Twp 3	60	549
MERTSCHLER			
William F*	Solano Benecia	69	316
MERTY			
Charles	Amador Twp 3	55	375
MERTZ			
---	San Francisco San Francisco 3 67		68
George*	Calaveras Twp 6	57	115
MERWIN			
Henry	Sacramento Ward 4	63	577
P T	San Joaquin Stockton	641	100
Samuel	Sacramento Ward 1	63	38
MERY			
Germanigue	Yuba Foster B	72	821
MERYAS			
J	Nevada Grass Valley	61	149
MERYHEW			
Levi	Tulara Twp 1	71	97
MERYMAN			
Jeremiah	San Joaquin Elkhorn	64	972
MES			
---	Tuolumne Twp 3	71	463
MESA			
Antonio	Santa Clara Alviso	65	399
Dolores	Santa Clara Alviso	65	399
Francisco	Los Angeles Los Angeles	59	518
Guadaloupe	Santa Inez	64	142
	San Bernardino		
Jose	Contra Costa Twp 1	57	508
Jose	Santa Clara San Jose	65	384
Jose D	Contra Costa Twp 1	57	483
Jose Jesus	Monterey Pajaro	601	014
Josefa	Santa Clara Alviso	65	412
Lucia	Santa Clara San Jose	65	302
Lucinana	Santa Clara Alviso	65	412
Lucinda	Santa Clara Alviso	65	412
Manuel*	San Francisco San Francisco 2 67		685
Nabor	Los Angeles Santa Ana	59	459
Ramon	Santa Clara Fremont	65	432
Rosalio	Los Angeles Santa Ana	59	459
MESALES			
Alex	Mariposa Twp 3	60	617
MESATOME			
---	Fresno Twp 3	59	39
MESCATA			
Maria	Santa Cruz Soguel	66	579
MESCESETS			
Louis	Sierra Downieville	661	019
MESCHANT			
C	Tuolumne Twp 1	71	235
MESCOL			
---	Tulara Twp 3	71	44
MESCUL			
---*	Tulara Sinks Te	71	44
MESE			
H	San Francisco San Francisco 10		272
		67	
Hermann	San Francisco San Francisco 7 681		385
Petra	Santa Clara San Jose	65	304
MESEANY			
Vincent*	Calaveras Twp 5	57	207
MESEAUX			
Vincent	Calaveras Twp 5	57	207
MESEHEL			
A	El Dorado Greenwood	58	721
MESENGER			
R M	Calaveras Twp 9	57	392
MESENGIN			
R M*	Calaveras Twp 9	57	392
MESENO			
Hosa*	Siskiyou Yreka	69	172
MESER			
Antone	El Dorado Salmon Falls	581	051
Cristy*	Sierra Downieville	66	957
MESERVE			
R	Sacramento Cosummes	63	402
MESEY			
John	Calaveras Twp 5	57	191
MESGHER			
Alphonso	El Dorado Big Bar	58	737

Name	County Locale	Roll	Page
MESH			
P*	San Francisco San Francisco	5 67	483
MESHAW			
J J	San Francisco San Francisco	5 67	496
MESHER			
George	Los Angeles Tejon	59	527
MESIA			
Baptisto	Mariposa Twp 3	60	594
MESIAH			
---	Mendocino Twp 1	60	891
MESICK			
Richard S	Yuba Marysville	72	863
MESIENO			
Jose	El Dorado Greenwood	58	714
MESIGANELIN			
John	El Dorado Greenwood	58	721
MESIL			
Asa	Calaveras Twp 6	57	142
MESITER			
August	Sacramento Ward 1	63	19
MESKER			
Chas*	San Francisco San Francisco	2 67	691
D E*	Butte Kimshaw	56	605
MESKETER			
Anesita	Monterey Alisal	60	1030
Auesita*	Monterey Alisal	60	1036
Ingracia	Monterey Alisal	60	1036
Jngracia*	Monterey Alisal	60	1036
Manuel	Monterey Alisal	60	1030
MESLER			
Charles	San Francisco San Francisco	4 68	1169
P	Sonoma Salt Point	69	691
MESMORE			
Solomon	Sonoma Petaluma	69	595
MESODUB			
---	Fresno Twp 3	59	24
MESOKE			
---	Fresno Twp 2	59	102
MESOKEK			
---	Fresno Twp 3	59	97
MESONA			
Victor	Los Angeles Azuza	59	278
MESOPOTA			
---	Fresno Twp 2	59	105
MESOTO			
Salvador	Santa Cruz Pescadero	66	642
MESOTOME			
---	Fresno Twp 3	59	23
MESRELL			
Edward*	San Francisco San Francisco	9 68	1097
MESS			
Henry	San Francisco San Francisco	6 67	446
MESSA			
Thomas*	Yuba Marysville	72	943
MESSAN			
Peter*	Tuolumne Big Oak	71	178
MESSBERTON			
James*	El Dorado Georgetown	58	706
MESSE			
Josiah*	Yuba Marysville	72	972
MESSEE			
---	Tulara Visalia	71	120
MESSEL			
Joseph	Calaveras Twp 6	57	148
MESSELFOSS			
Diedrich	Stanislaus Emory	70	752
MESSEN			
John H	San Bernardino San Salvador	64	649
MESSENBERG			
Pater F	Marin Bolinas	60	745
MESSENEY			
J	Nevada Nevada	61	284
MESSENGER			
H W	Butte Kimshaw	56	574
Hiram	Amador Twp 5	55	318
Simon	San Francisco San Francisco	2 67	718
Wm	Yuba Long Bar	72	773
Wm D	Sacramento Ward 1	63	88
Wm S*	Sacramento Ward 1	63	88
MESSENORE			
Isaac*	Yuba Marysville	72	977
MESSER			
Daniel	El Dorado Diamond	58	763
Daniel*	Placer Michigan	62	829
H S	Mariposa Twp 3	60	621
Kilian	Los Angeles Los Angeles	59	396
Lucinda H	Marin San Rafael	60	758
MESSEROE			
Wm J	Sacramento Ward 1	63	45
MESSERRE			
Theo*	San Francisco San Francisco	2 67	739
MESSERS			
John	San Bernardino San Bernadino	64	670
MESSERSMITH			
J L	Nevada Rough &	61	413
MESSERVE			
A K	Sacramento Granite	63	258

Name	County Locale	Roll	Page
MESSERVE			
Geo	Sacramento Ward 3	63	424
Jas	Sacramento Ward 3	63	450
Theo*	San Francisco San Francisco	2 67	739
Wm J*	Sacramento Ward 1	63	45
MESSES			
H S	Mariposa Twp 3	60	621
J	San Francisco San Francisco	2 67	781
MESSEY			
John A*	Napa Clear Lake	61	126
MESSIA			
Ewzeb	Amador Twp 2	55	295
MESSIC			
A K	Trinity Mouth Ca	70	1010
MESSICK			
G	El Dorado Salmon Falls	58	1060
James W	Solano Suisan	69	240
Jeptha	Sonoma Petaluma	69	550
William S	Yuba Bear Rvr	72	1013
MESSIE			
Chas	Santa Clara Santa Clara	65	481
MESSIEA			
Dana R	Colusa Monroeville	57	448
MESSIER			
J	San Francisco San Francisco	1 68	934
MESSING			
Benj*	San Francisco San Francisco	3 67	7
MESSINGER			
W L	El Dorado Diamond	58	809
MESSINORE			
Isaac	Yuba Marysville	72	977
MESSIO			
Jeseus	Calaveras Twp 4	57	331
Jessus	Calaveras Twp 4	57	331
Jesus	Calaveras Twp 4	57	331
MESSKELLY			
James	Yuba Suida	72	990
MESSLER			
James	El Dorado Eldorado	58	946
MESSMAKER			
Jacob	Sierra Pine Grove	66	821
MESSMITH			
B F	Sierra Downieville	66	1001
MESSMORE			
Isaac*	Yuba Marysville	72	977
MESSNER			
John*	Siskiyou Callahan	69	7
MESSNES			
John	Siskiyou Callahan	69	7
MESSONIER			
Victor	Los Angeles Los Angeles	59	332
MESSRAN			
J M	Placer Iona Hills	62	863
MESSY			
Daniel H	Tuolumne Twp 1	71	188
MEST			
Livsy*	Mariposa Coulterville	60	703
MESTAYER			
Rachel	Nevada Bridgeport	61	470
MESTIS			
Conrad*	Sierra Twp 5	66	917
MESTRE			
Eteeme	Plumas Meadow Valley	62	911
MESTRICK			
August	Amador Twp 4	55	243
MESTUYER			
Rachel*	Nevada Bridgeport	61	470
MET			
---	Amador Twp 6	55	433
---	San Francisco San Francisco	9 68	1096
Peter*	El Dorado Kelsey	58	1132
META			
Daniel	Calaveras Twp 9	57	381
METAGUE			
Henry	Butte Chico	56	567
METAR			
Juana N*	Calaveras Twp 6	57	136
METATORICH			
Andrew	Yuba Marysville	72	919
METATZ			
Henry*	San Francisco San Francisco	3 67	15
METCALF			
A	Placer Michigan	62	829
A	San Francisco San Francisco	5 67	529
A B	San Francisco San Francisco	1 68	877
Charles	Shasta Horsetown	66	708
David	Siskiyou Scott Va	69	53
Edward	Plumas Meadow Valley	62	900
G R	Siskiyou Yreka	69	177
Henry	Amador Twp 3	55	397
Isham	Napa Napa	61	98
J	San Francisco San Francisco	5 67	485
J J	San Francisco San Francisco	1 68	810
Jas	Placer Stewart	62	607
John	El Dorado Mud Springs	58	955
Lewis	Placer Iona Hills	62	887

Name	County Locale	Roll	Page
METCALF			
M	Nevada Grass Valley	61	161
Moses	Mariposa Twp 3	60	603
Nancy	Shasta Horsetown	66	711
Nancy R	Shasta Horsetown	66	711
O F	Siskiyou Yreka	69	171
Patrick	El Dorado Mud Springs	58	955
Peter	San Francisco San Francisco	8 68	1258
Saml A	San Francisco San Francisco	10 67	229
T	Nevada Nevada	61	269
Thos	Yolo Putah	72	554
W H	Trinity Steiner	70	1000
William	Plumas Quincy	62	955
METCH			
Remmy	Los Angeles Santa Ana	59	448
METEALF			
J J	San Francisco San Francisco	1 68	810
METER			
Meh	El Dorado Big Bar	58	735
METES			
Simon*	Calaveras Twp 5	57	241
METHAN			
---	El Dorado Coloma	58	1118
METHARAY			
M T	Tuolumne Twp 1	71	260
METHARVEY			
M T*	Tuolumne Twp 1	71	260
METHERNS			
Meta*	San Francisco San Francisco	3 67	63
METHEWS			
Leonard	Yuba Long Bar	72	773
Meta*	San Francisco San Francisco	3 67	63
METHIRNS			
Meta*	San Francisco San Francisco	3 67	63
METHRA			
Rotto*	Santa Cruz Soguel	66	590
METHSEN			
W	El Dorado Placerville	58	826
METHVEN			
D*	El Dorado Placerville	58	871
METHVIN			
D*	El Dorado Placerville	58	871
METLOCK			
Danl	Butte Chico	56	531
METMAN			
William	Calaveras Twp 5	57	210
METONAY			
Peter	Sierra Grizzly	66	1058
METRO			
Antonia	Amador Twp 3	55	376
Francisco	Los Angeles Los Angeles	59	501
METSGER			
Jacob	Sacramento Ward 4	63	512
METSON			
Eliza*	Placer Virginia	62	701
John E	Napa Napa	61	72
METSOW			
John E*	Napa Napa	61	72
METTE			
Felix J	San Francisco San Francisco	2 67	574
George	Santa Clara San Jose	65	348
METTICK			
Joseph	Los Angeles Santa Ana	59	440
METTLER			
Isaiah	Amador Twp 6	55	442
METTUS			
James*	Santa Cruz Santa Cruz	66	599
METTZGER			
Peter*	Tuolumne Big Oak	71	129
METU			
Francisco*	Los Angeles Los Angeles	59	501
METZ			
Geo	San Francisco San Francisco	10 67	259
Israel	San Joaquin O'Neal	64	1005
John M	Los Angeles Santa Ana	59	443
Mary	El Dorado Georgetown	58	677
Theodore	San Francisco San Francisco	7 68	1367
W T	Nevada Grass Valley	61	175
METZENBACH			
Jacob	Placer Michigan	62	814
METZER			
L J	San Francisco San Francisco	9 68	941
METZGAR			
William	Siskiyou Klamath	69	96
METZGER			
Charles L	Tuolumne Chinese	71	500
E D	Sacramento Granite	63	228
Peter	Tuolumne Twp 4	71	129
METZGUR			
William	Siskiyou Klamath	69	96
METZKER			
George	Los Angeles Los Angeles	59	332
Jacob	Los Angeles Los Angeles	59	332
L	Siskiyou Scott Va	69	30

California 1860 Census Index

Name	County Locale	M653 RollPage
METZLEE		
Wm*	Nevada Nevada	61 241
METZLER		
Caroline	Sacramento Ward 3	63 431
Ernest	Sacramento Ward 3	63 430
George	Placer Yankee J	62 781
M C	El Dorado Placerville	58 859
P	El Dorado Placerville	58 820
Wm	Sacramento Ward 4	63 518
Wm*	Nevada Nevada	61 241
Wm*	Sacramento Ward 1	63 37
METZNER		
Catharine	San Francisco San Francisco	7 681377
METZZER		
John	Sacramento Ward 1	63 77
Peter*	Tuolumne Big Oak	71 129
MEU		
Chu	San Francisco San Francisco	4 681176
Leong	San Francisco San Francisco	11 159 67
MEUBO		
Frederick*	Santa Cruz Pescadero	66 643
MEUDOZA		
Rawon	Merced Monterey	60 929
MEUGIS		
Agustin*	Los Angeles Tejon	59 539
MEULE		
Jacob*	San Francisco San Francisco	9 681105
MEULLY		
Michael*	Calaveras Twp 5	57 242
MEULTON		
J*	Butte Wyandotte	56 660
MEUMCAR		
----	Mendocino Round Va	60 883
MEUMER		
Barnard*	Calaveras Twp 4	57 339
Burnard	Calaveras Twp 4	57 339
MEUN		
----	Sacramento Cosumnes	63 392
G M*	San Francisco San Francisco	8 681297
MEUNEMU		
Edward*	Contra Costa Twp 1	57 511
MEUNG		
----	Sierra Twp 5	66 947
MEURING		
A	Nevada Nevada	61 260
MEURNRS		
Bernard*	Calaveras Twp 4	57 338
Julian	Calaveras Twp 4	57 338
MEURON		
Augusta*	San Francisco San Francisco	9 681061
MEUROS		
Jose	Monterey San Juan	60 985
MEURTIN		
Wm*	Sacramento Granite	63 246
MEUSDORFFER		
Howard*	Yuba Marysville	72 845
MEUSER		
Henry*	San Francisco San Francisco	9 681051
William*	Nevada Bridgeport	61 444
MEUSICE		
Hirr*	El Dorado Georgetown	58 689
MEUSING		
Rebecca*	San Francisco San Francisco	10 359 67
MEUTHEN		
Wm*	Butte Kimshaw	56 601
MEUTHER		
C F	Sacramento Granite	63 246
MEV		
----	Calaveras Twp 5	57 176
MEVELGET		
William T*	Calaveras Twp 6	57 152
MEVILLE		
James	Sierra Port Win	66 797
MEVLIN		
Joseph	Tulara Keyesville	71 62
MEVOLET		
Jon*	San Francisco San Francisco	2 67 662
MEW		
----	Butte Bidwell	56 709
----	Butte Ophir	56 815
----	Calaveras Twp 5	57 255
----	El Dorado Union	581090
----	Plumas Meadow Valley	62 910
----	Tuolumne Jamestown	71 439
----	Yolo No E Twp	72 684
----	Yuba Slate Ro	72 684
----	Yuba Long Bar	72 758
Ah	Butte Bidwell	56 709
Choy	Butte Ophir	56 815
Gogh	Plumas Quincy	62 947
Ing	Butte Bidwell	56 726
MEWAGNI		
A	El Dorado Greenwood	58 722
MEWER		
F M	Butte Ophir	56 781

Name	County Locale	M653 RollPage
MEWFER		
William*	San Francisco San Francisco	9 681031
MEWG		
Jacob*	San Francisco San Francisco	7 681325
MEWHAFF		
Frank	San Francisco San Francisco	10 195 67
MEWIT		
J M	Calaveras Twp 9	57 412
MEWMAN		
Chas L	San Francisco San Francisco	10 204 67
MEWSSDOFFER		
H	San Francisco San Francisco	5 67 488
MEWTHRA		
Rotto*	Santa Cruz Soguel	66 590
MEWTON		
R N	Nevada Red Dog	61 548
MEX		
Warren	San Francisco San Francisco	4 681165
MEXERS		
Jos	Trinity Minersville	70 968
MEXICAN		
----	Marin San Rafael	60 765
Juan	Amador Twp 2	55 266
MEXICO		
S	El Dorado Coloma	581107
T	El Dorado Coloma	581107
MEY		
----	Butte Ophir	56 817
----	El Dorado Georgetown	58 755
----	Mariposa Twp 5	60 564
----	Nevada Bridgeport	61 462
----	Plumas Meadow Valley	62 914
----	Plumas Quincy	62 950
----	Sacramento Cosumnes	63 392
Chee	Butte Ophir	56 810
Chew	Butte Ophir	56 809
Chew	Butte Ophir	56 813
Chey	Butte Ophir	56 811
MEYACHIM		
E	San Francisco San Francisco	5 67 515
MEYAN		
Antonie F	Calaveras Twp 4	57 331
MEYAR		
Antoine F	Calaveras Twp 4	57 331
MEYASSON		
Lecon	San Francisco San Francisco	8 681277
Leecon	San Francisco San Francisco	8 681277
MEYCE		
L*	Sacramento Alabama	63 412
MEYDENBER		
William	San Francisco San Francisco	8 681245
MEYED		
Chas*	Butte Oregon	56 620
MEYEN		
----	Shasta Horsetown	66 711
Andrew	Calaveras Twp 4	57 312
MEYER		
Aaron	San Francisco San Francisco	2 67 769
Adam	San Francisco San Francisco	10 220 67
Adolphus	Alameda Oakland	55 25
Albert	San Francisco San Francisco	10 331 67
Alfred	San Francisco San Francisco	1 68 814
Andrew	Calaveras Twp 4	57 312
Andrew	San Francisco San Francisco	7 681411
Antoine	Sacramento American	63 167
Arnold W	Yuba Rose Bar	72 802
August	San Francisco San Francisco	3 67 41
Augustus	Tuolumne Big Oak	71 177
Barclay	Alameda Oakland	55 47
Bennet	Tuolumne Shawsfla	71 413
Bernard	Tuolumne Shawsfla	71 405
C	Yolo Putah	72 598
Caspar	San Francisco San Francisco	7 681335
Casper	San Francisco San Francisco	7 681335
Catharine	San Francisco San Francisco	8 681288
Charles	Yuba Rose Bar	72 800
Charles W	Yuba Rose Bar	72 802
Chas	San Francisco San Francisco	10 279 67
Chas	San Francisco San Francisco	6 67 433
Chas	San Francisco San Francisco	2 67 721
Chas	San Francisco San Francisco	1 68 889
Chas	San Francisco San Francisco	1 68 927
Chas	San Francisco San Francisco	9 68 977
Chris	Tuolumne Twp 2	71 390
Christ	Alameda Brooklyn	55 152
Christopher	San Francisco San Francisco	7 681376
	San Francisco	
Chs	San Francisco San Francisco	6 67 433
D	San Francisco San Francisco	1 68 903
David	San Francisco San Francisco	4 681170
E	Sacramento Ward 4	63 607

Name	County Locale	M653 RollPage
MEYER		
Emanuel	San Francisco San Francisco	3 67 8
F	Shasta Millvill	66 756
Francis	San Francisco San Francisco	7 681398
Frank	Alameda Oakland	55 70
Frank	Sierra Downieville	66 968
Fred	San Francisco San Francisco	9 681068
Frederick	San Francisco San Francisco	4 681137
Fredk	San Francisco San Francisco	9 681037
Fredk	Trinity Weaverville	701064
G H	Nevada Nevada	61 244
Geo	San Francisco San Francisco	2 67 711
George	Alameda Brooklyn	55 142
George	San Francisco San Francisco	4 681110
George	San Francisco San Francisco	7 681423
George	Siskiyou Yreka	69 156
George	Siskiyou Yreka	69 157
George	Tuolumne Twp 5	71 487
George H	Yuba Rose Bar	72 801
George W	San Francisco San Francisco	7 681423
Geroge	Tuolumne Chinese	71 487
H	San Francisco San Francisco	3 67 33
H	San Francisco San Francisco	5 67 485
Helen	San Francisco San Francisco	2 67 660
Henry	San Francisco San Francisco	3 67 12
Henry	San Francisco San Francisco	3 67 48
Henry	Santa Clara Santa Clara	65 497
Henry	Shasta Shasta	66 757
Henry	Tuolumne Twp 5	71 494
Henry	Yuba Fosters	72 832
Henry H	San Francisco San Francisco	7 681342
Herny	Tuolumne Chinese	71 494
Isaac	Los Angeles Los Nieto	59 430
J	Calaveras Twp 9	57 409
J	San Francisco San Francisco	1 68 923
Jacob	Klamath Liberty	59 236
Jacob	San Joaquin Stockton	641015
Jacob	San Joaquin Elkhorn	64 985
Jacob F	Alameda Brooklyn	55 195
James	San Francisco San Francisco	9 68 969
James	Yuba Rose Bar	72 788
Jane	San Francisco San Francisco	2 67 749
Jno	Butte Hamilton	56 527
Jno	Sacramento Ward 4	63 595
Joanna	San Francisco San Francisco	7 681376
Johan H	San Francisco San Francisco	11 102 67
John	Los Angeles Los Angeles	59 366
John	Los Angeles Los Angeles	59 36
John	San Francisco San Francisco	3 67 2
John	Tulara Twp 1	71 79
John A	San Joaquin Castoria	64 872
John Henry	Alameda Oakland	55 10
John*	San Francisco San Francisco	7 681432
Jos A	San Francisco San Francisco	2 67 790
Joseph	Calaveras Twp 5	57 180
Joseph	San Francisco San Francisco	2 67 708
Joseph*	Yuba Marysville	72 952
Kate	Alameda Brooklyn	55 162
L C	Sacramento Ward 4	63 495
Leonard	Tuolumne Shawsfla	71 386
Leopold	Sacramento Ward 4	63 555
Lewis	San Francisco San Francisco	6 67 400
Louis	Alameda Oakland	55 7
Louis	San Francisco San Francisco	9 681027
Louis	San Francisco San Francisco	6 67 461
Mark	Sierra Downieville	66 968
Mathew	Tuolumne Sonora	71 210
Mathias	Tuolumne Twp 1	71 210
Melchior	Siskiyou Yreka	69 183
Nathan	San Francisco San Francisco	2 67 620
O	San Francisco San Francisco	10 251 67
P	Sacramento Ward 4	63 607
Peter	Butte Kimshaw	56 584
Richard	San Joaquin Stockton	641047
Robert	San Francisco San Francisco	3 67 26
Rosalie	Alameda Oakland	55 12
S M	San Mateo Twp 1	65 65
Saml	Sacramento Brighton	63 193
Saml	San Francisco San Francisco	2 67 701
Saml	San Francisco San Francisco	1 68 930
Samuel	Los Angeles Los Angeles	59 327
T	El Dorado Georgetown	58 704
T H	San Francisco San Francisco	6 67 463
T Lemmen	San Francisco	6 67 452
T R	San Francisco	
T R	Yuba Foster B	72 828
T*	El Dorado Georgetown	58 704
W	El Dorado Placerville	58 918
W	Merced Twp 1	60 895
William	Alameda Oakland	55 43
William	San Francisco San Francisco	11 136 67
William	San Joaquin Castoria	64 902
William	Tulara Twp 3	71 57

California 1860 Census Index

Name	County Locale	M653 RollPage
MEYER		
Wm	Alameda Brooklyn	55 212
Wm	Sacramento Granite	63 243
Wm	San Francisco San Francisco 10	220 67
Wm	San Francisco San Francisco 6	67 414
Wm H	San Francisco San Francisco 3	67 67
Wm H	San Francisco San Francisco 2	67 730
MEYERCK		
Frederic	Alameda Oakland	55 25
MEYERFELDT		
Moses	San Francisco San Francisco 9	68 980
MEYERHOFER		
F V	San Francisco San Francisco 10	193 67
MEYERHOFFER		
Killion	Sacramento Ward 1	63 14
MEYERHOFFEV		
Killion*	Sacramento Ward 1	63 14
MEYERHOLTY		
Christ*	Alameda Brooklyn	55 127
MEYERHOLZ		
Wm H	Sacramento Ward 4	63 555
MEYERHOTTY		
Christ*	Alameda Brooklyn	55 127
MEYERS		
A	Sacramento Dry Crk	63 375
A	San Joaquin Stockton	641054
Aaron	San Francisco San Francisco 4	681221
Adolph	San Francisco San Francisco 9	68 972
Alfred	Plumas Quincy	62 988
Andrew	San Joaquin Castoria	64 873
C	San Francisco San Francisco 2	67 701
Cathrine	Plumas Quincy	62 925
Charles	San Joaquin Oneal	64 936
Chas	Trinity E Weaver	701058
Christian	Fresno Twp 2	59 19
D	Tuolumne Twp 4	71 128
Edw	Siskiyou Cottonwoood	69 98
F	Del Norte Crescent	58 645
F B	Merced Twp 2	60 924
Frank	San Francisco San Francisco 2	67 713
Frederick	Calaveras Twp 6	57 127
Frederick	Calaveras Twp 5	57 143
Hannse	Sacramento Ward 4	63 571
Hariford	San Joaquin Castoria	64 905
Heman	Calaveras Twp 5	57 215
Henry	Plumas Quincy	62 975
Henry	Sacramento Ward 1	63 14
Henry	Sacramento Alabama	63 411
Henry	San Joaquin O'Neal	641003
Henry	Siskiyou Klamath	69 86
J	Calaveras Twp 9	57 410
J	San Joaquin Stockton	641042
Jacob	Plumas Quincy	62 924
Jacob	San Francisco San Francisco 4	681220
Jacob	Shasta French G	66 722
Jacob	Yuba Marysville	72 847
Jacob K	San Joaquin Castoria	64 873
John	Calaveras Twp 4	57 329
John	Nevada Red Dog	61 540
John	San Francisco San Francisco 7	681432
John	San Joaquin Castoria	64 894
John	Sierra St Louis	66 812
John	Yuba Fosters	72 829
John	Yuba Suida	72 985
John*	San Francisco San Francisco 7	681432
Joseph	San Joaquin Elkhorn	64 963
Josiah	Butte Kimshaw	56 576
L	Sacramento Ward 4	63 508
Leon R	San Francisco San Francisco 5	67 499
Louisa	Plumas Meadow Valley	62 913
M	San Francisco San Francisco 5	67 485
M	San Francisco San Francisco 2	67 758
M J	El Dorado Georgetown	58 701
Mary	San Joaquin Castoria	64 873
Mary Am	San Francisco San Francisco 2	67 576
Mary Ann*	San Francisco 2	67 576
	San Francisco	
P	Sacramento Granite	63 234
Peter	Sacramento Brighton	63 202
Robt	El Dorado White Oaks	581031
Saml	Nevada Nevada	61 298
Samuel	San Joaquin Castoria	64 873
Saul	Nevada Nevada	61 298
Thos*	Sacramento San Joaquin	63 350
W F	Siskiyou Scott Ri	69 75
W G	Butte Oregon	56 644
W R	Butte Wyandotte	56 664
Walter	Plumas Quincy	62 998
William	San Joaquin Oneal	64 913
William	Tulara Keyesville	71 57
William	Yuba Bear Rvr	721000
Wm	Alameda Brooklyn	55 196
Wm	San Francisco San Francisco 2	67 784
MEYERSTEIN		
Henry	San Francisco San Francisco 7	681405

Name	County Locale	M653 RollPage
MEYERT		
Chas	Butte Oregon	56 620
MEYET		
Morris	Alameda Murray	55 218
MEYHAN		
Francis	San Francisco San Francisco 9	681100
MEYHARE		
Francis	San Francisco San Francisco 9	681100
MEYHER		
Daniel*	Sierra La Porte	66 765
Wm	San Francisco San Francisco 2	67 738
MEYHOOD		
John	San Joaquin Castoria	64 907
MEYLAR		
F	Sacramento Cosumnes	63 400
MEYLE		
Jacob	Yuba Marysville	72 958
MEYN		
---	San Francisco San Francisco 9	681088
MEYNWALL		
Jas	Tehama Antelope	70 888
MEYOR		
Antoine F	Calaveras Twp 4	57 331
MEYORS		
M	El Dorado Kelsey	581129
MEYROL		
Chas*	Butte Oregon	56 620
MEYRON		
W A*	Yuba Rose Bar	72 788
MEYSTERS		
John	Sacramento American	63 167
MEZDENBER		
William*	San Francisco San Francisco 8	681245
MEZENER		
S A	San Joaquin Stockton	641063
MEZES		
David	San Mateo Twp 3	65 92
MEZORA		
Antonio	Alameda Brooklyn	55 160
MEZOTE		
Antonio	Alameda Brooklyn	55 202
MEZZERAR		
Peter	San Francisco San Francisco 8	681292
MFARLAND		
Dennis*	Plumas Quincy	621002
Thos*	Napa Yount	61 55
MG GUS		
Angus*	Solano Benecia	69 302
MGDALENE		
---	Mariposa Twp 1	60 630
MGE		
Sam	Butte Cascade	56 700
MGEE		
Andrew*	Plumas Quincy	62 940
MGEHEE		
M*	Tuolumne Twp 4	71 130
MGILTON		
Thomas	Tuolumne Twp 2	71 318
MGLIM		
James*	Placer Iona Hills	62 864
MGLINE		
James*	Placer Iona Hills	62 864
MGOFF		
Alvin	Yuba Marysville	72 939
MH		
Meoi*	San Francisco San Francisco 4	681195
Moi*	San Francisco San Francisco 4	681195
MHERG		
C H*	Sacramento Ward 3	63 488
MHIEG		
C H*	Sacramento Ward 3	63 488
MHUG		
C H*	Sacramento Ward 3	63 488
MI MA CHICK KEE		
---*	San Francisco San Francisco 9	681062
MI		
---	Calaveras Twp 10	57 259
---	El Dorado Salmon Falls	581042
---	El Dorado Coloma	581110
---	Nevada Bridgeport	61 457
---	Sacramento Granite	63 259
---	Sierra Downieville	661026
---	Tuolumne Twp 3	71 436
Boke	Yuba Long Bar	72 756
Choi	San Francisco San Francisco 4	681190
Chung	Butte Cascade	56 692
Gee	El Dorado Mud Springs	58 971
Ho	Sacramento Granite	63 268
Kong	San Francisco San Francisco 4	681204
Oh	Sacramento Granite	63 259
Sam	Calaveras Twp 8	57 83
Teh*	Alameda Oakland	55 57
MIA		
---	Mariposa Twp 3	60 607
MIAAND		
Wm*	Calaveras Twp 9	57 354

Name	County Locale	M653 RollPage
MIABLA		
Hose M	Fresno Twp 1	59 81
MIABLE		
Hose M	Fresno Twp 1	59 81
MIADELDO		
Enid*	Mariposa Coulterville	60 703
MIADEW		
T J	Tuolumne Sonora	71 211
MIAH		
---	Placer Auburn	62 576
MIAHLEISON		
Mike	Tuolumne Twp 1	71 197
MIAM		
---	Sacramento Cosummes	63 406
MIAMS		
S H W	Tuolumne Twp 2	71 288
MIANG		
John	Placer Iona Hills	62 861
MIANS		
R	Sutter Sutter	70 817
W	Sutter Sutter	70 817
MIARS		
Calvin	Mendocino Big Rvr	60 848
Elijah	Sierra Twp 2	66 865
Henry	El Dorado Georgetown	58 761
MIATER		
John*	Mariposa Twp 1	60 666
MIBELLI		
L	San Francisco San Francisco 3	67 83
MIBHY		
J*	Placer Dutch Fl	62 714
MIBILLI		
L*	San Francisco San Francisco 3	67 83
MICAELA		
---	San Bernardino Santa Barbara	64 159
MICALA		
Orneta	Calaveras Twp 9	57 373
MICAUL		
Dedrick	Tuolumne Sonora	71 241
MICCSA		
---*	Tulara Visalia	71 39
MICE		
---	Tulara Twp 3	71 56
Abram*	Nevada Red Dog	61 542
Augustus	Amador Twp 5	55 335
F	Calaveras Twp 9	57 416
MICERAVER		
Henry*	Nevada Red Dog	61 541
MICH		
---	San Bernardino San Bernadino	64 667
George	El Dorado Georgetown	58 691
MICHAEL		
---	Calaveras Twp 7	57 2
---	Calaveras Twp 7	57 3
---	Mendocino Twp 1	60 892
---	Tulara Keyesville	71 55
Alfred	San Francisco San Francisco 4	681153
C E	San Francisco San Francisco 5	67 480
Casamer	Santa Cruz Santa Cruz	66 633
Caspar	San Francisco San Francisco 10	203 67
Charles	Fresno Twp 2	59 19
Cunningham	San Mateo Twp 3	65 107
Cunningham	Sierra Downieville	66 963
Davis	Alameda Murray	55 223
E D	Colusa Monroeville	57 443
Elias	Amador Twp 2	55 270
Franklin	San Francisco San Francisco 9	681080
Gensen*	San Francisco San Francisco 3	67 23
Henry*	Alameda Brooklyn	55 177
J	Sacramento Granite	63 238
J	San Francisco San Francisco 10	168 67
J	Yolo Washington	72 568
James C	San Francisco San Francisco 8	681289
Jno	Butte Kimshaw	56 592
John	Alameda Brooklyn	55 127
John	Calaveras Twp 7	57 22
Joseph	Calaveras Twp 6	57 125
Joseph	San Francisco San Francisco 4	681149
Julius	Sierra Downieville	66 987
Lines	Sierra La Porte	66 783
M	San Francisco San Francisco 4	681160
Roney	Sierra La Porte	66 783
S	Shasta French G	66 715
W B	Butte Kimshaw	56 592
MICHAELINI		
Santiago	San Francisco San Francisco 2	67 764
MICHAELS		
A F	Butte Kimshaw	56 590
B	San Francisco San Francisco 2	67 705
Christ	San Francisco San Francisco 2	67 652
F J	San Francisco San Francisco 5	67 495
George	Placer Yankee J	62 775
George	Placer Michigan	62 853
George	San Francisco San Francisco 2	67 576

Name	County Locale	M653 Roll	Page
MICHAELS			
George	Sonoma Washington	69	678
V	Sacramento Ward 1	63	18
MICHAELSON			
---	Mariposa Twp 3	60	606
Henry	Sierra Twp 7	66	914
MICHAGEE			
F	San Francisco San Francisco 2	67	627
MICHAH			
---	Tulara Twp 2	71	40
MICHAILINE			
Santiago	San Francisco San Francisco 2	67	764
MICHAL			
Grhald	Amador Twp 5	55	361
Nicholas	Sierra Downieville	66	972
P	San Francisco San Francisco 5	67	519
Thomas	Sierra Twp 7	66	877
MICHALIS			
Frederick*	San Francisco 7	681	390
	San Francisco		
MICHALL			
Henry*	Alameda Brooklyn	55	177
S	Tuolumne Twp 2	71	326
MICHAN			
Thos	San Mateo Twp 3	65	76
MICHAND			
Pierre	Sacramento Ward 3	63	442
MICHANS			
Hermann	San Francisco San Francisco 4	681	158
MICHEALEM			
A*	San Francisco San Francisco 3	67	33
MICHEL			
A W	Sutter Butte	70	792
A*	Nevada Grass Valley	61	201
Adolph	Yuba Rose Par	72	794
Carl	San Francisco San Francisco 7	681	384
Frigola	Sierra Twp 5	66	944
George	Nevada Bridgeport	61	467
Jagnes	Siskiyou Yreka	69	176
Jaques	Siskiyou Yreka	69	176
John	El Dorado Georgetown	58	755
John	Nevada Rough &	61	406
John*	Yuba Marysville	72	911
MICHELDOCK			
M	Yolo Washington	72	568
MICHELE			
John	Sacramento Ward 1	63	75
Robt	Sacramento Ward 3	63	447
Roland T	Sacramento Ward 3	63	484
MICHELHAN			
Daniel	San Francisco San Francisco 4	681	213
MICHELHANSEN			
Louis	San Francisco San Francisco 10		188
		67	
MICHELL			
C	El Dorado Diamond	58	816
Franklin	Sacramento Natonia	63	273
John	Shasta Cottonwood	66	736
Robt	Tehama Tehama	70	941
Schollastegih	San Francisco 6	67	426
	San Francisco		
Schollastegue*	San Francisco 6	67	426
	San Francisco		
Wm H	Solano Suisan	69	213
MICHELLER			
George*	Calaveras Twp 9	57	390
O	Calaveras Twp 9	57	401
MICHELLOR			
George	Calaveras Twp 9	57	390
MICHELLRENA			
Jesus*	Sacramento Ward 1	63	99
MICHELLRRENA			
Jesus*	Sacramento Ward 1	63	99
MICHELS			
Herman	San Francisco San Francisco 10		223
		67	
Michels	Siskiyou Yreka	69	184
MICHELSON			
E	San Francisco San Francisco 5	67	520
Leo	Santa Clara San Jose	65	340
M	San Francisco San Francisco 10		289
		67	
Martha	San Francisco San Francisco 7	681	414
Mathas*	San Francisco San Francisco 7	681	414
Nicholas H	Yuba Bear Rvr	721	001
MICHELTRAN			
Daniel*	San Francisco San Francisco 4	681	213
MICHENER			
W P	Sacramento Ward 1	63	84
MICHESHAFFER			
Geo	San Joaquin Stockton	641	043
MICHETHRENA			
Jesus*	Sacramento Ward 1	63	99
MICHHELITCH			
Juan	Plumas Meadow Valley	62	934
MICHIE			
Antone	Trinity East For	701	027

Name	County Locale	M653 Roll	Page
MICHIE			
P D	Sierra Twp 7	66	890
MICHIGAN			
---	Solano Benecia	69	315
C	San Francisco San Francisco 9	681	092
MICHIL			
John	Yuba Marysville	72	911
MICHILLANTS			
J*	San Francisco San Francisco 5	67	491
MICHILLER			
O	Calaveras Twp 9	57	401
MICHIR			
P D	Sierra Twp 7	66	890
MICHL			
Andrew	Tulara Twp 3	71	60
MICHLEN			
Frances	Sierra Port Win	66	795
MICHLER			
N	San Francisco San Francisco 5	67	478
W	San Francisco San Francisco 5	67	478
William	Calaveras Twp 7	57	17
MICHLIM			
J J*	Butte Kimshaw	56	603
MICHLIN			
J J*	Butte Kimshaw	56	603
MICHLINE			
J J*	Butte Kimshaw	56	603
MICHLING			
Micheal	El Dorado Coloma	581	080
MICHOLAS			
---	San Bernardino San Bernadino	64	682
John H	Placer Dutch Fl	62	723
Thos J	Placer Dutch Fl	62	714
MICHOLS			
William	San Francisco San Francisco 3	67	43
MICHON			
Adolph	Tuolumne Sonora	71	214
MICHOU			
Adolph	Tuolumne Twp 1	71	214
MICHRABES			
Fred	Sacramento Sutter	63	300
MICI			
Abram*	Nevada Red Dog	61	542
MICIO			
Antonio*	El Dorado Casumnes	581	176
MICK			
---	Yuba Slate Ro	72	708
---*	Tulara Visalia	71	37
Andrew	Contra Costa Twp 1	57	536
Anton	Sacramento Ward 3	63	444
John	Yolo Slate Ra	72	688
N G	Sierra Twp 7	66	874
MICKALE			
Joseph	Calaveras Twp 8	57	58
MICKEL			
---	Fresno Twp 3	59	97
Daniel	Sierra Pine Grove	66	834
Fugola	Sierra Twp 5	66	944
J A	Sutter Sutter	70	812
M	El Dorado Newtown	58	777
MICKELER			
Peter S	Yuba Marysville	72	977
MICKELNATE			
R	Siskiyou Cottonwoood	69	101
MICKELS			
Warren	San Francisco San Francisco 2	67	694
MICKEN			
Jacob	San Bernardino San Bernadino	64	627
Patrick	San Bernardino San Bernadino	64	670
MICKER			
Catherine	San Francisco San Francisco 3	67	6
MICKERSEN			
Fred	Shasta Shasta	66	663
MICKERSON			
Chas	San Francisco San Francisco 9	681	061
Ensign A	San Bernardino San Bernadino	64	622
Fred	Shasta Shasta	66	663
Samuel	Calaveras Twp 9	57	383
William	Santa Cruz Santa Cruz	66	619
MICKEY			
James	Placer Michigan	62	851
MICKIMENSENI			
Lewis	San Francisco San Francisco 2	67	748
MICKLE			
Peter	San Joaquin Elkhorn	64	964
William	Marin Cortemad	60	779
Wm	Sierra Downieville	661	011
MICKLERESON			
John	San Joaquin Elkhorn	64	969
MICKLESON			
Jno*	Alameda Brooklyn	55	146
MICKLEY			
John	Tuolumne Big Oak	71	133
MICKLING			
Michael	El Dorado Coloma	581	080
MICKLINS			
John	Del Norte Happy Ca	58	667

Name	County Locale	M653 Roll	Page
MICKOTOP			
---	Fresno Twp 2	59	60
MICO			
---	Tulara Keyesville	71	64
MICOLINE			
Antone	Sierra Twp 7	66	897
Antonio	Sierra Twp 7	66	897
MICOUL			
Didrick	Tuolumne Twp 1	71	241
MICOVICH			
Christopher	San Francisco 3	67	39
	San Francisco		
MICTHELL			
John H	Placer Stewart	62	606
MICUT			
William*	San Francisco San Francisco 9	68	993
MICY			
---*	Butte Ophir	56	814
MIDALGO			
Eugenio	Los Angeles Los Angeles	59	300
MIDAND			
Wm*	Calaveras Twp 9	57	354
MIDANDO			
Aele*	Sacramento Ward 1	63	13
MIDAUDO			
Adele*	Sacramento Ward 1	63	13
MIDAY			
Jacob	Sierra Cox'S Bar	66	950
MIDBERRY			
Thomas	Tuolumne Twp 3	71	429
MIDDATER			
John*	Mariposa Twp 3	60	611
MIDDERHILL			
Virginia	El Dorado Placerville	58	909
MIDDERTIN			
John*	Mariposa Twp 3	60	611
MIDDERTON			
John*	Mariposa Twp 3	60	611
MIDDICK			
Hella M*	Placer Auburn	62	569
MIDDIX			
George H	Sierra Pine Grove	66	826
MIDDLE			
John	Sierra La Porte	66	775
Wm	Sierra Twp 7	66	869
MIDDLECOM			
Hiram	Yuba New York	72	721
MIDDLEHOFF			
Gerrard*	San Francisco San Francisco 7	681	362
MIDDLEMISO			
James*	Colusa Grand Island	57	468
MIDDLEMIST			
A	Yolo Slate Ra	72	698
MIDDLEMOST			
A	Yuba Slate Ro	72	698
MIDDLESWORTH			
D	Tuolumne Twp 1	71	211
J R	Tuolumne Twp 1	71	234
M	Tuolumne Sonora	71	234
MIDDLETON			
A H	Nevada Bridgeport	61	454
Amelia	Sonoma Healdsbu	69	476
Amos	San Joaquin Elkhorn	64	989
Arch	Tuolumne Chinese	71	492
Eleanor	Yuba Marysville	72	860
Eleanor	Yuba Marysville	72	860
Frank	Plumas Meadow Valley	62	899
Frank	San Francisco San Francisco 1	68	830
G A	Tuolumne Twp 1	71	230
George	Plumas Quincy	62	941
J C	Tuolumne Twp 4	71	144
J T	El Dorado Placerville	58	885
James	Trinity Lewiston	70	957
James A	San Joaquin Stockton	641	021
Jessee	Butte Chico	56	564
Jno	San Francisco San Francisco 9	681	068
John	Amador Twp 3	55	369
John	Calaveras Twp 6	57	160
John	San Francisco San Francisco 4	681	141
John	San Francisco San Francisco 1	68	896
John	Yuba Rose Bar	72	815
Jos H	Tuolumne Twp 4	71	126
R G	Yolo Cache	72	635
Richd	Tuolumne Twp 1	71	192
Richl	Tuolumne Sonora	71	192
Saml	Trinity Rearings	70	990
Thos	Amador Twp 2	55	295
Thos	Amador Twp 6	55	434
Thos	Trinity Hay Fork	70	994
W O	Butte Ophir	56	762
William	Siskiyou Yreka	69	154
William	Solano Vallejo	69	244
Wm	Sonoma Vallejo	69	614
Wm H	Sonoma Healdsbu	69	476
Z	Sonoma Santa Rosa	69	394
MIDDLSTON			
Jessee*	Butte Chico	56	564

California 1860 Census Index

Name	County Locale	M653 Roll	Page
MIDDLTON			
Joseph	El Dorado Placerville	58	924
MIDDOHOFF			
Geneva*	San Francisco San Francisco	7	681361
MIDEL			
Antoine F	Calaveras Twp 5	57	240
MIDELLE			
John	Sierra La Porte	66	775
MIDEN			
Enoch M	Los Angeles Los Angeles	59	321
MIDENCOURT			
J M	Yolo Washington	72	572
MIDENHAMER			
Alex*	Sacramento Ward 1	63	91
MIDER			
John*	El Dorado White Oaks	58	1027
MIDERHILL			
Geo L*	El Dorado Placerville	58	909
MIDERSILLE			
B*	Calaveras Twp 8	57	51
MIDERVA			
Jacob*	Sierra Cox'S Bar	66	951
MIDGE			
Theodore	San Francisco San Francisco	8	681286
MIDGETT			
B	Napa Napa	61	70
MIDHELLAND			
Henry	Sierra Twp 7	66	908
MIDHOLLAND			
Frank J*	Yuba Marysville	72	906
MIDICROFT			
Mary A	Santa Clara San Jose	65	384
MIDIMAN			
Frederick E*	Yuba Marysville	72	937
MIDINGTON			
James	Calaveras Twp 6	57	116
MIDLEMISS			
Joseph	Humbolt Eureka	59	173
MIDLETON			
Arch	Tuolumne Twp 5	71	492
John M	Humbolt Bucksport	59	155
MIDLEWROTH			
Andrew Van*	Sierra St Louis	66	814
MIDLEY			
A J	Sonoma Petaluma	69	578
J	Santa Clara Santa Clara	65	490
MIDLIN			
Middleton	San Joaquin Elkhorn	64	993
MIDMOST			
Tho	Siskiyou Cottonwoood	69	100
MIDZSTER			
Joseph	San Francisco San Francisco 2	67	747
MIE			
---	Tuolumne Jacksonville	71	168
August	Alameda Brooklyn	55	197
MIEBER			
Joseph F	San Francisco San Francisco	7	681329
MIEBES			
Joseph F*	San Francisco San Francisco	7	681329
	San Francisco		
MIEBIS			
Joseph F*	San Francisco San Francisco	7	681329
	San Francisco		
MIEBSON			
Henry*	Mariposa Coulterville	60	684
MIEBSOR			
Henry	Mariposa Coulterville	60	684
MIEH			
George	El Dorado Georgetown	58	691
MIEK			
Christophr	Placer Iona Hills	62	861
MIEL			
Juan	Calaveras Twp 9	57	351
MIELER			
John*	El Dorado White Oaks	58	1027
MIELIKEN			
Frances M	Calaveras Twp 6	57	122
MIELL			
Emerson E	Yuba Marysville	72	891
MIELLER			
E	Siskiyou Yreka	69	187
MIEN			
Henry*	San Francisco San Francisco 11		101 67
Peter	San Francisco San Francisco 11		100 67
Richard	Tuolumne Shawsfla	71	410
MIENECKE			
Chas	San Francisco San Francisco 2	67	591
MIENECKIE			
Edward*	Calaveras Twp 9	57	354
MIENECKIR			
Edward*	Calaveras Twp 9	57	354
MIENECKIS			
Edward*	Calaveras Twp 9	57	354
MIENO			
Antonino*	Sierra Downieville	66	972

Name	County Locale	M653 Roll	Page
MIER			
Adam*	Butte Oregon	56	629
Daniel	San Francisco San Francisco	7	681364
Henry	San Francisco San Francisco 11		139 67
J T	Sacramento Ward 1	63	10
Jacob	Tuolumne Twp 1	71	194
Jno	Sacramento Ward 3	63	445
Peter*	San Francisco San Francisco 11		100 67
MIERDERKS			
C	San Francisco San Francisco	8	681274
MIERDIFRAID			
P	Tuolumne Twp 3	71	465
MIERS			
J M	Shasta Millvill	66	756
Jas	Sacramento Granite	63	251
Jno	Sacramento Ward 1	63	150
P	Sierra Downieville	66	964
MIESEGAES			
Alfred	Tuolumne Big Oak	71	129
H	Tuolumne Twp 4	71	151
MIESEGEUS			
H	Tuolumne Big Oak	71	151
MIEW			
W M	Marin Bolinas	60	746
W W*	Marin Bolinas	60	746
MIFENCHER			
Fred*	Alameda Brooklyn	55	148
MIFFALL			
James H*	Mendocino Calpella	60	829
MIFNER			
Fletcher	San Joaquin Elkhorn	64	958
MIFS			
Ko*	Sacramento Ward 1	63	52
MIG			
F	Del Norte Happy Ca	58	669
MIGAEE			
Antonio	Santa Cruz Soguel	66	583
MIGAEL			
Antonio	Santa Cruz Soguel	66	583
MIGAN			
Kate	San Joaquin Stockton	64	1016
Mary*	Sacramento Ward 1	63	121
MIGANT			
John	San Bernardino San Bernadino	64	626
MIGART			
Wm H*	Solano Vallejo	69	252
MIGE			
---	El Dorado Mud Springs	58	970
MIGEN			
Fernon*	Sierra Downieville	66	965
MIGENT			
John*	San Francisco San Francisco 2	67	713
Richard	Santa Cruz Santa Cruz	66	612
T C	El Dorado Placerville	58	854
Wm H	Solano Vallejo	69	252
MIGER			
John	El Dorado Greenwood	58	716
T*	El Dorado Georgetown	58	704
MIGET			
---	El Dorado Placerville	58	836
MIGETTE			
B	San Francisco San Francisco 4		681170
MIGGAL			
Jacob	Calaveras Twp 7	57	48
MIGGINS			
Charles	Calaveras Twp 7	57	1
George W	Calaveras Twp 7	57	1
John*	San Francisco San Francisco 1	68	880
MIGGUERA			
Pea	Los Angeles Los Angeles	59	360
MIGHELL			
Richard	Los Angeles Los Angeles	59	334
William H	San Francisco San Francisco	8	681282
MIGHEROL			
Miguel	Los Angeles Los Angeles	59	293
MIGHES			
Daniel	Sierra La Porte	66	765
MIGHT			
A	Calaveras Twp 9	57	407
Jennet B	Santa Clara San Jose	65	313
Jerry	Solano Vallejo	69	255
Joseph	Calaveras Twp 6	57	142
MIGHTON			
Ezra	Solano Vallejo	69	244
Geo	San Francisco San Francisco	9	681031
MIGIEN			
John	San Francisco San Francisco	7	681327
MIGILLO			
Juan M	Los Angeles Los Nieto	59	429
Poloma	Los Angeles Los Angeles	59	360
MIGIN			
James	Nevada Bridgeport	61	454
MIGLER			
John	Shasta Millvill	66	739

Name	County Locale	M653 Roll	Page
MIGLIAVACA			
Jack	Mariposa Twp 1	60	630
MIGNDERBER			
Mary*	San Francisco San Francisco	8	681246
MIGONO			
Pedro	Alameda Oakland	55	14
MIGOR			
Gregory	Los Angeles Los Angeles	59	510
Joquin	Los Angeles Los Angeles	59	510
MIGRAM			
Samuel*	Yuba Linda	72	989
MIGUEL			
---	Fresno Twp 1	59	54
---	Los Angeles Los Angeles	59	383
---	Monterey San Juan	60	1000
---	Monterey San Juan	60	1005
---	Monterey San Juan	60	1010
---	Monterey Alisal	60	1026
---	Monterey Monterey	60	929
---	San Bernardino Santa Inez	64	143
---	San Bernardino S Timate	64	693
---	San Bernardino S Timate	64	697
---	San Bernardino S Timate	64	698
---	San Bernardino S Timate	64	699
---	San Bernardino S Timate	64	701
---	San Bernardino S Timate	64	703
---	San Bernardino S Timate	64	708
---	San Bernardino S Timate	64	710
---	San Bernardino S Timate	64	732
---	San Bernardino S Timate	64	734
---	San Bernardino S Timate	64	736
---	San Bernardino S Timate	64	748
---	San Bernardino S Timate	64	749
---	San Bernardino S Timate	64	750
---	San Bernardino S Timate	64	755
---	San Bernardino S Timate	64	756
---	San Diego San Diego	64	773
---	San Diego San Diego	64	774
---	San Diego Agua Caliente	64	864
Antonio	Santa Cruz Soguel	66	583
Hise	Alameda Brooklyn	55	106
Hose	Alameda Brooklyn	55	106
Hosea	Alameda Brooklyn	55	207
Jose	Marin Cortemad	60	789
Jose	San Bernardino S Timate	64	691
Jose	San Diego Agua Caliente	64	818
Jose	San Diego Agua Caliente	64	819
Juan	Los Angeles Tejon To	59	535
Juan	Santa Cruz Pajaro	66	576
Peter	Alameda Oakland	55	42
MIGUELA			
Maria	Los Angeles Santa Ana	59	451
MIGUELITA			
---	San Bernardino S Timate	64	695
MIGUELITO			
---	San Bernardino S Timate	64	701
MIGUELLA			
---	San Bernardino San Bernadino	64	678
---	San Bernardino San Bernadino	64	682
MIGUERA			
Domingo	Los Angeles San Gabriel	59	416
Doroteo	Los Angeles San Pedro	59	479
Jose J	Los Angeles San Gabriel	59	416
MIGUERALA			
Teresa	Los Angeles Los Angeles	59	323
MIGUIL			
---	San Bernardino Santa Inez	64	138
---	San Bernardino S Buenav	64	222
MIGUS			
Stephen*	San Francisco San Francisco 1	68	862
MIHE			
Eugene	San Francisco San Francisco 2	67	801
Henry	Yuba Marysville	72	865
MIHEIN			
Eugene	Calaveras Twp 5	57	198
MIHEN			
James	Sierra St Louis	66	810
MIHESTON			
Wm H	San Francisco San Francisco	9	681083
MIHLIS			
Michael	Santa Clara San Jose	65	289
MIHOR			
A	Los Angeles Tejon	59	526
MIHOTENS			
Anna*	San Francisco San Francisco 10		331 67
MIIRCANS			
George*	Yuba Marysville	72	863
MIJADO			
Aldagracia*	Napa Napa	61	114
Aldajracia	Napa Napa	61	114
MIJAH			
Herronia	Los Angeles Elmonte	59	255
MIJELLO			
Refugio	Los Angeles Los Angeles	59	300
MIJILLO			
Maria G	Los Angeles San Gabriel	59	416

Name	County Locale	M653 Roll	Page
MIJOE			
---	Tulara Twp 2	71	36
MIK			
---	Calaveras Twp 5	57	233
MIKE			
---	Butte Bidwell	56	710
---	El Dorado Salmon Hills	58	1053
---	El Dorado Coloma	58	1110
---	El Dorado Mud Springs	58	984
---	Mendocino Round Va	60	880
---	Trinity Bates	70	967
---	Yolo No E Twp	72	680
---	Yuba North Ea	72	680
Ah	Butte Bidwell	56	710
Antonio	Butte Oro	56	678
Edorah	Placer Auburn	62	574
George	Nevada Rough &	61	424
I	Calaveras Twp 9	57	389
Indian*	Sacramento Centre	63	181
J	Calaveras Twp 9	57	398
John	San Mateo Twp 3	65	109
Joseph	Contra Costa Twp 1	57	520
Lee	Butte Bidwell	56	714
Peter	El Dorado Coloma	58	1122
MIKEN			
Jacob	San Bernardino San Bernadino	64	627
MIKENS			
Richard	Placer Secret R	62	613
MIKESELL			
J C	Yolo Slate Ra	72	710
N C	Yuba Slate Ro	72	710
MIKKELSAN			
R	San Francisco San Francisco 5	67	515
MIKKLETON			
John	San Francisco San Francisco 4	68	1141
MIKLESON			
Jacob	Alameda Oakland	55	17
MILAGAN			
John B	Napa Napa	61	97
MILAIN			
John*	Calaveras Twp 5	57	205
MILAJAN			
John B*	Napa Napa	61	97
MILAKIN			
A S	Napa Napa	61	58
H L*	Napa Napa	61	58
MILAN			
A B	Nevada Grass Valley	61	182
J	Nevada Grass Valley	61	196
Jesus	Tuolumne Twp 2	71	284
John	Calaveras Twp 5	57	205
Mary	Nevada Little Y	61	537
R	Nevada Grass Valley	61	164
Thomas	Los Angeles Azuza	59	272
MILBER			
A H	Sutter Butte	70	798
MILBOARN			
Robert*	Yuba Suida	72	992
MILBONE			
C E	Nevada Nevada	61	287
MILBORNE			
Jonah	Sacramento Ward 1	63	100
Sarah	Sacramento Ward 1	63	100
MILBOURN			
B P	Butte Oro	56	686
Joseph*	Nevada Bridgeport	61	474
MILBURG			
M	El Dorado Diamond	58	770
MILBURN			
Albert	San Francisco San Francisco 7	68	1437
Henry	Yuba Rose Bar	72	788
John	Mariposa Twp 3	60	572
Thomas	Santa Cruz Pescadero	66	651
MILBURY			
Samuel	Alameda Brooklyn	55	92
MILCARES			
---	San Bernardino Santa Ba	64	219
MILCHA			
---	Mendocino Twp 1	60	892
MILCHAUST			
William*	San Francisco San Francisco 8	68	1282
MILCHER			
F G*	Los Angeles Los Angeles	59	491
MILCO			
John	San Joaquin Stockton	64	1043
N	San Joaquin Stockton	64	1043
MILD			
Henry	Calaveras Twp 6	57	127
MILDEN			
Theresa	Sierra Port Win	66	796
MILDES			
Jonathan	Siskiyou Yreka	69	181
MILDWATER			
George	Marin Saucileto	60	751
Mary	Marin San Rafael	60	757
MILE			
T	Sutter Vernon	70	843

Name	County Locale	M653 Roll	Page
MILEGAN			
George	Siskiyou Yreka	69	143
MILEHAUST			
William	San Francisco San Francisco 8	68	1282
MILEM			
Mary*	Nevada Red Dog	61	537
MILEN			
Matthias	Sierra Downieville	66	953
MILER			
Albert	Tuolumne Twp 1	71	215
Aug	Stanislaus Buena Village	70	723
Charly	Yuba Marysville	72	958
Hirram	Napa Yount	61	45
James T	Tuolumne Twp 2	71	413
S	El Dorado Placerville	58	864
MILERN			
Mary*	Nevada Little Y	61	537
MILERS			
Henry	Calaveras Twp 7	57	40
MILES			
A	Placer Virginia	62	683
A C*	Nevada Nevada	61	329
Albert	Tuolumne Sonora	71	215
Alfred	Placer Goods	62	697
Anderson	Butte Bidwell	56	716
Andrew	Sonoma Mendocino	69	463
Burk	Sonoma Mendocino	69	463
Catherine	Sonoma Mendocino	69	463
Chas S	Trinity Weaverville	70	1052
Cornitus	Yolo Washington	72	570
E F	El Dorado Mud Springs	58	997
Elbridge	Placer Goods	62	697
G C	El Dorado Kelsey	58	1154
Geo	El Dorado White Oaks	58	1001
George	Nevada Little Y	61	535
H A	San Francisco San Francisco 5	67	545
Henry	Placer Iona Hills	62	876
Henry	San Francisco San Francisco 2	67	716
Henry W	Tulara Twp 1	71	101
Hugh	San Francisco San Francisco 8	68	1288
I*	San Francisco San Francisco 1	68	921
J	Siskiyou Klamath	69	79
J A	El Dorado White Oaks	58	1011
J W	Sierra Downieville	66	1001
James	San Francisco San Francisco 6	67	414
James	Solano Montezuma	69	368
James E	Tuolumne Sonora	71	196
James L	Solano Montezuma	69	368
Jane	Sonoma Mendocino	69	463
Jane*	Nevada Grass Valley	61	236
John	San Francisco San Francisco 6	67	460
John	Sonoma Mendocino	69	463
Joseph	Del Norte Happy Ca	58	669
L	Siskiyou Klamath	69	79
M	Calaveras Twp 9	57	409
Martin	Santa Clara San Jose	65	281
Mary S	Placer Goods	62	697
Milton	El Dorado Spanish	58	1125
Morgan	Santa Clara San Jose	65	331
Patrick	Placer Michigan	62	841
Patrick	Santa Clara Santa Clara	65	502
R	El Dorado Newtown	58	776
Ridney	Tehama Tehama	70	937
S M	Sierra Twp 7	66	882
S W	Sierra Twp 7	66	882
Thomas	Calaveras Twp 8	57	94
Thos	San Francisco San Francisco 1	68	866
W	El Dorado Kelsey	58	1149
W J	El Dorado Diamond	58	767
W J	San Francisco San Francisco 6	67	468
Walter	El Dorado Mud Springs	58	953
Wm	Sacramento Natonia	63	280
Wm	San Francisco San Francisco 2	67	740
Wm	Tehama Moons	70	852
Wm H	Colusa Grand Island	57	481
MILEY			
Andrew	Yuba Bear Rvr	72	1014
Martin	Siskiyou Scott Va	69	51
MILGATE			
Thos	Sacramento American	63	163
Wm	Sacramento Natonia	63	276
MILHBERG			
Gustar	San Francisco San Francisco 2	67	676
MILHOLAND			
Patrick	Calaveras Twp 4	57	314
MILHOLLAND			
James	Alameda Oakland	55	50
MILHOLUND			
John	Calaveras Twp 4	57	314
Patrick	Calaveras Twp 4	57	314
MILIANA			
---	Monterey San Juan	60	1010
MILICAN			
M	Siskiyou Scott Ri	69	75
MILICENT			
John H	Calaveras Twp 6	57	156

Name	County Locale	M653 Roll	Page
MILICON			
J	Amador Twp 3	55	393
MILIEN			
John	Calaveras Twp 5	57	205
MILIGAN			
Frank	Mariposa Coulterville	60	702
Henry	Sonoma Petaluma	69	579
MILINA			
Joqunida*	Calaveras Twp 4	57	331
MILINDUZ			
Juan	Monterey Monterey	60	954
MILINER			
Alfred	Nevada Rough &	61	405
MILIOR			
A*	Los Angeles Tejon	59	526
MILISICH			
Antonia*	Trinity Weaverville	70	1063
MILITON			
---	Monterey Monterey	60	954
---	Monterey Monterey	60	957
MILKEN			
S W	Placer Dutch Fl	62	719
MILKEY			
Wm	Sierra Twp 7	66	896
MILKINS			
Charles*	El Dorado Placerville	58	914
MILKLE			
Jared	Placer Forest H	62	773
MILKS			
E	Placer Michigan	62	842
MILL			
E W	Nevada Bridgeport	61	444
Ferdinand	Butte Ophir	56	779
J	Yolo Cottonwoood	72	555
Peter	El Dorado Coloma	58	1120
Quartz	Siskiyou Yreka	69	146
Questz	Siskiyou Yreka	69	146
Sill	Butte Bidwell	56	708
William	Placer Iona Hills	62	882
William	San Francisco San Francisco 8	68	1237
MILLA			
James	Sierra Downieville	66	976
MILLALY			
Joseph	San Bernardino San Bernadino	64	635
MILLAN			
Braman	Sierra Twp 7	66	875
D H	Yuba Long Bar	72	753
John	San Joaquin Stockton	64	1021
Simon	Los Angeles Azuza	59	272
MILLAR			
Caspar	San Francisco San Francisco 11	67	98
Richard M	Stanislaus Oatvale	70	718
Samuel	San Francisco San Francisco 11	67	136
MILLARD			
Alfred	Santa Clara Redwood	65	446
G	Tuolumne Columbia	71	328
G R	Butte Kimshaw	56	605
Henry	Los Angeles San Gabriel	59	408
Huldah	Sacramento Dry Crk	63	369
John	Santa Cruz Pescadero	66	645
Jsa	Contra Costa Twp 2	57	548
Levi	Santa Clara Redwood	65	448
Lewis	Tuolumne Twp 1	71	220
N	San Joaquin Stockton	64	1097
N	Amador Twp 7	55	419
R	El Dorado Casumnes	58	1174
R	El Dorado Newtown	58	778
W	Amador Twp 7	55	419
W M	Tehama Tehama	70	947
William	San Mateo Twp 3	65	77
MILLBIER			
Frank	Sierra Downieville	66	994
MILLBUR			
Frank	Sierra Downieville	66	994
MILLCOXOW			
C E	Sutter Yuba	70	772
MILLEGAN			
Alfred*	Calaveras Twp 6	57	148
MILLEL			
Antoine F*	Calaveras Twp 5	57	240
MILLEN			
---*	Placer Dutch Fl	62	730
Amelia	Nevada Bridgeport	61	465
Francis	San Joaquin O'Neal	64	1001
Fred	Placer Todds Va	62	763
George	Placer Iona Hills	62	889
George*	Placer Todds Va	62	763
James	Sierra Twp 7	66	877
John	Sacramento Granite	63	260
L	Shasta Millvill	66	725
M F	Sierra Gibsonville	66	852
P A	Butte Kimshaw	56	595
Peter	Mariposa Twp 3	60	621
Richard M	Sierra La Porte	66	783

California 1860 Census Index

Name	County Locale	M653 Roll Page
MILLEN		
W*	San Francisco San Francisco 5	67 524
W S*	Nevada Red Dog	61 544
MILLENDEN		
H P*	San Francisco San Francisco 1	68 905
MILLENS		
Frank	Sacramento Ward 1	63 14
James	Santa Cruz Pescadero	66 650
MILLEOW		
Joel*	Napa Napa	61 73
MILLER PHILIP		
Scott	Shasta Shasta	66 653
MILLER		
---	Amador Twp 3	55 374
---	Placer Ophirville	62 659
---	San Francisco San Francisco 7	681408
---	San Francisco San Francisco 7	681419
---	Siskiyou Scott Va	69 40
---*	Placer Dutch Fl	62 730
A	Butte Cascade	56 690
A	Butte Ophir	56 824
A	El Dorado Diamond	58 807
A	Nevada Eureka	61 359
A	Placer Dutch Fl	62 728
A	San Francisco San Francisco 4	681222
A	San Francisco San Francisco 5	67 542
A	San Francisco San Francisco 5	67 552
A	Santa Clara San Jose	65 353
A	Shasta Millvill	66 739
A	Trinity Weaverville	701075
A G	Sierra Twp 5	66 929
A H	Sierra Twp 7	66 891
A J	Merced Twp 2	60 918
A M	Mariposa Twp 3	60 595
A M	Tuolumne Twp 1	71 241
A O	Del Norte Crescent	58 671
A S	Colusa Muion	57 458
A W	Tuolumne Twp 4	71 161
Ad	Nevada Red Dog	61 548
Adam	Alameda Brooklyn	55 210
Adam	El Dorado Coloma	581111
Adam	Shasta Horsetown	66 693
Adolph	Alameda Oakland	55 13
Adolph	Tuolumne Twp 2	71 283
Albert	Mendocino Big Rvr	60 852
Albert	San Francisco San Francisco 6	67 406
Albert	Yuba New York	72 737
Alenn	Placer Iona Hills	62 870
Alex	El Dorado Gold Hill	581097
Alex	El Dorado Casumnes	581174
Alex	San Francisco San Francisco 10	67 326
Alex	Siskiyou Scott Va	69 54
Alex C	Calaveras Twp 5	57 210
Alexander	Calaveras Twp 4	57 364
Alexander	Colusa Spring Valley	57 429
Alfred	Placer Forest H	62 797
Allen	Mendocino Little L	60 835
Allen C	Calaveras Twp 9	57 210
Alonas*	Calaveras Twp 9	57 367
Alonso	Calaveras Twp 9	57 367
Alonzo*	Calaveras Twp 9	57 367
Amelia	Sacramento Ward 4	63 570
And Graf	Sacramento Ward 4	63 507
Andrew	Alameda Brooklyn	55 153
Andrew	Plumas Meadow Valley	62 931
Ann	El Dorado Mud Springs	58 959
Ann	San Francisco San Francisco 3	67 14
Anna	Yuba Marysville	72 936
Anton	Sacramento Ward 3	63 444
Antone	Placer Michigan	62 851
Antoney	Yuba Timbucto	72 787
Antoni	Butte Cascade	56 694
Antonie	Butte Cascade	56 694
Antony	Yuba Timbucto	72 787
Aoliver	Solano Vacaville	69 362
Archibald	Tuolumne Twp 1	71 187
August	Sacramento Ward 1	63 46
August	San Francisco San Francisco 9	681100
Augustas	Calaveras Twp 5	57 203
Augustus	Calaveras Twp 5	57 203
Augustus	Napa Napa	61 98
Augustus	Placer Michigan	62 820
Augustus W	Calaveras Twp 4	57 322
Avis	Napa Napa	61 100
B	Amador Twp 4	55 242
B	San Mateo Twp 3	65 110
B S	Mariposa Twp 3	60 592
Barbary	Tuolumne Twp 2	71 319
Barther	Santa Cruz Santa Cruz	66 628
Benj	Marin Bolinas	60 740
Benj	San Francisco San Francisco 2	67 627
Benj	Siskiyou Scott Va	69 52
Benjamin	Yuba Bear Rvr	72 996
Bennet	San Francisco San Francisco 7	681380

Name	County Locale	M653 Roll Page
MILLER		
C	El Dorado Placerville	58 822
C	Mariposa Coulterville	60 694
C	Nevada Nevada	61 247
C	Nevada Nevada	61 276
C	Sacramento Ward 3	63 456
C	Shasta Millvill	66 739
C	Siskiyou Klamath	69 94
C	Trinity Minersville	70 969
C	Yolo Cache	72 627
C A	Mariposa Twp 1	60 624
C C	Tehama Moons	70 851
C D	Butte Oro	56 677
C D	Tehama Lassen	70 865
C F	Santa Clara San Jose	65 375
C H	Siskiyou Scott Ri	69 63
C H	Sonoma Armally	69 482
C M	El Dorado Union	581089
C S	Marin Tomales	60 776
C W	Butte Wyandotte	56 665
C W	Tehama Lassen	70 867
Catharie	Sonoma Armally	69 516
Catharine	Sierra La Porte	66 783
Catharine	Tuolumne Twp 2	71 340
Catherine	Sonoma Mendocino	69 466
Ce	Nevada Grass Valley	61 175
Cefhis	Santa Cruz Santa Cruz	66 618
Celia	Sonoma Mendocino	69 467
Cephis	Santa Cruz Santa Cruz	66 618
Ceplies*	Santa Cruz Santa Cruz	66 618
Chancy	Placer Todds Va	62 783
Charels	Sierra Downieville	661010
Charles	Humbolt Eel Rvr	59 144
Charles	Los Angeles San Pedro	59 482
Charles	Placer Michigan	62 810
Charles	Plumas Quincy	62 916
Charles	Plumas Quincy	62 940
Charles	San Francisco San Francisco 9	681103
Charles	San Francisco San Francisco 11	67 149
Charles	San Joaquin Stockton	641063
Charles	San Mateo Twp 3	65 76
Charles	Sierra Downieville	661010
Charles	Sierra Excelsior	661033
Charles	Sierra Twp 7	66 869
Charles	Sierra Downieville	66 963
Charles	Siskiyou Yreka	69 148
Charles	Tuolumne Twp 2	71 280
Charles	Tuolumne Twp 3	71 442
Charles	Tuolumne Twp 5	71 509
Charles	Yolo No E Twp	72 672
Charles	Yuba North Ea	72 672
Charles	Yuba Fosters	72 823
Charles B	San Francisco San Francisco 7	681357
Charles C	Tuolumne Chinese	71 501
Charles F	Santa Cruz Pajaro	66 573
Charles S	Solano Vacaville	69 356
Charles*	Tuolumne Twp 5	71 501
Charley	Yuba Marysville	72 958
Charly	Tuolumne Twp 2	71 280
Chas	Butte Ophir	56 794
Chas	Mariposa Twp 3	60 593
Chas	Nevada Nevada	61 239
Chas	Nevada Eureka	61 370
Chas	Placer Rattle Snake	62 635
Chas	Placer Virginia	62 668
Chas	Placer Virginia	62 675
Chas	Sacramento Mississipi	63 188
Chas	Sacramento Ward 3	63 421
Chas	Sacramento Ward 1	63 79
Chas	San Francisco San Francisco 10	67 305
Chas	San Francisco San Francisco 2	67 755
Chas	San Francisco San Francisco 1	68 825
Chas	San Francisco San Francisco 1	68 890
Chas	Sonoma Vallejo	69 625
Chas	Trinity Weaverville	701068
Chas H	Sacramento Ward 1	63 73
Chris	El Dorado Mud Springs	58 957
Chrishan	Calaveras Twp 6	57 159
Christian	Calaveras Twp 6	57 159
Christian	Calaveras Twp 5	57 248
Christopher	Placer Folsom	62 647
Christopher	Santa Cruz Santa Cruz	66 621
Christopher	Santa Cruz Santa Cruz	66 623
Christopher	Solano Benecia	69 317
Chs	San Francisco San Francisco 5	67 494
Clint	Sierra Downieville	661029
Clinton	Alameda Brooklyn	55 106
Conrad	Sacramento Ward 4	63 600
Conrad	Sierra St Louis	66 811
Constine	San Francisco San Francisco 4	681130
Cyrus	San Joaquin Elkhorn	64 972
D	Calaveras Twp 9	57 404
D	Sacramento Brighton	63 196
D A	Butte Bidwell	56 732

Name	County Locale	M653 Roll Page
MILLER		
D R	Amador Twp 5	55 335
Dan C	Sacramento Ward 1	63 21
Daniel	Napa Yount	61 44
Daniel	Santa Cruz Santa Cruz	66 633
Daniel	Sierra Gibsonville	66 859
Daniel	Siskiyou Yreka	69 193
Daniel S	Yuba Bear Rvr	721008
Danl	Monterey Pajaro	601020
Danl	Santa Clara Alviso	65 401
Danl	Santa Clara Santa Clara	65 477
David	El Dorado Mud Springs	58 953
David	El Dorado Mud Springs	58 959
David	San Francisco San Francisco 9	681063
David	Santa Cruz Santa Cruz	66 628
David	Tuolumne Twp 6	71 542
David	Yolo Putah	72 585
David B	Butte Oregon	56 636
David D	San Luis Obispo San Luis Obispo 65	10
David S*	Yuba Bear Rvr	721000
David T*	Yuba Bear Rvr	721000
Dell	Santa Cruz Watsonville	66 539
Dewight*	El Dorado Georgetown	58 754
Diedrich	Tuolumne Montezuma	71 509
Diedrick	Tuolumne Twp 5	71 509
E	El Dorado Coloma	581071
E	Los Angeles Tejon	59 524
E	Sacramento Cosumnes	63 389
E	Santa Clara San Jose	65 352
E	Tuolumne Big Oak	71 153
E A	Sierra Downieville	661011
E B	Nevada Bloomfield	61 514
E B	Yolo Slate Ra	72 718
E B	Yuba New York	72 718
E D	Sierra Downieville	66 978
E J	Sacramento San Joaquin	63 350
E J	Sierra Twp 7	66 893
E J	Trinity E Weaver	701058
E S	San Francisco San Francisco 6	67 449
E S	Siskiyou Scott Va	69 39
E V	Marin Bolinas	60 745
Ed	Sacramento Ward 1	63 81
Edward	El Dorado Salmon Falls	581042
Edward	Monterey San Juan	60 995
Edward	San Francisco San Francisco 3	67 69
Edward	San Joaquin Douglass	64 921
Edward	San Mateo Twp 3	65 79
Edward	Santa Cruz Pescadero	66 649
Edward	Sierra Whiskey	66 850
Ej	Sierra Twp 7	66 893
Eli	Yuba New York	72 735
Eli	Yuba Marysville	72 852
Eli	Yuba Marysville	72 857
Elias	Sonoma Bodega	69 532
Elisha	El Dorado Placerville	58 926
Eliza	San Francisco San Francisco 3	67 26
Elizabeth	San Francisco San Francisco 7	681356
Elizabeth	San Francisco San Francisco 2	67 737
Elizabeth	Sonoma Santa Rosa	69 387
Enoch	Yuba Bear Rvr	72 996
Erastus G	Santa Cruz Watsonville	66 536
Estha	Marin Bolinas	60 744
F	Sacramento Ward 1	63 14
F	Sacramento Alabama	63 414
F	Sacramento Alabama	63 415
F	Tehama Tehama	70 946
F A	El Dorado Newtown	58 776
F K	Tuolumne Twp 1	71 192
F L	Yolo Cache Crk	72 665
F L	Yuba Parks Ba	72 775
F P	San Francisco San Francisco 5	67 545
Fanny	Butte Ophir	56 767
Fanny Jane	Alameda Brooklyn	55 174
Ferdinand	Calaveras Twp 5	57 143
Flose	Calaveras Twp 10	57 277
Francis	Amador Twp 2	55 261
Francis	San Francisco San Francisco 7	681036
Francis	San Francisco San Francisco 7	681436
Francis	El Dorado Coloma	581104
Frank	Marin Point Re	60 730
Frank	Sierra Pine Grove	66 834
Franklin	Marin Bolinas	60 727
Franklin	Placer Auburn	62 560
Franklin	San Francisco San Francisco 4	681162
Franklin	San Francisco San Francisco 4	681217
Franklin	San Francisco San Francisco 7	681353
Franklin	San Luis Obispo San Luis Obispo 65	28
Fred	Calaveras Twp 9	57 343
Fred	Calaveras Twp 9	57 353
Fred	Placer Yankee J	62 781
Fred	Sacramento San Joaquin	63 349
Fred	Sacramento Ward 4	63 597
Fred	Sacramento Ward 4	63 604
Fred	Tuolumne Twp 1	71 241
Fred A	Calaveras Twp 9	57 373
Fred*	Placer Michigan	62 809

Name	County Locale	M653 Roll Page
MILLER		
Frederick	San Francisco San Francisco	4 681147
Fredrick	Plumas Meadow Valley	62 932
Fredrick	Plumas Meadow Valley	62 933
Fredrick	Tuolumne Twp 5	71 495
G	Nevada Eureka	61 353
G	Nevada Bridgeport	61 469
G	San Francisco San Francisco	6 67 463
G A	Sacramento Ward 4	63 560
G B	Siskiyou Scott Va	69 21
G L	San Francisco San Francisco	1 68 922
G T	Yolo Cache Crk	72 663
G W	Amador Twp 1	55 482
G W	Siskiyou Scott Va	69 36
Geo	Butte Bidwell	56 707
Geo	El Dorado Placerville	58 912
Geo	Napa Napa	61 105
Geo	Sacramento Granite	63 258
Geo	Sacramento Franklin	63 319
Geo	Sacramento Ward 1	63 85
Geo	San Francisco San Francisco	10 217 67
Geo	San Francisco San Francisco	2 67 709
Geo	Siskiyou Scott Ri	69 71
Geo	Siskiyou Klamath	69 84
Geo	Siskiyou Klamath	69 96
Geo B	Sacramento Centre	63 180
Geo F	Sierra Twp 7	66 901
Geo R	Sonoma Santa Rosa	69 406
Geo W	San Francisco San Francisco	10 273 67
Geo W	Sonoma Petaluma	69 587
Georg	Yuba Rose Bar	72 819
George	Amador Twp 3	55 391
George	Calaveras Twp 5	57 240
George	Humbolt Eureka	59 164
George	Placer Auburn	62 568
George	Plumas Quincy	62 989
George	Sacramento Ward 1	63 128
George	San Francisco San Francisco	4 681119
George	San Francisco San Francisco	7 681416
George	San Francisco San Francisco	3 67 66
George	San Mateo Twp 3	65 85
George	Sierra Twp 7	66 889
George	Sierra Downieville	66 956
George	Sierra Downieville	66 997
George	Sonoma Mendocino	69 456
George	Sonoma Mendocino	69 467
George	Tehama Lassen	70 866
George	Trinity Rattle Snake	701029
George	Trinity Weaverville	701071
George	Tuolumne Twp 1	71 228
George	Yuba Rose Bar	72 802
George	Yuba Marysville	72 931
George F	Plumas Quincy	62 960
George H*	Sierra Pine Grove	66 826
George W	Santa Clara Gilroy	65 249
George W	Siskiyou Yreka	69 171
Gilbert	Stanislaus Branch	70 712
Giles D*	Placer Virginia	62 662
Grundy	Tulara Twp 1	71 83
Gustave	San Francisco San Francisco	3 67 71
Gustave	Yuba Marysville	72 968
Gustave*	San Francisco San Francisco	3 67 71
H	Butte Ophir	56 796
H	El Dorado Salmon Falls	581054
H	El Dorado Georgetown	58 760
H	El Dorado Placerville	58 912
H	El Dorado Placerville	58 933
H	Sacramento Ward 4	63 557
H	Santa Clara San Jose	65 279
H	Shasta Cottonwood	66 724
H	Siskiyou Cottonwoood	69 99
H	Stanislaus Emory	70 739
H	Tuolumne Twp 4	71 146
H A	Sierra Eureka	661044
H H	Nevada Eureka	61 378
H H	Sutter Butte	70 795
H S	Sacramento Dry Crk	63 379
H S	Tuolumne Columbia	71 335
H W	Sierra Twp 7	66 879
H Z	El Dorado Mud Springs	58 980
Hans	San Francisco San Francisco	9 681034
Hans	San Francisco San Francisco	11 147 67
Harper	Placer Mountain	62 708
Harry	Sacramento Ward 1	63 67
Henry	Alameda Oakland	55 12
Henry	Amador Twp 2	55 278
Henry	Amador Twp 3	55 376
Henry	Amador Twp 6	55 433
Henry	Amador Twp 6	55 435
Henry	Butte Mountain	56 738
Henry	Calaveras Twp 10	57 290
Henry	Calaveras Twp 8	57 85
Henry	Calaveras Twp 8	57 90
MILLER		
Henry	Contra Costa Twp 3	57 611
Henry	El Dorado Coloma	581070
Henry	El Dorado Casumnes	581170
Henry	El Dorado Newtown	58 780
Henry	Humbolt Bucksport	59 161
Henry	Mariposa Coulterville	60 696
Henry	Mendocino Big Rvr	60 851
Henry	Mendocino Anderson	60 866
Henry	Nevada Rough &	61 403
Henry	Nevada Rough &	61 434
Henry	Nevada Red Dog	61 551
Henry	Placer Folsom	62 641
Henry	Plumas Quincy	62 956
Henry	Sacramento Ward 1	63 124
Henry	Sacramento Franklin	63 312
Henry	Sacramento Cosummes	63 383
Henry	San Francisco San Francisco	11 103 67
Henry	San Francisco San Francisco	10 326 67
Henry	San Francisco San Francisco	3 67 82
Henry	Santa Clara Santa Clara	65 493
Henry	Sierra Downieville	661011
Henry	Sierra Twp 7	66 908
Henry	Sierra Twp 7	66 909
Henry	Siskiyou Yreka	69 150
Henry	Siskiyou Klamath	69 97
Henry	Siskiyou Cottonwood	69 99
Henry	Tuolumne Big Oak	71 145
Henry	Tuolumne Twp 1	71 239
Henry	Yuba Bear Rvr	72 997
Henry T	Nevada Bridgeport	61 477
Henry W	San Francisco San Francisco	10 206 67
Henry W	San Francisco San Francisco	9 68 974
Henry*	Sierra Poverty	66 800
Herman	Yuba Marysville	72 935
Hiram	Napa Yount	61 45
Howard B	San Joaquin Oneal	64 936
Hu	Tuolumne Big Oak	71 146
I P*	Nevada Red Dog	61 542
Isaac	Sacramento Ward 1	63 128
Isaac	San Francisco San Francisco	7 681419
Isaac	Solano Benecia	69 317
Isaac	Sonoma Russian	69 442
Isaac Jun	Sonoma Russian	69 442
J	Butte Oregon	56 639
J	Butte Mountain	56 734
J	Colusa Grand Island	57 469
J	El Dorado Diamond	58 787
J	El Dorado Diamond	58 803
J	El Dorado Placerville	58 824
J	El Dorado Placerville	58 854
J	Nevada Grass Valley	61 203
J	Nevada Grass Valley	61 214
J	Sacramento Brighton	63 194
J	Sacramento Ward 4	63 607
J	San Francisco San Francisco	5 67 491
J	San Francisco San Francisco	5 67 549
J	Santa Clara San Jose	65 372
J	Santa Clara Santa Clara	65 469
J	Siskiyou Scott Ri	69 67
J	Siskiyou Callahan	69 6
J	Solano Vacaville	69 325
J	Solano Montezuma	69 375
J	Sutter Yuba	70 761
J	Sutter Bear Rvr	70 819
J A	Butte Ophir	56 755
J A	San Francisco San Francisco	3 67 52
J A	Sutter Butte	70 779
J B	El Dorado Coloma	581071
J B	San Francisco San Francisco	5 67 543
J C	El Dorado Coloma	581080
J D	Shasta Millvill	66 739
J E	Sacramento Ward 3	63 481
J E	San Joaquin Ward 4	641045
J F	Sacramento Ward 1	63 114
J F	Sierra Eureka	661044
J H	Calaveras Twp 9	57 411
J H	Mariposa Twp 3	60 597
J H	Yolo Cottonwood	72 656
J H P E	Nevada Nevada	61 291
J J	San Joaquin Stockton	641099
J J A	Nevada Bridgeport	61 503
J M	Marin Tomales	60 723
J M	Sacramento Georgian	63 335
J M	Sacramento Ward 4	63 527
J P	Nevada Red Dog	61 542
J R	Shasta Millvill	66 752
J T	Sacramento Ward 1	63 114
J W	San Francisco San Francisco	9 681080
J W	San Francisco San Francisco	6 67 462
J W	Yolo Cottonwood	72 656
J W P E	Nevada Nevada	61 291
Jack	Mariposa Coulterville	60 686
MILLER		
Jacob	Butte Kimshaw	56 580
Jacob	El Dorado Georgetown	58 673
Jacob	Mariposa Twp 3	60 565
Jacob	Plumas Quincy	62 954
Jacob	Sacramento Franklin	63 314
Jacob	San Francisco San Francisco	7 681418
Jacob	Shasta Shasta	66 732
Jacob	Sierra Forest C	66 909
Jacob	Trinity North Fo	701023
Jacob	Trinity Honest B	701043
Jacob	Yuba Marysville	72 865
Jacob	Yuba Marysville	72 939
Jacob F	Placer Stewart	62 605
Jacob F	San Francisco San Francisco	3 67 63
Jacob F*	Siskiyou Shasta Rvr	69 112
Jacob L	Santa Clara San Jose	65 337
Jacob T	Siskiyou Shasta Rvr	69 112
Jad	Tuolumne Columbia	71 334
James	Alameda Brooklyn	55 147
James	Amador Twp 3	55 403
James	Calaveras Twp 4	57 320
James	Calaveras Twp 4	57 335
James	Colusa Grand Island	57 476
James	Humbolt Eureka	59 173
James	Humbolt Eureka	59 176
James	Marin Novato	60 734
James	Nevada Nevada	61 253
James	Plumas Meadow Valley	62 930
James	San Francisco San Francisco	9 681053
James	San Francisco San Francisco	3 67 35
James	Santa Cruz Pajaro	66 553
James	Santa Cruz Pajaro	66 572
James	Sierra Downieville	66 976
James	Solano Fremont	69 382
James	Sonoma Mendocino	69 447
James	Tuolumne Columbia	71 298
James	Yolo Cottonwood	72 655
James C	Tuolumne Jamestown	71 442
James C	Yuba Marysville	72 886
James H	El Dorado Mud Springs	58 988
James H	Plumas Meadow Valley	62 930
James H	San Joaquin Castoria	64 910
James J	Tuolumne Twp 2	71 357
James L	San Francisco San Francisco	8 681293
James T	Tuolumne Shawsfla	71 413
Jane	San Francisco San Francisco	4 681218
Jane	San Francisco San Francisco	8 681237
Jane	San Francisco San Francisco	1 68 869
Jane	Solano Benecia	69 310
Jane	Tehama Antelope	70 887
Jas	Amador Twp 2	55 285
Jas	Butte Ophir	56 795
Jas	Placer Virginia	62 689
Jas	Sacramento Granite	63 246
Jas	Sacramento Natonia	63 278
Jas	Sonoma Santa Rosa	69 397
Jas	Sonoma Petaluma	69 583
Jas M	Santa Clara San Jose	65 321
Jas S	Sonoma Santa Rosa	69 397
Jas T	Trinity East For	701027
Jasper	Nevada Red Dog	61 555
Jerome	Placer Iona Hills	62 891
Jerome	Santa Clara San Jose	65 360
Jerrie	Sacramento Ward 1	63 127
Jessie	Sacramento Ward 1	63 127
Jno	Alameda Brooklyn	55 198
Jno	Butte Chico	56 560
Jno	Sacramento Ward 3	63 478
Jno	Sacramento Ward 4	63 500
Jno	Sacramento Ward 4	63 587
Jno	San Francisco San Francisco	9 681089
Jno	San Joaquin Stockton	641011
Jno E	Butte Kimshaw	56 581
Jno T	Sacramento Ward 1	63 49
Jno W	Sacramento Ward 4	63 535
Joab	Sonoma Cloverdale	69 679
Johanna	Sacramento Ward 3	63 488
John	Alameda Washington	55 174
John	Alameda Oakland	55 61
John	Amador Twp 2	55 295
John	Amador Twp 2	55 320
John	Amador Twp 3	55 392
John	Butte Ophir	56 756
John	Calaveras Twp 6	57 118
John	Calaveras Twp 6	57 172
John	Colusa Spring Valley	57 430
John	Del Norte Crescent	58 628
John	Del Norte Crescent	58 650
John	El Dorado Salmon Hills	581065
John	El Dorado Casumnes	581173
John	El Dorado Diamond	58 765
John	El Dorado Placerville	58 897
John	El Dorado Placerville	58 904
John	Los Angeles Los Nieto	59 435
John	Monterey Monterey	60 925

Name	County Locale	M653 RollPage
MILLER		
John	Monterey Monterey	60 964
John	Nevada Bridgeport	61 453
John	Placer Michigan	62 836
John	Placer Michigan	62 842
John	Placer Iona Hills	62 890
John	Plumas Quincy	62 939
John	Sacramento Ward 1	63 26
John	Sacramento Natonia	63 276
John	Sacramento Ward 4	63 517
John	Sacramento Ward 4	63 519
John	San Francisco San Francisco 9	681090
John	San Francisco San Francisco 3	67 12
John	San Francisco San Francisco 7	681346
John	San Francisco San Francisco 7	681364
John	San Francisco San Francisco 6	67 444
John	San Francisco San Francisco 5	67 513
John	San Francisco San Francisco 2	67 640
John	San Francisco San Francisco 2	67 685
John	San Francisco San Francisco 2	67 733
John	San Francisco San Francisco 3	67 76
John	San Francisco San Francisco 1	68 817
John	San Francisco San Francisco 1	68 855
John	San Francisco San Francisco 1	68 909
John	San Francisco San Francisco 1	68 910
John	San Mateo Twp 2	65 131
John	Santa Clara San Jose	65 384
John	Santa Clara Santa Clara	65 475
John	Santa Cruz Soguel	66 583
John	Santa Cruz Santa Cruz	66 621
John	Santa Cruz Santa Cruz	66 622
John	Santa Cruz Santa Cruz	66 624
John	Shasta Shasta	66 730
John	Shasta Millvill	66 739
John	Shasta Millvill	66 755
John	Sierra La Porte	66 776
John	Sierra La Porte	66 787
John	Siskiyou Yreka	69 127
John	Siskiyou Yreka	69 131
John	Siskiyou Yreka	69 139
John	Siskiyou Yreka	69 143
John	Siskiyou Scott Va	69 48
John	Siskiyou Scott Va	69 55
John	Solano Suisan	69 204
John	Sonoma Sonoma	69 652
John	Stanislaus Branch	70 713
John	Stanislaus Emory	70 741
John	Trinity Taylor'S	701036
John	Tulara Sinks Te	71 42
John	Tulara Keeneysburg	71 47
John	Tulara Keyesville	71 53
John	Tulara Visalia	71 90
John	Tuolumne Twp 1	71 190
John	Tuolumne Twp 2	71 289
John	Yolo Cache Crk	72 639
John	Yolo Cottonwood	72 649
John	Yuba Marysville	72 905
John	Yuba Linda	72 995
John	Yuba Bear Rvr	72 997
John B	Tuolumne Jamestown	71 451
John E	Sacramento Sutter	63 295
John H	Plumas Quincy	62 964
John H	San Francisco San Francisco 3	67 86
John L	Plumas Quincy	62 942
John L	Tuolumne Twp 1	71 254
John P	Tuolumne Twp 1	71 264
John S	San Francisco San Francisco 8	681245
John S	San Francisco San Francisco 9	68 984
John S	Solano Suisan	69 209
John S	Tuolumne Twp 1	71 187
John W	Sierra Monte Crk	661039
John W	Tuolumne Twp 2	71 273
John W	Yuba Bear Rvr	72 996
Joil	Sonoma Santa Rosa	69 392
Jos	Butte Ophir	56 755
Jos	Sacramento Ward 1	63 19
Jos	Sacramento Ward 4	63 594
Jos B	Amador Twp 1	55 481
Joseph	Calaveras Twp 5	57 224
Joseph	El Dorado Georgetown	58 707
Joseph	El Dorado Greenwood	58 718
Joseph	El Dorado Placerville	58 930
Joseph	Marin Tomales	60 722
Joseph	Placer Iona Hills	62 885
Joseph	San Diego Agua Caliente	64 855
Joseph	San Francisco San Francisco 10	173 67
Joseph	Santa Cruz Santa Cruz	66 637
Joseph	Tulara Visalia	71 21
Joseph	Yolo Washington	72 573
Joseph	Yuba Rose Bar	72 808
Joseph	Yuba Bear Rvr	72 996
Joseph	Yuba Bear Rvr	72 999
Joseph A	Alameda Oakland	55 48
Josephine	Yolo Washington	72 574
Julius J	San Francisco San Francisco 4	681142

Name	County Locale	M653 RollPage
MILLER		
Kate L	San Francisco San Francisco 10	317 67
L	Sacramento Lee	63 218
L	San Mateo Twp 3	65 103
L	Siskiyou Cottonwoood	69 98
L	Trinity Douglas	70 978
L D	Butte Bidwell	56 720
L D	Sacramento Casmunes	63 381
L W	Sacramento Ward 4	63 502
L W	Sonoma Armally	69 493
L W	Tehama Pasakent	70 859
Lamel	Sierra Gibsonville	66 859
Larry	Placer Virginia	62 668
Lawrence	Calaveras Twp 6	57 115
Lewis	Mariposa Coulterville	60 689
Lewis	Plumas Quincy	62 936
Lewis W	Plumas Quincy	62 939
Louis	Amador Twp 3	55 383
Louis	Nevada Bloomfield	61 525
Louis	Placer Rattle Snake	62 604
Louis	Placer Rattle Snake	62 632
Louis	San Francisco San Francisco 7	681364
Louis	San Francisco San Francisco 11	154 67
Louis	Siskiyou Scott Va	69 26
Louis	Siskiyou Scott Va	69 53
Louis E	Placer Rattle Snake	62 598
Louiya	Nevada Bloomfield	61 519
Louiza	Nevada Bloomfield	61 519
Lucy	Sacramento Ward 4	63 580
Luis	Mariposa Coulterville	60 689
Luis	Santa Clara San Jose	65 290
M	Colusa Monroeville	57 440
M	El Dorado Greenwood	58 712
M	El Dorado Placerville	58 862
M	Nevada Grass Valley	61 214
M	San Francisco San Francisco 10	215 67
M	San Mateo Twp 3	65 92
M	Sonoma Cloverdale	69 682
M B	Butte Mountain	56 736
M F	Sacramento Ward 1	63 6
M K	San Francisco San Francisco 11	103 67
M L	Sonoma Armally	69 496
M R	El Dorado Placerville	58 883
M R	Marin Novato	60 735
M W	Nevada Eureka	61 367
Margaret	San Francisco San Francisco 5	67 481
Margaret	Santa Clara Alviso	65 402
Martin	Alameda Oakland	55 59
Martin	Calaveras Twp 10	57 267
Martin	Plumas Quincy	62 996
Martin B*	Marin Tomales	60 774
Martin J	Calaveras Twp 4	57 312
Mary	Contra Costa Twp 1	57 511
Mary	Plumas Quincy	62 920
Mary	San Francisco San Francisco 2	67 785
Mary	San Francisco San Francisco 9	68 972
Mary	Shasta Millvill	66 740
Mary	Sierra Whiskey	66 849
Mary	Sonoma Mendocino	69 456
Mary A	Santa Clara Santa Clara	65 480
Mary F	Sonoma Mendocino	69 456
Meredith R	Solano Vacaville	69 358
Merritt	Nevada Rough &	61 410
Mich	Sacramento Ward 3	63 456
Michael	Contra Costa Twp 1	57 510
Mickl	Sierra Downieville	66 978
Milton	San Joaquin Castoria	64 886
Miner	San Francisco San Francisco 7	681442
Mn	Butte Oregon	56 618
Morg	Sacramento Ward 1	63 36
Morris	San Joaquin Castoria	64 904
Mr	Marin San Rafael	60 764
N C	Nevada Bridgeport	61 467
N C	Nevada Bridgeport	61 473
N C*	Nevada Bridgeport	61 467
N E	Tuolumne Twp 1	71 192
N H	Siskiyou Yreka	69 190
N M	Sutter Nicolaus	70 834
N N	Sonoma Sonoma	69 636
N W	El Dorado Georgetown	58 682
Nicholas	Los Angeles San Gabriel	59 411
Nicholas	Placer Forest H	62 799
Noah	Colusa Butte Crk	57 465
Noel	El Dorado Kelsey	581139
O	Sacramento Georgian	63 335
Oliver	Solano Vacaville	69 362
Oscar	Butte Oro	56 674
Oscar	Tulara Visalia	71 106
P	El Dorado Newtown	58 776
P	El Dorado Newtown	58 778
P	Sacramento American	63 164
P	Siskiyou Scott Va	69 40

Name	County Locale	M653 RollPage
MILLER		
P	Sutter Sutter	70 812
P	Tuolumne Twp 4	71 165
P A	Tuolumne Twp 2	71 364
P M	San Francisco San Francisco 9	681089
P P	San Francisco San Francisco 5	67 481
Patrick	Shasta Shasta	66 731
Pelter*	Alameda Brooklyn	55 156
Percilla	San Francisco San Francisco 2	67 748
Pery	Stanislaus Emory	70 748
Peter	Butte Bidwell	56 721
Peter	El Dorado Coloma	581123
Peter	Klamath S Fork	59 200
Peter	Plumas Quincy	62 942
Peter	Sacramento Ward 4	63 603
Peter	San Francisco San Francisco 8	681293
Peter	San Francisco San Francisco 2	67 713
Peter	Sierra Downieville	66 976
Peter	Trinity Weaverville	701051
Peter	Tuolumne Jamestown	71 441
Peter	Yolo Merritt	72 581
Peter	Yolo Putah	72 587
Petter*	Alameda Brooklyn	55 156
Phil	Nevada Rough &	61 423
Philip	Santa Cruz Pescadero	66 653
Phillip	San Francisco San Francisco 3	67 3
Phillip	San Francisco San Francisco 2	67 616
Phillip	Siskiyou Yreka	69 139
Phillips	Amador Twp 5	55 359
R	Trinity Weaverville	701078
R B	Tuolumne Sonora	71 200
R C	Sutter Yuba	70 767
R H	El Dorado Georgetown	58 682
R H	Yuba Timbucto	72 787
R S	Mariposa Twp 3	60 592
R S	San Francisco San Francisco 5	67 481
R W	San Joaquin Stockton	641015
Raft	San Francisco San Francisco 1	68 898
Rawson	Santa Cruz Santa Cruz	66 618
Richard	Contra Costa Twp 1	57 511
Richard	Marin Cortemad	60 756
Richard	Plumas Quincy	62 964
Richard	Sierra Pine Grove	66 831
Richard	Sierra Pine Grove	66 834
Richard	Yuba Rose Bar	72 802
Richard	Yuba Marysville	72 905
Richard C	Solano Suisan	69 205
Rober*	Sierra St Louis	66 807
Robert	Calaveras Twp 4	57 299
Robert	San Mateo Twp 3	65 100
Robert	Shasta Shasta	66 734
Robert	Sierra St Louis	66 807
Robert	Sierra St Louis	66 809
Robert	Solano Green Valley	69 242
Robert	Tulara Twp 2	71 15
Robt	Napa Clear Lake	61 138
Robt	Sacramento Sutter	63 295
Robt	Sacramento Ward 4	63 562
Robt	Tuolumne Twp 2	71 340
Rodolph	Solano Vallejo	69 260
Rosa	Sacramento Ward 3	63 444
Ruben	Siskiyou Scott Va	69 56
S	El Dorado Diamond	58 810
S	Siskiyou Cottonwoood	69 98
S B	Placer Dutch Fl	62 715
S D	Sacramento Dry Crk	63 372
S H	Sierra Gibsonville	66 859
S K	Calaveras Twp 9	57 375
S K	El Dorado Georgetown	58 675
S K*	Calaveras Twp 9	57 375
S L	Butte Ophir	56 824
S R	El Dorado Georgetown	58 675
S W	Butte Wyandotte	56 663
S Y*	Sacramento Brighton	63 197
Sam	El Dorado Georgetown	58 673
Sam	San Joaquin Stockton	641012
Saml	Alameda Brooklyn	55 187
Saml	Sacramento Dry Crk	63 372
Saml	Sacramento Ward 4	63 553
Saml R	Amador Twp 6	55 445
Samuel	El Dorado White Oaks	581017
Samuel	El Dorado Cold Spring	581100
Samuel	Marin Cortemad	60 782
Samuel	Mariposa Twp 1	60 632
Samuel	Siskiyou Klamath	69 84
Samuel	Stanislaus Empire	70 728
Samuel	Tulara Twp 2	71 14
Samuel C	Sierra Twp 5	66 917
Samuel E	Sonoma Russian	69 442
Samuel I*	Sonoma Russian	69 442
Samul	Siskiyou Klamath	69 84
Sarah	Yuba Bear Rvr	72 998
Sidney	Yuba New York	72 737
Simeon	Sierra Scales D	66 803
Solomon M	Tuolumne Chinese	71 490
Sophia	Sacramento Ward 4	63 547

Name	County Locale	M653 RollPage
MILLER		
Stephen	Butte Mountain	56 741
Susan	San Francisco San Francisco 6	67 440
Susan	Tuolumne Twp 5	71 527
T	Nevada Grass Valley	61 170
T	Siskiyou Scott Va	69 40
T A	Butte Ophir	56 755
T A	Sonoma Sonoma	69 651
T F	Butte Ophir	56 762
T G	Butte Cascade	56 692
T H	Sonoma Sonoma	69 651
T S	Tehama Antelope	70 892
Theo	Nevada Rough &	61 405
Theodore	San Francisco San Francisco 3	67 67
Thomas	Calaveras Twp 6	57 148
Thomas	El Dorado Gold Hill	581096
Thomas	El Dorado Georgetown	58 679
Thomas	Monterey San Juan	601003
Thomas	San Joaquin Stockton	641018
Thomas	Solano Suisan	69 219
Thomas A	Calaveras Twp 8	57 82
Thomas L	Tuolumne Sonora	71 239
Thos	Alameda Washington	55 170
Thos	Butte Kimshaw	56 571
Thos	Butte Oregon	56 619
Thos	Butte Oro	56 683
Thos	Mariposa Coulterville	60 677
Thos	Sacramento Georgian	63 337
Thos	Sacramento Ward 4	63 573
Thos	Sacramento Ward 1	63 97
Thos	San Francisco San Francisco 12	385 67
Thos	San Francisco San Francisco 1	68 854
Thos B	Sonoma Washington	69 669
Thos H	Sierra Morristown	661052
Thos L	Trinity Bates	70 967
Thos S	San Francisco San Francisco 9	68 990
U K	San Francisco San Francisco 11	103 67
U U*	Sonoma Sonoma	69 636
Ulrich	Siskiyou Yreka	69 150
Uriah	Sonoma Armally	69 494
Uriah	Tuolumne Columbia	71 471
V	Sutter Butte	70 797
Valentine	San Francisco San Francisco 7	681362
Valentine	Sonoma Mendocino	69 466
Valentine	Yolo No E Twp	72 674
Valentine	Yuba North Ea	72 674
Vincenta	San Francisco San Francisco 2	67 761
W	Butte Oregon	56 614
W	Calaveras Twp 9	57 404
W	Sacramento Lee	63 217
W	Sutter Yuba	70 775
W	Sutter Sutter	70 817
W	Yolo Cache Crk	72 621
W	Yolo Cache Crk	72 645
W A	El Dorado Cold Spring	581099
W A	Tuolumne Twp 2	71 286
W B	Siskiyou Callahan	69 16
W B	Sutter Bear Rvr	70 821
W C	Nevada Bridgeport	61 473
W D	Del Norte Crescent	58 626
W F	Sacramento Ward 1	63 6
W L G	Sierra Eureka	661044
W P	San Francisco San Francisco 9	681062
W R	Marin Bolinas	60 745
W S	Butte Kimshaw	56 573
Wade	Tulara Visalia	71 2
Warren P	Yuba Marysville	72 890
Wash	Sacramento Ward 1	63 134
William	Calaveras Twp 5	57 190
William	Calaveras Twp 4	57 299
William	Colusa Colusi	57 422
William	El Dorado White Oaks	581009
William	El Dorado Spanish	581125
William	Marin Cortemad	60 781
William	Monterey Monterey	60 931
William	Plumas Quincy	62 977
William	San Francisco San Francisco 4	681113
William	San Francisco San Francisco 4	681146
William	San Francisco San Francisco 4	681167
William	San Francisco San Francisco 4	681217
William	San Francisco San Francisco 7	681356
William	San Francisco San Francisco 9	68 956
William	San Joaquin Elkhorn	64 971
William	San Mateo Twp 3	65 93
William	Sierra La Porte	66 781
William	Sierra La Porte	66 784
William	Siskiyou Yreka	69 135
William	Siskiyou Callahan	69 15
William	Siskiyou Scott Va	69 50
William	Solano Suisan	69 223
William	Tuolumne Twp 1	71 203
William	Tuolumne Twp 2	71 286
William	Tuolumne Twp 2	71 311
William	Yuba Bear Rvr	721001

Name	County Locale	M653 RollPage
MILLER		
William C	Plumas Quincy	62 986
William C	San Joaquin Stockton	641015
William F	Nevada Rough &	61 410
William G	Sierra Poker Flats	66 841
William H	San Francisco San Francisco 7	681410
William J*	Yuba Marysville	72 926
William K	Calaveras Twp 8	57 53
William P	San Joaquin Stockton	641089
Wliam	Tuolumne Twp 2	71 286
Wm	Alameda Brooklyn	55 188
Wm	Amador Twp 1	55 506
Wm	Butte Kimshaw	56 598
Wm	Butte Oregon	56 618
Wm	Calaveras Twp 6	57 144
Wm	El Dorado Kelsey	581149
Wm	El Dorado Placerville	58 924
Wm	Fresno Twp 2	59 3
Wm	Mariposa Twp 1	60 629
Wm	Napa Napa	61 108
Wm	Sacramento Centre	63 174
Wm	Sacramento Ward 3	63 433
Wm	Sacramento Ward 1	63 84
Wm	Sacramento Ward 1	63 87
Wm	San Francisco San Francisco 2	67 558
Wm	San Francisco San Francisco 2	67 624
Wm	San Francisco San Francisco 2	67 711
Wm	San Francisco San Francisco 2	67 802
Wm	Tuolumne Twp 2	71 329
Wm	Yuba Rose Bar	72 816
Wm C	Yuba Marysville	72 971
Wm E	Placer Dutch Fl	62 754
Wm H	Alameda Brooklyn	55 163
Wm H	Del Norte Crescent	58 642
Wm H	Plumas Quincy	62 945
Wm H	Sacramento Georgian	63 347
Wm H	San Francisco San Francisco 2	67 620
Wm Kilz	Butte Oro	56 685
Wm Kitz	Butte Oro	56 685
Wm O*	Butte Kimshaw	56 571
Wm P	Klamath Trinidad	59 220
Zacanah	Tulara Visalia	71 17
Zacariah	Tulara Twp 2	71 17
Zelow	Placer Virginia	62 662
MILLERCHARLES		
Goodale	Sierra Downieville	66 963
MILLEREDWARD		
Cahill	Sierra Whiskey	66 850
MILLERMAN		
Chas	Trinity Lewiston	70 961
N	Sacramento Ward 4	63 511
MILLERS		
Fred*	Placer Michigan	62 809
MILLERTON		
---	Fresno Twp 1	59 55
MILLES		
C	Mariposa Coulterville	60 694
Henry	Sierra Scales D	66 800
J M	Sonoma Armally	69 506
Jack	Mariposa Coulterville	60 686
Joseph	Marin Tomales	60 722
R B	Tuolumne Twp 1	71 200
Saml R	Amador Twp 6	55 445
Samuel	El Dorado Cold Spring	581100
Thos	Mariposa Coulterville	60 677
MILLET		
Erastus B	Santa Cruz Watsonville	66 536
Erastus G	Santa Cruz Watsonville	66 536
Mary J	San Francisco San Francisco 9	681009
MILLETT		
Edgar A	San Joaquin Elliott	641102
Harrison*	Mariposa Coulterville	60 693
Hiram	Mendocino Calpella	60 829
Jas H	Placer Dutch Fl	62 714
Jesse	Placer Sacramento	62 646
Ortimiro*	San Bernadino	64 634
	San Bernardino	
Ortuniro*	San Bernadino	64 634
	San Bernardino	
Solomon P	Contra Costa Twp 2	57 550
MILLETTE		
P C	Sacramento Ward 3	63 427
MILLEUS		
Frank*	Sacramento Ward 1	63 14
MILLEW		
James	Sierra Twp 7	66 877
MILLEY		
P	Siskiyou Callahan	69 14
William	Merced Monterey	60 931
MILLEYAN		
Alfred	Calaveras Twp 6	57 148
MILLHAM		
J	Yolo Cottonwood	72 648
MILLHENCH		
Elisabeth	Yuba Long Bar	72 756

Name	County Locale	M653 RollPage
MILLHENCH		
Elizabeth	Yuba Long Bar	72 756
MILLHOLLAND		
Frank	San Francisco San Francisco 1	68 917
MILLHOUSE		
G	San Bernardino Santa Barbara	64 154
MILLIARD		
Chancy	Placer Iona Hills	62 885
Elisha	Amador Twp 2	55 307
Mrs	Amador Twp 2	55 307
Stephen	Santa Cruz Pajaro	66 526
W	San Francisco San Francisco 9	681074
MILLICAN		
George	Siskiyou Yreka	69 143
MILLIE		
Archibald	San Francisco San Francisco 11	137 67
D	El Dorado Greenwood	58 724
MILLIES		
Charles	Mendocino Ukiah	60 800
Charly	Mendocino Ukiah	60 800
MILLIET		
Alenis*	San Francisco San Francisco 3	67 80
MILLIGAN		
A	San Francisco San Francisco 5	67 484
David	Alameda Brooklyn	55 145
J W	Santa Clara Gilroy	65 232
Jas B	Amador Twp 1	55 475
John	Placer Iona Hills	62 879
John	Sierra Pine Grove	66 819
Michael	Solano Benecia	69 317
Phillip	Placer Illinois	62 738
Richard	Santa Clara Alviso	65 410
Robt	Stanislaus Branch	70 712
Wm	Sacramento Ward 1	63 37
MILLIKEN		
Georgian J	Sacramento Ward 3	63 453
Joe	Fresno Twp 3	59 32
John	San Francisco San Francisco 1	68 905
John	Santa Clara Fremont	65 440
John M	Sacramento Ward 3	63 450
T J	Sacramento Ward 3	63 450
MILLIMAN		
Frederick*	San Francisco 3	67 15
S W	San Francisco	
	San Francisco 7	681333
MILLINDEN		
H P*	San Francisco San Francisco 1	68 905
MILLINER		
J J	San Francisco San Francisco 5	67 478
John D	San Francisco San Francisco 7	681338
MILLINGTON		
James	Alameda Oakland	55 66
John	Tuolumne Columbia	71 342
Samuel J	San Francisco San Francisco 7	681339
MILLINS		
Geo	Sacramento Granite	63 241
MILLINZ		
William*	San Francisco San Francisco 7	681433
MILLION		
Joel*	Napa Napa	61 73
MILLIS		
C	El Dorado Greenwood	58 711
Calvin*	Siskiyou Yreka	69 143
E	Shasta Shasta	66 684
F K	Tuolumne Sonora	71 192
H	El Dorado Placerville	58 837
J*	Siskiyou Klamath	69 87
MILLISON		
M	Napa Napa	61 87
MILLITT		
Hiram	Mendocino Calpella	60 829
MILLMAN		
M G	Sacramento Ward 3	63 423
MILLMARKER		
H	Santa Clara San Jose	65 322
MILLNER		
Casper	Mariposa Twp 1	60 647
Geo	Amador Twp 2	55 266
MILLOBY		
Marry	Tuolumne Sonora	71 209
MILLON		
John*	Sierra La Porte	66 780
Marcel	Calaveras Twp 4	57 338
Robt	Sacramento Ward 4	63 507
S	San Francisco San Francisco 2	67 625
Thomas*	Placer Iona Hills	62 881
Wm	Tuolumne Sonora	71 224
MILLONE		
H C	Santa Clara San Jose	65 280
MILLOR		
C	Santa Clara Redwood	65 452
T*	Sutter Sutter	70 815
Thomas	El Dorado Georgetown	58 679
MILLOY		
J	Nevada Grass Valley	61 215

California 1860 Census Index

Name	County Locale	M653 RollPage
MILLR		
Anaren	Placer Forest H	62 771
C W	Placer Dutch Fl	62 710
MILLS		
---	Nevada Eureka	61 355
A	San Francisco San Francisco 5	67 541
A	Sutter Butte	70 798
A J	Sonoma Santa Rosa	69 408
A L	Sacramento Ward 1	63 49
Alex	Yolo Cache Crk	72 607
Alex*	Yolo Cache	72 608
Andrew	Colusa Monroeville	57 451
Andrew	Marin Tomales	60 722
Benjamin	Placer Todds Va	62 787
Boardman	Santa Cruz Pajaro	66 557
C C	Tuolumne Twp 4	71 142
C H	Napa Clear Lake	61 137
Charles	Humbolt Pacific	59 130
Charles	Marin Cortemad	60 783
Charles	Placer Iona Hills	62 896
Charls	Marin Cortemad	60 783
Chester	Contra Costa Twp 2	57 547
Chilian*	Monterey San Juan	601004
Christopher	San Francisco 10	198
		67
D	Shasta Millvill	66 755
D O	Nevada Rough &	61 410
D O	Sacramento Ward 4	63 608
Daniel S	Alameda Brooklyn	55 211
E	Nevada Grass Valley	61 236
E L	Napa Napa	61 64
E L C	Napa Napa	61 64
E W	Calaveras Twp 9	57 410
Easton	San Francisco San Francisco 12	379
		67
Ed	Nevada Rough &	61 418
Edward	San Francisco San Francisco 3	67 41
Edward T	Los Angeles Elmonte	59 266
Emory	Contra Costa Twp 2	57 568
Francis	El Dorado Mud Springs	58 965
Frank	San Bernardino San Bernadino	64 636
Freeman	San Joaquin Elkhorn	64 976
Geo W	Sonoma Mendocino	69 447
George M	Alameda Brooklyn	55 158
H	Calaveras Twp 9	57 399
H A	Nevada Nevada	61 269
H C	Nevada Nevada	61 275
Henry	Plumas Quincy	62 947
Henry	Sierra Downieville	66 970
Hiram	Contra Costa Twp 1	57 535
I	El Dorado Placerville	58 912
J	El Dorado Union	581094
J P	Nevada Rough &	61 413
J P	Sacramento Ward 4	63 546
J S	Napa Clear Lake	61 139
J*	San Francisco San Francisco 1	68 921
James	Marin Bolinas	60 746
James	Sacramento Franklin	63 320
James	San Francisco San Francisco 11	132
		67
James A	Santa Clara San Jose	65 349
James E	Tuolumne Twp 1	71 196
James L	San Joaquin Stockton	641055
James O	Trinity Weaverville	701071
James P	San Francisco San Francisco 3	67 37
Jane	Nevada Grass Valley	61 236
Jas	Sacramento Granite	63 229
Jas	Sacramento Granite	63 251
Jesse	Yolo Washington	72 600
Jhilian*	Monterey San Juan	601004
Job	Sierra Twp 7	66 888
John	El Dorado Kelsey	581129
John	Marin Cortemad	60 791
John	Placer Forest H	62 806
John	San Mateo Twp 3	65 99
John	Santa Clara San Jose	65 374
John	Sonoma Armally	69 513
John C	San Francisco San Francisco 10	346
		67
John C	Yuba Marysville	72 959
John J	Sacramento Ward 3	63 454
John Y	Colusa Spring Valley	57 433
L R	San Francisco San Francisco 3	67 74
Lenoci	Calaveras Twp 5	57 209
Lenoco	Calaveras Twp 5	57 209
Lhilian*	Monterey San Juan	601004
Lydia A	San Francisco San Francisco 10	349
		67
M M	Yolo Cache	72 613
Martha	Nevada Red Dog	61 540
Marvin E	Placer Auburn	62 559
Mary Ann	Yuba Rose Bar	72 789
Mathew	Sierra Downieville	661019
Melisa	Napa Hot Springs	61 27
N B	Calaveras Twp 9	57 396

Name	County Locale	M653 RollPage
MILLS		
Niles	San Francisco San Francisco 12	368
		67
O D	San Francisco San Francisco 10	193
		67
Owen	Tulara Yule Rvr	71 24
P	El Dorado Placerville	58 864
Perry	San Joaquin Elkhorn	64 988
Philo	San Francisco San Francisco 3	67 29
Rich	Sacramento Ward 4	63 525
Robert	Calaveras Twp 10	57 282
Robert	Mendocino Calpella	60 818
Robert	San Francisco San Francisco 3	67 34
Robert	San Francisco San Francisco 3	67 66
Robert	Yuba Long Bar	72 753
Robt	Santa Clara Gilroy	65 245
S	Nevada Eureka	61 372
S B	San Francisco San Francisco 3	67 74
S T	Sacramento Cosummes	63 404
Saml	Sacramento Natonia	63 280
Saml L	San Francisco San Francisco 2	67 719
Samuel	Klamath Klamath	59 224
Samuel C	San Francisco San Francisco 8	681309
Senoce*	Calaveras Twp 5	57 209
Senoci*	Calaveras Twp 5	57 209
Thomas	San Bernardino Santa Ba	64 218
Thomas	San Bernardino S Buenav	64 219
Thomas	Shasta Horsetown	66 695
Thomas B	San Diego Colorado	64 807
Thomas J	Sierra Twp 7	66 867
Thomas*	Mendocino Big Rvr	60 853
Thos	Nevada Bloomfield	61 515
Thos J	Nevada Bloomfield	61 515
W	Tuolumne Sonora	71 192
W B	Calaveras Twp 9	57 396
W L	Sacramento Ward 1	63 49
Walter	Contra Costa Twp 1	57 510
William	Calaveras Twp 5	57 182
William	Klamath Orleans	59 217
William	Nevada Bridgeport	61 468
William	Placer Iona Hills	62 875
William	Tulara Twp 2	71 13
William B	San Joaquin Stockton	641045
William C	Calaveras Twp 5	57 239
William E	Yuba Marysville	72 904
Wm	Alameda Brooklyn	55 139
Wm	Amador Twp 3	55 407
Wm	Mariposa Twp 1	60 668
Wm	Nevada Grass Valley	61 151
Wm	Sacramento Ward 4	63 505
Wm	Sacramento Ward 4	63 583
Wm	Sacramento Ward 1	63 74
Wm C	Nevada Nevada	61 315
Wm R	Colusa Spring Valley	57 433
MILLSAP		
G	Yolo Cottonwood	72 656
Hiram	Colusa Monroeville	57 444
Joseph	Colusa Monroeville	57 445
R T	Placer Michigan	62 845
W	Yolo Cache Crk	72 635
W R	Solano Vallejo	69 248
MILLSAPY		
A J	Colusa Monroeville	57 445
MILLSLIGER		
Andrew	Colusa Grand Island	57 468
MILLSPAUGH		
C W	Nevada Nevada	61 258
MILLUM		
Henry	Yuba Rose Bar	72 788
MILLUS		
M C W	Placer Dutch Fl	62 731
MILLWARD		
E	Siskiyou Scott Ri	69 72
MILLWORK		
E	Siskiyou Scott Ri	69 75
MILLY		
Michael	Calaveras Twp 5	57 196
MILNER		
John F	Tuolumne Twp 5	71 499
N	Tuolumne Twp 2	71 391
MILNES		
B	Calaveras Twp 9	57 417
John	Calaveras Twp 7	57 13
MILNIPSY		
---	Mendocino Big Rvr	60 853
MILO		
---	Fresno Twp 1	59 54
MILON		
Matthias	Sierra Downieville	66 953
MILONE		
Mary*	San Francisco San Francisco 12	380
		67
MILONEY		
Abbey	Santa Clara San Jose	65 316
Briget	Santa Clara San Jose	65 305
MILOON		
John	Monterey San Juan	601004

Name	County Locale	M653 RollPage
MILORE		
Wm	Santa Clara San Jose	65 350
MILOT		
John	Calaveras Twp 6	57 179
MILOY		
John	Sierra Downieville	661017
MILPA		
---	Tulara Keyesville	71 68
MILPO		
---	Tulara Keyesville	71 71
MILR		
Samuel	Plumas Quincy	62 953
MILSON		
Charles C*	Mendocino Big Rvr	60 843
Peter	Mendocino Big Rvr	60 851
MILTAN		
Chas*	Mendocino Big Rvr	60 850
MILTEN		
James*	Placer Iona Hills	62 892
MILTETT		
Harrison*	Mariposa Coulterville	60 693
MILTIM		
Chas*	Mendocino Big Rvr	60 850
MILTOBY		
Marry*	Tuolumne Twp 1	71 209
MILTON		
A	El Dorado Grizzly	581182
C E	Nevada Nevada	61 287
Charles	Yuba Marysville	72 959
Charles F*	Santa Cruz Pajaro	66 573
Henry	Sonoma Petaluma	69 613
J C	Sierra Excelsior	661033
James*	Placer Iona Hills	62 892
James*	Sonoma Petaluma	69 614
Jas H	Amador Twp 4	55 256
Jeremiah	Placer Auburn	62 588
John	El Dorado Grizzly	581182
John	Marin Tomales	60 720
John	Nevada Bridgeport	61 448
John*	Sierra La Porte	66 780
Joseph	Tuolumne Shawsfla	71 391
L R*	Sacramento San Joaquin	63 348
S R*	Sacramento San Joaquin	63 348
Sandson	Santa Cruz Pescadero	66 647
Thomas*	Placer Iona Hills	62 881
William	Calaveras Twp 5	57 205
William	Nevada Red Dog	61 555
William	Plumas Meadow Valley	62 903
Wm	Alameda Brooklyn	55 181
Wm*	Tuolumne Twp 1	71 224
MILTS		
J S*	Napa Clear Lake	61 139
Jacob	San Joaquin Elliott	64 941
MILTZ		
Jacob	Shasta Shasta	66 654
Jacob	Trinity Weaverville	701062
Jacob*	Shasta Shasta	66 654
MILUMBY		
Michael*	Alameda Brooklyn	55 139
MILWAIN		
Sciler	Placer Dutch Fl	62 724
MIM		
---	El Dorado Diamond	58 806
John*	Mariposa Coulterville	60 695
MIMENEAH		
---*	Tulara Visalia	71 39
MIMGUEL		
---	San Bernardino S Timate	64 694
MIMIAM		
A D	Tuolumne Twp 2	71 420
MIMICKS		
G	Calaveras Twp 9	57 411
MIMOKAK		
---	Tulara Twp 1	71 118
MIMSHONER		
Nicholas*	Santa Clara Alviso	65 412
MIMSHOWER		
Nicholas*	Santa Clara Alviso	65 412
MIMSO		
Thomas*	Yuba Slate Ro	72 694
MIMSON		
J	Calaveras Twp 9	57 410
Josoiah	Sierra Downieville	66 967
MIN CHOW		
---	Nevada Nevada	61 302
MIN		
---	Amador Twp 2	55 311
---	Amador Twp 5	55 335
---	Amador Twp 5	55 360
---	Amador Twp 6	55 428
---	Butte Hamilton	56 530
---	Butte Kimshaw	56 582
---	Butte Bidwell	56 713
---	Butte Mountain	56 741
---	Calaveras Twp 5	57 146
---	Calaveras Twp 5	57 234

California 1860 Census Index

Name	County Locale	M653 Roll	Page
MIN			
---	Calaveras Twp 5	57	244
---	Calaveras Twp 5	57	258
---	Calaveras Twp 4	57	305
---	Calaveras Twp 4	57	306
---	El Dorado Big Bar	58	737
---	Mariposa Twp 3	60	571
---	Mariposa Twp 1	60	663
---	Mariposa Coulterville	60	692
---	Nevada Grass Valley	61	230
---	Nevada Nevada	61	299
---	Placer Dutch Fl	62	721
---	Placer Illinois	62	754
---	San Francisco San Francisco 5	67	507
---	San Francisco San Francisco 3	67	50
---	San Francisco San Francisco 3	67	9
---	Shasta French G	66	712
---	Sierra Downieville	66	985
---*	Butte Hamilton	56	530
---*	Butte Kimshaw	56	605
---*	Calaveras Twp 5	57	234
---*	Mariposa Twp 3	60	607
---*	Nevada Eureka	61	385
Ah	Butte Bidwell	56	713
Catharine*	Del Norte Crescent	58	619
Chow	Nevada Grass Valley	61	227
Choy	Nevada Grass Valley	61	230
Fred*	Sacramento Ward 3	63	422
Gee	El Dorado Georgetown	58	704
Ha	Butte Oro	56	686
High	Mariposa Twp 3	60	620
Kee*	Mariposa Twp 3	60	582
See	Mariposa Twp 3	60	620
Sing	Mariposa Coulterville	60	682
Son Se	Mariposa Coulterville	60	692
Too	Amador Twp 2	55	312
Too	Butte Kimshaw	56	582
Warren*	Amador Twp 2	55	314
Wash	Amador Twp 5	55	335
Yaw	Mariposa Coulterville	60	682
MIN'GY			
L T*	Mariposa Twp 3	60	608
MINA			
Sing	San Francisco San Francisco 3	67	60
MINAGUS			
John*	Calaveras Twp 9	57	370
MINAJUS			
John*	Calaveras Twp 9	57	370
MINALY			
John*	Sierra La Porte	66	766
MINAN			
Jeremiah	San Francisco San Francisco 2	67	651
MINANDEZ			
Joseph	Tuolumne Twp 1	71	211
MINANER			
Juan	Mariposa Twp 1	60	629
MINARD			
Wm	Yuba Rose Bar	72	816
MINAS			
Anestacia	Yuba Marysville	72	948
MINAVERA			
Rafael	Marin Cortemad	60	780
MINAVESA			
Rafael	Marin Cortemad	60	780
MINAY			
Francisco	Santa Clara San Jose	65	328
MINAYIS			
John	Calaveras Twp 9	57	370
MINCANS			
George*	Yuba Marysville	72	863
MINCAPAN			
M F	Siskiyou Scott Va	69	59
MINCE			
---	El Dorado Salmon Hills	58	1058
Henry	Alameda Brooklyn	55	159
MINCFEE			
C*	El Dorado Placerville	58	852
MINCH			
Carl	Santa Clara Santa Clara	65	481
MINCHALL			
George	Calaveras Twp 6	57	172
MINCHAM			
Hamson	Sonoma Petaluma	69	548
MINCHARRINNE			
D	San Francisco San Francisco 3	67	51
MINCHEL			
Dasuris*	Yolo Putah	72	546
MINCHELL			
May	Solano Suisan	69	233
MINCHING			
Wm H	Butte Bidwell	56	727
MINCHOUSE			
M*	San Francisco San Francisco 5	67	518
MINCHULL			
George	Calaveras Twp 5	57	172
MINCI			
---*	El Dorado Salmon Falls	58	1058

Name	County Locale	M653 Roll	Page
MINCO			
H	Shasta Shasta	66	679
MINCY			
C C	Marin Novato	60	736
MIND			
Raymund	Sacramento Granite	63	244
MINDDORO			
D L*	El Dorado Placerville	58	875
MINDER			
R*	San Francisco San Francisco 5	67	543
MINDEZ			
Jose*	Santa Clara San Jose	65	390
MINDIA			
Ascension	Santa Cruz Watsonville	66	540
MINDINES			
Francisco*	Santa Clara Santa Clara	65	494
MINDIRAGO			
Hosea*	Alameda Murray	55	219
MINDON			
H	Sutter Nicolaus	70	827
MINDOSA			
Jesus	Marin Cortemad	60	788
MINDOZA			
Jaan	Mariposa Twp 1	60	641
Manuel	Tuolumne Sonora	71	481
MINDWYLER			
Jacob*	San Francisco San Francisco 7	68	1389
MINE			
---	Placer Illinois	62	753
Daniel	Calaveras Twp 6	57	161
Frederick*	Yuba New York	72	737
M A	Sutter Sutter	70	803
Prosper	San Francisco San Francisco 2	67	694
Thomas	San Francisco San Francisco 7	68	1399
MINEA			
William*	San Mateo Twp 2	65	123
MINEAH			
---*	Tularа Visalia	71	39
MINEAHE			
---	Tulara Twp 2	71	39
MINEAM			
George*	Yuba Marysville	72	863
MINEANS			
George*	Yuba Marysville	72	863
MINEAR			
Nathan	Calaveras Twp 8	57	83
MINECK			
Daniel	Sierra St Louis	66	812
F	Sacramento Ward 4	63	607
Henry M*	Sierra St Louis	66	811
MINEED			
---	San Bernardino S Timate	64	700
MINEHAN			
Timothy E	San Francisco San Francisco 7	68	1353
MINEKITN			
Santiago*	Calaveras Twp 6	57	164
MINEKITU			
Santiago	Calaveras Twp 6	57	164
MINELO			
T*	Tehama Red Bluff	70	926
MINEMAH			
---*	Tulara Visalia	71	40
MINEMAHO			
---	Tulara Twp 2	71	40
MINEO			
N	Shasta Shasta	66	679
MINER			
---*	Amador Twp 4	55	242
Adam	Siskiyou Scott Va	69	53
Andrew	Siskiyou Scott Va	69	27
Avinia	San Francisco San Francisco 10	67	289
C H	Solano Suisan	69	207
C L	Nevada Nevada	61	284
D W	Nevada Bloomfield	61	508
Frank	Placer Todds Va	62	789
Frank*	Amador Twp 2	55	321
G F	Sacramento Georgian	63	339
G R	Solano Suisan	69	208
Garner	Colusa Grand Island	57	468
Geo	Butte Oregon	56	623
George	Plumas Meadow Valley	62	900
Hamar*	Amador Twp 4	55	255
Hamas*	Amador Twp 4	55	255
Hugh C	Tulara Visalia	71	105
Isaac	Klamath Trinidad	59	223
J	Nevada Grass Valley	61	204
J H	San Francisco San Francisco 5	67	505
Jacob	El Dorado Georgetown	58	750
Jacob	Yuba Marysville	72	938
James	Placer Michigan	62	820
James D	Plumas Quincy	62	938
James P	Sierra St Louis	66	864
Jane	Placer Yankee J	62	779
Jard	El Dorado Georgetown	58	686
Jno	Sacramento Granite	63	230

Name	County Locale	M653 Roll	Page
MINER			
John	Marin San Rafael	60	765
John	Placer Todds Va	62	784
Jolhn	El Dorado Big Bar	58	738
M	El Dorado Coloma	58	1107
M E	Alameda Oakland	55	53
M E	Marin Bolinas	60	726
Matthew	Siskiyou Yreka	69	188
Napoleon	Yuba Parke Ba	72	786
Napoleon	Yuba Marysville	72	882
Richard H	Calaveras Twp 4	57	318
S B	Tuolumne Jamestown	71	425
T J	Siskiyou Scott Ri	69	68
Thomas	Placer Forest H	62	768
Thos	Tuolumne Big Oak	71	126
Thos	Tuolumne Twp 4	71	128
V L	Tehama Red Bluff	70	922
W S	Amador Twp 5	55	348
William	Santa Cruz Santa Cruz	66	603
William	Siskiyou Callahan	69	19
Wm	Butte Chico	56	555
Wm	Sacramento Dry Crk	63	379
Wm	San Francisco San Francisco 6	67	465
MINERO			
Chas	San Francisco San Francisco 2	67	748
MINERS			
J*	Nevada Grass Valley	61	207
MINERT			
J	Nevada Grass Valley	61	207
MINERVA			
M*	Nevada Grass Valley	61	193
MINES			
---*	Yuba Marysville	72	895
J T*	Mariposa Twp 3	60	587
Wm L	Colusa Muion	57	462
MINET			
---	Tulara Visalia	71	113
MINETT			
Charles	Placer Michigan	62	840
MINEY			
J L	El Dorado Placerville	58	893
J P	Sutter Vernon	70	842
John*	Sierra Downieville	66	1022
T	El Dorado Placerville	58	823
MINEYUS			
John*	Calaveras Twp 9	57	370
MINFORD			
John	Amador Twp 2	55	263
MING CHANG			
---	San Joaquin Stockton	64	1056
MING			
---	Amador Twp 2	55	312
---	Amador Twp 2	55	315
---	Amador Twp 2	55	326
---	Amador Twp 2	55	327
---	Amador Twp 6	55	425
---	Amador Twp 6	55	430
---	Amador Twp 6	55	450
---	Amador Twp 1	55	497
---	Amador Twp 1	55	506
---	Butte Kimshaw	56	606
---	Butte Ophir	56	807
---	Butte Ophir	56	814
---	Calaveras Twp 5	57	181
---	Calaveras Twp 5	57	205
---	Calaveras Twp 5	57	257
---	Calaveras Twp 10	57	269
---	Calaveras Twp 10	57	270
---	Calaveras Twp 10	57	271
---	Calaveras Twp 4	57	300
---	Calaveras Twp 4	57	306
---	Calaveras Twp 4	57	320
---	Calaveras Twp 4	57	333
---	Calaveras Twp 4	57	334
---	Calaveras Twp 9	57	349
---	Calaveras Twp 9	57	362
---	Calaveras Twp 9	57	375
---	Calaveras Twp 7	57	39
---	Calaveras Twp 7	57	47
---	Calaveras Twp 7	57	48
---	Calaveras Twp 8	57	59
---	Calaveras Twp 8	57	76
---	Calaveras Twp 8	57	82
---	Calaveras Twp 8	57	84
---	Calaveras Twp 8	57	87
---	Del Norte Crescent	58	633
---	Del Norte Crescent	58	651
---	Del Norte Crescent	58	659
---	El Dorado Salmon Falls	58	1043
---	El Dorado Salmon Falls	58	1046
---	El Dorado Salmon Falls	58	1052
---	El Dorado Salmon Falls	58	1067
---	El Dorado Coloma	58	1085
---	El Dorado Coloma	58	1109
---	El Dorado Coloma	58	1114
---	El Dorado Coloma	58	1122

California 1860 Census Index

Name	County Locale	M653 RollPage
MING		
---	El Dorado Kelsey	58 1130
---	El Dorado Kelsey	58 1155
---	El Dorado Casumnes	58 1160
---	El Dorado Casumnes	58 1176
---	El Dorado Mountain	58 1178
---	El Dorado Mountain	58 1186
---	El Dorado Greenwood	58 714
---	El Dorado Diamond	58 794
---	El Dorado Diamond	58 795
---	El Dorado Placerville	58 829
---	El Dorado Placerville	58 870
---	El Dorado Placerville	58 874
---	El Dorado Placerville	58 904
---	El Dorado Eldorado	58 940
---	El Dorado Eldorado	58 945
---	El Dorado Mud Springs	58 952
---	El Dorado Mud Springs	58 981
---	Mariposa Twp 3	60 569
---	Mariposa Twp 3	60 607
---	Mariposa Twp 1	60 659
---	Nevada Bridgeport	61 460
---	Nevada Bridgeport	61 493
---	Placer Virginia	62 684
---	Placer Illinois	62 740
---	Placer Illinois	62 748
---	Placer Illinois	62 749
---	Placer Illinois	62 750
---	Plumas Meadow Valley	62 913
---	San Francisco San Francisco 4	68 1183
---	San Francisco San Francisco 11	67 146
---	San Francisco San Francisco 11	67 161
---	Stanislaus Branch	70 714
---	Stanislaus Buena Village	70 724
---	Trinity Cox'S Bar	70 1037
---	Tuolumne Twp 3	71 468
---	Yolo No E Twp	72 685
---	Yolo Slate Ra	72 711
---	Yuba North Ea	72 685
---	Yuba Slate Ro	72 711
---	Yuba Long Bar	72 759
---	Yuba Long Bar	72 767
---	Yuba Marysville	72 927
---*	Los Angeles Los Angeles	59 321
---*	Nevada Bridgeport	61 460
---*	Stanislaus Branch	70 714
---*	Trinity Big Flat	70 1041
A*	Nevada Bridgeport	61 460
Ah	Calaveras Twp 7	57 36
Choy	Butte Ophir	56 820
Fee	San Francisco San Francisco 11	67 160
Foo	Yuba New York	72 735
Han Ping	Calaveras Twp 6	57 151
Hee	San Francisco San Francisco 11	67 159
Herm	Mariposa Coulterville	60 682
John*	Yuba Fosters	72 836
L	Mariposa Twp 3	60 608
Lee	San Francisco San Francisco 11	67 159
Lee	Yuba Foster B	72 830
Lo	Butte Eureka	56 652
No	San Francisco San Francisco 11	67 159
Pak	Stanislaus Emory	70 752
Sing	Del Norte Crescent	58 633
Ti	San Francisco San Francisco 11	67 159
Tong	San Francisco San Francisco 11	67 160
Wal	San Francisco San Francisco 1	68 925
MINGARD		
Jack	Trinity Lewiston	70 961
MINGES		
John	San Joaquin Castoria	64 885
MINGG		
---	El Dorado Georgetown	58 680
MINGIRA		
Jose	Calaveras Twp 7	57 11
MINGIS		
A	Solano Fremont	69 379
MINGLE		
Isaac	Calaveras Twp 7	57 18
M B	Mariposa Twp 3	60 584
Thomas	Contra Costa Twp 2	57 539
MINGLETON		
Bernard	San Francisco San Francisco 7	68 1325
MINGMUIN		
J*	Calaveras Twp 9	57 397
MINGO		
---	Alameda Oakland	55 24
---	Tulara Twp 3	71 64
Chas	Trinity Weaverville	70 1073

Name	County Locale	M653 RollPage
MINGOON		
---	Trinity Trinindad Rvr	70 1047
---	Trinity Weaverville	70 1075
MINGUE		
Mary	Sierra Downieville	66 968
MINGUS		
John A	Calaveras Twp 9	57 375
MINICK		
Daniel	Sierra St Louis	66 812
Marion	Butte Ophir	56 746
Mitchel	Sierra St Louis	66 815
Mitchell	Sierra St Louis	66 815
MINIFEE		
Fred	Santa Clara Santa Clara	65 513
MINIFER		
Robert*	Sacramento Ward 1	63 94
MINIG		
---	Sacramento Centre	63 182
MINIHAN		
F	San Francisco San Francisco 4	68 1165
MINIMOND		
R	Calaveras Twp 9	57 406
MINIRO		
Chas	San Francisco San Francisco 2	67 748
MINIROLE		
W*	San Francisco San Francisco 6	67 406
MINIS		
John	Yuba Bear Rvr	72 1006
Richd	Napa Clear Lake	61 137
W	Yolo Putah	72 598
MINISAY		
Patrick	Santa Cruz Santa Cruz	66 634
MINIUM		
Abraham	Plumas Quincy	62 957
George*	Plumas Meadow Valley	62 908
MINJ		
---	Amador Twp 2	55 302
MINJEA		
Manuell	Amador Twp 5	55 336
MINK		
H C	Sutter Sutter	70 810
MINKE		
Edward	San Francisco San Francisco 6	67 455
MINKES		
Henry	Calaveras Twp 4	57 318
MINKIS		
Henry	Calaveras Twp 4	57 318
MINKLE		
John*	El Dorado Placerville	58 916
MINKS		
J	Sacramento Ward 3	63 433
MINLEOFA		
---	Mendocino Calpella	60 823
MINLOTTA		
Carlotta*	El Dorado Georgetown	58 684
MINLTIN		
James	Sierra Twp 7	66 865
MINN		
---	Butte Oregon	56 629
---	Butte Ophir	56 818
---	Mariposa Twp 3	60 620
---*	Amador Twp 4	55 242
A	Sacramento Granite	63 250
Ah	Butte Oregon	56 629
Patrick	Sierra Downieville	66 1021
Silas B	El Dorado Big Bar	58 739
MINNE		
---	Tulara Twp 2	71 39
---*	Tulara Visalia	71 40
MINNEANTONINO		
Wilcox	Sierra Downieville	66 972
MINNEGAN		
Jas	San Francisco San Francisco 12	67 385
MINNEHAM		
John	Santa Clara San Jose	65 287
MINNELITO		
---	San Diego Agua Caliente	64 843
MINNENEAH		
---	Tulara Twp 2	71 39
MINNER		
Perry	San Mateo Twp 3	65 88
Toachmen	Butte Mountain	56 741
Tvachmen*	Butte Mountain	56 741
MINNETT		
George	Sierra Twp 7	66 903
MINNIMOND		
J	Calaveras Twp 9	57 406
MINNOCK		
John	Yolo Cache	72 590
MINNRIKILO		
Matilda	Calaveras Twp 6	57 133
MINNS		
George W	San Francisco San Francisco 7	68 1397
William	San Francisco San Francisco 7	68 1347
MINNY		
Clement*	San Francisco San Francisco 5	67 495

Name	County Locale	M653 RollPage
MINO		
---*	Nevada Nevada	61 305
Juan	Santa Clara San Jose	65 373
MINOAS		
Guadalupe*	Napa Napa	61 102
MINOGUE		
J	Nevada Eureka	61 357
MINOLA		
John	Mariposa Twp 1	60 625
MINOLD		
T	Tehama Red Bluff	70 916
MINOLO		
S	Tehama Red Bluff	70 928
MINOLS		
Nicholas	Mariposa Twp 1	60 666
Nicholos	Mariposa Twp 1	60 666
MINOMY		
Jno B	Monterey Pajaro	60 1025
MINON		
Margaret	San Francisco San Francisco 10	67 334
MINONNY		
Jno B	Monterey Pajaro	60 1025
MINONS		
Guadalupe*	Napa Napa	61 102
MINOQUE		
J*	Nevada Eureka	61 357
MINOR		
C	San Francisco San Francisco 2	67 752
Ellen	San Francisco San Francisco 3	67 72
Ernst*	San Francisco San Francisco 1	68 825
H B	Butte Bidwell	56 705
Israel	Sacramento Ward 4	63 612
J	Nevada Grass Valley	61 236
James P	Sierra Twp 7	66 864
Jessi G	Calaveras Twp 6	57 126
Morris	Napa Napa	61 71
P O	Santa Clara San Jose	65 280
Seth	Sonoma Vallejo	69 620
Terence	Sacramento Ward 1	63 37
W C	San Francisco San Francisco 3	67 72
Willie	Tuolumne Columbia	71 320
Wm	San Francisco San Francisco 6	67 465
MINORT		
Jesse	San Joaquin Elkhorn	64 982
MINORY		
Guadalupe*	Napa Napa	61 102
MINOT		
H B	Butte Bidwell	56 705
Jacob	Nevada Little Y	61 535
P J	Tuolumne Sonora	71 216
MINOUY		
Guadalupe	Napa Napa	61 102
MINOX		
Baron	Sonoma Petaluma	69 546
Seth	Sonoma Vallejo	69 620
MINP		
---	Mariposa Twp 3	60 552
MINR		
Alex*	San Francisco San Francisco 2	67 625
MINRAL		
A*	San Francisco San Francisco 2	67 684
MINROE		
R W	Nevada Nevada	61 271
MINROSE		
George	San Bernardino San Bernadino	64 675
MINSELL		
J F	Shasta Cottonwoood	66 724
MINSER		
Wm	Yolo Slate Ra	72 695
MINSES		
John	Mariposa Coulterville	60 693
MINSHALL		
Geo	Humbolt Bucksport	59 155
MINSLER		
Leopold	San Francisco San Francisco 2	67 791
MINSON		
James	Amador Twp 2	55 319
Wm	Yuba Slate Ro	72 695
MINSSHEY		
D*	Nevada Nevada	61 292
MINSSORO		
D L*	El Dorado Placerville	58 875
MINT		
S*	Nevada Grass Valley	61 192
MINTA		
Julia	San Francisco San Francisco 6	67 462
MINTE		
Nattianiel	Colusa Monroeville	57 452
P	Amador Twp 2	55 308
MINTEER		
Wm	Trinity Indian C	70 988
MINTEIRN		
W T	Calaveras Twp 9	57 393
MINTER		
J C	Tuolumne Twp 2	71 324

California 1860 Census Index

Name	County Locale	M653 RollPage
MINTER		
James*	Contra Costa Twp 2	57 557
John S	San Diego Agua Caliente	64 843
Nilhelmura*	Stockton	641017
	San Joaquin	
MINTERN		
W	San Francisco San Francisco 5	67 544
MINTES		
Delores	El Dorado Placerville	58 896
J C*	Tuolumne Columbia	71 324
MINTEY		
Franklin*	Sierra Cox'S Bar	66 952
MINTI		
P*	Amador Twp 2	55 308
MINTIRN		
W*	San Francisco San Francisco 5	67 544
MINTO		
John	Tuolumne Sonora	71 229
M*	San Francisco San Francisco 5	67 480
MINTON		
Hugh	Santa Clara Santa Clara	65 510
James	Santa Clara Santa Clara	65 510
Victor	Sierra Twp 5	66 921
MINTRUM		
M*	Sacramento Alabama	63 416
MINTRY		
Franklin	Sierra Cox'S Bar	66 952
Jacob*	El Dorado Placerville	58 918
MINTURD		
Chas	Sacramento Granite	63 254
MINTURM		
Jno	Sacramento Franklin	63 321
MINTURN		
Chas	Sacramento Granite	63 254
Chas*	San Francisco San Francisco 1	68 873
H P	Sacramento Franklin	63 316
John	San Francisco San Francisco 1	68 932
W T	Calaveras Twp 9	57 393
MINTZER		
Miner	San Francisco San Francisco 6	67 436
MINUIMO		
---	Tulara Twp 2	71 39
MINUR		
Alfd*	Butte Oregon	56 627
MINUS		
W J	El Dorado Placerville	58 872
MINVAL		
A*	San Francisco San Francisco 2	67 684
MINVLER		
Leopold	San Francisco San Francisco 2	67 791
MINWIIIMO		
---*	Tulara Visalia	71 39
MINX		
S*	Nevada Grass Valley	61 192
MINY		
---	Amador Twp 5	55 354
---	Calaveras Twp 10	57 269
---	Calaveras Twp 4	57 300
---	Calaveras Twp 4	57 302
---	Calaveras Twp 4	57 306
---	Calaveras Twp 8	57 75
---	Calaveras Twp 8	57 79
MINZER		
Wm	Tuolumne Twp 1	71 248
MIOLDA		
Fermin*	Los Angeles Los Angeles	59 352
Ferwin*	Los Angeles Los Angeles	59 352
MIOLOVI		
F*	San Francisco San Francisco 5	67 503
MION		
Manuel	San Bernardino San Bernadino	64 675
MIOR		
R	Sierra Downieville	661012
MIORALLES		
Amelia	San Francisco San Francisco 4	681157
MIORS		
John D*	Mariposa Twp 3	60 586
MIOT		
Alexr	Sierra Downieville	66 967
MIP KO		
---	Sacramento Ward 1	63 52
MIP		
---	Placer Illinois	62 745
MIPER		
Eliza*	San Francisco San Francisco 7	681353
MIPMANN		
Christian	San Francisco San Francisco 8	681282
MIPRO		
Albert*	Mariposa Twp 3	60 593
D A	Colusa Butte Crk	57 464
MIPTRATE		
F	Tuolumne Twp 2	71 283
MIQUEL		
---	Los Angeles Los Angeles	59 369
---	Los Angeles Los Nieto	59 433
---	San Diego San Diego	64 775

Name	County Locale	M653 RollPage
MIQUEL		
---	San Diego Temecula	64 804
Hancock	Los Angeles Los Angeles	59 370
MIQUES		
M*	Tuolumne Columbia	71 338
MIR SO		
---	Sierra Twp 7	66 889
MIR		
---	Amador Twp 2	55 328
---	El Dorado Big Bar	58 733
Lanus	El Dorado Mud Springs	58 984
MIRAL		
James	Placer Yankee J	62 760
MIRALAS		
Navara	Santa Clara San Jose	65 302
MIRALD		
O*	Calaveras Twp 9	57 418
MIRAMON		
John	Tuolumne Twp 3	71 470
MIRAN		
John	San Francisco San Francisco 10	67 209
		67
MIRANAN		
William*	Siskiyou Scott Va	69 43
MIRANCHO		
Francisco*	Contra Costa Twp 3	57 601
MIRANDA		
---*	Yuba Marysville	72 948
Antonio*	Contra Costa Twp 3	57 599
Chonita	Monterey Monterey	60 946
Cruz	Monterey Monterey	60 962
F	El Dorado Placerville	58 821
Francisco	Marin S Antoni	60 707
Guadalupa	Contra Costa Twp 1	57 529
Joaquin	Contra Costa Twp 3	57 599
Jose	Plumas Quincy	62 988
Josefa	Los Angeles Los Angeles	59 407
Juana	Santa Clara Fremont	65 436
Manuel	Contra Costa Twp 2	57 579
Mario	Trinity North Fo	701023
Polidore	Monterey Pajaro	601011
Polidoro*	Monterey Pajaro	601011
Polonio	Los Angeles Santa Ana	59 449
Rafail	Santa Clara Burnett	65 258
Ramon	Contra Costa Twp 3	57 599
Ramon	Los Angeles Los Angeles	59 404
Ramona	Los Angeles Los Angeles	59 300
Ramone	Monterey Pajaro	601011
Satos	Contra Costa Twp 2	57 563
Servillo	Los Angeles Los Angeles	59 304
Silvian	Los Angeles San Gabriel	59 417
Tomas	Los Angeles Tejon	59 541
MIRANDER		
Domingo*	Calaveras Twp 5	57 198
MIRANDEZ		
Pascual	Los Angeles Santa Ana	59 445
MIRANDI		
Casase*	Marin Cortemad	60 757
Casuse	Marin Cortemad	60 757
Francisco	Marin Novato	60 739
MIRANDO		
Angel	San Diego S Luis R	64 780
Concelpion	San Diego Temecula	64 792
Guadalupe	Santa Clara San Jose	65 358
Joaquin	Calaveras Twp 5	57 198
Joayuin	Calaveras Twp 5	57 198
Jose	San Bernardino Santa Barbara	64 149
Ramon	Monterey Alisal	601041
MIRANDOE		
Antonio*	Contra Costa Twp 3	57 599
Domingo*	Calaveras Twp 5	57 198
MIRAR		
Peter	Sierra Downieville	66 977
MIRAUY		
Charlotte*	Calaveras Twp 5	57 179
MIRCED		
---	San Bernardino S Timate	64 697
MIRCELINA		
---	San Bernardino San Bernadino	64 678
MIRCHANS		
Manseen	Contra Costa Twp 3	57 585
MIRCHANT		
George	San Mateo Twp 3	65 80
MIRCHIRISE		
Jno	Nevada Nevada	61 287
MIRCHISON		
A	Tuolumne Twp 1	71 243
S	Tuolumne Sonora	71 243
MIRE		
Frederick	Yuba New York	72 737
MIREER		
Charles	Solano Suisan	69 231
MIREHEAD		
Samuel*	Alameda Brooklyn	55 139
MIRELES		
Rumaldo	Los Angeles Santa Ana	59 457

Name	County Locale	M653 RollPage
MIRELES		
Silvestre	Los Angeles Santa Ana	59 458
MIREMAN		
Samuel*	Alameda Murray	55 218
MIREN		
Mary*	San Francisco San Francisco 7	681418
MIRERS		
Charles	Sierra La Porte	66 769
MIRESOL		
Jose M	Los Angeles Los Angeles	59 346
MIREY		
John	Calaveras Twp 5	57 191
MIRFAN		
James*	El Dorado Georgetown	58 753
MIRGAN		
Ann*	Alameda Brooklyn	55 93
MIRGINS		
John A	Calaveras Twp 9	57 375
MIRGMUIN		
J*	Calaveras Twp 9	57 397
MIRIAM		
A J	San Francisco San Francisco 3	67 18
MIRICE		
Phillipe	Mariposa Twp 1	60 628
MIRICK		
Caroline	Santa Clara San Jose	65 318
MIRIER		
August	Tuolumne Twp 2	71 282
MIRILL		
Phillipe	Mariposa Twp 1	60 628
MIRINO		
Gabrial	Los Angeles Los Angeles	59 510
Urusla	Los Angeles Los Angeles	59 510
MIRIX		
Heputel*	Sierra Eureka	661049
MIRKLE		
W S	Sierra Twp 5	66 938
MIRLET		
John	Calaveras Twp 5	57 207
MIRLLOY		
James	San Francisco San Francisco 3	67 56
MIRLTEN		
Thos	Santa Clara San Jose	65 335
MIRMOSE		
F	Tuolumne Sonora	71 214
MIRMOSO		
F	Tuolumne Twp 1	71 214
MIRN		
---*	Nevada Grass Valley	61 228
---*	Sacramento Granite	63 249
Marco	Sacramento Ward 1	63 34
Pat	Sacramento Ward 1	63 83
MIRNAIO		
Agno	Santa Clara San Jose	65 299
MIRNEY		
---	El Dorado Kelsey	581155
MIRNSON		
Robt H	Nevada Bridgeport	61 472
MIRO		
Anson	El Dorado Georgetown	58 697
R	Sierra Downieville	661012
MIROIS		
Chales	Sierra La Porte	66 769
MIROLET		
Jon*	San Francisco San Francisco 2	67 662
MIRON		
Chas	Placer Virginia	62 673
MIRONDI		
Augustus	Marin San Rafael	60 766
MIRONO		
Gabrial	Los Angeles Los Angeles	59 510
MIROR		
Andrew*	Sacramento Ward 1	63 116
MIROW		
G M*	Sierra Twp 5	66 940
MIRPAL		
C*	Nevada Grass Valley	61 157
MIRRALY		
John*	Sierra La Porte	66 766
MIRRE		
David	San Francisco San Francisco 2	67 618
MIRRER		
Anna M	Mariposa Coulterville	60 678
MIRRFER		
William*	San Francisco San Francisco 9	681031
MIRRIAM		
A D	Tuolumne Shawsfla	71 420
MIRRIASN		
George	San Francisco San Francisco 3	67 51
MIRRIFER		
Robert*	Sacramento Ward 1	63 94
MIRRIL		
Frank*	Yuba Rose Bar	72 819
MIRRING		
Michael	Yuba Slate Ro	72 689
MIRRIS		
Richd*	Napa Clear Lake	61 137

California 1860 Census Index

Name	County Locale	M653 Roll Page
MIRROGUE		
J*	Nevada Eureka	61 357
MIRROQUE		
J*	Nevada Eureka	61 357
MIRROR		
Ernst*	San Francisco San Francisco 1	68 825
Fred	Stanislaus Branch	70 702
MIRROW		
Joseph*	Sierra Downieville	66 969
MIRS		
Mary A*	Sierra Eureka	661042
MIRSE		
Nathaniel H	Calaveras Twp 6	57 147
MIRTCHUM		
J	Butte Bidwell	56 710
MIRTE		
A A	San Francisco San Francisco 4	681129
MIRTON		
William*	Calaveras Twp 8	57 85
MIRUFH		
Patrick*	Mariposa Twp 3	60 585
MIRUS		
William	San Francisco San Francisco 7	681347
MIRY		
---	Amador Twp 2	55 302
---	Amador Twp 2	55 315
---	Amador Twp 5	55 355
---	Amador Twp 5	55 356
MISA		
Antonio	Santa Clara Almaden	65 274
Carlos	Santa Clara Gilroy	65 223
Chino	Santa Clara San Jose	65 384
Francisco	Los Angeles Los Angeles	59 518
Jose	Santa Clara San Jose	65 303
Jose	Santa Clara San Jose	65 369
Manuel	Los Angeles Los Angeles	59 511
Manuel*	San Francisco San Francisco 2	67 685
Pedro	Santa Clara San Jose	65 383
Ramona	Trinity Weaverville	701081
Simon	Santa Clara San Jose	65 305
MISAL		
Casper	Amador Twp 1	55 478
MISALD		
O*	Calaveras Twp 9	57 418
MISAMORE		
Peter	Yuba Bear Rvr	721012
MISANDO		
Joayuin*	Calaveras Twp 5	57 198
MISCHANT		
C F	Tuolumne Sonora	71 235
MISE		
Christopher	Sonoma Sonoma	69 643
H	San Francisco San Francisco 10	272 67
MISEH		
L	El Dorado Placerville	58 871
MISEHEAD		
Samuel*	Alameda Brooklyn	55 139
MISEN		
Mary*	San Francisco San Francisco 7	681418
MISENDO		
Pand	El Dorado Greenwood	58 730
MISEO		
---	Fresno Twp 2	59 108
MISER		
Aaron	Humbolt Pacific	59 132
F S	Shasta Horsetown	66 693
H R	Butte Kimshaw	56 588
John	Placer Dutch Fl	62 728
Solomon*	Sacramento Cosumnes	63 404
MISERIS		
Joseph	Calaveras Twp 4	57 335
MISERMAN		
Diedrick	Yuba Marysville	72 923
MISERSERY		
John	El Dorado Greenwood	58 711
MISGUILE		
Joseph*	Yuba Marysville	72 952
MISH		
P	San Francisco San Francisco 5	67 488
P*	San Francisco San Francisco 5	67 483
William	Calaveras Twp 6	57 127
Wm*	San Bernardino San Bernadino	64 631
MISHEHIEM		
Wm*	Napa Clear Lake	61 132
MISHIHIEM		
Wm*	Napa Clear Lake	61 132
MISHLER		
Peter B	El Dorado Coloma	581103
MISHON		
James	Santa Cruz Santa Cruz	66 634
MISHOR		
George	Los Angeles Tejon	59 527
MISHRHRIM		
Wm M*	Napa Clear Lake	61 132
MISIN		
George*	El Dorado Georgetown	58 702
MISING		
---	Sierra Downieville	661026
MISION		
George	El Dorado Georgetown	58 702
Messee*	Tulara Twp 1	71 120
MISKELL		
John	San Francisco San Francisco 2	67 778
MISKILL		
Robt	Sierra Twp 7	66 867
MISKLE		
W S*	Sierra Twp 5	66 938
MISLER		
B	Butte Ophir	56 776
MISLETIE		
Carlotta	El Dorado Georgetown	58 684
MISMER		
A S	Tuolumne Twp 2	71 315
MISNER		
A S	Tuolumne Columbia	71 315
C H	Amador Twp 5	55 363
John	Placer Michigan	62 837
Lansing	San Francisco San Francisco 9	681046
N L	El Dorado Salmon Falls	581050
MISOR		
A J	Calaveras Twp 9	57 393
H R*	Butte Kimshaw	56 588
MISS		
Chas	Alameda Brooklyn	55 107
Ko*	Sacramento Ward 1	63 52
MISSELBROOK		
Joseph	Tuolumne Sonora	71 245
MISSELL		
J	San Francisco San Francisco 5	67 525
MISSENHEUMER		
R M	Trinity Indian C	70 988
MISSENO		
W N	Sierra Downieville	66 953
MISSERK		
Joseph	San Joaquin Douglass	64 920
MISSERVE		
Theo*	San Francisco San Francisco 2	67 739
MISSIC		
J G	Trinity Weaverville	701080
MISSIDA		
Leo*	El Dorado Georgetown	58 747
MISSIMER		
J D	Stanislaus Emory	70 750
MISSING		
H	Santa Clara San Jose	65 291
P	Stanislaus Buena Village	70 721
MISSINGER		
Joseph	Santa Clara San Jose	65 294
MISSION		
J J	San Francisco San Francisco 1	68 823
Monangete*	Tulara Twp 1	71 120
Old*	Tulara Twp 1	71 120
Yennellitch*	Tulara Twp 1	71 120
MISSIRN		
George*	Calaveras Twp 10	57 281
MISSIVE		
W N*	Sierra Downieville	66 953
MISSURN		
George	Calaveras Twp 10	57 281
MISSWE		
W N*	Sierra Downieville	66 953
MISTADE		
Wm	Sierra Downieville	661018
MISTADO		
Wm	Sierra Downieville	661018
MISTCHUM		
J	Butte Bidwell	56 710
MISTE		
Charles	Calaveras Twp 8	57 64
MISTELHUM		
Jacob*	Placer Auburn	62 588
MISTELI		
John	El Dorado White Oaks	581014
MISTER		
Christopher	San Francisco 8	681256
	San Francisco	
MISTETULL		
W H*	Placer Iona Hills	62 867
MISTMOSO		
T	Calaveras Twp 9	57 418
MISTON		
Fred	Sonoma Armally	69 482
MISTRE		
L	San Francisco San Francisco 1	68 934
MISULA		
Leo*	El Dorado Georgetown	58 747
MISURIS		
Juan	Santa Clara San Jose	65 300
MISYAN		
James	Calaveras Twp 6	57 143
MITATZ		
Henry*	San Francisco San Francisco 3	67 15
MITCALF		
Reuben	San Joaquin Elkhorn	64 961
Saml A	San Francisco San Francisco 10	229 67
MITCELL		
Peter	Tuolumne Sonora	71 210
MITCH		
John*	Sacramento San Joaquin	63 368
MITCHAEL		
Mary	Mariposa Coulterville	60 701
Thomas	Mariposa Coulterville	60 701
Wm	Mariposa Coulterville	60 701
MITCHAL		
John	Tuolumne Twp 2	71 398
MITCHAMA		
---	San Diego Agua Caliente	64 815
MITCHEAL		
Thos	Amador Twp 2	55 290
MITCHEL		
---	Yuba Marysville	72 867
A H	Sutter Yuba	70 764
A M	Tuolumne Jamestown	71 422
Adolphus	Tulara Visalia	71 77
Armstead	Tulara Visalia	71 106
B N	Sutter Nicolaus	70 835
Butram	San Francisco San Francisco 4	681171
C	Nevada Grass Valley	61 179
D F	San Francisco San Francisco 4	681111
David	Calaveras Twp 4	57 329
Dora	Tuolumne Visalia	71 95
E	Nevada Grass Valley	61 218
Elias	Klamath S Fork	59 203
Felix	San Francisco San Francisco 1	68 825
Francisco	Alameda Brooklyn	55 180
Fred	Tuolumne Twp 3	71 443
G	Tuolumne Jamestown	71 427
G V	Tehama Tehama	70 941
Geo S	San Joaquin O'Neal	641001
George	San Mateo Twp 3	65 110
Goodman	Tuolumne Columbia	71 356
H	Nevada Grass Valley	61 172
Henry C	Calaveras Twp 6	57 152
J	Sutter Bear Rvr	70 826
J R	Nevada Bridgeport	61 453
J R	Sutter Nicolaus	70 832
John	Amador Twp 3	55 380
John	Sierra Pine Grove	66 822
John	Sierra Poker Flats	66 839
John	Tuolumne Shawsfla	71 398
Julius	Marin San Rafael	60 763
L T	Sacramento Alabama	63 414
Levi	Tulara Visalia	71 103
Lucy	Marin Bolinas	60 742
M	Nevada Grass Valley	61 191
Maria	Humbolt Bucksport	59 162
Miler M	Calaveras Twp 4	57 318
Miles M	Calaveras Twp 4	57 318
N	Sutter Nicolaus	70 830
R W	San Francisco San Francisco 9	681069
Robert	Tulara Visalia	71 107
Saml	Tuolumne Twp 3	71 427
Samuel	Tuolumne Big Oak	71 133
T	Nevada Grass Valley	61 218
Thomas	Marin Tomales	60 717
Thomas	Marin Cortemad	60 779
Thos*	Solano Benecia	69 317
William	Klamath Trinidad	59 223
William Mc S	Calaveras Twp 6	57 150
Z	El Dorado Newtown	58 777
MITCHELDOCK		
M	Yolo Washington	72 568
MITCHELE		
Blaise D	Calaveras Twp 7	57 7
George	Calaveras Twp 7	57 7
Joseph	Calaveras Twp 7	57 1
MITCHELL		
---	Yuba Marysville	72 867
A	Trinity Weaverville	701065
A B	Nevada Red Dog	61 538
A C	El Dorado Newtown	58 779
A W	Butte Chico	56 554
A Y	San Joaquin Stockton	641073
Adolphus	Tulara Twp 1	71 77
Alex	San Francisco San Francisco 10	250 67
Alex	Yolo Putah	72 585
Alexander H	Yolo No E Twp	72 668
Alfred	Placer Michigan	62 818
Alfred*	Placer Michigan	62 807
Andrew	Sierra St Louis	66 805
Andrew	Solano Suisan	69 225
Andrew	Solano Vacaville	69 362
Andrew	Yolo No E Twp	72 672
Andrew	Yuba North Ea	72 672
Anne	Solano Vallejo	69 250
Augustus	San Francisco San Francisco 7	681378

MITCHELL -
MITCHLANU

California 1860 Census Index

Name	County Locale	M653 RollPage
MITCHELL		
Authur	El Dorado Mud Springs	58 953
B J	Sacramento Ward 1	63 116
B S	El Dorado White Oaks	581012
Ben W	Yuba Marysville	72 901
Benjamin	Yolo Slate Ra	72 691
Benjamin	Yuba Slate Ro	72 691
Bernard	Sacramento Granite	63 267
Bernard	Sacramento Natonia	63 284
Bernut	Sacramento Granite	63 267
Bery	Los Angeles Tejon	59 537
C	Stanislaus Emory	70 748
C L	Shasta Shasta	66 686
Caroline	San Francisco San Francisco 3	67 50
Cashman	Santa Cruz Pajaro	66 551
Casper	Sierra Gibsonville	66 858
Charles	El Dorado Coloma	581082
Charles	San Francisco San Francisco 6	67 414
Charles	Sierra Gibsonville	66 853
Charles	Yuba Fosters	72 840
Charles E	Monterey San Juan	60 995
Charles L	San Joaquin Elkhorn	64 951
Chas	San Francisco San Francisco 2	67 716
Chas	Santa Clara San Jose	65 362
Chas T	San Francisco San Francisco 7	681444
Consider	San Joaquin Elkhorn	64 986
D	El Dorado Diamond	58 770
D	Siskiyou Scott Ri	69 72
D A	Sacramento Ward 4	63 580
D C	Placer Dutch Fl	62 729
D C	San Francisco San Francisco 1	68 808
D M	Mendocino Ukiah	60 796
D S	Butte Oro	56 680
D S	Butte Ophir	56 787
D Sw	Butte Oro	56 680
D W	Sierra Eureka	661044
Dan	Placer Virginia	62 677
David	Sacramento Alabama	63 413
David	Stanislaus Emory	70 746
Dora	Tulara Twp 1	71 95
E	Siskiyou Yreka	69 152
E A	San Francisco San Francisco 1	68 897
E A	Tuolumne Twp 1	71 204
E F	Calaveras Twp 9	57 407
Elimm	Santa Clara Almaden	65 278
Elisha	Sonoma Healdsbu	69 475
Elizabeth	El Dorado Coloma	581069
Elizabeth	Sonoma Petaluma	69 576
Emma Miss	San Francisco San Francisco 10	181 67
Emma Sister*	San Francisco San Francisco 10	181 67
F	Siskiyou Scott Ri	69 73
F E	Sacramento Sutter	63 297
F K	San Francisco San Francisco 10	199 67
Franar	Amador Twp 4	55 259
Frances	Sacramento Cosummes	63 401
Francis	San Francisco San Francisco 7	681347
Francis K	San Francisco San Francisco 7	681347
Frank	San Francisco San Francisco 2	67 739
Franklin	Placer Michigan	62 814
Frederick	Monterey San Juan	60 994
G	Butte Chico	56 541
G B	Butte Kimshaw	56 580
G M	El Dorado White Oaks	581031
Genas	Sonoma Petaluma	69 546
Geo	El Dorado White Oaks	581026
Geo	San Francisco San Francisco 2	67 769
Geo	San Francisco San Francisco 1	68 886
George	Amador Twp 4	55 236
George	Calaveras Twp 7	57 7
George	Plumas Quincy	62 980
George	Yuba North Ea	72 676
Geroge	Yolo No E Twp	72 676
H	El Dorado Placerville	58 817
H	San Francisco San Francisco 3	67 23
H	Sonoma Bodega	69 522
H M	Butte Hamilton	56 528
Harriet	Nevada Bloomfield	61 508
Henry	Butte Bidwell	56 725
Henry	San Francisco San Francisco 10	228 67
Henry	Shasta French G	66 714
Henry C	Calaveras Twp 6	57 152
Henry K	Yuba Marysville	72 896
Henry*	San Francisco San Francisco 1	68 854
Isaac	Placer Virginia	62 666
Isaac	Placer Goods	62 695
Isaac	Shasta Millvill	66 746
J	El Dorado Diamond	58 783
J	El Dorado Diamond	58 791
J	Sutter Nicolaus	70 830
J	Yolo Putah	72 553
J C	Butte Ophir	56 797
J C	Sierra Twp 5	66 923
MITCHELL		
J C	Tuolumne Big Oak	71 135
J C	Yolo No E Twp	72 679
J D	Butte Oro	56 674
J E	Napa Yount	61 49
J E	San Francisco San Francisco 10	165 67
J H	Sacramento Ward 4	63 496
J H	Yolo Putah	72 614
J J	Sacramento Ward 1	63 116
J L	Yuba North Ea	72 679
J S	Tuolumne Twp 4	71 172
J W	Mariposa Twp 3	60 558
J W	Placer Michigan	62 814
J W	Siskiyou Scott Va	69 20
Jacob	San Joaquin Stockton	641020
Jacob	Yuba Linda	72 987
James	Calaveras Twp 7	57 19
James	Contra Costa Twp 1	57 535
James	Contra Costa Twp 2	57 563
James	Monterey S Antoni	60 967
James	Placer Todds Va	62 789
James	Plumas Meadow Valley	62 901
James	San Francisco San Francisco 7	681440
James	San Joaquin Elkhorn	64 956
James	Santa Cruz Santa Cruz	66 637
James	Shasta Millvill	66 726
James	Shasta Cottonwoood	66 736
James	Sonoma Vallejo	69 626
James S	Solano Vacaville	69 359
Jas	Merced Twp 1	60 896
Jas	Stanislaus Branch	70 709
Jas W	San Bernardino San Bernadino	64 676
Jasper	Plumas Quincy	621006
Jasper	Plumas Quincy	621007
Jerry	Tuolumne Columbia	71 321
Jesse A	San Joaquin Oneal	64 931
Jno	San Francisco San Francisco 9	681056
John	Butte Mountain	56 740
John	Calaveras Twp 9	57 360
John	Contra Costa Twp 3	57 595
John	Monterey Pajaro	601019
John	Nevada Bloomfield	61 512
John	Placer Auburn	62 593
John	Sacramento Ward 1	63 96
John	San Francisco San Francisco 8	681274
John	San Francisco San Francisco 1	68 870
John	San Joaquin Elkhorn	64 967
John	San Joaquin Elkhorn	64 986
John	Santa Clara Almaden	65 275
John	Santa Cruz Pajaro	66 533
John	Santa Cruz Watsonville	66 535
John	Sierra Pine Grove	66 822
John	Solano Suisan	69 239
John	Solano Benecia	69 317
John	Trinity W Weaver	701054
John	Trinity Grass Valley	70 962
John	Trinity Minersville	70 969
John	Trinity Steiner	70 999
John	Tulara Petersburg	71 51
John	Tulara Keyesville	71 62
John	Yolo No E Twp	72 679
John	Yuba North Ea	72 679
John	Yuba Rose Bar	72 793
John C	San Francisco San Francisco 2	67 586
John H	Nevada Bloomfield	61 508
John*	Solano Benecia	69 317
Jos	Merced Twp 1	60 896
Joseph	San Francisco San Francisco 3	67 20
Joseph	Santa Clara San Jose	65 291
Josiah	Plumas Quincy	621002
Julius	San Francisco San Francisco 8	681287
L	Nevada Eureka	61 392
Lewis	Alameda Brooklyn	55 91
Lewis	Merced Twp 2	60 924
Louis	San Francisco San Francisco 11	126 67
Lyman	Solano Vallejo	69 262
M	Nevada Grass Valley	61 204
M	Santa Clara San Jose	65 290
M	Tehama Moons	70 852
M B	Siskiyou Scott Va	69 28
M E	Siskiyou Scott Ri	69 76
Ma	San Joaquin Stockton	641091
Marceles	Humbolt Table Bl	59 141
Martin	Amador Twp 4	55 258
Mary	Los Angeles Los Angeles	59 315
Mary	San Francisco San Francisco 8	681270
Mary	San Francisco San Francisco 2	67 690
Mary E	San Francisco San Francisco 2	67 669
Mat	Placer Folsom	62 641
Medora	Sacramento Ward 1	63 98
Mornan	San Francisco San Francisco 7	681393
Mos	San Joaquin Stockton	641020
N	San Francisco San Francisco 9	681073
Oliver	Sierra Twp 5	66 948
MITCHELL		
Olivert	Sierra Twp 5	66 948
P	El Dorado Coloma	581068
P	El Dorado Placerville	58 821
P	Sacramento Dry Crk	63 377
P H	Nevada Eureka	61 374
P W	Mariposa Twp 3	60 558
Pasqual	Contra Costa Twp 1	57 533
Patrick	Sierra Twp 5	66 948
Peter	Butte Wyandotte	56 664
Peter	Sierra Pine Grove	66 828
Peter	Siskiyou Callahan	69 3
Peter	Siskiyou Callahan	69 4
R	Calaveras Twp 9	57 401
R P	San Francisco San Francisco 5	67 550
Richard	Los Angeles Los Angeles	59 317
Richd W	San Francisco San Francisco 9	68 988
Robert	Solano Vacaville	69 349
Robt L	Sonoma Russian	69 446
Robt T	Sonoma Russian	69 446
S	Butte Wyandotte	56 664
S	Butte Bidwell	56 719
Samuel	Contra Costa Twp 2	57 565
Sister Emma*	San Francisco San Francisco 10	181 67
Smith	Solano Fairfield	69 202
Smith	Tuolumne Twp 1	71 193
T A	San Francisco San Francisco 2	67 731
T E	Sacramento Sutter	63 297
T S	San Francisco San Francisco 6	67 431
Tabb*	Placer Auburn	62 560
Thomas	El Dorado Coloma	581119
Thomas	El Dorado Placerville	58 908
Thomas	Placer Michigan	62 811
Thomas	Placer Iona Hills	62 870
Thomas	Plumas Quincy	62 981
Thomas	Santa Cruz Watsonville	66 535
Thomas	Sierra Downieville	661016
Thomas	Solano Benecia	69 300
Thomas	Tulara Twp 3	71 54
Thomas	Yuba Fosters	72 837
Thomas	Yuba Fosters	72 838
Thoms	Sierra Downieville	661016
Thos	Sacramento Ward 1	63 120
Thos	San Francisco San Francisco 10	343 67
W	El Dorado Placerville	58 853
W P	Sacramento San Joaquin	63 367
W S	Mendocino Big Rvr	60 843
W W	Trinity New Rvr	701030
Wanen	Sierra Downieville	661029
Willia R	Tuolumne Twp 5	71 501
William	Contra Costa Twp 2	57 565
William	Placer Forest H	62 796
William	Siskiyou Yreka	69 150
William	Sonoma Washington	69 672
William H	San Francisco San Francisco 7	681345
William Mc S	Calaveras Twp 6	57 150
William R	Tuolumne Chinese	71 501
Wm	Butte Ophir	56 824
Wm	El Dorado Mud Springs	58 956
Wm	Placer Virginia	62 673
Wm	Sacramento Alabama	63 416
Wm	Sacramento Ward 4	63 514
Wm	San Francisco San Francisco 9	681061
Wm	Santa Clara Almaden	65 275
Wm	Santa Clara San Jose	65 336
Wm	Yuba Rose Bar	72 814
Wm J	Mariposa Twp 3	60 559
Wm P	Mariposa Twp 3	60 559
Wm R	Plumas Meadow Valley	62 906
Wm S	Mendocino Big Rvr	60 843
MITCHELLING		
Gustave	San Francisco San Francisco 8	681320
Instave	San Francisco San Francisco 8	681320
MITCHELTREE		
J	Shasta Horsetown	66 700
MITCHELTRES		
J	Shasta Horsetown	66 700
MITCHER		
Wm	Amador Twp 3	55 392
MITCHESEN		
Fredk	San Francisco San Francisco 12	361 67
MITCHIL		
A H	Calaveras Twp 9	57 413
MITCHILL		
Emma	San Francisco San Francisco 10	181 67
MITCHINER		
J	El Dorado Placerville	58 897
MITCHLANIE		
Pedro	Calaveras Twp 6	57 136
MITCHLANN		
Pedro	Calaveras Twp 5	57 136
MITCHLANU		
Pedro*	Calaveras Twp 6	57 136

California 1860 Census Index

Name	County Locale	M653 RollPage
MITCHLEN		
G	San Francisco San Francisco	4 681147
MITCHLER		
Margaret	San Francisco San Francisco	10 277 67
MITCHLIN		
G*	San Francisco San Francisco	4 681147
MITCHNER		
J S	Colusa Colusi	57 426
James	Colusa Colusi	57 426
MITCHSNILL		
S	Calaveras Twp 9	57 414
MITCHULL		
J	El Dorado Newtown	58 779
MITCHUM		
A G	Colusa Grand Island	57 471
MITE		
Peter	El Dorado Coloma	581122
MITEHILE		
D F	San Francisco San Francisco	4 681111
MITES		
M	Calaveras Twp 9	57 409
MITFORD		
T J	Sacramento Natonia	63 279
MITHCEL		
Fred	Tuolumne Jamestown	71 443
MITHCELL		
Wm	Santa Clara San Jose	65 311
MITHEHEIM		
Wm*	Napa Clear Lake	61 132
MITHERALD		
J*	Siskiyou Klamath	69 86
MITHERS		
John*	San Francisco San Francisco	9 68 966
MITHERTON		
E	Butte Hamilton	56 521
S	Butte Hamilton	56 521
MITHLUY		
Mich	Sacramento Granite	63 254
MITHS		
Rosina	San Francisco San Francisco	8 681308
MITLAR		
Louis*	Siskiyou Scott Va	69 26
MITLEL		
Antoine F*	Calaveras Twp 5	57 240
MITLET		
H	Tehama Red Bluff	70 910
MITONDO		
Miguel	Santa Clara San Jose	65 329
MITT		
John C*	San Francisco San Francisco	10 322 67
MITTALL		
George	San Joaquin Stockton	641071
Jno*	Sacramento Natonia	63 278
MITTAR		
Louis	Siskiyou Scott Va	69 26
MITTEL		
Antoine F*	Calaveras Twp 5	57 240
MITTEN		
Geo A	Napa Clear Lake	61 122
John	Nevada Nevada	61 241
Richard	Calaveras Twp 8	57 73
MITTING		
Albert	Nevada Red Dog	61 550
MITTINGTON		
Lewis	Placer Forest H	62 796
MITTON		
James*	Sonoma Petaluma	69 614
John*	Sierra La Porte	66 780
MITTOR		
William M	Nevada Rough &	61 421
MITTS		
J	Sutter Nicolaus	70 837
Thos	Merced Twp 1	60 913
MITTY		
Nicolas	Mendocino Ukiah	60 801
MITTZ		
Jacob*	Shasta Shasta	66 654
MITU		
Francisco*	Los Angeles Los Angeles	59 501
MITULA		
Leo*	El Dorado Georgetown	58 747
MITUMBY		
Michael*	Alameda Brooklyn	55 139
MITZ		
Ettinis*	Stanislaus Branch	70 700
Geo	San Francisco San Francisco	10 259 67
MITZGER		
W	Nevada Grass Valley	61 211
MITZKER		
Fredk	San Francisco San Francisco	2 67 767
Ramon	Monterey Alisal	601037
MITZLER		
Thomas	Sierra Monte Crk	661039

Name	County Locale	M653 RollPage
MITZLER		
Wm	Sacramento Ward 1	63 37
Wm*	Nevada Nevada	61 241
Wm*	Sacramento Ward 1	63 37
MITZZER		
John	Sacramento Ward 1	63 77
MIU		
---	San Francisco San Francisco	11 160 67
MIUNER		
Toachmen*	Butte Mountain	56 741
MIUR		
Alex	San Francisco San Francisco	2 67 625
Jos	Sacramento Ward 1	63 61
MIVEN		
Wm	Butte Chico	56 560
MIVN		
A*	San Francisco San Francisco	10 309 67
MIVOLET		
Jon*	San Francisco San Francisco	2 67 662
Jose*	San Francisco San Francisco	2 67 663
MIVORY		
Edward	Contra Costa Twp 1	57 533
MIW		
---	Calaveras Twp 5	57 234
---	Calaveras Twp 5	57 244
---	Tuolumne Twp 3	71 439
---*	Butte Hamilton	56 530
MIWHURIL		
A	Sierra La Porte	66 785
MIX		
A A	San Francisco San Francisco	9 681106
Caroline	Yuba Fosters	72 830
Dana S	Santa Cruz Pescadero	66 645
G J	Yuba Fosters	72 829
George	Yolo Slate Ra	72 706
George	Yuba Slate Ro	72 706
Gustavus L	Los Angeles Los Angeles	59 365
J D	Shasta Shasta	66 657
Joseph	El Dorado Salmon Falls	581055
P	Butte Cascade	56 691
S	Siskiyou Klamath	69 84
MIXEAH		
---*	Tulara Visalia	71 40
MIXEAHO		
---	Tulara Twp 2	71 40
MIXER		
George H	Sacramento Ward 1	63 142
Henry	Butte Kimshaw	56 590
John	Sacramento Ward 1	63 112
Wm	Sacramento Ward 1	63 48
MIXLEY		
Charles	Yuba Marysville	72 910
MIXOAH		
---*	Tulara Visalia	71 39
MIXOM		
Maria	El Dorado Coloma	581072
MIXOMENAH		
---	Tulara Twp 2	71 39
MIXON		
P P	El Dorado Coloma	581072
Wm	Amador Twp 3	55 406
MIXONIENAH		
---*	Tulara Visalia	71 39
MIY		
---	Amador Twp 2	55 289
---	El Dorado Mud Springs	58 971
---	Mariposa Twp 3	60 544
---*	Butte Ophir	56 819
MIYERS		
J	Nevada Eureka	61 346
MIYES		
B F*	Mariposa Twp 3	60 596
MIZANO		
J*	Sutter Vernon	70 847
MIZANOS		
J*	Sutter Vernon	70 847
MIZE		
Merrel	Sonoma Santa Rosa	69 406
Merrol	Sonoma Santa Rosa	69 406
MIZEN		
Fernon*	Sierra Downieville	66 965
MIZENHAURER		
Hartwell	San Joaquin Elliott	64 945
MIZER		
H C	Sonoma Santa Rosa	69 415
MIZNER		
John	Contra Costa Twp 2	57 555
MIZON		
Juan Jose	Del Norte Crescent	58 650
MJES		
Onofrio	Los Angeles Los Angeles	59 346
MJESSON		
T	Calaveras Twp 9	57 395
MKELVEY		
Chas*	Napa Yount	61 51

Name	County Locale	M653 RollPage
MLAFLIN		
Jas	San Francisco San Francisco	1 68 907
MLASHAMELE		
---*	Mendocino Big Rvr	60 854
MLAUGHLIN		
William*	Yuba Marysville	72 943
MLENOTH		
Artemtes*	Nevada Bloomfield	61 510
MLERMEN		
Donald*	Napa Yount	61 55
MLON		
---*	San Francisco San Francisco	9 681087
MLONI		
J	Nevada Nevada	61 274
MLORY		
J M*	Nevada Eureka	61 373
MMENDERHILL		
J H	Yolo Cache Crk	72 640
MMOON		
---	Yuba Marysville	72 916
MMORE		
William	Santa Cruz Santa Cruz	66 613
MMULDER		
Loraina M	Colusa Butte Crk	57 464
MNDRERS		
Lyman*	Yuba New York	72 738
MNIE		
J H*	San Francisco San Francisco	4 681167
MNIGHT		
John J	Solano Vallejo	69 258
MNY		
---	Calaveras Twp 5	57 240
MNYER		
Hugh	Contra Costa Twp 1	57 527
MO HO		
---	Sierra Twp 7	66 876
MO LO		
---	Sierra St Louis	66 816
MO		
---	Amador Twp 1	55 479
---	Calaveras Twp 5	57 193
---	Calaveras Twp 10	57 259
---	Calaveras Twp 10	57 283
---	Calaveras Twp 4	57 305
---	Calaveras Twp 4	57 310
---	Mariposa Twp 1	60 659
---	Placer Illinois	62 745
---	San Francisco San Francisco	4 681203
---	Sierra Downieville	661030
---	Sierra Poker Flats	66 839
---	Sierra St Louis	66 861
---*	Mariposa Twp 3	60 560
Ah	Butte Eureka	56 649
Bem*	Stanislaus Branch	70 713
Fo	San Francisco San Francisco	4 681185
Ginn	Placer Iona Hills	62 898
Ha	San Francisco San Francisco	4 681175
Han*	Butte Oregon	56 626
Ho	San Francisco San Francisco	4 681175
Hun*	Butte Oregon	56 626
Kee	Calaveras Twp 5	57 220
Ko	Sierra Twp 7	66 876
Ku	Calaveras Twp 5	57 220
Lo	Sierra St Louis	66 816
Lo	Sierra Pine Grove	66 825
Lo	Sierra Poker Flats	66 840
Ping	El Dorado Coloma	581076
Rey	San Francisco San Francisco	2 67 743
Sam	Calaveras Twp 10	57 275
See	El Dorado Diamond	58 807
So	Sierra Poker Flats	66 840
Su	Tuolumne Twp 4	71 182
Yonay	Sacramento Granite	63 268
MO???		
Joseph*	Calaveras Twp 5	57 205
MOA		
---	Calaveras Twp 4	57 333
---	El Dorado Kelsey	581131
---	El Dorado Placerville	58 831
---	Yuba Marysville	72 925
MOADEY		
Orren	Santa Clara Gilroy	65 249
MOAK		
Boltis	Sonoma Armally	69 482
Hans	Yuba Marysville	72 940
MOALTON		
William*	Nevada Bridgeport	61 447
MOAN		
C	Butte Kimshaw	56 602
MOAPH		
Patrick*	Mariposa Twp 3	60 585
MOAR		
Mary A*	Contra Costa Twp 3	57 607
MOARY		
Chas	Nevada Bloomfield	61 526
MOAS		
William	Sierra Port Win	66 793

Name	County Locale	M653 Roll Page
MOASPLAIN		
Grul*	El Dorado Greenwood	58 718
MOAT		
James	Alameda Brooklyn	55 133
MOATH		
Peter	Placer Mountain	62 708
MOATS		
Wm D	Tehama Lassen	70 883
MOBAR		
Joseph	San Francisco San Francisco 11	118 67
MOBERRY		
Geo	Sacramento Granite	63 258
MOBIER		
C	San Francisco San Francisco 6 67	470
MOBILA		
Frank	Los Angeles Tejon To	59 535
MOBLE		
Arthur D	San Francisco San Francisco 8	681 296
MOBLEY		
F F	Nevada Bridgeport	61 445
James R	San Joaquin Tulare	64 870
MOBLO		
James	Placer Michigan	62 814
MOBOM		
P	Yolo Putah	72 554
MOBRAY		
Thos J	Klamath Klamath	59 228
MOCALE		
---*	Tulara Visalia	71 4
MOCALL		
---	Tulara Twp 2	71 4
MOCBUS		
Fred*	San Joaquin Stockton	641 010
MOCE		
Saml H*	Placer Virginia	62 672
MOCELINE		
Patrick	Calaveras Twp 5	57 238
MOCH		
J D	El Dorado Placerville	58 855
MOCHACHO		
---*	Tulara Visalia	71 37
MOCHEE		
---	Tulara Twp 2	71 31
MOCHOLE		
---	Tulara Twp 2	71 4
MOCHOLO		
---*	Tulara Visalia	71 4
MOCK		
---	Mariposa Twp 3	60 590
---	Mariposa Coulterville	60 682
---	Plumas Meadow Valley	62 913
---	Plumas Quincy	62 947
Abraham	Tuolumne Twp 1	71 213
Adam	Plumas Meadow Valley	62 903
Chas	Sonoma Sonoma	69 646
Flora	Sonoma Petaluma	69 600
J L	Sonoma Petaluma	69 600
John	Tulara Visalia	71 33
Myron*	Sacramento Dry Crk	63 378
Wesly	Sonoma Santa Rosa	69 418
Wm	Sonoma Sonoma	69 646
MOCKA		
Francisco*	Calaveras Twp 6	57 135
MOCKE		
John	Tulara Twp 2	71 33
MOCKEE		
---*	Tulara Visalia	71 34
MOCKEL		
G B	Calaveras Twp 6	57 118
MOCKER		
Fredk W	San Francisco San Francisco 10	171 67
W	San Francisco San Francisco 5 67	535
MOCKLER		
Michael	Calaveras Twp 8	57 70
MOCKLIN		
Janes M	Mariposa Coulterville	60 683
MOCKRIDGE		
A	Butte Ophir	56 794
MOCKROW		
---	Tulara Twp 2	71 34
MOCO		
Autin*	El Dorado Mud Springs	58 974
James M	Calaveras Twp 6	57 153
MOCTROVICH		
Peter	San Francisco San Francisco 3 67	51
MODALIO		
Pancho*	Calaveras Twp 6	57 178
MODAN		
Abraham	Santa Clara Santa Clara	65 466
W C	Klamath S Fork	59 198
MODE		
J	Sutter Yuba	70 761
MODELEY		
Harry	Butte Ophir	56 782

Name	County Locale	M653 Roll Page
MODENA		
Moses	Amador Twp 1	55 452
MODENO		
Esperodeon*	Calaveras Twp 5	57 250
MODENS		
Andrew	Mariposa Coulterville	60 698
MODER		
Sopare	Mariposa Coulterville	60 675
MODESTA		
---	Mariposa Twp 1	60 644
MODESTE		
Chas	San Francisco San Francisco 12	396 67
MODESTER		
---	Mariposa Twp 1	60 644
MODEYINE		
Carma*	Alameda Brooklyn	55 131
MODIC		
T W*	Napa Napa	61 100
MODIE		
L W	Napa Napa	61 100
Rebecca	Napa Yount	61 49
T W*	Napa Napa	61 100
MODIN		
Gabriel	Solano Vallejo	69 275
MODINA		
John Maria*	San Mateo Twp 1	65 47
MODISTA		
---	Los Angeles Tejon	59 529
MODKIRD		
Danl	Sacramento Dry Crk	63 375
MODRIX		
Geo W*	Placer Virginia	62 701
MODRY		
Marcus*	San Francisco San Francisco 3 67	3
MODSY		
Marcus	San Francisco San Francisco 3 67	3
MODUS		
Marea	San Francisco San Francisco 6 67	448
Maria	San Francisco San Francisco 6 67	448
MODY		
Edwad T	Del Norte Happy Ca	58 661
MOE		
---	El Dorado Placerville	58 832
---	Tuolumne Montezuma	71 509
S	Tehama Tehama	70 945
MOEBUS		
Fred*	San Joaquin Stockton	641 010
MOECK		
Chris	Sacramento Ward 1	63 12
MOEHR		
Joseph	El Dorado Big Bar	58 738
Louis	Sacramento Ward 4	63 536
MOELLER		
Charles	Los Angeles Los Angeles	59 374
MOENHANEN		
Alex*	Sacramento Ward 1	63 91
MOERE		
I*	El Dorado Placerville	58 877
MOERY		
Germanique*	Yuba Fosters	72 821
MOESO		
Agustine	Alameda Brooklyn	55 191
MOETROVICH		
Peter*	San Francisco San Francisco 3 67	51
MOEY		
---	Butte Ophir	56 812
---	San Francisco San Francisco 9	681 096
---	San Francisco San Francisco 4	681 178
---	San Francisco San Francisco 4	681 186
---	San Francisco San Francisco 4	681 197
---	San Francisco San Francisco 4	681 200
---	Trinity Mouth Ca	701 016
MOEYES		
T*	Calaveras Twp 9	57 396
MOFF		
Julius	Sierra Downieville	66 972
MOFFAIR		
Jno A	Sacramento Ward 4	63 532
MOFFAT		
Albert	Amador Twp 2	55 297
Alex	Santa Clara Santa Clara	65 521
Andrew	Sonoma Santa Rosa	69 416
E D	Solano Vacaville	69 344
Elizabeth	Amador Twp 1	55 495
Henry	Sonoma Santa Rosa	69 414
J	Placer Folsom	62 640
W G	San Francisco San Francisco 1 68	878
W H	Sacramento San Joaquin	63 349
Wm	Sacramento San Joaquin	63 348
Wm B	Placer Rattle Snake	62 632
MOFFATT		
Elijah	Amador Twp 2	55 297
Geo	Sacramento Ward 4	63 547
James	Mendocino Little L	60 829
Jane	San Francisco San Francisco 7	681 337

Name	County Locale	M653 Roll Page
MOFFATT		
Joseph	Tuolumne Twp 4	71 143
Marg	Sacramento Ward 4	63 547
Margaret	San Francisco San Francisco 7	681 429
Patrick	San Francisco San Francisco 8	681 311
Thomas G	San Joaquin Elkhorn	641 000
W S	Nevada Bloomfield	61 525
MOFFAY		
John	Amador Twp 5	55 349
MOFFET		
C C	Siskiyou Scott Ri	69 83
James	Alameda Brooklyn	55 82
John	Sacramento Georgian	63 343
Robert	Sierra St Louis	66 816
William	Siskiyou Callahan	69 1
MOFFETT		
J F	Amador Twp 6	55 424
Orson	Sacramento Ward 4	63 526
MOFFEY		
Daniel	Tehama Antelope	70 893
MOFFIN		
Flamingo C	Calaveras Twp 4	57 308
MOFFIT		
F	Shasta Shasta	66 680
G	Butte Eureka	56 653
John	San Francisco San Francisco 10	311 67
John B*	Placer Secret R	62 619
Robert	Sierra St Louis	66 816
William	San Francisco San Francisco 11	162 67
Wm	Amador Twp 2	55 290
MOFFITT		
Ben	Tuolumne Twp 1	71 262
Elizabeth	Contra Costa Twp 3	57 609
Jas	Amador Twp 3	55 401
Jno	Sonoma Vallejo	69 612
John	Del Norte Happy Ca	58 663
Samuel	Contra Costa Twp 3	57 586
Thomas	Santa Clara Gilroy	65 245
MOFFORD		
Sidney J*	Calaveras Twp 8	57 79
MOFIS		
Patrick	Calaveras Twp 7	57 23
MOG		
---	Placer Illinois	62 746
---	Placer Illinois	62 752
MOGAINIS		
Michael*	Calaveras Twp 10	57 299
MOGAL		
---	Fresno Twp 3	59 96
MOGAMIS		
Michael*	Calaveras Twp 10	57 299
MOGAN		
A	San Mateo Twp 1	65 47
Maggie	San Francisco San Francisco 10	183 67
Majjie	San Francisco San Francisco 10	183 67
Thomas	Solano Vallejo	69 279
MOGEL		
George H*	Sierra Pine Grove	66 835
MOGEN		
Jno	San Francisco San Francisco 10	205 67
MOGER		
Stillman L	Calaveras Twp 6	57 125
MOGLER		
Abram	San Francisco San Francisco 2 67	598
MOGLIN		
J P	Butte Ophir	56 762
MOGLURR		
Peter*	Calaveras Twp 4	57 345
MOGNIHAN		
Andrew	Sierra Twp 7	66 894
MOGRIDGE		
Henry	San Bernardino San Salvador	64 649
MOGUEL		
Ulisea*	Stanislaus Branch	70 705
Ulosea*	Stanislaus Branch	70 705
MOGUL		
---	Fresno Twp 2	59 44
MOH		
---	Alameda Oakland	55 57
---	Siskiyou Scott Ri	69 66
MOHAILANY		
Wm*	Calaveras Twp 5	57 178
MOHAN		
James	Los Angeles Azuza	59 274
MOHARK		
---	Mendocino Twp 1	60 890
MOHARTER		
James	Nevada Rough &	61 407
MOHARVE		
---	Fresno Twp 2	59 74
MOHEIT		
Charles	Siskiyou Yreka	69 146

California 1860 Census Index

Name	County Locale	M653 Roll	Page
MOHEKA			
Ramon	San Mateo Twp 3	65	98
MOHER			
James	San Francisco San Francisco 1	68	919
MOHERS			
Antonia	Mariposa Twp 1	60	660
MOHINDA			
Hiram	Sacramento Ward 4	63	536
MOHINEU			
Joguvinlia*	Calaveras Twp 4	57	331
MOHINIE			
Sebatin	Sierra La Porte	66	784
MOHINU			
Pebatin	Sierra La Porte	66	784
MOHLER			
M	Nevada Eureka	61	381
Marx	Solano Fremont	69	379
P L	Sacramento Ward 4	63	508
Phlillipe	El Dorado Big Bar	58	734
MOHN			
Arnold	Tuolumne Springfield	71	373
Charles*	San Francisco San Francisco 7	68	1436
John	Yuba Parks Ba	72	778
MOHNA			
Louis	Mariposa Twp 3	60	600
MOHO			
---	Amador No 6	55	432
MOHOALE			
Augustus	Sierra Twp 5	66	935
MOHONEY			
Timothy	Amador Twp 4	55	240
William	Amador Twp 4	55	131
MOHONY			
Chas	Amador Twp 3	55	393
MOHOONEY			
John	Calaveras Twp 9	57	402
MOHR			
Albert	San Francisco San Francisco 7	68	1335
August	Klamath Liberty	59	231
Charles*	San Francisco San Francisco 7	68	1436
George	Tuolumne Twp 2	71	277
Geroge	Tuolumne Twp 1	71	277
John	Contra Costa Twp 1	57	534
Joseph*	Yuba Rose Bar	72	796
MOHRALE			
Augustus*	Sierra Twp 5	66	935
MOHRIG			
C F	San Francisco San Francisco 3	67	12
MOHUKA			
Pabblin*	San Mateo Twp 2	65	114
MOHVALE			
Augustus*	Sierra Twp 5	66	935
MOI			
---	Calaveras Twp 8	57	60
---	Calaveras Twp 8	57	82
---	Calaveras Twp 8	57	87
---	Tuolumne Chinese	71	526
---	Tuolumne Don Pedro	71	538
---	Tuolumne Twp 6	71	539
---	Yuba Long Bar	72	757
---	Yuba Marysville	72	896
---*	San Francisco San Francisco 4	68	1195
MOIA			
Charles	Mariposa Twp 3	60	594
MOIBERG			
E*	Klamath S Fork	59	197
MOIBERY			
E*	Klamath S Fork	59	197
MOIGG			
Joseph	Tuolumne Montezuma	71	506
MOIGS			
George	Mariposa Twp 1	60	668
MOIL			
Enno*	Yolo Putah	72	545
MOIN			
Jane*	Sacramento Ward 1	63	86
John*	Alameda Brooklyn	55	143
Thomas*	Sierra Poker Flats	66	838
MOIO			
Frederick*	Sierra Twp 7	66	870
MOIRE			
Wm*	Placer Virginia	62	688
MOIRR			
Jane*	Sacramento Ward 1	63	86
MOIS			
J N	Placer Auburn	62	578
MOISA			
Merejildo	Los Angeles Los Nieto	59	429
MOISE			
Henry	San Francisco San Francisco 6	67	451
Martha E	San Francisco San Francisco 6	67	406
MOISER			
J	El Dorado Georgetown	58	707
MOISES			
J	El Dorado Georgetown	58	707
MOIST			
Thos P	Trinity E Weaver	70	1058
MOIT			
Joseph K	Calaveras Twp 9	57	347
MOJARE			
---	Tulara Twp 1	71	118
MOJON			
Antonio	Los Angeles San Pedro	59	480
MOK			
---	El Dorado Georgetown	58	701
---	El Dorado Georgetown	58	755
---	El Dorado Georgetown	58	756
---	Placer Virginia	62	665
---	Sacramento Ward 1	63	70
---	San Francisco San Francisco 9	68	1094
---	San Francisco San Francisco 9	68	1095
---	San Francisco San Francisco 4	68	1199
---	Siskiyou Scott Ri	69	66
---*	San Francisco San Francisco 9	68	1093
Ar	Trinity Lewiston	70	955
Le*	San Francisco San Francisco 9	68	1094
MOKADEL			
---*	San Francisco San Francisco 5	67	543
MOKAKE			
---	San Francisco San Francisco 5	67	543
MOKE			
---	Amador Twp 6	55	432
---	Butte Ophir	56	812
---	El Dorado White Oaks	58	1032
---	El Dorado Salmon Falls	58	1053
---	El Dorado Salmon Hills	58	1061
---	El Dorado Coloma	58	1110
---	El Dorado Diamond	58	805
---	Tuolumne Don Pedro	71	535
---	Tuolumne Twp 6	71	540
John O	Sacramento Ward 1	63	33
Pant	El Dorado White Oaks	58	1017
Sul	Sacramento Ward 3	63	493
MOKEL KAWHA			
---	Mendocino Big Rvr	60	855
MOKI			
---	Tuolumne Twp 6	71	535
---*	Amador Twp 6	55	432
MOKIAS			
Wm*	Calaveras Twp 9	57	360
MOKISE			
---	Tulara Twp 1	71	115
MOKISHE			
---	Tulara Twp 1	71	119
MOKLY			
John*	Sonoma Armally	69	507
MOKOLOMKE			
---	Fresno Twp 2	59	48
MOKOPE			
---	Fresno Twp 2	59	116
MOL			
---	Tulara Visalia	71	121
MOLALIO			
Pancho*	Calaveras Twp 6	57	178
MOLAN			
Edward	Santa Cruz Santa Cruz	66	604
Roman*	Sacramento Granite	63	244
Romem*	Sacramento Granite	63	244
Romeur*	Sacramento Granite	63	244
Romian	Sacramento Granite	63	244
MOLAND			
H	Nevada Eureka	61	343
MOLAR			
Andrew	Yolo No E Twp	72	675
Andrew	Yuba North Ea	72	675
MOLARD			
H	Nevada Eureka	61	343
J	Nevada Eureka	61	343
MOLARN			
John	Calaveras Twp 5	57	223
MOLARU			
John	Calaveras Twp 5	57	223
MOLASHI			
Tonsaut	Del Norte Crescent	58	641
MOLAT			
Charly	Alameda Brooklyn	55	191
MOLAY			
Catharin	Sonoma Vallejo	69	629
Matharin	Sonoma Vallejo	69	629
MOLBERT			
---	San Bernardino S Timate	64	695
MOLBRITH			
---	San Bernardino S Timate	64	697
MOLBRLGEMURT			
Mox*	Napa Clear Lake	61	129
MOLBY			
William	Sierra Port Win	66	791
MOLDES			
---	Tulara Twp 3	71	65
MOLDING			
Joseph B	Los Angeles Los Angeles	59	305
Joseph B	Los Angeles Los Angeles	59	365
MOLDRUFF			
August	San Francisco San Francisco 3	67	57
MOLDRUP			
A	San Francisco San Francisco 5	67	539
MOLDUFF			
August	San Francisco San Francisco 3	67	57
MOLE			
Saml	Yolo Washington	72	570
MOLECIA			
Jose	San Luis Obispo San Luis Obispo	65	11
MOLEECHEY			
Michael*	Calaveras Twp 5	57	229
MOLEICHEY			
Michael	Calaveras Twp 5	57	229
MOLEN			
E M	El Dorado Placerville	58	853
James	Santa Clara Gilroy	65	245
MOLENA			
Chas	Napa Napa	61	99
Hosea	Alameda Brooklyn	55	210
Peralta	Alameda Brooklyn	55	213
Sircaco	Monterey San Juan	60	1001
MOLENARA			
J	Amador Twp 1	55	491
MOLENCE			
Victir*	Alameda Murray	55	223
MOLEND			
Chas*	Napa Napa	61	99
MOLENIS			
A T*	Butte Oregon	56	609
MOLENO			
Carlo	Napa Napa	61	115
Pape	Calaveras Twp 6	57	141
Pepe	Calaveras Twp 6	57	141
Wm	El Dorado Georgetown	58	704
MOLEON			
H	San Joaquin Stockton	64	1091
MOLER			
Henry	San Diego Colorado	64	807
MOLES			
Jos	Butte Cascade	56	701
MOLESTO			
---	San Diego Temecula	64	786
MOLESWORTH			
J G	Solano Benecia	69	297
MOLETER			
A	San Francisco San Francisco 3	67	9
MOLETOR			
M	El Dorado Newtown	58	780
MOLETT			
Fred	Santa Clara Gilroy	65	248
MOLEY			
Eugene L	Siskiyou Scott Ri	69	70
J	Nevada Eureka	61	372
MOLHAREN			
P	El Dorado Coloma	58	1113
MOLHASTI			
Martin*	Calaveras Twp 5	57	178
MOLILER			
M*	Nevada Eureka	61	381
MOLIN			
John	Yuba Parks Ba	72	778
Mary	San Francisco San Francisco 4	68	1156
MOLINA			
Angel	Los Angeles Santa Ana	59	448
Antonio	Alameda Brooklyn	55	94
Charles	Amador Twp 1	55	468
George	Contra Costa Twp 1	57	493
Jesusa	San Diego Colorado	64	811
Joquvida*	Calaveras Twp 4	57	331
Juanna	Alameda Brooklyn	55	196
Louis	Mariposa Twp 3	60	600
Manuel	Contra Costa Twp 1	57	509
Maria C	Los Angeles San Juan	59	470
Ramon	Calaveras Twp 6	57	177
Ramon	Calaveras Twp 4	57	335
MOLINAIRA			
Peter*	Mariposa Twp 3	60	604
MOLINANI			
Peter	Mariposa Twp 3	60	604
MOLINCE			
J P*	Shasta Shasta	66	675
Victor*	Alameda Murray	55	223
MOLIND			
Joquvider	Calaveras Twp 4	57	331
Ramon	Calaveras Twp 5	57	177
MOLINE			
Francis	Butte Oregon	56	637
MOLINES			
Mercede	Tuolumne Twp 2	71	321
MOLINEUR			
M	Sierra Twp 7	66	880
MOLINEUX			
H	Sierra Twp 7	66	880
MOLINIER			
Jean	San Diego San Diego	64	758
MOLINIS			
A T	Butte Oregon	56	609

California 1860 Census Index

Name	County Locale	M653 Roll Page
MOLINO		
---	Tulara Twp 3	71 64
---	Tulara Twp 3	71 66
Angel	Los Angeles Santa Ana	59 448
Antonio	Solano Montezuma	69 369
Crus	Contra Costa Twp 1	57 501
Jasus	Los Angeles Los Nieto	59 428
Jesus	Los Angeles Los Nieto	59 428
Jesus	Santa Cruz Pajaro	66 544
Pablo	Los Angeles Los Angeles	59 323
Pedro	Santa Cruz Pajaro	66 577
Petro	Santa Cruz Pajaro	66 577
Reyes	San Diego Colorado	64 811
MOLIO		
---	Tulara Keyesville	71 63
MOLION		
Martin	Calaveras Twp 6	57 133
MOLITER		
A*	San Francisco San Francisco 3	67 9
MOLITOR		
A*	San Francisco San Francisco 3	67 9
MOLITRON		
S*	San Francisco San Francisco 5	67 505
MOLIUS		
Cruz	Los Angeles Tejon	59 539
MOLKALKIES		
---	Fresno Twp 1	59 51
MOLL		
Peter D	San Francisco San Francisco 7	681371
MOLLA		
Santiago	San Bernardino Santa Inez	64 140
MOLLAON		
Adelaide	San Francisco San Francisco 2	67 769
MOLLARD		
James	Los Angeles Los Angeles	59 519
MOLLARLGERNUTH		
Mox*	Napa Clear Lake	61 129
MOLLATESTA		
E	San Francisco San Francisco 2	67 682
MOLLAVA		
Adelarde	San Francisco San Francisco 2	67 769
MOLLAY		
Patrick	Sonoma Armally	69 515
MOLLEMS		
H	San Francisco San Francisco 1	68 923
MOLLEN		
H	San Francisco San Francisco 4	681156
Nicholas*	Sacramento Ward 3	63 486
MOLLENARA		
M	Yolo Merritt	72 584
MOLLER		
Jas P H	Humbolt Pacific	59 138
Nicholas*	Sacramento Ward 3	63 486
P C*	San Francisco San Francisco 9	681099
P E	San Francisco San Francisco 9	681099
Panllo*	Calaveras Twp 7	57 11
MOLLES		
Petro	Calaveras Twp 7	57 11
MOLLET		
N J*	Sacramento Cosumnes	63 382
MOLLINEUSE		
Maria	San Francisco San Francisco 1	68 877
MOLLIR		
Adam	Sacramento Brighton	63 206
MOLLISON		
H P	Sonoma Mendocino	69 447
MOLLITER		
A P	San Francisco San Francisco 3	67 64
MOLLONARA		
M*	Yolo Merritt	72 584
MOLLOY		
A B	Napa Yount	61 48
Honora	San Francisco San Francisco 7	681349
Hugh	San Francisco San Francisco 10	263 67
J	Nevada Nevada	61 294
Michael	Santa Cruz Pescadero	66 647
Patrick	San Francisco San Francisco 3	67 23
MOLLY		
E R	Sacramento Ward 4	63 541
Geo D	Sacramento Ward 4	63 541
John*	Sonoma Armally	69 507
MOLN		
Henry	Placer Forest H	62 768
MOLOCK		
James	San Joaquin Castoria	64 902
MOLONA		
S J	Yolo Cache Crk	72 617
MOLONEY		
Charlott M	Humbolt Eureka	59 165
Edwd	San Francisco San Francisco 10	261 67
H P	Tuolumne Twp 4	71 146
Hu Pu*	Tuolumne Big Oak	71 146
Wm	Trinity Whites Crk	701028
MOLONY		
Jas E	Sacramento Ward 1	63 75

Name	County Locale	M653 Roll Page
MOLONY		
Jos E	Sacramento Ward 1	63 75
Martin	Calaveras Twp 2	57 145
Thomas	Sierra La Porte	66 786
MOLOY		
William*	San Francisco San Francisco 3	67 21
MOLRERTO		
---	San Bernardino S Timate	64 690
MOLRUM		
Robert	Sierra Poker Flats	66 842
MOLS		
J	Trinity Weaverville	701081
MOLSEN		
Fred	Alameda Brooklyn	55 152
MOLSERY		
Theodore*	El Dorado Placerville	58 924
MOLSEY		
Theadore	El Dorado Placerville	58 924
MOLT		
Elijah	San Francisco San Francisco 1	68 920
Jno	Alameda Brooklyn	55 159
John	San Francisco San Francisco 10	306 67
MOLTBY		
Charles	Yolo Washington	72 569
Thomas	El Dorado Coloma	581108
MOLTER		
Adam	Sacramento Ward 4	63 604
Phillip	Amador Twp 7	55 412
MOLTHAM		
W	Sutter Yuba	70 762
MOLTON		
A	San Francisco San Francisco 4	681151
Alick	Napa Napa	61 87
Aluk	Napa Napa	61 87
Garner	Sacramento Cosummes	63 384
Josiah*	Mariposa Twp 3	60 602
MOLU		
John	Placer Michigan	62 829
MOLY		
Eugene L	Siskiyou Scott Ri	69 70
MOLZUEADES		
Jose	Monterey San Juan	60 986
MOM		
---	Amador Twp 2	55 315
---	Mariposa Twp 3	60 563
---	Placer Virginia	62 679
Jenson*	Sacramento Mississipi	63 188
John*	Alameda Brooklyn	55 143
MOMAL		
A B	Nevada Grass Valley	61 215
MOMEN		
Michael	San Francisco San Francisco 2	67 641
MOMENT		
Wescribber	El Dorado Greenwood	58 717
MOMER		
George	San Francisco San Francisco 4	681154
MOMESE		
Dfuroro*	Nevada Bloomfield	61 519
MOMJAIES		
Jose*	Monterey Monterey	60 955
MOMS		
Martin	Los Angeles Los Angeles	59 359
MOMSEN		
J B	Siskiyou Scott Va	69 43
MOMSON		
Geo	Sacramento Ward 4	63 504
Hans	Alameda Brooklyn	55 126
R	Butte Oregon	56 611
MOMSSOY		
James*	Sierra Poker Flats	66 841
MON A ME		
---	Mariposa Twp 3	60 612
MON		
---	Amador Twp 2	55 318
---	Amador Twp 5	55 347
---	Amador Twp 5	55 348
---	Amador Twp 5	55 352
---	Amador Twp 6	55 439
---	Calaveras Twp 5	57 167
---	Calaveras Twp 5	57 191
---	Calaveras Twp 5	57 204
---	Calaveras Twp 10	57 269
---	Calaveras Twp 10	57 271
---	Calaveras Twp 4	57 317
---	Calaveras Twp 4	57 322
---	Calaveras Twp 4	57 327
---	Calaveras Twp 8	57 59
---	El Dorado Salmon Falls	581042
---	El Dorado Salmon Falls	581043
---	El Dorado Salmon Falls	581045
---	El Dorado Salmon Falls	581046
---	El Dorado Salmon Falls	581053
---	El Dorado Salmon Falls	581060
---	El Dorado Salmon Falls	581065
---	El Dorado Salmon Falls	581066

Name	County Locale	M653 Roll Page
MON		
---	El Dorado Salmon Falls	581067
---	El Dorado Coloma	581077
---	El Dorado Coloma	581086
---	El Dorado Coloma	581106
---	El Dorado Coloma	581110
---	El Dorado Coloma	581111
---	El Dorado Coloma	581115
---	El Dorado Coloma	581116
---	El Dorado Coloma	581120
---	El Dorado Coloma	581122
---	El Dorado Kelsey	581130
---	El Dorado Kelsey	581144
---	El Dorado Indian D	581159
---	El Dorado Georgetown	58 673
---	El Dorado Georgetown	58 700
---	El Dorado Greenwood	58 731
---	El Dorado Big Bar	58 740
---	El Dorado Georgetown	58 755
---	El Dorado Diamond	58 796
---	El Dorado Placerville	58 831
---	El Dorado Placerville	58 922
---	El Dorado Mud Springs	58 958
---	El Dorado Mud Springs	58 971
---	El Dorado Mud Springs	58 976
---	Mariposa Twp 3	60 560
---	Mariposa Twp 3	60 563
---	Mariposa Twp 3	60 564
---	Mariposa Twp 3	60 580
---	Mariposa Twp 3	60 607
---	Mariposa Twp 3	60 608
---	Mariposa Twp 1	60 627
---	Mariposa Twp 1	60 650
---	Nevada Nevada	61 299
---	Nevada Nevada	61 302
---	Nevada Rough &	61 426
---	Placer Auburn	62 582
---	Placer Rattle Snake	62 602
---	Placer Virginia	62 665
---	Placer Virginia	62 670
---	Placer Virginia	62 677
---	Placer Virginia	62 679
---	Placer Illinois	62 751
---	Placer Illinois	62 752
---	Placer Illinois	62 754
---	Plumas Quincy	62 947
---	Plumas Quincy	62 949
---	Sacramento Granite	63 231
---	Sacramento Ward 1	63 55
---	Sacramento Ward 4	63 612
---	San Francisco San Francisco 9	681087
---	San Francisco San Francisco 9	681095
---	San Francisco San Francisco 3	681096
---	San Francisco San Francisco 4	681188
---	San Francisco San Francisco 4	681200
---	San Francisco San Francisco 4	681208
---	San Francisco San Francisco 11	144
---		67
---	San Francisco San Francisco 3	67 50
---	Shasta Horsetown	66 706
---	Shasta Horsetown	66 711
---	Sierra Downieville	661008
---	Sierra La Porte	66 780
---	Sierra La Porte	66 782
---	Stanislaus Branch	70 714
---	Trinity Eastman	70 960
---	Tuolumne Twp 5	71 515
---	Yolo No E Twp	72 676
---	Yuba North Ea	72 676
---	Yuba New York	72 739
---	Yuba Long Bar	72 758
---	Yuba Long Bar	72 766
---	Yuba Marysville	72 925
---*	Calaveras Twp 8	57 93
---*	Mariposa Twp 3	60 582
---*	Plumas Meadow Valley	62 914
---*	Sacramento Cosumnes	63 392
---*	San Francisco San Francisco 9	681088
---*	San Francisco San Francisco 9	681096
---*	Yuba Long Bar	72 749
Ah Fe*	San Francisco San Francisco 4	681202
Aigh	El Dorado Georgetown	58 761
Ceo	Trinity Lewiston	70 953
Chan	Amador Twp 2	55 290
Chiang	San Francisco San Francisco 5	67 509
Chick	Stanislaus Emory	70 743
Chow	Nevada Grass Valley	61 229
Chow	Nevada Nevada	61 302
Choy	San Francisco San Francisco 4	681204
Fe*	San Francisco San Francisco 4	681202
Fee*	Mariposa Twp 3	60 582
Fing	San Francisco San Francisco 4	681177
Free*	Mariposa Twp 3	60 582
Gang	El Dorado Placerville	58 866
Hon	Yuba Long Bar	72 760
J*	Sacramento Ward 1	63 81

California 1860 Census Index

MON -
MONG

Name	County Locale	M653 RollPage
MON		
Jon	Shasta Horsetown	66 711
Kee	Mariposa Twp 3	60 582
Ko	San Francisco San Francisco 4	681175
Lan	San Francisco San Francisco 4	681189
Lau	San Francisco San Francisco 4	681189
Lee	El Dorado Georgetown	58 755
Lee	San Francisco San Francisco 4	681194
Lin	Amador Twp 2	55 285
Ling	San Francisco San Francisco 4	681177
Low	Placer Auburn	62 592
Lu	San Francisco San Francisco 4	681194
Mary J*	San Francisco San Francisco 10	237 67
Nang*	Sacramento Ward 1	63 71
Nim	Nevada Rough &	61 425
Pong	San Francisco San Francisco 4	681204
R G R	El Dorado Placerville	58 853
Riti	Butte Cascade	56 699
See	El Dorado Georgetown	58 700
Sing	Sacramento Ward 1	63 71
So	Mariposa Twp 3	60 620
Teo	San Francisco San Francisco 4	681188
Ter	Alameda Oakland	55 35
Ther	San Francisco San Francisco 4	681177
Thou	San Francisco San Francisco 4	681188
Tio	San Francisco San Francisco 4	681188
Ton	Shasta Horsetown	66 711
Top	Calaveras Twp 5	57 255
Tou	San Francisco San Francisco 4	681191
Tow	San Francisco San Francisco 4	681191
Wong	El Dorado Greenwood	58 711
Yan	Amador Twp 5	55 334
You	Sacramento Granite	63 231
MONA		
A	El Dorado Placerville	58 893
Jose*	Mariposa Twp 1	60 645
MONACHO		
Lewis	Amador Twp 2	55 303
Louis	Amador Twp 2	55 303
MONACTON		
G	Calaveras Twp 9	57 406
MONAGHAN		
Awen*	Sierra Twp 7	66 892
Danl	San Francisco San Francisco 12	384 67
E	San Francisco San Francisco 5	67 511
Frederic	Los Angeles Los Angeles	59 372
Owen	Sierra Twp 7	66 892
Rosa	San Francisco San Francisco 11	123 67
Thos	Butte Mountain	56 737
Wm	San Francisco San Francisco 12	382 67
MONAHAM		
Ed	Alameda Brooklyn	55 123
Rosanna	San Joaquin Castoria	64 910
MONAHAN		
Cath	San Francisco San Francisco 9	68 971
Cathl	San Francisco San Francisco 9	68 971
Edward	Alameda Oakland	55 27
Hugh	San Francisco San Francisco 7	681333
James	Alameda Oakland	55 15
James	Monterey San Juan	60 980
John	Tuolumne Twp 1	71 221
Pat	Sacramento Ward 1	63 82
Wm	San Francisco San Francisco 2	67 794
MONAHON		
Danl	Trinity Raabs Ba	701020
John	Solano Vacaville	69 335
Pat	Sacramento Ward 1	63 82
Wm	San Francisco San Francisco 2	67 794
MONAHUR		
John	Nevada Bridgeport	61 494
MONAL		
J W*	Nevada Nevada	61 320
MONALLS		
John	Yolo Merritt	72 578
MONAN		
Catharine	Placer Michigan	62 838
Patrick*	Placer Michigan	62 838
MONANGETE		
---*	Tulara Twp 1	71 120
MONAR		
D	Siskiyou Scott Ri	69 81
MONARCO		
Antonio	Tuolumne Twp 2	71 286
MONATATER		
Joseph	Calaveras Twp 5	57 197
MONATCH		
---	Tulara Twp 2	71 31
MONATTE		
Peter	Tuolumne Twp 2	71 279
MONAY		
Jose	San Diego Colorado	64 810
MONBOCKER		
J	Yolo Cottonwood	72 652

Name	County Locale	M653 RollPage
MONBS		
Jesus*	Yuba Marysville	72 936
MONCALLO		
Rago*	San Bernardino Slmaden	64 272
Razo*	Santa Clara Almaden	65 272
MONCAYO		
Manuel S*	Yuba Marysville	72 917
MONCHAMP		
Julius	Amador Twp 2	55 295
MONCHEL		
S	Nevada Eureka	61 365
MONCHES		
---	Trinity Weaverville	701074
MONCHIA		
Appolinia*	Yuba Marysville	72 918
Appolonia*	Yuba Marysville	72 918
MONCHO		
---	Tulara Twp 2	71 31
MONCREAF		
E*	Shasta Horsetown	66 702
MONCREOF		
E	Shasta Horsetown	66 702
MOND		
Raymond*	Sacramento Granite	63 244
MONDARO		
Antonio	San Joaquin Stockton	641074
MONDAY		
Albert	San Francisco San Francisco 1	68 891
D S	Sacramento Ward 3	63 435
Edward	El Dorado Mud Springs	58 984
James	Santa Clara Santa Clara	65 485
N J	El Dorado Placerville	58 909
Nicholas	Contra Costa Twp 1	57 505
P H	El Dorado White Oaks	581030
Patrick	Placer Auburn	62 566
Saml	Sacramento Ward 3	63 436
MONDAZ		
Carmel	Tehama Red Bluff	70 931
MONDE		
Victor	Colusa Grand Island	57 473
MONDEGO		
Colio	Alameda Brooklyn	55 142
MONDEIJA		
Louis*	Alameda Brooklyn	55 142
MONDELET		
F	San Francisco San Francisco 4	681171
MONDELL		
I	San Francisco San Francisco 5	67 537
J	San Francisco San Francisco 5	67 537
L	San Francisco San Francisco 5	67 518
MONDERHILL		
John	Sonoma Santa Rosa	69 406
MONDEYA		
Louis*	Alameda Brooklyn	55 142
MONDIA		
Jose	Los Angeles Los Angeles	59 386
MONDIL		
John	Plumas Quincy	62 972
MONDIN		
John*	Calaveras Twp 6	57 127
MONDIRAGO		
Hosea*	Alameda Murray	55 219
MONDITET		
F*	San Francisco San Francisco 4	681171
MONDOCK		
Amoli*	Calaveras Twp 5	57 226
Arnold	Calaveras Twp 5	57 226
MONDON		
Mc Neill	Tuolumne Sonora	71 484
MONDONIR		
John B	Calaveras Twp 10	57 289
MONDOSA		
Manuel	Marin Cortemad	60 755
MONDRAN		
F V C	San Bernardino Santa Barbara	64 203
MONDS		
Chas	Sacramento Ward 1	63 151
P	San Joaquin Stockton	641097
MONDSALE PECULA		
B*	El Dorado Diamond	58 803
MONDY		
Permain*	Amador Twp 2	55 296
MONE		
---	Amador Twp 1	55 507
---	El Dorado Kelsey	581143
---	El Dorado Casumnes	581174
---	El Dorado Mud Springs	58 984
---	Mariposa Twp 3	60 553
---*	Mariposa Twp 3	60 578
Geo W*	Sacramento Ward 3	63 454
Jaques*	El Dorado Georgetown	58 750
John*	Yuba New York	72 721
Thomas*	Sierra Forest C	66 910
MONEDA		
Joseph	Los Angeles Los Angeles	59 300
MONEGAN		
Hugh	Solano Vallejo	69 271

Name	County Locale	M653 RollPage
MONEGHAN		
Eliza	San Francisco San Francisco 2	67 661
MONEGRAN		
Patrick	Placer Secret R	62 612
MONEHAN		
Anne	Solano Vallejo	69 278
MONEHOS		
Francis*	Santa Clara Santa Clara	65 482
MONEIL		
J W*	Nevada Nevada	61 320
MONEL		
John	El Dorado White Oaks	581033
Jose	San Bernardino S Buenav	64 216
MONELL		
Charles	San Francisco San Francisco 8	681275
Chas	San Francisco San Francisco 2	67 562
E	El Dorado Mud Springs	58 984
Geo	Nevada Nevada	61 321
H B	Amador Twp 7	55 411
Phillip	Butte Oregon	56 615
MONEN		
Patrick*	Placer Michigan	62 837
W T	Sutter Yuba	70 760
MONENES		
Feliciana*	Calaveras Twp 6	57 113
MONENO		
A*	El Dorado Placerville	58 917
MONER		
T	San Francisco San Francisco 5	67 477
MONES		
H P*	Sierra Eureka	661050
Hosea	Alameda Brooklyn	55 179
MONET		
B	El Dorado Diamond	58 783
Francis	Sierra Twp 5	66 942
H A*	Shasta Shasta	66 654
MONETT		
L	Siskiyou Yreka	69 184
MONEWEG		
Tim	Alameda Brooklyn	55 93
MONEY		
Cornelia	Sonoma Santa Rosa	69 411
Cornelius	Sonoma Santa Rosa	69 411
Ellen	San Francisco San Francisco 2	67 681
John	Yuba Foster B	72 835
Mary	San Francisco San Francisco 2	67 564
O	Yolo Cache	72 640
Patrick	San Francisco San Francisco 2	67 564
Pilia*	Los Angeles Los Angeles	59 492
William	Los Angeles Los Angeles	59 368
MONFRA		
Jean	Calaveras Twp 7	57 14
MONG SO		
---*	San Francisco San Francisco 4	681203
MONG		
---	Alameda Oakland	55 64
---	Calaveras Twp 8	57 106
---	Calaveras Twp 10	57 260
---	Calaveras Twp 10	57 280
---	Calaveras Twp 9	57 358
---	Calaveras Twp 7	57 39
---	Calaveras Twp 8	57 62
---	Calaveras Twp 8	57 91
---	El Dorado Salmon Falls	581052
---	El Dorado Salmon Hills	581065
---	El Dorado Salmon Hills	581066
---	El Dorado Coloma	581077
---	El Dorado Coloma	581122
---	El Dorado Casumnes	581160
---	El Dorado Mud Springs	58 969
---	El Dorado Mud Springs	58 988
---	Mariposa Twp 3	60 550
---	Mariposa Twp 3	60 569
---	Mariposa Twp 1	60 650
---	Mariposa Twp 1	60 652
---	Mariposa Twp 1	60 657
---	Mariposa Twp 1	60 658
---	Mariposa Twp 1	60 669
---	Mariposa Coulterville	60 699
---	Nevada Rough &	61 424
---	Placer Auburn	62 573
---	Placer Rattle Snake	62 637
---	Placer Horseshoe	62 650
---	Placer Virginia	62 662
---	Placer Virginia	62 671
---	Placer Virginia	62 674
---	Placer Virginia	62 678
---	Placer Virginia	62 683
---	Placer Virginia	62 701
---	Placer Dutch Fl	62 732
---	Placer Illinois	62 740
---	Placer Illinois	62 741
---	Placer Illinois	62 746
---	Placer Illinois	62 747
---	Placer Illinois	62 748
---	Placer Illinois	62 749

Copyright 1999 by Heritage Quest, a division of AGLL, Inc., Bountiful, UT 84011. All rights reserved

California 1860 Census Index

Name	County Locale	M653 Roll	Page
MONG			
---	Placer Illinois	62	752
---	Plumas Meadow Valley	62	910
---	Plumas Meadow Valley	62	914
---	Plumas Quincy	62	926
---	Plumas Quincy	62	950
---	Plumas Quincy	62	969
---	Sacramento Centre	63	182
---	Sacramento Cosumnes	63	392
---	San Francisco San Francisco 9	681	095
---	San Francisco San Francisco 4	681	173
---	San Francisco San Francisco 4	681	182
---	San Francisco San Francisco 4	681	201
---	San Francisco San Francisco 4	681	212
---	San Francisco San Francisco 11	67	158
---	San Francisco San Francisco 1	68	925
---	San Francisco San Francisco 1	68	926
---	Shasta Horsetown	66	710
---	Sierra Downieville	661	004
---	Stanislaus Branch	70	713
---	Tuolumne Big Oak	71	150
---	Tuolumne Sonora	71	477
---	Tuolumne Knights	71	528
---	Yolo Slate Ra	72	708
---	Yuba New York	72	740
---	Yuba Long Bar	72	763
---	Yuba Long Bar	72	767
---*	Nevada Rough &	61	424
---*	Shasta Shasta	66	670
Ah	Calaveras Twp 7	57	33
Ah	Calaveras Twp 7	57	36
Fee	San Francisco San Francisco 4	681	201
Fu	San Francisco San Francisco 4	681	201
He*	Yuba New York	72	740
High	El Dorado Georgetown	58	693
Jerry	El Dorado Kelsey	581	151
Kate	Yuba Long Bar	72	762
Ko	San Francisco San Francisco 1	68	925
Lay	Mariposa Twp 3	60	550
Lee	Mariposa Twp 3	60	550
Lee	San Francisco San Francisco 4	681	202
Lu	San Francisco San Francisco 4	681	202
Nof	San Francisco San Francisco 9	681	093
So	San Francisco San Francisco 4	681	203
War	Placer Auburn	62	583
Yaw	Placer Auburn	62	578
Yong	San Francisco San Francisco 1	68	926
MONGANTA			
Francisco	Santa Inez San Bernardino	64	141
MONGARA			
August	San Bernardino Santa Inez	64	139
MONGAY			
---	Trinity Weaverville	701	073
MONGCOT			
John	Yuba Long Bar	72	751
MONGEL			
John	San Francisco San Francisco 8	681	287
MONGELLA			
Juan	Mariposa Twp 3	60	570
MONGEOT			
John	Yuba Long Bar	72	751
MONGER			
Bollen	San Francisco San Francisco 4	681	214
N D	Sutter Butte	70	794
MONGFONG			
---	Trinity Lewiston	70	954
MONGG			
---	El Dorado Mud Springs	58	988
MONGIES			
James	Sierra Twp 5	66	940
MONGILLA			
Juan	Mariposa Twp 3	60	570
MONGLAND			
David	Yolo Washington	72	567
MONGLANTE			
John	Tuolumne Twp 1	71	255
MONGLER			
---	Plumas Quincy	62	949
MONGLIE			
R B	Nevada Nevada	61	279
MONGLIR			
R B	Nevada Nevada	61	279
MONGOLLE			
J	San Francisco San Francisco 2	67	690
MONGOMERY			
B W	Sierra Twp 7	66	866
John	Amador Twp 5	55	339
Mary	Santa Clara San Jose	65	318
MONGON			
Guiseppe	Tuolumne Chinese	71	497
MONGORA			
Sam	Mariposa Twp 1	60	639
San	Mariposa Twp 1	60	639
MONGOS			
Appolevia*	Yuba Marysville	72	917

Name	County Locale	M653 Roll	Page
MONGOS			
Appolonia	Yuba Marysville	72	917
MONGREN			
John	Placer Yankee J	62	757
MONGRENOND			
Robert*	Siskiyou Callahan	69	9
MONGREWOND			
Robert*	Siskiyou Callahan	69	9
MONGRINER			
Jacques	Tuolumne Twp 2	71	363
MONGSEMOND			
Robert	Siskiyou Callahan	69	9
MONGSEN			
John	Siskiyou Callahan	69	8
MONGUA			
L	El Dorado Diamond	58	801
MONGUE			
Mary	Sierra Downieville	66	968
MONGUILLIARD			
P	Calaveras Twp 9	57	377
MONGUS			
James*	Sierra Twp 5	66	940
MONHALE			
J*	Sacramento Ward 3	63	428
MONHALL			
J*	Sacramento Ward 3	63	428
MONHARA			
Andres	Mariposa Twp 1	60	641
Andris	Mariposa Twp 1	60	641
Andus*	Mariposa Twp 1	60	641
MONHART			
Frederick	Placer Michigan	62	852
MONHEAD			
Benj	Butte Ophir	56	783
MONHER			
---	Trinity Trininad Rvr	701	045
MONHOUSE			
J J*	Placer Todds Va	62	787
MONI			
---	Amador Twp 5	55	353
Liz	Sacramento Granite	63	256
MONIBRAY			
William*	San Francisco San Francisco 4	681	127
MONICA			
---	Monterey San Juan	60	992
MONIE			
C	Klamath S Fork	59	197
MONIER			
George	San Francisco San Francisco 11	67	111
Robert	San Joaquin Tulare	64	871
Wm	Placer Auburn	62	584
MONIET			
J L A	San Francisco San Francisco 2	67	689
MONIEUR			
Bakes*	Nevada Bloomfield	61	518
Balies*	Nevada Bloomfield	61	518
Baties	Nevada Bloomfield	61	518
MONIGAN			
Hugh	Solano Vallejo	69	271
MONIGHAN			
John	Plumas Meadow Valley	62	912
MONILL			
Benj	Placer Virginia	62	673
MONILLA			
Pallolla*	San Mateo Twp 2	65	111
MONILS			
Randolph	San Francisco San Francisco 9	68	944
MONIN			
Harrison*	San Francisco San Francisco 1	68	909
Jeremiah*	Alameda Oakland	55	76
MONIO			
Hosa*	Nevada Bloomfield	61	512
MONIS			
Manuel*	Solano Benecia	69	285
MONISEY			
James	Santa Cruz Santa Cruz	66	634
Thomas	Solano Vallejo	69	268
MONISON			
Charles*	Solano Benecia	69	292
Pat	Yolo Merritt	72	577
R B	Solano Eureka	61	369
Robert	San Francisco San Francisco 7	681	332
Thomas	Solano Suisan	69	231
MONISY			
Thomas	Solano Vallejo	69	268
MONITHER			
John	Sierra Twp 7	66	865
MONITT			
John	Sierra Morristown	661	051
MONJASS			
Jesse*	San Joaquin O'Neal	641	006
MONJOS			
Dominga	Yuba Marysville	72	920
MONK			
---	Shasta French G	66	713

Name	County Locale	M653 Roll	Page
MONK			
---	Trinity Eastman	70	960
C H	Mariposa Twp 1	60	635
Celestina	Merced Monterey	60	941
Celestina	Monterey Monterey	60	941
E P	Nevada Nevada	61	320
George*	Mendocino Ukiah	60	800
Henry	El Dorado Kelsey	581	146
MONKARD			
Maria	San Mateo Twp 1	65	62
MONKER			
Peter	Alameda Brooklyn	55	98
MONKEY			
---	Fresno Twp 2	59	109
Edw	Napa Napa	61	84
MONKGEL			
Santiago	Contra Costa Twp 1	57	514
MONKHOUSE			
T A	San Francisco San Francisco 6	67	431
MONKIN			
Peter	Alameda Brooklyn	55	98
MONKLEY			
Owen	Yuba Bear Rvr	721	007
MONKNEGRO			
P	Sacramento Ward 1	63	34
MONKS			
Eliza	San Francisco San Francisco 2	67	667
John	San Joaquin Elkhorn	64	954
Samuel	San Francisco San Francisco 4	681	156
MONKTON			
D	Yolo Cottonwooood	72	652
MONLAN			
Mary	Sacramento Ward 1	63	144
MONLANA			
Thomas*	Placer Damascus	62	846
MONLANG			
H	Sutter Butte	70	794
MONLARACHE			
A*	El Dorado Georgetown	58	685
MONLDER			
Peter*	Butte Chico	56	548
MONLIN			
Hetor	Santa Clara San Jose	65	292
Martel	Butte Kimshaw	56	597
MONLTIN			
James*	Sierra Twp 7	66	865
MONLTON			
A B	Butte Bidwell	56	729
William	Nevada Bridgeport	61	447
MONMAN			
J	Yolo Putah	72	586
MONMAND			
F	San Francisco San Francisco 2	67	796
MONNAS			
Banasua*	Marin Bolinas	60	728
MONNET			
Claude*	Alameda Oakland	55	5
MONNIN			
J	San Francisco San Francisco 6	67	468
MONNOT			
Claude*	Alameda Oakland	55	5
MONNT			
Sarah*	Yuba Fosters	72	823
MONNTATER			
Joseph	Calaveras Twp 5	57	197
MONNTONI			
J J	Yolo Putah	72	549
MONNY			
Bridget	San Francisco San Francisco 2	67	758
Wm	Sierra Downieville	661	022
MONO			
---	Tulara Twp 2	71	31
---	Tulara Twp 2	71	4
---	Tulara Keyesville	71	64
---	Tulara Keyesville	71	71
---	Tulara Keyesville	71	72
---*	Tulara Yule Rvr	71	31
---*	Tulara Visalia	71	4
John	Tuolumne Twp 1	71	228
Jose	Los Angeles Azuza	59	273
Louis	Amador Twp 3	55	372
Maria	Siskiyou Yreka	69	147
MONOGSEMOND			
Robert	Siskiyou Callahan	69	9
MONOHAN			
Hisey*	Solano Vallejo	69	245
Huey	Solano Vallejo	69	245
Hugh	San Francisco San Francisco 7	681	333
P	San Francisco San Francisco 6	67	463
Thos	Sacramento Ward 1	63	63
MONOIN			
E F*	Nevada Bridgeport	61	486
MONOMAR			
Joseph	Siskiyou Klamath	69	89
MONOMENEN			
---*	Tulara Visalia	71	38

California 1860 Census Index

Name	County Locale	M653 Roll	Page
MONOMENEU			
---	Tulara Twp 2	71	38
MONON			
Harvey	Placer Rattle Snake	62	626
W R	Nevada Eureka	61	353
MONOREAF			
E*	Shasta Horsetown	66	702
MONORO			
Harry	Placer Rattle Snake	62	628
MONOS			
Francisco	Calaveras Twp 5	57	227
Juan	Los Angeles Los Angeles	59	323
Michael	Tuolumne Twp 1	71	228
MONOTTE			
Fredk	San Francisco San Francisco 10	67	175
MONOTTI			
Peter*	Tuolumne Twp 2	71	279
Vincent	Santa Cruz Pajaro	66	531
MONOTTO			
F	San Mateo Twp 1	65	48
Peter	San Mateo Twp 1	65	48
MONOW			
G H*	Nevada Nevada	61	322
MONOWEG			
Tim	Alameda Brooklyn	55	93
MONOY			
Eloena*	Yuba Marysville	72	917
Elvina	Yuba Marysville	72	917
MONPE			
C*	San Francisco San Francisco 10	67	359
MONQUE			
Juan	Contra Costa Twp 1	57	497
MONREE			
Danl*	Santa Clara Santa Clara	65	467
MONRO			
Peter	San Francisco San Francisco 2	67	714
MONROE			
A	Nevada Grass Valley	61	182
A	San Francisco San Francisco 10	67	311
A C	Nevada Nevada	61	289
A J	Nevada Nevada	61	288
A L	Nevada Grass Valley	61	175
Alonzo	Humbolt Eureka	59	165
Amelia	San Francisco San Francisco 10	67	253
Andrew	Mendocino Little L	60	832
Anneta	San Francisco San Francisco 2	67	693
Annita	San Francisco San Francisco 2	67	693
Arthur	Santa Clara San Jose	65	284
C	San Francisco San Francisco 5	67	530
Chas	Santa Clara San Jose	65	337
Chas	Santa Clara San Jose	65	393
Danl	Placer Virginia	62	700
David	Tuolumne Twp 1	71	232
F M	Shasta French G	66	722
Francisca	Santa Clara San Jose	65	303
Frederick	San Francisco San Francisco 7	68	1436
G V	Nevada Eureka	61	351
George	San Diego Agua Caliente	64	855
George	San Francisco San Francisco 1	68	891
George	Siskiyou Shasta Valley	69	120
Gyeur*	Nevada Grass Valley	61	176
Ishmael	San Joaquin Castoria	64	881
J	Nevada Eureka	61	364
J	Nevada Eureka	61	375
J A	San Francisco San Francisco 6	67	474
J B	Trinity Trinity	70	975
J*	Nevada Grass Valley	61	224
James	Alameda Brooklyn	55	99
James	Nevada Nevada	61	246
James	San Joaquin Castoria	64	911
James	Solano Suisan	69	217
James	Yuba New York	72	737
Jas	San Francisco San Francisco 1	68	824
John	Calaveras Twp 8	57	90
John	Humbolt Pacific	59	135
John	Tuolumne Twp 2	71	288
John	Tuolumne Twp 2	71	300
L	El Dorado Kelsey	58	1153
Louis*	Mariposa Twp 3	60	584
Louis*	Mariposa Twp 3	60	616
Luke	San Francisco San Francisco 5	67	494
Mary	Tuolumne Twp 2	71	366
Merdock	Tuolumne Twp 1	71	262
Murdo	Tuolumne Twp 1	71	223
Norton	Alameda Brooklyn	55	176
R	Nevada Grass Valley	61	194
R W	Nevada Nevada	61	271
Robt	San Francisco San Francisco 1	68	813
Timothy	Yuba Marysville	72	877
W	Nevada Eureka	61	375
W	San Francisco San Francisco 9	68	1058
W A	Nevada Nevada	61	319

Name	County Locale	M653 Roll	Page
MONROE			
W W	Butte Ophir	56	784
William	Sonoma Armally	69	509
William*	Placer Forest H	62	805
Wm	Monterey San Juan	60	995
Wm	Yuba Rose Bar	72	791
Wm B	Mendocino Little L	60	832
Wm H	Placer Virginia	62	689
Wm J	Monterey San Juan	60	984
Zeur*	Nevada Grass Valley	61	176
MONROL			
Andrew	Mendocino Little L	60	832
MONROO			
Mary*	Tuolumne Columbia	71	366
MONROR			
John*	Tuolumne Columbia	71	300
MONROW			
A	San Mateo Twp 3	65	89
B F	El Dorado Diamond	58	784
J	El Dorado Placerville	58	852
Jos	San Mateo Twp 3	65	107
Marcela	Placer Auburn	62	574
Marshall E*	Placer Auburn	62	569
Micheal	Nevada Bridgeport	61	501
William	Calaveras Twp 8	57	65
MONROWS			
Marshall E	Placer Auburn	62	569
MONROY			
Carlolo*	Yuba Marysville	72	918
Juan	Santa Clara San Jose	65	368
MONRVE			
Amelia	San Francisco San Francisco 10	67	253
MONS			
Peter*	Siskiyou Yreka	69	125
MONSE			
A*	Nevada Nevada	61	288
Harry	Tuolumne Twp 2	71	289
Lenord	San Francisco San Francisco 1	68	810
Peter	Sierra Downieville	66	1022
MONSER			
S M*	Sacramento Ward 4	63	572
MONSERRAT			
Diego	El Dorado Georgetown	58	701
MONSESSAT			
Diego	El Dorado Georgetown	58	701
MONSEY			
Henry	Nevada Bridgeport	61	473
MONSHOLDER			
H	Yolo Cache	72	606
MONSINCA			
Basto	Calaveras Twp 8	57	68
MONSLER			
J A	Nevada Nevada	61	286
J R	Nevada Nevada	61	286
MONSLY			
H	Nevada Nevada	61	278
MONSON			
A C	Sacramento Ward 1	63	155
B H	Sacramento Ward 1	63	45
Edwin R	Calaveras Twp 5	57	243
Eliza C	Sacramento Ward 1	63	46
Enmonte	Calaveras Twp 6	57	156
J L	Nevada Bridgeport	61	451
James	Amador Twp 2	55	319
Jno*	Butte Oregon	56	630
John*	Tuolumne Columbia	71	300
Joseph*	Amador Twp 2	55	328
Leonard	San Joaquin Douglass	64	922
Peter	Calaveras Twp 10	57	282
R H	Nevada Bridgeport	61	489
T	Sutter Butte	70	790
Uriah	Nevada Rough &	61	414
W	Sutter Butte	70	791
Wriah	Nevada Rough &	61	414
MONSTON			
A*	Santa Clara Redwood	65	452
Ole	Sierra Twp 5	66	947
W	Yolo Washington	72	599
W H	Sonoma Armally	69	508
MONT			
Mureal	Calaveras Twp 6	57	128
Sefrat	Placer Virginia	62	664
MONTA			
Henry*	Tuolumne Big Oak	71	139
MONTADANECO			
Joseph	Amador Twp 4	55	248
MONTAFT			
Antin	Tuolumne Columbia	71	333
MONTAGA			
Pancho	Napa Napa	61	115
William	Solano Suisan	69	212
MONTAGE			
Santiago	Los Angeles Elmonte	59	254
MONTAGIO			
Charles*	Contra Costa Twp 1	57	509

Name	County Locale	M653 Roll	Page
MONTAGOUE			
Edward	Nevada Bridgeport	61	488
MONTAGUE			
Cayetano	Los Angeles Los Angeles	59	321
E	El Dorado Diamond	58	783
Edward	Nevada Bridgeport	61	488
F M	Yuba Rose Bar	72	815
Geo	Sacramento Ward 4	63	526
Giles E	Humbolt Pacific	59	134
J	Nevada Grass Valley	61	157
J	Nevada Eureka	61	371
Joel S	Yuba Marysville	72	969
Kate	San Francisco San Francisco 4	68	1222
L D	Butte Kimshaw	56	591
Mike	Sacramento Ward 1	63	83
Rodney	Los Angeles Los Angeles	59	372
Saml S	Placer Virginia	62	685
T B	San Bernardino San Bernardino	64	625
W W	San Francisco San Francisco 5	67	484
MONTAHI			
Hosea*	Alameda Brooklyn	55	137
MONTAIGUE			
Barny	Los Angeles Tejon	59	539
MONTAINE			
Ponche	Calaveras Twp 10	57	291
MONTAJO			
Curriacion	San Joaquin Castoria	64	900
MONTALLO			
Jose	El Dorado Georgetown	58	702
MONTALN			
Dennis	Los Angeles Los Angeles	59	347
MONTANA			
Jose	Santa Clara Alviso	65	400
Jose V	Santa Clara Gilroy	65	224
Maria P	Los Angeles San Juan	59	462
Mercurio	Los Angeles Los Angeles	59	350
Thomas*	Placer Damascus	62	846
MONTANDEN			
Wm*	Sacramento Ward 4	63	552
MONTANDON			
A E	Amador Twp 2	55	278
Mary	Amador Twp 2	55	278
MONTANE			
Fredrico*	Calaveras Twp 6	57	135
MONTANEGRO			
Ygnacio	Tuolumne Chinese	71	498
MONTANG			
F	Sutter Yuba	70	777
MONTANI			
Antonio	Calaveras Twp 6	57	135
Fredrico*	Calaveras Twp 6	57	135
MONTANIA			
J	Merced Twp 1	60	900
L	Merced Twp 1	60	900
MONTANIO			
Polonio	Los Angeles San Pedro	59	478
MONTANO			
Jose C	Los Angeles San Gabriel	59	411
Nestor**	Monterey San Juan	60	1002
MONTANS			
Nestor	Monterey San Juan	60	1002
MONTANYA			
A De La*	San Francisco San Francisco 7	68	1437
H De La	San Francisco San Francisco 2	67	786
J L	San Francisco San Francisco 10	67	173
MONTAQUE			
Bernard	Los Angeles Tejon	59	521
J	Nevada Eureka	61	371
Rodney	Los Angeles Los Angeles	59	372
MONTARA			
A	Amador Twp 1	55	500
MONTARACHE			
A*	El Dorado Georgetown	58	685
MONTARIA			
Antonio	Santa Clara San Jose	65	371
MONTARIO			
Pedro	Los Angeles Los Angeles	59	404
MONTAYO			
Celarai	Alameda Brooklyn	55	180
MONTE			
---	Fresno Twp 2	59	108
---	Fresno Twp 2	59	61
---	Tulara Twp 3	71	68
---	Tulara Twp 3	71	71
Eliher*	Yuba Marysville	72	948
Jose	Los Angeles Los Angeles	59	389
MONTEGO			
Jesus	Alameda Murray	55	227
MONTEGRAN			
Nicols	Santa Clara San Jose	65	305
MONTEGUE			
Edward	El Dorado Georgetown	58	704
Elwood	El Dorado Georgetown	58	704
MONTEITH			

California 1860 Census Index

Name	County Locale	M653 Roll	Page
MONTEITH			
Randolph	San Francisco San Francisco 12	386	
		67	
MONTEJO			
Ygnacio	Los Angeles Los Angeles	59	399
MONTEKO			
---	Fresno Twp 2	59	103
MONTEL			
Pedro	Yuba Marysville	72	948
MONTELL			
Frederick	Yuba Bear Rvr	72	998
MONTEMEGO			
Antonio	Santa Clara San Jose	65	299
MONTENCHO			
Joaquin*	Contra Costa Twp 3	57	599
MONTENDIER			
M	San Francisco San Francisco 4	681	160
MONTENEGRO			
Anita	Los Angeles San Juan	59	461
Eugene	Los Angeles Santa Ana	59	453
M	Merced Twp 1	60	900
P	Sacramento Ward 1	63	34
MONTENER			
B	Merced Twp 1	60	900
MONTENETIO			
Joaquin*	Contra Costa Twp 3	57	599
MONTENITTE			
C	Nevada Nevada	61	291
MONTENO			
Gregorio	Los Angeles Los Angeles	59	309
MONTEPON			
Francisco	San Diego Colorado	64	811
MONTER			
Henry*	Tuolumne Big Oak	71	139
Manuel	Alameda Brooklyn	55	210
MONTERCIDE			
L	Trinity Indian C	70	988
MONTERCODE			
Louis	Trinity Indian C	70	988
MONTERO			
Maria	San Francisco San Francisco 5	67	490
MONTERSILLE			
C	Nevada Nevada	61	291
MONTERULLA			
Ramond	Calaveras Twp 4	57	333
MONTERULLEN			
Francisco	Calaveras Twp 4	57	333
MONTES			
---	Tulara Twp 3	71	66
Eliha	Yuba Marysville	72	948
Elihn*	Yuba Marysville	72	948
Guadalooupe	Yuba Marysville	72	948
Guadaloupe	Yuba Marysville	72	948
Jose M	Los Angeles San Pedro	59	478
Pablo	San Diego Temecula	64	801
Zgnacio	Santa Clara Gilroy	65	245
MONTEVERDE			
G B	Tuolumne Big Oak	71	130
MONTFERANT			
John*	Siskiyou Callahan	69	4
Salvd*	Siskiyou Callahan	69	4
MONTFORD			
Henry	Sacramento Ward 4	63	577
MONTGOMERY			
A	Colusa Grand Island	57	468
A	Mendocino Ukiah	60	797
A	Sacramento Ward 1	63	50
A	Trinity Redding	70	985
A	Yolo Putah	72	550
A	Yolo Cottonwoood	72	659
A W	Tuolumne Jamestown	71	432
Acom	San Francisco San Francisco 2	67	597
Alex	Napa Napa	61	112
B W	Sierra Twp 7	66	866
C	El Dorado Coloma	581	070
C	El Dorado Georgetown	58	703
C	Siskiyou Scott Ri	69	72
Ch	Solano Fremont	69	384
Charles	El Dorado Kelsey	581	148
Charles	Tehama Tehama	70	943
E	San Francisco San Francisco 9	681	101
E	San Francisco San Francisco 4	681	215
E L	Butte Oro	56	682
Elizabeth	San Francisco San Francisco 9	681	105
F	Tuolumne Twp 2	71	353
F P	Nevada Rough &	61	414
Francis	Colusa Monroeville	57	444
Frank	Napa Clear Lake	61	136
G A	Nevada Grass Valley	61	173
G B	Santa Clara San Jose	65	306
G W	Sacramento Ward 1	63	29
Geo E	Sacramento Ward 1	63	38
Geo H	Sacramento Ward 1	63	3
George W	Yuba Marysville	72	915
Grace	Yuba Marysville	72	899
H	San Francisco San Francisco 5	67	500

Name	County Locale	M653 Roll	Page
MONTGOMERY			
H	Sutter Butte	70	781
H C	El Dorado Union	581	088
H F	Sacramento Ward 4	63	500
I L	Siskiyou Cottonwood	69	100
Isaac S	Sierra St Louis	66	812
J	Merced Twp 2	60	924
J	Nevada Nevada	61	295
J	Nevada Eureka	61	373
J	Sutter Yuba	70	768
J B	Shasta Shasta	66	678
J F	Sacramento Ward 4	63	552
J L	Yolo Cottonwoood	72	658
J M	Merced Twp 2	60	924
James	Calaveras Twp 6	57	116
James	Humbolt Eureka	59	171
James	Nevada Red Dog	61	553
James	Siskiyou Yreka	69	190
James	Yuba New York	72	738
James S	Nevada Rough &	61	402
Jas	Butte Chico	56	552
Jas	Butte Chico	56	554
Jas	Yolo Cottonwoood	72	658
Jno	Butte Chico	56	557
Jno	Merced Twp 2	60	924
Jno	Sacramento Ward 1	63	47
Jno	Sacramento Ward 1	63	76
John	Calaveras Twp 5	57	229
John	Napa Napa	61	106
John	Nevada Bridgeport	61	453
John	Placer Michigan	62	810
John	Sonoma Armally	69	489
John	Yuba Bear Rvr	721	010
John	Yuba Marysville	72	907
Johnson	Butte Kimshaw	56	587
Joseph	Nevada Rough &	61	404
Laura	Butte Ophir	56	761
M	Sutter Yuba	70	768
Mat S	Mendocino Little L	60	831
O	Calaveras Twp 9	57	399
Philip	San Mateo Twp 2	65	120
R C	Sacramento Ward 4	63	529
R T	Napa Napa	61	82
Robert	Plumas Quincy	62	943
Robert C	Plumas Quincy	62	989
Saml	Calaveras Twp 5	57	229
Thomas	San Joaquin Oneal	64	912
Thomas*	Plumas Quincy	62	981
Thos	Stanislaus Oatvale	70	717
W	Tehama Lassen	70	871
W	Yolo Putah	72	550
W C	Nevada Nevada	61	272
W G	Sierra Morristown	661	054
W J	Butte Kimshaw	56	599
W T	San Francisco San Francisco 3	67	73
Washington	Yuba Marysville	72	894
William	San Francisco San Francisco 9	68	952
Wm	Butte Oro	56	678
Wm	Napa Napa	61	92
Wm	Nevada Nevada	61	288
Wm	San Francisco San Francisco 2	67	770
Wm	Sierra Downieville	66	968
Wm G	Sierra St Louis	66	810
Wm H	Sierra St Louis	66	810
Z	Sutter Yuba	70	770
MONTGOMEY			
Z	Calaveras Twp 9	57	399
MONTGOMORY			
Charles	El Dorado Kelsey	581	148
Elizabeth	San Francisco San Francisco 9	681	105
MONTGOMREY			
R T	Napa Napa	61	82
MONTGOND			
Charles	El Dorado Salmon Hills	581	065
MONTGONE			
Lury	Tehama Tehama	70	946
MONTGONEY			
Thomas*	Plumas Quincy	62	981
MONTGUILLEARD			
P	Calaveras Twp 9	57	377
MONTGUILLIARD			
Louis	Calaveras Twp 9	57	377
MONTGUMRAY			
Alex	Napa Napa	61	112
MONTH			
Joseph	El Dorado Casumnes	581	170
MONTHENAY			
W Deha*	San Bernadino	64	619
	San Bernardino		
MONTHENIEY			
W Deha*	San Bernadino	64	619
	San Bernardino		
MONTHOS			
Francis*	Santa Clara Santa Clara	65	482
MONTICENO			
Manuell	Amador Twp 5	55	332

Name	County Locale	M653 Roll	Page
MONTICO			
Lucus	Los Angeles Elmonte	59	258
MONTIFO			
M	San Francisco San Francisco 5	67	513
MONTIGA			
Jose	El Dorado Georgetown	58	694
MONTIGNO			
Morjeles	Calaveras Twp 10	57	286
MONTIGO			
Jesus	San Joaquin Castoria	64	891
MONTIJO			
Amada	Los Angeles Los Angeles	59	400
Jesus	Santa Clara Almaden	65	268
Palinario*	Los Angeles Santa Ana	59	456
Palmario	Los Angeles Santa Ana	59	456
Ramon	Los Angeles Santa Ana	59	452
Ugnacio	Los Angeles Los Angeles	59	399
MONTILLO			
Jose	El Dorado Georgetown	58	702
MONTIMA			
Jose*	Solano Vacaville	69	335
MONTIMER			
B S	Siskiyou Scott Ri	69	75
MONTINAGO			
E*	Napa Hot Springs	61	2
MONTINEGRO			
M*	Merced Twp 1	60	900
MONTINER			
B	Merced Twp 1	60	900
MONTINO			
Burtolina	Calaveras Twp 8	57	87
MONTION			
Agustus	Los Angeles Los Angeles	59	337
MONTIVILLE			
Antone	Amador Twp 4	55	241
MONTJERANT			
John	Siskiyou Callahan	69	3
MONTJO			
Pancho	Los Angeles Azuza	59	274
MONTJOY			
C W	El Dorado Placerville	58	864
MONTKIN			
John	Santa Cruz Santa Cruz	66	604
MONTMAQUETT			
Peter	Placer Michigan	62	809
MONTNELIEF			
---	Mendocino Calpella	60	822
MONTO			
Jas	Amador Twp 3	55	380
MONTOGNO			
Morjeles*	Calaveras Twp 10	57	286
MONTOGO			
Jose	San Bernardino San Salvador	64	662
Rifugio	San Bernardino San Salvador	64	662
MONTOGOMERY			
C R	San Joaquin Elkhorn	64	988
G	Santa Clara San Jose	65	361
MONTOGUE			
T C	El Dorado Kelsey	581	127
MONTOLLE			
A	Merced Twp 1	60	903
MONTOME			
Joseph A	Santa Clara San Jose	65	295
MONTOMERY			
H	Amador Twp 5	55	334
MONTON			
Calistra	Los Angeles Los Angeles	59	518
MONTONIA			
Jose	Solano Vacaville	69	335
MONTOR			
Vicor	Yolo Slate Ra	72	690
Victor	Yuba Slate Ro	72	690
MONTORY			
Edward	San Joaquin Elkhorn	64	997
MONTOSS			
Jose	Contra Costa Twp 1	57	509
MONTOYA			
Baltazar	Los Angeles Los Angeles	59	317
Francisco	Monterey San Juan	601	001
Francisco	Monterey San Juan	601	001
Jose	Los Angeles Los Angeles	59	387
Jose C	Los Angeles Los Angeles	59	387
Joseph	Nevada Red Dog	61	552
Patricio	Marin Cortemad	60	786
Patrick	Marin Cortemad	60	786
MONTOYNO			
Morjelies*	Calaveras Twp 10	57	286
MONTPENNE			
Adriele	Siskiyou Callahan	69	3
Adriele	Siskiyou Callahan	69	4
MONTPERAT			
Pierre	Yuba Parks Ba	72	782
MONTREGOS			
Joel	Alameda Brooklyn	55	104
Jose	Alameda Brooklyn	55	104
MONTRELLER			
Henry	San Francisco San Francisco 2	67	691

California 1860 Census Index

Name	County Locale	M653 Roll	Page
MONTREVILLE			
C	San Francisco San Francisco 6	67	465
MONTRUDIN			
M	San Francisco San Francisco 4	681	160
MONTRY			
Franklin*	Sierra Cox'S Bar	66	952
MONTSON			
John	Placer Yankee J	62	777
MONTSSERAT			
Pierre*	Yuba Parke Ba	72	782
MONTT			
C	San Francisco San Francisco 10	324 67	
MONTTHROP			
John L	San Francisco San Francisco 8	681	249
MONTTIN			
James*	Sierra Twp 7	66	865
MONTY			
D C	Butte Chico	56	562
John	Calaveras Twp 5	57	227
MONTYO			
Palinario*	Los Angeles Santa Ana	59	456
MONUAS			
Banasna*	Marin Bolinas	60	728
Banasua	Marin Bolinas	60	728
MONUT			
Jas	Sacramento Granite	63	264
MONY			
---	Calaveras Twp 5	57	192
---	Calaveras Twp 10	57	260
---	Calaveras Twp 10	57	270
---	Calaveras Twp 10	57	280
---	El Dorado Coloma	581	122
---*	Nevada Rough &	61	424
Michael	Tuolumne Sonora	71	228
MONYA			
Jose	San Diego Agua Caliente	64	863
Mary	San Francisco San Francisco 3	67	47
MONYAR			
Martinez	San Francisco San Francisco 3	67	3
MONYAS			
Martinez	San Francisco San Francisco 3	67	3
MONYOI			
Phil*	Tuolumne Twp 2	71	284
MONYOR			
Phil	Tuolumne Twp 2	71	284
MONZ			
---	Mariposa Twp 1	60	650
MOO			
---	Amador Twp 2	55	291
---	Calaveras Twp 5	57	257
---	Del Norte Happy Ca	58	664
---	El Dorado Coloma	581	120
---	El Dorado Diamond	58	801
---	Sacramento Ward 3	63	492
---	Sacramento Ward 3	63	493
---	Sacramento Ward 1	63	53
---	Sacramento Ward 1	63	54
---	Sacramento Ward 1	63	71
---	San Francisco San Francisco 4	681	175
---	San Francisco San Francisco 4	681	193
---	San Francisco San Francisco 4	681	195
---	San Francisco San Francisco 4	681	198
---	Tuolumne Don Pedro	71	533
---	Yuba Long Bar	72	761
---*	Calaveras Twp 6	57	181
Ah	San Francisco San Francisco 4	681	198
Jim	Tuolumne Twp 3	71	441
John	Yolo No E Twp	72	677
Lee	Amador Twp 2	55	312
Loss	San Francisco San Francisco 4	681	211
MOOBLEY			
F F	Nevada Bridgeport	61	445
MOOBSTAIG			
R*	Nevada Grass Valley	61	178
MOOD			
Thos	Tehama Antelope	70	890
W B	Shasta Shasta	66	729
MOODAY			
Andrew	San Francisco San Francisco 4	681	163
MOODEY			
Andrew J	Santa Clara Santa Clara	65	483
D R	Nevada Little Y	61	532
V D	Santa Clara San Jose	65	313
MOODIC			
G W	Santa Clara Santa Clara	65	464
MOODIE			
Sandford W	Fresno Twp 2	59	50
Stiles B	Fresno Twp 2	59	50
MOODSWORTH			
P B	Sutter Butte	70	792
MOODY			
A	Nevada Grass Valley	61	183
Abram	Mariposa Twp 1	60	635
Albert J	San Francisco San Francisco 7	681	338
Alexander	Mendocino Arrana	60	863

Name	County Locale	M653 Roll	Page
MOODY			
Alexr	Plumas Quincy	62	959
Barton	Santa Clara Fremont	65	421
Bridget	San Francisco San Francisco 9	681	079
Charles C	Solano Fairfield	69	200
Chas	Santa Clara San Jose	65	317
D R	Nevada Nevada	61	291
Dan	Calaveras Twp 6	57	160
Danl	Calaveras Twp 6	57	160
Danl	Santa Clara Fremont	65	422
Edwin	San Francisco San Francisco 3	67	32
Emma F	Sacramento Ward 1	63	143
Francis	Yolo Slate Ra	72	691
Francis	Yuba Slate Ro	72	691
Fred	El Dorado Greenwood	58	726
Frederick	Placer Iona Hills	62	895
Geo P	Sacramento Ward 1	63	115
George	Colusa Monroeville	57	454
George	San Francisco San Francisco 4	681	114
George	San Francisco San Francisco 11	99 67	
H	Sutter Yuba	70	775
H A	Placer Folsom	62	640
J	Yolo Washington	72	599
J A	San Francisco San Francisco 4	681	114
J W	Shasta Shasta	66	686
Jacob	Los Angeles Los Angeles	59	504
James	El Dorado Georgetown	58	758
James	Los Angeles Los Angeles	59	403
James	Monterey Monterey	60	965
James E	Yuba Marysville	72	862
John	El Dorado Placerville	58	891
John	Santa Clara Fremont	65	422
John	Siskiyou Yreka	69	149
John F	Placer Dutch Fl	62	717
Jonathen	Yolo Slate Ra	72	691
Jonathen	Yuba Slate Ro	72	691
Joseph	Placer Auburn	62	596
L	Nevada Grass Valley	61	153
L	Nevada Grass Valley	61	177
L	Nevada Grass Valley	61	178
L	Yolo Cottonwooood	72	555
Lucy A	Santa Clara Fremont	65	422
M	Tuolumne Twp 1	71	244
M O	Del Norte Happy Ca	58	661
Peter	San Francisco San Francisco 11	103 67	
R A	Tuolumne Twp 3	71	462
R P	Santa Clara San Jose	65	317
R P	Tuolumne Columbia	71	361
S	Los Angeles Tejon	59	524
S R	Nevada Grass Valley	61	165
Salmon	Yuba Rose Bar	72	794
Salnon*	Yuba Rose Bar	72	794
Samuel	Placer Forest H	62	801
Sarah	San Francisco San Francisco 4	681	228
T	Los Angeles Tejon	59	524
T	Nevada Grass Valley	61	153
T F	Yuba Long Bar	72	745
Thomas	Humbolt Mattole	59	126
W H	Butte Bidwell	56	719
Wash	Santa Clara Fremont	65	422
Wiliam	Placer Yankee J	62	781
William	San Diego Temecula	64	793
William	San Francisco San Francisco 3	67	81
William	Shasta Shasta	66	666
Wm	Calaveras Twp 9	57	356
Wm B	Solano Fairfield	69	200
Wm E	San Francisco San Francisco 1	68	863
MOOE			
Mary J*	San Francisco San Francisco 10	237 67	
MOOFS			
Jennette*	San Francisco San Francisco 9	681	007
MOOGAN			
P*	Nevada Grass Valley	61	224
MOOHECUT			
---	Tulara Twp 1	71	121
MOOHER			
H*	San Francisco San Francisco 9	681	079
MOOK			
---	Amador Twp 4	55	252
---	Placer Iona Hills	62	893
---	San Francisco San Francisco 4	681	186
---	Yuba Bear Rvr	721	000
Abram	Butte Oregon	56	613
Ah	Yuba Bear Rvr	721	000
Hans	Yuba Marysville	72	940
Jackson*	Mariposa Coulterville	60	693
MOOKE			
---	Fresno Twp 2	59	60
MOOKUM			
---	Plumas Quincy	62	969
MOOLA			
H*	Nevada Grass Valley	61	187
MOOLASE			
T	Nevada Grass Valley	61	148

Name	County Locale	M653 Roll	Page
MOOLD			
H*	Nevada Grass Valley	61	187
MOOLENER			
William	Siskiyou Klamath	69	86
MOOLEY			
R	Nevada Grass Valley	61	162
William*	Siskiyou Yreka	69	177
MOOM			
Etchguow*	Del Norte Klamath	58	658
MOON EYE			
---	Tulara Twp 3	71	56
MOON			
---	Amador Twp 2	55	308
---	Amador Twp 2	55	310
---	Amador Twp 2	55	312
---	Calaveras Twp 5	57	225
---	El Dorado Salmon Hills	581	063
---	El Dorado Coloma	581	085
---	Mariposa Twp 3	60	579
---	Mariposa Twp 3	60	590
---	Mariposa Twp 3	60	608
---	Mariposa Twp 3	60	613
---	Nevada Rough &	61	397
---	Nevada Rough &	61	434
---	Nevada Bridgeport	61	461
---	Nevada Bridgeport	61	492
---	Placer Illinois	62	741
---	Placer Iona Hills	62	897
---	San Francisco San Francisco 4	681	187
---	Tuolumne Columbia	71	347
---	Tuolumne Twp 2	71	409
---	Tuolumne Twp 2	71	416
---	Tuolumne Jamestown	71	435
---	Tuolumne Twp 3	71	446
---	Tuolumne Sonora	71	476
---	Tuolumne Jacksonville	71	515
---	Yuba Long Bar	72	767
---	Yuba Marysville	72	868
---	Yuba Marysville	72	921
---*	Tuolumne Twp 3	71	435
---*	Yuba Marysville	72	916
A	San Francisco San Francisco 10	309 67	
A B	Nevada Eureka	61	344
A D	Marin Cortemad	60	752
A S	Siskiyou Klamath	69	85
Ah	Tuolumne Twp 2	71	347
Ah	Tuolumne Twp 2	71	386
Ann	San Francisco San Francisco 8	681	313
C	Butte Ophir	56	794
C A	San Joaquin Oneal	64	931
Chak	San Francisco San Francisco 5	67	507
Charles	Tuolumne Green Springs	71	519
D	Amador Twp 1	55	488
David	Amador Twp 4	55	243
Dionecea*	Calaveras Twp 5	57	170
Dionecen*	Calaveras Twp 6	57	170
Dioneceu*	Calaveras Twp 5	57	170
Eli	Del Norte Crescent	58	647
Elijah R	Del Norte Klamath	58	653
Ellen E	San Francisco San Francisco 3	67	10
Fow	Shasta Horsetown	66	704
Francis	Sacramento Ward 1	63	129
Francis	Yuba Rose Bar	72	815
H	Butte Kimshaw	56	588
H	Nevada Washington	61	338
Henry*	Siskiyou Yreka	69	150
Horatho T	Tuolumne Green Springs	71	519
Hy Lan	El Dorado Georgetown	58	748
Jacob	San Bernardino S Timate	64	689
James	Santa Clara Santa Clara	65	493
James A	Plumas Quincy	621	005
John	Butte Bidwell	56	722
John	El Dorado Placerville	58	928
John	Sacramento Cosumnes	63	408
John	Shasta Shasta	66	728
L	Mariposa Twp 3	60	613
La	Tehama Lassen	70	872
Leep	Yuba Suida	72	991
M	El Dorado Placerville	58	928
Martha	San Bernardino San Bernardino	64	621
Mary	San Francisco San Francisco 4	681	141
P L	Amador Twp 2	55	308
Patrick	Tuolumne Twp 3	71	449
Patrick*	San Francisco San Francisco 2	67	584
R	Nevada Grass Valley	61	165
R	Nevada Grass Valley	61	191
Richard	Alameda Brooklyn	55	161
Richard	Contra Costa Twp 1	57	485
T R	Nevada Eureka	61	379
W	Nevada Grass Valley	61	182
W	Shasta Shasta	66	734
W S	Butte Ophir	56	754
Walter	Tuolumne Twp 2	71	314
Wm	Amador Twp 1	55	489
Wm	Sacramento Natonia	63	280

Name	County Locale	M653 RollPage
MOON		
Wm Jr	Tehama Moons	70 851
Wm Sr	Tehama Moons	70 851
Z B*	Nevada Grass Valley	61 202
MOONAU		
J	Nevada Eureka	61 354
MOONAY		
Wm	Sacramento Ward 4	63 553
MOONE		
---	Sierra Downieville	66 979
Gideon	Sacramento Natonia	63 274
H	San Francisco San Francisco 5	67 537
John	Sierra Chappare	661040
Thos*	Placer Secret R	62 614
MOONEN		
Michael	San Francisco San Francisco 2	67 641
MOONEY		
B	Tehama Antelope	70 892
Barney	El Dorado Mud Springs	58 997
Benj	Sierra Twp 7	66 867
Benny	Sierra Twp 7	66 867
C M	Nevada Grass Valley	61 194
Charles	Tuolumne Twp 2	71 280
Chs	Stanislaus Emory	70 738
E	Nevada Eureka	61 365
Eduard	San Francisco San Francisco 1	68 908
Elizaabeth	Tuolumne Twp 2	71 281
H	Nevada Nevada	61 244
H	Placer Virginia	62 690
Haywood B	Fresno Twp 3	59 14
Henry	Placer Ophirville	62 655
Hugh	Tehama Tehama	70 947
J	Calaveras Twp 9	57 413
J	El Dorado Georgetown	58 705
J	Nevada Grass Valley	61 182
J	San Francisco San Francisco 10	314 67
J	San Francisco San Francisco 2	67 775
J B	Nevada Eureka	61 360
J C*	Placer Illinois	62 739
J F	Sierra Downieville	661003
James	San Francisco San Francisco 3	67 66
James	Solano Benecia	69 312
James	Solano Benecia	69 313
James	Yuba Bear Rvr	721004
Jno	Sacramento Granite	63 240
John	Amador Twp 4	55 239
John	Calaveras Twp 9	57 352
John	Sierra St Louis	66 817
John	Solano Fremont	69 380
John	Tuolumne Jamestown	71 443
John F	Calaveras Twp 9	57 355
Joseph	Tuolumne Twp 1	71 272
Joseph	Tuolumne Twp 2	71 281
M H	Nevada Nevada	61 291
Mat	Amador Twp 4	55 235
Michael	Calaveras Twp 9	57 365
Michael	Yuba Bear Rvr	721009
Michiel	Calaveras Twp 9	57 365
Mike	San Joaquin Oneal	64 929
O*	Nevada Grass Valley	61 198
P	Nevada Washington	61 332
Pat	El Dorado Georgetown	58 677
Pat	Santa Clara Santa Clara	65 463
Patrick	Sierra St Louis	66 817
Peter P	Siskiyou Scott Va	69 39
Petr P	Siskiyou Scott Va	69 39
R	Nevada Grass Valley	61 177
S B	Sierra Downieville	661003
Samuel	Sierra Downieville	661003
Thomas	Yuba Rose Bar	72 816
Thos	Butte Mountain	56 737
Thos	Placer Dutch Fl	62 710
Thos	Sacramento Granite	63 229
Thos	San Francisco San Francisco 12	382 67
Wheeler	Plumas Quincy	62 957
Wm	Amador Twp 3	55 384
Wm	Solano Benecia	69 304
MOONING		
---	Mariposa Twp 3	60 607
MOONMAD		
John	Placer Forest H	62 768
MOONS		
William*	Mendocino Big Rvr	60 846
MOONY		
---	Nevada Bridgeport	61 462
Alexander	Calaveras Twp 5	57 147
Bridget	San Francisco San Francisco 2	67 758
J	Nevada Eureka	61 392
L	Nevada Grass Valley	61 190
Mary	San Francisco San Francisco 2	67 757
O*	Nevada Grass Valley	61 198
Pat	El Dorado Georgetown	58 677
W W	Butte Ophir	56 766
MOOON		
---	Tuolumne Twp 1	71 476

Name	County Locale	M653 RollPage
MOOP		
N C	Tehama Lassen	70 865
MOOR		
---	San Francisco San Francisco 4	681179
---	San Francisco San Francisco 4	681195
---	Tuolumne Shawsfla	71 386
---*	San Francisco San Francisco 4	681195
B	Sacramento Ward 1	63 85
B F	Sacramento Ward 1	63 107
C A	Tehama Red Bluff	70 916
Carolina	Santa Clara San Jose	65 377
Catherine	Santa Clara San Jose	65 377
Daniel T	San Mateo Twp 3	65 78
Ellen	Solano Vacaville	69 332
F J	Sacramento Ward 1	63 111
G*	Nevada Grass Valley	61 178
H	San Francisco San Francisco 1	68 920
Henry C*	Mendocino Big Rvr	60 853
Isaac	Trinity Sturdiva	701006
J C	Tehama Antelope	70 892
James	Contra Costa Twp 1	57 489
James	Tehama Lassen	70 879
John	Solano Vacaville	69 319
John	Tehama Antelope	70 894
John G	San Mateo Twp 3	65 78
Jonn G*	Mendocino Big Rvr	60 849
Joseph	Tehama Antelope	70 897
Mary A	Contra Costa Twp 3	57 607
Patrick	San Mateo Twp 3	65 107
William	Tulara Keeneysburg	71 48
William A	Contra Costa Twp 2	57 558
Wm	Los Angeles Los Angeles	59 503
Z B*	Nevada Grass Valley	61 202
MOORCROFT		
Thos C	San Francisco San Francisco 10	355 67
MOORE		
---	Mariposa Twp 3	60 592
A	Butte Chico	56 538
A	Sutter Sutter	70 805
A	Yolo Slate Ra	72 705
A	Yuba Slate Ro	72 705
A B	Nevada Eureka	61 344
A B	Placer Todds Va	62 789
A C	Mendocino Big Rock	60 873
A C	Siskiyou Scott Ri	69 83
A D	Siskiyou Scott Ri	69 66
A E	Tuolumne Twp 4	71 151
A F	Sacramento Ward 1	63 107
A N	Sacramento Ward 3	63 432
A P	San Francisco San Francisco 10	234 67
Adalph	Calaveras Twp 6	57 120
Adolph*	Calaveras Twp 6	57 120
Albert	Amador Twp 1	55 493
Albert	Siskiyou Yreka	69 149
Albert	Tulara Visalia	71 81
Albert	Yolo Slate Ra	72 700
Albert*	Yuba Slate Ro	72 700
Alex	Klamath Liberty	59 241
Alex	Merced Twp 1	60 903
Alex	Placer Forest H	62 800
Alex	Placer Forest H	62 801
Alex	San Francisco San Francisco 2	67 712
Alexander	Plumas Meadow Valley	62 934
Alexander	San Joaquin Elkhorn	64 955
Alexander	Santa Cruz Pescadero	66 644
Alford	Butte Kimshaw	56 583
Alfred	Butte Kimshaw	56 583
Alfred	Sierra Downieville	661012
Allen	San Francisco San Francisco 9	681019
Allen	Yolo No E Twp	72 673
Allen	Yuba North Ea	72 673
Alonzo	Alameda Oakland	55 45
Alx	El Dorado Georgetown	58 706
Amanda J	Tuolumne Twp 2	71 349
Ambrose J	Siskiyou Yreka	69 139
Ambrosia	Fresno Twp 1	59 82
Amos	Santa Cruz Pajaro	66 543
Amos H	San Francisco San Francisco 2	67 727
Ampledro	Santa Cruz Pajaro	66 541
Andrew	San Francisco San Francisco 1	68 866
Andrew	San Francisco San Francisco 1	68 879
Andrew	Santa Cruz Pajaro	66 541
Andrew	Siskiyou Klamath	69 88
Andw	Monterey Alisal	601035
Andw J	Monterey Alisal	601035
Anebrase*	Siskiyou Yreka	69 139
Ann	San Francisco San Francisco 8	681313
Anthen*	Solano Vacaville	69 366
Archy	Nevada Bridgeport	61 445
Armstrong	Plumas Quincy	62 915
Arthur	Sierra Twp 5	66 925
Arthur	Solano Vacaville	69 366
Augustus	Santa Cruz Soguel	66 594
B	Sacramento Ward 1	63 85

Name	County Locale	M653 RollPage
MOORE		
B C	San Francisco San Francisco 9	68 989
B F	Tuolumne Twp 1	71 231
B P	San Francisco San Francisco 1	68 816
B*	Sacramento Ward 1	63 85
Bas*	San Francisco San Francisco 11	107 67
Bat	San Francisco San Francisco 11	107 67
Ben	Napa Clear Lake	61 127
Benj	Solano Suisan	69 218
Benj F	San Francisco San Francisco 3	67 20
Berry	Sacramento Ward 3	63 458
Berry	Tuolumne Don Pedro	71 534
Betherel C	San Francisco	67
Bethuel C	San Francisco San Francisco 10	270 67
Buck	El Dorado Mud Springs	58 954
C	El Dorado Placerville	58 847
C	Nevada Nevada	61 313
C A	Nevada Grass Valley	61 214
C C	San Francisco San Francisco 5	67 547
C F	Shasta Horsetown	66 709
C P	Sonoma Washington	69 668
Cafein	El Dorado Coloma	581102
Calein	El Dorado Coloma	581102
Calvin	Sonoma Bodega	69 537
Catharine	San Francisco San Francisco 11	91 67
Cela	Napa Clear Lake	61 134
Charles	El Dorado Casumnes	581166
Charles	Humbolt Eureka	59 174
Charles	Los Angeles Los Angeles	59 352
Charles	Los Angeles San Juan	59 461
Charles	Nevada Rough &	61 422
Charles	Placer Forest H	62 796
Charles	San Francisco San Francisco 8	681313
Charles	San Francisco San Francisco 7	681371
Charles	San Francisco San Francisco 7	681443
Charles	San Francisco San Francisco 3	67 66
Charles	Sierra Eureka	661050
Charles	Siskiyou Yreka	69 173
Charles C	Yuba Rose Bar	72 809
Charlie	Alameda Brooklyn	55 140
Chas	Alameda Brooklyn	55 132
Chas	Placer Sacramento	62 645
Chas	San Francisco San Francisco 9	681060
Cynis*	Butte Hamilton	56 529
Cyrus	Butte Hamilton	56 529
D	Siskiyou Scott Ri	69 64
D	Sutter Sutter	70 811
D C	San Mateo Twp 1	65 56
D D	Nevada Bridgeport	61 498
D M	San Francisco San Francisco 7	681423
D Z	Sacramento Ward 3	63 431
Dan	Tehama Red Bluff	70 916
Daniel	Calaveras Twp 6	57 161
Daniel	Yolo Putah	72 588
David	El Dorado Placerville	58 913
David	San Francisco San Francisco 10	286 67
David Z	Sacramento Ward 4	63 502
Dick	Nevada Eureka	61 356
E	Butte Hamilton	56 516
E	Butte Kimshaw	56 578
E	Merced Twp 1	60 903
E	Nevada Grass Valley	61 206
E	Sacramento Ward 1	63 23
E	Sacramento Sutter	63 289
E	Siskiyou Scott Va	69 29
E D	Siskiyou Scott Va	69 40
E L	Tuolumne Columbia	71 360
E N	Yolo Cache Crk	72 593
E R	Yuba Rose Par	72 796
Ebin	Yolo Putah	72 588
Edward H	Yolo Slate Ra	72 692
Edward H	Yuba Slate Ro	72 692
Eli	Stanislaus Branch	70 705
Elizabeth	Amador Twp 1	55 506
Elizabeth	Nevada Red Dog	61 551
Elizabeth	Santa Cruz Santa Cruz	66 615
Elizabeth	Sonoma Armally	69 503
Elvin	Mariposa Twp 3	60 565
Enoch	Tulara Twp 3	71 61
Ervin	Mariposa Twp 3	60 565
F	Butte Wyandotte	56 658
F	San Francisco San Francisco 8	681102
F A	San Francisco San Francisco 5	67 548
F B*	Sacramento Lee	63 210
F G	Sacramento Ward 1	63 25
F??Niar C*	Tuolumne Sonora	71 209
Finias*	Tuolumne Twp 1	71 209
Florance	Yuba Marysville	72 853
Florence	Yuba Marysville	72 858
Francis	Sacramento Ward 1	63 129

Name	County Locale	M653 Roll	Page
MOORE			
Frank	El Dorado Placerville	58	913
Frank	Nevada Nevada	61	290
Franklin	San Joaquin Elkhorn	64	967
Frenchman	Amador Twp 3	55	382
G	Nevada Grass Valley	61	151
G C	Butte Ophir	56	763
G H	Yolo Cache Crk	72	633
G M	Tuolumne Twp 2	71	396
G N	Yolo Cache	72	633
G W	El Dorado Salmon Falls	581	035
G W	Nevada Bridgeport	61	482
G W	San Joaquin Stockton	641	093
G W	Sonoma Santa Rosa	69	390
G W	Tuolumne Shawsfla	71	396
Gabriel	Fresno Twp 3	59	6
Ganl	Solano Vacaville	69	366
Gaul*	Solano Vacaville	69	366
Gedeon	Sacramento Natonia	63	274
Geo	Amador Twp 5	55	357
Geo	Amador Twp 3	55	402
Geo	El Dorado Mud Springs	58	965
Geo	Sacramento Ward 1	63	62
Geo	Stanislaus Empire	70	730
Geo B	San Francisco San Francisco 6	67	433
Geo G	Sacramento Ward 4	63	590
Geo R	Sacramento Ward 3	63	472
Geo W	Sacramento Franklin	63	332
Georg	Yuba Rose Bar	72	790
George	Plumas Meadow Valley	62	912
George	San Francisco San Francisco 3	67	76
George	San Mateo Twp 3	65	108
George	Sonoma Bodega	69	527
George A	Monterey San Juan	60	995
George H	San Francisco San Francisco 7	681	346
George W	San Salvador San Bernardino	64	654
Goff	Amador Twp 4	55	237
Gorham H	Butte Ophir	56	799
H	Butte Kimshaw	56	588
H	Nevada Washington	61	338
H A	Butte Oregon	56	623
H C	San Francisco San Francisco 9	681	080
H G	Yuba New York	72	728
H H	San Bernardino Santa Barbara	64	171
H H	San Francisco San Francisco 10	234	67
H J	Butte Kimshaw	56	588
H J	Calaveras Twp 8	57	65
H M	Nevada Eureka	61	351
H M	Yolo Cache Crk	72	644
Hannah	San Francisco San Francisco 10	357	
Harrison	El Dorado Casumnes	581	163
Henry	Napa Napa	61	108
Henry	Napa Clear Lake	61	128
Henry	Sacramento Casumnes	63	381
Henry	San Joaquin Castoria	64	873
Henry	San Joaquin Elkhorn	64	983
Henry	San Luis Obispo San Luis Obispo	65	32
Henry	Siskiyou Cottonwoood	69	107
Henry	Yuba Marysville	72	906
Henry J	San Francisco San Francisco 10	267	67
Horace H	San Francisco San Francisco 11	98	67
Horatio N	Tuolumne Twp 5	71	519
Hugh	Shasta Horsetown	66	702
Hugh	Yuba Bear Rvr	721	008
I	Nevada Nevada	61	318
I*	El Dorado Placerville	58	877
Isabela	Amador Twp 1	55	494
J	Butte Hamilton	56	528
J	El Dorado Placerville	58	867
J	Nevada Grass Valley	61	149
J	Nevada Grass Valley	61	150
J	Nevada Grass Valley	61	202
J	Nevada Nevada	61	318
J	Placer Dutch Fl	62	721
J	San Francisco San Francisco 5	67	495
J	Shasta Millvill	66	739
J	Solano Fremont	69	376
J	Sutter Butte	70	785
J	Sutter Butte	70	793
J	Sutter Butte	70	794
J	Sutter Bear Rvr	70	825
J	Trinity Trinity	70	970
J A	El Dorado Salmon Falls	581	065
J B	Nevada Nevada	61	247
J B	Sacramento Granite	63	222
J B	Sacramento Granite	63	229
J B	San Francisco San Francisco 10	327	67
J B	San Francisco San Francisco 6	67	456
J B	San Francisco San Francisco 3	67	46
MOORE			
J C	San Francisco San Francisco 10	200	67
J D	Merced Twp 1	60	910
J F	Santa Clara San Jose	65	336
J F	Yolo Cache Crk	72	663
J G	Butte Hamilton	56	514
J H	Santa Clara San Jose	65	293
J H	Yolo Cache Crk	72	663
J H	Yuba New York	72	746
J L	Tuolumne Twp 1	71	211
J M	Siskiyou Scott Ri	69	81
J M	Solano Vallejo	69	251
J S	Butte Bidwell	56	727
J S	Tuolumne Twp 2	71	365
J S	Yuba Rose Bar	72	788
J T	El Dorado Kelsey	581	145
J W	Amador Twp 7	55	420
J W	Butte Wyandotte	56	661
J W	Sacramento San Joaquin	63	356
J W	Sonoma Santa Rosa	69	390
J*	Nevada Grass Valley	61	150
Jacke	Tuolumne Twp 3	71	441
Jackson	Mariposa Coulterville	60	693
Jacob	Amador Twp 1	55	474
Jacob	Butte Cascade	56	694
James	Alameda Oakland	55	51
James	Amador Twp 7	55	415
James	Mendocino Ukiah	60	804
James	Napa Hot Springs	61	7
James	Nevada Bridgeport	61	478
James	Sacramento San Joaquin	63	355
James	San Francisco San Francisco 9	681	048
James	San Francisco San Francisco 4	681	137
James	San Francisco San Francisco 3	67	82
James	San Francisco San Francisco 9	68	942
James	San Francisco San Francisco 9	68	966
James	San Joaquin Elliott	64	941
James	Santa Cruz Watsonville	66	538
James	Santa Cruz Pajaro	66	574
James	Santa Cruz Santa Cruz	66	639
James	Siskiyou Scott Va	69	29
James	Sonoma Armally	69	497
James	Trinity E Weaver	701	060
James	Yolo Cache	72	630
James	Yuba Rose Bar	72	792
James	Yuba Marysville	72	845
James A	San Francisco San Francisco 7	681	356
James M	Contra Costa Twp 2	57	559
Jaques*	El Dorado Georgetown	58	750
Jas	Amador Twp 3	55	382
Jas	Butte Oro	56	675
Jas	Placer Ophirville	62	653
Jas	Placer Illinois	62	705
Jas	Sacramento Granite	63	239
Jas	Sacramento Ward 1	63	37
Jas	Santa Clara Alviso	65	401
Jerome	Alameda Brooklyn	55	150
Jerry	Mendocino Ukiah	60	800
Jesse	Sonoma Petaluma	69	564
Jl J	Sacramento Ward 4	63	502
Jno	Butte Chico	56	545
Jno	Fresno Twp 3	59	15
Jno	Klamath Salmon	59	208
Jno	Klamath Klamath	59	224
Jno	Sacramento Franklin	63	318
Jno	Sacramento Ward 4	63	504
Jno	Sacramento Ward 4	63	529
Jno	Tehama Lassen	70	867
Jno E	San Joaquin Stockton	641	088
Jno R S	San Francisco San Francisco 10	323	67
Jno T	Klamath Liberty	59	242
John	Amador Twp 1	55	472
John	Butte Wyandotte	56	672
John	Calaveras Twp 7	57	19
John	Del Norte Crescent	58	659
John	El Dorado Kelsey	581	148
John	Humbolt Mattole	59	124
John	Los Angeles Elmonte	59	250
John	Los Angeles Los Angeles	59	399
John	Mariposa Coulterville	60	694
John	Placer Virginia	62	663
John	Placer Michigan	62	830
John	Plumas Meadow Valley	62	900
John	San Diego Colorado	64	808
John	San Francisco San Francisco 4	681	146
John	San Francisco San Francisco 7	681	356
John	San Francisco San Francisco 2	67	610
John	San Joaquin Tulare	64	871
John	San Joaquin Castoria	64	875
John	San Joaquin Elkhorn	64	992
John	Santa Cruz Pescadero	66	649
John	Shasta Shasta	66	687
John	Sierra Scales D	66	803
John	Solano Suisan	69	232
MOORE			
John	Solano Vacaville	69	357
John	Solano Fremont	69	382
John	Sonoma Santa Rosa	69	397
John	Sonoma Sonoma	69	657
John	Trinity Weaverville	701	063
John	Tuolumne Columbia	71	472
John	Yolo New York	72	720
John	Yuba New York	72	720
John	Yuba New York	72	721
John A	San Francisco San Francisco 7	681	402
John C	Yuba Marysville	72	977
John F	Sierra Downieville	66	989
John J	Marin San Rafael	60	757
John K	San Francisco San Francisco 9	681	102
John L*	Sacramento Cosummes	63	395
John S	Butte Mountain	56	739
John S*	Sacramento Cosummes	63	395
John W	San Francisco San Francisco 1	68	893
John W	Yuba Marysville	72	846
Johnathan	Placer Auburn	62	580
Jos	Amador Twp 2	55	299
Jos	San Mateo Twp 2	65	125
Joseph	Colusa Monroeville	57	455
Joseph	El Dorado Georgetown	58	675
Joseph	El Dorado Mud Springs	58	979
Joseph	Sacramento Ward 4	63	499
Josephene	Yuba Marysville	72	898
Josephine	Yuba Marysville	72	898
Justin	Mendocino Big Rvr	60	840
Jw	Santa Clara San Jose	65	383
K M	Yolo Cache	72	644
L	El Dorado Union	581	094
L	Klamath S Fork	59	205
L	Mariposa Twp 3	60	575
L	Sacramento Georgian	63	337
L	San Francisco San Francisco 9	681	104
L	Tehama Moons	70	854
L G	Siskiyou Scott Va	69	24
L L	San Francisco San Francisco 5	67	544
L W	Butte Chico	56	555
Lavina	Yuba Marysville	72	950
Leroy	Nevada Grass Valley	61	167
Leroy	Yolo Cache Crk	72	663
Levi P	Napa Yount	61	46
Levy*	Yolo Cache Crk	72	663
Lewis	Butte Ophir	56	772
Lewis W	Butte Chico	56	559
Louis W	Butte Chico	56	559
Louisa	San Francisco San Francisco 6	67	408
Lucias B	Yuba Marysville	72	900
Lucinda	Sacramento Ward 4	63	604
Luke	Santa Clara Santa Clara	65	522
Lyman	Butte Kimshaw	56	572
Lyman	Placer Michigan	62	830
M	Sacramento Lee	63	216
M	Shasta Millvill	66	751
M P	Sacramento Ward 3	63	443
Margaret	Placer Todds Va	62	789
Marge	Santa Clara San Jose	65	287
Maria	Santa Cruz Soguel	66	594
Mary	El Dorado Kelsey	581	145
Mary A	Sacramento Ward 4	63	568
Melton	Monterey Pajaro	601	018
Milton	Monterey Pajaro	601	018
Mirnivra	Napa Clear Lake	61	128
N	El Dorado Diamond	58	797
Nelson	Yuba Linda	72	985
Nelson S	Contra Costa Twp 2	57	560
Newell	Sacramento Cosummes	63	383
Nich	Sacramento Ward 1	63	42
Olive M	Humbolt Union	59	192
Oliver	Santa Clara Santa Clara	65	474
Oliver	Tuolumne Twp 4	71	144
Orlando	San Diego San Diego	64	766
P R	Sacramento Centre	63	178
Pat	Sonoma Bodega	69	521
Patrick	San Francisco San Francisco 4	681	132
Patrick	Yuba Rose Bar	72	819
Patrick C	San Francisco San Francisco 7	681	334
Patrick*	San Francisco San Francisco 2	67	584
Perry	Sacramento Granite	63	235
Peter	Calaveras Twp 8	57	85
Peter	Calaveras Twp 8	57	89
Peter	Sierra Gibsonville	66	858
Peter L*	San Francisco San Francisco 2	67	726
Peter S	San Francisco San Francisco 2	67	726
Phil	Nevada Nevada	61	239
Phil	San Francisco San Francisco 9	681	067
Philip	Sacramento Georgian	63	337
R	El Dorado Placerville	58	850
R	Nevada Grass Valley	61	168
R	Siskiyou Cottonwoood	69	109
R	Sutter Butte	70	799
R A	Mariposa Twp 3	60	591
R A	Nevada Grass Valley	61	146

Name	County Locale	M653 Roll	Page
MOORE			
R A	Nevada Nevada	61	288
R A	Siskiyou Yreka	69	170
R A S	Nevada Nevada	61	288
R A*	Mariposa Twp 3	60	591
R B	Butte Hamilton	56	529
R M	Nevada Grass Valley	61	197
R P	Sierra Downieville	66	1030
R V	Sacramento American	63	166
R W	Colusa Grand Island	57	477
Ransom B	Los Angeles Elmonte	59	253
Reuben	Mendocino Big Rock	60	876
Reuben	San Francisco San Francisco 9	68	1066
Reuben C	San Francisco San Francisco 9	68	1066
Richard	Humbolt Eel Rvr	59	153
Richd	Napa Napa	61	74
Robert	Marin Tomales	60	714
Robert	Nevada Bloomfield	61	525
Robert	San Joaquin Stockton	64	1059
Robt	Sonoma Armally	69	497
Robt	Sonoma Sonoma	69	652
Ruben P	Calaveras Twp 4	57	301
Rudolph	San Francisco San Francisco 8	68	1314
S	El Dorado Placerville	58	851
S	Nevada Eureka	61	350
S	San Francisco San Francisco 5	67	526
S	Siskiyou Klamath	69	93
S	Sutter Bear Rvr	70	819
S	Trinity New Rvr	70	1030
S B	Santa Clara San Jose	65	283
S C	El Dorado Cold Spring	58	1100
S D	Yolo Cache	72	636
S H	Sutter Sutter	70	814
S L	Yuba Rose Bar	72	798
S M	Nevada Grass Valley	61	197
S Q	Sacramento Ward 1	63	28
S S	Yuba Rose Bar	72	798
Sam	Sacramento Ward 1	63	67
Saml	Sacramento Ward 1	63	73
Saml H	Sacramento Cosummes	63	382
Saml H*	Placer Virginia	62	672
Samnda J	Tuolumne Columbia	71	349
Samuel	Placer Forest H	62	800
Samuel	San Francisco San Francisco 3	67	78
Samuel W	San Francisco San Francisco 8	68	1287
Sarah	El Dorado Kelsey	58	1141
Sarah	San Joaquin Castoria	64	873
Sarah J	San Francisco San Francisco 4	68	1131
Serrnule	San Francisco San Francisco 3	67	78
Shelly	Yolo Cache Crk	72	663
Simeon	Butte Chico	56	560
Solen	Contra Costa Twp 2	57	560
Stephen	Santa Clara San Jose	65	321
Stuart	Sonoma Petaluma	69	599
Sucretia D	Alameda Brooklyn	55	188
Susan	Siskiyou Cottonwoood	69	107
Susan	Siskiyou Cottonwood	69	108
Susan H	Alameda Brooklyn	55	206
Susan H	Sacramento Ward 4	63	576
T	Butte Wyandotte	56	658
T B*	Sacramento Lee	63	210
T J	Butte Oro	56	676
T K	San Francisco San Francisco 3	67	44
T R	Nevada Eureka	61	379
T S	El Dorado Gold Hill	58	1096
Tho	Siskiyou Callahan	69	12
Thomas	Calaveras Twp 8	57	93
Thomas	Santa Cruz Pescadero	66	641
Thomas	Shasta Millvill	66	742
Thomas	Sierra Twp 7	66	910
Thomas	Sierra Twp 5	66	943
Thomas	Sonoma Bodega	69	522
Thomas	Tuolumne Twp 2	71	303
Thomas	Yuba Marysville	72	962
Thomas E*	Mendocino Round Va	60	877
Thomas P	Calaveras Twp 7	57	25
Thomas W	San Bernardino Santa Barbara	64	171
Thomas*	Sierra Forest C	66	910
Thos	Calaveras Twp 8	57	102
Thos	Klamath Klamath	59	224
Thos	Sacramento American	63	167
Thos	Sacramento Sutter	63	296
Thos J	San Francisco San Francisco 7	68	1397
Thos*	Placer Secret R	62	614
Vincent	Yuba Parke Ba	72	781
Vincent	Yuba Marysville	72	976
Vincent W	Yuba Parks Ba	72	781
W	San Francisco San Francisco 9	68	1070
W	San Francisco San Francisco 5	67	499
W	San Francisco San Francisco 5	67	547
W	Shasta Millvill	66	751
W	Tuolumne Twp 4	71	176
W A J	Del Norte Ferry P O	58	665
W D	Tuolumne Twp 2	71	302
MOORE			
W G	Sierra Grizzly	66	1057
W T	Napa Clear Lake	61	126
W W	Amador Twp 6	55	437
W W	Colusa Monroeville	57	441
Walter	Tuolumne Columbia	71	314
Warren	Humbolt Eureka	59	175
Watson J	Sacramento Ward 3	63	471
Wesley	Sonoma Bodega	69	528
Willaim	Yuba Bear Rvr	72	1007
William	Los Angeles Los Angeles	59	373
William	Nevada Bloomfield	61	525
William	Plumas Quincy	62	958
William	San Francisco San Francisco 4	68	1147
William	San Francisco San Francisco 7	68	1356
William	San Francisco San Francisco 7	68	1377
William	San Francisco San Francisco 3	67	69
William	San Joaquin Elkhorn	64	957
William	Santa Cruz Santa Cruz	66	613
William	Shasta Millvill	66	740
William	Yuba Bear Rvr	72	1007
William	Yuba Marysville	72	976
William A	Solano Fairfield	69	198
William G	Napa Hot Springs	61	24
William*	Mendocino Big Rvr	60	846
William*	Santa Cruz Santa Cruz	66	613
Wm	Alameda Brooklyn	55	155
Wm	Amador Twp 6	55	421
Wm	Butte Chico	56	560
Wm	Napa Yount	61	50
Wm	Placer Virginia	62	689
Wm	San Francisco San Francisco 1	68	851
Wm	Santa Clara Burnett	65	258
Wm	Tehama Pasakent	70	858
Wm	Trinity Minersville	70	968
Wm	Yuba New York	72	729
Wm	Yuba Parke Ba	72	784
Wm	Yuba Rose Bar	72	807
Wm	Yuba Rose Bar	72	809
Wm B	Mariposa Twp 1	60	633
Wm H	Napa Clear Lake	61	128
Wm H	Sacramento Ward 1	63	27
Wm H	Yuba Rose Bar	72	788
Wm K	Tuolumne Columbia	71	303
Wm W	Alameda Brooklyn	55	206
Wm*	Placer Virginia	62	688
Wm*	Yuba Rose Bar	72	809
Wyatt	Tuolumne Columbia	71	472
MOOREHEAD			
Andrew	Placer Forest H	62	797
MOOREHOUSE			
Daniel	Yuba Marysville	72	882
Georg	Tuolumne Columbia	71	306
George	Tuolumne Twp 2	71	306
S J	Placer Forest H	62	795
MOORELARACHE			
A*	El Dorado Georgetown	58	685
MOORER			
Charles B	Amador Twp 4	55	255
MOORES			
Chas	Santa Clara Burnett	65	254
H C	Shasta Millvill	66	755
J E	Siskiyou Scott Va	69	38
Jerry*	Tuolumne Twp 6	71	534
Stephen	Siskiyou Yreka	69	147
MOOREWOOD			
Thomas	Mariposa Coulterville	60	699
MOORHAKE			
Frederick	San Francisco San Francisco 8	68	1318
MOORING			
Burni	Napa Clear Lake	61	127
Burrie	Napa Clear Lake	61	127
MOORIS			
William*	Mendocino Big Rvr	60	846
MOORISON			
Harrison	Alameda Brooklyn	55	205
R B	Nevada Eureka	61	370
Wm	Sacramento Ward 1	63	40
MOORISS			
J*	El Dorado Coloma	58	1069
MOORO			
Thomas E*	Mendocino Round Va	60	877
MOORS			
John D*	Mariposa Twp 3	60	586
W T	Napa Clear Lake	61	126
MOORSE			
Geo	Sacramento Cosummes	63	391
MOOS			
Henry C*	Mendocino Big Rvr	60	853
James*	Contra Costa Twp 1	57	489
Jonn G*	Mendocino Big Rvr	60	849
Patrick	San Francisco San Francisco 2	67	584
MOOSE			
D D	Nevada Bridgeport	61	498
G	El Dorado Georgetown	58	699
J	Nevada Grass Valley	61	147
MOOSE			
J L	Nevada Rough &	61	417
J*	Nevada Grass Valley	61	150
L	El Dorado Georgetown	58	699
Mary*	Siskiyou Yreka	69	152
R	Siskiyou Cottonwoood	69	109
R A	Siskiyou Yreka	69	170
MOOSEHEAD			
P*	Shasta Shasta	66	656
MOOSER			
Wm*	San Francisco San Francisco 3	67	18
MOOSHAKE			
Frederick*	San Francisco San Francisco 8	68	1318
MOOSICK			
William S	Los Angeles Los Angeles	59	355
MOOSS			
Jennette*	San Francisco San Francisco 9	68	1007
MOOSTER			
L*	Calaveras Twp 9	57	374
MOOSTES			
L*	Calaveras Twp 9	57	374
MOOTHIS			
Chris*	Sacramento Ward 1	63	26
MOOTHUS			
Chris	Sacramento Ward 1	63	26
MOOTIM			
---*	Mendocino Big Rvr	60	854
MOOTUN			
---*	Mendocino Big Rvr	60	854
MOOVER			
Leonce	Los Angeles Los Angeles	59	391
MOOY			
---	Nevada Bridgeport	61	462
---	Sacramento Ward 1	63	52
---	Sacramento Ward 1	63	53
MOOYAN			
P*	Nevada Grass Valley	61	224
MOOYER			
Frank	Nevada Bridgeport	61	482
MOP			
---	Mariposa Twp 3	60	618
---	San Francisco San Francisco 4	68	1181
---	San Francisco San Francisco 4	68	1199
---*	Fresno Twp 2	59	70
Charles A	Solano Vallejo	69	278
J	Sacramento Ward 1	63	47
James S	Tuolumne Sonora	71	192
John	Tuolumne Twp 1	71	192
Joseph	Santa Clara Redwood	65	457
Joseph	Tuolumne Sonora	71	238
Lysander	San Francisco San Francisco 8	68	1320
Newton*	Napa Napa	61	93
T J*	San Francisco San Francisco 8	68	1318
MOPE			
---	Mariposa Coulterville	60	688
MOPEY			
J G	Tuolumne Sonora	71	243
MOPNAYRE			
Antone	Sierra Gibsonville	66	854
MOPOGET			
Philenn	Sonoma Petaluma	69	543
MOPPER			
John	Calaveras Twp 10	57	266
MOPPIT			
John B*	Placer Secret R	62	619
MOPREL			
George*	Nevada Red Dog	61	554
MOR			
---	Amador Twp 2	55	328
---	Sacramento Granite	63	231
---	Tuolumne Twp 5	71	526
---*	Mariposa Twp 3	60	582
Caroline*	Sacramento Ward 4	63	545
So	Sierra Twp 7	66	889
MORA			
---	El Dorado Salmon Falls	58	1043
Antonio	Los Angeles Los Nieto	59	426
Baldo	Santa Clara San Jose	65	300
Bridget	Solano Vallejo	69	252
Charles	Mariposa Twp 3	60	594
D	San Francisco San Francisco 9	68	993
Domingo	Monterey San Juan	60	985
Francis	Monterey San Juan	60	986
Gabriel	Placer Forest H	62	773
Giovanni	San Francisco San Francisco 11	67	154
J H	San Francisco San Francisco 4	68	1167
Josefa	Monterey San Juan	60	985
Josifa	Monterey San Juan	60	985
M	Merced Twp 1	60	900
Manuel	Placer Yankee J	62	781
Nicholas	San Francisco San Francisco 1	68	815
Rafael	San Mateo Twp 2	65	118
MORAA			
Chaly	Mariposa Twp 1	60	636

California 1860 Census Index

Name	County Locale	M653 Roll	Page
MORAEO			
Pedro	Mariposa Twp 1	60	660
MORAFEN			
Hosea*	Mariposa Twp 1	60	666
MORAGA			
Duringo	Los Angeles San Juan	59	475
Felipi	San Luis Obispo San Luis Obispo	65	10
Inocencia*	Contra Costa Twp 1	57	491
Jnocencia	Contra Costa Twp 1	57	491
Jose	San Bernardino Santa Ba	64	210
Maria	Los Angeles Los Angeles	59	331
Pablo	Contra Costa Twp 3	57	612
Rafael	Solano Suisan	69	222
MORAGGA			
Josapa	Contra Costa Twp 2	57	556
Jose	Contra Costa Twp 2	57	554
MORAGO			
B	Alameda Brooklyn	55	208
MORAGON			
S	Mariposa Twp 3	60	606
MORAILES			
Deonicia	Santa Cruz Pajaro	66	547
MORAL			
Antonio	Santa Clara San Jose	65	327
Mary*	Alameda Brooklyn	55	121
MORALAS			
Ignacio	Los Angeles Los Angeles	59	497
MORALE			
Phillister	Calaveras Twp 10	57	287
MORALEN			
Hosea	Mariposa Twp 1	60	666
MORALERS			
Hosea*	Mariposa Twp 1	60	666
MORALES			
Alejo	Los Angeles San Gabriel	59	413
Alen	Mariposa Twp 3	60	617
Alijo	Los Angeles San Gabriel	59	413
Allen	Mariposa Twp 3	60	602
Antonio	Monterey Alisal	60	1044
Antonio	Santa Clara Almaden	65	275
Antonio	Tuolumne Twp 5	71	497
Antonio	Tuolumne Twp 5	71	511
Ascencion	Los Angeles San Gabriel	59	413
Augustine	Santa Cruz Pajaro	66	531
Benito	Merced Monterey	60	933
Benito	Monterey Monterey	60	933
Carlito	Siskiyou Scott Ri	69	63
Carmel*	San Joaquin Stockton	64	1077
Carmen	San Bernardino Santa Inez	64	140
Carrnel*	San Joaquin Stockton	64	1077
Cassais	Calaveras Twp 5	57	178
Cassan*	Calaveras Twp 6	57	178
Cassau*	Calaveras Twp 6	57	178
Cesilio	Los Angeles San Juan	59	462
E	Tuolumne Sonora	71	224
Feliciano	San Bernardino Santa Inez	64	140
Francisco	Los Angeles Los Nieto	59	437
Francisco	Los Angeles San Juan	59	460
Francisco	Los Angeles Los Angeles	59	495
Francisco	Santa Cruz Pescadero	66	649
Gomacindo	San Bernardino Santa Ba	64	214
Harmon*	Yuba Marysville	72	936
Hermon*	Yuba Marysville	72	936
Herrmon*	Yuba Marysville	72	937
Jacinto	Santa Cruz Santa Cruz	66	640
Jesus	Los Angeles Tejon	59	539
Jesus	San Bernardino S Timate	64	688
Jesus	Santa Cruz Pajaro	66	546
Jose J	Los Angeles Los Angeles	59	315
Juan	San Bernardino San Bernadino	64	669
Keenir*	Mariposa Coulterville	60	691
L	San Francisco San Francisco 5	67	542
Loretto	San Joaquin Stockton	64	1078
Louise	Tuolumne Sonora	71	228
Magarito	San Bernardino San Bernardino	64	639
Manello	San Bernardino Santa Barbara	64	178
Manuel	Monterey Alisal	60	1039
Manuel	Monterey Alisal	60	1044
Manuel	San Bernardino S Buenav	64	208
Maria	Yuba Marysville	72	858
Maria	Yuba Marysville	72	860
Martias	Los Angeles Los Angeles	59	508
Mary	San Francisco San Francisco 6	67	446
Peter	Contra Costa Twp 1	57	519
Phillisto	Calaveras Twp 10	57	287
Reenir P	Mariposa Coulterville	60	691
Reevis*	Mariposa Coulterville	60	691
Roman	Los Angeles Los Angeles	59	385
Romualdo	San Bernardino Santa Inez	64	140
Salvador	Santa Clara Almaden	65	273
Serapio	San Bernardino San Bernardino	64	670
Simon	San Mateo Twp 2	65	113
Theodore	Los Angeles Santa Ana	59	451
Wancisco	Los Angeles Los Angeles	59	311
MORALIO			
Pancho	Calaveras Twp 5	57	178
MORALIS			
E	Tuolumne Twp 1	71	224
Francisco	Los Angeles Los Angeles	59	495
Jesus	Los Angeles Los Angeles	59	519
Juan	Los Angeles Los Angeles	59	508
Juan	Santa Clara Burnett	65	259
Juna	Los Angeles Los Angeles	59	508
L	Tuolumne Twp 2	71	373
Louise	Tuolumne Twp 1	71	228
Martha	Tuolumne Springfield	71	373
Martias	Los Angeles Los Angeles	59	508
MORALL			
John	Shasta French G	66	718
Robert	Yuba Marysville	72	907
William*	Mendocino Ukiah	60	798
MORALLAS			
Cosmer	Mariposa Twp 1	60	637
MORALLE			
Joaquin*	Calaveras Twp 6	57	179
Joaquin*	Calaveras Twp 6	57	179
MORALLES			
Amelia	San Francisco San Francisco 4	68	1157
Juan*	Santa Cruz Pajaro	66	555
Mal	Calaveras Twp 10	57	283
MORALLIS			
Ramone	Los Angeles Elmonte	59	262
MORALLO			
Joaquin*	Calaveras Twp 5	57	179
MORALS			
Cyprian	San Mateo Twp 2	65	113
MORAM			
Marear	Mariposa Twp 1	60	628
Morear	Mariposa Twp 1	60	628
MORAN			
A	Nevada Grass Valley	61	225
Biddy	San Francisco San Francisco 11	67	121
Bridget	Solano Benecia	69	310
C W	Nevada Grass Valley	61	218
Chaly	Mariposa Twp 1	60	636
Chas	San Francisco San Francisco 2	67	692
Daniel	Yolo Washington	72	566
David	San Francisco San Francisco 3	67	81
Delia	Alameda Brooklyn	55	78
Deloros	Napa Yount	61	50
Domini K	Sierra La Porte	66	790
Dominick	Sierra La Porte	66	790
Edwd	San Francisco San Francisco 2	67	763
Edwd	San Francisco San Francisco 2	67	763
Francis	San Francisco San Francisco 11	67	109
Frank	Alameda Brooklyn	55	120
G	Nevada Grass Valley	61	218
H*	El Dorado Placerville	58	870
Hugh	Colusa Butte Crk	57	465
Isaac	Tehama Red Bluff	70	920
J	Nevada Grass Valley	61	163
J	Nevada Grass Valley	61	221
J	Shasta Millvill	66	752
James	Los Angeles Tejon	59	522
James	Sierra Downieville	66	1002
Jas	Santa Clara Santa Clara	65	509
John	Alameda Brooklyn	55	124
John	Calaveras Twp 7	57	4
John	Los Angeles Los Angeles	59	389
John	Sacramento San Joaquin	63	360
John	San Francisco San Francisco 8	68	1276
John	San Francisco San Francisco 12	67	363
John	San Mateo Twp 1	65	58
John	Tuolumne Twp 1	71	265
John H	Napa Napa	61	91
John M	Calaveras Twp 7	57	3
John*	San Francisco San Francisco 10	67	209
Joseph	Amador Twp 3	55	406
Josiah	Sonoma Armally	69	499
Julia	Alameda Oakland	55	27
Julian	Tuolumne Twp 3	71	445
Louis	Tuolumne Twp 3	71	445
M	Sacramento Ward 4	63	529
M	San Francisco San Francisco 5	67	537
Manuel	Mendocino Big Rock	60	874
Marg*	San Francisco San Francisco 2	67	739
Margaret	Mariposa Twp 3	60	563
Margaret	San Francisco San Francisco 6	67	418
Maria	San Francisco San Francisco 9	68	1086
Mary	Alameda Oakland	55	26
Mary	Sacramento Ward 1	63	63
Mary	San Francisco San Francisco 4	68	1223
Mary	San Francisco San Francisco 2	67	739
Mary	San Mateo Twp 1	65	64
Mary	Santa Cruz Pajaro	66	525
Mary C	Sacramento Ward 1	63	94
MORAN			
Mary*	San Francisco San Francisco 2	67	739
Michael	Shasta Shasta	66	732
Michael	Yuba Rose Bar	72	808
O	Sacramento Cosummes	63	383
P	Solano Suisan	69	231
Patrick	San Francisco San Francisco 12	67	386
Patrick	San Francisco San Francisco 1	68	922
Patrick*	Placer Michigan	62	838
Philip	Mendocino Big Rvr	60	847
Philomene	San Francisco San Francisco 2	67	661
R	Nevada Grass Valley	61	148
Silram*	Solano Vallejo	69	250
T	Shasta Millvill	66	752
T	Tuolumne Twp 4	71	158
Thomas	Contra Costa Twp 3	57	602
Thomas	Los Angeles Tejon	59	522
Thomas	Sonoma Santa Rosa	69	393
Thos	Nevada Bridgeport	61	499
Thos A	Sacramento Ward 3	63	427
MORANA			
C	Merced Twp 1	60	914
Pedro	Santa Cruz Soguel	66	593
Philas*	Alameda Murray	55	228
MORAND			
Aurora	Yuba Marysville	72	917
Lewis	Mendocino Little L	60	834
Louis	Mendocino Little L	60	834
MORANDA			
Tomas	Monterey San Juan	60	999
MORANDES			
Juan	Contra Costa Twp 3	57	600
MORANDI			
Angelina	San Francisco San Francisco 2	67	700
MORANDO			
Cathrine	San Mateo Twp 2	65	115
L	Merced Twp 2	60	924
Theresa	Sacramento Ward 1	63	16
Ysidro	Contra Costa Twp 1	57	497
MORANE			
H*	El Dorado Placerville	58	870
Lemore	Mariposa Twp 1	60	636
MORANG			
Charlotta*	Calaveras Twp 6	57	179
MORANGO			
Charlata*	Calaveras Twp 6	57	179
Charlotta*	Calaveras Twp 6	57	179
MORANI			
Joseph	San Francisco San Francisco 11	67	129
MORANO			
Aurera**	Yuba Marysville	72	917
Francisco	Mariposa Twp 1	60	653
Ignacia	Mariposa Twp 1	60	654
Ignacio	Mariposa Twp 1	60	654
Jesus	Marin Cortemad	60	780
Joaquin	Tuolumne Columbia	71	337
Joaquin	Tuolumne Shawsfla	71	390
Juan	Los Angeles Los Angeles	59	516
Lenobin*	Calaveras Twp 5	57	182
Lenore	Mariposa Twp 1	60	636
Maraquita	Yuba Marysville	72	949
Martin	Calaveras Twp 5	57	210
Martin	Calaveras Twp 5	57	211
Maynel	Mariposa Twp 1	60	645
Philas*	Alameda Murray	55	228
Rues	Calaveras Twp 10	57	261
Ruis	Calaveras Twp 10	57	261
Senobia	Calaveras Twp 6	57	182
Siliam	Solano Vallejo	69	250
Silram*	Solano Vallejo	69	250
Tomas	San Bernardino San Bernadino	64	639
Tomax	San Bernardino San Salvador	64	639
MORANS			
P	El Dorado Placerville	58	876
MORANT			
Edward	San Francisco San Francisco 2	67	585
J	Nevada Grass Valley	61	165
Jno	Nevada Nevada	61	297
John	San Francisco San Francisco 2	67	566
MORANTA			
Jose	Merced Twp 1	60	909
MORANTES			
Panlecia*	Yuba Marysville	72	932
Paulecia*	Yuba Marysville	72	932
Paulina	Yuba Marysville	72	932
MORAR			
Margaret	Mariposa Twp 3	60	563
MORARCO			
Antonio	Tuolumne Twp 2	71	286
MORARDO			
Theresa	Sacramento Ward 1	63	16
MORARY			
Christian	San Francisco San Francisco 2	67	694

Name	County Locale	M653 RollPage
MORASCHR		
Anton*	El Dorado Georgetown	58 703
MORASCO		
Antonio	Tuolumne Twp 2	71 284
MORAT		
Volentine	San Joaquin Stockton	641027
MORATORIO		
L	San Francisco San Francisco 5	67 511
MORATZ		
J	San Francisco San Francisco 10	313 67
MORAVY		
Christian*	San Francisco San Francisco 2	67 694
MORAY		
Nelson	Mendocino Big Rock	60 873
W	Mariposa Twp 1	60 635
MORAZ		
Christian*	San Francisco San Francisco 2	67 694
MORAZA		
Jose*	San Bernardino S Buenav	64 210
MORBAC		
Nicholas*	San Francisco San Francisco 2	67 700
MORBACKE		
---	San Francisco San Francisco 7	681400
MORBAIGA		
Domingo	Santa Clara San Jose	65 298
MORBECK		
Henry	San Francisco San Francisco 8	681302
MORBID		
Henry	Sonoma Sonoma	69 658
MORCA		
Martin	Yuba Marysville	72 925
MORCAL		
John C	Butte Ophir	56 767
Jose	Solano Vallejo	69 250
MORCALLES		
R*	Shasta Horsetown	66 699
MORCAUX		
Vincent	Plumas Meadow Valley	62 933
MORCE		
Charles*	Santa Cruz Soguel	66 597
Henry	Humbolt Eel Rvr	59 151
MORCHOUSE		
Joseph	Yuba Marysville	72 861
MORCIER		
Leopold	Yuba Fosters	72 835
MORCINIS		
Lofrixes*	Calaveras Twp 5	57 226
MORCINS		
Lofrircs*	Calaveras Twp 5	57 226
MORCLAY		
Jeremiah	Tulara Visalia	71 98
MORCO		
Jose E	Los Angeles Los Angeles	59 363
MORCOM		
Edmund	Trinity Weaverville	701075
MORCOND		
Pierre	Calaveras Twp 5	57 239
MORCOUD		
Pierre*	Calaveras Twp 5	57 239
MORCUO		
Jose	Los Angeles Los Nieto	59 426
MORDAND		
Anna	Tuolumne Twp 1	71 203
MORDANT		
G	San Joaquin Stockton	641093
MORDEM		
Esperodeon*	Calaveras Twp 5	57 250
MORDEN		
Smith	Placer Goods	62 693
MORDERA		
Marie	Tuolumne Twp 1	71 275
MORDERS		
Maria	Tuolumne Twp 2	71 275
MORDOFF		
H	El Dorado Placerville	58 845
MORDRANN		
Augelir*	San Bernardino Santa Barbara	64 203
MORDSLEY		
Edward*	Placer Michigan	62 857
MORDY		
I*	Nevada Red Dog	61 547
J M M	Tuolumne Sonora	71 201
J*	Nevada Red Dog	61 547
James	Monterey Monterey	60 965
MORE		
C E	Yolo Cache Crk	72 621
Caroline	El Dorado Diamond	58 773
Charles	San Bernardino S Buenav	64 214
Chas	Santa Clara San Jose	65 336
Ed*	Siskiyou Klamath	69 96
Edwin	Marin Tomales	60 775
Enna*	Yolo Putah	72 545
Enns	Yolo Putah	72 545
Hoop	Tuolumne Columbia	71 292
J	El Dorado Diamond	58 797

Name	County Locale	M653 RollPage
MORE		
John	Sacramento Natonia	63 280
Joseph F	Fresno Twp 2	59 48
Mary J*	San Francisco San Francisco 10	237 67
T W	San Mateo Twp 2	65 132
Thomas*	Tulara Visalia	71 98
W H	San Francisco San Francisco 5	67 487
William H	San Francisco San Francisco 9	681015
Wm	Sonoma Santa Rosa	69 401
MOREA		
Galerd	El Dorado Mud Springs	58 966
H	El Dorado Placerville	58 870
H	El Dorado Placerville	58 875
Hosa	El Dorado Coloma	581119
Joseph	El Dorado Placerville	58 918
M	Mariposa Twp 1	60 639
Manuel	Yuba Marysville	72 925
Quartins	Los Angeles San Jose	59 292
Ramon	Alameda Oakland	55 56
MOREAH		
Rafael	Los Angeles Elmonte	59 259
MOREAL		
Jose	Solano Vallejo	69 250
MOREALLES		
R*	Shasta Horsetown	66 699
MOREAN		
A	San Francisco San Francisco 6	67 452
MOREAR		
Hosa	Mariposa Twp 1	60 628
Manwell	Mariposa Twp 1	60 628
Pedro*	Mariposa Twp 1	60 660
MOREARTY		
J	El Dorado Diamond	58 787
MOREAU		
A	San Francisco San Francisco 6	67 452
MOREBACK		
A H	Tehama Red Bluff	70 923
MOREDA		
Mary	San Francisco San Francisco 2	67 728
MOREGA		
Alenent	Santa Cruz Santa Cruz	66 621
MOREHANT		
Joseph*	Sierra La Porte	66 769
MOREHAWT		
Joseph*	Sierra La Porte	66 769
MOREHEAD		
James	Siskiyou Yreka	69 192
Jas	San Bernardino S Timate	64 687
Jno	Trinity Lewiston	70 953
P	Shasta Shasta	66 656
Saml	San Francisco San Francisco 1	68 930
Wm	Trinity Minersville	70 968
MOREHOME		
Thos	Trinity Weaverville	701080
MOREHOUS		
Legrand	San Francisco San Francisco 7	681342
MOREHOUSE		
C D	Sonoma Washington	69 672
E W	Nevada Nevada	61 240
G W	San Francisco San Francisco 8	681255
Henry	Calaveras Twp 7	57 8
J J*	Placer Todds Va	62 787
Jno	Nevada Nevada	61 287
Jno	San Francisco San Francisco 9	681052
John	Stanislaus Empire	70 735
John B	San Joaquin Stockton	641059
Le Roy*	Alameda Brooklyn	55 119
N B	Sonoma Washington	69 672
Wm P	Tuolumne Sonora	71 219
MOREID		
Louis	Contra Costa Twp 2	57 554
MOREIN		
Romuind*	Calaveras Twp 10	57 296
MOREL		
Owra	El Dorado Coloma	581119
Theophel	Plumas Meadow Valley	62 911
MORELAN		
Jane	Yolo Cache	72 635
W	Yolo Cache Crk	72 623
MORELAND		
A H	Yolo Cache Crk	72 607
A H	Yolo Cache	72 608
Anna	Tuolumne Twp 1	71 203
F M	Santa Clara Santa Clara	65 490
James B	Yuba New York	72 726
Louisa	Santa Clara Gilroy	65 251
P	San Joaquin Stockton	641093
Sidney	Santa Clara Gilroy	65 241
T H	Nevada Nevada	61 323
T H	Tuolumne Big Oak	71 154
Thos	Santa Clara Gilroy	65 251
William	Calaveras Twp 8	57 54
William	Plumas Quincy	62 976
Wm	Nevada Nevada	61 246
Zacariah	Tulara Yule Rvr	71 24

Name	County Locale	M653 RollPage
MORELEM		
Esperodeon*	Calaveras Twp 5	57 250
MORELES		
Calishe	San Luis Obispo San Luis Obispo	65 37
Francisco	Fresno Twp 1	59 76
Juan	San Joaquin Stockton	641074
Rumaldo	Los Angeles Santa Ana	59 457
MORELL		
Bryan	Yuba Marysville	72 889
David	Stanislaus Emory	70 739
Horace	Stanislaus Branch	70 703
John	El Dorado Coloma	581115
N S	Tuolumne Twp 2	71 322
MORELLER		
George	Placer Todds Va	62 786
MORELLO		
Augustine	San Diego San Diego	64 763
Eugenio	San Diego San Diego	64 772
Jose	San Diego Agua Caliente	64 861
MOREMAN		
Samuel*	Alameda Murray	55 218
MORENA		
???	Calaveras Twp 5	57 221
Anastatia	Alameda Brooklyn	55 199
Antonio	San Diego Colorado	64 812
B	Sacramento Ward 4	63 536
Bicenta	Calaveras Twp 5	57 221
Bicento	Calaveras Twp 5	57 221
Jesus	San Diego S Luis R	64 779
Reyes	San Diego S Luis R	64 779
Saladonia	Los Angeles Los Angeles	59 503
MORENAS		
Dolores*	Calaveras Twp 6	57 150
MORENEA		
Joseana	San Joaquin Stockton	641078
MORENEBRE		
P	Tuolumne Big Oak	71 151
MORENHANT		
Antonio	Los Angeles Los Angeles	59 332
Jacob A	Los Angeles Los Angeles	59 332
MORENI		
John	Calaveras Twp 5	57 198
MORENO		
A	El Dorado Placerville	58 898
A*	El Dorado Placerville	58 917
Anistacio	Los Angeles Los Angeles	59 511
Antonio	Santa Clara Gilroy	65 252
Bautista	Los Angeles Los Angeles	59 294
Benito	Los Angeles Los Angeles	59 396
Carisano*	Calaveras Twp 6	57 183
Carmes	Santa Clara San Jose	65 324
Carmino*	Calaveras Twp 6	57 183
Carssieno*	Calaveras Twp 6	57 183
Demecio	Los Angeles Los Angeles	59 395
Dolores	Santa Clara San Jose	65 335
Ebano	Los Angeles Tejon	59 539
Felipe	Los Angeles Santa Ana	59 456
Filipe	Los Angeles Santa Ana	59 456
Frances	Calaveras Twp 7	57 8
Francisco	Marin Cortemad	60 780
Gore	Alameda Brooklyn	55 113
Grinidad	Los Angeles Los Nieto	59 430
Ingracia	San Francisco San Francisco 2	67 605
Injracia	San Francisco San Francisco 2	67 605
Jesus	San Diego Agua Caliente	64 862
Jesus	Santa Clara San Jose	65 368
John	Calaveras Twp 5	57 198
John	Solano Benecia	69 289
Jose	San Bernardino Santa Barbara	64 194
Jose	San Francisco San Francisco 7	681380
Jose	Santa Clara Almaden	65 271
Jose Antonio	San Diego Temecula	64 801
Jose M	San Diego San Diego	64 757
Jose R	Los Angeles San Juan	59 463
Josefa	Merced Monterey	60 933
Josefa	Monterey Monterey	60 933
Juan	Los Angeles Los Angeles	59 362
Juan	Tuolumne Chinese	71 497
Juan J	Los Angeles Los Angeles	59 295
Julian	Los Angeles Los Angeles	59 370
Lucos	Mariposa Twp 1	60 656
Maguel	Mariposa Twp 1	60 645
Maracia	San Francisco San Francisco 2	67 605
Maria	Los Angeles Los Angeles	59 516
Marie	Sacramento Ward 3	63 439
Maynel	Mariposa Twp 1	60 645
Michael	San Mateo Twp 3	65 84
Pio	San Bernardino Santa Barbara	64 154
Refugio	Plumas Quincy	62 995
Rosano	San Bernardino Santa Barbara	64 189
Rufiag	Los Angeles Los Nieto	59 426
Rufino	Los Angeles Los Nieto	59 426
S	El Dorado Placerville	58 848
Tomas	Santa Clara Gilroy	65 228
Trindad	Los Angeles Los Nieto	59 430
MORENSEAN		
P	Tuolumne Twp 1	71 482

California 1860 Census Index

Name	County Locale	M653 Roll	Page
MORENT			
Sarah*	Yuba Fosters	72	823
MORENY			
Juan	Los Angeles Los Angeles	59	510
MOREO			
Jese	San Joaquin Stockton	64	1080
Jose E*	Los Angeles Los Angeles	59	363
MOREORON			
John	Mariposa Twp 1	60	634
MOREOYA			
Manito*	Calaveras Twp 5	57	207
Munito*	Calaveras Twp 5	57	207
MOREOYER			
Manito*	Calaveras Twp 5	57	207
Munito*	Calaveras Twp 5	57	207
MOREROR			
John*	Tuolumne Columbia	71	300
MORERY			
James A	San Mateo Twp 3	65	92
MORES			
James	Mendocino Little L	60	837
Maria F	Los Angeles Los Angeles	59	323
MORESTANT			
Adolph	Sonoma Petaluma	69	571
MORETA			
Hosea*	Alameda Murray	55	227
MORETAGUE			
Joel S	Yuba Marysville	72	969
MORETO			
Adela	Sacramento Ward 1	63	16
Geo E*	Sacramento Ward 1	63	14
Juan	Solano Vallejo	69	250
Lucy	Sacramento Ward 1	63	17
MORETON			
Seth	Santa Clara Fremont	65	421
MORETRO			
Geo E	Sacramento Ward 1	63	14
MORETT			
Wm	Trinity Readings	70	996
MORETTA			
G	San Francisco San Francisco 2	67	702
MORETTE			
G P*	Shasta Shasta	66	675
Gule*	Marin S Antoni	60	710
MORETTI			
Gale	Marin S Antoni	60	710
MOREUGA			
Manito	Calaveras Twp 5	57	207
Maruto	Calaveras Twp 5	57	207
MOREUO			
John*	Solano Benecia	69	289
Lorenzo	Los Angeles Los Angeles	59	295
MOREVER			
C*	Nevada Eureka	61	352
MOREY			
E J	Sacramento Cosumnes	63	389
E R	El Dorado Mountain	58	1186
Frederick	Yuba Parks Ba	72	776
Lemon B	San Francisco San Francisco 10	67	253
M A	San Francisco San Francisco 12	67	394
R D	Mendocino Twp 1	60	892
Reiben	Monterey Monterey	60	956
Reuben	Monterey Monterey	60	956
Simon B	San Francisco San Francisco 10	67	253
MORFEN			
J	Butte Chico	56	549
MORFFOT			
S P	El Dorado Kelsey	58	1135
MORG			
Ah	Tuolumne Twp 4	71	150
MORGAH			
James	Santa Cruz Santa Cruz	66	634
MORGAIN			
B H	Sierra Poker Flats	66	837
MORGAN			
---	San Francisco San Francisco 3	67	54
---	Tulara Keyesville	71	56
---*	San Francisco San Francisco 3	67	54
A	Amador Twp 3	55	385
A	Placer Michigan	62	838
A	San Francisco San Francisco 5	67	515
A S	Calaveras Twp 8	57	70
Abram	Nevada Bridgeport	61	440
Abram H	Nevada Bridgeport	61	440
Alex	El Dorado Coloma	58	1110
Alex	Stanislaus Empire	70	731
Andrew	Placer Michigan	62	847
Andrew	Sacramento American	63	161
Andrew	San Mateo Twp 3	65	104
Andrew	Santa Cruz Pescadero	66	646
Andrew	Tuolumne Twp 3	71	441
Ann	Alameda Brooklyn	55	93
Anne	Sacramento Granite	63	262
Annie	Sacramento Granite	63	262
B F	Humbolt Eureka	59	174
B H*	Sierra Poker Flats	66	837
B P	Butte Eureka	56	648
Bartlett	Placer Michigan	62	853
Benj	Sacramento Ward 4	63	523
Benj	San Francisco San Francisco 5	67	517
Benjamin	Sierra Monte Crk	66	1035
Brayett*	Sonoma Petaluma	69	585
Breyett*	Sonoma Petaluma	69	585
Brogett*	Sonoma Petaluma	69	585
C	Nevada Grass Valley	61	176
C	Nevada Grass Valley	61	177
C	Nevada Grass Valley	61	190
C	Nevada Grass Valley	61	194
C	Siskiyou Scott Ri	69	68
C A	Nevada Nevada	61	288
C H	Yolo Cottonwood	72	658
C Stuart	El Dorado Greenwood	58	723
Catherine	Solano Vacaville	69	343
Charles	San Francisco San Francisco 7	68	1402
Charles	Tuolumne Twp 2	71	304
Charles	Tuolumne Shawsfla	71	378
Charles D	Contra Costa Twp 1	57	486
Charles E	San Joaquin Elkhorn	64	956
Chas	Nevada Rough &	61	415
Chas	Sonoma Mendocino	69	451
Clara M	San Francisco San Francisco 6	67	439
D H	El Dorado Coloma	58	1080
D H	Siskiyou Yreka	69	177
D P	Butte Cascade	56	697
D W C	Sierra Whiskey	66	846
Dan	Siskiyou Klamath	69	90
Daniel	Sonoma Armally	69	503
Danl	Sacramento Ward 1	63	112
Danl P	San Francisco San Francisco 2	67	731
Danl R	San Francisco San Francisco 2	67	731
Dannie	Santa Cruz Pescadero	66	647
David	Butte Bidwell	56	725
David	Sierra Port Win	66	796
David	Sierra Port Win	66	797
Davis	Butte Ophir	56	768
Dennis	Santa Clara San Jose	65	335
Doris E	Calaveras Twp 5	57	208
E	Siskiyou Cottonwoood	69	107
E	Siskiyou Cottonwoood	69	108
E	Siskiyou Klamath	69	85
E D	Sierra Downieville	66	1023
E P	Sierra Pine Grove	66	827
E P	Sierra Poker Flats	66	837
Eben	Nevada Bridgeport	61	469
Ebenezer	Sierra Port Win	66	796
Edward	Alameda Brooklyn	55	121
Edward	El Dorado Greenwood	58	723
Elisabeth T	Yolo Slate Ra	72	699
Elizabeth S*	San Francisco 2	67	737
	San Francisco		
Eneas	Sierra Twp 7	66	892
Eynes	Marin Tomales	60	714
F	Amador Twp 1	55	478
F	Shasta Horsetown	66	699
F A	Butte Ophir	56	789
Francis	El Dorado Coloma	58	1108
Fredk	Amador Twp 5	55	361
G	Nevada Grass Valley	61	183
G A	Amador Township	55	467
G G	Sacramento Ward 4	63	565
G J	Yolo Putah	72	615
Geo	Butte Chico	56	539
Geo	San Francisco San Francisco 10	67	310
Geo	Santa Clara Fremont	65	442
Geo D	San Francisco San Francisco 9	68	1028
George	Tehama Lassen	70	863
George	Tuolumne Twp 2	71	334
George J	Yuba Long Bar	72	748
H	Butte Kimshaw	56	603
H H	Nevada Grass Valley	61	144
H W	Butte Kimshaw	56	592
Harold	El Dorado Big Bar	58	736
Henry	Calaveras Twp 9	57	371
Henry	Napa Clear Lake	61	119
Henry	Nevada Bloomfield	61	513
Henry	San Francisco San Francisco 9	68	1005
Henry	Shasta Horsetown	66	699
Henry	Sierra Excelsior	66	1033
Henry	Tulara Visalia	71	98
Henry O	Sacramento Sutter	63	297
Hy	San Francisco San Francisco 2	67	671
I B*	Nevada Bridgeport	61	482
Ira	Tulara Twp 3	71	58
Isaac	Marin Bolinas	60	749
Isaac	Placer Stewart	62	607
Isaac	Sacramento Franklin	63	327
J	El Dorado Placerville	58	866
J	Nevada Grass Valley	61	154
J	Nevada Eureka	61	378
J	San Francisco San Francisco 5	67	525
J	Siskiyou Scott Ri	69	69
J A	Amador Twp 1	55	467
J A	Nevada Grass Valley	61	221
J A	San Francisco San Francisco 9	68	973
J B	Nevada Bridgeport	61	482
J B	Siskiyou Cottonwoood	69	107
J B*	Nevada Bridgeport	61	482
J C	Nevada Grass Valley	61	195
J Day	Yolo Cottonwood	72	556
J G	Humbolt Mattole	59	124
J H	Butte Chico	56	552
J H	Butte Chico	56	557
J H	San Francisco San Francisco 9	68	973
J H	Santa Clara Santa Clara	65	466
J L	Nevada Grass Valley	61	180
J W	Amador Twp 5	55	334
Jacob	Nevada Little Y	61	534
Jacob	Sierra Monte Crk	66	1036
Jacob S	Contra Costa Twp 2	57	560
James	Calaveras Twp 5	57	143
James	Contra Costa Twp 1	57	504
James	Contra Costa Twp 3	57	605
James	El Dorado Coloma	58	1110
James	Los Angeles Los Angeles	59	315
James	Nevada Washington	61	334
James	Nevada Little Y	61	531
James	Placer Michigan	62	831
James	San Francisco San Francisco 9	68	1073
James	San Francisco San Francisco 10	67	297
James	San Joaquin O'Neal	64	1006
James	Santa Cruz Pajaro	66	544
James	Santa Cruz Pajaro	66	572
James	Santa Cruz Santa Cruz	66	615
James	Santa Cruz Santa Cruz	66	634
James	Tuolumne Shawsfla	71	378
James W	Santa Cruz Watsonville	66	538
Jas	San Francisco San Francisco 2	67	572
Jas B	Fresno Millerto	59	1
Jas*	San Francisco San Francisco 9	68	1074
Javis R*	Sierra Twp 5	66	922
Jeremiah	Contra Costa Twp 3	57	602
Jesse	Tulara Twp 3	71	46
Jessee	Contra Costa Twp 3	57	602
Jno	Tehama Moons	70	852
Jno A	San Francisco San Francisco 10	67	306
John	Butte Ophir	56	748
John	Del Norte Happy Ca	58	663
John	Nevada Bridgeport	61	441
John	Nevada Little Y	61	533
John	Placer Virginia	62	677
John	Placer Michigan	62	838
John	Sacramento Ward 1	63	105
John	San Francisco San Francisco 9	68	1053
John	San Francisco San Francisco 2	67	706
John	San Joaquin Oneal	64	913
John	Santa Cruz Pajaro	66	525
John	Shasta Shasta	66	662
John	Shasta Shasta	66	677
John	Sierra Twp 7	66	872
John	Sierra Cox'S Bar	66	952
John	Tehama Lassen	70	869
John	Tehama Red Bluff	70	906
John	Tuolumne Columbia	71	290
John F	San Bernardino San Bernadino	64	666
John F	Sierra Twp 5	66	938
John Sen	San Joaquin Oneal	64	913
John W	Santa Cruz Soguel	66	598
John*	San Francisco San Francisco 5	67	545
Jolm*	San Francisco San Francisco 5	67	545
Jon	Tuolumne Twp 2	71	290
Jos	Butte Ophir	56	760
Jos	San Francisco San Francisco 9	68	1074
Jos	San Francisco San Francisco 2	67	572
Joseph	Contra Costa Twp 1	57	528
Joseph	Fresno Twp 3	59	32
Joseph	Solano Vallejo	69	243
Joseph	Tehama Tehama	70	945
Joshua	Santa Clara Santa Clara	65	513
L	Sierra Scales D	66	804
L A	Nevada Grass Valley	61	177
L B	Nevada Grass Valley	61	223
L E	Yolo No E Twp	72	678
L E	Yuba North Ea	72	678
L M	Nevada Nevada	61	283
Levi	San Francisco San Francisco 12	67	393
Lewis	Sacramento Franklin	63	312
Lewis R	Sierra Twp 5	66	922
Linus	Amador Twp 1	55	488
Louis E	Calaveras Twp 5	57	208

Name	County Locale	M653 Roll	Page
MORGAN			
Louis E	Contra Costa Twp 1	57	523
Louis R*	Sierra Twp 5	66	922
M	Amador Twp 2	55	307
M	El Dorado Georgetown	58	675
M L	San Francisco San Francisco 10	214	67
M W	Yolo Cache Crk	72	642
Margaret	San Francisco San Francisco 12	383	67
Margaret	Santa Clara Santa Clara	65	473
Margaret A	San Francisco	8	681280
Mary	Sacramento Ward 1	63	77
Mary B	San Francisco San Francisco 2	67	660
Mary E	Sacramento Sutter	63	298
Morgan	Placer Stewart	62	607
N	Butte Wyandotte	56	664
N L	Siskiyou Cottonwoood	69	98
Nelson	El Dorado Georgetown	58	687
O A	Nevada Nevada	61	288
O E	Los Angeles Los Angeles	59	501
O H	San Francisco San Francisco 10	284	67
Oliver	Calaveras Twp 8	57	80
Ottis	Alameda Brooklyn	55	187
P	Nevada Grass Valley	61	224
Patrick	Contra Costa Twp 1	57	532
Peter	Butte Wyandotte	56	657
Peter	San Francisco San Francisco 9	681074	
Phillip*	San Francisco San Francisco 9	68	946
R	Nevada Grass Valley	61	178
R A	Nevada Grass Valley	61	144
R A	Nevada Grass Valley	61	193
Richd	San Francisco San Francisco 10	216	67
Robert	Calaveras Twp 8	57	63
Ruth	San Francisco San Francisco 10	198	67
S	Nevada Grass Valley	61	146
S	Nevada Grass Valley	61	148
S	Sacramento Cosumnes	63	394
S	Sierra Scales D	66	804
S	Sierra Pine Grove	66	827
Saml	Sonoma Petaluma	69	546
Samuel	Solano Benecia	69	318
Shedrick*	Placer Michigan	62	830
Susan	Calaveras Twp 8	57	55
Susan	San Francisco San Francisco 6	67	440
T	Yolo Slate Ra	72	694
T	Yuba Slate Ro	72	694
T G	Butte Kimshaw	56	580
Theron	Plumas Quincy	62	938
Thomas	Calaveras Twp 6	57	133
Thomas	Placer Michigan	62	828
Thomas	Solano Vallejo	69	279
Thomas	Tuolumne Twp 5	71	505
Thomas B	San Francisco San Francisco 4	681280	
Thos	Alameda Brooklyn	55	77
Thos	Butte Oregon	56	627
Thos	Placer Stewart	62	607
Thos W	Sacramento Ward 1	63	45
Tlavere	Sierra Port Win	66	796
Tylor	Tuolumne Columbia	71	313
W	Butte Wyandotte	56	664
W D	Del Norte Happy Ca	58	663
W H	Sierra Twp 7	66	897
W H	Siskiyou Callahan	69	19
W J	Nevada Grass Valley	61	192
W J	Yolo Putah	72	588
W W	Butte Oro	56	676
Washington	Sierra Cold Can	66	836
Wesley*	Contra Costa Twp 3	57	588
William	Contra Costa Twp 3	57	589
William	El Dorado Coloma	581103	
William	El Dorado Kelsey	581139	
William	El Dorado Kelsey	581103	
William	Placer Forest H	62	765
William	Placer Michigan	62	819
William	San Francisco San Francisco 8	681280	
William	Sierra Pine Grove	66	835
William	Siskiyou Scott Va	69	31
William	Tulara Visalia	71	102
William	Tulara Twp 1	71	98
William B	Sierra St Louis	66	814
Wisley*	Contra Costa Twp 3	57	588
Wm	Butte Oregon	56	621
Wm	Butte Oro	56	678
Wm	Mariposa Twp 3	60	563
Wm	Nevada Nevada	61	274
Wm	San Francisco San Francisco 10	175	67
Wm	San Francisco San Francisco 12	389	67
Wm	San Francisco San Francisco 2	67	636
Wm	San Francisco San Francisco 2	67	671
MORGAN			
Wm	Solano Benecia	69	309
MORGANB			
Ruth	San Francisco San Francisco 10	198	67
MORGANE			
Joseph*	Calaveras Twp 5	57	205
MORGANS			
Margaret	Santa Clara San Jose	65	374
Morgan	Amador Twp 4	55	235
Phillip*	San Francisco San Francisco 9	68	946
MORGANSTAND			
S	San Francisco San Francisco 3	67	28
MORGANSTEIN			
A	San Francisco San Francisco 3	67	57
MORGANT			
C	Nevada Grass Valley	61	217
O	Nevada Grass Valley	61	217
MORGBROCKER			
J*	Yolo Cottonwoood	72	652
MORGE			
W*	Siskiyou Scott Ri	69	76
MORGEARTY			
J	San Francisco San Francisco 5	67	534
MORGIN			
David	Mariposa Twp 1	60	629
MORGO			
Joseph*	Mariposa Coulterville	60	697
MORGON			
David	Mariposa Twp 1	60	629
Elisabeth T	Yuba Slate Ro	72	699
MORGROW			
George*	Placer Michigan	62	824
MORGUIS			
Victorio	Contra Costa Twp 1	57	518
MORGUN			
William	Los Angeles Azuza	59	279
MORHAM			
James*	Klamath S Fork	59	198
MORHER			
H	San Francisco San Francisco 9	681079	
MORHMAN			
Chas	Tuolumne Big Oak	71	137
Olias	Tuolumne Twp 4	71	137
MORHO			
Uneh	Fresno Twp 1	59	76
MORHY			
Anna	San Francisco San Francisco 10	178	67
MORI			
---	Calaveras Twp 6	57	148
Jose	Alameda Brooklyn	55	137
Louis	Plumas Meadow Valley	62	932
Peter	Plumas Meadow Valley	62	932
MORIA			
Cosa	Mariposa Twp 1	60	645
Cosar	Mariposa Twp 1	60	645
MORIAH			
Casuse	Mariposa Twp 1	60	672
MORIAN			
Louisanae	Fresno Twp 1	59	83
MORIARTY			
J	San Francisco San Francisco 5	67	534
MORIAS			
D	Siskiyou Scott Ri	69	81
MORIATI			
Emillio*	Stanislaus Branch	70	699
MORICA			
J	El Dorado Placerville	58	894
MORICO			
---	Fresno Twp 1	59	85
MORIDOSE			
Manuel	Marin Cortemad	60	755
MORIE			
John*	Yuba Marysville	72	904
MORIGE			
Juan	Los Angeles Los Angeles	59	330
MORIGNEU			
Foster	San Francisco San Francisco 7	681378	
MORILL			
George	Yuba Marysville	72	904
John	El Dorado Mud Springs	58	968
N S	Tuolumne Columbia	71	322
MORILLO			
Brigido	Los Angeles Santa Ana	59	458
Jose A	Los Angeles Santa Ana	59	458
Lojia	Los Angeles Los Angeles	59	363
Manuel	Los Angeles San Juan	59	476
MORIM			
Eliza*	Amador Twp 6	55	429
MORIN			
Alex	Stanislaus Branch	70	700
C*	Tehama Red Bluff	70	912
Counter	Santa Cruz Pescadero	66	647
Frank*	Alameda Brooklyn	55	178
Harrison*	San Francisco San Francisco 1	68	909
MORIN			
James	Santa Cruz Watsonville	66	539
M	El Dorado Placerville	58	825
Manl	Mariposa Twp 1	60	644
MORINA			
Saladonia	Los Angeles Los Angeles	59	503
T G	Yolo Fremont	72	605
MORINE			
C D	Yolo Cache Crk	72	621
Eliza*	Amador Twp 6	55	429
Elizer	Amador Twp 6	55	429
M*	El Dorado Newtown	58	778
MORINEBRE			
P	Tuolumne Twp 4	71	151
MORINES			
Francisco	Calaveras Twp 10	57	287
MORINGTON			
Charles	Santa Cruz Soguel	66	590
MORINO			
Anistacio	Los Angeles Los Angeles	59	511
Baloino*	Santa Cruz Santa Cruz	66	617
Balomo	Santa Cruz Santa Cruz	66	617
Balonio	Santa Cruz Santa Cruz	66	617
Balvino*	Santa Cruz Santa Cruz	66	617
Carmina*	Calaveras Twp 5	57	183
Dolores	Tuolumne Twp 2	71	314
Goudulupo	Calaveras Twp 6	57	132
Juan	Los Angeles Los Angeles	59	516
M	El Dorado Coloma	581113	
Maria*	Los Angeles Los Angeles	59	516
Santiago	San Luis Obispo	65	14
MORINOS			
Normon	Marin Bolinas	60	745
MORINRS			
Heancisa	Calaveras Twp 10	57	287
MORIO			
---	Tulara Keyesville	71	68
---	Tulara Keyesville	71	71
Hosa	Nevada Bloomfield	61	512
John	Calaveras Twp 10	57	261
Jose*	Mariposa Twp 1	60	645
MORION			
H R	Nevada Eureka	61	353
Peter	Calaveras Twp 5	57	189
MORIPE			
C*	San Francisco San Francisco 10	359	67
MORIS			
A	San Francisco San Francisco 4	681156	
James	Mendocino Little L	60	837
L	Nevada Grass Valley	61	150
Robert	Monterey Pajaro	601018	
William G	Tulara Twp 1	71	95
MORISER			
Jerry*	Nevada Bridgeport	61	500
S M*	Sacramento Ward 4	63	572
MORISIN			
Saml	Napa Clear Lake	61	134
MORISON			
B	Mariposa Twp 1	60	672
Enmonte	Calaveras Twp 6	57	156
Howard	San Francisco San Francisco 3	67	86
J J	Nevada Bridgeport	61	505
J L	Tuolumne Twp 4	71	174
James	Napa Yount	61	37
Joseph*	Amador Twp 2	55	328
R	Nevada Bridgeport	61	489
Saml	Napa Clear Lake	61	134
Z	Sutter Bear Rvr	70	824
MORISSY			
John	Calaveras Twp 8	57	64
MORITENARIO			
M	Tuolumne Twp 1	71	270
MORITO			
Hiram	Placer Yankee J	62	760
MORITON			
Hugh*	Stanislaus Branch	70	705
MORITY			
J	Mariposa Twp 1	60	643
MORITZ			
Gab	Sacramento Ward 4	63	511
J	Mariposa Twp 1	60	643
John C	San Francisco San Francisco 2	67	625
MORIUO			
Baloino*	Santa Cruz Santa Cruz	66	617
Balvino*	Santa Cruz Santa Cruz	66	617
MORJAN			
Elizabeth*	San Francisco San Francisco 2	67	737
MORJES			
R B*	Nevada Eureka	61	392
MORK			
---	El Dorado Georgetown	58	756
MORKEN			
H F	San Francisco San Francisco 5	67	514

Name	County Locale	M653 RollPage
MORKEN		
Martin	San Francisco San Francisco 2	67 625
MORKEO		
W	Placer Ophirville	62 657
MORLA		
Joseph	Calaveras Twp 5	57 201
MORLAND		
John	Placer Auburn	62 589
S	El Dorado Diamond	58 794
MORLEIR		
A	San Francisco San Francisco 4	681156
MORLENER		
William	Siskiyou Klamath	69 86
MORLENIE		
Natali	Calaveras Twp 5	57 135
MORLEY		
A	Merced Twp 1	60 896
A P	Sierra Twp 7	66 902
Charles*	Yuba Marysville	72 910
George	Sierra La Porte	66 771
George W	Sierra La Porte	66 772
J D	Stanislaus Branch	70 707
Paul	Del Norte Crescent	58 642
William	San Francisco San Francisco 4	681156
MORLIN		
A	San Francisco San Francisco 4	681156
MORLINA		
G	San Francisco San Francisco 1	68 880
MORLIR		
Frank*	Alameda Brooklyn	55 178
MORLOCK		
Chris	Sacramento Ward 3	63 435
Preston*	Sacramento Ward 3	63 452
MORLOTH		
Antonea*	Mariposa Twp 1	60 631
MORLREY		
John	El Dorado Big Bar	58 741
MORLS		
William*	Calaveras Twp 6	57 141
MORLY		
Chas M	Trinity Trinity	70 974
MORMAN		
Anslon*	Placer Michigan	62 840
Henry*	San Francisco San Francisco 4	681155
MORMAND		
Eugene	Calaveras Twp 6	57 151
MORMEN		
Dick	Mariposa Coulterville	60 685
MORMODAS		
Jesus	Calaveras Twp 4	57 331
MORMON		
Dick*	Mariposa Coulterville	60 685
F	San Francisco San Francisco 2	67 791
Richard	Mariposa Twp 1	60 638
Thomas	Tulara Twp 2	71 30
MORMONE		
Thomas	Tulara Visalia	71 30
MORMTAIN		
James	Shasta French G	66 717
Jno*	Butte Kimshaw	56 605
MORN		
---	Placer Virginia	62 680
---	Shasta Horsetown	66 710
G*	Nevada Grass Valley	61 178
Jane*	Sacramento Ward 1	63 86
Liz*	Sacramento Granite	63 256
MORNAY		
Carloto	Yuba Marysville	72 918
MORNCE		
Samuel C*	Tuolumne Big Oak	71 134
MORNEG		
J	San Francisco San Francisco 2	67 775
MORNER		
T	San Francisco San Francisco 5	67 477
MORNEY		
John	Tuolumne Twp 3	71 443
M H	Nevada Nevada	61 291
R J	Merced Twp 1	60 911
Thos	Butte Mountain	56 737
MORNING		
B	El Dorado Kelsey	581136
L M	Yolo Cache	72 623
MORNINGSTAR		
Chas	Butte Cascade	56 693
G	Tuolumne Twp 2	71 348
Jacob	El Dorado Mud Springs	58 956
MORNON		
Mary	Santa Clara San Jose	65 308
MORNORNG		
F	San Francisco San Francisco 9	681080
MORNS		
Jerome	Alameda Brooklyn	55 183
John	Alameda Washington	55 170
MORNSJA		
Abraham	Placer Sacramento	62 643
MORNSON		
Joseph*	Amador Twp 2	55 328

Name	County Locale	M653 RollPage
MORNSON		
Wm	Alameda Brooklyn	55 200
MORNWOOD		
C	Yolo Cache	72 627
MORNY		
Wm	Sierra Downieville	661022
MORO		
---	Amador Twp 5	55 348
---	Yuba Long Bar	72 749
Ed	Siskiyou Klamath	69 96
Jose Maria	San Diego Agua Caliente	64 821
MOROE		
J H*	San Francisco San Francisco 4	681167
MOROFO		
Jerome	Calaveras Twp 5	57 221
MOROGON		
S*	Mariposa Twp 3	60 606
MOROLRA		
Felix*	San Mateo Twp 1	65 50
MORON		
Jacob*	Tuolumne Twp 3	71 425
MORONEY		
Ella	Yuba Marysville	72 965
Frank	Yuba Marysville	72 978
Margaret	Yuba Marysville	72 965
Mark	Yuba Marysville	72 978
Paul	Yuba Marysville	72 964
MORONI		
Daivd	San Joaquin Oneal	64 940
MORONIL		
Jose	Santa Clara Gilroy	65 245
MORONO		
Maynel*	Mariposa Twp 1	60 645
MORONY		
John	Alameda Oakland	55 66
Paul	Yuba Marysville	72 964
MOROON		
H	Los Angeles Tejon	59 524
MOROSS		
Jerome*	Calaveras Twp 5	57 221
MOROSUNG		
---	Sacramento Ward 1	63 71
MOROW		
G M	Sierra Twp 5	66 940
Jacob	Tuolumne Jamestown	71 425
MORPHEY		
John	Contra Costa Twp 1	57 492
MORPHIN		
James	Santa Cruz Santa Cruz	66 624
James	Santa Cruz Santa Cruz	66 626
MORPHY		
James	Calaveras Twp 5	57 215
John	Calaveras Twp 8	57 75
John	San Francisco San Francisco 3	67 44
Patrick	Calaveras Twp 5	57 215
Paul*	Marin S Antoni	60 711
Puid	Marin S Antoni	60 711
W F	El Dorado Placerville	58 909
Wm*	San Francisco San Francisco 1	68 917
MORPHYN		
Jose	Santa Cruz Pajaro	66 547
MORPLEY		
James	Calaveras Twp 5	57 215
MORR		
---	Calaveras Twp 9	57 375
G*	Nevada Grass Valley	61 178
J M B*	Nevada Bridgeport	61 473
Jerimiah	Nevada Little Y	61 534
Mary I	San Francisco San Francisco 10	237 67
MORRA		
H	El Dorado Newtown	58 780
Jose Del	San Luis Obispo	65 36
	San Luis Obispo	
MORRAGE		
Eli*	Plumas Quincy	62 994
MORRALES		
Antonio	Santa Cruz Pajaro	66 576
Ascension	Santa Cruz Santa Cruz	66 639
Deonicio*	Santa Cruz Pajaro	66 547
Dionicia	Santa Cruz Pajaro	66 547
Francisco	Santa Cruz Pescadero	66 644
Jacinto	Santa Cruz Santa Cruz	66 640
Jose	Santa Cruz Pajaro	66 572
Manuel	Santa Cruz Pajaro	66 542
MORRALLES		
Juan	Santa Cruz Pajaro	66 555
MORRAN		
Bridget	Solano Vallejo	69 252
John	San Francisco San Francisco 2	67 799
Mary	Tuolumne Sonora	71 237
Opeter*	Calaveras Twp 5	57 189
MORRANNY		
John	Del Norte Crescent	58 634
John*	Del Norte Crescent	58 633
MORRATY		
J	San Francisco San Francisco 10	313

Name	County Locale	M653 RollPage
MORRCEY		
Timothy	Sierra Twp 5	66 920
MORRCY		
Timothy*	Sierra Twp 5	66 920
MORRE		
C F	Shasta Horsetown	66 709
Catharine	San Francisco San Francisco 11	91 67
Cela	Napa Clear Lake	61 134
Chas	Calaveras Twp 10	57 276
E R*	Yuba Rose Bar	72 796
F H*	Sierra Twp 7	66 908
H	San Francisco San Francisco 9	681061
Horace H	San Francisco San Francisco 11	98 67
James	Nevada Bridgeport	61 478
Jno F	Alameda Oakland	55 16
Jno M	Alameda Brooklyn	55 188
John K	San Francisco San Francisco 9	681102
John W	Alameda Brooklyn	55 204
John*	Yuba New York	72 721
Joseh	Shasta Millvill	66 738
Joseph	Shasta Millvill	66 738
Justin	Mendocino Big Rvr	60 840
Thomas	El Dorado Kelsey	581142
Wm*	Yuba Rose Bar	72 809
MORREAN		
Vincent	Sierra Port Win	66 795
MORREAU		
Antone*	Placer Michigan	62 840
MORREL		
Augustus	Calaveras Twp 10	57 266
Chas	Calaveras Twp 10	57 276
David S	Calaveras Twp 6	57 127
Ephraim	Sierra Scales D	66 800
Frank	Yuba Rose Bar	72 819
George*	Placer Michigan	62 844
Henry	Sierra La Porte	66 774
J C	Butte Chico	56 559
Theokop*	Sierra Port Win	66 794
Theokoss	Sierra Port Win	66 794
MORRELL		
A G	Nevada Grass Valley	61 182
A J	Sacramento Ward 1	63 47
A*	Sacramento Ward 1	63 135
Abert	Napa Clear Lake	61 117
Augustus	Calaveras Twp 10	57 266
C	Sacramento Granite	63 230
Chas	San Francisco San Francisco 3	67 32
Chas*	San Francisco San Francisco 2	67 562
Dolan	Nevada Grass Valley	61 175
E	San Francisco San Francisco 5	67 483
E H	Placer Folsom	62 639
F L	San Francisco San Francisco 9	681056
G J N	Sacramento Ward 4	63 509
Geo	Nevada Nevada	61 321
George	San Francisco San Francisco 3	67 8
H B	Amador Twp 7	55 411
Hiram P*	El Dorado Georgetown	58 705
I H	Nevada Nevada	61 320
Isaac S	San Joaquin Elliott	64 943
J C	Santa Clara San Jose	65 385
J K	Sacramento Ward 1	63 74
Jane	San Francisco San Francisco 2	67 693
Jno C	San Francisco San Francisco 9	681016
John F	San Francisco San Francisco 1	68 897
Joseph	San Francisco San Francisco 2	67 714
June	San Francisco San Francisco 2	67 693
L	Mariposa Twp 3	60 561
L	Nevada Nevada	61 290
Lewis	Amador Twp 2	55 264
Samuel	Placer Auburn	62 578
Thos	San Francisco San Francisco 9	681063
MORREO		
Gualupe	Alameda Oakland	55 57
Marcus	Santa Cruz Pajaro	66 565
MORRES		
Ellen	San Francisco San Francisco 8	681287
T J	Sonoma Bodega	69 538
MORRESEY		
Timothy	Humbolt Eel Rvr	59 144
MORREY		
J C	San Francisco San Francisco 3	67 46
W R	San Francisco San Francisco 5	67 524
MORRI		
Liz*	Sacramento Granite	63 256
MORRIA		
Juan	Santa Cruz Santa Cruz	66 620
MORRIAH		
John	Sonoma Vallejo	69 626
MORRIAY		
Llane	Butte Oregon	56 618
MORRICE		
John	El Dorado Mud Springs	58 995
Juan	Santa Cruz Santa Cruz	66 620
MORRICEUX		
G	San Francisco San Francisco 6	67 468

67

California 1860 Census Index

Name	County Locale	M653 RollPage
MORRIEGA		
J Angel	San Francisco San Francisco 2	67 790
MORRIGA		
J Angel	San Francisco San Francisco 2	67 790
MORRIHAM		
John	Yolo Putah	72 585
MORRIL		
Elisa	Alameda Oakland	55 20
Wm	Napa Napa	61 75
MORRILE		
B G	Sacramento Ward 1	63 74
Mary*	Nevada Bridgeport	61 465
Mons	San Francisco San Francisco 12	388 67
MORRILL		
A	Sacramento Ward 1	63 135
A J	Sacramento Ward 1	63 47
A W	El Dorado Coloma	581071
A*	Sacramento Ward 1	63 135
B G	Sacramento Ward 1	63 74
Benjamin	Placer Yankee J	62 760
C F	Yolo Washington	72 566
C H*	Yolo Washington	72 566
Caroline	Sacramento Ward 1	63 138
E C	El Dorado Coloma	581071
Ebenezer	San Francisco San Francisco 2	67 557
Elizabet	Santa Cruz Pajaro	66 550
Elizabeth	Santa Cruz Pajaro	66 550
F	El Dorado Placerville	58 865
F T*	El Dorado Newtown	58 776
G	Nevada Grass Valley	61 160
G	Sacramento Ward 4	63 530
G P	El Dorado Placerville	58 828
G W	Mendocino Ukiah	60 801
Geo	San Francisco San Francisco 1	68 909
Geo E	Sacramento Ward 4	63 495
J P	Sacramento Ward 1	63 143
Jesse	Sacramento Ward 1	63 103
John A	San Francisco San Francisco 1	68 884
Joseph	El Dorado Mud Springs	58 987
Joseph	San Francisco San Francisco 4	681139
L	Mariposa Twp 3	60 561
L	Nevada Grass Valley	61 195
Mary*	Nevada Bridgeport	61 465
Oliver C	Yuba Marysville	72 877
Oliver L	San Francisco San Francisco 8	681255
Rufus G	Placer Stewart	62 606
S	Nevada Grass Valley	61 182
S H	Santa Clara San Jose	65 354
Waren*	Sacramento Ward 1	63 135
William*	Mendocino Ukiah	60 798
MORRILLO		
Anastacio	Plumas Quincy	62 974
MORRIN		
Frank	San Francisco San Francisco 1	68 898
Jeremiah*	Alameda Oakland	55 76
Stephen*	San Francisco San Francisco 1	68 891
MORRINE		
T G	Yolo Washington	72 605
MORRIO		
Marcus	Santa Cruz Pajaro	66 565
MORRIS		
---	Amador Twp 2	55 301
---	Solano Benecia	69 315
A	Butte Kimshaw	56 588
A	El Dorado Diamond	58 793
A	Sacramento Ward 4	63 511
A	San Francisco San Francisco 4	681156
A	San Francisco San Francisco 2	67 685
A	Sonoma Petaluma	69 585
A C	Marin Cortemad	60 756
A H	Butte Hamilton	56 527
A W	San Francisco San Francisco 7	681367
A W	Yolo Cache Crk	72 611
Abrah	Tuolumne Twp 5	71 488
Abraham	San Francisco San Francisco 7	681365
Abram	Tuolumne Chinese	71 488
Agnes	Sacramento Ward 4	63 512
Alex	El Dorado White Oaks	581003
Alfred	El Dorado Kelsey	581153
Anderson	Contra Costa Twp 2	57 565
Ann	Nevada Eureka	61 390
Archibald W	Elkhorn San Joaquin	64 949
Austin	Colusa Muion	57 463
B	Sacramento Ward 1	63 25
B F	Mariposa Twp 3	60 565
Barnett	Marin S Antoni	60 710
Barnette	Marin S Antoni	60 710
Ben	Napa Clear Lake	61 117
Benjamin	Placer Forest H	62 794
Benjamin	San Joaquin Castoria	64 886
Bernard	Yuba Marysville	72 913
Bersalon	Mariposa Twp 3	60 590
Bersalou*	Mariposa Twp 3	60 590
Bertha	Yuba Marysville	72 915

Name	County Locale	M653 RollPage
MORRIS		
C	Calaveras Twp 9	57 374
C A	Nevada Grass Valley	61 145
Carlton	San Francisco San Francisco 10	268 67
Cassandra	San Joaquin Stockton	641027
Catharine	San Francisco San Francisco 9	68 981
Charles	Humbolt Mattole	59 125
Charles	Yuba Fosters	72 834
Charles M	Calaveras Twp 7	57 9
Chas	San Francisco San Francisco 12	386 67
Chas	San Francisco San Francisco 2	67 787
Chas	Santa Clara San Jose	65 356
Chas	Sonoma Petaluma	69 616
D	Siskiyou Callahan	69 2
D	Sutter Nicolaus	70 831
D C	Sierra Cox'S Bar	66 952
Daniel	Sierra Eureka	661043
David	Placer Forest H	62 803
David	Sacramento Georgian	63 340
David	San Francisco San Francisco 9	681063
Dorcas	Del Norte Crescent	58 619
E	Nevada Grass Valley	61 222
Edward	San Joaquin Oneal	64 934
Edward	Sonoma Washington	69 676
Edward	Tulara Visalia	71 32
Edwin B	Contra Costa Twp 3	57 593
Eliza	San Francisco San Francisco 10	179 67
Eliza	Yolo Cache Crk	72 636
Elles	Yuba Marysville	72 888
Ellis	Yuba Marysville	72 888
F	El Dorado Kelsey	581154
F	Siskiyou Yreka	69 191
F	Tuolumne Big Oak	71 144
Francis	Santa Clara Santa Clara	65 514
Frank	Yuba Marysville	72 904
Frederick	San Mateo Twp 3	65 93
Frederick	Tuolumne Twp 1	71 270
G W	Yuba Marysville	72 978
Geo	Del Norte Happy Ca	58 662
Geo	Nevada Nevada	61 244
Geo	Nevada Nevada	61 266
Geo	San Francisco San Francisco 9	681030
Geo F	San Francisco San Francisco 1	68 886
George	Calaveras Twp 7	57 42
George	Los Angeles Tejon	59 539
George	Santa Clara San Jose	65 292
George H	Yuba Bear Rvr	721006
George W	Siskiyou Yreka	69 140
H	Nevada Grass Valley	61 193
H	Nevada Eureka	61 372
H	Sacramento Ward 1	63 38
H	Tuolumne Twp 4	71 172
H P*	Sierra Eureka	661050
Helen	Butte Wyandotte	56 670
Henry	Calaveras Twp 8	57 69
Henry	San Francisco San Francisco 3	67 38
Henry	Sonoma Petaluma	69 590
Henry	Yuba Fosters	72 832
Herman	Los Angeles Los Angeles	59 345
Hetz*	San Francisco San Francisco 7	681374
Hitz*	San Francisco San Francisco 7	681374
Homer	Calaveras Twp 4	57 344
Isaac	Marin Cortemad	60 784
J	El Dorado Diamond	58 798
J	Nevada Grass Valley	61 208
J	Nevada Grass Valley	61 210
J	Nevada Grass Valley	61 212
J	Nevada Nevada	61 254
J	Nevada Nevada	61 313
J	Nevada Eureka	61 382
J	Sacramento Ward 1	63 30
J	Sacramento Franklin	63 310
J	San Francisco San Francisco 5	67 539
J	San Francisco San Francisco 5	67 550
J	Tehama Tehama	70 946
J	Tuolumne Garrote	71 175
J	Yuba Slate Ro	72 693
J C	Amador Twp 2	55 265
J Carter	El Dorado Diamond	58 775
J D	El Dorado Placerville	58 845
J F	Sutter Vernon	70 843
J H	Nevada Grass Valley	61 222
J H	Sonoma Armally	69 504
J H	Yolo Cache	72 634
J J	Amador Twp 6	55 438
J R	Mariposa Twp 3	60 573
J S	Amador Twp 6	55 438
J W	Butte Cascade	56 691
J W	Mariposa Twp 3	60 556
J W	San Francisco San Francisco 5	67 538
J W	Sonoma Santa Rosa	69 393
Jacob	Yuba Marysville	72 894
Jacob S	Plumas Quincy	62 943

Name	County Locale	M653 RollPage
MORRIS		
James	Contra Costa Twp 3	57 613
James	El Dorado Placerville	58 901
James	Humbolt Union	59 192
James	Los Angeles Los Angeles	59 494
James	Marin San Rafael	60 763
James	San Francisco San Francisco 8	681243
James	Santa Cruz Santa Cruz	66 635
James	Solano Vacaville	69 351
James	Trinity Weaverville	701070
James	Trinity Indian C	70 987
James	Tuolumne Columbia	71 342
James B	Tuolumne Shawsfla	71 391
James B	Plumas Meadow Valley	62 900
James R	Sierra Excelsior	661033
James W	Calaveras Twp 7	57 9
Jane	Butte Wyandotte	56 670
Jas	Placer Christia	62 736
Jas	Sacramento Franklin	63 316
Jas	San Francisco San Francisco 2	67 692
Jas	San Francisco San Francisco 1	68 932
Jas	Tehama Lassen	70 884
Jeremiah	San Francisco San Francisco 7	681427
Jesse	Butte Ophir	56 800
Jno	Sonoma Sonoma	69 657
Jno D	Alameda Brooklyn	55 172
Jno N	Sacramento Ward 1	63 30
Jno W	Mendocino Ukiah	60 800
Jno W	San Francisco San Francisco 9	68 951
John	Alameda Brooklyn	55 170
John	Los Angeles Los Angeles	59 519
John	Marin Cortemad	60 790
John	Marin Cortemad	60 791
John	Mariposa Twp 3	60 557
John	Napa Yount	61 48
John	Nevada Bridgeport	61 501
John	Placer Michigan	62 831
John	San Francisco San Francisco 3	67 30
John	San Francisco San Francisco 10	336 67
John	San Francisco San Francisco 2	67 639
John	San Francisco San Francisco 1	68 890
John	Shasta Horsetown	66 691
John	Sierra Twp 7	66 908
John	Siskiyou Scott Ri	69 65
John	Sonoma Washington	69 676
John	Yolo Merritt	72 584
John H	Tuolumne Jamestown	71 451
John K	Tulara Twp 1	71 90
John S	Butte Wyandotte	56 669
John W	Alameda Oakland	55 4
Jonathan	Placer Virginia	62 661
Jonathan*	Placer Virginia	62 683
Jophn	Placer Michigan	62 808
Jos E	Yolo Washington	72 602
Joseph	Contra Costa Twp 3	57 598
Joseph	Napa Napa	61 58
Joseph	Sierra Port Win	66 792
Joseph	Sierra Twp 5	66 924
Joseph	Tulara Visalia	71 33
Julius	San Francisco San Francisco 6	67 462
Julius L	Los Angeles Los Angeles	59 345
Julius*	Yuba Marysville	72 899
L	Nevada Grass Valley	61 144
L	Sacramento Ward 1	63 81
L	Solano Vacaville	69 330
L G	Nevada Grass Valley	61 195
Len	Yuba Slate Ro	72 694
Lenis	Yolo Slate Ra	72 694
Leo	Contra Costa Twp 2	57 568
Levi	Plumas Quincy	62 971
Levi	Yolo Slate Ra	72 694
Levy	Los Angeles Los Angeles	59 359
Lewid	Tehama Lassen	70 883
Lewis	San Francisco San Francisco 10	203 67
Lewis	Yuba Slate Ro	72 694
Louis	Los Angeles San Jose	59 284
Luke	El Dorado Big Bar	58 735
M	Monterey Monterey	60 946
M	San Francisco San Francisco 6	67 464
M	San Francisco San Francisco 5	67 547
M	San Francisco San Francisco 5	67 553
M	Trinity Cox'S Bar	701038
M	Yolo Slate Ra	72 707
M	Yuba Slate Ro	72 707
M A	Nevada Eureka	61 382
M W	Mendocino Ukiah	60 800
Manuel	Solano Benecia	69 285
Manuel	Solano Benecia	69 297
Manuel*	Solano Benecia	69 285
Martin	Los Angeles Los Angeles	59 359
Mary	Klamath Liberty	59 236
Mary	San Francisco San Francisco 10	250 67

California 1860 Census Index

Name	County Locale	M653 RollPage
MORRIS		
Mary	San Francisco San Francisco	10 266
		67
Mary F	Butte Ophir	56 770
Mary J	Monterey Alisal	601031
Matt	Klamath Liberty	59 230
Mellon	Napa Hot Springs	61 22
Micheal	El Dorado Mud Springs	58 977
Milton	Napa Hot Springs	61 22
Moritz	San Francisco San Francisco	8 681287
Moutz	San Francisco San Francisco	8 681287
Owzier*	Sierra Downieville	66 963
Peter	Calaveras Twp 5	57 228
Peter	Sacramento Granite	63 230
Peter	San Francisco San Francisco	4 681168
Pingus	San Francisco San Francisco	3 67 36
Polly	Sonoma Sonoma	69 638
Preston	Calaveras Twp 6	57 115
R	Sutter Yuba	70 765
R H	El Dorado Casumnes	581160
R N	Yolo Cache	72 611
R R	El Dorado Placerville	58 877
R R	Santa Clara San Jose	65 289
R*	Nevada Grass Valley	61 162
Rachael	San Francisco San Francisco	2 67 601
Rafeal	Mariposa Twp 3	60 556
Rafel	Mariposa Twp 3	60 556
Randolph	Sonoma Santa Rosa	69 406
Randoph	Sonoma Santa Rosa	69 406
Richard	Calaveras Twp 5	57 240
Richard	Placer Ophirville	62 658
Richard	Siskiyou Callahan	69 8
Richard	Yuba Marysville	72 913
Richd*	Napa Clear Lake	61 137
Robert	Monterey Pajaro	601018
Robert E	San Joaquin Elliott	64 944
Robt	San Francisco San Francisco	2 67 672
Rrachael	San Francisco San Francisco	2 67 601
S	Nevada Grass Valley	61 148
S	Nevada Grass Valley	61 150
S	Nevada Grass Valley	61 175
S	Sacramento Ward 1	63 81
S	Sonoma Santa Rosa	69 391
Saml	Stanislaus Empire	70 735
Saml D	Calaveras Twp 6	57 126
Saml G	Placer Rattle Snake	62 599
Samuel	Santa Clara San Jose	65 294
Samuel F	San Francisco San Francisco	10 180
		67
Sarah	San Francisco San Francisco	6 67 459
Seth	Colusa Monroeville	57 443
Stephen	Santa Cruz Pajaro	66 575
Stephen	Siskiyou Yreka	69 147
Steven	Amador Twp 4	55 258
Thomas	Colusa Monroeville	57 440
Thomas	San Francisco San Francisco	2 67 680
Thomas	Solano Suisan	69 217
Thomas	Tuolumne Twp 1	71 270
Thomas	Tuolumne Columbia	71 355
Thos	Placer Dutch Fl	62 710
Thos	Sacramento Franklin	63 311
Thos	Sacramento San Joaquin	63 362
Thos	San Francisco San Francisco	1 68 904
Thos	Trinity W Weaver	701054
Toomey	Amador Twp 2	55 266
Virot	San Francisco San Francisco	11 134
		67
W	Calaveras Twp 6	57 112
W	El Dorado Newtown	58 781
W	Sacramento Franklin	63 311
W	Yolo Putah	72 598
W D	Butte Hamilton	56 527
W D	San Francisco San Francisco	5 67 539
W E	Siskiyou Scott Va	69 25
W H	Sierra Twp 7	66 911
W J	Solano Suisan	69 209
W M	San Joaquin Stockton	641043
William	Calaveras Twp 7	57 25
William	Napa Clear Lake	61 138
William	San Francisco San Francisco	11 118
		67
William	Sierra Scales D	66 801
William	Siskiyou Scott Va	69 50
William F	Sierra Scales D	66 801
William G	Tulara Visalia	71 95
Wilson G	Calaveras Twp 7	57 9
Wldern A	Colusa Monroeville	57 452
Wm	Colusa Monroeville	57 445
Wm	Nevada Eureka	61 371
Wm	San Francisco San Francisco	10 194
		67
Wm	San Francisco San Francisco	10 201
		67
Wm	San Francisco San Francisco	1 68 906
Wm T	Yolo Slate Ra	72 702
Wm T	Yuba Slate Ro	72 702

Name	County Locale	M653 RollPage
MORRISA		
Jerry*	Nevada Bridgeport	61 500
MORRISANA		
Anterano	Fresno Twp 1	59 81
Aulerano	Fresno Twp 1	59 81
MORRISEY		
Henry	Trinity Douglas	70 980
James	Santa Cruz Santa Cruz	66 634
John	Sierra La Porte	66 766
John	Sierra Twp 5	66 925
P	Sacramento Cosummes	63 399
Patrick	Santa Cruz Santa Cruz	66 634
MORRISH		
Thos J	Sacramento Ward 4	63 535
MORRISIN		
Chas Wm*	San Francisco 1	68 843
	San Francisco	
MORRISOIN		
Carrol	Yuba Bear Rvr	721005
MORRISON		
A G	Stanislaus Branch	70 715
A J	Tuolumne Columbia	71 326
A L	Yuba Rose Bar	72 810
A M	Mendocino Ukiah	60 806
Adalbert	Klamath S Fork	59 203
Adam	Calaveras Twp 6	57 118
Agnes	San Francisco San Francisco	2 67 644
Anges	Shasta Cottonwood	66 723
Augus	Shasta Cottonwoood	66 723
B	Sutter Vernon	70 845
Benj	Nevada Red Dog	61 538
C A	Nevada Nevada	61 328
Carrol	Yuba Bear Rvr	721005
Charles	Solano Benecia	69 292
Charles	Yuba Foster B	72 833
Charles*	Solano Benecia	69 292
Chas	Placer Auburn	62 580
Chas Wm*	San Francisco 1	68 843
	San Francisco	
Cyrus W	Humbolt Pacific	59 130
D	San Francisco San Francisco	4 681231
D	San Francisco San Francisco	10 314
		67
D S	San Francisco San Francisco	3 67 53
D*	San Francisco San Francisco	4 681231
David	Contra Costa Twp 2	57 572
Donald	Humbolt Eureka	59 178
Duncan	Calaveras Twp 4	57 305
E	Trinity Minersville	70 969
Eduard*	Yuba Rose Bar	72 799
Edward	Santa Cruz Pescadero	66 643
Edward	Yuba Rose Bar	72 799
Elijah*	Plumas Quincy	62 994
Ewd	Santa Clara Freemont	65 416
F F	Butte Chico	56 536
F J	Butte Ophir	56 795
Frank	Sierra Downieville	661007
Franklin	Sierra Downieville	66 963
Fredrick	Plumas Quincy	62 982
G B	Butte Oregon	56 639
Geo	San Francisco San Francisco	9 68 997
Geo	Siskiyou Cottonwoood	69 99
George	Placer Iona Hills	62 873
George	Yuba Fosters	72 840
H	Nevada Grass Valley	61 186
H J	Butte Oregon	56 629
Hector	San Francisco San Francisco	2 67 592
Henry	Tehama Red Bluff	70 912
Hugh	Yuba Bear Rvr	721005
Isaac	Nevada Bridgeport	61 441
Israel D	San Joaquin Castoria	64 897
J	Calaveras Twp 9	57 410
J	El Dorado Placerville	58 877
J	Sacramento Lee	63 212
J	San Francisco San Francisco	10 190
		67
J	San Francisco San Francisco	5 67 489
J	Sutter Butte	70 795
J	Yolo Cache Crk	72 606
J B	Siskiyou Scott Va	69 43
J H	Stanislaus Emory	70 740
J J	San Francisco San Francisco	4 681150
J L	San Francisco San Francisco	3 67 9
J M	Shasta Shasta	66 679
J S	Mariposa Twp 3	60 561
James	San Francisco San Francisco	7 681354
James	Santa Clara San Jose	65 320
Jane	Nevada Bloomfield	61 510
Jasper	Colusa Butte Crk	57 466
Jerry	Nevada Bridgeport	61 500
Jno A	Klamath Salmon	59 208
Jno C	San Francisco San Francisco	10 327
		67
John	Amador Twp 5	55 349
John	Plumas Meadow Valley	62 906
John	Sacramento Brighton	63 204

Name	County Locale	M653 RollPage
MORRISON		
John	Santa Clara Fremont	65 432
John	Sierra Twp 7	66 890
John	Solano Suisan	69 220
John	Solano Vallejo	69 262
John C	Siskiyou Yreka	69 149
John H	Humbolt Eel Rvr	59 149
Jos H	San Francisco San Francisco	12 363
		67
Josepe*	Amador Twp 2	55 328
Joseph	Alameda Brooklyn	55 205
Joseph	Contra Costa Twp 2	57 573
Joseph*	Amador Twp 2	55 328
Josiah	Sierra Downieville	66 967
Kate	Alameda Brooklyn	55 184
L	Nevada Grass Valley	61 165
L	Yolo Cache	72 606
Margt	San Francisco San Francisco	2 67 675
Mary	San Francisco San Francisco	10 184
		67
Mary	Santa Clara Santa Clara	65 513
Mary A	Napa Napa	61 87
McHenry	Contra Costa Twp 1	57 490
Merlton	Yolo Washington	72 599
Mich	Sacramento Ward 1	63 14
Michael	Placer Auburn	62 587
Mick*	Sacramento Ward 1	63 14
Milton	Yolo Washington	72 599
Murray	San Francisco San Francisco	7 681331
N G	Sacramento Ward 3	63 429
P	Siskiyou Cottonwoood	69 101
Pat	Yolo Merritt	72 577
Patrick	Alameda Brooklyn	55 112
Patrick	San Francisco San Francisco	9 681002
Perry	Alameda Brooklyn	55 207
R	Butte Oregon	56 611
R	Trinity Trinity	70 972
R B	Nevada Eureka	61 369
R B	Nevada Eureka	61 370
R F	Sacramento Ward 1	63 44
Remile*	San Francisco San Francisco	2 67 686
Richard	El Dorado Eldorado	58 941
Richard	Yuba Marysville	72 866
Richd	Butte Ophir	56 781
Richd	Butte Ophir	56 784
Robert	Mariposa Twp 3	60 601
Robert	Santa Cruz Santa Cruz	66 607
Robert	Solano Benecia	69 302
Robt H	Nevada Bridgeport	61 472
S	Marin Novato	60 739
S	San Francisco San Francisco	10 190
		67
S L	Santa Clara Gilroy	65 238
S P	Nevada Bridgeport	61 504
Saml	Placer Secret R	62 618
Saml	Santa Clara Santa Clara	65 507
Saml A	San Francisco San Francisco	6 67 422
Sarah	Sacramento Ward 1	63 63
T	San Francisco San Francisco	5 67 553
T H	San Francisco San Francisco	5 67 500
Thomas	Yolo No E Twp	72 673
Thomas M	Yuba North Ea	72 673
Thos	Yolo Washington	72 568
W	Butte Oregon	56 619
W	Shasta Millvill	66 755
W P	San Mateo Twp 3	65 81
Walter	Yolo Washington	72 599
William	Yuba Rose Bar	72 814
William A	Tuolumne Jamestown	71 450
William E	Yuba Fosters	72 830
Wm	Butte Oregon	56 619
Wm	Mendocino Ukiah	60 796
Wm	Sacramento Ward 1	63 40
Wm J	Mendocino Ukiah	60 796
Wm P	San Francisco San Francisco	10 280
		67
MORRISS		
F T	El Dorado Newtown	58 776
J	El Dorado Coloma	581069
L B	Nevada Grass Valley	61 149
S B	Nevada Grass Valley	61 149
MORRISSE		
C*	San Francisco San Francisco	10 359
		67
MORRISSEY		
James	Sierra Poker Flats	66 841
Mary	San Francisco San Francisco	9 681047
Michael	Yolo Slate Ra	72 689
MORRISSON		
Robert	Santa Cruz Santa Cruz	66 607
MORRISSOY		
James*	Sierra Poker Flats	66 841
MORRISSY		
Danl	Tuolumne Sonora	71 210
James	Tuolumne Twp 2	71 310
John	Tuolumne Twp 1	71 195

MORRISTON

Name	County Locale	M653 Roll Page
Robert*	Santa Cruz Santa Cruz	66 607

MORRISY

Name	County Locale	Roll Page
Chris	Sacramento Natonia	63 277
John	Sierra La Porte	66 766

MORRIT

R*	Nevada Grass Valley	61 162

MORRITT

David*	Nevada Red Dog	61 548
James	Placer Michigan	62 836

MORRITZ

M	San Francisco San Francisco 10	266 67

MORRIW

Juan*	Calaveras Twp 8	57 92

MORRIXON

Hector	San Francisco San Francisco 2	67 592

MORRIYMAR

Richard	Yuba Slate Ro	72 711

MORROER

C*	Nevada Eureka	61 352

MORRON

B	El Dorado Placerville	58 849
James	Placer Forest H	62 773
James	Sacramento Franklin	63 312
John	Plumas Quincy	62 976
M*	Nevada Eureka	61 353
Peter	Siskiyou Klamath	69 91
Tillman	Yuba Parks Ba	72 774

MORRONE

J	El Dorado Kelsey	581153

MORROS

James B	Plumas Quincy	62 957

MORROVIACH

John	San Diego Agua Caliente	64 819

MORROW

A D	Yuba Parks Ba	72 774
Alice	Amador Twp 1	55 486
Almerin	Tulara Visalia	71 109
Almesin	Tulara Twp 1	71 109
Andrew	Alameda Brooklyn	55 189
C	Nevada Eureka	61 352
Charles	Placer Yankee J	62 775
Charles	Tuolumne Twp 1	71 195
Charly	Tuolumne Sonora	71 195
D S	Butte Oregon	56 632
F W	Butte Oro	56 686
G H	Nevada Nevada	61 322
H D	Nevada Bridgeport	61 496
Harrison B	Los Angeles Los Angeles	59 335
J	El Dorado Casumnes	581164
J C	Nevada Eureka	61 371
J H	Yolo Cache Crk	72 607
James	Amador Twp 2	55 320
James	El Dorado Coloma	581080
James	Nevada Red Dog	61 544
James	Sonoma Armally	69 500
Jesse	Fresno Twp 3	59 9
Jno	Sacramento Ward 1	63 43
Jno B	Sacramento Ward 4	63 602
John	Plumas Meadow Valley	62 907
John	Plumas Quincy	62 991
John	Yuba Rose Bar	72 803
Joseph	Calaveras Twp 8	57 107
Joseph	Los Angeles Elmonte	59 250
Joseph	Sierra Downieville	66 969
Joshua	El Dorado Casumnes	581161
L J	Stanislaus Buena Village	70 725
Lyle	Klamath S Fork	59 199
Mahalia A	Calaveras Twp 8	57 65
Mary A	Stanislaus Buena Village	70 725
Otis	Yolo Slate Ra	72 696
Otis	Yuba Slate Ro	72 696
Peter	Calaveras Twp 5	57 189
Peter	Siskiyou Klamath	69 91
Peter*	Calaveras Twp 5	57 189
Robert	Calaveras Twp 8	57 65
Samuel	Amador Twp 4	55 332
Thomas H	Yuba Marysville	72 876
Thos	San Francisco San Francisco 2	67 581
Thos H	Sacramento Ward 1	63 49
Tillman	Yuba Parks Ba	72 774
W	Yolo Cache	72 627
W R	Nevada Eureka	61 353
William	Calaveras Twp 4	57 318
William	Solano Suisan	69 215
William S	Los Angeles Los Angeles	59 334
Wm	Santa Clara Redwood	65 444
Wm M	Sonoma Santa Rosa	69 392

MORROWS

Jacques	Yuba New York	72 723
Otis	Yuba Slate Ro	72 696

MORROWTT

John*	El Dorado Diamond	58 792

MORRPLEY

Daniel	Butte Oregon	56 621

MORRSON

J S	Mariposa Twp 3	60 561

MORRTIMA

Jose*	Solano Vacaville	69 335

MORRY

J W	Mariposa Twp 3	60 556

MORS

Petr*	Siskiyou Yreka	69 125

MORSCH

F	San Francisco San Francisco 10	175 67

MORSE

A	Siskiyou Callahan	69 12
A C	Tehama Tehama	70 946
Abner	San Joaquin Oneal	64 939
Agustus	Yolo No E Twp	72 668
Amos	Marin Tomales	60 726
Andrew L	Siskiyou Yreka	69 185
B	Siskiyou Yreka	69 151
Benj	Amador Twp 3	55 406
Benjamin	Placer Yankee J	62 776
C L	Tuolumne Big Oak	71 153
C W	Sacramento Natonia	63 273
Chancy	Calaveras Twp 7	57 33
Charles	El Dorado Salmon Falls	581049
Charles	Santa Cruz Pajaro	66 543
Chas	Butte Wyandotte	56 666
Chas	Sacramento Granite	63 230
Chas	Sacramento Granite	63 243
Chas E G	Placer Rattle Snake	62 629
Chus*	Sacramento Granite	63 243
David	San Francisco San Francisco 2	67 618
David	Santa Cruz Santa Cruz	66 622
David	Santa Cruz Santa Cruz	66 624
David	Siskiyou Yreka	69 158
David	Siskiyou Yreka	69 165
Davis	Santa Cruz Pescadero	66 643
Dominick	Calaveras Twp 6	57 116
E	Nevada Nevada	61 244
E	Sonoma Washington	69 663
E C	Butte Ophir	56 779
E E	San Francisco San Francisco 10	189 67
E F	Nevada Grass Valley	61 192
Ebbice*	Santa Cruz Pescadero	66 644
Ebbin*	Santa Cruz Pescadero	66 644
Ebbue*	Santa Cruz Pescadero	66 644
Eben	Sacramento Ward 4	63 519
Elijah A	Humbolt Eureka	59 163
Elizabeth	San Bernardino San Bernardino	64 621
Emery	Humbolt Eel Rvr	59 150
Ephraim W	San Diego Agua Caliente	64 834
F H*	Sierra Twp 7	66 908
Frank	Nevada Bridgeport	61 480
Frank	Santa Cruz Santa Cruz	66 636
Franklin	Placer Folsom	62 639
H M	Siskiyou Scott Va	69 40
Harris	Tuolumne Columbia	71 289
Harvey C	San Bernardino	64 620
Heeman	Sonoma Mendocino	69 459
Henry	San Bernardino San Bernardino	64 634
Henry	Sonoma Armally	69 512
Henry	Yuba Marysville	72 870
Henry N	Alameda Oakland	55 29
J	Calaveras Twp 9	57 412
J	Nevada Grass Valley	61 147
J	Siskiyou Klamath	69 93
J B	San Francisco San Francisco 5	67 481
J B	Sonoma Santa Rosa	69 400
J F	Sacramento Ward 1	63 74
J H	Yuba Rose Par	72 797
J S	Tehama Tehama	70 945
J T*	Sacramento Ward 1	63 74
Ja	El Dorado Eldorado	58 939
James	Calaveras Twp 8	57 103
James	Humbolt Eel Rvr	59 152
James	Yuba Fosters	72 834
Jno	Tehama Lassen	70 869
John	Calaveras Twp 7	57 13
John	Calaveras Twp 7	57 42
John	Santa Cruz Soguel	66 582
John	Siskiyou Klamath	69 92
John	Stanislaus Branch	70 697
John H	San Francisco San Francisco 3	67 10
John J	Sierra Pine Grove	66 823
Julius G	Mendocino Arrana	60 858
Justice	San Bernardino San Bernardino	64 633
L E	Butte Oro	56 686
L M	San Joaquin Elkhorn	64 973
Loranzo	Tuolumne Twp 2	71 390
Lorenzo	Tuolumne Shawsfla	71 390
Lucius A	Calaveras Twp 6	57 151
M H	Tuolumne Twp 2	71 327
M H	Tuolumne Twp 2	71 339
Mary	Siskiyou Yreka	69 152

MORSE

Mary	Sonoma Mendocino	69 459
Mary*	Siskiyou Yreka	69 152
Moses	San Bernardino San Bernardino	64 628
Nathaniel H	Calaveras Twp 5	57 147
O W	Sacramento Natonia	63 273
Randolph W	Castoria	64 892
S	San Joaquin	
S	Siskiyou Klamath	69 80
S F	Yolo Merritt	72 581
Salnie*	Mendocino Ukiah	60 801
Salnu*	Mendocino Ukiah	60 801
Salvie*	Mendocino Ukiah	60 801
Thomas	Calaveras Twp 10	57 294
Thomas	San Francisco San Francisco 1	68 885
Thomas A	El Dorado Eldorado	58 943
Thos	San Francisco San Francisco 1	68 891
W H	Siskiyou Scott Va	69 59
William	San Francisco San Francisco 9	681089
William*	Mendocino Big Rvr	60 846
Wm B	Solano Benecia	69 282
Wm H	Calaveras Twp 9	57 417

MORSEHEAD

P*	Shasta Shasta	66 656

MORSGIE

J	San Francisco San Francisco 9	681076

MORSHAND

Joshua	Contra Costa Twp 2	57 546

MORSI

John H	San Francisco San Francisco 3	67 10

MORSON

H	Los Angeles Tejon	59 524
James*	Placer Michigan	62 824
Richd	San Francisco San Francisco 10	295 67

MORSSE

Jacob	San Joaquin Elliott	64 943

MORSSHY

Paul*	Marin S Antoni	60 711

MORSTARACHE

A*	El Dorado Georgetown	58 685

MORT

Elizabeth	Calaveras Twp 7	57 19
Peter	San Francisco San Francisco 6	67 462
Thomas	Calaveras Twp 7	57 28

MORTA

Antonio	Monterey Alisal	601029
Jesus	Yuba Marysville	72 949

MORTAGE

Eli*	Plumas Quincy	62 994

MORTAL

Elizabeth	San Joaquin Oneal	64 937

MORTALDO

Geo Butta	Calaveras Twp 6	57 167

MORTAN

D	Nevada Washington	61 332

MORTAT

Doff	Yuba New York	72 737

MORTE

Rose	San Joaquin Stockton	641090

MORTEMAS

William*	Calaveras Twp 5	57 210

MORTEN

John	Mariposa Coulterville	60 685
Thos	Alameda Brooklyn	55 181

MORTENAZ

Juan	Yuba Marysville	72 936

MORTENEE

Natalie	Calaveras Twp 6	57 135

MORTENER

Martel*	Mariposa Twp 3	60 605
Natali*	Calaveras Twp 6	57 135

MORTENSELL

Peter	Yolo Slate Ra	72 718

MORTENU

Natali	Calaveras Twp 6	57 135

MORTHER

A W	Napa Napa	61 113

MORTHERWELL

E	Trinity Oregon G	701009

MORTHES

Chris*	Sacramento Ward 1	63 26

MORTHIS

Chris*	Sacramento Ward 1	63 26

MORTIMAN

William	Calaveras Twp 5	57 210

MORTIMER

B S*	Siskiyou Scott Ri	69 75
H T*	Butte Kimshaw	56 585
H*	Butte Kimshaw	56 585
Henry	Tulara Visalia	71 102
Louis	San Francisco San Francisco 2	67 757
Margaret	Solano Benecia	69 281

MORTIMORE

Christ	Butte Bidwell	56 729

MORTIN

A	Stanislaus Oatvale	70 716

Name	County Locale	M653 Roll	Page
MORTIN			
B	San Mateo Twp 1	65	66
Charles	Marin Point Re	60	730
James	Placer Forest H	62	802
Joseph	Santa Clara Alviso	65	396
Nelson	San Mateo Twp 2	65	120
R	Shasta Millvill	66	751
Thomas	Shasta Shasta	66	732
Thomas	Sierra Twp 7	66	896
William*	Placer Iona Hills	62	895
MORTINER			
Marlet*	Mariposa Twp 3	60	605
MORTINI			
Mickael	Calaveras Twp 8	57	90
MORTINIS			
Antonio*	Calaveras Twp 5	57	248
MORTINO			
Joseph	Calaveras Twp 8	57	87
MORTINORE			
P*	Siskiyou Cottonwoood	69	103
MORTINUS			
Ambrose	Calaveras Twp 10	57	259
MORTISE			
Jesus	San Luis Obispo San Luis Obispo	65	1
MORTIZA			
Pedro	Santa Clara San Jose	65	368
MORTLAND			
John	Trinity Weaverville	70	1052
MORTMAN			
William*	Calaveras Twp 5	57	210
MORTO			
Peter	San Mateo Twp 3	65	91
MORTOMAN			
William	Calaveras Twp 5	57	210
MORTON			
A G	San Francisco San Francisco 6	67	428
A W	Stanislaus Buena Village	70	724
A W	Trinity Bates	70	967
Albert	Sierra Pine Grove	66	826
Alfred	Sacramento Ward 1	63	13
B	El Dorado Placerville	58	866
Bacary	Marin S Antoni	60	707
Barry	San Francisco San Francisco 10	67	248
Bennet	Tuolumne Twp 2	71	279
Bridget	Sacramento Ward 1	63	139
Charles C	San Francisco San Francisco 4	68	1214
Charles*	Marin Point Re	60	730
D	Nevada Washington	61	332
D C	Tuolumne Shawsfla	71	411
Danl	Sonoma Petaluma	69	554
E	Tuolumne Columbia	71	473
E G	Mariposa Twp 1	60	636
E S	Tuolumne Jamestown	71	425
Edward	Santa Clara San Jose	65	317
Edwd H	San Francisco San Francisco 2	67	556
Eliza	Butte Oregon	56	634
Freeman	San Joaquin Stockton	64	1022
Geo H	Tuolumne Shawsfla	71	382
George	Tuolumne Twp 1	71	480
Geroge	Tuolumne Sonora	71	480
H	Yolo Putah	72	554
Harvey	Mendocino Ukiah	60	794
Henry J	Amador Twp 4	55	236
Henry J	San Francisco San Francisco 10	67	199
Isaac	Mariposa Twp 3	60	548
J	Calaveras Twp 9	57	404
J	San Francisco San Francisco 9	68	1058
J W	Tuolumne Shawsfla	71	386
James A	Mariposa Twp 1	60	636
James H	Mariposa Twp 1	60	636
Jas	San Francisco San Francisco 1	68	880
John	Alameda Brooklyn	55	213
John	Marin Cortemad	60	755
John	Mariposa Twp 3	60	572
John	Mariposa Coulterville	60	685
John	San Francisco San Francisco 8	68	1260
John	Sierra Downieville	66	971
John	Tuolumne Columbia	71	353
Josiah	Mariposa Twp 3	60	602
Kate	San Francisco San Francisco 6	67	448
Malinda	Sonoma Petaluma	69	568
Michael	San Francisco San Francisco 2	67	594
N	Solano Benecia	69	288
Nathan S	Placer Rattle Snake	62	633
Nathaneil	Solano Benecia	69	281
Nathaniel	Marin San Rafael	60	758
Nathaniel	Solano Benecia	69	281
P	El Dorado Diamond	58	771
P	El Dorado Diamond	58	810
Philander*	Stanislaus Branch	70	708
Reuben	San Francisco San Francisco 8	68	1260
Richard	Alameda Brooklyn	55	132
Robert H	Tuolumne Big Oak	71	180
Robert N	Tuolumne Twp 4	71	180

Name	County Locale	M653 Roll	Page
MORTON			
Saml	Tehama Pasakent	70	858
Sargant	San Francisco San Francisco 8	68	1279
T M	Sacramento Ward 3	63	480
Thomas	Shasta Shasta	66	732
Thomas	Sierra Twp 7	66	896
Thomas H	Solano Suisan	69	209
Thos	Nevada Bridgeport	61	451
W	Calaveras Twp 8	57	55
W	Mariposa Twp 3	60	552
W	San Francisco San Francisco 5	67	527
W H	El Dorado Greenwood	58	718
Wfry	Sierra Pine Grove	66	832
William	Calaveras Twp 8	57	85
William	Klamath Trinidad	59	222
William	San Joaquin Elkhorn	64	967
William	Siskiyou Yreka	69	180
William L	Sierra Pine Grove	66	832
Wm	Sacramento Ward 1	63	62
Wm	San Francisco San Francisco 10	67	254
Wm H	Humbolt Union	59	193
Zacary	Marin S Antoni	60	707
MORTONSELL			
Peter	Yuba New York	72	718
MORTOTH			
Antonea*	Mariposa Twp 1	60	631
MORTOTT			
Antonea	Mariposa Twp 1	60	631
MORTULDO			
Gio Butta	Calaveras Twp 6	57	167
MORUCE			
Samuel	Tuolumne Twp 4	71	134
Samuel C*	Tuolumne Big Oak	71	134
MORUEL			
Balonie	Santa Cruz Santa Cruz	66	617
MORUESE			
Dfuroro*	Nevada Bloomfield	61	519
Djuroro*	Nevada Bloomfield	61	519
MORUIS			
Julius*	Yuba Marysville	72	899
MORULL			
G W	Mendocino Ukiah	60	801
W	Yolo Washington	72	561
MORULLO			
Joaquin*	Calaveras Twp 5	57	179
MORUR			
Awzier*	Sierra Downieville	66	963
MORUS			
Francisco	Calaveras Twp 5	57	227
J	Nevada Nevada	61	254
MORVEL			
W*	Nevada Grass Valley	61	158
MORWER			
C*	Nevada Eureka	61	352
MORWO			
J C*	Nevada Eureka	61	371
MORX			
Sebastian	Alameda Brooklyn	55	147
MORY			
---	Butte Ophir	56	814
---	Calaveras Twp 10	57	271
---	San Francisco San Francisco 4	68	1173
---	San Francisco San Francisco 5	67	510
---	Sierra La Porte	66	780
---	Placer Nicolaus	62	692
Katy	Solano Montezuma	69	373
Richard			
MORYER			
Frank	Nevada Bridgeport	61	482
MORZET			
Geo	Sacramento Ward 4	63	518
MOS			
---*	Mariposa Twp 3	60	582
Caroline*	Sacramento Ward 4	63	545
MOSANO ATTE			
P*	El Dorado Placerville	58	833
MOSAS			
E	El Dorado Placerville	58	853
MOSBY			
L B	San Francisco San Francisco 1	68	919
MOSCHALDD			
Henry	San Francisco San Francisco 2	67	724
MOSCISETA			
Louis	Sierra Downieville	66	1019
MOSCLY			
Wade	Yolo Washington	72	602
MOSCOSO			
Frank	Tuolumne Twp 2	71	320
Marykita*	Tuolumne Columbia	71	320
MOSCOUD			
Pierre*	Calaveras Twp 5	57	239
MOSCRIPT			
Andrew	Humbolt Eureka	59	172
MOSE			
---	Mendocino Round Va	60	881
Andrew	Tuolumne Green Springs	71	519

Name	County Locale	M653 Roll	Page
MOSE			
Thomas	Tulara Twp 1	71	98
MOSEAR			
Pedro*	Mariposa Twp 1	60	660
MOSEAUX			
Vincent	Calaveras Twp 5	57	207
MOSEBY			
Benj	Sacramento Ward 1	63	98
MOSEL			
Font	Nevada Grass Valley	61	224
MOSELAND			
Zacariah*	Tulara Twp 2	71	24
MOSELAY			
John	Humbolt Table Bl	59	141
MOSELEY			
Charles	Solano Vallejo	69	251
D P	Butte Ophir	56	824
Jas O	Butte Bidwell	56	712
MOSELLE			
Rob	Yolo Cache Crk	72	641
MOSELY			
A	Del Norte Crescent	58	633
A	Del Norte Crescent	58	634
Thomas	San Joaquin Stockton	64	1011
MOSEN			
E	San Francisco San Francisco 2	67	804
MOSENO			
Bineta	Calaveras Twp 5	57	221
MOSER			
A	Tehama Tehama	70	937
Andrew B	Calaveras Twp 6	57	145
Christian	Sierra Downieville	66	959
Cristy	Sierra Downieville	66	957
E	San Francisco San Francisco 2	67	804
Elizabeth	San Francisco San Francisco 2	67	652
F S	Shasta Horsetown	66	693
Ferdenand	Tuolumne Don Pedro	71	540
Fred	El Dorado Grizzly	58	1181
Frederick	San Francisco San Francisco 3	67	71
Jacob	San Francisco San Francisco 3	67	6
MOSERAS			
R*	El Dorado Placerville	58	870
MOSERES			
R*	El Dorado Placerville	58	870
MOSES			
---	Mendocino Round Va	60	878
---	San Joaquin Stockton	64	1098
---	Sonoma Salt Point	69	695
A	El Dorado Placerville	58	882
Adalaid W*	Siskiyou Yreka	69	167
Agustus	San Francisco San Francisco 2	67	798
Ambros	Santa Cruz Soguel	66	585
Ambrose	Santa Cruz Soguel	66	585
Andrew B	Calaveras Twp 6	57	145
Augustus	San Francisco San Francisco 2	67	798
Caroline	Sacramento Ward 4	63	534
Christian	Sierra Downieville	66	959
Daniel	Siskiyou Scott Va	69	56
Edwd	San Francisco San Francisco 5	67	487
G*	San Francisco San Francisco 1	68	814
H A	El Dorado Greenwood	58	714
H A	Sacramento Ward 1	63	120
Henry	San Francisco San Francisco 12	67	385
Hiram	Sacramento Natonia	63	281
Hiran*	Sacramento Natonia	63	281
Hirem*	Sacramento Natonia	63	281
Horatio	Alameda Brooklyn	55	96
J J	El Dorado Placerville	58	856
Jacob H	Yuba Marysville	72	883
James	Tehama Tehama	70	937
John	Tuolumne Chinese	71	521
Jonathan	Santa Clara San Jose	65	389
L*	San Francisco San Francisco 1	68	814
Meyer	San Francisco San Francisco 2	67	763
Phillip	Nevada Little Y	61	531
S	Amador Twp 1	55	482
Tom	El Dorado Kelsey	58	1132
William S	Siskiyou Yreka	69	166
Wm F	Calaveras Twp 6	57	120
MOSFUN			
Peter*	Calaveras Twp 4	57	345
MOSGROVE			
J D*	Shasta Shasta	66	681
MOSGUEDA			
Jesus*	Los Angeles Los Angeles	59	388
MOSH			
---	Butte Bidwell	56	719
Ah	Butte Bidwell	56	719
MOSHBERGER			
Christian*	San Francisco San Francisco 7	68	1325
MOSHE			
Henry	El Dorado Greenwood	58	708
MOSHEIMER			
Jos	San Francisco San Francisco 10	67	247

California 1860 Census Index

Name	County Locale	M653 Roll Page
MOSHEINIER		
Jas	San Francisco San Francisco 10	247 67
MOSHER		
C	Nevada Grass Valley	61 169
J	Tuolumne Twp 4	71 147
Treeman P*	Humbolt Eureka	59 178
MOSHIER		
M	San Francisco San Francisco 5	67 548
MOSHIRE		
W H	San Francisco San Francisco 5	67 552
MOSIA		
Hosea*	Mariposa Twp 3	60 574
MOSIER		
Abraham	San Francisco San Francisco 8	681262
E	Shasta Shasta	66 674
Geo	Sacramento San Joaquin	63 364
Joel O	Sacramento Georgian	63 337
John	Sacramento Dry Crk	63 371
John	Yuba Marysville	72 974
Joseph	Yuba Marysville	72 962
Sam	Del Norte Klamath	58 656
Saml	Sacramento Ward 4	63 514
MOSIES		
W M	Tuolumne Twp 1	71 247
MOSIN		
Amos	Placer Iona Hills	62 870
Joseph	Yuba Marysville	72 962
MOSINGS		
John	Sacramento Ward 4	63 518
MOSINIA		
Salino	Calaveras Twp 5	57 139
MOSINO		
Frank	Calaveras Twp 10	57 289
Maria*	Los Angeles Los Angeles	59 516
MOSKER		
Treeman P	Humbolt Eureka	59 178
MOSKIMAN		
Robert	San Francisco San Francisco 2	67 612
MOSKINAN		
R H	San Francisco San Francisco 2	67 611
MOSLEY		
Augashi	El Dorado Georgetown	58 688
Augasta	El Dorado Georgetown	58 688
J	El Dorado Placerville	58 821
James	El Dorado Mud Springs	58 970
MOSLNO		
Jesus	San Francisco San Francisco 2	67 779
MOSLOCK		
Preston*	Sacramento Ward 3	63 452
MOSOI		
J J	El Dorado Greenwood	58 716
MOSOKEEK		
---	Fresno Twp 3	59 97
MOSOKET		
---	Fresno Twp 2	59 66
MOSPETO		
---	Fresno Twp 2	59 65
MOSQUEDA		
Jesus	Los Angeles Los Angeles	59 388
MOSRES		
John	Calaveras Twp 8	57 78
MOSS		
---*	Fresno Twp 2	59 70
A	Napa Napa	61 65
A B	Nevada Bloomfield	61 511
Abburn	San Francisco San Francisco 7	681442
Alexander	Contra Costa Twp 2	57 540
Charles A	Solano Vallejo	69 278
Chas	Alameda Brooklyn	55 107
Chas	Sacramento Georgian	63 344
Churchill	Mariposa Twp 3	60 551
D B	Tuolumne Twp 3	71 449
D H T	San Francisco San Francisco 6	67 470
Danl	Calaveras Twp 10	57 299
E	San Francisco San Francisco 5	67 498
E W	Solano Vacaville	69 329
Edward	Colusa Monroeville	57 443
Ella J	San Francisco San Francisco 10	268 67
Frank	El Dorado Diamond	58 764
Franklin	Yuba Marysville	72 729
George W	El Dorado Georgetown	58 682
Henry	Plumas Quincy	621003
Hiram W	San Joaquin Castoria	64 895
J	Sacramento Ward 1	63 47
J H	Yuba New York	72 730
J M	Sierra Downieville	661031
J Mora	San Francisco San Francisco 6	67 436
J S	Nevada New York	61 380
J S	Yuba New York	72 730
James	El Dorado Coloma	581102
James	El Dorado Placerville	58 904
James	Mariposa Twp 3	60 567
James	Placer Michigan	62 817
Jas	Butte Hamilton	56 519
MOSS		
John	El Dorado Kelsey	581152
John	Mariposa Twp 3	60 565
John	Placer Michigan	62 823
John A	Sierra Gibsonville	66 860
Joseph	Tuolumne Twp 1	71 238
Jss	Nevada Eureka	61 380
L	El Dorado Diamond	58 767
Lewis	Sacramento Granite	63 222
Louis	Calaveras Twp 5	57 209
Lysander	San Francisco San Francisco 8	681320
Manly	Tuolumne Twp 1	71 244
Nathaniel H	Calaveras Twp 6	57 147
Newton	Napa Napa	61 93
Orris	Sonoma Vallejo	69 630
P	Siskiyou Cottonwoood	69 97
T	El Dorado Georgetown	58 707
T J	San Francisco San Francisco 8	681318
Theodore	El Dorado Placerville	58 910
Thomas	Monterey San Juan	601000
W	San Joaquin Stockton	641052
W E	Butte Kimshaw	56 600
Wm A	Sierra Eureka	661048
Woodsen	Butte Hamilton	56 519
MOSSE		
D A T	San Francisco San Francisco 11	98 67
D H T	San Francisco San Francisco 11	98 67
W B	El Dorado Placerville	58 870
MOSSENEY		
J*	Nevada Nevada	61 284
MOSSERREY		
J*	Nevada Nevada	61 284
MOSSEY		
J W	El Dorado Kelsey	581144
MOSSIAS		
Jahena	Fresno Twp 1	59 76
MOSSIEURS		
Theodore	Fresno Twp 1	59 83
MOSSLANDER		
Thomas	Placer Yankee J	62 759
MOSSMAN		
F	Yolo Washington	72 603
Geo	San Francisco San Francisco 5	67 480
MOSSNAYRE		
Antone*	Sierra Gibsonville	66 854
MOSSOYD		
Philena	Sonoma Petaluma	69 543
MOST		
Goerge W	El Dorado Georgetown	58 682
Henry J*	Yuba Marysville	72 976
John	San Francisco San Francisco 10	306 67
Linsy*	Mariposa Coulterville	60 703
MOSTE		
G B	Sierra La Porte	66 777
MOSTHER		
Me*	Calaveras Twp 10	57 293
Mil*	Calaveras Twp 10	57 293
Nie*	Calaveras Twp 10	57 293
MOSTHIE		
Abil*	Calaveras Twp 10	57 293
MOSTHIR		
Neil*	Calaveras Twp 10	57 293
MOSTNO		
Manerela*	San Salvador	64 659
	San Bernardino	
MOSTON		
Charles*	Marin Point Re	60 730
D	Shasta Millvill	66 743
MOSTRUN		
Axel*	Santa Cruz Santa Cruz	66 637
MOSTS		
Henry J*	Yuba Marysville	72 976
MOSTYEN		
Thomas	Sierra Twp 7	66 864
MOSUR		
Ira	San Joaquin Elkhorn	64 985
MOSURE		
G W	San Francisco San Francisco 10	251 67
James	Los Angeles Azuza	59 277
MOSY		
---	Fresno Twp 2	59 108
MOT		
Ming	San Francisco San Francisco 4	681188
Pee	Butte Ophir	56 809
Pin	Butte Ophir	56 809
MOTA		
Maxemiano	Monterey Pajaro	601025
Maximiano*	Monterey Pajaro	601025
Maxinnano*	Monterey Pajaro	601025
Maxnnano*	Monterey Pajaro	601025
MOTANIA		
Mocario	Tulara Twp 3	71 41
MOTANIS		
Mocario*	Tulara Keeneysburg	71 41
MOTAR		
A*	Yuba North Ea	72 686
MOTARES		
A*	Yuba North Ea	72 686
MOTARS		
A*	Yolo Slate Ra	72 686
MOTE		
Adam	El Dorado Greenwood	58 729
Jeremiah W*	Arrana	60 859
	Mendocino	
Jeremiah*	Mendocino Arrana	60 859
MOTHERSEAD		
A J	Sonoma Russian	69 438
MOTHERWOOD		
T N*	Mariposa Twp 1	60 670
MOTHEWSON		
D T	San Mateo Twp 3	65 102
MOTHIAN		
Leonard	Yuba Long Bar	72 773
MOTIA		
N	El Dorado Placerville	58 821
MOTICEL		
Rumcenio	Napa Napa	61 114
MOTIE		
Charles E	Yuba Marysville	72 904
MOTIESS		
---	Mendocino Little L	60 839
MOTITLETO		
Geore	El Dorado Georgetown	58 705
Gerges*	El Dorado Georgetown	58 705
MOTITTETO		
Gerger*	El Dorado Georgetown	58 705
MOTLBY		
Thomas	El Dorado Coloma	581108
MOTO		
Jeremiah W*	Arrana	60 859
	Mendocino	
Pasqual	Monterey S Antoni	60 968
MOTOMOT		
---	San Diego Agua Caliente	64 863
MOTRELO		
Maria C	Los Angeles San Juan	59 473
MOTRESS		
---	Mendocino Little L	60 839
MOTRETO		
Maria C*	Los Angeles San Juan	59 473
MOTRO		
---	Tulara Twp 3	71 63
MOTROYET		
---	Tulara Twp 1	71 117
MOTT		
---	Calaveras Twp 9	57 358
Charles	Sierra Twp 7	66 874
E B	Sacramento Ward 4	63 496
Elijah	San Francisco San Francisco 6	67 410
F N	Yolo Cache Crk	72 665
Gordon N	Yuba Marysville	72 850
Henry D*	Yuba Marysville	72 945
J	Nevada Grass Valley	61 167
M	Sacramento Franklin	63 321
M H	Butte Chico	56 533
Mary J	San Francisco San Francisco 6	67 411
R F	Colusa Monroeville	57 452
T N	Yolo Cache Crk	72 665
Thomas D	Los Angeles Los Angeles	59 332
Thos	Shasta Shasta	66 682
W A	Sonoma Armally	69 509
Wm A	Placer Virginia	62 690
MOTTER		
James	Calaveras Twp 5	57 191
MOTTESLY		
Henry	Butte Ophir	56 784
MOTTEY		
Claude	Amador Twp 1	55 488
MOTTLER		
Henry	Tuolumne Twp 2	71 284
MOTTO		
Antonia	San Francisco San Francisco 3	67 63
MOTTON		
A*	San Francisco San Francisco 4	681151
Josiah*	Mariposa Twp 3	60 602
MOTTS		
Phillip	Calaveras Twp 9	57 347
MOTZ		
Henry	Sierra Twp 7	66 866
Mary	El Dorado Georgetown	58 677
MOTZLER		
Wm*	Nevada Nevada	61 241
MOU		
---	Calaveras Twp 5	57 191
---	Calaveras Twp 5	57 257
---	Calaveras Twp 10	57 269
---	Calaveras Twp 10	57 271
---	El Dorado White Oaks	581025

California 1860 Census Index

Name	County Locale	M653 RollPage
MOU		
---	El Dorado Salmon Falls	581041
---	Mariposa Twp 3	60 608
---	San Francisco San Francisco 4	681186
---	San Francisco San Francisco 4	681188
---	San Francisco San Francisco 4	681192
---	San Francisco San Francisco 4	681194
---*	Placer Auburn	62 582
Ah Fe	San Francisco San Francisco 4	681202
Fa	San Francisco San Francisco 4	681198
Fok	San Francisco San Francisco 4	681199
Kok	San Francisco San Francisco 4	681199
Po	San Francisco San Francisco 4	681192
Po	San Francisco San Francisco 4	681201
Shall	El Dorado Georgetown	58 756
MOUAHAN		
John	Tuolumne Sonora	71 221
MOUAL		
Joseph	Tuolumne Big Oak	71 140
MOUCHEL		
S*	Nevada Eureka	61 365
MOUCHIA		
Appolonia*	Yuba Marysville	72 918
MOUD		
John	Butte Ophir	56 784
Raymond*	Sacramento Granite	63 244
MOUDAY		
S L	El Dorado Placerville	58 843
MOUDY		
Permain*	Amador Twp 2	55 296
MOUE		
---*	Mariposa Twp 3	60 578
MOUFGOND		
Charles*	El Dorado Salmon Falls	581065
MOUGER		
Bollen	San Francisco San Francisco 4	681214
R C	Amador Twp 1	55 454
MOUGHER		
A	El Dorado Newtown	58 776
MOUGHLANTE		
John	Tuolumne Twp 1	71 255
MOUGONT		
J F	Tuolumne Twp 4	71 157
MOUGRINER		
Jacques	Tuolumne Columbia	71 363
MOUGUS		
James*	Sierra Twp 5	66 940
MOUH		
---	Calaveras Twp 10	57 286
MOUIO		
Hosa*	Nevada Bloomfield	61 512
MOUK		
---	Shasta French G	66 713
C H	Marin Point Re	60 732
MOUKEY		
Edw*	Napa Napa	61 84
MOUL		
Joseh	Calaveras Twp 4	57 340
Joseph	Calaveras Twp 4	57 340
P	El Dorado Placerville	58 833
MOULAN		
W	Yolo Cache	72 623
MOULBY		
Calib C	Butte Ophir	56 800
MOULD		
G*	Nevada Grass Valley	61 188
W	Yuba Parks Ba	72 776
MOULDER		
And J	San Francisco San Francisco 3	67 18
G W	Nevada Grass Valley	61 171
H	Nevada Grass Valley	61 153
J M*	Nevada Grass Valley	61 205
Joseph	Sacramento American	63 165
Peter*	Butte Chico	56 548
W P	Sierra Cox'S Bar	66 951
MOULERALLA		
Francisco	Calaveras Twp 4	57 333
MOULES		
Jesus*	Yuba Marysville	72 936
Jesus*	Yuba Marysville	72 937
MOULLEN		
David	Siskiyou Scott Va	69 31
MOULSON		
John	Sacramento Granite	63 234
MOULTHIOP		
John L*	San Francisco San Francisco 8	681249
MOULTIN		
David	Siskiyou Scott Va	69 31
MOULTON		
A B	Butte Bidwell	56 729
Asa	Sonoma Armally	69 510
Asa	Sonoma Armally	69 513
B T	San Francisco San Francisco 1	68 823
Bedal	Los Angeles Los Angeles	59 326
Charles	San Francisco San Francisco 4	681213
Charles S	San Francisco San Francisco 4	681213

Name	County Locale	M653 RollPage
MOULTON		
David	Siskiyou Scott Va	69 31
Elijah	Los Angeles Los Angeles	59 392
H	Los Angeles Tejon	59 525
H H	Sierra Twp 7	66 903
J	San Francisco San Francisco 5	67 528
J B	Butte Kimshaw	56 586
J H	Sierra Twp 7	66 913
James	San Francisco San Francisco 11	147 67
James B	San Francisco San Francisco 11	131 67
John	Calaveras Twp 7	57 1
John	Sacramento Ward 1	63 32
Jos	San Francisco San Francisco 9	681049
L F	Colusa Muion	57 463
Martin	San Joaquin Castoria	64 901
Peter	Tuolumne Columbia	71 340
Thos	Stanislaus Emory	70 752
Toran	Sierra La Porte	66 787
U F*	Sacramento Ward 3	63 454
Vinness	Tuolumne Twp 1	71 263
W F*	Sacramento Ward 3	63 454
W H	Sierra Twp 7	66 903
William	Nevada Bridgeport	61 447
MOULTZUN		
Alex	Sacramento Ward 1	63 101
MOUN		
---	Mariposa Twp 3	60 609
MOUNAKE		
Chas	San Francisco San Francisco 1	68 818
MOUNAS		
Dolores	Calaveras Twp 6	57 150
MOUNCE		
Absolem	Los Angeles Tejon	59 521
Absolim	Los Angeles Tejon	59 521
MOUND		
Jose M	San Francisco San Francisco 7	681397
M	El Dorado Newtown	58 778
MOUNDEN		
Amanda*	Yolo Putah	72 551
MOUNEY		
Susan	Tehama Moons	70 853
MOUNO		
J C*	Nevada Eureka	61 371
MOUNS		
J C*	Nevada Eureka	61 371
MOUNT		
A	Sacramento Granite	63 224
Charles	San Francisco San Francisco 4	681170
Emery	Napa Napa	61 77
Francis	Del Norte Crescent	58 641
Geo	Sacramento Ward 4	63 579
J Henry	San Francisco San Francisco 7	681356
John	Santa Clara Fremont	65 435
Joseph	Napa Napa	61 77
L	San Joaquin Stockton	641091
Liberty	Nevada Bridgeport	61 496
M	San Francisco San Francisco 9	681058
Sarah	Yuba Foster B	72 823
T	Napa Napa	61 60
Tilton S	Napa Napa	61 61
Wm	San Francisco San Francisco 1	68 810
MOUNTAIN		
Benectus*	Plumas Quincy	62 956
J I	El Dorado Georgetown	58 702
Jno	Butte Kimshaw	56 605
Juan	Santa Clara San Jose	65 327
MOUNTFORD		
W E	Trinity Sturdiva	701006
MOUNTFORK		
E	Trinity Sturdiva	701006
MOUNTFOY		
E*	Santa Clara Santa Clara	65 523
MOUNTON		
Isaac	San Joaquin Stockton	641069
MOUNTPEY		
E*	Santa Clara Santa Clara	65 523
MOUNTROY		
Theodore	Calaveras Twp 5	57 171
MOUNTS		
Charles*	San Francisco San Francisco 3	67 31
Cyrus	Plumas Meadow Valley	62 913
MOUNY		
Nicholas	Placer Ophirville	62 657
MOUOW		
G H*	Nevada Nevada	61 322
MOUR		
Jenson*	Sacramento Mississipi	63 188
John*	Yuba New York	72 721
MOURAE		
Louis*	Mariposa Twp 3	60 584
MOURD		
Antonio C	Calaveras Twp 7	57 5
Davis*	Mariposa Twp 3	60 584
John	Butte Ophir	56 782

Name	County Locale	M653 RollPage
MOURE		
Thomas	San Bernardino Santa Barbara	64 173
MOURELL		
W	Yolo Washington	72 561
MOURER		
William	San Francisco San Francisco 8	681235
MOURESSEY		
Lawrence	Humbolt Bucksport	59 160
MOURGAN		
Aman J*	Nevada Bloomfield	61 526
Amany*	Nevada Bloomfield	61 526
Anrany*	Nevada Bloomfield	61 526
Arnany*	Nevada Bloomfield	61 526
MOURILL		
C H*	Yolo Washington	72 566
MOURIS		
Liberty	Nevada Bridgeport	61 496
MOURN		
Jas	San Francisco San Francisco 1	68 909
MOUROY		
Carlolo*	Yuba Marysville	72 918
MOURRTIN		
M	El Dorado Placerville	58 821
MOURTON		
Casius	Santa Clara San Jose	65 320
MOUS		
Nah*	Tuolumne Big Oak	71 150
Wah*	Tuolumne Big Oak	71 150
MOUSE		
Alex	El Dorado Georgetown	58 676
Joseph	Contra Costa Twp 1	57 510
Joseph	Tuolumne Twp 4	71 140
Lenoard	San Francisco San Francisco 1	68 810
Peter	Sierra Downieville	661022
MOUSER		
S M*	Sacramento Ward 4	63 572
MOUSHORN		
John	Yolo Putah	72 585
MOUSLY		
H	Nevada Nevada	61 278
MOUSMER		
J A	El Dorado Greenwood	58 713
MOUSON		
J L*	Nevada Bridgeport	61 451
McNeill	Tuolumne Twp 1	71 484
MOUSSAND		
R	Tuolumne Twp 1	71 216
MOUSSIAN		
V	Tuolumne Columbia	71 349
MOUSTON		
A*	Santa Clara Redwood	65 452
Ole*	Sierra Twp 5	66 947
MOUTIS		
Terevia	Calaveras Twp 6	57 125
MOUTKIN		
John*	Santa Cruz Santa Cruz	66 604
MOUTON		
Dinniss	Tuolumne Twp 1	71 263
Filnean	Colusa Muion	57 463
MOUTTENS		
Samuel S	El Dorado Greenwood	58 727
MOUTTIN		
James*	Sierra Twp 7	66 865
MOUY		
---	Plumas Meadow Valley	62 910
MOUZE		
Henry	Tuolumne Columbia	71 332
MOVARKY		
Wm	San Francisco San Francisco 10	357 67
MOVATRURCH		
Antonio	Sacramento Ward 1	63 100
MOVATWICH		
Antonio	Sacramento Ward 1	63 100
MOVDAY		
Andrew	San Francisco San Francisco 4	681163
MOVEALLIS		
R	Shasta Horsetown	66 699
MOVER		
Alen*	El Dorado Georgetown	58 676
MOVERS		
---	Stanislaus Empire	70 734
MOVICH		
Joseph	Tuolumne Twp 4	71 133
MOVILE		
J B*	Sacramento Natonia	63 277
MOVLASE		
T	Nevada Grass Valley	61 148
MOVLENER		
William*	Siskiyou Klamath	69 86
MOVOREY		
H O*	Nevada Eureka	61 361
MOVULL		
G*	Nevada Grass Valley	61 160
MOW KEE		
---	Nevada Bridgeport	61 457

Name	County Locale	M653 Roll	Page
MOW KEE			
---	Tuolumne Green Springs	71	521
MOW NANG			
---	Sacramento Ward 1	63	71
MOW WAH			
---	Sacramento Ward 1	63	71
MOW			
---	Butte Hamilton	56	530
---	Butte Bidwell	56	717
---	Butte Bidwell	56	726
---	Butte Mountain	56	741
---	Butte Mountain	56	742
---	Calaveras Twp 5	57	148
---	Calaveras Twp 5	57	181
---	Calaveras Twp 5	57	203
---	Calaveras Twp 5	57	224
---	Calaveras Twp 5	57	234
---	Calaveras Twp 5	57	237
---	Calaveras Twp 5	57	248
---	Calaveras Twp 5	57	251
---	Calaveras Twp 5	57	252
---	Calaveras Twp 5	57	254
---	Calaveras Twp 5	57	257
---	Calaveras Twp 10	57	259
---	Calaveras Twp 10	57	261
---	Calaveras Twp 10	57	272
---	Calaveras Twp 10	57	273
---	Calaveras Twp 10	57	295
---	Calaveras Twp 4	57	304
---	Calaveras Twp 4	57	322
---	Calaveras Twp 4	57	334
---	Calaveras Twp 9	57	348
---	El Dorado Salmon Falls	58	1046
---	El Dorado Salmon Falls	58	1047
---	El Dorado Salmon Falls	58	1052
---	El Dorado Salmon Falls	58	1056
---	El Dorado Salmon Falls	58	1058
---	El Dorado Salmon Falls	58	1065
---	El Dorado Salmon Falls	58	1067
---	El Dorado Coloma	58	1077
---	El Dorado Coloma	58	1078
---	El Dorado Coloma	58	1084
---	El Dorado Coloma	58	1085
---	El Dorado Union	58	1089
---	El Dorado Coloma	58	1105
---	El Dorado Coloma	58	1109
---	El Dorado Coloma	58	1111
---	El Dorado Coloma	58	1114
---	El Dorado Coloma	58	1116
---	El Dorado Coloma	58	1121
---	El Dorado Kelsey	58	1135
---	El Dorado Kelsey	58	1143
---	El Dorado Indian D	58	1159
---	El Dorado Casumnes	58	1177
---	El Dorado Mountain	58	1178
---	El Dorado Diamond	58	784
---	El Dorado Diamond	58	795
---	El Dorado Diamond	58	802
---	El Dorado Diamond	58	805
---	El Dorado Placerville	58	832
---	El Dorado Placerville	58	834
---	El Dorado Placerville	58	886
---	El Dorado Placerville	58	902
---	El Dorado Placerville	58	923
---	El Dorado Eldorado	58	941
---	El Dorado Eldorado	58	944
---	El Dorado Eldorado	58	948
---	El Dorado Mud Springs	58	950
---	El Dorado Mud Springs	58	972
---	El Dorado Mud Springs	58	987
---	El Dorado Mud Springs	58	991
---	Mariposa Twp 3	60	569
---	Mariposa Twp 1	60	651
---	Mariposa Coulterville	60	700
---	Merced Twp 1	60	914
---	Nevada Nevada	61	305
---	Nevada Little Y	61	533
---	Placer Auburn	62	576
---	Placer Auburn	62	583
---	Placer Rattle Snake	62	602
---	Placer Rattle Snake	62	626
---	Placer Rattle Snake	62	637
---	Placer Folsom	62	648
---	Placer Ophirville	62	658
---	Placer Virginia	62	669
---	Placer Virginia	62	671
---	Placer Virginia	62	672
---	Placer Virginia	62	674
---	Placer Virginia	62	676
---	Placer Virginia	62	677
---	Placer Virginia	62	682
---	Placer Virginia	62	687
---	Placer Illinois	62	738
---	Placer Illinois	62	741
---	Placer Illinois	62	745
---	Placer Illinois	62	746

Name	County Locale	M653 Roll	Page
MOW			
---	Placer Illinois	62	748
---	Placer Illinois	62	749
---	Placer Illinois	62	751
---	Placer Illinois	62	753
---	Placer Illinois	62	754
---	Sacramento Mississipi	63	190
---	Sacramento Granite	63	251
---	Sacramento Cosummes	63	397
---	Sacramento Ward 1	63	60
---	Sacramento Ward 4	63	610
---	Sacramento Ward 1	63	67
---	San Francisco San Francisco 9	681	087
---	San Francisco San Francisco 9	681	088
---	San Francisco San Francisco 9	681	095
---	San Francisco San Francisco 9	681	096
---	San Francisco San Francisco 4	681	186
---	San Francisco San Francisco 4	681	192
---	San Francisco San Francisco 4	681	194
---	Shasta Shasta	66	669
---	Shasta Horsetown	66	704
---	Shasta Horsetown	66	706
---	Shasta French G	66	720
---	Sierra Downieville	661	003
---	Sierra Downieville	661	008
---	Sierra Downieville	661	025
---	Sierra Downieville	661	030
---	Sierra La Porte	66	782
---	Sierra Downieville	66	996
---	Trinity Weaverville	701	072
---	Trinity Lewiston	70	956
---	Tuolumne Chinese	71	525
---	Yolo No E Twp	72	679
---	Yuba North Ea	72	679
---	Yuba New York	72	739
---	Yuba Long Bar	72	752
---	Yuba Long Bar	72	757
---	Yuba Long Bar	72	766
---	Yuba Parks Ba	72	777
---*	Calaveras Twp 6	57	181
---*	Calaveras Twp 10	57	273
---*	Mariposa Twp 3	60	578
---*	Nevada Nevada	61	305
---*	Sacramento Cosummes	63	392
---*	San Francisco San Francisco 9	681	088
---*	Yuba Long Bar	72	749
Ah	Butte Bidwell	56	717
Ching	Butte Bidwell	56	727
Ching	Butte Mountain	56	741
Cling	Butte Cascade	56	690
Fa	San Francisco San Francisco 4	681	198
Fim	Butte Bidwell	56	725
Fok	San Francisco San Francisco 4	681	199
Frederick*	Sierra Twp 7	66	870
High	Butte Bidwell	56	717
Hom	Yuba Long Bar	72	760
Hong	Butte Bidwell	56	709
J	Sacramento Ward 1	63	81
J M B*	Nevada Bridgeport	61	473
J*	Sacramento Ward 1	63	81
Kee	Nevada Bridgeport	61	457
Kiew	Sierra Poker Flats	66	838
Ko	San Francisco San Francisco 4	681	175
Kok	San Francisco San Francisco 4	681	199
Ku	Tuolumne Twp 5	71	521
L G*	Nevada Grass Valley	61	217
Lee	San Francisco San Francisco 9	681	096
Ling	Butte Bidwell	56	707
Nang*	Sacramento Ward 1	63	71
On	San Francisco San Francisco 9	681	096
Po	San Francisco San Francisco 4	681	192
Po	San Francisco San Francisco 4	681	201
Quo	El Dorado Mud Springs	58	949
Sin	El Dorado Georgetown	58	761
Sing	Butte Bidwell	56	731
Sing	Butte Mountain	56	735
Sing*	Sacramento Ward 1	63	71
Theo	San Francisco San Francisco 4	681	177
Wah	Sacramento Ward 1	63	71
Yon	San Francisco San Francisco 9	681	096
MOWANT			
C N	Sierra Morristown	661	054
MOWATT			
Commodore	San Francisco 10		326
	San Francisco	67	
MOWBRAY			
Thomas	Plumas Quincy	62	916
William	San Francisco San Francisco 4	681	127
MOWBRIDGE			
L	Nevada Grass Valley	61	216
MOWE			
---	El Dorado Salmon Hills	581	066
---	El Dorado Coloma	581	110
---	El Dorado Coloma	581	120
Geo W*	Sacramento Ward 3	63	454
W	El Dorado Diamond	58	788

Name	County Locale	M653 Roll	Page
MOWER			
B W	Butte Bidwell	56	705
Cornelius	Alameda Brooklyn	55	143
David	Butte Cascade	56	696
George	San Francisco San Francisco 4	681	154
Sarah Jo	San Francisco San Francisco 2	67	681
MOWERS			
Henry	Alameda Brooklyn	55	143
MOWERY			
C	Sutter Bear Rvr	70	826
Lyman	Butte Ophir	56	752
Syman	Butte Ophir	56	752
MOWESE			
Dfuroro*	Nevada Bloomfield	61	519
MOWEY			
George E	Sierra Downieville	661	012
MOWHOY			
James T	Calaveras Twp 4	57	317
MOWIN			
Stephen*	San Francisco San Francisco 1	68	891
MOWLAND			
Enos	Solano Green Valley	69	241
MOWLEY			
A A	Sierra Twp 7	66	902
MOWN			
---	Calaveras Twp 10	57	297
---	Calaveras Twp 4	57	333
George	El Dorado Georgetown	58	749
MOWNAN			
J*	Yolo Putah	72	586
MOWNURD			
A*	Sierra La Porte	66	785
MOWNUREL			
A*	Sierra La Porte	66	785
MOWREE			
Danl*	Santa Clara Santa Clara	65	467
MOWREY			
H O	Nevada Eureka	61	361
Peter	San Joaquin Stockton	641	031
MOWRY			
Albert	Calaveras Twp 5	57	204
Barton	Alameda Brooklyn	55	204
C	Amador Twp 5	55	358
Cath	Alameda Oakland	55	38
Charles	San Joaquin Oneal	64	932
Davenport	San Diego Colorado	64	808
David A	Calaveras Twp 5	57	204
Jervis	Sacramento Ward 1	63	55
Mary A	San Francisco San Francisco 7	681	343
Silvester*	San Francisco San Francisco 2	67	647
MOWSER			
John	Tuolumne Twp 1	71	197
MOWSON			
Edwin R	Calaveras Twp 5	57	243
MOWTROY			
James T	Calaveras Twp 4	57	317
MOWWY			
George E*	Sierra Downieville	661	012
MOWY			
Sing	Sacramento Mississipi	63	190
MOX			
---	Sacramento Cosummes	63	398
---	San Francisco San Francisco 9	681	088
Henrietta	Yuba Marysville	72	880
Warren	San Francisco San Francisco 4	681	165
MOXEY			
James W*	Contra Costa Twp 2	57	563
MOXHAM			
C	Trinity Minersville	70	968
James*	Klamath S Fork	59	198
M M	Yolo Merritt	72	583
MOXINE			
Henry W	San Francisco San Francisco 4	681	224
MOXIR			
Jos	San Francisco San Francisco 3	67	78
MOXLEY			
Charles*	Yuba Marysville	72	910
MOXTON			
D	Shasta Millvill	66	743
MOXWELL			
J W*	Napa Clear Lake	61	134
MOXWILL			
J W*	Napa Clear Lake	61	134
MOY LEI LUNG			
---*	San Francisco San Francisco 3	67	26
MOY			
---	Amador Twp 5	55	354
---	Butte Ophir	56	771
---	Butte Ophir	56	807
---	Butte Ophir	56	810
---	Butte Ophir	56	812
---	Butte Ophir	56	816
---	Butte Ophir	56	819
---	Butte Ophir	56	820
---	Calaveras Twp 4	57	304

Name	County Locale	M653 Roll	Page
MOY			
---	Calaveras Twp 8	57	60
---	El Dorado Salmon Falls	58	1046
---	El Dorado Salmon Falls	58	1060
---	El Dorado Mud Springs	58	987
---	Mariposa Twp 1	60	673
---	Nevada Rough &	61	437
---	Placer Virginia	62	666
---	Placer Virginia	62	674
---	Plumas Quincy	62	1008
---	Sacramento Ward 1	63	54
---	San Francisco San Francisco 9	68	1092
---	San Francisco San Francisco 9	68	1094
---	San Francisco San Francisco 4	68	1151
---	San Francisco San Francisco 4	68	1173
---	San Francisco San Francisco 4	68	1175
---	San Francisco San Francisco 4	68	1178
---	San Francisco San Francisco 4	68	1179
---	San Francisco San Francisco 4	68	1180
---	San Francisco San Francisco 4	68	1190
---	San Francisco San Francisco 4	68	1192
---	San Francisco San Francisco 4	68	1193
---	San Francisco San Francisco 4	68	1194
---	San Francisco San Francisco 4	68	1195
---	San Francisco San Francisco 4	68	1198
---	San Francisco San Francisco 5	67	1207
---	San Francisco San Francisco 4	68	1208
---	San Francisco San Francisco 4	68	1211
---	Siskiyou Yreka	69	195
---	Stanislaus Branch	70	713
---	Tuolumne Twp 3	71	433
---	Tuolumne Twp 3	71	440
---	Tuolumne Twp 3	71	442
---	Tuolumne Twp 3	71	457
---	Tuolumne Twp 3	71	467
---	Tuolumne Twp 1	71	478
Ah	Yuba Suida	72	991
Chew	Butte Ophir	56	787
Chew	Butte Ophir	56	818
Chow	Butte Ophir	56	819
Chu	San Francisco San Francisco 4	68	1185
Foo	El Dorado Mud Springs	58	986
Fung	Butte Ophir	56	807
George	Yuba Slate Ro	72	695
Geroge	Yolo Slate Ra	72	695
Ha	San Francisco San Francisco 4	68	1175
Ho	San Francisco San Francisco 4	68	1175
Ho	San Francisco San Francisco 4	68	1187
Kee	San Francisco San Francisco 9	68	1093
Koru	San Francisco San Francisco 4	68	1175
Kow	San Francisco San Francisco 4	68	1175
Lee	Butte Ophir	56	820
Lin	Butte Ophir	56	816
Long	San Francisco San Francisco 6	67	468
We	San Francisco San Francisco 9	68	1092
MOYA			
---	El Dorado Diamond	58	787
Ramon	Los Angeles Los Angeles	59	360
Trinidad	Los Angeles Los Angeles	59	359
MOYAN			
Elizabeth*	San Francisco 2	67	737
	San Francisco		
MOYASHAN			
Andrew	Sierra Twp 7	66	894
MOYAUNUN			
Jamis	Calaveras Twp 6	57	126
MOYBROCKER			
J*	Yolo Cottonwood	72	652
MOYCE			
---	Mariposa Coulterville	60	698
MOYE			
---	Amador Twp 6	55	433
---	Amador Twp 1	55	458
---	Sacramento Cosumnes	63	387
MOYEL			
George A	Sierra Pine Grove	66	835
George H	Sierra Pine Grove	66	835
MOYER			
A	Trinity Weaverville	70	1080
Bicenti	Calaveras Twp 5	57	204
Carminie	Calaveras Twp 6	57	128
John	San Francisco San Francisco 11	67	89
			67
John	Sierra Twp 7	66	875
Susan	Calaveras Twp 6	57	165
Thos C	Napa Napa	61	107
MOYERS			
Henry	Tulara Twp 1	71	3
J	Nevada Eureka	61	346
Jacob	Shasta French G	66	722
MOYES			
B F	Mariposa Twp 3	60	596
Bicenti	Calaveras Twp 5	57	204
J M	Butte Cascade	56	701
Juan	Mariposa Twp 3	60	570
R B	Nevada Eureka	61	392

Name	County Locale	M653 Roll	Page
MOYES			
T	Calaveras Twp 9	57	396
Wm	Alameda Brooklyn	55	113
MOYHEW			
James	Calaveras Twp 5	57	206
MOYISES			
E W	Calaveras Twp 9	57	407
MOYLAN			
Mary*	Sacramento Ward 1	63	144
Timothy	Sacramento Ward 4	63	506
MOYLAW			
Mary*	Sacramento Ward 1	63	144
MOYLE			
C J	Tuolumne Shawsfla	71	400
James W	Sierra Pine Grove	66	832
Jamse W	Sierra Pine Grove	66	832
Matthew	Tuolumne Twp 1	71	251
MOYLEN			
Marhl*	Butte Kimshaw	56	597
MOYLUN			
Peter	Calaveras Twp 4	57	345
MOYLURR			
Peter*	Calaveras Twp 4	57	345
MOYNICE			
Phillip	Sierra Twp 7	66	916
MOYNS			
N	Yolo Cache Crk	72	642
MOYODOE			
Jose	Fresno Twp 1	59	83
MOYOMUKS			
---	Tulara Twp 1	71	117
MOYOMULE			
---	Mendocino Big Rvr	60	854
MOYOS			
Dolones	Los Angeles Los Angeles	59	300
MOYOSE			
Manuel	Calaveras Twp 5	57	216
MOYRE			
Manuel	Calaveras Twp 5	57	216
MOYS			
George	Mariposa Twp 1	60	668
MOYSE			
John	Sierra Twp 7	66	875
MOYSER			
Manuel*	Calaveras Twp 5	57	216
Peter	Calaveras Twp 5	57	197
MOYUIN			
Eugene	Calaveras Twp 4	57	317
MOYUR			
Leon*	Calaveras Twp 6	57	157
MOYWINIS			
Michael*	Calaveras Twp 4	57	299
MOZANTE			
Joseph	Calaveras Twp 4	57	333
MOZEL			
J	El Dorado Diamond	58	804
MOZES			
Juan*	Mariposa Twp 3	60	570
MOZGRAP			
J	San Francisco San Francisco 1	68	810
MOZGRASS			
J	San Francisco San Francisco 1	68	810
MOZICE			
A	El Dorado Diamond	58	798
MOZIER			
John	Placer Michigan	62	855
Thomas M	Plumas Quincy	62	924
MOZL			
Jose*	Santa Clara Fremont	65	435
Pedro*	Santa Clara Fremont	65	435
MOZO			
Iraquinn	San Bernardino San Bernadino	64	665
Isidro	San Bernardino San Salvador	64	659
Jose J	San Bernardino San Salvador	64	659
Jose J	San Bernardino San Salvador	64	660
MOZRA			
Browly	Solano Montezuma	69	370
MPA			
Manly	Tuolumne Sonora	71	244
MRADDOCK			
Elira J	Nevada Bridgeport	61	486
MRETROVICH			
Peter*	San Francisco San Francisco 3	67	51
MRGAN			
E D	Sierra Downieville	66	1023
MRIANDES			
Manuel*	Contra Costa Twp 1	57	514
MRICHEN			
Emile*	Calaveras Twp 4	57	319
MRICHIN			
Emile*	Calaveras Twp 4	57	319
MRIDELL			
Frank A*	Calaveras Twp 6	57	168
MRITQUINB			
Ma*	San Francisco San Francisco 4	68	1224
MROLLERY			
Joseph*	Sierra Excelsior	66	1034

Name	County Locale	M653 Roll	Page
MROT			
Alexr*	Sierra Downieville	66	967
MROWN			
F T	Tuolumne Twp 1	71	207
MRRILL			
Saml*	Tuolumne Twp 1	71	266
MRUDOCK			
Horace	Calaveras Twp 10	57	290
MRYERS			
Henry	El Dorado Coloma	58	1068
J*	Nevada Eureka	61	346
MSITH			
Thomas	Tuolumne Twp 5	71	503
MU TULIEF			
---	Mendocino Calpella	60	822
MU			
---	Calaveras Twp 5	57	192
---	Calaveras Twp 5	57	193
---	Calaveras Twp 5	57	224
---	Calaveras Twp 5	57	244
---	Calaveras Twp 5	57	258
---	Calaveras Twp 10	57	259
---	Calaveras Twp 10	57	268
---	Calaveras Twp 10	57	269
---	Sacramento Ward 1	63	54
---	Sacramento Ward 1	63	59
---*	Nevada Rough &	61	432
A	Sacramento Natonia	63	286
Gu	Calaveras Twp 10	57	269
Hu	San Francisco San Francisco 4	68	1201
John*	San Francisco San Francisco 7	68	1393
Kunk	San Francisco San Francisco 4	68	1189
Lan	Yuba Rose Bar	72	800
Lee	Sacramento Granite	63	243
Ling	Tuolumne Twp 6	71	537
Moy	San Francisco San Francisco 4	68	1211
Thoy	San Francisco San Francisco 4	68	1211
Top	Calaveras Twp 5	57	255
Tuck	Calaveras Twp 5	57	192
Yu	Sacramento Granite	63	269
MUA			
---	Sierra Twp 5	66	933
MUASON			
Horatio	San Joaquin Castoria	64	885
MUC CHAW			
---*	Tulara Visalia	71	4
MUC			
---	Tulara Twp 2	71	33
---	Tulara Twp 2	71	37
---*	Tulara Visalia	71	33
---	Tulara Visalia	71	37
Chaw*	Tulara Visalia	71	4
MUCALY			
John*	Sierra La Porte	66	766
MUCCE			
Robert W*	Yuba Marysville	72	882
MUCH			
James*	Santa Cruz Santa Cruz	66	598
John*	San Francisco San Francisco 1	68	920
MUCHAN			
---*	Tulara Visalia	71	34
---*	Tulara Visalia	71	37
MUCHANE			
Hannah*	San Francisco San Francisco 9	68	1014
MUCHANELI			
Phillip	Calaveras Twp 5	57	225
MUCHAU			
---	Tulara Twp 2	71	34
---	Tulara Twp 2	71	37
MUCHAVILLI			
Phillip	Calaveras Twp 5	57	225
MUCHCHAW			
---	Tulara Twp 2	71	40
MUCHCHOWM			
---	Tulara Twp 2	71	36
MUCHCHOWME			
---*	Tulara Visalia	71	36
MUCHELL			
B	Butte Hamilton	56	513
MUCHET			
Joseph	San Francisco San Francisco 2	67	712
MUCHIN			
Emile*	Calaveras Twp 4	57	319
MUCHINGHUE			
D	Mariposa Twp 3	60	622
MUCHN			
Alex*	Yolo Cache	72	608
MUCHO			
---	Tulara Twp 2	71	39
---	Tulara Keyesville	71	64
---*	Tulara Visalia	71	39
MUCHOMUCK			
---	Tulara Twp 3	71	70
MUCHOW			
---	Tulara Twp 2	71	33
---	Tulara Twp 2	71	35

California 1860 Census Index

Name	County Locale	M653 Roll	Page
MUCHOW			
---*	Tulara Visalia	71	33
MUCIANA			
Salvador	Alameda Brooklyn	55	157
MUCK MUCK			
---	Fresno Twp 1	59	55
---	Fresno Twp 2	59	64
MUCK			
---	Amador Twp 2	55	292
---	Sacramento Ward 1	63	51
---	Sacramento Ward 1	63	55
George	Yuba Bear Rvr	72	1010
Slowe	Sierra Eureka	66	1047
MUCKAMUCK			
---	Fresno Twp 2	59	111
MUCKCHOW			
---	Tulara Twp 2	71	35
---*	Tulara Visalia	71	38
MUCKLEY			
Michael	Placer Secret R	62	619
MUCKOMUCK			
---	Tulara Keyesville	71	70
MUCKOW			
---*	Tulara Visalia	71	35
MUCULINO			
---	Los Angeles Los Angeles	59	495
MUD			
Anthony	Placer Yankee J	62	777
Ellen	El Dorado Salmon Hills	58	1056
MUDBY			
M	El Dorado Greenwood	58	721
MUDEHO			
Pachas	Fresno Twp 1	59	76
MUDEN			
John Ed*	Calaveras Twp 4	57	323
John Ev*	Calaveras Twp 4	57	323
Thomas B*	Sierra Pine Grove	66	830
MUDEY			
Wm	Alameda Brooklyn	55	163
MUDGE			
F	Sacramento Ward 4	63	557
MUDGET			
Almira	Fresno Twp 1	59	33
Elvin	Fresno Twp 1	59	33
Nelson	San Bernardino San Bernadino	64	674
MUDGETT			
H	Sacramento Brighton	63	200
John	Napa Napa	61	95
MUDGITT			
John*	Napa Napa	61	95
MUDGLIN			
Eliza	San Joaquin Castoria	64	882
MUDIA			
John	Calaveras Twp 5	57	207
MUDIAR			
D*	Calaveras Twp 9	57	392
MUDID			
John*	Calaveras Twp 5	57	207
MUDIE			
Robert	Tuolumne Twp 5	71	505
MUDLEN			
Wilson*	San Joaquin Elkhorn	64	997
MUDLEY			
F	El Dorado Placerville	58	873
J	El Dorado Mud Springs	58	983
MUDLIN			
Wilson*	San Joaquin Elkhorn	64	997
MUDLISWORTH			
J	Calaveras Twp 9	57	408
MUDLLIN			
James*	El Dorado Georgetown	58	755
MUDOR			
Manuel*	Alameda Brooklyn	55	139
MUDRERES			
Lyman	Yuba New York	72	738
MUDRONA			
Jas	Placer Virginia	62	677
MUDYER			
William T	Calaveras Twp 6	57	152
MUE			
Aj Kim	El Dorado Big Bar	58	733
Sing	Calaveras Twp 5	57	255
MUEDITH			
Wm	Nevada Eureka	61	370
MUEL			
---	Fresno Twp 2	59	62
MUELEN			
Thomas B*	Sierra Pine Grove	66	830
MUELLER			
Charles	Los Angeles Los Angeles	59	374
MUELLY			
Michael*	Calaveras Twp 5	57	242
MUEN			
---	Tuolumne Twp 5	71	524
MUENER			
Toachmen*	Butte Mountain	56	741

Name	County Locale	M653 Roll	Page
MUER			
Frank	Sacramento Ward 3	63	465
MUERTAS			
Rafael	Los Angeles Los Angeles	59	401
MUEY			
---	Del Norte Crescent	58	651
MUFAN			
Albert	El Dorado Georgetown	58	755
MUFCAL			
C*	Nevada Grass Valley	61	157
MUFFATT			
James H	Mendocino Calpella	60	829
MUFFEN			
A	Mariposa Twp 3	60	567
MUFFIN			
Ellen	Yolo Cache Crk	72	593
Francis	Sacramento Ward 4	63	510
MUFFLER			
Fred	Yuba Rose Bar	72	814
MUFFLEY			
W N	El Dorado Diamond	58	763
MUFHONN			
Shap	Calaveras Twp 9	57	380
MUFHONR			
Thos*	Calaveras Twp 9	57	380
MUFHORN			
Thos*	Calaveras Twp 9	57	380
MUFLER			
Fred	Alameda Brooklyn	55	103
MUG			
---	Placer Rattle Snake	62	637
---*	Sacramento Ward 1	63	59
Wan	Yuba Marysville	72	895
MUGAN			
---*	San Francisco San Francisco 3	67	54
Cath	Sacramento Ward 1	63	133
John*	San Francisco San Francisco 5	67	545
Mary*	Sacramento Ward 1	63	121
Thomas R	San Francisco San Francisco 4	68	1219
MUGARA			
Manuella	Tuolumne Twp 1	71	221
Manvilla	Tuolumne Sonora	71	221
MUGEE			
John*	Yuba Rose Bar	72	818
MUGENT			
A*	Nevada Grass Valley	61	196
MUGERN			
Mary	Sacramento Ward 1	63	121
MUGGETT			
W B	Sutter Butte	70	791
MUGGINS			
---	Tulara Keyesville	71	55
Madame	Tehama Lassen	70	865
MUGGRIDGE			
Benj	Solano Vallejo	69	253
Thos S	San Francisco San Francisco 3	67	25
MUGGS			
J*	Nevada Grass Valley	61	149
MUGHAN			
P J*	El Dorado Diamond	58	771
Patrick	Sierra Morristown	66	1053
MUGINS			
---	Tulara Twp 3	71	55
MUGLE			
G A*	Butte Mountain	56	739
MUGLER			
C	Merced Twp 2	60	919
Charley	Mariposa Twp 3	60	573
MUGLES			
Charley*	Mariposa Twp 3	60	573
MUH			
---	Calaveras Twp 4	57	301
Nicholas	San Francisco San Francisco 2	67	788
MUHAN			
M*	Solano Suisan	69	204
William	Yuba Marysville	72	961
MUHANY			
Mary*	San Francisco San Francisco 4	68	1120
MUHARD			
Antin	Sacramento Natonia	63	273
MUHEL			
S*	Sacramento Granite	63	265
MUHEN			
Edward	San Francisco San Francisco 2	67	706
MUHLANBRINK			
Wm	San Francisco San Francisco 2	67	590
MUHLE			
Tefti	San Francisco San Francisco 3	67	78
Tofe*	San Francisco San Francisco 3	67	78
Toft*	San Francisco San Francisco 3	67	78
MUHN			
Anna	San Francisco San Francisco 8	68	1299
MUHO			
Deis	Alameda Brooklyn	55	160
MUHU			
Anna*	San Francisco San Francisco 8	68	1299

Name	County Locale	M653 Roll	Page
MUICFEE			
C*	El Dorado Placerville	58	852
MUIER			
A*	Sacramento Granite	63	250
W	Tuolumne Twp 4	71	163
MUILER			
John Ed*	Calaveras Twp 4	57	323
MUILIPO			
B*	Tehama Red Bluff	70	932
MUINIEN			
James*	Calaveras Twp 4	57	313
MUINS			
G	Sutter Butte	70	795
MUIOR			
Ernst*	San Francisco San Francisco 1	68	825
MUIR			
Adam	Sierra Twp 5	66	939
Andrew	Sacramento Ward 1	63	116
Bartly*	Alameda Oakland	55	48
Bartty*	Alameda Oakland	55	48
James	El Dorado Georgetown	58	690
John	San Francisco San Francisco 11	67	90
Jos*	Sacramento Ward 1	63	61
Presley	Napa Napa	61	74
W	Tuolumne Don Pedro	71	163
MUIRE			
James	Sierra St Louis	66	817
MUIRHEID			
Wm	Sacramento Ward 3	63	427
MUIS			
James	El Dorado Georgetown	58	690
MUISON			
Eugene	San Francisco San Francisco 2	67	615
MUITY			
A*	Yuba Foster B	72	833
MUJARAH			
M	Tuolumne Twp 2	71	293
MUJINE			
Sam	El Dorado Georgetown	58	706
MUJS			
James	Santa Clara San Jose	65	292
MUK			
---	El Dorado Georgetown	58	761
---	San Francisco San Francisco 4	68	1182
---	San Francisco San Francisco 4	68	1209
---	San Francisco San Francisco 5	67	510
E G	Nevada Nevada	61	257
Mrs C	Butte Ophir	56	790
MUKAKA			
---	Fresno Twp 2	59	101
MUKAMUK			
---	Fresno Twp 2	59	47
MUKE			
Peter	Tuolumne Twp 3	71	427
MUKER			
D E*	Butte Kimshaw	56	605
Geo	Nevada Nevada	61	264
Mary	San Francisco San Francisco 1	68	932
Melvin	Tuolumne Twp 3	71	462
O*	Nevada Washington	61	334
Thomas*	Sierra Pine Grove	66	834
MUKKEIK			
---	Fresno Twp 3	59	97
MUKLER			
John	Colusa Muion	57	462
MUKLLIM			
John F*	Placer Virginia	62	677
MUKS			
John*	Yuba New York	72	734
MUKUTEKS			
---	Tulara Twp 1	71	119
MUL			
Sony	Calaveras Twp 5	57	255
MULA FA			
---	Mendocino Calpella	60	823
MULACHA			
---	Butte Chico	56	550
MULADDY			
John	Butte Chico	56	567
MULAGAN			
James	Siskiyou Scott Ri	69	82
MULAHA			
Mathew	Contra Costa Twp 1	57	492
MULAN			
James	Sonoma Santa Rosa	69	398
MULAND			
O*	Nevada Eureka	61	391
P	Nevada Eureka	61	391
MULANEY			
Patrick	Solano Benecia	69	296
MULARKEY			
John	Tehama Antelope	70	893
MULATTO			
John	San Francisco San Francisco 5	67	477
MULAY			
Chaes*	El Dorado Georgetown	58	706

Name	County Locale	M653 Roll/Page
MULAY		
Chals*	El Dorado Georgetown	58 706
MULBALL		
Thomas	Yuba Linda	72 986
MULBAUGH		
John	Placer Yankee J	62 756
MULBIN		
J	Calaveras Twp 9	57 408
MULBURY		
Joseph B L	Alameda Brooklyn	55 93
MULCAGLY		
Patrick*	Contra Costa Twp 3	57 592
MULCAHAY		
J	Nevada Nevada	61 249
Jno	Nevada Nevada	61 249
MULCAHEY		
Thos	San Francisco San Francisco 1	68 894
MULCAHY		
Ed	Sacramento Natonia	63 280
Ellen	San Francisco San Francisco 5	67 491
J	San Francisco San Francisco 5	67 537
Jas	Mariposa Twp 1	60 663
Jus	Mariposa Twp 1	60 663
Morris	Sacramento Natonia	63 281
MULCATZ		
W	Shasta Millvill	66 752
MULCAY		
Lott	San Francisco San Francisco 9	68 947
William	San Francisco San Francisco 9	68 946
MULCAYLY		
Patrick*	Contra Costa Twp 3	57 592
MULCHAY		
Cornelius	Nevada Bridgeport	61 456
I	Nevada Nevada	61 318
J	Nevada Nevada	61 318
Mary	Solano Benecia	69 310
P	Nevada Nevada	61 315
MULCHINS		
Cornelius*	Nevada Bridgeport	61 456
MULCHY		
Michael	Yuba Marysville	72 935
MULCREEVY		
Martin	San Francisco San Francisco 10	174 67
MULDETES		
---	Tulara Twp 3	71 66
MULDOM		
James	Solano Suisan	69 222
MULDON		
Pat R	Placer Rattle Snake	62 625
MULDOON		
Barney	Amador Twp 1	55 465
D	Shasta Shasta	66 687
John	Tuolumne Big Oak	71 139
John	Tuolumne Twp 1	71 484
P	Amador Twp 1	55 509
Wm	Sacramento Ward 1	63 26
MULDREN		
Jas	Sacramento Sutter	63 290
MULDROM		
Wm	Sacramento Sutter	63 292
MULDRON		
John P	Yuba Marysville	72 956
Peter	Tuolumne Columbia	71 308
Wm	Sacramento Sutter	63 292
Wm*	Sacramento Ward 1	63 26
MULDROON		
James	Solano Suisan	69 222
MULDROW		
Wm Col	Marin Tomales	60 776
Wm*	Sacramento Ward 1	63 26
MULE		
---	Mendocino Twp 1	60 892
S J	El Dorado Georgetown	58 676
MULEE		
Wm	Amador Twp 1	55 494
MULEGAN		
A	Nevada Grass Valley	61 167
Peter	Sierra Downieville	66 994
MULEHY		
Mathew	Contra Costa Twp 1	57 492
Michael	Alameda Brooklyn	55 90
MULEN		
Alixcander*	Tuolumne Twp 3	71 459
John	Tulara Twp 3	71 44
MULENS		
A	El Dorado Placerville	58 900
MULER		
Abram*	Calaveras Twp 6	57 124
William	Placer Forest H	62 772
MULET		
Abram*	Calaveras Twp 6	57 124
Emile	Sacramento Ward 4	63 553
MULEY		
Amile	Sacramento Ward 1	63 8
MULFERD		
John*	Placer Michigan	62 853
MULFORD		
J	Nevada Grass Valley	61 157
Jacob M D	Solano Suisan	69 204
L Burnett	Yuba Rose Bar	72 803
P H	Sacramento Franklin	63 332
Prentice	Tuolumne Twp 3	71 425
Samuel B	Yuba Marysville	72 876
T W	Alameda Brooklyn	55 126
MULGREW		
Felix	Sonoma Healdsbu	69 474
Susannah	Sonoma Healdsbu	69 474
MULGROVE		
Elicia	San Francisco San Francisco 9	68 990
MULGUEENY		
James	Sierra Whiskey	66 849
MULHA		
Jose Mario	Yuba Rose Bar	72 810
Yose Mario	Yuba Rose Bar	72 810
MULHADEN		
Hannah	San Francisco San Francisco 10	316 67
MULHADER		
Hannah*	San Francisco San Francisco 10	316 67
MULHALL		
John*	San Francisco San Francisco 3	67 46
P	Tuolumne Sonora	71 244
Patrick	Tuolumne Twp 1	71 259
MULHALLANT		
Hugh	Placer Secret R	62 613
MULHALLARD		
R	San Joaquin Stockton	641094
MULHAM		
Alexander	Sierra Downieville	661031
MULHAN		
John	San Francisco San Francisco 2	67 742
Mary	Yuba Rose Bar	72 810
MULHARE		
James	Marin Cortemad	60 788
Jas	San Francisco San Francisco 6	67 434
Jos	San Francisco San Francisco 6	67 434
Joseph	San Diego Colorado	64 808
Mary*	Yuba Rose Bar	72 810
MULHARKY		
Michael	Alameda Oakland	55 73
MULHE		
W	San Francisco San Francisco 3	67 78
MULHERREN		
Pat*	San Francisco San Francisco 9	68 986
MULHERRIN		
Pat	San Francisco San Francisco 9	68 986
MULHIE		
Martin	Alameda Brooklyn	55 103
Mathew	Alameda Brooklyn	55 103
MULHOAN		
D B	Mendocino Big Rvr	60 847
MULHOLDEN		
W	Yolo Washington	72 563
MULHOLDIN		
W	Yolo Washington	72 563
MULHOLLAM		
R S	Sierra Grizzly	661058
MULHOLLAN		
Jas	San Francisco San Francisco 2	67 721
MULHOLLAND		
Frank J*	Yuba Marysville	72 906
Henry	Sierra Twp 7	66 908
James	San Diego San Diego	64 766
James	San Francisco San Francisco 11	90 67
P	San Francisco San Francisco 5	67 476
MULHOLY		
Francis	San Francisco San Francisco 3	67 75
MULIAN		
D	Calaveras Twp 9	57 392
MULICH		
W W	Yolo Putah	72 552
MULICK		
M W	Yolo Putah	72 552
MULIDA		
Bridget	Alameda Oakland	55 42
MULIGAN		
Peter	Sierra Downieville	66 994
Thomas	Nevada Bridgeport	61 499
Wm	Sierra Downieville	66 994
MULKAHA		
C	Tuolumne Twp 2	71 271
MULKAHAY		
C	Tuolumne Twp 1	71 271
MULKEEN		
Margt	San Francisco San Francisco 2	67 673
MULKINS		
Andrew	San Diego Agua Caliente	64 814
Jane	San Diego Agua Caliente	64 855
MULL		
A	Sacramento Lee	63 215
MULL		
Emerson E*	Yuba Marysville	72 891
Geo	El Dorado Cold Spring	581100
Geo	El Dorado Placerville	58 897
M J	San Francisco San Francisco 7	681402
William	San Francisco San Francisco 8	681316
Wm A	Tuolumne Twp 2	71 324
MULLA		
Jacob	San Francisco San Francisco 2	67 756
MULLAN		
Edward	Plumas Meadow Valley	62 904
Elizabeth	Yuba Rose Bar	72 819
Patrick	Plumas Quincy	62 961
MULLAND		
Mathew	San Francisco San Francisco 4	681166
MULLANEY		
Patrick	Solano Benecia	69 296
MULLAR		
Emele	Tuolumne Twp 2	71 287
MULLARD		
James	Fresno Twp 1	59 82
Jas	Los Angeles Tejon	59 539
MULLARKY		
James	Trinity Price'S	701019
MULLAY		
C H	Nevada Nevada	61 272
J*	Nevada Eureka	61 390
R*	Nevada Grass Valley	61 223
MULLBUT		
H C	Yolo Cache	72 639
MULLE		
Mary M	El Dorado Georgetown	58 699
MULLEGAN		
S*	Nevada Grass Valley	61 161
MULLEN		
A	Mariposa Twp 3	60 567
A	Nevada Grass Valley	61 224
Adrew	San Francisco San Francisco 9	681057
Allen	Nevada Bloomfield	61 528
Andrew	San Francisco San Francisco 9	68 947
Andrew	Solano Vallejo	69 251
Barchay	Placer Auburn	62 561
C	Tuolumne Sonora	71 220
C J	Nevada Nevada	61 315
Catharine	San Francisco San Francisco 8	681239
Charles	Yuba Marysville	72 934
Chas W	Butte Oregon	56 616
D	El Dorado Diamond	58 801
Daniel	Placer Forest H	62 801
Daniel S	Yuba Bear Rvr	721008
Danl	San Francisco San Francisco 10	241 67
David S*	Yuba Marysville	72 931
David T	Yuba Bear Rvr	721000
E F*	Butte Oregon	56 624
E P	Butte Oregon	56 624
E T	Butte Oregon	56 624
E*	Nevada Nevada	61 261
Edmond	Placer Illinois	62 739
Edward	Placer Auburn	62 580
Enoch	Yuba Bear Rvr	72 996
Frank	Placer Michigan	62 831
Helena*	San Francisco San Francisco 1	68 823
Hugh	Butte Bidwell	56 710
J	Nevada Grass Valley	61 224
James	Mariposa Twp 3	60 616
James	San Francisco San Francisco 10	296 67
James*	Napa Hot Springs	61 5
Jas	Sacramento Granite	63 246
Jas	San Francisco San Francisco 1	68 840
Jerome	Yuba Marysville	72 850
Jno	Amador Twp 2	55 282
John	Calaveras Twp 7	57 14
John	Sacramento Ward 1	63 123
John	Sacramento Ward 1	63 37
John	Sacramento Ward 4	63 541
John	San Joaquin Elliott	64 942
John	Santa Clara Fremont	65 430
John	Sierra Port Win	66 791
John	Tuolumne Sonora	71 237
John	Yuba Rose Bar	72 808
John	Yuba Bear Rvr	72 997
Joseph	El Dorado Kelsey	581130
Joseph	Yuba Bear Rvr	72 999
K	Nevada Washington	61 335
Kate	San Joaquin Castoria	64 904
L	Nevada Nevada	61 276
L	Shasta Millvill	66 725
M	Nevada Grass Valley	61 170
M E	San Francisco San Francisco 10	269 67
M*	El Dorado Georgetown	58 699
Martin	El Dorado Georgetown	58 706
Mary	San Francisco San Francisco 2	67 569
Mary	Tuolumne Twp 2	71 277

Name	County Locale	M653 RollPage
MULLEN		
Mary*	San Francisco San Francisco 2	67 569
Mathew	Butte Hamilton	56 518
Nathaniel	Sierra Whiskey	66 847
Neil	Sierra La Porte	66 766
P	Nevada Eureka	61 350
P	Yolo Putah	72 554
Patrick	Calaveras Twp 10	57 274
Patrick	Solano Benecia	69 316
Patrick	Tuolumne Shawsfla	71 397
Peter	Amador Twp 2	55 316
Peter	Mariposa Twp 3	60 557
Peter	Mariposa Twp 3	60 621
Peter	Placer Secret R	62 612
Peter	Placer Secret R	62 614
Peter	Placer Virginia	62 688
Peter	Plumas Quincy	62 990
Retsick	Calaveras Twp 10	57 290
Rob	Tuolumne Twp 2	71 277
Robt	Tuolumne Twp 1	71 277
S	Mariposa Twp 3	60 568
Samuel	Sierra La Porte	66 774
T*	Nevada Grass Valley	61 178
Thomas	San Francisco San Francisco 5	67 494
Thomas	Tuolumne Twp 1	71 246
Thomas	Tuolumne Twp 1	71 272
Thomas	Tuolumne Columbia	71 363
Thomas	Yuba Rose Bar	72 801
Thomas B	Sierra Pine Grove	66 830
Thos	Mariposa Twp 3	60 606
Thos	San Mateo Twp 1	65 69
W	Shasta Shasta	66 682
W	Shasta Shasta	66 758
William	Marin San Rafael	60 771
Wm	El Dorado Georgetown	58 706
Wm H	Butte Bidwell	56 731
Wm J	Del Norte Crescent	58 621
Wm P	Solano Vallejo	69 264
MULLENN		
Alice*	San Francisco San Francisco 4	681119
MULLER		
A*	Nevada Washington	61 334
Dewight*	El Dorado Georgetown	58 754
E	Nevada Nevada	61 261
E T	San Francisco San Francisco 1	68 916
E*	Nevada Nevada	61 261
Fred	Alameda Brooklyn	55 103
Fred	Sonoma Petaluma	69 563
Fredrick	Plumas Quincy	62 986
Fritz	Alameda Murray	55 221
George	Alameda Brooklyn	55 144
George	Alameda Brooklyn	55 181
H	Amador Twp 1	55 452
H J	Butte Oregon	56 615
Henry	Yuba Bear Rvr	72 997
Henry R	Alameda Brooklyn	55 162
Hurlbart*	Mendocino Big Rvr	60 852
Hurlhart*	Mendocino Big Rvr	60 852
J	El Dorado Placerville	58 879
James	Mariposa Twp 3	60 616
James F	Monterey San Juan	60 984
Jas	Sacramento Brighton	63 191
Jas	San Francisco San Francisco 9	681072
Jeremiah	San Francisco San Francisco 2	67 646
John	Sacramento Ward 1	63 148
Jos	San Francisco San Francisco 9	681072
Louis	Los Angeles Los Angeles	59 353
M	El Dorado Placerville	58 873
Mary*	San Francisco San Francisco 2	67 569
Michael	San Mateo Twp 1	65 48
O*	Nevada Washington	61 334
Patrick	San Francisco San Francisco 11	107
		67
Peter	San Francisco San Francisco 9	681089
Robert	El Dorado Georgetown	58 691
Rodolph	San Francisco San Francisco 6	67 431
T*	Nevada Grass Valley	61 178
Thomas	Calaveras Twp 6	57 148
Thomas*	Monterey San Juan	601003
Timothy	Nevada Bridgeport	61 442
W	Sacramento Ward 4	63 525
William	San Francisco San Francisco 4	681152
William*	Alameda Brooklyn	55 142
Wm	Sacramento Ward 4	63 526
Wm	San Francisco San Francisco 2	67 711
MULLERE		
John	Tulara Sinks Te	71 44
MULLERIN		
Alice*	San Francisco San Francisco 4	681119
MULLERON		
Alice*	San Francisco San Francisco 4	681119
MULLERS		
Thomas	Tuolumne Twp 2	71 272
MULLET		
James	Sacramento Centre	63 174
MULLEY		
Annie	Alameda Oakland	55 39

Name	County Locale	M653 RollPage
MULLEY		
J S*	Nevada Grass Valley	61 223
MULLFORD		
D	San Francisco San Francisco 6	67 448
MULLHAREN		
Henry	Sacramento Ward 4	63 554
MULLICAN		
R F	Mendocino Big Rvr	60 847
MULLIDAY		
Michael	Butte Kimshaw	56 592
MULLIGAN		
A	Nevada Eureka	61 391
Angela	San Francisco San Francisco 2	67 661
B	Sacramento Sutter	63 293
Barney	Tuolumne Twp 2	71 308
Bridget	San Francisco San Francisco 10	201
		67
C	Nevada Nevada	61 246
Cath	Sacramento Ward 3	63 439
G	Los Angeles Tejon	59 537
J	El Dorado Greenwood	58 723
J*	Yolo Cache	72 596
James	Sierra Twp 7	66 912
John	Butte Ophir	56 768
M	Tuolumne Big Oak	71 156
Mary	San Francisco San Francisco 7	681335
Mary	Sonoma Vallejo	69 627
Michael	Sierra Port Win	66 796
Mike	Trinity Weaverville	701064
Owen	Tuolumne Twp 2	71 295
P	Nevada Grass Valley	61 167
P	Nevada Nevada	61 246
Partick	Calaveras Twp 5	57 195
Patrick	Calaveras Twp 5	57 195
R A	San Francisco San Francisco 10	220
		67
S	Nevada Grass Valley	61 161
S	Sonoma Armally	69 503
S*	Nevada Grass Valley	61 161
T	Yolo Cache Crk	72 596
Thomas	San Diego Temecula	64 792
Thomas	San Joaquin Castoria	64 905
Thomas	Sierra Twp 7	66 868
Thos	Nevada Eureka	61 374
Thos	San Francisco San Francisco 1	68 835
W L N	Sierra Downieville	66 957
William	Calaveras Twp 5	57 196
MULLIGUN		
Patrick	Calaveras Twp 5	57 195
MULLIN		
A J	Shasta Horsetown	66 706
Barney	Tuolumne Columbia	71 333
Benj	San Francisco San Francisco 6	67 456
C	Nevada Nevada	61 297
Charles	Yuba Marysville	72 950
Dewight*	El Dorado Georgetown	58 754
Helena*	San Francisco San Francisco 1	68 823
J	Calaveras Twp 5	57 408
J H	Sierra Morristown	661053
James	Santa Cruz Pescadero	66 644
James	Sierra Morristown	661053
John	Plumas Quincy	62 992
John	Sacramento Ward 1	63 37
John	San Mateo Twp 3	65 109
John	Shasta French G	66 722
Mike	Amador Twp 2	55 293
P	Yolo Putah	72 554
Patrick	Plumas Quincy	621002
Patrick	Tuolumne Columbia	71 333
Robert	Tuolumne Columbia	71 333
T	Sutter Vernon	70 845
Thos	Trinity Bates	70 967
W H	Butte Oregon	56 616
MULLINEAUR		
John*	Del Norte Happy Ca	58 669
MULLINEAUS		
John*	Del Norte Happy Ca	58 669
MULLINEAUX		
John*	Del Norte Happy Ca	58 669
MULLING		
George W	Yuba Rose Bar	72 792
MULLINGTON		
Charles	Alameda Oakland	55 41
J E	El Dorado Greenwood	58 715
MULLINS		
A W	Tuolumne Twp 4	71 128
B F	Sierra Downieville	66 987
Geo	Butte Oro	56 682
James	Los Angeles Tejon	59 523
James*	Placer Iona Hills	62 860
Jams*	Placer Iona Hills	62 860
Jerry	Yuba Suida	72 984
John	Napa Yount	61 52
Lawrence	Plumas Quincy	621001
Mary	San Francisco San Francisco 9	681011
MULLION		
J M	El Dorado Georgetown	58 699

Name	County Locale	M653 RollPage
MULLIS		
James	Marin Cortemad	60 785
John W	Sonoma Russian	69 433
MULLIUN		
Alice*	San Francisco San Francisco 4	681119
MULLMAN		
Fredk	San Francisco San Francisco 9	68 970
MULLOB		
Lewis*	San Francisco San Francisco 2	67 796
MULLOCK		
William	Los Angeles Los Angeles	59 405
MULLON		
Jane F	Humbolt Table Bl	59 140
John	El Dorado Grizzly	581182
Moses J*	Yuba Bear Rvr	72 999
MULLONE		
James	Nevada Bridgeport	61 488
Niles	Nevada Bridgeport	61 494
MULLONY		
Michael	Sacramento Ward 1	63 75
MULLOON		
Jno	San Francisco San Francisco 9	681074
MULLORY		
J	Nevada Eureka	61 390
MULLOT		
Lewis	San Francisco San Francisco 2	67 796
Sebastian	Yuba Fosters	72 821
Sebastian	Yuba Foster B	72 821
MULLOWAY		
Edward	Sierra Morristown	661052
MULLOY		
Charles	San Francisco San Francisco 11	147
		67
H	Nevada Grass Valley	61 215
H D	Nevada Grass Valley	61 218
J	Nevada Grass Valley	61 156
J K	El Dorado Georgetown	58 746
James	San Francisco San Francisco 3	67 56
Jas	San Francisco San Francisco 2	67 721
Jas	San Francisco San Francisco 1	68 942
Maria	San Francisco San Francisco 8	681287
Patrick	San Francisco San Francisco 9	68 952
T	Nevada Grass Valley	61 206
MULLROLY		
Francis	San Francisco San Francisco 3	67 75
MULMARY		
Joseph	Tuolumne Twp 4	71 127
MULNARY		
Joseph	Tuolumne Big Oak	71 125
MULNONEY		
Bernard*	Nevada Bridgeport	61 473
MULOANY		
Chas	San Francisco San Francisco 10	290
		67
MULOCOGER		
Daniel*	Yuba Marysville	72 892
MULON		
---	Calaveras Twp 4	57 300
---	Calaveras Twp 4	57 300
James	Sonoma Santa Rosa	69 398
MULONE		
James*	Calaveras Twp 6	57 139
William	Calaveras Twp 4	57 312
MULONG		
John*	Calaveras Twp 5	57 245
MULONNEY		
Bernard*	Nevada Bridgeport	61 473
MULONSKI		
Antionio*	Los Angeles Los Angeles	59 366
Antonio	Los Angeles Los Angeles	59 366
MULONY		
David	Calaveras Twp 6	57 168
John	Calaveras Twp 5	57 245
Peter	Tuolumne Twp 2	71 284
MULOY		
Barnard	Sierra Twp 5	66 918
James	Nevada Bridgeport	61 465
John	Calaveras Twp 5	57 187
Mary*	San Francisco San Francisco 9	68 961
MULPAH		
M	Nevada Eureka	61 367
MULQUEEN		
Denis	Sierra Whiskey	66 845
MULQUEENY		
James	Sierra Whiskey	66 849
MULRAMY		
Mary	San Francisco San Francisco 4	681120
MULRANY		
Edwd	Sonoma Sonoma	69 654
Mary*	San Francisco San Francisco 4	681120
MULRAP		
G W	Colusa Monroeville	57 444
MULREINE		
David	San Francisco San Francisco 6	67 449
MULREY		
Jos	San Francisco San Francisco 9	681074

California 1860 Census Index

Name	County Locale	M653 Roll/Page
MULRINE		
Peter	Tulara Petersburg	71 51
MULRON		
James	Placer Iona Hills	62 885
MULRONEY		
Bernard*	Nevada Bridgeport	61 473
MULRONY		
Edward	Plumas Quincy	62 979
Thomas	Plumas Meadow Valley	62 903
MULROONEY		
Bernard	Nevada Bridgeport	61 473
MULROY		
James	Placer Yankee J	62 778
MULRY		
Mary*	San Francisco San Francisco 9	68 961
MULSEN		
H*	San Francisco San Francisco 2	67 674
MULSTAY		
P	San Francisco San Francisco 12	394 67
MULTEN		
Peter	Mariposa Twp 3	60 557
MULTER		
Jesse	Sierra St Louis	66 805
MULTHER		
Thos*	San Francisco San Francisco 1	68 841
MULTINO		
Hanna	San Francisco San Francisco 8	681276
MULUY		
Chas	El Dorado Georgetown	58 706
MULVANEY		
E	Tuolumne Twp 2	71 345
Frank	Klamath S Fork	59 199
MULVANY		
Chas	San Francisco San Francisco 10	290 67
Edwd	Sonoma Sonoma	69 654
John	San Francisco San Francisco 10	172 67
MULVAY		
Patrick	Tuolumne Twp 2	71 364
MULVENY		
John	Klamath S Fork	59 199
MULVEY		
P H	San Francisco San Francisco 7	681375
MULVILLE		
George F	Yuba Marysville	72 871
Michael	San Francisco San Francisco 2	67 580
MULVY		
Mary	San Francisco San Francisco 9	68 961
MULY		
Henry	Sonoma Santa Rosa	69 393
MUM		
---	Butte Oregon	56 629
---	Mariposa Twp 3	60 582
---	Nevada Nevada	61 305
---	Sacramento Centre	63 182
---	Sacramento Mississipi	63 190
---	Tuolumne Don Pedro	71 538
---	Tuolumne Twp 6	71 539
---*	Mariposa Twp 3	60 582
A L	Sierra La Porte	66 771
Wm	Amador Twp 5	55 342
MUMBO		
---	Mendocino Round Va	60 886
MUMFORD		
David	Butte Oregon	56 619
MUMFORT		
Wm	Yuba Rose Bar	72 818
MUMFRD		
James	Plumas Meadow Valley	62 902
MUMFRET		
Wm*	Yuba Rose Bar	72 818
MUMKERBECK		
Jacob	San Francisco San Francisco 7	681329
MUMO		
---	Tulara Twp 2	71 38
MUMPHEAD		
---	Tulara Twp 3	71 56
MUMSTER		
Martin*	Mariposa Coulterville	60 695
MUN CHOW		
---*	Nevada Nevada	61 306
MUN CHUN		
---	Tuolumne Green Springs	71 521
MUN		
---	Amador Twp 4	55 247
---	Amador Twp 2	55 293
---	Amador Twp 5	55 347
---	Amador Twp 7	55 414
---	Amador Twp 6	55 432
---	Butte Kimshaw	56 582
---	Calaveras Twp 5	57 254
---	Calaveras Twp 10	57 275
---	Calaveras Twp 4	57 327
---	El Dorado Georgetown	58 687

Name	County Locale	M653 Roll/Page
MUN		
---	Mariposa Twp 3	60 582
---	Mariposa Twp 3	60 612
---	Mariposa Coulterville	60 681
---	Nevada Grass Valley	61 227
---	Nevada Grass Valley	61 228
---	Nevada Grass Valley	61 230
---	Nevada Nevada	61 302
---	Nevada Nevada	61 305
---	Nevada Nevada	61 306
---	Placer Virginia	62 670
---	Placer Illinois	62 753
---	Placer Iona Hills	62 898
---	San Francisco San Francisco 4	681182
---	Sierra Twp 5	66 947
---	Tuolumne Jacksonville	71 514
---	Tuolumne Don Pedro	71 538
---	Tuolumne Twp 6	71 539
---	Tuolumne Don Pedro	71 541
---	Yuba North Ea	72 681
---*	Nevada Grass Valley	61 228
---*	Nevada Nevada	61 305
---*	Stanislaus Emory	70 743
Ali	Butte Oregon	56 636
Chin	Yuba Slate Ro	72 684
Chow	Nevada Eureka	61 385
Chun	Tuolumne Twp 5	71 521
Chung	Tuolumne Don Pedro	71 541
Huo	Calaveras Twp 10	57 274
John	Mariposa Coulterville	60 695
Ling	San Francisco San Francisco 11	146 67
Lu	El Dorado Greenwood	58 730
Sing	San Francisco San Francisco 11	161 67
Sing	Tuolumne Don Pedro	71 537
Song	San Francisco San Francisco 11	161 67
Yin	Mariposa Coulterville	60 682
MUNA		
A	El Dorado Placerville	58 833
MUNAK		
Leopold	Sacramento Granite	63 244
MUNAS		
Nicholas	El Dorado Greenwood	58 709
MUNAY		
Abner	Tuolumne Shawsfla	71 386
C B	Yolo Putah	72 548
James	Sierra Twp 7	66 893
John	Santa Cruz Soguel	66 592
Michael*	San Francisco San Francisco 8	681271
Thomas	Sierra Twp 7	66 913
Thos*	San Francisco San Francisco 9	681090
Wm	Sierra Downieville	661018
MUNCE		
Fred	El Dorado Georgetown	58 698
Robert W*	Yuba Marysville	72 882
Thul	El Dorado Georgetown	58 698
MUNCER		
Henry	Sierra Twp 5	66 929
MUNCH		
Adam G	Sierra Pine Grove	66 823
Anthony	Yuba Marysville	72 967
Henry	San Francisco San Francisco 4	681217
Jacob	San Francisco San Francisco 10	287 67
John	Sierra Poker Flats	66 841
S	Yolo Cottonwoood	72 655
MUNCHANSER		
Clemens	Mendocino Big Rock	60 876
MUNCHO		
Ramone	Los Angeles Azuza	59 277
MUNCK		
Heny*	San Francisco San Francisco 4	681217
S	Sutter Yuba	70 776
MUNCY		
Jno	Klamath S Fork	59 203
MUND		
Nicholas	Calaveras Twp 6	57 119
O A	Napa Clear Lake	61 140
MUNDAY		
Samuel	San Joaquin Elkhorn	64 994
Thomas	Sierra Downieville	66 963
W	Calaveras Twp 9	57 418
MUNDEIS		
H	El Dorado Diamond	58 813
MUNDELL		
J W	Trinity Bates	70 967
MUNDERS		
John	Tuolumne Sonora	71 209
MUNDERY		
Charles	Tuolumne Twp 1	71 262
MUNDEY		
Charles	Tuolumne Twp 1	71 262
MUNDHEIM		
H	San Francisco San Francisco 5	67 483

Name	County Locale	M653 Roll/Page
MUNDIE		
Mack	Tuolumne Green Springs	71 543
MUNDIGEL		
Teresa	San Francisco San Francisco 10	192 67
MUNDLY		
Pat O	Plumas Quincy	62 915
MUNDORE		
Mary	Tuolumne Twp 1	71 226
MUNDT		
A	San Francisco San Francisco 5	67 519
J	San Francisco San Francisco 5	67 519
MUNDY		
E J	Sierra Downieville	66 958
E L	Sierra Downieville	66 958
Hugh	Tuolumne Twp 3	71 455
J J	Sacramento Casumnes	63 380
John	Sacramento Cosumnes	63 390
L S	Sacramento Lee	63 218
Lawrence	Trinity Lewiston	70 964
Peter	San Francisco San Francisco 11	103 67
Thomas	Sierra Downieville	661012
Thoms	Sierra Downieville	661012
Wm	Sacramento Brighton	63 198
MUNE		
---	Tulara Twp 2	71 36
MUNEBERG		
Fredrick	Plumas Meadow Valley	62 929
MUNECKE		
Chas*	San Francisco San Francisco 2	67 591
MUNEER		
Henry*	Sierra Twp 5	66 929
MUNELLA		
Aggiuttu	Sierra La Porte	66 785
MUNER		
Louis*	Butte Kimshaw	56 604
MUNES		
Julian	Fresno Twp 1	59 76
MUNEZ		
Jose	Yuba Marysville	72 948
MUNFEA		
D	El Dorado Diamond	58 801
MUNFIETO		
Marks C*	San Francisco San Francisco 2	67 767
MUNFORD		
Eldredge J*	Calaveras Twp 6	57 160
MUNFREY		
William*	San Francisco San Francisco 8	681318
MUNG KO		
---*	San Francisco San Francisco 4	681202
MUNG		
---	Alameda Oakland	55 63
---	Amador Twp 4	55 233
---	Amador Twp 1	55 458
---	Amador Twp 1	55 508
---	Butte Kimshaw	56 586
---	Butte Kimshaw	56 600
---	Butte Ophir	56 808
---	Calaveras Twp 8	57 107
---	Calaveras Twp 6	57 182
---	Calaveras Twp 10	57 285
---	Calaveras Twp 10	57 295
---	Calaveras Twp 10	57 297
---	El Dorado Salmon Hills	581058
---	El Dorado Georgetown	58 702
---	Mariposa Twp 1	60 659
---	Merced Twp 2	60 916
---	Placer Folsom	62 649
---	Placer Virginia	62 674
---	Placer Virginia	62 681
---	Placer Virginia	62 684
---	Sacramento Ward 1	63 51
---	Sacramento Ward 1	63 52
---	Sacramento Ward 4	63 613
---	San Francisco San Francisco 9	681088
---	San Francisco San Francisco 4	681186
---	San Francisco San Francisco 4	681212
---	San Francisco San Francisco 6	67 470
---	Sierra Twp 5	66 947
---	Sierra Downieville	66 983
---	Tuolumne Columbia	71 350
---	Tuolumne Twp 3	71 434
---	Tuolumne Sonora	71 478
---	Tuolumne Twp 5	71 523
---	Tuolumne Twp 6	71 529
---	Yuba Long Bar	72 761
---	Yuba Fosters	72 826
---*	Butte Kimshaw	56 586
---*	Plumas Meadow Valley	62 914
---*	Stanislaus Branch	70 714
---*	Yuba Foster B	72 826
---*	Yuba Fosters	72 842
Ah	Tuolumne Twp 2	71 350
Guet	Sacramento Ward 3	63 492
Ko	San Francisco San Francisco 4	681202

California 1860 Census Index

Name	County Locale	M653 RollPage
MUNG		
Pan	Calaveras Twp 5	57 220
Peter	Placer Rattle Snake	62 634
MUNGAN		
David*	Mariposa Coulterville	60 702
MUNGER		
C	Sacramento Sutter	63 305
L M	Sierra Pine Grove	66 831
MUNHAN		
George	Calaveras Twp 5	57 144
MUNICH		
Jacob	Santa Clara Alviso	65 415
MUNIJO		
Rapelto	Napa Napa	61 114
MUNIOUS		
Warlopy	Mariposa Twp 1	60 667
MUNJEE		
G	San Joaquin Stockton	641096
MUNK		
B F	Sierra Downieville	661013
Thos K	Sacramento Ward 1	63 125
MUNKETRICK		
Charles	Calaveras Twp 5	57 229
MUNKITRICK		
Charles	Calaveras Twp 5	57 229
MUNLOTTA		
Corlotta*	El Dorado Georgetown	58 684
MUNN		
---	Sacramento Mississipi	63 190
A L	Sierra La Porte	66 771
Alfc*	Butte Oregon	56 627
Alfd*	Butte Oregon	56 627
Anna	San Francisco San Francisco 8	681299
Chas	Santa Clara San Jose	65 367
Chas	Sonoma Sonoma	69 643
D	Tuolumne Twp 4	71 164
Geo*	Butte Oregon	56 623
Jno W	Butte Chico	56 563
P C	Butte Chico	56 568
Thomas R	Fresno Twp 3	59 10
Wm	San Francisco San Francisco 10	311 67
MUNNAY		
O	Siskiyou Klamath	69 93
MUNNCY		
R*	Yolo Washington	72 561
MUNNELS		
Louis*	Calaveras Twp 9	57 354
MUNNERY		
George	Calaveras Twp 4	57 336
MUNNES		
Alen T	Calaveras Twp 6	57 160
Alere T*	Calaveras Twp 6	57 160
Alex T*	Calaveras Twp 6	57 160
MUNNEY		
R*	Yolo Washington	72 561
MUNNING		
Peter	Nevada Bridgeport	61 468
MUNNTUN		
J F	El Dorado Georgetown	58 702
MUNO		
---	Tulara Twp 3	71 65
Antonino*	Sierra Downieville	66 972
MUNOS		
Ancela	San Francisco San Francisco 2	67 788
Manuel	Los Angeles San Gabriel	59 422
Ramiga	Los Angeles Los Angeles	59 509
Trinidad	Los Angeles Los Angeles	59 332
Uncela*	San Francisco San Francisco 2	67 788
MUNOZ		
Francisco	Santa Clara Fremont	65 437
Inez	Santa Clara Almaden	65 274
MUNRAL		
Catarina	Monterey Monterey	60 947
MUNRAS		
Catarina	Monterey Monterey	60 947
MUNRESE		
Joseph	Yuba Parks Ba	72 782
MUNRIETTA		
---	Tulara Keyesville	71 69
MUNRO		
David	Yolo Slate Ra	72 694
David	Yuba Slate Ro	72 694
Thomas	Yolo Slate Ra	72 694
Thomas*	Yuba Slate Ra	72 694
Wm	San Francisco San Francisco 10	311 67
MUNROE		
Alexander	Yolo Slate Ra	72 694
Alexander	Yuba Slate Ro	72 694
C F	San Francisco San Francisco 3	67 81
Geo	San Francisco San Francisco 1	68 860
Geo	San Francisco San Francisco 9	68 980
Geo	Tuolumne Twp 4	71 138
George	Amador Twp 1	55 488
H	San Francisco San Francisco 1	68 928

Name	County Locale	M653 RollPage
MUNROE		
H V	Nevada Eureka	61 351
J	Sacramento Lee	63 210
J*	Nevada Grass Valley	61 224
James	San Francisco San Francisco 2	67 670
John	Fresno Twp 1	59 82
John	Placer Yankee J	62 776
John	Solano Benecia	69 313
John	Tulara Petersburg	71 52
Jos	Sacramento Ward 4	63 514
Mary E	Alameda Oakland	55 71
Robert	Sierra Gibsonville	66 857
Robt	Santa Clara Santa Clara	65 492
W A	Nevada Nevada	61 319
William	San Francisco San Francisco 11	156 67
MUNROO		
Geo	San Francisco San Francisco 1	68 894
MUNROW		
W C	Nevada Bridgeport	61 496
MUNRY		
Abraham*	Sierra Pine Grove	66 835
MUNS		
---	Butte Ophir	56 804
MUNSAS		
Carsuel*	San Mateo Twp 1	65 52
MUNSAY		
Joe B	Yuba Long Bar	72 747
MUNSE		
Hermon*	Humbolt Union	59 183
MUNSELL		
James	Placer Auburn	62 567
Jas	Placer Ophir	62 651
MUNSEY		
Isaac	Sierra Gibsonville	66 857
John	Nevada Little Y	61 534
Jonathan	Placer Yankee J	62 779
MUNSFIELD		
John T	Calaveras Twp 5	57 147
MUNSON		
---	Sierra Twp 5	66 945
Chas	Santa Clara Santa Clara	65 491
D	Sacramento Brighton	63 209
E	Butte Oregon	56 634
G R	San Francisco San Francisco 3	67 79
H L	Butte Kimshaw	56 597
Ira	San Francisco San Francisco 10	307 67
J	Nevada Grass Valley	61 163
J A	Calaveras Twp 9	57 407
James	Sierra Pine Grove	66 825
James H	San Francisco San Francisco 7	681409
Jno	Butte Oregon	56 630
Jno	San Francisco San Francisco 9	681079
Jno*	Butte Oregon	56 630
Joel	San Joaquin Castoria	64 886
John	El Dorado White Oaks	581030
John	Sierra St Louis	66 814
Jones	El Dorado Cold Spring	581099
Joseph	El Dorado Cold Spring	581099
Margetta	Nevada Bridgeport	61 482
Marion	Tulara Twp 3	71 52
Mary	El Dorado Cold Spring	581100
Maryetta	Nevada Bridgeport	61 482
O D	San Francisco San Francisco 2	67 648
Peter	San Joaquin Castoria	64 894
Robert	Nevada Bridgeport	61 496
T	San Francisco San Francisco 1	68 811
MUNSONEY		
F	Nevada Washington	61 337
T*	Nevada Washington	61 337
MUNSS		
Fredk	El Dorado Coloma	581117
MUNSTER		
A	San Joaquin Stockton	641036
Elija	Nevada Bridgeport	61 470
John	Trinity Weaverville	701052
Marcus*	Yuba Marysville	72 894
Martin	Mariposa Coulterville	60 695
MUNT		
John	San Francisco San Francisco 3	67 70
Richard	Yolo Slate Ra	72 705
MUNTER		
Marcus*	Yuba Marysville	72 894
MUNTZ		
Joshua	Yolo Slate Ra	72 691
Joshua	Yuba Slate Ro	72 691
MUNUK		
Leopold*	Sacramento Granite	63 244
MUNUSALES		
Jose	Colusa Colusi	57 425
MUNY		
---	Calaveras Twp 5	57 254
---	Calaveras Twp 10	57 295
---	Calaveras Twp 10	57 297
Pan	Calaveras Twp 5	57 220

Name	County Locale	M653 RollPage
MUNYASE		
R	Amador Twp 1	55 499
MUNYO		
Jose M	San Francisco San Francisco 2	67 783
MUNZER		
---	El Dorado Georgetown	58 747
---	Sierra Pine Grove	66 831
L M	Sierra Pine Grove	66 831
MUOLAY		
J*	Nevada Eureka	61 350
MUORSEN		
Jacob*	Yuba Marysville	72 939
MUOS		
Emmanuel	Alameda Brooklyn	55 108
MUOY		
---	Plumas Quincy	62 969
MUP		
---	Mariposa Twp 3	60 569
---	Mariposa Twp 3	60 576
---	Mariposa Twp 3	60 609
MUPAL		
C*	Nevada Grass Valley	61 157
MUPER		
Charles	Solano Fairfield	69 203
F	Nevada Nevada	61 255
MUPHUBURG		
A O*	Placer Michigan	62 852
MUPHY		
John L	Amador Twp 4	55 235
MUPSLEAD		
Charles*	El Dorado Salmon Falls	581056
MUPSTEAD		
Charles	El Dorado Salmon Hills	581056
MUR		
---	Butte Cascade	56 699
---	Placer Illinois	62 746
---	San Francisco San Francisco 4	681212
See	San Francisco San Francisco 4	681201
Su	San Francisco San Francisco 4	681201
MURA		
Frank	Tuolumne Twp 3	71 459
Jose	Alameda Brooklyn	55 101
MURAFIELD		
Daniel	Mendocino Little L	60 839
MURALY		
John*	Sierra La Porte	66 766
MURAN		
Edward F	Calaveras Twp 5	57 248
MURAND		
Jerry	Sierra Whiskey	66 845
P	Mariposa Twp 3	60 556
MURANDA		
Cuiz	Monterey Monterey	60 962
MURASKY		
Chas	San Francisco San Francisco 2	67 629
Mina	San Francisco San Francisco 10	310 67
MURAT		
Joseph	Los Angeles Los Angeles	59 353
MURATT		
Christ	Butte Ophir	56 798
MURAY		
J	Siskiyou Scott Ri	69 70
Patrick	Santa Clara San Jose	65 328
MURBUR		
W*	Nevada Grass Valley	61 202
MURCH		
Arthur B	Klamath Klamath	59 228
B	Sacramento Granite	63 228
Caleb	San Francisco San Francisco 2	67 755
Leonard H	Klamath Orleans	59 216
MURCHEN		
Dedrick	Plumas Quincy	62 939
MURCHIE		
John C*	Yuba Foster B	72 829
MURCHY		
John	San Joaquin Tulare	64 869
MURCINIS		
Lofinis	Calaveras Twp 5	57 226
MURCO		
Antonio	San Francisco San Francisco 1	68 916
MURCOCK		
Henry V	San Mateo Twp 1	65 56
MURDEN		
Peter	Placer Michigan	62 844
MURDICK		
Gawn	Butte Chico	56 532
MURDITH		
John	Sierra St Louis	66 864
MURDOCK		
A	Butte Chico	56 538
A H	Nevada Grass Valley	61 213
A P	Sacramento Ward 3	63 432
Albert H	Humbolt Union	59 183
Alex	San Francisco San Francisco 2	67 702
C	Calaveras Twp 9	57 391
Elijah	Tuolumne Twp 2	71 378

California 1860 Census Index

Name	County Locale	M653 Roll	Page
MURDOCK			
F B	Santa Clara San Jose	65	334
Gawn	Butte Chico	56	532
Geo	El Dorado Casumnes	581	165
Geo L	Stanislaus Branch	70	703
George L	San Francisco San Francisco 7	681	341
Harrison	Calaveras Twp 6	57	147
Horace	Calaveras Twp 10	57	290
Hugh M	San Francisco San Francisco 7	681	427
J	El Dorado Placerville	58	835
J	Sutter Sutter	70	802
J	Sutter Sutter	70	806
J B	San Francisco San Francisco 5	67	545
James	El Dorado Georgetown	58	747
James	San Joaquin Elkhorn	64	976
John	San Francisco San Francisco 10	67	191
John C	Yuba Marysville	72	940
Lenard	El Dorado Gold Hill	581	095
Mary	Butte Chico	56	538
McKinsey	Amador Twp 3	55	378
R	El Dorado Placerville	58	836
Rubicon	Siskiyou Scott Va	69	35
S	Sutter Sutter	70	801
S B	Sutter Sutter	70	807
Samuel	Colusa Mansville	57	438
Samuel	Colusa Monroeville	57	457
Sarah	Sutter Sutter	70	807
W	Sutter Sutter	70	807
William	San Francisco San Francisco 9	68	983
Wm	Colusa Muion	57	458
Wm	San Francisco San Francisco 10	67	243
MURDOF			
A	Nevada Grass Valley	61	149
MURDRUP			
William*	Fresno Twp 2	59	49
MURDY			
R	Sutter Bear Rvr	70	820
MURE			
---	El Dorado Salmon Falls	581	045
James	Santa Clara San Jose	65	358
MUREGAN			
David*	Mariposa Coulterville	60	702
MUREHEAD			
John	Placer Michigan	62	841
MUREHINE			
Gaeteno*	Sierra Poker Flats	66	839
MURETTA			
Francisco	Amador Twp 3	55	376
MUREY			
Jno	Alameda Brooklyn	55	101
MURFREY			
William	San Francisco San Francisco 8	681	318
MURG			
Jacob	San Francisco San Francisco 7	681	325
MURGALTEN			
H C*	El Dorado Placerville	58	874
MURGATTEN			
H C*	El Dorado Placerville	58	874
MURGE			
Christian	San Francisco San Francisco 1	68	808
MURGIA			
Antonia*	San Francisco San Francisco 2	67	738
MURGINS			
Reuben*	Santa Cruz Soguel	66	583
MURGOLD			
M	El Dorado Diamond	58	788
MURGRAVE			
A L	Nevada Nevada	61	284
MURGROVE			
L	Nevada Grass Valley	61	150
R*	Nevada Grass Valley	61	159
MURGUIR			
Reuben	Santa Cruz Soguel	66	583
MURHIT			
R	Alameda Oakland	55	17
MURICH			
N*	Sacramento Ward 1	63	4
MURICL			
N*	Sacramento Ward 1	63	4
MURID			
N*	Sacramento Ward 1	63	4
MURIEL			
N	Sacramento Ward 1	63	4
MURIENA			
Jerry*	Sierra Whiskey	66	845
MURIETTA			
---	Tulara Twp 3	71	44
---	Tulara Keyesville	71	63
---	Tulara Keyesville	71	65
---	Tulara Keyesville	71	66
---	Tulara Twp 3	71	69
---	Tulara Keyesville	71	72
---*	Tulara Sinks Te	71	44
MURIFEE			
T	El Dorado Diamond	58	799

Name	County Locale	M653 Roll	Page
MURIGAN			
David*	Mariposa Coulterville	60	702
MURIGH			
Phillip J	El Dorado Georgetown	58	707
MURILLO			
---	Fresno Twp 2	59	64
MURIN			
Geo*	Butte Oregon	56	623
Joing	San Francisco San Francisco 6	67	466
MURINE			
Cecelia*	Amador Twp 4	55	240
MURINGER			
Harry*	Calaveras Twp 8	57	103
MURK			
Fred	Sacramento Ward 1	63	33
MURKINS			
M	Sutter Butte	70	795
MURKRY			
Patrick*	Siskiyou Scott Va	69	31
MURKS			
Zadock	Yolo Cottonwood	72	558
MURLAY			
J	Nevada Eureka	61	350
MURLCAY			
William*	San Francisco San Francisco 9	68	946
MURMAIN			
Thomas	Tuolumne Twp 1	71	236
MURMAN			
Peter	Sierra Twp 5	66	947
MURMTHEW			
M W*	Butte Ophir	56	793
MURN			
Wm*	Amador Twp 5	55	342
MURNEY			
Jas	Butte Bidwell	56	725
MURNNA			
Jerry*	Sierra Whiskey	66	845
MUROE			
John	Tulara Twp 3	71	52
MUROES			
F	El Dorado Placerville	58	876
MUROS			
Pablo	Solano Suisan	69	228
MURPE			
---*	Mariposa Twp 3	60	582
MURPH			
Patrick*	Mariposa Twp 3	60	585
MURPHE			
Jas	Amador Twp 2	55	322
MURPHERY			
E	Solano Vacaville	69	322
MURPHEY			
A	El Dorado White Oaks	581	016
A	Tuolumne Twp 1	71	263
B	El Dorado Placerville	58	856
B	Nevada Washington	61	335
C T	El Dorado Placerville	58	863
Chas	Napa Napa	61	89
Con	Nevada Nevada	61	298
D	Nevada Nevada	61	292
D	Nevada Eureka	61	372
D J	Napa Napa	61	73
Danl	Napa Napa	61	65
E	Solano Vacaville	69	322
Edw	Nevada Rough &	61	407
Eli	Los Angeles Tejon	59	526
Elitia	El Dorado Coloma	581	080
Elitica	El Dorado Coloma	581	080
G	El Dorado Kelsey	581	156
H	Los Angeles Tejon	59	524
H F	Napa Napa	61	110
Henry	Napa Napa	61	77
J	Nevada Grass Valley	61	155
J B	Nevada Bridgeport	61	451
J S	Napa Yount	61	31
James	El Dorado White Oaks	581	012
James	El Dorado White Oaks	581	018
James	El Dorado Kelsey	581	132
Jhn	Nevada Red Dog	61	554
John	Contra Costa Twp 1	57	516
John	El Dorado Salmon Hills	581	056
John	El Dorado Kelsey	581	131
John	Nevada Rough &	61	420
M	El Dorado Placerville	58	819
M	Nevada Grass Valley	61	152
M	Nevada Grass Valley	61	209
M	Nevada Eureka	61	354
M G	Nevada Eureka	61	346
M W	Napa Napa	61	109
Mich	Nevada Rough &	61	396
Michiel	Nevada Red Dog	61	548
Miko	El Dorado Mud Springs	58	970
Mk	Nevada Eureka	61	354
Pat	Nevada Rough &	61	430
Pat	Nevada Bridgeport	61	471
Pat	Nevada Red Dog	61	543

Name	County Locale	M653 Roll	Page
MURPHEY			
Patrick	Napa Napa	61	85
Peter	El Dorado Kelsey	581	127
R	Nevada Grass Valley	61	200
Silvester	Nevada Bridgeport	61	488
Thos	Napa Napa	61	76
Thos	Napa Napa	61	99
Wm	Yuba New York	72	727
MURPHI			
Jas	Amador Twp 2	55	322
MURPHLY			
Demis*	Butte Eureka	56	649
Dennis*	Butte Eureka	56	649
MURPHPY			
Chas	Trinity Mouth Ca	701	013
T	Amador Twp 1	55	462
MURPHT			
M	San Francisco San Francisco 5	67	551
MURPHY			
A	Tuolumne Sonora	71	207
A J	Tuolumne Twp 1	71	207
A S	San Francisco San Francisco 3	67	44
Agnes	Yuba Marysville	72	945
Andrew	San Francisco San Francisco 9	68	952
Andrew	Santa Clara San Jose	65	368
Ann	Placer Auburn	62	561
Ann	Sacramento Ward 3	63	425
Anna	San Francisco San Francisco 10	67	178
Anna	San Francisco San Francisco 10	67	218
Anthey	Sierra Twp 5	66	918
Arthur	Sacramento Georgian	63	346
Arthur	San Francisco San Francisco 9	681	042
Authey	Sierra Twp 5	66	918
B	Trinity Evans Ba	701	002
B A	Calaveras Twp 9	57	390
B F	Sutter Sutter	70	816
Barny	Placer Yankee J	62	759
Bartholoman	Butte Eureka	56	650
Benard	Sacramento Natonia	63	281
Bendit	Amador Twp 4	55	259
Bennut*	Sacramento Natonia	63	281
Bernard	San Francisco San Francisco 1	68	870
Bernard	Tuolumne Columbia	71	358
Bernrut*	Sacramento Natonia	63	281
Bridget	San Francisco San Francisco 9	681	026
Bridget	San Francisco San Francisco 10	67	246
Bridget	Shasta Shasta	66	675
Briget	Calaveras Twp 8	57	51
C P	San Joaquin Elkhorn	64	986
C P	Tehama Red Bluff	70	925
Cath	Sacramento Ward 4	63	521
Catharine	San Francisco San Francisco 8	681	273
Catharine	San Francisco San Francisco 10	67	231
Catharine	San Francisco San Francisco 9	68	979
Catharine	San Francisco San Francisco 4	681	156
Catherine	San Francisco San Francisco 6	67	466
Catherine	Santa Clara Gilroy	65	252
Charles	San Francisco San Francisco 9	68	975
Charlie	Alameda Brooklyn	55	89
Chas	Trinity Mouth Ca	701	013
Chas A	Napa Napa	61	62
Clement	Santa Clara Gilroy	65	252
Con	Nevada Nevada	61	298
Conreleus	Sierra Whiskey	66	844
Cornelius	San Francisco San Francisco 12	67	374
Cornelius	Santa Cruz Santa Cruz	66	621
Cornelius	Sierra Whiskey	66	844
Cornelius	Sierra Twp 5	66	943
Cyrus	Tuolumne Twp 1	71	482
D	Butte Chico	56	539
D	Butte Wyandotte	56	665
D	Mariposa Twp 3	60	556
D	Merced Twp 1	60	913
D	Nevada Grass Valley	61	213
D	Nevada Nevada	61	287
D	Nevada Eureka	61	372
D	Sacramento Ward 3	63	428
D	Tehama Tehama	70	943
D	Trinity Lewiston	70	957
D J	San Francisco San Francisco 10	67	189
D J*	Napa Napa	61	73
D R	Trinity Big Flat	701	040
D S	San Francisco San Francisco 5	67	546
D*	Sierra St Louis	66	809
Daniel	Butte Oregon	56	621
Daniel	San Francisco San Francisco 7	681	371
Daniel	San Francisco San Francisco 10	67	171
Daniel	San Francisco San Francisco 9	68	947
Daniel	San Francisco San Francisco 9	68	987

California 1860 Census Index

Name	County Locale	M653 RollPage
MURPHY		
Daniel	Santa Clara Gilroy	65 249
Daniel	Santa Clara Santa Clara	65 522
Daniel	Shasta French G	66 714
Daniel	Yuba Rose Bar	72 791
Daniel	Yuba Rose Bar	72 804
Daniel J	San Francisco San Francisco 10 174	67
Danl	Butte Oregon	56 616
Danl	Merced Twp 1	60 898
Danl	Napa Napa	61 65
Danl	Placer Virginia	62 674
Danl	San Francisco San Francisco 10 310	67
Danl	San Francisco San Francisco 1 68 836
Danl	San Francisco San Francisco 1 68 897
Danl J	Placer Dutch Fl	62 732
Danl*	Butte Oregon	56 616
David	Butte Chico	56 537
David	Butte Ophir	56 759
David	Sacramento Ward 1	63 62
David	Solano Benecia	69 285
David	Solano Vacaville	69 344
David	Solano Vacaville	69 344
Davis	Solano Vacaville	69 344
Delia	San Francisco San Francisco 2 67 662
Denis	Solano Vacaville	69 359
Dennis	Butte Eureka	56 649
Dennis	San Francisco San Francisco 12 385	67
Dennis	San Francisco San Francisco 1 68 844
Dennis	San Francisco San Francisco 9 68 966
Dennis	Siskiyou Scott Va	69 42
E	Calaveras Twp 9	57 392
E	Shasta Horsetown	66 690
E	Shasta French G	66 717
E H	Sierra Morristown	661054
Ed	Tuolumne Columbia	71 326
Ed M	Tuolumne Columbia	71 315
Edrd	San Francisco San Francisco 1 68 905
Edward	Alameda Brooklyn	55 154
Edward	Calaveras Twp 9	57 352
Edward	Calaveras Twp 9	57 370
Edward	Del Norte Crescent	58 628
Edward	Plumas Quincy	62 996
Edward	Sierra Pine Grove	66 822
Edward	Sierra Twp 7	66 912
Edward	Solano Vallejo	69 277
Edward	Tuolumne Columbia	71 314
Edward P	San Joaquin Douglass	64 923
Eliza	San Francisco San Francisco 4 681119
Eliza	San Francisco San Francisco 10 338	67
Elizabeth	Calaveras Twp 5	57 231
Ellen	Alameda Brooklyn	55 121
Ellen	Alameda Murray	55 220
Ellen	Sacramento Ward 1	63 133
Ellen	San Francisco San Francisco 9 681077
Ellen	San Francisco San Francisco 8 681259
Ellen	Santa Cruz Santa Cruz	66 604
Ellen	Santa Cruz Santa Cruz	66 640
Ellen M	San Francisco San Francisco 9 68 993
F	San Francisco San Francisco 9 681072
F	Tuolumne Springfield	71 373
F M	Sutter Sutter	70 807
Fanny	Colusa Colusi	57 423
Fanny	San Francisco San Francisco 9 68 945
Frances	Sierra Pine Grove	66 833
Francis	San Francisco San Francisco 9 681066
Francis	San Francisco San Francisco 9 68 946
Francis	Sierra Pine Grove	66 833
Frank	San Francisco San Francisco 9 68 944
G H	San Francisco San Francisco 3 67 39
G W	Yolo Slate Ra	72 693
Garrett	Tuolumne Big Oak	71 139
Geo	San Francisco San Francisco 9 681071
Geo H	Calaveras Twp 5	57 230
George	San Francisco San Francisco 4 681133
George	Solano Vacaville	69 344
George H	Solano Vacaville	69 344
H	Los Angeles Tejon	59 524
H	Shasta Millvill	66 752
H	Sutter Nicolaus	70 838
H	Tehama Red Bluff	70 915
H S	San Francisco San Francisco 3 67 44
Hannah	San Francisco San Francisco 4 681112
Hannah	San Francisco San Francisco 10 184	67
Hannah	Tuolumne Columbia	71 364
Harvey	San Francisco San Francisco 10 211	67
Henry	Calaveras Twp 9	57 356
Henry	El Dorado Placerville	58 926
Henry	Napa Napa	61 77
Henry	Sacramento Ward 1	63 26
Henry	Sacramento Ward 3	63 430
Henry	Tehama Tehama	70 943

Name	County Locale	M653 RollPage
MURPHY		
Henry F	San Francisco San Francisco 6 67 458
Honora	San Francisco San Francisco 10 229	67
Hugh	Calaveras Twp 4	57 328
Hugh	Sacramento Ward 4	63 524
Hugh	Sonoma Petaluma	69 579
Hugh	Yuba Fosters	72 837
Hugh S	San Francisco San Francisco 9 681041
Hugh*	Calaveras Twp 4	57 328
J	Amador Twp 3	55 380
J	Nevada Grass Valley	61 190
J	Nevada Eureka	61 391
J	San Francisco San Francisco 5 67 516
J	San Francisco San Francisco 5 67 538
J	San Joaquin Stockton	641046
J	Siskiyou Cottonwood	69 100
J	Siskiyou Scott Ri	69 73
J	Sutter Yuba	70 775
J	Yolo Putah	72 552
J C	El Dorado Placerville	58 877
J C	Yolo Cottonwood	72 558
J H	Yolo Washington	72 563
J J	Sacramento Ward 1	63 86
J N	Yolo Washington	72 563
J P*	Sacramento Brighton	63 192
J T	Tehama Red Bluff	70 906
J W	Sacramento Sutter	63 298
J*	San Francisco San Francisco 5 67 538
Jack	Nevada Bridgeport	61 500
Jacob	Plumas Quincy	62 954
James	Calaveras Twp 5	57 196
James	El Dorado White Oaks	581033
James	El Dorado Union	581093
James	Humbolt Eureka	59 166
James	Klamath Liberty	59 242
James	Marin San Rafael	60 767
James	Placer Iona Hills	62 882
James	Placer Iona Hills	62 886
James	Plumas Meadow Valley	62 911
James	San Francisco San Francisco 3 67 10
James	San Francisco San Francisco 7 681334
James	San Joaquin Stockton	641075
James	Santa Cruz Santa Cruz	66 637
James	Santa Cruz Santa Cruz	66 639
James	Sierra La Porte	66 787
James	Sierra Downieville	66 972
James	Siskiyou Scott Va	69 52
James	Solano Vallejo	69 269
James	Solano Vallejo	69 279
James	Tuolumne Twp 1	71 272
James	Tuolumne Columbia	71 345
James	Tuolumne Don Pedro	71 534
Jane	San Francisco San Francisco 7 681333
Jas	Amador Twp 1	55 454
Jas	Butte Cascade	56 694
Jas	Calaveras Twp 9	57 380
Jas	Calaveras Twp 9	57 381
Jas	Placer Virginia	62 678
Jas	Placer Illinois	62 706
Jas	Placer Dutch Fl	62 719
Jas	Sacramento Granite	63 257
Jas	Sacramento Ward 4	63 600
Jas	San Francisco San Francisco 10 258	67
Jas	San Francisco San Francisco 10 300	67
Jas	San Joaquin Elliott	641104
Jas	San Mateo Twp 1	65 58
Jas	Santa Clara San Jose	65 386
Jas	Trinity Sturdiva	701007
Jas C	Sacramento Ward 3	63 473
Jas R	Placer Auburn	62 584
Jasper N	Fresno Twp 2	59 3
Jeremiah	Amador Twp 1	55 466
Jeremiah	Tuolumne Jamestown	71 430
Jerh	San Francisco San Francisco 2 67 713
Jerry	Amador Twp 3	55 386
Jerry	San Francisco San Francisco 1 68 836
Jerry	Sierra Morristown	661053
Jno	Butte Kimshaw	56 592
Jno	Butte Kimshaw	56 598
Jno	Butte Kimshaw	56 607
Jno	Nevada Nevada	61 315
Jno	Sacramento Franklin	63 308
Jno	Sacramento Ward 4	63 590
Jno	San Francisco San Francisco 9 681072
Jno F	Trinity State Ba	701001
Jno J	San Francisco San Francisco 9 68 995
Jno L	Butte Oregon	56 641
Jno R	Mendocino Calpella	60 810
Joanna	Alameda Brooklyn	55 100
Joanna M	Sacramento Ward 4	63 542
Joarma	Alameda Brooklyn	55 100
Johanna	San Francisco San Francisco 2 67 662
Johanna	San Francisco San Francisco 1 68 847

Name	County Locale	M653 RollPage
MURPHY		
John	Alameda Brooklyn	55 156
John	Alameda Brooklyn	55 165
John	Amador Twp 3	55 376
John	Amador Twp 3	55 380
John	Amador Twp 1	55 471
John	Butte Ophir	56 746
John	Calaveras Twp 7	57 24
John	Calaveras Twp 4	57 299
John	Calaveras Twp 4	57 300
John	Calaveras Twp 7	57 37
John	Humbolt Eel Rvr	59 152
John	Marin Cortemad	60 754
John	Mariposa Twp 3	60 557
John	Mariposa Twp 3	60 558
John	Mariposa Twp 3	60 663
John	Nevada Bridgeport	61 499
John	Placer Secret R	62 614
John	Placer Virginia	62 673
John	Placer Michigan	62 816
John	Plumas Quincy	62 939
John	Plumas Quincy	62 955
John	Sacramento Franklin	63 322
John	Sacramento Ward 1	63 92
John	San Diego Colorado	64 806
John	San Francisco San Francisco 7 681335
John	San Francisco San Francisco 10 200	67
John	San Francisco San Francisco 6 67 450
John	San Francisco San Francisco 3 67 64
John	San Francisco San Francisco 1 68 827
John	San Joaquin Stockton	641062
John	San Mateo Twp 3	65 100
John	San Mateo Twp 3	65 106
John	San Mateo Twp 3	65 109
John	San Mateo Twp 3	65 96
John	Santa Clara Alviso	65 411
John	Santa Cruz Pajaro	66 525
John	Sierra Twp 5	66 930
John	Sierra Downieville	66 995
John	Siskiyou Scott Va	69 43
John	Solano Vallejo	69 253
John	Sonoma Petaluma	69 577
John	Sonoma Sonoma	69 649
John	Tehama Lassen	70 875
John	Trinity Oregon G	701009
John	Trinity Weaverville	701077
John	Trinity Ferry	70 977
John	Tuolumne Big Oak	71 143
John	Tuolumne Twp 1	71 254
John	Tuolumne Twp 2	71 302
John	Tuolumne Twp 2	71 311
John	Tuolumne Columbia	71 359
John	Yuba Marysville	72 889
John	Yuba Marysville	72 898
John	Yuba Marysville	72 922
John A	Yuba Marysville	72 856
John A	Yuba Marysville	72 861
John C	Tuolumne Twp 6	71 538
John D	Tuolumne Don Pedro	71 538
John E	Yuba Marysville	72 887
John H	Monterey San Juan	60 989
John J	Los Angeles Elmonte	59 257
John J	San Joaquin Elkhorn	64 969
John L	Sacramento Ward 1	63 120
John L	Tuolumne Twp 4	71 130
John M	Santa Clara San Jose	65 390
John P	Alameda Brooklyn	55 101
John S*	Amador Twp 4	55 235
John W	Yuba New York	72 723
Johnson	Amador Twp 3	55 381
Jos	San Francisco San Francisco 10 258	67
Jos	San Francisco San Francisco 10 300	67
Joseph	Calaveras Twp 8	57 69
Joseph	Plumas Quincy	62 972
Joseph	San Francisco San Francisco 9 681005
Julia	Nevada Nevada	61 242
Julia	San Francisco San Francisco 9 681091
Julia	San Francisco San Francisco 9 68 986
Kate	Sacramento Ward 1	63 23
Kate	San Francisco San Francisco 10 185	67
Kate	Santa Clara San Jose	65 385
L	Sierra St Louis	66 809
Lewis	San Francisco San Francisco 9 681091
Luke	Merced Twp 2	60 916
M	Nevada Grass Valley	61 189
M	Nevada Eureka	61 354
M	Nevada Eureka	61 363
M	Sacramento Ward 1	63 2
M	San Francisco San Francisco 5 67 517
M	San Francisco San Francisco 5 67 551
M	San Francisco San Francisco 1 68 848
M	Sutter Bear Rvr	70 819

Name	County Locale	M653 RollPage
MURPHY		
M A	Tehama Red Bluff	70 909
M K	Sacramento Ward 1	63 118
Margaret	El Dorado Coloma	581068
Margaret	San Francisco San Francisco 4	681155
Margaret	San Francisco San Francisco 8	681320
Margaret	San Francisco San Francisco 10	244 67
Martin	Santa Clara Fremont	65 438
Martin	Santa Cruz Santa Cruz	66 637
Martin	Tuolumne Twp 2	71 300
Martin D	Yuba Parks Ba	72 778
Martin J	Yuba Parks Ba	72 778
Mary	Sacramento Ward 3	63 444
Mary	Sacramento Ward 4	63 574
Mary	Sacramento Ward 4	63 584
Mary	San Francisco San Francisco 9	681079
Mary	San Francisco San Francisco 10	240 67
Mary	San Francisco San Francisco 5	67 491
Mary	San Francisco San Francisco 2	67 562
Mary	San Joaquin Castoria	64 909
Mary	Yolo Cache Crk	72 606
Mary A	San Francisco San Francisco 10	233 67
Mary A B	San Francisco San Francisco 10	335 67
Mary E	Santa Clara San Jose	65 326
Mary Emly Siste	Solano Benecia	69 300
Mary Emsy Siste	Solano Benecia	69 300
Mary H	Alameda Oakland	55 49
Mary M	San Francisco San Francisco 10	186 67
Mary Raimond Si	Solano Benecia	69 300
Mathew	Alameda Brooklyn	55 141
Mathew	Alameda Brooklyn	55 92
Mathew	Placer Michigan	62 830
Mathew	San Francisco San Francisco 11	122 67
Menry F	San Francisco San Francisco 6	67 458
Michael	Colusa Monroeville	57 453
Michael	El Dorado Greenwood	58 720
Michael	Klamath Klamath	59 228
Michael	Placer Auburn	62 588
Michael	San Francisco San Francisco 5	1 68 908
Michael	San Francisco San Francisco 9	68 987
Michael	Santa Cruz Pajaro	66 558
Michael	Santa Cruz Santa Cruz	66 604
Michael	Sierra Excelsior	661034
Michael	Sierra Downieville	66 972
Michael	Sierra Downieville	66 977
Michael	Solano Suisan	69 222
Michael	Solano Fremont	69 380
Michael	Stanislaus Branch	70 698
Michael	Tuolumne Twp 2	71 311
Michael	Tuolumne Shawsfla	71 387
Michael J	San Francisco San Francisco 10	207 67
Michael*	San Francisco San Francisco 1	68 930
Michal	San Bernardino San Bernadino	64 626
Morris	Calaveras Twp 5	57 230
Morris	Santa Clara Fremont	65 439
Mosehughes	San Mateo Twp 3	65 107
Mr	Sonoma Sonoma	69 647
N	Stanislaus Emory	70 745
N N	Yolo Putah	72 614
Nellie	San Francisco San Francisco 10	185 67
Norah	Santa Cruz Pajaro	66 551
Noriah*	Santa Cruz Pajaro	66 551
Oliver	Sacramento Ward 4	63 513
Orrin	Butte Oroville	56 823
Owen	Yuba Marysville	72 855
Owen	Yuba Marysville	72 860
P	San Francisco San Francisco 5	67 494
P	San Francisco San Francisco 2	67 705
P	Siskiyou Scott Ri	69 75
P	Trinity Weaverville	701064
P	Tuolumne Jacksonville	71 172
P	Yuba New York	72 738
P A	Sacramento Ward 4	63 544
Paddy	Mariposa Coulterville	60 678
Pat	Butte Eureka	56 650
Pat	Butte Oro	56 688
Pat	Calaveras Twp 9	57 379
Pat	El Dorado Georgetown	58 679
Pat	El Dorado Georgetown	58 705
Pat	Mariposa Twp 2	60 664
Pat	Napa Hot Springs	61 17
Pat	Placer Secret R	62 620
Pat	Sacramento Granite	63 263
Pat	San Francisco San Francisco 9	68 988
Pat	Sonoma Petaluma	69 603
Pat	Tehama Pasakent	70 858
Pat F	Sacramento Natonia	63 273

Name	County Locale	M653 RollPage
MURPHY		
Patk	San Francisco San Francisco 10	193 67
Patk	San Francisco San Francisco 12	382 67
Patk	Tuolumne Big Oak	71 143
Patrick	Alameda Brooklyn	55 114
Patrick	Alameda Oakland	55 72
Patrick	Calaveras Twp 5	57 215
Patrick	Calaveras Twp 7	57 35
Patrick	Calaveras Twp 8	57 68
Patrick	Calaveras Twp 8	57 85
Patrick	Calaveras Twp 8	57 87
Patrick	Sacramento Ward 4	63 596
Patrick	San Francisco San Francisco 9	681030
Patrick	San Francisco San Francisco 7	681403
Patrick	San Francisco San Francisco 1	68 812
Patrick	San Francisco San Francisco 1	68 835
Patrick	San Francisco San Francisco 1	68 902
Patrick	Sierra Twp 7	66 891
Patrick	Sierra Twp 5	66 920
Patrick	Tuolumne Twp 3	71 436
Patrick	Yuba New York	72 723
Patrick	Yuba Marysville	72 967
Peter	Alameda Oakland	55 28
Peter	Monterey Alisal	601033
Peter	San Francisco San Francisco 2	67 738
Peter	Sierra Twp 7	66 874
Peter	Yuba Rose Bar	72 805
Philip	San Francisco San Francisco 11	102 67
Pions	Solano Benecia	69 314
Pious O P	Solano Benecia	69 314
R	El Dorado Placerville	58 891
R	Sacramento Brighton	63 207
R	San Mateo Twp 3	65 105
R	Siskiyou Scott Ri	69 70
R M	El Dorado Placerville	58 866
Richard	El Dorado Georgetown	58 682
Richard	Nevada Red Dog	61 544
Richard	San Francisco San Francisco 11	96 67
Richd	Yuba Marysville	72 865
Richd	Sonoma Mendocino	69 461
Robert	Solano Vacaville	69 345
Rose	San Joaquin Stockton	641040
Rose	Sonoma Petaluma	69 590
S	Calaveras Twp 9	57 413
S	El Dorado Placerville	58 865
S P*	Sacramento Brighton	63 192
S W	Yuba Slate Ro	72 693
Sam	Klamath S Fork	59 203
Saml	Klamath S Fork	59 203
Sarah	San Francisco San Francisco 11	123 67
Stephen	Placer Secret R	62 623
Stephen	Santa Cruz Pajaro	66 574
Stephen	Sierra Twp 7	66 913
Stephen	Yuba Rose Bar	72 807
T	Amador Twp 1	55 462
T	Sacramento Ward 1	63 2
T	Sacramento Ward 4	63 606
T D	Tuolumne Twp 2	71 398
Therese	Alameda Oakland	55 22
Thomas	Alameda Oakland	55 40
Thomas	Calaveras Twp 7	57 48
Thomas	Colusa Monroeville	57 452
Thomas	Fresno Twp 1	59 82
Thomas	San Francisco San Francisco 3	67 85
Thomas	San Joaquin Castoria	64 897
Thomas	Sierra Eureka	661048
Thomas	Tuolumne Columbia	71 302
Thomas	Tuolumne Springfield	71 368
Thomas	Tuolumne Montezuma	71 508
Thomas	Yuba Marysville	72 958
Thos	Nevada Nevada	61 249
Thos	Placer Auburn	62 588
Thos	Placer Auburn	62 589
Thos	Placer Ophir	62 651
Thos	Sacramento Sutter	63 290
Thos	San Francisco San Francisco 9	681031
Thos	San Francisco San Francisco 7	681330
Thos	Santa Clara San Jose	65 332
Thos	Tehama Antelope	70 897
Timothy	Alameda Oakland	55 56
Timothy	San Francisco San Francisco 7	681367
Timothy	San Joaquin Oneal	64 938
Timothy	San Mateo Twp 2	65 126
Timothy	Siskiyou Yreka	69 178
Timothy	Sonoma Armally	69 507
W	Marin Sauciteto	60 751
W	Nevada Eureka	61 375
W	Yolo Putah	72 588
W M*	Trinity Weaverville	701080
W T	Tehama Antelope	70 887
W V	Shasta Horsetown	66 696

Name	County Locale	M653 RollPage
MURPHY		
Walter	Tuolumne Twp 2	71 273
William	Marin Novato	60 736
William	Marin Cortemad	60 779
William	Mendocino Round Va	60 880
William	Placer Michigan	62 816
William	San Francisco San Francisco 9	681082
William	San Francisco San Francisco 4	681167
William	San Francisco San Francisco 7	681350
William	San Mateo Twp 3	65 103
William	Santa Cruz Santa Cruz	66 601
William	Tulara Visalia	71 11
Wm	Alameda Brooklyn	55 128
Wm	Alameda Brooklyn	55 134
Wm	Marin San Rafael	60 769
Wm	Santa Clara Santa Clara	65 474
Wm	Siskiyou Callahan	69 5
Wm	Sonoma Petaluma	69 559
Wm	Stanislaus Empire	70 729
Wm	Tehama Moons	70 852
Wm	Tehama Red Bluff	70 921
Wm	Tehama Tehama	70 947
Wm	Tuolumne Big Oak	71 125
Wm	Tuolumne Twp 4	71 127
Wm	Yuba New York	72 727
Wm D	Sierra Forest C	66 910
Wm H	Calaveras Twp 5	57 230
MURPHYL		
Leon	El Dorado Big Bar	58 733
MURPHYS		
Pat	Calaveras Twp 9	57 379
MURPLY		
Bartholomew	Butte Eureka	56 650
Michael*	San Francisco San Francisco 1	68 930
Thos	San Francisco San Francisco 1	68 913
Wm*	San Francisco San Francisco 1	68 917
MURPY		
D*	Sierra St Louis	66 809
L*	Sierra St Louis	66 809
MURR		
---	Tuolumne Twp 5	71 514
Charles	San Francisco San Francisco 8	681274
Chris	San Francisco San Francisco 9	681054
John	Sierra Downieville	661007
John*	Mariposa Coulterville	60 695
Louis*	Calaveras Twp 5	57 209
M	Siskiyou Scott Va	69 56
W H*	Nevada Grass Valley	61 200
MURRA		
Miguel	Santa Clara San Jose	65 315
MURRAG		
Michael	Butte Wyandotte	56 666
MURRAH		
W	Sutter Butte	70 782
MURRAN		
J D	Siskiyou Scott Va	69 57
MURRAY		
A	Butte Bidwell	56 725
A C	Sierra Twp 7	66 878
A G*	Nevada Grass Valley	61 182
A J	Sacramento Alabama	63 411
A R	Tuolumne Big Oak	71 151
Abner	Tuolumne Twp 2	71 386
Abner	Tuolumne Shawsfla	71 390
Abrah	Tulara Twp 1	71 79
Abram	Tulara Visalia	71 79
Alex	Placer Virginia	62 688
Alexander	Marin Cortemad	60 785
Alexander	San Luis Obispo	65 38
Amelia	Del Norte Crescent	58 619
Andrew	Plumas Meadow Valley	62 905
Ann	Placer Illinois	62 706
Ann	San Francisco San Francisco 9	681065
Ann	San Francisco San Francisco 4	681165
Ann	San Francisco San Francisco 8	681273
Annie	San Francisco San Francisco 2	67 744
Arch	Merced Twp 2	60 915
B	Nevada Grass Valley	61 213
B	Sacramento Lee	63 216
Benjamin W	Sierra St Louis	66 811
Bridget	Alameda Brooklyn	55 198
Bridget	San Francisco San Francisco 2	67 734
Bridget	San Francisco San Francisco 1	68 880
C	San Francisco San Francisco 5	67 539
C B	Yolo Putah	72 548
Calvin A	San Francisco San Francisco 11	121 67
Cash	Sacramento Ward 3	63 466
Catharine	Del Norte Crescent	58 636
Ceeswell	Siskiyou Yreka	69 154
Charles	Alameda Oakland	55 56
Chas	Sacramento Ward 4	63 525
Cloda	Mendocino Anderson	60 871
Cornelius	Marin San Rafael	60 772
Cuswell	Siskiyou Yreka	69 154

California 1860 Census Index

Name	County Locale	M653 Roll	Page
MURRAY			
D	Nevada Grass Valley	61	152
D Mc C	Sonoma Healdsbu	69	477
D W	Mendocino Ukiah	60	799
David	Siskiyou Scott Va	69	37
Davidson	Sacramento Ward 1	63	133
Dennis	San Francisco San Francisco 11	67	104
Dennis	Trinity McGillev	70	1021
E	San Francisco San Francisco 1	68	825
Edwd	Butte Kimshaw	56	569
Eliza	San Francisco San Francisco 4	68	1150
Ellen	Alameda Brooklyn	55	187
Ellen	San Francisco San Francisco 1	68	828
F	San Joaquin Stockton	64	1100
F	Trinity Trinity	70	973
F J	Tuolumne Springfield	71	368
Fanny	San Francisco San Francisco 10	67	259
Fanny	San Francisco San Francisco 2	67	791
Francis	San Francisco San Francisco 2	67	681
Frank L	Yolo Slate Ra	72	691
Frank L	Yuba Slate Ro	72	691
Frederick	Siskiyou Scott Va	69	22
G H	Klamath S Fork	59	203
Geo	San Francisco San Francisco 10	67	213
Geo	Siskiyou Callahan	69	11
George	Plumas Quincy	62	1007
George	Yuba Marysville	72	935
Hannah	San Francisco San Francisco 6	67	419
Henry A	Yuba Marysville	72	880
Hugh	San Francisco San Francisco 7	68	1403
Hugh	Santa Clara San Jose	65	294
Isaac	Mendocino Anderson	60	871
J	Nevada Eureka	61	394
J	Sacramento Ward 3	63	449
J	Siskiyou Scott Ri	69	70
J	Tuolumne Big Oak	71	152
J	Yolo No E Twp	72	675
J	Yuba North Ea	72	675
J B	Santa Clara San Jose	65	295
J D	Siskiyou Scott Va	69	57
J E	Alameda Brooklyn	55	187
Jack	Sonoma Petaluma	69	601
Jack	Sonoma Vallejo	69	630
James	Calaveras Twp 5	57	148
James	El Dorado Georgetown	58	701
James	Monterey Pajaro	60	1012
James	San Francisco San Francisco 11	67	103
James	San Francisco San Francisco 7	68	1339
James	Sierra Port Win	66	794
James	Sierra Twp 7	66	893
James	Siskiyou Yreka	69	123
James	Sonoma Armaly	69	510
James	Tuolumne Twp 2	71	360
James W	Sacramento Ward 4	63	509
Jane	Yuba Marysville	72	890
Jarah A	Napa Napa	61	105
Jas	Butte Ophir	56	775
Jas	Sacramento Granite	63	236
Jas	Sacramento Granite	63	267
Jas	Sacramento Ward 4	63	515
Jeannette	San Francisco San Francisco 10	67	185
Jno	Alameda Murray	55	227
Jno	Sacramento Granite	63	240
Jno	San Francisco San Francisco 9	68	1074
Jno D	Mendocino Big Rvr	60	847
Joaquin	Tuolumne Shawsfla	71	391
John	Humbolt Pacific	59	129
John	San Bernardino Santa Barbara	64	173
John	San Diego Agua Caliente	64	847
John	San Francisco San Francisco 9	68	1042
John	San Francisco San Francisco 11	67	108
John	San Francisco San Francisco 8	68	1259
John	San Francisco San Francisco 7	68	1383
John	San Francisco San Francisco 10	67	301
John	San Francisco San Francisco 5	67	496
John	San Francisco San Francisco 1	68	836
John	San Francisco San Francisco 1	68	871
John	Santa Clara Redwood	65	457
John	Santa Cruz Soguel	66	592
John	Siskiyou Scott Va	69	22
John	Sonoma Sonoma	69	636
John	Tulara Yule Rvr	71	23
John	Tulara Keeneysburg	71	46
John	Tuolumne Big Oak	71	135
John	Tuolumne Big Oak	71	177
John	Yuba Rose Bar	72	808
John C	Solano Fairfield	69	199
John H *	Colusa Monroeville	57	448
John L *	Humbolt Eureka	59	169

Name	County Locale	M653 Roll	Page
MURRAY			
John S	Santa Clara Alviso	65	403
John S *	Humbolt Eureka	59	169
John*	Santa Cruz Soguel	66	592
Jos	Amador Twp 3	55	399
Joshua	Tulara Visalia	71	79
Julia	San Francisco San Francisco 6	67	425
Julia	Yuba Marysville	72	873
K	Sierra Eureka	66	1049
Kate	Sacramento Ward 1	63	92
L	Calaveras Twp 9	57	409
Lawrence	Trinity Lewiston	70	964
Lizzie	San Francisco San Francisco 10	67	184
M	Sacramento Lee	63	216
M	Siskiyou Scott Va	69	60
M	Yuba Bear Rvr	72	1009
M*	Tuolumne Big Oak	71	152
Madalene	San Francisco San Francisco 2	67	661
Margare	San Francisco San Francisco 8	68	1241
Margaret	San Francisco San Francisco 8	68	1241
Margaret	Santa Clara San Jose	65	279
Margt	San Francisco San Francisco 2	67	645
Margt T	San Francisco San Francisco 9	68	1085
Mark*	Amador Twp 2	55	302
Mary	San Francisco San Francisco 9	68	1041
Mary	San Francisco San Francisco 4	68	1117
Mary	San Francisco San Francisco 12	67	381
Mary	San Francisco San Francisco 6	67	437
Mary	San Joaquin Stockton	64	1078
Mary	Sonoma Petaluma	69	551
Mary Anne	San Francisco 11	67	101
	San Francisco	67	
Math*	Amador Twp 2	55	302
Michael	Alameda Murray	55	226
Michael	Marin Cortemad	60	781
Michael	San Francisco San Francisco 8	68	1271
Michael	Solano Benecia	69	311
Michael W	Yuba Marysville	72	861
Michael*	Butte Wyandotte	56	666
Michael*	San Francisco San Francisco 8	68	1271
Michl	Sacramento Mississipi	63	187
Michl	San Francisco San Francisco 9	68	1076
Morris	San Francisco San Francisco 7	68	1381
Mth	Amador Twp 2	55	302
O	Siskiyou Callahan	69	2
O	Siskiyou Klamath	69	93
Olson	Calaveras Twp 5	57	209
Orson*	Calaveras Twp 5	57	209
Owen	San Francisco San Francisco 6	67	450
Owen	Tuolumne Twp 2	71	367
Owin	San Francisco San Francisco 6	67	450
P	Sacramento Ward 1	63	76
P	Trinity Mouth Ca	70	1010
Patric C	Alameda Oakland	55	14
Patrick	Alameda Murray	55	226
Patrick	Sacramento Ward 3	63	475
Patrick	Sacramento Ward 1	63	91
Pembroke	Siskiyou Yreka	69	180
Perry	Siskiyou Yreka	69	123
Peter	Alameda Murray	55	223
Peter	Siskiyou Shasta Rvr	69	113
Peter	Tuolumne Columbia	71	334
Petrick	Tuolumne Columbia	71	345
Q	Calaveras Twp 9	57	409
R	Yolo Washington	72	561
Reta	San Francisco San Francisco 6	67	445
Robert	Solano Benecia	69	315
Sarah	Sonoma Healdsbu	69	477
Sarah A	Napa Napa	61	105
Siland	Butte Oregon	56	618
Stephen	Mariposa Twp 3	60	571
Sylvester	Tulara Twp 2	71	22
Tho	Siskiyou Klamath	69	79
Thomas	Calaveras Twp 5	57	148
Thomas	Contra Costa Twp 2	57	570
Thomas	Klamath Liberty	59	239
Thomas	Marin Cortemad	60	784
Thomas	Shasta Shasta	66	732
Thomas	Sierra Twp 7	66	913
Thomas	Siskiyou Shasta Valley	69	120
Thos	Alameda Oakland	55	61
Thos	Klamath Liberty	59	233
Thos	San Francisco San Francisco 9	68	1090
Thos	Sonoma Petaluma	69	561
Thos	Sonoma Petaluma	69	606
Thos*	San Francisco San Francisco 9	68	1090
Timothy	Sacramento Georgian	63	347
Timothy	San Francisco San Francisco 8	68	1305
W	Sacramento Granite	63	229
W	Shasta Millvill	66	755
W	Solano Vacaville	69	321
W	Sutter Yuba	70	762
W E	Alameda Brooklyn	55	179
W O	Butte Ophir	56	746

Name	County Locale	M653 Roll	Page
MURRAY			
W R	Butte Ophir	56	797
Walter	San Luis Obispo San Luis Obispo	65	35
William	Klamath Liberty	59	240
William	Marin San Rafael	60	769
William	Monterey Alisal	60	1037
William	San Francisco San Francisco 4	68	1145
William	San Francisco San Francisco 7	68	1410
William	San Joaquin Oneal	64	936
William*	San Francisco San Francisco 8	68	1305
Wm	Sacramento Centre	63	178
Wm	Alameda Murray	55	223
Wm	Alameda Oakland	55	7
Wm	San Francisco San Francisco 6	67	441
Wm	San Francisco San Francisco 2	67	733
Wm	San Francisco San Francisco 1	68	853
Wm	Santa Clara San Jose	65	390
Wm	Yuba Rose Bar	72	801
Wm H	Placer Sacramento	62	644
Z	Nevada Grass Valley	61	157
MURRAZ			
Jose M	San Luis Obispo San Luis Obispo	65	20
MURRELL			
Calvin	El Dorado Placerville	58	903
J W H	Sonoma Petaluma	69	578
MURREN			
Dennis	Sierra Twp 7	66	903
MURREY			
B	Tuolumne Twp 4	71	161
C	San Joaquin Stockton	64	1059
M	Tuolumne Twp 4	71	152
Mary	San Francisco San Francisco 10	67	249
Orson	Calaveras Twp 5	57	209
Thomas	Shasta Shasta	66	732
MURRGAN			
David*	Mariposa Coulterville	60	702
MURRIER			
John A	Plumas Quincy	62	978
MURRIETTA			
E	Merced Twp 1	60	906
MURRILL			
Hugh	Butte Cascade	56	696
Manuell	Amador Twp 5	55	332
MURRINE			
M*	Nevada Grass Valley	61	235
MURRIO			
---	Tulara Twp 2	71	38
MURRIS			
J	Nevada Grass Valley	61	159
MURRME			
M*	Nevada Grass Valley	61	235
MURROW			
Dennis	Sierra Twp 7	66	903
H S	Nevada Bridgeport	61	496
James	San Francisco San Francisco 3	67	59
MURROY			
Orson*	Calaveras Twp 5	57	209
MURRPH			
Patrick*	Mariposa Twp 3	60	585
MURRPHY			
Danl*	Butte Oregon	56	616
MURRRY			
John	El Dorado Mud Springs	58	995
MURRU			
---	Stanislaus Branch	70	715
MURRY			
---*	San Francisco San Francisco 2	67	638
A J	Nevada Bloomfield	61	528
Abraham*	Sierra Pine Grove	66	835
Alexander	Marin Cortemad	60	785
B F	El Dorado Placerville	58	872
C	Nevada Grass Valley	61	149
C	Nevada Grass Valley	61	189
Charles	El Dorado White Oaks	58	1027
Charles	El Dorado Mud Springs	58	966
Chas	Merced Twp 1	60	913
E E	Tehama Tehama	70	946
George	Placer Iona Hills	62	890
H	El Dorado Placerville	58	838
H	San Joaquin Stockton	64	1099
Hugh	El Dorado Casumnes	58	1175
J	El Dorado Placerville	58	826
J	El Dorado Placerville	58	876
J	Shasta French G	66	717
J C	Merced Twp 1	60	899
J W	Placer Todds Va	62	762
Jackson	San Francisco San Francisco 2	67	670
Jacob	Shasta Horsetown	66	693
John	Amador Twp 1	55	471
John	El Dorado Mud Springs	58	972
John	Placer Forest H	62	769
John	Placer Michigan	62	857
John	San Mateo Twp 3	65	96
John	Sierra Morristown	66	1054
John C	Sonoma Santa Rosa	69	411

Name	County Locale	M653 Roll	Page
MURRY			
Joseph	El Dorado Salmon Falls	58	1050
K	El Dorado Placerville	58	931
L	San Francisco San Francisco 5	67	552
L L	Tehama Lassen	70	865
Laurence*	Stanislaus Branch	70	702
Lizzie	San Francisco San Francisco 10	67	184
M J	Calaveras Twp 9	57	382
Nathen	San Mateo Twp 3	65	73
Owen	San Francisco San Francisco 2	67	787
Owen	Siskiyou Callahan	69	10
P	Sutter Yuba	70	760
Pat	Sonoma Petaluma	69	604
Peter	San Francisco San Francisco 1	68	922
Peter	Tuolumne Twp 2	71	334
R	Nevada Grass Valley	61	208
Robert J	Alameda Oakland	55	13
T	El Dorado Placerville	58	824
T	Shasta French G	66	717
Thomas	El Dorado White Oaks	58	1019
Thomas	El Dorado Mountain	58	1190
Thomas	San Francisco San Francisco 9	68	983
Thomas	Shasta French G	66	717
Thos	Butte Ophir	56	783
W	Sutter Yuba	70	761
W D	Tuolumne Twp 1	71	260
William	Nevada Little Y	61	533
MURRYFIELD			
F A	Tuolumne Shawsfla	71	394
MURS			
Louis	Calaveras Twp 5	57	209
MURSH			
T	Nevada Bridgeport	61	472
MURSILY			
D T*	San Francisco San Francisco 5	67	503
MURSLY			
J	Sutter Butte	70	794
MURSTON			
C A*	Nevada Red Dog	61	540
MURTAGH			
P	Tuolumne Big Oak	71	179
MURTAH			
John*	Plumas Quincy	62	999
MURTAUGH			
Thos	Amador Twp 3	55	391
MURTEN			
A B*	Siskiyou Scott Ri	69	67
MURTHA			
Barnette	Marin S Antoni	60	734
Burnette*	Marin S Antoni	60	734
Marg*	San Francisco San Francisco 2	67	569
P J	Marin Novato	60	738
William O	San Francisco San Francisco 7	68	1344
MURTHY			
Timothy	Tuolumne Twp 1	71	230
MURTIN			
A B*	Siskiyou Scott Ri	69	67
George*	Calaveras Twp 5	57	240
MURTINEY			
---*	Mariposa Twp 1	60	644
MURTIS			
Jas	Calaveras Twp 9	57	366
N B	Sacramento Sutter	63	297
MURTNESS			
Francis	Sacramento Ward 1	63	100
MURTO			
James	Amador Twp 1	55	488
Michael	Mendocino Big Rvr	60	845
MURTY			
A	Yuba Fosters	72	833
Michael	Mendocino Big Rvr	60	845
MURUNA			
Jerry*	Sierra Whiskey	66	845
MURUNCE			
Jerry*	Sierra Whiskey	66	845
MURVEL			
Peter	Sacramento Natonia	63	279
MURVZEN			
Jas	Sacramento Natonia	63	271
MURY			
---	Amador Twp 5	55	347
Eveline	San Joaquin Stockton	64	1075
Jeremiah	Contra Costa Twp 3	57	585
Mary A	Sonoma Armally	69	509
MURZEN			
Jas	Sacramento Natonia	63	271
MUS			
---	Nevada Eureka	61	385
Day*	Sacramento Granite	63	243
Dery*	Sacramento Granite	63	243
Dory*	Sacramento Granite	63	243
John	El Dorado White Oaks	58	1015
MUSANDER			
John	El Dorado Greenwood	58	727
MUSBESTON			
James	El Dorado Georgetown	58	706

Name	County Locale	M653 Roll	Page
MUSCALE			
Phil	Alameda Brooklyn	55	101
MUSCARTER			
Frank	San Francisco San Francisco 1	68	930
MUSCOT			
Arnst	Sonoma Petaluma	69	554
MUSCOTT			
Thomas	Sierra Twp 7	66	895
MUSCOVITCH			
Lireos*	Sacramento Ward 1	63	84
Lueoo*	Sacramento Ward 1	63	84
Sireoo*	Sacramento Ward 1	63	84
Sireos*	Sacramento Ward 1	63	84
Sneos*	Sacramento Ward 1	63	84
Sueoo*	Sacramento Ward 1	63	84
Sueos*	Sacramento Ward 1	63	84
MUSE			
---	Mendocino Twp 1	60	892
Eliza F	Yuba Marysville	72	973
F H	Sierra Twp 7	66	908
James	Siskiyou Scott Va	69	29
Joseah*	Yuba Marysville	72	972
Joseph	San Francisco San Francisco 9	68	1079
Josiah*	Yuba Marysville	72	972
Louis*	Calaveras Twp 5	57	209
MUSEGOES			
Alford	Tuolumne Twp 4	71	129
MUSEOKA			
---	Fresno Twp 2	59	101
MUSETT			
S P	Butte Ophir	56	792
MUSGRAVE			
A J	Butte Chico	56	531
A L*	Nevada Nevada	61	284
Alfred	Napa Hot Springs	61	19
Calvin	Napa Hot Springs	61	18
Louis H*	Napa Hot Springs	61	1
MUSGROVE			
Calvin	Napa Hot Springs	61	18
J D*	Shasta Shasta	66	681
Louis H*	Napa Hot Springs	61	1
R	Nevada Grass Valley	61	159
S	Nevada Grass Valley	61	150
Thomas	Mendocino Calpella	60	812
MUSH			
Ellen	Alameda Oakland	55	67
Jacob	San Francisco San Francisco 3	67	71
MUSHAL			
Joseph*	Alameda Brooklyn	55	125
MUSHAMMER			
Wm	Santa Clara Gilroy	65	239
MUSHAN			
D N*	Yolo Cache	72	609
MUSHAT			
John	Amador Twp 1	55	494
MUSHAWAY			
Peter L	Yuba Bear Rvr	72	1002
MUSHBITH			
Julius	Santa Clara San Jose	65	283
MUSHER			
D N*	Yolo Cache	72	609
MUSIC			
Clanson	Napa Clear Lake	61	123
E L	Napa Clear Lake	61	129
E S*	Napa Clear Lake	61	129
Elanson	Napa Clear Lake	61	123
J J	Napa Clear Lake	61	121
Wm L	Colusa Mansville	57	439
MUSICK			
Abram	Sacramento Sutter	63	295
Lameo F	Colusa Colusi	57	422
MUSIE			
J J	Napa Clear Lake	61	121
MUSIER			
Peter	Butte Ophir	56	777
MUSIETTE			
Jose	El Dorado Greenwood	58	716
MUSINO			
P	El Dorado Georgetown	58	746
MUSKELL			
Robt	Sierra Twp 7	66	867
MUSKEY			
Abraham	San Francisco San Francisco 11	67	103
MUSKIN			
George	Contra Costa Twp 1	57	507
MUSLONE			
James	Nevada Bridgeport	61	488
MUSLOTTA			
Carlotta	El Dorado Georgetown	58	684
MUSON			
Alva	Nevada Bloomfield	61	529
MUSOT			
Catherine	San Francisco San Francisco 3	67	66
MUSOYAM			
---	Mendocino Big Rvr	60	853

Name	County Locale	M653 Roll	Page
MUSQUAL			
---	Fresno Twp 2	59	70
MUSSAL			
C*	Nevada Grass Valley	61	157
MUSSAN			
Thomas	Nevada Bridgeport	61	499
MUSSARY			
B A	Tuolumne Twp 2	71	384
MUSSAY			
B A	Tuolumne Shawsfla	71	384
MUSSCHE			
Andrew	Tuolumne Twp 3	71	424
MUSSCHI			
Charles	Tuolumne Twp 1	71	211
MUSSEAN			
Shoes	Sierra Scales D	66	804
MUSSEAR			
---	Del Norte Klamath	58	657
MUSSEER			
Henry*	Sierra Twp 5	66	929
MUSSELMAN			
David	San Francisco San Francisco 2	67	578
MUSSEN			
Peter	Humbolt Mattole	59	122
MUSSENG			
Antony*	Sierra St Louis	66	817
MUSSER			
Charles*	Solano Fairfield	69	203
Chris	Sacramento Ward 4	63	533
F	Nevada Nevada	61	255
J	El Dorado Kelsey	58	1137
P G	Yuba Parks Ba	72	780
MUSSERS			
Wm M	Santa Clara San Jose	65	279
MUSSERY			
J	El Dorado Placerville	58	898
MUSSES			
L*	Sacramento Granite	63	242
S*	Sacramento Granite	63	242
MUSSETT			
Fredericka	San Francisco 2	67	693
	San Francisco		
MUSSEY			
A W	El Dorado White Oaks	58	1003
E W	Sierra Whiskey	66	847
James	El Dorado Georgetown	58	701
Nelson	San Francisco San Francisco 2	67	748
MUSSIC			
Ellen	Alameda Oakland	55	17
MUSSING			
Anthony	Sierra St Louis	66	817
Antony	Sierra St Louis	66	817
MUSSLEAD			
Charles*	El Dorado Salmon Falls	58	1056
MUSSLER			
Leopold	Placer Iona Hills	62	893
MUSSLES			
A	El Dorado Placerville	58	834
MUSSNOR			
C*	El Dorado Georgetown	58	677
MUSSO			
John*	Sierra Downieville	66	968
MUSTARD			
George	Marin Point Re	60	729
J D	El Dorado Eldorado	58	936
J D	El Dorado Eldorado	58	946
MUSTER			
Chas	Butte Hamilton	56	523
MUSTERS			
Geo	Sacramento Granite	63	253
MUSTERTION			
Stephen	Calaveras Twp 5	57	217
MUSTNEP			
Francis*	Sacramento Ward 1	63	100
MUSTNESS			
Francis*	Sacramento Ward 1	63	100
MUSTON			
James	El Dorado Georgetown	58	703
MUTA			
---	Fresno Twp 2	59	104
MUTAH			
William	Los Angeles Tejon	59	536
MUTALL			
Jno	Sacramento Natonia	63	276
MUTCHINGS			
Thenston	Monterey San Juan	60	995
MUTCHINSON			
Charles G	Los Angeles San Gabriel	59	411
MUTE			
John	Marin Bolinas	60	748
MUTHALL			
John*	San Francisco San Francisco 3	67	46
MUTHIAS			
---	Sacramento Granite	63	249
MUTHOL			
John*	San Francisco San Francisco 9	68	1064

Name	County Locale	M653 Roll Page
MUTHRA		
Rollo*	Santa Cruz Soguel	66 590
Rotto*	Santa Cruz Soguel	66 590
MUTHROLY		
Francis*	San Francisco San Francisco 3	67 75
MUTNOP		
H	San Francisco San Francisco 4	681162
MUTQUINB		
Ma	San Francisco San Francisco 4	681224
MUTSCHMAR		
Victor	San Francisco San Francisco 1	68 861
MUTSON		
William	Calaveras Twp 4	57 311
MUTTALL		
Sarah*	San Francisco San Francisco 1	68 931
MUTTIGAN		
Mar	Sonoma Vallejo	69 627
MUTTINE		
Hanna	San Francisco San Francisco 8	681276
MUTTLEBERRY		
H	Tuolumne Twp 1	71 193
MUTTON		
Thos	Placer Stewart	62 607
MUTY		
Henry	Sonoma Santa Rosa	69 393
MUTYER		
John	Alameda Brooklyn	55 193
MUTZ		
George*	Calaveras Twp 6	57 115
MUTZENBECKER		
John	San Francisco San Francisco 7	681341
MUTZKIE		
Fredk	San Francisco San Francisco 2	67 767
MUUAS		
---*	Mendocino Big Rvr	60 853
MUUSEY		
Jaques	San Joaquin Castoria	64 895
MUUSOW		
Charles	San Joaquin Castoria	64 886
MUW		
---	Sacramento Cosumnes	63 392
---*	Calaveras Twp 10	57 273
Chow	Nevada Eureka	61 385
MUXEY		
Daniel*	Butte Oregon	56 639
MUXMENE		
---*	Tulara Visalia	71 38
MUXMERIC		
---	Tulara Twp 2	71 38
MUY		
---	Butte Ophir	56 817
---	Calaveras Twp 5	57 257
---	San Francisco San Francisco 1	68 924
---*	Trinity Taylor'S	701033
J*	Siskiyou Scott Ri	69 75
Pie	Butte Ophir	56 817
MUYFOE		
John*	San Francisco San Francisco 3	67 85
MUYHART		
J W*	Siskiyou Scott Ri	69 76
MUYHUE		
James	El Dorado Coloma	581123
MUZ		
J*	Siskiyou Scott Ri	69 75
L	Siskiyou Scott Ri	69 75
MUZEL		
Fred	Calaveras Twp 6	57 117
MUZZY		
E L	Trinity Lewiston	70 963
Jos*	Klamath Orleans	59 216
Lorenzo	Solano Vacaville	69 334
MUZZZ		
E L*	Trinity Lewiston	70 963
MY		
---	Amador Twp 2	55 274
---	Amador Twp 5	55 365
---	Amador Twp 7	55 412
---	Amador Twp 6	55 432
---	Butte Kimshaw	56 603
---	Calaveras Twp 10	57 268
---	El Dorado Coloma	581106
---	El Dorado Placerville	58 830
---	El Dorado Placerville	58 886
---	El Dorado Eldorado	58 939
---	El Dorado Mud Springs	58 966
---	Sacramento Ward 4	63 610
---	Shasta Shasta	66 669
Ah	Butte Oregon	56 626
Ah	Butte Oregon	56 642
Fou	El Dorado Coloma	581077
He	El Dorado Georgetown	58 700
Hin	Mariposa Coulterville	60 682
Kee	Butte Oregon	56 630
Kim	El Dorado Georgetown	58 701
Ku	San Francisco San Francisco 5	671207
Lee	El Dorado Georgetown	58 702
MY		
Lee	Sacramento Granite	63 243
Ne	El Dorado Georgetown	58 700
Ree	San Francisco San Francisco 5	671207
Slim*	El Dorado Greenwood	58 729
MYALETA		
Mary	El Dorado Kelsey	581132
MYALL		
Albert	Tuolumne Twp 2	71 398
MYANA		
Gilmore*	Santa Cruz Soguel	66 592
MYARS		
H	Tuolumne Sonora	71 189
MYCE		
C*	Sacramento Alabama	63 412
Charles	Siskiyou Yreka	69 155
Henry*	Sacramento Alabama	63 412
MYCHAEL		
---*	Mariposa Twp 3	60 563
MYCKOFF		
Wm	Tuolumne Twp 1	71 203
MYDRICK		
Jos	Sacramento Ward 1	63 129
MYE		
---	El Dorado Coloma	581121
---	El Dorado Placerville	58 831
---	Fresno Twp 3	59 31
---	San Francisco San Francisco 4	681182
---	San Francisco San Francisco 4	681200
L*	Sacramento Brighton	63 194
Mias	Colusa Mansville	57 438
S*	Sacramento Brighton	63 194
MYENS		
O*	Calaveras Twp 9	57 366
MYER		
---	San Francisco San Francisco 9	681088
Adam	Sacramento Mississipi	63 186
Antone	Sierra Gibsonville	66 855
August	San Francisco San Francisco 2	67 651
C*	Sacramento Alabama	63 412
Caroline	Yuba Marysville	72 938
Charles N	Alameda Brooklyn	55 108
Chris	San Francisco San Francisco 11	129 67
Christian	Calaveras Twp 9	57 361
Christian	Yuba Marysville	72 956
Clemens	Tuolumne Twp 1	71 236
Clocis	Yuba Suida	72 994
Cloeis*	Yuba Linda	72 994
Clous*	Yuba Linda	72 994
Daniel	San Francisco San Francisco 2	67 592
David	San Francisco San Francisco 4	681170
E	Nevada Nevada	61 248
Frank	Yuba Marysville	72 859
Frank	Yuba Marysville	72 860
Franklin	San Francisco San Francisco 4	681217
Fred	Alameda Brooklyn	55 147
Fred	Placer Virginia	62 677
Frederick	Marin San Rafael	60 766
G M	San Francisco San Francisco 5	67 520
George	San Francisco San Francisco 7	681329
George	San Francisco San Francisco 1	68 932
Henry	Calaveras Twp 7	57 18
Henry*	Sacramento Alabama	63 412
J	Los Angeles Tejon	59 524
J	San Francisco San Francisco 5	67 527
J	Siskiyou Scott Ri	69 69
J H	Siskiyou Scott Ri	69 73
J H	Sutter Butte	70 786
James A	Tuolumne Twp 2	71 473
John	San Mateo Twp 2	65 112
Jonas	San Francisco San Francisco 2	67 666
Joseph	El Dorado Casumnes	581177
Joseph	Yuba Marysville	72 877
Joseph	Yuba Marysville	72 880
Joseph	Yuba Marysville	72 952
Kate	San Francisco San Francisco 10	359 67
L*	Sacramento Alabama	63 412
Lenna*	San Francisco San Francisco 4	681162
Lenora	San Francisco San Francisco 4	681162
Lewis	Tehama Lassen	70 884
Louis	San Francisco San Francisco 9	681019
Michael M	Yuba Marysville	72 862
P	El Dorado Diamond	58 784
P	El Dorado Diamond	58 799
Peter	San Francisco San Francisco 9	68 990
Rositta F	Santa Clara San Jose	65 294
S	San Francisco San Francisco 3	67 64
T	San Francisco San Francisco 3	67 64
T R*	Yuba Fosters	72 828
Theadore	Humbolt Bucksport	59 157
W B	San Francisco San Francisco 9	681084
William	San Francisco San Francisco 11	112 67
William	Yuba Linda	72 987
MYER		
Wm	Alameda Oakland	55 18
Wm	San Francisco San Francisco 5	67 514
MYERA		
Beneto	Santa Cruz Santa Cruz	66 616
MYERFEILD		
M*	San Francisco San Francisco 5	67 551
MYERFRILD		
M	San Francisco San Francisco 5	67 551
MYERICK		
Jos*	Sacramento Ward 1	63 129
MYERLE		
Beneto*	Santa Cruz Santa Cruz	66 616
Lewis	San Joaquin Elliott	641103
Philip	San Joaquin Elliott	641103
MYERS JACOB		
Jacob	Colusa Grand Island	57 477
MYERS		
---	Yolo Cache Crk	72 593
A	Tuolumne Twp 1	71 262
A J	Trinity Trinity	70 974
Abner J	Tuolumne Jacksonville	71 516
Abraham H	Alameda Oakland	55 75
Agnes	San Francisco San Francisco 4	681172
Albert	Mariposa Twp 3	60 593
Alex	Sonoma Bodega	69 541
Alexander	Placer Iona Hills	62 888
Andrew	Colusa Spring Valley	57 429
Andrew	Colusa Grand Island	57 478
Andrew	Santa Cruz Pajaro	66 528
Andrew	Tulara Twp 2	71 6
Andrew	Yolo Cache	72 643
B E	San Francisco San Francisco 4	681146
B F	Amador Twp 1	55 457
B K	Sacramento Ward 4	63 497
B T	Solano Montezuma	69 373
Benj	Nevada Little Y	61 535
Benj F	Placer Auburn	62 571
Bernard	Yuba Marysville	72 862
C	Nevada Grass Valley	61 149
C	San Francisco San Francisco 3	67 51
C	San Mateo Twp 2	65 129
C	Shasta Shasta	66 731
C	Yolo Putah	72 552
C A	Mariposa Twp 3	60 590
Catharine	San Francisco San Francisco 7	681442
Charles	Contra Costa Twp 3	57 602
Charles	Placer Michigan	62 839
Charles	Sierra Gibsonville	66 855
Charles	Yuba Long Bar	72 754
Charles	Yuba Marysville	72 868
Charles A	Yuba Marysville	72 888
Chas	Sacramento Ward 3	63 469
Chas	Santa Cruz Santa Cruz	66 636
Chas M	Placer Secret R	62 616
Christian	Calaveras Twp 10	57 292
Christopher	Mendocino Anderson	60 865
D	Amador Twp 2	55 310
D	Amador Twp 2	55 312
D D	Amador Twp 7	55 416
D	Alameda Brooklyn	55 152
David	Amador Twp 1	55 474
David	Butte Ophir	56 780
David	Mariposa Twp 1	60 671
David	Sacramento Ward 3	63 482
David H	San Luis Obispo San Luis Obispo	65 31
David*	Placer Virginia	62 669
Dudley	Sonoma Santa Rosa	69 389
Dudley D	Sonoma Santa Rosa	69 389
Edw	Siskiyou Cottonwoood	69 98
Edward	Tuolumne Chinese	71 488
Elharman	Humbolt Pacific	59 137
Eli	Amador Twp 5	55 363
Elizabeth	Trinity Douglas	70 980
Emily*	Contra Costa Twp 2	57 572
Eugene	San Francisco San Francisco 10	231 67
F	Yolo Putah	72 615
Frank	El Dorado Georgetown	58 673
Frank	El Dorado Mud Springs	58 998
Frank	Nevada Bloomfield	61 509
Frank	Yuba Marysville	72 927
Frank E	El Dorado Georgetown	58 752
Frank*	Sonoma Petaluma	69 588
Franklin	San Francisco San Francisco 9	681084
Fred	Sacramento Natonia	63 284
Fred	Sierra Twp 7	66 885
Fred	Tuolumne Sonora	71 196
Fredk	San Francisco San Francisco 10	256 67
G	El Dorado Placerville	58 817
Geo	El Dorado White Oaks	581008
Geo	El Dorado White Oaks	581018
George	Tuolumne Don Pedro	71 534
George F	Sierra Monte Crk	661037
George L	Yuba Marysville	72 907

California 1860 Census Index

Name	County Locale	M653 Roll	Page
MYERS			
H	El Dorado Placerville	58	834
H	El Dorado Placerville	58	858
H	Placer Dutch Fl	62	710
H	San Francisco San Francisco 5	67	493
H B	San Francisco San Francisco 12	67	366
H Jp	San Joaquin Elkhorn	64	994
H L	San Francisco San Francisco 2	67	669
H R	Butte Ophir	56	792
H R	Nevada Grass Valley	61	179
Harris	San Francisco San Francisco 8	681	269
Henry	Amador Twp 2	55	326
Henry	Calaveras Twp 7	57	17
Henry	Calaveras Twp 4	57	311
Henry	Del Norte Happy Ca	58	670
Henry	El Dorado White Oaks	581	006
Henry	El Dorado Kelsey	581	129
Henry	Mariposa Coulterville	60	684
Henry	Placer Yankee J	62	782
Henry	Placer Iona Hills	62	861
Henry	San Francisco San Francisco 7	681	378
Henry	Sierra Monte Crk	661	037
Henry	Siskiyou Yreka	69	175
Henry	Siskiyou Scott Va	69	21
Henry	Siskiyou Scott Va	69	49
Henry	Tehama Moons	70	852
Henry	Tulara Visalia	71	3
Henry T*	Tuolumne Twp 5	71	516
Henry*	Mariposa Coulterville	60	684
Ignatins*	Yuba Marysville	72	863
Ignatius	Yuba Marysville	72	863
Isaac C	Yuba Marysville	72	901
J	Calaveras Twp 9	57	377
J	El Dorado Placerville	58	822
J	Nevada Eureka	61	358
J	Nevada Eureka	61	363
J	Sacramento American	63	172
J	Sacramento Ward 1	63	4
J	Tehama Red Bluff	70	912
J G	Sacramento American	63	172
J H	Siskiyou Scott Ri	69	73
J H	Siskiyou Klamath	69	94
J H	Tuolumne Twp 1	71	196
J N	Placer Auburn	62	565
J P	Shasta Millvill	66	725
J S	Butte Wyandotte	56	664
J*	Nevada Eureka	61	346
Jackson	Sonoma Russian	69	444
Jacob	Alameda Brooklyn	55	147
Jacob	Amador Twp 2	55	220
Jacob	Colusa Grand Island	57	481
Jacob	Santa Clara San Jose	65	388
Jacob	Siskiyou Klamath	69	93
Jacob	Yuba Rose Bar	72	794
Jacob	Yuba Marysville	72	847
Jacob	Yuba Marysville	72	867
Jacob D	Humbolt Table Bl	59	142
Jacob*	Yuba Rose Bar	72	794
Jameds	Siskiyou Shasta Rvr	69	114
James	Alameda Brooklyn	55	80
James	Humbolt Eel Rvr	59	150
James	Santa Clara Alviso	65	399
James	Siskiyou Shasta Rvr	69	114
James	Solano Suisan	69	219
James	Yuba Long Bar	72	748
James*	Mendocino Ukiah	60	793
James*	Nevada Little Y	61	534
Jerome	San Joaquin Stockton	641	074
Jesse	Alameda Brooklyn	55	115
Jno	San Francisco San Francisco 10	67	231
Jno	San Francisco San Francisco 10	67	333
John	Amador Twp 3	55	386
John	Calaveras Twp 7	57	30
John	Contra Costa Twp 2	57	569
John	Mariposa Twp 1	60	644
John	Merced Monterey	60	942
John	Monterey Monterey	60	942
John	Sacramento Franklin	63	321
John	Sacramento Ward 3	63	484
John	San Francisco San Francisco 11	67	110
John	San Francisco San Francisco 2	67	659
John	San Mateo Twp 1	65	71
John	Santa Cruz Pajaro	66	551
John	Sierra St Louis	66	807
John	Siskiyou Klamath	69	84
John	Solano Suisan	69	233
John	Solano Benecia	69	316
John	Sonoma Petaluma	69	563
John	Stanislaus Branch	70	703
John	Trinity Taylor'S	701	034
John	Yolo Slate Ra	72	689
John	Yuba Slate Ro	72	689

Name	County Locale	M653 Roll	Page
MYERS			
John L	Yuba Linda	72	985
John L	Mariposa Twp 3	60	586
John P	Colusa Grand Island	57	477
John W	Calaveras Twp 8	57	91
Joseph	El Dorado Grizzly	581	181
Joseph	Placer Auburn	62	578
Joseph	San Francisco San Francisco 9	681	097
Joseph	San Mateo Twp 1	65	71
Joseph	Solano Vacaville	69	364
Joseph M	Alameda Oakland	55	50
L	Nevada Grass Valley	61	186
L D	Tuolumne Twp 2	71	371
L*	Sacramento Brighton	63	198
Lemuel	Sierra Gibsonville	66	851
Leonard N	Sacramento Ward 3	63	483
Leonora	Amador Twp 2	55	278
Levi	Sierra Twp 7	66	885
Lewis	Tehama Lassen	70	882
Louis	San Francisco San Francisco 9	681	003
M	El Dorado Placerville	58	879
M	El Dorado Placerville	58	888
M	Nevada Grass Valley	61	192
M	San Francisco San Francisco 4	681	165
M	San Francisco San Francisco 5	67	550
M	San Francisco San Francisco 1	68	878
M E	Sacramento Georgian	63	341
Margt	San Francisco San Francisco 2	67	697
Maris	San Francisco San Francisco 4	681	149
Mathewson	Twp 1	57	499
	Contra Costa		
Michael	Placer Secret R	62	612
Michael	Sierra Gibsonville	66	856
Milton	Trinity New Rvr	701	031
Mitchell	San Francisco San Francisco 6	67	449
Morris	San Francisco San Francisco 4	681	149
Moses	San Francisco San Francisco 10	67	351
Nathan	Placer Iona Hills	62	897
O*	Calaveras Twp 9	57	366
P	Calaveras Twp 9	57	376
P	Nevada Nevada	61	243
P	San Francisco San Francisco 4	681	230
Peter	Contra Costa Twp 3	57	599
Peter	El Dorado Mud Springs	58	998
Reuben	Santa Cruz Santa Cruz	66	616
Richard	San Francisco San Francisco 10	67	169
Robert	San Francisco San Francisco 9	681	053
Robert	Yolo Cache	72	645
S	Calaveras Twp 9	57	401
S	El Dorado Placerville	58	843
S	Nevada Eureka	61	358
S A	Trinity W Weaver	701	054
S C	Mendocino Ukiah	60	804
S M	Sacramento American	63	158
S*	Sacramento Brighton	63	198
Saml	San Francisco San Francisco 10	67	231
Sampson	San Francisco San Francisco 9	681	007
Samuel	El Dorado White Oaks	581	014
Stephen G	Solano Cosummes	69	364
Stranton	Sacramento American	63	170
Susan	El Dorado White Oaks	581	010
T	El Dorado Mountain	581	184
T	El Dorado Placerville	58	894
T	Sacramento Cosummes	63	403
T	San Francisco San Francisco 1	68	878
Thomas	Del Norte Crescent	58	644
Thos B	Butte Wyandotte	56	667
Thos E	Sacramento Franklin	63	326
Thos*	Sacramento San Joaquin	63	350
W	Butte Wyandotte	56	664
W	Siskiyou Cottonwood	69	101
W A	Trinity Minersville	70	969
W F	Siskiyou Scott Ri	69	75
W H	Siskiyou Scott Ri	69	62
W M	Siskiyou Scott Ri	69	62
W*	Nevada Grass Valley	61	192
Wash	Sacramento Ward 3	63	473
Wesley	Placer Rattle Snake	62	625
William	El Dorado Placerville	58	899
William	Nevada Bridgeport	61	486
William	Plumas Quincy	621	005
William	Sierra Gibsonville	66	854
William	Solano Vacaville	69	358
William	Yuba Bear Rvr	721	000
William J	San Francisco San Francisco 11	67	155
Willian	Nevada Bridgeport	61	486
Wm	Butte Bidwell	56	705
Wm	Del Norte Crescent	58	623
Wm	Placer Virginia	62	684
Wm	San Francisco San Francisco 1	68	920
Wm	Tehama Red Bluff	70	909
Wm	Tuolumne Twp 1	71	234

Name	County Locale	M653 Roll	Page
MYERS			
Wm	Yuba New York	72	723
Wm	Yuba Rose Bar	72	788
Wm	Yuba Rose Bar	72	799
Wm	Yuba Fosters	72	841
MYGANT			
J	El Dorado Diamond	58	803
MYINS			
J	Calaveras Twp 9	57	377
MYKINS			
Danl	Sacramento Ward 4	63	553
MYLAR			
Romas	Calaveras Twp 7	57	29
MYLER			
James L	Mariposa Coulterville	60	702
MYLES			
Henry R	Los Angeles Los Angeles	59	334
Wm T	Alameda Oakland	55	5
MYLETT			
James	Yuba Rose Bar	72	790
MYMA			
Gilmore	Santa Cruz Soguel	66	592
MYMER			
Gilmore*	Santa Cruz Soguel	66	592
MYNCE			
N	Sacramento Alabama	63	415
MYNCK			
C G	Marin Cortemad	60	755
MYNES			
Henry*	San Francisco San Francisco 1	68	932
MYNNE			
James	Santa Cruz Pajaro	66	577
MYON			
W A*	Yuba Rose Bar	72	788
MYOR			
Adolf	Los Angeles Tejon	59	526
MYORS			
B T	Solano Montezuma	69	373
MYR			
---	Mariposa Twp 1	60	643
---	San Francisco San Francisco 4	681	182
H N	Tuolumne Twp 2	71	363
MYRAHAM			
Newton	Calaveras Twp 10	57	279
MYRAL			
Esperancio	Santa Cruz Santa Cruz	66	605
MYRAND			
Guadelupe	Santa Cruz Pajaro	66	556
Henry	Santa Cruz Pajaro	66	556
Ontino	Santa Cruz Pajaro	66	556
Outino*	Santa Cruz Pajaro	66	556
MYRANDO			
Raphael	Santa Cruz Pajaro	66	541
MYRANDS			
Raphael	Santa Cruz Pajaro	66	541
MYRAS			
G	Sutter Yuba	70	765
MYRD			
Esperanceo*	Santa Cruz Santa Cruz	66	605
Esperancio*	Santa Cruz Santa Cruz	66	605
MYRE			
---	Placer Rattle Snake	62	635
MYREA			
Geo	Santa Clara Fremont	65	431
MYRES			
Antone	Amador Twp 4	55	254
Daniel	Amador Twp 4	55	237
David G	Placer Dutch Fl	62	716
Emily*	Contra Costa Twp 2	57	572
G	Sutter Yuba	70	759
H	Placer Auburn	62	565
Henry*	San Francisco San Francisco 1	68	932
J W	Marin San Rafael	60	757
Jas	San Francisco San Francisco 1	68	904
John	Marin S Antoni	60	712
L	El Dorado Diamond	58	783
L M	El Dorado Mud Springs	58	988
Robert	Marin San Rafael	60	757
Robert	Marin San Rafael	60	766
MYRICK			
C G	Marin Cortemad	60	755
C M	San Francisco San Francisco 12	67	392
D B	Sonoma Washington	69	675
H M	Tehama Red Bluff	70	914
Jos	Sacramento Ward 1	63	129
Reuben C	Calaveras Twp 4	57	337
Samuel	Santa Cruz Santa Cruz	66	603
Thomas	San Francisco San Francisco 7	681	350
Thomas S	San Francisco San Francisco 7	681	350
MYRINE			
James	Santa Cruz Pajaro	66	577
MYRING			
Wm	Sonoma Russian	69	439
MYRON			
James	Calaveras Twp 8	57	104

California 1860 Census Index

Name	County Locale	M653 Roll	Page
MYRRICK			
J N	Placer Yankee J	62	756
MYSBY			
G*	Napa Hot Springs	61	7
MYSICK			
J W	Placer Iona Hills	62	870
Reuben C*	Calaveras Twp 4	57	337
MYSLY			
G*	Napa Hot Springs	61	7
MYSTER			
Joseph	Sacramento Sutter	63	303
MYSTRELLY			
Peter	Tuolumne Twp 2	71	284
MYSTY			
G*	Napa Hot Springs	61	7
MYTHOS			
Charles	San Francisco San Francisco 4	681	217
MYUE			
---*	Tulara Visalia	71	36
MYY			
---*	Trinity Taylor'S	701	033
N E			
---*	Sierra Downieville	661	009
N K			
---	Sierra Downieville	66	998
N R			
---	Sierra Downieville	66	999
N W			
---	Butte Oregon	56	638
N			
E*	Sierra Downieville	661	009
Vaginia	Amador Twp 6	55	428
Way	Sierra St Louis	66	815
NA CA TO			
---	Mendocino Calpella	60	824
NA			
---	Amador Twp 2	55	293
---	Calaveras Twp 10	57	261
---	El Dorado Diamond	58	808
---	Mariposa Twp 1	60	666
---*	Calaveras Twp 10	57	261
Hi	Yuba Long Bar	72	756
Sli	Yuba Long Bar	72	756
NAAGLE			
Jno	Sacramento Natonia	63	285
NAAL			
Warren	San Francisco San Francisco 1	68	928
NAAU			
---	Sacramento Natonia	63	283
NAAVARRO			
Juan	San Diego San Diego	64	770
NAB			
---	Sacramento Ward 1	63	55
NABA			
Marciana	San Francisco San Francisco 2	67	767
NABB			
Richd	Sonoma Healdsbu	69	472
NABELE			
Chas	Santa Clara Santa Clara	65	482
W*	Calaveras Twp 9	57	394
NABER			
F	Shasta Shasta	66	683
NABERS			
Martin	San Joaquin Elkhorn	64	995
NABIS			
John	El Dorado White Oaks	581	026
NABLE			
C A*	Sacramento Centre	63	177
H	Sutter Yuba	70	759
NABLES			
Moses G	Santa Clara Gilroy	65	238
NABOR			
F*	Shasta Shasta	66	683
NABOT			
Elisha	Sacramento Granite	63	260
NABRETTE			
Frank*	Sierra Poker Flats	66	840
NACA			
---	Fresno Twp 1	59	27
NACER			
Joquin	Santa Clara San Jose	65	299
NACHE			
John	Mariposa Twp 3	60	545
NACHMAN			
A	El Dorado Placerville	58	828
NACHTINGALE			
H	San Francisco San Francisco 5	67	497
NACIO			
H	San Mateo Twp 2	65	114
NACK			
---	Sierra Downieville	661	015
NACKLER			
Ernest	Tuolumne Twp 2	71	322
NACLIS			
Bertha*	Sacramento Ward 1	63	34
NACOUSTA			
---	Fresno Twp 2	59	74

Name	County Locale	M653 Roll	Page
NACTONDO			
Pedro	Santa Clara San Jose	65	297
NAD DORN			
A V	San Francisco San Francisco 10		242
		67	
NADA			
Marco	Alameda Oakland	55	31
NADAL			
Catalina	Los Angeles Los Angeles	59	296
NADDEN			
John	Siskiyou Callahan	69	3
NADDY			
Robert	Napa Clear Lake	61	121
NADEN			
Clement	Calaveras Twp 4	57	304
P	Siskiyou Scott Ri	69	75
NADER			
James	San Francisco San Francisco 9	681	067
NADLEIGH			
W E	Butte Eureka	56	655
NADO			
E	Amador Twp 4	55	245
NADREWS			
Rebecca P	Calaveras Twp 4	57	338
NAEFF			
John M	San Francisco San Francisco 9	681	106
Wm J	San Francisco San Francisco 2	67	604
NAEL			
Peter*	Siskiyou Scott Va	69	49
NAELIS			
Bertha	Sacramento Ward 1	63	34
NAES			
Bernado	Calaveras Twp 7	57	1
NAFE			
I	Nevada Washington	61	337
J	Nevada Washington	61	337
NAFF			
John	Santa Clara San Jose	65	360
NAFSARIO			
---	San Diego Temecula	64	789
NAG			
---	Sacramento Ward 1	63	61
Kee	Mariposa Twp 3	60	544
NAGA			
Jacob	Yuba New York	72	733
NAGAR			
Jose	Plumas Quincy	62	988
NAGEL			
Christ	Sacramento Granite	63	260
Eugene	San Francisco San Francisco 7	681	334
Jacob	San Francisco San Francisco 7	681	416
NAGENT			
Jas	Calaveras Twp 9	57	371
NAGER			
Claus	Tuolumne Shawsfla	71	410
R	Calaveras Twp 9	57	384
Syus	Yolo Cache	72	637
NAGES			
Claus	Tuolumne Twp 2	71	410
David*	Nevada Bridgeport	61	478
NAGG			
Jas	Yolo Putah	72	551
NAGLE			
Anna E	Contra Costa Twp 1	57	536
B A	Siskiyou Scott Va	69	58
C	Mariposa Coulterville	60	677
Chas	El Dorado Greenwood	58	710
Edwd	San Francisco San Francisco 10		258
		67	
Jacob	San Francisco San Francisco 2	67	795
Jacob	Yuba New York	72	733
James	Contra Costa Twp 3	57	592
John	Placer Rattle Snake	62	603
John	San Francisco San Francisco 7	681	334
John	San Francisco San Francisco 2	67	723
Mary	Contra Costa Twp 3	57	607
Mary	San Francisco San Francisco 11		113
		67	
Mary J	San Francisco San Francisco 10		182
		67	
N	San Francisco San Francisco 2	67	723
P B	Stanislaus Branch	70	697
Richard	San Francisco San Francisco 11		93
		67	
Richard	Sierra Morristown	661	052
William	San Francisco San Francisco 7	681	347
William	Tuolumne Twp 1	71	212
William	Tuolumne Twp 1	71	245
Wm	San Francisco San Francisco 2	67	784
NAGLEY			
Charles	Contra Costa Twp 1	57	502
NAGNALL			
John*	Santa Cruz Santa Cruz	66	600
NAGNSERER			
F*	Siskiyou Callahan	69	5

Name	County Locale	M653 Roll	Page
NAGNSERES			
F*	Siskiyou Callahan	69	5
NAGOR			
R	Calaveras Twp 9	57	384
NAGUS			
David*	Nevada Bridgeport	61	478
NAGUSERE			
F	Siskiyou Callahan	69	5
NAGY			
Alexander	Santa Clara San Jose	65	289
NAH			
---	Calaveras Twp 5	57	242
---	Tuolumne Don Pedro	71	536
Ah Le	Sacramento Ward 1	63	145
NAHL			
Bridget	Yuba Marysville	72	955
Chas	San Francisco San Francisco 1	68	813
NAHLEE			
---	Tuolumne Twp 5	71	504
NAHOO			
---	Tulara Twp 2	71	4
NAHOR			
---*	Tulara Visalia	71	4
Joseph	Placer Iona Hills	62	885
NAHUN			
Robert G*	Sierra La Porte	66	770
NAIAR			
Henry	Sierra Downieville	66	997
NAIFF			
John M*	San Francisco San Francisco 9	681	106
NAIGHBON			
Geo	Butte Ophir	56	791
NAIL			
Isaac	Siskiyou Scott Va	69	57
J W	Butte Oro	56	679
M	El Dorado Mountain	581	183
N	El Dorado Mountain	581	183
P	Siskiyou Scott Va	69	57
NAILE			
S	Tuolumne Twp 4	71	149
NAILL			
C	Tuolumne Twp 4	71	161
NAILLY			
John*	Calaveras Twp 9	57	387
NAILO			
Pedro	Calaveras Twp 9	57	376
NAILOR			
George	Yuba Marysville	72	883
Martin	Marin Bolinas	60	742
W	Siskiyou Scott Ri	69	71
William	Calaveras Twp 4	57	318
NAILS			
George	San Joaquin Elliott	641	102
Pedro	Calaveras Twp 9	57	376
NAIM			
---	El Dorado Georgetown	58	762
NAIND			
Joseph*	Calaveras Twp 5	57	186
NAINS			
Joseph	Contra Costa Twp 1	57	486
NAIRED			
Joseph	Calaveras Twp 5	57	186
NAIRTHGRAVE			
W	Butte Kimshaw	56	568
NAITH			
Jane*	Nevada Nevada	61	328
NAJA			
M	Tehama Red Bluff	70	931
Pas*	San Mateo Twp 2	65	132
NAK			
---	Mariposa Twp 3	60	608
NALAN			
Mary A	Siskiyou Yreka	69	194
NALDER			
F*	Butte Eureka	56	649
NALDMAN			
Abraham	Alameda Brooklyn	55	81
NALE			
D	San Francisco San Francisco 9	681	086
M	Siskiyou Cottonwoood	69	98
Milling	Napa Napa	61	88
NALELE			
W*	Calaveras Twp 9	57	394
NALEN			
B F*	Siskiyou Scott Va	69	36
NALENCA			
Hosa	El Dorado Coloma	581	075
Hose	El Dorado Coloma	581	075
NALENCIO			
Cereno	Calaveras Twp 7	57	9
NALES			
Franklin R	San Francisco San Francisco 4	681	131
NALF			
---*	Mariposa Twp 3	60	564
Jacob	Butte Oregon	56	641
NALGOMOT			
James	Sacramento San Joaquin	63	361

California 1860 Census Index

Name	County Locale	M653 Roll	Page
NALIO			
---	Tulara Keyesville	71	64
NALL			
---	Yuba Marysville	72	895
H N	El Dorado Placerville	58	822
James	San Francisco San Francisco 8	681	284
John	Yuba Fosters	72	839
Melling*	Napa Napa	61	88
Milling*	Napa Napa	61	88
W	Sutter Butte	70	794
NALLA			
---	Sierra Downieville	66	998
NALLEUYNELA			
Juan	Contra Costa Twp 1	57	537
NALLOIS			
Juluos	Calaveras Twp 5	57	198
NALLSON			
N E	Sacramento Georgian	63	344
NALLY			
A B	Sonoma Santa Rosa	69	393
James	Klamath Liberty	59	236
Nangasa	Alameda Brooklyn	55	208
NALNMA			
---	Mendocino Big Rvr	60	853
NALOR			
Thomles*	Calaveras Twp 4	57	319
NALSH			
M*	Butte Kimshaw	56	596
NALUM			
Halley	El Dorado Kelsey	581	133
NALUMA			
---*	Mendocino Big Rvr	60	853
NALUMCO			
---*	Mendocino Big Rvr	60	853
NAM			
---	Calaveras Twp 10	57	260
---	El Dorado Salmon Falls	581	054
---	El Dorado Casumnes	581	176
---	El Dorado Diamond	58	785
---	Nevada Rough &	61	431
---	Sierra Pine Grove	66	827
Chi	Calaveras Twp 5	57	255
Heny	Calaveras Twp 10	57	295
Tis	Calaveras Twp 5	57	246
NAMAKUEA			
---	Fresno Twp 2	59	60
NAMARE			
Lasser	Mariposa Twp 1	60	660
NAMARO			
Lasser	Mariposa Twp 1	60	660
NAME			
---	Calaveras Twp 6	57	151
---	Tuolumne Twp 5	71	521
NAMED			
Jno	Sonoma Mendocino	69	466
Jos	Sonoma Salt Point	69	689
Nat	Sonoma Cloverdale	69	686
Not	Sonoma Salt Point	69	689
Not	Sonoma Salt Point	69	690
Not	Sonoma Salt Point	69	692
NAMEHTO			
O H	Nevada Eureka	61	374
NAMEHTS			
O H*	Nevada Eureka	61	374
NAMELYS			
---	Mariposa Twp 3	60	601
NAMER			
Joaquin*	Calaveras Twp 10	57	276
Patrick W	San Francisco San Francisco 3	67	81
NAMES			
Jose	Tehama Red Bluff	70	930
NAMI			
---	Calaveras Twp 6	57	151
NAMO			
L Y*	Yuba Slate Ro	72	701
NAMSEY			
Theodore	Contra Costa Twp 2	57	569
NAMUR			
N	Sacramento Ward 1	63	15
NAN			
---	Butte Kimshaw	56	599
---	Butte Eureka	56	652
---	Calaveras Twp 5	57	209
---	El Dorado Salmon Falls	581	045
---	El Dorado Casumnes	581	163
---	Mariposa Twp 3	60	564
---	Sierra St Louis	66	812
---	Stanislaus Emory	70	752
---*	Calaveras Twp 8	57	93
Edward*	Alameda Oakland	55	2
J	Sutter Nicolaus	70	841
Qua	San Francisco San Francisco 5	67	514
Yonk	Trinity Lewiston	70	955
NANALSTIRE			
N	Sutter Bear Rvr	70	818
NANARSDEN			
A*	Yolo Putah	72	550

Name	County Locale	M653 Roll	Page
NANC			
W*	Butte Oregon	56	642
NANCE			
Benj	Butte Hamilton	56	517
Benj T	Butte Hamilton	56	519
George	Nevada Bridgeport	61	480
J P	Butte Hamilton	56	525
J S	Butte Hamilton	56	525
John	Butte Bidwell	56	707
NANCI			
George*	Nevada Bridgeport	61	480
NANCIORVIS			
Thos*	Nevada Bridgeport	61	497
NANCKE			
Fred	Del Norte Crescent	58	624
NANCOLLANS			
William	Nevada Bridgeport	61	497
NANCURVIR			
Thos*	Nevada Bridgeport	61	497
NANCURVIS			
Thos*	Nevada Bridgeport	61	497
NANCY			
---	Del Norte Klamath	58	655
---	Fresno Twp 2	59	42
---	Mendocino Calpella	60	822
---	Mendocino Calpella	60	828
---	San Francisco San Francisco 2	67	673
---	Tulara Twp 1	71	119
NANDALSUN			
H	Santa Clara San Jose	65	374
NANDEAS			
Francisco	Contra Costa Twp 1	57	491
NANDEBERG			
Charles*	Tuolumne Twp 2	71	298
NANDES			
Jose	Amador Twp 1	55	508
NANDEVIA			
Antonio*	Yuba Marysville	72	946
NANDINO			
Francisco	Calaveras Twp 10	57	260
NANDINS			
Francisco	Calaveras Twp 10	57	260
NANDON			
J G	Tuolumne Jamestown	71	432
NANEPWAY			
---*	Mendocino Big Rvr	60	853
NANERRO			
Pierro*	Mariposa Twp 3	60	553
NANERT			
Fritz	Sonoma Petaluma	69	571
NANES			
J T*	Mariposa Twp 3	60	587
NANETH			
John H	Yuba Marysville	72	926
NANEZ			
Sebastiano*	Monterey San Juan	60	998
NANG			
---	Calaveras Twp 4	57	328
---	El Dorado Casumnes	581	176
---	Mariposa Twp 1	60	662
---	Mariposa Twp 1	60	666
---	Placer Folsom	62	647
---	Sacramento Ward 1	63	61
---	Shasta Horsetown	66	705
---	Tuolumne Shawsfla	71	416
---	Tuolumne Twp 3	71	468
---	Tuolumne Sonora	71	475
---	Tuolumne Sonora	71	477
---	Yuba Long Bar	72	764
Name	Yuba Long Bar	72	763
NANGLE			
Ellen F*	San Francisco San Francisco 8	681	296
NANI			
---	Calaveras Twp 10	57	269
NANIS			
John	Calaveras Twp 4	57	345
NANKLEN			
L P	Marin Novato	60	738
NANMAN			
Chas T*	Sierra St Louis	66	806
Henry	Sacramento Ward 3	63	437
NANNAN			
Michael	Solano Benecia	69	285
NANNEN			
John B	Sacramento Ward 3	63	421
NANO			
Ramon	San Bernardino San Salvador	64	638
NANPELS			
Danl	Santa Clara San Jose	65	336
NANTER			
Fred*	Sacramento Ward 3	63	445
NANTY			
Issac	Calaveras Twp 8	57	92
NANTZ			
Allen	Calaveras Twp 10	57	264
NANUS			
Larnise*	Sacramento Natonia	63	279

Name	County Locale	M653 Roll	Page
NANY			
---	Calaveras Twp 4	57	328
---	Mariposa Twp 1	60	666
---*	Yuba Foster B	72	827
NAOMAN			
Chas W*	San Francisco San Francisco 3	67	86
NAPA			
---	Mendocino Calpella	60	824
Andrew	Shasta Shasta	66	655
NAPARIO			
---*	San Diego Temecula	64	789
NAPHHALY			
H	San Francisco San Francisco 9	68	967
NAPHTRALY			
H*	San Francisco San Francisco 9	68	967
NAPIER			
G	San Francisco San Francisco 4	681	225
J H	El Dorado Placerville	58	868
John	San Francisco San Francisco 7	681	442
S	Siskiyou Cottonwoood	69	103
Step	Siskiyou Cottonwoood	69	102
NAPLEY			
Peter C	Los Angeles Los Angeles	59	490
NAPOLEAN			
G	San Francisco San Francisco 5	67	545
G	Tuolumne Twp 1	71	219
NAPOLEON			
---	Mendocino Calpella	60	825
---	San Francisco San Francisco 12	67	392
Jean	Santa Clara Redwood	65	452
Louis	Klamath S Fork	59	202
Louis	Marin Cortemad	60	788
NAPP			
M	Yolo Putah	72	551
NAPPA			
Leon	San Bernardino San Salvador	64	661
NAPPER			
Thomas	Sierra Downieville	66	989
NAPPIN			
William	Nevada Red Dog	61	546
NAPPS			
Harrance	Nevada Bloomfield	61	529
NAPRA			
J	El Dorado Diamond	58	804
NAPTHALIF			
H*	San Francisco San Francisco 9	68	967
NAPTHALY			
H*	San Francisco San Francisco 9	68	967
NAR			
---	El Dorado Salmon Falls	581	045
---	Sacramento Natonia	63	283
Joseph*	Yuba Marysville	72	941
Sew	El Dorado Mud Springs	58	972
NARADUS			
Gill*	Siskiyou Yreka	69	149
NARAH			
Jose Maria	San Mateo Twp 2	65	118
NARAMORE			
Andrew	Placer Secret R	62	617
NARANGA			
Reducinda*	San Francisco 2	67	605
	San Francisco		
NARANJ?			
Reducinda*	San Francisco 2	67	605
	San Francisco		
NARANJA			
Redncinda*	San Francisco 2	67	605
	San Francisco		
NARANJR			
Redercinda*	San Francisco 2	67	605
	San Francisco		
NARANO			
Antonio	San Bernardino S Buenav	64	209
NARANY			
Redacinda	San Francisco San Francisco 2	67	605
NARAR			
Henry	Sierra Downieville	66	997
NARARETE			
Fernando	San Francisco San Francisco 2	67	562
NARARO			
Antonia	Mariposa Twp 1	60	628
NARARRO			
Bernardo	Los Angeles Los Angeles	59	310
Serapio	Los Angeles Los Angeles	59	313
NARAWO			
Pedro*	Fresno Twp 1	59	83
NARBOE			
John*	Tulara Sinks Te	71	43
NARBOLD			
Phillip	El Dorado Coloma	581	104
NARBONNE			
Nathaniel	Los Angeles San Pedro	59	480
NARCESSA			
---	San Bernardino Santa Inez	64	137
NARCIS			
Francisco	Contra Costa Twp 1	57	498

California 1860 Census Index

Name	County Locale	M653 Roll	Page
NARCISA			
Botiller	Los Angeles Los Angeles	59	368
NARCISNS			
S*	El Dorado Placerville	58	822
NARCISO			
---*	Los Angeles Tejon	59	529
Jose	Santa Cruz Pajaro	66	528
NARCISSA			
Jose	Santa Cruz Pajaro	66	554
NARD			
Phillip J*	Calaveras Twp 5	57	252
NARDEMAN			
Patrick	Santa Clara Fremont	65	438
NARDO			
Nre*	Sierra Downieville	66	1012
Ure*	Sierra Downieville	66	1012
NAREISO			
---*	Los Angeles Tejon	59	529
NARGREN			
H	Santa Clara Redwood	65	450
NARH			
Patrick	Solano Suisan	69	232
Peter*	Butte Eureka	56	654
NARING			
F	El Dorado Diamond	58	815
NARIRO			
J	Tuolumne Twp 4	71	162
NARJUCA			
William*	San Mateo Twp 3	65	81
NARK			
John	Sacramento Ward 4	63	548
NARMAN			
John*	Nevada Red Dog	61	540
NARMIAN			
John	El Dorado Georgetown	58	760
NARNEHTO			
O H*	Nevada Eureka	61	374
NARNUN			
Henry*	El Dorado Georgetown	58	760
NARO			
Anton	Tuolumne Jamestown	71	455
NAROM			
Felix	Alameda Brooklyn	55	129
NAROO			
John*	Calaveras Twp 5	57	202
NARR			
Jno*	Klamath S Fork	59	197
NARRA			
Jesus	San Francisco San Francisco 2	67	752
NARRIO			
Angel	Yuba Marysville	72	974
NARRIRIO			
----	Tulara Keyesville	71	69
NARRISON			
James*	San Francisco San Francisco 2	67	603
NARS			
G N	Tuolumne Twp 3	71	465
NARSH			
Lewis*	Calaveras Twp 4	57	326
NARSINO			
---	Tulara Twp 3	71	69
NARSON			
Frederick*	Placer Iona Hills	62	897
NARTAL			
L**	El Dorado Placerville	58	925
NARTH			
Jane*	Nevada Nevada	61	328
NARTHING			
James	Amador Twp 3	55	397
NARTHUG			
Orarye*	Shasta Shasta	66	728
NARTMAN			
Andrew	Nevada Bridgeport	61	489
NARTREVEDORE			
Nanwell	Sacramento Ward 3	63	449
NARUGOMES			
Isadora*	Calaveras Twp 4	57	318
Isadore	Calaveras Twp 4	57	318
NARUIS			
Larnier*	Sacramento Natonia	63	279
NARURRO			
Pedro*	Fresno Twp 1	59	83
NARVAEZ			
Antonio	Santa Clara Alviso	65	403
Jose	Santa Clara Alviso	65	400
Jose A*	Santa Clara Alviso	65	396
Jose D*	Santa Clara Alviso	65	396
Jose J	Santa Clara Alviso	65	400
Juan	Santa Clara Alviso	65	400
Slvador	Santa Clara San Jose	65	360
NARVARETTO			
Fernando	San Francisco San Francisco 6	67	431
NARVO			
John	Calaveras Twp 5	57	202
NARVOE			
John*	Tulara Twp 3	71	43

Name	County Locale	M653 Roll	Page
NARWOOD			
Wm	Sacramento Cosumnes	63	410
NARY			
John	Calaveras Twp 8	57	81
Patrick	Placer Todds Va	62	785
Thos	Nevada Rough &	61	430
William	Shasta Millvill	66	750
NASAGOMOS			
Isadora*	Calaveras Twp 4	57	318
NASANDO			
---	San Bernardino S Timate	64	712
NASANE			
E	Sacramento Cosumnes	63	404
NASARIA			
---	San Bernardino S Timate	64	715
NASARIO			
---	Los Angeles San Pedro	59	486
---	San Bernardino S Timate	64	706
---	San Bernardino S Timate	64	718
---	San Bernardino S Timate	64	725
---	San Bernardino S Timate	64	726
---	San Bernardino S Timate	64	728
---	San Bernardino S Timate	64	733
---	San Bernardino S Timate	64	740
---	San Bernardino S Timate	64	741
---	San Bernardino S Timate	64	749
---	San Bernardino S Timate	64	750
---	San Bernardino S Timate	64	752
---	Tulara Keyesville	71	65
---	Tulara Keyesville	71	72
Antonio	San Bernardino Santa Ba	64	209
NASEMANN			
Haman	Monterey San Juan	60	981
NASEN			
Job*	Sacramento Alabama	63	417
NASETON			
F*	Calaveras Twp 8	57	95
NASEUS			
James*	Nevada Nevada	61	318
NASH			
---	Calaveras Twp 5	57	222
Caleb	Nevada Bloomfield	61	524
E M	Sutter Nicolaus	70	831
E W	Nevada Grass Valley	61	179
Edwin	Yolo Slate Ra	72	717
Fred	Alameda Brooklyn	55	177
George	Sierra Twp 7	66	865
George H	Sierra Twp 7	66	865
H A	San Francisco San Francisco 5	67	478
I	Nevada Eureka	61	357
J	Nevada Eureka	61	357
J	Sutter Nicolaus	70	831
J H	El Dorado Placerville	58	862
J M	Butte Ophir	56	796
J N	Butte Oregon	56	637
James	San Francisco San Francisco 3	67	6
James	Yuba Long Bar	72	753
Jno	Sacramento Ward 3	63	456
Jno C	Klamath Liberty	59	238
Joel H	San Francisco San Francisco 11	67	152
John	Placer Lisbon	62	733
John	San Joaquin Castoria	64	878
John	Yuba Marysville	72	896
Lizzie	San Francisco San Francisco 10	67	185
Mary	Yuba Parks Ba	72	776
Nelson	Siskiyou Scott Va	69	41
P J	Butte Eureka	56	653
Patrick	Contra Costa Twp 2	57	573
Patrick	Solano Suisan	69	232
Peter	Butte Eureka	56	654
R	Sutter Butte	70	785
Robert	Yuba Marysville	72	865
Robt H	San Francisco San Francisco 12	67	361
Roswell	San Francisco San Francisco 2	67	589
S B	Sutter Nicolaus	70	831
Shaw	Alameda Brooklyn	55	171
T	El Dorado Placerville	58	860
T	San Francisco San Francisco 3	67	43
Thomas	Contra Costa Twp 2	57	573
Tontalbee	Sierra Downieville	66	1012
Tontatha	Sierra Downieville	66	1012
Vanburton L	Sierra Scales D	66	804
W	Shasta Horsetown	66	706
W H	Napa Hot Springs	61	11
Warren	Tuolumne Twp 1	71	221
William	San Bernardino Santa Ba	64	218
William	San Bernardino Buenav	64	219
William	Tulara Visalia	71	98
William C	Yuba Marysville	72	963
William D	Yuba Marysville	72	963
Wm	San Bernardino Santa Barbara	64	173
NASIL			
---	San Bernardino San Bernadino	64	682

Name	County Locale	M653 Roll	Page
NASK			
Edwin	Yuba Slate Ro	72	717
J N	Butte Oregon	56	637
NASON			
C C	Placer Michigan	62	834
Edmund	Marin Tomales	60	716
Henry	Placer Forest H	62	800
J H	Calaveras Twp 9	57	367
J H	Calaveras Twp 9	57	370
R H*	Butte Kimshaw	56	579
R N	Butte Kimshaw	56	579
Saml C	Calaveras Twp 10	57	294
Samuel L	Sierra St Louis	66	817
NASOR			
J H*	Calaveras Twp 9	57	367
NASORIO			
---	San Bernardino S Timate	64	709
NASS			
G N	Tuolumne Twp 3	71	465
Henry J	San Francisco San Francisco 9	68	1097
NASSA			
Andrew*	Shasta Shasta	66	655
NASTERIDAD			
---*	San Bernardino S Timate	64	749
NASTRAMEL			
William Vas*	Sierra Pine Grove	66	832
NASTRAMIL			
William Vas*	Sierra Pine Grove	66	832
NASUIEN			
P*	El Dorado Placerville	58	843
NAT			
---	El Dorado Georgetown	58	702
NATCH			
Henry*	Nevada Bridgeport	61	483
NATCHEZ			
Jose	Los Angeles Los Angeles	59	333
NATEH			
Henry	Nevada Bridgeport	61	483
NATER			
W	Tehama Antelope	70	890
NATERIDAD			
---	San Bernardino S Timate	64	707
NATH			
Jane*	Nevada Nevada	61	328
NATHAM			
G M*	Nevada Nevada	61	323
Marks*	San Francisco San Francisco 9	68	1053
NATHAN			
B	Nevada Grass Valley	61	177
B	Nevada Eureka	61	381
C	Nevada Grass Valley	61	177
E P	Sacramento Ward 1	63	113
Ike	Los Angeles Los Angeles	59	345
Isaac	Butte Kimshaw	56	595
J B	Yolo Cache Crk	72	666
J G	Butte Oregon	56	625
Jack	Sacramento Ward 4	63	545
John	Amador Twp 1	55	465
L	San Francisco San Francisco 9	68	955
Lena	San Francisco San Francisco 9	68	964
Leva	San Francisco San Francisco 9	68	964
Luois	Siskiyou Yreka	69	155
Marks*	San Francisco San Francisco 9	68	1053
Mary	San Francisco San Francisco 7	68	1348
Nathaniel	Los Angeles Los Angeles	59	345
Philip	Siskiyou Yreka	69	155
Rosina	Sacramento Ward 4	63	544
Saml	Sacramento Ward 3	63	422
Saml	San Francisco San Francisco 1	68	899
Solomon*	San Francisco San Francisco 9	68	1052
NATHANIEL			
---	Tulara Twp 3	71	48
NATHANS			
G M*	Nevada Nevada	61	323
G W	Nevada Nevada	61	323
NATHARE			
B*	Nevada Eureka	61	381
NATHERPP			
Chas H*	San Francisco San Francisco 4	68	1226
NATHERTON			
John	Contra Costa Twp 2	57	550
NATHEWS			
Justice	Butte Bidwell	56	706
NATHON			
S*	Nevada Grass Valley	61	177
NATHRUP			
D B	San Francisco San Francisco 3	67	74
NATHUPP			
Chas H*	San Francisco San Francisco 4	68	1226
NATHY			
John*	Placer Michigan	62	849
NATIN			
W B*	San Mateo Twp 1	65	71
NATINIDAD			
---*	San Bernardino S Timate	64	735
NATION			
S	Shasta Cottonwood	66	736

Name	County Locale	M653 Roll Page
NATIONS		
George	Nevada Bridgeport	61 444
Saml	Nevada Bridgeport	61 466
W B	Nevada Bridgeport	61 446
NATIOUS		
W B*	Nevada Bridgeport	61 446
NATIRIDAD		
---	San Bernardino S Timate	64 710
Anisette	San Bernardino Cecelio	64 136
NATIVIDAD		
---	San Bernardino S Timate	64 702
Arros	San Bernardino Santa Barbara	64 165
NATKINS		
Charles*	Butte Eureka	56 655
NATON		
Charles	El Dorado Placerville	58 931
NATONIDAD		
---	San Bernardino S Timate	64 731
NATRETTE		
Frank	Sierra Poker Flats	66 840
NATRONS		
Jeff	Yolo Slate Ra	72 704
NATSH		
Jacob	Santa Clara Alviso	65 413
NATT		
Geo	San Joaquin Stockton	641033
NATTER		
B	Sonoma Washington	69 675
John	Tehama Red Bluff	70 918
William M*	Nevada Rough &	61 421
NATTERRES		
P	Sacramento Ward 4	63 607
NATTERWOOD		
T H N	Mariposa Twp 1	60 670
NATTINI		
Emanuel	Santa Clara Santa Clara	65 481
NATTRAN		
S C*	San Francisco San Francisco 1	68 828
NATTSON		
Otto	Sierra Downieville	661016
NATUS		
Thomas*	Calaveras Twp 8	57 97
NATYYAH		
---	Mendocino Twp 1	60 887
NAU		
---	Calaveras Twp 5	57 209
---	Calaveras Twp 5	57 251
---	Mariposa Twp 1	60 626
Emill	Amador Twp 1	55 490
NAUAGAN		
Kate*	Tuolumne Sonora	71 200
NAUBANER		
D	El Dorado Placerville	58 817
NAUC		
W	Butte Oregon	56 642
NAUCE		
J W	Butte Cascade	56 701
NAUDERBILT		
W H	San Francisco San Francisco 9	681070
NAUDON		
J G	Tuolumne Twp 3	71 432
NAUGHAN		
Jos	San Francisco San Francisco 9	681068
NAUGHTEN		
Malachi	San Francisco San Francisco 10	196 67
Nalachi	San Francisco San Francisco 10	196 67
NAUGHTON		
A M*	Napa Napa	61 56
Henry	Yuba New York	72 735
NAUGLE		
Ellen F	San Francisco San Francisco 8	681296
Jno	Sacramento Natonia	63 285
NAUL		
Henery	Colusa Monroeville	57 453
J C	Colusa Monroeville	57 455
NAULT		
Thomas	Shasta Millvill	66 738
NAULTY		
N	San Francisco San Francisco 9	68 946
NAUMAN		
Chas S	Sierra St Louis	66 806
Chas T*	Sierra St Louis	66 806
Jacob	San Diego San Diego	64 763
John*	Alameda Brooklyn	55 147
NAUMEL		
Matilda	San Francisco San Francisco 10	196 67
NAUMEN		
Gustave	Sierra St Louis	66 806
NAUN		
Jacob*	Napa Hot Springs	61 8
NAUNBURY		
J H	Butte Wyandotte	56 671
NAUTER		
Fred*	Sacramento Ward 3	63 445
NAUX		
Henry	Sacramento Ward 1	63 22
NAV		
---	Calaveras Twp 5	57 181
NAVADA		
Francisco	Tuolumne Twp 1	71 227
NAVADO		
Rosa	Tuolumne Twp 2	71 320
NAVADUS		
Gill	Siskiyou Yreka	69 149
NAVAL		
John	Amador Twp 6	55 435
NAVANITE		
Jese	Sierra Downieville	66 968
Jose*	Sierra Downieville	66 968
NAVARA		
Peter	San Mateo Twp 3	65 93
NAVARETE		
Fernando*	San Francisco San Francisco 2	67 562
---	San Francisco	
NAVARI		
Francis	San Luis Obispo San Luis Obispo	65 36
NAVARNA		
W	Napa Napa	61 111
NAVARO		
Antonia*	Mariposa Twp 1	60 628
Mererde	Tuolumne Twp 2	71 407
Pedro	Santa Cruz Watsonville	66 536
NAVARR		
Mercede	Tuolumne Shawsfla	71 407
NAVARRA		
Angel	Contra Costa Twp 1	57 488
NAVARRE		
Luis	Del Norte Crescent	58 625
NAVARRITE		
Jose*	Sierra Downieville	66 968
NAVARRO		
Carlos	Los Angeles Los Angeles	59 393
Clemente	Los Angeles Los Angeles	59 404
Concepcion	Los Angeles Los Angeles	59 318
Diego	Marin Cortemad	60 781
Feodoro*	Los Angeles Santa Ana	59 457
Hernique*	San Francisco San Francisco 2	67 664
---	San Francisco	
Jose T	Los Angeles Los Angeles	59 394
Maguijl	San Bernardino Santa Barbara	64 167
Manuel	Tuolumne Big Oak	71 125
Manuel	Tuolumne Twp 4	71 127
Rafael	Tuolumne Twp 5	71 495
Teodoro	Los Angeles Santa Ana	59 457
NAVAWO		
Diego	Marin Cortemad	60 781
NAVE		
Daul J	Plumas Quincy	621001
Solomon	Sierra Gibsonville	66 856
NAVEL		
Louis	San Francisco San Francisco 4	681166
NAVELATHE		
V*	San Francisco San Francisco 5	67 500
NAVENS		
Riley D	Yuba Bear Rvr	721006
NAVERINA G		
Santo	Mariposa Twp 3	60 554
NAVERINA		
Antonia	Mariposa Twp 3	60 554
NAVERRO		
Pierre*	Mariposa Twp 3	60 553
Pierro*	Mariposa Twp 3	60 553
NAVIEN		
M	Tuolumne Twp 1	71 276
NAVIGO		
Brimo	Los Angeles Los Angeles	59 513
Primo	Los Angeles Los Angeles	59 513
NAVILL		
Wm	Butte Ophir	56 782
NAVIMETS		
---*	Mariposa Twp 3	60 614
NAVIN		
William	El Dorado Placerville	58 902
NAVIS		
Frank	Placer Yankee J	62 758
NAVISU		
M	Tuolumne Twp 2	71 276
NAVRA		
S	Sacramento Ward 4	63 506
NAVURRO		
Rafael	Tuolumne Chinese	71 495
NAVUT		
Caslesto	Calaveras Twp 6	57 130
NAVY		
Thos*	Nevada Rough &	61 430
William*	Shasta Millvill	66 750
NAW		
---	Butte Kimshaw	56 599
---	Nevada Bloomfield	61 528
Hing	Calaveras Twp 10	57 295
NAW		
Ho	Sierra Twp 7	66 875
NAWA		
---	Sierra Twp 5	66 945
NAWN		
Jacob*	Napa Hot Springs	61 8
NAWNAN		
Michael*	Solano Benecia	69 285
NAXEMERIAH		
---	Tulara Twp 2	71 37
NAXON		
Saml	Sacramento Ward 1	63 82
NAY		
---	Mariposa Twp 1	60 666
---	Nevada Bridgeport	61 466
D	Sutter Sutter	70 811
S A	Marin San Rafael	60 766
Samuel	Solano Vacaville	69 338
William	Tulara Twp 1	71 74
NAYALLOR		
Saml	Santa Clara Gilroy	65 239
NAYER		
Wm	Nevada Eureka	61 390
NAYES		
Phillip*	Klamath S Fork	59 198
NAYLER		
Kate*	Alameda Brooklyn	55 201
W F S	Siskiyou Scott Va	69 51
W T S	Siskiyou Scott Va	69 51
NAYLOCKES		
Henry	Yolo Putah	72 546
NAYLOF		
Danl	Santa Clara Santa Clara	65 516
NAYLOR		
Franklin	Los Angeles Elmonte	59 248
John	Los Angeles Elmonte	59 268
Kate*	Alameda Brooklyn	55 201
Margt	San Francisco San Francisco 1	68 888
N W	Santa Clara San Jose	65 306
W T S	Siskiyou Scott Va	69 51
NAYMAN		
William	Santa Cruz Santa Cruz	66 631
NAYMIRE		
Samuel	Siskiyou Yreka	69 148
NAYNE		
W*	Siskiyou Callahan	69 2
NAYNIRE		
Nancy*	Siskiyou Yreka	69 148
NAYNOLLA		
---	Del Norte Klamath	58 657
NAYU		
---	Nevada Bridgeport	61 460
NAZLE		
C	Sacramento Brighton	63 197
NCCARDLE		
Michael	Tuolumne Twp 2	71 352
NCCOL		
James*	Mariposa Twp 3	60 609
NCK		
---	Sierra Downieville	661008
NCKAY		
W Y	Amador Twp 2	55 302
NDERSON		
Chas	Merced Twp 1	60 898
James	San Diego San Diego	64 766
NE CARTNEY		
Cyrus*	San Francisco San Francisco 8	681300
NE SAY		
---	Mariposa Twp 1	60 667
NE WAH		
See*	Sacramento Ward 1	63 59
NE		
---	Calaveras Twp 6	57 147
---	Calaveras Twp 6	57 150
---	Calaveras Twp 5	57 249
---	Mariposa Twp 1	60 673
---	Sierra Twp 5	66 942
---*	Butte Kimshaw	56 607
Ching	Butte Oro	56 686
Cum	Siskiyou Yreka	69 194
Hah	El Dorado Big Bar	58 740
Ja	Mariposa Twp 3	60 618
Koy	Sierra Downieville	661026
Say	Mariposa Twp 1	60 667
Wa	Calaveras Twp 5	57 254
NEA		
---	Calaveras Twp 5	57 148
---*	Mariposa Twp 1	60 659
---*	Yolo No E Twp	72 680
Kuow	Placer Auburn	62 577
Sam	Butte Ophir	56 779
NEACE		
B W	Calaveras Twp 9	57 403
NEAD		
John	Los Angeles San Pedro	59 485
John*	Santa Clara Santa Clara	65 486

California 1860 Census Index

Name	County Locale	M653 Roll	Page
NEADER			
Charles*	Placer Forest H	62	803
NEADHAM			
Foster	Nevada Bloomfield	61	512
NEADHAW			
Foster	Nevada Bloomfield	61	512
NEADIRO			
Damaso	San Francisco San Francisco 3	67	6
NEADOR			
Thos*	Napa Clear Lake	61	123
NEAGLE			
Mary	San Francisco San Francisco 10	67	288
NEAH			
---	Fresno Twp 3	59	32
Nsy	El Dorado Georgetown	58	702
NEAHR			
David	San Diego Colorado	64	812
NEAKER			
G	San Francisco San Francisco 3	67	12
NEAL			
A J	Tehama Red Bluff	70	907
Alexander	Solano Suisan	69	221
Aron	Calaveras Twp 7	57	29
Bathinda	Sacramento Granite	63	248
C	Tehama Red Bluff	70	912
Charles	San Luis Obispo San Luis Obispo	65	36
Chas	Butte Chico	56	566
Chas	Sacramento Ward 1	63	87
Dan	Sacramento Ward 3	63	431
Danl C	Sierra St Louis	66	805
Duncan	Butte Chico	56	549
Elizabeth	Santa Clara Santa Clara	65	461
Fann	Tehama Tehama	70	946
George	Yuba New York	72	726
H A	El Dorado Greenwood	58	708
H H	El Dorado Georgetown	58	708
H W	Sacramento Ward 4	63	496
Harry	Mendocino Big Rvr	60	850
Henry O*	Santa Cruz Pajaro	66	526
Henry R	San Francisco San Francisco 8	681	260
Henry R	San Francisco San Francisco 8	681	323
J A	Butte Kimshaw	56	605
J D	Sierra Eureka	661	047
J E	Butte Oregon	56	623
J H*	Nevada Grass Valley	61	180
J O*	Siskiyou Scott Ri	69	73
James W	Humbolt Pacific	59	131
Jas	Placer Rattle Snake	62	631
Jas	Sacramento Granite	63	248
Jas	San Francisco San Francisco 9	681	063
Jas	Santa Clara Santa Clara	65	481
Jno O*	Nevada Nevada	61	253
John	Calaveras Twp 6	57	124
John	Sacramento Sutter	63	300
John	Santa Clara Santa Clara	65	513
John	Sonoma Petaluma	69	565
John C	San Francisco San Francisco 5	67	546
John H*	Calaveras Twp 6	57	114
John*	Santa Clara Santa Clara	65	486
L N	El Dorado Placerville	58	910
Lem*	Sacramento Ward 1	63	120
Lene*	Sacramento Ward 1	63	120
M	Sacramento Granite	63	241
M	Sacramento Ward 3	63	435
M	San Mateo Twp 1	65	71
M M	San Francisco San Francisco 5	67	553
M O*	Butte Eureka	56	646
Margaret	San Francisco San Francisco 10	67	304
Martha*	Mendocino Calpella	60	815
P J	Sutter Butte	70	793
Robert	Plumas Quincy	62	993
S	Sutter Butte	70	793
Saml B	San Francisco San Francisco 12	67	385
Saml*	Sacramento Ward 1	63	155
Sen*	Sacramento Ward 1	63	120
Spencer	Nevada Rough &	61	407
Tho	Siskiyou Scott Ri	69	72
Uriah	Tehama Tehama	70	939
W	San Francisco San Francisco 3	67	59
W B	Sutter Butte	70	787
W R	San Francisco San Francisco 3	67	59
William	Nevada Rough &	61	407
William C	Sierra La Porte	66	787
William H	San Joaquin Stockton	641	071
William W	San Francisco San Francisco 8	681	248
	San Francisco		
Wm	Tehama Red Bluff	70	912
Y H	Tehama Tehama	70	942
NEALAN			
Cath*	Sacramento Ward 1	63	139
Mary A	Siskiyou Yreka	69	194
Sarah	Humbolt Table Bl	59	139
NEALAND			
M	Siskiyou Cottonwoood	69	101

Name	County Locale	M653 Roll	Page
NEALAW			
Cath	Sacramento Ward 1	63	139
NEALE			
John H	Plumas Quincy	62	982
Wm J	Sierra Twp 7	66	904
NEALIS			
Thos J	Sacramento Ward 1	63	13
NEALL			
Jack M	San Joaquin Stockton	641	071
James	San Francisco San Francisco 8	681	284
James	San Francisco San Francisco 3	67	32
Jos P	San Joaquin Stockton	641	014
NEALON			
David	Tuolumne Twp 4	71	139
NEALOR			
David*	Tuolumne Big Oak	71	139
NEALY			
Robert	Santa Clara San Jose	65	340
NEAM			
---	El Dorado Casumnes	581	175
NEAMOR			
Luke M	Yolo Cache	72	592
NEAN			
---	Amador Twp 1	55	457
Conard	Calaveras Twp 6	57	148
Conrad	Calaveras Twp 5	57	148
NEANES			
J	El Dorado Placerville	58	843
NEANRRIN			
John	San Francisco San Francisco 2	67	796
NEANS			
Young	El Dorado Big Bar	58	739
NEANSCOPOLE			
---	Fresno Twp 2	59	57
NEANSON			
F	Calaveras Twp 9	57	389
NEANWIN			
John*	San Francisco San Francisco 2	67	796
NEAR			
John*	Yolo Cottonwoood	72	651
NEARBOP			
Christine*	Solano Fremont	69	381
NEARBOSS			
Christine	Solano Fremont	69	381
NEARENS			
James	Nevada Nevada	61	318
NEARY			
Michl	Sacramento Ward 1	63	94
O S	Yuba Suida	72	982
O S	Yuba Linda Twp	72	984
Patrick	San Francisco San Francisco 10	67	345
R	Siskiyou Cottonwoood	69	104
Thomas	Calaveras Twp 8	57	52
NEASE			
John C	Humbolt Bucksport	59	157
NEASON			
David*	Nevada Rough &	61	415
Samuel	San Diego Agua Caliente	64	854
NEASTROM			
Chs	San Francisco San Francisco 6	67	456
NEAT			
---	Calaveras Twp 6	57	167
Jos M	San Francisco San Francisco 9	681	089
NEATE			
John	Solano Benecia	69	291
NEATUN			
Robt	San Francisco San Francisco 3	67	44
NEAUMAN			
Henry	Sacramento Ward 4	63	507
NEAVER			
A G	Nevada Eureka	61	366
NEBDEN			
Catherine*	Yuba Linda	72	983
NEBLAS			
Margeta	Mariposa Twp 1	60	631
NEBLETT			
E	Trinity Weaverville	701	070
NEBSON			
Robert	Yuba Slate Ro	72	696
NECHAN			
---	Sierra La Porte	66	780
NECHARD			
L	El Dorado Newtown	58	776
NECHEUMENE			
---	Tulara Twp 2	71	35
NED			
---	Butte Oregon	56	619
---	Fresno Twp 3	59	38
---	Santa Clara Fremont	65	430
---	Tulara Twp 2	71	37
---	Yuba Bear Rvr	721	014
---*	Fresno Twp 1	59	78
---*	Tulara Visalia	71	37
NEDA			
Ka*	Placer Auburn	62	574

Name	County Locale	M653 Roll	Page
NEDAL			
Estesan	San Francisco San Francisco 3	67	6
NEDAR			
Frederick	Contra Costa Twp 1	57	490
NEDCHUHELT			
F*	Yolo Cache Crk	72	620
NEDDEN			
Catherine	Yuba Linda	72	983
NEDDREIN			
Henry F*	Yuba Marysville	72	867
NEDEVER			
John*	San Bernardino Santa Barbara	64	177
NEDGER			
S	San Joaquin Stockton	641	029
NEDSCHIHDT			
F	Yolo Cache	72	620
NEE			
---	Amador Twp 4	55	251
---	Amador Twp 4	55	252
---	Amador Twp 4	55	255
---	Amador Twp 4	55	332
---	Butte Kimshaw	56	600
---	Calaveras Twp 6	57	145
---	Calaveras Twp 6	57	167
---	Calaveras Twp 5	57	236
---	El Dorado Kelsey	581	144
---	El Dorado Placerville	58	894
---	El Dorado Mud Springs	58	971
---	El Dorado Mud Springs	58	972
---	Sacramento Ward 1	63	69
---	San Francisco San Francisco 9	681	095
---	San Francisco San Francisco 4	681	182
---	San Francisco San Francisco 11	67	159
---	Yolo Slate Ra	72	710
---*	Butte Kimshaw	56	600
---*	Fresno Twp 1	59	27
---*	Nevada Red Dog	61	549
Joy	San Francisco San Francisco 5	671	206
Kain*	San Francisco San Francisco 11	67	159
Kam*	San Francisco San Francisco 11	67	159
Long	San Francisco San Francisco 11	67	160
Michael	Amador Twp 4	55	254
Mon	San Francisco San Francisco 11	67	159
Pan	San Francisco San Francisco 5	67	509
Ran	San Francisco San Francisco 11	67	160
Scow*	Tuolumne Chinese	71	525
Sum	Placer Auburn	62	581
You	Tuolumne Twp 4	71	150
NEECE			
Charles	Sierra Downieville	661	012
NEED			
Joseph*	Santa Clara Santa Clara	65	488
Michael	Sacramento Dry Crk	63	370
NEEDHAM			
Cyrus	Santa Clara Fremont	65	422
John	Siskiyou Yreka	69	166
S B	Santa Clara San Jose	65	380
Wm	Colusa Colusi	57	426
Wm L	San Joaquin Stockton	641	046
NEEDLE			
L	Yolo Cottonwoood	72	646
NEEDNEAR			
---	Fresno Twp 2	59	52
NEEDON			
John	Santa Cruz Santa Cruz	66	630
NEEE			
Amander	Amador Twp 6	55	445
NEEF			
Dawn*	Klamath Liberty	59	230
NEEHAN			
M	Solano Suisan	69	204
NEEL			
J J	Trinity Cox'S Bar	701	037
Wm	Mariposa Coulterville	60	702
NEELAN			
R A	Nevada Nevada	61	290
NEELAND			
Gertrude	El Dorado Coloma	581	080
NEELEN			
J C	Siskiyou Cottonwoood	69	99
NEELEND			
David	Tuolumne Big Oak	71	137
NEELEY			
Henry	Santa Clara Santa Clara	65	492
J	El Dorado Salmon Hills	581	066
J S	El Dorado Coloma	581	108
John	Amador Twp 5	55	345
John	San Francisco San Francisco 11	67	118
L	San Joaquin Elkhorn	64	976

California 1860 Census Index

Name	County Locale	M653 Roll Page
NEELEY		
Mary L	Tuolumne Twp 1	71 217
Wm*	Amador Twp 2	55 281
Wm*	Sacramento Ward 1	63 19
NEELY		
A L	Sonoma Healdsbu	69 474
David	San Francisco San Francisco 10 67	324
Green A	Plumas Quincy	62 958
James	San Francisco San Francisco 11 67	125
James	Sonoma Bodega	69 535
John	Sacramento Dry Crk	63 369
Morgan	Sierra Twp 7	66 881
N	Klamath Trinidad	59 219
Robert	Sonoma Mendocino	69 447
Thomas	Shasta Millvill	66 727
Wm	Sacramento Ward 1	63 19
NEENAN		
John	San Francisco San Francisco 2	67 802
NEEOMAN		
John	Yuba Marysville	72 969
NEERECK		
Geo*	San Francisco San Francisco 9	681075
NEERRSE		
---	San Mateo Twp 1	65 50
NEESE		
Robert	Humbolt Eel Rvr	59 147
Samuel	Tuolumne Big Oak	71 141
NEESIA		
Mariana	Colusa Monroeville	57 453
NEETAU		
R A*	Nevada Nevada	61 290
NEETE		
Warren*	Nevada Rough &	61 412
NEETZ		
Ernest*	San Francisco San Francisco 3	67 42
NEEVEASCHEVANDE		
Frdk*	Yuba Linda Twp	72 983
NEEVENSCHEVANDE		
Frdk*	Yuba Linda Twp	72 983
NEFF		
---	Mariposa Twp 3	60 555
Albert N	Alameda Oakland	55 52
Amador	Amador Twp 6	55 445
Benjamin N	Placer Secret R	62 612
C I	Mariposa Twp 3	60 561
C S	Mariposa Twp 3	60 561
Cef*	Mariposa Twp 3	60 561
Charles	San Francisco San Francisco 7	681398
Dan	Trinity Eastman	70 960
Emma S	Sacramento Ward 3	63 481
Jacob	Placer Iona Hills	62 867
Jas W	Sacramento Ward 3	63 480
John	Placer Virginia	62 677
John J	Amador Twp 6	55 442
Joseph	Marin Cortemad	60 787
Rachel N	Solano Vacaville	69 349
NEFOLO		
Cruz*	Santa Clara Burnett	65 260
NEFT		
Fred	El Dorado Mud Springs	58 953
NEGAL		
John*	San Francisco San Francisco 1	68 885
Miki	Butte Ophir	56 823
NEGENAR		
Theodore*	Mariposa Twp 3	60 583
NEGENAS		
Theodore*	Mariposa Twp 3	60 583
NEGERS		
G S	Mariposa Twp 1	60 629
NEGEUAR		
Theodore*	Mariposa Twp 3	60 583
NEGLE		
Geo D	San Francisco San Francisco 9	681017
Michael	Butte Ophir	56 777
T	San Francisco San Francisco 6	67 436
NEGLEY		
Simon	Contra Costa Twp 1	57 501
NEGLI		
Peter	Tuolumne Twp 5	71 500
NEGRA		
Reuben	Fresno Twp 1	59 33
NEGRO		
---	San Bernardino S Timate	64 736
---*	San Bernardino S Timate	64 733
NEHANT		
C	San Joaquin Stockton	641092
NEHEMIAH		
F	San Joaquin Stockton	641013
NEHNORF		
Rudelph*	Sierra Eureka	661044
Rudolph*	Sierra Eureka	661044
NEHNWF		
Rudolph*	Sierra Eureka	661044
NEI		
---	Calaveras Twp 6	57 145

Name	County Locale	M653 Roll Page
NEI		
---	Yuba Slate Ro	72 710
NEIAL		
Pat O*	Sacramento Natonia	63 272
NEICE		
Charles*	Placer Michigan	62 814
John	Yuba Bear Rvr	721012
NEID		
Michael	Placer Michigan	62 849
NEIDHARDT		
Fred	Sacramento Ward 3	63 431
NEIDHOLT		
F	Yolo Putah	72 550
NEIDIG		
Henry	San Francisco San Francisco 11 67	104
NEIDY		
Henry	San Francisco San Francisco 11 67	104
John	El Dorado White Oaks	581007
NEIELCIA		
---	San Diego Agua Caliente	64 857
NEIFF		
Jacob*	Sacramento Ward 4	63 497
NEIGH		
---	Placer Secret R	62 621
NEIGHBOR		
Henry	San Joaquin Elkhorn	641000
Jacob	Tuolumne Montezuma	71 506
NEIGHER		
William*	Sierra St Louis	66 806
NEIGHLY		
Nellie	San Francisco San Francisco 10 67	198
Nettie	San Francisco San Francisco 10 67	198
NEIHER		
George	Calaveras Twp 7	57 32
NEIL		
Anna O*	Napa Napa	61 90
Chas O*	Calaveras Twp 8	57 103
D O	Yuba Long Bar	72 768
David	Shasta Shasta	66 686
David H	Santa Clara Gilroy	65 231
Elijah	Yuba Fosters	72 828
Elizabeth	Mendocino Little L	60 833
H	El Dorado Placerville	58 818
J K	Nevada Grass Valley	61 157
James	Sacramento Cosumnes	63 401
James O*	Stanislaus Buena Village	70 723
M	Nevada Nevada	61 322
Margaret O*	Nevada Nevada	61 257
Marther	Amador Twp 2	55 266
Mary	Sacramento Ward 3	63 476
Mathew	Nevada Rough &	61 409
P O*	Yuba Foster B	72 836
R N	Yolo Merritt	72 583
Robert	Yuba Marysville	72 969
Robt	Sacramento Ward 3	63 427
T	Nevada Grass Valley	61 213
W O	Nevada Eureka	61 369
William	Los Angeles Los Angeles	59 344
NEILAND		
Peter	San Joaquin Douglass	64 921
NEILE		
Fo	El Dorado Greenwood	58 719
NEILEN		
J C	Siskiyou Cottonwoood	69 99
John	Siskiyou Shasta Valley	69 119
NEILL		
Anthur C*	Placer Auburn	62 593
Authur C*	Placer Auburn	62 593
Charles O*	Monterey San Juan	60 989
Harvey	Monterey San Juan	60 989
Henry	Merced Twp 1	60 898
J A	Merced Twp 1	60 898
J G	Sacramento Granite	63 235
James M	Mendocino Calpella	60 810
Jno	Klamath Klamath	59 228
John	Monterey Monterey	60 926
John*	Yolo Cache Crk	72 647
Magaret J	Shasta Millvill	66 739
Mallad S	Monterey Alisal	601035
Samuel	Mendocino Calpella	60 810
Stoddard	Mendocino Calpella	60 810
W N	Merced Twp 1	60 898
NEILLER		
Charles*	Tuolumne Twp 5	71 501
NEILLY		
A	Nevada Eureka	61 393
NEILSON		
M	Tuolumne Twp 2	71 279
NEILY		
---	Mariposa Twp 3	60 616
NEIM		
Charles	Sierra Twp 5	66 925

Name	County Locale	M653 Roll Page
NEIN		
---	Calaveras Twp 5	57 234
NEINHAM		
Z*	San Francisco San Francisco 2	67 796
NEINSTADLER		
Agnes	San Francisco San Francisco 10 67	358
NEIOMAN		
Schooly D	Calaveras Twp 5	57 208
NEIONES		
Prfeto*	El Dorado Diamond	58 813
NEIOPIT		
Parker	Butte Wyandotte	56 658
NEIPP		
Jacob*	Sacramento Ward 4	63 497
NEIPPAL		
William	Sierra St Louis	66 818
NEIRA		
Valentine	Marin Cortemad	60 779
Valentino*	Marin Cortemad	60 779
Maria	San Francisco San Francisco 2	67 685
NEIRRA		

NEISERANDER		
John*	Plumas Quincy	62 986
NEISERMAN		
Dadrich*	Yuba Marysville	72 923
NEISWANDER		
J	Del Norte Crescent	58 642
John*	Plumas Quincy	62 986
NEIT		
A*	El Dorado Placerville	58 871
NEITHER		
Morrel	Sacramento Franklin	63 314
NEITZEL		
Frank	Solano Suisan	69 235
NEJAR		
Maria P	Los Angeles Los Angeles	59 388
NEKAL		
Christian	Alameda Brooklyn	55 206
NEL		
Yet	San Francisco San Francisco 4	681174
NELBRECH		
Hennan*	Siskiyou Yreka	69 148
NELCON		
John P	San Francisco San Francisco 10 67	240
NELDEN		
Albert*	Sacramento Cosumnes	63 391
NELDON		
Ambros	El Dorado Kelsey	581153
David S	Calaveras Twp 6	57 141
NELE		
Henry R	San Francisco San Francisco 9	681092
NELEM		
Y*	Siskiyou Scott Ri	69 82
NELERAM		
E*	Sutter Yuba	70 776
NELFENT		
James*	Calaveras Twp 10	57 288
NELICK		
Christina	El Dorado Coloma	581074
NELIGAN		
Patrick	Solano Vallejo	69 272
NELL		
---	Sierra Downieville	661026
Henry H*	Sacramento Granite	63 249
Heny H*	Sacramento Granite	63 249
NELLCOSO		
R*	Yolo Cache	72 626
NELLEL		
Geo	El Dorado Placerville	58 820
NELLER		
Gothfrid*	San Francisco San Francisco 1	68 825
Michael	Sacramento Centre	63 180
Robert*	Sierra St Louis	66 807
NELLEY		
T	Yolo Washington	72 600
NELLIE		
Geo	Sacramento Granite	63 258
NELLIGAN		
W	El Dorado Placerville	58 869
NELLINGTON		
Edmond	Tuolumne Twp 2	71 395
NELLIS		
Emery	Calaveras Twp 7	57 17
James	Calaveras Twp 7	57 17
John	Siskiyou Yreka	69 146
Stephen	Tuolumne Springfield	71 373
T	Calaveras Twp 9	57 355
Walter	Tuolumne Twp 2	71 373
NELLITY		
Geo D	San Francisco San Francisco 9	68 982
NELLNER		
Casper*	Mariposa Twp 1	60 647
NELLS		
L	San Francisco San Francisco 1	68 906

Name	County Locale	M653 Roll	Page
NELLSON			
Samuel	Alameda Brooklyn	55	79
NELLVILLE			
Henry	Mariposa Coulterville	60	678
NELLY			
---	Yuba Marysville	72	866
P	San Joaquin Stockton	64	1091
NELM			
N R*	Yolo Cottonwood	72	656
NELOH			
Stephen	San Francisco San Francisco 1	68	927
NELON			
Richard O*	Yolo Putah	72	552
NELSEN			
Adan	Sacramento Granite	63	247
F O	Amador Twp 2	55	306
G R	San Francisco San Francisco 3	67	48
H C	Colusa Muion	57	462
John	Sacramento Sutter	63	307
Wm	Sacramento Franklin	63	308
NELSENSHALL			
P	El Dorado Georgetown	58	686
NELSN			
E	San Francisco San Francisco 1	68	923
Frank	Mariposa Twp 3	60	573
NELSON			
---	Mariposa Twp 3	60	594
---	Placer Dutch Fl	62	718
A	Los Angeles Los Angeles	59	499
A	Sacramento Ward 3	63	429
A	San Francisco San Francisco 9	68	1059
A	San Francisco San Francisco 5	67	495
A	San Francisco San Francisco 5	67	529
A	San Mateo Twp 2	65	124
A	San Mateo Twp 2	65	125
A G	San Joaquin Douglass	64	928
A H	San Francisco San Francisco 10	67	174
A J	Sacramento Ward 4	63	611
A O	Klamath S Fork	59	198
A T	Sacramento Ward 1	63	150
A W	Santa Clara San Jose	65	389
Abram	Tuolumne Twp 2	71	280
Abrams	Tuolumne Twp 2	71	280
Adam	Sacramento Granite	63	247
Admiral	Placer Iona Hills	62	866
Albert	Sierra La Porte	66	778
Alex	San Francisco San Francisco 1	68	897
Alfred D	Yuba Marysville	72	977
Allan	Sonoma Armally	69	511
Allen	Plumas Quincy	62	995
Ambros	El Dorado Kelsey	58	1153
Amence	Butte Chico	56	533
Anderson	Santa Cruz Santa Cruz	66	636
Andrew	Contra Costa Twp 3	57	599
Andrew	San Francisco San Francisco 7	68	1398
Andrew	San Francisco San Francisco 10	67	292
Andrew	San Francisco San Francisco 12	67	363
Andrew	San Joaquin Oneal	64	934
Anton	Tuolumne Jamestown	71	432
Antone	Mariposa Twp 1	60	639
Antoni	Mariposa Twp 1	60	639
Arthur	Siskiyou Yreka	69	169
August	Placer Yankee J	62	780
Augustus	San Francisco San Francisco 1	68	899
Auton	Tuolumne Twp 3	71	432
B	Butte Oregon	56	638
B	Santa Clara San Jose	65	346
B	Solano Suisan	69	235
B	Sutter Sutter	70	812
Bridget	San Francisco San Francisco 6	67	402
C	El Dorado Oakland	58	769
C	Sacramento Ward 4	63	607
C	San Francisco San Francisco 10	67	261
C	Shasta Shasta	66	681
C	Siskiyou Klamath	69	90
C	Trinity Turner'S	70	997
C	Yolo Cache Crk	72	594
C C	Merced Twp 2	60	922
C*	Butte Hamilton	56	517
Caroline F	Trinity Turner'S	70	997
Charles	Alameda Oakland	55	9
Charles	Calaveras Twp 9	57	348
Charles	Nevada Rough &	61	430
Charles	Placer Michigan	62	852
Charles	Plumas Meadow Valley	62	899
Charles	Sacramento Franklin	63	313
Charles	San Mateo Twp 3	65	96
Charles	Tuolumne Columbia	71	312
Charles	Yolo New York	72	720
Charles	Yuba New York	72	720
Charles R	Yuba Marysville	72	971
Chas	Klamath Orleans	59	215

Name	County Locale	M653 Roll	Page
NELSON			
Chas	Placer Virginia	62	685
Chas	Sacramento Ward 4	63	606
Chas	Trinity Mouth Ca	70	1012
Chris	Mariposa Twp 3	60	604
Chris	Mariposa Twp 3	60	617
Christian	Klamath Trinidad	59	220
Cyrus F	Siskiyou Yreka	69	139
D	Mariposa Twp 1	60	630
D S	Monterey Monterey	60	959
D W	Mariposa Twp 3	60	597
Darius	Sacramento Ward 1	63	1
David	San Francisco San Francisco 9	68	1004
David	San Francisco San Francisco 3	67	64
David	San Francisco San Francisco 1	68	922
Dennis	San Mateo Twp 3	65	103
E	Nevada Nevada	61	280
E	Tuolumne Twp 4	71	149
E C*	Butte Hamilton	56	517
E Y	Sierra Gibsonville	66	858
Edwin	San Joaquin O'Neal	64	1007
Eliza	Yuba Marysville	72	898
Elizabeth	San Francisco San Francisco 8	68	1293
Emma	Yuba Marysville	72	890
F	Siskiyou Callahan	69	5
F D	Sutter Sutter	70	816
F L	Amador Twp 2	55	306
Frances*	Tuolumne Twp 1	71	203
Francis	Mendocino Big Rock	60	873
Frank	Mariposa Twp 3	60	573
Frank	Placer Michigan	62	824
Frank	Placer Michigan	62	826
Frank	San Francisco San Francisco 1	68	930
Frank	San Joaquin Oneal	64	937
Fred	Placer Goods	62	698
G R	San Francisco San Francisco 3	67	48
G W	Mariposa Twp 3	60	612
G Y	Sierra Gibsonville	66	858
Geo	Monterey Pajaro	60	1020
Geo	Sacramento Brighton	63	200
Geo	San Francisco San Francisco 2	67	753
Geo	San Francisco San Francisco 1	68	895
Geo M	Butte Kimshaw	56	590
Geo W	Calaveras Twp 10	57	289
George	Calaveras Twp 5	57	190
George	Sacramento Ward 1	63	39
George	San Luis Obispo San Luis Obispo	65	36
George	Sierra Poker Flats	66	837
George D	Sierra Poker Flats	66	838
George H	San Francisco San Francisco 8	68	1253
George W	Sierra Eureka	66	1046
George W	Yuba Marysville	72	917
Gilman	San Joaquin Elkhorn	64	968
H	El Dorado Diamond	58	790
H	Shasta Shasta	66	676
H	Sutter Butte	70	785
H	Sutter Nicolaus	70	839
H B	El Dorado Georgetown	58	707
H C	Sacramento Georgian	63	344
H C	San Francisco San Francisco 9	68	1055
H C*	San Francisco San Francisco 1	68	888
H W C	Colusa Monroeville	57	456
Hans P	Alameda Brooklyn	55	153
Henry	Contra Costa Twp 3	57	585
Henry	Mendocino Big Rvr	60	849
Henry	Plumas Meadow Valley	62	929
Henry	Plumas Quincy	62	960
Henry	Sacramento Sutter	63	290
Henry	San Francisco San Francisco 9	68	1018
Henry	San Francisco San Francisco 3	67	55
Henry	Sonoma Armally	69	495
Henry	Tuolumne Twp 2	71	427
Henry	Tuolumne Twp 3	71	453
Herman	Alameda Brooklyn	55	73
Hiram	Siskiyou Yreka	69	124
Isaac	San Francisco San Francisco 6	67	433
Isaac M	San Francisco San Francisco 3	67	56
Isham	Tuolumne Twp 2	71	370
J	Butte Ophir	56	768
J	Nevada Eureka	61	348
J	Sacramento Cosumnes	63	396
J	San Francisco San Francisco 9	68	1059
J	San Francisco San Francisco 10	67	228
J	San Francisco San Francisco 10	67	313
J	San Francisco San Francisco 5	67	529
J	San Francisco San Francisco 5	67	540
J	Siskiyou Scott Ri	69	82
J H	San Joaquin Oneal	64	930
J M	Siskiyou Cottonwood	69	109
Jacob	Marin Bolinas	60	742
Jacob	Mendocino Big Rvr	60	847
Jacob	San Francisco San Francisco 9	68	1066
Jacob	San Francisco San Francisco 10	67	297

Name	County Locale	M653 Roll	Page
NELSON			
Jacob	Yuba Parks Ba	72	777
Jacob W	Mendocino Big Rvr	60	847
James	Mariposa Twp 3	60	574
James	Nevada Bridgeport	61	449
James	Plumas Meadow Valley	62	905
James	Sierra St Louis	66	815
James D	Humbolt Eel Rvr	59	151
James L	Sierra St Louis	66	806
Jane W	Yuba Marysville	72	931
Jas	San Francisco San Francisco 10	67	304
Jas	San Francisco San Francisco 2	67	779
Jas	San Francisco San Francisco 1	68	915
Jas T	Yolo Cottonwoood	72	662
Jno	San Francisco San Francisco 9	68	1091
John	Alameda Oakland	55	29
John	El Dorado White Oaks	58	1029
John	El Dorado White Oaks	58	1032
John	El Dorado Salmon Falls	58	1041
John	El Dorado Placerville	58	920
John	Marin Bolinas	60	733
John	Marin Tomales	60	774
John	Marin Cortemad	60	780
John	Napa Clear Lake	61	134
John	Nevada Rough &	61	435
John	Nevada Bridgeport	61	502
John	Nevada Bloomfield	61	518
John	Plumas Meadow Valley	62	900
John	Sacramento Ward 1	63	27
John	Sacramento Sutter	63	289
John	Sacramento Cosumnes	63	399
John	San Francisco San Francisco 10	67	178
John	San Francisco San Francisco 10	67	189
John	Santa Clara Santa Clara	65	519
John	Sierra Downieville	66	1013
John	Solano Vallejo	69	276
John	Trinity Ferry	70	977
John	Tuolumne Columbia	71	343
John B	Yuba New York	72	736
John G	San Francisco San Francisco 7	68	1433
John P	San Francisco San Francisco 10	67	240
John S	Plumas Quincy	62	936
John*	Placer Todds Va	62	783
Jos	San Francisco San Francisco 10	67	304
Jos	San Francisco San Francisco 2	67	779
Joseph	Alameda Brooklyn	55	178
Kate	San Francisco San Francisco 10	67	357
L	San Francisco San Francisco 1	68	923
L C	Placer Dutch Fl	62	718
Laura M	Tuolumne Twp 2	71	331
Lewis	Plumas Meadow Valley	62	902
Lyman	El Dorado Salmon Falls	58	1037
M	San Mateo Twp 3	65	80
M	Sierra St Louis	66	818
Martin	Santa Cruz Pescadero	66	648
Mary	Alameda Oakland	55	68
Mary	San Francisco San Francisco 2	67	595
Miles	Tuolumne Twp 2	71	384
Mily	Tuolumne Shawsfla	71	384
Morton	Sacramento San Joaquin	63	348
N	Calaveras Twp 8	57	108
N	Nevada Eureka	61	348
N R	El Dorado Georgetown	58	707
Napoleon B	Yuba Marysville	72	975
Nathaniel	San Joaquin Elkhorn	64	961
Nelse	Plumas Meadow Valley	62	902
Nelse	Sierra La Porte	66	778
Newton	Tulara Twp 2	71	32
O	Siskiyou Scott Ri	69	82
Obeg*	Solano Benecia	69	298
Obey	Solano Benecia	69	298
Ole	Yolo Putah	72	560
P	Sutter Nicolaus	70	835
P	Tuolumne Jacksonville	71	168
P	Yolo Putah	72	615
Patrick	Sierra Downieville	66	957
Peter	Alameda Brooklyn	55	115
Peter	Amador Twp 1	55	467
Peter	El Dorado Mountain	58	1186
Peter	El Dorado Georgetown	58	691
Peter	Mariposa Twp 3	60	574
Peter	San Francisco San Francisco 1	68	896
Peter	Trinity Steiner	70	1000
Peter	Trinity Rearings	70	990
Peter	Tuolumne Twp 2	71	284
R H	Butte Hamilton	56	524
Ralph	San Francisco San Francisco 1	68	807
Rheuben	Sonoma Vallejo	69	619
Richard	Yolo Putah	72	552
Robert	Yolo Slate Ra	72	696

California 1860 Census Index

Name	County Locale	M653 Roll	Page
NELSON			
Robt	Santa Clara San Jose	65	383
Rosa	Sacramento Ward 4	63	585
S	Colusa Monroeville	57	455
S	Klamath Liberty	59	235
S	Shasta Horsetown	66	702
S E	Sutter Butte	70	793
Sam	Mariposa Twp 3	60	566
Saml	Butte Kimshaw	56	592
Saml	Placer Dutch Fl	62	728
Saml B*	Napa Napa	61	112
Samuel	San Francisco San Francisco 3	67	70
Silas	Solano Fairfield	69	202
Sophea	Alameda Brooklyn	55	100
Sophia	Alameda Brooklyn	55	100
Spence	Plumas Meadow Valley	62	902
Swinerton	Sierra Gibsonville	66	852
T	Nevada Eureka	61	348
T H	Nevada Washington	61	336
Thomas	Placer Auburn	62	596
Thomas	San Francisco San Francisco 7	68	1333
Thomas	San Joaquin Oneal	64	933
Thomas	Sierra Gibsonville	66	852
Thomas	Sierra Twp 2	66	887
Thomas	Sierra Downieville	66	995
Thomas	Solano Fremont	69	376
Thomas	Tuolumne Twp 1	71	254
Thomas*	Calaveras Twp 4	57	319
Thos	Sacramento Granite	63	236
Thos	Sacramento Ward 4	63	607
Thos	Trinity Trinity	70	972
Thos M	Del Norte Happy Ca	58	668
Volney S	Trinity Trinity	70	975
W	Mariposa Coulterville	60	676
W F	Sutter Sutter	70	816
W F	Trinity Rush Crk	70	965
W L	San Francisco San Francisco 5	67	486
W M	Merced Twp 1	60	901
W T	Mariposa Twp 3	60	621
W W	Butte Oro	56	676
William	El Dorado Georgetown	58	693
William	El Dorado Georgetown	58	760
William	Nevada Bloomfield	61	522
William	San Francisco San Francisco 9	68	1031
William	San Francisco San Francisco 8	68	1235
William	Sierra Poker Flats	66	839
William	Siskiyou Scott Va	69	37
William	Solano Vacaville	69	361
Wm	Butte Bidwell	56	725
Wm	Butte Ophir	56	791
Wm	Merced Twp 1	60	914
Wm	Sacramento Sutter	63	292
Wm	San Francisco San Francisco 2	67	565
Wm H	Mariposa Twp 3	60	562
Wm L	Colusa Grand Island	57	471
Wm M	Tuolumne Twp 2	71	354
Z C*	Butte Hamilton	56	517
NELSPEIR			
Peter	San Francisco San Francisco 9	68	1063
NELSTER			
William P	San Joaquin Tulare	64	870
NELTON			
J	Sacramento Sutter	63	306
NEM			
---	Calaveras Twp 8	57	71
---	El Dorado Mountain	58	1189
---	Nevada Rough &	61	409
---	Nevada Bridgeport	61	459
NEMAN			
Gabarial	El Dorado White Oaks	58	1010
Timothy*	San Francisco San Francisco 6	67	425
NEMANDE			
Epetacio	Yuba Marysville	72	936
NEMANN			
Henry	San Francisco San Francisco 3	67	67
NEMANTRE			
Nicholas*	San Francisco San Francisco 2	67	711
NEMINS			
John	San Joaquin Elliott	64	944
NEMMETT			
Ann	San Francisco San Francisco 2	67	772
NEMON			
Jacob*	Yolo Slate Ra	72	689
NEN			
---	Calaveras Twp 6	57	148
---*	Yolo No E Twp	72	680
Gah	Amador Twp 2	55	291
You	San Francisco San Francisco 4	68	1200
NENA			
---	San Bernardino S Timate	64	724
NENARS			
Henry	Tuolumne Twp 2	71	334
NENBER			
Adam	Yolo Putah	72	554
NENEE			
Andrew	El Dorado Mud Springs	58	982

Name	County Locale	M653 Roll	Page
NENICO			
Mary*	San Francisco San Francisco 10	182	67
NENIS			
Atronia	Amador Twp 5	55	365
NENL			
Bartho C*	Alameda Brooklyn	55	81
NENLS			
Owen*	Sonoma Petaluma	69	595
NENNALLLY			
H S Jr	Trinity Weaverville	70	1081
NENNETT			
Joseph C	Calaveras Twp 10	57	265
NENS			
Youn G	El Dorado Big Bar	58	739
NENSAELAER			
E	Tehama Tehama	70	949
NENSHAW			
J B*	Yolo Cache Crk	72	607
NENSSIS			
L	Sacramento Granite	63	242
NENSTADT			
C*	Sacramento Ward 4	63	573
NENSTATT			
Adolph	Tuolumne Sonora	71	207
NENTER			
John	Mariposa Coulterville	60	690
NENTOIME			
Edward*	San Francisco San Francisco 3	67	80
NENTRE			
Franklin*	Siskiyou Yreka	69	125
NENTZEL			
C	Siskiyou Scott Ri	69	72
NENTZELL			
C	Siskiyou Scott Va	69	22
NENUSNOKE			
---	Tulara Twp 1	71	120
NEOA			
---	El Dorado Salmon Falls	58	1040
NEOBET			
Tho	Siskiyou Scott Ri	69	64
NEODLE			
James	Mariposa Twp 3	60	563
NEOGE			
P*	Yolo Washington	72	561
NEOME			
J	Sacramento Granite	63	225
NEOPOLEAN			
---	Mendocino Calpella	60	825
NEOR			
Abe	Santa Clara Gilroy	65	247
NEPELRADE			
N*	Siskiyou Scott Ri	69	81
NEPER			
Chas*	Sacramento Brighton	63	200
NEPET			
Felex	San Francisco San Francisco 2	67	800
NEPHAN			
John	El Dorado Placerville	58	844
NEPIER			
M R	Yolo Slate Ra	72	698
M R	Yuba Slate Ro	72	698
NEPIT			
Felix	San Francisco San Francisco 2	67	800
NEPOLIAN			
Martin	Mariposa Coulterville	60	702
NEPOMACENO			
Juan	Los Angeles Los Angeles	59	338
NEPOMESENA			
Juan	San Mateo Twp 2	65	118
NEPOOR			
Agustus	El Dorado Grizzly	58	1181
NEPPEN			
O H	Sonoma Sonoma	69	636
NEPTON			
John B	San Francisco San Francisco 8	68	1296
NEQUENENNE			
---	Tulara Twp 2	71	34
NEQUIRES			
Geo	Yolo Cache	72	637
NER			
---	Calaveras Twp 5	57	145
---	Calaveras Twp 6	57	166
NERA			
J N	Butte Ophir	56	762
NERACK			
Ellen	San Francisco San Francisco 4	68	1152
NERAMY			
---	San Diego Agua Caliente	64	814
NERARINE			
C	Mariposa Twp 1	60	630
NERAW			
R	Sacramento Sutter	63	306
NERDLER			
Joseph*	Calaveras Twp 5	57	238
NERGE			
P*	Yolo Washington	72	561

Name	County Locale	M653 Roll	Page
NERGET			
Wm*	San Francisco San Francisco 3	67	65
NERHOOD			
John	Sierra Downieville	66	991
NERIL			
Bartho C*	Alameda Brooklyn	55	81
Richard	Nevada Bridgeport	61	504
NERILAS			
Felix	San Francisco San Francisco 2	67	768
NERILLE			
John M	Solano Benecia	69	295
NERILLI			
John	Amador Twp 6	55	429
NERILLO			
C*	Shasta Shasta	66	656
NERIN			
Margaret*	Yuba Rose Bar	72	813
Thomas*	Yuba Rose Bar	72	803
NERIO			
Trinidad	Los Angeles Los Angeles	59	295
NERIS			
Antoine	Yuba Parks Ba	72	784
Jose*	San Bernardino S Buenav	64	218
NERISON			
David	Nevada Rough &	61	415
NERL			
J K	Nevada Grass Valley	61	157
NERLL			
John	Monterey Monterey	60	926
NERM			
Thomas	San Francisco San Francisco 11	67	107
NERMETA			
George	Amador Twp 3	55	376
NERNCK			
Ellen*	San Francisco San Francisco 4	68	1152
NERNEY			
Agapita*	Sierra La Porte	66	773
NERON			
Clayton	San Joaquin Elkhorn	64	991
NEROUNDA			
---	Tulara Visalia	71	105
NERRIAM			
Josiph*	Nevada Rough &	61	420
NERSEHEM			
A*	Marin S Antoni	60	707
NERSEL			
Adam	Sacramento Ward 1	63	36
NERSTRAMMER			
Lewis*	Alameda Murray	55	219
NERTNIS			
William*	Nevada Bridgeport	61	472
NERTON			
B	Shasta Cottonwoood	66	724
C	Siskiyou Scott Ri	69	72
NERTZEL			
C	Siskiyou Scott Ri	69	72
NERVAEZ			
Francisco	Santa Clara San Jose	65	361
NERVELL			
James	Marin San Rafael	60	764
NERVILLE			
J N	San Bernardino Santa Barbara	64	151
Wm W	San Francisco San Francisco 3	67	87
NERVMAN			
E	Marin Cortemad	60	752
NERYBAUGH			
T	Calaveras Twp 9	57	373
NESBET			
Tho	Siskiyou Scott Ri	69	64
Thomas	Yuba Linda	72	988
NESBETH			
---	Siskiyou Yreka	69	149
NESBIL			
Geo*	San Francisco San Francisco 1	68	890
NESBIT			
Alex	Sacramento Sutter	63	300
Benj R	Alameda Oakland	55	35
Geo*	San Francisco San Francisco 1	68	890
James	San Francisco San Francisco 8	68	1294
James	Yuba Bear Rvr	72	1013
Jos	San Mateo Twp 3	65	107
Wm	San Francisco San Francisco 2	67	626
NESBITT			
A J	San Francisco San Francisco 4	68	1224
Jane A	Siskiyou Yreka	69	158
Jane A	Siskiyou Yreka	69	165
Jno	Butte Oregon	56	633
John	Solano Suisan	69	234
Samuel	San Francisco San Francisco 9	68	938
Wm	Butte Chico	56	563
Wm	Butte Kimshaw	56	583
Wm G	Butte Oregon	56	621
NESBOR			
Chona*	Contra Costa Twp 3	57	615
NESCIMO			
---	San Diego Agua Caliente	64	822

California 1860 Census Index

Name	County Locale	M653 RollPage
NESCOM		
N	Amador Twp 3	55 374
NESDAIL		
P	Nevada Grass Valley	61 154
NESDAIR		
J*	Nevada Grass Valley	61 154
NESETITLER		
J M	Santa Clara Gilroy	65 229
NESEY		
Parker	Butte Cascade	56 690
NESGUE		
Eugene*	Tuolumne Twp 5	71 512
NESHE		
Henry	Trinity Soldiers	701005
NESHIE		
Geo	Sacramento San Joaquin	63 364
NESHITT		
Jno*	Butte Oregon	56 633
NESHORA		
---	Mendocino Calpella	60 822
NESIEL		
Henry*	Sacramento Ward 1	63 24
NESISON		
David*	Nevada Rough &	61 415
NESKIE		
Joe	Sacramento Sutter	63 298
NESLEY		
John*	Yolo Putah	72 547
NESMITH		
A	El Dorado Coloma	581069
J S	Sacramento Ward 1	63 16
Thomas*	Placer Yankee J	62 781
NESMORN		
Florenthecina*	Twp 2	65 115
	San Mateo	
NESOPOTA		
---	Fresno Twp 1	59 75
NESQUE		
Eugene	Tuolumne Montezuma	71 512
NESS		
George	El Dorado Greenwood	58 720
J L	El Dorado Georgetown	58 684
Sally	Sierra Eureka	661047
NESSART		
P	San Francisco San Francisco 9	681105
NESSEL		
Harry	Sacramento Ward 1	63 24
Henry*	Sacramento Ward 1	63 24
NESSELRODE		
N*	Siskiyou Scott Ri	69 81
NESSEN		
M C	San Francisco San Francisco 9	681084
NESSER		
Chas*	Sacramento Brighton	63 200
NESSLER		
Lorenzo	Sierra Downieville	66 958
NESSNER		
John*	Siskiyou Callahan	69 7
NESSON		
A M*	Placer Dutch Fl	62 711
Thomas	Placer Iona Hills	62 890
NESSTLERADE		
N*	Siskiyou Scott Ri	69 81
NESTER		
B D	Calaveras Twp 9	57 366
George	Marin Cortemad	60 791
M	Calaveras Twp 9	57 369
NESTOM		
James	El Dorado Georgetown	58 706
NESTON		
A M*	Placer Dutch Fl	62 711
NESTOR		
---	San Bernardino Santa Inez	64 138
Chona*	Contra Costa Twp 3	57 615
NESUS		
Jasus*	Los Angeles Los Angeles	59 489
NESUYA		
---	Butte Chico	56 551
NESWANGER		
Wm	Nevada Nevada	61 285
NET		
Yet	San Francisco San Francisco 4	681174
NETH		
Eliza	Sonoma Mendocino	69 452
NETHA		
Carmal	San Mateo Twp 3	65 99
NETHER		
Catherine	San Francisco San Francisco 3	67 9
NETHERCOTT		
Alfred	Sacramento Ward 4	63 601
NETHERHOYG		
J*	Nevada Grass Valley	61 235
NETHERLAND		
Samuel	Solano Vacaville	69 339
NETHERLY		
F	Trinity Readings	70 996

Name	County Locale	M653 RollPage
NETHERTON		
James W	Tulara Twp 1	71 76
John	Shasta Horsetown	66 699
NETHERWOOD		
T N*	Mariposa Twp 1	60 670
NETHORTON		
John	Shasta Horsetown	66 699
NETIGAN		
Joanna*	San Francisco San Francisco 9	681024
NETO		
Jesus	San Francisco San Francisco 10	280
		67
NETRONS		
Jeff*	Yuba Slate Ro	72 704
NETSEFS		
Cathlest	El Dorado Greenwood	58 715
NETSON		
Peter	El Dorado Mountain	581186
NETTART		
John*	San Francisco San Francisco 1	68 922
NETTINGHAM		
John	Sierra Twp 5	66 917
NETTLE		
John	Calaveras Twp 8	57 64
NETTLES		
Elijah	Tuolumne Green Springs	71 518
Mary	Calaveras Twp 8	57 54
NEU		
---	Calaveras Twp 6	57 148
---	Yuba North Ea	72 680
NEUBERGER		
Wm	San Francisco San Francisco 3	67 15
NEUCTREAUN		
Andrew*	Placer Michigan	62 837
NEUGHES		
Charles E	San Luis Obispo 65	40
	San Luis Obispo	
NEUHAM		
H	San Francisco San Francisco 2	67 591
NEUHANS		
H*	San Francisco San Francisco 2	67 591
NEUHAUS		
H	San Francisco San Francisco 2	67 591
NEUL		
John H	Calaveras Twp 6	57 114
NEUMAN		
C	El Dorado Placerville	58 869
Edwd	San Francisco San Francisco 10	256
		67
Emanuel	San Francisco San Francisco 10	256
		67
J B*	Nevada Nevada	61 247
J M	Placer Goods	62 697
Jno	Nevada Nevada	61 256
John	Napa Hot Springs	61 25
T A	Nevada Nevada	61 296
NEUMER		
Barnard	Calaveras Twp 4	57 339
NEUN		
---	San Francisco San Francisco 4	681188
NEUNJ		
---	Amador Twp 6	55 449
NEUNY		
---	Amador Twp 6	55 449
NEUSON		
Darrit*	Nevada Rough &	61 415
David*	Nevada Rough &	61 415
NEUSTADHER		
H	San Francisco San Francisco 5	67 522
NEUSTADT		
Adolph	Tuolumne Twp 1	71 207
C*	Sacramento Ward 4	63 573
Isador	Tuolumne Sonora	71 206
NEUTOIME		
Edward*	San Francisco San Francisco 3	67 80
NEUTOIMI		
Edward*	San Francisco San Francisco 3	67 80
NEUTONNI		
Edward*	San Francisco San Francisco 3	67 80
NEUTZELL		
C	Siskiyou Scott Va	69 22
NEUWARD		
Andrew	Marin San Rafael	60 757
NEVADA BOB		
---	Fresno Twp 3	59 24
NEVADA		
Francis	Yuba Parke Ba	72 786
Mary	Sonoma Santa Rosa	69 416
Mary	Sonoma Healdsbu	69 478
Sierra	Sonoma Mendocino	69 450
Sierra	Yuba Long Bar	72 744
NEVAL		
Louis	Calaveras Twp 7	57 13
NEVALES		
Sebastian	Los Angeles Los Nieto	59 430
NEVAN		
Harvey	Santa Cruz Watsonville	66 536

Name	County Locale	M653 RollPage
NEVAN		
J*	Nevada Grass Valley	61 180
S*	Nevada Grass Valley	61 180
NEVANS		
Harvey	Santa Cruz Watsonville	66 536
NEVARES		
Juan	Santa Clara Almaden	65 266
Nevar	Monterey San Juan	60 985
NEVARINE		
C	Mariposa Twp 1	60 630
NEVARIO		
Eland	Yuba Marysville	72 951
NEVARIS		
Eland	Yuba Marysville	72 951
Nevar	Monterey San Juan	60 985
NEVEES		
Jesee	Fresno Twp 1	59 75
NEVEL		
Richard*	Nevada Red Dog	61 544
Thos*	Nevada Bridgeport	61 495
NEVELL		
Partrick	Calaveras Twp 7	57 13
NEVELLE		
Richd	Nevada Bridgeport	61 454
NEVELT		
Jos H*	Sacramento Ward 1	63 87
NEVEN		
Theodore	Los Angeles Los Angeles	59 313
NEVENS		
Ann	Sierra La Porte	66 777
NEVER		
Wadaloupe*	Mariposa Twp 3	60 611
Wadoloupe*	Mariposa Twp 3	60 611
NEVERS		
P K*	Mariposa Twp 3	60 611
NEVES		
Wadaloupe*	Mariposa Twp 3	60 611
NEVETT		
Jos H*	Sacramento Ward 1	63 87
NEVIL		
Richard*	Nevada Bridgeport	61 504
NEVILL		
James	Sierra La Porte	66 774
NEVILLE		
C	Shasta Shasta	66 656
James	Mariposa Twp 3	60 563
John	Amador Twp 6	55 429
John M	Solano Benecia	69 295
Richd*	Nevada Bridgeport	61 454
Thomas J*	San Francisco 8	681281
	San Francisco	
NEVILLES		
James	San Francisco San Francisco 3	67 19
NEVILLO		
Thomas J	San Francisco San Francisco 8	681281
NEVIN		
Eduard	Yuba Rose Bar	72 801
Edward	Yuba Rose Bar	72 801
Henry	Yuba Fosters	72 839
Margaret*	Yuba Rose Bar	72 813
Martin	Yuba Rose Bar	72 813
Michael	Colusa Monroeville	57 452
Thomas	San Francisco San Francisco 11	107
		67
Thomas	Yuba Rose Bar	72 803
NEVINS		
A H	San Francisco San Francisco 10	304
		67
J	San Joaquin Stockton	641099
Jas S	Sacramento Franklin	63 315
L S	Sacramento Franklin	63 315
Thos J	Alameda Oakland	55 70
W R	San Francisco San Francisco 7	681332
NEVIO		
Fredrick	Sierra Twp 7	66 870
NEVIS		
Antoine*	Yuba Parke Ba	72 784
F*	Alameda Brooklyn	55 128
Phillip*	Alameda Brooklyn	55 128
NEVISON		
John	San Francisco San Francisco 12	366
		67
NEVITT		
Frank	Placer Yankee J	62 780
NEVIUS		
John*	Yuba Marysville	72 904
NEW HOUSE		
M	Sierra Gibsonville	66 854
NEW SHAM		
B*	El Dorado Georgetown	58 752
NEW YORK		
---	Nevada Rough &	61 438
NEW		
---	El Dorado Union	581090
---	El Dorado Greenwood	58 728
---	El Dorado Placerville	58 832

California 1860 Census Index

Name	County Locale	M653 RollPage
NEW		
---	El Dorado Mud Springs	58 972
---	Mariposa Twp 3	60 546
---	Mariposa Twp 1	60 658
---	Sierra St Louis	66 861
---	Yuba Fosters	72 843
James	Stanislaus Emory	70 749
James S	Calaveras Twp 5	57 238
John	Tuolumne Twp 3	71 461
Phillip	San Francisco San Francisco 9	681073
Pierre C	Tuolumne Twp 3	71 461
Pum C	Tuolumne Twp 3	71 461
York	Nevada Rough &	61 438
NEWA		
---	El Dorado White Oaks	581021
---	El Dorado Salmon Falls	581042
---	El Dorado Salmon Falls	581054
---	El Dorado Placerville	58 839
---	El Dorado Mud Springs	58 949
Hu	El Dorado Diamond	58 785
NEWAD		
Henry	Solano Fremont	69 385
NEWAH		
---	Mariposa Twp 1	60 658
NEWAL		
R	Nevada Grass Valley	61 237
NEWART		
P	San Francisco San Francisco 9	681105
NEWBANER		
Adam*	Sacramento Ward 1	63 82
Leonard*	Sacramento Ward 4	63 599
NEWBANES		
Leonard*	Sacramento Ward 4	63 599
NEWBARIER		
Adam*	Sacramento Ward 1	63 82
NEWBARN		
Ed	Calaveras Twp 9	57 389
NEWBAUER		
Adam	Sacramento Ward 1	63 82
H	Amador Twp 1	55 455
NEWBAUGH		
G	Yolo Cottonwoood	72 652
T	Calaveras Twp 9	57 373
NEWBAUM		
F*	Butte Kimshaw	56 579
NEWBAUMER		
Henry	Tuolumne Sonora	71 186
NEWBAURN		
F*	Butte Kimshaw	56 579
NEWBEGIN		
David	Trinity Douglas	70 979
NEWBERG		
John	San Francisco San Francisco 3	67 70
NEWBERGER		
Ed	San Francisco San Francisco 9	68 980
Maria	Yuba Marysville	72 898
Sarah	Yuba Marysville	72 873
Solomon	Contra Costa Twp 2	57 564
NEWBERN		
J	Shasta French G	66 718
NEWBERRY		
Benjamin	Yolo Slate Ra	72 697
Charles	Solano Benecia	69 304
Henry	Yolo Slate Ra	72 697
NEWBERT		
Charles	Yuba Marysville	72 875
J W	Solano Vallejo	69 279
Leander	Yuba Rose Bar	72 799
Rodolph*	San Francisco San Francisco 3	67 4
Sophia	Yuba Marysville	72 875
T A*	Yuba Rose Bar	72 796
NEWBEST		
Rodolph	San Francisco San Francisco 3	67 4
Sophia*	Yuba Marysville	72 875
NEWBOLT		
Frank	Sonoma Sonoma	69 633
NEWBOP		
Christine*	Solano Fremont	69 381
NEWBRYHEN		
A*	Calaveras Twp 6	57 119
H*	Calaveras Twp 6	57 119
NEWBUGHER		
Henrietta	Calaveras Twp 6	57 116
NEWBURG		
John	Sacramento Franklin	63 327
NEWBURGHER		
Abraham	Calaveras Twp 6	57 114
NEWBURRYH		
G*	Yolo Cottonwood	72 652
NEWBURY		
Henry	Sierra La Porte	66 787
J	El Dorado Coloma	581071
Joseph	Sierra Poker Flats	66 842
NEWBY		
Alex W	Sierra Scales D	66 802
C	Stanislaus Emory	70 737

Name	County Locale	M653 RollPage
NEWBY		
Sarah	San Francisco San Francisco 4	681159
Zmri	Stanislaus Emory	70 747
NEWCANMER		
Hen Ry	Tuolumne Twp 1	71 186
NEWCASTLE		
James	Solano Vacaville	69 319
NEWCIS		
H	El Dorado Placerville	58 851
NEWCOM		
Solomon	San Francisco San Francisco 3	67 17
NEWCOMB		
Amelia	Sacramento Ward 1	63 148
C J	San Joaquin Stockton	641036
Geo	Sacramento Ward 1	63 48
Geo	San Joaquin Stockton	641099
Geo H	Tuolumne Twp 3	71 459
George Jr	Sacramento Ward 1	63 49
J W	Sierra Twp 7	66 895
Martin	San Francisco San Francisco 2	67 575
Solomon D	Contra Costa Twp 3	57 598
W	Calaveras Twp 9	57 404
Wesley	Alameda Oakland	55 28
Wm	Alameda Oakland	55 9
NEWCOMER		
Furry	Tuolumne Jamestown	71 429
L	Tehama Pasakent	70 858
NEWCONB		
C	Sutter Yuba	70 775
NEWDIKE		
N	Yolo Cottonwood	72 656
NEWEB		
George	Mariposa Twp 1	60 660
NEWEILES		
John	Tuolumne Sonora	71 205
NEWEL		
E	Sutter Sutter	70 808
Phoebe N	Calaveras Twp 6	57 152
NEWELL		
A M	Yuba New York	72 732
D K	Sonoma Santa Rosa	69 389
Danial S	Humbolt Union	59 188
E	Placer Goods	62 694
Eddiseon	Santa Cruz Santa Cruz	66 616
Eddison	Santa Cruz Santa Cruz	66 616
Eddisson	Santa Cruz Santa Cruz	66 616
Edward L	Humbolt Eel Rvr	59 149
Elzy	San Joaquin Castoria	64 902
F	Amador Twp 3	55 390
F W	Placer Michigan	62 857
Frank T	Alameda Oakland	55 73
Fredk	San Francisco San Francisco 2	67 772
G B	Nevada Bridgeport	61 442
H P	El Dorado Gold Hill	581095
H T	Sacramento Ward 1	63 28
Henry	Amador Twp 3	55 400
James	Marin San Rafael	60 764
James	Sierra Twp 7	66 937
Jno M	Butte Oregon	56 618
John	Los Angeles Los Angeles	59 344
John	Placer Michigan	62 858
John	Siskiyou Scott Va	69 47
John J	Los Angeles Los Angeles	59 391
Jos	Sonoma Petaluma	69 604
L	Siskiyou Scott Ri	69 77
M	San Joaquin Stockton	641093
Martin	San Francisco San Francisco 2	67 745
Mary	Butte Ophir	56 770
Milton	Santa Cruz Santa Cruz	66 614
Mitlon*	Santa Cruz Santa Cruz	66 614
Nathan	Santa Cruz Santa Cruz	66 614
Norman	Butte Ophir	56 753
P O C	Sonoma Petaluma	69 606
Spaulding	Plumas Quincy	62 991
Sydn Ey	San Joaquin Stockton	641021
Sydney	San Joaquin Stockton	641045
Tho	Siskiyou Callahan	69 10
Thomas	Santa Clara Gilroy	65 246
Tim	San Joaquin Stockton	641021
W	San Francisco San Francisco 3	67 42
W F	Tehama Antelope	70 892
W P	El Dorado Gold Hill	581095
William	San Francisco San Francisco 9	681041
Wm	Napa Napa	61 68
Wm W	San Francisco San Francisco 3	67 87
NEWELS		
Milton*	Santa Cruz Santa Cruz	66 614
NEWENSCHANDER		
Frdk	Yuba Suida	72 982
NEWER		
W M	Amador Twp 3	55 388
NEWERY		
Thomas	Santa Cruz Soguel	66 583
NEWETT		
Jos	Sonoma Petaluma	69 604
NEWFELT		
H	San Francisco San Francisco 2	67 766

Name	County Locale	M653 RollPage
NEWFETT		
H	San Francisco San Francisco 2	67 766
NEWFIELD		
Louis*	San Francisco San Francisco 2	67 655
NEWFRAND		
Jno	San Francisco San Francisco 12	382 67
NEWGIN		
D	Sutter Bear Rvr	70 819
NEWHAFF		
Frank	San Francisco San Francisco 10	195 67
NEWHALL		
A B	Yolo Washington	72 565
Allen	Santa Cruz Pescadero	66 651
D B	Tuolumne Twp 4	71 158
Frank	Sonoma Sonoma	69 640
Geo W	Butte Eureka	56 651
Hiser	Nevada Rough &	61 400
J	Tuolumne Twp 4	71 147
J D	Butte Hamilton	56 519
James C	Calaveras Twp 6	57 152
W M	San Francisco San Francisco 5	67 520
NEWHAM		
Ed*	Calaveras Twp 9	57 389
NEWHARD		
Samuel F	Colusa Muion	57 459
Wm H	Colusa Muion	57 458
NEWHAUM		
F	Butte Kimshaw	56 579
NEWHAUS		
Charles	San Francisco San Francisco 7	681434
James	Sierra Twp 5	66 929
NEWHER		
Henry	El Dorado Kelsey	581145
NEWHOLT		
Fred	Sacramento American	63 163
NEWHOME		
Martin	Placer Virginia	62 684
NEWHOUSE		
Charles	San Francisco San Francisco 4	681150
Jacob	Santa Clara San Jose	65 345
K	Santa Clara Redwood	65 448
M	Sierra Gibsonville	66 854
Saml	Plumas Meadow Valley	62 931
NEWIMS		
J*	El Dorado Georgetown	58 683
NEWINES		
Henry*	El Dorado Kelsey	581145
NEWITT		
George	El Dorado Greenwood	58 726
NEWKERSH		
John	Sonoma Salt Point	69 694
NEWKIRK		
Isaac J	Humbolt Union	59 181
Saml	Plumas Quincy	62 959
NEWKIRSH		
John	Sonoma Salt Point	69 694
NEWL		
John	Calaveras Twp 6	57 158
NEWLAND		
Aguilla	Colusa Colusi	57 424
Alfred	Colusa Colusi	57 424
Andrew	Sacramento Ward 4	63 505
Danius	Colusa Colusi	57 424
Edward	Alameda Oakland	55 32
James	Colusa Colusi	57 424
Jose F	Colusa Colusi	57 424
P	San Francisco San Francisco 5	67 539
Patrick	San Francisco San Francisco 8	681240
T	Sutter Butte	70 785
Thomas J	Humbolt Pacific	59 136
William	Napa Yount	61 38
William H	Plumas Quincy	62 972
NEWLAW		
Ed*	Calaveras Twp 9	57 389
NEWLERT		
Leander*	Yuba Rose Bar	72 799
T A*	Yuba Rose Par	72 796
NEWLIN		
James	Plumas Quincy	62 959
John	Calaveras Twp 8	57 95
NEWLINS		
James	Siskiyou Scott Va	69 48
NEWLY		
Patrick	Solano Vallejo	69 279
NEWMAN		
---	El Dorado Diamond	58 813
A	Tuolumne Twp 2	71 386
Alfred	San Bernardino San Bernadino	64 685
Ang	Sonoma Petaluma	69 556
August	Tuolumne Twp 2	71 282
Awen*	Sierra Downieville	66 957
B F	Stanislaus Branch	70 709
Barnabas	Los Angeles Elmonte	59 253
Bleistein	Sonoma Healdsbu	69 471

Name	County Locale	M653 Roll	Page
NEWMAN			
C	Sacramento Cosumnes	63	409
Cath	San Francisco San Francisco 9	681	067
Catherine	San Francisco San Francisco 3	67	59
Catherine	San Joaquin Stockton	641	065
Charles	San Francisco San Francisco 4	681	160
Charles	Tuolumne Jamestown	71	431
Charles*	San Joaquin Stockton	641	032
Chas	Alameda Brooklyn	55	215
Chas L	San Francisco San Francisco 10		204
		67	
Chas W	Sacramento Ward 4	63	533
Clarke	Plumas Meadow Valley	62	907
D M	Amador Twp 2	55	290
David D	Plumas Quincy	62	992
E	Marin Cortemad	60	752
Edward	Butte Ophir	56	777
Edward	El Dorado White Oaks	581	018
Edward	Sacramento Mississipi	63	185
Eliza	San Joaquin Stockton	641	069
Emanuel*	San Francisco San Francisco 10		256
		67	
Ewing	Yolo Merritt	72	583
Fernando	Tuolumne Jamestown	71	438
Frederick	Sacramento Centre	63	176
G	Nevada Eureka	61	363
G	San Francisco San Francisco 10		357
		67	
G R	Nevada Grass Valley	61	176
George	Amador Twp 1	55	470
George T*	Sierra Downieville	66	988
George W	Plumas Quincy	62	957
Gomer C	Placer Stewart	62	606
Henrietta	Santa Clara San Jose	65	318
Henry	San Francisco San Francisco 7	681	433
Henry	San Francisco San Francisco 3	67	19
Henry*	Sacramento Ward 3	63	437
Herman	El Dorado Coloma	581	074
Isaac	Sacramento Centre	63	176
J	Nevada Grass Valley	61	202
J	San Francisco San Francisco 3	67	73
J	Trinity North Fo	701	023
J B	Nevada Nevada	61	247
J W	Tehama Lassen	70	877
Jacob	Placer Christia	62	736
James	Napa Hot Springs	61	10
James	Sierra Twp 7	66	912
Jno	Merced Twp 1	60	906
Jno	Nevada Nevada	61	256
Jno T	San Francisco San Francisco 10		323
		67	
John	Napa Hot Springs	61	25
John	Sacramento Sutter	63	305
John	San Joaquin Stockton	641	066
John	Trinity Weaverville	701	067
John	Trinity Indian C	70	983
John	Tuolumne Big Oak	71	180
John	Yuba Marysville	72	969
John A	Nevada Rough &	61	418
John H	Alameda Brooklyn	55	137
John R	Placer Ophirville	62	657
Jonathan	Santa Cruz Soquel	66	595
Jonathon	Santa Cruz Soquel	66	595
Joseph	Humbolt Mattole	59	124
Joseph	San Francisco San Francisco 3	67	52
Joshua	Solano Vacaville	69	356
Julia	Shasta French G	66	716
Julius N	Tuolumne Twp 3	71	437
Kate	San Francisco San Francisco 2	67	667
Kusky	Butte Ophir	56	799
L	Nevada Grass Valley	61	194
L B	Amador Twp 6	55	424
Leobold	Placer Iona Hills	62	862
Lewis W	San Francisco San Francisco 10		225
		67	
M	Sacramento Ward 1	63	26
M	Sacramento Ward 4	63	548
M R	El Dorado Casumnes	581	164
Mathew	San Francisco San Francisco 4	681	114
Moms*	Sierra Downieville	66	987
Morris	Sierra Downieville	66	987
Moses	Tuolumne Sonora	71	239
N	San Francisco San Francisco 9	681	102
N K	El Dorado Casumnes	581	164
Nonathon	Santa Cruz Soquel	66	595
Otto	Sierra Twp 7	66	877
Otts	Sierra Twp 7	66	877
Owen	Sierra Downieville	66	957
Patrick	Sierra Twp 5	66	917
Paul	Calaveras Twp 5	57	174
Peter	Sierra Twp 5	66	947
Peter	Sierra Downieville	66	964
Pleasant	Yolo Cache Crk	72	592
Q*	Yolo Putah	72	553
Reuban	Sacramento Ward 4	63	592
Richd	Plumas Quincy	62	916

Name	County Locale	M653 Roll	Page
NEWMAN			
S	San Francisco San Francisco 10		357
		67	
S	Tehama Red Bluff	70	909
S B	Amador Twp 6	55	424
S T	Napa Napa	61	64
Smith	Yuba Bear Rvr	721	006
Solomon	Sacramento Centre	63	176
T A	Nevada Nevada	61	296
Thomas	El Dorado Placerville	58	925
Thomas	San Francisco San Francisco 7	681	438
W	Klamath Klamath	59	225
W	Sacramento Ward 4	63	581
William	Contra Costa Twp 2	57	571
William	Contra Costa Twp 3	57	596
William	Placer Iona Hills	62	890
Wm	Butte Bidwell	56	712
Wm	Humbolt Union	59	186
Wm	Mendocino Ukiah	60	798
Wm	Sacramento Sutter	63	301
Wm	Sierra Eureka	661	048
Wm	Tuolumne Twp 2	71	317
NEWMANN			
William	Tuolumne Twp 2	71	353
NEWMARK			
Harris	Los Angeles Los Angeles	59	361
J S	Sacramento Ward 4	63	502
M	Sacramento Ward 1	63	38
Myers J	Los Angeles Los Angeles	59	361
Narris	Los Angeles Los Angeles	59	361
S	Sacramento Ward 1	63	47
Valentine	Solano Benecia	69	317
NEWMARTS			
S*	Sacramento Ward 1	63	47
NEWMAYER			
C	Sacramento Ward 1	63	74
NEWMES			
Henry*	El Dorado Kelsey	581	145
NEWMEYER			
Meria	San Francisco San Francisco 10		177
		67	
Mina	San Francisco San Francisco 10		177
		67	
Wm	San Francisco San Francisco 12		390
		67	
NEWMILLER			
C	San Joaquin Stockton	641	100
NEWMIRNA			
---	Fresno Twp 2	59	58
NEWMONDS			
Bernard	San Mateo Twp 2	65	115
NEWNHAN			
B	El Dorado Diamond	58	792
NEWNIARK			
Joseph	Los Angeles Los Angeles	59	341
NEWNOBLE			
Peter	San Joaquin Stockton	641	036
NEWNOL			
Joseph	Santa Clara Gilroy	65	246
NEWORN			
J W	Tuolumne Twp 4	71	150
NEWPIT			
Packer	Butte Wyandotte	56	658
NEWRAN			
H B	Butte Oro	56	688
NEWSBAUM			
A B C	Tehama Red Bluff	70	930
NEWSBURY			
J H*	Butte Wyandotte	56	671
NEWSOM			
Amos	Napa Napa	61	94
B	San Francisco San Francisco 4	681	229
J W	Tuolumne Big Oak	71	150
W	San Francisco San Francisco 5	67	494
Wm	Sacramento Ward 1	63	16
NEWSOME			
John	Stanislaus Empire	70	733
NEWSON			
E	Tehama Antelope	70	892
E	Tehama Antelope	70	893
George	Calaveras Twp 4	57	337
John	San Francisco San Francisco 9	681	046
NEWSTADT			
Ferdinand	San Francisco San Francisco 3	67	29
NEWSTEAD			
Chas	San Francisco San Francisco 10		291
		67	
John	Contra Costa Twp 2	57	558
NEWT			
---	El Dorado Union	581	090
---	Mendocino Round Va	60	878
NEWTEN			
M	El Dorado Georgetown	58	699
NEWTERN			
J	Shasta French G	66	718
NEWTHORNE			
William	Yuba Bear Rvr	721	007

Name	County Locale	M653 Roll	Page
NEWTOH			
Wesley	Amador Twp 2	55	319
NEWTOLE			
Wesley*	Amador Twp 2	55	319
NEWTON			
A	Sacramento Ward 1	63	18
Adolph	Marin Cortemad	60	780
Alfred	Sacramento Georgian	63	338
Andrew J	Placer Auburn	62	583
C	El Dorado Kelsey	581	156
C C	Sutter Nicolaus	70	841
Charles	Calaveras Twp 7	57	35
D S	El Dorado Placerville	58	847
Edward	Yuba Linda Twp	72	982
G	Sutter Yuba	70	760
G L	Sierra Downieville	66	961
Geo	Butte Kimshaw	56	586
Geo	Nevada Eureka	61	357
George	Calaveras Twp 5	57	213
George	Placer Michigan	62	839
George	Tuolumne Knights	71	529
George W	El Dorado Georgetown	58	705
Gerge W	El Dorado Georgetown	58	705
H	Sacramento Ward 4	63	565
H B	Butte Oro	56	688
Hallis	Placer Virginia	62	689
Haratio W	Sierra Pine Grove	66	825
Horatio W	Sierra Pine Grove	66	825
J	Nevada Eureka	61	357
J	Sutter Nicolaus	70	839
J B	Nevada Eureka	61	343
J B	Nevada Eureka	61	357
Jabey	Amador Twp 2	55	272
Jackson	Amador Twp 3	55	383
James	Amador Twp 7	55	419
James	Calaveras Twp 7	57	38
James	Plumas Quincy	62	997
Jas	Butte Chico	56	538
Jas	Butte Cascade	56	693
Jas L	Trinity Ferry	70	977
Jno	Sonoma Petaluma	69	587
John	Calaveras Twp 7	57	42
John	Calaveras Twp 8	57	69
John	Plumas Meadow Valley	62	928
John	Siskiyou Callahan	69	3
John S	Tuolumne Twp 2	71	289
L	El Dorado Kelsey	581	152
Levy	Tulara Twp 2	71	28
Lewis A	Siskiyou Shasta Rvr	69	115
M Arshall	Sierra Pine Grove	66	830
Marshall	Sierra Pine Grove	66	830
Mary	Sutter Nicolaus	70	841
Mary Jane	Yuba Long Bar	72	771
O H	Sutter Sutter	70	801
Otis J	Calaveras Twp 8	57	103
R S	Yuba Marysville	72	931
Reuben	Sierra Downieville	66	961
Rev	Solano Vallejo	69	278
Russell	Napa Napa	61	69
Saml	Sonoma Santa Rosa	69	419
Thomas	El Dorado Big Bar	58	743
Thos	San Francisco San Francisco 9	68	975
Thos	Trinity Lewiston	70	957
W B	Merced Twp 2	60	922
W F	Merced Twp 2	60	921
W H	Merced Twp 2	60	921
W O	Tuolumne Twp 3	71	436
Warren	Nevada Bridgeport	61	489
William	Calaveras Twp 7	57	40
William D	Sierra Gibsonville	66	856
Wm G	Los Angeles Elmonte	59	250
NEWTOTE			
Wesley*	Amador Twp 2	55	319
NEWVICK			
Sam	Butte Ophir	56	765
NEWY			
---	Mariposa Twp 1	60	662
NEWZ			
---	Mariposa Twp 1	60	662
NEX			
J T*	Sacramento San Joaquin	63	350
NEXFORD			
Dolorus	Contra Costa Twp 2	57	542
NEXT			
Ro	Yolo Putah	72	554
NEY GONZALOS			
Jose	Solano Vacaville	69	335
NEY			
D A	San Francisco San Francisco 5	67	542
George	Placer Yankee J	62	759
J	Nevada Nevada	61	260
Peter	Humbolt Union	59	181
S M	Sierra St Louis	66	864
NEYENAR			
Theodore*	Mariposa Twp 3	60	583
NEYER			
Christian*	Yuba Marysville	72	956

California 1860 Census Index

Name	County Locale	M653 Roll Page
NEYER		
Joseph*	Yuba Marysville	72 952
NEYERS		
Henry*	El Dorado Coloma	581068
NEYINAR		
Giacomo	Sacramento Ward 1	63 23
NEYLAND		
James	Alameda Oakland	55 36
NEYMAR		
Giacomo	Sacramento Ward 1	63 23
NEYMER		
Henry	Calaveras Twp 5	57 198
NEYURER		
Henry	Calaveras Twp 5	57 198
NEZET		
Peter	Humbolt Union	59 190
NGAN		
---	San Francisco San Francisco 6	67 466
NHANSO		
Michael*	San Francisco San Francisco 2	67 784
NHY		
Coo	Butte Ophir	56 816
NI CANG		
---	Nevada Bridgeport	61 460
NI HANNAH		
Mn M*	San Francisco San Francisco 2	67 739
Mon*	San Francisco San Francisco 2	67 739
NI		
---	Calaveras Twp 4	57 305
---	El Dorado Placerville	58 829
---	Sacramento Ward 1	63 69
Ling	Butte Bidwell	56 708
Low	Stanislaus Emory	70 753
Qui	Calaveras Twp 9	57 406
Yang	Calaveras Twp 8	57 93
NIALIVNO		
Pablo*	Mariposa Twp 3	60 611
NIANA		
---	San Diego Agua Caliente	64 815
NIARDIS		
W L*	Yolo Cottonwoood	72 650
NIAVES		
Wancisco	Los Angeles Los Angeles	59 300
NIBBLE		
John	San Mateo Twp 3	65 86
NIBBLY		
John	San Mateo Twp 1	65 48
Mary C	San Mateo Twp 1	65 48
NIBELA		
Henrico*	Calaveras Twp 7	57 24
NIBER		
Henry	El Dorado White Oaks	581015
NIBLE		
P A*	Siskiyou Yreka	69 143
NIBLES		
John*	Siskiyou Yreka	69 131
NIBY		
W H	Sacramento Georgian	63 342
NICALHOS		
Almoro	Tuolumne Twp 2	71 281
NICARKOS		
Elnioro*	Tuolumne Twp 2	71 281
NICBLES		
Lorenzo	Santa Clara Almaden	65 272
NICBLOS		
Panchor*	Mariposa Twp 3	60 545
NICCOLEE		
Fred*	Placer Ophirville	62 658
NICCSA		
---	Tulara Twp 2	71 39
NICE		
M	Sierra Port Win	66 796
Sydney*	San Bernardino San Bernadino	64 644
NICEOVONDER		
J L*	Calaveras Twp 9	57 383
NICEWANDER		
D	Calaveras Twp 9	57 410
NICEWANER		
Henry*	Nevada Red Dog	61 541
NICEWONDER		
J L	Calaveras Twp 9	57 383
NICHAL		
Edwin	San Francisco San Francisco 9	681019
NICHALAS		
Martin*	Siskiyou Shasta Valley	69 120
NICHALS		
E	Nevada Washington	61 337
John	Butte Bidwell	56 728
Wallace	Placer Dutch Fl	62 730
William	Contra Costa Twp 3	57 586
NICHALSON		
Andrew	Calaveras Twp 10	57 264
James	Tuolumne Jamestown	71 422
Lem	Tuolumne Twp 1	71 243
Peter	Siskiyou Scott Ri	69 66
NICHELSON		
J	Siskiyou Scott Ri	69 71

Name	County Locale	M653 Roll Page
NICHELSON		
John	El Dorado Coloma	581123
NICHER		
Betty*	Alameda Brooklyn	55 139
NICHERSON		
Jno	Monterey Alisal	601036
Wm H	Alameda Brooklyn	55 145
NICHILA		
Rasar	Amador Twp 5	55 332
NICHLEN		
Francis	Sierra Port Win	66 795
NICHLESS		
Sarah J*	Sacramento Ward 1	63 132
NICHLOS		
Amey	El Dorado Placerville	58 924
Pancho	Mariposa Twp 3	60 545
R J	El Dorado Placerville	58 933
NICHOL		
Amanda	Sonoma Petaluma	69 561
Andrew	Tulara Keyesville	71 60
H F	Sierra Twp 3	66 936
Henry	Plumas Quincy	62 938
James	Tuolumne Twp 2	71 292
John C	Tuolumne Jamestown	71 448
P	Calaveras Twp 9	57 389
P	Calaveras Twp 9	57 398
S	San Joaquin Stockton	641054
NICHOLA		
John	Contra Costa Twp 1	57 510
John	San Francisco San Francisco 5	67 503
NICHOLAS		
---	El Dorado Big Bar	58 744
---	Los Angeles Tejon	59 522
---	Nevada Bloomfield	61 511
---	Placer Dutch Fl	62 729
---	San Bernardino S Timate	64 690
---	San Bernardino S Timate	64 710
---	San Bernardino S Timate	64 711
---	San Bernardino S Timate	64 714
---	San Bernardino S Timate	64 716
---	San Bernardino S Timate	64 722
---	San Bernardino S Timate	64 723
---	San Bernardino S Timate	64 724
---	San Bernardino S Timate	64 727
---	San Bernardino S Timate	64 728
---	San Bernardino S Timate	64 738
---	San Bernardino S Timate	64 739
---	San Bernardino S Timate	64 742
---	San Bernardino S Timate	64 744
---	San Bernardino S Timate	64 745
---	San Bernardino S Timate	64 751
---	San Bernardino S Timate	64 753
---	San Bernardino S Timate	64 754
---	San Mateo Twp 3	65 108
---	San Mateo Twp 1	65 48
---	Tulara Twp 3	71 62
---*	Placer Dutch Fl	62 729
A	Sacramento Casumnes	63 381
A J	Sonoma Bodega	69 522
Alexander J	Yuba Marysville	72 958
Benj	Amador Twp 6	55 441
C	San Joaquin Stockton	641092
Charles	Siskiyou Yreka	69 182
Edwin	Amador Twp 2	55 286
Eliza	Siskiyou Yreka	69 157
Esta	El Dorado Coloma	581068
Francis	Butte Kimshaw	56 582
Francis	Calaveras Twp 6	57 133
Geo	Amador Twp 6	55 441
Geo	El Dorado Cold Spring	581100
H M	Sacramento Sutter	63 300
Henry	Siskiyou Yreka	69 179
Henry*	El Dorado White Oaks	581022
J S	San Francisco San Francisco 9	681086
Jacob	Amador Twp 6	55 441
James	Nevada Washington	61 331
James	Nevada Washington	61 341
James	Tuolumne Twp 2	71 280
Jas	Nevada Washington	61 331
John	Sacramento Sutter	63 298
John	San Francisco San Francisco 3	67 60
John	Trinity S Fork	701032
John	Tuolumne Twp 2	71 282
Jose	San Francisco San Francisco 3	67 2
Lewis	Amador Twp 6	55 441
Louis	Nevada Bloomfield	61 518
Louis	Tuolumne Twp 1	71 259
M	Amador Twp 6	55 437
M J	Sacramento Sutter	63 308
Manuel	Placer Michigan	62 850
Mariana*	San Francisco San Francisco 3	67 4
Martin	Siskiyou Shasta Valley	69 120
Peter	Butte Eureka	56 654
Peter	Placer Christia	62 736
Thomas	Sierra Twp 5	66 926
Vere	Alameda Brooklyn	55 95

Name	County Locale	M653 Roll Page
NICHOLAS		
Wm	Tehama Antelope	70 894
NICHOLASA		
---	San Bernardino S Timate	64 726
---	San Bernardino S Timate	64 730
---	San Bernardino S Timate	64 731
NICHOLASKY		
Louis	San Francisco San Francisco 4	681158
NICHOLAUS		
Charles	San Francisco San Francisco 3	67 4
Mariana	San Francisco San Francisco 3	67 4
NICHOLDS		
E	Marin Bolinas	60 728
Edwin	Marin San Rafael	60 773
NICHOLER		
D	San Francisco San Francisco 2	67 574
NICHOLES		
D*	San Francisco San Francisco 2	67 574
Henry	Siskiyou Scott Va	69 37
Henry*	El Dorado White Oaks	581022
Samuel	Nevada Nevada	61 298
NICHOLHOUSON		
Hiram*	Mendocino Calpella	60 816
NICHOLIE		
John	Yuba Fosters	72 835
NICHOLINI		
Eapron*	Sierra Whiskey	66 843
NICHOLLS		
Jacob	Sierra Twp 7	66 899
Robert	Tulara Visalia	71 5
NICHOLOS		
Frank	El Dorado Coloma	581082
Geo	El Dorado Cold Spring	581100
J P	El Dorado Kelsey	581147
NICHOLS		
---	Siskiyou Yreka	69 156
A B	Nevada Bloomfield	61 527
A C	San Francisco San Francisco 6	67 421
A J	El Dorado White Oaks	581017
A N	San Francisco San Francisco 5	67 479
A R	Sonoma Vallejo	69 631
A W	San Francisco San Francisco 5	67 479
Amber	Nevada Bloomfield	61 515
Anderson	Butte Oregon	56 609
Andrew	Butte Oregon	56 609
Andrw S	San Francisco San Francisco 12 67	390
B F	Butte Kimshaw	56 596
B S	Sacramento Ward 1	63 103
Benjamin	Santa Cruz Soguel	66 588
Bridget	San Francisco San Francisco 7	681415
C R	Klamath S Fork	59 198
Calvin L	Mendocino Calpella	60 812
Charles	San Francisco San Francisco 3	67 31
Chas	Klamath S Fork	59 202
Chas	Mendocino Big Rvr	60 848
Chas	Sacramento Ward 3	63 429
Chas	San Francisco San Francisco 1	68 895
Cornelius	San Francisco San Francisco 3	67 37
D	San Francisco San Francisco 9	681059
D	San Francisco San Francisco 2	67 670
Danl	Trinity Evans Ba	701002
E	Nevada Washington	61 331
Eli L	Placer Rattle Snake	62 629
Elisha	Colusa Muion	57 459
Ella F	San Francisco San Francisco 6	67 421
Elton	Plumas Quincy	62 976
Ezra	Tuolumne Twp 2	71 284
Ezra	Tuolumne Twp 2	71 284
Felicita E	Fresno Twp 1	59 33
Fred	Tuolumne Columbia	71 303
Geo	Calaveras Twp 10	57 277
Geo	San Francisco San Francisco 5	67 537
George	Humbolt Pacific	59 130
George	Nevada Red Dog	61 553
George	Santa Clara Gilroy	65 239
Granville	Sacramento Ward 1	63 151
Gulle	San Francisco San Francisco 2	67 777
Gutte	San Francisco San Francisco 2	67 777
H	Siskiyou Scott Va	69 43
H C	San Francisco San Francisco 5	67 495
H D	Siskiyou Scott Va	69 43
H M	Sacramento Franklin	63 328
Hannah	Sacramento Ward 3	63 455
Henry	Amador Twp 1	55 488
Henry	Siskiyou Scott Va	69 37
Henry	Yuba Rose Bar	72 818
Henry W	Alameda Oakland	55 73
Howard	Contra Costa Twp 3	57 606
Isaac J	Trinity North Fo	701004
J F	Sacramento Granite	63 228
J L	Shasta Shasta	66 731
J M	Napa Napa	61 91
J R	Alameda Brooklyn	55 199
J S	San Francisco San Francisco 5	67 480
Jacob	San Francisco San Francisco 7	681436

California 1860 Census Index

Name	County Locale	M653 Roll	Page
NICHOLS			
Jacob L	Napa Napa	61	89
James	San Diego San Diego	64	760
James	San Joaquin Elkhorn	64	962
James	Santa Clara San Jose	65	389
James	Shasta Shasta	66	733
James	Tuolumne Twp 2	71	280
James	Tuolumne Twp 2	71	367
James	Tuolumne Twp 2	71	380
James F W	Calaveras Twp 6	57	187
Jas C	Sacramento Ward 1	63	68
Jatoh L	Napa Napa	61	89
Jno	Merced Twp 1	60	906
Jno	Sacramento Ward 3	63	433
John	Amador Twp 1	55	493
John	Butte Bidwell	56	728
John	Calaveras Twp 10	57	277
John	San Joaquin Stockton	64	1055
John	Trinity Price'S	70	1019
John	Tulara Keyesville	71	55
John	Tuolumne Twp 2	71	282
John G	Los Angeles Los Angeles	59	348
John R	Fresno Twp 1	59	33
Joseph	Alameda Brooklyn	55	205
L	San Joaquin Elkhorn	64	991
Lawrence P	San Francisco San Francisco 7	68	1389
Leslie	Humbolt Eureka	59	174
Luther R	Siskiyou Yreka	69	134
Manda	Amador Twp 2	55	300
Martin N	Shasta Shasta	66	734
Martin V*	Shasta Shasta	66	734
Mary	Contra Costa Twp 1	57	510
Mary E	San Francisco San Francisco 8	68	1296
Moses	Butte Oregon	56	611
Moses	Butte Oregon	56	612
Moses	San Francisco San Francisco 9	68	1044
Nells	Calaveras Twp 5	57	182
Ory	Trinity Mouth Ca	70	1014
P M	Sacramento American	63	170
Peter	Butte Eureka	56	649
Peter	Marin Cortemad	60	779
R	Amador Twp 1	55	507
R	San Francisco San Francisco 6	67	467
R H	Nevada Grass Valley	61	172
S	Shasta Millvill	66	749
S S	Placer Iona Hills	62	872
S S	Sacramento Ward 4	63	530
Saml	Butte Kimshaw	56	577
Setti C	San Francisco San Francisco 1	68	924
T	Nevada Grass Valley	61	163
Theodore	El Dorado Greenwood	58	723
Thomas	Tuolumne Columbia	71	303
Thomas E	Calaveras Twp 5	57	241
Thos	Butte Mountain	56	737
Thos	El Dorado Big Bar	58	738
Thos	Sonoma Petaluma	69	556
Tobiar	Mendocino Big Rvr	60	843
Tobias	Mendocino Big Rvr	60	843
W H	Solano Benecia	69	289
W W	Nevada Bloomfield	61	510
Watson	Sacramento Ward 1	63	103
Wells	Calaveras Twp 6	57	182
William	Calaveras Twp 4	57	299
William	San Francisco San Francisco 3	67	43
William	San Joaquin Oneal	64	940
William	San Joaquin Elliott	64	945
William	San Joaquin Elkhorn	64	993
William	Siskiyou Cottonwood	69	109
William	Siskiyou Cottonwoood	69	99
William	Tuolumne Sonora	71	202
William H	San Joaquin Elkhorn	64	965
William I	Plumas Quincy	62	963
Wm	Humbolt Bucksport	59	162
Wm	Sacramento Natonia	63	272
Wm	Sacramento Ward 4	63	555
Wm	San Francisco San Francisco 5	67	552
Wm	Sierra Twp 7	66	903
Wm	Trinity Soldiers	70	1005
Wm F	Napa Napa	61	59
Wm M	Butte Ophir	56	775
Wm N	Sacramento Ward 1	63	142
Wm W	Alameda Brooklyn	55	199
NICHOLSEN			
J	Sacramento Sutter	63	304
Theod	Mendocino Big Rvr	60	848
Thos	Nevada Nevada	61	261
NICHOLSON			
Alex	San Francisco San Francisco 6	67	450
Andrew	Tulara Keyesville	71	54
Andrew	Yuba Marysville	72	852
Andrew	Yuba Marysville	72	857
Anton	Tuolumne Shawsfla	71	404
B F	Shasta Millvill	66	748
B H	Shasta Millvill	66	748
Catherine	Solano Benecia	69	297
NICHOLSON			
E S	Sierra Downieville	66	960
George	Yuba Marysville	72	948
J	Sacramento Sutter	63	304
J	Siskiyou Scott Ri	69	71
J J	San Francisco San Francisco 7	68	1436
J W	Sierra Downieville	66	960
James	Los Angeles Elmonte	59	253
James	Napa Hot Springs	61	20
James	Tuolumne Twp 3	71	422
Jas A	San Bernardino San Salvador	64	644
John	San Francisco San Francisco 2	67	659
John	Santa Clara San Jose	65	370
John H	Contra Costa Twp 2	57	570
John Y	San Francisco San Francisco 2	67	737
Jsh	Yolo Slate Ra	72	704
Jsh*	Yuba Slate Ro	72	704
Keneth	Tuolumne Twp 2	71	385
Lem	Tuolumne Sonora	71	243
Malcomb	Yuba Marysville	72	962
Mary J	San Francisco San Francisco 10	67	277
Mecal	Alameda Oakland	55	17
Michael	Santa Clara San Jose	65	316
O F	Sutter Sutter	70	812
Parker	San Mateo Twp 2	65	119
Patrick	Yuba Marysville	72	879
Peter	San Francisco San Francisco 1	68	855
Peter	Siskiyou Scott Ri	69	66
Peter	Yolo No E Twp	72	669
Sher*	Mendocino Big Rvr	60	848
Sherd*	Mendocino Big Rvr	60	848
Suton	Tuolumne Twp 2	71	404
Thos	Nevada Nevada	61	255
Thos	Nevada Nevada	61	261
W C	Shasta Horsetown	66	705
W E	Sacramento American	63	161
W W	Tuolumne Jacksonville	71	167
William	Contra Costa Twp 2	57	571
Wm C	Sacramento Ward 3	63	459
Wm M	Nevada Nevada	61	283
Y	San Francisco San Francisco 2	67	752
NICHOLSTON			
Kate	San Francisco San Francisco 2	67	673
NICHONS			
J H	Shasta Millvill	66	750
NICHSON			
Franklin	Alameda Brooklyn	55	79
NICK			
George*	Alameda Brooklyn	55	147
NICKALAS			
Paris	Calaveras Twp 7	57	6
NICKALE			
John	Tuolumne Jamestown	71	443
NICKALES			
George	Calaveras Twp 7	57	6
Micheal	Calaveras Twp 7	57	6
Nichalas	Calaveras Twp 7	57	1
NICKALLS			
Nichalas*	Calaveras Twp 7	57	1
NICKALSON			
Andrew	Calaveras Twp 10	57	264
NICKE			
---	Tulara Twp 2	71	37
NICKEL			
H	Nevada Grass Valley	61	189
NICKELER			
Peter S	Yuba Marysville	72	977
NICKELL			
Saml	Placer Dutch Fl	62	730
NICKELLS			
A	Butte Cascade	56	694
NICKELS			
Dopen	Butte Bidwell	56	705
Dossen	Butte Bidwell	56	705
Margaret	Sierra La Porte	66	772
NICKELSON			
P R	San Francisco San Francisco 4	68	1165
NICKENBOTHAM			
Edwin	San Joaquin Stockton	64	1052
NICKERBACKER			
George	San Mateo Twp 3	65	87
NICKERSEN			
Mulford	San Francisco San Francisco 10	67	357
NICKERSON			
Benjamin Q*	Amador Twp 4	55	234
Benjamin Z*	Amador Twp 4	55	234
Byron	Solano Fairfield	69	200
Charles	San Francisco San Francisco 4	68	1150
Chas*	Trinity Big Flat	70	1040
Cornelius G	Humbolt Pacific	59	138
J B	Sacramento Ward 1	63	141
James	Colusa Grand Island	57	474
Jas R	Placer Virginia	62	700
M	El Dorado Placerville	58	859
NICKERSON			
Mulford*	San Francisco San Francisco 10	67	357
Richard M	Placer Virginia	62	670
William	Santa Cruz Santa Cruz	66	619
NICKES			
Edith M*	Del Norte Crescent	58	644
NICKET			
Edith M*	Del Norte Crescent	58	644
NICKEY			
T	Calaveras Twp 9	57	405
NICKHAL			
Sarah	Sutter Vernon	70	842
NICKHAM			
J	Siskiyou Scott Va	69	52
NICKLEP			
Sarah J*	Sacramento Ward 1	63	132
NICKLESON			
Jno*	Alameda Brooklyn	55	146
NICKLESS			
Sarah J*	Sacramento Ward 1	63	132
NICKMANN			
Robt	Tuolumne Columbia	71	320
NICKO			
Jack	Tuolumne Twp 1	71	270
NICKOL			
James	Tuolumne Columbia	71	292
NICKOLANS			
J	Sutter Sutter	70	804
NICKOLD			
Ann	San Francisco San Francisco 2	67	617
NICKOLS			
Anderson W	Los Angeles Los Angeles	59	347
George	Yuba Marysville	72	965
Henry	Yuba Bear Rvr	72	1002
J T	El Dorado Diamond	58	813
Jeramiah	El Dorado Eldorado	58	947
John	Tulara Visalia	71	98
Louisa	Tulara Visalia	71	98
Margaret	Sierra La Porte	66	772
Ory	Trinity Mouth Ca	70	1014
Richard	Plumas Quincy	62	982
Robert	San Francisco San Francisco 11	67	120
William B	San Francisco San Francisco 11	67	99
NICKOLSON			
Benjamin	Tulara Twp 1	71	84
John	San Francisco San Francisco 8	68	1293
NICKONIO			
Whan	Amador Twp 5	55	355
NICKS			
Jack	Tuolumne Twp 1	71	270
Moses*	Butte Eureka	56	645
NICKSON			
Henry	Santa Cruz Pajaro	66	531
Edith M*	Del Norte Crescent	58	644
NICKY			
William	San Joaquin Elkhorn	64	976
NICLESON			
Elijah	Santa Clara San Jose	65	340
NICLOA			
Peter	Calaveras Twp 7	57	7
NICLOAS			
P	Siskiyou Scott Ri	69	65
NICOCHAYA			
Jose M	San Diego San Diego	64	764
NICOL			
J H	Amador Twp 2	55	301
Mary A	Monterey Pajaro	60	1014
William	San Francisco San Francisco 3	67	48
William	San Francisco San Francisco 3	67	49
NICOLA			
A	Shasta Shasta	66	676
Jasper	Calaveras Twp 7	57	7
NICOLAI			
L	Nevada Grass Valley	61	170
NICOLAS			
---	Los Angeles San Juan	59	465
---	Los Angeles San Pedro	59	486
---	Monterey San Juan	60	994
---	San Diego Temecula	64	784
---	San Diego Temecula	64	791
Erastus	Santa Cruz Santa Cruz	66	601
J W	Sutter Sutter	70	809
Joseph	San Francisco San Francisco 11	67	94
Julia	Santa Cruz Soguel	66	594
Leonardo	Los Angeles San Juan	59	462
William	Santa Cruz Soguel	66	592
William	Santa Cruz Soguel	66	594
NICOLAUS			
T	Nevada Grass Valley	61	158
NICOLS			
Wm	Mariposa Twp 3	60	586

Name	County Locale	M653 Roll	Page
NICOLS			
Wm*	Nevada Grass Valley	61	151
Wm*	Mariposa Twp 3	60	586
NICOLSON			
J	Mariposa Twp 3	60	612
NICOTTO			
Charles A	San Joaquin Castoria	64	895
NICSON			
J	Calaveras Twp 9	57	415
NICT			
Lena	San Francisco San Francisco 7	68	1374
NICTMAN			
Victor W*	Alameda Brooklyn	55	206
NICUBO			
Frederick*	Santa Cruz Pescadero	66	643
NIDER			
E	San Bernardino Santa Barbara	64	190
J S	Sutter Yuba	70	760
NIDEVER			
George	San Bernardino Santa Barbara	64	164
John*	San Bernardino Santa Barbara	64	177
NIDGE			
J	Calaveras Twp 9	57	413
NIDIE			
Barthio*	Santa Cruz Santa Cruz	66	626
NIDO			
Wancisco	Los Angeles Los Angeles	59	308
NIE			
---	El Dorado White Oaks	58	1021
---	Sacramento Ward 1	63	70
---	Shasta Horsetown	66	708
---*	Mariposa Twp 3	60	569
John	Shasta Shasta	66	679
P	Calaveras Twp 9	57	408
NIEBLES			
Cuperts	Mariposa Twp 3	60	549
Francisco	Mariposa Twp 3	60	549
NIEBOHR			
Wm	San Francisco San Francisco 9	68	1053
NIECE			
Adam M	Mendocino Ukiah	60	807
Henry	Amador Twp 2	55	309
Mary Ann	Mendocino Ukiah	60	807
NIED			
Jacob*	Shasta Shasta	66	663
NIEL			
---	Amador Twp 2	55	327
C O	Nevada Eureka	61	377
Charles*	Los Angeles Los Angeles	59	491
Danl	Sacramento Ward 4	63	572
J O	Nevada Grass Valley	61	235
Jos	Amador Twp 2	55	310
Jos	Amador Twp 2	55	312
T	Nevada Grass Valley	61	213
William*	Siskiyou Yreka	69	143
NIELLSON			
Capt	Mariposa Twp 3	60	610
NIELR			
Michael	Calaveras Twp 6	57	136
NIELS			
Edgar*	Sacramento Ward 4	63	613
NIELSEN			
John*	Siskiyou Shasta Valley	69	119
NIEM			
Charles*	Sierra Twp 5	66	925
NIEMAN			
Herman	San Francisco San Francisco 10	67	209
W	Shasta Shasta	66	728
NIEMON			
Jacob	Yuba Slate Ro	72	689
NIEN			
---*	Sacramento Ward 1	63	67
Edward	Yuba New York	72	728
NIEPPAL			
William*	Sierra St Louis	66	818
NIER			
Patrick H	Solano Suisan	69	226
NIEREAS			
---	San Bernardino S Timate	64	719
NIERECK			
Geo	San Francisco San Francisco 9	68	1075
NIETE			
Warren	Nevada Rough &	61	412
NIETO			
Peregeino*	Santa Clara Gilroy	65	224
Petra	Los Angeles Los Nieto	59	429
NIETZ			
Ernest	San Francisco San Francisco 3	67	42
NIEVES			
---	San Diego San Diego	64	774
NIG			
---	Mariposa Twp 3	60	551
Lee	Butte Cascade	56	692
NIGAL			
John*	San Francisco San Francisco 1	68	885
NIGARY			
Joseph	Santa Clara Alviso	65	414
NIGER			
Micholas	Yuba Slate Ro	72	702
Nicholas	Yolo Slate Ra	72	702
NIGERS			
M	Calaveras Twp 9	57	396
NIGGEE			
John*	Nevada Red Dog	61	537
NIGGER			
Mrs	San Francisco San Francisco 11	67	101
Urs	San Francisco San Francisco 11	67	101
NIGGINS			
George W*	Calaveras Twp 7	57	1
NIGH			
Henry*	Yuba Marysville	72	902
J*	Nevada Eureka	61	387
NIGHOLAS			
C	San Joaquin Stockton	64	1042
NIGHT			
Arther	Marin Novato	60	736
Augustus	Los Angeles Elmonte	59	263
G W	Sacramento Sutter	63	308
Jno L	Sacramento Ward 4	63	530
John	Contra Costa Twp 1	57	503
John	Marin San Rafael	60	770
R A	Butte Mountain	56	738
William	Nevada Little Y	61	534
Wm	Tehama Red Bluff	70	918
NIGHTAYILL			
Gideon	Yuba Marysville	72	885
NIGHTENGALE			
James	Placer Michigan	62	847
Wm	San Francisco San Francisco 1	68	917
NIGHTHART			
George*	Placer Forest H	62	800
NIGHTINGALE			
C E	Amador Twp 3	55	385
John	San Francisco San Francisco 8	68	1237
John	San Joaquin Douglass	64	923
William	Calaveras Twp 8	57	58
Wm J*	San Francisco San Francisco 7	68	1443
NIGHTINGILL			
Gideon R	Yuba Marysville	72	885
NIGHTMAYE			
---	Mendocino Big Rvr	60	854
NIGHTNIGALE			
John	San Francisco San Francisco 8	68	1237
NIGINIA			
Spencer*	Yuba Rose Bar	72	791
NIGLE			
J*	Nevada Eureka	61	387
NIGO LI			
---*	Nevada Red Dog	61	539
NIGO LO			
---*	Nevada Red Dog	61	539
NIGRAM			
Samuel*	Yuba Linda	72	989
NIGRO			
---	Tulara Keyesville	71	68
---	Tulara Keyesville	71	71
NIHAN			
Jas*	San Francisco San Francisco 1	68	899
NIHART			
Daniel	Plumas Quincy	62	942
NIHCALS			
H D	Siskiyou Scott Va	69	43
NIHEN			
David	San Mateo Twp 3	65	90
NIHON			
J	Tehama Lassen	70	877
NIHONS			
Edwarrd	Alameda Brooklyn	55	182
NIHOOF			
Peter	Tuolumne Big Oak	71	128
NILAN			
Catharine	San Francisco San Francisco 9	68	961
Michael*	San Francisco San Francisco 1	68	859
NILE			
Henry R*	San Francisco San Francisco 9	68	1092
Mary	San Francisco San Francisco 9	68	979
Peter	Calaveras Twp 7	57	40
NILEM			
Wm	San Francisco San Francisco 2	67	565
NILENS			
Philip	Yolo Washington	72	563
NILES			
A W	Siskiyou Cottonwoood	69	98
A*	San Francisco San Francisco 9	68	1045
Andrew	Marin Tomales	60	713
C G	Yolo Cottonwoood	72	654
E	San Mateo Twp 1	65	48
Henry W	Tulara Visalia	71	101
M S	Sacramento Sutter	63	303
NILES			
O G	Yolo Cottonwoood	72	654
Patrick	Sierra Twp 7	66	881
Paul	Tuolumne Twp 6	71	539
Paul J	Tuolumne Don Pedro	71	539
Peter	San Mateo Twp 3	65	90
T J	Siskiyou Cottonwoood	69	98
T S	Siskiyou Cottonwoood	69	98
W S	Sacramento Sutter	63	303
Walter S	San Francisco San Francisco 7	68	1443
NILEY			
P	Butte Eureka	56	654
NILIO			
---	Tulara Twp 3	71	64
NILKE			
N C	San Joaquin Stockton	64	1052
NILLCAUS			
Farlow M*	Nevada Bridgeport	61	447
NILLIA			
Francisco	Los Angeles Los Angeles	59	495
Francisco*	Los Angeles Los Angeles	59	495
NILLIN			
Samuel*	Alameda Brooklyn	55	79
NILLION			
Samuel*	Alameda Brooklyn	55	79
NILLIS			
G S*	Calaveras Twp 9	57	406
R J*	Sacramento Ward 3	63	466
NILLNER			
Casper	Mariposa Twp 1	60	647
NILLON			
John*	Placer Todds Va	62	783
NILLSON			
Samuel*	Alameda Brooklyn	55	79
NILON			
J	Yolo Putah	72	552
NILSEN			
David	San Mateo Twp 3	65	89
NILSON			
Frances*	Tuolumne Twp 1	71	203
James	Siskiyou Yreka	69	145
Jas	Butte Ophir	56	791
Joseph	Marin Tomales	60	713
M	Tuolumne Twp 2	71	279
P S*	Sacramento Cosumnes	63	391
R L*	Sacramento Dry Crk	63	375
Rufus*	Sacramento Dry Crk	63	371
S E*	Sacramento Alabama	63	415
Wm*	San Francisco San Francisco 9	68	1055
NIM CHI			
---*	Calaveras Twp 8	57	59
NIM			
---	Amador Twp 6	55	428
---	Amador Twp 1	55	501
---	Butte Wyandotte	56	666
---	Butte Oro	56	688
---	Butte Cascade	56	699
---	Butte Bidwell	56	714
---	Butte Bidwell	56	715
---	Butte Bidwell	56	731
---	Butte Mountain	56	740
---	Butte Mountain	56	742
---	Butte Mountain	56	744
---	Butte Ophir	56	759
---	Calaveras Twp 5	57	139
---	Calaveras Twp 5	57	147
---	El Dorado Coloma	58	1085
---	El Dorado Diamond	58	787
---	Mariposa Twp 1	60	673
---	Nevada Rough &	61	426
---	Nevada Bloomfield	61	522
---	Placer Illinois	62	746
Ah	Butte Oro	56	688
Ah	Butte Bidwell	56	708
Ah	Butte Bidwell	56	731
Bloke	Butte Oro	56	675
Clim	Butte Bidwell	56	711
Fee	Butte Ophir	56	816
Ha	Butte Oro	56	686
Han	Butte Mountain	56	744
Hay	Butte Mountain	56	744
Hife	Butte Oro	56	686
Hip	Butte Oro	56	686
Hon	Butte Mountain	56	744
Hoo	Butte Ophir	56	816
How	Butte Bidwell	56	708
Hoy	Butte Ophir	56	788
Jenesse*	Butte Cascade	56	699
Lee	Butte Wyandotte	56	672
Lee	Butte Oro	56	675
Lee	Butte Oro	56	677
Lee	Butte Oro	56	682
Lee	Butte Ophir	56	760
Lu	Butte Ophir	56	760
Sim	Butte Bidwell	56	711
Wan	Butte Oro	56	677
Wareen*	Amador Twp 2	55	314

Name	County Locale	M653 Roll	Page
NIM			
Warren*	Amador Twp 2	55	314
Warun*	Amador Twp 2	55	314
Wha	Butte Cascade	56	701
NIMA			
---	Fresno Twp 1	59	28
NIMAN			
Feliciana	Santa Clara San Jose	65	357
NIMCO			
---*	Butte Chico	56	550
NIMER			
Jacob	Sierra La Porte	66	776
NIMES			
Elin	San Joaquin Elkhorn	64	964
Hosea	Alameda Brooklyn	55	199
NIMETH			
Andrew	Contra Costa Twp 3	57	616
NIMIE			
---	Tulara Twp 2	71	40
NIMJ			
---	Nevada Bloomfield	61	522
NIMON			
Jacob*	Yolo Slate Ra	72	689
NIMS			
Clinton	Sierra Twp 7	66	888
Daniel	San Joaquin Stockton	64	1090
Noah	Placer Yankee J	62	760
NIN SHUNG			
---*	Mariposa Twp 1	60	671
NIN			
---	Amador Twp 2	55	290
---	Amador Twp 5	55	349
---	Amador Twp 3	55	382
---	Calaveras Twp 6	57	139
---	Calaveras Twp 5	57	205
---	Calaveras Twp 10	57	272
---	Calaveras Twp 4	57	320
---	El Dorado Salmon Falls	58	1047
---	El Dorado Salmon Hills	58	1053
---	El Dorado Salmon Falls	58	1058
---	El Dorado Kelsey	58	1133
---	El Dorado Georgetown	58	700
---	El Dorado Placerville	58	842
---	El Dorado Eldorado	58	944
---	Sacramento Natonia	63	283
---	Yuba New York	72	739
A	Sonoma Sonoma	69	639
Crew*	Butte Ophir	56	806
See	El Dorado Georgetown	58	702
NINA			
A	Nevada Washington	61	335
NINAN			
Samuel*	Santa Cruz Santa Cruz	66	607
NINCAMP			
Felix	Placer Iona Hills	62	886
NINCINESLY			
Steccino	Butte Ophir	56	766
NINCO			
---	Calaveras Twp 8	57	59
NINDITH			
W C*	Calaveras Twp 9	57	408
NINE			
---	Placer Secret R	62	621
---	Sierra Downieville	66	954
Adonis*	El Dorado Greenwood	58	722
Barthol	Alameda Brooklyn	55	81
J	Calaveras Twp 9	57	391
NINEHALL			
R F	El Dorado Greenwood	58	712
NINEMAKER			
Fred	Amador Twp 6	55	441
NINERA			
---	Tulara Twp 3	71	64
NINEVA			
---	Tulara Keyesville	71	64
NINFIELD			
Louis*	San Francisco San Francisco 2	67	655
NING DI			
---	Solano Suisan	69	205
NING			
---	Amador Twp 4	55	247
---	Butte Wyandotte	56	665
---	Calaveras Twp 6	57	165
---	El Dorado White Oaks	58	1022
---	El Dorado Salmon Falls	58	1041
---	El Dorado Salmon Falls	58	1053
---	El Dorado Coloma	58	1085
---	El Dorado Coloma	58	1106
---	El Dorado Casumnes	58	1173
---	El Dorado Georgetown	58	695
---	Tuolumne Twp 2	71	410
---	Tuolumne Shawsfla	71	416
---	Tuolumne Twp 3	71	433
---	Tuolumne Jamestown	71	434
---	Tuolumne Jamestown	71	439
---	Tuolumne Twp 3	71	468

Name	County Locale	M653 Roll	Page
NING			
---	Tuolumne Sonora	71	475
---	Tuolumne Sonora	71	478
---	Tuolumne Jacksonville	71	515
---	Tuolumne Twp 6	71	540
---*	Butte Ophir	56	814
---*	Sacramento Ward 1	63	59
Charles B*	Calaveras Twp 8	57	78
Cun	Siskiyou Yreka	69	195
Goy	Butte Ophir	56	819
Hoe	Siskiyou Yreka	69	194
Kehoy	Siskiyou Yreka	69	194
Name	Yuba Long Bar	72	763
Ri	Solano Suisan	69	205
NINGO			
J D	Amador Twp 2	55	309
NINO			
---	Fresno Twp 2	59	102
Juan N	Alameda Oakland	55	55
Santa	San Diego Agua Caliente	64	867
NINOMISS			
---	Del Norte Klamath	58	657
NINON			
---	El Dorado Georgetown	58	692
NINOTT			
Gordon	Yuba Marysville	72	850
NINSLOW			
Benj F	Marin Bolinas	60	727
NINSMAKER			
Fred*	Amador Twp 6	55	441
NINTHOL			
John*	San Francisco San Francisco 9	68	1064
NINTRAN			
Peter	San Francisco San Francisco 9	68	1067
NIOBE			
Henry	San Francisco San Francisco 3	67	15
NIOM			
Jane*	Sacramento Ward 1	63	86
NIONE			
Jane*	Sacramento Ward 1	63	86
NIONTKIN			
John*	Santa Cruz Santa Cruz	66	604
NIOR			
E	Nevada Nevada	61	289
NIOREER			
Anna M	Mariposa Coulterville	60	678
NIOUR			
Jane*	Sacramento Ward 1	63	86
NIP			
---	Butte Mountain	56	744
---	El Dorado Cold Spring	58	1101
NIPLE			
---	Siskiyou Scott Va	69	51
Martin	Siskiyou Scott Va	69	51
NIPPAL			
William	Sierra St Louis	66	818
NIPPE			
John	Tuolumne Twp 3	71	425
NIPPER			
A B	Butte Oro	56	686
Hugh	Yuba New York	72	727
NIPPIN			
William	Calaveras Twp 8	57	80
NIPPLER			
Geo*	San Francisco San Francisco 1	68	825
NIPPON			
Ott	Sonoma Sonoma	69	636
NIPTRATE			
F	Tuolumne Twp 2	71	283
NIR			
---	Calaveras Twp 5	57	205
---	El Dorado Greenwood	58	719
NIREON			
Melinda	Santa Clara San Jose	65	368
NIRGHLEY			
Robt	Santa Clara Santa Clara	65	465
NIROMAN			
Chas W	San Francisco San Francisco 3	67	86
NIRRHANS			
James	Sierra Twp 5	66	929
NIRTON			
Charles	Calaveras Twp 5	57	200
NIRU			
Hay	Butte Ophir	56	811
Lee	Butte Ophir	56	811
NIS			
Bo	San Francisco San Francisco 4	68	1187
NISBITT			
James	El Dorado Greenwood	58	710
John	El Dorado Greenwood	58	710
NISBRATH			
Philip*	San Joaquin Stockton	64	1034
NISCHEL			
A*	Nevada Grass Valley	61	201
NISEMAN			
Henry	Plumas Quincy	62	991

Name	County Locale	M653 Roll	Page
NISEMAN			
Henry W	Plumas Quincy	62	991
NISEN			
Andrew	Contra Costa Twp 1	57	524
NISERD			
Patrick*	Tuolumne Don Pedro	71	538
NISH			
Wm	San Bernardino San Bernadino	64	631
Wm*	San Joaquin San Bernadino	64	629
NISHER			
James	El Dorado Salmon Hills	58	1065
NISHOLS			
J L	Shasta Shasta	66	731
NISLEY			
P W	Siskiyou Scott Va	69	31
NISMANGER			
William	Los Angeles Elmonte	59	245
NISMITH			
---	San Mateo Twp 3	65	107
NISS			
---	Nevada Bridgeport	61	463
J	Calaveras Twp 9	57	413
NISSHFELD			
C*	San Joaquin Stockton	64	1040
NISSON			
C	Alameda Brooklyn	55	128
Peter	Humbolt Eel Rvr	59	145
NISUS			
Jasus*	Los Angeles Los Angeles	59	489
Jesus	Los Angeles Los Angeles	59	489
NITE			
John*	Nevada Red Dog	61	545
NITEN			
David	El Dorado Placerville	58	904
NITENGALE			
James	El Dorado Mud Springs	58	989
NITILE			
John*	San Bernardino San Bernadino	64	636
NITKOSKY			
M*	Sacramento Ward 1	63	74
NITLE			
Peter	Siskiyou Scott Ri	69	64
NITO			
John*	Nevada Red Dog	61	545
NITSON			
P	El Dorado Diamond	58	800
NITTIS			
Wm	Sierra Eureka	66	1050
NITTON			
Wm*	Mariposa Coulterville	60	674
NITTS			
Robert	Nevada Bloomfield	61	514
NITTUCK			
G*	Calaveras Twp 9	57	404
NITZ			
Henry	Sacramento San Joaquin	63	353
NIU			
---	Calaveras Twp 5	57	205
NIUTRAN			
Peter*	San Francisco San Francisco 9	68	1067
NIVA			
A*	Nevada Washington	61	335
NIVEL			
Richard*	Nevada Red Dog	61	544
NIVELA			
Henrico*	Calaveras Twp 7	57	24
NIVEN			
A	Nevada Eureka	61	352
NIVENS			
A*	Nevada Eureka	61	352
D	Nevada Eureka	61	352
Joseph	Plumas Quincy	62	954
NIVER			
Adam*	Butte Oregon	56	629
NIVVIAN			
Nartrun*	Calaveras Twp 4	57	319
NIW			
---	El Dorado Salmon Falls	58	1047
NIX			
C M	Yolo Slate Ra	72	704
C M*	Yuba Slate Ro	72	704
Dana S*	Santa Cruz Pescadero	66	645
F	Nevada Eureka	61	369
J T*	Sacramento San Joaquin	63	350
Mark D L	Yuba Marysville	72	871
R	Calaveras Twp 9	57	417
NIXEN			
J R	Yolo Cottonwoood	72	648
NIXER			
Harriett*	Yolo Cache	72	608
Saml*	Yolo Cache	72	607
NIXON			
Alex B	Sacramento Ward 4	63	560
Charles	Plumas Quincy	62	980
David W	Humbolt Eureka	59	167
Geo	Sacramento Ward 3	63	441

California 1860 Census Index

Name	County Locale	M653 Roll	Page
NIXON			
J	Calaveras Twp 9	57	412
J	Nevada Eureka	61	390
J	San Francisco San Francisco 5	67	539
J B	Yolo Cache	72	606
J B	Yolo Cottonwoood	72	648
J M*	Nevada Nevada	61	274
James	Siskiyou Scott Va	69	20
Jane	San Francisco San Francisco 8	681	251
Jesse	Nevada Bloomfield	61	525
John	Placer Rattle Snake	62	631
Patrick	Solano Vallejo	69	248
R	Sacramento Brighton	63	192
R L	Tehama Red Bluff	70	905
Robt	Sacramento Ward 3	63	431
Robt B	Santa Clara San Jose	65	368
Saml	Sacramento Ward 4	63	500
Saml	Sacramento Ward 1	63	82
Sarah	Humbolt Union	59	186
Thomas	Sierra Twp 7	66	896
Wm	Amador Twp 3	55	406
Wm	Sacramento Ward 4	63	583
NKY			
---	El Dorado Greenwood	58	730
NNE			
---	Tuolumne Chinese	71	521
NNONMEL			
Matilda	San Francisco San Francisco 10	67	196
NNOYES			
Al	Sutter Butte	70	787
NO LEE			
Ma*	Yuba Fosters	72	843
NO SAB REE			
---	Yuba Parke Ba	72	782
NO			
---	Butte Kimshaw	56	586
---	Butte Oregon	56	618
---	Calaveras Twp 5	57	245
---	Calaveras Twp 5	57	246
---	Fresno Twp 2	59	20
---	Sacramento Cosumnes	63	397
---	San Francisco San Francisco 4	681	193
---	Yuba Long Bar	72	757
---*	Butte Kimshaw	56	586
---*	El Dorado Georgetown	58	701
Ah	Butte Oregon	56	618
Ah	Tuolumne Twp 2	71	307
Kee	El Dorado Georgetown	58	687
Non	Nevada Rough &	61	409
Sab Bee	Yuba Parks Ba	72	782
Yan*	San Francisco San Francisco 9	681	096
Yaw*	San Francisco San Francisco 9	681	096
Yeck	Sacramento Granite	63	269
NO??S			
S W*	San Francisco San Francisco 5	67	547
NOA			
---	Fresno Twp 1	59	28
NOAB			
Jaque*	Colusa Monroeville	57	444
NOAH			
Joel	San Francisco San Francisco 3	67	20
M M	San Francisco San Francisco 6	67	439
Wm B	San Francisco San Francisco 2	67	726
NOAKES			
James T	Fresno Twp 3	59	32
John	Tulara Twp 5	71	59
John H	San Bernardino San Salvador	64	653
NOAMEK			
---	Fresno Twp 2	59	90
NOARA			
David*	Nevada Bridgeport	61	472
J	Sutter Sutter	70	808
NOATH			
Amos	Tehama Tehama	70	935
NOAVA			
David	Nevada Bridgeport	61	472
NOAY			
Cassius	San Francisco San Francisco 11	67	124
NOBB			
James	Yuba Rose Bar	72	815
NOBBS			
Joseph	Los Angeles Los Angeles	59	338
Stephen B*	Napa Clear Lake	61	119
Thos*	Sonoma Armally	69	482
NOBE			
Michael	Yolo Putah	72	551
NOBEL			
R	Sacramento Ward 4	63	548
NOBELETT			
Robt	San Francisco San Francisco 3	67	10
NOBLE			
Albert L	Yuba Marysville	72	927
Arthur D	San Francisco San Francisco 8	681	296
Augustus	Santa Cruz Soguel	66	590
NOBLE			
C A*	Sacramento Centre	63	177
C H	San Francisco San Francisco 9	681	099
Charles	Solano Suisan	69	204
Chas	Trinity Redding	70	985
Donald G	Plumas Quincy	62	960
E	Trinity Minersville	70	968
E J	Nevada Eureka	61	382
Edwin	San Joaquin Stockton	641	010
Edwin	San Joaquin Stockton	641	074
Frank	San Joaquin Elkhorn	64	978
Fredrik	Plumas Meadow Valley	62	932
G W	Sierra Gibsonville	66	851
Geo	Butte Cascade	56	694
H A	Sonoma Mendocino	69	448
Hana	Butte Ophir	56	768
Harra*	Butte Ophir	56	768
Hiram H	Tuolumne Twp 1	71	199
J	Nevada Eureka	61	382
J H	Tehama Lassen	70	878
J N	Nevada Eureka	61	382
J W	Sacramento Ward 4	63	517
James	Yuba Rose Bar	72	815
Jane	San Francisco San Francisco 1	68	821
Jefsee*	Marin San Rafael	60	773
Jessee	Marin San Rafael	60	773
John	Butte Oroville	56	746
John	San Francisco San Francisco 2	67	747
Newton	San Bernardino San Bernadino	64	675
Nicholas	Siskiyou Yreka	69	145
P A	Nevada Eureka	61	382
P A*	Siskiyou Yreka	69	143
P C	Butte Oregon	56	626
Robert	Placer Iona Hills	62	887
Robert W	San Joaquin Castoria	64	875
Robt	Nevada Bridgeport	61	503
S	El Dorado Mud Springs	58	974
Saml J	Tuolumne Twp 1	71	323
Stephen	Trinity New Rvr	701	030
T E	Nevada Eureka	61	382
Thos	San Francisco San Francisco 1	68	820
Thos M	San Mateo Twp 3	65	86
W	Calaveras Twp 9	57	394
W	Tuolumne Twp 1	71	233
W N	Nevada Nevada	61	273
William	San Francisco San Francisco 7	681	441
Zebadee	Contra Costa Twp 2	57	545
NOBLES			
A M	Sutter Yuba	70	767
Alonzo T	San Francisco San Francisco 11	67	121
Andrew	Santa Cruz Watsonville	66	539
E J	Siskiyou Scott Ri	69	66
George	Placer Iona Hills	62	897
H R	Mendocino Arrana	60	861
John	Mariposa Twp 3	60	543
John	Siskiyou Yreka	69	131
M M	Mendocino Arrana	60	859
Mary	San Joaquin Stockton	641	022
Shphen B*	Napa Clear Lake	61	119
Stephen B*	Napa Clear Lake	61	119
Washington	Trinity Minersvlle	70	968
NOBLET			
Maria	San Francisco San Francisco 2	67	775
Peter	Yuba Marysville	72	904
NOBLETT			
I M*	Nevada Bridgeport	61	476
J M	Nevada Bridgeport	61	476
NOBLIS			
Stephen B	Napa Clear Lake	61	119
NOBMAN			
John	San Francisco San Francisco 2	67	555
NOBMANN			
John	San Francisco San Francisco 12	67	376
NOBO			
Dionicio	Tuolumne Twp 5	71	498
NOBOR			
William	Shasta Horsetown	66	705
NOBRUSON			
R A	Stanislaus Emory	70	740
NOBUT			
Nelwn*	Yolo Putah	72	598
NOC			
Geacme	Amador Twp 1	55	481
NOCH			
Dominique	Tuolumne Twp 1	71	269
NOCHA			
Gerolomo	Amador Twp 4	55	248
NOCHE			
Carlo	Calaveras Twp 7	57	9
Girana	Calaveras Twp 7	57	9
John	Calaveras Twp 7	57	42
John	Mariposa Twp 3	60	545
Phephu	Calaveras Twp 7	57	9
Stephen	Calaveras Twp 7	57	45
NOCHIN			
Jose Ma	San Bernardino Santa Barbara	64	203
NOCIN			
---	Fresno Twp 1	59	27
NOCK			
Dominigas	Tuolumne Twp 1	71	269
NOCKE			
Joannah	Contra Costa Twp 1	57	527
NOCKER			
Peter	San Joaquin Oneal	64	935
NOCKERSON			
Charles	San Francisco San Francisco 4	681	150
NOCKOLD			
Ann	San Francisco San Francisco 2	67	617
NOCOLS			
Jales	Sierra Twp 7	66	868
NOCRICK			
Jack	Del Norte Klamath	58	655
NODE			
D H	Tuolumne Twp 1	71	263
NODEGO			
Hosa	Yolo Washington	72	605
NODINA			
Paul*	Amador Twp 2	55	306
NODINCE			
Paul	Amador Twp 2	55	306
NODON			
Lucy	Santa Cruz Soguel	66	596
NOE			
---	Amador Twp 2	55	326
---	El Dorado Coloma	581	116
---	Trinity Mouth Ca	701	017
Bart L	Yuba Marysville	72	951
E	San Francisco San Francisco 2	67	713
J B	Sutter Butte	70	781
James G	Tuolumne Twp 5	71	513
N W	El Dorado Placerville	58	856
Nimirod C	San Joaquin Castoria	64	880
R	Sutter Butte	70	779
Stephen	San Francisco San Francisco 3	67	18
Thomas	Contra Costa Twp 2	57	570
W A	Siskiyou Scott Va	69	27
NOEL			
A E	Sacramento San Joaquin	63	363
Alphonse	San Francisco San Francisco 7	681	390
Arnold D	Tuolumne Shawsfla	71	393
Felix	Stanislaus Branch	70	702
J T	Solano Vacaville	69	347
John	Alameda Oakland	55	45
L	El Dorado Placerville	58	820
Lewis	Plumas Meadow Valley	62	904
M	El Dorado Placerville	58	868
Peter	Placer Yankee J	62	778
Peter	Siskiyou Scott Va	69	49
Samuel	Tuolumne Twp 2	71	411
William*	Siskiyou Yreka	69	143
NOELS			
J R	Yolo Cache	72	609
NOER			
Juan B	San Bernardino Santa Ba	64	211
NOES			
Bernado	Calaveras Twp 7	57	1
W B	Napa Hot Springs	61	16
NOESSELLER			
E B	Tuolumne Twp 2	71	322
NOFELL			
John	Sierra Twp 5	66	921
NOFF			
---	Mariposa Twp 3	60	564
John	El Dorado Mud Springs	58	966
NOFILL			
John*	Sierra Twp 5	66	921
NOGAL			
Jos	San Francisco San Francisco 10	67	313
NOGALES			
---	Monterey Alisal	601	040
NOGES			
S W*	San Francisco San Francisco 5	67	547
NOGGETT			
David	Klamath S Fork	59	203
NOGGINS			
Alexcir	Tuolumne Twp 1	71	247
Alexis	Tuolumne Twp 1	71	247
NOGGS			
J W*	Mariposa Twp 1	60	642
NOGHFORD			
Harry	Calaveras Twp 10	57	289
NOGLE			
Vinick	Mendocino Calpella	60	821
NOGNES			
John	Yuba Marysville	72	874
NOGSITT			
M	Placer Forest H	62	794
NOGUES			
John	Yuba Marysville	72	874

California 1860 Census Index

Name	County Locale	M653 RollPage
NOGUEZ		
Antonio	San Francisco San Francisco	10 190 67
Mad*	San Francisco San Francisco	10 175 67
NOH		
---	Calaveras Twp 4	57 301
---	Calaveras Twp 4	57 305
NOHEIRS		
Frederick*	Calaveras Twp 6	57 127
NOHL		
H A	El Dorado Placerville	58 825
NOHLER		
Michael	Sacramento Ward 3	63 474
NOHR		
Leno	San Francisco San Francisco	10 348 67
NOI		
---	San Francisco San Francisco	4 681183
NOICE		
Charles S	Humbolt Eureka	59 176
NOILLY		
Frietel*	Calaveras Twp 9	57 347
John*	Calaveras Twp 9	57 387
Westel	Calaveras Twp 9	57 347
Witztil*	Calaveras Twp 9	57 347
Wortel*	Calaveras Twp 9	57 347
NOILS		
J N	Yolo Cache Crk	72 609
NOILY		
John*	Calaveras Twp 9	57 387
NOIM		
---	Butte Bidwell	56 708
NOIR		
Juan B*	San Bernardino S Buenav	64 211
NOIRJEAN		
Piere	Del Norte Crescent	58 625
NOIS		
---	Del Norte Klamath	58 654
NOISE		
Barnard	San Joaquin Elkhorn	64 963
Enoch	San Mateo Twp 1	65 69
Henry	San Mateo Twp 1	65 69
Thos	San Mateo Twp 1	65 72
NOLAN		
Bridget	Solano Benecia	69 287
Bridget	Solano Benecia	69 313
Caleb	Tuolumne Twp 1	71 246
Charles F	San Francisco San Francisco	7 681410
Daniel	Stanislaus Emory	70 749
David	San Francisco San Francisco	5 67 546
Delia*	San Francisco San Francisco	10 310 67
Dilia	San Francisco San Francisco	10 310 67
Edward	Santa Cruz Santa Cruz	66 604
Edward	Tulara Twp 3	71 47
F J	Sacramento Granite	63 222
F J	Sacramento Granite	63 228
Frank	Sacramento Ward 1	63 142
Ignatius	San Francisco San Francisco	2 67 661
J	Nevada Eureka	61 366
J	Solano Vallejo	69 271
James	Placer Auburn	62 577
James	San Francisco San Francisco	11 116 67
James	San Joaquin Elkhorn	64 956
James	Stanislaus Emory	70 749
James	Tuolumne Sonora	71 221
James H	Tuolumne Twp 6	71 536
Jas	Sacramento Ward 4	63 591
Jno	Butte Chico	56 531
John	Stanislaus Emory	70 751
Joseph	San Francisco San Francisco	2 67 742
Lawrence	Sierra Twp 5	66 936
Luke	Stanislaus Emory	70 749
M	San Francisco San Francisco	9 68 946
M	Tehama Tehama	70 949
Mary	Alameda Oakland	55 26
Mary	San Francisco San Francisco	6 67 433
Mary	San Francisco San Francisco	2 67 760
Michael	San Francisco San Francisco	10 168 67
P	Nevada Nevada	61 313
P	San Francisco San Francisco	12 379 67
Patrick	San Francisco San Francisco	7 681372
Patrick	Tuolumne Columbia	71 361
Pierce	Sacramento Ward 4	63 535
Robt	Tuolumne Columbia	71 361
Stephen	Alameda Oakland	55 39
Stephen	Tuolumne Twp 1	71 246
Thomas	San Francisco San Francisco	11 149 67
William	Solano Vallejo	69 258
William	Yuba Marysville	72 962

Name	County Locale	M653 RollPage
NOLAND		
Alfred	San Francisco San Francisco	7 681443
Ann	San Francisco San Francisco	1 68 828
Ann	San Francisco San Francisco	1 68 903
C H	Tehama Red Bluff	70 911
Ellen	San Francisco San Francisco	8 681283
Frank	Sacramento Ward 1	63 79
George	Mendocino Ukiah	60 808
Iwlliam	Sierra Poker Flats	66 838
James	Sierra Monte Crk	661038
James H	Tuolumne Don Pedro	71 536
Jno	Sacramento Ward 4	63 523
John	Contra Costa Twp 3	57 609
John	Sacramento Ward 1	63 79
John	San Mateo Twp 1	65 51
John	Sierra Downieville	66 963
Joseph	San Francisco San Francisco	1 68 828
Lawrence	Sierra Twp 5	66 936
Mary	Solano Suisan	69 221
P	Napa Napa	61 58
Patrick	Solano Suisan	69 226
Patrick	Solano Vacaville	69 361
S H	Tehama Red Bluff	70 927
T	San Francisco San Francisco	1 68 922
Thomas	Alameda Oakland	55 73
Thomas	Los Angeles Azuza	59 274
Thomas	Tuolumne Twp 3	71 422
Thos	Sacramento Ward 4	63 539
Thos	Tehama Tehama	70 935
W S	Amador Twp 3	55 409
William	Sierra Poker Flats	66 838
Wm	Butte Chico	56 559
NOLANDS		
J W	Sierra Downieville	661028
NOLANE		
Jo	Butte Eureka	56 651
NOLANI		
Jo	Butte Eureka	56 651
NOLAY		
John	San Joaquin Oneal	64 933
NOLBERTA		
---*	San Bernardino S Timate	64 738
NOLBERTO		
---	San Bernardino S Timate	64 703
---	San Bernardino S Timate	64 736
---	San Bernardino S Timate	64 749
---	San Bernardino S Timate	64 753
---	San Bernardino S Timate	64 754
---*	San Bernardino S Timate	64 736
NOLBS		
Thos*	Sonoma Armally	69 482
NOLD		
Fred	Sacramento Ward 4	63 591
NOLDE		
Rodolph	Plumas Quincy	621005
NOLE		
Ellen	San Francisco San Francisco	4 681144
NOLEN		
B F	Siskiyou Scott Va	69 36
Benton	Siskiyou Scott Va	69 32
Daniel	Siskiyou Callahan	69 6
Frank	Sacramento Ward 1	63 142
James	Siskiyou Scott Va	69 58
M S	Yuba Rose Bar	72 791
Martin	Sonoma Bodega	69 540
Matthew	San Francisco San Francisco	9 681027
Thos	Sacramento Ward 4	63 524
NOLENBERG		
J	Tuolumne Twp 4	71 146
NOLES		
A F	Tuolumne Twp 1	71 204
Christian	Contra Costa Twp 2	57 559
John	Shasta Shasta	66 728
Richard	Placer Michigan	62 809
S	San Francisco San Francisco	9 681022
NOLF		
Jacob*	Butte Oregon	56 641
NOLFF		
William	Siskiyou Yreka	69 145
NOLIN		
J W	Sutter Butte	70 800
Luke	El Dorado Salmon Falls	581039
NOLINE		
Miguel C	Yuba Marysville	72 957
NOLK		
Phillip	Sierra Downieville	661011
NOLL		
Louis	Calaveras Twp 6	57 115
NOLLAND		
James	Tehama Lassen	70 877
NOLLENBURN		
John*	Tulara Twp 3	71 54
NOLLINER		
E P	Shasta Millvill	66 750
NOLMANLL		
Napoleon*	Sierra Port Win	66 794

Name	County Locale	M653 RollPage
NOLMARILL		
Napoleon	Sierra Port Win	66 794
NOLMAUEL		
Napoleon*	Sierra Port Win	66 794
NOLONB		
Luke	El Dorado Big Bar	58 733
NOLSE		
Jacob	Amador Twp 1	55 484
NOLT		
James*	Alameda Oakland	55 64
Joseph*	Placer Todds Va	62 790
NOLTBY		
N	Calaveras Twp 9	57 398
NOLTE		
Rudolph	San Francisco San Francisco	2 67 624
NOLTER		
William	San Francisco San Francisco	7 681353
NOLTING		
Caroline	San Francisco San Francisco	7 681385
Henry W	Alameda Oakland	55 16
NOLTON		
Jefferson	Plumas Quincy	62 963
Marcus	San Francisco San Francisco	11 136 67
NOLTY		
Lewis H	San Francisco San Francisco	2 67 588
NOLTZ		
Frederick*	Yuba Marysville	72 901
NOM		
---	Amador Twp 3	55 410
---	Amador Twp 1	55 452
---	El Dorado White Oaks	581024
---	El Dorado White Oaks	581033
---	El Dorado Salmon Falls	581062
---	El Dorado Kelsey	581133
---	El Dorado Kelsey	581136
---	El Dorado Mountain	581189
---	El Dorado Greenwood	58 727
---	El Dorado Georgetown	58 746
---	El Dorado Diamond	58 784
---	El Dorado Diamond	58 795
---	Shasta French G	66 712
---*	Amador Twp 6	55 431
Otto	Sacramento Natonia	63 283
Sin	El Dorado Mud Springs	58 958
NOMALIN		
Peter	Tuolumne Columbia	71 317
NOMAN		
China	San Joaquin Stockton	641098
Dennis*	San Francisco San Francisco	9 681028
J	Calaveras Twp 9	57 411
W B	San Joaquin Stockton	641088
NOMARES		
Jesus	Contra Costa Twp 1	57 491
NOMBLE		
J R*	Sacramento Ward 1	63 78
NOMBRE		
Sin	San Diego Temecula	64 804
NOMDEAS		
Jesus*	Mariposa Twp 1	60 629
NOMDIAS		
Jesus	Mariposa Twp 1	60 629
NOME		
---	El Dorado Mountain	581189
Oscar F	Placer Dutch Fl	62 725
NOMEN		
Frank	Alameda Brooklyn	55 212
NOMEOMIS		
C	Calaveras Twp 9	57 387
NOMERO		
Louis	Contra Costa Twp 1	57 537
NOMEZ		
Sebastiano	Monterey San Juan	60 998
NOMIORRIS		
C*	Calaveras Twp 9	57 387
NOMOY		
---	Humbolt Union	59 182
NOMROD		
Eduard	San Francisco San Francisco	1 68 914
NOMTA		
---	Fresno Twp 1	59 27
NON		
---	Amador Twp 5	55 353
---	Calaveras Twp 6	57 168
---	El Dorado Salmon Falls	581046
---	El Dorado Salmon Falls	581051
---	El Dorado Salmon Falls	581053
---	Nevada Rough &	61 342
---	Yolo No E Twp	72 684
---	Yuba Slate Ro	72 684
---*	Nevada Rough &	61 399
John	Placer Auburn	62 573
Tek	San Francisco San Francisco	11 159 67
NONA		
B E	El Dorado Kelsey	581143

California 1860 Census Index

Name	County Locale	M653 RollPage
NONAL		
Mary*	Alameda Brooklyn	55 121
NONANDEN		
Miguel	San Francisco San Francisco 3	67 8
NONARO		
Padro*	Calaveras Twp 6	57 179
NONCUSRIS		
Thos*	Nevada Bridgeport	61 497
NONCUSVIS		
Thos*	Nevada Bridgeport	61 497
NONDY		
A F*	Tuolumne Sonora	71 481
NONE		
---	El Dorado Mountain	581188
---	Mariposa Coulterville	60 681
---	Yolo No E Twp	72 676
---	Yuba North Ea	72 676
How	Butte Cascade	56 690
Otto	Sacramento Natonia	63 283
NONEINMON		
Charles	Alameda Brooklyn	55 197
NONELLA		
Frank*	Calaveras Twp 7	57 25
NONEPWAY		
---*	Mendocino Big Rvr	60 853
NONG		
---	Amador Twp 5	55 354
---	Amador Twp 1	55 479
---	Del Norte Crescent	58 643
---	El Dorado White Oaks	581024
---	El Dorado Coloma	581085
---	El Dorado Georgetown	58 674
---	Mariposa Twp 1	60 667
---	Mariposa Twp 1	60 673
---	Nevada Red Dog	61 549
---	Sacramento Ward 1	63 70
---	San Francisco San Francisco 11	162 67
---	Trinity Cox'S Bar	701037
---	Yuba Long Bar	72 764
Fong	San Francisco San Francisco 11	161 67
Tie*	Placer Auburn	62 570
Tri	Sacramento Ward 3	63 494
NONGUE		
Joseph*	Sierra Twp 5	66 918
NONGUES		
Joseph*	Sacramento Ward 4	63 589
NONIOUS		
Frederick*	Contra Costa Twp 3	57 606
NONKLEA		
E A	El Dorado Placerville	58 869
NONNAN		
Peter	San Francisco San Francisco 9	681099
NONNES		
W	San Francisco San Francisco 5	67 499
NONNICH		
Augustus	San Francisco San Francisco 9	681002
NONO		
Santo	Amador Twp 5	55 360
NONSEEA		
---	Fresno Twp 1	59 28
NONTRE		
Franklin*	Siskiyou Yreka	69 125
NONUE		
Larnise*	Sacramento Natonia	63 279
NONURI		
Padro	Calaveras Twp 5	57 179
NONURO		
Padro*	Calaveras Twp 6	57 179
NOO		
---	Amador Twp 2	55 326
---	Butte Kimshaw	56 587
---	Calaveras Twp 6	57 149
---	Nevada Bloomfield	61 528
Song	San Francisco San Francisco 11	159 67
NOOD		
Joel*	Yolo Cottonwood	72 656
NOOGREN		
Fred	Placer Dutch Fl	62 719
NOOI		
---	Shasta French G	66 713
NOOK		
---	Yuba Marysville	72 895
NOOKE		
---	Plumas Quincy	62 949
NOOKS		
Milton	Contra Costa Twp 2	57 542
NOOLY		
Thomas*	Shasta Millvill	66 727
NOOMLEMEAR		
G	Siskiyou Klamath	69 86
NOON		
---	El Dorado Union	581090
---	Mariposa Coulterville	60 699

Name	County Locale	M653 RollPage
NOON		
---*	Nevada Rough &	61 434
---*	Amador Twp 6	55 430
---*	Amador Twp 6	55 431
George	Plumas Quincy	62 960
J J	Tehama Red Bluff	70 923
James	Nevada Rough &	61 412
Mark	San Francisco San Francisco 7	681360
R P A	Tuolumne Sonora	71 482
R P*	Tuolumne Twp 1	71 482
NOONAN		
---*	San Francisco San Francisco 9	68 959
Dennis	San Francisco San Francisco 1	68 894
George	Trinity North Fo	701024
J	Nevada Eureka	61 354
J	San Francisco San Francisco 5	67 512
J*	Nevada Eureka	61 354
James	Santa Cruz Pajaro	66 573
John	San Francisco San Francisco 8	681233
John	Sierra Whiskey	66 844
John	Tuolumne Sonora	71 229
Margaret	San Francisco San Francisco 10	182 67
Martin	Sierra Twp 5	66 917
Mary	San Francisco San Francisco 2	67 593
Patrick	San Francisco San Francisco 9	68 959
Sarah	San Francisco San Francisco 11	93 67
NOONARE		
J*	Nevada Eureka	61 354
NOONAW		
Martin	Sierra Twp 5	66 917
NOONEN		
Ann	Sacramento Ward 4	63 552
B	Sacramento Ward 3	63 447
C	Sacramento Ward 1	63 39
J R	Sacramento Ward 4	63 535
James	Marin San Rafael	60 763
Julia	Sacramento Ward 3	63 447
Kate	San Francisco San Francisco 2	67 592
NOONON		
J M	Yolo Cache Crk	72 626
NOONS		
Frances*	Nevada Rough &	61 424
Francis*	Nevada Rough &	61 424
Grancis*	Nevada Rough &	61 424
Manuel	Calaveras Twp 6	57 166
NOONUN		
Irwin	Solano Benecia	69 317
Simon	Solano Benecia	69 317
NOOR		
---	Mariposa Coulterville	60 681
NOORE		
William	Santa Cruz Santa Cruz	66 613
NOOTEN		
J P	Butte Ophir	56 795
NOOTON		
J P	Butte Ophir	56 795
NOOTRAM PLANE		
---	Mendocino Big Rvr	60 853
NOOWAN		
John	San Francisco San Francisco 8	681233
NOP		
---*	Nevada Bridgeport	61 459
William	San Francisco San Francisco 8	681323
NOPANNY		
---	Butte Chico	56 551
NOPARRNY		
---*	Butte Chico	56 551
NOPE		
---	Placer Auburn	62 582
NOQAES		
Juan	Contra Costa Twp 1	57 496
NOQUILLIA		
Stephen*	Tuolumne Big Oak	71 125
NOR		
---	Nevada Bridgeport	61 463
---	Placer Illinois	62 752
NORA		
Pamguisa*	Calaveras Twp 5	57 211
Pamyuiro	Calaveras Twp 5	57 211
Pamyuiso*	Calaveras Twp 5	57 211
NORAL		
Anthony	Plumas Quincy	62 936
NORAN		
Ann	San Francisco San Francisco 8	681301
Anna*	San Francisco San Francisco 8	681301
NORANA		
Clyisha*	Mariposa Twp 3	60 559
NORBERG		
Andrew	Plumas Quincy	62 954
NORBERGE		
William*	Plumas Quincy	62 975
NORBERTINE		
Sister	Santa Clara San Jose	65 373
NORBERTO		
Dupont	Santa Clara Fremont	65 428

Name	County Locale	M653 RollPage
NORBOE		
Catherine	Tulara Twp 3	71 46
John*	Tulara Twp 3	71 43
NORBUS		
Peter D	San Joaquin Douglass	64 924
NORCAGO		
Thos	Amador Twp 5	55 358
NORCERIO		
J	Tuolumne Twp 4	71 157
NORCESTER		
Morran	Calaveras Twp 5	57 189
NORCET		
John	Calaveras Twp 5	57 253
NORCHROP		
Thomas T	Tuolumne Twp 5	71 516
NORCRASS		
C D*	Santa Clara San Jose	65 317
NORCROFS		
Nelson F*	Calaveras Twp 6	57 127
NORCROP		
Daniel	San Francisco San Francisco 8	681239
John	Yuba Marysville	72 941
NORCROSS		
C D*	Santa Clara San Jose	65 317
Daniel	San Francisco San Francisco 8	681239
Geo	Sacramento Ward 3	63 484
Nelson F*	Calaveras Twp 6	57 127
Thomas W	Humbolt Eureka	59 165
Wesley F	Placer Auburn	62 564
Wm	El Dorado Big Bar	58 741
NORD		
---	Trinity Weaverville	701052
John H	Calaveras Twp 5	57 227
Phillip J*	Calaveras Twp 5	57 252
NORDEHOLDT		
B	Tuolumne Big Oak	71 149
NORDEN		
Henry M*	Yolo Cache	72 594
T	Amador Twp 3	55 401
W M*	Yolo Cache	72 593
NORDENHOLDT		
B	Tuolumne Twp 4	71 149
NORDEW		
Tew	Amador Twp 3	55 400
NORDHEIMER		
Arnold	Klamath S Fork	59 203
B	Klamath Trinidad	59 222
NORDIKE		
B	Sutter Sutter	70 801
NORDSIDE		
E G*	San Francisco San Francisco 7	681406
NORDSON		
H*	Butte Oregon	56 642
NORDSTRONE		
P Q	Sacramento Ward 1	63 62
NORDYKE		
C	Yuba Fosters	72 840
Jacob*	Alameda Brooklyn	55 150
Wm H	Humbolt Bucksport	59 158
NOREGA		
Alenail	Santa Cruz Santa Cruz	66 621
Alenent*	Santa Cruz Santa Cruz	66 621
Aleneut*	Santa Cruz Santa Cruz	66 621
NOREIGA		
Jose	Santa Clara San Jose	65 322
NORELL		
C*	Yolo Washington	72 601
Olof	Plumas Meadow Valley	62 902
NORELLA		
Frank*	Calaveras Twp 7	57 25
NOREN		
Joseph*	Sacramento Franklin	63 311
NOREOGER		
Jose	Calaveras Twp 6	57 161
NORET		
Joseph	Mariposa Twp 1	60 648
NORFLEET		
B	El Dorado Mud Springs	58 951
NORFUNDING		
B M*	Yuba Slate Ro	72 703
NORGAN		
James	San Francisco San Francisco 10	297 67
NORGET		
Jus	Sacramento Ward 4	63 582
Wm	San Francisco San Francisco 3	67 65
NORGHTON		
Patrick	Trinity Mouth Ca	701018
NORHEN		
Henry	Tuolumne Sonora	71 194
NORIAGO		
---	Tulara Keyesville	71 63
NORIDER		
A F*	Tuolumne Twp 1	71 481
NORIDIN		
Louis*	Calaveras Twp 6	57 160

Name	County Locale	M653 Roll	Page
NORIEGA			
A	Santa Clara San Jose	65	323
Juan	Los Angeles Los Nieto	59	428
NORIGO			
---	Tulara Twp 3	71	63
NORINA			
Chrish'N	Mariposa Twp 3	60	559
NORINER			
Christ'A*	Mariposa Twp 3	60	559
NORING			
Albert	San Francisco San Francisco 7	681	386
NORIO			
Santiago*	San Mateo Twp 1	65	61
NORIS			
Maria	Calaveras Twp 6	57	125
NORITZKEY			
H	Nevada Grass Valley	61	171
NORKEL			
Michael	Placer Virginia	62	700
NORLAN			
D R*	Calaveras Twp 9	57	407
NORLEY			
Stephen	Nevada Rough &	61	412
Wm	Sonoma Sonoma	69	634
NORLINGER			
Babbit*	San Francisco San Francisco 7	681	365
Babbitt	San Francisco San Francisco 7	681	365
NORLLIN			
Richd*	Napa Clear Lake	61	123
NORMA N			
George	San Francisco San Francisco 3	67	16
NORMA			
Jo*	Tehama Red Bluff	70	919
NORMAIS			
R B*	Sacramento Ward 4	63	584
NORMAN			
A D	Calaveras Twp 8	57	80
A J	Yuba Marysville	72	930
Anne	San Francisco San Francisco 1	68	813
Billy	Tehama Tehama	70	939
C C	Calaveras Twp 8	57	80
Dennis	Tuolumne Twp 2	71	271
E	Trinity Big Flat	701	039
Edward	Yuba Marysville	72	961
Ewing	Yolo Merritt	72	583
F G	El Dorado Diamond	58	763
G W	Napa Hot Springs	61	11
George	Plumas Quincy	62	962
Gus	Mariposa Twp 1	60	663
H	Shasta Shasta	66	730
Henry	Amador Twp 2	55	302
Henry	Calaveras Twp 5	57	213
Henry M*	Calaveras Twp 5	57	213
J	Calaveras Twp 9	57	411
J C	Solano Suisan	69	218
M	Siskiyou Yreka	69	171
Mr	Sonoma Vallejo	69	626
O	Siskiyou Yreka	69	189
P	Tuolumne Twp 4	71	164
P	Tuolumne Twp 4	71	176
Patrick	Contra Costa Twp 1	57	527
R B*	Sacramento Ward 4	63	584
Schooly D	Calaveras Twp 5	57	208
Thos	Placer Secret R	62	611
William	Contra Costa Twp 1	57	527
William	Siskiyou Scott Va	69	43
Wm	Los Angeles Tejon	59	527
Wm	Trinity Big Flat	701	039
Wm A	Amador Twp 6	55	444
NORMAND			
Victor	San Francisco San Francisco 2	67	598
NORMANDY			
John	San Francisco San Francisco 1	68	926
NORMER			
Christiam	Mariposa Twp 3	60	559
NORMILE			
Michael	Humbolt Eureka	59	165
NORMON			
James	Tehama Lassen	70	879
NORMORDER			
Mary Ann	Alameda Oakland	55	13
NORN			
---	El Dorado Coloma	581	085
---*	Amador Twp 6	55	430
---*	Amador Twp 6	55	431
Foo	El Dorado Mud Springs	58	972
NORNAN			
Margaret	San Francisco San Francisco 10	67	182
NORNEN			
C*	Sacramento Ward 1	63	39
NORONA			
Francisco	San Francisco San Francisco 2	67	767
NORR			
Jeremiah	Nevada Little Y	61	534
NORRBERGER			
Nicholas	Amador Twp 4	55	247
NORREL			
Henry	Sierra La Porte	66	790
NORREN			
Kate	San Francisco San Francisco 2	67	592
NORRICK			
Edward	El Dorado Coloma	581	119
NORRIL			
Henry	Sierra La Porte	66	790
NORRILL			
Oliver L	San Francisco San Francisco 8	681	255
NORRIN			
David	Sierra Eureka	661	045
NORRIS			
Andrew	Tuolumne Big Oak	71	177
B	Tuolumne Twp 2	71	288
C H	Calaveras Twp 9	57	387
Carlos	Los Angeles Los Angeles	59	326
Carlos	Los Angeles Los Angeles	59	390
Catharine	San Francisco San Francisco 6	67	456
Charles	El Dorado Coloma	581	082
Chas	Calaveras Twp 9	57	350
Chas	Sacramento Ward 1	63	15
Chas	Sonoma Santa Rosa	69	402
Christopher	Calaveras Twp 5	57	195
D	Sacramento Ward 1	63	17
Edmond	Yuba New York	72	729
Edward	San Mateo Twp 3	65	78
Edward	Yuba New York	72	729
Ellen	Sacramento Ward 4	63	583
Fances*	Nevada Rough &	61	424
Francis*	Nevada Rough &	61	424
Geo	Amador Twp 3	55	401
Geo	Sacramento Ward 3	63	429
Geo S	Klamath Orleans	59	219
George	Marin San Rafael	60	764
H	Siskiyou Callahan	69	6
Henry C	Sacramento Granite	63	253
Heny C	Sacramento Granite	63	253
Hiram	Placer Secret R	62	612
Hosea M*	Placer Auburn	62	591
J	Sacramento Alabama	63	416
J N	El Dorado Union	581	088
J R	Mariposa Twp 3	60	573
Jacob	Los Angeles Los Angeles	59	341
James	Sacramento Granite	63	251
James	San Francisco San Francisco 8	681	245
James	San Joaquin Oneal	64	940
James	Sonoma Santa Rosa	69	406
James S	Tuolumne Twp 1	71	246
Jas	Sacramento Granite	63	236
Jeremiah	San Francisco San Francisco 7	681	427
John	Butte Ophir	56	753
John S	Butte Ophir	56	753
Joseph	Placer Auburn	62	591
Larnier	Sacramento Natonia	63	279
Laura M	Sacramento Brighton	63	206
Martin	Tulara Twp 3	71	41
Mary	Contra Costa Twp 1	57	527
Morris	Butte Ophir	56	800
N	Nevada Grass Valley	61	200
N E	Yolo Washington	72	604
Peter	Calaveras Twp 8	57	81
Phillip	Santa Clara Gilroy	65	246
R	El Dorado Newtown	58	779
R E	Yolo Fremont	72	604
Rob	Sacramento Ward 1	63	12
Saml	Sacramento American	63	172
Samuel	El Dorado Mountain	581	186
Samuel R	Sierra Pine Grove	66	823
Stephen	Monterey Alisal	601	036
Theo	Mariposa Twp 3	60	601
Thio*	Mariposa Twp 3	60	601
Thomas A B	Sierra Pine Grove	66	827
Washington	Siskiyou Yreka	69	140
William	El Dorado Mud Springs	58	978
William	Klamath Klamath	59	225
William	Santa Cruz Pescadero	66	645
William	Siskiyou Callahan	69	1
Wm	Butte Cascade	56	703
Wm	Santa Clara San Jose	65	283
Wm B	Plumas Quincy	62	959
NORRLIN			
W	Napa Napa	61	114
NORRY			
David	Nevada Rough &	61	410
NORSE			
George	Sierra Pine Grove	66	833
NORSH			
U	Calaveras Twp 9	57	408
NORST			
C	Calaveras Twp 9	57	408
NORT			
Augustus	Calaveras Twp 8	57	95
NORTAN			
Agnes	El Dorado Georgetown	58	684
Jim	El Dorado Georgetown	58	674
NORTELL			
Frederick*	Yuba Bear Rvr	72	998
Robt	El Dorado Placerville	58	934
NORTEN			
Geo	Butte Eureka	56	656
Michael	San Francisco San Francisco 9	68	947
NORTH			
Charles	Calaveras Twp 9	57	388
Charles	Calaveras Twp 8	57	78
Chas	Santa Clara Santa Clara	65	501
Edmund	San Francisco San Francisco 6	67	410
Francis	Calaveras Twp 9	57	380
Geo	Butte Oregon	56	617
Geo	Butte Eureka	56	647
George	Yuba Marysville	72	870
H	Mariposa Twp 3	60	556
J H	Tehama Red Bluff	70	910
J M	San Joaquin O'Neal	641	001
James	Calaveras Twp 7	57	42
Jane*	Nevada Nevada	61	328
Jno G	San Francisco San Francisco 10	67	235
John	Los Angeles Los Angeles	59	356
John	Los Angeles San Pedro	59	481
John	Solano Vallejo	69	247
Patrick	Sacramento Ward 4	63	611
Samuel	Siskiyou Yreka	69	182
Samuel	Siskiyou Yreka	69	190
William	Calaveras Twp 8	57	69
NORTHAM			
Daniel*	Amador Twp 4	55	237
G*	Nevada Red Dog	61	553
Stephan	Tuolumne Jamestown	71	448
Stephen	Tuolumne Twp 3	71	448
NORTHAN			
G*	Nevada Red Dog	61	553
NORTHBAUGHER			
J C*	Butte Ophir	56	796
NORTHBAUGHN			
J C	Butte Ophir	56	796
NORTHCUT			
Maddison	Placer Michigan	62	827
Philip	Trinity Taylor'S	701	034
NORTHEMEN			
F	San Francisco San Francisco 2	67	774
NORTHEMER			
F*	San Francisco San Francisco 2	67	774
NORTHEN			
J P*	Sutter Yuba	70	773
NORTHER			
H W	Napa Napa	61	113
NORTHERMAN			
William	Yuba Marysville	72	939
NORTHERN			
A	Mariposa Twp 1	60	642
H	Mariposa Twp 1	60	642
NORTHERNER			
F*	San Francisco San Francisco 2	67	774
NORTHEY			
N	Alameda Brooklyn	55	78
T W	Tuolumne Sonora	71	236
NORTHFIELD			
J R	Tuolumne Twp 4	71	128
NORTHGRAVE			
W	Butte Chico	56	558
W*	Butte Kimshaw	56	568
NORTHHOUSC			
C G F	San Joaquin Stockton	641	046
NORTHING			
D	Nevada Eureka	61	374
Geo	Nevada Eureka	61	374
Jno	Butte Chico	56	567
NORTHINGPOTH			
A*	Napa Yount	61	33
NORTHINGTON			
T H	Yuba New York	72	737
NORTHINTON			
B F	Mariposa Twp 3	60	548
NORTHIRP			
Perrin G*	Del Norte Crescent	58	640
NORTHNEY			
Orange*	Shasta Shasta	66	728
NORTHNIG			
Wm	Butte Chico	56	567
NORTHOLD			
William	Los Angeles Los Angeles	59	329
NORTHORP			
James	Napa Hot Springs	61	23
NORTHOUSE			
Henry	El Dorado Casumnes	581	161
NORTHRAP			
C F*	Shasta Shasta	66	658
NORTHRIPP			
Chas H	San Francisco San Francisco 4	681	226
NORTHROP			
A F	Amador Twp 2	55	317

California 1860 Census Index

Name	County Locale	M653 Roll Page
NORTHROP		
C F	Shasta Shasta	66 658
Darvin	Contra Costa Twp 2	57 575
Joseph	Calaveras Twp 6	57 166
Thomas J	Tuolumne Jacksonville	71 516
NORTHRUP		
B C	Sacramento Ward 1	63 15
Charles	Yolo Slate Ra	72 707
Charles	Yuba Slate Ro	72 707
D B	San Francisco San Francisco 3	67 74
Edward	Solano Suisan	69 205
Giles	San Joaquin Elkhorn	64 998
Johln	Siskiyou Yreka	69 146
John	Siskiyou Yreka	69 146
Moses	Mariposa Twp 1	60 637
O F*	Shasta Shasta	66 658
S	Calaveras Twp 9	57 410
S W	San Joaquin O'Neal	641003
NORTHUEY		
Orange*	Shasta Shasta	66 728
NORTHUOY		
Orarye*	Shasta Shasta	66 728
NORTHUP		
Ames	Colusa Colusi	57 425
B C	Sacramento Ward 1	63 15
Edred	Nevada Bridgeport	61 493
Edward	Solano Suisan	69 205
Elred	Nevada Bridgeport	61 493
John	Amador Twp 1	55 469
Perrin G*	Del Norte Crescent	58 640
R G	Tuolumne Columbia	71 342
S	Calaveras Twp 9	57 410
NORTHY		
David	Mendocino Big Rvr	60 850
Geo R	Mendocino Big Rvr	60 849
Henry*	Mariposa Twp 3	60 558
NORTIN		
Corbin	Nevada Bridgeport	61 496
Corbui	Nevada Bridgeport	61 496
J B	Placer Iona Hills	62 869
NORTLY		
Henry*	Mariposa Twp 3	60 558
NORTMAN		
Fredk	Plumas Meadow Valley	62 900
NORTMIER		
Eliza	San Francisco San Francisco 6	67 415
NORTO		
M	San Francisco San Francisco 4	681231
NORTOM		
James*	El Dorado Georgetown	58 706
NORTON		
A H	Placer Goods	62 699
A W	Napa Napa	61 93
Abram	Amador Twp 4	55 131
Agnes	El Dorado Georgetown	58 684
Alfred	Calaveras Twp 7	57 11
Almonzo	Klamath Klamath	59 225
Andrew A	Calaveras Twp 9	57 349
Andrus A*	Calaveras Twp 9	57 349
Anna	San Francisco San Francisco 2	67 656
B	Shasta Cottonwoood	66 724
Bridget	San Joaquin Stockton	641024
C	Shasta Horsetown	66 702
C A	Sacramento Ward 3	63 446
Charles	Calaveras Twp 5	57 200
Charles	Los Angeles San Juan	59 460
Chas*	San Francisco San Francisco 9	681046
Cysus*	El Dorado Greenwood	58 723
D A	Sacramento Ward 4	63 507
D E	El Dorado Eldorado	58 936
D E	Monterey San Juan	60 990
D V	Napa Yount	61 38
Daniel C	San Joaquin Castoria	64 873
Danl*	Placer Goods	62 695
Feorge	Calaveras Twp 8	57 64
Frank	Calaveras Twp 5	57 199
Franklus	Del Norte Crescent	58 621
Geo	Butte Eureka	56 656
Geo M	San Francisco San Francisco 9	681030
George	Calaveras Twp 8	57 52
George	Calaveras Twp 8	57 54
George W	Mariposa Twp 1	60 653
Henry	Placer Mountain	62 708
Henry	Solano Benecia	69 286
Horatio	Contra Costa Twp 3	57 589
J	Sacramento Sutter	63 294
J	San Francisco San Francisco 5	67 525
J	Sutter Bear Rvr	70 820
J	Trinity Weaverville	701056
J B	Tehama Red Bluff	70 927
J C	San Francisco San Francisco 9	681062
J G	Solano Vallejo	69 250
J M	El Dorado Mountain	581185
Jacob	Calaveras Twp 7	57 38
Jacob	Santa Clara Santa Clara	65 519
Jacob	Yuba Marysville	72 866
NORTON		
James	Contra Costa Twp 3	57 591
James	San Francisco San Francisco 4	681228
James	Sierra Twp 5	66 935
James H	Plumas Quincy	62 976
Jas J	San Francisco San Francisco 2	67 560
Jeremiah	Plumas Quincy	62 990
Jno W	San Francisco San Francisco 9	681052
John	Monterey Alisal	601034
John	San Francisco San Francisco 9	681063
John	San Joaquin Stockton	641082
John	San Joaquin Elkhorn	64 962
John C	El Dorado Big Bar	58 742
John P	Sierra Downieville	66 959
John R	San Francisco San Francisco 7	681438
Jos J	San Francisco San Francisco 2	67 560
Joseph	San Francisco San Francisco 12	370 67
Joseph	San Joaquin Elkhorn	64 962
Josiah	Mariposa Twp 3	60 597
Julia	San Francisco San Francisco 10	289 67
Julia L	San Francisco San Francisco 9	681015
K C	El Dorado Placerville	58 821
K E	El Dorado Mud Springs	58 970
L	Calaveras Twp 7	57 40
Latti*	Yolo Cache Crk	72 590
Latts*	Yolo Cache Crk	72 590
Lewis A	Sonoma Healdsbu	69 471
Lott	Yolo Cache	72 590
M	El Dorado Placerville	58 921
M	San Francisco San Francisco 4	681231
M	Yolo Cache Crk	72 634
M L	Merced Twp 2	60 917
M S	Calaveras Twp 8	57 73
M S	Merced Twp 2	60 917
Martin	Napa Napa	61 76
Mary	Marin San Rafael	60 764
Mary A	Yolo Cache Crk	72 589
Maryu A	Yolo Cache	72 589
Michael	Calaveras Twp 9	57 369
Michael	Santa Clara Almaden	65 266
Micheal	Calaveras Twp 9	57 369
Moses	Los Angeles Los Angeles	59 340
Mr	Sonoma Vallejo	69 627
Myron	Los Angeles Los Angeles	59 367
Myron	San Francisco San Francisco 7	681332
Myron	Siskiyou Scott Va	69 53
N	Yolo Putah	72 554
Nelson	Sonoma Petaluma	69 594
Orloff	Los Angeles San Gabriel	59 419
P	San Francisco San Francisco 1	68 907
P C	Napa Yount	61 32
P I*	Nevada Bridgeport	61 483
P J	Nevada Bridgeport	61 483
P N	Placer Yankee J	62 776
P N	Sacramento Ward 4	63 512
Patrick	Marin Tomales	60 721
Patrick	Sierra Poker Flats	66 842
Patrick	Tuolumne Columbia	71 312
Peter	Nevada Rough A	61 432
Peter	San Francisco San Francisco 3	67 65
Philander*	Stanislaus Branch	70 708
R C	Amador Twp 3	55 385
Raymundo	Los Angeles Los Angeles	59 367
Roger	San Francisco San Francisco 7	681342
S B	Trinity Weaverville	701046
Sam	El Dorado Georgetown	58 674
Saml	El Dorado Georgetown	58 673
Saml	El Dorado Greenwood	58 714
Samuel	Los Angeles San Juan	59 460
Samuel	Plumas Quincy	62 987
Samuel	San Francisco San Francisco 3	67 45
Thadeu	Sierra Pine Grove	66 828
Thadeus	Sierra Pine Grove	66 828
Thomas	Calaveras Twp 8	57 50
Thomas B	San Joaquin Castoria	64 909
Thomas B	San Joaquin Castoria	64 910
Thos	Sacramento Ward 4	63 598
Thos J	Santa Clara San Jose	65 332
W	El Dorado Casumnes	581173
W	San Joaquin Stockton	641045
W	Santa Clara San Jose	65 381
W	Yolo Putah	72 549
W H	Mendocino Big Rvr	60 845
William	El Dorado Greenwood	58 725
Wilson	Sonoma Petaluma	69 594
Wm	Alameda Brooklyn	55 177
Wm	Butte Eureka	56 654
Wm H	San Francisco San Francisco 3	67 37
NORTONS		
W	Yolo Putah	72 549
NORTORN		
James*	El Dorado Georgetown	58 706
NORTSRAUGHT		
Charles*	Alameda Murray	55 226
NORTSROUGHT		
Charles**	Alameda Murray	55 226
NORTTE		
David G	El Dorado Mud Springs	58 996
NORTTY		
Henry	Mariposa Twp 3	60 558
NORTWELL		
J	Nevada Eureka	61 360
NORTWOOD		
William	Placer Forest H	62 767
NORU		
---*	Placer Virginia	62 671
Pamguire*	Calaveras Twp 5	57 211
Pamguiso*	Calaveras Twp 5	57 211
Pamyuiso*	Calaveras Twp 5	57 211
Paniyuiso*	Calaveras Twp 5	57 211
NORVAL		
Hanson E	San Francisco San Francisco 7	681363
R	El Dorado Georgetown	58 690
NORVALD		
D R	San Francisco San Francisco 5	67 477
NORVALL		
D R	San Francisco San Francisco 5	67 477
NORVELL		
William*	Sierra Pine Grove	66 831
NORVER		
T J*	Solano Vacaville	69 330
NORVILL		
T E	Yolo No E Twp	72 675
William	Sierra Pine Grove	66 831
NORWALL		
H A	Alameda Brooklyn	55 163
NORWOOD		
Saml	Tuolumne Sonora	71 186
Thomas	Tuolumne Sonora	71 185
NORWOOOD		
Joseph	Santa Clara Fremont	65 419
NORY		
---	Amador Twp 6	55 428
---	Sierra La Porte	66 780
NORYES		
Hosea M	Alameda Brooklyn	55 199
NOSA		
Antonio*	Tuolumne Big Oak	71 140
NOSARIO		
---	Tulara Twp 3	71 65
NOSERO		
Sanovera*	Mariposa Twp 1	60 628
NOSESO		
Samovera	Mariposa Twp 1	60 628
NOSETO		
Sanovera*	Mariposa Twp 1	60 628
NOSHOSO		
---	Mendocino Big Rvr	60 854
NOSHUM		
Anee*	Santa Cruz Santa Cruz	66 634
Ariee*	Santa Cruz Santa Cruz	66 634
NOSISO		
Sanovera*	Mariposa Twp 1	60 628
NOSKIS		
George	Contra Costa Twp 3	57 592
NOSLER		
Thomas	Placer Auburn	62 565
NOSRILL		
T E	Yuba North Ea	72 675
NOSS		
William	San Francisco San Francisco 8	681323
William	San Francisco San Francisco 7	681406
NOSTER		
H	El Dorado Georgetown	58 706
NOSTLY		
Henry*	Mariposa Twp 3	60 558
NOSTOM		
James*	El Dorado Georgetown	58 706
NOSTORN		
James*	El Dorado Georgetown	58 706
NOSTRANES		
D Van	San Francisco San Francisco 9	681102
NOSTROM		
Isaac Van*	San Diego Colorado	64 811
NOSTRUM		
Arice*	Santa Cruz Santa Cruz	66 634
NOT		
---	El Dorado Georgetown	58 702
---	Tulara Twp 2	71 31
Joseph*	Placer Todds Va	62 790
NOTAR		
Francisco*	Marin Bolinas	60 728
NOTARY		
Adrain	San Francisco San Francisco 2	67 646
NOTCH		
Mary*	San Francisco San Francisco 9	681001
NOTE		
Ling	El Dorado Greenwood	58 708
Long*	El Dorado Georgetown	58 708
Lony*	El Dorado Georgetown	58 708

California 1860 Census Index

Name	County Locale	M653 Roll	Page
NOTE			
Wm	El Dorado Greenwood	58	708
NOTEWAN			
C M	El Dorado Placerville	58	857
NOTHACIN			
Caroline*	San Francisco San Francisco 10		175
		67	
NOTHAM			
Daniel*	Amador Twp 4	55	237
William	Calaveras Twp 6	57	164
NOTHAN			
Daniel*	Amador Twp 4	55	237
NOTHBY			
N	Calaveras Twp 9	57	389
NOTHORN			
F	San Mateo Twp 1	65	61
NOTING			
John	San Mateo Twp 1	65	48
NOTN			
Antonio*	Alameda Brooklyn	55	107
NOTRE			
Antonio	Alameda Brooklyn	55	107
Mary	Sierra La Porte	66	778
NOTRIS			
Thomas*	Calaveras Twp 8	57	97
NOTRO			
Antonio*	Alameda Brooklyn	55	107
H	Calaveras Twp 9	57	405
NOTSON			
Wm	Plumas Meadow Valley	62	904
NOTT			
Hiram J	Marin Bolinas	60	746
James*	Alameda Oakland	55	64
John	San Francisco San Francisco 11		102
		67	
Thos	Nevada Red Dog	61	550
NOTTERWOOD			
T H	Mariposa Twp 1	60	670
NOTTINGHAM			
Comodore	Contra Costa Twp 2	57	548
John	Sierra Twp 5	66	917
M J	Butte Chico	56	538
Thos	San Francisco San Francisco 12		363
		67	
NOTTLES			
Elijah	Tuolumne Twp 5	71	518
NOTTS			
P	San Joaquin Stockton	641093	
NOTTY			
---	Fresno Twp 2	59	91
NOU			
---	El Dorado Diamond	58	808
---	Mariposa Coulterville	60	683
---	San Francisco San Francisco 4	681180	
---	San Francisco San Francisco 4	681194	
---*	Mariposa Twp 3	60	576
---*	Nevada Rough &	61	399
Chi	San Francisco San Francisco 5	671205	
NOUA			
---	El Dorado Diamond	58	787
NOUDEN			
Louis	Calaveras Twp 6	57	160
NOUDIN			
Louis*	Calaveras Twp 6	57	160
NOUELL			
C*	Yolo Washington	72	601
NOUG			
---	El Dorado Placerville	58	898
---	El Dorado Mud Springs	58	956
NOUGERS			
M	San Francisco San Francisco 5	67	548
NOUGHTON			
Wm A	Amador Twp 1	55	455
NOUGON			
---	Del Norte Happy Ca	58	667
NOUGUES			
Joseph*	Sacramento Ward 4	63	589
NOUNG			
---	Butte Ophir	56	807
NOUQUE			
Joseph*	Sierra Twp 5	66	918
NOURAN			
Dennis*	San Francisco San Francisco 9	681028	
NOURSE			
A J	Tuolumne Twp 1	71	252
George F	Calaveras Twp 7	57	23
J E	Tuolumne Twp 4	71	165
Joseph	Sierra Twp 7	66	900
NOUSHA			
Aawn	Yolo Cache	72	621
NOUSSO			
A J*	Tuolumne Twp 1	71	252
NOUTHMAY			
F	Trinity Trinity	70	971
NOV			
---	Nevada Bloomfield	61	528

Name	County Locale	M653 Roll	Page
NOVA			
Peter	Nevada Rough &	61	411
NOVAIR			
Francisco	Contra Costa Twp 3	57	613
NOVAL			
John	Amador Twp 6	55	435
NOVAN			
Anna*	San Francisco San Francisco 8	681301	
NOVCROSS			
D C	Sacramento Sutter	63	300
NOVDYKE			
Jacob*	Alameda Brooklyn	55	150
NOVEL			
Charles	San Mateo Twp 1	65	47
Thos	Nevada Bridgeport	61	495
NOVELL			
C*	Yolo Washington	72	601
NOVEN			
Joseph*	Sacramento Franklin	63	311
Trinadad	Placer Auburn	62	579
NOVERJA			
Aterago	Mariposa Twp 3	60	612
Sterago*	Mariposa Twp 3	60	612
NOVICE			
C	San Mateo Twp 1	65	48
NOVILL			
James	Sierra La Porte	66	774
NOVROUS			
Frederick*	Contra Costa Twp 3	57	606
NOW			
---	Amador Twp 6	55	447
---	Calaveras Twp 5	57	211
---	Calaveras Twp 5	57	234
---	Calaveras Twp 5	57	242
---	Calaveras Twp 10	57	259
---	El Dorado White Oaks	581023	
---	El Dorado Salmon Falls	581044	
---	El Dorado Salmon Falls	581058	
---	El Dorado Coloma	581084	
---	El Dorado Union	581090	
---	El Dorado Mountain	581188	
---	El Dorado Mountain	581189	
---	El Dorado Big Bar	58	736
---	Mariposa Twp 3	60	546
---	Mariposa Twp 3	60	550
---	Mariposa Twp 3	60	569
---	Mariposa Coulterville	60	681
---	Mariposa Coulterville	60	683
---	Mariposa Coulterville	60	684
---	Nevada Rough &	61	398
---	Nevada Rough &	61	399
---	Nevada Bridgeport	61	462
---	Placer Virginia	62	671
---	Placer Virginia	62	678
---	Placer Illinois	62	752
---	San Francisco San Francisco 4	681194	
---	Shasta Horsetown	66	704
---	Sierra Whiskey	66	849
---	Sierra St Louis	66	861
---	Sierra Downieville	66	979
---	Tuolumne Twp 5	71	515
---	Yolo No E Twp	72	681
---	Yuba North Ea	72	681
---*	Mariposa Twp 1	60	651
Chi	San Francisco San Francisco 5	671205	
Ching	Butte Bidwell	56	709
Hong	Butte Bidwell	56	709
Ki	San Francisco San Francisco 9	681096	
Long	Butte Bidwell	56	720
Loriano	Calaveras Twp 7	57	3
NOWDIKE			
H	Yolo Cottonwoood	72	656
NOWEL			
Charles	San Mateo Twp 1	65	47
Louis*	San Francisco San Francisco 4	681166	
Peter	El Dorado Kelsey	581139	
NOWELL			
A E	El Dorado White Oaks	581001	
NOWER			
B	Sonoma Bodega	69	529
S J	Solano Vacaville	69	330
T J*	Solano Vacaville	69	330
NOWLAN			
J F J	Sacramento American	63	167
Johanah Sr	Solano Benecia	69	300
NOWLAND			
Charles	Mariposa Twp 1	60	671
Edwr H	San Francisco San Francisco 9	68	988
Hiram N	Butte Oregon	56	620
NOWLE			
J C	El Dorado Gold Hill	581098	
NOWLIN			
B	El Dorado White Oaks	581010	
J P	El Dorado Diamond	58	791
James	El Dorado White Oaks	581010	
NOWLS			
William	Shasta Millvill	66	747

Name	County Locale	M653 Roll	Page
NOWN			
---	Calaveras Twp 10	57	297
NOWREY			
Origon	Alameda Brooklyn	55	185
NOWRY			
Silvester*	San Francisco San Francisco 2	67	647
NOY			
---	Butte Oro	56	688
---	Butte Cascade	56	690
---	Butte Cascade	56	702
---	Butte Mountain	56	743
---	Calaveras Twp 4	57	313
---	San Francisco San Francisco 4	681174	
---	Trinity Big Flat	701042	
---	Yuba Long Bar	72	765
---*	Nevada Nevada	61	303
Ah	Butte Oro	56	688
Ah	Butte Cascade	56	690
Hop	Butte Ophir	56	804
NOYA			
Theodore	El Dorado Kelsey	581134	
Theordore	El Dorado Kelsey	581134	
NOYAGOR			
Maryketa	Tuolumne Twp 1	71	241
NOYAQOR			
Maryketa	Tuolumne Sonora	71	241
NOYCE			
Mittel*	Mariposa Coulterville	60	698
W T	Tehama Red Bluff	70	911
William	San Francisco San Francisco 3	67	36
NOYD			
Mittel*	Mariposa Coulterville	60	698
NOYE			
George W	Yuba Long Bar	72	773
Jose M	Alameda Brooklyn	55	117
Michael	San Francisco San Francisco 11		152
		67	
NOYEE			
Mittel*	Mariposa Coulterville	60	698
Mittet*	Mariposa Coulterville	60	698
NOYES			
Abraham	Mariposa Twp 3	60	549
Amos	San Francisco San Francisco 10		242
		67	
C G	Tuolumne Twp 1	71	220
E	El Dorado Salmon Falls	581052	
E	El Dorado Placerville	58	882
Ellen	San Francisco San Francisco 8	681287	
George	San Francisco San Francisco 7	681390	
H*	Sutter Butte	70	787
J D	San Francisco San Francisco 7	681443	
J W	Placer Iona Hills	62	866
James	Trinity Trinity	70	973
Jas M	San Francisco San Francisco 10		220
		67	
Jonathan	Plumas Quincy	62	936
M	Sonoma Salt Point	69	695
Moody	San Francisco San Francisco 10		270
		67	
Moody	Sonoma Mendocino	69	457
Patrick	Mariposa Twp 3	60	615
S W*	San Francisco San Francisco 5	67	547
Sct*	Trinity E Weaver	701060	
Wil W*	San Bernardino San Bernardino	64	619
Wild W*	San Bernardino San Bernadino	64	619
William H	San Diego San Diego	64	763
Wils W*	San Bernardino San Bernadino	64	619
NOYILLIA			
Stephen	Tuolumne Twp 4	71	127
NOYLAND			
Angela	San Francisco San Francisco 10		181
		67	
Angela Sister	San Francisco 10		181
	San Francisco	67	
Angela Sister*	San Francisco 10		181
	San Francisco	67	
Sister Angela*	San Francisco 10		181
	San Francisco	67	
NOYMAN			
George	San Francisco San Francisco 11		120
		67	
NOYS			
George W	Yuba Long Bar	72	773
NOYSE			
Henry A	Yuba Marysville	72	967
NOYUS			
N	Yolo Cache	72	642
NOZAGEN			
Nicolo*	Calaveras Twp 5	57	219
NOZARET			
S*	Trinity Weaverville	701071	
NOZERMAN			
Henry	Calaveras Twp 4	57	340
NOZEYIN			
Nicolo	Calaveras Twp 5	57	219
NOZZS			
I W	Mariposa Twp 1	60	642

Name	County Locale	M653 RollPage
NOZZS		
J W	Mariposa Twp 1	60 642
NP		
---*	Butte Kimshaw	56 586
NRA		
---	Tuolumne Don Pedro	71 538
NRAGOR		
M J*	El Dorado Georgetown	58 685
NREENE		
Patrick*	Mariposa Twp 3	60 567
NRGE		
---	Sierra Downieville	66 983
NROVILE		
J B	Sacramento Natonia	63 277
NROVILL		
J B*	Sacramento Natonia	63 277
NRSE		
D A	Solano Montezuma	69 367
NS		
Charles	Santa Cruz Soguel	66 591
NSAWHER		
Whaner*	Mariposa Coulterville	60 702
NSOELS		
Matilda*	Yuba Bear Rvr	721004
NTALE		
Edmond*	Calaveras Twp 8	57 64
NU		
---	Amador Twp 2	55 314
---	Calaveras Twp 5	57 252
---	Calaveras Twp 10	57 269
---	El Dorado Diamond	58 798
---	Mariposa Twp 3	60 551
---	Nevada Bridgeport	61 448
---	San Francisco San Francisco 4	681182
---	Sierra Downieville	661020
---	Tuolumne Twp 3	71 460
Foy	San Francisco San Francisco 5	671206
Gow	Calaveras Twp 5	57 202
Hong	San Francisco San Francisco 5	67 506
Lu	Sacramento Granite	63 268
Saw	Sacramento Natonia	63 286
See*	Sacramento Granite	63 268
NUA		
---	Placer Horseshoe	62 650
NUACUI		
Strause	Amador Twp 1	55 468
NUAL		
Pat O*	Sacramento Natonia	63 272
NUAPP		
W	El Dorado Georgetown	58 758
NUAR		
Wm*	Stanislaus Branch	70 709
NUBAT		
Elisha	Sacramento Granite	63 260
NUBBACK		
Adalade*	Mariposa Twp 1	60 668
NUBER		
---	Mendocino Twp 1	60 890
NUBILL		
S D	Sonoma Armally	69 518
NUBY		
George	El Dorado Big Bar	58 744
NUCI		
Abram*	Nevada Red Dog	61 542
NUCKCHOW		
---	Tulara Twp 2	71 38
NUCKENBOTHAM		
John T	San Joaquin Stockton	641049
NUCKINS		
Oliver	Nevada Bridgeport	61 503
NUCKLER		
James N	Mendocino Calpella	60 818
James W*	Mendocino Calpella	60 818
NUCKOLDS		
James N	Mendocino Calpella	60 816
NUCOMB		
B F	Tuolumne Jamestown	71 437
NUCOTT		
Gordon*	Yuba Marysville	72 850
NUCUT		
William*	San Francisco San Francisco 9	68 993
NUD		
Joseph*	Santa Clara Santa Clara	65 488
S	Calaveras Twp 9	57 409
NUDD		
B F	San Francisco San Francisco 8	681239
H J	Calaveras Twp 9	57 411
W P	San Francisco San Francisco 3	67 60
NUDDEN		
John	Siskiyou Callahan	69 3
NUDENHAMER		
Alex*	Sacramento Ward 1	63 91
NUDENHAUM		
Alex*	Sacramento Ward 1	63 91
NUDGET		
L A*	Sacramento Brighton	63 199
NUDGET		
S A*	Sacramento Brighton	63 199
NUDZSTER		
Joseph	San Francisco San Francisco 2	67 747
NUE		
---	El Dorado White Oaks	581023
NUEMAKARA		
---	Fresno Twp 2	59 46
NUEMAN		
Peter	Sierra Downieville	66 964
NUES		
Geo	Siskiyou Cottonwood	69 105
NUFEUCHER		
Fred*	Alameda Brooklyn	55 148
NUG		
---	Placer Rattle Snake	62 638
Ye	Tuolumne Twp 5	71 512
NUGEAT		
Mary	San Francisco San Francisco 2	67 676
NUGENT		
A S	Nevada Bloomfield	61 515
Bridget	San Francisco San Francisco 3	67 81
Danl	San Francisco San Francisco 1	68 855
E J	Trinity Grass Valley	70 962
Edwd	San Francisco San Francisco 10	358 67
George	Solano Vallejo	69 260
Henry	Butte Oro	56 673
James	Marin San Rafael	60 763
James	San Francisco San Francisco 12	385 67
James	Santa Clara Santa Clara	65 511
James	Tuolumne Twp 3	71 454
Jas	Calaveras Twp 9	57 371
Jas	San Francisco San Francisco 5	67 501
John	Amador Twp 5	55 347
John	Sacramento Sutter	63 294
John	San Francisco San Francisco 8	681295
John	San Francisco San Francisco 2	67 713
John S	Tuolumne Twp 2	71 322
John*	San Francisco San Francisco 2	67 713
Mary	Contra Costa Twp 2	57 582
Mathew	Santa Cruz Pajaro	66 525
Mathew P	San Francisco San Francisco 3	67 81
Michael	Calaveras Twp 7	57 1
Peter	San Francisco San Francisco 5	67 546
Ricd N	San Francisco San Francisco 2	67 730
Richard	Santa Cruz Santa Cruz	66 612
T	Sutter Yuba	70 761
William	San Francisco San Francisco 11	153 67
NUGER		
Adolphus*	San Francisco 8 San Francisco	681289
Albert	Sonoma Petaluma	69 560
Wm*	Del Norte Happy Ca	58 670
NUGFORD		
John	Sacramento Natonia	63 272
NUGGLES		
L R	Yolo Cache Crk	72 597
NUGHTON		
Thomas	Sierra Twp 5	66 941
NUGLES		
Amands	Yolo Cache Crk	72 597
NUGNET		
James	Tuolumne Jamestown	71 454
NUGUTS		
Laura	Yolo Washington	72 564
NUHAM		
Fred	Amador Twp 5	55 338
NUHARD		
Antne*	Sacramento Natonia	63 273
Anton*	Sacramento Natonia	63 273
Autne*	Sacramento Natonia	63 273
NUJENT		
Francis	El Dorado Greenwood	58 725
NUJNEY		
---	El Dorado Kelsey	581131
NUK		
---	Alameda Oakland	55 52
NUKERMAN		
John	Butte Wyandotte	56 666
NUKS		
Jacob*	Yuba Slate Ro	72 703
NUL		
Charles*	Los Angeles Los Angeles	59 491
NULFORD		
F J	Sacramento Natonia	63 279
NULICK		
George	Tuolumne Twp 6	71 534
NULL		
J	San Joaquin Stockton	641091
James	Tuolumne Shawsfla	71 406
John	Shasta Millvill	66 744
John	Sierra St Louis	66 816
Leonard	Colusa Grand Island	57 472
NULL		
R	Sutter Sutter	70 805
Richard	Yolo Cottonwoood	72 557
William	Tulara Twp 2	71 22
NULLER		
Jas*	Sacramento Granite	63 246
John W*	Yuba Bear Rvr	72 996
Wm O*	Butte Kimshaw	56 571
NULLES		
Thos	Mariposa Coulterville	60 677
NULLETT		
Ortimiro*	San Bernadino San Bernardino	64 634
NULLON		
Moses J*	Yuba Bear Rvr	72 999
NULLS		
Henry	Humbolt Union	59 181
NULSE		
A P	Klamath S Fork	59 198
J L	Klamath S Fork	59 198
NULTER		
A P*	Butte Kimshaw	56 607
Enusa*	Santa Cruz Pescadero	66 643
NULTY		
Mary	Amador Twp 2	55 272
NULTZ		
Hafer	San Francisco San Francisco 10	311 67
Xafer*	San Francisco San Francisco 10	311 67
NUM		
---	Amador Twp 5	55 329
---	Amador Twp 5	55 346
---	Calaveras Twp 10	57 275
---	Calaveras Twp 10	57 284
---	El Dorado Georgetown	58 692
---	Mariposa Twp 1	60 659
---	Trinity Big Flat	701041
---	Trinity Trinindad Rvr	701044
---	Trinity Lewiston	70 955
Ah*	Placer Secret R	62 620
San	Siskiyou Scott Ri	69 66
Yin	Mariposa Coulterville	60 682
NUMAKER		
Isaac	Siskiyou Klamath	69 87
NUMAN		
Henry*	Napa Hot Springs	61 14
Maurice	Mariposa Twp 3	60 550
NUMAS		
Rose	Calaveras Twp 4	57 336
NUMEE		
B F*	Sierra La Porte	66 777
B V	Sierra La Porte	66 777
NUMER		
Alfd*	Butte Oregon	56 627
Jacob	Sierra La Porte	66 776
NUMES		
Augustin	San Diego Temecula	64 785
NUMIE		
B F*	Sierra La Porte	66 777
NUN		
---	Amador Twp 5	55 340
---	Calaveras Twp 8	57 107
---	Mariposa Twp 3	60 571
---	Mariposa Twp 3	60 607
A	Amador Twp 4	55 314
Charles	Sierra Downieville	661012
Edward	Yuba New York	72 728
Hing	Calaveras Twp 6	57 126
See	Mariposa Twp 3	60 607
Warren*	Amador Twp 2	55 314
NUNA		
Alecia	Los Angeles San Jose	59 288
NUNALLY		
Thos C	Placer Virginia	62 661
NUNAN		
James	Placer Michigan	62 815
Maggi	San Francisco San Francisco 10	183 67
Maggie	San Francisco San Francisco 10	183 67
Timothy	San Francisco San Francisco 6	67 425
NUNANS		
David G	San Francisco San Francisco 9	68 955
NUNCO		
---*	Butte Chico	56 550
NUNCY		
John	Sierra Downieville	661022
NUNDIVAS		
Chapeto	Yuba Linda Twp	72 980
NUNE		
---	El Dorado Coloma	581105
NUNES		
Hosea	Alameda Brooklyn	55 118
Hosea Maria	Alameda Brooklyn	55 199
J*	El Dorado Placerville	58 841

California 1860 Census Index

Name	County Locale	M653 Roll	Page
NUNES			
Manuel	Placer Michigan	62	850
Manuel	Placer Michigan	62	851
Narciso	Los Angeles Santa Ana	59	447
Pedro	Tuolumne Twp 5	71	498
Ramon	Los Angeles Santa Ana	59	444
T	Calaveras Twp 9	57	407
NUNEY			
Agapita	Sierra La Porte	66	773
John*	Sierra Downieville	66	1022
Pedro	Santa Clara Almaden	65	262
NUNEZ			
Basilio	Santa Clara Burnett	65	261
Jose*	Yuba Marysville	72	948
Ricardo	Santa Clara San Jose	65	365
NUNG			
---	Sierra Downieville	66	983
---	Tuolumne Twp 2	71	410
---	Tuolumne Jamestown	71	433
---	Tuolumne Jamestown	71	434
---	Tuolumne Twp 3	71	468
---	Tuolumne Twp 1	71	475
---	Tuolumne Twp 1	71	477
---	Tuolumne Don Pedro	71	540
---	Yuba Long Bar	72	760
---	Yuba Long Bar	72	767
---	Yuba Fosters	72	841
NUNIES			
Anestacia*	Yuba Marysville	72	948
Clara	Los Angeles San Jose	59	288
NUNINGER			
George*	Calaveras Twp 8	57	51
NUNIS			
B L	Calaveras Twp 9	57	408
B S	Calaveras Twp 9	57	408
Frank	Tuolumne Shawsfla	71	384
John	Calaveras Twp 4	57	345
NUNLZ			
Andrica	Calaveras Twp 6	57	123
NUNN			
Ah*	Placer Secret R	62	620
H	Butte Oro	56	677
Henry	Mendocino Anderson	60	864
Noah	Mendocino Anderson	60	865
Sylvester	Mendocino Anderson	60	865
Tinaton M*	Mendocino Anderson	60	864
Truaton M*	Mendocino Anderson	60	864
NUNNALLY			
W A	Trinity Weaverville	70	1081
NUNP			
---*	Mariposa Twp 3	60	552
NUNRZ			
Toyasola	Calaveras Twp 6	57	130
NUNY			
---	El Dorado Kelsey	58	1131
---	Yuba Long Bar	72	760
A	Yuba Foster B	72	827
NUO			
Paulo	Tuolumne Chinese	71	498
NUON			
---	El Dorado Union	58	1090
NUPER			
Thomas	Sierra Downieville	66	1011
NUPPS			
Harrana*	Nevada Bloomfield	61	529
Harrance*	Nevada Bloomfield	61	529
NUR			
---	Sierra Downieville	66	979
Henry	San Francisco San Francisco 2	67	695
NURANDA			
Cinz*	Monterey Monterey	60	962
NUREMBERG			
Augutt	Tuolumne Twp 2	71	308
NURETER			
Wm*	San Francisco San Francisco 3	67	13
NURIENS			
J*	El Dorado Georgetown	58	683
NURIMS			
J*	El Dorado Georgetown	58	683
NURIR			
Andrew*	Sacramento Ward 1	63	116
NURL			
H*	San Francisco San Francisco 5	67	495
NURLCAY			
William*	San Francisco San Francisco 9	68	946
NURN			
---*	Sacramento Granite	63	249
---*	Sacramento Granite	63	250
NURNS			
John	San Francisco San Francisco 3	67	75
NUROHAR			
Patrick	Santa Cruz Santa Cruz	66	626
NURPHY			
Jno	Butte Kimshaw	56	607
Patrick	Tuolumne Jamestown	71	436
NURRE			
---	Sacramento Granite	63	249

Name	County Locale	M653 Roll	Page
NURRILL			
Rufus R*	Yuba Marysville	72	880
Rufus*	Yuba Marysville	72	880
NURSE			
A	Siskiyou Cottonwoood	69	106
D A	Solano Montezuma	69	367
J P*	San Francisco San Francisco 8	68	1291
R	Amador Twp 6	55	445
Wm B	Solano Benecia	69	282
NURSO			
J P	San Francisco San Francisco 8	68	1291
NUSE			
---	El Dorado Greenwood	58	711
George	Sierra Pine Grove	66	833
NUSEHEM			
A*	Marin S Antoni	60	707
NUSNEHANEN			
Alex*	Sacramento Ward 1	63	91
NUSO			
Anton	Tuolumne Twp 3	71	455
NUSON			
W	Tuolumne Twp 1	71	256
NUSSBAUM			
William	Siskiyou Cottonwoood	69	97
NUSSUL			
R	El Dorado Georgetown	58	690
NUSTRAMMER			
Lewis*	Alameda Murray	55	219
NUT			
---	Tuolumne Twp 5	71	523
NUTALL			
Alice	Sacramento Natonia	63	277
G	Shasta Horsetown	66	699
G	Shasta Horsetown	66	699
James	Nevada Bloomfield	61	507
John	Yolo No E Twp	72	676
NUTALS			
James	Nevada Bloomfield	61	507
NUTE			
H	Contra Costa Twp 1	57	535
Warren*	Nevada Rough &	61	412
NUTEE			
John*	Amador Twp 5	55	329
NUTER			
John	Amador Twp 5	55	329
NUTFIELD			
Thomas	San Francisco San Francisco 3	67	79
NUTHRA			
Rotto*	Santa Cruz Soguel	66	590
NUTLER			
Thomas*	Santa Cruz Santa Cruz	66	640
NUTLEY			
Gustavus*	Marin Novato	60	737
NUTMAN			
Victor W*	Alameda Brooklyn	55	206
NUTOX			
B	Tuolumne Twp 4	71	145
NUTT			
Henry	Stanislaus Empire	70	731
Jno	Alameda Brooklyn	55	210
John C*	San Francisco San Francisco 10	67	322
N M	Placer Yankee J	62	778
NUTTALE			
Jno	Sacramento Natonia	63	278
NUTTALL			
Jno*	Sacramento Natonia	63	278
John	Yuba North Ea	72	676
R K	San Francisco San Francisco 5	67	497
NUTTEN			
Geo A*	Napa Clear Lake	61	122
Henry	Calaveras Twp 10	57	274
NUTTENTON			
R M	Shasta Horsetown	66	694
NUTTER			
A P	Butte Kimshaw	56	607
Emisa*	Santa Cruz Pescadero	66	643
Euisa*	Santa Cruz Pescadero	66	643
Francis	Butte Ophir	56	752
George	Santa Cruz Santa Cruz	66	634
Henry	Calaveras Twp 10	57	274
Joh P	Humbolt Eureka	59	177
John	Marin Bolinas	60	733
John	Santa Cruz Santa Cruz	66	636
N P	Butte Kimshaw	56	598
Richard*	Calaveras Twp 10	57	274
Thomas J	Yuba Marysville	72	928
Thomas*	Santa Cruz Santa Cruz	66	640
Thos W*	San Francisco San Francisco 3	67	20
William M	Nevada Rough &	61	421
Wm	San Francisco San Francisco 1	68	837
Wm	Yuba New York	72	738
NUTTES			
Thos W*	San Francisco San Francisco 3	67	20
NUTTING			
A	Sonoma Salt Point	69	694

Name	County Locale	M653 Roll	Page
NUTTING			
Calvin	San Francisco San Francisco 12	67	367
Daniel	Sonoma Bodega	69	519
H	Nevada Bloomfield	61	517
Harris	Sonoma Armally	69	510
J E	San Francisco San Francisco 6	67	419
John	San Francisco San Francisco 11	67	150
Julia	Sierra Twp 7	66	897
Wm	San Francisco San Francisco 9	68	1091
NUTTINGHAM			
James	Mendocino Round Va	60	877
NUTTLE			
Geo W	Sacramento Natonia	63	277
Thomas	Siskiyou Yreka	69	123
Tomas	Siskiyou Yreka	69	123
NUTTOR			
William M*	Nevada Rough &	61	421
NUTTS			
Christian	Placer Yankee J	62	756
NUTYHORN			
John	Tuolumne Chinese	71	494
NUTZ			
Ernest*	San Francisco San Francisco 3	67	42
NUTZHORN			
John	Tuolumne Twp 5	71	494
NUVEOMER			
Furry*	Tuolumne Twp 3	71	429
NUVIMS			
J*	El Dorado Georgetown	58	683
NUVNING			
J	El Dorado Diamond	58	808
NUWELL			
Henry	El Dorado Greenwood	58	723
NUYES			
Gotlick	Del Norte Crescent	58	660
NWMAN			
J	Yolo Putah	72	553
NY CHUN			
---	Mariposa Twp 3	60	612
NY			
---	Butte Kimshaw	56	600
---	Butte Kimshaw	56	605
---	Butte Oregon	56	626
---	Butte Ophir	56	812
---	Butte Ophir	56	817
---	Calaveras Twp 5	57	233
---	El Dorado Greenwood	58	727
---	Mariposa Twp 3	60	581
---	Mariposa Coulterville	60	684
Chun	Mariposa Twp 3	60	612
Kee	San Francisco San Francisco 11	67	146
Lef	Sacramento Natonia	63	283
Ling	Butte Ophir	56	806
Pong	San Francisco San Francisco 11	67	146
Ree	San Francisco San Francisco 11	67	146
Tuk	San Francisco San Francisco 11	67	146
NYARS			
Michael J*	Yuba Marysville	72	931
NYATE			
Jn	Sacramento Natonia	63	284
NYE			
---	Butte Mountain	56	743
---	Calaveras Twp 4	57	324
---	Mariposa Twp 1	60	643
---	Placer Rattle Snake	62	638
A R	Tuolumne Jamestown	71	425
Adam	Amador Twp 5	55	363
Albert	Tuolumne Twp 3	71	449
B F	El Dorado Greenwood	58	724
Benjamin	Santa Cruz Pajaro	66	534
Chas	San Francisco San Francisco 1	68	912
D B	Amador Twp 2	55	324
D B	Nevada Grass Valley	61	151
David B	Calaveras Twp 4	57	337
David Jr	Butte Ophir	56	798
Frank	Nevada Washington	61	332
G H	Napa Hot Springs	61	2
George	San Francisco San Francisco 5	67	549
George W	Plumas Quincy	62	941
H M	Tuolumne Columbia	71	363
Hyram*	San Francisco San Francisco 9	68	1049
Jack	Colusa Mansville	57	438
Jno	Nevada Washington	61	332
John	Placer Auburn	62	583
John	Sacramento Granite	63	262
John	San Joaquin Elkhorn	64	1000
John B	San Joaquin Stockton	64	1064
Jones	San Joaquin Elkhorn	64	984
Lynman	Tuolumne Shawsfla	71	393
Mary J	Sacramento Ward 1	63	136

California 1860 Census Index

Name	County Locale	M653 Roll	Page
NYE			
Michael C	Yuba Marysville	72	911
Michael O	Yuba Marysville	72	911
Pearson*	El Dorado Greenwood	58	723
Perelan*	El Dorado Greenwood	58	723
Peter	Tuolumne Sonora	71	480
Po	San Francisco San Francisco 11		146
		67	
Rodolphus S	San Gabriel	59	412
	Los Angeles		
S F	Tuolumne Twp 2	71	359
S O	El Dorado Georgetown	58	681
S T	San Joaquin Stockton	641	038
Sam	Butte Bidwell	56	708
Samuel	El Dorado Georgetown	58	704
Saul	Sacramento Sutter	63	300
Sum	Placer Rattle Snake	62	631
Symman	Tuolumne Twp 2	71	393
T F	Tuolumne Shawsfla	71	397
T H	Tuolumne Twp 2	71	397
Thomas	San Joaquin Stockton	641	084
Walter	Placer Iona Hills	62	894
William	Tuolumne Columbia	71	342
Wm F	San Francisco San Francisco 3	67	86
NYERS			
James	Nevada Little Y	61	534
John*	Sierra St Louis	66	807
NYLE			
Henry	Yuba Marysville	72	902
NYMAN			
Alfred P	Nevada Rough &	61	416
F L	Tuolumne Twp 2	71	321
Frank	Klamath Liberty	59	237
NYMANN			
G B	Tuolumne Jamestown	71	422
NYN			
William	Tuolumne Twp 2	71	342
NYNG			
---	Yuba Fosters	72	827
NYNNT			
William*	San Francisco San Francisco 9	68	991
NYO			
A R	Tuolumne Twp 3	71	425
Lee	San Francisco San Francisco 4	681	187
Lu	San Francisco San Francisco 4	681	187
Oh	San Francisco San Francisco 11		159
		67	
Wis	San Francisco San Francisco 4	681	187
NYON			
---	San Francisco San Francisco 11		146
		67	
NYS			
John	Sacramento Granite	63	262
Louis	Calaveras Twp 6	57	116
NYSTRON			
J H	Siskiyou Klamath	69	80
NYUNT			
William*	San Francisco San Francisco 9	68	991
NZUSBACK			
John M	Placer Forest H	62	765
O CHUM			
---*	Fresno Twp 3	59	7
O CO CHAW			
---*	Mendocino Calpella	60	826
O			
---	Sierra Downieville	66	998
Ger	Sierra Downieville	661	006
Henry	San Francisco San Francisco 9	68	953
How	Sierra Downieville	66	992
James	San Francisco San Francisco 9	68	949
James	San Francisco San Francisco 9	68	950
James	San Francisco San Francisco 9	68	952
K*	Sierra Downieville	661	008
Sing	Sierra Downieville	66	998
Soyoy	Sierra Downieville	661	015
Thomas	San Francisco San Francisco 9	68	952
Yo	Sierra Downieville	661	026
O'OAKLEY			
Robert*	San Francisco San Francisco 11		104
		67	
O'OPISH			
---	Tulara Twp 1	71	118
OA			
---	El Dorado Eldorado	58	939
OAGAN			
T	Tuolumne Twp 4	71	145
OAGWE			
W B	Nevada Rough &	61	408
OAH			
---	Sacramento Ward 3	63	490
Wah	San Francisco San Francisco 11		144
		67	
OAHA			
P E*	Shasta Shasta	66	679
OAHER			
P E*	Shasta Shasta	66	679

Name	County Locale	M653 Roll	Page
OAIRE			
Joseph*	Tuolumne Twp 2	71	279
OAK			
---	Nevada Rough &	61	437
OAKER			
P E*	Shasta Shasta	66	679
OAKERMAN			
F	Yolo Putah	72	552
OAKES			
A G	Sonoma Sonoma	69	659
Charles	Yuba Marysville	72	873
D M	Solano Fremont	69	378
F G	Sacramento Ward 1	63	4
James	El Dorado Placerville	58	896
John	Tuolumne Twp 1	71	247
Margt	Butte Kimshaw	56	576
OAKEY			
G	Nevada Eureka	61	377
OAKLESS			
E C	San Joaquin Stockton	641	097
OAKLEY			
Amasa W*	Yuba Bear Rvr	721	007
C C	Sacramento American	63	164
C L*	Sacramento Centre	63	175
C S*	Sacramento Centre	63	175
Edward	Yuba Bear Rvr	721	009
Edwd D	San Francisco San Francisco 10		231
		67	
H D	El Dorado Placerville	58	918
Henry	Santa Clara Fremont	65	434
John	El Dorado Placerville	58	931
O B	San Francisco San Francisco 8	681	265
Peter	Monterey Alisal	601	028
Robert O*	San Francisco		104
		67	
Robet O	San Francisco San Francisco 11		104
		67	
Saml E	San Francisco San Francisco 10		230
		67	
OAKLY			
David	El Dorado Placerville	58	905
J	San Francisco San Francisco 5	67	540
W	San Francisco San Francisco 5	67	496
OAKMAN			
O	Nevada Eureka	61	370
OAKOLAND			
John	Shasta Cottonwood	66	737
OAKS			
D B	Nevada Eureka	61	345
David C	Napa Napa	61	73
J	Nevada Washington	61	333
John	Yuba Rose Bar	72	820
Levi	Sacramento American	63	169
M	San Francisco San Francisco 6	67	437
N D	Placer Dutch Fl	62	726
Nathan	El Dorado Salmon Falls	581	034
Omar	Santa Clara Santa Clara	65	512
Russell	Placer Folsom	62	641
Samuel	Nevada Little Y	61	536
Thomas	Santa Clara Almaden	65	270
OAKSON			
Ardolph	San Joaquin Tulare	64	871
OAKSOP			
---	Mendocino Big Rvr	60	854
OAKY			
A G	Sonoma Sonoma	69	659
John	Tuolumne Twp 1	71	247
OALISON			
John	Nevada Bridgeport	61	495
OALLEY			
G B	Nevada Nevada	61	240
OALLMAN			
Thos	Nevada Nevada	61	260
OALLONE			
George	Yolo Merritt	72	580
OAM			
Ah	Tuolumne Twp 4	71	179
OAN			
---	Sacramento Ward 1	63	52
---*	Sacramento Ward 1	63	71
---*	Tuolumne Big Oak	71	179
Lee*	Sacramento Ward 1	63	71
Wan*	Sacramento Ward 1	63	71
Waw*	Sacramento Ward 1	63	71
OANGHEN			
George	Yolo Merritt	72	579
OANN			
---*	Sacramento Ward 1	63	56
OAP			
---	Sacramento Natonia	63	286
OAPOTO			
---	Tulara Twp 1	71	121
OAQULIN			
David*	Santa Cruz Pescadero	66	641
OARFIDA			
Michael	Tuolumne Twp 6	71	531

Name	County Locale	M653 Roll	Page
OARID			
---	Mendocino Calpella	60	827
OARN			
---	Sacramento Ward 1	63	56
OART			
---	Sierra Downieville	66	998
OARTUS			
John	Santa Cruz Soguel	66	588
OASLEY			
Lecta	Santa Clara Gilroy	65	241
OASTRO			
Lucina	Los Angeles San Jose	59	282
OATCEL			
Gobletz*	Calaveras Twp 6	57	147
OATES			
Arthur	San Francisco San Francisco 1	68	816
J	El Dorado Placerville	58	863
OATIRO			
Fernando	Los Angeles Los Angeles	59	517
OATLE			
Henry	San Diego Colorado	64	808
OATLEY			
G B	Nevada Nevada	61	240
OATMAN			
C	Nevada Eureka	61	370
E J	Calaveras Twp 9	57	410
Henry	San Joaquin Douglass	64	916
Ira E	Sacramento Ward 3	63	461
J	Calaveras Twp 9	57	408
M	Mariposa Coulterville	60	703
T R	San Francisco San Francisco 5	67	545
William	Yuba Foster B	72	832
OATS			
Charles	Tuolumne Shawsfla	71	387
Ferando	Santa Clara Alviso	65	404
James	El Dorado Salmon Falls	581	041
James	El Dorado Coloma	581	107
M G	Nevada Nevada	61	266
Mary	San Francisco San Francisco 8	681	275
Phela	Sonoma Petaluma	69	590
S O	Nevada Nevada	61	263
Wm	Mariposa Coulterville	60	703
OATTEE			
Ohio*	Yolo Cottonwoood	72	646
OATUNAN			
Lyman*	Colusa Grand Island	57	469
OAU LEE			
---	Sacramento Ward 1	63	71
OAU SE			
---	Sacramento Ward 1	63	70
OAU WAN			
---	Sacramento Ward 1	63	71
OAUN			
---*	Sacramento Ward 1	63	56
OAW			
---	Sacramento Ward 1	63	71
---	Sierra Downieville	661	000
---*	Sacramento Ward 1	63	52
---*	Sacramento Ward 1	63	71
Le	Sacramento Ward 1	63	70
Lee*	Sacramento Ward 1	63	71
Se*	Sacramento Ward 1	63	70
OB			
Hing	San Francisco San Francisco 5	67	510
Hox	San Francisco San Francisco 5	67	509
Kim	San Francisco San Francisco 5	67	509
OB?RHETE			
Mary A*	Yuba Marysville	72	924
OBAHAM			
J K*	Siskiyou Klamath	69	84
OBAIN			
John	Yuba Marysville	72	929
OBAKER			
John*	Butte Wyandotte	56	668
OBANION			
D	Sutter Sutter	70	809
OBANNON			
Yeburton*	Yuba Long Bar	72	769
OBAR			
A J*	Mendocino Anderson	60	864
OBARSHAW			
L*	Shasta Shasta	66	680
Q	Shasta Shasta	66	680
OBATES			
Geo*	Sacramento San Joaquin	63	366
OBAY			
Michael*	El Dorado Georgetown	58	678
OBAYLEY			
James*	El Dorado Casumnes	581	177
OBBINS			
Isaah*	Nevada Red Dog	61	546
Isauh*	Nevada Red Dog	61	546
OBDHAM			
J K*	Siskiyou Klamath	69	84
OBE			
Louis	Siskiyou Klamath	69	97

Name	County Locale	M653 Roll	Page
OBEALS			
Henry*	San Francisco San Francisco 6	67	422
OBEANT			
Thomas	Sierra Twp 5	66	943
OBEL			
---	San Francisco San Francisco 4	68	1173
OBELEY			
R T*	Nevada Grass Valley	61	196
OBELMAN			
W	Nevada Eureka	61	361
OBER			
Andrew	Mariposa Twp 1	60	648
Benjm	San Francisco San Francisco 8	68	1308
C H	San Joaquin Elkhorn	64	977
Cha M	San Francisco San Francisco 10	67	236
Chas	Butte Kimshaw	56	583
Chas M	San Francisco San Francisco 10	67	236
Henry	Butte Kimshaw	56	583
Isaac	El Dorado Placerville	58	896
Jacob	San Joaquin Stockton	64	1057
William	Yuba Marysville	72	896
OBERDINE			
Willie	Tehama Red Bluff	70	930
OBERDUNER			
M	Trinity Weaverville	70	1069
OBERFELDT			
Andrew	San Diego Colorado	64	808
OBERHETE			
Mary A*	Yuba Marysville	72	924
OBERKETE			
Mary A*	Yuba Marysville	72	924
OBERLANDER			
Samuel*	Humbolt Union	59	190
OBERLE			
John	Sierra St Louis	66	808
OBERLIN			
William R	Siskiyou Yreka	69	124
OBERLUTE			
Frederick O*	Yuba Marysville	72	910
OBERLY			
Enoch	Calaveras Twp 7	57	14
William N	Calaveras Twp 8	57	92
OBERMAYER			
S	Trinity Mouth Ca	70	1017
OBERMAZER			
S	Trinity Mouth Ca	70	1017
OBERMULLER			
E	San Francisco San Francisco 9	68	1054
OBERRY			
Peter	Sierra Downieville	66	963
OBERSHAW			
L*	Shasta Shasta	66	680
OBERSON			
Matthew	Siskiyou Scott Va	69	42
OBERT			
J	Nevada Grass Valley	61	191
OBHINE			
---	Sacramento Cosumnes	63	408
OBIA			
Chris	Sacramento Granite	63	263
Jose	Tuolumne Twp 5	71	498
OBIRDEN			
Patrick*	Tuolumne Twp 2	71	295
OBIREN			
John	Marin Cortemad	60	786
OBIRNE			
Mary*	San Francisco San Francisco 4	68	1138
OBISTWIG			
Abbia	Tuolumne Twp 1	71	221
OBIZE			
L	Nevada Eureka	61	389
OBLACK			
---	Mendocino Twp 1	60	888
OBLEGER			
George*	Yuba Marysville	72	966
OBLEYER			
George*	Yuba Marysville	72	966
OBNEAR			
G	San Francisco San Francisco 2	67	766
OBOOKE			
William	San Francisco San Francisco 8	68	1268
OBOOTS			
Jack	Del Norte Klamath	58	655
OBOURNE			
P	Sutter Butte	70	798
OBOY			
Margarett*	Placer Michigan	62	821
OBRACKET			
George*	Humbolt Eel Rvr	59	144
OBREIN			
Peter	Contra Costa Twp 2	57	555
OBRIAN			
Burnard	Placer Auburn	62	586
C	San Francisco San Francisco 5	67	534
Daniel	Nevada Bridgeport	61	505
Danl	San Francisco San Francisco 6	67	467
Eddward	Amador Twp 4	55	240
Ellen	Alameda Brooklyn	55	122
H	San Francisco San Francisco 5	67	537
Henry	Butte Oregon	56	615
James	San Francisco San Francisco 5	67	546
James C*	El Dorado Coloma	58	1104
Jas	Calaveras Twp 9	57	368
Jas	Calaveras Twp 9	57	369
Jas	San Francisco San Francisco 9	68	1068
Jas B	Calaveras Twp 9	57	367
John	Amador Twp 4	55	235
John	Placer Rattle Snake	62	626
John	San Francisco San Francisco 6	67	407
John	San Francisco San Francisco 6	67	425
Jos	San Francisco San Francisco 9	68	1068
Jos	San Francisco San Francisco 1	68	810
Kate	San Francisco San Francisco 6	67	442
M	Butte Chico	56	549
Mich	San Francisco San Francisco 6	67	407
Michael	Placer Rattle Snake	62	604
P	San Francisco San Francisco 5	67	537
Patk*	Napa Napa	61	99
Patrick	Santa Clara San Jose	65	283
Patrick	Siskiyou Yreka	69	137
Patrick	Siskiyou Yreka	69	138
Peter	San Francisco San Francisco 9	68	1070
Thos	Alameda Brooklyn	55	96
Thos	Napa Napa	61	97
Thos	Nevada Bridgeport	61	446
Ths	San Francisco San Francisco 6	67	407
Timothy	San Francisco San Francisco 3	67	65
William	Placer Michigan	62	839
William	San Francisco San Francisco 6	67	402
Wm	Placer Rattle Snake	62	599
OBRIANT			
John	Sierra Twp 7	66	908
John	Sierra Twp 7	66	911
John*	Sierra Twp 7	66	908
OBRIEN			
Alexis	Calaveras Twp 7	57	40
Amelia	San Francisco San Francisco 10	67	185
Ann	Trinity Lewiston	70	953
Anna	Sacramento Ward 3	63	447
Anne	Sacramento Ward 3	63	464
Barnard	San Francisco San Francisco 7	68	1335
C W	Merced Twp 4	60	920
Cath	Alameda Brooklyn	55	106
Cath	Alameda Oakland	55	36
Cath	Sacramento Ward 4	63	584
Catharine	Contra Costa Twp 3	57	596
Catharine	San Francisco San Francisco 8	68	1280
Catharine	San Francisco San Francisco 8	68	1323
Catharine	San Francisco San Francisco 10	67	233
Catharine	San Francisco San Francisco 10	67	284
Catharine L	San Francisco San Francisco 7	68	1383
Charles	Alameda Brooklyn	55	181
Charles	San Mateo Twp 2	65	132
Charles*	Alameda Oakland	55	57
Chris	Santa Cruz Santa Cruz	66	600
Cornelius	Nevada Bridgeport	61	499
D	Nevada Eureka	61	367
D	Sacramento Ward 4	63	555
Daivd	Klamath Liberty	59	233
Dan	Sacramento Ward 1	63	43
Daniel	Nevada Bridgeport	61	499
Daniel	Nevada Bridgeport	61	501
Daniel	San Francisco San Francisco 8	68	1322
Daniel	San Francisco San Francisco 2	67	746
Danl	Alameda Brooklyn	55	168
Danl	San Francisco San Francisco 10	67	189
David	Klamath Liberty	59	239
Dennis	Klamath Liberty	59	233
Dennis	San Francisco San Francisco 7	68	1355
Dennis	Siskiyou Callahan	69	3
Dennis	Solano Suisan	69	221
Dennis	Tuolumne Jamestown	71	470
E	Butte Cascade	56	693
Ed	Sacramento Ward 1	63	31
Edelfonda	San Luis Obispo San Luis Obispo	65	26
Edelfrida	San Bernardino Santa Inez	64	140
Edward	San Francisco San Francisco 7	68	1390
Edward	San Francisco San Francisco 7	68	1406
Edward	San Francisco San Francisco 5	67	528
Edward	San Francisco San Francisco 1	68	852
Edward	San Francisco San Francisco 1	68	922
Edward	Solano Vallejo	69	267
Edward	Tuolumne Springfield	71	369
Edward	Yuba Bear Rvr	72	1006
Edward O	Yuba Bear Rvr	72	1006
Eliza	Sacramento Ward 1	63	134
Elizabeth	San Francisco San Francisco 10	67	218
Ellen	Alameda Oakland	55	6
Ellen	Sacramento Ward 3	63	447
Ellen	San Francisco San Francisco 8	68	1277
Ellen	San Francisco San Francisco 7	68	1382
Ellen	San Francisco San Francisco 10	67	282
Ellen	Yuba Marysville	72	845
Ellen	Yuba Marysville	72	908
F*	San Francisco San Francisco 9	68	937
Felix	San Francisco San Francisco 1	68	868
Florence	San Francisco San Francisco 8	68	1241
Frances	San Francisco San Francisco 8	68	1264
Francis	Santa Cruz Pescadero	66	646
H	Nevada Washington	61	338
H	Santa Clara Santa Clara	65	522
Henry	Sacramento Ward 4	63	553
Hugh	San Francisco San Francisco 8	68	1288
J	Nevada Grass Valley	61	238
J	Tuolumne Big Oak	71	149
James	Alameda Brooklyn	55	101
James	Alameda Brooklyn	55	90
James	Alameda Brooklyn	55	93
James	Marin Bolinas	60	745
James	Marin San Rafael	60	763
James	Mariposa Twp 3	60	616
James	Plumas Quincy	62	1002
James	Sacramento Georgian	63	345
James	Sacramento San Joaquin	63	359
James	Shasta French G	66	717
James	Sierra La Porte	66	775
James	Sierra St Louis	66	817
James	Sonoma Healdsbu	69	476
James	Tuolumne Sonora	71	232
James	Tuolumne Twp 1	71	232
James C*	El Dorado Coloma	58	1104
James O	Alameda Brooklyn	55	101
James*	Alameda Brooklyn	55	93
Jane	Nevada Nevada	61	283
Jas	Nevada Grass Valley	61	218
Jas	San Francisco San Francisco 2	67	785
Jas	San Francisco San Francisco 1	68	810
Jas	San Francisco San Francisco 1	68	910
Jas*	Butte Ophir	56	767
Jeremeah	San Francisco San Francisco 11	67	107
Jeremiah	Alameda Oakland	55	72
Jeremiah	San Francisco San Francisco 11	67	107
Jerome	San Francisco San Francisco 10	67	310
Jno	Klamath Salmon	59	208
Jno	Sacramento Ward 1	63	151
Jno	Sonoma Sonoma	69	641
Johanna	San Francisco San Francisco 2	67	747
John	Alameda Murray	55	220
John	Amador Twp 2	55	306
John	Marin Bolinas	60	741
John	Marin Cortemad	60	786
John	Napa Napa	61	73
John	Nevada Nevada	61	246
John	Plumas Meadow Valley	62	900
John	San Bernardino Santa Barbara	64	170
John	San Francisco San Francisco 8	68	1244
John	San Francisco San Francisco 7	68	1405
John	San Francisco San Francisco 10	67	294
John	San Francisco San Francisco 2	67	672
John	San Francisco San Francisco 1	68	810
John	San Francisco San Francisco 1	68	873
John	San Francisco San Francisco 1	68	909
John	San Francisco San Francisco 11	67	96
John	Sierra St Louis	66	816
John	Solano Vallejo	69	243
John	Tuolumne Shawsfla	71	415
John	Yuba Marysville	72	929
John	Yuba Marysville	72	953
John C	Contra Costa Twp 3	57	595
John F	San Francisco San Francisco 2	67	749
John T	Nevada Red Dog	61	554
John T	Sacramento Georgian	63	345
Jon	Yuba Marysville	72	953
Jos	San Francisco San Francisco 9	68	1075
Jos	San Francisco San Francisco 2	67	785
Josefa	San Bernardino Santa Barbara	64	203
Julia	San Francisco San Francisco 8	68	1252
Kate	Alameda Oakland	55	
Kate	Alameda Oakland	55	9
Kate	Nevada Nevada	61	255
Lake*	Yuba Marysville	72	880

California 1860 Census Index

Name	County Locale	M653 Roll Page
OBRIEN		
Luke	Yuba Marysville	72 880
M	Nevada Grass Valley	61 225
M	Sacramento Granite	63 233
M A	Alameda Oakland	55 26
Marg	Sacramento Ward 1	63 46
Margarett	Placer Iona Hills	62 881
Margt	Sacramento Ward 1	63 46
Margt	San Francisco San Francisco 7	681329
Margt*	San Francisco San Francisco 7	681329
Martin	San Francisco San Francisco 10	166 67
Mary	Alameda Brooklyn	55 177
Mary	Alameda Oakland	55 29
Mary	Placer Forest H	62 766
Mary	Placer Iona Hills	62 860
Mary	Sacramento Ward 3	63 472
Mary	San Francisco San Francisco 10	182 67
Mary	San Francisco San Francisco 10	244 67
Mary	San Francisco San Francisco 2	67 573
Mary	San Francisco San Francisco 2	67 590
Mary	San Francisco San Francisco 2	67 654
Mary	San Francisco San Francisco 1	68 844
Mary	San Francisco San Francisco 11	89 67
Mary	San Francisco San Francisco 1	68 911
Mary	Shasta Shasta	66 667
Mary	Sonoma Sonoma	69 657
Mary X	San Francisco San Francisco 2	67 661
Mary*	Sonoma Sonoma	69 657
Michael	Sacramento Dry Crk	63 379
Michael	San Francisco San Francisco 10	327 67
Michael	San Francisco San Francisco 3	67 45
Michael	San Joaquin Douglass	64 921
Michael	Santa Cruz Soguel	66 581
Michael	Sierra Scales D	66 804
Michael	Sierra St Louis	66 816
Michael	Siskiyou Callahan	69 8
Michael	Tuolumne Twp 4	71 136
Michael*	Sierra St Louis	66 816
Michl	Sacramento Georgian	63 338
Minna	San Francisco San Francisco 8	681246
Mortimer	San Francisco San Francisco 11	125 67
Nicholas	San Francisco San Francisco 1	68 909
Niel	Alameda Brooklyn	55 119
Owen	San Joaquin Douglass	64 919
P	Sacramento San Joaquin	63 368
P	Sacramento Ward 4	63 589
P	Sutter Bear Rvr	70 824
Patk	Klamath Liberty	59 233
Patk	Napa Napa	61 99
Patk*	Napa Napa	61 99
Patrick	Alameda Brooklyn	55 117
Patrick	Alameda Oakland	55 3
Patrick	Colusa Mansville	57 439
Patrick	Contra Costa Twp 3	57 609
Patrick	Placer Auburn	62 585
Patrick	San Francisco San Francisco 8	681260
Patrick	San Francisco San Francisco 9	68 943
Patrick	San Francisco San Francisco 9	68 959
Patrick	Yuba Bear Rvr	721006
Patrick	Yuba Marysville	72 943
Patrick*	Amador Twp 5	55 329
Patrick*	Yuba Bear Rvr	721006
Peter	Alameda Oakland	55 48
Peter	San Diego San Diego	64 767
Philip	Yuba Rose Bar	72 805
Phillip	San Francisco San Francisco 4	681168
Robt	San Francisco San Francisco 2	67 773
S	Nevada Nevada	61 320
S	Sacramento Ward 3	63 488
Smith	Butte Oro	56 688
Susan	San Francisco San Francisco 10	166 67
T	Sacramento Ward 3	63 488
T	Sutter Butte	70 794
T	Tuolumne Shawsfla	71 389
T*	El Dorado Newtown	58 777
Terlew	Tuolumne Twp 1	71 277
Teslew	Tuolumne Twp 2	71 277
Thomas	Yuba Marysville	72 926
Thos	Calaveras Twp 8	57 85
Thos	Placer Dutch Fl	62 727
Thos	Santa Cruz Santa Cruz	66 600
Thos	Sierra Morristown	661052
Thos S	Butte Oregon	56 642
Timothy	Alameda Oakland	55 67
Timothy	Plumas Quincy	621002
Timothy	San Francisco San Francisco 9	681311
W	San Francisco San Francisco 9	681082
W P	Sacramento Cosumnes	63 385
William	Alameda Brooklyn	55 122
OBRIEN		
William	Klamath Orleans	59 215
William	Santa Cruz Santa Cruz	66 598
William	Santa Cruz Pescadero	66 643
Wm	Sacramento Ward 1	63 120
Wm	Sacramento Ward 1	63 147
Wm	San Francisco San Francisco 2	67 752
Wm	San Francisco San Francisco 1	68 874
Wm	Tuolumne Twp 4	71 126
Wm	Tuolumne Big Oak	71 137
Wm	Tuolumne Twp 4	71 137
Wm C	Sonoma Healdsbu	69 472
Wm*	Yuba Slate Ro	72 697
OBRIER		
Ann*	Alameda Oakland	55 76
Charles*	Alameda Oakland	55 57
Patric	Alameda Oakland	55 45
OBRIETA		
Antonio	San Luis Obispo San Luis Obispo	65 34
OBRIN		
Patrick	Amador Twp 5	55 329
OBRINE		
Jacob	Los Angeles Los Angeles	59 491
James*	Yolo Cache Crk	72 595
John	Amador Twp 5	55 358
John	Yolo Cache Crk	72 595
Mary*	San Francisco San Francisco 4	681138
OBRION		
James C	El Dorado Coloma	581104
Patrick*	El Dorado Coloma	581104
T*	Butte Cascade	56 690
OBROWN		
William	San Francisco San Francisco 9	681065
OBRY		
Margarett*	Placer Michigan	62 821
OBRYAN		
Catherine	San Francisco San Francisco 3	67 28
Henry	San Francisco San Francisco 4	681123
Henry	San Mateo Twp 1	65 64
Henry*	San Francisco San Francisco 4	681123
James	San Francisco San Francisco 9	681085
James	San Francisco San Francisco 9	68 950
James	Santa Clara San Jose	65 341
Jerry	San Francisco San Francisco 9	681032
Jno	San Francisco San Francisco 9	681037
John	Calaveras Twp 5	57 178
John*	Calaveras Twp 6	57 178
Mary	San Francisco San Francisco 6	67 459
Michael	San Francisco San Francisco 3	67 23
Michael*	San Francisco San Francisco 3	67 49
Pat	San Francisco San Francisco 9	681053
Patrick	San Francisco San Francisco 9	681020
Patrick	San Francisco San Francisco 3	67 40
Susan P	Siskiyou Yreka	69 182
Thos	San Mateo Twp 3	65 87
William	San Francisco San Francisco 9	681034
William	San Mateo Twp 2	65 124
OBRYANT		
Dennis	Sierra Twp 5	66 918
Henry*	Monterey Alisal	601033
James	Sonoma Santa Rosa	69 392
Jno W	Sonoma Santa Rosa	69 401
John	Sonoma Santa Rosa	69 398
OBRYEN		
Thomas*	El Dorado Salmon Falls	581054
OBRYENT		
W J*	Yuba Slate Ro	72 703
OBSLEY		
Nuber	Santa Clara Santa Clara	65 522
OBURTON		
Wilson*	Mariposa Twp 1	60 640
OBYRNE		
Rodger	Tuolumne Columbia	71 352
Rodger	Tuolumne Twp 2	71 352
Sarah	Tuolumne Twp 2	71 316
OC		
Wan	Calaveras Twp 6	57 181
Wao*	Calaveras Twp 6	57 181
OCALLAGHAN		
Catharine	San Francisco San Francisco 2	67 663
Danl	Merced Monterey	60 937
Danl	Monterey Monterey	60 937
H H	Sacramento Ward 1	63 144
H H*	Sacramento Ward 1	63 144
OCALLAHAN		
D J	San Francisco San Francisco 2	67 763
OCAMFU		
Wancisca	Los Angeles Los Angeles	59 320
OCAMPO		
Camillo	Los Angeles San Pedro	59 485
Dolores	San Francisco San Francisco 2	67 763
Dolores	San Francisco San Francisco 2	67 763
OCANA		
Bartola Leon	Los Angeles	59 303
	Los Angeles	
Jose M	Los Angeles Los Angeles	59 303
OCANNAN		
M*	Nevada Washington	61 338
OCANNER		
Thomas	Shasta French G	66 716
OCAR		
Wm*	San Francisco San Francisco 1	68 841
OCARROLL		
W	Solano Vallejo	69 249
OCARTER		
J	Nevada Eureka	61 379
S*	Nevada Eureka	61 379
OCASEY		
Rafael	San Francisco San Francisco 2	67 613
OCCENE		
L	Yuba Slate Ro	72 701
OCEEN		
Jas*	Napa Napa	61 71
OCERD		
J*	Nevada Eureka	61 343
OCH		
---	Amador Twp 5	55 342
OCHA		
Francisco	Calaveras Twp 5	57 248
OCHACA		
John	Calaveras Twp 5	57 183
OCHADO		
Julean	San Diego Agua Caliente	64 854
OCHAGNACH		
Jacob	San Joaquin Oneal	64 930
OCHARA		
Jose Maria	Santa Cruz Pajaro	66 574
OCHARROW		
John	Contra Costa Twp 3	57 584
OCHARTER		
John*	Calaveras Twp 6	57 119
OCHAYA		
Manuel	San Diego S Luis R	64 777
OCHEE		
John*	Alameda Brooklyn	55 105
OCHEL		
Peter	Sacramento Ward 3	63 445
OCHELLE		
John	Mariposa Twp 3	60 558
OCHELTREE		
M D	Trinity Douglas	70 978
OCHIO		
Casiniro	Tuolumne Twp 3	71 438
Jacinto	Tuolumne Twp 3	71 438
OCHIR		
Jacinto	Tuolumne Jamestown	71 438
OCHNOU		
Juan	Calaveras Twp 7	57 28
OCHO		
---	Mendocino Calpella	60 828
Bisihito*	Tuolumne Twp 3	71 443
Bisitito	Tuolumne Jamestown	71 443
Jno	San Francisco San Francisco 9	681072
R	Merced Twp 1	60 901
Raphael	Tuolumne Twp 5	71 511
OCHOA		
Manuel	San Francisco San Francisco 8	681253
Vincenta	San Bernardino San Bernadino	64 639
OCHOBA		
Ramono	Los Angeles Azuza	59 276
OCHOCA		
John*	Calaveras Twp 5	57 183
OCHOE		
Raphael	Tuolumne Twp 5	71 497
OCHOER		
Frank	San Joaquin Stockton	641055
OCHOIN		
Frank	Calaveras Twp 10	57 292
OCHOIR		
Vincenta	San Bernardino San Salvador	64 639
OCHOIS		
Jesus	Calaveras Twp 10	57 292
OCHONE		
Rafael	Calaveras Twp 7	57 24
OCHORA		
Hustar	Placer Secret R	62 608
OCHORO		
Phillippe	Los Angeles Elmonte	59 254
OCHOVA		
Phillippe	Los Angeles Azuza	59 278
OCHRA		
F	Stanislaus Emory	70 737
Jose Maria*	Santa Cruz Pajaro	66 574
OCHRIA		
Juan	Santa Cruz Pajaro	66 576
OCHS		
S	San Francisco San Francisco 5	67 529
OCHSENBIEN		
Louise*	San Francisco San Francisco 3	67 17
OCHT		
Jacob	El Dorado Casumnes	581161
OCHUM		
---	Amador Twp 3	55 410

Name	County Locale	M653 Roll Page
OCHUN		
---	Amador Twp 1	55 501
OCHUNE		
---	Amador Twp 1	55 499
---	Amador Twp 1	55 510
---	Amador Twp 1	55 511
OCHURN		
---	Amador Twp 3	55 410
OCIA		
Antonia*	San Mateo Twp 3	65 98
Antonio*	San Mateo Twp 3	65 98
OCIEAJERU		
Antonia*	Calaveras Twp 8	57 61
OCK		
---	Calaveras Twp 5	57 191
---	El Dorado White Oaks	58 1008
---	El Dorado Salmon Falls	58 1054
---	El Dorado Salmon Falls	58 1063
---	El Dorado Kelsey	58 1128
---	El Dorado Casumnes	58 1164
---	El Dorado Diamond	58 801
---	El Dorado Diamond	58 804
---	El Dorado Placerville	58 886
---*	Nevada Red Dog	61 549
---*	Shasta Shasta	66 669
Che	El Dorado Coloma	58 1109
J*	Nevada Red Dog	61 549
OCKANE		
Joseph*	Siskiyou Shasta Valley	69 118
OCKEITT		
Moses	Sierra Twp 7	66 884
OCKERTT		
Moses*	Sierra Twp 7	66 884
OCKMA		
---	Fresno Twp 1	59 28
OCKUTT		
Moses*	Sierra Twp 7	66 884
OCLETREO		
A J	Marin San Rafael	60 770
OCNNELLY		
James	San Joaquin Castoria	64 889
OCNNER		
Michael	Calaveras Twp 5	57 194
OCOMNEL		
Donegal*	Napa Napa	61 105
OCONE		
John*	Monterey Monterey	60 941
OCONEL		
T	Sutter Butte	70 781
OCONELL		
Margaret	Alameda Oakland	55 18
OCONER		
D	Tuolumne Twp 4	71 172
Jane	Marin San Rafael	60 764
Louisa*	San Francisco San Francisco 4	68 1115
P O	Sutter Sutter	70 814
T	Sutter Nicolaus	70 840
OCONI		
John	Calaveras Twp 7	57 34
OCONIO		
James	Calaveras Twp 8	57 82
John	Calaveras Twp 8	57 82
OCONN		
---*	Nevada Grass Valley	61 197
John	Alameda Oakland	55 45
OCONNE		
Thomas	Alameda Oakland	55 74
OCONNEL		
D*	San Francisco San Francisco 5	67 534
Donegal*	Napa Napa	61 105
Donejal	Napa Napa	61 105
John	San Joaquin Stockton	64 1067
L	Shasta Shasta	66 662
Martin	Tuolumne Twp 2	71 278
Mary	San Joaquin Elkhorn	64 987
Q	San Francisco San Francisco 5	67 534
Wm	Santa Clara Redwood	65 448
OCONNELL		
Anthony F	San Francisco 2	67 611
	San Francisco	
Benjamin	Siskiyou Yreka	69 149
C	Shasta French G	66 717
D	San Francisco San Francisco 5	67 534
D S	Shasta French G	66 717
Daniel	Siskiyou Scott Ri	69 77
David	Yuba Bear Rvr	72 1003
Eliza	San Joaquin Stockton	64 1095
Hannorah	Sacramento Ward 3	63 454
James	Sacramento Ward 3	63 454
Jas	Solano Vacaville	69 360
Jas	Sacramento Ward 4	63 588
Jas	San Francisco San Francisco 9	68 1085
Jno	Butte Oregon	56 641
John	Sacramento Ward 1	63 43
John	San Francisco San Francisco 10	226 67

Name	County Locale	M653 Roll Page
OCONNELL		
John	San Francisco San Francisco 12	370 67
John*	San Francisco San Francisco 10	226 67
Jos	San Francisco San Francisco 9	68 1085
Lawrence	San Francisco San Francisco 10	268 67
Lucy	San Francisco San Francisco 7	68 1359
M*	Sacramento Georgian	63 339
M*	Sacramento Ward 1	63 13
Martin	Tuolumne Twp 1	71 278
Mary	San Diego Colorado	64 811
Mary	San Francisco San Francisco 8	68 1297
Mary	San Francisco San Francisco 6	67 439
Michael	Butte Oregon	56 626
Michael	San Francisco San Francisco 10	296 67
Michael*	Butte Oregon	56 626
Morris	Alameda Brooklyn	55 77
Timohty	San Francisco San Francisco 10	226 67
William	Contra Costa Twp 1	57 493
William*	Contra Costa Twp 1	57 525
OCONNER		
B	San Joaquin Stockton	64 1095
B*	San Francisco San Francisco 9	68 1103
Briget	Santa Clara San Jose	65 328
Cas*	Napa Napa	61 85
Catharine	San Francisco San Francisco 10	175 67
Cathe	San Francisco San Francisco 2	67 798
Catherine	Calaveras Twp 9	57 385
Chas*	Napa Napa	61 85
D	Nevada Eureka	61 355
D	Nevada Eureka	61 378
Daniel	San Joaquin Stockton	64 1095
Danl	San Francisco San Francisco 10	321 67
Edward	Yolo Slate Ra	72 709
F	Santa Clara San Jose	65 386
Geo	Santa Clara Gilroy	65 224
Henry	Calaveras Twp 9	57 385
J B	Tehama Pasakent	70 858
J C	Nevada Eureka	61 379
J*	Nevada Grass Valley	61 211
James	San Francisco San Francisco 8	68 1279
James	Shasta French G	66 718
James	Sierra Twp 5	66 923
Jas	Sacramento Lee	63 211
Jas	Yolo Putah	72 585
Johanna	Alameda Oakland	55 5
John	Alameda Brooklyn	55 211
John	Napa Napa	61 98
John	Nevada Nevada	61 317
John	Placer Secret R	62 618
John	Placer Ophir	62 652
John	Placer Dutch Fl	62 734
John	San Francisco San Francisco 7	68 1360
John	San Francisco San Francisco 2	67 664
John	Sierra Pine Grove	66 821
John	Tuolumne Twp 3	71 457
John*	Alameda Oakland	55 50
John*	El Dorado Salmon Falls	58 1034
John*	Stanislaus Buena Village	70 724
Joseph	Santa Clara San Jose	65 359
Louisa	San Francisco San Francisco 4	68 1115
M	San Francisco San Francisco 9	68 960
M	Sonoma Bodega	69 539
M	Sonoma Bodega	69 540
M	Tuolumne Twp 1	71 246
M*	Nevada Grass Valley	61 178
Margaret*	San Francisco 4	68 1144
	San Francisco	
Margt	San Francisco San Francisco 9	68 1013
Margt	San Francisco San Francisco 8	68 1308
Mary	Alameda Washington	55 170
Mary	San Francisco San Francisco 6	67 428
Mary*	Sacramento Ward 1	63 73
Michael	Calaveras Twp 5	57 186
Michael	Calaveras Twp 5	57 194
Michael	Los Angeles San Gabriel	59 413
Michael	San Francisco San Francisco 10	243 67
Michael*	Calaveras Twp 6	57 186
Micheal	El Dorado Greenwood	58 717
Morris	Sacramento Ward 3	63 445
P	Nevada Washington	61 334
Patrick	San Francisco San Francisco 10	322 67
Patrick*	Tulara Twp 3	71 52
Patrik	Plumas Meadow Valley	62 912
Peter	Yolo No E Twp	72 679
Sarah	San Francisco San Francisco 10	181 67

Name	County Locale	M653 Roll Page
OCONNER		
Sarah Miss	San Francisco	10 181 67
Susan	San Francisco San Francisco 1	68 931
T	Sacramento Ward 1	63 18
Thomas	Calaveras Twp 6	57 151
Thomas	San Francisco San Francisco 8	68 1245
Thomas	Shasta French G	66 716
Thomas	Tuolumne Twp 2	71 363
Thos	Butte Chico	56 536
Thos	Butte Bidwell	56 707
Thos	Tehama Cottonwood	70 898
W	San Francisco San Francisco 5	67 520
Wm	Placer Secret R	62 614
Wm	Sacramento Ward 1	63 9
Wm	San Francisco San Francisco 1	68 868
OCONNNELL		
Benjamin	Siskiyou Yreka	69 149
OCONNOL		
Patrick	Sacramento Ward 4	63 584
OCONNOLL		
Jno	Sacramento Ward 4	63 523
OCONNOR		
---	Merced Twp 2	60 917
Ann	San Francisco San Francisco 2	67 633
B	San Francisco San Francisco 9	68 1103
B*	San Francisco San Francisco 9	68 1103
Bridget	San Francisco San Francisco 10	355 67
Bridget	San Francisco San Francisco 9	68 979
C	San Francisco San Francisco 9	68 943
Cathe	San Francisco San Francisco 2	67 798
Catherine	Calaveras Twp 6	57 128
Charles	Placer Michigan	62 835
Charles	Yuba Marysville	72 881
Daniel	Solano Vallejo	69 270
Edwd	Santa Clara Santa Clara	65 482
Ellen	San Francisco San Francisco 2	67 743
Francis	San Francisco San Francisco 7	68 1333
George	Amador Twp 1	55 480
H	Trinity Lewiston	70 966
Hannah	San Francisco San Francisco 9	68 1046
Hannah	San Francisco San Francisco 6	67 415
Hugh	San Francisco San Francisco 8	68 1257
J	Trinity Trinity	70 972
James	El Dorado Georgetown	58 679
James	San Diego Colorado	64 808
James	San Francisco San Francisco 11	130 67
James	San Francisco San Francisco 9	68 942
James	Santa Clara Burnett	65 254
James	Siskiyou Klamath	69 84
James	Trinity Weaverville	70 1066
James*	Siskiyou Klamath	69 84
Joanna	San Francisco San Francisco 2	67 661
Johanna	San Francisco San Francisco 2	67 739
John	Calaveras Twp 6	57 140
John	Placer Auburn	62 570
John	San Francisco San Francisco 11	134 67
John	San Francisco San Francisco 2	67 582
John	Sierra La Porte	66 790
John	Sierra Pine Grove	66 821
John	Siskiyou Yreka	69 140
Joseph	Yuba Marysville	72 959
L P	Placer Iona Hills	62 867
M	San Joaquin Stockton	64 1037
Margaret	San Francisco San Francisco 4	68 1144
Margaret	San Francisco San Francisco 4	68 1222
Margaret	Yuba Marysville	72 975
Margt	San Francisco San Francisco 9	68 979
Mariah	San Francisco San Francisco 11	127 67
Mary	San Francisco San Francisco 11	104 67
Mary	San Francisco San Francisco 7	68 1413
Mary	Yuba Marysville	72 960
Michael	Calaveras Twp 4	57 313
Michael	San Francisco San Francisco 7	68 1348
Michael	San Francisco San Francisco 11	140 67
Michael	San Francisco San Francisco 11	162 67
Michael	San Francisco San Francisco 9	68 944
Michael	Yuba Marysville	72 858
Michael*	San Francisco San Francisco 9	68 944
Michael*	Yuba Marysville	72 858
Morris	San Francisco San Francisco 2	67 739
Moses	San Francisco San Francisco 2	67 581
P	Sacramento Ward 1	63 92
P J	San Francisco San Francisco 8	68 1258
P S	Santa Clara Santa Clara	65 522
Pat	San Francisco San Francisco 9	68 966
Patrick	Placer Dutch Fl	62 734
Patrick	Sierra Whiskey	66 843
Patrick	Trinity Honest B	70 1043

California 1860 Census Index

Name	County Locale	M653 Roll	Page
OCONNOR			
Patrick	Tulara Petersburg	71	52
Peter	San Francisco San Francisco 1	68	865
Peter	Tulara Keyesville	71	58
Peter	Tulara Twp 3	71	58
Peter	Yuba North Ea	72	679
Peter	Yuba Marysville	72	955
R	Nevada Grass Valley	61	235
Richard	El Dorado Coloma	58	1116
Richd	Sacramento Ward 1	63	93
T	San Francisco San Francisco 1	68	891
Thomas	San Francisco San Francisco 8	68	1245
Thomas M	San Francisco	11	123
	San Francisco	67	
Thos	San Francisco San Francisco 1	68	891
Thos	San Francisco San Francisco 9	68	980
Thos	Trinity E Weaver	70	1060
Timothy	Klamath Liberty	59	239
Timothy	San Francisco San Francisco 10		226
		67	
Timothy	San Francisco San Francisco 9	68	948
Timothy	Sierra Whiskey	66	843
William	San Mateo Twp 3	65	95
Wm	Placer Secret R	62	619
OCONOR			
D	Sutter Yuba	70	763
D	Tuolumne Jacksonville	71	172
D O	Tuolumne Twp 4	71	158
Denis	Placer Forest H	62	774
Michael	Sierra Pine Grove	66	829
Thomas	Placer Iona Hills	62	877
OCONTA			
---	Mendocino Big Rvr	60	853
OCOR			
Alphozo	Alameda Brooklyn	55	150
OCORENER			
Michael*	Calaveras Twp 5	57	186
OCORROL			
J A	Los Angeles Tejon	59	524
OCOUD			
O	Nevada Eureka	61	367
OCRAN			
Wm C	Nevada Nevada	61	321
OCRAU			
Wm C*	Nevada Nevada	61	321
OCRAW			
Wm C*	Nevada Nevada	61	321
OCROWELL			
---*	El Dorado Coloma	58	1082
OCRTER			
Henry	Tuolumne Montezuma	71	513
OCSAR			
J	San Francisco San Francisco 2	67	777
OCSTING			
Paul*	San Francisco San Francisco 2	67	596
OCTARIO			
---	Tulara Keyesville	71	67
---	Tulara Keyesville	71	70
OCTAVIA			
Ignaci*	Mariposa Twp 3	60	611
Ignacio	Mariposa Twp 3	60	611
OCTAVIO			
---	Tulara Twp 3	71	67
---	Tulara Twp 3	71	70
OCTHUMAN			
J	Yolo Putah	72	553
OCTITREO			
A J*	Marin San Rafael	60	770
OCTTIMAN			
J*	Yolo Putah	72	553
OCUINER			
Sarah	Solano Vallejo	69	278
OD			
---	Tuolumne Jamestown	71	446
ODA			
Thos	Sacramento Georgian	63	338
ODAIN			
James H	Yuba Bear Rvr	72	996
ODAIR			
Boden*	Yuba Bear Rvr	72	997
ODAM			
Walter	San Francisco San Francisco 9	68	1089
ODANIEL			
Manuel	Santa Clara Almaden	65	273
ODARR			
Michael*	San Francisco San Francisco 3	67	57
ODAUGHERTY			
Michael	Santa Clara Fremont	65	440
Patrick	Santa Clara San Jose	65	359
ODAUGHLITTLE			
Wm*	Tuolumne Twp 1	71	208
ODAUGHTERY			
Geo	Santa Clara San Jose	65	334
ODAVIS			
Coleman*	Sierra Scales D	66	804
ODAY			
Bridget*	San Francisco San Francisco 2	67	772

Name	County Locale	M653 Roll	Page
ODAY			
Dennis J*	San Francisco San Francisco 10		288
		67	
Michl	San Francisco San Francisco 9	68	1063
Pat*	Sacramento Granite	63	260
Thos	San Francisco San Francisco 2	67	782
ODD			
---	Tuolumne Columbia	71	350
---	Tuolumne Twp 3	71	457
---	Tuolumne Twp 3	71	467
---	Tuolumne Twp 1	71	477
Ah	Tuolumne Twp 2	71	350
ODDE			
Bridges	San Francisco San Francisco 10		222
		67	
Bridget	San Francisco San Francisco 10		222
		67	
ODE			
Edward	San Francisco San Francisco 2	67	569
ODEAS			
Ollaannce*	Calaveras Twp 7	57	24
ODEL			
William	Nevada Bridgeport	61	505
ODELL			
A	Mariposa Twp 3	60	554
Chancey E	Humbolt Bucksport	59	161
Cornelius M	Humbolt Pacific	59	129
Daniel	San Joaquin O'Neal	64	1002
Daniel	Tuolumne Montezuma	71	502
David	Sonoma Washington	69	668
E L	Sacramento Cosumnes	63	391
E L*	Sacramento Cosumnes	63	388
Geo E	Calaveras Twp 5	57	227
H W	Sacramento Georgian	63	335
Isaac	Shasta French G	66	720
J*	Sacramento Cosumnes	63	390
James	El Dorado Casumnes	58	1165
James F	Sierra Twp 5	66	925
James T	Sierra Twp 5	66	925
Jno P	Sacramento Ward 3	63	443
John*	Nevada Nevada	61	311
Latham	Butte Chico	56	558
Mary	San Joaquin Stockton	64	1023
Oscar	Sacramento American	63	162
S G	Sonoma Washington	69	666
S*	Sacramento Cosumnes	63	390
Saml	Napa Yount	61	52
Steven*	Sonoma Petaluma	69	591
T B	Sacramento Ward 3	63	487
T*	Sacramento Cosumnes	63	390
W	Shasta Millvill	66	756
William H	Siskiyou Yreka	69	149
Wm H	Calaveras Twp 5	57	227
ODEM			
Bennett*	Monterey San Juan	60	994
ODEMPSIE			
Francis*	El Dorado Coloma	58	1079
ODENDEFF			
James*	Sierra Twp 5	66	923
ODENEAL			
Johnson	El Dorado Kelsey	58	1126
ODENG			
---*	Mariposa Coulterville	60	700
ODER			
Louis*	Amador Twp 5	55	333
ODERK			
Adam*	Placer Virginia	62	664
ODERKIRK			
Peter	Tulara Twp 1	71	112
ODERN			
Bennett	Monterey San Juan	60	994
ODES			
Samuel	Sonoma Bodega	69	525
ODEUYER			
Edward*	Alameda Brooklyn	55	140
ODFERS			
Thomas	Placer Iona Hills	62	873
ODGERS			
James	Sierra Twp 7	66	874
Thomas*	Placer Michigan	62	819
William	Sierra Poker Flats	66	842
ODHEE			
John*	Alameda Brooklyn	55	105
ODIAGO			
Santiago	Monterey San Juan	60	1010
ODILUDA			
Chas	Placer Twp 2	62	660
ODION			
Mary A	San Francisco San Francisco 6	67	445
ODLE			
Calon J*	Yuba Bear Rvr	72	1010
Cellon J*	Yuba Bear Rvr	72	1010
Sellon J	Yuba Bear Rvr	72	1010
ODLUM			
Ellen	San Francisco San Francisco 2	67	628
ODMAN			
Ferdnand	San Francisco San Francisco 2	67	687

Name	County Locale	M653 Roll	Page
ODNEWLAND			
Joseph	Calaveras Twp 7	57	33
ODOCK			
Adam*	Placer Virginia	62	664
ODOHERTY			
John	San Francisco San Francisco 2	67	582
ODON			
Carlos	Los Angeles Los Angeles	59	513
ODONAHOE			
E M	Nevada Nevada	61	294
ODONALD			
Anne	Klamath Liberty	59	236
Bridget	Butte Ophir	56	823
Charles*	Contra Costa Twp 1	57	514
Coleman	Yuba Marysville	72	955
Daniel	Amador Twp 1	55	509
H	Butte Ophir	56	791
J	Nevada Eureka	61	356
M C	San Francisco San Francisco 2	67	593
Patrick	Contra Costa Twp 2	57	553
Theadore*	Sierra St Louis	66	807
Theodore	Sierra St Louis	66	807
Wm	Calaveras Twp 9	57	385
Wm	Nevada Eureka	61	361
Wm*	Nevada Eureka	61	361
ODONCO			
---	San Bernardino Santa Inez	64	137
ODONDER			
Thomas	San Francisco San Francisco 11		132
		67	
ODONELL			
J	El Dorado Placerville	58	869
James	El Dorado Coloma	58	1079
John	San Francisco San Francisco 2	67	626
ODONGHERTY			
J*	Sacramento Ward 1	63	8
ODONNAL			
Johnson	El Dorado Kelsey	58	1126
M C	Nevada Grass Valley	61	235
ODONNALL			
Festy*	Placer Auburn	62	580
Pat	Nevada Nevada	61	243
ODONNEL			
Conn	Tuolumne Twp 3	71	444
Ezra	Plumas Quincy	62	1000
Francis	Plumas Quincy	62	940
James	Sierra La Porte	66	769
John	Santa Clara Alviso	65	402
John	Tuolumne Jamestown	71	425
John	Tuolumne Jamestown	71	444
Joseph	San Joaquin Douglass	64	917
M	Nevada Nevada	61	320
Margt	San Francisco San Francisco 9	68	990
Mary	Nevada Nevada	61	239
Mary	San Francisco San Francisco 5	67	488
P*	Nevada Nevada	61	324
Pat	Yolo Putah	72	586
Pierce	Tuolumne Jamestown	71	422
Sarah	San Francisco San Francisco 8	68	1307
William	Plumas Quincy	62	982
ODONNELE			
John	San Francisco San Francisco 1	68	904
ODONNELL			
Anthony	San Francisco San Francisco 2	67	568
Bernard	San Francisco San Francisco 2	67	623
Chas	Sacramento Ward 1	63	20
Chas	Sacramento Granite	63	256
Comr	Tuolumne Twp 3	71	435
D C	Butte Ophir	56	768
Daniel	Alameda Brooklyn	55	80
Elizabeth	San Francisco San Francisco 10		256
		67	
Frank	Yuba Bear Rvr	72	997
Hannah	Nevada Nevada	61	241
Hugh*	San Francisco San Francisco 2	67	769
James	Calaveras Twp 6	57	157
James	Plumas Quincy	62	981
James	Sacramento Ward 1	63	131
James	Solano Benecia	69	291
Jas	Butte Oregon	56	610
Jas	Butte Oro	56	683
Jas*	San Francisco San Francisco 10		267
		67	
John	Calaveras Twp 5	57	175
John	Calaveras Twp 5	57	175
John	Calaveras Twp 9	57	356
John	Plumas Quincy	62	960
John	San Francisco San Francisco 2	67	521
John	Siskiyou Shasta Valley	69	119
John	Solano Vallejo	69	255
John	Solano Vallejo	69	276
John	Tuolumne Columbia	71	336
John	Tuolumne Jamestown	71	435
John*	Alameda Brooklyn	55	102
John*	Solano Vallejo	69	276
Julia	Sacramento Ward 4	63	610

Name	County Locale	M653 Roll	Page
ODONNELL			
M	Nevada Nevada	61	295
M	Yolo Cottonwood	72	648
Margt	San Francisco San Francisco 8	68	1291
Martin	San Francisco San Francisco 7	68	1435
Mary Mrs	Siskiyou Yreka	69	167
Michael	San Francisco San Francisco 10	67	235
Michael	Tuolumne Twp 3	71	458
Mrs Mary	Siskiyou Yreka	69	167
Neil	Yuba Rose Bar	72	801
Pat	Nevada Nevada	61	243
Patrick	Alameda Brooklyn	55	102
Patrick	Sacramento Ward 1	63	131
Patrick	Sierra Twp 7	66	885
Pedro	Yuba Bear Rvr	72	1004
Peter	Calaveras Twp 5	57	197
R	Tuolumne Twp 3	71	428
Richd	Trinity Weaverville	70	1062
Wm	San Francisco San Francisco 12	67	364
Wm	Santa Clara San Jose	65	339
Wm	Tuolumne Twp 4	71	138
Wm*	Tuolumne Big Oak	71	138
ODONNELLY			
James	San Francisco San Francisco 3	67	40
ODONNER			
Daniel*	Placer Michigan	62	830
David*	Placer Michigan	62	830
Michl	San Francisco San Francisco 9	68	1040
ODONNILL			
M	Nevada Nevada	61	295
ODONOHOE			
E M	Nevada Nevada	61	294
M	Nevada Nevada	61	261
ODORE			
Benjn	San Francisco San Francisco 9	68	989
ODORICO			
---	San Luis Obispo San Luis Obispo	65	14
ODOUGHERTY			
T*	Nevada Eureka	61	367
ODOWD			
John	San Francisco San Francisco 1	68	836
ODOWE			
Michael*	San Francisco San Francisco 3	67	4
ODOWELL			
Eliza	Santa Clara San Jose	65	283
ODRANT			
Hayest*	Alameda Murray	55	218
Hayrst*	Alameda Murray	55	218
ODRENDA			
John	Marin San Rafael	60	767
ODREW			
Chas*	Napa Yount	61	35
ODWAY			
Julius	San Francisco San Francisco 9	68	1053
Mary	San Francisco San Francisco 4	68	1172
ODWYER			
Mary B	San Francisco San Francisco 2	67	660
OEBRIECHER			
Frederick	San Francisco San Francisco 7	68	1366
OEE			
---	Sierra Cox'S Bar	66	950
OEGESTEN			
L*	San Francisco San Francisco 3	67	46
OEHEE			
John*	Alameda Brooklyn	55	105
OEHO			
Orgorn*	Contra Costa Twp 1	57	513
OEHOI			
Jesus*	Calaveras Twp 10	57	292
OEIFS			
---	Sacramento Natonia	63	286
OELER			
Louis*	Amador Twp 5	55	333
OELHOLL			
Jacob	San Francisco San Francisco 3	67	49
OEQUINA			
Francis	Calaveras Twp 7	57	22
OERTLE			
Frank	Sacramento Sutter	63	289
OESTING			
Paul	San Francisco San Francisco 4	68	1221
OESTRICHER			
T*	Tuolumne Columbia	71	315
OETEUM			
J D*	Nevada Eureka	61	348
OETZMANN			
Emile	Yuba Marysville	72	902
OFARNEL			
John*	Placer Auburn	62	586
OFARRALL			
Bridget	Sierra Downieville	66	962
OFARREL			
John*	Placer Auburn	62	586
OFARRELL			
Francis*	San Francisco San Francisco 9	68	982

Name	County Locale	M653 Roll	Page
OFARRELL			
Henry	San Francisco San Francisco 2	67	662
Jas O	Amador Twp 3	55	406
John	Placer Iona Hills	62	882
M*	Siskiyou Scott Va	69	50
Michael	San Francisco San Francisco 8	68	1240
Michael	San Francisco San Francisco 11	67	156
Michael	Yuba Fosters	72	833
Michael*	Yuba Foster B	72	833
Patrick	San Francisco San Francisco 2	67	627
Peter	Butte Ophir	56	758
OFARREN			
James	San Francisco San Francisco 9	68	952
OFARWELL			
Oel*	San Francisco San Francisco 11	67	140
OFEA			
Proguata*	Alameda Murray	55	218
OFEINOND			
Fitz J*	Mariposa Twp 3	60	573
OFERRAL			
Peter*	Butte Oregon	56	642
OFERRALL			
Bridget	Sierra Downieville	66	962
OFERREL			
R H	Butte Chico	56	549
OFERRELL			
R	Butte Chico	56	564
OFF THE CROS			
Alocio*	Yuba Marysville	72	961
OFFELT			
Chas*	Sonoma Petaluma	69	598
OFFER			
---	Butte Kimshaw	56	579
OFFERMAN			
John	Tuolumne Twp 5	71	493
OFFERMANN			
John	Tuolumne Chinese	71	493
OFFETT			
Chas*	Sonoma Petaluma	69	598
OFFICE			
W	Siskiyou Scott Ri	69	76
OFFICER			
James	Yuba Bear Rvr	72	1012
OFFIEL			
W	Siskiyou Scott Ri	69	76
OFFIELD			
John D	Sierra Downieville	66	1029
OFFITT			
Chas	Sonoma Petaluma	69	598
James	San Joaquin Elkhorn	64	961
OFFLING			
C C	Sutter Bear Rvr	70	819
OFFNER			
Jacob	Yuba Rose Bar	72	819
OFFO			
---	Sacramento Ward 1	63	60
OFFORD			
Robert	Tuolumne Twp 3	71	464
OFFUTT			
Z	Nevada Eureka	61	376
OFIELD			
R	Sacramento Lee	63	213
OFIRTZ			
F*	Sacramento Ward 1	63	24
OFLAHERTY			
L	Solano Benecia	69	308
Patrick	Sonoma Mendocino	69	457
Rodger*	Alameda Brooklyn	55	94
OFLARETY			
Richard	Calaveras Twp 7	57	22
OFLARITY			
Thos	San Francisco San Francisco 9	68	1068
OFLYNN			
David	San Francisco San Francisco 2	67	567
OFOY			
Charles	San Francisco San Francisco 8	68	1277
OFRADY			
James	Sierra La Porte	66	789
OFRIJO			
Candido	San Mateo Twp 2	65	134
OFRITZ			
F*	Sacramento Ward 1	63	24
OFUEN			
Frank*	Calaveras Twp 5	57	177
OFULLER			
Julius*	Monterey Alisal	60	1034
OG			
---	El Dorado Coloma	58	1109
Ravade	Sierra Downieville	66	963
OGA			
Manuel	Los Angeles Los Angeles	59	504
OGAN			
Alex	Santa Clara San Jose	65	353
D P W	Sonoma Armally	69	504

Name	County Locale	M653 Roll	Page
OGAN			
James S	Santa Clara San Jose	65	381
John M	Santa Clara San Jose	65	380
Michael	San Francisco San Francisco 7	68	1403
Milly A	Santa Clara San Jose	65	380
OGARD			
Wm B	San Francisco San Francisco 1	68	820
OGARY			
Thos	Amador Twp 2	55	267
OGBORN			
John C	Yolo Putah	72	554
Mary W	Yolo Putah	72	554
OGBURN			
John	Shasta Millvill	66	745
OGDEN			
---	Yuba Marysville	72	850
A J	Yolo Cache Crk	72	631
Chas	Sacramento Ward 1	63	9
D E	Sacramento Ward 4	63	537
Edward	San Mateo Twp 2	65	121
Fred	Napa Napa	61	86
Henry	Sierra Twp 7	66	883
Horace W	Placer Virginia	62	661
J	Nevada Grass Valley	61	195
James	Marin Cortemad	60	792
Jas	Placer Sacramento	62	646
Jesse	Colusa Monroeville	57	446
John	Nevada Nevada	61	247
M	Sierra Pine Grove	66	820
Mary	San Francisco San Francisco 9	68	1074
Randolph	Placer Yankee J	62	778
Richd	San Francisco San Francisco 12	67	396
Robt	Nevada Red Dog	61	538
Rosa	Sacramento Ward 4	63	570
Saml P	Placer Ophir	62	652
Samuel	Sierra St Louis	66	812
Stephen	Placer Forest H	62	798
William C	Yuba Marysville	72	861
Wm	Colusa Grand Island	57	477
Wm	Nevada Nevada	61	273
OGDERS			
William	Sierra Poker Flats	66	842
OGDON			
Aron	Sonoma Bodega	69	537
OGELSBY			
James	San Francisco San Francisco 5	67	486
OGEO			
Jaroel	Yuba Marysville	72	947
OGERA			
Pat	Amador Twp 2	55	261
OGERREL			
R H	Butte Chico	56	549
OGG			
James	Marin Tomales	60	722
John	Santa Clara Santa Clara	65	512
Samuel	Sierra Poker Flats	66	842
OGGEL			
B F	Tuolumne Columbia	71	309
OGIER			
Isaac S K	Los Angeles Los Angeles	59	405
Jas H*	Santa Clara San Jose	65	389
Marcello	Tuolumne Jamestown	71	431
OGILBY			
Samuel	Alameda Brooklyn	55	126
OGILE			
Martha	Sonoma Santa Rosa	69	427
OGILIVIA			
Wm*	San Francisco San Francisco 9	68	1061
OGILLIARDE			
Joseph*	Monterey Alisal	60	1033
OGILVEE			
John	San Francisco San Francisco 7	68	1385
OGILVIE			
F	Calaveras Twp 9	57	409
Mary	San Francisco San Francisco 10	67	235
OGILVIO			
F	Calaveras Twp 9	57	409
OGIN			
Jjosaphine	Contra Costa Twp 1	57	520
OGLE			
David	Santa Clara Gilroy	65	223
David	Trinity Weaverville	70	1078
David A	Tuolumne Twp 2	71	283
Henry	Santa Clara Santa Clara	65	515
J	Sutter Yuba	70	771
Jasper	Solano Vacaville	69	346
Manuala	Placer Michigan	62	814
Martha	Sonoma Santa Rosa	69	427
OGLEBY			
H	Los Angeles Tejon	59	524
OGLESBBY			
James	San Francisco San Francisco 6	67	407
OGLESBY			
William	Placer Michigan	62	825

Name	County Locale	M653 Roll/Page
OGLETHORP		
Louis	Yuba Slate Ro	72 710
OGLETHORPE		
Louis	Yolo Slate Ra	72 710
OGLEY		
Wm G	Tuolumne Sonora	71 237
OGLIVIES		
Alise	Tuolumne Jamestown	71 436
OGLIVIRS		
Alise	Tuolumne Twp 3	71 436
OGLOVER		
Jacob*	Calaveras Twp 10	57 266
OGOUGH		
Henry	San Francisco San Francisco 7	681406
OGRADY		
Colman	San Francisco San Francisco 8	681245
J H	San Joaquin Stockton	641099
James	Sierra La Porte	66 789
Michael	Alameda Oakland	55 1
Ptk	San Francisco San Francisco 10	208 67
William*	Sierra La Porte	66 789
Winfred	San Joaquin Douglass	64 914
OGRE		
Lawrence	Yolo Washington	72 568
OGREN		
John	San Francisco San Francisco 3	67 69
OGRISOL		
John*	Sierra Twp 7	66 912
OGRO		
Jarul	Yuba Marysville	72 947
OGRUDY		
William*	Sierra La Porte	66 789
OGUE		
Hanson	Yuba New York	72 739
OGUIKO		
Michael	Calaveras Twp 6	57 122
OGUR		
Jas H*	Santa Clara San Jose	65 389
OH		
---	Amador Twp 6	55 449
---	Calaveras Twp 5	57 257
---	Calaveras Twp 4	57 306
---	Sacramento Ward 1	63 66
---	San Francisco San Francisco 9	681093
---	Shasta Horsetown	66 702
Chee*	Mariposa Twp 1	60 626
Cher	Mariposa Twp 1	60 626
Gi*	Mariposa Twp 1	60 651
Hing	San Francisco San Francisco 5	67 490
Liu	San Francisco San Francisco 11	160 67
Moy*	Butte Ophir	56 815
Muiz	San Francisco San Francisco 11	159 67
Op	Mariposa Twp 3	60 544
Sally*	Mendocino Big Rock	60 876
Sing	San Francisco San Francisco 11	146 67
Sung	San Francisco San Francisco 11	159 67
Tak	San Francisco San Francisco 5	67 526
Wee	San Francisco San Francisco 11	161 67
Yoa	Yuba Marysville	72 916
OHA		
---	El Dorado Placerville	58 904
OHAIR		
Patrick	El Dorado White Oaks	581027
OHALE		
Ed	Tuolumne Sonora	71 236
Ed	Tuolumne Twp 1	71 236
Henry	Tuolumne Sonora	71 236
Henry	Tuolumne Twp 1	71 236
OHALERAN		
P	Siskiyou Cottonwood	69 108
OHALL		
Daniel*	Monterey Pajaro	601025
S	Nevada Eureka	61 381
OHALLARAN		
D	Tuolumne Jacksonville	71 172
D	Tuolumne Twp 4	71 172
OHALLORAN		
M*	Sacramento Ward 1	63 140
OHAM		
---	Nevada Bridgeport	61 460
Mary	Solano Benecia	69 304
OHAN		
---	El Dorado Kelsey	581131
OHANCOCK		
Francis	San Francisco San Francisco 9	681086
OHANKAY		
John*	Santa Cruz Santa Cruz	66 604
OHANLIN		
Thomas	Contra Costa Twp 1	57 512
OHANLON		
Thomas	Plumas Quincy	62 923

Name	County Locale	M653 Roll/Page
OHANLOW		
Robert T*	Yuba Marysville	72 897
OHAR		
A J*	Mendocino Anderson	60 864
OHARA		
Charles	Yolo Slate Ra	72 703
Charles	Yuba Slate Ro	72 703
Daniel*	Placer Michigan	62 841
Edwd	San Francisco San Francisco 10	284 67
Ellen	Santa Clara Gilroy	65 252
I	Merced Twp 1	60 902
J D	Butte Ophir	56 755
James	Calaveras Twp 8	57 93
James	Tuolumne Twp 4	71 126
James	Yuba Bear Rvr	721002
Jas	Sacramento Natonia	63 286
Jno	Sacramento Ward 4	63 607
John	Solano Benecia	69 316
Margt	San Francisco San Francisco 2	67 666
Mary	San Francisco San Francisco 2	67 675
May A	Sonoma Petaluma	69 617
Mich*	Sacramento Granite	63 267
Michael	Sacramento Granite	63 248
Michael	Sierra Twp 7	66 907
Michael	Yuba Marysville	72 904
Peter	Plumas Quincy	621000
Peter	Plumas Quincy	62 991
Thomas	San Francisco San Francisco 12	362 67
William	Plumas Quincy	62 958
OHARE		
Charles	Alameda Brooklyn	55 134
Edward	Tuolumne Columbia	71 366
Ellen	Colusa Monroeville	57 449
Jas*	Sonoma Petaluma	69 593
John	Sacramento Franklin	63 312
John	San Francisco San Francisco 11	115 67
John	Santa Clara San Jose	65 312
John	Tuolumne Columbia	71 366
Lem	Plumas Quincy	62 965
Michael	San Francisco San Francisco 2	67 662
Patrick	Calaveras Twp 4	57 342
Thomas*	Yolo No E Twp	72 667
OHARN		
Mary*	Solano Benecia	69 304
OHARO		
Jose	San Bernardino San Bernadino	64 670
OHARR		
Patrick	Calaveras Twp 4	57 342
Patrick*	Calaveras Twp 4	57 342
OHARRA		
James	Calaveras Twp 4	57 324
John	Sonoma Vallejo	69 627
John	Tuolumne Columbia	71 348
John	Tuolumne Twp 2	71 350
Pat	Sonoma Petaluma	69 616
Wiliam	Tuolumne Twp 2	71 305
William	Tuolumne Columbia	71 305
OHARRAS		
Alise	Tuolumne Twp 2	71 387
OHARRY		
Bryan	Napa Clear Lake	61 123
OHASSA		
D S	Nevada Nevada	61 268
OHASTI		
John	Calaveras Twp 7	57 47
OHAVE LIM		
---*	Plumas Quincy	62 969
OHAYS		
Jacob*	Siskiyou Yreka	69 151
OHE		
---	Plumas Meadow Valley	62 910
Sow	Shasta Shasta	66 680
OHEAL		
John	Sierra Downieville	66 955
OHEARN		
John	Tuolumne Twp 4	71 150
OHEARNE		
Mary	San Joaquin Stockton	641018
OHEENY		
Michael*	San Francisco San Francisco 1	68 920
OHEILL		
John W	San Francisco San Francisco 2	67 741
OHEINY		
Michael*	San Francisco San Francisco 1	68 920
OHEN		
---	Sierra Twp 7	66 898
Poblo	Tehama Lassen	70 882
OHEONG		
---	Plumas Quincy	62 926
OHERE		
Patrick*	Calaveras Twp 4	57 342
Thomas*	Yolo No E Twp	72 667
OHERN		
J	Nevada Eureka	61 366

Name	County Locale	M653 Roll/Page
OHERN		
J*	Nevada Eureka	61 366
OHERON		
J	Sutter Yuba	70 775
Timothy	San Francisco San Francisco 4	681130
Timothy*	San Francisco San Francisco 4	681130
OHERREN		
Thos*	Butte Ophir	56 764
OHERRIN		
Thomas	San Francisco San Francisco 9	68 952
Thos	Butte Ophir	56 764
OHERSON		
G W	Sonoma Santa Rosa	69 415
OHET		
John	Calaveras Twp 10	57 281
OHIDA		
Maria A	Merced Monterey	60 933
Maria A	Monterey Monterey	60 933
OHILLA		
Juez*	Santa Clara San Jose	65 389
Tues*	Santa Clara San Jose	65 389
OHIM		
J*	Nevada Grass Valley	61 203
OHIN		
Louis	San Francisco San Francisco 8	681304
OHINS		
Francisco*	Monterey Alisal	601043
OHIO		
Mary*	San Francisco San Francisco 1	68 809
OHIRN		
J*	Nevada Grass Valley	61 203
OHIS		
Daniel	Mendocino Big Rvr	60 846
Jacob	Tuolumne Twp 2	71 372
OHLEGER		
George*	Yuba Marysville	72 966
OHLER		
Robert	Solano Vacaville	69 362
OHLEYER		
George*	Yuba Marysville	72 966
OHM		
Chas	Santa Clara Fremont	65 434
Edward F	San Francisco San Francisco 8	681304
Frederick	San Francisco San Francisco 7	681335
Louis*	San Francisco San Francisco 8	681304
OHMEN		
John	Alameda Brooklyn	55 147
OHN		
---	Placer Secret R	62 622
Ting	El Dorado Georgetown	58 756
OHNBUCK		
H T	Siskiyou Scott Ri	69 65
OHNY		
---	Amador Twp 5	55 351
OHO		
---	Placer Secret R	62 624
OHOGK		
---	Placer Virginia	62 665
OHOLLAND		
---*	Nevada Grass Valley	61 179
OHOM		
---*	Placer Rattle Snake	62 602
OHON		
---	Nevada Washington	61 342
OHONE		
---	El Dorado Coloma	581109
Michael	Placer Nicolaus	62 692
OHOVA		
Fanstina	Los Angeles San Jose	59 286
OHOWELL		
Reed	Sonoma Santa Rosa	69 390
OHPENHEIM		
R	Sacramento Ward 1	63 25
OHRAS		
Carolina*	S Buenav	64 210
	San Bernardino	
OHRN		
Fred	San Francisco San Francisco 5	67 494
OHS		
F*	Nevada Eureka	61 347
OHSHANE		
J B	Siskiyou Yreka	69 188
OHUGHES		
---*	San Francisco San Francisco 9	681075
OHUNDLY		
Pat*	Plumas Quincy	62 915
OHUNT		
Thos*	Fresno Twp 3	59 22
OHUR		
Louis*	San Francisco San Francisco 8	681304
OHVAY		
Thomas T	Sacramento Ward 1	63 132
OI		
Win	Yuba Long Bar	72 762
OIBLE		
Julius	Sacramento Ward 3	63 474

California 1860 Census Index

Name	County Locale	M653 RollPage
OICI		
---	Calaveras Twp 6	57 137
OIE		
---	Placer Rattle Snake	62 627
OIHOA		
Manuel*	Contra Costa Twp 3	57 601
OIK		
Charles*	Yuba Marysville	72 911
OILER		
John L	Solano Fairfield	69 197
OILHOLL		
Jacob	San Francisco San Francisco 3	67 49
OIMICK		
C*	Stanislaus Branch	70 700
OIN		
---	Calaveras Twp 6	57 176
---	San Francisco San Francisco 9	681094
OIRISH		
Henry*	Mendocino Arrana	60 856
OISTER		
S	Siskiyou Klamath	69 94
OIVEN		
Patrick	Sierra Twp 7	66 912
OIY		
---*	Amador Twp 2	55 328
OJABERS		
Victor	Tuolumne Twp 2	71 335
OJEDA		
Bernarbel	Los Angeles Los Angeles	59 356
Florencio	San Bernardino Santa Barbara	64 170
Jesus	Los Angeles Los Angeles	59 303
OJO		
Brcenta	Los Angeles Azuza	59 277
OK		
---	San Francisco San Francisco 4	681189
---	San Francisco San Francisco 4	681199
---	Sierra Downieville	661008
---	Sierra Cox'S Bar	66 951
---*	Sierra Downieville	661008
George	Sierra Gibsonville	66 859
Sun	San Francisco San Francisco 4	681208
OKANE		
John	San Francisco San Francisco 7	681349
John	San Francisco San Francisco 5	67 493
John*	San Francisco San Francisco 7	681385
Joseph	Siskiyou Shasta Valley	69 118
OKEAF		
David	Sonoma Petaluma	69 557
Denis	Nevada Rough &	61 395
M	El Dorado Placerville	58 869
OKEEF		
D*	Nevada Eureka	61 361
Isabella	Nevada Eureka	61 361
John*	Contra Costa Twp 1	57 486
Wm	Sierra Downieville	661006
OKEEFA		
Mich*	Sacramento Granite	63 267
OKEEFE		
---	San Francisco San Francisco 10	254 67
Andrew	Yuba Marysville	72 958
Arthur	Solano Vallejo	69 256
C	Tuolumne Twp 2	71 367
Catherine	Los Angeles Los Angeles	59 336
Danl	San Francisco San Francisco 10	254 67
Danl	San Francisco San Francisco 10	258 67
Danl	Trinity Weaverville	701069
Dennis	Trinity Weaverville	701067
Ellen	Solano Vallejo	69 270
Geronomo	Santa Barbara San Bernardino	64 204
H K	San Francisco San Francisco 6	67 446
Honora	Los Angeles Los Angeles	59 392
Jas	San Francisco San Francisco 1	68 855
Jeremiah	San Francisco San Francisco 11	131 67
Jeremiah	Siskiyou Callahan	69 7
Johanna	San Francisco San Francisco 2	67 751
John	Alameda Oakland	55 53
John	Tuolumne Montezuma	71 503
John M	Tuolumne Columbia	71 328
John M*	Tuolumne Twp 2	71 328
Maj	Sacramento Ward 1	63 18
Margt	San Francisco San Francisco 9	681029
Mary	San Francisco San Francisco 10	167 67
Mary	Solano Vallejo	69 256
Mary C	Yuba Marysville	72 959
May	Sacramento Ward 1	63 18
Mich*	Sacramento Granite	63 267
P B	Trinity Weaverville	701079
Patrick	San Joaquin Castoria	64 891
Thomas	San Francisco San Francisco 8	681252
Timothy	San Francisco San Francisco 2	67 583

Name	County Locale	M653 RollPage
OKEEFEE		
Ann*	Sacramento Ward 1	63 76
OKEEFER		
Ann*	Sacramento Ward 1	63 76
OKEEFFE		
Jeremiah	Siskiyou Callahan	69 7
OKEEFS		
C*	Tuolumne Springfield	71 367
OKEEN		
Jas*	Napa Napa	61 71
OKEEPE		
John M*	Tuolumne Twp 2	71 328
OKEFFE		
John	Trinity Douglas	70 979
Timothy	El Dorado Kelsey	581132
OKEIF		
Catharine	San Francisco San Francisco 6	67 473
D	Nevada Eureka	61 361
Joseph	San Francisco San Francisco 7	681394
OKEIFF		
Dennis	Sierra Monte Crk	661037
OKEITH		
Bridget	San Francisco San Francisco 9	681015
Bridget	San Francisco San Francisco 9	68 942
Daniel	San Francisco San Francisco 1	68 937
OKELLY		
James*	Tuolumne Twp 6	71 534
OKEY		
H B	Siskiyou Cottonwoood	69 107
Thom Jason*	Nevada Bridgeport	61 466
Thompson	Nevada Bridgeport	61 466
OKILEY		
C	Nevada Grass Valley	61 160
OKMAR		
---	Fresno Twp 1	59 27
OKOSO		
---	Fresno Twp 1	59 118
OKOUKE		
Wm	Tuolumne Twp 2	71 277
OKUFA		
Mich	Sacramento Granite	63 267
OL		
Chee*	Mariposa Twp 1	60 626
Sneden	Tuolumne Twp 1	71 201
OLA		
Ocova	Los Angeles San Jose	59 284
OLACHE		
Otaliano	San Bernardino San Bernadino	64 666
OLAHAM		
J K	Siskiyou Klamath	69 84
OLAIG		
J B*	Nevada Nevada	61 320
OLAIY		
J B*	Nevada Nevada	61 320
OLALL		
S	Amador Twp 6	55 437
OLANDO		
Peter	Tuolumne Twp 2	71 291
Rengio	Contra Costa Twp 1	57 495
OLANDTE		
Nicholas	San Francisco San Francisco 4	681123
OLANSKY		
---	Sacramento San Joaquin	63 355
OLARE		
Jesus	Santa Clara San Jose	65 309
OLARTE		
Ygnacio	Monterey Monterey	60 939
Ygnasio	Merced Monterey	60 939
OLARY		
J B	Nevada Nevada	61 320
OLAS		
F*	Nevada Eureka	61 347
William	Calaveras Twp 8	57 79
OLATTE		
Juan	Contra Costa Twp 1	57 493
OLAUGHLAN		
Mary	San Francisco San Francisco 11	156 67
OLAUGHLIN		
John	Sierra Downieville	66 963
Stephen*	Butte Oregon	56 630
Thos	Alameda Brooklyn	55 202
OLAY		
Alender*	San Francisco San Francisco 9	681089
Aleuder*	San Francisco San Francisco 9	681089
Samuel*	Placer Iona Hills	62 894
OLBIS		
H	El Dorado Placerville	58 865
OLBORDAKA		
---	Fresno Twp 2	59 59
OLBRICHT		
A	San Francisco San Francisco 7	681374
OLCALF		
Robert	Sacramento Franklin	63 329
OLCELLO		
Morea	Tuolumne Twp 5	71 495

Name	County Locale	M653 RollPage
OLCOMB		
B	El Dorado Georgetown	58 688
OLCOTT		
Raswell	Siskiyou Yreka	69 136
Roswell	Siskiyou Yreka	69 136
OLD ANDRES		
---	Tulara Visalia	71 114
OLD BEADS		
---	Tulara Visalia	71 114
OLD BILL		
---	Tulara Twp 2	71 40
OLD BUCKSKIN		
---	Tulara Twp 1	71 115
OLD CHARLEY		
---	Tulara Twp 2	71 19
---*	Tulara Visalia	71 3
OLD DOC		
---	Sacramento Cosumnes	63 406
OLD ELK		
---	Tulara Twp 1	71 119
OLD FOX		
---	Tulara Twp 1	71 119
OLD HARDY		
---	Tulara Twp 2	71 37
OLD MAN		
---	Fresno Twp 1	59 53
---	Sacramento Cosumnes	63 407
OLD MISSION		
---	Tulara Visalia	71 120
OLD NICK		
---	Fresno Twp 3	59 8
OLD NUSSION		
---	Tulara Twp 1	71 120
OLD SAL		
---	Fresno Twp 3	59 7
OLD SERAPIPE		
---	Tulara Twp 1	71 119
OLD SERAPPA		
---	Tulara Twp 1	71 119
OLD STURGEON		
---	Tulara Twp 1	71 121
OLD WASH		
---	Tulara Twp 1	71 117
OLD		
C E E	Sierra Downieville	66 975
Charley*	Tulara Visalia	71 3
W D*	Nevada Grass Valley	61 192
OLDBAR		
Moile*	Calaveras Twp 6	57 155
OLDBRAS		
Moile*	Calaveras Twp 6	57 155
OLDEMAN		
Jas N	Napa Napa	61 85
Oscar*	Yuba Long Bar	72 752
OLDEN		
Ida	San Francisco San Francisco 4	681218
Joseph	San Mateo Twp 3	65 87
OLDENBATTLE		
George	San Francisco San Francisco 3	67 65
OLDERNAN		
Oscar*	Yuba Long Bar	72 752
OLDESMAN		
Oscar	Yuba Long Bar	72 752
OLDFELDT		
Sally	Sacramento Ward 1	63 119
OLDFIELD		
Colin	Butte Hamilton	56 526
F H	San Francisco San Francisco 2	67 587
Jonathan	Sierra Downieville	661020
Mary A	Yuba Marysville	72 929
Salley	Sacramento Ward 1	63 119
OLDFRED		
C C	Calaveras Twp 9	57 415
OLDHAM		
Alice	Yuba Rose Bar	72 813
C W	San Francisco San Francisco 2	67 805
Chas	San Francisco San Francisco 2	67 795
Frank	Santa Clara Fremont	65 423
G W	Santa Clara Santa Clara	65 503
J D	Yuba Long Bar	72 750
James	Yuba Marysville	72 941
Jno T	San Joaquin Stockton	641047
John	Calaveras Twp 7	57 35
John	Siskiyou Shasta Valley	69 119
Mary	Nevada Bloomfield	61 523
Patrick	Santa Cruz Santa Cruz	66 629
S	Siskiyou Scott Va	69 26
OLDHAN		
Caleb	Calaveras Twp 8	57 86
OLDIN		
John	Butte Bidwell	56 713
S J	El Dorado Georgetown	58 689
OLDMAN		
Isaac	San Francisco San Francisco 2	67 761
Jas W	Napa Napa	61 85
OLDMER		
Martin	San Francisco San Francisco 3	67 12

California 1860 Census Index

Name	County Locale	M653 Roll	Page
OLDRICH			
John N	Tuolumne Chinese	71	494
OLDS			
B S	Butte Cascade	56	693
Chena	Yolo Cache Crk	72	617
China	Yolo Cache	72	617
Daniel	Marin Bolinas	60	732
Daniel	Marin Bolinas	60	733
Edward	Yuba Marysville	72	905
James	Contra Costa Twp 3	57	605
Julia	San Francisco San Francisco 2	67	715
Levis	Yolo Cache Crk	72	617
Lewis	Yolo Cache	72	617
Louis	Mendocino Arrana	60	859
N H	Marin Bolinas	60	733
Orlando	Napa Hot Springs	61	21
W H	Solano Vacaville	69	340
William	Contra Costa Twp 1	57	484
OLDSON			
G W	San Francisco San Francisco 5	67	482
Jno	Alameda Brooklyn	55	188
N	San Francisco San Francisco 5	67	536
OLDSTONE			
Samuel	San Francisco San Francisco 4	681160	
OLDTRAN			
Moile	Calaveras Twp 6	57	155
OLDWAY			
Robert J	San Francisco San Francisco 7	681336	
OLE LEE			
---	Sierra Twp 7	66	916
OLEA			
Ceseno	Calaveras Twp 4	57	332
OLEARY			
Daniel	Sierra Whiskey	66	845
Dennis	San Francisco San Francisco 8	681275	
Dennis*	San Francisco San Francisco 8	681275	
J	Sacramento Ward 1	63	80
J*	Sacramento Ward 1	63	80
James	Plumas Meadow Valley	62	928
John	Placer Yankee J	62	758
John	Santa Clara Santa Clara	65	512
John*	El Dorado Coloma	581078	
John*	El Dorado Diamond	58	765
M*	San Francisco San Francisco 10	313 67	
Mary	Butte Ophir	56	770
Mary	Santa Clara Alviso	65	405
Patrick	San Francisco San Francisco 7	681367	
T	Merced Twp 2	60	917
Thomas	Alameda Brooklyn	55	102
Thomas	Alameda Brooklyn	55	103
OLEAS			
Cesario	Calaveras Twp 4	57	332
OLEC			
---	Del Norte Klamath	58	656
OLECSE			
George*	Mariposa Twp 1	60	636
OLEE			
---	Yuba Bear Rvr	721014	
---	Yuba Bear Rvr	721015	
OLEESE			
Andrew	Mariposa Twp 1	60	636
OLEMER			
Antonio	Marin Cortemad	60	754
OLEN			
C W	Placer Michigan	62	839
Nobut	Yolo Cottonwoood	72	557
Robert	Yolo Cottonwoood	72	557
OLENADA			
Felix	San Francisco San Francisco 2	67	798
OLENDER			
F*	Tehama Red Bluff	70	914
OLENDROF			
W D	Tehama Red Bluff	70	914
OLENGHLEN			
M	Siskiyou Scott Va	69	54
OLENSE			
P	Siskiyou Scott Ri	69	74
OLENSTEAD			
Sarah	Sacramento Granite	63	263
OLEOADI			
Bernado	Calaveras Twp 5	57	203
OLEOMER			
Catherine*	Calaveras Twp 6	57	128
OLEONNIS			
Patrick	Calaveras Twp 6	57	118
OLEOUNOR			
Bridget*	Calaveras Twp 6	57	118
OLEPHANT			
H D	Butte Oro	56	683
OLEPHUNT			
James	Solano Fremont	69	385
OLER			
---	Trinity Lewiston	70	961
OLERADA			
Felix	San Francisco San Francisco 2	67	798

Name	County Locale	M653 Roll	Page
OLERARES			
Benereta	San Francisco San Francisco 4	681155	
OLERELL			
Wm Geo*	San Francisco San Francisco 2	67	723
OLESERA			
Marcos	San Bernardino Santa Ba	64	216
Marcos	San Bernardino S Buenav	64	217
OLESERIO			
Manano	Santa Inez	64	144
	San Bernardino		
OLESON			
Antroph*	Sierra Downieville	66	957
Autroph	Sierra Downieville	66	957
OLESTERMAN			
J	Siskiyou Scott Ri	69	69
OLEUSE			
P*	Siskiyou Scott Ri	69	74
OLEVA			
Gatriel	Monterey San Juan	60	977
Jacob*	Yuba Long Bar	72	747
OLEVADE			
Manuel	Mariposa Coulterville	60	690
OLEVADO			
Bernado	Calaveras Twp 5	57	203
OLEVELL			
Wm Geo*	San Francisco San Francisco 2	67	723
OLEVER			
Jacob*	Yuba Long Bar	72	747
OLEVERA			
Jose	San Mateo Twp 2	65	134
OLEVES			
Bernardo	Santa Cruz Pajaro	66	565
Carnacion	Santa Cruz Pajaro	66	565
OLEVIR			
John	San Francisco San Francisco 3	67	79
OLEWA			
Emily	Mariposa Twp 1	60	625
OLFENY			
John	Sacramento Natonia	63	283
OLFERD			
M C	San Francisco San Francisco 7	681399	
OLFFIN			
C	Tuolumne Big Oak	71	145
OLFIELD			
John	El Dorado Placerville	58	928
OLGBACKER			
Martin	Yuba Marysville	72	957
OLGER			
Maria A	San Luis Obispo San Luis Obispo	65	35
OLH			
W	Shasta Shasta	66	677
OLHAL			
---	Mendocino Round Va	60	883
OLHICK			
W D	El Dorado Coloma	581082	
OLIE			
---	Sierra Twp 5	66	932
OLIEM			
Frank	Mariposa Twp 1	60	651
OLIF			
Eugene M	San Francisco San Francisco 9	681020	
OLIMPA			
---	Marin San Rafael	60	772
OLIN			
C H	Nevada Grass Valley	61	217
L B	Nevada Grass Valley	61	217
Simeon	Nevada Eureka	61	345
Simon	Nevada Eureka	61	345
OLINDER			
F*	Tehama Red Bluff	70	914
OLINGEN			
Arch*	Nevada Bloomfield	61	508
OLINGER			
A F	Santa Clara Santa Clara	65	488
Arch*	Nevada Bloomfield	61	508
George	Solano Vacaville	69	321
J W*	Nevada Red Dog	61	557
James	Nevada Bloomfield	61	513
OLINGS			
William	Placer Forest H	62	804
OLINSKO			
---	Sacramento Cosumnes	63	407
OLINSTEAD			
O A	Sonoma Bodega	69	534
OLIO			
---*	Sierra Twp 5	66	932
OLIPHANT			
H D	Butte Oro	56	683
Henry	Stanislaus Emory	70	753
James	Solano Fremont	69	385
James	Tuolumne Montezuma	71	508
OLIRAS			
Carolina	San Bernardino Santa Ba	64	210
Felipe*	San Bernardino S Buenav	64	217
Getindes*	Santa Barbara	64	174
	San Bernardino		

Name	County Locale	M653 Roll	Page
OLIRAS			
Jose	San Bernardino Santa Barbara	64	184
Louis	San Bernardino Santa Barbara	64	174
Ramundo*	S Buenav	64	216
	San Bernardino		
OLIRD			
A S*	Nevada Nevada	61	241
OLIRSUM			
John*	Shasta Shasta	66	682
OLIRUNN			
John*	Shasta Shasta	66	682
OLIS			
F	Nevada Eureka	61	347
OLISASHER			
W	Nevada Eureka	61	378
OLISBY			
John*	El Dorado Coloma	581076	
OLIVA			
Caesar	San Francisco San Francisco 10	257 67	
Dominico	San Francisco San Francisco 11	124 67	
OLIVAI			
Elyjo*	Contra Costa Twp 3	57	615
OLIVANTE			
G	Shasta Millvill	66	756
OLIVARA			
Gaudalope	Los Angeles Elmonte	59	246
Walupa	Los Angeles Elmonte	59	260
OLIVARD			
Ramondo	Contra Costa Twp 1	57	495
OLIVARES			
Jesus	San Luis Obispo San Luis Obispo	65	6
Jose V	Los Angeles Azuza	59	277
OLIVAS			
Antonia	Los Angeles Santa Ana	59	459
Antonio	San Bernardino Santa Ba	64	218
Antonio	San Bernardino S Buenav	64	219
Dominga	Los Angeles Los Angeles	59	314
Getindes*	Santa Barbara	64	174
	San Bernardino		
Guadalupe	Santa Clara Gilroy	65	229
Guellermo	Santa Inez	64	140
	San Bernardino		
Jose	Los Angeles Los Angeles	59	400
Jose	San Bernardino S Timate	64	687
Jose	Santa Clara Gilroy	65	228
Jose	Santa Clara Almaden	65	275
Jose A	Los Angeles Los Angeles	59	299
Jose D	Los Angeles San Gabriel	59	419
Jose De La Cruz	San Gabriel	59	416
	Los Angeles		
Jose M	Los Angeles Los Nieto	59	428
Juan	Los Angeles Azuza	59	274
Juan	Los Angeles Los Angeles	59	373
Juan	San Bernardino Santa Barbara	64	185
Louis	San Bernardino Santa Ba	64	216
Maria De Los A	San Gabriel	59	420
	Los Angeles		
Maria J	San Francisco San Francisco 2	67	690
Matias	Los Angeles San Juan	59	476
Nicolas	San Bernardino Santa Ba	64	216
Pedro	Los Angeles San Jose	59	285
Ramon	Los Angeles Los Angeles	59	299
Ramundo	Santa Ba	64	216
	San Bernardino		
OLIVATO			
Jesus	Santa Clara San Jose	65	296
OLIVE			
A S	Nevada Nevada	61	241
Ellen	San Francisco San Francisco 2	67	763
Geo	Klamath Trinidad	59	221
Josephine	Yuba Marysville	72	903
Maria	Santa Cruz Watsonville	66	540
T	Sacramento Cosumnes	63	393
OLIVELL			
Wm Geo	San Francisco San Francisco 2	67	723
OLIVER			
A	El Dorado Diamond	58	804
A	Siskiyou Scott Va	69	40
A	Yolo Washington	72	601
A J	Stanislaus Branch	70	706
A R	Sierra Poker Flats	66	841
Allen	Tuolumne Twp 3	71	422
C F	Sacramento Ward 3	63	425
C H	Nevada Grass Valley	61	193
Chas F	Sacramento Ward 1	63	18
D	Butte Chico	56	531
D B	El Dorado White Oaks	581009	
Daniel	Tuolumne Twp 3	71	422
David	Sacramento Ward 3	63	460
David	Solano Vacaville	69	354
Dennis J	San Francisco San Francisco 8	681298	
Dixon	Butte Chico	56	532
Domingo	Tuolumne Twp 2	71	314
E	Sacramento Cosumnes	63	404

Name	County Locale	M653 RollPage
OLIVER		
F	Nevada Nevada	61 276
Fisher	Los Angeles San Gabriel	59 413
G B	El Dorado Coloma	581071
Geo	Merced Monterey	60 932
Geo	Monterey Monterey	60 932
Geo W	Del Norte Crescent	58 628
H R	Sierra Poker Flats	66 841
H S	Shasta Millvill	66 755
J	Nevada Nevada	61 276
J B	Butte Kimshaw	56 589
J M	Sonoma Armally	69 508
J P	El Dorado Salmon Falls	581049
J W	Siskiyou Scott Va	69 40
J Y	Butte Oregon	56 632
Jacob	Tuolumne Twp 1	71 259
James	Colusa Monroeville	57 453
James	Mendocino Arrana	60 858
James	Siskiyou Yreka	69 141
James	Solano Suisan	69 207
Jas	Sacramento Franklin	63 309
Jas R	Butte Oregon	56 640
Jno G	Butte Chico	56 540
John	Sacramento Sutter	63 307
John	San Bernardino San Bernadino	64 674
John	San Francisco San Francisco 9	681082
John	San Francisco San Francisco 11	158
		67
John	San Francisco San Francisco 3	67 79
John	Sierra Downieville	661011
John	Sierra Pine Grove	66 835
John	Solano Vacaville	69 367
John	Tehama Red Bluff	70 915
John	Yuba Marysville	72 854
John B	San Francisco San Francisco 8	681298
Joseph	Sierra Downieville	661023
Juan Maria	Tulara Twp 3	71 43
L	El Dorado Diamond	58 804
L	Sutter Bear Rvr	70 826
Lizzie	Sacramento Ward 1	63 147
Louis	Shasta Millvill	66 744
M	San Francisco San Francisco 5	67 538
Malcom	Tuolumne Twp 4	71 422
Manuel	Mariposa Twp 3	60 611
Martin	Santa Cruz Pajaro	66 571
McKinney	San Francisco San Francisco 7	681340
Owen	Alameda Oakland	55 49
P Y	Butte Oregon	56 632
Pierre	Amador Twp 3	55 403
R	Trinity Lewiston	70 953
Richard	Plumas Quincy	621006
Robert	Sierra Twp 7	66 894
Robrt	San Francisco San Francisco 1	68 921
Robt	Butte Mountain	56 739
Robt	Napa Clear Lake	61 135
Saml	Los Angeles Tejon	59 536
Sarah	Sacramento Sutter	63 309
Solomon	Tuolumne Twp 2	71 418
Spartiria	San Luis Obispo	65 41
	San Luis Obispo	
Thomas	El Dorado Union	581090
Thomas	San Francisco San Francisco 5	67 550
Thomas E	Tuolumne Twp 5	71 520
Thomas N	Tuolumne Chinese	71 520
Ths	San Francisco San Francisco 5	67 480
W C	Napa Clear Lake	61 124
Wallie	Plumas Meadow Valley	62 933
Warren	Siskiyou Scott Va	69 40
William	El Dorado Coloma	581121
William	Mendocino Arrana	60 859
William	Plumas Quincy	62 947
William	San Francisco San Francisco 4	681164
William	Santa Cruz Soguel	66 591
William	Tuolumne Sonora	71 245
William H	Sierra La Porte	66 765
William J	Yuba Bear Rvr	721003
William M	San Joaquin Elkhorn	64 956
Wm	San Francisco San Francisco 1	68 920
Wm A	Tuolumne Twp 3	71 422
OLIVERA		
---	Tulara Twp 3	71 67
---	Tulara Keyesville	71 70
Benuto	Marin Cortemad	60 781
Besuto	Marin Cortemad	60 781
Cencoon	Alameda Oakland	55 3
Cencoun*	Alameda Oakland	55 3
Concepcion	Santa Barbara	64 164
	San Bernardino	
Delores*	Tulara Twp 3	71 43
Diego	San Bernardino Santa Inez	64 139
Esterim	San Bernardino Santa Barbara	64 195
Faurtivir	San Luis Obispo	65 45
	San Luis Obispo	
Jesus	San Bernardino Santa Barbara	64 192
Jose	San Luis Obispo San Luis Obispo	65 38
Jose An	San Bernardino Santa Barbara	64 194

Name	County Locale	M653 RollPage
Jose R	San Mateo Twp 2	65 133
Juan	San Bernardino Santa Barbara	64 180
Juan De D	Los Angeles Santa Ana	59 455
Juan M	Los Angeles Los Angeles	59 381
Juan Ma	San Bernardino Santa Barbara	64 199
Juan Maria	Tulara Sinks Te	71 43
Juima	Santa Clara San Jose	65 323
Louis	Alameda Brooklyn	55 77
Manuel	Alameda Oakland	55 48
Martin	Los Angeles Los Angeles	59 384
Pedro	San Bernardino Santa Inez	64 141
Rafail	San Bernardino Santa Barbara	64 165
Ramon	San Bernardino Santa Barbara	64 193
OLIVERAS		
Ascension	Los Angeles San Pedro	59 478
Faliz*	San Francisco San Francisco 3	67 3
Jose	Los Angeles Santa Ana	59 458
Maria J	Los Angeles San Juan	59 471
Pulgueria	Los Angeles Los Angeles	59 311
OLIVERES		
Maria A	Los Angeles San Juan	59 471
OLIVERI		
Elyjo*	Contra Costa Twp 3	57 615
OLIVERJOSEPH		
Hoyt	Sierra Downieville	661023
OLIVERO		
John	Tuolumne Twp 1	71 255
OLIVERS		
John	Yuba Marysville	72 859
OLIVES		
Jno G*	Butte Chico	56 540
John	San Francisco San Francisco 2	67 672
John	Shasta Shasta	66 757
OLIVGER		
I W*	Nevada Red Dog	61 557
OLIVIA		
F	Tuolumne Twp 2	71 402
OLIVIER		
George	Yuba Marysville	72 906
OLIVIRAS		
Falez	San Francisco San Francisco 3	67 3
OLIVIS		
Tomas	Los Angeles Los Angeles	59 509
OLIVO		
A S*	Nevada Nevada	61 241
John H	Stanislaus Emory	70 757
OLIVORA		
Jesus	San Bernardino Santa Barbara	64 192
OLIVRA		
Juan P	San Mateo Twp 2	65 131
OLK		
W*	Shasta Shasta	66 677
OLKAIVETT		
Joseph	San Bernardino San Salvador	64 661
OLLASSON		
Peter	Tuolumne Sonora	71 194
OLLAY		
Benjamin	Santa Cruz Pescadero	66 648
OLLER		
J	Solano Vacaville	69 332
OLLEY		
S G	Nevada Grass Valley	61 150
OLLGEA		
Alexis*	Yuba New York	72 722
OLLGEN		
Alexis*	Yuba New York	72 722
OLLINGER		
Margret	Santa Cruz Pajaro	66 534
Thomas	Santa Cruz Soguel	66 582
OLLIVER		
A	Amador Twp 6	55 425
M B	Amador Twp 7	55 419
OLLMAN		
George	Marin S Antoni	60 711
OLLNER		
Margaret*	San Mateo Twp 3	65 85
OLLO		
Auswa	Tuolumne Twp 2	71 283
OLLSTON		
Peter	San Francisco San Francisco 9	681080
OLLY		
C T	Nevada Grass Valley	61 217
OLLYEA		
Pierre	Yuba New York	72 722
OLLYEN		
Alexis*	Yuba New York	72 722
Perri	Yuba New York	72 722
OLMAN		
Harris	San Francisco San Francisco 1	68 908
OLMEDO		
Feiliciano	Santa Clara Almaden	65 267
OLMER		
A	Nevada Nevada	61 252
Behenio	Marin Cortemad	60 755
OLMSEAD		
A	Mariposa Twp 1	60 629

Name	County Locale	M653 RollPage
OLMSTEAD		
Cornelius	Contra Costa Twp 2	57 545
Eliphalet	Sacramento Centre	63 178
J	Sacramento Granite	63 229
James	Yuba Rose Bar	72 788
John	San Francisco San Francisco 1	68 914
Marvin	Yuba Long Bar	72 754
O	Sacramento Ward 4	63 515
Plaffet*	Siskiyou Yreka	69 136
Plasset*	Siskiyou Yreka	69 136
Rachael	Yuba Rose Bar	72 812
Sarah	Sacramento Granite	63 263
W C	Amador Twp 3	55 407
Wm T	Humbolt Eel Rvr	59 151
OLMSTED		
James M	San Francisco San Francisco 7	681338
Robt B	San Luis Obispo San Luis Obispo	65 6
Sarah	Napa Napa	61 65
OLNEY		
---	San Francisco San Francisco 9	681067
Augustus	Mariposa Coulterville	60 686
H	San Francisco San Francisco 9	681067
James N	San Francisco San Francisco 8	681318
OLNGRAY		
Charles*	San Francisco San Francisco 7	681386
OLODON		
Lucy*	Santa Cruz Soguel	66 596
OLOFLIN		
James	Sierra Twp 7	66 911
OLOGLIN		
James	Sierra Twp 7	66 911
OLOMER		
Catherine*	Calaveras Twp 6	57 128
OLOMONS		
F R	San Joaquin Stockton	641094
OLONE		
John	Merced Monterey	60 941
John*	Monterey Monterey	60 941
OLOUGHLIN		
John*	Sierra Poker Flats	66 838
OLOVER		
J M	El Dorado Diamond	58 765
OLOY		
Alender	San Francisco San Francisco 9	681089
Aleuder*	San Francisco San Francisco 9	681089
OLPHERE		
H	San Francisco San Francisco 1	68 934
OLRANY		
Thos W*	Trinity Cox'S Bar	701038
OLRICH		
William	Tuolumne Chinese	71 501
OLRIS		
Daniel*	Mendocino Blg Rvr	60 846
OLSALER		
Miguel	Stanislaus Emory	70 754
OLSCK		
August*	Mendocino Big Rvr	60 849
OLSEN		
A	Siskiyou Cottonwoood	69 107
A S	Sacramento Sutter	63 300
Alex	Trinity Minersville	70 969
E	Sacramento Brighton	63 200
Elias	Siskiyou Scott Va	69 39
Hasper*	Butte Bidwell	56 729
J	Trinity Trinity	70 974
J L	Sacramento Ward 1	63 41
J S	Sacramento Ward 1	63 41
John	Trinity S Fork	701032
L	Sutter Butte	70 794
Lawrence	San Francisco San Francisco 9	681055
Ludwick	Klamath Klamath	59 225
N	San Francisco San Francisco 9	681059
Peter	Alameda Brooklyn	55 136
S	San Joaquin Stockton	641093
OLSON		
A	Siskiyou Cottonwoood	69 108
Alex	Santa Clara Redwood	65 457
Andrew	Nevada Rough &	61 405
Aul*	El Dorado Placerville	58 910
Christine	Plumas Quincy	62 971
Deidrick	Yuba Marysville	72 898
Edwd	San Francisco San Francisco 1	68 809
Edwin D*	San Francisco San Francisco 1	68 809
Edwin*	San Francisco San Francisco 1	68 809
Edwind*	San Francisco San Francisco 1	68 809
H S	Nevada Bloomfield	61 523
Hans	Santa Clara Redwood	65 460
John	Placer Todds Va	62 783
Lewis	Plumas Meadow Valley	62 902
Magmes*	Sierra Pine Grove	66 828
Magnus	Sierra Pine Grove	66 828
Mangus	Sierra Pine Grove	66 827
Maynus*	Sierra Pine Grove	66 828
Oleg*	El Dorado Coloma	581074
Oley	El Dorado Coloma	581074
Peter	El Dorado White Oaks	581025

California 1860 Census Index

Name	County Locale	M653 RollPage
OLSON		
Peter	El Dorado Kelsey	581130
Saml	Sierra Twp 5	66 947
OLSONN		
H	Siskiyou Klamath	69 85
OLSTEAD		
Adam	Napa Napa	61 61
OLSTON		
G	El Dorado Mud Springs	58 992
Joel	El Dorado Georgetown	58 687
Joll	El Dorado Georgetown	58 687
Leslie	El Dorado Georgetown	58 687
Lidire*	El Dorado Georgetown	58 687
Lusire*	El Dorado Georgetown	58 687
Susin*	El Dorado Georgetown	58 687
OLT		
John*	Plumas Quincy	62 939
Martin	Sacramento Natonia	63 274
OLTEN		
W	Sonoma Bodega	69 534
OLTMAN		
George	Marin S Antoni	60 711
OLTOR		
Peter	Solano Suisan	69 233
OLU		
Said*	San Francisco San Francisco 4	681224
OLUGRAY		
Charles*	San Francisco San Francisco 7	681386
OLUNEY		
---	Yuba Bear Rvr	721000
OLVANY		
Thos W*	Trinity Cox'S Bar	701038
OLVENS		
C	Sacramento San Joaquin	63 354
OLVERA		
Agustin	Los Angeles Los Angeles	59 294
Ignacio	San Luis Obispo San Luis Obispo	65 30
Manuel	Mariposa Twp 3	60 602
OLVERAS		
Louisa	San Luis Obispo San Luis Obispo	65 22
OLVERO		
Manuel	Mariposa Twp 3	60 602
OLVESTEAD		
R H	Sacramento Granite	63 263
OLVIS		
Daniel	Mendocino Big Rvr	60 846
OLWAY		
Thomas*	Sacramento Ward 1	63 132
OLYDA		
John	Placer Virginia	62 665
OLYEN		
Alexis*	Yuba New York	72 722
OLYHALBENSON		
Oley*	Sierra Twp 5	66 941
OLYHALBEUSON		
Alex	Sierra Twp 5	66 941
OM		
---	Tuolumne Big Oak	71 149
Andrew	Mariposa Twp 1	60 635
Bang Le	Sacramento Ward 3	63 493
Joseph	El Dorado Georgetown	58 682
OMAHNA		
Louis*	Mariposa Twp 3	60 600
OMAKEA		
---	Fresno Twp 3	59 40
OMALERY		
Rich	El Dorado White Oaks	581019
OMALLA		
J	San Joaquin Stockton	641092
OMALLEY		
John	San Joaquin Stockton	641077
Pat	Sacramento Ward 1	63 140
Wm	San Francisco San Francisco 12	384 67
OMALLY		
James	Calaveras Twp 5	57 196
Jno*	Sonoma Petaluma	69 600
Patrick	Calaveras Twp 7	57 21
Thos	San Francisco San Francisco 2	67 785
OMALTY		
Jno*	Sonoma Petaluma	69 600
OMALY		
Austin	San Mateo Twp 2	65 122
Patrick	Solano Vallejo	69 274
OMANN		
Asa*	Mendocino Little L	60 830
OMANS		
G W	Sonoma Vallejo	69 622
George	Sonoma Santa Rosa	69 390
George*	Sonoma Santa Rosa	69 390
OMAPOKA		
---	Fresno Twp 2	59 67
OMAR		
---	Mendocino Big Rvr	60 855
Maria	Santa Cruz Pajaro	66 554
Ramon*	El Dorado Placerville	58 921

Name	County Locale	M653 RollPage
OMARA		
Lucy*	Calaveras Twp 5	57 231
Michael	Del Norte Crescent	58 659
William	San Francisco San Francisco 3	67 37
OMARN		
Lucy*	Calaveras Twp 5	57 231
OMAUS		
George*	Sonoma Santa Rosa	69 390
OMEALLY		
Peter	Calaveras Twp 4	57 312
OMEALY		
Louisa E	Humbolt Union	59 185
OMEARA		
Anna	San Francisco San Francisco 8	681252
Edward	San Francisco San Francisco 2	67 752
John	San Francisco San Francisco 2	67 727
Margaret	San Francisco San Francisco 6	67 459
Margaret	San Francisco San Francisco 2	67 727
Marjaret	San Francisco San Francisco 2	67 727
Michael	Sacramento Ward 3	63 475
Michael	San Francisco San Francisco 10	208 67
OMEAULLY		
Peter	Calaveras Twp 4	57 312
OMEDA		
Eugenta	Calaveras Twp 7	57 45
OMEE		
Manuel*	Sacramento Granite	63 254
OMEGA		
M	Sutter Yuba	70 772
OMELIA		
Michael*	San Francisco San Francisco 7	681379
OMELLEY		
Thos*	San Francisco San Francisco 9	681007
OMENAH		
John	Siskiyou Callahan	69 8
OMENDEZ		
Sacramenta	Los Angeles Los Angeles	59 300
OMENS		
J P	Tehama Red Bluff	70 907
OMERA		
Benj	San Francisco San Francisco 9	681012
Corneleus	Sierra Whiskey	66 849
Cornelius	Sierra Whiskey	66 849
Elizabeth	San Francisco San Francisco 2	67 622
James	Calaveras Twp 6	57 168
Mary	San Francisco San Francisco 2	67 718
OMEREAH		
John*	Siskiyou Callahan	69 8
OMERER		
Pat	Nevada Bridgeport	61 442
OMERICA		
Wm	Amador Twp 5	55 341
OMERN		
James	Calaveras Twp 6	57 168
OMERO		
---	Monterey San Juan	60 977
OMIANANCE		
---	Mendocino Big Rvr	60 853
OMIARA		
John	San Francisco San Francisco 2	67 727
OMIKE		
C	Sutter Bear Rvr	70 824
OMILLER		
Wm*	Butte Kimshaw	56 571
OMIN		
Joseph	Sacramento Natonia	63 272
OMITTS		
Jruins	Yolo Merritt	72 579
OMM		
---	Amador Twp 1	55 477
OMOKE		
---	Tulara Twp 1	71 119
OMOPETHE		
---	Tulara Twp 1	71 119
OMPONE		
---	Mendocino Big Rvr	60 853
OMR		
Andrew*	Mariposa Twp 1	60 635
OMRE		
Domingo	Mariposa Twp 3	60 577
OMSBERG		
Calvin*	Nevada Bridgeport	61 476
OMSLEY		
Wm	Santa Clara Santa Clara	65 522
OMSTEAD		
C K	Nevada Bridgeport	61 483
I P*	Nevada Bridgeport	61 474
J P	Nevada Bridgeport	61 474
Joshua	Los Angeles Tejon	59 527
Joshue	Los Angeles Tejon	59 527
OMTILE		
Myna*	San Bernardino San Bernadino	64 629
OMTOH		
Mynan	San Joaquin San Bernardino	64 629
OMTOTE		
Mynane	San Bernardino San Bernadino	64 629

Name	County Locale	M653 RollPage
OMUKHUYITS		
---	Tulara Visalia	71 120
OMULLY		
James	Calaveras Twp 5	57 196
OMUNN		
Asa	Mendocino Little L	60 830
Asa*	Mendocino Little L	60 830
OMURTHA		
William	San Francisco San Francisco 7	681344
OMUT		
---	Tulara Twp 1	71 116
OMY		
---	Amador Twp 6	55 449
ON AUK		
---*	Yuba Long Bar	72 767
ON FALLY		
---	Tuolumne Montezuma	71 511
ON SANG		
---*	Yuba Long Bar	72 752
ON		
---	Amador Twp 5	55 350
---	Calaveras Twp 5	57 192
---	Calaveras Twp 5	57 208
---	Calaveras Twp 5	57 214
---	Calaveras Twp 5	57 225
---	Calaveras Twp 5	57 232
---	Calaveras Twp 5	57 233
---	Calaveras Twp 5	57 236
---	Calaveras Twp 5	57 237
---	Calaveras Twp 10	57 270
---	Calaveras Twp 10	57 285
---	Calaveras Twp 10	57 287
---	Calaveras Twp 10	57 297
---	Calaveras Twp 4	57 315
---	Calaveras Twp 4	57 321
---	Calaveras Twp 4	57 323
---	El Dorado White Oaks	581011
---	El Dorado White Oaks	581021
---	El Dorado Salmon Falls	581042
---	El Dorado Salmon Falls	581058
---	El Dorado Coloma	581120
---	El Dorado Coloma	581121
---	El Dorado Kelsey	581142
---	El Dorado Diamond	58 785
---	El Dorado Diamond	58 788
---	El Dorado Diamond	58 789
---	El Dorado Diamond	58 797
---	El Dorado Diamond	58 815
---	El Dorado Placerville	58 830
---	El Dorado Eldorado	58 941
---	Mariposa Twp 1	60 668
---	Placer Auburn	62 579
---	Placer Forest H	62 792
---	Sacramento Ward 3	63 492
---	Sacramento Ward 1	63 56
---	San Francisco San Francisco 4	681185
---	Sierra Downieville	66 999
---	Siskiyou Scott Va	69 47
---	Trinity Mouth Ca	701011
---	Trinity E Weaver	701061
---	Trinity Eastman	70 960
---	Tuolumne Green Springs	71 517
---*	El Dorado Kelsey	581142
---*	Sierra Twp 5	66 934
An	Amador Twp 2	55 285
Ank	Yuba Long Bar	72 767
Auk*	Yuba Long Bar	72 767
Chaw	Tuolumne Twp 5	71 515
Gin	Calaveras Twp 5	57 237
Low	Calaveras Twp 5	57 202
Nue	El Dorado Mud Springs	58 972
Sang	Yuba Long Bar	72 752
Sin	El Dorado Kelsey	581141
Tally*	Tuolumne Twp 5	71 511
Tow	Calaveras Twp 5	57 202
Une	El Dorado White Oaks	581010
Ye	El Dorado Diamond	58 808
ONA		
---	El Dorado Salmon Falls	581055
John*	Tuolumne Columbia	71 291
ONALOT		
Wm*	Yuba New York	72 741
ONASA		
---	Fresno Twp 1	59 27
ONASTEN		
John J	Yolo Cache Crk	72 638
ONASTON		
John L	Yolo Cache	72 638
ONATO		
Mike	Tuolumne Twp 1	71 269
Miko	Tuolumne Twp 1	71 269
ONAY		
---	El Dorado Mud Springs	58 960
ONBDO		
Dioncio	Tuolumne Montezuma	71 511

Name	County Locale	M653 RollPage
ONBO		
---	Sierra Downieville	66 998
ONC		
---	El Dorado Diamond	58 801
Ah	Tuolumne Twp 4	71 149
ONCEY		
Milbon	San Joaquin Castoria	64 874
ONDER		
E F G*	San Francisco San Francisco 10	236 67
ONDERDONK		
Peter	Sacramento Natonia	63 288
ONDERFULLEN		
C	Yolo Washington	72 572
ONDERTS		
Sebastian	Santa Clara San Jose	65 335
ONDOERES		
P*	Amador Twp 2	55 303
ONDON		
Lucy*	Santa Cruz Soguel	66 596
ONDUFULLIN		
C	Yolo Washington	72 572
ONDVERES		
P	Amador Twp 2	55 303
ONE		
---	Amador Twp 4	55 246
---	Amador Twp 2	55 319
---	Calaveras Twp 9	57 362
---	Nevada Rough &	61 432
---	Nevada Rough &	61 434
---	Nevada Bridgeport	61 439
---	Shasta French G	66 713
---	Tuolumne Big Oak	71 150
---	Tuolumne Twp 5	71 525
---	Tuolumne Knights	71 529
---*	Calaveras Twp 9	57 362
---*	Nevada Rough &	61 434
Ah	Tuolumne Twp 4	71 150
J	Nevada Rough &	61 434
See	Yuba Foster B	72 834
ONEAL		
Andrew	Mariposa Twp 3	60 601
Ann	San Francisco San Francisco 7	681 352
Benjamin	Sierra St Louis	66 805
Bernard	San Mateo Twp 1	65 67
Bridget	San Francisco San Francisco 1	68 868
Catharine	Marin San Rafael	60 759
Catharine	San Francisco San Francisco 1	68 868
Chas	San Francisco San Francisco 2	67 563
Constantin	Placer Michigan	62 843
D	Nevada Eureka	61 366
Daniel	Alameda Oakland	55 63
Daniel	Solano Vacaville	69 334
Danl	San Francisco San Francisco 10	339 67
Danl	Solano Benecia	69 305
David	San Francisco San Francisco 7	681 382
Dennia	Tuolumne Twp 1	71 188
Dennis	San Francisco San Francisco 8	681 279
Dennis	Tuolumne Sonora	71 188
E	Sacramento Ward 1	63 18
Ed W	Sacramento Ward 1	63 133
Edmund	San Francisco San Francisco 9	681 063
Edw	Sacramento Ward 1	63 133
Edward	Solano Benecia	69 297
Ellen	Sacramento Ward 1	63 23
Ellen	San Francisco San Francisco 9	68 966
Ellen	San Joaquin Castoria	64 896
Francis	Placer Michigan	62 834
George	Sierra St Louis	66 863
George	Sierra Twp 7	66 863
H R	Butte Oregon	56 620
Henry	Solano Vallejo	69 254
Henry*	Santa Cruz Pajaro	66 526
Hezekiah	Tulara Visalia	71 100
J	Siskiyou Scott Ri	69 73
J H	San Francisco San Francisco 3	67 85
J*	Siskiyou Scott Ri	69 73
Jackson	Siskiyou Scott Va	69 44
Jackson*	Siskiyou Scott Va	69 44
James	Calaveras Twp 4	57 313
James	Placer Iona Hills	62 880
James	San Francisco San Francisco 7	681 380
James	San Francisco San Francisco 7	681 393
James	San Francisco San Francisco 9	68 987
James	San Joaquin Stockton	641 060
James	San Joaquin Oneal	64 933
James	Tehama Cottonwoood	70 900
James	Tuolumne Knights	71 529
Jas	San Francisco San Francisco 9	68 939
Jeremiah	San Joaquin Castoria	64 888
Jno*	Nevada Nevada	61 253
John	Alameda Brooklyn	55 101
John	Amador Twp 4	55 252
John	Amador Twp 6	55 426
John	Los Angeles Los Angeles	59 365

Name	County Locale	M653 RollPage
ONEAL		
John	Marin Tomales	60 720
John	Sacramento Ward 1	63 126
John	San Francisco San Francisco 7	681 387
John	San Francisco San Francisco 5	67 546
John	Sierra Port Win	66 798
John	Solano Vallejo	69 243
John B	Calaveras Twp 5	57 147
John B	Calaveras Twp 6	57 147
John W	San Joaquin Stockton	641 014
Joseph	Marin Cortemad	60 788
M	Butte Eureka	56 646
M	Sacramento Ward 1	63 18
M	Trinity Lewiston	70 964
M*	Butte Eureka	56 646
Margaret	San Francisco San Francisco 7	681 330
Mary	Amador Twp 3	55 405
Mary	Calaveras Twp 6	57 116
Mary S	San Francisco San Francisco 9	68 958
Melinda	Stanislaus Emory	70 748
Michael	Calaveras Twp 5	57 229
Michael	San Francisco San Francisco 7	681 334
Morris	Sierra St Louis	66 864
Morris	Sierra Twp 7	66 864
N	San Francisco San Francisco 6	67 484
O H	Solano Vacaville	69 325
Oskar	Amador Twp 3	55 391
Owen	Sierra Twp 5	66 926
P	San Joaquin Stockton	641 100
Pat	Sacramento Natonia	63 272
Pat	San Joaquin Stockton	641 068
Patk	Klamath Liberty	59 234
Patric	Calaveras Twp 4	57 315
Patrick	Calaveras Twp 5	57 137
Patrick	Calaveras Twp 5	57 137
Patrick	Calaveras Twp 4	57 315
R	Mariposa Twp 3	60 577
Richard	San Francisco San Francisco 7	681 343
Robt	Klamath Trinidad	59 222
Thomas	San Francisco San Francisco 8	681 324
Thomas J	Mendocino Arrana	60 862
Thomas*	Yolo No E Twp	72 667
Thonas	San Francisco San Francisco 8	681 290
Thos	San Francisco San Francisco 9	681 069
Tim	El Dorado Mud Springs	58 964
W	Marin S Antoni	60 712
W	San Joaquin Stockton	641 092
Wheeler	San Francisco San Francisco 8	681 324
William	Alameda Oakland	55 46
William B	San Joaquin Elkhorn	64 980
William*	Shasta Shasta	66 728
Wm	San Joaquin Stockton	641 099
Wm	Tuolumne Twp 4	71 126
Wm G	San Francisco San Francisco 2	67 572
Wm H	San Francisco San Francisco 2	67 572
ONEALE		
William T	Yuba Marysville	72 847
ONEAWL		
Peter	Sierra Port Win	66 797
ONED		
Manuel*	Sacramento Granite	63 254
ONEE		
---	Shasta French G	66 713
ONEEL		
Francis W*	Mariposa Twp 3	60 587
Tim	Sierra Twp 5	66 942
ONEFY		
---	Shasta Horsetown	66 704
ONEGA		
---	Sacramento Cosummes	63 408
ONEIAL		
Pat*	Sacramento Natonia	63 272
ONEIL		
Allice	San Mateo Twp 1	65 49
Aloysia Sister	Solano Benecia	69 300
And	Mariposa Twp 3	60 599
Anna	Napa Napa	61 90
Annie	San Francisco San Francisco 10	182 67
Benard	Solano Benecia	69 305
Bernard*	Solano Benecia	69 305
Bridget	San Francisco San Francisco 12	394 67
C	Nevada Eureka	61 377
C	Shasta Horsetown	66 690
Cath	Alameda Brooklyn	55 126
Charles	Colusa Grand Island	57 471
Charles	Santa Clara Gilroy	65 236
Chas	Sonoma Bodega	69 529
Chas	Sonoma Bodega	69 531
Chas*	Calaveras Twp 8	57 103
D	Sacramento Ward 4	63 524
D	Yuba Long Bar	72 768
D F	Sacramento Ward 1	63 79
Dan	Solano Benecia	69 305
Daniel	San Francisco San Francisco 3	67 71

Name	County Locale	M653 RollPage
ONEIL		
David	Nevada Rough &	61 413
E	Solano Benecia	69 285
E J	Sutter Yuba	70 770
Ed	Sacramento Sutter	63 298
Edwin	Yolo Cache	72 595
Eugene	San Mateo Twp 3	65 85
F	Tuolumne Twp 4	71 179
Fern	Sierra Twp 5	66 942
Francis	Mariposa Twp 3	60 587
Francis	Nevada Nevada	61 315
Henry	Calaveras Twp 8	57 103
J	Nevada Grass Valley	61 159
James	Napa Yount	61 32
James	Nevada Bridgeport	61 505
James	San Francisco San Francisco 9	68 949
James	Yuba Foster B	72 833
James	Yuba Fosters	72 833
James*	Stanislaus Buena Village	70 723
Jas	Calaveras Twp 9	57 370
Jno	Nevada Nevada	61 245
Jno	Nevada Nevada	61 253
Jno	Sacramento Ward 3	63 473
John	Calaveras Twp 9	57 381
John	Placer Auburn	62 565
John	San Mateo Twp 2	65 120
John	Siskiyou Yreka	69 145
Jos	Amador Twp 1	55 468
M	Nevada Grass Valley	61 155
M	Yolo Putah	72 549
M	Yolo Slate Ra	72 687
M	Yuba North Ea	72 687
M J	San Francisco San Francisco 3	67 23
Margaret	Nevada Nevada	61 257
Margaret	San Mateo Twp 3	65 96
Margaret R J	Fresno Twp 2	59 5
Margaret*	Nevada Nevada	61 257
Mary	Alameda Oakland	55 8
Michael	Calaveras Twp 9	57 402
P	Yuba Fosters	72 836
P*	Yuba Foster B	72 836
Pat Jas	Sacramento Granite	63 263
Patrick	Calaveras Twp 6	57 137
Patrick	Calaveras Twp 9	57 358
Patrick	San Diego S Luis R	64 777
Patrick	San Mateo Twp 2	65 132
Patrick	Sierra Port Win	66 791
Peter	Butte Ophir	56 781
Peter	Shasta Shasta	66 668
Peter	Sierra Port Win	66 797
Peter B	Fresno Twp 2	59 5
Philip	Sacramento Granite	63 251
R C	Placer Dutch Fl	62 711
Richard	Los Angeles Tejon	59 522
Robt	Butte Ophir	56 764
S	San Francisco San Francisco 1	68 851
S	San Mateo Twp 3	65 88
Thomas	Calaveras Twp 9	57 370
Thomas	Contra Costa Twp 1	57 503
Thomas	San Francisco San Francisco 3	67 24
Thomas	Yolo No E Twp	72 667
Thomas*	Yolo No E Twp	72 667
Thos	San Mateo Twp 3	65 105
Thos O P Revd	Solano Benecia	69 314
Thos Rev D	Solano Benecia	69 314
Tim	Sacramento Granite	63 246
Timothy	Trinity Whites Crk	701 028
Timothy D	Placer Rattle Snake	62 638
W	Nevada Eureka	61 369
W	Shasta Horsetown	66 690
William	Alameda Oakland	55 43
Wm	Alameda Brooklyn	55 205
ONEILE		
John	Tuolumne Jamestown	71 456
ONEILL		
Barney	Santa Clara Alviso	65 411
Can	Tuolumne Twp 2	71 351
Carr	Tuolumne Columbia	71 351
Charles*	Monterey San Juan	60 989
E W	San Francisco San Francisco 1	68 917
Edward	San Francisco San Francisco 11	129 67
Elizabeth	San Francisco San Francisco 10	275 67
F	Tuolumne Big Oak	71 179
Henry	Santa Clara San Jose	65 386
Hugh	Plumas Quincy	62 999
Hugh	San Francisco San Francisco 11	139 67
Hugh	Solano Vacaville	69 360
I	San Francisco San Francisco 2	67 742
J	San Francisco San Francisco 2	67 742
James	San Francisco San Francisco 11	95 67
James	Tuolumne Columbia	71 308
James	Tuolumne Twp 3	71 457

Name	County Locale	M653 RollPage
ONEILL		
John	San Francisco San Francisco	3 67 6
John	Santa Clara San Jose	65 333
John	Tuolumne Twp 3	71 422
John	Tuolumne Twp 3	71 456
John F	Plumas Quincy	62 926
John M	Monterey Monterey	60 966
M	San Francisco San Francisco	12 394 67
Michael	San Francisco San Francisco	10 206 67
Michael	Santa Clara San Jose	65 390
Patrick	Tuolumne Twp 2	71 340
Peter	Santa Clara San Jose	65 333
Thomas	San Francisco San Francisco	11 91 67
Wm	Tuolumne Twp 1	71 270
Wm	Tuolumne Columbia	71 324
ONEILS		
John	Butte Oro	56 680
ONEL		
Wm	Yolo Slate Ra	72 710
Wm	Yuba Slate Ro	72 710
ONELA		
John	Marin Tomales	60 720
ONELIA		
T	San Francisco San Francisco	5 67 537
ONELL		
Thomas	San Francisco San Francisco	11 91 67
ONELON		
Richard*	Yolo Putah	72 552
ONEMAN		
Barny*	Alameda Brooklyn	55 147
ONENS		
E S	Butte Oro	56 680
F*	Yuba Rose Bar	72 796
J S	Butte Ophir	56 787
Robert*	Calaveras Twp 8	57 92
ONEPY		
---	Shasta Horsetown	66 704
ONERBACK		
Fred*	Sierra La Porte	66 776
ONERLIN		
Martin*	San Francisco San Francisco	9 68 947
ONERTON		
Jas M*	Calaveras Twp 9	57 347
ONESLY		
---	Shasta Shasta	66 670
ONET		
Antonio	Amador Twp 1	55 485
ONETO		
John	Calaveras Twp 8	57 105
Joseph	Los Angeles Los Angeles	59 310
ONETT		
---	Butte Oro	56 675
Andrew	Calaveras Twp 5	57 220
John	Calaveras Twp 5	57 220
Leander	Calaveras Twp 5	57 226
Leuniler	Calaveras Twp 5	57 226
Lorenzo	Calaveras Twp 5	57 220
ONETTA		
Carl	Calaveras Twp 5	57 228
Nicholas	Calaveras Twp 5	57 217
ONETTIE		
James	Calaveras Twp 5	57 217
ONETTO		
James*	Calaveras Twp 5	57 217
Nicholas	Calaveras Twp 5	57 217
ONETTU		
Earl	Calaveras Twp 5	57 228
ONFRAY		
Mitchel	San Francisco San Francisco	7 681395
ONG KANG		
---	Nevada Red Dog	61 549
ONG		
---	Amador Twp 2	55 289
---	Amador Twp 1	55 496
---	Calaveras Twp 5	57 192
---	Calaveras Twp 5	57 245
---	Calaveras Twp 4	57 333
---	El Dorado White Oaks	581024
---	El Dorado Salmon Falls	581047
---	El Dorado Salmon Falls	581061
---	El Dorado Salmon Falls	581062
---	El Dorado Coloma	581082
---	El Dorado Georgetown	58 692
---	El Dorado Big Bar	58 738
---	El Dorado Diamond	58 801
---	El Dorado Placerville	58 823
---	El Dorado Placerville	58 917
---	El Dorado Mud Springs	58 959
---	El Dorado Mud Springs	58 971
---	Mariposa Twp 3	60 544
---	Mariposa Twp 1	60 667
---	Nevada Washington	61 342

Name	County Locale	M653 RollPage
ONG		
---	Nevada Rough &	61 437
---	Nevada Bridgeport	61 460
---	Nevada Bridgeport	61 461
---	Nevada Bridgeport	61 463
---	Sacramento Ward 1	63 70
---	San Francisco San Francisco	5 67 508
---	Siskiyou Scott Ri	69 67
---	Yuba Fosters	72 842
---	Yuba Marysville	72 917
---*	Nevada Bridgeport	61 461
---*	Yuba Marysville	72 917
Cho	Siskiyou Scott Ri	69 67
Gow	Butte Oregon	56 631
J*	Nevada Bridgeport	61 461
Kong	Mariposa Twp 3	60 544
Le	Sacramento Ward 4	63 609
Low	El Dorado Mud Springs	58 953
Peck	El Dorado Salmon Hills	581066
Rockaway	El Dorado Coloma	581082
Sam*	Yuba Long Bar	72 763
Seong	Plumas Quincy	62 950
Won	Plumas Meadow Valley	62 914
ONGE		
---	San Francisco San Francisco	9 68 963
ONGEN		
Birenta	Alameda Brooklyn	55 190
ONGERN		
M	El Dorado Diamond	58 800
ONGICH		
Charles*	El Dorado Diamond	58 765
ONGIN		
Jose	Monterey San Juan	601003
ONGON		
Jose*	Monterey San Juan	601003
ONGULICE		
David*	Santa Cruz Pescadero	66 641
ONGULIO		
David*	Santa Cruz Pescadero	66 641
ONGYE		
---	Amador Twp 3	55 410
ONI		
---	Nevada Rough &	61 432
ONICE		
Edward	Calaveras Twp 8	57 70
ONIDO		
---	Sacramento Cosumnes	63 408
ONIEL		
Arthur	Sacramento Ward 4	63 606
B	Sacramento Lee	63 215
C	Nevada Eureka	61 377
C P	Sacramento Ward 1	63 20
Cath	Sacramento Ward 3	63 480
Chas*	San Francisco San Francisco	1 68 847
Cornelius	Calaveras Twp 7	57 10
Cornlius	San Joaquin Castoria	64 895
Daniel	Calaveras Twp 8	57 82
Daniel	San Francisco San Francisco	3 67 71
E M	San Francisco San Francisco	1 68 918
Edward*	Calaveras Twp 8	57 70
Hannah	Sacramento Ward 3	63 451
Hugh	San Francisco San Francisco	2 67 802
I R*	Mariposa Twp 3	60 591
J R	Mariposa Twp 3	60 591
J*	Nevada Grass Valley	61 235
James	Calaveras Twp 7	57 41
James	Santa Cruz Soguel	66 599
Jas	Sacramento Ward 1	63 20
Jas	Sacramento Ward 4	63 533
Jno	Sacramento Ward 1	63 91
John	Butte Oro	56 680
John	Calaveras Twp 8	57 75
John	San Francisco San Francisco	1 68 890
John	San Francisco San Francisco	1 68 891
Joseph	Sacramento Ward 4	63 559
Laurence	San Mateo Twp 3	65 79
Mary	San Francisco San Francisco	1 68 809
Michael	San Francisco San Francisco	2 67 802
Pat	Sacramento Ward 4	63 606
Pat Jas	Sacramento Granite	63 263
Patrick	San Francisco San Francisco	1 68 869
Phillip	San Francisco San Francisco	2 67 575
S	Sutter Butte	70 797
Saml	Sacramento Ward 4	63 602
Sarah	Sacramento Ward 1	63 112
T	Sacramento Ward 4	63 607
Thomas	Calaveras Twp 8	57 57
Thomas	Contra Costa Twp 1	57 500
Thomas	Sacramento Ward 1	63 33
Thos	San Francisco San Francisco	1 68 880
Tim	Sacramento Ward 4	63 568
William	Calaveras Twp 7	57 10
William	Calaveras Twp 7	57 23
ONIELL		
Chas	Santa Clara Santa Clara	65 468
Francis W	Mariposa Twp 3	60 587

Name	County Locale	M653 RollPage
ONEILL		
John	Los Angeles San Pedro	59 481
John G	Los Angeles Los Angeles	59 354
ONIELS		
John	Butte Oro	56 680
ONIN		
Cath*	Sacramento Ward 1	63 91
ONIQUIS		
John	Tuolumne Columbia	71 292
ONIRDOLPHS		
John*	Los Angeles Los Angeles	59 365
ONIRLAN		
Jno	San Francisco San Francisco	9 681070
ONIS		
Charles	Solano Vallejo	69 251
Jacob*	Tuolumne Springfield	71 372
ONISISNA		
---	Monterey Monterey	60 961
ONISPO		
---	Sacramento Franklin	63 333
ONISQUE		
Jose	Los Angeles Los Angeles	59 381
ONIZ		
Jesus*	Los Angeles San Gabriel	59 423
ONJ		
---	Amador Twp 7	55 415
ONK		
Lee	Yolo No E Twp	72 676
ONLDEN		
Thomas*	Santa Cruz Santa Cruz	66 621
ONLEY		
Wallace*	Solano Vacaville	69 323
ONLSEN		
Wm*	San Francisco San Francisco	3 67 65
ONLY		
William	Tuolumne Twp 1	71 259
ONM		
---	Amador Twp 1	55 499
ONMKUTE		
---	Tulara Twp 1	71 118
ONN		
---	Calaveras Twp 8	57 60
---	Calaveras Twp 8	57 91
---	Calaveras Twp 8	57 94
---	Placer Folsom	62 648
---	Shasta Horsetown	66 698
---	Yuba Bear Rvr	721000
---*	Calaveras Twp 5	57 237
ONNAUPER		
Henry*	Del Norte Crescent	58 622
ONNELLO		
Peter	Calaveras Twp 5	57 221
ONNIAH		
---	Fresno Twp 1	59 27
ONNKEN		
Wm*	Sierra Twp 5	66 924
ONNKIN		
Wm	Sierra Twp 5	66 924
ONO		
---	Sierra Downieville	66 980
John*	Tuolumne Columbia	71 291
ONOKA		
---	Mendocino Big Rvr	60 853
ONOMINCE		
---*	Mendocino Big Rvr	60 854
ONONS		
Anne*	San Francisco San Francisco	2 67 573
ONOUS		
Anne*	San Francisco San Francisco	2 67 573
ONREO		
Mary	San Francisco San Francisco	1 68 809
ONRIOL		
Nicholas*	Contra Costa Twp 1	57 488
ONRMAN		
Barny*	Alameda Brooklyn	55 147
ONRWASHER		
Fred*	Placer Iona Hills	62 885
ONSLEY		
Henry*	Napa Hot Springs	61 12
John*	Nevada Grass Valley	61 150
ONSMONE		
Henry	Los Angeles Santa Ana	59 444
ONSTED		
G	Trinity Mouth Ca	701014
ONSTEM		
Wm	Fresno Millerto	59 2
ONSTOL		
Philip*	Yuba Marysville	72 975
ONSTOT		
J A	Yuba Long Bar	72 741
Philip*	Yuba Marysville	72 975
ONTIOEROS		
John*	Yuba Marysville	72 873
ONTIREROS		
Ferdera	San Francisco San Francisco	2 67 698
ONTIVERAS		
Frank P	San Luis Obispo San Luis Obispo	65 32

California 1860 Census Index

Name	County Locale	M653 RollPage
ONTIVERAS		
Juan	Los Angeles Santa Ana	59 445
Patricio	Los Angeles Santa Ana	59 445
ONTIVEROS		
John*	Yuba Marysville	72 873
ONTOD		
Jno*	San Francisco San Francisco 9	681080
ONTON		
Jno	San Francisco San Francisco 9	681080
ONTONE		
Manuel	Monterey Monterey	60 965
ONTONIO		
Sam	San Bernardino S Timate	64 690
ONTRARAY		
Gaston	Los Angeles San Gabriel	59 421
ONTREMENT		
A B*	Mariposa Twp 3	60 577
ONUILA		
Thomasf*	Sacramento Ward 1	63 128
ONULL		
Wm	Tuolumne Twp 1	71 270
ONULLEY		
Thos*	San Francisco San Francisco 9	681007
ONURRA		
James	Calaveras Twp 4	57 324
ONVMINCE		
---*	Mendocino Big Rvr	60 854
ONWARD		
Henry	San Francisco San Francisco 2	67 750
ONY		
---	Calaveras Twp 5	57 192
---	Calaveras Twp 5	57 224
---	Calaveras Twp 5	57 235
---	Calaveras Twp 5	57 245
---	Calaveras Twp 4	57 314
---	Calaveras Twp 4	57 333
---	San Francisco San Francisco 4	681177
---*	Sacramento Ward 1	63 54
E	Calaveras Twp 9	57 403
Louisa	Calaveras Twp 9	57 403
ONYEA		
---	Amador Twp 1	55 499
ONYETT		
Betty	Butte Ophir	56 748
John	Butte Ophir	56 748
OO YA		
---*	Yuba Long Bar	72 761
OO		
---	Amador Twp 2	55 301
---	Amador Twp 6	55 422
Van Que	Yuba Long Bar	72 762
Win	Yuba Long Bar	72 762
Ya	Yuba Long Bar	72 761
Yeng	Yuba Long Bar	72 763
Yeny	Yuba Long Bar	72 763
OOAKENITT		
---	Tulara Twp 1	71 119
OOH		
---	Sacramento Ward 1	63 59
OOLAK		
---*	Mendocino Big Rvr	60 855
OOLOHA		
---*	Mendocino Big Rvr	60 854
OOLOLAM		
---*	Mendocino Big Rvr	60 854
OOLOLARN		
---*	Mendocino Big Rvr	60 854
OOLPISH		
---	Tulara Twp 1	71 120
OOMOPOOTUX		
---	Tulara Twp 1	71 117
OON		
---	Placer Iona Hills	62 896
---	Sacramento Ward 1	63 50
OONER		
William	Tuolumne Twp 2	71 290
OOSHA		
---	Mendocino Big Rvr	60 855
OOT		
---*	Mariposa Coulterville	60 692
OOTOOLAM		
---	Mendocino Big Rvr	60 855
OOTVUTS		
---	Tulara Twp 1	71 117
OOWENS		
William*	Mendocino Anderson	60 867
OP		
---	Calaveras Twp 5	57 234
Sing	Sierra Twp 5	66 928
OPAL		
G	Nevada Eureka	61 393
OPANHAM		
B	Mariposa Twp 1	60 623
OPARTERN		
Maria*	Tuolumne Twp 1	71 221
OPATRICK		
---*	Nevada Grass Valley	61 197

Name	County Locale	M653 RollPage
OPE		
Augustus	Sacramento Sutter	63 295
OPEA		
Proguata*	Alameda Murray	55 218
OPELVIN		
Minnie	Santa Clara San Jose	65 313
OPEN		
Samuel	Santa Cruz Santa Cruz	66 634
OPENCIS		
Oliver	Tuolumne Twp 1	71 250
OPENHEIM		
Cecilia*	San Francisco San Francisco 2	67 658
OPENHEIMER		
David	Tuolumne Columbia	71 356
Henry	San Joaquin Stockton	641018
Henry	Tuolumne Twp 1	71 205
OPENNEUR		
Geo	San Francisco San Francisco 2	67 755
OPENSAFF		
J	Nevada Nevada	61 285
OPENSOFF		
J	Nevada Nevada	61 285
OPERTE		
Manuel	Sacramento Granite	63 254
OPESTEN		
Maria	Tuolumne Sonora	71 221
OPEZ		
Cristoval	San Diego San Diego	64 773
OPFER		
J H	Sacramento Franklin	63 333
OPFORD		
Robert	Tuolumne Twp 3	71 464
OPHAM		
Abjah	Klamath Orleans	59 216
OPHANIA		
Pauline	San Joaquin Stockton	641079
OPHENHAN		
Michael	San Francisco San Francisco 4	681130
OPHER		
Henry	San Joaquin Douglass	64 918
OPHILIPS		
W*	Mendocino Big Rvr	60 845
OPHISTULA		
---	Del Norte Ferry P O	58 665
OPIAJE		
Louis*	San Mateo Twp 1	65 67
OPIE		
Thomas	Alameda Oakland	55 66
Wm	Trinity Weaverville	701056
OPIEN		
Frank*	Calaveras Twp 5	57 177
OPIL		
David	El Dorado Placerville	58 892
OPIRTERN		
Maria*	Tuolumne Twp 1	71 221
OPITZ		
F	Sacramento Ward 1	63 24
OPIU		
---	Calaveras Twp 5	57 256
OPKINS		
Peter	Nevada Rough &	61 430
OPOE		
Robt	Sacramento Ward 4	63 539
OPOO		
---	Monterey Monterey	60 959
OPOST		
Mary*	Yuba Marysville	72 947
OPP		
Henry	Placer Forest H	62 772
OPPDYKE		
George	Yuba New York	72 718
Geroge	Yolo Slate Ra	72 718
OPPEBHEIM		
A	San Joaquin Stockton	641097
OPPEMAN		
C	Tehama Red Bluff	70 916
OPPENBARGER		
Joseph*	Placer Iona Hills	62 886
OPPENEIM		
Michael*	San Francisco San Francisco 4	681130
OPPENHAN		
Adolph	Butte Ophir	56 755
OPPENHEIM		
Joseph	San Francisco San Francisco 8	681273
R	Sacramento Ward 1	63 25
OPPENHEIMER		
A	El Dorado Georgetown	58 688
Julius	San Joaquin Stockton	641037
Myer	Siskiyou Yreka	69 182
P	Nevada Eureka	61 392
OPPENHEM		
Michael*	San Francisco San Francisco 4	681130
OPPENHERMIN		
P*	Nevada Eureka	61 392
OPPENHIEM		
N	Mariposa Twp 3	60 548

Name	County Locale	M653 RollPage
OPPENSHAW		
James	Placer Michigan	62 823
OPPERMAN		
Christian	San Francisco San Francisco 2	67 614
E F	Tehama Tehama	70 946
OPPIMAN		
Julius	Humbolt Bucksport	59 161
OPPINHAN		
Adolph*	Butte Ophir	56 755
OPPINHEM		
Michael*	San Francisco San Francisco 4	681130
OPPINHUN		
Michael*	San Francisco San Francisco 4	681130
OPPIUHAN		
Adolph*	Butte Ophir	56 755
OPPLETON		
Morris*	Yuba Marysville	72 926
OPPUSHAN		
John	Placer Michigan	62 817
Joseph	Placer Michigan	62 818
OPT		
Henry	Sierra Downieville	66 961
OPUP		
---	Sierra Downieville	66 979
OR		
---	Sierra Downieville	661005
Hen	Sierra Downieville	66 973
Hew	Sierra Downieville	66 973
Nancy W*	San Francisco 10	227
---	San Francisco	67
ORA		
Josa	Amador Twp 5	55 339
ORADO		
Julius	San Francisco San Francisco 4	681215
ORAFFERTY		
Bernard*	Butte Oregon	56 628
Jackson	Placer Michigan	62 825
ORAGA		
Rosaria	Monterey Monterey	60 965
ORAGAN		
Sampson*	Tuolumne Twp 3	71 449
T*	Nevada Nevada	61 252
T*	Nevada Nevada	61 317
William	San Francisco San Francisco 3	67 27
ORALE		
Mamoria	San Joaquin Stockton	641072
ORAM		
Charles	Marin Bolinas	60 749
ORAMA		
Jas	San Francisco San Francisco 1	68 818
Jos*	San Francisco San Francisco 1	68 818
ORAMPSON		
Jesus	Tehama Red Bluff	70 919
ORANDALL		
R M	Amador Twp 1	55 456
ORANE		
John*	Calaveras Twp 8	57 102
ORANGE		
Wm	Sacramento Ward 3	63 456
ORANGES		
James	Siskiyou Klamath	69 84
ORANKE		
D	Amador Twp 3	55 380
ORANTE		
Jaes	Monterey San Juan	60 982
James	Monterey San Juan	60 982
ORANTES		
James	Santa Cruz Pajaro	66 571
ORAPESA		
Vicente	Santa Clara Almaden	65 275
ORASCO		
Fecanda	Santa Clara Almaden	65 274
Jose	Santa Cruz Pajaro	66 566
ORASEI		
Jose	Calaveras Twp 5	57 178
ORASER		
Jose	Calaveras Twp 6	57 178
ORASIS		
Jesus	San Bernardino San Bernardino	64 663
ORAST		
W A	Nevada Eureka	61 354
ORATER		
Amas	Siskiyou Yreka	69 152
ORATES		
Juan	Tehama Tehama	70 938
Margareto	Tehama Tehama	70 938
ORAUK		
P	Nevada Grass Valley	61 225
P*	Nevada Grass Valley	61 225
ORBDO		
Dionico*	Tuolumne Twp 5	71 511
ORBIY		
John*	Contra Costa Twp 1	57 487
ORBY		
Henry	Tuolumne Twp 1	71 245
ORCHARD		
Geo	Sacramento Ward 4	63 517

California 1860 Census Index

Name	County Locale	M653 RollPage
ORCONI		
Estaphue	Mariposa Twp 3	60 545
ORCUCANO		
Masador*	Santa Cruz Santa Cruz	66 617
ORCULL		
Geo	San Francisco San Francisco 10	234
		67
ORCUTT		
Geo	San Francisco San Francisco 10	234
		67
H L	Klamath S Fork	59 204
Moses	Sierra Twp 7	66 878
Saml S	Tuolumne Columbia	71 313
ORD		
James L	San Bernardino Santa Barbara	64 149
John	Santa Cruz Soguel	66 584
John	Sierra Monte Crk	661038
John J	Santa Cruz Soguel	66 584
John S	Santa Cruz Soguel	66 584
John S*	Santa Cruz Soguel	66 594
Pacipcus	Colusa Monroeville	57 456
Robert B	Colusa Monroeville	57 455
Wm	Butte Hamilton	56 516
ORDARAY		
A O	Sutter Sutter	70 811
ORDAZ		
Vicente	San Bernardino Santa Barbara	64 181
Vincente	San Mateo Twp 2	65 131
ORDEAS		
Juprane	Amador Twp 5	55 332
ORDEMAN		
Mary	San Francisco San Francisco 10	192
		67
ORDEN		
C	San Mateo Twp 1	65 66
George	Los Angeles San Pedro	59 484
L Van*	Butte Ophir	56 767
Maria M	Los Angeles San Pedro	59 485
ORDENAY		
E W	San Francisco San Francisco 5	67 506
ORDIN		
D T Van*	San Francisco San Francisco 6	67 457
ORDINIO		
Julio*	Marin Cortemad	60 786
ORDNAY		
Amos	Tulara Visalia	71 78
N F	Tuolumne Twp 2	71 300
ORDON		
Bernardo	Los Angeles Los Angeles	59 513
Birnardo	Los Angeles Los Angeles	59 513
ORDONS		
Dolores*	San Francisco San Francisco 2	67 790
ORDUM		
Mary	Siskiyou Scott Ri	69 63
ORDUNCO		
Julio	Marin Cortemad	60 786
ORDUNO		
Elizia	Los Angeles Los Angeles	59 315
Henry	Siskiyou Scott Ri	69 63
Mary	Siskiyou Scott Ri	69 63
ORDWAN		
Wm*	Sonoma Petaluma	69 603
ORDWART		
Wm*	Sonoma Petaluma	69 603
ORDWAY		
David K	Humbolt Eureka	59 174
John	Sonoma Sonoma	69 649
Nehemiah	Tuolumne Columbia	71 302
Pimers*	Tulara Twp 1	71 78
Wm	Sonoma Petaluma	69 603
ORE		
---	Sierra Twp 5	66 931
Jacob Saml*	Mendocino Calpella	60 820
Peitra	Calaveras Twp 8	57 69
OREA		
Gengo	Alameda Brooklyn	55 208
OREAL		
William	Shasta Shasta	66 728
OREAN		
Isaac	Yolo Merritt	72 581
OREAR		
Benjamin*	Yuba Bear Rvr	721004
Isaac*	Yolo Merritt	72 581
W E	Nevada Rough &	61 403
OREAS		
Juan	Monterey San Juan	60 984
OREGENAR		
Theodore*	Mariposa Twp 3	60 583
OREGG		
James M*	Sierra Twp 5	66 938
OREGH		
T*	Nevada Eureka	61 370
OREGON		
Alexander	S Timate	64 688
	San Bernardino	
Jose	San Diego Agua Caliente	64 855

Name	County Locale	M653 RollPage
OREGTON		
---	Amador Twp 2	55 290
OREIL		
F M	Butte Kimshaw	56 593
OREILEY		
James	Yolo Merritt	72 584
OREILL		
G	San Francisco San Francisco 5	67 500
OREILLY		
H A	San Francisco San Francisco 2	67 774
John	Sierra St Louis	66 817
Jos	Sacramento Brighton	63 193
Lorence	Solano Benecia	69 316
Mich	San Francisco San Francisco 2	67 770
Patrick	Monterey Alisal	601026
Patrick	San Francisco San Francisco 11	93
		67
William	San Francisco San Francisco 7	681370
OREILY		
Chas	El Dorado Georgetown	58 675
Chas*	El Dorado Georgetown	58 675
P S	Sacramento Ward 3	63 440
Robt	San Francisco San Francisco 2	67 705
OREITZ		
Robt*	San Francisco San Francisco 2	67 705
ORELL		
Patrick	Sierra Downieville	661017
ORELLA		
Bruno	San Bernardino Santa Barbara	64 150
OREMIRE		
J D	Shasta French G	66 721
OREMOKL		
H*	Trinity E Weaver	701060
OREN		
---	Siskiyou Scott Ri	69 73
---	Tulara Twp 3	71 50
Ah	Siskiyou Scott Ri	69 73
ORENDAYA		
Hepolite*	San Francisco San Francisco 2	67 769
Hupolite*	San Francisco San Francisco 2	67 769
ORENDER		
Wm	Mendocino Calpella	60 817
ORENDORF		
F H	Butte Cascade	56 691
ORENDORFF		
Isaac	Napa Napa	61 69
ORENDOST		
F H	Butte Cascade	56 691
ORENNIE		
G	Siskiyou Scott Ri	69 74
ORENSA		
Bermudo	San Bernardino Santa Barbara	64 149
ORENTES		
Jose D	Los Angeles Santa Ana	59 455
ORERLY		
Chas*	El Dorado Georgetown	58 675
ORERSHINER		
George*	Nevada Red Dog	61 555
ORERTRULF		
Jocob*	Yuba Fosters	72 825
ORESA		
Francisco	Monterey San Juan	60 986
ORESER		
Francisco	Monterey San Juan	60 986
ORESTOREN		
---	Monterey Alisal	601044
ORETHAS		
Juan A	Los Angeles Elmonte	59 259
ORETORIA		
Sister	Yuba Marysville	72 961
ORETTE		
C*	Shasta Shasta	66 656
ORETTI		
C*	Shasta Shasta	66 656
ORETTO		
C	Shasta Shasta	66 656
OREUTTORFF		
Isaac*	Napa Napa	61 69
OREVES		
Jerenema	Tuolumne Twp 5	71 499
Jeronemo	Tuolumne Chinese	71 499
OREVORLON		
Frank*	San Francisco San Francisco 3	67 2
OREW		
---	Sacramento Granite	63 245
OREWELA		
Henry	Butte Wyandotte	56 658
OREWELER		
Henry*	Butte Wyandotte	56 658
OREY		
Samuel*	Tuolumne Green Springs	71 532
OREZARSA		
Jose M	Los Angeles Santa Ana	59 446
ORF		
Henry	Colusa Butte Crk	57 464
ORFAR		
Gormasso	Calaveras Twp 6	57 128

Name	County Locale	M653 RollPage
ORFFIN		
C	Tuolumne Twp 4	71 145
ORFILA		
Antonio	San Bernardino Santa Barbara	64 160
ORG		
---	San Francisco San Francisco 4	681177
---*	Amador Twp 2	55 328
ORGAIN		
Joseph	San Mateo Twp 1	65 63
ORGAN		
Eli	San Francisco San Francisco 4	681126
Jas	Butte Oregon	56 644
Michael	San Francisco San Francisco 1	68 846
T V	El Dorado Eldorado	58 945
Thomas	El Dorado Kelsey	581126
ORGGO		
Wm	Sonoma Bodega	69 537
ORGIDO		
Joaqain*	Santa Cruz Santa Cruz	66 610
ORGNIS		
Jesus*	Los Angeles Los Angeles	59 494
ORGON		
P	Calaveras Twp 9	57 406
ORGOOD		
Luther E	Alameda Brooklyn	55 186
ORGUIS		
Tomas	Los Angeles Los Angeles	59 519
ORHAM		
Daris	Yuba Long Bar	72 750
Davis	Yuba Long Bar	72 750
ORHITAKER		
L	Yolo Cache	72 620
ORI		
---	Calaveras Twp 6	57 166
ORIAN		
Benjamin	Yuba Bear Rvr	721004
ORICK		
B	Sacramento American	63 163
Jane	Los Angeles Los Nieto	59 436
Thomas	Los Angeles Los Nieto	59 436
ORICUS		
Wm	Amador Twp 5	55 368
ORIELLEY		
Teresa	San Francisco San Francisco 2	67 615
ORIELY		
Chas*	El Dorado Georgetown	58 675
Falfonsa	Sacramento Ward 4	63 571
ORILEY		
August	Placer Forest H	62 796
David	Klamath S Fork	59 207
James	Trinity Indian C	70 989
James	Yolo Merritt	72 584
Jas	Placer Auburn	62 581
Lawrence*	Placer Auburn	62 566
M	San Francisco San Francisco 6	67 463
P	Sacramento Ward 1	63 33
Patrick	Trinity Weaverville	701081
Peter	San Francisco San Francisco 9	681025
Peter*	Calaveras Twp 5	57 219
Phillip	Trinity Browns C	70 984
Wallace	Solano Vacaville	69 323
Wm	Sonoma Santa Rosa	69 393
ORILLE		
Owen*	Plumas Quincy	621002
ORILSEN		
Wm	San Francisco San Francisco 3	67 65
ORIMONE		
Juan J	Los Angeles Los Angeles	59 514
ORIMONI		
Juan J	Los Angeles Los Angeles	59 514
ORIMRVILL		
E*	Calaveras Twp 9	57 401
ORIN		
Jessie	Nevada Bridgeport	61 488
John	San Francisco San Francisco 4	681117
S	Nevada Bridgeport	61 445
ORINE		
James	Yolo Cache	72 595
John	Yolo Cache	72 595
ORINGHT		
W*	Yolo Putah	72 549
ORINNVILL		
E*	Calaveras Twp 9	57 401
ORINSTAN		
James	El Dorado Mountain	581183
ORIOLA		
Felipa	Los Angeles Los Angeles	59 311
ORION		
---	Tulara Keyesville	71 63
---	Tulara Keyesville	71 65
---	Tulara Twp 3	71 69
ORIRIAL		
Nicholas	Contra Costa Twp 1	57 488
ORIS		
Jacob*	Tuolumne Springfield	71 372
ORISELL		
William	Siskiyou Yreka	69 152

California 1860 Census Index

Name	County Locale	M653 Roll	Page
ORISMONE			
Henry*	Los Angeles Santa Ana	59	444
ORISPEN			
C	El Dorado Kelsey	58	1146
ORISTONI			
G	Monterey Monterey	60	925
ORITO			
Sebero	Tuolumne Twp 5	71	497
ORITT			
H W*	Nevada Bridgeport	61	448
ORIVES			
Dolores	Los Angeles San Juan	59	476
Jose M	Los Angeles Santa Ana	59	455
Juana M*	Los Angeles San Pedro	59	484
ORIVEZ			
William	San Luis Obispo San Luis Obispo	65	29
ORK			
---	Trinity Grass Valley	70	962
ORKEDAS			
Jesus	Monterey Pajaro	60	1014
ORKLER			
M*	Sonoma Washington	69	674
ORKNS			
Frank	Tuolumne Montezuma	71	508
ORKUS			
Frank	Tuolumne Twp 5	71	508
ORLADES			
Morallino*	Mariposa Twp 3	60	605
William	Mariposa Twp 3	60	605
ORLANDES			
Henry	Tuolumne Shawsfla	71	413
ORLAVICH			
P	San Francisco San Francisco 5	67	539
ORLIN			
---	Trinity China Bar	70	959
ORLOONE			
Chas*	Butte Bidwell	56	713
ORLORIN			
Francisco	Santa Cruz Santa Cruz	66	607
ORLOVECH			
P	San Francisco San Francisco 5	67	539
ORLOVICH			
Peter	San Francisco San Francisco 3	67	61
ORM			
---	El Dorado Placerville	58	933
ORMAN			
Cecelia	Calaveras Twp 4	57	313
John	Nevada Bloomfield	61	529
ORMAND			
Louis	Yuba Marysville	72	875
ORMAT			
Joaquin	San Bernardino Santa Barbara	64	147
ORMAUPER			
Henry*	Del Norte Crescent	58	622
ORME			
E	Siskiyou Cottonwoood	69	105
ORMELLO			
Peter*	Calaveras Twp 5	57	221
ORMESGAN			
Turindad*	Yuba Marysville	72	936
ORMIJO			
Justo*	Monterey San Juan	60	1003
ORMRVILL			
E*	Calaveras Twp 9	57	401
ORMSBEY			
M	El Dorado Placerville	58	839
ORMSBY			
C	Nevada Grass Valley	61	219
Geo	Napa Clear Lake	61	138
Henry	El Dorado Casumnes	58	1168
J	Calaveras Twp 9	57	400
Jacob	El Dorado Eldorado	58	946
John	Alameda Brooklyn	55	165
John	Nevada Eureka	61	361
John S	Sonoma Healdsbu	69	478
Johns S	Sonoma Healdsbu	69	478
Oliver	Placer Dutch Fl	62	728
ORMSLEY			
C	Nevada Grass Valley	61	219
H	El Dorado Indian D	58	1157
Wm*	Sierra Twp 7	66	912
ORMSTEAD			
Nelson	San Bernardino S Timate	64	690
Thos	Napa Clear Lake	61	122
ORMWELL			
E	Calaveras Twp 9	57	401
ORN			
Joseph	El Dorado Georgetown	58	682
Thomas	El Dorado Placerville	58	924
ORNACES			
Theodore	Marin San Rafael	60	765
ORNAL			
T	Siskiyou Scott Ri	69	65
ORNALLIS			
Levisio	Yuba Marysville	72	947
Tevisco*	Yuba Marysville	72	947
Tevisio*	Yuba Marysville	72	947
ORNBURN			
Jno*	Mendocino Anderson	60	870
ORNE			
Wm	Tehama Cottonwoood	70	901
ORNELES			
Fimon	Merced Monterey	60	934
Simon	Monterey Monterey	60	934
ORNET			
Sarah Ann	Sierra La Porte	66	783
ORNETH			
Carlos	Calaveras Twp 8	57	82
ORNETO			
John	Calaveras Twp 8	57	61
ORNETTE			
John	Tuolumne Twp 1	71	270
ORNETTI			
Carlos*	Calaveras Twp 8	57	82
ORNETTO			
Joseph	Calaveras Twp 5	57	217
ORNSLEY			
Wm	Sierra Twp 7	66	912
ORNSTOCK			
Samuel	Santa Cruz Pajaro	66	574
ORO			
---	Amador Twp 2	55	290
OROCK			
Jno*	Nevada Nevada	61	260
OROIK			
Jno*	Nevada Nevada	61	260
OROIS			
Jouqquin*	Santa Cruz Soguel	66	584
ORONARK			
Patrick	Alameda Brooklyn	55	211
ORONAT			
Francisco	Santa Barbara San Bernardino	64	178
ORONDER			
John*	Sonoma Bodega	69	533
ORONDES			
John*	Sonoma Bodega	69	533
OROOKE			
Jeremiah	San Joaquin Oneal	64	940
L*	Nevada Grass Valley	61	166
OROS			
Raimon	Tuolumne Twp 5	71	527
OROSCO			
Augustin	San Diego S Luis R	64	778
Dolores	Los Angeles Los Angeles	59	506
Doloris*	Los Angeles Los Angeles	59	506
Gregorio	Monterey Alisal	60	1041
J J	Merced Twp 1	60	910
Jose	Santa Cruz Pajaro	66	542
Julian	Los Angeles Santa Ana	59	444
Luis	Los Angeles Los Angeles	59	517
Rosano	Los Angeles Los Nieto	59	436
Rosario*	Los Angeles Los Nieto	59	436
Simon	Los Angeles Santa Ana	59	453
OROSCOE			
Ramon*	Marin Cortemad	60	784
OROSCR			
Rosario*	Los Angeles Los Nieto	59	436
OROSEO			
Eathean	Mariposa Twp 1	60	660
Eatthean	Mariposa Twp 1	60	660
OROSER			
Jose	Santa Cruz Pajaro	66	542
OROSO			
Guadalupe	Santa Clara San Jose	65	327
OROUKE			
Cath	San Francisco San Francisco 2	67	673
Dennis	Trinity Hay Fork	70	991
Mary	Santa Clara Santa Clara	65	512
Morgan	Tuolumne Twp 2	71	367
Patrick	San Francisco San Francisco 2	67	583
Patrick	Yuba Bear Rvr	72	999
Patrick*	Yuba Bear Rvr	72	999
OROURK			
Anne	San Francisco San Francisco 10	67	270
J	Nevada Eureka	61	366
John	Trinity Ferry	70	977
Patrick	Yuba Rose Bar	72	810
Patrick*	Yuba Rose Bar	72	810
OROURKE			
B	San Francisco San Francisco 12	67	387
Daniel	Placer Iona Hills	62	889
Hugh	San Francisco San Francisco 3	67	59
James	Placer Forest H	62	800
John	Yuba Rose Bar	72	808
John*	Yuba Rose Bar	72	808
Laurence	San Francisco San Francisco 11	67	112
Mary J	Sacramento Ward 4	63	571
OROURKE			
Michael	Placer Yankee J	62	757
Michael	Tuolumne Twp 4	71	143
P*	San Francisco San Francisco 5	67	532
Patrick	Sierra Twp 7	66	913
Thomas*	Siskiyou Yreka	69	141
ORPIGA			
A	Tuolumne Twp 1	71	229
ORPOR			
Gormasso	Calaveras Twp 6	57	128
ORQUIAS			
Maria B	Los Angeles Tejon	59	539
ORQUIS			
Candilario	Los Angeles Los Angeles	59	519
Candilaro	Los Angeles Los Angeles	59	519
Jesus	Los Angeles Los Angeles	59	494
Jose Ma*	Los Angeles Los Angeles	59	519
Tomas	Los Angeles Los Angeles	59	519
ORR			
---	Calaveras Twp 10	57	287
A S	Mariposa Twp 1	60	648
Alex	Sacramento Natonia	63	278
Andrew	Mariposa Twp 1	60	635
C	Nevada Eureka	61	343
Chamber	Calaveras Twp 8	57	102
David	Placer Yankee J	62	777
E	Sonoma Salt Point	69	694
Edward	Napa Napa	61	102
Franklin J	San Joaquin Elliott	64	945
George	Placer Forest H	62	804
George	Placer Michigan	62	843
H S	Mariposa Twp 1	60	648
J C	Tehama Red Bluff	70	924
J H	Siskiyou Scott Va	69	35
J W	El Dorado Casumnes	58	1164
Jacob Saml*	Mendocino Calpella	60	820
James	El Dorado Salmon Falls	58	1037
James	Mendocino Big Rvr	60	850
James	San Francisco San Francisco 7	68	1383
Jas	San Francisco San Francisco 1	68	819
John	Shasta French G	66	714
John	Sonoma Salt Point	69	694
John	Tuolumne Sonora	71	191
John	Tuolumne Shawsfla	71	404
John S	Siskiyou Yreka	69	125
John*	Tuolumne Twp 2	71	404
Joseh	El Dorado Georgetown	58	683
Joseph	El Dorado Georgetown	58	683
Julia	Sacramento Ward 4	63	590
Letetia	Yuba Marysville	72	847
M N	Tuolumne Twp 2	71	297
Matthew	Siskiyou Yreka	69	125
Nancy W	San Francisco San Francisco 10	67	227
Peter	Sierra La Porte	66	768
Robert	Siskiyou Shasta Rvr	69	111
S M	Tuolumne Twp 2	71	474
Saml	Mendocino Calpella	60	820
Sarah E	Napa Napa	61	103
Sarah J	Sacramento Ward 4	63	562
Susan	Siskiyou Shasta Rvr	69	111
Tally*	Tuolumne Twp 5	71	511
Thomas	El Dorado Salmon Falls	58	1037
Thomas	Siskiyou Yreka	69	123
W	Butte Kimshaw	56	601
Walker	Sacramento Ward 1	63	107
Walkr	Sacramento Ward 1	63	107
Walter*	Sacramento Ward 1	63	107
William	Mendocino Calpella	60	809
William	Siskiyou Shasta Rvr	69	111
William	Siskiyou Yreka	69	125
William*	Contra Costa Twp 2	57	543
Wm	Butte Kimshaw	56	601
Wm	Sacramento Ward 1	63	137
Wm H	Placer Auburn	62	591
ORRAN			
Jno	Sacramento Granite	63	253
ORRANO			
Homobono	Santa Cruz Santa Cruz	66	607
ORRATO			
Antonio	Calaveras Twp 7	57	12
ORRATTO			
Andrea	Calaveras Twp 7	57	12
ORRENWELL			
Wm	Sierra Twp 5	66	931
ORRICK			
Thomas	Los Angeles Azuza	59	272
W G	Sierra Gibsonville	66	852
ORRIELLA			
Ylana	San Bernardino Santa Barbara	64	196
ORRINDER			
John*	Plumas Quincy	62	985
ORRINO			
Roberts*	San Mateo Twp 3	65	103
ORRIS			
Charles	Solano Vallejo	69	251

California 1860 Census Index

Name	County Locale	M653 Roll	Page
ORRIS			
Geo	Santa Clara Santa Clara	65	496
ORRIYA			
E*	Sacramento Ward 1	63	5
ORRNSTUN			
James	El Dorado Mountain	58	1183
ORROCH			
Edgar	Yuba Linda Twp	72	982
ORRONG			
---	Sacramento Ward 1	63	50
ORRSLEY			
G*	Nevada Grass Valley	61	236
ORRVILA			
Thomas*	Sacramento Ward 1	63	128
ORSAN			
James*	Sierra Twp 7	66	901
ORSANNA			
Jose	Yuba Marysville	72	960
ORSAR			
J	San Francisco San Francisco 2	67	777
ORSBEM			
Silas	Siskiyou Scott Ri	69	63
Splas*	Siskiyou Scott Ri	69	63
ORSBON			
Thomas	Nevada Bridgeport	61	439
ORSBURN			
Gould	Placer Auburn	62	559
John	Contra Costa Twp 3	57	596
R	El Dorado Coloma	58	1069
William	Placer Auburn	62	559
ORSEA			
Concepcion	Monterey San Juan	60	986
ORSININGER			
W T*	Yuba Long Bar	72	743
ORSNDER			
Wm	Mendocino Calpella	60	817
ORSO			
Preston	Santa Cruz Pajaro	66	574
ORSOIN			
James*	Sierra Twp 7	66	901
ORSTON			
Thomas*	Nevada Bridgeport	61	439
ORSULA			
Tomasa	Santa Clara San Jose	65	302
ORT			
A*	El Dorado Placerville	58	820
ORTAGA			
Jose Ma	San Bernardino Santa Ba	64	207
ORTARESS			
Fellepe*	Santa Cruz Santa Cruz	66	605
Fellesse*	Santa Cruz Santa Cruz	66	605
Tellefse*	Santa Cruz Santa Cruz	66	605
Tellepe	Santa Cruz Santa Cruz	66	605
Tellesse*	Santa Cruz Santa Cruz	66	605
Yellepe	Santa Cruz Santa Cruz	66	605
ORTEGA			
Cervasio	Los Angeles Los Angeles	59	298
Cristoval	Los Angeles Los Nieto	59	428
Diego	San Bernardino Santa Inez	64	139
Dolores	San Bernardino Santa Barbara	64	155
Dolores	San Bernardino Santa Barbara	64	161
Elgor	Tehama Red Bluff	70	926
Emidgio	San Bernardino Santa Ba	64	209
Francisco	Los Angeles Los Angeles	59	360
Francisco	San Diego S Luis R	64	780
Gabriel	Los Angeles Los Angeles	59	296
Guadelup*	San Bernardino Santa Barbara	64	155
H S	Calaveras Twp 9	57	364
Jesusmorron	San Diego San Diego	64	769
Joaquin	San Diego S Luis R	64	779
Jose	Monterey San Juan	60	993
Jose	San Bernardino Santa Inez	64	140
Jose	San Bernardino Santa Barbara	64	197
Jose	San Bernardino S Buenav	64	209
Jose	Santa Clara San Jose	65	371
Jose An	San Bernardino Santa Barbara	64	200
Jose Ma	San Bernardino Santa Barbara	64	195
Jose Manuel	San Mateo Twp 2	65	131
Jose Q	Monterey San Juan	60	993
Jose R	San Bernardino Santa Barbara	64	198
Juanna	San Bernardino Santa Inez	64	140
Madelinia	San Bernardino Santa Barbara	64	154
Manuela	San Bernardino Santa Barbara	64	203
Maria	San Mateo Twp 2	65	131
Maria G	Los Angeles San Gabriel	59	419
Martin	Los Angeles Los Nieto	59	428
Pacifico	San Bernardino Santa Barbara	64	199
Pedro	San Bernardino Santa Inez	64	144
Plastina	Santa Clara San Jose	65	302
Quintin	Santa Clara San Jose	65	361
Rafaila	San Bernardino Santa Inez	64	140
Rafaila	San Bernardino Santa Barbara	64	203
Ram A	Los Angeles Los Angeles	59	317
Ramon	San Bernardino Santa Inez	64	140
ORTEGA			
Refugio	Los Angeles Los Angeles	59	316
Reyes	San Bernardino Santa Inez	64	141
Stephen	San Luis Obispo San Luis Obispo	65	9
Thos	El Dorado Georgetown	58	745
Ucente	San Bernardino Santa Inez	64	144
Uzalo	Santa Clara San Jose	65	297
Vencente	San Bernardino S Buenav	64	212
Vicente	San Bernardino Santa Barbara	64	180
Victor	Marin Novato	60	738
Wat	Santa Clara San Jose	65	301
Ygnacio	San Bernardino Santa Barbara	64	197
ORTEGO			
D	Stanislaus Branch	70	697
Jose	Monterey San Juan	60	1005
Joseph	Marin San Rafael	60	769
ORTEGUE			
Encarnatcon	Yuba Marysville	72	948
ORTEJA			
Gregoreo	San Francisco San Francisco 2	67	768
Gregorio	San Francisco San Francisco 2	67	768
Ignacio	San Luis Obispo San Luis Obispo	65	8
Jesus	Santa Clara Almaden	65	270
ORTEL			
Joseph	San Francisco San Francisco 2	67	747
Jsoeph	San Francisco San Francisco 2	67	747
ORTELA			
---	Marin San Rafael	60	772
ORTELL			
B	San Francisco San Francisco 5	67	500
ORTELLY			
Francis	Tuolumne Twp 5	71	507
ORTEN			
Ralph	Placer Mealsburg	62	702
Susan	Santa Clara Redwood	65	447
ORTERBY			
John J*	Santa Clara Alviso	65	412
ORTERO			
Amelio	Tuolumne Chinese	71	495
Fernando*	Los Angeles Los Angeles	59	517
ORTES			
Domingo	Los Angeles Los Angeles	59	497
Nicholas	Los Angeles Tejon	59	521
Peter	San Francisco San Francisco 2	67	743
ORTESA			
Lunard	Los Angeles Elmonte	59	259
ORTESE			
Jose Marie	Calaveras Twp 6	57	162
Josi Marin*	Calaveras Twp 6	57	162
ORTEVARO			
Pamphilo	Los Angeles Azuza	59	277
ORTEY			
John*	Sacramento Ward 4	63	502
ORTEZ			
Arran	Monterey San Juan	60	983
Chono	San Diego Agua Caliente	64	847
Doleres	Monterey San Juan	60	975
Elana	Monterey San Juan	60	986
Elaria	Monterey San Juan	60	986
Sacramento	San Diego San Diego	64	768
ORTEZE			
Jose Marie*	Calaveras Twp 6	57	162
ORTH			
Jno W	Sacramento American	63	158
Jos	Sacramento Ward 1	63	88
ORTHESO			
Paletho*	San Mateo Twp 1	65	57
ORTHIS			
Domingo	San Mateo Twp 3	65	100
ORTICE			
Adel	Amador Twp 5	55	337
ORTIES			
Joseph	Napa Napa	61	84
ORTIGO			
Lamons*	Napa Napa	61	111
Samono	Napa Napa	61	111
Samons*	Napa Napa	61	111
ORTIN			
A	El Dorado Placerville	58	841
John	Siskiyou Cottonwoood	69	103
Thomas	Tulara Twp 1	71	76
ORTIS			
Antonie	Los Angeles Los Angeles	59	503
Antonio	Los Angeles Los Angeles	59	503
Domingo	Los Angeles Los Angeles	59	497
Francisco	Los Angeles Tejon	59	521
Franicsco	Los Angeles Tejon	59	521
Jose	San Luis Obispo San Luis Obispo	65	42
Nicholas	Los Angeles Tejon	59	521
ORTISANO			
---	Los Angeles Los Angeles	59	514
ORTISH			
Edward	Santa Cruz Pajaro	66	535
ORTIVERES			
Salvado	San Bernardino Santa Inez	64	141
ORTIZ			
Avelado	Los Angeles San Juan	59	461
Bicinte	Del Norte Crescent	58	650
Felipa	Los Angeles Los Angeles	59	297
J	Sacramento Ward 1	63	4
Jose	Los Angeles San Pedro	59	485
Juan	San Bernardino Santa Barbara	64	150
Miguel	Los Angeles Los Angeles	59	306
ORTLEP			
Geo	San Francisco San Francisco 10	67	341
ORTMAN			
Fredk	San Francisco San Francisco 2	67	603
ORTON			
John	Yuba Marysville	72	957
Prolo	Sonoma Petaluma	69	615
Proto	Sonoma Vallejo	69	615
Thomas	Plumas Meadow Valley	62	928
Thomas	Tulara Visalia	71	76
ORTOONE			
Chas*	Butte Bidwell	56	713
ORTRARAT			
Gaston	Los Angeles San Gabriel	59	421
ORTRUP			
Martin	Placer Yankee J	62	781
ORTTEZ			
Julio	El Dorado Georgetown	58	675
ORTTINYR			
Henry*	Calaveras Twp 6	57	113
ORTURNA			
J	Yuba Bear Rvr	72	1016
ORTURUA			
---*	Yuba Bear Rvr	72	1016
ORTZ			
J	Sacramento Ward 1	63	4
ORUNS			
Fernidad	Santa Cruz Santa Cruz	66	608
N C	Tuolumne Columbia	71	363
ORVIN			
W F	Mariposa Twp 1	60	646
ORVIS			
Jougguin	Santa Cruz Soguel	66	584
ORVSCO			
Simon*	Los Angeles Santa Ana	59	453
ORVUON			
Catharine*	San Francisco San Francisco 7	68	1414
ORWAN			
R H	Shasta Shasta	66	686
ORWENS			
William*	Mendocino Anderson	60	867
ORX			
Chas	Sacramento Ward 4	63	587
ORY			
---	Amador Twp 5	55	360
---	Amador Twp 6	55	449
ORYAN			
James	San Francisco San Francisco 1	68	929
Patrick	Solano Vallejo	69	274
Wm	Butte Oregon	56	631
OSA			
---	San Bernardino S Timate	64	693
---	Tulara Keyesville	71	65
OSAGUIDA			
Dolores	Tuolumne Sonora	71	228
Doloris	Tuolumne Twp 1	71	228
OSALIJES			
Onlahan*	Calaveras Twp 7	57	14
OSAPOTER			
Laboro	Mariposa Twp 1	60	646
OSAPUTER			
Laboro	Mariposa Twp 1	60	646
OSAPUTIR			
Saboro*	Mariposa Twp 1	60	646
Saburo	Mariposa Twp 1	60	646
OSARA			
Daniel*	Placer Michigan	62	841
OSARLIS			
Paul	Calaveras Twp 7	57	31
OSATHA			
---	Napa Napa	61	84
Francis	Napa Napa	61	84
Francy	Napa Napa	61	84
OSBECK			
Charles	Plumas Quincy	62	956
OSBERMAN			
William	Santa Cruz Pajaro	66	558
OSBERN			
S	El Dorado Kelsey	58	1138
OSBERT			
C P	Sacramento Lee	63	215
OSBERTS			
J T	Sacramento Lee	63	215
OSBIY			
John*	Contra Costa Twp 1	57	487
OSBON			
Julian Gonzales	Santa Clara San Jose	65	307

California 1860 Census Index

Name	County Locale	M653 Roll	Page
OSBOOW			
Louis	Butte Kimshaw	56	571
OSBORN TURNER			
Jim*	Humbolt Union	59	179
OSBORN			
---	San Joaquin Tulare	64	871
Anthony	Alameda Brooklyn	55	179
B F	Yolo Washington	72	569
B T	Solano Fairfield	69	197
C	San Francisco San Francisco 5	67	547
Charles	Sacramento Sutter	63	296
Charles	Tuolumne Twp 4	71	129
Charles	Yuba Marysville	72	943
Charles I	Calaveras Twp 5	57	200
Charles L	Calaveras Twp 5	57	200
Charles S*	Calaveras Twp 5	57	200
Chas	Sacramento Ward 1	63	58
D	Nevada Eureka	61	380
D C	Shasta Millvill	66	726
David	Sacramento Franklin	63	331
Edward	Calaveras Twp 7	57	8
Eli	Sierra Pine Grove	66	832
F	Sacramento Sutter	63	308
G E W	San Francisco San Francisco 9	68	970
Geo W	San Francisco San Francisco 9	68	970
George	Calaveras Twp 8	57	99
H	Butte Kimshaw	56	583
H B	Sacramento Sutter	63	301
H P	Placer Nicolaus	62	691
Henry	Butte Ophir	56	756
Henry	Humbolt Pacific	59	131
Henry	San Joaquin Elkhorn	64	967
Henry	Santa Cruz Pajaro	66	556
Henry	Stanislaus Empire	70	733
J B	Alameda Brooklyn	55	94
J B	San Francisco San Francisco 6	67	430
J B	Sonoma Salt Point	69	689
J L	San Francisco San Francisco 5	67	534
James	San Francisco San Francisco 3	67	83
James B	Calaveras Twp 7	57	8
James J	Yuba Marysville	72	891
Jas	Butte Kimshaw	56	578
Jas	Calaveras Twp 9	57	401
John	San Francisco San Francisco 10	345 67	
John B	Sierra Twp 7	66	867
Louis	Butte Kimshaw	56	571
M	Calaveras Twp 9	57	402
Martin	Placer Mealsburg	62	702
Melzer	Marin Tomales	60	718
Nelson	Stanislaus Branch	70	710
Oscar	Butte Oregon	56	611
R	Nevada Eureka	61	355
Saml	San Joaquin O'Neal	641007	
T C	San Joaquin Stockton	641088	
Thos	Tehama Antelope	70	890
W	Nevada Nevada	61	317
W	Tuolumne Garrote	71	174
W F	Sutter Yuba	70	768
William	Plumas Quincy	62	942
Woodworth	Plumas Quincy	62	959
OSBORNE			
A	El Dorado Greenwood	58	724
C M	Solano Benecia	69	295
Chas	Sacramento Ward 1	63	19
Chas	Sacramento Ward 4	63	553
Enoch	Sacramento Ward 1	63	149
Enoch	Sacramento Ward 1	63	4
Geo	Butte Mountain	56	738
H	Butte Kimshaw	56	583
Hattie M	Sacramento Ward 3	63	463
Henry	Sacramento Ward 4	63	510
Henry	Sierra Twp 7	66	879
Homer	Sacramento Ward 4	63	502
I N	Amador Twp 5	55	347
J	Alameda Brooklyn	55	186
James	Klamath Orleans	59	217
James	San Francisco San Francisco 11	151 67	
Jno	Sacramento Ward 1	63	76
Jos	San Francisco San Francisco 10	310 67	
Milo	Sacramento Ward 1	63	21
Minnie	Sacramento Ward 3	63	462
R F	Sacramento Ward 4	63	574
Robert	San Francisco San Francisco 2	67	605
Thos P	Trinity E Weaver	701059	
William	Sonoma Healdsbu	69	476
William T	Fresno Twp 3	59	32
OSBORNN			
Asa*	Mendocino Little L	60	830
OSBOURNE			
D H	Sierra Pine Grove	66	834
Francis	Stanislaus Branch	70	701
John	Yuba Bear Rvr	721003	
Stephen	Trinity North Fo	701026	

Name	County Locale	M653 Roll	Page
OSBOURNE			
Wm	San Bernardino San Bernadino	64	630
OSBREY			
William S	Tuolumne Don Pedro	71	539
William T	Tuolumne Twp 6	71	539
OSBRONE			
Wm A	Alameda Oakland	55	54
OSBURN			
Arch P	Mendocino Big Rvr	60	840
Avareto*	Los Angeles Santa Ana	59	457
Avaristo	Los Angeles Santa Ana	59	457
Avarito*	Los Angeles Santa Ana	59	457
D	Nevada Eureka	61	380
David	Tehama Red Bluff	70	910
Deptha*	Sonoma Armally	69	505
Eli	Sierra Pine Grove	66	832
Henry	Santa Clara San Jose	65	390
I W	Napa Napa	61	67
J W	Napa Napa	61	67
John	San Francisco San Francisco 3	67	1
Oeptha*	Sonoma Armally	69	505
Peptha*	Sonoma Armally	69	505
S B	Butte Ophir	56	790
Silas K	Mendocino Big Rvr	60	849
Sullivan	Colusa Monroeville	57	443
W G	San Francisco San Francisco 9	68	941
William B	Los Angeles Los Angeles	59	296
OSBURNE			
Wm*	San Bernardino San Bernadino	64	630
OSCANDABOURN			
J	Tuolumne Sonora	71	239
OSCAR			
David	Santa Cruz Santa Cruz	66	615
Eliza	Sacramento Ward 1	63	115
Geo	Mendocino Big Rvr	60	848
OSCER			
Thos	Mariposa Twp 3	60	593
OSCOE			
Jos	Sacramento Ward 3	63	432
OSCOTT			
A	Tuolumne Twp 4	71	166
OSEARY			
J*	Sacramento Ward 1	63	80
OSEHEIMER			
Isaac*	Sacramento Ward 4	63	603
OSEIR			
Charles*	Sierra Downieville	66	955
OSEMON			
Sabrana	Tehama Lassen	70	882
OSENBECK			
Matilda	San Joaquin Stockton	641017	
OSENBERG			
V	San Joaquin Stockton	641038	
OSENBURY			
Jno*	Alameda Brooklyn	55	177
OSER			
---	Sacramento Natonia	63	280
Louis	San Joaquin Stockton	641017	
OSERALL			
Charity*	Tulara Visalia	71	78
OSERNA			
Camula*	Los Angeles Tejon	59	540
OSET			
---	Tulara Visalia	71	117
OSEUBURY			
Jno*	Alameda Brooklyn	55	177
OSEVALL			
Charity*	Tulara Visalia	71	78
OSEVORLON			
Frank*	San Francisco San Francisco 3	67	2
OSFORD			
Catherine	San Joaquin Stockton	641084	
OSGOOD			
Archer	San Francisco San Francisco 10	256 67	
Benjamin	Humbolt Mattole	59	128
D	Tehama Tehama	70	949
D F	Trinity Weaverville	701078	
E H	Tuolumne Twp 1	71	267
Frank	San Francisco San Francisco 10	188 67	
Frank P	Yuba Marysville	72	892
G	Butte Wyandotte	56	662
G W	San Francisco San Francisco 9	681080	
George	San Francisco San Francisco 8	681324	
George	San Francisco San Francisco 7	681352	
H C	Trinity Whites Crk	701028	
H P	San Francisco San Francisco 6	67	443
Haza Jr	Tuolumne Columbia	71	309
J	Amador Twp 5	55	389
J F	Mendocino Big Rvr	60	848
J H	Marin Tomales	60	717
J H	Sierra Poker Flats	66	840
J N R*	Alameda Oakland	55	26
J W	Tuolumne Twp 2	71	323
James	Yuba Rose Bar	72	791

Name	County Locale	M653 Roll	Page
OSGOOD			
Jno K*	Alameda Oakland	55	26
John S	San Francisco San Francisco 3	67	86
Joseph	Yolo No E Twp	72	674
Joseph	Yuba North Ea	72	674
L	Nevada Washington	61	332
L H	Sierra Poker Flats	66	840
L*	Nevada Washington	61	332
P	Nevada Grass Valley	61	174
Porter	Yuba Marysville	72	861
R E	Tuolumne Columbia	71	323
Richard	Sierra Pine Grove	66	832
Rufus W	Marin Novato	60	734
W R	Butte Ophir	56	791
Warren	San Francisco San Francisco 10	188 67	
Wm	Alameda Oakland	55	26
OSGOORE			
Richard*	Sierra Pine Grove	66	832
OSGORD			
G W	San Francisco San Francisco 9	681080	
OSHA			
Ferdinan	Tehama Tehama	70	948
OSHAE			
Martin	Butte Kimshaw	56	578
OSHARLEN			
Henry*	Placer Forest H	62	767
OSHATTUCK			
David*	San Francisco San Francisco 11	100 67	
OSHAUGHY			
James	Solano Fremont	69	383
OSHEA			
Catharine	San Francisco San Francisco 11	112 67	
Catharine	San Francisco San Francisco 7	681330	
M	Shasta Shasta	66	662
Richard	Los Angeles Azuza	59	276
Robrt	San Francisco San Francisco 1	68	839
Thomas	Shasta Shasta	66	730
Wm	Butte Ophir	56	777
OSHER			
L	El Dorado Placerville	58	912
OSHINN			
John	Sonoma Russian	69	438
OSHON			
P	Tehama Moons	70	854
OSHST			
John	Sacramento Ward 3	63	431
OSHUNGHY			
James	Solano Fremont	69	383
OSHURNE			
Wm*	San Bernardino San Bernadino	64	630
OSIER			
Eliza	Sacramento Ward 1	63	115
Jas	Sacramento Ward 3	63	467
OSIMO			
Leonada	Alameda Brooklyn	55	208
OSIN			
Charles	Sierra Downieville	66	955
OSINCLAIR			
Adam*	Sacramento Ward 1	63	46
OSIO			
Josefa	Los Angeles Los Angeles	59	315
Marie C	Monterey Alisal	601030	
Salvado	Merced Monterey	60	939
Salvador	Monterey Monterey	60	939
OSIT			
---	Tulara Twp 1	71	117
OSLARLEN			
Henry*	Placer Forest H	62	767
OSMEN			
Sarah*	Del Norte Crescent	58	619
OSMENT			
J A	Trinity Readings	70	996
OSMER			
Chas	San Francisco San Francisco 9	681066	
George	San Francisco San Francisco 3	67	61
Isa	El Dorado Georgetown	58	674
J	El Dorado Grizzly	581182	
N A*	El Dorado Placerville	58	884
Sarah*	Del Norte Crescent	58	619
Thos	Sacramento Ward 1	63	10
OSMES			
N A*	El Dorado Placerville	58	884
OSMITH			
Robt	Napa Clear Lake	61	127
OSMOS			
F	Yolo Merritt	72	584
Orson	Butte Bidwell	56	708
OSMUM			
Orson	Butte Bidwell	56	708
OSMUS			
F	Yolo Merritt	72	584
OSNER			
Chas	San Francisco San Francisco 2	67	774

California 1860 Census Index

Name	County Locale	M653 Roll	Page
OSO			
---	Mendocino Calpella	60	824
---	Mendocino Big Rock	60	876
---	Tulara Keyesville	71	56
---	Tulara Keyesville	71	57
---	Tulara Twp 3	71	63
---	Tulara Keyesville	71	66
---	Tulara Keyesville	71	67
---	Tulara Keyesville	71	69
---	Tulara Twp 3	71	70
---	Tulara Keyesville	71	72
OSOLIO			
---	San Francisco San Francisco 2	67	791
Lucinda	San Francisco San Francisco 2	67	791
OSOO			
---*	Nevada Rough &	61	399
John	Siskiyou Yreka	69	134
OSOOL			
Clementine*	Alameda Oakland	55	31
OSORIA			
Mariana	Napa Napa	61	114
OSORIO			
Baimon	Tuolumne Montezuma	71	507
OSORIR			
Raimon*	Tuolumne Twp 5	71	507
OSPENCER			
A*	San Francisco San Francisco 1	68	921
OSPENSER			
Richard*	San Francisco San Francisco 3	67	1
OSPINSER			
Richard*	San Francisco San Francisco 3	67	1
OSS SING			
---	Sierra Twp 5	66	928
OSSBURN			
R*	El Dorado Coloma	58	1069
OSSELIN			
Peter	San Mateo Twp 1	65	60
OSSENHEIM			
Cecilia*	San Francisco San Francisco 2	67	658
OSSEO			
---	Amador Twp 2	55	327
OSSHEIMER			
Isaac*	Sacramento Ward 4	63	603
OSSITER			
E J	Sierra La Porte	66	777
OSSUNA			
Francisca	San Diego San Diego	64	768
Innocencia	San Diego San Diego	64	773
Juliana	San Diego San Diego	64	768
Julio*	San Diego San Diego	64	768
OST			
Julius	Colusa Colusi	57	424
OSTAVE			
Trinidad*	Tehama Tehama	70	941
OSTEGA			
Encarnation	Yuba Marysville	72	948
OSTEJA			
Jesus	San Luis Obispo San Luis Obispo	65	37
OSTEN			
John	Amador Twp 1	55	470
OSTENADER			
J	El Dorado Georgetown	58	695
OSTENBECK			
Henry	Nevada Little Y	61	533
OSTEND			
---	Fresno Twp 1	59	80
OSTENDING			
Gustanew	Solano Fairfield	69	199
OSTENDURF			
Gustanis*	Solano Fairfield	69	199
Gustarus*	Solano Fairfield	69	199
OSTER			
Henry	San Francisco San Francisco 12	67	396
OSTERAURP			
Henry	Sierra Twp 7	66	878
OSTERBROOKS			
D	Siskiyou Scott Va	69	58
OSTERBY			
John J*	Santa Clara Alviso	65	412
OSTERCAMP			
Henry	Sierra Twp 7	66	878
OSTERHOLTZ			
Fred	Tuolumne Springfield	71	369
OSTERHOUT			
C*	Sutter Butte	70	788
George	Tuolumne Twp 1	71	192
OSTERMAN			
Francis	Del Norte Klamath	58	653
Martin	Sierra Twp 7	66	870
William	Santa Cruz Pajaro	66	558
OSTHOFF			
Henry	Trinity Oregon G	70	1009
OSTIRE			
J	Nevada Eureka	61	366
OSTORN			
J*	San Joaquin Stockton	64	1099
OSTOSKE			
S	Butte Ophir	56	764
OSTOSKI			
S	Butte Ophir	56	764
OSTRAM			
Chas	Santa Clara Santa Clara	65	477
OSTRANDER			
George	Alameda Brooklyn	55	98
H J	Merced Twp 1	60	912
Henry	El Dorado Georgetown	58	695
Peter	San Francisco San Francisco 12	67	389
Stephen	San Francisco San Francisco 3	67	20
Wm	Merced Twp 2	60	916
OSTRANDIR			
H J	Merced Twp 1	60	912
OSTRAVDER			
George	Alameda Brooklyn	55	98
OSTRIC			
J*	Nevada Eureka	61	366
OSTRICH			
H	Amador Twp 6	55	441
OSTRICHER			
T*	Tuolumne Columbia	71	315
OSTRIM			
Jno	Nevada Nevada	61	266
OSTROM			
J D	Nevada Eureka	61	348
J F	Amador Twp 6	55	429
Jno	Nevada Nevada	61	266
Tobiar*	Amador Twp 4	55	258
Tobias*	Amador Twp 4	55	258
OSTRON			
L*	Nevada Grass Valley	61	175
OSTROON			
J D*	Nevada Eureka	61	348
OSTROUR			
J D*	Nevada Eureka	61	348
OSTRUS			
G	Nevada Nevada	61	248
OSTSOOD			
Henry M	San Luis Obispo San Luis Obispo	65	29
OSTUC			
J*	Nevada Eureka	61	366
OSTUE			
M*	Nevada Eureka	61	366
OSTURA			
J	Yuba Bear Rvr	72	1016
OSTURUA			
---*	Yuba Bear Rvr	72	1016
OSULIVAN			
Geo*	Placer Rattle Snake	62	626
T W	Nevada Rough &	61	408
OSULLIVAN			
Cornelius	San Francisco San Francisco 8	68	1250
Cornelius*	San Francisco San Francisco 8	68	1250
Delia	San Francisco San Francisco 2	67	569
Ellen	San Francisco San Francisco 2	67	723
Fras	San Francisco San Francisco 12	67	386
James	Tuolumne Twp 3	71	443
Michael	Sierra Twp 7	66	912
Michael	Tuolumne Twp 3	71	432
Pat	Tuolumne Twp 3	71	443
Simon	Yuba Rose Bar	72	808
Simon*	Yuba Rose Bar	72	808
T W	Nevada Rough &	61	408
OSUM			
N C	Tuolumne Twp 2	71	363
OSUNA			
A H*	Napa Hot Springs	61	2
Josefer	San Francisco San Francisco 2	67	763
Mareial	Santa Clara Almaden	65	267
OSUND			
Josefa	San Francisco San Francisco 2	67	763
OSUNDGREEN			
Peter*	San Francisco San Francisco 3	67	69
OSUNDGRUN			
Peter*	San Francisco San Francisco 3	67	69
OSUNO			
Antonio	Santa Clara Almaden	65	262
OSVIS			
Jougguiss	Santa Cruz Soguel	66	584
OSWALD			
Benjamin	Los Angeles Los Angeles	59	402
Frank	Trinity Mouth Ca	70	1013
John	Sacramento Ward 4	63	549
R	Alameda Oakland	55	39
OSWELL			
James	San Francisco San Francisco 11	67	137
OSWINICE			
Jean*	Calaveras Twp 7	57	8
OT			
---	El Dorado Mud Springs	58	950
Seen	San Francisco San Francisco 11	67	146
OTADOR			
Nicascoen	Calaveras Twp 6	57	150
Nicaswea*	Calaveras Twp 6	57	150
Nicaswen*	Calaveras Twp 6	57	150
OTAGO			
Fumusco*	Calaveras Twp 5	57	226
OTAH			
H	El Dorado Placerville	58	833
OTAN			
Clocis	Yuba Suida	72	994
Clous*	Yuba Linda	72	994
OTARDO			
Jose Maria	Calaveras Twp 6	57	150
OTARGA			
Eugenina	Santa Clara San Jose	65	305
OTARO			
Facund	Tuolumne Shawsfla	71	380
OTASCIO			
Rosetta	Contra Costa Twp 1	57	497
OTASSA			
Maria	Contra Costa Twp 1	57	496
OTAYLOR			
---*	El Dorado Cold Spring	58	1101
OTAYO			
Tomusoo	Calaveras Twp 5	57	226
Tomusso	Calaveras Twp 5	57	226
OTELL			
Louis	Sacramento Ward 3	63	485
Mariah	San Francisco San Francisco 11	67	136
OTELO			
Jesus	Monterey Alisal	60	1041
OTEN			
Vicente A	Monterey San Juan	60	983
OTERE			
Fernando	San Luis Obispo San Luis Obispo	65	24
OTEREZ			
Jose M	Santa Cruz Santa Cruz	66	621
Jose W	Santa Cruz Santa Cruz	66	623
OTERO			
Clemente	Santa Cruz Pescadero	66	642
Clemento	Santa Cruz Pescadero	66	642
Jesus	San Francisco San Francisco 5	67	513
Juan	Santa Cruz Santa Cruz	66	601
Lorenzo	Los Angeles Santa Ana	59	442
Maximo	Monterey San Juan	60	1003
Vicente A*	Monterey San Juan	60	983
OTESEA			
Rebecca*	San Francisco San Francisco 2	67	762
OTESEN			
Rebecca	San Francisco San Francisco 2	67	762
OTESO			
Mariaca	San Luis Obispo San Luis Obispo	65	24
OTEY			
Morris T	Napa Hot Springs	61	27
OTH			
J J*	Nevada Nevada	61	266
OTHEL			
George*	Calaveras Twp 6	57	155
OTHEMAN			
A H	Nevada Eureka	61	390
OTHER			
John	Sacramento Natonia	63	286
T*	Nevada Grass Valley	61	181
OTHET			
T*	Nevada Grass Valley	61	181
OTHICK			
E	Sacramento Ward 3	63	458
W D	El Dorado Coloma	58	1082
OTHO			
---	Mendocino Calpella	60	828
Andrew	Sacramento Granite	63	259
Bernard	Nevada Rough &	61	425
OTHOA			
Manuel*	San Francisco San Francisco 8	68	1253
OTIEN			
August	Shasta Shasta	66	682
OTILS			
Mary	San Francisco San Francisco 7	68	1343
OTILZ			
Mary	San Francisco San Francisco 7	68	1343
OTIS			
C C	Sacramento Lee	63	212
Chas	San Francisco San Francisco 10	67	201
Isaac	Nevada Rough &	61	405
Isaac B	Nevada Rough &	61	406
Jas	San Francisco San Francisco 10	67	244
John	Calaveras Twp 5	57	203
Jos	San Francisco San Francisco 10	67	244

California 1860 Census Index

Name	County Locale	M653 Roll	Page	Name	County Locale	M653 Roll	Page	Name	County Locale	M653 Roll	Page
OTIS				**OTTO**				**OULY**			
Mitchell	Fresno Twp 2	59	4	Anthony	Placer Iona Hills	62	888	William	Tuolumne Twp 1	71	259
Stephen	San Francisco San Francisco 6	67	422	Benedict	Sierra Twp 5	66	937	**OUM**			
Thomas	Tulara Twp 3	71	61	Charles	Placer Forest H	62	796	---	Amador Twp 1	55	502
Thomas P	Yuba Marysville	72	873	Charles	San Francisco San Francisco 7	68	1348	---	Amador Twp 1	55	510
OTIZE				George	Santa Cruz Santa Cruz	66	614	---	Amador Twp 1	55	511
L*	Nevada Eureka	61	389	Gustavus	San Francisco San Francisco 3	67	3	---	Sierra Twp 5	66	926
OTLER				Gustuvus	San Francisco San Francisco 3	67	3	**OUN**			
Chas	Santa Clara Santa Clara	65	470	Henry	Siskiyou Yreka	69	174	---	Calaveras Twp 8	57	106
OTMAN				Philipene	Siskiyou Yreka	69	175	---	Calaveras Twp 4	57	306
Hoeman*	San Mateo Twp 1	65	70	Wm	Humbolt Union	59	190	Yup	Nevada Washington	61	342
OTNAS				Wm	San Francisco San Francisco 1	68	923	**OUNKEN**			
John	Placer Virginia	62	673	**OTTOMEN**				Wm*	Sierra Twp 5	66	924
OTO				Frank	San Francisco San Francisco 3	67	70	**OUO**			
---	Sierra St Louis	66	816	**OTTOSI**				---	Amador Twp 3	55	410
Benj	Nevada Bridgeport	61	439	Jean	San Francisco San Francisco 2	67	689	---	Placer Auburn	62	568
OTOOL				**OTTS**				**OUR**			
Clementine*	Alameda Oakland	55	31	Peter	Los Angeles Los Angeles	59	511	---	Amador Twp 3	55	410
Thos	Yolo Merritt	72	584	Petro	Los Angeles Los Angeles	59	511	---	Calaveras Twp 5	57	181
OTOOLE				William B	Los Angeles Los Angeles	59	370	**OURIN**			
Adeline	Tuolumne Columbia	71	472	**OTTU**				John	El Dorado White Oaks	58	1018
Adeline	Tuolumne Twp 2	71	472	Joseph*	Placer Michigan	62	807	**OURIOL**			
Hery	Plumas Quincy	62	916	**OTUL**				Nicholas*	Contra Costa Twp 1	57	488
M	Butte Ophir	56	781	Pablis	Calaveras Twp 6	57	150	**OURMAN**			
Martin	Butte Ophir	56	761	Pablo	Calaveras Twp 6	57	150	Barny*	Alameda Brooklyn	55	147
Wm	Santa Clara Alviso	65	408	**OTURDS**				**OURNS**			
OTRO				Jose Maria	Calaveras Twp 6	57	150	B W	San Joaquin Stockton	64	1058
Jesus	Napa Napa	61	84	**OTURRAT**				J	Calaveras Twp 9	57	403
OTSON				Greyoin	Calaveras Twp 6	57	123	**OUROUX**			
M	Nevada Nevada	61	298	**OTWAY**				Edward	Alameda Oakland	55	66
OTT				Thomas*	Sacramento Ward 1	63	132	**OUSAN**			
Chas B	Sacramento Ward 4	63	554	**OTWOOD**				Manuel	Contra Costa Twp 1	57	496
George	Sierra Gibsonville	66	859	Francis	San Francisco San Francisco 8	68	1252	**OUSLEY**			
J J	Nevada Nevada	61	266	**OTY**				E	Nevada Grass Valley	61	237
Jacob	San Francisco San Francisco 9	68	1055	Robt	Santa Clara San Jose	65	354	G*	Nevada Grass Valley	61	236
John	Mariposa Twp 3	60	568	**OTYBACKER**				Henry*	Napa Hot Springs	61	12
John G	Tuolumne Columbia	71	312	Martin	Yuba Marysville	72	957	John*	Nevada Grass Valley	61	150
John*	Plumas Quincy	62	939	**OU**				Jordan	Nevada Grass Valley	61	236
Julius	Tuolumne Twp 1	71	261	---	Amador Twp 2	55	280	L	Nevada Grass Valley	61	237
Maak	El Dorado Casumnes	58	1174	---	Amador Twp 6	55	445	M	Nevada Grass Valley	61	237
Mack*	El Dorado Casumnes	58	1174	---	Calaveras Twp 10	57	270	R C	Nevada Grass Valley	61	196
Martin	Tuolumne Twp 2	71	312	---	El Dorado Salmon Falls	58	1041	W*	Nevada Grass Valley	61	171
V G	Placer Michigan	62	852	---	El Dorado Georgetown	58	682	**OUSLY**			
OTTEGA				---	Sierra Twp 7	66	898	Y	Nevada Grass Valley	61	236
Manuel	Calaveras Twp 8	57	70	---	Sierra Downieville	66	999	**OUSTON**			
OTTEL				---	Siskiyou Scott Va	69	47	L H	El Dorado White Oaks	58	1007
George	Calaveras Twp 6	57	155	---	Yuba Linda	72	991	**OUTCEL**			
OTTEMAN				---*	El Dorado Kelsey	58	1142	Gabletz	Calaveras Twp 6	57	147
Susan	Nevada Nevada	61	290	---*	Siskiyou Scott Va	69	47	Gobletz	Calaveras Twp 5	57	147
OTTEN				Ah	Yuba Suida	72	991	**OUTHOUSE**			
Carson	Klamath Liberty	59	231	Chong	Plumas Quincy	62	945	Jas*	Sacramento Cosumnes	63	405
Chas	Klamath Liberty	59	231	Fang	Plumas Quincy	62	945	Jos*	Sacramento Cosumnes	63	405
H	San Mateo Twp 1	65	63	Su	Sacramento Granite	63	268	**OUTHWAIT**			
Henry	Klamath S Fork	59	203	Wa	Calaveras Twp 5	57	256	---	Placer Secret R	62	615
Henry	San Francisco San Francisco 9	68	1054	**OUDIN**				**OUTIOEROS**			
J H	Amador Twp 1	55	461	Frank	Santa Clara Burnett	65	260	John*	Yuba Marysville	72	873
John	Tulara Visalia	71	33	**OUDVERES**				**OUTIS**			
V	Trinity Prices B	70	1019	P*	Amador Twp 2	55	303	John	Colusa Muion	57	462
OTTENHEIM				**OUENR**				**OUTMAN**			
Daniel	Los Angeles Los Angeles	59	344	James*	Mariposa Twp 1	60	673	Harman	Calaveras Twp 10	57	265
OTTENHEIMER				**OUGE**				Husman	Calaveras Twp 10	57	265
J B	Siskiyou Scott Va	69	50	---	Amador Twp 3	55	410	**OUTOD**			
William	Siskiyou Yreka	69	185	---	San Francisco San Francisco 9	68	963	Jno*	San Francisco San Francisco 9	68	1080
OTTENWELDER				**OUGH**				**OUTON**			
Martin	Butte Hamilton	56	516	T	Nevada Eureka	61	370	Jno*	San Francisco San Francisco 9	68	1080
OTTER				**OUGHTELL**				**OUY**			
Antone*	Mariposa Twp 1	60	647	P	San Joaquin Elkhorn	64	991	---	Sacramento Ward 1	63	54
David	El Dorado Salmon Falls	58	1035	**OUGNLICE**				**OVALLES**			
J	El Dorado Diamond	58	814	David*	Santa Cruz Pescadero	66	641	Hosea T	Alameda Brooklyn	55	131
John	Tulara Twp 2	71	33	**OUHER**				**OVASE**			
Louis	Mariposa Twp 1	60	647	---	Sacramento Granite	63	264	Minailla*	Alameda Brooklyn	55	151
Peter	Solano Suisan	69	233	**OUI**				**OVEFIELD**			
Wm	Santa Clara San Jose	65	333	---	Calaveras Twp 5	57	138	George	Contra Costa Twp 1	57	528
OTTERMAN				**OUID**				**OVELA**			
J*	Yolo Putah	72	553	Manuel	Sacramento Granite	63	254	P*	Nevada Grass Valley	61	166
OTTERSON				**OUIGUIS**				**OVEMIRE**			
G W	Sonoma Santa Rosa	69	415	John	Tuolumne Twp 2	71	292	Charles	Shasta French G	66	721
Henry	Sacramento Ward 4	63	502	**OUINGOCHAPA**				J D	Shasta French G	66	721
James	Santa Clara Fremont	65	430	Antonio	Los Angeles San Juan	59	470	**OVENBERG**			
OTTERSTATTER				**OUINGUCHAPA**				Henry	Nevada Rough &	61	396
John	Del Norte Crescent	58	633	Narciso*	Los Angeles San Juan	59	470	**OVENDELL**			
John	Del Norte Crescent	58	634	**OUIRLAN**				Jas	Sonoma Sonoma	69	638
OTTESMAN				Jno*	San Francisco San Francisco 9	68	1070	**OVENDILL**			
Susan	Nevada Nevada	61	290	**OUITTENDEN**				Jas	Sonoma Sonoma	69	638
OTTING				Giles E	Yuba Bear Rvr	72	1003	**OVENDIVI**			
Charles	Humbolt Eel Rvr	59	154	**OULD**				Elizabeth	San Joaquin Castoria	64	884
Frederick	San Francisco San Francisco 7	68	1358	J	Nevada Grass Valley	61	207	**OVENIDICK**			
Rich	Sacramento Granite	63	267	**OULDEN**				Fredk*	Del Norte Crescent	58	631
Rick	Sacramento Granite	63	267	Thomas	Santa Cruz Santa Cruz	66	621	**OVEOLS**			
OTTIS				**OULLAMAN**				Ysidro	San Bernardino Santa Ba	64	211
A	Nevada Eureka	61	370	D J	San Joaquin Stockton	64	1060	**OVER**			
Mary J	Marin Point Re	60	731	**OULLEN**				John M	Sierra St Louis	66	810
Michael*	San Francisco San Francisco 1	68	836	J*	Nevada Eureka	61	369	**OVERACRE**			
OTTIWELL				**OULLER**				Phillip	Amador Twp 3	55	401
Thos	Nevada Rough &	61	419	J*	Nevada Eureka	61	369	**OVERACRO**			
OTTMAN				**OULPEPPER**				Phillip	Amador Twp 3	55	401
Chris	Nevada Bridgeport	61	451	G	Siskiyou Klamath	69	88				

California 1860 Census Index

Name	County Locale	M653 Roll	Page
OVERACTER			
Howard	Alameda Brooklyn	55	209
Michael	Alameda Brooklyn	55	209
OVERAKE			
Phillipp	Amador Twp 3	55	395
OVERALL			
Charity	Tulara Twp 1	71	78
Charles	Shasta Millvill	66	756
OVERAND			
J A T	San Francisco San Francisco 1	68	875
OVERBACK			
Fred	Sierra La Porte	66	776
OVERBRUCK			
Gustave	Placer Forest H	62	806
OVERCOTT			
Julius	Tuolumne Twp 2	71	379
OVERFET			
W C	Santa Clara San Jose	65	378
OVERFIELD			
Geo	Sacramento Georgian	63	340
OVERHILL			
Martin	Butte Oregon	56	641
OVERHOLSER			
Jacob	Alameda Brooklyn	55	103
OVERHOLT			
D D*	Napa Yount	61	33
D G	Napa Yount	61	40
Wm G	Napa Yount	61	38
OVERHOUSE			
R B	Solano Vacaville	69	360
William	Solano Vacaville	69	360
OVERLAND			
Jacob	Plumas Quincy	62	954
Jacob	Plumas Quincy	62	972
OVERLANDER			
Samuel*	Humbolt Union	59	190
OVERLY			
A	Sutter Butte	70	792
OVERMAN			
William	El Dorado Kelsey	58	1149
OVERMIER			
F	Tuolumne Twp 2	71	288
OVERMILLER			
George	Alameda Brooklyn	55	141
OVERMIRE			
Q	Sacramento Brighton	63	198
OVERMYER			
Solomon	Sierra La Porte	66	775
OVERSHINN			
G J	Yolo Cottonwood	72	652
OVERSON			
Matthew	Siskiyou Scott Va	69	42
Peter	San Francisco San Francisco 9	68	1089
R	Sacramento Brighton	63	200
OVERSTREET			
J H	Santa Clara Santa Clara	65	487
OVERTAN			
William L	San Joaquin Oneal	64	934
OVERTON			
A P	Sonoma Petaluma	69	543
Amos A	Fresno Twp 1	59	34
Ann	El Dorado Salmon Falls	58	1049
Anna	Santa Cruz Soguel	66	593
Aura	Santa Cruz Soguel	66	593
E G	San Joaquin Stockton	64	1085
E P	Butte Ophir	56	780
Edward	Siskiyou Cottonwood	69	104
Emma	Santa Cruz Pajaro	66	542
Harris	Sonoma Santa Rosa	69	421
J	Butte Wyandotte	56	670
J W	Calaveras Twp 9	57	348
Jas M	Calaveras Twp 9	57	347
John B	Plumas Quincy	62	952
L H	Nevada Grass Valley	61	183
M*	Calaveras Twp 7	57	13
Robert	Calaveras Twp 6	57	160
Wm	Sierra Twp 7	66	883
OVERTULF			
Jocob*	Yuba Fosters	72	825
OVERTUN			
M*	Calaveras Twp 7	57	13
OVERTWOLF			
Jacob*	Yuba Foster B	72	825
OVERUNGER			
Solomon	Sierra La Porte	66	775
OVERY			
Eliza	San Francisco San Francisco 4	68	1144
S D*	Nevada Grass Valley	61	184
OVERYMA			
Jas*	Butte Bidwell	56	726
OVERYMITS			
Jas	Butte Bidwell	56	726
OVERYRIA			
Jas*	Butte Bidwell	56	726
OVETON			
Anna	Santa Cruz Soguel	66	593
OVEZIDER			
Wm	Mendocino Calpella	60	817
OVHEAT			
Jas*	Yolo Merritt	72	581
OVIEDO			
Rucos	Sacramento Ward 1	63	57
OVIGEO			
Guctan	Calaveras Twp 5	57	217
Guitan	Calaveras Twp 5	57	217
OVINGHT			
W*	Yolo Putah	72	549
OVIRT			
Saml	Calaveras Twp 5	57	243
OVIST			
Saml	Calaveras Twp 5	57	243
OVITT			
H W	Nevada Bridgeport	61	448
OVREN			
E F	Sierra Downieville	66	995
OVTIES			
Joseph*	Napa Napa	61	84
OVUHOLT			
D D*	Napa Yount	61	33
OW			
---	Calaveras Twp 10	57	287
---	Calaveras Twp 10	57	297
---	Nevada Bridgeport	61	466
---	Placer Illinois	62	754
---	Placer Iona Hills	62	891
---	Sierra Downieville	66	1005
---	Sierra Downieville	66	983
---*	Nevada Bridgeport	61	461
---*	Nevada Bridgeport	61	466
---*	Siskiyou Scott Va	69	47
J*	Nevada Bridgeport	61	461
J*	Nevada Bridgeport	61	466
Sin	Sacramento Natonia	63	286
Sou	San Francisco San Francisco 5	67	485
Whong	San Francisco San Francisco 5	67	485
OWADO			
Juana*	San Francisco San Francisco 3	67	1
OWAN			
---	El Dorado Placerville	58	904
---	Sierra Downieville	66	1003
OWANICINO			
J	Sacramento Ward 1	63	110
OWANICINS			
J	Sacramento Ward 1	63	110
OWANS			
Geo S	Tuolumne Sonora	71	219
OWD			
W J	Tuolumne Twp 3	71	460
OWDON			
Lucy	Santa Cruz Soguel	66	596
OWE			
---	Amador Twp 2	55	319
---	Amador Twp 5	55	356
---	El Dorado Diamond	58	795
---	Sierra Downieville	66	1003
---	Siskiyou Scott Ri	69	76
Ock	Amador Twp 5	55	355
OWEAL			
J*	Nevada Grass Valley	61	170
OWEN			
---	Siskiyou Scott Ri	69	67
Addison	Mariposa Twp 1	60	647
Ah	Siskiyou Scott Ri	69	67
Alonzo	San Francisco San Francisco 9	68	1021
Alonzo W	San Francisco San Francisco 8	68	1234
Aristne*	Alameda Oakland	55	48
Austin*	Alameda Oakland	55	48
B F	El Dorado Placerville	58	918
Benj	Butte Chico	56	540
Benj	El Dorado Mud Springs	58	978
C E	Shasta Millvill	66	756
C E	Yuba Parks Ba	72	778
Chas	Napa Napa	61	72
Comolly*	Amador Twp 1	55	454
Connelly*	Amador Twp 1	55	454
Eben	Sacramento Ward 3	63	476
Edward	Tuolumne Sonora	71	233
Eliaha	Tuolumne Sonora	71	206
Elisha	Tuolumne Twp 1	71	206
Eliza	San Francisco San Francisco 4	68	1144
Evan	San Francisco San Francisco 3	67	68
F H	Yolo No E Twp	72	670
F H	Yuba North Ea	72	670
Francis	San Francisco San Francisco 3	67	68
George	Calaveras Twp 7	57	30
Isaac	Santa Clara Santa Clara	65	491
J	El Dorado Georgetown	58	690
J Carroll	Solano Suisan	69	205
J N	San Francisco San Francisco 5	67	551
J S	Sonoma Armally	69	507
James	Alameda Brooklyn	55	103
James	Placer Yankee J	62	782
OWEN			
James	Siskiyou Yreka	69	146
James	Siskiyou Klamath	69	92
James H	Santa Clara Gilroy	65	253
Jno	Sacramento Granite	63	253
John	Amador Twp 5	55	358
John	Nevada Bridgeport	61	469
John F	Sierra Excelsior	66	1033
John W	Solano Suisan	69	209
Joshua	Tulara Twp 1	71	94
Joshua	Tuolumne Visalia	71	94
Kate	Solano Vallejo	69	266
L	Shasta Shasta	66	734
Lytle	Tulara Twp 1	71	93
Lytle	Tuolumne Visalia	71	93
M W	San Francisco San Francisco 4	68	1225
Meloin*	Amador Twp 7	55	419
Melorn*	Amador Twp 7	55	419
Melvin	Amador Twp 7	55	419
N	Shasta Horsetown	66	699
Patrick*	Sierra Twp 7	66	912
Randolph R	San Joaquin Elkhorn	64	949
Richard	Sacramento San Joaquin	63	349
Richard	Sierra Downieville	66	1028
Richard	Yuba Marysville	72	979
Richard*	Yuba Marysville	72	932
Robert	Sierra Twp 7	66	866
Robert	Yuba Marysville	72	857
Robert*	Sierra Twp 7	66	866
S W	Amador Twp 2	55	269
Saml	Amador Twp 2	55	308
Samuel	Calaveras Twp 4	57	319
Samuel	Sierra Twp 7	66	878
Samuel	Sierra Twp 7	66	884
Samuel	Sierra Twp 7	66	892
Sanford	Siskiyou Callahan	69	1
Silas	Shasta Shasta	66	672
Thomas	Sierra Cold Can	66	836
Thomas H	Solano Suisan	69	213
W	San Francisco San Francisco 2	67	631
W F	Mariposa Twp 1	60	646
W P	San Francisco San Francisco 9	68	981
Watson	El Dorado Placerville	58	901
William	Contra Costa Twp 2	57	543
William C	Tulara Twp 1	71	99
William H	Tulara Visalia	71	99
William R	Tulara Visalia	71	86
William R	Tulara Twp 1	71	94
William R	Tuolumne Visalia	71	94
William W	Sierra Gibsonville	66	860
Wilson	Tulara Visalia	71	107
Wm	Alameda Brooklyn	55	134
Wm	Placer Virginia	62	700
Woodford	Solano Suisan	69	206
OWENES			
William*	Tuolumne Don Pedro	71	540
OWENS			
Alex	Siskiyou Scott Va	69	51
Anna	San Joaquin Stockton	64	1045
Anne	San Francisco San Francisco 2	67	573
Benjamin	El Dorado Greenwood	58	720
Briget	San Francisco San Francisco 3	67	53
Brigit	San Francisco San Francisco 3	67	53
C	San Francisco San Francisco 9	68	1090
Calvin	Tehama Cottonwoood	70	901
Cathrene	San Francisco San Francisco 2	67	729
Cathrine	San Francisco San Francisco 2	67	729
Charles	Los Angeles Los Angeles	59	360
Charles	Santa Cruz Soguel	66	591
D	El Dorado Placerville	58	864
D W	Sierra Eureka	66	1042
David	Amador Twp 2	55	274
E S	Butte Oro	56	680
Edward	Tuolumne Twp 1	71	233
Edward	Tuolumne Twp 6	71	541
Edward	Yuba Marysville	72	955
Elisha	Tuolumne Twp 1	71	256
Elizabeth	Sacramento Ward 3	63	438
F	Yuba Rose Par	72	796
F A	Tehama Antelope	70	886
F*	Yuba Rose Bar	72	796
H	San Francisco San Francisco 5	67	537
Henry	San Francisco San Francisco 8	68	1235
Hugh	Tulara Twp 1	71	100
Isaac	Del Norte Crescent	58	621
J	Calaveras Twp 9	57	403
J	Siskiyou Klamath	69	87
J B	Sacramento Ward 1	63	46
J M	Siskiyou Scott Ri	69	64
J R	Santa Clara Alviso	65	402
J W	Trinity Weaverville	70	1062
Ja	Sacramento Ward 1	63	40
James	Mariposa Twp 1	60	673
James	Siskiyou Klamath	69	92
James A	Santa Clara Gilroy	65	251
James J	Humbolt Eureka	59	170

California 1860 Census Index

Name	County Locale	M653 Roll	Page
OWENS			
James K	Tuolumne Twp 2	71	384
James M	Napa Yount	61	48
Jas	Butte Wyandotte	56	668
Jas H	San Francisco San Francisco 9	68	1077
Jehil	Santa Clara Gilroy	65	244
Jno	Trinity Trinity	70	974
John	Nevada Washington	61	333
John	Sacramento Franklin	63	319
John	San Francisco San Francisco 7	68	1351
John	San Joaquin Elliott	64	1104
John	Sierra Twp 7	66	899
John	Tehama Cottonwood	70	898
John	Tuolumne Twp 6	71	541
John B	Sacramento Ward 3	63	438
Joseph L	Napa Yount	61	36
Joseph S	Napa Yount	61	36
K	Tehama Cottonwoood	70	898
L	Amador Twp 1	55	452
Lemuel	Humbolt Eureka	59	167
Lewis	Sierra Excelsior	66	1033
Lizzie	San Joaquin Stockton	64	1063
M	Siskiyou Scott Va	69	48
Martha	San Bernardino San Bernadino	64	623
Mary	San Francisco San Francisco 8	68	1250
Mary	Santa Cruz Santa Cruz	66	600
Mason	San Diego San Diego	64	766
Michiel	Nevada Bridgeport	61	454
Mr	San Francisco San Francisco 10	67	311
Nancy	Sacramento San Joaquin	63	355
Nelson	El Dorado Georgetown	58	685
O	Amador Twp 2	55	269
O C	Calaveras Twp 9	57	386
Orland	Butte Ophir	56	756
Orlando	Butte Bidwell	56	722
Owen	Tehama Moons	70	854
Owen	Yuba Fosters	72	821
Pater	San Francisco San Francisco 9	68	1056
Patrick	San Francisco San Francisco 3	67	54
Patrick H	San Francisco San Francisco 8	68	1261
Perry	Tuolumne Don Pedro	71	538
R A	San Francisco San Francisco 9	68	998
Robert	Los Angeles Los Angeles	59	293
Robert	Los Angeles Los Angeles	59	364
Robert	Siskiyou Klamath	69	88
Robert*	Calaveras Twp 8	57	92
Terry	Tuolumne Twp 6	71	540
Thomas	El Dorado Greenwood	58	721
Thomas	Mendocino Ukiah	60	801
Thomas	Tulara Twp 3	71	46
Thos	Klamath Orleans	59	215
Virginia	Napa Napa	61	58
W P	San Francisco San Francisco 9	68	1083
W W	Amador Twp 1	55	470
W W	Placer Forest H	62	795
William	Placer Todds Va	62	763
William	Placer Michigan	62	811
William	Plumas Quincy	62	983
William	Tuolumne Twp 6	71	540
Williams	Calaveras Twp 8	57	70
Wm	San Francisco San Francisco 10	67	306
Wm	Sierra Monte Crk	66	1036
OWENSET			
H*	San Francisco San Francisco 5	67	537
OWEY			
---	Del Norte Crescent	58	641
---	El Dorado Salmon Falls	58	1044
OWHALING			
Julia*	San Francisco San Francisco 8	68	1248
OWHITNEY			
Jno*	Butte Kimshaw	56	575
OWI			
---*	Stanislaus Buena Village	70	722
OWILLIAMS			
C W	San Francisco San Francisco 5	67	478
Eliza	San Francisco San Francisco 3	67	19
OWIN			
Bridget	San Francisco San Francisco 6	67	434
OWINE			
John	Yuba Marysville	72	963
OWINGS			
John T	Placer Virginia	62	675
William	Placer Damascus	62	846
OWIRDOLPHO			
John	Los Angeles Los Angeles	59	365
OWL			
---*	Mendocino Twp 1	60	890
OWLSON			
Jents*	San Francisco San Francisco 1	68	895
OWN			
---	Amador Twp 5	55	341
---	Shasta Shasta	66	680
---	Shasta Horsetown	66	702
---	Sierra Twp 5	66	945

Name	County Locale	M653 Roll	Page
OWN			
---	Sierra Downieville	66	974
---	Sierra Downieville	66	979
---	Sierra Downieville	66	998
Ah	Yuba Bear Rvr	72	1000
OWNANS			
Catharine*	San Francisco 7	68	1414
	San Francisco		
OWNE			
John*	Calaveras Twp 8	57	102
OWNEN			
Alexander*	Sierra Twp 5	66	918
OWNES			
John	El Dorado Mud Springs	58	968
OWNIN			
Alexander	Sierra Twp 5	66	918
OWNON			
Catharine*	San Francisco 7	68	1414
	San Francisco		
OWNONS			
Catharine*	San Francisco 7	68	1414
	San Francisco		
OWNSBY			
James P	Los Angeles Los Angeles	59	381
OWOCK			
Edgar	Yuba Suida	72	982
OWON			
---	Siskiyou Scott Ri	69	67
OWRIOL			
Nichalas*	Contra Costa Twp 1	57	488
OWRS			
John*	Yuba New York	72	736
OWSBY			
L	Napa Clear Lake	61	126
W A	Napa Clear Lake	61	126
OWSLEY			
John A*	Napa Clear Lake	61	126
T	Napa Clear Lake	61	126
W A	Napa Clear Lake	61	126
OWUANS			
Catharine*	San Francisco 7	68	1414
	San Francisco		
OWUN			
James K	Tuolumne Shawsfla	71	384
OWUOL			
Nichalas*	Contra Costa Twp 1	57	488
OWYETT			
John*	Butte Ophir	56	748
OX			
E	San Francisco San Francisco 6	67	453
J	Tuolumne Twp 1	71	239
OXANDABOURN			
OXEBY			
Christopher	San Joaquin Douglass	64	916
Christopher	San Joaquin Douglass	64	922
OXENDINE			
S C	San Joaquin Stockton	64	1074
OXENDUIL			
Chs*	Stanislaus Emory	70	753
OXENHEIMER			
Geo	San Joaquin Stockton	64	1051
OXENTINE			
John	Placer Todds Va	62	785
OXLERY			
M*	Calaveras Twp 9	57	395
OXLEY			
James	Amador Twp 6	55	438
M*	Calaveras Twp 9	57	395
OY			
---	El Dorado Eldorado	58	941
---	El Dorado Eldorado	58	948
---	El Dorado Mud Springs	58	950
---*	Shasta Shasta	66	670
OYE			
---	Amador Twp 2	55	318
---	Tuolumne Twp 5	71	524
OYER			
P	El Dorado Diamond	58	806
OYG			
---	Sierra Downieville	66	999
OYO			
---	Amador Twp 2	55	318
OYOCOTITSH			
---	Tulara Twp 1	71	120
OYSTERMAN			
D	Klamath Liberty	59	230
OZANE			
Charlene	Sierra Pine Grove	66	821
Charles	Sierra Pine Grove	66	821
OZENCRANTZ			
John	San Francisco San Francisco 7	68	1370
OZMAN			
A P	Butte Oregon	56	621
OZREN			
John*	San Francisco San Francisco 3	67	69
P DE ARCE			
Lucas*	San Francisco San Francisco 10	67	355

Name	County Locale	M653 Roll	Page
P E			
---	Sierra Downieville	66	1003
---	Sierra Downieville	66	1029
PA KAU ME			
---	Plumas Quincy	62	970
PA US UM			
---	Plumas Quincy	62	969
PA			
---	Sierra Downieville	66	1007
---	Sierra Downieville	66	1026
---	Sierra La Porte	66	782
---	Sierra Twp 5	66	927
---	Tuolumne Chinese	71	524
---	Yuba Marysville	72	917
Hum	San Francisco San Francisco 4	68	1175
K	Tuolumne Twp 2	71	406
Latt	Yuba Long Bar	72	756
Tate	Yuba Long Bar	72	763
Tuck	Amador Twp 2	55	292
PABAS			
Peter	Amador Twp 2	55	290
PABBLOW			
Manuel	San Mateo Twp 3	65	75
Pedrow	San Mateo Twp 3	65	75
PABEDA			
Qirila*	Yuba Marysville	72	917
PABILO			
---	San Bernardino S Timate	64	703
PABLA			
---	Monterey S Antoni	60	972
---	San Bernardino S Timate	64	756
Maria	San Diego Temecula	64	788
PABLE			
Augustus	Yuba Marysville	72	919
PABLER			
Edward	El Dorado Diamond	58	764
PABLO			
---	Los Angeles Los Angeles	59	377
---	Los Angeles San Gabriel	59	414
---	Los Angeles Santa Ana	59	456
---	Mariposa Twp 1	60	627
---	Mariposa Twp 1	60	628
---	Mendocino Round Va	60	886
---	San Bernardino Santa Barbara	64	200
---	San Bernardino San Bernadino	64	669
---	San Bernardino San Bernadino	64	677
---	San Bernardino San Bernadino	64	679
---	San Bernardino S Timate	64	700
---	San Bernardino S Timate	64	704
---	San Bernardino S Timate	64	707
---	San Bernardino S Timate	64	708
---	San Bernardino S Timate	64	710
---	San Bernardino S Timate	64	711
---	San Bernardino S Timate	64	712
---	San Bernardino S Timate	64	714
---	San Bernardino S Timate	64	715
---	San Bernardino S Timate	64	716
---	San Bernardino S Timate	64	717
---	San Bernardino S Timate	64	718
---	San Bernardino S Timate	64	719
---	San Bernardino S Timate	64	720
---	San Bernardino S Timate	64	723
---	San Bernardino S Timate	64	724
---	San Bernardino S Timate	64	725
---	San Bernardino S Timate	64	726
---	San Bernardino S Timate	64	727
---	San Bernardino S Timate	64	728
---	San Bernardino S Timate	64	729
---	San Bernardino S Timate	64	733
---	San Bernardino S Timate	64	737
---	San Bernardino S Timate	64	740
---	San Bernardino S Timate	64	742
---	San Bernardino S Timate	64	743
---	San Bernardino S Timate	64	744
---	San Bernardino S Timate	64	745
---	San Bernardino S Timate	64	746
---	San Bernardino S Timate	64	747
---	San Bernardino S Timate	64	748
---	San Bernardino S Timate	64	749
---	San Bernardino S Timate	64	750
---	San Bernardino S Timate	64	751
---	San Bernardino S Timate	64	752
---	San Bernardino S Timate	64	753
---	San Bernardino S Timate	64	755
---	San Diego Agua Caliente	64	815
---	San Diego Agua Caliente	64	827
---	San Diego Agua Caliente	64	850
---	San Diego Agua Caliente	64	856
---	San Diego Agua Caliente	64	866
---	Tulara Visalia	71	121
---	Tulara Keeneysburg	71	50
---	Tulara Keyesville	71	56
---	Tulara Keyesville	71	65
---	Tulara Keyesville	71	67
---	Tulara Keyesville	71	69
---	Tulara Keyesville	71	70

California 1860 Census Index

Name	County Locale	M653 Roll	Page
PABLO			
Antonio	Calaveras Twp 7	57	25
Jose	Los Angeles Tejon	59	529
Jose	San Diego Agua Caliente	64	818
Juan	Los Angeles Los Angeles	59	405
Juan	San Diego Temecula	64	790
Juan	San Diego Agua Caliente	64	846
Juan	San Diego Agua Caliente	64	864
Juan	Santa Cruz Pescadero	66	650
Maria	San Diego Agua Caliente	64	851
Panga	Amador Twp 1	55	508
Paro	El Dorado Placerville	58	930
Pedro	Los Angeles Santa Ana	59	441
Pedro	San Diego S Luis R	64	781
Pedro	San Diego S Luis R	64	782
Pedro	San Diego Temecula	64	789
Pedro	San Diego Temecula	64	801
Pedro	San Diego Agua Caliente	64	838
Surita	San Bernardino Santa Barbara	64	201
PABLOS			
Ignateo*	Yuba Marysville	72	936
Ignatio	Yuba Marysville	72	937
PABTISTE			
Jean	Santa Clara Alviso	65	406
PACCAND			
Louis	Placer Dutch Fl	62	723
PACCASSO			
Stephen	Tuolumne Sonora	71	229
PACE			
Jonathan	San Joaquin Elkhorn	64	996
Julia Ann	San Francisco San Francisco 2	67	562
Woodford M	Klamath S Fork	59	197
PACEY			
Edward H	Yuba Marysville	72	955
PACHCO			
Morid*	Los Angeles Los Angeles	59	497
Moriel*	Los Angeles Los Angeles	59	497
PACHE			
G	San Francisco San Francisco 5	67	500
PACHEA			
Vincent*	Mariposa Twp 3	60	601
PACHECE			
Victor*	Mariposa Twp 3	60	600
Vincent*	Mariposa Twp 3	60	601
PACHECI			
Mariano	San Luis Obispo San Luis Obispo	65	26
Vincent*	Mariposa Twp 3	60	601
PACHECO			
A	Amador Twp 3	55	395
Antonio*	San Francisco San Francisco 9	68	1072
Ascension	Yuba Parke Ba	72	786
Axension*	Yuba Parks Ba	72	786
Conception	Alameda Brooklyn	55	143
Davoles	Fresno Twp 1	59	84
Fernando	Contra Costa Twp 3	57	614
Gabriel	Los Angeles San Juan	59	471
Hosea M*	Alameda Murray	55	217
Irwin	Yolo Slate Ra	72	714
Jose	Contra Costa Twp 3	57	614
Jose R	Los Angeles San Gabriel	59	413
Juan	Yuba Slate Ro	72	714
Juana	Los Angeles Los Angeles	59	324
Magdelena*	Santa Clara Alviso	65	414
Malesia	Alameda Brooklyn	55	201
Mani L	Alameda Brooklyn	55	131
Mariano	San Francisco San Francisco 2	67	574
Pantaleona	Contra Costa Twp 3	57	616
Sacramento	Fresno Twp 1	59	84
Salvio	Contra Costa Twp 3	57	615
Vicento	Fresno Twp 1	59	84
Wm	Sacramento Granite	63	243
PACHECV			
Victor*	Mariposa Twp 3	60	600
PACHEER			
Leno*	Contra Costa Twp 1	57	527
PACHERELL			
B	San Francisco San Francisco 2	67	796
PACHERO			
Juana	Santa Clara San Jose	65	303
Rafael	Santa Clara San Jose	65	302
PACHES			
Och*	Mariposa Twp 3	60	548
Oih*	Mariposa Twp 3	60	548
PACHET			
---	Shasta French G	66	713
PACHETO			
Cancino	Los Angeles Azuza	59	275
PACHEW			
Victor*	Mariposa Twp 3	60	600
Vincent*	Mariposa Twp 3	60	601
PACHI			
Marie*	Stanislaus Branch	70	703
PACHICE			
Hosea M*	Alameda Murray T	55	217
PACHICO			
Antonio	San Francisco San Francisco 9	68	1072

Name	County Locale	M653 Roll	Page
PACHICO			
Egnasia	Marin San Rafael	60	761
Magdelena*	Santa Clara Alviso	65	414
Miguil	Santa Clara Santa Clara	65	495
Petra Sato	Santa Clara San Jose	65	288
PACHIEO			
Banto	Santa Clara San Jose	65	297
PACHINA			
P	Amador Twp 1	55	507
PACHINTA			
Cushing	San Francisco San Francisco 2	67	688
PACHIO			
Frncis	Fresno Twp 1	59	76
PACHIRO			
Encarnacion	Santa Clara San Jose	65	303
PACHITA			
---	San Diego Agua Caliente	64	841
PACHOT			
---	Shasta French G	66	713
PACHTA			
Frederick	Sierra Twp 5	66	942
PACIENCIO			
Manuel	Marin Cortemad	60	788
PACIENCIS			
Manuel	Marin Cortemad	60	788
PACIFIC			
---	Solano Vacaville	69	347
PACIFICO			
---	San Diego Temecula	64	790
PACITAS			
---	Mendocino Calpella	60	823
PACITOS			
---	Mendocino Calpella	60	823
PACK			
---	El Dorado White Oaks	58	1032
---	El Dorado Coloma	58	1083
---	El Dorado Kelsey	58	1136
---	El Dorado Mud Springs	58	958
---	Sierra Downieville	66	974
---*	Yuba Slate Ro	72	711
Ah	Tuolumne Twp 4	71	158
Aun	Sacramento Granite	63	250
Eugene	Nevada Bridgeport	61	441
Francis	Santa Clara San Jose	65	318
Horace	Plumas Quincy	62	945
Joseph	El Dorado Indian D	58	1158
Low	Yuba Long Bar	72	762
R C	Sierra Twp 7	66	906
R R	Calaveras Twp 6	57	120
PACKAR			
Peter	Trinity New Rvr	70	1030
PACKARD			
A	San Bernardino Santa Barbara	64	155
A A	Butte Chico	56	545
Benjamin F M	Castoria	64	872
C C	San Joaquin Amador Twp 2	55	319
C C	El Dorado Mountain	58	1186
Chs	San Francisco San Francisco 6	67	409
E	Tuolumne Twp 2	71	330
Eugen	Sacramento Natonia	63	280
Francisca	Santa Barbara	64	155
George L	San Bernardino San Francisco 3	67	32
H A	Tuolumne Twp 2	71	309
Jno	Sacramento Natonia	63	280
John D	Yuba Marysville	72	946
John Q	Yuba Marysville	72	946
Martin	San Joaquin Oneal	64	931
Martin	Solano Suisan	69	205
N L	Tuolumne Garrote	71	173
P	El Dorado Coloma	58	1073
P W	Napa Napa	61	57
R	Butte Kimshaw	56	598
S	San Mateo Twp 3	65	80
Stephen	Contra Costa Twp 1	57	533
William	Tulara Petersburg	71	52
Wm R	Tuolumne Columbia	71	309
PACKE			
---	Fresno Twp 1	59	25
PACKEN			
George	Sierra Twp 5	66	941
PACKER			
---	Sierra Twp 5	66	941
A H	Nevada Nevada	61	241
Elias	El Dorado Placerville	58	919
Elizabeth	San Francisco San Francisco 2	67	743
Geo F	Colusa Monroeville	57	450
George	Sierra Twp 5	66	941
J J	El Dorado Placerville	58	871
J J	Sacramento Ward 1	63	6
Jno	San Francisco San Francisco 12	386 67	
L H	El Dorado Placerville	58	909
Lewis	Tuolumne Columbia	71	300
W F	Sierra Downieville	66	988

Name	County Locale	M653 Roll	Page
PACKERBURY			
Benjamin	San Joaquin Elkhorn	64	952
George	San Joaquin Elkhorn	64	950
PACKERD			
Eugene	Sacramento Natonia	63	280
Mary A	Placer Goods	62	694
PACKES			
Och	Mariposa Twp 3	60	548
PACKET			
Edmund	San Francisco San Francisco 9	68	1023
Prosper	Amador Twp 1	55	506
Samuel	Placer Forest H	62	801
PACKETT			
D	Shasta Millvill	66	754
L	Shasta Millvill	66	754
Thomas*	Amador Twp 4	55	237
Wm R	Butte Oregon	56	637
PACKHAM			
C C	El Dorado Newtown	58	781
PACKHAN			
Henry	San Francisco San Francisco 9	68	1020
PACKI			
Frank*	Stanislaus Branch	70	703
PACKMIRE			
G N	Calaveras Twp 9	57	375
PACKRAY			
John	Sierra Twp 7	66	895
PACKSHER			
Alex	Humbolt Union	59	179
PACKSON			
General	Tulara Twp 3	71	56
PACKUS			
Gorgonia	Santa Clara Almaden	65	270
PACKWOOD			
---	Tulara Twp 2	71	4
Daniel	Solano Suisan	69	214
Elisha	Santa Clara San Jose	65	311
Elisha	Santa Clara San Jose	65	367
Henderson	Tulara Visalia	71	5
PACO			
H	El Dorado Placerville	58	833
Jose	Los Angeles Los Angeles	59	303
PACOBY			
John F*	Tulara Visalia	71	100
PACOFF			
Frank	Sierra Whiskey	66	850
PACOLA			
---	El Dorado Kelsey	58	1133
PACRAGR			
William	Tuolumne Twp 6	71	534
PACTCHETT			
T P*	Napa Hot Springs	61	2
PACTER			
Peter	Sierra Cox'S Bar	66	950
PACUNDO			
---	San Bernardino S Timate	64	720
PADATRETTE			
A	El Dorado Placerville	58	823
PADDAN			
D	Nevada Nevada	61	258
PADDEN			
Patrick	Mendocino Big Rvr	60	846
PADDERTZ			
Henry	Los Angeles Santa Ana	59	440
PADDISON			
E	Santa Clara Santa Clara	65	467
PADDLEFORD			
Frank	San Joaquin Elliott	64	942
G F	Yolo Cache Crk	72	635
J G	Nevada Eureka	61	378
T	Amador Twp 1	55	469
PADDOCK			
B H	Tehama Lassen	70	860
Geo W	Sonoma Mendocino	69	452
J	San Francisco San Francisco 4	68	1156
J E	Santa Clara Redwood	65	456
James	Amador Twp 3	55	382
James H	Siskiyou Yreka	69	139
James J	Siskiyou Yreka	69	139
O	Tehama Lassen	70	860
Robt*	El Dorado White Oaks	58	1008
PADDOCKS			
---	Amador Twp 3	55	405
PADDOR			
William*	Placer Iona Hills	62	859
PADDOX			
William*	Placer Iona Hills	62	859
PADDY			
Jarrus	San Joaquin Oneal	64	930
Rowland	Tuolumne Sonora	71	200
PADELFORD			
W H	Trinity Browns C	70	984
PADEM			
Isaac*	Placer Michigan	62	851
PADEN			
Abram	Klamath S Fork	59	197

California 1860 Census Index

Name	County Locale	M653 Roll	Page
PADEN			
John	Trinity North Fo	70	1023
Joseph	Colusa Monroeville	57	451
Thos	Sacramento Ward 1	63	40
Thos	Sacramento Ward 1	63	9
PADENS			
Jose	Santa Clara Fremont	65	432
PADER			
Calisti	El Dorado Mud Springs	58	970
M	Trinity Dead Wood	70	958
PADESTA			
John*	Tuolumne Columbia	71	341
Louise*	Tuolumne Columbia	71	341
PADFIELD			
R	Sacramento Brighton	63	191
PADGEN			
Owen	Butte Kimshaw	56	573
PADGET			
George W	San Francisco San Francisco 3	67	18
PADGETT			
E	Sutter Yuba	70	766
F M	Calaveras Twp 9	57	349
PADGITT			
F M*	Calaveras Twp 9	57	349
PADIA			
Manuel	Monterey San Juan	60	1001
Pedro	Monterey San Juan	60	1002
PADIALA			
Jose M	Los Angeles San Gabriel	59	420
Juan	Los Angeles Los Angeles	59	402
Maria L	Los Angeles Los Angeles	59	363
PADIEN			
Owen	Butte Kimshaw	56	607
PADILLA			
Jose M	Los Angeles San Gabriel	59	420
Juan	Los Angeles Los Angeles	59	402
Juan N	Los Angeles Los Angeles	59	362
Maria L	Los Angeles Los Angeles	59	363
PADILLO			
Bicente	Santa Clara San Jose	65	368
Inasanea	Santa Clara San Jose	65	324
Jose	Monterey San Juan	60	1010
PADINI			
Joseph	Santa Clara Santa Clara	65	481
PADIS			
Stephen	Calaveras Twp 8	57	90
PADISTA			
John	Tuolumne Twp 2	71	341
PADISTTA			
Bartollo*	Calaveras Twp 7	57	12
PADLER			
James	El Dorado White Oaks	58	1030
PADMAN			
Lucy	Placer Iona Hills	62	864
PADMORE			
Samuel	Santa Cruz Soguel	66	595
PADNA			
Andrew*	Calaveras Twp 7	57	10
PADO			
---	Mendocino Little L	60	839
---	Mendocino Twp 1	60	891
PADRE			
---	Fresno Twp 2	59	70
---	Tulara Twp 3	71	56
PADREA			
Jose	Los Angeles San Jose	59	285
PADREAS			
Rafucio	Los Angeles Azuza	59	276
PADRERYASO			
---	San Francisco San Francisco 4	68	1157
PADRES			
J M	Merced Twp 1	60	909
PADRIS			
J M	Merced Twp 1	60	909
PADRO			
---	Mariposa Twp 1	60	635
---	Tulara Twp 2	71	32
Panca	Amador Twp 5	55	332
PADROW JUDUTO			
---	San Mateo Twp 3	65	99
PADRUYASO			
---	San Francisco San Francisco 4	68	1157
PADSO			
---*	Tulara Visalia	71	32
PAE			
---	El Dorado Mud Springs	58	958
---	Sierra Twp 5	66	932
---	Yuba Long Bar	72	761
Mary	San Joaquin Elkhorn	64	957
PAECADO			
Rafall	Alameda Brooklyn	55	210
PAEG			
---	Yuba Marysville	72	896
PAEK			
---	El Dorado Mud Springs	58	978
PAENDLETON			
John	Shasta Shasta	66	757

Name	County Locale	M653 Roll	Page
PAERCIOS			
Calistra	Santa Clara Almaden	65	268
PAERSON			
George	Tuolumne Green Springs	71	532
PAESON			
Thos	Butte Ophir	56	786
PAESONS			
Cyntha E	Santa Clara Santa Clara	65	511
PAETA			
Francisco	Santa Barbara	64	156
	San Bernardino		
PAGANI			
Jean	Calaveras Twp 7	57	31
Joseph	Calaveras Twp 7	57	47
PAGANNI			
T	San Francisco San Francisco 5	67	539
PAGANO			
Francisco	San Francisco San Francisco 2	67	686
PAGATTE			
Norbert*	Amador Twp 4	55	245
PAGE			
---	Placer Secret R	62	622
---	Siskiyou Yreka	69	124
A B	Trinity Evans Ba	70	1002
A T	Sierra Eureka	66	1050
B	Yuba Long Bar	72	747
Benj	Siskiyou Scott Ri	69	75
Charles	Calaveras Twp 8	57	54
Charles	Calaveras Twp 8	57	64
Charles	Tulara Visalia	71	7
Chars	Calaveras Twp 7	57	38
Chas	Calaveras Twp 6	57	155
Cw	Calaveras Twp 7	57	38
E	San Francisco San Francisco 6	67	438
E M	San Francisco San Francisco 6	67	438
Edward	San Francisco San Francisco 7	68	1342
Elijah	Santa Clara Santa Clara	65	493
Elizabeth	Calaveras Twp 5	57	220
Emily	Santa Clara San Jose	65	392
Emma N	San Francisco San Francisco 2	67	693
Enos	Placer Secret R	62	616
Erastus	San Francisco San Francisco 3	67	66
F	Sacramento Sutter	63	300
Frances M	Sacramento Ward 3	63	447
Francis	Humbolt Mattole	59	128
Frank	El Dorado Placerville	58	827
Frank	Yuba Marysville	72	920
Freeman	San Diego Colorado	64	811
G P	Sacramento Ward 1	63	87
G W	Sacramento Ward 3	63	435
George	Placer Michigan	62	811
George	San Francisco San Francisco 2	67	570
H F	El Dorado Placerville	58	822
Henry	Sierra Pine Grove	66	833
Hiram	Siskiyou Yreka	69	155
J	El Dorado Placerville	58	824
J	Shasta Horsetown	66	697
J C	Yolo Cache Crk	72	623
J C Fred	Sacramento Ward 1	63	38
J D	San Francisco San Francisco 5	67	484
J E	Placer Forest H	62	795
J H*	Placer Michigan	62	834
J T	Yolo Washington	72	601
J W	Sonoma Washington	69	676
James	Nevada Bloomfield	61	523
James H	Napa Hot Springs	61	1
John B*	Calaveras Twp 5	57	231
John O	San Francisco San Francisco 11	67	156
Johnathan	Sacramento Ward 4	63	508
Joseph	Mariposa Twp 1	60	654
Joseph	San Francisco San Francisco 2	67	582
Joseph*	Mariposa Twp 1	60	654
L T	Yolo Washington	72	601
Lizzie	San Francisco San Francisco 10	67	185
M	Calaveras Twp 8	57	53
M C	Siskiyou Scott Va	69	57
Milo	San Bernardino San Bernardino	64	686
Mitchell	Yuba Fosters	72	822
Nathl	San Francisco San Francisco 9	68	1005
Orlando	Calaveras Twp 10	57	292
Pitta	Mariposa Twp 1	60	654
Polly*	Sonoma Santa Rosa	69	414
Prince B	Humbolt Eureka	59	176
R	Yuba New York	72	747
Reuben F	Yuba New York	72	726
Reylon T	Yuba New York	72	726
Robert	San Francisco San Francisco 4	68	1158
Robert	Yolo Merritt	72	583
Robert C	San Francisco San Francisco 8	68	1281
Robt	Sacramento Ward 3	63	434
S P	Amador Twp 2	55	272
S P	Sacramento Sutter	63	298
Saml	Amador Twp 1	55	467
Sarah A	San Francisco San Francisco 4	68	1155

Name	County Locale	M653 Roll	Page
PAGE			
Soloman	Sonoma Mendocino	69	463
W D	Siskiyou Scott Va	69	57
W F	El Dorado Big Bar	58	739
Warren S	Santa Clara Santa Clara	65	498
William	Mendocino Big Rvr	60	840
William	Placer Iona Hills	62	895
William	San Francisco San Francisco 8	68	1257
William	San Mateo Twp 3	65	80
Wm	Sacramento Ward 1	63	62
Wm	Sonoma Washington	69	665
Wm R	Sonoma Salt Point	69	694
Wordbing*	Placer Auburn	62	587
PAGEL			
August	San Francisco San Francisco 11	67	141
PAGELLO			
Simon*	Mariposa Twp 3	60	568
PAGENT			
J	El Dorado Placerville	58	835
PAGER			
E	Sacramento Lee	63	215
PAGGA			
---	Tulara Keyesville	71	68
PAGGAENIMS			
Antony*	Calaveras Twp 5	57	197
PAGGAMINI			
Antony*	Calaveras Twp 5	57	197
PAGGANINNI			
Louis*	Calaveras Twp 5	57	197
PAGGANINNIE			
Louis	Calaveras Twp 5	57	197
PAGGANINNIN			
Antony*	Calaveras Twp 5	57	197
PAGGARNIMI			
Antony*	Calaveras Twp 5	57	197
PAGGARNINI			
Antony*	Calaveras Twp 5	57	197
PAGGATT			
L	San Francisco San Francisco 1	68	934
PAGGEN			
Catharine	Alameda Oakland	55	4
PAGGER			
Catharine	Alameda Oakland	55	4
PAGGETT			
Geo	San Francisco San Francisco 9	68	1005
PAGGON			
Louis	San Francisco San Francisco 4	68	1161
PAGIN			
John	Placer Michigan	62	837
PAGIO			
Giovanni	Tuolumne Twp 5	71	499
PAGJA			
---	Tulara Keyesville	71	71
PAGNARO			
Joseph	San Joaquin Stockton	64	1052
PAGNINO			
L	San Francisco San Francisco 5	67	499
PAGO			
Robert C	San Francisco San Francisco 8	68	1281
PAGONTELLA			
---*	Mariposa Twp 1	60	628
PAGOTT			
Jno C	Nevada Nevada	61	289
PAGOTTE			
Norbert*	Amador Twp 4	55	245
PAGR			
Chas	Calaveras Twp 6	57	155
PAGRANDE			
---	Tulara Keyesville	71	56
PAGSLEY			
Elias T	Tuolumne Sonora	71	188
PAGUA			
John*	Calaveras Twp 6	57	161
PAGUILLOR			
Julius	Nevada Bloomfield	61	516
PAGUITA			
---	Fresno Twp 2	59	92
PAH LOUK			
---*	Plumas Quincy	62	970
PAH POW			
---	Tuolumne Jacksonville	71	515
PAH SE TUCK			
---	Plumas Quincy	62	970
PAH			
---	Alameda Oakland	55	16
---	Alameda Oakland	55	64
---	Sacramento Ward 3	63	492
---	Sacramento Ward 3	63	494
---	Shasta Shasta	66	669
---	Shasta Horsetown	66	703
---	Sierra La Porte	66	774
---	Tuolumne Shawsfla	71	410
---	Tuolumne Twp 3	71	439
---	Tuolumne Twp 3	71	468
---	Tuolumne Twp 6	71	529

California 1860 Census Index

Name	County Locale	M653 Roll	Page
PAH			
---	Tuolumne Green Springs	71	531
---	Yuba Long Bar	72	757
Cheong	San Francisco San Francisco 5	671	207
Ching*	San Francisco San Francisco 5	671	207
Dery	Amador Twp 3	55	401
Fommer*	Plumas Quincy	62	970
Fommu*	Plumas Quincy	62	970
Lee	San Francisco San Francisco 4	681	207
Long	Amador Twp 3	55	401
Lu	San Francisco San Francisco 4	681	207
See	El Dorado Georgetown	58	755
Soy*	San Francisco San Francisco 5	671	207
Tow	Tuolumne Twp 5	71	515
PAHAD			
Frank	Calaveras Twp 7	57	29
PAHAN			
Jack	Sonoma Sonoma	69	659
PAHERTE			
Jose	San Bernardino San Salvador	64	641
PAHINE			
Joseph	Yuba New York	72	732
PAHINI			
Joseph	Yuba New York	72	732
PAHIRTE			
Jose*	San Bernardino San Bernadino	64	641
PAHNCE			
D R*	Mariposa Twp 3	60	621
PAHR			
John*	Yuba Marysville	72	908
PAHREN			
William H*	El Dorado Georgetown	58	698
PAHRIA			
J R*	Mariposa Twp 3	60	621
PAHRICE			
J R*	Mariposa Twp 3	60	621
PAHULLEN			
Emile	San Francisco San Francisco 11	119 67	
PAHUTO			
Jose*	San Bernardino San Bernardino	64	622
PAI			
---	Calaveras Twp 6	57	149
PAICE			
David H	Yuba Marysville	72	903
Edward F*	Yuba Bear Rvr	721	011
PAIDE			
Justo	Calaveras Twp 6	57	155
PAIDLEY			
W G*	San Francisco San Francisco 5	67	543
PAIE			
Fredrick	Amador Twp 4	55	246
PAIGE			
A J	Nevada Rough &	61	420
James	Tuolumne Twp 2	71	367
John	Sierra Twp 5	66	935
Louis	Tuolumne Twp 2	71	380
Peter*	San Francisco San Francisco 4	681	167
Thomas	Tuolumne Twp 2	71	367
Timothy	San Joaquin Stockton	641	034
Wm T	Tuolumne Twp 1	71	237
PAIKER			
Martin	Siskiyou Scott Va	69	34
PAIKN			
Nemiah	Siskiyou Shasta Valley	69	121
PAILE			
Wm	Butte Oregon	56	639
PAILOR			
Jas	San Francisco San Francisco 1	68	854
PAIN			
---	San Francisco San Francisco 4	681	178
Chas	Sonoma Petaluma	69	588
E	El Dorado Diamond	58	810
Fred	Siskiyou Yreka	69	145
Nemiah	Siskiyou Shasta Valley	69	121
S	Sutter Yuba	70	762
Thomas H	San Joaquin Tulare	64	871
PAINE			
---	Placer Rattle Snake	62	629
Amos	San Francisco San Francisco 7	681	338
B T	Yuba Parks Ba	72	781
C	Monterey San Juan	601	007
Chas F	Calaveras Twp 4	57	337
Daniel D	San Joaquin Castoria	64	874
Edward P	Alameda Brooklyn	55	204
Elizabeth	Mariposa Twp 3	60	609
Eunice	Yolo Cache Crk	72	665
G C	Sierra Downieville	661	031
Geo	Trinity Whites Crk	701	028
George*	Mariposa Twp 3	60	573
J	Nevada Grass Valley	61	151
J J*	Mariposa Twp 1	60	623
J M	Calaveras Twp 9	57	382
J R	Nevada Bloomfield	61	515
Ja R	Nevada Bloomfield	61	515
Jacob	El Dorado Georgetown	58	748
PAINE			
James	Sierra St Louis	66	811
James	Sonoma Petaluma	69	576
John	San Francisco San Francisco 1	68	913
John	Santa Clara Gilroy	65	242
John A	Yuba New York	72	727
Joseph	Calaveras Twp 5	57	249
M H*	Nevada Rough &	61	411
Mary	Calaveras Twp 6	57	170
Mary	Mariposa Twp 3	60	609
Mary*	Calaveras Twp 5	57	170
Michl	Sierra Downieville	661	019
P C	Tehama Pasakent	70	859
T T	Mariposa Twp 1	60	623
Thos	Mariposa Twp 3	60	568
W H	Nevada Rough &	61	411
W H	Santa Clara Gilroy	65	231
W H*	Nevada Rough &	61	411
Wm	Mariposa Twp 3	60	609
PAINER			
Gonleo*	Calaveras Twp 6	57	135
PAINES			
Gonler	Calaveras Twp 6	57	135
Gouleo*	Calaveras Twp 6	57	135
PAINGLE			
Charles	Sacramento Sutter	63	294
PAINIO			
Francisco	Calaveras Twp 10	57	260
PAINO			
Amos	San Francisco San Francisco 7	681	338
PAINR			
Mary*	Calaveras Twp 5	57	170
PAINTER			
A J	Sacramento Ward 4	63	503
Adolph	Tuolumne Twp 1	71	199
Benj B	Plumas Quincy	62	981
David	Placer Iona Hills	62	895
George	Nevada Rough &	61	415
George	Sierra La Porte	66	786
J B	San Francisco San Francisco 2	67	636
J J	Butte Oregon	56	640
Jno H	Butte Oregon	56	633
John	Placer Todds Va	62	786
Joseph M	Plumas Quincy	62	986
Levi	Sacramento Franklin	63	331
Mariah*	Santa Clara Santa Clara	65	471
P*	Trinity E Weaver	701	059
Richd	Amador Twp 2	55	315
Robert	Humbolt Eureka	59	177
Samuel	Plumas Quincy	62	981
Thos	Sacramento Ward 1	63	62
W	El Dorado Placerville	58	874
PAINTGO			
Radolph*	Calaveras Twp 4	57	338
PAINTON			
Baryan	Shasta Millvill	66	749
M	Shasta Horsetown	66	695
Maryan	Shasta Millvill	66	749
Richard*	Amador Twp 4	55	238
PAINTOR			
Mariah*	Santa Clara Santa Clara	65	471
PAIPOINT			
D W*	Yuba Linda	72	993
PAIR			
---	Amador Twp 5	55	352
---	Amador Twp 6	55	422
---*	Amador Twp 7	55	419
B F	Mariposa Twp 1	60	638
PAIRE			
George*	Mariposa Twp 3	60	573
Louis	Tuolumne Twp 2	71	285
PAIRSONS			
E	Calaveras Twp 9	57	401
PAISE			
Louis	Tuolumne Twp 2	71	285
PAISH			
Charles	Yuba Marysville	72	891
PAISHLEY			
Wm H	Alameda Brooklyn	55	97
PAISONS			
M E*	Santa Clara Alviso	65	412
PAISTON			
Ildefona	Yuba Marysville	72	918
PAIT			
---	Tuolumne Twp 6	71	536
PAITEE			
Wm*	Nevada Eureka	61	346
PAITEN			
R*	Nevada Nevada	61	292
PAITER			
Wm*	Nevada Eureka	61	346
PAITROMAN			
Stephen	Tuolumne Twp 3	71	465
PAITRONIAN			
Stephen	Tuolumne Twp 3	71	465
PAITSHEKO			
William*	San Francisco San Francisco 7	681	353
PAIUR			
Mary*	Calaveras Twp 5	57	170
PAJE			
Edward*	San Francisco San Francisco 3	67	82
PAJELLO			
Simion*	Mariposa Twp 3	60	568
Simon	Mariposa Twp 3	60	568
PAJIS			
James	Amador Twp 3	55	371
PAK			
---	Calaveras Twp 6	57	139
---	Calaveras Twp 6	57	149
---	Calaveras Twp 8	57	59
---	El Dorado Greenwood	58	732
---	El Dorado Big Bar	58	734
---	San Francisco San Francisco 4	681	177
---	Stanislaus Branch	70	715
---	Tuolumne Twp 2	71	410
---	Tuolumne Jamestown	71	439
---	Tuolumne Knights	71	529
---	Alameda Oakland	55	24
Coh			
Kong	San Francisco San Francisco 5	671	206
Koug	San Francisco San Francisco 5	671	206
Man	San Francisco San Francisco 5	671	206
Mon	San Francisco San Francisco 5	671	206
Yea	San Francisco San Francisco 11	160 67	
PAKE			
---	Sierra St Louis	66	813
---	Yolo Slate Ra	72	713
E T	Trinity Mouth Ca	701	015
PAKES			
John	Tuolumne Twp 1	71	265
PAKETA			
---	Fresno Twp 2	59	116
PAKI			
---	Calaveras Twp 5	57	245
PAKIN			
Phillip	Sierra Twp 7	66	872
PAKO			
Jose Ma*	Los Angeles Los Angeles	59	519
PAL			
John T	Amador Twp 2	55	290
PALACHIE			
E	Calaveras Twp 9	57	389
PALACIAS			
Tifano	Santa Clara Almaden	65	269
PALACIO			
Francisco	Merced Monterey	60	943
Francisco	Monterey Monterey	60	943
Icedro*	Monterey San Juan	60	975
Trinidad	Monterey San Juan	60	982
Ycidro*	Monterey San Juan	60	976
PALACIOS			
Pedro	Santa Clara Almaden	65	262
PALACIOUS			
Leno	Napa Napa	61	102
PALACIS			
Ycidro	Monterey San Juan	60	976
PALACROEES			
Leno*	Napa Napa	61	102
PALACROUS			
Leno*	Napa Napa	61	102
Seno*	Napa Napa	61	102
PALAFSEZ			
Manuel*	Sacramento Ward 1	63	75
PALAGO			
---	San Diego Agua Caliente	64	817
PALAGOSA			
Leonardo	Los Angeles Santa Ana	59	446
PALAICO			
Umercindo	San Francisco 2	67	782
	San Francisco		
PALAMARE			
Andrea	Calaveras Twp 7	57	27
PALAMENA			
Dolores	San Luis Obispo San Luis Obispo	65	43
PALAMO			
Juan	Sierra La Porte	66	784
PALAMYRA			
Ignatio	Los Angeles San Jose	59	291
PALAMYRAS			
Barva	Los Angeles San Jose	59	291
Louis	Los Angeles San Jose	59	291
PALAN			
Peter	Siskiyou Scott Va	69	33
Thomas	Marin S Antoni	60	707
PALANA			
Thomas	Sierra Downieville	66	977
PALANGUR			
Jno	Sacramento Granite	63	252
PALARAN			
Andrew*	Calaveras Twp 6	57	116
PALARINO			
Bernard*	Calaveras Twp 6	57	116
PALASETRA			
---	Mariposa Twp 1	60	625

Name	County Locale	M653 RollPage
PALASKI		
Estanislans*	San Diego Colorado	64 807
PALASSES		
Manuel	Sacramento Ward 1	63 75
PALASSEZ		
Manuel*	Sacramento Ward 1	63 75
PALAVATARI		
J	Tuolumne Jamestown	71 456
PALBACK		
Elia	Butte Ophir	56 766
PALCOMO		
Juan	Sierra La Porte	66 784
PALD		
A	Calaveras Twp 9	57 391
PALDUNAN		
D	Tuolumne Twp 4	71 160
PALE CUNA		
---	Plumas Quincy	62 969
PALE		
A J	Siskiyou Scott Va	69 48
Eleanor*	Sacramento American	63 161
PALEAT		
Carlden	Amador Twp 1	55 495
PALECERTE		
Andres	Alameda Brooklyn	55 143
PALENCIA		
Jose	Tuolumne Chinese	71 498
PALENSON		
B B	Nevada Bridgeport	61 446
PALERSON		
John	Nevada Red Dog	61 547
PALETO		
---	Monterey San Juan	60 999
PALFRICNIVICK		
---	San Bernardino San Bernadino	64 667
PALGARO		
Gartano	Tuolumne Twp 1	71 239
PALGRIN		
Anaram*	Placer Iona Hills	62 870
PALHECO		
Victor	Mariposa Twp 3	60 600
PALHEMUS		
J L*	Sacramento Ward 3	63 424
PALICO		
John	Calaveras Twp 5	57 201
PALINA		
Hosea*	Alameda Brooklyn	55 207
PALINER		
Geo	Butte Oregon	56 620
J B	Butte Kimshaw	56 583
PALING		
C	El Dorado Diamond	58 764
PALIRS		
Saml*	El Dorado Georgetown	58 749
PALISIO		
---	Los Angeles Los Angeles	59 515
PALISO		
H	Tuolumne Twp 2	71 310
PALISSE		
---	Butte Chico	56 550
---	Butte Chico	56 551
PALISTANI		
Jose	San Bernardino San Bernadino	64 678
PALITANA		
---	San Bernardino S Timate	64 723
---	San Bernardino S Timate	64 742
PALITANO		
---	San Bernardino S Timate	64 716
---	San Bernardino S Timate	64 719
---	San Bernardino S Timate	64 728
PALITTE		
James	Mariposa Twp 1	60 666
PALK		
John	Placer Michigan	62 845
John	Tuolumne Springfield	71 370
PALL		
Cuna	Plumas Quincy	62 965
J H	Trinity Weaverville	701077
John	Amador Twp 1	55 458
PALLADEN		
Gillermo*	Contra Costa Twp 1	57 526
PALLAHOSE		
Besenta	Mariposa Coulterville	60 699
Besento	Mariposa Coulterville	60 699
PALLARD		
D	Placer Dutch Fl	62 727
E	Tuolumne Twp 1	71 251
John G	Calaveras Twp 10	57 283
William	Tuolumne Twp 2	71 388
PALLART		
E	Tuolumne Twp 1	71 251
PALLATE		
John	Solano Suisan	69 240
PALLEAR		
Bernard	Calaveras Twp 4	57 324
PALLEDINE		
John G	Solano Benecia	69 288

Name	County Locale	M653 RollPage
PALLENHIGH		
Andrew	San Francisco San Francisco 2	67 756
PALLENHYLE		
Andrew	San Francisco San Francisco 2	67 756
PALLET		
Manes	Alameda Murray	55 228
PALLETT		
G W	Mendocino Ukiah	60 802
PALLEY		
J A	Siskiyou Klamath	69 88
PALLHAUS		
F	San Francisco San Francisco 12	367 67
PALLICK		
Joseph	El Dorado White Oaks	581010
PALLIER		
John	San Francisco San Francisco 2	67 794
PALLIES		
V	Tuolumne Jacksonville	71 165
PALLIMER		
W*	Butte Kimshaw	56 592
PALLIMRE		
W*	Butte Kimshaw	56 592
PALLIN		
---	Tulara Keyesville	71 56
J A	Sierra Twp 7	66 886
PALLOCK		
J	El Dorado Casumnes	581172
PALLORE		
Louis	Yuba New York	72 725
PALLOW		
Antonia	Amador Twp 3	55 379
PALLRIR		
John*	San Francisco San Francisco 2	67 794
PALLS		
I	Nevada Nevada	61 317
J	Nevada Nevada	61 317
PALLSAMONIO		
---	Mariposa Twp 3	60 557
PALLULES		
Paron*	Placer Dutch Fl	62 712
PALLUNER		
W*	Butte Kimshaw	56 592
PALLUNN		
W*	Butte Kimshaw	56 592
PALLY		
W	El Dorado Diamond	58 809
PALM		
Eduard	San Francisco San Francisco 8	681294
Edward	San Francisco San Francisco 8	681294
Edward	San Francisco San Francisco 2	67 682
Edward*	San Francisco San Francisco 8	681294
PALMA Y MESA		
Morcieles	Santa Barbara San Bernardino	64 195
PALMA		
Bosaria	Tuolumne Twp 5	71 499
E O	Butte Bidwell	56 705
E V	Butte Bidwell	56 705
Edward	San Francisco San Francisco 2	67 685
Juan	Santa Clara San Jose	65 309
Maguil	San Bernardino Santa Barbara	64 152
Wm	Trinity Steiner	701000
PALMAN		
James	San Francisco San Francisco 4	681133
PALMARIO		
---	San Bernardino S Timate	64 701
PALME		
John	Yuba Long Bar	72 755
PALMEIR		
Louis*	San Francisco San Francisco 7	681391
PALMEN		
Jhn	Mariposa Twp 1	60 634
PALMER		
A	El Dorado Diamond	58 771
A B	El Dorado Placerville	58 846
A D	Calaveras Twp 9	57 397
Ananias	Contra Costa Twp 2	57 568
Andrew	Alameda Brooklyn	55 101
Antone	Placer Todds Va	62 787
Asa	San Francisco San Francisco 1	68 901
B R	Sacramento Ward 4	63 612
Bennett	Sonoma Petaluma	69 605
C	Sierra Downieville	661016
C H	Amador Twp 1	55 468
C L H	Sacramento Granite	63 242
C M	Nevada Nevada	61 247
C S	Solano Benecia	69 297
C S H	Sacramento Granite	63 242
Charles T	Placer Auburn	62 564
Clinton	San Francisco San Francisco 4	681225
D	Nevada Eureka	61 376
Daniel	Placer Michigan	62 811
Domingo	Alameda Brooklyn	55 119
E	Amador Twp 6	55 441
E	El Dorado Newtown	58 779

Name	County Locale	M653 RollPage
PALMER		
E	Sutter Sutter	70 810
E C	Amador Twp 1	55 467
E C	San Francisco San Francisco 4	681226
Ed H	San Francisco San Francisco 6	67 404
Edwin	San Francisco San Francisco 3	67 85
Elias B	Calaveras Twp 5	57 199
Elisha	Butte Oregon	56 615
Emanuel	Sacramento Georgian	63 342
Frank C	San Luis Obispo San Luis Obispo	65 5
Fred	El Dorado White Oaks	581016
Geo	Butte Oregon	56 620
Geo	Butte Eureka	56 655
Geo	Placer Auburn	62 566
Geo W	Trinity Hay Fork	70 993
George	Calaveras Twp 5	57 251
Gideon	Sierra Gibsonville	66 856
Green	San Joaquin Elkhorn	64 994
H	Siskiyou Scott Va	69 43
H D	El Dorado Big Bar	58 740
Hannah	Plumas Quincy	62 915
Harry	San Mateo Twp 3	65 110
Henry	Placer Michigan	62 836
Henry	San Francisco San Francisco 12	67 371
Henry	Solano Suisan	69 240
Henry	Stanislaus Emory	70 738
Henry	Yuba Marysville	72 875
Henry Jr	Mendocino Arrana	60 862
Hiram	Butte Ophir	56 757
Hiram	El Dorado Mountain	581186
I W D	Amador Twp 2	55 310
I W D	Amador Twp 2	55 312
Isaac	Tuolumne Jamestown	71 470
Isabella	Del Norte Crescent	58 619
J	Trinity Redding	70 985
J A	Calaveras Twp 9	57 382
J A	Tuolumne Twp 2	71 329
J B	Butte Kimshaw	56 583
J C	Tuolumne Big Oak	71 126
J C	Tuolumne Twp 4	71 128
J D	El Dorado Georgetown	58 673
J H	Tuolumne Sonora	71 482
J K	Calaveras Twp 9	57 417
J M Smiths*	Butte Ophir	56 753
J W	Sacramento Ward 4	63 509
J W	Sonoma Bodega	69 519
J W D	Amador Twp 2	55 310
Jacob	Calaveras Twp 5	57 205
Jacob	Sonoma Petaluma	69 584
James	Marin Saucileto	60 750
James	Napa Yount	61 39
James	Sierra Eureka	661049
James	Sonoma Mendocino	69 467
Jas	Sonoma Petaluma	69 608
Jas G	Butte Kimshaw	56 581
Jasper	Plumas Quincy	62 968
Jhn	Mariposa Twp 1	60 634
Jhn	Napa Hot Springs	61 4
Jhn*	Mariposa Twp 1	60 634
John	Amador Twp 5	55 333
John	Placer Virginia	62 666
John	San Francisco San Francisco 3	67 67
John	Shasta Horsetown	66 708
John	Siskiyou Yreka	69 167
John	Sonoma Salt Point	69 692
John	Yuba Long Bar	72 755
John	Yuba Parks Ba	72 779
John	Yuba Rose Bar	72 808
John F	Butte Ophir	56 753
John T	Marin Cortemad	60 782
John*	Placer Michigan	62 826
Jos	Placer Mountain	62 707
Jos	Sonoma Petaluma	69 608
Jos	Trinity Weaverville	701066
Jos A	Alameda Brooklyn	55 156
Jos C	Alameda Brooklyn	55 181
Joseph	Calaveras Twp 8	57 93
Joseph	Mariposa Twp 1	60 632
Joseph	Mendocino Big Rvr	60 841
Joseph H	Calaveras Twp 7	57 15
L	Nevada Nevada	61 264
L	San Mateo Twp 3	65 78
L A	Nevada Nevada	61 265
L W	San Francisco San Francisco 5	67 531
Leander	Sierra La Porte	66 779
Lizzie	San Francisco San Francisco 2	67 589
Lutrie	Tuolumne Don Pedro	71 534
Lydia	San Francisco San Francisco 2	67 665
M	Calaveras Twp 9	57 379
M	Tehama Red Bluff	70 916
M I C	San Francisco San Francisco 2	67 727
M J C	San Francisco San Francisco 2	67 727
M K	Los Angeles Elmonte	59 247
M L	Butte Oregon	56 620
M S	Butte Oregon	56 620

Name	County Locale	M653 Roll	Page
PALMER			
M S	Butte Eureka	56	655
Marvin C	Siskiyou Shasta Rvr	69	114
Mary	Sacramento Ward 4	63	559
Mary	San Francisco San Francisco 9	68	1014
Mary	San Francisco San Francisco 10		181
		67	
N C	Alameda Brooklyn	55	211
N W	Alameda Oakland	55	70
Noah	Santa Clara Santa Clara	65	477
O L	San Francisco San Francisco 5	67	525
Odalf*	Yolo Washington	72	571
Phillip	Solano Suisan	69	215
Phillipa	San Francisco San Francisco 2	67	557
Pollpa	San Joaquin Stockton	64	1084
R L	Butte Kimshaw	56	586
R R	Sierra Eureka	66	1045
R W	Amador Twp 2	55	305
Rich	Yuba Rose Bar	72	814
Richard	Contra Costa Twp 1	57	500
Richard	San Francisco San Francisco 2	67	556
Richard	Solano Vallejo	69	279
Richard	Yuba Rose Bar	72	803
Robert	Sierra Twp 7	66	911
Robert	Yuba Marysville	72	961
S A	Sacramento Ward 4	63	504
S R	Sierra Twp 7	66	900
Sam	El Dorado Georgetown	58	687
Samuel	Humbolt Table Bl	59	139
Samuel	Santa Cruz Pajaro	66	571
Samuel	Sierra La Porte	66	768
Samuel	Siskiyou Yreka	69	184
Samuel L	San Francisco San Francisco 7	68	1327
Samul	Siskiyou Yreka	69	184
Sarah B	Sonoma Bodega	69	519
Seancler	Sierra La Porte	66	779
Smauel	Sierra La Porte	66	768
Smith	Alameda Brooklyn	55	176
Solomon	Sierra Twp 5	66	921
Solomon	Yolo Slate Ra	72	700
Solomon	Yuba Slate Ro	72	700
Susan	San Francisco San Francisco 2	67	578
Sutue*	Tuolumne Twp 6	71	534
T	Tuolumne Twp 4	71	166
T E	Tuolumne Twp 1	71	247
Thomas	Plumas Quincy	62	986
Thomas	San Francisco San Francisco 3	67	21
Thos	Calaveras Twp 6	57	152
Vah*	El Dorado Georgetown	58	760
W	El Dorado Mud Springs	58	979
W	Nevada Eureka	61	376
W C	San Mateo Twp 3	65	92
W C	Solano Montezuma	69	374
W H	Butte Ophir	56	753
W J	Calaveras Twp 9	57	386
W R	Butte Ophir	56	785
W S	Calaveras Twp 9	57	386
William A	San Francisco San Francisco 9	68	1013
William C	Santa Cruz Pajaro	66	534
William G	San Joaquin Stockton	64	1066
William H*	El Dorado Georgetown	58	698
Wilmer	Amador Twp 5	55	334
Wm	Humbolt Table Bl	59	139
Wm	Sacramento Ward 1	63	154
Wm	Sonoma Petaluma	69	594
Wm A	Napa Napa	61	112
PALMERE			
Nicholas	Nevada Bloomfield	61	526
PALMES			
M S	Butte Eureka	56	655
PALMESTHAM			
P G	Mendocino Big Rvr	60	845
PALMIRA			
---	Tulara Keyesville	71	64
PALMIREZ			
Jose R	Sacramento Ward 4	63	555
PALMO			
Nignetra*	Placer Michigan	62	840
PALMORE			
Andrew	Alameda Brooklyn	55	101
Nicholas*	Nevada Bloomfield	61	526
PALMORES			
Nicholas*	Nevada Bloomfield	61	526
PALMTREE			
Charles	San Bernardino Santa Barbara	64	179
PALMYRA			
Jose	Santa Cruz Pajaro	66	567
Robert	Santa Cruz Pajaro	66	564
PALNEN			
William H*	El Dorado Georgetown	58	698
PALNER			
Odalf*	Yolo Washington	72	571
PALNICE			
J R	Mariposa Twp 3	60	621
PALNODE			
J	Sacramento Brighton	63	201
PALOENIN			
John*	Calaveras Twp 8	57	88
PALOHER			
P*	Nevada Nevada	61	246
PALOMA			
---	San Bernardino S Timate	64	721
---	San Bernardino S Timate	64	726
---	San Bernardino S Timate	64	731
---	San Bernardino S Timate	64	747
Lucas	Santa Clara Santa Clara	65	478
PALOMARES			
Dolores	San Bernardino Santa Barbara	64	158
Francisco	Santa Clara Alviso	65	403
PALOMARIS			
Jose	Santa Clara Alviso	65	403
PALONIA			
---	San Bernardino S Timate	64	693
---	San Bernardino S Timate	64	706
PALONIO			
---	San Diego Agua Caliente	64	817
PALONO			
---	San Diego Agua Caliente	64	838
PALOS			
Mary	Tuolumne Columbia	71	345
PALPE			
David	Sacramento Ward 3	63	433
PALPEY			
Alexander	Yuba Linda Twp	72	981
PALPHINSE			
Geo*	San Francisco San Francisco 2	67	803
PALPHMSE			
Geo*	San Francisco San Francisco 2	67	803
PALPHOUSE			
Geo	San Francisco San Francisco 2	67	803
PALPINNNIVICK			
---	San Bernardino San Bernadino	64	667
PALSMIRE			
Henry	El Dorado Grizzly	58	1182
PALSON			
John	Nevada Bridgeport	61	499
Odolf	Yolo Washington	72	571
PALSUN			
J D	El Dorado Big Bar	58	741
PALTEN			
F W	El Dorado Mud Springs	58	999
PALTER			
S*	Mariposa Twp 3	60	574
PALTESS			
Fred	El Dorado Coloma	58	1122
PALTIN			
---	Tulara Twp 3	71	56
PALTON			
John*	San Francisco San Francisco 5	67	483
PALUCIO			
Trinidad	Monterey San Juan	60	982
PALURAN			
Andrew*	Calaveras Twp 6	57	116
PALZ			
Jacob W	Yuba Marysville	72	899
PAM			
---	Amador Twp 5	55	336
---	Amador Twp 1	55	495
---	Amador Twp 1	55	499
---	Amador Twp 1	55	502
---	Amador Twp 1	55	503
---	Amador Twp 1	55	510
---	Amador Twp 1	55	511
---	El Dorado Mud Springs	58	971
---	Placer Rattle Snake	62	626
---	Yuba North Ea	72	682
Mary*	Alameda Oakland	55	36
PAMACENO			
---	San Bernardino San Bernadino	64	679
PAMAHO			
---	Butte Chico	56	550
PAMALY			
N S	Siskiyou Scott Ri	69	73
PAMAN			
H	Yolo Cache Crk	72	664
PAMER			
J*	El Dorado Placerville	58	882
PAMES			
J*	El Dorado Placerville	58	882
PAMLGO			
Radolph*	Calaveras Twp 4	57	338
PAMMEL			
Fields*	Mendocino Little L	60	830
PAMMER			
John R*	Tulara Twp 1	71	100
PAMONE			
---*	Tulara Twp 2	71	38
PAMOONA			
---	San Mateo Twp 3	65	99
PAMPIA			
Julias	Alameda Oakland	55	10
PAMQEA			
Simon P	Yuba Marysville	72	966
PAMS			
Um	Plumas Quincy	62	965
PAMSETT			
Adan	Sacramento Granite	63	264
PAMSGALY			
Francisca*	Sacramento Ward 1	63	99
PAMTES			
Jno H	Butte Oregon	56	633
PAMYEN			
Simon P	Yuba Marysville	72	966
PAN FINKE			
John	Calaveras Twp 7	57	13
PAN JIM			
---	Sacramento Ward 1	63	70
PAN KEE			
---	Nevada Rough & Nevada Bridgeport	61	434
---	Nevada Rough & Nevada Bridgeport	61	462
PAN			
---	Amador Twp 2	55	315
---	Amador Twp 2	55	326
---	Amador Twp 2	55	327
---	Amador Twp 2	55	328
---	Amador Twp 5	55	330
---	Amador Twp 5	55	342
---	Amador Twp 5	55	349
---	Amador Twp 3	55	398
---	Amador Twp 3	55	410
---	Amador Twp 6	55	445
---	Amador Twp 6	55	450
---	Amador Twp 1	55	477
---	Calaveras Twp 8	57	106
---	Calaveras Twp 6	57	176
---	Calaveras Twp 6	57	181
---	Calaveras Twp 5	57	245
---	Calaveras Twp 10	57	284
---	Calaveras Twp 4	57	300
---	Calaveras Twp 4	57	321
---	Calaveras Twp 8	57	63
---	Del Norte Crescent	58	631
---	El Dorado White Oaks	58	1021
---	El Dorado Salmon Falls	58	1047
---	El Dorado Salmon Falls	58	1060
---	El Dorado Salmon Falls	58	1067
---	El Dorado Coloma	58	1109
---	El Dorado Coloma	58	1116
---	El Dorado Kelsey	58	1144
---	El Dorado Casumnes	58	1160
---	El Dorado Mountain	58	1187
---	El Dorado Big Bar	58	734
---	El Dorado Diamond	58	787
---	El Dorado Diamond	58	790
---	El Dorado Placerville	58	894
---	El Dorado Placerville	58	930
---	El Dorado Eldorado	58	939
---	El Dorado Eldorado	58	940
---	El Dorado Mud Springs	58	959
---	El Dorado Mud Springs	58	973
---	El Dorado Mud Springs	58	981
---	El Dorado Mud Springs	58	992
---	Fresno Twp 2	59	19
---	Mariposa Twp 3	60	608
---	Mariposa Twp 1	60	646
---	Mariposa Twp 1	60	664
---	Nevada Rough & Nevada Bridgeport	61	437
---	Nevada Bridgeport	61	458
---	Nevada Bridgeport	61	492
---	Sacramento Cosumnes	63	387
---	Sacramento Cosumnes	63	397
---	Sacramento Ward 4	63	609
---	Shasta Horsetown	66	711
---	Sierra Downieville	66	1000
---	Sierra Downieville	66	1026
---	Sierra Downieville	66	1029
---	Sierra La Porte	66	774
---	Sierra Twp 5	66	927
---	Sierra Twp 5	66	942
---	Sierra Downieville	66	974
---	Sierra Downieville	66	981
---	Sierra Downieville	66	984
---	Sierra Downieville	66	990
---	Sierra Downieville	66	999
---	Siskiyou Klamath	69	78
---	Stanislaus Emory	70	743
---	Tuolumne Columbia	71	347
---	Tuolumne Twp 2	71	409
---	Tuolumne Shawsfla	71	416
---	Tuolumne Twp 3	71	433
---	Tuolumne Twp 3	71	439
---	Tuolumne Twp 3	71	440
---	Tuolumne Twp 3	71	446
---	Tuolumne Sonora	71	477
---	Tuolumne Montezuma	71	504
---	Tuolumne Jacksonville	71	515
---	Tuolumne Twp 6	71	536
---	Yolo No E Twp	72	681
---	Yolo No E Twp	72	682

Name	County Locale	Roll	Page
PAN			
---	Yuba Long Bar	72	761
---*	Amador Twp 2	55	315
A	Sierra Downieville	66	981
Ah	Sacramento San Joaquin	63	353
Ah	Sacramento Cosumnes	63	390
Ah	Tuolumne Twp 2	71	347
Chi	San Francisco San Francisco 5	671	207
Due	Nevada Bloomfield	61	520
Far	El Dorado Mud Springs	58	962
Hard*	Sonoma Sonoma	69	662
Im*	Sacramento Ward 1	63	70
Jin	Sacramento Ward 1	63	70
Jose	San Diego Agua Caliente	64	843
Kee	Nevada Rough &	61	434
Kee	Nevada Bridgeport	61	462
Kung	San Francisco San Francisco 4	681	179
L B	Yuba Parks Ba	72	786
Lou	San Francisco San Francisco 5	671	206
On	San Francisco San Francisco 5	67	508
Tuck	Calaveras Twp 5	57	246
PANACER			
Casus	Mariposa Twp 1	60	624
PANAN			
---	Sonoma Sonoma	69	640
A	Sonoma Sonoma	69	640
PANANA			
Manuel	Marin Saucileto	60	749
PANASUALED			
Peabody*	Mariposa Twp 3	60	596
PANCE			
Hand	Sierra Downieville	66	957
Hinid*	Sierra Downieville	66	957
PANCH			
---	Butte Chico	56	550
---	Merced Twp 1	60	896
Billy	Butte Chico	56	550
F*	Nevada Eureka	61	348
PANCHA			
---	Tulara Keyesville	71	64
PANCHETE			
---	Tulara Keyesville	71	67
PANCHITA			
---	Fresno Twp 2	59	102
PANCHITO			
---	Tulara Twp 3	71	67
PANCHITTA			
---	Tulara Keyesville	71	70
PANCHO			
---	Butte Chico	56	551
---	Merced Twp 1	60	896
---	Tulara Keyesville	71	56
---	Tulara Keyesville	71	64
Antonio	Tuolumne Sonora	71	479
Francisco	Tuolumne Sonora	71	475
PANCHOND			
Lewis*	Calaveras Twp 4	57	340
PANCHORED			
Lewis*	Calaveras Twp 4	57	340
PANCHOUD			
Lewis	Calaveras Twp 4	57	340
PANCIS			
---	Monterey San Juan	60	992
PANCKMANN			
Anna	San Francisco San Francisco 9	68	954
PANCOAST			
Franklin	Alameda Oakland	55	70
PANCOST			
W M	Sonoma Petaluma	69	589
PANCQUA			
---	Fresno Twp 2	59	91
PANDER			
Henry*	Stanislaus Emory	70	739
Johnson	Butte Chico	56	561
PANDOLO			
Antonio	Calaveras Twp 8	57	82
Lorenza	Calaveras Twp 8	57	82
PANDON			
Walter J	El Dorado Greenwood	58	727
PANDORA			
Antonia	Calaveras Twp 7	57	34
PANE			
---	El Dorado Casumnes	581	160
---	El Dorado Mountain	581	188
---	El Dorado Placerville	58	923
Chas	Tehama Lassen	70	874
F A	Siskiyou Cottonwoood	69	106
Gecsjo*	Mariposa Twp 3	60	573
George	Mariposa Twp 3	60	573
Kung	Fresno Twp 2	59	19
Sarah	Tuolumne Twp 2	71	341
Wm	Butte Kimshaw	56	606
Wm	Tehama Lassen	70	871
Wm	Tehama Red Bluff	70	919
PANER			
Batise	El Dorado White Oaks	581	033

Name	County Locale	Roll	Page
PANER			
Charles A*	Mendocino Ukiah	60	807
PANERS			
George	Amador Twp 2	55	315
PANETT			
Eugene	Yolo Cache Crk	72	613
PANG			
---	Calaveras Twp 8	57	101
---	Calaveras Twp 8	57	102
---	Calaveras Twp 5	57	138
---	Calaveras Twp 5	57	219
---	Calaveras Twp 5	57	256
---	Calaveras Twp 4	57	315
---	Calaveras Twp 9	57	352
---	Calaveras Twp 7	57	47
---	Calaveras Twp 8	57	56
---	Calaveras Twp 8	57	82
---	Calaveras Twp 8	57	84
---	Calaveras Twp 8	57	91
---	Calaveras Twp 8	57	94
---	Del Norte Happy Ca	58	668
---	El Dorado Salmon Falls	581	042
---	El Dorado Salmon Falls	581	046
---	El Dorado Salmon Falls	581	064
---	El Dorado Salmon Falls	581	066
---	El Dorado Coloma	581	078
---	El Dorado Cold Spring	581	101
---	El Dorado Coloma	581	122
---	El Dorado Diamond	58	774
---	El Dorado Mud Springs	58	958
---	El Dorado Mud Springs	58	966
---	Mariposa Twp 1	60	650
---	Mariposa Twp 1	60	670
---	Mariposa Twp 1	60	671
---	Mariposa Coulterville	60	687
---	Mariposa Coulterville	60	688
---	Placer Rattle Snake	62	638
---	Placer Sacramento	62	646
---	Placer Horseshoe	62	650
---	Placer Virginia	62	666
---	Placer Virginia	62	674
---	Placer Virginia	62	676
---	Placer Virginia	62	677
---	Placer Virginia	62	686
---	Placer Illinois	62	742
---	San Joaquin Stockton	641	088
---	Shasta Horsetown	66	704
---	Sierra Downieville	66	982
---	Sierra Downieville	66	996
--*	Trinity E Weaver	701	059
---	Tuolumne Columbia	71	347
---	Tuolumne Shawsfla	71	408
---	Tuolumne Shawsfla	71	409
---	Tuolumne Twp 2	71	416
---	Tuolumne Twp 3	71	433
---	Tuolumne Jamestown	71	434
---	Tuolumne Jamestown	71	435
---	Tuolumne Jamestown	71	439
---	Tuolumne Twp 3	71	440
---	Tuolumne Twp 3	71	442
---	Tuolumne Jamestown	71	446
---	Tuolumne Twp 3	71	457
---	Tuolumne Twp 3	71	460
---	Tuolumne Twp 1	71	475
---	Tuolumne Twp 1	71	477
---	Tuolumne Sonora	71	478
---	Tuolumne Twp 5	71	525
---	Tuolumne Twp 6	71	528
---	Tuolumne Don Pedro	71	536
---	Tuolumne Don Pedro	71	538
---	Tuolumne Twp 6	71	539
---	Yuba Slate Ro	72	711
---	Yuba Long Bar	72	758
---	Yuba Fosters	72	831
---	Yuba Marysville	72	885
---*	Yuba Foster B	72	831
Ah	Calaveras Twp 7	57	14
Ah	Calaveras Twp 7	57	32
Ah	Calaveras Twp 7	57	35
Ah	Tuolumne Twp 2	71	347
Chan G	Tuolumne Twp 4	71	181
Chong	Tuolumne Big Oak	71	181
PANGAN			
Charles	Fresno Twp 3	59	32
PANGBORN			
James L	San Francisco San Francisco 3	67	33
PANGBRAN			
Joseph P	Yuba Long Bar	72	771
PANGE			
Traosa*	Calaveras Twp 6	57	161
Traosee*	Calaveras Twp 6	57	161
PANGER			
James	Amador Twp 3	55	373
PANGR			
Taosu*	Calaveras Twp 6	57	161
PANGRU			
W C*	Stanislaus Oatvale	70	717

Name	County Locale	Roll	Page
PANHAO			
Iniovel	Fresno Twp 1	59	76
PANHURST			
William*	San Francisco San Francisco 9	681	040
PANICA			
R	San Mateo Twp 2	65	118
PANINO			
Franciso	San Francisco San Francisco 3	67	16
PANIO			
D*	El Dorado Georgetown	58	704
PANIR			
D*	El Dorado Georgetown	58	704
PANIRS			
L*	Nevada Grass Valley	61	204
PANIS			
Eugene*	Marin Cortemad	60	787
Thomas*	Sierra Downieville	661	006
PANISGALY			
Francisca*	Sacramento Ward 1	63	99
PANIX			
George	Yuba Marysville	72	962
PANK			
---	Alameda Oakland	55	63
---	Sierra Twp 5	66	931
---	Yuba Long Bar	72	758
PANKETO			
---	Fresno Twp 2	59	114
PANKO			
---	Fresno Twp 3	59	100
PANLET			
John	Amador Twp 1	55	492
PANLEY			
Benjamin	Sierra Downieville	66	978
PANLL			
Henry*	Tuolumne Big Oak	71	144
PANLSON			
Henry	Yuba Fosters	72	831
PANLY			
Aron	Yuba Long Bar	72	745
Eliza A*	Napa Napa	61	99
Nicholas*	Sierra Gibsonville	66	858
PANN			
---	Tuolumne Twp 2	71	416
---	Tuolumne Jamestown	71	446
---	Tuolumne Twp 1	71	476
---	Yolo No E Twp	72	682
PANNALY			
R S*	Siskiyou Scott Ri	69	73
PANNAN			
H*	Yolo Cache Crk	72	664
PANNANF			
A	El Dorado Placerville	58	906
PANNEL			
Thos	Placer Goods	62	697
PANNELL			
S S	El Dorado Georgetown	58	745
PANNER			
C F*	Solano Vacaville	69	328
PANNIE			
Oscar*	Butte Oregon	56	627
PANNY			
---	Amador Twp 5	55	360
PANOLINO			
Jose	Santa Cruz Pajaro	66	554
PANQUITA			
---	Fresno Twp 3	59	98
PANS			
J B	San Francisco San Francisco 4	681	218
Jean*	Sacramento Ward 1	63	85
John	Sacramento Ward 1	63	11
Wm	Plumas Quincy	62	965
PANSE			
Adelaide	Del Norte Crescent	58	620
Manuel	Tuolumne Chinese	71	498
PANSEN			
J*	San Francisco San Francisco 9	681	060
PANSHEN			
---	Plumas Quincy	62	965
PANSIA			
Peter	Sierra Downieville	661	022
PANSKARD			
Allen*	Colusa Monroeville	57	451
PANSMAN			
William*	Yuba Marysville	72	902
PANT			
---	Sierra Downieville	66	981
William P	Siskiyou Yreka	69	180
PANTA			
John	Amador Twp 1	55	494
PANTALONES			
---	San Bernardino Santa Ba	64	219
PANTARA			
---	Fresno Twp 2	59	104
PANTATONES			
---	San Bernardino S Buenav	64	220
PANTHON			
Thos	Amador Twp 5	55	360

California 1860 Census Index

Name	County Locale	M653 RollPage
PANTIN		
William L	Sierra Whiskey	66 845
PANTO		
Jose	San Diego San Diego	64 773
Jose	San Diego Agua Caliente	64 843
PANTON		
Peter*	Amador Twp 4	55 234
PANTOS		
Jese	Sierra La Porte	66 781
Jose	Sierra La Porte	66 781
PANTOYA		
Yguacio	Los Angeles Los Angeles	59 330
PANTRO		
---	Tulara Keyesville	71 68
---	Tulara Keyesville	71 71
PANTUCO		
---	Fresno Twp 2	59 90
PANY		
---	Calaveras Twp 5	57 219
---	Calaveras Twp 5	57 256
---	Calaveras Twp 10	57 285
---	Calaveras Twp 4	57 315
---	Sacramento Granite	63 266
---	Sacramento Granite	63 268
---	Tuolumne Twp 2	71 408
---*	Sacramento Granite	63 266
Chemt*	Placer Stewart	62 606
PANYH		
---	Sacramento Granite	63 259
PANZZA		
Geovanni	San Francisco San Francisco 11	109 67
Giovanni	San Francisco San Francisco 11	109 67
PAO		
---	Calaveras Twp 4	57 300
---	El Dorado Salmon Falls	581067
PAOG		
Elijah	Calaveras Twp 6	57 157
PAOLE		
E A*	San Francisco San Francisco 1	68 917
PAP		
---	Mariposa Coulterville	60 693
J W*	Nevada Nevada	61 240
PAPA		
J	El Dorado Diamond	58 789
Jasper	San Francisco San Francisco 3	67 75
Jasper J*	San Francisco San Francisco 3	67 75
PAPARD		
Robert	Tulara Visalia	71 100
PAPAS		
---	Tulara Twp 1	71 114
PAPE		
Charles*	Siskiyou Yreka	69 134
Christopher	Nevada Little Y	61 537
Ed	Siskiyou Cottonwood	69 107
Edmund*	Butte Oregon	56 613
Geo	Sonoma Salt Point	69 689
J	San Francisco San Francisco 5	67 537
J C	El Dorado Placerville	58 899
John	Tuolumne Twp 1	71 265
M S	Butte Kimshaw	56 601
Minna*	San Francisco San Francisco 7	681434
Peter W	Tuolumne Twp 2	71 390
Saml*	Siskiyou Cottonwoood	69 107
PAPEL		
Colorado	Tulara Visalia	71 120
PAPELCOLVRADO		
---	Tulara Twp 1	71 120
PAPER		
Jasper J*	San Francisco San Francisco 3	67 75
PAPHAM		
Geo	Siskiyou Scott Ri	69 74
PAPI		
M S*	Butte Kimshaw	56 601
PAPIA		
Paul	Alameda Brooklyn	55 142
PAPILLAN		
Adam*	Yuba New York	72 732
Jean	Yuba New York	72 732
PAPILLAS		
---	Los Angeles San Pedro	59 479
PAPIN		
Joseph	Yuba Foster B	72 822
PAPO		
---	Tulara Keyesville	71 67
---	Tulara Keyesville	71 70
PAPON		
Pierre	Santa Clara Fremont	65 439
PAPPA		
C	El Dorado Diamond	58 811
PAPPE		
Agelin*	Calaveras Twp 6	57 135
Agielina*	Calaveras Twp 5	57 135
Agneline	Calaveras Twp 6	57 135
Agrelime*	Calaveras Twp 6	57 135

Name	County Locale	M653 RollPage
PAPPE		
Agulina	Calaveras Twp 6	57 135
Aqulina*	Calaveras Twp 5	57 135
C L	San Francisco San Francisco 5	67 526
PAPPY		
Adolph	Sonoma Sonoma	69 633
Mrs	Sonoma Sonoma	69 633
PAPSON		
Wm	Santa Clara San Jose	65 379
PAQATTE		
Nobert*	Amador Twp 4	55 245
PAQUENNO		
---	Tulara Twp 1	71 118
PAQUETTS		
J B	Placer Iona Hills	62 866
PAR		
---	Amador Twp 1	55 503
---	Calaveras Twp 5	57 149
---	Calaveras Twp 10	57 275
---	El Dorado Salmon Hills	581067
---	Sierra Twp 5	66 921
---	Sierra Downieville	66 984
---	Sierra Downieville	66 997
Yar	Mariposa Twp 1	60 651
PARA		
Diego	Los Angeles San Juan	59 469
PARACAN		
Lewis	Yolo Washington	72 574
PARACCO		
Jas*	Amador Twp 3	55 384
PARACHO		
Hosea	Alameda Brooklyn	55 191
PARACIO		
Ygnacia*	Contra Costa Twp 1	57 497
PARACO		
F	El Dorado Placerville	58 860
PARADEE		
William	Plumas Quincy	621003
PARADES		
A	Nevada Grass Valley	61 180
P	Merced Twp 1	60 899
PARADI		
Jose	Tuolumne Twp 3	71 460
PARAH		
Paul	San Francisco San Francisco 2	67 709
PARALA		
R	Solano Fremont	69 383
PARALGO		
Rodolph	Calaveras Twp 4	57 338
PARALLIS		
Rais	Calaveras Twp 5	57 206
Ruir	Calaveras Twp 5	57 206
PARALO		
Sephia	San Joaquin Stockton	641079
PARALSON		
W	Siskiyou Scott Va	69 49
PARALTA		
Ignacro*	Contra Costa Twp 1	57 525
J	Tuolumne Big Oak	71 154
PARALTO		
Juan	Marin San Rafael	60 768
Rosetha*	San Mateo Twp 3	65 99
PARALYO		
Rodolph*	Calaveras Twp 4	57 338
PARAMENA		
A	Amador Twp 1	55 483
Wm*	Los Angeles Tejon To	59 535
PARAND		
Joseph	Tuolumne Jamestown	71 438
PARANE		
P*	Sacramento Ward 1	63 5
PARANNO		
Chemeng*	Calaveras Twp 5	57 216
Chemuny*	Calaveras Twp 5	57 216
PARANO		
Augustin	Calaveras Twp 5	57 217
Augustine	Calaveras Twp 5	57 217
Chemuny	Calaveras Twp 5	57 216
John	Calaveras Twp 5	57 217
Joseph	Calaveras Twp 5	57 216
Joseph Jr	Calaveras Twp 5	57 216
PARANS		
John	Calaveras Twp 5	57 217
John	Calaveras Twp 5	57 228
Joseph	Calaveras Twp 5	57 217
Julins	Calaveras Twp 5	57 217
Julius	Calaveras Twp 5	57 217
PARAQU		
Juan	Alameda Brooklyn	55 171
PARARA		
John	Tuolumne Twp 3	71 424
PARARAN		
Lewis	Yolo Washington	72 574
PARARGUA		
Joseph	San Joaquin Stockton	641069

Name	County Locale	M653 RollPage
PARARIE		
P	Sacramento Ward 1	63 5
PARARINTE		
Alex	Sierra La Porte	66 768
PARAS		
Carmelita	Yuba Marysville	72 933
Pabloccino	Yuba Marysville	72 936
Pedro	Yuba Marysville	72 949
Ramon	Yuba Marysville	72 936
Ramon	Yuba Marysville	72 937
PARASE		
Ah	Butte Cascade	56 699
PARASI		
---	Butte Cascade	56 699
PARATA		
Jack	Tuolumne Twp 1	71 190
John	El Dorado Placerville	58 926
PARATO		
Gustavus	Calaveras Twp 6	57 128
PARATTO		
Juan	Marin San Rafael	60 768
PARAUD		
Joseph	Tuolumne Twp 3	71 438
PARAUS		
John	Calaveras Twp 5	57 228
PARAZETT		
M B	Nevada Eureka	61 353
PARAZITT		
M B*	Nevada Eureka	61 353
PARBER		
Joseph*	Monterey S Antoni	60 973
PARBURG		
W M	El Dorado Newtown	58 777
PARBURT		
George R	San Francisco San Francisco 2	67 588
PARBY		
Nicholas*	San Francisco San Francisco 1	68 918
PARCE		
Frederick	Yuba Marysville	72 913
Josa	Amador Twp 5	55 332
Thomas J	Yuba Marysville	72 975
PARCEL		
Cyrus	Yuba Suida	72 988
Enora	San Francisco San Francisco 2	67 741
PARCELL		
Norah	Yuba Marysville	72 912
PARCELLE		
O	Sacramento Granite	63 239
PARCELLS		
Jno J	San Francisco San Francisco 9	68 999
PARCELS		
Stephen D	Humbolt Pacific	59 138
PARCHANNCHA		
---	Mendocino Calpella	60 828
PARCHANUCHA		
---	Mendocino Calpella	60 828
PARCHET		
Z*	El Dorado Placerville	58 912
PARCHO		
Calenda	Alameda Brooklyn	55 189
PARCID		
---	San Bernardino San Bernadino	64 677
PARCKER		
P	Siskiyou Callahan	69 6
PARCO		
John	Sierra Downieville	661006
PARD		
Manuel	El Dorado Coloma	581086
PARD?SSUS		
Rene	Sacramento Granite	63 244
PARDAS		
Vicente	Los Angeles Los Angeles	59 321
PARDDSSUS		
Rene*	Sacramento Granite	63 244
PARDEA		
Antoio	Yuba Marysville	72 925
Antonio	Yuba Marysville	72 925
PARDEE		
E H	San Francisco San Francisco 6	67 404
F F	Sacramento Sutter	63 297
F T	Sacramento Sutter	63 297
Geo	San Francisco San Francisco 9	681063
James V	Amador Twp 1	55 480
Jas	San Francisco San Francisco 2	67 694
Joseph	Sierra Whiskey	66 843
Lewis	Humbolt Union	59 185
Maria B	Sacramento Ward 4	63 597
P W	Tuolumne Twp 3	71 458
R S	Amador Twp 2	55 262
Thomas	Yuba Marysville	72 852
Thomas	Yuba Marysville	72 857
PARDEER		
Gregorio	Contra Costa Twp 1	57 491
PARDEL		
Stephen	San Luis Obispo	65 26
	San Luis Obispo	

Name	County Locale	M653 Roll	Page
PARDEN			
J	Placer Secret R	62	611
John	Placer Michigan	62	820
PARDENHAMER			
Nicholas*	Sierra Poker Flats	66	837
PARDENHEEMER			
Nicholas*	Sierra Poker Flats	66	837
Nicholus*	Sierra Poker Flats	66	837
PARDENHEEMES			
Nicholas*	Sierra Poker Flats	66	837
PARDENHUMER			
Nicholas*	Sierra Poker Flats	66	837
PARDENKEEMES			
Nicholas*	Sierra Poker Flats	66	837
PARDENO			
Benito	Santa Cruz Pajaro	66	552
PARDENS			
Edward	Calaveras Twp 5	57	206
PARDER			
William	Yuba Marysville	72	882
PARDERO			
Benito	Santa Cruz Pajaro	66	552
PARDEUS			
Edward	Calaveras Twp 5	57	206
PARDEVANT			
G	Tuolumne Shawsfla	71	406
PARDEVART			
G*	Tuolumne Twp 2	71	406
PARDIALO			
Francisco	San Mateo Twp 2	65	132
PARDINO			
Benito	Santa Cruz Pajaro	66	550
PARDIO			
Anthony	Contra Costa Twp 2	57	564
PARDIS			
Theis	Sierra Grizzly	66	1058
PARDISSUS			
Rerre	Sacramento Granite	63	244
PARDLOW			
Isaac	Mendocino Anderson	60	870
PARDO			
Ruben	Santa Cruz Pajaro	66	559
PARDONS			
William	Nevada Rough &	61	437
PARDOW			
Emma	Santa Cruz Pajaro	66	564
PARDTSSUS			
Rene*	Sacramento Granite	63	244
PARDUS			
Kene Jr	Sacramento Granite	63	244
Rene Jr*	Sacramento Granite	63	244
PARDY			
Ben	Yuba Rose Bar	72	812
J C	Tuolumne Twp 2	71	346
Wm	Sierra Downieville	66	964
PARE			
Manuel	Placer Michigan	62	832
Richd	Tuolumne Sonora	71	238
PAREA			
F	El Dorado Placerville	58	841
Jesus	Monterey Pajaro	60	1013
PARECH			
F*	Nevada Eureka	61	348
PAREDES			
Gabriel	San Diego San Diego	64	761
PAREMPO			
---	Fresno Twp 2	59	115
PAREMSSO			
---	Fresno Twp 2	59	115
PARENT			
Chas	San Francisco San Francisco 9	68	1035
Fred	Siskiyou Scott Va	69	49
Joseph	Tuolumne Twp 2	71	380
Jred	Siskiyou Scott Va	69	49
PARER			
F*	Sacramento Brighton	63	196
PARES			
Juan	San Joaquin Tulare	64	869
Rosana	San Francisco San Francisco 2	67	626
PARET			
Joseph	Tuolumne Shawsfla	71	380
PAREVANA			
Louis	Sacramento Ward 3	63	426
PAREY			
Marcus*	San Luis Obispo	65	33
	San Luis Obispo		
PAREZ			
Domingo	Contra Costa Twp 2	57	565
Luacana	San Francisco San Francisco 2	67	783
Luanana*	San Francisco San Francisco 2	67	783
PARG			
---	Mariposa Twp 1	60	665
PARGANETE			
Nicholas	San Francisco San Francisco 7	68	1397
PARGAT			
Faustan	San Francisco San Francisco 2	67	613

Name	County Locale	M653 Roll	Page
PARGAT			
Trese	San Francisco San Francisco 2	67	613
PARGE			
A J*	Nevada Rough &	61	420
John	Sierra Twp 5	66	935
PARGMAN			
Joseph	Siskiyou Klamath	69	93
PARGON			
---	Sierra Downieville	66	984
PARHAM			
Jno B*	Nevada Nevada	61	285
PARHAW			
Jno B*	Nevada Nevada	61	285
PARIA			
Phidel*	San Joaquin O'Neal	64	1004
PARIAR			
Louis	Siskiyou Yreka	69	178
PARIBLO			
Pedro	Calaveras Twp 7	57	11
PARICA			
Padro	Amador Twp 5	55	332
PARICINS			
G B	San Francisco San Francisco 7	68	1400
PARICIOO			
---	San Bernardino S Timate	64	701
PARIDE			
Justo	Calaveras Twp 6	57	155
PARIERS			
George*	Amador Twp 2	55	315
PARIG			
---	Tuolumne Twp 6	71	536
PARIIER			
Louis*	Siskiyou Yreka	69	178
PARILL			
Henry*	Tuolumne Big Oak	71	144
PARILLA			
Magnus*	El Dorado Georgetown	58	747
PARIN			
Frank	Calaveras Twp 5	57	226
Peter	Nevada Bloomfield	61	516
PARING			
John A	Yuba New York	72	727
PARIO			
Allicano	Calaveras Twp 7	57	10
Vandanson*	Mariposa Coulterville	60	696
PARIS			
Augustus	Mariposa Twp 3	60	588
Charlotte	San Francisco San Francisco 1	68	807
Chas	Alameda Oakland	55	36
D H	Sacramento Cosummes	63	383
George*	Tuolumne Twp 6	71	534
Indreas*	Plumas Quincy	62	967
J	San Francisco San Francisco 2	67	472
J	San Francisco San Francisco 2	67	795
J B*	San Francisco San Francisco 4	68	1218
Jack	Calaveras Twp 6	57	161
Jean*	Sacramento Ward 1	63	85
John	Calaveras Twp 6	57	160
Lyman	Santa Cruz Santa Cruz	66	630
Ramon	Los Angeles Los Angeles	59	518
S	Mariposa Twp 3	60	588
Tulena	El Dorado Placerville	58	897
Vincento	Sacramento Ward 1	63	110
PARISH			
Charles	Placer Iona Hills	62	887
Daniel	San Joaquin Stockton	64	1090
James	Napa Clear Lake	61	133
Jas	Sacramento Ward 3	63	458
Joseph	Calaveras Twp 8	57	93
Nathl	San Francisco San Francisco 9	68	1035
S H	San Francisco San Francisco 5	67	543
Thos	Butte Chico	56	565
PARISTA			
Jacob	Calaveras Twp 5	57	220
PARISTO			
Jacob	Calaveras Twp 5	57	220
PARJETTA			
Joseph*	Yuba Parks Ba	72	780
PARK			
---	Mariposa Twp 1	60	662
---	Sierra Twp 5	66	931
---	Trinity Mouth Ca	70	1018
---	Yolo No E Twp	72	683
---	Yuba Slate Ro	72	683
A D	El Dorado Diamond	58	773
Albert	Fresno Twp 3	59	32
Caroline	San Francisco San Francisco 10	67	232
Chas	Nevada Bloomfield	61	529
Chris*	Nevada Bloomfield	61	529
D	Shasta Millvill	66	744
D H	San Francisco San Francisco 6	67	413
E	Sonoma Salt Point	69	692
E W	San Francisco San Francisco 1	68	900
Eliz S	San Francisco San Francisco 2	67	690
F A	Sacramento Sutter	63	308

Name	County Locale	M653 Roll	Page
PARK			
Fred	Placer Todds Va	62	786
G C	Sonoma Salt Point	69	692
G W	Yolo Cache Crk	72	645
J W	Sacramento Ward 4	63	607
James	San Bernardino Santa Ba	64	218
James	San Bernardino S Buenav	64	219
John	Calaveras Twp 4	57	330
John	Sonoma Bodega	69	521
John C	San Francisco San Francisco 3	67	36
L D	Sacramento Ward 1	63	28
Laura*	Siskiyou Yreka	69	158
Lawra*	Siskiyou Yreka	69	158
Mary	Sacramento Ward 1	63	147
R C	Sierra Twp 7	66	906
Robert	Calaveras Twp 7	57	17
S D	Sacramento Ward 1	63	28
Samuel	Placer Michigan	62	851
Stephen	Shasta Millvill	66	743
T B	San Francisco San Francisco 5	67	499
T W	Mariposa Twp 3	60	546
T W	San Francisco San Francisco 6	67	421
T W*	Mariposa Twp 3	60	546
Thomas	Calaveras Twp 4	57	330
Thomas B	Sierra Twp 5	66	946
W H	Sonoma Santa Rosa	69	400
William	Calaveras Twp 4	57	330
William	Siskiyou Yreka	69	158
William	Siskiyou Yreka	69	165
William	Sonoma Bodega	69	536
Wm	Sonoma Bodega	69	521
PARKAM			
Jno B*	Nevada Nevada	61	285
PARKAW			
Jno B	Nevada Nevada	61	285
PARKBURST			
Daniel W	Yuba Marysville	72	901
PARKE			
Charles	Calaveras Twp 5	57	210
Frank	El Dorado Eldorado	58	945
Ha	El Dorado Eldorado	58	945
J A	Alameda Brooklyn	55	145
James W	Sacramento Ward 1	63	130
James W	Sacramento Ward 1	63	131
L C	El Dorado Eldorado	58	945
R	Amador Twp 2	55	315
R F	San Francisco San Francisco 5	67	552
R F	Sutter Butte	70	788
Silas	San Francisco San Francisco 10	67	238
PARKEN			
George	El Dorado Greenwood	58	726
PARKER			
---	Sierra St Louis	66	812
A	Santa Clara San Jose	65	347
A H	Amador Twp 4	55	237
A H	Nevada Nevada	61	241
A R	Nevada Grass Valley	61	192
Adison	El Dorado Kelsey	58	1147
Albert	Calaveras Twp 7	57	10
Albert	Placer Folsom	62	639
Alex	San Francisco San Francisco 1	68	909
Alexander*	Siskiyou Callahan	69	1
Allel	Colusa Monroeville	57	456
Alongon*	Yuba Bear Rvr	72	1008
Alonzon	Yuba Bear Rvr	72	1008
Alougon*	Yuba Bear Rvr	72	1008
Ambrose	Butte Oregon	56	626
Angeline C	San Francisco 6	67	421
	San Francisco		
Anthony	Calaveras Twp 4	57	326
Arthur	Nevada Rough &	61	429
Arthur D	Nevada Rough &	61	429
B E	Shasta Millvill	66	749
B M	Shasta Horsetown	66	694
Basel G	Tulara Twp 1	71	108
Benjamin	Placer Forest H	62	799
Benjamine	Tuolumne Twp 5	71	502
Benjmine	Tuolumne Montezuma	71	502
Bill	Alameda Oakland	55	56
C	San Joaquin Stockton	64	1038
C A	Placer Dutch Fl	62	709
C B	Siskiyou Scott Va	69	54
C F*	El Dorado Placerville	58	885
C O	El Dorado Georgetown	58	679
Carlton	Placer Michigan	62	857
Caroline	San Francisco San Francisco 3	67	76
Charles	Calaveras Twp 5	57	210
Charles	Sierra Downieville	66	987
Chas	Mariposa Twp 3	60	558
Chas	San Francisco San Francisco 2	67	701
Chas F	Sacramento Ward 1	63	20
Chas F	San Francisco San Francisco 10	67	273
D	Stanislaus Buena Village	70	720
D P	Butte Chico	56	533

Name	County Locale	M653 RollPage
PARKER		
Daniel	Calaveras Twp 7	57 39
Daniel B	Tuolumne Twp 6	71 531
David	Tuolumne Twp 2	71 328
Davis	Yuba Bear Rvr	721007
E	El Dorado Kelsey	581130
E	Sacramento Cosummes	63 402
E A	Sacramento Ward 4	63 587
E F	Stanislaus Emory	70 745
E G	Sacramento Granite	63 230
Edward	Butte Ophir	56 789
Edward	Placer Michigan	62 855
Edward D	San Francisco San Francisco 3	67 36
Edwd M	San Francisco San Francisco 9	681035
Edwd W	San Francisco San Francisco 10	304 67
Edwin	Tuolumne Twp 2	71 283
Eldredge	Calaveras Twp 6	57 172
Eliah	Mendocino Big Rvr	60 841
Elijah	Mendocino Big Rvr	60 841
Elizabeth	San Francisco San Francisco 12	363 67
Ellen	Alameda Oakland	55 27
Emily E	San Francisco San Francisco 2	67 716
Eustace	Calaveras Twp 10	57 288
Eustoce	Calaveras Twp 10	57 288
F A	Tuolumne Twp 1	71 221
F W	San Francisco San Francisco 1	68 903
Ford	Del Norte Happy Ca	58 669
Francis	Contra Costa Twp 1	57 511
Francis	Siskiyou Cottonwoood	69 107
Francis L	San Francisco San Francisco 2	67 616
Frank	Marin Cortemad	60 753
Fred	Amador Twp 2	55 305
Fred	Sonoma Petaluma	69 608
Freeman	Sonoma Petaluma	69 605
G H	El Dorado Kelsey	581154
G M	Sacramento Ward 1	63 111
G M	Sacramento Ward 1	63 136
G W	Alameda Brooklyn	55 139
G W	Sacramento Ward 1	63 111
G W H	Calaveras Twp 9	57 355
Geo	Butte Oro	56 678
Geo	San Francisco San Francisco 10	258 67
Geo	Trinity Rush Crk	70 965
Geo D	Napa Clear Lake	61 132
Geo F	Sacramento Ward 1	63 79
Geo F	Santa Clara San Jose	65 366
Geo F*	Sacramento Ward 1	63 79
Geo H	Sacramento Ward 1	63 147
Geo H	Santa Clara Alviso	65 409
Geo T*	Sacramento Ward 1	63 79
George	Nevada Red Dog	61 541
George	Sacramento Granite	63 266
George	San Francisco San Francisco 4	681126
Gustaves	Tuolumne Twp 2	71 279
Gustavey	Tuolumne Twp 2	71 279
H	Butte Oregon	56 627
H	San Francisco San Francisco 9	681060
H	Siskiyou Yreka	69 185
H A	Trinity Grass Valley	70 962
H C	San Francisco San Francisco 4	681126
H G	El Dorado Salmon Hills	581065
H J	San Bernardino San Salvador	64 648
H L	El Dorado White Oaks	581009
H P	San Francisco San Francisco 4	681110
H T	Shasta Cottonwoood	66 723
Harry	Nevada Eureka	61 355
Harry	Sacramento Granite	63 264
Harry D	San Francisco San Francisco 3	67 19
Henry	Calaveras Twp 10	57 266
Henry	Fresno Twp 2	59 49
Hiram	San Joaquin Castoria	64 898
Israel	Tuolumne Twp 1	71 484
J	El Dorado Kelsey	581146
J	Nevada Grass Valley	61 110
J	Nevada Eureka	61 351
J	Sutter Nicolaus	70 832
J	Sutter Vernon	70 845
J C	Calaveras Twp 9	57 362
J F	Calaveras Twp 9	57 407
J G	Butte Oregon	56 627
J L	Yuba Long Bar	72 748
J M	Napa Napa	61 91
J M	Nevada Rough &	61 433
J M	San Joaquin Elkhorn	64 994
J N	Placer Todds Va	62 783
Jackson	Los Angeles Azuza	59 273
Jackson	Tulara Visalia	71 10
James	Contra Costa Twp 2	57 573
James	Los Angeles Elmonte	59 263
James	Nevada Rough &	61 412
James	Placer Michigan	62 842
James	Placer Michigan	62 856
James	San Luis Obispo San Luis Obispo	65 8

Name	County Locale	M653 RollPage
PARKER		
James	Santa Cruz Pajaro	66 572
James	Santa Cruz Pajaro	66 574
James	Sierra Port Win	66 792
James	Sierra Twp 7	66 891
James	Sierra Twp 7	66 895
James E	Plumas Quincy	62 980
Jas	Butte Oro	56 684
Jas	Sacramento San Joaquin	63 359
Jas	Sonoma Petaluma	69 543
Jas E	Sacramento Ward 3	63 442
Jasper	Tulara Yule Rvr	71 22
Jeremiah	Shasta Millvill	66 744
Jeremiah	Tulara Twp 1	71 108
Jno	Nevada Nevada	61 243
Jno	Nevada Washington	61 333
Jno	San Francisco San Francisco 9	681028
Jno D	Napa Clear Lake	61 132
Jno E	Sacramento Ward 3	63 472
Jno*	Nevada Washington	61 333
John	Calaveras Twp 8	57 80
John	Colusa Muion	57 459
John	El Dorado Greenwood	58 719
John	El Dorado Mud Springs	58 992
John	Marin Tomales	60 721
John	Marin Cortemad	60 752
John	Plumas Quincy	62 991
John	Sacramento Granite	63 225
John	Sacramento Franklin	63 324
John	San Joaquin Douglass	64 928
John	Santa Cruz Santa Cruz	66 602
John	Solano Suisan	69 205
John	Sonoma Sonoma	69 647
John	Tuolumne Don Pedro	71 534
John	Yolo Putah	72 588
John G	Tulara Twp 1	71 99
John L	Sierra La Porte	66 784
John M	Sierra La Porte	66 784
John S	Butte Ophir	56 793
John S	Calaveras Twp 5	57 231
John S	San Mateo Twp 3	65 73
John S	Sierra La Porte	66 784
John V	Santa Cruz Pajaro	66 525
John W	Calaveras Twp 5	57 171
Jos	Sonoma Petaluma	69 544
Jos B	Calaveras Twp 6	57 119
Joseph	Sonoma Armally	69 518
Joseph C	Tulara Twp 1	71 99
Jsnol*	Tuolumne Sonora	71 484
Julia A	Sierra Downieville	66 958
Julia N	Sierra Downieville	66 958
L	El Dorado Placerville	58 932
L F	Santa Clara San Jose	65 366
L M	Tehama Pasakent	70 855
Lafayette	San Joaquin Elkhorn	64 972
Levi	El Dorado Georgetown	58 753
Lewis R	Siskiyou Yreka	69 132
Lilas	Sonoma Armally	69 482
Louise	Sacramento Ward 1	63 148
Lozino	Sonoma Santa Rosa	69 403
M	San Mateo Twp 3	65 108
M	Siskiyou Cottonwoood	69 99
M	Solano Montezuma	69 370
Martha	Napa Clear Lake	61 128
Martin	Siskiyou Scott Va	69 34
Mary	El Dorado Georgetown	58 683
Mary	San Francisco San Francisco 10	216 67
Mary	San Joaquin Stockton	641009
Mary	Siskiyou Yreka	69 174
Mary Jane	Yuba New York	72 727
Milton	Santa Clara San Jose	65 366
Milton	Siskiyou Yreka	69 139
Mr	Marin Bolinas	60 747
Nancy C	Tulara Twp 1	71 87
Nius*	San Francisco San Francisco 7	681410
O W	El Dorado Placerville	58 877
Orrin	Placer Todds Va	62 762
P C	Sacramento Ward 4	63 527
P*	Siskiyou Callahan	69 6
Peter	Butte Ophir	56 793
R	El Dorado Salmon Hills	581061
R	San Francisco San Francisco 12	391 67
R B	San Joaquin Stockton	641055
R D	Tuolumne Columbia	71 356
R W	Solano Montezuma	69 374
Raufus	Sierra Cox'S Bar	66 949
Richard	San Francisco San Francisco 7	681338
Richard	Tulara Twp 1	71 108
Richard	Yolo Merritt	72 579
Richard B	San Francisco San Francisco 8	681252
Robert	Alameda Brooklyn	55 99
Robert	Tulara Visalia	71 30
Robert	Yuba Parks Ba	72 780

Name	County Locale	M653 RollPage
PARKER		
Robt A	San Francisco San Francisco 10	281 67
Robt F	Klamath Trinidad	59 220
Rufus	Sierra Cox'S Bar	66 949
S H	San Francisco San Francisco 7	681445
S W	El Dorado White Oaks	581012
Sam	Sacramento Ward 1	63 64
Saml	Butte Chico	56 532
Saml D	Butte Chico	56 531
Saml N	Calaveras Twp 5	57 148
Samuel	Amador Twp 6	55 439
Samuel	El Dorado Georgetown	58 696
Samuel	Placer Michigan	62 826
Samuel	Santa Cruz Pajaro	66 558
Seth A	Yuba Bear Rvr	721007
Silas	San Francisco San Francisco 10	238 67
Silas	Sonoma Armally	69 482
Simon	Del Norte Crescent	58 627
Stephen	Santa Cruz Santa Cruz	66 635
T	Siskiyou Klamath	69 79
T D	San Francisco San Francisco 6	67 445
Tharon	Stanislaus Buena Village	70 724
Thomas	Plumas Meadow Valley	62 899
Thomas	San Francisco San Francisco 4	681165
Thomas	San Francisco San Francisco 7	681339
Thomas B	San Joaquin Elliott	641103
Thos	Nevada Eureka	61 363
Thos	Yolo Washington	72 570
Timothy	San Francisco San Francisco 11	152 67
W	Calaveras Twp 9	57 389
W	Calaveras Twp 9	57 398
W	Calaveras Twp 9	57 406
W	Shasta Shasta	66 666
W	Solano Vacaville	69 330
W	Sutter Nicolaus	70 827
W C	San Francisco San Francisco 4	681225
W E	Sacramento Ward 3	63 431
W F	Mariposa Twp 3	60 603
W H	Sonoma Armally	69 508
W K	Marin Bolinas	60 740
W S	Marin San Rafael	60 758
W T	Marin San Rafael	60 758
W T*	Mariposa Twp 3	60 603
W W	Amador Twp 3	55 374
Washington	San Joaquin Elkhorn	64 972
William	Los Angeles Elmonte	59 246
William	Los Angeles San Pedro	59 480
William	Mendocino Calpella	60 810
William	San Francisco San Francisco 7	681326
William	Siskiyou Cottonwoood	69 101
William	Stanislaus Oatvale	70 717
William	Tulara Twp 2	71 11
William	Tulara Twp 1	71 41
William C	San Luis Obispo	65 33
	San Luis Obispo	
William E	San Francisco San Francisco 7	681428
William E	Sierra Poker Flats	66 837
William S	Sierra Pine Grove	66 823
Wm	El Dorado Mud Springs	58 990
Wm	Nevada Eureka	61 366
Wm	Sacramento San Joaquin	63 349
Wm	San Francisco San Francisco 10	323 67
Wm	San Francisco San Francisco 1	68 905
Wm	Santa Clara Gilroy	65 247
Wm	Santa Clara Burnett	65 256
Wm	Santa Clara San Jose	65 288
Wm	Sierra Downieville	661016
Wm	Sonoma Armally	69 479
Wm	Sonoma Petaluma	69 606
Wm E	San Francisco San Francisco 10	166 67
Wm F	Sierra Twp 5	66 923
Wm H	Fresno Millerto	59 2
Wm R	Napa Napa	61 106
PARKERFIELD		
Henny F	Calaveras Twp 5	57 210
PARKERSON		
Geo	San Francisco San Francisco 6	67 446
Saml	Tuolumne Twp 3	71 469
Sarah	Yolo Cache Crk	72 663
PARKES		
Alexander	Siskiyou Callahan	69 1
Chas	Mariposa Twp 3	60 558
PARKHAM		
G W	Sacramento Ward 1	63 141
PARKHARST		
H	Shasta French G	66 715
PARKHERT		
Sophia	Tuolumne Sonora	71 188
PARKHIRST		
O	El Dorado Placerville	58 883
PARKHURST		
H	Shasta French G	66 715

California 1860 Census Index

Name	County Locale	M653 RollPage
PARKHURST		
John	Calaveras Twp 10	57 276
M A	San Mateo Twp 3	65 78
M F	Sacramento Sutter	63 300
Mary H	Yuba Marysville	72 892
R	Placer Forest H	62 794
Sophia	Tuolumne Twp 1	71 188
W	Sacramento Granite	63 230
William	El Dorado Big Bar	58 741
PARKHUTE		
Theodore	Placer Dutch Fl	62 716
PARKIN		
George*	El Dorado Greenwood	58 727
John	El Dorado Placerville	58 910
Margarin*	El Dorado Greenwood	58 726
Samuel	San Joaquin Elkhorn	64 972
PARKINGTON		
Tho	Sonoma Sonoma	69 658
PARKINS		
James	San Mateo Twp 3	65 93
PARKINSON		
D F*	Shasta Millvill	66 752
D W	Shasta Millvill	66 752
E A	Mendocino Anderson	60 867
Jno	Sacramento Ward 4	63 505
John	Placer Iona Hills	62 895
Sarah	Yolo Cache Crk	72 663
William	Placer Michigan	62 853
Wm K	Placer Auburn	62 566
PARKLEY		
Jos	San Francisco San Francisco 9	681076
PARKMAN		
A	Sutter Butte	70 796
PARKNET		
Joshua	El Dorado Kelsey	581135
PARKO		
Oliver	San Diego Colorado	64 806
PARKRSON		
Saml	Tuolumne Jamestown	71 469
PARKS		
Ada	Napa Napa	61 100
Albert W	San Francisco San Francisco 7	681371
Alonzo	San Francisco San Francisco 10	352
		67
Andrew H	San Joaquin Castoria	64 907
Arthur	San Bernardino San Bernadino	64 631
C L	Nevada Bloomfield	61 510
Charles	Amador Twp 1	55 488
Charles	Tuolumne Twp 1	71 197
Chas	Placer Nicolaus	62 692
D B	Napa Napa	61 111
D H	Sonoma Armally	69 510
Danl	Santa Clara Redwood	65 445
David	Siskiyou Cottonwoood	69 103
David C	Calaveras Twp 7	57 2
E A	Sierra Eureka	661046
Edward	Tuolumne Twp 5	71 505
Edwd	Butte Kimshaw	56 596
G W	Yolo Cache	72 645
G W	Yuba New York	72 725
Geo G	Napa Napa	61 111
George	Shasta Horsetown	66 691
H	Butte Ophir	56 795
H	Santa Clara Redwood	65 444
H G	Sonoma Bodega	69 532
Hough	Butte Bidwell	56 719
Hugh	Butte Bidwell	56 719
Hugh	Calaveras Twp 9	57 372
J C	Placer Forest H	62 759
J E	Santa Clara San Jose	65 346
J N	Butte Ophir	56 761
J W	Solano Vacaville	69 356
James	Placer Michigan	62 843
James	Sierra Port Win	66 792
Jane	Tuolumne Twp 6	71 528
Jas	Santa Clara Redwood	65 445
Jno	Butte Hamilton	56 527
Joel	Santa Clara Santa Clara	65 513
John	Butte Ophir	56 754
John	Santa Clara San Jose	65 392
John	Shasta Horsetown	66 699
John	Solano Suisan	69 230
L	Merced Twp 1	60 911
M R	Sierra Twp 7	66 891
Mr	Sonoma Vallejo	69 615
N A	Solano Vacaville	69 325
Narmon	Amador Twp 3	55 381
R H	Del Norte Crescent	58 633
R W	Del Norte Crescent	58 633
Rebecca	Solano Benecia	69 290
Richard	Napa Napa	61 81
Robert	San Joaquin Elkhorn	64 950
Robt F*	Fresno Twp 3	59 22
Robt T*	Fresno Twp 3	59 22
Sam	El Dorado Placerville	58 895
Samuel	El Dorado Kelsey	581135

Name	County Locale	M653 RollPage
PARKS		
Samuel	San Joaquin Castoria	64 907
Stephen	San Francisco San Francisco 9	68 970
T C	Tuolumne Twp 1	71 256
W H	Sutter Butte	70 788
PARKUD		
Joshua	El Dorado Kelsey	581135
PARKY		
Ada	Napa Napa	61 100
PARLA		
Marcelia	Los Angeles Los Angeles	59 297
PARLAM		
Oldham	Tuolumne Sonora	71 484
PARLE		
John	Tuolumne Twp 1	71 270
PARLER		
Keziah	Amador Twp 3	55 381
PARLETT		
N*	Amador Twp 2	55 310
PARLIER		
John	Nevada Nevada	61 327
PARLIN		
Eugene	Yolo No E Twp	72 674
Eugene	Yuba North Ea	72 674
Frank	Yuba Long Bar	72 744
Harlow	Amador Twp 3	55 382
John	Sierra Twp 7	66 892
Jos	Butte Cascade	56 689
L F	Sierra Twp 5	66 923
W W	Amador Twp 2	55 298
PARLINE		
Rachel	Sacramento Ward 1	63 134
PARLING		
Cyrus	Mendocino Big Rvr	60 843
PARLLSIN		
Peter	Trinity Readings	70 996
PARLLUCH		
John*	Santa Cruz Soguel	66 593
PARLMELL		
John*	Santa Cruz Soguel	66 593
PARLMELS		
John*	Santa Cruz Soguel	66 593
PARLMER		
John	Yuba Rose Bar	72 808
PARLMETI		
John	Santa Cruz Soguel	66 593
PARLOCK		
Mary	Tuolumne Twp 4	71 147
PARLOW		
N	El Dorado Placerville	58 885
PARLSON		
Peter	San Francisco San Francisco 1	68 895
PARLUIE		
Rachel*	Sacramento Ward 1	63 134
PARLVER		
J	San Joaquin Stockton	641096
PARLY		
Manuel	San Francisco San Francisco 2	67 688
PARMALY		
R S	Siskiyou Scott Ri	69 73
PARMAN		
Wm	Tehama Tehama	70 948
PARMEKE		
Justin*	Santa Cruz Pescadero	66 648
PARMELEE		
Emeline	Yuba Marysville	72 957
Justin	Santa Cruz Pescadero	66 648
PARMELLE		
Justin*	Santa Cruz Pescadero	66 648
PARMEN		
Ed*	Nevada Bridgeport	61 475
PARMENTS		
A	El Dorado Diamond	58 766
PARMER		
Abram	Nevada Bloomfield	61 518
C F	Solano Vacaville	69 328
E	San Francisco San Francisco 4	681230
Ed*	Nevada Bridgeport	61 475
Fred	Siskiyou Callahan	69 9
Geo	Sacramento Ward 3	63 297
Geo	Siskiyou Scott Va	69 43
Henry	Trinity Lewiston	70 964
J C	Nevada Bridgeport	61 501
John	San Francisco San Francisco 3	67 39
John R	Tulara Visalia	71 100
L	Siskiyou Callahan	69 9
N	San Francisco San Francisco 6	67 437
O S	El Dorado Grizzly	581179
T H	Siskiyou Scott Va	69 58
W	San Francisco San Francisco 6	67 437
PARMERTER		
J E	El Dorado White Oaks	581018
PARMESA		
Stepham	San Francisco San Francisco 11	156
		67
PARMETER		
John	Sonoma Bodega	69 519

Name	County Locale	M653 RollPage
PARMILEE		
Geo E	San Francisco San Francisco 6	67 442
PARMIN		
Henry	San Francisco San Francisco 8	681259
PARMLEE		
Geo E	San Francisco San Francisco 6	67 442
Walter	Placer Michigan	62 849
PARMLER		
Henry*	Placer Michigan	62 838
PARMLEY		
Amos*	San Joaquin Elkhorn	64 999
PARN		
Mary*	Alameda Oakland	55 36
PARNEL		
---	Sacramento Granite	63 249
PARNELEY		
Lamos*	San Joaquin Elkhorn	64 999
PARNELL		
Edmond	Tuolumne Jamestown	71 424
Edward*	San Francisco San Francisco 1	68 869
George	Tulara Visalia	71 112
H H	San Francisco San Francisco 3	67 76
John	Calaveras Twp 8	57 98
Mark	Tuolumne Twp 3	71 424
PARNEY		
L	Nevada Eureka	61 388
William*	San Francisco San Francisco 4	681172
PARNGLE		
Charles	Sacramento Sutter	63 294
PARNIER		
Fred	Tuolumne Twp 2	71 292
PARNIX		
L*	Nevada Eureka	61 388
PARNULER		
Emeline	Yuba Marysville	72 957
PARNUS		
Fred	Tuolumne Columbia	71 292
PARO		
Alex	Calaveras Twp 4	57 316
Crosanchi	Calaveras Twp 6	57 129
Fabro	Mariposa Twp 1	60 647
Jynacio	Calaveras Twp 6	57 129
Z	El Dorado Placerville	58 837
PAROD		
Paul	Sacramento Ward 4	63 531
PARODEN		
Charles*	Tuolumne Twp 1	71 257
Charly	Tuolumne Twp 1	71 257
PARODI		
Alfred	Sacramento Centre	63 175
John B	San Francisco San Francisco 11	156
		67
PARODIN		
Charles	Tuolumne Twp 1	71 257
PARODY		
Jas	Sacramento American	63 167
PAROINS		
Henry	Santa Cruz Santa Cruz	66 626
PAROLLA		
Wm	Trinity East For	701027
PAROLLETTE		
Lucia	San Francisco San Francisco 2	67 775
PAROLTO		
Lorenzo	Calaveras Twp 10	57 289
PARON		
Ar	Sierra Downieville	66 984
William H	San Francisco San Francisco 7	681421
Wm*	Los Angeles Tejon To	59 535
PARONER		
Abrow	Nevada Bloomfield	61 518
PARONO		
Augustin	Calaveras Twp 5	57 217
PAROS		
Edurado	Tehama Red Bluff	70 915
Ricento	Sacramento Ward 1	63 48
PAROT		
Andre	Sacramento Ward 1	63 15
Francisco	Calaveras Twp 5	57 219
L	Nevada Grass Valley	61 144
PAROTT		
John	Sacramento Georgian	63 339
PAROUCH		
Peter	San Francisco San Francisco 1	68 893
PAROZ		
L	Nevada Grass Valley	61 144
PARPAN		
L	San Francisco San Francisco 12	395
		67
PARPOINT		
D W	Yuba Suida	72 993
PARQUETTE		
John	Yolo Slate Ra	72 687
John	Yuba North Ea	72 687
PARR		
---	Amador Twp 1	55 494
---	Tuolumne Shawsfla	71 409

California 1860 Census Index

Name	County Locale	M653 Roll	Page
PARR			
---*	Amador Twp 2	55	315
Chas	Santa Clara Santa Clara	65	470
Danil	San Joaquin Elkhorn	64	977
E	Nevada Grass Valley	61	207
H E	Tuolumne Twp 1	71	265
Henry	Sierra Twp 7	66	894
Jonathan	Santa Clara Santa Clara	65	495
L B*	Yuba Parke Ba	72	786
Madison	Nevada Bloomfield	61	513
Nicholas	Tuolumne Big Oak	71	131
Nicholas	Tuolumne Twp 4	71	131
Noah	Santa Clara Burnett	65	260
Simpson	Santa Clara Fremont	65	424
W	Nevada Grass Valley	61	207
PARRA			
Alejo	Los Angeles San Juan	59	468
Alijo	Los Angeles San Juan	59	468
Diego	Los Angeles San Juan	59	469
Francisco	Santa Clara Santa Clara	65	507
Jose	Los Angeles San Juan	59	468
Juan	Santa Clara Almaden	65	267
Miguela	Los Angeles San Juan	59	467
PARRAH			
Michael	San Mateo Twp 3	65	84
William H	Yuba Marysville	72	867
PARRAIS			
Colostide	Mariposa Twp 1	60	628
PARRAN			
J	Sacramento Franklin	63	334
PARRANT			
Frank	Sierra Downieville	66	1023
PARRARA			
Charles	Tuolumne Twp 3	71	443
Louis	Tuolumne Jamestown	71	443
Louis*	Tuolumne Twp 3	71	458
Peter	Tuolumne Twp 3	71	443
PARRAS			
Florencio	San Bernardino Santa Barbara	64	190
Juan	San Bernardino Santa Inez	64	141
Julian	Santa Clara Gilroy	65	224
Neives*	Los Angeles Los Angeles	59	385
Nieves	Los Angeles Los Angeles	59	385
Refugio	Los Angeles Los Angeles	59	386
PARRAZ			
Ramon	San Bernardino Santa Inez	64	135
PARRCE			
Nicholita*	Santa Clara Santa Clara	65	507
PARRE			
Miguel	Alameda Oakland	55	74
Peter*	San Francisco San Francisco 2	67	721
PARREL			
E*	Calaveras Twp 9	57	353
PARRELL			
J B P	Sacramento Ward 1	63	155
PARRENT			
Albert	Sonoma Mendocino	69	468
J H	Santa Clara Santa Clara	65	474
PARRERS			
George*	Amador Twp 2	55	315
PARRES			
Francisco	Santa Clara Alviso	65	413
Juan	Santa Cruz Soguel	66	595
PARRET			
E*	Calaveras Twp 9	57	353
Margt*	San Francisco San Francisco 2	67	698
S H	Calaveras Twp 9	57	362
PARRETT			
Charles	Yolo Cache Crk	72	637
Eugene	Yolo Cache	72	613
John	San Diego San Diego	64	769
PARREZ			
Romir	Tuolumne Jamestown	71	431
PARRICIO			
---	San Bernardino S Timate	64	707
PARRIE			
John	Nevada Eureka	61	358
Oscar*	Butte Oregon	56	627
PARRIL			
Oscar	Butte Oregon	56	627
PARRIMORE			
John	Calaveras Twp 7	57	25
PARRIS			
A	Mariposa Twp 3	60	588
B	Siskiyou Scott Ri	69	73
C	San Joaquin Stockton	64	1046
Damingo	Santa Cruz Pajaro	66	547
Domingo	Santa Cruz Pajaro	66	547
Eugene*	Marin Cortemad	60	787
Fanny	San Joaquin Stockton	64	1024
George W	Contra Costa Twp 3	57	617
Herman	San Francisco San Francisco 9	68	1090
Jas*	San Francisco San Francisco 9	68	1081
Joe	Sierra Downieville	66	1011
Jose M	Marin S Antoni	60	709
Juan	Santa Cruz Soguel	66	595
PARRIS			
Lee	Sierra Downieville	66	1011
Newman	San Francisco San Francisco 9	68	1090
Samuel	Sierra Downieville	66	968
Thomas	Sierra Downieville	66	1006
Thomas	Sierra Morristown	66	1052
Thomas*	Sierra Downieville	66	1006
Westley	San Joaquin Stockton	64	1062
PARRISH			
A A	Tuolumne Jamestown	71	429
A H	Trinity Rattle Snake	70	1029
B F	Nevada Bridgeport	61	481
Barney	Yuba Rose Bar	72	795
C L	Amador Twp 1	55	463
Daniel	San Francisco San Francisco 4	68	1167
E C	Los Angeles Elmonte	59	247
Edward	Yuba Marysville	72	955
Ellen	Yuba Marysville	72	956
Ezra	San Bernardino San Salvador	64	653
H A	Tuolumne Twp 3	71	429
H E	El Dorado Coloma	58	1078
Henry S	San Bernardino San Salvador	64	654
Jack	San Francisco San Francisco 4	68	1167
Josiah	Santa Cruz Soguel	66	590
Josuah	Santa Cruz Soguel	66	590
Louis	San Francisco San Francisco 4	68	1124
Peter	Plumas Quincy	62	996
Reuben	Nevada Red Dog	61	550
Richard M	Placer Dutch Fl	62	725
S G	Siskiyou Callahan	69	8
S J	Siskiyou Callahan	69	8
Sally	San Diego San Diego	64	757
William A	Tuolumne Twp 3	71	429
PARRISS			
Aniseto	Santa Clara Almaden	65	267
PARRNER			
Fred*	Siskiyou Callahan	69	9
Geo*	Siskiyou Scott Va	69	43
PARRO			
Antonia	Mariposa Twp 1	60	653
H A	Calaveras Twp 9	57	364
PARRON			
Adolph	Tuolumne Twp 2	71	287
PARRONS			
J E	Tuolumne Twp 2	71	331
PARROS			
Carnulita	Tuolumne Big Oak	71	134
Juan*	San Bernardino Santa Inez	64	135
PARROT			
Charles	Tuolumne Twp 1	71	255
Charly	Tuolumne Twp 1	71	255
E*	Calaveras Twp 9	57	353
Fredk	San Francisco San Francisco 2	67	678
Gustave	Los Angeles Shaffer	59	397
Louis	Plumas Meadow Valley	62	931
Mathew	Marin Bolinas	60	744
PARROTO			
C C*	Solano Fremont	69	380
PARROTT			
---	San Francisco San Francisco 7	68	1375
Betsy	Sacramento San Joaquin	63	350
C C	Solano Fremont	69	380
Charles	Yolo Cache	72	637
Corneleus	San Francisco San Francisco 4	68	1145
Cornelius	San Francisco San Francisco 4	68	1145
John	San Francisco San Francisco 10		290 67
John	San Joaquin Elkhorn	64	991
John	Santa Cruz Pajaro	66	550
W L	Trinity Mouth Ca	70	1012
W S	Trinity Mouth Ca	70	1012
William	Mendocino Big Rvr	60	850
PARRP			
John	Los Angeles Los Angeles	59	366
PARRRA			
Antonio	Contra Costa Twp 1	57	497
PARRS			
Jean*	Sacramento Ward 1	63	85
Joseph	Nevada Rough &	61	411
PARRUER			
Fred*	Siskiyou Callahan	69	9
PARRUILLON			
L	Yuba North Ea	72	686
PARRUILON			
L	Yolo Slate Ra	72	686
PARRUX			
L*	Nevada Eureka	61	388
PARRY			
---*	Sacramento Granite	63	266
A M	Napa Napa	61	82
Antonie	Amador Twp 5	55	332
Augusta	San Joaquin Stockton	64	1066
Chemt*	Placer Stewart	62	606
Hugh	Plumas Quincy	62	940
J*	Napa Hot Springs	61	7
James	Humbolt Bucksport	59	161
PARRY			
John	Los Angeles Los Angeles	59	366
John Jr	San Francisco San Francisco 2	67	621
Marcus	Alameda Washington	55	174
S M	Nevada Bridgeport	61	450
PARSAND			
A E	El Dorado Georgetown	58	686
PARSEBARG			
S W*	Nevada Bridgeport	61	448
PARSEBAY			
S W*	Nevada Bridgeport	61	448
PARSEL			
Remington	Sonoma Mendocino	69	462
PARSELARG			
S W*	Nevada Bridgeport	61	448
PARSELAY			
S W	Nevada Bridgeport	61	448
PARSELY			
Jas J	Butte Oregon	56	632
Jos J	Butte Oregon	56	632
PARSENS			
Geo	Amador Twp 2	55	267
Jose	Amador Twp 2	55	298
PARSHAL			
Chester	San Mateo Twp 3	65	81
PARSHLEY			
W M	El Dorado Salmon Falls	58	1048
Wm H	Alameda Brooklyn	55	97
PARSIA			
Jean*	Tuolumne Twp 2	71	297
PARSICK			
John	Siskiyou Yreka	69	140
PARSILEY			
Hartnell	Monterey San Juan	60	990
PARSINS			
H	San Francisco San Francisco 1	68	815
PARSLEY			
George*	Yuba Marysville	72	897
James R	San Joaquin Castoria	64	898
Richard	Fresno Twp 1	59	34
W H	Solano Vacaville	69	320
William	El Dorado Salmon Falls	58	1051
PARSLORN			
M	San Francisco San Francisco 5	67	529
PARSMANO			
T	San Joaquin Stockton	64	1090
PARSON			
---	Tulara Keyesville	71	56
---	Tulara Keyesville	71	63
B F	Sacramento Ward 4	63	512
G A	Nevada Eureka	61	351
Geo	Alameda Brooklyn	55	84
George	San Joaquin Elkhorn	64	982
Hans	San Francisco San Francisco 7	68	1426
Joel	Fresno Twp 2	59	4
John	Butte Cascade	56	692
Joseph	Sierra Twp 7	66	888
Lawrence	Sacramento Ward 3	63	487
Levin*	Calaveras Twp 5	57	240
R	San Francisco San Francisco 9	68	1058
Seoin*	Calaveras Twp 5	57	240
Seom*	Calaveras Twp 5	57	240
Sevin*	Calaveras Twp 5	57	240
William	Yuba Marysville	72	897
PARSONS			
Adney	San Francisco San Francisco 9	68	1043
Amelia J	Los Angeles Los Nieto	59	436
Benj F	San Bernardino San Bernadino	64	624
C A	San Francisco San Francisco 5	67	526
C A	Tuolumne Columbia	71	345
C H	Tuolumne Columbia	71	339
Caloa*	Yuba Marysville	72	889
Calone	Yuba Marysville	72	889
Charles	Marin Bolinas	60	732
D	Trinity Lewiston	70	966
Darius	Plumas Quincy	62	940
E	Calaveras Twp 9	57	401
E	San Francisco San Francisco 6	67	465
E	Shasta Millvill	66	725
Edward	Yuba Long Bar	72	754
Emma L	Santa Cruz Santa Cruz	66	626
Erastus	Sacramento Ward 4	63	605
Geo	El Dorado Coloma	58	1111
Geo W	Alameda Oakland	55	42
George	El Dorado Georgetown	58	683
George	El Dorado Georgetown	58	694
George W	Santa Cruz Santa Cruz	66	620
Gerge	El Dorado Georgetown	58	683
H	San Francisco San Francisco 1	68	815
Henry	Santa Cruz Santa Cruz	66	632
Isaac	Sierra Gibsonville	66	851
Isaac	Sierra Gibsonville	66	860
J C	Tuolumne Twp 2	71	294
J E	Tuolumne Columbia	71	331
Jacob	Santa Cruz Soguel	66	579
James	Placer Michigan	62	839

Name	County Locale	M653 RollPage
PARSONS		
James	San Joaquin Elkhorn	64 971
James	Santa Cruz Santa Cruz	66 639
James	Tuolumne Twp 1	71 243
James B	Tuolumne Twp 3	71 428
James R	Tuolumne Jamestown	71 428
Jas	Sacramento Ward 3	63 421
Jas	Sacramento Ward 3	63 427
Jejerrenva*	San Francisco 6 San Francisco	67 449
Jemima	San Francisco 6 San Francisco	67 449
Jeremiah	Santa Clara San Jose	65 370
Jerry	Yuba Bear Rvr	721011
John	Amador Twp 1	55 462
John A	Yuba Marysville	72 908
John R	Calaveras Twp 5	57 185
Joseph	Santa Clara Alviso	65 401
Joseph	Santa Clara Redwood	65 453
L A	San Mateo Twp 3	65 91
Levy	San Francisco 6 San Francisco	67 434
Lewis	Alameda Oakland	55 62
Lewis	El Dorado Mud Springs	58 960
Lewis*	Yolo Merritt	72 583
Louis	Yolo Merritt	72 583
M E*	Santa Clara Alviso	65 412
M W	Tuolumne Twp 2	71 339
Marion	Santa Cruz Santa Cruz	66 622
Marion	Santa Cruz Santa Cruz	66 624
Mark	Mendocino Ukiah	60 802
Mart*	Mendocino Ukiah	60 802
Mary A	Yolo Cache	72 596
Mob*	El Dorado Greenwood	58 721
Nathan	Sierra Grizzly	661058
Nathaniel	Amador Twp 4	55 251
Oliver	Los Angeles Los Nieto	59 436
P	Butte Eureka	56 656
P H	Yolo Cache Crk	72 596
P N	Yolo Cache	72 596
Pearson	Santa Clara Redwood	65 453
S C	Calaveras Twp 8	57 77
Sam	Sonoma Petaluma	69 602
Saml	Calaveras Twp 9	57 383
Saml	Sacramento Ward 1	63 37
T	El Dorado Kelsey	581150
Thomas	Santa Cruz Santa Cruz	66 626
Thomas	Santa Cruz Santa Cruz	66 628
Thos	Yolo Putah	72 614
W E	Mendocino Big Rock	60 876
Warren	Sonoma Armally	69 495
Wickliff	San Francisco 10 San Francisco	319 67
William	Los Angeles Los Angeles	59 364
William	Marin Tomales	60 775
William	Nevada Rough &	61 437
William	Tuolumne Columbia	71 339
Wm H	Los Angeles Tejon	59 527
PARSONY		
Edmons*	Tuolumne Twp 2	71 274
PARSOR		
Simon	Santa Clara Redwood	65 456
PARSORY		
Edmond	Tuolumne Twp 1	71 274
PARSTINO		
Benih	Santa Cruz Pajaro	66 550
Benito*	Santa Cruz Pajaro	66 550
PART		
---	Sierra Twp 5	66 948
---	Tuolumne Chinese	71 525
---	Tuolumne Don Pedro	71 536
Ar	Sierra Twp 5	66 948
James	San Francisco 4 San Francisco	681146
PARTANDO		
Marco	Calaveras Twp 7	57 9
PARTEE		
Geo	Santa Clara Santa Clara	65 492
PARTEK		
Christian	Contra Costa Twp 1	57 537
PARTELL		
N	Amador Twp 2	55 310
N	Amador Twp 2	55 312
N*	Amador Twp 2	55 310
PARTEN		
R*	Nevada Nevada	61 292
William	Calaveras Twp 6	57 143
PARTENS		
Charles	Tuolumne Springfield	71 367
PARTEO		
C C	El Dorado White Oaks	581009
PARTER		
Caroline	Santa Clara San Jose	65 279
Clark	El Dorado Kelsey	581139
Edgar	Amador Twp 3	55 379
George	Tuolumne Twp 3	71 459
James	El Dorado Mud Springs	58 990
Lewis	El Dorado Casumnes	581165
Nath	El Dorado Mud Springs	58 988

Name	County Locale	M653 RollPage
PARTER		
Wm *	El Dorado Mud Springs	58 988
Wm*	Nevada Eureka	61 346
PARTEU		
R	Nevada Nevada	61 292
PARTEUW		
Patro	Calaveras Twp 6	57 131
PARTHECHE		
B	Sacramento Sutter	63 299
PARTHIA		
Pedro	Calaveras Twp 9	57 354
PARTHOW		
Amos	Sonoma Healdsbu	69 471
PARTIAL		
Jas	Mariposa Twp 3	60 597
PARTICE		
J	Nevada Nevada	61 292
PARTICH		
Estephe*	Mariposa Twp 3	60 584
PARTICIO		
Lugardo	Tuolumne Twp 1	71 228
Lujardo	Tuolumne Sonora	71 228
PARTICK		
Estephen*	Mariposa Twp 3	60 584
PARTIDGE		
Wm	Sierra Twp 7	66 879
PARTIN		
J	Nevada Nevada	61 292
William L*	Sierra Whiskey	66 845
PARTING		
---	Amador Twp 2	55 280
PARTLOW		
Amos	Sonoma Healdsbu	69 471
PARTMAN		
Thos	Sacramento Ward 1	63 32
PARTON		
B F	Calaveras Twp 9	57 406
B G	Calaveras Twp 9	57 406
F L	Amador Twp 5	55 348
H B	Trinity Minersville	70 969
Hugh	Butte Chico	56 551
James	Mendocino Calpella	60 829
Thomas Sr	Mendocino Little L	60 839
PARTOSY		
Charles	Tuolumne Shawsfla	71 390
PARTOW		
Thomas Sr	Mendocino Little L	60 839
PARTRICO		
Spiro	Placer Michigan	62 829
PARTRIDGE		
Antonie	Sacramento Ward 1	63 30
F W	Sierra Downieville	661032
H C	Sacramento Ward 1	63 30
Jackson	Calaveras Twp 6	57 159
John	Calaveras Twp 6	57 127
John D	Plumas Meadow Valley	62 927
Peter	San Francisco 9 San Francisco	68 972
Prescot	Yuba Long Bar	72 752
Prescott	Yuba Long Bar	72 752
Richd	San Francisco 9 San Francisco	681077
Thomas	Tuolumne Columbia	71 314
Wm	Sierra Twp 7	66 879
Wm J	Yuba New York	72 737
PARTRO		
Juan	Yolo No E Twp	72 685
Juan	Yuba North Ea	72 685
PARTSHEKO		
William*	San Francisco 7 San Francisco	681353
PARTTE		
Michal	Alameda Oakland	55 45
PARTWELL		
Mary*	Yuba Marysville	72 862
PARU		
Alex*	Calaveras Twp 4	57 316
PARULTOR		
Loranzo*	Calaveras Twp 10	57 289
PARUN		
John	Sacramento Sutter	63 295
PARUTO		
Gustavus	Calaveras Twp 6	57 128
PARUTTEN		
Loranzo*	Calaveras Twp 10	57 289
PARVAY		
J G	Marin Cortemad	60 756
PARVILL		
Daniel	Tuolumne Columbia	71 312
PARVIN		
Oliver R	Humbolt Mattole	59 127
W S	Sierra La Porte	66 771
PARVY		
J*	Napa Hot Springs	61 7
PARY		
---	Amador Twp 5	55 342
---	Amador Twp 5	55 354
---	Mariposa Coulterville	60 687
---*	Amador Twp 5	55 340

Name	County Locale	M653 RollPage
PARY		
A	Sacramento Granite	63 268
James	Shasta Horsetown	66 693
PARYEAR		
---	Trinity Weaverville	701052
PARZA		
Leon	Amador Twp 4	55 245
PAS		
---	Stanislaus Branch	70 714
Custodia	San Francisco 8 San Francisco	681309
PASADO		
---	Mendocino Calpella	60 823
PASANO		
B	El Dorado Diamond	58 802
Joseph Jr*	Calaveras Twp 5	57 216
PASANOGNT		
Joseph*	Calaveras Twp 5	57 216
PASANS		
John*	Calaveras Twp 5	57 228
PASATA		
Jack	Tuolumne Sonora	71 190
PASAUS		
John*	Calaveras Twp 5	57 228
PASBERG		
Betty	San Francisco 1 San Francisco	68 825
PASBT		
Deitrich*	Alameda Brooklyn	55 138
PASBURG		
J L	El Dorado Newtown	58 777
PASCAIS		
Antonine	Amador Twp 2	55 303
Antonio	Amador Twp 2	55 303
PASCAL		
Amiel	San Francisco 2 San Francisco	67 588
C	San Francisco 4 San Francisco	681162
H	Nevada Eureka	61 365
Henry	San Francisco 2 San Francisco	67 696
Jas	Sacramento Brighton	63 202
John	Santa Clara Santa Clara	65 482
PASCALL		
J H	Sacramento Cosumnes	63 410
PASCAR		
Ans	Humbolt Eureka	59 172
PASCDDO		
---	Tulara Twp 1	71 117
PASCE		
Charles H	Yuba Marysville	72 950
PASCHA		
---	Fresno Twp 1	59 117
PASCHAL		
---	Tulara Keyesville	71 66
---	Tulara Keyesville	71 72
Charles*	Sierra Twp 7	66 882
Pet	Sacramento Granite	63 265
Walter	El Dorado Georgetown	58 746
PASCHALL		
D P	Los Angeles Elmonte	59 250
J	Siskiyou Scott Ri	69 73
PASCHAN		
John D	Plumas Meadow Valley	62 927
PASCHANCIO		
Pan	Sierra Downieville	66 987
PASCHELL		
David	Yuba New York	72 729
PASCHUL		
Fluter	Calaveras Twp 6	57 137
PASCI		
J C	Placer Iona Hills	62 870
PASCKER		
P	Siskiyou Callahan	69 6
PASCO		
B	Tuolumne Twp 2	71 333
B W	Tuolumne Columbia	71 298
John	Sierra Downieville	661006
Joseph	Sierra Excelsior	661035
William	Placer Iona Hills	62 870
PASCOE		
H	Santa Clara Fremont	65 438
J	Nevada Grass Valley	61 208
J C	Nevada Grass Valley	61 208
Jeptha	Tulara Keeneysburg	71 41
W	Nevada Grass Valley	61 209
W	Nevada Nevada	61 319
William	Nevada Bloomfield	61 529
William P	Yuba Bear Rvr	721011
William S*	Yuba Bear Rvr	721011
William T*	Yuba Bear Rvr	721011
PASCOLL		
Sarah R	Alameda Brooklyn	55 85
PASCON		
Frederick	Tuolumne Sonora	71 205
PASCUAL		
---	Los Angeles Los Angeles	59 398
PASCUALA		
---	Los Angeles San Gabriel	59 414
Maria	Los Angeles Los Angeles	59 350

California 1860 Census Index

Name	County Locale	M653 Roll	Page
PASCUALA			
Maria	Los Angeles Los Angeles	59	364
PASE			
A M	San Joaquin Stockton	64	1059
M	Nevada Eureka	61	346
PASED			
Emily	San Francisco San Francisco 2	67	650
PASEO			
B W	Tuolumne Twp 2	71	298
PASEY			
Moses	San Francisco San Francisco 1	68	838
Thos	Tehama Red Bluff	70	927
PASGERLI			
C*	Calaveras Twp 9	57	395
PASGUE			
John	Sacramento Franklin	63	334
PASGULI			
C	Calaveras Twp 9	57	395
PASH			
W	El Dorado Placerville	58	851
PASILLA			
Magnus*	El Dorado Georgetown	58	747
PASILOM			
Louis	Tuolumne Twp 1	71	254
PASINALA			
---	San Bernardino San Bernadino	64	680
PASIS			
Vicento	Sacramento Ward 1	63	110
PASKA			
Blas*	San Mateo Twp 2	65	116
PASKEL			
John	Tuolumne Twp 1	71	195
John A S	Tuolumne Sonora	71	195
PASKER			
Alexander	Siskiyou Callahan	69	1
Lewis R*	Siskiyou Yreka	69	132
PASKILL			
John	Tuolumne Sonora	71	195
PASKIN			
B F	Calaveras Twp 9	57	415
Thos	Santa Clara San Jose	65	317
PASKS			
Hugh	Calaveras Twp 9	57	372
PASLAM			
Oldham	Tuolumne Twp 1	71	484
PASLIN			
Frank	Yuba New York	72	744
PASLISNAR			
Isadore*	Calaveras Twp 5	57	186
PASLISNUT			
Isadore*	Calaveras Twp 5	57	186
PASLIT			
Deitrich*	Alameda Brooklyn	55	138
PASLOCK			
Mary	Tuolumne Big Oak	71	147
PASLOT			
Deitrich*	Alameda Brooklyn	55	138
PASMAN			
Andrew	Tuolumne Chinese	71	501
PASMER			
J C	Nevada Bridgeport	61	501
PASO			
Eceso	Amador Twp 5	55	339
PASONA			
B	El Dorado Diamond	58	801
Jos	Amador Twp 3	55	394
PASQNAL			
---	Fresno Twp 3	59	21
PASQUAH			
B	San Francisco San Francisco 3	67	8
PASQUAL			
---	Fresno Twp 2	59	93
---	Los Angeles Los Angeles	59	497
---	Monterey Pajaro	60	1024
---	San Diego Temecula	64	798
---	San Luis Obispo San Luis Obispo	65	9
---	Tulara Keyesville	71	71
---	Tulara Keyesville	71	72
Prener	Mariposa Twp 1	60	631
S B	Los Angeles Tejon To	59	535
Santana	El Dorado White Oaks	58	1007
Trover	Amador Twp 2	55	282
PASQUALA			
---	San Diego Temecula	64	801
PASQUALE			
B	San Francisco San Francisco 3	67	8
PASQUALL			
---	Tulara Keyesville	71	64
---	Tulara Keyesville	71	65
---	Tulara Keyesville	71	68
---	Tulara Keyesville	71	69
PASQUALLAR			
---	Mariposa Twp 1	60	629
PASQUEAL			
Jean	Calaveras Twp 7	57	27
PASQUEL			
Zeth	Butte Ophir	56	795
PASQUERS			
Peter	Sierra Downieville	66	1001
PASQUETT			
Jerry*	Nevada Bloomfield	61	519
PASQUIRS			
Peter*	Sierra Downieville	66	1001
PASQUITT			
Jerry	Nevada Bloomfield	61	519
PASS			
J W	Nevada Nevada	61	240
PASSA			
Jacob	Tuolumne Twp 4	71	146
Nicholas	San Francisco San Francisco 1	68	895
PASSAGE			
J	Sacramento Granite	63	230
Mary	Trinity Weaverville	70	1081
PASSAHO			
---	Tulara Twp 3	71	64
PASSAMENTO			
Frank	Tuolumne Shawsfla	71	420
PASSEMAN			
John	Tuolumne Sonora	71	242
PASSER			
Joseph	Tuolumne Jamestown	71	470
PASSEY			
---	Mendocino Calpella	60	821
Marg	Yolo Cache	72	606
PASSIA			
Jean*	Tuolumne Columbia	71	297
PASSIMAN			
John	Tuolumne Twp 1	71	242
PASSIMAR			
Isadon	Calaveras Twp 5	57	186
Isadore	Calaveras Twp 5	57	186
PASSIME			
John	Calaveras Twp 5	57	212
PASSISNAR			
Isadon	Calaveras Twp 6	57	186
PASSMAN			
D	San Francisco San Francisco 9	68	1071
PASSMORE			
John	Tuolumne Big Oak	71	126
John	Tuolumne Twp 4	71	128
S E C	San Francisco San Francisco 2	67	697
Thomas	Sierra Morristown	66	1054
Wm	San Francisco San Francisco 1	68	890
PASSO			
P	Tuolumne Big Oak	71	153
PASSON			
Young	Calaveras Twp 5	57	240
PASSTELL			
Peter	San Francisco San Francisco 3	67	23
PAST			
Francis	Sonoma Petaluma	69	576
John	San Francisco San Francisco 1	68	810
N	Amador Twp 1	55	452
R	Nevada Nevada	61	240
William H	Calaveras Twp 5	57	142
PASTA			
Jno	Butte Oregon	56	636
PASTANI			
Franc??Er*	Alameda Murray	55	219
Francner*	Alameda Murray	55	219
PASTEL			
Gartavus	Tuolumne Columbia	71	314
PASTEN			
William*	Calaveras Twp 6	57	143
PASTER			
Charles W	El Dorado White Oaks	58	1001
J S*	El Dorado Diamond	58	764
PASTERS			
Mary	San Francisco San Francisco 4	68	1149
PASTIN			
---	San Bernardino S Timate	64	691
PASTIRER			
R L	Tuolumne Sonora	71	215
PASTIUR			
R L	Tuolumne Twp 1	71	215
PASTLE			
John	Napa Clear Lake	61	138
PASTMINE			
Wm	San Francisco San Francisco 1	68	814
PASTMONE			
Wm	San Francisco San Francisco 1	68	814
PASTO			
Mary	Santa Clara San Jose	65	299
PASTON			
---*	San Mateo Twp 1	65	65
H G	Butte Hamilton	56	523
PASTONIA			
---	Butte Ophir	56	792
PASTOR			
Copt	Contra Costa Twp 3	57	614
Tomas	Contra Costa Twp 1	57	533
PASTORE			
---*	San Mateo Twp 1	65	65
PASTORS			
Mary*	San Francisco San Francisco 4	68	1149
PASTRA			
James	Calaveras Twp 8	57	81
PASTRIDGE			
Thomas	Tuolumne Twp 2	71	314
PASTTO			
John*	Napa Clear Lake	61	138
PASTY			
Jno	Butte Oregon	56	636
PASVELL			
Daniel	Tuolumne Twp 2	71	312
PAT			
---	Amador Twp 2	55	275
---	Amador Twp 5	55	345
---	Amador Twp 5	55	354
---	Amador Twp 7	55	413
---	Amador Twp 6	55	447
---	Amador Twp 1	55	449
---	Calaveras Twp 6	57	139
---	Calaveras Twp 6	57	149
---	Calaveras Twp 5	57	234
---	Calaveras Twp 5	57	245
---	Calaveras Twp 4	57	342
---	El Dorado White Oaks	58	1009
---	El Dorado Union	58	1089
---	El Dorado Georgetown	58	756
---	El Dorado Eldorado	58	942
---	El Dorado Mud Springs	58	972
---	El Dorado Mud Springs	58	986
---	Sacramento Ward 3	63	493
---	Sacramento Ward 3	63	494
---	Sacramento Ward 1	63	55
---	Sacramento Ward 1	63	56
---	Sacramento Ward 1	63	59
---	Sacramento Ward 1	63	61
---	Sacramento Ward 1	63	71
---	San Francisco San Francisco 4	68	1187
---	San Francisco San Francisco 4	68	1208
---	Sierra Morristown	66	1056
---	Tuolumne Twp 5	71	512
---	Tuolumne Twp 5	71	516
---	Yuba Marysville	72	921
---*	San Francisco San Francisco 4	68	1187
---*	San Francisco San Francisco 5	67	509
Hou	San Francisco San Francisco 5	67	1206
How	San Francisco San Francisco 5	67	1206
Kon	San Francisco San Francisco 1	68	925
Ling	El Dorado Georgetown	58	692
Sing	El Dorado Big Bar	58	736
PATA			
Morris	Calaveras Twp 8	57	86
PATASDO			
John	Tuolumne Shawsfla	71	388
PATCH			
Geo	San Francisco San Francisco 9	68	980
George W	San Francisco San Francisco 8	68	1298
Sam	Humbolt Eel Rvr	59	144
Samuel	El Dorado White Oaks	58	1015
Samuel	Marin Cortemad	60	782
Samuel	Placer Goods	62	694
Wm	San Francisco San Francisco 1	68	910
Wm Y	San Francisco San Francisco 10	67	326
PATCHELL			
Chas W	Placer Rattle Snake	62	628
J	El Dorado White Oaks	58	1002
J	El Dorado White Oaks	58	1016
John	San Joaquin Castoria	64	879
PATCHEN			
T	Nevada Grass Valley	61	164
PATCHENST			
Mary H*	Yuba Marysville	72	892
PATCHER			
B	Nevada Washington	61	333
Clinton H	Sierra Twp 7	66	909
E L	Sutter Nicolaus	70	836
PATCHET			
John	Napa Napa	61	90
PATCHETT			
M A	Napa Hot Springs	61	3
T P*	Napa Hot Springs	61	2
PATCHIN			
Clinton G	Sierra Twp 7	66	909
Clinton H	Sierra Forest C	66	909
George	Del Norte Crescent	58	626
Thos A	Sacramento Ward 3	63	473
PATDEL			
George	Sierra Downieville	66	1006
PATE			
---	Tuolumne Twp 5	71	505
A J	Siskiyou Scott Va	69	48
Adam	San Joaquin Elkhorn	64	996
Alexander	Tulara Visalia	71	95
David	Colusa Butte Crk	57	466
David	Solano Fairfield	69	201

Name	County Locale	M653 RollPage
PATE		
Edward	San Joaquin Elkhorn	64 992
Eligah	Tuolumne Don Pedro	71 540
Elijah	Tuolumne Twp 6	71 540
F M	Mariposa Twp 1	60 652
J	Siskiyou Scott Va	69 58
John	Santa Clara San Jose	65 349
Peterson	Tuolumne Don Pedro	71 538
Reuben	Amador Twp 3	55 389
Saml	Tuolumne Twp 4	71 144
William	Plumas Meadow Valley	62 901
PATEA		
Alen	Mariposa Twp 3	60 583
Alex*	Mariposa Twp 3	60 583
PATEAS		
Alex*	Mariposa Twp 3	60 583
PATEN		
Charles	Sierra Downieville	661017
John	Nevada Red Dog	61 551
PATER		
J	El Dorado Diamond	58 811
Jane	Calaveras Twp 7	57 35
John	Yuba Marysville	72 939
Jonathan	Sierra Twp 5	66 918
Jonn	Yuba Marysville	72 939
Maria	Calaveras Twp 7	57 35
Wm*	Butte Wyandotte	56 670
PATERMO		
Matter	Alameda Brooklyn	55 193
PATERN		
Marie	Sacramento Ward 1	63 80
PATERSON		
C O	Amador Twp 2	55 309
George	Plumas Quincy	62 992
James	Nevada Rough &	61 426
Jas	San Mateo Twp 1	65 59
John	Napa Clear Lake	61 140
Joseph	Nevada Rough &	61 424
Peter A	El Dorado Greenwood	58 720
R	Calaveras Twp 9	57 397
Robert	Calaveras Twp 8	57 100
Robt	Nevada Rough &	61 417
Thos	Nevada Little Y	61 531
William	Nevada Bridgeport	61 490
PATES		
A W	Nevada Nevada	61 256
N H	Sonoma Washington	69 665
PATEW		
Alex*	Mariposa Twp 3	60 583
PATHA		
Peter	Plumas Meadow Valley	62 908
PATHEL		
Johu	Tehama Tehama	70 942
PATHEN		
Robt	Placer Rattle Snake	62 626
PATHENSON		
Alex*	San Francisco San Francisco 1	68 867
PATHERSON		
John	San Francisco San Francisco 1	68 901
PATHESON		
Henry	San Joaquin Stockton	641057
PATHEWELL		
Thomas	Alameda Oakland	55 20
PATHILL		
William	Tuolumne Sonora	71 234
PATHO		
Jose	Solano Vacaville	69 322
PATHS		
J	Calaveras Twp 9	57 394
Joe*	Mariposa Twp 3	60 600
PATICIO		
Jose	Los Angeles Los Angeles	59 402
PATIDA		
Qirila*	Yuba Marysville	72 917
PATIMA		
---	Monterey San Juan	60 991
PATIN		
M	Sacramento Ward 1	63 4
PATINARIO		
---	San Bernardino S Timate	64 696
PATINI		
A	Tuolumne Twp 4	71 159
PATISE		
M	Nevada Grass Valley	61 168
PATISON		
John*	Nevada Bridgeport	61 495
Mellecent F	Yuba Marysville	72 942
Mellecent P	Yuba Marysville	72 942
PATISTO		
Margurtte*	Placer Michigan	62 840
PATITE		
---	San Bernardino S Timate	64 691
PATITTA		
James	Mariposa Twp 1	60 666
PATITTE		
James	Mariposa Twp 1	60 666

Name	County Locale	M653 RollPage
PATMAN		
Oscar	Mariposa Twp 3	60 565
PATMARIO		
---	San Bernardino San Bernadino	64 680
PATMEK		
W T	Calaveras Twp 9	57 395
PATMENTE		
Alx	Sierra La Porte	66 768
PATMER		
Edwin	San Francisco San Francisco 3	67 85
PATNAM		
Anne	San Francisco San Francisco 10	228 67
PATO		
---	Mendocino Little L	60 839
PATODE		
S	Amador Twp 2	55 302
PATODI		
P	Amador Twp 2	55 302
PATOENIN		
John*	Calaveras Twp 8	57 88
PATON		
J D	Sonoma Sonoma	69 660
Jennete*	San Francisco San Francisco 9	681024
Joseph	Yuba New York	72 728
PATONIA		
---	San Bernardino S Timate	64 721
PATONICA		
---	San Bernardino S Timate	64 719
PATRA		
Juan	Alameda Oakland	55 31
PATRADGE		
Lyman	El Dorado Mud Springs	58 995
PATRAL		
Jannary	El Dorado Mud Springs	58 967
PATRE		
Maria	San Francisco San Francisco 4	681170
PATREK		
Abram*	Sacramento American	63 161
PATRIA		
Bertrand	Tuolumne Twp 1	71 241
PATRICA		
---	San Bernardino S Timate	64 700
PATRICAN		
Bactolomy	Calaveras Twp 4	57 327
Bartolomy	Calaveras Twp 4	57 327
PATRICE		
Patrick	San Francisco San Francisco 9	681068
PATRICIA		
---	Mendocino Twp 1	60 889
---	San Bernardino Santa Barbara	64 202
---	San Bernardino San Bernadino	64 678
---	San Bernardino San Bernadino	64 682
Mary Sister	Santa Clara San Jose	65 373
PATRICIO		
---	San Diego Agua Caliente	64 832
---	San Diego Agua Caliente	64 843
---	San Diego Agua Caliente	64 853
Jose	Los Angeles Los Angeles	59 402
PATRICK		
---	Placer Nicolaus	62 692
---	Placer Lisbon	62 733
---	Sierra Downieville	66 995
---	Solano Benecia	69 290
---	Yuba Marysville	72 967
A	El Dorado Kelsey	581152
Abram*	Sacramento American	63 161
B	El Dorado Salmon Hills	581052
C H	El Dorado Union	581087
Daniel	Siskiyou Yreka	69 172
Ellen	Sonoma Santa Rosa	69 391
Fras	San Francisco San Francisco 10	273 67
G	Nevada Washington	61 335
G W	Tuolumne Sonora	71 204
Geo	El Dorado Coloma	581072
Geo	Sacramento Franklin	63 323
Geo B	Sierra Downieville	66 968
H M*	Yolo Cache	72 626
Hull	Yolo Cache Crk	72 626
J D	Amador Twp 2	55 285
J F	Sonoma Washington	69 674
J M	Sonoma Washington	69 675
James	Sacramento Granite	63 243
Jarvis	Sacramento Granite	63 243
Jas	Napa Napa	61 60
Jas C	San Francisco San Francisco 9	681003
John B	Tuolumne Twp 2	71 395
John W	Amador Twp 4	55 235
John W	Tuolumne Shawsfla	71 395
Joseph	Tuolumne Montezuma	71 506
K M*	Yolo Cache	72 626
Lakim	Contra Costa Twp 1	57 484
M Fritz	Sacramento Ward 1	63 30
M G	Butte Chico	56 564
M L	Butte Chico	56 564

Name	County Locale	M653 RollPage
PATRICK		
Morrison	Sierra Downieville	66 963
N C	San Joaquin Stockton	641022
Nehemiah	Humbolt Pacific	59 132
Nicholas	San Francisco San Francisco 3	67 86
Nicholas	Trinity Indian C	70 987
O*	Nevada Grass Valley	61 197
Richard	Placer Dutch Fl	62 732
Rider	San Mateo Twp 1	65 51
Sarah M	Sacramento Ward 3	63 453
Thomas	Tuolumne Columbia	71 311
Thomas Kirk	Calaveras Twp 8	57 80
W T	Calaveras Twp 9	57 395
Wm	Amador Twp 2	55 262
Wm	Sacramento Granite	63 246
Wm	San Francisco San Francisco 2	68 921
Wm H	San Francisco San Francisco 7	67 589
Wm M	San Francisco San Francisco 9	681079
Wm M*	Napa Napa	61 60
PATRICKERR		
---*	Calaveras Twp 9	57 369
PATRIDGE		
Alden	Calaveras Twp 7	57 18
B F	Calaveras Twp 7	57 18
Edward	Sierra Pine Grove	66 820
Ejra	Calaveras Twp 7	57 18
H C	Sacramento Ward 1	63 30
James H	Sierra Gibsonville	66 859
M	Placer Illinois	62 703
R K	San Francisco San Francisco 4	681113
Wm	Nevada Eureka	61 371
PATRIGINI		
P*	El Dorado Georgetown	58 675
PATRINO		
Manuel	San Francisco San Francisco 1	68 816
PATRO		
---	Marin San Rafael	60 768
---	Mariposa Twp 1	60 628
PATROCINDA		
---	San Diego S Luis R	64 782
PATROM		
Temeo*	Tuolumne Twp 1	71 210
PATRON		
Felis	San Bernardino San Bernadino	64 668
Feliz	Los Angeles Santa Ana	59 448
Temeo	Tuolumne Sonora	71 210
PATRONCER		
M	Sierra La Porte	66 772
PATRONE		
Temeo*	Tuolumne Twp 1	71 210
PATRONEA		
M	Sierra La Porte	66 772
PATRONO		
Manul	San Francisco San Francisco 1	68 816
San Francisco*	Amador Twp 2	55 282
PATRONS		
Gregorid*	Sacramento Ward 3	63 449
Gregoris*	Sacramento Ward 3	63 449
San Francisco*	Amador Twp 2	55 282
PATRY		
Peter	Santa Clara San Jose	65 323
PATS		
G	El Dorado Diamond	58 809
T	Calaveras Twp 9	57 412
Wheeler	El Dorado Placerville	58 919
PATSIGIM		
P*	El Dorado Georgetown	58 675
PATSIGINI		
P*	El Dorado Georgetown	58 675
PATSJACK		
William*	Yuba Marysville	72 886
PATT		
---	Nevada Rough &	61 436
PATTECK		
Joseph	San Francisco San Francisco 9	68 976
PATTEE		
Louis	San Francisco San Francisco 9	681063
Ohio*	Yolo Cottonwoood	72 646
PATTEER		
Decateer*	Yuba Linda	72 984
Peter*	Tuolumne Twp 3	71 465
PATTEN		
A*	Mariposa Twp 3	60 574
Allen	Tuolumne Chinese	71 501
B A	San Francisco San Francisco 9	68 967
Decateer*	Yuba Linda	72 984
E	Yolo Washington	72 604
Edward*	Mendocino Ukiah	60 793
Elizabeth T	Placer Auburn	62 565
F W	Santa Clara San Jose	65 331
G M	Tuolumne Springfield	71 373
G R	Yuba Marysville	72 878
George C	Monterey San Juan	60 995
Gepken*	Sacramento Ward 4	63 549
Gessken H*	Sacramento Ward 4	63 549
Grace	Monterey Monterey	60 965

Name	County Locale	M653 Roll	Page
PATTEN			
H B*	Butte Oregon	56	641
Helen	San Francisco San Francisco 2	67	703
Hiram	Amador Twp 1	55	481
I E	Calaveras Twp 9	57	403
J	El Dorado Placerville	58	822
J A	Yolo Merritt	72	579
J C	Siskiyou Scott Ri	69	64
J E	Calaveras Twp 9	57	403
Jas	Placer Ophirville	62	653
Joel C	Santa Clara San Jose	65	294
John	Butte Hamilton	56	514
John	Placer Forest H	62	803
John	San Francisco San Francisco 10	67	168
John	Siskiyou Yreka	69	139
John	Sonoma Armally	69	512
John R	San Francisco San Francisco 3	67	39
John W	San Bernardino San Bernardino	64	630
Joseph	Santa Cruz Pescadero	66	641
Julia	San Mateo Twp 1	65	57
Lelia L	San Francisco San Francisco 10	67	176
Marie	Sacramento Ward 1	63	80
Mary	Sonoma Santa Rosa	69	387
Mary A	Sonoma Santa Rosa	69	411
Mary Ann	Sonoma Santa Rosa	69	412
Mathew	Klamath S Fork	59	202
Nathan	Sacramento Brighton	63	205
O G	Stanislaus Empire	70	731
Oscatun	Yuba Suida	72	984
P A	El Dorado Georgetown	58	686
Pamelia G	San Francisco San Francisco 10	67	176
Patrick	Santa Clara Gilroy	65	245
Phebe A	Tuolumne Twp 2	71	332
R C	Tuolumne Columbia	71	325
Robert	San Mateo Twp 1	65	57
S	Nevada Eureka	61	368
S*	Mariposa Twp 3	60	574
Samuel	Alameda Brooklyn	55	102
T	Tehama Red Bluff	70	928
T J	Tuolumne Twp 2	71	297
Thomas	El Dorado Georgetown	58	673
Thomas	Yuba Marysville	72	878
Thomas	Yuba Marysville	72	931
W H	Santa Clara San Jose	65	334
William	Alameda Brooklyn	55	81
William	Marin San Rafael	60	773
William	Tuolumne Twp 3	71	442
Wm H	San Francisco San Francisco 10	67	217
PATTENS			
J	Butte Oro	56	681
P A	El Dorado Georgetown	58	686
PATTENSON			
Alex*	San Francisco San Francisco 1	68	867
PATTEOR			
J S*	Siskiyou Scott Ri	69	75
PATTER			
A	Mariposa Twp 3	60	574
Absolne	San Joaquin Oneal	64	934
David C	El Dorado Mud Springs	58	991
E R	Tuolumne Twp 1	71	270
G L	Tehama Red Bluff	70	912
George	Nevada Bridgeport	61	448
Henry	Shasta Shasta	66	760
Hiram	Calaveras Twp 10	57	293
Ira	Nevada Red Dog	61	541
J S*	Siskiyou Scott Ri	69	75
J W	Tuolumne Twp 3	71	460
James D	Solano Suisan	69	238
Thomas	Tuolumne Twp 2	71	374
Wm*	Placer Virginia	62	667
PATTERE			
D C*	Stanislaus Buena Village	70	720
PATTERFORD			
John	Nevada Bridgeport	61	447
PATTERRIUS			
Benj	Solano Benecia	69	298
PATTERSEN			
Joseph R*	Siskiyou Shasta Valley	69	121
Wm H	San Francisco San Francisco 3	67	44
PATTERSON			
---	Amador Twp 1	55	474
---	San Francisco San Francisco 5	68	1080
---	Tulara Visalia	71	110
A	San Francisco San Francisco 5	67	550
A D	Sacramento Granite	63	221
A D	Siskiyou Scott Ri	69	82
A J	Stanislaus Oatvale	70	719
A S	Sonoma Armally	69	512
Albert	Siskiyou Scott Va	69	39
Alex*	San Francisco San Francisco 1	68	867
Alexander	Los Angeles Los Angeles	59	369
Alice	El Dorado Indian D	58	1159
PATTERSON			
Alise	Santa Clara Gilroy	65	224
Andrew	Alameda Brooklyn	55	215
Archibald	Santa Clara Santa Clara	65	485
C B	El Dorado Placerville	58	863
C B	Sonoma Washington	69	675
C H*	Stanislaus Emory	70	756
C P	San Francisco San Francisco 1	68	922
Capt	Sonoma Sonoma	69	655
Carlisle P	Alameda Oakland	55	26
Charles	Calaveras Twp 6	57	112
Charles	Marin Bolinas	60	749
Charles	Tuolumne Columbia	71	357
Charles E	Del Norte Crescent	58	625
Charles M	Yuba Marysville	72	853
Charles M	Yuba Marysville	72	858
Chas	Sacramento Brighton	63	192
Crosby	San Francisco San Francisco 2	67	580
D	Butte Oregon	56	615
D	Merced Twp 2	60	916
D W	San Francisco San Francisco 10	67	192
David	Butte Hamilton	56	524
David	Butte Ophir	56	792
David	Plumas Quincy	62	992
David	San Francisco San Francisco 2	67	658
David	San Francisco San Francisco 2	67	723
Eaber	Contra Costa Twp 1	57	519
Ed C	Calaveras Twp 6	57	121
Elisabeth	San Francisco San Francisco 1	68	812
Elizabeth	San Francisco San Francisco 1	68	812
Elizabeth	Sonoma Mendocino	69	467
F	Siskiyou Yreka	69	184
Fred	Tuolumne Twp 2	71	314
G T	Nevada Nevada	61	242
Geo	El Dorado Salmon Falls	58	1035
Geo	Sacramento San Joaquin	63	366
Geo	Sonoma Mendocino	69	467
Geo	Trinity Indian C	70	983
Geo W	Amador Twp 2	55	309
George	Alameda Brooklyn	55	191
George	San Francisco San Francisco 2	67	575
Gilbert	Yuba Long Bar	72	770
Green*	Alameda Murray	55	221
Griffith	San Francisco San Francisco 1	68	922
H S	Tuolumne Sonora	71	212
Henry	Contra Costa Twp 2	57	571
Henry	Tuolumne Twp 4	71	143
Hugh	Butte Cascade	56	696
Humphrey	San Francisco San Francisco 3	67	30
Ira	El Dorado Salmon Falls	58	1048
Isaac	Santa Cruz Pajaro	66	527
J	El Dorado Diamond	58	792
J	Mariposa Twp 1	60	642
J	Sacramento Brighton	63	199
J	Sacramento Cosumnes	63	409
J	Shasta Millvill	66	751
J	Sutter Sutter	70	811
J A	Tehama Antelope	70	888
J B	Santa Clara Santa Clara	65	480
J D	Tuolumne Twp 1	71	207
J E	Sacramento Brighton	63	202
J H	Nevada Eureka	61	376
J H	Stanislaus Emory	70	750
J L	Calaveras Twp 8	57	66
J N	Amador Twp 5	55	374
J R	Nevada Nevada	61	239
J W	Sutter Sutter	70	812
James	Mendocino Calpella	60	811
James	Mendocino Arrana	60	860
James	San Francisco San Francisco 7	68	1350
James	San Francisco San Francisco 9	68	995
James	Santa Cruz Santa Cruz	66	636
James	Sierra Downieville	66	956
Jas	Placer Rattle Snake	62	602
Jas	San Francisco San Francisco 10	67	193
Jas M	Santa Clara San Jose	65	370
Jesse	Siskiyou Yreka	69	148
Jno	Alameda Brooklyn	55	215
Jno	Sacramento Lee	63	212
Jno P	San Francisco San Francisco 9	68	1080
Jno W	San Francisco San Francisco 9	68	1000
John	El Dorado White Oaks	58	1017
John	El Dorado Casumnes	58	1160
John	Placer Michigan	62	847
John	San Francisco San Francisco 7	68	1390
John	San Francisco San Francisco 3	67	36
John	San Joaquin Douglass	64	927
John	Santa Clara San Jose	65	348
John	Siskiyou Callahan	69	17
John	Solano Green Valley	69	242
John	Solano Benecia	69	317
John	Solano Vacaville	69	363
John A	Fresno Twp 3	59	10
PATTERSON			
John A	Solano Benecia	69	317
John B	Yuba Parks Ba	72	786
John R	Santa Cruz Santa Cruz	66	613
John R	Yuba Parke Ba	72	786
Jos	San Francisco San Francisco 9	68	1064
Jos	San Francisco San Francisco 10	67	193
Joseph	Sacramento Ward 1	63	39
Joseph	San Joaquin Elliott	64	945
Joseph	Siskiyou Yreka	69	131
Joseph R	Siskiyou Shasta Valley	69	121
Lew	Sacramento Franklin	63	310
Louisa	Del Norte Crescent	58	624
Lucy	Tehama Antelope	70	888
M	Colusa Monroeville	57	446
M	Shasta Horsetown	66	689
M	Sutter Yuba	70	767
Margaret	San Francisco San Francisco 10	67	255
Margt	San Francisco San Francisco 1	68	886
Mary	Sacramento Ward 1	63	153
Matt	Klamath Liberty	59	242
Mimmie	El Dorado Casumnes	58	1166
Munnie*	El Dorado Casumnes	58	1166
N C	San Francisco San Francisco 3	67	48
N C	San Francisco San Francisco 3	67	49
N H*	Stanislaus Emory	70	756
Nancy	San Francisco San Francisco 10	67	192
Nath G	Alameda Murray	55	229
Orilias	Placer Secret R	62	620
P	Mariposa Twp 1	60	642
P G	Sonoma Cloverdale	69	685
Pane	Santa Clara Gilroy	65	244
Paul	Sacramento Georgian	63	344
Paul	San Francisco San Francisco 9	68	1055
Paul	Santa Cruz Pajaro	66	525
R	Merced Twp 1	60	907
R	Sacramento Brighton	63	199
R T	Sierra Cox'S Bar	66	951
R W	Sonoma Vallejo	69	619
Racheal	Fresno Twp 3	59	15
Robt	Solano Benecia	69	304
Robt	Tehama Cottonwood	70	902
S	Yolo Cache Crk	72	621
T	Amador Twp 5	55	348
T	Sutter Sutter	70	816
Thomas	Placer Iona Hills	62	875
Thomas R	Sierra Twp 7	66	865
W	El Dorado Cold Spring	58	1099
W	Shasta Shasta	66	656
W L	Santa Clara San Jose	65	296
W P	El Dorado Salmon Falls	58	1035
W W	Tuolumne Columbia	71	357
Webb	Santa Clara San Jose	65	342
William	Los Angeles Los Angeles	59	354
William	Placer Michigan	62	841
William	Sierra Poker Flats	66	837
William	Sierra Poker Flats	66	840
William	Siskiyou Callahan	69	17
Wm	Alameda Brooklyn	55	77
Wm	Sacramento Brighton	63	197
Wm	San Francisco San Francisco 9	68	1090
Wm	Sierra Twp 7	66	885
Wm	Sierra Forest C	66	910
Wm	Sonoma Mendocino	69	466
Wm	Trinity Cox'S Bar	70	1038
Wm	Trinity China Bar	70	959
Wm	Tuolumne Twp 2	71	354
Wm H	San Francisco San Francisco 3	67	44
Wm R	Placer Auburn	62	588
PATTERSONL			
J A*	Nevada Nevada	61	239
PATTES			
---	Mendocino Round Va	60	884
E R	Tuolumne Twp 1	71	270
PATTESON			
A B*	Siskiyou Scott Ri	69	80
A D	Siskiyou Scott Ri	69	82
Edward	Los Angeles Los Angeles	59	359
J	Shasta Millvill	66	751
James	Mendocino Calpella	60	811
Jno	Nevada Nevada	61	256
John	Trinity Trinity	70	971
PATTICE			
Robt B	Sonoma Santa Rosa	69	390
PATTIE			
J	Nevada Eureka	61	353
Ohio	Yolo Cottonwoood	72	646
PATTIES			
V*	Tuolumne Jacksonville	71	165
PATTILLOW			
T	Tuolumne Twp 4	71	173
PATTIN			
D R	San Francisco San Francisco 3	67	45

Name	County Locale	M653 Roll	Page
PATTIN			
Jno	Sacramento Ward 1	63	79
Marie*	Sacramento Ward 1	63	80
Thos	Amador Twp 5	55	362
PATTINDEN			
Leander	El Dorado Big Bar	58	739
PATTINSON			
Edward	San Joaquin Stockton	64	1027
PATTIRON			
Edward	Los Angeles Los Angeles	59	359
PATTISON			
A B	Siskiyou Klamath	69	80
Albert	Siskiyou Scott Va	69	39
Harriett	Siskiyou Scott Va	69	29
Jno*	Nevada Nevada	61	256
John	Shasta Millvill	66	750
Silas	Siskiyou Callahan	69	16
Thos	Trinity Taylor'S	70	1034
PATTIT			
Asa	Yolo Cache	72	622
PATTON			
A	Butte Chico	56	562
A	Mendocino Big Rvr	60	850
Archd	Napa Napa	61	81
Benjamin	Mendocino Calpella	60	820
D R	San Francisco San Francisco 3	67	45
David	Tehama Lassen	70	866
Dina	Napa Napa	61	113
Dona	Napa Napa	61	113
E	Yolo Fremont	72	604
Edward	Mendocino Ukiah	60	793
Edward	Placer Iona Hills	62	865
George	San Luis Obispo San Luis Obispo	65	16
H	Solano Suisan	69	219
H G	San Francisco San Francisco 2	67	579
Henry R	Butte Ophir	56	797
J A	Sierra Twp 7	66	886
J D	Sonoma Sonoma	69	660
Jno	Sonoma Sonoma	69	643
John	Mendocino Ukiah	60	801
John	Sonoma Santa Rosa	69	411
John	Sonoma Petaluma	69	600
John A	Placer Virginia	62	665
John*	San Francisco San Francisco 5	67	483
Joseph	Sonoma Mendocino	69	461
Louisa	Sonoma Mendocino	69	461
M	Mendocino Big Rvr	60	840
Martha C	Sonoma Sonoma	69	660
Mary	Sonoma Armally	69	510
Mary Ann	Sonoma Santa Rosa	69	412
R L	Butte Ophir	56	748
Redman	Sonoma Santa Rosa	69	420
Richd	Sonoma Sonoma	69	634
Richd*	Napa Napa	61	81
Robert	Placer Iona Hills	62	875
Sarah F	Sonoma Mendocino	69	468
T P	Mendocino Arrana	60	862
Thomas	Mendocino Ukiah	60	807
Thomas	Placer Michigan	62	835
Thomas	Siskiyou Scott Va	69	23
Thomas S	Marin Tomales	60	718
Thoms	Mendocino Ukiah	60	807
Thos	Napa Napa	61	72
Thos	Sonoma Vallejo	69	612
Thos B	Sonoma Mendocino	69	468
W A	Nevada Grass Valley	61	152
William	Contra Costa Twp 3	57	590
William	Placer Iona Hills	62	874
Wm E	Mendocino Ukiah	60	807
PATTOW			
Auhd*	Napa Napa	61	81
M	Mendocino Big Rvr	60	840
Richd*	Napa Napa	61	81
PATTRE			
Hiram*	Calaveras Twp 10	57	293
PATTRO			
Bernard	Santa Cruz Soquel	66	584
Jose	Solano Vacaville	69	322
PATTS			
J	Santa Clara Redwood	65	456
Levi	Nevada Rough &	61	434
Lydia J	Santa Clara San Jose	65	347
Margaret	Santa Clara San Jose	65	347
PATTUR			
Peter	Tuolumne Twp 3	71	465
PATTY			
Isaac	Humbolt Pacific	59	134
John	Yuba Rose Bar	72	813
Joseph	Yuba Marysville	72	882
PATUKA			
---	Fresno Twp 2	59	101
PATURTE			
Jose*	San Bernardino San Bernadino	64	641
PATURTO			
Jose*	San Bernardino San Bernadino	64	622
PATWELL			
Chas	Butte Kimshaw	56	591

Name	County Locale	M653 Roll	Page
PATY			
Robt	San Francisco San Francisco 2	67	741
William	Tuolumne Twp 2	71	389
PATZER			
Lewis	San Francisco San Francisco 1	68	898
PAU			
---	Calaveras Twp 5	57	245
---	Calaveras Twp 10	57	275
---	San Francisco San Francisco 4	68	1185
---	Tuolumne Twp 2	71	416
PAUCE			
Himd*	Sierra Downieville	66	957
PAUCH			
F	Nevada Eureka	61	348
PAUCHOUD			
Lewis*	Calaveras Twp 4	57	340
PAUDLANDER			
David	Placer Secret R	62	612
PAUDOLO			
Antoinu	Calaveras Twp 8	57	82
Lorenja	Calaveras Twp 8	57	82
PAUENGER			
Louise*	Alameda Brooklyn	55	142
PAUERS			
J W	Amador Twp 3	55	382
PAUGH			
---	Amador Twp 5	55	351
---	Sacramento Granite	63	259
---	Trinity Mouth Ca	70	1014
---	Trinity Mouth Ca	70	1015
---	Trinity Lewiston	70	956
W J	Amador Twp 1	55	462
PAUHORST			
William B*	San Francisco 9	68	1040
---	San Francisco		
PAUIS			
Thomas*	Sierra Downieville	66	1006
PAUL			
C	San Francisco San Francisco 10		354
		67	
C W	El Dorado White Oaks	58	1006
Colin	Napa Napa	61	67
Ebzg M*	Yuba Marysville	72	883
Ebzgell*	Yuba Marysville	72	883
Ebzy M	Yuba Marysville	72	883
Fred	Butte Hamilton	56	529
G	Sacramento Sutter	63	293
Geo	Santa Clara San Jose	65	386
Geo R	San Francisco San Francisco 2	67	740
George	Solano Suisan	69	222
Henry	Butte Oregon	56	642
J	Solano Montezuma	69	374
Jacob	Klamath Liberty	59	234
James	El Dorado Georgetown	58	754
James	Fresno Twp 1	59	76
James	Humbolt Eureka	59	169
James	San Francisco San Francisco 11		157
		67	
James	Trinity Weaverville	70	1062
Jas	Sonoma Sonoma	69	647
Jean Le*	Sacramento Ward 1	63	149
John	Calaveras Twp 7	57	18
John	Marin Bolinas	60	748
John	Placer Michigan	62	809
John	Sierra Twp 7	66	883
John	Siskiyou Yreka	69	145
John	Yuba Parks Ba	72	783
John E	Tuolumne Twp 2	71	304
John*	Siskiyou Callahan	69	4
Kate V	San Francisco San Francisco 2	67	559
King	Alameda Murray	55	223
Lake	Sonoma Vallejo	69	623
M	Calaveras Twp 9	57	392
Mary	Calaveras Twp 6	57	116
Nelson	Alameda Brooklyn	55	87
Otto	Sierra Monte Crk	66	1036
Peter	Calaveras Twp 7	57	7
Richard	Amador Twp 4	55	233
Richard	Placer Forest H	62	800
Robert H	Calaveras Twp 6	57	131
Romset J	San Francisco San Francisco 8	68	1238
Rousset J	San Francisco San Francisco 8	68	1238
S F	Nevada Grass Valley	61	199
Saml	Placer Secret R	62	612
Sarah	Tuolumne Columbia	71	341
Thomas	Calaveras Twp 6	57	116
Wen	Yuba Foster B	72	829
William	San Francisco San Francisco 11		110
		67	
William P	Siskiyou Yreka	69	180
Wm	San Frncisco San Francisco 10		293
		67	
Wm	Santa Clara Fremont	65	430
Wm	Sonoma Cloverdale	69	685
Wm	Yuba Fosters	72	829
PAULALEON			
---*	Los Angeles San Juan	59	460

Name	County Locale	M653 Roll	Page
PAULDING			
C W	Sacramento Ward 1	63	30
PAULE			
Fancisco	Los Angeles Los Angeles	59	392
Francisco	Los Angeles Los Angeles	59	392
PAULETT			
Joseph*	San Joaquin Stockton	64	1052
PAULEY			
John	Alameda Brooklyn	55	162
PAULIA			
---	San Bernardino S Timate	64	745
PAULINA			
---	San Bernardino S Timate	64	696
---	San Bernardino S Timate	64	699
---	San Bernardino S Timate	64	700
---	San Bernardino S Timate	64	703
---	San Bernardino S Timate	64	704
---	San Bernardino S Timate	64	705
---	San Bernardino S Timate	64	706
---	San Bernardino S Timate	64	709
---	San Bernardino S Timate	64	710
---	San Bernardino S Timate	64	712
---	San Bernardino S Timate	64	713
---	San Bernardino S Timate	64	714
---	San Bernardino S Timate	64	715
---	San Bernardino S Timate	64	716
---	San Bernardino S Timate	64	718
---	San Bernardino S Timate	64	719
---	San Bernardino S Timate	64	723
---	San Bernardino S Timate	64	724
---	San Bernardino S Timate	64	725
---	San Bernardino S Timate	64	728
---	San Bernardino S Timate	64	729
---	San Bernardino S Timate	64	731
---	San Bernardino S Timate	64	732
---	San Bernardino S Timate	64	734
---	San Bernardino S Timate	64	735
---	San Bernardino S Timate	64	736
---	San Bernardino S Timate	64	740
---	San Bernardino S Timate	64	741
---	San Bernardino S Timate	64	742
---	San Bernardino S Timate	64	743
---	San Bernardino S Timate	64	744
---	San Bernardino S Timate	64	749
---	San Bernardino S Timate	64	752
---	San Bernardino S Timate	64	753
---	San Bernardino S Timate	64	754
PAULINE			
---	San Bernardino S Timate	64	729
Eugene	Sacramento Ward 4	63	500
PAULINO			
---	Los Angeles San Pedro	59	478
PAULK			
John	Tuolumne Big Oak	71	132
Richard*	Calaveras Twp 9	57	360
PAULKINHAUSER			
Richard*	Calaveras Twp 9	57	360
PAULKONHAUSER			
Richard*	Calaveras Twp 9	57	360
PAULLACK			
Jas	San Francisco San Francisco 2	67	668
PAULLEY			
J P	Sierra Twp 5	66	943
P P	Sierra Twp 5	66	943
PAULLIN			
James R	San Francisco San Francisco 8	68	1294
PAULLY			
C C	Sierra Excelsior	66	1033
John	Sierra Excelsior	66	1033
PAULMAN			
Henry	Napa Napa	61	113
PAULSEH			
Jon	San Francisco San Francisco 9	68	1069
PAULSELL			
Calvin	San Joaquin Castoria	64	880
PAULSEN			
C P	San Francisco San Francisco 5	67	478
F C	Nevada Eureka	61	378
Henry	Yuba Foster B	72	831
Jacob	Trinity Turner'S	70	997
Jno	San Francisco San Francisco 9	68	1069
W	Santa Clara Santa Clara	65	469
PAULSIN			
---	Tulara Keyesville	71	56
John	Trinity Readings	70	996
PAULSON			
John	Calaveras Twp 9	57	356
PAULY			
Benjamin	Sierra Downieville	66	978
Eliza A	Napa Napa	61	99
Nicholas*	Sierra Gibsonville	66	858
PAULZ			
Henry	Tuolumne Twp 4	71	144
PAUS			
Jean*	Sacramento Ward 1	63	85
John*	Sacramento Ward 1	63	11
PAUSELEY			
Hartnett	Monterey San Juan	60	990

Name	County Locale	M653 RollPage
PAUSEN		
Hans	Alameda Brooklyn	55 153
J*	San Francisco San Francisco 9	681060
PAUSHUM		
---	Plumas Quincy	62 969
PAUST		
E E	El Dorado Greenwood	58 708
PAUSTIN		
Joshua	San Joaquin Castoria	64 903
PAUTALEON		
---*	Los Angeles San Juan	59 460
PAUTATEON		
---*	Los Angeles San Juan	59 460
PAUTEN		
P*	Nevada Grass Valley	61 170
PAVATT		
P	Tuolumne Twp 1	71 216
PAVEL		
Howel	Nevada Bridgeport	61 470
PAVELSON		
James	Sacramento Ward 4	63 546
PAVER		
F*	Sacramento Brighton	63 196
PAVEY		
Bumieo	El Dorado Eldorado	58 945
Charles	El Dorado Eldorado	58 943
W H	El Dorado Eldorado	58 943
PAVIO		
Marco	Amador Twp 1	55 476
PAVNIYANT		
James H	El Dorado Big Bar	58 739
PAVRET		
Margt*	San Francisco San Francisco 2	67 698
PAW TUCK		
---	Fresno Twp 1	59 117
PAW		
---	Amador Twp 2	55 289
---	Amador Twp 2	55 315
---	Amador Twp 4	55 332
---	Amador Twp 5	55 336
---	Amador Twp 5	55 340
---	Amador Twp 6	55 423
---	Calaveras Twp 8	57 109
---	Calaveras Twp 10	57 261
---	Calaveras Twp 8	57 87
---	El Dorado Salmon Falls	581044
---	El Dorado Salmon Falls	581054
---	Nevada Bridgeport	61 461
---	Placer Virginia	62 687
---	Sierra Twp 5	66 942
---	Sierra Twp 5	66 948
---	Sierra Downieville	66 982
---	Sierra Downieville	66 984
---	Sierra Downieville	66 991
---	Stanislaus Buena Village	70 724
---	Trinity Mouth Ca	701014
---	Tuolumne Jamestown	71 444
---	Tuolumne Twp 3	71 460
---	Tuolumne Columbia	71 474
---	Tuolumne Twp 1	71 475
Alex*	Calaveras Twp 4	57 316
Cham	Fresno Twp 3	59 31
Fer	Nevada Bridgeport	61 461
PAWELL		
E	El Dorado Kelsey	581156
PAWLING		
T M	Amador Twp 1	55 455
PAWOY		
Morris	Tuolumne Twp 1	71 236
PAWTE		
Wm	Santa Clara San Jose	65 285
PAWTTER		
Loranzo*	Calaveras Twp 10	57 289
PAXDDO		
---	Tulara Visalia	71 117
PAXON		
Francis	San Francisco San Francisco 7	681443
Joseph	San Francisco San Francisco 7	681345
Richard	San Francisco San Francisco 7	681345
PAXTOA		
Adolph	Yuba Marysville	72 870
John A*	Yuba Marysville	72 870
PAXTON		
Adolph	Yuba Marysville	72 870
Alex	Nevada Red Dog	61 550
D A	Sonoma Washington	69 679
David W	Calaveras Twp 10	57 288
George	Plumas Quincy	62 952
Jno	Sonoma Sonoma	69 659
John A*	Yuba Marysville	72 870
Robert	Tuolumne Twp 3	71 508
Thomas	Siskiyou Yreka	69 140
Thoms	Siskiyou Yreka	69 140
Walter	Plumas Quincy	621000
PAXTOW		
David W*	Calaveras Twp 10	57 288

Name	County Locale	M653 RollPage
PAY		
---	Amador Twp 2	55 323
---	Amador Twp 2	55 328
---	Amador Twp 5	55 341
---	Amador Twp 5	55 355
---	Amador Twp 5	55 367
---	Amador Twp 3	55 408
---	Calaveras Twp 4	57 304
---	Calaveras Twp 4	57 323
---	El Dorado White Oaks	581032
---	El Dorado White Oaks	581033
---	El Dorado Salmon Falls	581048
---	El Dorado Big Bar	58 734
---	El Dorado Eldorado	58 940
---	Mariposa Twp 3	60 620
---	Mariposa Coulterville	60 693
---	Nevada Rough &	61 436
---	Placer Virginia	62 666
---	Sacramento Ward 1	63 51
---	Sacramento Ward 1	63 52
---	Sacramento Ward 1	63 60
---	San Francisco San Francisco 4	681174
---	San Francisco San Francisco 11	144 67
---	Shasta French G	66 712
---	Sierra Downieville	66 984
C*	Nevada Grass Valley	61 182
Fon	El Dorado Placerville	58 829
Michael	Alameda Brooklyn	55 77
PAYDAY		
William	Tuolumne Twp 1	71 481
PAYE		
---	Amador Twp 6	55 428
Edward*	San Francisco San Francisco 3	67 82
Saml	Amador Township	55 467
PAYELLO		
Simion*	Mariposa Twp 3	60 568
Simon*	Mariposa Twp 3	60 568
PAYEN		
Marven	Sacramento Natonia	63 282
PAYER		
L	El Dorado Placerville	58 833
PAYET		
Antoine	Siskiyou Yreka	69 142
PAYETTE		
Joseph	Yuba Parks Ba	72 780
PAYJA		
---	Tulara Twp 3	71 71
PAYLEY		
L	Nevada Grass Valley	61 144
S	Nevada Grass Valley	61 144
PAYLOR		
John	Calaveras Twp 9	57 353
Wm*	Solano Suisan	69 236
PAYM		
Geo H*	Amador Twp 2	55 325
PAYMULE		
Julius	San Francisco San Francisco 2	67 775
PAYN		
P E	El Dorado Placerville	58 860
PAYNA		
John*	Calaveras Twp 6	57 161
Wm	Sacramento Ward 4	63 525
PAYNE		
Alduch	Calaveras Twp 8	57 102
Amelia	Mariposa Twp 3	60 602
Aron	San Mateo Twp 3	65 83
Benj	Plumas Quincy	62 923
Bettio*	San Joaquin Stockton	641015
Cathrin	Butte Ophir	56 769
Charles	El Dorado Coloma	581117
E	El Dorado Diamond	58 771
E	El Dorado Placerville	58 848
Edward	Sacramento Sutter	63 301
Elisha	Calaveras Twp 6	57 149
Frank B	Amador Twp 4	55 259
Frederick	San Francisco San Francisco 7	681358
G	Sacramento Ward 1	63 147
G A	Nevada Rough &	61 404
G G	Sacramento Ward 1	63 147
Geo	Amador Twp 3	55 396
Geo H	Amador Twp 2	55 325
Geo W	San Francisco San Francisco 2	67 695
George	San Francisco San Francisco 7	681407
George	Yuba Fosters	72 839
George C	Calaveras Twp 7	57 30
H	El Dorado Placerville	58 817
H B	Sacramento Ward 4	63 522
Henry	Amador Twp 6	55 448
Henry	El Dorado Mud Springs	58 965
Henry	Sacramento Ward 1	63 147
Horace J	San Francisco San Francisco 8	681294
J	Sutter Nicolaus	70 834
J B	Siskiyou Scott Va	69 58
James	Plumas Quincy	62 964
Jas H	Santa Clara Thomas	65 443

Name	County Locale	M653 RollPage
PAYNE		
Jerry	Placer Iona Hills	62 859
Joseph	Merced Twp 1	60 907
Joseph	Placer Yankee J	62 775
Joseph	Yuba Long Bar	72 773
Jospeh	Merced Twp 1	60 907
M	San Mateo Twp 1	65 64
Manin*	Placer Nicolaus	62 691
Martha	San Joaquin Stockton	641073
Moses	El Dorado Casumnes	581175
N	El Dorado Salmon Falls	581041
Noah N	Sierra La Porte	66 771
Norman	Sacramento Natonia	63 282
O	Nevada Eureka	61 376
P A*	Nevada Rough &	61 404
R	Amador Twp 1	55 489
R	Sacramento Ward 1	63 80
S K	Sacramento Granite	63 233
Saml	Shasta Millvill	66 738
T	Nevada Eureka	61 381
T A*	Nevada Rough &	61 404
Thos	Alameda Brooklyn	55 121
Thos	Mariposa Twp 3	60 599
Thos	Sacramento San Joaquin	63 357
Tim	Nevada Bridgeport	61 449
W	Sacramento Ward 1	63 79
W H	Sacramento Ward 4	63 499
W W	Sacramento Natonia	63 282
W W	San Luis Obispo San Luis Obispo	65 31
W*	Siskiyou Callahan	69 2
William	San Francisco San Francisco 5	67 546
William	San Joaquin Elkhorn	64 975
William	Shasta Horsetown	66 707
Willis	Amador Twp 2	55 273
Wm	Butte Chico	56 551
Wm	Sacramento Natonia	63 282
Wm	Santa Clara Thomas	65 443
Wm	Sonoma Petaluma	69 568
PAYNO		
John*	Calaveras Twp 6	57 161
PAYNSE		
---*	Mendocino Round Va	60 881
PAYO		
---	Amador Twp 2	55 280
---*	Los Angeles Los Angeles	59 493
Francis	San Francisco San Francisco 2	67 719
PAYOH		
Antone	Siskiyou Yreka	69 177
PAYOR		
Henry	San Francisco San Francisco 3	67 86
PAYORY		
---	Amador Twp 3	55 374
PAYOT		
Henry	San Francisco San Francisco 3	67 86
PAYOUS		
Simin	Calaveras Twp 5	57 198
Simon	Calaveras Twp 5	57 198
PAYPE		
---	Butte Chico	56 550
PAYR		
Edward	San Francisco San Francisco 3	67 82
PAYRAN		
Steven	Sonoma Petaluma	69 604
PAYSANT		
J	Sacramento Ward 1	63 85
PAYSER		
M W	El Dorado Placerville	58 864
PAYSMO		
Daniel W	Alameda Brooklyn	55 211
PAYTEN		
H	Yolo Cache Crk	72 623
Y	Yolo Cache Crk	72 623
PAYTES		
G W	Amador Twp 3	55 395
PAYTON		
Benj	El Dorado Placerville	58 924
H B	Tuolumne Twp 4	71 172
James	Amador Twp 4	55 255
James	Tehama Antelope	70 893
John W	Tuolumne Shawsfla	71 407
N	Yolo Cache	72 623
William	Amador Twp 4	55 257
William	Fresno Twp 3	59 9
Wm	Tehama Red Bluff	70 919
Y	Yolo Cache	72 623
PAYUSE		
---*	Mendocino Round Va	60 881
PAYWELL		
Lewis	Siskiyou Klamath	69 85
PAZ		
Custodia	San Francisco San Francisco 8	681309
PAZORANO		
Manuel	San Bernardino San Salvador	64 660
PAZZO		
Antonio	Santa Clara San Jose	65 331
J	Santa Clara San Jose	65 325

Name	County Locale	M653 Roll	Page
PE CHING			
---	Nevada Bridgeport	61	458
PE			
Ching	Nevada Bridgeport	61	458
Chong	Alameda Oakland	55	14
Lung	Alameda Oakland	55	14
Mang	Yuba Long Bar	72	763
Tee	Yuba North Ea	72	675
Tong	Calaveras Twp 6	57	125
PEA			
---	Calaveras Twp 4	57	305
---	Mendocino Calpella	60	825
Peter	Santa Clara San Jose	65	304
PEAARTS			
Julius	San Francisco San Francisco 1	68	896
PEABODDY			
Saml	Tuolumne Sonora	71	483
PEABODY			
A	Mariposa Twp 1	60	631
Andrew J	Yuba Marysville	72	926
B F	Sacramento San Joaquin	63	350
Enos	Trinity Hay Fork	70	994
F W	Colusa Spring Valley	57	435
Feo	Nevada Nevada	61	279
G A*	San Francisco San Francisco 5	67	532
Geo	Nevada Nevada	61	279
George	Calaveras Twp 7	57	32
Henry G	San Francisco San Francisco 8	681	322
J A	San Francisco San Francisco 5	67	532
James	Calaveras Twp 8	57	85
Jane	Nevada Nevada	61	274
John T	Solano Fairfield	69	197
Joseph	Calaveras Twp 8	57	96
Joseph	Sacramento Ward 4	63	533
Lunian	San Joaquin Elkhorn	64	950
S J	Sacramento Ward 1	63	78
T J	Sacramento Ward 1	63	17
Wm	Sacramento Ward 1	63	153
Wm F	Solano Benecia	69	281
PEACE			
J P	Tuolumne Twp 2	71	399
PEACH			
Amos	Tuolumne Twp 1	71	270
Augustus L	San Francisco	67	143
	San Francisco	67	
Benj	Alameda Brooklyn	55	128
Eliza	Santa Clara San Jose	65	321
James	San Francisco San Francisco 11	67	110
John	Tuolumne Columbia	71	325
Joseph	Sierra Twp 7	66	890
Patrick	Mendocino Ukiah	60	805
Steward	Butte Oregon	56	616
William	Marin Bolinas	60	740
PEACHAM			
George	Sonoma Petaluma	69	566
PEACHEY			
A J	Siskiyou Scott Va	69	33
Geo W	San Joaquin Stockton	641	053
PEACHY			
A C	San Francisco San Francisco 3	67	73
Bonaparte*	Mendocino Calpella	60	812
Bonaport	Mendocino Calpella	60	812
J B	San Francisco San Francisco 3	67	74
William	El Dorado Coloma	581	121
Williams	El Dorado Coloma	581	121
PEACK			
John*	Tuolumne Twp 2	71	325
PEACOCK			
Allen	Siskiyou Shasta Valley	69	118
Chas	Nevada Eureka	61	374
Daniel	Nevada Bloomfield	61	518
David	Nevada Bloomfield	61	529
E A	Siskiyou Yreka	69	156
Geo	Del Norte Crescent	58	650
Geo W	Santa Clara Alviso	65	406
George W	Sierra Pine Grove	66	821
J	Sonoma Washington	69	675
J A	Butte Bidwell	56	705
John	Santa Clara Santa Clara	65	500
John	Yuba Fosters	72	835
John R	Tuolumne Twp 6	71	541
Joseph	Santa Clara San Jose	65	361
Joseph	Siskiyou Scott Va	69	27
Mary	San Francisco San Francisco 8	681	316
S A	Nevada Grass Valley	61	210
T B	El Dorado Salmon Falls	581	063
Thomas	Sierra Downieville	66	971
Wm	Tuolumne Columbia	71	293
PEACORD			
Joseph	Solano Benecia	69	299
PEADAN			
Albert	Contra Costa Twp 2	57	567
PEADRO			
Tarta	Placer Michigan	62	832
PEAHL			
George	Calaveras Twp 9	57	374

Name	County Locale	M653 Roll	Page
PEAI			
Albert*	Yuba Marysville	72	907
PEAK			
---	Yuba Long Bar	72	760
---*	Stanislaus Branch	70	713
Abram	Napa Clear Lake	61	128
Chas A	Sacramento Ward 4	63	564
F M	Butte Chico	56	534
F M	Butte Chico	56	539
L R	San Joaquin Douglass	64	917
Luke	Contra Costa Twp 2	57	541
Robert B	Plumas Quincy	62	945
Wm	Napa Clear Lake	61	128
PEAKE			
Albert A	San Francisco San Francisco 9	68	989
E T	Trinity Mouth Ca	701	015
Jas M	San Francisco San Francisco 12	67	389
N W	Santa Clara San Jose	65	293
Saml	Napa Hot Springs	61	2
W F	Sacramento Dry Crk	63	370
Wm	Sacramento San Joaquin	63	348
Wm B	San Francisco San Francisco 1	68	821
PEAKS			
Amess	Sierra Twp 7	66	899
Amos	Sierra Twp 7	66	899
R P	San Mateo Twp 3	65	109
PEAL			
Chas	Butte Ophir	56	799
James W	San Joaquin Elkhorn	64	965
PEALER			
B	Yolo Cottonwood	72	655
Measer	Amador Twp 5	55	332
PEALONGEOT			
Francis	Calaveras Twp 6	57	151
PEALOS			
Barna	Tulara Yule Rvr	71	25
PEALSTICKER			
Wm	Butte Cascade	56	697
PEANCE			
Joseph	Amador Twp 3	55	378
PEANCHEND			
Fred	Siskiyou Klamath	69	93
PEANG			
---	Amador Twp 7	55	415
PEANON			
Rowona	Tuolumne Twp 5	71	519
PEANOY			
Paul	Butte Bidwell	56	723
PEAR			
---	Amador Twp 5	55	351
---	Mariposa Coulterville	60	681
J	Trinity Dead Wood	70	958
PEARC			
Miriane*	Sacramento Ward 1	63	113
PEARCE			
Andrew	Colusa Spring Valley	57	432
Ann	Yolo Slate Ra	72	689
Ann	Yuba Slate Ro	72	689
Ann	Yuba Slate Ro	72	700
Charles	Sierra Monte Crk	661	038
Chas	Sonoma Petaluma	69	591
Douglass	Yuba New York	72	738
Edwin	Yolo Washington	72	563
Ellen	San Francisco San Francisco 11	67	142
Geo	Sonoma Petaluma	69	588
George	San Francisco San Francisco 8	681	260
George W	Sacramento Ward 1	63	106
H	San Francisco San Francisco 10	67	338
H	Sonoma Santa Rosa	69	417
Henry	Nevada Bloomfield	61	521
J F	Yuba North Ea	72	670
J M	Yolo Washington	72	605
J T	Yolo No E Twp	72	670
J*	El Dorado Placerville	58	895
James	Alameda Oakland	55	19
James	Amador Twp 7	55	420
James	Yolo No E Twp	72	678
James	Yuba North Ea	72	678
James P	Yuba Rose Bar	72	806
James*	San Joaquin Stockton	641	012
John	Yolo Slate Ra	72	699
John	Yuba Slate Ro	72	699
Jos	Sonoma Sonoma	69	636
Lewis	Monterey Pajaro	601	018
Mariam W*	Yuba Marysville	72	875
Mary	San Francisco San Francisco 4	681	225
Moses	Sierra St Louis	66	864
Nedea	Tehama Tehama	70	946
Peter H	San Francisco San Francisco 10	67	194
Richard	Sierra Downieville	66	960
Thos	Nevada Nevada	61	255
William	Siskiyou Cottonwoood	69	101

Name	County Locale	M653 Roll	Page
PEARCE			
Willm	Sacramento Lee	63	217
Wm	Tuolumne Twp 1	71	264
Wm	Yolo No E Twp	72	684
PEARCEFIELD			
R H	Yolo Slate Ra	72	692
PEARCIFIELD			
R H	Yuba Slate Ro	72	692
PEARDO			
Bennit	Santa Clara Santa Clara	65	482
PEARE			
M	Trinity Lewiston	70	963
Miriane*	Sacramento Ward 1	63	113
Thomas	San Francisco San Francisco 8	681	238
PEARELES			
Rose	El Dorado Georgetown	58	677
PEARER			
Riley	San Joaquin Oneal	64	940
PEAREY			
J J*	Butte Oregon	56	609
PEARIE			
J*	El Dorado Placerville	58	895
PEARINE			
Atinacia*	El Dorado Placerville	58	908
PEARIS			
R A*	Sacramento Ward 3	63	455
PEARL			
Ben*	Sacramento Ward 1	63	81
Benf	Solano Benecia	69	314
Benj	Solano Benecia	69	314
Charles	Alameda Brooklyn	55	111
George	Calaveras Twp 9	57	374
H A	San Francisco San Francisco 7	681	437
John H	Santa Clara San Jose	65	368
John L	Santa Clara San Jose	65	281
Rosa	Alameda Brooklyn	55	96
S	Sacramento Ward 1	63	152
Syb*	Sacramento Ward 1	63	40
Syl	Sacramento Ward 1	63	40
Wm D	Alameda Brooklyn	55	175
Wm M	Yuba Rose Bar	72	791
PEARLBERG			
A	San Francisco San Francisco 3	67	50
PEARLE			
M	Santa Clara San Jose	65	368
PEARLRY			
A C*	San Francisco San Francisco 3	67	73
J B*	San Francisco San Francisco 3	67	74
PEARMAN			
Samuel	Siskiyou Shasta Rvr	69	114
PEARNCY			
S*	San Francisco San Francisco 5	67	524
PEARNEY			
William*	San Francisco San Francisco 4	681	172
PEARS			
William	Nevada Rough &	61	414
PEARSALL			
Daniel	Tuolumne Sonora	71	188
Solomon	San Joaquin Stockton	641	063
PEARSE			
Henry*	Nevada Bloomfield	61	521
R A	Nevada Bloomfield	61	524
Thos	Nevada Nevada	61	255
W J*	Nevada Red Dog	61	540
William L*	Nevada Rough &	61	395
PEARSEN			
W A	Amador Twp 2	55	325
PEARSI			
W J*	Nevada Red Dog	61	540
PEARSO			
N	Amador Twp 6	55	449
PEARSON			
---	Amador Twp 2	55	266
Alice	San Francisco San Francisco 9	68	979
Bowona*	Tuolumne Green Springs	71	519
C	San Francisco San Francisco 3	67	22
C A	Sacramento Brighton	63	209
Charles	San Joaquin Oneal	64	912
Charles	Sierra Twp 5	66	941
David	Sierra Pine Grove	66	826
E A	Butte Oregon	56	630
Frank	Napa Yount	61	39
Frank	San Joaquin Oneal	64	932
Geo	El Dorado Diamond	58	810
Geo	San Francisco San Francisco 10	67	268
George	San Joaquin Stockton	641	069
George A	Del Norte Ferry P O	58	666
George P	San Francisco San Francisco 9	681	045
Ginger	El Dorado Georgetown	58	694
H	San Francisco San Francisco 3	67	46
H H	Nevada Bridgeport	61	486
Herman	San Francisco San Francisco 7	681	436
J B	Placer Michigan	62	821
J F	Sierra Grizzly	661	058
J O	Tuolumne Shawsfla	71	402

California 1860 Census Index

Name	County Locale	M653 RollPage
PEARSON		
J W	Amador Twp 6	55 449
J W	Tuolumne Twp 2	71 400
Jack	Nevada Red Dog	61 552
James	Calaveras Twp 7	57 40
James	Colusa Spring Valley	57 432
James	San Joaquin Stockton	641051
James	San Joaquin Stockton	641052
James	Santa Clara Redwood	65 453
Jas	Calaveras Twp 9	57 389
Joana	San Francisco San Francisco 6	67 428
John	Amador Twp 1	55 509
John	Calaveras Twp 8	57 83
John	San Francisco San Francisco 12	67 372
John K	San Francisco San Francisco 11	67 136
Jonna	San Francisco San Francisco 6	67 428
Leander	Tuolumne Chinese	71 490
Marry E	Yolo Washington	72 567
Mary	Amador Twp 1	55 469
Mary E	Yolo Washington	72 567
Mathew	San Joaquin O'Neal	641002
Matilda	Napa Yount	61 35
Noah	Amador Twp 3	55 400
Peter	Nevada Bloomfield	61 526
Philip T	Tuolumne Twp 1	71 400
Richard	Colusa Spring Valley	57 432
S M	Calaveras Twp 9	57 375
S P	Amador Twp 2	55 279
Thomas C	San Joaquin Elkhorn	64 968
Thos	Sacramento San Joaquin	63 352
W	Shasta Millvill	66 750
W A	Amador Twp 2	55 325
William	Sonoma Russian	69 439
William R	San Joaquin Elkhorn	64 957
Wm	San Francisco San Francisco 5	67 480
Wm	Sierra Twp 7	66 891
Wm	Yolo Slate Ra	72 689
Wm	Yuba Slate Ro	72 689
PEARSONS		
Daniel	Santa Cruz Pajaro	66 574
Geo A	Butte Chico	56 556
James	Santa Cruz Santa Cruz	66 632
PEART		
Ben	Sacramento Ward 1	63 81
PEARTRY		
A C*	San Francisco San Francisco 3	67 73
J B*	San Francisco San Francisco 3	67 74
PEARUCY		
S*	San Francisco San Francisco 5	67 524
PEAS		
Elijah	Contra Costa Twp 1	57 500
John	Contra Costa Twp 1	57 500
John	Contra Costa Twp 2	57 577
L S	San Francisco San Francisco 4	681227
William C	Contra Costa Twp 2	57 542
PEASE		
C B*	Mendocino Arrana	60 856
Chas S	Tuolumne Twp 1	71 246
E T	San Francisco San Francisco 10	67 198
Eli	San Francisco San Francisco 10	67 198
Elija Jr	Nevada Bridgeport	61 443
Elijah	Nevada Bridgeport	61 442
George	Placer Yankee J	62 778
Gilbert	Santa Cruz Santa Cruz	66 633
James	San Francisco San Francisco 9	68 978
John	Placer Yankee J	62 778
L	Napa Hot Springs	61 20
L D	Alameda Brooklyn	55 190
L M	San Francisco San Francisco 5	67 518
Miriam*	Sacramento Ward 1	63 113
Nelson L	San Francisco San Francisco 8	681241
P A	El Dorado Georgetown	58 745
Richmond	Amador Twp 4	55 249
T B	Nevada Bloomfield	61 523
W C	San Francisco San Francisco 1	68 924
W S	Tuolumne Twp 4	71 176
Wm C	San Francisco San Francisco 2	67 772
PEASELY		
J	Yuba New York	72 724
John	San Francisco San Francisco 8	681251
PEASLEE		
Wm	Yuba New York	72 744
PEASLEY		
Aaron W	Humbolt Union	59 191
J	Nevada Eureka	61 362
Jn O	Sacramento Ward 4	63 516
John	Calaveras Twp 5	57 209
Oliver	Tuolumne Twp 1	71 268
Olvier	Tuolumne Twp 1	71 268
Sophia W	Yuba Marysville	72 978
PEASTER		
Geo	Tuolumne Twp 1	71 252
PEAT		
Ellen	Sacramento Ward 3	63 470
Geo	Yolo Putah	72 553
J Fred	San Francisco San Francisco 8	681264
PEATERSON		
Jackson	Contra Costa Twp 3	57 606
PEATES		
Geo	Yolo Putah	72 553
PEATFIELD		
John	San Francisco San Francisco 9	68 975
PEATREES		
David	Amador Twp 5	55 362
PEATRENS		
I A	Amador Twp 2	55 313
PEATRERS		
J A	Amador Twp 2	55 313
PEATRO		
Margene*	Placer Michigan	62 840
Rodena*	Placer Michigan	62 840
Rosetta	Placer Michigan	62 832
PEATROSS		
Wm W	Sonoma Bodega	69 529
PEATRS		
John	Amador Twp 3	55 382
PEATZY		
Charles*	Calaveras Twp 4	57 340
PEAUCHEND		
Fred*	Siskiyou Klamath	69 93
PEAVEE		
Mary*	San Francisco San Francisco 4	681225
PEAVEY		
J J	Butte Oregon	56 609
Sophia	San Francisco San Francisco 12	67 380
PEAVY		
May B	Yuba Marysville	72 908
PEBBERSON		
Stickney	Mariposa Twp 1	60 663
PEBBETT		
Edward F*	Yuba Linda	72 990
Edward*	Yuba Linda	72 990
PEBBLES		
Jac	Butte Eureka	56 654
PEBBS		
Thos	Mariposa Twp 3	60 600
PEBERTY		
E A	Tuolumne Columbia	71 309
PEBETIE		
J	El Dorado Placerville	58 851
PEBFRETT		
Robert*	San Bernardino San Bernadino	64 621
PEBLER		
Fredk	San Francisco San Francisco 2	67 800
PEBODY		
Franklin	Amador Twp 5	55 343
PECANDO		
---*	San Bernardino S Timate	64 750
PECART		
N	San Francisco San Francisco 1	68 927
PECECK		
Thos	Amador Twp 2	55 319
PECH		
---	Placer Auburn	62 563
PECHACO		
Jose	Contra Costa Twp 2	57 565
PECHEM		
Charles	Yuba Foster B	72 835
PECHERN		
Charles*	Yuba Fosters	72 835
PECHICE		
Francisco	Alameda Brooklyn	55 189
PECHILLA		
---	San Diego Agua Caliente	64 840
PECHLER		
Joseph*	Tuolumne Twp 6	71 538
PECIAS		
W	El Dorado Kelsey	581134
PECIEO		
S	El Dorado Placerville	58 867
PECINDO		
---	San Bernardino S Timate	64 719
PECIRNDO		
---	San Bernardino S Timate	64 700
---	San Bernardino S Timate	64 702
PECK		
---	Calaveras Twp 6	57 149
---	Calaveras Twp 10	57 259
---	Nevada Bridgeport	61 492
---*	Stanislaus Branch	70 713
A J	El Dorado Placerville	58 884
A J	Yolo Cache Crk	72 591
A M	Sierra La Porte	66 765
A W	Tuolumne Twp 4	71 144
Aaron B	Sierra Twp 7	66 866
Andrus	El Dorado White Oaks	581014
Benj F	Placer Rattle Snake	62 628
PECK		
Bradley	Sacramento San Joaquin	63 352
C	Amador Twp 6	55 431
C A	Nevada Bridgeport	61 483
C F	El Dorado Casumnes	581166
Catherine	Santa Clara San Jose	65 329
Charles	Tuolumne Twp 2	71 394
Charles*	Placer Michigan	62 823
Clouse	Siskiyou Yreka	69 192
Danl*	Butte Kimshaw	56 572
Daul	Butte Kimshaw	56 572
E S	Calaveras Twp 8	57 70
Edmond W	Contra Costa Twp 3	57 590
Edward	Solano Suisan	69 238
Edward T	Santa Cruz Watsonville	66 535
Eli	Plumas Quincy	62 992
Erastus	Monterey San Juan	601004
F	Merced Twp 1	60 895
Frank	Butte Chico	56 567
Frederick	Calaveras Twp 4	57 337
Geo	Butte Chico	56 566
Geo	San Francisco San Francisco 10	67 340
Geo H	San Francisco San Francisco 6	67 459
Geo W	Calaveras Twp 4	57 337
George	Sonoma Mendocino	69 464
George W N	San Francisco San Francisco 3	67 13
Henry	Amador Twp 2	55 313
Henry	Amador Twp 7	55 414
Henry	Calaveras Twp 6	57 127
Henry	El Dorado White Oaks	581022
Henry	Tuolumne Sonora	71 245
Henry M	San Luis Obispo San Luis Obispo	65 40
Henry W	Santa Cruz Pescadero	66 651
Henry*	Tuolumne Twp 1	71 245
J	Nevada Eureka	61 371
J S	Siskiyou Klamath	69 96
James	Calaveras Twp 4	57 325
James	Calaveras Twp 7	57 41
James	Santa Cruz Soguel	66 599
James H	Santa Clara Fremont	65 430
Jas A	Santa Clara Fremont	65 433
Jesse D	San Francisco San Francisco 4	681114
Jno A	San Francisco San Francisco 9	681008
Jno M	San Francisco San Francisco 10	67 200
Jno R	Sonoma Mendocino	69 464
Joel	Sonoma Sonoma	69 636
John S	Siskiyou Yreka	69 170
Joseph	Plumas Quincy	62 972
Juster	Santa Cruz Watsonville	66 539
L P	Butte Cascade	56 696
Leon	Trinity Bates	70 967
Levi P	Santa Clara San Jose	65 280
Lewis	San Francisco San Francisco 4	681114
Lnemda	Yolo Washington	72 565
Lucinda	Yolo Washington	72 565
M W	Alameda Oakland	55 67
M W	Alameda Oakland	55 75
Maria	Santa Clara San Jose	65 329
Mary	San Francisco San Francisco 10	67 176
Nancy	Sonoma Mendocino	69 464
Nathan R*	Placer Ophirville	62 653
Nathaniel	Marin Tomales	60 723
Nicholas	Contra Costa Twp 2	57 559
Nicholas	Placer Auburn	62 585
O A	Napa Hot Springs	61 19
Oscar	Plumas Quincy	62 923
R H	Butte Cascade	56 695
S S B	Nevada Bridgeport	61 465
Sallie M	San Francisco San Francisco 10	67 185
Samuel	Yuba Rose Bar	72 789
Sarah	Placer Forest H	62 794
Sidley	Sierra La Porte	66 786
Solon	Butte Oregon	56 609
Stephen	Placer Forest H	62 796
Sulley	Sierra La Porte	66 786
Theodore	Siskiyou Yreka	69 151
Thomas	Calaveras Twp 4	57 337
Thomas	Santa Cruz Pescadero	66 650
Thomas	Sierra Twp 7	66 899
William	San Francisco San Francisco 3	67 10
William A	Calaveras Twp 4	57 338
William H	Calaveras Twp 4	57 338
Wm	Napa Napa	61 100
Wm D	Colusa Monroeville	57 447
Wm R	Plumas Meadow Valley	62 932
PECKER		
Hariet	San Francisco San Francisco 10	67 287
Harriet	San Francisco San Francisco 10	67 287

California 1860 Census Index

Name	County Locale	M653 Roll	Page
PECKER			
Mary	San Francisco San Francisco	10 67	287
PECKET			
E	San Francisco San Francisco	5 67	536
PECKETT			
J L	Sonoma Petaluma	69	577
PECKHAM			
Asha R	San Francisco San Francisco	7 68	1402
B F	Sacramento Ward 1	63	104
E P	San Francisco San Francisco	12 67	367
George	Yuba Marysville	72	954
George W	Yuba Rose Bar	72	817
Robert F	Santa Cruz Pajaro	66	527
Sarah	Santa Cruz Pajaro	66	527
PECKINPON			
Robt*	Sonoma Washington	69	670
PECKINSSON			
Robt*	Sonoma Washington	69	670
PECO			
---	Fresno Twp 2	59	73
J M	Sutter Vernon	70	843
Pio	Amador Twp 5	55	332
PECOCK			
Thos	Amador Twp 2	55	319
PECON			
James	Nevada Rough &	61	407
PECORO			
James*	Nevada Rough &	61	407
PECULA			
B Mondsale*	El Dorado Diamond	58	803
PECUNDO			
---	San Bernardino S Timate	64	698
---	San Bernardino S Timate	64	699
---	San Bernardino S Timate	64	712
---	San Bernardino S Timate	64	721
---	San Bernardino S Timate	64	736
---*	San Bernardino S Timate	64	734
PED			
Robert*	Mendocino Little L	60	837
PEDANCES			
Francis	Monterey San Juan	60	974
PEDDLEFORD			
A F	San Joaquin Castoria	64	902
B A	Mendocino Big Rvr	60	845
PEDDLER			
George	San Joaquin Elkhorn	64	965
Margt	San Francisco San Francisco	9 68	968
PEDDLN			
H	Yolo Washington	72	603
PEDEGRASS			
Harry B	Siskiyou Yreka	69	178
PEDENBOYL			
Henry*	Placer Virginia	62	661
PEDERS			
Hermann	San Francisco San Francisco	2 67	793
PEDFORT			
Henry	San Francisco San Francisco	2 67	689
PEDIC			
James	Marin Bolinas	60	745
PEDIE			
James	Marin Bolinas	60	745
PEDISTO			
Joseph*	Calaveras Twp 9	57	372
PEDLAR			
John	Placer Dutch Fl	62	725
PEDLER			
Franklin	Yolo Cottonwood	72	660
Jones	El Dorado Mud Springs	58	974
Mike	El Dorado White Oaks	58	1006
Sarah	Yolo Cottonwoood	72	660
Thos	Placer Dutch Fl	62	715
PEDNEGER			
James*	Nevada Bridgeport	61	471
PEDNIGER			
James	Nevada Bridgeport	61	471
PEDRAGGINI			
Lewis	Marin S Antoni	60	710
PEDREGGINE			
Lewis	Marin S Antoni	60	710
PEDRICANO			
Maria	Napa Napa	61	115
PEDRICK			
William	San Francisco San Francisco	11 67	143
PEDRO			
---	Amador Twp 2	55	282
---	Los Angeles Los Angeles	59	389
---	Los Angeles San Gabriel	59	411
---	Los Angeles San Gabriel	59	414
---	Los Angeles San Gabriel	59	423
---	Los Angeles Santa Ana	59	442
---	Los Angeles Santa Ana	59	445
---	Los Angeles San Juan	59	462
---	Los Angeles San Juan	59	475
PEDRO			
---	Los Angeles San Juan	59	477
---	Los Angeles Los Angeles	59	517
---	Mariposa Twp 1	60	645
---	Monterey San Juan	60	1000
---	Monterey S Antoni	60	969
---	Monterey S Antoni	60	971
---	Monterey S Antoni	60	972
---	Monterey San Juan	60	974
---	Nevada Bridgeport	61	471
---	San Bernardino Santa Inez	64	143
---	San Bernardino Santa Barbara	64	204
---	San Bernardino Santa Ba	64	219
---	San Bernardino S Buenav	64	220
---	San Bernardino San Bernadino	64	669
---	San Bernardino San Bernardino	64	678
---	San Bernardino San Bernardino	64	679
---	San Bernardino San Bernardino	64	682
---	San Bernardino S Timate	64	692
---	San Bernardino S Timate	64	695
---	San Bernardino S Timate	64	696
---	San Bernardino S Timate	64	697
---	San Bernardino S Timate	64	698
---	San Bernardino S Timate	64	699
---	San Bernardino S Timate	64	700
---	San Bernardino S Timate	64	704
---	San Bernardino S Timate	64	705
---	San Bernardino S Timate	64	707
---	San Bernardino S Timate	64	708
---	San Bernardino S Timate	64	711
---	San Bernardino S Timate	64	714
---	San Bernardino S Timate	64	715
---	San Bernardino S Timate	64	721
---	San Bernardino S Timate	64	724
---	San Bernardino S Timate	64	725
---	San Bernardino S Timate	64	726
---	San Bernardino S Timate	64	727
---	San Bernardino S Timate	64	729
---	San Bernardino S Timate	64	730
---	San Bernardino S Timate	64	731
---	San Bernardino S Timate	64	732
---	San Bernardino S Timate	64	734
---	San Bernardino S Timate	64	739
---	San Bernardino S Timate	64	740
---	San Bernardino S Timate	64	741
---	San Bernardino S Timate	64	744
---	San Bernardino S Timate	64	745
---	San Bernardino S Timate	64	747
---	San Bernardino S Timate	64	748
---	San Bernardino S Timate	64	749
---	San Bernardino S Timate	64	753
---	San Bernardino S Timate	64	755
---	San Diego San Diego	64	773
---	San Diego S Luis R	64	782
---	San Diego S Luis R	64	783
---	San Diego Temecula	64	787
---	San Diego Temecula	64	788
---	San Diego Temecula	64	799
---	San Diego Temecula	64	803
---	San Diego Temecula	64	805
---	San Diego Agua Caliente	64	848
---	San Diego Agua Caliente	64	860
---	San Diego Agua Caliente	64	863
---	San Diego Agua Caliente	64	864
---	San Luis Obispo San Luis Obispo	65	32
---	San Mateo Twp 2	65	134
---	Santa Clara Santa Clara	65	462
---	Tulara Twp 1	71	121
---	Tulara Twp 3	71	55
---	Tulara Twp 3	71	57
---	Tulara Twp 3	71	66
---	Tulara Twp 3	71	72
---	Tulara Twp 2	71	8
---	Yuba Marysville	72	963
---*	Mariposa Twp 1	60	645
Anastasi	Fresno Twp 1	59	33
Antone	Siskiyou Yreka	69	147
Don	Tulara Twp 1	71	113
Hawela	Yuba Bear Rvr	72	1016
Ivan	Tulara Visalia	71	5
John	San Francisco San Francisco	3 67	75
Jose	San Diego Temecula	64	784
Jose	San Diego Temecula	64	801
Juan	Los Angeles Elmonte	59	255
Juan	San Bernardino Santa Inez	64	145
Juan	San Diego San Diego	64	775
Juan	San Diego S Luis R	64	779
Juan	San Diego Agua Caliente	64	818
Juan	San Diego Agua Caliente	64	829
Juan	San Diego Agua Caliente	64	864
Juan	Tulara Twp 2	71	5
Manuel	Alameda Brooklyn	55	149
Torras	San Bernardino Santa Barbara	64	155
PEDROLI			
Gyorano	San Joaquin Oneal	64	933
PEDRON			
Arthur	Tuolumne Twp 5	71	507
PEDRONCINI			
Basilio	San Francisco San Francisco	2 67	687
PEDRONICO			
Andress	Los Angeles Los Angeles	59	491
PEDRORENA			
---	San Diego Agua Caliente	64	842
Miguel	San Diego San Diego	64	764
PEDROW			
M	San Mateo Twp 3	65	74
PEDRUCY			
S*	San Francisco San Francisco	5 67	524
PEDULON			
Ami*	Calaveras Twp 5	57	145
PEDURN			
Charles*	Yuba Fosters	72	835
PEDUTON			
Ami*	Calaveras Twp 5	57	145
PEE A			
---	Sierra Twp 5	66	932
PEE			
---	Amador Twp 5	55	366
---	Calaveras Twp 8	57	84
---	San Francisco San Francisco	4 68	1186
---	Sierra Cox'S Bar	66	951
---	Sierra Downieville	66	986
---	Tuolumne Green Springs	71	517
---	Yolo Slate Ra	72	708
A*	Sierra Twp 5	66	932
Robert	Mendocino Little L	60	837
Sung	Mariposa Twp 3	60	620
Tung*	Calaveras Twp 6	57	169
PEEBE			
Joseph	Sierra La Porte	66	789
PEEBLER			
Jane*	San Francisco San Francisco	9 68	1015
PEEBLES			
J L	Butte Eureka	56	647
W	Trinity Oregon G	70	1009
PEED			
Frank	Plumas Meadow Valley	62	912
PEEG			
Peter	Siskiyou Klamath	69	95
PEEHOUR			
John	Tuolumne Twp 2	71	321
PEEK			
Charles N	San Mateo Twp 1	65	68
Edward T	Santa Cruz Watsonville	66	535
Jepe D	San Francisco San Francisco	4 68	1114
Nathan R*	Placer Ophirville	62	653
Ong	El Dorado Salmon Falls	58	1066
P N	Amador Twp 3	55	380
Smith	Santa Clara San Jose	65	394
William	Calaveras Twp 6	57	132
PEEKEHAM			
James	Marin Novato	60	738
PEEKHAM			
James	Marin Novato	60	738
PEEL			
Bolard	Yuba Marysville	72	940
Bosard	Yuba Marysville	72	940
H	Siskiyou Callahan	69	7
Jno	San Francisco San Francisco	9 68	1009
John J L	Plumas Quincy	62	935
T T	Sacramento Ward 3	63	487
Wm	Mariposa Twp 3	60	560
Wm	Napa Napa	61	100
PEELATON			
Ami*	Calaveras Twp 6	57	145
PEELER			
---	Yuba Linda Twp	72	982
J B	Sierra Twp 7	66	909
PEELIR			
J B*	Sierra Forest C	66	909
PEELY			
Edwd	San Francisco San Francisco	1 68	896
PEEN			
---	Nevada Rough &	61	436
Derry*	Mariposa Twp 3	60	621
Francisco*	Calaveras Twp 6	57	125
PEEPEY			
A S*	Nevada Eureka	61	369
PEEPLES			
C T	Sonoma Washington	69	669
PEEPLL			
D C*	Nevada Eureka	61	379
PEEPNICKER			
Henry	Tuolumne Sonora	71	191
PEER			
John	Placer Michigan	62	840
T A	Tehama Tehama	70	949
Thomas*	Mariposa Twp 3	60	606
PEERA			
Jm H	Sutter Sutter	70	810
PEERCE			
J W*	San Francisco San Francisco	5 67	533
PEERS			
Alex	Santa Clara San Jose	65	333

Name	County Locale	M653 RollPage
PEERS		
Derry*	Mariposa Twp 3	60 621
L	Santa Clara Santa Clara	65 515
PEERSON		
George	Tuolumne Twp 6	71 532
PEES		
P M	Siskiyou Klamath	69 84
PEESE		
James	San Mateo Twp 2	65 111
PEESEE		
Frank	Mariposa Twp 3	60 559
PEESSLL		
D C*	Nevada Eureka	61 379
PEET		
Francis	Mariposa Twp 3	60 606
Thomas*	Mariposa Twp 3	60 606
PEETRO		
James	Tulara Keeneysburg	71 47
PEEVEY		
D C	Siskiyou Cottonwoood	69 106
PEFFEINS		
Peter	Placer Dutch Fl	62 730
PEFFER		
Fredrick	Plumas Quincy	62 956
George	Los Angeles Los Angeles	59 344
PEFFIER		
Dominich	Yuba Fosters	72 835
PEFFIN		
Chas	Placer Dutch Fl	62 720
Dominick	Yuba Foster B	72 835
PEFFREY		
E*	Nevada Grass Valley	61 169
PEFLEIR		
J M	Santa Clara Santa Clara	65 490
PEG LEG		
---	Fresno Twp 2	59 20
PEG		
---	Fresno Twp 1	59 80
---	Trinity Lewiston	70 964
PEGAMALL		
John	Mariposa Coulterville	60 678
PEGARD		
C	Butte Bidwell	56 714
PEGER		
Elizabeth	Calaveras Twp 5	57 220
PEGG		
Lewis	Sierra Cox'S Bar	66 951
PEGGS		
Catharine	San Francisco San Francisco 9	68 994
Chatharine	San Francisco San Francisco 9	68 994
Rosanna	San Francisco San Francisco 10	230 67
PEGIRA		
J	Nevada Grass Valley	61 187
PEGNENNO		
---	Tulara Twp 1	71 118
PEGO		
Estapheu	Mariposa Twp 3	60 545
PEGOTT		
Robert	Nevada Bloomfield	61 529
PEGRAMALL		
John*	Mariposa Coulterville	60 678
PEGUENNO		
---	Tulara Visalia	71 118
PEGUENOT		
E*	San Francisco San Francisco 2	67 699
PEH		
Tung	El Dorado Georgetown	58 692
PEHET		
Alex	Del Norte Crescent	58 635
PEHHAM		
J M*	San Bernardino San Bernadino	64 628
PEHLPS		
Jeremiah	Los Angeles Elmonte	59 248
PEHNABB		
Gustavus*	Calaveras Twp 7	57 12
Jacob	Calaveras Twp 7	57 12
PEHNABLE		
Gustavus*	Calaveras Twp 7	57 12
Jacob*	Calaveras Twp 7	57 12
PEIATTII		
C*	Santa Clara Burnett	65 256
PEIATTU		
C*	Santa Clara Burnett	65 256
PEICE		
E*	Nevada Eureka	61 375
PEICELY		
Amy	Yuba Marysville	72 899
PEICON		
Jonas	Nevada Rough &	61 398
PEILER		
John*	San Francisco San Francisco 2	67 683
Oscar	Placer Iona Hills	62 880
PEIN		
J N	Del Norte Crescent	58 640

Name	County Locale	M653 RollPage
PEINE		
S C	El Dorado Kelsey	581146
PEINLEY		
Kena	Alameda Oakland	55 26
PEINO		
Aicholat	Amador Township	55 467
Nicholas	Amador Twp 1	55 467
PEIR		
H	Santa Clara Redwood	65 444
PEIRCE		
---	Mariposa Twp 3	60 556
A C S	Butte Kimshaw	56 595
Alfred	Alameda Oakland	55 42
C	Nevada Nevada	61 270
Chas	Butte Oregon	56 618
Geo	Butte Oregon	56 624
Geo E	Butte Oregon	56 634
Gudhik	El Dorado Georgetown	58 683
Isaac	Placer Sacramento	62 644
Isaac	Santa Cruz Santa Cruz	66 620
J M	San Francisco San Francisco 5	67 535
J W	Solano Suisan	69 206
Jno	Butte Oregon	56 624
Jno B	Alameda Oakland	55 37
John	El Dorado Placerville	58 932
John	Tulara Visalia	71 3
John*	Napa Napa	61 81
Lewellyn	Tuolumne Shawsfla	71 401
M	Butte Oregon	56 624
M	El Dorado Placerville	58 876
M	Nevada Eureka	61 347
M*	Butte Oregon	56 624
O	San Francisco San Francisco 4	681231
Susan	Placer Ophirville	62 655
William	Tulara Twp 2	71 2
Wm	Alameda Brooklyn	55 137
Wm	Yuba Slate Ro	72 684
PEIRNISH		
Louis	San Francisco San Francisco 4	681124
PEIRSON		
Arthur C	Siskiyou Yreka	69 178
Barnard	San Francisco San Francisco 5	67 477
Cordilia	Butte Ophir	56 761
D M	El Dorado Kelsey	581135
E	El Dorado Placerville	58 873
Elizabeth*	Stanislaus Empire	70 726
F M	Butte Kimshaw	56 595
Geo	Butte Oro	56 673
George W	Siskiyou Yreka	69 178
H	Sutter Sutter	70 815
Jno D	Butte Kimshaw	56 579
John	El Dorado Placerville	58 873
Phineas	Santa Cruz Santa Cruz	66 605
Phineus*	Santa Cruz Santa Cruz	66 605
R M	Butte Kimshaw	56 595
Thomas	Calaveras Twp 4	57 316
PEISER		
Eliza	San Francisco San Francisco 6	67 439
PEITCH		
Solomon	Sacramento Ward 1	63 61
PEITRONE		
Joseph	Marin Novato	60 736
PEIVER		
James	San Francisco San Francisco 4	681115
PEIW		
---	Placer Rattle Snake	62 629
PEJEN		
Theodore	Calaveras Twp 5	57 175
PEJER		
Theodore	Calaveras Twp 6	57 175
PEK		
---	San Francisco San Francisco 4	681174
---	San Francisco San Francisco 4	681184
Harar	San Luis Obispo San Luis Obispo 65	8
PEKE		
George	Colusa Muion	57 462
J D	Sierra Twp 7	66 874
Mary	Tehama Lassen	70 861
PEKKKKKKKKARE		
Miriam	Sacramento Ward 1	63 113
PEKO		
J J	Solano Suisan	69 204
PELAGOSA		
Dolores*	Santa Clara Alviso	65 413
PELAJOSA		
Dolores*	Santa Clara Alviso	65 413
PELCHER		
Jos	Sacramento Ward 1	63 51
M	El Dorado Casumnes	581173
Samuel	El Dorado Gold Hill	581097
PELECAN		
Jacob	El Dorado Salmon Falls	581050
PELEG		
C	Amador Twp 5	55 361
PELEGAN		
John	Amador Twp 4	55 248

Name	County Locale	M653 RollPage
PELEGAN		
Oliver*	Sierra Twp 7	66 913
PELEGRINO		
---	San Diego Agua Caliente	64 825
PELENGER		
E M	San Francisco San Francisco 4	681121
H	San Francisco San Francisco 6	67 464
PELERSON		
George*	San Francisco San Francisco 9	681097
PELESSIER		
Joseph	Monterey Pajaro	601013
PELESTRE		
Rafael	Los Angeles Los Angeles	59 389
PELETEAUX		
Edwd	San Francisco San Francisco 2	67 698
PELETS		
Maria	San Diego Agua Caliente	64 818
PELETTE		
Julian	Los Angeles Los Angeles	59 342
PELEY		
Henry	Tuolumne Columbia	71 357
PELGARIE		
Wan	El Dorado Gold Hill	581098
PELHAM		
E A	Shasta Shasta	66 658
W A	Nevada Rough &	61 403
W H	Nevada Rough &	61 403
PELIA		
Frank	Sierra Downieville	661019
John	Colusa Butte Crk	57 464
PELIAN		
Thomas	Calaveras Twp 10	57 292
PELIAR		
Thomas	Calaveras Twp 10	57 292
PELICAN		
B	San Francisco San Francisco 12	395 67
PELIGAN		
Oliver*	Sierra Twp 7	66 913
PELINGE		
Wm S	San Francisco San Francisco 10	321 67
PELINGER		
E M	San Francisco San Francisco 4	681121
H	San Francisco San Francisco 6	67 464
PELINGTIN		
Walter	Sacramento Granite	63 245
PELIT		
John*	Butte Mountain	56 741
Peter*	Butte Mountain	56 741
PELKEY		
Joseph	Napa Yount	61 46
PELL		
J A	San Francisco San Francisco 3	67 42
Martha W	San Francisco San Francisco 12	361 67
Mick	Sierra Twp 7	66 910
Samuel	Colusa Monroeville	57 449
Seba	San Francisco San Francisco 12	389 67
Thos J	San Francisco San Francisco 10	357 67
Unche	Placer Rattle Snake	62 604
William	Contra Costa Twp 3	57 613
PELLA		
Alexander	Contra Costa Twp 2	57 543
PELLAN		
Joseph	Yuba New York	72 722
PELLAR		
Joseph	Yuba New York	72 722
PELLARD		
Sarah R	Sierra Twp 5	66 924
PELLATON		
Eugene	Calaveras Twp 7	57 1
PELLATOU		
Eujene	Calaveras Twp 7	57 1
PELLECHE		
Pelipi*	Marin Cortemad	60 790
PELLECHI		
Pelipi*	Marin Cortemad	60 790
PELLEKER		
Harry*	Nevada Bloomfield	61 514
PELLEREN		
Frank	Nevada Bloomfield	61 522
PELLERTON		
Ami*	Calaveras Twp 6	57 145
PELLESSIER		
Joseph	Monterey Pajaro	601013
PELLET		
H A	Napa Napa	61 86
Julia	Del Norte Crescent	58 622
Saml	Napa Napa	61 86
PELLETER		
Julius	Nevada Bloomfield	61 516
PELLETIER		
Harry*	Nevada Bloomfield	61 514

Name	County Locale	M653 RollPage
PELLETRER		
John	San Francisco San Francisco	4 681 156
PELLETRN		
John*	San Francisco San Francisco	4 681 156
PELLEY		
W D	Sierra Eureka	661 048
PELLIEIOX		
Emma*	San Francisco San Francisco	6 67 425
PELLIER		
Francisca	S Buenav	64 209
	San Bernardino	
Louis P	Alameda Brooklyn	55 169
Peter	Alameda Brooklyn	55 169
PELLIEUX		
Emma	San Francisco San Francisco	6 67 425
PELLIEWX		
Emma*	San Francisco San Francisco	6 67 425
PELLING		
Sidney	San Francisco San Francisco	2 67 573
PELLISIER		
John B	San Francisco San Francisco	11 133
		67
PELLIT		
C*	Sacramento Brighton	63 192
R H	Calaveras Twp 9	57 403
PELLITER		
Julius*	Nevada Bloomfield	61 516
PELLIUOX		
Emma*	San Francisco San Francisco	6 67 425
PELLMAN		
B*	Sacramento Lee	63 214
PELLNAE		
John*	Mariposa Coulterville	60 676
PELLON		
Cassimer A	Calaveras Twp 4	57 339
John*	San Francisco San Francisco	1 68 860
Latrobe R	Yuba Suida	72 988
Luis	Santa Clara Almaden	65 267
Satrobe R*	Yuba Linda	72 988
PELLOW		
K B	Santa Clara Gilroy	65 242
PELLOWMAN		
W	El Dorado Diamond	58 809
PELLSE		
Charles*	Alameda Brooklyn	55 111
PELLTIER		
James	Yuba Long Bar	72 751
PELLUAO		
John	Mariposa Coulterville	60 676
PELLUER		
Charles	San Luis Obispo San Luis Obispo	65 36
PELLUTON		
Ami*	Calaveras Twp 6	57 145
PELMER		
M	Calaveras Twp 9	57 379
P	Calaveras Twp 9	57 379
PELO		
Andrew D	Tuolumne Big Oak	71 140
PELON		
---	San Bernardino Santa Barbara	64 200
PELONA		
---	Mendocino Round Va	60 886
Rigina	Santa Clara San Jose	65 304
PELONIA		
---	San Bernardino S Timate	64 695
PELOPEN		
Felin	Mariposa Coulterville	60 688
Felix	Mariposa Coulterville	60 688
Ielire	Mariposa Coulterville	60 688
PELOYON		
Felix*	Mariposa Coulterville	60 688
PELSTIN		
Martin*	Placer Iona Hills	62 887
PELT		
D F Van	San Francisco San Francisco	4 681 142
E	Mariposa Twp 1	60 633
Edwin	Sacramento San Joaquin	63 348
Everett	Sonoma Santa Rosa	69 423
Van	Siskiyou Yreka	69 184
PELTER		
Joseph	Amador Twp 3	55 389
PELTERS		
R*	Sacramento Cosumnes	63 410
PELTERSON		
P*	Mariposa Twp 3	60 558
PELTICE		
Alex	Nevada Bloomfield	61 518
PELTIER		
Stephen	Amador Twp 2	55 297
PELTON		
E	El Dorado Kelsey	581 151
Henry	Calaveras Twp 4	57 299
Henry	Calaveras Twp 4	57 300
Henry	Los Angeles Los Angeles	59 406
Henry T	San Joaquin Elkhorn	64 987
Horatra	El Dorado White Oaks	581 003

Name	County Locale	M653 RollPage
PELTON		
Lester	Yolo Slate Ra	72 688
Lester	Yuba Slate Ro	72 688
P W	El Dorado Mud Springs	58 987
S B	El Dorado White Oaks	581 003
S W	El Dorado White Oaks	581 004
PELTREAN		
A	Trinity Taylor'S	701 036
PELTSETT		
William	Tuolumne Twp 1	71 193
PELTY		
Alex	Butte Hamilton	56 517
E*	Mariposa Twp 1	60 633
PELUMO		
Joseph*	Calaveras Twp 8	57 103
PELWELL		
Adam	El Dorado Mud Springs	58 970
PELY		
Wm	Santa Clara San Jose	65 289
PEM		
---	Sacramento Ward 1	63 56
PEMBERTON		
James	Tulara Visalia	71 26
Jasper	Tulara Twp 2	71 28
Jef	Placer Auburn	62 588
John	Amador Twp 4	55 249
John	Tulara Twp 2	71 26
Thomas	San Joaquin Douglass	64 923
PEMBORTON		
James*	Tulara Twp 2	71 26
PEMBROKE		
Jas	Sacramento Ward 1	63 48
PEMDEL		
J L*	Sacramento Granite	63 248
PEMEL		
Walter	Calaveras Twp 9	57 384
PEMEN		
Joseph	Sierra Twp 7	66 909
PEMINRA		
---	San Bernardino San Bernadino	64 681
PEMMINGTUN		
Joel*	Calaveras Twp 8	57 62
PEMMY		
Alfred	Mariposa Coulterville	60 677
PEMNING		
Alfred*	Mariposa Coulterville	60 677
PEMOLT		
W	Santa Clara San Jose	65 335
PEMROCK		
Ann	Sacramento Natonia	63 275
PEMRY		
H*	Siskiyou Scott Va	69 38
PEMSA		
Jaquin	Alameda Brooklyn	55 172
PEMSDILL		
E B*	Nevada Bridgeport	61 482
PEN		
---	Calaveras Twp 5	57 219
---	El Dorado Georgetown	58 745
---	Mariposa Twp 1	60 651
---	Monterey Monterey	60 959
---	Sacramento Ward 1	63 56
---	Sierra Twp 7	66 886
---	Sierra Twp 7	66 927
---	Sierra Downieville	66 983
---	Tuolumne Twp 5	71 512
---	Tuolumne Knights	71 529
Kin	Sierra Downieville	66 983
Lee	Butte Bidwell	56 720
Lei	El Dorado Greenwood	58 731
Ling*	Butte Ophir	56 808
PENA		
Amado	Santa Clara Almaden	65 262
C	Solano Fremont	69 378
Carmel	Los Angeles Los Angeles	59 309
D	Solano Vacaville	69 325
Felipe	San Bernardino Santa Barbara	64 160
Feresadela	Monterey San Juan	601 003
Gudalupe	San Francisco San Francisco	2 67 695
Jose	San Bernardino Santa Barbara	64 153
Ramon	San Luis Obispo San Luis Obispo	65 36
PENADA		
Victor	Monterey San Juan	601 002
PENAGE		
J	Siskiyou Scott Va	69 58
PENAGOT		
---	San Diego Agua Caliente	64 863
PENAL		
---	Butte Ophir	56 771
PENALDS		
F*	Calaveras Twp 9	57 404
T	Calaveras Twp 9	57 404
PENALONG		
---	Nevada Bloomfield	61 511
PENALOUG		
---*	Nevada Bloomfield	61 511

Name	County Locale	M653 RollPage
PENAN		
Chas	Santa Clara Santa Clara	65 480
PENANCE		
A J*	Placer Todds Va	62 789
PENARED		
P	Trinity Browns C	70 984
PENARO		
Hosea*	Calaveras Twp 9	57 357
PENAS		
Lorenzo	Santa Clara San Jose	65 301
PENASS		
Samuell	Amador Twp 5	55 357
PENBELLAN		
Wm	Butte Oregon	56 640
PENBERTHY		
I	Tuolumne Twp 3	71 442
J	Tuolumne Jamestown	71 442
PENBROOK		
---	Napa Clear Lake	61 123
PENCE		
John	Napa Napa	61 81
M R *	Tuolumne Big Oak	71 154
M*	Butte Oregon	56 624
Peter	Amador Twp 5	55 348
T A	Amador Twp 5	55 342
PENCELS		
Ellen	Monterey Monterey	60 950
PENCEST		
A	San Francisco San Francisco	4 681 156
PENCHEL		
Emma	San Francisco San Francisco	4 681 149
PENCHU		
Fong*	San Francisco San Francisco	4 681 180
PENCIL		
P	Siskiyou Scott Va	69 53
PENCIR		
C	Sierra Twp 7	66 881
PENCOTT		
Filix	Mendocino Calpella	60 813
PENCRE		
Pedre*	Alameda Oakland	55 7
PENCUS		
H	San Francisco San Francisco	6 67 449
PEND		
Charles H	Los Angeles San Jose	59 281
PENDAGRAP		
M S*	Nevada Nevada	61 317
PENDAGRASS		
M S	Nevada Nevada	61 317
PENDAL		
J	Amador Twp 6	55 427
PENDALS		
Nichol*	San Joaquin O'Neal	641 004
PENDANT		
Mon*	Nevada Bridgeport	61 452
Mori	Nevada Bridgeport	61 452
PENDARDEST		
R	Siskiyou Scott Ri	69 77
PENDE		
John	El Dorado White Oaks	581 017
Joseph	El Dorado White Oaks	581 017
PENDEGAS		
Michael	San Francisco San Francisco	1 68 900
PENDEGAST		
P J	Calaveras Twp 9	57 387
PENDEGRASS		
Eliza	San Francisco San Francisco	2 67 644
Geo	San Francisco San Francisco	1 68 817
J N	Yolo Cache Crk	72 596
W W	Yolo Cache Crk	72 593
PENDEL		
August	San Francisco San Francisco	11 124
		67
PENDELON		
Henry	Mariposa Twp 3	60 548
PENDER		
August*	Nevada Bloomfield	61 516
John	Shasta Horsetown	66 692
John H	Yuba Marysville	72 881
M	San Joaquin Stockton	641 092
Macker	Alameda Brooklyn	55 143
Thos R	Amador Twp 6	55 434
William	Yuba Marysville	72 882
William A	Sierra St Louis	66 812
PENDERGAST		
W	San Francisco San Francisco	5 67 532
PENDERGRASS		
William	Calaveras Twp 6	57 143
William	Solano Vacaville	69 351
William*	Calaveras Twp 5	57 143
PENDERGRAST		
Ellen	San Francisco San Francisco	8 681 269
J	San Francisco San Francisco	5 67 490
Michael	Placer Forest H	62 800
Thos	San Francisco San Francisco	9 681 090
PENDERGROSS		
William	Calaveras Twp 5	57 143

California 1860 Census Index

Name	County Locale	M653 RollPage
PENDERGROST		
J C	Santa Clara Santa Clara	65 477
PENDERINI		
Jesus	Los Angeles San Pedro	59 478
PENDERUIS		
Jesus	Los Angeles San Pedro	59 478
PENDERYROND		
William	Calaveras Twp 6	57 143
PENDEY		
Geo	Yolo Cottonwoood	72 646
PENDIER		
Gregorio	Contra Costa Twp 1	57 491
PENDIN		
Joseph	Yolo Merritt	72 578
PENDLE		
W F	Sacramento Cosumnes	63 393
PENDLEBURY		
Isaac*	Yuba Rose Bar	72 810
Thomas*	Yuba Rose Bar	72 799
PENDLELURY		
Isaac*	Yuba Rose Bar	72 810
Thomas	Yuba Rose Bar	72 799
PENDLEMD		
George	Siskiyou Shasta Rvr	69 111
PENDLEOTN		
George A	San Diego San Diego	64 763
PENDLETON		
B F	Amador Twp 4	55 255
Elisha	Butte Hamilton	56 525
Eliza	Nevada Bloomfield	61 512
G E	Sierra Twp 7	66 886
H	Tuolumne Twp 4	71 169
I	Nevada Nevada	61 292
J	Nevada Nevada	61 292
James	San Joaquin Elkhorn	64 985
John	Shasta Shasta	66 757
L	Tehama Lassen	70 872
L J	Sierra Twp 7	66 914
Sofronia	Santa Clara Gilroy	65 232
U	Tuolumne Jacksonville	71 169
William C	San Joaquin Douglass	64 926
PENDLINANE		
L	Santa Clara San Jose	65 350
PENDLUND		
George	Siskiyou Shasta Rvr	69 111
PENDO		
Govani	Tuolumne Twp 5	71 498
Govoni	Tuolumne Chinese	71 498
PENDOLA		
B	Mariposa Twp 3	60 555
Bantislo	San Bernardino Santa Barbara	64 177
Bautislo*	Santa Barbara	64 177
	San Bernardino	
Steven	Tuolumne Chinese	71 499
PENDORA		
Lorenza	Calaveras Twp 8	57 96
PENDORO		
Dominic	Tuolumne Twp 5	71 498
PENDRO		
Lefefsen*	Mariposa Twp 3	60 547
Peouse	Mariposa Twp 1	60 669
Sefefpen*	Mariposa Twp 3	60 547
Tefefpen	Mariposa Twp 3	60 547
PENE		
---	Plumas Quincy	62 949
PENEAOR		
Patricia*	Monterey San Juan	60 996
PENEGAND		
Alfonso	Calaveras Twp 9	57 347
PENEGO		
M L	San Francisco San Francisco 5	67 533
PENENAN		
A	El Dorado Coloma	581116
PENER		
E B	San Francisco San Francisco 2	67 707
PENERIL		
I W	Amador Twp 2	55 303
J W	Amador Twp 2	55 303
PENET		
Jeremiah	Santa Cruz Soquel	66 579
PENEX		
Jeremiah	Santa Cruz Soquel	66 579
PENEY		
Gaiging*	El Dorado Greenwood	58 723
PENFIELD		
Lewis	Plumas Quincy	62 958
T**	San Francisco San Francisco 3	67 5
Wm	El Dorado Georgetown	58 745
PENFOLD		
John	Alameda Oakland	55 34
Stephen	Alameda Oakland	55 34
PENG FOO		
Sam*	Yuba Long Bar	72 756
PENG		
---	Amador Twp 2	55 262
---	Amador Twp 2	55 292

Name	County Locale	M653 RollPage
PENG		
---	Calaveras Twp 8	57 107
---	El Dorado Coloma	581076
---	Sacramento Ward 1	63 66
---	Sierra Downieville	66 993
---	Yolo Slate Ra	72 710
---	Yolo Slate Ra	72 715
---	Yuba Slate Ro	72 710
---	Yuba Long Bar	72 756
---	Yuba Long Bar	72 763
---	Yuba Long Bar	72 767
Ah	Calaveras Twp 7	57 30
Ah	Calaveras Twp 7	57 32
Ah	Calaveras Twp 7	57 33
Sam*	Yuba Long Bar	72 760
PENGDLEY		
J*	Nevada Grass Valley	61 207
PENGER		
Chas	Mariposa Twp 3	60 594
PENGIN		
Antoine	Calaveras Twp 8	57 88
PENGRA		
W	Siskiyou Klamath	69 84
PENGSA		
W	Siskiyou Klamath	69 84
PENHELLAN		
Wm	Butte Oregon	56 640
PENHERT		
Benordire*	Placer Auburn	62 569
Benordue*	Placer Auburn	62 569
PENIA		
Carmel	San Mateo Twp 2	65 114
Francisco	Monterey San Juan	601002
Mouicha	Yuba Marysville	72 918
PENICAARTE		
---	Tulara Twp 2	71 31
PENICARTE		
---*	Tulara Yule Rvr	71 31
PENICK		
D	Sutter Yuba	70 767
PENILLEU		
Eugene*	San Francisco San Francisco 11	140
		67
PENIN		
Mary*	San Francisco San Francisco 4	681128
PENINK		
Charles*	San Mateo Twp 3	65 86
PENIR		
D	El Dorado Georgetown	58 704
PENJO		
F	Shasta Shasta	66 674
PENKE		
Christen*	Alameda Brooklyn	55 147
PENKENS		
L A	Sacramento Granite	63 227
W H	Nevada Grass Valley	61 177
PENKER		
Saml C	Calaveras Twp 6	57 126
PENKEY		
William	El Dorado Georgetown	58 693
PENKILT		
C*	Nevada Grass Valley	61 155
PENKITH		
C	Nevada Grass Valley	61 155
PENKITT		
C*	Nevada Grass Valley	61 155
PENKNEY		
W J	San Francisco San Francisco 5	67 534
PENKUS		
Louis	Tuolumne Twp 4	71 131
PENLAND		
Isaac R	Napa Hot Springs	61 17
PENLANT		
Isaac R*	Napa Hot Springs	61 17
PENM		
Mary*	San Francisco San Francisco 4	681128
PENMAN		
Geo*	Butte Oro	56 678
Robert*	Plumas Quincy	62 991
Saml*	Sonoma Vallejo	69 624
PENMAY		
Saml	Sonoma Vallejo	69 624
PENMOREAN		
Delia	San Francisco San Francisco 4	681127
PENMORIAN		
Delia	San Francisco San Francisco 4	681127
PENN		
---	Sierra Whiskey	66 849
E A	Tuolumne Big Oak	71 155
George	Shasta Shasta	66 760
Henry	Nevada Bridgeport	61 487
J	San Francisco San Francisco 5	67 540
James	Plumas Quincy	62 989
Jas	Sonoma Petaluma	69 568
Joseph	Napa Napa	61 68
Mary	San Francisco San Francisco 4	681128

Name	County Locale	M653 RollPage
PENNA		
---	Sonoma Bodega	69 542
Harriet	Amador Twp 1	55 470
PENNARD		
Jos*	San Francisco San Francisco 2	67 670
PENNAY		
Saml*	Sonoma Vallejo	69 624
PENNEB		
Harry*	Sacramento Ward 1	63 40
PENNEL		
Harry*	Sacramento Ward 1	63 40
PENNELE		
I C	Napa Napa	61 93
PENNELEA		
Mary*	Yuba Marysville	72 923
PENNELL		
A	El Dorado Georgetown	58 677
S T	San Francisco San Francisco 9	681054
W W	Calaveras Twp 9	57 366
Wm	Solano Suisan	69 211
PENNEPECKER		
Henry	Butte Mountain	56 741
PENNER		
Robert	San Francisco San Francisco 3	67 66
PENNERLA		
R	Nevada Grass Valley	61 158
PENNERLD		
R*	Nevada Grass Valley	61 158
PENNEY		
Jas T	San Francisco San Francisco 9	68 998
Lorenzo	Tuolumne Twp 2	71 289
Norman	Plumas Quincy	62 999
R H*	Tuolumne Shawsfla	71 404
R M	El Dorado Mud Springs	58 951
PENNEYBECKER		
W R	Butte Ophir	56 754
PENNEYBICKS		
W H	Butte Bidwell	56 729
PENNFEATHER		
Geo*	Butte Chico	56 567
PENNFIELD		
J V W	Nevada Nevada	61 240
PENNFOLD		
Jefsee C	Los Angeles Elmonte	59 256
John	Los Angeles Elmonte	59 256
PENNICKS		
M	Shasta Millvill	66 752
PENNIE		
---	San Diego Agua Caliente	64 865
James C	Los Angeles Los Angeles	59 309
William	San Francisco San Francisco 4	681171
PENNIGBECKER		
W R*	Butte Ophir	56 754
PENNIGTON		
Robert	Sonoma Bodega	69 523
PENNILIA		
Mary*	Yuba Marysville	72 923
PENNIMAN		
Nathaniel	Yuba Bear Rvr	721006
Thos	San Francisco San Francisco 1	68 931
PENNING		
Alfred*	Mariposa Coulterville	60 677
PENNINGS		
M	Nevada Grass Valley	61 156
PENNINGTON		
B	Siskiyou Scott Va	69 59
E H	San Francisco San Francisco 4	681110
G	Amador Twp 3	55 370
George	Tulara Visalia	71 106
Jocl*	Calaveras Twp 8	57 106
John	San Joaquin Stockton	641029
Joseph	Marin Tomales	60 721
Joseph	Tuolumne Twp 4	71 180
Samuel	Plumas Quincy	62 992
Wm	Trinity Lewiston	70 957
PENNISON		
Wm	Sacramento Ward 4	63 498
PENNIX		
E H	San Francisco San Francisco 5	67 504
Edward*	Yuba Marysville	72 957
George	Yuba Marysville	72 962
PENNOCK		
Ann	Sacramento Natonia	63 275
PENNOYER		
Alonzo	San Francisco San Francisco 1	68 892
John*	Sierra Twp 5	66 920
PENNY		
C G*	Nevada Grass Valley	61 196
Geo	Placer Secret R	62 619
George	Trinity Taylor'S	701036
H*	Siskiyou Scott Va	69 38
J D	San Francisco San Francisco 5	67 497
Jas	Sacramento Ward 4	63 567
Jas	San Francisco San Francisco 1	68 921
Jose	Sacramento Ward 1	63 110
L	Sacramento Sutter	63 291

Name	County Locale	M653 Roll	Page
PENNY			
Norton	Plumas Quincy	62	960
S S	Nevada Nevada	61	251
S V	Sacramento Ward 1	63	78
Thos*	Sacramento Ward 4	63	575
W M	Sacramento Granite	63	237
PENNYBACK			
John	Butte Bidwell	56	730
PENNYBECK			
George	Monterey Alisal	60	1038
PENNYBECKER			
George	Monterey Alisal	60	1038
George F*	Monterey Alisal	60	1038
PENNYBICKS			
W H	Butte Bidwell	56	729
PENNYCOOK			
Gas	Sacramento Ward 1	63	30
James	Tuolumne Twp 2	71	281
Jas	Sacramento Ward 1	63	30
Jas	Sacramento Ward 4	63	527
PENNYMAN			
Arthur	Contra Costa Twp 2	57	560
Hiram	Contra Costa Twp 3	57	592
PENNYPACKER			
J J	Sonoma Petaluma	69	577
PENNYSON			
Wm	Sacramento Ward 1	63	87
PENNYWEALTHIE			
Geo	Nevada Nevada	61	270
PENNYWEATHER			
Geo	Nevada Nevada	61	270
PENOCH			
John	Santa Clara San Jose	65	387
PENOCIA			
Eso*	Sierra Downieville	66	987
PENOLDS			
Adaline*	Siskiyou Shasta Rvr	69	117
PENOLM			
Joseph	Yolo Merritt	72	578
PENON			
Jean	Santa Clara Almaden	65	270
PENOR			
Aiyst*	Mariposa Twp 1	60	648
Aryst	Mariposa Twp 1	60	648
Augst	Mariposa Twp 1	60	648
PENORAMA			
H	Santa Clara San Jose	65	359
PENOS			
Franciss	Monterey San Juan	60	988
PENOSA			
Jaquin	Alameda Washington	55	172
PENOST			
Paul B	Yuba Marysville	72	890
PENOTTIAS			
Ramon	Placer Secret R	62	608
PENPRAISE			
P	Nevada Eureka	61	375
PENRO			
Jacomo*	San Francisco San Francisco 11		124
		67	
PENROSE			
Elijah	Nevada Bloomfield	61	525
Eyrus	Sierra Excelsior	66	1033
Isaac	Nevada Bridgeport	61	452
John	Nevada Bloomfield	61	526
Richard	Nevada Bridgeport	61	480
W	El Dorado Coloma	58	1114
PENSAGERO			
Catherina	Calaveras Twp 6	57	151
PENSAIN			
Jno J*	San Francisco San Francisco 10		345
		67	
PENSAYERS			
Catherine	Calaveras Twp 6	57	151
PENSCIA			
Eso	Sierra Downieville	66	987
PENSE			
Charles*	Alameda Brooklyn	55	111
Saml	Alameda Brooklyn	55	156
PENSHAW			
Henry	Siskiyou Yreka	69	147
PENSIGER			
Dan	San Francisco San Francisco 9	68	1102
PENSON			
D	Santa Clara Santa Clara	65	509
PENSR			
Alunzi	Calaveras Twp 6	57	124
PENT			
---	Calaveras Twp 5	57	204
Lenard	Placer Ophir	62	652
PENTACOSTA			
Magnil	Contra Costa Twp 1	57	494
PENTEL			
Conception	Tuolumne Sonora	71	219
Conciption	Tuolumne Twp 1	71	219
PENTENMEYER			
Adolph	Calaveras Twp 6	57	143

Name	County Locale	M653 Roll	Page
PENTER			
Henry	Amador Twp 2	55	298
Wm	El Dorado Mud Springs	58	989
PENTERMEYER			
Aadolph	Calaveras Twp 6	57	143
PENTERY			
Bernard	El Dorado Georgetown	58	676
PENTEY			
Sol	Amador Twp 2	55	298
PENTILO			
---	Tulara Keyesville	71	64
PENTISY			
Bernard	El Dorado Georgetown	58	676
PENTITO			
---	Tulara Twp 3	71	64
PENTON			
A	Tehama Moons	70	852
PENTWOOD			
J	Calaveras Twp 9	57	417
PENTZEA			
John	Placer Iona Hills	62	894
PENTZY			
Charles*	Calaveras Twp 4	57	340
PENUELEA			
Mary*	Yuba Marysville	72	923
PENUELLER			
A*	Butte Bidwell	56	723
PENWELL			
J C	Napa Napa	61	93
PENWELLER			
A	Butte Bidwell	56	723
PENWIX			
Edward*	Yuba Marysville	72	957
PENWRIGHT			
C J	Merced Twp 1	60	913
PENY			
B	Calaveras Twp 9	57	396
Fuson	Amador Twp 6	55	438
J*	Nevada Eureka	61	348
R H*	Sierra Twp 5	66	920
Robert	Calaveras Twp 5	57	207
Wm	Sonoma Sonoma	69	650
PENYA			
Rainonds	Calaveras Twp 6	57	134
PENZANGER			
J	Tuolumne Twp 2	71	327
PENZINGER			
J	Tuolumne Columbia	71	327
PENZIRE			
Amiel*	El Dorado Casumnes	58	1175
Arniel*	El Dorado Casumnes	58	1175
PEO			
---	San Bernardino S Timate	64	743
---	San Francisco San Francisco 11		144
		67	
---	Sierra La Porte	66	780
Robert*	Mendocino Little L	60	837
PEOBLES			
Jerome	Tuolumne Jamestown	71	470
PEOBODY			
M Y	Napa Hot Springs	61	2
PEOHE			
---	Tulara Twp 2	71	4
PEOHI			
---*	Tulara Visalia	71	4
PEOMAT			
W	Santa Clara Almaden	65	270
PEON			
---	Amador Twp 6	55	434
PEONA			
Guadalupe	San Diego Colorado	64	810
PEONCA			
Nicholas*	Amador Twp 4	55	241
PEONCE			
Nicholas*	Amador Twp 4	55	241
PEONE			
---	Amador Twp 1	55	503
PEONG			
---	El Dorado White Oaks	58	1025
---	El Dorado Diamond	58	797
PEOPLES			
Abraham	Tulara Keeneysburg	71	47
Andrew	Marin Tomales	60	716
Geo	Nevada Nevada	61	240
J	Nevada Nevada	61	240
Jno	Sacramento Ward 4	63	524
Thos	San Francisco San Francisco 2	67	778
PEOY			
---	Amador Twp 6	55	450
PEPE			
Francisco	Monterey Alisal	60	1035
PEPEON			
George	Contra Costa Twp 1	57	516
PEPER			
R	Yolo Putah	72	553
PEPES			
Ferdinand	San Francisco San Francisco 2	67	653

Name	County Locale	M653 Roll	Page
PEPETOE			
Isaac	Sonoma Santa Rosa	69	410
PEPHAM			
J M	San Bernardino San Bernadino	64	628
PEPIN			
J B	Sierra Twp 7	66	913
Sarah	Tuolumne Twp 5	71	502
PEPIO			
Palinoilo	Calaveras Twp 4	57	312
PEPIR			
N*	Yolo Putah	72	553
PEPPER			
Augustus	Placer Secret R	62	610
Charles	San Joaquin Elkhorn	64	971
Charles	Yolo Cache	72	637
E S	Sonoma Petaluma	69	579
Ed D	Sacramento Ward 1	63	80
Edd D	Sacramento Ward 1	63	80
G B	San Francisco San Francisco 9	68	958
G B	Yuba Fosters	72	837
G B	Yuba Fosters	72	838
Hart	Placer Auburn	62	580
Henry	Butte Oregon	56	636
J M	Sierra Whiskey	66	849
James	Sierra Pine Grove	66	819
James	Solano Vacaville	69	358
John	Yuba Marysville	72	962
John W	Sierra Whiskey	66	846
Manuel	Los Angeles Los Angeles	59	338
Shelby	Tulara Twp 3	71	49
Sophie	San Francisco San Francisco 9	68	1062
Thelby	Tulara Keeneysburg	71	49
Wm	Sacramento Ward 1	63	101
Wm	Sonoma Petaluma	69	552
PEPPERDINE			
---	San Mateo Twp 3	65	108
PEPPIN			
George	Sierra Twp 7	66	875
PEPPLE			
H	Shasta Millvill	66	751
PEQUE			
Edward*	San Francisco San Francisco 4	68	1218
PEQUINIA			
Jos	Amador Twp 3	55	380
PER			
---	Sierra Twp 5	66	948
PERA			
---	San Bernardino S Timate	64	729
Balvanada	Los Angeles Los Angeles	59	294
Pedro	Yuba Marysville	72	893
PERAFOLO			
Peter	Sonoma Petaluma	69	560
PERAIR			
Anto Victor	Twp 1	57	508
	Contra Costa		
PERAJJI			
Joseph*	Calaveras Twp 8	57	61
PERALDO			
Pablo	Napa Napa	61	114
PERALLA			
Cerano	Alameda Brooklyn	55	210
PERALTA			
Anfela	Alameda Oakland	55	56
Desidrio	Monterey San Juan	60	1002
Desidris*	Monterey San Juan	60	1002
Felipe	Los Angeles Santa Ana	59	448
Francisco	Alameda Brooklyn	55	99
Gertrudes	Los Angeles Santa Ana	59	450
Hosea A Artatl	Alameda Brooklyn	55	97
Hosea Artalito	Alameda Brooklyn	55	97
Ignatio	Alameda Brooklyn	55	105
Ignatis*	Alameda Brooklyn	55	105
Jesus	Los Angeles Los Nieto	59	438
Juan	Alameda Brooklyn	55	190
Juan	San Bernardino Santa Barbara	64	197
Juan	San Bernardino Santa Barbara	64	203
Julian	Los Angeles San Gabriel	59	412
Louisa	Santa Clara Santa Clara	65	478
Luis	Los Angeles Los Angeles	59	357
Miguel	Alameda Brooklyn	55	105
Nieves L	Los Angeles Santa Ana	59	449
Rafael	Los Angeles Santa Ana	59	450
Ramon	Los Angeles Los Nieto	59	438
Snaw	San Luis Obispo San Luis Obispo	65	37
Vecenta	Alameda Oakland	55	57
PERALTI			
Juan	Santa Cruz Watsonville	66	540
Maria	Santa Cruz Santa Cruz	66	607
PERALTO			
Luciano	Tulara Sinks Te	71	43
Maria	Santa Cruz Santa Cruz	66	607
PERAN			
James	Calaveras Twp 8	57	68
John	Calaveras Twp 8	57	93
Joseph	Calaveras Twp 8	57	58
Juan	Marin Cortemad	60	792

Name	County Locale	M653 Roll	Page
PERANE			
Antonio	Calaveras Twp 8	57	92
PERANO			
Angel	Calaveras Twp 7	57	39
Angel	Calaveras Twp 7	57	43
Angel	Calaveras Twp 8	57	87
Antomi	Calaveras Twp 7	57	39
Jackoma	Calaveras Twp 7	57	61
John	Calaveras Twp 7	57	35
John	Calaveras Twp 8	57	51
John	Calaveras Twp 8	57	82
Joseph	Calaveras Twp 7	57	43
Joseph	Calaveras Twp 8	57	52
Michael	Calaveras Twp 7	57	46
Michael*	Calaveras Twp 7	57	6
Michal	Calaveras Twp 7	57	6
Micheale*	Calaveras Twp 8	57	102
Micheil*	Calaveras Twp 7	57	6
PERANU			
Angel	Calaveras Twp 7	57	35
John	Calaveras Twp 8	57	61
Michael	Calaveras Twp 8	57	68
PERASO			
Louisa	Mariposa Twp 3	60	547
Palo G	Mariposa Twp 3	60	547
Palo T	Mariposa Twp 3	60	547
PERATH			
Josefa	Santa Clara San Jose	65	301
PERATO			
Antonio	Calaveras Twp 8	57	52
PERATTA			
Hosea A ArtatlAlameda Brooklyn		55	97
PERAZZA			
Joseph	Calaveras Twp 8	57	105
PERAZZO			
Giovanni San Francisco San Francisco 11		67	110
PERB			
Henry	Los Angeles San Gabriel	59	408
PERBLES			
Carey	Santa Clara Santa Clara	65	509
PERCE			
Edwin	Solano Montezuma	69	375
Rayman San Francisco San Francisco 9		68	965
PERCEGER			
Henry	Plumas Quincy	62	962
PERCEL			
James	Tuolumne Twp 2	71	283
Jas San Francisco San Francisco 1		68	864
Michael* San Francisco San Francisco 3		67	31
PERCELL			
George	Plumas Quincy	62	980
J C	Sonoma Armally	69	507
John San Francisco San Francisco 4		68	1141
PERCEOAL			
H	Amador Twp 2	55	302
PERCEY			
C N San Bernardino San Bernadino		64	627
William	Plumas Quincy	62	997
PERCH			
Jno H	Klamath Orleans	59	215
PERCHARD			
Charles	Placer Forest H	62	772
PERCIL			
James*	Tuolumne Twp 2	71	283
PERCIOAC			
Martin*	Stanislaus Buena Village	70	721
PERCIVAL			
Camelia	Napa Napa	61	65
Egbert D	Placer Auburn	62	591
Hector	Calaveras Twp 5	57	215
Henry	Amador Twp 2	55	322
Henry San Francisco San Francisco 10		67	290
James	El Dorado Big Bar	58	735
Jean San Francisco San Francisco 2		67	626
Joseph	Placer Michigan	62	843
PERCON			
Jonas*	Nevada Rough &	61	398
PERCONT			
Peter	Alameda Brooklyn	55	180
PERCY			
A J	Sutter Sutter	70	810
John	Yuba Marysville	72	855
John	Yuba Marysville	72	860
Peel	Plumas Quincy	62	918
Richard C	Sierra Morristown	66	1051
PERDENELLE			
Manuel*	Alameda Oakland	55	3
PERDENILLE			
Manuel*	Alameda Oakland	55	3
PERDER			
Aimede*	Mariposa Twp 3	60	594
PERDEVINSKY			
FerdinandSan Francisco San Francisco 7		68	1416
PERDICILLE			
Bernard*	Alameda Oakland	55	3

Name	County Locale	M653 Roll	Page
PERDIEILKLE			
Bernard*	Alameda Oakland	55	3
PERDIMONTE			
DomingoSan Bernardino Santa Barbara		64	193
PERDIN			
Thomas	Marin San Rafael	60	763
PERDU			
Hosa	Los Angeles Elmonte	59	268
William	Los Angeles Elmonte	59	268
PERDUE			
M	El Dorado Georgetown	58	703
W H	Sutter Sutter	70	801
PERE			
---	Yolo Slate Ra	72	711
Antonio	San Francisco San Francisco 2	67	768
Leon	San Francisco San Francisco 2	67	795
PEREA			
Agupito	Monterey San Juan	60	1001
Domingo	Monterey San Juan	60	1002
Joaquin	Monterey San Juan	60	983
Jose	Los Angeles Los Nieto	59	434
Patricia*	Monterey San Juan	60	996
PERECE			
M R*	Tuolumne Big Oak	71	154
PERECHE			
Ferdinand*	Sierra Downieville	66	977
PEREED			
--- San Bernardino San Bernadino		64	681
PEREGAND			
Alfonso	Calaveras Twp 9	57	347
PEREGO			
Juan	Alameda Brooklyn	55	157
PEREGORY			
C E	Mariposa Twp 3	60	578
PEREGS			
Juan*	Alameda Brooklyn	55	157
PEREIGO			
Frank	Calaveras Twp 9	57	347
PEREILE			
Francis	El Dorado Greenwood	58	721
PEREIVAL			
Hector	Calaveras Twp 5	57	215
PERELBERRG			
A* San Francisco San Francisco 3		67	82
PERELBING			
Dowisso San Francisco San Francisco 3		67	82
PERELBURG			
A* San Francisco San Francisco 3		67	82
PERELL			
Chancey	Marin Cortemad	60	792
PERENCE			
Andrew	El Dorado Coloma	58	1104
PERER			
J J San Francisco San Francisco 4		68	1125
Manuel	Mariposa Twp 3	60	545
PERERO			
Antonio	Santa Clara San Jose	65	349
PERES			
Antoni	Alameda Oakland	55	7
Enagento	Calaveras Twp 7	57	39
Euogenti*	Calaveras Twp 7	57	35
Helena San Francisco San Francisco 10		67	210
Hosia M	Tuolumne Twp 4	71	133
Joseph	Calaveras Twp 7	57	35
Joseph	Calaveras Twp 7	57	39
Juan	Santa Clara Almaden	65	263
Lewis San Francisco San Francisco 10		67	209
Louis	Tuolumne Twp 4	71	131
Maria A San Bernardino San Bernadino		64	663
Mosia M	Tuolumne Big Oak	71	133
Viente San Francisco San Francisco 1		68	814
PERESO			
A	Tuolumne Twp 4	71	160
PERESOR			
J T*	Shasta Shasta	66	662
PERET			
Louis	Mariposa Twp 3	60	606
PEREY			
Diego	Sierra La Porte	66	784
L San Francisco San Francisco 6		67	464
PEREZ			
Anche	Tuolumne Shawsfla	71	420
Antonie San Francisco San Francisco 2		67	768
Antonio	Los Angeles Los Nieto	59	425
Antonio	Monterey Alisal	60	1035
Auche	Tuolumne Twp 2	71	420
Buenaventura	San Gabriel Los Angeles	59	420
Cesto* San Francisco San Francisco 2		67	688
Cisto* San Francisco San Francisco 2		67	688
Craig San Luis Obispo San Luis Obispo		65	33
Enrique	Los Angeles Los Angeles	59	327
Fernando	Los Angeles San Juan	59	475
Francisca	Los Angeles San Gabriel	59	416

Name	County Locale	M653 Roll	Page
PEREZ			
Francisco	Los Angeles Los Nieto	59	434
Francisco JLos Angeles Los Nieto		59	434
Jean	San Francisco San Francisco 2	67	767
Jose	Los Angeles Los Angeles	59	397
Juan	Santa Clara San Jose	65	302
L	San Francisco San Francisco 6	67	464
Louisa San Francisco San Francisco 1		68	865
Louisa	Yuba Long Bar	72	748
Lucien	Calaveras Twp 4	57	341
Mancisca	Los Angeles San Gabriel	59	416
Manuel	Monterey Pajaro	60	1013
Maria	Los Angeles San Gabriel	59	421
Miguel	San Diego San Diego	64	768
Miguela	Los Angeles Los Angeles	59	304
Nicorio	San Diego Colorado	64	810
Pedro	Los Angeles Los Nieto	59	433
Policarpio	Los Angeles Los Angeles	59	363
Ramon	Butte Oregon	56	614
Romedo	Tuolumne Chinese	71	499
Romeds	Tuolumne Twp 5	71	499
Santas	Santa Clara Almaden	65	273
Simon	San Diego San Diego	64	766
Sucien*	Calaveras Twp 4	57	341
PERFICTA			
---	Monterey S Antoni	60	972
PERGE			
John	El Dorado Georgetown	58	699
PERGEL			
John	Alameda Brooklyn	55	81
Michael	Calaveras Twp 6	57	158
PERGER			
G San Francisco San Francisco 6		67	451
PERHAM			
Hiram	Klamath Trinidad	59	219
Liberty	Alameda Brooklyn	55	154
PERI			
Albert*	Yuba Marysville	72	907
John	Calaveras Twp 10	57	291
S	Trinity Browns C	70	984
PERIA			
Francisco	San Luis Obispo San Luis Obispo	65	18
Francisco*	Monterey San Juan	60	1002
Jose	Santa Clara Gilroy	65	224
Jose MSan Luis Obispo San Luis Obispo		65	25
ToedadSan Luis Obispo San Luis Obispo		65	36
PERICE			
AdolphusSan Francisco San Francisco 3		67	60
Cha	Butte Oregon	56	618
Chas	Sacramento San Joaquin	63	359
Geo E	Butte Oregon	56	634
M R	Tuolumne Twp 4	71	154
PERICHE			
Ferdinand*	Sierra Downieville	66	977
PERICON			
Jonas	Nevada Rough &	61	398
PERICUS			
Isaac	Trinity Weaverville	70	1063
PERIDES			
Rosa	El Dorado Georgetown	58	677
PERIE			
--- San Francisco San Francisco 10		67	358
PERIER			
Zeam*	Yuba Parks Ba	72	781
Zean	Yuba Parke Ba	72	781
Zeans*	Yuba Parks Ba	72	781
PERIES			
Zeam	Yuba Parks Ba	72	781
PERIGANT			
Alfonse	Calaveras Twp 9	57	388
PERIGAUT			
Alfonse*	Calaveras Twp 9	57	388
PERIGO			
Amos	Butte Chico	56	534
Amos T	Colusa Colusi	57	420
F	Shasta Shasta	66	674
Frank	Calaveras Twp 9	57	347
Geo	Butte Chico	56	534
Geo W	Colusa Colusi	57	425
Orsiann	Colusa Colusi	57	425
Z A	Colusa Colusi	57	425
PERIM			
Lonis	Monterey S Antoni	60	973
Louis	Monterey S Antoni	60	973
PERIN			
Harm	Solano Benecia	69	292
Isaac	Amador Twp 1	55	451
Lucy	Solano Benecia	69	292
PERINE			
A S	Sonoma Bodega	69	520
Charles	Calaveras Twp 7	57	48
F A	Calaveras Twp 7	57	9
James M	Solano Suisan	69	205
S B	Trinity North Fo	70	1024

California 1860 Census Index

Name	County Locale	M653 RollPage
PERINE		
S C	El Dorado Kelsey	581146
PERING		
France	Alameda Oakland	55 1
W	Nevada Grass Valley	61 175
PERINTEON		
Wm F	Sierra Twp 5	66 946
PERIS		
Carmel	Contra Costa Twp 1	57 519
Jose	San Joaquin Stockton	641071
Joseph	Amador Twp 4	55 259
Paricio	San Joaquin Stockton	641071
PERISE		
Joseph	Santa Clara Santa Clara	65 482
PERISI		
Joseph*	Santa Clara Santa Clara	65 482
PERISON		
Geo*	Butte Oro	56 673
PERIT		
Louis*	Mariposa Twp 3	60 606
PERIZ		
Francisco	Contra Costa Twp 1	57 509
PERK		
George	Calaveras Twp 6	57 132
PERKENS		
Brice A	Yuba Marysville	72 896
PERKEY		
John W	San Joaquin Elliott	64 942
PERKHAM		
Charles	San Francisco San Francisco 3	67 44
PERKIN		
H	El Dorado Diamond	58 799
Samuel	El Dorado Georgetown	58 696
Wm	Tehama Red Bluff	70 907
PERKINPINE		
John	Shasta Horsetown	66 707
PERKINS		
A B	San Francisco San Francisco 8	681319
A K	Trinity Indian C	70 986
A T	Mendocino Ukiah	60 793
Agustus	Yolo Slate Ra	72 691
Agustus	Yuba Slate Ro	72 691
Albert	Yuba New York	72 723
Alonzo	Alameda Oakland	55 44
Ann L	Sacramento Ward 4	63 539
Anna	Tuolumne Twp 2	71 329
Anthony	San Francisco San Francisco 9	68 997
B	El Dorado Georgetown	58 697
Bettes	Mariposa Twp 1	60 662
Bettos	Mariposa Twp 1	60 662
Brook	Siskiyou Yreka	69 147
Bruce A*	Yuba Marysville	72 896
C	Solano Vacaville	69 358
C P	Sacramento Ward 3	63 432
Charles	El Dorado Mountain	581186
Charles	San Francisco San Francisco 11	152 67
Charles C	Yuba Timbucto	72 787
Charles H	San Francisco San Francisco 7	681338
Chas	Mariposa Twp 1	60 663
Chas C	Alameda Brooklyn	55 100
D B	Solano Suisan	69 212
D H	Sacramento Franklin	63 316
Daniel	Tulara Keyesville	71 60
Daniel S	Alameda Oakland	55 68
Davins*	Tulara Visalia	71 110
Davius*	Tulara Visalia	71 110
Davus	Tulara Twp 1	71 110
E	Butte Cascade	56 692
E	Butte Ophir	56 786
E E	Yolo Cache Crk	72 636
E J	El Dorado Mud Springs	58 968
E S	San Francisco San Francisco 2	67 667
Edwd	San Francisco San Francisco 10	295 67
Edwd	San Francisco San Francisco 6	67 448
Edwin	Yolo Cottonwoood	72 650
Eliphales	Calaveras Twp 4	57 328
Eliphalet	Calaveras Twp 4	57 328
F	El Dorado Placerville	58 900
F	Sacramento Alabama	63 416
F C	Mariposa Twp 1	60 636
Frank	Solano Vacaville	69 326
Fred	Yuba Parks Ba	72 774
G L	El Dorado Placerville	58 872
G R	Sonoma Petaluma	69 587
Geo	Sacramento Centre	63 174
Geo C	Butte Ophir	56 764
Geo R	Del Norte Happy Ca	58 669
George	San Francisco San Francisco 11	120 67
H	Siskiyou Scott Ri	69 71
H C	Merced Twp 1	60 897
Harris	Butte Chico	56 561
Harry	San Mateo Twp 3	65 106
Henry	Shasta Shasta	66 758

Name	County Locale	M653 RollPage
PERKINS		
Henry W	Humbolt Eureka	59 170
Hiram	Calaveras Twp 5	57 243
Hiram	Siskiyou Yreka	69 151
Hiram	Tulara Twp 3	71 60
Hunner*	Calaveras Twp 5	57 243
Isaac	Sacramento Ward 1	63 103
Isaiah S	Humbolt Eureka	59 177
J	Klamath Trinidad	59 221
J	Nevada Grass Valley	61 170
J	San Francisco San Francisco 3	67 15
J	Siskiyou Scott Ri	69 81
J	Sutter Butte	70 798
J B	Butte Chico	56 538
J C	Mariposa Twp 1	60 636
J C	Placer Damascus	62 846
J D*	Sacramento Cosummes	63 387
J F	Butte Chico	56 561
J L	Yuba Rose Bar	72 820
J N	San Joaquin Stockton	641013
J R	Colusa Muion	57 458
J S	Nevada Eureka	61 379
Jacob	El Dorado Kelsey	581154
James	Siskiyou Cottonwoood	69 99
James	Tuolumne Twp 1	71 356
Jas	Sacramento Ward 3	63 442
Jas*	Placer Lisbon	62 735
Jesse	Stanislaus Empire	70 728
Jesse	Yuba Marysville	72 950
Jessie	Butte Oro	56 684
Jno J	Mendocino Anderson	60 870
John	Contra Costa Twp 1	57 514
John	Santa Cruz Pajaro	66 528
John	Shasta Shasta	66 757
John L	Tuolumne Twp 3	71 436
John S	Tuolumne Jamestown	71 436
Jonathan	Placer Michigan	62 851
Jos*	Placer Lisbon	62 735
Joseph	Solano Vallejo	69 262
Lorenzo	San Joaquin Douglass	64 921
Luke H	San Francisco San Francisco 9	68 939
Manie*	Placer Auburn	62 578
Maria	Tuolumne Sonora	71 217
Mary	Alameda Brooklyn	55 162
Mary	Sacramento Franklin	63 318
Mary E	San Francisco San Francisco 2	67 568
Mathew	Sierra Whiskey	66 850
N	San Francisco San Francisco 4	681231
N B	Mendocino Ukiah	60 793
O M	San Francisco San Francisco 6	67 434
Oliver	Alameda Brooklyn	55 153
P	El Dorado Placerville	58 899
P	Tuolumne Twp 4	71 175
P B	San Francisco San Francisco 6	67 437
P H	Placer Todds Va	62 785
R F	San Francisco San Francisco 2	67 803
R H	Sutter Butte	70 797
Ralph	San Francisco San Francisco 9	68 953
Robert G	San Francisco San Francisco 11	120 67
Robt	Sacramento Franklin	63 317
Russel C	San Francisco San Francisco 11	135 67
Sam*	Butte Oregon	56 621
Saml	San Francisco San Francisco 10	230 67
Samuel	San Francisco San Francisco 11	120 67
Samuel A	Napa Hot Springs	61 23
Solomon D	Contra Costa Twp 2	57 557
Susan E	Nevada Red Dog	61 553
T L	San Francisco San Francisco 12	375 67
Tho	Siskiyou Scott Ri	69 82
Thos	Butte Wyandotte	56 657
Thos	Sacramento Brighton	63 193
Thos	Santa Clara San Jose	65 338
W	El Dorado Georgetown	58 699
W	Sutter Butte	70 792
William	El Dorado Coloma	581074
William	Yuba Marysville	72 906
Wm	Mariposa Twp 3	60 577
Wm	Napa Napa	61 103
Wm	Placer Stewart	62 607
Wm	Sacramento Ward 1	63 81
Wm A	Plumas Meadow Valley	62 930
Wm D	Placer Secret R	62 611
PERKISN		
J	Sacramento Cosummes	63 387
PERKNES		
Wm	Sierra Morristown	661054
PERLE		
John	Placer Michigan	62 845
PERLEY		
D W	San Francisco San Francisco 5	67 505
G A	Tuolumne Twp 2	71 339

Name	County Locale	M653 RollPage
PERLEY		
James E	San Joaquin Elkhorn	64 955
Jas	Mariposa Twp 3	60 605
John C	Tuolumne Twp 2	71 286
John C	Tuolumne Columbia	71 339
Jos	Mariposa Twp 3	60 605
R H	San Joaquin Elkhorn	64 993
PERLLIN		
Growell	Monterey San Juan	60 995
PERLY		
John	Placer Michigan	62 826
PERMAK		
---	Fresno Twp 2	59 58
PERMAN		
Alexander*	Placer Michigan	62 853
David*	Placer Michigan	62 852
James	Mariposa Twp 1	60 636
PERMEB		
Harry*	Sacramento Ward 1	63 40
PERMEL		
Harry*	Sacramento Ward 1	63 40
PERMFEACHER		
Geo	Butte Chico	56 567
PERMFEATHER		
Geo*	Butte Chico	56 567
PERMIE		
William*	San Francisco San Francisco 4	681171
PERMILLA		
H*	San Mateo Twp 1	65 63
PERNANCE		
A J*	Placer Todds Va	62 789
PERNCOUGH		
A	Tuolumne Twp 2	71 301
A K*	Tuolumne Columbia	71 301
A*	Tuolumne Columbia	71 301
PERNE		
Thos	Calaveras Twp 9	57 400
PERNEL		
Harry*	Sacramento Ward 1	63 40
PERNELL		
Insiah	Siskiyou Yreka	69 138
Johln	Siskiyou Yreka	69 145
John	Sonoma Armally	69 513
John*	Siskiyou Yreka	69 145
Josiah	Siskiyou Yreka	69 137
Jusiah*	Siskiyou Yreka	69 138
Santa	San Francisco San Francisco 4	681231
PERNERONE		
Manuel	Alameda Brooklyn	55 204
PERNET		
Saml	Plumas Quincy	621001
PERNETZ		
Fred	Alameda Brooklyn	55 153
PERNEY		
William*	San Francisco San Francisco 4	681172
PERNICK		
John D	Monterey San Juan	60 995
PERNIE		
G	Sutter Sutter	70 811
PERNIS		
A*	Calaveras Twp 9	57 392
PERNSDELL		
E B	Nevada Bridgeport	61 482
PERNY		
Hen	Placer Secret R	62 624
PERO		
Francis	Monterey San Juan	60 977
Francisco*	Monterey San Juan	601001
Franicisco	Monterey San Juan	601001
Gerow	Sacramento Ward 1	63 48
Isaac De*	Nevada Rough &	61 420
J	El Dorado Placerville	58 823
John	El Dorado Coloma	581086
Jose	Monterey San Juan	601002
Simino	Alameda Brooklyn	55 132
Tomias	Monterey San Juan	60 977
PEROKO		
---	Fresno Twp 2	59 67
PEROLLER		
Jose	San Bernardino Santa Barbara	64 190
PEROLLO		
Domingo	Alameda Oakland	55 55
PEROM		
Juan*	Marin Cortemad	60 792
PERON		
Andrew	Sacramento Ward 4	63 544
John	Calaveras Twp 7	57 33
Juan*	Marin Cortemad	60 792
PERONA		
Hosea	Alameda Brooklyn	55 202
PERORY		
P	Mariposa Twp 3	60 571
PEROS		
Andraes	Amador Twp 4	55 249
Enogenta	Calaveras Twp 8	57 88
PEROSON		
L F*	Yolo Putah	72 560

Name	County Locale	M653 Roll	Page
PEROT			
Joan	San Francisco San Francisco	11 67	151
PEROTO			
Romero	Alameda Brooklyn	55	165
PEROUSE			
Vicor	San Francisco San Francisco	11 67	135
PEROY			
Alex	Sacramento Ward 1	63	35
PERPELY			
Patricio	San Francisco San Francisco 2	67	712
PERPLES			
Thos	San Francisco San Francisco 2	67	778
PERR			
Madison*	Nevada Bloomfield	61	513
PERRALTO			
Lubine	Tulara Sinks Te	71	42
Subine	Tulara Twp 3	71	42
PERRANO			
Jackoma*	Calaveras Twp 8	57	105
PERRARA			
Carlos	Mariposa Twp 3	60	554
PERRAULT			
J	San Francisco San Francisco 3	67	48
Julian	San Francisco San Francisco 6	67	410
PERRCIL			
P	Siskiyou Scott Va	69	53
PERREGANA			
Alfonzo*	Calaveras Twp 9	57	347
PERREGAND			
Alfonzo*	Calaveras Twp 9	57	347
PERREGAUD			
Alfonso*	Calaveras Twp 9	57	347
PERREGO			
Frank*	Calaveras Twp 9	57	347
PERREIS			
A*	Calaveras Twp 9	57	392
PERREN			
Edwin	Sacramento San Joaquin	63	352
John	Tuolumne Twp 5	71	522
Pedre*	Alameda Oakland	55	7
PERRENT			
Albt	Sonoma Vallejo	69	612
PERRER			
Frank	San Francisco San Francisco 1	68	845
PERRES			
Caroline	Santa Cruz Watsonville	66	540
Cornelia	Santa Cruz Santa Cruz	66	616
J N B	Sacramento Mississipi	63	188
Juan	Calaveras Twp 9	57	347
PERRET			
T H	Calaveras Twp 9	57	362
PERRETTZO			
Vincent	San Francisco San Francisco 2	67	679
PERREZ			
Marcellena	Contra Costa Twp 1	57	509
PERRICK			
Patk	Trinity Mouth Ca	70	1016
PERRIE			
Frank	Santa Cruz Pajaro	66	545
PERRIER			
C	El Dorado Casumnes	58	1173
Joseph	Sierra La Porte	66	769
PERRIF			
Frank*	San Francisco San Francisco 2	67	687
PERRIFS			
A*	Calaveras Twp 9	57	392
PERRIGREN			
James	Tuolumne Sonora	71	481
PERRIL			
P	Nevada Grass Valley	61	187
PERRILL			
E*	Trinity E Weaver	70	1057
PERRIN			
Albert	Mariposa Twp 1	60	664
E	Trinity Rearings	70	990
Francis	Calaveras Twp 10	57	263
Granville	Amador Twp 1	55	467
Gustave	Plumas Meadow Valley	62	911
Gustavi*	Plumas Meadow Valley	62	933
J	Nevada Grass Valley	61	211
J A	Amador Twp 1	55	456
James F	Nevada Little Y	61	537
Lyman	San Francisco San Francisco 2	67	775
Mary	San Francisco San Francisco 4	68	1152
O	Tuolumne Twp 4	71	173
Orlando	Sierra Twp 5	66	921
Warron	Mariposa Twp 1	60	663
PERRINE			
Armell	San Francisco San Francisco 4	68	1131
PERRINGER			
David	Sonoma Petaluma	69	569
Leonard	Sierra Twp 7	66	880
PERRINGTON			
Stephen	Yolo Slate Ra	72	691

Name	County Locale	M653 Roll	Page
PERRINGTON			
Stephen	Yuba Slate Ro	72	691
PERRINS			
Elizabeth*	El Dorado Spanish	58	1125
Ellizabeth*	El Dorado Spanish	58	1125
PERRIS			
Caroline	Santa Cruz Watsonville	66	540
Casons*	Butte Chico	56	532
Casous	Butte Chico	56	532
Charolotte	San Francisco 1	68	807
	San Francisco		
Feliciano	Contra Costa Twp 3	57	608
Gujery	Amador Twp 5	55	332
Juan	Calaveras Twp 9	57	347
N	Amador Twp 1	55	483
R A*	Sacramento Ward 3	63	455
Rose	San Mateo Twp 3	65	98
Simion	Santa Cruz Santa Cruz	66	606
Simon	Santa Cruz Santa Cruz	66	606
PERRISH			
Martha	Sacramento Ward 1	63	146
Martin	Sacramento Ward 1	63	146
PERRISTER			
A	Trinity Indian C	70	987
PERRIUN			
J T	Mariposa Twp 3	60	561
J T**	Mariposa Twp 3	60	561
PERRIXS			
A*	Calaveras Twp 9	57	392
PERROCHAD			
Andrew	San Francisco San Francisco 10 67		358
PERROLE			
Amajohn	Butte Bidwell	56	730
PERRON			
Louis*	Siskiyou Callahan	69	9
P L	Siskiyou Callahan	69	9
PERRORA			
Manuel	San Francisco San Francisco 1	68	864
PERROST			
David*	Nevada Rough &	61	407
PERROT			
Franciss	Monterey San Juan	60	988
Frank	Plumas Meadow Valley	62	934
Jas	San Francisco San Francisco 10 67		200
T H*	Calaveras Twp 9	57	362
PERRT			
Wm	Siskiyou Callahan	69	10
PERRUM			
J T*	Mariposa Twp 3	60	561
PERRUS			
Elizabeth	El Dorado Spanish	58	1125
PERRUSEE			
John P	Tuolumne Sonora	71	230
PERRY			
---	Amador Twp 2	55	327
---	Amador Twp 5	55	365
---	Calaveras Twp 4	57	320
---	Sierra St Louis	66	812
A B	Butte Kimshaw	56	578
A C	Sacramento Franklin	63	311
Adna E	Yolo No E Twp	72	673
Adna E	Yuba North Ea	72	673
Alex	Sacramento Ward 1	63	35
Allen	Amador Twp 3	55	378
Andrew	Siskiyou Scott Va	69	30
B	Calaveras Twp 9	57	396
Bartholemew	Twp 1	57	518
	Contra Costa		
C	San Joaquin Stockton	64	1067
C	Tuolumne Columbia	71	313
C S	Sonoma Petaluma	69	593
Charles	Amador Twp 1	55	451
Charles	Plumas Quincy	62	991
Charles	San Joaquin Elkhorn	64	972
Chas	Sacramento Ward 1	63	34
Chester	Amador Twp 6	55	438
D	Marin Tomales	60	725
D	Sacramento Cosumnes	63	409
Daniel	Mendocino Big Rvr	60	852
Daniel	Santa Clara Almaden	65	275
Daniel	Siskiyou Scott Va	69	31
David	Nevada Bloomfield	61	511
E A	Amador Twp 1	55	451
E A	Santa Clara Redwood	65	459
E F	Sutter Butte	70	798
E H	El Dorado Casumnes	58	1165
Elija	San Francisco San Francisco 10 67		258
Elijah	Amador Twp 6	55	429
Elizabeth V	Yuba Marysville	72	860
Elizabeth V	Yuba Marysville	72	860
Ellen*	Calaveras Twp 9	57	355
Eran	Placer Michigan	62	815
F R	Solano Montezuma	69	371

Name	County Locale	M653 Roll	Page
PERRY			
Francis	Butte Hamilton	56	526
Frank	Yuba Marysville	72	866
Fuson	Amador Twp 6	55	438
G O	Amador Twp 1	55	451
Geo	Solano Benecia	69	314
Geo B	El Dorado Casumnes	58	1166
Geo O P	Solano Benecia	69	314
Geo W	Trinity Indian C	70	987
Geo*	San Francisco San Francisco 2	67	674
George	Humbolt Eureka	59	178
Greenleaf	Placer Ophirville	62	654
Guillirno*	El Dorado Georgetown	58	746
H	El Dorado Placerville	58	855
H	Sacramento Cosumnes	63	405
H	San Francisco San Francisco 6	67	465
H C	Tehama Red Bluff	70	917
H E	San Francisco San Francisco 2	67	735
Hampton	Amador Twp 7	55	411
Henry	Placer Michigan	62	814
Henry	Placer Michigan	62	819
Henry	Placer Iona Hills	62	861
Henry A	Nevada Washington	61	333
Henry J	San Francisco San Francisco 4	68	1121
Hugh	Sierra Scales D	66	803
J	Nevada Grass Valley	61	159
J	Nevada Grass Valley	61	221
J	Nevada Eureka	61	348
J	San Francisco San Francisco 3	67	43
J	Siskiyou Scott Ri	69	70
J D	Amador Twp 6	55	439
J H	Sacramento San Joaquin	63	363
J M	Napa Clear Lake	61	134
J S	Butte Chico	56	556
J S	San Joaquin Stockton	64	1043
James	Los Angeles San Gabriel	59	422
James	Sacramento Centre	63	176
James	San Francisco San Francisco 7	68	1364
James	Shasta Millvill	66	742
James	Solano Vallejo	69	249
James A	Humbolt Eureka	59	167
Jerome	Santa Cruz Pajaro	66	533
Jessie L	Placer Virginia	62	661
Jno	Sacramento Ward 4	63	578
Jno R	Nevada Nevada	61	280
John	Butte Wyandotte	56	665
John	Butte Cascade	56	690
John	Butte Ophir	56	759
John	Calaveras Twp 9	57	355
John	Nevada Grass Valley	61	149
John	Nevada Bridgeport	61	453
John	Placer Auburn	62	585
John	Placer Michigan	62	843
John	Santa Cruz Santa Cruz	66	603
John	Yuba Marysville	72	896
John H	Nevada Bridgeport	61	443
John Jr	San Francisco San Francisco 2	67	621
John L	San Francisco San Francisco 2	67	675
John N	Nevada Bridgeport	61	443
John W	Humbolt Bucksport	59	157
Johnathan	Humbolt Pacific	59	138
Jose John A	Santa Clara San Jose	65	279
Julius	Placer Iona Hills	62	875
L B	Sacramento Franklin	63	311
L C	Nevada Grass Valley	61	221
Manuel	San Mateo Twp 1	65	52
Marcus*	San Luis Obispo	65	33
Marg I	Sacramento Ward 1	63	118
Margt	Sacramento Ward 1	63	118
Martha J	Humbolt Bucksport	59	157
Menoa	Napa Napa	61	79
Minna	San Francisco San Francisco 1	68	880
Moses	San Bernardino Santa Inez	64	141
N	Sacramento Franklin	63	315
N	San Francisco San Francisco 9	68	1071
N A	Sonoma Santa Rosa	69	419
Newton C	Placer Secret R	62	609
O	Trinity Indian C	70	986
O A	Calaveras Twp 7	57	10
O S	Siskiyou Cottonwoood	69	103
Oliver H	San Joaquin Castoria	64	875
Pat*	Siskiyou Scott Va	69	56
Peter	Solano Suisan	69	226
Peter R	Fresno Twp 3	59	12
R H	Sierra Twp 5	66	920
Rascom	San Francisco San Francisco 8	68	1271
Richard	Solano Montezuma	69	371
Richd	Santa Clara Gilroy	65	246
Rob	Sacramento Granite	63	249
Robert	Calaveras Twp 5	57	207
Robert	Marin Tomales	60	720
Robt	Sacramento Granite	63	249
S	Nevada Nevada	61	264
S	Sonoma Armally	69	508
S H	Sonoma Armally	69	508
S J	Sacramento Ward 3	63	426

Name	County Locale	M653 Roll	Page
PERRY			
S M	Nevada Bridgeport	61	450
S R	Solano Montezuma	69	371
Samuel	Alameda Oakland	55	41
Samuel B	Fresno Twp 3	59	12
Sarah	San Francisco San Francisco 5	67	543
Sarah S	San Francisco San Francisco 1	68	808
Silas W	Contra Costa Twp 2	57	543
Solomon	Siskiyou Scott Va	69	49
Stephen	Sacramento Franklin	63	310
Sullivan*	El Dorado Georgetown	58	746
T	Sutter Butte	70	779
T E	Yuba Long Bar	72	749
Thomas	Colusa Monroeville	57	452
Thomas	El Dorado Coloma	58	1068
Thomas	Marin Cortemad	60	791
Thomas	Tulara Visalia	71	108
Thos W	San Francisco San Francisco 1	68	924
W	El Dorado Eldorado	58	946
W	Nevada Grass Valley	61	209
W E	El Dorado Eldorado	58	936
W T	El Dorado Placerville	58	867
Wathew	El Dorado Coloma	58	1116
William	Contra Costa Twp 1	57	529
William	Nevada Bridgeport	61	453
William	Placer Iona Hills	62	874
William	Placer Iona Hills	62	884
William	Plumas Quincy	62	1001
William	San Luis Obispo San Luis Obispo	65	26
William	Sierra Scales D	66	803
William	Tuolumne Shawsfla	71	388
William	Yuba Marysville	72	911
William	Yuba Marysville	72	965
William H	Los Angeles Los Angeles	59	326
William S	Yuba Marysville	72	911
Wm	Amador Twp 3	55	403
Wm	Nevada Eureka	61	369
Wm	Siskiyou Callahan	69	10
Wm	Solano Suisan	69	238
Wm	Sonoma Sonoma	69	650
PERRYMAN			
John	Calaveras Twp 8	57	67
John*	Solano Benecia	69	284
Joseph	Calaveras Twp 8	57	67
PERRYN			
Francis	San Joaquin Elkhorn	64	977
PERSALL			
E	Stanislaus Oatvale	70	719
PERSAND			
A E	El Dorado Georgetown	58	686
PERSANEL			
John	Siskiyou Scott Va	69	60
PERSAO			
J	Tuolumne Twp 4	71	157
PERSAWEL			
John	Siskiyou Scott Va	69	60
PERSAWL			
John	Siskiyou Scott Va	69	60
PERSE			
John N	Butte Cascade	56	702
John Y	Butte Cascade	56	702
PERSEL			
Mike*	Yolo Slate Ra	72	687
Mike*	Yuba North Ea	72	687
PERSELL			
Josh	Contra Costa Twp 1	57	526
PERSENTON			
Wm F*	Sierra Twp 5	66	946
PERSET			
J	Siskiyou Callahan	69	2
PERSHBAKER			
Helen	Yuba Marysville	72	847
PERSIAN			
James	Tulara Visalia	71	80
PERSIGAMON			
Henry	Calaveras Twp 5	57	203
PERSIGARNON			
Henry	Calaveras Twp 5	57	203
PERSIGIA			
Francisco	S Buenav	64	221
	San Bernardino		
PERSING			
W G	El Dorado Placerville	58	885
PERSIYAMON			
Henry	Calaveras Twp 5	57	203
PERSOLL			
Lewis	Sierra St Louis	66	808
PERSOMETTE			
M W	Trinity Douglas	70	980
PERSON			
Danl	Butte Ophir	56	793
Henry	Solano Vallejo	69	278
James	Sierra Twp 7	66	885
Wilson	Sierra Twp 7	66	890
Witson*	Sierra Twp 7	66	890
Wm	Sierra Twp 7	66	888

Name	County Locale	M653 Roll	Page
PERSONS			
George J	El Dorado Spanish	58	1125
Lewis*	Yolo Merritt	72	583
Rudolph	Nevada Bridgeport	61	446
Wm	Sacramento Ward 1	63	49
PERSUANO			
Francis	Tuolumne Twp 4	71	127
PERSY			
C F	El Dorado Big Bar	58	740
N B	El Dorado Big Bar	58	739
PERT			
Michael	Siskiyou Scott Va	69	49
PERTCHARD			
J	Yolo Cache	72	621
PERTEAS			
Joseph	Calaveras Twp 5	57	225
PERTENS			
Joseph*	Calaveras Twp 5	57	225
PERTER			
Frank	Monterey S Antoni	60	973
J	Mariposa Coulterville	60	675
PERTESA			
Hosa Mercar	Mariposa Twp 1	60	628
Hosa Merear	Mariposa Twp 1	60	628
PERTICA			
Angel	San Bernardino Santa Barbara	64	152
PERTINS			
Saml	Butte Oregon	56	621
PERTIUS			
Saml*	Butte Oregon	56	621
PERTOES			
James	Calaveras Twp 7	57	28
PERTON			
Jonas*	Nevada Rough &	61	398
PERTY			
Ben	Sacramento Natonia	63	282
PERU			
Henry	Los Angeles San Gabriel	59	408
Joseph H	Los Angeles Los Angeles	59	337
Richard	Santa Clara Almaden	65	275
PERUANA			
Francis	Tuolumne Big Oak	71	125
PERUGO			
Frank*	Calaveras Twp 9	57	347
PERULTA			
Maria*	Santa Cruz Santa Cruz	66	607
PERUNA			
John	Calaveras Twp 8	57	105
PERVINES			
Alex*	Sacramento Brighton	63	191
PERVIS			
James	Sonoma Petaluma	69	552
PERVOST			
David*	Nevada Rough &	61	407
PERWELLER			
A*	Butte Bidwell	56	723
PERY			
---	Amador Twp 5	55	347
---	Amador Twp 5	55	356
Erastus	Napa Yount	61	39
Gouri*	Shasta Horsetown	66	701
Warren	Yuba Marysville	72	926
PES			
Kim	El Dorado Greenwood	58	713
PESADA			
Ramon	Santa Clara Almaden	65	270
PESANO			
John	Sonoma Vallejo	69	630
PESARO			
Bernodo	Calaveras Twp 8	57	50
PESBUY			
Francis	Placer Ophirville	62	657
PESCELL			
Wm	Tuolumne Sonora	71	235
PESCHIN			
Regroun*	El Dorado Georgetown	58	705
Reuban	El Dorado Georgetown	58	705
PESCHKE			
Wm	Trinity State Ba	70	1001
PESCO			
John	Fresno Twp 1	59	76
PESCOTT			
Chals	El Dorado Georgetown	58	686
PESECUD			
M	El Dorado Georgetown	58	703
PESERTE			
Antonio	San Bernardino Santa Barbara	64	151
PESGUAL			
Prener	Mariposa Twp 1	60	631
PESH			
John*	Alameda Brooklyn	55	97
PESIAL			
Usia	Santa Clara Almaden	65	275
PESINE			
James M	Solano Suisan	69	205
PESISH			
H	El Dorado Greenwood	58	713

Name	County Locale	M653 Roll	Page
PESLAFESCE			
Joseph	Calaveras Twp 10	57	292
PESLAFIRCE			
Joseph	Calaveras Twp 10	57	292
PESLERBE			
John*	Calaveras Twp 6	57	153
PESLERK			
John*	Calaveras Twp 6	57	153
PESLEY			
John C	Tuolumne Twp 2	71	286
PESQUIERA			
Miguel	Los Angeles Los Angeles	59	332
PESR			
---	El Dorado Greenwood	58	729
PESRIUN			
J T*	Mariposa Twp 3	60	561
PESRUM			
J T*	Mariposa Twp 3	60	561
PESSEDY			
John	San Francisco San Francisco 2	67	682
PESSEL			
Mike*	Yuba North Ea	72	687
PESSER			
John	San Francisco San Francisco 5	67	481
PESSEY			
J M	Tuolumne Columbia	71	343
PESSINS			
Chas H	El Dorado Big Bar	58	739
PESSNS			
Chas H	El Dorado Big Bar	58	739
PEST			
Michael	Siskiyou Scott Va	69	49
W O	Sierra Downieville	66	975
PESTER			
John	Placer Virginia	62	674
PESTERTR			
John	Calaveras Twp 6	57	153
PESTNER			
E	Shasta Shasta	66	659
PESTRILLO			
John S	Tuolumne Sonora	71	188
PESTROY			
W	Nevada Grass Valley	61	209
PESTUER			
E	Shasta Shasta	66	659
PET			
---	El Dorado Diamond	58	807
---	Sierra St Louis	66	815
PETALES			
Malto	Alameda Brooklyn	55	202
PETANS			
William	Sierra Port Win	66	794
PETATIO			
---	San Bernardino Santa Inez	64	139
PETAX			
John	Mariposa Coulterville	60	678
PETCAR			
Louis	Humbolt Union	59	192
PETCH			
Richard	San Francisco San Francisco 6	67	444
PETCHICKAWN			
---	Del Norte Klamath	58	657
PETE			
---	Butte Chico	56	558
---	Sacramento Granite	63	250
---	Sacramento Georgian	63	346
---	Sacramento Cosummes	63	406
---	Sacramento Cosummes	63	407
---	Sacramento Cosummes	63	408
---	Yolo No E Twp	72	682
---	Yuba North Ea	72	682
Danl E*	Calaveras Twp 6	57	142
Hon	Yuba New York	72	740
PETEE			
Rosa*	Yolo Cottonwoood	72	649
PETEGAN			
Oliver	Sierra Twp 7	66	913
PETEGRERO			
C	Tuolumne Sonora	71	481
PETEGREW			
John H	Yuba Bear Rvr	72	999
PETELIN			
Louis	San Francisco San Francisco 2	67	804
PETELIS			
Louis	San Francisco San Francisco 2	67	804
PETENAN			
Alfred*	Merced Twp 2	60	916
PETENSON			
C L	San Francisco San Francisco 5	67	536
C*	San Francisco San Francisco 5	67	536
Jno*	San Francisco San Francisco 5	67	537
PETER			
---	Butte Chico	56	558
---	Mendocino Calpella	60	822
---	Mendocino Calpella	60	827
---	Mendocino Round Va	60	878

California 1860 Census Index

Name	County Locale	M653 Roll	Page
PETER			
---	Mendocino Twp 1	60	886
---	Sacramento Ward 1	63	7
---	San Francisco San Francisco 12	67	387
---	San Francisco San Francisco 3	67	49
---	San Francisco San Francisco 3	67	56
---	San Mateo Twp 2	65	122
---	San Mateo Twp 2	65	126
---	San Mateo Twp 3	65	99
---	Tulara Twp 1	71	4
Antone	Klamath Salmon	59	209
Antone	Trinity Rush Crk	70	965
Antonia	Siskiyou Yreka	69	137
Antonia	Siskiyou Yreka	69	138
Antonio	Sierra Poker Flats	66	839
Blasweek*	Sierra Whiskey	66	850
Brow	Amador Twp 4	55	238
Christopher	San Joaquin Elkhorn	64	961
Dan E	Calaveras Twp 6	57	142
Danl E*	Calaveras Twp 6	57	142
David	Tuolumne Twp 1	71	246
Denning	Calaveras Twp 5	57	189
Ferras	Contra Costa Twp 3	57	612
G	San Joaquin Stockton	64	1070
George	Calaveras Twp 4	57	318
George	Sierra Downieville	66	1011
George	Siskiyou Yreka	69	155
George	Sonoma Santa Rosa	69	426
Hannah	Sonoma Mendocino	69	454
Henrie	Alameda Brooklyn	55	102
Henry	Tuolumne Shawsfla	71	406
Herman	Solano Vacaville	69	353
Horace	Sonoma Mendocino	69	454
Hug E	Tuolumne Columbia	71	366
Hugh	Tuolumne Twp 2	71	366
Jesse	Yolo Washington	72	575
John	Alameda Brooklyn	55	158
John	Calaveras Twp 6	57	187
John	Mariposa Coulterville	60	678
John	Sacramento Granite	63	265
John	San Bernardino San Bernadino	64	670
John	Santa Cruz Pescadero	66	645
John	Sierra Downieville	66	1028
John	Sierra Twp 7	66	871
John	Sierra Downieville	66	987
John	Sierra Downieville	66	991
John	Solano Benecia	69	316
John	Sonoma Petaluma	69	547
John	Yuba Fosters	72	837
Joseph	Sacramento Natonia	63	273
K M	Sierra Downieville	66	953
Liton	Tuolumne Twp 2	71	375
M	San Francisco San Francisco 2	67	689
M	Sonoma Petaluma	69	547
Maldere	Sierra Whiskey	66	843
Mantei	Butte Ophir	56	824
Manuel	Yuba Fosters	72	833
Martin	El Dorado White Oaks	58	1015
Mary	Calaveras Twp 6	57	135
Rosa	Yolo Cottonwood	72	649
Rosk*	Yolo Cottonwoood	72	649
Saml	Tuolumne Twp 1	71	256
Silas	Napa Hot Springs	61	16
Spelman	Sierra Downieville	66	963
W	San Mateo Twp 3	65	86
PETERA			
Albert	Placer Rattle Snake	62	633
PETERAN			
J	Sierra Twp 5	66	919
PETERCROSS			
O H*	Trinity Weaverville	70	1079
PETERGREW			
C	Tuolumne Twp 1	71	481
PETERHANSON			
F	Tuolumne Sonora	71	484
PETERLAND			
John	Siskiyou Yreka	69	137
PETERLCALF			
Allen	Yuba Marysville	72	902
PETERMAN			
John C	Placer Secret R	62	621
John R	Stanislaus Empire	70	727
PETERMORE			
Peter	El Dorado Grizzly	58	1182
PETERS DANL			
Barnes	Tuolumne Twp 1	71	201
PETERS			
A	Santa Clara San Jose	65	291
Adolphus	San Francisco San Francisco 9	68	1063
Agustus	Yolo Slate Ra	72	708
Amual*	Sierra Port Win	66	797
Andrew	Solano Fremont	69	383
Anneal*	Sierra Port Win	66	797
Annial	Sierra Port Win	66	797
Antone	Sierra St Louis	66	817
PETERS			
Augustus	Yuba Slate Ro	72	708
B	San Francisco San Francisco 1	68	903
Bridget	Tehama Tehama	70	940
C	San Francisco San Francisco 9	68	1090
C	Sonoma Bodega	69	526
C B	Tuolumne Twp 3	71	466
C D	Siskiyou Klamath	69	96
C H	Sierra Scales D	66	804
Carrie	San Francisco San Francisco 1	68	846
Carson	Klamath Liberty	59	237
Cartron*	Alameda Brooklyn	55	140
Cass	Sierra La Porte	66	780
Ch	Sierra Scales D	66	804
Charles	Amador Twp 1	55	489
Charles	Siskiyou Yreka	69	189
Charles O	Solano Vacaville	69	356
Chas	Sacramento Ward 1	63	29
Chas R	San Francisco San Francisco 10	67	349
Chris	Sierra Excelsior	66	1033
Clara	Solano Vacaville	69	351
Danl	Tuolumne Sonora	71	201
David	Trinity Hay Fork	70	992
Ed	Sacramento Natonia	63	271
Francis*	Solano Benecia	69	297
Frank	Butte Eureka	56	645
Frank	San Francisco San Francisco 3	67	9
Frederick	Sierra Twp 5	66	920
G E	Tuolumne Twp 2	71	417
G H	Nevada Grass Valley	61	150
Geo	Siskiyou Scott Ri	69	67
George	Yuba Marysville	72	857
Henry	Klamath Liberty	59	237
Henry	Mendocino Ukiah	60	794
Henry	Placer Yankee J	62	782
Henry	San Francisco San Francisco 9	68	1089
Henry	Solano Vacaville	69	355
Henry	Tuolumne Twp 2	71	406
Henry F	Tuolumne Columbia	71	362
Herman	Placer Todds Va	62	763
Hermann	San Francisco San Francisco 2	67	793
Isaac	Placer Michigan	62	811
Isaacs	Amador Twp 2	55	278
J	San Francisco San Francisco 5	67	482
J D	San Joaquin Stockton	64	1023
J D	San Joaquin Stockton	64	1038
J R	Siskiyou Cottonwoood	69	104
Jacob	Butte Hamilton	56	526
Jacob	Butte Kimshaw	56	581
Jacob	Sacramento Granite	63	254
Jacob	San Joaquin Douglass	64	928
James	El Dorado Coloma	58	1080
James	Placer Iona Hills	62	870
James	San Joaquin Elkhorn	64	991
James	Yolo Slate Ra	72	687
James	Yuba North Ea	72	687
James R	Napa Hot Springs	61	14
Jesse	Mendocino Round Va	60	877
Jno	Mendocino Big Rvr	60	849
Jno	Sacramento Ward 3	63	456
Jno	Tehama Red Bluff	70	922
Joel	Plumas Quincy	62	937
John	Placer Dutch Fl	62	720
John	Placer Iona Hills	62	881
John	Sacramento Ward 3	63	422
John	Sacramento Ward 3	63	487
John	San Francisco San Francisco 2	67	559
John	San Francisco San Francisco 2	67	685
John	San Joaquin Oneal	64	912
John	Shasta Shasta	66	730
John	Sierra Poker Flats	66	842
John	Tulara Keyesville	71	59
John	Tuolumne Twp 1	71	272
John*	Mariposa Coulterville	60	678
Jonas	El Dorado White Oaks	58	1011
Jones	El Dorado White Oaks	58	1017
Joseph	Sacramento Natonia	63	273
Joseph	Tuolumne Twp 1	71	251
Lawrence	Tuolumne Columbia	71	362
Manuel	San Francisco San Francisco 1	68	919
Martin	Klamath Liberty	59	237
Mary E	Sonoma Armally	69	517
Michael	Placer Michigan	62	857
N	El Dorado Georgetown	58	694
O F	Nevada Grass Valley	61	164
P	Sutter Nicolaus	70	838
P Melin*	Mariposa Twp 3	60	571
P S	Tuolumne Columbia	71	362
Pehelin*	Mariposa Twp 3	60	571
Peter	Mariposa Twp 3	60	571
Peter	Plumas Quincy	62	995
Peter	Sacramento Ward 1	63	28
R	Trinity Readings	70	996
R J	El Dorado Salmon Falls	58	1035
R L	Butte Oregon	56	634
PETERS			
Sam	Sacramento American	63	165
Simon	Mendocino Big Rvr	60	848
Thomas	Calaveras Twp 5	57	140
Thomas	Calaveras Twp 5	57	142
Thomas	Monterey San Juan	60	1008
Thomas	San Francisco San Francisco 7	68	1438
Timothy	Yuba Rose Bar	72	789
W B	Klamath S Fork	59	205
W C	San Mateo Twp 2	65	131
William	Tulara Visalia	71	105
William	Tuolumne Sonora	71	196
Wm	Sacramento Granite	63	243
Wm	Yolo Slate Ra	72	708
Wm	Yuba Slate Ro	72	708
Wm J	San Francisco San Francisco 7	68	1373
PETERSEN			
C H	Amador Twp 5	55	358
Nick	El Dorado Georgetown	58	760
O	Amador Twp 2	55	309
T A	San Francisco San Francisco 3	67	44
William	Shasta Shasta	66	675
PETERSON			
A	Calaveras Twp 9	57	405
A	El Dorado Kelsey	58	1155
A	Marin San Rafael	60	766
A	San Francisco San Francisco 2	67	738
A	Trinity Trinity	70	972
A J	Sonoma Santa Rosa	69	419
Albert	San Francisco San Francisco 1	68	909
Alex	Siskiyou Scott Ri	69	64
Allen	Santa Cruz Santa Cruz	66	611
Andrew	El Dorado White Oaks	58	1012
Andrew	El Dorado Union	58	1093
Andrew	El Dorado Mountain	58	1186
Andrew	San Francisco San Francisco 9	68	1044
Andrew	Sierra Whiskey	66	846
Andrew	Trinity Evans Ba	70	1002
Anne S	El Dorado Greenwood	58	710
Arthur	Amador Twp 4	55	239
Augustin	Sonoma Petaluma	69	557
Augustus	Sonoma Santa Rosa	69	419
Augustus	Yuba Marysville	72	975
Author S	Placer Stewart	62	607
B F	Sonoma Bodega	69	533
C	San Francisco San Francisco 9	68	1057
C	San Francisco San Francisco 5	67	536
C A	Tehama Moons	70	851
C G	Calaveras Twp 9	57	410
C H	Trinity Weaverville	70	1064
C L	San Francisco San Francisco 5	67	536
C*	San Francisco San Francisco 5	67	536
Charles	Alameda Brooklyn	55	104
Charles	Calaveras Twp 8	57	108
Charles	Calaveras Twp 6	57	137
Charles	Calaveras Twp 5	57	211
Charles	Colusa Monroeville	57	142
Charles	Colusa Monroeville	57	442
Charles	Placer Michigan	62	851
Charles	San Francisco San Francisco 3	67	40
Charles	San Mateo Twp 3	65	85
Charles	Sonoma Russian	69	440
Charles	Tuolumne Twp 1	71	271
Charles	Tuolumne Twp 1	71	479
Charles J	San Francisco San Francisco 7	68	1354
Charly	Tuolumne Sonora	71	479
Chas	Placer Virginia	62	664
Chas	Sacramento Ward 1	63	149
Chas	San Francisco San Francisco 3	67	82
Chas	San Francisco San Francisco 1	68	916
Chas F	Butte Kimshaw	56	585
Chas J	Trinity Point Ba	70	976
Chris	El Dorado Greenwood	58	712
Christ	Nevada Bloomfield	61	511
Christian	Placer Rattle Snake	62	630
Christian	Placer Folsom	62	640
Christian	Sonoma Armally	69	487
Christopher	Placer Virginia	62	665
D C	Siskiyou Klamath	69	80
E J	Tuolumne Garrote	71	176
Edwin	Sonoma Petaluma	69	543
Elias	Yolo Cottonwoood	72	648
Ellen	Sonoma Healdsbu	69	472
Filepena	Yolo Cottonwoood	72	558
Floyd	Solano Fremont	69	377
Fred	Plumas Quincy	62	923
Fred	Tuolumne Twp 2	71	292
Fredk	San Francisco San Francisco 10	67	284
Fredrick	Plumas Quincy	62	991
G	San Francisco San Francisco 3	67	29
G H	Sonoma Healdsbu	69	472
G K	Mariposa Twp 1	60	638
Geo	Alameda Oakland	55	36
Geo	San Francisco San Francisco 1	68	906

California 1860 Census Index

Name	County Locale	M653 RollPage
PETERSON		
George	Plumas Meadow Valley	62 904
George	San Francisco San Francisco 9	681097
George	San Mateo Twp 2	65 122
George*	San Francisco San Francisco 9	681097
H	Trinity Trinity	70 972
Henry	Placer Auburn	62 571
Henry	San Francisco San Francisco 9	681064
Henry	San Francisco San Francisco 9	681084
Henry	San Joaquin Elkhorn	64 982
Henry	Solano Vacaville	69 354
Henry	Tuolumne Sonora	71 192
J	Calaveras Twp 8	57 81
J	Los Angeles Tejon	59 528
J	Nevada Eureka	61 374
J	San Francisco San Francisco 9	681058
J	San Francisco San Francisco 9	681059
J	Sierra Twp 5	66 919
J	Yolo Cottonwoood	72 559
J A	San Joaquin Stockton	641094
J F	Tuolumne Twp 2	71 284
J J	Tuolumne Twp 2	71 284
Jacob	Sierra Twp 5	66 920
James	San Francisco San Francisco 2	67 574
James	Siskiyou Scott Va	69 36
James	Siskiyou Scott Va	69 43
Jno	Butte Eureka	56 655
Jno	San Francisco San Francisco 9	681081
Jno*	San Francisco San Francisco 5	67 537
John	Alameda Brooklyn	55 136
John	Alameda Oakland	55 28
John	Calaveras Twp 4	57 336
John	Calaveras Twp 7	57 40
John	El Dorado Casumnes	581173
John	Nevada Rough &	61 413
John	Nevada Bloomfield	61 526
John	Placer Auburn	62 567
John	Placer Folsom	62 640
John	San Francisco San Francisco 3	67 32
John	San Francisco San Francisco 10	336
		67
John	San Francisco San Francisco 2	67 656
John	San Francisco San Francisco 2	67 749
John	Sierra Excelsior	661033
John	Siskiyou Callahan	69 19
John	Tehama Cottonwood	70 900
John	Tuolumne Twp 3	71 448
John A	Placer Rattle Snake	62 632
Jos	Sacramento Ward 1	63 153
L	Nevada Rough &	61 408
L	Yolo Cottonwoood	72 557
Lewis	Sacramento Franklin	63 326
Lewis	Tuolumne Twp 1	71 186
Louis	Los Angeles San Pedro	59 481
Louis	Placer Folsom	62 640
Louis	Placer Michigan	62 837
Mary	Sacramento Ward 1	63 129
Mary	Sonoma Sonoma	69 643
N P	El Dorado Kelsey	581156
Nicholas	El Dorado Greenwood	58 710
Nicholus	El Dorado Georgetown	58 760
Niels P	Los Angeles Los Angeles	59 328
O	Amador Twp 2	55 309
O	Sacramento Georgian	63 344
Ole	Tuolumne Sonora	71 230
Orlim*	El Dorado Casumnes	581172
Orlnn	El Dorado Casumnes	581172
Orlun*	El Dorado Casumnes	581172
Otto	Trinity Evans Ba	701002
P	Butte Bidwell	56 711
P	Nevada Eureka	61 374
P	San Francisco San Francisco 9	681060
P	San Francisco San Francisco 3	67 55
P	Siskiyou Scott Ri	69 70
P	Yolo Cottonwoood	72 559
P S	Santa Clara Santa Clara	65 485
Paul	Sonoma Sonoma	69 656
Peter	Alameda Brooklyn	55 112
Peter	Alameda Brooklyn	55 152
Peter	Alameda Brooklyn	55 88
Peter	El Dorado Coloma	581122
Peter	El Dorado Mountain	581186
Peter	El Dorado Greenwood	58 720
Peter	Humbolt Bucksport	59 155
Peter	Marin San Rafael	60 771
Peter	Placer Yankee J	62 775
Peter	San Francisco San Francisco 3	67 62
Peter	San Francisco San Francisco 1	68 909
Peter	San Joaquin Stockton	641066
Peter	Santa Clara San Jose	65 389
Peter	Sierra Downieville	661010
Peter	Sonoma Santa Rosa	69 427
Peter	Sonoma Petaluma	69 573
Peter	Yuba Rose Bar	72 803
Peter W	Alameda Brooklyn	55 140
Raymond	El Dorado Georgetown	58 757

Name	County Locale	M653 RollPage
PETERSON		
Rebeca	Napa Yount	61 45
Rebecca	Napa Yount	61 45
Robert	San Mateo Twp 3	65 79
S	El Dorado Georgetown	58 707
S B	San Francisco San Francisco 10	352
		67
Samuel	Sierra Downieville	661028
Sarah	San Francisco San Francisco 4	681114
Sarah A	San Francisco San Francisco 10	307
		67
Sophia	Tuolumne Twp 2	71 271
T A	San Francisco San Francisco 3	67 44
T A	San Francisco San Francisco 3	67 79
T E	Sacramento Mississipi	63 187
Theadore	San Francisco San Francisco 3	67 68
Theodore	San Francisco San Francisco 3	67 68
Tho	Siskiyou Scott Ri	69 82
Thomas	Marin S Antoni	60 706
Thomas	San Francisco San Francisco 3	67 67
Thomas	Yolo No E Twp	72 668
Thos	Sonoma Vallejo	69 628
Wesley	Plumas Quincy	62 941
Wiliam	Placer Forest H	62 767
William	Shasta Shasta	66 675
William H	Los Angeles Los Angeles	59 336
Wm	Sonoma Santa Rosa	69 414
PETERY		
---	Mendocino Calpella	60 822
PETES		
Joseph	Yuba Marysville	72 936
Sevese	Colusa Spring Valley	57 436
PETET		
Charles	Sierra Whiskey	66 843
Henry	Tuolumne Twp 2	71 280
John	Alameda Oakland	55 1
PETETE		
Anderson	Tuolumne Twp 1	71 233
PETETER		
Caroline	San Francisco San Francisco 2	67 625
PETEY		
Sampson	Yuba Bear Rvr	721008
PETEYSEN		
John H*	Yuba Bear Rvr	72 999
PETEZE		
Henry	Sonoma Bodega	69 536
PETH		
---	Sierra St Louis	66 805
PETHALAGE		
Geo	Del Norte Crescent	58 634
Geo*	Del Norte Crescent	58 633
PETHALAJE		
Geo	Del Norte Crescent	58 633
PETHAM		
J M*	San Bernardino San Bernadino	64 628
PETHELL		
Peter G	Tuolumne Sonora	71 199
PETHERLY		
Henry	San Francisco San Francisco 4	681118
PETIER		
Henrie	Alameda Brooklyn	55 102
PETIGI		
George	Alameda Brooklyn	55 205
PETIGNY		
Chas	San Francisco San Francisco 10	190
		67
PETIGO		
Meredith	Tulara Visalia	71 82
PETIJEN		
D	Nevada Washington	61 334
PETIL		
James P	Yuba Marysville	72 918
PETIONS		
Mary L	San Francisco San Francisco 7	681383
PETIRE		
William	Yolo Putah	72 551
PETISMAN		
O	Calaveras Twp 9	57 414
PETIT JEAN		
---*	Yuba Parke Ba	72 786
PETIT		
Amos	Sonoma Armally	69 515
August	Santa Clara San Jose	65 370
Charles	San Francisco San Francisco 8	681247
Charles	Sierra Whiskey	66 843
J L	Butte Ophir	56 750
J S	Butte Ophir	56 750
James P	Yuba Marysville	72 918
Jas E	Butte Ophir	56 771
John	Alameda Oakland	55 1
John*	Butte Mountain	56 741
Joseph	Solano Benecia	69 285
Lewis	Butte Ophir	56 759
Margaret	Sonoma Armally	69 510
Peter	Butte Mountain	56 741
Z A	Butte Bidwell	56 714

Name	County Locale	M653 RollPage
PETIT		
Z A	Butte Bidwell	56 715
PETLETIER		
Harry*	Nevada Bloomfield	61 514
PETMON		
Peter	Sierra Downieville	661010
PETNEL		
---	San Bernardino S Timate	64 693
PETNER		
Wilson	Colusa Monroeville	57 451
PETNES		
Frederick*	Sierra Twp 5	66 920
PETO		
---	Fresno Twp 2	59 68
PETOMEY		
W	El Dorado Grizzly	581180
PETON		
Frank	El Dorado Kelsey	581134
PETOS		
Pihelin*	Mariposa Twp 3	60 571
Pipelin*	Mariposa Twp 3	60 571
PETR		
---	Sacramento Granite	63 250
PETRA		
---	Los Angeles Los Angeles	59 371
---	Los Angeles San Gabriel	59 414
---	Los Angeles S Nieto	59 436
---	Los Angeles Santa Ana	59 442
---	San Bernardino Santa Inez	64 139
---	San Bernardino S Buenav	64 222
---	San Bernardino S Timate	64 695
---	San Bernardino S Timate	64 706
---	San Bernardino S Timate	64 710
---	San Bernardino S Timate	64 723
---	San Bernardino S Timate	64 727
---	San Bernardino S Timate	64 729
---	San Bernardino S Timate	64 736
---	San Bernardino S Timate	64 739
---	San Bernardino S Timate	64 746
---	San Bernardino S Timate	64 750
---	San Bernardino S Timate	64 754
---	San Diego San Diego	64 771
---	San Diego Temecula	64 798
---	San Diego Agua Caliente	64 832
---	San Diego Agua Caliente	64 843
Adolph	Calaveras Twp 6	57 143
August	Calaveras Twp 5	57 143
M	San Francisco San Francisco 2	67 702
Peter	Colusa Spring Valley	57 432
PETRAN		
Gudrich	El Dorado Georgetown	58 683
PETRAY		
Columbus	Sonoma Russian	69 433
Geo	Sonoma Russian	69 440
Geo W	Sonoma Russian	69 440
Martha	Sonoma Russian	69 438
PETRAYS		
R A	Sonoma Russian	69 438
PETRE		
---	San Bernardino San Bernadino	64 680
---	San Bernardino S Timate	64 734
Gerard	Alameda Brooklyn	55 180
PETREAM		
Charles	Amador Twp 1	55 465
PETREANE		
Charles	Amador Twp 1	55 465
PETREE		
---	San Bernardino San Bernadino	64 681
---	San Bernardino S Timate	64 699
---	San Bernardino S Timate	64 700
---	San Bernardino S Timate	64 707
---	San Bernardino S Timate	64 714
---	San Bernardino S Timate	64 717
---	San Bernardino S Timate	64 726
---	San Bernardino S Timate	64 730
---	San Bernardino S Timate	64 732
---	San Bernardino S Timate	64 741
---	San Bernardino S Timate	64 749
A	Siskiyou Klamath	69 86
Jno	Sacramento Ward 4	63 573
Robt	El Dorado Mud Springs	58 981
Webster*	Tulara Keyesville	71 59
PETREL		
---	San Bernardino San Bernadino	64 678
---	San Bernardino San Bernadino	64 679
Webster*	Tulara Keyesville	71 59
PETRENE		
Juliana	San Francisco San Francisco 2	67 570
PETRER		
---	San Bernardino S Timate	64 696
PETRICE		
---	San Bernardino S Timate	64 696
PETRIE		
Benjamin	Yolo Slate Ra	72 711
Benjamin	Yuba Slate Ro	72 711
F C	Sacramento Centre	63 174

California 1860 Census Index

Name	County Locale	M653 Roll	Page
PETRIE			
G C	Sacramento Centre	63	174
Wm	Yuba New York	72	734
PETRINE			
Juliana*	San Francisco San Francisco 2	67	570
PETRO			
---	Los Angeles Los Angeles	59	402
---	San Bernardino S Timate	64	697
---	San Bernardino S Timate	64	703
---	San Bernardino S Timate	64	712
---*	San Bernardino Santa Inez	64	143
Don	Stanislaus Oatvale	70	719
Jesse*	Yolo Washington	72	575
Juan	Yuba New York	72	734
Polandro*	Placer Michigan	62	832
Treama	Tuolumne Chinese	71	495
PETRONE			
Peter	San Francisco San Francisco 2	67	570
PETRONELLA			
---	San Bernardino Santa Barbara	64	199
PETRONILLA			
---*	Monterey San Juan	60	999
PETROS			
Francis	Solano Benecia	69	297
PETRSON			
S	El Dorado Georgetown	58	707
PETRUO			
A*	Placer Virginia	62	677
PETRY			
C B	Tuolumne Twp 3	71	466
Peter	San Luis Obispo San Luis Obispo	65	36
PETT			
---	Yolo Slate Ra	72	712
---	Yuba Slate Ro	72	712
David	Calaveras Twp 4	57	299
George L	Sierra Downieville	661	023
James	Sierra Eureka	661	044
Thomas	Calaveras Twp 4	57	299
PETTAN			
Amanda M	El Dorado Mountain	581	183
PETTE			
John	San Diego Agua Caliente	64	814
PETTEES			
Alfred	Amador Twp 2	55	302
PETTEL			
A M	San Francisco San Francisco 9	68	945
PETTER			
Clark	El Dorado Georgetown	58	699
J	El Dorado Newtown	58	778
PETTERS			
I	El Dorado Placerville	58	924
Ira	Sonoma Mendocino	69	450
J*	El Dorado Placerville	58	924
R*	Sacramento Cosummes	63	410
PETTERSON			
Alva	Siskiyou Yreka	69	171
Andrew	Siskiyou Scott Va	69	22
Chas	Sierra St Louis	66	813
Chas P	Sierra St Louis	66	813
Jas	San Francisco San Francisco 2	67	696
Jerry	Mariposa Twp 3	60	561
Landrew	Siskiyou Scott Va	69	22
O H	Placer Iowa Hills	62	861
P	Mariposa Twp 3	60	558
Perry	Mariposa Twp 3	60	561
William	Sierra Poker Flats	66	837
PETTES			
John	San Diego S Luis R	64	778
Trinidad	San Diego Agua Caliente	64	835
PETTET JEAN			
Marie*	Yuba Fosters	72	821
PETTET			
Edwd	San Francisco San Francisco 10	261 67	
Thomas	Yuba Marysville	72	976
PETTETT			
John	Mariposa Twp 1	60	671
PETTEY			
John	Calaveras Twp 4	57	343
PETTIBONE			
S J	Sierra Twp 7	66	894
PETTIER			
A	Amador Twp 1	55	492
Alex	Nevada Bloomfield	61	524
F X	Amador Twp 5	55	362
PETTIG			
John*	Calaveras Twp 4	57	343
PETTIGROVE			
Harrison K	Mendocino Arrana	60	862
Jno	Mendocino Arrana	60	859
PETTIL			
Charles	Sierra Downieville	66	972
PETTING			
H H	Sierra Downieville	661	020
PETTING			
J F	Sierra Downieville	661	020
John	Calaveras Twp 4	57	343
John F	Sierra Downieville	66	989
Wm	Sierra Downieville	66	997
PETTINGER			
Frank	Sierra Poker Flats	66	841
John	Plumas Quincy	62	971
PETTINGILL			
Samuel B	Sierra Gibsonville	66	855
PETTINGLL			
William W	Sierra Gibsonville	66	855
PETTINGS			
George	Sierra La Porte	66	767
PETTINOS			
J A	San Francisco San Francisco 10	282 67	
W T	Placer Damascus	62	846
PETTIS			
A	Nevada Grass Valley	61	152
B F	El Dorado Placerville	58	851
F W	Butte Chico	56	561
George H	San Francisco San Francisco 7	681	358
J E	San Francisco San Francisco 5	67	535
Joseph	Santa Clara Santa Clara	65	480
Thos	Santa Clara Redwood	65	446
PETTIT			
A P	Sacramento Ward 1	63	79
Antoin Ette	Sonoma Russian	69	440
Antoinette	Sonoma Russian	69	440
Asa	Yolo Cache Crk	72	622
C B	El Dorado Placerville	58	861
C*	Sacramento Brighton	63	192
Charles	Sierra Downieville	66	972
Horatio N	San Francisco San Francisco 11	105 67	
I H	Mariposa Twp 3	60	592
J H	Mariposa Twp 3	60	592
N S	San Francisco San Francisco 6	67	413
Thomas	Yuba Marysville	72	976
PETTITS			
John	Tulara Twp 3	71	54
PETTIZ			
W R	Butte Ophir	56	792
PETTONOS			
P	San Francisco San Francisco 10	234 67	
PETTRESLAND			
Samuel*	Solano Vacaville	69	339
PETTRY			
John*	Calaveras Twp 4	57	343
PETTS			
Henry A*	San Francisco San Francisco 3	67	31
J M*	Yuba Marysville	72	950
Wm W	Sierra Twp 7	66	915
PETTSELL			
William	Tuolumne Sonora	71	193
PETTUS			
James E	Mendocino Twp 1	60	892
PETTY			
A	Amador Twp 3	55	387
A J	Trinity Minersville	70	968
Alex	Butte Hamilton	56	517
B A*	Mariposa Twp 1	60	633
C M	Amador Twp 1	55	476
E	Mariposa Twp 1	60	633
E John	San Joaquin Stockton	641	020
E*	Mariposa Twp 1	60	633
Geo L*	Alameda Brooklyn	55	93
Geo S	Alameda Washington	55	214
Geo S*	Alameda Brooklyn	55	93
George	Sonoma Russian	69	433
J A	Shasta Horsetown	66	692
J E	Amador Twp 6	55	436
J W	Stanislaus Buena Village	70	721
Jas A	Sacramento Natonia	63	283
Jno	Klamath Liberty	59	243
Jno W	Mendocino Calpella	60	816
John	Amador Twp 3	55	392
John	San Francisco San Francisco 11	143 67	
Jonathan	Marin Tomales	60	718
Jonathon	Marin Tomales	60	718
Mary	Santa Cruz Pajaro	66	559
N	Merced Twp 1	60	910
O S	Sutter Bear Rvr	70	824
S A*	Mariposa Twp 1	60	633
S P*	Alameda Oakland	55	71
Walter	San Joaquin Elkhorn	64	972
William	Plumas Quincy	62	962
William	San Joaquin Oneal	64	936
Wm	Tuolumne Columbia	71	323
Wm H	San Francisco San Francisco 10	255 67	
PETTYBINE			
James*	Amador Twp 7	55	416
PETTYBORN			
James*	Amador Twp 7	55	416
PETTYJOHN			
C C	Trinity Rush Crk	70	965
PETTYTONE			
James	Amador Twp 7	55	416
PETUES			
Frederick*	Sierra Twp 5	66	920
PETUS			
J	El Dorado Diamond	58	796
Jesse*	Yolo Washington	72	575
PETUTE			
Polite	Amador Twp 1	55	494
PETVA			
Jascuitho	Santa Cruz Santa Cruz	66	612
PETZER			
Augustes	Yuba Marysville	72	898
Augustus*	Yuba Marysville	72	898
PEÜ			
---	Calaveras Twp 4	57	305
---	Sierra La Porte	66	780
---	Yuba Slate Ro	72	711
PEUDERGRAST			
Thos*	San Francisco San Francisco 9	681	090
PEUDRO			
Sefefpen*	Mariposa Twp 3	60	547
PEUET			
Jeremiah*	Santa Cruz Soguel	66	579
PEUETEER			
Harry*	Nevada Bloomfield	61	514
PEUÉTIER			
Harry*	Nevada Bloomfield	61	514
PEUGH			
---	Calaveras Twp 4	57	306
Theophilas	Mariposa Coulterville	60	693
Theophilos	Mariposa Coulterville	60	693
PEUILLEU			
Eugene*	San Francisco San Francisco 11	140 67	
PEUILON			
Monore	Los Angeles Los Angeles	59	298
PEUJADAUX			
Louis	Calaveras Twp 7	57	24
PEUKE			
Christen*	Alameda Brooklyn	55	147
PEUMDO			
---	San Bernardino S Timate	64	708
PEUNDO			
---	San Bernardino S Timate	64	700
---	San Bernardino S Timate	64	748
PEUNG			
Ah	Sacramento Ward 1	63	156
PEURO			
Jacomo*	San Francisco San Francisco 11	124 67	
PEURS			
C*	Calaveras Twp 9	57	393
William*	Nevada Rough &	61	414
PEURSON			
J C	Tuolumne Twp 2	71	402
PEUSAM			
Jno J*	San Francisco San Francisco 10	345 67	
PEUSE			
Elijah*	Nevada Bridgeport	61	442
PEUSON			
Cordilea	Butte Ophir	56	761
PEUT			
Louis*	Mariposa Twp 3	60	606
PEUTLAND			
James D*	Stanislaus Buena Village	70	723
PEUTZY			
Charles	Calaveras Twp 4	57	340
PEVELES			
Peter H	Del Norte Happy Ca	58	662
PEVER			
E B	San Francisco San Francisco 2	67	707
PEVERTH			
Layarnus	Calaveras Twp 7	57	6
PEVETKINS			
Isruel	El Dorado Greenwood	58	729
PEVICHE			
Ferdinand	Sierra Downieville	66	977
PEVONTAIN			
Al	Yolo Cache Crk	72	611
PEVONTAN			
Al	Yolo Cache	72	611
PEVRANTH			
Caler	Yuba Suida	72	983
PEVRANTT			
Calix*	Yuba Linda	72	983
PEVRAUTT			
Calix*	Yuba Linda	72	983
PEVRIF			
Frank*	San Francisco San Francisco 2	67	687
PEVRY			
Geo*	San Francisco San Francisco 2	67	674

Name	County Locale	M653 Roll Page
PEW FIR		
---*	Nevada Bridgeport	61 461
PEW		
---	El Dorado Salmon Hills	581055
---	El Dorado Salmon Hills	581060
---	El Dorado Salmon Hills	581062
---	El Dorado Union	581090
---	Placer Folsom	62 640
---	Placer Illinois	62 742
---	Sierra Twp 5	66 927
---	Sierra Twp 5	66 928
---	Sierra Downieville	66 983
---	Tuolumne Twp 5	71 522
---	Tuolumne Twp 6	71 530
---	Tuolumne Twp 6	71 536
B F	El Dorado Placerville	58 886
Grandvill*	San Mateo Twp 3	65 85
Kin	Sierra Downieville	66 983
W H	El Dorado Placerville	58 914
PEWEOST		
A	San Francisco San Francisco 4	681156
PEWET		
Ephiam	Sacramento Ward 3	63 482
PEWINES		
Alex*	Sacramento Brighton	63 191
PEWMAN		
Geo	Butte Oro	56 678
PEWS		
Edmund	Santa Cruz Soguel	66 585
Edward	Santa Cruz Soguel	66 585
PEWTER		
Patk	Klamath Liberty	59 230
PEWWELL		
S A	El Dorado Gold Hill	581097
PEXLEY		
Geo	El Dorado Diamond	58 793
PEY		
---	Nevada Bridgeport	61 461
---*	Calaveras Twp 6	57 176
PEYE		
Edward*	San Francisco San Francisco 3	67 82
Sarah A*	San Francisco San Francisco 4	681155
PEYEL		
Michael*	Calaveras Twp 6	57 158
PEYLOU		
V M	San Joaquin Stockton	641072
PEYNA		
Martin	Tuolumne Columbia	71 291
PEYNE		
F	San Francisco San Francisco 5	67 534
PEYON		
P	Yolo Cache	72 595
PEYRAN		
Pauline	Calaveras Twp 6	57 131
PEYRAND		
Peter	Yuba Marysville	72 925
PEYRASEME		
Beltand*	Siskiyou Callahan	69 9
Beltaud*	Siskiyou Callahan	69 9
PEYRASOME		
Beltand*	Siskiyou Callahan	69 9
Beltaud*	Siskiyou Callahan	69 9
PEYREINE		
B	Siskiyou Callahan	69 3
PEYRON		
Jerome	Tuolumne Green Springs	71 527
PEYSEINE		
B	Siskiyou Callahan	69 3
PEYSEN		
Jno*	Sacramento Ward 1	63 86
PEYSER		
Jno	Sacramento Ward 1	63 86
Philip	Sacramento Ward 4	63 506
PEYSON		
Jerome	Tuolumne Twp 5	71 527
PEYSTER		
W De*	San Francisco San Francisco 10	218 67
PEYTAN		
T B	Stanislaus Oatvale	70 720
PEYTON		
Ann	Sonoma Sonoma	69 645
Bernard	San Mateo Twp 1	65 49
J A	Sonoma Petaluma	69 573
J B	Trinity Mouth Ca	701015
Jno	Sonoma Sonoma	69 645
John A	Solano Suisan	69 216
John R	Yuba Marysville	72 978
William	Placer Michigan	62 837
William	Placer Michigan	62 838
PEZET		
John Wm	San Francisco San Francisco 2	67 609
PEZGONE		
Juliana*	San Francisco San Francisco 2	67 570
PEZZONE		
Juliana*	San Francisco San Francisco 2	67 570

Name	County Locale	M653 Roll Page
PFAAR		
Philip	Plumas Quincy	62 939
PFAFF		
January	San Francisco San Francisco 11	129 67
PFEIFER		
A W	San Francisco San Francisco 10	302 67
John	San Francisco San Francisco 8	681308
Josephine	San Francisco San Francisco 8	681314
PFEIFEX		
A W	San Francisco San Francisco 10	302 67
PFEIFFER		
Chas	Del Norte Crescent	58 622
Lorenzo	Sacramento Ward 4	63 554
M	Solano Vacaville	69 329
Moses	Yolo Cache Crk	72 666
PFENNINGER		
H	Siskiyou Klamath	69 93
PFERFFER		
M	Solano Vacaville	69 329
PFFEIFFER		
Lawry	San Francisco San Francisco 2	67 689
PFFERS		
Thos	Tuolumne Big Oak	71 140
PFFLES		
A	Siskiyou Klamath	69 93
PFIASTAR		
C	El Dorado Newtown	58 778
PFIEFER		
Josephine	San Francisco San Francisco 8	681314
PFIEFFER		
George	San Francisco San Francisco 7	681352
J E	San Francisco San Francisco 2	67 640
PFIEL		
Conrad	Colusa Butte Crk	57 465
PFIFE		
August	Placer Forest H	62 772
PFIFER		
John	San Francisco San Francisco 7	681395
PFINTER		
J	San Francisco San Francisco 5	67 523
PFIPER		
Charles	Placer Iona Hills	62 875
PFISTER		
Joseph	Colusa Spring Valley	57 431
PFLANG		
George	Solano Benecia	69 316
PFLANZ		
George	Solano Benecia	69 316
PFOOR		
Frederica	San Francisco San Francisco 7	681382
PFORE		
Christian*	Tuolumne Don Pedro	71 542
PFORGHEISEN		
Isaac*	Yuba Marysville	72 905
PFORR		
Christian*	Tuolumne Don Pedro	71 542
John	San Francisco San Francisco 7	681416
PFORZHEIMER		
Isaac	Yuba Marysville	72 905
PFOUTS		
J	Sierra Twp 7	66 885
PFRISTER		
A P	Santa Clara San Jose	65 316
PFURER		
William	San Francisco San Francisco 7	681433
PGO		
Mary*	Placer Iona Hills	62 876
PGOMEZ		
Maria S	Los Angeles Los Nieto	59 434
PHACE		
Nora*	Alameda Brooklyn	55 93
PHAENG		
---	San Francisco San Francisco 5	67 508
PHAH		
---	El Dorado Georgetown	58 675
PHAIR		
Nora	Alameda Brooklyn	55 93
PHALAN		
James	Sierra Downieville	661011
PHALANSA		
Antonio	San Joaquin Stockton	641086
PHALAR		
W	Merced Twp 2	60 920
PHALEN		
M	Tuolumne Jacksonville	71 172
Michael	Placer Forest H	62 794
PHALEY		
Michal	Napa Napa	61 67
PHALPS		
R C	Amador Twp 3	55 408
PHAN		
---	Calaveras Twp 9	57 363

Name	County Locale	M653 Roll Page
PHAN		
Chow	San Francisco San Francisco 10	356 67
Richd*	Tuolumne Twp 1	71 238
PHARE		
Thos	San Francisco San Francisco 10	330 67
PHARO		
Jos	Sacramento Ward 1	63 76
Richd*	Tuolumne Twp 1	71 238
PHARR		
Phillip	Sierra St Louis	66 808
PHAZELL		
M	Sutter Bear Rvr	70 822
PHEASANT		
Henry	Tulara Twp 2	71 32
William	Tulara Twp 2	71 33
PHEBBOTT		
Wm*	Nevada Nevada	61 292
PHEE		
---*	Yuba Marysville	72 908
Arthur*	San Mateo Twp 1	65 48
PHEENEY		
Mary	San Francisco San Francisco 12	395 67
PHEHN		
Kim*	Nevada Bridgeport	61 501
PHEIFFER		
George	San Francisco San Francisco 7	681352
PHEILE		
Mons	San Francisco San Francisco 11	119 67
PHEIPP		
Ann M	San Francisco San Francisco 9	681035
PHEK		
John	Yuba Slate Ro	72 699
PHELAN		
A J F	Sacramento Ward 3	63 439
Ab	Klamath Orleans	59 217
Dennis	Stanislaus Branch	70 715
Edward	Tuolumne Sonora	71 484
Edwd	San Francisco San Francisco 10	213 67
Ellen	San Francisco San Francisco 11	149 67
G J	Sacramento Ward 3	63 466
Geoffery	San Luis Obispo San Luis Obispo	65 3
I J	San Mateo Twp 3	65 79
J	San Francisco San Francisco 6	67 473
James	Marin San Rafael	60 764
James	San Francisco San Francisco 8	681233
Jas	Butte Oregon	56 611
John	Del Norte Crescent	58 660
John	San Francisco San Francisco 4	681118
John	Tuolumne Twp 3	71 466
John J	San Francisco San Francisco 4	681118
M	Nevada Eureka	61 375
Mary	San Francisco San Francsco 2	67 663
Mary	San Francisco San Francisco 2	67 717
O T	Butte Oregon	56 617
Patrick	San Francisco San Francisco 10	294 67
Richard	San Francisco San Francisco 7	681328
PHELANI		
Even	Placer Secret R	62 609
PHELAR		
Z P	Butte Bidwell	56 714
PHELESAMEA		
Galean	Siskiyou Yreka	69 140
PHELESANNA		
Galean*	Siskiyou Yreka	69 140
PHELESANUA		
Galean*	Siskiyou Yreka	69 140
PHELHOTT		
Wm*	Nevada Nevada	61 292
PHELISIANO		
Jose*	San Francisco San Francisco 2	67 664
PHELLA		
Patrick	Tuolumne Big Oak	71 138
PHELLE		
Patrick	Tuolumne Twp 4	71 138
PHELLEN		
D M*	Butte Cascade	56 696
PHELLIPS		
I*	Mariposa Twp 3	60 602
W L*	Napa Hot Springs	61 26
PHELLON		
D M	Butte Cascade	56 696
PHELM		
Kim*	Nevada Bridgeport	61 501
PHELPLACE		
H	Sutter Sutter	70 812
PHELPLS		
Eugene	Placer Iona Hills	62 878
PHELPO		
A F	Mariposa Twp 1	60 660

Name	County Locale	M653 Roll	Page
PHELPS			
A F	Mariposa Twp 1	60	660
A M	Mariposa Twp 1	60	660
A T	Yolo Putah	72	549
Abner	San Francisco San Francisco 11	67	137
Alma	Sonoma Bodega	69	529
Andrew	Solano Vallejo	69	247
Argalie	Amador Twp 5	55	332
Asa W	San Francisco San Francisco 11	67	155
Augustus	San Francisco San Francisco 4	68	1215
Bella	San Francisco San Francisco 10	67	182
C	Nevada Grass Valley	61	155
C	Yolo Slate Ra	72	697
C	Yuba Slate Ro	72	697
C W	Sonoma Armally	69	497
Casper	Santa Clara San Jose	65	309
Charles	Siskiyou Cottonwood	69	102
Chas	Alameda Brooklyn	55	100
Corrin	Yolo Slate Ra	72	700
D D	Solano Vallejo	69	277
Daniel	Sacramento Georgian	63	347
Daniel	Sacramento Ward 4	63	513
Danl	Plumas Quincy	62	951
David	Placer Auburn	62	595
David	San Mateo Twp 1	65	69
David	Sierra Downieville	66	989
E	Amador Twp 1	55	471
E	Solano Vacaville	69	328
E A	Yolo Cache Crk	72	633
Ebner	Sacramento Georgian	63	345
Edward	Contra Costa Twp 1	57	487
Edward	Marin Cortemad	60	754
Edward	Solano Vacaville	69	319
Elisha	Stanislaus Branch	70	703
G H	Siskiyou Cottonwoood	69	106
G W	Sierra Downieville	66	988
Geo	Butte Eureka	56	651
Geo F	Butte Oregon	56	625
H C	Sacramento Ward 3	63	463
Harriet*	San Joaquin Stockton	641	069
Henry	Santa Clara San Jose	65	353
J	Yolo Putah	72	554
J B	Amador Twp 1	55	454
John P	San Francisco San Francisco 4	68	1171
Joseph	Tuolumne Sonora	71	198
K	Siskiyou Cottonwoood	69	102
L J	Yolo Putah	72	549
L M	Sonoma Petaluma	69	593
L P	Butte Kimshaw	56	598
L P	Butte Kimshaw	56	607
Lamon H	San Francisco San Francisco 4	68	1215
M D	Tuolumne Twp 4	71	138
Mary	Sonoma Bodega	69	531
N D	Tuolumne Big Oak	71	138
O	Solano Vacaville	69	319
Orvil	Amador Twp 1	55	480
R	Yolo Cache Crk	72	641
R E	Tuolumne Big Oak	71	125
R E	Tuolumne Twp 4	71	127
R M	Butte Bidwell	56	723
Rm	Butte Bidwell	56	723
S	Sacramento Cosummes	63	395
T	Solano Vallejo	69	272
T E	El Dorado Diamond	58	801
T J	Amador Twp 6	55	429
T M	Colusa Grand Island	57	481
Thomas	Marin Point Re	60	730
Thos J	Butte Ophir	56	785
W W	El Dorado Placerville	58	888
Wells	Tuolumne Shawsfla	71	393
William	San Diego Colorado	64	808
William	Tuolumne Jamestown	71	423
William S	San Francisco San Francisco 4	68	1215
Wm	Colusa Monroeville	57	446
PHELSON			
P*	Sacramento Ward 4	63	516
PHELSTOTT			
Wm*	Nevada Nevada	61	292
PHELY			
Samuel	San Francisco San Francisco 11	67	109
PHENIX			
James	Marin Tomales	60	713
James	Sacramento Ward 1	63	109
Jas	Sonoma Petaluma	69	546
John	Siskiyou Cottonwood	69	102
PHENMARBECK			
P	Sutter Sutter	70	814
PHENOT			
Autro*	Calaveras Twp 9	57	353
PHEONIX			
Edwrd	San Francisco San Francisco 1	68	907
PHEPPEN			
John*	Napa Napa	61	107

Name	County Locale	M653 Roll	Page
PHEPPS			
John*	Napa Clear Lake	61	134
PHERFF			
G*	San Francisco San Francisco 3	67	78
PHEW			
---	El Dorado Diamond	58	787
PHFERFFER			
Phil	Sacramento Ward 3	63	430
PHIBBEE			
---	Sierra La Porte	66	782
PHIBY			
Edward*	Tuolumne Twp 3	71	464
Edwrd	Tuolumne Twp 3	71	464
PHIEFFER			
Thos	Sacramento Ward 1	63	13
PHIERIE			
Edward	Marin Cortemad	60	792
PHIFER			
Chas	Trinity Indian C	70	988
Fred	Sacramento Ward 1	63	35
John	Butte Wyandotte	56	657
John	Colusa Butte Crk	57	467
PHIFFER			
Fred	Sacramento Ward 1	63	35
P B*	Colusa Mansville	57	438
PHIFING			
John	Sonoma Petaluma	69	567
PHIIPS			
B	San Mateo Twp 3	65	106
PHIK			
John	Yolo Slate Ra	72	699
Su	Calaveras Twp 5	57	220
PHIL			
---	Amador Twp 4	55	242
Su	Calaveras Twp 5	57	220
PHILAN			
Edwd	San Francisco San Francisco 10	67	213
Ella	San Francisco San Francisco 10	67	294
Hy C	San Francisco San Francisco 1	68	931
John	Tuolumne Twp 3	71	466
Mary	San Francisco San Francisco 1	68	931
Ncholus	Napa Clear Lake	61	124
Nicholas	Napa Clear Lake	61	124
Patrick	San Francisco San Francisco 10	67	294
T	Calaveras Twp 9	57	403
PHILAND			
Catharin	Sonoma Sonoma	69	659
PHILANF			
T	Calaveras Twp 9	57	403
PHILAR			
Z P	Butte Bidwell	56	715
PHILBE			
James	Sonoma Santa Rosa	69	422
PHILBRICK			
A C	Placer Todds Va	62	789
Allen	Amador Twp 3	55	396
J C	Shasta Horsetown	66	694
John	Sacramento Ward 1	63	32
L G	Tuolumne Twp 1	71	206
M H	Amador Twp 3	55	369
Sarah E	Calaveras Twp 10	57	279
Squire	Trinity Weaverville	701	079
T C	Mendocino Ukiah	60	793
William	Placer Forest H	62	798
PHILBROCK			
Edward	Placer Forest H	62	805
PHILBROOK			
---	San Francisco San Francisco 10	67	175
Chas E	Trinity Cox'S Bar	701	038
E M	Trinity East For	701	027
Geo	Stanislaus Emory	70	757
J M	San Francisco San Francisco 5	67	498
J P	Sacramento Ward 1	63	87
J W	Trinity Mouth Ca	701	010
Jos A	San Francisco San Francisco 12	67	390
M	Shasta Horsetown	66	698
PHILBROOKS			
Lefonda	San Mateo Twp 1	65	53
PHILBRUCK			
Sarah E*	Calaveras Twp 10	57	279
PHILBURN			
John	Los Angeles Los Angeles	59	495
PHILDERS			
Joseph	Yuba Rose Bar	72	818
PHILEPY			
Alex	Tuolumne Twp 2	71	280
PHILESIANO			
Jose*	San Francisco San Francisco 2	67	664
PHILFLIPS			
Robt	Sacramento Ward 4	63	592
PHILICE			
---	Marin San Rafael	60	768

Name	County Locale	M653 Roll	Page
PHILILS			
Nathan	Shasta Shasta	66	729
PHILINGBER			
Jonas	San Joaquin Elkhorn	64	959
PHILIP			
---	Placer Virginia	62	666
---	Placer Dutch Fl	62	725
---	San Mateo Twp 3	65	110
Austin	San Joaquin Elliott	64	947
Gonzales	Tuolumne Twp 2	71	375
Jart*	San Joaquin O'Neal	641	001
John Y*	Napa Yount	61	43
Jos	San Francisco San Francisco 1	68	890
M	Siskiyou Yreka	69	186
Thomas	Yolo No E Twp	72	680
Thomas	Yuba North Ea	72	680
Warner	San Joaquin Elliott	64	946
PHILIPE			
Jalencie*	Napa Napa	61	84
PHILIPI			
Gustan	Alameda Brooklyn	55	142
PHILIPPS			
David	Plumas Quincy	62	962
Louisa J	Contra Costa Twp 2	57	571
Picot*	Plumas Meadow Valley	62	927
PHILIPS LUCIAS			
Araando	Tuolumne Twp 2	71	375
PHILIPS			
---	Placer Dutch Fl	62	731
A	Placer Dutch Fl	62	728
A	Placer Dutch Fl	62	731
A	Shasta Millvill	66	753
Abner	San Francisco San Francisco 11	67	155
Albert	Santa Cruz Pescadero	66	647
August	Nevada Bloomfield	61	518
B W	Siskiyou Cottonwoood	69	100
C B	San Joaquin Stockton	641	047
E	Shasta Shasta	66	656
E	Sonoma Vallejo	69	619
Edgar	Yuba Marysville	72	939
Edward	Nevada Bridgeport	61	455
Egby	San Mateo Twp 3	65	109
Elisha	Yuba Marysville	72	903
Elizabeth	Solano Vacaville	69	356
Francis	San Francisco San Francisco 11	67	90
Frank	Nevada Rough &	61	425
Fred	Siskiyou Scott Va	69	51
G	San Joaquin Stockton	641	092
Geo	Placer Dutch Fl	62	732
George	Sierra La Porte	66	784
George	Tuolumne Twp 1	71	265
George	Yuba Marysville	72	862
Geroge	Tuolumne Twp 1	71	265
Gideon	Yuba Bear Rvr	72	999
Green	San Joaquin Elliott	64	942
H	Siskiyou Cottonwoood	69	108
H G	Nevada Bloomfield	61	515
Harland	Tuolumne Twp 1	71	262
Henry	Contra Costa Twp 2	57	565
Henry	Yolo Washington	72	602
Isaac	Shasta Millvill	66	742
J	Yuba Slate Ro	72	710
James	Amador Twp 4	55	234
James	Nevada Red Dog	61	545
James	Plumas Meadow Valley	62	904
James	Solano Vacaville	69	367
James	Yuba Bear Rvr	721	007
Jas	Santa Clara San Jose	65	337
John	Contra Costa Twp 3	57	617
John	Mariposa Twp 1	60	633
John	Napa Yount	61	43
John	San Mateo Twp 1	65	64
John	Shasta Shasta	66	760
John D	San Francisco San Francisco 1	68	922
Jonathan	Yolo Cache Crk	72	607
Jonathan	Yolo Cache	72	608
Kate	San Francisco San Francisco 1	68	921
L	Nevada Grass Valley	61	192
L D	Calaveras Twp 9	57	396
L S	Yolo Putah	72	550
L T	Yolo Putah	72	550
Lewis	Merced Twp 1	60	896
Limon R	Merced Twp 2	60	924
Louis	Nevada Bloomfield	61	524
Louis	Tuolumne Twp 1	71	253
Lucins B*	Tuolumne Springfield	71	375
Lucius B*	Tuolumne Springfield	71	375
M	El Dorado Placerville	58	825
M	Siskiyou Cottonwoood	69	107
M B	Del Norte Happy Ca	58	664
Manuel	Contra Costa Twp 1	57	520
Mary	Yolo Washington	72	602
Michael	San Francisco San Francisco 11	67	148

Name	County Locale	M653 RollPage
PHILIPS		
N	Calaveras Twp 9	57 410
Nathan	Shasta Shasta	66 729
P	Sutter Nicolaus	70 836
Perry	Solano Vacaville	69 356
Philip	Placer Secret R	62 617
Philip	Tuolumne Columbia	71 314
Randelph	Tuolumne Columbia	71 324
Randolph	Tuolumne Twp 2	71 324
Richard	Contra Costa Twp 1	57 499
Robt	Butte Kimshaw	56 596
S	Nevada Grass Valley	61 209
S H	Nevada Grass Valley	61 197
Simon R	Merced Twp 2	60 924
T	Amador Twp 1	55 475
T	Calaveras Twp 9	57 416
Theodore	Merced Twp 2	60 922
Thomas	Yuba Long Bar	72 772
Thomas	Yuba Marysville	72 979
Thomas S	Tuolumne Twp 3	71 447
Thos	San Francisco San Francisco 9	681058
Thos	San Francisco San Francisco 1	68 892
Valencio	Napa Napa	61 84
W	Placer Dutch Fl	62 710
W	Placer Dutch Fl	62 714
W O	Mendocino Big Rvr	60 845
Wells	Tuolumne Twp 2	71 393
William	Contra Costa Twp 3	57 597
PHILIPSON		
A	Shasta Shasta	66 658
John	Napa Hot Springs	61 9
PHILIPY		
Alexc	Tuolumne Twp 2	71 280
PHILIS		
J	Yolo Slate Ra	72 710
PHILL		
M	Napa Yount	61 48
PHILLBROOK		
J P	Sacramento Ward 1	63 87
PHILLEPS		
John	Nevada Bridgeport	61 439
PHILLGES		
Henry*	El Dorado Georgetown	58 708
PHILLGIS		
Henry*	El Dorado Georgetown	58 708
PHILLIMINI		
Pescossu	Calaveras Twp 5	57 198
PHILLIMIUR		
Percosso	Calaveras Twp 5	57 198
PHILLINUSNI		
Percussn*	Calaveras Twp 5	57 198
PHILLIP		
Adam	San Francisco San Francisco 7	681397
Amas G	Calaveras Twp 4	57 335
Amos G	Calaveras Twp 4	57 335
B R*	Mariposa Twp 3	60 578
Bonafarle*	Alameda Brooklyn	55 106
Bonapade	Alameda Brooklyn	55 106
Catharine	San Francisco San Francisco 8	681306
Erchel	Sierra Poker Flats	66 837
J W	Trinity Lewiston	70 953
Jesus	Alameda Murray	55 227
John	Sierra Downieville	661020
L	El Dorado Placerville	58 869
Lewis	Sierra Downieville	661020
Lewis	Sierra Twp 7	66 885
Lungo*	Calaveras Twp 9	57 358
Lunzo*	Calaveras Twp 9	57 358
Lurgo*	Calaveras Twp 9	57 358
Martin	Stanislaus Branch	70 702
Phillipe	Alameda Murray	55 227
Samuel	San Francisco San Francisco 3	67 55
Sarah*	Sacramento Granite	63 243
Sungo*	Calaveras Twp 9	57 358
Thos	San Francisco San Francisco 9	681074
Wm	Mariposa Twp 3	60 589
PHILLIPE		
John	San Francisco San Francisco 10	202 67
Louis	Yuba New York	72 746
Mark	Yuba Foster B	72 835
Thomas	Calaveras Twp 7	57 15
PHILLIPES		
Wm S	Calaveras Twp 9	57 386
PHILLIPI		
Anthony	San Francisco San Francisco 10	343 67
Sarah	Sacramento Granite	63 243
PHILLIPINE		
Carlo	Calaveras Twp 7	57 2
Martin	Calaveras Twp 7	57 2
PHILLIPP		
John W	San Francisco San Francisco 3	67 25
Samuel	San Francisco San Francisco 9	68 966
PHILLIPPI		
---	Mariposa Twp 1	60 644

Name	County Locale	M653 RollPage
PHILLIPPI		
P	San Francisco San Francisco 2	67 795
PHILLIPPS		
J P	Tehama Lassen	70 876
PHILLIPS		
---	San Francisco San Francisco 7	681336
---	San Francisco San Francisco 10	173 67
---	San Francisco San Francisco 5	67 518
A	San Francisco San Francisco 5	67 531
A	Trinity Rush Crk	70 965
A C	El Dorado Kelsey	581156
A E	Monterey Monterey	60 925
A H	Sierra Twp 7	66 903
A R	Amador Twp 2	55 264
A R	Amador Twp 5	55 366
A S	Butte Bidwell	56 712
Alexr	Sierra Downieville	661019
Allen H	Alameda Brooklyn	55 124
Amos G	Calaveras Twp 4	57 335
Amtilda	San Francisco San Francisco 2	67 714
Ann	San Francisco San Francisco 6	67 440
Ann	San Francisco San Francisco 6	67 445
Anton	Placer Iona Hills	62 878
Antone	Placer Forest H	62 806
Archibald	Sonoma Russian	69 433
Ayer	Sierra Pine Grove	66 822
Ayes	Sierra Pine Grove	66 822
B B*	Napa Napa	61 98
B R	Mariposa Twp 3	60 578
Benj	El Dorado Grizzly	581180
Bermond	Los Angeles San Pedro	59 478
C	Sacramento Granite	63 246
C A	Sacramento Lee	63 217
C C	Tehama Antelope	70 894
C E	El Dorado Salmon Falls	581036
C H	Sacramento American	63 158
C R	San Francisco San Francisco 3	67 75
Catharine	Los Angeles Los Angeles	59 362
Catharine	San Francisco San Francisco 8	681306
Catherine	Los Angeles Los Angeles	59 362
Charles	Merced Monterey	60 941
Charles	Monterey Monterey	60 941
Charles	San Diego San Diego	64 767
Charles	San Francisco San Francisco 8	681261
Charles	Sierra Downieville	661016
Charles R	Alameda Brooklyn	55 145
Chas	Santa Clara Santa Clara	65 509
Christopher	San Diego San Diego	64 767
Corrum	Yuba Slate Ro	72 700
Cyrus	Sierra Downieville	66 962
D D	Sierra Twp 7	66 904
David	Calaveras Twp 6	57 123
Duval D	Sonoma Mendocino	69 462
E	San Francisco San Francisco 5	67 527
Edmund	Sonoma Mendocino	69 462
Eduard*	San Francisco San Francisco 7	681435
Edward*	San Francisco San Francisco 7	681435
Edwin J	San Francisco San Francisco 8	681258
Elizabeth	Mariposa Twp 3	60 589
Em	Butte Kimshaw	56 581
F	Butte Chico	56 555
F	Sacramento Cosumnes	63 398
F A	Sacramento Ward 1	63 9
Fetel	San Francisco San Francisco 8	681314
Fetil	San Francisco San Francisco 8	681314
Frank	Fresno Twp 2	59 4
Frank	Nevada Rough &	61 425
G	Sutter Bear Rvr	70 818
G I*	Nevada Bridgeport	61 449
G J	Nevada Bridgeport	61 449
G S	Santa Clara Santa Clara	65 476
G T	Nevada Bridgeport	61 449
Geo	Amador Twp 2	55 309
Geo W	Sierra Twp 7	66 910
George	Mendocino Ukiah	60 803
George	San Francisco San Francisco 11	153 67
George	San Francisco San Francisco 3	67 41
George	Siskiyou Shasta Valley	69 119
George	Yuba Long Bar	72 769
H	El Dorado Georgetown	58 707
H	Nevada Nevada	61 330
H	Nevada Washington	61 334
H D	Tehama Lassen	70 866
H G	Nevada Nevada	61 275
Harlow	San Diego San Diego	64 767
Henry	Calaveras Twp 6	57 141
Henry	El Dorado Greenwood	58 708
Henry	San Francisco San Francisco 2	67 782
Henry	Santa Clara Santa Clara	65 521
Henry	Trinity Weaverville	701052
I B	Amador Twp 2	55 294
Isaac	Calaveras Twp 6	57 153
Isaac	Colusa Colusi	57 419
Isaac	Tehama Lassen	70 882

Name	County Locale	M653 RollPage
PHILLIPS		
J	Mariposa Twp 3	60 602
J	Nevada Nevada	61 319
J	San Francisco San Francisco 5	67 523
J B	Amador Twp 6	55 439
J B	Merced Monterey	60 931
J B	Monterey Monterey	60 931
J H	Mariposa Twp 3	60 558
J H	San Francisco San Francisco 7	681336
J H	Sierra Twp 7	66 903
J I	Mariposa Twp 3	60 558
J M	Sonoma Armally	69 517
J S	Mariposa Twp 3	60 558
J W	Calaveras Twp 9	57 363
J W	Placer Forest H	62 791
J W	Trinity North Fo	701023
J W	Trinity Lewiston	70 953
J W D	El Dorado Kelsey	581156
J*	Mariposa Twp 3	60 602
Jac	Sacramento Ward 1	63 37
Jacob	Los Angeles Los Angeles	59 365
Jacob	Santa Clara Gilroy	65 235
Jacob	Sonoma Healdsbu	69 472
James	Calaveras Twp 6	57 140
James	Marin Cortemad	60 781
James	Monterey Pajaro	601016
James	Plumas Quincy	62 943
James	Plumas Quincy	62 944
James	Santa Cruz Pajaro	66 559
James	Solano Vallejo	69 267
James B	Trinity Oregon G	701009
James E	El Dorado Mud Springs	58 963
James F	Santa Cruz Pajaro	66 570
Jane	San Francisco San Francisco 2	67 586
Jas	Butte Ophir	56 746
Jas	Calaveras Twp 9	57 389
Jas	Sacramento Ward 3	63 443
Jas F	Sacramento Granite	63 266
Jno	Sacramento Ward 1	63 10
Jno	Sacramento Franklin	63 327
Jno	Sacramento Ward 4	63 552
Jno W	Sonoma Mendocino	69 462
John	Calaveras Twp 10	57 261
John	Calaveras Twp 8	57 98
John	El Dorado Salmon Falls	581065
John	El Dorado Casumnes	581164
John	Monterey Monterey	60 966
John	Nevada Bridgeport	61 439
John	Placer Forest H	62 774
John	Placer Michigan	62 831
John	Sacramento San Joaquin	63 351
John	Sacramento Dry Crk	63 369
John	San Francisco San Francisco 11	145 67
John	San Francisco San Francisco 11	162 67
John	San Francisco San Francisco 2	67 609
John	Sierra Downieville	661020
John D	San Francisco San Francisco 7	681357
John F	Tulara Visalia	71 109
Jos	Trinity Trinity	70 975
Jos W	San Francisco San Francisco 10	236 67
Joseph	El Dorado Coloma	581107
Joseph	San Francisco San Francisco 11	141 67
Joseph	Siskiyou Yreka	69 137
Joseph	Siskiyou Yreka	69 138
Joseph	Yuba Linda Twp	72 982
L	El Dorado Mud Springs	58 984
L	San Francisco San Francisco 10	222 67
L D	Calaveras Twp 9	57 396
L P	San Francisco San Francisco 3	67 54
Lewis	Sierra Twp 7	66 885
Louis	Los Angeles Los Angeles	59 406
Louis	Sacramento Ward 1	63 14
Louis	San Francisco San Francisco 1	68 937
Louis*	Yuba Long Bar	72 746
M	El Dorado Casumnes	581168
Manuel	Santa Clara Santa Clara	65 485
Mary A	San Francisco San Francisco 4	681146
N T	El Dorado Placerville	58 871
Nat	El Dorado Casumnes	581164
Nathan	El Dorado Casumnes	581166
Nathl	San Francisco San Francisco 7	681371
Nellie	El Dorado Coloma	581123
O	Butte Oro	56 677
O	Klamath S Fork	59 203
O	Trinity Trinity	70 975
Oliver H	Siskiyou Yreka	69 152
Patrick	El Dorado Coloma	581082
Q	Klamath S Fork	59 203
R	San Francisco San Francisco 5	67 540
R B	Napa Napa	61 98
R R	El Dorado Mountain	581184

PHILLIPS

Name	County Locale	M653 Roll	Page
Rich	Nevada Bridgeport	61	446
Rich'D	El Dorado Kelsey	58	1150
Richard	San Francisco San Francisco 2	67	599
Richd	El Dorado Kelsey	58	1150
Robert	Los Angeles Los Nieto	59	435
Robert	Nevada Little Y	61	531
Robert R	Tulara Visalia	71	99
Robt	Klamath Trinidad	59	223
Rufus	Humbolt Union	59	192
S W	Santa Clara San Jose	65	341
Sally	San Francisco San Francisco 4	68	1225
Samual	San Francisco San Francisco 2	67	573
Samuel	Mendocino Big Rvr	60	843
Samuel	San Francisco San Francisco 3	67	55
Samuel	San Francisco San Francisco 2	67	573
Samuel S	San Francisco San Francisco 8	68	1320
Sarah*	Nevada Red Dog	61	550
Sarah*	Sacramento Granite	63	243
Simon E	Humbolt Eel Rvr	59	145
Susan	San Francisco San Francisco 10	67	184
T B	San Francisco San Francisco 5	67	543
T B	Amador Twp 2	55	264
Theadore	Placer Virginia	62	668
Thomas	Calaveras Twp 9	57	374
Thomas	San Francisco San Francisco 11	67	126
Thomas	Sierra Twp 7	66	863
Thomas	Sierra Twp 7	66	864
Thomas	Solano Benecia	69	290
Thomas	Solano Benecia	69	294
Thos	Amador Twp 3	55	373
Thos	Nevada Washington	61	331
Thos	Nevada Washington	61	341
Thos	Sacramento San Joaquin	63	363
Thos	San Francisco San Francisco 7	68	1443
Thos	San Francisco San Francisco 1	68	913
Travis	Santa Clara San Jose	65	367
W L	Napa Hot Springs	61	26
W L	Nevada Nevada	61	288
W L*	Napa Hot Springs	61	26
Walter G	Sierra Cox'S Bar	66	952
William	Placer Michigan	62	856
William	Sierra Port Win	66	792
William	Sonoma Russian	69	433
Wm	Butte Kimshaw	56	581
Wm	Colusa Muion	57	463
Wm	Mariposa Twp 1	60	672
Wm	Nevada Rough &	61	422
Wm	Sierra Twp 7	66	904
Wm	Sierra Downieville	66	995
Wm	Yuba Rose Bar	72	808
Wm E	Humbolt Union	59	192
Wm S	Calaveras Twp 9	57	386

PHILLIPSON

Thos	El Dorado Greenwood	58	724

PHILLIS

Antonio	Calaveras Twp 5	57	250
Joce M*	Calaveras Twp 5	57	249
Jose M	Calaveras Twp 5	57	249

PHILLMAN

John*	Placer Michigan	62	856

PHILLO

Louis	Klamath Liberty	59	231

PHILLPIN

Walter*	Sierra Cox'S Bar	66	952

PHILLRICK

T C*	Mendocino Ukiah	60	793

PHILLSIN

Walter*	Sierra Cox'S Bar	66	952

PHILLSSON

Walter	Sierra Cox'S Bar	66	952

PHILLY

John	Contra Costa Twp 2	57	577

PHILLYES

Henry*	El Dorado Georgetown	58	708

PHILLYIS

Henry*	El Dorado Georgetown	58	708

PHILOMENA

---	San Bernardino Santa Inez	64	139

PHILOPONELL

A	San Joaquin Stockton	64	1091

PHILOPT

Adison*	Napa Hot Springs	61	19

PHILPOT

A C	Trinity Hay Fork	70	991
Adism	Napa Hot Springs	61	19

PHILPOTT

Rebecca A	Mendocino Ukiah	60	797

PHILPRTT

Rebecca A*	Mendocino Ukiah	60	797

PHILPS

Alex	Sacramento Granite	63	253
Andrew	Solano Vallejo	69	247
David N	Alameda Brooklyn	55	206
Edward	Contra Costa Twp 1	57	487
Edward	Marin Cortemad	60	754
Geo G	Butte Oregon	56	625
H G	Placer Iona Hills	62	885
J B	Amador Twp 1	55	454
John P	San Francisco San Francisco 4	68	1171
T G	San Mateo Twp 3	65	104

PHILRU

Kuir*	Nevada Bridgeport	61	501
Kun*	Nevada Bridgeport	61	501

PHILSSOT

Adison*	Napa Hot Springs	61	19

PHIM

---	El Dorado Georgetown	58	680
---	Sierra St Louis	66	813

PHIN

Joseph	Calaveras Twp 7	57	22

PHINA

Sein*	Sacramento Granite	63	263

PHINANDES

---	Nevada Little Y	61	535

PHINDERS

S P*	Nevada Eureka	61	358

PHINEBERGER

J M	Nevada Nevada	61	277

PHINEDOLLAR

John*	Tuolumne Big Oak	71	137

PHINEVOLLEN

John	Tuolumne Twp 4	71	137

PHINEY

John	Sacramento Granite	63	248

PHINKETT

Elizabeth*	San Francisco 10		310
---	San Francisco	67	

PHINKITE

James	Sacramento Ward 1	63	148

PHINNY

John*	Sacramento Granite	63	248
Randall	Sonoma Vallejo	69	616

PHINOT

Antro*	Calaveras Twp 9	57	353
Autro*	Calaveras Twp 9	57	353

PHINS

Sim	Sacramento Granite	63	263

PHIPHER

John*	Tuolumne Shawsfla	71	378

PHIPHIS

John	Tuolumne Twp 2	71	378
Kjohn*	Tuolumne Shawsfla	71	378

PHIPPEN

John	Napa Napa	61	107

PHIPPENS

C L*	Sacramento Brighton	63	198
C S*	Sacramento Brighton	63	198

PHIPPIN

John*	Napa Napa	61	107

PHIPPS

E K	Siskiyou Yreka	69	169
George	Tuolumne Twp 2	71	324
H M	Butte Ophir	56	762
Isaac	Santa Clara San Jose	65	344
J	El Dorado Placerville	58	822
J C	Sonoma Vallejo	69	622
John	Napa Clear Lake	61	134
Simon	Santa Clara San Jose	65	345
Wm	El Dorado Georgetown	58	686
Wm R	Santa Clara Gilroy	65	239

PHIPS

Elizabeth*	Sacramento Georgian	63	338
J*	Sacramento Georgian	63	337
John W	San Francisco San Francisco 7	68	1339
Wm*	Sacramento Georgian	63	337

PHIRFFER

Thos*	Sacramento Ward 1	63	13

PHIRHES

Felix*	Santa Cruz Santa Cruz	66	633

PHISEMAN

Chas*	Nevada Bridgeport	61	469

PHISHES

Felix*	Santa Cruz Santa Cruz	66	633

PHISS

Elizabeth*	Sacramento Georgian	63	338
J*	Sacramento Georgian	63	337
Wm*	Sacramento Georgian	63	337

PHISTER

S	Butte Kimshaw	56	595

PHITCIRNE

Ogden*	Siskiyou Yreka	69	150

PHITENNE

Ogden*	Siskiyou Yreka	69	150

PHITHES

Felix*	Santa Cruz Santa Cruz	66	633

PHITSET

William C*	Siskiyou Yreka	69	126

PHLISSER

D*	El Dorado Placerville	58	855

PHLLIPE

Mark	Yuba Fosters	72	835

PHLLIPS

Louis	San Francisco San Francisco 1	68	907
T	San Francisco San Francisco 5	67	543

PHNE

D H*	San Francisco San Francisco 9	68	1091

PHO

---*	Placer Auburn	62	563

PHOEY

---	San Francisco San Francisco 4	68	1185

PHONING

Joseph*	Shasta Shasta	66	657

PHOO

---	Calaveras Twp 8	57	65
---	Calaveras Twp 8	57	83
Ah	Calaveras Twp 7	57	32
Ah	Calaveras Twp 7	57	34

PHOON

---*	Mariposa Twp 3	60	590

PHORFF

G	San Francisco San Francisco 3	67	78

PHOW

---	San Francisco San Francisco 9	68	1096

PHOY

---	Nevada Bridgeport	61	458
---	San Francisco San Francisco 5	67	508

PHU

---	El Dorado Georgetown	58	691
Sul	El Dorado Georgetown	58	746

PHUBBUCK

E C	El Dorado Placerville	58	852

PHUE

D H	San Francisco San Francisco 9	68	1091

PHUG

---	San Francisco San Francisco 4	68	1187
---*	San Francisco San Francisco 4	68	1188

PHULECHI

Casto Carlo	Calaveras Twp 6	57	164

PHULER

Chas*	Siskiyou Yreka	69	147

PHUN

---	El Dorado Georgetown	58	747
---	Sierra St Louis	66	813

PHUNG

War	Placer Dutch Fl	62	732

PHUNNE

---	El Dorado Georgetown	58	691

PHURNNER

John	Yuba North Ea	72	678

PHY

---	Placer Illinois	62	752

PHYAH

---	El Dorado Greenwood	58	732

PHYFE

William	San Bernardino Santa Barbara	64	178

PHYLEPS

M C	Siskiyou Scott Ri	69	62

PHYLESS

M C*	Siskiyou Scott Ri	69	62

PHYMES

James	Tulara Keeneysburg	71	46

PI

---	Alameda Oakland	55	63
---	Amador Twp 2	55	310
---	Calaveras Twp 5	57	233
---	Fresno Twp 1	59	28
---	Mariposa Twp 1	60	652

PI?DY

G R*	El Dorado Coloma	58	1104

PIA

---	Los Angeles San Gabriel	59	414

PIAISTO

Joseph	Calaveras Twp 9	57	372

PIANDY

G R*	El Dorado Coloma	58	1104

PIANER

Edward*	Yuba Marysville	72	957

PIARE

M	Trinity Lewiston	70	963

PIARNEY

William*	San Francisco San Francisco 4	68	1172

PIASE

C B*	Mendocino Arrana	60	856

PIATT

O R	Tuolumne Twp 1	71	247

PIBALS

Susan	Los Angeles Tejon	59	523

PICANI

Charles	Calaveras Twp 7	57	2
Ross	Calaveras Twp 7	57	2

PICARD

H	Yuba Long Bar	72	752
Louis	Yuba Long Bar	72	771
Louis	Yuba Parks Ba	72	779

PICARDO

A	Tuolumne Twp 1	71	255

Name	County Locale	M653 RollPage
PICARO		
Louis	San Francisco San Francisco	7 681416
PICARRO		
Andreas	Tuolumne Twp 2	71 284
Andrew	Tuolumne Twp 2	71 284
PICAYNNE		
---	Mendocino Calpella	60 827
PICAYNORE		
---	Mendocino Calpella	60 827
PICCKO		
---*	Tulara Visalia	71 38
PICE		
---	Yolo Slate Ra	72 710
Nicholas	El Dorado Big Bar	58 735
Santos*	Yuba Fosters	72 828
PICER		
J	Shasta French G	66 722
PICH		
---	Alameda Oakland	55 53
PICHARD		
C H	Mariposa Twp 1	60 655
PICHE		
Louis	Siskiyou Scott Ri	69 67
PICHEL		
Julius	Los Angeles Los Angeles	59 369
PICHEREAU		
Pierre	Yuba Rose Bar	72 794
PICHLER		
Joseph	Tuolumne Don Pedro	71 538
PICHNEY		
Isaac*	Tuolumne Twp 5	71 516
PICHO		
Gustrus	Calaveras Twp 7	57 39
PICHUSE		
---	Tulara Twp 2	71 31
PICI		
---	Yuba Slate Ro	72 710
PICIAS		
W	El Dorado Kelsey	581134
PICILANS		
H	El Dorado Diamond	58 813
PICIMDO		
---	San Bernardino S Timate	64 706
PICK		
---	Stanislaus Branch	70 715
---	Tuolumne Columbia	71 347
---	Tuolumne Twp 2	71 416
---	Tuolumne Twp 3	71 440
---	Tuolumne Twp 3	71 468
---	Tuolumne Sonora	71 475
---*	Tuolumne Montezuma	71 511
Aaron B	Sierra Twp 7	66 866
Ah	Tuolumne Twp 2	71 347
Charles	Placer Michigan	62 823
Erastus	Monterey San Juan	601004
Henry*	Tuolumne Twp 1	71 245
Hugh*	Colusa Monroeville	57 440
William	San Francisco San Francisco 3	67 10
PICKA		
---	Mendocino Big Rock	60 874
John W	Placer Auburn	62 582
PICKARD		
A	Nevada Bloomfield	61 520
Danial	Humbolt Eureka	59 177
PICKARDS		
William*	Yuba Marysville	72 926
PICKAYUNE		
---	Mendocino Round Va	60 883
PICKEL		
Martin	Tuolumne Twp 2	71 287
Moses	Amador Twp 1	55 462
PICKELL		
Moses	Amador Twp 1	55 451
PICKELVILLE		
Frances*	Sierra Downieville	66 994
Francis	Sierra Downieville	66 994
PICKEN		
Jaes E	Sierra Downieville	661021
James E	Sierra Downieville	661021
PICKENHERD		
---*	Mendocino Round Va	60 881
PICKENS		
A	Tuolumne Springfield	71 374
C H	Siskiyou Scott Ri	69 78
Cyrus	Siskiyou Scott Ri	69 77
PICKER		
Thos	San Mateo Twp 1	65 67
PICKERATAFF		
John*	Marin Cortemad	60 753
PICKERELL		
James H	Mendocino Arrana	60 863
PICKERING		
Abram B	Calaveras Twp 6	57 158
Hiram B	Calaveras Twp 6	57 158
J	Siskiyou Scott Ri	69 74
John	Placer Iona Hills	62 889

Name	County Locale	M653 RollPage
PICKERING		
Wm	San Francisco San Francisco 2	67 681
PICKERNELL		
Timothy	Sacramento Cosumnes	63 398
PICKERSTAFF		
John	Marin Cortemad	60 753
PICKERSVILLE		
W	Tuolumne Jamestown	71 455
PICKET		
Alex	Calaveras Twp 10	57 294
B H	Tehama Antelope	70 897
Garret	Placer Dutch Fl	62 722
Mary A	San Francisco San Francisco 5	67 489
PICKETT		
---	Monterey Alisal	601032
A J	Amador Twp 4	55 245
C E	San Francisco San Francisco 6	67 448
D L	Yolo Cache Crk	72 607
Daniel	Placer Goods	62 695
James	Mendocino Calpella	60 820
James M	Trinity W Weaver	701054
James W	Plumas Quincy	621005
Jas	San Francisco San Francisco 10	352 67
John	Sacramento Ward 1	63 66
John	Shasta Shasta	66 674
Michael	San Francisco San Francisco 3	67 31
S H	Tuolumne Twp 2	71 330
Vincent	Monterey San Juan	60 991
William	Los Angeles Los Angeles	59 380
Wm	San Francisco San Francisco 2	67 600
PICKHAM		
Marian	Nevada Little Y	61 535
Marrian	Nevada Little Y	61 535
PICKHEART		
Wm	Santa Clara San Jose	65 288
PICKINPON		
Robt	Sonoma Washington	69 670
PICKINS		
A	Tuolumne Twp 2	71 374
PICKINSON		
Richard	Sierra Eureka	661046
PICKLE		
C G	Sonoma Russian	69 435
Geo	Sonoma Russian	69 430
J	Nevada Eureka	61 362
Wm	Nevada Eureka	61 362
PICKLETTE		
---	Tulara Twp 1	71 121
PICKOLA		
Jno	Klamath S Fork	59 203
PICKRING		
James	Nevada Bridgeport	61 482
PICKSON		
W	Shasta Millvill	66 752
PICKSTON		
H M	Butte Oregon	56 641
PICO		
---	San Diego Agua Caliente	64 824
---	San Diego Agua Caliente	64 831
---	Tulara Visalia	71 117
Andress	Los Angeles Los Angeles	59 514
Andrew	Santa Cruz Pajaro	66 553
Andriss	Los Angeles Los Angeles	59 514
Chla	Sacramento Ward 1	63 81
Chlo*	Sacramento Ward 1	63 81
Cristom	Monterey Monterey	60 960
Custan*	Monterey Monterey	60 960
Custom*	Monterey Monterey	60 960
Estefana	San Bernardino Santa Barbara	64 153
Francisco	Santa Barbara San Bernardino	64 156
Gregorio	San Bernardino Santa Barbara	64 175
Griselda	Los Angeles San Juan	59 446
John Jnato*	Santa Barbara San Bernardino	64 162
Jose Antonio	San Diego S Luis R	64 780
Juan Antonio	San Diego S Luis R	64 780
Juan De La Cruz	Los Nieto	59 426
Juana	Los Angeles Merced Monterey	60 934
Juana	Monterey Monterey	60 934
Mariano	San Bernardino Santa Barbara	64 201
Pio	Los Angeles Los Nieto	59 426
Ramon	San Bernardino Santa Inez	64 139
Ramona	San Bernardino Santa Barbara	64 153
Tomas	Los Angeles San Pedro	59 478
Ventura	San Bernardino Santa Barbara	64 156
Victorino	Contra Costa Twp 2	57 549
Vincente	San Bernardino Santa Barbara	64 153
PICOHT		
Dioret*	Yuba Long Bar	72 771
PICOLET		
Diviet	Yuba Long Bar	72 771
PICOLI		
Angelo	Calaveras Twp 7	57 1

Name	County Locale	M653 RollPage
PICORETA		
Francisco	Los Angeles San Juan	59 476
PICOT		
Alexion	Calaveras Twp 5	57 135
Rose	Amador Twp 3	55 383
PICTEHAN		
S	Sutter Yuba	70 768
PICTO		
Alexion	Calaveras Twp 6	57 135
PICTORIOUS		
Godfrey*	San Francisco San Francisco 7	681357
PIDD		
Jesse	San Francisco San Francisco 2	67 632
PIDDY		
G R	El Dorado Coloma	581104
PIDE		
Timothy*	Solano Fremont	69 384
PIDGE		
John S	Sierra Twp 5	66 923
Peter	Placer Forest H	62 798
Samuel	Sierra Twp 7	66 866
PIDGEON		
Fred	Amador Twp 6	55 442
PIDGION		
Fred	Amador Twp 6	55 442
PIDGO		
D P	Santa Clara San Jose	65 307
PIDK		
---	Tuolumne Twp 3	71 468
PIDKAT		
Charles	Tuolumne Twp 2	71 413
PIDSO		
James	Placer Forest H	62 773
PIE		
---	Amador Twp 6	55 431
---	Butte Kimshaw	56 595
---	Calaveras Twp 5	57 215
---	El Dorado Salmon Falls	581041
---	San Francisco San Francisco 4	681189
Ah	Sacramento Ward 3	63 492
Gory	San Francisco San Francisco 4	681188
Herman	San Mateo Twp 3	65 106
Loey	San Francisco San Francisco 4	681188
PIEBLE		
Samuel	Siskiyou Klamath	69 96
PIEBLER		
Jane*	San Francisco San Francisco 9	681015
PIEESON		
Willard H*	Butte Oro	56 674
PIEGEUT		
Nicholas*	Amador Twp 2	55 304
PIEGUET		
Nicholas*	Amador Twp 2	55 304
PIEGUIT		
Nicholas	Amador Twp 2	55 304
PIEKET		
Louis*	El Dorado Placerville	58 914
PIEKRING		
James	Nevada Bridgeport	61 482
PIEKSEN		
W*	Shasta Millvill	66 752
PIEN		
---	Sierra Downieville	66 997
PIEPNICKER		
Henry	Tuolumne Twp 1	71 191
PIEQUET		
Nicholas*	Amador Twp 2	55 304
PIER		
A G	Nevada Nevada	61 252
H	Solano Benecia	69 286
PIERAL		
W R	El Dorado Georgetown	58 683
PIERAN		
Gudrich	El Dorado Georgetown	58 683
PIERCAL		
G*	Nevada Grass Valley	61 163
PIERCE		
A	Nevada Washington	61 331
Andrew	Tuolumne Twp 2	71 292
Asa	Colusa Colusi	57 423
B W	Amador Twp 3	55 372
Barney	Calaveras Twp 7	57 17
Burlin	Tulara Visalia	71 97
Burtin*	Tulara Twp 1	71 97
C	Nevada Nevada	61 270
C	San Francisco San Francisco 5	67 499
C W	San Francisco San Francisco 5	67 520
Charles	Calaveras Twp 8	57 73
Charles	San Mateo Twp 3	65 78
Charles B	Solano Vacaville	69 356
Charles H	Yuba Marysville	72 950
D A	Calaveras Twp 6	57 114
D B	Tuolumne Sonora	71 193
David H	Yuba Marysville	72 903
E	Nevada Eureka	61 375
E	Nevada Eureka	61 378

Name	County Locale	M653 Roll	Page
PIERCE			
E E	Siskiyou Klamath	69	86
E*	Nevada Eureka	61	375
Edward F	Yuba Bear Rvr	72	1011
Elishaq	Plumas Quincy	62	917
Ellen	Napa Napa	61	102
Elzy	Santa Clara Santa Clara	65	513
Eugene	El Dorado Georgetown	58	683
F M	Sonoma Armally	69	493
Ferdinand C	San Francisco San Francisco 7	68	1395
Francis E	San Mateo Twp 1	65	57
Frank	Mariposa Twp 3	60	559
Frank	San Joaquin Oneal	64	935
Franklin	Placer Michigan	62	845
Fussell	Plumas Quincy	62	935
G	Nevada Eureka	61	378
G W	Tehama Lassen	70	876
Galen A	Sierra La Porte	66	765
Galson A	Sierra La Porte	66	765
Geo	El Dorado Salmon Falls	58	1040
Geo E	Butte Oregon	56	634
George	San Francisco San Francisco 7	68	1398
George A	Solano Vacaville	69	330
George D	Tuolumne Shawsfla	71	381
George L	Contra Costa Twp 2	57	562
H	Nevada Washington	61	334
H	Tehama Red Bluff	70	910
H B	El Dorado Coloma	58	1071
H L	Tehama Moons	70	852
Harrison	Napa Napa	61	80
Henry	San Mateo Twp 1	65	57
Henry D	San Francisco San Francisco 9	68	983
Hiram D	Tuolumne Sonora	71	203
Hiram D	Tuolumne Sonora	71	245
Horace	San Francisco San Francisco 7	68	1333
Ira*	San Francisco San Francisco 3	67	16
Irving	Calaveras Twp 5	57	210
Isa*	San Francisco San Francisco 3	67	16
Isaac	Amador Twp 2	55	324
Isabella	San Joaquin Elkhorn	64	962
J	Mariposa Twp 3	60	606
J A	Tehama Red Bluff	70	924
J L	Sutter Sutter	70	815
J M	El Dorado Diamond	58	773
J M	San Francisco San Francisco 5	67	551
J S	Solano Vacaville	69	324
J W	San Francisco San Francisco 5	67	533
J W	Solano Suisan	69	206
Jack	San Mateo Twp 1	65	57
Jacob	Tuolumne Twp 2	71	376
James	Nevada Nevada	61	266
James	Trinity Mouth Ca	70	1013
James H	Los Angeles Elmonte	59	263
Jas	Nevada Nevada	61	257
Jno	Klamath Trinidad	59	223
John	Del Norte Crescent	58	650
John	Humbolt Union	59	185
John	Placer Todds Va	62	785
John	Sacramento Granite	63	251
John	San Diego Agua Caliente	64	816
John	Tuolumne Big Oak	71	125
John	Tuolumne Twp 4	71	127
John	Tuolumne Shawsfla	71	378
John B	Siskiyou Shasta Rvr	69	114
John F	Butte Ophir	56	774
John M	Solano Vacaville	69	347
John T	Solano Montezuma	69	373
Jos	Butte Mountain	56	740
Jos	San Francisco San Francisco 5	67	514
Joshua	San Francisco San Francisco 2	67	715
Lewellyn	Tuolumne Twp 2	71	401
Louis	San Francisco San Francisco 2	67	690
Luther	Sacramento Ward 1	63	48
Luther	Sacramento Ward 1	63	64
M	Nevada Eureka	61	347
M A	Los Angeles Tejon	59	536
M K	Trinity Minersville	70	969
Mariam W*	Yuba Marysville	72	875
Mary C	Siskiyou Shasta Valley	69	117
Mary E*	Siskiyou Shasta Valley	69	117
N T	Solano Vacaville	69	355
Nathaniel	Santa Clara Santa Clara	65	522
Noah	Santa Clara Santa Clara	65	520
O	Nevada Washington	61	341
O	Siskiyou Klamath	69	86
O S	San Francisco San Francisco 5	67	514
O*	Nevada Washington	61	331
Oliver A	Tuolumne Shawsfla	71	381
Patk	Sacramento Mississipi	63	187
Patrick	Trinity Mouth Ca	70	1015
Perry	Santa Clara San Jose	65	362
R	Nevada Washington	61	331
R	Nevada Washington	61	341
R	Nevada Eureka	61	378
R	Trinity Readings	70	996

Name	County Locale	M653 Roll	Page
PIERCE			
Ricard	Tuolumne Twp 1	71	264
Richard	Tuolumne Big Oak	71	177
Richd	Tuolumne Twp 1	71	264
Ruel	Tuolumne Big Oak	71	136
S D	Sacramento Ward 4	63	518
Seth L	Yuba Long Bar	72	742
Seth S	Yuba Long Bar	72	742
Solomon	Marin Point Re	60	731
Solomon	Yuba Marysville	72	947
Thomas	El Dorado Placerville	58	925
Thomas	San Francisco San Francisco 11	67	149
Thomas	Yuba Marysville	72	857
Thos	Sacramento Ward 1	63	32
Wilber	Contra Costa Twp 1	57	529
William	Plumas Quincy	62	999
William	San Francisco San Francisco 7	68	1414
William	Tulara Twp 1	71	28
Wm	Alameda Brooklyn	55	137
Wm	Butte Cascade	56	697
Wm	Butte Cascade	56	701
Wm	Sacramento Brighton	63	196
Wm	Sacramento Granite	63	251
Wm	Sacramento Georgian	63	340
Wm	Sacramento Ward 3	63	452
Wm S	Santa Clara Gilroy	65	230
PIERCEY			
C N	San Bernardino San Bernadino	64	627
PIERCOR			
John*	Santa Clara Alviso	65	405
PIERCY			
C L	Butte Wyandotte	56	664
Saml*	Napa Yount	61	51
Sanl*	Napa Yount	61	51
PIERD			
A F	Santa Clara Santa Clara	65	510
J	Nevada Grass Valley	61	151
PIERFORT			
F H	San Francisco San Francisco 6	67	448
F H J	San Francisco San Francisco 6	67	448
PIERILL			
Elijah	Tuolumne Shawsfla	71	399
PIERMAN			
John	Tuolumne Sonora	71	231
PIERNEY			
Patrick	Siskiyou Scott Va	69	39
PIERO			
Ellen*	Sacramento Ward 1	63	135
PIERPOINT			
Eliza J*	Napa Napa	61	104
PIERPONT			
Noah	San Joaquin Stockton	64	1019
PIERPOURT			
Eliza J*	Napa Napa	61	104
PIERRE			
---	San Francisco San Francisco 12	67	388
Austin	Tuolumne Twp 2	71	410
Bart	San Francisco San Francisco 11	67	139
Eophil*	Sierra Downieville	66	1023
Esphil*	Sierra Downieville	66	1023
Fangnirose*	Siskiyou Callahan	69	3
Fangrirore*	Siskiyou Callahan	69	3
Fangurore	Siskiyou Callahan	69	3
John	Sacramento Ward 1	63	15
Mary	San Francisco San Francisco 2	67	722
Peter	San Francisco San Francisco 2	67	721
Ruch*	Sierra Downieville	66	963
Thos W	San Francisco San Francisco 2	67	748
PIERRER			
Luc	San Francisco San Francisco 10	67	329
PIERRIE			
L	Nevada Grass Valley	61	168
PIERRO			
Jesns	Sierra La Porte	66	773
Jesus	Sierra La Porte	66	773
PIERRON			
J W J	San Francisco San Francisco 9	68	1012
PIERSALL			
Saml W*	Calaveras Twp 6	57	124
Solomon	San Joaquin Stockton	64	1020
PIERSEN			
Bill	Alameda Brooklyn	55	144
PIERSOLL			
Lewis	Sierra St Louis	66	808
PIERSON			
Abel	Napa Napa	61	112
Abraham	Napa Napa	61	85
Adam	El Dorado Georgetown	58	745
Amond	San Francisco San Francisco 2	67	631
Annond*	San Francisco San Francisco 2	67	631
Armond*	San Francisco San Francisco 2	67	631
Arthur S	Tuolumne Columbia	71	357

Name	County Locale	M653 Roll	Page
PIERSON			
Awnond*	San Francisco San Francisco 2	67	631
B H	Sacramento Ward 3	63	424
B H	Sacramento Ward 4	63	576
C	El Dorado Placerville	58	849
C	Siskiyou Callahan	69	5
Charles	Solano Vacaville	69	353
E	Siskiyou Callahan	69	6
Edwar*	Placer Michigan	62	820
Edward	Placer Michigan	62	809
Edward	San Francisco San Francisco 2	67	556
Eleagor M	Yuba Marysville	72	888
Eleazor M	Yuba Marysville	72	888
Eliza	Sacramento Ward 4	63	576
Ester J	San Francisco San Francisco 2	67	704
Fred	Placer Rattle Snake	62	625
Geo	Alameda Brooklyn	55	84
Geo*	Butte Oro	56	673
George	Yuba Marysville	72	885
Godfrey	Placer Michigan	62	847
H H	Sacramento Ward 4	63	544
H H	San Francisco San Francisco 4	68	1130
Harlow	Plumas Quincy	62	915
Henry	Tuolumne Twp 4	71	177
Isaac N	Solano Vacaville	69	342
J	Sacramento Ward 4	63	598
J C	Napa Napa	61	104
J G	San Francisco San Francisco 6	67	436
J S	Solano Vacaville	69	353
James	San Francisco San Francisco 7	68	1337
James	Santa Cruz Pajaro	66	530
James	Shasta Shasta	66	666
James*	Sacramento Ward 1	63	1
Jas H	Amador Twp 6	55	444
John	Placer Forest H	62	791
John	San Francisco San Francisco 11	67	119
John	Tuolumne Big Oak	71	132
Jos I*	San Francisco San Francisco 2	67	801
Jos J*	San Francisco San Francisco 2	67	801
Jos T	San Francisco San Francisco 2	67	801
Joseph D	San Francisco San Francisco 8	68	1315
Leandrow	San Mateo Twp 1	65	56
Martin B	San Bernardino San Bernadino	64	622
Perre	San Francisco San Francisco 2	67	788
R	Sacramento Ward 4	63	575
Richard	Placer Michigan	62	811
S A	San Joaquin Elkhorn	64	1000
S J	Sacramento Ward 4	63	611
Samuel	Calaveras Twp 5	57	190
Thomas*	Calaveras Twp 4	57	316
Thos Dexter	Alameda Brooklyn	55	107
Willard H	Butte Oro	56	674
William	Siskiyou Cottonwoood	69	103
William D	San Francisco San Francisco 7	68	1336
William*	Placer Michigan	62	842
Wm S	San Francisco San Francisco 10	67	316
PIERSONS			
B F*	Sacramento American	63	168
Chas	Sacramento American	63	167
PIERSOR			
James*	Sacramento Ward 1	63	1
PIERTY			
Martin S	Tuolumne Twp 2	71	292
PIESCHI			
Joseph	El Dorado Greenwood	58	729
PIESSALL			
Saml W*	Calaveras Twp 6	57	124
PIESSEN			
C*	Siskiyou Callahan	69	5
PIESSON			
C*	Siskiyou Callahan	69	5
PIESTO			
Peter*	Yuba Marysville	72	872
PIETRO			
---	San Bernardino S Timate	64	703
PIEVER			
James	San Francisco San Francisco 4	68	1115
PIFFER			
E G	Butte Oregon	56	637
PIFIFER			
And	Butte Oregon	56	644
PIG			
---	Nevada Bridgeport	61	461
PIGEN			
---	Placer Auburn	62	592
PIGENTI			
John	Placer Dutch Fl	62	726
PIGEON TOES			
---	Fresno Twp 2	59	94
PIGEON			
---	San Diego Agua Caliente	64	858
PIGG			
T M	Siskiyou Scott Ri	69	64
PIGGINS			
Pat	Yuba Rose Bar	72	819

Name	County Locale	M653 Roll	Page
PIGGOT			
A H	Sonoma Bodega	69	522
PIGGOTT			
William	Mendocino Big Rvr	60	847
PIGLE			
Orran*	Sonoma Sonoma	69	652
PIGMAN			
J R*	Nevada Red Dog	61	540
PIGOTT			
J	El Dorado Greenwood	58	723
Robert	Nevada Bloomfield	61	529
PIGUENOT			
E*	San Francisco San Francisco 2	67	699
PIGUILLER			
Frank	Alameda Brooklyn	55	169
PIHON			
Paul	Contra Costa Twp 1	57	521
PIHTIN			
Catharin*	Sonoma Sonoma	69	653
PIJCER			
M L	El Dorado Big Bar	58	743
PIKE			
---	El Dorado Union	58	1090
---	Fresno Twp 2	59	95
---	Mendocino Calpella	60	826
---	Mendocino Twp 1	60	891
---	Merced Twp 1	60	908
---	San Mateo Twp 3	65	106
---	Siskiyou Shasta Rvr	69	111
A C	Siskiyou Callahan	69	10
B F	Butte Ophir	56	753
B F	Sacramento Franklin	63	325
B H	Klamath S Fork	59	206
C B	Butte Bidwell	56	706
Charles	San Mateo Twp 2	65	125
Charles M	Yolo No E Twp	72	673
Charles M	Yuba North Ea	72	673
Chas R	San Francisco San Francisco 10	67	275
Delos	Placer Goods	62	695
Eirje*	Shasta Shasta	66	759
Elias W	San Francisco San Francisco 10	67	215
G	El Dorado Placerville	58	847
G	Nevada Red Dog	61	546
George	Shasta Shasta	66	759
George H	San Francisco San Francisco 7	68	1409
H A	Colusa Colusi	57	419
H G	Mendocino Big Rock	60	874
J	Sacramento Ward 1	63	90
J C	Siskiyou Callahan	69	10
J D	Nevada Eureka	61	347
J D	Sierra Twp 7	66	874
J R	San Joaquin Stockton	64	1051
Jacob	Calaveras Twp 8	57	66
James E	San Bernardino San Bernadino	64	636
James F	San Francisco San Francisco 8	68	1314
James M	Sierra Scales D	66	802
Jas	San Francisco San Francisco 1	68	810
Jervis S	San Bernardino San Bernadino	64	636
John	El Dorado Placerville	58	892
John	Santa Cruz Pajaro	66	561
Jos	San Francisco San Francisco 1	68	810
Nathan	Yuba Rose Bar	72	803
S	Colusa Monroeville	57	446
Saml T	Tuolumne Jamestown	71	446
Schooler	Plumas Quincy	62	944
T	San Francisco San Francisco 5	67	504
Ward	Tuolumne Twp 2	71	382
Ward C	Tuolumne Twp 2	71	397
William A	Colusa Colusi	57	419
Wm	Butte Chico	56	563
Z H	Trinity Weaverville	70	1051
PIKEL			
---	Tulara Visalia	71	113
PIKER			
August	Nevada Bloomfield	61	514
George	Marin Point Re	60	730
Gerrac	Marin Point Re	60	730
Saml T	Tuolumne Twp 3	71	446
PIKETER			
John	San Francisco San Francisco 12	67	392
PIKTIN			
Catharin	Sonoma Sonoma	69	653
PILAND			
J	Nevada Grass Valley	61	166
PILAR			
Jose	Santa Clara Almaden	65	272
PILASTER			
James	El Dorado Mud Springs	58	970
PILAY			
Pauline	Trinity North Fo	70	1023
PILCHER			
Samuel	El Dorado Gold Hill	58	1097
PILDORPE			
William Von*	San Diego Colorado	64	807

Name	County Locale	M653 Roll	Page
PILE			
Edward	Santa Clara Gilroy	65	240
J	Shasta Horsetown	66	699
J R	Shasta Horsetown	66	699
John F	Santa Clara San Jose	65	347
W	Sacramento Brighton	63	195
William	Siskiyou Klamath	69	96
Wm	Amador Twp 1	55	489
Wm	Amador Twp 1	55	493
PILER			
John L	Solano Fairfield	69	197
PILERD			
Petre	Siskiyou Yreka	69	126
PILES			
Edward	Santa Clara Santa Clara	65	521
Edwd	Santa Clara San Jose	65	378
S C	Marin Bolinas	60	742
William	Contra Costa Twp 2	57	573
PILESS			
Erksim	Tuolumne Columbia	71	289
Ertsine*	Tuolumne Twp 2	71	289
PILGRIM			
Charles	San Joaquin Elkhorn	64	998
Thomas	San Diego Colorado	64	812
PILHAM			
W H	Nevada Rough &	61	403
PILIGRENE			
---	Calaveras Twp 7	57	2
PILITIN			
Catharin*	Sonoma Sonoma	69	653
PILKIN			
William	Calaveras Twp 6	57	154
PILKINGLER			
Emily E*	San Francisco San Francisco 8	68	1296
John B	San Francisco San Francisco 8	68	1296
PILKINGTON			
Josephine	Sonoma Armally	69	479
Josephine	Sonoma Armally	69	479
PILKINTON			
M	Sacramento San Joaquin	63	359
PILLBRICK			
Saml W	Placer Rattle Snake	62	638
PILLEANUX			
J	Tuolumne Twp 4	71	131
PILLEAUX			
J	Tuolumne Big Oak	71	131
PILLER			
Gabarial	El Dorado Mud Springs	58	968
PILLEY			
Robert	Calaveras Twp 7	57	14
PILLIER			
William	Sonoma Santa Rosa	69	410
PILLING			
J	Calaveras Twp 9	57	410
John	San Francisco San Francisco 3	67	55
John	Sierra Twp 7	66	879
Sidney*	San Francisco San Francisco 2	67	573
T	San Joaquin Stockton	64	1095
PILLINGS			
George	Sierra La Porte	66	767
PILLMAN			
B*	Sacramento Lee	63	214
Wm	San Francisco San Francisco 1	68	927
PILLON			
G*	Calaveras Twp 9	57	402
John*	San Francisco San Francisco 1	68	860
PILLOW			
G	Calaveras Twp 9	57	402
John*	San Francisco San Francisco 1	68	860
PILLSBERRY			
James*	Mariposa Twp 1	60	655
PILLSBURY			
Danl H	Calaveras Twp 5	57	212
Geo	Sacramento Ward 1	63	64
James	Mariposa Twp 1	60	655
S	San Francisco San Francisco 5	67	529
PILSBURY			
---*	Yolo Putah	72	551
Asa	Tuolumne Twp 6	71	543
R J	Yolo Putah	72	551
PILTON			
G*	Calaveras Twp 9	57	402
PILTRETT			
Peter G	Tuolumne Twp 1	71	199
PIM			
---	Nevada Bridgeport	61	466
---	Sierra Downieville	66	993
---	Yuba North Ea	72	682
---*	Sierra Downieville	66	997
PIMDLE			
Jno*	Nevada Washington	61	333
PIMENTO			
Hannah	Tuolumne Twp 2	71	339
Joana	Tuolumne Columbia	71	320
Josephna	Tuolumne Twp 2	71	320
PIMER			
Gondolph*	Calaveras Twp 6	57	167

Name	County Locale	M653 Roll	Page
PIMES			
Gondolph*	Calaveras Twp 6	57	167
PIMG			
---	Sacramento Ward 1	63	66
PIMINTERO			
Loretto	Fresno Twp 1	59	76
PIMKHAM			
Geo	Tuolumne Twp 2	71	287
PIMMONS			
L	El Dorado Placerville	58	877
PIMTREAD			
Sopen	Tulara Twp 2	71	31
PIMU			
Raphael	San Joaquin Stockton	64	1072
PIMUCHEE			
---	Tulara Twp 1	71	119
PIN			
---	Amador Twp 2	55	283
---	Amador Twp 2	55	328
---	Amador Twp 5	55	333
---	Amador Twp 5	55	356
---	Butte Oregon	56	640
---	Calaveras Twp 6	57	126
---	Calaveras Twp 6	57	149
---	Calaveras Twp 5	57	170
---	Calaveras Twp 5	57	224
---	Calaveras Twp 5	57	256
---	Calaveras Twp 4	57	303
---	Calaveras Twp 4	57	304
---	Calaveras Twp 4	57	322
---	Calaveras Twp 4	57	342
---	El Dorado Coloma	58	1084
---	El Dorado Kelsey	58	1144
---	El Dorado Georgetown	58	746
---	El Dorado Diamond	58	797
---	El Dorado Placerville	58	923
---	El Dorado Mud Springs	58	986
---	Mariposa Coulterville	60	700
---	Sacramento Ward 1	63	51
---	San Francisco San Francisco 4	68	1173
---	Sierra Downieville	66	1003
---	Sierra Downieville	66	1005
---	Sierra Downieville	66	1008
---	Sierra Downieville	66	1014
---	Sierra Downieville	66	1015
---	Sierra Downieville	66	1027
---	Sierra Downieville	66	1032
---	Sierra Poker Flats	66	838
---	Sierra Twp 5	66	931
---	Sierra Downieville	66	954
---	Sierra Downieville	66	982
---	Sierra Downieville	66	983
---	Sierra Downieville	66	991
---	Sierra Downieville	66	996
---	Sierra Downieville	66	997
---	Tuolumne Sonora	71	477
---	Tuolumne Twp 6	71	529
---	Yuba Marysville	72	895
---*	Sierra Downieville	66	1008
---*	Sierra Downieville	66	1031
---*	Sierra Downieville	66	983
Tuck	Amador Twp 2	55	292
You	San Francisco San Francisco 4	68	1175
PINA			
Antonie*	Los Angeles Los Angeles	59	495
Antonio	Los Angeles Los Angeles	59	495
Blas	Sonoma Santa Rosa	69	423
Defonsn	San Francisco San Francisco 2	67	789
Defonsu	San Francisco San Francisco 2	67	789
Frances	Sonoma Mendocino	69	462
Jesus	Mendocino Ukiah	60	797
Jose	Los Angeles Los Angeles	59	370
Jose	Los Angeles Santa Ana	59	454
Josefa	Mendocino Ukiah	60	797
Lonos*	Mendocino Ukiah	60	796
PINAP			
L	Tuolumne Twp 4	71	148
PINARCO			
John	Santa Clara Santa Clara	65	481
PINARD			
Esdras	Santa Clara San Jose	65	305
PINARO			
Hosea*	Calaveras Twp 9	57	357
PINATSTER			
Geo	El Dorado Mud Springs	58	970
PINCE			
Adolphus*	San Francisco 3	67	60
	San Francisco		
Geo	Butte Cascade	56	693
W*	Yolo Washington	72	568
PINCH			
John	Sierra La Porte	66	765
John	Sierra La Porte	66	777
PINCHARD			
J B	Tuolumne Twp 1	71	200
V	Tuolumne Twp 2	71	320

California 1860 Census Index

Name	County Locale	M653 RollPage
PINCHEY		
Y	Tehama Lassen	70 864
PINCHINER		
Jacob	Sacramento Ward 4	63 511
PINCHORE		
Henry	San Luis Obispo San Luis Obispo	65 4
PINCHU		
Fong*	San Francisco San Francisco 4	681180
PINCK		
Peter	Placer Todds Va	62 763
PINCKMAN		
Seth	San Francisco San Francisco 7	681409
PINCOM		
John*	Napa Yount	61 46
PINCON		
John	Napa Yount	61 46
PINCUS		
H	San Francisco San Francisco 6	67 449
PINDER		
George	Tuolumne Shawsfla	71 379
William*	Yuba Marysville	72 882
PINDLE		
Charles	Siskiyou Scott Ri	69 66
J	Shasta Shasta	66 657
Peter	Mariposa Coulterville	60 686
PINDRES		
Pindres	Tulara Twp 1	71 114
PINDY		
J L	Nevada Eureka	61 387
PINE		
---	Shasta Shasta	66 677
---	Shasta Horsetown	66 708
Charles A	Humbolt Eel Rvr	59 150
Dudley	San Bernardino San Bernadino	64 684
Elijah H	Siskiyou Yreka	69 130
Elijah W	Siskiyou Yreka	69 130
Hiram	Humbolt Eel Rvr	59 150
Horace A	Mendocino Ukiah	60 794
James	Yuba Rose Bar	72 790
Joseph	Sierra Downieville	661031
Joseph	Yuba Fosters	72 823
Lafayette	San Joaquin Castoria	64 882
Lonos*	Mendocino Ukiah	60 796
Nelson*	El Dorado Georgetown	58 758
Phebe L	San Francisco San Francisco 2	67 704
Saml	San Bernardino San Bernadino	64 684
PINEA		
Jacinto	Solano Vallejo	69 252
Monielia	Yuba Marysville	72 918
PINEHOR		
---*	San Francisco San Francisco 7	681413
PINELL		
P	Stanislaus Oatvale	70 719
PINELU		
Baiseilo	Calaveras Twp 6	57 129
PINENTER		
J I	San Francisco San Francisco 2	67 781
PINENTO		
Joana	Tuolumne Twp 2	71 320
PINER		
Charles A*	Mendocino Ukiah	60 807
John	Mendocino Ukiah	60 801
L*	Nevada Grass Valley	61 185
W	El Dorado Placerville	58 833
PINERO		
Manen*	Marin Cortemad	60 779
Marien	Marin Cortemad	60 779
PINERY		
J	Sutter Nicolaus	70 837
PINES		
Joseph	Sierra Downieville	661006
L*	Nevada Grass Valley	61 185
W	Yolo Washington	72 568
Wm*	San Francisco San Francisco 1	68 874
PINET		
J	Mariposa Coulterville	60 688
PINFIELD		
T	San Francisco San Francisco 3	67 5
PING HANG		
Chou*	Yuba Long Bar	72 748
PING		
---	Amador Twp 4	55 246
---	Amador Twp 4	55 256
---	Amador Twp 2	55 280
---	Amador Twp 2	55 307
---	Amador Twp 2	55 308
---	Amador Twp 2	55 311
---	Amador Twp 2	55 312
---	Amador Twp 2	55 314
---	Amador Twp 2	55 327
---	Amador Twp 3	55 403
---	Amador Twp 6	55 430
---	Amador Twp 6	55 449
---	Amador Twp 1	55 499
---	Amador Twp 1	55 501
---	Calaveras Twp 5	57 192

Name	County Locale	M653 RollPage
PING		
---	Calaveras Twp 5	57 219
---	Calaveras Twp 5	57 232
---	Calaveras Twp 4	57 313
---	Calaveras Twp 4	57 320
---	Calaveras Twp 4	57 328
---	Calaveras Twp 4	57 339
---	Calaveras Twp 7	57 40
---	Calaveras Twp 7	57 42
---	Calaveras Twp 7	57 45
---	Calaveras Twp 8	57 63
---	Calaveras Twp 8	57 75
---	Calaveras Twp 8	57 83
---	Calaveras Twp 8	57 87
---	Del Norte Happy Ca	58 669
---	El Dorado White Oaks	581021
---	El Dorado White Oaks	581032
---	El Dorado Salmon Falls	581043
---	El Dorado Salmon Falls	581044
---	El Dorado Salmon Falls	581053
---	El Dorado Coloma	581076
---	El Dorado Union	581090
---	El Dorado Coloma	581106
---	El Dorado Coloma	581109
---	El Dorado Coloma	581110
---	El Dorado Casumnes	581160
---	El Dorado Casumnes	581177
---	El Dorado Mountain	581178
---	El Dorado Big Bar	58 737
---	El Dorado Diamond	58 795
---	El Dorado Diamond	58 815
---	El Dorado Placerville	58 842
---	El Dorado Placerville	58 933
---	El Dorado Eldorado	58 939
---	El Dorado Eldorado	58 940
---	El Dorado Mud Springs	58 964
---	El Dorado Mud Springs	58 992
---	Mariposa Twp 1	60 665
---	Mariposa Coulterville	60 682
---	Nevada Bridgeport	61 460
---	Nevada Bridgeport	61 461
---	Placer Rattle Snake	62 635
---	Placer Virginia	62 665
---	Placer Virginia	62 669
---	Sierra Downieville	661015
---	Sierra Twp 5	66 924
---	Sierra Twp 5	66 926
---	Sierra Downieville	66 971
---	Sierra Downieville	66 993
---	Sierra Downieville	66 996
---	Tuolumne Jamestown	71 433
---	Tuolumne Twp 3	71 467
---	Tuolumne Don Pedro	71 537
---	Yolo Slate Ra	72 715
---	Yuba Slate Ro	72 712
---	Yuba Slate Ro	72 715
---	Yuba Long Bar	72 758
---*	Calaveras Twp 8	57 109
---*	Shasta French G	66 713
Abraham	Sierra Excelsior	661033
Ah	Calaveras Twp 7	57 33
Ah	Sacramento Ward 1	63 156
Chang	Yuba Long Bar	72 755
Chang	Yuba Long Bar	72 755
Chong	Yuba Long Bar	72 759
Fong	Yuba Long Bar	72 762
Hong	Yuba Long Bar	72 762
Hop*	San Francisco San Francisco 9	681093
Leek	Yuba Long Bar	72 766
Mo	El Dorado Coloma	581076
Taong	El Dorado Eldorado	58 939
PINGE		
W*	Yolo Washington	72 568
PINGGOLD		
G H	San Francisco San Francisco 10	285 67
PINGHIMBAUGH		
Gideon*	Tulara Twp 1	71 90
PINGJ		
---	Amador Twp 2	55 308
PINGLE		
John O	Contra Costa Twp 2	57 579
Joseph	Sierra Twp 5	66 946
Peter	Butte Mountain	56 734
Wm	Sierra Twp 7	66 913
PINGLEY		
Robert	Sierra La Porte	66 782
PINGLLA		
Antonio	San Francisco San Francisco 2	67 697
PINHO		
Jesus	Solano Vallejo	69 250
PINI		
J B	Stanislaus Branch	70 703
PINIE		
Adolphus*	San Francisco 3	67 60
	San Francisco	

Name	County Locale	M653 RollPage
PINJ		
---	Amador Twp 2	55 307
PINK		
---	Mendocino Calpella	60 821
Franklin	Calaveras Twp 7	57 35
Henry	Sacramento Ward 1	63 38
Joseph	Santa Clara San Jose	65 313
P L*	Yolo Putah	72 550
Saml R	Calaveras Twp 10	57 268
Saml W	Calaveras Twp 10	57 268
Simon	Calaveras Twp 7	57 34
Simon P	Calaveras Twp 8	57 86
PINKAN		
Peter*	Mariposa Twp 3	60 611
PINKARD		
Allen*	Colusa Monroeville	57 451
PINKEM		
Peter*	Mariposa Twp 3	60 611
PINKENSTEIN		
H	San Francisco San Francisco 5	67 525
PINKERSTAFF		
John*	Marin Cortemad	60 753
PINKHAM		
Augusta	Tehama Red Bluff	70 923
Barnum	San Francisco San Francisco 11	140 67
Benjamin F	San Francisco 11	114 67
Charles	San Francisco San Francisco 3	67 44
Chet	Santa Clara San Jose	65 348
D W	Tuolumne Twp 2	71 284
F W	San Francisco San Francisco 6	67 449
Jonathan C	San Francisco 11	143 67
Rush*	Santa Cruz Soguel	66 600
Rust	Santa Cruz Santa Cruz	66 600
S N	Siskiyou Scott Va	69 39
Sameus*	Yuba Marysville	72 898
Samner	Yuba Marysville	72 898
Sean	Santa Clara San Jose	65 321
PINKHAMN		
S N	Siskiyou Scott Va	69 39
PINKHURST		
Mengel	San Francisco San Francisco 7	681417
PINKINGTON		
James	Amador Twp 1	55 460
PINKMAN		
Peter*	Mariposa Twp 3	60 611
PINKNEY		
D W	Solano Vacaville	69 360
Richd	Sonoma Petaluma	69 592
PINKSTON		
Sarah*	Stanislaus Branch	70 710
PINKTON		
Sarah	Stanislaus Branch	70 710
PINKUN		
Peter*	Mariposa Twp 3	60 611
PINN		
---	Sierra Whiskey	66 849
---	Yolo No E Twp	72 682
Blas	Sonoma Santa Rosa	69 423
Saladonia*	Stanislaus Branch	70 704
PINNARD		
Jos*	San Francisco San Francisco 2	67 670
PINNE		
Morris*	San Francisco San Francisco 7	681382
P R*	Nevada Nevada	61 239
PINNELL		
Wallis	Del Norte Crescent	58 659
PINNER		
Isaac H	San Francisco San Francisco 3	67 61
PINNEY		
Moses	Sacramento Ward 4	63 537
R H	Placer Dutch Fl	62 722
R H	Tuolumne Twp 2	71 404
PINNON		
---	Tulara Twp 2	71 4
PINNOYER		
John*	Sierra Twp 5	66 920
PINO		
Cerildro	San Bernardino S Timate	64 687
Francisco	Los Angeles Santa Ana	59 455
Louis	Mendocino Ukiah	60 796
Pepa	San Joaquin Stockton	641055
Saladonia*	Stanislaus Branch	70 704
PINOLINI		
Frank	Calaveras Twp 4	57 331
PINOLL		
Lacota	Santa Clara San Jose	65 337
PINOON		
---	Trinity Weaverville	701073
PINOR		
Stephen	Mendocino Ukiah	60 806
PINORD		
Jas	Amador Twp 1	55 492
PINORES		
Loretto	San Bernardino Santa Barbara	64 188

Name	County Locale	M653 Roll	Page
PINOS			
Cassus*	Sierra Downieville	66	963
PINOSA			
Jose	Tuolumne Shawsfla	71	375
Manl	Tuolumne Shawsfla	71	375
PINOSE			
Velviate	El Dorado Greenwood	58	730
PINOT			
Cahrles A	Mendocino Ukiah	60	807
Stephen*	Mendocino Ukiah	60	806
PINPHAM			
Rush*	Santa Cruz Soguel	66	600
PINROSE			
John	Sonoma Bodega	69	539
PINSCHOVER			
S*	El Dorado Diamond	58	763
PINSON			
D D	Yolo Cache Crk	72	594
PINSTON			
S J	Marin Novato	60	735
T	Calaveras Twp 9	57	416
PINTA			
---	Mendocino Round Va	60	885
PINTEL			
Vactura	Tuolumne Twp 1	71	219
Ventura	Tuolumne Sonora	71	219
PINTER			
Edward	El Dorado White Oaks	58	1007
PINTO			
---	Mendocino Calpella	60	821
---	Tulara Twp 1	71	114
---	Tulara Twp 1	71	32
---	Tulara Keyesville	71	56
---	Tulara Keyesville	71	67
---	Tulara Keyesville	71	70
---*	Tulara Visalia	71	32
Francisco	Merced Monterey	60	942
Francisco	Monterey Monterey	60	942
Maria	Santa Clara Almaden	65	271
Maria Y	Merced Monterey	60	939
Maria Y	Monterey Monterey	60	939
Paulina	Santa Clara San Jose	65	331
Peter	Yuba Marysville	72	872
Rafael	Merced Monterey	60	936
Rafael	Monterey Monterey	60	936
Rafael	Santa Cruz Pajaro	66	577
Stephen	Santa Clara San Jose	65	331
PINTYMAN			
A C	Nevada Nevada	61	251
PINVUES			
Juan	Tehama Red Bluff	70	930
PINY			
---	Amador Twp 5	55	365
---	Calaveras Twp 4	57	320
---	Calaveras Twp 4	57	328
PINYON			
---*	Tulara Visalia	71	4
PIO CUNG			
---	Tuolumne Green Springs	71	517
PIO			
---	Los Angeles Los Angeles	59	515
---	San Bernardino San Bernadino	64	680
---	San Bernardino S Timate	64	714
---	San Bernardino S Timate	64	716
---	San Bernardino S Timate	64	717
---	San Bernardino S Timate	64	722
---	San Bernardino S Timate	64	723
---	San Bernardino S Timate	64	726
---	San Bernardino S Timate	64	740
---	San Bernardino S Timate	64	744
---	San Bernardino S Timate	64	753
---	San Diego Agua Caliente	64	822
---	Tuolumne Shawsfla	71	409
---	Tuolumne Twp 3	71	433
---	Tuolumne Jamestown	71	440
---	Tuolumne Jamestown	71	446
---	Tuolumne Twp 3	71	467
---	Tuolumne Sonora	71	477
---*	Yuba Marysville	72	917
Morino	Los Angeles Los Angeles	59	516
Peco	Amador Twp 5	55	332
PIOCKE			
Louis	Yuba Long Bar	72	772
PIODA			
Paul*	Solano Benecia	69	313
PIODER			
Paul*	Solano Benecia	69	313
PIOLA			
Bernard	Santa Clara San Jose	65	298
PION			
Alex	Sierra Downieville	66	1002
Alexr	Sierra Downieville	66	1002
PIPE			
William	Del Norte Happy Ca	58	669
PIPER			
A	Sacramento Sutter	63	306

Name	County Locale	M653 Roll	Page
PIPER			
A D	Placer Auburn	62	593
Asa G	Los Angeles Los Angeles	59	333
Catharine	San Francisco San Francisco 7	68	1434
Chas	Butte Bidwell	56	716
Chas	Butte Bidwell	56	727
Daniel	Sierra Cox'S Bar	66	952
E	El Dorado Diamond	58	808
Francis	Sacramento Granite	63	248
Fredk	Calaveras Twp 10	57	265
George A	Plumas Meadow Valley	62	911
Henry	Butte Mountain	56	734
Henry	San Francisco San Francisco 10	67	187
Henry	San Francisco San Francisco 3 67		52
Henry	Shasta Shasta	66	760
Huston	Nevada Rough &	61	416
J S	Marin Novato	60	738
James	Calaveras Twp 7	57	21
Jas	Butte Mountain	56	734
John	San Francisco San Francisco 10	67	187
John G	Sonoma Healdsbu	69	476
John J	Sonoma Healdsbu	69	476
Robt	Trinity E Weaver	70	1057
S W	Nevada Rough &	61	410
Stephen L	San Francisco San Francisco 6 67		407
T E*	San Francisco San Francisco 3 67		4
William	Sierra Whiskey	66	844
William*	Calaveras Twp 5	57	137
Wm	Nevada Washington	61	336
PIPES			
Ferdinand*	San Francisco 2 67		653
	San Francisco		
Jas	San Francisco San Francisco 1	68	879
Jas	San Mateo Twp 1	65	67
John	El Dorado Newtown	58	777
PIPIN			
J B	Sierra Twp 7	66	913
Sarah	Tuolumne Montezuma	71	502
PIPIR			
Henry	San Francisco San Francisco 3 67		52
T E	San Francisco San Francisco 3 67		4
PIPNE			
Eliyah*	Sacramento Natonia	63	278
PIPPER			
A G	Butte Oregon	56	637
And	Butte Oregon	56	644
PIPPY			
Henry J	San Francisco San Francisco 10	67	270
PIPTSIR			
Catharin*	Sonoma Sonoma	69	653
PIPUR			
Elijah	Sacramento Natonia	63	278
PIQUE			
Edward	San Francisco San Francisco 4	68	1218
PIR			
---	Amador Twp 5	55	366
---	San Francisco San Francisco 4	68	1173
---	Tuolumne Jamestown	71	433
PIRA			
Lutira*	Los Angeles Los Angeles	59	493
Michael	Santa Clara Fremont	65	440
Sutua	Los Angeles Los Angeles	59	493
PIRALTO			
Julio	San Bernardino Santa Ba	64	208
Luciano	Tulara Twp 3	71	43
Victor	San Bernardino Santa Ba	64	208
PIRAN			
Jones	Alameda Brooklyn	55	91
Louis	Alameda Brooklyn	55	91
PIRANNO			
Joseph	Tuolumne Twp 1	71	254
PIRAS			
Alise	Santa Clara San Jose	65	326
Manuel	San Francisco San Francisco 4	68	1215
PIRATTO			
Victor	San Bernardino S Buenav	64	208
PIRCEL			
Michael*	San Francisco San Francisco 3 67		31
PIRCHE			
Alfred	San Francisco San Francisco 10	67	318
PIRDFOLEY			
Robt	Tuolumne Columbia	71	331
PIREC			
Nelson*	El Dorado Georgetown	58	758
PIRIERA			
Francis	Tuolumne Twp 1	71	226
PIRK			
John	El Dorado White Oaks	58	1014
PIRKE			
John	Santa Cruz Pajaro	66	561
PIRKSEN			
W*	Shasta Millvill	66	752

Name	County Locale	M653 Roll	Page
PIRN			
---	Sierra Downieville	66	1031
Pon	Tulara Twp 1	71	115
PIRNES			
Gonitalph*	Calaveras Twp 6	57	167
PIROLA			
Antonio	San Francisco San Francisco 11	67	116
PIRR			
---	Amador Twp 2	55	328
H	Calaveras Twp 6	57	118
PIRRE			
Lorida	Santa Clara Almaden	65	270
PIRREHOR			
---*	San Francisco San Francisco 7	68	1413
PIRRELL			
Chancey*	Marin Cortemad	60	792
PIRRIS			
Manuel	Contra Costa Twp 1	57	514
PIRRLES			
Joseph	El Dorado Placerville	58	913
PIRRUSEE			
John P	Tuolumne Twp 1	71	230
PIRY			
---	Amador Twp 5	55	365
---	Amador Twp 5	55	366
PIS			
---	Calaveras Twp 5	57	204
PISALES			
Juan	Butte Chico	56	561
PISARO			
Benetio*	Butte Chico	56	540
Beneto*	Butte Chico	56	540
Peter	Calaveras Twp 7	57	47
PISCA			
---	Tulara Keyesville	71	68
---	Tulara Keyesville	71	71
PISCADA			
---	Tulara Keyesville	71	64
PISCADOLE			
Francis	San Francisco San Francisco 3 67		63
PISCHCHAR			
Charles	Solano Benecia	69	290
PISCHE			
Alfred*	San Francisco San Francisco 10	67	318
PISCOLINI			
John*	Calaveras Twp 7	57	48
PISCONI			
William H	Calaveras Twp 7	57	16
PISCONS			
William H*	Calaveras Twp 7	57	16
PISCORO			
Petro	Calaveras Twp 7	57	31
PISEADOLE			
Francis	San Francisco San Francisco 3 67		63
PISEALINI			
John*	Calaveras Twp 7	57	48
PISER			
Louis	Placer Michigan	62	807
PISHING			
James	El Dorado Placerville	58	891
PISING			
Theodore	San Francisco San Francisco 8	68	1283
PISKEL			
Anthony	El Dorado Coloma	58	1114
PISNER			
J*	El Dorado Georgetown	58	686
PISSY			
---	El Dorado Georgetown	58	755
PISTEE			
Dominigue	Tuolumne Twp 2	71	399
PISTER			
Dominigen	Tuolumne Shawsfla	71	399
PISUTIN			
---	San Bernardino S Timate	64	693
PIT			
---*	Mariposa Twp 3	60	581
PITCH			
John	Santa Clara Santa Clara	65	514
PITCHER			
E M	Sacramento American	63	159
Henry	Sacramento American	63	159
Henry S	San Mateo Twp 2	65	123
Hiram	Amador Twp 1	55	486
Hitcher	Amador Twp 3	55	383
John	San Francisco San Francisco 6	67	402
R L	Solano Vacaville	69	330
Unis	Contra Costa Twp 2	57	549
Wm	Placer Mountain	62	708
PITCHETT			
J C*	Yolo Cottonwood	72	656
PITCHFORD			
W H	El Dorado Placerville	58	906
PITCOM			
Isaac	Siskiyou Scott Va	69	60

Name	County Locale	M653 Roll	Page
PITERNIC			
T J*	El Dorado Placerville	58	908
PITERSON			
D C	Tuolumne Twp 1	71	230
PITES			
M M	Tuolumne Twp 1	71	201
PITGEN			
Merers	El Dorado Greenwood	58	709
PITHALAGE			
Geo**	Del Norte Crescent	58	633
PITHMAN			
Hosen G	Calaveras Twp 6	57	185
PITIGREW			
Jackson	Placer Michigan	62	826
PITKIN			
William	Calaveras Twp 6	57	154
PITLAR			
John	Santa Clara Santa Clara	65	508
PITLEY			
Jonath	Napa Clear Lake	61	132
PITMAN			
A J	Santa Clara Fremont	65	433
Alfred	Merced Twp 2	60	916
C J	Solano Suisan	69	234
Elias	Tulara Twp 1	71	78
G L	Sacramento Ward 4	63	525
Jas	Sacramento Cosummes	63	405
John A	Placer Dutch Fl	62	711
L W	Sierra Twp 7	66	886
Spencer	Tuolumne Chinese	71	489
PITNER			
S H	Yolo Putah	72	552
PITNERS			
Damarcus	Tulara Visalia	71	110
PITNEY			
S H	Tehama Tehama	70	948
Saml	Trinity Minersville	70	968
PITOYER			
George*	Calaveras Twp 7	57	13
PITOYEUR			
George*	Calaveras Twp 7	57	13
PITRES			
Wm	Mariposa Twp 3	60	610
PITREY			
Charles	Solano Benecia	69	286
PITRNAN			
Alfred*	Merced Twp 2	60	916
PITRON			
E	Nevada Grass Valley	61	185
PITT			
Andw J	Sonoma Sonoma	69	652
George	Siskiyou Shasta Rvr	69	116
John H	San Francisco San Francisco 9	681	036
Ralph S	Yuba Rose Bar	72	816
Robt	Shasta Shasta	66	761
Thomas	Calaveras Twp 10	57	299
Umis	Tehama Tehama	70	936
Walter	Siskiyou Yreka	69	148
Willie	Sacramento Ward 1	63	134
Wm	Amador Twp 1	55	462
Wm	Santa Clara Santa Clara	65	509
PITTCHETT			
J C	Yolo Cottonwoood	72	656
PITTENOS			
J A	San Francisco San Francisco 10	67	282
PITTEY			
Jonath	Napa Clear Lake	61	132
PITTIBONE			
S J	Sierra Twp 7	66	894
PITTIER			
Alex	Nevada Bloomfield	61	524
PITTIS			
John Jr	Sacramento Ward 3	63	429
PITTMAN			
A J	Tuolumne Sonora	71	186
Hosea G	Calaveras Twp 5	57	185
Hosen G	Calaveras Twp 5	57	185
John R	Amador Twp 1	55	482
William	Stanislaus Branch	70	707
PITTMORE			
A	Tuolumne Twp 1	71	186
PITTON			
Henry	Butte Ophir	56	793
PITTORPP			
Valentine	Tuolumne Twp 2	71	413
PITTOSFF			
Valentine	Tuolumne Shawsfla	71	413
PITTS			
Abner	Tuolumne Sonora	71	201
Albt	Butte Oregon	56	638
E	Trinity E Weaver	701	057
G B	Siskiyou Scott Va	69	55
Henry A*	San Francisco San Francisco 3	67	31
Isaac	Marin Tomales	60	774
J M*	Yuba Marysville	72	950

Name	County Locale	M653 Roll	Page
PITTS			
S G	San Mateo Twp 1	65	53
S W	Tuolumne Columbia	71	310
W R	San Francisco San Francisco 1	68	863
Washington	San Francisco San Francisco 1	68	919
William	Marin Tomales	60	774
Wm	Fresno Twp 3	59	15
Wm O	Mendocino Calpella	60	816
PITZER			
Augustes*	Yuba Marysville	72	898
Augustus	Yuba Marysville	72	898
Christopher C	Yuba Bear Rvr	721	000
D K	Mariposa Twp 1	60	640
J S	Trinity Weaverville	701	076
Sarilda	Mariposa Twp 1	60	640
PITZR			
D R	Mariposa Twp 1	60	640
PIUCK			
Lewis*	Sierra Downieville	66	970
PIUMBO			
John*	Tuolumne Twp 1	71	254
PIUMBS			
John	Tuolumne Twp 1	71	254
PIUSON			
Wilard H	Butte Oro	56	674
PIVER			
L*	Nevada Grass Valley	61	185
William	San Francisco San Francisco 4	681	143
PIVET			
J*	Mariposa Coulterville	60	688
PIVETAZ			
Nicholas	Tuolumne Jamestown	71	454
PIVITA			
Nicholas	Tuolumne Twp 3	71	454
PIW			
---	Calaveras Twp 5	57	244
---	Calaveras Twp 4	57	304
PIX			
Hiram	San Francisco San Francisco 2	67	670
William	Solano Benecia	69	316
Wm	San Bernardino San Bernadino	64	670
PIXBY			
Theron	San Joaquin Elkhorn	64	983
PIXLEY			
Alonzo	Nevada Bridgeport	61	483
Calvin	Del Norte Happy Ca	58	670
Frank M	San Francisco San Francisco 12	67	379
M	Colusa Monroeville	57	448
Mark	Nevada Bridgeport	61	482
Wm B	San Joaquin Stockton	641	044
PIXON			
Franklinb	El Dorado Placerville	58	933
PIY			
---	Nevada Bridgeport	61	461
PIYLE			
Orran	Sonoma Sonoma	69	652
PIZA			
E	San Francisco San Francisco 6	67	452
PIZANNA			
---	Fresno Twp 1	59	53
PIZANO			
Frank	San Francisco San Francisco 2	67	719
Frank	Sierra Downieville	661	011
PIZAR			
Louis	San Francisco San Francisco 4	681	158
PIZARRI			
John	Plumas Quincy	62	944
PIZARRO			
Juan F	Sacramento Ward 1	63	17
PIZER			
G	San Francisco San Francisco 10	67	170
PIZON			
Pedro	Los Angeles Los Angeles	59	360
PIZZANO			
J T	Sacramento Ward 1	63	105
PIZZARO			
Augustin	Santa Clara Alviso	65	414
PIZZARRO			
J T*	Sacramento Ward 1	63	105
PJALICERIO			
---	San Bernardino S Timate	64	692
PLA			
---	Calaveras Twp 4	57	300
---*	Calaveras Twp 4	57	300
Ah	Calaveras Twp 7	57	31
PLACCE			
Layer*	Tuolumne Twp 1	71	235
PLACCIA			
Bernave	Los Angeles Los Angeles	59	295
PLACE			
C L	San Francisco San Francisco 9	681	033
C L	San Francisco San Francisco 9	681	054

Name	County Locale	M653 Roll	Page
PLACE			
Cap G J*	San Francisco San Francisco 11	67	113
Emma	Sacramento Ward 1	63	16
G J Cap	San Francisco San Francisco 11	67	113
Henry	San Francisco San Francisco 2	67	697
James H	Nevada Bridgeport	61	496
John	San Diego Agua Caliente	64	834
Maria	San Diego Temecula	64	793
Nancey	Amador Twp 2	55	269
P E	San Francisco San Francisco 9	68	951
Thomas	El Dorado Kelsey	581	155
William	San Bernardino Santa Barbara	64	199
Wm	Sacramento Granite	63	257
PLACEADE			
Metario	Alameda Brooklyn	55	177
PLACEDEN			
G	Mariposa Twp 3	60	555
PLACEE			
Layer	Tuolumne Sonora	71	235
PLACENCIA			
Vicente	Monterey Monterey	60	961
PLACENTIO			
Yguacio	Los Angeles Los Angeles	59	310
PLACER			
Layer*	Tuolumne Twp 1	71	235
Loto	Calaveras Twp 4	57	340
Sato*	Calaveras Twp 4	57	340
Tate*	Calaveras Twp 4	57	340
Tuto*	Calaveras Twp 4	57	340
Vincent	Calaveras Twp 6	57	138
PLACES			
Raymond*	San Joaquin Stockton	641	048
Vincent	Calaveras Twp 6	57	138
PLACHE			
James	Calaveras Twp 8	57	76
PLACHET			
Louisa	San Francisco San Francisco 8	681	294
PLACIDE			
Edmond	Yuba Foster B	72	821
PLACIR			
Martin	Placer Forest H	62	791
PLAFF			
J N	Trinity Weaverville	701	077
W	Tuolumne Jacksonville	71	169
PLAGEMAN			
Frederick	San Francisco San Francisco 4	681	146
PLAGERMAN			
Henry	San Francisco San Francisco 2	67	721
PLAHARTY			
Dennis	San Francisco San Francisco 2	67	703
PLAIN			
George H	Santa Cruz Soguel	66	596
Morris	Calaveras Twp 7	57	6
PLAINHAMER			
F	Tuolumne Twp 1	71	259
PLAINHAMN			
F	Tuolumne Twp 1	71	259
PLAMER			
A J	Trinity Indian C	70	986
PLANCE			
James*	Yuba Marysville	72	905
PLANCHARD			
Louis	San Francisco San Francisco 2	67	796
Louisa	San Francisco San Francisco 2	67	796
PLANCHE			
J R	Sacramento Ward 1	63	108
PLANCHO			
Jose	Tuolumne Jamestown	71	470
PLANE			
Aegane	Siskiyou Callahan	69	7
Aszane*	Siskiyou Callahan	69	7
V	Siskiyou Callahan	69	7
PLANER			
B	San Francisco San Francisco 5	67	506
Wm	Calaveras Twp 9	57	368
PLANJEATCH			
Jno*	Sacramento Ward 1	63	81
PLANJECETCH			
Jno*	Sacramento Ward 1	63	81
PLANJECITCH			
Jno	Sacramento Ward 1	63	81
PLANK			
D	Sutter Bear Rvr	70	825
Daniel K	Sierra Pine Grove	66	835
L J	Butte Cascade	56	689
Mary	San Francisco San Francisco 2	67	557
Phillip	San Francisco San Francisco 2	67	583
W	Nevada Washington	61	333
PLANKET			
Rob	Amador Twp 5	55	330
Rob'	Amador Twp 5	55	330
PLANN			
Mary	San Francisco San Francisco 4	681	216
PLANNADY			
P	Yolo No E Twp	72	673

California 1860 Census Index

Name	County Locale	M653 Roll	Page
PLANNELL			
Peter	Sacramento Dry Crk	63	368
PLANNETT			
Chas	Sacramento Granite	63	222
PLANOR			
Wm	Calaveras Twp 9	57	368
PLANT			
Essex	El Dorado Georgetown	58	700
H T	El Dorado Coloma	58	1070
L J	Butte Cascade	56	689
PLANTO			
M*	El Dorado Placerville	58	866
PLANTS			
J S	Sacramento Lee	63	219
PLARIE			
V	Siskiyou Callahan	69	7
PLAROIR			
Wm*	Calaveras Twp 9	57	369
PLARSONS			
James*	Santa Cruz Santa Cruz	66	632
PLASANT			
Charles	Los Angeles Los Angeles	59	373
John	Los Angeles Los Angeles	59	373
PLASER			
Manuel	Placer Auburn	62	583
PLASHETT			
Joseph*	Yuba New York	72	723
PLASKETT			
Joseph	Yuba New York	72	723
Peter	Yolo No E Twp	72	675
Peter	Yuba North Ea	72	675
Peter	Yuba North Ea	72	721
Wm L	Mendocino Anderson	60	869
PLASS			
B	El Dorado White Oaks	58	1015
Chs W	Napa Napa	61	71
Joseph L*	El Dorado Placerville	58	931
Peter V N	San Mateo Twp 3	65	86
Wm	Napa Napa	61	71
PLASSA			
---	San Mateo Twp 3	65	99
Louis	San Mateo Twp 3	65	98
PLASSON			
Gabriel	Tuolumne Green Springs	71	527
PLASTER			
Charles	San Francisco San Francisco 7	68	1366
PLATA			
---	Tulara Twp 3	71	66
Maria	Alameda Oakland	55	14
PLATARCE			
San Juan	Amador Twp 2	55	300
PLATCHEK			
Joseph	San Francisco San Francisco 3	67	15
PLATE			
A F	Butte Kimshaw	56	573
D	San Francisco San Francisco 5	67	538
Frank	San Joaquin Stockton	64	1032
H	San Francisco San Francisco 2	67	780
James	San Francisco San Francisco 9	68	943
PLATENO			
---	Monterey San Juan	60	999
PLATES			
Antone	El Dorado Salmon Hills	58	1052
PLATET			
G B	Tuolumne Columbia	71	364
PLATISHICK			
S	San Francisco San Francisco 5	67	501
PLATO			
---	Tulara Twp 3	71	72
A J	San Francisco San Francisco 8	68	1265
D*	San Francisco San Francisco 5	67	538
PLATONI			
Jean Baptisti*	Yuba New York	72	725
Jeom Baptiste	Yuba New York	72	725
PLATSHEK			
Julius	San Francisco San Francisco 8	68	1314
PLATT			
A	Tuolumne Twp 1	71	264
A F	Butte Kimshaw	56	573
Alonzao	Sierra Downieville	66	971
Alonzo	Sierra Downieville	66	971
Arvilla	Placer Grizzly	62	755
Benj	Tuolumne Twp 1	71	263
Benja	Tuolumne Twp 1	71	263
C W	El Dorado Placerville	58	851
Conrad	Calaveras Twp 6	57	119
D M	Sutter Butte	70	788
E W	El Dorado Georgetown	58	754
Edward	San Francisco San Francisco 3	67	56
Elliotte	Siskiyou Scott Va	69	46
F	Mendocino Big Rvr	60	845
F C	El Dorado Placerville	58	862
F T	Marin San Rafael	60	757
F*	Mendocino Big Rvr	60	845
George	San Francisco San Francisco 2	67	694
H	Nevada Eureka	61	390

Name	County Locale	M653 Roll	Page
PLATT			
H	San Francisco San Francisco 2	67	780
H G	Tuolumne Sonora	71	204
Henry	Placer Stewart	62	606
Henry B	San Francisco San Francisco 7	68	1359
Hiram	Amador Twp 2	55	283
Hiram	Tulara Twp 3	71	62
J C	Colusa Muion	57	461
J R	Marin San Rafael	60	757
J W	Colusa Muion	57	461
James	Placer Michigan	62	835
James	San Francisco San Francisco 9	68	943
Jetta	Yuba Marysville	72	911
John	Placer Ophirville	62	659
John	Sierra Downieville	66	964
Joseph	Mariposa Twp 3	60	617
Joseph B	Sierra St Louis	66	806
Joseph R	Sierra St Louis	66	806
Nelson	Plumas Quincy	62	965
Peter	Los Angeles Tejon	59	539
Philip	Contra Costa Twp 2	57	542
R G	Butte Oregon	56	637
Robrt	San Francisco San Francisco 1	68	909
Sam	Nevada Bridgeport	61	447
Sam	San Francisco San Francisco 9	68	1060
Saml	San Francisco San Francisco 9	68	816
Samuel	San Francisco San Francisco 9	68	816
Samuel	Tuolumne Twp 1	71	263
Sophia	San Joaquin Stockton	64	1044
Thomas	Calaveras Twp 7	57	28
W	Yolo Putah	72	552
Wm	Amador Twp 2	55	305
PLATTA			
---	Tulara Keyesville	71	72
PLATTE			
Henry	Yuba Marysville	72	926
Jos	Mariposa Twp 3	60	603
Joseph	Mariposa Twp 3	60	617
PLATTER			
Hiram	Santa Clara San Jose	65	348
PLATTNER			
Henry	Yuba Marysville	72	939
PLATTO			
---	Tulara Keyesville	71	66
Henry	Yuba Marysville	72	926
PLATURO			
---*	Monterey San Juan	60	999
PLAUCHE			
J R*	Sacramento Ward 1	63	108
PLAUK			
W*	Nevada Washington	61	333
PLAULER			
Chas*	Siskiyou Yreka	69	147
PLAUNT			
H*	Tuolumne Twp 1	71	216
PLAUUT			
H*	Tuolumne Twp 1	71	216
PLAWIN			
W	Calaveras Twp 9	57	369
Wm	Calaveras Twp 9	57	369
PLAY			
H	Shasta Shasta	66	683
PLAYEMAN			
Frederick	San Francisco San Francisco 4	68	1146
PLAYER			
John	Siskiyou Cottonwoood	69	105
PLAYET			
Henry	El Dorado Coloma	58	1114
PLAYFAIR			
Saml	Tuolumne Sonora	71	219
PLAYTER			
E W	San Francisco San Francisco 5	67	479
PLAZA			
Peter	Amador Twp 4	55	238
PLE			
Edward	San Francisco San Francisco 2	67	652
PLEANCO			
Pleanco	Sutter Vernon	70	842
PLEANNON			
James R	Sonoma Santa Rosa	69	418
PLEARMANY			
W	Sierra Twp 7	66	865
PLEAS			
Obediah	San Joaquin Stockton	64	1014
PLEASANT			
Benj	Marin Novato	60	737
Buford	Calaveras Twp 9	57	370
Byford	Calaveras Twp 9	57	370
Edward	Los Angeles Los Angeles	59	401
Ellen	San Francisco San Francisco 10	232 67	
George	San Joaquin Oneal	64	931
M C	Calaveras Twp 9	57	399
M C	Calaveras Twp 9	57	408
Mike	Calaveras Twp 9	57	408
William	Plumas Quincy	62	1000

Name	County Locale	M653 Roll	Page
PLEASANTS			
Charles	Siskiyou Yreka	69	166
Henry	San Francisco San Francisco 10	335 67	
Jacob A*	Solano Vacaville	69	358
James M	Solano Vacaville	69	358
Nancy M	San Francisco San Francisco 10	258 67	
Tacoh A*	Solano Vacaville	69	358
William	Solano Vacaville	69	358
PLEASENTS			
J T	El Dorado Newtown	58	781
PLECH			
Frederick*	Yuba Linda	72	994
PLECK			
Frederick	Yuba Suida	72	994
P	Siskiyou Klamath	69	97
PLEDGER			
James	Sierra Monte Crk	66	1039
PLEEGG			
G*	Nevada Washington	61	337
PLEEH			
Frederick*	Yuba Linda	72	994
PLEGE			
Henry	San Francisco San Francisco 2	67	607
Lewis	San Francisco San Francisco 2	67	607
PLEGRAMI			
Stephen	Alameda Oakland	55	13
PLEIFIELD			
Susan*	Nevada Bloomfield	61	523
PLEIGG			
G*	Nevada Washington	61	337
PLEMENS			
Charles	El Dorado White Oaks	58	1019
PLEMING			
Patrick	Mariposa Twp 3	60	567
PLEMPTON			
Plenny	San Mateo Twp 3	65	101
PLEN			
Eunice*	San Francisco San Francisco 6	67	401
PLENEKLETT			
Jos C*	San Francisco San Francisco 9	68	944
PLENKET			
Wm*	Amador Twp 5	55	331
PLENTER			
Chas*	Siskiyou Yreka	69	147
PLENUSE			
John	Solano Suisan	69	230
PLEROW			
Clinton	San Joaquin Castoria	64	879
PLERREKLETT			
Jos C*	San Francisco San Francisco 9	68	944
PLESSEKLETT			
Jos C*	San Francisco San Francisco 9	68	944
PLETT			
S	El Dorado Greenwood	58	722
PLETTER			
Henry*	San Francisco San Francisco 9	68	1064
PLETZ			
Charles*	San Francisco San Francisco 5	67	495
PLEVEKLETT			
Jos C	San Francisco San Francisco 9	68	944
PLEVER			
D	El Dorado Cold Spring	58	1101
PLEY			
F	Siskiyou Scott Ri	69	61
PLIFFNER			
James	Siskiyou Klamath	69	96
PLILIAS			
---	Marin San Rafael	60	768
PLIMA			
Sim*	Sacramento Granite	63	263
PLIMKITE			
James*	Sacramento Ward 1	63	148
PLIMPTON			
Dwigh	Napa Hot Springs	61	27
Dwight*	Napa Hot Springs	61	27
PLIN			
---	Sierra Downieville	66	1015
Eunice*	San Francisco San Francisco 6	67	401
PLINEKLITT			
Jos C	San Francisco San Francisco 9	68	944
PLING			
Ah	Calaveras Twp 7	57	32
PLINKER			
Wm*	Amador Twp 5	55	331
PLINKET			
Wm*	Amador Twp 5	55	331
PLINNER			
Simon*	Tulara Visalia	71	105
PLINNIR			
Simon*	Tulara Visalia	71	105
PLIRNSKET			
Isaac	Amador Twp 7	55	411
PLISKIE			
Frank	Placer Rattle Snake	62	632

California 1860 Census Index

Name	County Locale	M653 Roll	Page
PLISS			
Frederick	Santa Clara Alviso	65	410
PLISTER			
S*	Butte Kimshaw	56	595
PLITCHET			
Gabrell	Amador Twp 3	55	373
PLITES			
W H	Sonoma Washington	69	665
PLITTER			
Henry*	San Francisco San Francisco 9	68	1064
PLITZ			
Charles*	San Francisco San Francisco 5	67	495
PLIUNIR			
Simon*	Tulara Visalia	71	105
PLIVENS			
Jacksen	Sacramento Granite	63	256
Jackson*	Sacramento Granite	63	256
PLIVEUS			
Jackson*	Sacramento Granite	63	256
PLOBB			
Nathan C	Tuolumne Green Springs	71	519
Nathan G	Tuolumne Twp 5	71	519
PLOCHBERGER			
Henry	Sierra Gibsonville	66	851
PLOM			
Christian*	Calaveras Twp 10	57	281
PLOMB			
John	Trinity Rearings	70	990
PLOMO			
Hosa	Los Angeles Azuza	59	273
PLOMOSOR			
Gorgonia	Tuolumne Twp 1	71	224
PLONE			
Christian*	Calaveras Twp 10	57	281
PLONER			
Wm*	Calaveras Twp 9	57	368
PLORE			
Christian*	Calaveras Twp 10	57	281
PLORKBERGER			
Henry*	Sierra Gibsonville	66	851
PLORR			
Christian	Tuolumne Twp 6	71	542
PLORY			
John	Yolo No E Twp	72	676
John*	Yuba North Ea	72	676
PLOS			
Reymond	Amador Twp 1	55	507
PLOSBROW			
Richard	Alameda Brooklyn	55	167
PLOTT			
Hiram	Tulara Keyesville	71	62
PLOUGH			
Amos	Alameda Brooklyn	55	192
Valentine	Tuolumne Twp 2	71	367
PLOUGHMAN			
K P	Trinity Weaverville	70	1068
PLOVER			
Wm	Sacramento Granite	63	233
PLOW			
J I	Shasta Millvill	66	740
PLOWER			
Patrick	San Francisco San Francisco 2	67	790
PLRENING			
Joseph*	Shasta Shasta	66	657
PLRONING			
Joseph*	Shasta Shasta	66	657
PLUCER			
Futo	Calaveras Twp 4	57	340
Tuto*	Calaveras Twp 4	57	340
PLUCKER			
B	El Dorado Mountain	58	1178
PLUGG			
G*	Nevada Washington	61	337
PLUGHOFF			
Hannah*	Yuba Marysville	72	849
Heanch*	Yuba Marysville	72	849
Henneh*	Yuba Marysville	72	849
Hermah*	Yuba Marysville	72	849
Hinuch*	Yuba Marysville	72	849
PLUINE			
Wm*	Nevada Eureka	61	345
PLUKET			
James	Amador Twp 6	55	433
PLUM			
---*	Butte Ophir	56	816
Chas	Napa Napa	61	108
Chas M	San Francisco San Francisco 10	215 67	
George H	Santa Cruz Soguel	66	596
J	Shasta French G	66	716
Patrick	Yolo Cache Crk	72	612
T	Shasta French G	66	716
Wm	Nevada Eureka	61	358
PLUMA			
C	Solano Fremont	69	377
PLUMADO			
F H	El Dorado Placerville	58	909
PLUMAS			
Geo	Nevada Eureka	61	370
Kgeo	Nevada Eureka	61	370
PLUMB			
Charles	Tuolumne Shawsfla	71	420
D	Calaveras Twp 9	57	392
Madison	Butte Ophir	56	749
N B	Butte Oro	56	680
Orin	Calaveras Twp 7	57	23
PLUMBER			
Chas B	Placer Dutch Fl	62	711
D	El Dorado Gold Hill	58	1098
Geo W	Tuolumne Twp 2	71	288
PLUMBERGER			
J M	Nevada Nevada	61	277
PLUMBEY			
Geo W	Tuolumne Twp 2	71	288
PLUMBY			
KI	Nevada Eureka	61	363
L	Nevada Eureka	61	363
PLUME			
A*	Nevada Nevada	61	320
H	Nevada Grass Valley	61	219
Kate	San Francisco San Francisco 2	67	715
O	Nevada Nevada	61	320
Wm	Nevada Eureka	61	345
PLUMER			
Chas W	San Francisco San Francisco 9	68	951
Daniel A	Santa Cruz Pajaro	66	558
George H	Santa Cruz Soguel	66	596
H	Nevada Nevada	61	247
H L	Sutter Bear Rvr	70	825
J	Sutter Sutter	70	801
John	El Dorado Gold Hill	58	1097
John B	Siskiyou Yreka	69	151
Mary	San Francisco San Francisco 9	68	951
Nathan	Stanislaus Emory	70	744
Robt	Sacramento Granite	63	266
Thomas	Sierra Downieville	66	1000
W	Tuolumne Twp 1	71	267
PLUMERICH			
Robert*	El Dorado Coloma	58	1079
PLUMERICK			
Robert*	El Dorado Coloma	58	1079
PLUMIER			
H	Nevada Nevada	61	247
PLUMKALL			
J W	Shasta Millvill	66	741
PLUMKETT			
James	San Francisco San Francisco 2	67	745
PLUMLEY			
Alonzo	Contra Costa Twp 3	57	602
PLUMLY			
A	Nevada Eureka	61	363
H	Nevada Eureka	61	363
Kh	Nevada Eureka	61	363
PLUMME			
Levi	Santa Clara Alviso	65	400
PLUMMER			
A	Sacramento Brighton	63	204
Andrew Z	Santa Clara Alviso	65	397
C	San Francisco San Francisco 5	67	541
C	Sonoma Petaluma	69	587
C*	Sacramento Lee	63	212
Charles	Contra Costa Twp 3	57	604
D A	Sutter Bear Rvr	70	825
Danl A	Alameda Brooklyn	55	83
E	Amador Twp 2	55	284
F W	San Mateo Twp 3	65	92
Geo	San Francisco San Francisco 6	67	401
Geo	San Francisco San Francisco 5	67	546
H G	San Francisco San Francisco 4	68	1131
Henry	Tuolumne Columbia	71	343
J C	San Francisco San Francisco 6	67	472
J H	Butte Chico	56	543
J H	Tuolumne Twp 2	71	343
J S	Nevada Rough &	61	416
Jas G	Sacramento Ward 1	63	81
John	Santa Clara Santa Clara	65	501
John A	Humbolt Table Bl	59	141
John L	San Francisco San Francisco 6	67	472
John W	Sierra Twp 2	66	867
John*	Yolo No E Twp	72	678
Marshall D	Alameda Brooklyn	55	84
Mary A	Sierra Downieville	66	972
Merril	San Mateo Twp 3	65	106
Miles	San Mateo Twp 3	65	106
Nathan	Plumas Quincy	62	987
O*	Sacramento Lee	63	212
Susan	San Joaquin Stockton	64	1086
Thomas	Sierra Downieville	66	1000
W	Nevada Washington	61	333
W	Tuolumne Twp 1	71	267
Wm	San Francisco San Francisco 3	67	34
PLUMMES			
D T	Calaveras Twp 9	57	418
E H	El Dorado Placerville	58	862
PLUMMOR			
Danl A	Alameda Brooklyn	55	83
PLUMOFF			
Wm	Nevada Nevada	61	294
PLUMRICK			
Robert	El Dorado Coloma	58	1079
PLUMTON			
H	El Dorado Placerville	58	892
PLUN			
Patrick	Yolo Cache	72	612
PLUNA			
Sein*	Sacramento Granite	63	263
PLUNDERS			
S P*	Nevada Eureka	61	358
PLUNK			
Asa	Placer Rattle Snake	62	599
PLUNKARD			
Richd	Santa Clara Fremont	65	442
Thos M	San Francisco San Francisco 1	68	885
PLUNKET			
Alex	Klamath Liberty	59	233
Celia	Alameda Oakland	55	68
G W	Tehama Red Bluff	70	919
Margt	San Francisco San Francisco 9	68	1013
Mathew	Nevada Bridgeport	61	495
PLUNKETT			
Alex	Klamath Salmon	59	208
Elizabeth	San Francisco San Francisco 10	310 67	
James	San Francisco San Francisco 2	67	745
John	Sonoma Bodega	69	528
Jos	Klamath S Fork	59	207
Jos	San Francisco San Francisco 10	204 67	
Mary	San Francisco San Francisco 9	68	1012
P	Solano Vallejo	69	265
Thomas	Solano Benecia	69	299
PLUNKY			
---	Fresno Twp 2	59	112
PLUNNER			
Robt*	Sacramento Granite	63	266
PLUNSKET			
Isaac	Amador Twp 7	55	411
PLUNSOM			
Paul	San Francisco San Francisco 3	67	20
PLUNTREE			
N	El Dorado Union	58	1089
PLURNGARIN			
N*	El Dorado Placerville	58	925
PLUSHMAN			
Charles	San Francisco San Francisco 7	68	1366
PLUTARCO			
---	Fresno Twp 1	59	85
PLUTO			
---	Fresno Twp 2	59	61
PLUTRU			
---	Tulara Visalia	71	114
PLUTS			
---	Tulara Twp 1	71	114
PLUTT			
F T	Marin San Rafael	60	757
PLYMATE			
J	Nevada Washington	61	332
PLYMUTE			
J*	Nevada Washington	61	332
PMRA			
John*	Siskiyou Scott Va	69	49
PNIK			
John	Nevada Bridgeport	61	480
PNINTER			
J T*	San Francisco San Francisco 2	67	781
PNIOST			
John*	Calaveras Twp 7	57	2
PO			
---	Amador Twp 2	55	293
---	Amador Twp 2	55	312
---	Calaveras Twp 5	57	244
---	Del Norte Crescent	58	633
---	Nevada Rough &	61	437
---	Sacramento Cosumnes	63	390
---	Sacramento Cosumnes	63	391
---	Sacramento Ward 1	63	50
---	Sacramento Ward 1	63	56
---	Sacramento Ward 1	63	61
---	Sacramento Ward 1	63	66
---	San Francisco San Francisco 4	68	1179
---	Sierra Downieville	66	1007
---*	Tuolumne Big Oak	71	181
Ah	Sacramento Ward 1	63	152
Ah	Tuolumne Twp 4	71	181
Henn	San Francisco San Francisco 4	68	1173
Hom	Calaveras Twp 5	57	254
John	Del Norte Crescent	58	633
Ry	Sierra Twp 7	66	875

California 1860 Census Index

Name	County Locale	M653 Roll	Page
PO			
Wit	Sacramento Ward 1	63	156
Wu	San Francisco San Francisco 5	67	510
Yan	Sacramento Granite	63	268
POA			
---	El Dorado Casumnes	58	1162
POAG			
Elijah	Calaveras Twp 6	57	157
James*	Mendocino Little L	60	833
Peter	Yolo Cache	72	609
POAGE			
Joseph C	San Francisco San Francisco 11	67	148
POALTER			
Thomas A	Yuba Marysville	72	860
Thomas A*	Yuba Marysville	72	860
POAR			
Caroline*	Sacramento Natonia	63	282
POATT			
Wm H	El Dorado Georgetown	58	682
POBIN			
Chris*	Mariposa Twp 3	60	585
POBITA			
---	San Bernardino San Bernadino	64	680
POBLA			
Miguel	Mariposa Twp 3	60	543
POBPETT			
Robert*	San Bernardino San Bernadino	64	621
POBST			
Mathias	Plumas Meadow Valley	62	934
POBUARIO			
---	San Bernardino S Timate	64	698
POC			
Ah	Yuba Bear Rvr	72	1000
POCALOVICH			
P	San Francisco San Francisco 5	67	543
POCHECO			
Antonio*	San Francisco San Francisco 9	68	1072
POCK			
---	Calaveras Twp 10	57	291
---	Placer Michigan	62	836
Leon*	Trinity Bates	70	967
Thomas B	San Joaquin Stockton	64	1071
POCKENHEND			
---*	Mendocino Round Va	60	881
POCKENHERD			
---*	Mendocino Round Va	60	881
POCKINS			
Charles G*	Yuba Marysville	72	890
POCKMAN			
F C	Yolo Cache	72	592
H C	Yolo Cache Crk	72	624
Mary	Yolo Cache	72	645
N C	Yolo Cache	72	624
T C	Yolo Cache Crk	72	592
POCKMIRE			
G N	Calaveras Twp 9	57	375
POCL			
---	Placer Iona Hills	62	894
POCOL			
---	Fresno Twp 2	59	70
POCOLA			
John	Calaveras Twp 7	57	43
POCTTHROP			
C W	San Francisco San Francisco 2	67	571
POCTTHROSS			
C W*	San Francisco San Francisco 2	67	571
PODALCO			
Francisco	San Mateo Twp 2	65	113
PODD			
Jesse	San Francisco San Francisco 2	67	632
PODDEN			
Patrick	Mendocino Big Rvr	60	846
PODE			
Edwarde*	San Joaquin San Bernadino	64	645
PODESTA			
John*	Tuolumne Columbia	71	341
Louise*	Tuolumne Columbia	71	341
PODESTCA			
Bartola	Calaveras Twp 7	57	45
PODFREY			
Jas	Tuolumne Twp 4	71	137
PODISTA			
Frank	Amador Twp 3	55	369
PODLEY			
R	Nevada Grass Valley	61	166
PODLY			
R*	Nevada Grass Valley	61	166
PODT			
John*	Tuolumne Twp 5	71	518
POE			
---	El Dorado Salmon Falls	58	1041
---	El Dorado Coloma	58	1078
---	Sacramento Ward 4	63	613
---	Sierra Downieville	66	1026
A P	Napa Napa	61	63
POE			
Ah	Yuba Suida	72	990
Francis	San Francisco San Francisco 6	67	460
John	Shasta Horsetown	66	703
Lee	Tuolumne Jamestown	71	433
Mary E	Sonoma Mendocino	69	467
Robert	Mendocino Little L	60	837
POEHLMAN			
Martin	Sonoma Petaluma	69	591
POER			
Mele*	Placer Damascus	62	846
POETHE			
C	Shasta Shasta	66	659
POETZ			
John C	San Francisco San Francisco 7	68	1426
POEY			
---	Amador Twp 4	55	251
---	Fresno Twp 2	59	4
---	San Francisco San Francisco 4	68	1182
---	San Francisco San Francisco 4	68	1185
---	Tuolumne Twp 5	71	522
---*	San Francisco San Francisco 4	68	1182
POFF			
Anthony	Placer Forest H	62	797
Charles	Placer Michigan	62	828
POFFETTA			
Louis	Mariposa Twp 3	60	557
POG			
---	Amador Twp 3	55	401
POGARTH			
N*	Stanislaus Branch	70	702
POGE			
Elizabeth	Calaveras Twp 5	57	220
Joseph	Mariposa Twp 1	60	654
Pitta*	Mariposa Twp 1	60	654
Polly	Sonoma Santa Rosa	69	414
POGGAINIM???			
Antony*	Calaveras Twp 5	57	197
POGIO			
Giovanni	Tuolumne Chinese	71	499
POGUE			
John	Sonoma Santa Rosa	69	416
POH			
---	Sacramento Ward 1	63	53
---	Sacramento Ward 1	63	54
---	Shasta Horsetown	66	697
---*	Sacramento Ward 1	63	53
POHCOIN			
---	Tulara Twp 3	71	56
POHLEY			
Joseph	San Francisco San Francisco 2	67	721
POHLKER			
J H	San Francisco San Francisco 10	67	288
J St*	San Francisco San Francisco 10	67	288
POHN			
A	El Dorado Placerville	58	869
Charles*	Nevada Nevada	61	267
POHNER			
Jas	Sonoma Vallejo	69	629
POI			
---	Calaveras Twp 6	57	146
---	Yuba Bear Rvr	72	1000
---	Yuba Linda	72	990
POIBLE			
Sam*	Mariposa Coulterville	60	697
POIER			
Jonah	Sacramento Sutter	63	307
POIFLE			
Sam*	Mariposa Coulterville	60	697
POIKER			
John*	Tuolumne Twp 6	71	534
POILE			
Wm	Butte Oregon	56	639
POILLE			
Sam*	Mariposa Coulterville	60	697
POIN			
---	El Dorado White Oaks	58	1023
POINDETH			
J R	Nevada Nevada	61	296
POINDEXTER			
F H	Siskiyou Klamath	69	94
G W	Siskiyou Klamath	69	97
J R	Butte Chico	56	539
P H	Siskiyou Klamath	69	94
William G	Tulara Visalia	71	107
POINER			
Gonleo	Calaveras Twp 5	57	135
POINEROY			
Geo*	Butte Kimshaw	56	590
POING			
---	Butte Kimshaw	56	606
POINSELT			
Wm*	Alameda Oakland	55	51
POINTON			
Richard*	Amador Twp 4	55	238
POINTS			
Frank	Sacramento Franklin	63	322
Frank	Sacramento San Joaquin	63	350
POIPLE			
Sam*	Mariposa Coulterville	60	697
POISAL			
J	Sutter Sutter	70	814
POISE			
Francis	San Joaquin Elkhorn	64	969
POITY			
J C	San Francisco San Francisco 6	67	463
POIW			
Ah	Butte Oregon	56	640
POJ			
---*	Calaveras Twp 6	57	176
POJAN			
George	Shasta Shasta	66	757
POJOR			
Adolph*	Calaveras Twp 6	57	156
POK			
---	San Francisco San Francisco 9	68	1087
---	San Francisco San Francisco 9	68	1088
---	Shasta Horsetown	66	708
---*	Shasta Shasta	66	670
F	San Francisco San Francisco 9	68	1094
Fo	San Francisco San Francisco 9	68	1094
Ko	San Francisco San Francisco 4	68	1207
POKA			
---	Butte Chico	56	566
POKE			
---	Calaveras Twp 5	57	245
---	El Dorado Union	58	1090
---	Tuolumne Jacksonville	71	514
POKEL			
---	Tulara Twp 1	71	116
POKER			
---	Fresno Twp 2	59	61
---	Fresno Twp 2	59	93
Jose	Calaveras Twp 6	57	136
POKHUMMING			
---*	Mendocino Big Rvr	60	854
POKHUMMONY			
---*	Mendocino Big Rvr	60	854
POKU			
---	Calaveras Twp 8	57	84
POLACK			
John	Butte Ophir	56	756
POLADSOE			
John	Shasta Millvill	66	741
POLAMYER			
Jno*	Sacramento Granite	63	252
POLANA			
Thomas	Sierra Downieville	66	977
POLANCO			
T	Merced Twp 2	60	921
POLAND			
And	Sacramento Ward 4	63	562
David	San Francisco San Francisco 12	67	391
H H*	San Francisco San Francisco 4	68	1137
Jeremiah	Placer Michigan	62	858
John	Sierra Whiskey	66	845
John T	Placer Rattle Snake	62	627
Joseph	Placer Forest H	62	773
Kate	Sacramento Ward 1	63	82
Nahur	Alameda Oakland	55	67
R C	Placer Auburn	62	565
Robert C	Placer Auburn	62	559
William	San Francisco San Francisco 9	68	975
POLANDER			
Wm	San Francisco San Francisco 2	67	784
POLAR			
---	Mendocino Round Va	60	886
Micke	Calaveras Twp 7	57	5
POLARD			
Lewis	Sacramento American	63	162
Thoma	Sonoma Armally	69	487
POLATE			
Zaer P*	Butte Ophir	56	751
Zaw P*	Butte Ophir	56	751
POLATSEK			
E	San Francisco San Francisco 10	67	272
POLBENARIA			
---	San Bernardino S Timate	64	704
POLCHIER			
L	Shasta French G	66	718
POLCHIN			
L	Shasta French G	66	718
POLDER			
Julia	San Luis Obispo San Luis Obispo	65	36
POLE			
C	Sacramento Granite	63	241
Eleanor*	Sacramento American	63	161
Mary A	Nevada Bridgeport	61	469
R H	San Francisco San Francisco 4	68	1148

California 1860 Census Index

Name	County Locale	M653 Roll	Page
POLE			
Wm	Sacramento American	63	163
Wm	Sacramento American	63	172
Zibalon	Nevada Bridgeport	61	474
Zibulon*	Nevada Bridgeport	61	474
POLEEKI			
Joseph	Sonoma Petaluma	69	558
POLELA			
Saml*	San Francisco San Francisco 9	68	940
POLEMAN			
Lewis	Sierra Twp 7	66	878
POLERTA			
Arbeta*	Alameda Brooklyn	55	215
POLES			
Hyram	Mariposa Twp 1	60	648
POLET			
Wyram	Mariposa Twp 1	60	648
POLETEBES			
E	Alameda Brooklyn	55	210
POLEWYN			
Jno*	Sacramento Granite	63	252
POLEY			
S	San Francisco San Francisco 6	67	438
POLHEMUS			
C B	San Francisco San Francisco 5	67	514
Isaac Jr	San Diego Colorado	64	812
J L*	Sacramento Ward 3	63	424
Thomas	San Francisco San Francisco 11	67	102
POLI			
Mary A*	Nevada Bridgeport	61	469
S	San Francisco San Francisco 2	67	689
POLICARPIO			
---	Los Angeles Los Angeles	59	400
---	Los Angeles San Juan	59	469
---	Monterey S Antoni	60	972
POLIMO			
Juan	Plumas Quincy	62	971
POLINARIA			
---	San Bernardino S Timate	64	694
---*	San Bernardino S Timate	64	749
POLINARIO			
---	Los Angeles San Juan	59	460
---	San Bernardino S Timate	64	698
---	San Bernardino S Timate	64	706
---	San Diego Agua Caliente	64	863
POLININIO			
---	Los Angeles Los Angeles	59	515
POLINO			
Theodore	Calaveras Twp 5	57	221
POLISI			
H	Tuolumne Columbia	71	310
POLIT			
William	El Dorado White Oaks	58	1026
POLITA			
---	San Bernardino S Timate	64	690
Mongelda*	Amador Twp 2	55	280
Monjelda*	Amador Twp 2	55	280
POLITANA			
---	San Bernardino S Timate	64	714
POLITE			
Jesus	Santa Cruz Pajaro	66	551
POLITO			
Jesus	Santa Cruz Pajaro	66	551
Jesus	Santa Cruz Santa Cruz	66	638
POLITZ			
J	Sacramento Ward 4	63	576
POLK			
Bruce R	Plumas Quincy	62	942
Robt T	San Francisco San Francisco 12	67	366
T A	Amador Twp 1	55	463
William	Plumas Quincy	62	942
POLKIMUS			
Pornihus*	El Dorado Georgetown	58	696
Pornilius*	El Dorado Georgetown	58	696
Pornilun*	El Dorado Georgetown	58	696
POLL			
Emmet	Siskiyou Callahan	69	3
Mick	Sierra Forest C	66	910
POLLACK			
A	El Dorado Coloma	58	1102
A C	San Francisco San Francisco 5	67	502
J	San Francisco San Francisco 6	67	671
J S	San Francisco San Francisco 6	67	454
Robert	San Francisco San Francisco 2	67	697
S	San Francisco San Francisco 5	67	512
S	San Francisco San Francisco 5	67	518
POLLAIN			
Christian	San Francisco San Francisco 2	67	788
POLLAIR			
Christian*	San Francisco San Francisco 2	67	788
POLLAN			
Christian*	San Francisco San Francisco 2	67	788
Christianb	San Francisco San Francisco 2	67	788
POLLAND			
J	Nevada Nevada	61	318
POLLAND			
J*	Nevada Grass Valley	61	144
Jeramiah	Nevada Bridgeport	61	449
Wm*	Tehama Pasakent	70	857
POLLARD			
A	Butte Mountain	56	740
Aaron	San Mateo Twp 1	65	48
B P	Klamath Liberty	59	240
C H	Siskiyou Scott Va	69	47
C J	Nevada Nevada	61	311
Charles	Nevada Bridgeport	61	456
Charles P	Yuba Marysville	72	879
D F	El Dorado Georgetown	58	759
Dann	Klamath Trinidad	59	220
E	San Francisco San Francisco 6	67	444
I	Nevada Nevada	61	318
I H*	Siskiyou Callahan	69	5
Isaac	San Francisco San Francisco 7	68	1407
J	Nevada Grass Valley	61	144
J D	Butte Kimshaw	56	593
J H	Siskiyou Callahan	69	5
J T	Solano Vacaville	69	321
J*	Nevada Grass Valley	61	144
Jeramiah	Nevada Bridgeport	61	449
Jno C	San Francisco San Francisco 5	67	478
John	Contra Costa Twp 3	57	598
John	Nevada Bridgeport	61	488
John	Sacramento American	63	158
John	San Francisco San Francisco 7	68	1403
John	San Joaquin Stockton	64	1011
John M	San Francisco San Francisco 8	68	1265
Joseph	San Francisco San Francisco 7	68	1420
Joseph	Tuolumne Jamestown	71	446
Laurence	Santa Cruz Soguel	66	593
Lawrence*	Santa Cruz Soguel	66	593
Manuel A	San Luis Obispo San Luis Obispo	65	28
Massy	Contra Costa Twp 1	57	522
Sarah R	Sierra Twp 5	66	924
W	Calaveras Twp 9	57	409
William	El Dorado Mud Springs	58	970
William	Mendocino Calpella	60	821
William	San Francisco San Francisco 3	67	43
William	Tuolumne Shawsfla	71	388
Wm	San Francisco San Francisco 1	68	916
Wm*	Tehama Moons	70	857
POLLARDE			
Thos	Mariposa Twp 3	60	571
POLLARENA			
Juan	Los Angeles Los Nieto	59	435
POLLASDE			
Thos	Mariposa Twp 3	60	571
POLLECHI			
Polipi*	Marin Cortemad	60	790
POLLET			
Flora M	Alameda Brooklyn	55	195
Peter	Tuolumne Montezuma	71	512
POLLETE			
Chas	Napa Napa	61	110
Mary	Napa Napa	61	111
POLLETT			
Jas	Yolo Washington	72	568
POLLETTA			
C	Calaveras Twp 9	57	377
POLLEY			
F M	Sierra Eureka	66	1046
G P	Tuolumne Big Oak	71	140
L N	Sierra Eureka	66	1049
Low	Butte Mountain	56	735
S	San Francisco San Francisco 6	67	438
Wm	Napa Napa	61	105
Wm	Sacramento Ward 1	63	73
POLLEYS			
Samuel	San Joaquin Elkhorn	64	958
POLLI			
Louis	San Francisco San Francisco 3	67	15
POLLICK			
C	El Dorado Placerville	58	822
Margaret	San Mateo Twp 3	65	88
William	San Mateo Twp 3	65	109
POLLIN			
Ann	Los Angeles Los Angeles	59	501
POLLING			
John	Sierra Twp 7	66	879
POLLINS			
Saml	El Dorado Georgetown	58	745
POLLIS			
A	Los Angeles Tejon	59	523
POLLISTRA			
Louis*	Placer Michigan	62	857
POLLO			
J	San Francisco San Francisco 2	67	791
POLLOCK			
A	El Dorado Coloma	58	1102
J	Sacramento Lee	63	216
James	Solano Benecia	69	295
POLLOCK			
Jas	Sacramento Cosumnes	63	380
Periander	Plumas Quincy	62	980
Pierce	El Dorado Kelsey	58	1131
Samuel	Humbolt Mattole	59	127
POLLORENA			
Edwardo	Los Angeles Los Nieto	59	435
Joaquina	Los Angeles Los Nieto	59	430
Juan	Los Angeles Los Nieto	59	435
Maria A	Los Angeles Los Angeles	59	295
POLLORENIA			
Joaquina*	Los Angeles Los Nieto	59	430
POLLY			
---	Butte Chico	56	558
---	Del Norte Klamath	58	654
---	Mariposa Twp 1	60	626
---	Mendocino Calpella	60	827
---	Mendocino Calpella	60	828
---	Mendocino Round Va	60	878
---	Mendocino Round Va	60	881
---	Mendocino Arrana	60	862
Henry	Sierra Pine Grove	66	828
John	Butte Oregon	56	623
Saml	Sutter Butte	70	794
W			
POLMONTER			
R	Sutter Yuba	70	776
POLNO			
Jms R	Klamath S Fork	59	207
POLOLA			
Saml	San Francisco San Francisco 9	68	940
POLOMA			
---	San Bernardino S Timate	64	737
---	San Bernardino S Timate	64	738
POLOMARA			
M H	Tuolumne Sonora	71	215
POLOMARES			
Cristobal	Santa Clara Alviso	65	403
Refugia	San Bernardino Santa Barbara	64	154
POLONIA			
---	Los Angeles Los Angeles	59	373
---	San Bernardino S Timate	64	710
---	San Bernardino S Timate	64	713
---	San Bernardino S Timate	62	734
---*	San Bernardino S Timate	64	733
POLONIO			
---	San Bernardino Santa Ba	64	208
POLONK			
Mary*	Alameda Oakland	55	64
POLOPS			
---	Fresno Twp 2	59	60
POLORUPE			
Jose	San Luis Obispo San Luis Obispo	65	23
POLOSKI			
A	Sacramento Ward 3	63	480
POLOUK			
Mary*	Alameda Oakland	55	64
POLOZO			
---	San Bernardino Santa Inez	64	138
POLSON			
Chris	Mariposa Twp 3	60	585
David	Del Norte Crescent	58	659
F	Alameda Brooklyn	55	144
John	Nevada Bridgeport	61	499
POLSTIN			
Martin*	Placer Iona Hills	62	887
POLTEC			
Abraham	Colusa Butte Crk	57	466
POLTER			
Jno H*	Mendocino Arrana	60	856
William*	Mendocino Calpella	60	813
POLTS			
James	Solano Benecia	69	289
POLUILDOVER			
Julia*	Yuba Marysville	72	956
POLYURE			
Clement*	Calaveras Twp 6	57	124
POLYURO			
Clement*	Calaveras Twp 6	57	124
POM			
---	El Dorado Greenwood	58	719
---	Placer Virginia	62	674
---	Yuba North Ea	72	682
William*	San Francisco San Francisco 9	68	1081
POMAN			
William*	Placer Forest H	62	769
POMASAMA			
---	Alameda Oakland	55	49
POMASANO			
---	Mariposa Twp 1	60	624
POMASENO			
---	San Bernardino S Timate	64	749
POMBER			
Luis	Monterey Pajaro	60	1015
POMDETHE			
J R*	Nevada Nevada	61	296
POME			
---	Mendocino Big Rvr	60	854

Name	County Locale	M653 Roll	Page
POMEIN			
William*	Placer Forest H	62	769
POMELLER			
Pedro	San Bernardino Santa Barbara	64	156
POMERAY			
A	El Dorado Georgetown	58	695
POMEROY			
A	Sacramento Ward 1	63	40
A D	Sacramento Ward 1	63	17
C H	Sacramento Cosumnes	63	383
David	San Francisco San Francisco 9	681	079
Geo	Butte Kimshaw	56	590
Hiram	Santa Clara Alviso	65	401
Isabella*	Del Norte Crescent	58	619
Jas	Sonoma Petaluma	69	590
John	Sierra Chappare	661	040
Peter	Tulara Twp 3	71	58
S	San Francisco San Francisco 5	67	549
T S	Del Norte Crescent	58	619
Thos M	Sacramento Natonia	63	276
Warren	Santa Clara Alviso	65	409
POMESBY			
A	El Dorado Georgetown	58	695
POMESENO			
---	San Bernardino S Timate	64	733
POMG			
---*	Butte Kimshaw	56	606
POMICATES			
M	Shasta Millvill	66	752
POMID			
Jno W*	Mendocino Anderson	60	871
POMISE			
P	Nevada Eureka	61	365
POMMIER			
Fred*	Sacramento Mississipi	63	188
POMMIES			
Fred*	Sacramento Mississipi	63	188
POMNEY			
S*	San Francisco San Francisco 5	67	549
POMNIER			
Jane*	Siskiyou Yreka	69	174
Janne*	Siskiyou Yreka	69	174
Jaune*	Siskiyou Yreka	69	174
POMONOFF			
F	San Francisco San Francisco 9	681	061
POMOROY			
Geo*	Butte Kimshaw	56	590
POMPANELLI			
Salvadore	Sacramento Ward 1	63	113
POMPEISRELOR			
Jesus	El Dorado Greenwood	58	718
POMPHIRT			
Richard	Calaveras Twp 10	57	282
POMPIAN			
Victor	Mariposa Twp 3	60	556
POMPOSA			
---	San Francisco San Francisco 3	67	4
POMPOSO			
---	Los Angeles Tejon	59	529
POMPY			
---	Fresno Twp 2	59	115
POMRD			
Jno W*	Mendocino Anderson	60	871
POMROY			
A	Santa Clara Gilroy	65	238
C W	Santa Clara San Jose	65	340
Chas	Santa Clara Gilroy	65	232
E	Santa Clara San Jose	65	286
E H	Nevada Rough &	61	417
J T	Santa Clara San Jose	65	353
John	San Mateo Twp 1	65	70
Mack	Santa Clara Alviso	65	400
O L	Merced Twp 1	60	898
O S	Merced Twp 1	60	898
S S	San Francisco San Francisco 5	67	525
POMSELT			
Wm*	Alameda Oakland	55	51
POMSEN			
Wm	Sacramento Granite	63	261
POMSON			
Wm*	Sacramento Granite	63	261
POMTOPLE			
S	Amador Twp 1	55	486
POMTOR			
C	Sutter Bear Rvr	70	821
PON PUN			
---	Tulara Twp 1	71	115
PON			
---	Amador Twp 6	55	445
---	Calaveras Twp 5	57	244
---	Calaveras Twp 10	57	270
---	Calaveras Twp 9	57	371
---	Del Norte Crescent	58	631
---	Del Norte Crescent	58	632
---	El Dorado Salmon Falls	581	048
---	El Dorado Coloma	581	105

Name	County Locale	M653 Roll	Page
PON			
---	El Dorado Coloma	581	107
---	El Dorado Kelsey	581	141
---	Nevada Red Dog	61	539
---	San Francisco San Francisco 4	681	182
---	San Francisco San Francisco 4	681	185
---	San Francisco San Francisco 4	681	186
---	San Francisco San Francisco 4	681	191
---	Sierra Downieville	661	010
---	Sierra Downieville	661	014
---	Sierra Twp 5	66	925
---	Sierra Twp 5	66	928
---	Sierra Twp 5	66	948
---	Sierra Downieville	66	983
---	Sierra Downieville	66	996
---	Sierra Downieville	66	998
---	Tuolumne Twp 3	71	457
---	Tuolumne Sonora	71	477
---	Tuolumne Chinese	71	524
---	Tuolumne Twp 6	71	536
---	Yuba Long Bar	72	759
---*	Mariposa Twp 3	60	562
---*	San Francisco San Francisco 9	681	093
An	Del Norte Crescent	58	631
Chu	San Francisco San Francisco 4	681	180
James H*	Sierra Twp 7	66	913
Kie	El Dorado Diamond	58	797
Lang	San Francisco San Francisco 4	681	208
Que	Sierra Downieville	661	004
Sing*	Butte Ophir	56	808
Tucks	Calaveras Twp 5	57	246
PONA			
A A	Placer Todds Va	62	790
PONAIA			
---	San Bernardino S Timate	64	719
PONARO			
Hosea	Calaveras Twp 9	57	357
PONCCO			
Manuel	Tuolumne Montezuma	71	511
PONCE DE LION			
Loura*	San Bernardino Santa Barbara	64	193
PONCE			
John	Alameda Brooklyn	55	91
John	Alameda Brooklyn	55	97
Jose	Santa Clara Alviso	65	397
Louis	San Bernardino Santa Barbara	64	183
Romeo	Alameda Murray	55	223
Rommo*	Alameda Murray	55	223
W	Calaveras Twp 9	57	414
PONCEANO			
Reanda*	San Francisco San Francisco 11	67	156
Reauda	San Francisco San Francisco 11	67	156
PONCER			
Peyton	Placer Todds Va	62	785
PONCHES			
Samuel	Yuba Rose Bar	72	814
PONCHET			
Cath	San Francisco San Francisco 2	67	661
PONCHO			
Antonio	Tuolumne Twp 1	71	479
Francisco	Tuolumne Shawsfla	71	410
Francisco	Tuolumne Twp 1	71	475
Frank	Trinity Mouth Ca	701	017
Mercede	Tuolumne Twp 1	71	479
PONCIA			
---	San Bernardino S Timate	64	712
---	San Bernardino S Timate	64	716
---	San Bernardino S Timate	64	722
---	San Bernardino S Timate	64	723
---	San Bernardino S Timate	64	730
---	San Bernardino S Timate	64	740
---	San Bernardino S Timate	64	751
PONCIN			
---	San Bernardino San Bernadino	64	681
PONCO			
Manuel*	Tuolumne Twp 5	71	511
POND			
A R	Solano Vacaville	69	355
Ambrose	San Francisco San Francisco 11	67	162
Balam	Tuolumne Twp 2	71	472
Clark	Butte Oregon	56	617
Daniel	Yuba Marysville	72	893
Donald	Sierra Forest C	66	910
Doneld*	Sierra Twp 7	66	910
E B	Butte Hamilton	56	528
E S	San Francisco San Francisco 6	67	408
Elijah*	Mendocino Arrana	60	859
George H	Tuolumne Twp 1	71	262
George H	Tuolumne Twp 1	71	262
J E	Napa Napa	61	93
James M	Sierra Scales D	66	803
John P	San Diego San Diego	64	772
Mary	San Diego San Diego	64	761

Name	County Locale	M653 Roll	Page
POND			
P	Sutter Butte	70	787
S P	Yolo Cache Crk	72	592
Summer	Sacramento Ward 3	63	484
William	San Francisco San Francisco 9	681	081
William	Solano Suisan	69	204
Wm C	Sierra Downieville	66	958
PONDERFAST			
Michael	El Dorado Big Bar	58	735
PONDO			
Donald	Sierra Twp 7	66	910
Giovani B	Tuolumne Twp 5	71	498
PONDOE			
E*	El Dorado Placerville	58	879
PONDOL			
E*	El Dorado Placerville	58	879
PONDOLA			
Bautesto*	Santa Barbara	64	193
	San Bernardino		
PONDS			
G W	Yuba New York	72	744
PONDY			
J L*	Nevada Eureka	61	387
PONE			
---	El Dorado Mountain	581	187
---	Shasta Shasta	66	677
---	Sierra Downieville	661	004
PONELA			
---*	Alameda Brooklyn	55	114
PONEMA			
---	San Bernardino S Timate	64	711
PONER			
Lee	Butte Bidwell	56	720
PONERS			
John*	San Francisco San Francisco 1	68	905
John*	Yuba New York	72	739
PONES			
Jacob	Sacramento Ward 4	63	497
Jeshua	Sierra Downieville	661	006
Wm*	San Francisco San Francisco 1	68	874
PONETT			
J	Sutter Nicolaus	70	828
PONEY			
Pong	San Francisco San Francisco 5	67	510
PONEZ			
John D	San Joaquin Stockton	641	082
PONG CAY			
---	Nevada Red Dog	61	556
PONG			
---	Amador Twp 2	55	290
---	Amador Twp 3	55	403
---	Amador Twp 7	55	414
---	Calaveras Twp 8	57	100
---	Calaveras Twp 5	57	191
---	Calaveras Twp 5	57	232
---	Calaveras Twp 4	57	339
---	El Dorado White Oaks	581	021
---	El Dorado Salmon Falls	581	042
---	El Dorado Salmon Falls	581	064
---	El Dorado Coloma	581	083
---	El Dorado Union	581	089
---	El Dorado Union	581	093
---	El Dorado Coloma	581	110
---	El Dorado Placerville	58	839
---	El Dorado Placerville	58	923
---	El Dorado Eldorado	58	939
---	El Dorado Mud Springs	58	958
---	El Dorado Mud Springs	58	959
---	Marin Cortemad	60	783
---	Marin Cortemad	60	791
---	Mariposa Coulterville	60	682
---	Nevada Rough &	61	431
---	Nevada Bridgeport	61	464
---	Nevada Bridgeport	61	493
---	Nevada Bridgeport	61	505
---	Placer Rattle Snake	62	598
---	Placer Ophirville	62	659
---	Placer Virginia	62	670
---	Placer Virginia	62	679
---	Placer Virginia	62	680
---	Placer Virginia	62	681
---	Placer Virginia	62	682
---	Placer Virginia	62	687
---	Placer Virginia	62	688
---	Placer Dutch Fl	62	732
---	Placer Illinois	62	740
---	Placer Michigan	62	835
---	Placer Iona Hills	62	881
---	Plumas Quincy	62	948
---	Sacramento Ward 3	63	493
---	Sacramento Ward 1	63	52
---	Sacramento Ward 4	63	613
---	Sacramento Ward 1	63	68
---	San Francisco San Francisco 9	681	096
---	San Francisco San Francisco 4	681	197

Name	County Locale	M653 Roll Page
PONG		
---	San Francisco San Francisco 11	144
		67
---	Shasta French G	66 713
---	Shasta French G	66 720
---	Sierra Downieville	661029
---	Sierra Twp 5	66 924
---	Sierra Downieville	66 993
---	Trinity Mouth Ca	701016
---	Trinity Mouth Ca	701018
---	Trinity Trinidad Rvr	701044
---	Trinity Trinidad Rvr	701048
---	Trinity Rearings	70 990
---	Tuolumne Twp 2	71 409
---	Tuolumne Twp 2	71 410
---	Tuolumne Twp 3	71 433
---	Tuolumne Twp 3	71 440
---	Tuolumne Jamestown	71 446
---	Tuolumne Twp 3	71 457
---	Tuolumne Twp 3	71 467
---	Tuolumne Twp 3	71 468
---	Tuolumne Sonora	71 476
---	Tuolumne Twp 1	71 477
---	Tuolumne Jacksonville	71 514
---*	Placer Auburn	62 563
---*	Placer Virginia	62 680
---*	Tuolumne Twp 1	71 476
Ah	Alameda Murray	55 223
Ah	Sacramento Ward 3	63 491
Ah	Trinity Indian C	70 983
Ah	Tuolumne Twp 2	71 386
Eliza	Trinity Weaverville	701073
Ghu	Placer Iona Hills	62 896
Gick	Placer Iona Hills	62 897
Hung	Tuolumne Twp 2	71 347
James	Mendocino Little L	60 833
Long Ah*	Marin Cortemad	60 780
Sing	Nevada Bloomfield	61 530
Sung	Placer Michigan	62 858
PONGELE		
C*	San Francisco San Francisco 10	343
		67
PONGTONG		
Fred*	Nevada Bloomfield	61 510
PONGUE		
J A	El Dorado Union	581088
PONIFRANELLI		
Salvadore	Sacramento Ward 1	63 113
PONIG		
---	Butte Kimshaw	56 599
---	Butte Eureka	56 651
Ah	Butte Eureka	56 651
PONIS		
B	Siskiyou Scott Ri	69 73
Joseph	Sierra Downieville	661006
Joshua*	Sierra Downieville	661006
PONISELT		
Wm*	Alameda Oakland	55 51
PONJAE		
J	San Francisco San Francisco 12	393
		67
PONKHAM		
Susan W	San Joaquin Stockton	641056
PONKINS		
D	San Francisco San Francisco 4	681231
PONKNEY		
W J*	San Francisco San Francisco 5	67 534
PONKS		
---	Plumas Quincy	62 948
PONLAIN		
Augustin	Los Angeles Los Angeles	59 375
PONLEY		
Henry	Yolo Merritt	72 583
PONLZE		
Louis	San Francisco San Francisco 11	104
		67
PONMARAT		
Victor	Butte Kimshaw	56 602
PONNARD		
Komk*	Mariposa Coulterville	60 696
PONOOIUR		
Jas*	San Francisco San Francisco 2	67 709
PONORD		
Jno W*	Mendocino Anderson	60 871
PONOVIUR		
Jas	San Francisco San Francisco 2	67 709
PONPUN		
---	Tulara Visalia	71 115
PONREAU		
Pierre*	Plumas Meadow Valley	62 934
PONRIE		
John	Shasta Shasta	66 671
PONRISE		
P*	Nevada Eureka	61 365
PONRSET		
Canchi	San Francisco San Francisco 2	67 789

Name	County Locale	M653 Roll Page
PONRSET		
Carichi	San Francisco San Francisco 2	67 789
PONS		
Bart	Siskiyou Yreka	69 130
C	San Francisco San Francisco 5	67 496
Theo	Siskiyou Yreka	69 130
PONSA		
Rafael	San Bernardino San Bernadino	64 639
PONSCHI		
Theodore	Calaveras Twp 5	57 218
PONSE		
Juan	Tuolumne Chinese	71 497
Manuel	Tuolumne Twp 5	71 498
PONSET		
George	Marin Bolinas	60 746
PONSO		
Juan	Tuolumne Twp 5	71 497
PONT		
---	Sierra Morristown	661056
Fred	Sacramento Ward 4	63 503
PONTACOPA		
George*	Amador Twp 4	55 258
PONTAI		
Roma	Alameda Oakland	55 61
PONTEN		
Henry*	Butte Oregon	56 618
Robt J	San Francisco San Francisco 2	67 768
PONTERRA		
---	Fresno Twp 2	59 115
PONTES		
Peter	Tuolumne Sonora	71 236
PONTHOI		
---	Tulara Twp 1	71 115
PONTIAS		
Saml	Butte Oregon	56 611
PONTIER		
Vickland*	San Joaquin Tulare	64 871
PONTIN		
Henry*	Butte Oregon	56 618
PONTIS		
Peter	Tuolumne Twp 1	71 236
PONTO		
Frank	Amador Twp 1	55 467
Samuel	Calaveras Twp 10	57 278
PONTON		
Henry*	Butte Oregon	56 618
Peter*	Amador Twp 4	55 234
Robt J	San Francisco San Francisco 2	67 768
PONTRAO		
Alhen*	Alameda Oakland	55 56
PONY		
---	Amador Twp 2	55 275
---	Amador Twp 5	55 364
---	Calaveras Twp 5	57 192
---	Calaveras Twp 4	57 309
---	Del Norte Klamath	58 656
---	Shasta French G	66 713
Say Fong	San Francisco San Francisco 5	67 510
PONYA		
Frank	Tuolumne Twp 1	71 255
POO FAH LEE		
---	Plumas Quincy	62 970
POO FOO		
---	Nevada Red Dog	61 538
POO MOH		
---	Sacramento Ward 3	63 490
POO		
---	Amador Twp 4	55 233
---	Amador Twp 4	55 251
---	Amador Twp 4	55 256
---	Amador Twp 6	55 444
---	Amador Twp 6	55 445
---	Calaveras Twp 6	57 165
---	Calaveras Twp 6	57 167
---	Calaveras Twp 5	57 214
---	Calaveras Twp 10	57 274
---	Calaveras Twp 4	57 332
---	Calaveras Twp 8	57 50
---	Calaveras Twp 8	57 63
---	El Dorado Big Bar	58 737
---	El Dorado Eldorado	58 940
---	Fresno Twp 2	59 19
---	Fresno Twp 1	59 27
---	Fresno Twp 2	59 4
---	Mariposa Twp 3	60 562
---	Nevada Rough &	61 399
---	Nevada Red Dog	61 538
---	Placer Iona Hills	62 893
---	Siskiyou Klamath	69 80
---	Stanislaus Branch	70 713
---	Tuolumne Twp 3	71 433
---	Tuolumne Twp 3	71 457
---	Tuolumne Twp 6	71 535
---	Tuolumne Twp 6	71 536
---	Tuolumne Don Pedro	71 537
---	Tuolumne Twp 6	71 539

Name	County Locale	M653 Roll Page
POO		
---	Yuba Slate Ro	72 711
---	Yuba Fosters	72 842
---	Yuba Marysville	72 868
---*	Nevada Red Dog	61 538
---*	Yuba Fosters	72 842
A*	Sierra Twp 5	66 932
Ah	Calaveras Twp 7	57 36
Ah	Sacramento Ward 1	63 152
Ching*	San Francisco San Francisco 5	67 514
Chung	Fresno Twp 2	59 20
Foy	Butte Bidwell	56 709
Goon	Calaveras Twp 5	57 252
Ham	El Dorado Greenwood	58 727
J*	Nevada Red Dog	61 538
Lee	Plumas Quincy	62 946
Otigh	Fresno Twp 1	59 33
Thon	San Francisco San Francisco 4	681196
Thou	San Francisco San Francisco 4	681196
Ton	San Francisco San Francisco 4	681175
Tow	San Francisco San Francisco 4	681175
Wam*	San Francisco San Francisco 5	67 514
POOCATRU		
---	Tulara Twp 1	71 121
POODNOW		
Lincoln	Tuolumne Twp 4	71 143
POOE		
---	Butte Bidwell	56 709
POOER		
Daniel	Tulara Keeneysburg	71 47
POOEY		
---	Del Norte Happy Ca	58 668
POOH		
---	Calaveras Twp 8	57 49
POOING		
---	Plumas Quincy	621008
POOK		
---	Marin Cortemad	60 792
---	Mariposa Twp 3	60 620
---	San Francisco San Francisco 5	67 510
---	San Francisco San Francisco 5	67 532
A	San Francisco San Francisco 5	67 532
POOL		
---	Yuba Linda	72 993
Ah	Yuba Suida	72 993
Alexander	Marin Point Re	60 732
Amini*	Siskiyou Yreka	69 179
Annie*	Siskiyou Yreka	69 179
Arien*	Placer Auburn	62 589
Chas*	San Francisco San Francisco 1	68 902
D	Nevada Nevada	61 254
D M	Mariposa Twp 1	60 660
Edward	Santa Cruz Watsonville	66 538
Ellen	San Francisco San Francisco 9	68 986
Henry	El Dorado White Oaks	581032
Henry B	El Dorado Mud Springs	58 956
Isaac K	Tuolumne Big Oak	71 125
Isaac K	Tuolumne Twp 4	71 127
J H	San Francisco San Francisco 6	67 420
Jacob	Mariposa Coulterville	60 696
Jesse J	Siskiyou Scott Va	69 31
Jno	Mendocino Arrana	60 861
Jno	Monterey Alisal	601033
Joseph	Plumas Meadow Valley	62 912
Joshua B	Monterey Alisal	601033
Nathan	Contra Costa Twp 1	57 508
Orien*	Placer Auburn	62 589
Susan M	Mariposa Coulterville	60 696
Tho B	Monterey Alisal	601045
Thomas	Tuolumne Big Oak	71 136
Thos B	Monterey Alisal	601045
W	Shasta French G	66 714
W	Yolo Washington	72 599
W P	Siskiyou Scott Va	69 31
Walter	Sierra Downieville	66 988
William	El Dorado Salmon Falls	581052
Wm	Nevada Grass Valley	61 159
Wm	Nevada Grass Valley	61 169
Z	El Dorado Salmon Falls	581036
POOLE		
A W	Placer Damascus	62 846
Edward*	San Bernardino San Bernadino	64 645
Francis	Yuba Rose Bar	72 811
Geo W	Sacramento Cosummes	63 382
Henry J	Sonoma Russian	69 440
Hiram	Calaveras Twp 8	57 70
J H	San Francisco San Francisco 1	68 922
James	Santa Cruz Pajaro	66 541
John	Santa Cruz Pajaro	66 545
Josiah	Sacramento Georgian	63 341
Kennedy	Sonoma Russian	69 431
Leonard	Plumas Meadow Valley	62 932
Lycargus	Sonoma Russian	69 431
Lycurgus	Sonoma Russian	69 431
M	Sacramento Ward 3	63 436
Robt	Sacramento Brighton	63 196

Name	County Locale	M653 RollPage
POOLE		
W	San Francisco San Francisco 9	681058
William	Placer Iona Hills	62 885
William	San Francisco San Francisco 4	681131
Wm	Amador Twp 1	55 455
Wm	San Francisco San Francisco 3	67 52
POOLER		
Henry	San Francisco San Francisco 2	67 564
POOLEY		
S N	Tuolumne Twp 2	71 343
S W	Tuolumne Columbia	71 343
Wm	Butte Kimshaw	56 607
POOLIS		
William	Placer Forest H	62 774
POOLONG		
---	San Joaquin Stockton	641087
POOLUS		
A*	Nevada Grass Valley	61 154
POOLY		
William	Placer Michigan	62 845
POOMETS		
---	Tulara Twp 1	71 117
POOMOVCOTUT		
---	Tulara Twp 1	71 116
POON		
---	Amador Twp 5	55 360
---	Amador Twp 5	55 366
---	Amador Twp 1	55 477
---	Amador Twp 1	55 501
---	Calaveras Twp 6	57 181
---	Calaveras Twp 5	57 226
---	Placer Virginia	62 665
G A	Tehama Pasakent	70 860
Hay	San Francisco San Francisco 5	67 507
POONNACE		
Gifes	Sacramento Ward 4	63 512
POOP		
Emry*	Alameda Brooklyn	55 195
Ermy*	Alameda Brooklyn	55 195
POOR		
Anna	San Francisco San Francisco 3	67 10
B V	Tuolumne Twp 2	71 284
B W	Tuolumne Twp 2	71 284
C	Calaveras Twp 9	57 405
Carolin	Sacramento Natonia	63 282
Caroline*	Sacramento Natonia	63 282
Flavius	Sonoma Healdsbu	69 475
George	Solano Benecia	69 286
Guilford	Nevada Little Y	61 536
John	Siskiyou Shasta Rvr	69 114
Richard	Shasta Horsetown	66 702
S C	Calaveras Twp 9	57 408
She*	Calaveras Twp 9	57 408
William	El Dorado Kelsey	581154
William	San Francisco San Francisco 3	67 62
POORE		
J J	Tuolumne Twp 2	71 341
Walter	San Francisco San Francisco 4	681153
POORRY		
T*	San Francisco San Francisco 4	681231
POOSER		
Daniel	Tulara Twp 3	71 47
POOSEY		
J	San Joaquin Elkhorn	64 994
POOSS		
Emry*	Alameda Brooklyn	55 195
Ermy*	Alameda Brooklyn	55 195
POOT		
T	El Dorado Placerville	58 834
POOTMAN		
T J	Mariposa Twp 3	60 574
POOTOK		
---	Fresno Twp 2	59 101
POP		
---	Calaveras Twp 10	57 272
---*	Sacramento Ward 1	63 53
Alexander	San Francisco San Francisco 9	68 9057
Kasby	Sierra Twp 7	66 880
Ko Lee	San Francisco San Francisco 4	681176
POPCORN		
---	Tulara Keyesville	71 56
POPE		
---	Solano Benecia	69 310
A J	San Francisco San Francisco 10	232 67
Andrew	San Francisco San Francisco 9	681032
Catherine	Solano Vallejo	69 258
Charles	San Mateo Twp 1	65 65
Charles	Siskiyou Yreka	69 134
Charles*	Siskiyou Yreka	69 134
Chas A	Sonoma Russian	69 446
Christopher*	Nevada Red Dog	61 537
Cord	San Francisco San Francisco 7	681390
E	San Francisco San Francisco 9	681022
E R	Tuolumne Twp 1	71 200
Ed	Siskiyou Cottonwoood	69 108
POPE		
Edward	Butte Oregon	56 613
Gales*	Sacramento Lee	63 218
Gates*	Sacramento Lee	63 218
Harry	Butte Ophir	56 770
Henry	Siskiyou Yreka	69 182
Henry	Yuba Marysville	72 918
Horace	Santa Cruz Santa Cruz	66 618
J	San Francisco San Francisco 5	67 537
J H	Colusa Monroeville	57 451
James	Trinity E Weaver	701057
John	Plumas Quincy	62 978
Jose	San Bernardino San Bernardino	64 676
Peter W	Tuolumne Shawsfla	71 390
R P S	Tuolumne Twp 2	71 287
Richard	Calaveras Twp 8	57 77
Robert	Calaveras Twp 5	57 191
Saml	Siskiyou Cottonwoood	69 108
Saml*	Siskiyou Cottonwoood	69 107
Thos	Alameda Murray	55 222
W C	Nevada Grass Valley	61 202
W J	Alameda Brooklyn	55 101
William	San Francisco San Francisco 9	681054
Wm	San Francisco San Francisco 2	67 779
POPER		
Wm	Nevada Washington	61 336
POPERT		
Nathan D	Yuba Marysville	72 883
POPES		
Francisco	Merced Twp 2	60 921
Gates	El Dorado White Oaks	581001
POPHAM		
Geo	Siskiyou Scott Ri	69 74
POPI		
---	Mendocino Round Va	60 878
POPNIA		
---	San Bernardino S Timate	64 690
POPP		
H	San Francisco San Francisco 2	67 659
POPPA		
---	Tulara Twp 2	71 37
POPPE		
Bernard	San Joaquin Elkhorn	64 960
Henry	San Joaquin Elkhorn	64 980
Peter	Mariposa Coulterville	60 701
POPPEN		
Fanny	Sonoma Sonoma	69 652
POPPER		
Charles	Yolo Cache Crk	72 637
Chas	Placer Rattle Snake	62 599
Chas	San Francisco San Francisco 10	191 67
Fanny	Sonoma Sonoma	69 652
Leon	Alameda Brooklyn	55 181
POPPERTY		
James	Solano Benecia	69 311
POPPEY		
Henry	Butte Oregon	56 634
POPPIN		
Thos	El Dorado Georgetown	58 748
POPPLE		
H	Shasta Millvill	66 751
W H	Yuba Parke Ba	72 785
POPPY		
Adolph	Sonoma Sonoma	69 633
POPUR		
Elijah*	Sacramento Natonia	63 278
POPUT		
Nathan D*	Yuba Marysville	72 883
POQUILLOR		
Julius	Nevada Bloomfield	61 516
POR LOW		
---*	Tuolumne Don Pedro	71 537
POR		
---	Amador Twp 6	55 432
---	Calaveras Twp 6	57 182
---	Calaveras Twp 5	57 204
---	Mariposa Twp 3	60 562
---*	Shasta Shasta	66 670
Chee	Tuolumne Green Springs	71 532
Chu	Tuolumne Twp 6	71 532
Low	Tuolumne Twp 6	71 537
Thon	San Francisco San Francisco 4	681176
PORA		
---	Los Angeles Tejon	59 529
PORAN		
---	San Francisco San Francisco 9	681093
PORAW		
---	San Francisco San Francisco 9	681093
PORBURN		
Mistress*	Siskiyou Yreka	69 144
PORCH		
John	San Joaquin Elkhorn	64 976
T S	Sacramento Franklin	63 316
PORCHARD		
A	Sutter Sutter	70 807
PORCHES		
A	El Dorado Placerville	58 871
PORCHINTZ		
Otto*	Alameda Oakland	55 72
PORDIA		
Garcia	Santa Clara San Jose	65 304
PORE		
Casper	Mariposa Twp 1	60 638
Domingo*	Monterey San Juan	601002
John*	El Dorado Kelsey	581140
William	Tulara Visalia	71 101
POREILL		
Wm	Tuolumne Twp 1	71 235
PORETTI		
P	El Dorado Diamond	58 802
POREZ		
Louisa*	Yuba Long Bar	72 748
PORGSES		
Louis*	Mariposa Coulterville	60 695
Lous	Mariposa Coulterville	60 695
PORH		
---	Siskiyou Yreka	69 146
PORHORST		
Joseph	Nevada Bridgeport	61 441
PORIER		
Richd	Sacramento Ward 1	63 47
PORIG		
---	Nevada Bridgeport	61 505
PORIR		
Jonah	Sacramento Sutter	63 307
PORITIO		
---	San Bernardino San Bernadino	64 680
PORITO		
S*	Amador Twp 4	55 245
PORITRAO		
Alhen*	Alameda Oakland	55 56
PORK		
A Q	Sutter Nicolaus	70 829
PORKER		
C B	Siskiyou Scott Va	69 54
PORKINSON		
D F*	Shasta Millvill	66 752
PORKS		
George	Marin Point Re	60 729
PORLANVER		
J	Butte Oregon	56 614
PORLE		
Edward	San Bernardino San Salvador	64 645
Edwarde*	San Salvador / San Bernardino	64 645
PORLEY		
Edward	San Francisco San Francisco 3	67 47
PORLUS		
A	Nevada Grass Valley	61 154
PORN		
---	El Dorado White Oaks	581024
PORNISE		
P*	Nevada Eureka	61 365
PORNSETT		
Adam	Sacramento Granite	63 264
PORNY		
Mary	Yolo Cache Crk	72 606
PORO		
---	Placer Rattle Snake	62 598
---	Sierra La Porte	66 767
POROCKLE		
James	Sacramento Ward 4	63 515
PORR		
---	San Francisco San Francisco 5	67 510
John	El Dorado Kelsey	581140
PORRA		
France	Alameda Brooklyn	55 178
PORRELL		
G N L	San Francisco San Francisco 2	67 557
PORRER		
David	San Francisco San Francisco 2	67 663
Richard	San Francisco San Francisco 2	67 662
PORRES		
Jose	Tuolumne Twp 5	71 498
PORRETEL		
G	Mariposa Twp 1	60 635
PORRIER		
Frank	Nevada Bloomfield	61 516
PORRITOL		
G	Mariposa Twp 1	60 635
PORSENS		
Amelia	El Dorado Georgetown	58 694
PORSIER		
John Baptiste	Alameda Oakland	55 54
PORSONS		
Amilia	El Dorado Georgetown	58 694
PORSSET		
George*	Alameda Oakland	55 29
PORT		
---	Sierra Morristown	661055
Anton	Sacramento Ward 4	63 541

California 1860 Census Index

Name	County Locale	M653 Roll	Page
PORT			
B F	El Dorado Placerville	58	861
Jacob*	Sacramento Franklin	63	331
John M	Amador Twp 4	55	236
Peter	Placer Dutch Fl	62	709
PORTA			
Francisco	Alameda Brooklyn	55	151
Geo	Alameda Oakland	55	45
Nicholas	San Francisco San Francisco 2	67	618
PORTAL			
Jacinto	Monterey Alisal	60	1034
PORTANZA			
Pasquale*	Marin Cortemad	60	789
Pasquals	Marin Cortemad	60	789
PORTCHARD			
David*	Placer Michigan	62	817
PORTE			
Augustine*	San Francisco San Francisco 3	67	17
PORTEEGAESE			
John*	Yuba Marysville	72	852
PORTEEGUESE			
John*	Yuba Marysville	72	852
PORTEGAE			
Joseph*	Siskiyou Yreka	69	146
PORTER			
---	San Francisco San Francisco 10	67	228
A	Nevada Grass Valley	61	148
A	Nevada Eureka	61	356
A	Placer Dutch Fl	62	725
A B	San Francisco San Francisco 6	67	466
A C	Solano Vacaville	69	346
A G	Nevada Little Y	61	534
Abel	Calaveras Twp 6	57	160
Abrel*	Calaveras Twp 6	57	160
Acy E	Tulara Twp 1	71	75
Aichel*	San Francisco San Francisco 8	68	1313
Alex	Placer Dutch Fl	62	719
Alfred	San Joaquin Elkhorn	64	959
Alrel*	Calaveras Twp 6	57	160
Ambrose J	Contra Costa Twp 3	57	608
Andrew	Amador Twp 4	55	251
Archel	San Francisco San Francisco 8	68	1313
Arthur	Alameda Brooklyn	55	190
Benj	Siskiyou Scott Va	69	23
Charles	San Joaquin Tulare	64	869
Charles A*	Calaveras Twp 5	57	237
Chas A	Placer Dutch Fl	62	714
Christopher	Plumas Meadow Valley	62	929
Clark	El Dorado Kelsey	58	1139
Clayton	Placer Yankee J	62	778
D B	Nevada Nevada	61	286
D C	San Francisco San Francisco 3	67	58
D J	Tuolumne Big Oak	71	144
D W	San Francisco San Francisco 7	68	1442
Danforth	Santa Cruz Pajaro	66	550
David	San Francisco San Francisco 9	68	1049
David	San Francisco San Francisco 2	67	609
David	Tulara Keyesville	71	60
David A	Napa Yount	61	44
David M	Los Angeles Los Angeles	59	334
David M	San Bernardino San Bernadino	64	635
De Witt C	Sacramento Centre	63	179
E J	Placer Michigan	62	853
E L	Placer Rattle Snake	62	634
Edward	Santa Cruz Soguel	66	589
Edward	Solano Suisan	69	206
Elizabeth	San Francisco San Francisco 1	68	841
Ellen	Sacramento Ward 3	63	439
F C	Sonoma Petaluma	69	590
Fanny	Sacramento Ward 3	63	446
Fanny	Sacramento Ward 4	63	530
Frank	Monterey S Antoni	60	973
Franklin	Los Angeles Santa Ana	59	441
G F	San Francisco San Francisco 5	67	552
Geo	San Francisco San Francisco 6	67	415
Geo S	San Francisco San Francisco 10	67	278
Geo W	Calaveras Twp 6	57	151
Geor W	Calaveras Twp 6	57	151
George	Santa Cruz Soguel	66	583
George	Sierra Twp 5	66	923
George	Solano Vacaville	69	319
George	Tuolumne Twp 3	71	459
George C	Solano Vacaville	69	319
George F	San Mateo Twp 1	65	53
Gooding*	El Dorado Georgetown	58	751
H	El Dorado Georgetown	58	678
H	Nevada Washington	61	333
H B	Merced Twp 2	60	916
H C	Solano Vacaville	69	346
Harriet	San Joaquin Stockton	64	1059
Hazzard	Calaveras Twp 5	57	186
Hazzard W	Calaveras Twp 5	57	186
Henry	Nevada Bloomfield	61	514

Name	County Locale	M653 Roll	Page
PORTER			
Henry	Sacramento Mississipi	63	183
Henry	Santa Clara Burnett	65	257
Horace	San Francisco San Francisco 6	67	473
Ira	Santa Clara Alviso	65	406
J	El Dorado Georgetown	58	701
J	San Francisco San Francisco 5	67	552
J	Sutter Sutter	70	813
J	Tuolumne Twp 4	71	173
J A C	Sonoma Armally	69	479
J B	Napa Hot Springs	61	13
J C	Sierra Twp 7	66	909
J G	Nevada Grass Valley	61	189
J H	Butte Hamilton	56	515
J M	Tuolumne Twp 3	71	470
J S*	El Dorado Diamond	58	764
J W	Mariposa Coulterville	60	675
J W	Sonoma Petaluma	69	593
James	San Francisco San Francisco 9	68	1041
James	San Francisco San Francisco 7	68	1355
James	Sierra Downieville	66	977
James	Solano Vacaville	69	348
James	Sonoma Mendocino	69	457
James L	Sonoma Mendocino	69	459
Jas	Butte Kimshaw	56	574
Jas	Sonoma Vallejo	69	628
Jerome	Santa Cruz Pajaro	66	534
Jno	Alameda Brooklyn	55	171
Jno S	Amador Twp 2	55	272
John	Placer Virginia	62	683
John	Placer Iona Hills	62	883
John	Plumas Quincy	62	955
John	Sacramento Ward 1	63	18
John	San Francisco San Francisco 7	68	1403
John	Santa Cruz Watsonville	66	540
John	Sonoma Santa Rosa	69	400
John K	Contra Costa Twp 2	57	558
John T	Santa Cruz Santa Cruz	66	611
Jos	Napa Yount	61	40
Joseph	Sierra Whiskey	66	849
Josiah	Contra Costa Twp 2	57	564
L	Tuolumne Twp 4	71	176
L D	Yuba Fosters	72	829
L J	Tuolumne Twp 1	71	215
L P	Yuba Foster B	72	829
Lewis	Sierra Whiskey	66	844
Lewis C	Sierra Whiskey	66	844
Lozino	Sonoma Santa Rosa	69	403
Lucinda	Contra Costa Twp 2	57	558
M	Nevada Nevada	61	271
M	San Francisco San Francisco 5	67	476
M	Sonoma Salt Point	69	695
Martin	Placer Todds Va	62	763
Mary	Santa Cruz Watsonville	66	540
Mary J	Santa Clara Alviso	65	401
Missouri A	Sonoma Mendocino	69	459
Myles I	El Dorado Greenwood	58	718
Nathan	San Francisco San Francisco 6	67	419
Nathan	Solano Vacaville	69	346
O	Nevada Grass Valley	61	194
R	Nevada Grass Valley	61	209
R M	Tuolumne Big Oak	71	129
R S	Shasta French G	66	722
Raft	Santa Clara San Jose	65	284
Richard	Contra Costa Twp 3	57	589
Robert	Humbolt Eureka	59	172
Robert	San Francisco San Francisco 11	67	126
Robert	Siskiyou Yreka	69	191
Robert	Tulara Twp 3	71	60
S A	Yolo Slate Ra	72	700
S A	Yuba Slate Ro	72	700
S J	Tuolumne Sonora	71	215
Stephen	San Francisco San Francisco 7	68	1327
T	Tuolumne Garrote	71	176
T C	San Francisco San Francisco 9	68	1055
T M	El Dorado Georgetown	58	678
Thom	El Dorado Greenwood	58	726
Thomas	Marin Tomales	60	724
Thornton	Contra Costa Twp 3	57	608
Thos A D	Sonoma Mendocino	69	459
Thos F*	Sacramento American	63	159
Thos J*	Sacramento American	63	159
Thos N	Placer Illinois	62	703
V	Amador Twp 1	55	472
W	Sacramento Granite	63	242
W D	Calaveras Twp 9	57	394
W J	Tehama Antelope	70	890
Wad	San Francisco San Francisco 6	67	464
William	Klamath Liberty	59	230
William	Placer Forest H	62	766
William	Shasta Shasta	66	673
William	Siskiyou Yreka	69	178
William S	Amador Twp 4	55	254
Wm	Alameda Brooklyn	55	165
Wm	Butte Wyandotte	56	670

Name	County Locale	M653 Roll	Page
PORTER			
Wm	Humbolt Mattole	59	126
Wm	Los Angeles Los Angeles	59	495
Wm	Mariposa Coulterville	60	696
Wm	Nevada Eureka	61	346
Wm C	Sacramento Ward 3	63	487
Wm H	San Francisco San Francisco 2	67	586
Wm J	Solano Vallejo	69	276
Wm T	Sacramento Ward 4	63	566
Wm W	Calaveras Twp 6	57	127
Wm W	Calaveras Twp 6	57	148
Wm W	Tuolumne Twp 4	71	145
Wm Wa*	Tuolumne Big Oak	71	145
Wm*	Butte Wyandotte	56	670
Wm*	Nevada Eureka	61	346
PORTERCHENS			
Baptiste*	Calaveras Twp 5	57	225
PORTERCHINE			
Baptist	Calaveras Twp 5	57	225
PORTERCHIR			
Buptista	Calaveras Twp 5	57	225
PORTERFIELD			
H	Napa Napa	61	58
J W	Yolo Cottonwoood	72	662
Kenny F*	Calaveras Twp 5	57	210
Plenny	Calaveras Twp 5	57	210
Plenny F	Calaveras Twp 5	57	210
Plinny F*	Calaveras Twp 5	57	210
Robert*	Plumas Quincy	62	924
PORTERGAESE			
John*	Yuba Marysville	72	852
PORTERRIER			
Pierre	San Francisco San Francisco 2	67	700
PORTERS			
John	Santa Clara Gilroy	65	242
Samuel	Solano Benecia	69	290
PORTES			
H*	Nevada Washington	61	336
J M	Amador Twp 3	55	377
Pedro	San Diego Temecula	64	801
PORTEZEE			
Joseph*	Siskiyou Yreka	69	146
PORTHAIST			
Daniel W*	Yuba Marysville	72	901
PORTI			
Josepha	Alameda Brooklyn	55	124
PORTIA			
Gresida	Los Angeles Los Angeles	59	338
Maria F	Los Angeles Los Angeles	59	338
PORTIBS			
Estepher*	Mariposa Twp 3	60	584
PORTICHS			
Estepher	Mariposa Twp 3	60	584
PORTICO			
George	San Joaquin Castoria	64	905
PORTIDES			
Estephes*	Mariposa Twp 3	60	584
PORTIER			
L	San Francisco San Francisco 5	67	497
PORTILES			
Estelber*	Mariposa Twp 3	60	584
PORTILLA			
Rosano S	Los Angeles Los Angeles	59	293
Sosten	Los Angeles San Juan	59	463
PORTILLO			
T	Trinity Big Flat	70	1039
PORTIMAN			
Joseph	Sierra Downieville	66	1032
PORTIS			
Wm	San Francisco San Francisco 10	67	194
PORTLAND			
A A	Stanislaus Branch	70	710
PORTLER			
Charles A*	Calaveras Twp 5	57	237
PORTLOCK			
John	Siskiyou Cottonwood	69	108
PORTMAN			
Frank	Sierra Gibsonville	66	860
J H C	San Francisco San Francisco 10	67	253
PORTOSI			
Sylvestre	San Diego Agua Caliente	64	820
PORTRON			
Victor	Calaveras Twp 6	57	163
PORTUFIELD			
Robert*	Plumas Quincy	62	924
PORTUGAESE			
John*	Yuba Marysville	72	852
PORTUGAL			
Adolph	Los Angeles Los Angeles	59	341
PORTUGEESE			
John	Yuba Marysville	72	857
PORTUGRE			
John*	Yolo Washington	72	573
PORTUGSE			
John*	Yolo Washington	72	573

California 1860 Census Index

Name	County Locale	M653 Roll	Page
PORTUGU			
John	Yolo Washington	72	573
PORTY			
J C	San Francisco San Francisco 6	67	463
PORVEN			
Cath*	Sacramento Ward 1	63	124
PORVENS			
Cath	Sacramento Ward 1	63	124
PORVERS			
W	San Francisco San Francisco 5	67	480
PORVERTS			
Sylvester	Sonoma Washington	69	678
PORY			
---	Amador Twp 5	55	354
---	Amador Twp 3	55	403
---*	Tuolumne Twp 1	71	476
Tom	Amador Twp 5	55	347
POS TO MIAH			
---	Plumas Quincy	62	969
POSER			
John	Yuba Marysville	72	944
POSETA			
---	Fresno Twp 1	59	29
POSEY			
Henry	Yuba New York	72	724
Lewis	Butte Hamilton	56	519
Lewis	Tuolumne Twp 1	71	218
Louis	Butte Hamilton	56	519
POSH			
John*	Alameda Brooklyn	55	97
POSHNONA			
---*	Mendocino Round Va	60	883
POSHUONA			
---*	Mendocino Round Va	60	883
POSIER			
H	Butte Oro	56	680
POSKA			
Jacob	San Francisco San Francisco 6	67	447
POSS			
Alexander*	San Francisco San Francisco 9	68	957
POSSIME			
John	Calaveras Twp 5	57	212
POSSIMEN			
John	Calaveras Twp 5	57	212
POSSTELL			
Peter*	San Francisco San Francisco 3	67	23
POST			
A J	Tehama Lassen	70	874
A V V	El Dorado Salmon Falls	58	1038
Adelaide	Sonoma Russian	69	429
B J	El Dorado Georgetown	58	699
Caroline	Sonoma Mendocino	69	447
David	Santa Cruz Santa Cruz	66	608
Emily	San Francisco San Francisco 7	68	1352
Geo	Sonoma Russian	69	431
H B	San Joaquin Stockton	64	1009
H J	San Francisco San Francisco 5	67	553
H M	Merced Twp 1	60	906
J	El Dorado Diamond	58	810
J	Nevada Grass Valley	61	215
J C	Trinity Hay Fork	70	994
J M	Shasta French G	66	720
Jacob*	Sacramento Franklin	63	331
Jerome	San Francisco San Francisco 11	67	133
Jerome	Santa Cruz Pajaro	66	563
John M*	Amador Twp 4	55	236
Louis	Butte Chico	56	541
Lovisa	Santa Clara San Jose	65	321
Lucius	Sacramento Ward 4	63	536
M	Shasta Horsetown	66	700
Mary	Yuba Marysville	72	851
Mary	Yuba Marysville	72	947
Mary O*	Yuba Marysville	72	947
R J	El Dorado Georgetown	58	699
V B	Sonoma Petaluma	69	581
W F	Calaveras Twp 9	57	383
W O	Sierra Downieville	66	975
William H	San Joaquin Elkhorn	64	968
Wm	San Francisco San Francisco 2	67	675
Wm F	Calaveras Twp 9	57	383
Wm K	Sierra Downieville	66	967
POSTE			
Augustine*	San Francisco San Francisco 3	67	17
POSTEGEE			
Joseph*	Siskiyou Yreka	69	146
POSTEGRE			
Joseph*	Siskiyou Yreka	69	146
POSTEL			
Blas	Solano Benecia	69	297
POSTER			
Isaac	Alameda Brooklyn	55	116
POSTEWART			
John T	Sierra Scales D	66	800

Name	County Locale	M653 Roll	Page
POSTLES			
Charles	Tehama Tehama	70	947
POSTLEWAIT			
John D	Sierra Scales D	66	800
POSTLEWART			
John D	Sierra Scales D	66	800
John T	Sierra Scales D	66	800
John*	Sierra Scales D	66	800
POSTLOCK			
John	Siskiyou Cottonwoood	69	107
POSTOBA			
---	Fresno Twp 2	59	66
POSTOMIAH			
---	Plumas Quincy	62	965
POSTON			
Eugenia	Yuba Marysville	72	891
Jerry	Yuba Bear Rvr	72	1000
POSTTO			
John*	Napa Clear Lake	61	138
POSUN			
O P*	Napa Hot Springs	61	13
POT			
---	Calaveras Twp 8	57	105
---	Del Norte Crescent	58	651
---	El Dorado White Oaks	58	1022
---	El Dorado Union	58	1089
---	El Dorado Kelsey	58	1133
---	El Dorado Kelsey	58	1135
---	San Francisco San Francisco 9	68	1094
---	San Francisco San Francisco 4	68	1176
---	Sierra Downieville	66	1007
---	Trinity Lewiston	70	954
Lun	San Francisco San Francisco 5	67	1205
Pho	San Francisco San Francisco 5	67	1206
Tek	San Francisco San Francisco 11	67	160
Wing	San Francisco San Francisco 4	68	1207
You	San Francisco San Francisco 5	67	1205
POTAND			
William	San Francisco San Francisco 9	68	975
POTANS			
William	Sierra Port Win	66	794
POTARD			
Manuel	Shasta French G	66	720
POTE			
---	El Dorado Diamond	58	808
POTEA			
Alex	Mariposa Twp 3	60	583
POTEET			
Fancis M	Los Angeles Los Angeles	59	377
Francis M	Los Angeles Los Angeles	59	377
POTEKO			
---	Fresno Twp 2	59	116
POTEO			
Pomato	Yolo Washington	72	573
Ponrato	Yolo Washington	72	573
POTEOR			
Boder	Alameda Oakland	55	48
POTER			
Israel	Tuolumne Twp 2	71	299
M	San Francisco San Francisco 5	67	476
Saml	Sonoma Santa Rosa	69	416
POTERSON			
Jacob	Sierra Twp 5	66	920
POTHAM			
Frank*	Mariposa Twp 3	60	567
POTHIM			
Frank*	Mariposa Twp 3	60	567
POTHNATHO			
Christopher	Contra Costa Twp 3	57	588
POTHOMUS			
Thomas C*	San Francisco San Francisco 11	67	102
POTHS			
Joe	Mariposa Twp 3	60	600
POTHUN			
Frank	Mariposa Twp 3	60	567
POTIER			
M O	San Francisco San Francisco 4	68	1138
POTILLER			
Pascual	San Bernardino Santa Barbara	64	175
POTITANO			
---	San Bernardino S Timate	64	754
POTKIM			
Frank*	Mariposa Twp 3	60	567
POTKUN			
Frank	Mariposa Twp 3	60	567
POTMER			
Fredk	San Francisco San Francisco 2	67	714
POTON			
Manuel	Shasta French G	66	720
POTRO			
---	Tulara Twp 3	71	71
POTSIN			
Chris*	Mariposa Twp 3	60	585

Name	County Locale	M653 Roll	Page
POTT			
George L	Sierra Downieville	66	1023
James	Sierra Eureka	66	1044
POTTE			
A W	Sierra Downieville	66	964
POTTELL			
James	Yolo Washington	72	566
POTTEN			
A B*	Butte Oregon	56	641
Geo W*	Butte Kimshaw	56	594
H B*	Butte Oregon	56	641
Jefferson*	Tulara Keeneysburg	71	49
POTTER			
A F	Amador Twp 2	55	265
A G	Sacramento Ward 3	63	432
A J	San Francisco San Francisco 5	67	480
Abner	Stanislaus Emory	70	745
Alvin	Mendocino Little L	60	832
Andrew C	Monterey Alisal	60	1034
Andrew P	Monterey Alisal	60	1034
Angel R	Plumas Quincy	62	972
C D	Sacramento Ward 1	63	84
Charles	San Francisco San Francisco 2	67	603
Charles	Sonoma Armally	69	489
Charles A	San Joaquin Castoria	64	900
Charles B	Contra Costa Twp 2	57	581
Charles J	Contra Costa Twp 2	57	581
Chas S	Alameda Oakland	55	39
Clark	Butte Kimshaw	56	582
Clark	El Dorado Georgetown	58	699
Crancis M	Mendocino Calpella	60	813
D B	Sierra Whiskey	66	844
Daniel	Plumas Quincy	62	978
David	Butte Oro	56	688
David D	Solano Benecia	69	298
E R	Shasta Horsetown	66	702
E S	Sacramento Alabama	63	418
Edward	San Joaquin Stockton	64	1068
Elisha	Nevada Red Dog	61	547
Elisha	Sierra Twp 7	66	888
Elizabeth	San Joaquin O'Neal	64	1001
Ephraim	Colusa Grand Island	57	477
Floyd	Sacramento Ward 1	63	10
Fristan D	San Joaquin Oneal	64	938
Geo	Sacramento Alabama	63	417
Geo W	Butte Kimshaw	56	594
George	Nevada Bridgeport	61	448
George	Yuba Rose Bar	72	805
H B*	Butte Oregon	56	641
H C	Calaveras Twp 9	57	413
Harry	Sacramento Georgian	63	340
Henry	Sacramento Ward 1	63	91
Henry	San Joaquin Stockton	64	1083
Henry	Trinity Mouth Ca	70	1015
Henry B	San Francisco San Francisco 11	67	154
Henry N	Sacramento Ward 1	63	34
Isaac J	Tuolumne Columbia	71	299
J	Nevada Eureka	61	382
J	Sacramento Ward 4	63	606
J A	Yolo Merritt	72	579
J B	Shasta Shasta	66	732
J C	Butte Wyandotte	56	664
J F	Butte Cascade	56	701
J G	Butte Cascade	56	701
J H	El Dorado Eldorado	58	935
J H	Nevada Eureka	61	378
James	San Joaquin Douglass	64	927
James D*	Solano Suisan	69	238
James T	San Francisco San Francisco 1	68	989
Jas	San Francisco San Francisco 1	68	903
Jefferson*	Tulara Keeneysburg	71	49
Jennie	San Francisco San Francisco 4	67	434
Jeremiah	San Joaquin Stockton	64	1045
Jeremiah	San Joaquin Castoria	64	902
Jesse S	San Francisco San Francisco 10	67	326
Jesse S	San Mateo Twp 1	65	62
Jno	San Francisco San Francisco 2	67	750
Jno H*	Mendocino Arrana	60	856
John	Alameda Oakland	55	17
John	Sierra Pine Grove	66	829
John	Yuba Marysville	72	941
John C	Napa Hot Springs	61	7
Jonas G	Yuba Marysville	72	931
Jos	Butte Wyandotte	56	662
Joseph	Alameda Brooklyn	55	84
Joseph	Tulara Visalia	71	14
Joseph	Yuba Parks Ba	72	778
Joseph F	Yuba Marysville	72	931
Joseph H	San Joaquin Douglass	64	925
L B	Sierra Whiskey	66	844
L D	Butte Wyandotte	56	662
L M	Tehama Red Bluff	70	923
Lizzett	San Francisco San Francisco 6	67	439
Louisa	Shasta Cottonwood	66	736

Name	County Locale	M653 RollPage
POTTER		
Martin	San Bernardino San Salvador	64 656
Nehemiah A	Los Angeles	59 334
	Los Angeles	
Nelson	Amador Twp 2	55 317
Nelson	Amador Twp 2	55 326
Ohio	Yolo Cache Crk	72 646
Perin A	Monterey Alisal	601033
Phebe A	Tuolumne Columbia	71 332
R	El Dorado Diamond	58 811
R G	Sacramento Ward 1	63 148
S D	Butte Wyandotte	56 662
S W	Sierra Twp 7	66 904
Sam	Sonoma Bodega	69 521
Saml	Sacramento Granite	63 254
Sizyett	San Francisco San Francisco 6	67 439
Starlina	Mendocino Ukiah	60 801
Starling	Mendocino Ukiah	60 801
T F Jr*	San Francisco San Francisco 3	67 24
Thomas	Solano Vallejo	69 267
Thomas	Tuolumne Springfield	71 374
Thos	Amador Twp 2	55 324
Tom	Yolo Slate Ra	72 699
Tom	Yuba Slate Ro	72 699
W	El Dorado Placerville	58 887
W	Sacramento Granite	63 234
W	San Francisco San Francisco 3	67 45
W E	Sierra Twp 7	66 892
W F	Sierra Downieville	661001
W F	Tehama Moons	70 851
W H	Yolo Washington	72 600
W R	Butte Ophir	56 755
W W	Yolo Washington	72 600
William	Colusa Colusi	57 419
William	Los Angeles Los Angeles	59 331
William	Mendocino Calpella	60 813
William G	Los Angeles Azuza	59 277
William M	Napa Hot Springs	61 15
William R	Sierra Whiskey	66 845
William*	Mendocino Calpella	60 813
Wm	San Francisco San Francisco 2	67 690
Wm	Sonoma Petaluma	69 579
Wm*	Placer Virginia	62 667
POTTERS		
Joseph F	Yuba Marysville	72 931
POTTES		
A M	Nevada Nevada	61 256
Henry	Sacramento Ward 1	63 91
T F Jr*	San Francisco San Francisco 3	67 24
William R*	Sierra Whiskey	66 845
POTTHOFF		
N*	El Dorado Placerville	58 879
W*	El Dorado Placerville	58 879
POTTIE		
Jennie	San Francisco San Francisco 6	67 434
POTTIER		
J	San Francisco San Francisco 2	67 678
POTTIGREW		
James	Santa Clara San Jose	65 366
POTTING		
H H	Sierra Downieville	661020
John F	Sierra Downieville	66 989
Wm	Sierra Downieville	66 997
POTTLE		
Wm	Los Angeles Tejon	59 523
POTTS		
A W	Sierra Downieville	66 964
Benjamin	San Francisco San Francisco 7	681333
Daniel S	Marin Cortemad	60 781
David	Tulara Twp 3	71 53
Davis	Tulara Keyesville	71 53
Edwin	Colusa Monroeville	57 455
George	Mariposa Twp 3	60 610
H	Shasta Cottonwood	66 724
Harry	San Joaquin Stockton	641075
J	San Francisco San Francisco 2	67 791
J D	Shasta Cottonwoood	66 724
J W	Sutter Butte	70 793
J W	Yuba Marysville	72 950
James	Solano Benecia	69 289
John	Sierra Downieville	661000
John	Solano Fremont	69 379
John H	Napa Hot Springs	61 1
Levi	Nevada Rough &	61 434
Martha A	Monterey Alisal	601030
Sarah	Napa Hot Springs	61 26
Thomas	El Dorado Placerville	58 927
Wm W	Sierra Twp 7	66 915
POTTSJOHN		
Thatcher	Sierra Downieville	661000
POTWIN		
George T	Contra Costa Twp 3	57 590
POTZEE		
L	Trinity North Fo	701026
POU		
---	Calaveras Twp 5	57 252

Name	County Locale	M653 RollPage
POU		
---	Calaveras Twp 10	57 270
---	Calaveras Twp 4	57 332
---	El Dorado Kelsey	581141
---	El Dorado Kelsey	581144
---	San Francisco San Francisco 4	681184
---	San Francisco San Francisco 4	681185
---	San Francisco San Francisco 4	681186
---	San Francisco San Francisco 4	681190
---	San Francisco San Francisco 4	681191
---	San Francisco San Francisco 4	681193
---	San Francisco San Francisco 5	671206
---	San Francisco San Francisco 4	681208
---	San Francisco San Francisco 4	681212
---	San Francisco San Francisco 2	67 754
---	Sierra Twp 5	66 932
---	Tuolumne Don Pedro	71 536
Ah	Calaveras Twp 7	57 32
Long	San Francisco San Francisco 4	681208
POUCHO		
Francisco	Tuolumne Twp 2	71 410
POUCOTT		
H*	El Dorado Georgetown	58 673
POUD		
J L	Butte Ophir	56 823
POUELL		
Dick*	Mariposa Twp 3	60 578
Mathias*	Yuba Fosters	72 840
POUG		
---	Amador Twp 2	55 291
POUGE		
Frank*	Tuolumne Twp 1	71 255
POUGELE		
C*	San Francisco San Francisco 10	343 67
POUGH		
---	El Dorado Placerville	58 924
---	Trinity Trinindad Rvr	701049
---	Trinity China Bar	70 959
---	Trinity Eastman	70 960
POUIG		
---*	Butte Kimshaw	56 599
POUILA		
---*	Alameda Brooklyn	55 114
POUIS		
Joshua*	Sierra Downieville	661006
POUJA		
Chire	San Francisco San Francisco 3	67 5
Chise	San Francisco San Francisco 3	67 5
POULAIF		
Augustin	Los Angeles Los Angeles	59 375
POULARD		
Guls*	Trinity Big Flat	701039
POULE		
Edward*	San Bernardino San Bernadino	64 645
POULER		
Wm Henry*	Alameda Brooklyn	55 112
POULETT		
John	Placer Iona Hills	62 890
POULEUR		
B	Trinity Big Flat	701040
POULEY		
Henry	Yolo Merritt	72 583
POULI		
G P	Sonoma Sonoma	69 638
POULSTER		
Geo	San Francisco San Francisco 1	68 929
POULTERER		
Minna	San Francisco San Francisco 2	67 715
Thos J	San Francisco San Francisco 2	67 714
POULTERIR		
Thos J*	San Francisco San Francisco 2	67 714
POULTNEY		
Geo	San Francisco San Francisco 10	246 67
POULTRY		
James*	Amador Twp 4	55 244
POULZE		
Louis	San Francisco San Francisco 11	104 67
POUNARD		
Komk*	Mariposa Coulterville	60 696
POUND		
Daniel	Los Angeles Tejon	59 529
Harvey M	Plumas Quincy	62 995
John	Santa Clara Thomas	65 443
POUNDSTONE		
Clarance	Amador Twp 4	55 258
POUPLONA		
A	El Dorado Placerville	58 821
POUR		
William*	San Francisco San Francisco 9	681081
POURCET		
John	Calaveras Twp 5	57 231
POURCH		
Ann	San Francisco San Francisco 7	681416

Name	County Locale	M653 RollPage
POURDEATHE		
J R*	Nevada Nevada	61 296
POUREAU		
Pierre*	Plumas Meadow Valley	62 934
POURIE		
John	Shasta Shasta	66 671
POURLAND		
Chs B	Solano Benecia	69 309
POURLINIER		
Henry	Nevada Bridgeport	61 452
POURRY		
T*	San Francisco San Francisco 4	681231
POURSILLE		
Adrican	San Francisco San Francisco 7	681425
POURSILLO		
Adrican	San Francisco San Francisco 7	681425
POURVERY		
J G	Marin Cortemad	60 756
POUS		
J W	Los Angeles Elmonte	59 245
POUSA		
Rafael	San Bernardino San Salvador	64 639
POUSCET		
John	Calaveras Twp 5	57 231
POUSON		
James*	El Dorado Kelsey	581133
POUTACOPA		
George*	Amador Twp 4	55 258
POUTEN		
P*	Nevada Grass Valley	61 170
POUTIER		
Vickland**	San Joaquin Tulare	64 871
POUTO		
S*	Amador Twp 4	55 245
POUTON		
Henry*	Butte Oregon	56 618
POUY		
---	Sacramento Cosumnes	63 392
POVERS		
J	Nevada Grass Valley	61 226
POVIRS		
Joseph*	Nevada Rough &	61 411
POVOCA		
Jose O	Contra Costa Twp 2	57 571
POW YIE		
Toouy	Yuba Marysville	72 895
POW		
---	Amador Twp 4	55 252
---	Amador Twp 7	55 412
---	Butte Bidwell	56 717
---	Calaveras Twp 5	57 146
---	Calaveras Twp 5	57 209
---	Calaveras Twp 5	57 235
---	Calaveras Twp 5	57 244
---	Calaveras Twp 5	57 252
---	Calaveras Twp 5	57 258
---	Calaveras Twp 10	57 268
---	Calaveras Twp 10	57 297
---	Calaveras Twp 4	57 322
---	Calaveras Twp 9	57 371
---	Calaveras Twp 7	57 44
---	El Dorado White Oaks	581009
---	El Dorado Salmon Falls	581045
---	El Dorado Salmon Falls	581046
---	El Dorado Salmon Falls	581059
---	El Dorado Salmon Falls	581062
---	El Dorado Coloma	581075
---	El Dorado Coloma	581077
---	El Dorado Union	581089
---	El Dorado Coloma	581109
---	El Dorado Coloma	581122
---	El Dorado Kelsey	581144
---	El Dorado Mountain	581188
---	El Dorado Greenwood	58 731
---	El Dorado Greenwood	58 732
---	El Dorado Georgetown	58 750
---	El Dorado Diamond	58 784
---	El Dorado Diamond	58 785
---	El Dorado Diamond	58 798
---	El Dorado Diamond	58 806
---	El Dorado Placerville	58 886
---	El Dorado Placerville	58 898
---	El Dorado Mud Springs	58 977
---	El Dorado Mud Springs	58 982
---	El Dorado Mud Springs	58 986
---	Fresno Twp 1	59 28
---	Marin Cortemad	60 786
---	Mariposa Twp 1	60 627
---	Mariposa Coulterville	60 683
---	Placer Auburn	62 573
---	Placer Rattle Snake	62 600
---	Placer Virginia	62 663
---	Placer Virginia	62 674
---	Placer Virginia	62 676
---	Placer Virginia	62 679
---	Placer Virginia	62 681

Name	County Locale	M653 Roll	Page
POW			
---	Placer Virginia	62	684
---	Placer Virginia	62	686
---	Placer Virginia	62	687
---	Placer Dutch Fl	62	732
---	Placer Illinois	62	740
---	Placer Illinois	62	746
---	Placer Illinois	62	752
---	Placer Illinois	62	754
---	Plumas Quincy	62	948
---	Sacramento Centre	63	182
---	Sacramento Cosumnes	63	388
---	Sacramento Ward 1	63	60
---	San Francisco San Francisco 9	681	087
---	San Francisco San Francisco 9	681	093
---	San Francisco San Francisco 9	681	094
---	San Francisco San Francisco 4	681	182
---	San Francisco San Francisco 4	681	184
---	San Francisco San Francisco 4	681	190
---	San Francisco San Francisco 4	681	191
---	San Francisco San Francisco 4	681	193
---	San Francisco San Francisco 4	681	200
---	San Francisco San Francisco 5	671	206
---	San Francisco San Francisco 4	681	208
---	San Francisco San Francisco 4	681	212
---	San Francisco San Francisco 2	67	754
---	Sierra Chinese	661	003
---	Sierra Downieville	661	004
---	Sierra Downieville	661	005
---	Sierra Downieville	661	009
---	Sierra Downieville	661	010
---	Sierra Downieville	661	015
---	Sierra La Porte	66	767
---	Sierra Gibsonville	66	860
---	Sierra Twp 5	66	931
---	Sierra Twp 5	66	932
---	Sierra Twp 5	66	948
---	Sierra Downieville	66	980
---	Sierra Downieville	66	982
---	Sierra Downieville	66	983
---	Sierra Downieville	66	990
---	Trinity Mouth Ca	701	016
---	Trinity Trinindad Rvr	701	049
---	Tuolumne Twp 5	71	509
---	Tuolumne Twp 5	71	512
---	Tuolumne Jacksonville	71	516
---	Tuolumne Twp 5	71	521
---	Tuolumne Twp 6	71	531
---	Tuolumne Don Pedro	71	533
---	Tuolumne Don Pedro	71	535
---	Tuolumne Don Pedro	71	536
---	Yolo Slate Ra	72	717
---	Yuba Slate Ro	72	717
---*	Calaveras Twp 5	57	235
---*	Marin Cortemad	60	786
---*	Sierra Downieville	66	980
Ah	Butte Bidwell	56	717
James	Calaveras Twp 7	57	29
James H*	Sierra Twp 7	66	913
James Jh	Sierra Twp 7	66	913
Long	San Francisco San Francisco 4	681	208
Reuben	Colusa Butte Crk	57	467
Sang	San Francisco San Francisco 4	681	208
Tan	San Francisco San Francisco 10	356	67
Ten	Sierra Downieville	66	998
Yin Tong	Yuba Marysville	72	895
POWALL			
W	Sutter Butte	70	784
POWCIS			
Ansen H	Calaveras Twp 4	57	345
POWDEM			
---*	Mendocino Twp 1	60	887
POWDERN			
---*	Mendocino Twp 1	60	887
POWDSON			
Henry	Yuba Bear Rvr	721	011
POWEFORD			
Ellison L	El Dorado Greenwood	58	712
POWEL			
James M	Sierra Scales D	66	803
Jaseph	Santa Clara Redwood	65	453
John	Nevada Bridgeport	61	490
L M	Solano Montezuma	69	375
Lewis	Marin Bolinas	60	733
Lowis	Marin Bolinas	60	733
Martha	Marin Bolinas	60	733
Mary	Solano Montezuma	69	375
W	Marin San Rafael	60	771
Walter	Tuolumne Jamestown	71	445
Whet*	Yuba Bear Rvr	721	007
Whit	Yuba Bear Rvr	721	007
William	Nevada Bridgeport	61	466
POWELDON			
Wm	San Francisco San Francisco 2	67	784
POWELL			
---	Calaveras Twp 8	57	104

Name	County Locale	M653 Roll	Page
POWELL			
---	Siskiyou Yreka	69	193
A	Butte Cascade	56	693
A	Mariposa Twp 3	60	578
A E	El Dorado Newtown	58	781
A Jr	Solano Vallejo	69	263
Aaron	El Dorado White Oaks	581	020
Chas	San Francisco San Francisco 2	67	671
Chas W	Alameda Brooklyn	55	115
Chas W	Sacramento Ward 1	63	58
Chasw	Sacramento Ward 1	63	58
Christ	El Dorado Salmon Falls	581	037
D	Tuolumne Twp 4	71	167
David	Nevada Bridgeport	61	440
E B	Trinity Browns C	70	984
Frank	Sacramento Ward 4	63	516
Frank	Sonoma Sonoma	69	645
Fred*	San Francisco San Francisco 1	68	829
G N L	San Francisco San Francisco 2	67	557
G W	Butte Bidwell	56	716
Geo	Yolo Putah	72	588
Geo N L	San Francisco San Francisco 12	393	67
George	San Joaquin Oneal	64	930
George W	Tuolumne Twp 5	71	487
George W	Tuolumne Twp 5	71	492
Geroge W	Tuolumne Chinese	71	492
Henry	Nevada Bridgeport	61	440
I	Nevada Washington	61	331
J	Nevada Washington	61	331
J	Nevada Washington	61	341
J M	Butte Bidwell	56	722
Jacob	Butte Bidwell	56	715
James	Alameda Brooklyn	55	129
James H	Colusa Grand Island	57	472
Jerrimiah	Colusa Grand Island	57	473
Jno	Alameda Brooklyn	55	189
Jno	Sonoma Vallejo	69	610
Jno J	Sacramento Ward 1	63	152
Jno L	Sacramento Ward 4	63	527
John	Mendocino Ukiah	60	802
John	Sacramento Ward 1	63	32
John	Siskiyou Cottonwoood	69	104
John M	Sierra Downieville	661	007
John*	San Francisco San Francisco 1	68	908
Jona L	Sacramento Natonia	63	276
Joseph	Sacramento Ward 1	63	126
Joseph	San Joaquin Oneal	64	939
L	Butte Bidwell	56	718
L H	Colusa Monroeville	57	445
Lizzie	San Francisco San Francisco 10	244	67
Louis	Siskiyou Cottonwoood	69	104
Luther	Yolo Slate Ra	72	707
Luther	Yuba Slate Ro	72	707
M	Butte Bidwell	56	722
M	El Dorado Placerville	58	881
M B	Yolo Cottonwoood	72	655
Margaret	Sonoma Sonoma	69	649
Mary	Sonoma Mendocino	69	453
Mathews	Yuba Fosters	72	840
Mathias*	Yuba Fosters	72	840
Michael	Placer Auburn	62	586
Michael	Tuolumne Twp 5	71	489
Michael	Yuba Rose Bar	72	810
Myron	Sierra Eureka	661	046
Obediah	San Joaquin O'Neal	641	002
P	Butte Eureka	56	653
P S	San Joaquin Stockton	641	027
Patrick	San Francisco San Francisco 2	67	611
R F*	Butte Kimshaw	56	594
R J	Butte Kimshaw	56	594
R N	Butte Bidwell	56	715
R T*	Butte Kimshaw	56	594
R Y	Butte Bidwell	56	715
Rachael	Sonoma Healdsbu	69	474
Ransom	Sonoma Mendocino	69	453
Richd C	San Francisco San Francisco 10	322	67
Roche*	Plumas Meadow Valley	62	906
Rosemon	El Dorado Gold Hill	581	096
Russell B	Alameda Brooklyn	55	116
S	Butte Bidwell	56	718
S	Butte Ophir	56	756
Saml*	Amador Twp 5	55	357
Samuel T	Alameda Brooklyn	55	116
Sanil*	Amador Twp 5	55	357
Sarah L	Solano Vallejo	69	263
Stephen	Butte Kimshaw	56	600
Thomas	San Joaquin O'Neal	641	002
Thos	Butte Oregon	56	639
Thos C	Butte Ophir	56	762
W	Yolo Cache	72	611
W S	Sacramento San Joaquin	63	355
W T	Butte Ophir	56	782
Walter	Tulara Keyesville	71	59

Name	County Locale	M653 Roll	Page
POWELL			
Walter	Tulara Keyesville	71	61
William	Calaveras Twp 8	57	100
William	Contra Costa Twp 1	57	527
William	El Dorado Mud Springs	58	994
William	Nevada Rough &	61	418
William	Siskiyou Yreka	69	169
William S	Tulara Visalia	71	104
William W	Tuolumne Chinese	71	501
Wm	Sonoma Healdsbu	69	474
POWELLEO			
A	Tuolumne Twp 4	71	160
POWELSON			
Andrew	Marin Tomales	60	774
H	Sutter Nicolaus	70	827
Heny	Yuba Bear Rvr	721	011
J	El Dorado Kelsey	581	151
Peter	San Francisco San Francisco 8	681	246
Wm	San Francisco San Francisco 2	67	784
Wm L	San Francisco San Francisco 10	358	67
POWELT			
Rosemon	El Dorado Gold Hill	581	096
POWEN			
C P	Placer Dutch Fl	62	726
POWER			
A	San Joaquin Stockton	641	096
A J	Santa Clara Redwood	65	457
Adam	Monterey Pajaro	601	021
Chas	Sacramento Ward 1	63	12
Francis	Nevada Red Dog	61	539
Jas	Sacramento Ward 3	63	437
John	Santa Clara San Jose	65	366
John	Tuolumne Sonora	71	221
Mike	Tuolumne Twp 2	71	277
Morris	Tuolumne Sonora	71	236
O P*	Butte Oregon	56	628
R	Mariposa Coulterville	60	674
Robert	Sierra Twp 5	66	918
Robert	Yuba Marysville	72	912
Thomas	Sierra La Porte	66	765
Thomas	Tulara Visalia	71	109
Thos	Calaveras Twp 8	57	88
Thos	Sacramento Ward 4	63	534
W	Siskiyou Scott Ri	69	70
Wm J	San Francisco San Francisco 1	68	854
POWEREY			
Thos M	Sacramento Natonia	63	276
POWERS			
A B	Nevada Nevada	61	269
A W	Alameda Brooklyn	55	117
Adam	Monterey Pajaro	601	021
Albert	Contra Costa Twp 2	57	562
Amelia*	El Dorado Georgetown	58	694
Anson H*	Calaveras Twp 4	57	345
Anthony	Calaveras Twp 7	57	5
Bridget	San Francisco San Francisco 7	681	365
C E	Nevada Bridgeport	61	474
C P*	Butte Oregon	56	628
Catharine	San Francisco San Francisco 9	681	004
Chas	San Francisco San Francisco 4	681	118
Chas	San Francisco San Francisco 2	67	691
Chas	San Francisco San Francisco 9	68	966
Chas	Trinity East For	701	027
Chas	Trinity Rearings	70	990
Christen	El Dorado Mud Springs	58	966
Chs	San Francisco San Francisco 5	67	480
Chs H	San Francisco San Francisco 6	67	414
Clarisse B	Alameda Oakland	55	72
Cyrus	Siskiyou Cottonwoood	69	107
Daniel	Santa Cruz Pajaro	66	529
Daniel	Siskiyou Yreka	69	187
Daniel	Tuolumne Springfield	71	367
E S	El Dorado Placerville	58	818
Edward	Amador Twp 4	55	235
Edward	Nevada Bridgeport	61	446
Eliza	Napa Napa	61	85
Elizabeth	San Francisco San Francisco 2	67	579
Ellen	Sacramento Ward 4	63	535
Elya	Napa Napa	61	85
F	El Dorado White Oaks	581	001
Francis G	Tuolumne Columbia	71	317
Frank	San Francisco San Francisco 9	68	988
George	Placer Michigan	62	826
H	Sutter Nicolaus	70	841
H	Trinity Rearings	70	990
H C	Butte Mountain	56	734
Ira F	Sierra Gibsonville	66	857
J	Nevada Grass Valley	61	226
J C	El Dorado Mountain	581	178
J S	Shasta Shasta	66	679
J T	Shasta Shasta	66	662
James	Sierra La Porte	66	788
James	Solano Benecia	69	312
James	Tehama Red Bluff	70	934
James G	Tuolumne Twp 3	71	445

California 1860 Census Index

Name	County Locale	M653 RollPage
POWERS		
Jas	Sacramento Granite	63 234
Jno W	Mendocino Calpella	60 815
John	Los Angeles Los Angeles	59 344
John	Monterey Pajaro	601019
John	Placer Michigan	62 815
John	San Francisco San Francisco 8 681253	
John	San Francisco San Francisco 2 67 801	
John	San Francisco San Francisco 1 68 905	
John	Shasta Horsetown	66 698
John	Sierra Twp 5	66 938
John	Siskiyou Callahan	69 16
John	Trinity Cox'S Bar	701037
John J	Yuba Rose Bar	72 820
John L	San Francisco San Francisco 10 325	
		67
John S	Yuba Rose Bar	72 820
John*	Yuba New York	72 739
Johnn	Monterey Pajaro	601019
Lewis	San Francisco San Francisco 9 68 975	
Lewis	Yuba Marysville	72 976
Linus	Placer Virginia	62 664
Lucius	Sacramento Ward 4	63 590
M	Mariposa Twp 3	60 556
M	Tuolumne Twp 4	71 156
M*	Nevada Grass Valley	61 155
Marcy	Yuba Marysville	72 885
Margret	Sacramento Franklin	63 332
Mary	San Francisco San Francisco 3 67 9	
Mary	Yuba Marysville	72 885
Michael	Contra Costa Twp 1	57 504
Michael	San Joaquin Oneal	64 934
Michael	San Mateo Twp 3	65 75
Michael	Sierra Scales D	66 803
Michael	Sierra Twp 5	66 930
O	Siskiyou Scott Va	69 55
O B	Solano Suisan	69 208
O C	Placer Dutch Fl	62 732
O P	Butte Oregon	56 628
P R	Nevada Rough &	61 417
Patrick	San Diego Colorado	64 807
Patrick	San Francisco San Francisco 10 354	
		67
Peter	Yuba Rose Bar	72 812
Pierce	Solano Vallejo	69 271
Rhewben	Santa Clara Santa Clara	65 511
Richard	Siskiyou Callahan	69 5
Richd	Amador Twp 3	55 389
Richd	Amador Twp 3	55 389
Robert	Placer Michigan	62 826
Robert	Nevada Grass Valley	61 210
S D	Nevada Grass Valley	61 210
S T	Sonoma Armally	69 507
Talbert P	Solano Vacaville	69 337
Theodore	Tuolumne Twp 5	71 492
Thomas	Plumas Quincy	62 982
Thomas	Sierra La Porte	66 776
Thomas	Tulara Twp 3	71 61
Thomas	Yolo No E Twp	72 674
Thomas	Yuba North Ea	72 674
Thomas J	Yuba Marysville	72 869
Thomas T	San Joaquin Stockton	641077
Thos	Alameda Brooklyn	55 90
Thos	San Francisco San Francisco 10 314	
		67
W J	San Francisco San Francisco 9 681081	
W W	Siskiyou Yreka	69 177
Walter	Yuba Bear Rvr	721009
Wayne	Amador Twp 5	55 345
William	El Dorado Salmon Falls	581038
William	Nevada Bloomfield	61 512
Wm	Sacramento Granite	63 254
POWERY		
M	Nevada Grass Valley	61 155
POWESS		
Aaron H	Calaveras Twp 4	57 345
Anson H*	Calaveras Twp 4	57 345
POWETT		
Patrick	San Francisco San Francisco 2 67 611	
POWL		
Ah	Sacramento Mississipi	63 190
POWLE		
J F	Calaveras Twp 7	57 14
POWLEY		
Celipo	Calaveras Twp 8	57 89
POWLSON		
J	El Dorado Placerville	58 838
POWNALE		
Joseph	Tuolumne Twp 2	71 330
POWNALL		
Joseph	Tuolumne Columbia	71 330
POWORD		
Jno W*	Mendocino Anderson	60 871
POWROS		
Richard	Nevada Bridgeport	61 480
POWSON		
A W	San Francisco San Francisco 9 681079	

Name	County Locale	M653 RollPage
POWSONS		
William*	Nevada Rough &	61 437
POWY		
---	San Francisco San Francisco 4 681182	
POX		
William	Solano Benecia	69 316
POY		
---	Amador Twp 1	55 478
---	Amador Twp 1	55 479
---	Calaveras Twp 5	57 176
---	Calaveras Twp 5	57 191
---	Calaveras Twp 4	57 302
---	Calaveras Twp 4	57 304
---	El Dorado Salmon Falls	581045
---	El Dorado Salmon Falls	581063
---	El Dorado Big Bar	58 737
---	Mariposa Twp 1	60 673
---	Nevada Nevada	61 302
---	Sacramento Ward 1	63 51
---	Sacramento Ward 1	63 53
---	Sacramento Ward 1	63 54
---	Sacramento Ward 1	63 60
---	San Francisco San Francisco 4 681174	
---	San Francisco San Francisco 4 681178	
---	San Francisco San Francisco 4 681183	
---	Sierra La Porte	66 780
---	Sierra St Louis	66 861
---	Trinity Big Flat	701042
---	Tuolumne Montezuma	71 512
---	Tuolumne Chinese	71 524
---	Yolo Slate Ra	72 711
---*	Calaveras Twp 6	57 176
Ah	Sacramento Ward 1	63 152
C*	Nevada Grass Valley	61 182
Lee	Butte Bidwell	56 709
POYD		
Elijah*	Mendocino Arrana	60 859
POYE		
John B*	Calaveras Twp 5	57 231
POYER		
John	Nevada Nevada	61 328
POYES		
John B	Calaveras Twp 5	57 231
POYLE		
Wm	Butte Kimshaw	56 579
POYNE		
Elisha	Calaveras Twp 5	57 149
John*	Sonoma Santa Rosa	69 416
William	Calaveras Twp 10	57 282
POYNER		
Jesse D	San Joaquin Castoria	64 880
POYON		
J	Calaveras Twp 9	57 381
POYONS		
Simon	Calaveras Twp 5	57 198
POYOR		
Adolph*	Calaveras Twp 6	57 156
POZEDA		
M	San Francisco San Francisco 9 681058	
POZER		
T	Trinity Steiner	701000
POZNTON		
A W Jr	Trinity Trinity	70 974
POZOS		
Jas	Calaveras Twp 9	57 380
PPENETON		
Joseph	Los Angeles Los Angeles	59 342
PPONG		
Sing	Nevada Bloomfield	61 530
PPURINTON		
C M	Amador Twp 6	55 441
PRAAG		
A J	San Francisco San Francisco 3 67 2	
Sam Van*	Sacramento Ward 1	63 64
PRACAFRIO		
M	Santa Clara Burnett	65 258
PRACE		
Herman	San Diego Colorado	64 808
PRACHT		
F	Trinity Turner'S	70 997
PRACIA		
Bonifacis	San Diego S Luis R	64 782
PRACKLER		
Jacob*	Siskiyou Yreka	69 140
PRACTER		
William	Mendocino Anderson	60 867
PRACTERS		
Isaac	Alameda Brooklyn	55 88
PRACY		
George	San Francisco San Francisco 7 681356	
PRADER		
Antone	Tuolumne Twp 2	71 388
Frank	Tuolumne Twp 2	71 389
Jas	Sacramento Cosummes	63 402
Jos	Sacramento Ward 3	63 430
Manuel	Tuolumne Twp 2	71 388

Name	County Locale	M653 RollPage
PRADER		
Manuel	Tuolumne Shawsfla	71 389
N	San Francisco San Francisco 2 67 642	
PRADES		
Antone	Tuolumne Shawsfla	71 388
Frank	Tuolumne Shawsfla	71 389
Manuel	Tuolumne Shawsfla	71 388
PRADY		
William	Solano Fremont	69 379
PRAETTO		
---	Tulara Twp 1	71 113
PRAG		
James*	Mendocino Little L	60 833
Martin	San Francisco San Francisco 2 67 582	
PRAGER		
Charles	Los Angeles San Pedro	59 481
L	San Francisco San Francisco 5 67 517	
Samuel	Los Angeles Los Angeles	59 345
PRAHER		
R	Alameda Brooklyn	55 215
Ryan	Alameda Washington	55 215
PRAHL		
C	Yuba Foster B	72 828
E	Yuba Fosters	72 828
PRAIDER		
G	San Francisco San Francisco 1 68 901	
Geo W	Merced Twp 1	60 904
PRAIN		
F	Shasta Shasta	66 668
PRAIRINA		
Frank*	Sacramento Ward 1	63 23
PRAITHER		
A	Shasta Millvill	66 748
PRALONGEOT		
Francis*	Calaveras Twp 6	57 151
PRAMBERY		
Charles	Contra Costa Twp 3	57 594
PRAMMEL		
Frilds	Mendocino Little L	60 830
PRANAN		
Patrick	Tuolumne Don Pedro	71 539
PRANDO		
Leatro*	Mariposa Twp 3	60 558
PRANKELL		
Ramon*	Marin Cortemad	60 792
PRAP		
C H F*	Tuolumne Shawsfla	71 417
PRAPPINE		
Henry	Calaveras Twp 7	57 20
PRARA		
Joseph	Tuolumne Twp 2	71 389
PRARIA		
A R	San Francisco San Francisco 1 68 831	
PRARIE		
John	San Francisco San Francisco 1 68 885	
Joseph	San Francisco San Francisco 1 68 861	
PRARNEY		
William*	San Francisco San Francisco 4 681172	
PRARY		
A*	Nevada Grass Valley	61 185
PRASBERY		
Horace	San Francisco San Francisco 7 681353	
PRASLORN		
M	San Francisco San Francisco 5 67 529	
PRASS		
C H F*	Tuolumne Shawsfla	71 417
PRASSA		
F A	Tuolumne Twp 1	71 188
PRASSEN		
A	San Francisco San Francisco 5 67 500	
PRASSER		
John	Tuolumne Twp 3	71 470
PRASTEN		
J	Shasta Shasta	66 673
PRASTER		
A J	Yolo Cache Crk	72 623
Peter	Sierra Cox'S Bar	66 950
PRASTOL		
Peter	San Francisco San Francisco 1 68 901	
PRASTON		
A L	Yolo Cache	72 623
Simon	Plumas Quincy	62 938
PRAT		
---	Sierra Morristown	661056
PRATE		
James*	San Francisco San Francisco 10 262	
		67
Miller W	Solano Suisan	69 205
William	Colusa Monroeville	57 454
Wm A	Colusa Monroeville	57 453
PRATER		
Alfred	Amador Twp 2	55 273
Chas	Santa Clara Santa Clara	65 504
J	Nevada Grass Valley	61 207
M W	Trinity E Weaver	701059
Thos	Amador Twp 3	55 370

Name	County Locale	M653 RollPage
PRATER		
W H	Trinity Arkansas	701004
William B	San Joaquin Elliott	641101
PRATHER		
Abraham*	San Joaquin Douglass	64 926
Ashfora*	Amador Twp 2	55 279
James J	San Joaquin Douglass	64 921
Philip	Yolo Cache Crk	72 626
Squire H	Calaveras Twp 10	57 293
Sqyire H	Calaveras Twp 10	57 293
W J	Yolo Cache	72 632
William	San Joaquin Douglass	64 920
PRATHERON		
S W	Sacramento Cosummes	63 381
PRATHEROW		
S W	Sacramento Casumnes	63 381
PRATHN		
Philip	Yolo Cache	72 626
PRATO		
Antonio	Calaveras Twp 4	57 340
PRATOR		
Z	El Dorado White Oaks	581022
PRATORA		
F G	Stanislaus Oatvale	70 718
PRATT		
A	El Dorado Placerville	58 873
A	Nevada Grass Valley	61 318
A P	Sacramento Ward 1	63 48
Addison	San Bernardino San Salvador	64 658
Albert*	San Francisco San Francisco 2	67 647
Allen	Yolo Putah	72 554
Amos	San Francisco San Francisco 3	67 74
Ancell	Siskiyou Scott Va	69 31
Ann	San Francisco San Francisco 10	263 67
Arcell	Siskiyou Scott Va	69 31
Arville C	San Francisco San Francisco 4	681222
Asa	Klamath Klamath	59 225
Benjamin	San Francisco San Francisco 7	681396
C	El Dorado Placerville	58 860
C C	Tehama Pasakent	70 857
C F	Colusa Grand Island	57 469
C N	San Joaquin Castoria	64 900
Calvin B	Sierra Pine Grove	66 821
Calvin R	Sierra Pine Grove	66 821
Charles	Marin Cortemad	60 784
Chas	San Francisco San Francisco 2	67 693
Christopher	Mariposa Coulterville	60 701
Clarind E	Yuba Marysville	72 979
D	Yuba Rose Bar	72 795
David	Yuba Parks Ba	72 774
E	Sacramento Cosummes	63 409
E A	Sacramento Granite	63 257
E E	Tuolumne Twp 2	71 369
E W	Tuolumne Twp 2	71 384
Edward	San Joaquin Castoria	64 899
Edward M	Mariposa Coulterville	60 674
Enoch	Yolo No E Twp	72 674
Enoch	Yuba North Ea	72 674
Enos	Amador Twp 4	55 255
Frank	Sacramento Ward 1	63 15
Franklin	Placer Michigan	62 841
Franklin G	San Francisco San Francisco 7	681349
G	Nevada Grass Valley	61 157
George	San Joaquin Elliott	64 944
George H	San Francisco San Francisco 7	681327
George R	Tuolumne Big Oak	71 145
H	El Dorado Casumnes	581172
H	Solano Fremont	69 376
H G	San Francisco San Francisco 3	67 54
Hantrell	Yolo Slate Ra	72 689
Henry	Calaveras Twp 7	57 26
Henry	Nevada Rough &	61 404
Henry	Nevada Red Dog	61 550
Henry	San Francisco San Francisco 3	67 11
Henry	San Francisco San Francisco 1	68 826
Hintrebt*	Yuba Slate Ro	72 689
Hiram	Tulara Twp 3	71 58
Ida	Yuba Marysville	72 957
J	Siskiyou Scott Va	69 59
J	Yuba Rose Par	72 795
J Davis	Placer Rattle Snake	62 635
J S	El Dorado Eldorado	58 947
J T	San Joaquin Stockton	641038
James	Calaveras Twp 7	57 4
James	San Francisco San Francisco 10	262 67
James	Yuba Parks Ba	72 774
James N	San Francisco San Francisco 7	681349
James S	San Francisco San Francisco 3	67 77
John	Calaveras Twp 9	57 372
John	Sierra Twp 7	66 914
John F	Yuba Marysville	72 945
Joseph	Contra Costa Twp 1	57 514
Joseph	Sacramento Georgian	63 339
Joseph	San Joaquin Castoria	64 900

Name	County Locale	M653 RollPage
PRATT		
Joseph	Yuba North Ea	72 674
L	Nevada Grass Valley	61 220
L M	Nevada Grass Valley	61 218
Lenell*	Yuba Rose Bar	72 816
Lewis B	Tuolumne Shawsfla	71 399
Lorenzo	Calaveras Twp 6	57 130
Martin	Nevada Bloomfield	61 527
N	Siskiyou Scott Va	69 26
Nathan	Santa Clara Fremont	65 438
Noah N	Yuba Marysville	72 978
Noah U	Yuba Marysville	72 978
O	El Dorado Kelsey	581148
Orville C	San Francisco San Francisco 4	681222
Peter	Sonoma Bodega	69 530
R H	Sonoma Santa Rosa	69 405
Richard F	Yuba Marysville	72 978
Rudolph	San Francisco San Francisco 9	681004
Sam B	Tuolumne Twp 1	71 268
Senell*	Yuba Rose Bar	72 816
Sevell*	Yuba Rose Bar	72 816
Sewell*	Yuba Rose Bar	72 816
Simmion	Calaveras Twp 8	57 104
Solomon	Tuolumne Springfield	71 369
W	San Francisco San Francisco 2	67 663
W P	San Francisco San Francisco 5	67 478
W P	San Francisco San Francisco 5	67 527
Walter	San Francisco San Francisco 7	681417
William	Plumas Quincy	62 981
William	San Bernardino Santa Barbara	64 173
Wm	Santa Clara Alviso	65 399
Wm	Solano Vallejo	69 280
Wm C	Amador Twp 2	55 276
Wm H	El Dorado Georgetown	58 682
Wm H H	Sacramento Ward 1	63 121
Wm W	Santa Clara Redwood	65 459
PRATTICE		
Robt B	Sonoma Santa Rosa	69 390
PRATTON		
Ann	San Francisco San Francisco 4	681124
PRAUMJATT		
James H	El Dorado Big Bar	58 739
PRAVINA		
Frank*	Sacramento Ward 1	63 23
PRAVUNA		
Frank	Sacramento Ward 1	63 23
PRAWINA		
Frank*	Sacramento Ward 1	63 23
PRAY		
A	El Dorado Casumnes	581163
A	Sutter Vernon	70 768
A D	El Dorado Mountain	581184
Ira W	Plumas Meadow Valley	62 906
J	Calaveras Twp 7	57 30
J W	Butte Bidwell	56 720
Joseph*	Sacramento Franklin	63 311
Manuel	Tuolumne Columbia	71 310
Many*	San Francisco San Francisco 9	68 995
Marry*	San Francisco San Francisco 9	68 995
Mary	San Francisco San Francisco 9	68 995
Mary	Tuolumne Columbia	71 313
Mary Lu	Sonoma Bodega	69 524
O D	El Dorado Mountain	581184
Octavia W	San Francisco San Francisco 7	681415
	San Francisco	
PRAYER		
S	Amador Twp 2	55 302
PRAZ		
Isaac C	Tuolumne Twp 4	71 139
PRAZA		
Juan	San Bernardino San Bernadino	64 668
PRE		
---*	Sierra Twp 5	66 932
PREACHER		
James	Sonoma Mendocino	69 458
John	Sonoma Mendocino	69 458
Lewis	Yolo Merritt	72 584
PREAST		
Josiah	San Joaquin Oneal	64 929
PREAWEN		
Mk*	Nevada Eureka	61 377
PREBBLE		
Chas	Placer Goods	62 699
S	San Mateo Twp 1	65 51
PREBLE		
A J	Tuolumne Twp 2	71 325
Augustus*	Yuba Marysville	72 919
Chas	Placer Lisbon	62 733
Chas E	Fresno Twp 3	59 16
L W	Marin Tomales	60 713
Leander	Klamath S Fork	59 204
Letrus*	Nevada Little Y	61 532
Lutius	Nevada Little Y	61 532
S W	Marin Tomales	60 713
Samuel	Siskiyou Klamath	69 96
PRECH		
Philip	Tuolumne Don Pedro	71 539

Name	County Locale	M653 RollPage
PRECIADO		
Jose	Los Angeles San Gabriel	59 423
Juan J	San Bernardino San Bernadino	64 667
PRECK		
Antonio	San Bernardino San Bernadino	64 667
Philip*	Tuolumne Twp 6	71 539
PREDHAM		
George	Amador Twp 1	55 452
PREDOCIO		
---	San Bernardino S Timate	64 696
PREDOCK		
Benj	Trinity Weaverville	701073
PREDOM		
Moses	Placer Auburn	62 569
PREE		
John	Calaveras Twp 7	57 44
PREENE		
John H	Alameda Oakland	55 35
PREETTO		
---	Tulara Keyesville	71 68
---	Tulara Keyesville	71 71
PREFALD		
Martin	San Francisco San Francisco 8	681237
PREFFENBERGER		
Louis	Siskiyou Yreka	69 192
PREFOIN		
Lorain*	Plumas Meadow Valley	62 928
PREFOOM		
Guiseppe	San Francisco San Francisco 11	156 67
PREFOOTAM		
A	Yolo Cache	72 626
PREFORTAIN		
A	Yolo Cache Crk	72 626
PREFREANT		
C	San Francisco San Francisco 4	681166
PREFSEY		
Benj F*	San Francisco San Francisco 10	275 67
PREGNELL		
Wm	Amador Twp 3	55 372
PREICADO		
Manello	Fresno Twp 1	59 84
PREICE		
E*	Nevada Eureka	61 375
William*	Alameda Brooklyn	55 126
PREICHT		
Frederick	Marin Novato	60 737
PREICOTE		
C	Colusa Monroeville	57 445
PREILEY		
Geo V	Tuolumne Twp 4	71 145
PREISE		
William*	Alameda Brooklyn	55 126
PREIST		
Janas*	Plumas Quincy	62 972
PREITO		
L	San Francisco San Francisco 2	67 719
PREITON		
Henry*	Butte Kimshaw	56 604
PREJSEY		
Benj F	San Francisco San Francisco 10	275 67
PRELILE		
A J	Tuolumne Columbia	71 362
PRELLEN		
Eli	Yolo Cache	72 592
PREMAN		
A	Sacramento Cosummes	63 408
PREMENTEL		
Francis	Calaveras Twp 4	57 325
PREMINGTON		
W T	San Mateo Twp 1	65 69
PREMORE		
Lera B	Placer Auburn	62 593
PRENDERGAST		
John	San Francisco San Francisco 11	130 67
PRENECHT		
Henry	San Francisco San Francisco 7	681393
PRENITT		
Thomas*	Yuba Fosters	72 836
PRENOR		
Jacob	Santa Cruz Santa Cruz	66 602
PRENOS		
Jacob	Santa Cruz Santa Cruz	66 602
PRENTICE		
Edward	Colusa Butte Crk	57 467
Edward	Sacramento Sutter	63 298
Fred	Sacramento Ward 1	63 13
Fredk	Sacramento Ward 4	63 574
Henry*	San Francisco San Francisco 1	68 905
Jno	Sacramento Ward 4	63 573
Thos	Sonoma Washington	69 673
PRENTINO		
H*	Mariposa Twp 1	60 623

California 1860 Census Index

Name	County Locale	M653 RollPage
PRENTIS		
Geo	Sacramento Sutter	63 298
W D	Nevada Grass Valley	61 199
PRENTISS		
Adam	Mariposa Twp 1	60 642
E D	Sacramento Ward 4	63 565
Geo*	San Francisco San Francisco 3	67 87
George	San Francisco San Francisco 8	681324
H	San Francisco San Francisco 9	681073
J H	San Francisco San Francisco 9	681073
Moses	Plumas Quincy	62 987
W H	Sacramento American	63 159
PRENTNO		
H	Mariposa Twp 1	60 623
PRENTUO		
H	Mariposa Twp 1	60 623
PRENTUR		
H*	Mariposa Twp 1	60 623
PREPEY		
John B	Solano Suisan	69 209
PREPIANT		
C	San Francisco San Francisco 4	681166
PRERGON		
Wm	Butte Bidwell	56 729
PRERO		
Ellen	Sacramento Ward 1	63 135
PRERSON		
B F*	Sacramento American	63 168
James	Sacramento Ward 1	63 1
PRESBARY		
William W	Yuba Marysville	72 845
PRESBURRY		
M*	Sutter Butte	70 780
PRESBURY		
Ella	San Joaquin Elliott	64 948
William	San Joaquin Elliott	64 948
PRESBY		
Elijah	San Francisco San Francisco 10	332 67
Milton H	Plumas Quincy	62 977
PRESCAR		
Isaac	Santa Clara San Jose	65 309
PRESCHMAKER		
Chas	San Francisco San Francisco 1	68 846
PRESCOT		
Geo W	Yuba Marysville	72 902
James	Klamath Salmon	59 208
PRESCOTT		
---	Monterey San Juan	60 976
A	Nevada Nevada	61 313
A H	Sonoma Bodega	69 519
C	Sonoma Bodega	69 534
Cyrus	Siskiyou Scott Va	69 33
Danforth	Yuba Bear Rvr	721004
Derins	Amador Twp 1	55 465
Derins	Amador Twp 1	55 475
Derius	Amador Twp 1	55 465
Eleaner	San Francisco San Francisco 10	312 67
Eleanor	San Francisco San Francisco 10	312 67
Ezekiel	San Joaquin Elkhorn	64 959
Geo	Calaveras Twp 9	57 401
Geo W	San Francisco San Francisco 2	67 578
Geo W	Yuba Marysville	72 902
George	Yuba Fosters	72 833
George W	San Francisco San Francisco 7	681342
H	San Francisco San Francisco 5	67 547
H	San Francisco San Francisco 9	68 984
J W	San Francisco San Francisco 10	187 67
Jacob	Placer Forest H	62 792
Jno	San Francisco San Francisco 9	681077
John	Placer Dutch Fl	62 734
John	Sacramento Franklin	63 314
L	San Francisco San Francisco 5	67 480
L H	Sacramento Ward 4	63 499
Margaret	Tuolumne Columbia	71 301
N J	Napa Napa	61 102
S L	Sierra La Porte	66 771
S R	San Joaquin Stockton	641031
Sal	El Dorado Georgetown	58 754
Samuel	El Dorado Georgetown	58 681
T A	San Joaquin Stockton	641027
Theron	Tuolumne Columbia	71 361
Theuben	Santa Clara Gilroy	65 245
Thos	El Dorado Georgetown	58 673
W	San Francisco San Francisco 9	681102
William	Monterey San Juan	60 991
William	San Francisco San Francisco 4	681110
William	San Francisco San Francisco 9	68 985
Wm	San Bernardino San Salvador	64 660
PRESCOTTE		
John W	San Francisco San Francisco 1	68 911
PRESCUX		
Ed*	Alameda Oakland	55 54

Name	County Locale	M653 RollPage
PRESEAL		
Isaac	Santa Clara San Jose	65 330
PRESENG		
Fred*	Alameda Brooklyn	55 148
PRESENS		
John	Santa Cruz Santa Cruz	66 634
PRESENT		
John*	Santa Cruz Santa Cruz	66 634
PRESENTACION		
---	San Diego San Diego	64 774
PRESENTON		
Wm F*	Sierra Twp 5	66 946
PRESEUG		
Fred*	Alameda Brooklyn	55 148
PRESFRE		
Baynere	Siskiyou Callahan	69 4
John	Siskiyou Callahan	69 4
PRESGON		
Wm	Butte Bidwell	56 729
PRESHO		
Solomon	San Francisco San Francisco 10	348 67
William	Calaveras Twp 10	57 288
William M	Calaveras Twp 7	57 16
PRESINDO		
Francisco	S Buenav	64 221
	San Bernardino	
PRESIRDO		
Francisco	Tuolumne Sonora	71 211
PRESLEY		
A	Amador Twp 1	55 505
Hugh	Yuba Rose Bar	72 806
Jas F	Sacramento Ward 1	63 40
Jas T	Sacramento Ward 1	63 40
John	San Francisco San Francisco 1	68 907
PRESLUNE		
---	Mendocino Calpella	60 824
PRESON		
P S	Sierra Downieville	66 955
PRESRON		
J	Sutter Bear Rvr	70 819
PRESSER		
William	Sierra Scales D	66 802
PRESSEY		
Benj F*	San Francisco San Francisco 10	275 67
John B	Solano Suisan	69 209
PRESSITT		
Thomas*	Yuba Fosters	72 836
PREST		
Paul	Trinity E Weaver	701059
PRESTA		
Victor	Yuba Parks Ba	72 786
PRESTCOFF		
S R	Nevada Eureka	61 376
PRESTCOTT		
L R	Nevada Eureka	61 376
PRESTEN		
A	Mariposa Twp 3	60 606
Mary	Tuolumne Sonora	71 237
S	Mariposa Twp 3	60 606
S H*	Shasta Shasta	66 682
PRESTER		
Augusta	San Francisco San Francisco 2	67 719
John	Calaveras Twp 9	57 386
T L	El Dorado Diamond	58 782
Victor	Yuba Parke Ba	72 786
PRESTIMONI		
L*	Sacramento Ward 1	63 15
PRESTIN		
Andrew	Fresno Twp 1	59 34
PRESTLY		
Chas	San Francisco San Francisco 9	681089
PRESTMOIN		
L	Sacramento Ward 1	63 15
PRESTON		
A	Nevada Nevada	61 328
A	San Francisco San Francisco 4	681225
A B	Tuolumne Twp 3	71 430
Alex M	Humbolt Union	59 187
Benjamin	Yuba Bear Rvr	721000
C H	Sonoma Mendocino	69 457
Catherine R	Humbolt Union	59 187
Danl H	Placer Stewart	62 607
Edward*	Placer Iona Hills	62 895
Elijah	Monterey Pajaro	601021
Elijah J	Monterey Pajaro	601021
Enoch	San Joaquin Stockton	641038
Fred A	Tuolumne Big Oak	71 133
Geo	Placer Stewart	62 607
George H	Yuba Marysville	72 878
H L	Del Norte Crescent	58 633
H L	Del Norte Crescent	58 634
Henry	Los Angeles Los Angeles	59 404
Henry*	Butte Kimshaw	56 604
J	Sacramento Ward 4	63 516

Name	County Locale	M653 RollPage
PRESTON		
J	Shasta Shasta	66 673
J	Solano Vacaville	69 335
J S	Sierra Downieville	66 955
James*	El Dorado Spanish	581124
Jefferson	Sierra Pine Grove	66 832
John	Monterey Pajaro	601012
John	Placer Iona Hills	62 890
John C	Humbolt Union	59 187
Lewis	Tulara Twp 1	71 109
Mary	Tuolumne Twp 1	71 237
O J	San Francisco San Francisco 8	681272
Philip	Tuolumne Twp 6	71 528
R	Mariposa Twp 3	60 577
R	Sierra Cox'S Bar	66 951
R J	Marin Tomales	60 724
Richard S	Sierra Downieville	66 955
Royal	Sacramento Ward 4	63 595
S	Solano Vacaville	69 319
S H	Shasta Shasta	66 682
Samuel	Contra Costa Twp 2	57 548
W H	San Francisco San Francisco 5	67 521
William	Sierra St Louis	66 808
Wm	Sacramento Ward 4	63 527
Wm	Santa Clara San Jose	65 371
PRESTONE		
T	Solano Vacaville	69 319
PRESTTO		
---	Tulara Twp 3	71 71
PRESTUNONI		
L*	Sacramento Ward 1	63 15
PRETCHARD		
John	San Francisco San Francisco 5	67 554
PRETE		
Chas Victor	Sacramento Ward 3	63 442
PRETH		
Paul*	Trinity E Weaver	701059
PRETILE		
A J	Tuolumne Twp 2	71 362
PRETORIOUS		
Godfrey*	San Francisco San Francisco 7	681357
PRETTTYMAN		
Wm P	Tuolumne Twp 1	71 193
PRETTYMAN		
Painter	Tuolumne Sonora	71 197
Wm P	Tuolumne Sonora	71 193
PREUITT		
Thomas*	Yuba Fosters	72 836
PREVA		
Pa Meir	Nevada Nevada	61 296
Patten	Nevada Nevada	61 296
PREVAST		
S	Santa Clara San Jose	65 335
PREVEASO		
Henry	Alameda Oakland	55 48
PREVENX		
Ed*	Alameda Oakland	55 54
PREVOST		
J B	Tuolumne Columbia	71 309
Leopold	Alameda Oakland	55 51
PREWELL		
Elizah*	Sacramento Mississipi	63 183
John	Sonoma Russian	69 432
Samul A	Sonoma Russian	69 432
PREWETT		
Edward	Sacramento Mississipi	63 188
Edward	Sonoma Russian	69 443
Elizah*	Sacramento Mississipi	63 183
James	Sonoma Russian	69 435
John	Sonoma Russian	69 432
Samul A	Sonoma Russian	69 432
Sarah E	Sonoma Russian	69 432
PREWIT		
Alex	Sacramento Ward 3	63 479
PREWITT		
Thomas	Yuba Fosters	72 836
PREWS		
Conrad*	San Mateo Twp 1	65 69
PREWSTER		
Clemen T	Fresno Twp 3	59 32
PREY		
Joseph*	Sacramento Franklin	63 311
PREYMAND		
E	Amador Twp 3	55 394
PREZZO		
Vencio	Tuolumne Chinese	71 500
PRGONTELLA		
---	Mariposa Twp 1	60 628
PRHBERG		
Joseph*	San Francisco San Francisco 7	681337
PRIATO		
Mathew	El Dorado White Oaks	581028
PRIBBLE		
Elim P	Placer Rattle Snake	62 633
Jerutha	San Francisco San Francisco 9	68 995
PRIBEANSE		
John	Tuolumne Shawsfla	71 401

California 1860 Census Index

Name	County Locale	M653 Roll	Page

PRIBEAUSE
| John | Tuolumne Twp 2 | 71 | 401 |

PRIBELL
| Frank* | El Dorado Salmon Falls | 58 | 1055 |

PRIBLE
| G O | Siskiyou Klamath | 69 | 96 |

PRICDE
| Edmond | Tuolumne Twp 2 | 71 | 298 |

PRICE
A	Butte Mountain	56	737
A	Sacramento Brighton	63	207
A D	El Dorado Newtown	58	781
A G	Trinity Mouth Ca	70	1018
A J	Stanislaus Branch	70	701
Abner	San Francisco San Francisco 9	68	1065
Adelaide	San Francisco San Francisco 8	68	1249
Alfred	San Francisco San Francisco 9	68	975
Alier	El Dorado White Oaks	58	1005
Alongo*	Siskiyou Yreka	69	142
Ann	San Francisco San Francisco 2	67	597
Ann	Sonoma Vallejo	69	630
Anna	Siskiyou Scott Va	69	26
Augustin*	Napa Napa	61	59
Augustus	Napa Napa	61	59
B	Mariposa Twp 1	60	671
B	San Francisco San Francisco 10	67	264
Benj	San Joaquin Stockton	64	1048
Benja	Calaveras Twp 5	57	255
Benjamin	Yuba Bear Rvr	72	1003
Benjamin	Yuba Marysville	72	975
Calvin	Tuolumne Twp 2	71	297
Cath	Sacramento Ward 3	63	460
Charles L	Sacramento Ward 4	63	549
Chas	Sacramento Ward 4	63	519
David	Amador Twp 3	55	392
David	Sacramento Centre	63	175
David	Yuba Slate Ro	72	697
David	Yuba Slate Ro	72	700
David Jr	Del Norte Crescent	58	627
David T	Yolo Slate Ra	72	700
E H	Sutter Yuba	70	777
E H	Yuba North Ea	72	670
E L	El Dorado Georgetown	58	689
E W	Nevada Bridgeport	61	468
Edward	San Joaquin Oneal	64	912
Edward	Santa Cruz Santa Cruz	66	626
Edward	Santa Cruz Santa Cruz	66	628
Edward	Sierra Chappare	66	1041
Edward	Siskiyou Scott Va	69	21
Edward D	Yuba Slate Ro	72	697
Elizabeth	San Francisco San Francisco 2	67	647
F M	Yolo Cache	72	624
F R	Trinity Trinity	70	1022
Frank*	Santa Cruz Santa Cruz	66	627
Franklin F	Siskiyou Yreka	69	123
G H	Yolo No E Twp	72	670
Geo*	Butte Cascade	56	693
George F	Siskiyou Yreka	69	188
H	Butte Wyandotte	56	658
H	Shasta Horsetown	66	690
Henry	San Francisco San Francisco 2	67	681
Henry	Santa Cruz Santa Cruz	66	636
Henry J	Butte Hamilton	56	521
Ira	Santa Clara San Jose	65	391
Isaac	Humbolt Pacific	59	132
J	Merced Twp 2	60	918
J	Nevada Eureka	61	356
J A	Sonoma Washington	69	666
J A	Yolo Cache Crk	72	628
J B	Mendocino Ukiah	60	802
J B	Santa Clara San Jose	65	314
J C	San Francisco San Francisco 1	68	898
J J	San Francisco San Francisco 4	68	1151
J P	Butte Hamilton	56	527
Jacob	El Dorado Kelsey	58	1155
Jacob	Plumas Quincy	62	1004
Jacob	Sonoma Vallejo	69	629
Jacob	Yuba Marysville	72	959
James	Nevada Nevada	61	266
James	San Francisco San Francisco 7	68	1422
James	San Francisco San Francisco 2	67	658
James	Siskiyou Callahan	69	10
James	Tuolumne Twp 1	71	249
James E*	Calaveras Twp 4	57	328
Janes E*	Calaveras Twp 4	57	328
Jas	Butte Chico	56	532
Jas	Placer Dutch Fl	62	730
Jas	San Francisco San Francisco 2	67	786
Jno	Butte Kimshaw	56	580
Jo	Napa Yount	61	37
Joel	Solano Suisan	69	211
John	El Dorado Coloma	58	1080
John	El Dorado Coloma	58	1103
John	San Joaquin Elkhorn	64	964
John	Sonoma Washington	69	664

Name	County Locale	M653 Roll	Page

PRICE
John	Tulara Visalia	71	112
John	Tulara Visalia	71	98
John B	Butte Oro	56	683
John B	El Dorado Grizzly	58	1179
John M	Marin Cortemad	60	787
John M	Tuolumne Twp 3	71	448
John N	El Dorado Big Bar	58	738
John R	Solano Vallejo	69	249
Johnson	Sacramento Ward 3	63	437
Joice	San Francisco San Francisco 1	68	896
Jos	Butte Chico	56	532
Jos	San Francisco San Francisco 2	67	786
Joseph M	Yuba Marysville	72	904
Joseph W	Yuba Marysville	72	904
K H	Alameda Brooklyn	55	138
L	Calaveras Twp 9	57	380
M	Sutter Nicolaus	70	832
Mannella	San Francisco San Francisco 10	67	228
Manuella	San Francisco San Francisco 10	67	228
Margaret	Del Norte Crescent	58	628
Margaret	Nevada Eureka	61	356
Mary	Siskiyou Scott Va	69	21
Merare F	Sierra Whiskey	66	846
Michael	San Francisco San Francisco 7	68	1433
Nat	El Dorado Grizzly	58	1182
Ned	Siskiyou Callahan	69	16
Priscal	Placer Secret R	62	611
R F	Tuolumne Twp 1	71	234
Richard	El Dorado Kelsey	58	1142
Richd	Sonoma Santa Rosa	69	425
Robert	San Francisco San Francisco 9	68	951
S	Butte Ophir	56	795
S J	Sonoma Washington	69	664
Sam	Butte Kimshaw	56	569
Saml	Butte Kimshaw	56	569
Saml G	Tuolumne Twp 3	71	470
Saml W	Butte Hamilton	56	525
Simeon	Tuolumne Sonora	71	484
Smith	Merced Twp 2	60	916
Solomon	Yuba Marysville	72	947
T	Sacramento American	63	162
T G	San Francisco San Francisco 3	67	68
T J	Tehama Cottonwoood	70	898
T J	Tuolumne Twp 1	71	249
Tho	Nevada Eureka	61	356
Tho	Siskiyou Klamath	69	88
Thomas	Merced Twp 2	60	918
Thomas L	Tuolumne Twp 6	71	539
Thos	Sacramento Ward 4	63	524
Thos H	Sacramento Ward 1	63	64
W	Santa Clara Fremont	65	426
W	Yuba Rose Bar	72	809
W E	Siskiyou Scott Va	69	25
W W	Sacramento Ward 1	63	47
Walter	Butte Oregon	56	621
Watkin	Nevada Bridgeport	61	441
William	Calaveras Twp 4	57	309
William	El Dorado Eldorado	58	935
William	San Francisco San Francisco 4	68	1143
William	Santa Cruz Pajaro	66	560
William	Sierra Pine Grove	66	820
Wm	Placer Secret R	62	612
Wm D	Sierra Twp 7	66	869
Wm E	El Dorado Placerville	58	928
Wm H	Butte Ophir	56	791
Wm W	Placer Virginia	62	675

PRICER
| F | Siskiyou Callahan | 69 | 10 |

PRICHAD
| A* | Placer Ophirville | 62 | 656 |

PRICHARD
Danl	Butte Oregon	56	636
James	Humbolt Hawksport	59	158
John	Nevada Eureka	61	355
M	Tehama Red Bluff	70	916
Richard	San Joaquin Stockton	64	1053
T	San Francisco San Francisco 10	67	357
William S	Yuba Marysville	72	963

PRICHET
| J C | Butte Ophir | 56 | 760 |

PRICHIT
| J C* | Butte Ophir | 56 | 760 |

PRICHT
| Augustus | San Francisco San Francisco 8 | 68 | 1309 |

PRICIDDLE
| Edwardo | Tulara Twp 3 | 71 | 43 |

PRICIDDO
| Edward* | Tulara Sinks Te | 71 | 43 |

PRICK
| --- | Calaveras Twp 10 | 57 | 284 |
| F | Tehama Antelope | 70 | 892 |

Name	County Locale	M653 Roll	Page

PRICKETT
| Joel | San Diego Colorado | 64 | 808 |
| Saml | Trinity Weaverville | 70 | 1066 |

PRICKTOR
| --- | Siskiyou Yreka | 69 | 156 |

PRICO
| Louis* | San Francisco San Francisco 4 | 68 | 1219 |

PRICSTLY
| John* | San Mateo Twp 1 | 65 | 48 |

PRICTOR
| --- | San Bernardino S Timate | 64 | 696 |

PRIDAUH
| Wm* | Trinity E Weaver | 70 | 1059 |

PRIDE
Bamche*	Sierra Downieville	66	989
Baniche*	Sierra Downieville	66	989
John	San Francisco San Francisco 10	67	242
Nelson	San Joaquin Castoria	64	897
Parrick	Plumas Quincy	62	996
Richard	Tuolumne Columbia	71	298
Tho	Nevada Eureka	61	356

PRIDEANSE
| F | Tuolumne Shawsfla | 71 | 412 |

PRIDEAUSE
| F | Tuolumne Twp 2 | 71 | 412 |

PRIDGEN
| A J* | Nevada Bridgeport | 61 | 446 |
| Johnson | Calaveras Twp 6 | 57 | 154 |

PRIDGON
| F M | Nevada Bridgeport | 61 | 456 |

PRIEBATCH
| W | Sacramento Ward 1 | 63 | 35 |

PRIEDERMEINES
| Charles* | San Francisco San Francisco 7 | 68 | 1355 |

PRIEFF
| Henry* | San Francisco San Francisco 8 | 68 | 1282 |

PRIEO
| Louis* | San Francisco San Francisco 4 | 68 | 1219 |

PRIER
Ann*	San Francisco San Francisco 3	67	68
John B	Butte Oro	56	683
M	Tuolumne Big Oak	71	145
T G	San Francisco San Francisco 3	67	68

PRIERSON
| W J | Yolo Cache Crk | 72 | 666 |

PRIEST
C B	Placer Iona Hills	62	868
Clearana*	Sacramento Franklin	63	324
Cleavana*	Sacramento Franklin	63	324
D Q	Placer Iona Hills	62	875
Edward	San Francisco San Francisco 9	68	1102
J G	Alameda Washington	55	174
J J	Placer Iona Hills	62	875
J S	Placer Iona Hills	62	875
Jas	Amador Twp 1	55	476
Joseph	San Francisco San Francisco 9	68	1103
Nathan	San Joaquin Douglass	64	922
Samuel	Nevada Nevada	61	275
T	Solano Vacaville	69	330
W C	Tuolumne Twp 4	71	176

PRIESTLY
| John | San Mateo Twp 1 | 65 | 48 |

PRIETA
| Maria A | Monterey San Juan | 60 | 1008 |

PRIETO
| --- | San Bernardino S Timate | 64 | 709 |
| --- | San Bernardino S Timate | 64 | 726 |

PRIETOR
| Daniel* | Alameda Brooklyn | 55 | 111 |

PRIETTO
| --- | Tulara Twp 3 | 71 | 68 |

PRIGER
| Silas* | Mariposa Twp 3 | 60 | 565 |

PRIGGE
| John | San Francisco San Francisco 3 | 67 | 65 |

PRIGGETT
| Enos | Calaveras Twp 7 | 57 | 23 |
| Jacob | Calaveras Twp 7 | 57 | 23 |

PRIGGI
| John | San Francisco San Francisco 3 | 67 | 65 |

PRIGH
| Lawrence | San Francisco San Francisco 7 | 68 | 1333 |

PRIGMORE
| Ephraim | Humbolt Union | 59 | 189 |
| James | Humbolt Union | 59 | 189 |

PRIGRA
| Josep | Sacramento San Joaquin | 63 | 352 |

PRIGUET
| Peter F | Colusa Butte Crk | 57 | 467 |

PRIJER
| Silas* | Mariposa Twp 3 | 60 | 565 |

PRIKNDLE
| Saml S | Calaveras Twp 6 | 57 | 155 |

PRILATA
| Francis | Santa Clara Santa Clara | 65 | 481 |

Name	County Locale	M653 Roll	Page
PRILET			
Paul*	Sacramento Ward 1	63	87
PRILFEMAKAR			
F*	San Francisco San Francisco 4	681	134
PRILLMAN			
A	Nevada Grass Valley	61	235
PRIME			
P R	Nevada Nevada	61	239
PRIMER			
Henry	Sacramento Ward 1	63	11
PRIMERE			
S	Siskiyou Scott Va	69	53
PRIMERS			
S	Siskiyou Scott Va	69	53
PRIMESE			
S	Siskiyou Scott Va	69	53
PRIMGRU			
W C*	Stanislaus Oatvale	70	717
PRIMLY			
Frederick	Solano Vacaville	69	346
PRIMM			
G*	Nevada Eureka	61	392
PRIMMER			
Honora	San Francisco San Francisco 9	681	026
PRIMROSE			
John	Placer Forest H	62	804
T	Nevada Grass Valley	61	157
PRINCE			
A E	San Francisco San Francisco 10		177 67
August	Sierra Pine Grove	66	825
B R	Calaveras Twp 8	57	103
E L	El Dorado Georgetown	58	689
Edward	Sierra Twp 5	66	925
Francis	Mariposa Coulterville	60	674
G	El Dorado Diamond	58	795
Geo	Calaveras Twp 8	57	107
Geo	San Francisco San Francisco 2	67	688
James	Shasta Horsetown	66	699
James E	Calaveras Twp 4	57	328
Jas	Butte Hamilton	56	521
Jno	San Francisco San Francisco 10		180 67
John	Amador Twp 5	55	363
John	Yuba Foster B	72	822
Jos	Sonoma Sonoma	69	636
Jule	Alameda Oakland	55	46
Julius F	Yuba Foster B	72	824
Julius F	Yuba Fosters	72	824
Lewis	Mariposa Twp 1	60	625
N J	Marin Tomales	60	717
O	San Francisco San Francisco 4	681	231
Peter	Placer Secret R	62	616
Rupertio	San Francisco San Francisco 2	67	702
Silas S	Contra Costa Twp 2	57	580
Swing*	Calaveras Twp 5	57	210
T	Shasta French G	66	718
T R	Marin Tomales	60	717
Thomas P	Humbolt Union	59	188
Thos	San Francisco San Francisco 2	67	598
W A	Shasta Cottonwood	66	723
William	Contra Costa Twp 3	57	609
William	San Mateo Twp 1	65	53
PRINCELY			
Wm	Tuolumne Columbia	71	314
PRINCETON			
E	Butte Oregon	56	614
PRINCPL			
Stephen*	San Francisco San Francisco 4	681	168
PRINDELL			
Edwin	Santa Clara Fremont	65	417
S	Siskiyou Scott Va	69	48
Wm	Santa Clara Fremont	65	417
PRINDH			
Charles T	Yolo No E Twp	72	669
PRINDLE			
Charles T	Yolo No E Twp	72	669
David S	San Francisco San Francisco 8	681	297
George	Shasta Shasta	66	759
J L	Sacramento Granite	63	248
Saml S	Calaveras Twp 6	57	155
Wm	Placer Mountain	62	707
PRINDLES			
George	Shasta Shasta	66	759
PRINE			
John	Siskiyou Yreka	69	151
PRINELL			
Sarah	Santa Clara Santa Clara	65	468
PRINEPL			
Stephen	San Francisco San Francisco 4	681	168
PRING			
---	Placer Folsom	62	640
PRINGH			
Jno	Butte Oregon	56	612
PRINGLE			
H T	Solano Suisan	69	214

Name	County Locale	M653 Roll	Page
PRINGLE			
Jno*	Butte Oregon	56	612
Joseph	Sierra Twp 5	66	946
M B	Mariposa Twp 3	60	584
Puehade*	Santa Clara Fremont	65	419
R D	Solano Suisan	69	227
Richd	San Francisco San Francisco 1	68	838
W	San Francisco San Francisco 5	67	539
W	San Mateo Twp 2	65	117
Wm	Nevada Eureka	61	356
PRINGTE			
H T	Solano Suisan	69	214
PRINIFL			
Stephen*	San Francisco San Francisco 4	681	168
PRINM			
Henry	Sonoma Petaluma	69	605
PRINODIA			
Frank	Calaveras Twp 4	57	331
PRINT			
Chals	El Dorado Georgetown	58	685
Chas	El Dorado Georgetown	58	685
PRINTA			
Jose	Contra Costa Twp 1	57	518
PRINTEP			
Geo	San Francisco San Francisco 3	67	87
PRINTH			
Charles T*	Yolo No E Twp	72	669
PRINTIP			
Geo*	San Francisco San Francisco 3	67	87
PRINTY			
Geo W	Butte Ophir	56	790
PRINTZ			
L H	Siskiyou Cottonwood	69	107
PRIOK			
John*	Nevada Bridgeport	61	480
PRIOR			
Benjamin	Amador Twp 4	55	250
Charles	San Mateo Twp 3	65	90
H	Nevada Nevada	61	282
J A	Sierra Twp 7	66	869
J H	Merced Twp 1	60	909
J W	Tuolumne Twp 2	71	329
John	Placer Michigan	62	823
John	San Francisco San Francisco 11		104 67
John*	Nevada Bridgeport	61	480
Mary	San Mateo Twp 3	65	94
Nathaniel	Santa Cruz Watsonville	66	536
Rosanna J	Colusa Colusi	57	419
Simon	Contra Costa Twp 2	57	549
W C	Tehama Cottonwoood	70	898
PRIP			
William	Siskiyou Yreka	69	127
PRIPETH			
J B	Nevada Nevada	61	240
PRIPITH			
J B	Nevada Nevada	61	240
PRIPLETT			
Paten	Sierra Downieville	661	011
PRIRR			
John	San Francisco San Francisco 11		104 67
PRIRRE			
---	Sacramento Granite	63	249
PRISAL			
James	Calaveras Twp 8	57	89
PRISBURRY			
M*	Sutter Butte	70	780
PRISCH			
---*	Tulara Yule Rvr	71	31
PRISCHE			
---	Tulara Twp 2	71	31
PRISCOTT			
---	Monterey San Juan	60	976
Theron	Tuolumne Twp 2	71	361
PRISEN			
Jno	Butte Oregon	56	618
PRISIRDO			
Francisco	Tuolumne Twp 1	71	211
PRISOE			
William	El Dorado Grizzly	581	179
PRISON			
A	Placer Rattle Snake	62	638
D D	Yolo Cache	72	594
PRISSEE			
Miguel	Santa Clara San Jose	65	300
PRISSIR			
R	El Dorado Diamond	58	808
PRIST			
John P	Trinity E Weaver	701	059
PRISTELLO			
John	Tuolumne Twp 1	71	188
PRISTLY			
A*	Calaveras Twp 9	57	389
PRISTO			
Peter*	Yuba Marysville	72	872

Name	County Locale	M653 Roll	Page
PRISTON			
A	San Francisco San Francisco 4	681	225
Ildefona	Yuba Marysville	72	918
James	El Dorado Spanish	581	124
PRISTY			
John*	Nevada Eureka	61	374
PRIT			
---*	Sacramento Ward 1	63	61
PRITCHARD			
E J	El Dorado Kelsey	581	146
Elisha	Butte Kimshaw	56	599
Emanuel	Napa Napa	61	74
Emmanuel	Napa Napa	61	74
Ira W	Yolo Slate Ra	72	703
Ira W	Yuba Slate Ro	72	703
J	San Francisco San Francisco 3	67	24
J	Yolo Cache Crk	72	621
James	Los Angeles Elmonte	59	256
James A	San Francisco San Francisco 11		114 67
John	Plumas Quincy	62	944
John	San Joaquin Elliott	64	945
John*	San Francisco San Francisco 5	67	554
L*	Sacramento Brighton	63	195
Richard	Yolo Slate Ra	72	701
Richard	Yuba Slate Ro	72	701
Robt	Shasta Shasta	66	662
S H	San Francisco San Francisco 6	67	433
S*	Sacramento Brighton	63	195
T	San Francisco San Francisco 5	67	548
Thomas	Calaveras Twp 5	57	214
Thomas	Yolo Slate Ra	72	701
Thomas	Yuba Slate Ro	72	701
Thomas L	Sierra Twp 7	66	877
Thomas*	Calaveras Twp 5	57	214
W J	San Francisco San Francisco 10		261 67
William	Sierra Port Win	66	797
Wm	Napa Napa	61	82
Wm	Sacramento Ward 4	63	538
Wm	Yolo Slate Ra	72	700
Wm	Yolo Slate Ro	72	701
Wm	Yuba Slate Ro	72	701
PRITCHARE			
Calvin	Calaveras Twp 7	57	20
PRITCHELL			
Elizabeth	Sonoma Mendocino	69	461
James H	Sonoma Mendocino	69	461
PRITCHEN			
John	Plumas Quincy	62	980
PRITCHER			
Manuel	Calaveras Twp 5	57	249
Phillisciano*	Calaveras Twp 5	57	250
PRITCHET			
James	Nevada Rough &	61	403
PRITCHETT			
J C*	Yolo Cottonwoood	72	656
Jacob H	Yuba Timbucto	72	787
James H	Sonoma Mendocino	69	461
PRITCHEY			
George L	Napa Hot Springs	61	16
PRITCHFIELD			
Jno	Sacramento Ward 4	63	538
PRITCHORD			
Thomas*	Calaveras Twp 5	57	214
PRITOIS			
J	Amador Twp 1	55	487
PRITRA			
Andrew*	Calaveras Twp 7	57	37
PRITSELLS			
C	El Dorado Diamond	58	786
PRITSL			
L	El Dorado Diamond	58	788
PRITTING			
George	Tuolumne Twp 5	71	493
Geroge	Tuolumne Chinese	71	493
PRITTMAN			
A	Nevada Grass Valley	61	235
PRIUM			
Henry*	Sonoma Petaluma	69	605
PRIUTT			
A*	Merced Twp 1	60	898
PRIVERS			
John	Siskiyou Callahan	69	16
PRIVOST			
J B	Tuolumne Twp 2	71	309
PRIZER			
Fred	Siskiyou Callahan	69	9
PROAG			
Richard*	Mariposa Coulterville	60	696
PROAL			
J L*	Nevada Eureka	61	358
J S	Nevada Eureka	61	358
Oliver	Butte Chico	56	549
PROBART			
William	El Dorado Casumnes	581	165

Name	County Locale	M653 RollPage
PROBASCO		
George WSan Francisco San Francisco 11		143 67
Jas	Sacramento Georgian	63 337
PROBER		
Locwood S	Calaveras Twp 9	57 356
Locwood*	Calaveras Twp 9	57 356
PROBES		
Locwood S*	Calaveras Twp 9	57 356
Locwood*	Calaveras Twp 9	57 356
PROBIT		
John	Stanislaus Emory	70 742
PROBOBO		
Baptisto	Mariposa Twp 3	60 547
PROBOCO		
Domingo	Mariposa Twp 3	60 547
Givani	Mariposa Twp 3	60 547
Pedro	Mariposa Twp 3	60 547
PROBOR		
Locwood*	Calaveras Twp 9	57 356
PROBST		
Fredrick	Tuolumne Twp 6	71 530
PROBURN		
Mistress*	Siskiyou Yreka	69 144
Thomas*	Siskiyou Yreka	69 144
PROCHER		
Mary	El Dorado Georgetown	58 683
PROCHOLD		
Charles San Francisco San Francisco 8 681309		
PROCIDO		
Mary	Tuolumne Twp 1	71 202
PROCISE		
J R	Marin Tomales	60 775
PROCKET		
Chas	San Francisco San Francisco 10	261 67
PROCKTER		
---*	Siskiyou Yreka	69 156
PROCKTOR		
---	Siskiyou Yreka	69 156
PROCTER		
Joshua M	Alameda Brooklyn	55 165
Wm H	Tuolumne Twp 6	71 296
PROCTOR		
Ann	Placer Michigan	62 807
Benj	Tuolumne Columbia	71 331
Chas B	Sonoma Mendocino	69 455
D W	Alameda Brooklyn	55 157
Daniel	Alameda Brooklyn	55 111
Francis	El Dorado Placerville	58 909
Frank	Solano Suisan	69 219
Franklin	El Dorado Placerville	58 920
G M*	Amador Twp 3	55 400
G W	Sacramento Ward 4	63 532
G W*	Amador Twp 3	55 400
J	Butte Oro	56 685
J	Butte Ophir	56 795
J M	Siskiyou Klamath	69 84
Jno	Alameda Brooklyn	55 186
John	San Mateo Twp 1	65 49
John W	Amador Twp 3	55 401
L G	Calaveras Twp 8	57 79
M	Calaveras Twp 9	57 391
Mary A	Sonoma Mendocino	69 455
Reuben	Amador Twp 2	55 301
Samuel	Alameda Oakland	55 51
Thos	Napa Napa	61 76
W F	Butte Ophir	56 754
William	Placer Michigan	62 819
PRODFIT		
F	Calaveras Twp 9	57 391
PRODGER		
J H	Nevada Grass Valley	61 178
PRODMORE		
J H	Shasta Millvill	66 755
PROEL		
Edwd*	Sacramento Mississipi	63 183
PROETOR		
Frank	Solano Suisan	69 219
PROFFAT		
A	Merced Twp 1	60 907
PROFFER		
E	Nevada Nevada	61 259
PROFFET		
A	Merced Twp 1	60 907
PROFFITT		
John B	Solano Montezuma	69 369
John R	Solano Montezuma	69 369
PROFING		
John	El Dorado Casumnes	581161
PROG		
Conrad*	Calaveras Twp 6	57 174
PROGAN		
William	Siskiyou Yreka	69 143
PROGAR		
M	San Joaquin Stockton	641094

Name	County Locale	M653 RollPage
PROLEANA		
G	Amador Twp 3	55 372
PROLERY		
John	El Dorado Kelsey	581135
PROLL		
H	San Francisco San Francisco 5 67 492	
John	San Francisco San Francisco 7 681420	
Lewis	San Francisco San Francisco 10	260 67
PROLUS		
A*	Nevada Grass Valley	61 154
PROM		
Frederick	San Mateo Twp 1	65 65
PROMER		
Saml	Sacramento Ward 1	63 22
PRONARO		
Francisco	Mariposa Twp 1	60 667
PRONAVO		
Cloraindo*	Mariposa Twp 1	60 667
Clorando*	Mariposa Twp 1	60 667
Elvarado	Mariposa Twp 1	60 667
PRONBBS		
Sylvester	Siskiyou Scott Va	69 22
PRONG		
---	Sacramento Ward 1	63 60
PRONMONGER		
C*	Alameda Oakland	55 1
PRONOFIT		
James*	San Joaquin Stockton	641036
PRONT		
Amanda	El Dorado Georgetown	58 685
Cath*	Sacramento Ward 3	63 454
George*	Placer Michigan	62 807
Mary	Sacramento Ward 1	63 120
PRONTY		
Jackson*	Tulara Twp 1	71 102
James	Stanislaus Buena Village	70 722
PROOE		
Frank*	Nevada Nevada	61 324
PROOG		
Richard	Mariposa Coulterville	60 696
PROOLE		
Sylvester*	Sonoma Washington	69 678
PROP		
John	Trinity East For	701027
PROPELL		
H A	Sonoma Bodega	69 530
PROPER		
E*	Sutter Butte	70 782
W F	Trinity Mouth Ca	701016
W T	Trinity Mouth Ca	701016
PROPHY		
Master	Alameda Brooklyn	55 186
PRORCE		
August*	Tuolumne Twp 5	71 522
PRORINE		
F*	Napa Hot Springs	61 4
PRORL		
Edwd*	Sacramento Mississipi	63 183
PROROINES		
Geo*	El Dorado Mountain	581185
PRORONCHAR		
Eliza	Solano Vallejo	69 259
Manuel*	Solano Vallejo	69 259
PROSO		
Louis	Solano Benecia	69 316
PROSPE		
Valdimora	Monterey Monterey	60 956
PROSPER		
---	San Francisco San Francisco 2 67 640	
Beagle	Humbolt Union	59 192
Guy	Plumas Meadow Valley	62 932
Henry	El Dorado Eldorado	58 942
O	Nevada Nevada	61 284
Peter	San Luis Obispo San Luis Obispo 65 17	
Valdimora	Monterey Monterey	60 956
PROSSAR		
James	Alameda Brooklyn	55 174
PROSSER		
Watkin	Sierra Port Win	66 796
William	Sierra Scales D	66 802
Wm J	Sacramento Centre	63 177
PROTER		
Jos	Napa Yount	61 40
PROTERIO		
Eledric	San Mateo Twp 1	65 60
PROTEST		
Charles	Tuolumne Twp 2	71 383
PROTHEN		
Peter*	San Mateo Twp 1	65 60
PROTHERN		
Wm	Sacramento Cosumnes	63 382
PROTHERO		
Joseph	Tulara Visalia	71 84
PROTHERON		
F	Sacramento Cosumnes	63 385

Name	County Locale	M653 RollPage
PROTHEROW		
Alonzo	Sacramento Cosumnes	63 385
Ann	Sacramento Casumnes	63 380
PROTHERS		
Edwd	Fresno Twp 3	59 16
Joseph	Tulara Twp 1	71 84
PROTO		
---	San Diego Agua Caliente	64 864
M	El Dorado Diamond	58 800
PROUBBS		
Sylvester	Siskiyou Scott Va	69 22
PROUD		
Palmer	Plumas Quincy	621007
PROUL		
Cath*	Sacramento Ward 3	63 454
Edwd*	Sacramento Mississipi	63 183
Frank	Nevada Nevada	61 284
PROULE		
Sylvester*	Sonoma Washington	69 678
PROUSE		
Alma	Sonoma Mendocino	69 465
Julia	Sonoma Washington	69 678
Saml	Nevada Grass Valley	61 195
Sylvester	Sonoma Mendocino	69 465
William	Tuolumne Twp 5	71 508
PROUSENER		
P H*	Tuolumne Big Oak	71 152
PROUSINER		
P H	Tuolumne Twp 4	71 152
PROUST		
David W	Placer Virginia	62 677
PROUT		
George*	Placer Michigan	62 807
James	Plumas Quincy	621007
Mary	Sacramento Ward 1	63 120
PROUTY		
Jackson	Tulara Visalia	71 102
John	San Francisco San Francisco 1 68 858	
PROUTZ		
C C	Amador Twp 2	55 269
Jos	Amador Twp 2	55 269
Simon	Amador Twp 2	55 269
PROVE		
Frank*	Nevada Nevada	61 324
John	Marin S Antoni	60 712
PROVEAN		
Louis*	Yuba Parks Ba	72 785
PROVEAU		
Louis	Yuba Parke Ba	72 785
PROVEAW		
Louis*	Yuba Parks Ba	72 785
PROVELLA		
Guarderloupe*	Yuba Marysville	72 920
PROVENA		
Quarderloupe*	Yuba Marysville	72 920
PROVENCE		
Geo	Tuolumne Garrote	71 175
PROVERLY		
Luca	Alameda Brooklyn	55 152
PROVIDO		
Mary	Tuolumne Sonora	71 202
PROVIM		
F*	Napa Hot Springs	61 4
PROVINA		
Guadalupe	Yuba Marysville	72 920
PROVINCE		
Geo	Tuolumne Twp 4	71 175
Wm	San Francisco San Francisco 10	228 67
PROVINE		
F*	Napa Hot Springs	61 4
PROVINES		
R R	San Francisco San Francisco 5 67 483	
PROVINGE		
Wm*	Napa Yount	61 41
PROVINGER		
Wm*	Napa Yount	61 41
PROVINGS		
Wm*	Napa Yount	61 41
PROVINYE		
Wm*	Napa Yount	61 41
PROVIS		
W	Nevada Grass Valley	61 151
PROVIZZU		
John	Contra Costa Twp 1	57 506
PROVO		
Frank*	Nevada Nevada	61 324
Louie	Amador Twp 2	55 264
PROVONCHAR		
Manuel*	Solano Vallejo	69 259
PROVOST		
Daniel B	Alameda Oakland	55 27
F J	Tuolumne Sonora	71 198
George	Nevada Bloomfield	61 522
John W	San Francisco San Francisco 8 681237	
Jule	Sierra Port Win	66 797

Name	County Locale	M653 Roll	Page
PROVOST			
Paul B	Yuba Marysville	72	890
R M	Solano Suisan	69	229
PROW			
---	Sierra Downieville	66	980
Charles	Yolo Cache	72	609
PROWA			
John	Siskiyou Scott Va	69	49
PROWBBS			
Sylvester*	Siskiyou Scott Va	69	22
PROWBRIDGE			
Geroge	Tuolumne Green Springs	71	519
PROWINES			
Geo	El Dorado Mountain	581	185
PROWN			
J	Yolo Cache Crk	72	645
PROWSE			
F A	Nevada Nevada	61	277
PROY			
Conrad	Calaveras Twp 5	57	174
PRROE			
Frank*	Nevada Nevada	61	324
PRROOA			
John*	Siskiyou Scott Va	69	49
PRSCHANCIO			
Pan	Sierra Downieville	66	987
PRUCEY			
Johnson	Sierra Downieville	661	013
PRUCK			
---*	Calaveras Twp 10	57	259
Leo	Yuba Marysville	72	894
Loo	Yuba Marysville	72	894
PRUCONRER			
A P*	San Francisco San Francisco 7	681	437
PRUCOURER			
A P*	San Francisco San Francisco 7	681	437
PRUCOWRER			
A P*	San Francisco San Francisco 7	681	437
PRUDDES			
S	Calaveras Twp 9	57	413
PRUDDIVENT			
P L*	Sacramento Ward 1	63	40
PRUDENT			
Marcar	Sierra Twp 5	66	925
Marear*	Sierra Twp 5	66	925
Morcar*	Sierra Twp 5	66	925
PRUDERMEINES			
Charles*	San Francisco San Francisco 7	681	355
PRUDEY			
Geo	Yolo Cache Crk	72	646
PRUDHOMME			
F	Tuolumne Twp 4	71	172
Leon V	Los Angeles Los Angeles	59	343
PRUDON			
P L	San Francisco San Francisco 2	67	758
P S	San Francisco San Francisco 2	67	758
PRUDY			
Stephen	Santa Clara Redwood	65	448
PRUELL			
Sarnes*	San Luis Obispo	65	5
	San Luis Obispo		
PRUENGER			
Louise*	Alameda Brooklyn	55	142
PRUENTES			
Manuel	Santa Clara Alviso	65	407
PRUERS			
John D*	Mariposa Twp 3	60	586
PRUETT			
S A	Siskiyou Callahan	69	14
PRUETTE			
J*	Siskiyou Klamath	69	87
PRUEUGER			
Louise*	Alameda Brooklyn	55	142
PRUFF			
Henry	San Francisco San Francisco 8	681	282
PRUISE			
D C	Sacramento Granite	63	241
PRUIT			
Geo	Yolo Washington	72	599
PRUITO			
A	Trinity New Rvr	701	031
PRUITT			
A	Merced Twp 1	60	898
Lemuel	Trinity Lewiston	70	957
Samuel	Trinity Lewiston	70	957
PRUKETT			
Edwd	Sonoma Petaluma	69	616
PRUME			
James*	Sonoma Petaluma	69	576
PRUMO			
James*	Sonoma Petaluma	69	576
PRUNE			
W	El Dorado Diamond	58	787
PRUNER			
Charles	Amador Twp 3	55	379
PRUNG			
Ho	San Francisco San Francisco 9	681	096

Name	County Locale	M653 Roll	Page
PRUNNS			
G	Nevada Eureka	61	392
PRUNTY			
Jas	Stanislaus Buena Village	70	721
PRUP			
C H F*	Tuolumne Twp 2	71	417
PRUSE			
Isadore*	San Francisco San Francisco 2	67	557
PRUSH			
Henry	Santa Clara San Jose	65	348
PRUST			
E E	El Dorado Georgetown	58	708
T	El Dorado Diamond	58	811
PRUTCHARD			
Wm	Yuba Slate Ro	72	683
PRUTEHARD			
Wm	Yolo No E Twp	72	683
PRUTH			
Joseph*	Tuolumne Twp 6	71	539
PRUTYMAN			
A C*	Nevada Nevada	61	251
PRUTZEL			
John	San Francisco San Francisco 7	681	430
PRUX			
Isadore	San Francisco San Francisco 2	67	557
PRUZZO			
John	Sonoma Vallejo	69	630
PRWERS			
Pierce	Solano Vallejo	69	271
PRY			
---*	Mariposa Twp 3	60	581
Wapht	El Dorado Big Bar	58	736
PRYDE			
Geo	El Dorado Placerville	58	923
Wm*	El Dorado Placerville	58	921
PRYEL			
Michael*	Calaveras Twp 6	57	158
PRYER			
N A	Calaveras Twp 9	57	414
William*	Placer Michigan	62	839
PRYERS			
John L*	Mariposa Twp 3	60	586
PRYON			
C	San Francisco San Francisco 5	67	533
Mary	San Francisco San Francisco 10	184 67	
PRYOR			
C	San Francisco San Francisco 5	67	533
Caroline	Alameda Oakland	55	28
D	Sacramento Ward 1	63	20
E B	Nevada Nevada	61	277
Elijah	Mendocino Ukiah	60	802
J	Sacramento Ward 1	63	20
Jas	Calaveras Twp 9	57	380
Jas	Calaveras Twp 9	57	381
Joseph	Shasta Horsetown	66	695
Michael	Yuba Rose Bar	72	800
Paul	Los Angeles San Juan	59	466
Paula	Los Angeles Shaffer	59	397
R A	El Dorado Mud Springs	58	980
Rebecca	Nevada Bridgeport	61	484
Susan	Nevada Nevada	61	278
William*	Placer Michigan	62	839
Wm	Alameda Brooklyn	55	107
Wm	Solano Suisan	69	232
Wm	Tehama Tehama	70	935
Wm	Tuolumne Twp 2	71	408
PRYS			
Henry E*	San Francisco San Francisco 3	67	86
PRYSON			
Mary	San Francisco San Francisco 10	184 67	
PSEILDO			
Frank	Sierra Downieville	66	971
PSEILDS			
Frank	Sierra Downieville	66	971
PSIYER			
Fred	Siskiyou Callahan	69	9
PSUNO			
Poncianno*	Yuba Marysville	72	917
PTETCHEY			
Williamson*	Yuba Bear Rvr	72	996
PTIT			
J	Mariposa Twp 1	60	655
PTOCKNELL			
Thompson*	San Francisco 1	68	916
	San Francisco		
PTOPINCH			
Bayilles*	Calaveras Twp 7	57	5
PTTER			
Ephraim	Colusa Grand Island	57	468
PU FOY			
See*	Sacramento Ward 1	63	52
PU RES			
John	Sierra Twp 7	66	868
PU TOY			
See*	Sacramento Ward 1	63	52

Name	County Locale	M653 Roll	Page
PU US UN			
---	Plumas Quincy	62	969
PU			
---	Mariposa Twp 1	60	662
---	San Francisco San Francisco 4	681	186
---	Sierra Downieville	66	986
---	Tuolumne Twp 5	71	517
---*	Shasta Shasta	66	670
---*	Sierra Twp 5	66	932
Ah	Calaveras Twp 7	57	32
Tung*	Calaveras Twp 6	57	169
Ung	Calaveras Twp 5	57	254
Uny	Calaveras Twp 5	57	254
PUADSELL			
James W	Tuolumne Montezuma	71	512
PUAMSENO			
---	San Bernardino S Timate	64	749
PUATTU			
Liberata*	Santa Clara Burnett	65	257
PUBART			
William	El Dorado Casumnes	581	165
PUBELL			
Frank*	El Dorado Salmon Falls	581	055
PUBLE			
Augustus*	Yuba Marysville	72	919
PUBSTOCK			
H	Shasta Millvill	66	752
PUBUB			
Charles	San Francisco San Francisco 7	681	395
PUCALES			
H*	El Dorado Placerville	58	840
PUCH			
Philip*	Tuolumne Twp 6	71	539
PUCHAL			
Charles*	Sierra Twp 7	66	882
PUCHCO			
Morod*	Los Angeles Los Angeles	59	497
PUCHI			
Marie*	Stanislaus Branch	70	703
PUCHTER			
Frederick	Sierra Twp 5	66	942
PUCI			
David*	Yolo Slate Ra	72	697
Edward D	Yolo Slate Ra	72	697
PUCK			
---	Amador Twp 5	55	365
---	Calaveras Twp 6	57	168
---	Calaveras Twp 10	57	259
---	Calaveras Twp 10	57	271
---	Calaveras Twp 10	57	284
---	Mendocino Calpella	60	824
---	Placer Iona Hills	62	898
PUCKER			
Elmore	Humbolt Eel Rvr	59	146
Tho	Siskiyou Scott Va	69	41
PUCKET			
Geo S	Tuolumne Twp 2	71	400
PUCKETT			
Edwd	Sonoma Vallejo	69	616
S A	Nevada Bridgeport	61	455
Thomas*	Amador Twp 4	55	237
PUCKEY			
Walter	Tuolumne Twp 1	71	251
PUCKHABER			
John	San Francisco San Francisco 8	681	255
PUCON			
Martin	San Luis Obispo San Luis Obispo	65	24
PUDD			
Benjamin	Tulara Twp 2	71	29
PUDE			
Ramche	Sierra Downieville	66	989
PUDNEY			
William	San Francisco San Francisco 9	681	037
PUDOMAR			
---	Mendocino Round Va	60	885
PUDTIN			
Edward*	Placer Iona Hills	62	895
PUE			
---	Fresno Twp 1	59	28
---	Sierra Downieville	661	025
---	Sierra Downieville	661	031
---	Sierra Downieville	66	959
---	Sierra Downieville	66	991
---*	Sacramento Ward 1	63	56
---*	Sierra Downieville	661	031
---*	Sierra Downieville	66	983
PUEBLA			
Andrew	San Francisco San Francisco 2	67	699
PUEBLO			
---	Tulara Twp 3	71	67
---	Tulara Twp 3	71	70
PUECH			
D	San Francisco San Francisco 2	67	728
PUEDE			
---	Fresno Twp 1	59	55
PUELAN			
E	Sacramento Ward 4	63	528

California 1860 Census Index

Name	County Locale	M653 Roll	Page
PUENTEZ			
Manuel	San Francisco San Francisco	11	153
		67	
PUERTO			
Andres	Santa Clara Almaden	65	271
PUESON			
Cordilia	Butte Ophir	56	761
PUFF			
John	Amador Twp 4	55	244
PUFFER			
Wilson	Alameda Oakland	55	42
PUG			
---	Sierra Downieville	66	985
---	Sierra Downieville	66	999
PUGER			
Silas	Mariposa Twp 3	60	565
PUGH			
---	El Dorado Big Bar	58	740
---	Fresno Twp 2	59	18
Anne	San Francisco San Francisco 9		681062
E	Sutter Butte	70	787
Edmund	San Francisco San Francisco 1	68	852
Edward	San Francisco San Francisco 7		681444
Edward W	San Bernadino	64	620
	San Bernardino		
Fred	Sacramento San Joaquin	63	349
H	Siskiyou Klamath	69	88
Hugh	Shasta Shasta	66	681
Isaac	Alameda Brooklyn	55	175
J	Sutter Butte	70	787
J T	Sierra Twp 7	66	898
J W	Sacramento Ward 3	63	454
James	Shasta Millvill	66	725
James	Sierra Eureka		661048
James	Sierra Eureka		661049
James	Siskiyou Cottonwoood	69	100
James	Sonoma Santa Rosa	69	420
John	Mariposa Coulterville	60	694
John	Tulara Twp 1	71	112
John A	Sonoma Santa Rosa	69	411
Lawrence	San Francisco San Francisco 7		681333
Malvina	Sonoma Santa Rosa	69	421
Margaret	San Francisco San Francisco 4		681214
N	Sutter Butte	70	784
R	Shasta Millvill	66	752
William	Nevada Bridgeport	61	487
PUGJA			
---	Tulara Twp 3	71	68
PUGREE			
G	Calaveras Twp 9	57	396
PUGRU			
G*	Calaveras Twp 9	57	396
PUGSLEY			
Elias	Tuolumne Sonora	71	188
PUH			
Soy*	San Francisco San Francisco 5		671207
PUHIV			
Law*	Calaveras Twp 8	57	88
Lou*	Calaveras Twp 8	57	88
PUI			
---	Sierra Downieville		661030
---*	Sierra Downieville		661031
PUICK			
---*	Calaveras Twp 10	57	259
Lewis*	Sierra Downieville	66	970
PUIGER			
Mary	San Francisco San Francisco 9	68	979
PUIL			
M*	San Mateo Twp 3	65	78
PUIN			
---	Calaveras Twp 5	57	233
PUIR			
Francisco*	Calaveras Twp 6	57	125
PUIRG			
---	Placer Rattle Snake	62	629
PUIS			
Maria	Los Angeles Los Angeles	59	506
PUISON			
Jos*	Butte Ophir	56	780
PUIST			
Edward*	San Francisco San Francisco 9		681102
Joseph*	San Francisco San Francisco 9		681103
PUJAR			
Jule	San Francisco San Francisco 2	67	761
Magdaline	San Francisco San Francisco 2	67	761
PUJEN			
Magdalion	San Francisco 2	67	761
	San Francisco		
PUK			
Lum	Tuolumne Don Pedro	71	537
PUL			
---	Tuolumne Jacksonville	71	514
---	Yuba Slate Ro	72	712
PULACHER			
Fredrick	Nevada Bloomfield	61	511
PULACROUS			
Leno*	Napa Napa	61	102

Name	County Locale	M653 Roll	Page
PULAMYRAS			
Thomas	Los Angeles San Jose	59	290
PULAND			
Frank	Yuba Long Bar	72	751
PULANN			
Andech	Tuolumne Chinese	71	492
Andeoh*	Tuolumne Twp 5	71	492
PULANS			
---	Tulara Twp 2	71	32
PULARINO			
Bernard*	Calaveras Twp 6	57	116
PULARKI			
Lewis	Monterey Monterey	60	944
PULASKI			
J M	Napa Napa	61	99
Lewis	Merced Monterey	60	944
PULASKIE			
P	Nevada Eureka	61	346
PULE			
---	Yolo Slate Ra	72	712
C M	Siskiyou Scott Va	69	50
PULER			
John*	San Francisco San Francisco 2	67	683
PULES			
George	Tehama Red Bluff	70	908
PULET			
Paul	Sacramento Ward 1	63	87
PULFCHER			
David	Alameda Brooklyn	55	167
PULFEMAHAR			
F	San Francisco San Francisco 4		681134
PULFEMAKAR			
F*	San Francisco San Francisco 4		681134
PULGAREO			
C	Tuolumne Sonora	71	229
PULGARIS			
C	Tuolumne Twp 1	71	229
PULIR			
J B*	Sierra Forest C	66	909
PULISKI			
Jno	Sacramento Georgian	63	344
PULISSE			
---	Butte Chico	56	551
---*	Butte Chico	56	550
PULISSO			
---*	Butte Chico	56	550
PULKENHORN			
William	Placer Michigan	62	825
PULLAN			
William	Siskiyou Scott Ri	69	67
PULLARD			
C H	Siskiyou Scott Va	69	47
PULLEARN			
M R C*	Butte Oregon	56	624
PULLEN			
Augs F	San Francisco San Francisco 10		275
		67	
Chas	Alameda Brooklyn	55	153
James	Sacramento Ward 1	63	147
William A	Calaveras Twp 10	57	263
PULLET			
Felix	Amador Twp 4	55	245
PULLEUN			
Bernard*	Calaveras Twp 4	57	324
PULLEY			
E H	Siskiyou Cottonwoood	69	106
George	Nevada Bloomfield	61	511
PULLIAM			
Howard	Solano Vallejo	69	244
M R C*	Butte Oregon	56	624
Natter*	Butte Oregon	56	642
Walter	Butte Oregon	56	642
PULLIARN			
M R C*	Butte Oregon	56	624
PULLIN			
Eli	Yolo Cache Crk	72	592
Grandl	Monterey San Juan	60	995
James	El Dorado Eldorado	58	946
PULLINAN			
J	El Dorado Placerville	58	837
PULLING			
J	El Dorado White Oaks		581007
James	Tuolumne Twp 2	71	387
PULLINN			
W*	Butte Kimshaw	56	592
PULLMAN			
J B	Nevada Bridgeport	61	440
PULLOY			
George	Nevada Bloomfield	61	511
PULLRN			
William	Calaveras Twp 10	57	263
PULM			
Chas	Napa Napa	61	108
PULMER			
George	Calaveras Twp 5	57	251
John	Yuba Parks Ba	72	779

Name	County Locale	M653 Roll	Page
PULS			
Fred	Placer Illinois	62	705
PULSE			
Tedick*	Placer Illinois	62	740
PULSER			
John	Sacramento Ward 1	63	125
PULSIFER			
John W	Plumas Quincy	62	964
Joseph	Colusa Spring Valley	57	436
PULSIPHER			
J P	Yolo Putah	72	585
Sarah	Sacramento Ward 4	63	528
PULTING			
G F	Nevada Nevada	61	264
PULTRUG			
Nelson*	Placer Iona Hills	62	886
PULTS			
Isaac	Yolo No E Twp	72	680
Isaac	Yuba North Ea	72	680
PULTY			
W	Yolo Putah	72	549
PULTZEL			
Peter*	San Francisco San Francisco 7		681429
PULTZET			
Peter*	San Francisco San Francisco 7		681429
PULYAMERS			
Maria	Fresno Twp 1	59	83
PULZARO			
Gartano	Tuolumne Sonora	71	239
PUMAN			
Alexander*	Placer Michigan	62	853
PUMEY			
Tho*	Siskiyou Callahan	69	2
PUMFOY			
Geo*	Sacramento Ward 1	63	90
PUMIT			
---	Tulara Twp 1	71	113
PUMLEY			
William	Del Norte Ferry P O	58	665
PUMM			
---	Tuolumne Shawsfla	71	386
PUMMARES			
Michael*	El Dorado Georgetown	58	692
PUMMER			
Chas	Sacramento Ward 1	63	27
PUMPER			
---	Tulara Twp 2	71	38
PUMPHREY			
Absolom	Humbolt Pacific	59	130
PUN CHEE			
---	Tuolumne Jacksonville	71	516
PUN			
---	Amador Twp 4	55	256
---	Amador Twp 2	55	315
---	Amador Twp 5	55	364
---	Nevada Rough &	61	436
---	Sierra Downieville		661004
---	Sierra Twp 5	66	927
---	Sierra Downieville	66	985
---	Sierra Downieville	66	993
---	Sierra Downieville	66	997
---	Tuolumne Jamestown	71	438
---	Tuolumne Twp 3	71	439
---	Tuolumne Twp 3	71	440
---*	Sierra Downieville	66	997
Ah	Calaveras Twp 7	57	16
Ar	Sierra Downieville	66	985
Chu	Tuolumne Twp 5	71	516
Francisco*	Calaveras Twp 6	57	125
La	Tuolumne Big Oak	71	181
Low	San Francisco San Francisco 5		671206
Sing	El Dorado Georgetown	58	756
Young	Fresno Twp 2	59	19
PUNADIERO			
Francisco	Plumas Quincy	62	988
PUNAT			
Frederick	Tuolumne Sonora	71	191
PUNCH			
---	Mendocino Round Va	60	880
PUNDLEBURY			
Isaac	Yuba Rose Bar	72	810
PUNDY			
Stephen	San Joaquin Elkhorn	64	981
PUNE			
Eopel	Sierra Downieville		661023
PUNEROY			
A	Sacramento Ward 1	63	40
PUNFOY			
Geo	Sacramento Ward 1	63	90
PUNG			
---	Alameda Oakland	55	38
---	Amador Twp 3	55	402
---	Amador Twp 1	55	511
---	Calaveras Twp 8	57	108
---	Calaveras Twp 6	57	137
---	Calaveras Twp 5	57	138

California 1860 Census Index

Name	County Locale	M653 Roll	Page
PUNG			
---	Calaveras Twp 5	57	173
---	Calaveras Twp 5	57	192
---	Calaveras Twp 7	57	40
---	Calaveras Twp 8	57	82
---	El Dorado Eldorado	58	939
---	Mariposa Twp 1	60	650
---	Mariposa Twp 1	60	661
---	Mariposa Twp 1	60	662
---	Mariposa Coulterville	60	688
---	Nevada Bridgeport	61	460
---	Nevada Bridgeport	61	461
---	Placer Auburn	62	583
---	Placer Folsom	62	648
---	Placer Horseshoe	62	650
---	Placer Virginia	62	669
---	Placer Virginia	62	677
---	Placer Virginia	62	678
---	Sacramento Ward 1	63	51
---	Sacramento Ward 1	63	66
---	Sierra St Louis	66	812
---	Sierra Downieville	66	996
---	Tuolumne Columbia	71	347
---	Tuolumne Shawsfla	71	386
---	Tuolumne Twp 3	71	409
---	Tuolumne Twp 3	71	435
---	Tuolumne Twp 3	71	439
---	Tuolumne Jamestown	71	440
---	Tuolumne Twp 3	71	442
---	Tuolumne Twp 3	71	446
---	Tuolumne Twp 3	71	457
---	Tuolumne Twp 3	71	467
---	Tuolumne Sonora	71	476
---	Tuolumne Twp 1	71	478
---	Tuolumne Chinese	71	525
---	Tuolumne Knights	71	529
---	Tuolumne Green Springs	71	531
---	Tuolumne Twp 6	71	533
---	Tuolumne Don Pedro	71	536
---	Tuolumne Don Pedro	71	538
---*	Tuolumne Big Oak	71	179
Ah	Calaveras Twp 7	57	33
Ah	Calaveras Twp 7	57	34
Ah	Tuolumne Twp 4	71	179
Ah	Tuolumne Twp 2	71	347
Ho	San Francisco San Francisco 9	68	1096
Way	Siskiyou Yreka	69	195
PUNGKOP			
Ching	San Francisco San Francisco 9	68	1093
PUNGOS			
---	Mendocino Twp 1	60	889
PUNISONINO			
---	Mendocino Calpella	60	824
PUNKEE			
---	Fresno Twp 2	59	69
PUNN			
---	Tuolumne Columbia	71	350
---	Tuolumne Twp 2	71	409
---	Tuolumne Shawsfla	71	416
---	Tuolumne Twp 3	71	467
---	Tuolumne Sonora	71	476
A	Tuolumne Twp 2	71	350
Ah	Tuolumne Twp 2	71	386
PUNNDO			
---*	San Bernardino S Timate	64	732
PUNNELL			
D	Calaveras Twp 9	57	415
PUNNEY			
J A	Del Norte Crescent	58	659
PUNNINGTON			
Joseph	Tuolumne Big Oak	71	180
PUNT			
---	Sierra Downieville	66	981
PUNTACHESLER			
John	Amador Twp 1	55	468
PUNTER			
Thomas	Tuolumne Twp 1	71	236
PUNTICE			
Henry*	San Francisco San Francisco 1	68	905
PUNY			
---	Stanislaus Branch	70	714
PUOCK			
---	Sacramento Ward 1	63	51
PUOG			
---	Calaveras Twp 5	57	253
PUOY			
---	Calaveras Twp 5	57	253
PUP			
---	Yuba Long Bar	72	758
PUR			
---	Sierra Downieville	66	1030
---	Sierra Downieville	66	998
Chy	Sacramento Natonia	63	280
Pan	Tuolumne Twp 5	71	511
PURAMINS			
Michael*	El Dorado Georgetown	58	692
PURAMIRS			
Michael*	El Dorado Georgetown	58	692
PURAT			
John	Calaveras Twp 8	57	68
PURCE			
J M	San Francisco San Francisco 5	67	535
PURCEL			
Saml	Shasta Shasta	66	685
PURCELL			
Abner L	Yuba Marysville	72	868
D J	Mendocino Ukiah	60	805
David	Sierra Twp 7	66	893
E J	Mendocino Ukiah	60	805
Feliz	Mendocino Calpella	60	813
John	Sacramento Ward 1	63	125
John	San Mateo Twp 2	65	118
John D	Plumas Quincy	62	985
Joseph	Sierra Twp 7	66	913
M C	Sacramento Ward 4	63	612
Martin	Stanislaus Buena Village	70	722
Mary A	Placer Virginia	62	685
Norah	Yuba Marysville	72	912
Pat	Placer Virginia	62	685
Patrick	Sacramento Ward 4	63	561
Thos	San Francisco San Francisco 1	68	913
PURCEVILLE			
J	Sacramento Lee	63	212
PURCEY			
Johnson	Sierra Downieville	66	1013
PURCHASE			
Geo	El Dorado Kelsey	58	1145
PURCHY			
Edward F	Calaveras Twp 8	57	63
PURCIL			
Michael	Tulara Twp 3	71	47
PURCILL			
Mike	Klamath Liberty	59	230
PURCO			
---	Tulara Twp 3	71	63
PURD			
Thimas	San Francisco San Francisco 3	67	43
Thomas	San Francisco San Francisco 3	67	43
PURDAY			
James	Amador Twp 1	55	468
PURDER			
William*	Yuba Marysville	72	882
PURDEY			
Jenny	Alameda Oakland	55	26
PURDEZ			
John	El Dorado Placerville	58	844
PURDY			
B K	Napa Napa	61	56
Ben	Yuba Rose Bar	72	812
Edwin	Santa Clara Gilroy	65	249
G	Sutter Vernon	70	842
Geo	Sonoma Petaluma	69	561
H D	Butte Chico	56	532
H H	Sierra Downieville	66	968
Henry	San Joaquin Douglass	64	916
J C	Tuolumne Columbia	71	346
J L*	Nevada Eureka	61	387
J W	Tuolumne Sonora	71	239
James	San Francisco San Francisco 4	68	1151
Joel	Sonoma Vallejo	69	621
John H	Alameda Oakland	55	74
Jos G	Trinity Taylor'S	70	1036
Jos Y	Trinity Taylor'S	70	1036
Morris	Siskiyou Callahan	69	15
Nathl	Plumas Quincy	62	979
Philip	Tuolumne Twp 4	71	134
S	San Francisco San Francisco 5	67	501
S F	Sierra Downieville	66	966
Solomon	Sierra Downieville	66	960
Thomas	Calaveras Twp 7	57	321
W	Sacramento Ward 4	63	611
Wm	Sierra Downieville	66	960
PUREE			
Frank	Mariposa Twp 3	60	559
Henry	Santa Clara Almaden	65	278
PUREEY			
Robert	Santa Clara Almaden	65	277
PUREHOR			
---*	San Francisco San Francisco 7	68	1413
PUREY			
John C	Santa Clara San Jose	65	391
PURG			
Hop*	San Francisco San Francisco 9	68	1093
PURGER			
Marry	San Francisco San Francisco 9	68	979
PURGHON			
Samuel	El Dorado Placerville	58	928
PURGHOSE			
Robert W	Yuba New York	72	738
PURIER			
James	Sierra Twp 7	66	884
Samuel	El Dorado Mud Springs	58	983
PURINTON			
C U	Amador Twp 6	55	441
PURKERD			
Enoch	Sierra La Porte	66	787
S D	Sierra La Porte	66	787
PURKEREL			
S D	Sierra La Porte	66	787
PURKISS			
John	Yuba Long Bar	72	752
PURKSS			
John*	Yuba Long Bar	72	752
PURLATE			
Frank*	El Dorado Placerville	58	905
PURLIDGE			
George	Tuolumne Twp 5	71	519
PURMEN			
Ed	Nevada Bridgeport	61	475
PURMEYER			
John	Sierra Twp 5	66	920
PURNELL			
J	San Francisco San Francisco 2	67	756
J W	Merced Twp 1	60	904
Jas R	San Francisco San Francisco 2	67	599
Jos R	San Francisco San Francisco 2	67	599
Joseph	Plumas Meadow Valley	62	899
PURNEY			
Tho*	Siskiyou Callahan	69	2
PURNILL			
J W*	Merced Twp 1	60	904
PUROCIA			
Eso*	Sierra Downieville	66	987
PURPLE			
Edwin R	San Diego Colorado	64	812
PURRE			
---	Sacramento Granite	63	249
Eopel	Sierra Downieville	66	1023
PURRIE			
James	Sierra St Louis	66	811
PURRIS			
Jas*	San Francisco San Francisco 9	68	1081
Jos	San Francisco San Francisco 9	68	1081
PURROCKE			
Eustanna	Calaveras Twp 7	57	12
PURSE			
James	Sierra Twp 5	66	936
PURSELL			
J	Alameda Oakland	55	63
Jefferson	San Joaquin Douglass	64	918
PURSER			
Jacob	San Francisco San Francisco 7	68	1433
PURSLEY			
Bridget	San Francisco San Francisco 9	68	1037
Jas	Napa Napa	61	56
PURSON			
Elizabeth*	Stanislaus Empire	70	726
William*	Placer Michigan	62	842
PURSOW			
Robt M	Del Norte Crescent	58	621
PURT			
J	Sierra Twp 7	66	886
PURTAH			
Frank*	El Dorado Placerville	58	905
PURTAK			
Frank*	El Dorado Placerville	58	905
PURTEN			
Mary	San Francisco San Francisco 2	67	745
PURTMAN			
A G	El Dorado Placerville	58	826
PURTYMAN			
A C*	Nevada Nevada	61	251
PURVINE			
Chas	Sonoma Petaluma	69	554
PURY			
---	Amador Twp 5	55	355
---	Amador Twp 5	55	363
PURYMAN			
Anthony	Nevada Eureka	61	359
PUS			
---	Stanislaus Branch	70	714
PUSAL			
James*	Calaveras Twp 8	57	89
PUSALL			
Sarah R	Alameda Brooklyn	55	85
PUSBERRY			
E H	Sacramento Alabama	63	412
PUSCH			
Marcus	El Dorado Georgetown	58	702
PUSELONE			
James	Amador Twp 2	55	325
PUSELONS			
James*	Amador Twp 2	55	325
PUSELOW			
James*	Amador Twp 2	55	325
PUSENTON			
Wm F*	Sierra Twp 5	66	946
PUSH			
Fred	Sierra Downieville	66	994

Name	County Locale	M653 Roll Page
PUSHAL		
Charles	Sierra Twp 7	66 882
PUSINTON		
Wm F*	Sierra Twp 5	66 946
PUSLEIRAN		
William*	Calaveras Twp 7	57 14
PUSLEIVAN		
William*	Calaveras Twp 7	57 14
PUSSET		
George*	Alameda Oakland	55 29
PUSSON		
John	Tuolumne Twp 1	71 254
PUSTLY		
A	Calaveras Twp 9	57 398
A*	Calaveras Twp 9	57 389
PUT		
---	El Dorado Georgetown	58 748
---	Sacramento Ward 1	63 61
---	San Francisco San Francisco 4	681 208
---*	San Francisco San Francisco 5	67 509
Sun	Placer Rattle Snake	62 629
PUTACHER		
Fredrick*	Nevada Bloomfield	61 511
PUTCH		
Thos	Santa Clara San Jose	65 347
PUTCHARD		
Elleanor	Yolo Slate Ra	72 699
Elleanor	Yuba Slate Ro	72 699
PUTE		
F M	Mariposa Twp 1	60 652
PUTER		
Stephen	San Francisco San Francisco 7	681 327
PUTH		
Joseph	Tuolumne Don Pedro	71 539
PUTHAM		
Rush*	Santa Cruz Soguel	66 600
PUTIMAN		
C E	Nevada Rough &	61 427
Lucretia	Nevada Rough &	61 428
PUTKA		
Patrick	Siskiyou Yreka	69 136
PUTMAN		
Benjamin	Santa Cruz Pajaro	66 532
Calvin	San Mateo Twp 2	65 125
Eijah*	Los Angeles Los Angeles	59 514
Esjah*	Los Angeles Los Angeles	59 514
J	Calaveras Twp 9	57 396
James	El Dorado Placerville	58 897
Joseph	San Joaquin Elliott	641 104
Oscar	Mariposa Twp 3	60 565
P S	Tuolumne Jamestown	71 445
R	Calaveras Twp 9	57 396
Samuel	El Dorado Casumnes	581 168
Thos	Sacramento Ward 1	63 32
V B	Amador Twp 4	55 236
PUTMANN		
V B	Amador Twp 1	55 484
PUTNAM		
A A	Nevada Bridgeport	61 503
A F	Amador Twp 2	55 274
A J	Nevada Bloomfield	61 507
A W	Solano Vacaville	69 358
Adelaide	San Francisco San Francisco 9	681 033
Anne	San Francisco San Francisco 10	228 67
Charles	Tulara Twp 3	71 59
Chas E	Calaveras Twp 6	57 125
E	San Francisco San Francisco 5	67 484
Geo	Sacramento Ward 1	63 138
J	Shasta Millvill	66 755
John H	Alameda Brooklyn	55 91
Porter	Tulara Visalia	71 28
Royal	Tulara Keyesville	71 59
Rufus	Nevada Rough &	61 415
S	El Dorado Georgetown	58 698
V C	Nevada Bridgeport	61 454
PUTNER		
David	Placer Iona Hills	62 889
PUTNERY		
Aurther	Calaveras Twp 7	57 2
PUTNEY		
A H	Calaveras Twp 9	57 390
A S	Sacramento Dry Crk	63 379
Asa E	Alameda Brooklyn	55 195
Aurther	Calaveras Twp 7	57 2
C M	Santa Clara San Jose	65 340
David	Sacramento Granite	63 221
Obediah	Sierra St Louis	66 810
Obedina	Sierra St Louis	66 810
PUTODO		
Paschal	Fresno Twp 1	59 75
PUTREWEST		
A B*	Mariposa Twp 3	60 577
PUTRO		
---	Tulara Twp 3	71 68
---	Tulara Keyesville	71 71

Name	County Locale	M653 Roll Page
PUTSMAN		
C E*	Nevada Rough &	61 417
PUTTER		
Charles A	Calaveras Twp 5	57 237
PUTTERMAN		
Sarah Jane	Trinity North Fo	701 024
PUTTING		
G F	Nevada Nevada	61 264
R	Nevada Eureka	61 378
PUTTOCK		
H	Shasta Millvill	66 752
PUTTRUG		
Nelson*	Placer Iona Hills	62 886
PUTTZEL		
Peter*	San Francisco San Francisco 7	681 429
PUTU		
Sam	Plumas Quincy	62 970
PUTZMAN		
Fred	Sacramento Ward 4	63 499
PUU		
---	Amador Twp 2	55 315
PUVEL		
Howel*	Nevada Bridgeport	61 470
PUVOLL		
Jesse	Sierra Port Win	66 797
PUW		
Ah	Calaveras Twp 7	57 15
PUY		
---	Placer Virginia	62 677
---*	Shasta Horsetown	66 701
PUYENE		
P S*	Stanislaus Oatvale	70 716
PUYH		
Henry E*	San Francisco San Francisco 3	67 86
PUYK		
Henry E*	San Francisco San Francisco 3	67 86
PUZZLE		
Willard	San Mateo Twp 2	65 121
PWETEN		
Mary*	San Francisco San Francisco 2	67 745
PWROA		
John*	Siskiyou Scott Va	69 49
PY		
---	El Dorado Greenwood	58 727
Wing	El Dorado Georgetown	58 700
Zong	Alameda Oakland	55 34
PYATT		
John	El Dorado Georgetown	58 685
Thos H	Sonoma Santa Rosa	69 387
PYBURN		
Sarah	Monterey Monterey	60 946
PYBURNE		
Edward	Tulara Twp 3	71 46
PYE		
Lee	Butte Bidwell	56 728
PYER		
M	San Francisco San Francisco 5	67 487
PYGALL		
George	Calaveras Twp 9	57 365
PYGAS		
George	Yuba Bear Rvr	721 008
PYLE		
Barnett W	Los Angeles Los Angeles	59 341
John H	Los Angeles Elmonte	59 257
Samuel	Solano Vacaville	69 354
William	Solano Vacaville	69 354
PYLES		
Nathl	Plumas Quincy	621 005
PYNG		
---	San Francisco San Francisco 11	144 67
PYRSEME		
Beltand	Siskiyou Callahan	69 9
PYSER		
S	San Francisco San Francisco 5	67 487
PYZER		
H	San Francisco San Francisco 9	68 968
Q		
---	Sierra Downieville	661 009
QA		
---	Mariposa Coulterville	60 684
QAFT		
C C*	Nevada Nevada	61 266
QAIR		
---*	Mariposa Twp 3	60 579
QAM		
---*	Nevada Nevada	61 308
QANDEP		
Francis*	Calaveras Twp 8	57 96
QANG		
---	El Dorado Salmon Hills	581 066
QAO		
---*	Calaveras Twp 5	57 242
QASTRO		
Ambrose	Fresno Twp 1	59 33
QAUT		
---	Sierra Downieville	66 996

Name	County Locale	M653 Roll Page
QAY		
---*	Nevada Nevada	61 309
Chi	Amador Twp 2	55 312
QECUTT		
A L	Klamath S Fork	59 204
QEE		
---	Yolo No E Twp	72 682
S W*	Mariposa Twp 3	60 577
QEIE?VRA		
Joseph	Mariposa Twp 3	60 548
QEINECHA		
Fred	San Joaquin O'Neal	641 005
QENG		
---	Mariposa Coulterville	60 690
QEP		
---	Placer Virginia	62 701
QEROY		
Lusgood*	San Francisco San Francisco 4	681 148
QHICK		
John	Humbolt Eel Rvr	59 150
QI		
Qi	Calaveras Twp 5	57 220
QIBURCIA		
Maria*	Los Angeles San Juan	59 465
QIE		
Ang	Sacramento Ward 3	63 491
QIEAGADO		
Jose*	Los Angeles Santa Ana	59 459
QIER		
---	Calaveras Twp 4	57 306
QIGNOGA		
Pascual	Los Angeles Los Angeles	59 343
QIH		
---*	El Dorado Georgetown	58 692
QIM SING		
---	Butte Kimshaw	56 587
QIMMEL		
Louis	Los Angeles Santa Ana	59 443
QINCE		
M*	Nevada Nevada	61 290
QINEN		
---	Yuba North Ea	72 685
QING		
Cathering	Calaveras Twp 8	57 84
Jebrues*	Sierra Cox'S Bar	66 952
QINO		
---	El Dorado Salmon Hills	581 059
QIROY		
Lusgood*	San Francisco San Francisco 4	681 148
QIURE		
Raphael*	Alameda Murray	55 219
QIVE		
---	Nevada Bridgeport	61 506
QLGANS		
Ignacio	Amador Twp 3	55 387
QMI		
---*	El Dorado Salmon Falls	581 059
QMOST		
Jno*	Sacramento Ward 1	63 149
QNANG		
---*	Calaveras Twp 7	57 41
QOG		
---	Nevada Washington	61 341
QOIE		
---	Sierra Downieville	661 006
QONAKE		
---	Fresno Twp 2	59 52
QONY		
---	Yuba Slate Ro	72 712
Gin	Calaveras Twp 5	57 202
QOO		
---	San Francisco San Francisco 4	681 191
QOU		
---	Calaveras Twp 10	57 275
---	El Dorado Mud Springs	58 985
---*	Nevada Nevada	61 308
QOW		
---	Yolo No E Twp	72 677
---	Yolo Slate Ra	72 710
---	Yuba Slate Ro	72 710
QOY		
---	Placer Forest H	62 771
---*	Nevada Nevada	61 308
---*	Nevada Nevada	61 309
---*	Nevada Nevada	61 310
QOZ		
---*	Nevada Nevada	61 309
QSICI		
R	Calaveras Twp 9	57 413
QU		
---	Calaveras Twp 5	57 209
---	Mariposa Twp 1	60 661
---	Nevada Bridgeport	61 462
---	San Francisco San Francisco 4	681 194
---	Sierra Downieville	661 015
Cum	San Francisco San Francisco 2	67 689

Name	County Locale	M653 RollPage
QU		
You	Nevada Bridgeport	61 491
QUA HANG		
---	Sacramento Ward 1	63 71
QUA LA		
---	Sacramento Ward 1	63 65
QUA		
---	Amador Twp 4	55 256
---	Butte Ophir	56 787
---	Butte Ophir	56 816
---	Calaveras Twp 5	57 241
---	Calaveras Twp 5	57 257
---	Calaveras Twp 10	57 261
---	Calaveras Twp 10	57 267
---	Calaveras Twp 10	57 269
---	Calaveras Twp 10	57 275
---	Calaveras Twp 10	57 285
---	Calaveras Twp 10	57 295
---	Calaveras Twp 10	57 297
---	Calaveras Twp 4	57 300
---	El Dorado Diamond	58 815
---	Mariposa Twp 3	60 550
---	Mariposa Twp 3	60 551
---	Mariposa Twp 3	60 553
---	Mariposa Twp 3	60 560
---	Mariposa Twp 3	60 561
---	Mariposa Twp 3	60 562
---	Mariposa Twp 3	60 564
---	Mariposa Twp 3	60 569
---	Mariposa Twp 3	60 571
---	Mariposa Twp 3	60 572
---	Mariposa Twp 3	60 576
---	Mariposa Twp 1	60 643
---	Mariposa Twp 1	60 653
---	Mariposa Twp 1	60 658
---	Mariposa Twp 1	60 659
---	Mariposa Twp 1	60 660
---	Mariposa Twp 1	60 661
---	Mariposa Twp 1	60 665
---	Mariposa Coulterville	60 683
---	Mariposa Coulterville	60 684
---	Mariposa Coulterville	60 689
---	Mariposa Coulterville	60 690
---	Mariposa Coulterville	60 697
---	Placer Horseshoe	62 650
---	Placer Iona Hills	62 881
---	Sierra Downieville	661027
---	Sierra Downieville	66 973
---	Siskiyou Yreka	69 194
---	Siskiyou Scott Va	69 32
---	Stanislaus Buena Village	70 724
---	Yuba Long Bar	72 761
---*	Butte Ophir	56 811
---*	Butte Ophir	56 818
---*	Mariposa Twp 3	60 576
---*	Mariposa Twp 3	60 607
---*	Mariposa Coulterville	60 684
Camella	Calaveras Twp 9	57 368
Camilla	Calaveras Twp 9	57 368
Fa	Butte Ophir	56 819
Hang	Sacramento Ward 1	63 71
La	Sacramento Ward 1	63 65
Rum*	Placer Auburn	62 576
Rurr*	Placer Auburn	62 576
QUABIS		
Merialdo	Calaveras Twp 7	57 26
QUACHINBURCH		
Catherine	Santa Clara San Jose	65 377
QUACK TI		
---	Sacramento Ward 1	63 70
QUACK		
Ti	Sacramento Ward 1	63 70
QUACKINBURK		
Hiram	Humbolt Mattole	59 124
QUACY		
Dauy	Yuba Marysville	72 895
QUAD		
Charly	Shasta Shasta	66 669
Henry	Calaveras Twp 8	57 108
San Domingo	San Francisco 2	67 642
	San Francisco	
QUADE		
Andrew	El Dorado Coloma	581121
QUAE		
---	Fresno Twp 3	59 32
---*	Yuba Marysville	72 893
QUAEL		
James	Amador Twp 1	55 487
QUAEY		
---	Fresno Twp 3	59 31
QUAG		
---	El Dorado Salmon Falls	581064
---	Nevada Bridgeport	61 457
QUAGADO		
Jose*	Los Angeles Santa Ana	59 459
QUAH		
---	Sacramento Ward 1	63 60

Name	County Locale	M653 RollPage
QUAH		
---	Sacramento Ward 1	63 65
QUAHALU		
James*	El Dorado Georgetown	58 760
QUAI		
---*	Yuba Marysville	72 893
QUAID		
William	Siskiyou Callahan	69 8
QUAIG		
H	Calaveras Twp 9	57 395
QUAIL		
Frank	San Mateo Twp 1	65 50
H	San Francisco San Francisco 3	67 61
P	San Francisco San Francisco 5	67 537
S F	Calaveras Twp 9	57 357
S W	Calaveras Twp 9	57 357
William	Tuolumne Twp 1	71 248
QUAILS		
Fanshus	San Luis Obispo	65 8
	San Luis Obispo	
QUAIN		
A H	Tuolumne Springfield	71 368
Mary M	Calaveras Twp 9	57 405
QUAIT		
B C*	Siskiyou Cottonwoood	69 106
QUAJADO		
Jose*	Los Angeles Santa Ana	59 459
QUAK		
Cew	Sierra Cox'S Bar	66 951
QUAKNER		
Peter	San Francisco San Francisco 4	681161
QUAKNN		
Peter*	San Francisco San Francisco 4	681161
QUALEY		
John F	Yuba Marysville	72 880
QUALL		
P	San Francisco San Francisco 5	67 528
QUALLA		
Andrez	San Bernardino Santa Ba	64 214
QUALLES		
---	Tulara Twp 1	71 121
QUALLS		
James	Los Angeles Tejon	59 526
QUAM		
---	El Dorado Salmon Falls	581064
---	Sierra Downieville	66 982
---*	Calaveras Twp 8	57 93
Lip	Calaveras Twp 4	57 313
Liss	Calaveras Twp 4	57 313
QUAN		
---	Amador Twp 2	55 285
---	Amador Twp 6	55 427
---	Amador Twp 6	55 434
---	Amador Twp 1	55 502
---	Amador Twp 1	55 507
---	Calaveras Twp 6	57 166
---	Calaveras Twp 5	57 254
---	Calaveras Twp 5	57 256
---	Calaveras Twp 10	57 286
---	Calaveras Twp 10	57 295
---	Calaveras Twp 4	57 315
---	Calaveras Twp 4	57 339
---	Del Norte Crescent	58 640
---	El Dorado White Oaks	581023
---	El Dorado Georgetown	58 678
---	El Dorado Diamond	58 787
---	El Dorado Placerville	58 832
---	El Dorado Placerville	58 841
---	El Dorado Mud Springs	58 957
---	El Dorado Mud Springs	58 976
---	Fresno Twp 3	59 31
---	Mariposa Twp 3	60 564
---	Mariposa Twp 3	60 569
---	Mariposa Twp 1	60 662
---	Nevada Rough &	61 434
---	Nevada Rough &	61 437
---	Nevada Rough &	61 459
---	Nevada Bridgeport	61 506
---	Nevada Bloomfield	61 528
---	Placer Iona Hills	62 891
---	Shasta French G	66 720
---	Sierra St Louis	66 861
---	Sierra Twp 5	66 947
---	Trinity Mouth Ca	701018
---	Yuba Bear Rvr	721000
---	Yuba Fosters	72 830
---	Yuba Fosters	72 841
---*	Amador Twp 6	55 434
---*	Yuba Foster B	72 830
---*	Yuba Fosters	72 841
Ah	Yuba Bear Rvr	721000
Kise	El Dorado Placerville	58 821
Ring	Yuba Long Bar	72 764
Seing	Shasta Horsetown	66 701
Yemy	Shasta Shasta	66 670
Yomg*	Shasta Shasta	66 670

Name	County Locale	M653 RollPage
QUAN		
Young*	Shasta Shasta	66 670
QUANCE		
Jarvis*	Tulara Visalia	71 101
QUANCHI		
D	Sacramento Ward 1	63 38
Jno	Sacramento Ward 1	63 25
QUANG		
---	Amador Twp 2	55 285
---	Amador Twp 2	55 286
---	Amador Twp 2	55 320
---	Amador Twp 1	55 507
---	Calaveras Twp 8	57 71
---	Calaveras Twp 8	57 83
---	Calaveras Twp 8	57 94
---	Del Norte Crescent	58 631
---	El Dorado Diamond	58 785
---	El Dorado Diamond	58 787
---	El Dorado Diamond	58 797
---	El Dorado Placerville	58 832
---	Mariposa Twp 3	60 579
---	Mariposa Twp 1	60 626
---	Mariposa Twp 1	60 655
---	Mariposa Twp 1	60 658
---	Mariposa Twp 1	60 661
---	Mariposa Twp 1	60 665
---	Nevada Bridgeport	61 457
---	Nevada Bridgeport	61 459
---	Sacramento Ward 3	63 491
---	Sacramento Ward 3	63 492
---	Shasta Horsetown	66 701
---	Shasta Horsetown	66 705
---	Shasta French G	66 712
---	Sierra Pine Grove	66 827
---	Stanislaus Branch	70 713
---	Yolo Slate Ra	72 713
---	Yolo Slate Ra	72 715
Ah	Calaveras Twp 7	57 36
An	Del Norte Crescent	58 631
Huey	Yuba Marysville	72 895
Man	Shasta Horsetown	66 702
QUANKEE		
---	Shasta Shasta	66 671
QUANLAN		
Maggie	San Francisco San Francisco 2	67 609
QUANNEN		
Jesus	Calaveras Twp 10	57 259
QUANT		
F I	Solano Vallejo	69 249
F J	Solano Vallejo	69 249
Susan	Napa Napa	61 87
QUANTE		
---	San Bernardino S Timate	64 749
QUANTIAREN		
Ignacio*	Calaveras Twp 5	57 208
QUANTIARM		
Ignacio*	Calaveras Twp 5	57 208
QUANTRAIS		
Doce	Calaveras Twp 7	57 28
QUANTRARIM		
Ignacio*	Calaveras Twp 5	57 208
QUANTRARIN		
Ignacio*	Calaveras Twp 5	57 208
QUANTS		
---*	San Bernardino S Timate	64 751
QUANY		
---	Calaveras Twp 4	57 320
---	Shasta Horsetown	66 705
Man	Shasta Horsetown	66 702
QUAONY		
---	Calaveras Twp 4	57 320
QUAORIS		
Elovsin	Calaveras Twp 5	57 204
Elvusin	Calaveras Twp 5	57 204
QUAR		
---	Amador Twp 6	55 428
---	Amador Twp 1	55 497
---	Mariposa Twp 3	60 564
---	Mariposa Twp 3	60 569
---	Mariposa Twp 6	60 626
---	Mariposa Twp 1	60 657
---	Sierra Cox'S Bar	66 951
QUARCIA		
C	Amador Twp 6	55 437
QUARDA		
Ramon	San Luis Obispo San Luis Obispo	65 34
QUAREL		
Alexander	Calaveras Twp 6	57 153
QUARES		
Banjamin	Santa Barbara	64 154
	San Bernardino	
QUAREZ		
Trinidad	Santa Clara San Jose	65 360
QUARIA		
Nicholas	Amador Twp 4	55 248
QUARIECE		
C*	Amador Twp 6	55 437

Name	County Locale	M653 Roll	Page
QUARKEN			
---	Placer Rattle Snake	62	629
QUARLES			
Archy	San Joaquin Elkhorn	64	976
Eliza	San Francisco San Francisco 8	681	307
William*	San Francisco San Francisco 8	681	248
QUARNCE			
C*	Amador Twp 6	55	437
QUARNEY			
J	Solano Benecia	69	297
QUARNOW			
Jose	Los Angeles Azuza	59	274
QUAROLO			
Joseph	Amador Twp 1	55	481
QUAROVA			
John	Amador Twp 1	55	466
QUARTA			
---	San Bernardino S Timate	64	703
QUARTE			
---	San Bernardino S Timate	64	691
---	San Bernardino S Timate	64	695
---	San Bernardino S Timate	64	697
---	San Bernardino S Timate	64	701
---	San Bernardino S Timate	64	705
QUARTEL			
R	Tuolumne Twp 3	71	432
QUARTERMAN			
William	San Mateo Twp 3	65	97
QUARTO			
---	San Bernardino S Timate	64	695
QUARTRO			
Vaneto	Marin Saucileto	60	751
QUARY			
---	Amador Twp 2	55	320
QUAST			
Chas	San Francisco San Francisco 5	67	546
QUASTE			
Charles	Yuba Foster B	72	834
QUASTI			
Charles*	Yuba Fosters	72	834
QUATA			
Maria	San Diego Agua Caliente	64	858
QUATE			
---	Mariposa Twp 1	60	652
---	Yolo No E Twp	72	683
---	Yuba Slate Ro	72	683
QUATIC			
---	Mariposa Twp 1	60	652
QUATIS			
Joseph	Calaveras Twp 8	57	108
QUATIUS			
Genaro*	Placer Auburn	62	578
QUAVER			
Manuel	Marin Cortemad	60	755
QUAVO			
Donecia	Amador Twp 1	55	495
QUAW			
---	El Dorado Salmon Hills	581	064
---	El Dorado Salmon Falls	581	066
---	Trinity Weaverville	701	074
QUAY			
---	Del Norte Crescent	58	630
---	Del Norte Happy Ca	58	668
---	El Dorado Salmon Falls	581	041
---	El Dorado Salmon Falls	581	058
---	El Dorado Eldorado	58	939
---	Mariposa Twp 3	60	581
---	Mariposa Twp 1	60	665
---	Mariposa Coulterville	60	682
---	Nevada Rough &	61	431
---	Nevada Bridgeport	61	457
---	Nevada Bridgeport	61	462
---	Nevada Bloomfield	61	528
---	Trinity Taylor'S	701	033
---	Trinity Trinidad Rvr	701	044
---	Trinity Trinindad Rvr	701	045
---	Yuba Long Bar	72	761
---*	Nevada Rough &	61	431
An	Del Norte Crescent	58	630
An	Del Norte Crescent	58	631
Orlando	Calaveras Twp 9	57	402
Wm	Sacramento Ward 1	63	54
QUAYAAN			
---	Calaveras Twp 5	57	253
QUAYL			
Wm	Yolo Slate Ra	72	687
Wm	Yuba North Ea	72	687
QUAYLE			
J	Tuolumne Twp 4	71	164
QUDING			
---	Calaveras Twp 8	57	106
QUDLER			
Michael*	Sierra Downieville	66	967
QUDSON			
G*	Calaveras Twp 9	57	413
QUDU			
---*	Calaveras Twp 5	57	193

Name	County Locale	M653 Roll	Page
QUDY			
---*	Nevada Rough &	61	431
QUE			
---	Alameda Oakland	55	59
---	Butte Hamilton	56	530
---	Butte Oregon	56	644
---	Butte Cascade	56	699
---	Calaveras Twp 6	57	146
---	El Dorado Mud Springs	58	985
---	El Dorado Mud Springs	58	986
---	El Dorado Mud Springs	58	988
---	Mariposa Twp 3	60	552
---	Mariposa Twp 3	60	581
---	Nevada Bridgeport	61	485
---	Nevada Bridgeport	61	506
---	Placer Auburn	62	582
---	Sacramento Cosummes	63	392
---	Sierra Downieville	661	004
---	Sierra Downieville	661	006
---	Sierra Downieville	661	015
---	Sierra Downieville	661	027
---	Sierra La Porte	66	780
---	Sierra Twp 5	66	927
---	Sierra Twp 5	66	931
---	Sierra Downieville	66	973
---	Sierra Downieville	66	974
---	Sierra Downieville	66	981
---	Sierra Downieville	66	982
---	Sierra Downieville	66	983
---	Sierra Downieville	66	986
---	Sierra Downieville	66	993
---	Tuolumne Don Pedro	71	163
---	Tuolumne Jamestown	71	434
---	Tuolumne Jamestown	71	436
---	Tuolumne Sonora	71	477
---	Tuolumne Twp 6	71	539
---	Yolo Slate Ra	72	711
---	Yolo Slate Ra	72	712
---	Yuba Bear Rvr	721	000
---	Yuba Slate Ro	72	711
---	Yuba Slate Ro	72	712
---*	Nevada Bridgeport	61	485
---*	Tuolumne Big Oak	71	178
Ah	Butte Cascade	56	699
Ah	Tuolumne Twp 4	71	163
Ah	Tuolumne Twp 4	71	178
Ah	Tuolumne Twp 4	71	182
Ah	Yuba Bear Rvr	721	000
Cho	El Dorado Coloma	581	079
George	Placer Rattle Snake	62	637
QUEAR			
Lewis	Humbolt Eureka	59	169
QUEBEDO			
Diego	Santa Clara Almaden	65	269
QUEE			
---	Sierra St Louis	66	812
QUEEN			
---	Del Norte Klamath	58	654
---	Fresno Twp 1	59	25
---	Mariposa Coulterville	60	692
G	El Dorado Georgetown	58	690
James	Sacramento Ward 1	63	17
Sarah	San Francisco San Francisco 2	67	692
QUEENEY			
W	San Francisco San Francisco 5	67	529
QUEIN			
---*	San Francisco San Francisco 5	67	506
QUEL			
Yang	Mariposa Coulterville	60	682
QUELCH			
J T	Sacramento Franklin	63	307
QUELLIEN			
Wm	Mariposa Twp 1	60	635
QUELPORT			
W	El Dorado Coloma	581	116
QUELRO			
G	Tuolumne Twp 4	71	157
QUEN			
---	El Dorado Georgetown	58	747
---	Sierra Downieville	66	980
---	Yolo Slate Ra	72	715
---	Yuba Slate Ro	72	715
---	Yuba Fosters	72	843
Chee	Yuba Long Bar	72	763
Hubbard	Calaveras Twp 5	57	141
Michael*	Sierra Downieville	661	031
QUENG			
---	Alameda Oakland	55	38
---	Yuba Long Bar	72	765
---*	Placer Illinois	62	738
QUENIN			
Thresa	San Francisco San Francisco 4	681	150
QUENJ			
Henry*	Santa Clara Fremont	65	434
QUENTE			
F	Tuolumne Twp 2	71	306

Name	County Locale	M653 Roll	Page
QUENTERA			
Ambrosio	San Diego S Luis R	64	778
QUENTI			
Joseph M*	Calaveras Twp 4	57	341
QUERALLO			
Joseph	Tuolumne Twp 1	71	270
QUEREDA			
Rosano	Los Angeles Los Angeles	59	395
QUERILLACGU			
John	San Francisco San Francisco 7	681	332
QUERO			
---	Yolo No E Twp	72	684
QUEROS			
Doleres	Alameda Murray	55	219
QUERTEI			
Hosea	Mariposa Twp 3	60	545
QUERY			
A	Nevada Eureka	61	354
A J	Nevada Eureka	61	354
QUESERBURY			
Moses	Sonoma Armally	69	482
QUESPERANCE			
Frank*	Stanislaus Branch	70	704
QUEST			
Edmond	Sierra Twp 5	66	938
Edmund	Sierra Twp 5	66	938
QUESTE			
Jos	Amador Twp 3	55	408
Jose	Alameda Brooklyn	55	93
QUESTI			
Jos	Amador Twp 3	55	380
QUESTO			
John	Amador Twp 5	55	361
Jos	Amador Twp 3	55	408
QUESTON			
Chas O	Sierra Gibsonville	66	857
QUET LA			
---	Sacramento Ward 3	63	491
QUEVAS			
Josefa	Monterey Alisal	601	044
QUEVEDA			
Rosario	Los Angeles Los Angeles	59	395
QUEW			
---	El Dorado Salmon Falls	581	062
---	Yuba Slate Ro	72	684
---	Yuba Fosters	72	830
---	Yuba Fosters	72	843
---*	Yuba Foster B	72	830
QUEXOTIS			
Antone*	San Francisco San Francisco 7	681	440
QUEY			
---	El Dorado Salmon Falls	581	045
---	Sierra Twp 7	66	881
QUG			
---	El Dorado Salmon Hills	581	059
---	El Dorado Diamond	58	803
QUGE			
---	El Dorado Coloma	581	111
QUI YOUNG			
---	Siskiyou Scott Ri	69	67
QUI			
---	Amador Twp 2	55	290
---	Amador Twp 5	55	335
---	Amador Twp 5	55	336
---	Amador Twp 5	55	351
---	Amador Twp 5	55	353
---	Amador Twp 7	55	355
---	Amador Twp 7	55	414
---	Amador Twp 6	55	428
---	Amador Twp 6	55	430
---	Amador Twp 6	55	449
---	Amador Twp 6	55	450
---	Amador Twp 1	55	458
---	Amador Twp 1	55	492
---	Amador Twp 1	55	501
---	Butte Ophir	56	807
---	Calaveras Twp 5	57	146
---	Calaveras Twp 6	57	165
---	Calaveras Twp 5	57	176
---	Calaveras Twp 5	57	208
---	Calaveras Twp 5	57	215
---	Calaveras Twp 5	57	224
---	Calaveras Twp 5	57	236
---	Calaveras Twp 5	57	248
---	Calaveras Twp 5	57	250
---	Calaveras Twp 5	57	254
---	Calaveras Twp 5	57	257
---	Calaveras Twp 10	57	259
---	Calaveras Twp 10	57	260
---	Calaveras Twp 10	57	267
---	Calaveras Twp 10	57	274
---	Calaveras Twp 10	57	286
---	Calaveras Twp 10	57	287
---	Calaveras Twp 10	57	296
---	Calaveras Twp 4	57	299
---	Calaveras Twp 4	57	300

California 1860 Census Index

Name	County Locale	M653 Roll	Page
QUI			
---	Calaveras Twp 4	57	303
---	Calaveras Twp 4	57	310
---	Calaveras Twp 4	57	333
---	Calaveras Twp 4	57	334
---	Calaveras Twp 9	57	363
---	Calaveras Twp 8	57	84
---	Mariposa Twp 3	60	562
---	Mariposa Twp 3	60	571
---	Mariposa Twp 3	60	579
---	Mariposa Twp 3	60	589
---	Mariposa Coulterville	60	681
---	Mariposa Coulterville	60	682
---	Monterey Alisal	60	1035
---	Nevada Rough &	61	431
---	Placer Rattle Snake	62	601
---	San Francisco San Francisco 9	68	1094
---	San Francisco San Francisco 4	68	1173
---	San Francisco San Francisco 4	68	1174
---	San Francisco San Francisco 11	67	144
---	San Francisco San Francisco 10	67	356
---	Sierra Downieville	66	1015
---	Sierra Downieville	66	1025
---	Siskiyou Yreka	69	195
---	Stanislaus Branch	70	714
---	Stanislaus Emory	70	744
---	Tuolumne Columbia	71	350
---	Tuolumne Twp 3	71	436
---	Yuba Marysville	72	895
---	Yuba Marysville	72	896
---	Yuba Marysville	72	921
---*	Calaveras Twp 6	57	173
---*	El Dorado Salmon Falls	58	1058
---*	Yuba Marysville	72	916
Ah	Calaveras Twp 7	57	34
Ah	Tuolumne Twp 2	71	350
Buck	Calaveras Twp 4	57	307
Chee	San Francisco San Francisco 4	68	1186
Chu	San Francisco San Francisco 4	68	1186
E	San Francisco San Francisco 2	67	689
Eng	Yuba Long Bar	72	766
Eny	Yuba Long Bar	72	766
Far	Calaveras Twp 6	57	176
Far	Calaveras Twp 5	57	193
Ho	Amador Twp 5	55	335
Hong	El Dorado Placerville	58	832
Kee	Calaveras Twp 5	57	254
Kong	Yuba Marysville	72	921
L	Mariposa Twp 3	60	552
Ni	Calaveras Twp 9	57	406
See*	Mariposa Twp 3	60	578
Tar	Calaveras Twp 4	57	334
Tur	Calaveras Twp 4	57	334
Yang	Mariposa Coulterville	60	682
Young	Siskiyou Scott Ri	69	67
QUIADA			
Lauridus	San Francisco San Francisco 3	67	84
Sanridus*	San Francisco San Francisco 3	67	84
QUIAE			
---	Fresno Twp 1	59	30
QUIAL			
Frederick	Yuba Marysville	72	854
QUIAN			
---	Nevada Rough &	61	434
QUIAQUE			
Charles	Santa Clara Almaden	65	270
QUIATO			
---	Mendocino Calpella	60	824
QUIBIDO			
Juan	Santa Clara Almaden	65	270
QUIBLY			
Peter	Santa Clara San Jose	65	337
QUICE			
M	Nevada Nevada	61	290
QUICK			
---	El Dorado Salmon Falls	58	1064
E	Placer Dutch Fl	62	727
E A	Nevada Red Dog	61	550
E H	Mariposa Twp 3	60	604
G A	Sierra Poker Flats	66	842
J	Nevada Grass Valley	61	170
J S	Sacramento Ward 4	63	612
J W	Trinity Lewiston	70	963
James	Amador Twp 4	55	332
James	Placer Michigan	62	856
James*	Sierra Twp 5	66	926
John	Sierra Gibsonville	66	852
L L	Siskiyou Scott Va	69	45
Luther L	San Francisco San Francisco 9	68	988
M W	Mariposa Twp 3	60	593
Paul	Nevada Bridgeport	61	449
Thomas	El Dorado Cold Spring	58	1099
Wm	Solano Suisan	69	214
QUICK			
Wm G	San Francisco San Francisco 10	67	191
QUICKLY			
James	Alameda Brooklyn	55	127
QUIDIN			
Wm	Solano Vallejo	69	276
QUIE			
---	Calaveras Twp 4	57	334
---	El Dorado White Oaks	58	1011
---	El Dorado Salmon Falls	58	1058
---	El Dorado Coloma	58	1078
---	El Dorado Placerville	58	832
---	El Dorado Mud Springs	58	976
---	El Dorado Mud Springs	58	985
---	El Dorado Mud Springs	58	992
---	Placer Rattle Snake	62	638
Sin	Klamath Liberty	59	235
QUIETO			
---	Fresno Twp 2	59	93
QUIFADA			
Juan	Monterey San Juan	60	985
QUIG			
Jebrnes*	Sierra Cox'S Bar	66	952
Jebrues*	Sierra Cox'S Bar	66	952
Saml B	San Francisco San Francisco 5	67	477
QUIGBY			
T	Calaveras Twp 9	57	412
QUIGG			
Charles	Solano Benecia	69	311
Michael	Solano Benecia	69	304
QUIGGLEY			
M	Yolo Cottonwoood	72	649
QUIGLEY			
Andrew J	Sierra La Porte	66	767
Ann	San Francisco San Francisco 9	68	977
B	Sonoma Petaluma	69	612
B C	Sacramento Granite	63	227
Bemirs H	Tulara Visalia	71	88
C C	Tuolumne Twp 2	71	389
Cath	Sacramento Ward 1	63	143
Catharine	San Francisco San Francisco 9	68	978
Chas	Amador Twp 5	55	404
Chas	Trinity Point Ba	70	976
Danl	San Francisco San Francisco 10	67	224
David	San Joaquin Tulare	64	869
E H	Sonoma Armally	69	509
Edmond	Sierra La Porte	66	765
Edward	Sierra La Porte	66	765
Edward	Tuolumne Twp 2	71	387
Edward	Tuolumne Twp 3	71	425
Ellen	San Francisco San Francisco 10	67	310
Ellis	San Francisco San Francisco 1	68	858
H	Sacramento Ward 1	63	149
Jack	Santa Clara Alviso	65	406
James	Tuolumne Twp 4	71	138
John	Siskiyou Scott Va	69	20
Marcel	San Francisco San Francisco 8	68	1265
Margaret	Mariposa Twp 3	60	584
Margt	San Francisco San Francisco 1	68	902
May	Sierra La Porte	66	768
Michael	Alameda Oakland	55	23
Michael	Alameda Oakland	55	9
Michael	San Francisco San Francisco 12	67	374
Michael	Tuolumne Twp 3	71	430
P	Calaveras Twp 9	57	411
P	Tuolumne Garrote	71	174
Pat	Amador Twp 5	55	343
Pat	Sonoma Petaluma	69	594
Patrick	San Francisco San Francisco 8	68	1243
Patrick	Yuba Rose Bar	72	800
R V	Sutter Yuba	70	771
Rumus H	Tulara Twp 1	71	88
Sarah	Nevada Rough &	61	427
Thomas	Sierra Eureka	66	1043
Wm	Tuolumne Shawsfla	71	401
QUIGLY			
John	San Francisco San Francisco 2	67	580
John	Sierra Twp 7	66	893
John	Sierra Twp 7	66	894
John	Sierra Downieville	66	997
Margaret	Mariposa Twp 3	60	584
Thomas	Sierra Twp 7	66	909
QUIGNANDEN			
L	Siskiyou Scott Ri	69	72
QUIGUANDEN			
L*	Siskiyou Scott Ri	69	72
QUIJADA			
Yelipe	San Bernardino Santa Barbara	64	176
QUIJANA			
Maria Y	Los Angeles Los Angeles	59	313
QUILDER			
Laurence	Mariposa Twp 3	60	559
QUILES			
---	Los Angeles Tejon	59	541
QUILIN			
Miles	San Francisco San Francisco 2	67	616
QUILL			
---	Sierra Downieville	66	982
James	Humbolt Pacific	59	133
John	Tuolumne Columbia	71	305
John	Yolo Washington	72	605
T	Tuolumne Twp 4	71	169
QUILLAN			
B M	San Francisco San Francisco 5	67	501
QUILLER			
Hal	El Dorado Georgetown	58	689
QUILLIN			
C	Sutter Sutter	70	811
QUILLMAN			
R M	Tehama Red Bluff	70	899
QUILMA			
Hosea	Alameda Brooklyn	55	199
QUILON			
---	Shasta Shasta	66	670
QUILOW			
---	Shasta Shasta	66	670
QUILT			
Charles	Placer Michigan	62	854
QUIM			
---	Nevada Bloomfield	61	528
---*	Placer Iona Hills	62	862
B B	Siskiyou Klamath	69	90
QUIMAN			
P W	Mendocino Big Rvr	60	841
QUIMBY			
Augustus	Tuolumne Shawsfla	71	418
E W	San Francisco San Francisco 9	68	944
QUIMES			
Alexander*	Calaveras Twp 6	57	177
Theodore	San Luis Obispo San Luis Obispo	65	16
QUIMLAN			
Catharine	Trinity Weaverville	70	1053
P B	San Francisco San Francisco 5	67	502
QUIMLEY			
Augustey	Tuolumne Twp 2	71	418
C S*	Butte Hamilton	56	522
QUIMLY			
Aaron	San Bernardino Santa Barbara	64	181
QUIMMBY			
E V	San Francisco San Francisco 9	68	944
QUIMSLY			
Samuel	Mariposa Coulterville	60	686
QUIMTON			
John B	San Francisco San Francisco 4	68	1121
QUIN O K			
---*	Butte Kimshaw	56	587
QUIN			
---	Alameda Oakland	55	24
---	Amador Twp 2	55	291
---	Amador Twp 5	55	347
---	Amador Twp 5	55	360
---	Amador Twp 5	55	365
---	Amador Twp 7	55	414
---	Butte Ophir	56	814
---	Calaveras Twp 5	57	181
---	Calaveras Twp 5	57	233
---	Calaveras Twp 10	57	296
---	Calaveras Twp 4	59	303
---	Calaveras Twp 4	57	306
---	Calaveras Twp 4	57	310
---	Calaveras Twp 4	57	320
---	Calaveras Twp 4	57	323
---	Del Norte Crescent	58	630
---	Del Norte Crescent	58	633
---	El Dorado White Oaks	58	1023
---	El Dorado Diamond	58	816
---	El Dorado Mud Springs	58	991
---	Mariposa Twp 3	60	559
---	Nevada Rough &	61	399
---	Nevada Bridgeport	61	458
---	Nevada Bridgeport	61	464
---	Placer Auburn	62	574
---	Placer Virginia	62	670
---	Placer Illinois	62	746
---	Placer Illinois	62	752
---	Placer Iona Hills	62	861
---	San Francisco San Francisco 4	68	1198
---	Sierra Morristown	66	1056
---	Sierra Downieville	66	982
---	Sierra Downieville	66	985
---	Sierra Downieville	66	994
---	Sierra Downieville	66	999
---	Siskiyou Yreka	69	195
---	Sonoma Sonoma	69	639
---	Yuba Fosters	72	826
---	Yuba Marysville	72	928
---*	Butte Chico	56	545

California 1860 Census Index

Name	County Locale	M653 Roll	Page
QUIN			
---*	Nevada Nevada	61	303
A	Sonoma Sonoma	69	639
Alex	Monterey San Juan	60	982
Alexr	Monterey San Juan	60	982
Andrew	Sacramento Ward 1	63	20
Ann	El Dorado Mud Springs	58	976
Bridget	Alameda Brooklyn	55	87
Bridget	Sacramento Ward 3	63	451
Buck	Calaveras Twp 4	57	307
Cath*	Sacramento Ward 1	63	91
D H	Sacramento Ward 1	63	90
Elizabeth	Alameda Oakland	55	15
Fee	San Francisco San Francisco 4	681	203
Fred*	Santa Clara Alviso	65	412
Fu*	San Francisco San Francisco 4	681	203
Hannah	Sacramento Ward 1	63	155
J*	Butte Chico	56	545
James	El Dorado Mud Springs	58	976
Jno	Sacramento Ward 3	63	449
John	Butte Ophir	56	796
John	El Dorado Salmon Falls	581	049
John	Nevada Rough &	61	430
John	Nevada Rough &	61	432
John	Sacramento Granite	63	269
John E	Sacramento Ward 3	63	461
John*	Nevada Rough &	61	432
Jose*	Butte Chico	56	545
Lee	Amador Twp 2	55	289
Nich	Sacramento Ward 4	63	525
Nn	Yuba Marysville	72	895
Ock	Butte Kimshaw	56	587
Pat	Placer Virginia	62	680
Patrick	Marin Cortemad	60	754
Patrick	Sacramento Ward 1	63	33
Patrick	San Francisco San Francisco 11		90
		67	
Peter	Tehama Red Bluff	70	910
Rich	Sacramento Ward 4	63	504
Sam	Sacramento Ward 1	63	60
Sing	Butte Kimshaw	56	587
Thomas	San Francisco San Francisco 3	67	24
Thos	Sacramento Granite	63	267
Tin	Amador Twp 2	55	292
Wm	Merced Monterey	60	937
Wm	Monterey Monterey	60	937
QUINA			
Alexander	Contra Costa Twp 3	57	590
QUINAN			
Christian*	Contra Costa Twp 3	57	595
Pascal A	San Francisco San Francisco 1	68	931
QUINANES			
Margaret	Santa Clara Almaden	65	272
QUINBY			
David	Placer Michigan	62	821
QUINCE			
Jarvis*	Tulara Twp 1	71	101
QUINCEY			
John	Monterey San Juan	601	007
QUINCHARD			
Julias	San Francisco San Francisco 10		266
		67	
Julius	San Francisco San Francisco 10		266
		67	
QUINCY			
A*	Sutter Yuba	70	763
Leander	Siskiyou Scott Va	69	50
QUINDOJA			
Manuel	San Luis Obispo San Luis Obispo	65	38
QUINE			
---	Fresno Twp 3	59	31
Thos M	Trinity Lewiston	70	957
Thos W	Trinity Lewiston	70	957
W A	Trinity Lewiston	70	957
QUINEY			
Leander	Siskiyou Scott Va	69	50
QUING WO			
---	Solano Suisan	69	221
QUING			
---	Calaveras Twp 10	57	285
---	El Dorado Eldorado	58	941
---	El Dorado Mud Springs	58	955
---	Nevada Bridgeport	61	439
---	Placer Forest H	62	791
---	Plumas Meadow Valley	62	910
---	Sierra Downieville	66	981
---	Yolo Slate Ra	72	708
---	Yolo Slate Ra	72	716
---	Yolo Slate Ra	72	718
---	Yuba North Ea	72	685
---	Yuba Slate Ro	72	708
---	Yuba Slate Ro	72	713
---	Yuba Slate Ro	72	716
John	Yuba North Ea	72	677
Patrick	Amador Twp 5	55	350
QUINGUE			
Frank	Siskiyou Yreka	69	179

Name	County Locale	M653 Roll	Page
QUINIAN			
P W	Mendocino Big Rvr	60	841
QUINIHAN			
John	San Francisco San Francisco 11		107
		67	
QUININ			
B	Siskiyou Klamath	69	87
Thresa*	San Francisco San Francisco 4	681	150
QUINIR			
Anton	Tuolumne Jamestown	71	435
QUINK			
Catharine	San Joaquin Stockton	641	061
QUINLAN			
Ellen	Solano Vallejo	69	267
Jerry	Yolo Slate Ra	72	717
John	Tuolumne Twp 1	71	271
Margaret	Los Angeles Los Angeles	59	365
QUINLAND			
D P	Amador Twp 3	55	397
John	Trinity Sturdiva	701	007
M	Trinity Taylor'S	701	036
QUINLAR			
Jerry	Yuba Slate Ro	72	717
QUINLEN			
Anna	Yolo No E Twp	72	670
QUINLEY			
J M	Colusa Colusi	57	422
Jno	San Francisco San Francisco 9	681	055
QUINLIN			
Patrick	Sonoma Bodega	69	526
QUINLIVEN			
Michael	Mendocino Calpella	60	809
QUINLON			
Anna	Yuba North Ea	72	670
QUINLY			
John	Stanislaus Empire	70	730
QUINN			
---	Sacramento Ward 3	63	490
---	Yuba Fosters	72	841
A	Siskiyou Scott Va	69	37
A B	Placer Illinois	62	703
A H	Tuolumne Twp 2	71	368
Aeneus	San Bernardino San Bernadino	64	628
Aeneus*	San Joaquin San Bernadino	64	628
Amelia	San Francisco San Francisco 10		183
		67	
Ann	Humbolt Eel Rvr	59	145
Ann	San Francisco San Francisco 10		261
		67	
Arthur	San Francisco San Francisco 11		128
		67	
B	Siskiyou Klamath	69	87
Bernard	Plumas Quincy	621	000
Bridget	Yolo Putah	72	614
Charles	San Francisco San Francisco 4	681	112
Chas	San Francisco San Francisco 9	681	039
Chas	San Francisco San Francisco 9	68	985
Cornelius	Placer Illinois	62	750
D	Yolo Fremont	72	604
Dennis	San Francisco San Francisco 10		270
		67	
Duncan	Placer Michigan	62	831
Edward	San Francisco San Francisco 4	681	134
Edward	San Francisco San Francisco 2	67	634
Edward	Yuba Marysville	72	867
Elizabeth	San Francisco San Francisco 10		351
		67	
Ellen	Alameda Oakland	55	49
Ellen	San Francisco San Francisco 5	67	491
Frank	Placer Rattle Snake	62	628
Frank	Sacramento Brighton	63	193
Frank	Sacramento Brighton	63	204
Geo C	Tuolumne Twp 2	71	284
H	Nevada Nevada	61	240
H	Nevada Eureka	61	379
Hugh	Tuolumne Twp 2	71	400
Hugh	Tuolumne Shawsfla	71	401
Hugh Jr	Tuolumne Twp 2	71	400
Isaac	Yolo Cache	72	609
J	San Francisco San Francisco 2	67	785
J	Santa Clara Santa Clara	65	505
J	Yolo Putah	72	588
J	Yolo Cache	72	609
J B	Siskiyou Scott Va	69	46
J M	Calaveras Twp 8	57	77
James	Alameda Oakland	55	49
James	Contra Costa Twp 3	57	591
James	El Dorado Mud Springs	58	982
James	Klamath Klamath	59	228
James	Placer Illinois	62	750
James	San Francisco San Francisco 9	681	029
James	San Francisco San Francisco 10		166
		67	
James	San Mateo Twp 3	65	73
James	Sierra Twp 5	66	938
James	Solano Benecia	69	311

Name	County Locale	M653 Roll	Page
QUINN			
James C	Yuba Parks Ba	72	778
James F	San Francisco San Francisco 11		123
		67	
James*	Mariposa Twp 1	60	673
Jas	Butte Oregon	56	619
Jas	San Francisco San Francisco 10		171
		67	
Jas	San Francisco San Francisco 10		299
		67	
Jas	San Francisco San Francisco 1	68	854
Jas H	San Francisco San Francisco 1	68	902
Jas R	Sacramento Ward 3	63	461
Jerry	Klamath Trinidad	59	220
Jno	Mendocino Big Rvr	60	843
Jno	San Joaquin Stockton	641	051
John	Alameda Oakland	55	23
John	Sacramento Granite	63	269
John	San Francisco San Francisco 8	681	300
John	San Joaquin Douglass	64	919
John	Sierra Downieville	661	019
John	Yolo Fremont	72	603
John	Yuba Parks Ba	72	778
Jos	San Francisco San Francisco 10		299
		67	
Joseph	Contra Costa Twp 3	57	597
Joseph	Tuolumne Twp 2	71	290
Joseph	Tuolumne Twp 2	71	313
Km	Nevada Eureka	61	364
L	Sacramento Ward 3	63	428
M	Nevada Eureka	61	364
M	Nevada Eureka	61	393
M F	San Francisco San Francisco 5	67	491
M F	Los Angeles Elmonte	59	245
Marc	San Francisco San Francisco 9	68	971
Margaret	San Francisco San Francisco 10		233
		67	
Mark	San Francisco San Francisco 9	68	971
Martin	Fresno Twp 2	59	5
Mary	San Francisco San Francisco 10		184
		67	
Michael	El Dorado Spanish	581	125
Michael	Placer Virginia	62	672
Michael	Santa Clara Santa Clara	65	473
Michael	Tuolumne Shawsfla	71	398
Michiel	Nevada Bridgeport	61	449
Michiell	Nevada Bridgeport	61	449
N P	Solano Benecia	69	282
P	Nevada Nevada	61	240
P	San Francisco San Francisco 5	67	535
Pat	Nevada Bridgeport	61	441
Patrick	Alameda Brooklyn	55	93
Patrick	Contra Costa Twp 2	57	542
Patrick	Humbolt Bucksport	59	161
Patrick	San Francisco San Francisco 1	68	825
Patrick	Tuolumne Shawsfla	71	401
Patrick	Yuba Marysville	72	943
Patrick*	Mariposa Twp 3	60	617
Peter	Plumas Quincy	62	999
Peter	San Francisco San Francisco 1	68	902
Peter	Trinity Rush Crk	70	965
Peter	Yuba Rose Bar	72	799
Qmelia	San Francisco San Francisco 10		183
		67	
Robert*	El Dorado Georgetown	58	676
Stephen	San Francisco San Francisco 1	68	858
Thomas	Amador Twp 3	55	399
Thomas	Contra Costa Twp 3	57	594
Thomas	Marin Bolinas	60	744
Thomas	San Francisco San Francisco 11		128
		67	
Thomas	Tuolumne Twp 2	71	400
Thomas	Yuba Marysville	72	954
Thos	Sacramento Granite	63	248
Thos	San Francisco San Francisco 7	681	347
Thos	Tehama Cottonwood	70	900
Thrisa	San Francisco San Francisco 4	681	150
W	San Francisco San Francisco 6	67	463
W	Yolo Cache	72	595
William	Contra Costa Twp 2	57	541
William	San Francisco San Francisco 9	68	993
William	San Joaquin Elkhorn	64	959
William	Sierra Gibsonville	66	858
William H	Yuba Marysville	72	899
Wm	Alameda Brooklyn	55	137
Wm	Butte Chico	56	539
Wm	Tehama Cottonwoood	70	900
QUINNA			
M*	San Francisco San Francisco 5	67	532
QUINNACE			
Patk	Klamath Klamath	59	228
QUINNAN			
John	San Joaquin Douglass	64	925
QUINNBY			
Elizabeth	Yuba Marysville	72	909
QUINNELL			
Jno	San Francisco San Francisco 9	68	946

California 1860 Census Index

Name	County Locale	M653 RollPage
QUINNELL		
Margt	San Francisco San Francisco	9 681056
QUINNNNNLIA		
Joseph*	Sierra Downieville	661021
QUINO		
Giovanno	Calaveras Twp 7	57 9
QUINOGUE		
J*	Nevada Eureka	61 357
QUINOLL		
John	Tuolumne Jamestown	71 432
QUINOME		
Hasap La	San Francisco San Francisco	4 681155
Hasapha	San Francisco San Francisco	4 681155
QUINQUE		
Frank	Siskiyou Yreka	69 179
QUINROLE		
Angelina	Tuolumne Twp 4	71 140
QUINS		
O*	Calaveras Twp 9	57 415
QUINSAN		
P W*	Mendocino Big Rvr	60 841
QUINSBY		
C S	Butte Hamilton	56 522
QUINSENERS		
Polonila	Tuolumne Twp 4	71 137
QUINT		
Frederick	Yuba Marysville	72 854
G W	San Francisco San Francisco	12 376 67
Geo	Siskiyou Cottonwood	69 100
Jas	Sacramento Natonia	63 284
Leander	Tuolumne Sonora	71 207
QUINTA		
Gaudalupa	Tuolumne Sonora	71 228
Juana	Los Angeles Los Angeles	59 403
QUINTAL		
Peter	San Francisco San Francisco 2	67 780
Peter Sr	San Francisco San Francisco 2	67 780
QUINTANA		
Esteven San Bernardino	Santa Barbara	64 147
Jeromino	San Salvador San Bernardino	64 661
Jesus	Santa Clara Alviso	65 403
Jesus M San Bernardino	San Salvador	64 662
Jose M San Francisco	San Francisco 2	67 781
QUINTANER		
Francisco	Santa Clara Gilroy	65 250
QUINTANN		
Jose M San Luis Obispo	San Luis Obispo	65 22
QUINTANORO		
Poncho	Yuba Suida	72 980
Poucho	Yuba Linda Twp	72 980
QUINTARO		
Ascencion	Yuba Marysville	72 919
John	Tuolumne Shawsfla	71 408
QUINTEAN		
Frank	Amador Twp 1	55 491
QUINTEANO		
---	San Diego Temecula	64 792
QUINTEN		
Francisco	Los Angeles Los Angeles	59 379
Richd	Nevada Bridgeport	61 481
QUINTERO		
Francisco	Los Angeles Los Angeles	59 379
Jose D San Luis Obispo	San Luis Obispo	65 36
QUINTERY		
D	Tuolumne Twp 2	71 405
QUINTEVES		
D	Tuolumne Shawsfla	71 405
QUINTILL		
Wm	Santa Clara Redwood	65 454
QUINTON		
James	Santa Clara Fremont	65 424
Jas	San Francisco San Francisco 1	68 922
Jas M	Calaveras Twp 9	57 347
John B San Francisco	San Francisco 4	681121
Wm	Solano Suisan	69 226
QUINTOO		
---	Trinity Mouth Ca	701011
QUINTRELL		
James	Tuolumne Twp 2	71 372
QUINUS		
S M*	El Dorado Placerville	58 887
QUINUSLY		
Samuel	Mariposa Coulterville	60 686
QUIOST		
Jno*	Sacramento Ward 1	63 149
QUIRADO		
Jesus	Los Angeles San Juan	59 466
QUIRALLO		
B	Calaveras Twp 8	57 95
QUIRATO		
---*	Mendocino Calpella	60 824
QUIRCTERO		
Fansite San Luis Obispo	San Luis Obispo	65 8
QUIRDSON		
Mary E*	Nevada Rough &	61 395
QUIRE		
---	Sierra Downieville	66 979
Frank	Sacramento Ward 1	63 13
Raphael*	Alameda Murray	55 219
QUIRES		
Henry D	Santa Clara Almaden	65 263
QUIRINO		
P	Stanislaus Emory	70 737
QUIRK		
Bridget	Alameda Brooklyn	55 139
I	Nevada Eureka	61 358
J	Nevada Eureka	61 358
James	Alameda Oakland	55 70
John	San Joaquin Oneal	64 938
John	Solano Benecia	69 317
John	Yuba Rose Bar	72 798
Jos	Placer Lisbon	62 733
Michael	Santa Cruz Pajaro	66 573
P	Sacramento Ward 1	63 63
Peter	Plumas Meadow Valley	62 903
Richd	Sacramento Ward 4	63 555
S G	Nevada Grass Valley	61 167
Thomas	El Dorado Cold Spring	581099
Thomas*	Sacramento Ward 1	63 128
William	Nevada Red Dog	61 545
Wm	Nevada Eureka	61 356
QUIRLA		
Thomas*	Sacramento Ward 1	63 128
QUIRNOS		
Alexander	Calaveras Twp 5	57 177
QUIRO		
Josh	Amador Twp 1	55 468
QUIROA		
Felipe*	Los Angeles Santa Ana	59 441
Filipe	Los Angeles Santa Ana	59 441
QUIROLES		
Angelina	Tuolumne Big Oak	71 140
QUIROLO		
Joseph	Amador Twp 1	55 482
QUIRON		
Felipe*	Los Angeles Santa Ana	59 441
QUIROS		
Felipe	Los Angeles Santa Ana	59 445
Jose	Los Angeles Santa Ana	59 453
Santiago	Los Angeles Los Nieto	59 434
QUIRR		
James	Sierra Twp 5	66 936
QUIS		
---	Calaveras Twp 5	57 173
---	Calaveras Twp 5	57 240
---	Calaveras Twp 4	57 303
---	Siskiyou Yreka	69 195
---*	Calaveras Twp 6	57 173
Yang	Mariposa Coulterville	60 682
QUISADA		
Jesus San Francisco	San Francisco 2	67 789
QUISALLE		
Joseph	Tuolumne Twp 1	71 270
QUISDOLPHS		
John*	Los Angeles Los Angeles	59 365
QUISK		
Michael	Santa Cruz Pajaro	66 573
QUISMAN		
---	Sutter Butte	70 780
QUISROLL		
John	Tuolumne Twp 3	71 432
QUIT		
---	Calaveras Twp 4	57 303
Me	Placer Illinois	62 752
QUITMERE		
Christian*	Sierra Downieville	661031
QUITZ		
Andrew	Sacramento Brighton	63 194
QUITZON		
Albert Van*	Santa Ana Los Angeles	59 440
QUIU		
---*	Butte Chico	56 545
Cruix*	Butte Chico	56 545
QUIUT		
Leander*	Tuolumne Twp 1	71 207
QUIVER		
Patrick	Sierra La Porte	66 785
QUIVERS		
E	Merced Twp 2	60 916
Manuel	Mariposa Twp 3	60 555
QUIYOW		
---	Klamath Liberty	59 235
QUIZGO		
Castro	Tuolumne Columbia	71 338
QUKE		
---	El Dorado Georgetown	58 680
QULLEY		
J*	Nevada Eureka	61 344
QULLINGHAM		
Wm K	Sonoma Mendocino	69 455
QULLY		
J*	Nevada Eureka	61 354
QUM CHOW		
---*	Nevada Nevada	61 308
QUM		
---	Nevada Washington	61 341
---	Placer Virginia	62 679
---*	Nevada Rough &	61 399
---*	San Francisco San Francisco 4	681198
---*	Yuba Foster B	72 826
QUMAN		
J*	El Dorado Diamond	58 796
QUMER		
E	El Dorado Diamond	58 805
QUMG		
---	Yuba Slate Ro	72 711
---	Yuba Fosters	72 831
QUMIS		
Leonce*	Calaveras Twp 6	57 163
QUMONT		
Jord A	Calaveras Twp 6	57 141
QUN CHOW		
---*	Nevada Nevada	61 308
QUN		
---	Calaveras Twp 10	57 297
---	El Dorado Kelsey	581135
---	Mariposa Twp 1	60 659
---	Mariposa Twp 1	60 661
---	Nevada Nevada	61 309
---	Nevada Nevada	61 310
---	Placer Virginia	62 666
---	San Francisco San Francisco 4	681200
---*	Nevada Nevada	61 308
---*	Nevada Nevada	61 310
Ann	Shasta Millvill	66 750
Choy	Calaveras Twp 4	57 304
QUNAN		
Iglaze*	Sierra Downieville	661022
QUNDSON		
Mary E*	Nevada Rough &	61 395
QUNE		
---	Calaveras Twp 6	57 181
---	El Dorado Georgetown	58 690
---	Sierra Downieville	66 979
QUNETARO		
Asceacion*	Yuba Marysville	72 919
QUNG		
---	Nevada Bridgeport	61 439
---	Plumas Quincy	62 950
---	Yolo Slate Ra	72 711
---	Yuba Long Bar	72 758
---*	Yuba Foster B	72 831
QUNIOLE		
Charles	Santa Cruz Santa Cruz	66 626
QUNIOTE		
Charles*	Santa Cruz Santa Cruz	66 626
QUNKY		
Marinte	Amador Twp 3	55 398
QUNLAP		
Samuel	Solano Vacaville	69 362
QUNN		
C	Calaveras Twp 9	57 384
QUNNBY		
E W*	San Francisco San Francisco 9	68 944
QUNNG		
---	Yuba Long Bar	72 762
---	Yuba Parks Ba	72 780
QUNNY		
J M*	Butte Hamilton	56 517
QUNORIS		
Elousin*	Calaveras Twp 5	57 204
QUNOTARO		
Asceacion*	Yuba Marysville	72 919
QUNPHY		
Michael San Bernardino	San Bernadino	64 626
QUNRAS		
Jose	Calaveras Twp 8	57 77
QUNSAY		
---*	Placer Auburn	62 562
QUNTAR		
Santus*	Calaveras Twp 5	57 198
QUNTARD		
Santrus	Calaveras Twp 5	57 198
QUNTIUS		
Genaro*	Placer Auburn	62 578
QUO		
---	Amador Twp 6	55 446
---	Calaveras Twp 6	57 181
---	Calaveras Twp 5	57 220
---	Calaveras Twp 5	57 241
---	Calaveras Twp 5	57 242
---	Calaveras Twp 10	57 275
---	Calaveras Twp 10	57 295
---	Placer Virginia	62 679
---	San Francisco San Francisco 4	681191

California 1860 Census Index

Name	County Locale	M653 Roll	Page
QUO			
---	Tuolumne Sonora	71	477
---	Yuba Marysville	72	921
Lee	San Francisco San Francisco 7	681	395
Yong	Placer Dutch Fl	62	722
QUOCK			
---	El Dorado Diamond	58	815
---	Sacramento Ward 1	63	51
QUODIOSS			
Ramon	Calaveras Twp 5	57	206
QUOEK			
---	El Dorado Mud Springs	58	961
QUOGOAN			
---*	Calaveras Twp 5	57	253
QUOGUAN			
---*	Calaveras Twp 5	57	253
QUOH			
---	Sacramento Ward 1	63	51
QUOI			
---	San Francisco San Francisco 11	146 67	
---	Tuolumne Twp 6	71	529
---	Tuolumne Green Springs	71	531
QUOIRIS			
Elousin*	Calaveras Twp 5	57	204
QUOKE			
---	Plumas Quincy	62	949
QUON			
---	Amador Twp 6	55	444
---	Calaveras Twp 5	57	193
---	Calaveras Twp 5	57	245
---	Calaveras Twp 5	57	247
---	Del Norte Happy Ca	58	663
---	El Dorado Salmon Falls	581	040
---	El Dorado Salmon Falls	581	052
---	El Dorado Salmon Falls	581	055
---	El Dorado Salmon Hills	581	059
---	El Dorado Coloma	581	084
---	El Dorado Kelsey	581	144
---	El Dorado Diamond	58	795
---	El Dorado Eldorado	58	948
---	El Dorado Mud Springs	58	954
---	El Dorado Mud Springs	58	959
---	Nevada Red Dog	61	549
---	Placer Rattle Snake	62	636
---	Placer Iona Hills	62	893
---	Placer Iona Hills	62	894
---	Sacramento Ward 1	63	112
---	Sierra Downieville	66	980
---	Yolo No E Twp	72	681
---	Yolo Slate Ra	72	711
---	Yuba Slate Ro	72	711
---	Yuba Long Bar	72	752
---	Yuba Long Bar	72	760
---	Yuba Long Bar	72	766
---	Yuba Long Bar	72	763
Chee	Santa Clara San Jose	65	392
Emille	Placer Iona Hills	62	869
Hen	El Dorado Mud Springs	58	961
Heu	Yuba Long Bar	72	764
Ring	Calaveras Twp 5	57	193
See	El Dorado Placerville	58	830
Shi	El Dorado Mud Springs	58	971
Sin	Calaveras Twp 5	57	193
Sri	Calaveras Twp 5	57	193
Su			
QUONE			
---	El Dorado Kelsey	581	141
---	El Dorado Mud Springs	58	960
QUONG SE			
---	Sacramento Ward 1	63	70
QUONG			
---	Amador Twp 2	55	274
---	Amador Twp 1	55	506
---	Amador Twp 1	55	510
---	Calaveras Twp 5	57	192
---	Calaveras Twp 5	57	219
---	Calaveras Twp 10	57	271
---	Calaveras Twp 10	57	275
---	Del Norte Happy Ca	58	668
---	El Dorado White Oaks	581	025
---	El Dorado White Oaks	581	032
---	El Dorado Salmon Falls	581	047
---	El Dorado Salmon Falls	581	058
---	El Dorado Salmon Falls	581	059
---	El Dorado Coloma	581	078
---	El Dorado Coloma	581	084
---	El Dorado Coloma	581	106
---	El Dorado Mountain	581	188
---	El Dorado Mountain	581	189
---	El Dorado Diamond	58	787
---	El Dorado Diamond	58	816
---	El Dorado Placerville	58	825
---	El Dorado Placerville	58	829
---	El Dorado Placerville	58	842
---	El Dorado Placerville	58	844
---	El Dorado Placerville	58	902

Name	County Locale	M653 Roll	Page
QUONG			
---	El Dorado Placerville	58	911
---	El Dorado Eldorado	58	939
---	El Dorado Eldorado	58	941
---	El Dorado Eldorado	58	942
---	El Dorado Mud Springs	58	953
---	El Dorado Mud Springs	58	962
---	El Dorado Mud Springs	58	975
---	El Dorado Mud Springs	58	976
---	Mariposa Twp 3	60	581
---	Mariposa Twp 1	60	626
---	Nevada Bridgeport	61	439
---	Placer Horseshoe	62	650
---	Placer Virginia	62	669
---	Placer Virginia	62	671
---	Placer Virginia	62	674
---	Placer Virginia	62	676
---	Placer Virginia	62	679
---	Placer Virginia	62	687
---	Placer Dutch Fl	62	721
---	Placer Dutch Fl	62	737
---	Placer Illinois	62	738
---	Placer Illinois	62	739
---	Placer Iona Hills	62	881
---	Plumas Quincy	62	920
---	Plumas Quincy	62	926
---	Sacramento Ward 3	63	489
---	Sacramento Ward 3	63	490
---	Sacramento Ward 1	63	50
---	Sacramento Ward 1	63	60
---	Sacramento Ward 4	63	612
---	San Francisco San Francisco 4	681	203
---	San Francisco San Francisco 11	144 67	
---	San Francisco San Francisco 5	67	490
---	Tuolumne Don Pedro	71	162
---	Tuolumne Chinese	71	521
---	Tuolumne Knights	71	529
---	Yolo No E Twp	72	675
---	Yolo Slate Ra	72	711
---	Yuba Bear Rvr	721	000
---	Yuba North Ea	72	682
---	Yuba Slate Ro	72	711
---	Yuba Slate Ro	72	715
---	Yuba Long Bar	72	757
---	Yuba Long Bar	72	762
---	Yuba Long Bar	72	763
---	Yuba Long Bar	72	765
---	Yuba Long Bar	72	766
---	Yuba Fosters	72	826
---	Yuba Fosters	72	831
---	Yuba Fosters	72	841
---	Yuba Linda	72	991
---*	Yuba Foster B	72	826
---*	Yuba Foster B	72	831
---*	Yuba Fosters	72	841
Ah	Sacramento Ward 1	63	152
Ah	Sacramento Ward 3	63	492
Ah	Tuolumne Twp 4	71	162
Ah	Yuba Bear Rvr	721	000
Ah	Yuba Suida	72	991
Be Too*	Sacramento Ward 1	63	152
Chu	Yuba Fosters	72	827
Chun	Placer Michigan	62	858
Chung	Calaveras Twp 4	57	306
Ci	Placer Forest H	62	771
Foo	Yuba Foster B	72	830
G	El Dorado Placerville	58	834
Kang	El Dorado Mud Springs	58	953
Long	El Dorado Eldorado	58	939
Mou	Calaveras Twp 5	57	202
Sam	Yolo Slate Ra	72	715
Sam*	Yuba Slate Ro	72	715
Se	Sacramento Ward 1	63	70
QUONTER			
J	El Dorado Kelsey	581	155
QUONY			
---	Calaveras Twp 5	57	192
---	Calaveras Twp 5	57	219
---	Calaveras Twp 5	57	226
---	Calaveras Twp 10	57	271
---	Calaveras Twp 5	57	323
---	Yuba North Ea	72	681
Chuy	Calaveras Twp 4	57	306
Mor	Calaveras Twp 5	57	202
QUOON			
---	El Dorado Salmon Hills	581	059
---	El Dorado Coloma	581	078
QUORTER			
Benj F M*	Calaveras Twp 9	57	359
Biy F M*	Calaveras Twp 9	57	359
Buj F M*	Calaveras Twp 9	57	359
QUORTERN			
J*	Calaveras Twp 9	57	378
QUORTERR			
J*	Calaveras Twp 9	57	378

Name	County Locale	M653 Roll	Page
QUOST			
Jno	Sacramento Ward 1	63	149
QUOT			
---	Calaveras Twp 5	57	235
QUOTO			
Ramone	Amador Twp 1	55	504
QUOVIRS			
Nicholas	Calaveras Twp 5	57	141
QUOW			
---	Yuba North Ea	72	681
---	Yuba Long Bar	72	766
QUOY HAN			
---*	San Francisco San Francisco 4	681	175
QUOY			
---	Amador Twp 2	55	287
---	Calaveras Twp 10	57	261
---	Calaveras Twp 10	57	275
---	Calaveras Twp 10	57	284
---	El Dorado Kelsey	581	144
---	Sacramento Ward 3	63	492
---	San Francisco San Francisco 4	681	175
---	San Francisco San Francisco 4	681	179
---	Tuolumne Jacksonville	71	516
---	Yolo Slate Ra	72	710
---	Yuba Slate Ro	72	710
---	Yuba Fosters	72	841
Han	San Francisco San Francisco 4	681	175
QUR			
---	Calaveras Twp 4	57	333
QURAN			
---*	Yolo No E Twp	72	681
QURAY			
---	Yolo No E Twp	72	681
QURCK			
James	Sierra Twp 5	66	926
QUREM			
---	Yolo No E Twp	72	685
QUREN			
---	Calaveras Twp 4	57	302
QUREW			
---	Yuba North Ea	72	681
QUREY			
---	Sierra Twp 7	66	881
QURIN			
---	Calaveras Twp 10	57	285
QURING			
---	Yolo Slate Ra	72	708
John	Yolo No E Twp	72	677
QURLEY			
D	El Dorado Placerville	58	892
QURNTAMORS			
Polonier*	Tuolumne Big Oak	71	137
QURNTEMORS			
Polonia*	Tuolumne Big Oak	71	137
QURNTI			
Joseph M	Calaveras Twp 4	57	341
QUROL			
John	Calaveras Twp 6	57	164
QURON			
John	Calaveras Twp 6	57	167
QURONG			
---	Yolo No E Twp	72	682
QUROR			
John	Calaveras Twp 6	57	167
QUROY			
Lusgood	San Francisco San Francisco 4	681	148
QURRO			
Julian	Santa Clara Almaden	65	267
QURT			
J	Sierra Twp 7	66	886
QURTIUS			
Genaro*	Placer Auburn	62	578
QURY			
---	Amador Twp 5	55	336
---	El Dorado Kelsey	581	144
QUSLIA			
George*	Placer Michigan	62	850
QUSTARUS			
A	Trinity Browns C	70	984
QUSTIA			
George*	Placer Michigan	62	850
QUSTO			
---*	San Bernardino Santa Ba	64	219
QUUDIOSS			
Ramon	Calaveras Twp 5	57	206
QUUN			
---	Calaveras Twp 10	57	286
QUUNG			
---	Yuba New York	72	718
QUVER			
A P*	Calaveras Twp 9	57	397
QUY YE LOW			
---	Sacramento Ward 1	63	66
QUY			
---	Sacramento Ward 1	63	65
---	Sacramento Ward 1	63	66

California 1860 Census Index

Name	County Locale	M653 RollPage
QUY		
---	Trinity Weaverville	70 1074
Lan	Sacramento Ward 1	63 58
Mi	Amador Twp 5	55 333
Ye Low	Sacramento Ward 1	63 66
Yow	Sacramento Ward 1	63 58
QUYADA		
Juan	Monterey San Juan	60 985
QWA		
---*	Nevada Rough &	61 434
QWAN		
---*	Nevada Rough &	61 437
QWANG		
---	Butte Chico	56 543
QWAY		
---	Nevada Bridgeport	61 458
QWEEN		
---	Nevada Rough &	61 437
---	Nevada Bridgeport	61 463
---	Nevada Red Dog	61 556
---*	Nevada Rough &	61 437
QWOCK		
---	Placer Forest H	62 771
R GO		
---	Sierra Downieville	66 954
R GUN		
---	Sierra Twp 7	66 881
R M		
---	Sierra Twp 7	66 898
R MARK		
---*	Sierra Downieville	661007
R UMEBE		
Joseph M	Los Angeles Los Angeles	59 340
R		
Go	Sierra Downieville	66 954
Gun	Sierra Twp 7	66 881
Gun	Sierra Downieville	66 992
Lee	Sierra Downieville	66 992
M	Sierra Twp 7	66 898
Mark*	Sierra Downieville	661007
Yong	Sierra Downieville	66 992
R?UN??		
P G*	Tuolumne Twp 1	71 243
RA		
Ly	Mariposa Twp 3	60 618
RAAB		
Louis	Trinity Raabs Ba	701020
RAABE		
Otto	San Francisco San Francisco 8	681286
RAACH		
Dennis*	San Francisco San Francisco 9	68 941
John	San Francisco San Francisco 9	681102
RAAL		
John	San Francisco San Francisco 3	67 46
RAB		
Gue	Sierra Twp 7	66 889
Son	Sierra Twp 7	66 889
RABALEL		
Rosalie	Alameda Oakland	55 5
RABAN		
C	Amador Twp 2	55 294
RABANAL		
Ramon	Santa Clara Fremont	65 434
RABAR		
Victor	Sacramento Ward 4	63 557
RABB		
Wm	Nevada Nevada	61 323
RABBERDY		
Rafael	Monterey San Juan	60 982
RABBET		
Frank	Tuolumne Columbia	71 366
RABBIT		
E	Trinity Douglas	70 980
Frank	Tuolumne Twp 2	71 366
Patrick	Placer Michigan	62 851
RABBITS		
Nicholas	Amador Twp 4	55 242
RABBITT		
H R	Butte Ophir	56 793
John	Yolo Washington	72 574
RABBLE		
Frank	Tuolumne Twp 2	71 362
RABBLS		
Frank	Tuolumne Columbia	71 362
RABE		
A	Sierra Pine Grove	66 832
Andrew	Amador Twp 3	55 370
Anne	San Francisco San Francisco 12	374 67
Conrad	San Joaquin Elliott	641102
RABEL		
Adolph	Del Norte Happy Ca	58 661
Frank	Sacramento Ward 3	63 488
RABEN		
Charles	Placer Michigan	62 817
RABENY		
Phillip*	Calaveras Twp 6	57 164

Name	County Locale	M653 RollPage
RABER		
Chas	Amador Twp 5	55 346
J A	Sutter Yuba	70 772
Martin	San Francisco San Francisco 3	67 75
RABEROLT		
Leopuld*	Amador Twp 4	55 237
RABEUX		
Louis	San Francisco San Francisco 2	67 679
RABIA		
Augustine	Siskiyou Yreka	69 177
RABING		
A*	San Francisco San Francisco 7	681414
A???	San Francisco San Francisco 7	681414
RABINSON		
H W	Tuolumne Jamestown	71 421
RABINY		
Phillip*	Calaveras Twp 6	57 164
RABLAM		
Geo	Yolo Putah	72 587
RABLAN		
Geo	Yolo Putah	72 587
RABLE		
Domnick	Amador Twp 3	55 390
RABLEIN		
Richard*	Yuba Marysville	72 878
RABLEIR		
Richard*	Yuba Marysville	72 878
RABLES		
Ramond	Amador Twp 5	55 354
RABLIN		
Richard	Yuba Marysville	72 878
RABLINS		
Nathan	Placer Forest H	62 803
RABLO		
Fred	Yolo Washington	72 573
RABO		
T P	Butte Mountain	56 734
RABOLLET		
John	San Francisco San Francisco 3	67 3
RABOUE		
J*	Nevada Grass Valley	61 169
RABOW		
J*	Nevada Grass Valley	61 169
RABOYN		
H	El Dorado Salmon Falls	581052
RABRE		
Felix	Tuolumne Twp 2	71 292
RABSON		
N*	El Dorado Georgetown	58 689
RABULES		
Francisco	Calaveras Twp 10	57 277
RACA		
---	San Bernardino S Timate	64 730
Joshua*	Tuolumne Twp 3	71 429
RACAIO		
Frank	Amador Twp 3	55 372
RACANO		
Frank	San Francisco San Francisco 3	67 63
RACAS		
Thomseo	San Diego Agua Caliente	64 861
RACE		
Hosa	El Dorado Coloma	581118
Hose	El Dorado Coloma	581118
J	Sacramento Ward 1	63 8
John	San Francisco San Francisco 8	681278
RACEARO		
Leverona	El Dorado Placerville	58 896
RACER		
---	Tulara Twp 1	71 122
RACH		
Eliza	Sierra Eureka	661044
RACHARD		
Zarer	San Francisco San Francisco 2	67 801
Zaver	San Francisco San Francisco 2	67 801
RACHBURN		
John	Sierra Eureka	661047
RACHELLE		
John	Mariposa Twp 3	60 558
RACHES		
Juan	San Bernardino San Bernadino	64 677
RACHI		
Frank*	Stanislaus Branch	70 703
John*	Stanislaus Branch	70 698
RACHIA		
Salono*	Calaveras Twp 7	57 45
RACHO		
Patk	Klamath Liberty	59 230
RACICH		
Michael	San Francisco San Francisco 3	67 39
RACINCT		
August	San Joaquin Stockton	641067
RACINE		
Henry	Butte Chico	56 531
Henry	Sierra Downieville	661002
RACINI		
Henry	Sierra Downieville	661002

Name	County Locale	M653 RollPage
RACIO		
Elmana	Los Angeles San Jose	59 282
RACK		
B	Sutter Nicolaus	70 836
Wilhelm*	Nevada Bridgeport	61 467
RACKABY		
Cintha A	Yolo Cache Crk	72 619
Cinthia A	Yolo Cache	72 619
RACKER		
James	San Francisco San Francisco 4	681145
John	Placer Yankee J	62 759
RACKERLY		
J J	Yolo Cache Crk	72 618
RACKETT		
Catharine	Yuba Rose Bar	72 808
William	Yuba Rose Bar	72 808
RACKIER		
J A	Nevada Rough &	61 428
RACKLE		
Charles	San Diego San Diego	64 767
RACKLIFF		
Alden	Placer Auburn	62 559
John	Yuba Slate Ro	72 700
RACKLIFFE		
John	Yolo Slate Ra	72 700
RACLEN		
Frasir	Amador Twp 2	55 279
RACLET		
Wm*	San Francisco San Francisco 2	67 700
RACO		
Carlos	San Francisco San Francisco 2	67 719
RACOCK		
J C*	Stanislaus Branch	70 711
RACOLOM		
H	San Francisco San Francisco 4	681154
RACOLOUR		
H	San Francisco San Francisco 4	681154
RACOSON		
E B	Tehama Lassen	70 868
RACRIDH		
Joseph*	San Mateo Twp 1	65 60
RACUIS		
---	Napa Napa	61 78
RAD		
Abner	Tulara Visalia	71 28
RADAM		
Wm	Nevada Grass Valley	61 154
RADARICH		
Rufus	San Francisco San Francisco 3	67 61
RADBY		
Mary	Alameda Washington	55 172
RADCLIFF		
C M	Tuolumne Twp 1	71 217
Jas	Placer Rattle Snake	62 603
T	Sacramento Ward 1	63 106
Wright	Calaveras Twp 5	57 187
RADCLIFFE		
Saml*	Alameda Brooklyn	55 81
Saney A*	Yuba Marysville	72 909
T	Sacramento Ward 1	63 106
Wm M	Sacramento Ward 1	63 10
RADDING		
J	Sonoma Bodega	69 519
RADDLE		
Thos	Butte Ophir	56 790
RADDLER		
Charles*	Placer Michigan	62 834
RADDOCK		
Robt*	El Dorado White Oaks	581008
RADDY		
John	Siskiyou Scott Va	69 59
RADEGENFKI		
Jacob*	Sacramento Ward 3	63 433
RADEGEWFKI		
Jacob*	Sacramento Ward 3	63 433
RADEL		
E	Trinity North Fo	701026
RADEMAKER		
Jeo	Sacramento Ward 4	63 529
RADENBACK		
Mary*	San Francisco San Francisco 3	67 30
RADER		
John	El Dorado Grizzly	581181
John	Sacramento Cosumnes	63 402
RADES		
Facondo	Calaveras Twp 5	57 203
Facondr	Calaveras Twp 5	57 203
J C	Tehama Tehama	70 935
RADET		
Wm*	San Francisco San Francisco 2	67 700
RADFORD		
M J	Siskiyou Scott Va	69 20
Michael	San Francisco San Francisco 6	67 402
Robert	Amador Twp 4	55 241
Thomas	Calaveras Twp 6	57 143
Ths	San Francisco San Francisco 6	67 402

California 1860 Census Index

Name	County Locale	M653 Roll	Page
RADFORD			
W J*	Siskiyou Callahan	69	20
Wm	Colusa Monroeville	57	450
RADGEFORD			
M	Shasta Shasta	66	672
RADGEP			
Roper	Tehama Tehama	70	944
RADGER			
John	Amador Twp 1	55	491
RADGERS			
G W	Tuolumne Jamestown	71	444
Josiah B	Alameda Brooklyn	55	205
RADICK			
Leonard	Yuba Marysville	72	975
RADINGER			
Elisa	Yuba Long Bar	72	771
RADIPOT			
August	San Francisco San Francisco 3	67	82
RADISH			
Frank	Mariposa Coulterville	60	697
Nicholas	Tuolumne Sonora	71	243
Thomas	San Francisco San Francisco 7	68	1411
RADKY			
Mary	Alameda Brooklyn	55	172
RADLE			
Henry	San Mateo Twp 1	65	53
RADLIFFE			
Saml	Sacramento Ward 4	63	505
RADMAN			
Chas*	Santa Clara Alviso	65	411
RADMER			
Perry	Calaveras Twp 5	57	198
RADMEYER			
Aug F*	Mendocino Little L	60	838
RADMOND			
Mathew	Sierra Downieville	66	994
RADODALE			
Mathew	Alameda Brooklyn	55	103
RADOFF			
Sarah	Santa Clara Redwood	65	451
RADOKEY			
Wm	Alameda Brooklyn	55	186
RADOLIFFE			
Landy A*	Yuba Marysville	72	909
RADONA			
Jose	Los Angeles Los Angeles	59	305
RADONICH			
T W	San Francisco San Francisco 5	67	479
RADORVICH			
T W*	San Francisco San Francisco 5	67	479
RADRIFUES			
Jose	San Bernardino San Bernadino	64	669
RADSDALE			
Mathew	Alameda Brooklyn	55	103
RADSEFORD			
M	Shasta Shasta	66	672
RADSENBERY			
Fred	Tuolumne Twp 3	71	453
RADSENBEY			
Fred	Tuolumne Jamestown	71	453
RADSNAN			
L	Solano Fairfield	69	197
RADSOW			
Habbell W N*	Yuba Marysville	72	858
RADSTONE			
Jacob	San Francisco San Francisco 8	68	1295
RADTEK			
C A	Tuolumne Twp 2	71	283
RADY			
Louis	Placer Iona Hills	62	882
Sarah	Sacramento Lee	63	219
RAE			
August	Colusa Monroeville	57	447
Chas	Alameda Brooklyn	55	124
Chas	Alameda Brooklyn	55	149
Ching	Butte Bidwell	56	717
D M	San Francisco San Francisco 5	67	505
RAEANO			
Frank*	San Francisco San Francisco 3	67	63
RAEB			
A*	San Francisco San Francisco 5	67	503
RAEGG			
Ester	San Francisco San Francisco 2	67	793
RAEHR			
Wm	Trinity Weaverville	70	1068
RAELZ			
A*	San Francisco San Francisco 5	67	503
RAENBUY			
John	Siskiyou Klamath	69	94
RAENHBRY			
John	Siskiyou Klamath	69	94
RAEUIS			
---	Napa Napa	61	78
RAFACE			
Fontam	Calaveras Twp 7	57	39
RAFAEL			
---	Los Angeles Los Angeles	59	386
---	Los Angeles Los Angeles	59	388
---	Los Angeles San Juan	59	464
---	Los Angeles San Pedro	59	485
---	Mendocino Twp 1	60	889
---	Monterey San Juan	60	1000
---	Monterey Pajaro	60	1011
---	Monterey S Antoni	60	970
---	Monterey S Antoni	60	972
---	San Bernardino S Timate	64	696
---	San Bernardino S Timate	64	706
---	San Bernardino S Timate	64	720
---	San Bernardino S Timate	64	721
---	San Bernardino S Timate	64	723
---	San Bernardino S Timate	64	728
---	San Bernardino S Timate	64	730
---	San Bernardino S Timate	64	749
---	San Bernardino S Timate	64	750
---	San Bernardino S Timate	64	755
---	San Diego Temecula	64	790
---	San Diego Agua Caliente	64	844
---	Tulara Keyesville	71	67
---	Tulara Keyesville	71	70
Francis	Siskiyou Yreka	69	145
J Thos	San Francisco San Francisco 2	67	789
John	Calaveras Twp 4	57	340
Sanlo	Mariposa Twp 3	60	597
Saulo*	Mariposa Twp 3	60	597
W*	San Francisco San Francisco 5	67	496
RAFAELA			
---	San Bernardino S Timate	64	702
---	San Bernardino S Timate	64	743
---	San Bernardino S Timate	64	747
---	San Bernardino S Timate	64	748
---	San Diego Temecula	64	803
Maria	San Diego San Diego	64	776
RAFAID			
---	San Bernardino Santa Inez	64	137
Feliz	San Bernardino Santa Barbara	64	165
RAFAIL			
---	San Bernardino Santa Barbara	64	200
B	San Bernardino San Bernadino	64	681
---	El Dorado Georgetown	58	696
RAFAL			
Antone*	Mendocino Round Va	60	877
RAFALL			
John	El Dorado Georgetown	58	699
RAFEAL			
Aaron	Yuba Marysville	72	896
Fontana	Calaveras Twp 8	57	85
RAFEE			
Augustus	Trinity Whites Crk	70	1028
RAFEIL			
---	Monterey S Antoni	60	972
RAFEL			
---	Butte Chico	56	550
---	Los Angeles Los Angeles	59	515
Antone*	Mendocino Round Va	60	877
Jose	Los Angeles Los Angeles	59	513
RAFELL			
---	San Mateo Twp 2	65	115
RAFETTA			
L	El Dorado Diamond	58	804
RAFFAEL			
---*	Mariposa Twp 1	60	643
RAFFE			
G	San Joaquin Stockton	64	1040
Paul Revd*	San Francisco	10 67	317
RAFFEE			
Atal*	Calaveras Twp 7	57	12
RAFFENBERY			
Louis	Placer Forest H	62	799
RAFFER			
Jos*	Santa Cruz Pescadero	66	646
Paul	San Francisco San Francisco 10 67		317
RAFFERD			
D*	Nevada Eureka	61	350
RAFFERTY			
Bernard O	Butte Oregon	56	628
Catharine	San Francisco San Francisco 10 67		187
Daniel	Sierra Morristown	66	1053
Eliz	Sacramento Ward 1	63	91
James	Shasta Horsetown	66	688
John R	San Joaquin Castoria	64	898
M K	Butte Kimshaw	56	603
Mathew	Placer Forest H	62	792
Michael	Placer Forest H	62	772
Patrick	Placer Michigan	62	833
T C	Calaveras Twp 8	57	89
Thomas	San Francisco San Francisco 3	67	84
Thomas	San Joaquin Stockton	64	1077
Thomas	Sierra Twp 5	66	917
Wm	San Francisco San Francisco 7	68	1373
RAFFEY			
Michael	Sierra Twp 7	66	912
RAFFIRD			
D*	Nevada Eureka	61	350
RAFFLE			
Atal*	Calaveras Twp 7	57	12
M	Nevada Eureka	61	394
RAFFO			
Paul Revd	San Francisco San Francisco 10 67		317
RAFFORD			
D	Nevada Eureka	61	350
G	Nevada Eureka	61	346
R	Nevada Eureka	61	346
RAFFUEL			
---	Mariposa Twp 1	60	643
RAFIL			
---	Los Angeles Los Angeles	59	515
RAFLEY			
Michael	Sierra Twp 7	66	912
RAFO			
Louis	San Bernardino Santa Barbara	64	180
RAFOOFA			
---	San Mateo Twp 2	65	115
RAFRIONA			
---	San Diego Agua Caliente	64	835
RAFRITTO			
Alexander	Los Angeles Los Angeles	59	495
RAFS			
Joseph*	Shasta Shasta	66	679
Wm	San Francisco San Francisco 1	68	907
RAFSLER			
H*	Nevada Grass Valley	61	166
RAFT			
Joseph	Shasta Shasta	66	679
Marcus	Nevada Rough &	61	425
RAFTER			
Geo	Alameda Brooklyn	55	117
George	Alameda Brooklyn	55	116
RAFUEL			
John	Calaveras Twp 4	57	340
RAGALES			
Jose	Santa Clara Alviso	65	403
RAGAN			
Bridget	Los Angeles Los Angeles	59	344
C	Nevada Grass Valley	61	176
Dennis	Yuba Long Bar	72	754
Emily	Tehama Red Bluff	70	926
G*	Nevada Grass Valley	61	186
George	Tulara Twp 3	71	42
J	Nevada Washington	61	333
James	Yuba Marysville	72	929
James D	Napa Hot Springs	61	11
John	Nevada Little Y	61	531
M E	Tehama Tehama	70	949
Martin	Trinity Mouth Ca	70	1010
Michael*	Santa Clara Alviso	65	406
P	Nevada Eureka	61	381
P*	Nevada Grass Valley	61	206
T C	Placer Iona Hills	62	882
T O	Nevada Nevada	61	252
T O	Nevada Nevada	61	317
T O*	Nevada Nevada	61	252
T O*	Nevada Nevada	61	317
RAGANA			
John	Sierra Downieville	66	1002
RAGARD			
Gardner G*	Yuba Rose Bar	72	812
RAGARDO			
Jose	Contra Costa Twp 1	57	509
RAGARIA			
John*	Sierra Downieville	66	1002
RAGAVA			
John*	Sierra Downieville	66	1002
RAGDON			
Rheuben	Santa Clara San Jose	65	317
RAGEE			
A	Solano Vacaville	69	327
G F*	Butte Oregon	56	625
G F*R	Butte Oregon	56	625
George*	Solano Vacaville	69	366
RAGEN			
Jas	Tehama Lassen	70	869
John	Yuba Marysville	72	970
Patrick	Solano Suisan	69	232
RAGER			
August	Nevada Rough &	61	423
G F*	Butte Oregon	56	625
J	El Dorado Diamond	58	808
James A	Del Norte Crescent	58	648
RAGERT			
Louis*	San Francisco San Francisco 7	68	1369
RAGGENS			
Henry	San Francisco San Francisco 9	68	1062
RAGGIO			
Antonia	Amador Twp 3	55	376

California 1860 Census Index

Name	County Locale	M653 Roll	Page
RAGGIS			
A	Tuolumne Twp 4	71	159
L	Tuolumne Twp 4	71	159
RAGGIZONE			
Jos	San Francisco San Francisco 2	67	684
RAGGLE			
M	Nevada Grass Valley	61	150
RAGGNET			
Michael	Tuolumne Twp 4	71	177
RAGGRO			
Jose	San Luis Obispo San Luis Obispo	65	18
RAGHOLDS			
John	Butte Ophir	56	786
RAGHUNN			
Asa	El Dorado Georgetown	58	745
RAGLAN D			
Lard	Tehama Tehama	70	949
RAGLAND			
John	Tehama Red Bluff	70	904
Lewis	Tehama Red Bluff	70	904
Wm*	Tehama Red Bluff	70	918
RAGLE			
E L	Sonoma Armally	69	495
G J	Sonoma Armally	69	495
Wm C	Sonoma Armally	69	495
RAGLIN			
James	Shasta Horsetown	66	701
John	Shasta Horsetown	66	701
RAGLINA			
Pauline	San Francisco San Francisco 2	67	648
RAGNAN			
Arvite*	Amador Twp 1	55	469
RAGNOLD			
John S	Butte Ophir	56	768
RAGNOLDS			
L C	El Dorado Mud Springs	58	978
RAGON			
Geo	Butte Bidwell	56	713
Riychael*	Mariposa Twp 3	60	566
W B	Yuba Rose Bar	72	812
RAGOO			
Joseph	Calaveras Twp 7	57	29
RAGOON			
Rheuben	Santa Clara Alviso	65	401
RAGOTTE			
Leon	Siskiyou Klamath	69	91
Levi	Siskiyou Klamath	69	91
RAGS			
Henderson	Amador Twp 1	55	489
RAGSA			
Pedro*	Mariposa Twp 3	60	570
RAGSDAIL			
James	Siskiyou Scott Va	69	42
RAGSDALE			
Jesse	Mariposa Twp 1	60	636
John	San Joaquin Castoria	64	905
Wm	Santa Clara Redwood	65	457
RAGSO			
Pedro*	Mariposa Twp 3	60	570
RAGU			
G F*	Butte Oregon	56	625
George	Solano Vacaville	69	366
RAGULMA			
Miguel*	Alameda Oakland	55	3
RAGUN			
John	Sierra Twp 5	66	941
RAH			
Loo	Yuba Long Bar	72	763
RAHAL			
M	Sutter Yuba	70	765
RAHAN			
Martin*	Santa Clara San Jose	65	390
Romaldo	San Diego Agua Caliente	64	862
RAHANS			
N	San Francisco San Francisco 9	68	1080
RAHARS			
N*	San Francisco San Francisco 9	68	1080
RAHDERS			
Henry	San Francisco San Francisco 3	67	25
RAHEL			
Emily R	San Bernardino San Salvador	64	650
Henry	San Bernardino San Salvador	64	649
RAHILL			
Thomas	Yuba Marysville	72	959
RAHLENBERG			
John	Napa Napa	61	102
RAHLER			
John	Tuolumne Twp 2	71	274
RAHLS			
Henry*	Sierra Pine Grove	66	820
RAHM			
M A	Yolo Cache	72	641
RAHMIN			
Jose*	Santa Cruz Soguel	66	587
RAHN			
Fred	Mariposa Twp 3	60	548
RAHO			
Blas	Los Angeles Los Angeles	59	310
RAHRER			
Fred	Sonoma Sonoma	69	651
RAHWIN			
Jose*	Santa Cruz Soguel	66	587
RAICE			
Mariam W*	Yuba Marysville	72	875
RAICHE			
Frederick*	San Francisco 3 San Francisco	67	8
RAID			
W	Tuolumne Twp 4	71	151
RAIDLINGER			
Charles	Solano Suisan	69	232
RAIEDER			
J H	Sierra Twp 7	66	868
RAIEL			
W*	Tuolumne Big Oak	71	151
RAIERSON			
Christopher	Tuolumne Twp 5	71	504
RAIEZ			
Jauen	Fresno Twp 1	59	76
RAIG			
George*	Plumas Meadow Valley	62	932
RAIGA			
Ramajo*	Contra Costa Twp 1	57	501
RAIL			
E B	Butte Ophir	56	766
RAILA			
Hosea*	Stanislaus Empire	70	729
RAILLEY			
Francis	Placer Auburn	62	589
J H	Mariposa Twp 1	60	664
RAILLIY			
J H*	Mariposa Twp 1	60	664
RAILLNY			
J H	Mariposa Twp 1	60	664
RAILLON			
M	El Dorado Diamond	58	799
RAILSBACK			
Wm	Sonoma Petaluma	69	548
RAILTS			
Marrinio	Calaveras Twp 6	57	134
RAIM			
Colah*	Santa Clara Santa Clara	65	472
RAIMOND			
Charles	Humbolt Eureka	59	175
RAIMUNDO			
---	San Bernardino Santa Inez	64	137
RAIN			
---	Nevada Bridgeport	61	464
David	Yuba Marysville	72	914
George	San Francisco San Francisco 4	68	1166
John	Alameda Oakland	55	13
John	Placer Iona Hills	62	892
RAINALDE			
R*	Shasta Shasta	66	667
RAINALDI			
R	Shasta Shasta	66	667
RAINBOW			
J P M	Sacramento Ward 1	63	23
RAINBRIDGE			
G W*	Shasta Horsetown	66	693
Levi	Yuba New York	72	739
RAINDLER			
Gustave	San Francisco San Francisco 4	68	1224
RAINEN			
Ja*	El Dorado Placerville	58	911
RAINER			
H	El Dorado Placerville	58	892
RAINERG			
Cafsamirea*	Mariposa Twp 3	60	545
RAINERY			
Cassaminea	Mariposa Twp 3	60	545
RAINES			
Ellen	Alameda Oakland	55	35
G	El Dorado Placerville	58	848
G	El Dorado Placerville	58	873
John	Placer Forest H	62	800
Josiah	Placer Michigan	62	842
Manford	Placer Goods	62	696
W	Shasta Horsetown	66	703
Wm	Sonoma Russian	69	433
RAINEY			
A	Nevada Grass Valley	61	153
Cafsamirea*	Mariposa Twp 3	60	545
Chas	San Francisco San Francisco 9	68	939
Elizabeth	San Francisco San Francisco 9	68	1022
Felix	Santa Clara Santa Clara	65	512
James	Klamath Liberty	59	234
M	Nevada Grass Valley	61	225
Patrick	Tuolumne Twp 3	71	452
Ralph	Alameda Oakland	55	71
Robert	Santa Cruz Pajaro	66	557
Roberty	Santa Cruz Pajaro	66	557
RAINEY			
Samuel	Solano Vallejo	69	265
T	El Dorado Placerville	58	892
William	Santa Cruz Pajaro	66	565
RAINFROW			
Jas	Placer Sacramento	62	643
RAINICKE			
C	Shasta Millvill	66	754
RAINIE			
William	Nevada Bridgeport	61	496
RAINING			
Lucia	Yuba Marysville	72	929
RAINISFORD			
James*	Sacramento Ward 1	63	64
RAINMONS			
Elihue*	Siskiyou Yreka	69	190
RAINONE			
Cassimero	Mariposa Twp 3	60	545
RAINOR			
Bernado	Calaveras Twp 5	57	248
RAINORETT			
H P R	Tuolumne Twp 1	71	220
RAINOS			
Bernado*	Calaveras Twp 5	57	248
RAINS			
B	Nevada Nevada	61	288
B	Sutter Yuba	70	762
B	Sutter Butte	70	782
Gabriel J	Humbolt Bucksport	59	160
Gallant	Sonoma Petaluma	69	601
Gallant	Sonoma Cloverdale	69	685
J F	Tuolumne Columbia	71	315
John	San Bernardino San Bernadino	64	641
John	Yolo Cache Crk	72	645
M	Amador Twp 5	55	368
Silas	Siskiyou Shasta Valley	69	120
Syrus	Yolo Cottonwoood	72	655
Thomas	Alameda Oakland	55	1
Warren	Tuolumne Twp 1	71	261
RAINWONS			
Elihue*	Siskiyou Yreka	69	190
RAINY			
M	Nevada Grass Valley	61	226
Mc Kee	Calaveras Twp 9	57	372
RAIRA			
Andrew	Sierra Downieville	66	1020
RAIRDEN			
M	Yolo Putah	72	560
RAIRE			
Bansivam*	Sierra Downieville	66	1021
Banswam*	Sierra Downieville	66	1021
RAIREN			
J A*	El Dorado Placerville	58	911
RAIRHARD			
T N*	San Francisco San Francisco 9	68	971
RAIS			
---	Mariposa Coulterville	60	685
Pedro	Fresno Twp 1	59	84
RAISE			
Bansovam*	Sierra Downieville	66	1021
RAISER			
Andrew	Sierra Downieville	66	1020
Joseph	San Francisco San Francisco 7	68	1363
RAISH			
Charles	Yuba Marysville	72	891
RAISON			
John	El Dorado Kelsey	58	1150
RAITO			
Louis	Sacramento Ward 4	63	508
RAIVEN			
J A*	El Dorado Placerville	58	911
RAIVIR			
Thos*	Shasta Horsetown	66	699
RAIVIS			
Thos*	Shasta Horsetown	66	699
RAIYO			
Peter	Amador Twp 1	55	508
RAJAN			
Timothy	Placer Iona Hills	62	879
RAJOS			
Maria	Sacramento Ward 1	63	110
RAJSA			
Pedro*	Mariposa Twp 3	60	570
RAJSSA			
Pedro*	Mariposa Twp 3	60	570
RAKER			
Anthro	Mariposa Twp 1	60	672
Chas	Butte Bidwell	56	721
RAKIN			
John	Yolo Slate Ra	72	709
John	Yuba Slate Ro	72	709
RAKKAEL			
Edward*	Tuolumne Twp 2	71	284
RAKOW			
J	San Francisco San Francisco 2	67	734
RAKSTIN			
Richard*	Siskiyou Cottonwoood	69	107

Name	County Locale	M653 Roll Page
RALAMATUS		
Demier	Calaveras Twp 9	57 364
RALAND		
Alexander	Placer Auburn	62 568
V	El Dorado Placerville	58 844
Wm	Nevada Washington	61 337
RALBER		
Irreas*	Alameda Oakland	55 1
Issac*	Alameda Oakland	55 1
RALDIN		
L	Nevada Eureka	61 390
RALDN		
L	Nevada Eureka	61 390
RALDWIN		
Johnson	Tuolumne Montezuma	71 511
RALEIGH		
L B	Nevada Grass Valley	61 150
S B	Nevada Grass Valley	61 150
RALER		
J	Nevada Nevada	61 247
S	Nevada Nevada	61 247
RALES		
Augustus*	Placer Forest H	62 767
Joseph	Placer Ophirville	62 654
RALEY		
Daniel	Solano Benecia	69 285
W C	Nevada Bridgeport	61 474
Watson	Tuolumne Columbia	71 348
Westley	Tuolumne Columbia	71 348
Wm H	Tuolumne Twp 2	71 284
Wm H	Tuolumne Twp 2	71 284
RALF		
N*	Nevada Grass Valley	61 156
W	Nevada Grass Valley	61 156
RALIANS		
N*	San Francisco San Francisco 9	681080
RALIARS		
N*	San Francisco San Francisco 9	681080
RALIM		
Jas	Amador Twp 2	55 306
RALINE		
Jas*	Amador Twp 2	55 306
RALKER		
Henry*	Placer Ophir	62 652
RALKEY		
H	El Dorado Spanish	581124
RALL		
J*	Nevada Grass Valley	61 166
RALLERSON		
J A	Amador Twp 7	55 420
RALLETT		
G W	Mendocino Ukiah	60 802
RALLI		
John	Yuba Foster B	72 835
RALLO		
C C	Tuolumne Twp 3	71 464
RALLSTEN		
Margaret*	Shasta Shasta	66 679
RALLSTON		
A P	San Francisco San Francisco 1	68 846
John	Placer Michigan	62 841
John	Shasta Horsetown	66 703
Margarette	Shasta Shasta	66 679
Thomas	Placer Michigan	62 841
RALM		
Fred	Mariposa Twp 3	60 548
M R	Yolo Cache Crk	72 641
RALMAKE		
James	San Joaquin Elkhorn	64 981
RALMESTHAM		
P G	Mendocino Big Rvr	60 845
RALMORE		
Geroge	Tuolumne Twp 2	71 284
RALPH		
Adolph	San Joaquin Stockton	641064
Calvin R	San Joaquin Castoria	64 876
H	Solano Vacaville	69 319
Henry	Yuba Marysville	72 928
J	Nevada Grass Valley	61 149
J F	Tuolumne Twp 1	71 260
Joseph	Alameda Brooklyn	55 199
R	Butte Chico	56 553
Richd	San Bernardino San Salvador	64 657
Smithand W	Elkhorn San Joaquin	64 964
Thomas	El Dorado Placerville	58 928
W	San Francisco San Francisco 5	67 543
Wm	San Francisco San Francisco 2	67 601
RALPLEY		
John	Placer Mountain	62 708
RALSLER		
H*	Nevada Grass Valley	61 166
RALSOM		
Wm*	Sacramento Georgian	63 343
RALSON		
N	Yuba Timbucto	72 787
RALSTAN		
S W*	Sacramento Georgian	63 343
RALSTIN		
Richard	Siskiyou Cottonwoood	69 107
RALSTON		
J A	San Francisco San Francisco 12	393 67
J B	Nevada Grass Valley	61 221
J N	Sacramento Sutter	63 291
Jos	Sacramento Sutter	63 291
N	Amador Twp 1	55 488
S W*	Sacramento Georgian	63 343
W C	San Francisco San Francisco 5	67 500
RALSTONE		
R	San Francisco San Francisco 1	68 921
RALT		
N*	Nevada Grass Valley	61 156
RALWEY		
Levi P	Tuolumne Jamestown	71 421
RALYEN		
L B*	Sacramento Granite	63 222
S B*	Sacramento Granite	63 222
RAM		
---	San Francisco San Francisco 4	681209
---	Yuba Slate Ro	72 713
RAMA		
Francio*	San Mateo Twp 1	65 60
RAMAGE		
J	San Francisco San Francisco 5	67 490
M	Siskiyou Scott Va	69 23
Samuel	Siskiyou Yreka	69 156
RAMAKA		
---	Fresno Twp 2	59 113
RAMALUE		
Peter	Siskiyou Yreka	69 173
RAMAN		
David	Nevada Bridgeport	61 478
George	Humbolt Union	59 185
John	San Francisco San Francisco 2	67 770
RAMANDEZ		
Ramon	Placer Forest H	62 772
RAMANDO		
---	Monterey S Antoni	60 970
RAMANE		
M	Nevada Eureka	61 366
RAMANO		
Redro	Los Angeles Los Angeles	59 493
RAMARA		
Antonio	Tuolumne Jamestown	71 426
RAMARES		
Jesus	Contra Costa Twp 1	57 491
Jose Mane	Calaveras Twp 6	57 160
RAMAREZ		
Carmine	Calaveras Twp 4	57 332
RAMARIO		
Josa*	Santa Cruz Soguel	66 596
RAMARISS		
Jose Marie	Calaveras Twp 6	57 160
RAMARO		
Antonio	Tuolumne Twp 3	71 426
B	El Dorado Placerville	58 840
J	Sacramento Ward 1	63 124
Josepha	San Joaquin Stockton	641050
RAMAS		
Juan	Marin Cortemad	60 785
RAMASISS		
Jose Mario*	Calaveras Twp 6	57 160
RAMAUE		
M	Nevada Eureka	61 366
RAMAZZI		
Dominigue	Marin Cortemad	60 781
Dominue*	Marin Cortemad	60 781
RAMBATI		
D	San Francisco San Francisco 3	67 83
RAMBEAN		
C	Sacramento Ward 1	63 106
RAMBER		
Calvin	Tehama Red Bluff	70 927
RAMBLE		
G	Sacramento Cosummes	63 404
RAMBO		
Isaac	Sonoma Vallejo	69 618
Jacob	Sonoma Armally	69 499
Jas H	Napa Napa	61 62
Joel M	Siskiyou Yreka	69 131
RAMBON		
J P M	Sacramento Ward 1	63 23
RAMBOS		
Jose	Santa Cruz Pescadero	66 644
RAMBOY		
Peirre	Sacramento Ward 1	63 103
RAMBRAN		
C*	Sacramento Ward 1	63 106
RAMCE		
Victor*	Mariposa Twp 3	60 585
RAMDAY		
Levi*	Stanislaus Empire	70 730
RAMECIO		
A	San Mateo Twp 2	65 122
RAMEL		
Victor	Mariposa Twp 3	60 585
RAMELLO		
Vincenta	Tuolumne Twp 1	71 225
RAMEN		
Michael*	Yuba Bear Rvr	721000
RAMENTO		
---	Tulara Twp 3	71 63
RAMEO		
Simon*	Sacramento Ward 1	63 137
RAMER		
J	El Dorado Casumnes	581175
Simon*	Sacramento Ward 1	63 137
V*	Sutter Yuba	70 766
Washington*	Placer Forest H	62 770
RAMERA		
Gaudalupe	Alameda Brooklyn	55 177
Hermenfallio*	Plumas Quincy	62 995
RAMERAS		
N	San Mateo Twp 1	65 48
RAMERES		
Amarala	Alameda Brooklyn	55 143
Caazar	Tuolumne Twp 1	71 235
Jesusa	Tuolumne Sonora	71 235
Matilda	Alameda Oakland	55 57
RAMEREZ		
Anita	San Diego San Diego	64 763
Anna	Sacramento Ward 1	63 99
Candelerea	Santa Barbara San Bernardino	64 152
Felix	Tuolumne Twp 2	71 275
Herculanio	Sacramento Ward 1	63 105
Honasa	Los Angeles Elmonte	59 259
Joaquin	Plumas Quincy	62 988
Jose	Santa Clara Fremont	65 434
Lazaro	Santa Clara San Jose	65 369
RAMERIA		
Jesus	Mariposa Twp 3	60 549
RAMERIEZ		
Severo	Santa Clara San Jose	65 300
RAMERIS		
Jose	Los Angeles Los Angeles	59 516
Rafael	San Diego S Luis R	64 780
RAMERIZ		
Alaca	Tuolumne Twp 5	71 490
Alaco	Tuolumne Chinese	71 490
Carmileto	Tuolumne Twp 5	71 490
Horincia	Santa Clara Almaden	65 277
Victoria	Tuolumne Twp 5	71 491
RAMERO		
B R*	Nevada Grass Valley	61 167
Bartoleo	San Francisco San Francisco 3	67 84
Bartolio	San Francisco San Francisco 3	67 84
F	Tuolumne Shawsfla	71 420
Jose	Santa Clara Fremont	65 436
Jose	Tuolumne Jamestown	71 437
Pedros	Sacramento Ward 1	63 149
Quoeencio*	Santa Clara Fremont	65 436
RAMEROS		
Jisusa	Tuolumne Twp 1	71 235
Walonpa	Tuolumne Sonora	71 475
Waloupa*	Tuolumne Twp 1	71 475
RAMERS		
B R	Nevada Grass Valley	61 167
C	Nevada Grass Valley	61 238
RAMERT		
B R*	Nevada Grass Valley	61 167
RAMERY		
Felise	Tuolumne Twp 1	71 275
RAMES		
John	El Dorado Greenwood	58 712
RAMESE		
John*	El Dorado Greenwood	58 717
RAMEV		
Simon*	Sacramento Ward 1	63 137
RAMEY		
B	Nevada Grass Valley	61 188
George	Tulara Twp 2	71 24
J	El Dorado Casumnes	581175
James	Sonoma Cloverdale	69 681
Johnathan	Tuolumne Twp 2	71 348
Robt*	Sacramento Centre	63 179
Titus	Humbolt Bucksport	59 156
Wm	Amador Twp 7	55 413
RAMEZ		
Francisco	Calaveras Twp 4	57 337
RAMEZEZ		
Berriona*	San Francisco San Francisco 2	67 700
RAMFIELD		
J	Yolo Washington	72 563
RAMFIN		
Frank	Yolo Slate Ra	72 687
RAMFORD		
J	Nevada Washington	61 336

California 1860 Census Index

Name	County Locale	M653 RollPage
RAMGUIN		
Francis	Contra Costa Twp 1	57 517
RAMIDOS		
V	Merced Twp 1	60 909
RAMIE		
Victor	Mariposa Twp 3	60 585
RAMIEG		
Julien*	Marin Cortemad	60 786
RAMIEZ		
Julien	Marin Cortemad	60 786
RAMILES		
Anastacio	Calaveras Twp 10	57 289
RAMILLA		
Fenlina San Luis Obispo	San Luis Obispo	65 11
RAMILLARD		
Riorsa*	Calaveras Twp 4	57 321
Riosa*	Calaveras Twp 4	57 321
RAMILLES		
J	Sacramento Ward 1	63 4
RAMILLO		
Vicenta	Tuolumne Sonora	71 225
RAMINEZ		
Antonio	Marin Cortemad	60 780
RAMINS		
R	Merced Twp 1	60 915
RAMIR		
Edward*	Yuba Marysville	72 957
RAMIRAS		
Manuel	Calaveras Twp 5	57 241
RAMIRES		
Jesus	Los Angeles Los Angeles	59 492
Rafael	Santa Clara Almaden	65 273
RAMIREZ		
Andres	Los Angeles Los Angeles	59 359
Antonio	Yuba Marysville	72 858
Antonio	Yuba Marysville	72 860
Antonio*	Marin Cortemad	60 780
Augustus	Yuba Marysville	72 950
Bartolo	Los Angeles Los Nieto	59 432
Benedita	Los Angeles Los Angeles	59 310
Carmel	Los Angeles Los Angeles	59 309
Conception	San Francisco 11	101
	San Francisco	67
Cruz	Sacramento Ward 1	63 110
Custodio	Los Angeles Los Nieto	59 434
Eiculano	Sacramento Ward 1	63 110
Evanlano	Sacramento Ward 1	63 110
F	Sacramento Ward 1	63 8
Feliciana	Los Angeles Los Nieto	59 426
Filipe	Mendocino Arrana	60 861
Francisco	Los Angeles Los Nieto	59 437
Guadalupe	Los Angeles Los Angeles	59 386
Herculamo*	Sacramento Ward 1	63 105
Hercularno*	Sacramento Ward 1	63 105
Isabella	San Francisco San Francisco 2	67 768
Jesus	Los Angeles San Juan	59 460
Jose	Los Angeles Los Nieto	59 434
Jose	Marin Cortemad	60 782
Jose	San Diego Colorado	64 811
Jose M	Los Angeles Los Nieto	59 426
Jose M	Los Angeles Los Nieto	59 433
Jose M	Yuba Marysville	72 957
Juan	Los Angeles Los Angeles	59 390
Juan	San Bernardino Santa Inez	64 141
Lantaro	San Francisco San Francisco 11	101
		67
Lucia	Los Angeles Los Angeles	59 378
Madalina	Yuba Marysville	72 946
Manuel	Monterey Monterey	60 957
Maria	Los Angeles Los Nieto	59 432
Maria R C	Los Angeles San Juan	59 464
Pascual	Los Angeles Los Angeles	59 302
RAMIRIS		
Jose	Los Angeles Los Angeles	59 516
Jose A	Los Angeles Los Angeles	59 511
RAMIRIZ		
Manuel	Monterey Monterey	60 957
RAMIRO		
Wm	El Dorado Georgetown	58 675
RAMIRRES		
Philip	Contra Costa Twp 1	57 513
RAMIRUS		
Manuel*	Calaveras Twp 5	57 241
RAMISFORD		
James	Sacramento Ward 1	63 64
RAMISH		
J*	Nevada Grass Valley	61 176
RAMIUS		
Manuel*	Calaveras Twp 5	57 241
RAMKIN		
Walker	Tulara Twp 1	71 74
RAMLE		
M	Amador Twp 3	55 384
RAMLON		
W*	Nevada Eureka	61 370
RAMMA		
E H	Siskiyou Yreka	69 180

Name	County Locale	M653 RollPage
RAMMELSBERG		
Alfred*	Contra Costa Twp 1	57 524
RAMMERS		
John	Siskiyou Yreka	69 187
RAMNANS		
John*	Sacramento Ward 1	63 42
RAMO		
Francisco	San Diego Temecula	64 785
RAMON		
---	Los Angeles Los Angeles	59 383
---	Los Angeles San Gabriel	59 413
---	Marin Bolinas	60 728
---	Mendocino Calpella	60 826
---	Monterey Monterey	60 962
---	San Bernardino Santa Barbara	64 160
---	San Bernardino San Bernardino	64 673
---	San Bernardino San Bernardino	64 678
---	San Bernardino S Timate	64 692
---	San Bernardino S Timate	64 693
---	San Bernardino S Timate	64 695
---	San Bernardino S Timate	64 696
---	San Bernardino S Timate	64 701
---	San Bernardino S Timate	64 702
---	San Bernardino S Timate	64 703
---	San Bernardino S Timate	64 705
---	San Bernardino S Timate	64 707
---	San Bernardino S Timate	64 708
---	San Bernardino S Timate	64 710
---	San Bernardino S Timate	64 712
---	San Bernardino S Timate	64 713
---	San Bernardino S Timate	64 717
---	San Bernardino S Timate	64 718
---	San Bernardino S Timate	64 720
---	San Bernardino S Timate	64 724
---	San Bernardino S Timate	64 727
---	San Bernardino S Timate	64 728
---	San Bernardino S Timate	64 729
---	San Bernardino S Timate	64 730
---	San Bernardino S Timate	64 731
---	San Bernardino S Timate	64 732
---	San Bernardino S Timate	64 733
---	San Bernardino S Timate	64 736
---	San Bernardino S Timate	64 738
---	San Bernardino S Timate	64 740
---	San Bernardino S Timate	64 742
---	San Bernardino S Timate	64 744
---	San Bernardino S Timate	64 745
---	San Bernardino S Timate	64 746
---	San Bernardino S Timate	64 749
---	San Bernardino S Timate	64 750
---	San Bernardino S Timate	64 752
---	San Bernardino S Timate	64 753
---	San Diego Agua Caliente	64 815
---	San Diego Agua Caliente	64 845
---	San Mateo Twp 2	65 133
---	Tulara Twp 1	71 118
---	Tulara Keeneysburg	71 50
---	Tulara Keyesville	71 63
---	Tulara Keyesville	71 65
---	Tulara Keyesville	71 66
---	Tulara Keyesville	71 67
---	Tulara Keyesville	71 69
---	Tulara Keyesville	71 70
---	Tulara Keyesville	71 72
Antomi	Calaveras Twp 4	57 331
Antonie	Calaveras Twp 4	57 331
Antonio	Calaveras Twp 7	57 29
Antonio	Calaveras Twp 4	57 331
Baptiste	Calaveras Twp 7	57 20
Don	Stanislaus Oatvale	70 719
Felipe	Los Angeles Los Angeles	59 306
Guadaloupe	Plumas Meadow Valley	62 933
Jesus	San Diego Temecula	64 791
Jesus	Santa Cruz Pescadero	66 651
John	Tuolumne Shawsfla	71 420
Jose	Contra Costa Twp 1	57 494
Jose	Los Angeles Los Angeles	59 382
Jose	San Luis Obispo San Luis Obispo	65 12
Jose	Tuolumne Twp 2	71 414
Juan	Santa Cruz Santa Cruz	66 601
Leonardo	Los Angeles Shaffer	59 396
Leonardo	Los Angeles Los Angeles	59 397
Luno	Tulara Keyesville	71 66
Perfectar	Contra Costa Twp 3	57 600
Thos	Mariposa Twp 1	60 639
RAMONA JUNA		
---*	Los Angeles Los Angeles	59 495
RAMONA		
---	Los Angeles Los Angeles	59 497
---	San Bernardino Santa Ba	64 221
---	San Bernardino San Bernadino	64 673
---	San Bernardino S Timate	64 692
---	San Bernardino S Timate	64 694
---	San Bernardino S Timate	64 697
---	San Bernardino S Timate	64 704
---	San Bernardino S Timate	64 713

Name	County Locale	M653 RollPage
RAMONA		
---	San Bernardino S Timate	64 718
---	San Bernardino S Timate	64 721
---	San Bernardino S Timate	64 735
---	San Bernardino S Timate	64 741
---	San Bernardino S Timate	64 752
---	San Bernardino S Timate	64 754
---*	San Bernardino S Buenav	64 221
Ramon	San Diego Colorado	64 810
RAMOND		
Bernard	Calaveras Twp 4	57 334
C	San Mateo Twp 3	65 92
Joseph P	Yuba Suida	72 982
Joseph S	Yuba Linda Twp	72 982
RAMONDA		
---	San Bernardino S Timate	64 750
RAMONDO		
---	San Bernardino San Bernadino	64 669
---	San Bernardino S Timate	64 701
---	San Bernardino S Timate	64 717
---	San Bernardino S Timate	64 720
---	San Bernardino S Timate	64 722
---	San Bernardino S Timate	64 723
---	San Bernardino S Timate	64 724
---	San Bernardino S Timate	64 730
---	San Bernardino S Timate	64 745
---	San Bernardino S Timate	64 749
RAMONDS		
---	San Bernardino S Timate	64 738
RAMONE		
---*	Mariposa Twp 3	60 614
G	Nevada Grass Valley	61 224
Guadalupa*	Napa Napa	61 115
Ignacio	Mariposa Twp 3	60 571
Ihgacio	Mariposa Twp 3	60 571
Lenaeio*	Mariposa Twp 3	60 571
Y*	Nevada Grass Valley	61 224
RAMONO		
Guadalupa	Napa Napa	61 115
Manl*	Mariposa Twp 1	60 644
RAMONS		
J	Siskiyou Scott Ri	69 73
RAMORDIS		
Hagartus	Calaveras Twp 4	57 330
Hayartus	Calaveras Twp 4	57 330
RAMORES		
Jacques*	Yuba New York	72 734
RAMOREZ		
Cristorae	San Bernardino Santa Ba	64 216
Cristorae	San Bernardino S Buenav	64 217
Cusmine	Calaveras Twp 4	57 332
Juan	Los Angeles Los Angeles	59 390
RAMORIA		
---*	San Bernardino S Buenav	64 221
RAMORIS		
Frando	Amador Twp 5	55 332
RAMORO		
Joquin	Los Angeles Los Angeles	59 512
Manl	Mariposa Twp 1	60 644
RAMOS		
Andres	Santa Clara Fremont	65 431
Annita	San Francisco San Francisco 2	67 683
Annita	San Francisco San Francisco 2	67 790
Antonio	San Francisco San Francisco 2	67 688
Bartolo	Los Angeles Los Nieto	59 427
Carmina	Calaveras Twp 4	57 336
Domingo	Los Angeles Los Angeles	59 379
Eurebia	Calaveras Twp 6	57 128
Eusebia	Calaveras Twp 6	57 128
Frances	San Francisco San Francisco 2	67 686
Jesus	Santa Clara Alviso	65 408
Jesus	Santa Clara Fremont	65 431
Jose	Calaveras Twp 7	57 31
Jose	San Francisco San Francisco 2	67 795
Jose	Tuolumne Columbia	71 337
Jose M	Santa Clara Gilroy	65 227
Juan	Marin Cortemad	60 785
Maria	San Francisco San Francisco 2	67 581
Maria	San Francisco San Francisco 2	67 683
Mary	Tuolumne Columbia	71 320
Maryneta	Sacramento Ward 1	63 99
Marysuta	Sacramento Ward 1	63 99
Papias	Santa Clara Alviso	65 408
Theodore	Tuolumne Sonora	71 227
Thomas	Yuba Marysville	72 948
RAMOT		
L	Nevada Grass Valley	61 150
RAMOUD		
Bernard*	Calaveras Twp 4	57 334
RAMOULIS		
Augustus	Calaveras Twp 4	57 330
RAMP		
James*	San Francisco San Francisco 3	67 72
RAMPENDAHL		
Henry	Napa Hot Springs	61 23
RAMPER		
Ranna*	Placer Auburn	62 580

California 1860 Census Index

Name	County Locale	M653 Roll	Page
RAMPTON			
R L	Yolo Washington	72	567
RAMRENSTOB			
Charles J*	San Francisco San Francisco 7	68	1345
RAMRES			
Jacques	Yuba New York	72	734
RAMREZ			
Annette*	Sacramento Ward 1	63	78
RAMRITZ			
Armetre*	Sacramento Ward 1	63	78
RAMROEZ			
Madalina	Yuba Marysville	72	946
RAMS			
Gullant	Sonoma Petaluma	69	601
Saml	Napa Clear Lake	61	123
RAMSAY			
Dominick	San Francisco San Francisco 11	67	162
G	Stanislaus Buena Village	70	721
Geo R	Stanislaus Emory	70	740
James W	Sierra Poker Flats	66	840
Lafayette	San Luis Obispo San Luis Obispo	65	42
Levi*	Stanislaus Empire	70	730
William	Monterey S Antoni	60	972
RAMSBOTTOM			
David	Stanislaus Emory	70	752
Robert	Stanislaus Emory	70	752
RAMSDALE			
A G	San Francisco San Francisco 4	68	1130
Benj	San Francisco San Francisco 1	68	826
George W	Yuba Marysville	72	860
George W	Yuba Marysville	72	860
J	Calaveras Twp 9	57	399
S C	Tuolumne Columbia	71	309
RAMSDELL			
C B	Butte Bidwell	56	716
Geo	Nevada Nevada	61	290
James	Sierra Downieville	66	957
T M	Sierra Downieville	66	966
RAMSDEN			
Joseph	Siskiyou Yreka	69	143
RAMSEE			
G M	Nevada Grass Valley	61	156
RAMSEL			
G M*	Nevada Grass Valley	61	156
RAMSELL			
C H*	San Francisco San Francisco 3	67	44
Chas	Butte Bidwell	56	723
Chas	Butte Bidwell	56	730
T L*	Calaveras Twp 9	57	355
RAMSER			
Jno	Sacramento Ward 4	63	521
RAMSEY			
A	El Dorado Placerville	58	860
Alex	El Dorado White Oaks	58	1008
Alexander	Colusa Grand Island	57	478
Andrew	Plumas Quincy	62	964
Augustus	Yuba Marysville	72	950
B J	Sacramento Georgian	63	339
B M	Sonoma Cloverdale	69	686
Charles	Solano Suisan	69	237
D C	Solano Suisan	69	221
Edwd	San Francisco San Francisco 12	67	392
F	Sacramento Ward 1	63	8
Geo	El Dorado Coloma	58	1105
Geo	Sacramento Cosummes	63	390
Geo	San Francisco San Francisco 2	67	693
Geo H	San Francisco San Francisco 9	68	1020
H	Sacramento Ward 1	63	1
H F*	Nevada Nevada	61	296
J M	Yuba New York	72	737
James	Klamath S Fork	59	205
James	Tulara Twp 2	71	20
James D	San Francisco San Francisco 6	67	400
Jas	Placer Lisbon	62	733
Jill	Yuba New York	72	737
John B	Colusa Grand Island	57	468
Lackman	El Dorado Georgetown	58	690
Lockwood	El Dorado Georgetown	58	690
M	Calaveras Twp 9	57	416
Mary	Yuba Rose Bar	72	791
N F	Marin S Antoni	60	709
Robert T	Yuba Marysville	72	911
Sam	Merced Twp 1	60	909
Saml	Sacramento Georgian	63	347
W	Butte Kimshaw	56	604
W	Nevada Nevada	61	261
W F	Marin S Antoni	60	709
W T	Nevada Nevada	61	296
William	Nevada Bloomfield	61	515
William	Solano Green Valley	69	241
Wm	Butte Kimshaw	56	604
Wm	Butte Oregon	56	620
RAMSEY			
Wm	Humbolt Eureka	59	165
Wm	Placer Secret R	62	612
Wm H	Sonoma Mendocino	69	449
RAMSHILL			
Algeroy	Tuolumne Don Pedro	71	539
RAMSILL			
C H*	San Francisco San Francisco 3	67	44
RAMSLER			
James	San Francisco San Francisco 4	68	1171
RAMSON			
E	Butte Kimshaw	56	604
RAMSPECK			
H J	Trinity E Weaver	70	1061
RAMSPORT			
Owen	Yuba Bear Rvr	72	1006
RAMSY			
E T	Amador Twp 2	55	274
RAMUN			
David	Nevada Bridgeport	61	478
RAMUNDO			
---	Monterey S Antoni	60	972
RAMUS			
J	San Joaquin Stockton	64	1099
Porfelto	Los Angeles Elmonte	59	258
RAMUZ			
Annette*	Sacramento Ward 1	63	78
RAMVENSTOB			
Charles J*	San Francisco San Francisco 7	68	1345
RAMY			
A*	Napa Hot Springs	61	3
W F	Yuba New York	72	725
RAN			
---	Amador Twp 5	55	333
---	El Dorado Placerville	58	919
---	Mariposa Twp 1	60	646
---	Mariposa Coulterville	60	685
---	San Francisco San Francisco 4	68	1194
---*	Mariposa Twp 3	60	553
---*	Stanislaus Branch	70	714
Chou	San Francisco San Francisco 4	68	1181
Lewis	Los Angeles Elmonte	59	256
Long	Stanislaus Branch	70	713
Thomas	Calaveras Twp 4	57	314
RANABERGER			
D	El Dorado Placerville	58	855
RANAHAN			
Edmund	San Francisco San Francisco 9	68	1005
RANAN			
Thomas	Solano Suisan	69	204
RANARD			
Jas	Sonoma Petaluma	69	570
Thos	Sonoma Petaluma	69	569
RANBZ			
William*	Plumas Quincy	62	975
RANCCA			
John	Butte Mountain	56	736
RANCE			
Eliz	Sacramento Ward 3	63	472
RANCH			
Frank	Mariposa Twp 3	60	601
Sarah	Yuba Foster B	72	823
W	San Francisco San Francisco 5	67	511
RANCHER			
August	El Dorado Mud Springs	58	966
RANCHIRIO			
---	Tulara Keyesville	71	64
RANCHLEY			
A R	Nevada Grass Valley	61	162
RANCICH			
Martin*	Sacramento Ward 3	63	426
RANCICK			
Martin*	Sacramento Ward 3	63	426
RANCK			
Isaac	Siskiyou Yreka	69	176
RANCKER			
Jas	San Francisco San Francisco 2	67	801
Jos	San Francisco San Francisco 2	67	801
RANCKMANN			
Anna*	San Francisco San Francisco 9	68	954
RANCO			
Peter	Calaveras Twp 7	57	34
RANCON			
Robt	Klamath Liberty	59	230
RANCOR			
O W	Marin Cortemad	60	752
RANCT			
Alexander*	Placer Rattle Snake	62	633
RANCY			
Patrick*	Tuolumne Twp 3	71	454
RAND			
Charles	Calaveras Twp 10	57	294
Chas W	San Francisco San Francisco 2	67	647
D H*	San Francisco San Francisco 5	67	522
Edward	Solano Vallejo	69	261
RAND			
Elizabeth	Santa Clara San Jose	65	362
Geo	San Francisco San Francisco 2	67	693
Hanson	Butte Chico	56	531
Jasper	Yuba Linda	72	990
Jno H	Klamath S Fork	59	198
John	Yolo Slate Ra	72	690
Joseph	San Mateo Twp 1	65	55
L H*	San Francisco San Francisco 5	67	522
Mary A	San Francisco San Francisco 7	68	1347
N B	Shasta Horsetown	66	689
O	Trinity Mouth Ca	70	1013
O H	Solano Vallejo	69	280
Thomas	Placer Iona Hills	62	884
Thomas H	Contra Costa Twp 2	57	546
Vincent	Tuolumne Jamestown	71	441
Wm	Amador Twp 1	55	470
RANDABUSH			
Abram	Contra Costa Twp 2	57	544
RANDAL			
A C	Nevada Bridgeport	61	488
A W	Siskiyou Scott Ri	69	64
Amos	Yuba Marysville	72	900
C	San Joaquin Stockton	64	1086
Edmin	Napa Yount	61	44
Edmun	Napa Yount	61	44
H	Butte Cascade	56	697
H B	Siskiyou Scott Ri	69	64
W E	Marin Bolinas	60	740
Welcm	Nevada Bridgeport	61	503
RANDALE			
William L	San Francisco San Francisco 8	68	1308
RANDALL			
A J	San Joaquin Stockton	64	1091
Adelia	San Francisco San Francisco 7	68	1330
Amos A	Yuba Marysville	72	900
Arthur A	San Francisco San Francisco 2	67	659
Augustus	Sacramento Ward 1	63	139
B	Calaveras Twp 8	57	86
Benjamine	Tuolumne Twp 6	71	542
C B	San Francisco San Francisco 6	67	449
C H	Tuolumne Sonora	71	214
Charles	Calaveras Twp 4	57	308
Curtis	Sierra St Louis	66	812
D	Butte Kimshaw	56	589
Daniel	Tuolumne Sonora	71	205
David	Tuolumne Twp 1	71	205
E	San Francisco San Francisco 9	68	1102
Ephraim	San Francisco San Francisco 10	67	213
F	Butte Eureka	56	651
F	San Francisco San Francisco 9	68	1059
F	San Francisco San Francisco 5	67	553
Francis	Calaveras Twp 6	57	121
Frank	Santa Clara Redwood	65	457
G	Nevada Grass Valley	61	165
Geo	Nevada Eureka	61	371
Geo	Sacramento Ward 4	63	516
Geo	San Francisco San Francisco 2	67	746
Geo	San Francisco San Francisco 1	68	890
George	San Francisco San Francisco 3	67	34
H	Butte Oregon	56	644
Henry	Klamath S Fork	59	200
Henry	Sacramento Ward 1	63	103
Henry A	Sacramento Granite	63	252
Isiah	Amador Twp 3	55	401
J	Nevada Nevada	61	291
J	Nevada Eureka	61	367
James B	San Francisco San Francisco 7	68	1361
Jas	Butte Oregon	56	628
Jas	Placer Rattle Snake	62	600
Jno	Butte Oregon	56	628
John	Yolo Merritt	72	581
John N	San Joaquin Douglass	64	925
Jos	Amador Twp 3	55	374
Mary	San Francisco San Francisco 2	67	669
Mary	San Francisco San Francisco 1	68	893
Mary P	Alameda Oakland	55	47
N	Tuolumne Columbia	71	354
Newel	Tuolumne Columbia	71	471
P M	Amador Twp 4	55	255
Perry	Tulara Twp 1	71	88
R R	Butte Mountain	56	740
Rhodes B	Tuolumne Don Pedro	71	542
Robert	Calaveras Twp 6	57	178
Robt B	Del Norte Crescent	58	622
S	El Dorado Placerville	58	847
S F	Nevada Grass Valley	61	183
S I*	Placer Damascus	62	846
S S	Napa Yount	61	45
Saml	Shasta Millvill	66	725
Saml G	Tuolumne Twp 2	71	393
Samuel	Napa Yount	61	43
Samuel	Placer Forest H	62	804
Samuel	San Diego San Diego	64	757

California 1860 Census Index

Name	County Locale	M653 RollPage
RANDALL		
Samuel	San Francisco San Francisco 11	162
		67
T S	Napa Yount	61 45
Thomas	San Joaquin Stockton	641066
Timothy	Contra Costa Twp 1	57 519
W T	Sacramento Georgian	63 346
William L	San Francisco San Francisco 8	681308
Wm	Nevada Grass Valley	61 175
Wm F	San Francisco San Francisco 3	67 9
Y C	El Dorado Greenwood	58 725
RANDALMAN		
Henry	Sacramento Dry Crk	63 376
RANDEAS		
Francisco	Contra Costa Twp 1	57 491
RANDELL		
A	Placer Todds Va	62 764
Benj	Alameda Brooklyn	55 190
Elizabeth	Alameda Brooklyn	55 203
G	Calaveras Twp 9	57 376
Geo	Santa Clara Redwood	65 456
H D	El Dorado Placerville	58 897
Irah*	Alameda Oakland	55 47
Isah*	Alameda Oakland	55 47
J B	Santa Clara Redwood	65 458
Jacob	Alameda Brooklyn	55 94
James	Alameda Brooklyn	55 94
Theophilus	Siskiyou Yreka	69 150
Thesphilus*	Siskiyou Yreka	69 150
Willis	San Joaquin Stockton	641031
RANDEN		
M	Yolo Putah	72 560
RANDENEL		
Caroline	Yuba Marysville	72 919
RANDENOR		
Mary*	Mariposa Twp 1	60 635
RANDETADDLER		
George	Placer Yankee J	62 758
RANDEZ		
C	Calaveras Twp 9	57 389
RANDHALT		
Deithrh*	San Francisco San Francisco 3	67 65
Deittrich*	San Francisco San Francisco 3	67 65
Dertheh*	San Francisco San Francisco 3	67 65
RANDHORIO		
---	Tulara Twp 3	71 64
RANDLE		
Albert	Sierra Twp 5	66 936
Joseph	Yolo Putah	72 588
K T	Mendocino Big Rvr	60 844
M A	El Dorado Casumnes	581172
Miles	San Mateo Twp 3	65 83
O A	El Dorado Placerville	58 874
P W	Alameda Brooklyn	55 83
Thomas	Sonoma Armally	69 480
RANDLEMAN		
Jane	Sacramento Dry Crk	63 371
RANDLER		
William	Santa Cruz Santa Cruz	66 630
RANDLETI		
Charles*	Placer Forest H	62 796
RANDLETT		
Adaline	Mendocino Calpella	60 812
Henry A	Mendocino Calpella	60 812
Ranson*	Placer Forest H	62 799
RANDNEZ		
C	Calaveras Twp 9	57 398
RANDOHE		
Francis	Yuba Marysville	72 874
RANDOLER		
Francis*	Yuba Marysville	72 874
RANDOLHR		
Francis*	Yuba Marysville	72 874
RANDOLPH		
B H	San Francisco San Francisco 6	67 460
B M	Sacramento Granite	63 221
Chas	Amador Twp 2	55 320
E	Nevada Nevada	61 326
Edmund	San Francisco San Francisco 2	67 744
George	Plumas Quincy	62 984
H	Nevada Washington	61 332
Hamilton	Sonoma Petaluma	69 607
Henry	San Francisco San Francisco 8	681287
Henry	Siskiyou Scott Va	69 30
Isaac	Yolo Cache	72 591
J	Sonoma Bodega	69 539
J F	Nevada Nevada	61 257
J N	Amador Twp 4	55 242
J N	Shasta Horsetown	66 695
J W	Shasta Horsetown	66 695
James	Del Norte Crescent	58 659
John	Placer Michigan	62 858
John	San Francisco San Francisco 1	68 915
John	Tuolumne Twp 1	71 266
L*	Placer Michigan	62 831
P	El Dorado Placerville	58 847

Name	County Locale	M653 RollPage
RANDOLPH		
P C	Napa Yount	61 37
Rachael	Sonoma Petaluma	69 607
Reuben	Solano Benecia	69 301
Ruben T	Solano Benecia	69 301
S*	Placer Michigan	62 831
Saml S	Sacramento Dry Crk	63 368
Stephen	Placer Todds Va	62 785
Thomas C	Yuba Marysville	72 881
W C	Nevada Nevada	61 252
William	Santa Cruz Santa Cruz	66 636
Wm	Nevada Eureka	61 363
Wm	Sacramento Dry Crk	63 373
RANDOPLAS		
E	El Dorado Kelsey	581144
RANDRUP		
William	San Francisco San Francisco 7	681346
RANDS		
Vincent	Tuolumne Twp 3	71 441
RANDULL		
Charles	Calaveras Twp 4	57 308
RANDY		
G W	Yolo Cache	72 630
J	El Dorado Placerville	58 845
RANE		
Antone	El Dorado Mud Springs	58 966
Frederick	Calaveras Twp 7	57 19
James*	San Francisco San Francisco 3	67 66
M	Sacramento Sutter	63 300
Michael*	Solano Benecia	69 296
Patrick	Contra Costa Twp 1	57 525
RANEIREZ		
Isabella*	San Francisco San Francisco 2	67 768
RANERMEYER		
Adolph	San Francisco San Francisco 3	67 38
RANERY		
A J*	Napa Yount	61 47
RANES		
Camelia	El Dorado White Oaks	581017
RANETTE		
John*	Nevada Red Dog	61 556
RANEVY		
A J	Napa Yount	61 47
RANEY		
A J*	Napa Yount	61 47
A*	Napa Hot Springs	61 3
Alexander	Monterey Monterey	60 925
Alexr	Monterey Monterey	60 956
Crisa	Yolo Washington	72 573
Crist	Yolo Washington	72 573
Geroge W	Tuolumne Twp 1	71 461
John B	Sonoma Healdsbu	69 471
L C	Butte Oregon	56 617
Patrick	Tuolumne Jamestown	71 454
Peter	Butte Chico	56 552
Robt	Sonoma Sonoma	69 635
Robt*	Sacramento Centre	63 179
Robt*	Sonoma Sonoma	69 635
S H	Nevada Eureka	61 377
Sulivan	Nevada Rough &	61 413
RANFT		
H	San Francisco San Francisco 2	67 640
Henry*	San Francisco San Francisco 5	67 494
Hy	San Francisco San Francisco 2	67 640
RANG LA		
---	Mariposa Twp 3	60 607
RANG		
Georgej	Plumas Meadow Valley	62 932
RANGDON		
I	Amador Twp 2	55 309
J*	Amador Twp 2	55 309
RANGEL		
Andres	Los Angeles Los Nieto	59 438
Francisco*	Los Angeles Los Nieto	59 425
Gabriel	Los Angeles Los Nieto	59 426
Jesus	Los Angeles Los Nieto	59 438
RANGELL		
John	Del Norte Crescent	58 622
RANGER		
Henry	Placer Ophirville	62 657
RANGO		
Dominigas	Tuolumne Twp 2	71 281
Dominique	Tuolumne Twp 2	71 281
RANGUIES		
Joseph*	Sacramento Ward 4	63 575
RANHALE		
Ramora	Los Angeles San Jose	59 289
RANHARD		
F N	San Francisco San Francisco 9	68 971
RANHER		
Jno H G*	Alameda Oakland	55 41
RANIER		
Simon	Sacramento Ward 1	63 137
RANIERES		
Jose	San Diego Temecula	64 785
RANIES		
W*	Shasta Horsetown	66 703

Name	County Locale	M653 RollPage
RANIR		
Thos*	Shasta Horsetown	66 699
RANIRA		
Savon*	Placer Auburn	62 580
RANITT		
W C	Yolo Cottonwoood	72 652
RANIY		
Robt*	Sonoma Sonoma	69 635
RANK		
Cyrus P	San Francisco San Francisco 3	67 25
J	Sutter Butte	70 796
Thomas	Sierra St Louis	66 806
Vahntrini*	El Dorado Greenwood	58 724
Washington	Yuba Parks Ba	72 780
Wm*	Napa Napa	61 81
RANKAN		
A A	El Dorado Placerville	58 836
J D	El Dorado Casumnes	581166
RANKE		
And*	Sacramento Ward 3	63 424
RANKEL		
Ignacio	Santa Cruz Pajaro	66 564
Ignasia	Santa Cruz Pajaro	66 564
Ignasio	Santa Cruz Pajaro	66 564
RANKELL		
Ramon	Marin Cortemad	60 792
RANKEN		
Amos*	Yuba Linda	72 984
Ellen*	Marin S Antoni	60 706
RANKER		
Henry*	Calaveras Twp 4	57 342
Ignasia	Santa Cruz Pajaro	66 526
RANKEY		
William	El Dorado Georgetown	58 693
RANKII		
Amos*	Yuba Linda	72 984
RANKIM		
Tell*	Tuolumne Columbia	71 348
RANKIN		
---	Tulara Visalia	71 110
A P	Butte Hamilton	56 519
A V	Alameda Washington	55 214
A?*	Alameda Brooklyn	55 93
Ag*	Alameda Brooklyn	55 93
Amos	Yuba Suida	72 984
Aq*	Alameda Brooklyn	55 93
B	San Mateo Twp 3	65 101
Charles	Mendocino Arrana	60 857
Chas	Amador Twp 5	55 358
Curd*	Del Norte Happy Ca	58 661
Daniel	Nevada Bridgeport	61 494
Ellen	Marin S Antoni	60 706
Francis	Sierra Downieville	661016
G	Nevada Eureka	61 343
H	Nevada Eureka	61 343
H	San Francisco San Francisco 10	328
		67
H*	Nevada Eureka	61 343
Henry	Calaveras Twp 4	57 342
J	Nevada Eureka	61 343
J W	Tuolumne Columbia	71 340
James	Sierra La Porte	66 782
Jas	Sacramento Ward 1	63 67
Jno P	Calaveras Twp 9	57 401
John	San Francisco San Francisco 1	68 917
John	Tuolumne Twp 6	71 534
Oroville*	San Francisco San Francisco 11	133
		67
P L	Solano Vallejo	69 252
R	El Dorado Placerville	58 819
T	San Francisco San Francisco 9	681081
Tell	Tuolumne Twp 2	71 348
W	Santa Clara Alviso	65 401
Walker	Tulara Visalia	71 74
Wm	Amador Twp 3	55 403
Wm	Nevada Eureka	61 355
Wm	Nevada Eureka	61 372
Wm	San Francisco San Francisco 2	67 619
Wm*	Nevada Eureka	61 372
RANKING		
A P	Colusa Mansville	57 437
RANKINS		
Antonio	Santa Clara Alviso	65 403
Davis V	Sierra Whiskey	66 845
John	San Francisco San Francisco 1	68 913
Tell*	Tuolumne Columbia	71 348
Wm	Sierra Twp 7	66 916
RANKIR		
Henry*	Calaveras Twp 4	57 342
RANKLE		
John*	Calaveras Twp 6	57 136
RANKS		
J	Sutter Nicolaus	70 830
N H	El Dorado Mud Springs	58 970
T	Sutter Bear Rvr	70 821
RANLAND		
John*	Shasta Shasta	66 677

California 1860 Census Index

Name	County Locale	M653 Roll	Page
RANLIF			
Albt	Sonoma Sonoma	69	636
RANMANS			
John	Sacramento Ward 1	63	42
RANMAUS			
John*	Sacramento Ward 1	63	42
RANML			
Welcome*	Nevada Bridgeport	61	504
RANN			
Colah*	Santa Clara Santa Clara	65	472
E T	Sacramento Ward 1	63	49
John	Stanislaus Emory	70	738
RANNA			
Charles	Calaveras Twp 5	57	231
RANNAR			
Morris*	Siskiyou Yreka	69	144
RANNARY			
Annetta	San Francisco San Francisco 2	67	661
RANNAS			
Morris	Siskiyou Yreka	69	144
RANNBRAR			
Martin S	Calaveras Twp 10	57	292
RANNELS			
H J	Solano Benecia	69	294
RANNEN			
Michael*	Yuba Bear Rvr	72	1000
RANNENSTOB			
Charles J	San Francisco San Francisco 7	68	1345
RANNEP			
Thompson	Napa Clear Lake	61	131
RANNER			
P	El Dorado Kelsey	58	1156
RANNESS			
Thompson*	Napa Clear Lake	61	131
RANNEY			
A	El Dorado Placerville	58	894
B*	Nevada Grass Valley	61	188
Cary	Yolo Cache Crk	72	611
Geo	El Dorado Placerville	58	894
J	Sutter Butte	70	779
Joseph	El Dorado Coloma	58	1118
RANNEZ			
Annette*	Sacramento Ward 1	63	78
RANNIS			
Robert	Mendocino Little L	60	837
RANNISH			
J*	Nevada Grass Valley	61	176
RANNISS			
Thompson*	Napa Clear Lake	61	131
RANNITEN			
James	Calaveras Twp 5	57	230
RANNNNNDLETT			
John	Placer Forest H	62	799
RANNSES			
Jacques*	Yuba New York	72	734
RANO			
---	Placer Rattle Snake	62	598
P	El Dorado Placerville	58	843
P	San Joaquin Stockton	64	1099
RANOLDS			
Bridget	Solano Vallejo	69	246
J	Nevada Eureka	61	363
RANONGAN			
John*	San Mateo Twp 3	65	94
RANONS			
Francis M	Siskiyou Yreka	69	167
Francis W*	Siskiyou Yreka	69	167
H W*	Yolo Cache Crk	72	664
John H	Yuba Marysville	72	872
RANPINGTH			
John*	Placer Dutch Fl	62	728
RANREGOUR			
Lenart S	Alameda Oakland	55	12
RANSE			
Sarah	San Bernardino San Salvador	64	657
Wario	Amador Twp 5	55	360
RANSELL			
Chas	Butte Bidwell	56	723
RANSEN			
Michael	Yuba Bear Rvr	72	1000
RANSEY			
Alex	El Dorado White Oaks	58	1017
RANSFORD			
John	El Dorado Kelsey	58	1129
RANSILOR			
G	San Mateo Twp 3	65	86
RANSLEY			
M J*	Tehama Red Bluff	70	909
RANSMAN			
Wm*	Nevada Eureka	61	352
RANSMORE			
A	Sonoma Bodega	69	534
RANSOM			
A N	Trinity Eastman	70	960
David	Sacramento Franklin	63	334
H	Alameda Oakland	55	14
RANSOM			
Habbell W	Yuba Marysville	72	853
Harry I	Yuba Marysville	72	873
J	El Dorado Placerville	58	886
J W	Trinity Lewiston	70	953
James	Alameda Brooklyn	55	132
John	Amador Twp 1	55	473
Jos	Alameda Murray	55	218
Leander	San Francisco San Francisco 8	68	1281
Legman W*	Yuba Marysville	72	891
Lguran W*	Yuba Marysville	72	891
Squian W	Yuba Marysville	72	891
T	Tuolumne Twp 2	71	289
Wm	San Francisco San Francisco 2	67	603
RANSON			
---	Tulara Keyesville	71	66
D	Nevada Eureka	61	351
H	Yuba Rose Bar	72	800
J	San Francisco San Francisco 2	67	741
J	San Francisco San Francisco 2	67	741
Leander	San Francisco San Francisco 8	68	1281
R S	Monterey San Juan	60	1004
RANSONE			
Habbell W N*	Yuba Marysville	72	858
Harry I	Yuba Marysville	72	873
RANSOW			
Habbell W N*	Yuba Marysville	72	858
RANSY			
A J*	Napa Yount	61	47
RANT			
Bennett*	San Joaquin Castoria	64	892
RANTEQS			
David*	Yuba Marysville	72	847
RANTEY			
David*	Yuba Marysville	72	847
RANTEYS			
David*	Yuba Marysville	72	847
RANTRY			
W D	El Dorado Placerville	58	932
RANTS			
Adison	El Dorado Placerville	58	878
RANTZ			
Anna	Sacramento Ward 4	63	595
RANTZAN			
Chas H	Trinity Lewiston	70	963
RANUEZ			
Juan	Tehama Red Bluff	70	931
RANVIOT			
Ernest*	Stanislaus Branch	70	701
RANWENSTOB			
Charles*	San Francisco 7	68	1345
	San Francisco		
RANY			
David	Calaveras Twp 5	57	172
Orpha	San Joaquin Castoria	64	901
RANYDON			
J*	Amador Twp 2	55	309
RAODEN			
John*	Sacramento Ward 1	63	132
RAOHI			
Peter	Stanislaus Branch	70	702
RAOIZER			
Louis	Calaveras Twp 5	57	205
RAOMER			
Perry	Calaveras Twp 5	57	198
RAORZER			
Louis	Calaveras Twp 5	57	205
RAOSNER			
Perry	Calaveras Twp 5	57	198
RAP			
Don	Tehama Red Bluff	70	899
Donald	Tuolumne Twp 2	71	382
Edward*	Placer Ophirville	62	655
Philip*	Shasta Horsetown	66	707
RAPALA			
Nepalita	Alameda Brooklyn	55	207
RAPEE			
John	Yolo Washington	72	565
RAPEILL			
G	Butte Cascade	56	696
RAPELL			
Richard	Calaveras Twp 5	57	190
RAPELYE			
Abraham W	Tulara Visalia	71	104
RAPELYS			
Abraham W	Tulara Visalia	71	104
RAPENEA			
Nicholas	Placer Secret R	62	610
RAPER			
E C	Sutter Yuba	70	760
Thomas	Sierra Twp 7	66	901
Thos*	Butte Hamilton	56	527
RAPETT			
Thomas	Shasta Cottonwood	66	723
RAPETTO			
Alexander	Los Angeles Los Angeles	59	495
RAPHAD			
A*	Butte Oro	56	679
RAPHAEL			
A	Butte Oro	56	679
Jas M	San Francisco San Francisco 10		339 67
John	Amador Twp 1	55	507
Jose	Calaveras Twp 6	57	170
Lewis	Butte Oro	56	679
Meyer	Calaveras Twp 6	57	131
Morris	San Francisco San Francisco 7	68	1348
Ramon	Tulara Visalia	71	28
Sam	Amador Twp 1	55	495
RAPHAIL			
A*	Butte Oro	56	679
RAPHAM			
J	El Dorado Diamond	58	771
RAPHEAT			
---	Fresno Twp 3	59	21
RAPHEL			
A	El Dorado Diamond	58	801
H D	El Dorado Placerville	58	855
Isaac	San Francisco San Francisco 3	67	38
RAPHINA			
Francisco	San Francisco San Francisco 11		135 67
RAPHINE			
Joseph	Amador Twp 4	55	131
RAPILY			
C G*	Shasta Millvill	66	738
RAPITY			
C G*	Shasta Millvill	66	738
RAPLEY			
J W*	El Dorado Placerville	58	911
R	Santa Clara Fremont	65	441
RAPOTTE			
Lewis	Tuolumne Twp 4	71	146
RAPOTTO			
Lewis	Tuolumne Big Oak	71	146
RAPP			
---	Tehama Tehama	70	937
A H	San Francisco San Francisco 6	67	469
Amos	San Francisco San Francisco 1	68	813
Andrew	Butte Kimshaw	56	597
Charles	Yuba Marysville	72	945
Charles W	Yuba Marysville	72	945
Dan	Tehama Tehama	70	937
Eastman	Stanislaus Oatvale	70	718
F	Los Angeles Tejon	59	524
Fred	Alameda Brooklyn	55	134
Geo	Placer Rattle Snake	62	603
Julius	San Francisco San Francisco 1	68	813
Leonard	Yuba Suida	72	990
Peter	Nevada Rough &	61	411
Phillip	Santa Clara Gilroy	65	243
RAPPAY			
M	San Francisco San Francisco 5	67	478
RAPPAZ			
M	San Francisco San Francisco 5	67	478
Morris	San Francisco San Francisco 2	67	781
RAPPLEYE			
J S	Tuolumne Twp 4	71	126
RAPPOLD			
C	Trinity Prices B	70	1019
RAPPS			
Mathias	Contra Costa Twp 2	57	562
RAPSELL			
G	Butte Cascade	56	696
RAPTLY			
O G	Shasta Millvill	66	738
RAPUR			
Wm	Amador Twp 5	55	348
RAQER			
Clara	Amador Twp 1	55	499
RAR SON			
---	Sierra Twp 7	66	889
RAR			
Sin	Sierra Downieville	66	979
RARADE			
Pune*	Sierra Downieville	66	963
RARAMRE			
Leonard	San Francisco San Francisco 2	67	747
RARANO			
Frank*	San Francisco San Francisco 3	67	63
RARCE			
Mariam W*	Yuba Marysville	72	875
RARCHE			
Frederick*	San Francisco 3	67	8
	San Francisco		
RARCHI			
Frederick	San Francisco San Francisco 3	67	8
RARDEN			
John*	Sacramento Ward 1	63	132
RARELES			
Lucio	San Francisco San Francisco 1	68	815
RARELIA			
Stano*	Calaveras Twp 7	57	11

California 1860 Census Index

Name	County Locale	M653 RollPage
RAREN		
Christian*	Solano Vallejo	69 244
J	Nevada Grass Valley	61 222
RARGNAR		
Peter	Sierra Downieville	661021
RARLSBACK		
Caleb	Sonoma Petaluma	69 569
RARMICKEL		
Jacob*	Trinity Rattle Snake	701029
RARNEY		
A	Nevada Grass Valley	61 153
M	Nevada Grass Valley	61 225
RARNS		
Saml*	Napa Clear Lake	61 123
RARO		
Becinta	El Dorado Gold Hill	581098
RARON		
Phillip*	Sierra Pine Grove	66 820
RARONSENFT		
W*	Shasta Shasta	66 671
RARR		
A*	Siskiyou Callahan	69 6
RARREY		
A*	Napa Hot Springs	61 3
RARRNANS		
John*	Sacramento Ward 1	63 42
RARRSEO		
Jesus*	Placer Secret R	62 608
RARUD		
A	Trinity Browns C	70 984
RARUNAUS		
John*	Sacramento Ward 1	63 42
RARVIR		
Thos*	Shasta Horsetown	66 699
RARY		
John	Sonoma Armally	69 503
RARYNAR		
Peter	Sierra Downieville	661021
RASA		
Antone*	San Francisco San Francisco 9	681098
Pauline	San Francisco San Francisco 1	68 901
Peter	Santa Clara Almaden	65 278
RASAFE		
Hanah	Santa Clara San Jose	65 309
RASALA		
Charles*	El Dorado Coloma	581104
RASALES		
Louis	Calaveras Twp 6	57 185
RASALO		
Charles*	El Dorado Coloma	581104
RASAR		
Nichila	Amador Twp 5	55 332
RASBERRY		
Bonego	Calaveras Twp 8	57 52
H	Sutter Butte	70 797
J R*	Siskiyou Yreka	69 173
W	Butte Oregon	56 639
Wm	Butte Oregon	56 639
RASCEAS		
L	Amador Twp 3	55 393
RASCH		
Manuel	San Mateo Twp 1	65 60
RASCHER		
Horatio	San Francisco San Francisco 7	681407
RASCHI		
Frederick	San Francisco San Francisco 3	67 8
RASCOS		
Loreso*	Amador Twp 2	55 301
Lorezo*	Amador Twp 2	55 301
RASCOVITCH		
Auguste	San Francisco San Francisco 11	126 67
RASDELL		
A	Mariposa Coulterville	60 699
RASE		
A*	Siskiyou Callahan	69 11
Antonio	Los Angeles San Jose	59 285
H	San Francisco San Francisco 5	67 503
Henry	Placer Virginia	62 661
Henry	San Francisco San Francisco 4	681134
Innocencia	Los Angeles Elmonte	59 255
Philip	Tuolumne Sonora	71 219
Walton*	Siskiyou Callahan	69 16
Wm	Santa Clara San Jose	65 298
RASENBAUM		
J	San Francisco San Francisco 5	67 529
RASENBURG		
M*	Siskiyou Scott Va	69 54
Victor	Calaveras Twp 10	57 278
RASENKIMS		
John*	Amador Twp 2	55 323
RASENKINES		
John*	Amador Twp 2	55 323
RASENKINS		
John	Amador Twp 2	55 323
RASENTERE		
A T*	Nevada Grass Valley	61 198

Name	County Locale	M653 RollPage
RASENTESE		
A F*	Nevada Grass Valley	61 198
RASER		
Louis*	Yuba Marysville	72 938
RASERER		
Joseph	Placer Dutch Fl	62 724
RASERY		
Ddanl	Tuolumne Twp 1	71 273
RASEWARREN		
H*	Nevada Grass Valley	61 209
RASH		
Peter	Santa Clara Santa Clara	65 473
RASHEE		
Victor H	Solano Vallejo	69 246
RASHEL		
Victor H	Solano Vallejo	69 246
RASING		
George*	Nevada Red Dog	61 541
RASINSTOCK		
S	San Francisco San Francisco 5	67 518
RASKA		
Wm R*	Tuolumne Sonora	71 187
RASKEN		
Anna	Yolo Washington	72 566
RASKETT		
R	Yolo Cache	72 623
RASKIN		
John	San Mateo Twp 2	65 125
RASLER		
M*	San Francisco San Francisco 3	67 72
RASMASSEON		
George	San Bernardino San Bernadino	64 631
RASMASSON		
George	San Bernardino San Bernadino	64 631
RASMER		
Leana	San Francisco San Francisco 4	681151
RASMEYERS		
R A	San Joaquin Stockton	641093
RASMIS		
Ellen*	Alameda Brooklyn	55 142
RASMODEL		
F	San Francisco San Francisco 4	681172
RASMON		
J V*	Los Angeles Tejon	59 528
RASMTRAN		
Martin S	Calaveras Twp 10	57 292
RASMUS		
John	Butte Ophir	56 745
RASMUSSON		
R	Solano Vacaville	69 324
RASNUS		
Ellen*	Alameda Brooklyn	55 142
RASO		
Jose M	Monterey Alisal	601042
RASON		
J	San Francisco San Francisco 9	681057
RASONER		
Benj	Nevada Bloomfield	61 525
L K	Nevada Bloomfield	61 525
RASONS		
Nelson	Yolo Washington	72 570
RASPBERRY		
P	El Dorado Casumnes	581169
RASPEE		
Charles	Tuolumne Jamestown	71 424
RASPEL		
Edward	Tuolumne Twp 2	71 338
RASPER		
Charles	Tuolumne Twp 3	71 424
RASPILLI		
Charles	San Joaquin Elkhorn	64 950
RASS		
A	San Francisco San Francisco 4	681231
J*	Calaveras Twp 7	57 398
James	Calaveras Twp 7	57 28
John	Tuolumne Twp 2	71 310
Jose M	Monterey Alisal	601042
Joseph*	Shasta Shasta	66 679
Joshua	Calaveras Twp 7	57 28
Philip*	Shasta Horsetown	66 707
W	Siskiyou Scott Va	69 54
RASSA		
Frank	Santa Cruz Soguel	66 597
Pedro	Mariposa Twp 3	60 570
RASSAKRANTZ		
Hiram D	Siskiyou Yreka	69 129
RASSEAN		
Antoine*	Calaveras Twp 4	57 340
RASSEDAR		
James*	Amador Twp 4	55 235
RASSEK		
H	El Dorado Big Bar	58 739
RASSELL		
Jas	Santa Clara Santa Clara	65 505
RASSEN		
Peter	El Dorado Kelsey	581134

Name	County Locale	M653 RollPage
RASSENNET		
Auguste	Siskiyou Yreka	69 130
RASSER		
James	Siskiyou Klamath	69 92
Thos*	Butte Hamilton	56 527
RASSEY		
Wm	Butte Ophir	56 775
RASSITA		
Dominico*	Amador Twp 3	55 401
Domnico*	Amador Twp 3	55 401
RASSO		
P	Tuolumne Twp 4	71 153
RASSON		
W H	Nevada Bridgeport	61 465
RAST		
A	Siskiyou Callahan	69 6
Jacob	Placer Auburn	62 574
John*	Nevada Washington	61 331
William*	Calaveras Twp 5	57 228
RASTER		
J	Nevada Grass Valley	61 160
RASTING		
James	Napa Hot Springs	61 17
RASTNER		
John Bates	Alameda Brooklyn	55 98
RASTNIE		
John Bates*	Alameda Brooklyn	55 98
RASTON		
W	Napa Hot Springs	61 4
RASTURY		
James	Napa Hot Springs	61 17
RASY		
James	Tehama Lassen	70 877
RAT		
---	Calaveras Twp 5	57 245
---	Yuba New York	72 740
B	Amador Township	55 466
RATALLIOT		
Leraphina*	Calaveras Twp 7	57 4
Seraphina	Calaveras Twp 7	57 4
RATALONGO		
Lorenza	Monterey San Juan	60 981
RATAMATAS		
Demier*	Calaveras Twp 9	57 364
RATCHKE		
Chas	Alameda Brooklyn	55 184
RATCLIFF		
Henry	San Francisco San Francisco 3	67 36
James	Calaveras Twp 8	57 94
Julia	San Francisco San Francisco 3	67 36
Samuel	Los Angeles Los Angeles	59 332
William	Calaveras Twp 7	57 40
RATE		
---	Mariposa Coulterville	60 680
RATEAST		
Thomas	Marin Cortemad	60 754
RATEKIN		
James	Siskiyou Cottonwoood	69 101
RATES		
Blap	Tehama Tehama	70 943
RATH		
C	Trinity Evans Ba	701002
Dan	Nevada Rough &	61 424
Elias	Sacramento Ward 4	63 594
Francis	Tuolumne Twp 1	71 209
John*	San Francisco San Francisco 1	68 861
RATHAM		
Keres	San Francisco San Francisco 3	67 64
RATHBINS		
M C	Shasta Shasta	66 760
RATHBONE		
G	Santa Clara Alviso	65 405
J H	Placer Dutch Fl	62 731
RATHBORN		
Jeremiah	Contra Costa Twp 2	57 577
RATHBUM		
Johathan*	Placer Iona Hills	62 863
RATHBUN		
Charles S*	San Diego San Diego	64 759
Geo S	Sacramento Ward 1	63 67
H B	Sacramento Ward 3	63 421
J S	Amador Twp 3	55 371
Jas	Sonoma Petaluma	69 594
Steven	Sonoma Vallejo	69 621
RATHBURN		
Dan C	San Bernardino San Salvador	64 638
Danl	San Bernardino San Bernadino	64 638
Enskine*	Mendocino Ukiah	60 794
Erskine	Mendocino Ukiah	60 794
F U*	Los Angeles Tejon	59 528
F V*	Los Angeles Tejon	59 528
G	Sacramento Ward 1	63 145
Jonathan*	Placer Iona Hills	62 863
L D	Nevada Bloomfield	61 507
RATHEMES		
Cornilius	El Dorado Georgetown	58 696

Name	County Locale	M653 Roll	Page
RATHER			
Jacob	Santa Clara Gilroy	65	253
S*	Nevada Grass Valley	61	172
William T	Monterey Pajaro	60	1024
RATHERFORD			
Frank	Santa Clara Santa Clara	65	513
RATHERS			
William T	Monterey Pajaro	60	1024
RATHLIN			
Geo S	Sacramento Ward 1	63	67
RATHMAN			
Edward	Solano Benecia	69	298
RATIL			
V	El Dorado Diamond	58	800
RATILLAND			
F	El Dorado Placerville	58	817
RATIMEAN			
M	Calaveras Twp 7	57	7
RATIMEM			
M*	Calaveras Twp 7	57	7
RATISHOUSE			
John U*	Sierra Scales D	66	801
RATIUNO			
Jose*	Santa Cruz Soguel	66	587
RATLEY			
Frank	Butte Ophir	56	764
RATLIFF			
Elizabeth	Plumas Quincy	62	973
RATO			
B	Calaveras Twp 7	57	12
John	Calaveras Twp 7	57	23
Joseph	Calaveras Twp 8	57	85
Vincent	Calaveras Twp 7	57	2
RATON			
---	Nevada Grass Valley	61	229
RATOVICH			
Edw	San Francisco San Francisco 10	67	215
Ewd*	San Francisco San Francisco 10	67	215
RATS			
J B	Amador Twp 3	55	372
RATSKIN			
James*	Siskiyou Cottonwoood	69	101
RATTEGAN			
Tim*	San Francisco San Francisco 11	67	106
Tine*	San Francisco San Francisco 11	67	106
RATTEN			
Geo L	Sonoma Sonoma	69	653
RATTENBAM			
Henry*	Contra Costa Twp 2	57	557
RATTENBURG			
Wm H	Sacramento Ward 3	63	450
RATTENHAM			
Henry*	Contra Costa Twp 2	57	557
RATTENIUS			
Benj	Solano Benecia	69	298
RATTER			
James	Sacramento San Joaquin	63	356
S*	Nevada Grass Valley	61	172
T	El Dorado Diamond	58	802
RATTERSON			
John	El Dorado Casumnes	58	1160
RATTERY			
Agnes	San Francisco San Francisco 1	68	867
Donald	San Francisco San Francisco 11	67	132
RATTEY			
Frank	Butte Ophir	56	764
RATTIGAN			
Tim	San Francisco San Francisco 11	67	106
RATTLE SNAKE			
---	Tulara Twp 1	71	116
RATTLE			
John S	Placer Virginia	62	675
O	Siskiyou Scott Ri	69	73
RATTLEMILLER			
Leonard	Siskiyou Yreka	69	137
RATTLER			
T P	Nevada Grass Valley	61	197
RATTO			
John	Calaveras Twp 7	57	45
Joseph	Calaveras Twp 7	57	38
Louis	Tuolumne Twp 4	71	130
RATZ			
Antoine	Calaveras Twp 6	57	164
William	Calaveras Twp 6	57	119
RAU			
Tah	San Francisco San Francisco 11	67	160
RAUB			
Andrew	Plumas Quincy	62	1000
RAUCKMANN			
Anna*	San Francisco San Francisco 9	68	954

Name	County Locale	M653 Roll	Page
RAUCT			
Alexander*	Placer Rattle Snake	62	633
RAUDALE			
David	Colusa Butte Crk	57	464
RAUDEE			
J H	Sierra Twp 7	66	868
RAUDOLPH			
J F	Nevada Nevada	61	257
RAUGEL			
Francisco*	Los Angeles Los Nieto	59	425
Gabriel	Los Angeles Los Nieto	59	426
RAUGH			
Santa	Calaveras Twp 8	57	90
Wm M	Trinity Steiner	70	1000
RAUHAND			
J H	Calaveras Twp 9	57	378
Peter	Calaveras Twp 9	57	378
Z	Calaveras Twp 9	57	378
RAUHER			
Jno H G*	Alameda Oakland	55	41
RAUK			
Wm*	Napa Napa	61	81
RAUKE			
And*	Sacramento Ward 3	63	424
RAUKIN			
H*	Nevada Eureka	61	343
Oroville*	San Francisco San Francisco 11	67	133
T*	San Francisco San Francisco 9	68	1081
Wm*	Nevada Eureka	61	372
RAUKIR			
Henry*	Calaveras Twp 4	57	342
RAUL			
Bennett*	San Joaquin Castoria	64	892
RAULAND			
John*	Shasta Shasta	66	677
RAULETT			
Joseph*	San Joaquin Stockton	64	1052
RAUN			
Et*	Sacramento Ward 1	63	49
RAUS?TT?			
Amvil*	Calaveras Twp 9	57	353
Anvil*	Calaveras Twp 9	57	353
RAUSETT			
Anvil*	Calaveras Twp 9	57	353
RAUSETTE			
Amril*	Calaveras Twp 9	57	353
Amvil*	Calaveras Twp 9	57	353
Anvil*	Calaveras Twp 9	57	353
RAUSH			
Wm	Los Angeles Tejon	59	526
RAUSOTTE			
Amril*	Calaveras Twp 9	57	353
Anvil*	Calaveras Twp 9	57	353
RAUTER			
Len	Sacramento Ward 4	63	497
RAUTEY			
David*	Yuba Marysville	72	847
RAUTHEMEL			
L	Tehama Antelope	70	894
RAUX			
Elder	Napa Napa	61	105
RAVADE			
Piene*	Sierra Downieville	66	963
RAVALESES			
Ramona	Los Angeles Elmonte	59	259
RAVAN			
Martin	Sacramento Ward 1	63	28
RAVARIO			
Alphonse	Placer Iona Hills	62	870
RAVDEN			
John*	Sacramento Ward 1	63	132
RAVE			
C	Sacramento Ward 4	63	496
Cornelius*	Calaveras Twp 6	57	136
RAVEL			
Marcuse	Tuolumne Jamestown	71	437
RAVELES			
Lucio	San Francisco San Francisco 1	68	815
RAVELY			
S W	Yolo Cache Crk	72	610
RAVEN			
Carl	Butte Hamilton	56	515
Charles	El Dorado Big Bar	58	743
Christian*	Solano Vallejo	69	244
RAVENA			
Manuel	Los Angeles Los Angeles	59	346
RAVENI			
Jose*	Los Angeles Los Angeles	59	491
RAVENNA			
V	San Francisco San Francisco 3	67	21
RAVENSCROFT			
W	Shasta Shasta	66	671
RAVER			
---	Tulara Keeneysburg	71	50
John	Tuolumne Twp 2	71	370

Name	County Locale	M653 Roll	Page
RAVESON			
L	Tuolumne Twp 4	71	162
RAVETTI			
John*	Nevada Red Dog	61	556
RAVIEL			
Peates	Amador Twp 3	55	392
RAVINE			
Frederick	San Francisco San Francisco 4	68	1218
RAVING			
James*	Alameda Brooklyn	55	158
RAVINGER			
G	San Francisco San Francisco 5	67	550
RAVINI			
Frederick	San Francisco San Francisco 4	68	1218
RAVINY			
James*	Alameda Brooklyn	55	158
RAVIS			
John	Calaveras Twp 7	57	9
RAVIX			
John	Contra Costa Twp 1	57	502
RAVNO			
Daniel	Yolo Cache	72	590
RAVONA			
Marcus	El Dorado Kelsey	58	1136
RAVORINE			
D*	San Francisco San Francisco 3	67	51
RAVORINI			
L	San Francisco San Francisco 3	67	51
RAW			
---	Calaveras Twp 10	57	261
---	Mariposa Coulterville	60	685
---	Placer Illinois	62	742
---	Placer Illinois	62	748
RAWAND			
T*	San Francisco San Francisco 5	67	544
RAWAS			
Kapping*	Mendocino Big Rvr	60	850
RAWDEN			
John	Sacramento Ward 1	63	132
Wm	Sierra Twp 7	66	900
RAWDON			
Wm	Sierra Twp 7	66	900
RAWE			
A F	Tuolumne Twp 1	71	209
W	San Francisco San Francisco 5	67	533
RAWELL			
H H	Tuolumne Twp 1	71	275
RAWFORD			
J	Nevada Washington	61	336
RAWKIN			
D	Amador Twp 3	55	381
P L	Solano Vallejo	69	252
RAWL			
John	San Francisco San Francisco 3	67	46
Solomon	Amador Twp 1	55	474
RAWLER			
Margaret	Placer Stewart	62	605
Wm E	Placer Stewart	62	605
RAWLES			
John	Plumas Quincy	62	1006
RAWLEY			
A C	El Dorado Georgetown	58	689
J C	Siskiyou Scott Va	69	47
Levi P	Tuolumne Twp 3	71	421
Lewis A	Yuba Marysville	72	879
R	Santa Clara Fremont	65	420
S B	Santa Clara Alviso	65	409
RAWLING			
A C C	Tuolumne Twp 1	71	266
Francis	San Bernardino San Bernardino	64	633
RAWLINGS			
L	Sierra Downieville	66	976
Thomas G	Tuolumne Shawsfla	71	388
RAWLINS			
A	Calaveras Twp 9	57	395
C W	Stanislaus Buena Village	70	724
John	Shasta Shasta	66	735
M C	Tuolumne Sonora	71	482
RAWLSON			
John	Plumas Quincy	62	996
RAWNAR			
Morris*	Siskiyou Yreka	69	144
RAWOLF			
Wm	Tehama Lassen	70	870
RAWONS			
Francis W*	Siskiyou Yreka	69	167
RAWORTH			
Joseph	Tuolumne Twp 5	71	505
RAWS			
W	San Francisco San Francisco 5	67	533
RAWSDALE			
S C	Tuolumne Twp 2	71	309
RAWSEY			
H F*	Nevada Nevada	61	296
RAWSON			
Ace W	Santa Cruz Santa Cruz	66	618

California 1860 Census Index

Name	County Locale	M653 Roll/Page
RAWSON		
Benj	Plumas Quincy	62 922
Caleb	Plumas Quincy	62 963
Chas	Plumas Quincy	62 918
H A	Tehama Lassen	70 868
J A	San Francisco San Francisco 6	67 449
N	San Francisco San Francisco 3	67 74
N	Sutter Nicolaus	70 829
RAWSPORT		
Oliver	Yuba Bear Rvr	721006
RAY		
---	Calaveras Twp 9	57 388
---	El Dorado Placerville	58 842
---	Nevada Grass Valley	61 229
Albert M	Santa Clara Redwood	65 444
Alexis	Calaveras Twp 7	57 41
B B	Sonoma Salt Point	69 690
C	Nevada Grass Valley	61 153
C	Siskiyou Scott Va	69 28
Chas	Santa Cruz Soguel	66 591
D	Sutter Nicolaus	70 837
Danl B	Napa Napa	61 61
David	San Joaquin Elkhorn	64 993
David	San Joaquin Elkhorn	64 995
David P	Colusa Colusi	57 427
E	Sacramento Dry Crk	63 373
Edward	Solano Benecia	69 302
Edwd H	Butte Oregon	56 632
Edwin R	Calaveras Twp 6	57 127
Elijah	Mendocino Ukiah	60 805
Emily	Yuba Marysville	72 887
Ezekiel	Siskiyou Shasta Rvr	69 114
F	Butte Bidwell	56 719
Felix G	Calaveras Twp 5	57 185
Francis	El Dorado Georgetown	58 749
G	Tehama Red Bluff	70 929
G W	Santa Clara San Jose	65 341
Gilbert	Butte Bidwell	56 722
H B	Butte Kimshaw	56 593
H F	Siskiyou Scott Va	69 52
H P	Nevada Red Dog	61 541
H R	Butte Kimshaw	56 593
Henry	San Francisco San Francisco 7	681330
Henry	San Francisco San Francisco 7	681390
Horace	Calaveras Twp 6	57 127
I S	Amador Twp 3	55 379
J	Mariposa Twp 3	60 622
J C	Yolo Merritt	72 577
J F	Butte Chico	56 553
J G	Butte Chico	56 553
J H	El Dorado Diamond	58 808
J R	Sacramento Ward 1	63 121
James	El Dorado Mud Springs	58 991
James	Placer Forest H	62 801
James	Sacramento Sutter	63 306
James	Santa Clara San Jose	65 356
James	Shasta Horsetown	66 707
James	Sierra Twp 5	66 924
James L	Calaveras Twp 5	57 184
James S	Calaveras Twp 5	57 184
James*	San Francisco San Francisco 7	681411
Jas	San Francisco San Francisco 1	68 929
Jefferson	Sacramento Franklin	63 323
John	Calaveras Twp 8	57 70
John	Colusa Colusi	57 425
John	El Dorado White Oaks	581016
John	El Dorado Kelsey	581130
John	Sacramento American	63 170
John	Sacramento Franklin	63 327
John	Yuba Marysville	72 943
John	Yuba Linda	72 991
John C	Sonoma Washington	69 673
John J	Sonoma Russian	69 441
L	Nevada Grass Valley	61 155
L J	El Dorado Placerville	58 885
Lerania	Amador Twp 2	55 313
Levania	Amador Twp 2	55 313
Lewis	Sacramento Franklin	63 326
Lewis	Siskiyou Shasta Valley	69 119
Louis	Calaveras Twp 8	57 49
M	El Dorado Placerville	58 830
Major	Placer Secret R	62 609
Manuel	Placer Michigan	62 851
Martin	Humbolt Eureka	59 168
Mary	Contra Costa Twp 1	57 520
Mecales	Sacramento Ward 3	63 439
O	El Dorado Placerville	58 867
P	Mariposa Twp 3	60 622
Parrella	San Francisco San Francisco 6	67 399
Pat	Nevada Eureka	61 361
Patrick	Los Angeles Los Angeles	59 370
Peter	El Dorado Mountain	581186
R	San Francisco San Francisco 5	67 530
Rachel	Sacramento Ward 1	63 93
S	Nevada Grass Valley	61 155
S A	El Dorado Placerville	58 831

Name	County Locale	M653 Roll/Page
RAY		
Saml	Butte Oregon	56 639
Saml	Nevada Bridgeport	61 450
Saml J	Placer Stewart	62 606
Samuel	San Joaquin Elkhorn	64 993
Samuel	Solano Vallejo	69 277
Thomas	Placer Forest H	62 802
Thomas	Plumas Quincy	62 989
W B	Tuolumne Shawsfla	71 399
William	Placer Forest H	62 771
William	Plumas Quincy	62 954
William	San Francisco San Francisco 9	681081
William	Shasta Shasta	66 731
William	Yolo Merritt	72 578
Wm	Butte Bidwell	56 716
Wm	El Dorado Eldorado	58 936
RAY??		
J*	Nevada Grass Valley	61 223
RAYA		
A	Tuolumne Twp 1	71 229
RAYAIR		
J*	Nevada Eureka	61 389
RAYAN		
G W	Nevada Nevada	61 262
G*	Nevada Grass Valley	61 186
J	Nevada Eureka	61 350
J	Nevada Eureka	61 389
P*	Nevada Grass Valley	61 206
RAYBOLD		
E	Solano Vacaville	69 330
RAYBURN		
C S	Nevada Washington	61 335
J B	El Dorado Kelsey	581157
RAYBURNS		
Spence K	Nevada Bridgeport	61 455
RAYCROFT		
S	Tehama Red Bluff	70 916
RAYE		
Rosa	San Francisco San Francisco 8	681255
RAYEE		
Emma J	Yolo Washington	72 565
Emona J	Yolo Washington	72 565
RAYERS		
A	El Dorado Newtown	58 776
RAYES		
Francisco	Los Angeles Los Angeles	59 373
J	San Francisco San Francisco 9	681082
Maria	Amador Twp 1	55 500
RAYESDALE		
Jn	Sutter Nicolaus	70 832
RAYHARD		
Jacob	Yolo Putah	72 547
RAYLAND		
A M	Nevada Eureka	61 344
RAYLE		
P W S	Sacramento Ward 1	63 16
RAYLESS		
E	Nevada Eureka	61 369
RAYLIN		
Chas	Sonoma Sonoma	69 636
RAYLOR		
James	San Francisco San Francisco 3	67 56
John	Tuolumne Twp 5	71 522
Ramon*	Tulara Twp 2	71 30
RAYMAN		
Freeman	Tulara Keeneysburg	71 49
Geo	Butte Oregon	56 624
M	Butte Ophir	56 764
RAYMAND		
John	Sierra Twp 5	66 944
RAYMO		
Dapre	Tuolumne Twp 3	71 461
Dupre	Tuolumne Twp 3	71 461
RAYMOBND		
Giom*	Calaveras Twp 6	57 144
RAYMON		
Herman	Santa Cruz Soguel	66 597
John	Santa Cruz Santa Cruz	66 639
Josa	Amador Twp 3	55 408
Jozu	Amador Twp 3	55 408
RAYMOND		
---	Sacramento Granite	63 244
---	San Francisco San Francisco 7	681339
A	El Dorado Placerville	58 892
A	Siskiyou Scott Va	69 57
A	Sutter Bear Rvr	70 822
Albert	Siskiyou Yreka	69 124
Alfred	Siskiyou Yreka	69 124
Amos E	Tuolumne Jamestown	71 424
Armona	Napa Napa	61 114
August	Tuolumne Twp 1	71 482
C	Nevada Grass Valley	61 183
C A	Nevada Grass Valley	61 163
Cara	Shasta Millvill	66 727
Charles	Sierra Poker Flats	66 839
Chas H	San Francisco San Francisco 2	67 669

Name	County Locale	M653 Roll/Page
RAYMOND		
Cora	Shasta Millvill	66 727
D T	San Francisco San Francisco 5	67 483
D T	Trinity Mouth Ca	701010
F	Sacramento Sutter	63 296
F	San Francisco San Francisco 5	67 504
F S	Tuolumne Twp 1	71 264
G L	Nevada Nevada	61 257
G M	El Dorado Placerville	58 874
Geo	Butte Ophir	56 778
Geo	Nevada Grass Valley	61 146
Geo	Siskiyou Scott Ri	69 71
Geom	Calaveras Twp 5	57 144
George	Siskiyou Yreka	69 170
Gertrude	San Francisco San Francisco 2	67 661
Gwen	Calaveras Twp 6	57 144
H	Sierra Twp 7	66 906
H A	Sierra Twp 7	66 904
H H	San Francisco San Francisco 5	67 478
J	Amador Twp 3	55 392
J	Nevada Grass Valley	61 207
J	Nevada Nevada	61 294
J	Sacramento Granite	63 230
J	San Francisco San Francisco 1	68 867
J A	Siskiyou Scott Va	69 47
J H	Santa Clara Alviso	65 405
J P	San Francisco San Francisco 5	67 536
J S	Nevada Nevada	61 242
James	Mendocino Big Rock	60 873
James	Placer Michigan	62 817
Jas M	San Francisco San Francisco 12	67 371
Jno	Sacramento Natonia	63 281
John	Del Norte Happy Ca	58 670
John	Los Angeles Los Angeles	59 511
John	Sierra Twp 5	66 944
L	Nevada Grass Valley	61 157
L A	Nevada Nevada	61 286
Martin	Santa Cruz Santa Cruz	66 638
Martin	Solano Benecia	69 314
Philip	Plumas Quincy	62 940
Phocison	San Francisco San Francisco 2	67 571
R	San Francisco San Francisco 6	67 465
R G	Nevada Grass Valley	61 220
R H	Nevada Nevada	61 269
R J	Nevada Nevada	61 269
R S	Tuolumne Twp 1	71 200
S	Nevada Grass Valley	61 207
Saml	San Francisco San Francisco 3	67 8
Samuel	San Francisco San Francisco 3	67 85
Spence K*	Nevada Bridgeport	61 455
V R	Tuolumne Columbia	71 336
William	San Francisco San Francisco 9	681037
William	Solano Vacaville	69 324
Wm	Nevada Nevada	61 327
Wm	Santa Clara San Jose	65 349
RAYMONDK		
J S	Nevada Nevada	61 242
RAYMOUNDO		
Jose Carr	Santa Clara San Jose	65 390
RAYMUND		
Jn	Sacramento Natonia	63 281
RAYNALDS		
Elizabeth	El Dorado Kelsey	581127
RAYNAN		
Arvite	Amador Township	55 469
RAYNE		
J*	Nevada Grass Valley	61 223
RAYNEON		
Herman*	Santa Cruz Soguel	66 597
RAYNES		
A E	Siskiyou Yreka	69 185
John	San Francisco San Francisco 1	68 846
R	El Dorado Placerville	58 853
Reuben	Nevada Rough &	61 418
Reuben	Sacramento Ward 4	63 608
RAYNEY		
Ale	Sutter Bear Rvr	70 818
RAYNOLD		
R B	Nevada Nevada	61 260
RAYNOLDS		
Benj	Butte Ophir	56 799
Geo	El Dorado Placerville	58 908
J L	Nevada Grass Valley	61 154
J T	Nevada Grass Valley	61 154
RAYNOLDSAH		
Pin	Sierra Poker Flats	66 838
RAYNOR		
A B	San Joaquin Stockton	641057
Bery	Butte Ophir	56 783
John	Santa Cruz Pescadero	66 645
John	Santa Cruz Pescadero	66 646
William	San Francisco San Francisco 4	681116
William	Santa Cruz Pescadero	66 646
William	Santa Cruz Pescadero	66 646
RAYO		
Rosa	San Francisco San Francisco 8	681255

Name	County Locale	M653 RollPage
RAYOIS		
J*	Nevada Grass Valley	61 223
RAYON		
James	El Dorado White Oaks	581014
Miguel	Los Angeles Los Angeles	59 404
W B	Yuba Rose Bar	72 812
RAYR		
Ebra*	Calaveras Twp 6	57 130
RAYS		
James	Contra Costa Twp 2	57 555
Martin	Santa Cruz Pajaro	66 546
Wm	San Francisco San Francisco 1	68 914
RAYSDALE		
Edward B	San Francisco San Francisco 3	67 84
RAYSDALL		
A E	Nevada Grass Valley	61 214
RAYSDUE		
S G*	Nevada Grass Valley	61 165
RAYSETALE		
Edward B	San Francisco San Francisco 3	67 84
RAYWOOD		
James	Placer Todds Va	62 786
RAZEN		
Mike*	Trinity Taylor'S	701034
RAZER		
Mike	Trinity Taylor'S	701034
RAZOR		
John	Amador Twp 2	55 287
RCHERSON		
John*	Mariposa Coulterville	60 684
RE MY		
---*	Butte Kimshaw	56 606
RE		
---	Sierra Twp 7	66 887
Lahier	Nevada Bridgeport	61 452
Wey*	Butte Kimshaw	56 606
REA		
---	Placer Virginia	62 679
---	Sierra Twp 5	66 926
Joseph	El Dorado Placerville	58 906
Saml	Santa Clara Gilroy	65 232
Thos	Santa Clara Gilroy	65 232
REACE		
S	Calaveras Twp 9	57 416
T	Nevada Grass Valley	61 218
REACH		
Elden	Butte Chico	56 532
J O	Siskiyou Scott Va	69 45
John	San Francisco San Francisco 2	67 575
REACOCK		
J C*	Stanislaus Branch	70 711
READ		
---	Placer Auburn	62 574
A	Calaveras Twp 9	57 414
A G	Placer Todds Va	62 790
Abe	El Dorado Georgetown	58 759
Abner	Tulara Twp 2	71 28
Ann	Tuolumne Columbia	71 361
Bradford B	Tuolumne Twp 6	71 532
Charles A	Siskiyou Yreka	69 147
Christ	Sacramento Ward 4	63 545
D	Calaveras Twp 9	57 414
E B	Sierra Twp 7	66 892
Eliza	Sacramento Ward 3	63 489
Elizabeth	Yuba Marysville	72 854
Elizabeth	Yuba Marysville	72 859
Emaline	Sonoma Petaluma	69 596
F	Nevada Grass Valley	61 207
F	Nevada Grass Valley	61 218
F	San Francisco San Francisco 5	67 504
Fayette	Sonoma Armally	69 481
G N	Yolo Cache	72 612
G W	Yolo Cache Crk	72 612
Garden	Amador Twp 5	55 343
George	Calaveras Twp 4	57 326
H	Calaveras Twp 9	57 410
Henry	Sacramento Ward 4	63 554
J	San Joaquin Stockton	641096
J B	Tuolumne Big Oak	71 177
J M	Napa Napa	61 99
James	Los Angeles Azuza	59 271
James	Tuolumne Jamestown	71 448
John	Del Norte Klamath	58 655
John	Los Angeles Elmonte	59 268
John A	Tuolumne Twp 3	71 448
John H	Tuolumne Jamestown	71 448
Jos B	San Francisco San Francisco 12	377 67
Joseph	Napa Napa	61 69
Louis	San Joaquin Castoria	64 967
M M	Sacramento Ward 4	63 566
N L	Placer Michigan	62 831
Peter	Alameda Brooklyn	55 135
Q	Calaveras Twp 9	57 418
R	Sacramento Ward 3	63 488
Richard	Calaveras Twp 5	57 213
READ		
Samuel	Yuba Marysville	72 862
T	Sutter Vernon	70 845
Thos T*	Sacramento Ward 3	63 455
Thos Y*	Sacramento Ward 3	63 455
Tildon	Tulara Twp 2	71 13
W T	Sacramento Ward 1	63 99
Walter	Sonoma Bodega	69 523
William	El Dorado Georgetown	58 759
William D	San Joaquin Elkhorn	64 988
Wm	Sacramento Ward 3	63 489
Wm A	San Francisco San Francisco 1	68 898
Wm B	Alameda Brooklyn	55 194
Wm M	Sonoma Armally	69 485
READDY		
James	Yolo Cache Crk	72 664
READE		
John	Sacramento Ward 1	63 40
READER		
John	San Diego Temecula	64 793
Saml	Amador Twp 1	55 484
Saml	Klamath Liberty	59 234
READEY		
Wm	Tuolumne Twp 1	71 268
READFREED		
J	Butte Ophir	56 764
READFRUD		
J*	Butte Ophir	56 764
READING		
James	San Joaquin Douglass	64 921
John	Alameda Brooklyn	55 101
John	Sierra Pine Grove	66 835
Mary Jane	Butte Ophir	56 780
P B	Shasta Shasta	66 761
READON		
Mary	Butte Ophir	56 756
READONEL		
Frank	Sierra Downieville	661002
READY		
Daniel	Humbolt Eel Rvr	59 150
Francis	San Francisco San Francisco 5	67 546
J	San Joaquin Stockton	641083
John	Shasta Horsetown	66 698
M	Trinity Oregon G	701008
Martin	Los Angeles Los Angeles	59 357
Mary	San Francisco San Francisco 2	67 645
Philip	San Joaquin Oneal	64 935
Sarah	Sacramento Ward 3	63 483
W B*	Sacramento Ward 3	63 483
REAGAN		
James	Shasta Horsetown	66 703
James	Trinity Weaverville	701064
James	Yuba Rose Bar	72 806
Jno	Sacramento Ward 1	63 76
Thomas	Sierra Downieville	66 957
Thomas J	San Francisco San Francisco 7	681350
REAGEN		
John*	Yuba Marysville	72 928
Martin A	Colusa Monroeville	57 456
Thomas	San Francisco San Francisco 7	681335
REAGER		
William	Amador Twp 2	55 319
REAGNE		
Geo*	Siskiyou Klamath	69 94
REAGUE		
Geo	Siskiyou Klamath	69 94
REAL		
Adam	El Dorado Grizzly	581181
Diego	Monterey San Juan	60 983
Frank	Stanislaus Empire	70 726
John	Siskiyou Yreka	69 189
Jose	Contra Costa Twp 3	57 614
Jose M	Monterey San Juan	601003
Josefa	Monterey San Juan	60 960
Joseph	Tuolumne Twp 1	71 211
Josifa	Monterey Monterey	60 960
Manuel	Monterey San Juan	60 980
Manuel*	Monterey San Juan	601001
Maria	Monterey Monterey	60 962
Pedro Antonio	San Jose	65 390
	Santa Clara	
Rose	Sierra La Porte	66 773
Theodore	Calaveras Twp 4	57 335
REALDIS		
Jesus*	Los Angeles Los Angeles	59 490
REALE		
Paolo	San Francisco San Francisco 11	134 67
REALIN		
J R	Nevada Nevada	61 279
REALY		
Samuel T	Mariposa Twp 1	60 667
REALYENSTEIN		
Gust	Sierra Downieville	66 976
REAM		
Ben*	Yuba New York	72 719
REAM		
Calvim*	Napa Clear Lake	61 118
Calvin	Napa Clear Lake	61 118
D	Siskiyou Scott Va	69 61
J L*	Sacramento San Joaquin	63 354
Jacob	Yuba Bear Rvr	721004
N	Sutter Yuba	70 761
REAMARD		
Andre*	Shasta Shasta	66 661
REAMER		
A	Yolo Putah	72 588
J	Yolo Washington	72 568
R L	Yolo Cache	72 593
Ralph	Nevada Bridgeport	61 467
REAMOND		
Andre	Shasta Shasta	66 661
REAMS		
Jas	Butte Kimshaw	56 606
REAN		
J M	Nevada Nevada	61 240
William*	San Mateo Twp 3	65 100
REANCHAMP		
Elmira	Sierra Twp 5	66 936
REAND		
S	Calaveras Twp 9	57 406
REANDO		
Antonio*	San Francisco San Francisco 2	67 687
REANDRO		
Andrew	San Mateo Twp 1	65 48
REANIN		
A	Yolo Putah	72 588
REANLON		
James	Calaveras Twp 5	57 229
REANLT		
J	Yolo Slate Ra	72 688
S	Yuba Slate Ro	72 688
REANM		
Simon*	Calaveras Twp 7	57 36
REANN		
Jade	Calaveras Twp 7	57 40
REANNA		
J	Yolo Washington	72 568
Joseph	Calaveras Twp 7	57 2
REANNO		
Joseph	Calaveras Twp 7	57 2
REANO		
P W	Butte Ophir	56 751
REANOY		
Paul	Butte Bidwell	56 723
REANREPAN		
Louis*	Contra Costa Twp 1	57 521
REANY		
Wm	Sacramento Ward 1	63 39
REAPIN		
H	Butte Ophir	56 792
REAR		
Ben J O*	Yuba Slate Ro	72 717
Ben T A	Yolo Slate Ra	72 717
Benjamin O*	Yuba Bear Rvr	721004
Thoms	Sierra Downieville	661019
Thos	Tehama Red Bluff	70 912
REARDAN		
Henry	Yuba Marysville	72 871
James	Yuba Marysville	72 871
Thomas B	Yuba Marysville	72 871
REARDEN		
L O	Sacramento Franklin	63 326
Michael	Solano Vallejo	69 248
Michael*	Calaveras Twp 6	57 151
Owen	Klamath Liberty	59 233
REARDON		
Barney	San Francisco San Francisco 11	162 67
Catharine	San Francisco San Francisco 10	181 67
Catharine	Solano Vacaville	69 336
D	San Francisco San Francisco 6	67 467
Danl	San Francisco San Francisco 10	237 67
Francis	San Francisco San Francisco 10	236 67
Gordon	Solano Vallejo	69 260
Henry	Placer Forest H	62 804
Henry W	Yuba Slate Ro	72 691
James	Calaveras Twp 5	57 229
James	San Francisco San Francisco 11	118 67
Jas	San Francisco San Francisco 10	214 67
Jas	San Francisco San Francisco 2	67 800
Jhn	Trinity Raabs Ba	701020
John	San Francisco San Francisco 4	681165
John	San Francisco San Francisco 8	681302
John	San Francisco San Francisco 2	67 674
John	San Joaquin Castoria	64 883
John	Trinity Raabs Ba	701020

California 1860 Census Index

Name	County Locale	M653 RollPage
REARDON		
Jos	San Francisco San Francisco 2	67 800
Kate	San Francisco San Francisco 1	68 813
Martin*	Sacramento Granite	63 255
Mary	Sacramento Ward 1	63 94
Michael	Shasta Horsetown	66 689
P	San Joaquin Stockton	641099
Patrick*	Sierra St Louis	66 809
Philip	San Joaquin Douglass	64 914
Richd	San Francisco San Francisco 2	67 630
Thomas	Yuba Rose Bar	72 804
Thos	San Francisco San Francisco 10	214 67
Timothy	San Francisco San Francisco 10	189 67
Timothy*	San Mateo Twp 1	65 72
REARDOW		
Martin	Sacramento Granite	63 255
REAREY		
W B*	Sacramento Ward 3	63 483
REARNEY		
Phillip	Solano Vallejo	69 271
REARNS		
Jas*	Butte Kimshaw	56 606
REARS		
John	San Mateo Twp 3	65 84
Josa	Amador Twp 5	55 337
REARSEN		
Helen*	San Francisco San Francisco 2	67 559
REARTEN		
Michael	Monterey Alisal	601037
REAS		
Dewitt C	Humbolt Pacific	59 134
Peter W	Humbolt Pacific	59 134
REASANER		
Antone	San Francisco San Francisco 3	67 13
REASLER		
A J	Stanislaus Branch	70 697
REASNER		
Nelson	Siskiyou Callahan	69 16
REASON		
Guillaance J*	Yuba Marysville	72 936
Guillarmo J	Yuba Marysville	72 937
John J	Monterey Alisal	601034
Reuben	Calaveras Twp 7	57 3
REASONER		
Elizabeth	Tulara Visalia	71 74
L K	Nevada Bloomfield	61 525
REASORY		
John J*	Monterey Alisal	601034
REAT		
---	Placer Auburn	62 582
REATA		
Antonio	Alameda Brooklyn	55 195
REATHON		
---	San Francisco San Francisco 4	681225
REATHS		
Geo	Butte Cascade	56 695
REATYENSTEIN		
Gust	Sierra Downieville	66 976
REAUDRO		
Andrew	San Mateo Twp 1	65 48
REAUN		
Lenroux	Calaveras Twp 8	57 92
REAVES		
Chas S	Calaveras Twp 8	57 104
D M*	Butte Chico	56 541
J	El Dorado Placerville	58 838
John E	Amador Twp 4	55 253
REAVIS		
D M	Butte Chico	56 541
REAVY		
Margt*	San Francisco San Francisco 2	67 688
REAWARD		
Andre*	Shasta Shasta	66 661
REAY		
A W	San Francisco San Francisco 5	67 523
Lucy M	San Francisco San Francisco 10	258 67
REAZ		
Robt	Trinity Mouth Ca	701010
REBAND		
R	Sacramento Ward 1	63 12
REBE		
Fred	Alameda Brooklyn	55 143
REBEAN		
Clotina	San Francisco San Francisco 2	67 626
REBEAU		
Clotina	San Francisco San Francisco 2	67 626
REBEINSKIN		
J F	Sacramento Ward 1	63 34
REBEINSTEIN		
J F	Sacramento Ward 1	63 34
REBEN		
Jacob	Nevada Bridgeport	61 497
REBER		
Wm	Nevada Nevada	61 297

Name	County Locale	M653 RollPage
REBERA		
Rumone	Los Angeles Azuza	59 279
REBEREDA		
Diego	Placer Secret R	62 623
REBORD		
Just	Sacramento Ward 1	63 78
REBOUL		
Frances A	Yuba Marysville	72 933
REBUS		
---	Fresno Twp 2	59 110
REC		
Lere	Yuba Parks Ba	72 786
RECABEMAN		
A Domingo*	Sierra Downieville	66 965
RECAHNA		
Geo	Sacramento Ward 1	63 110
Gr*	Sacramento Ward 1	63 110
RECALAN		
Hosea*	Calaveras Twp 9	57 354
RECALINA		
Gr*	Sacramento Ward 1	63 110
RECARD		
Mathew	Marin San Rafael	60 769
RECART		
Jacob*	Tulara Visalia	71 91
RECARTHE		
Mr	Sonoma Sonoma	69 636
RECAST		
Jacob	Tuolumne Visalia	71 91
RECEIVER		
Henry	Sierra Downieville	661017
RECENBACHER		
J	El Dorado Georgetown	58 698
RECER		
Aaron	San Francisco San Francisco 2	67 786
RECH		
Wm*	Sierra Twp 5	66 919
RECHENPACH		
Ferdinand*	Calaveras Twp 6	57 160
RECHENPACK		
Ferdinand	Calaveras Twp 6	57 160
RECHENPOCH		
Ferinand*	Calaveras Twp 6	57 160
RECHEUPUCH		
Ferdinand*	Calaveras Twp 6	57 160
RECHLL		
Jose J*	Los Angeles Los Angeles	59 489
RECHMAN		
Wm*	Napa Napa	61 101
RECHMAW		
J B*	Napa Napa	61 97
RECI		
Wm*	Napa Napa	61 72
RECIER		
Prahadio*	Yuba Marysville	72 919
RECK		
David H	Alameda Brooklyn	55 213
Lewis	San Francisco San Francisco 8	681293
RECKER		
T	Trinity Lewiston	70 966
RECKETTS		
Alfred	Sonoma Armally	69 480
RECKMAN		
Ann E*	Napa Napa	61 69
RECKORD		
A	Shasta French G	66 718
RECO		
Hosa	El Dorado Mud Springs	58 974
RECOE		
R	Shasta Millvill	66 727
RECON		
W C*	Monterey Alisal	601044
RECORD		
George	Solano Suisan	69 232
James	Mendocino Anderson	60 869
Marion	San Francisco San Francisco 6	67 449
W C	Monterey Alisal	601044
W*	Monterey Alisal	601044
RECORDS		
Ben	Nevada Red Dog	61 545
RECT		
Henry*	Butte Oregon	56 640
RECTIR		
L	Siskiyou Cottonwoood	69 107
RECTON		
James*	Amador Twp 2	55 275
RECTOR		
E G	Merced Twp 1	60 895
Geo	Napa Yount	61 33
H	Shasta Millvill	66 726
H H	Sacramento Franklin	63 321
Hasan	Amador Twp 2	55 297
Jacob J	Napa Yount	61 30
James*	Amador Twp 2	55 275
Jno	Mendocino Big Rvr	60 847
L	Siskiyou Cottonwoood	69 108

Name	County Locale	M653 RollPage
RECTOR		
Mary	Napa Hot Springs	61 28
R P	Napa Hot Springs	61 28
R T	Napa Hot Springs	61 28
Thos H	Klamath Liberty	59 242
W A*	Napa Hot Springs	61 28
RECUBOUM		
Thomas	Calaveras Twp 6	57 133
RECUE		
R*	Shasta Millvill	66 727
RECURTHE		
Mr	Sonoma Sonoma	69 636
RED HEAD		
---	Fresno Twp 2	59 50
RED SHORT		
---	Fresno Twp 2	59 18
RED		
Charles	El Dorado Mud Springs	58 985
J J	Colusa Monroeville	57 456
R	San Francisco San Francisco 9	681075
REDA		
Jose	Sacramento Ward 1	63 57
REDCLIFF		
Miles	Calaveras Twp 10	57 265
Saml*	Alameda Brooklyn	55 81
REDCLIFFE		
Saml*	Alameda Brooklyn	55 81
REDD		
Oliver	Napa Napa	61 81
Wm*	El Dorado Georgetown	58 691
REDDECK		
James*	San Francisco San Francisco 7	681412
REDDELL		
Julius*	Napa Napa	61 67
REDDEN		
Charles	Marin Point Re	60 732
Jonathan	Tuolumne Twp 1	71 195
T	Shasta French G	66 717
REDDER		
Geo B*	Napa Napa	61 105
REDDICH		
John	Santa Clara San Jose	65 346
REDDICK		
A M*	Mendocino Ukiah	60 798
Andrew	Tuolumne Jamestown	71 423
Hardin	Solano Vacaville	69 362
James	Tuolumne Jamestown	71 423
John	Tuolumne Jamestown	71 432
Susan	Solano Vacaville	69 362
William	Calaveras Twp 5	57 218
REDDING		
Andrew	San Francisco San Francisco 9	681007
Anna	San Francisco San Francisco 6	67 454
Ben B	Sacramento Ward 1	63 138
Cornelius	Sierra Twp 7	66 901
Eliza	Placer Auburn	62 562
Enoch	El Dorado Casumnes	581166
F W	Sacramento American	63 167
Felix	Plumas Meadow Valley	62 903
Fritz W	Sacramento Ward 1	63 145
Geo C	Sacramento Ward 4	63 551
John A	Yolo Putah	72 546
Mary	Sacramento Ward 1	63 145
Pat	San Francisco San Francisco 9	681063
Patrick	San Francisco San Francisco 7	681426
Robert	Siskiyou Yreka	69 126
William	Marin Tomales	60 774
William	Tuolumne Twp 6	71 542
Wm	Sacramento Sutter	63 295
REDDINGTON		
Alfred	Sacramento Ward 3	63 455
N A	Tuolumne Sonora	71 223
Wm	San Francisco San Francisco 2	67 611
REDDISH		
Peter	Sacramento Ward 4	63 500
REDDLE		
Dewitt C	Fresno Twp 2	59 49
REDDLEFORD		
B A	Mendocino Big Rvr	60 845
REDDLER		
M	Yolo Fremont	72 603
REDDY		
B*	Siskiyou Callahan	69 7
Benj H	Butte Oregon	56 631
Michael	San Francisco San Francisco 12	391 67
Peter	Los Angeles San Pedro	59 483
REDEMEYER		
Aug F	Mendocino Little L	60 838
REDENGTON		
Mathew*	San Francisco San Francisco 1	68 903
REDER		
Fred	El Dorado White Oaks	581017
H M*	San Francisco San Francisco 3	67 76
REDFELD		
O F	Yuba Rose Bar	72 789

Name	County Locale	M653 Roll	Page
REDFERN			
Alfred	Calaveras Twp 6	57	133
REDFIELD			
Joel	Tulara Twp 3	71	54
Leonard	Tulara Twp 3	71	45
O F	Yuba Rose Bar	72	789
REDFISH			
John	Yolo Washington	72	602
REDFORD			
J F*	Shasta Shasta	66	685
John	San Francisco San Francisco 11		154
		67	
REDGEWAY			
R	San Francisco San Francisco 6	67	446
REDHEAD			
B B	Amador Twp 1	55	462
B B	Amador Twp 1	55	487
REDICK			
David	Humbolt Union	59	189
REDIN			
F	San Francisco San Francisco 2	67	797
REDINGS			
E J	El Dorado Salmon Falls	581	065
REDINGTON			
A A	Sacramento Ward 1	63	151
C	Tuolumne Twp 4	71	165
J	Nevada Eureka	61	389
Jacob	El Dorado Eldorado	58	947
John	Yuba Rose Bar	72	818
REDITH			
L	San Francisco San Francisco 3	67	64
REDKER			
W	Shasta Horsetown	66	699
REDKIN			
Richard	Contra Costa Twp 1	57	498
REDLEAN			
C	Sacramento Sutter	63	309
REDLER			
A	Amador Twp 7	55	417
REDLICK			
S	San Francisco San Francisco 5	67	501
REDMAN			
Barney	Placer Michigan	62	849
C	Mariposa Twp 1	60	642
E H	Mariposa Twp 1	60	649
Eli	San Francisco San Francisco 3	67	73
H B	Mariposa Twp 1	60	649
Harrison	Butte Oregon	56	637
Henrietta	San Francisco San Francisco 10		329
		67	
Henry	Tulara Visalia	71	11
Henry*	Butte Kimshaw	56	602
Hugh	San Joaquin Castoria	64	888
James	Sierra Twp 5	66	920
James	Yuba Rose Bar	72	804
James*	El Dorado Casumnes	581	162
John	Tuolumne Shawsfla	71	381
L	Mariposa Twp 3	60	557
Le	Mariposa Twp 3	60	557
Margaret	Yuba Marysville	72	874
Mary Ann	Alameda Murray	55	224
Mathew	Yuba Rose Bar	72	814
Pero	Tuolumne Twp 2	71	278
R A	Santa Clara San Jose	65	311
Robert M	Calaveras Twp 5	57	252
Thomas	Tuolumne Columbia	71	292
W	El Dorado Casumnes	581	160
W	Tehama Red Bluff	70	916
Wm G	Alameda Oakland	55	32
Wm M	Napa Napa	61	86
REDMAND			
Mary*	San Francisco San Francisco 8	681	298
REDMARSON			
Stokely R	Sonoma Mendocino	69	467
REDMOND			
Agatha	San Francisco San Francisco 10		183
		67	
Catherine	Solano Benecia	69	296
Frank	Sacramento Centre	63	173
J B	San Francisco San Francisco 6	67	417
James	Placer Forest H	62	767
James	Tuolumne Sonora	71	214
Jos G	San Francisco San Francisco 10		235
		67	
Jos H	San Francisco San Francisco 10		235
		67	
Mary	San Francisco San Francisco 8	681	298
Mary	San Joaquin Stockton	641	017
Mary L	San Francisco San Francisco 10		183
		67	
N	Tuolumne Big Oak	71	145
REDMUND			
Mary*	San Francisco San Francisco 8	681	298
REDNAW			
C	Butte Oro	56	683
REDOLPH			
Charles*	Solano Vacaville	69	365
REDON			
Louis	San Francisco San Francisco 4	681	171
REDONDA			
Manuel	San Bernardino Santa Barbara	64	190
REDONDO			
Francisa	Los Angeles San Juan	59	477
Francisca	Los Angeles San Juan	59	477
Jesus	Los Angeles Los Angeles	59	305
REDPAND			
William	Yuba Marysville	72	968
REDPATH			
Jas J	Placer Virginia	62	700
REDRIGUEZ			
Juan	San Bernardino S Buenav	64	217
REDRINGTON			
J	Nevada Eureka	61	389
REDRO			
Don*	Stanislaus Oatvale	70	718
REDSON			
Guillanme J*	Yuba Marysville	72	936
John	Amador Twp 5	55	342
John	Amador Twp 5	55	348
REDULLO			
Mateo	San Francisco San Francisco 7	681	411
REDUNEYER			
Aug F*	Mendocino Little L	60	838
REDWIN			
Jno	Sonoma Petaluma	69	549
REDWINE			
Fred A	Placer Auburn	62	587
L P	Marin Cortemad	60	786
REDWITH			
C	San Joaquin Stockton	641	055
REDWOOD			
Thomas	San Francisco San Francisco 11		107
		67	
REDY			
John	Trinity East For	701	027
REE			
---	Butte Oregon	56	631
---	Butte Oregon	56	642
---	El Dorado Georgetown	58	680
---	Placer Auburn	62	592
---	Sierra Twp 5	66	927
---	Sierra Twp 5	66	932
---	Yolo Slate Ra	72	719
---	Yuba Slate Ro	72	708
---	Yuba Long Bar	72	757
---	Yuba Long Bar	72	767
---*	Calaveras Twp 6	57	181
---*	Sacramento Ward 1	63	56
Ah	Butte Oregon	56	631
Ah	Butte Oregon	56	642
Dj S	Santa Clara Fremont	65	420
Lere*	Yuba Parke Ba	72	786
Too*	San Francisco San Francisco 11		146
		67	
Winn	El Dorado Georgetown	58	756
Yan	El Dorado Coloma	581	078
REEAN			
Thos*	San Francisco San Francisco 9	681	027
REEB			
Eli	Tuolumne Twp 1	71	209
Lewis	Tuolumne Sonora	71	209
Mons	Tuolumne Twp 1	71	209
REEBBS			
J L	Butte Eureka	56	647
REEBE			
John R	Tuolumne Twp 2	71	378
REEBER			
J*	Sacramento Ward 3	63	434
REEBS			
John R	Tuolumne Shawsfla	71	378
REECE			
A W	Nevada Rough &	61	420
David	Calaveras Twp 8	57	69
George	Nevada Bloomfield	61	516
J T	Nevada Little Y	61	533
Jhs	Yolo Washington	72	601
John S	Sierra Twp 7	66	867
Louis	Del Norte Crescent	58	649
N W*	Nevada Rough &	61	420
T N	Yolo Cache	72	590
T W	Yolo Cache Crk	72	590
Thos	Yolo Washington	72	601
REED			
A	Butte Ophir	56	770
A	Siskiyou Callahan	69	10
A B	Amador Twp 3	55	370
A C	Merced Twp 1	60	903
A H	San Francisco San Francisco 5	67	533
A H	Sierra Twp 7	66	874
A J	Nevada Nevada	61	240
A J	Trinity Sturdiva	701	006
A T	Trinity Weaverville	701	063
Abner	Tuolumne Twp 2	71	383
REED			
Ada	Placer Dutch Fl	62	726
Adam	San Francisco San Francisco 9	681	099
Adam	San Francisco San Francisco 4	681	224
Alexander	Placer Auburn	62	594
Amanda	El Dorado Kelsey	581	148
Annie	Humbolt Bucksport	59	155
Azel	Siskiyou Yreka	69	171
B	El Dorado Kelsey	581	140
B	Nevada Nevada	61	247
Benj	Trinity Lewiston	70	966
Benj H	San Francisco San Francisco 6	67	406
Bradford B	Tuolumne Green Springs	71	532
Bridget	San Francisco San Francisco 9	681	008
Bruce	Amador Twp 2	55	297
C	San Francisco San Francisco 10		332
		67	
C	Santa Clara Gilroy	65	245
C C	San Francisco San Francisco 5	67	541
C G	Tehama Red Bluff	70	913
C H	Yolo Cache	72	609
C W	Yolo Washington	72	565
Caleb	El Dorado Placerville	58	916
Charles	San Francisco San Francisco 8	681	241
Charles	San Francisco San Francisco 10		353
		67	
Charles	San Francisco San Francisco 3	67	67
Charles	San Francisco San Francisco 3	67	70
Chas	Calaveras Twp 9	57	369
Chas	Sacramento Ward 3	63	23
Chas	Sierra St Louis	66	814
Chas W	Alameda Oakland	55	64
Chauncy	Sacramento Ward 3	63	485
Constance	Sacramento Centre	63	175
Daniel	Calaveras Twp 9	57	356
Daniel	Plumas Quincy	62	980
Danl	Mariposa Twp 1	60	664
David	El Dorado White Oaks	581	016
David	Sierra Twp 5	66	947
David	Tuolumne Columbia	71	306
David C	Calaveras Twp 7	57	15
Demcuo*	Mariposa Twp 3	60	571
Dencen	Mariposa Twp 3	60	571
Denpero	Mariposa Twp 3	60	571
Duncin*	Mariposa Twp 3	60	571
E	Sacramento Brighton	63	193
E	Santa Clara San Jose	65	294
E	Sutter Yuba	70	774
E L	Marin Tomales	60	714
E L	Sonoma Santa Rosa	69	424
E P	Santa Clara San Jose	65	294
E S	Sonoma Santa Rosa	69	424
Edward	Sierra Port Win	66	797
Elijah	El Dorado Mountain	581	185
Eliza	San Francisco San Francisco 6	67	437
Elizabeth	San Francisco San Francisco 2	67	605
Elizabeth	Yuba Marysville	72	854
Elizah	El Dorado Mountain	581	185
Ellen	San Francisco San Francisco 9	681	105
F	Sacramento Sutter	63	306
F	Sacramento Sutter	63	307
Francis	Siskiyou Yreka	69	158
Francis	Siskiyou Yreka	69	165
Francis L	Sacramento Granite	63	260
Frank	San Francisco San Francisco 12		378
		67	
Frank	Tuolumne Twp 2	71	292
Frank	Tuolumne Columbia	71	293
G K	Nevada Bloomfield	61	525
G W	Sonoma Petaluma	69	575
G W	Sonoma Washington	69	677
G W	Tehama Red Bluff	70	917
Geo	Butte Mountain	56	740
Geo	Stanislaus Empire	70	735
Geo E	Del Norte Crescent	58	649
Geo H	San Francisco San Francisco 1	68	828
George	Calaveras Twp 9	57	347
George	Calaveras Twp 8	57	73
George	Sacramento Franklin	63	333
George	San Diego San Diego	64	765
George	San Francisco San Francisco 5	67	484
George	Tuolumne Twp 4	71	178
George A	Calaveras Twp 9	57	364
George K	Monterey S Antoni	60	967
George W	Humbolt Eel Rvr	59	151
George W	Siskiyou Yreka	69	152
George*	Placer Michigan	62	853
H	Butte Chico	56	531
H A	San Francisco San Francisco 4	681	165
H B	Solano Vacaville	69	325
H R	San Francisco San Francisco 3	67	48
H R	San Francisco San Francisco 3	67	49
Harrison	Yolo Washington	72	565
Helen	San Francisco San Francisco 4	681	147
Henry	Los Angeles Los Angeles	59	327
Henry	Placer Secret R	62	624

California 1860 Census Index

Name	County Locale	M653 Roll	Page
REED			
Henry	Siskiyou Scott Ri	69	63
Henry	Yolo Merritt	72	582
Henry	Yolo Merritt	72	584
Henry	Yuba Bear Rvr	72	1003
Henry M	Siskiyou Yreka	69	193
Hilara	Marin Sauciteto	60	751
Hy	San Francisco San Francisco 1	68	904
Isaac	San Francisco San Francisco 9	68	1071
Isaac	Yolo Merritt	72	582
J	El Dorado Placerville	58	860
J	El Dorado Eldorado	58	946
J	Nevada Nevada	61	269
J	Nevada Eureka	61	372
J	Sacramento Brighton	63	193
J	San Francisco San Francisco 5	67	529
J	Tehama Lassen	70	868
J	Trinity Mouth Ca	70	1013
J	Tuolumne Twp 4	71	158
J A	Sacramento Sutter	63	306
J B	Mariposa Twp 3	60	549
J C	Solano Fremont	69	384
J F	Butte Ophir	56	794
J J	El Dorado Placerville	58	856
J Lucien	San Francisco San Francisco 8	68	1318
J N	Calaveras Twp 9	57	405
J P	El Dorado Coloma	58	1082
J W	Mariposa Twp 3	60	552
Jackiar	Colusa Muion	57	463
Jacob T	Contra Costa Twp 2	57	572
Jame B	Mariposa Twp 3	60	571
James	Contra Costa Twp 2	57	542
James	Nevada Eureka	61	355
James	San Francisco San Francisco 7	68	1350
James	San Francisco San Francisco 2	67	729
James	Santa Cruz Santa Cruz	66	612
James	Sierra Twp 7	66	893
James	Solano Vacaville	69	360
James*	Yolo Washington	72	564
James*	Placer Michigan	62	849
Jane	San Francisco San Francisco 2	67	729
Jane B	Mariposa Twp 3	60	571
Jas	Butte Oro	56	681
Jas	San Francisco San Francisco 1	68	858
Jas B	Santa Clara San Jose	65	342
Jno	Mendocino Big Rvr	60	848
Jno C	Mendocino Calpella	60	819
Jno S	Klamath Liberty	59	235
Job	Alameda Oakland	55	51
John	Butte Kimshaw	56	607
John	Butte Wyandotte	56	667
John	El Dorado White Oaks	58	1018
John	El Dorado Mountain	58	1185
John	Humbolt Mattole	59	126
John	Mariposa Twp 3	60	548
John	Nevada Red Dog	61	545
John	Placer Secret R	62	618
John	Sacramento Cosumnes	63	393
John	San Francisco San Francisco 2	67	632
John	San Francisco San Francisco 1	68	837
John	San Francisco San Francisco 1	68	892
John	Santa Clara Fremont	65	420
John	Shasta Horsetown	66	695
John	Sierra Twp 5	66	917
John	Siskiyou Yreka	69	177
John	Solano Vacaville	69	357
John	Stanislaus Emory	70	740
John	Trinity Trinity	70	972
John	Yolo Slate Ra	72	702
John	Yolo Slate Ra	72	717
John	Yuba Slate Ro	72	717
John B	Alameda Oakland	55	65
John B	Sierra Downieville	66	975
John J	Solano Vacaville	69	359
John L	Humbolt Union	59	183
John L	Tuolumne Shawsfla	71	417
John M	Butte Cascade	56	702
John R*	Sierra La Porte	66	778
John T	Placer Auburn	62	560
John W*	San Francisco San Francisco 1	68	878
John*	Butte Kimshaw	56	607
John*	Placer Iona Hills	62	877
John*	Solano Vacaville	69	357
Joseh	San Francisco San Francisco 2	67	621
Joseph	Mariposa Coulterville	60	697
Joseph	San Francisco San Francisco 2	67	621
Joseph	Sonoma Washington	69	677
Joseph	Tuolumne Twp 2	71	343
Joseph A	San Luis Obispo San Luis Obispo	65	45
Josephus	Siskiyou Yreka	69	177
June	Alameda Oakland	55	12
K	Mariposa Twp 3	60	558
L	Butte Kimshaw	56	588
L E	Alameda Brooklyn	55	118
L F	Sacramento Ward 4	63	585

Name	County Locale	M653 Roll	Page
REED			
L J	Tuolumne Twp 4	71	158
L M	Nevada Nevada	61	293
L*	Butte Kimshaw	56	588
Lenord	Mariposa Coulterville	60	687
Lewis	Calaveras Twp 7	57	15
Louis	Yuba Long Bar	72	773
Martha	Colusa Grand Island	57	473
Mary	San Francisco San Francisco 10	67	317
Mary	Yuba Marysville	72	886
Mathew*	San Francisco San Francisco 1	68	878
Matthew	Yuba Marysville	72	941
Mons	Tuolumne Sonora	71	209
N R	Sierra Twp 7	66	905
O J	Nevada Eureka	61	355
O L	Yolo Cache	72	607
Oth	Marin Cortemad	60	755
Otto	Marin Cortemad	60	755
Oz	Tehama Antelope	70	895
Patrick	Sierra Twp 7	66	912
Peter	Yuba Marysville	72	924
Peter B	Alameda Brooklyn	55	189
Phil	Shasta Shasta	66	674
Philip	Tuolumne Green Springs	71	519
R	Mariposa Twp 3	60	558
R	San Francisco San Francisco 5	67	480
R C	San Francisco San Francisco 3	67	71
R*	San Francisco San Francisco 5	67	491
Ralph	Nevada Red Dog	61	545
Reuben	Butte Ophir	56	748
Rhoda	Colusa Mansville	57	437
Robert	Calaveras Twp 8	57	106
Robert	Calaveras Twp 8	57	62
Robert	San Francisco San Francisco 5	67	545
Robt	Alameda Oakland	55	70
Robt	Amador Twp 2	55	271
Robt	Sacramento Cosumnes	63	387
Robt M	Sonoma Mendocino	69	449
S	El Dorado Placerville	58	892
S D C	Amador Twp 2	55	288
S L	Solano Fremont	69	384
Saml	Butte Chico	56	559
Saml	Placer Ophirville	62	655
Saml	San Bernardino San Salvador	64	648
Saml	San Francisco San Francisco 5	67	544
Saml B	San Francisco San Francisco 12	67	366
Saml P	Placer Auburn	62	597
Samuel	El Dorado Placerville	58	921
Samuel	Solano Vacaville	69	347
Samuel	Yuba Rose Bar	72	805
Sarah	Los Angeles Elmonte	59	250
Silas A	Tuolumne Twp 1	71	203
T	Tuolumne Twp 4	71	151
T B	Nevada Red Dog	61	540
T L	Solano Fremont	69	384
Thomas	El Dorado Mud Springs	58	982
Thomas	Tuolumne Columbia	71	295
Thomas	Yuba Bear Rvr	72	1009
Thos	Butte Eureka	56	653
Thos	Butte Ophir	56	799
Thos	Sacramento Brighton	63	200
Thos	Sacramento Casumnes	63	380
Thos	Sacramento Cosumnes	63	383
Thos	Sacramento Cosumnes	63	385
Thos	San Francisco San Francisco 6	67	441
Thos	San Francisco San Francisco 2	67	710
Thos	Solano Vallejo	69	249
Thos*	Butte Eureka	56	653
Timothy	Tuolumne Montezuma	71	506
Victoria	Los Angeles San Gabriel	59	419
W	Butte Ophir	56	800
W C	Sacramento Ward 4	63	588
W C	San Francisco San Francisco 10	67	279
W D*	Sacramento Lee	63	218
W H	San Francisco San Francisco 3	67	46
W H	San Mateo Twp 1	65	53
W J	Yolo Cache	72	607
W L	El Dorado Kelsey	58	1138
W R	Sierra Twp 7	66	905
W S	Los Angeles Azuza	59	276
Warren	El Dorado Mud Springs	58	982
Warren L	Tuolumne Twp 1	71	203
Wilburn	Yuba Bear Rvr	72	1000
William	El Dorado Mud Springs	58	973
William	Nevada Bridgeport	61	450
William	Siskiyou Klamath	69	95
William	Yuba Bear Rvr	72	1000
William	Yuba Rose Bar	72	814
William A	Sierra La Porte	66	778
William H	Sierra La Porte	66	778
William J	San Francisco San Francisco 11	67	152
William*	San Francisco San Francisco 7	68	1361

Name	County Locale	M653 Roll	Page
REED			
William*	Yuba Rose Bar	72	814
Wilson	Solano Fremont	69	384
Wm	Mariposa Coulterville	60	702
Wm	San Francisco San Francisco 10	67	193
Wm C	Tuolumne Sonora	71	234
Wm F	Plumas Meadow Valley	62	927
Wm H	Nevada Nevada	61	240
Wm J	Humbolt Eureka	59	171
Wm M	San Francisco San Francisco 10	67	279
Wm*	Alameda Brooklyn	55	122
Wm*	San Francisco San Francisco 1	68	875
X*	San Francisco San Francisco 5	67	491
Zelotus	Contra Costa Twp 2	57	556
REEDA			
J*	Nevada Nevada	61	317
REEDE			
W	Tuolumne Twp 4	71	157
William	Calaveras Twp 7	57	25
REEDEN			
C	El Dorado Diamond	58	803
REEDER			
Henry	Tuolumne Sonora	71	231
John	Nevada Rough &	61	436
John M	Nevada Bridgeport	61	456
John*	Nevada Rough &	61	436
W H*	Sacramento Cosumnes	63	389
Wm	Sacramento Cosumnes	63	382
REEDES			
Henry	Tuolumne Twp 1	71	231
REEDIN			
F G	Colusa Monroeville	57	454
REEDING			
Wm	Santa Clara San Jose	65	337
REEDLE			
L	Yolo Cache Crk	72	646
REEDMAN			
Daniel	Placer Auburn	62	588
REEDS			
Joseph	San Francisco San Francisco 2	67	645
REEDSHAW			
William*	Nevada Bridgeport	61	467
REEF			
Dann*	Klamath Liberty	59	230
REEFER			
Abram	Yuba Rose Bar	72	820
REEGAN			
R	Nevada Eureka	61	360
REEGUAR			
Marsele*	San Francisco San Francisco 2	67	703
REEIER			
Prahadio*	Yuba Marysville	72	919
REEIS			
Manuela*	Yuba Marysville	72	951
REEK			
George	San Diego San Diego	64	765
REEKETT			
Alfred	Sonoma Armally	69	480
REEKINS			
John	El Dorado Georgetown	58	689
REEKMAN			
A*	San Francisco San Francisco 3	67	51
REEL			
Barton	Sierra St Louis	66	818
D G	Amador Twp 5	55	346
John	Sacramento Ward 4	63	521
John	Sierra Poverty	66	799
Wilson C	Sierra Pine Grove	66	827
REELIA			
Louis*	Calaveras Twp 6	57	137
REELIN			
Louis	Calaveras Twp 5	57	137
REELL			
James*	Yuba Long Bar	72	768
REELLER			
John*	Stanislaus Emory	70	739
REELLY			
Jas F*	San Francisco San Francisco 10	67	266
REEM			
J	Nevada Eureka	61	351
REEMS			
Alex	Sacramento Alabama	63	413
REEN			
Chas	San Francisco San Francisco 2	67	737
D	San Francisco San Francisco 5	67	551
J	Siskiyou Scott Ri	69	75
Jas O*	Napa Napa	61	71
REENAHER			
Patk*	Napa Napa	61	102
REENAKER			
Patk*	Napa Napa	61	102
REENE			
George	Calaveras Twp 7	57	7

California 1860 Census Index

Name	County Locale	M653 Roll	Page
REENER			
J	Nevada Grass Valley	61	237
REENOLD			
John	San Joaquin Castoria	64	890
REEPELL			
Wm S*	San Francisco San Francisco 3	67	83
REEQUAR			
Marsele*	San Francisco San Francisco 2	67	703
REERES			
John Jr	San Francisco San Francisco 2	67	639
REERS			
Remon	Mariposa Twp 1	60	672
REES			
Ely	Calaveras Twp 9	57	363
Humphry*	Amador Twp 4	55	250
Jasen*	Amador Twp 5	55	334
Jeseus	Amador Twp 5	55	334
Jisens*	Amador Twp 5	55	334
Leopold*	Alameda Murray	55	225
Manuel	Calaveras Twp 5	57	173
Patrick	Sierra Twp 7	66	912
Stephen	Colusa Spring Valley	57	436
Thomas	Sierra Pine Grove	66	835
Wm	Sierra Monte Crk	66	1037
REESA			
Jacob	San Francisco San Francisco 5	67	494
REESE			
Adonmis*	Calaveras Twp 7	57	45
Ann B	San Francisco San Francisco 10	67	238
Aven	Sierra Port Win	66	794
Avon	Sierra Port Win	66	794
Catharine	San Francisco San Francisco 2	67	793
Catherine	San Francisco San Francisco 2	67	793
Chas	Calaveras Twp 9	57	369
Conrad	El Dorado Kelsey	58	1142
D	San Francisco San Francisco 5	67	505
D	Solano Vallejo	69	279
David	Plumas Meadow Valley	62	934
David	San Francisco San Francisco 1	68	890
David	Solano Vallejo	69	254
E L	Shasta Shasta	66	673
Elder*	Sonoma Petaluma	69	575
Elias	Los Angeles Elmonte	59	247
Ely	Calaveras Twp 9	57	363
Ernest	San Francisco San Francisco 7	68	1391
Frederick	Calaveras Twp 9	57	364
George	Mendocino Round Va	60	879
Gustavus	Sierra Downieville	66	1011
H	Mariposa Twp 3	60	602
H	Butte Wyandotte	56	664
H	San Francisco San Francisco 5	67	543
H	San Francisco San Francisco 5	67	551
Henry	Plumas Meadow Valley	62	901
Henry Halcomb*	Yuba Marysville	72	859
Henry Halcomb*	Yuba Marysville	72	858
Henry Holcomb*	Yuba Marysville	72	858
Isaac	Sacramento Ward 1	63	77
J C	Tuolumne Twp 1	71	250
J M D	Placer Virginia	62	673
James	Sacramento Ward 1	63	32
James	Yuba Rose Bar	72	814
James M	Yuba Marysville	72	978
Joel	Shasta Shasta	66	760
John	El Dorado Coloma	58	1072
John	El Dorado Casumnes	58	1161
John	Merced Twp 1	60	905
John J	Sierra Pine Grove	66	830
Jose M*	Yuba Marysville	72	922
Joseph	Tulara Visalia	71	2
Joseph	Yuba Parks Ba	72	779
L L	Tehama Red Bluff	70	905
Leonard	Yolo Cache Crk	72	642
M M	Tuolumne Sonora	71	221
M N	Nevada Nevada	61	275
Margaret	El Dorado Coloma	58	1072
Philip	Tuolumne Twp 1	71	219
R	Tuolumne Jamestown	71	445
Rebecca	San Francisco San Francisco 2	67	737
Reese	Sierra Port Win	66	798
Robert P	Los Angeles Los Angeles	59	333
W	San Francisco San Francisco 9	68	1076
W M	Tuolumne Twp 1	71	221
William	Sierra Port Win	66	793
Wm	Sonoma Bodega	69	519
Wm	Yolo Slate Ra	72	702
Wm	Yuba Slate Ro	72	702
Wm N	Sacramento Ward 4	63	532
Wm S	San Francisco San Francisco 10	67	279
REESER			
J W	Sacramento Ward 1	63	142
Wm Ah	Yolo Slate Ra	72	701
REESES			
D D	Solano Suisan	69	204
Samuel	Tulara Visalia	71	105

Name	County Locale	M653 Roll	Page
REESH			
C D*	Sierra Twp 7	66	903
REESIR			
Poahadio*	Yuba Marysville	72	919
REESLER			
Wm*	Sacramento Natonia	63	284
REESO			
H*	Mariposa Twp 3	60	602
REESS			
Danl	Stanislaus Emory	70	741
REETH			
John*	Sacramento Franklin	63	313
REEVE			
Alice	Sacramento Ward 4	63	573
Allan	Sacramento American	63	167
Ferdinand	Amador Twp 4	55	258
Henry P	Napa Yount	61	36
John	Alameda Brooklyn	55	114
R	Nevada Grass Valley	61	202
Robt	Santa Clara Santa Clara	65	475
REEVER			
Annie	Sacramento American	63	160
REEVES			
---	Stanislaus Emory	70	741
A B	Stanislaus Buena Village	70	723
Amos	Plumas Quincy	62	963
Bartlett	Placer Virginia	62	689
Charles	Contra Costa Twp 3	57	589
Charles	Tuolumne Twp 6	71	541
Christ	Napa Napa	61	80
D D	Solano Suisan	69	204
Elija	Napa Clear Lake	61	121
Geo*	Napa Napa	61	77
George	Napa Napa	61	62
George	Yolo Cottonwoood	72	555
George*	Napa Napa	61	62
Grundy	Tulara Twp 1	71	82
Henry	Santa Clara Gilroy	65	229
Henry C	Plumas Quincy	62	996
J C	Napa Clear Lake	61	125
J K	Siskiyou Scott Ri	69	76
J W	Sacramento Ward 1	63	41
Jasper	Fresno Twp 3	59	22
John	El Dorado Salmon Falls	58	1042
John Jr	San Francisco San Francisco 2	67	639
John M	Plumas Quincy	62	974
John M	Yuba Marysville	72	968
L	Butte Hamilton	56	521
L L	Los Angeles Elmonte	59	266
Luke	El Dorado White Oaks	58	1015
M	El Dorado Newtown	58	779
Margaret	Placer Virginia	62	685
Mary A	San Francisco San Francisco 8	68	1303
Peter	Placer Michigan	62	854
Philip	Solano Benecia	69	312
Robert C	Plumas Quincy	62	952
Rundy	Tulara Visalia	71	82
Samuel	Tulara Visalia	71	105
W	Trinity Sturdiva	70	1007
W B	Siskiyou Klamath	69	78
Wesle*	Napa Napa	61	80
Wm	Alameda Brooklyn	55	213
Wm	San Francisco San Francisco 6	67	434
REEVIS			
John M	Yuba Marysville	72	968
REFA			
Rufina*	Monterey San Juan	60	997
REFELVER			
Fanareo	Mariposa Twp 1	60	653
Fancirco*	Mariposa Twp 1	60	653
Fancireo*	Mariposa Twp 1	60	653
Fancisco	Mariposa Twp 1	60	653
Faneirer	Mariposa Twp 1	60	653
REFFERN			
Michael	Solano Vallejo	69	269
REFFEY			
E T*	Napa Clear Lake	61	134
REFFOR			
H	Siskiyou Klamath	69	84
REFINGIN			
---	San Bernardino S Timate	64	698
REFUGEA			
---	San Bernardino S Timate	64	707
---	San Bernardino S Timate	64	721
REFUGIA			
---	San Bernardino Santa Inez	64	137
---	San Bernardino San Bernadino	64	678
---	San Bernardino S Timate	64	696
---	San Bernardino S Timate	64	734
---	San Bernardino S Timate	64	735
---	San Bernardino S Timate	64	737
---	San Bernardino S Timate	64	747
---	San Diego San Diego	64	771
---	San Diego Colorado	64	812
Maria	San Diego Agua Caliente	64	839
Maria	Santa Cruz Santa Cruz	66	617

Name	County Locale	M653 Roll	Page
REFUGIA			
Masador	Santa Cruz Santa Cruz	66	617
REFUGIO			
---	Monterey San Juan	60	991
---	San Bernardino S Timate	64	731
---	San Bernardino S Timate	64	749
Maria	Los Angeles San Juan	59	465
REFUGO			
---	Los Angeles Los Angeles	59	495
REFUIGE			
Nicholas*	Santa Cruz Pajaro	66	542
REFUIGI			
Nicholas	Santa Cruz Pajaro	66	542
REGA			
Jose	Santa Clara Alviso	65	408
REGALADO			
Antonio	Los Angeles Los Nieto	59	437
Victor	Los Angeles Los Angeles	59	306
REGALAY			
Louis	San Francisco San Francisco 11	67	156
REGALIS			
Antoine	Calaveras Twp 5	57	232
REGALON			
Jose	Sacramento Ward 1	63	110
REGALORO			
Jose	Sacramento Ward 1	63	110
REGAN			
Alfred	Mendocino Little L	60	838
Annie	Alameda Oakland	55	2
B	Nevada Grass Valley	61	177
Cornelius	Alameda Brooklyn	55	83
David	San Francisco San Francisco 11	67	99
E	Sacramento Ward 4	63	607
Edward	Sacramento Ward 1	63	122
Hannah	San Francisco San Francisco 9	68	1016
Isaac L	Sacramento Ward 3	63	482
James	San Francisco San Francisco 4	68	1157
James	San Francisco San Francisco 3	67	46
James	San Francisco San Francisco 11	67	90
Jeremiah	Alameda Brooklyn	55	113
Jeremiah	San Francisco San Francisco 7	68	1421
Jno	Alameda Brooklyn	55	210
Joanna	San Francisco San Francisco 7	68	1422
Joel	Sonoma Mendocino	69	461
John	San Francisco San Francisco 7	68	1421
John	San Francisco San Francisco 3	67	82
John	San Mateo Twp 3	65	74
John	Shasta Horsetown	66	698
Julius	San Francisco San Francisco 11	67	120
Kate	San Francisco San Francisco 2	67	643
Mary A	Alameda Oakland	55	8
Orrin	San Francisco San Francisco 5	67	490
P	Nevada Grass Valley	61	197
Pat	Placer Virginia	62	675
Patrick	Monterey Pajaro	60	1025
Patrick	San Francisco San Francisco 10	67	225
Patrick	San Francisco San Francisco 1	68	899
Patrick O	Solano Vallejo	69	274
Robt	San Francisco San Francisco 1	68	890
Sames	San Francisco San Francisco 3	67	46
T	El Dorado Diamond	58	774
T	Nevada Grass Valley	61	179
Thomas	Sierra La Porte	66	784
Thos	Sacramento Ward 1	63	12
William	San Francisco San Francisco 11	67	116
Wm	San Francisco San Francisco 10	67	251
Wm	San Francisco San Francisco 1	68	900
REGELBUTH			
Elizabeth	Yuba Marysville	72	943
REGELHEETH			
Elizabeth*	Yuba Marysville	72	943
REGELHKBIRTH			
Elezabeth	Yuba Marysville	72	943
REGEN			
John	Siskiyou Callahan	69	7
John	Yuba Marysville	72	970
Simon	San Francisco San Francisco 7	68	1344
Simon	San Francisco San Francisco 7	68	1351
REGENBENGER			
J*	San Francisco San Francisco 4	68	1149
REGENBURGER			
J	San Francisco San Francisco 4	68	1149
REGENSBERGER			
Melvin	San Francisco San Francisco 8	68	1299
REGENSBURGHER			
Amelia	San Francisco San Francisco 10	67	228
REGER			
Louis	San Francisco San Francisco 2	67	763

California 1860 Census Index

Name	County Locale	M653 Roll	Page
REGERIA			
Genseppe	Amador Twp 3	55	376
REGES			
Jose	Butte Oregon	56	612
Miguel	Santa Clara Santa Clara	65	521
Peter	Santa Clara Gilroy	65	235
Phillip	Santa Clara Santa Clara	65	520
REGETTA			
Carmetta	Tuolumne Columbia	71	321
REGGEN			
Wm	Tuolumne Twp 1	71	185
REGGET			
Henry*	Contra Costa Twp 3	57	593
REGGS			
Rosanna	San Francisco San Francisco 10	67	230
REGIELNIA			
Meguel*	Alameda Oakland	55	3
REGIER			
Thomas	Yuba Suida	72	989
REGIES			
Thomas*	Yuba Linda	72	989
REGILNIA			
Miguel*	Alameda Oakland	55	3
REGINE			
Michael	Calaveras Twp 5	57	232
REGIS			
Jose	Santa Clara Santa Clara	65	513
Nicholas	Yuba Marysville	72	925
Nickolos	Yuba Marysville	72	925
REGIVE			
Michael*	Calaveras Twp 5	57	232
REGLA			
Rufina*	Monterey San Juan	60	997
REGLE			
John	Yuba Marysville	72	865
REGLHUT			
Conrad	San Francisco San Francisco 2	67	634
REGLOS			
Rufina	Monterey San Juan	60	997
REGNA			
Alfred*	Mendocino Little L	60	838
C	Butte Bidwell	56	715
Issac L*	Sacramento Ward 4	63	558
J B	Siskiyou Scott Va	69	38
J E	Tuolumne Sonora	71	211
Jno*	Sacramento Ward 4	63	557
REGNAR			
Joel	Santa Clara Alviso	65	402
REGNER			
Jacob	Yuba Marysville	72	872
Peter	Sacramento Granite	63	240
REGNIER			
John	San Francisco San Francisco 11	67	138
REGO			
Jose	Amador Twp 5	55	336
REGOEVA			
Francisco	Calaveras Twp 5	57	198
REGOI			
Antonia	El Dorado Placerville	58	932
REGOLLS			
Danl	Mariposa Coulterville	60	694
REGUA			
Alfred	Mendocino Little L	60	838
Issac L*	Sacramento Ward 4	63	558
J E	Tuolumne Twp 1	71	211
Jno*	Sacramento Ward 4	63	557
REGUD			
Jaques*	Butte Hamilton	56	526
REGUENA			
Antonio M	Los Angeles Los Angeles	59	322
Manuel	Los Angeles Los Angeles	59	328
REGULIS			
Antoine	Calaveras Twp 5	57	232
REGUTTEL			
Louisa	Yuba Marysville	72	933
REHBURG			
Walter	Trinity Trinity	70	971
REHE			
Jas	Butte Cascade	56	698
REHEAR			
John	Mariposa Twp 3	60	586
REHER			
L	El Dorado Placerville	58	882
REHIAR			
John*	Mariposa Twp 3	60	586
REHIAS			
John	Mariposa Twp 3	60	586
REHILL			
John	San Francisco San Francisco 8	68	1323
John	San Francisco San Francisco 7	68	1406
REHL			
Eugene	Yuba Marysville	72	849
Jas	Butte Cascade	56	698
REHLFN			
C*	Yuba Long Bar	72	750
REHOE			
Michael	Monterey San Juan	60	974
REHOG			
Ning	Siskiyou Yreka	69	194
REHOS			
Lorenzo	Sonoma Mendocino	69	462
REHR			
John C	Humbolt Eel Rvr	59	145
REHRS			
F	San Francisco San Francisco 2	67	583
REIAS			
Jose Many	Placer Auburn	62	580
REIB			
Michael	Mariposa Twp 1	60	660
REIBSCHAL			
Henry*	San Francisco San Francisco 1	68	827
REICARDIA			
Jose	Santa Cruz Santa Cruz	66	609
REICART			
Jacob*	Tulara Twp 1	71	91
REICE			
Geo W	Klamath Orleans	59	216
Peo Kentho*	San Mateo Twp 1	65	56
Robart	Mariposa Twp 3	60	555
Roilcart*	Mariposa Twp 3	60	555
Rolcart*	Mariposa Twp 3	60	555
William	Fresno Twp 3	59	15
REICHE			
Theodore	Los Angeles Los Angeles	59	340
REICHELL			
Wm	San Francisco San Francisco 2	67	694
REICHERT			
J A	San Francisco San Francisco 10	67	334
REICHLEY			
John*	Solano Vacaville	69	345
REICHNAAGEN			
William*	Yuba Marysville	72	896
REICHORD			
Charles	Marin Cortemad	60	755
REICHOW			
Charles	Marin Cortemad	60	755
REICK			
Lewis	Sierra Downieville	66	970
REID			
A C	Merced Twp 1	60	903
A H	El Dorado Placerville	58	852
A J	Shasta Millvill	66	727
Albert	Plumas Quincy	62	952
Alexander	Tulara Keeneysburg	71	47
Andrew	Fresno Twp 3	59	13
Charles	San Francisco San Francisco 3	67	67
Charles*	Alameda Oakland	55	13
Danl	Mariposa Twp 1	60	664
E A	Shasta Millvill	66	727
F L Van	San Francisco San Francisco 2	67	573
F W	Trinity Prices B	70	1019
Francis	Sierra La Porte	66	787
Frans*	Sierra La Porte	66	787
Fraus*	Sierra La Porte	66	787
H	Nevada Grass Valley	61	188
H B	Solano Vacaville	69	325
H D*	Calaveras Twp 8	57	100
H F	Yolo Putah	72	587
Hester	San Francisco San Francisco 11	67	133
I	Calaveras Twp 9	57	389
I N	Calaveras Twp 9	57	405
J	Calaveras Twp 9	57	398
J	Nevada Eureka	61	372
J B	Sacramento Ward 4	63	512
J D	Yolo Cache Crk	72	644
James	Contra Costa Twp 2	57	556
James H	Tuolumne Twp 1	71	260
Jno	Butte Oregon	56	620
Jno	Mendocino Anderson	60	869
John	San Francisco San Francisco 7	68	1356
John	Siskiyou Yreka	69	177
John	Yuba Slate Ro	72	702
John A	Trinity New Rvr	70	1030
John B	Sierra La Porte	66	778
John C	Tulara Twp 1	71	96
John J*	Solano Vacaville	69	359
John R*	Sierra La Porte	66	778
John*	Butte Kimshaw	56	607
John*	Solano Vacaville	69	357
Jose M	Fresno Twp 1	59	76
L	Nevada Grass Valley	61	195
Lafayette L	San Joaquin Castoria	64	906
Paul	San Francisco San Francisco 7	68	1400
R	Monterey S Antoni	60	973
R	Nevada Grass Valley	61	195
R C	San Francisco San Francisco 3	67	71
R H	San Joaquin Stockton	64	1012
Robert C	Siskiyou Yreka	69	153
Robt	Sacramento Ward 3	63	427
REID			
S*	Nevada Grass Valley	61	195
Samuel	Tulara Petersburg	71	51
Thomas	Tuolumne Twp 2	71	295
Thos	San Mateo Twp 3	65	104
Thos*	Butte Eureka	56	653
U F	Yolo Putah	72	587
V A	Tehama Lassen	70	875
W	San Joaquin Stockton	64	1092
W D*	Sacramento Lee	63	218
William	Nevada Bridgeport	61	450
William*	Yuba Rose Bar	72	814
Wm*	Alameda Brooklyn	55	122
REIDD			
C F	Butte Oregon	56	619
REIDER			
Jacob	Tuolumne Twp 1	71	186
John M*	Nevada Bridgeport	61	456
W H*	Sacramento Cosumnes	63	389
REIDES			
Jacob	Tuolumne Sonora	71	186
REIDEY			
James*	Calaveras Twp 5	57	216
REIEHMAN			
Henry	Santa Clara Fremont	65	421
REIERSEN			
Helen*	San Francisco San Francisco 2	67	559
REIFENSTALL			
Drod*	Alameda Brooklyn	55	140
REIFER			
Abram*	Yuba Rose Bar	72	820
REIFERRSTALL			
Drod*	Alameda Brooklyn	55	140
REIFF			
L	Sacramento Dry Crk	63	376
REIFFER			
W J	Santa Clara Santa Clara	65	511
REIFONEATH			
P	Yolo Cache	72	641
REIFUIL			
B	El Dorado Georgetown	58	696
REIG			
Henry	Amador Twp 1	55	461
REIGHLEY			
Henry	El Dorado Mud Springs	58	967
REIK			
---	Sierra Downieville	66	984
REIL			
Conrad	Butte Kimshaw	56	569
Frederick	San Francisco San Francisco 11	67	120
REILEY			
Catharine	San Francisco San Francisco 2	67	651
Eliza*	Napa Napa	61	95
Ellen	Santa Cruz Pajaro	66	551
Geo V	Tuolumne Big Oak	71	145
Jas	San Francisco San Francisco 1	68	888
Patrick	Santa Cruz Pajaro	66	550
Phillip	Marin Cortemad	60	791
Thos	Santa Clara Santa Clara	65	509
W A	Butte Oregon	56	629
Wm A*	Butte Oregon	56	629
REILFENEATH			
P	Yolo Cache Crk	72	641
REILL			
James*	Yuba Long Bar	72	768
REILLEY			
Ellen	Santa Cruz Pajaro	66	551
Thomas	Mendocino Little L	60	834
REILLY			
Alfred Wm	San Francisco 11	67	126
James	San Francisco San Francisco 10	67	290
Jane	San Francisco San Francisco 10	67	240
Jas F	San Francisco San Francisco 10	67	266
John	Sacramento Sutter	63	290
John	San Francisco San Francisco 10	67	197
Joseph	San Luis Obispo San Luis Obispo	65	5
Joseph*	Placer Yankee J	62	757
Mary Sybilena S	Solano Benecia	69	300
Owen	San Francisco San Francisco 11	67	122
Thos	San Francisco San Francisco 12	67	382
REILY			
Elizabeth	San Francisco San Francisco 2	67	661
Jno	Mendocino Big Rvr	60	843
John	Solano Benecia	69	304
John C	San Francisco San Francisco 7	68	1435
REIM			
Sam	Yuba New York	72	719
REIMAN			
Henry	San Francisco San Francisco 6	67	415

California 1860 Census Index

Name	County Locale	M653 Roll Page
REIMAN		
Mary	San Francisco San Francisco	6 67 415
REIMANE		
Lizzie	San Francisco San Francisco	10 262 67
REIMAS		
J T	Sacramento Granite	63 234
REIMCKE		
G*	Sacramento Ward 1	63 27
REIMELS		
Charles	San Francisco San Francisco	7 681385
REIMER		
Edward	San Francisco San Francisco	11 115 67
John	Plumas Quincy	62 923
Washington*	Placer Forest H	62 770
REIMLEY		
H*	Butte Cascade	56 696
REIN		
Ed	Stanislaus Emory	70 738
Felix	Calaveras Twp 9	57 402
Hannorah	Sacramento Ward 4	63 570
J W	Sonoma Bodega	69 524
REINA		
Meed*	San Francisco San Francisco	1 68 814
Mud*	San Francisco San Francisco	1 68 814
REINAKER		
Patk*	Napa Napa	61 102
REINAN		
John*	Placer Forest H	62 802
REINARD		
Charles	San Francisco San Francisco	8 681263
REINCLOUX		
Pierre	Sierra La Porte	66 768
REINE		
Albert	Tulara Visalia	71 86
Mathew	Calaveras Twp 8	57 95
REINECKE		
G*	Sacramento Ward 1	63 25
REINER		
Augustus	Sacramento Ward 1	63 25
J	Calaveras Twp 8	57 62
REINERS		
John H	San Francisco San Francisco	7 681365
REINES		
Joseph	San Diego San Diego	64 765
REINETER		
Lena*	San Francisco San Francisco	7 681391
REINETZKER		
A	San Francisco San Francisco	5 67 504
REINEY		
C J	Napa Yount	61 52
T F	Napa Napa	61 80
REINFELDT		
Charles	San Francisco San Francisco	11 114 67
REINHADT		
Jesse	Tuolumne Twp 5	71 501
REINHANS		
Richard	Tuolumne Chinese	71 497
REINHARDT		
Jesse	Tuolumne Chinese	71 501
John B	San Francisco San Francisco	10 217 67
REINHART		
Chas	San Francisco San Francisco	1 68 912
D W	Solano Benecia	69 287
E B	Calaveras Twp 9	57 370
Edward	Solano Benecia	69 281
Eli	Yuba Marysville	72 875
Ellnora	San Francisco San Francisco	7 681399
Henry	Santa Clara Santa Clara	65 502
Jacob	El Dorado Kelsey	581130
Lina	Santa Clara Santa Clara	65 470
M	Nevada Eureka	61 377
Rosa	San Francisco San Francisco	2 67 647
Rosa L	Santa Clara Santa Clara	65 469
William P	San Diego Colorado	64 808
Wm	San Francisco San Francisco	2 67 592
REINHAUS		
Richard	Tuolumne Twp 5	71 497
REINHEART		
Charles	Yolo Cottonwoood	72 658
REINICKE		
G*	Sacramento Ward 1	63 25
REINS		
Frederic	Siskiyou Yreka	69 171
Frederica	Siskiyou Yreka	69 171
James	Siskiyou Yreka	69 178
John W	Siskiyou Yreka	69 176
Marion	Calaveras Twp 10	57 280
Warren	Tuolumne Twp 1	71 261
REINSHEGN		
Conrad	Tuolumne Chinese	71 487
REINSON		
Henry*	Calaveras Twp 4	57 318

Name	County Locale	M653 Roll Page
REINSTEIN		
Marcus	Tulara Visalia	71 103
Oscar	Tulara Visalia	71 104
REINSTERN		
Oscar	Tulara Visalia	71 104
REINWALD		
Mary Allice*	Siskiyou Scott Ri	69 65
W	Siskiyou Scott Ri	69 65
REINX		
Alonso	San Francisco San Francisco	2 67 703
REIR		
Lawrence*	Yuba Long Bar	72 756
REIRSERMAN		
John*	Contra Costa Twp 2	57 572
REIRVS		
Frederica*	Siskiyou Yreka	69 171
REIS		
A D	Butte Ophir	56 761
A L	Butte Oregon	56 618
C	El Dorado Placerville	58 895
C	Sierra Downieville	66 960
D	Butte Eureka	56 654
Donis	Fresno Twp 3	59 22
F	Tehama Pasakent	70 860
Isabell	Butte Ophir	56 785
L	Butte Oregon	56 616
Leopold*	Alameda Murray	55 225
W D	Butte Ophir	56 761
REISE		
H	El Dorado Placerville	58 928
James	Tuolumne Twp 1	71 475
M	El Dorado Diamond	58 813
REISER		
Augustus	Siskiyou Yreka	69 173
George	Siskiyou Yreka	69 186
Jacob	Sierra La Porte	66 767
Wm	Amador Twp 7	55 411
REISES		
Jos*	San Mateo Twp 1	65 66
REISH		
Geo*	Siskiyou Callahan	69 7
Wm	Sacramento Granite	63 248
REISKER		
Henry	Solano Vacaville	69 361
REISMUSSER		
Christen*	Alameda Brooklyn	55 145
REISS		
Elize	Yuba Marysville	72 873
REIST		
Chrisstian	Tuolumne Twp 3	71 444
Christian	Tuolumne Jamestown	71 444
REISTA		
Manual	Amador Twp 2	55 294
REISTER		
John	Tuolumne Twp 2	71 357
REIT		
John	Tehama Tehama	70 942
REITHLEY		
John	Solano Vacaville	69 345
REITNREYER		
Wm	Sacramento Ward 3	63 487
REITZ		
Benj	Siskiyou Scott Ri	69 67
E	Butte Oregon	56 614
John K	Tuolumne Chinese	71 490
REIUGIO		
---	San Bernardino S Timate	64 699
REIVA		
Meed	San Francisco San Francisco	1 68 814
Mich*	San Francisco San Francisco	1 68 814
REIVE		
Oliver	Monterey Alisal	601026
REIVES		
Wesley	Napa Napa	61 80
REJER		
Lujarda	San Luis Obispo San Luis Obispo	65 34
REJES		
Jose	Los Angeles Los Angeles	59 355
Pablo	Los Angeles Los Angeles	59 370
REJOS		
Juan	Sacramento Ward 1	63 58
Snarr	Sacramento Ward 1	63 58
REK		
Lei	El Dorado Greenwood	58 731
REKENS		
Bartholomew*	Yuba Rose Bar	72 819
Henry*	Tuolumne Don Pedro	71 540
REKER		
B H	Yolo Washington	72 563
Harry*	Mariposa Twp 1	60 672
REKERS		
Thomas*	Tuolumne Twp 6	71 540
REKINS		
Henry*	Tuolumne Don Pedro	71 540
REKU		
Mary*	Calaveras Twp 6	57 135

Name	County Locale	M653 Roll Page
RELAY		
Franklin*	San Francisco San Francisco	9 681076
J H	San Francisco San Francisco	6 67 449
J P*	San Francisco San Francisco	9 681081
J R	San Francisco San Francisco	9 681081
Jno	San Francisco San Francisco	9 681072
RELD		
C F	Yolo Cache Crk	72 609
RELDAN		
Luisa	Los Angeles Los Angeles	59 298
RELEKEE		
Jacob*	Sierra Downieville	66 965
RELEY		
Ann	San Francisco San Francisco	2 67 631
B J*	Sacramento Ward 1	63 147
Patrick	Sierra Twp 7	66 891
Robert	Alameda Brooklyn	55 190
RELEZ		
Marcelina	Santa Ba San Bernardino	64 214
RELFRO		
John G*	Sierra Twp 7	66 915
RELGELLET		
Louisa*	Yuba Marysville	72 933
RELINGHE		
W*	El Dorado Georgetown	58 753
RELIRPHE		
W*	El Dorado Georgetown	58 753
RELLA		
Refripa*	Mariposa Twp 3	60 595
Refrissa*	Mariposa Twp 3	60 595
RELLERO		
J W	Yolo Cache Crk	72 626
R	Yolo Cache Crk	72 626
RELLEY		
John*	Solano Benecia	69 285
RELLEYHAN		
John	Contra Costa Twp 1	57 498
RELLIEN		
F	Siskiyou Scott Va	69 45
RELLMBUY		
Hayden	Yolo Cache Crk	72 640
RELLUM		
Z	Solano Montezuma	69 368
RELLY		
John C	San Francisco San Francisco	3 67 75
M	Nevada Grass Valley	61 212
RELSEY		
R A	San Francisco San Francisco	4 681172
RELTOGTIOLIS		
Henry*	Calaveras Twp 6	57 163
RELTON		
Georg	Mariposa Twp 1	60 638
RELTOYTIOLIS		
Henry*	Calaveras Twp 6	57 163
RELTY		
T	Calaveras Twp 9	57 391
RELUITZ		
J J	Nevada Nevada	61 254
RELVILLE		
J	Yolo Cache	72 624
RELWITZ		
J J	Nevada Nevada	61 254
RELYEA		
Louis	Sacramento Ward 3	63 477
REM		
Peter*	Del Norte Crescent	58 660
William*	Solano Vacaville	69 323
REMA		
A	San Joaquin Stockton	641099
REMACH		
James	Calaveras Twp 8	57 90
REMACK		
Julim*	Sonoma Petaluma	69 585
Julins*	Sonoma Petaluma	69 585
REMALS		
F	Siskiyou Callahan	69 9
REMAN		
---	Sonoma Salt Point	69 694
Geo	Sonoma Salt Point	69 694
Iglaze*	Sierra Downieville	661022
REMARY		
Romena	Mariposa Twp 1	60 634
REMAS		
James*	El Dorado Georgetown	58 674
Lance*	El Dorado Georgetown	58 674
Laraca*	El Dorado Georgetown	58 674
Larien*	El Dorado Georgetown	58 674
Lurica*	El Dorado Georgetown	58 674
REMBLE		
Honora	Tuolumne Twp 1	71 483
REMBY		
J S	Sacramento Ward 4	63 512
REMENAS		
Rafael	Tulara Keyesville	71 54
REMER		
Edson	Placer Virginia	62 675

Name	County Locale	M653 RollPage
REMER		
W R	Sutter Sutter	70 809
REMEREZ		
Alfonzo	Monterey San Juan	60 974
REMERIZ		
Alfonzo	Monterey San Juan	60 974
REMERO		
Hosea	Alameda Brooklyn	55 189
REMERTERIA		
Mary Agness	Solano Benecia	69 300
REMERTINA		
Mary Agnes S	Solano Benecia	69 300
REMEY		
John*	Alameda Brooklyn	55 128
REMI		
Julien	Plumas Meadow Valley	62 927
REMIAS		
Joanna*	Calaveras Twp 7	57 20
REMICK		
J	Yolo Slate Ra	72 707
J	Yuba Slate Ro	72 707
John	Placer Forest H	62 792
John	Placer Forest H	62 798
John	Placer Iona Hills	62 884
John San Luis Obispo San Luis Obispo		65 16
REMICKE		
G	Sacramento Ward 1	63 25
G*	Sacramento Ward 1	63 27
REMIES		
L	Yuba Foster B	72 834
REMIGNI		
Maria	Los Angeles Los Angeles	59 350
REMIJAN		
---* San Bernardino Santa Inez		64 138
REMIJIO		
---	San Diego Agua Caliente	64 851
REMINAS		
Rafael	Tulara Twp 3	71 54
REMINGTON		
D C	Trinity Big Flat	701040
Estella San Francisco San Francisco 10		237 67
J B	Yuba Parks Ba	72 776
Jonathan	Alameda Brooklyn	55 82
M L	Nevada Eureka	61 364
Martha	Plumas Quincy	62 959
REMIS		
Jacob	Placer Todds Va	62 763
REMLON		
T	Nevada Eureka	61 370
W	Nevada Eureka	61 370
REMMEL		
Jacob	Sacramento Ward 4	63 518
REMMINGTON		
Chas San Francisco San Francisco 12		380 67
I C*	Nevada Red Dog	61 549
J C*	Nevada Red Dog	61 549
Judson	Siskiyou Yreka	69 153
Judson D	Siskiyou Yreka	69 153
Reuben*	Nevada Red Dog	61 541
REMOND		
George	Calaveras Twp 9	57 383
REMPSTEAD		
Jno	Mendocino Ukiah	60 795
REMRALS		
F	Siskiyou Callahan	69 9
REMRIS		
L*	Yuba Fosters	72 834
REMSDILL		
E B*	Nevada Bridgeport	61 482
REMSHART		
John San Joaquin Stockton		641061
REMSON		
Henry*	Calaveras Twp 4	57 318
REMSY		
H	Siskiyou Scott Va	69 38
REMTZ		
Jacob	Mendocino Calpella	60 819
REMUNDA		
---	San Mateo Twp 2	65 127
REMUNDO		
---	San Mateo Twp 2	65 113
REMUS		
L*	Yuba Fosters	72 834
REMUSAT		
Dennis	Yuba Foster B	72 833
REMUT		
A*	Butte Oregon	56 638
REMY		
Damas*	El Dorado Georgetown	58 690
REN		
--- San Francisco San Francisco 4		681 209
--- San Francisco San Francisco 4		681 210
---	Yuba Long Bar	72 759
Alexander San Joaquin Elkhorn		64 957
REN		
Besutho* San Mateo Twp 3		65 93
Charlotte E*	San Francisco 3	67 15
San Francisco		
Fo San Francisco San Francisco 4		681 207
John Colusa Spring Valley		57 429
P	Sutter Nicolaus	70 838
Peter	Siskiyou Callahan	69 3
Peter	Siskiyou Callahan	69 4
REN'G		
---	Mariposa Twp 3	60 608
RENA		
John San Francisco San Francisco 2		67 671
Stephen	Placer Ophirville	62 654
RENAJIA		
--- San Bernardino Santa Inez		64 142
RENALDI		
Rafael San Francisco San Francisco 2		67 707
RENALDO		
B San Francisco San Francisco 10		341 67
G San Francisco San Francisco 5		67 542
RENALDS		
T*	Calaveras Twp 9	57 404
RENALS		
E	Siskiyou Scott Ri	69 66
William	Siskiyou Scott Va	69 52
RENAN		
Fred*	Sacramento Ward 4	63 551
RENAND		
Antonio San Francisco San Francisco 10		318 67
G*	Sacramento Ward 3	63 428
Julian	Alameda Brooklyn	55 169
RENARD		
H	Amador Twp 3	55 374
Mary San Francisco San Francisco 4		681 172
RENARK		
Oziah	Plumas Quincy	62 971
RENARKE		
Richard	Sierra Downieville	661021
RENAUD		
Antonio* San Francisco San Francisco 10		318 67
G*	Sacramento Ward 3	63 428
T* San Francisco San Francisco 5		67 544
RENAW		
Fred*	Sacramento Ward 4	63 551
RENBEL		
John	Tulara Twp 2	71 8
RENCE		
F	Siskiyou Yreka	69 187
RENCH		
Frank*	Mariposa Twp 3	60 601
Jno M*	Butte Kimshaw	56 577
RENCHE		
Angus San Francisco San Francisco 4		681 217
Augus San Francisco San Francisco 4		681 217
RENCILL		
Paul	Amador Twp 2	55 302
RENCON		
Jose	Tuolumne Jamestown	71 430
REND		
Jno	Butte Oregon	56 620
RENDALL		
Caroline	Yuba Slate Ro	72 703
RENDER		
Jake*	Trinity North Fo	701026
RENDFIELD		
Charles C	Calaveras Twp 4	57 343
RENDING		
Francis San Francisco San Francisco 4		681 154
RENDON		
Alejo	Los Angeles Los Angeles	59 346
F* San Francisco San Francisco 1		68 924
Jesus	Tuolumne Sonora	71 225
Mariaciana Los Angeles Los Angeles		59 351
RENDOSA		
Colstnon*	San Mateo Twp 1	65 62
RENE		
Augustir San Bernardino Santa Barbara		64 152
John E* San Francisco San Francisco 3		67 18
Simon	Los Angeles Los Angeles	59 399
Tomber	Sierra Downieville	661011
RENEAN		
P	Tuolumne Big Oak	71 150
RENEE		
Esmille*	Yuba Parks Ba	72 781
RENEN		
D*	Yolo Cache Crk	72 591
RENEY		
Patrick	Plumas Quincy	62 945
RENFERT		
Henry Contra Costa Twp 1		57 503
RENFIELD		
Charels C	Calaveras Twp 4	57 343
RENFIELD		
Charles	Calaveras Twp 4	57 343
Sarah	Amador Twp 2	55 282
RENFRAND		
William*	Yuba Marysville	72 968
RENFRO		
James H	Amador Twp 4	55 236
John G*	Sierra Twp 7	66 915
RENFROW		
D K	Trinity Sturdiva	701006
RENGALDO		
Charles*	Calaveras Twp 9	57 353
RENGENBERG		
Albert	Nevada Bloomfield	61 511
RENGENSBERGER		
H San Francisco San Francisco 5		67 475
RENHAM		
Ira	Siskiyou Scott Va	69 33
RENHARD		
F N* San Francisco San Francisco 9		68 971
RENHART		
J*	Sacramento American	63 167
RENICK		
A S	Sonoma Washington	69 672
Alfred B	Sonoma Washington	69 672
Richard Contra Costa Twp 2		57 548
Robert	Plumas Quincy	62 916
RENIDAY		
A M San Francisco San Francisco 3		67 75
RENIG		
Conrad San Francisco San Francisco 2		67 679
RENIKLER		
William*	Calaveras Twp 8	57 85
RENKEN		
J H	Alameda Oakland	55 8
RENKIN		
Wm	Yuba New York	72 729
RENKVOS		
August	Sierra Poker Flats	66 841
RENL		
Theodore*	Calaveras Twp 4	57 335
RENLANDS		
John	Nevada Bridgeport	61 490
RENLEN		
A*	Siskiyou Scott Ri	69 71
RENLICK		
J	Nevada Nevada	61 270
RENLOT		
Wm*	Sacramento Brighton	63 196
RENLSTRUN		
L T	Sacramento Granite	63 266
RENLY		
J	Siskiyou Scott Ri	69 74
RENMERS		
Herman*	Alameda Brooklyn	55 108
RENNALS		
Bernard	Siskiyou Callahan	69 10
F	Siskiyou Callahan	69 9
RENNDER		
T*	El Dorado Diamond	58 798
RENNER		
Wm	Butte Ophir	56 755
RENNESAT		
Dennis*	Yuba Fosters	72 833
RENNET		
A*	Butte Oregon	56 638
RENNEY		
Hugh	Sierra Downieville	661016
RENNIC		
James B	Plumas Quincy	62 956
RENNICK		
William	Marin Cortemad	60 788
RENNICKE		
G	Sacramento Ward 1	63 27
RENNIE		
Chas E* San Francisco San Francisco 2		67 693
S*	Sacramento Granite	63 221
William San Francisco San Francisco 11		102 67
RENNIR		
John	El Dorado White Oaks	581018
RENNISON		
Wm* San Francisco San Francisco 1		68 883
RENNIT		
A	Butte Oregon	56 638
RENNO		
Nelson	Yolo Washington	72 570
RENNOLDS		
Ellen San Francisco San Francisco 6		67 404
F B San Francisco San Francisco 5		67 487
Geo San Francisco San Francisco 6		67 440
Geo W San Francisco San Francisco 6		67 455
Jas H San Francisco San Francisco 6		67 458
Jos H San Francisco San Francisco 6		67 458
Joseph	Amador Twp 4	55 254
RENNOLS		
William	Nevada Bridgeport	61 485

California 1860 Census Index

Name	County Locale	M653 Roll	Page
RENNON			
F	San Francisco San Francisco 2	67	795
RENNY			
H	Siskiyou Scott Va	69	38
Jose	Sacramento Ward 1	63	110
William*	Shasta French G	66	715
RENO			
Joseph	San Mateo Twp 1	65	49
Matterson	Sierra La Porte	66	783
RENOLDS			
Adaline	Siskiyou Shasta Rvr	69	117
Cornelious	Yolo Merritt	72	579
Edward	Sierra Gibsonville	66	851
RENONEL			
F*	San Francisco San Francisco 6	67	455
RENOSA			
Jesus	Monterey San Juan	60	985
Juana*	Monterey San Juan	60	979
Juanna	Monterey San Juan	60	979
Juarma	Monterey San Juan	60	979
RENOUEL			
F*	San Francisco San Francisco 6	67	455
RENOUIL			
F	San Francisco San Francisco 6	67	455
RENPO			
L C	Yolo Cottonwoood	72	652
S W	Nevada Bridgeport	61	496
RENSCPH			
L	San Francisco San Francisco 2	67	588
RENSEHLER			
Benj	Nevada Rough &	61	417
RENSEPH			
L*	San Francisco San Francisco 2	67	588
RENSEY			
W P	Nevada Nevada	61	297
RENSHA			
Aaron	Yolo Cache Crk	72	621
RENSHEN			
Henry*	San Francisco San Francisco 7	68	1442
RENSOR			
J	Yolo Putah	72	614
RENSTER			
Jerry*	San Francisco San Francisco 2	67	584
RENSY			
William	Shasta French G	66	715
RENT			
W	Nevada Grass Valley	61	191
RENTAGEN			
Charles	Yolo Merritt	72	579
RENTERIA			
Francisco	Los Angeles Los Nieto	59	436
RENTEVIA			
Juan*	Santa Clara Alviso	65	404
RENTON			
A B	Siskiyou Scott Va	69	39
Morris	Tuolumne Twp 1	71	277
R J	Sacramento Brighton	63	196
RENTRY			
Geo	El Dorado Placerville	58	924
RENTSTEIN			
S T	Sacramento Granite	63	266
RENTZ			
Julias	Klamath Liberty	59	231
RENUER			
Andrew	El Dorado White Oaks	58	1027
RENUET			
A*	Butte Oregon	56	638
RENWALS			
Bernard	Siskiyou Callahan	69	10
RENWICK			
A L	Sacramento Ward 4	63	510
John	Nevada Bridgeport	61	494
Walter	Contra Costa Twp 2	57	551
RENY			
C	Siskiyou Scott Va	69	28
Henry A	Nevada Washington	61	333
Jas*	San Francisco San Francisco 1	68	861
RENYALDO			
Charles*	Calaveras Twp 9	57	353
RENYOLDS			
Stepen	Mariposa Coulterville	60	678
RENYONDS			
Stephen	Mariposa Coulterville	60	678
RENYSTRAM			
A	Sonoma Sonoma	69	656
RENZ			
F	Siskiyou Scott Va	69	43
REO			
---	Amador Twp 5	55	334
---	Placer Auburn	62	571
REOCHNER			
B W*	San Francisco San Francisco 4	68	1222
REODER			
Peter	Trinity Mouth Ca	70	1013
REODITZ			
C F*	Butte Kimshaw	56	602

Name	County Locale	M653 Roll	Page
REOETT			
Peter	Mariposa Twp 1	60	653
REOLY			
Victor	San Francisco San Francisco 10	67	358
REOMON			
C	Sutter Yuba	70	775
REON			
James	Solano Fremont	69	384
REONDEN			
Michael*	Calaveras Twp 6	57	151
REONHARDT			
John B	San Francisco San Francisco 10	67	217
REOOS			
Francisco*	Yuba Marysville	72	946
Luceanna*	Yuba Marysville	72	946
REOUGH			
John	Solano Benecia	69	285
REOYER			
J J	San Francisco San Francisco 4	68	1162
REPAYRE			
V	Trinity Weaverville	70	1070
REPDGE			
Jeromar*	Yuba Marysville	72	870
Jeromer*	Yuba Marysville	72	870
REPELGE			
Jerome*	Yuba Marysville	72	870
REPELJE			
Jerome*	Yuba Marysville	72	870
REPELLA			
John	Mariposa Twp 3	60	545
REPEN			
William	Yuba Bear Rvr	72	1009
REPENN			
R	San Francisco San Francisco 5	67	488
REPENSKY			
Tobias	Yuba Marysville	72	872
REPER			
William	Yuba Bear Rvr	72	1009
REPETOE			
O Badiah	Sonoma Santa Rosa	69	394
REPETOR			
O Budiah	Sonoma Santa Rosa	69	394
REPETTO			
John	Tuolumne Big Oak	71	131
REPEUSKY			
Tobias*	Yuba Marysville	72	872
REPHEMIA			
R	Nevada Washington	61	337
REPHENNA			
R*	Nevada Washington	61	337
REPHENUS			
R*	Nevada Washington	61	337
REPITA			
Jose	San Diego Agua Caliente	64	864
REPP			
Henry	Yuba Marysville	72	944
Philip	Amador Twp 1	55	470
REPPER			
H*	San Francisco San Francisco 5	67	519
REPPERT			
Daniel	Siskiyou Scott Va	69	31
H H	Siskiyou Scott Va	69	41
John	Siskiyou Klamath	69	92
REPPEY			
G C	Solano Vacaville	69	320
REPPIGE			
J A	San Francisco San Francisco 9	68	945
REPSEIN			
Jacob	Trinity Canon Crk	70	1018
REPSEON			
Jacob	Trinity Mouth Ca	70	1018
REQUA			
Issac L*	Sacramento Ward 4	63	558
Jaques*	Butte Hamilton	56	526
REQUD			
Jaques*	Butte Hamilton	56	526
RERASA			
Louisa	Mariposa Twp 3	60	547
RERCRE			
August*	Tuolumne Twp 5	71	522
RERD			
J D	Yolo Cache	72	644
RERDON			
John N*	San Francisco San Francisco 9	68	1034
REREE			
Charles	San Bernardino Santa Barbara	64	171
RERERE			
Auguste	Tuolumne Chinese	71	522
RERICO			
Richard	El Dorado Gold Hill	58	1098
RERIG			
Damus*	El Dorado Georgetown	58	690
RERIUCKE			
G*	Sacramento Ward 1	63	27

Name	County Locale	M653 Roll	Page
RERL			
Louquin	Calaveras Twp 5	57	205
RERMIUN			
P	Nevada Eureka	61	345
RERN			
William*	Solano Vacaville	69	323
RERNEY			
John*	Alameda Brooklyn	55	128
RERNICK			
John D	Monterey San Juan	60	995
RERNICKE			
G*	Sacramento Ward 1	63	27
RERORS			
William	Calaveras Twp 5	57	218
RERRA			
Jose*	Los Angeles Los Angeles	59	334
RERRICK			
Harrison*	Tuolumne Twp 5	71	517
RERRIGAN			
Michael	Calaveras Twp 7	57	7
Micheal*	Calaveras Twp 7	57	7
RERRINS			
Margaret	Mariposa Twp 3	60	593
RERRIS			
Simon	Santa Cruz Santa Cruz	66	606
RERROLE			
Amajohn	Butte Bidwell	56	730
RERSKARD			
Andrew	El Dorado Mud Springs	58	966
RERSON			
Jarvis	San Francisco San Francisco 2	67	584
RERT			
Henry*	Mendocino Big Rvr	60	847
RERVES			
George*	Napa Napa	61	62
RERVIS			
George*	Napa Napa	61	62
William	Calaveras Twp 5	57	218
RERX			
Henry*	Mendocino Big Rvr	60	847
RESAS			
Donzingeu*	Sierra Downieville	66	1011
RESBRITZ			
D	Sacramento Ward 3	63	429
RESCARDIA			
Jose	Santa Cruz Santa Cruz	66	609
RESDDEN			
Ann*	Yuba Marysville	72	904
RESDER			
Maria T	Alameda Brooklyn	55	202
RESE			
J	Nevada Nevada	61	240
James*	Sierra St Louis	66	805
John*	El Dorado Georgetown	58	746
Joseph	Sierra Downieville	66	1001
N	Amador Twp 7	55	420
Richard	El Dorado Spanish	58	1125
Rise*	El Dorado Georgetown	58	746
Timothy	Sierra Twp 7	66	899
RESEMER			
Andrew	Alameda Brooklyn	55	102
RESER			
Fred*	Yuba Marysville	72	932
RESERT			
Juan*	Alameda Washington	55	171
RESERVERE			
Manuel	Alameda Brooklyn	55	107
RESH			
Wm G	Placer Goods	62	698
Wm*	San Francisco San Francisco 1	68	872
RESHLEMANN			
Jacob	Yuba Suida	72	989
RESIADO			
Maria A	Los Angeles Los Angeles	59	309
RESIN			
Christian	Sierra Twp 7	66	901
RESING			
D B*	San Francisco San Francisco 12	67	393
RESIRDO			
Gregarda*	Calaveras Twp 7	57	24
RESIRE			
August	El Dorado Big Bar	58	733
RESLER			
W R	Butte Ophir	56	760
RESLEY			
D A	Tuolumne Jacksonville	71	171
Harriet M	Yuba Marysville	72	975
RESLOR			
W R	Butte Ophir	56	760
RESMAN			
Paldi	Calaveras Twp 8	57	86
RESMASSER			
Erasmus	Alameda Brooklyn	55	153
RESMIRON			
P	Nevada Eureka	61	345

California 1860 Census Index

Name	County	Locale	M653 Roll	Page
RESMONDE				
Louis*	San Francisco	San Francisco 3	67	50
RESO				
Bortollo*	Calaveras	Twp 7	57	11
RESORTH				
John*	Mariposa	Twp 1	60	666
RESPAZIE				
Mary	San Francisco	San Francisco 2	67	796
RESS				
---*	San Francisco	San Francisco 2	67	669
Arrin	Sierra	Twp 7	66	908
John	Sierra	Twp 7	66	907
RESSEN				
G F	Yuba	Marysville	72	979
RESSER				
John	San Francisco	San Francisco 2	67	639
RESSETTO				
John*	Tuolumne	Twp 4	71	131
RESSIGNEE				
Adam	Amador	Twp 5	55	348
RESSIRA				
Robt*	Santa Clara	Redwood	65	452
RESSLER				
George	Alameda	Brooklyn	55	150
Peter	Yolo	Slate Ra	72	704
William	Tuolumne	Chinese	71	523
RESSPER				
H*	San Francisco	San Francisco 5	67	519
RESSS				
Robert*	San Francisco	San Francisco 3	67	44
RESSTER				
Jacob	Placer	Michigan	62	811
RESTAVE				
Frank	San Francisco	San Francisco 11	67	134
RESTEN				
W	Nevada	Eureka	61	367
RESTERA				
J	El Dorado	Diamond	58	811
RESTERSON				
John J	Solano	Fremont	69	383
RESTINGH				
Thomas	Sierra	Twp 5	66	943
RET				
---	El Dorado	Casumnes	58	1160
RETA				
Mary	Calaveras	Twp 5	57	135
RETALIA				
Antonio	Amador	Twp 1	55	491
RETCHE				
Mary*	Nevada	Bridgeport	61	479
RETCHER				
Jacob*	Sierra	Downieville	66	965
RETCHEY				
Williamson*	Yuba	Bear Rvr	72	996
RETCHLER				
Mary S	San Francisco	San Francisco 4	68	1160
RETCHUM				
A	Nevada	Eureka	61	364
RETDOGTIOLIS				
Henry*	Calaveras	Twp 6	57	163
RETEBIE				
Alexander	Yuba	Linda	72	995
RETEKER				
Jacob	Sierra	Downieville	66	965
RETER				
Mary*	Calaveras	Twp 6	57	135
RETERMITCH				
Peter	San Francisco	San Francisco 2	67	756
RETERMITELI				
Peter*	San Francisco	San Francisco 2	67	756
RETERMITELO				
Peter*	San Francisco	San Francisco 2	67	756
RETFOR				
H*	Siskiyou	Klamath	69	84
RETHERFORD				
D	Amador	Twp 2	55	319
RETILLIC				
James	Solano	Fremont	69	384
RETIRA				
Juan J	Los Angeles	Los Angeles	59	298
RETON				
Elizabith	Placer	Auburn	62	559
RETTAN				
John*	Napa	Clear Lake	61	141
RETTLEYET				
John	Amador	Twp 4	55	245
RETTOGTIOLIS				
Henry*	Calaveras	Twp 6	57	163
RETTON				
Georg	Mariposa	Twp 1	60	638
George	Mariposa	Twp 1	60	638
RETTZ				
Conrad*	Sacramento	Ward 4	63	581
RETU				
Mary	Calaveras	Twp 6	57	135
RETY				
E*	Calaveras	Twp 8	57	55
RETZ				
Andrew	San Bernardino	Santa Barbara	64	177
RETZIEN				
Chas*	Butte	Ophir	56	795
RETZION				
Chas	Butte	Ophir	56	795
REUBEE				
John	Tulara	Yule Rvr	71	8
REUBEN				
---	Tulara	Twp 3	71	50
---	Tulara	Twp 3	71	55
Charles	Amador	Twp 2	55	318
G S	Tuolumne	Twp 1	71	202
Geo	San Francisco	San Francisco 10	67	297
REUBN				
G S	Tuolumne	Sonora	71	202
REUDON				
Jesus*	Tuolumne	Twp 1	71	225
REUELLE				
Amele	Tuolumne	Twp 3	71	465
REUERS				
Rose	Sierra	Twp 7	66	887
REUFRAND				
William*	Yuba	Marysville	72	968
REUFRO				
John G	Sierra	Twp 7	66	915
REUFUS				
Charley	Sacramento	Sutter	63	294
REUGER				
Justin	Sierra	Twp 7	66	867
REUIRLL				
Paul	Amador	Twp 2	55	302
REUK				
---	Yuba	Long Bar	72	760
REUL				
Rose	Sierra	La Porte	66	773
Theodore*	Calaveras	Twp 4	57	335
REULEN				
A	Siskiyou	Scott Ri	69	71
Charles	Amador	Twp 2	55	318
REULIN				
Joseph	Shasta	Millvill	66	741
REULO				
Manels	Calaveras	Twp 8	57	86
REULON				
John C	Yuba	New York	72	745
REULOT				
Wm*	Sacramento	Brighton	63	196
REUMAN				
Robert M	Calaveras	Twp 5	57	252
REUMERS				
Herman	Alameda	Brooklyn	55	108
REUN				
---	Calaveras	Twp 5	57	230
REUNAS				
Joanna*	Calaveras	Twp 7	57	20
REUNDER				
J*	El Dorado	Diamond	58	802
REUNIE				
S*	Sacramento	Granite	63	221
REURDON				
Henry W	Yolo	Slate Ra	72	691
REUSCPH				
L*	San Francisco	San Francisco 2	67	588
REUSHERD				
Henry*	San Francisco	San Francisco 7	68	1442
REUSHEW				
Henry*	San Francisco	San Francisco 7	68	1442
REUSS				
Michael	San Francisco	San Francisco 12	67	384
REUTENA				
Francisco*	Los Angeles	Los Nieto	59	436
REUXPH				
L*	San Francisco	San Francisco 2	67	588
REVAER				
Habacio	Mariposa	Twp 1	60	654
REVARD				
Louis	Yolo	Merritt	72	582
REVARRE				
Leon	San Francisco	San Francisco 11	67	139
REVARUS				
Jose	Napa	Napa	61	115
REVAULT				
Theodore	Monterey	Monterey	60	966
REVAUNT				
H	Calaveras	Twp 9	57	394
REVAURT				
H	Calaveras	Twp 9	57	394
REVCHNER				
B W*	San Francisco	San Francisco 4	68	1222
REVEAL				
G*	Nevada	Grass Valley	61	163
REVEHNER				
B W	San Francisco	San Francisco 4	68	1222
REVEITO				
Juan	Alameda	Brooklyn	55	171
REVEL				
Joseph	Nevada	Rough &	61	408
Pedro	San Bernardino	Santa Inez	64	140
REVELL				
Joanna*	Sacramento	Ward 1	63	152
REVELLE				
Joanna*	Sacramento	Ward 1	63	152
REVELLI				
Nicolas	San Luis Obispo	San Luis Obispo	65	37
REVEN				
Catharina	Tuolumne	Twp 2	71	282
Joseph	Tuolumne	Twp 1	71	269
REVER				
Delourus	Mariposa	Twp 1	60	655
Delovrus	Mariposa	Twp 1	60	655
Habacio	Mariposa	Twp 1	60	655
Halacio	Mariposa	Twp 1	60	655
Loreser	Mariposa	Twp 1	60	655
Nelson	Amador	Twp 1	55	454
REVERA				
Antonio	Monterey	San Juan	60	999
E D	San Francisco	San Francisco 5	67	478
REVERAR				
E	Mariposa	Twp 1	60	640
REVERDY				
E C	Mariposa	Twp 1	60	663
REVERE				
Andrew	Calaveras	Twp 5	57	216
August	Tuolumne	Twp 3	71	465
George	Tuolumne	Twp 3	71	465
Joseph	Tuolumne	Twp 1	71	269
Wm	Sacramento	Ward 4	63	542
REVEREZ				
Jesus*	Yuba	Marysville	72	858
REVERIE				
Gormor*	El Dorado	Salmon Falls	58	1064
REVERO				
Fernando	Los Angeles	Los Angeles	59	517
Jose M	Marin	Bolinas	60	728
P	Merced	Twp 1	60	900
REVERRI				
Gormor*	El Dorado	Salmon Falls	58	1064
REVERS				
Jose M*	Marin	Bolinas	60	728
Rose*	Sierra	Twp 7	66	887
REVERT				
Juan*	Alameda	Washington	55	171
REVERTEGAS				
E	San Francisco	San Francisco 2	67	674
REVERTO				
Juan*	Alameda	Washington	55	171
REVERZ				
James*	Yuba	Long Bar	72	742
REVES				
Charles	Tuolumne	Don Pedro	71	541
Frank	Tehama	Tehama	70	947
John J	El Dorado	Georgetown	58	698
William*	San Mateo	Twp 3	65	110
REVESE				
Jerratus	Yuba	Marysville	72	914
REVETT				
Chas D*	Sacramento	Ward 1	63	50
REVIFF				
Asa	Sacramento	Ward 3	63	474
REVIN				
Augusti	Tuolumne	Sonora	71	245
REVINE				
Saml*	Sacramento	Franklin	63	333
REVIRO				
Fernando	Los Angeles	Los Angeles	59	517
REVIS				
E M	Los Angeles	Azuza	59	277
Jas	Amador	Twp 6	55	447
John J	El Dorado	Georgetown	58	698
Jos	Amador	Twp 6	55	447
Newton	Amador	Twp 7	55	412
REVIT				
John	Calaveras	Twp 4	57	311
REVOIR				
Francois	San Francisco	San Francisco 8	68	1291
REVONA				
John	El Dorado	Kelsey	58	1136
REVOS				
Luceanna*	Yuba	Marysville	72	946
REW				
---	Calaveras	Twp 10	57	285
---	Tuolumne	Twp 6	71	533
Peter*	Siskiyou	Callahan	69	4
REWARK				
Robert T	San Joaquin	Douglass	64	916
REWCASTLE				
James	Solano	Vacaville	69	319

California 1860 Census Index

Name	County Locale	M653 Roll	Page
REWEB			
George	Mariposa Twp 1	60	660
REWIS			
George*	Napa Napa	61	62
W S*	Nevada Grass Valley	61	184
REWOLDS			
Adaline*	Siskiyou Shasta Rvr	69	117
REWSEHLER			
Benj*	Nevada Rough &	61	417
REXEN			
Clorise	San Francisco San Francisco 3	67	70
Clouse*	San Francisco San Francisco 3	67	70
REY			
---	Yuba Long Bar	72	766
---*	Sierra Downieville	66	992
A	Trinity Trinity	70	970
Del	Butte Eureka	56	655
Elisabeth	Sacramento Ward 4	63	578
F C	San Francisco San Francisco 3	67	17
Hin	Mariposa Coulterville	60	682
Hope	El Dorado Coloma	58	1077
J J	San Francisco San Francisco 2	67	587
Joseph	Mendocino Big Rvr	60	842
Mo*	San Francisco San Francisco 2	67	743
W H	Mendocino Big Rvr	60	842
REYAN			
A	Nevada Nevada	61	277
L	Nevada Nevada	61	277
L C	Nevada Grass Valley	61	153
REYBURN			
G	Nevada Grass Valley	61	235
Joseph	Santa Clara Fremont	65	419
L C	Sonoma Petaluma	69	588
Wayne	Sonoma Petaluma	69	552
REYDEN			
John	Yuba Marysville	72	905
REYE			
Anus A	Tuolumne Twp 2	71	284
REYER			
Frank*	Yuba Parke Ba	72	786
Wm*	El Dorado Georgetown	58	681
REYERS			
Charles	Alameda Brooklyn	55	93
REYES			
Andreas	San Diego Temecula	64	793
B	Calaveras Twp 9	57	410
Carmen	Alameda Oakland	55	28
Frank	Yuba Parks Ba	72	786
Inaria	San Bernardino S Buenav	64	211
Jose	Los Angeles Los Angeles	59	355
Jose	San Bernardino Santa Ba	64	208
Jose D	Los Angeles Los Angeles	59	340
Jose M	San Bernardino S Buenav	64	211
Juan	Los Angeles Tejon To	59	535
Juan D	Los Angeles Santa Ana	59	444
Manuel	San Bernardino Santa Ba	64	216
Maria	San Bernardino Santa Ba	64	211
Maria A M	Los Angeles Los Angeles	59	369
Merced	Los Angeles Los Angeles	59	314
Refugia	San Diego S Luis R	64	778
Santon	Yuba Parke Ba	72	786
Stephen	Alameda Oakland	55	10
Usidro	Los Angeles Los Angeles	59	382
Wm*	El Dorado Georgetown	58	681
Ysidro	Los Angeles Los Angeles	59	382
REYHO			
Jack	Contra Costa Twp 3	57	590
REYHOLDS			
A*	Mariposa Twp 3	60	592
REYIVE			
Michael*	Calaveras Twp 5	57	232
REYL			
John	El Dorado Coloma	58	1108
REYLA			
M*	San Francisco San Francisco 1	68	934
REYLAND			
Philip J	Tuolumne Sonora	71	243
REYLER			
John*	Tulara Twp 2	71	8
REYLEY			
A	Napa Napa	61	98
REYMER			
Lewis	El Dorado Mountain	58	1185
REYMOND			
A C	El Dorado Placerville	58	887
L M	El Dorado Placerville	58	887
REYNA			
Angel	Los Angeles Santa Ana	59	455
Caledoneo	Los Angeles Los Nieto	59	434
Jose	Los Angeles Los Nieto	59	433
Jose	Los Angeles Santa Ana	59	450
REYNALD			
E	Sonoma Bodega	69	522
REYNALDS			
W	Amador Twp 2	55	317
Wiles	Tuolumne Twp 1	71	255

Name	County Locale	M653 Roll	Page
REYNARD			
Mary	San Francisco San Francisco 4	68	1164
Peter*	Siskiyou Klamath	69	86
REYNAUD			
Fredrick	Plumas Meadow Valley	62	932
Joseph*	Plumas Meadow Valley	62	932
REYNAULD			
Justin	Stanislaus Branch	70	702
REYNER			
Fred	Sacramento Sutter	63	293
REYNEY			
Martin	Calaveras Twp 6	57	157
REYNLDS			
J W B	Napa Yount	61	32
REYNOLD			
Edwd	San Francisco San Francisco 10	208	67
Elsey*	Contra Costa Twp 2	57	560
Sarah A	San Francisco San Francisco 8	68	1302
REYNOLDS			
A	Amador Twp 3	55	377
A	Mariposa Twp 3	60	592
A B	El Dorado Georgetown	58	698
A*	Mariposa Twp 3	60	592
Add	Marin Cortemad	60	792
Albart	Mariposa Twp 1	60	663
Albert	Mariposa Twp 1	60	663
Albert	Santa Cruz Pajaro	66	543
Alex	Sonoma Petaluma	69	569
Allen	Colusa Grand Island	57	478
Ann	San Francisco San Francisco 3	67	22
B J	Yolo Cache	72	612
Belle	Sonoma Sonoma	69	654
Ben	Del Norte Crescent	58	628
Benj E	Calaveras Twp 5	57	142
Benj R	Calaveras Twp 6	57	142
Benja R	Calaveras Twp 6	57	142
C	Nevada Nevada	61	321
C	San Francisco San Francisco 1	68	821
C C	Yuba Marysville	72	965
C D	Calaveras Twp 8	57	67
Caroline	Sierra Downieville	66	988
Charles	San Francisco San Francisco 4	68	1163
Charles H	Yuba Marysville	72	879
Chas	San Francisco San Francisco 9	68	1082
Chas O	San Francisco San Francisco 9	68	999
Cornelia	San Francisco San Francisco 9	68	996
Cornlius	Yolo Merritt	72	579
Cov	Yolo Merritt	72	581
D	Alameda Brooklyn	55	192
D	San Francisco San Francisco 4	68	1217
D	San Francisco San Francisco 2	67	663
D	Sutter Sutter	70	817
David	El Dorado Placerville	58	913
David	San Joaquin Castoria	64	890
E A	Monterey San Juan	60	988
E A	Shasta Shasta	66	686
E T	Santa Clara Santa Clara	65	494
Edwd	Del Norte Crescent	58	641
Edwd	San Francisco San Francisco 10	208	67
Edwd	San Francisco San Francisco 2	67	639
Edwd B	San Francisco San Francisco 10	203	67
Elisha	Calaveras Twp 7	57	18
Elizabeth	Sonoma Mendocino	69	460
Ellen	Trinity Trinity	70	975
Elsey*	Contra Costa Twp 2	57	560
Eugene	Butte Hamilton	56	522
Ezekiel G	Sonoma Mendocino	69	460
F	Sacramento Ward 4	63	541
F H	Mariposa Twp 1	60	629
Fanny	Sacramento Ward 3	63	422
Francis	San Francisco San Francisco 9	68	993
Fred	San Francisco San Francisco 3	67	4
Fredk	San Francisco San Francisco 2	67	591
Fredrick	Sierra Poker Flats	66	838
Geo	Butte Oro	56	682
Geo	San Francisco San Francisco 1	68	894
Geo A	San Francisco San Francisco 10	287	67
Geo A	San Francisco San Francisco 1	68	895
Geo W	Santa Clara San Jose	65	368
Geo W	Tuolumne Twp 1	71	482
George	Humbolt Eel Rvr	59	150
George	Sierra Excelsior	66	1034
George	Tuolumne Twp 1	71	480
George A	Yuba Marysville	72	879
George L	San Francisco San Francisco 4	68	1132
Georgiana	Tuolumne Twp 4	71	132
Geroge	Tuolumne Sonora	71	480
Gilbert	San Joaquin Oneal	64	939
H	Sutter Butte	70	786
Hannah	Yuba Marysville	72	885
Henry	Calaveras Twp 7	57	22
Henry	Mendocino Big Rvr	60	845

Name	County Locale	M653 Roll	Page
REYNOLDS			
Henry	Trinity Trinity	70	973
Henry D	San Francisco San Francisco 10	217	67
Horace	Plumas Meadow Valley	62	901
J	Nevada Grass Valley	61	209
J	Nevada Eureka	61	364
J	Placer Illinois	62	705
J	Sutter Yuba	70	768
J A	Sonoma Santa Rosa	69	389
J B	San Francisco San Francisco 5	67	526
J H	Calaveras Twp 8	57	66
J J	El Dorado Placerville	58	850
J M	Nevada Nevada	61	313
J S	Sierra Twp 7	66	891
J V	El Dorado Mountain	58	1186
J W B	Napa Yount	61	32
J*	Nevada Grass Valley	61	219
Jackson	Nevada Red Dog	61	546
James	Colusa Butte Crk	57	465
James	Marin Tomales	60	719
James	Plumas Quincy	62	996
James	San Francisco San Francisco 4	68	1134
James	San Joaquin Castoria	64	890
James	Sonoma Bodega	69	539
Jane	San Francisco San Francisco 11	100	67
Jas	Butte Chico	56	563
Jas	Sacramento Lee	63	214
Jas	Sonoma Petaluma	69	600
Jas S	Sacramento Franklin	63	333
Jessee	Tulara Twp 2	71	26
Jno	Tehama Red Bluff	70	932
John	Amador Twp 4	55	250
John	Amador Twp 1	55	414
John	Amador Twp 1	55	472
John	Butte Cascade	56	695
John	Butte Mountain	56	737
John	Humbolt Eel Rvr	59	145
John	Marin San Rafael	60	759
John	Marin Cortemad	60	786
John	Nevada Rough &	61	430
John	San Francisco San Francisco 9	68	1057
John	San Francisco San Francisco 4	68	1120
John	San Francisco San Francisco 2	67	686
John	Yolo Cache	72	625
John	Yolo Cache	72	633
John	Yuba Rose Bar	72	801
John B	Calaveras Twp 6	57	141
John P	San Francisco San Francisco 11	93	67
Jos	Sacramento Ward 3	63	456
Jos	Tehama Red Bluff	70	908
Joseph	Yuba Marysville	72	931
L	Tehama Antelope	70	890
Lawrence	Solano Vacaville	69	340
Levi	Trinity Trinity	70	975
Lewais	Sacramento Ward 3	63	437
Louis	Contra Costa Twp 1	57	522
Louisa	Tuolumne Twp 4	71	132
M	Calaveras Twp 9	57	406
Mart	Sacramento Cosummes	63	389
Mary	San Joaquin Castoria	64	892
Mary A	San Francisco San Francisco 10	252	67
Michael	San Francisco San Francisco 2	67	591
N N	Yolo Cottonwoood	72	653
Nicholas	San Francisco San Francisco 2	67	625
Nicolas	Los Angeles Los Angeles	59	348
Orin	Marin San Rafael	60	769
P I	Solano Benecia	69	304
P T	Solano Benecia	69	304
Patk	San Francisco San Francisco 10	300	67
Peter	Marin Cortemad	60	786
Peter	Stanislaus Branch	70	706
R	Nevada Grass Valley	61	222
R B	Nevada Nevada	61	260
R E	Sutter Sutter	70	816
R V	Nevada Nevada	61	240
Reuben	Fresno Twp 3	59	15
Richard	Shasta Shasta	66	680
Robert	San Joaquin Elliott	64	941
Robt	Klamath Trinidad	59	222
Robt T	San Francisco San Francisco 9	68	980
S	Santa Clara Santa Clara	65	490
S	Tehama Red Bluff	70	908
S G	Sacramento Ward 4	63	499
S W	Amador Twp 3	55	369
Saml*	Napa Napa	61	85
Samuel	San Francisco San Francisco 8	68	1267
Samuel F	Los Angeles Los Angeles	59	337
Samuel F	San Francisco San Francisco 4	68	1145
Sanl	Napa Napa	61	85
Sarah A	San Francisco San Francisco 8	68	1302
Stephen*	Mariposa Coulterville	60	678

Name	County Locale	M653 Roll Page
REYNOLDS		
Story	Shasta Shasta	66 731
T	Calaveras Twp 8	57 81
T H	Yolo Cache Crk	72 607
Thomas	Contra Costa Twp 1	57 511
Thomas	Marin Cortemad	60 791
Thomas	Santa Cruz Watsonville	66 535
Thomas	Sierra Eureka	661049
Thomas	Yuba Parks Ba	72 777
Thos	Nevada Rough &	61 430
Thos	San Francisco San Francisco 6	67 424
Thos	San Francisco San Francisco 2	67 590
W C	Sierra Downieville	66 975
W J	Sacramento Dry Crk	63 375
Wesley	Napa Yount	61 39
William	Contra Costa Twp 1	57 534
William	Nevada Bridgeport	61 485
William	San Francisco San Francisco 4	681127
William	Sierra Poker Flats	66 842
William	Yuba Marysville	72 883
William	Yuba Marysville	72 924
William A	Tuolumne Twp 1	71 192
Wm	Alameda Brooklyn	55 119
Wm	Marin Tomales	60 721
Wm	Plumas Quincy	62 925
Wm	Sacramento Ward 4	63 524
Wm	Sacramento Ward 4	63 533
Wm	Sacramento Ward 4	63 598
Wm	San Francisco San Francisco 3	67 38
Wm	San Francisco San Francisco 5	67 554
Wm	San Francisco San Francisco 1	68 924
Wm	Santa Clara San Jose	65 337
Wm	Santa Clara Fremont	65 435
Wm O	San Francisco San Francisco 12	374 67
Wm P	Los Angeles Los Angeles	59 510
Wm P	Sonoma Sonoma	69 653
Wm P*	Los Angeles Los Angeles	59 510
Wm R	Calaveras Twp 10	57 264
REYNR		
Elicha	Calaveras Twp 6	57 149
REYO		
Angus A	Tuolumne Twp 2	71 284
REYOLLI		
Joseph	Calaveras Twp 5	57 226
REYOLLIS		
Joseph	Calaveras Twp 5	57 226
REYON		
J M	Yolo Putah	72 545
REYOWA		
Francisco	Calaveras Twp 5	57 198
REYSER		
P B	Tuolumne Twp 2	71 285
REYWARD		
Peter	Siskiyou Klamath	69 86
RFFLER		
A*	Siskiyou Klamath	69 93
RGO		
Mary*	Placer Iona Hills	62 876
RHADES		
Chas*	Mariposa Twp 3	60 593
RHAM		
Charles	Siskiyou Yreka	69 187
RHAWL		
Mary A	San Francisco San Francisco 10	273 67
RHEA		
Irevin	Calaveras Twp 9	57 364
Irwin W	Calaveras Twp 9	57 364
J D	Tuolumne Shawsfla	71 390
R H	Sonoma Cloverdale	69 682
RHEHM		
Chas*	Sacramento Ward 1	63 82
RHEIM		
Benedict	Yuba Parks Ba	72 782
Jacob	San Francisco San Francisco 9	68 950
RHEIMERS		
Henry	San Francisco San Francisco 11	157 67
RHEIMS		
Rosario	Los Angeles Los Angeles	59 353
RHEINCLEIN		
Samuel*	Placer Michigan	62 808
RHEINER		
Adolph	San Francisco San Francisco 7	681325
RHEINHARD		
E*	San Francisco San Francisco 5	67 498
RHEIRN		
Jacob	San Francisco San Francisco 9	68 950
RHELUN		
Chas*	Sacramento Ward 1	63 82
RHEM		
M J	Tuolumne Twp 2	71 345
William	Nevada Bloomfield	61 508
RHEMHART		
J	El Dorado Georgetown	58 688
RHENIS		
Rosano	Los Angeles Los Angeles	59 353
RHEUTER		
Anton	San Francisco San Francisco 10	275 67
RHEW		
William	Nevada Bloomfield	61 508
RHIDES		
J P	Butte Cascade	56 696
RHIENHART		
J*	El Dorado Georgetown	58 679
John	Santa Clara Santa Clara	65 467
RHIME		
John	Placer Rattle Snake	62 633
RHINARD		
Frank	San Mateo Twp 1	65 71
RHINE		
Frederick	Sacramento Sutter	63 300
John	Yuba Parks Ba	72 777
Liftal	Sierra Morristown	661052
Nathan	El Dorado Eldorado	58 935
Richard	Plumas Quincy	62 999
RHINEDOLLAR		
John*	Tuolumne Big Oak	71 137
RHINEDOLLEN		
John*	Tuolumne Big Oak	71 137
RHINEHART		
B	Sacramento Cosumnes	63 393
B	Sacramento Cosumnes	63 396
David B	Siskiyou Yreka	69 154
F	El Dorado Placerville	58 826
James	Colusa Grand Island	57 472
Wm	Amador Twp 3	55 399
RHINHART		
John	Plumas Quincy	62 944
RHINHEART		
J	El Dorado Georgetown	58 678
RHINHURT		
J	El Dorado Georgetown	58 678
RHOADS		
D H	Sierra Twp 7	66 892
Danial	Humbolt Union	59 191
Thomas F	Tuolumne Montezuma	71 508
Wm J	Amador Twp 1	55 508
Wm P	Sierra Twp 7	66 863
RHOCUS		
Augusten	Tuolumne Twp 2	71 405
Augustun	Tuolumne Shawsfla	71 405
RHODAS		
J	San Joaquin Stockton	641067
RHODDA		
R M*	Nevada Grass Valley	61 186
RHODE		
Geo	San Francisco San Francisco 10	282 67
Henry	Tuolumne Twp 2	71 348
RHODEFOR		
D	Mariposa Twp 3	60 550
RHODEGO		
Antonio	Alameda Brooklyn	55 132
Hesus	Alameda Brooklyn	55 131
RHODEHALD		
---	Nevada Bloomfield	61 511
RHODER		
L	San Francisco San Francisco 5	67 554
W*	Nevada Eureka	61 370
RHODERICK		
John	San Joaquin Stockton	641090
RHODES		
A	El Dorado Kelsey	581137
A	El Dorado Placerville	58 818
A	Sacramento Ward 1	63 48
A	Yuba Marysville	72 907
Abraham	Yuba Marysville	72 934
Abram	Yuba Marysville	72 966
Adam	Sacramento Ward 1	63 19
Ann M	San Francisco San Francisco 9	68 998
Anthony	San Francisco San Francisco 8	681257
Charles W	Tuolumne Twp 5	71 491
Chas	Mariposa Twp 3	60 593
D	Sutter Bear Rvr	70 819
Danl	Santa Clara San Jose	65 308
E	Sacramento Ward 1	63 18
E J	Napa Napa	61 104
E S	Santa Clara San Jose	65 280
Edward	San Joaquin Oneal	64 930
Frank W	San Francisco San Francisco 7	681325
G	Nevada Grass Valley	61 187
G H	El Dorado Kelsey	581153
Geo	Nevada Grass Valley	61 146
George	Placer Michigan	62 849
George	Santa Clara Gilroy	65 231
H	El Dorado Diamond	58 813
H	Nevada Grass Valley	61 189
H	Nevada Grass Valley	61 236
H C	Butte Oregon	56 611
RHODES		
H N	Stanislaus Emory	70 754
Harvey	Los Angeles Los Angeles	59 304
Henry	Butte Hamilton	56 524
Henry	Yolo Cottonwoood	72 657
Henry*	Butte Hamilton	56 524
Henry*	Placer Michigan	62 837
Henz*	Placer Michigan	62 837
Isaac	Sacramento Lee	63 217
Isaac	Sacramento San Joaquin	63 359
Isaac	Solano Vacaville	69 349
Isaac	Solano Vacaville	69 365
J	Nevada Grass Valley	61 188
J	Siskiyou Callahan	69 9
J H	El Dorado Kelsey	581153
J M	Yolo Cottonwoood	72 657
J P	Butte Cascade	56 696
J P	Sacramento Lee	63 214
J T	Sacramento Cosumnes	63 405
Jacob	Yolo Cottonwoood	72 657
James	San Joaquin Castoria	64 877
James	San Joaquin Castoria	64 907
James M	San Francisco San Francisco 11	124 67
James M	San Joaquin Stockton	641014
James S	Los Angeles Los Angeles	59 293
John	Sacramento Granite	63 248
John	Siskiyou Callahan	69 12
John	Yolo Slate Ra	72 714
John	Yuba Slate Ro	72 714
John W	Plumas Quincy	62 943
Joseph	Tuolumne Columbia	71 293
L	El Dorado Diamond	58 813
M	Nevada Nevada	61 245
Mary A	Sacramento Granite	63 248
Mary M	San Joaquin Oneal	64 930
May A*	Sacramento Granite	63 248
N H	Placer Lisbon	62 735
O M	Siskiyou Callahan	69 2
R	El Dorado Placerville	58 880
R G	Nevada Eureka	61 344
R M	Sacramento Ward 4	63 519
R W	El Dorado Mud Springs	58 975
Ralpheal	Fresno Twp 2	59 3
S	Nevada Grass Valley	61 188
Saml	Butte Hamilton	56 521
Samuel	Amador Twp 5	55 363
Thomas	El Dorado Kelsey	581150
Thomas	Tuolumne Twp 3	71 460
W	Nevada Eureka	61 370
W	San Francisco San Francisco 5	67 512
W H	Calaveras Twp 9	57 401
W K*	Calaveras Twp 9	57 401
W V*	Calaveras Twp 9	57 401
W*	Nevada Eureka	61 370
William	San Joaquin Castoria	64 899
William	Siskiyou Scott Va	69 42
William	Tulara Visalia	71 16
William H	Yolo Cottonwoood	72 657
Wm	Yolo No E Twp	72 679
Wm	Yuba North Ea	72 679
Wm H	Butte Ophir	56 799
RHODESTRON		
Angal	Alameda Brooklyn	55 210
RHODIS		
Henry	Santa Clara Gilroy	65 231
Wm B	Santa Clara Gilroy	65 231
RHODY		
Henry*	Butte Hamilton	56 524
RHOJO		
Leandro	Del Norte Crescent	58 629
RHOLLEY		
C	Nevada Grass Valley	61 183
RHOLSON		
M W	Sierra Pine Grove	66 830
RHONE		
John	Yuba Parks Ba	72 777
RHONER		
Henry	Humbolt Eel Rvr	59 145
RHONN		
C M S	Yolo Cache	72 616
RHOO		
---	Calaveras Twp 8	57 109
---*	Calaveras Twp 7	57 46
RHORER		
Cyrus	Sonoma Petaluma	69 581
John	Siskiyou Yreka	69 129
RHORES		
John*	Siskiyou Yreka	69 129
RHORICH		
H	Butte Oregon	56 636
RHORICK		
H*	Butte Oregon	56 636
RHOTE		
Theo	Sonoma Petaluma	69 580
RHOTIS		
Joel	Plumas Quincy	62 993

Name	County Locale	M653 Roll	Page
RHULE			
John	Napa Napa	61	93
Margaret*	Napa Napa	61	92
RHUM			
John	San Francisco San Francisco	11	97
			67
RHUNHARD			
E*	San Francisco San Francisco	5 67	498
RHUNHART			
J*	El Dorado Georgetown	58	679
RHYMES			
James	Tulara Twp 3	71	46
RHYNE			
P	Nevada Grass Valley	61	212
RI COY			
T	Tuolumne Twp 2	71	325
RI			
---	Amador Twp 5	55	346
---	Calaveras Twp 4	57	305
RIA *			
Jian*	Monterey Pajaro	601	018
Juan*	Monterey Pajaro	601	018
RIAD			
H L*	Placer Michigan	62	831
RIAGAN			
John	Yuba Marysville	72	928
RIAGENER			
Jas	Mariposa Twp 3	60	594
RIAL			
Manuel	Monterey San Juan	601	001
RIALDES			
Jesus	Los Angeles Los Angeles	59	490
RIALDIS			
Jesus*	Los Angeles Los Angeles	59	490
RIALES			
Augustus*	Placer Forest H	62	767
RIALIS			
Ramonda	Los Angeles Los Angeles	59	504
RIALO			
Elcaro	Sacramento Ward 1	63	105
Elearo*	Sacramento Ward 1	63	105
RIALS			
David	Amador Twp 6	55	424
David Jr	Amador Twp 6	55	424
RIAMOR			
Fred B	Sacramento Ward 3	63	430
RIAN			
Camp	Nevada Bridgeport	61	453
Comp*	Nevada Bridgeport	61	453
E	Tehama Red Bluff	70	914
John	Nevada Bridgeport	61	450
Wm	Merced Twp 2	60	922
RIANDO			
Antonio*	San Francisco San Francisco	2 67	687
RIAPATH			
Peter	Santa Clara San Jose	65	382
RIAR			
John	Nevada Bridgeport	61	450
RIARDEN			
C	Tuolumne Twp 1	71	231
RIAS			
Francisco	Monterey San Juan	601	000
Sylvanio	Napa Napa	61	84
Sylvario	Napa Napa	61	84
Wancisco	Los Angeles Los Angeles	59	304
RIASDEN			
C	Tuolumne Sonora	71	231
RIASON			
Henry	Los Angeles Los Angeles	59	492
RIASS			
Joshua R*	Yuba Marysville	72	929
RIAST			
Susan	San Francisco San Francisco	10	194
			67
RIATO			
Franco	Calaveras Twp 7	57	31
RIATOR			
W A*	Napa Hot Springs	61	28
RIBARD			
Anthony	Contra Costa Twp 1	57	492
Clanes*	Contra Costa Twp 1	57	491
Claud	Contra Costa Twp 1	57	491
Edwardo	Contra Costa Twp 1	57	521
Josephine	Sacramento Ward 3	63	426
RIBAY			
John*	San Francisco San Francisco	9 681	101
RIBBE			
C*	Nevada Grass Valley	61	185
RIBBINS			
F R	San Francisco San Francisco	6 67	423
Francis	Siskiyou Shasta Rvr	69	111
William B	Siskiyou Yreka	69	152
RIBBLE			
M	San Francisco San Francisco	4 681	111
RIBBS			
Wm*	Placer Secret R	62	612

Name	County Locale	M653 Roll	Page
RIBBT			
A	El Dorado Placerville	58	823
RIBLER			
Marvin*	Placer Michigan	62	841
RIBLET			
J A	El Dorado Placerville	58	849
RIBOLT			
Ramon	Los Angeles Los Angeles	59	502
RIBONCE			
Wm A*	Calaveras Twp 9	57	371
RIBOND			
Wm A*	Calaveras Twp 9	57	371
RIBONNIE			
Wederic	Los Angeles Los Angeles	59	330
RIBONSON			
Samuel	Yuba New York	72	721
RIBORD			
Just*	Sacramento Ward 1	63	78
Wm A*	Calaveras Twp 9	57	371
RIBOTT			
Ramon	Los Angeles Los Angeles	59	502
RIBOVER			
Just*	Sacramento Ward 1	63	78
RIBSTOCK			
John	San Francisco San Francisco	8 681	291
Ljohn	San Francisco San Francisco	8 681	291
RIC			
K*	Nevada Red Dog	61	553
RICA			
---	San Bernardino S Timate	64	711
Adam	Tuolumne Twp 2	71	340
Antonio	Alameda Brooklyn	55	143
Maria	San Diego Temecula	64	784
Refoell*	El Dorado Placerville	58	896
RICABEMAN			
A Domingo*	Sierra Downieville	66	965
RICALAN			
Hosea*	Calaveras Twp 9	57	354
RICALDU			
Hosea*	Calaveras Twp 9	57	354
RICALTON			
Robert*	Sierra Morristown	661	052
RICAND			
Frank	Yuba Long Bar	72	751
RICARD			
George	Nevada Rough &	61	429
Nicholas	Tuolumne Jamestown	71	452
RICARDO			
---	Mendocino Calpella	60	826
---	Monterey S Antoni	60	967
---	Tulara Twp 3	71	63
Antonio	Tuolumne Twp 3	71	468
Joaquin	Tuolumne Twp 2	71	321
RICARDS			
Ben*	Nevada Red Dog	61	545
Wm	Sacramento Dry Crk	63	376
RICARDY			
---	Mendocino Calpella	60	826
RICARO			
B	Tuolumne Twp 3	71	463
Domingo	Tuolumne Twp 1	71	255
RICAS			
Olivia	Yuba Marysville	72	925
RICATTON			
Robert*	Sierra Morristown	661	052
RICCO			
Benjamin*	Yuba Marysville	72	975
RICE			
A	Amador Twp 3	55	407
A A	Butte Kimshaw	56	607
A C	Solano Vacaville	69	326
A J	Nevada Nevada	61	279
A W	San Mateo Twp 1	65	54
Aaron	Napa Napa	61	88
Abraham	San Francisco San Francisco	10	187
			67
Alfred	Alameda Brooklyn	55	188
Amos	San Mateo Twp 1	65	55
And	Sacramento Ward 4	63	595
Archibald	Plumas Quincy	62	935
B	San Francisco San Francisco	3 67	33
Barton	Sierra St Louis	66	818
Benjn A	San Francisco San Francisco	7 681	374
Bzo	San Bernardino San Bernadino	64	678
C C	Napa Clear Lake	61	132
C F	San Francisco San Francisco	5 67	538
C N	Merced Twp 1	60	914
C P	Tehama Tehama	70	937
Calvin	Plumas Quincy	62	922
Calvin	Tuolumne Columbia	71	297
Catherine	Yuba Marysville	72	869
Charles	El Dorado Placerville	58	920
Charles	Placer Illinois	62	738
Charles	Placer Yankee J	62	758
Charles	Placer Iona Hills	62	890
Charles	San Francisco San Francisco	7 681	409

Name	County Locale	M653 Roll	Page
RICE			
Chas	Placer Virginia	62	688
Chas R	San Francisco San Francisco	10	211
			67
Conrad	Sierra Twp 5	66	931
Cornelius	Sonoma Mendocino	69	454
D M	Nevada Grass Valley	61	180
Daniel A	Placer Rattle Snake	62	599
David	Amador Twp 7	55	420
David	Plumas Quincy	62	939
David	Sonoma Bodega	69	532
David	Sonoma Bodega	69	540
David B	Amador Twp 4	55	245
Dewit C	Yuba Marysville	72	884
Edward	Plumas Meadow Valley	62	903
Edward E	Yuba Marysville	72	894
Edward W	Amador Twp 4	55	241
Elizaa	San Joaquin Oneal	64	933
Elizabeth	Yolo Cache	72	619
Emmet E	Yuba Marysville	72	894
Ephraim	Sacramento Franklin	63	314
F H	Butte Kimshaw	56	605
F M	Colusa Monroeville	57	448
F M	Tehama Moons	70	853
F*	Sacramento Brighton	63	194
Francis	Sierra Twp 5	66	921
Frank	San Bernardino San Bernadino	64	633
Franklin E	San Francisco San Francisco	4 681	119
Fred	Yolo Slate Ra	72	686
Fred	Yuba North Ea	72	686
Frederick	San Francisco San Francisco	7 681	388
G	Nevada Washington	61	338
G F	San Francisco San Francisco	9 681	091
Geo	Siskiyou Scott Va	69	33
Geo H	Alameda Brooklyn	55	150
George	Nevada Bloomfield	61	515
George	Santa Cruz Soguel	66	591
George	Siskiyou Yreka	69	194
George	Tulara Twp 2	71	15
H	El Dorado Coloma	581	070
H A	Butte Kimshaw	56	602
H B	Solano Vacaville	69	338
H L	Plumas Quincy	62	942
H P	El Dorado Coloma	581	081
H S	Sacramento Georgian	63	347
Hairy	Santa Cruz Santa Cruz	66	603
Haron	Napa Napa	61	88
Harrey W	Alameda Brooklyn	55	189
Harry	El Dorado Coloma	581	083
Harsey	Solano Suisan	69	227
Harvey W	Alameda Brooklyn	55	115
Henry	Santa Cruz Santa Cruz	66	603
Henry	Santa Cruz Santa Cruz	66	636
Henry	Yuba Bear Rvr	721	011
Henry B	Sacramento Ward 4	63	495
Henry H	Sierra Twp 5	66	938
Hiram	Del Norte Crescent	58	659
Hiram	Santa Cruz Soguel	66	592
Horace*	Placer Forest H	62	793
Ian	San Mateo Twp 3	65	109
Isaac	Colusa Spring Valley	57	435
Isaac	El Dorado Mud Springs	58	979
Isaac R	Napa Clear Lake	61	122
J	Nevada Nevada	61	294
J	Yolo Cache Crk	72	618
J	Yolo Cache	72	641
J D	Siskiyou Klamath	69	87
J J	Yolo Cache	72	638
J J	Yolo Cache Crk	72	641
J L	Sacramento Ward 1	63	16
J M	Amador Twp 5	55	357
J S	Siskiyou Scott Ri	69	69
J V	Mendocino Big Rvr	60	851
J W	Klamath Trinidad	59	223
Jacob	Sonoma Armally	69	482
James	El Dorado Salmon Hills	581	066
James	El Dorado Georgetown	58	699
James	El Dorado Mud Springs	58	996
James	Nevada Bridgeport	61	466
James	San Francisco San Francisco	8 681	319
James	San Francisco San Francisco	7 681	428
James	Siskiyou Shasta Valley	69	119
James	Sonoma Armally	69	512
James	Yuba Long Bar	72	755
James	Yuba Long Bar	72	756
James W	San Joaquin Oneal	64	934
Jane	Colusa Monroeville	57	449
Jane*	Napa Clear Lake	61	133
Jas	Placer Stewart	62	605
Jas	Sacramento Granite	63	235
Jas	San Francisco San Francisco	1 68	906
Jas H	Napa Napa	61	67
Jason C	Alameda Brooklyn	55	115
Jno	Mendocino Big Rvr	60	846
Jno	Sacramento Ward 4	63	601
John	Butte Wyandotte	56	663

California 1860 Census Index

Name	County Locale	M653 Roll/Page
RICE		
John	Butte Wyandotte	56 664
John	Butte Oro	56 674
John	El Dorado Kelsey	581137
John	El Dorado Georgetown	58 750
John	Mariposa Twp 3	60 570
John	Mariposa Twp 3	60 574
John	Solano Suisan	69 239
John	Sonoma Sonoma	69 637
John C	Tuolumne Twp 1	71 272
John H	San Francisco San Francisco 8	681279
Jose Antonio	San Pedro Los Angeles	59 484
Joseph	Amador Twp 5	55 343
Joseph	Colusa Grand Island	57 469
Joseph	Los Angeles Tejon	59 529
Joseph	Santa Clara Gilroy	65 225
Joseph	Tulara Twp 2	71 20
K*	Nevada Red Dog	61 553
L	San Francisco San Francisco 9	68 948
L S	El Dorado Salmon Falls	581054
L*	Sacramento Brighton	63 192
L*	San Mateo Twp 3	65 110
Lawrence	Yuba Long Bar	72 756
Lewetten	San Joaquin Elkhorn	64 973
Lewis	Butte Oro	56 674
Louis	Mendocino Big Rvr	60 841
Lucy	Sacramento Franklin	63 328
M D	Siskiyou Scott Ri	69 69
M M	Yolo Cache Crk	72 619
Margaret	San Joaquin Stockton	641082
Maria	San Bernardino Santa Barbara	64 203
Martin M	Monterey San Juan	60 979
Mathew	El Dorado Placerville	58 918
Matilde	San Francisco San Francisco 2	67 618
Migel	Calaveras Twp 7	57 26
Moses	Napa Hot Springs	61 1
Nathan	Yuba Rose Bar	72 816
Nelson	Butte Kimshaw	56 607
Nigly	El Dorado Georgetown	58 677
Orrin	Plumas Meadow Valley	62 899
Oscar	El Dorado White Oaks	581001
P	Nevada Grass Valley	61 224
P Felix	Sacramento Ward 4	63 510
Pasqual	Tuolumne Twp 2	71 284
Pat	Sonoma Petaluma	69 616
Patrick	San Francisco San Francisco 9	681056
Patrick	Yolo Washington	72 562
Peter	Alameda Brooklyn	55 208
Peter	Butte Wyandotte	56 664
Peter	Yuba Parks	72 781
Phillip	El Dorado Greenwood	58 720
R	Sutter Sutter	70 817
R J	Sacramento Lee	63 217
Richard	Mendocino Round Va	60 880
Richard	San Luis Obispo San Luis Obispo 65	28
Robert	Colusa Butte Crk	57 465
Robert	San Francisco San Francisco 11	150 67
Rosa	San Francisco San Francisco 10	267 67
S C	Tuolumne Twp 1	71 276
S S	Siskiyou Scott Va	69 33
S*	Sacramento Brighton	63 192
S*	San Mateo Twp 3	65 110
Saml E	Butte Wyandotte	56 665
Samuel	Yuba New York	72 731
Samuel W	Calaveras Twp 5	57 218
Santos	Yuba Foster B	72 828
Sarah	Sonoma Washington	69 671
Spencer	Santa Cruz Soguel	66 580
T D	El Dorado Kelsey	581134
T J	Mariposa Twp 3	60 601
T*	Sacramento Brighton	63 194
Thompson	Yolo Washington	72 602
Thram	Santa Cruz Soguel	66 592
Tolaver C	San Joaquin Elkhorn	641000
W	Shasta Horsetown	66 707
W B	Sacramento Ward 1	63 2
W L	Sonoma Washington	69 672
W M	Trinity Lewiston	70 966
W W	Butte Hamilton	56 530
William	Klamath Salmon	59 209
William	Placer Michigan	62 837
William	Placer Michigan	62 838
William	San Diego San Diego	64 765
William	San Joaquin Stockton	641050
William	Sierra Gibsonville	66 859
William	Tuolumne Shawsfla	71 403
William	Yuba New York	72 735
William	Yuba Parke Ba	72 781
William G	Yuba New York	72 735
Wm	Alameda Brooklyn	55 189
Wm	Napa Napa	61 72
Wm H	Tuolumne Columbia	71 308
Wm M	Colusa Monroeville	57 449
RICE		
Wm P	Placer Illinois	62 705
Wm V	Plumas Quincy	62 957
Wm*	Napa Napa	61 72
RICED		
Patrick	Solano Vallejo	69 249
RICH		
A G	Santa Clara Fremont	65 427
Abel	Siskiyou Yreka	69 186
B	Nevada Eureka	61 381
Bernard	San Francisco San Francisco 8	681297
Catharin N*	San Francisco San Francisco 8	681296
Chas	Fresno Twp 1	59 76
D	Nevada Nevada	61 270
D	Nevada Eureka	61 381
E	San Francisco San Francisco 5	67 496
Eldridge	Humbolt Union	59 190
Francis	Yuba Marysville	72 908
Fred	San Francisco San Francisco 2	67 765
George B	San Francisco San Francisco 3	67 15
Harras*	Yuba Marysville	72 908
Henry	San Francisco San Francisco 3	67 71
Henry	Solano Benecia	69 295
J J	Butte Cascade	56 690
J J	Placer Iona Hills	62 867
Jacob	San Francisco San Francisco 10	200 67
James	Sacramento Franklin	63 310
Jas	Calaveras Twp 9	57 353
Jas	Sacramento Ward 4	63 516
Jas	San Joaquin Stockton	641015
Jno	Sacramento Brighton	63 198
John	El Dorado Kelsey	581153
John	Napa Napa	61 69
John	San Joaquin Castoria	64 905
John	Sierra Morristown	661055
John	Yuba Marysville	72 969
Joseph	San Francisco San Francisco 8	681296
Joseph	Tehama Tehama	70 947
Lucius	Sierra Poker Flats	66 837
P M	Sonoma Bodega	69 530
Rachael	San Francisco San Francisco 10	201 67
Renton*	San Francisco San Francisco 9	681073
Reubon*	San Francisco San Francisco 9	681073
Reuton*	San Francisco San Francisco 9	681073
Saml	Sacramento Sutter	63 299
Solomon	San Francisco San Francisco 8	681294
T	Nevada Eureka	61 357
T J	Butte Bidwell	56 720
Thomas	Plumas Meadow Valley	62 903
Timothy	Sacramento Mississipi	63 188
William	Placer Iona Hills	62 866
Wm	Sierra Twp 5	66 919
Wm Walter	Alameda Oakland	55 1
RICHA		
Francisco	Monterey Pajaro	601024
RICHALS		
Chas	Mendocino Big Rvr	60 848
RICHAND		
Nathaniel*	San Francisco San Francisco 7	681338
RICHANS		
Nathaniel*	San Francisco San Francisco 7	681338
RICHARD		
---	Mendocino Round Va	60 877
---	Tulara Twp 1	71 50
A	Sacramento Ward 1	63 15
Ambro*	Santa Cruz Pajaro	66 548
Amby*	Santa Cruz Pajaro	66 548
Amly	Santa Cruz Pajaro	66 548
Anna E	Tuolumne Sonora	71 205
B	Calaveras Twp 9	57 375
Clara	San Francisco San Francisco 8	681257
D F	Tehama Red Bluff	70 909
Dal	Napa Napa	61 61
David	San Francisco San Francisco 7	681341
Edmond	San Francisco San Francisco 4	681224
George	Placer Michigan	62 845
Henry	Calaveras Twp 6	57 160
Hyer	Santa Cruz Santa Cruz	66 633
Isaac M	Monterey Pajaro	601025
J	Sutter Yuba	70 772
J J	San Francisco San Francisco 7	681441
Jacob	Sacramento Franklin	63 324
John	Amador Twp 3	55 393
John	Placer Iona Hills	62 866
John	Sierra Eureka	661044
John	Tuolumne Sonora	71 220
John	Yolo Cache	72 635
Julius	San Francisco San Francisco 11	103 67
Louis	Contra Costa Twp 2	57 552
RICHARD		
Louis	San Francisco San Francisco 11	126 67
Louisa	Santa Clara San Jose	65 305
Nathaniel	San Francisco San Francisco 7	681338
T	Nevada Nevada	61 240
Thos	Tehama Red Bluff	70 910
Tilmon	Yuba Marysville	72 979
West	Santa Cruz Santa Cruz	66 634
William	Calaveras Twp 8	57 49
William	Placer Forest H	62 806
William S	Yuba Marysville	72 963
Wm	Trinity North Fo	701055
Wm C	Placer Dutch Fl	62 711
Wm H	Tuolumne Big Oak	71 125
Wm H	Tuolumne Twp 4	71 127
RICHARDLY		
Jebez	Butte Eureka	56 652
RICHARDO		
B	Tuolumne Twp 1	71 255
RICHARDS		
A	San Mateo Twp 1	65 55
A D	Siskiyou Klamath	69 87
A H	El Dorado Salmon Falls	581034
Alex	San Francisco San Francisco 1	68 818
Amly*	Santa Cruz Pajaro	66 548
Amty*	Santa Cruz Pajaro	66 548
Anna E	Tuolumne Twp 1	71 205
Anson	El Dorado Big Bar	58 736
August	Plumas Quincy	62 918
B	Sonoma Salt Point	69 691
B	Tuolumne Twp 1	71 255
Benj J	Sacramento Ward 4	63 611
Brastin*	San Mateo Twp 3	65 84
Braxtin*	San Mateo Twp 3	65 84
C	Nevada Grass Valley	61 168
C	San Francisco San Francisco 6	67 455
C H	Trinity Indian C	70 988
Charles	Calaveras Twp 5	57 231
Charles	Santa Cruz Pajaro	66 561
Charles	Tuolumne Jamestown	71 430
Charles F	Siskiyou Yreka	69 192
Charles W	Humbolt Pacific	59 131
D J	Stanislaus Emory	70 749
Daniel	Sierra Eureka	661047
Daniel	Tuolumne Twp 4	71 139
Danl	Napa Napa	61 107
David	San Francisco San Francisco 7	681341
David	Sierra Eureka	661044
David M	San Francisco San Francisco 8	681263
David W	Sierra Whiskey	66 845
Dick	San Mateo Twp 2	65 124
E	Siskiyou Cottonwoood	69 104
E S	Tuolumne Twp 1	71 240
Elijah	Tuolumne Twp 1	71 215
Evan	Butte Oregon	56 638
Ezra	San Francisco San Francisco 7	681351
G A	Santa Clara Santa Clara	65 463
G A	Tuolumne Jamestown	71 429
G W	Shasta Horsetown	66 696
George	Sacramento Franklin	63 334
George	Santa Cruz Santa Cruz	66 633
H	Nevada Grass Valley	61 179
H	Tehama Antelope	70 890
Henry	Marin Tomales	60 718
Henry	Placer Virginia	62 675
Henry	Sierra Twp 5	66 936
Isaac M	Monterey Pajaro	601025
J	Amador Twp 5	55 340
J	El Dorado Placerville	58 833
J	Nevada Grass Valley	61 167
J	Nevada Grass Valley	61 209
J	Nevada Nevada	61 316
J	San Francisco San Francisco 6	67 461
J	Sutter Sutter	70 808
J	Sutter Bear Rvr	70 821
J B	Del Norte Klamath	58 653
J J*	San Francisco San Francisco 7	681441
J M	Butte Wyandotte	56 668
J R	Nevada Little Y	61 534
Jack	Yolo Slate Ra	72 714
Jack	Yuba Slate Ro	72 714
Jacob	San Francisco San Francisco 4	681132
Jacob	Tuolumne Twp 2	71 284
Jacob	Tuolumne Twp 2	71 284
James	El Dorado Salmon Falls	581051
James	Placer Iona Hills	62 870
James	San Joaquin Castoria	64 879
James	Tulara Twp 1	71 95
James	Tuolumne Twp 1	71 265
James	Tuolumne Visalia	71 95
Jas	Butte Ophir	56 790
Jenkins	Placer Dutch Fl	62 719
Jms M	Klamath Liberty	59 230
Job	Plumas Quincy	62 954

Name	County Locale	M653 Roll/Page
RICHARDS		
John	El Dorado Coloma	581116
John	El Dorado Georgetown	58 689
John	Nevada Rough &	61 430
John	Plumas Meadow Valley	62 930
John	Sacramento Lee	63 211
John	San Mateo Twp 3	65 74
John	Santa Clara Redwood	65 447
John	Siskiyou Callahan	69 11
John	Sonoma Santa Rosa	69 390
John	Tuolumne Twp 1	71 262
John	Tuolumne Twp 1	71 265
John	Tuolumne Twp 2	71 371
Joseph	Yuba Rose Bar	72 798
L D	Calaveras Twp 8	57 67
Lucinda	San Joaquin Stockton	641024
M	Sutter Yuba	70 761
M A	El Dorado Placerville	58 821
Mann	Klamath Orleans	59 216
Martha	Placer Iona Hills	62 884
Mathew	Nevada Little Y	61 533
Mathew	Placer Forest H	62 804
Mattew	Nevada Little Y	61 533
O B	Butte Oro	56 674
Oliver	San Francisco San Francisco 2	67 643
Oliver	Yolo Slate Ra	72 704
Oliver	Yuba Slate Ro	72 704
Oswald	Sonoma Santa Rosa	69 388
P W	Sutter Bear Rvr	70 820
Pat S	Sacramento Granite	63 265
Paul	Butte Ophir	56 746
Peril	Alameda Brooklyn	55 204
Pet	Sacramento Granite	63 265
Peter	Los Angeles Los Angeles	59 356
Philip	Tuolumne Jamestown	71 424
R	El Dorado Coloma	581110
R	Sacramento Sutter	63 301
R	Santa Clara San Jose	65 359
R M	El Dorado Big Bar	58 736
R S	Tuolumne Twp 1	71 250
Robt	Tuolumne Twp 1	71 253
S L	Sierra Eureka	661045
Sam	San Francisco San Francisco 3	67 67
Saml	San Francisco San Francisco 3	67 67
Saml	Tuolumne Twp 1	71 253
Saml	Tuolumne Twp 2	71 359
Sewell	Santa Cruz Pajaro	66 532
Stephen	Trinity Trinity	70 973
Sylvester	Tuolumne Twp 4	71 141
T	Amador Twp 3	55 371
T	Nevada Grass Valley	61 209
T	Nevada Nevada	61 240
Thos	Butte Ophir	56 795
Thos	San Francisco San Francisco 2	67 803
Thos	Trinity E Weaver	701057
Thos C	Napa Yount	61 52
Thos G	San Francisco San Francisco 2	67 697
Tobias	Tuolumne Twp 1	71 263
W	El Dorado Placerville	58 829
W	El Dorado Placerville	58 833
W	Nevada Nevada	61 316
W B	Sierra Twp 7	66 891
W E	Sonoma Petaluma	69 594
W H	San Francisco San Francisco 6	67 421
W S	Butte Ophir	56 766
William	San Francisco San Francisco 3	67 65
William	Tuolumne Twp 1	71 221
William*	Yuba Marysville	72 926
Wm	Butte Ophir	56 773
Wm	Mariposa Twp 1	60 668
Wm	Sacramento Sutter	63 297
Wm	Sacramento Georgian	63 335
Wm	Tuolumne Twp 1	71 253
Wm S	Calaveras Twp 9	57 373
RICHARDSEN		
Harry	Butte Wyandotte	56 669
John*	Siskiyou Yreka	69 133
RICHARDSON		
A	Butte Wyandotte	56 662
A	Del Norte Klamath	58 654
A	Placer Michigan	62 818
A C	Sacramento Franklin	63 331
A C	Yuba Long Bar	72 773
A E	Sierra Twp 7	66 887
A G	Sacramento Ward 1	63 140
A S	Amador Twp 5	55 331
Achillis	Mendocino Big Rock	60 873
Adolphus	San Francisco San Francisco 11	112 67
Albert	Alameda Brooklyn	55 126
Albert	Contra Costa Twp 3	57 586
Alfred	Monterey Alisal	601028
Alonzo	Plumas Quincy	62 994
Alpheus*	Contra Costa Twp 3	57 603
Andrew	El Dorado White Oaks	581010
Ann	San Francisco San Francisco 6	67 442

Name	County Locale	M653 Roll/Page
RICHARDSON		
C	Nevada Grass Valley	61 164
C	San Joaquin Stockton	641090
C C	Mariposa Coulterville	60 703
C E	Butte Kimshaw	56 589
C O	Mariposa Coulterville	60 703
Charles	Humbolt Eureka	59 176
D M	San Joaquin Elliott	64 944
David	Solano Suisan	69 230
E	El Dorado Newtown	58 777
E H	Placer Iona Hills	62 872
E H	Siskiyou Callahan	69 6
Edward	El Dorado Casumnes	581167
Edward	Marin San Rafael	60 773
Edward	Sierra Pine Grove	66 828
Eligah	Plumas Quincy	62 994
Elisha P	Alameda Oakland	55 69
Esward	El Dorado Casumnes	581167
Eugene	Butte Hamilton	56 526
Franklin	Sonoma Petaluma	69 571
G P	Sutter Vernon	70 842
G W	El Dorado Placerville	58 873
Geo	Butte Eureka	56 647
Geo	San Francisco San Francisco 2	67 794
George	Placer Michigan	62 811
George	Yuba Marysville	72 948
George H	San Joaquin Castoria	64 892
George M	Solano Suisan	69 230
H F	Santa Clara Santa Clara	65 483
H J	Butte Bidwell	56 724
H M	El Dorado Mountain	581178
Harriett F	San Joaquin Elliott	64 944
Harry	Butte Wyandotte	56 669
Horace	Sonoma Mendocino	69 456
J	Butte Wyandotte	56 664
J	Nevada Nevada	61 256
J	Nevada Nevada	61 272
J	Sonoma Bodega	69 527
J	Sonoma Bodega	69 540
J B	El Dorado Eldorado	58 935
J E	El Dorado White Oaks	581002
J F	El Dorado Salmon Falls	581061
J F	Siskiyou Scott Va	69 37
J G	El Dorado Kelsey	581152
J G	Tehama Red Bluff	70 922
J H J	Sonoma Santa Rosa	69 388
J L	El Dorado Salmon Hills	581061
J R	Nevada Nevada	61 252
J S	El Dorado Salmon Falls	581061
James	Santa Clara Fremont	65 427
James	Sonoma Petaluma	69 558
Jas	Santa Clara San Jose	65 369
Jas	Santa Clara Fremont	65 421
Jno	Klamath Salmon	59 209
Jno	Sacramento American	63 164
Jno	San Francisco San Francisco 10	258 67
Jno H	Sonoma Petaluma	69 606
John	Colusa Muion	57 462
John	Contra Costa Twp 1	57 526
John	Del Norte Happy Ca	58 661
John	El Dorado White Oaks	581001
John	El Dorado White Oaks	581006
John	Los Angeles Los Angeles	59 503
John	Sacramento Cosummes	63 393
John	San Francisco San Francisco 1	68 854
John	San Francisco San Francisco 1	68 903
John	Sonoma Sonoma	69 640
John	Tehama Lassen	70 877
John	Tulara Visalia	71 105
John T	El Dorado Georgetown	58 749
John*	Siskiyou Yreka	69 133
Jonathan	Santa Clara Fremont	65 426
Josefa	Merced Monterey	60 934
Josefa	Monterey Monterey	60 934
Joseph	Calaveras Twp 9	57 363
Joseph	Santa Cruz Pajaro	66 558
L	El Dorado Placerville	58 851
L B	El Dorado Placerville	58 860
L D	Trinity Trinity 2	70 986
L F	El Dorado Mud Springs	581000
L S*	Siskiyou Yreka	69 184
Larkin	Solano Fairfield	69 201
Lorenzo	Calaveras Twp 4	57 336
M M	Solano Suisan	69 212
Margaret	Sonoma Petaluma	69 557
Mary A	San Francisco San Francisco 9	68 986
Mary J	San Francisco San Francisco 9	68 986
Mathew	San Francisco San Francisco 4	681121
Michael	San Francisco San Francisco 1	68 855
Michael	Sierra Pine Grove	66 827
Mike	Del Norte Crescent	58 659
N W	Solano Suisan	69 225
O P	Sutter Bear Rvr	70 821
Olira	Sierra Morristown	661052
P S	Sutter Nicolaus	70 829

Name	County Locale	M653 Roll/Page
RICHARDSON		
Pat	Tuolumne Twp 2	71 400
Prescott V	San Francisco 11	126
	San Francisco	67
R	El Dorado Placerville	58 863
R	Sacramento Cosummes	63 399
Richard B	Alameda Brooklyn	55 159
Richard B	Contra Costa Twp 2	57 559
Robert	Placer Forest H	62 802
S	El Dorado Diamond	58 805
S	Nevada Eureka	61 381
S	Sacramento Ward 1	63 6
S	Santa Clara San Jose	65 382
S	Santa Clara Redwood	65 447
S C	Nevada Grass Valley	61 181
S D	Calaveras Twp 9	57 371
S J	Siskiyou Cottonwoood	69 104
S S*	Siskiyou Yreka	69 184
Saml S	San Francisco San Francisco 3	67 16
Samuel	Napa Yount	61 41
Samuel	Yuba Bear Rvr	721005
Sarah	San Francisco San Francisco 10	201 67
Sarah H	Sonoma Mendocino	69 456
Silas	Yolo Cache	72 635
Sol	Alameda Brooklyn	55 128
Soloman	Alameda Brooklyn	55 118
Sophia	El Dorado White Oaks	581029
Stephen	Marin Sauciteto	60 750
Stephen	Placer Iona Hills	62 872
T	El Dorado Diamond	58 806
T H	Yuba New York	72 729
Thomas	Sierra Twp 7	66 899
Thos	Nevada Rough &	61 415
Thos	Sacramento Granite	63 222
Thos	Sacramento Ward 1	63 73
Thos	Sonoma Sonoma	69 657
Thos	Stanislaus Oatvale	70 718
W	San Francisco San Francisco 5	67 534
W H	Tuolumne Sonora	71 198
Wendell	San Francisco San Francisco 10	165 67
William	Marin S Antoni	60 708
William	Mendocino Little L	60 833
William	Mendocino Round Va	60 878
William	San Luis Obispo San Luis Obispo	65 44
William	Yuba Marysville	72 975
Wm	El Dorado Big Bar	58 744
Wm	Humbolt Bucksport	59 156
Wm	San Francisco San Francisco 2	67 729
Wm B	Monterey Monterey	60 954
Wm R	Alameda Brooklyn	55 89
Y W	El Dorado Big Bar	58 744
RICHARDTON		
Alfred*	Monterey Alisal	601028
RICHARSOM		
J C*	El Dorado Georgetown	58 697
RICHARSON		
J C*	El Dorado Georgetown	58 697
RICHART		
A	El Dorado Kelsey	581152
George	Los Angeles Los Angeles	59 335
RICHARZ		
---	Sierra Downieville	661014
RICHASON		
Joseph*	El Dorado Big Bar	58 744
RICHASSON		
W H	El Dorado Georgetown	58 697
RICHD		
Hock*	Amador Twp 5	55 333
RICHE		
Caleb	Monterey S Antoni	60 967
Geo	Butte Wyandotte	56 669
H	Santa Clara San Jose	65 314
J	Shasta Shasta	66 678
Robert	Tulara Visalia	71 110
RICHEANT		
D*	Nevada Rough &	61 395
RICHEART		
D	Nevada Rough &	61 395
RICHEE		
W T	Trinity Mouth Ca	701017
RICHEL		
A	Nevada Eureka	61 392
Robert*	Santa Cruz Santa Cruz	66 636
RICHELLING		
F	Calaveras Twp 9	57 382
RICHEN		
Wm	Alameda Brooklyn	55 212
RICHER		
A	Amador Twp 7	55 420
Gristan	Sacramento Ward 1	63 39
Gustar	Sacramento Ward 1	63 39
Gustav*	Sacramento Ward 1	63 39
Louis	San Mateo Twp 3	65 107
M D*	Napa Hot Springs	61 7

Name	County Locale	M653 RollPage
RICHERBERGER		
D	Tuolumne Twp 2	71 375
RICHERBOIR		
August	Butte Bidwell	56 723
RICHERBOIS		
August	Butte Bidwell	56 723
RICHERDSON		
Alfred	Placer Secret R	62 618
Henry	El Dorado Mud Springs	58 960
Orril	El Dorado Mud Springs	58 984
RICHERO		
B G	Tuolumne Twp 1	71 254
RICHERS		
B G*	Tuolumne Twp 1	71 254
Geo	San Francisco San Francisco 9	681081
RICHERSON		
David	Butte Ophir	56 753
J J	El Dorado Diamond	58 769
RICHERT		
Elizabeth	Del Norte Crescent	58 620
John	Del Norte Crescent	58 621
RICHESON		
L A	Solano Vacaville	69 331
M	Solano Vacaville	69 327
RICHET		
C	San Francisco San Francisco 2	67 784
N F	San Francisco San Francisco 4	681152
RICHEWOOD		
George*	Yuba Marysville	72 926
RICHEY		
A	Amador Twp 3	55 382
E*	Sacramento San Joaquin	63 360
James	Del Norte Crescent	58 640
James	San Francisco San Francisco 7	681342
John	Calaveras Twp 10	57 294
John Jr	Calaveras Twp 10	57 291
Margant*	Butte Ophir	56 761
Margaret	Butte Ophir	56 761
RICHFORD		
George	Placer Michigan	62 820
Thomas	Sierra Twp 7	66 910
RICHHOFER		
Jos	Amador Twp 7	55 412
RICHIE		
A	Shasta Horsetown	66 708
F	El Dorado Kelsey	581139
Harvey A	Yuba Bear Rvr	72 997
Leon M	Tulara Visalia	71 101
M D*	Napa Hot Springs	61 7
Milton	Napa Napa	61 67
Robert	Santa Cruz Santa Cruz	66 636
W A	Placer Michigan	62 857
W T	Trinity Mouth Ca	701017
Wm	Napa Napa	61 112
Wm S	Placer Ophirville	62 655
RICHINS		
Bartholomen	Yuba Rose Bar	72 819
RICHISON		
Frank	Amador Twp 2	55 265
N	Butte Oregon	56 642
S	Butte Oregon	56 642
RICHL		
Geo	Butte Wyandotte	56 669
RICHLEN		
John*	Calaveras Twp 5	57 203
RICHLER		
John	Calaveras Twp 5	57 203
Paul	Placer Forest H	62 793
RICHLES		
Martin	Tuolumne Shawsfla	71 404
RICHLIRY		
F	Amador Twp 3	55 383
RICHLY		
John	San Luis Obispo San Luis Obispo	65 11
RICHMAN		
Chas	Calaveras Twp 5	57 195
Frank	Santa Clara San Jose	65 366
Henry	San Francisco San Francisco 9	681065
Henry F	San Joaquin Castoria	64 893
J B*	Napa Napa	61 97
RICHMARD		
Walters	Amador Twp 3	55 373
RICHMAW		
J B*	Napa Napa	61 97
RICHMOND		
Asbury B	Humbolt Mattole	59 125
B	Nevada Grass Valley	61 201
B M	Merced Twp 4	60 917
Charles	Santa Clara Burnett	65 257
E	Shasta Shasta	66 654
Ed	Tehama Red Bluff	70 922
Ernest	Siskiyou Scott Va	69 46
George	Yuba Marysville	72 926
Horace	Plumas Meadow Valley	62 901
J	Sacramento Sutter	63 307
Jno	Sacramento Ward 4	63 597

Name	County Locale	M653 RollPage
RICHMOND		
Mary	San Francisco San Francisco 8	681285
Thos	Butte Hamilton	56 526
RICHNER		
Daniel	Siskiyou Callahan	69 14
Robert	Calaveras Twp 6	57 155
RICHNEY		
Isaac*	Tuolumne Twp 5	71 516
RICHNOR		
Jno*	Santa Cruz Santa Cruz	66 629
RICHOLDS		
John	San Joaquin Elliott	64 941
RICHOLOS		
J W	El Dorado Kelsey	581156
RICHOM		
Annelole	San Francisco San Francisco 2	67 781
RICHON		
N	San Francisco San Francisco 5	67 487
RICHOR		
T	Amador Twp 3	55 380
RICHSON		
J	Yolo Putah	72 553
RICHSTER		
John	San Francisco San Francisco 3	67 87
RICHTER		
H	San Francisco San Francisco 4	681217
Martin	Tuolumne Twp 2	71 404
Samuel*	Solano Vacaville	69 365
W H	San Francisco San Francisco 10	321 67
Wm	Del Norte Crescent	58 659
RICHTINGER		
Ben	Amador Twp 5	55 334
RICHTOR		
Samuel	Solano Vacaville	69 365
RICHUSON		
H T	Butte Ophir	56 774
RICHWAGEN		
William	Yuba Marysville	72 896
RICHWAH		
Chas	Butte Bidwell	56 712
RICI		
C C*	Napa Clear Lake	61 132
James	Nevada Bloomfield	61 527
Jane*	Napa Clear Lake	61 133
RICIDE		
Josea Mam*	Alameda Oakland	55 3
RICIDI		
Jose Maim*	Alameda Oakland	55 3
Josea Mam*	Alameda Oakland	55 3
RICIT		
John*	Shasta French G	66 719
RICK		
---	Sierra Downieville	66 984
A D	El Dorado Georgetown	58 689
Carris	Amador Twp 4	55 258
F	Sonoma Petaluma	69 574
G	El Dorado Diamond	58 794
Hanes*	San Francisco San Francisco 1	68 894
Harris*	San Francisco San Francisco 1	68 894
Henry	Amador Twp 4	55 246
Henry	Placer Michigan	62 825
Jacob	Santa Clara San Jose	65 290
James	San Francisco San Francisco 8	681319
John	San Francisco San Francisco 2	67 605
John M*	Sierra Twp 7	66 913
John*	Plumas Quincy	621001
Joseph	Sierra Downieville	66 954
RICKANYON		
B	Sutter Sutter	70 811
RICKARD		
Jacob	Yuba Marysville	72 880
James	San Francisco San Francisco 11	155 67
RICKARDS		
William	Yuba Marysville	72 926
RICKART		
Geo	El Dorado Newtown	58 780
John	El Dorado Newtown	58 780
RICKATTY		
John	Sierra Pine Grove	66 821
RICKE		
F*	Siskiyou Callahan	69 7
John	Humbolt Mattole	59 125
RICKEG		
John*	Nevada Rough &	61 405
RICKELER		
M	El Dorado White Oaks	581015
RICKELLING		
F*	Calaveras Twp 9	57 382
RICKEN		
Wm	Tuolumne Shawsfla	71 417
RICKENS		
Geo*	San Francisco San Francisco 9	681081
RICKER		
A	Amador Twp 7	55 420

Name	County Locale	M653 RollPage
RICKER		
Alexander	Tulara Twp 3	71 45
Benjamin	San Mateo Twp 2	65 127
George	Sacramento Ward 1	63 41
J M	El Dorado Diamond	58 770
James	Placer Forest H	62 772
Martin	Napa Napa	61 68
Monroe	Calaveras Twp 10	57 267
Moses	Yuba Linda Twp	72 980
N H	Butte Kimshaw	56 569
Thos	Alameda Brooklyn	55 195
W H	Butte Kimshaw	56 569
W J*	Napa Napa	61 95
RICKERBANGH		
Bistin	Napa Clear Lake	61 121
RICKERBY		
Samuel	Solano Suisan	69 216
RICKERS		
Geo*	San Francisco San Francisco 9	681081
William	Yuba Marysville	72 858
RICKERSON		
John*	Mariposa Coulterville	60 684
W W	Tuolumne Twp 4	71 158
RICKERT		
John	Amador Twp 1	55 457
RICKES		
R A	Placer Illinois	62 704
RICKETS		
E	Sutter Yuba	70 768
Jas A	Calaveras Twp 9	57 363
Susan	Butte Chico	56 545
RICKETT		
Martha	San Diego Colorado	64 809
RICKETTS		
D L	Yolo Cache	72 608
RICKEY		
D B	Amador Twp 2	55 269
E*	Sacramento San Joaquin	63 360
Frank	Amador Twp 1	55 484
James	Amador Twp 2	55 316
John	Calaveras Twp 10	57 294
John	Nevada Rough &	61 405
Josphns	Amador Twp 2	55 277
N	Santa Clara Gilroy	65 247
Thos	Amador Twp 2	55 277
Wm	Amador Twp 2	55 272
Wm	Tuolumne Twp 2	71 417
RICKFORD		
L	Calaveras Twp 9	57 409
RICKHOLT		
J W	Sutter Butte	70 779
RICKINBER		
Geo	El Dorado Gold Hill	581096
RICKLIFF		
Peter	Sonoma Petaluma	69 551
RICKLIFFS		
P H	Sonoma Armally	69 483
RICKMAN		
Chas	Calaveras Twp 5	57 195
D	Butte Cascade	56 697
David H	Sonoma Mendocino	69 447
J	San Francisco San Francisco 5	67 525
J W	Butte Oro	56 673
RICKNER		
Daniel*	Siskiyou Callahan	69 14
RICKNEY		
Jno K	San Francisco San Francisco 9	68 975
RICKOR		
Pardon	Napa Yount	61 39
RICKS		
C	Calaveras Twp 9	57 392
Casper L*	Humbolt Eureka	59 171
Casper S*	Humbolt Eureka	59 171
Celia	San Joaquin O'Neal	641007
E	Siskiyou Scott Va	69 38
Henry	Nevada Rough &	61 398
J A	Shasta French G	66 718
J H	Calaveras Twp 8	57 106
John	Amador Twp 4	55 246
John	Sonoma Washington	69 669
John E	Solano Vacaville	69 360
Lucy J	Stanislaus Branch	70 708
Thomas	Humbolt Eureka	59 171
RICKSON		
Wm	Placer Goods	62 694
RICKSTRAN		
Elwood	Plumas Quincy	62 977
RICKSWARTZ		
Fredk	Plumas Quincy	62 953
RICKTER		
Vel	Amador Twp 2	55 267
RICKWARD		
Thos	Amador Twp 4	55 253
RICKWELL		
A W	Amador Twp 6	55 434
RICL		
Cyrus	Yuba North Ea	72 674

RICLEHOUSE - RIDMOND

California 1860 Census Index

Name	County Locale	M653 Roll	Page
RICLEHOUSE			
C	El Dorado Newtown	58	777
RICO			
Francisco	Merced Monterey	60	935
Francisco	Monterey Monterey	60	935
Francisco	Monterey San Juan	60	978
Jane*	Napa Clear Lake	61	133
Jesus	Yuba Marysville	72	948
Jose	Merced Twp 1	60	913
Jose	Tuolumne Sonora	71	227
Jose Jesus	San Luis Obispo San Luis Obispo	65	39
Joseph	San Francisco San Francisco 2	67	699
M H	Tuolumne Twp 2	71	308
Moses	Napa Hot Springs	61	8
P	El Dorado Placerville	58	821
Pasquel	Tuolumne Twp 2	71	284
W M	Trinity Lewiston	70	966
RICORA			
R	Stanislaus Buena Village	70	722
RICORD			
C G	Placer Forest H	62	794
Clarinda	San Francisco San Francisco 9	68	1022
Henry	Amador Twp 2	55	293
J W	Tuolumne Twp 2	71	378
Jos	Mariposa Twp 3	60	556
RICORDA			
Senor	Calaveras Twp 5	57	188
RICORDER			
Senor*	Calaveras Twp 6	57	188
RICORDO			
Antonio	Tuolumne Twp 3	71	468
Senor	Calaveras Twp 5	57	188
RICOS			
Don	Stanislaus Oatvale	70	719
RICOUGH			
Thomas*	Tuolumne Twp 2	71	271
RICOZ			
John P	Yolo Washington	72	563
RICR			
Danl K	Calaveras Twp 6	57	131
RICT			
S	Marin Bolinas	60	743
William	Placer Iona Hills	62	893
RICTBURG			
H*	Los Angeles Tejon	59	524
RICTHERY			
H*	Los Angeles Tejon	59	524
RICTHING			
H*	Los Angeles Tejon	59	524
RICTINGER			
Stephens	Amador Twp 5	55	334
RICTLEY			
S*	Calaveras Twp 9	57	391
RICTMEER			
Stephens*	Amador Twp 5	55	334
RICTMLER			
Stephens*	Amador Twp 5	55	334
RICTOR			
W A	Napa Hot Springs	61	28
RICUT			
John	Shasta French G	66	719
RICYANDIERO			
Pier	Calaveras Twp 8	57	92
RID			
R	San Francisco San Francisco 9	68	1075
RIDA			
---	San Bernardino S Timate	64	722
RIDAN			
Morel	Los Angeles Los Angeles	59	516
RIDD			
Pelig	Sonoma Russian	69	434
R H	El Dorado Placerville	58	866
Wm*	El Dorado Georgetown	58	691
RIDDEL			
John E	San Francisco San Francisco 11	67	105
Jos	Sacramento Ward 3	63	458
RIDDELL			
Geo	San Francisco San Francisco 10	67	330
George H	Solano Benecia	69	287
Julias	Napa Napa	61	67
Julius*	Napa Napa	61	67
Phillip	Sacramento Ward 1	63	142
Robt A	San Francisco San Francisco 12	67	390
Sarah	Solano Benecia	69	313
RIDDELS			
Sarah	Solano Benecia	69	313
RIDDEN			
Jonathan	Tuolumne Sonora	71	195
RIDDER			
A J	Siskiyou Scott Va	69	54
Ross	Sierra La Porte	66	781
RIDDICH			
M S	Sutter Yuba	70	778

Name	County Locale	M653 Roll	Page
RIDDICK			
A M	Mendocino Ukiah	60	798
James*	San Francisco San Francisco 7	68	1412
Joseph	Placer Todds Va	62	788
RIDDIL			
Edward A	Calaveras Twp 7	57	9
RIDDING			
Jeremiah	Los Angeles Los Angeles	59	498
John	San Francisco San Francisco 1	68	835
RIDDINGTON			
N A	Tuolumne Twp 1	71	223
RIDDLE			
Anderson	Tuolumne Twp 2	71	310
Daniel	Solano Vacaville	69	345
David	San Francisco San Francisco 7	68	1343
Ebenizar	Contra Costa Twp 2	57	569
F S	Nevada Bloomfield	61	517
George	Plumas Quincy	62	937
Isaac	Santa Clara Alviso	65	406
J G	Colusa Monroeville	57	449
J L	Amador Twp 1	55	463
James W	Siskiyou Yreka	69	185
Jas	Placer Rattle Snake	62	628
Jas	Stanislaus Branch	70	704
Kate	Placer Yankee J	62	781
Mer*	Marin Point Re	60	730
Mes*	Marin Point Re	60	730
Mr*	Marin Point Re	60	730
Ms*	Marin Point Re	60	730
P	Calaveras Twp 9	57	415
R P	Sierra Eureka	66	1046
Robert	Contra Costa Twp 2	57	575
Robert	Plumas Meadow Valley	62	901
Spear	San Francisco San Francisco 10	67	260
Taswell	Siskiyou Yreka	69	144
Thomas	Plumas Quincy	62	960
Walter	Placer Yankee J	62	781
William	Calaveras Twp 8	57	102
William	San Francisco San Francisco 7	68	1342
RIDDLER			
Michael	San Francisco San Francisco 7	68	1408
RIDDLES			
R W	El Dorado Mud Springs	58	974
RIDDLEY			
J P	Sacramento Sutter	63	297
RIDDLINGTON			
Thos	Sacramento Ward 4	63	496
RIDDON			
Robt	El Dorado White Oaks	58	1030
RIDDOR			
A J	Siskiyou Scott Va	69	54
RIDE			
Abner*	Sonoma Armally	69	515
RIDEM			
Thos	Solano Vallejo	69	265
RIDEN			
Chas S*	San Francisco San Francisco 1	68	846
RIDENCOMB			
T M*	Yolo Washington	72	572
RIDENCONETT			
T M*	Yolo Washington	72	572
RIDENHONR			
Lewis	Sonoma Mendocino	69	458
RIDENHOUR			
Lewis	Sonoma Mendocino	69	458
Mary	Sonoma Mendocino	69	458
RIDEON			
Thos	Solano Vallejo	69	265
RIDEONT			
N J	Yolo Slate Ra	72	697
RIDEOUS			
James R	Yolo Slate Ra	72	692
RIDEOUT			
Cyrus E	Yolo Slate Ra	72	693
Cyrus E	Yuba Slate Ro	72	693
N J	Yuba Slate Ro	72	697
RIDER			
B H	Nevada Nevada	61	242
B H	Nevada Nevada	61	248
D A	Sutter Nicolaus	70	837
F W	Nevada Eureka	61	369
George	San Francisco San Francisco 9	68	1100
George	San Francisco San Francisco 3	67	76
H M	San Francisco San Francisco 3	67	76
J	Nevada Grass Valley	61	201
James	Siskiyou Cottonwoood	69	109
Jno	Butte Oregon	56	617
Jno B	San Francisco San Francisco 6	67	410
Jos A	Butte Mountain	56	733
L	Calaveras Twp 9	57	409
Reuben	Alameda Brooklyn	55	98
S W	Nevada Eureka	61	369
T	Tuolumne Twp 4	71	158
T W	Nevada Eureka	61	369
Vincent	Calaveras Twp 9	57	365

Name	County Locale	M653 Roll	Page
RIDER			
W	San Francisco San Francisco 5	67	549
William	Siskiyou Klamath	69	85
William*	Nevada Rough &	61	436
William*	Siskiyou Klamath	69	85
RIDERT			
James*	Siskiyou Cottonwood	69	109
RIDES			
W M	Sonoma Armally	69	497
RIDFEARER			
Wm	Sierra Twp 7	66	897
RIDFIARA			
Wm	Sierra Twp 7	66	897
RIDGE			
Jacob	Butte Oregon	56	619
John R	Yuba Marysville	72	940
Robert	Butte Oregon	56	622
RIDGELEY			
William F	Monterey San Juan	60	1007
RIDGELY			
Hebbert	Yuba Marysville	72	902
Marcelus W	Napa Hot Springs	61	12
RIDGENAY			
Garet M*	Mariposa Twp 3	60	588
RIDGENEY			
Garet M	Mariposa Twp 3	60	588
RIDGES			
Gilford	Klamath S Fork	59	202
RIDGEWAY			
Calif*	Napa Yount	61	46
Culif*	Napa Yount	61	46
Jeremiah P	Fresno Twp 2	59	18
John	Nevada Bridgeport	61	465
Michael	Placer Secret R	62	614
R	San Francisco San Francisco 6	67	446
RIDGIELD			
Dzle	Sutter Nicolaus	70	838
RIDGILL			
Wm	Del Norte Crescent	58	642
RIDGLEY			
James	Yuba Marysville	72	944
Wm	Marin Cortemad	60	785
RIDGLY			
Hilbert	Yuba Marysville	72	902
RIDGRAY			
T John	San Francisco San Francisco 7	68	1426
RIDGUAY			
T John	San Francisco San Francisco 7	68	1426
RIDGWAY			
Henry	Solano Benecia	69	289
S S	Yolo Cottonwoood	72	660
W P	San Francisco San Francisco 7	68	1330
RIDH			
B	Nevada Eureka	61	381
J	Nevada Eureka	61	381
RIDHARDSON			
S	Nevada Eureka	61	381
RIDINGER			
A	Sacramento Cosummes	63	400
G	El Dorado Diamond	58	786
RIDINGTON			
Mathew	San Francisco San Francisco 1	68	903
RIDINOR			
Mary*	Mariposa Twp 1	60	635
RIDIONT			
James R	Yuba Slate Ro	72	692
RIDLAN			
John	Sierra Gibsonville	66	856
RIDLE			
David M	San Francisco San Francisco 1	68	928
William	Nevada Rough &	61	436
RIDLER			
N	Amador Twp 7	55	417
RIDLES			
Samuel	El Dorado Kelsey	58	1156
RIDLEY			
Charles A	San Francisco San Francisco 4	68	1141
Chris	Sacramento Ward 1	63	149
Edward	San Bernardino San Bernadino	64	630
Elizabeth	San Francisco San Francisco 9	68	1078
Jacob	Butte Ophir	56	796
James	Calaveras Twp 5	57	216
Jas	Butte Cascade	56	703
Nich	Napa Napa	61	67
Robt	Butte Mountain	56	741
Robt	El Dorado Mud Springs	58	970
S*	Calaveras Twp 9	57	391
RIDMAN			
C	Mariposa Twp 1	60	642
Dennis	Sierra Eureka	66	1042
Harrison*	Butte Oregon	56	637
Henry	Butte Kimshaw	56	602
Horace	Plumas Quincy	62	1000
James*	El Dorado Cosumnes	58	1162
RIDMOND			
James	Tuolumne Twp 1	71	214

Copyright 1999 by Heritage Quest, a division of AGLL, Inc., Bountiful, UT 84011. All rights reserved

366

California 1860 Census Index

Name	County Locale	M653 RollPage
RIDMONS		
W C	El Dorado White Oaks	581013
RIDMORE		
Charles	Yuba Fosters	72 836
RIDNAUEL		
C*	Butte Ophir	56 786
RIDNEGER		
Saml*	Nevada Red Dog	61 545
RIDNEY		
John Jr	Calaveras Twp 10	57 291
RIDNIGER		
Saml*	Nevada Red Dog	61 545
RIDO		
B	San Francisco San Francisco 4	681166
M Wolf*	San Francisco San Francisco 4	681166
RIDOLPH		
Charles	Solano Vacaville	69 365
RIDONY		
Anson	Santa Clara San Jose	65 316
RIDR		
Abner*	Sonoma Armally	69 515
RIDRO		
Don*	Stanislaus Oatvale	70 718
RIDWELL		
A	Sutter Yuba	70 768
RIE		
---	El Dorado Union	581092
---	El Dorado Coloma	581123
---	Stanislaus Branch	70 713
---*	El Dorado Coloma	581084
Ah	Calaveras Twp 7	57 14
RIEALMA		
Jose	Santa Clara Santa Clara	65 470
RIECHER		
James C	Calaveras Twp 7	57 19
RIECHLING		
P	Amador Twp 1	55 455
RIECKE		
A W	Tuolumne Twp 2	71 272
RIECKER		
Margaret*	Monterey Alisal	601031
RIED		
Cyrus	Yolo No E Twp	72 674
John W*	San Francisco San Francisco 1	68 878
RIEDEL		
Walter*	San Francisco San Francisco 3	67 53
Walters*	San Francisco San Francisco 3	67 53
Waltur	San Francisco San Francisco 3	67 53
Waltus*	San Francisco San Francisco 3	67 53
RIEDIL		
Waltris*	San Francisco San Francisco 3	67 53
RIEE		
Michael*	Calaveras Twp 8	57 57
RIEF		
Peter	Mariposa Twp 3	60 603
RIEFER		
Lewis	Calaveras Twp 7	57 22
RIEFF		
Anna	Sacramento Ward 4	63 577
W C	Sacramento Ward 4	63 602
RIEFFER		
Louis	Calaveras Twp 7	57 12
RIEGO		
Pablo	San Francisco San Francisco 11	154 67
RIEHNOR		
Jno*	Santa Cruz Santa Cruz	66 629
RIEKE		
F	Siskiyou Callahan	69 7
RIEKER		
W J*	Napa Napa	61 95
RIEKMAN		
A	San Francisco San Francisco 3	67 51
RIELEY		
Eliza*	Napa Napa	61 95
Jno	Sacramento Ward 4	63 520
John	Alameda Oakland	55 2
Joseph	Tuolumne Twp 4	71 134
RIELLAN		
John*	Sierra Gibsonville	66 856
RIELLEY		
James*	Calaveras Twp 5	57 216
RIELLY		
T	Calaveras Twp 9	57 391
Thos	Sacramento Ward 1	63 5
RIELSY		
Joseph	Tuolumne Big Oak	71 134
RIEN		
August*	Shasta Shasta	66 682
Samuel	Sonoma Bodega	69 522
RIENER		
Charles	Calaveras Twp 8	57 63
Charles P	Calaveras Twp 7	57 10
RIENHART		
Eli	Yuba Marysville	72 875
RIENS		
Klaus	Butte Ophir	56 793

Name	County Locale	M653 RollPage
RIEORDA		
Senor	Calaveras Twp 5	57 188
RIEQUAR		
Marsele	San Francisco San Francisco 2	67 703
RIER		
G	El Dorado Placerville	58 868
RIERA		
---	Los Angeles San Gabriel	59 414
Suz	Los Angeles Los Angeles	59 294
RIERDON		
Ellen	San Francisco San Francisco 7	681350
John P	San Francisco San Francisco 8	681280
M	Amador Twp 2	55 308
RIES		
George	San Diego San Diego	64 767
Isabella	Butte Ophir	56 785
John	Santa Clara Fremont	65 427
Leopold*	Alameda Murray	55 225
S	Sutter Yuba	70 770
Wyly*	El Dorado Georgetown	58 677
RIESIN		
Henry	Yuba Marysville	72 976
RIESS		
Clara	Yuba Marysville	72 925
Henry	San Francisco San Francisco 6	67 458
Peter*	Mariposa Twp 3	60 603
RIET		
S*	Marin Bolinas	60 743
RIETA		
Prospier*	San Francisco San Francisco 2	67 650
RIETBERG		
H*	Los Angeles Tejon	59 524
RIETHERY		
H*	Los Angeles Tejon	59 524
RIEUT		
John*	Shasta French G	66 719
RIEVES		
Christ*	Napa Napa	61 80
Elija*	Napa Clear Lake	61 121
Geo*	Napa Napa	61 77
Wesley*	Napa Napa	61 80
RIEW		
August*	Shasta Shasta	66 682
RIEYNHAGAN		
Edward*	Contra Costa Twp 2	57 542
RIFASMO		
Gertudes	Santa Clara Almaden	65 277
RIFAY		
T S	Marin San Rafael	60 761
RIFDAY		
J Phillips*	Butte Oregon	56 619
RIFE		
John	Santa Clara San Jose	65 353
Rebecca	Santa Clara San Jose	65 383
S B	Calaveras Twp 9	57 397
S B	Placer Todds Va	62 789
Samuel	Placer Yankee J	62 782
RIFENROD		
G	El Dorado Diamond	58 790
RIFFAL		
Absalom	Plumas Quincy	62 940
RIFFE		
P H	Siskiyou Scott Va	69 34
RIFFER		
John*	San Joaquin Stockton	641009
RIFFES		
John*	San Joaquin Stockton	641009
RIFFEY		
E T	Napa Clear Lake	61 134
RIFFINS		
Owen	Contra Costa Twp 1	57 522
RIFFLE		
Chas F	Sacramento American	63 168
RIFRUGE		
Nicholas	Santa Cruz Pajaro	66 542
RIFUGEE		
---	San Bernardino S Timate	64 702
RIFUGEN		
---	San Bernardino S Timate	64 693
RIFUGIA		
---	San Bernardino San Bernadino	64 677
---	San Bernardino S Timate	64 701
RIFUGIO		
---	San Bernardino S Timate	64 705
Maria	San Bernardino San Bernadino	64 683
RIFUGO		
---	Los Angeles Los Angeles	59 495
RIG		
J J	San Francisco San Francisco 2	67 587
RIGAL		
Alexis	Sacramento Ward 4	63 541
RIGAN		
J	San Francisco San Francisco 5	67 518
Margaret	San Francisco San Francisco 7	681402
RIGBEY		
Edward*	El Dorado Gold Hill	581097

Name	County Locale	M653 RollPage
RIGBY		
A J	Sierra La Porte	66 777
J A	Sutter Sutter	70 810
J W	Yolo Slate Ra	72 709
J W	Yuba Slate Ro	72 709
RIGDON		
Rufus	San Joaquin Elkhorn	64 961
RIGELENHAUSE		
August	Sacramento Ward 4	63 522
RIGENAY		
A	El Dorado Placerville	58 865
RIGENSBERGER		
Melvin*	San Francisco San Francisco 8	681299
RIGES		
Jose	Santa Clara Almaden	65 271
RIGETTS		
Charles	Tuolumne Twp 3	71 460
RIGG		
John	Tehama Tehama	70 949
John L	Del Norte Crescent	58 649
RIGGENS		
Jas	Sacramento Franklin	63 315
RIGGERS		
William F	Placer Illinois	62 740
RIGGIN		
Henry	Yolo Cottonwoood	72 654
RIGGINS		
Mary	Colusa Grand Island	57 474
RIGGIO		
Gorrence	Mariposa Coulterville	60 674
Larrence	Mariposa Coulterville	60 674
Lorrence*	Mariposa Coulterville	60 674
RIGGOLD		
Charles	San Francisco San Francisco 9	681101
RIGGS		
B	Calaveras Twp 9	57 396
Charles	Siskiyou Yreka	69 153
Columbus	Colusa Monroeville	57 450
Edward	Humbolt Bucksport	59 161
Edward A	San Francisco San Francisco 2	67 751
Edwin A*	San Francisco San Francisco 2	67 751
Eli	San Joaquin Elkhorn	64 967
Irvin	Mariposa Twp 3	60 573
Isaac	Sierra Downieville	66 976
J J	Sacramento Ward 4	63 527
J K	El Dorado Union	581089
J R	El Dorado Union	581089
John	San Joaquin Douglass	64 926
L M	El Dorado Placerville	58 925
Louis	Mariposa Twp 3	60 573
Louisa	San Francisco San Francisco 2	67 751
R N	Tehama Antelope	70 889
S A	Sutter Yuba	70 773
Silas	Santa Clara San Jose	65 346
Thomas	Monterey San Juan	601007
Thomas	Shasta Shasta	66 683
Thomas	Siskiyou Yreka	69 151
Troin*	Mariposa Twp 3	60 573
Washington	Contra Costa Twp 2	57 541
William A	Contra Costa Twp 2	57 570
Z A	Santa Clara Redwood	65 459
RIGGSLEY		
Andrew	Yolo Cache Crk	72 640
RIGHERS		
John	Placer Virginia	62 661
RIGHERTY		
Martin	San Francisco San Francisco 1	68 865
RIGHEY		
Edward*	El Dorado Gold Hill	581097
RIGHT		
Joseph	San Mateo Twp 1	65 71
L D	Calaveras Twp 9	57 389
L D	Calaveras Twp 9	57 398
Lucy*	Contra Costa Twp 1	57 504
Romero	Contra Costa Twp 3	57 587
Samuel	San Mateo Twp 2	65 119
Suey*	Contra Costa Twp 1	57 504
Thos	Sonoma Vallejo	69 612
William	Calaveras Twp 5	57 242
RIGHTER		
Richd	El Dorado Mud Springs	58 991
RIGHTMAN		
John	Sacramento American	63 170
RIGHTMEYER		
A	Butte Hamilton	56 526
James	Tulara Twp 1	71 77
RIGHTMIN		
A	Nevada Nevada	61 260
RIGHTMIRE		
A D	Sacramento Ward 4	63 542
A*	Nevada Nevada	61 260
RIGHTMYER		
James	Tulara Visalia	71 77
RIGITTS		
Charles	Tuolumne Twp 3	71 460

Name	County Locale	M653 Roll	Page
RIGLER			
F	Siskiyou Yreka	69	186
Jacob	Yuba Fosters	72	837
John	Yolo Putah	72	587
RIGLEY			
Geo	Siskiyou Scott Ri	69	64
John	Yuba Foster B	72	825
Larry	Placer Virginia	62	663
Peter	Siskiyou Yreka	69	139
RIGLHUT			
Conrad	San Francisco San Francisco 2	67	634
RIGNER			
Charles	Trinity E Weaver	70	1061
RIGNEY			
Jas	San Francisco San Francisco 10		176
		67	
Jas	San Francisco San Francisco 1	68	870
Las	San Francisco San Francisco 10		176
		67	
Wm	San Francisco San Francisco 1	68	931
RIGON			
H Van*	San Francisco San Francisco 3	67	68
RIGOT			
Jagues	Tuolumne Big Oak	71	129
Jaques	Tuolumne Twp 4	71	129
RIGSDALE			
J D	Shasta Millvill	66	753
RIGUERMES			
Juan J	Los Angeles Los Angeles	59	393
RIGUM			
Joseph*	El Dorado Georgetown	58	751
RIGWAY			
Martin	Calaveras Twp 6	57	157
RIHELL			
Dennis C	San Francisco San Francisco 7	68	1359
RIHL			
Adam*	San Francisco San Francisco 10		287
		67	
RIHLE			
Fred	Placer Yankee J	62	756
Jacob	Placer Yankee J	62	756
RIJJS			
Edwin A*	San Francisco San Francisco 2	67	751
RIKANC			
S	Calaveras Twp 9	57	406
RIKAR			
Chas	Placer Ophir	62	652
RIKAY			
Robt	San Francisco San Francisco 9	68	1075
RIKE			
Minty*	San Mateo Twp 2	65	124
RIKER			
Ann C	Sacramento Natonia	63	279
Harrison H	Siskiyou Yreka	69	158
Harrison H	Siskiyou Yreka	69	165
Harry*	Mariposa Twp 1	60	672
John	Butte Bidwell	56	716
Mary	San Francisco San Francisco 7	68	1429
Saml	Sacramento Natonia	63	279
Thos	Sacramento Ward 4	63	515
RIKHAM			
Ruch	Santa Cruz Santa Cruz	66	600
RIKL			
Adam*	San Francisco San Francisco 10		287
		67	
RIKY			
Jas	Sacramento Alabama	63	411
RILAND			
B*	Nevada Grass Valley	61	147
Be*	Nevada Grass Valley	61	147
Bee	Nevada Grass Valley	61	147
G	Nevada Grass Valley	61	157
RILATA			
Charlie	Alameda Brooklyn	55	118
RILAY			
Franklin	San Francisco San Francisco 9	68	1076
J P*	San Francisco San Francisco 9	68	1081
Jno*	San Francisco San Francisco 9	68	1072
John	San Francisco San Francisco 9	68	1101
RILE			
F	Tehama Red Bluff	70	910
RILEL			
Martin	El Dorado Big Bar	58	733
RILEOX			
James*	Stanislaus Empire	70	732
RILEY			
A	Nevada Grass Valley	61	235
A	Sonoma Cloverdale	69	685
A T Eisen*	San Francisco San Francisco 8	68	1280
	San Francisco		
Ada	San Francisco San Francisco 4	68	1111
Alfred	Solano Fairfield	69	198
Alpedalias*	Yuba Marysville	72	910
Andrew	Calaveras Twp 5	57	238
Andrew	San Francisco San Francisco 1	68	807
Andrew	Tuolumne Twp 2	71	312

Name	County Locale	M653 Roll	Page
RILEY			
Ann	Humbolt Eel Rvr	59	151
Ann	San Francisco San Francisco 2	67	631
Ann	Shasta Shasta	66	658
Ann	Shasta Millvill	66	727
Anna	Sierra Twp 7	66	906
B	El Dorado White Oaks	58	1001
B	San Francisco San Francisco 2	67	640
B J	Sacramento Ward 1	63	147
Barnard	Yuba Rose Bar	72	801
Bridget	San Francisco San Francisco 4	68	1121
Bridget	Santa Clara Gilroy	65	246
C	Nevada Eureka	61	346
C C	San Francisco San Francisco 9	68	971
C R	Tuolumne Big Oak	71	125
C R	Tuolumne Twp 4	71	127
C W	Solano Montezuma	69	372
Catharine	San Francisco San Francisco 8	68	1320
Chas	San Francisco San Francisco 1	68	854
Christapher C*	Siskiyou Yreka	69	139
Christopher	San Francisco San Francisco 9	68	1032
	San Francisco		
Christopher C	Siskiyou Yreka	69	139
Chs	Los Angeles Tejon To	59	535
Cornelius	San Francisco San Francisco 3	67	32
D D	El Dorado Placerville	58	896
D P	San Francisco San Francisco 5	67	534
Daniel	Calaveras Twp 7	57	46
Daniel	Tuolumne Twp 2	71	387
Danl	Tuolumne Twp 2	71	277
David	Yolo Merritt	72	579
Delia	San Francisco San Francisco 4	68	1122
E	Merced Twp 2	60	921
E W	Yuba Rose Bar	72	788
Ed	Sacramento Natonia	63	285
Edward	Butte Ophir	56	794
Edward	Calaveras Twp 5	57	178
Edward	Placer Iona Hills	62	877
Edward	San Joaquin Stockton	64	1057
Edward	San Joaquin Castoria	64	905
Edward	Santa Cruz Santa Cruz	66	629
Edward	Tulara Yule Rvr	71	23
Edward	Tulara Petersburg	71	52
Edwd	Sonoma Vallejo	69	627
Elizabeth	San Francisco San Francisco 10		283
		67	
Elizabeth	San Francisco San Francisco 10		349
		67	
Elizabeth	San Francisco San Francisco 2	67	598
F	El Dorado Placerville	58	855
F S	Marin San Rafael	60	761
Frances	Tuolumne Twp 2	71	324
Francis	Calaveras Twp 8	57	54
Francis	Siskiyou Yreka	69	152
Frank	Monterey Alisal	60	1029
Franklin	San Francisco San Francisco 9	68	1068
Franklin	San Luis Obispo San Luis Obispo	65	3
G	Nevada Grass Valley	61	166
Garrett	Placer Virginia	62	685
Geo	Sacramento Ward 1	63	23
Geo	San Francisco San Francisco 9	68	1054
George	San Joaquin Elkhorn	64	976
George	Tuolumne Twp 1	71	226
H	Nevada Grass Valley	61	154
H	Nevada Grass Valley	61	225
H	Shasta Shasta	66	673
H B	Tuolumne Twp 2	71	400
H B	Tuolumne Twp 2	71	413
Hannah	Del Norte Crescent	58	625
Henry	San Francisco San Francisco 9	68	1008
Hugh	Nevada Red Dog	61	546
Isaac	San Francisco San Francisco 9	68	978
J	Nevada Grass Valley	61	203
J	Nevada Grass Valley	61	226
J	Sacramento Brighton	63	198
J	Sacramento Sutter	63	306
J	San Francisco San Francisco 5	67	522
J	San Francisco San Francisco 5	67	541
J	Sonoma Washington	69	664
J B	Siskiyou Scott Va	69	41
J G	San Francisco San Francisco 1	68	894
J L	San Francisco San Francisco 9	68	1053
J S	Nevada Grass Valley	61	215
J S	Tuolumne Sonora	71	198
J S F	Colusa Spring Valley	57	436
J W	El Dorado Grizzly	58	1181
J W	Nevada Grass Valley	61	185
James	Calaveras Twp 6	57	142
James	Calaveras Twp 4	57	313
James	Colusa Monroeville	57	452
James	Los Angeles Los Angeles	59	333
James	Nevada Rough &	61	430
James	Nevada Red Dog	61	550
James	Placer Michigan	62	849
James	Placer Iona Hills	62	896
James	Plumas Quincy	62	953

Name	County Locale	M653 Roll	Page
RILEY			
James	San Francisco San Francisco 7	68	1403
James	San Francisco San Francisco 9	68	957
James	San Francisco San Francisco 9	68	959
James	San Francisco San Francisco 9	68	988
James	Tuolumne Columbia	71	323
James	Tuolumne Columbia	71	353
James	Tuolumne Twp 2	71	353
James	Tuolumne Columbia	71	356
James	Tuolumne Jamestown	71	428
James	Tuolumne Sonora	71	480
James	Yuba Marysville	72	959
James A	Del Norte Crescent	58	621
Jane	Santa Clara San Jose	65	319
Jas	Butte Cascade	56	698
Jas	Butte Bidwell	56	724
Jas	San Francisco San Francisco 1	68	876
Jas	San Mateo Twp 1	65	56
Jno	Mendocino Big Rock	60	876
Jno	Nevada Nevada	61	239
Jno	Sacramento Brighton	63	192
Jno R	San Joaquin Stockton	64	1046
Jno W	Butte Kimshaw	56	596
John	Amador Twp 4	55	258
John	Amador Twp 2	55	322
John	El Dorado White Oaks	58	1005
John	El Dorado Mud Springs	58	979
John	Nevada Eureka	61	349
John	San Francisco San Francisco 9	68	1020
John	San Francisco San Francisco 11		148
		67	
John	San Francisco San Francisco 1	68	890
John	Santa Clara Gilroy	65	242
John	Santa Clara Almaden	65	278
John	Sierra Downieville	66	994
John	Solano Vallejo	69	259
John	Sonoma Petaluma	69	564
John	Sonoma Petaluma	69	583
John	Sonoma Vallejo	69	616
John	Tuolumne Twp 2	71	297
John	Tuolumne Twp 2	71	312
John	Tuolumne Twp 2	71	351
John	Tuolumne Twp 2	71	367
John	Yolo Slate Ra	72	718
John	Yuba New York	72	718
John W	Calaveras Twp 9	57	363
Jos	Tehama Red Bluff	70	928
Jos	Tehama Red Bluff	70	931
Joseph	Siskiyou Shasta Rvr	69	112
Julia	Yuba Marysville	72	912
Kasa*	San Francisco San Francisco 7	68	1403
L O	Nevada Grass Valley	61	189
Lawrence	Marin Novato	60	738
Lawrence O*	Placer Auburn	62	566
Luke	El Dorado Coloma	58	1068
Luke	El Dorado Coloma	58	1118
Luke	Santa Clara Gilroy	65	242
M	El Dorado Kelsey	58	1130
M	El Dorado Placerville	58	848
M	El Dorado Placerville	58	861
M	Nevada Grass Valley	61	191
M	Nevada Washington	61	333
M	San Francisco San Francisco 9	68	1099
M O	San Francisco San Francisco 6	67	463
Major	Contra Costa Twp 1	57	524
Marcos	Santa Clara San Jose	65	305
Margaret	San Francisco San Francisco 10		255
		67	
Margaret	Yuba Marysville	72	864
Mary	Sacramento Ward 1	63	124
Mary	San Francisco San Francisco 9	68	1011
Mary	San Francisco San Francisco 4	68	1123
Mary	San Francisco San Francisco 8	68	1310
Mary	San Francisco San Francisco 10		178
		67	
Mary	Santa Clara San Jose	65	355
Mary	Yuba Marysville	72	890
Mary B	San Francisco San Francisco 2	67	726
Mathew	Sacramento Dry Crk	63	372
Mathew	Santa Clara Santa Clara	65	523
Michael	Butte Ophir	56	775
Michael	Del Norte Crescent	58	650
Michael	Del Norte Klamath	58	653
Michael	San Francisco San Francisco 8	68	1237
Michael	San Francisco San Francisco 2	67	575
Michael	San Francisco San Francisco 2	67	610
Michael	San Mateo Twp 1	65	55
Michael	Solano Benecia	69	305
Michael	Stanislaus Branch	70	715
Michael	Yuba Rose Bar	72	808
Michael	Yuba Bear Rvr	72	998
Michal	Alameda Brooklyn	55	106
Morris	Del Norte Klamath	58	653
N J	Sutter Sutter	70	816
Oscar	Amador Twp 2	55	296
Owen	Butte Cascade	56	704

Name	County Locale	M653 Roll	Page
RILEY			
Owen	San Diego San Diego	64	767
P	Mariposa Twp 3	60	561
P	Nevada Grass Valley	61	158
P	Shasta Shasta	66	673
P	Yolo Putah	72	550
P	Yolo Cache	72	595
P D	Siskiyou Scott Ri	69	77
P O	Sacramento Ward 1	63	33
Pat	Nevada Grass Valley	61	215
Pat	Nevada Little Y	61	534
Pat	San Francisco San Francisco 9	68	1056
Pat	Siskiyou Callahan	69	13
Patrick	Alameda Oakland	55	13
Patrick	Alameda Brooklyn	55	99
Patrick	Plumas Meadow Valley	62	931
Patrick	San Francisco San Francisco 2	67	593
Patrick	San Francisco San Francisco 2	67	643
Patrick	San Francisco San Francisco 1	68	839
Patrick	San Francisco San Francisco 1	68	856
Patrick	San Francisco San Francisco 9	68	940
Patrick	Santa Clara Almaden	65	268
Patrick	Santa Clara Almaden	65	274
Patrick	Sierra Twp 7	66	891
Patrick	Sierra Downieville	66	994
Patrick	Trinity Taylor'S	70	1036
Patrick	Yuba New York	72	722
Peter	Calaveras Twp 4	57	338
Peter	Sacramento Dry Crk	63	376
Peter	San Francisco San Francisco 7	68	1338
Peter	San Francisco San Francisco 1	68	912
Peter	Tuolumne Twp 1	71	401
Peter O	Calaveras Twp 5	57	219
Peter S	Calaveras Twp 6	57	156
Petere	San Joaquin Elkhorn	64	963
Philip	Placer Yankee J	62	757
Philip	Tuolumne Columbia	71	351
Phillip	Marin Cortemad	60	791
Phillip	Nevada Bridgeport	61	446
Presley	Colusa Butte Crk	57	466
R	Trinity Weaverville	70	1080
R A	Nevada Grass Valley	61	164
R C	Nevada Eureka	61	350
Richard	Calaveras Twp 5	57	186
Richard	San Francisco San Francisco 8	68	1316
Richard	San Francisco San Francisco 7	68	1350
Richd	San Francisco San Francisco 1	68	870
Rose	San Francisco San Francisco 8	68	1316
Rose	San Francisco San Francisco 9	68	982
Ruben	Yolo Washington	72	572
S	Nevada Grass Valley	61	188
S	Nevada Grass Valley	61	225
S	Placer Dutch Fl	62	720
S B	Calaveras Twp 9	57	374
Sarah	Alameda Oakland	55	25
Sife	Santa Clara San Jose	65	329
Stephen	Napa Hot Springs	61	22
Sun	Santa Clara San Jose	65	374
T	Butte Chico	56	562
T	Nevada Grass Valley	61	225
T	Tuolumne Columbia	71	325
Terance*	Tuolumne Columbia	71	324
Terence	San Francisco San Francisco 11		96
		67	
Terrence	San Francisco San Francisco 2	67	794
Thomas	Alameda Brooklyn	55	162
Thomas	Del Norte Crescent	58	650
Thomas	Los Angeles Los Angeles	59	362
Thomas	Placer Auburn	62	559
Thomas	San Francisco San Francisco 9	68	1103
Thomas	San Francisco San Francisco 8	68	1280
Thos	Nevada Rough &	61	430
Thos	Sacramento American	63	169
Thos	San Francisco San Francisco 9	68	1069
Thos	San Francisco San Francisco 1	68	823
Thos	Santa Clara Alviso	65	409
Thos	Solano Suisan	69	234
Thos D	Butte Ophir	56	770
Thos P	Butte Ophir	56	775
Tim	Mariposa Twp 3	60	558
Tiranco*	Tuolumne Twp 2	71	324
Trance*	Tuolumne Columbia	71	324
W	El Dorado Diamond	58	809
W	Tehama Red Bluff	70	920
W R	Shasta Shasta	66	730
Walker	Butte Oro	56	688
Walter	Butte Wyandotte	56	672
Wen	Butte Ophir	56	786
William	Calaveras Twp 4	57	312
William	Siskiyou Shasta Rvr	69	112
William	Trinity W Weaver	70	1054
Wm	Amador Twp 2	55	270
Wm	El Dorado Placerville	58	930
Wm	Mariposa Twp 1	60	663
Wm	Tehama Red Bluff	70	921
Wm	Tehama Red Bluff	70	922

Name	County Locale	M653 Roll	Page
RILEY			
Wm E	Sierra Twp 7	66	872
Wm G	Nevada Eureka	61	394
Wm H	Tehama Red Bluff	70	922
RILEYS			
Daniel*	Yolo Merritt	72	579
RILFE			
M J	Santa Clara Fremont	65	417
RILHENNY			
Mary	Solano Benecia	69	291
RILI			
Francis*	Yuba New York	72	722
RILL			
---	El Dorado Diamond	58	774
RILLANDS			
Thomas	Yuba Parks Ba	72	777
RILLEY			
Daniel	Calaveras Twp 7	57	4
Dann	Klamath Liberty	59	242
John	Calaveras Twp 7	57	4
Patk	Klamath Liberty	59	242
RILLGORD			
C H	Tuolumne Twp 2	71	284
RILLIN			
Francis*	Alameda Brooklyn	55	137
RILLING			
Thos*	San Francisco San Francisco 9	68	950
RILLINGBY			
William	Solano Montezuma	69	371
RILLINGLEY			
William	Solano Montezuma	69	371
RILLINGS			
Alfred W*	Monterey Alisal	60	1032
RILLLMAN			
A	Butte Wyandotte	56	657
RILLM			
Francis*	Alameda Brooklyn	55	137
RILLMAN			
Thos*	Nevada Red Dog	61	555
RILLSNIAN			
A	Butte Wyandotte	56	657
RILLY			
Jas A	San Bernardino San Bernadino	64	628
Pat	Yuba North Ea	72	678
W M*	Butte Kimshaw	56	594
RILPEY			
William	El Dorado Kelsey	58	1126
RILSER			
G F	Yuba Marysville	72	979
RILSEY			
R A	San Francisco San Francisco 4	68	1172
RILTAN			
John*	Napa Clear Lake	61	141
RILTER			
F S	Nevada Red Dog	61	546
Frankling	San Joaquin Elliott	64	943
John*	Sonoma Petaluma	69	554
RILTON			
John*	El Dorado Placerville	58	933
RILTSTON			
Richd	San Francisco San Francisco 1	68	851
RILY			
Anthony	San Francisco San Francisco 1	68	887
Bernard	Placer Iona Hills	62	884
John	Placer Iona Hills	62	884
Martin	Placer Forest H	62	793
Michael	Humbolt Union	59	191
RIM			
---	Amador Twp 2	55	312
---	Sierra Downieville	66	992
John*	Nevada Bridgeport	61	500
RIMALL			
David*	Nevada Bridgeport	61	442
RIMAS			
Kapping*	Mendocino Big Rvr	60	850
RIMBOL			
Charles	Plumas Meadow Valley	62	933
RIMBOUGER			
John	Santa Clara San Jose	65	391
RIMDLE			
Jno*	Nevada Washington	61	333
R T*	Mendocino Big Rvr	60	844
RIMEY			
Peter	Marin San Rafael	60	763
RIMG			
---*	San Francisco San Francisco 4	68	1194
RIMHEROTT			
A	Los Angeles Tejon	59	524
RIMLER			
Leonard	Placer Todds Va	62	787
RIMMELL			
John	Fresno Twp 2	59	17
RIMMER			
F	El Dorado White Oaks	58	1027
John	Plumas Quincy	62	964
RIMMINGTON			
Reuben*	Nevada Red Dog	61	541

Name	County Locale	M653 Roll	Page
RIMMULL			
John*	Yuba Marysville	72	928
RIMNICH			
Thos*	Yolo Cache Crk	72	626
RIMPO			
Albert	Los Angeles Los Angeles	59	502
James	Los Angeles Los Angeles	59	501
RIMSON			
Henry*	Calaveras Twp 4	57	318
RIMTON			
Jose*	San Diego Agua Caliente	64	857
RIMYAN			
Jas	Butte Chico	56	556
RIN			
---	Amador Twp 5	55	347
---	Tuolumne Big Oak	71	144
---	Yuba Long Bar	72	758
Ah	Tuolumne Twp 4	71	147
Charlotte E*	San Francisco San Francisco 3	67	15
John	Placer Iona Hills	62	875
Tonso	Sierra Twp 7	66	898
Tou	Tuolumne Twp 4	71	147
RINAGO			
P T	Amador Twp 3	55	393
RINAL			
Abraham*	Colusa Monroeville	57	454
Jacob	Del Norte Crescent	58	649
RINALDO			
G*	San Francisco San Francisco 5	67	542
RINARKE			
Richard	Sierra Downieville	66	1021
RINAS			
Manuel*	San Francisco San Francisco 3	67	77
RINCAPAW			
Robert W*	Siskiyou Yreka	69	155
RINCH			
John L	Sierra Pine Grove	66	825
RINCHU			
Fong	San Francisco San Francisco 4	68	1180
RINCK			
Frederick	San Francisco San Francisco 3	67	8
RINCKLE			
Eduard	Butte Ophir	56	782
Edward	Butte Ophir	56	782
RINCLIFF			
R	Calaveras Twp 9	57	409
RINCON			
---	Tulara Twp 3	71	63
RIND			
C P*	Placer Iona Hills	62	881
RINDAL			
Saml	Contra Costa Twp 2	57	557
RINDALL			
F	Butte Eureka	56	651
G D	Nevada Nevada	61	241
RINDGE			
Hiram	Tulara Keyesville	71	54
RINDON			
F*	San Francisco San Francisco 1	68	924
RINE			
Catharin	Sonoma Sonoma	69	653
Catharine	Nevada Bridgeport	61	441
Edward	Sacramento Franklin	63	330
F	Nevada Eureka	61	373
George	Nevada Bridgeport	61	448
Jacob P	Sierra Pine Grove	66	829
John	Nevada Bridgeport	61	500
John E*	San Francisco San Francisco 3	67	18
John*	Nevada Bridgeport	61	500
M	Amador Twp 2	55	308
Mary	Sierra La Porte	66	783
T	Nevada Eureka	61	373
Tomlin	Sierra Downieville	66	1011
William	Nevada Bloomfield	61	511
RINED			
Edward*	Alameda Oakland	55	43
RINEHARD			
Jno	Sacramento Ward 4	63	519
RINEHART			
A	Tuolumne Twp 2	71	310
Agnes	Siskiyou Klamath	69	94
James	Siskiyou Klamath	69	94
W	Sacramento Sutter	63	291
RINEHERDT			
A*	Los Angeles Tejon	59	524
RINEHUDT			
A*	Los Angeles Tejon	59	524
RINEL			
Stephen	Calaveras Twp 7	57	15
RINEMAN			
P	Trinity State Ba	70	1001
RINERS			
Rose*	Sierra Twp 7	66	887
RINERSON			
W L	Amador Twp 1	55	454

Name	County Locale	M653 Roll/Page
RINES		
J P	San Francisco San Francisco	5 67 492
RINETON		
Jose*	San Diego Agua Caliente	64 857
RING		
---	Butte Mountain	56 742
---	San Francisco San Francisco	4 681188
---	Yolo Slate Ra	72 715
---	Yuba Slate Ro	72 715
---*	Nevada Bridgeport	61 466
---*	San Francisco San Francisco	4 681183
Ah	Calaveras Twp 7	57 8
B L	El Dorado Placerville	58 882
C	Solano Vacaville	69 330
Charles B	San Francisco San Francisco	9 68 953
David	San Francisco San Francisco	12 383 67
Dennis	Placer Iona Hills	62 880
Edward	San Mateo Twp 2	65 124
G	San Francisco San Francisco	1 68 923
Geo W*	Siskiyou Cottonwoood	69 101
Hannah	San Francisco San Francisco	4 681227
Henry	Placer Michigan	62 857
Henry	Yuba Fosters	72 834
Ho	San Francisco San Francisco	4 681211
Hos	Yuba Long Bar	72 764
Hoy	Yuba Long Bar	72 764
J H	Solano Vacaville	69 325
James	Sacramento Mississipi	63 184
James	San Joaquin Tulare	64 869
Jane	San Francisco San Francisco	4 681142
Jno	Sacramento Ward 4	63 500
John U	El Dorado Georgetown	58 751
John*	Yuba Slate Ro	72 706
Joseph	El Dorado Salmon Falls	581052
Joseph	Plumas Quincy	62 955
L R*	Nevada Grass Valley	61 187
Lee	Butte Mountain	56 743
Margt	San Francisco San Francisco	9 68 987
Marris*	Placer Iona Hills	62 886
Mary	San Francisco San Francisco	10 344 67
Mary F*	Nevada Red Dog	61 546
Michael	San Joaquin Stockton	641065
Morris*	Placer Iona Hills	62 886
Nora	San Francisco San Francisco	10 338 67
Richard	San Francisco San Francisco	9 68 981
Sam	Yolo Slate Ra	72 708
Thomas	Santa Cruz Pajaro	66 571
Timothy	Calaveras Twp 10	57 274
RINGALDO		
Charles*	Calaveras Twp 9	57 353
RINGAR		
Charley	Alameda Brooklyn	55 152
RINGE		
Fritz	Siskiyou Yreka	69 176
RINGELL		
C	San Francisco San Francisco	10 348 67
RINGEN		
John*	Yuba Marysville	72 928
RINGER		
Christopher	San Francisco	3 67 44
Moses*	Amador Twp 2	55 297
RINGES		
James	Amador Twp 3	55 387
RINGET		
Joseph	San Francisco San Francisco	8 681251
RINGGOLD		
Chas	Sacramento Ward 1	63 5
G H	San Francisco San Francisco	10 285 67
RINGLE		
Aget	Siskiyou Yreka	69 125
RINGMAN		
P*	Sacramento American	63 164
R G*	Nevada Grass Valley	61 182
RINGMON		
P*	Sacramento American	63 164
RINGNER		
B F	Yolo Merritt	72 579
Z F	Yolo Merritt	72 579
RINGNETT		
Eli H*	Tuolumne Twp 2	71 292
RINGOLD		
C S K	Mariposa Twp 3	60 615
Geo	Amador Twp 7	55 416
Saml	Butte Kimshaw	56 603
RINGOYNE		
Alfred	Yuba Foster B	72 825
RINGSBURY		
Milow	Calaveras Twp 7	57 14
RINGSDAFF		
Henry	Santa Clara Fremont	65 428

Name	County Locale	M653 Roll/Page
RINGSLEY		
Wm*	Solano Benecia	69 288
RINGSLY		
Wm	Solano Benecia	69 288
RINGUETT		
Eli H	Tuolumne Columbia	71 292
RINGWOOD		
Sam	Klamath Liberty	59 230
RINHART		
E B	Calaveras Twp 9	57 370
RINIS		
Joseph	Calaveras Twp 4	57 330
RINJER		
Moses*	Amador Twp 2	55 297
RINKER		
Casper	Butte Ophir	56 773
RINNE		
Hans*	Placer Auburn	62 585
Haus*	Placer Auburn	62 585
RINNER		
Wm*	Yuba New York	72 724
RINNERT		
C P	Nevada Nevada	61 268
RINNEY		
G W	Tuolumne Sonora	71 480
Hugh	Sierra Downieville	661016
RINNI		
Ah	Calaveras Twp 7	57 16
RINNIE		
Chas E	San Francisco San Francisco	2 67 693
RINNIS		
Robert	Mendocino Little L	60 837
RINNMAN		
G	Butte Eureka	56 652
RINNUTZ		
James*	El Dorado Georgetown	58 675
RINO		
Benjamin*	Yuba Marysville	72 975
C P*	Placer Iona Hills	62 881
Francisca	Calaveras Twp 4	57 337
Henry	Calaveras Twp 4	57 337
Henry	Placer Forest H	62 797
Jas	Butte Kimshaw	56 605
RINSE		
Thos	Amador Twp 3	55 399
RINSINGER		
Joseph	Placer Rattle Snake	62 633
RINSLEY		
Anne	Klamath Liberty	59 242
RINSS		
Joshua R*	Yuba Marysville	72 929
RINT		
A Ed*	Stanislaus Branch	70 704
RINTHY		
G*	Yolo Putah	72 550
RINTO		
Richard*	Placer Iona Hills	62 881
RINY		
Jas*	San Francisco San Francisco	1 68 861
John*	San Mateo Twp 2	65 132
S R*	Nevada Grass Valley	61 187
RINYMAN		
R G*	Nevada Grass Valley	61 182
RINYOLD		
Geo*	Amador Twp 7	55 416
RINYSER		
Bradford	Butte Ophir	56 751
RIO		
---	Calaveras Twp 6	57 121
---*	Calaveras Twp 5	57 232
Francis	Siskiyou Yreka	69 168
RIOAS		
Celena	Yuba Marysville	72 925
RIODEN		
Mary	Sacramento Ward 4	63 515
RIOER		
John B	Calaveras Twp 5	57 197
RIOHLER		
Joseph	Tuolumne Twp 6	71 540
RIOKER		
Geo	Butte Ophir	56 760
RION		
John B*	Calaveras Twp 5	57 197
RIOOS		
Francisco*	Yuba Marysville	72 946
RIORDAN		
Danl S	Tuolumne Sonora	71 213
David	Sierra Twp 7	66 868
RIORDE		
James	Tuolumne Twp 2	71 313
RIORDEN		
Jno	San Francisco San Francisco	10 269 67
RIORN		
John B*	Calaveras Twp 5	57 197
RIOS		
Augustina	Yuba Marysville	72 948

Name	County Locale	M653 Roll/Page
RIOS		
Benancio	Los Angeles San Juan	59 464
Fermon	Santa Clara Santa Clara	65 462
Francisco	Los Angeles Los Angeles	59 326
Garamel	San Luis Obispo	65 7
Gregorio	Los Angeles San Juan	59 461
Gregorio	Los Angeles San Juan	59 472
Ignacio	Los Angeles San Juan	59 462
Ignacio	Los Angeles San Juan	59 466
Jose	Plumas Quincy	62 988
Jose	San Luis Obispo San Luis Obispo	65 27
Jose	Santa Clara Fremont	65 429
Jose Usabia	Tulara Sinks Te	71 43
Leando	Yuba Marysville	72 949
Leonardi	San Luis Obispo	65 27
Lozaro	Santa Clara San Jose	65 331
Luciano	Santa Clara Almaden	65 268
Luganta	Los Angeles Los Angeles	59 371
Lugonla*	Los Angeles Los Angeles	59 371
Manuela	Los Angeles San Juan	59 473
Maria De Los N	San Juan (Los Angeles)	59 475
Maria Helena	San Luis Obispo	65 6
Marie A	Monterey Monterey	60 952
Miguel	Los Angeles Los Angeles	59 369
Miquil	San Mateo Twp 2	65 132
Narcisa	Los Angeles Los Angeles	59 368
Patricio	Los Angeles San Juan	59 463
Petromillo	San Luis Obispo	65 6
Romona	Santa Clara Almaden	65 266
Santiago	Los Angeles San Juan	59 464
RIOUS		
Juan	Calaveras Twp 6	57 138
RIOVIA		
Jose J	Los Angeles Los Angeles	59 489
RIOX		
Edward	Santa Cruz Santa Cruz	66 630
RIP		
---	Amador Twp 5	55 366
John	El Dorado White Oaks	581029
Rea	Butte Mountain	56 743
Yow	Stanislaus Emory	70 745
RIPEN		
James Van	San Francisco	4 681110
RIPER		
Henry	Siskiyou Scott Ri	69 81
William	Calaveras Twp 6	57 137
RIPETOE		
Joseph	Sonoma Santa Rosa	69 417
RIPETUE		
Isaac	Sonoma Santa Rosa	69 410
RIPLAY		
J Phillips	Butte Oregon	56 619
RIPLEY		
A B	Trinity Lewiston	70 963
Aunice L	San Francisco San Francisco	9 681024
C J	Tuolumne Twp 1	71 248
C*	Tuolumne Twp 1	71 248
Calvin	Tuolumne Twp 1	71 254
Charles	Tuolumne Twp 1	71 480
Christopher	Yuba Marysville	72 897
David	Napa Napa	61 60
Francis L	Monterey Monterey	60 947
G C	El Dorado Mud Springs	58 996
H W	Sacramento Ward 1	63 88
Henry	Sacramento Ward 1	63 93
J	Shasta Cottonwood	66 724
J M	Sacramento Ward 3	63 425
J Phillips	Butte Oregon	56 619
Joseph	Humbolt Table Bl	59 141
M M	Butte Kimshaw	56 595
Richd	Trinity Minersville	70 968
S H	Tuolumne Twp 1	71 254
Samuel	El Dorado Cold Spring	581099
William	El Dorado Kelsey	581126
Wm	San Francisco San Francisco	1 68 905
RIPLIS		
Charles	El Dorado Placerville	58 931
RIPLY		
V	Tuolumne Big Oak	71 152
RIPON		
Wm	San Francisco San Francisco	10 265 67
RIPOND		
Wm A*	Calaveras Twp 9	57 371
RIPP		
Henry	Yuba Marysville	72 944
RIPPEN		
Andrew	Mendocino Round Va	60 879
RIPPER		
Chas W	Del Norte Crescent	58 640

Name	County Locale	M653 RollPage
RIPPER		
H*	San Francisco San Francisco 5	67 519
RIPPERDAM		
Henry	Tuolumne Twp 1	71 267
Isaac	Tuolumne Sonora	71 481
RIPPERDAN		
James*	Stanislaus Empire	70 729
RIPPERSAM		
James*	Stanislaus Empire	70 729
RIPPERTON		
Joel	San Joaquin Castoria	64 879
RIPPEY		
G C	Solano Vacaville	69 320
James	El Dorado Indian D	581158
Robert	San Francisco San Francisco 9	681098
RIPPINBURY		
Wm	Butte Bidwell	56 716
RIPPINS		
S E	Sonoma Bodega	69 531
RIPPLE		
Jeremiah	San Francisco San Francisco 7	681328
L	Calaveras Twp 9	57 416
W	Stanislaus Empire	70 735
RIPPON		
Jno*	Sacramento Ward 3	63 477
Samuel*	Sacramento Ward 3	63 478
Wm	San Francisco San Francisco 10	265 67
RIPSEY		
---	Butte Bidwell	56 717
Ah	Butte Bidwell	56 717
RIPSON		
C	Siskiyou Klamath	69 91
J A	Siskiyou Klamath	69 91
W E	El Dorado Mud Springs	58 984
RIPSTEIN		
John	Trinity E Weaver	701061
RIPTOE		
Wm	Amador Twp 2	55 297
RIQUERMES		
Juan J	Los Angeles Los Angeles	59 393
RIQUIGE		
Nicholas*	Santa Cruz Pajaro	66 542
RIRARO		
Jose M	Monterey Alisal	601031
RIRCRYDER		
Jos	San Francisco San Francisco 5	67 479
RIRDON		
John N*	San Francisco San Francisco 9	681034
RIRERA		
Miguel*	Alameda Brooklyn	55 93
RIRET		
Israel*	Alameda Oakland	55 43
RIRHSTER		
John*	San Francisco San Francisco 3	67 87
RIRITT		
Philip*	San Joaquin O'Neal	641003
RIRK		
Isaac	Butte Eureka	56 654
RIRKER		
George	San Joaquin Elliott	64 945
RIRLEY		
Ricard*	Santa Cruz Santa Cruz	66 604
RIRNAN		
Bernard	Butte Bidwell	56 716
RIRSON		
James	San Francisco San Francisco 2	67 584
RIRY		
---	Amador Twp 2	55 294
RIRYER		
Christopher	San Francisco San Francisco 3	67 44
	San Francisco	
RIS		
Augustus	San Francisco San Francisco 9	68 973
RISBY		
E	Butte Chico	56 561
Miss	Napa Hot Springs	61 21
RISCT		
Israel*	Alameda Oakland	55 43
RISDON		
Jelin	Santa Cruz Pajaro	66 560
RISE		
---*	El Dorado Georgetown	58 746
John	El Dorado Georgetown	58 750
John*	El Dorado Georgetown	58 746
John*	El Dorado Georgetown	58 750
Lewis	Solano Benecia	69 317
M	San Francisco San Francisco 5	67 552
RISEMAY		
Fred	Tuolumne Twp 2	71 380
RISEN		
Frances	El Dorado Mud Springs	58 963
Joseph T	Sierra Chappare	661040
RISENCRANTS		
Harry*	Mariposa Twp 3	60 621
RISENCRONTZ		
Harris	Mariposa Twp 3	60 621

Name	County Locale	M653 RollPage
RISER		
Benj	Tehama Lassen	70 877
J W	Solano Montezuma	69 375
John J	Alameda Brooklyn	55 187
RISH		
Rodolph	Santa Clara San Jose	65 281
Wm*	San Francisco San Francisco 1	68 872
RISHBERGER		
Henry	Tuolumne Twp 1	71 268
RISHLUNDRA		
---*	San Bernardino S Timate	64 752
RISHNER		
H*	El Dorado Eldorado	58 938
RISHNES		
H*	El Dorado Eldorado	58 938
RISIN		
Richd	Los Angeles Tejon To	59 535
RISING		
D B*	San Francisco San Francisco 12	393 67
Laurence	Butte Mountain	56 741
Richard	Sierra Downieville	66 955
RISK		
Alfred	San Francisco San Francisco 8	681296
Catharin N*	San Francisco San Francisco 8	681296
	San Francisco	
Emily E	San Francisco San Francisco 8	681296
RISLER		
Thomas C	Humbolt Pacific	59 132
RISLEY		
D A	Tuolumne Twp 4	71 171
H	Napa Hot Springs	61 5
Harriet M	Yuba Marysville	72 975
J B	Napa Hot Springs	61 23
Mary E	Napa Hot Springs	61 6
RISMONDE		
Louis*	San Francisco San Francisco 3	67 50
RISPINE		
C	Sacramento Ward 1	63 149
RISR		
Jesus	Calaveras Twp 6	57 124
RISS		
---*	San Francisco San Francisco 2	67 669
RISSELL		
Calven	Santa Clara Santa Clara	65 471
RISSIFNGER		
Henry	Yuba Marysville	72 958
RISSINGER		
Henry	Yuba Marysville	72 958
RISSNONDE		
Lowis	San Francisco San Francisco 3	67 50
RISSO		
Robert*	San Francisco San Francisco 3	67 44
RISSON		
J A*	Siskiyou Klamath	69 91
Jno*	Sacramento Ward 3	63 477
Samuel*	Sacramento Ward 3	63 478
W R	El Dorado Newtown	58 779
RISSPER		
H*	San Francisco San Francisco 5	67 519
RIST		
Wm	Sacramento Ward 4	63 500
RISTE		
Benjamin	Tuolumne Twp 3	71 429
J H	Tuolumne Jamestown	71 429
J H	Tuolumne Twp 3	71 429
RISTER		
John	Butte Cascade	56 703
RISTINE		
John	Yolo Washington	72 572
Wm	Sacramento Ward 1	63 154
RISTLER		
John J	Stanislaus Emory	70 737
RISTON		
E R	Sacramento Dry Crk	63 372
Ransom	Sacramento Dry Crk	63 372
S E	Sacramento Dry Crk	63 372
RISTOVIO		
Tubusia	Los Angeles Los Angeles	59 513
RISUT		
John*	Shasta French G	66 719
RIT		
---	Amador Twp 2	55 311
---*	El Dorado Casumnes	581160
Benjamin*	Yuba New York	72 735
RITA		
---	Los Angeles San Gabriel	59 414
---	San Bernardino San Bernardino	64 679
---	San Bernardino S Timate	64 692
---	San Bernardino S Timate	64 711
---	San Bernardino S Timate	64 716
---	San Bernardino S Timate	64 717
---	San Bernardino S Timate	64 723
---	San Bernardino S Timate	64 739
---	San Bernardino S Timate	64 743
---	San Bernardino S Timate	64 754

Name	County Locale	M653 RollPage
RITA		
---	San Diego Agua Caliente	64 843
RITCH		
H H	Nevada Bridgeport	61 476
John*	Sacramento San Joaquin	63 368
Peter	Butte Chico	56 560
RITCHARD		
Chas	Nevada Bridgeport	61 502
RITCHARDS		
Chas	Nevada Bridgeport	61 502
Joseph	San Mateo Twp 3	65 107
RITCHARDSON		
Foswill	Tulara Twp 3	71 61
Roswell	Tulara Keyesville	71 61
RITCHE		
J B	San Joaquin Stockton	641093
Mary	Nevada Bridgeport	61 479
RITCHEL		
Peter	Yolo Putah	72 598
Samuel	Sierra La Porte	66 784
RITCHEN		
C	Tehama Red Bluff	70 899
RITCHENS		
J	Calaveras Twp 9	57 395
RITCHER		
Geo	El Dorado Georgetown	58 673
George A	El Dorado Georgetown	58 674
James	San Francisco San Francisco 7	681399
Peter	Butte Chico	56 560
RITCHERSON		
Edward	San Mateo Twp 1	65 65
Jacob	San Mateo Twp 1	65 62
RITCHERY		
Henry*	Yolo Putah	72 550
RITCHEY		
Henry	Yolo Putah	72 550
Hiram D	Napa Yount	61 39
Isaac	Napa Hot Springs	61 12
Jas	San Francisco San Francisco 10	276 67
Jos	San Francisco San Francisco 10	276 67
Silas	Napa Yount	61 39
Williamson	Yuba Bear Rvr	72 996
Wm	El Dorado Placerville	58 878
RITCHI		
Bery	Stanislaus Branch	70 703
Mary*	Nevada Bridgeport	61 479
RITCHIE		
Abbie	San Francisco San Francisco 9	681079
Anthony C	Fresno Twp 3	59 37
Archy	Santa Clara Gilroy	65 249
Crawford	Placer Auburn	62 586
David	Plumas Quincy	621006
Franklin	Placer Auburn	62 582
Frederick	San Francisco San Francisco 11	133 67
Geo	El Dorado Georgetown	58 673
George	Plumas Quincy	621004
George	Plumas Meadow Valley	62 900
George A	El Dorado Georgetown	58 674
James	Yuba New York	72 747
Jane	San Diego San Diego	64 760
Jas	Placer Rattle Snake	62 600
Jeff	Yolo Slate Ra	72 693
Jeff	Yuba Slate Ro	72 693
Jno	Mendocino Big Rvr	60 850
John	Plumas Quincy	62 922
John	Plumas Quincy	62 942
Jos H	Amador Twp 2	55 300
M H	San Francisco San Francisco 10	243 67
Robt	Butte Ophir	56 780
Robt	Sierra Monte Crk	661038
Samuel	Sierra La Porte	66 784
Vital C	San Diego Temecula	64 792
W C	Amador Twp 2	55 297
William	San Francisco San Francisco 7	681403
William	Siskiyou Yreka	69 144
RITCHINS		
Alexander	Yuba Suida	72 995
RITCHISON		
Thos	Nevada Bloomfield	61 510
RITCHOY		
Henry*	Yolo Putah	72 550
RITE		
Mon	Butte Cascade	56 699
RITER		
C	Siskiyou Klamath	69 96
O*	Siskiyou Klamath	69 96
RITH		
James	Santa Clara San Jose	65 290
RITHERS		
William	Siskiyou Cottonwoood	69 98
RITHIL		

California 1860 Census Index

Name	County Locale	M653 Roll	Page
RITHIL			
M H	San Francisco San Francisco	10	243
		67	
RITHURMAND			
W F*	El Dorado Salmon Falls	58	1035
RITIAS			
Maria J	Los Angeles Los Angeles	59	496
RITJER			
L	El Dorado Newtown	58	781
RITLY			
Jas A	San Bernardino San Bernadino	64	628
RITMER			
J A*	Sacramento Georgian	63	341
RITNER			
J A*	Sacramento Georgian	63	341
J P	Klamath S Fork	59	199
M M	Tuolumne Twp 2	71	283
RITOUP			
Hans Peter	Del Norte Crescent	58	637
RITRE			
John	Nevada Bloomfield	61	507
RITSON			
Edwd	San Francisco San Francisco	10	268
		67	
RITT			
Barbary	Sacramento Sutter	63	298
J	Nevada Nevada	61	271
Philip N	Sacramento Sutter	63	296
RITTAN			
John	Napa Clear Lake	61	141
RITTBERG			
Julius	San Joaquin Oneal	64	913
RITTDE			
Christophr*	Yuba Long Bar	72	751
RITTELE			
Christopher*	Yuba Long Bar	72	751
Christophr*	Yuba Long Bar	72	751
RITTER			
C M	Trinity Grass Valley	70	962
Charles	Siskiyou Yreka	69	184
F	El Dorado Big Bar	58	744
F S*	Nevada Red Dog	61	546
J S	Sacramento San Joaquin	63	362
Jacob	Fresno Twp 3	59	9
John*	Sonoma Petaluma	69	554
Mons L E	Calaveras Twp 7	57	1
P	El Dorado Placerville	58	880
Thos	Sacramento Ward 3	63	486
Wm	Amador Twp 5	55	358
RITTGER			
John	Tehama Pasakent	70	857
RITTLE			
Virginia*	Yolo No E Twp	72	674
RITTON			
John*	El Dorado Placerville	58	933
RITTS			
George	Yuba Long Bar	72	743
RITUARES			
Agapito	Los Angeles Los Angeles	59	326
RITY			
Charles	Yolo Washington	72	570
Chas	Sacramento San Joaquin	63	350
L	El Dorado Diamond	58	811
RITZ			
Charles	Yolo Washington	72	570
Peter	El Dorado Georgetown	58	759
RITZEWOLLER			
S	Tuolumne Twp 1	71	230
RITZGERALD			
John	Los Angeles Los Angeles	59	390
RITZGERALDS			
Patrick	Calaveras Twp 10	57	282
RITZLOFF			
William	Calaveras Twp 4	57	308
RIUG			
Maria*	Santa Cruz Santa Cruz	66	608
Mary F*	Nevada Red Dog	61	546
RIURE			
Frank*	Sacramento Ward 1	63	13
RIUS			
N	Merced Twp 1	60	900
Saliormna*	S Buenav	64	216
	San Bernardino		
Sameormna*	S Buenav	64	216
	San Bernardino		
RIUSS			
Joshua R	Yuba Marysville	72	929
RIUZ			
Dionicio	Monterey Monterey	60	948
RIVAL			
Abraham*	Colusa Monroeville	57	454
Augustus	Calaveras Twp 10	57	264
RIVALGS			
Chico	Calaveras Twp 5	57	198
RIVALYO			
Chico	Calaveras Twp 5	57	198

Name	County Locale	M653 Roll	Page
RIVARD			
Ed	Sacramento Ward 4	63	555
RIVARDS			
Louis	Plumas Meadow Valley	62	913
RIVAS			
Amago	Tuolumne Twp 3	71	468
Benja F	Calaveras Twp 10	57	279
Dolores	Merced Twp 1	60	900
Feliz	Yuba Marysville	72	945
Manuel	San Francisco San Francisco 9	68	1101
Manuel	San Francisco San Francisco 3	67	77
R	Merced Twp 1	60	902
Rafaele	San Francisco San Francisco 11		127
		67	
Ramon	San Diego S Luis R	64	777
Ramon	San Diego Temecula	64	792
William	San Francisco San Francisco 3	67	81
RIVE			
Catharine	Nevada Bridgeport	61	441
George	Nevada Bridgeport	61	448
RIVEAN			
----*	Tulara Visalia	71	40
RIVEAU			
---	Tulara Twp 2	71	40
RIVEIO			
Sacramento*	Sierra La Porte	66	778
RIVELES			
George	Marin Cortemad	60	785
RIVENS			
Peter	San Francisco San Francisco 9	68	1069
RIVER			
Delourus	Mariposa Twp 1	60	655
Franklin E	San Francisco San Francisco 4	68	1119
James	Solano Fremont	69	384
John B	Calaveras Twp 5	57	197
RIVERA			
Bes*	Mariposa Coulterville	60	688
Cherino	Marin Cortemad	60	779
E D	San Francisco San Francisco 5	67	478
Estanislans*	San Francisco 2	67	593
F	San Francisco		
Estanislaus	San Francisco 2	67	593
F	San Francisco		
Fernando	Los Angeles Los Angeles	59	311
Francisco	Marin Cortemad	60	779
Franco	Los Angeles Tejon	59	536
Jesus	Los Angeles Los Angeles	59	301
Jose J	Los Angeles Los Angeles	59	489
Juan	Mariposa Twp 3	60	595
Miguel*	Alameda Brooklyn	55	93
Ramon	Los Angeles Los Angeles	59	393
Sonisa*	Calaveras Twp 5	57	214
RIVERAS			
Ramon	Los Angeles Los Angeles	59	394
Ygnacia	Los Angeles Los Angeles	59	297
RIVERCOMB			
George*	Fresno Twp 3	59	7
RIVERCOMBS			
George*	Fresno Twp 3	59	7
RIVERDY			
E C	Mariposa Twp 1	60	663
RIVERE			
Irving	San Francisco San Francisco 4	68	1123
Jerratus	Yuba Marysville	72	914
RIVERES			
Dolores	Los Angeles Los Angeles	59	338
RIVEREZ			
Jesus	Yuba Marysville	72	860
Jesus*	Yuba Marysville	72	858
RIVERI			
Augusti	Tuolumne Twp 1	71	245
RIVERIA			
Remegio	Santa Clara Gilroy	65	224
RIVERIE			
Ben	Mariposa Coulterville	60	688
Ber*	Mariposa Coulterville	60	688
Bes*	Mariposa Coulterville	60	688
RIVERNS			
Jesus*	Calaveras Twp 6	57	188
RIVERO			
Jose	San Bernardino San Bernadino	64	615
Juan J	Los Angeles Tejon	59	521
Sacramento*	Sierra La Porte	66	778
RIVERRI			
Gormon	El Dorado Salmon Hills	58	1064
RIVERS			
Catharine	Tuolumne Twp 2	71	282
Charles	Tuolumne Twp 1	71	265
Chas	San Francisco San Francisco 1	68	905
Danl G	Tuolumne Jacksonville	71	515
David	Tuolumne Twp 5	71	515
Geo B	San Francisco San Francisco 9	68	1086
Jesus	Calaveras Twp 5	57	188
Jos	Trinity Texas Ba	70	981
Jose	San Bernardino San Bernadino	64	615
Jose	Santa Cruz Pajaro	66	542

Name	County Locale	M653 Roll	Page
RIVERS			
Louis	Fresno Twp 1	59	26
Lucindat	San Francisco San Francisco 11		155
		67	
Manuel	San Francisco San Francisco 1	68	831
Peter	San Francisco San Francisco 9	68	1069
Wm	Trinity E Weaver	70	1057
RIVERU			
Bes*	Mariposa Coulterville	60	688
RIVERUS			
Jesus	Calaveras Twp 5	57	188
RIVES			
Jose	Santa Cruz Pajaro	66	542
RIVETT			
Chas D	Sacramento Ward 1	63	50
RIVEY			
Joseph	Placer Rattle Snake	62	603
RIVIERE			
Edward	Sierra Port Win	66	795
Francisco	Los Angeles Los Angeles	59	353
Frank	Los Angeles Los Angeles	59	392
John	Amador Twp 2	55	299
Wancisco*	Los Angeles Los Angeles	59	353
RIVIERS			
Edward	Sierra Port Win	66	795
RIVIES			
Joseph	Calaveras Twp 4	57	330
RIVIN			
Augusti	Tuolumne Twp 1	71	245
RIVIS			
Burtin	Los Angeles Los Angeles	59	504
W H	Sacramento Ward 3	63	422
RIVIT			
Wiliam	Placer Todds Va	62	763
RIVOIS			
Juan	Solano Vacaville	69	361
RIVOLET			
Solomon	Amador Twp 1	55	488
RIVORIE			
Louisa	Calaveras Twp 5	57	214
RIVORO			
Juan J	Los Angeles Tejon	59	521
RIVORU			
Sruiso*	Calaveras Twp 5	57	214
RIVOS			
Benja F	Calaveras Twp 10	57	279
F	Solano Fremont	69	377
John	Calaveras Twp 5	57	221
Louisa	Solano Fremont	69	377
Luciana	Yuba Marysville	72	946
RIVUAL			
Jesus	Calaveras Twp 5	57	188
RIX			
A O	Alameda Brooklyn	55	176
Cecilia	San Francisco San Francisco 2	67	638
Edward	Alameda Brooklyn	55	185
Edward	San Francisco San Francisco 11		130
		67	
Hale	San Francisco San Francisco 7	68	1401
Ira O	Stanislaus Emory	70	743
J	Nevada Nevada	61	313
M	San Francisco San Francisco 5	67	552
Timothy	Alameda Brooklyn	55	185
RIXBY			
Alonzo	Nevada Bridgeport	61	483
RIXEN			
Clouse*	San Francisco San Francisco 3	67	70
RIXER			
Harriett*	Yolo Cache	72	608
Saml*	Yolo Cache	72	607
RIXFORD			
E A	Sonoma Petaluma	69	591
RIXON			
Harriett*	Yolo Cache	72	608
RIXTER			
Gustar	San Francisco San Francisco 2	67	565
Gustav	San Francisco San Francisco 2	67	565
RIYIS			
B*	Calaveras Twp 9	57	410
RIYNOLDS			
Wm P*	Los Angeles Los Angeles	59	510
RIYOLLI			
Joseph	Calaveras Twp 5	57	226
RIZER			
W	Shasta Millvill	66	751
RLANCE			
James*	Yuba Marysville	72	905
RLIDSON			
Saml	Tuolumne Twp 1	71	484
RLIRA			
---*	Mariposa Twp 3	60	613
RLO			
---*	Calaveras Twp 5	57	232
RLYMATE			
J*	Nevada Washington	61	332
RNBERG			
T	El Dorado Diamond	58	763

Name	County Locale	M653 Roll	Page
RNI			
Ah	Calaveras Twp 7	57	16
RNIS			
Manuela*	Yuba Marysville	72	951
RNOCH			
L*	Nevada Nevada	61	254
RNYAN			
H L	Sonoma Russian	69	435
RO			
---	San Francisco San Francisco 4	68	1176
Fan	San Francisco San Francisco 4	68	1156
Fju	San Francisco San Francisco 4	68	1156
Low	San Francisco San Francisco 4	68	1174
Yoke	Butte Ophir	56	814
Yoke	Butte Ophir	56	818
RO??			
Jacob*	Siskiyou Callahan	69	17
ROA			
Wederic W	Los Angeles Los Angeles	59	333
ROABLE			
Perez*	Calaveras Twp 6	57	138
ROACH			
A	Sacramento Brighton	63	209
A	Tuolumne Twp 4	71	159
Adaline	Alameda Oakland	55	65
Alen	Mariposa Twp 3	60	587
Alex	Mariposa Twp 3	60	587
Amos	Sacramento Ward 4	63	516
Anna	Sacramento Ward 1	63	137
C F	Sacramento Ward 1	63	103
C T	Sacramento Ward 1	63	103
Cathe	San Francisco San Francisco 9	68	972
Cathl	San Francisco San Francisco 9	68	972
Chas	San Francisco San Francisco 1	68	890
D*	Nevada Grass Valley	61	156
D*	San Francisco San Francisco 5	67	543
David	Contra Costa Twp 1	57	524
Dennis*	San Francisco San Francisco 9	68	941
Edmond	Siskiyou Callahan	69	3
Edmond	Siskiyou Callahan	69	4
Edward	Placer Michigan	62	831
Edward	San Joaquin Douglass	64	925
Ellen	San Francisco San Francisco 4	68	1159
Eve	San Francisco San Francisco 7	68	1362
F	San Francisco San Francisco 6	67	446
Frederick	San Bernadino	64	625
	San Bernardino		
Garet*	Placer Iona Hills	62	877
Geo	San Joaquin Stockton	64	1050
Hannah	San Francisco San Francisco 2	67	653
Hannah	San Francisco San Francisco 9	68	991
J	Nevada Grass Valley	61	165
J	Nevada Grass Valley	61	206
J	Siskiyou Scott Ri	69	81
J	Sutter Nicolaus	70	841
J B	Siskiyou Cottonwood	69	102
J H	Shasta Shasta	66	671
James	Nevada Bridgeport	61	501
James	San Francisco San Francisco 9	68	958
James	Sierra Poker Flats	66	840
Jno F	Sacramento Ward 3	63	482
John	Calaveras Twp 5	57	197
John	Mariposa Twp 3	60	566
John	San Francisco San Francisco 9	68	1102
John	San Francisco San Francisco 11	67	131
John	San Francisco San Francisco 10	67	342
John	San Francisco San Francisco 2	67	575
John	Shasta Horsetown	66	700
John	Tuolumne Twp 2	71	273
John	Tuolumne Twp 4	71	460
John*	Shasta Horsetown	66	700
L	Nevada Grass Valley	61	174
L R	Sacramento Cosumnes	63	391
Lawrence	San Francisco San Francisco 10	67	324
Lawrence	Yuba Marysville	72	970
M	Nevada Grass Valley	61	219
M	Nevada Washington	61	333
M	San Francisco San Francisco 1	68	921
M	Shasta Millvill	66	752
M J	Sacramento Ward 3	63	430
M*	Nevada Grass Valley	61	199
Margt	San Francisco San Francisco 2	67	637
Mary	San Francisco San Francisco 3	67	28
Mary	San Francisco San Francisco 3	67	582
Mary A	San Francisco San Francisco 2	67	693
Michael	Calaveras Twp 5	57	195
Michael	San Bernardino San Bernadino	64	636
Michael	San Joaquin Oneal	64	929
Michael	Siskiyou Scott Va	69	59
Michael	Yolo Merritt	72	577
Michael*	Calaveras Twp 5	57	195
Michl	San Francisco San Francisco 9	68	1070
Morris	San Francisco San Francisco 3	67	47

Name	County Locale	M653 Roll	Page
ROACH			
P	Sacramento Cosumnes	63	383
Pat	Nevada Little Y	61	534
Patricia*	Sacramento Ward 4	63	571
Patrick	Alameda Oakland	55	66
Patrick	Mendocino Ukiah	60	805
Philip	San Joaquin Douglass	64	918
Phillip	Santa Clara San Jose	65	362
Phillip A	San Francisco San Francisco 2	67	584
Richael	Yolo Merritt	72	577
Sawrena	Yuba Marysville	72	970
T	Nevada Grass Valley	61	187
T P	Butte Oregon	56	618
Thoas	Sacramento Natonia	63	278
Thomas	Sierra Poker Flats	66	840
Thos	Nevada Bridgeport	61	501
Thos	Sacramento Natonia	63	278
Tobias M	San Francisco San Francisco 7	68	1420
W	Nevada Grass Valley	61	156
W	Sacramento Brighton	63	194
W	Shasta Millvill	66	752
W*	Nevada Grass Valley	61	156
William	Santa Cruz Pajaro	66	541
Wm C	San Francisco San Francisco 1	68	840
ROACK			
Ed*	Nevada Red Dog	61	546
Mark	Calaveras Twp 9	57	387
ROACKLER			
Jacob	Siskiyou Yreka	69	140
ROACT			
M*	Nevada Grass Valley	61	199
ROAD			
E	Sonoma Washington	69	672
Saml	Sierra Grizzly	66	1057
ROADES			
G	Nevada Grass Valley	61	167
ROADFIELD			
J H	El Dorado Coloma	58	1104
ROADHAMEL			
W	Shasta Shasta	66	666
ROADHOME			
Joseph*	Monterey Pajaro	60	1022
ROADHORESE			
Joseph*	Monterey Pajaro	60	1022
ROADHORUE			
Joseph*	Monterey Pajaro	60	1022
ROADHOUSE			
Joseph	Monterey Pajaro	60	1022
ROADS			
Alonzo	Calaveras Twp 9	57	366
John	Humbolt Eureka	59	177
ROAFLE			
Perez*	Calaveras Twp 6	57	138
ROAGAN			
Patk	San Francisco San Francisco 12	67	382
ROAK			
M J	Nevada Rough &	61	404
Washington*	Yuba Marysville	72	865
Wm J*	Nevada Rough &	61	404
ROAKA			
John	Yuba Bear Rvr	72	1009
ROAKE			
Morgan	Tuolumne Columbia	71	361
Timothy T	San Francisco 1	68	874
	San Francisco		
ROAKEY			
Jacob*	Nevada Red Dog	61	538
ROAKS			
Chas	Butte Chico	56	562
ROALFE			
Wm	San Francisco San Francisco 10	67	247
ROAN			
Charles	San Mateo Twp 3	65	95
Jno	Sonoma Sonoma	69	659
P H	El Dorado White Oaks	58	1002
T	Nevada Grass Valley	61	166
ROANE			
James	Mariposa Twp 3	60	566
ROANVILLE			
Louis*	San Mateo Twp 1	65	63
ROAR			
J	Siskiyou Cottonwood	69	98
ROARCK			
J	Napa Hot Springs	61	6
ROARK			
D W	Mariposa Twp 3	60	546
J W	Mariposa Twp 3	60	546
James	Nevada Rough &	61	403
P H	Sacramento Alabama	63	414
ROARKE			
Michael*	San Francisco San Francisco 3	67	22
ROAS			
K*	Siskiyou Cottonwoood	69	98
ROASTER			
Peter	Placer Auburn	62	593

Name	County Locale	M653 Roll	Page
ROAYO			
Jaim*	Mariposa Twp 3	60	545
ROB			
David	Butte Bidwell	56	721
H	San Joaquin Stockton	64	1039
ROBAL			
---*	Placer Auburn	62	576
ROBARDS			
Fletcher	Santa Clara Fremont	65	433
J B	Tuolumne Twp 2	71	286
ROBASCO			
John	Mariposa Twp 3	60	599
ROBASON			
William	Tuolumne Twp 5	71	487
ROBAT			
---*	Placer Auburn	62	576
ROBB			
A	San Francisco San Francisco 5	67	513
F M	Sierra Downieville	66	1002
Henry	Nevada Red Dog	61	547
J S	Mariposa Twp 3	60	565
John	Santa Clara San Jose	65	284
John	Santa Cruz Soguel	66	579
John W	Nevada Bloomfield	61	512
Mary	Yolo Cottonwoood	72	649
Saml	San Francisco San Francisco 10	67	173
U T*	Amador Twp 7	55	420
W	San Francisco San Francisco 9	68	1071
W T	Sacramento Sutter	63	302
William	San Joaquin Stockton	64	1052
ROBBARDS			
John E	Santa Clara San Jose	65	367
ROBBE			
C	Nevada Grass Valley	61	185
ROBBENSON			
Stickney	Mariposa Twp 1	60	663
ROBBERSON			
Alexander	Napa Hot Springs	61	20
Stickney	Mariposa Twp 1	60	663
ROBBERTS			
E	Tuolumne Twp 4	71	176
Edwin	Santa Cruz Pajaro	66	577
Geo	Amador Twp 5	55	349
Hank	El Dorado Big Bar	58	742
M	Napa Yount	61	32
S W	El Dorado Greenwood	58	726
W	Tuolumne Twp 4	71	176
ROBBET			
Charles*	Calaveras Twp 5	57	227
ROBBETS			
Wm M	Nevada Nevada	61	239
ROBBIN			
Enrib	Sonoma Sonoma	69	639
Isaac	Amador Twp 2	55	321
ROBBINETT			
M	El Dorado Georgetown	58	685
Signett	El Dorado Georgetown	58	685
ROBBINS			
A	Nevada Nevada	61	277
A	Tuolumne Twp 1	71	265
A D	Sacramento Ward 4	63	595
Alfred	San Francisco San Francisco 9	68	1050
Benj	Siskiyou Scott Va	69	22
C E	Siskiyou Cottonwoood	69	109
C F	San Francisco San Francisco 6	67	456
C H	Butte Chico	56	549
Chareles B*	Sierra Gibsonville	66	856
Charles	Contra Costa Twp 3	57	596
Charles B	Sierra Gibsonville	66	856
D B	Siskiyou Scott Va	69	39
D M	Nevada Nevada	61	241
D S	Siskiyou Scott Va	69	39
Daniel P	San Joaquin Elkhorn	64	980
E	San Bernardino San Bernadino	64	619
E Camillo	Santa Barbara	64	148
	San Bernardino		
Ebenezer	Butte Oregon	56	611
Edgar	Solano Benecia	69	294
Ezekiel	Nevada Rough &	61	423
Francis*	Siskiyou Shasta Rvr	69	111
G	Nevada Nevada	61	322
Griffin	Los Angeles Los Angeles	59	333
Henry	Nevada Red Dog	61	537
Henry	Nevada Red Dog	61	552
Henry	San Joaquin Stockton	64	1055
J	Tehama Tehama	70	948
James	Calaveras Twp 5	57	238
Jno	Alameda Brooklyn	55	192
Jno	Sacramento Ward 4	63	500
John	El Dorado Greenwood	58	726
John	El Dorado Georgetown	58	757
John	Trinity Indian C	70	988
Joseh	Sacramento Natonia	63	274
Joseph	Sacramento Natonia	63	274
L	Tuolumne Twp 2	71	410

Name	County Locale	M653 Roll	Page
ROBBINS			
Lawrence	Calaveras Twp 8	57	76
Lot R	Solano Benecia	69	293
Lot S	Solano Benecia	69	293
Lucinda	Amador Twp 2	55	316
M	Nevada Nevada	61	321
N	El Dorado Placerville	58	858
N W	Sacramento Ward 4	63	504
O	Siskiyou Cottonwoood	69	109
P	Sacramento Ward 3	63	477
Peter	Sacramento Ward 4	63	530
R W	Nevada Nevada	61	271
Rual	Solano Suisan	69	225
S B	Sacramento Ward 1	63	145
Saml	Nevada Nevada	61	261
Saml	Sacramento Sutter	63	306
Saml	Sacramento Sutter	63	307
Samuel P	El Dorado Greenwood	58	729
Siynitt	El Dorado Georgetown	58	685
Thomas	Calaveras Twp 8	57	75
Thomas	Santa Cruz Pescadero	66	651
Thos	Sacramento Ward 4	63	526
Thos	Stanislaus Emory	70	740
Thos J	Sonoma Vallejo	69	619
William	Plumas Quincy	62	993
William	Santa Cruz Pajaro	66	571
William B	Siskiyou Yreka	69	152
William J	San Francisco San Francisco 8	68	1255
Williams	Santa Cruz Pajaro	66	531
Wm	Sierra Downieville	66	1013
ROBBINSON			
Clayton	Calaveras Twp 7	57	27
Edward	El Dorado Georgetown	58	749
George	Siskiyou Shasta Rvr	69	114
George	Siskiyou Yreka	69	130
Henry	Calaveras Twp 8	57	77
Jacob	Placer Michigan	62	854
M	El Dorado Georgetown	58	751
Peter	Calaveras Twp 7	57	27
Thomas	Placer Forest H	62	805
ROBBISTI			
Edwin	Santa Cruz Pajaro	66	577
ROBBIT			
Charles	Calaveras Twp 5	57	227
ROBBITS			
Wm N	Nevada Nevada	61	239
ROBBS			
Juan	El Dorado Georgetown	58	705
ROBBT			
Charles	Calaveras Twp 5	57	227
ROBE			
John W	Yuba Bear Rvr	72	1003
Michael	Yolo Putah	72	551
William	San Francisco San Francisco 4	68	1121
ROBECK			
Az	Sierra Downieville	66	956
ROBECO			
F	Tuolumne Twp 4	71	169
ROBEEELY			
James	San Joaquin Stockton	64	1053
ROBEL			
John	Siskiyou Scott Va	69	36
William	Siskiyou Scott Va	69	36
ROBELETT			
Robt	San Francisco San Francisco 3	67	10
ROBELIS			
L	El Dorado Placerville	58	841
ROBELS			
S	San Joaquin Stockton	64	1099
ROBEN			
G	Shasta Shasta	66	676
ROBENO			
Franco	Marin Cortemad	60	787
ROBENSON			
Janl	Napa Napa	61	89
ROBER			
John	Yuba Marysville	72	908
ROBEROLT			
Leopold*	Amador Twp 4	55	237
ROBERON			
John	Sierra Downieville	66	1021
ROBERSON			
Andrew	San Joaquin Elkhorn	64	958
D	Shasta Cottonwoood	66	737
D	Tuolumne Shawsfla	71	385
George	Napa Clear Lake	61	132
J S*	Sonoma Petaluma	69	581
Jacob	Shasta Shasta	66	759
John	Mariposa Coulterville	60	684
John	Sierra Downieville	66	1021
Nancy	Sonoma Mendocino	69	451
R	Tuolumne Twp 1	71	267
Robert	Alameda Brooklyn	55	128
S	Sacramento Granite	63	241
Saml	Sonoma Mendocino	69	451
Thomas	San Francisco San Francisco 7	68	1430
ROBERSON			
W D	Shasta Shasta	66	734
Warren	San Joaquin Oneal	64	912
ROBERSTONE			
John	San Francisco San Francisco 1	68	836
ROBERSTOON			
G W	Yuba Rose Bar	72	797
ROBERT S			
Dennis	San Mateo Twp 3	65	103
ROBERT			
---	Del Norte Klamath	58	658
---	Mendocino Round Va	60	878
---	Mendocino Twp 1	60	889
---	Placer Dutch Fl	62	719
---	Placer Dutch Fl	62	731
---	San Francisco San Francisco 3	67	2
---	Tulara Twp 3	71	50
A	Shasta Shasta	66	673
Andrea*	Shasta Shasta	66	671
Andrew*	Shasta Shasta	66	671
Auguste	Yuba Foster B	72	834
Bastille*	Alameda Murray	55	223
Camill	Plumas Meadow Valley	62	934
Chas J	Amador Twp 6	55	447
D E	San Francisco San Francisco 5	67	515
D W	San Francisco San Francisco 2	67	796
E D	Tuolumne Twp 2	71	369
Feny	Santa Cruz Santa Cruz	66	633
Henry	Napa Napa	61	64
J C	Butte Oregon	56	619
James	Amador Twp 2	55	261
Lazar	Plumas Meadow Valley	62	931
Nelson	Yolo Putah	72	598
Reed*	Alameda Murray	55	223
Robert	Sierra Chappare	66	1041
T S	Monterey Monterey	60	927
ROBERTS			
Elijah	Los Angeles Tejon	59	536
Ellis	Yolo Slate Ra	72	701
Ellis	Yuba Slate Ro	72	701
F M	Butte Chico	56	560
F M	El Dorado Placerville	58	859
Francis M	Los Angeles Los Angeles	59	354
G	Klamath Orleans	59	217
G	Nevada Eureka	61	382
G	San Francisco San Francisco 10	67	216
G D	Sutter Bear Rvr	70	826
G D	Nevada Grass Valley	61	173
G G	San Francisco San Francisco 10	67	216
Geo	Amador Twp 6	55	426
Geo	Butte Hamilton	56	525
Geo	Mariposa Twp 4	60	650
Geo	San Francisco San Francisco 1	68	904
Geo 2	Butte Hamilton	56	525
George	Marin Cortemad	60	780
George	San Francisco San Francisco 11	67	111
George	Sierra Downieville	66	1020
George	Siskiyou Yreka	69	179
George	Tulara Keeneysburg	71	47
George	Yolo No E Twp	72	669
George	Yuba North Ea	72	669
George M	Contra Costa Twp 2	57	548
George W	San Francisco San Francisco 7	68	1362
Griffin	Yuba Slate Ro	72	701
Griffis	Yolo Slate Ra	72	701
Griffith	Nevada Bridgeport	61	469
Griffith	Yolo Slate Ra	72	701
Griffith	Yuba Slate Ro	72	701
H	Nevada Grass Valley	61	155
H H	Sonoma Sonoma	69	637
H M	Nevada Grass Valley	61	176
H Q	Nevada Rough &	61	422
H W	Placer Iona Hills	62	862
Hardin	Sonoma Russian	69	440
Harma*	Mariposa Twp 3	60	559
Harman	Mariposa Twp 3	60	559
Harmon	Mariposa Twp 3	60	559
Harrison	El Dorado Salmon Falls	58	1050
Hellen	Santa Cruz Santa Cruz	66	621
Henry	Nevada Rough &	61	412
Henry	Nevada Bloomfield	61	510
Henry	San Francisco San Francisco 9	68	1102
Henry	San Francisco San Francisco 2	67	603
Henry C	Los Angeles Azuza	59	274
Hiram	San Joaquin Oneal	64	929
Hugh	Nevada Bridgeport	61	487
I	Siskiyou Cottonwoood	69	102
Isaac	Calaveras Twp 10	57	282
Isabel D	Calaveras Twp 10	57	288
Isahl D*	Calaveras Twp 10	57	288
Isatel D*	Calaveras Twp 10	57	288
J	El Dorado Casumnes	58	1161
J	Nevada Grass Valley	61	151
ROBERTS			
J	Nevada Grass Valley	61	208
J	Siskiyou Cottonwoood	69	102
J	Siskiyou Scott Va	69	57
J E	El Dorado Casumnes	58	1176
J E	Sacramento Ward 4	63	523
J M	Butte Ophir	56	783
J S	Sonoma Bodega	69	528
J W	Sierra Downieville	66	961
J W	Sutter Nicolaus	70	841
Jackson	Nevada Bridgeport	61	447
Jacob	Alameda Brooklyn	55	154
James	Mendocino Little L	60	838
James	Plumas Quincy	62	990
James	Sacramento Ward 1	63	153
James	San Francisco San Francisco 11	67	109
James	San Francisco San Francisco 7	68	1380
James	San Francisco San Francisco 9	68	988
James	Sierra Scales D	66	801
James	Sonoma Santa Rosa	69	413
James	Tulara Visalia	71	99
James A	Tulara Twp 1	71	99
James M	Alameda Oakland	55	14
James R	Mendocino Little L	60	838
James W	Los Angeles Tejon	59	527
Jno M	Butte Chico	56	552
Jno T	Sacramento Ward 4	63	603
Johanun	Tuolumne Twp 1	71	198
John	Amador Twp 5	55	484
John	Calaveras Twp 5	57	149
John	Marin Cortemad	60	781
John	Monterey Pajaro	60	1023
John	Placer Michigan	62	819
John	Plumas Meadow Valley	62	934
John	San Bernardino San Salvador	64	642
John	San Francisco San Francisco 10	67	226
John	Santa Clara Burnett	65	256
John	Sierra La Porte	66	786
John	Sierra Poverty	66	799
John	Sierra Pine Grove	66	821
John	Sierra Cold Can	66	836
John	Siskiyou Scott Va	69	26
John	Siskiyou Scott Ri	69	72
John	Siskiyou Scott Ri	69	82
John	Solano Suisan	69	221
John	Tulara Visalia	71	76
John	Tuolumne Twp 1	71	208
John	Tuolumne Twp 5	71	503
John	Tuolumne Twp 5	71	505
John	Yolo Slate Ra	72	702
John	Yuba Slate Ro	72	702
John F	San Francisco San Francisco 10	67	297
John J	Humbolt Bucksport	59	159
John M	Sonoma Vallejo	69	629
John R	Napa Yount	61	33
John W	San Francisco San Francisco 7	68	1341
John W	San Joaquin Castoria	64	879
Joseph	San Diego Colorado	64	808
Joseph	San Joaquin O'Neal	64	1003
Joseph	Santa Clara Almaden	65	276
Joseph	Santa Cruz Soguel	66	596
Joseph	Sierra St Louis	66	817
Joseph	Sonoma Santa Rosa	69	420
Joseph	Tulara Twp 3	71	57
Joseph D	San Mateo Twp 2	65	125
Josiah	Shasta Horsetown	66	708
L A	Merced Twp 1	60	908
Lewis	Marin Bolinas	60	746
M	Sacramento Ward 4	63	500
Margaret	San Francisco San Francisco 4	68	1170
Margeret	San Francisco San Francisco 4	68	1170
Maria E	San Luis Obispo San Luis Obispo	65	26
Mary	Calaveras Twp 5	57	247
Mary	Placer Michigan	62	815
Mary	Sonoma Santa Rosa	69	394
Matilda	Sacramento Ward 1	63	104
Michael	Tulara Twp 3	71	59
N M	San Francisco San Francisco 5	67	504
N P	Yuba Rose Bar	72	802
N S	Butte Cascade	56	690
Nelson	Solano Fremont	69	376
Owen	Tulara Twp 1	71	100
P	Nevada Grass Valley	61	146
Parlaski	El Dorado Big Bar	58	739
Patrick	El Dorado Big Bar	58	739
R B	Mariposa Twp 3	60	559
R P	Siskiyou Cottonwoood	69	103
R T	Nevada Bridgeport	61	444
R T	Solano Vallejo	69	252
Rich	Sacramento Ward 4	63	523
Richard	Los Angeles Santa Ana	59	441
Richard	San Francisco San Francisco 11	67	136

California 1860 Census Index

Name	County Locale	M653 Roll	Page
ROBERTS			
Richard	Santa Cruz Pajaro	66	564
Rob R	Humbolt Mattole	59	126
Robert	Calaveras Twp 10	57	277
Robert	Humbolt Pacific	59	137
Robert	Sierra Excelsior	66	1033
Robert	Tuolumne Sonora	71	244
Robert	Yolo Slate Ra	72	701
Robert	Yuba Slate Ro	72	701
Robt	Napa Napa	61	64
Robt	Shasta Horsetown	66	691
Robt	Solano Vacaville	69	342
S	Nevada Grass Valley	61	198
S	Siskiyou Scott Va	69	27
S	Sutter Nicolaus	70	835
S A	San Joaquin Stockton	64	1011
S J	El Dorado Casumnes	58	1176
S*	El Dorado Casumnes	58	1161
Samuel	El Dorado Placerville	58	916
Sarah	San Joaquin Stockton	64	1090
Stephen	Fresno Twp 1	59	76
Stephen	San Francisco San Francisco 7	68	1490
T*	El Dorado Casumnes	58	1161
Thomas	Plumas Quincy	62	1000
Thomas	San Francisco San Francisco 3	67	68
Thomas	Solano Suisan	69	207
Thomas J	Humbolt Mattole	59	123
Thos	Butte Kimshaw	56	574
Thos	Sacramento Franklin	63	325
Thos	San Bernardino San Bernadino	64	641
Thos	San Francisco San Francisco 9	68	966
Thos	San Joaquin Elkhorn	64	998
Thos	Santa Clara Almaden	65	275
Thos R	Sacramento Ward 1	63	149
Thos R*	Nevada Bridgeport	61	495
Tom	Sacramento Ward 1	63	110
V B	Sacramento Ward 4	63	597
W	Calaveras Twp 9	57	408
W	El Dorado Placerville	58	833
W	El Dorado Placerville	58	860
W	San Joaquin Stockton	64	1062
W	Siskiyou Scott Ri	69	72
W	Tehama Lassen	70	880
W G	Mariposa Twp 3	60	572
W G	Trinity Mouth Ca	70	1013
W H	Amador Twp 7	55	419
W H	Sierra Twp 7	66	886
W J	Mendocino Calpella	60	821
W P	Calaveras Twp 9	57	405
W T	Mendocino Calpella	60	821
W W	Sierra Twp 7	66	886
William	Alameda Brooklyn	55	147
William	Calaveras Twp 5	57	246
William	El Dorado Coloma	58	1103
William	El Dorado Mud Springs	58	966
William	Monterey Pajaro	60	1023
William	Nevada Rough &	61	422
William	Nevada Bridgeport	61	470
William	Nevada Red Dog	61	557
William	Santa Cruz Santa Cruz	66	621
William	Sonoma Santa Rosa	69	413
William	Yuba Fosters	72	837
William	Yuba Fosters	72	838
William	Yuba Marysville	72	866
William M	Nevada Bridgeport	61	455
Wm	Amador Twp 1	55	510
Wm	Butte Kimshaw	56	572
Wm	Colusa Colusi	57	426
Wm	Colusa Monroeville	57	452
Wm	Humbolt Mattole	59	126
Wm	Humbolt Bucksport	59	159
Wm	Trinity Taylor'S	70	1036
Wm E	Placer Nicolaus	62	692
Wm G	Nevada Nevada	61	247
Wm H	Tuolumne Sonora	71	218
Wm M	Sonoma Santa Rosa	69	424
Wm W	Yolo Slate Ra	72	691
Wm W	Yuba Slate Ro	72	691
Y Houston	Yuba Marysville	72	865
ROBERTSEN			
Jas	Tehama Lassen	70	871
ROBERTSON			
A	Siskiyou Callahan	69	9
Alex	Sacramento Ward 1	63	24
Alexd	San Francisco San Francisco 7	68	1438
Anna M	San Francisco San Francisco 7	68	1409
C	Calaveras Twp 9	57	408
C O	San Francisco San Francisco 3	67	68
Chas	San Francisco San Francisco 3	67	70
D	Amador Twp 1	55	506
D M	San Francisco San Francisco 9	68	979
Elisha B	Calaveras Twp 6	57	154
Ellen	San Francisco San Francisco 4	68	1154
F	Sacramento Ward 4	63	528
F	San Francisco San Francisco 5	67	549
Geo	Sacramento Granite	63	233

Name	County Locale	M653 Roll	Page
ROBERTSON			
H	Shasta Shasta	66	673
Henry	Siskiyou Scott Va	69	29
Isabel	Sonoma Santa Rosa	69	414
Isabella	Amador Twp 1	55	506
Isarol	Tuolumne Twp 1	71	252
Israel	Tuolumne Twp 1	71	252
J	Calaveras Twp 9	57	379
J	Calaveras Twp 9	57	403
J	Mariposa Twp 3	60	557
J	Mariposa Twp 1	60	639
J	Tuolumne Twp 1	71	250
J W	Merced Twp 1	60	895
Jacob	San Francisco San Francisco 10	213	67
James	Sierra Twp 7	66	884
James	Siskiyou Yreka	69	174
James	Tuolumne Springfield	71	368
James	Yolo Slate Ra	72	694
James	Yuba Marysville	72	965
James W	Colusa Mansville	57	439
Jas	Merced Twp 1	60	899
Jas	Sacramento Granite	63	226
Jas	San Francisco San Francisco 10	189	67
John	Calaveras Twp 5	57	230
John	Mariposa Coulterville	60	694
John	Placer Michigan	62	855
John	San Francisco San Francisco 8	68	1268
John	San Francisco San Francisco 7	68	1352
John	Sierra La Porte	66	778
John	Siskiyou Yreka	69	179
Jonn	San Francisco San Francisco 7	68	1352
Jos	San Francisco San Francisco 10	189	67
Joseph	Santa Clara San Jose	65	372
L M	Tuolumne Twp 4	71	178
M	Calaveras Twp 9	57	389
M	Calaveras Twp 9	57	398
Margaret	Amador Twp 1	55	505
Martha	San Francisco San Francisco 7	68	1393
Mary A	San Francisco San Francisco 9	68	1007
Patrick	Tuolumne Shawsfla	71	379
Q	Colusa Mansville	57	439
R	San Francisco San Francisco 9	68	1059
R L	Sacramento Ward 3	63	459
Robert	Alameda Brooklyn	55	138
Robert	Calaveras Twp 7	57	311
Robert	Nevada Bridgeport	61	467
Robert	San Francisco San Francisco 7	68	1440
Robert	San Mateo Twp 1	65	70
Robrt	San Francisco San Francisco 1	68	855
Robt	Amador Twp 2	55	303
Robt	San Francisco San Francisco 9	68	988
S S	Sierra Twp 7	66	909
Saml	San Francisco San Francisco 1	68	865
Saml	Sonoma Vallejo	69	628
Stanly L	Tuolumne Knights	71	529
Thomas	Tulara Visalia	71	110
Thos	Alameda Brooklyn	55	107
W	El Dorado Kelsey	58	1156
W	Nevada Bloomfield	61	507
W D	Siskiyou Scott Va	69	61
W G	Mariposa Twp 3	60	572
W J	Sacramento Ward 4	63	504
William	San Joaquin Castoria	64	910
William	Solano Montezuma	69	368
Wm	Butte Oregon	56	638
Wm	Colusa Spring Valley	57	436
Wm	Sacramento Ward 1	63	8
ROBERTSS			
Thos	Stanislaus Oatvale	70	717
ROBERTY			
Johanem	Tuolumne Sonora	71	198
L A	Merced Twp 1	60	908
ROBERY			
Chs	Stanislaus Branch	70	707
ROBES			
Antonia	El Dorado White Oaks	58	1017
Edward	San Francisco San Francisco 1	68	815
ROBESON			
G*	Solano Vacaville	69	330
J*	Solano Vacaville	69	332
W	Solano Vacaville	69	329
ROBETARO			
Magil*	Tuolumne Columbia	71	295
ROBETH			
Louis	Yuba Marysville	72	939
ROBEY			
Benj	Tuolumne Sonora	71	241
F C	Butte Oregon	56	619
H L*	Sacramento Ward 1	63	45
H S	Sacramento Ward 1	63	45
ROBICE			
F	Tuolumne Jacksonville	71	169
ROBIDAUX			
Chouis*	San Bernardino San Bernadino	64	639

Name	County Locale	M653 Roll	Page
ROBIDAUX			
Clouis*	San Bernardino San Bernadino	64	639
Guadalupa G	San Salvador	64	640
	San Bernardino		
Louis	San Bernardino San Salvador	64	639
ROBIE			
L H	San Francisco San Francisco 2	67	736
ROBILLIAD			
Joseph	Alameda Oakland	55	43
ROBIN			
Barret	Solano Vacaville	69	355
Barrett	Solano Vacaville	69	355
Chas	Sacramento Ward 3	63	437
E	Tuolumne Big Oak	71	150
Edmund	Sacramento Ward 3	63	438
Eugene	Yuba Parks Ba	72	781
John	Calaveras Twp 4	57	325
R	Tuolumne Big Oak	71	147
ROBINES			
Moses*	Yuba Fosters	72	821
ROBINET			
Sam	Sacramento Ward 4	63	512
ROBINETT			
Ely	Napa Hot Springs	61	28
J C	Sutter Nicolaus	70	832
ROBINETTE			
Coleman	Amador Twp 3	55	377
ROBINGER			
Henry	Butte Ophir	56	772
ROBINNUTTE			
Ed F*	Butte Oregon	56	625
ROBINS			
Alden	Placer Iona Hills	62	894
Alexander B	Tulara Visalia	71	106
B	El Dorado Mountain	58	1187
B H	El Dorado Kelsey	58	1154
Charles H	Sacramento Ward 1	63	149
Charlotte	Sacramento Ward 1	63	149
Claude	San Joaquin Stockton	64	1069
E	Trinity Oregon G	70	1009
F	Del Norte Happy Ca	58	670
G B	Tuolumne Columbia	71	320
H C	Nevada Red Dog	61	547
Henry	Napa Napa	61	88
J	Nevada Grass Valley	61	158
John	San Francisco San Francisco 11	106	67
Josiah	Tuolumne Twp 2	71	313
L	Siskiyou Scott Ri	69	70
Moses	Yuba Foster B	72	821
Nathan	El Dorado Salmon Falls	58	1035
Sarah B	San Joaquin Elkhorn	64	977
Steph	Tehama Red Bluff	70	929
W W	Yuba New York	72	728
ROBINS??			
B H*	El Dorado Kelsey	58	1154
ROBINSEN			
Henry	Butte Wyandotte	56	663
John	Sacramento Granite	63	265
John*	San Francisco San Francisco 7	68	1431
Wm	Sacramento Natonia	63	276
ROBINSIN			
Jas S	Sacramento Natonia	63	282
John*	Sacramento Granite	63	265
ROBINSON			
---	Monterey Pajaro	60	1019
A	Nevada Nevada	61	323
A	Nevada Eureka	61	345
A	Sacramento Cosumnes	63	396
A	Sacramento Ward 3	63	426
A	San Francisco San Francisco 4	68	1231
A	Butte Oro	56	677
A E	Sacramento Ward 1	63	86
A F	Napa Napa	61	96
A J	El Dorado Union	58	1087
A J	El Dorado Coloma	58	1119
A S	El Dorado Union	58	1087
A Y	Nevada Bridgeport	61	496
Aaron	San Francisco San Francisco 10	260	67
Aaron W	Yuba Marysville	72	947
Albert W	Alameda Brooklyn	55	97
Aleck	Yolo Slate Ra	72	687
Aleck	Yuba North Ea	72	687
Alex	Del Norte Crescent	58	636
Alex	San Francisco San Francisco 12	383	67
Alex	Sierra Twp 7	66	901
Alexander	San Joaquin O'Neal	64	1005
Alexr	Sierra Twp 7	66	901
Anderson	El Dorado Placerville	58	912
Andrew	Plumas Meadow Valley	62	902
B	Butte Ophir	56	759
B	El Dorado White Oaks	58	1033
B	El Dorado Georgetown	58	704
B	Merced Twp 2	60	917

California 1860 Census Index

Name	County Locale	M653 RollPage
ROBINSON		
B H*	El Dorado Kelsey	581154
Bebe	Napa Napa	61 90
Benjamin	Tulara Twp 3	71 49
Benjamin	Tulara Twp 3	71 55
Bete*	Napa Napa	61 90
C G	Yolo Cottonwood	72 556
C J	Sonoma Petaluma	69 572
C M	El Dorado Coloma	581072
Charles	Humbolt Pacific	59 137
Charles	Humbolt Table Bl	59 140
Charles	Nevada Nevada	61 274
Charles	Sierra Downieville	661013
Chas	Butte Kimshaw	56 596
Chas	Calaveras Twp 9	57 361
Chas	El Dorado Georgetown	58 760
Chas	San Francisco San Francisco 1	68 895
Chas H	San Francisco San Francisco 1	68 895
Chas W	Placer Folsom	62 641
Chas W	Placer Virginia	62 678
Cyrus D	Mendocino Arrana	60 859
D G	San Francisco San Francisco 1	68 895
D Y	Nevada Bridgeport	61 496
Daniel	Placer Auburn	62 568
Daniel	Sacramento Ward 4	63 524
Daniel	Sierra La Porte	66 788
Daniel	Yolo Cottonwood	72 555
David	Amador Twp 3	55 388
David	El Dorado Mud Springs	58 997
David	San Diego Colorado	64 811
David	Yuba Marysville	72 927
David V	Tuolumne Twp 4	71 135
David V	Tuolumne Twp 5	71 489
Dorcas	San Francisco San Francisco 10	260 67
Dorcus	San Francisco San Francisco 2	67 628
Duncan	Plumas Quincy	62 917
E	Nevada Nevada	61 247
E	Santa Clara Santa Clara	65 507
E K	Yuba Rose Bar	72 791
E M	El Dorado Diamond	58 783
E R	Nevada Grass Valley	61 192
E R	Sacramento Lee	63 213
E*	Nevada Nevada	61 247
Ed	Butte Kimshaw	56 571
Ed	San Francisco San Francisco 9	681031
Edward	San Mateo Twp 1	65 57
Elijah	Sacramento Ward 1	63 15
Eliza	San Bernardino San Bernadino	64 636
Eliza	San Francisco San Francisco 11	133 67
Elizabeth	Contra Costa Twp 1	57 529
Ellen	Santa Cruz Santa Cruz	66 613
Ezekiel	Monterey Pajaro	601012
F	El Dorado Placerville	58 822
F H	San Francisco San Francisco 12	392 67
Frank	San Francisco San Francisco 4	681138
Frank D	Mendocino Anderson	60 870
Franklin	Calaveras Twp 5	57 184
Franklin C	Los Angeles Los Angeles	59 369
Frederick	Calaveras Twp 9	57 386
G	Mariposa Twp 3	60 567
G	Nevada Eureka	61 350
G	San Francisco San Francisco 9	681059
G H	Yuba Rose Bar	72 791
G N	Tuolumne Columbia	71 332
Geo	Amador Twp 2	55 278
Geo	Trinity North Fo	701024
Geo F	Trinity Weaverville	701051
Geo W	Butte Wyandotte	56 657
George	El Dorado Big Bar	58 742
George	Nevada Rough &	61 404
George	Plumas Quincy	62 983
George	Tuolumne Twp 5	71 508
George	Yuba Rose Bar	72 802
George	Yuba Rose Bar	72 814
George	Yuba Fosters	72 821
George	Yuba Fosters	72 825
George	Yuba Marysville	72 868
George F	Humbolt Pacific	59 137
George S	Monterey Pajaro	601021
Geroge	Tuolumne Montezuma	71 508
H	Santa Clara San Jose	65 349
H	Tehama Red Bluff	70 925
H C	Sierra Downieville	661011
H F	Tuolumne Twp 2	71 284
H L	San Joaquin Elkhorn	64 984
H O	San Francisco San Francisco 7	681341
H W	Tuolumne Twp 3	71 421
Hany*	Sierra Downieville	66 995
Harrison	Tulara Visalia	71 91
Hary	Sierra Downieville	66 995
Henry	Alameda Oakland	55 67
Henry	Amador Twp 4	55 241
Henry	Butte Wyandotte	56 663

Name	County Locale	M653 RollPage
ROBINSON		
Henry	El Dorado Mud Springs	58 967
Henry	Humbolt Eel Rvr	59 147
Henry	Plumas Quincy	62 954
Henry	San Francisco San Francisco 7	681382
Henry	San Francisco San Francisco 2	67 605
Henry	San Joaquin Elkhorn	64 962
Henry	Santa Clara Burnett	65 256
Henry	Santa Clara San Jose	65 386
Henry E	Sacramento Ward 1	63 17
Henry F	Placer Auburn	62 585
Henry*	Sierra Downieville	66 995
Hugh	Amador Twp 1	55 482
I	San Francisco San Francisco 3	67 21
I H	Calaveras Twp 9	57 400
I P	Amador Twp 3	55 305
Isaac	Calaveras Twp 7	57 10
Isabella	Humbolt Pacific	59 137
J	Amador Twp 3	55 369
J	El Dorado Kelsey	581149
J	El Dorado Indian D	581159
J	El Dorado Mountain	581186
J	Nevada Grass Valley	61 202
J	Nevada Grass Valley	61 208
J	Sacramento Granite	63 238
J	Sacramento Cosummes	63 397
J	Sacramento Ward 3	63 428
J	San Francisco San Francisco 4	681227
J	San Francisco San Francisco 5	67 512
J	San Francisco San Francisco 5	67 539
J	San Francisco San Francisco 2	67 689
J	San Francisco San Francisco 3	67 72
J	Siskiyou Klamath	69 88
J	Sonoma Bodega	69 530
J B	El Dorado Placerville	58 870
J B	Merced Twp 2	60 917
J H	Calaveras Twp 9	57 400
J H	Tuolumne Twp 1	71 199
J L C	San Francisco San Francisco 3	67 26
J M	Calaveras Twp 9	57 386
J M	El Dorado Placerville	58 847
J M	Siskiyou Scott Ri	69 77
J P	Amador Twp 2	55 305
J P	Sacramento Ward 3	63 438
J R	Nevada Grass Valley	61 193
J R	Sonoma Petaluma	69 587
J S	Santa Clara Santa Clara	65 476
J S*	Sonoma Petaluma	69 581
J W	Nevada Eureka	61 345
Jack	San Joaquin Stockton	641076
Jacob	Colusa Monroeville	57 452
Jacob	Humbolt Eureka	59 177
Jacob	Placer Sacramento	62 645
James	Alameda Brooklyn	55 126
James	Contra Costa Twp 1	57 488
James	Contra Costa Twp 3	57 586
James	Del Norte Klamath	58 654
James	Placer Michigan	62 821
James	Plumas Quincy	62 989
James	Sacramento Ward 1	63 140
James	San Diego Agua Caliente	64 855
James	San Joaquin Elkhorn	64 971
James	Santa Clara Alviso	65 397
James	Santa Clara Fremont	65 441
James	Santa Cruz Santa Cruz	66 613
James	Sierra Poker Flats	66 841
James E	Monterey Pajaro	601012
James E	San Francisco San Francisco 11	141 67
James M	Solano Vacaville	69 358
James P	Plumas Quincy	62 944
Jane	San Joaquin Elkhorn	64 986
Jarison	Tulara Twp 3	71 91
Jas	Butte Hamilton	56 521
Jas	Sacramento Ward 4	63 521
Jas	Sacramento Ward 1	63 83
Jas	San Francisco San Francisco 9	681073
Jas	San Mateo Twp 3	65 77
Jas S S	Sacramento Natonia	63 282
Jeremiah	Tulara Twp 3	71 61
Jerry	El Dorado Union	581093
Jesse R	Calaveras Twp 6	57 145
Jessee B	Napa Clear Lake	61 129
Jessie B	Napa Clear Lake	61 129
Jim*	Alameda Brooklyn	55 93
Jiw*	Alameda Brooklyn	55 93
Jno	Alameda Washington	55 214
Jno	Butte Kimshaw	56 577
Jno	Sonoma Petaluma	69 590
Jno B	San Francisco San Francisco 2	67 755
Jno C	Tuolumne Twp 4	71 144
Joh	Alameda Brooklyn	55 168
John	Butte Ophir	56 774
John	Colusa Monroeville	57 448
John	Contra Costa Twp 3	57 602
John	El Dorado White Oaks	581017

Name	County Locale	M653 RollPage
ROBINSON		
John	El Dorado Placerville	58 913
John	El Dorado Mud Springs	58 980
John	El Dorado Mud Springs	58 998
John	Fresno Twp 1	59 35
John	Fresno Twp 2	59 50
John	Marin Cortemad	60 788
John	Mariposa Coulterville	60 684
John	Monterey Monterey	60 947
John	Nevada Eureka	61 360
John	Nevada Rough &	61 398
John	Nevada Rough &	61 411
John	Nevada Bloomfield	61 516
John	Nevada Bloomfield	61 519
John	Nevada Red Dog	61 546
John	Placer Virginia	62 689
John	Placer Todds Va	62 785
John	Plumas Quincy	62 955
John	Plumas Quincy	62 956
John	Plumas Quincy	62 962
John	Sacramento Cosummes	63 398
John	San Francisco San Francisco 9	681056
John	San Francisco San Francisco 11	150 67
John	San Francisco San Francisco 2	67 688
John	San Francisco San Francisco 1	68 855
John	San Joaquin Elliott	64 946
John	Santa Clara Burnett	65 254
John	Santa Cruz Pajaro	66 573
John	Sierra Port Win	66 793
John	Sierra St Louis	66 809
John	Sierra Twp 7	66 901
John	Sierra Twp 5	66 920
John	Sonoma Petaluma	69 578
John	Trinity Weaverville	701051
John	Yuba New York	72 736
John C	San Francisco San Francisco 4	681143
John C	San Francisco San Francisco 8	681239
John D	Merced Monterey	60 944
John D	Monterey Monterey	60 944
John K	San Francisco San Francisco 7	681402
John M	San Francisco San Francisco 2	67 754
John N	Placer Goods	62 693
John P	El Dorado Greenwood	58 716
John T	Santa Cruz Watsonville	66 536
John W	Napa Yount	61 33
John*	Sacramento Granite	63 265
John*	San Francisco San Francisco 7	681431
Johnathan	Yuba Fosters	72 840
Johnathon E	Yuba Fosters	72 840
Jon	Yuba New York	72 736
Jos	Butte Mountain	56 740
Jos	San Francisco San Francisco 9	681056
Jos*	Butte Mountain	56 740
Jose R	Calaveras Twp 5	57 145
Joseph	Plumas Quincy	62 995
Joseph	Sacramento Granite	63 244
Joseph	Sacramento Ward 4	63 562
Joseph	San Francisco San Francisco 8	681024
Joseph	San Francisco San Francisco 8	681285
Joseph	San Francisco San Francisco 3	67 62
Joseph A	San Francisco San Francisco 4	681148
Joshua	El Dorado Georgetown	58 690
Joshua	Nevada Bridgeport	61 449
Josiah	San Luis Obispo San Luis Obispo	65 7
Julia	Del Norte Klamath	58 652
Julius	San Francisco San Francisco 5	67 476
Kate	Butte Oro	56 676
L	Sacramento Ward 4	63 604
L	Santa Clara Santa Clara	65 470
L L	Yuba North Ea	72 670
Laura V	Humbolt Table Bl	59 139
Locke	Tuolumne Twp 1	71 482
Loring	Yuba Long Bar	72 742
Louis	Calaveras Twp 9	57 386
Louis	Calaveras Twp 8	57 49
Louisa	Calaveras Twp 9	57 386
Lydia	Humbolt Eel Rvr	59 147
M	Butte Kimshaw	56 598
M	San Francisco San Francisco 6	67 452
M	Santa Clara San Jose	65 319
M	Santa Clara San Jose	65 371
M	Santa Clara Santa Clara	65 521
M	Sonoma Bodega	69 531
M	Tuolumne Twp 2	71 364
M E	San Francisco San Francisco 4	681225
M F	Napa Napa	61 59
M M	Placer Iona Hills	62 872
M S	El Dorado Diamond	58 789
Marcus D	Fresno Twp 3	59 10
Maria	San Francisco San Francisco 7	681326
Mark	Sacramento Ward 3	63 427
Martha	Alameda Oakland	55 10
Mary	El Dorado Georgetown	58 690
Mary	San Bernardino San Bernadino	64 636
Mary	San Francisco San Francisco 9	681014

California 1860 Census Index

Name	County Locale	M653 Roll	Page
ROBINSON			
Mary	San Francisco San Francisco 12	67	364
Mary	San Francisco San Francisco 2	67	695
Mary	San Joaquin Douglass	64	926
Mary L	Yolo Cache Crk	72	642
Millington	San Bernardino San Bernardino	64	620
N	San Francisco San Francisco 9	68	1082
N W	San Francisco San Francisco 2	67	670
Nancy	Mariposa Coulterville	60	703
Neil	Mariposa Twp 3	60	610
Nelson	Plumas Quincy	62	955
Niel	Mariposa Twp 3	60	610
P	El Dorado Placerville	58	854
Patrick	Placer Secret R	62	611
Perry	El Dorado Mud Springs	58	954
Peter	Mariposa Coulterville	60	697
Peter	Sacramento Dry Crk	63	378
Peter	San Francisco San Francisco 2	67	739
Philip R	Marin Cortemad	60	792
Prescott	Sacramento Ward 4	63	575
R	Butte Kimshaw	56	600
R	Butte Wyandotte	56	665
R	Calaveras Twp 9	57	389
R	Calaveras Twp 9	57	398
R	Santa Clara San Jose	65	292
R	Tuolumne Twp 1	71	267
R A	Sierra Morristown	66	1051
R B	Tuolumne Twp 4	71	133
R G	Calaveras Twp 9	57	354
R P	San Francisco San Francisco 2	67	586
R P S	San Francisco San Francisco 2	67	586
R R	Sacramento Cosummes	63	395
R S	Calaveras Twp 9	57	354
Rascal	San Bernardino San Bernadino	64	675
Richard	Napa Napa	61	66
Richard	Yolo Putah	72	587
Robert	San Francisco San Francisco 11	67	123
Robert	San Francisco San Francisco 2	67	659
Robert J	San Diego Colorado	64	807
Robt	Sacramento Ward 3	63	476
Robt	San Francisco San Francisco 10	67	295
S	San Francisco San Francisco 6	67	445
S	San Francisco San Francisco 5	67	541
S G	Marin Cortemad	60	790
S G	Placer Auburn	62	595
S L	Yolo No E Twp	72	670
Saml	Placer Folsom	62	649
Saml	San Francisco San Francisco 2	67	783
Saml C	Calaveras Twp 6	57	145
Saml H	Alameda Oakland	55	8
Saml*	Napa Napa	61	89
Samuel	Amador Twp 4	55	241
Samuel	Sierra Downieville	66	1017
Samuel	Sierra St Louis	66	818
Samuel	Yuba New York	72	721
Sanl*	Napa Napa	61	89
Sarah V*	San Diego San Diego	64	763
Sibbert J	San Francisco San Francisco 8	68	1286
Silvanus	Placer Ophirville	62	655
Simon	Plumas Quincy	62	938
Susan	San Francisco San Francisco 9	68	958
T	Sacramento Ward 3	63	457
T D	El Dorado Coloma	58	1076
T J	Amador Twp 2	55	264
T J	Shasta French G	66	722
Thomas	Amador Twp 4	55	247
Thomas	Nevada Bloomfield	61	517
Thomas	Sierra Downieville	66	1017
Thomas	Yuba Rose Bar	72	788
Thomas	Yuba Rose Bar	72	801
Thomas*	Yuba Rose Bar	72	788
Thomasj	Nevada Bloomfield	61	517
Thos	Nevada Bloomfield	61	516
Thos	San Francisco San Francisco 1	68	896
Thos	Yolo Cache	72	639
Thos C	Amador Twp 4	55	250
Thos P	San Francisco San Francisco 2	67	630
Tod	Sacramento Ward 4	63	602
Uger	Calaveras Twp 9	57	381
Uges	Calaveras Twp 9	57	381
V	Nevada Eureka	61	394
W	Nevada Grass Valley	61	161
W	Siskiyou Scott Ri	69	64
W C	Butte Chico	56	566
W H	Butte Oregon	56	620
W H	Sacramento Brighton	63	208
W H	San Francisco San Francisco 6	67	465
W H	San Francisco San Francisco 5	67	522
W J	Siskiyou Scott Va	69	47
W J X	San Francisco San Francisco 3	67	25
W L	San Francisco San Francisco 9	68	1022
W W	Mariposa Twp 3	60	548
Walter	El Dorado Placerville	58	913
Walter	San Francisco San Francisco 1	68	910
Westmore	Mariposa Twp 3	60	555
William	Amador Twp 4	55	245
William	Calaveras Twp 5	57	209
William	El Dorado Salmon Hills	58	1058
William	Mendocino Ukiah	60	797
William	Placer Michigan	62	825
William	Placer Iona Hills	62	867
William	Plumas Quincy	62	953
William	San Francisco San Francisco 11	67	116
William	San Francisco San Francisco 8	68	1239
William	San Joaquin Stockton	64	1063
William	San Joaquin Elkhorn	64	994
William D	Monterey Monterey	60	950
William H	Calaveras Twp 8	57	104
Willin	Sacramento Centre	63	177
Wilson	Placer Virginia	62	684
Wm	Alameda Brooklyn	55	128
Wm	Alameda Brooklyn	55	78
Wm	Butte Eureka	56	650
Wm	Calaveras Twp 4	57	342
Wm	Humbolt Bucksport	59	159
Wm	Humbolt Union	59	181
Wm	Klamath Trinidad	59	221
Wm	Nevada Eureka	61	360
Wm	Sacramento Ward 1	63	116
Wm	Sacramento Ward 1	63	135
Wm	Sacramento Natonia	63	276
Wm	Sacramento Ward 1	63	36
Wm	San Bernardino San Bernadino	64	636
Wm	San Francisco San Francisco 9	68	1036
Wm	San Francisco San Francisco 9	68	1085
Wm	San Francisco San Francisco 3	67	66
Wm	San Francisco San Francisco 2	67	765
Wm	San Francisco San Francisco 1	68	860
Wm	San Francisco San Francisco 1	68	895
Wm	Sonoma Bodega	69	519
Wm	Sonoma Bodega	69	539
Wm B	Alameda Oakland	55	73
Wm E	Sacramento Ward 1	63	27
Wm H	Placer Virginia	62	668
Wm J	Sierra Twp 7	66	894
Wm J	Trinity Whites Crk	70	1028
Wm R	San Francisco San Francisco 9	68	988
Wm S	San Francisco San Francisco 10	67	343
Wm T	Sierra Twp 7	66	894
ROBINSONT			
E*	Nevada Nevada	61	247
ROBINY			
Henry	Napa Napa	61	88
Phillip	Calaveras Twp 6	57	164
ROBIRMUTTE			
Ed F*	Butte Oregon	56	625
ROBISON			
A C	Mariposa Twp 3	60	558
Arvin	Marin Tomales	60	717
B H	Marin Tomales	60	714
B K	Marin Tomales	60	714
C	Sutter Butte	70	783
Charles	Sonoma Russian	69	432
G	Solano Vacaville	69	330
G D	Marin Saucileto	60	749
G D W	Marin Saucileto	60	749
G*	Solano Vacaville	69	330
J	Solano Vacaville	69	332
J	Sutter Yuba	70	765
J H	Shasta Shasta	66	666
J S	Shasta Shasta	66	666
J*	Solano Vacaville	69	332
John	Sonoma Washington	69	666
Marion	Shasta Shasta	66	666
N B	Shasta Shasta	66	666
N S	Solano Vacaville	69	360
Neil	Mariposa Twp 3	60	616
P	Sutter Vernon	70	842
S C	Mariposa Twp 3	60	558
Samuel	Marin Point Re	60	731
W	Solano Vacaville	69	329
W	Sutter Yuba	70	777
W B	Shasta Shasta	66	666
W E	Shasta Shasta	66	666
Wm	Marin S Antoni	60	710
Wm	Sonoma Russian	69	443
Wm	Sonoma Cloverdale	69	680
ROBITAN			
Magil	Tuolumne Twp 2	71	295
ROBITCHECK			
H	San Francisco San Francisco 5	67	512
ROBLEDO			
Mercedes*	San Francisco San Francisco 2	67	683
ROBLES			
Antonia	Monterey San Juan	60	1003
Cutan	San Francisco San Francisco 6	67	427
F	Merced Twp 2	60	919
Gabriel	Monterey Monterey	60	959
Gabril	Monterey Monterey	60	959
Guadaloupe	San Bernardino Santa Barbara	64	194
Guadelupe	Santa Cruz Pajaro	66	548
John	San Mateo Twp 1	65	72
Jose	San Luis Obispo San Luis Obispo	65	20
Loretta	Napa Napa	61	84
Manuel	Contra Costa Twp 2	57	583
P	Sacramento Ward 1	63	5
Pedro	Napa Napa	61	114
Rafael	Santa Clara San Jose	65	309
Rague	Santa Clara Alviso	65	399
Rufino	Santa Clara Burnett	65	261
ROBLET			
John P	El Dorado Placerville	58	930
ROBLEY			
Bonetha	San Mateo Twp 2	65	117
Incanation	Napa Napa	61	111
John	Napa Napa	61	111
Loretta	Napa Napa	61	84
ROBLEZ			
Leeandino*	Santa Clara Fremont	65	428
ROBLIN			
Isaac	Amador Twp 2	55	321
J	Sutter Bear Rvr	70	826
John	Placer Dutch Fl	62	723
ROBLIS			
Ceetan*	San Francisco San Francisco 6	67	427
Cietan	San Francisco San Francisco 6	67	427
F	Merced Twp 2	60	919
Rafarla	Tuolumne Twp 1	71	226
ROBLY			
Incanation	Napa Napa	61	111
ROBNISON			
Jos*	Butte Mountain	56	740
ROBONL			
C*	Tuolumne Garrote	71	173
ROBOUL			
C	Tuolumne Twp 4	71	173
ROBOURDEN			
Charles	San Francisco San Francisco 3	67	1
ROBOURDIN			
Charles*	San Francisco San Francisco 3	67	1
ROBRIAUX			
Emily	El Dorado Eldorado	58	945
ROBRIMETH			
Ed F	Butte Oregon	56	625
ROBRITS			
John	Calaveras Twp 6	57	149
ROBRST			
Wm*	Calaveras Twp 6	57	135
ROBRTS			
Thos R	Nevada Bridgeport	61	495
ROBRTSON			
James	Yuba Slate Ro	72	694
ROBRURAE			
Barbara	Alameda Brooklyn	55	211
ROBSON			
George	Sierra Pine Grove	66	832
Henry	Sacramento Ward 3	63	429
Henry	Sacramento Ward 4	63	523
John	El Dorado Placerville	58	926
Joseph	Sierra Pine Grove	66	832
N*	El Dorado Georgetown	58	689
W	El Dorado Georgetown	58	689
ROBT			
Gust*	Trinity North Fo	70	1026
U T	Amador Twp 7	55	420
Yow	El Dorado Coloma	58	1082
ROBULY			
Thomas	Calaveras Twp 5	57	206
ROBURGER			
Bernard	Alameda Brooklyn	55	141
ROBUS			
Seasten	Los Angeles Elmonte	59	260
ROBUTS			
James	Monterey Monterey	60	959
William	Monterey San Juan	60	993
ROBY			
Deel	Yolo Washington	72	572
H C	Yolo No E Twp	72	669
J C	Butte Oregon	56	617
J T	Nevada Eureka	61	357
J Y	Nevada Eureka	61	357
John P	Yuba Bear Rvr	72	1003
John S	Yuba Bear Rvr	72	1003
Milten	Calaveras Twp 10	57	276
Walter	Calaveras Twp 10	57	276
ROC			
David*	Humbolt Union	59	191
ROCA			
---	San Bernardino San Bernadino	64	685

Name	County Locale	M653 Roll	Page
ROCA			
---	San Bernardino S Timate	64	739
---	San Bernardino S Timate	64	744
---	San Bernardino S Timate	64	746
---	San Diego Temecula	64	802
Joseph	Sacramento Granite	63	265
ROCAL			
Ucanio	Butte Kimshaw	56	573
ROCCA			
Francisco	Amador Twp 1	55	456
ROCCE			
Alfred	Colusa Monroeville	57	453
Frederick	Yuba Bear Rvr	72	997
ROCCHICCIOLI			
R F	San Francisco San Francisco 6	67	460
ROCCO			
Jean*	Calaveras Twp 7	57	24
ROCCU			
Jean*	Calaveras Twp 7	57	24
ROCERO			
L	Mariposa Twp 1	60	623
ROCH			
---	Plumas Meadow Valley	62	910
Am*	Mariposa Twp 3	60	604
Arn*	Mariposa Twp 3	60	604
C	El Dorado Newtown	58	780
William*	Tuolumne Twp 3	71	461
Wm*	Sierra Twp 5	66	919
ROCHA			
Antonio	Los Angeles Los Angeles	59	384
Feliz	Los Angeles Los Angeles	59	305
Jacinto	Los Angeles San Pedro	59	485
Jacinto A	Los Angeles San Pedro	59	485
Juan	Los Angeles San Gabriel	59	417
ROCHAMAN			
J*	Sacramento Brighton	63	196
ROCHDESLER			
Conrad	Tuolumne Montezuma	71	513
ROCHE			
---	San Francisco San Francisco 12		388 67
Edward	San Francisco San Francisco 2	67	690
Forester	San Francisco San Francisco 7	681396	
John	Sierra Poker Flats	66	837
P M	San Francisco San Francisco 2	67	597
Thomas	Yolo Slate Ra	72	688
Wm	San Francisco San Francisco 9	681069	
ROCHEBURNE			
Alfred	San Francisco San Francisco 8	681240	
ROCHEE			
Moses Des	Plumas Meadow Valley	62	912
ROCHELLE			
John	Mariposa Twp 3	60	558
ROCHENE			
F	San Joaquin Stockton	641095	
ROCHER			
Francis	Plumas Meadow Valley	62	932
ROCHES			
M	Sacramento Ward 1	63	4
ROCHESTER			
B	Nevada Grass Valley	61	184
John	San Francisco San Francisco 8	681324	
ROCHETTO			
Manuel	Tuolumne Twp 2	71	281
P	Sacramento Ward 1	63	28
ROCHFORD			
Patric	Tuolumne Twp 2	71	375
Thos	Sonoma Petaluma	69	564
ROCHI			
Wm*	San Francisco San Francisco 9	681069	
ROCHIBACK			
Lewis	Santa Clara San Jose	65	294
ROCHICU			
Antonia	Calaveras Twp 8	57	88
ROCHINGES			
Frederick	San Francisco San Francisco 7	681380	
ROCHINI			
Mared	Los Angeles San Jose	59	290
ROCHINO			
Jesus	Santa Clara San Jose	65	300
ROCHIO			
Charles	Calaveras Twp 7	57	43
Jean	Calaveras Twp 7	57	39
ROCHIS			
Augustino	Calaveras Twp 7	57	45
ROCHL			
Julius	San Francisco San Francisco 7	681424	
ROCHO			
Jose	Los Angeles Los Angeles	59	509
ROCHOM			
Annelole	San Francisco San Francisco 2	67	781
ROCHON			
Alex	San Francisco San Francisco 2	67	678
Napoleon	Placer Todds Va	62	790
O	Amador Twp 7	55	414
Octave	Sacramento Ward 4	63	550
ROCINTO			
---	San Diego Temecula	64	795
ROCK			
A D	El Dorado Georgetown	58	689
Anna	Yolo Putah	72	550
Bridget	San Francisco San Francisco 6	67	455
Charles	San Mateo Twp 3	65	74
David	Shasta Shasta	66	735
David	Sonoma Armally	69	488
F S	San Mateo Twp 1	65	71
Francis	San Joaquin Tulare	64	870
G	Nevada Eureka	61	350
Henry	Tuolumne Jamestown	71	426
Henry O	San Francisco San Francisco 9	68	953
Israel S*	San Mateo Twp 1	65	70
J	Nevada Eureka	61	350
J	Nevada Eureka	61	375
James	Mendocino Little L	60	833
Jas F*	Butte Eureka	56	651
Jno F*	Butte Eureka	56	651
Jno O*	Nevada Nevada	61	260
Jno W	Sacramento Ward 1	63	10
John	San Francisco San Francisco 2	67	605
John J	Placer Auburn	62	567
John M*	Sierra Twp 7	66	913
John*	Plumas Quincy	621001	
Joseph	Sierra La Porte	66	769
Josph	Sierra Downieville	66	954
Jsoeph	Sierra La Porte	66	769
Kate	Alameda Oakland	55	14
Lorenzo	Sierra Twp 5	66	941
Margaret	San Francisco San Francisco 6	67	431
Mark	Calaveras Twp 9	57	387
Martha	San Francisco San Francisco 4	681170	
Marthew	San Francisco San Francisco 4	681170	
Mary	San Francisco San Francisco 1	68	879
Michael*	Placer Secret R	62	615
Pedrow	San Mateo Twp 3	65	74
R	El Dorado Diamond	58	792
Robert W	Monterey Monterey	60	926
Rose	San Francisco San Francisco 10		250 67
Stephano	Calaveras Twp 8	57	92
Stephen	Calaveras Twp 7	57	39
V S	San Francisco San Francisco 2	67	559
Wilhelm	Nevada Bridgeport	61	467
William	Tuolumne Twp 3	71	461
William*	Tuolumne Twp 3	71	283
William*	Tuolumne Twp 3	71	461
Wm*	Sierra Twp 5	66	919
ROCKA			
Francisa	Calaveras Twp 9	57	360
Francisca	Calaveras Twp 9	57	360
ROCKAFELLER			
J F*	Santa Clara Redwood	65	452
ROCKAFFELL			
Danl	Sacramento Ward 1	63	141
ROCKAMAN			
J*	Sacramento Brighton	63	196
ROCKAN			
Peter	Calaveras Twp 4	57	304
ROCKAR			
Peter	Calaveras Twp 4	57	304
ROCKAWAY			
S H	El Dorado Coloma	581082	
ROCKE			
Thomas	Yuba Slate Ro	72	688
ROCKEN			
Joseph	Sierra Downieville	66	957
ROCKER			
Charles	Yuba Marysville	72	975
Joseph	Sacramento Granite	63	245
ROCKES			
M*	Sacramento Ward 1	63	4
ROCKET			
---	Fresno Twp 2	59	106
ROCKETHER			
Alonzo	Placer Michigan	62	825
ROCKETTO			
Manuel	Tuolumne Twp 2	71	281
ROCKEYFELLOW			
Hiram	Contra Costa Twp 1	57	523
R	San Mateo Twp 2	65	115
ROCKFORD			
G	Yolo Putah	72	560
Luke	Sacramento Ward 3	63	473
Mary	Yuba Marysville	72	965
Patrick	Tuolumne Shawsfla	71	375
Thos	Sonoma Petaluma	69	563
Wm H	Tehama Antelope	70	890
ROCKHELD			
H L	Shasta Horsetown	66	704
ROCKHOLD			
H L	Shasta Horsetown	66	704
R	Sutter Butte	70	794
ROCKHOLT			
F	Yolo Cache Crk	72	611
ROCKINGFIELD			
John	Colusa Grand Island	57	471
ROCKINS			
Charles G*	Yuba Marysville	72	890
ROCKINTAUND			
Matthew*	Yuba Marysville	72	923
ROCKLAYO			
Jno B	Tuolumne Big Oak	71	140
ROCKLESS			
Charles	Yolo Merritt	72	584
ROCKLIN			
Charles	Yolo Merritt	72	584
ROCKMAN			
J M	Yolo Cache Crk	72	665
ROCKOFELLER			
J F*	Santa Clara Redwood	65	452
ROCKORD			
A	Shasta French G	66	718
ROCKS			
Bridget	San Joaquin Castoria	64	902
John	San Joaquin Stockton	641053	
ROCKWAL			
A W	Amador Twp 6	55	421
ROCKWAY			
P P	Sacramento Ward 4	63	514
ROCKWELL			
A W*	Amador Twp 6	55	421
A W*	Amador Twp 6	55	434
Chas	Plumas Meadow Valley	62	905
Elijah A	San Francisco San Francisco 4	681220	
Elisha	Plumas Quincy	62	961
Geo	El Dorado Placerville	58	819
H	Butte Wyandotte	56	666
Henry	Solano Vacaville	69	332
Horace	Alameda Brooklyn	55	212
J	Nevada Grass Valley	61	146
Jethred	Alameda Brooklyn	55	95
Jethrid	Alameda Brooklyn	55	95
John	Plumas Quincy	62	940
R	El Dorado Placerville	58	838
T K	El Dorado Placerville	58	838
W R	Calaveras Twp 9	57	392
W R C	Nevada Nevada	61	324
Wm M	San Francisco San Francisco 10		350 67
ROCKWITH			
W	Calaveras Twp 9	57	392
ROCKWOOD			
Geo	El Dorado Placerville	58	919
H C	Amador Twp 1	55	465
Jas S	Sacramento Ward 3	63	487
ROCKY			
---	Fresno Twp 2	59	91
J N	Sutter Bear Rvr	70	823
ROCO			
Giseppa	Amador Twp 3	55	387
P	El Dorado Placerville	58	870
ROCOO			
Orrlli*	El Dorado Eldorado	58	944
ROCOS			
Ceezer	Calaveras Twp 4	57	331
Ceizer	Calaveras Twp 4	57	331
Propina	Tuolumne Shawsfla	71	405
ROCSING			
E L*	San Francisco San Francisco 6	67	464
ROCTHE			
Chas W	Tuolumne Twp 4	71	138
ROCTHER			
Charles	Yuba Marysville	72	975
ROCULES			
Mariana	Calaveras Twp 6	57	131
ROCUS			
Clara	Humbolt Eureka	59	168
Juan	Monterey San Juan	60	978
Timothy	Tuolumne Twp 2	71	405
ROD			
Anne	San Francisco San Francisco 10		259 67
RODA			
---	Del Norte Klamath	58	655
RODAM			
Wm	Nevada Grass Valley	61	154
RODANHAFAL			
Christian	Trinity Whites Crk	701028	
RODARICH			
Rufus	San Francisco San Francisco 3	67	61
RODAW			
James	Placer Iona Hills	62	870
RODAY			
W	San Francisco San Francisco 3	67	64
RODBECK			
Conrod	Sierra Downieville	66	994
RODBRUY			
Christian*	Calaveras Twp 6	57	180
RODCHILD			
H	San Francisco San Francisco 6	67	443

California 1860 Census Index

Name	County Locale	M653 Roll	Page
RODCLIFFE			
Saml*	Alameda Brooklyn	55	81
RODD			
Alvin	San Francisco San Francisco 3	67	48
J	San Francisco San Francisco 5	67	551
RODDA			
E	Nevada Grass Valley	61	199
John	Sacramento Natonia	63	273
Josiah	Placer Iona Hills	62	869
R	Nevada Grass Valley	61	199
RODDEN			
Chas F	San Francisco San Francisco 1	68	856
G L	Tuolumne Sonora	71	482
William	Tuolumne Twp 5	71	511
William	Tuolumne Montezuma	71	511
Wm H	Merced Monterey	60	944
Wm H	Monterey Monterey	60	944
RODDESLER			
Conrad	Tuolumne Twp 5	71	513
RODDIN			
G B	Tuolumne Twp 1	71	266
G C	Tuolumne Twp 1	71	266
RODDING			
Robert	Siskiyou Yreka	69	126
William	Placer Iona Hills	62	891
RODDOCK			
Benj*	Calaveras Twp 9	57	353
Bnj*	Calaveras Twp 9	57	353
Buj*	Calaveras Twp 9	57	353
RODDS			
Andrew	Tuolumne Twp 2	71	351
RODDY			
B	Siskiyou Callahan	69	7
Sarah	San Francisco San Francisco 10	340 67	
William	Nevada Bridgeport	61	465
RODE			
Jas	Sonoma Sonoma	69	636
RODEAIN			
Pourlu	Calaveras Twp 6	57	131
RODEAN			
August	Yuba Foster B	72	835
RODEBANGH			
Jacob	Butte Mountain	56	737
RODEBAUGK			
Jacob	Butte Mountain	56	737
RODECKER			
Elias	San Francisco San Francisco 7	681428	
RODEGO			
Mosa	Yolo Fremont	72	605
RODEHAVEN			
Harry	Sonoma Petaluma	69	548
RODEMAKE			
Joseph	Tuolumne Twp 2	71	334
RODEMAN			
Geo*	Humbolt Union	59	182
Gor*	Humbolt Union	59	182
RODEN			
A G	San Francisco San Francisco 5	67	523
Allen	Tehama Lassen	70	871
Augustin	Sonoma Petaluma	69	615
D	Sacramento San Joaquin	63	356
RODENA			
Ferdenand*	Placer Michigan	62	832
RODENBACK			
Mary*	San Francisco San Francisco 3	67	30
RODENBURG			
D	Siskiyou Klamath	69	86
RODENGO			
Pablo	Calaveras Twp 8	57	107
RODENGURS			
Iswaldo	Calaveras Twp 10	57	289
RODENIYORS			
Augustine	Calaveras Twp 10	57	290
RODEO			
Frank	El Dorado Salmon Falls	581051	
RODER			
Antonia	San Francisco San Francisco 1	68	895
John	Stanislaus Emory	70	752
Paul	Solano Benecia	69	313
Wash	Tehama Lassen	70	870
RODEREGEZ			
Cause*	Mariposa Twp 1	60	624
RODEREGIS			
Marcos	Alameda Brooklyn	55	149
RODEREGOG			
Cause	Mariposa Twp 1	60	624
RODEREGUE			
M	San Francisco San Francisco 6	67	467
RODEREGUES			
Conception	Santa Cruz Soguel	66	589
Iswaldo	Calaveras Twp 10	57	289
RODERGISS			
Roman*	Santa Cruz Santa Cruz	66	607
RODERGUES			
Conception	Santa Cruz Soguel	66	589

Name	County Locale	M653 Roll	Page
RODERGUES			
Fecilin	Santa Cruz Santa Cruz	66	608
Forcenria	Santa Cruz Santa Cruz	66	616
Forcona	Santa Cruz Santa Cruz	66	616
Jose*	Santa Cruz Santa Cruz	66	607
Manuel	Santa Cruz Soguel	66	587
Margrecia	Santa Cruz Soguel	66	588
Margrecin	Santa Cruz Soguel	66	588
Marrin	Santa Cruz Pajaro	66	548
Miguel	Santa Cruz Soguel	66	582
Refugio	Santa Cruz Soguel	66	586
Roman	Santa Cruz Santa Cruz	66	607
Yorconir*	Santa Cruz Santa Cruz	66	616
RODERGUEZ			
Deisdarci	San Luis Obispo	65	33
	San Luis Obispo		
RODERGUIS			
Jose	Santa Cruz Santa Cruz	66	639
Juan	Santa Cruz Pajaro	66	570
RODERICK			
Frank	Mendocino Arrana	60	861
J	Amador Twp 3	55	378
Jacob	Solano Vacaville	69	347
James	Placer Forest H	62	770
John	Placer Forest H	62	770
Maria	Amador Twp 5	55	337
Peter	Alameda Brooklyn	55	97
Thomas	Placer Stewart	62	606
RODERICKS			
John	Solano Vacaville	69	348
Manuel	Contra Costa Twp 1	57	520
RODERIEGUIS			
Elvisa	Calaveras Twp 5	57	249
RODERIGAES			
Pedro	Santa Cruz Pajaro	66	552
RODERIGE			
Prospero	Sacramento Ward 1	63	110
RODERIGO			
Prospero	Sacramento Ward 1	63	110
RODERIGOES			
Juan	Santa Cruz Pajaro	66	552
RODERIGUES			
Benjamin	Santa Cruz Pajaro	66	554
Brigados*	Sacramento Ward 1	63	7
Brijador	Sacramento Ward 1	63	7
Brijados*	Sacramento Ward 1	63	7
Escolata	Santa Cruz Pajaro	66	556
Francisco	Santa Cruz Pajaro	66	556
Franciser	Santa Cruz Pajaro	66	556
Galores	Calaveras Twp 10	57	277
Guadelupe	Santa Cruz Pajaro	66	543
Joaquin	Santa Cruz Pescadero	66	651
Jose	Santa Cruz Pajaro	66	561
Juan	Santa Cruz Pajaro	66	552
Maria	Santa Cruz Pajaro	66	556
Marvin	Santa Cruz Pajaro	66	548
Pedro	Santa Cruz Pajaro	66	552
RODERIGUS			
Elvison	Calaveras Twp 5	57	249
RODERIQUES			
Galoris	Calaveras Twp 10	57	277
RODERNOUT			
Henry	El Dorado White Oaks	581026	
RODERQUES			
Fecilin*	Santa Cruz Santa Cruz	66	608
Jose*	Santa Cruz Santa Cruz	66	607
Roman*	Santa Cruz Santa Cruz	66	607
RODERREGEUS			
Elvisa*	Calaveras Twp 5	57	249
RODERRIGER			
Raphael*	Calaveras Twp 5	57	201
Ruphael*	Calaveras Twp 5	57	201
RODERSIYER			
Raphael	Calaveras Twp 5	57	201
RODERUGUIS			
Augustine	Calaveras Twp 10	57	290
RODES			
H	El Dorado Diamond	58	813
H*	Nevada Washington	61	336
Martha	Placer Ophirville	62	659
Saml	Butte Hamilton	56	521
Wm	Tehama Lassen	70	877
RODEY			
John	San Francisco San Francisco 10	302 67	
John	San Francisco San Francisco 3	67	67
RODFELDT			
P R	San Francisco San Francisco 5	67	494
RODFISH			
Henry N	Yolo No E Twp	72	674
RODFORD			
Thomas	Calaveras Twp 6	57	143
RODGAN			
Z*	San Mateo Twp 3	65	76
RODGER			
Charles	Plumas Meadow Valley	62	927

Name	County Locale	M653 Roll	Page
RODGER			
Chas	Plumas Meadow Valley	62	904
D J	Shasta Millvill	66	753
RODGERGO			
Eunice	Santa Cruz Pajaro	66	542
RODGERGUIS			
Juan	Santa Cruz Pajaro	66	570
RODGERIGUES			
Guadalupe*	Santa Cruz Pajaro	66	543
Guadelupe*	Santa Cruz Pajaro	66	542
RODGERS W			
Squiri	San Francisco San Francisco 3	67	73
RODGERS			
---	San Mateo Twp 3	65	95
A	Sacramento Franklin	63	334
A	San Francisco San Francisco 1	68	920
A E	Tuolumne Twp 1	71	222
A S	Trinity Hay Fork	70	993
Albert	Mariposa Twp 1	60	636
Alfred	San Francisco San Francisco 11	100 67	
Alick	Napa Yount	61	52
Aloan*	Calaveras Twp 4	57	326
Alvan	Calaveras Twp 4	57	326
Ann	Yuba Long Bar	72	756
Anna	San Francisco San Francisco 2	67	770
Antone	Trinity New Rvr	701030	
B	Sacramento Lee	63	210
Benj	Sacramento Georgian	63	336
Benj	Tuolumne Twp 1	71	251
Benjamin	San Joaquin Elkhorn	64	985
C	Nevada Grass Valley	61	164
C F	Shasta Shasta	66	678
Charles	Amador Twp 3	55	394
Chas P	Butte Kimshaw	56	598
Danl H	Los Angeles Elmonte	59	251
Danl L	Tuolumne Twp 2	71	396
David	Alameda Brooklyn	55	86
David	Plumas Quincy	621004	
E	San Francisco San Francisco 5	67	542
E A	El Dorado Greenwood	58	716
E A	Tuolumne Twp 1	71	242
E K	San Francisco San Francisco 1	68	851
Edward	Tuolumne Twp 2	71	396
Elijah	Amador Twp 4	55	249
Elisha P	San Francisco San Francisco 1	68	874
Ellen	San Francisco San Francisco 10	245 67	
Eugene C	Placer Goods	62	695
Eunice	Santa Cruz Pajaro	66	542
Ffjfohn*	El Dorado Georgetown	58	759
Frank	Alameda Brooklyn	55	149
G H	Nevada Eureka	61	380
G W	San Mateo Twp 3	65	92
G W	Tuolumne Twp 3	71	444
Geland	Santa Cruz Pajaro	66	560
Geo	Nevada Grass Valley	61	147
George E	Alameda Oakland	55	65
Gland*	Santa Cruz Pajaro	66	560
Gos M*	Placer Rattle Snake	62	633
Grand	Santa Cruz Pajaro	66	560
H	Amador Twp 2	55	308
H	Butte Kimshaw	56	595
Hayden*	Stanislaus Emory	70	747
Henry	El Dorado Georgetown	58	695
Henry	Placer Secret R	62	610
Henry	Placer Iona Hills	62	872
Henry	San Francisco San Francisco 3	67	43
Henry	San Joaquin Douglass	64	921
Henry A	Placer Secret R	62	610
Henry M	San Francisco San Francisco 3	67	43
J	Calaveras Twp 9	57	418
J	Nevada Nevada	61	275
J	Nevada Nevada	61	314
J	Sacramento Sutter	63	291
J	Sutter Butte	70	780
J E	Tehama Red Bluff	70	906
J L	Nevada Nevada	61	290
J S*	El Dorado Georgetown	58	695
Jacob	San Francisco San Francisco 1	68	834
James	Amador Twp 5	55	367
James	Calaveras Twp 6	57	114
James	San Francisco San Francisco 3	67	81
James	Solano Vallejo	69	270
James	Tulara Visalia	71	21
James A	San Joaquin Castoria	64	875
James B	Tuolumne Twp 1	71	264
Jas	Napa Hot Springs	61	26
Jas	San Francisco San Francisco 1	68	934
Jas B	Butte Oregon	56	643
Jas C	Sacramento Ward 4	63	566
Jas N	San Mateo Twp 3	65	77
Jerry	Butte Oregon	56	522
Jno	Nevada Nevada	61	327
Jno G	Butte Kimshaw	56	586
Jno R	Alameda Oakland	55	30

Name	County Locale	M653 Roll	Page
RODGERS			
Jno T	Butte Kimshaw	56	586
John	Amador Twp 4	55	241
John	Calaveras Twp 4	57	321
John	El Dorado Georgetown	58	685
John	Fresno Twp 1	59	34
John	Los Angeles San Pedro	59	483
John	Merced Twp 2	60	924
John	Placer Goods	62	695
John	Plumas Meadow Valley	62	907
John	Santa Cruz Pajaro	66	541
John	Shasta Millvill	66	740
John	Solano Vallejo	69	271
John	Stanislaus Buena Village	70	725
John	Trinity Oregon G	70	1009
John	Tuolumne Twp 2	71	396
John	Tuolumne Twp 2	71	401
John	Tuolumne Twp 3	71	441
Jon	Solano Vallejo	69	271
Jos M*	Placer Rattle Snake	62	633
Joseph	Calaveras Twp 10	57	290
Joseph	Santa Cruz Pajaro	66	558
Joseph	Shasta Shasta	66	682
Joseph	Tuolumne Columbia	71	327
Joseph	Yolo Washington	72	574
Josiah B	Alameda Brooklyn	55	205
Julius	San Francisco San Francisco 3	67	60
L	Nevada Grass Valley	61	196
L	Trinity Price'S	70	1019
Lane	San Luis Obispo San Luis Obispo	65	5
Lovely	Mariposa Twp 1	60	671
M	Shasta Shasta	66	682
M B	San Francisco San Francisco 2	67	777
Manuel	Alameda Brooklyn	55	128
Martha	Sierra Morristown	66	1054
Mary	Sierra Pine Grove	66	820
Mary A	Yolo Cache Crk	72	596
Maybell	San Francisco San Francisco 6	67	456
Michael	San Mateo Twp 2	65	123
Miguel	Santa Cruz Soguel	66	582
Moses	Mariposa Twp 1	60	638
Nancy	Alameda Oakland	55	5
Nathan	Tuolumne Twp 2	71	327
Ourn	Calaveras Twp 4	57	317
Owen	Calaveras Twp 4	57	317
P B	San Francisco San Francisco 9	68	1100
P W	Sacramento Ward 4	63	524
Patrick	Tuolumne Shawsfla	71	378
Phillip	Alameda Oakland	55	41
R M	Alameda Oakland	55	65
Robert	Tulara Visalia	71	12
S	Amador Twp 3	55	404
S	Trinity Prices B	70	1019
S T	Butte Kimshaw	56	575
Sam	Tuolumne Shawsfla	71	378
Saml	Placer Virginia	62	663
Samuel	Alameda Washington	55	172
Sylvester	Amador Twp 4	55	286
Thomas	Napa Hot Springs	61	23
Thomas	Tuolumne Twp 2	71	412
Thos	Amador Twp 2	55	300
Thos	San Francisco San Francisco 1	68	862
Thos	Stanislaus Emory	70	753
Thos	Trinity Lewiston	70	964
Uriah	Sierra Pine Grove	66	823
W	Placer Illinois	62	705
W C	Mariposa Twp 1	60	667
W C	Sacramento Franklin	63	334
W K	Sacramento Ward 1	63	44
W L	Del Norte Crescent	58	645
William B	Contra Costa Twp 2	57	561
Wm	Alameda Brooklyn	55	151
Wm	Sacramento Cosummes	63	396
Wm A	Placer Dutch Fl	62	728
Wm B	Alameda Brooklyn	55	124
Wm H	Napa Yount	61	45
Wm Henry	Alameda Brooklyn	55	194
Wm R	Amador Twp 4	55	249
RODGERSON			
James	Del Norte Klamath	58	654
RODGES			
D J*	Shasta Millvill	66	753
RODGESEY			
H	El Dorado Placerville	58	855
RODGINS			
Henry	San Francisco San Francisco 3	67	43
RODGOTH			
Carlo	Calaveras Twp 7	57	29
John	Calaveras Twp 7	57	29
RODGRS			
Patrick	Tuolumne Twp 2	71	378
RODIANO			
John	Calaveras Twp 7	57	31
RODICINDA			
Maria	San Diego San Diego	64	773
RODIE			
M	Yolo Merritt	72	581

Name	County Locale	M653 Roll	Page
RODIEN			
Jose	Calaveras Twp 5	57	172
RODIER			
Jose	Calaveras Twp 6	57	172
RODIGICT			
Licke	Alameda Oakland	55	15
RODIGUES			
Marcelina	Santa Clara San Jose	65	325
RODIHAVEN			
John	Sonoma Petaluma	69	548
RODIN			
Augustus	Sonoma Vallejo	69	615
F	San Francisco San Francisco 2	67	797
RODINQUES			
F	Tuolumne Sonora	71	225
RODINQUS			
F*	Tehama Red Bluff	70	930
RODIREGUES			
R	Tuolumne Columbia	71	337
RODIREQUE			
M	San Francisco San Francisco 6	67	467
RODIRGUEZ			
Mary S*	San Francisco San Francisco 2	67	661
RODIRIGAS			
Ysadora	Tuolumne Sonora	71	224
RODIRIGAUS			
Antonio	Tuolumne Twp 1	71	225
RODIRIGIOUS			
Jose	Tuolumne Twp 3	71	432
RODIRIGOUS			
Jose	Tuolumne Jamestown	71	432
RODIRIGUES			
Jose	Tuolumne Twp 3	71	460
Manvilla	Tuolumne Sonora	71	225
T	Tuolumne Twp 1	71	225
RODIRIGUIS			
Manwella	Tuolumne Twp 1	71	225
RODIRIGUS			
Ysadora	Tuolumne Twp 1	71	224
RODIRIQUES			
Antonio	Tuolumne Sonora	71	225
R	Tuolumne Twp 2	71	337
RODISES			
Trinedadud*	Calaveras Twp 4	57	311
Trinidadad	Calaveras Twp 4	57	311
RODISINA			
J	Calaveras Twp 7	57	3
Martin	Calaveras Twp 7	57	1
RODITZ			
A	Butte Eureka	56	652
RODIX			
Manuel	Klamath Salmon	59	209
RODIZ			
E F*	Butte Kimshaw	56	602
RODLER			
Wm	Trinity Rearings	70	990
RODMAN			
Alfred	Butte Ophir	56	754
Chas*	Santa Clara Alviso	65	411
E N	Tuolumne Columbia	71	349
R D	Yuba New York	72	737
Solman	San Joaquin Stockton	64	1053
RODMARK			
A	El Dorado Coloma	58	1122
RODMON			
R D	Yuba New York	72	737
RODNGALZ			
Relijan	San Luis Obispo San Luis Obispo	65	34
RODNGNEY			
M A	San Francisco San Francisco 2	67	645
RODNGUEY			
M A	San Francisco San Francisco 2	67	645
RODNURT			
John*	El Dorado Placerville	58	917
RODNUTT			
John*	El Dorado Placerville	58	917
RODOIGUEZ			
Appo	Marin Cortemad	60	782
RODOLPH			
Charles	Placer Michigan	62	840
Godfrey	Yolo Cache	72	644
James	Tehama Red Bluff	70	922
S F	Yolo Cache Crk	72	625
RODOM			
Alexander*	Placer Michigan	62	832
RODONDO			
Jesus	San Bernardino S Timate	64	688
RODONI			
Alexander*	Placer Michigan	62	832
J*	El Dorado Georgetown	58	696
RODONX			
Joseph*	Nevada Rough &	61	424
RODOUX			
Joseph	Nevada Rough &	61	424
RODOVITCH			
N	San Francisco San Francisco 3	67	62

Name	County Locale	M653 Roll	Page
RODREEDES			
Polonia	San Mateo Twp 2	65	113
RODREGAS			
Juan	Mariposa Twp 1	60	644
RODREGEZ			
C	San Joaquin Stockton	64	1099
RODREGO			
Francisco	Mariposa Twp 1	60	631
Fransisca	Mariposa Twp 1	60	631
Fransisco	Mariposa Twp 1	60	631
RODREGOS			
Kylanix*	Mariposa Twp 1	60	644
RODREGUEZ			
Antonio D	Santa Barbara	64	153
	San Bernardino		
RODREGUUSE			
D*	Amador Twp 1	55	453
RODRICAS			
Juan	Los Angeles Azuza	59	279
RODRICK			
Hermann	San Francisco San Francisco 3	67	44
Jno	Sonoma Petaluma	69	557
Peter	Mariposa Twp 1	60	653
RODRIGAES			
Artelana	Yuba Marysville	72	948
RODRIGAS			
Juan	Mariposa Twp 1	60	644
Margarita	Merced Monterey	60	937
Margarita	Monterey Monterey	60	937
Maria	San Mateo Twp 2	65	117
Mathis	San Mateo Twp 2	65	117
RODRIGAZ			
Jacinto	Merced Monterey	60	939
Lancici	San Luis Obispo San Luis Obispo	65	37
RODRIGEIUSE			
D*	Amador Twp 1	55	453
RODRIGES			
Jose A	Contra Costa Twp 1	57	489
Tavereio*	Contra Costa Twp 1	57	483
RODRIGIEUSE			
D	Amador Twp 1	55	453
RODRIGO			
---	Siskiyou Yreka	69	183
Mrs	Siskiyou Yreka	69	183
RODRIGOS			
Ignacio	Los Angeles Los Angeles	59	508
RODRIGUE			
A	Siskiyou Scott Ri	69	61
RODRIGUES			
Alfonzo	Yuba Marysville	72	946
Balbanada	Monterey Monterey	60	944
F	Merced Twp 1	60	901
Francisco	Los Angeles Santa Ana	59	442
Gertrude	Yuba Marysville	72	946
J M	Merced Twp 1	60	899
Jesus	Santa Clara Almaden	65	275
Jose	Contra Costa Twp 1	57	517
Jose Maria	Yuba Marysville	72	858
Jose Maria	Yuba Marysville	72	860
Lorette	San Bernardino Santa Barbara	64	151
Mariana	Santa Clara San Jose	65	331
P	Merced Twp 1	60	911
Raphael	Calaveras Twp 5	57	201
RODRIGUEZ			
A	Stanislaus Emory	70	737
Alonzo	Yuba Marysville	72	946
Anastaco	Santa Cruz Santa Cruz	66	627
Antonio	San Bernardino Santa Ba	64	213
Appo	Marin Cortemad	60	782
Bicente	Santa Clara Fremont	65	434
Carlos	San Bernardino Santa Barbara	64	196
Carmel	Mariposa Twp 3	60	611
Clara	Monterey S Antoni	60	969
Deonicia	Monterey San Juan	60	978
Felipe	San Francisco San Francisco 2	67	698
Francisco	Fresno Twp 1	59	76
Francisco	Los Angeles Santa Ana	59	442
Francisco	Los Angeles San Juan	59	467
Francisco	Santa Ba	64	216
Francisco	San Bernardino		
Francisco	San Francisco San Francisco 2	67	758
Frutosa*	Placer Damascus	62	846
Gertrude	Yuba Marysville	72	946
J	Santa Clara San Jose	65	324
J F	San Francisco San Francisco 2	67	694
Jacinto	Monterey Monterey	60	939
Jesus	Santa Clara Fremont	65	433
Jose	Marin Cortemad	60	787
Jose	Monterey S Antoni	60	973
Jose	San Bernardino Santa Barbara	64	191
Jose	San Francisco San Francisco 2	67	757
Jose M	Los Angeles Los Angeles	59	384
Jose M	Monterey S Antoni	60	971
Juan	San Bernardino Santa Ba	64	212
Juan	San Bernardino Santa Ba	64	216
Juan	San Bernardino S Buenav	64	222

Name	County Locale	M653 RollPage
RODRIGUEZ		
Leonardo	Los Angeles San Pedro	59 481
Leonardo	Los Angeles San Pedro	59 483
Lorenza	Monterey Monterey	60 942
Luis	Monterey S Antoni	60 972
Maefonso*	Los Angeles Los Angeles	59 304
Maria	San Diego San Diego	64 764
Maria A	Los Angeles Santa Ana	59 455
Martin	Del Norte Crescent	58 626
Martin	Marin Cortemad	60 785
Nella	Placer Todds Va	62 790
Octeland*	Yuba Marysville	72 948
Pablo	Los Angeles Santa Ana	59 441
Permin*	Del Norte Crescent	58 641
Ramon	San Diego San Diego	64 758
Severeana	Los Angeles Santa Ana	59 445
Simona	San Bernardino Santa Barbara	64 158
RODRIGUIEZ		
Antonio	San Bernardino S Buenav	64 213
RODRIGUIS		
F	Merced Twp 1	60 901
J M	Merced Twp 1	60 899
Ygnacio	Contra Costa Twp 3	57 615
RODRIGUIZ		
Jose	San Luis Obispo San Luis Obispo	65 42
Jose M	Contra Costa Twp 3	57 614
RODRIGUS		
E*	Tehama Red Bluff	70 930
Lorenza	Merced Monterey	60 942
RODRIGUZ		
Balbanada	Merced Monterey	60 944
RODRIQUES		
Delio	Contra Costa Twp 1	57 509
Jose	Tehama Red Bluff	70 926
Juan	San Diego S Luis R	64 781
RODRIQUEZ		
Basilio	Santa Clara Almaden	65 273
Jose	Marin Cortemad	60 787
Juan	San Bernardino S Buenav	64 212
Julian	Los Angeles Los Angeles	59 330
Maria	San Bernardino Santa Barbara	64 182
Marino	Santa Clara San Jose	65 291
Trinidad	San Diego Agua Caliente	64 856
Uatea	Los Angeles Los Angeles	59 348
RODRYNEZ		
Nolane	San Luis Obispo San Luis Obispo	65 1
RODSFORD		
W S	Butte Ophir	56 786
RODSHENYER		
Frederick	San Francisco San Francisco 7	681410
RODUGUEZ		
Deonicia	Monterey San Juan	60 978
J F*	San Francisco San Francisco 2	67 694
RODUNI		
J*	El Dorado Georgetown	58 696
RODVELL		
Johnathan	Amador Twp 5	55 364
RODVICK		
Peter	Mariposa Twp 1	60 653
RODY		
Catharine	San Francisco San Francisco 8	681266
Nich	Sacramento Granite	63 266
Nick	Sacramento Granite	63 266
RODYET		
George*	Calaveras Twp 10	57 280
ROE		
Augustus	Sierra La Porte	66 782
Augustus	Yuba Marysville	72 854
Augustus	Yuba Marysville	72 859
C F*	San Francisco San Francisco 3	67 526
David*	Humbolt Union	59 191
Edward	Nevada Bridgeport	61 467
Elmina A	Amador Twp 4	55 253
Frank	Colusa Mansville	57 437
George	Sonoma Armally	69 494
J M	Tuolumne Twp 4	71 178
James*	Contra Costa Twp 3	57 598
John	Tulara Twp 1	71 94
John	Tuolumne Visalia	71 94
Long	Butte Bidwell	56 709
Lyman B	San Francisco San Francisco 3	67 18
M N	Sutter Bear Rvr	70 820
Ranson	Solano Vacaville	69 363
Richard	El Dorado Georgetown	58 747
Richard	El Dorado Georgetown	58 758
Richard	Placer Goods	62 698
W	Butte Wyandotte	56 662
Wm H	Mariposa Twp 3	60 555
ROEBENG		
Christian*	Calaveras Twp 6	57 180
ROEBENY		
Christian*	Calaveras Twp 6	57 180
ROECK		
Fred*	Sonoma Petaluma	69 576
ROEDER		
Louis	Los Angeles Los Angeles	59 353

Name	County Locale	M653 RollPage
ROEDER		
Peter	Trinity Mouth Ca	701013
ROEEK		
Fred*	Sonoma Petaluma	69 576
ROEEL		
Joaquin*	Calaveras Twp 5	57 205
ROEHERLE		
Charles	San Francisco San Francisco 11	141 67
ROEHL		
Julius*	San Francisco San Francisco 7	681424
ROEHLBERG		
Saml	Amador Twp 3	55 369
ROEHOW		
O	Amador Twp 7	55 414
ROELKER		
Philip	Trinity Trinity	701022
ROEMARD		
Joseph*	El Dorado Placerville	58 910
ROENA		
Dolores	San Diego Colorado	64 811
ROENTHAL		
Davis	Mariposa Twp 1	60 623
ROEPKE		
Edwd	San Francisco San Francisco 10	321 67
ROER		
Manuel	Contra Costa Twp 1	57 496
Peter	Sacramento Ward 4	63 538
ROERCHUS		
Francico	Butte Ophir	56 766
Francisco	Butte Ophir	56 766
ROERL		
Joaquin	Calaveras Twp 5	57 205
ROESING		
E L	San Francisco San Francisco 6	67 464
ROETH		
Israel S*	San Mateo Twp 1	65 70
ROETHE		
C*	Shasta Shasta	66 659
ROFALIA		
Wm	El Dorado Coloma	581075
ROFAS		
Francisco*	Merced Monterey	60 940
Manuela	San Francisco San Francisco 1	68 815
Pedro	Calaveras Twp 7	57 4
ROFE		
Danl	Tuolumne Twp 2	71 279
ROFERTY		
Peter	San Francisco San Francisco 9	681067
ROFETY		
J*	El Dorado Placerville	58 863
ROFF		
Hy	San Francisco San Francisco 5	67 547
Isaac	Marin Bolinas	60 745
J S	Mariposa Twp 3	60 565
James L	Nevada Little Y	61 536
Louis	Yolo Washington	72 574
Nathan J	Yolo Slate Ra	72 696
Nathan J	Yuba Slate Ro	72 696
S	El Dorado Georgetown	58 689
Susanna	Sacramento Ward 4	63 536
W H	Sierra Twp 5	66 929
William	San Francisco San Francisco 11	121 67
William	Yuba Marysville	72 974
ROFFES		
John	Calaveras Twp 10	57 293
ROFFIN		
J F	El Dorado Coloma	581121
ROFFING		
Henry	El Dorado White Oaks	581028
ROFFINO		
John	Tuolumne Twp 1	71 210
ROFING		
John*	El Dorado Casumnes	581161
ROFINOUGH		
W	El Dorado Kelsey	581138
ROFS		
Alexr*	Sierra Downieville	661023
E*	Sacramento Ward 1	63 3
Saml	Butte Ophir	56 800
ROFSA		
Pedro*	Mariposa Twp 3	60 570
ROFUS		
Robt	Napa Napa	61 84
ROG		
---	El Dorado Georgetown	58 746
ROGA		
John*	Calaveras Twp 6	57 155
ROGABLE		
Perez	Calaveras Twp 6	57 138
ROGAN		
Briget	Sonoma Sonoma	69 649
Dougal*	Plumas Quincy	621007
John	Placer Auburn	62 589

Name	County Locale	M653 RollPage
ROGAN		
John	Placer Yankee J	62 775
Kate	Sacramento Ward 1	63 138
Michael*	Santa Clara Alviso	65 406
ROGAR		
Saml	Trinity Weaverville	701070
ROGARS		
Hale	Sacramento Ward 1	63 138
ROGART		
Wm	Sonoma Bodega	69 533
ROGARTH		
N*	Stanislaus Branch	70 702
ROGAS		
Felipe	Solano Suisan	69 228
Ignacis	Solano Suisan	69 228
Jynacis*	Solano Suisan	69 228
ROGEL		
Louis	San Francisco San Francisco 2	67 793
Mary	Alameda Oakland	55 16
Morris	San Francisco San Francisco 6	67 460
R	San Francisco San Francisco 4	681222
ROGEN		
John	Siskiyou Callahan	69 7
Nathan	Sonoma Petaluma	69 556
ROGENS		
Ann*	San Francisco San Francisco 9	68 993
ROGER		
---	Fresno Twp 1	59 85
A	San Francisco San Francisco 5	67 549
Adele	Calaveras Twp 10	57 262
Aire*	Tuolumne Twp 1	71 255
Amuel Z	Colusa Grand Island	57 481
Francis*	Mendocino Ukiah	60 801
John	Calaveras Twp 5	57 170
John	Santa Cruz Santa Cruz	66 609
John*	Calaveras Twp 6	57 170
M	San Francisco San Francisco 7	681442
Matilda	Sonoma Mendocino	69 451
ROGERJUEZ		
Barbara	San Luis Obispo San Luis Obispo	65 26
ROGERO		
L	Mariposa Twp 1	60 623
ROGEROONEY		
John	Amador Twp 4	55 247
ROGERR		
Maria*	San Francisco San Francisco 2	67 702
ROGERS		
A	El Dorado Newtown	58 780
A	Nevada Nevada	61 258
A F	Sonoma Vallejo	69 628
A H	Sierra Whiskey	66 849
A W	Sonoma Petaluma	69 589
Abraham T	San Francisco San Francisco 7	681418
Alexander	San Francisco	
Alexander	Calaveras Twp 7	57 44
Alvaro	Tulara Visalia	71 103
Andrew	Calaveras Twp 5	57 248
Andrew	Tulara Twp 3	71 45
Andrew M	Tulara Visalia	71 103
Ann	San Francisco San Francisco 9	68 993
Anna	Yuba Marysville	72 950
Antoine	Calaveras Twp 6	57 135
Antonio	Calaveras Twp 8	57 103
Augusta	Sierra La Porte	66 772
Benjamin	Calaveras Twp 7	57 2
Benjamon	Calaveras Twp 7	57 2
C	Calaveras Twp 8	57 108
C	Nevada Grass Valley	61 174
C	Nevada Grass Valley	61 191
C	San Francisco San Francisco 2	67 694
C	Sonoma Sonoma	69 656
C	Tuolumne Twp 4	71 157
C A	El Dorado Casumnes	581164
C B	Santa Clara San Jose	65 282
C F	Butte Bidwell	56 729
Charles	Calaveras Twp 7	57 40
Charles	Placer Michigan	62 826
Charles	Siskiyou Yreka	69 189
Charles T	Mendocino Ukiah	60 801
Chas	Butte Bidwell	56 721
Chas E	Butte Ophir	56 755
Cornelius	Contra Costa Twp 3	57 617
D	Calaveras Twp 9	57 412
D F	Sacramento Brighton	63 202
Daniel	Nevada Rough &	61 403
Daniel	Santa Clara San Jose	65 286
Daniel	Siskiyou Scott Va	69 51
Danl	San Francisco San Francisco 10	352 67
Danl	San Francisco San Francisco 1	68 833
David	El Dorado Kelsey	581140
David	Sacramento Ward 1	63 111
David	San Francisco San Francisco 3	67 62
David F	Yuba Marysville	72 877
E P	Calaveras Twp 7	57 3
E P	Sierra Downieville	66 961

California 1860 Census Index

Name	County Locale	M653 Roll	Page
ROGERS			
E S	Calaveras Twp 7	57	3
Edward	Calaveras Twp 8	57	77
Edward	Humbolt Eureka	59	165
F A	Siskiyou Scott Va	69	48
F R	Sierra Twp 7	66	871
Florance	Amador Twp 4	55	239
Frank	Sacramento Granite	63	248
Frank	Sonoma Petaluma	69	567
G H	Butte Bidwell	56	706
G W	Merced Twp 2	60	923
Geo	Butte Cascade	56	696
Geo	Napa Napa	61	116
Geo	Siskiyou Scott Ri	69	70
Geo C	Solano Vacaville	69	331
George	San Diego Agua Caliente	64	835
George	Solano Fremont	69	383
George	Tulara Twp 1	71	97
George	Yuba Suida	72	984
George F	Tuolumne Big Oak	71	133
George S	San Francisco San Francisco 4	68	1143
H	Calaveras Twp 9	57	368
H	El Dorado Placerville	58	879
H	Nevada Grass Valley	61	187
H A	Siskiyou Scott Ri	69	70
H C	Butte Cascade	56	696
H D	Santa Clara San Jose	65	374
H S	Tuolumne Twp 1	71	233
Hamilton	San Joaquin Stockton	64	1036
Harry	Humbolt Eureka	59	168
Henry	Humbolt Eel Rvr	59	145
Henry	Humbolt Eureka	59	168
Horatio	San Joaquin Elkhorn	64	966
Isabel	El Dorado Greenwood	58	717
J	Nevada Grass Valley	61	149
J	Nevada Grass Valley	61	179
J	Nevada Grass Valley	61	185
J	Nevada Grass Valley	61	217
J	Tuolumne Big Oak	71	154
J A	Nevada Eureka	61	375
J A	Sacramento Ward 1	63	104
J A	Sacramento Ward 1	63	7
J F	Butte Mountain	56	738
J G	Marin Bolinas	60	747
J G	Sierra Twp 7	66	880
J H	El Dorado Eldorado	58	947
J K	Colusa Grand Island	57	468
J W	San Joaquin Elkhorn	64	1036
J W	Sierra Downieville	66	956
Jacob	Sierra Morristown	66	1053
James	Calaveras Twp 6	57	171
James	Colusa Monroeville	57	451
James	El Dorado Diamond	58	789
James	San Francisco San Francisco 3	67	81
James	San Joaquin Elkhorn	64	1000
James	Santa Clara Santa Clara	65	480
James	Solano Vacaville	69	346
James	Solano Vacaville	69	363
James	Tulara Twp 1	71	75
James	Yolo No E Twp	72	682
James	Yuba Bear Rvr	72	1004
James	Yuba North Ea	72	682
James D	Sonoma Santa Rosa	69	411
James K	Colusa Grand Island	57	477
James M	San Joaquin O'Neal	64	1003
Jane	San Francisco San Francisco 10	67	244
Jas	Butte Bidwell	56	712
Jas H	San Francisco San Francisco 1	68	824
Jas M	Sacramento Granite	63	260
Jas R	Placer Rattle Snake	62	631
Jno	Klamath S Fork	59	207
Jno	Sacramento Ward 3	63	483
John	Butte Wyandotte	56	659
John	Calaveras Twp 7	57	40
John	Calaveras Twp 7	57	47
John	El Dorado Georgetown	58	685
John	El Dorado Placerville	58	931
John	Nevada Bridgeport	61	471
John	Nevada Bridgeport	61	484
John	San Francisco San Francisco 8	68	1238
John	Yolo Slate Ra	72	701
John	Yuba Slate Ro	72	701
John	Yuba New York	72	724
John A	Sierra Twp 7	66	866
John J	Marin S Antoni	60	705
John P	San Francisco San Francisco 7	68	1347
Jos	Butte Ophir	56	750
Jos	Butte Ophir	56	799
Jos	Sacramento Ward 1	63	122
Joseph	Calaveras Twp 5	57	217
Joseph	Placer Rattle Snake	62	633
Joseph P	Siskiyou Yreka	69	170
Joseph T	Siskiyou Yreka	69	170
L	Mariposa Twp 1	60	623
L B	Nevada Grass Valley	61	182
ROGERS			
Lester	Butte Wyandotte	56	659
Lewis	Sierra Twp 7	66	892
M A	Siskiyou Scott Ri	69	70
M A B	San Francisco San Francisco 4	68	1159
M C	Butte Cascade	56	703
M E	Butte Oro	56	680
Madeline	San Francisco San Francisco 7	68	1329
Mannah	Fresno Twp 3	59	37
Margaret	San Francisco San Francisco 9	68	954
Margaret*	San Mateo Twp 3	65	87
Mary	Calaveras Twp 5	57	217
Mary	San Francisco San Francisco 7	68	1409
Mary	San Francisco San Francisco 6	67	437
Mary	San Francisco San Francisco 1	68	860
Mrs	Napa Napa	61	116
N	Solano Montezuma	69	369
Nelson*	Calaveras Twp 9	57	367
O	Solano Vacaville	69	330
O G	Sonoma Petaluma	69	573
Owen	Solano Vacaville	69	319
P	Nevada Grass Valley	61	154
P K	San Francisco San Francisco 7	68	1392
Patrick	San Francisco San Francisco 3	67	61
Patrick T	San Francisco San Francisco 3	67	61
Peter	El Dorado Kelsey	58	1145
Peter	Siskiyou Yreka	69	129
Peuvai*	Santa Clara Santa Clara	65	498
Phillip	San Francisco San Francisco 7	68	1433
R B	Nevada Eureka	61	344
Richd R	San Francisco San Francisco 2	67	777
Robert	Sacramento Ward 1	63	48
Robt	El Dorado Casumnes	58	1168
Robt C	San Francisco San Francisco 10	67	246
Robt*	Nevada Red Dog	61	544
Ruben	Siskiyou Yreka	69	152
Russel K	San Francisco San Francisco 11	67	130
S	El Dorado Placerville	58	844
S F	El Dorado Eldorado	58	945
S W*	Nevada Grass Valley	61	217
Sage P	San Francisco San Francisco 6	67	426
Sam	Yolo Slate Ra	72	687
Sam	Yuba North Ea	72	687
Samuel	Fresno Twp 1	59	76
Sarah	San Francisco San Francisco 9	68	1017
Stephen	San Joaquin Elkhorn	64	964
T B	El Dorado Mud Springs	58	1000
T J	El Dorado Indian D	58	1157
T P J	San Francisco San Francisco 3	67	20
Thomas	Marin Cortemad	60	780
Thomas	Nevada Bridgeport	61	442
Thomas	Sierra La Porte	66	769
Thomas	Solano Vacaville	69	331
Thomas John*	Twp 6	57	171
	Calaveras		
Thomas*	Marin Cortemad	60	780
Thos	Nevada Bridgeport	61	454
Thos	Nevada Bridgeport	61	470
W B	Santa Clara San Jose	65	362
W K	Sacramento Ward 4	63	495
W M	Siskiyou Scott Ri	69	67
William	Marin Point Re	60	730
William	Marin Cortemad	60	780
William	San Francisco San Francisco 9	68	1051
William	Tulara Petersburg	71	51
William H	San Francisco San Francisco 3	67	11
William N	Yuba Marysville	72	974
William S	San Joaquin Castoria	64	909
Wm	Colusa Colusi	57	427
Wm	Sacramento Ward 1	63	92
Wm	San Francisco San Francisco 1	68	879
Wm	Yolo No E Twp	72	680
Wm	Yuba North Ea	72	680
Wm A	Amador Twp 1	55	498
Wm H	Sonoma Armally	69	484
Wm M*	Tuolumne Twp 2	71	313
Y W	Nevada Grass Valley	61	217
Zachariah	San Francisco San Francisco 3	67	34
ROGERY			
Mrs*	Napa Napa	61	116
ROGESS			
Thomas*	Marin Cortemad	60	780
ROGESSEN			
Charles	San Francisco San Francisco 7	68	1434
ROGET			
J	San Francisco San Francisco 5	67	538
ROGEY			
Mrs*	Napa Napa	61	116
ROGGERS			
Frank	El Dorado Salmon Falls	58	1051
J	El Dorado Placerville	58	822
N H	El Dorado Placerville	58	900
Nelson	Calaveras Twp 9	57	389
ROGIER			
Wm M	Tuolumne Columbia	71	313
ROGINE			
L	Solano Benecia	69	285
ROGINS			
Ferdinand*	Twp 3	57	592
	Contra Costa		
ROGIRS			
James D	Sonoma Santa Rosa	69	411
ROGIS			
M	Amador Twp 6	55	427
ROGIYO			
Jana*	Mariposa Twp 3	60	545
ROGNEY			
Thos*	Calaveras Twp 9	57	402
ROGNIN			
V M	Sacramento Ward 1	63	6
ROGORS			
Nelson	Calaveras Twp 9	57	367
ROGUE			
---	Los Angeles San Gabriel	59	414
Antepio*	Calaveras Twp 7	57	6
Antipio	Calaveras Twp 7	57	6
John	Tuolumne Sonora	71	226
Martin	Los Angeles Los Angeles	59	382
ROGUES			
Auguste	Sierra La Porte	66	772
ROGUIES			
Manuel	Contra Costa Twp 1	57	495
ROGUIS			
Ferdinand*	Twp 3	57	592
	Contra Costa		
ROGULMA			
Miguel*	Alameda Oakland	55	3
ROGUM			
V M	Sacramento Ward 1	63	6
ROGYO			
Jama*	Mariposa Twp 3	60	545
Jana*	Mariposa Twp 3	60	545
ROH			
John	Yuba Marysville	72	917
ROHAN			
Martin*	Santa Clara San Jose	65	390
Michel	Sierra Downieville	66	957
Patrick	Calaveras Twp 5	57	197
ROHDE			
Henry	Mendocino Big Rvr	60	845
ROHDER			
A M	Tuolumne Twp 2	71	364
Fred	Alameda Brooklyn	55	148
ROHDERS			
H	San Francisco San Francisco 5	67	525
ROHDO			
Henry	Mendocino Big Rvr	60	845
ROHERING			
Henry*	Napa Yount	61	30
ROHERS			
Antonia	Mariposa Twp 1	60	660
ROHES			
Ankel	Sierra La Porte	66	773
ROHL			
James*	Santa Cruz Soguel	66	599
John	Placer Iona Hills	62	888
ROHLFS			
C	Yuba Long Bar	72	750
ROHLLFFS			
Charles	Tuolumne Montezuma	71	506
Ernest	Tuolumne Chinese	71	490
ROHMANGER			
Fredk*	San Francisco San Francisco 9	68	1003
ROHNS			
Calvin	Sonoma Petaluma	69	583
ROHO			
Padro	Amador Twp 6	55	427
ROHR			
Flora*	Yuba Marysville	72	918
John	Yuba Marysville	72	930
John*	Yuba Marysville	72	908
Padro	Amador Twp 6	55	427
ROHRER			
Fred	Sonoma Sonoma	69	651
Swan	Sonoma Petaluma	69	583
Xarier	Yolo Slate Ra	72	703
Xavier	Yuba Slate Ro	72	703
ROHRLE			
Chas	San Francisco San Francisco 10	67	343
ROHRRANGER			
Fredk*	San Francisco San Francisco 9	68	1003
ROHT			
Gust*	Trinity North Fo	70	1026
ROHUING			
Henry*	Napa Yount	61	30
ROHWELL			
Hans	Solano Vacaville	69	355
ROI			
C F*	San Francisco San Francisco 5	67	526
ROIA			
John	Tuolumne Sonora	71	237

California 1860 Census Index

Name	County Locale	M653 Roll	Page
ROIBRAY			
Christian	Calaveras Twp 5	57	180
ROIBRUY			
Christian*	Calaveras Twp 6	57	180
ROICE			
Henry	San Francisco San Francisco 7	68	1428
ROIDE			
Louis	Yuba Marysville	72	959
ROILES			
H*	Nevada Washington	61	336
ROILGERS			
Alvan*	Calaveras Twp 4	57	326
ROILYERS			
Alvan*	Calaveras Twp 4	57	326
ROISEN			
Wm O	Sierra Downieville	66	1000
ROISEUN			
Charles	Calaveras Twp 4	57	325
ROITES			
H	Nevada Washington	61	336
ROJA			
John	Calaveras Twp 6	57	155
ROJAR			
Antonio	Tuolumne Twp 3	71	460
Casamon	Tuolumne Twp 1	71	229
Y	Tuolumne Sonora	71	187
ROJAS			
Josfa	Tuolumne Columbia	71	320
Jospa	Tuolumne Twp 2	71	320
Manuel	Marin Cortemad	60	787
Marinero	San Luis Obispo San Luis Obispo	65	35
Serarha	San Luis Obispo San Luis Obispo	65	26
Y	Tuolumne Twp 1	71	187
ROJE			
Jesus	San Francisco San Francisco 2	67	767
ROJES			
Ramon	Sacramento Ward 1	63	57
ROJJO			
Manuel	Tuolumne Twp 5	71	490
ROJO			
A	Tuolumne Twp 4	71	157
J G	Tuolumne Twp 4	71	156
Jesus	San Francisco San Francisco 2	67	767
Pedro	Plumas Quincy	62	995
ROJOH			
Austin	Tuolumne Shawsfla	71	414
ROK			
Lee	San Francisco San Francisco 10	67	355
Lu*	San Francisco San Francisco 10	67	355
ROKA			
Manuel	San Mateo Twp 1	65	49
ROKE			
John	Tuolumne Twp 1	71	191
ROKENS			
Batholomew*	Yuba Rose Bar	72	819
ROKES			
John	Yuba Marysville	72	906
Juan	San Bernardino San Salvador	64	661
ROKESA			
Manuel	San Francisco San Francisco 1	68	865
ROKHALDEE			
Jacob*	San Francisco San Francisco 7	68	1421
ROKLER			
Michael	Yuba New York	72	722
ROL			
James*	Contra Costa Twp 3	57	598
ROLAFF			
R C	Placer Todds Va	62	764
ROLAN			
Charles	El Dorado Placerville	58	844
Jos	Tehama Red Bluff	70	921
ROLAND			
A H	Mariposa Twp 1	60	649
A R	Nevada Grass Valley	61	183
C	Nevada Grass Valley	61	153
Chas	San Francisco San Francisco 3	67	37
Christopher	Placer Secret R	62	624
F	San Francisco San Francisco 10	67	354
Francis	Siskiyou Yreka	69	137
Francis	Siskiyou Yreka	69	138
G R	Sonoma Armally	69	490
Geo	Nevada Grass Valley	61	165
Geo	San Francisco San Francisco 1	68	849
H	Nevada Grass Valley	61	187
H C	Mariposa Twp 1	60	648
J	Nevada Grass Valley	61	163
J	Nevada Eureka	61	372
J B	Nevada Grass Valley	61	175
J H	Mariposa Twp 1	60	649
J H	Mariposa Twp 1	60	949
J M	Siskiyou Yreka	69	158
J M	Siskiyou Yreka	69	165
ROLAND			
Jacob	Tuolumne Sonora	71	245
James	Placer Yankee J	62	758
James	Sierra Downieville	66	978
Jas	San Francisco San Francisco 2	67	737
Jno	San Francisco San Francisco 10	67	188
Patrick	Tuolumne Twp 2	71	354
Peter	Trinity Indian C	70	986
Polcena	Trinity Indian C	70	986
R	Nevada Grass Valley	61	182
Robert	Nevada Bridgeport	61	482
S B	Nevada Grass Valley	61	176
Sarah J	Calaveras Twp 9	57	349
T B	El Dorado Diamond	58	776
Thomas A	Yuba Marysville	72	933
Thos	Placer Folsom	62	649
William	Del Norte Crescent	58	641
William	San Francisco San Francisco 11	67	93
William	San Mateo Twp 2	65	121
ROLANDE			
David	Nevada Bridgeport	61	478
ROLANDS			
A G	Sacramento Ward 1	63	105
M	Calaveras Twp 9	57	417
ROLANS			
John R	Yuba Marysville	72	972
ROLARI			
Jas	Sacramento Ward 3	63	435
ROLBERT			
Richard	Sierra St Louis	66	813
ROLBERTO			
Joseph	Calaveras Twp 8	57	86
ROLCEILS			
Elizabeth	Colusa Monroeville	57	444
ROLDS			
Joseph	Mendocino Anderson	60	869
ROLDSON			
W	El Dorado Mountain	58	1184
ROLEN			
W B	Nevada Bridgeport	61	490
ROLER			
A C	Nevada Bloomfield	61	525
Flora*	Yuba Marysville	72	918
Jno	Tehama Lassen	70	871
John*	Yuba Marysville	72	917
Joseph	Calaveras Twp 7	57	30
ROLERSTAD			
Geo*	Mariposa Twp 3	60	605
ROLERSTODT			
Geo	Mariposa Twp 3	60	605
ROLERSTOON			
G W*	Yuba Rose Bar	72	797
ROLES			
David	Tehama Lassen	70	876
James	Tehama Red Bluff	70	917
John	Tehama Lassen	70	876
Patrick	Tehama Lassen	70	873
William	San Francisco San Francisco 3	67	45
ROLESWEB			
Henry	Yuba Marysville	72	976
ROLEY			
---	Nevada Red Dog	61	546
Daniel	Colusa Butte Crk	57	466
Edward	San Bernardino San Bernadino	64	630
H L*	Sacramento Ward 1	63	45
ROLF			
Agustus	Yuba Long Bar	72	750
Asa T	San Francisco San Francisco 2	67	775
C H	Siskiyou Callahan	69	15
G	El Dorado Diamond	58	791
Israel	San Joaquin Stockton	64	1032
J T	Mendocino Little L	60	839
John	El Dorado Mud Springs	58	987
Joseph	El Dorado Diamond	58	770
Nelson	Merced Twp 2	60	918
William	Sierra Gibsonville	66	856
ROLFE			
Alfred	Amador Twp 4	55	234
Charles	Solano Suisan	69	226
Horace	San Bernardino San Bernadino	64	634
Horace C	San Bernardino San Bernadino	64	634
I J	Nevada Nevada	61	329
J J	Nevada Nevada	61	329
T H	Nevada Nevada	61	329
ROLFO			
O D	Amador Twp 4	55	250
ROLIGAN			
L B	Placer Auburn	62	565
ROLIMAN			
T L	Yolo Cache Crk	72	639
Thos	Yolo Cache Crk	72	639
ROLIMON			
T L	Yolo Cache	72	639
ROLIN			
W B	Nevada Bridgeport	61	490
ROLINA			
---	Mariposa Twp 3	60	548
ROLING			
G H	Sierra Twp 7	66	866
ROLINGER			
Geroge	Yolo Slate Ra	72	710
ROLINGSON			
Charles	San Mateo Twp 3	65	85
ROLINN			
P C	Yolo Cache Crk	72	637
ROLINS			
W W	Yuba New York	72	728
ROLINSON			
John*	Nevada Rough &	61	411
Thomas*	Yuba Rose Bar	72	788
ROLINSORO			
Charles	San Bernardino Santa Barbara	64	180
ROLIS			
Peter	El Dorado Coloma	58	1104
William*	San Francisco San Francisco 3	67	45
ROLL			
Charles*	Tuolumne Twp 5	71	513
Israel	Sierra Gibsonville	66	860
Nicholas S	Sierra Gibsonville	66	856
ROLLA			
Frank	Mariposa Twp 1	60	656
ROLLAND			
Abram	Amador Twp 6	55	443
Ferdinand	Yuba Fosters	72	821
Furdinan*	Yuba Foster B	72	821
Rudolph N*	Siskiyou Shasta Rvr	69	111
Rudolph W	Siskiyou Shasta Rvr	69	111
Yardinan N*	Yuba Foster B	72	821
ROLLANDS			
Francis E	Los Angeles Tejon	59	523
O P	Los Angeles Tejon	59	523
ROLLANZI			
Giosue	Amador Twp 1	55	456
ROLLBERG			
Henry	Colusa Colusi	57	425
ROLLEN			
Chas	Sonoma Sonoma	69	635
ROLLENS			
C	Nevada Nevada	61	249
ROLLEO			
John	Amador Twp 4	55	245
ROLLER			
J F	Klamath S Fork	59	197
ROLLEY			
D	Tuolumne Twp 2	71	300
J	Amador Twp 1	55	478
ROLLIN			
C	Sacramento Ward 1	63	85
Chas	Sonoma Sonoma	69	635
E S	Sacramento Ward 1	63	33
Ed	Sacramento Ward 1	63	33
Emma	Napa Napa	61	64
Fred	Santa Clara San Jose	65	284
J W	Mariposa Twp 3	60	548
W P	Mariposa Twp 3	60	602
ROLLINET			
Colman	Amador Twp 3	55	381
ROLLINGS			
Chas	Tuolumne Twp 2	71	364
Jacob	Nevada Red Dog	61	550
ROLLINGSTONE			
Samuel	Yuba New York	72	727
ROLLINS			
A	Placer Dutch Fl	62	734
A	Sacramento Cosummes	63	403
Albert S	Humbolt Eureka	59	170
C	Butte Wyandotte	56	657
C	El Dorado Placerville	58	835
C	Nevada Nevada	61	249
C J	Nevada Grass Valley	61	221
E B	Mariposa Twp 3	60	566
E J	Butte Hamilton	56	523
E S	Mariposa Twp 3	60	566
E V	Colusa Colusi	57	424
Fredk	San Francisco San Francisco 3	67	66
George W	Yuba Marysville	72	878
H	Nevada Nevada	61	249
H B C	Colusa Colusi	57	424
H P	Tuolumne Twp 4	71	144
Harry C	Calaveras Twp 7	57	4
Henry C	San Francisco San Francisco 11	67	153
Hiram	Butte Cascade	56	690
Hiram	Yolo No E Twp	72	674
Hiram	Yuba North Ea	72	674
Holman C	Tuolumne Big Oak	71	140
Holsincer	Tuolumne Twp 4	71	140
Irzen	Alameda Brooklyn	55	200
J A	Tuolumne Twp 4	71	175

Name	County Locale	M653 Roll	Page
ROLLINS			
Joe	Butte Ophir	56	824
John A	Yuba Parks Ba	72	781
Joseph	El Dorado Salmon Falls	58	1034
Levi	Amador Twp 2	55	288
Lloyd	Butte Hamilton	56	517
M B	Amador Twp 3	55	407
Malissa	Nevada Rough &	61	400
Mallissu*	Nevada Rough &	61	400
Marry C	Calaveras Twp 7	57	4
N C	Solano Suisan	69	207
N R	Nevada Eureka	61	387
P J	Butte Ophir	56	776
R J	Tuolumne Twp 1	71	266
Samuel B	Tuolumne Twp 4	71	140
Sophia	Sacramento Natonia	63	276
Sophia A	Los Angeles Los Angeles	59	372
Thomas	San Joaquin Douglass	64	924
Walter	Tulara Keyesville	71	59
William	Nevada Bridgeport	61	445
Wm	Sacramento Ward 4	63	505
Wm	San Francisco San Francisco 10		333
		67	
Zenaphon	Sonoma Petaluma	69	591
ROLLO			
C C	Tuolumne Twp 3	71	464
Geo	San Francisco San Francisco 10		258
		67	
ROLLS			
Cath	Sacramento Ward 1	63	23
James	Los Angeles Tejon	59	526
John	Tuolumne Twp 2	71	400
Robert	Yuba Rose Bar	72	789
ROLO			
Felecicon	Amador Twp 6	55	427
Felicicon	Amador Twp 6	55	427
ROLOFF			
John	Solano Vallejo	69	269
ROLOSS			
S I	Amador Twp 2	55	309
S J	Amador Twp 2	55	309
ROLP			
Charles	Tuolumne Montezuma	71	513
ROLPH			
John	San Francisco San Francisco 5	67	548
ROLS			
Jesse	Tehama Lassen	70	876
ROLSE			
John*	Yuba Marysville	72	930
ROLSON			
Morrice	El Dorado Gold Hill	58	1097
ROLSTEIN			
J T*	Sacramento Brighton	63	200
T T*	Sacramento Brighton	63	200
ROLSTON			
A W	Sierra Pine Grove	66	835
J B	Nevada Grass Valley	61	221
John	Amador Twp 1	55	482
ROLTON			
Henry	El Dorado Big Bar	58	736
ROLUT			
W J	Yolo Cache Crk	72	617
ROLY			
H C	Yolo No E Twp	72	669
ROM			
---	El Dorado Coloma	58	1085
---	Yolo No E Twp	72	681
---	Yolo Slate Ra	72	711
---	Yuba North Ea	72	681
---	Yuba Slate Ro	72	711
Top*	Placer Michigan	62	831
ROMADO			
Jesus	Calaveras Twp 6	57	173
ROMAIF			
Doleac	Los Angeles San Gabriel	59	416
ROMAIN			
Doleac	Los Angeles San Gabriel	59	416
Leon*	Yuba Marysville	72	897
ROMALOS			
Agustus	El Dorado White Oaks	58	1017
ROMAM			
Jno	Mendocino Little L	60	829
ROMAN			
---	Siskiyou Yreka	69	184
Anthony	San Francisco San Francisco 8	68	1253
Antonia	Mariposa Twp 1	60	653
Antonio	Amador Twp 2	55	322
F	San Francisco San Francisco 5	67	550
F	Siskiyou Yreka	69	187
Fa	Siskiyou Yreka	69	184
Henry	San Francisco San Francisco 7	68	1344
Iglaze*	Sierra Downieville	66	1022
J B	Nevada Grass Valley	61	208
J D	Siskiyou Cottonwood	69	102
James	Amador Twp 4	55	233
Jeremiah	Tehama Tehama	70	936

Name	County Locale	M653 Roll	Page
ROMAN			
Jno	Mendocino Calpella	60	829
John	Shasta Millvill	66	742
John	Tuolumne Shawsfla	71	411
Mary	San Francisco San Francisco 4	68	1127
Pedro	Yuba Marysville	72	917
Richard	San Francisco San Francisco 9	68	1104
ROMANCE			
Thomas	El Dorado Casumnes	58	1168
ROMANDA			
Ferdanand	Mariposa Twp 1	60	672
ROMANE			
Joseph	El Dorado Coloma	58	1118
ROMANO			
Pedro	Los Angeles Los Angeles	59	493
ROMANS			
Fleming	Tuolumne Twp 1	71	257
Samuel	Sierra Poker Flats	66	842
William	Los Angeles Los Angeles	59	344
ROMARA			
Ramord	Placer Secret R	62	608
ROMAREZ			
Curmine	Calaveras Twp 4	57	332
ROMARIA			
Guadalupe	Santa Cruz Pajaro	66	562
Guadelupe	Santa Cruz Pajaro	66	562
ROMARIO			
Jose	Santa Cruz Soguel	66	596
Nuavo	Tuolumne Shawsfla	71	414
ROMARIS			
Jose*	Santa Cruz Soguel	66	596
ROMARO			
Lasser	Mariposa Twp 1	60	660
R	El Dorado Placerville	58	870
Rainono	Contra Costa Twp 3	57	587
ROMARTO			
Jose*	Santa Cruz Soguel	66	596
ROMARY			
Romena	Mariposa Twp 1	60	634
ROMAS			
---	Tulara Twp 3	71	66
Tomas	Los Angeles San Juan	59	465
ROMASA			
---	Fresno Twp 2	59	107
ROMAY			
Byron*	Tuolumne Twp 3	71	449
ROMBACK			
R	El Dorado Placerville	58	854
ROMBERK			
John	San Francisco San Francisco 11		129
		67	
ROMBI			
Edward	San Francisco San Francisco 2	67	712
ROMBLINS			
George	Marin Cortemad	60	790
ROMBO			
Henry	El Dorado Coloma	58	1105
ROMBOLOR			
S*	Nevada Grass Valley	61	198
ROMCE			
J	Shasta Horsetown	66	690
ROME			
---	Siskiyou Cottonwood	69	103
Cutter	San Francisco San Francisco 2	67	713
John W	Colusa Colusi	57	419
ROMEA			
W	El Dorado Placerville	58	875
ROMEE			
Mary	Santa Clara Santa Clara	65	488
ROMELDO			
---	Los Angeles Los Angeles	59	392
ROMEN			
Guadalupe	Los Angeles Santa Ana	59	439
Jesus	Los Angeles Shaffer	59	397
Maria J	Los Angeles San Gabriel	59	416
ROMEO			
Antonio	Los Angeles Elmonte	59	258
Antonio	Tuolumne Jamestown	71	432
Francisco	Napa Napa	61	116
Francisco	Tehama Red Bluff	70	914
H	Yolo Putah	72	614
John	Tuolumne Shawsfla	71	414
Julia*	Sacramento American	63	170
Luce	Tuolumne Sonora	71	210
Ramon	Tuolumne Twp 2	71	413
Raphael	Sierra St Louis	66	818
ROMEORRIS			
C*	Calaveras Twp 9	57	387
ROMER			
Charles	Sierra Twp 5	66	942
Edward	Calaveras Twp 6	57	152
Elwood	Calaveras Twp 6	57	152
Frances*	Solano Green Valley	69	242
Frdk	San Francisco San Francisco 2	67	767
Fredk	San Francisco San Francisco 2	67	767
J	Shasta Horsetown	66	690

Name	County Locale	M653 Roll	Page
ROMER			
Julia*	Sacramento American	63	170
Raphael	Sierra St Louis	66	818
Thomas	Sierra Pine Grove	66	819
ROMERA			
Antonia	Monterey San Juan	60	1003
Cristovala	Los Angeles San Gabriel	59	419
Josaphine	Yuba Marysville	72	919
Josephine	Yuba Marysville	72	919
Luis	Monterey S Antoni	60	971
Maria A	Monterey Alisal	60	1041
Rafaela	Los Angeles Los Angeles	59	325
Rafaela	Los Angeles Los Angeles	59	401
Ramone*	Placer Auburn	62	576
Susana	Los Angeles Los Angeles	59	343
Wancisca	Los Angeles Los Angeles	59	315
ROMERER			
Peter	Mariposa Twp 1	60	654
ROMERES			
Peter	Mariposa Twp 1	60	654
ROMEREZ			
Antonio	Monterey S Antoni	60	968
Jose	San Mateo Twp 2	65	132
ROMERIO			
Mary	Sacramento Ward 1	63	55
Mateo	Los Angeles San Juan	59	464
ROMERO			
Anastacia	Santa Barbara	64	183
Aneseto	San Bernardino		
	Mendocino Ukiah	60	805
Antonia	Monterey San Juan	60	1003
Augustina	Monterey Monterey	60	949
Augustino	Monterey Monterey	60	949
Clemente	Los Angeles Tejon	59	542
Cruz	Santa Clara Almaden	65	262
Demecio	San Bernardino Santa Barbara	64	179
Dolores	Los Angeles Los Angeles	59	382
Esteban*	Yuba Marysville	72	918
Estoban	Yuba Marysville	72	918
F	Tuolumne Twp 2	71	420
Feliz	Los Angeles San Juan	59	472
Foreria*	Monterey San Juan	60	982
Francisco	Los Angeles Los Angeles	59	371
Guadalupe	Los Angeles Los Nieto	59	439
Guadalupe	Los Angeles Santa Ana	59	455
Haviel*	Contra Costa Twp 1	57	489
Havrel*	Contra Costa Twp 1	57	489
Havul*	Contra Costa Twp 1	57	489
Inocent	Los Angeles Tejon	59	522
Inocente	San Bernardino Santa Barbara	64	185
Jacento	Mariposa Twp 1	60	647
Jacinto	Mariposa Twp 1	60	647
Jesus	Los Angeles Los Angeles	59	397
Jesus	Los Angeles Los Nieto	59	433
Jose	Los Angeles Los Angeles	59	386
Jose	San Bernardino Santa Barbara	64	197
Jose	Santa Cruz Pajaro	66	561
Juan	Monterey S Antoni	60	967
Juan	San Bernardino Santa Barbara	64	181
Juan	San Bernardino Santa Barbara	64	183
Juan	Santa Clara Gilroy	65	224
Juan J	Contra Costa Twp 3	57	602
Juana	Los Angeles Los Angeles	59	367
Kylaner	Mariposa Twp 1	60	644
L W	Yolo Cache	72	609
Lacaria	San Bernardino Santa Barbara	64	185
Magurt	Mariposa Twp 1	60	647
Manuel	Los Angeles Los Angeles	59	308
Manuel	Los Angeles Los Nieto	59	439
Manuela	San Bernardino Santa Barbara	64	184
Maria	San Diego Agua Caliente	64	814
Maria A	Monterey Alisal	60	1040
Maria J	Los Angeles San Gabriel	59	416
Matias J	Los Angeles Los Angeles	59	358
Mayeil	Mariposa Twp 1	60	647
Nicolas	Los Angeles Los Angeles	59	397
P	San Francisco San Francisco 6	67	442
Pedro	Monterey S Antoni	60	967
R	Santa Clara Burnett	65	258
Rafael	Los Angeles Los Angeles	59	305
Rafaela	Los Angeles Los Angeles	59	401
Ramon	Los Angeles Los Nieto	59	428
Refugio	Monterey Monterey	60	963
Refussio	Monterey Monterey	60	963
Santiago	Sierra La Porte	66	773
Thos	Napa Napa	61	114
Tomas	San Bernardino Santa Barbara	64	184
Toreria	Monterey San Juan	60	982
Wm	El Dorado Georgetown	58	675
ROMERR			
Juan	San Luis Obispo San Luis Obispo	65	43
ROMERRO			
D	El Dorado Coloma	58	1080
ROMES			
Antony	Sierra St Louis	66	812
Frances*	Solano Green Valley	69	242

Name	County Locale	M653 RollPage
ROMES		
Francisco	Napa Napa	61 116
Julia*	Sacramento American	63 170
ROMEY		
John*	Siskiyou Callahan	69 14
Michael	Sacramento Ward 4	63 605
ROMEZ		
Antoine	Yuba New York	72 730
ROMIDTUE		
John*	Monterey San Juan	60 975
ROMIE		
Ernish	San Luis Obispo San Luis Obispo	65 22
ROMIER		
Saml*	Sacramento Ward 1	63 22
ROMIG		
Simeon	Solano Fairfield	69 198
ROMIGEZ		
Ignacio*	Tuolumne Twp 3	71 430
ROMINCO		
Garciano*	San Bernadino	64 641
	San Bernardino	
ROMINE		
H	Shasta Horsetown	66 707
M	Siskiyou Klamath	69 90
Semuel	Sierra Poker Flats	66 839
ROMINES		
Garciano*	San Bernadino	64 641
	San Bernardino	
ROMINGER		
Michael	Yuba Marysville	72 856
Michael	Yuba Marysville	72 861
ROMINI		
H*	Shasta Horsetown	66 707
Lemuel	Sierra Poker Flats	66 839
ROMIO		
Joaquin	Tuolumne Twp 2	71 414
John	Tuolumne Twp 2	71 414
Luce	Tuolumne Twp 1	71 210
Peter	Tuolumne Twp 2	71 307
ROMIR		
Autonie	Tuolumne Twp 3	71 432
ROMIRES		
Garciano*	San Bernadino	64 641
	San Bernardino	
ROMIREZ		
Lucia	Yuba Marysville	72 929
Trinidad	Santa Clara Almaden	65 269
ROMIRIZ		
Ignacio	Tuolumne Jamestown	71 430
ROMIRO		
Mazal	Mariposa Twp 1	60 647
ROMKIN		
Jos*	Sacramento Ward 1	63 67
ROMLOF		
L	Tuolumne Twp 4	71 146
Le*	Tuolumne Big Oak	71 146
ROMMIREZ		
Corez	Sacramento Ward 1	63 110
ROMNAN		
G*	Butte Kimshaw	56 600
ROMO		
Antonio	Los Angeles Azuza	59 275
Felipa	Los Angeles Los Angeles	59 317
Francisco	Los Angeles Santa Ana	59 444
Francisco	Santa Barbara	64 158
	San Bernardino	
Jose M	Monterey Monterey	60 965
Manuel	Los Angeles Los Nieto	59 424
Pedro	Los Angeles Shaffer	59 397
Ramom	Los Angeles Azuza	59 275
Simon	Los Angeles Los Angeles	59 294
Teresa	Los Angeles Los Nieto	59 426
ROMON		
Jose	San Bernardino Santa Barbara	64 188
ROMONA		
---	San Bernardino San Bernadino	64 678
ROMONIO		
Garciano	San Bernardino San Salvador	64 641
ROMORO		
Joquin	Los Angeles Los Angeles	59 512
ROMP		
H D	El Dorado Kelsey	581136
ROMPIN		
Frank	Yuba North Ea	72 687
ROMPON		
Ceazer	Calaveras Twp 5	57 226
Ceuzer	Calaveras Twp 5	57 226
ROMPOR		
Ceuzer	Calaveras Twp 5	57 226
ROMPORD		
Henry*	Tuolumne Twp 3	71 453
ROMRIO		
Joaquin	Tuolumne Shawsfla	71 414
ROMS		
R	El Dorado Placerville	58 870
ROMSBY		
M J*	Tehama Red Bluff	70 909

Name	County Locale	M653 RollPage
ROMSEY		
Mary*	Yuba Rose Bar	72 791
ROMTOF		
Le*	Tuolumne Big Oak	71 146
ROMULUS		
---	Fresno Twp 2	59 112
RON		
---	Mariposa Coulterville	60 683
---*	Mariposa Twp 3	60 576
---*	Yuba Long Bar	72 766
Annie Judy*	San Mateo Twp 1	65 65
RONA		
Delarus	El Dorado Kelsey	581136
RONALDSON		
Catharine	San Francisco San Francisco 11	131 67
Wm	Trinity East For	701027
RONAN		
James	San Francisco San Francisco 11	138 67
Thomas*	Solano Suisan	69 204
Timothy	Tuolumne Shawsfla	71 411
RONARK		
John	Tuolumne Twp 4	71 125
RONBIA		
Mready*	Placer Auburn	62 576
RONBIER		
M*	Nevada Eureka	61 365
RONBORN		
J R*	Nevada Eureka	61 370
RONCE		
George*	El Dorado Georgetown	58 680
Richard*	Solano Vacaville	69 343
RONCHART		
W	Sacramento Sutter	63 291
ROND		
John	Yuba Slate Ro	72 690
RONDEL		
Edward	San Francisco San Francisco 8	681234
RONDENA		
Louy	Mariposa Twp 1	60 672
RONDER		
Michael	Calaveras Twp 6	57 151
RONDERIA		
Louy	Mariposa Twp 1	60 672
RONDEY		
Albert	Marin Cortemad	60 789
RONDOE		
Chas	Klamath S Fork	59 202
RONDON		
Juana	Los Angeles Los Angeles	59 302
RONDONA		
Domingo	San Bernardino Santa Barbara	64 193
RONDOVILLE		
Charles	Sacramento Ward 1	63 111
RONE		
J	Placer Dutch Fl	62 728
M*	Nevada Grass Valley	61 176
RONEANO		
Mary	Amador Twp 5	55 337
RONEARRO		
Mary	Amador Twp 5	55 337
RONEG		
John*	Mariposa Coulterville	60 676
RONELL		
J W	Placer Todds Va	62 784
Joseph	San Francisco San Francisco 2	67 557
RONEN		
David*	Placer Iona Hills	62 870
John	Yuba Parks Ba	72 777
Ma A	San Diego San Diego	64 766
RONER		
Geo	Yolo Cache	72 612
RONERRO		
D	El Dorado Coloma	581080
RONERS		
Thos	Mariposa Coulterville	60 677
RONEY		
A S	Napa Napa	61 60
Christ	El Dorado Mud Springs	58 991
J M	Nevada Eureka	61 361
James	San Francisco San Francisco 2	67 727
John	Sierra La Porte	66 783
John	Solano Vallejo	69 243
John	Tuolumne Sonora	71 186
John A*	Napa Napa	61 73
John*	Mariposa Coulterville	60 676
John*	Nevada Red Dog	61 555
Joseph	Stanislaus Empire	70 734
Nicholas	Solano Vallejo	69 274
Peter	Sierra La Porte	66 783
Sulivan*	Nevada Rough &	61 413
William	Los Angeles Los Angeles	59 347
RONG		
---	Amador Twp 2	55 293
---	San Francisco San Francisco 4	681176

Name	County Locale	M653 RollPage
RONG		
---	Yuba New York	72 739
---	Yuba Long Bar	72 766
---*	San Francisco San Francisco 4	681199
Sam*	Yuba Long Bar	72 753
Torn	Marin Cortemad	60 783
Wa	San Francisco San Francisco 10	355 67
RONGA		
---	San Francisco San Francisco 4	681203
RONGE		
Pake	Yuba Slate Ro	72 713
RONGEAN		
Louis	Sierra Port Win	66 791
RONGEN		
Henry	San Francisco San Francisco 2	67 773
RONGER		
John	Yuba Long Bar	72 750
RONGET		
Chas	San Francisco San Francisco 10	219 67
RONGLE		
Aget	Siskiyou Yreka	69 125
RONGOR		
John	Yuba Long Bar	72 750
RONIG		
Henry	Yuba North Ea	72 679
RONILL		
George	Amador Twp 6	55 445
RONILLARD		
Prosper	Merced Monterey	60 943
Prosper	Monterey Monterey	60 943
RONING		
Simon	Solano Fairfield	69 198
RONIO		
Jesus	Los Angeles Los Angeles	59 330
RONKENRERE		
Alfred	San Francisco San Francisco 2	67 777
RONKENREVE		
Alfred*	San Francisco San Francisco 2	67 777
RONKER		
J*	Sacramento Brighton	63 195
RONKIN		
James	Yolo Slate Ra	72 689
James	Yuba Slate Ro	72 689
Wm	Yuba New York	72 729
RONLAND		
Peter*	Solano Benecia	69 291
RONLANDS		
John*	Nevada Bridgeport	61 490
Thiros*	Yuba Slate Ro	72 701
RONLEY		
---	Siskiyou Scott Va	69 48
John	Placer Michigan	62 807
RONLO		
Chas*	Sacramento Ward 4	63 554
RONMAN		
G*	Butte Kimshaw	56 600
RONNSA		
J P	Yolo Washington	72 600
RONNSER		
J P	Yolo Washington	72 600
RONNTHAL		
Lewis*	Sierra Downieville	66 968
RONON		
J	Yolo Putah	72 614
RONP		
H D	El Dorado Kelsey	581136
RONSE		
George*	El Dorado Georgetown	58 680
John*	Sacramento Dry Crk	63 373
Jos	Butte Oregon	56 620
RONSETT		
Anvil*	Calaveras Twp 9	57 353
RONSINE		
Catharine A*	Placer Auburn	62 561
Edward*	Siskiyou Yreka	69 125
RONSK		
RONSLER		
Peter*	Sacramento Ward 1	63 41
RONSTRO		
J	El Dorado Placerville	58 823
RONTENBRG		
Abraham*	San Francisco 7	681411
	San Francisco	
RONTET		
Mattias	Los Angeles Los Angeles	59 320
RONTILLON		
Lewis	Stanislaus Branch	70 698
RONTOIN		
J R*	Nevada Eureka	61 370
RONTOM		
J R*	Nevada Eureka	61 370
RONTORN		
J R*	Nevada Eureka	61 370
RONTOUN		
J R*	Nevada Eureka	61 370

California 1860 Census Index

Name	County Locale	M653 RollPage
RONUS		
Antonio	Yuba New York	72 730
RONZEAN		
Lewis	Sierra Port Win	66 791
ROO		
---	Butte Oregon	56 612
---	Calaveras Twp 6	57 136
---	Calaveras Twp 6	57 165
---	Calaveras Twp 6	57 167
---	Placer Auburn	62 592
---	Stanislaus Branch	70 715
---*	Butte Oregon	56 612
Ca*	Butte Kimshaw	56 592
Lee	Butte Mountain	56 741
ROOB		
Charles	Placer Auburn	62 566
ROOBAL		
J	Nevada Nevada	61 257
ROOCH		
John	Tuolumne Twp 1	71 273
Michael*	Calaveras Twp 5	57 195
ROOD		
A N	San Francisco San Francisco 7	681435
Davinport	Placer Yankee J	62 776
E	Sonoma Washington	69 672
R N	Sacramento Ward 1	63 44
T J	Sonoma Santa Rosa	69 402
Wm	Sonoma Santa Rosa	69 403
ROODS		
Daniel	Sonoma Cloverdale	69 683
Dariel	Sonoma Cloverdale	69 683
ROOF		
Henry	San Bernardino San Bernadino	64 625
ROOFLE		
Perez	Calaveras Twp 5	57 138
ROOK		
Beman	Napa Napa	61 112
Bernard	Napa Napa	61 112
Christian	El Dorado Mud Springs	58 980
F S	San Mateo Twp 1	65 63
G	Nevada Grass Valley	61 164
Wm	Butte Bidwell	56 710
ROOKE		
L C*	Nevada Grass Valley	61 166
Valentine	Tuolumne Columbia	71 312
ROOKER		
B	Butte Oro	56 680
B	Butte Bidwell	56 713
Geo	Butte Ophir	56 760
Henry J	Solano Suisan	69 234
Wm	Butte Kimshaw	56 581
ROOKMAN		
J	Nevada Grass Valley	61 238
ROOKWITZ		
Jas	San Mateo Twp 1	65 55
ROOL		
John	Sierra Downieville	661018
ROOLES		
Antonia	Monterey San Juan	601003
ROOLEY		
P	Nevada Grass Valley	61 163
Wm	Butte Kimshaw	56 607
ROOLS		
George R*	Calaveras Twp 6	57 140
ROOMBS		
Peter	Los Angeles Tejon	59 525
ROOME		
Edward	Alameda Brooklyn	55 151
Oakley	Monterey S Antoni	60 969
ROON		
---	Butte Oregon	56 612
---	El Dorado Coloma	581078
George	San Bernardino Santa Barbara	64 185
J J*	Yolo Cache Crk	72 623
J L	Yolo Cache	72 623
Joseph	Sacramento Granite	63 265
ROONER		
John	Sacramento Brighton	63 193
ROONEY		
Ann	San Francisco San Francisco 4	681213
Bridget	San Francisco San Francisco 9	681082
C	Sutter Bear Rvr	70 823
Catherine	Sacramento San Joaquin	63 352
G	Nevada Grass Valley	61 144
Garret	Calaveras Twp 9	57 383
Garrit	Calaveras Twp 9	57 383
John	Nevada Eureka	61 375
John	Siskiyou Callahan	69 14
John	Solano Vallejo	69 274
Joseph	Yuba Bear Rvr	721006
Julia T	Yuba Marysville	72 850
Luke	Tuolumne Twp 3	71 446
M	Sacramento Ward 4	63 606
Michael	Plumas Quincy	621002
Pat	Placer Auburn	62 589
Patrick	Tuolumne Columbia	71 305

Name	County Locale	M653 RollPage
ROONEY		
Patrick	Yolo Merritt	72 584
Peter	Butte Chico	56 534
Peter	Colusa Colusi	57 423
R H	Butte Kimshaw	56 599
Richard	Sacramento Franklin	63 320
S B	Sacramento Ward 1	63 47
Samuel	Santa Cruz Pajaro	66 563
Thos	Butte Hamilton	56 522
Thos	Calaveras Twp 9	57 387
Thos	Calaveras Twp 9	57 402
Thos	Sacramento Ward 1	63 130
Thos	Sacramento Ward 1	63 131
Thos	Sonoma Bodega	69 540
William	Yuba Marysville	72 869
Winnie	Sacramento Ward 4	63 572
Winnifred	Sacramento Ward 4	63 601
Wm	Trinity Lewiston	70 953
ROONEZ		
Llas*	Calaveras Twp 9	57 387
Thos*	Calaveras Twp 9	57 387
ROONY		
Thomas	Calaveras Twp 8	57 89
ROOP		
Geo	Tehama Red Bluff	70 909
George	Santa Clara Gilroy	65 237
John	Monterey San Juan	601006
John	Monterey San Juan	60 980
Randolph	Plumas Quincy	62 940
ROORK		
Thomas	Tulara Visalia	71 83
ROOS		
---	Stanislaus Buena Village	70 722
Anton J	Tuolumne Columbia	71 473
Charles	San Francisco San Francisco 3	67 51
F G*	Sacramento Ward 1	63 28
Joseph	Tuolumne Columbia	71 473
Lyman	Sacramento Sutter	63 300
Nicholas	Sierra Pine Grove	66 827
ROOSBROOK		
L	Sacramento Sutter	63 297
ROOSE		
Joseph	Tuolumne Shawsfla	71 392
ROOSH		
Thomas	Tulara Twp 1	71 83
ROOSS		
John*	Solano Benecia	69 288
ROOST		
Josephus	San Francisco San Francisco 11	157 67
ROOSTER		
Wm	Butte Kimshaw	56 581
ROOT		
---	Plumas Meadow Valley	62 913
A	El Dorado Placerville	58 817
A W	San Joaquin Stockton	641033
Adams	San Francisco San Francisco 7	681409
Albert	Plumas Quincy	62 937
Albert	Sonoma Santa Rosa	69 404
Almarian	Alameda Brooklyn	55 167
Asa	Alameda Brooklyn	55 132
Botiver	Yolo Washington	72 571
Catharine	Sonoma Santa Rosa	69 426
Datus E	San Francisco San Francisco 7	681347
David	Solano Fremont	69 380
Elliott M	Yuba Marysville	72 877
George	Alameda Brooklyn	55 167
George R	Calaveras Twp 5	57 140
George W	Siskiyou Shasta Rvr	69 116
Harry	San Francisco San Francisco 6	67 448
Henry*	Mendocino Big Rvr	60 847
J	Shasta Millvill	66 746
J	Solano Vacaville	69 334
James	San Francisco San Francisco 10	216 67
James M	Tuolumne Twp 1	71 240
Jeremiah	Alameda Brooklyn	55 132
Jeremiah	Sonoma Santa Rosa	69 426
John	San Joaquin Stockton	641033
John	Sierra Downieville	661018
John	Sonoma Santa Rosa	69 427
John S	Plumas Quincy	621007
Jon	Sonoma Santa Rosa	69 427
Lemuel	Calaveras Twp 5	57 140
Lemuel G	Calaveras Twp 6	57 140
Leonidar*	Contra Costa Twp 1	57 491
Leonidas	Contra Costa Twp 1	57 491
Nathan	Calaveras Twp 4	57 329
Nathan T	Calaveras Twp 4	57 329
Orin	Napa Yount	61 46
Richd	Amador Twp 2	55 320
Richd G	Sacramento Ward 1	63 63
Saml J	Butte Kimshaw	56 596
Samuel	Siskiyou Scott Va	69 56
Van Dork	Yuba New York	72 733
W	El Dorado Placerville	58 922

Name	County Locale	M653 RollPage
ROOT		
W	Yolo No E Twp	72 671
W	Yuba North Ea	72 671
W H	Nevada Eureka	61 379
W J	El Dorado Kelsey	581144
W J	Siskiyou Scott Va	69 22
W J	Yolo Cache	72 639
W J	Yolo Cache Crk	72 639
Wm D	Amador Twp 2	55 324
Wm H	Amador Twp 2	55 324
ROOTHLY		
Hanson	Yolo Merritt	72 583
ROOTS		
Abram	Calaveras Twp 10	57 287
James	El Dorado Georgetown	58 694
ROOVE		
Ira*	Yolo Cottonwoood	72 651
ROP		
A	Trinity Dead Wood	70 958
A	Trinity Douglas	70 980
A J	Trinity Lewiston	70 953
Albert*	Plumas Quincy	621004
G C	Marin Tomales	60 714
Geo A	Butte Bidwell	56 716
Geo*	Trinity Lewiston	70 964
George	Tehama Red Bluff	70 916
H	Sacramento Ward 4	63 503
Hugh	Butte Cascade	56 697
Hugh	Butte Bidwell	56 729
J W	Sacramento Ward 1	63 45
James	San Francisco San Francisco 10	302 67
John	Butte Bidwell	56 719
John	Tehama Tehama	70 941
John	Tuolumne Twp 4	71 144
John	Tuolumne Twp 2	71 288
John E	Santa Clara Redwood	65 460
John M	Trinity Lewiston	70 957
Joseph	San Francisco San Francisco 8	681264
M	Trinity Dead Wood	70 958
Philip	Shasta Horsetown	66 707
Robt	Trinity East For	701027
S H P	Merced Twp 1	60 897
Simon C	San Francisco San Francisco 7	681338
Sing	Butte Ophir	56 807
Thomas	San Francisco San Francisco 10	354 67
Wm	Butte Cascade	56 697
ROPAS		
Maniela	San Francisco San Francisco 1	68 815
ROPE		
Chas	Trinity Trinity	70 972
John B	Sierra Twp 7	66 865
ROPEMAN		
John	El Dorado Mud Springs	581000
ROPER		
---	Fresno Twp 2	59 44
Daniel	San Francisco San Francisco 5	67 518
Edwd	San Francisco San Francisco 10	258 67
Edwin	Calaveras Twp 5	57 250
Horace	Plumas Quincy	62 916
J	Shasta Millvill	66 754
J E	Sutter Yuba	70 774
J L	Sierra Downieville	66 988
J M	Merced Twp 1	60 902
James M	Sacramento Ward 1	63 31
M A	Siskiyou Scott Ri	69 64
Wm P*	San Francisco San Francisco 2	67 651
ROPES		
R	Calaveras Twp 9	57 377
ROPETS		
William	Monterey San Juan	60 993
ROPITAR		
Thomas	Solano Fremont	69 382
ROPLIS		
James	Placer Iona Hills	62 889
ROPOENS		
J	El Dorado Placerville	58 822
ROPP		
C	Sutter Yuba	70 766
Lenine	Sierra St Louis	66 814
Leonard*	Yuba Linda	72 990
Loriene	Sierra St Louis	66 814
ROPPS		
Adam	Contra Costa Twp 1	57 505
ROPPY		
John	San Francisco San Francisco 9	68 939
ROPUKA		
---	Fresno Twp 2	59 50
ROPY COFF		
Chas*	Calaveras Twp 4	57 314
ROPYLOFF		
Chas	Calaveras Twp 4	57 314
ROQUE		
---	San Diego Temecula	64 795

California 1860 Census Index

Name	County Locale	M653 Roll	Page
ROQUE			
Antepio*	Calaveras Twp 7	57	6
Martin	Los Angeles Los Angeles	59	382
ROQUES			
Francisco	Contra Costa Twp 1	57	508
Jose	Contra Costa Twp 1	57	496
Juan	Contra Costa Twp 1	57	496
Maria	Contra Costa Twp 1	57	509
ROR			
John	San Francisco San Francisco 10	67	179
RORAL			
J*	Nevada Grass Valley	61	193
RORCE			
Frederick	Yuba Bear Rvr	72	997
RORCKIN			
John*	Santa Clara Santa Clara	65	521
RORERA			
Miguel*	Alameda Brooklyn	55	93
RORGIRS			
Margaret*	San Mateo Twp 3	65	87
RORHER			
Richard	Tuolumne Twp 1	71	212
RORHO			
Bil	San Francisco San Francisco 3	67	82
RORICK			
F	El Dorado Diamond	58	814
RORICKE			
Hugh O	San Francisco San Francisco 3	67	59
RORISA			
James	Placer Yankee J	62	760
RORK			
Michael*	Placer Secret R	62	615
RORKE			
Barney	Calaveras Twp 4	57	311
John*	Sierra Poker Flats	66	837
RORKER			
J E	Sutter Sutter	70	811
RORKS			
James R	Mendocino Big Rvr	60	840
RORLEY			
Ricard*	Santa Cruz Santa Cruz	66	604
RORLY			
Richard*	Yuba New York	72	744
RORMER			
Saml*	Sacramento Ward 1	63	22
RORMEROS			
Malaupa*	Tuolumne Twp 1	71	475
RORNIER			
Saml*	Sacramento Ward 1	63	22
RORP			
John	Monterey San Juan	60	980
RORRE			
C L	San Francisco San Francisco 5	67	512
RORSH			
George	Calaveras Twp 5	57	251
RORST			
George*	Calaveras Twp 5	57	251
RORTES			
H*	Nevada Washington	61	336
RORURIG			
G H	Sierra Twp 7	66	866
RORY			
---	San Francisco San Francisco 4	68	1176
---	Tulara Twp 1	71	119
ROS			
---	Sierra Twp 5	66	939
ROSA			
---	Mendocino Calpella	60	821
---	Monterey San Juan	60	1000
---	San Bernardino Santa Inez	64	138
---	San Bernardino Santa Inez	64	142
---	San Bernardino Santa Inez	64	143
---	San Bernardino Santa Ba	64	216
---	San Bernardino San Bernadino	64	681
---	San Bernardino S Timate	64	693
---	San Bernardino S Timate	64	694
---	San Bernardino S Timate	64	695
---	San Bernardino S Timate	64	696
---	San Bernardino S Timate	64	698
---	San Bernardino S Timate	64	701
---	San Bernardino S Timate	64	702
---	San Bernardino S Timate	64	703
---	San Bernardino S Timate	64	706
---	San Bernardino S Timate	64	707
---	San Bernardino S Timate	64	709
---	San Bernardino S Timate	64	717
---	San Bernardino S Timate	64	718
---	San Bernardino S Timate	64	720
---	San Bernardino S Timate	64	721
---	San Bernardino S Timate	64	728
---	San Bernardino S Timate	64	729
---	San Bernardino S Timate	64	731
---	San Bernardino S Timate	64	734
---	San Bernardino S Timate	64	736
---	San Bernardino S Timate	64	737
---	San Bernardino S Timate	64	743
---	San Bernardino S Timate	64	744
---	San Bernardino S Timate	64	748
---	San Bernardino S Timate	64	749
---	San Bernardino S Timate	64	750
---	San Bernardino S Timate	64	752
---	San Diego Temecula	64	805
---	San Diego Agua Caliente	64	846
Ambrosio*	Monterey San Juan	60	981
Andrew	Santa Clara Santa Clara	65	511
Antoine	San Francisco San Francisco 11	67	124
Antone	San Francisco San Francisco 9	68	1098
Antonio	Tuolumne Twp 4	71	140
Antonio	Tuolumne Columbia	71	310
Antonio*	Tuolumne Big Oak	71	140
C G	Yolo Cottonwood	72	650
Hosea Martinas	Calaveras Twp 9	57	353
Jacob*	Siskiyou Callahan	69	17
Janacio	Amador Twp 1	55	490
Jose	Calaveras Twp 6	57	144
Juana	Amador Twp 1	55	469
Manuel	Monterey Monterey	60	961
Manuel	Tuolumne Columbia	71	357
Orr	Sierra Downieville	66	972
Pedro*	Mariposa Twp 3	60	570
Roberto	San Francisco San Francisco 2	67	702
W	Amador Twp 3	55	379
William	Nevada Rough &	61	413
William	San Francisco San Francisco 3	67	66
ROSAE			
Juan	Alameda Brooklyn	55	107
ROSAIRO			
Jose	Contra Costa Twp 1	57	514
ROSAKEK			
---	Fresno Twp 1	59	51
ROSAL			
Joran	Alameda Brooklyn	55	107
Manel	Alameda Brooklyn	55	170
Manuel	Alameda Washington	55	170
ROSALA			
Jauganes	Amador Twp 5	55	332
ROSALEE			
R	San Mateo Twp 2	65	127
ROSALES			
Antonio	Merced Monterey	60	933
Antonio	Monterey Monterey	60	933
Lantos	Merced Monterey	60	935
Louis	Calaveras Twp 5	57	185
Polano	Monterey San Juan	60	982
Santo	Merced Monterey	60	935
Santo	Monterey Monterey	60	935
Santos	Monterey Monterey	60	935
ROSALIO			
Mana	Yuba Marysville	72	951
Maria	Yuba Marysville	72	951
ROSALLES			
Aicurro	Calaveras Twp 6	57	125
Brano	Santa Cruz Pajaro	66	554
ROSAMSON			
Andrew	El Dorado Union	58	1092
Morrice	El Dorado Union	58	1092
ROSAN			
Nickolos	El Dorado White Oaks	58	1012
ROSANNA			
Margt	San Francisco San Francisco 2	67	683
ROSANTHAL			
F	San Francisco San Francisco 5	67	516
ROSAR			
Antonio*	Tuolumne Twp 1	71	238
John*	Tuolumne Twp 1	71	210
ROSARI			
---	San Mateo Twp 3	65	99
ROSARIA			
---	Los Angeles San Pedro	59	478
ROSARIO			
---	Los Angeles San Pedro	59	485
---	San Bernardino San Bernardino	64	679
---	San Diego Agua Caliente	64	851
Ignacio*	Los Angeles Santa Ana	59	441
Jose	Los Angeles Santa Ana	59	441
Maria	San Bernardino San Bernardino	64	683
Ramon	Calaveras Twp 5	57	208
ROSAS			
Adelaida	Los Angeles Los Angeles	59	297
Ambrosio	Monterey San Juan	60	981
Antonio	Tuolumne Sonora	71	238
Beatrice	Monterey San Juan	60	982
Dalia	Monterey Alisal	60	1027
Donzingue	Sierra Downieville	66	1011
F M	Marin Cortemad	60	789
Felicita	Los Angeles Los Angeles	59	335
John	Tuolumne Sonora	71	210
Jose	Monterey San Juan	60	1000
Lanila*	Tuolumne Big Oak	71	134
Lauila	Tuolumne Twp 4	71	134
Licenise*	San Francisco San Francisco 2	67	696
Manuela	Santa Clara San Jose	65	371
Marallan	San Francisco San Francisco 4	68	1216
Maria L	Los Angeles San Gabriel	59	421
Ramon	Los Angeles Los Nieto	59	435
Serafina	Los Angeles Los Angeles	59	331
Sesophrosa	Los Angeles Elmonte	59	259
Vicente	Los Angeles San Pedro	59	484
ROSASCO			
Paul	Alameda Oakland	55	41
ROSASIO			
Ramon	Calaveras Twp 5	57	208
ROSATES			
Louis	Calaveras Twp 5	57	185
ROSATHA			
---	Napa Napa	61	84
ROSBACK			
H	Sacramento Ward 4	63	503
ROSBOUROUGH			
Judge	Siskiyou Yreka	69	194
ROSBURY			
J R*	Siskiyou Yreka	69	173
ROSCE			
Frederick*	Yuba Bear Rvr	72	997
ROSCHE			
Jacob	Sacramento Ward 4	63	550
ROSCOD			
Manl	Mariposa Twp 1	60	644
ROSCOE			
Eli	Placer Forest H	62	803
Manl	Mariposa Twp 1	60	644
Wm	San Francisco San Francisco 3	67	43
ROSDE			
Louis	Yuba Marysville	72	959
ROSE			
---	Butte Bidwell	56	711
---	Fresno Twp 1	59	85
A	El Dorado Mud Springs	58	964
A	Siskiyou Callahan	69	11
A W	Amador Twp 4	55	257
A*	Siskiyou Callahan	69	11
Adam	Siskiyou Klamath	69	96
Ah	Butte Bidwell	56	711
Allen E	San Joaquin Castoria	64	891
Alley	Alameda Brooklyn	55	125
Anderson	San Joaquin Elkhorn	64	989
Andy	Mariposa Twp 3	60	600
Ann	Tuolumne Springfield	71	367
Antone	Alameda Brooklyn	55	127
Antone	El Dorado Salmon Hills	58	1055
Antonio M	Los Angeles San Jose	59	286
Augustus	Yuba Marysville	72	970
Austen	Alameda Brooklyn	55	184
Autin*	Sacramento Granite	63	246
Autur*	Sacramento Granite	63	246
B	Yolo Cache	72	609
B F	Sacramento Cosumnes	63	388
Catharine	Butte Bidwell	56	726
Charles	Amador Twp 1	55	471
Charles	El Dorado Placerville	58	907
Charles	Tulara Twp 2	71	24
Charles W	San Francisco San Francisco 7	68	1405
Chas	Sacramento Natonia	63	285
Cornelius*	Calaveras Twp 6	57	136
Danl	Tuolumne Twp 2	71	279
David	San Francisco San Francisco 8	68	1269
E	Butte Chico	56	533
E	El Dorado Mud Springs	58	983
E B	Yuba Foster B	72	828
E L	Solano Benecia	69	309
Edwar	Tuolumne Jamestown	71	452
Edward	Sierra Twp 5	66	939
Emanuel	Trinity State Ba	70	1001
Fank	El Dorado Big Bar	58	735
Frank	Nevada Rough &	61	424
Frank	San Francisco San Francisco 2	67	720
Frank H	El Dorado Mud Springs	58	980
Frank S	Alameda Brooklyn	55	209
Fred	San Francisco San Francisco 2	67	788
Frederick	San Francisco San Francisco 3	67	48
Frederick	San Francisco San Francisco 3	67	66
Fredrick	San Francisco San Francisco 3	67	66
G	Sacramento Ward 4	63	512
G	Sutter Yuba	70	778
Geo	Nevada Grass Valley	61	151
Geo H	Napa Napa	61	90
George	Los Angeles Los Angeles	59	335
George	Trinity Hay Fork	70	991
George W	San Francisco San Francisco 4	68	1159
H	Sacramento Ward 1	63	4
H P	Shasta Millvill	66	741
H T	Amador Twp 3	55	393

California 1860 Census Index

Name	County Locale	M653 RollPage
ROSE		
Haroly	El Dorado Georgetown	58 759
Henry	Sacramento Lee	63 211
Henry	San Francisco San Francisco 4	681 134
Henry	San Francisco San Francisco 7	681 335
Henry	San Francisco San Francisco 9	68 955
Henry C*	Stanislaus Branch	70 698
Isaac	Calaveras Twp 5	57 146
Isaac	Sacramento Georgian	63 347
J	Nevada Eureka	61 375
J	Shasta Shasta	66 673
J	Sutter Sutter	70 809
J	Sutter Sutter	70 812
J C	Napa Napa	61 75
J C	Nevada Nevada T	61 326
J C	Yolo Putah	72 614
J M	Tuolumne Columbia	71 307
J P	Sutter Nicolaus	70 830
Jacob	Nevada Bloomfield	61 516
Jacob	Siskiyou Callahan	69 17
James	Sierra St Louis	66 805
James	Solano Suisan	69 220
James*	Sierra St Louis	66 805
Jell	Tuolumne Twp 2	71 307
Jesse	Los Angeles Los Angeles	59 512
John	Alameda Brooklyn	55 141
John	Amador Twp 1	55 468
John	El Dorado Casumnes	581 162
John	El Dorado Mud Springs	58 991
John	Napa Yount	61 38
John	Nevada Nevada T	61 327
John	Placer Rattle Snake	62 600
John	Sacramento Georgian	63 335
John	San Francisco San Francisco 9	681 106
John	San Francisco San Francisco 5	67 477
John	San Francisco San Francisco 2	67 773
John	San Mateo Twp 3	65 78
John	Sierra Twp 7	66 884
John	Tuolumne Twp 2	71 288
John	Yolo Cache Crk	72 643
Jose	Calaveras Twp 5	57 144
Joseph	Alameda Brooklyn	55 125
Joseph	Nevada Bloomfield	61 526
Joseph	Sierra Downieville	661 001
Joseph	Trinity Texas Ba	70 981
Joseph	Yolo Merritt	72 577
Josiah	San Francisco San Francisco 11	104 67
Julius K	San Francisco San Francisco 8	681 271
L	Amador Twp 3	55 396
L	Nevada Grass Valley	61 211
L	Yuba Fosters	72 828
Lewis	Solano Benecia	69 317
Lewis*	Solano Benecia	69 316
Louis	San Bernardino San Bernadino	64 670
Louis	San Diego San Diego	64 760
Lucy	Colusa Monroeville	57 440
Lyrus	Napa Napa	61 73
M	Nevada Nevada	61 290
M	Nevada Washington	61 333
M P	Napa Napa	61 56
Manuel	Alameda Brooklyn	55 100
Manuel	Tuolumne Twp 4	71 140
Marshal R	Sacramento Ward 4	63 518
Mary	Shasta French G	66 714
Mary A	Yolo Washington	72 573
Mary E	Napa Napa	61 59
Meillon	Sacramento Granite	63 226
Merllon*	Sacramento Granite	63 226
Miguel	Alameda Brooklyn	55 150
Milten	Sacramento Granite	63 252
Milton	Sacramento Granite	63 252
Monl*	Nevada Bridgeport	61 441
Mons*	Nevada Bridgeport	61 441
Mont	Nevada Bridgeport	61 441
Moul*	Nevada Bridgeport	61 441
Mous*	Nevada Bridgeport	61 441
N D	Solano Vacaville	69 348
N P	San Mateo Twp 1	65 68
Paul	Yuba New York	72 736
Peter*	Nevada Red Dog	61 549
R C	Butte Oregon	56 643
Racula	Los Angeles San Jose	59 285
Richard	San Francisco San Francisco 11	147 67
Robert H	Sierra La Porte	66 784
Robt	Del Norte Crescent	58 631
Robt	Del Norte Crescent	58 632
S R	Sacramento Ward 3	63 485
Saml	Placer Dutch Fl	62 715
Saml D	Solano Suisan	69 226
Saml De	Solano Suisan	69 226
Syrus	Napa Napa	61 73
T	Sutter Sutter	70 809
Terrence	San Francisco San Francisco 1	68 845
Thoms	Yolo Merritt	72 578
ROSE		
W	Amador Twp 7	55 420
W	Nevada Grass Valley	61 164
W J	El Dorado Kelsey	581 141
W L	Butte Ophir	56 758
Walton	Siskiyou Callahan	69 16
Whany	Sierra La Porte	66 773
William	Calaveras Twp 6	57 115
William	Yolo Cottonwoood	72 655
Wm	Sacramento Ward 1	63 106
Wm	Sacramento Ward 3	63 458
Wm	Sierra Twp 7	66 899
ROSEA		
F	El Dorado Placerville	58 841
J W	Mariposa Twp 3	60 585
ROSEANA		
Charles	Marin San Rafael	60 767
ROSEBAUM		
William*	Alameda Oakland	55 57
ROSEBERG		
John	Sonoma Santa Rosa	69 388
ROSEBERRY		
Wm	Sierra Monte Crk	661 037
ROSEBERY		
John	Butte Wyandotte	56 667
ROSEBOON		
Gilbert	Butte Ophir	56 745
ROSEBROOK		
L D	Sacramento Ward 3	63 481
ROSEBROUGH		
J H	Yolo Cache Crk	72 635
J N	Yolo Cache	72 635
ROSEBUON		
Gilbert	Butte Ophir	56 745
ROSEBURG		
Henry	Alameda Brooklyn	55 148
ROSEBURRY		
E R	Nevada Grass Valley	61 220
J	Nevada Grass Valley	61 220
ROSEBURY		
J*	Nevada Grass Valley	61 220
ROSECOM		
Wm	San Francisco San Francisco 1	68 811
ROSECRONS		
Eli*	Sierra Twp 5	66 929
ROSECROUS		
Columbus	Sierra Twp 7	66 866
Eli*	Sierra Twp 5	66 929
ROSECROUSE		
Columbus	Sierra Twp 7	66 866
ROSEE		
Ickolas	Plumas Meadow Valley	62 929
ROSEFELD		
J N	Sacramento Ward 1	63 87
ROSEFERN		
Frank	Nevada Rough &	61 424
ROSEL		
Geo	Butte Oregon	56 635
ROSELA		
Ana R	Los Angeles Santa Ana	59 445
ROSELAP		
L	El Dorado Mud Springs	58 993
ROSELAUM		
William*	Alameda Oakland	55 57
ROSELES		
Manti*	Plumas Quincy	62 971
ROSELL		
Joel	Alameda Brooklyn	55 138
W A	El Dorado Placerville	58 874
ROSELLS		
John	Placer Yankee J	62 759
ROSELY		
William	El Dorado Coloma	581 113
ROSEMAIRRD		
Hannah*	San Francisco San Francisco 9	68 979
ROSEMAMD		
Hannah*	San Francisco San Francisco 9	68 979
ROSEMAN		
Custavus	Placer Michigan	62 842
F	San Joaquin Stockton	641 057
Jacob	Calaveras Twp 6	57 175
ROSEMANN		
Hannah*	San Francisco San Francisco 9	68 979
ROSEMAUN		
Hannah	San Francisco San Francisco 9	68 979
ROSEMENSE		
James*	Shasta Horsetown	66 707
ROSEMER		
Andrew	Alameda Brooklyn	55 102
ROSEMERSE		
James*	Shasta Horsetown	66 707
ROSEMIRE		
Jno	Klamath Trinidad	59 223
ROSEMONSE		
Jamesa	Shasta Horsetown	66 707
ROSEN		
George	Tuolumne Shawsfla	71 404
J W	Mariposa Twp 3	60 585
ROSENANSE		
James*	Shasta Horsetown	66 707
ROSENBAMER		
M J*	Butte Kimshaw	56 597
ROSENBANIN		
John*	Nevada Bridgeport	61 486
ROSENBAUM		
Abraham	San Francisco San Francisco 7	681 372
F H	San Francisco San Francisco 10	221 67
H	Tuolumne Columbia	71 332
J L*	Tehama Red Bluff	70 916
J S	San Francisco San Francisco 5	67 526
J S*	Tehama Red Bluff	70 916
J W	Tehama Red Bluff	70 913
John	Nevada Bridgeport	61 486
John H	Placer Virginia	62 665
Jos	San Francisco San Francisco 2	67 799
Joseph	Yuba Marysville	72 847
M J	Butte Kimshaw	56 597
Morris	San Francisco San Francisco 2	67 799
S	Butte Ophir	56 792
ROSENBAWER		
M J*	Butte Kimshaw	56 597
ROSENBENG		
Souis*	Calaveras Twp 10	57 294
ROSENBERG		
Benjamin	Yuba Marysville	72 910
Elisha	Sonoma Santa Rosa	69 390
G C	Nevada Bridgeport	61 502
George	San Francisco San Francisco 8	681 297
Harriet	San Francisco San Francisco 7	681 364
Henry	Yuba Marysville	72 930
Herman	San Francisco San Francisco 2	67 590
James	Yuba Marysville	72 878
John	Sonoma Santa Rosa	69 388
K	San Francisco San Francisco 2	67 755
Lewis	San Francisco San Francisco 2	67 590
Louis	Sacramento Casumnes	63 381
Marcus J	Sonoma Russian	69 436
Marks	Sonoma Santa Rosa	69 388
Meyer G	Sonoma Russian	69 436
Nathan	San Francisco San Francisco 8	681 322
Otto	Marin Bolinas	60 749
P	Sacramento Ward 1	63 31
Sorris*	Calaveras Twp 10	57 294
Victor	Calaveras Twp 10	57 278
ROSENBERRY		
Morris*	Placer Iona Hills	62 859
ROSENBERY		
James	Yuba Marysville	72 878
Marcus J	Sonoma Russian	69 436
ROSENBLUME		
Joseph	Tuolumne Twp 5	71 488
ROSENBOGHER		
John*	San Francisco San Francisco 3	67 26
ROSENBURG		
Jacob	San Francisco San Francisco 2	67 799
Jacob	Yuba Marysville	72 908
Larrie	Alameda Oakland	55 12
Lius	Los Angeles San Juan	59 477
Louis	Calaveras Twp 10	57 294
Luis	Los Angeles San Juan	59 477
M	Siskiyou Scott Va	69 54
Morris*	Placer Iona Hills	62 859
Myer	San Francisco San Francisco 2	67 629
Samuel	Siskiyou Yreka	69 188
Thomas	Plumas Quincy	62 962
ROSENBURGER		
A	El Dorado Mud Springs	58 949
ROSENBURGH		
Maria	San Francisco San Francisco 4	681 148
Marie	San Francisco San Francisco 4	681 148
ROSENCRANTR		
Harris	Mariposa Twp 3	60 621
ROSENCRANZ		
J	Stanislaus Oatvale	70 718
ROSENDAL		
Charles*	Nevada Bridgeport	61 448
ROSENDALE		
Max	San Francisco San Francisco 9	68 990
ROSENEN		
George	Calaveras Twp 5	57 141
ROSENER		
George*	Calaveras Twp 6	57 141
L	San Francisco San Francisco 5	67 512
ROSENERANDS		
Henry M	San Francisco San Francisco 2	67 763
ROSENFELD		
J N	Sacramento Ward 1	63 87
ROSENFELDT		
John	San Francisco San Francisco 10	350 67

Name	County Locale	M653 RollPage
ROSENFELDT		
Rosa	San Francisco San Francisco	10 228 67
Rosn	San Francisco San Francisco	10 228 67
ROSENFELT		
Ann S	San Francisco San Francisco	7 681348
Catharine*	San Francisco San Francisco	7 681417
Simon	Sacramento Ward 1	63 37
ROSENFIELD		
M	San Francisco San Francisco	5 67 520
Simon*	Sacramento Ward 1	63 151
ROSENHEIM		
Aaron	San Francisco San Francisco	7 681383
Joel	Santa Cruz Pajaro	66 532
M	Siskiyou Yreka	69 188
ROSENIARD		
Joseph*	El Dorado Placerville	58 910
ROSENKRANTZ		
Hiram D	Siskiyou Yreka	69 129
ROSENKROW		
Richard	Placer Dutch Fl	62 718
ROSENORAND		
Henry M	San Francisco San Francisco	2 67 763
ROSENSTINGAL		
Charles	Yuba Long Bar	72 755
ROSENSTOCK		
S W	San Francisco San Francisco	5 67 475
Saml	San Francisco San Francisco	5 67 476
ROSENSTUGAL		
Charles	Yuba Long Bar	72 755
ROSENTHAL		
A	San Francisco San Francisco	5 67 519
Bendson	San Francisco San Francisco	8 681297
Benson*	San Francisco San Francisco	8 681297
Frank	Sierra Monte Crk	661035
Jacob	San Francisco San Francisco	9 681052
Jacob	San Francisco San Francisco	2 67 696
Lewis	Sierra Downieville	66 968
Louis	San Joaquin Stockton	641026
Nancy	San Francisco San Francisco	8 681297
S	Nevada Nevada	61 257
Simon R	Butte Ophir	56 761
ROSENTHALL		
A	Nevada Nevada	61 253
L	San Joaquin Stockton	641045
Max	Santa Clara Gilroy	65 238
S	Nevada Nevada	61 257
ROSENTHAT		
Dora	San Francisco San Francisco	5 67 519
ROSENTHEL		
Joseph	Mariposa Twp 1	60 656
ROSERONS		
Eli	Sierra Twp 5	66 929
ROSES		
Vinuntio*	El Dorado Georgetown	58 749
Zenobia	Tuolumne Twp 1	71 225
Zenolia	Tuolumne Sonora	71 225
ROSETA		
---	Monterey San Juan	60 992
ROSETAUM		
William*	Alameda Oakland	55 57
ROSEVI		
Manl	Mariposa Twp 1	60 644
ROSEWARREN		
H*	Nevada Grass Valley	61 209
ROSEWTHAL		
Benson*	San Francisco San Francisco	8 681297
ROSEY		
Danl	Tuolumne Twp 2	71 273
Louis	Placer Secret R	62 617
ROSGRASS		
J R	Sonoma Petaluma	69 589
ROSHU		
---	Fresno Twp 2	59 65
ROSI		
Peter*	Nevada Red Dog	61 549
ROSIA		
Lour	Contra Costa Twp 1	57 509
ROSIAS		
Domingues*	Yuba Parke Ba	72 782
ROSIDER		
John W	Sierra La Porte	66 777
ROSIER		
Levi	Nevada Bloomfield	61 510
ROSIERS		
Domingues*	Yuba Parke Ba	72 782
ROSIL		
Geo*	Butte Oregon	56 635
ROSILES		
Marti*	Plumas Quincy	62 971
ROSIN		
J*	El Dorado Georgetown	58 760
ROSINDALE		
Charles*	Nevada Bridgeport	61 448

Name	County Locale	M653 RollPage
ROSINER		
Elhannan*	Calaveras Twp 6	57 141
George	Calaveras Twp 6	57 141
ROSINFIELD		
Simon*	Sacramento Ward 1	63 151
ROSINGTON		
T B	El Dorado Diamond	58 783
ROSINI		
John*	San Francisco San Francisco	4 681216
ROSINO		
Austin	Sacramento Ward 1	63 110
Christin	Sacramento Ward 1	63 110
ROSINS		
Antonio	Yuba New York	72 730
ROSINSKY		
Simon	Los Angeles Los Angeles	59 333
ROSINSTOCK		
Saml	San Francisco San Francisco	5 67 476
ROSITA		
---	San Bernardino S Timate	64 694
---	San Bernardino S Timate	64 715
ROSIUS		
Domingues	Yuba Parks Ba	72 782
ROSKE		
Barney	Calaveras Twp 4	57 311
Barney Jr	Calaveras Twp 4	57 311
ROSLEMEYER		
V	San Francisco San Francisco	4 681156
ROSLER		
M	Yolo Merritt	72 581
ROSLOUGH		
Thomas	Sierra Twp 5	66 943
ROSMER		
G	Tuolumne Columbia	71 326
ROSMON		
J A*	Los Angeles Tejon	59 528
ROSMOSEN		
Ja	Sonoma Salt Point	69 691
ROSNER		
Levy	San Francisco San Francisco	5 67 476
Manuel	Shasta Shasta	66 682
ROSNEY		
P	Napa Napa	61 76
ROSO		
---*	Fresno Millerto	59 2
ROSONA		
John	Calaveras Twp 4	57 328
ROSONDAL		
Charles	Nevada Bridgeport	61 448
ROSONDALE		
Charles*	Nevada Bridgeport	61 448
ROSONDUL		
Charles*	Nevada Bridgeport	61 448
ROSOS		
Lorenzo	Calaveras Twp 4	57 316
ROSOSCO		
A	Tuolumne Twp 1	71 269
ROSROSTH		
Edwin C*	Calaveras Twp 5	57 206
ROSS		
A	Amador Twp 3	55 372
A	Marin Tomales	60 715
A	Sacramento Sutter	63 306
A	Sacramento Sutter	63 307
A	San Francisco San Francisco	6 67 463
A	Trinity Dead Wood	70 958
A	Yuba New York	72 733
A J	Trinity Lewiston	70 953
A M	Placer Michigan	62 830
A P	Siskiyou Scott Ri	69 68
Aaron	Sacramento Granite	63 239
Abraham	Sacramento Granite	63 248
Adam	San Francisco San Francisco	6 67 458
Adam	Solano Suisan	69 222
Albert*	Plumas Quincy	621004
Alex	Sacramento Franklin	63 316
Alexander	San Francisco San Francisco	11 152 67
Alexr	Sierra Downieville	661023
Alfred G	Calaveras Twp 6	57 158
Andrew	Alameda Brooklyn	55 199
Anton	Sacramento Ward 3	63 456
Antonio	Tuolumne Columbia	71 290
Asa	Sonoma Sonoma	69 651
Banjamin F	Monterey San Juan	60 994
Benjamin F	Monterey San Juan	60 994
Bery	Amador Twp 3	55 369
C	San Francisco San Francisco	9 681057
Catherine	Calaveras Twp 4	57 305
Cha	Sonoma Sonoma	69 651
Charles	Los Angeles San Pedro	59 481
Charles	San Joaquin Oneal	64 937
Charles	Tulara Keyesville	71 58
Charles A	Yuba Marysville	72 893
Charles L	San Francisco San Francisco	7 681422
Chas	Mariposa Twp 3	60 571

Name	County Locale	M653 RollPage
ROSS		
Chas	Sacramento Franklin	63 314
Chas	San Francisco San Francisco	2 67 757
Chas Frank	Calaveras Twp 6	57 159
D	El Dorado Greenwood	58 720
D	Sacramento Brighton	63 193
D	San Mateo Twp 3	65 76
D	Yuba Rose Bar	72 797
D B	Butte Wyandotte	56 666
D L	Sonoma Salt Point	69 692
D S	Sacramento Ward 3	63 466
Daniel	Butte Oregon	56 619
Daniel	Monterey Monterey	60 958
Daniel	San Francisco San Francisco	8 681242
Danl	Sacramento Sutter	63 290
Davd	Sonoma Salt Point	69 692
David	Napa Napa	61 94
David	Napa Napa	61 99
David	Nevada Rough &	61 421
David	Sacramento Ward 3	63 476
David	Sierra Twp 7	66 867
David	Sonoma Salt Point	69 692
David	Yuba New York	72 733
E	Sacramento Ward 1	63 3
E	Siskiyou Cottonwoood	69 105
E K	El Dorado Georgetown	58 754
E L	Sierra Downieville	661016
Edridge*	Yuba Marysville	72 893
Edward	Alameda Brooklyn	55 189
Edward	Sierra Twp 5	66 939
Elbridge	Yuba Marysville	72 945
Eldridge	Yuba Marysville	72 945
Ellridge	Yuba Marysville	72 893
F	Tuolumne Twp 3	71 421
F G	Sacramento Ward 1	63 28
Fernando	Contra Costa Twp 1	57 513
Francis	Monterey Monterey	60 958
Frank	Amador Twp 4	55 243
Frank	Calaveras Twp 5	57 229
Frank	El Dorado Salmon Falls	581049
Frank	Sierra Morristown	661053
Frank H	San Joaquin Castoria	64 886
Fredk	Calaveras Twp 4	57 315
G B	Sierra Twp 7	66 905
G C	Marin Tomales	60 714
Geo	Sacramento Natonia	63 277
Geo	Sonoma Petaluma	69 543
Geo	Sonoma Petaluma	69 544
Geo	Trinity Lewiston	70 964
Geo A	Butte Bidwell	56 716
George	Calaveras Twp 8	57 77
George H	Calaveras Twp 8	57 49
H B	Sacramento Dry Crk	63 373
H C	El Dorado Union	581087
H F	San Francisco San Francisco	10 224 67
H F	Shasta Millvill	66 754
Harry	Placer Forest H	62 804
Henry	Nevada Bloomfield	61 519
Henry	Solano Vacaville	69 321
Honald	Tuolumne Shawsfla	71 382
Hugh	Butte Cascade	56 697
Hugh	Butte Bidwell	56 729
Hugh	Sonoma Bodega	69 537
Hugh M	Calaveras Twp 4	57 322
I	Sacramento Ward 1	63 3
Igek	Mariposa Coulterville	60 686
Isaac	San Joaquin Douglass	64 922
J	Calaveras Twp 9	57 389
J	El Dorado Placerville	58 905
J	Marin Bolinas	60 745
J A	El Dorado Placerville	58 882
J B	Sacramento Georgian	63 345
J D	Marin Tomales	60 726
J G	Siskiyou Scott Ri	69 66
J H	Sacramento Franklin	63 315
J L	Sierra Downieville	661016
J M	Butte Kimshaw	56 604
J R	Marin Tomales	60 722
J W	Sacramento Ward 1	63 45
J W	San Francisco San Francisco	10 268 67
J*	Calaveras Twp 9	57 398
Jack	Mariposa Coulterville	60 686
James	Calaveras Twp 4	57 317
James	Calaveras Twp 8	57 67
James	Placer Iona Hills	62 890
James	Sacramento Ward 1	63 19
James	San Francisco San Francisco	9 681053
James	San Joaquin Stockton	641088
James	Santa Clara San Jose	65 393
James	Tuolumne Twp 2	71 289
James	Yuba Rose Bar	72 801
James	Yuba Marysville	72 914
James B	Humbolt Pacific	59 136
James M	Tuolumne Twp 1	71 244

California 1860 Census Index

Name	County Locale	M653 RollPage
ROSS		
James*	San Francisco San Francisco 10	302 67
Jane	Napa Napa	61 113
Jas	Amador Twp 3	55 391
Jas	Sacramento Ward 3	63 436
Jas	San Francisco San Francisco 2 67 784
Jas	San Francisco San Francisco 1 68 821
Jesse B	Fresno Twp 1	59 35
Jno	Sacramento Ward 3	63 435
John	Butte Bidwell	56 719
John	Calaveras Twp 9	57 352
John	Calaveras Twp 7	57 41
John	Calaveras Twp 8	57 70
John	El Dorado Placerville	58 898
John	Merced Monterey	60 940
John	Monterey Monterey	60 940
John	Nevada Red Dog	61 545
John	San Francisco San Francisco 10	251 67
John	San Francisco San Francisco 6 67 429
John	Sierra Gibsonville	66 857
John	Sierra Twp 7	66 869
John	Sierra Twp 7	66 884
John	Sierra Twp 7	66 907
John	Sierra Twp 5	66 920
John	Tuolumne Big Oak	71 144
John	Tuolumne Twp 2	71 288
John	Tuolumne Columbia	71 310
John	Yuba Marysville	72 910
John H	Tuolumne Sonora	71 190
John H	Tuolumne Twp 1	71 190
John M	Trinity Lewiston	70 957
John P	Trinity Weaverville	701081
Jos	San Francisco San Francisco 2 67 784
Joseph	Monterey Monterey	60 956
Joseph	Placer Michigan	62 825
Joseph	Placer Michigan	62 840
Joseph	San Francisco San Francisco 8 681264
Joseph	Stanislaus Branch	70 697
Joseph W	Calaveras Twp 5	57 223
Joseph*	Shasta Shasta	66 679
Julis*	San Francisco San Francisco 10	268 67
L D	Nevada Nevada	61 272
Lawson	Sonoma Armally	69 499
Lorenzo	Sierra Gibsonville	66 856
Lyman	Sacramento Sutter	63 300
M	Nevada Grass Valley	61 193
M	Trinity Dead Wood	70 958
M W	Nevada Grass Valley	61 201
Marion	Amador Twp 1	55 489
Mary E	Sonoma Petaluma	69 603
Nahini R	San Francisco San Francisco 2 67 581
Nahuni R	San Francisco San Francisco 2 67 581
Nancy	Alameda Brooklyn	55 171
Orrin	Sierra Twp 7	66 908
Peter	El Dorado Cold Spring	581101
Peter	Placer Yankee J	62 760
Peter	San Francisco San Francisco 2 67 605
Philip*	Shasta Horsetown	66 707
Revd J W	Siskiyou Yreka	69 193
Richard	San Francisco San Francisco 2 67 804
Robert	Plumas Quincy	62 971
Robert	San Francisco San Francisco 2 67 557
S A	Merced Twp 1	60 898
S B	Sierra Twp 7	66 905
S H P	Merced Twp 1	60 897
Sam	Butte Wyandotte	56 671
Saml F	San Francisco San Francisco 10	282 67
Samuel	San Francisco San Francisco 11	150 67
Samuel	San Joaquin Douglass	64 916
Samuel D	Humbolt Mattole	59 126
Simon C	San Francisco San Francisco 7 681338
T G	El Dorado Greenwood	58 720
Thomas	El Dorado Big Bar	58 742
Thomas	San Francisco San Francisco 9 68 966
Thomas	Siskiyou Yreka	69 153
Thomas*	San Francisco San Francisco 10	354 67
Thos	Placer Virginia	62 662
Thos	Sacramento Granite	63 266
Thos	Sacramento Ward 3	63 476
Thos	Sacramento Ward 4	63 561
W	Siskiyou Scott Va	69 54
William	Del Norte Happy Ca	58 670
William	San Francisco San Francisco 9 68 943
William	Sonoma Armally	69 500
William B	Fresno Twp 2	59 19
William S	San Francisco San Francisco 8 681240
Wm	Butte Cascade	56 697
Wm	Butte Ophir	56 775
Wm	Humbolt Mattole	59 125
Wm	Nevada Nevada	61 243

Name	County Locale	M653 RollPage
ROSS		
Wm	Santa Clara San Jose	65 350
Wm G	Calaveras Twp 10	57 279
Wm G	San Francisco San Francisco 2 67 734
Wm H	Sierra Twp 7	66 911
Wm N	Sierra Twp 5	66 935
Wm R	Sierra Twp 7	66 911
Wm T	San Francisco San Francisco 1 68 821
Wm W	Yuba Rose Bar	72 791
ROSSA		
Frank	Santa Cruz Soguel	66 597
ROSSAR		
Francisco*	Merced Monterey	60 940
ROSSATER		
A	Sonoma Russian	69 434
ROSSE		
Nicholas	San Francisco San Francisco 7 681410
ROSSEAN		
Chas	San Francisco San Francisco 2 67 802
ROSSEBAR		
Andrew*	Calaveras Twp 6	57 164
ROSSENA		
Andrew*	Calaveras Twp 6	57 164
ROSSER		
E H	Sutter Yuba	70 760
Wm P*	San Francisco San Francisco 2 67 651
ROSSERA		
Andrea*	Calaveras Twp 6	57 164
ROSSES		
Rosena	Contra Costa Twp 1	57 508
ROSSET		
James	Stanislaus Branch	70 700
ROSSETAR		
Thomas*	Solano Fremont	69 382
ROSSETER		
Jas	San Francisco San Francisco 2 67 739
Thomas*	Solano Fremont	69 382
ROSSETES		
John	Amador Twp 2	55 302
ROSSETIA		
Martino*	Placer Michigan	62 832
ROSSETTER		
J H	Sonoma Bodega	69 521
ROSSEUN		
Charles	Calaveras Twp 4	57 325
ROSSEVAL		
J	Nevada Grass Valley	61 158
ROSSI		
Antonia	Amador Twp 3	55 401
James	Monterey Monterey	60 949
John	San Francisco San Francisco 2 67 691
Joseph	Tuolumne Sonora	71 225
Micholas	Tuolumne Twp 3	71 425
Nicholas	Tuolumne Jamestown	71 425
Theodore	Siskiyou Yreka	69 187
ROSSIDAR		
James*	Amador Twp 4	55 235
ROSSIN		
Jerome	El Dorado Mud Springs	581000
Morgan	El Dorado Mud Springs	581000
ROSSING		
John*	El Dorado Casumnes	581161
ROSSITER		
Jas	San Francisco San Francisco 2 67 739
Jno S	Mendocino Calpella	60 811
John W	Sierra La Porte	66 777
M S	Mendocino Calpella	60 811
N	El Dorado Diamond	58 806
ROSSLER		
Simpson	Tulara Visalia	71 103
ROSSMAN		
George	Amador Twp 4	55 239
ROSSON		
Antonio	Santa Cruz Pajaro	66 542
ROSSONE		
Alphonso	Santa Cruz Santa Cruz	66 620
ROSSOREIGH		
Edward	San Joaquin Elkhorn	64 953
ROSSOUGH		
A B	Calaveras Twp 6	57 183
H B	Calaveras Twp 5	57 183
ROST		
August	Yuba Marysville	72 893
Jacob	Yuba Marysville	72 958
John	Nevada Washington	61 341
John*	Nevada Washington	61 331
Peter H	Calaveras Twp 10	57 293
William	Calaveras Twp 5	57 228
ROSTELLER		
Geo	Butte Oro	56 682
ROSTER		
Henning*	San Francisco San Francisco 10	224 67
J	Nevada Grass Valley	61 160
John	Nevada Eureka	61 361
ROSTHE		
C*	Shasta Shasta	66 659

Name	County Locale	M653 RollPage
ROSTRASKY		
Henry	San Francisco San Francisco 6 67 400
ROSUER		
Manuel	Shasta Shasta	66 682
ROT		
---	Calaveras Twp 5	57 254
ROTA		
A	El Dorado Diamond	58 800
Francis	Placer Iona Hills	62 888
ROTAMOTAS		
Demier*	Calaveras Twp 9	57 364
ROTCHFORD		
G P	Nevada Bloomfield	61 519
ROTE		
A	Santa Clara Alviso	65 409
ROTEN		
---	Nevada Nevada	61 303
ROTENBERG		
Fred	Tuolumne Twp 1	71 197
ROTENGI		
Antonio	Amador Twp 3	55 404
ROTGER		
G*	Mariposa Twp 3	60 603
ROTH		
A	Nevada Nevada	61 313
Adam	Sierra Twp 5	66 937
C	San Francisco San Francisco 12	387 67
C G	Sutter Vernon	70 843
Charles	Siskiyou Yreka	69 187
Chas	Sacramento Ward 1	63 74
Dan*	Nevada Rough &	61 424
Francis	Tuolumne Sonora	71 209
Geo G	Sacramento Ward 4	63 523
Hiram	Monterey Monterey	60 926
Isaac	San Luis Obispo San Luis Obispo 65 35
Jacob	Yolo Slate Ra	72 703
Jacob	Yuba Slate Ro	72 703
James	Tuolumne Shawsfla	71 387
John	Merced Monterey	60 938
John	Monterey Monterey	60 938
John	Sacramento Ward 4	63 511
John*	San Francisco San Francisco 1 68 861
Marris	Calaveras Twp 9	57 351
Morris	Calaveras Twp 9	57 351
Rinehart	Yolo Cache Crk	72 644
Rudolph*	Sacramento Ward 4	63 543
Simon	Sacramento Ward 4	63 583
ROTHBURN		
James	San Francisco San Francisco 7 681338
ROTHCAP		
Robert	San Francisco San Francisco 3 67 7
ROTHCASS		
Robert*	San Francisco San Francisco 3 67 7
ROTHCHILD		
A	Nevada Nevada	61 257
B	Sacramento Ward 4	63 533
J S	San Francisco San Francisco 2 67 669
ROTHE		
Chas W*	Tuolumne Big Oak	71 138
Herman F	Tuolumne Big Oak	71 138
Julius A	Santa Clara Fremont	65 424
Lemuel	San Francisco San Francisco 10	224 67
ROTHECHILD		
M	San Francisco San Francisco 5 67 552
ROTHENBUCHER		
John	Sacramento Ward 1	63 35
ROTHENBUCHIE		
John*	Sacramento Ward 1	63 35
ROTHENBUSH		
Jacob	Tuolumne Sonora	71 204
Pler*	San Joaquin Stockton	641012
ROTHENIT		
Ferdinand*	Butte Ophir	56 766
ROTHENTH		
Ferdinand	Butte Ophir	56 766
ROTHENTRICHER		
John*	Sacramento Ward 1	63 35
ROTHER		
Robert	San Francisco San Francisco 7 681377
William	Tuolumne Twp 1	71 206
ROTHERY		
B M T	Yolo Cottonwood	72 650
ROTHESETH		
Ferdinand*	Butte Ophir	56 766
ROTHESUT		
Ferdinand*	Butte Ophir	56 766
ROTHFAS		
J B	Siskiyou Yreka	69 185
ROTHFIELD		
J	San Francisco San Francisco 5 67 521
ROTHINETT		
M	El Dorado Georgetown	58 685
ROTHING		
B M T	Yolo Cottonwoood	72 650

California 1860 Census Index

Name	County Locale	M653 Roll	Page
ROTHNER			
C H*	San Francisco San Francisco 4	68	1161
ROTHNIR			
C H*	San Francisco San Francisco 4	68	1161
ROTHOR			
William	Tuolumne Sonora	71	206
ROTHROCK			
Geo	Butte Oregon	56	610
Lewis*	Sacramento Ward 4	63	594
ROTHRRIR			
C H	San Francisco San Francisco 4	68	1161
ROTHRUCK			
Lewis*	Sacramento Ward 4	63	594
ROTHSCHILD			
E	San Francisco San Francisco 10	67	180
M	San Francisco San Francisco 5	67	552
Thomas	Tulara Twp 3	71	47
ROTHSTEIN			
Charles	Tuolumne Twp 1	71	259
Charly	Tuolumne Twp 1	71	259
ROTHSTEM			
Wecker	Sonoma Sonoma	69	638
Wuker	Sonoma Sonoma	69	638
ROTHURMAND			
W F*	El Dorado Salmon Falls	58	1035
ROTHWELL			
H	Shasta Horsetown	66	692
Kt	Nevada Eureka	61	358
T	Nevada Eureka	61	358
ROTHWICK			
G A*	Sierra Downieville	66	987
ROTIN			
---	Nevada Nevada	61	303
ROTKOPF			
D*	Napa Hot Springs	61	4
ROTSFORD			
R M	Trinity Hay Fork	70	993
ROTTANZI			
Antonio	San Francisco San Francisco 2	67	698
Geosue	Amador Twp 1	55	456
Giosue	Amador Twp 1	55	456
ROTTER			
Charles	Siskiyou Yreka	69	184
ROTTERMAN			
H W	Sutter Nicolaus	70	835
ROTTGUP			
D	Yolo Washington	72	562
ROU			
---	San Francisco San Francisco 4	68	1177
---	San Francisco San Francisco 4	68	1184
---*	Mariposa Twp 3	60	576
ROUBIA			
Mready*	Placer Auburn	62	576
ROUBIER			
M	Nevada Eureka	61	365
ROUBLE			
Martin	Calaveras Twp 6	57	123
W H	Butte Chico	56	556
ROUBORN			
J R*	Nevada Eureka	61	370
ROUCAIER			
Leon*	Yuba Marysville	72	897
ROUCE			
Richard	Solano Vacaville	69	343
Susan	San Francisco San Francisco 6	67	444
ROUCH			
D*	San Francisco San Francisco 5	67	543
James	Sierra Poker Flats	66	840
John L	Sierra Pine Grove	66	825
John*	Shasta Horsetown	66	700
M	Nevada Grass Valley	61	212
T B	Nevada Grass Valley	61	198
Thomas	Sierra Pine Grove	66	819
Thos	Sonoma Petaluma	69	589
William	Sierra Whiskey	66	845
ROUCHE			
John	Monterey Alisal	60	1044
ROUCK			
Ed*	Nevada Red Dog	61	546
ROUD			
Jasper	Yuba Suida	72	990
ROUERS			
Thos	Mariposa Coulterville	60	677
ROUEY			
John A*	Napa Napa	61	73
ROUGEN			
Henry*	San Francisco San Francisco 2	67	773
ROUGENS			
H*	Stanislaus Buena Village	70	722
ROUGET			
Chas	San Francisco San Francisco 10	67	219
ROUGHTEN			
N	Siskiyou Callahan	69	9
ROUGHTENTHESTEL			
Ben*	Yuba Fosters	72	840
ROUGHTENTHISTET			
Ben*	Yuba Fosters	72	840
ROUGHTON			
N	Siskiyou Callahan	69	9
ROUILL			
George	Amador Twp 6	55	445
ROUILLARD			
Prosper*	Merced Mont	60	943
Prosper*	Monterey Monterey	60	943
ROUIS			
Domingo	Calaveras Twp 6	57	150
ROUISE			
Manuel	Calaveras Twp 10	57	277
ROUK			
T	Nevada Grass Valley	61	205
Washington	Yuba Marysville	72	865
ROUKE			
Christian	Tuolumne Jamestown	71	444
ROUKER			
J*	Sacramento Brighton	63	195
ROUKS			
John	Tuolumne Twp 2	71	284
ROULAND			
Peter*	Solano Benecia	69	291
ROULANDS			
John*	Nevada Bridgeport	61	490
Wm E	Yolo Slate Ra	72	699
ROULIN			
C	Nevada Grass Valley	61	151
Moses	Alameda Oakland	55	43
ROULO			
Chas*	Sacramento Ward 4	63	554
ROUN			
Jno*	Sonoma Sonoma	69	659
Louis	Santa Cruz Santa Cruz	66	629
ROUND			
Lewis	San Francisco San Francisco 1	68	895
ROUNDA			
J	Calaveras Twp 9	57	406
ROUNDALL			
Chas	Sonoma Vallejo	69	627
ROUNDELUSH			
Geo	Siskiyou Cottonwoood	69	99
ROUNDS			
Elizabeth	Siskiyou Yreka	69	128
James L	Siskiyou Yreka	69	126
Saml	San Francisco San Francisco 10	67	305
Samuel H	San Francisco San Francisco 11	67	127
Thas G	Calaveras Twp 10	57	283
Thos G	Calaveras Twp 10	57	283
ROUNDTON			
Catherine	Solano Vallejo	69	261
ROUNDTREE			
Almus L	Los Angeles Los Angeles	59	347
B F	San Francisco San Francisco 4	68	1116
Geo	San Francisco San Francisco 9	68	981
Henry	Solano Vallejo	69	261
J G	Tehama Lassen	70	878
John	Monterey San Juan	60	975
John	Tulara Visalia	71	28
John H	Santa Clara Gilroy	65	225
Jos	San Francisco San Francisco 9	68	1066
ROUNER			
J L	El Dorado Gold Hill	58	1098
ROUNTHAL			
Lewis*	Sierra Downieville	66	968
ROUNTICE			
John	Contra Costa Twp 1	57	534
ROUNTIN			
Fredrick	Placer Auburn	62	591
ROUNTINE			
G	Tehama Red Bluff	70	916
ROUNTREE			
Isadore	Sacramento Ward 3	63	460
Jasper	Contra Costa Twp 3	57	601
Michael	Alameda Oakland	55	56
ROUP			
A W	El Dorado Coloma	58	1119
ROUR			
Thomas	Sierra Downieville	66	1019
ROURK			
Edward	Siskiyou Yreka	69	125
J O	Nevada Eureka	61	366
John H	Humbolt Union	59	185
ROURKE			
Bernard	Placer Yankee J	62	758
Christian	Tuolumne Twp 3	71	444
Elizabeth	Alameda Oakland	55	60
James C	Yuba Marysville	72	901
Jeremiah	Alameda Oakland	55	72
John	San Francisco San Francisco 2	67	763
John	San Francisco San Francisco 2	67	763
John C	Solano Suisan	69	232
John O*	Yuba Rose Bar	72	808
ROURKE			
M	Trinity Weaverville	70	1064
Michael O	Tuolumne Big Oak	71	143
Michael*	San Francisco San Francisco 3	67	22
Owen O	Yolo No E Twp	72	667
P J*	San Francisco San Francisco 5	67	532
P O*	San Francisco San Francisco 5	67	532
Thomas O*	Siskiyou Yreka	69	141
ROUSE			
Almeda	San Bernardino San Bernadino	64	624
Crous	Butte Ophir	56	799
Geo	Nevada Nevada	61	320
Geo	Yolo Cache Crk	72	612
George	Calaveras Twp 9	57	387
George*	El Dorado Georgetown	58	680
Horace	Sacramento Sutter	63	300
J C	Tuolumne Twp 2	71	329
J L	Sacramento Sutter	63	300
J W	Sacramento Cosummes	63	398
John	Humbolt Pacific	59	136
John	Yuba Foster B	72	834
John*	Sacramento Dry Crk	63	373
Jos	Butte Oregon	56	620
L	Santa Clara Redwood	65	450
Lewis	Colusa Muion	57	460
Martha	Sonoma Petaluma	69	545
Thos	Stanislaus Empire	70	733
William	El Dorado Greenwood	58	712
William L	Nevada Rough &	61	395
Wm	Sonoma Cloverdale	69	679
ROUSER			
John*	El Dorado Greenwood	58	725
John*	El Dorado Georgetown	58	760
ROUSETT			
Juan	Los Angeles Los Angeles	59	388
ROUSH			
John	Yuba New York	72	737
ROUSHE			
William	El Dorado Greenwood	58	723
ROUSINE			
Catharine A*	Placer Auburn	62	561
ROUSK			
Edward*	Siskiyou Yreka	69	125
ROUSKE			
John C	Solano Suisan	69	232
ROUSLER			
Peter	Sacramento Ward 1	63	41
ROUSORE			
Joseph	San Francisco San Francisco 9	68	939
ROUSSE			
Eugene	Alameda Brooklyn	55	169
ROUSSEL			
Argamor	San Francisco San Francisco 8	68	1267
Argarmor	San Francisco San Francisco 8	68	1267
Augouste	Yuba Fosters	72	822
Auguste*	Yuba Foster B	72	822
Jack	Alameda Brooklyn	55	169
ROUSSIN			
Ann	El Dorado Eldorado	58	945
T M	El Dorado Eldorado	58	945
ROUSSINE			
Sylvester S*	Placer Auburn	62	561
ROUSSO			
Ann E	Placer Auburn	62	562
ROUT			
David	Solano Fremont	69	380
ROUTENBRG			
Abraham*	San Francisco 7	68	1411
ROUTOIN			
J R*	Nevada Eureka	61	370
ROUTORN			
J R	Nevada Eureka	61	370
ROUX			
Andrew	San Francisco San Francisco 3	67	50
F	San Francisco San Francisco 5	67	492
F H	Nevada Nevada	61	293
Joshua	Tuolumne Jamestown	71	429
M	Nevada Nevada	61	294
Michael	Amador Twp 4	55	248
Peter	Tuolumne Shawsfla	71	417
R	Nevada Nevada	61	294
ROV			
Chine	Yuba Slate Ro	72	708
ROVAND			
Louis	Yolo Merritt	72	582
ROVARRE			
Armel*	San Francisco San Francisco 11	67	158
ROVE			
Cornelius	Calaveras Twp 5	57	136
M*	Nevada Grass Valley	61	176
Thomas*	Shasta Shasta	66	685
ROVEN			
John*	Tuolumne Springfield	71	370
ROVER			
---	Tulara Twp 2	71	40

Name	County Locale	M653 Roll	Page
ROVER			
---	Tulara Twp 3	71	50
---*	Tulara Visalia	71	40
Jno	Sacramento Brighton	63	194
John	Marin Tomales	60	724
John	San Francisco San Francisco 1	68	895
John*	Tuolumne Springfield	71	370
Margaret	San Francisco San Francisco 2	67	731
Wm H	Alameda Oakland	55	25
ROVERS			
Thos*	Mariposa Coulterville	60	677
ROVERTS			
David	Calaveras Twp 9	57	373
Edward	Calaveras Twp 9	57	373
ROVEY			
John*	Nevada Red Dog	61	555
ROVINSON			
J	San Joaquin Stockton	64	1092
ROVIO			
Domingo	Calaveras Twp 7	57	30
ROVIRO			
Lanta*	Los Angeles Los Angeles	59	517
Santa	Los Angeles Los Angeles	59	517
ROVOGAS			
J*	El Dorado Placerville	58	841
ROVS			
Charles	San Francisco San Francisco 3	67	51
ROVT			
Samuel	Calaveras Twp 6	57	140
ROW			
---	Calaveras Twp 6	57	176
---	Calaveras Twp 5	57	234
---	El Dorado Mountain	58	1188
---	Mariposa Coulterville	60	683
---	Placer Auburn	62	582
---	Sierra Twp 7	66	915
---	Sierra Twp 5	66	934
---	Yolo No E Twp	72	684
---	Yuba Slate Ro	72	684
---*	Calaveras Twp 5	57	235
---*	San Francisco San Francisco 4	68	1200
Ah	Butte Cascade	56	699
Arthur	Sacramento Granite	63	246
Chee	San Francisco San Francisco 11	67	146
Fook	San Francisco San Francisco 4	68	1192
Geo	Tuolumne Twp 2	71	281
John	Sierra Downieville	66	993
W	San Mateo Twp 3	65	101
William H	Monterey Pajaro	60	1024
ROWAN			
F	Nevada Grass Valley	61	153
G W	Merced Twp 1	60	913
Geo N*	Butte Oregon	56	644
Geo W	Butte Oregon	56	644
Jas	Sacramento Ward 1	63	43
Jas	San Francisco San Francisco 10	67	192
Jos	San Francisco San Francisco 10	67	192
Peter	San Francisco San Francisco 3	67	14
ROWAND			
T*	San Francisco San Francisco 5	67	544
ROWAS			
Kapping*	Mendocino Big Rvr	60	850
ROWASK			
Wm	Tuolumne Twp 4	71	125
ROWAWD			
T*	San Francisco San Francisco 5	67	544
ROWBRON			
Edwd	Sonoma Petaluma	69	543
ROWCOFT			
Harry	Tuolumne Twp 1	71	188
ROWCROFT			
Job	Plumas Meadow Valley	62	905
ROWDELL			
J R	Shasta Shasta	66	731
ROWDEN			
Jacob	Butte Hamilton	56	527
ROWDER			
Geo S	Butte Oregon	56	642
ROWDON			
Jacob	Butte Ophir	56	752
ROWE			
---	Butte Cascade	56	699
A	Butte Cascade	56	690
A B	Napa Napa	61	98
A F	Tuolumne Sonora	71	209
A F	Tuolumne Twp 1	71	252
A R	Tuolumne Twp 1	71	252
Albert	San Francisco San Francisco 10	67	307
Andrew	Plumas Meadow Valley	62	907
B	Mariposa Twp 1	60	650
B F	San Joaquin Stockton	64	1036
Cutter	San Francisco San Francisco 2	67	713
ROWE			
E H	Butte Oregon	56	640
E W	Solano Vallejo	69	251
Edward	San Francisco San Francisco 11	67	138
Eward*	Placer Folsom	62	641
Franklin J	Fresno Twp 3	59	9
Freeman	Sierra Downieville	66	1018
Geo	Butte Cascade	56	695
Geo	Butte Bidwell	56	732
Geo H	San Francisco San Francisco 2	67	635
George	Plumas Quincy	62	991
George	Yuba Marysville	72	960
Henry	Tuolumne Columbia	71	351
Ira	Yolo Cottonwoood	72	651
Ira M	Stanislaus Empire	70	736
J	Nevada Grass Valley	61	156
J G	San Joaquin Stockton	64	1023
J*	Placer Dutch Fl	62	728
Jacob	Tulara Twp 1	71	73
Jacob S	Stanislaus Empire	70	730
James	Tuolumne Big Oak	71	136
Jas C	Placer Folsom	62	647
Jenne	San Francisco San Francisco 2	67	665
John	Marin S Antoni	60	712
John	Siskiyou Callahan	69	8
John	Sonoma Armally	69	480
John	Yolo Washington	72	572
John	Yolo Cache	72	630
Joseph	Calaveras Twp 6	57	115
Josiah	Fresno Twp 1	59	76
L	Tuolumne Twp 4	71	165
L L	Yolo Cache Crk	72	663
Lewis	San Francisco San Francisco 12	67	374
Lucian	Klamath Liberty	59	231
M	Trinity Indian C	70	989
R	El Dorado Placerville	58	833
Robert	Nevada Nevada	61	247
Thos	Stanislaus Empire	70	736
Thos N	Trinity Trinity	70	971
Titus	Amador Twp 5	55	367
W	Nevada Grass Valley	61	151
W	Nevada Grass Valley	61	194
W S	San Francisco San Francisco 5	67	478
William	Tuolumne Twp 3	71	449
Wm	San Francisco San Francisco 2	67	585
Wm	San Francisco San Francisco 2	67	803
ROWEL			
C D	Tuolumne Columbia	71	324
John O	Tuolumne Columbia	71	317
Sanford	Tuolumne Columbia	71	360
ROWELL			
Albert	Contra Costa Twp 1	57	519
C	San Francisco San Francisco 5	67	493
C A	Nevada Grass Valley	61	190
Chamberlin W C	Placer Auburn	62	559
Ebin	El Dorado Casumnes	58	1162
Geo	Nevada Eureka	61	394
H H	Tuolumne Twp 2	71	275
Isaac	San Francisco San Francisco 10	67	278
Isaak	San Francisco San Francisco 2	67	672
J	Nevada Grass Valley	61	162
J	Nevada Grass Valley	61	165
Joseph	San Francisco San Francisco 2	67	557
L F	Nevada Nevada	61	256
O*	Tuolumne Twp 1	71	278
W	San Francisco San Francisco 5	67	553
Wm K	Alameda Oakland	55	24
ROWEN			
Frank	Los Angeles Shaffer	59	398
J B	Siskiyou Scott Va	69	58
J W	Mariposa Twp 3	60	585
James	Los Angeles Los Angeles	59	356
John	Yuba Parks Ba	72	777
Maltin	Sierra Gibsonville	66	857
Mattin*	Sierra Gibsonville	66	857
Michael	Placer Iona Hills	62	865
Multin*	Sierra Gibsonville	66	857
Robt	Solano Benecia	69	302
ROWENS			
F	Butte Oro	56	676
John	Sierra Monte Crk	66	1039
ROWENY			
James	Los Angeles Los Angeles	59	356
ROWERS			
A W	Yolo Cache	72	608
J G	Yolo Cache	72	627
ROWEY			
John A*	Napa Napa	61	73
ROWFF			
C	San Joaquin Stockton	64	1100
ROWHARD			
Ed	Yolo Putah	72	614
T	San Francisco San Francisco 4	68	1154
ROWLAND			
Catharine	San Francisco San Francisco 10	67	201
Charles	El Dorado Eldorado	58	943
Daniel	Sierra Port Win	66	792
Francis	Plumas Quincy	62	994
G	Nevada Washington	61	335
Geo	Sacramento Ward 1	63	87
Geo	San Francisco San Francisco 2	67	644
J P	San Francisco San Francisco 5	67	540
James	Placer Yankee J	62	759
Jas	San Francisco San Francisco 10	67	295
John	Alameda Brooklyn	55	103
John	Los Angeles Elmonte	59	266
John	Los Angeles Elmonte	59	267
John	Tuolumne Sonora	71	192
Jos	San Francisco San Francisco 10	67	295
K	Siskiyou Yreka	69	171
P	Sacramento Granite	63	224
P	Sacramento Granite	63	226
Peter	Solano Benecia	69	291
Q H	Colusa Colusi	57	425
Richd	San Francisco San Francisco 6	67	424
Robt	Sacramento San Joaquin	63	363
S	Nevada Grass Valley	61	157
Thomas	Yuba Marysville	72	971
W P	Sacramento Ward 3	63	442
Wm	Sacramento Georgian	63	341
ROWLANDS			
Evan	Yuba Slate Ro	72	701
Even	Yolo Slate Ra	72	701
Trenn	Yolo Slate Ra	72	701
ROWLANDSON			
Thomas	San Francisco San Francisco 11	67	140
ROWLANSON			
Robert	Mendocino Little L	60	830
Wm D	Mendocino Little L	60	830
ROWLENS			
G	Mariposa Twp 1	60	660
ROWLER			
---	Sacramento Cosumnes	63	408
ROWLES			
Geo	Butte Oregon	56	622
Isaac*	Nevada Eureka	61	356
Jas	Butte Kimshaw	56	580
John	Placer Dutch Fl	62	732
Mark	Butte Oregon	56	622
ROWLETT			
J	San Francisco San Francisco 5	67	553
ROWLEY			
Byren	Solano Vacaville	69	337
C C	Siskiyou Scott Va	69	41
Geo	El Dorado Kelsey	58	1127
Geo	El Dorado Kelsey	58	1128
H D	Sacramento Granite	63	222
Henry	Sierra Poker Flats	66	839
John	Placer Michigan	62	818
Louis	Napa Napa	61	101
Lucien	Napa Yount	61	38
Manael	Alameda Brooklyn	55	149
N T*	Solano Vacaville	69	324
Robt	Nevada Red Dog	61	551
V T	Solano Vacaville	69	324
Wells	El Dorado Mud Springs	58	969
Wm	Calaveras Twp 9	57	416
Wm	Napa Napa	61	87
ROWLING			
Sal	Calaveras Twp 4	57	321
William	San Francisco San Francisco 7	68	1399
ROWLINS			
A	Calaveras Twp 9	57	395
ROWLINSON			
Robert	Mendocino Little L	60	830
Wm D	Mendocino Little L	60	830
ROWLSON			
Edwd	Sonoma Petaluma	69	544
ROWLY			
William F	Santa Cruz Watsonville	66	536
William G	Santa Cruz Watsonville	66	536
ROWMELLUS			
A	San Francisco San Francisco 9	68	1034
ROWMOSEN			
J	Sonoma Salt Point	69	691
ROWN			
E	Sutter Yuba	70	772
Wm	San Francisco San Francisco 2	67	741
ROWNE			
Robt	Placer Rattle Snake	62	632
ROWNER			
J L	El Dorado Gold Hill	58	1098
ROWORTH			
Edwin C	Calaveras Twp 5	57	206
ROWOW			
---	Tulara Twp 1	71	117

California 1860 Census Index

Name	County Locale	M653 RollPage
ROWR		
Thos*	Santa Clara Gilroy	65 234
W S	San Francisco San Francisco 5	67 478
ROWS		
John	Yolo Washington	72 572
ROWSE		
J	Nevada Grass Valley	61 163
ROWTON		
Nathan	Butte Chico	56 531
ROX		
Henry	Tulara Visalia	71 109
ROXBURG		
James*	Santa Cruz Santa Cruz	66 610
Joseph*	Santa Cruz Santa Cruz	66 609
ROXBURGH		
Joseph	Santa Cruz Santa Cruz	66 609
ROXBURGLE		
Joseph*	Santa Cruz Santa Cruz	66 609
ROXBURY		
James	Santa Cruz Santa Cruz	66 610
Robert	San Francisco San Francisco 8	681252
ROXBURY?		
Joseph	Santa Cruz Santa Cruz	66 609
ROXBURYLE		
Joseph*	Santa Cruz Santa Cruz	66 609
ROXMON		
R E	San Francisco San Francisco 4	681155
ROXUGIUS		
Francisco	Contra Costa Twp 2	57 555
ROXWELL		
M	El Dorado Placerville	58 854
ROY		
---	El Dorado Georgetown	58 748
---	Placer Yankee J	62 779
---	San Francisco San Francisco 4	681173
---	Yolo No E Twp	72 681
---	Yolo Slate Ra	72 715
---	Yuba North Ea	72 681
---	Yuba Slate Ro	72 715
---	Yuba Fosters	72 842
A	Sutter Butte	70 798
Cho	San Francisco San Francisco 4	681173
David	San Francisco San Francisco 10	176 67
H P	Nevada Red Dog	61 540
J	Mariposa Twp 3	60 622
J	San Francisco San Francisco 5	67 527
J	San Francisco San Francisco 5	67 531
J A	San Francisco San Francisco 10	330 67
James	Santa Cruz Soguel	66 588
John	Humbolt Eureka	59 170
Reabu*	Calaveras Twp 5	57 216
Reuben	Calaveras Twp 5	57 216
Rich*	Santa Cruz Pescadero	66 646
Rien*	Santa Cruz Pescadero	66 646
Riet*	Santa Cruz Pescadero	66 646
Sylvius	San Francisco San Francisco 3	67 17
Ung	Yuba Long Bar	72 766
ROYA		
John*	Calaveras Twp 6	57 155
Nicholas	San Francisco San Francisco 2	67 790
ROYAL		
Geo	San Francisco San Francisco 1	68 905
H	El Dorado Diamond	58 810
H W	Sierra Twp 5	66 922
John	Yolo Cottonwoood	72 648
John S	Tuolumne Twp 2	71 298
Josiah B*	Fresno Twp 2	59 5
ROYALL		
J P	Tuolumne Twp 3	71 464
ROYAN		
Bestalli*	Calaveras Twp 5	57 197
ROYAR		
Bertalli*	Calaveras Twp 5	57 197
ROYARI		
Bertallo*	Calaveras Twp 5	57 197
ROYAT		
Barthelemy	Yuba Parks Ba	72 783
Joseph	Yuba Parke Ba	72 783
Narcite	Yuba Parke Ba	72 783
Nascite*	Yuba Parks Ba	72 783
ROYCE		
Jasper	Colusa Spring Valley	57 435
John J	Colusa Spring Valley	57 434
S M	Amador Twp 4	55 242
W*	Yolo Cache Crk	72 618
ROYEN		
A F	Sonoma Vallejo	69 628
ROYER		
A C	San Francisco San Francisco 2	67 802
Arlele	Calaveras Twp 10	57 262
Charles	Contra Costa Twp 1	57 499
Francisco	San Francisco San Francisco 4	681155
John	Yuba Rose Bar	72 801
John*	Calaveras Twp 6	57 170

Name	County Locale	M653 RollPage
ROYER		
Joseph	Nevada Bloomfield	61 521
Uire*	Tuolumne Twp 1	71 255
William	Tuolumne Twp 2	71 305
Wm	Yuba Rose Bar	72 819
ROYERRE		
Jean	Sacramento Ward 3	63 458
ROYERS		
Andrew	Calaveras Twp 5	57 248
Antonio	Calaveras Twp 5	57 135
Mary	Calaveras Twp 5	57 217
S W*	Nevada Grass Valley	61 217
Thomas	Sierra La Porte	66 769
ROYKINS		
John	Placer Yankee J	62 759
ROYL		
John	El Dorado Coloma	581108
ROYLE		
P W S*	Sacramento Ward 1	63 16
Patrick*	Yuba Marysville	72 926
ROYLES		
James	Yuba Marysville	72 929
ROYNDTREE		
W A	Sacramento Ward 3	63 460
ROYNO		
Bertallo*	Calaveras Twp 5	57 197
ROYNR		
William	Calaveras Twp 10	57 282
ROYNTON		
Ebrn V	Calaveras Twp 5	57 175
ROYO		
John	Amador Twp 1	55 503
ROYP		
John	Sierra Downieville	66 970
ROYR		
Ebra*	Calaveras Twp 6	57 130
ROYSS		
John*	Sierra Downieville	66 970
ROYWI		
Bertalli*	Calaveras Twp 5	57 197
ROYWO		
Bertalli*	Calaveras Twp 5	57 197
ROZAL		
Josiah B*	Fresno Twp 2	59 5
ROZEN		
Maria*	San Francisco San Francisco 2	67 702
ROZI		
Henry	Stanislaus Branch	70 697
ROZIER		
Wm M*	Tuolumne Twp 2	71 313
ROZINE		
L	Solano Benecia	69 285
RRACH		
J B*	Siskiyou Cottonwoood	69 102
RRODIE		
John P	San Francisco San Francisco 2	67 615
RROSS		
John	Solano Benecia	69 288
RSEISER		
Levi*	San Francisco San Francisco 7	681404
RTNER		
Demarcus	Tulara Twp 1	71 110
RU DDELL		
E P	Sierra Twp 7	66 869
RU DGE		
John	Sierra Port Win	66 796
RU LA		
---*	Yuba Long Bar	72 763
RU		
---	Calaveras Twp 5	57 181
---	El Dorado Placerville	58 900
---	El Dorado Placerville	58 902
---	Yuba Slate Ro	72 711
---*	Calaveras Twp 6	57 181
---*	El Dorado Coloma	581084
La*	Yuba Long Bar	72 763
RUA		
---	Mariposa Twp 3	60 543
Adam	Tuolumne Columbia	71 340
Martin*	Stanislaus Emory	70 739
RUAN		
---	Fresno Twp 1	59 86
RUARK		
Peter	San Joaquin Elkhorn	64 959
RUAS		
Amamiela*	San Francisco 2	67 782
	San Francisco	
Amanuela	San Francisco San Francisco 2	67 782
RUAW		
Thos*	San Francisco San Francisco 9	681027
RUB		
H	Butte Eureka	56 654
RUBAH		
Chas	Calaveras Twp 9	57 353
RUBARTS		
J H	El Dorado Placerville	58 837

Name	County Locale	M653 RollPage
RUBE		
---	Tulara Twp 2	71 32
A	Sierra Pine Grove	66 832
Peter	Calaveras Twp 5	57 203
RUBEA		
Charles	El Dorado Casumnes	581166
RUBELL		
Frank	El Dorado Salmon Hills	581055
RUBEN		
Jacob	Nevada Bridgeport	61 497
RUBENT		
John	Placer Iona Hills	62 894
RUBEO		
Pedro	Tuolumne Big Oak	71 133
RUBER		
Adam	Yolo Putah	72 554
J*	Sacramento Ward 3	63 434
Maricino	Santa Clara San Jose	65 325
RUBERDER		
Dominca	El Dorado Indian D	581159
RUBHAM		
Rush	Santa Cruz Santa Cruz	66 600
RUBIA		
Martin	Monterey Monterey	60 960
RUBIE		
Jacob	Sierra Twp 5	66 921
RUBIN		
Jacob	Nevada Bloomfield	61 530
Jose	Los Angeles Los Angeles	59 402
Louis	Calaveras Twp 6	57 137
RUBINS		
Geo	San Francisco San Francisco 6	67 450
RUBINSON		
W J	Siskiyou Scott Va	69 47
RUBIO		
Czpriuno	San Bernardino Santa Barbara	64 203
Feliz	Los Angeles Los Angeles	59 385
Francisco	Los Angeles Santa Ana	59 441
John	Yuba Marysville	72 922
Jon	Yuba Marysville	72 922
Jose	Los Angeles Los Angeles	59 402
Luisa	Los Angeles Los Angeles	59 373
Manuel	Los Angeles San Gabriel	59 420
Maria S	Los Angeles Los Angeles	59 394
Nabor	Los Angeles San Juan	59 461
Pedro	Los Angeles Santa Ana	59 441
Pedro	Tuolumne Twp 4	71 133
Thomas	Los Angeles Los Angeles	59 393
Tomaas	Los Angeles Los Angeles	59 393
RUBIS		
T	El Dorado Placerville	58 876
RUBL		
Christopher	Colusa Spring Valley	57 431
RUBLE		
W H	Tehama Lassen	70 876
RUBLEDO		
Mercedes*	San Francisco 2	67 683
	San Francisco	
RUBLES		
Jose	Sierra La Porte	66 781
Teresa	San Francisco San Francisco 2	67 709
RUBORTOM		
W W	Los Angeles Elmonte	59 256
RUBOTTOM		
Emphry	Los Angeles Los Angeles	59 347
RUBRI		
F	San Francisco San Francisco 4	681216
RUBSCHAL		
Henry*	San Francisco San Francisco 1	68 827
RUBSUMEN		
Jacob	Sierra La Porte	66 776
RUBSUMIN		
Jacob	Sierra La Porte	66 776
RUBURT		
John P	Yolo Cache Crk	72 589
RUBURTS		
John D	Yolo Cache	72 589
RUBUS		
Geo	Placer Stewart	62 606
RUBY		
E	Sacramento Ward 1	63 4
J R	San Francisco San Francisco 2	67 692
James	Placer Michigan	62 838
James	Tuolumne Twp 1	71 220
Mariaunat*	San Francisco 11	155
	San Francisco	67
Wm	Sacramento Georgian	63 338
RUCARD		
Saml	Santa Cruz Santa Cruz	66 629
RUCATE		
---	Fresno Twp 2	59 113
RUCE		
John S	Sierra Twp 7	66 867
RUCH		
Carisse*	Alameda Oakland	55 1
Herman*	Sierra Downieville	66 963

Name	County Locale	M653 Roll Page
RUCH		
M	Trinity E Weaver	70 1058
RUCHER		
Julius	Santa Cruz Pajaro	66 562
RUCHHOFER		
Jos	Amador Twp 7	55 412
RUCHI		
John*	Stanislaus Branch	70 698
RUCHILL		
P T	Trinity Weaverville	70 1078
RUCIO		
Manuel	Los Angeles San Gabriel	59 420
RUCK		
---	Calaveras Twp 5	57 205
Lyman	Sierra Twp 7	66 866
RUCKA		
J*	Siskiyou Cottonwoood	69 101
RUCKE		
Margaret	Monterey Alisal	60 1031
RUCKER		
Alfred	Solano Vacaville	69 354
J E	Santa Clara Gilroy	65 240
J*	Siskiyou Cottonwoood	69 101
John	El Dorado Georgetown	58 701
John	Santa Clara Gilroy	65 240
Julius	Santa Cruz Pajaro	66 562
Margaret	Monterey Alisal	60 1031
S	Calaveras Twp 9	57 417
Valentine	Yuba Long Bar	72 744
Valentini	Yuba New York	72 744
W J	Santa Clara Santa Clara	65 486
RUCKERT		
A	Amador Twp 1	55 460
RUCKIER		
J A*	Nevada Rough &	61 428
RUCKLAND		
G	Yuba New York	72 719
RUCKLER		
M C*	San Francisco San Francisco 9	68 945
RUCKS		
Michael M	Calaveras Twp 6	57 147
RUCKWER		
George A	San Joaquin Oneal	64 939
RUCONNELL		
Ann M	San Francisco San Francisco 9	68 1039
RUCT		
Carisse*	Alameda Oakland	55 1
Herman*	Sierra Downieville	66 963
RUD		
---	Tuolumne Twp 5	71 514
George*	Placer Michigan	62 853
Geryr K*	Monterey S Antoni	60 967
J	Nevada Nevada	61 269
James	Solano Vacaville	69 360
James*	Placer Michigan	62 849
John	Placer Michigan	62 834
John*	Placer Iona Hills	62 877
Manilla	Placer Iona Hills	62 864
Mat	Placer Yankee J	62 757
Mathew*	San Francisco San Francisco 1	68 878
William*	San Francisco San Francisco 7	68 1361
Wm*	San Francisco San Francisco 1	68 875
RUDA		
I	Nevada Nevada	61 317
J*	Nevada Nevada	61 317
RUDARFF		
William	Tuolumne Twp 1	71 212
RUDBRICK		
Harmon	Placer Iona Hills	62 886
RUDD		
C F	Butte Oregon	56 619
C G	Sacramento Ward 1	63 73
Eliza	Sierra Twp 7	66 906
John	Yolo Cache Crk	72 616
RUDDELL		
E P	Sierra Twp 7	66 869
RUDDEN		
Charles	Marin Point Re	60 732
RUDDIA		
T	Sacramento San Joaquin	63 359
RUDDICK		
Elizabeth	San Joaquin Stockton	64 1061
James	San Joaquin Stockton	64 1057
Johanna	San Francisco San Francisco 11	133 67
Robt	Amador Twp 3	55 390
RUDDIN		
Ann*	Yuba Marysville	72 904
RUDDING		
John A	Yolo Putah	72 545
RUDDLE		
Alice	Merced Twp 1	60 897
J B	Merced Twp 1	60 897
John	Merced Twp 1	60 897
RUDDOCK		
Ablert	Santa Cruz Pajaro	66 562

Name	County Locale	M653 Roll Page
RUDDOCK		
Albert	Santa Cruz Pajaro	66 562
Patrick	San Francisco San Francisco 3	67 27
RUDDOFF		
P C	El Dorado Coloma	58 1123
RUDDY		
B*	Siskiyou Callahan	69 7
George	Yuba Long Bar	72 753
George	Yuba Long Bar	72 755
Mary	Santa Clara San Jose	65 320
RUDE		
David	Sierra Twp 5	66 947
Richd	Sacramento Cosummes	63 409
RUDEL		
Eliza	Sierra Twp 7	66 906
John	Yolo Cache	72 616
RUDENBURG		
H	San Francisco San Francisco 2	67 780
RUDER		
John*	Nevada Rough &	61 436
RUDERIL		
John*	Sonoma Petaluma	69 564
RUDFERD		
W J*	Siskiyou Scott Va	69 20
RUDFORD		
W J	Siskiyou Scott Va	69 20
RUDGE		
Fred	Sierra Monte Crk	66 1038
John*	Sierra Port Win	66 796
RUDGENS		
Chas	San Francisco San Francisco 2	67 692
RUDGERS		
H	Amador Twp 2	55 308
RUDGET		
George	Calaveras Twp 10	57 280
RUDIAR		
D*	Calaveras Twp 9	57 392
RUDIN		
Peter*	Sierra St Louis	66 813
RUDINGER		
Eliza	Yuba Long Bar	72 771
RUDINL		
John*	Sonoma Petaluma	69 564
RUDKINS		
Nicholas	El Dorado Greenwood	58 709
RUDLAND		
F	Yolo Cache	72 617
RUDLER		
John*	Humbolt Table Bl	59 141
Michael	Sierra Downieville	66 967
RUDNUS		
S L*	Yolo Washington	72 605
RUDOFF		
George	Calaveras Twp 6	57 127
RUDOIS		
Charles	San Francisco San Francisco 2	67 780
RUDOLF		
J	Calaveras Twp 9	57 413
RUDOLP		
Constadt	Solano Vallejo	69 247
RUDOLPH		
Charles*	Solano Vacaville	69 365
Constadt	Solano Vallejo	69 247
F	Nevada Nevada	61 319
Isaac	Yolo Cache Crk	72 591
Jacob	San Francisco San Francisco 12	379 67
James	Solano Montezuma	69 371
John	Stanislaus Branch	70 715
L	Nevada Grass Valley	61 172
William	San Francisco San Francisco 3	67 58
RUDSHAW		
William	Nevada Bridgeport	61 467
RUDVIS		
Charle	San Francisco San Francisco 2	67 780
RUDY		
John	Stanislaus Branch	70 704
Peter	Stanislaus Branch	70 699
RUE		
---	Calaveras Twp 5	57 232
---	Sierra Twp 5	66 931
Andrew	Napa Napa	61 79
Calim*	Butte Chico	56 559
Calom*	Butte Chico	56 559
Calvin	Butte Chico	56 559
Thomas	Shasta Shasta	66 685
W	El Dorado Placerville	58 862
William	Sierra Gibsonville	66 859
RUEBOS		
Jose	Calaveras Twp 7	57 11
RUECH		
Harman*	Placer Auburn	62 565
RUED		
J C	Yuba Long Bar	72 754
RUEDER		
Louis*	Los Angeles Los Angeles	59 353

Name	County Locale	M653 Roll Page
RUEEH		
Harman*	Placer Auburn	62 565
RUEFF		
Charles	Alameda Oakland	55 15
RUEGER		
John	Solano Benecia	69 290
RUEGG		
Ester	San Francisco San Francisco 2	67 793
RUEHL		
Frederick	San Francisco San Francisco 7	68 1420
RUELAS		
Jesus	Plumas Quincy	62 937
RUELGERS		
C B	El Dorado Greenwood	58 716
RUELLUS		
Manwell	Mariposa Coulterville	60 699
RUENEVIDES		
Jose	Marin Cortemad	60 781
RUER		
Ceair*	Mariposa Twp 3	60 595
Ceaw*	Mariposa Twp 3	60 595
Peaw*	Mariposa Twp 3	60 595
RUERO		
Adrian*	Tuolumne Twp 3	71 432
RUESETEE		
J*	Nevada Nevada	61 321
RUEST		
James	Monterey S Antoni	60 969
RUEY		
Cosarfa	Alameda Washington	55 172
Hosea	Alameda Washington	55 174
Maria	Alameda Washington	55 173
Marin*	Alameda Brooklyn	55 173
RUEZ		
Marin*	Alameda Brooklyn	55 173
Natividad	Mariposa Twp 3	60 612
Ramon	San Diego Colorado	64 812
RUFER		
A	Butte Bidwell	56 711
Bernard	Yuba Long Bar	72 769
S	San Francisco San Francisco 5	67 492
Tom*	Butte Chico	56 550
RUFESNIDER		
Isaac	San Joaquin Castoria	64 908
RUFF		
A	San Francisco San Francisco 3	67 45
C	San Francisco San Francisco 5	67 554
Charles	Yuba Foster B	72 836
Isaac	Marin Bolinas	60 745
J	Siskiyou Scott Ri	69 75
Jacob	Sacramento Ward 4	63 499
Marshall	Plumas Meadow Valley	62 934
RUFFA		
Columbus*	Calaveras Twp 10	57 266
RUFFAT		
Josephine	San Francisco San Francisco 2	67 623
Josephine	San Francisco San Francisco 3	67 80
Josephini	San Francisco San Francisco 3	67 80
RUFFEN		
C H	El Dorado Kelsey	58 1151
D	Nevada Eureka	61 366
RUFFENER		
Lucius H	Sierra St Louis	66 806
RUFFER		
Jos	Santa Cruz Pescadero	66 646
RUFFERN		
E W	Mariposa Twp 1	60 647
RUFFERTY		
A	Shasta Millvill	66 755
RUFFERTZ		
A	Shasta Millvill	66 755
RUFFIN		
D	Nevada Eureka	61 366
Frank	San Francisco San Francisco 11	134 67
J	Tuolumne Twp 1	71 257
John	Los Angeles Elmonte	59 246
Wm	Santa Clara San Jose	65 367
RUFFINIO		
Bernado	Tuolumne Twp 1	71 210
RUFFLE		
Charles	San Joaquin Castoria	64 902
RUFFLEY		
T E	San Francisco San Francisco 10	256 67
RUFFLY		
John	San Francisco San Francisco 11	144 67
RUFFNER		
Joseph	Santa Cruz Santa Cruz	66 615
Neil	Amador Twp 5	55 475
RUFFO		
Columbus*	Calaveras Twp 10	57 266
Francis	San Francisco San Francisco 9	68 1034
Nicholas	Calaveras Twp 10	57 266
RUFFU		
Columbus	Calaveras Twp 10	57 266

Name	County Locale	M653 RollPage
RUFFUS		
John	Calaveras Twp 10	57 293
RUFIN		
J	Tuolumne Twp 1	71 257
RUFINA		
---	Los Angeles San Juan	59 468
RUFINO		
---	San Diego Agua Caliente	64 833
---	San Diego Agua Caliente	64 850
Jose	Los Angeles Santa Ana	59 441
RUFLER		
William	Tuolumne Twp 5	71 523
RUFMACK		
Andrew	El Dorado White Oaks	581029
RUFS		
Ferdinard	Contra Costa Twp 3	57 618
RUFSELL		
J W	Sonoma Santa Rosa	69 418
William*	Calaveras Twp 6	57 172
RUFSIAN		
N	San Francisco San Francisco 9	681101
RUFUGIO		
Maria	Los Angeles San Juan	59 465
RUFUL		
John M	Calaveras Twp 6	57 116
RUFUS		
Chaley	Sacramento Sutter	63 294
RUG		
---	San Francisco San Francisco 4	681209
---	Sierra Downieville	66 996
RUGACHA		
Hypolit	Mariposa Twp 1	60 648
RUGACHER		
Hypolit	Mariposa Twp 1	60 648
RUGACHU		
Hukolip*	Mariposa Twp 1	60 648
RUGBIRT		
C C*	Calaveras Twp 9	57 412
RUGBUT		
C C*	Calaveras Twp 9	57 412
RUGEN		
H	San Francisco San Francisco 5	67 535
RUGER		
Charles	Solano Fremont	69 385
John	Santa Cruz Santa Cruz	66 609
Wm	Butte Kimshaw	56 583
RUGERT		
Louis*	San Francisco San Francisco 7	681369
RUGG		
C S	Nevada Eureka	61 382
Elisha	San Joaquin Elkhorn	64 966
G P	Sutter Butte	70 797
J F	Sonoma Petaluma	69 591
James	San Joaquin Elkhorn	64 964
William	Marin San Rafael	60 767
RUGGE		
Clarke E	Plumas Quincy	62 982
RUGGLES		
Amanda	Yolo Cache	72 597
Austin	Placer Secret R	62 618
B	Tehama Antelope	70 893
Charles	Contra Costa Twp 1	57 531
David	San Francisco San Francisco 6	67 436
E S	Butte Bidwell	56 718
E W	San Francisco San Francisco 2	67 628
F C	Yolo Cache Crk	72 594
G	Nevada Grass Valley	61 144
H B	Siskiyou Klamath	69 85
Jacob	Sacramento Georgian	63 344
John	Placer Secret R	62 618
John	Sacramento Ward 1	63 148
John B*	Placer Secret R	62 618
John E	San Francisco San Francisco 1	68 823
Lewis	Sacramento Cosumnes	63 399
RUGGLIS		
Andrew	Placer Yankee J	62 782
RUGGS		
J S	El Dorado Greenwood	58 720
RUGLERS		
D S	Sierra Downieville	66 994
RUGLESS		
D S	Sierra Downieville	66 994
RUGORIA		
John	Santa Cruz Pajaro	66 548
RUH		
M	Siskiyou Yreka	69 191
RUHARA		
Thos C*	Napa Yount	61 52
RUHARAS		
Thos C*	Napa Yount	61 52
RUHL		
Henry	Tuolumne Twp 2	71 272
Phillip C	Amador Twp 1	55 476
RUHLEY		
Charles	Siskiyou Yreka	69 191
RUHLS		
Henry*	Sierra Pine Grove	66 820

Name	County Locale	M653 RollPage
RUHMAN		
J B	Napa Napa	61 97
Wm	Napa Napa	61 101
RUHMANN		
Henry	San Francisco San Francisco 10	323 67
RUID		
Daris*	Amador Twp 5	55 339
Daus*	Amador Twp 5	55 339
Davis	Amador Twp 5	55 339
RUIDA		
Jose M Steward*	Quincy Plumas	62 941
Tadeo	Plumas Quincy	62 941
RUIDITE		
Lewis	Plumas Quincy	62 939
RUIG		
Chares*	Placer Michigan	62 845
Charles B	San Francisco San Francisco 9	68 953
Mary F*	Nevada Red Dog	61 546
RUIGASU		
Landalin*	Plumas Quincy	62 939
RUIPP		
Adam	Sonoma Salt Point	69 691
RUIRE		
Frank*	Sacramento Ward 1	63 13
RUIRSEN		
Helen	San Francisco San Francisco 2	67 559
RUIS		
Antonio	Los Angeles Los Angeles	59 504
Antonio	San Francisco San Francisco 1	68 823
Antonio M	Los Angeles Los Angeles	59 498
Cino F	Los Angeles Los Angeles	59 514
Doleres	San Francisco San Francisco 2	67 768
Dolores	San Francisco San Francisco 2	67 768
Enacio*	Contra Costa Twp 1	57 501
F	Merced Twp 1	60 909
Francisco	Los Angeles Los Angeles	59 509
Francisco	Merced Twp 1	60 900
Francisco	Santa Clara San Jose	65 309
Gogoni	Contra Costa Twp 3	57 600
Iringdio*	Los Angeles Los Nieto	59 439
Joaquin	Monterey Alisal	601034
Jose	Contra Costa Twp 3	57 584
Jose	Los Angeles Los Angeles	59 499
Jose	Los Angeles Los Angeles	59 514
Jose J	Los Angeles Los Angeles	59 498
Juan	San Luis Obispo San Luis Obispo	65 31
Manuel	Contra Costa Twp 1	57 503
Marcinus	Contra Costa Twp 3	57 600
Maria	Los Angeles Los Angeles	59 506
N*	Merced Twp 1	60 900
Pablo*	Contra Costa Twp 3	57 585
Pedro	Los Angeles Los Angeles	59 504
Pedro	Monterey San Juan	601003
Petronella	Fresno Twp 1	59 84
Rafael	Marin Cortemad	60 781
Repugia	Placer Dutch Fl	62 722
S B	Los Angeles Tejon	59 521
Salarinna*	Santa Ba San Bernardino	64 216
Tilano	Plumas Quincy	62 988
Tino	Santa Clara Alviso	65 404
Tomas	Contra Costa Twp 1	57 497
Ymisdio*	Los Angeles Santa Ana	59 440
Yringdia*	Los Angeles Los Nieto	59 439
Yungdio*	Los Angeles Santa Ana	59 439
RUISALES		
Francisco	San Mateo Twp 2	65 115
RUIZ		
Antonio	Los Angeles Los Nieto	59 433
Becuenta	Los Angeles Los Angeles	59 356
Bemada	San Bernardino Santa Barbara	64 170
Benjildo	San Bernardino Santa Barbara	64 162
Bicenta	Los Angeles Los Angeles	59 356
Carlos	San Bernardino Santa Barbara	64 165
Diego	San Bernardino Santa Barbara	64 157
Dolores	Los Angeles Los Angeles	59 319
Doloress	San Diego Colorado	64 812
Domitila	Los Angeles Los Angeles	59 311
Dronicia	Monterey Monterey	60 948
Francisca	Los Angeles San Pedro	59 482
Francisco	Los Angeles Los Angeles	59 395
Francisco	Los Angeles San Gabriel	59 413
Francisco	Los Angeles San Juan	59 471
Francisco Ant	Santa Ba San Bernardino	64 216
Franco	Los Angeles Tejon To	59 535
Gabriel	San Bernardino Santa Inez	64 142
Geronomo	Santa Barbara San Bernardino	64 196
Guadalupe	Los Angeles Santa Ana	59 459
Isabel*	San Diego San Diego	64 765
Jesus	Los Angeles Los Angeles	59 402
Jesus	Marin Cortemad	60 779
Jesus	Santa Clara San Jose	65 300

Name	County Locale	M653 RollPage
RUIZ		
Joe A	Los Angeles San Gabriel	59 411
Jose	San Bernardino Santa Barbara	64 189
Jose	San Francisco San Francisco 3	67 6
Jose Anto	Santa Barbara San Bernardino	64 164
Jose Carmel	Santa Barbara San Bernardino	64 164
Jose M	Los Angeles Los Angeles	59 354
Jose M	Los Angeles San Pedro	59 486
Juan	Los Angeles Santa Ana	59 458
Juan	Los Angeles San Pedro	59 481
Juan	San Bernardino Santa Inez	64 141
Juan	San Bernardino Santa Barbara	64 201
Juanna	San Bernardino Santa Barbara	64 160
Manuel	Los Angeles San Juan	59 469
Margarita	Los Angeles Los Angeles	59 377
Mariana	Los Angeles Tejon	59 539
Mariano	Los Angeles Los Angeles	59 377
Martin	Los Angeles Los Angeles	59 370
Nicholas	Los Angeles Santa Ana	59 456
Nicolas	Los Angeles Santa Ana	59 456
Nieves	Los Angeles Los Angeles	59 376
Nilves	Los Angeles Los Angeles	59 376
Pedro	San Bernardino Santa Barbara	64 165
Rugino	Los Angeles San Juan	59 461
Santiago	Marin Cortemad	60 790
Simon	San Bernardino Santa Barbara	64 168
Vallazar	San Bernardino Santa Barbara	64 164
Wancisca	Los Angeles Los Angeles	59 317
Ylario*	San Bernardino Santa Barbara	64 165
RUIZS		
Haris*	San Bernardino Santa Barbara	64 165
RUJY		
---*	Calaveras Twp 8	57 109
RUK		
---	El Dorado Greenwood	58 728
---	San Francisco San Francisco 4	681194
RUKAS		
Cossenth*	San Mateo Twp 1	65 62
RUKER		
Joseph	Alameda Brooklyn	55 174
W J	Napa Napa	61 95
RUKMAN		
A*	San Francisco San Francisco 3	67 51
Ann E	Napa Napa	61 69
RUKOW		
J*	San Francisco San Francisco 2	67 734
RULAFORD		
J W	Placer Iona Hills	62 867
RULAND		
John G	Solano Benecia	69 316
Saml	Yolo Cottonwoood	72 650
RULE		
Adam	Siskiyou Klamath	69 97
Austin	Sonoma Petaluma	69 560
Benj	Trinity E Weaver	701059
D K	Napa Napa	61 106
D N*	Nevada Red Dog	61 548
D R*	Napa Napa	61 106
Edward*	Yuba New York	72 733
F	Siskiyou Scott Ri	69 74
F	Siskiyou Scott Ri	69 77
Jacob	Napa Napa	61 93
James	Sierra Twp 7	66 897
Jas K	Santa Clara Gilroy	65 229
John	Sierra Twp 5	66 921
John	Siskiyou Scott Ri	69 74
John*	Yuba Marysville	72 969
Margaret	Napa Napa	61 92
Samuel	Solano Vallejo	69 261
Silas	Trinity E Weaver	701059
Thomas N	Tuolumne Twp 5	71 519
Wm	Sierra Twp 5	66 896
Wm	Trinity E Weaver	701059
RULEA		
Wm	El Dorado Placerville	58 896
RULEY		
Eliza	Napa Napa	61 95
J W	Siskiyou Scott Va	69 31
John*	San Francisco San Francisco 1	68 928
Martin*	San Francisco San Francisco 1	68 928
RULIA		
Louis*	Calaveras Twp 6	57 137
RULIAH		
Chas*	Calaveras Twp 9	57 353
RULIN		
A	San Francisco San Francisco 6	67 458
RULL		
S	Nevada Eureka	61 393
RULLAND		
F	Yolo Cache Crk	72 617
RULLARD		
F H	Trinity Indian C	70 988
H C	Yolo Cottonwoood	72 653
John	Yolo Cottonwoood	72 653

Name	County Locale	M653 RollPage
RULLEN		
Martin	Sierra Downieville	661021
RULLER		
John*	Stanislaus Emory	70 739
RULLEY		
Patrick	Marin San Rafael	60 758
RULLIDGE		
John*	San Joaquin Elkhorn	64 997
Mary	San Francisco San Francisco 2	67 787
RULLIN		
Newton	Sierra Downieville	661021
RULLINS		
Alex	Mendocino Big Rvr	60 847
Wm	El Dorado Greenwood	58 709
RULLY		
James	Tuolumne Twp 2	71 300
Jas F*	San Francisco San Francisco 10	266
		67
Thos	San Francisco San Francisco 1	68 917
RULOPSON		
Wm H	Tuolumne Sonora	71 203
RULP		
S	Amador Twp 5	55 359
RULPH		
H	Solano Vacaville	69 319
RULY		
Cosarfa	Alameda Brooklyn	55 172
RUM		
---	Amador Twp 2	55 287
---	Sierra Downieville	66 953
Jacobb*	Amador Twp 1	55 452
Jacobt	Amador Twp 1	55 452
RUMA BANG		
---	Sierra Twp 7	66 877
RUMALS		
Wm T*	Tuolumne Twp 1	71 485
RUMAN		
C	Sacramento Cosumnes	63 408
John	San Francisco San Francisco 2	67 770
RUMAS		
H	Yolo Putah	72 614
RUMBLE		
Phil	Sacramento Ward 3	63 487
William	Tuolumne Columbia	71 313
Wm T	Tuolumne Sonora	71 485
RUMBO		
Francisco	Sierra Downieville	661021
RUMBOLD		
Eugene	El Dorado Georgetown	58 704
RUMCE		
Victor*	Mariposa Twp 3	60 585
RUMELLS		
John	Yolo Slate Ra	72 689
John	Yuba Slate Ro	72 689
RUMERY		
Thomas	Yuba New York	72 730
RUMFORD		
Isaac B	Alameda Brooklyn	55 92
RUMILES		
Amastuein*	Calaveras Twp 10	57 289
RUMING		
Frank	Santa Cruz Pajaro	66 545
RUMIS		
Fritz	El Dorado Georgetown	58 760
RUMKIN		
Charles*	San Francisco San Francisco 4	681134
RUMLAN		
R G*	Nevada Grass Valley	61 165
RUMLENG		
M M*	Mariposa Twp 1	60 671
RUMLEY		
H	Butte Cascade	56 696
M M	Mariposa Twp 1	60 671
RUMMEL		
Charles	Humbolt Union	59 192
RUMMELS		
Edward	Sierra Port Win	66 796
RUMMY JACK		
---	Fresno Twp 1	59 30
RUMMY		
---	Fresno Twp 2	59 106
---	Fresno Twp 2	59 109
RUMOLD		
Harrison	El Dorado Mountain	581183
RUMONE		
Guadlupe	Napa Napa	61 115
RUMORO		
Manl	Mariposa Twp 1	60 644
RUMPF		
Jacob	Amador Twp 1	55 459
RUMSEY		
D C	Solano Suisan	69 221
Hiram	Plumas Quincy	62 936
J B	Solano Suisan	69 221
L W	El Dorado Placerville	58 922
Thos	Tehama Red Bluff	70 919

Name	County Locale	M653 RollPage
RUMSEY		
Wm H	Monterey Monterey	60 927
RUMSHOTERL		
R A	Tuolumne Twp 4	71 175
RUMSHOTUL		
R A	Tuolumne Garrote	71 175
RUMSILL		
Ayro	Contra Costa Twp 1	57 519
C H	San Francisco San Francisco 3	67 44
T L	Calaveras Twp 9	57 355
RUMSS		
Jacob*	Amador Twp 1	55 459
RUMTAN		
R G*	Nevada Grass Valley	61 165
RUN		
---	Placer Illinois	62 752
---	San Francisco San Francisco 4	681174
---	Sierra Twp 5	66 928
---	Sierra Downieville	66 981
---*	Stanislaus Branch	70 714
Ling	Mariposa Coulterville	60 682
Thomas	Calaveras Twp 4	57 314
RUNAHER		
Patk*	Napa Napa	61 102
RUNAKER		
Patk*	Napa Napa	61 102
RUNALDS		
Maria	El Dorado Mountain	581183
R	El Dorado Diamond	58 766
RUNAN		
Benard	Butte Bidwell	56 716
RUNBLE		
John	Calaveras Twp 6	57 136
RUNCHEON		
Jacob	Amador Twp 1	55 468
RUNCLOUX		
Pierre	Sierra La Porte	66 768
RUNCOR		
O M	Marin Cortemad	60 752
RUNCORDE		
Bartelemo	Calaveras Twp 6	57 187
RUNCORDO		
Bartelemo	Calaveras Twp 5	57 187
Bartetemo	Calaveras Twp 5	57 187
RUNDALL		
Robert	Calaveras Twp 5	57 178
RUNDELL		
Eli	Santa Clara Gilroy	65 239
RUNDLE		
Charles H	Humbolt Bucksport	59 161
Jno	Nevada Washington	61 333
R T*	Mendocino Big Rvr	60 844
RUNDLETT		
J A	Sacramento Ward 3	63 487
RUNE		
Morris*	San Francisco San Francisco 7	681382
RUNER		
J	Calaveras Twp 8	57 106
Thos	El Dorado Georgetown	58 679
RUNET		
N G	Calaveras Twp 9	57 383
RUNG		
---	San Francisco San Francisco 4	681185
---	San Francisco San Francisco 4	681194
---	San Francisco San Francisco 4	681212
---	Sierra Twp 5	66 921
---*	San Francisco San Francisco 4	681194
RUNGE		
J	San Joaquin Stockton	641096
RUNHART		
Wm	San Francisco San Francisco 2	67 592
RUNI		
Patrick*	Mariposa Twp 3	60 617
RUNIELS		
Eldridge	San Joaquin Castoria	64 890
RUNIN		
Thos	El Dorado Georgetown	58 679
RUNING		
Frank	Santa Cruz Pajaro	66 545
RUNINGTON		
George F*	Calaveras Twp 4	57 336
RUNIR		
Thos	El Dorado Georgetown	58 679
RUNIS		
Joseph	Calaveras Twp 4	57 330
Robert	Mendocino Little L	60 837
RUNIT		
N G	Calaveras Twp 9	57 383
RUNK		
Geo	Sonoma Petaluma	69 592
Mary	Sonoma Petaluma	69 596
William	Los Angeles Los Angeles	59 360
Wm	Napa Napa	61 81
RUNKEL		
Henry	Placer Dutch Fl	62 720
John M	Siskiyou Yreka	69 193

Name	County Locale	M653 RollPage
RUNKIL		
Gustav*	Calaveras Twp 6	57 119
Gustuv*	Calaveras Twp 6	57 119
RUNKIN		
Charles	San Francisco San Francisco 4	681134
RUNKLE		
George*	Yuba Long Bar	72 752
John	Calaveras Twp 5	57 136
RUNLINS		
J	Siskiyou Scott Ri	69 68
RUNLON		
W*	Nevada Eureka	61 370
RUNMAN		
G*	Butte Eureka	56 652
RUNMEY		
Aaron*	Sierra St Louis	66 809
RUNNANN		
Henry	Marin Cortemad	60 755
RUNNAY		
Aaron*	Sierra St Louis	66 809
RUNNELLS		
J K	Stanislaus Oatvale	70 719
L W*	Butte Kimshaw	56 588
S J*	Butte Kimshaw	56 588
S W*	Butte Kimshaw	56 588
RUNNELS		
Edward	Sierra Port Win	66 796
Evan	Tuolumne Sonora	71 193
S G	Los Angeles Tejon	59 536
RUNNER		
---	Fresno Twp 1	59 56
Fredk	San Francisco San Francisco 1	68 905
Thos	Yolo Washington	72 567
RUNNEY		
Aaron	Sierra St Louis	66 809
RUNNING		
Francis	Santa Cruz Pajaro	66 557
Francis	Santa Cruz Pajaro	66 564
RUNNOLS		
Martin	Tulara Keeneysburg	71 41
RUNOUFHS		
A*	El Dorado Big Bar	58 741
RUNRON		
John	Tehama Lassen	70 877
RUNSEY		
Andrew	El Dorado Salmon Falls	581059
E	El Dorado Diamond	58 793
RUNSFORD		
Isaac B	Alameda Brooklyn	55 92
RUNT		
Inle	San Francisco San Francisco 2	67 557
Jule	San Francisco San Francisco 2	67 557
RUNWOOD		
J	Nevada Grass Valley	61 155
RUNYAN		
F H	Sierra Twp 5	66 923
H L	Sonoma Russian	69 435
Samuel	Amador Twp 4	55 241
RUNYON		
A	Sacramento Franklin	63 332
Alex N	Sacramento Ward 1	63 44
Jared	Sacramento Franklin	63 331
Lewis	Sacramento Brighton	63 202
R J	Sacramento San Joaquin	63 364
Sally	Sacramento Ward 1	63 44
Solomon	Sacramento Franklin	63 332
RUO		
---	Mariposa Twp 1	60 655
RUOCH		
L	Nevada Nevada	61 254
RUODER		
Geo S*	Butte Oregon	56 642
RUOFFS		
Christiana*	San Joaquin Stockton	641052
RUORK		
Jno	Sacramento Ward 4	63 603
RUORTER		
John*	Mariposa Twp 1	60 666
RUP		
Charles	San Francisco San Francisco 7	681429
James*	Nevada Eureka	61 369
RUPBELL		
Fredk	San Francisco San Francisco 3	67 76
RUPE		
George	Plumas Quincy	62 953
Isaac	Sacramento Ward 1	63 77
John	Sierra Twp 5	66 938
Saml H	Sonoma Sonoma	69 650
RUPEL		
A	Sutter Butte	70 780
C T	Tehama Red Bluff	70 927
G W	Monterey San Juan	60 989
James	San Francisco San Francisco 4	681168
W A	Sonoma Santa Rosa	69 394
RUPELEY		
R	Tuolumne Twp 2	71 392

Name	County Locale	M653 RollPage
RUPELKEY		
R	Tuolumne Shawsfla	71 392
RUPELL		
Ada	Solano Suisan	69 218
Adelia	San Francisco San Francisco 7	681442
Alexander	Solano Suisan	69 215
E M	Nevada Nevada	61 297
Fredk W	San Francisco San Francisco 3	67 76
Henry	Solano Suisan	69 218
J	Nevada Nevada	61 240
James	San Francisco San Francisco 4	681158
John	Sacramento Ward 1	63 128
John*	Mariposa Coulterville	60 696
L M	Trinity Trinity	70 973
William R	San Francisco San Francisco 4	681122
William*	Calaveras Twp 5	57 172
Wm S	San Francisco San Francisco 3	67 83
RUPERT		
Charles	Sierra Gibsonville	66 853
George	Contra Costa Twp 3	57 613
John	San Francisco San Francisco 9	681024
Phil	Butte Chico	56 539
RUPFER		
John	San Francisco San Francisco 11	133 67
RUPHURT		
George	Sierra Twp 7	66 865
RUPIAN		
N*	San Francisco San Francisco 9	681101
RUPLE		
R P	Amador Twp 1	55 488
RUPLEY		
J	Yolo Fremont	72 603
J W*	El Dorado Placerville	58 911
RUPON		
Michael*	Solano Benecia	69 315
RUPORT		
G W*	El Dorado Georgetown	58 690
RUPPE		
John	Los Angeles Santa Ana	59 440
RUPPEL		
C	Trinity Raabs Ba	701020
RUPPENETH		
Martha	San Francisco San Francisco 8	681313
RUPPENTHAL		
J C	San Francisco San Francisco 10	227 67
RUPPERT		
Augustus	Yuba Marysville	72 970
George	Sierra Twp 7	66 865
RUPPESETH		
Martha*	San Francisco San Francisco 8	681313
RUPPSEITH		
Martha*	San Francisco San Francisco 8	681313
RUPSELT		
William*	Calaveras Twp 5	57 172
RUPWORM		
Asancis E*	Calaveras Twp 4	57 326
Francis E	Calaveras Twp 4	57 326
RUR		
---	San Francisco San Francisco 4	681174
RURA		
---	El Dorado Kelsey	581131
RURDAN		
Davis	Sierra Twp 7	66 868
RURERS		
Rose*	Sierra Twp 7	66 887
RURMANN		
Henry	Marin Cortemad	60 755
RURMODEL		
F	San Francisco San Francisco 4	681172
RURRD		
Edward*	Alameda Oakland	55 43
RURRILL		
Charles*	Santa Cruz Santa Cruz	66 618
RURRINGTON		
George F*	Calaveras Twp 4	57 336
RURS		
Remon*	Mariposa Twp 1	60 672
RURZ		
Adam F*	Amador Twp 1	55 461
RUS		
D*	Butte Eureka	56 654
Domingo	Santa Clara San Jose	65 390
Humphry*	Amador Twp 4	55 250
RUSA		
Antonio	Alameda Oakland	55 71
Wyan*	Sonoma Sonoma	69 636
RUSCH		
Washington	Yuba Parks Ba	72 780
RUSCOM		
Wm	San Francisco San Francisco 1	68 811
RUSE		
Andy*	Mariposa Twp 3	60 600
Aney*	Mariposa Twp 3	60 600
Conrad	El Dorado Kelsey	581142

Name	County Locale	M653 RollPage
RUSE		
D	Solano Vallejo	69 279
Elder*	Sonoma Petaluma	69 575
Eli	Calaveras Twp 9	57 352
H	Butte Wyandotte	56 664
J	El Dorado Diamond	58 811
John	Tuolumne Twp 1	71 262
John J*	Sierra Pine Grove	66 830
John*	Napa Hot Springs	61 7
Joseph	Yuba Parks Ba	72 779
L	Calaveras Twp 9	57 415
Lewis	Tuolumne Twp 2	71 383
M N	Nevada Nevada	61 275
T	El Dorado Georgetown	58 682
Walton*	Siskiyou Callahan	69 16
Wm Ah	Yuba Slate Ro	72 701
Y	El Dorado Georgetown	58 682
RUSELL		
Alexander	Solano Suisan	69 215
Jule	Alameda Oakland	55 62
RUSER		
Wyan	Sonoma Sonoma	69 636
RUSH		
C D	Sierra Twp 7	66 903
C W	Nevada Eureka	61 363
Catharine	San Francisco San Francisco 1	68 879
Charles A	Yuba Marysville	72 922
Coralde	Tuolumne Twp 5	71 492
Coralete	Tuolumne Chinese	71 492
David	Trinity Cox'S Bar	701037
Edwd	San Francisco San Francisco 10	258 67
Geo	Butte Eureka	56 647
Geo D	Calaveras Twp 8	57 102
Henry	Yuba Marysville	72 927
Hiram	Solano Suisan	69 217
Isaac	Tulara Twp 1	71 108
J	Nevada Grass Valley	61 237
J E	Butte Oregon	56 626
Joel	Humbolt Eel Rvr	59 150
John	Colusa Spring Valley	57 436
Jonas	Tuolumne Twp 3	71 441
Jonas	Tuolumne Twp 3	71 450
Lenard	El Dorado Kelsey	581130
Patrick	San Francisco San Francisco 12	369 67
Paul	El Dorado Salmon Falls	581055
Peter	Marin Novato	60 736
Peter	Trinity Oregon G	701008
Wm	Sierra Downieville	66 964
Wm*	Sacramento Granite	63 248
RUSHART		
B	Calaveras Twp 9	57 375
RUSHAW		
Henry	Siskiyou Yreka	69 147
RUSHE		
Law*	Butte Ophir	56 824
Saml*	Butte Ophir	56 824
RUSHEA		
John	Trinity Cox'S Bar	701038
RUSHEN		
Minor	Los Angeles Elmonte	59 257
RUSHER		
Wm	Amador Twp 2	55 299
RUSHING		
J P	San Mateo Twp 3	65 110
Robert	Plumas Quincy	62 951
RUSHMAN		
G A*	El Dorado Georgetown	58 686
RUSHMORE		
A	Sonoma Petaluma	69 594
Chas	Napa Hot Springs	61 26
RUSHNOM		
G H*	El Dorado Georgetown	58 686
RUSHORT		
Geo	Sonoma Sonoma	69 644
RUSHORUM		
G H*	El Dorado Georgetown	58 686
RUSI		
John*	Napa Hot Springs	61 7
RUSIALL		
John	Calaveras Twp 6	57 127
RUSIN		
Henry	Yuba Marysville	72 976
RUSK		
B W	Sutter Nicolaus	70 835
James	San Diego S Luis R	64 781
Robert	Nevada Bridgeport	61 495
Robert	Tuolumne Columbia	71 299
Samuel	Colusa Grand Island	57 476
RUSKE		
Frederick	Marin Cortemad	60 756
James C*	Yuba Marysville	72 901
RUSKUL		
Alex	Contra Costa Twp 3	57 595
RUSLAND		
Victoria	San Francisco San Francisco 9	681038

Name	County Locale	M653 RollPage
RUSLDY		
George*	Yuba Long Bar	72 755
RUSLER		
Wm	Sacramento Natonia	63 284
RUSMELS		
S G*	Los Angeles Tejon	59 536
RUSN		
Jacobb*	Amador Twp 1	55 452
RUSO		
Eli*	Calaveras Twp 9	57 352
John	Tuolumne Twp 1	71 262
RUSS		
Adolphus G	San Francisco	San Francisco 7 681432
Albert	Sacramento Natonia	63 280
Benj	Butte Oro	56 688
Chales	El Dorado Greenwood	58 719
Christiana	San Francisco San Francisco 10	341 67
Clara	Yuba Marysville	72 925
D	San Francisco San Francisco 3	67 78
George	Calaveras Twp 7	57 44
George	Yuba Marysville	72 963
Henry	San Francisco San Francisco 2	67 704
Hy	San Francisco San Francisco 1	68 927
Ignacio	San Joaquin Stockton	641095
J E	San Francisco San Francisco 9	681055
James	Nevada Eureka	61 369
Joseph	Humbolt Pacific	59 129
Joseph	San Francisco San Francisco 3	67 44
Robert*	San Francisco San Francisco 3	67 44
RUSSAM		
Thomas	San Joaquin Elkhorn	64 985
RUSSE		
Jacobb*	Amador Twp 1	55 452
John*	Sierra Twp 5	66 938
Saml H*	Sonoma Sonoma	69 650
RUSSEAN		
Antoine	Calaveras Twp 4	57 340
RUSSEAU		
Antoine*	Calaveras Twp 4	57 340
RUSSEL		
A	Shasta Shasta	66 760
A M	El Dorado Big Bar	58 741
B J	Shasta Shasta	66 728
C B M	El Dorado Placerville	58 872
Chas	Klamath Trinidad	59 221
Eli F	San Joaquin Elkhorn	64 967
F G	Yolo Cottonwoood	72 648
Frank	Shasta Horsetown	66 708
G C	Sacramento Franklin	63 312
H B	Yuba New York	72 746
H W	El Dorado Georgetown	58 697
Harlow	Sierra La Porte	66 774
Henry	Tuolumne Columbia	71 472
J	San Joaquin Stockton	641042
James	Amador Twp 3	55 382
James	Marin Cortemad	60 785
James	Tuolumne Twp 1	71 263
James J	Tuolumne Sonora	71 482
John	El Dorado Mud Springs	58 984
John	Marin Cortemad	60 780
John S	Tuolumne Sonora	71 482
John*	Marin Cortemad	60 780
Manuel	Alameda Brooklyn	55 87
N A	Shasta Shasta	66 734
P	Sacramento San Joaquin	63 356
Silas	Sacramento Ward 4	63 522
Stephen	San Francisco San Francisco 1	68 915
W A	Sonoma Santa Rosa	69 394
Warren	San Francisco San Francisco 1	68 852
William	Amador Twp 1	55 509
William H	San Joaquin Douglass	64 924
Wm F	Tuolumne Columbia	71 300
RUSSELL		
---*	Yolo Putah	72 547
Albert	Amador Twp 5	55 357
Albert	San Francisco San Francisco 3	68 993
Albert	Sierra Cox'S Bar	66 950
Almond	San Joaquin Tulare	64 870
Alvin	Sierra Downieville	661029
Andrew	El Dorado Georgetown	58 752
Andrew	Placer Secret R	62 612
Ann	San Francisco San Francisco 2	67 626
B H	San Joaquin Douglass	64 926
C	Tuolumne Jacksonville	71 170
C E	Butte Oregon	56 629
Charles C	Tuolumne Knights	71 528
Charlotte	San Joaquin Stockton	641042
Chas	Butte Kimshaw	56 593
Cornelius	Alameda Brooklyn	55 209
D	Nevada Eureka	61 366
Daniel	El Dorado Salmon Falls	581063
David	Amador Twp 4	55 235
David	Butte Bidwell	56 712
David	San Francisco San Francisco 9	68 990

RUSSELL

Name	County Locale	M653 RollPage
E	Merced Twp 2	60 922
E	San Francisco San Francisco 5	67 523
E A	El Dorado Newtown	58 779
E M	Nevada Nevada	61 297
Edward	Mendocino Ukiah	60 806
Evan	Santa Cruz Santa Cruz	66 621
Evan	Santa Cruz Santa Cruz	66 623
F	San Francisco San Francisco 1	68 904
F E	Yolo Putah	72 554
F H	Sacramento Ward 1	63 137
G W	El Dorado Placerville	58 849
G W	Monterey San Juan	60 989
Geo	Butte Ophir	56 793
Geo	Merced Twp 2	60 924
Geo	San Francisco San Francisco 6	67 468
Geo	San Francisco San Francisco 9	68 978
Geo	Yolo Putah	72 547
Geo W	Del Norte Crescent	58 631
Geo W	Del Norte Crescent	58 632
George	San Francisco San Francisco 7	681407
George	Santa Cruz Santa Cruz	66 620
George	Siskiyou Yreka	69 178
George	Tuolumne Don Pedro	71 542
George P	Yuba Suida	72 981
H B	Yuba Long Bar	72 746
H C	San Francisco San Francisco 2	67 685
H H	San Francisco San Francisco 10	325 67
Hains*	Sierra Twp 5	66 919
Harriet	Merced Twp 1	60 895
Harris	Sierra Twp 5	66 919
Henry	Contra Costa Twp 2	57 559
Henry	Plumas Quincy	621007
Henry	Solano Suisan	69 218
Henry	Tuolumne Columbia	71 307
Henry F	San Joaquin Elliott	64 941
Henry L	Sacramento Ward 3	63 461
Henry P	Plumas Quincy	62 925
Hiram	Del Norte Crescent	58 645
Hiram C	San Bernardino San Salvador	64 650
J	Solano Vacaville	69 332
J	Solano Fremont	69 382
J	Sonoma Armally	69 512
J B	El Dorado Kelsey	581135
J E	San Francisco San Francisco 2	67 688
J F	Placer Dutch Fl	62 721
J M	Sacramento Dry Crk	63 378
J W	Sonoma Santa Rosa	69 418
James	Alameda Brooklyn	55 162
James	Colusa Spring Valley	57 433
James F	San Francisco San Francisco 2	67 726
James M	Napa Clear Lake	61 127
Jas	Napa Napa	61 89
Jas	Placer Auburn	62 588
Jas H	San Francisco San Francisco 3	67 44
Jno	Mendocino Big Rvr	60 846
John	Amador Twp 1	55 462
John	Contra Costa Twp 3	57 613
John	Del Norte Klamath	58 653
John	El Dorado Georgetown	58 680
John	Mariposa Coulterville	60 696
John	Placer Auburn	62 575
John	Placer Michigan	62 824
John	Sacramento Ward 1	63 128
John	Santa Cruz Pescadero	66 644
John	Sonoma Vallejo	69 625
John	Tuolumne Twp 1	71 266
John A	San Francisco San Francisco 2	67 745
John A	San Francisco San Francisco 1	68 869
John A	San Joaquin Douglass	64 924
John L	San Joaquin Castoria	64 903
John*	Mariposa Coulterville	60 696
Jos S	Sacramento Natonia	63 270
Joseph	Placer Michigan	62 827
Joseph	Santa Cruz Santa Cruz	66 629
Joseph L	Sacramento Ward 4	63 571
L M	Del Norte Crescent	58 619
L M	Tuolumne Twp 1	71 260
Laura E	Del Norte Crescent	58 619
Lewis	Nevada Little Y	61 534
Louis	Nevada Little Y	61 534
M	Calaveras Twp 9	57 415
M	Siskiyou Cottonwoood	69 101
Manuel	Alameda Brooklyn	55 87
Maria	San Francisco San Francisco 12	386 67
Mark	Merced Twp 1	60 896
Mary	Alameda Brooklyn	55 215
Mary B	San Francisco San Francisco 2	67 660
Nancy C	Sacramento Ward 4	63 568
O	El Dorado Diamond	58 801
Oliver P	Tuolumne Shawsfla	71 395
P A J	San Francisco San Francisco 6	67 441
P B	Butte Eureka	56 647
P H	Sacramento Ward 3	63 460

RUSSELL

Name	County Locale	M653 RollPage
Peter	Sierra Twp 5	66 921
R	Amador Twp 3	55 386
R	San Francisco San Francisco 9	681083
Richard	Calaveras Twp 5	57 190
Richard	Colusa Colusi	57 426
Rob	Santa Clara Santa Clara	65 523
Robert	Plumas Quincy	621002
Robert	Plumas Quincy	621004
Robert H	Placer Dutch Fl	62 731
Rufus C	Sierra Cox'S Bar	66 950
S	San Francisco San Francisco 3	67 45
S S	Sutter Yuba	70 772
Saml O	Plumas Quincy	62 919
Samuel	Contra Costa Twp 2	57 559
Samuel	San Joaquin Castoria	64 895
Sarah	Del Norte Crescent	58 626
Selah	Sacramento Dry Crk	63 371
Silas	Sacramento Sutter	63 292
Simon	Solano Benecia	69 314
Simon O P	Solano Benecia	69 314
Stephen S	Colusa Grand Island	57 469
Sylvester	Sonoma Mendocino	69 452
T	Del Norte Happy Ca	58 670
Theresa	San Francisco San Francisco 8	681314
Thomas	Contra Costa Twp 3	57 591
Thomas	El Dorado Eldorado	58 943
Thomas	Santa Cruz Santa Cruz	66 629
Thomas	Sierra Twp 5	66 921
Thos	Yolo Washington	72 566
W	Calaveras Twp 9	57 400
W	San Francisco San Francisco 10	192 67
W	Siskiyou Scott Va	69 39
W	Siskiyou Scott Ri	69 68
W	Tuolumne Garrote	71 176
W R	Butte Ophir	56 798
Wallace	Butte Bidwell	56 725
William	Nevada Bloomfield	61 528
William	San Francisco San Francisco 9	681101
William	San Francisco San Francisco 7	681417
William	San Joaquin Elliott	64 943
William	Siskiyou Scott Ri	69 64
William	Yuba Marysville	72 910
William A	Tulara Visalia	71 102
William G	Tulara Visalia	71 105
William R*	San Francisco 4	681122
William*	San Francisco Calaveras Twp 6	57 172
Willis	Sonoma Sonoma	69 645
Wilson	Alameda Brooklyn	55 209
Wm	Amador Twp 2	55 320
Wm	Napa Napa	61 80
Wm	Placer Virginia	62 670
Wm	Sacramento Brighton	63 194
Wm	Sacramento San Joaquin	63 357
Wm	Santa Clara Gilroy	65 232
Wm	Yolo No E Twp	72 673
Wm	Yuba North Ea	72 673
Wm H	El Dorado Georgetown	58 689
Wm H	Napa Yount	61 53
Wm J A*	El Dorado Georgetown	58 689
Wm L	Placer Virginia	62 672

RUSSELLS

Name	County Locale	M653 RollPage
S J*	Butte Kimshaw	56 588

RUSSER

Name	County Locale	M653 RollPage
James	Siskiyou Klamath	69 92

RUSSETEE

Name	County Locale	M653 RollPage
J*	Nevada Nevada	61 321

RUSSETT

Name	County Locale	M653 RollPage
Henry	Butte Oregon	56 624
I D*	Nevada Rough &	61 397
J D	Nevada Rough &	61 397
Joseph	Placer Michigan	62 840
Martin	San Francisco San Francisco 9	681084

RUSSEUN

Name	County Locale	M653 RollPage
Charles*	Calaveras Twp 4	57 325

RUSSIAN

Name	County Locale	M653 RollPage
N*	San Francisco San Francisco 9	681101
William	Tuolumne Twp 2	71 283

RUSSILL

Name	County Locale	M653 RollPage
C	El Dorado Placerville	58 851
James M	Napa Clear Lake	61 127

RUSSITER

Name	County Locale	M653 RollPage
J*	Nevada Nevada	61 321

RUSSOL

Name	County Locale	M653 RollPage
N A	Shasta Shasta	66 734

RUSSUIR

Name	County Locale	M653 RollPage
Thomas	San Joaquin Elkhorn	64 985

RUSSWORM

Name	County Locale	M653 RollPage
Francis E*	Calaveras Twp 4	57 326

RUST

Name	County Locale	M653 RollPage
A	Sacramento Granite	63 235
Albert B	Sacramento Ward 1	63 41
Albert S	Placer Secret R	62 617
Benj	Butte Oro	56 688

RUST

Name	County Locale	M653 RollPage
Benj	Tuolumne Jamestown	71 437
Charles	Los Angeles Santa Ana	59 441
Geo	Amador Twp 6	55 421
Gustave	Tuolumne Chinese	71 495
Horrace	Sonoma Armally	69 499
John A	Tuolumne Twp 3	71 437
Lot M	Nevada Rough &	61 423
Richard	Calaveras Twp 6	57 115
William	Calaveras Twp 5	57 228
William	El Dorado White Oaks	581013
William*	Calaveras Twp 5	57 228
Wm	Sacramento Ward 3	63 486

RUSTER

Name	County Locale	M653 RollPage
E W	El Dorado Placerville	58 817

RUSWELL

Name	County Locale	M653 RollPage
---	Tulara Twp 3	71 50

RUTA

Name	County Locale	M653 RollPage
Prospier*	San Francisco San Francisco 2	67 650

RUTAM

Name	County Locale	M653 RollPage
John*	Sacramento Franklin	63 323

RUTAN

Name	County Locale	M653 RollPage
Isaac	Solano Vallejo	69 262

RUTANN

Name	County Locale	M653 RollPage
John*	Sacramento Franklin	63 323

RUTCHER

Name	County Locale	M653 RollPage
R*	Butte Kimshaw	56 591

RUTCI

Name	County Locale	M653 RollPage
J T	Nevada Bridgeport	61 486

RUTE

Name	County Locale	M653 RollPage
F	Siskiyou Scott Ri	69 77

RUTEI

Name	County Locale	M653 RollPage
J T*	Nevada Bridgeport	61 486

RUTELTS

Name	County Locale	M653 RollPage
Lewis	Alameda Brooklyn	55 192

RUTER

Name	County Locale	M653 RollPage
J T*	Nevada Bridgeport	61 486

RUTGER

Name	County Locale	M653 RollPage
Francis	Sierra Gibsonville	66 858
G	Mariposa Twp 3	60 603

RUTH

Name	County Locale	M653 RollPage
Eli	Sacramento Cosumnes	63 402
Francis*	Yuba Parks Ba	72 780
J	Sacramento Brighton	63 208
James	Tuolumne Twp 2	71 387
John*	Sacramento Franklin	63 313
M A	Nevada Nevada	61 271
Richard	Amador Twp 1	55 463
William	Contra Costa Twp 3	57 597

RUTHBONE

Name	County Locale	M653 RollPage
Ann	San Francisco San Francisco 9	68 941

RUTHBUN

Name	County Locale	M653 RollPage
Jas	Sonoma Petaluma	69 594

RUTHCART

Name	County Locale	M653 RollPage
Victor	Placer Iona Hills	62 888

RUTHCHEL

Name	County Locale	M653 RollPage
Andrew	Placer Auburn	62 579

RUTHEDGE

Name	County Locale	M653 RollPage
A S	Yolo Putah	72 560

RUTHER

Name	County Locale	M653 RollPage
Jacob	Santa Clara Fremont	65 419
Richard	Yolo Merritt	72 583

RUTHERFORD

Name	County Locale	M653 RollPage
A J	San Francisco San Francisco 10	308 67
Aaron J	Monterey Alisal	601036
Adam	Tuolumne Twp 1	71 246
Alexander	San Francisco San Francisco 3	67 48
Andrew	San Francisco San Francisco 8	681311
Benjamin R	Sierra Gibsonville	66 853
Benjamin R*	Sierra Gibsonville	66 853
Benjamin R*	Sierra Gibsonville	66 853
Chas B	San Francisco San Francisco 9	681000
Forney	Humbolt Eel Rvr	59 146
G	Sonoma Bodega	69 521
Geo	Plumas Meadow Valley	62 903
George	Sierra Pine Grove	66 821
H A	Sacramento Cosumnes	63 409
J F	Nevada Eureka	61 356
J T	Butte Wyandotte	56 668
J T	Nevada Eureka	61 351
J T	Sonoma Bodega	69 536
J W	San Francisco San Francisco 5	67 506
M	Los Angeles Los Angeles	59 519
Moses	Los Angeles Los Angeles	59 365
N	Sacramento Granite	63 240
R	Nevada Eureka	61 356
R P	Nevada Eureka	61 356
Richard H	Sierra Pine Grove	66 823
Robt	Butte Wyandotte	56 668
Sarah	San Francisco San Francisco 9	68 979
T	Shasta Millvill	66 754
T	Sutter Bear Rvr	70 819
Thomas	San Francisco San Francisco 4	681113
Thomas	Solano Montezuma	69 368
Thos	Sacramento Sutter	63 295

Name	County Locale	M653 Roll	Page
RUTHERFORD			
W W	Stanislaus Buena Village	70	724
Walter M	Sierra Port Win	66	797
RUTHFORD			
John	Placer Iona Hills	62	886
RUTHIRS			
Alex	Mendocino Big Rvr	60	847
RUTHLAND			
W T	Sacramento Georgian	63	336
RUTHMAN			
A	San Francisco San Francisco 2	67	633
RUTHRAUFF			
Julia	San Francisco San Francisco 10	67	190
RUTHROFF			
Wm	Calaveras Twp 6	57	127
RUTING			
Otto*	Contra Costa Twp 3	57	612
RUTISHOUSE			
John U*	Sierra Scales D	66	801
RUTLEDGE			
A S	Yolo Putah	72	560
Paschal	Tuolumne Twp 5	71	506
Paxchal	Tuolumne Montezuma	71	506
R	Santa Clara Fremont	65	417
Robert	Sacramento Franklin	63	316
RUTLER			
Ereline M	Solano Suisan	69	205
Eveline M	Solano Suisan	69	205
Peter*	San Francisco San Francisco 1	68	905
RUTLIDGE			
John*	San Joaquin Elkhorn	64	997
RUTLIGE			
Edward	El Dorado Gold Hill	58	1096
RUTO			
Angelo	Calaveras Twp 4	57	299
Augelo	Calaveras Twp 4	57	300
RUTON			
Samuel	San Joaquin Elkhorn	64	979
RUTT			
Theop D	San Francisco San Francisco 9	68	1104
Wm	Placer Secret R	62	615
RUTTEFF			
Catharine	Solano Fremont	69	383
RUTTER			
Diana	Sacramento Ward 3	63	470
George	Santa Cruz Santa Cruz	66	634
Isaac	Sierra Poverty	66	799
RUTTERS			
Thos	Mariposa Twp 3	60	557
RUTTIDGE			
Mary	San Francisco San Francisco 2	67	787
RUTTIFF			
Catherine	Solano Fremont	69	383
RUTTIGE			
Edward	El Dorado Gold Hill	58	1096
Robt	El Dorado Gold Hill	58	1097
RUTTLER			
William	Siskiyou Yreka	69	123
RUTTMAN			
John	San Francisco San Francisco 3	67	30
RUTTOFF			
P C	El Dorado Coloma	58	1123
RUTZ			
Antoini	Calaveras Twp 6	57	164
Antonio	Calaveras Twp 5	57	217
RUTZER			
Francis	Sierra Gibsonville	66	858
RUURDS			
John*	Monterey Monterey	60	965
RUVE			
Geo*	Placer Virginia	62	669
RUVIS			
William*	Calaveras Twp 5	57	218
RUXE			
George	San Francisco San Francisco 4	68	1156
RUXTON			
George	Del Norte Happy Ca	58	668
RUYIS			
B*	Calaveras Twp 9	57	410
RUYNUND			
---*	Sacramento Granite	63	244
RUYTES			
Ehucth	Amador Twp 3	55	382
RUZAN			
Linn L	Placer Dutch Fl	62	729
RUZZELL			
James	Shasta Horsetown	66	694
RVAS			
K*	Siskiyou Cottonwood	69	98
RVPELL			
Wm S	San Francisco San Francisco 3	67	83
RVRAS			
Manuel	San Francisco San Francisco 3	67	77
RWETT			
Chas D*	Sacramento Ward 1	63	50

Name	County Locale	M653 Roll	Page
RWO			
---	Tuolumne Twp 1	71	477
RY SAU			
---	Mariposa Twp 3	60	608
RY			
---	Sierra Twp 7	66	875
Sang	Placer Yankee J	62	779
Seng	El Dorado Greenwood	58	715
RYAD			
H	Tuolumne Twp 4	71	157
RYADERS			
Richd	Nevada Rough &	61	434
RYAER			
R	Klamath Liberty	59	243
RYAL			
M	Sacramento Ward 1	63	2
William	San Francisco San Francisco 9	68	950
RYAM			
H S	Yuba Rose Bar	72	789
John*	Tulara Keyesville	71	53
RYAN			
---	El Dorado Big Bar	58	740
A	Butte Kimshaw	56	596
A	Sacramento Ward 4	63	527
A	Siskiyou Cottonwood	69	100
A H	Tehama Tehama	70	947
A*	Butte Kimshaw	56	596
Agnes	San Francisco San Francisco 10	67	247
Andrew	Sacramento Franklin	63	310
Ann	Placer Virginia	62	663
Anna	Tuolumne Jacksonville	71	168
Anne	San Francisco San Francisco 11	67	94
Betty	San Francisco San Francisco 9	68	996
Bridget	Calaveras Twp 4	57	342
Bridget	San Francisco San Francisco 2	67	775
Bridget	Yuba Marysville	72	851
C	San Francisco San Francisco 5	67	497
C	Siskiyou Scott Va	69	53
Catharine	San Francisco San Francisco 8	68	1254
Catharine	San Francisco San Francisco 7	68	1349
Catharine	San Francisco San Francisco 10	67	182
Catharine	San Francisco San Francisco 9	68	982
Catharine	San Francisco San Francisco 9	68	983
Charles	Marin Cortemad	60	786
Charles	Sierra Pine Grove	66	829
Charles	Yuba Long Bar	72	755
Charles	Yuba Long Bar	72	755
Charles*	Marin Cortemad	60	786
Chas	San Francisco San Francisco 9	68	960
Cornelius	Placer Virginia	62	663
D	San Francisco San Francisco 5	67	552
Dan	Sacramento Ward 1	63	79
Daniel	San Francisco San Francisco 12	67	387
Danl	San Francisco San Francisco 1	68	878
Dennis	Placer Secret R	62	615
Dennis	San Francisco San Francisco 6	67	458
Dennis	San Francisco San Francisco 3	67	84
Dennis	Santa Cruz Soguel	66	589
Dennis	Tuolumne Sonora	71	228
Dennis*	Santa Cruz Soguel	66	583
E B	Sacramento Ward 3	63	438
E J	Santa Clara Santa Clara	65	491
Edmond	Santa Clara Santa Clara	65	498
Edward	Alameda Brooklyn	55	83
Edward	San Francisco San Francisco 4	68	1159
Edward	San Mateo Twp 2	65	120
Edward	Siskiyou Yreka	69	178
Edward W	San Francisco 7	68	1376
	San Francisco		
Eliza	San Francisco San Francisco 1	68	865
Elizabeth	San Francisco San Francisco 2	67	634
Ema	El Dorado Placerville	58	894
F	El Dorado Diamond	58	813
F	Sutter Yuba	70	772
Frank	Nevada Red Dog	61	541
G F	Tuolumne Twp 1	71	369
Gerald	Yuba Marysville	72	863
H	Nevada Grass Valley	61	196
H L	Yuba New York	72	724
Hannah	Calaveras Twp 6	57	165
Hannah	Sacramento Ward 3	63	426
Henry S	Solano Suisan	69	205
Hugh	Fresno Twp 2	59	3
J	Nevada Eureka	61	366
J	Siskiyou Scott Va	69	38
J E	Solano Vallejo	69	251
J F	Butte Oregon	56	643
J J	Butte Oregon	56	620
Jame	Calaveras Twp 5	57	194
James	Amador Twp 6	55	426
James	Calaveras Twp 5	57	194
James	Placer Michigan	62	858

Name	County Locale	M653 Roll	Page
RYAN			
James	Plumas Quincy	62	940
James	Sacramento Ward 1	63	67
James	San Francisco San Francisco 4	68	1214
James	San Francisco San Francisco 12	67	365
James	Sierra Monte Crk	66	1037
James	Sierra St Louis	66	806
James	Siskiyou Scott Ri	69	83
James	Solano Vallejo	69	276
James	Sonoma Santa Rosa	69	427
James	Sonoma Washington	69	674
James	Trinity Taylor'S	70	1036
James E	Solano Vallejo	69	279
James T	Humbolt Eureka	59	164
Jas	Napa Napa	61	109
Jas	Sacramento Ward 1	63	18
Jas	Sacramento Granite	63	266
Jas	Sacramento Ward 3	63	425
Jas	San Francisco San Francisco 12	67	386
Jellin*	El Dorado Georgetown	58	688
Jeremiah	Alameda Oakland	55	23
Jeremiah	San Francisco San Francisco 1	68	894
Jno	Alameda Brooklyn	55	199
Jno	Butte Kimshaw	56	606
Jno	Calaveras Twp 9	57	410
Jno	Sacramento Granite	63	266
Jno	Sacramento Ward 4	63	566
Jno	Sacramento Ward 4	63	587
Joana	Yuba Marysville	72	935
Joanna	Yuba Marysville	72	935
John	Alameda Brooklyn	55	176
John	Calaveras Twp 7	57	1
John	Calaveras Twp 4	57	334
John	Mariposa Twp 3	60	558
John	Mariposa Coulterville	60	699
John	Placer Iona Hills	62	873
John	Sacramento Ward 1	63	106
John	San Bernardino San Bernardino	64	670
John	San Diego San Diego	64	767
John	San Francisco San Francisco 9	68	1031
John	San Francisco San Francisco 4	68	1159
John	San Francisco San Francisco 10	67	275
John	San Francisco San Francisco 3	67	37
John	San Francisco San Francisco 2	67	780
John	San Francisco San Francisco 1	68	855
John	San Mateo Twp 2	65	124
John	Shasta Millvill	66	751
John	Sierra Downieville	66	1002
John	Solano Benecia	69	303
John	Solano Benecia	69	316
John	Sonoma Mendocino	69	452
John	Tulara Twp 3	71	53
John	Yuba New York	72	740
John	Yuba Marysville	72	926
John	Yuba Marysville	72	954
John*	Tulara Keyesville	71	53
Jon	Sierra Downieville	66	1002
Jonas	El Dorado Georgetown	58	748
Jos	Sacramento Ward 1	63	118
Jos	San Francisco San Francisco 9	68	1069
Joseph	Amador Twp 2	55	320
Josephine	Humbolt Eureka	59	175
Josh	Sacramento Brighton	63	197
Julia*	El Dorado Georgetown	58	688
Julin*	El Dorado Georgetown	58	688
Julius*	El Dorado Georgetown	58	688
Katy	Sacramento Ward 4	63	528
L	Nevada Grass Valley	61	176
L	Siskiyou Scott Va	69	43
L C*	Nevada Grass Valley	61	153
L*	Sacramento Brighton	63	196
Launna*	Solano Vallejo	69	268
Laurena	Solano Vallejo	69	268
Laurena	Solano Benecia	69	300
Lauuna*	Solano Vallejo	69	268
Lawrance	San Francisco San Francisco 2	67	749
Lawrence	San Francisco San Francisco 1	68	848
Lawrence	Solano Benecia	69	300
M	Nevada Washington	61	331
M	San Francisco San Francisco 5	67	551
M	San Francisco San Francisco 2	67	663
Margaret	San Francisco San Francisco 5	67	483
Margaret	Yuba Marysville	72	910
Margarey	Yuba Marysville	72	910
Martin	San Francisco San Francisco 11	67	124
Mary	Sacramento Ward 1	63	114
Mary	San Francisco San Francisco 10	67	184
Mary	San Francisco San Francisco 9	68	998
Mary	Yuba Parks Ba	72	777
Mary	Yuba Marysville	72	914
Mather	San Francisco San Francisco 1	68	865

Name	County Locale	M653 RollPage
RYAN		
Mathew	Sierra Downieville	66 997
Matt	Klamath Liberty	59 235
Matthew	Amador Twp 1	55 473
Michael	Alameda Brooklyn	55 185
Michael	Calaveras Twp 5	57 178
Michael	Plumas Meadow Valley	62 911
Michael	San Francisco San Francisco 10	295 67
Michael	San Francisco San Francisco 1	68 902
Michael	San Francisco San Francisco 1	68 919
Michael	Stanislaus Emory	70 749
Michael	Tuolumne Sonora	71 218
Michael	Yuba Rose Bar	72 803
Michael	Yuba Rose Bar	72 804
Michael	Yuba Marysville	72 907
Mike	Sacramento Ward 4	63 501
Mike	San Joaquin Castoria	64 905
Mike	Sonoma Petaluma	69 604
Moses	Amador Twp 2	55 300
P	Nevada Grass Valley	61 210
P	Nevada Grass Valley	61 213
P	Nevada Washington	61 331
P	Nevada Washington	61 341
P	Sacramento Granite	63 236
P G	El Dorado Georgetown	58 679
P L	Nevada Nevada	61 266
P L	Nevada Nevada	61 276
Pat	Sacramento Ward 3	63 434
Pat	Sacramento Ward 4	63 527
Pat	Sacramento Ward 1	63 73
Pat	Sacramento Ward 1	63 83
Pat	San Francisco San Francisco 9	681071
Pat	San Francisco San Francisco 11	116 67
Pat	San Francisco San Francisco 2	67 794
Patrick	Contra Costa Twp 1	57 511
Patrick	Mendocino Ukiah	60 801
Patrick	Placer Auburn	62 589
Patrick	San Francisco San Francisco 3	67 32
Patrick	San Francisco San Francisco 12	385 67
Patrick	San Francisco San Francisco 5	67 545
Patrick	San Francisco San Francisco 5	67 554
Patrick	San Francisco San Francisco 1	68 838
Patrick	San Francisco San Francisco 1	68 840
Patrick	San Francisco San Francisco 1	68 930
Patrick	Yuba Rose Bar	72 790
Patrick*	Mendocino Ukiah	60 801
Paul	Tuolumne Twp 2	71 302
Peter	El Dorado Georgetown	58 753
Peter	San Francisco San Francisco 8	681301
Peter	San Francisco San Francisco 7	681360
Phil	Amador Twp 6	55 445
Pierce	San Francisco San Francisco 8	681285
R	El Dorado Placerville	58 856
R	Trinity Weaverville	701067
R L	Nevada Nevada	61 276
R P	Santa Clara San Jose	65 287
Rodger	San Francisco San Francisco 2	67 642
S	San Francisco San Francisco 5	67 498
S	Siskiyou Scott Va	69 43
S	Sutter Yuba	70 760
S*	Sacramento Brighton	63 196
Sarah	Shasta Horsetown	66 688
Sarah	Shasta Millvill	66 752
Sylvia A	San Francisco San Francisco 10	255 67
T	El Dorado Placerville	58 845
T	Nevada Grass Valley	61 198
T	Nevada Eureka	61 350
T	San Francisco San Francisco 6	67 462
T P	San Francisco San Francisco 5	67 490
Thomas	El Dorado Placerville	58 905
Thomas	Marin Tomales	60 726
Thomas	Plumas Meadow Valley	62 911
Thomas	Sacramento Ward 1	63 63
Thomas	San Joaquin Stockton	641090
Thomas	Siskiyou Scott Ri	69 67
Thomas	Solano Vallejo	69 255
Thos	Amador Twp 4	55 251
Thos	Nevada Grass Valley	61 202
Thos	Placer Sacramento	62 642
Thos	Sacramento Ward 3	63 435
Thos	Sacramento Ward 4	63 507
Thos	Sacramento Ward 4	63 606
Thos	San Francisco San Francisco 2	67 778
Thos	San Francisco San Francisco 1	68 915
Tim	Klamath Liberty	59 233
Timothy	San Francisco San Francisco 4	681229
Timothy	San Francisco San Francisco 11	150 67
Timothy	San Francisco San Francisco 10	294 67
Timothy*	Placer Iona Hills	62 879
W	Shasta Shasta	66 687

Name	County Locale	M653 RollPage
RYAN		
W D	Butte Oregon	56 631
Wilhelmina	San Francisco	12 386
	San Francisco	67
William	Monterey Monterey	60 956
William	San Francisco San Francisco 11	111 67
Wm	San Francisco San Francisco 10	211 67
Wm	San Francisco San Francisco 10	251 67
Wm	Sierra Eureka	661046
Wm	Solano Vallejo	69 277
Wm	Sonoma Petaluma	69 563
Wm	Sonoma Sonoma	69 636
Wm	Trinity Sturdiva	701007
Wm	Yolo No E Twp	72 674
Wm	Yuba North Ea	72 674
Wm H	Nevada Nevada	61 320
RYANDON		
Michael	Calaveras Twp 5	57 214
RYANN		
Andrew	San Francisco San Francisco 11	139 67
RYANOR		
John	Santa Cruz Pescadero	66 646
RYANS		
David S	Yuba Marysville	72 948
Humas	Placer Iona Hills	62 878
John*	Tulara Keyesville	71 53
W	Yolo Cache Crk	72 618
RYANSON		
C C	San Joaquin Douglass	64 915
RYARDON		
Machael*	Calaveras Twp 5	57 214
Michael	Calaveras Twp 5	57 214
Muchael*	Calaveras Twp 5	57 214
RYASON		
J	El Dorado Placerville	58 882
RYBLES		
Lap*	El Dorado Georgetown	58 749
RYBURN		
G*	Nevada Grass Valley	61 235
Sarah*	Monterey Monterey	60 946
RYCKMAN		
Albert	San Francisco San Francisco 2	67 676
George C	San Francisco San Francisco 7	681442
Wm D	San Francisco San Francisco 3	67 87
Wm L	San Francisco San Francisco 3	67 87
RYDENHOUR		
W W	Santa Clara Gilroy	65 223
RYDER		
A F	Tuolumne Twp 2	71 283
Albert S	San Joaquin Tulare	64 870
Anson	Plumas Quincy	621005
B F	Tuolumne Columbia	71 340
Benjamin	San Francisco San Francisco 11	116 67
C B	Klamath Trinidad	59 221
Charity	Sacramento Ward 4	63 563
Charles	Humbolt Eureka	59 171
Charles	Santa Cruz Pajaro	66 557
Dan S	Sacramento Ward 1	63 28
Danl	Sacramento Ward 3	63 423
David	Alameda Oakland	55 57
E B	Yuba Slate Ro	72 710
Ed	Sacramento Ward 1	63 61
F J	San Francisco San Francisco 1	68 878
Feuben	Alameda Brooklyn	55 100
George W	San Francisco San Francisco 4	681216
Isaac	Plumas Quincy	621000
James	Siskiyou Scott Va	69 53
Jerome	Sacramento Ward 4	63 563
Jno	Sacramento Ward 3	63 482
John	Calaveras Twp 6	57 158
John	San Francisco San Francisco 11	122 67
John	San Francisco San Francisco 2	67 635
Josiah	Solano Benecia	69 301
O F	Tuolumne Twp 2	71 283
Reuben	Alameda Brooklyn	55 100
T E	Sacramento Ward 4	63 612
Thomas	San Francisco San Francisco 11	133 67
W	Siskiyou Scott Va	69 53
RYE		
---*	Mariposa Twp 3	60 578
By*	Mariposa Twp 3	60 603
H	San Francisco San Francisco 1	68 926
John	Stanislaus Emory	70 750
John C	Calaveras Twp 8	57 72
Long	Butte Mountain	56 736
RYEKMAN		
G	San Francisco San Francisco 3	67 45
G C	San Francisco San Francisco 3	67 45
RYELO		
Gregora	San Francisco San Francisco 2	67 795

Name	County Locale	M653 RollPage
RYELO		
Gregoria	San Francisco San Francisco 2	67 795
RYEN		
John	Shasta Millvill	66 751
John	Sierra Twp 7	66 872
Wm O*	Yuba Slate Ro	72 697
RYENS		
John*	San Francisco San Francisco 1	68 871
RYER		
Francis	Mendocino Ukiah	60 801
Washington M	Stockton	641064
	San Joaquin	
William T S	San Joaquin Tulare	64 869
RYERS		
Charles	Alameda Brooklyn	55 93
RYERSON		
A P	Solano Benecia	69 309
Nicholas	Placer Auburn	62 588
Nicholas P	Placer Auburn	62 586
S W	Sierra Downieville	661024
RYES		
Cristoval	Los Angeles Los Angeles	59 514
RYGOUTTE		
G*	Nevada Grass Valley	61 157
RYGOUTTR		
G*	Nevada Grass Valley	61 157
RYGOUTTS		
G*	Nevada Grass Valley	61 157
RYHE		
P	Nevada Grass Valley	61 218
RYHT		
Elizabeth	San Mateo Twp 3	65 91
RYIS		
Egnacio	Los Angeles Los Angeles	59 497
Ignacio	Los Angeles Los Angeles	59 497
RYLAND		
C T	Santa Clara San Jose	65 336
C T	Siskiyou Scott Va	69 53
Richard	San Francisco San Francisco 7	681333
RYLE		
Wm	Butte Ophir	56 771
RYLEY		
J	San Francisco San Francisco 5	67 502
James	San Joaquin Castoria	64 902
Mary	San Francisco San Francisco 6	67 472
R	Sutter Yuba	70 760
RYLMUTE		
J*	Nevada Washington	61 332
R*	Nevada Washington	61 332
RYMAN		
Daniel	Sierra Downieville	661024
Otter	San Francisco San Francisco 9	681019
RYME		
John	Sonoma Sonoma	69 657
RYMER		
H A	Siskiyou Yreka	69 172
RYNALDO		
Frederick	Placer Todds Va	62 790
RYNAR		
Samuel*	Shasta Shasta	66 686
RYNDERS		
Benj F	Alameda Brooklyn	55 78
Benj F*	Alameda Murray	55 220
Richd	Nevada Rough	61 434
Richd	Nevada Rough &	61 434
RYNER		
Samuel	Shasta Shasta	66 686
RYNO		
L	Sacramento Ward 4	63 537
RYNOLDS		
J	Nevada Grass Valley	61 219
N	El Dorado White Oaks	581025
RYNS		
S A	Yolo Cache Crk	72 619
RYON		
J	Calaveras Twp 9	57 406
J M	Yolo Putah	72 546
James	Nevada Bridgeport	61 442
M	Los Angeles Tejon	59 525
Micheal	El Dorado White Oaks	581013
Micheal	El Dorado White Oaks	581015
P	Yolo Cache Crk	72 595
Patrick*	Placer Iona Hills	62 896
T	Sutter Butte	70 787
RYOS		
Hulian	Fresno Twp 1	59 84
RYOT		
L P*	Stanislaus Branch	70 699
RYSEN		
Antoni	Contra Costa Twp 1	57 506
Hans	Tuolumne Twp 1	71 242
RYSON		
Ana	Yuba Marysville	72 905
J	El Dorado Placerville	58 882
RYUSON		
A P*	Solano Benecia	69 309

Name	County Locale	M653 RollPage
RYZER		
Wm*	Mariposa Twp 3	60 609
S KELLY		
Pat*	Amador Twp 2	55 296
S PAUL		
John	Siskiyou Callahan	69 4
S SIGU		
---*	Nevada Nevada	61 306
S TON		
---*	Nevada Nevada	61 305
S		
Sais	Mariposa Twp 1	60 643
Yuk	Nevada Nevada	61 300
S???		
James*	Yolo Cottonwood	72 648
S???TZ		
A*	Mariposa Twp 3	60 592
S??IDT		
F*	Sacramento Sutter	63 290
S??M		
J M*	Yolo Cottonwoood	72 647
S??NN		
J M*	Yolo Cottonwoood	72 647
S?BENDDINGS		
La Fayette	Sierra Whiskey	66 846
S?BURDOCK		
Cormil*	San Mateo Twp 1	65 59
S'AM		
---*	Tuolumne Chinese	71 526
S'OO		
Pond*	Tuolumne Chinese	71 526
Powo*	Tuolumne Chinese	71 526
SA CLERE		
Jean*	San Francisco San Francisco 2	67 735
SA LOU		
Apie	Placer Illinois	62 706
SA MOW		
---*	Nevada Nevada	61 304
SA RUE		
A	Sacramento Granite	63 235
SA SEE		
---	Mariposa Twp 3	60 613
SA TUCK		
---	Sacramento Ward 1	63 68
SA-O-YAH-MAH		
---	Butte Chico	56 550
SA		
---	Calaveras Twp 10	57 260
---	Mariposa Twp 1	60 659
---	Placer Rattle Snake	62 630
---	San Joaquin Stockton	641087
Chois	Calaveras Twp 6	57 179
Fee	Nevada Rough &	61 398
Foo	Sacramento Ward 3	63 489
Hin	Plumas Meadow Valley	62 914
How	Nevada Grass Valley	61 229
Hue	Plumas Quincy	62 947
Kay	Mariposa Twp 3	60 569
Kee	Mariposa Twp 3	60 576
Koy	Mariposa Twp 3	60 569
Lee	Nevada Rough &	61 397
Leg	Mariposa Twp 3	60 618
Lo Ching	San Francisco San Francisco 4	681209
Loop	Butte Eureka	56 652
Man	Tuolumne Don Pedro	71 162
Mow	Nevada Nevada	61 304
Sam	Calaveras Twp 8	57 105
See	Mariposa Twp 3	60 613
So	Sacramento Ward 1	63 152
Tie	Nevada Bloomfield	61 521
Wa	Mariposa Twp 3	60 553
Yon	Nevada Grass Valley	61 228
Yow	Nevada Grass Valley	61 228
Yu	Nevada Nevada	61 301
Yup	Nevada Nevada	61 300
Yup	Nevada Eureka	61 383
SA?ILA		
---*	Los Angeles Los Angeles	59 495
SAAL		
Geo*	Sacramento Ward 4	63 576
SAALBERG		
S	Sacramento Ward 4	63 528
SAALFELCH		
C*	San Francisco San Francisco 12	375 67
SAANEDRA		
Jose P*	Mariposa Twp 1	60 624
SAANEDVA		
Jose P	Mariposa Twp 1	60 624
SAANEDVER		
Jose*	Mariposa Twp 1	60 624
SAARK		
Isham	Tuolumne Sonora	71 484
SAARO		
John Mello*	Calaveras Twp 5	57 187
Pedro Mello*	Calaveras Twp 5	57 187

Name	County Locale	M653 RollPage
SAAT		
---	Tuolumne Twp 4	71 178
SAAVEDVA		
Jose*	Mariposa Twp 1	60 624
SABADIE		
Jesus	San Bernardino Santa Inez	64 136
SABADO		
---	Tulara Twp 3	71 66
SABALZA		
Ygnacia	Los Angeles San Gabriel	59 423
Ygnacio	Los Angeles San Gabriel	59 423
SABAN		
Peter*	Yuba Linda	72 993
SABAR		
Peter	Yuba Suida	72 993
SABASTIAN		
H	Shasta Shasta	66 678
SABASTIRAMO		
M*	El Dorado Georgetown	58 699
SABASTRAINO		
M*	El Dorado Georgetown	58 699
SABATIE		
Alexd F	San Francisco San Francisco 8	681302
SABATTA		
---	Tulara Twp 3	71 65
---	Tulara Keyesville	71 69
SABBADO		
---	Tulara Keyesville	71 66
SABBAR		
Irvan	Calaveras Twp 9	57 347
Juan	Calaveras Twp 9	57 347
SABBAS		
Juan	Calaveras Twp 9	57 347
SABE		
---	Nevada Bridgeport	61 492
SABEDRA		
Caroline	San Francisco San Francisco 2	67 685
SABEIN		
J	Tuolumne Twp 4	71 170
SABEL		
Chana	Santa Cruz Santa Cruz	66 601
Henry*	San Francisco San Francisco 1	68 854
Peter	San Francisco San Francisco 2	67 795
SABEN		
C	Calaveras Twp 7	57 30
SABENAUGH		
Thos*	Sacramento San Joaquin	63 349
SABENGTON		
Edson	Santa Clara San Jose	65 383
SABEOS		
Timothy B*	Yuba Marysville	72 928
SABER		
Lorenzo*	Sacramento Granite	63 262
Peter	Yuba Marysville	72 875
Peters*	Yuba Marysville	72 875
SABERANES		
Jose M	Merced Monterey	60 934
SABERS		
Timothy B	Yuba Marysville	72 928
SABERT		
Mary S	Solano Benecia	69 313
SABETOURE		
Cassimer*	Tuolumne Twp 4	71 132
SABICHI		
Matias	Los Angeles Los Angeles	59 295
SABIER		
Thos	Calaveras Twp 9	57 399
SABIN		
A B	Sacramento Ward 1	63 1
John	San Francisco San Francisco 10	310 67
Shenden P*	Elkhorn	64 999
	San Joaquin	
SABINE		
Abner M	Calaveras Twp 10	57 288
Chester	Calaveras Twp 6	57 163
SABINS		
A C	San Francisco San Francisco 6	67 449
SABIRANO		
Francisco	Contra Costa Twp 3	57 585
SABISH		
Charles	Santa Cruz Santa Cruz	66 606
SABLE		
Henry	San Francisco San Francisco 5	67 480
Louisa	San Francisco San Francisco 2	67 661
SABLES		
M	San Francisco San Francisco 6	67 464
SABLETT		
Willis*	Solano Vacaville	69 319
SABNER		
Anthony	Sacramento Ward 1	63 76
SABOLEP		
A	Sutter Sutter	70 815
SABOMA		
Carle	Calaveras Twp 5	57 216
SABOMO		
Cade	Calaveras Twp 5	57 216

Name	County Locale	M653 RollPage
SABOMO		
Cule	Calaveras Twp 5	57 216
SABONEY		
Wm H*	San Francisco San Francisco 1	68 890
SABOOS		
Dionisio	Monterey Monterey	60 937
SABORANA		
---	San Diego San Diego	64 771
SABORDE		
John C	Yuba Marysville	72 880
SABORI		
Peter	Siskiyou Yreka	69 144
SABRIEL		
---*	San Francisco San Francisco 12	395 67
SABRINE		
Chester	Calaveras Twp 6	57 163
SABS		
Antonio*	San Mateo Twp 2	65 133
Mose*	Santa Cruz Santa Cruz	66 633
SABSO		
Antonio	Alameda Brooklyn	55 78
SAC		
---	Amador Twp 2	55 314
---	Nevada Bridgeport	61 506
---*	Nevada Rough &	61 431
SACARIAS		
---	Monterey Monterey	60 937
SACARSE		
John	Tuolumne Columbia	71 321
SACCONE		
B	Sacramento Sutter	63 303
SACER		
David*	Nevada Nevada	61 247
SACH		
---*	Mariposa Twp 1	60 664
SACHAGA		
Juan	San Joaquin Stockton	641071
SACHALL		
Philip	Sacramento Granite	63 251
SACHAN		
John	Solano Vacaville	69 355
SACHAPPELLE		
Louis	Calaveras Twp 8	57 53
SACHEL		
S	El Dorado White Oaks	581017
SACHELL		
C T	Nevada Grass Valley	61 216
SACHELOUME		
---	Tulara Twp 2	71 35
SACHEME		
---	Tulara Twp 2	71 37
SACHEMELO		
---	Tulara Twp 2	71 34
SACHER		
I*	Nevada Washington	61 336
J	Nevada Washington	61 336
SACHET		
Pierre	San Francisco San Francisco 2	67 724
SACHEZ		
Sequeidma*	San Francisco 1	68 823
	San Francisco	
SACHS		
Louis	San Francisco San Francisco 8	681301
Samuel	San Francisco San Francisco 4	681159
SACHSEN		
John	Sierra Twp 7	66 872
SACK JIM		
---*	Mendocino Twp 1	60 886
SACK		
---	Del Norte Crescent	58 641
---	El Dorado Placerville	58 932
---	Placer Rattle Snake	62 602
---	Sierra Downieville	661004
---	Sierra Downieville	66 979
---	Sierra Downieville	66 996
Ah	Sacramento Cosummes	63 384
Conard*	Mariposa Twp 3	60 605
Demcus F	Siskiyou Shasta Rvr	69 115
J C	San Francisco San Francisco 8	681294
Jim*	Mendocino Twp 1	60 886
Philip	Nevada Bloomfield	61 514
Samuel	Placer Forest H	62 804
Smy	Sacramento Ward 3	63 494
Wy	Yuba New York	72 721
SACKANMAHAN		
F	Trinity Sturdiva	701007
SACKE		
Russell	Calaveras Twp 9	57 381
SACKEMANUMAN		
---	Tulara Twp 2	71 34
SACKEMEN		
---*	Tulara Visalia	71 37
SACKEMENUMAN		
---*	Tulara Visalia	71 34
SACKET		
H	El Dorado Diamond	58 811

Name	County Locale	M653 RollPage
SACKETO		
Kirk	Napa Napa	61 56
SACKETT		
A W*	Tuolumne Twp 1	71 204
B R	Solano Vacaville	69 359
Bressel	Calaveras Twp 9	57 381
C	Siskiyou Klamath	69 91
D	Yuba Rose Par	72 797
D A	Sonoma Petaluma	69 586
D*	Yuba Rose Bar	72 797
Hanan S	El Dorado Mountain	581183
Kirk*	Napa Napa	61 56
L A	Nevada Eureka	61 351
Mary	El Dorado Mountain	581186
Morton B	Solano Vacaville	69 336
R	Sacramento Ward 1	63 49
Russell	Los Angeles Los Angeles	59 374
S A	Nevada Eureka	61 351
SACKEY		
Thos*	Napa Napa	61 64
SACKIREY		
O	Nevada Eureka	61 374
SACKITT		
Bussil	Calaveras Twp 9	57 381
SACKLAND		
Wm*	Calaveras Twp 9	57 368
SACKMAN		
Geo	Siskiyou Klamath	69 84
SACKMONE		
---	Tulara Twp 2	71 36
SACKNEY		
J W*	Napa Yount	61 36
SACKRIDER		
Gilbert	Santa Clara Santa Clara	65 514
SACKS		
John	San Francisco San Francisco 7	681384
William	El Dorado Eldorado	58 947
SACKSAAW		
---	Tulara Twp 2	71 40
SACKSAW		
---*	Tulara Twp 2	71 40
SACLERA		
Francis*	Calaveras Twp 6	57 144
SACORTER		
Palonia	Mariposa Twp 1	60 638
SACOSTA		
Pirre	Calaveras Twp 5	57 200
SACOSTER		
Thomas	Mariposa Twp 1	60 638
SACOT		
Francis	Calaveras Twp 4	57 316
SACPEL		
Frederick San Francisco San Francisco 8		681304
SACRAMEM		
---	Fresno Twp 2	59 73
SACRAMENTA		
---	Monterey Monterey	60 953
SACRAMENTO		
---	Tulara Keyesville	71 64
---	Tulara Keyesville	71 67
---	Tulara Twp 3	71 70
---*	Mendocino Round Va	60 884
Peter	Siskiyou Shasta Rvr	69 112
SACRE		
David	Sonoma Santa Rosa	69 408
Sam	Mariposa Twp 3	60 601
Sem	Mariposa Twp 3	60 601
SACRIDER		
C	Sacramento Granite	63 230
SACRY		
Geo M	Sonoma Santa Rosa	69 420
James	Sonoma Santa Rosa	69 421
SACT		
---*	Mariposa Twp 1	60 664
SACTEM		
---	Fresno Twp 2	59 104
SACTERC		
Francis*	Calaveras Twp 6	57 144
SADA		
Perfecto	Napa Napa	61 115
SADBATTER		
Mary*	Sacramento Ward 1	63 97
SADBATTES		
Mary*	Sacramento Ward 1	63 97
SADDEN		
E A	El Dorado Georgetown	58 749
SADDLEMAN		
J J	San Francisco San Francisco 4	681114
SADDLEMEYER		
Wm	Butte Kimshaw	56 579
SADDLEMIRE		
Rufus	San Francisco San Francisco 12	364 67
SADDLER		
F A	Solano Benecia	69 286
Frederick	Solano Benecia	69 303

Name	County Locale	M653 RollPage
SADDLER		
George	Plumas Quincy	62 987
James	Marin Novato	60 739
James	San Joaquin Stockton	641038
SADEDRA		
Agapita	Santa Clara San Jose	65 298
SADEVORTH		
Nicholas*	Marin Point Re	60 731
SADIRIGTON		
C*	Alameda Oakland	55 32
SADLAR		
F A*	Shasta Horsetown	66 700
SADLER		
Alex	El Dorado Placerville	58 917
F A	Shasta Horsetown	66 700
J J	Nevada Nevada	61 271
J M	Nevada Rough &	61 402
J W	Nevada Eureka	61 382
Robert	Placer Secret R	62 613
T	Nevada Eureka	61 346
T M	Nevada Rough &	61 402
Warren	El Dorado White Oaks	581031
SADLINGOR		
Joseph*	Siskiyou Yreka	69 153
SADMA		
Cary	Yolo Cache Crk	72 639
SADNIGTON		
C*	Alameda Oakland	55 32
SADOR		
Frank	Amador Twp 4	55 245
SADOUK		
Charles*	Tuolumne Twp 1	71 211
SADOUSE		
Charles	Tuolumne Sonora	71 211
SADOW		
Stephen W*	Sierra Scales D	66 802
SADWICK		
G	Klamath S Fork	59 197
SAE		
---	Nevada Nevada	61 300
---	Nevada Rough &	61 431
Lee	San Francisco San Francisco 5	67 508
SAEANKS		
Henry*	Amador Twp 2	55 325
SAECONE		
B	Sacramento Sutter	63 303
SAEIR		
Theodore*	Calaveras Twp 5	57 207
SAELLY		
M F	San Francisco San Francisco 10	261 67
Mme La*	San Francisco San Francisco 10	261 67
Sme La*	San Francisco San Francisco 10	261 67
SAEN		
---*	Yuba Bear Rvr	721014
SAENER		
A	San Francisco San Francisco 4	681164
SAENZ		
Jesus	Los Angeles Los Angeles	59 348
Jose D	San Diego San Diego	64 762
Rufino	Santa Clara Fremont	65 442
SAENZEN		
P*	San Francisco San Francisco 1	68 923
SAENZER		
P*	San Francisco San Francisco 1	68 923
SAEPEL		
Frederick* San Francisco	San Francisco 8	681304
SAEPIL		
Frederick* San Francisco	San Francisco 8	681304
SAERIDER		
C*	El Dorado Eldorado	58 941
SAERIUGEU		
George*	Placer Michigan	62 816
SAFARIGNO		
J*	Amador Twp 4	55 245
SAFEY		
Charly*	Calaveras Twp 4	57 341
SAFF		
Jno	Klamath Trinidad	59 223
SAFFELL		
J	Sutter Butte	70 800
SAFFER		
Geo	Nevada Grass Valley	61 144
SAFFERHILL		
David	San Joaquin Stockton	641033
SAFFNER		
O O	Solano Suisan	69 206
SAFFORD		
Chas B	Sacramento Ward 1	63 76
D S*	Butte Wyandotte	56 662
Henry	Yolo New York	72 720
Henry	Yuba New York	72 720

Name	County Locale	M653 RollPage
SAFFORD		
I V H	Amador Twp 1	55 463
J V H	Amador Twp 1	55 463
James	Nevada Rough &	61 423
Jas R	Sacramento Ward 4	63 505
John	Trinity Douglas	70 978
L S	Butte Wyandotte	56 662
Man	Trinity Taylor'S	701036
Oliver	Klamath Orleans	59 216
W L	Butte Ophir	56 796
William	San Francisco San Francisco 7	681344
SAFFRON		
John	San Francisco San Francisco 5	67 495
SAFLER		
John R	Sierra Poker Flats	66 841
SAFLIN		
R	Sacramento Sutter	63 308
SAFONSE		
John	Siskiyou Callahan	69 3
John*	Siskiyou Callahan	69 4
SAFORD		
Margaret	Yuba Marysville	72 936
SAFPIN		
William	Yuba Marysville	72 955
SAFRANK		
Joseph*	Calaveras Twp 4	57 340
SAFUN		
---*	Del Norte Klamath	58 657
SAG		
---	Calaveras Twp 10	57 261
---	El Dorado Casumnes	581177
---	El Dorado Georgetown	58 692
---	El Dorado Georgetown	58 748
---	Placer Illinois	62 746
---*	El Dorado Casumnes	581177
SAGALLA		
Antone	Trinity Taylor'S	701034
SAGATA		
Pampoza	Tuolumne Sonora	71 226
SAGDAM		
Mary Ann	Yuba Marysville	72 911
SAGDEN		
F	Amador Twp 4	55 250
SAGE		
Chas	Sacramento Georgian	63 336
D S	Sierra Forest C	66 909
Delos	Santa Clara Freemont	65 416
F A	Napa Napa	61 109
Hanry	Napa Napa	61 104
Henry	Napa Napa	61 104
Henry	Placer Ophirville	62 656
Lewis P	San Francisco San Francisco 12	390 67
Louis	Mariposa Twp 3	60 596
Oliver	Yuba Long Bar	72 749
Robt	San Francisco San Francisco 1	68 812
Timothy	Solano Benecia	69 313
SAGELEY		
Redman	Tulara Visalia	71 106
SAGELIN		
Pierre H	Yuba Long Bar	72 750
SAGELY		
Ridman	Tulara Visalia	71 106
SAGER		
C A	Nevada Grass Valley	61 157
Cecile	Amador Twp 1	55 452
Henry	Sierra Twp 7	66 875
Solomon	Sacramento Ward 4	63 508
SAGERT		
Robert	Santa Clara San Jose	65 338
SAGET		
Joseph	Del Norte Crescent	58 642
SAGEWELL		
Thomas	Yuba Marysville	72 909
SAGGART		
John W	Contra Costa Twp 2	57 576
SAGGITT		
William	Contra Costa Twp 2	57 568
SAGGRET		
John	Placer Horseshoe	62 650
SAGLE		
Wm*	Sacramento Brighton	63 193
SAGNARD		
J E	El Dorado Placerville	58 821
SAGNER		
Mary	Alameda Brooklyn	55 183
SAGRANGE		
Luther*	Yuba Bear Rvr	721012
Luthur	Yuba Bear Rvr	721012
SAGUARIPA		
Juan	Los Angeles Los Angeles	59 405
SAGURE		
Hosea M*	Alameda Oakland	55 57
SAGUTA		
Pampoza	Tuolumne Twp 1	71 226
SAGUTTIE		
---	Del Norte Klamath	58 658

Name	County Locale	M653 Roll	Page
SAH			
---	Calaveras Twp 8	57	105
---	Calaveras Twp 4	57	343
---	Mariposa Twp 3	60	564
Gin	Sacramento Natonia	63	283
Low	San Joaquin Stockton	641053	
My	El Dorado Greenwood	58	710
Ye	Calaveras Twp 6	57	170
Yum	Butte Kimshaw	56	605
SAHANFILE			
Lewis	Sierra Twp 7	66	867
SAHEMANN			
Frank*	Yuba Marysville	72	936
SAHG			
S H	Nevada Nevada	61	242
SAHINNDIS			
Frank*	Mariposa Twp 3	60	570
SAHKETTER			
Clous*	Calaveras Twp 4	57	313
SAHL			
Henry*	Tuolumne Twp 1	71	272
SAHLING			
Henry	San Francisco San Francisco 10	67	299
SAHNDRUAN			
Francis*	Mendocino Little L	60	830
SAHNKE			
Herman G	Tuolumne Sonora	71	187
SAHNMDIS			
Frank*	Mariposa Twp 3	60	570
SAHNMUS			
Frank	Mariposa Twp 3	60	570
SAHNNON			
Ann	San Francisco San Francisco 1	68	816
SAHNWILLS			
Frank	Mariposa Twp 3	60	570
SAHOFF			
Geo	El Dorado Grizzly	581179	
SAHOOL			
---	Mendocino Big Rvr	60	853
SAHP			
---	El Dorado Georgetown	58	675
SAHR			
Magel	Amador Twp 6	55	427
SAHRNNDIS			
Frank*	Mariposa Twp 3	60	570
SAHU			
John*	Calaveras Twp 6	57	138
SAHUMUS			
Frank*	Mariposa Twp 3	60	570
SAHY			
Patrick	Marin Tomales	60	717
SAI			
---	Calaveras Twp 10	57	269
---	Calaveras Twp 10	57	295
---	Calaveras Twp 7	57	42
---	Yuba Bear Rvr	721000	
SAICHEN			
Peter*	Mariposa Twp 3	60	610
SAID			
---	Klamath Liberty	59	232
Bartlett	Plumas Meadow Valley	62	930
Elkenna	Sierra Twp 7	66	884
J H	Yolo Cache Crk	72	639
SAIDE			
Elkinna	Sierra Twp 7	66	884
SAIDING			
Ramsey	Sierra Whiskey	66	846
SAIE			
Cam*	Sierra Port Win	66	798
Sair	San Francisco San Francisco 1	68	925
SAIFT			
S	Nevada Eureka	61	367
SAIG			
---	Shasta French G	66	712
---	Yuba Marysville	72	896
---*	Shasta French G	66	712
SAIGE			
---	Sierra Twp 5	66	932
SAIGHT			
G M*	San Joaquin Stockton	641040	
SAIHIN			
J*	Nevada Eureka	61	376
SAIHS			
Samuel*	San Francisco San Francisco 4	681159	
SAIK E			
---	Mariposa Twp 3	60	607
SAIKIN			
John*	Tuolumne Sonora	71	218
SAILER			
Geo	Butte Hamilton	56	524
SAILERS			
Thos	Yolo Merritt	72	584
SAILES			
Emor T	Contra Costa Twp 3	57	594
SAILIER			
John*	Nevada Nevada	61	327

Name	County Locale	M653 Roll	Page
SAILION			
J*	Nevada Eureka	61	376
SAILLER			
Phillip	Sierra Downieville	661022	
SAILLIE			
Phillip	Sierra Downieville	661022	
SAILLOT			
Alphonse	Alameda Brooklyn	55	98
SAILOR			
E M	Klamath Liberty	59	237
I	Nevada Washington	61	337
J	Nevada Washington	61	337
John	Alameda Brooklyn	55	138
Lowry	Tulara Visalia	71	13
Sonry	Tulara Twp 2	71	13
W H	Yolo Slate Ra	72	693
W H	Yuba Slate Ro	72	693
SAILTH			
---*	Del Norte Klamath	58	657
SAILUN			
J*	Nevada Eureka	61	376
SAIM			
John*	San Francisco San Francisco 2	67	687
SAIMR			
Ah	Butte Oregon	56	644
SAIN			
---	Amador Twp 6	55	423
---	Calaveras Twp 5	57	202
---	Calaveras Twp 5	57	235
---	Nevada Rough &	61	399
---	Sacramento Granite	63	259
---	Sierra Downieville	661009	
---	Yuba Bear Rvr	721015	
---*	Nevada Rough &	61	399
Ah	Sacramento Granite	63	232
Ah	Yuba Bear Rvr	721000	
Long	Butte Cascade	56	700
Wa	Nevada Nevada	61	303
Young	Stanislaus Branch	70	714
SAINBRANO			
Martinez	Tuolumne Twp 2	71	319
SAING			
Gregorio	Santa Clara Santa Clara	65	520
SAINSBURY			
H G	Yuba Marysville	72	915
James*	Sacramento Ward 1	63	39
SAINT			
James	El Dorado Georgetown	58	694
SAINTA			
---	Fresno Twp 2	59	107
SAINTELLE			
A W*	Butte Oregon	56	611
SAINTEYER			
Victor	San Francisco San Francisco 2	67	725
SAINTRILLE			
A	Yolo Cache Crk	72	624
SAINTVILLE			
St Louis	Yolo Cache Crk	72	624
SAINZ			
Leandro	San Bernardino Santa Barbara	64	197
SAIOYEL			
J D*	Siskiyou Scott Va	69	34
SAIP			
E T	San Francisco San Francisco 6	67	443
SAIR			
---	Yuba Linda	72	991
John*	San Francisco San Francisco 2	67	687
SAIRSON			
Gunderson	Placer Todds Va	62	788
SAIS			
L	Mariposa Twp 1	60	643
Rafael	Monterey San Juan	601002	
S	Mariposa Twp 1	60	643
SAITOTO			
---	Butte Chico	56	550
SAITT			
Wm*	Nevada Nevada	61	323
SAIV			
---	Amador Twp 5	55	347
SAIVTELLE			
A W*	Butte Oregon	56	611
SAIY			
---	Mariposa Twp 3	60	564
SAIZ			
Pearo	Mariposa Twp 1	60	630
Pedro	Mariposa Twp 1	60	630
SAJ Z			
---	Mariposa Twp 3	60	607
SAJONS			
Jacques	Yuba Marysville	72	874
SAJOUS			
Jacques	Yuba Marysville	72	874
SAK			
---	Amador Twp 2	55	291
Henry*	Placer Michigan	62	844

Name	County Locale	M653 Roll	Page
SAK			
Tonn	Placer Dutch Fl	62	737
SAKA			
Phillip Lan*	Calaveras Twp 9	57	354
SAKE			
---	Amador Twp 5	55	331
---	Calaveras Twp 4	57	300
---	Mariposa Twp 1	60	626
Amos	Placer Forest H	62	773
C	Nevada Eureka	61	352
E	Trinity E Weaver	701057	
John*	Yuba New York	72	740
Saml	Trinity Big Flat	701039	
SAKEMAN			
H A	San Francisco San Francisco 2	67	586
SAKENOW			
---	Tulara Twp 2	71	39
SAKER			
Louis	Calaveras Twp 6	57	126
SAKKEL			
John	Tuolumne Sonora	71	236
SAKOULERUE			
---	Tulara Twp 2	71	38
SAKOWNIE			
---	Tulara Twp 2	71	36
SAKRE			
Gaspard*	San Francisco San Francisco 4	681167	
SAKRI			
Gaspard	San Francisco San Francisco 4	681167	
SAKS			
O A	El Dorado Georgetown	58	759
SAL RUK			
---	Fresno Twp 2	59	46
SAL			
---	Tulara Twp 1	71	119
SALA			
A J	Tuolumne Twp 4	71	146
Petro	Calaveras Twp 7	57	29
SALADA			
Fred	Tuolumne Twp 2	71	372
SALADAY			
Jacob	Sierra Pine Grove	66	830
SALADE			
Ramon	Tuolumne Twp 2	71	402
SALADO			
Ramon	Tuolumne Shawsfla	71	402
SALADONIO			
---	Los Angeles Los Angeles	59	519
SALAGARO			
Santus	El Dorado White Oaks	581011	
SALAGER			
Peter*	Nevada Rough &	61	430
SALAMANDA			
S	Tuolumne Twp 2	71	390
SALAMER			
---	Monterey Monterey	60	957
SALAMON			
Perficto	Stanislaus Branch	70	698
SALANO			
Narcisso*	Los Angeles Tejon	59	536
SALAR			
Sacrannta	Mariposa Twp 1	60	631
Sacrementa	Mariposa Twp 1	60	631
SALARIS			
Lerrifind	Calaveras Twp 6	57	123
SALARO			
Stephen	Amador Twp 1	55	485
SALARSAR			
Pedro	Tuolumne Big Oak	71	131
SALAS			
Armada	Stanislaus Branch	70	698
Jesas	Tuolumne Twp 2	71	221
Juan	Yuba Marysville	72	963
Marcellena	San Francisco San Francisco 10	67	183
Marcellina	San Francisco San Francisco 10	67	183
Mariano	Yuba Marysville	72	934
Quain	Yuba Marysville	72	963
SALASAR			
Delorus	Mariposa Twp 1	60	659
Edward	Siskiyou Yreka	69	140
Jesus M	San Bernardino San Salvador	64	660
Jose	Marin San Rafael	60	760
Jose	Santa Cruz Santa Cruz	66	640
Pedro	Monterey Pajaro	601017	
SALASARD			
Ferdinand	Los Angeles Elmonte	59	261
SALASON			
Antonio	San Bernardino San Bernadino	64	675
M	Merced Twp 1	60	899
SALASSETOS			
Rose	San Francisco San Francisco 10	67	182
SALATHA			
Wadalupa	Los Angeles Elmonte	59	264

Name	County Locale	M653 RollPage
SALAUO		
Vidal	Tehama Red Bluff	70 916
SALAVEA		
Chinda	Los Angeles San Jose	59 287
SALAVEN		
Isabel	Los Angeles Los Angeles	59 374
SALAVI		
Domica	Calaveras Twp 8	57 106
Joseph	Calaveras Twp 8	57 106
Micheal	Calaveras Twp 8	57 106
SALAWAY		
Frank	San Joaquin Oneal	64 935
SALAYA		
Esquipito	Tulara Sinks Te	71 43
SALAYAR		
Vicente	Monterey San Juan	601001
SALAZA		
Pedro	San Bernardino Santa Barbara	64 200
SALAZAR		
Antonio	San Bernardino San Salvador	64 662
Deonicia*	Santa Cruz Pajaro	66 567
Deonscia	Santa Cruz Pajaro	66 567
Deonscias*	Santa Cruz Pajaro	66 567
F	Santa Clara San Jose	65 323
Fagundo	Monterey San Juan	60 975
Florentino	Monterey San Juan	601006
Franco	Los Angeles Tejon	59 541
Gutrades	Santa Clara Santa Clara	65 495
Joaquin	Los Angeles Los Angeles	59 304
Joaquin	Los Angeles Santa Ana	59 458
Jose	Los Angeles San Gabriel	59 518
Juan	Los Angeles San Gabriel	59 417
Juan	Monterey San Juan	60 983
Juan J	Los Angeles Los Angeles	59 352
Lasan	Los Angeles San Pedro	59 486
Leandro	Los Angeles Santa Ana	59 449
Rafael	Los Angeles Los Angeles	59 400
Rafel	Los Angeles Los Angeles	59 518
Rafil	Los Angeles Los Angeles	59 518
Refugio	Los Angeles Santa Ana	59 449
Valentina	Los Angeles Tejon	59 541
Vincente*	Monterey San Juan	601001
Ygnacio	Los Angeles San Pedro	59 485
SALBACH		
Edward	Calaveras Twp 9	57 364
SALBADOR		
---	Monterey Monterey	60 961
SALBAR		
Peter	Calaveras Twp 9	57 352
SALBERT		
J R	Nevada Nevada	61 320
SALBY		
Mary A*	San Francisco San Francisco 2	67 668
SALCEDO		
Carmen	Tuolumne Chinese	71 492
Pedro	Mariposa Twp 3	60 614
Pedro*	Mariposa Twp 3	60 611
Ramon	Los Angeles Santa Ana	59 457
SALCER		
Maguil	Mariposa Twp 1	60 654
SALCIDA		
Jabira	Calaveras Twp 5	57 250
Jabiro*	Calaveras Twp 5	57 250
SALCIDE		
Francisco	Los Angeles Los Angeles	59 395
SALCIDO		
Pedro*	Mariposa Twp 3	60 611
Pedro*	Mariposa Twp 3	60 614
Ramon	Los Angeles Santa Ana	59 457
Vicente	Los Angeles Los Angeles	59 320
SALCOMB		
C	Butte Ophir	56 823
SALCORITCH		
George*	Placer Michigan	62 851
SALDES		
H S	Sierra Twp 7	66 883
SALDEVIA		
Padro	Contra Costa Twp 2	57 555
SALDIS		
H L	Sierra Twp 7	66 883
SALDIVA		
Louis	Tuolumne Sonora	71 227
SALDO		
Frank	San Francisco San Francisco 2	67 625
SALE		
Adam*	Siskiyou Callahan	69 7
Andrew	Sierra Gibsonville	66 853
Charles A	Yuba New York	72 720
Charles O	Yolo New York	72 720
Dudley	Trinity Weaverville	701062
Henry	Sacramento Ward 4	63 515
J	El Dorado Diamond	58 811
J K	Nevada Grass Valley	61 236
W L	Siskiyou Scott Va	69 34
SALEC		
Carlos	Los Angeles Los Angeles	59 403

Name	County Locale	M653 RollPage
SALEDONIO		
---	San Diego Agua Caliente	64 839
SALEE		
John	Sonoma Mendocino	69 468
SALEEDO		
Carman	Tuolumne Twp 5	71 492
SALEER		
Maguil	Mariposa Twp 1	60 654
SALEIDO		
Pedro*	Mariposa Twp 3	60 611
Pedro*	Mariposa Twp 3	60 614
SALEM		
A F*	Tuolumne Shawsfla	71 376
SALEMENE		
---*	Tulara Visalia	71 36
SALEMON		
---	Tulara Twp 2	71 36
SALEMY		
---	Fresno Twp 2	59 112
SALENA		
Hosea	Calaveras Twp 9	57 361
SALENSTEIN		
E	Sacramento Ward 3	63 469
SALENSWALLA		
Simon	Mariposa Twp 1	60 639
SALEO		
Francisco*	Marin Cortemad	60 781
SALER		
John*	Sonoma Mendocino	69 468
Joseph*	Sonoma Petaluma	69 597
Julia Ellen	Sonoma Mendocino	69 468
Throthus*	Mariposa Twp 1	60 646
SALERIS		
Michael	Calaveras Twp 5	57 197
SALES		
Antonio*	Monterey San Juan	60 999
Bertino	Los Angeles San Gabriel	59 410
Florenciamerimo	Twp 2	65 114
Francisco	Los Angeles San Gabriel	59 420
Geo	Sacramento Ward 3	63 478
Geo F	Sacramento Natonia	63 276
Geo R	Sacramento Ward 3	63 457
Henry	Yuba Long Bar	72 746
J	San Francisco San Francisco 5	67 517
Joseph	San Francisco San Francisco 2	67 606
Juan	Monterey Pajaro	601012
L C	Sacramento Cosumnes	63 383
Miguel	Los Angeles Santa Ana	59 446
Mose	Santa Cruz Santa Cruz	66 633
Samuel	Placer Michigan	62 831
T	Sacramento Ward 4	63 592
Timothy	Yuba New York	72 722
Ventora	El Dorado Coloma	581105
William	Sierra Pine Grove	66 825
Wm*	Sacramento Natonia	63 275
SALESBURY		
Edwin	San Francisco San Francisco 1	68 890
SALESMANN		
H N	Tuolumne Twp 1	71 189
H W	Tuolumne Sonora	71 189
SALESTIA		
Michael	Tehama Tehama	70 947
SALESTIENO		
---	Napa Napa	61 78
SALESUR		
Francis	Mariposa Twp 1	60 641
SALEZAR		
Canuto	Marin Cortemad	60 781
SALGADA		
Juan	San Diego San Diego	64 765
Teresa	Monterey San Juan	60 993
Tomas	Monterey San Juan	60 993
SALGADO		
Francisco	Santa Inez	64 141
	San Bernardino	
Michiela M	San Francisco San Francisco 2	67 597
	San Francisco	
Pedra	Yuba Marysville	72 913
Pedro	Yuba Marysville	72 913
SALGADRO		
Pedro	Placer Forest H	62 791
SALGARDO		
Juana	Alameda Brooklyn	55 131
SALGARO		
Jose	San Joaquin Stockton	641072
SALGOTAD		
Mary B	San Francisco San Francisco 10	181 67
Mary V	San Francisco San Francisco 10	181 67
SALIA		
Thoedosia	S Timate	64 687
	San Bernardino	
SALIAN		
Lorenzo	Calaveras Twp 10	57 260

Name	County Locale	M653 RollPage
SALIBURY		
D	Sacramento Granite	63 234
SALICE		
Peter	Sierra Port Win	66 792
SALIDAD		
---	San Bernardino San Bernadino	64 681
SALIGE		
John	Yolo Cache	72 642
SALIGER		
Peter	Nevada Rough &	61 430
SALINA		
---	Tulara Twp 3	71 66
---	Tulara Twp 3	71 72
Hosea	Calaveras Twp 9	57 361
SALINAS		
Carman	San Francisco San Francisco 1	68 819
Carmel	Los Angeles Los Angeles	59 353
SALINDO		
M P	Tehama Red Bluff	70 931
SALINE		
A F	Tuolumne Twp 2	71 376
Augustine*	Calaveras Twp 5	57 214
SALING		
---	Shasta Shasta	66 680
Henry	Napa Yount	61 35
SALINGER		
J	Sutter Yuba	70 760
Julius	San Francisco San Francisco 8	681303
William*	Napa Yount	61 34
SALINI		
A F*	Tuolumne Shawsfla	71 376
SALINOS		
Mary	Tuolumne Twp 2	71 321
Pedro	Calaveras Twp 8	57 95
SALIO		
---	Tulara Keyesville	71 66
Desedam	S Timate	64 687
	San Bernardino	
Francisco	Marin Cortemad	60 781
SALIS		
Antoine*	Yuba Slate Ro	72 713
Henry	Yuba New York	72 746
Manuel	Los Angeles San Gabriel	59 410
SALISAR		
F	Merced Twp 1	60 909
Francis	Mariposa Twp 1	60 641
SALISBURY		
Dexter	Tehama Lassen	70 873
J	Tehama Red Bluff	70 912
J	Tehama Red Bluff	70 916
John	Sierra Downieville	66 960
Marvil	Tehama Lassen	70 873
N J	El Dorado Placerville	58 849
SALISE		
Augustine*	Calaveras Twp 5	57 214
SALISPE		
George*	Calaveras Twp 5	57 210
SALISPS		
George*	Calaveras Twp 5	57 210
SALISSE		
George*	Calaveras Twp 5	57 210
SALISTIENO		
---	Napa Napa	61 78
SALISTRA		
---	Marin Cortemad	60 788
SALIVAR		
John	Sierra Downieville	661028
SALIVER		
Augustine*	Calaveras Twp 5	57 214
SALIZAR		
Joseph	Calaveras Twp 5	57 206
SALIZASAR		
Jose	Santa Cruz Pajaro	66 542
SALJADE		
Marcia	San Luis Obispo San Luis Obispo	65 33
SALL		
---	Yolo Slate Ra	72 708
---	Yuba Slate Ro	72 708
SALLA		
Benito	Marin Cortemad	60 791
SALLAE		
Loran	Alameda Oakland	55 18
SALLAMANT		
D*	Sacramento Ward 1	63 3
SALLAS		
Santiago	Los Angeles Elmonte	59 259
SALLASAR		
Jose	Marin S Antoni	60 708
SALLE		
Mahonet*	San Francisco San Francisco 4	681223
Mary	Placer Forest H	62 770
SALLEE		
Nancy Ann	Trinity Lewiston	70 963
SALLENEUVE		
Henri	Sacramento Ward 4	63 559
SALLENT		
Michael*	Yuba Bear Rvr	721006

Name	County Locale	M653 RollPage
SALLER		
Fredrick	Sierra Gibsonville	66 860
SALLERS		
William	Calaveras Twp 4	57 316
SALLEY		
Chas	Placer Auburn	62 565
SALLI		
Mahonet*	San Francisco San Francisco 4	681223
SALLIE		
Mahonet*	San Francisco San Francisco 4	681223
SALLIMER		
Henry	Los Angeles Elmonte	59 245
SALLIN		
Carlos	Los Angeles Los Angeles	59 362
SALLINGER		
Wm	Sonoma Armally	69 512
SALLIS		
Patro	Marin S Antoni	60 706
SALLISAN		
W*	Mariposa Twp 3	60 585
SALLISANT		
Joseph	Calaveras Twp 4	57 328
SALLISORT		
Joseph	Calaveras Twp 4	57 328
SALLIVAN		
Catherine	Yuba Marysville	72 903
Julia	San Francisco San Francisco 10	181 67
SALLON		
T*	Nevada Eureka	61 373
Victor	Yuba Fosters	72 835
SALLONE		
T	Nevada Eureka	61 373
SALLOSA		
Braha	Mariposa Twp 1	60 625
Breha	Mariposa Twp 1	60 625
SALLOWAY		
George	Yuba No E Twp	72 844
S	San Francisco San Francisco 5	67 480
SALLS		
Henry	Colusa Butte Crk	57 466
Joseph*	San Francisco San Francisco 2	67 606
SALLY OH		
---*	Mendocino Big Rock	60 876
SALLY		
---	Fresno Twp 2	59 43
---	Mendocino Calpella	60 822
---	Mendocino Calpella	60 824
---	Mendocino Calpella	60 827
---	Mendocino Calpella	60 828
---	Mendocino Round Va	60 882
---	Mendocino Round Va	60 885
---	Mendocino Twp 1	60 890
---	Mendocino Twp 1	60 891
---	San Bernardino San Bernadino	64 673
---	Siskiyou Yreka	69 131
---	Tulara Twp 1	71 114
---	Tulara Twp 1	71 116
B	Mariposa Twp 1	60 642
John	San Francisco San Francisco 11	153 67
John*	Amador Twp 2	55 268
Lizzie	San Francisco San Francisco 10	184 67
O B	Nevada Grass Valley	61 189
Pat*	Placer Sacramento	62 645
Peter	Sierra Whiskey	66 849
SALM		
Charles	Tuolumne Twp 2	71 417
SALMAN		
J	El Dorado Placerville	58 883
SALMASTRO		
---	San Diego Agua Caliente	64 827
SALMINA		
Baptis	Marin Novato	60 736
SALMINUS		
Frank	Mariposa Twp 3	60 570
SALMIS		
Aramena	San Joaquin Stockton	641024
Edson	San Joaquin Stockton	641024
SALMON		
A	San Francisco San Francisco 6	67 470
Alejo	San Bernardino Santa Barbara	64 204
Cutler	San Joaquin Castoria	64 888
Dionisio	San Bernardino Santa Barbara	64 151
F C	Sacramento Ward 1	63 87
Francis	San Francisco San Francisco 8	681301
Francisco	Santa Clara Almaden	65 271
H	El Dorado Placerville	58 883
J W	San Francisco San Francisco 12	364 67
James	San Joaquin Castoria	64 888
John	El Dorado Mud Springs	58 978
John	San Francisco San Francisco 2	67 597
Peter	Alameda Brooklyn	55 146
R	Tuolumne Twp 3	71 437

Name	County Locale	M653 RollPage
SALMON		
Rafaila	San Bernardino Santa Barbara	64 203
Thos	Klamath S Fork	59 207
Wm R	Napa Napa	61 82
Y C	Sacramento Ward 1	63 87
SALMS		
Peter	Nevada Bridgeport	61 490
SALMY		
---	El Dorado Mud Springs	58 957
SALN		
Augustine*	Calaveras Twp 5	57 214
SALNIRR		
J*	Calaveras Twp 9	57 392
SALNUN		
J*	Calaveras Twp 9	57 392
SALOHER		
P*	Nevada Nevada	61 246
SALOM		
Dominick	Calaveras Twp 6	57 135
SALOMAN		
Jacob	Placer Iona Hills	62 859
SALOME		
---	Los Angeles Santa Ana	59 443
---	San Bernardino Santa Ba	64 221
SALOMON		
---	Los Angeles San Juan	59 464
Mateo	San Francisco San Francisco 4	681133
SALONE		
Dominick	Calaveras Twp 5	57 135
Julius	San Francisco San Francisco 2	67 671
SALONER		
R A	Sutter Yuba	70 770
SALONEY		
Wm H*	San Francisco San Francisco 1	68 890
SALONI		
James	Shasta Millvill	66 749
SALONO		
John	Calaveras Twp 7	57 45
SALOR		
Joseph	Sonoma Petaluma	69 597
SALORI		
Michael	Calaveras Twp 5	57 197
SALORIS		
Michael	Calaveras Twp 5	57 197
SALOS		
Antine	Yolo Slate Ra	72 713
SALOVIS		
Peter	Calaveras Twp 8	57 96
SALOWSKEY		
S	Napa Napa	61 99
SALOYA		
Esgrifrito	Tulara Twp 3	71 43
SALOZAR		
Ramon	San Bernardino Santa Barbara	64 199
SALPH		
Frederick	Yuba Long Bar	72 750
SALRIS		
Stanishlaw*	Twp 3	57 611
	Contra Costa	
SALRUS		
---	Marin San Rafael	60 772
SALSADO		
Jose	San Joaquin Stockton	641073
SALSATHER		
Antonio	Los Angeles Azuza	59 277
SALSBERG		
James	San Joaquin Douglass	64 921
SALSBERRY		
A S	Tuolumne Twp 1	71 256
B J	Santa Clara Santa Clara	65 466
Richd	Trinity Indian C	70 987
SALSBURG		
A*	Tuolumne Twp 1	71 253
John	El Dorado Mud Springs	58 966
SALSBURY		
A	Tuolumne Twp 1	71 253
D L*	El Dorado Diamond	58 768
Ellen	Sonoma Armally	69 489
F	Alameda Brooklyn	55 186
J G	Sacramento Granite	63 261
J S	Butte Chico	56 532
John	Yuba Marysville	72 903
Thos	Alameda Brooklyn	55 95
SALSBUY		
I G	Sacramento Granite	63 261
SALSEL		
Henry	Yolo Putah	72 587
SALSETHA		
Padro	Mariposa Twp 1	60 653
SALSETHER		
Francisco	Los Angeles Elmonte	59 264
SALSETHO		
Padro	Mariposa Twp 1	60 653
SALSH		
William	Calaveras Twp 8	57 107

Name	County Locale	M653 RollPage
SALSIG		
Geo A	Placer Dutch Fl	62 710
Samuel	Placer Auburn	62 590
SALSIGUR		
Michel*	Tuolumne Twp 2	71 405
SALSIGUS		
Michel	Tuolumne Shawsfla	71 405
SALSITHA		
Padro	Mariposa Twp 1	60 653
SALTAN		
Frederick	Calaveras Twp 9	57 354
SALTAR		
Jose A	Los Angeles Los Angeles	59 494
SALTEN		
Johsua	Nevada Bridgeport	61 496
SALTENO		
---	San Diego Temecula	64 796
SALTER		
Collin	Butte Chico	56 561
Frederick	Tuolumne Twp 1	71 198
Jas	San Francisco San Francisco 2	67 699
Robt T	San Francisco San Francisco 3	67 20
SALTERS		
Frank*	Plumas Quincy	62 998
Thimothy*	San Francisco 2	67 716
	San Francisco	
SALTES		
Robt T*	San Francisco San Francisco 3	67 20
SALTHOUSE		
John	Monterey San Juan	60 991
SALTI		
Mahomt*	San Francisco San Francisco 4	681223
SALTICELLO		
Petra*	Stanislaus Branch	70 698
SALTILLO		
Ramon	Los Angeles Los Angeles	59 518
SALTIR		
C W	Stanislaus Branch	70 711
SALTIRE		
Domingo	Alameda Brooklyn	55 215
SALTMARSH		
John B	Placer Auburn	62 587
SALTOLUM		
---	Mendocino Round Va	60 883
SALTOMAN		
Anna L	Nevada Rough &	61 422
SALTSMAN		
Anna L*	Nevada Rough &	61 422
Anna S*	Nevada Rough &	61 422
D	Shasta Shasta	66 759
SALTUS		
John F	Plumas Quincy	62 976
SALTY		
---	Mendocino Calpella	60 822
SALUIG		
---*	Shasta Shasta	66 680
SALUS		
Stanishlaw*	Twp 3	57 611
	Contra Costa	
SALVA		
Manuel	Alameda Brooklyn	55 100
Mary E	Marin Bolinas	60 749
SALVADER		
---	Mendocino Calpella	60 824
SALVADO		
Theo	Mariposa Twp 3	60 611
SALVADOR		
---	Los Angeles San Gabriel	59 420
---	Los Angeles Tejon	59 529
---	Marin Novato	60 737
---	Marin San Rafael	60 772
---	Monterey Monterey	60 961
---	San Bernardino San Bernadino	64 669
---	San Bernardino San Bernadino	64 680
---	San Bernardino San Bernadino	64 681
---	San Bernardino S Timate	64 716
---	San Bernardino S Timate	64 717
---	San Bernardino S Timate	64 728
---	San Bernardino S Timate	64 729
---	San Bernardino S Timate	64 730
---	San Bernardino S Timate	64 739
---	San Bernardino S Timate	64 740
---	San Bernardino S Timate	64 744
---	San Bernardino S Timate	64 745
---	San Bernardino S Timate	64 751
---	San Bernardino S Timate	64 754
---	San Bernardino S Timate	64 755
---	San Diego Agua Caliente	64 824
---	San Diego Agua Caliente	64 829
---	Santa Cruz Pescadero	66 641
---	Sonoma Salt Point	69 694
---	Tulara Twp 3	71 68
---	Tulara Twp 3	71 71
Cordero	San Bernardino Santa Barbara	64 192
Jesus	Santa Cruz Santa Cruz	66 634
Jose	Los Angeles San Gabriel	59 414

Name	County Locale	M653 Roll	Page
SALVADOR			
Jose M	Santa Cruz Pajaro	66	548
Juan	San Diego San Diego	64	763
Peter	Tuolumne Twp 1	71	255
SALVADORA			
---	San Bernardino Santa Inez	64	137
Jose M	Santa Cruz Pajaro	66	548
SALVADORE			
---	Mariposa Twp 1	60	627
---	Mendocino Calpella	60	824
---	San Bernardino S Timate	64	743
SALVAGE			
James	Sonoma Bodega	69	530
SALVEBECKER			
Abram	Alameda Brooklyn	55	79
SALVER			
Lorance	Amador Twp 4	55	243
R V	Nevada Nevada	61	322
SALVERSA			
S	Siskiyou Scott Va	69	25
SALVERSER			
S*	Siskiyou Scott Va	69	25
SALVESTA			
S	Siskiyou Scott Va	69	25
SALVISA			
Marghilo*	Calaveras Twp 5	57	201
SALVISER			
Morghilo*	Calaveras Twp 5	57	201
SALVO			
Mary	San Francisco San Francisco 5	67	498
SALVOS			
Mary E	Marin Bolinas	60	749
SALY			
John*	Placer Ophirville	62	655
SALYAS			
Inineo	San Bernardino San Salvador	64	659
SALZ			
Jacob	Alameda Brooklyn	55	181
SALZE			
Francis*	Calaveras Twp 6	57	112
SAM CHE			
---	San Joaquin Stockton	64	1083
SAM CHON			
---*	Nevada Nevada	61	310
SAM CHOW			
---	Nevada Nevada	61	306
---	Nevada Nevada	61	307
---	Nevada Nevada	61	308
---	Nevada Nevada	61	309
---	Nevada Nevada	61	310
---	Nevada Washington	61	339
---	Nevada Washington	61	340
SAM COW			
---	Nevada Washington	61	339
---	Nevada Washington	61	340
---	Nevada Washington	61	341
SAM FOG			
---*	Nevada Washington	61	339
SAM FON			
---*	Nevada Nevada	61	308
SAM FOOK			
---	Butte Oregon	56	613
SAM HA			
---	Colusa Colusi	57	421
SAM HAM			
---	Nevada Bridgeport	61	457
SAM HIMG			
---*	Butte Oregon	56	612
SAM HUT			
---	Butte Kimshaw	56	588
SAM LA			
---	Butte Kimshaw	56	606
---	Sacramento Ward 1	63	65
SAM LAP			
---	Mariposa Twp 1	60	667
---	Mariposa Twp 1	60	669
---	Mariposa Twp 1	60	670
---	Mariposa Coulterville	60	690
SAM LAY			
---	Nevada Nevada	61	306
SAM LEE			
---	Butte Kimshaw	56	589
---	Nevada Bridgeport	61	465
SAM LEI			
---	Butte Kimshaw	56	602
---	Butte Kimshaw	56	608
SAM LING			
---	Butte Kimshaw	56	605
---	Sierra La Porte	66	785
---	Sierra Port Win	66	794
SAM LINY			
---	Sierra La Porte	66	782
SAM LUSS			
---*	Mariposa Coulterville	60	689
SAM PANE			
---	Plumas Quincy	62	969

Name	County Locale	M653 Roll	Page
SAM QON			
---*	Nevada Nevada	61	308
SAM QOY			
---*	Nevada Nevada	61	308
---*	Nevada Nevada	61	310
SAM QUIN			
---	Sacramento Ward 1	63	60
SAM SAP			
---	Sacramento Ward 1	63	52
SAM SEE			
---	Sacramento Ward 1	63	71
SAM SEEN			
---*	Nevada Rough &	61	436
SAM SIME			
---*	Nevada Bridgeport	61	462
SAM SIN			
---	Nevada Nevada	61	303
SAM SING			
---	Butte Kimshaw	56	586
---	Butte Kimshaw	56	600
---	Mariposa Twp 3	60	613
---	Nevada Nevada	61	308
---	Nevada Washington	61	339
---*	Nevada Nevada	61	303
SAM SON			
---	Nevada Nevada	61	303
SAM SOO			
Tong	San Francisco San Francisco 1	68	924
SAM SUN			
---*	Nevada Rough &	61	436
SAM TONG			
---	Butte Oregon	56	617
SAM TOW			
---	Nevada Nevada	61	303
---	Nevada Washington	61	340
SAM TOY			
---	Nevada Nevada	61	307
---	Nevada Washington	61	339
---	Nevada Washington	61	340
---	Nevada Nevada	61	341
---*	Nevada Nevada	61	307
SAM WA			
---	Nevada Nevada	61	303
---	Nevada Nevada	61	304
---	Nevada Nevada	61	306
---	Nevada Washington	61	340
---	Tuolumne Chinese	71	510
SAM WAM			
---	Santa Clara San Jose	65	374
SAM WOH			
---	Sacramento Ward 1	63	60
SAM WOO			
---	San Joaquin Stockton	64	1037
---	San Joaquin Stockton	64	1088
SAM YE			
Ah*	Sacramento Ward 1	63	156
SAM YON			
---*	Nevada Nevada	61	304
SAM YOU			
---*	Nevada Nevada	61	304
SAM YUP			
---	Nevada Nevada	61	302
---	Nevada Nevada	61	307
---	Nevada Nevada	61	308
---	Nevada Nevada	61	309
---	Nevada Nevada	61	310
---	Nevada Washington	61	339
---	Nevada Washington	61	340
---	Nevada Washington	61	341
SAM			
---	Alameda Oakland	55	59
---	Amador Twp 4	55	233
---	Amador Twp 4	55	247
---	Amador Twp 4	55	251
---	Amador Twp 2	55	256
---	Amador Twp 2	55	290
---	Amador Twp 2	55	292
---	Amador Twp 2	55	294
---	Amador Twp 2	55	314
---	Amador Twp 2	55	315
---	Amador Twp 2	55	323
---	Amador Twp 2	55	327
---	Amador Twp 2	55	328
---	Amador Twp 5	55	331
---	Amador Twp 4	55	332
---	Amador Twp 5	55	333
---	Amador Twp 5	55	334
---	Amador Twp 5	55	340
---	Amador Twp 5	55	349
---	Amador Twp 5	55	351
---	Amador Twp 5	55	352
---	Amador Twp 5	55	354
---	Amador Twp 5	55	355
---	Amador Twp 5	55	359
---	Amador Twp 5	55	363
---	Amador Twp 5	55	365

Name	County Locale	M653 Roll	Page
SAM			
---	Amador Twp 3	55	379
---	Amador Twp 3	55	410
---	Amador Twp 7	55	413
---	Amador Twp 7	55	415
---	Amador Twp 6	55	422
---	Amador Twp 6	55	423
---	Amador Twp 6	55	432
---	Amador Twp 6	55	449
---	Amador Twp 6	55	450
---	Amador Twp 1	55	452
---	Amador Twp 1	55	457
---	Amador Twp 1	55	458
---	Amador Twp 1	55	477
---	Amador Twp 1	55	480
---	Amador Twp 1	55	497
---	Amador Twp 1	55	500
---	Amador Twp 1	55	501
---	Amador Twp 1	55	502
---	Amador Twp 1	55	503
---	Amador Twp 1	55	504
---	Amador Twp 1	55	507
---	Amador Twp 1	55	508
---	Amador Twp 1	55	510
---	Amador Twp 1	55	511
---	Butte Chico	56	558
---	Butte Chico	56	563
---	Butte Chico	56	566
---	Butte Kimshaw	56	577
---	Butte Kimshaw	56	580
---	Butte Kimshaw	56	584
---	Butte Kimshaw	56	589
---	Butte Oregon	56	611
---	Butte Oro	56	687
---	Butte Cascade	56	699
---	Butte Bidwell	56	707
---	Butte Bidwell	56	714
---	Butte Mountain	56	735
---	Butte Ophir	56	779
---	Calaveras Twp 6	57	105
---	Calaveras Twp 6	57	137
---	Calaveras Twp 6	57	138
---	Calaveras Twp 6	57	139
---	Calaveras Twp 6	57	149
---	Calaveras Twp 6	57	151
---	Calaveras Twp 6	57	158
---	Calaveras Twp 6	57	165
---	Calaveras Twp 6	57	167
---	Calaveras Twp 5	57	181
---	Calaveras Twp 6	57	183
---	Calaveras Twp 5	57	202
---	Calaveras Twp 5	57	226
---	Calaveras Twp 5	57	232
---	Calaveras Twp 5	57	234
---	Calaveras Twp 5	57	235
---	Calaveras Twp 5	57	239
---	Calaveras Twp 5	57	241
---	Calaveras Twp 5	57	244
---	Calaveras Twp 5	57	245
---	Calaveras Twp 5	57	249
---	Calaveras Twp 5	57	251
---	Calaveras Twp 5	57	254
---	Calaveras Twp 5	57	255
---	Calaveras Twp 5	57	257
---	Calaveras Twp 10	57	268
---	Calaveras Twp 10	57	269
---	Calaveras Twp 10	57	271
---	Calaveras Twp 10	57	275
---	Calaveras Twp 10	57	284
---	Calaveras Twp 10	57	285
---	Calaveras Twp 10	57	291
---	Calaveras Twp 10	57	294
---	Calaveras Twp 10	57	296
---	Calaveras Twp 10	57	297
---	Calaveras Twp 4	57	300
---	Calaveras Twp 4	57	305
---	Calaveras Twp 4	57	306
---	Calaveras Twp 4	57	307
---	Calaveras Twp 4	57	342
---	Calaveras Twp 8	57	51
---	Calaveras Twp 8	57	59
---	Calaveras Twp 8	57	92
---	Calaveras Twp 8	57	93
---	Calaveras Twp 8	57	94
---	Del Norte Klamath	58	655
---	Del Norte Klamath	58	656
---	Del Norte Klamath	58	658
---	El Dorado White Oaks	58	1009
---	El Dorado Coloma	58	1078
---	El Dorado Coloma	58	1107
---	El Dorado Casumnes	58	1163
---	El Dorado Mountain	58	1188
---	El Dorado Georgetown	58	691
---	El Dorado Georgetown	58	695
---	El Dorado Greenwood	58	727
---	El Dorado Greenwood	58	728

California 1860 Census Index

SAM

Name	County Locale	M653 Roll	Page
---	El Dorado Georgetown	58	747
---	El Dorado Georgetown	58	761
---	El Dorado Diamond	58	785
---	El Dorado Diamond	58	789
---	El Dorado Diamond	58	790
---	El Dorado Diamond	58	815
---	El Dorado Placerville	58	829
---	El Dorado Placerville	58	839
---	El Dorado Placerville	58	843
---	El Dorado Placerville	58	932
---	El Dorado Mud Springs	58	955
---	El Dorado Mud Springs	58	991
---	Fresno Twp 2	59	106
---	Fresno Twp 2	59	17
---	Fresno Twp 2	59	19
---	Fresno Twp 1	59	30
---	Fresno Twp 3	59	32
---	Fresno Twp 2	59	49
---	Fresno Twp 2	59	4
---	Fresno Twp 2	59	5
---	Fresno Twp 1	59	88
---	Klamath Liberty	59	232
---	Klamath Liberty	59	235
---	Mariposa Twp 3	60	552
---	Mariposa Twp 3	60	560
---	Mariposa Twp 3	60	563
---	Mariposa Twp 3	60	569
---	Mariposa Twp 3	60	572
---	Mariposa Twp 3	60	576
---	Mariposa Twp 3	60	580
---	Mariposa Twp 3	60	581
---	Mariposa Twp 3	60	582
---	Mariposa Twp 3	60	588
---	Mariposa Twp 3	60	596
---	Mariposa Twp 3	60	608
---	Mariposa Twp 3	60	613
---	Mariposa Twp 3	60	618
---	Mariposa Twp 1	60	626
---	Mariposa Twp 1	60	639
---	Mariposa Twp 1	60	640
---	Mariposa Twp 1	60	656
---	Mariposa Twp 1	60	664
---	Mariposa Coulterville	60	681
---	Mariposa Coulterville	60	683
---	Mariposa Coulterville	60	692
---	Mariposa Coulterville	60	697
---	Mendocino Calpella	60	817
---	Mendocino Calpella	60	819
---	Mendocino Round Va	60	878
---	Mendocino Round Va	60	884
---	Mendocino Twp 1	60	888
---	Monterey Monterey	60	965
---	Nevada Grass Valley	61	230
---	Nevada Grass Valley	61	232
---	Nevada Nevada	61	304
---	Nevada Nevada	61	307
---	Nevada Nevada	61	308
---	Nevada Washington	61	339
---	Nevada Washington	61	340
---	Nevada Washington	61	341
---	Nevada Washington	61	342
---	Nevada Eureka	61	383
---	Nevada Eureka	61	384
---	Nevada Eureka	61	385
---	Nevada Eureka	61	386
---	Nevada Rough &	61	399
---	Nevada Rough &	61	426
---	Nevada Rough &	61	436
---	Nevada Bridgeport	61	457
---	Nevada Bridgeport	61	458
---	Nevada Bridgeport	61	459
---	Nevada Bridgeport	61	461
---	Nevada Bridgeport	61	485
---	Nevada Bridgeport	61	492
---	Nevada Bridgeport	61	505
---	Nevada Bloomfield	61	521
---	Nevada Red Dog	61	539
---	Placer Secret R	62	621
---	Placer Rattle Snake	62	638
---	Placer Illinois	62	746
---	Placer Illinois	62	751
---	Placer Illinois	62	754
---	Placer Michigan	62	837
---	Placer Iona Hills	62	892
---	Plumas Quincy	62	1008
---	Plumas Meadow Valley	62	914
---	Sacramento Ward 1	63	137
---	Sacramento Granite	63	232
---	Sacramento Granite	63	259
---	Sacramento Natonia	63	286
---	Sacramento Cosummes	63	384
---	Sacramento Cosummes	63	387
---	Sacramento Cosummes	63	392
---	Sacramento Cosummes	63	395
---	Sacramento Cosummes	63	397
---	Sacramento Cosummes	63	406
---	Sacramento Cosummes	63	407
---	Sacramento Ward 1	63	40
---	Sacramento Ward 3	63	424
---	Sacramento Ward 1	63	51
---	Sacramento Ward 1	63	54
---	Sacramento Ward 4	63	558
---	Sacramento Ward 1	63	56
---	Sacramento Ward 1	63	58
---	Sacramento Ward 1	63	59
---	Sacramento Ward 4	63	609
---	Sacramento Ward 1	63	61
---	Sacramento Ward 1	63	70
---	Sacramento Ward 1	63	71
---	San Francisco San Francisco 4	68	1182
---	San Francisco San Francisco 7	68	1341
---	San Francisco San Francisco 11	67	145
---	San Francisco San Francisco 5	67	528
---	Shasta Shasta	66	678
---	Sierra Downieville	66	1004
---	Sierra Downieville	66	1008
---	Sierra Downieville	66	1009
---	Sierra Downieville	66	1025
---	Sierra La Porte	66	767
---	Sierra La Porte	66	774
---	Sierra La Porte	66	782
---	Sierra St Louis	66	805
---	Sierra Pine Grove	66	827
---	Sierra St Louis	66	861
---	Sierra Twp 5	66	934
---	Sierra Downieville	66	953
---	Sierra Downieville	66	974
---	Sierra Downieville	66	979
---	Sierra Downieville	66	980
---	Sierra Downieville	66	983
---	Sierra Downieville	66	984
---	Sierra Downieville	66	990
---	Sierra Downieville	66	991
---	Sierra Downieville	66	992
---	Sierra Downieville	66	996
---	Siskiyou Scott Ri	69	76
---	Siskiyou Klamath	69	80
---	Sonoma Sonoma	69	640
---	Trinity Lewiston	70	955
---	Tulara Visalia	71	114
---	Tulara Twp 1	71	118
---	Tulara Twp 2	71	28
---	Tulara Twp 2	71	34
---	Tulara Twp 2	71	35
---	Tulara Keeneysburg	71	50
---	Tulara Keyesville	71	55
---	Tulara Visalia	71	96
---	Tuolumne Big Oak	71	150
---	Tuolumne Don Pedro	71	163
---	Tuolumne Columbia	71	346
---	Tuolumne Columbia	71	347
---	Tuolumne Springfield	71	369
---	Tuolumne Shawsfla	71	385
---	Tuolumne Twp 2	71	410
---	Tuolumne Twp 2	71	416
---	Tuolumne Twp 3	71	434
---	Tuolumne Jamestown	71	439
---	Tuolumne Jamestown	71	456
---	Tuolumne Twp 3	71	460
---	Tuolumne Twp 3	71	468
---	Tuolumne Columbia	71	474
---	Tuolumne Sonora	71	475
---	Tuolumne Sonora	71	477
---	Tuolumne Twp 5	71	509
---	Tuolumne Twp 5	71	510
---	Tuolumne Twp 5	71	512
---	Tuolumne Twp 5	71	513
---	Tuolumne Jacksonville	71	514
---	Tuolumne Twp 5	71	517
---	Tuolumne Twp 5	71	521
---	Tuolumne Twp 5	71	525
---	Tuolumne Twp 5	71	526
---	Tuolumne Green Springs	71	531
---	Tuolumne Don Pedro	71	533
---	Tuolumne Don Pedro	71	535
---	Tuolumne Twp 6	71	536
---	Yolo No E Twp	72	682
---	Yolo No E Twp	72	685
---	Yolo Slate Ra	72	712
---	Yolo Slate Ra	72	713
---	Yuba Bear Rvr	72	1000
---	Yuba Bear Rvr	72	1001
---	Yuba North Ea	72	682
---	Yuba Slate Ro	72	713
---	Yuba Long Bar	72	753
---	Yuba Fosters	72	831
---	Yuba Fosters	72	842
---	Yuba Marysville	72	867
---	Yuba Marysville	72	895
---	Yuba Marysville	72	921
---	Yuba Linda	72	991
---*	Amador Twp 5	55	349
---*	Amador Twp 3	55	410
---*	El Dorado Salmon Falls	58	1064
---*	Mariposa Twp 3	60	590
---*	Sierra Twp 5	66	932
---*	Sierra Twp 5	66	934
---*	Tulara Visalia	71	34
---*	Tulara Visalia	71	35
---*	Tulara Visalia	71	38
---*	Tuolumne Big Oak	71	182
---*	Tuolumne Chinese	71	525
---*	Tuolumne Chinese	71	526
---*	Yolo No E Twp	72	676
---*	Yuba Foster B	72	831
---*	Yuba Fosters	72	842
A	Sierra Downieville	66	974
A	Sierra Downieville	66	980
A	Sonoma Sonoma	69	640
A*	Sierra Twp 5	66	934
Ah	Butte Bidwell	56	707
Ah	Butte Bidwell	56	725
Ah	Butte Mountain	56	735
Ah	Sacramento Ward 1	63	156
Ah	Sacramento Cosummes	63	384
Ah	Sacramento Cosummes	63	401
Ah	Siskiyou Klamath	69	80
Ah	Tuolumne Twp 4	71	150
Ah	Tuolumne Twp 4	71	160
Ah	Tuolumne Twp 2	71	346
Ah	Tuolumne Twp 2	71	347
Ah	Tuolumne Twp 2	71	385
Ah	Yuba Suida	72	991
Ah*	Butte Oro	56	687
App	Nevada Grass Valley	61	234
Ar	Sierra Twp 7	66	890
Ar	Trinity Lewiston	70	955
Boo	Calaveras Twp 5	57	211
Bor	Calaveras Twp 5	57	211
Bou	Calaveras Twp 5	57	211
Chan	Nevada Grass Valley	61	232
Chick	Yuba Long Bar	72	770
Ching	Butte Oro	56	675
Ching	Yuba New York	72	740
Ching	Yuba Long Bar	72	755
Ching*	Yuba New York	72	740
Ching*	Yuba Long Bar	72	755
Chon	Nevada Washington	61	342
Chon	Yuba Long Bar	72	756
Chon	Yuba Long Bar	72	765
Chon	Yuba Long Bar	72	767
Chow	Nevada Grass Valley	61	227
Chow	Nevada Grass Valley	61	228
Chow	Nevada Grass Valley	61	231
Chow	Nevada Grass Valley	61	232
Chow	Nevada Grass Valley	61	234
Chow	Nevada Nevada	61	306
Chow	Nevada Nevada	61	307
Chow	Nevada Nevada	61	308
Chow	Nevada Nevada	61	309
Chow	Nevada Nevada	61	310
Chow	Nevada Washington	61	340
Chow	Nevada Washington	61	342
Chow	Nevada Eureka	61	383
Chow	Nevada Eureka	61	384
Chow	Nevada Eureka	61	385
Chow	Nevada Eureka	61	386
Chow*	Nevada Washington	61	339
Chow*	Yuba Long Bar	72	756
Chow*	Yuba Long Bar	72	765
Chow*	Yuba Long Bar	72	767
Choy	Placer Iona Hills	62	897
Choy*	San Francisco San Francisco 11	67	146
Chum	Nevada Washington	61	342
Chun	Nevada Washington	61	342
Coe	Tuolumne Big Oak	71	148
Con	Nevada Washington	61	339
Con	Nevada Eureka	61	383
Con	Yuba Long Bar	72	759
Cow	Nevada Washington	61	339
Cow	Nevada Washington	61	340
Cow	Nevada Washington	61	341
Cow	Nevada Eureka	61	383
Cow*	Yuba Long Bar	72	759
Coy	Nevada Eureka	61	386
Cum	Sacramento Ward 1	63	59
Du	Calaveras Twp 10	57	277
Faak	Butte Oregon	56	613
Fang	Yuba Parks Ba	72	780
Fay	Nevada Nevada	61	306
Fay	Nevada Eureka	61	384
Finn	Yuba Fosters	72	834
Fon	Nevada Nevada	61	303

Name	County Locale	Roll	Page
SAM			
Foo	Plumas Quincy	62	946
Foo	Plumas Quincy	62	948
Foo Choo	Yuba Long Bar	72	760
Fou	Nevada Grass Valley	61	231
Foy	Nevada Grass Valley	61	234
Foy	Nevada Washington	61	341
Foy	Nevada Eureka	61	383
Fu	San Francisco San Francisco 1	68	925
Fun	Nevada Eureka	61	383
Fung	Yuba Long Bar	72	764
Fung	Yuba Parks Ba	72	780
Gap	Mariposa Twp 1	60	659
Gap	Mariposa Twp 1	60	667
Gap	Mariposa Twp 1	60	669
Gap	Mariposa Twp 1	60	670
Gap	Sacramento Ward 1	63	52
Gap*	Mariposa Twp 1	60	659
Gee	Plumas Quincy	62	947
Gin*	Yuba Bear Rvr	72	1001
Ham	Nevada Bridgeport	61	457
Han	Yuba Slate Ro	72	713
Hang	Calaveras Twp 5	57	193
Hee	Calaveras Twp 6	57	182
Hee	Yolo No E Twp	72	667
Hee	Yuba North Ea	72	680
Hee	Yuba Fosters	72	830
Him	Calaveras Twp 5	57	244
Hing	Butte Oregon	56	612
Hing	Yuba Fosters	72	830
Ho	San Francisco San Francisco 1	68	925
Hok	Sierra Port Win	66	794
Hon	Yuba Long Bar	72	753
Hop	Sacramento Natonia	63	280
Hop*	Sacramento Ward 1	63	69
Hose Maria*	San Mateo Twp 2	65	129
Hose Marie*	San Mateo Twp 2	65	129
How	Trinity Lewiston	70	953
Hue	Yuba Fosters	72	836
Hut	Butte Kimshaw	56	588
Hy	Yuba Fosters	72	827
J*	Nevada Bridgeport	61	458
Jim	Sierra Twp 5	66	927
Ke	Nevada Bloomfield	61	521
Kem	Tuolumne Jamestown	71	441
Khiy*	Yuba Slate Ro	72	708
Ki	Placer Iona Hills	62	869
King	Mariposa Twp 3	60	609
Ko	San Francisco San Francisco 1	68	925
La	Butte Kimshaw	56	606
La	Sacramento Ward 1	63	65
Lanker	Nevada Bridgeport	61	506
Lap	Mariposa Twp 1	60	655
Lap	Mariposa Twp 1	60	656
Lap	Mariposa Twp 1	60	657
Lap	Mariposa Twp 1	60	661
Lap	Mariposa Twp 1	60	665
Lap	Mariposa Twp 1	60	666
Lap	Mariposa Twp 1	60	667
Lap	Mariposa Twp 1	60	669
Lap	Mariposa Twp 1	60	670
Lap	Mariposa Coulterville	60	690
Lap*	Mariposa Twp 1	60	659
Lass	Mariposa Coulterville	60	689
Lay	Nevada Washington	61	342
Lay	Nevada Bridgeport	61	491
Lay*	Nevada Washington	61	342
Leaf*	Mariposa Twp 1	60	666
Leap	Mariposa Twp 1	60	666
Lee	Amador Twp 5	55	366
Lee	Butte Kimshaw	56	584
Lee	Butte Kimshaw	56	589
Lee	Butte Kimshaw	56	602
Lee	Butte Kimshaw	56	608
Lee	Butte Oregon	56	625
Lee	Butte Mountain	56	735
Lee	Mariposa Twp 3	60	588
Lee	Sacramento Ward 1	63	71
Lee	San Francisco San Francisco 9	68	1094
Lee	Yuba Long Bar	72	756
Lee	Yuba Marysville	72	916
Lee*	Plumas Quincy	62	925
Lee*	Yuba Long Bar	72	756
Lee*	Yuba Marysville	72	916
Legg	Nevada Washington	61	342
Ling	Butte Kimshaw	56	605
Ling	Butte Oregon	56	625
Ling	Butte Oregon	56	642
Ling	Mariposa Twp 3	60	551
Ling	Nevada Washington	61	341
Ling	San Joaquin Stockton	64	1053
Ling	Sierra Port Win	66	794
Ling	Sierra Twp 5	66	947
Ling	Yuba Long Bar	72	755
Ling	Yuba Marysville	72	927
Ling*	Calaveras Twp 10	57	234
SAM			
Ling*	Yuba Long Bar	72	755
Linn*	Mariposa Twp 3	60	619
Lo	San Francisco San Francisco 4	68	1198
Long	Butte Bidwell	56	708
Low	Butte Eureka	56	652
Low	Butte Ophir	56	812
Low	Butte Ophir	56	817
Low*	Yuba New York	72	740
Lu	Butte Kimshaw	56	580
Lu	Butte Ophir	56	779
Lu	San Francisco San Francisco 9	68	1094
Lupe	Butte Kimshaw	56	605
May	Nevada Eureka	61	384
Mge	Butte Cascade	56	700
Ming	Mariposa Twp 3	60	572
Ong	Yuba Long Bar	72	763
Pacha	Alameda Brooklyn	55	176
Pae	Nevada Grass Valley	61	234
Pam	Plumas Quincy	62	965
Par	Nevada Grass Valley	61	234
Peng Foo*	Yuba Long Bar	72	756
Peng*	Yuba Long Bar	72	760
Ping	Yuba Long Bar	72	760
Ping Foo	Yuba Long Bar	72	756
Poo	Plumas Quincy	62	945
Quong	Yuba Slate Ro	72	715
Rong	Yuba Long Bar	72	753
Sap	Mariposa Twp 3	60	641
Say*	Nevada Washington	61	342
Se	Mariposa Twp 3	60	620
See	Butte Eureka	56	649
See	Calaveras Twp 5	57	211
See	Mariposa Twp 3	60	588
See	Plumas Meadow Valley	62	909
See*	Calaveras Twp 5	57	211
Seen	Nevada Rough &	61	436
Sego	Plumas Quincy	62	948
Ser	Calaveras Twp 10	57	277
Sim	Butte Kimshaw	56	582
Sim	Butte Bidwell	56	725
Sing	Butte Kimshaw	56	586
Sing	Butte Kimshaw	56	600
Sing	Butte Oregon	56	644
Sing	Calaveras Twp 5	57	234
Sing	Mariposa Twp 3	60	551
Sing	Mariposa Twp 3	60	563
Sing	Mariposa Twp 3	60	571
Sing	Mariposa Twp 3	60	572
Sing	Mariposa Twp 3	60	613
Sing	Nevada Grass Valley	61	233
Sing	Nevada Nevada	61	306
Sing	Nevada Nevada	61	308
Sing	Nevada Washington	61	339
Sing	Nevada Eureka	61	383
Sing	Nevada Eureka	61	384
Sing	Nevada Bridgeport	61	492
Sing	Nevada Bridgeport	61	506
Sing	Plumas Quincy	62	946
Sing	San Francisco San Francisco 4	68	1209
Sing	Sierra La Porte	66	782
Sing	Sierra La Porte	66	785
Sing	Siskiyou Yreka	69	195
Sing	Siskiyou Scott Ri	69	66
Sing	Yuba Marysville	72	927
Sing*	Calaveras Twp 10	57	234
Siny*	Tulara Visalia	71	105
Siny*	Calaveras Twp 5	57	234
Siung*	Mariposa Twp 3	60	545
So	San Francisco San Francisco 1	68	925
Son	Nevada Nevada	61	303
Sop	Mariposa Twp 1	60	641
Sow	Butte Eureka	56	652
Srimg*	Mariposa Twp 3	60	545
Sring	Mariposa Twp 3	60	571
Sring*	Mariposa Twp 3	60	580
Su	Butte Eureka	56	649
Su	Calaveras Twp 5	57	211
Sun	Butte Kimshaw	56	582
Sung	Nevada Bridgeport	61	506
Sung	Plumas Quincy	62	1009
Thigh	El Dorado Georgetown	58	701
Ti	San Francisco San Francisco 1	68	925
Tim	Mariposa Twp 1	60	637
Tony	Butte Oregon	56	617
Too	Butte Kimshaw	56	598
Too	Nevada Nevada	61	303
Tou	Nevada Grass Valley	61	231
Tow	Nevada Nevada	61	303
Tow	Nevada Nevada	61	308
Tow	Nevada Washington	61	340
Tow*	Yuba Rose Bar	72	790
Toy	Nevada Nevada	61	307
Toy	Nevada Nevada	61	308
Toy	Nevada Nevada	61	310
Toy	Nevada Washington	61	339
SAM			
Toy	Nevada Washington	61	340
Toy	Nevada Washington	61	341
Toy	Nevada Eureka	61	383
Toy	Nevada Eureka	61	386
Toy	Placer Iona Hills	62	897
Troy*	San Francisco San Francisco 11	67	146
Tung	Yuba Long Bar	72	764
Valentine	Yuba Marysville	72	946
Wa	Calaveras Twp 10	57	259
Wa	Nevada Nevada	61	303
Wa	Nevada Nevada	61	304
Wa	Nevada Nevada	61	306
Wa	Nevada Washington	61	340
Wa	Nevada Eureka	61	386
Wa	Tuolumne Twp 5	71	510
Wan	Placer Auburn	62	576
Wan	San Joaquin Stockton	64	1038
Wan*	Yuba New York	72	740
Waw	Yuba New York	72	740
Woh*	Sacramento Ward 1	63	60
Wong	San Francisco San Francisco 1	68	925
Wy	Yuba Fosters	72	830
Wye	Butte Bidwell	56	708
Yan	Nevada Grass Valley	61	233
Yip	San Francisco San Francisco 10	67	356
Yon	Nevada Nevada	61	304
Yon*	Nevada Eureka	61	385
You	Nevada Grass Valley	61	233
You	Nevada Eureka	61	385
Young	Yuba Long Bar	72	760
Yow	Calaveras Twp 5	57	257
Yow*	Placer Dutch Fl	62	722
Yun	Nevada Grass Valley	61	233
Yup	Nevada Grass Valley	61	228
Yup	Nevada Grass Valley	61	230
Yup	Nevada Grass Valley	61	231
Yup	Nevada Grass Valley	61	233
Yup	Nevada Grass Valley	61	234
Yup	Nevada Nevada	61	300
Yup	Nevada Nevada	61	302
Yup	Nevada Nevada	61	307
Yup	Nevada Nevada	61	308
Yup	Nevada Nevada	61	309
Yup	Nevada Nevada	61	310
Yup	Nevada Washington	61	339
Yup	Nevada Washington	61	340
Yup	Nevada Washington	61	341
Yup	Nevada Washington	61	342
Yup	Nevada Eureka	61	383
Yup	Nevada Eureka	61	384
Yup	Nevada Eureka	61	385
Yup	Nevada Eureka	61	386
Yupu	Nevada Grass Valley	61	230
Yut	Nevada Grass Valley	61	231
SAMAGNIN			
Ch	Santa Clara San Jose	65	302
SAMALY			
Adam	Contra Costa Twp 1	57	503
SAMAMMEL			
---*	Mendocino Big Rvr	60	854
SAMAN			
C W J	Nevada Nevada	61	283
Jno*	Nevada Nevada	61	320
SAMANUEL			
---*	Mendocino Big Rvr	60	854
SAMAR			
M M	Nevada Nevada	61	292
SAMAREE			
Cooper*	Contra Costa Twp 1	57	522
SAMARTIN			
Stephen*	Calaveras Twp 5	57	230
SAMASAR			
Jose	Marin San Rafael	60	760
SAMB			
Joshua E*	Sonoma Washington	69	668
M	Sierra St Louis	66	816
SAMBA			
Maria	Tuolumne Twp 4	71	134
SAMBE			
Samuel	Yuba Marysville	72	941
SAMBERT			
A S	Sierra Downieville	66	986
Fred	Sacramento Ward 1	63	67
Isaak*	Yuba Marysville	72	889
Jno	Butte Kimshaw	56	579
John	Tuolumne Twp 1	71	278
SAMBERTON			
A	Shasta Shasta	66	759
SAMBI			
Samuel	Yuba Marysville	72	941
SAMBING			
F*	Shasta Millvill	66	754
SAMBLEY			
Edward	Los Angeles Los Angeles	59	364

Name	County Locale	M653 Roll	Page
SAMBLOW			
Francis*	Stanislaus Branch	70	697
SAMBO			
---	Fresno Twp 2	59	63
---	Tulara Twp 1	71	113
---	Tulara Twp 3	71	57
Maria*	Tuolumne Big Oak	71	134
SAMBOCLITA			
Dominick*	Calaveras Twp 6	57	163
SAMBODITA			
Dominick*	Calaveras Twp 6	57	163
SAMBOHN			
George W*	Yuba Marysville	72	904
SAMBORN			
Charles	Tulara Twp 1	71	74
Henry	Yuba New York	72	720
Jno*	Butte Oregon	56	633
SAMBOUM			
Lewis*	Plumas Quincy	62	986
SAMBRANO			
Martinez	Tuolumne Columbia	71	319
SAMBRONE			
Gerome	Fresno Millerto	59	1
SAMBURN			
S	Sutter Butte	70	786
SAMBUT			
A S	Sierra Downieville	66	986
SAMCHEZ			
Antonio	San Francisco San Francisco 2	67	688
SAMDAM			
F T*	Sacramento Ward 1	63	28
SAMDEN			
J F*	Napa Napa	61	100
SAMDER			
H	Shasta Shasta	66	734
SAMDRIA			
F*	Shasta Shasta	66	677
SAME			
---	Calaveras Twp 6	57	181
---	Tulara Twp 2	71	38
---	Tuolumne Montezuma	71	512
---	Tuolumne Chinese	71	521
Bartolo	Monterey San Juan	60	981
Wm	Placer Dutch Fl	62	718
SAMEL			
W	Yolo Putah	72	545
SAMELL			
Andrew*	Placer Michigan	62	829
SAMELLE			
Joseph	Calaveras Twp 4	57	313
SAMELSON			
M	Sacramento Ward 4	63	495
SAMES			
Almina	San Francisco San Francisco 7	68	1349
SAMESTER			
William	Monterey San Juan	60	988
SAMEY			
P	Trinity Weaverville	70	1053
SAMFESON			
Camilla*	Yuba Marysville	72	912
SAMFURS			
---*	Sierra Twp 5	66	927
SAMG			
---*	San Francisco San Francisco 4	68	1178
Sing	Tulara Visalia	71	105
SAMGUIS			
---	Sierra Twp 5	66	927
SAMHILL			
Charles	Siskiyou Yreka	69	184
SAMI			
---	Nevada Eureka	61	385
SAMIELS			
W L	Butte Bidwell	56	719
SAMIETO			
Anculo*	Sacramento Ward 1	63	7
Arculo*	Sacramento Ward 1	63	7
Ariculo*	Sacramento Ward 1	63	7
SAMILLAND			
Brossa*	Calaveras Twp 4	57	321
SAMINE			
Josephine	Santa Clara San Jose	65	296
SAMINETTE			
Joseph	Tuolumne Twp 1	71	254
SAMIS			
Almina	San Francisco San Francisco 7	68	1349
SAMISON			
---*	Tulara Visalia	71	34
SAMISS			
John	Amador Twp 1	55	478
SAMITA			
Theodore	Calaveras Twp 10	57	287
SAMITER			
Theodore	Calaveras Twp 10	57	287
SAML B			
Thorn	Calaveras Twp 5	57	189
SAML			
---	Mendocino Calpella	60	821

Name	County Locale	M653 Roll	Page
SAML			
A	El Dorado Placerville	58	856
Peter	Alameda Brooklyn	55	103
SAMLE			
Joshua E*	Sonoma Washington	69	668
SAMLUEL			
Morgan	Santa Cruz Pescadero	66	647
SAMM			
Hellen	San Francisco San Francisco 2	67	737
SAMMAN			
Charles	Tuolumne Twp 4	71	150
SAMMANN			
L	Tuolumne Twp 4	71	151
SAMMEL			
W	Yolo Putah	72	545
SAMMIL			
Ehra*	San Francisco San Francisco 12	67	395
SAMMIS			
A	San Francisco San Francisco 10	67	337
SAMMON			
---*	Tulara Visalia	71	35
Squire	Sierra Twp 7	66	899
SAMMONS			
E	Nevada Bridgeport	61	484
Margaret*	Nevada Red Dog	61	546
O	Nevada Bridgeport	61	484
SAMMUELS			
Geo*	Nevada Eureka	61	379
SAMMY			
B	San Francisco San Francisco 12	67	395
SAMNEY			
Joel*	Shasta Millvill	66	756
SAMNON			
---	Tulara Twp 2	71	35
SAMO			
---	El Dorado Georgetown	58	675
SAMODEA			
Cecilia	Yuba Long Bar	72	745
SAMODIO			
Cecilia	Yuba Marysville	72	918
Ceilia	Yuba Marysville	72	918
SAMON			
Ferdinand*	Nevada Bridgeport	61	502
Pat*	Amador Twp 2	55	265
SAMONA			
John*	Siskiyou Shasta Rvr	69	116
SAMONE			
---	Tulara Twp 2	71	36
---*	Tulara Twp 2	71	38
SAMONSAM			
---	Mendocino Big Rvr	60	855
SAMONT			
C	Nevada Nevada	61	287
SAMONTON			
A	El Dorado Placerville	58	861
SAMOO SAME			
---	Mendocino Big Rvr	60	855
SAMORA			
Cancepcion	Merced Monterey	60	936
Concepcion	Monterey Monterey	60	936
Jose	Contra Costa Twp 1	57	488
Maria A	Monterey Monterey	60	952
Rafael	Calaveras Twp 4	57	341
Sylvaiss	Los Angeles Los Angeles	59	323
SAMORD			
Jose	Contra Costa Twp 1	57	488
SAMORTIN			
John	Calaveras Twp 5	57	228
Stephen	Calaveras Twp 5	57	230
SAMOSA			
Rafael	Calaveras Twp 4	57	341
SAMOTT			
V	Nevada Nevada	61	291
SAMOVEAUX			
Saml	San Francisco San Francisco 6	67	412
SAMOZA			
Matti	Calaveras Twp 4	57	324
SAMPE			
Thoodow*	Nevada Nevada	61	242
SAMPEKA			
---	Fresno Twp 2	59	114
SAMPEN			
Louis	Amador Twp 6	55	439
SAMPERT			
John	Sierra Poverty	66	799
SAMPHEAN			
Danl C	Calaveras Twp 6	57	154
SAMPHEAR			
Danl C*	Calaveras Twp 6	57	154
SAMPHIER			
G	Siskiyou Scott Ri	69	72
SAMPHIRE			
R	San Francisco San Francisco 5	67	548

Name	County Locale	M653 Roll	Page
SAMPIRAN			
Henry*	San Francisco San Francisco 7	68	1401
SAMPKIN			
Richard H*	Sierra Scales D	66	800
SAMPKINS			
John	Solano Benecia	69	304
SAMPLE			
D R	Butte Bidwell	56	722
Isreal*	Butte Oregon	56	611
James T	Los Angeles Los Angeles	59	364
Osreal*	Butte Oregon	56	611
Osreed*	Butte Oregon	56	611
S S	Butte Ophir	56	766
William	Plumas Quincy	62	1000
SAMPLES			
Asa	Los Angeles Elmonte	59	250
SAMPLIN			
S	El Dorado Grizzly	58	1180
SAMPMAN			
Randall*	Siskiyou Shasta Rvr	69	114
SAMPO			
---	Fresno Twp 2	59	116
---	Fresno Twp 1	59	27
SAMPRA			
---	Fresno Twp 2	59	107
SAMPRON			
---	Mendocino Calpella	60	821
---	Mendocino Calpella	60	827
SAMPSEL			
Jos	Sacramento Ward 4	63	609
SAMPSEN			
Robt	Shasta Shasta	66	735
SAMPSON			
---	Butte Oregon	56	623
---	Mendocino Calpella	60	821
---	Mendocino Calpella	60	827
---	Tulara Twp 2	71	40
A	El Dorado Diamond	58	773
A O	Shasta Shasta	66	735
Abram T	Placer Auburn	62	576
Anderson	Yuba Marysville	72	924
B	Sacramento Sutter	63	300
B C	Tuolumne Twp 2	71	286
C C	Amador Twp 7	55	416
Camilla B	Yuba Marysville	72	912
Charles	Amador Twp 2	55	296
Charles	Fresno Twp 1	59	26
Charles C	Yuba Marysville	72	960
Chas	Alameda Brooklyn	55	179
Doyt	Yolo Cache	72	643
Francis	Placer Auburn	62	559
Franklin	Sierra Pine Grove	66	832
Fred	Alameda Brooklyn	55	112
Frederick	Los Angeles Los Angeles	59	389
George	Calaveras Twp 9	57	364
Gephina	Contra Costa Twp 3	57	613
Harvey W	Tuolumne Twp 2	71	382
Henry	El Dorado Eldorado	58	937
Henry	Sacramento San Joaquin	63	364
Henry	San Francisco San Francisco 4	68	1112
Henry	San Francisco San Francisco 1	68	817
Isaac*	Alameda Brooklyn	55	178
James	El Dorado Placerville	58	895
Jo	Mariposa Coulterville	60	685
John	Marin Bolinas	60	728
John	San Francisco San Francisco 10	67	262
John	San Francisco San Francisco 2	67	599
John	San Mateo Twp 3	65	81
John	Siskiyou Yreka	69	123
John	Siskiyou Yreka	69	151
John A	Tuolumne Shawsfla	71	411
John D	Sierra Poker Flats	66	837
John*	San Francisco San Francisco 2	67	599
Joseph	Yuba Marysville	72	927
Levi	San Francisco San Francisco 2	67	704
M	Calaveras Twp 5	57	238
M	San Francisco San Francisco 4	68	1166
Margaret E	Yuba Suida	72	983
Mary	San Bernardino San Bernadino	64	629
Mary	San Joaquin O'Neal	64	1006
Milo J	Siskiyou Yreka	69	169
Obert	Siskiyou Yreka	69	170
Philip	Tuolumne Shawsfla	71	379
R	Nevada Grass Valley	61	235
R A	Butte Oregon	56	629
Ralph*	Tuolumne Twp 5	71	512
Richard	Sierra Twp 7	66	880
Robt	Shasta Shasta	66	735
Royal M	Tuolumne Twp 5	71	511
S	Shasta Shasta	66	653
S H	Nevada Grass Valley	61	191
Sarah	Stanislaus Emory	70	750
Thomas*	Shasta Millvill	66	727
Thos	San Bernardino San Bernadino	64	629
William	Plumas Quincy	62	995

		M653	
Name	County Locale	Roll	Page

SAMPSON
William H	Yuba Marysville	72	972
Wm	Calaveras Twp 5	57	238
Wm	San Francisco San Francisco 1	68	857
Wm	Tehama Lassen	70	875
Wm	Tehama Tehama	70	942
Z	Sacramento Georgian	63	341

SAMPTIN
| John* | Siskiyou Yreka | 69 | 123 |

SAMPUS
| ---* | Sierra Twp 5 | 66 | 927 |

SAMPUT
| ---* | Sierra Twp 5 | 66 | 927 |

SAMROW
| H | El Dorado Mud Springs | 58 | 964 |
| Robt | El Dorado Mud Springs | 58 | 964 |

SAMSBURY
| James | Sacramento Ward 1 | 63 | 39 |

SAMSEL
| Hiram | Sonoma Bodega | 69 | 521 |

SAMSHA
| --- | Trinity Mouth Ca | 70 | 1011 |

SAMSO
| F | Amador Twp 1 | 55 | 492 |

SAMSON
---	Del Norte Klamath	58	658
---	Fresno Twp 2	59	61
---	Fresno Twp 2	59	72
---	Fresno Twp 3	59	95
---	San Diego Agua Caliente	64	814
---	Tulara Twp 2	71	34
A B	San Francisco San Francisco 6	67	401
C B	Nevada Bridgeport	61	444
Charles	San Francisco San Francisco 4	68	1154
Hardy	Butte Kimshaw	56	588
Jas	Butte Oregon	56	634
O	Marin Cortemad	60	781
S	Nevada Bridgeport	61	473
William A	Los Angeles Los Angeles	59	369
Willilam A	Los Angeles Los Angeles	59	369

SAMSTAG
| Joseph | Tulara Visalia | 71 | 103 |

SAMT
| --- | Placer Virginia | 62 | 666 |

SAMTEYER
| Victor* | San Francisco San Francisco 2 | 67 | 725 |

SAMU
| Louis* | Trinity W Weaver | 70 | 1054 |

SAMUDEO
| Leonardo | Marin Cortemad | 60 | 781 |
| Sonardo* | Marin Cortemad | 60 | 781 |

SAMUEL
---	Mendocino Calpella	60	821
---	San Diego Temecula	64	794
---	San Diego Temecula	64	796
---	Tulara Keyesville	71	57
---	Tulara Twp 3	71	66
---*	Placer Auburn	62	566
A T*	Nevada Nevada	61	294
Armour	Sierra Downieville	66	972
David	Marin Cortemad	60	787
Edward	San Francisco San Francisco 9	68	1050
G	San Francisco San Francisco 5	67	516
J	Nevada Grass Valley	61	216
James	Yuba Marysville	72	923
John	San Joaquin Douglass	64	916
Joseph	Amador Twp 3	55	385
Joseph	Stanislaus Branch	70	698
Joseph	Stanislaus Branch	70	701
McWilliams	Amador Twp 4	55	238
N	Solano Vacaville	69	321
R	Nevada Grass Valley	61	236
R	San Francisco San Francisco 6	67	471
S	Nevada Nevada	61	330
S	San Francisco San Francisco 5	67	511
Samuel	Sutter Nicolaus	70	838
Wm J	Sacramento Georgian	63	345

SAMUELS
---	San Francisco San Francisco 3	67	53
Anton	Tuolumne Sonora	71	479
Aton	Tuolumne Twp 1	71	479
Columbus	Calaveras Twp 9	57	352
D	San Francisco San Francisco 2	67	639
Edward	Napa Yount	61	48
F	Sutter Butte	70	780
Frielias	El Dorado Greenwood	58	714
Geo	Nevada Eureka	61	379
George	Marin Cortemad	60	782
J	Solano Montezuma	69	373
Jacob	Sonoma Sonoma	69	635
John	Solano Suisan	69	222
John F	Napa Yount	61	48
John R	Plumas Meadow Valley	62	905
Joseph	San Francisco San Francisco 9	68	1019
Joseph	Tulara Twp 3	71	61
L	Nevada Nevada	61	243

SAMUELS
Mary	San Francisco San Francisco 8	68	1313
N	Solano Montezuma	69	375
R B	El Dorado Georgetown	58	703
S	Nevada Nevada	61	243
Samuel	El Dorado Greenwood	58	714
Susan	Placer Forest H	62	795
W	Solano Montezuma	69	375

SAMUELSON
| Chas | Sacramento Ward 4 | 63 | 499 |
| M | Sacramento Ward 1 | 63 | 146 |

SAMUL
| H B | Sierra Downieville | 66 | 955 |

SAMUS
| J | Nevada Eureka | 61 | 372 |

SAMWEL
| --- | Tulara Keyesville | 71 | 66 |

SAMYEE
| Gerome | Monterey San Juan | 60 | 1004 |

SAN ANTONIO
---	San Bernardino S Timate	64	719
---	San Bernardino S Timate	64	742
---	San Bernardino S Timate	64	750

SAN BLAS
| Juan | San Diego Colorado | 64 | 811 |

SAN DIEGO
---	San Bernardino San Bernadino	64	677
---	San Bernardino San Bernardino	64	684
---	San Bernardino S Timate	64	700
---	San Bernardino S Timate	64	704
---	San Bernardino S Timate	64	712
---	San Bernardino S Timate	64	714
---	San Bernardino S Timate	64	715
---	San Bernardino S Timate	64	717
---	San Bernardino S Timate	64	718
---	San Bernardino S Timate	64	719
---	San Bernardino S Timate	64	722
---	San Bernardino S Timate	64	724
---	San Bernardino S Timate	64	728
---	San Bernardino S Timate	64	729
---	San Bernardino S Timate	64	731
---	San Bernardino S Timate	64	737
---	San Bernardino S Timate	64	740
---	San Bernardino S Timate	64	741
---	San Bernardino S Timate	64	742
---	San Bernardino S Timate	64	744
---	San Bernardino S Timate	64	745
---	San Bernardino S Timate	64	748
---	San Bernardino S Timate	64	749
---	San Bernardino S Timate	64	750
---	San Bernardino S Timate	64	751
---	San Bernardino S Timate	64	754

SAN FANG
| Ah* | Sacramento Ward 1 | 63 | 152 |

SAN FOO
| --- | San Joaquin Elkhorn | 64 | 991 |

SAN FRANSISCO
| A | Sutter Butte | 70 | 779 |

SAN GON
| ---* | Sacramento Ward 1 | 63 | 55 |

SAN JON
| --- | Sacramento Ward 1 | 63 | 55 |

SAN LEE
| --- | Mariposa Twp 3 | 60 | 613 |

SAN LING
| --- | Mariposa Twp 3 | 60 | 608 |

SAN MATIN
| J | San Francisco San Francisco 2 | 67 | 788 |

SAN MOY
| --- | Sacramento Ward 1 | 63 | 71 |

SAN NUM
| --- | Siskiyou Scott Ri | 69 | 66 |

SAN SEE
| --- | Mariposa Twp 3 | 60 | 614 |

SAN SING
| --- | Mariposa Twp 3 | 60 | 608 |
| --- | Mariposa Twp 3 | 60 | 613 |

SAN TOY
| --- | Calaveras Twp 8 | 57 | 60 |

SAN YOY
| --- | Tuolumne Chinese | 71 | 523 |

SAN
---	Alameda Oakland	55	41
---	Alameda Oakland	55	59
---	Amador Twp 4	55	246
---	Amador Twp 5	55	344
---	Amador Twp 5	55	355
---	Amador Twp 3	55	398
---	Amador Twp 7	55	413
---	Amador Twp 6	55	434
---	Amador Twp 6	55	437
---	Amador Twp 6	55	439
---	Amador Twp 1	55	496
---	Amador Twp 1	55	507
---	Amador Twp 1	55	510
---	Calaveras Twp 5	57	226

SAN
---	Calaveras Twp 5	57	232
---	Calaveras Twp 5	57	245
---	Calaveras Twp 5	57	246
---	Calaveras Twp 5	57	257
---	Calaveras Twp 5	57	258
---	Calaveras Twp 10	57	259
---	Calaveras Twp 10	57	270
---	Calaveras Twp 10	57	286
---	Calaveras Twp 4	57	299
---	Calaveras Twp 4	57	307
---	Calaveras Twp 4	57	308
---	Calaveras Twp 4	57	327
---	Calaveras Twp 4	57	338
---	Calaveras Twp 4	57	342
---	Del Norte Happy Ca	58	668
---	El Dorado White Oaks	58	1032
---	El Dorado Coloma	58	1086
---	El Dorado Coloma	58	1102
---	El Dorado Coloma	58	1106
---	El Dorado Kelsey	58	1130
---	El Dorado Kelsey	58	1143
---	El Dorado Diamond	58	788
---	El Dorado Diamond	58	796
---	El Dorado Diamond	58	802
---	El Dorado Diamond	58	812
---	El Dorado Diamond	58	815
---	El Dorado Diamond	58	816
---	El Dorado Placerville	58	829
---	El Dorado Placerville	58	830
---	El Dorado Placerville	58	831
---	El Dorado Placerville	58	832
---	El Dorado Placerville	58	841
---	El Dorado Placerville	58	844
---	El Dorado Placerville	58	888
---	El Dorado Placerville	58	890
---	El Dorado Placerville	58	898
---	El Dorado Placerville	58	904
---	El Dorado Placerville	58	905
---	El Dorado Placerville	58	925
---	El Dorado Placerville	58	929
---	El Dorado Placerville	58	933
---	El Dorado Eldorado	58	940
---	El Dorado Mud Springs	58	952
---	El Dorado Mud Springs	58	953
---	El Dorado Mud Springs	58	954
---	El Dorado Mud Springs	58	962
---	El Dorado Mud Springs	58	965
---	El Dorado Mud Springs	58	987
---	El Dorado Mud Springs	58	992
---	Fresno Twp 1	59	30
---	Mariposa Twp 3	60	552
---	Mariposa Twp 3	60	560
---	Mariposa Twp 3	60	564
---	Mariposa Twp 3	60	581
---	Mariposa Twp 3	60	608
---	Mariposa Twp 3	60	613
---	Mariposa Twp 3	60	618
---	Mariposa Twp 3	60	619
---	Mariposa Twp 1	60	662
---	Nevada Washington	61	339
---	Nevada Rough &	61	399
---	Nevada Rough &	61	409
---	Nevada Bridgeport	61	462
---	Placer Auburn	62	576
---	Placer Illinois	62	745
---	Placer Iona Hills	62	898
---	Sacramento Granite	63	231
---	Sacramento Cosumnes	63	392
---	Sacramento Ward 3	63	490
---	Sacramento Ward 1	63	54
---	Sacramento Ward 1	63	59
---	San Francisco San Francisco 4	68	1174
---	San Francisco San Francisco 4	68	1179
---	San Francisco San Francisco 4	68	1185
---	San Francisco San Francisco 4	68	1197
---	San Francisco San Francisco 4	68	1200
---	San Francisco San Francisco 4	68	1204
---	San Francisco San Francisco 4	68	1210
---	Sierra La Porte	66	790
---	Sierra St Louis	66	813
---	Sierra Downieville	66	971
---	Sierra Downieville	66	980
---	Sierra Downieville	66	984
---	Siskiyou Klamath	69	89
---	Trinity Lewiston	70	956
---	Tuolumne Jacksonville	71	168
---	Tuolumne Twp 3	71	459
---	Tuolumne Chinese	71	523
---	Tuolumne Don Pedro	71	535
---	Tuolumne Don Pedro	71	536
---	Yuba Marysville	72	908
---*	El Dorado Diamond	58	807
---*	Sacramento Cosumnes	63	390
---*	Sacramento Ward 1	63	59
---*	Yuba Linda	72	993

California 1860 Census Index

SAN

Name	County Locale	M653 Roll Page
Ah	Calaveras Twp 7	57 36
Ak	Mariposa Twp 3	60 620
Ali	Sacramento Ward 4	63 530
Ar*	Sierra Downieville	66 971
At Pou	San Francisco San Francisco 4	681186
Bear	Mariposa Twp 3	60 620
By	Mariposa Twp 3	60 608
Cho	San Francisco San Francisco 9	681094
Chop	Calaveras Twp 5	57 254
Chow	Nevada Washington	61 342
Choy	Calaveras San Francisco 5	57 254
Cong	Amador Twp 1	55 495
Cow	Nevada Nevada	61 301
Cow	Nevada Nevada	61 304
De	Mariposa Twp 3	60 620
Dell	Yuba Fosters	72 830
Di	Yuba Bear Rvr	72 999
Fa	San Francisco San Francisco 4	681207
Fo	San Francisco San Francisco 4	681207
Fong	San Francisco San Francisco 4	681204
Fung	San Francisco San Francisco 4	681204
Gee	El Dorado Mud Springs	58 971
Gill	Mariposa Twp 3	60 619
Hay	El Dorado Eldorado	58 942
He	El Dorado Coloma	581084
He	San Francisco San Francisco 4	681210
Hee	San Francisco San Francisco 4	681202
Hing	San Francisco San Francisco 4	681185
Ho	San Francisco San Francisco 4	681211
Ho	San Francisco San Francisco 4	681212
Hoa	El Dorado Salmon Falls	581048
Hong	San Francisco San Francisco 4	681203
Hop*	Sacramento Ward 1	63 69
Hot	Sacramento Natonia	63 280
Hou	San Francisco San Francisco 4	681185
How	El Dorado Eldorado	58 942
Hoy	San Francisco San Francisco 4	681186
Hu	San Francisco San Francisco 4	681202
Hung	San Francisco San Francisco 5	671206
Hung	Tuolumne Don Pedro	71 538
Huon	San Francisco San Francisco 4	681211
Hurey*	Tuolumne Twp 6	71 539
Jon*	Sacramento Ward 1	63 55
Kaon	San Francisco San Francisco 4	681211
Kee	San Francisco San Francisco 4	681177
Kee	Yuba Marysville	72 925
Kii	Mariposa Twp 3	60 620
Ko	San Francisco San Francisco 4	681177
Ko	San Francisco San Francisco 4	681179
Ko	San Francisco San Francisco 4	681201
Koo	San Francisco San Francisco 4	681177
Kou	Mariposa Twp 3	60 620
Ku	San Francisco San Francisco 4	681185
Ku	San Francisco San Francisco 4	681210
Ku Soo	San Francisco San Francisco 4	681210
Kung*	San Francisco San Francisco 9	681096
Lan*	Mariposa Twp 3	60 578
Lee	Mariposa Twp 3	60 553
Lee	Mariposa Twp 3	60 576
Lee	Nevada Bridgeport	61 465
Lee*	Mariposa Twp 3	60 576
Ling	Mariposa Twp 3	60 613
Lo	San Francisco San Francisco 4	681198
Lon	Amador Twp 2	55 302
Lou	Mariposa Twp 3	60 578
Luong	Alameda Oakland	55 24
Migh	Mariposa Twp 3	60 619
Moy	San Francisco San Francisco 4	681210
Muoy	Sacramento Ward 1	63 71
Num	Siskiyou Scott Ri	69 66
O*	Nevada Eureka	61 367
Po	San Francisco San Francisco 4	681184
Que	Nevada Bloomfield	61 520
Ree	San Francisco San Francisco 4	681210
San	San Francisco San Francisco 5	671207
See	Mariposa Twp 3	60 553
See	Mariposa Twp 3	60 582
Sime	Nevada Bridgeport	61 462
Sin	El Dorado Placerville	58 823
Sing	Nevada Eureka	61 383
Sing	San Francisco San Francisco 4	681209
Su	Calaveras Twp 5	57 211
Tan	Nevada Grass Valley	61 227
Tand	Fresno Twp 3	59 31
Tee	Nevada Rough &	61 399
Tie	Mariposa Twp 3	60 613
Tie	Nevada Bridgeport	61 492
Tong	Fresno Twp 1	59 28
Tu	El Dorado Coloma	581078
Tune	Nevada Grass Valley	61 227
Wan	El Dorado Placerville	58 829
We	El Dorado Georgetown	58 693
Wong	San Francisco San Francisco 4	681201
Wop	Stanislaus Emory	70 745
Yap	Sacramento Granite	63 268

SAN

Name	County Locale	M653 Roll Page
Yo	Calaveras Twp 5	57 246
Yon	Yuba Marysville	72 920
You	Calaveras Twp 10	57 278
You	San Francisco San Francisco 4	681181
You	San Francisco San Francisco 4	681198
You	San Francisco San Francisco 4	681201
Young*	Mariposa Twp 3	60 578
Yow	Calaveras Twp 10	57 278
Yuh	Nevada Grass Valley	61 227
Yuh	Nevada Grass Valley	61 228
Yune	Nevada Grass Valley	61 227
Yup	Nevada Grass Valley	61 227
Yup	Nevada Grass Valley	61 230
Yup	Nevada Grass Valley	61 231
Yup	Nevada Washington	61 342
Yup	Sacramento Granite	63 268
Yut	Nevada Grass Valley	61 231

SANA
---	Calaveras Twp 5	57 235
---	El Dorado Coloma	581078
---	El Dorado Mud Springs	58 950

SANAGE
| Robt | Santa Clara Fremont | 65 441 |
| Wm | Santa Clara Fremont | 65 441 |

SANAGO
| --- | Los Angeles San Gabriel | 59 421 |

SANAHAN
| Fichd | Tuolumne Twp 2 | 71 411 |
| Richd | Tuolumne Shawsfla | 71 411 |

SANAKAR
| William | Placer Forest H | 62 765 |

SANALL
| J M | Yolo Cache Crk | 72 589 |

SANAMON
| Unas* | Yolo Cache Crk | 72 666 |

SANANE
| Thos* | Butte Cascade | 56 689 |

SANARA
| John* | Calaveras Twp 9 | 57 362 |

SANAS
| Feliciana | Los Angeles Los Angeles | 59 306 |

SANB
| Casper* | Shasta French G | 66 719 |

SANBARN
| Albert H* | Sierra Pine Grove | 66 829 |
| John L | Santa Clara San Jose | 65 339 |

SANBAT
| Philip | Plumas Quincy | 62 990 |

SANBERG
| Theodore | Tuolumne Jamestown | 71 427 |

SANBERN
| Lock | Placer Yankee J | 62 779 |

SANBERT
| J S | Nevada Nevada | 61 282 |
| Thos | Trinity New Rvr | 701030 |

SANBO
| --- | Fresno Twp 2 | 59 116 |

SANBOM
B*	Yolo Cache Crk	72 591
J B*	Trinity Weaverville	701051
J T	Trinity Lewiston	70 953
Jno*	Butte Oregon	56 633
John	Tuolumne Don Pedro	71 534
R	Siskiyou Scott Ri	69 73

SANBONE
| Bradbury | Humbolt Eureka | 59 167 |

SANBORN
A J	Humbolt Mattole	59 122
Abram	Sonoma Santa Rosa	69 407
B	Yolo Cache	72 591
B F	San Joaquin Stockton	641087
B S	Amador Twp 1	55 498
B*	Yolo Cache Crk	72 591
C	Shasta Shasta	66 668
Charles	Sierra Pine Grove	66 829
Charles	Tulara Visalia	71 74
Charles S	San Francisco San Francisco 7	681358
D B	Tehama Red Bluff	70 910
D W	Solano Benecia	69 282
Fred	Sierra Twp 7	66 916
Gilman*	Placer Michigan	62 827
Henry*	Yuba Parks Ba	72 774
Hilliard J	Calaveras Twp 5	57 199
Hilliard T	Calaveras Twp 5	57 199
Hilliurd	Calaveras Twp 5	57 199
J W	Solano Benecia	69 283
J W Jr	Solano Benecia	69 283
Jno	Butte Oregon	56 633
John	Shasta Horsetown	66 688
John	Sierra Pine Grove	66 829
John	Tuolumne Twp 6	71 534
John B	Tuolumne Chinese	71 487
John C	Calaveras Twp 10	57 279
Jud	Sierra Twp 7	66 916
L D	Solano Benecia	69 282

SANBORN
Name	County Locale	M653 Roll Page
L H	Tehama Tehama	70 945
Lucius	Santa Cruz Pajaro	66 534
Moses	Mendocino Big Rvr	60 849
Newman	Santa Cruz Pajaro	66 534
R	Siskiyou Scott Ri	69 73
T C	San Francisco San Francisco 6	67 447
Thomas S	Los Angeles San Pedro	59 485
True	San Francisco San Francisco 7	681338
Ture*	San Francisco San Francisco 7	681338
Vamip	Solano Green Valley	69 242
Vamiss	Solano Green Valley	69 242
W J	San Francisco San Francisco 5	67 516
William	Santa Cruz Pajaro	66 534
William	Santa Cruz Pajaro	66 551

SANBOURN
James	El Dorado White Oaks	581002
Lewis*	Plumas Quincy	62 986
N H	Tuolumne Shawsfla	71 388

SANBRANO
| S | Tehama Red Bluff | 70 931 |

SANBUM
| William R* | Siskiyou Yreka | 69 151 |

SANBURG
| R G | San Francisco San Francisco 3 | 67 69 |

SANBURN
Albert H	Sierra Pine Grove	66 829
J Q	Nevada Bridgeport	61 498
John G	Trinity S Fork	701032
R	Siskiyou Scott Ri	69 71
T D	Tuolumne Twp 2	71 371
William	Siskiyou Scott Va	69 56
William R*	Siskiyou Yreka	69 151

SANBURON
| J D* | Nevada Bridgeport | 61 498 |

SANBURY
| R G* | San Francisco San Francisco 3 | 67 69 |

SANCASTER
| A | Nevada Nevada | 61 326 |
| G R | Nevada Nevada | 61 239 |

SANCE
| H | Nevada Nevada | 61 265 |
| Peter | Yolo Cache | 72 641 |

SANCH
| J* | Nevada Grass Valley | 61 150 |

SANCHAS
| F | El Dorado Placerville | 58 863 |
| Manuel | Marin San Rafael | 60 759 |

SANCHE
| Piten | Yolo Cache Crk | 72 641 |

SANCHERS
| H* | El Dorado Georgetown | 58 760 |

SANCHES
---	Tulara Keyesville	71 63
---	Tulara Keyesville	71 66
---	Tulara Keyesville	71 67
---	Tulara Keyesville	71 70
---	Tulara Keyesville	71 72
Bernabe	Monterey San Juan	60 978
Ellen	San Mateo Twp 1	65 63
F	San Mateo Twp 1	65 63
Francisco	Los Angeles Los Angeles	59 514
General	San Bernardino San Bernadino	64 623
Guardeloupe	Yuba Marysville	72 949
Igntio*	Napa Yount	61 52
Iqutio*	Napa Yount	61 52
J Angles	Calaveras Twp 9	57 378
John	San Mateo Twp 1	65 63
Jose	Plumas Quincy	62 937
Juan	Tuolumne Big Oak	71 141
L	El Dorado Placerville	58 870
Luco	Contra Costa Twp 1	57 509
Lugardo	Alameda Oakland	55 7
Maria	Santa Cruz Pescadero	66 642
Pancho	Mariposa Twp 3	60 571
Pancho*	Mariposa Twp 3	60 570
Patricio	San Diego S Luis R	64 777
Rancho	Mariposa Twp 3	60 570
Raphael	Santa Cruz Pajaro	66 568
Rita	San Bernardino S Timate	64 687
T*	El Dorado Placerville	58 900
Victorio	San Diego S Luis R	64 780

SANCHEY
E	Sierra Pine Grove	66 822
Juan*	Nevada Bloomfield	61 512
Mariana	San Francisco San Francisco 6	67 428

SANCHEZ
---	Monterey Alisal	601039
A	Tuolumne Columbia	71 337
Andrea	Los Angeles Los Nieto	59 432
Antoka*	San Mateo Twp 2	65 112
Antonio	Alameda Murray	55 228
Antonio	Los Angeles Los Angeles	59 368
Antonio	Yuba Marysville	72 920
Bancho*	Mariposa Twp 3	60 570
Bensucia	San Francisco San Francisco 2	67 738

Name	County Locale	M653 Roll	Page
SANCHEZ			
Beusucia*	San Francisco	2 67	738
	San Francisco		
Cattina	San Francisco San Francisco	2 67	767
Charles	San Mateo Twp 3	65	99
D	Solano Montezuma	69	370
Dolores	Santa Clara Santa Clara	65	512
Don J	San Mateo Twp 1	65	63
Felix	San Francisco San Francisco	8 681	245
Filipe	San Diego San Diego	64	768
Francisco	Monterey San Juan	601	001
Francisco	Santa Barbara	64	204
	San Bernardino		
Francisco	San Mateo Twp 1	65	52
Frank	San Mateo Twp 3	65	98
Garines	Calaveras Twp 6	57	125
Gertrude	Sacramento Ward 1	63	105
Gib	Merced Monterey	60	940
Gidore	San Mateo Twp 2	65	112
Gil	Monterey Monterey	60	940
Guadaloupe	Yuba Marysville	72	949
Guilerino	Fresno Twp 1	59	84
Higinio	Santa Clara San Jose	65	288
Igntio*	Napa Yount	61	52
J S	San Francisco San Francisco	6 67	467
Jacinta	Los Angeles Los Angeles	59	506
Jesus	Calaveras Twp 6	57	151
Jesus	Calaveras Twp 5	57	212
Jesus	Santa Clara Gilroy	65	233
John	San Bernardino S Buenav	64	207
John	Tuolumne Twp 3	71	468
Jose	Los Angeles Los Angeles	59	385
Jose	Los Angeles Los Nieto	59	433
Jose	San Bernardino Santa Ba	64	217
Jose	San Bernardino S Buenav	64	218
Jose A	Los Angeles Los Angeles	59	380
Juan	Los Angeles Los Angeles	59	299
Juan	Nevada Bloomfield	61	512
Juan	San Diego Agua Caliente	64	847
Juan	Santa Cruz Pescadero	66	642
Juan Jr	San Bernardino Santa Ba	64	217
Juan Jr	San Bernardino S Buenav	64	218
Juan*	Nevada Bloomfield	61	512
Julian	Yuba Marysville	72	858
Julian	Yuba Marysville	72	860
Lawriano	Fresno Twp 1	59	84
Lorenzo	Monterey San Juan	60	999
Lorenzo	San Diego Agua Caliente	64	864
Mamal*	Yuba Marysville	72	921
Maneal*	Yuba Marysville	72	921
Manel	Monterey Alisal	601	041
Manuel	San Francisco San Francisco	2 67	738
Manuel	Tuolumne Twp 2	71	410
Maria	Santa Cruz Pescadero	66	642
Mariana	San Francisco San Francisco	6 67	428
Marquez	Los Angeles San Gabriel	59	422
Martin	Los Angeles Los Angeles	59	385
Matias	Monterey San Juan	601	002
Miguel	Monterey Alisal	601	041
Nicholas	Tulara Keyesville	71	60
Nicolas	Los Angeles Los Nieto	59	433
Pacifico	San Bernardino S Buenav	64	207
Pancho*	Mariposa Twp 3	60	570
Pedro	Monterey Monterey	60	959
Pedro	Monterey San Juan	60	996
Pedro	San Francisco San Francisco	11	154
		67	
Pedro	San Mateo Twp 1	65	63
Petra	Los Angeles Los Angeles	59	342
R B	San Francisco San Francisco	4 681	129
Rafael	Merced Monterey	60	939
Rafael	Monterey Monterey	60	939
Rameldo	Los Angeles Los Angeles	59	371
Ramon	Los Angeles Los Angeles	59	381
Ramon	Monterey San Juan	601	001
Rancho	Mariposa Twp 3	60	570
Refugio	Monterey San Juan	60	993
Romaldo	Los Angeles Los Angeles	59	371
Romona	Santa Clara Santa Clara	65	480
Santiago	Los Angeles Los Angeles	59	391
Santiago	San Bernardino Santa Ba	64	218
Santiago	San Bernardino S Buenav	64	219
Susan	Solano Montezuma	69	370
Tades	San Bernardino Santa Ba	64	207
Teresa	Santa Cruz Santa Cruz	66	632
Theodore	Tuolumne Twp 5	71	507
Thomas	Los Angeles Los Nieto	59	434
Thresa	Santa Cruz Santa Cruz	66	632
Tomas A	Los Angeles Los Angeles	59	320
Tranquilin	Santa Barbara	64	182
	San Bernardino		
Tranquilino	Santa Barbara	64	195
	San Bernardino		
V	Tuolumne Twp 1	71	224
Vicente	Los Angeles Los Angeles	59	321
Ygnacio	Monterey San Juan	60	982

Name	County Locale	M653 Roll	Page
SANCHIS			
Francisco	Los Angeles Los Angeles	59	514
J Anglis	Calaveras Twp 9	57	378
SANCHO			
---	Mendocino Big Rvr	60	854
Hosea	Alameda Brooklyn	55	116
Marcas	Yuba Marysville	72	920
SANCLAVAL			
Antone	Sierra Pine Grove	66	821
SANCOMEA			
---	Fresno Twp 2	59	52
SAND			
Emanuel	San Joaquin Elkhorn	64	993
Henry	Alameda Oakland	55	71
J	Sutter Nicolaus	70	839
J H	Yolo Cache	72	639
John	Marin San Rafael	60	764
John	San Francisco San Francisco	5 67	515
Thos	Yolo Cottonwoood	72	652
William	Placer Forest H	62	805
Wm	Sacramento Ward 1	63	30
SANDABA			
Phillip*	Calaveras Twp 9	57	354
SANDAGE			
John	Placer Forest H	62	772
Samuel	Placer Grizzly	62	755
SANDAGOIN			
Chals*	El Dorado Georgetown	58	757
SANDAJOIN			
Chals*	El Dorado Georgetown	58	757
SANDAJOIR			
Chals*	El Dorado Georgetown	58	757
SANDAN			
Betty	San Francisco San Francisco	4 681	166
SANDARAH			
Antonio	Yuba Marysville	72	858
SANDARAL			
Antonio	Yuba Marysville	72	860
SANDARAS			
Jose	El Dorado Georgetown	58	684
SANDARS			
James	Shasta Millvill	66	753
SANDATA			
Francisco	Alameda Brooklyn	55	151
SANDAVAL			
Antone*	Sierra Pine Grove	66	821
SANDAY			
James	Los Angeles Tejon	59	526
SANDBERG			
S	Sacramento Ward 1	63	38
SANDBORN			
Joseph	San Francisco San Francisco	6 67	429
SANDBOURN			
M	Trinity Douglas	70	978
SANDBUN			
Louis	Amador Twp 1	55	482
SANDBURN			
J Q*	Nevada Bridgeport	61	497
SANDEE			
Manuel*	Yolo Merritt	72	578
SANDEMS			
Leasem	Siskiyou Callahan	69	3
SANDEN			
Ellisen	Amador Twp 2	55	301
Learem*	Siskiyou Callahan	69	4
SANDENOW			
O W	Tuolumne Twp 4	71	173
SANDER			
A	Mariposa Twp 1	60	642
C	Tuolumne Twp 1	71	209
E W	Amador Twp 7	55	419
Frank	El Dorado Salmon Falls	581	035
Frank*	Santa Cruz Pescadero	66	645
Geo	San Francisco San Francisco	5 67	553
Helena	San Francisco San Francisco	12	391
		67	
James	Santa Cruz Pescadero	66	645
S D	Nevada Eureka	61	381
S Dk	Nevada Eureka	61	381
T	Sutter Swan	70	765
W E	Shasta Millvill	66	756
SANDERDALE			
B M	Merced Twp 1	60	905
SANDERHOUN			
Joseph*	Mariposa Twp 3	60	573
SANDERHOUSE			
John	Sierra Twp 5	66	936
Joseph*	Mariposa Twp 3	60	573
SANDERLAND			
Thomas E	Yuba Fosters	72	837
Thos	Sacramento Ward 3	63	447
SANDERLIN			
Johnathan	Trinity Eastman	70	960
Jonathan	Trinity Eastman	70	960
SANDERS			
A	Nevada Grass Valley	61	176

Name	County Locale	M653 Roll	Page
SANDERS			
A	Nevada Bridgeport	61	469
A D	Siskiyou Klamath	69	85
Albert	Yuba Rose Bar	72	806
Alfred	Siskiyou Yreka	69	142
Alfred D	Siskiyou Yreka	69	142
Amos A	Sacramento Ward 1	63	42
Andrew	Alameda Brooklyn	55	151
Augustus	Tulara Twp 2	71	26
B	Sacramento Ward 1	63	5
B	San Francisco San Francisco	10	204
		67	
Ben	San Joaquin Elkhorn	64	990
C C	Placer Virginia	62	667
C D	San Francisco San Francisco	9 68	976
C*	Sacramento Lee	63	213
Cath	Sacramento Ward 3	63	449
Charles	Los Angeles Azuza	59	276
Charles	Plumas Quincy	62	985
Charles	San Francisco San Francisco	3 67	19
Charles	Sierra Twp 5	66	923
Charles O	Colusa Spring Valley	57	430
Chas L	Klamath Orleans	59	215
Cyrus G	San Bernardino San Bernardino	64	624
D C	San Francisco San Francisco	9 68	976
Daniel	Siskiyou Callahan	69	13
David	Tulara Twp 1	71	82
David	Yuba Rose Bar	72	811
E J	Sacramento Ward 1	63	124
Eda	Sonoma Santa Rosa	69	390
Eli	Nevada Red Dog	61	551
Eliza	San Francisco San Francisco	4 681	149
F	San Francisco San Francisco	5 67	496
F	Tuolumne Twp 1	71	209
F E L	Sierra Twp 7	66	882
Fonntaine	Sierra Twp 5	66	920
Fred	Alameda Brooklyn	55	140
Fred	Colusa Colusi	57	424
Fredk	Amador Twp 3	55	373
G P	Marin Cortemad	60	752
G W	Amador Twp 2	55	323
Geo	Klamath Trinidad	59	222
Geo	Sierra Chappare	661	040
Geo M	Alameda Brooklyn	55	134
George	El Dorado Big Bar	58	743
George	Sierra Downieville	661	024
George	Sierra Gibsonville	66	858
George M	Sierra Twp 5	66	928
George S	Yuba Marysville	72	871
George W	Sierra Twp 5	66	928
H	San Francisco San Francisco	5 67	551
Hiram	San Francisco San Francisco	2 67	755
Holsi*	Alameda Brooklyn	55	207
J	Nevada Grass Valley	61	237
J B	Calaveras Twp 9	57	406
J G	Yolo Washington	72	572
J H	Butte Chico	56	551
J M	San Francisco San Francisco	2 67	744
J M	Tehama Tehama	70	936
J P	San Francisco San Francisco	5 67	536
J R	Sacramento Granite	63	222
J S	Sonoma Armally	69	490
J W	Tuolumne Columbia	71	323
Jacob	Nevada Rough &	61	418
James	Amador Twp 3	55	387
James	Napa Hot Springs	61	18
James	San Joaquin Elkhorn	64	973
James	Shasta Millvill	66	753
James D	Humbolt Mattole	59	128
James H	San Mateo Twp 3	65	106
James O	Solano Vallejo	69	272
Jas	Sacramento Ward 4	63	523
Jas	San Francisco San Francisco	1 68	919
Jason	Sierra Poker Flats	66	842
Jerrimiah	Humbolt Pacific	59	130
Jesus	Amador Twp 2	55	301
Jms	Klamath Liberty	59	238
John	Amador Twp 6	55	424
John	Nevada Bridgeport	61	453
John	Placer Iona Hills	62	859
John	San Francisco San Francisco	1 68	904
John	San Francisco San Francisco	1 68	919
John	Sierra Twp 7	66	866
John	Siskiyou Scott Va	69	33
John	Tulara Visalia	71	91
John H	Contra Costa Twp 3	57	601
John Jnr	Solano Benecia	69	309
John Jr	Solano Benecia	69	309
Jonas	Tuolumne Shawsfla	71	411
Joseph	Mariposa Twp 1	60	631
K	Nevada Eureka	61	353
L F	San Francisco San Francisco	9 681	067
Laura	San Francisco San Francisco	4 681	117
Learein*	Siskiyou Callahan	69	4
Lewis Jr	Sacramento Ward 1	63	134
Lewis*	Placer Auburn	62	571

Name	County Locale	M653 Roll	Page
SANDERS			
M	El Dorado Casumnes	58	1171
M	Mariposa Twp 1	60	668
M	Nevada Grass Valley	61	208
M	Nevada Grass Valley	61	237
M	Nevada Eureka	61	368
M C	Sierra Twp 5	66	920
M*	Mariposa Twp 1	60	668
Margarite M	Sonoma Santa Rosa	69	389
Mary	San Francisco San Francisco 9	68	1015
Mary	San Francisco San Francisco 9	68	1019
Mary	San Francisco San Francisco 4	68	1128
Mary Ann	Butte Ophir	56	748
O*	Sacramento Lee	63	213
Peter	El Dorado Eldorado	58	935
Pra J*	Alameda Brooklyn	55	207
R	Sierra St Louis	66	817
R T	Butte Hamilton	56	518
Robert	Calaveras Twp 5	57	187
Robert	Calaveras Twp 5	57	190
Rosina	San Francisco San Francisco 10		272
		67	
Royal	Siskiyou Yreka	69	129
Saml	Alameda Brooklyn	55	152
Saml	Shasta Millvill	66	741
Sarah M	Yuba Marysville	72	848
Stephen	Sierra Gibsonville	66	853
T A	Klamath Orleans	59	216
T A	Sacramento Brighton	63	205
T R	Tuolumne Twp 1	71	222
Thomas	Mendocino Big Rvr	60	840
Thomas	Plumas Quincy	62	955
Thos	Amador Twp 6	55	438
Thos	Sacramento Ward 4	63	499
Velina	San Francisco San Francisco 9	68	1001
W B	Amador Twp 1	55	465
W B	Siskiyou Scott Va	69	46
W B	Siskiyou Scott Ri	69	71
W B*	Amador Twp 1	55	465
W E	Siskiyou Scott Va	69	50
W H	Sierra Twp 7	66	874
William	Mendocino Ukiah	60	796
William	Plumas Quincy	62	955
William	San Francisco San Francisco 9	68	1045
William	Sierra Gibsonville	66	853
William	Tulara Twp 2	71	9
William	Tuolumne Twp 1	71	207
William C	Tuolumne Don Pedro	71	539
Wilshire	Sierra Gibsonville	66	857
Wm	Nevada Nevada T	61	327
Wm	Tuolumne Sonora	71	221
Wm	Tuolumne Twp 2	71	279
Wm A	San Francisco San Francisco 3	67	34
Wm J	Tuolumne Twp 2	71	362
SANDERSIN			
P	Siskiyou Cottonwoood	69	105
SANDERSON			
A L	El Dorado Placerville	58	838
E H	San Joaquin Stockton	64	1044
Elizabeth	San Francisco San Francisco 9	68	1033
F	El Dorado Placerville	58	866
Ford*	Placer Michigan	62	839
Fred	Placer Michigan	62	837
Fred*	Placer Michigan	62	839
Geo H	San Joaquin Stockton	64	1018
Geo L	San Joaquin Stockton	64	1042
George	San Francisco San Francisco 9	68	1005
George	San Francisco San Francisco 11		115
		67	
George	San Francisco San Francisco 3	67	52
George W	Calaveras Twp 6	57	158
Hamilton	Yuba Marysville	72	964
Henry	Yuba Marysville	72	902
Henry A	Placer Auburn	62	582
Isaac	Butte Ophir	56	780
J	Placer Dutch Fl	62	731
J B	San Francisco San Francisco 2	67	611
James	Alameda Oakland	55	2
James	Sierra Poverty	66	799
James S	Alameda Oakland	55	2
Kitty	Sierra St Louis	66	810
L	San Francisco San Francisco 2	67	564
Mary	Alameda Oakland	55	2
O W	Tuolumne Garrote	71	173
P	Siskiyou Cottonwoood	69	105
R B	Mariposa Twp 3	60	558
Rose	San Mateo Twp 3	65	103
S A	San Francisco San Francisco 10		223
		67	
S W	El Dorado Placerville	58	839
T	Nevada Eureka	61	393
Tomkins	Calaveras Twp 4	57	311
W	El Dorado Grizzly	58	1180
W	El Dorado Mountain	58	1184
W	Yolo Cottonwoood	72	659
W M	Alameda Brooklyn	55	86

Name	County Locale	M653 Roll	Page
SANDERSON			
William	Calaveras Twp 5	57	229
William	Calaveras Twp 5	57	311
William	San Joaquin Castoria	64	908
William*	Calaveras Twp 4	57	311
Wm G	Fresno Twp 3	59	13
SANDESBURY			
Hiram	Yuba Suida	72	986
SANDEZ			
Maria	San Luis Obispo San Luis Obispo	65	20
SANDFERA			
P*	San Mateo Twp 3	65	77
SANDFORD			
A	Trinity China Bar	70	959
A J	Butte Kimshaw	56	594
B	Yuba Rose Bar	72	817
Chas	Sacramento Ward 4	63	611
Fidella	Monterey San Juan	60	993
H	Butte Kimshaw	56	581
H H	Tuolumne Twp 1	71	222
Henry	Los Angeles San Pedro	59	480
Hulda	Los Angeles Elmonte	59	248
Israel	Sierra Whiskey	66	844
Jas	Butte Hamilton	56	524
Jas B	Butte Hamilton	56	524
Jason L	San Francisco San Francisco 8	68	1253
Josiah H	Sonoma Santa Rosa	69	408
Nathan	Yuba Rose Bar	72	818
P	San Mateo Twp 3	65	82
T	San Francisco San Francisco 6	67	438
William T B	Los Angeles San Pedro	59	480
Wm	Sacramento Ward 3	63	487
SANDGRIST			
E	Butte Ophir	56	765
SANDHEIMER			
Emanuel	Sonoma Healdsbu	69	477
SANDIAGO			
Jesus	Tuolumne Twp 3	71	468
SANDICH			
Jno	Klamath Trinidad	59	219
SANDIEGO			
Jesus	Tuolumne Twp 3	71	468
SANDIES			
Joseph	Placer Twp 2	62	660
SANDIEZ			
Lorenzo*	Monterey San Juan	60	999
SANDIRS			
N S	Calaveras Twp 9	57	415
SANDLE			
Manuel	Yolo Merritt	72	578
SANDLES			
Theadore M	Placer Secret R	62	608
Thos	Placer Stewart	62	607
SANDLIN			
Wm	Sonoma Petaluma	69	605
Wm	Sonoma Petaluma	69	608
SANDMAN			
Leonard	Placer Iona Hills	62	875
Meredith C	San Joaquin Castoria	64	882
SANDNINE			
M*	El Dorado Placerville	58	878
SANDOL			
Francis	Tuolumne Twp 1	71	264
SANDON			
C G	Butte Ophir	56	763
Jno	Sonoma Petaluma	69	552
SANDONS			
Learein*	Siskiyou Callahan	69	4
SANDORAL			
Julian	San Diego Agua Caliente	64	856
SANDOVAL			
Antonio	Santa Clara Fremont	65	442
John P	Los Angeles San Pedro	59	481
Mariano	Los Angeles Los Angeles	59	296
Niguena*	Los Angeles Tejon	59	541
Niquena	Los Angeles Tejon	59	541
P	Sonoma Armally	69	502
Pablo	Los Angeles Los Angeles	59	346
Pablo	San Diego Agua Caliente	64	856
SANDRANO			
Juan	Sierra Downieville	66	1022
SANDRANS			
Juan	Sierra Downieville	66	1022
SANDREAS			
Antoina	Merced Twp 1	60	911
SANDRES			
Antonio	Contra Costa Twp 3	57	615
Jos	Amador Twp 3	55	399
SANDREZ			
Ramon*	Monterey San Juan	60	1001
SANDROBEGS			
A*	Amador Twp 4	55	247
SANDROBIGS			
A*	Amador Twp 4	55	247
U*	Amador Twp 4	55	247
SANDRY			
Danl	San Francisco San Francisco 2	67	623

Name	County Locale	M653 Roll	Page
SANDS			
A J	El Dorado Salmon Hills	58	1061
Chas	Sacramento Dry Crk	63	375
Christopher C	Humbolt Union	59	192
David	Yuba Marysville	72	930
Eliza	San Francisco San Francisco 10		184
		67	
J	Nevada Grass Valley	61	237
Jno	Klamath Salmon	59	209
John	Marin San Rafael	60	764
Lamber	Alameda Brooklyn	55	188
Loyd	El Dorado Mud Springs	58	949
M E	Nevada Grass Valley	61	237
Patrick F	Sacramento Ward 1	63	96
R T	Nevada Nevada	61	311
Robt	Sacramento Franklin	63	323
Saml G	Yuba Marysville	72	889
Sarah	San Francisco San Francisco 10		183
		67	
W	Calaveras Twp 9	57	410
Wm	Calaveras Twp 9	57	407
Wm	Sacramento Ward 1	63	30
SANDSBURY			
Jesse	Los Angeles Los Angeles	59	491
SANDSCHOL			
Logardo	Alameda Brooklyn	55	208
SANDSON			
Monin*	Santa Cruz Pescadero	66	647
Morrin*	Santa Cruz Pescadero	66	647
SANDUN			
Betty	San Francisco San Francisco 4	68	1166
SANDUNN			
Reuben	Tulara Twp 1	71	84
SANDUVAL			
Antone*	Sierra Pine Grove	66	821
SANDUZ			
Refugeo	Monterey San Juan	60	993
SANDWICH			
Nicholas	Santa Clara Fremont	65	432
Salvadore	Tuolumne Twp 2	71	282
SANDY			
Michael	Sierra Twp 7	66	866
SANDYCOCK			
John*	Napa Yount	61	55
SANDYCORK			
John*	Napa Yount	61	55
SANDYS			
Henry C	San Mateo Twp 1	65	50
SANE HOP			
---	Sacramento Ward 1	63	69
SANE			
---	Mariposa Twp 3	60	551
---	Mariposa Twp 1	60	670
Ah	Yuba Bear Rvr	72	1000
Christian	Placer Dutch Fl	62	710
Daniel*	Tulara Twp 3	71	47
Danl S	Calaveras Twp 10	57	288
Edward*	Yuba Marysville	72	887
Jas R	Butte Kimshaw	56	583
John	San Francisco San Francisco 9	68	963
Lawrance	Alameda Brooklyn	55	101
Mary	Sierra Twp 7	66	866
Thos*	Sacramento Brighton	63	191
SANEBRANO			
Gabriel*	San Bernardino Almaden	64	269
SANEGA			
Chela	Monterey Monterey	60	943
SANEHEY			
E*	Sierra Pine Grove	66	822
SANEIS			
Lorenzo	Calaveras Twp 9	57	378
SANELAVAL			
Antone*	Sierra Pine Grove	66	821
SANELER			
Frank*	Santa Cruz Pescadero	66	645
SANELERS			
H*	El Dorado Georgetown	58	760
SANELLE			
Albert*	Calaveras Twp 6	57	148
Albrit B*	Calaveras Twp 6	57	148
SANEMIS			
M A	Sacramento Ward 1	63	16
SANEN			
T*	Nevada Grass Valley	61	237
SANER			
Conrad*	El Dorado Casumnes	58	1174
Jacob	San Francisco San Francisco 12		384
		67	
SANEY			
Jack*	Nevada Rough &	61	431
SANFERD			
E L	San Francisco San Francisco 5	67	546
SANFLE			
David	Yolo Slate Ra	72	688
SANFORD			
A	Nevada Nevada	61	279

Name	County Locale	M653 Roll	Page

SANFORD

Name	County Locale	Roll	Page
A A	Nevada Bloomfield	61	508
Andrew	Santa Cruz Pajaro	66	553
Anna	San Francisco San Francisco 7	681	350
Anna E	San Francisco San Francisco 7	681	350
Antony	Sierra Gibsonville	66	856
August	Nevada Little Y	61	537
B H	Sierra Poker Flats	66	837
C W	Tuolumne Twp 2	71	383
Charles	Santa Cruz Pajaro	66	553
Charles	Yuba Marysville	72	910
Chas	San Francisco San Francisco 9	681	086
Cyrus	Los Angeles Los Angeles	59	507
E	San Francisco San Francisco 5	67	548
E L	San Francisco San Francisco 5	67	546
E P	Alameda Oakland	55	20
Emalans	Contra Costa Twp 3	57	609
F	Shasta Shasta	66	734
Farmer	Contra Costa Twp 2	57	574
Frank	San Francisco San Francisco 2	67	714
George P	Contra Costa Twp 3	57	610
Henry	Contra Costa Twp 2	57	561
J B	Napa Napa	61	112
James	Calaveras Twp 7	57	13
John	Santa Clara Santa Clara	65	475
Joseph	Amador Twp 5	55	348
Mary	Contra Costa Twp 2	57	561
Michael	Fresno Twp 3	59	8
Philip	Shasta Shasta	66	733
R A	Nevada Nevada	61	286
Riled	Trinity Rearings	70	990
Rosolon	Contra Costa Twp 2	57	561
Sarah E	Nevada Bloomfield	61	508
Seth	Sacramento Franklin	63	326
T G	San Francisco San Francisco 5	67	518
William	San Francisco San Francisco 11		90
		67	
Wm	Marin Cortemad	60	791
Wm	Solano Vallejo	69	257

SANG FRAU

Name	County Locale	Roll	Page
---*	Mariposa Twp 3	60	611

SANG HOP

| --- | Sacramento Ward 3 | 63 | 491 |

SANG KEE

| Hen Pan | Nevada Bridgeport | 61 | 466 |

SANG LING

| --- | Mariposa Twp 3 | 60 | 613 |

SANG SEE

| --- | Mariposa Twp 3 | 60 | 613 |

SANG WA

| --- | Nevada Nevada | 61 | 304 |

SANG WAH

| --- | Tuolumne Chinese | 71 | 510 |

SANG WOO

| --- | San Joaquin Stockton | 641 | 087 |

SANG

Name	County Locale	Roll	Page
---	Alameda Oakland	55	24
---	Alameda Oakland	55	34
---	Alameda Oakland	55	35
---	Alameda Oakland	55	63
---	Amador Twp 4	55	256
---	Amador Twp 2	55	289
---	Amador Twp 2	55	314
---	Amador Twp 6	55	439
---	Calaveras Twp 6	57	122
---	Calaveras Twp 6	57	134
---	Calaveras Twp 6	57	151
---	Calaveras Twp 6	57	169
---	Calaveras Twp 6	57	173
---	Calaveras Twp 6	57	176
---	Calaveras Twp 5	57	195
---	Calaveras Twp 5	57	219
---	Calaveras Twp 5	57	226
---	Calaveras Twp 5	57	235
---	Calaveras Twp 5	57	236
---	Calaveras Twp 5	57	245
---	Calaveras Twp 5	57	251
---	Calaveras Twp 5	57	254
---	Calaveras Twp 5	57	255
---	Calaveras Twp 5	57	256
---	Calaveras Twp 10	57	259
---	Calaveras Twp 10	57	270
---	Calaveras Twp 10	57	272
---	Calaveras Twp 10	57	273
---	Calaveras Twp 10	57	276
---	Calaveras Twp 8	57	93
---	El Dorado Salmon Hills	581	059
---	El Dorado Salmon Falls	581	064
---	El Dorado Kelsey	581	141
---	El Dorado Casumnes	581	176
---	El Dorado Mountain	581	178
---	El Dorado Georgetown	58	755
---	El Dorado Georgetown	58	756
---	El Dorado Diamond	58	794
---	El Dorado Diamond	58	806
---	El Dorado Mud Springs	58	952

SANG

Name	County Locale	Roll	Page
---	El Dorado Mud Springs	58	958
---	Mariposa Twp 3	60	546
---	Mariposa Twp 3	60	551
---	Mariposa Twp 3	60	553
---	Mariposa Twp 3	60	560
---	Mariposa Twp 3	60	563
---	Mariposa Twp 3	60	564
---	Mariposa Twp 3	60	572
---	Mariposa Twp 3	60	576
---	Mariposa Twp 3	60	590
---	Mariposa Twp 3	60	609
---	Mariposa Twp 1	60	641
---	Mariposa Twp 1	60	659
---	Mariposa Twp 1	60	661
---	Mariposa Coulterville	60	687
---	Monterey Monterey	60	965
---	Nevada Grass Valley	61	230
---	Nevada Grass Valley	61	234
---	Nevada Nevada	61	300
---	Nevada Washington	61	341
---	Nevada Eureka	61	385
---	Nevada Rough &	61	423
---	Nevada Rough &	61	431
---	Nevada Bridgeport	61	462
---	Nevada Bridgeport	61	485
---	Placer Auburn	62	573
---	Placer Secret R	62	622
---	Placer Rattle Snake	62	627
---	Placer Horseshoe	62	650
---	Placer Virginia	62	671
---	Placer Illinois	62	745
---	Placer Illinois	62	746
---	Placer Illinois	62	753
---	Placer Forest H	62	772
---	Sacramento Centre	63	182
---	Sacramento Mississipi	63	186
---	Sacramento Mississipi	63	188
---	Sacramento Granite	63	231
---	Sacramento Ward 3	63	491
---	Sacramento Ward 4	63	609
---	Sacramento Ward 1	63	68
---	Sacramento Ward 1	63	69
---	Sacramento Ward 1	63	71
---	San Francisco San Francisco 4	681	195
---	San Francisco San Francisco 2	67	754
---	Shasta Horsetown	66	705
---	Shasta Horsetown	66	709
---	Shasta French G	66	712
---	Sierra Downieville	661	009
---	Sierra Twp 5	66	932
---	Siskiyou Klamath	69	90
---	Tehama Tehama	70	944
---	Trinity Mouth Ca	701	018
---	Tuolumne Big Oak	71	149
---	Tuolumne Don Pedro	71	163
---	Tuolumne Jacksonville	71	166
---	Tuolumne Jacksonville	71	167
---	Tuolumne Jamestown	71	433
---	Tuolumne Jamestown	71	439
---	Tuolumne Jamestown	71	446
---	Tuolumne Twp 1	71	475
---	Tuolumne Twp 1	71	478
---	Tuolumne Twp 5	71	509
---	Tuolumne Twp 5	71	522
---	Tuolumne Twp 6	71	537
---	Yuba Long Bar	72	753
---	Yuba Parks Ba	72	779
---	Yuba Fosters	72	843
---	Yuba Linda	72	990
---*	Alameda Oakland	55	63
---*	El Dorado Casumnes	581	176
---*	El Dorado Georgetown	58	700
---*	El Dorado Georgetown	58	705
---*	Nevada Nevada	61	303
---*	Nevada Nevada	61	304
---*	Siskiyou Klamath	69	90
Ah	Sacramento Mississipi	63	186
Ah	Tuolumne Twp 4	71	149
Chan	Nevada Grass Valley	61	234
Chow	Nevada Grass Valley	61	234
Chow	Nevada Nevada	61	309
Fee	Nevada Grass Valley	61	234
Gee	Nevada Rough &	61	425
High	Mariposa Twp 3	60	620
Hoy	Yuba Rose Bar	72	800
John	Contra Costa Twp 1	57	494
Kee	Nevada Bridgeport	61	466
L H	Nevada Nevada	61	242
Lan	Nevada Grass Valley	61	234
Led	Mariposa Twp 3	60	619
Ling	Mariposa Twp 3	60	613
Lup	Butte Hamilton	56	529
Martin	Yuba Marysville	72	872
Mee	San Francisco San Francisco 4	681	204
Mu	San Francisco San Francisco 4	681	204

SANG

Name	County Locale	Roll	Page
Sea	Stanislaus Branch	70	714
See	Mariposa Twp 3	60	613
See	Nevada Grass Valley	61	234
Son	Nevada Bridgeport	61	492
Sup*	Butte Hamilton	56	529
Thomas*	Amador Twp 4	55	234
Tok	Sacramento Ward 3	63	492
Wah	Tuolumne Twp 5	71	510
Wang	Yuba Marysville	72	895
Weng*	Mariposa Twp 1	60	641
Wing	Mariposa Twp 1	60	641
Wing	Sacramento Ward 4	63	610
Wong	Mariposa Twp 1	60	641
Yow	Yuba Marysville	72	921
Yoy*	Tuolumne Twp 5	71	523

SANGACT

| John | Tuolumne Columbia | 71 | 325 |

SANGAET

| John | Tuolumne Twp 2 | 71 | 325 |

SANGAMATI

| Santela* | Calaveras Twp 4 | 57 | 340 |

SANGAMETTIS

| John* | Calaveras Twp 5 | 57 | 216 |

SANGAMITA

| Benja* | Calaveras Twp 4 | 57 | 340 |

SANGANENETTI

| John | Calaveras Twp 5 | 57 | 221 |

SANGANES

| Rosala | Amador Twp 5 | 55 | 332 |

SANGANETTA

| B | Nevada Nevada | 61 | 276 |

SANGAR

| J J | Butte Oregon | 56 | 618 |

SANGARPIMO

| Juan | Mariposa Twp 3 | 60 | 570 |

SANGDEN

| Richd* | Napa Clear Lake | 61 | 134 |

SANGDIN

| Richd | Napa Clear Lake | 61 | 134 |

SANGDON

| Giles | Placer Iona Hills | 62 | 880 |
| Richd* | Napa Clear Lake | 61 | 134 |

SANGE

| --- | Calaveras Twp 8 | 57 | 61 |

SANGEATE

| James* | Tuolumne Twp 1 | 71 | 210 |

SANGEATI

| James | Tuolumne Sonora | 71 | 210 |

SANGENETTI

| J* | Tulara Big Oak | 71 | 153 |

SANGENFRINID

| Juan* | Mariposa Twp 3 | 60 | 570 |

SANGER

Name	County Locale	Roll	Page
Antonio	San Francisco San Francisco 3	67	83
Frederick*	Sacramento Franklin	63	309
Geo	Amador Twp 3	55	380
Josiah*	Placer Virginia	62	669
M*	Sacramento Ward 3	63	425
S M	Butte Chico	56	539

SANGERBURGER

| F | Los Angeles Tejon | 59 | 526 |

SANGERS

| Lewis | Yolo Cache Crk | 72 | 618 |

SANGFORD

| Frances | Sierra Gibsonville | 66 | 855 |
| Henry | Butte Bidwell | 56 | 716 |

SANGGLIN

| Thomas | Placer Iona Hills | 62 | 883 |

SANGHLIN

| Patrick M | San Francisco San Francisco 11 | | 95 |
| | | 67 | |

SANGHTER

| Henry* | Placer Goods | 62 | 696 |

SANGINNETTIS

| John* | Calaveras Twp 5 | 57 | 216 |

SANGLEY

| Danl | Butte Bidwell | 56 | 712 |

SANGMASTER

| Fred | Contra Costa Twp 1 | 57 | 500 |

SANGMENTER

| Benja* | Calaveras Twp 4 | 57 | 340 |

SANGNUTH

| Ahona* | Mariposa Coulterville | 60 | 674 |

SANGO

| John | Tuolumne Montezuma | 71 | 513 |

SANGORA

| J | San Joaquin Stockton | 641 | 087 |

SANGRE

| --- | Mendocino Twp 1 | 60 | 889 |

SANGSTER

| J | Marin Point Re | 60 | 729 |

SANGTVAE

| --- | Fresno Twp 1 | 59 | 28 |

SANGU

| John* | Calaveras Twp 5 | 57 | 221 |

Name	County Locale	M653 Roll Page
SANGUENATI		
Santela*	Calaveras Twp 4	57 340
Santelie*	Calaveras Twp 4	57 340
SANGUENETTI		
John B	Calaveras Twp 5	57 216
SANGUINETTE		
John B	Calaveras Twp 5	57 216
SANGUINETTIS		
John	Calaveras Twp 5	57 216
SANGUIT		
D*	Calaveras Twp 9	57 395
SANGUMNETTI		
John*	Calaveras Twp 5	57 221
SANGUNANETTI		
John*	Calaveras Twp 5	57 221
SANGUNEOTTIS		
Francisco	Calaveras Twp 5	57 216
SANGUNNETIS		
John*	Calaveras Twp 5	57 221
SANGUNTH		
Ahona	Mariposa Coulterville	60 674
SANGURATE		
Joseph	San Francisco San Francisco 2	67 686
SANGURPENIR		
Juan*	Mariposa Twp 3	60 570
SANGURPINIO		
Juan*	Mariposa Twp 3	60 570
SANGURSSENIO		
Juan	Mariposa Twp 3	60 570
SANGUS		
Lewis*	Yolo Cache	72 618
SANGUSTA		
Juan	Fresno Twp 1	59 76
Paschal	Fresno Twp 1	59 76
SANGY		
Le	Mariposa Twp 3	60 608
SANHEZ		
Marina*	Yuba Marysville	72 921
SANHOSEA		
Theo	Solano Montezuma	69 375
SANI		
---	Amador Twp 5	55 362
---	Calaveras Twp 5	57 232
---	Calaveras Twp 5	57 244
---	Calaveras Twp 5	57 249
---	Calaveras Twp 5	57 251
---	Calaveras Twp 10	57 268
---*	Amador Twp 5	55 349
Chung*	Placer Michigan	62 821
SANIAGO		
---	Tulara Twp 3	71 50
SANIELS		
Richard	Butte Bidwell	56 720
SANIFESON		
Camilla B*	Yuba Marysville	72 912
SANIGAN		
Wm	Butte Mountain	56 740
SANIK		
John	El Dorado Mud Springs	58 961
SANILEY		
James	El Dorado Mud Springs	58 999
SANINGLE		
Thomas*	El Dorado Salmon Falls	581050
SANIO		
Jesus	Yuba Marysville	72 938
SANIPE		
George	Solano Fremont	69 382
SANIPS		
Howd	Butte Eureka	56 651
SANISANO		
Gabriel*	Santa Clara Almaden	65 269
SANITELLS		
M A	Nevada Rough &	61 427
SANK		
---	Calaveras Twp 4	57 299
---	Calaveras Twp 4	57 300
At	Mariposa Twp 3	60 620
S M*	Nevada Grass Valley	61 161
SANKE		
Charles	Siskiyou Callahan	69 18
SANKEY		
Maurice*	Plumas Meadow Valley	62 933
SANKMAN		
Joel*	Los Angeles Tejon	59 528
SANKS		
F L	Santa Clara Gilroy	65 242
Isaac	Nevada Grass Valley	61 236
J	Nevada Grass Valley	61 236
SANKTON		
Jim	Santa Clara Fremont	65 425
SANKWIN		
M*	San Mateo Twp 3	65 109
SANL		
J B*	Sacramento Franklin	63 326
SANLANDIE		
Jennie	Los Angeles Los Angeles	59 348

Name	County Locale	M653 Roll Page
SANLES		
Peter	San Francisco San Francisco 2	67 723
SANLETT		
John	El Dorado Mud Springs	581000
SANLEY		
Catharine*	Yuba Marysville	72 953
SANLLEY		
John	Yolo Washington	72 564
SANLORN		
Henry	Yolo New York	72 720
Henry*	Yuba Parks Ba	72 774
SANLSBERY		
J	Merced Twp 1	60 914
SANMARTINE		
H*	El Dorado Diamond	58 796
SANN		
---	Butte Eureka	56 649
---	Calaveras Twp 6	57 181
---	Mariposa Twp 3	60 572
---	Sacramento Ward 1	63 58
---	Shasta Shasta	66 670
---	Tuolumne Twp 1	71 477
---*	Mariposa Twp 3	60 608
---*	Yolo No E Twp	72 676
Ah	Butte Eureka	56 649
R	Placer Dutch Fl	62 719
SANNANING		
James	Yuba Marysville	72 962
SANNDERS		
Jas M*	Napa Napa	61 99
Math	San Francisco San Francisco 1	68 838
W D*	Napa Napa	61 99
SANNEBAUM		
P*	San Francisco San Francisco 10	266 67
SANNICHSON		
Jno B	Klamath Klamath	59 224
SANNS		
John*	Yuba Fosters	72 832
SANNY		
James*	San Francisco San Francisco 9	68 954
SANO ANA		
---	Fresno Twp 2	59 73
SANO		
Anapema	Tuolumne Twp 5	71 495
Anapoma	Tuolumne Chinese	71 495
Paneus	El Dorado Placerville	58 917
SANOAGAN		
Z	El Dorado Mud Springs	58 994
SANOMA		
---	Mendocino Round Va	60 884
SANONETTE		
Nass*	Sacramento American	63 166
SANONG		
---	El Dorado Eldorado	58 940
SANOR		
---	Stanislaus Branch	70 702
Michael	Santa Clara Santa Clara	65 477
SANOS		
M A	Sacramento Ward 1	63 18
M F*	Sacramento Ward 1	63 18
SANOTE		
P	Nevada Grass Valley	61 226
SANPEN		
Benja C	Calaveras Twp 5	57 208
SANPKINS		
Charles H*	Yuba Marysville	72 854
SANQUIPINIO		
Juan	Mariposa Twp 3	60 570
SANQUODO		
---	Fresno Twp 2	59 102
SANRENCE		
A	Nevada Eureka	61 381
SANRIG		
Henry*	San Francisco San Francisco 2	67 683
SANS		
O*	Calaveras Twp 9	57 376
Seen	Nevada Rough &	61 436
SANSBERGER		
Charles	San Francisco San Francisco 3	67 78
W	San Francisco San Francisco 1	68 927
SANSBERRY		
Jno	Mendocino Ukiah	60 805
Jno R	Mendocino Ukiah	60 805
John B	Sonoma Cloverdale	69 686
W H	Sonoma Cloverdale	69 686
SANSBUERGER		
Charles	San Francisco San Francisco 3	67 78
SANSBURY		
L	El Dorado Mud Springs	58 973
SANSDALE		
Alfred*	Monterey Alisal	601044
SANSDON		
Robt	Sonoma Petaluma	69 552
SANSELL		
Thos	Sonoma Bodega	69 522

Name	County Locale	M653 Roll Page
SANSEVA		
Nicholas	Santa Clara Fremont	65 435
SANSEVAINE		
B	San Francisco San Francisco 10	320 67
Jeanne	Los Angeles Los Angeles	59 376
Louis	Los Angeles Los Angeles	59 375
SANSFIELD		
George*	Sacramento Ward 1	63 104
Jos	San Francisco San Francisco 6	67 401
SANSING		
G J	Nevada Eureka	61 381
J A	Nevada Eureka	61 379
J V	Nevada Eureka	61 379
Jas R*	Butte Oregon	56 634
SANSMAN		
A R*	San Francisco San Francisco 3	67 77
Geo B*	Calaveras Twp 5	57 190
Saml W	Sacramento San Joaquin	63 361
SANSOLA		
Augusta*	Amador Twp 5	55 339
SANSOME		
Alexander	Sonoma Santa Rosa	69 427
Elizabeth	Sonoma Santa Rosa	69 426
SANSON		
---	Mariposa Twp 3	60 545
J W	Mariposa Twp 3	60 556
Wm	Tehama Tehama	70 939
SANSONI		
Anthony J	Yuba Marysville	72 859
Anthony J	Yuba Marysville	72 860
SANSSKINS		
Charles H*	Yuba Marysville	72 854
SANT		
Amos*	Calaveras Twp 5	57 172
Casper	Shasta French G	66 719
SANTA ANNA		
---	Fresno Twp 2	59 62
---	Fresno Twp 2	59 72
---	Santa Cruz Santa Cruz	66 623
---*	Mendocino Big Rock	60 876
SANTA CRUZ		
Jose	Monterey San Juan	60 985
SANTA ROSA		
---	Mendocino Calpella	60 823
SANTA		
---	Marin Tomales	60 776
Anna	San Diego San Diego	64 775
Rafalla	San Bernardino Santa Barbara	64 187
Rosa*	Mendocino Calpella	60 823
SANTAANNA		
---	Mariposa Twp 1	60 653
SANTAGO		
---	Fresno Twp 3	59 38
SANTALMER		
Henry*	Mariposa Twp 1	60 623
SANTALNER		
Henry	Mariposa Twp 1	60 623
SANTALWER		
Henry*	Mariposa Twp 1	60 623
SANTAMONTE		
John	Calaveras Twp 4	57 340
SANTAMONTI		
John*	Calaveras Twp 4	57 340
SANTANA		
Domingo	Santa Clara Almaden	65 267
Francisco	Amador Twp 2	55 301
Jose Gregerio	Marin Cortemad	60 786
Jose Gregorio	Marin Cortemad	60 786
Juan	Tuolumne Green Springs	71 527
Tomas	Tuolumne Chinese	71 499
SANTANAS		
Manuela	San Francisco San Francisco 2	67 683
SANTANDEL		
Manuel	San Francisco San Francisco 1	68 811
SANTANNA		
J	El Dorado Placerville	58 861
SANTAS		
Manuel*	San Francisco San Francisco 1	68 857
SANTAUDER		
Manuel	San Francisco San Francisco 1	68 811
SANTE		
James	El Dorado Georgetown	58 751
Thomas	El Dorado Coloma	581107
SANTEAGO		
James	Marin Point Re	60 731
SANTEANES		
Francisco*	Monterey San Juan	601001
SANTELLS		
Mary F*	Nevada Rough &	61 427
SANTEN		
Elijah*	Sierra Downieville	66 976
SANTER		
Antone	Sierra Pine Grove	66 822
Frederck*	Sierra Pine Grove	66 822
Fredreck*	Sierra Pine Grove	66 822

Name	County Locale	M653 Roll	Page
SANTER			
Margaret*	Napa Hot Springs	61	5
SANTERARO			
Antonio	Sacramento Ward 1	63	47
SANTERN			
John	Shasta Horsetown	66	688
SANTERRE			
John	Yolo Slate Ra	72	692
John	Yuba Slate Ro	72	692
SANTES			
Dolores*	Los Angeles Los Angeles	59	499
SANTESAN			
Louisa*	Santa Clara Alviso	65	415
SANTESRUASSER			
Ftitz*	Contra Costa Twp 1	57	527
SANTETTIAN			
Simon	Calaveras Twp 10	57	281
SANTEY			
Catharine	Yuba Marysville	72	953
Catherine	Yuba Marysville	72	909
Catherine	Yuba Marysville	72	953
Mary	Yuba Marysville	72	953
SANTHER			
S P	Santa Clara Santa Clara	65	509
SANTHEZ			
Marry	Sacramento Ward 1	63	104
Mary	Sacramento Ward 1	63	104
SANTHON			
John	Calaveras Twp 8	57	87
SANTIAGO			
---	Fresno Twp 2	59	101
---	Fresno Twp 2	59	107
---	Los Angeles Los Angeles	59	380
---	Los Angeles Los Angeles	59	388
---	Los Angeles Los Angeles	59	402
---	Los Angeles Los Angeles	59	404
---	Los Angeles San Gabriel	59	413
---	Los Angeles Los Nieto	59	439
---	Los Angeles Tejon	59	529
---	San Bernardino Santa Barbara	64	160
---	San Diego Temecula	64	788
---	San Diego Temecula	64	791
---	San Diego Temecula	64	793
---	San Diego Agua Caliente	64	835
---	San Diego Agua Caliente	64	859
---	Tulara Twp 3	71	44
---	Tulara Keeneysburg	71	50
---	Tulara Twp 3	71	63
---	Tulara Twp 3	71	66
---	Tulara Twp 3	71	67
---	Tulara Twp 3	71	70
---	Tulara Twp 3	71	72
---	Yolo Washington	72	605
---*	Tulara Sinks Te	71	44
Gregorio	Los Angeles San Juan	59	465
Nich	Alameda Brooklyn	55	139
R	El Dorado Diamond	58	814
SANTIANA			
Anselmo	Tuolumne Twp 2	71	284
Ansilmo	Tuolumne Twp 2	71	284
SANTIEN			
Baptiste	Yuba Parke Ba	72	782
SANTILLIAN			
Simon	Calaveras Twp 10	57	281
SANTIN			
Elijah*	Sierra Downieville	66	976
SANTING			
F	Shasta Millvill	66	754
SANTINIE			
Catharine	San Francisco San Francisco 10	67	324
SANTIS			
Angelo	Los Angeles Los Angeles	59	509
Dolores*	Los Angeles Los Angeles	59	499
Doloris	Los Angeles Los Angeles	59	499
SANTLY			
Danl*	San Francisco San Francisco 9	68	1073
SANTMAN			
C	San Francisco San Francisco 2	67	676
SANTMAREAH			
Arriele*	Yolo Cache Crk	72	665
SANTO VASSAN			
E*	San Francisco San Francisco 2	67	768
SANTO			
---	Butte Chico	56	566
---	Mariposa Twp 3	60	611
Espirita	Los Angeles Los Angeles	59	317
Maria	Mariposa Twp 3	60	611
Theodore	Amador Twp 1	55	495
SANTOM			
J B*	Trinity Weaverville	70	1051
SANTOME			
Elizabeth	Sonoma Santa Rosa	69	426
SANTOMONTI			
John	Calaveras Twp 4	57	340
SANTON			
Elijah	Sierra Downieville	66	976
SANTON			
J T	Trinity Lewiston	70	953
SANTOON			
Edward	Alameda Brooklyn	55	199
SANTORSUN			
---	San Diego Agua Caliente	64	861
SANTOS			
---	Monterey San Juan	60	1000
---	Monterey Monterey	60	954
Guadalupe	San Francisco 8	68	1282
Jose	Monterey Monterey	60	925
Jose	San Diego Temecula	64	797
Jose	San Diego Agua Caliente	64	822
Jose	San Diego Agua Caliente	64	824
Jose	San Diego Agua Caliente	64	833
Jose	San Diego Agua Caliente	64	842
Jose Los	Contra Costa Twp 3	57	615
Jose Los*	Contra Costa Twp 1	57	495
Juan	San Francisco San Francisco 2	67	694
Lanrita	Tuolumne Twp 4	71	175
Laurla	Tuolumne Garrote	71	175
Pasquala	Tuolumne Montezuma	71	504
Quirina	San Francisco San Francisco 2	67	797
Quivera	San Francisco San Francisco 2	67	797
T	Merced Twp 2	60	919
Victimoiro	San Francisco San Francisco 2	67	702
SANTRY			
Andrew	San Francisco San Francisco 11	67	107
SANTSGIRN			
D	Nevada Nevada	61	262
SANTSGIVER			
D*	Nevada Nevada	61	262
SANTUAN			
Luis	Santa Clara Alviso	65	415
SANTUS			
G L	Yolo Cache	72	626
SANTY			
S H	Nevada Grass Valley	61	222
SANTZ			
Antonio	San Francisco San Francisco 3	67	41
SANU			
---	Sacramento Ward 1	63	40
SANUE			
---	Fresno Twp 1	59	28
SANVEDRIA			
Mariana	San Francisco San Francisco 2	67	699
SANWHAN			
---	San Mateo Twp 2	65	112
SANWORD			
F W	Tuolumne Twp 4	71	166
SANY			
---	Amador Twp 2	55	281
---	Amador Twp 2	55	294
---	Calaveras Twp 5	57	219
---	Calaveras Twp 5	57	254
---	Calaveras Twp 5	57	255
---	Calaveras Twp 5	57	256
---	Calaveras Twp 10	57	270
---	Calaveras Twp 10	57	272
---	Calaveras Twp 10	57	276
---	Mariposa Twp 3	60	609
---	Placer Rattle Snake	62	625
---	Placer Rattle Snake	62	627
John L*	Placer Dutch Fl	62	711
SANYDER			
M W	Nevada Nevada	61	271
SANYER			
---	Tulara Twp 1	71	122
SANYON			
H*	El Dorado Georgetown	58	754
N*	El Dorado Georgetown	58	754
SANZ			
Chas*	Sacramento Brighton	63	199
SANZBERGER			
Lena	San Francisco San Francisco 7	68	1366
SANZEHES			
Josefino*	Los Angeles Los Angeles	59	499
SANZIHIS			
Josifine	Los Angeles Los Angeles	59	499
SAOLT			
Wm*	Nevada Nevada	61	323
SAORGEONI			
Antoine*	Calaveras Twp 5	57	232
SAORGRONI			
Antoine*	Calaveras Twp 5	57	232
SAORYEONI			
Antoine*	Calaveras Twp 5	57	232
SAP SEE			
---	Sacramento Ward 1	63	66
SAP			
---	Amador Twp 5	55	348
---	Butte Kimshaw	56	586
---	Butte Kimshaw	56	604
SAP			
---	Butte Kimshaw	56	605
---	Butte Bidwell	56	728
---	Mariposa Twp 1	60	664
---	Mariposa Twp 1	60	669
---	Sacramento Granite	63	259
---	Sacramento Ward 1	63	68
---	Tuolumne Twp 6	71	531
Ah	Butte Bidwell	56	728
Chung	Sacramento Ward 3	63	492
Saf	El Dorado Georgetown	58	756
Sam*	Mariposa Twp 1	60	641
See	Sacramento Ward 1	63	66
Sher*	Mariposa Twp 1	60	641
Sun	Butte Ophir	56	806
Wee	Mariposa Twp 3	60	641
Wer	Mariposa Twp 1	60	641
SAPADA			
Pean	Santa Clara San Jose	65	330
SAPANK			
Joseph*	Calaveras Twp 4	57	340
SAPARGA			
Anton	Tuolumne Twp 3	71	469
SAPAT			
---	Sacramento Ward 1	63	52
SAPATA			
Magel	Tuolumne Jamestown	71	447
SAPATERO			
Jose	Los Angeles Tejon	59	532
SAPAUK			
Joseph*	Calaveras Twp 4	57	340
SAPE			
---*	Marin Cortemad	60	787
SAPEDA			
Antonio	Los Angeles San Juan	59	475
SAPER			
Jacob*	Amador Twp 4	55	237
SAPFGER			
Wm A	San Francisco San Francisco 10	67	221
SAPHAIN			
N*	Sacramento American	63	172
SAPHAR			
Jacob	Santa Cruz Santa Cruz	66	633
SAPHARN			
N*	Sacramento American	63	172
SAPHENS			
Thomas	Sierra Twp 7	66	900
SAPI			
---	Nevada Washington	61	341
SAPIA			
Nabor	San Luis Obispo San Luis Obispo	65	37
Remonda*	Santa Cruz Watsonville	66	538
SAPIAS			
Franciser	Amador Twp 5	55	332
SAPIDGE			
W F*	San Francisco San Francisco 9	68	1073
SAPIER			
Cecilia	Yuba Marysville	72	897
Felix	Yolo Slate Ra	72	706
SAPILL			
Charles D	Los Angeles Los Angeles	59	501
Charlis D	Los Angeles Los Angeles	59	501
SAPIN			
Jose	Santa Cruz Soguel	66	587
SAPINGTON			
J L	Placer Nicolaus	62	691
SAPIRS			
Cecilia*	Yuba Marysville	72	897
SAPITZ			
---	Tulara Twp 2	71	4
SAPLAZ			
Julian	Placer Forest H	62	791
SAPLETZ			
Lewis	San Francisco San Francisco 10	67	193
SAPOINT			
L*	Sacramento Granite	63	237
SAPOLGARA			
Joshua	Tuolumne Jamestown	71	445
SAPP			
B	Colusa Grand Island	57	470
B F	Nevada Nevada	61	281
John	Mendocino Calpella	60	812
SAPPAN			
P K	Trinity McGillev	70	1021
SAPPIN			
William	Yuba Marysville	72	955
SAPPING			
Benjamin*	Yuba Bear Rvr	72	1004
SAPPINGTON			
John	Solano Suisan	69	240
SAPRIS			
Suterio	Los Angeles Los Angeles	59	489
SAPTANTE			
Dennis	Sierra La Porte	66	768

Name	County Locale	M653 RollPage
SAPTON		
Harinah	El Dorado Georgetown	58 707
SAPUL		
John*	Stanislaus Branch	70 699
SAPULVRY		
Mary*	Marin San Rafael	60 759
SAPUS		
---*	Del Norte Klamath	58 657
SAR		
---	Calaveras Twp 5	57 205
---	Calaveras Twp 5	57 226
---	Calaveras Twp 4	57 300
---	Calaveras Twp 4	57 327
---	Tuolumne Chinese	71 523
---*	El Dorado Diamond	58 807
Ger	El Dorado Georgetown	58 684
SAR'K E		
---*	Mariposa Twp 3	60 607
SARA COMA		
---	Mendocino Calpella	60 825
SARA PINATO		
---	San Mateo Twp 2	65 127
SARA		
---	Sacramento Natonia	63 286
Bicente*	Los Angeles Los Nieto	59 436
Francis	San Francisco San Francisco 4 681171
Martines	Tulara Sinks Te	71 43
SARABELDA		
Davis*	Calaveras Twp 8	57 103
SARABY		
Samuel	Placer Forest H	62 806
SARACCO		
Jas*	Amador Twp 3	55 384
SARAGE		
Ann*	Nevada Grass Valley	61 204
J*	Nevada Grass Valley	61 204
SARAGGINS		
Wm*	Nevada Nevada	61 330
SARAGOSA		
Francisco	Los Angeles Los Angeles	59 371
Jesus	Los Angeles San Juan	59 463
SARAH C		
---	San Francisco San Francisco 10 199 67
SARAH		
---	Fresno Twp 2	59 63
---	San Francisco San Francisco 1 68 849
---	Trinity Weaverville	701075
Palonia	Alameda Oakland	55 7
SARAMO		
Juan	Santa Cruz Santa Cruz	66 625
SARAN		
Antonio	Contra Costa Twp 1	57 502
John	Calaveras Twp 4	57 340
SARANA		
Valen	Los Angeles Los Angeles	59 346
SARANO		
Loranzo	Tuolumne Jamestown	71 424
Lorenzo	Tuolumne Twp 3	71 424
SARANTON		
J S*	Shasta Shasta	66 654
SARAR		
John*	San Francisco San Francisco 2 67 696
SARASE		
W	Nevada Grass Valley	61 226
SARASON		
J	Yuba New York	72 725
L	Yuba New York	72 725
SARASTA		
---	Tulara Twp 2	71 31
SARAVOCIA		
V	Amador Twp 1	55 468
SARAY		
---	Mendocino Calpella	60 828
SARBINA		
Bristams	Yolo Washington	72 573
SARBONA		
Bustanis	Yolo Washington	72 573
SARBOTT		
James*	Santa Cruz Pajaro	66 577
SARCESO		
---	Sierra Twp 7	66 898
SARCHEN		
Peter	Mariposa Twp 3	60 610
SARCHER		
Eliah	Yuba Marysville	72 934
SARCHET		
J B	Alameda Brooklyn	55 199
SARCO		
A	Amador Twp 3	55 394
SARD		
Porter*	Tulara Twp 2	71 27
SARDE		
---	Placer Rattle Snake	62 627
James*	Tulara Twp 2	71 25
SARDID		
John	Tulara Visalia	71 28

Name	County Locale	M653 RollPage
SARDNER		
Ande*	Calaveras Twp 8	57 93
Saml	Sacramento Sutter	63 305
SARDO		
Ure	Sierra Downieville	661012
SARE CHUM		
---	Sacramento Ward 1	63 69
SARE		
Chinn*	Sacramento Ward 1	63 69
Chum*	Sacramento Ward 1	63 69
SAREBRIN		
Daniel*	Alameda Brooklyn	55 168
SARELL		
C P	San Francisco San Francisco 9 681098
SAREN		
Francisco	Calaveras Twp 4	57 331
SARENX		
Lewis	Alameda Brooklyn	55 78
SARERAS		
---	Marin San Rafael	60 772
SARESAS		
---	Marin San Rafael	60 772
SARESOLEE		
Augusta	Amador Twp 5	55 339
SARETE		
Joseph	Amador Twp 4	55 131
SARETERO		
F	Merced Twp 1	60 909
SARETSON		
Nathan H	Solano Benecia	69 301
SAREVAN		
Felix	Alameda Brooklyn	55 91
SARFT		
S*	Nevada Eureka	61 367
SARG		
W*	San Francisco San Francisco 9 681081
SARGANT		
A A	Nevada Nevada	61 329
B	San Francisco San Francisco 4 681229
E F	Tehama Cottonwoood	70 898
John	Tuolumne Twp 2	71 284
P	Nevada Eureka	61 362
SARGARD		
Peter	Amador Twp 4	55 243
SARGARET		
John	Tuolumne Twp 2	71 284
SARGEANT		
Edward	Calaveras Twp 6	57 147
Ezra P	Colusa Monroeville	57 457
Geo	Trinity Indian C	70 988
Geo W	Mendocino Little L	60 836
J M	Trinity Trinity	70 974
Robt	Trinity Mouth Ca	701013
SARGENT		
A A*	Nevada Nevada	61 329
A I	Amador Twp 5	55 343
A J	Amador Twp 1	55 495
A L	Santa Clara Santa Clara	65 521
A*	Nevada Bridgeport	61 501
Asa M	Fresno Twp 2	59 114
B F	San Francisco San Francisco 3 67 77
Bradford V	Monterey Monterey	60 953
E F	San Francisco San Francisco 5 67 551
Enos	Sacramento Sutter	63 300
F L	Sacramento Ward 1	63 80
F S	Sacramento Ward 3	63 435
F S	Sacramento Ward 1	63 80
G T	Nevada Nevada	61 329
Geo W	San Francisco San Francisco 12 391 67
H S	San Joaquin Stockton	641054
Henry	Sonoma Healdsbu	69 471
Horace	Nevada Rough &	61 427
J	Tuolumne Twp 4	71 172
J R	Tuolumne Twp 3	71 459
James	Santa Clara Gilroy	65 235
Jane	Amador Twp 5	55 278
John	Placer Michigan	62 821
John*	Plumas Quincy	62 960
Joshua C	Yuba Bear Rvr	721013
Phillip	Calaveras Twp 10	57 276
R C	San Joaquin Elkhorn	64 998
R F	San Francisco San Francisco 3 67 77
R K	Sacramento Ward 4	63 510
S	El Dorado Diamond	58 810
Taylor	Amador Twp 3	55 409
Timothy	San Francisco San Francisco 11 152 67
Violim*	Amador Twp 3	55 407
Violine*	Amador Twp 3	55 407
Violirn*	Amador Twp 3	55 407
William	Plumas Quincy	621004
William	Solano Vallejo	69 265
SARGERINT		
C F	Siskiyou Scott Va	69 61
SARGERNT		
C F	Siskiyou Scott Va	69 61

Name	County Locale	M653 RollPage
SARGERONT		
C F	Siskiyou Scott Va	69 61
SARGOMATES		
S	Amador Twp 3	55 394
SARGOMORCEUN		
John	Calaveras Twp 5	57 228
SARGOVIA		
Manuel*	Calaveras Twp 5	57 203
SARGT		
S*	Nevada Eureka	61 367
SARGU		
John*	Calaveras Twp 5	57 221
SARGUIT		
D*	Calaveras Twp 9	57 395
SARH		
---	Calaveras Twp 4	57 322
SARHAWK		
Stephen	Sierra Downieville	661006
SARIA		
Jose*	Merced Twp 1	60 906
Susan	Calaveras Twp 9	57 364
Tuson	Calaveras Twp 9	57 364
SARICHDER		
Henry	Amador Twp 1	55 461
SARICHELER		
Henry	Amador Twp 1	55 461
SARIDER		
Eazbulon*	Los Angeles Los Angeles	59 492
SARIE		
Susan	Calaveras Twp 9	57 364
SARIEN		
Jesus	Calaveras Twp 5	57 198
SARIERS		
G*	El Dorado Placerville	58 850
SARIGAN		
Mike*	Sacramento Mississipi	63 184
SARILLE		
Susan	Solano Fairfield	69 197
SARINGTON		
William*	Placer Michigan	62 823
SARIRN		
Jesus	Calaveras Twp 5	57 198
SARITAS		
Manuel*	San Francisco San Francisco 1 68 857
SARK		
---	Sacramento Ward 1	63 68
SARKET		
C C	San Francisco San Francisco 2 67 603
SARKIN		
Mary	San Francisco San Francisco 6 67 455
Michael	Contra Costa Twp 1	57 502
SARLE		
Jno	Alameda Oakland	55 42
R A*	Alameda Brooklyn	55 127
SARLER		
Geo*	Butte Hamilton	56 524
SARLES		
M A	Solano Benecia	69 310
P	San Joaquin Stockton	641088
SARLINA		
Joseph	Calaveras Twp 5	57 226
SARLING		
Rumsey	Sierra Whiskey	66 846
SARLINN		
Joseph	Calaveras Twp 5	57 226
SARLIS		
Alvino	Calaveras Twp 7	57 30
M A	Solano Benecia	69 310
SARLLIT		
Alphonse	Alameda Brooklyn	55 98
SARLO		
Martinan*	Calaveras Twp 5	57 211
SARM		
---	El Dorado Mountain	581188
SARMIEN		
---	Fresno Twp 2	59 52
SARN		
---	Calaveras Twp 10	57 284
---	El Dorado Mountain	581188
---*	Yuba Bear Rvr	721014
Ah	Tuolumne Twp 4	71 182
Sing*	Mariposa Twp 3	60 563
SARNE		
James B	Alameda Brooklyn	55 80
SARNIS		
Jose	Los Angeles Los Angeles	59 497
SARNO		
---	San Joaquin Stockton	641088
SARNORTEME		
John*	Calaveras Twp 5	57 228
SARO CARJO		
---	Mendocino Calpella	60 825
SARO CAYO		
---	Mendocino Calpella	60 825
SARO		
---	Sierra La Porte	66 774

Name	County Locale	M653 Roll	Page
SAROCCO			
A	Amador Twp 3	55	380
SARONSKY			
Fred*	San Francisco San Francisco 1	68	920
SAROSA			
Francisco	Contra Costa Twp 1	57	495
SARPIE			
Oscar	Alameda Washington	55	214
SARPU			
---	Del Norte Klamath	58	656
SARPUE			
Oscar	Alameda Brooklyn	55	93
SARR			
M	San Francisco San Francisco 5	67	513
SARRAIT			
T S	El Dorado Mud Springs	58	965
SARRASEY			
John*	Sacramento Ward 1	63	39
SARRATE			
Charles	Los Angeles Los Angeles	59	374
Manuel	Tuolumne Twp 4	71	126
SARRELLE			
Albert B*	Calaveras Twp 6	57	148
SARREN			
T	Nevada Grass Valley	61	237
SARRIBER			
J D	Santa Clara San Jose	65	288
SARRIFESON			
Jno*	Sacramento Ward 1	63	114
SARRNAN			
William	San Luis Obispo San Luis Obispo	65	16
SARROAL			
Trinidad*	Sacramento Ward 1	63	99
SARRTELLI			
A W*	Butte Oregon	56	611
SARS			
James*	Sacramento Ward 1	63	84
SARSEOY			
M	Yolo Putah	72	585
SARSFIELD			
C	San Francisco San Francisco 10	67	322
Georg*	Sacramento Ward 1	63	104
Georgna	Sacramento Ward 1	63	104
James	Solano Suisan	69	204
Patrick	Solano Vallejo	69	250
SARSIDNAY			
Jesus*	Merced Twp 1	60	911
SARSIDREAY			
Jesus	Merced Twp 1	60	911
SARSIDRIAY			
Jesus*	Merced Twp 1	60	911
SARSILLE			
Manuel	San Bernardino Santa Inez	64	141
SARSING			
M	Yolo Putah	72	585
SARSON			
J	Sacramento Ward 1	63	67
SARTAIN			
Alfd	Butte Hamilton	56	515
William	San Francisco San Francisco 4	68	1125
SARTAM			
William	San Francisco San Francisco 4	68	1125
SARTELL			
Obed H	Yuba Marysville	72	848
SARTER			
Harden J	Siskiyou Yreka	69	137
J G	Siskiyou Yreka	69	193
SARTERS			
Milome	Tehama Red Bluff	70	930
SARTHANES			
Ealand	San Francisco San Francisco 9	68	1045
SARTIATO			
Lousa*	Tuolumne Twp 1	71	257
SARTIER			
S	Sutter Yuba	70	761
SARTKKKKKKKRY			
Augusti	Santa Clara Fremont	65	439
SARTON			
Joseph	Calaveras Twp 4	57	330
SARTONIS			
Joseph	Calaveras Twp 5	57	142
SARTOR			
Joseph	Yuba Linda Twp	72	981
SARTUTO			
Laura	Tuolumne Twp 1	71	257
SARTWELL			
D S	Del Norte Crescent	58	626
Frederid	Sierra Poker Flats	66	837
Fredred W*	Sierra Poker Flats	66	837
Fredrid W*	Sierra Poker Flats	66	837
Mary	Yuba Marysville	72	862
SARTY			
Moore K*	Calaveras Twp 4	57	340
Moore R*	Calaveras Twp 4	57	340
SARU			
---	Calaveras Twp 5	57	254

Name	County Locale	M653 Roll	Page
SARUN			
John*	Calaveras Twp 4	57	340
SARVERS			
Geo	Siskiyou Cottonwoood	69	102
SARVES			
John A*	Tuolumne Columbia	71	295
SARVILLE			
Wm*	Napa Yount	61	33
SARVIN			
Sylvania	Yuba Marysville	72	931
SARVINIOS			
Margaret	Calaveras Twp 6	57	150
SARVINT			
C	Nevada Nevada	61	287
SARVIS			
Henry*	El Dorado Georgetown	58	704
SARY			
---	Amador Twp 2	55	314
---	Amador Twp 3	55	394
---	Amador Twp 6	55	430
---	Sacramento Granite	63	259
---*	Mariposa Twp 3	60	576
SARYOMOIDENS			
John*	Calaveras Twp 5	57	228
SARYOVIN			
Manuel	Calaveras Twp 5	57	203
SASANIA			
Dominga	Tuolumne Big Oak	71	137
SASAY			
---	Nevada Rough &	61	426
SASCO			
Antonio	Plumas Quincy	62	989
SASH			
John	Contra Costa Twp 1	57	516
SASIEN			
Jesus	Calaveras Twp 5	57	198
SASK			
Louis*	Yuba Marysville	72	900
SASLE			
R A *	Alameda Brooklyn	55	127
SASLEY			
A J*	Napa Yount	61	31
SASMAN			
J	San Francisco San Francisco 5	67	531
SASMICE			
Domiopa	Tuolumne Twp 4	71	137
SASMOZA			
Mathi*	Calaveras Twp 4	57	324
Mattie*	Calaveras Twp 4	57	324
SASN			
---	El Dorado Diamond	58	787
SASNETA			
Jose M	Del Norte Crescent	58	641
SASNTWELL			
G W	Los Angeles Tejon	59	536
SASPIRE			
J	Butte Oro	56	683
SASS			
Henry A	Del Norte Crescent	58	647
SASSAN			
Emanuel	Contra Costa Twp 1	57	536
SASSELLE			
Albert B	Calaveras Twp 5	57	148
SASSELLI			
Joseph	Calaveras Twp 5	57	217
SASSER			
A A *	Nevada Bridgeport	61	487
SASSIDGE			
W F*	San Francisco San Francisco 9	68	1073
SASSMAN			
D*	San Francisco San Francisco 9	68	1071
SASSON			
A*	Nevada Nevada	61	327
SASTAMECO			
Tomas*	Contra Costa Twp 3	57	599
SASTAMERO			
Tomas*	Contra Costa Twp 3	57	599
SASTERFIELD			
Edward P	Calaveras Twp 10	57	279
SASTIMAS			
Antonio	Los Angeles Los Angeles	59	378
SASTRO			
A	Tuolumne Shawsfla	71	399
SASTURAI			
Clemente	Los Angeles Los Nieto	59	426
SAT			
---	Calaveras Twp 4	57	326
---	El Dorado Placerville	58	911
---	Placer Secret R	62	623
---	Sacramento Granite	63	245
Ah	Sacramento Ward 3	63	468
Me	El Dorado Georgetown	58	755
Peet	San Francisco San Francisco 11	67	159
See	San Francisco San Francisco 4	68	1190
Su	San Francisco San Francisco 4	68	1190

Name	County Locale	M653 Roll	Page
SATA			
Elerro	Contra Costa Twp 3	57	600
SATAHE			
Alexd F	San Francisco San Francisco 8	68	1302
SATANG			
Elivado	Tuolumne Twp 2	71	375
SATARDIO			
Leonardo	El Dorado Kelsey	58	1135
SATARO			
B	Amador Twp 1	55	485
SATCHINYAKA			
---*	Mendocino Twp 1	60	887
SATCHMYAKA			
---*	Mendocino Twp 1	60	887
SATCIDA			
Francisca	Los Angeles Los Angeles	59	395
SATE			
---	El Dorado Placerville	58	830
---	Mariposa Coulterville	60	680
Catharine	San Francisco San Francisco 10	67	245
George*	Calaveras Twp 4	57	342
SATEL			
Hasa M	Siskiyou Yreka	69	140
SATEMER			
J	Los Angeles Tejon	59	523
SATER			
Domingo	Mariposa Twp 3	60	547
SATERINNE			
Jose	Santa Cruz Pajaro	66	564
SATERINNI			
Jose*	Santa Cruz Pajaro	66	564
SATERINORE			
Jose	Santa Cruz Pajaro	66	564
SATES			
G V*	Butte Oregon	56	629
SATGADO			
Juan	Monterey Monterey	60	955
SATHANZ			
Bibeana*	San Mateo Twp 2	65	118
SATHER			
Peder	Alameda Oakland	55	75
SATHIAN			
Micheal	El Dorado Mud Springs	58	977
SATHIFIELD			
J M	Tuolumne Twp 1	71	268
SATHORLAND			
Agus	Mendocino Big Rvr	60	841
SATHRFIELD			
J M	Tuolumne Twp 1	71	268
SATHROP			
Edwin	Contra Costa Twp 1	57	529
Saml	Nevada Nevada	61	240
SATIMES			
Daniel	Calaveras Twp 5	57	243
SATIMIR			
J	Los Angeles Tejon	59	523
SATINS			
Wm	Trinity Weaverville	70	1053
SATIO			
Felis	San Bernardino S Timate	64	687
SATIPIE			
Jas W	Butte Kimshaw	56	597
SATISTRO			
---	Marin Cortemad	60	788
SATNER			
Louis	El Dorado Greenwood	58	725
SATO			
---	Sierra Downieville	66	1026
A F	Napa Clear Lake	61	125
Andelino	Santa Clara Gilroy	65	252
Angel	Contra Costa Twp 1	57	496
Antonio	Amador Twp 5	55	332
Domingo	Santa Clara San Jose	65	351
Francisco	Santa Clara San Jose	65	365
Gabriel	Santa Clara San Jose	65	391
Jose	Santa Clara Fremont	65	433
Juan	Santa Clara Gilroy	65	249
Juan	Santa Clara San Jose	65	351
Juan	Santa Clara Fremont	65	431
Maria	Santa Clara San Jose	65	303
Pancho	Santa Clara Fremont	65	432
SATON			
Chancy	Calaveras Twp 6	57	175
James	Fresno Twp 2	59	3
SATORA			
---	San Diego Agua Caliente	64	814
Francis*	Calaveras Twp 5	57	227
SATORN			
Francis	Calaveras Twp 5	57	227
SATOUR			
James	Shasta Millvill	66	749
SATRELLO			
Frank	Calaveras Twp 5	57	207
SATRETTE			
Kline	San Francisco San Francisco 3	67	84

Name	County Locale	M653 Roll Page
SATRILTE		
John*	San Francisco San Francisco	3 67 84
SATRINMIO		
---	San Bernardino S Timate	64 695
SATRITTE		
John*	San Francisco San Francisco	3 67 84
SATSON		
A C*	Napa Napa	61 69
SATTELY		
A	Butte Kimshaw	56 572
SATTER		
Frederick	Tuolumne Sonora	71 198
John*	Yuba Rose Bar	72 791
SATTERE		
J*	Nevada Eureka	61 378
SATTERFIELD		
Edward P	Calaveras Twp 10	57 279
John	Siskiyou Cottonwood	69 107
John	Siskiyou Cottonwoood	69 108
SATTERLEE		
John*	San Francisco San Francisco	3 67 21
Wm	San Francisco San Francisco	6 67 416
SATTERLY		
A	Butte Kimshaw	56 572
SATTERS		
Frank*	Plumas Quincy	62 998
Leroy	Shasta Millvill	66 740
Thimothy	San Francisco San Francisco	2 67 716
SATTIMER		
Wm H	Calaveras Twp 5	57 194
SATTO		
Francisco*	Calaveras Twp 6	57 177
SATTON		
John	Sierra St Louis	66 864
SATTORNINO		
---	Los Angeles San Gabriel	59 410
SATUNG		
---	Shasta Shasta	66 680
SATURN		
Seth	Contra Costa Twp 1	57 505
SATURNER		
Sarah	Sutter Yuba	70 770
SATURNIUS		
---	Los Angeles Los Nieto	59 429
SATURRICO		
---	San Bernardino S Timate	64 690
SATWILEE		
Wm*	Alameda Brooklyn	55 121
SATWILLE		
Wm*	Alameda Brooklyn	55 121
SAU SE		
---	Mariposa Twp 3	60 612
SAU		
---	Calaveras Twp 5	57 234
---	Calaveras Twp 5	57 246
---	Calaveras Twp 10	57 261
---	El Dorado Mud Springs	58 992
---	Mariposa Twp 3	60 608
---	Nevada Nevada	61 302
---	Stanislaus Emory	70 743
Ching Ho	San Francisco San Francisco	4 681191
Ko	San Francisco San Francisco	4 681191
Lay	Nevada Washington	61 342
Lee*	Mariposa Twp 3	60 576
Yi	Calaveras Twp 5	57 246
SAUBERG		
Theodore	Tuolumne Twp 3	71 427
SAUBINNE		
A	Colusa Grand Island	57 468
SAUCH		
J*	Nevada Grass Valley	61 150
SAUCHAL		
A M*	Butte Oregon	56 633
SAUCHEZ		
Ana M	Los Angeles Los Angeles	59 294
SAUDERS		
L F*	San Francisco San Francisco	9 681067
Lewis*	Placer Auburn	62 571
SAUDERSON		
George W	Calaveras Twp 6	57 158
William	Calaveras Twp 4	57 311
SAUDUS		
J	Butte Bidwell	56 716
SAUERDRUP		
Jno*	Sacramento Ward 1	63 33
SAUG		
---	Nevada Nevada	61 300
SAUGEATE		
James*	Tuolumne Twp 1	71 210
SAUGHLIN		
M	Nevada Eureka	61 367
Thos	Nevada Eureka	61 374
SAUGHTER		
Henry*	Placer Goods	62 696
SAUI		
---	Calaveras Twp 5	57 255

Name	County Locale	M653 Roll Page
SAUI		
---*	Nevada Rough &	61 399
SAUKEY		
Maurice*	Plumas Meadow Valley	62 933
SAUL		
G M	Calaveras Twp 8	57 72
J B*	Sacramento Franklin	63 326
John	El Dorado Union	581092
M E*	Sacramento Lee	63 219
Obisco*	Sacramento Lee	63 219
Pater	Alameda Brooklyn	55 103
See	Mariposa Twp 3	60 613
SAULB		
John*	Yolo Slate Ra	72 710
SAULBERG		
S	Sacramento Ward 1	63 38
SAULE		
Paul	San Francisco San Francisco 10	331
		67
Saml S	San Francisco San Francisco	9 681001
SAULES		
A*	Mariposa Twp 3	60 597
SAULESBURY		
Hiram	Yuba Linda	72 986
SAULEY		
Catharine	Yuba Marysville	72 909
SAULIKER		
John	Sierra Gibsonville	66 858
SAULS		
---	Los Angeles San Gabriel	59 414
H	Butte Hamilton	56 524
SAULSBERY		
J	Merced Twp 1	60 914
SAULSBURY		
Isaac	San Francisco San Francisco	7 681361
Stephen	Yuba Parke Ba	72 782
SAULSBY		
Thomas*	Tuolumne Twp 1	71 261
SAULSGIVER		
D*	Nevada Nevada	61 262
SAULSMAN		
Wm	El Dorado Placerville	58 928
SAULTER		
W	San Francisco San Francisco	1 68 928
SAULY		
Nicholas	Sierra Gibsonville	66 858
SAUM		
---	Fresno Twp 1	59 26
Long	Butte Bidwell	56 720
SAUMESTER		
Leonard	San Joaquin O'Neal	641008
Louis*	San Joaquin O'Neal	641008
SAUMIE		
A T*	Nevada Nevada	61 294
SAUMONS		
Jno	Trinity Cox'S Bar	701038
SAUN		
---	Calaveras Twp 10	57 268
---	Mariposa Twp 3	60 572
---*	Shasta Shasta	66 670
SAUNDER		
John W	Sacramento Ward 1	63 114
Philorous	Plumas Quincy	62 940
SAUNDERS		
A J	Trinity Evans Ba	701002
A N	Alameda Brooklyn	55 201
A P	Santa Clara San Jose	65 353
Ackley	Calaveras Twp 7	57 27
Amasa	Alameda Brooklyn	55 161
C R	San Francisco San Francisco 10	293
		67
Chas F	Trinity Weaverville	701074
George	El Dorado Greenwood	58 720
Henry	Trinity Browns C	70 984
J	Del Norte Crescent	58 642
J	Nevada Nevada	61 273
James	San Francisco San Francisco	7 681359
Jas	Butte Ophir	56 750
Jas M*	Napa Napa	61 99
Jno S	Sacramento Ward 4	63 512
John	Butte Bidwell	56 718
John	Mariposa Twp 1	60 630
Joseph	Siskiyou Yreka	69 183
Joseph	Yuba Linda	72 985
M	Nevada Eureka	61 368
Madison	Tulara Visalia	71 5
Mary	San Francisco San Francisco 10	289
		67
Matilda*	San Francisco San Francisco	7 681430
N D	San Joaquin Stockton	641054
Phillip	San Francisco San Francisco	7 681371
Robt	San Francisco San Francisco 10	256
		67
Thos A	Placer Secret R	62 619
W	Santa Clara San Jose	65 362
W D	Napa Napa	61 99

Name	County Locale	M653 Roll Page
SAUNDERS		
William	San Bernardino Santa Barbara	64 202
Wm	Butte Oro	56 677
SAUNDERSON		
A	San Mateo Twp 1	65 55
L F	Santa Clara San Jose	65 389
S A	Santa Clara Santa Clara	65 489
Thomas	San Francisco San Francisco	8 681277
SAUNDERY		
Jas M*	Napa Napa	61 99
SAUNDEY		
Jas M*	Napa Napa	61 99
SAUNERIAS		
Vintras	Santa Clara San Jose	65 334
SAUNS		
John*	Yuba Fosters	72 832
SAUNSBURY		
Chas	Monterey San Juan	60 995
SAUR		
---	San Francisco San Francisco	4 681182
SAURENCE		
Henry	Trinity Weaverville	701052
SAURENEL		
F*	Nevada Eureka	61 374
SAURIANO		
---	Monterey Monterey	60 957
SAURIN		
Charles	Calaveras Twp 5	57 240
SAUS		
O	Calaveras Twp 9	57 376
SAUSA		
J N	Tuolumne Twp 2	71 284
SAUSING		
G J*	Nevada Eureka	61 381
SAUSMAN		
A R*	San Francisco San Francisco	3 67 77
Geo B	Calaveras Twp 5	57 190
S R	San Francisco San Francisco	3 67 77
SAUSMAW		
A R*	San Francisco San Francisco	3 67 77
SAUTALMER		
Henry*	Mariposa Twp 1	60 623
SAUTEINISAN		
John B*	Calaveras Twp 5	57 178
SAUTERNISAR		
John B*	Calaveras Twp 6	57 178
SAUTHY		
Danl	San Francisco San Francisco	9 681073
SAUTLY		
Danl*	San Francisco San Francisco	9 681073
SAUTO		
---*	Butte Chico	56 566
SAUTUNISAN		
John B*	Calaveras Twp 5	57 178
SAUUHLER		
Jacob	Sierra Gibsonville	66 858
SAUYER		
R	Mariposa Twp 3	60 567
SAVADE		
Jacob	San Francisco San Francisco	7 681419
SAVAGE		
A	Sutter Butte	70 790
A R	Tuolumne Twp 1	71 275
Abraham	Nevada Rough &	61 404
Alden*	Butte Kimshaw	56 604
Aldin	Butte Kimshaw	56 604
Andrew	Calaveras Twp 5	57 209
Andrew J	Calaveras Twp 10	57 266
Ashfel	Alameda Oakland	55 15
Austin	Yuba Rose Bar	72 810
Barny	Mariposa Twp 1	60 671
Chas	Napa Napa	61 70
D M	Tuolumne Columbia	71 355
E M	Nevada Nevada	61 292
Frederick J	San Joaquin Elkhorn	64 956
Geo C*	San Francisco San Francisco	1 68 855
Geo E*	San Francisco San Francisco	1 68 855
Geo M	Tuolumne Shawsfla	71 376
Hipolite	San Francisco San Francisco	2 67 690
J B	Nevada Nevada	61 292
J*	Nevada Grass Valley	61 204
James	San Francisco San Francisco	3 67 59
James	San Joaquin Stockton	641091
James	Yuba Marysville	72 864
James D	San Francisco San Francisco	3 67 59
James H	Tuolumne Twp 2	71 377
Jno	Sacramento Ward 4	63 603
John	Amador Twp 1	55 414
Joseph	Amador Twp 4	55 239
K	Shasta Shasta	66 685
L	Mendocino Big Rvr	60 845
M	Nevada Eureka	61 351
Mary	Nevada Bridgeport	61 465
Mary S	Amador Twp 4	55 239
Michael	Contra Costa Twp 2	57 552
N C	El Dorado Diamond	58 797

Name	County Locale	M653 Roll Page
SAVAGE		
Nich	Napa Napa	61 113
Patrick	El Dorado Mud Springs	58 949
Patrick	Santa Clara Santa Clara	65 482
R W	Amador Twp 2	55 304
Richard	Santa Cruz Soquel	66 580
Richd	Sacramento Ward 1	63 49
S	Mariposa Coulterville	60 696
S	San Joaquin Stockton	641093
Thomas	Calaveras Twp 6	57 128
Thomas	San Francisco San Francisco 8	681271
Thos	San Francisco San Francisco 1	68 879
Wm	Del Norte Crescent	58 629
Wm M	Sonoma Mendocino	69 460
SAVAGER		
Vako	Tuolumne Jamestown	71 454
SAVAGES		
Geo M	Tuolumne Twp 2	71 376
Vako	Tuolumne Twp 3	71 454
SAVAGIN		
D	Siskiyou Callahan	69 3
SAVAGO		
D M	Tuolumne Twp 2	71 355
Thomas	San Francisco San Francisco 8	681271
Wm F	Tuolumne Twp 1	71 274
SAVAID		
Patria	Tuolumne Sonora	71 241
SAVAL		
Stephen	Calaveras Twp 5	57 221
SAVALETA		
Paulalem	Los Angeles Los Angeles	59 298
Tomas	Los Angeles Santa Ana	59 448
SAVALLE		
Athanan	Yuba Marysville	72 920
SAVALLO		
Antonea*	Yuba Marysville	72 920
Antonia*	Yuba Marysville	72 920
SAVALSA		
Jesus	Los Angeles Los Angeles	59 301
SAVAR		
John*	San Francisco San Francisco 2	67 696
SAVARA		
John*	Calaveras Twp 9	57 362
SAVARES		
M	Sacramento Ward 1	63 5
SAVARETTA		
Juan	Sacramento Ward 1	63 93
SAVARGO		
Andrew*	Calaveras Twp 5	57 209
SAVARYO		
Andrew*	Calaveras Twp 5	57 209
SAVASGO		
Andrew*	Calaveras Twp 5	57 209
SAVBELL		
Madaline	Nevada Bridgeport	61 465
SAVEBRIN		
Daniel*	Alameda Brooklyn	55 168
SAVEDEN		
Chars	San Francisco San Francisco 3	67 83
SAVEENEG		
Jas	Sacramento Ward 4	63 532
SAVEL		
---	Mariposa Twp 1	60 631
SAVELL		
C P*	San Francisco San Francisco 9	681098
Madaline	Nevada Bridgeport	61 465
SAVELLA		
Mariano	Contra Costa Twp 1	57 494
SAVENA		
Belavin*	Calaveras Twp 9	57 352
Belavir*	Calaveras Twp 9	57 352
Bilavir*	Calaveras Twp 9	57 352
SAVENUA		
Francis*	Calaveras Twp 5	57 258
SAVER		
E S	Nevada Bridgeport	61 486
SAVERA		
Belavin*	Calaveras Twp 9	57 352
SAVERDRUP		
Jno*	Sacramento Ward 1	63 33
SAVERIS		
M A	Sacramento Ward 1	63 16
SAVERKRUP		
Jno	Sacramento Ward 1	63 33
SAVERS		
William	Tulara Twp 3	71 48
SAVERY		
Wm	Sacramento Ward 1	63 145
Wm G	Amador Twp 1	55 473
SAVIAID		
Patria	Tuolumne Twp 1	71 241
SAVICHA		
John	Amador Twp 4	55 241
SAVILE		
Palicufs	Calaveras Twp 6	57 161
Torris	Calaveras Twp 6	57 161
SAVILLAC		
Thomas	San Bernardino Santa Inez	64 136
SAVILLE		
David	San Francisco San Francisco 9	681056
Mesendo	El Dorado Georgetown	58 702
Peter K*	Amador Twp 4	55 235
Wm	Del Norte Crescent	58 619
SAVILS		
---	Placer Dutch Fl	62 732
SAVIN		
Thos*	Calaveras Twp 9	57 399
SAVINA		
Belavin*	Calaveras Twp 9	57 352
Bilavin*	Calaveras Twp 9	57 352
SAVIO		
Natalis	San Francisco San Francisco 10	317 67
SAVIS		
Natalis	San Francisco San Francisco 10	317 67
SAVODEO		
Anto	Fresno Twp 1	59 84
SAVONO		
Ramon	Monterey San Juan	60 997
SAVONS		
Ramon	Monterey San Juan	60 997
SAVORAL		
Trinidad	Sacramento Ward 1	63 99
SAVORDIS		
Francisco	Calaveras Twp 4	57 330
SAVORLIS		
Francisco	Calaveras Twp 4	57 330
SAVORY		
Benj L	San Francisco San Francisco 10	320 67
Benj L	San Francisco San Francisco 3	67 79
SAVOY		
---	Tuolumne Twp 3	71 466
SAVOYE		
Thomas	Calaveras Twp 6	57 128
SAVOYER		
Andrew J	Calaveras Twp 10	57 266
SAVUR		
Thos*	Calaveras Twp 9	57 399
SAW COW		
---	Nevada Nevada	61 301
SAW JON		
---*	Sacramento Ward 1	63 55
SAW TIE		
---*	Nevada Nevada	61 303
SAW TOO		
---	Nevada Nevada	61 303
SAW		
---	Amador Twp 2	55 289
---	Amador Twp 2	55 327
---	Calaveras Twp 8	57 109
---	Calaveras Twp 6	57 126
---	Calaveras Twp 6	57 151
---	Calaveras Twp 6	57 165
---	Calaveras Twp 5	57 215
---	Calaveras Twp 5	57 234
---	Calaveras Twp 5	57 255
---	Calaveras Twp 5	57 257
---	Calaveras Twp 10	57 259
---	Calaveras Twp 10	57 270
---	Calaveras Twp 10	57 271
---	Calaveras Twp 10	57 283
---	Calaveras Twp 10	57 284
---	Calaveras Twp 10	57 294
---	Calaveras Twp 10	57 295
---	Calaveras Twp 10	57 296
---	Calaveras Twp 10	57 297
---	Calaveras Twp 4	57 303
---	Calaveras Twp 4	57 305
---	Calaveras Twp 8	57 92
---	Colusa Colusi	57 420
---	El Dorado Placerville	58 831
---	Mariposa Twp 3	60 569
---	Nevada Nevada	61 301
---	Nevada Nevada	61 302
---	Nevada Washington	61 341
---	Nevada Washington	61 342
---	Nevada Eureka	61 383
---	Nevada Eureka	61 384
---	Nevada Rough &	61 433
---	Nevada Bridgeport	61 459
---	Nevada Bridgeport	61 493
---	Nevada Bloomfield	61 521
---	Placer Virginia	62 666
---	Placer Virginia	62 676
---	Sacramento Centre	63 182
---	Sacramento Cosummes	63 392
---	Sacramento Ward 1	63 52
---	Sacramento Ward 1	63 59
---	San Francisco San Francisco 4	681185
---	San Joaquin Stockton	641083
SAW		
---	Sierra Downieville	66 992
---	Sierra Downieville	66 997
---	Yolo No E Twp	72 680
---	Yuba Marysville	72 908
---*	Yuba Marysville	72 908
---*	Yuba Linda	72 993
A*	Nevada Eureka	61 367
Ah	Siskiyou Klamath	69 89
Ah	Yuba Suida	72 993
Ah*	Sacramento Cosummes	63 382
Ar*	Sierra Downieville	66 971
At	Tuolumne Twp 4	71 159
Cho*	San Francisco San Francisco 9	681094
Chuy Ho	San Francisco San Francisco 4	681191
Cow	Nevada Nevada	61 301
Fun	Nevada Eureka	61 383
Hing	San Francisco San Francisco 4	681185
How	Nevada Nevada	61 302
Ip	Placer Virginia	62 676
John	Placer Auburn	62 578
Jon	Sierra Twp 7	66 898
Kee Soo	San Francisco San Francisco 4	681210
Ko	San Francisco San Francisco 4	681191
Kung	San Francisco San Francisco 9	681096
Ligg	Nevada Washington	61 342
Low*	Amador Twp 2	55 302
Muoy*	Sacramento Ward 1	63 71
O	Nevada Eureka	61 367
Po	San Francisco San Francisco 4	681184
Sing	Nevada Nevada	61 303
Sing	Nevada Eureka	61 383
Sing	Nevada Eureka	61 384
Tong*	Fresno Twp 1	59 28
Tow	Nevada Nevada	61 308
Wa	Sacramento Natonia	63 286
Yep	Nevada Washington	61 342
Yuh	Nevada Grass Valley	61 228
Yung	San Francisco San Francisco 9	681099
Yup	Nevada Grass Valley	61 228
Yup	Nevada Nevada	61 310
Yup	Nevada Eureka	61 383
SAWALL		
J M	Yolo Cache	72 589
SAWBINE		
Augustus	Sonoma Armally	69 507
SAWCEE		
----	Sierra Twp 5	66 933
SAWCER		
---	Sierra Twp 5	66 933
SAWE		
---	Placer Auburn	62 581
Chow	Nevada Eureka	61 383
SAWER		
James	Tuolumne Twp 2	71 398
SAWERBREY		
M	Trinity Honest B	701043
SAWES		
James	Tuolumne Shawsfla	71 398
John A*	Tuolumne Columbia	71 295
SAWGER		
Louis	San Francisco San Francisco 7	681392
SAWGRASS		
Henry	Sierra Downieville	66 977
SAWIDEY		
J	Nevada Nevada	61 273
SAWILLE		
Wm*	Napa Yount	61 33
SAWIN		
Geo W	San Francisco San Francisco 2	67 701
Jabr	Butte Ophir	56 787
M H	Trinity Trinity	70 971
Reuben	Santa Cruz Santa Cruz	66 601
SAWINIOS		
Margaret	Calaveras Twp 6	57 150
SAWLER		
Cathatharien*	Tuolumne Shawsfla	71 383
L D	Nevada Eureka	61 381
SAWLERS		
George	Santa Clara Santa Clara	65 518
Henry*	San Bernardino Almaden	64 278
SAWLES		
Cathatharien*	Tuolumne Shawsfla	71 383
SAWLESS		
Bord	Tulara Twp 2	71 13
Walter	San Francisco San Francisco 7	681425
SAWLEY		
James A	San Francisco San Francisco 6	67 431
John	Napa Napa	61 94
L M*	Butte Oregon	56 630
SAWLPER		
Frank*	Mendocino Big Rvr	60 848
SAWN		
John A	Tuolumne Twp 2	71 295
SAWPBEAR		
George	Colusa Butte Crk	57 465

California 1860 Census Index

Name	County Locale	M653 Roll Page
SAWPE		
Thoodon*	Nevada Nevada	61 242
Thoodore*	Nevada Nevada	61 242
SAWPI		
Theodere*	Nevada Nevada	61 242
SAWPSON		
Isaac*	Alameda Brooklyn	55 178
SAWRENCE		
C M	Trinity Weaverville	701051
W H	Tuolumne Twp 3	71 445
SAWREY		
Henry*	San Francisco San Francisco 2	67 683
SAWRIX		
J	Nevada Eureka	61 372
SAWS		
R C	Nevada Washington	61 337
SAWSON		
H M	Nevada Nevada	61 321
James	San Joaquin Stockton	641045
Jane*	Plumas Quincy	62 978
John	Calaveras Twp 5	57 240
SAWTELL		
C	San Francisco San Francisco 10	190 67
Thomas	Siskiyou Yreka	69 174
SAWTELLE		
M A	Nevada Rough &	61 427
Mary F	Nevada Rough &	61 427
SAWTELLS		
M A*	Nevada Rough &	61 427
SAWTFER		
Mary*	Mendocino Anderson	60 871
SAWTILLE		
E P	Mendocino Anderson	60 871
SAWUNY		
Wm	Sierra Twp 5	66 936
SAWYER		
A	Nevada Bridgeport	61 472
A B	Siskiyou Scott Va	69 54
A F	San Francisco San Francisco 3	67 82
A K	Merced Twp 1	60 911
Albert	Plumas Quincy	62 957
Alex	Butte Chico	56 531
Charles	San Francisco San Francisco 2	67 559
E A	Sacramento San Joaquin	63 364
E A	San Francisco San Francisco 6	67 451
Ebenezer D	San Francisco 8	681253
	San Francisco	
Elbridge	Tulara Keeneysburg	71 45
Elbridgo*	Tulara Twp 3	71 45
Elizabeth	San Francisco San Francisco 3	67 82
Eugene	Monterey San Juan	60 995
Eugene	San Luis Obispo San Luis Obispo	65 16
F A	San Francisco San Francisco 5	67 501
F R	Yolo Washington	72 564
Feo	Amador Twp 1	55 452
Francisco*	Santa Cruz Santa Cruz	66 632
Frank	Mendocino Big Rvr	60 848
Frederick*	Sacramento Franklin	63 309
Geo	Amador Twp 3	55 386
Geo	Amador Twp 1	55 452
George	Nevada Little Y	61 536
Gerome*	Monterey San Juan	601004
H	Amador Twp 1	55 473
H M	Trinity Trinity	70 971
J	Sacramento Franklin	63 310
J	Sacramento Ward 4	63 495
J D	Siskiyou Scott Va	69 34
J M	Tuolumne Columbia	71 322
J M	Tuolumne Jamestown	71 453
Jackson	Humbolt Table Bl	59 141
James	Sacramento Granite	63 251
James F	Mendocino Calpella	60 820
Jessee	Solano Vallejo	69 278
John	Calaveras Twp 7	57 40
John	Sacramento Dry Crk	63 371
Joseph S	San Salvador	64 649
	San Bernardino	
Jossen	Solano Vallejo	69 278
L M	Calaveras Twp 9	57 362
L W	San Joaquin Stockton	641013
Leander	San Francisco San Francisco 11	122 67
Leonard	Placer Michigan	62 845
M*	Sacramento Ward 3	63 425
Mary*	Mendocino Anderson	60 871
Milton G	Calaveras Twp 6	57 122
Murick	Placer Forest H	62 799
N	Sacramento Granite	63 235
O H	Nevada Rough &	61 401
Otis V	San Francisco San Francisco 6	67 399
R H	Sacramento Ward 4	63 611
R*	Mariposa Twp 3	60 567
S	Calaveras Twp 9	57 389
Sam	Sacramento Ward 1	63 147
Saml	Sacramento Ward 1	63 139

Name	County Locale	M653 Roll Page
SAWYER		
Saml	San Francisco San Francisco 5	67 477
Samuel	Placer Forest H	62 765
Samuel	San Francisco San Francisco 3	67 38
Stephen	Yuba Linda	72 989
T	Calaveras Twp 9	57 389
T	San Francisco San Francisco 9	681082
Tho	Siskiyou Scott Va	69 57
Thomas	Mendocino Little L	60 830
Thos	Sacramento Cosumnes	63 394
Thos	San Francisco San Francisco 10	333 67
Thos	San Francisco San Francisco 1	68 922
Thos S	Sacramento Sutter	63 307
Wade H*	Mendocino Little L	60 831
William H	Siskiyou Shasta Rvr	69 111
Wm	Nevada Eureka	61 370
Wm H	Calaveras Twp 6	57 115
Woodbury	Plumas Quincy	62 916
SAWYERS		
J M	Tuolumne Twp 2	71 322
SAWZE		
Jas	Amador Twp 1	55 461
SAX		
Jonathan	Solano Fremont	69 379
Moses	El Dorado Coloma	581113
Stephen*	Nevada Nevada	61 287
SAXBY		
J T	Nevada Bridgeport	61 471
SAXE		
A W	Santa Clara Santa Clara	65 466
M C	Sierra Downieville	661023
SAXEN		
John	San Francisco San Francisco 1	68 928
SAXILD		
John	Siskiyou Cottonwoood	69 98
SAXLEIR		
Daniel	San Francisco San Francisco 3	67 79
SAXON		
Andrew	Placer Iona Hills	62 891
G P	El Dorado Newtown	58 777
Thos	San Joaquin Stockton	641025
SAXRAMENTO		
---*	Mendocino Round Va	60 884
SAXTATER		
A	El Dorado Placerville	58 905
SAXTON		
E D	Sacramento Ward 1	63 62
H A	El Dorado Big Bar	58 742
James	Nevada Rough &	61 411
Jesse B	Alameda Oakland	55 21
Joseph	Calaveras Twp 4	57 330
Patrick	San Joaquin Stockton	641035
W M	Nevada Bridgeport	61 489
W W	Amador Twp 3	55 405
William	San Joaquin Stockton	641035
SAXY		
William	Tulara Twp 2	71 5
SAY CHEU		
---	Mariposa Twp 3	60 607
SAY LOY		
---	Nevada Bridgeport	61 460
SAY Y		
---	Mariposa Twp 3	60 607
SAY		
---	Amador Twp 2	55 289
---	Amador Twp 2	55 294
---	Amador Twp 2	55 315
---	Amador Twp 2	55 319
---	Amador Twp 2	55 323
---	Amador Twp 2	55 327
---	Amador Twp 5	55 329
---	Amador Twp 5	55 340
---	Amador Twp 5	55 344
---	Amador Twp 5	55 349
---	Amador Twp 5	55 364
---	Amador Twp 3	55 394
---	Amador Twp 3	55 410
---	Amador Twp 1	55 490
---	Amador Twp 1	55 492
---	Calaveras Twp 6	57 148
---	Calaveras Twp 5	57 250
---	Calaveras Twp 5	57 256
---	Calaveras Twp 10	57 261
---	Calaveras Twp 10	57 270
---	Calaveras Twp 10	57 276
---	Calaveras Twp 10	57 278
---	Calaveras Twp 4	57 304
---	Calaveras Twp 8	57 63
---	Calaveras Twp 8	57 71
---	Calaveras Twp 8	57 83
---	Calaveras Twp 8	57 94
---	El Dorado Salmon Hills	581063
---	El Dorado Salmon Hills	581064
---	El Dorado Mountain	581190
---	El Dorado Big Bar	58 737

Name	County Locale	M653 Roll Page
SAY		
---	El Dorado Georgetown	58 755
---	El Dorado Georgetown	58 756
---	El Dorado Diamond	58 796
---	El Dorado Placerville	58 841
---	El Dorado Placerville	58 844
---	El Dorado Eldorado	58 939
---	El Dorado Eldorado	58 940
---	El Dorado Eldorado	58 944
---	Mariposa Twp 3	60 564
---	Mariposa Twp 3	60 576
---	Mariposa Twp 3	60 608
---	Mariposa Twp 3	60 613
---	Mariposa Twp 1	60 661
---	Mariposa Twp 1	60 669
---	Nevada Grass Valley	61 232
---	Nevada Nevada	61 299
---	Nevada Nevada	61 308
---	Nevada Rough &	61 398
---	Nevada Rough &	61 409
---	Nevada Rough &	61 435
---	Nevada Rough &	61 437
---	Nevada Bridgeport	61 439
---	Nevada Bridgeport	61 459
---	Nevada Bridgeport	61 460
---	Nevada Bridgeport	61 463
---	Nevada Bloomfield	61 521
---	Placer Auburn	62 572
---	Placer Folsom	62 648
---	Placer Folsom	62 649
---	Placer Virginia	62 671
---	Placer Virginia	62 687
---	Placer Dutch Fl	62 737
---	Placer Illinois	62 742
---	Plumas Quincy	62 949
---	Sacramento Mississipi	63 186
---	Sacramento Granite	63 232
---	Sacramento Ward 1	63 55
---	San Francisco San Francisco 2	67 801
---	Shasta Horsetown	66 709
---	Sierra Downieville	661023
---	Siskiyou Yreka	69 194
---	Siskiyou Yreka	69 195
---	Stanislaus Emory	70 743
---	Tuolumne Jacksonville	71 168
---	Tuolumne Jamestown	71 442
---*	Amador Twp 2	55 289
---*	El Dorado Salmon Falls	581064
---*	Mariposa Twp 3	60 576
---*	Nevada Nevada	61 308
---*	Plumas Meadow Valley	62 913
Ah	Calaveras Twp 7	57 8
Ah	Tuolumne Twp 4	71 168
Chung	Placer Dutch Fl	62 737
Chung	Placer Illinois	62 738
Dong	Nevada Bridgeport	61 506
Fye	Calaveras Twp 9	57 363
G	Sutter Butte	70 779
He	Mariposa Twp 3	60 620
J	Nevada Rough &	61 409
J N*	Sutter Yuba	70 766
James*	Nevada Bridgeport	61 450
Jay	Mariposa Twp 3	60 619
Jesse	Yuba Slate Ro	72 717
K	Calaveras Twp 4	57 304
Kee	Mariposa Twp 3	60 576
Kee	Mariposa Twp 3	60 586
Lan	Mariposa Twp 3	60 582
Lay	Nevada Rough &	61 397
Lay	Nevada Bridgeport	61 492
Le	Mariposa Twp 3	60 619
Lee	Nevada Rough &	61 409
Let	Nevada Rough &	61 409
Long	Nevada Bridgeport	61 506
Loo*	Mariposa Twp 3	60 582
Loy	Nevada Bridgeport	61 460
Ma	Mariposa Twp 3	60 618
Sing	Placer Illinois	62 738
So	Mariposa Twp 3	60 618
Toy	Nevada Washington	61 341
Wass	Tuolumne Twp 4	71 167
Wing	Calaveras Twp 4	57 308
Yay	Mariposa Twp 3	60 544
Young	Mariposa Twp 3	60 544
Your*	Placer Auburn	62 578
Yow	Placer Dutch Fl	62 737
Yung	Placer Illinois	62 738
SAYANG		
Wm	Los Angeles Tejon	59 524
SAYAUN		
Paul	Calaveras Twp 4	57 324
SAYCOCK		
Mary*	Napa Napa	61 96
Sarah*	Solano Vacaville	69 319
SAYDAM		
Mary Ann*	Yuba Marysville	72 911

Name	County Locale	M653 Roll	Page
SAYDAM			
William	Tuolumne Shawsfla	71	382
SAYER			
C A	Nevada Grass Valley	61	157
Geo	Nevada Nevada	61	325
George	Sierra Pine Grove	66	829
H	Trinity Taylor'S	70	1036
Hunting	San Francisco San Francisco 8	68	1268
Lud L	San Francisco San Francisco 9	68	1046
Reuben S	San Francisco San Francisco 10	67	188
SAYERE			
Albert G	Monterey Alisal	60	1037
SAYERS			
Chas T	San Francisco San Francisco 3	67	85
D	Sacramento Cosumnes	63	400
Ephrahan*	Nevada Red Dog	61	547
Ephraipan*	Nevada Red Dog	61	547
Frank	Alameda Brooklyn	55	107
Frank	San Francisco San Francisco 2	67	728
George	Marin Cortemad	60	789
H	Mariposa Twp 3	60	554
James	Siskiyou Scott Va	69	61
Jas H	San Francisco San Francisco 9	68	1089
John	San Francisco San Francisco 4	68	1167
John T	Mariposa Twp 1	60	638
Jos H	San Francisco San Francisco 9	68	1089
Joseph	San Francisco San Francisco 4	68	1143
Samuel	Tuolumne Chinese	71	522
SAYES			
Geo*	Nevada Nevada	61	325
SAYESS			
James	Siskiyou Scott Va	69	61
SAYESTER			
J	Butte Bidwell	56	722
SAYLE			
Claudine G	Fresno Twp 1	59	33
SAYLEIR			
Daniel*	San Francisco San Francisco 3	67	79
SAYLER			
Henry	Humbolt Eureka	59	166
N N	Siskiyou Callahan	69	7
SAYLES			
G W	Sacramento American	63	169
Henry	Sierra Poker Flats	66	838
Henry W	Sierra Poker Flats	66	838
James Jr	Fresno Twp 2	59	3
SAYLOR			
George E	Tulara Visalia	71	102
John	Yuba Marysville	72	950
N N	Siskiyou Callahan	69	7
Oscar*	San Francisco San Francisco 9	68	1071
SAYLORAND			
Jos	San Francisco San Francisco 10	67	260
SAYMAN			
Saml*	Calaveras Twp 4	57	324
SAYNE			
Jno A	Butte Chico	56	535
SAYRE			
Henry E	Sierra Whiskey	66	845
L	Tuolumne Twp 4	71	164
T	Tuolumne Jacksonville	71	164
William	Placer Michigan	62	837
Wooley	Monterey Alisal	60	1037
Worley*	Monterey Alisal	60	1037
SAYRES			
Edward	San Francisco San Francisco 9	68	1035
SAYS			
Patrick	San Joaquin Douglass	64	922
SAYWARD			
W F	San Francisco San Francisco 2	67	678
SAYWITH			
G*	Siskiyou Scott Va	69	60
SAZARA			
Maria*	Los Angeles Los Angeles	59	370
SAZER			
Cecile	Amador Twp 1	55	452
H*	Trinity Taylor'S	70	1036
SAZIER			
David*	Nevada Nevada	61	328
SAZUR			
David*	Nevada Nevada	61	328
SBARBARA			
Antonio	Tuolumne Twp 5	71	503
Bartolmo	Tuolumne Chinese	71	499
SBARBORA			
Madelina	Tuolumne Twp 5	71	499
SCAB			
Niposeum*	Yuba Marysville	72	917
SCADDEE			
G*	Nevada Grass Valley	61	144
SCADDEN			
T*	Nevada Grass Valley	61	173
W	Nevada Grass Valley	61	186
SCADDER			
G*	Nevada Grass Valley	61	144

Name	County Locale	M653 Roll	Page
SCAFINO			
Nicholas	San Francisco San Francisco 3	67	64
SCAHRERT			
Max	Alameda Brooklyn	55	180
SCAILE			
John	Monterey San Juan	60	976
SCALAHER			
Charles	Tuolumne Twp 5	71	513
SCALES			
A H	Sierra Scales D	66	800
A W*	Sierra Scales D	66	800
William M	San Francisco San Francisco 8	68	1243
SCALILS			
Anistel	Los Angeles Los Angeles	59	512
SCALIS			
Anistil	Los Angeles Los Angeles	59	512
SCALLARD			
Morris	Alameda Brooklyn	55	106
Moses	Alameda Brooklyn	55	106
SCALLEN			
Cath	San Francisco San Francisco 6	67	404
SCALLY			
Patrick	Tuolumne Columbia	71	349
Patrick	Yuba Marysville	72	912
SCALNE			
Wesley	San Bernardino San Bernadino	64	638
SCALOTT			
Fogustia	Sierra Twp 7	66	912
SCALRE			
Wesley	San Bernardino San Salvador	64	638
SCAM			
Valentine	Yuba Marysville	72	946
SCAMANDY			
T	Tuolumne Twp 1	71	269
SCAMBLIN			
Moses	El Dorado Grizzly	58	1182
SCAMMAN			
Benj*	Stanislaus Emory	70	754
Eliza*	Shasta Shasta	66	666
SCAMMEN			
Harry	Sierra Downieville	66	976
J F	Shasta Shasta	66	655
SCAMMON			
Charles	San Francisco San Francisco 6	67	423
Eliza	Shasta Shasta	66	666
Henry*	Sierra Downieville	66	976
Hurry*	Sierra Downieville	66	976
J F*	Shasta Shasta	66	655
J H	Tuolumne Twp 2	71	371
SCAMP			
---	Amador Twp 6	55	431
SCANASUALED			
Peabody*	Mariposa Twp 3	60	596
SCANCH			
Antonia	Sonoma Sonoma	69	636
SCANDER			
August	Tuolumne Twp 2	71	280
SCANDLE			
W	Nevada Eureka	61	356
SCANDLER			
Cornelius	San Francisco San Francisco 1	68	889
S P*	Stanislaus Branch	70	715
SCANE			
---	Sierra Twp 7	66	886
SCANER			
Charles*	Yuba Marysville	72	892
SCANERL			
George	Calaveras Twp 10	57	291
SCANG			
---	Calaveras Twp 5	57	235
SCANIRE			
George	Calaveras Twp 10	57	291
SCANLA			
John L	Mariposa Twp 3	60	568
SCANLAN			
Bridget	San Francisco San Francisco 4	68	1214
David	San Francisco San Francisco 12	67	386
J	San Joaquin Stockton	64	1100
M	Trinity Mouth Ca	70	1012
Orin*	Sacramento Natonia	63	286
W	Trinity Oregon G	70	1008
SCANLAND			
Jno	Sonoma Petaluma	69	607
SCANLAW			
Owen	Sacramento Natonia	63	286
SCANLIN			
Daniel	Tuolumne Big Oak	71	143
Michael	Contra Costa Twp 1	57	483
Michael	Placer Secret R	62	609
Thomas	Shasta French G	66	719
Wm	Amador Twp 1	55	509
SCANLINE			
P	Shasta French G	66	716
SCANLON			
Bartholomew	Sierra Twp 7	66	887

Name	County Locale	M653 Roll	Page
SCANLON			
Francis	San Francisco San Francisco 8	68	1250
James	Solano Green Valley	69	241
John L	Mariposa Twp 3	60	568
P*	Napa Hot Springs	61	1
Thos	Trinity Mouth Ca	70	1016
SCANLOW			
Batheolomew	Sierra Twp 7	66	887
SCANNEL			
David	Marin Cortemad	60	787
SCANNELL			
E	Santa Clara Almaden	65	277
John	San Francisco San Francisco 8	68	1234
SCANNON			
Daniel	Tuolumne Twp 2	71	371
SCANORIM			
D	Tuolumne Twp 1	71	255
SCANORIVER			
C*	Tuolumne Twp 1	71	255
SCANTER			
S P*	Stanislaus Branch	70	715
SCANTHLIN			
Tim*	Nevada Red Dog	61	540
SCANTON			
J	San Francisco San Francisco 9	68	1082
J S	San Francisco San Francisco 9	68	1082
SCANUCLUIE			
James	Los Angeles Los Angeles	59	347
SCANY			
---*	Calaveras Twp 5	57	235
SCAPER			
Henry	Plumas Meadow Valley	62	905
SCARFORD			
Adam	Siskiyou Yreka	69	127
SCARGE			
W	Sierra Twp 5	66	926
SCARIDLER			
S P*	Stanislaus Branch	70	715
SCARING			
S D*	Placer Todds Va	62	786
SCARLET			
Elizabeth	Alameda Brooklyn	55	135
SCARLETT			
Chas	Sacramento Georgian	63	338
John	San Francisco San Francisco 11	67	90
SCARLIN			
P	Shasta French G	66	716
SCARRY			
T S	San Francisco San Francisco 5	67	490
SCARY			
Achilles	San Luis Obispo San Luis Obispo	65	17
SCATENO			
Angel	San Francisco San Francisco 2	67	679
SCATETU			
G*	Nevada Grass Valley	61	144
SCATONE			
Joseph*	Tulara Twp 2	71	7
SCAULAN			
Orin*	Sacramento Natonia	63	286
SCAVER			
Thomas*	Calaveras Twp 4	57	340
SCAWARD			
John	Yuba Bear Rvr	72	1005
SCAWORD			
Geo	Klamath S Fork	59	203
SCAWTHORPE			
Thomas	Tuolumne Sonora	71	190
SCAY			
A G*	Tuolumne Twp 1	71	264
SCBAUGH			
Mr	Sonoma Sonoma	69	643
SCBOLD			
D C	Trinity Lewiston	70	964
Eli	Sacramento Ward 3	63	468
SCBRING			
Thomas*	Sonoma Armally	69	502
SCEARCE			
L	Colusa Monroeville	57	441
SCEEL			
D E*	Nevada Grass Valley	61	189
SCEERON			
Darin*	San Mateo Twp 1	65	65
David*	San Mateo Twp 1	65	65
SCEILS			
Daniel	Placer Folsom	62	639
SCEIPE			
W	San Francisco San Francisco 5	67	549
W F	San Francisco San Francisco 5	67	549
SCELBY			
Mary A*	San Francisco San Francisco 2	67	668
SCEREST			
Fred*	Siskiyou Yreka	69	124
SCERLS			
Robt	Klamath Trinidad	59	221
SCH?ARTS			
M*	Nevada Bridgeport	61	502

Name	County Locale	M653 Roll Page
SCHAAFELT		
William*	Yuba Linda	72 989
SCHAAP		
J M	San Francisco San Francisco 2	67 562
SCHAAR		
Augusta*	Sacramento Ward 4	63 548
SCHAARTR		
Theo*	Nevada Rough &	61 413
SCHAARTZ		
Theo*	Nevada Rough &	61 413
SCHABBER		
Adam	San Francisco San Francisco 1	68 844
SCHABEE		
P	Butte Bidwell	56 711
SCHABEN		
P*	Butte Bidwell	56 711
SCHABER		
J C	Trinity Indian C	70 988
SCHABERE		
P*	Butte Bidwell	56 711
SCHABGUE		
Mary*	San Francisco San Francisco 2	67 749
SCHABJUE		
Mary	San Francisco San Francisco 2	67 749
SCHACALFOOT		
D H*	Sacramento San Joaquin	63 360
SCHACALFORT		
D H*	Sacramento San Joaquin	63 360
SCHACH		
Henry	Sacramento Ward 1	63 82
SCHACXLBON		
R*	Nevada Grass Valley	61 202
SCHACXLBOR		
R*	Nevada Grass Valley	61 202
SCHADE		
Jno	Sacramento Ward 3	63 425
John	San Francisco San Francisco 7	681337
SCHAEFER		
C	San Francisco San Francisco 5	67 483
Chris	Sacramento Ward 4	63 497
Chris	Sacramento Ward 4	63 500
SCHAEFF		
F W	Yuba Long Bar	72 752
SCHAEFFER		
An	San Francisco San Francisco 2	67 802
Francis	Yuba Marysville	72 864
Francis J	Yuba Marysville	72 883
Frank	Yuba Marysville	72 902
Geo	Sacramento Ward 4	63 600
Henry	San Francisco San Francisco 11	104 67
Jacob	San Francisco San Francisco 2	67 797
T	San Joaquin Stockton	641039
SCHAENBERG		
W*	San Francisco San Francisco 1	68 825
SCHAETTGEN		
Joseph	Tuolumne Columbia	71 317
SCHAEXLLON		
R*	Nevada Grass Valley	61 202
SCHAFER		
A	El Dorado Diamond	58 806
A	El Dorado Diamond	58 814
A	Sacramento Ward 1	63 25
Bayard	Sacramento Ward 1	63 12
Caroline	San Francisco San Francisco 8	681314
Chas	Sacramento Ward 1	63 31
F	El Dorado Diamond	58 814
Fred	San Joaquin Stockton	641054
Henry	Sacramento Ward 1	63 34
Henry	Tuolumne Twp 4	71 130
John	Placer Ophirville	62 655
John	Tuolumne Twp 4	71 129
John T	San Francisco San Francisco 9	68 983
Karper*	Placer Dutch Fl	62 718
Martha	Placer Virginia	62 662
SCHAFFER		
A	Trinity Trinity	70 975
B	El Dorado White Oaks	581006
Banard*	Sacramento Ward 1	63 12
C	San Joaquin Stockton	641099
C	Tuolumne Columbia	71 315
Charles	Tuolumne Twp 3	71 463
Chas F	San Francisco San Francisco 2	67 559
David	Sacramento Ward 3	63 452
David	Sacramento Ward 4	63 503
E	Trinity Eastman	70 960
Fred	Amador Twp 1	55 461
Frederick	Santa Clara San Jose	65 280
Fredk	San Francisco San Francisco 2	67 618
Fredr	San Francisco San Francisco 2	67 618
G	San Joaquin Stockton	641099
Geo	Sacramento American	63 172
Geo	Sacramento Brighton	63 208
Geo	Sacramento Franklin	63 324
J S	Sacramento Cosumnes	63 391
John	Placer Michigan	62 831

Name	County Locale	M653 Roll Page
SCHAFFER		
John	Sierra La Porte	66 770
Lewis	Sacramento Sutter	63 293
P	Sacramento Ward 3	63 469
P F	Sacramento Ward 1	63 63
Pierre	Tuolumne Twp 3	71 465
Simon	Placer Michigan	62 827
T	Sacramento Brighton	63 210
William	Plumas Meadow Valley	62 932
William C	Yuba Marysville	72 856
William C	Yuba Marysville	72 861
Wm	Sacramento Georgian	63 343
SCHAFFERS		
Sophie	San Francisco San Francisco 2	67 577
SCHAFFNER		
Martin	Placer Yankee J	62 781
SCHAFT		
Aaron	San Francisco San Francisco 1	68 930
SCHAG		
J	Sutter Yuba	70 766
SCHAGANCH		
H*	San Francisco San Francisco 9	681063
SCHAICK		
W	Trinity Readings	70 996
SCHAIDAN		
Peter*	Yuba Marysville	72 874
SCHAIFER		
George*	San Francisco San Francisco 3	67 80
SCHAIFFER		
An	San Francisco San Francisco 2	67 802
SCHAIX		
Vincent*	Stanislaus Branch	70 702
SCHAKEA		
Christian	Marin S Antoni	60 712
SCHALER		
John	Yuba Long Bar	72 750
Thos	Sacramento Sutter	63 306
Thos	Sacramento Sutter	63 308
SCHALES		
Geo	Siskiyou Callahan	69 9
SCHALINE		
Mathew	San Francisco San Francisco 2	67 629
SCHALL		
Leonard*	Sierra St Louis	66 815
Lewis J	Humbolt Eureka	59 163
Wallace	Yuba Marysville	72 941
SCHALLA		
Fred	Placer Secret R	62 616
SCHALLENBERGER		
J	Siskiyou Klamath	69 86
SCHALOT		
F N	Los Angeles Tejon	59 526
SCHALSON		
Christian	Marin S Antoni	60 712
SCHAMMEL		
Edward	San Francisco San Francisco 4	681153
Henry	San Francisco San Francisco 2	67 576
SCHAMO		
---	Tulara Twp 2	71 36
SCHANDORVI		
John	Sacramento American	63 158
SCHANFELT		
William	Yuba Suida	72 989
SCHANFRAN		
Bertrand*	Sierra Port Win	66 795
Bestrand	Sierra Port Win	66 795
SCHANK		
Jno H	Klamath Dillins	59 214
John	El Dorado Cold Spring	581101
Joseph	Sacramento Ward 4	63 497
Philip	Sacramento Franklin	63 311
SCHANKER		
F	Siskiyou Cottonwoood	69 98
SCHANMEL		
Edward*	San Francisco San Francisco 4	681153
SCHANNAMANN		
Hawi*	Tuolumne Twp 2	71 294
SCHANNMANN		
Harvy	Tuolumne Columbia	71 294
SCHANTY		
J P	Yolo Cottonwoood	72 649
SCHANY		
---	El Dorado White Oaks	581030
SCHAODZ		
August	Solano Fremont	69 383
SCHAPH		
Wm	San Francisco San Francisco 2	67 781
SCHAPPER		
C	Tuolumne Twp 2	71 315
SCHARA		
Matehes*	Mariposa Twp 3	60 573
SCHARBARN		
Wm*	Mendocino Big Rvr	60 845
SCHARD		
Matches*	Mariposa Twp 3	60 573
SCHARDIN		
Joseph P	Yuba Bear Rvr	721002

Name	County Locale	M653 Roll Page
SCHAREE		
Matches*	Mariposa Twp 3	60 573
SCHARK		
Jacob	San Francisco San Francisco 7	681371
SCHARL		
C	San Francisco San Francisco 2	67 777
SCHARP		
M	Nevada Grass Valley	61 166
SCHARRPP		
C	Los Angeles Tejon	59 525
SCHARTS		
M*	Nevada Bridgeport	61 502
SCHARTZ		
Chris	Del Norte Klamath	58 654
SCHATT		
Ballz	Yuba Suida	72 982
Ballz	Yuba Linda Twp	72 983
SCHAUD		
Matches*	Mariposa Twp 3	60 573
SCHAUF		
Nich	Sacramento Ward 1	63 142
Nick	Sacramento Ward 1	63 142
SCHAUFER		
George	San Francisco San Francisco 3	67 80
Peter	Sacramento Ward 4	63 507
SCHAUFRAN		
Bertrand*	Sierra Port Win	66 795
SCHAUFT		
Elba	Placer Ophirville	62 654
SCHAUL		
Leonard	Sierra St Louis	66 815
SCHAUMEL		
Edward*	San Francisco San Francisco 4	681153
SCHAUPE		
John	San Francisco San Francisco 1	68 929
SCHAUPMULLER		
Josephine	Sacramento Ward 3	63 470
SCHAUR		
A	Amador Twp 7	55 415
SCHAW		
Andrew A	Sierra Twp 5	66 943
SCHEAGE		
Antoine*	Yuba Marysville	72 903
SCHEAMAN		
Theresa*	Yuba Marysville	72 858
SCHEAR		
N	Trinity New Rvr	701030
SCHEBER		
Estuart	El Dorado Salmon Hills	581055
SCHEBIA		
Nicholas*	Los Angeles Los Angeles	59 491
SCHECKELS		
J R	El Dorado Salmon Hills	581063
SCHEDDER		
Henry	Mendocino Little L	60 836
SCHEDDIS		
Henry	Mendocino Little L	60 836
SCHEDER		
Jos	Trinity Trinity	701022
SCHEDU		
---*	Tulara Visalia	71 36
SCHEELY		
Fredk*	Tuolumne Big Oak	71 140
SCHEER		
J H	Sacramento Ward 1	63 149
Jacob	Sacramento Ward 4	63 498
William	Sierra Port Win	66 795
SCHEFER		
Antonio	Calaveras Twp 9	57 364
SCHEFERLY		
Jacob	San Luis Obispo San Luis Obispo 65	40
SCHEFNER		
Andrew	Tuolumne Big Oak	71 180
SCHEIFERLY		
John J	San Luis Obispo San Luis Obispo 65	28
SCHEIMER		
Earnest*	Alameda Murray	55 225
SCHEISTER		
Frederich	Yuba Marysville	72 865
SCHEK		
---	Tuolumne Don Pedro	71 537
SCHELD		
Philip	Sacramento Ward 4	63 600
SCHELDER		
John	El Dorado Coloma	581103
SCHELEN		
Jas	Amador Twp 3	55 384
SCHELER		
Estuart*	El Dorado Salmon Falls	581055
SCHELERCHER		
J*	San Francisco San Francisco 5	67 513
SCHELHEIMER		
H	San Francisco San Francisco 10	175 67
SCHELINE		
Nathaniel*	Sierra Gibsonville	66 854

Name	County Locale	M653 RollPage
SCHELKLE		
M	El Dorado Placerville	58 835
SCHELL		
A J	El Dorado Kelsey	581146
A J	El Dorado Placerville	58 849
Augustus	Mariposa Twp 3	60 615
C	Siskiyou Scott Va	69 31
Chas	Sacramento Mississipi	63 188
D	El Dorado Newtown	58 776
Daniel	Tuolumne Twp 2	71 418
Eli	San Francisco San Francisco 5 67 478	
Frank M	San Francisco San Francisco 2 67 556	
George H	Yuba Marysville	72 926
Jacob	Sacramento San Joaquin	63 365
Joseph	Tuolumne Chinese	71 487
Saml	Santa Clara San Jose	65 389
Simon	Tuolumne Sonora	71 480
Theo	Sonoma Sonoma	69 637
Thos	Sonoma Sonoma	69 637
SCHELLHINE		
A F	Nevada Nevada	61 272
SCHELLHOUS		
E J	Placer Sacramento	62 644
Martin A	Placer Sacramento	62 644
Snows M	Placer Sacramento	62 643
SCHELLING		
William	Marin Bolinas	60 742
SCHELLINGER		
Hector	Yuba Long Bar	72 746
Isaac	Sierra Eureka	661045
SCHELLINO		
Angelo	Tuolumne Montezuma	71 503
SCHELSEDEE		
---	San Francisco San Francisco 7 681421	
SCHELTER		
Nicholas	Siskiyou Callahan	69 1
SCHEMAHORE		
John	Santa Cruz Soguel	66 592
SCHEMBEIN		
Thadeus*	Solano Benecia	69 309
SCHEMER		
I	Amador Twp 2	55 308
J	Amador Twp 2	55 308
SCHEMERHORN		
John	Santa Cruz Soguel	66 592
SCHEMERKOM		
H	Sacramento Granite	63 238
SCHEN		
G	San Francisco San Francisco 9 68 937	
Henry*	San Francisco San Francisco 7 681377	
Peter	San Joaquin Castoria	64 902
SCHENCK		
Joseph	Sacramento Sutter	63 308
Wm	San Francisco San Francisco 1 68 915	
SCHENDEMAN		
Joseph	Sacramento Franklin	63 310
SCHENEN		
Ernst*	Alameda Brooklyn	55 153
SCHENER		
L	San Francisco San Francisco 5 67 506	
SCHENFF		
John*	Yuba Marysville	72 955
SCHENIFF		
John	Yuba Marysville	72 955
SCHENK		
Chas	San Francisco San Francisco 1 68 820	
Fredrick	Tuolumne Chinese	71 487
H	Butte Chico	56 549
Hugo	San Francisco San Francisco 7 681368	
Michael	San Francisco San Francisco 2 67 723	
SCHENPELCHER		
Wm	Tuolumne Twp 2	71 342
SCHENPF		
George*	Yuba Marysville	72 943
SCHENTY		
J P*	Yolo Cottonwood	72 649
SCHENUER		
Chas*	Butte Eureka	56 646
SCHEOR		
P	Siskiyou Klamath	69 87
SCHEPACOSSA		
Stephen	Calaveras Twp 7	57 25
SCHERDENN		
C*	Siskiyou Scott Ri	69 71
SCHERER		
Jacob	Yuba Marysville	72 954
SCHERFF		
John	Contra Costa Twp 3	57 586
SCHERIZAN		
Louis	San Bernardino San Bernadino	64 673
SCHERJEO		
Willaim	Shasta Millvill	66 750
SCHERMAN		
Theresa*	Yuba Marysville	72 858
SCHERMER		
Chas*	Butte Eureka	56 646

Name	County Locale	M653 RollPage
SCHERMERBORN		
C	Tuolumne Big Oak	71 130
SCHERMERHORN		
C	Tuolumne Twp 4	71 130
S P	Sacramento Ward 4	63 564
SCHERPECOCH		
John*	San Francisco San Francisco 3 67 86	
SCHERPEL		
Rudolph	Mendocino Big Rvr	60 841
SCHERPIL		
Andolph	Mendocino Big Rvr	60 841
Rudolph	Mendocino Big Rvr	60 841
SCHERR		
Jos	San Francisco San Francisco 2 67 596	
Joseph	San Francisco San Francisco 11 97 67	
SCHERSSLCOCH		
John*	San Francisco San Francisco 3 67 86	
SCHERTTZ		
Louis	San Francisco San Francisco 4 681161	
SCHERYED		
William	Shasta Millvill	66 750
SCHETLER		
Henry	San Francisco San Francisco 11 139 67	
SCHETMAN		
Charles	San Francisco San Francisco 11 101 67	
SCHETTER		
Frederick	San Francisco San Francisco 11 100 67	
Nicholas	Siskiyou Callahan	69 1
SCHEUEN		
Ernst*	Alameda Brooklyn	55 153
SCHEUOCRER		
Elizabeth*	Yuba Marysville	72 885
SCHEUPF		
George*	Yuba Marysville	72 943
SCHEURMAN		
W*	Shasta Shasta	66 665
SCHEUSMAN		
W*	Shasta Shasta	66 665
SCHEVENINTER		
Louis	San Francisco San Francisco 7 681370	
SCHEVER		
Jacob*	Yuba Marysville	72 954
Jas	Sonoma Petaluma	69 569
SCHEVERRIA		
V	San Francisco San Francisco 2 67 713	
SCHEVOCREN		
John P	Yuba Marysville	72 875
SCHEVOERER		
John P	Yuba Marysville	72 875
SCHEWEM		
C	Siskiyou Scott Ri	69 71
SCHEWENN		
C	Siskiyou Scott Ri	69 71
SCHIACK		
Conrad*	Calaveras Twp 6	57 113
SCHIBYE		
C B	Siskiyou Scott Va	69 47
SCHICK		
Daniel	Los Angeles Los Angeles	59 348
SCHICKLY		
Chrisoper	Calaveras Twp 9	57 350
Christopher	Calaveras Twp 9	57 350
SCHIDOCHER		
John	Siskiyou Scott Va	69 49
SCHIDOCHOR		
John*	Siskiyou Scott Va	69 49
SCHIDOCKER		
John*	Siskiyou Scott Va	69 49
SCHIDU		
---	Tulara Twp 2	71 36
SCHIEBELL		
L*	Nevada Washington	61 336
SCHIEBILL		
L*	Nevada Washington	61 336
SCHIEDEL		
Christopher	Yuba Marysville	72 958
SCHIEFFER		
Robt	San Francisco San Francisco 2 67 718	
SCHIELHALL		
Harman	Sonoma Petaluma	69 571
SCHIENDAN		
Peter*	Yuba Marysville	72 874
SCHIER		
William*	Sierra Port Win	66 795
SCHIEVDAN		
Peter*	Yuba Marysville	72 874
SCHIEZKEN		
Jacob	San Francisco San Francisco 1 68 811	
SCHIFER		
Antonio	Calaveras Twp 9	57 364
SCHIFFTIAN		
Louis	Tuolumne Twp 2	71 287

Name	County Locale	M653 RollPage
SCHIFFTIAN		
Sanis*	Tuolumne Twp 2	71 287
SCHIFNER		
Andrew	Tuolumne Twp 4	71 180
SCHILE		
George	San Francisco San Francisco 7 681418	
SCHILES		
G W	El Dorado Placerville	58 859
SCHILL		
Abraham	Stanislaus Emory	70 757
Daniel	Tuolumne Shawsfla	71 418
Simon	Tuolumne Twp 1	71 480
SCHILLE		
Marcus	San Diego San Diego	64 762
SCHILLENGER		
H	Butte Oro	56 680
SCHILLER		
Joseph	Sacramento Georgian	63 346
Louis	Santa Clara Burnett	65 256
Peter	Placer Dutch Fl	62 721
SCHILLHIRN		
A F	Nevada Nevada	61 272
SCHILLING		
Fred	San Francisco San Francisco 3 67 72	
Frederick	San Francisco San Francisco 7 681330	
Jacob	Alameda Brooklyn	55 152
SCHILLINGER		
H	Butte Oro	56 680
Hestor	Yuba New York	72 746
SCHILLU		
Charles	Placer Forest H	62 800
SCHILY		
Adam*	Stanislaus Emory	70 741
SCHIMDT		
J C*	San Francisco San Francisco 2 67 732	
SCHIMIER		
Chas	Butte Eureka	56 646
SCHIMP		
Eliza	Sierra Whiskey	66 849
SCHINABLE		
Charles	Sierra Grizzly	661057
SCHINBERG		
Charles	Mendocino Ukiah	60 801
SCHINDLER		
C	Sacramento Ward 4	63 533
D	Yolo Cache Crk	72 637
John	Placer Yankee J	62 780
SCHINE		
Patrick	Siskiyou Callahan	69 3
SCHINEFFE		
Conrad	Plumas Quincy	62 952
SCHINFER		
J	El Dorado Placerville	58 898
SCHINGLER		
John	Placer Ophirville	62 658
SCHINIBEL		
Henry	Sierra Whiskey	66 847
SCHINIDT		
J C*	San Francisco San Francisco 2 67 732	
SCHINKEL		
Charles	Yuba Marysville	72 955
SCHINNER		
Jos*	Butte Oregon	56 638
SCHINSE		
Geo	El Dorado Coloma	581117
SCHINTLER		
P	Butte Kimshaw	56 570
SCHINTZ		
Alfred	San Francisco San Francisco 2 67 779	
Herman	San Francisco San Francisco 2 67 779	
Hermann	San Francisco San Francisco 2 67 779	
John J	Calaveras Twp 4	57 323
SCHIOERZ		
Jacob*	Sierra Downieville	66 972
SCHIOUZ		
Jacob*	Sierra Downieville	66 972
SCHIPMAN		
John	Placer Todds Va	62 762
SCHIRAB		
Adolph*	San Francisco San Francisco 8 681316	
SCHIRENOR		
P J*	Napa Hot Springs	61 20
SCHIRFFER		
Robt	San Francisco San Francisco 2 67 718	
SCHIRUZ		
Jacob*	Sierra Downieville	66 972
SCHISELOT		
J	Yolo Washington	72 599
SCHISER		
Gerdy	Amador Twp 2	55 326
Goody*	Amador Twp 2	55 326
SCHISES		
Geody*	Amador Twp 2	55 326
SCHISING		
George*	San Francisco San Francisco 3 67 32	
SCHISTER		
Henry	Nevada Red Dog	61 542

Name	County Locale	M653 RollPage
SCHISTRIDS		
George*	San Joaquin Douglass	64 917
SCHITDER		
Geo*	Butte Kimshaw	56 572
SCHITELER		
Geo	Butte Kimshaw	56 572
SCHITLEN		
David	Butte Eureka	56 645
SCHITTLER		
Jacob	Siskiyou Yreka	69 144
SCHIVATKA		
N F	Marin Tomales	60 719
SCHIVENOR		
P J	Napa Hot Springs	61 20
SCHIVER		
Frederick*	San Francisco San Francisco 3	67 80
SCHKETTER		
Clous*	Calaveras Twp 4	57 313
SCHLACTER		
Wm	Amador Twp 1	55 494
SCHLAD		
Geo	El Dorado Mud Springs	58 962
SCHLAGERT		
Herman	Contra Costa Twp 2	57 564
SCHLAHEDEN		
M	Yuba Foster B	72 836
SCHLAND		
Frank	San Francisco San Francisco 1	68 811
SCHLASSER		
A*	San Francisco San Francisco 9	681051
SCHLECHT		
George	Alameda Murray	55 222
SCHLECHTWEG		
Henry	Mendocino Twp 1	60 891
SCHLEGEL		
Francis	Siskiyou Klamath	69 93
SCHLEIDER		
Wm	San Francisco San Francisco 1	68 819
SCHLEIER		
Mary	Alameda Brooklyn	55 148
SCHLEIGH		
Charles	Tulara Twp 3	71 46
SCHLEMAN		
Ernest	Yolo Cache Crk	72 644
SCHLENK		
George*	El Dorado Georgetown	58 708
SCHLEPEN		
F	Trinity Mouth Ca	701013
SCHLERCHER		
J*	San Francisco San Francisco 5	67 513
SCHLESINGER		
Oscar	Mendocino Ukiah	60 799
SCHLESLER		
John	San Francisco San Francisco 8	681285
SCHLESTER		
John	San Francisco San Francisco 8	681285
SCHLEY		
Daniel	San Francisco San Francisco 7	681347
SCHLICH		
Andrew	El Dorado Casumnes	581174
SCHLICHT		
Charles	Siskiyou Yreka	69 135
SCHLICK		
Andrew	El Dorado Casumnes	581174
SCHLIER		
G	El Dorado Newtown	58 776
SCHLIGEL		
Francis	Siskiyou Klamath	69 93
SCHLINDER		
W F D	San Francisco San Francisco 7	681355
SCHLING		
Mike	Trinity Mouth Ca	701013
SCHLIPEN		
F	Trinity Mouth Ca	701013
SCHLISINGER		
Iscar	Mendocino Ukiah	60 799
Max	Santa Clara San Jose	65 290
SCHLITTLER		
H	Placer Ophirville	62 656
SCHLOP		
Lewis	Sacramento Ward 1	63 115
Louis	Sacramento Ward 1	63 115
SCHLOPER		
Theodore	Sonoma Petaluma	69 604
Thos*	Sonoma Petaluma	69 580
SCHLORSE		
Coroline	Alameda Oakland	55 9
SCHLOSS		
Benj	San Francisco San Francisco 9	68 971
Benjn	San Francisco San Francisco 9	68 971
SCHLOSSEN		
Eliza*	El Dorado Newtown	58 777
SCHLOSSER		
A*	San Francisco San Francisco 9	681051
Theodore	Sonoma Petaluma	69 604

Name	County Locale	M653 RollPage
SCHLOSSER		
Thos*	Sonoma Petaluma	69 580
SCHLOTZHIMER		
P	El Dorado Eldorado	58 937
SCHLUCKEBEER		
Wm*	Sacramento Ward 3	63 469
SCHLUCKEBUR		
Wm*	Sacramento Ward 3	63 469
SCHLUMON		
Ernest	Yolo Cache	72 644
SCHLUNT		
Charles	San Francisco San Francisco 7	681432
SCHLUTER		
Henry	San Joaquin Elkhorn	64 997
SCHLUTIUS		
A	Sacramento Franklin	63 317
H	Sacramento Franklin	63 317
SCHLYAR		
Francis	Calaveras Twp 5	57 147
SCHMAETZE		
Louis	Sacramento Ward 4	63 594
SCHMAHL		
Jacob	San Francisco San Francisco 2	67 675
SCHMALENBERGER		
George	Yuba Long Bar	72 755
SCHMALENMEYER		
George	Yuba Long Bar	72 755
SCHMALTS		
Adolphus	Contra Costa Twp 1	57 500
SCHMEDLEVY		
Peter*	San Francisco San Francisco 2	67 761
SCHMEDT		
William*	San Francisco San Francisco 9	681097
SCHMEIDELL		
J	San Francisco San Francisco 5	67 513
SCHMEIZER		
Geo	Sacramento Ward 4	63 503
SCHMELYER		
F M*	Yuba Foster B	72 829
SCHMERTY		
C	San Francisco San Francisco 6	67 441
SCHMIAT		
Feerainand	Tuolumne Columbia	71 294
SCHMIDLEY		
Peter*	San Francisco San Francisco 2	67 761
SCHMIDT		
---	San Francisco San Francisco 9	681097
Alex	Trinity Trinity	701022
Andrew	Yuba Long Bar	72 753
Anton	Tuolumne Jamestown	71 454
C	San Francisco San Francisco 4	681161
Carl	Humbolt Union	59 180
Charles	San Diego Colorado	64 812
Charles	San Francisco San Francisco 3	67 13
Charles	Tuolumne Twp 1	71 245
Charles	Tuolumne Twp 4	71 459
Conrad	Del Norte Klamath	58 654
Cyrus	Tuolumne Sonora	71 483
E	San Francisco San Francisco 2	67 752
E	Tuolumne Twp 2	71 332
E*	San Francisco San Francisco 5	67 491
F	Tuolumne Sonora	71 222
F	Tuolumne Twp 3	71 469
Ferdinand	Tuolumne Twp 2	71 294
Frederick	Alameda Oakland	55 27
Frederick	Tuolumne Twp 4	71 128
G*	Sacramento Alabama	63 412
Geo	San Francisco San Francisco 10	247 67
George	Nevada Rough &	61 408
H	Tuolumne Twp 2	71 279
H L D	Sacramento Ward 4	63 499
H W	San Francisco San Francisco 5	67 493
Henry	Sacramento Ward 4	63 600
Henry	San Joaquin Stockton	641017
Henry	Tuolumne Big Oak	71 144
Henry	Yolo Slate Ra	72 687
Henry	Yuba North Ea	72 687
Henry	Yuba Long Bar	72 751
I C	San Francisco San Francisco 2	67 752
J	San Francisco San Francisco 6	67 471
J	San Francisco San Francisco 2	67 630
J J	San Francisco San Francisco 10	324 67
Jacob	Nevada Bridgeport	61 452
Jacob	Tuolumne Twp 2	71 318
Jas	Sacramento Ward 3	63 458
Jas	Sacramento Ward 4	63 601
Jeremiah	Sacramento Ward 4	63 507
Jno	Nevada Nevada	61 281
Jno M	Sacramento Ward 1	63 147
John	Amador Twp 1	55 460
John	Nevada Bloomfield	61 522
John	San Francisco San Francisco 4	681161
John	San Francisco San Francisco 2	67 680
John	Tuolumne Twp 3	71 431

Name	County Locale	M653 RollPage
SCHMIDT		
Julius H	Yuba Bear Rvr	721009
Lerren	Stanislaus Branch	70 702
Louisa	San Francisco San Francisco 2	67 798
Morton	San Francisco San Francisco 7	681426
Moses	Sacramento Ward 4	63 600
Nicholas	San Francisco San Francisco 7	681426
Paul	San Francisco San Francisco 2	67 802
Peter	Tuolumne Twp 1	71 257
S C	San Francisco San Francisco 5	67 493
William	San Francisco San Francisco 9	681097
William	San Joaquin Castoria	64 905
Wm	San Francisco San Francisco 1	68 825
Wm	San Francisco San Francisco 1	68 930
Wm Von*	San Francisco San Francisco 1	68 915
	San Francisco	
SCHMIDTH		
Jacob	San Diego Agua Caliente	64 855
SCHMIED		
David M*	Del Norte Crescent	58 646
SCHMIER		
Phillip	Sacramento Ward 3	63 469
SCHMIGHT		
Casfar	Sacramento Ward 4	63 533
SCHMILYER		
F M	Yuba Fosters	72 829
SCHMIN		
Wm	Tuolumne Twp 1	71 193
SCHMISEKAMP		
John	Trinity Indian C	70 988
Peter	Trinity Weaverville	701062
SCHMIT		
Geo	Sonoma Petaluma	69 574
Henry	Sonoma Petaluma	69 560
John	Tuolumne Twp 4	71 137
SCHMITD		
Theadore	Amador Twp 1	55 478
SCHMITT		
Ernest	San Francisco San Francisco 2	67 653
Henry	San Francisco San Francisco 4	681224
Jacob	Placer Forest H	62 793
Mary	San Francisco San Francisco 2	67 795
SCHMITZ		
Rachael*	San Francisco San Francisco 7	681378
SCHMLIFFER		
Wm	Sacramento Ward 4	63 525
SCHMODLERY		
Peter*	San Francisco San Francisco 2	67 761
SCHMODUNY		
Peter*	San Francisco San Francisco 2	67 761
SCHMOLDT		
Albert	Colusa Butte Crk	57 464
SCHMUD		
David M*	Del Norte Crescent	58 646
SCHNABLA		
Chas H	Placer Ophirville	62 655
SCHNABLY		
Henry	Placer Ophirville	62 657
SCHNALIN		
A	El Dorado Eldorado	58 948
SCHNAPS		
John W	San Francisco San Francisco 4	681220
SCHNAUM		
H*	San Francisco San Francisco 9	681070
SCHNAVAL		
Louis	Trinity Trinity	701022
SCHNCHERDT		
Ernest*	Colusa Colusi	57 427
SCHNEIBOUG		
Danl*	Plumas Quincy	62 984
SCHNEIDEE		
Fred*	Nevada Bridgeport	61 499
SCHNEIDER		
Allen	El Dorado Placerville	58 914
Chas	San Francisco San Francisco 1	68 930
Edward	Colusa Spring Valley	57 432
Edward N	San Diego Colorado	64 811
Fred	El Dorado Kelsey	581147
Fred	El Dorado Grizzly	581182
Fred*	Nevada Bridgeport	61 499
Geo	El Dorado Placerville	58 882
Geo	El Dorado Placerville	58 895
Geo	Mendocino Big Rvr	60 843
George	Yuba Marysville	72 928
H	El Dorado Diamond	58 766
Henry	El Dorado Mud Springs	581000
Henry	San Francisco San Francisco 2	67 592
Henry	San Francisco San Francisco 1	68 835
Henry	Trinity Rattle Snake	701029
Henry	Tulara Visalia	71 103
James	El Dorado Casumnes	581166
John	El Dorado Diamond	58 763
John	El Dorado Placerville	58 898
Louis	El Dorado Coloma	581081
SCHNEIDT		
Erdman	El Dorado Mud Springs	58 968

Name	County Locale	M653 RollPage
SCHNEILELER		
Geo*	San Francisco San Francisco 2	67 679
SCHNELL		
Joseph G*	Mendocino Ukiah	60 801
Peter	Tuolumne Chinese	71 487
SCHNELLE		
Charles	Contra Costa Twp 2	57 553
SCHNERDER		
Geo	Mendocino Big Rvr	60 843
SCHNESTER		
Joseph	El Dorado Coloma	581117
SCHNIBER		
Frederick*	Yuba Marysville	72 858
SCHNICKER		
George	San Francisco San Francisco 7	681329
Joseph	San Francisco San Francisco 7	681329
SCHNIDER		
Chas	Sacramento Ward 4	63 500
Francis	Solano Benecia	69 317
Jno S	Alameda Oakland	55 37
John	Colusa Spring Valley	57 432
SCHNIDLER		
D	Yolo Cache	72 637
SCHNIDT		
F*	Sacramento Sutter	63 290
John	Amador Twp 1	55 460
SCHNIEDER		
Henry	San Francisco San Francisco 2	67 592
SCHNITLICK		
Fred	Sonoma Petaluma	69 583
SCHNOEDER		
J	Butte Oregon	56 642
SCHNOUFER		
William*	Placer Michigan	62 843
SCHNUDCE		
Fred	Nevada Bridgeport	61 499
SCHNUTD		
Caroline	San Francisco San Francisco 2	67 638
SCHNYAN		
Joseph	Tuolumne Twp 1	71 481
SCHNYDER		
Joseph	Tuolumne Sonora	71 481
SCHOAB		
Valentine	Yuba Marysville	72 888
SCHOADZ		
Anguss	Solano Fremont	69 383
SCHOAR		
Augusta*	Sacramento Ward 4	63 548
SCHOBER		
Josephina	Amador Township	55 463
Josephine	Amador Twp 1	55 463
SCHOBERG		
Herman	San Francisco San Francisco 2	67 762
John	Sierra Downieville	66 960
SCHOCK		
Hon	Sacramento Granite	63 232
M	Trinity Sturdiva	701006
SCHOCKEY		
W	El Dorado Diamond	58 789
SCHOD		
William	San Francisco San Francisco 3	67 13
SCHODER		
Horton	Amador Twp 5	55 357
M	Trinity Honest B	701043
SCHODY		
Geo	Sacramento Granite	63 230
SCHOE		
John	Yuba Bear Rvr	72 998
SCHOEFIELD		
Charles*	San Francisco San Francisco 7	681419
SCHOEL		
Henry	San Francisco San Francisco 4	681171
SCHOELKOFF		
Chris	Del Norte Happy Ca	58 661
SCHOELLGN		
T*	Placer Rattle Snake	62 628
SCHOELLYN		
T*	Placer Rattle Snake	62 628
SCHOEMANN		
Otto	Sierra Gibsonville	66 854
SCHOEMENAN		
H	San Francisco San Francisco 2	67 802
SCHOENFIELD		
S	Tehama Red Bluff	70 916
SCHOER		
Henry	Sacramento Ward 4	63 534
Lewis	Santa Clara San Jose	65 281
SCHOFF		
Aaron	San Joaquin Douglass	64 926
SCHOFFER		
Lewis	Sacramento Ward 1	63 75
Louis	Sacramento Ward 1	63 75
SCHOFIELD		
Ralph	Nevada Bloomfield	61 513
Tracey	Trinity Weaverville	701065
Wm	Butte Oregon	56 636

Name	County Locale	M653 RollPage
SCHOFNER		
Frederick	San Francisco San Francisco 7	681425
Friderick	San Francisco San Francisco 7	681425
SCHOL		
Adam	Yuba New York	72 719
SCHOLBER		
Josephina	Amador Twp 1	55 463
SCHOLDEN		
Henry	Amador Twp 2	55 310
Henry	Amador Twp 2	55 312
SCHOLDS		
P	Solano Benecia	69 303
SCHOLENG		
Herman*	San Francisco San Francisco 2	67 762
SCHOLER		
Jno	Butte Kimshaw	56 579
SCHOLERG		
Herman*	San Francisco San Francisco 2	67 762
SCHOLES		
Jane	Mariposa Twp 3	60 557
SCHOLFIELD		
Charles*	San Francisco San Francisco 7	681419
SCHOLL		
Adam	Yolo Slate Ra	72 719
Asabel	Sonoma Mendocino	69 461
Asahel	Sonoma Mendocino	69 461
Christian	Sierra Twp 5	66 943
Christian H	Yuba Marysville	72 876
Clenstcan H	Yuba Marysville	72 876
E	El Dorado Kelsey	581134
Henry	San Francisco San Francisco 4	681171
Louis	San Francisco San Francisco 7	681416
Margaret	San Francisco San Francisco 7	681416
Michael	San Francisco San Francisco 2	67 606
SCHOLLAIS		
Andrew*	El Dorado Cold Spring	581101
SCHOLLARS		
Andrew	El Dorado Cold Spring	581101
SCHOLLE		
Jacob	San Francisco San Francisco 2	67 607
Wm	San Francisco San Francisco 2	67 607
SCHOLLENBERGER		
J	Siskiyou Klamath	69 86
SCHOLLENBURGER		
F	San Francisco San Francisco 2	67 703
SCHOLLZ		
Herman*	San Francisco San Francisco 9	681071
SCHOLON		
Nelson	Santa Clara Redwood	65 450
SCHOLTY		
George	Nevada Bloomfield	61 522
Herman	San Francisco San Francisco 9	681071
SCHOLTZ		
Charles	San Francisco San Francisco 3	67 41
Herman*	San Francisco San Francisco 9	681071
SCHOLU		
Jno	Butte Kimshaw	56 579
SCHOLUKE		
Ralph	Nevada Bloomfield	61 513
SCHOLY		
Luis	Calaveras Twp 4	57 332
SCHOMACHER		
Lewis	San Francisco San Francisco 10	231
		67
SCHOMP		
J	Sacramento Ward 4	63 517
SCHONADIKA		
F	Del Norte Happy Ca	58 667
SCHONEMAN		
C W	Amador Twp 2	55 307
SCHONFD		
Jonas*	San Francisco San Francisco 7	681431
SCHONFELD		
Jonas	San Francisco San Francisco 7	681431
SCHONG		
---	Trinity Weaverville	701072
SCHONHOLCAR		
George	Yuba Long Bar	72 754
SCHONLIHT		
John	Santa Clara San Jose	65 294
SCHOOAB		
Valentine	Yuba Marysville	72 888
SCHOOBEY		
James P	Yuba Marysville	72 976
SCHOOCK		
John*	Sierra Scales D	66 802
SCHOOF		
J	El Dorado Placerville	58 851
SCHOOLAY		
James P	Yuba Marysville	72 976
SCHOOLBOUGH		
D A	Tuolumne Columbia	71 319
SCHOOLCRAFT		
Howard	Yolo Merritt	72 583
SCHOOLER		
Henry	Yolo Merritt	72 578

Name	County Locale	M653 RollPage
SCHOOLES		
Henry	Yolo Merritt	72 578
SCHOOLEY		
Daniel	Yuba Marysville	72 913
William	El Dorado Coloma	581080
SCHOOLING		
Ferry*	Colusa Monroeville	57 449
Jerry*	Colusa Monroeville	57 449
SCHOOLMAKER		
Isaac	Sacramento Dry Crk	63 373
SCHOOLMON		
Inctous*	Alameda Brooklyn	55 137
Metous*	Alameda Brooklyn	55 137
SCHOOLS		
Hall	Solano Benecia	69 284
SCHOOLY		
Daniel	Yuba Marysville	72 913
SCHOOMBS		
Wm	San Francisco San Francisco 1	68 855
SCHOONER		
John	Los Angeles Los Angeles	59 392
Louis	Calaveras Twp 9	57 390
SCHOONMAKER		
Jas	Sacramento Ward 4	63 502
SCHOONONER		
S	El Dorado Kelsey	581156
SCHOORN		
John H*	San Diego Colorado	64 808
SCHOPH		
Jos	Nevada Nevada	61 290
SCHOPPE		
Chas	Trinity Steiner	701000
SCHOPPMAN		
Henry	Tuolumne Big Oak	71 144
Kmary	Napa Napa	61 92
Mary	Napa Napa	61 92
Wm	Tuolumne Twp 4	71 144
SCHORARTZ		
Lewis	Santa Cruz Santa Cruz	66 614
SCHORF		
Anton	San Bernardino San Bernadino	64 623
SCHORHOEAR		
George	Yuba Long Bar	72 754
SCHORMAN		
Anaeil*	Nevada Bridgeport	61 455
SCHORMN		
Anaeil*	Nevada Bridgeport	61 455
SCHORMY		
Robt*	El Dorado Coloma	581082
SCHORNM		
Anaeil	Nevada Bridgeport	61 455
SCHORNY		
Robt*	El Dorado Coloma	581082
SCHORR		
Peter	Trinity Trinity	701022
SCHOSINGER		
Joseph	Yuba Marysville	72 961
SCHOSSER		
Eliza*	El Dorado Newtown	58 777
SCHOTCHBAM		
Henry J	San Francisco San Francisco 5	67 515
SCHOTCHLER		
Jos B	San Francisco San Francisco 9	681030
SCHOTPITCH		
Godfrey	Placer Todds Va	62 762
SCHOTT		
Conrad*	Sierra St Louis	66 817
John	Placer Grizzly	62 755
SCHOTTE		
J	Sacramento Ward 4	63 551
SCHOTTERS		
Stephen	San Francisco San Francisco 9	681054
SCHOUFELD		
E	San Francisco San Francisco 5	67 495
SCHOUFER		
George*	San Francisco San Francisco 3	67 80
SCHOUMAN		
Hanse	Tuolumne Twp 2	71 294
SCHOUNAN		
Theresa*	Yuba Marysville	72 853
SCHOUNONER		
S	El Dorado Kelsey	581156
SCHOVARTZ		
Lewis*	Santa Cruz Santa Cruz	66 614
SCHOVIK		
John*	Sierra Scales D	66 802
SCHOWARTZ		
S	Tuolumne Twp 2	71 287
SCHOWIAN		
Theresa*	Yuba Marysville	72 853
SCHOWLER		
H	El Dorado Placerville	58 817
SCHOYER		
Francis	San Francisco San Francisco 8	681252
SCHRABER		
S	El Dorado Placerville	58 824

California 1860 Census Index

Name	County Locale	M653 Roll	Page
SCHRACK			
Eavin G	Calaveras Twp 4	57	329
Edwin G	Calaveras Twp 4	57	329
John	San Joaquin Stockton	64	1038
SCHRACKER			
C	San Joaquin Stockton	64	1066
SCHRADA			
Harman	Contra Costa Twp 1	57	486
SCHRADER			
Charles*	Tuolumne Twp 1	71	241
Charly	Tuolumne Sonora	71	241
Chas	Sacramento Ward 1	63	12
Chas	Sacramento Ward 3	63	468
Chorles*	Tuolumne Twp 1	71	241
George F	Solano Vacaville	69	344
John	Plumas Quincy	62	992
Joseph	El Dorado Mud Springs	58	981
Sophie	San Francisco San Francisco 2	67	660
SCHRAEBER			
John	Sacramento Ward 3	63	430
SCHRAEDER			
William	San Francisco San Francisco 7	68	1333
SCHRAGE			
Antoine	Yuba Marysville	72	903
SCHRAGER			
Gustav	Sacramento Ward 4	63	587
SCHRAIDER			
Jacob	El Dorado Kelsey	58	1126
Joseph	Santa Clara San Jose	65	383
William	San Francisco San Francisco 7	68	1333
SCHRAIN			
Jacob*	Napa Napa	61	108
SCHRALER			
Charles	Tuolumne Twp 3	71	441
SCHRALL			
Jacob	Stanislaus Oatvale	70	716
SCHRAM			
F	San Francisco San Francisco 5	67	513
Jacob	Napa Napa	61	108
SCHRAN			
Jas	Sacramento Ward 1	63	73
SCHRANCK			
Fred*	San Francisco San Francisco 1	68	893
SCHRANDA			
John	San Francisco San Francisco 2	67	722
SCHRARDER			
C	Shasta French G	66	722
SCHRATH			
Foley	Sacramento Ward 1	63	29
SCHRAUCK			
Fred*	San Francisco San Francisco 1	68	893
SCHRBU			
Phillilp	Butte Ophir	56	764
Phillip	Butte Ophir	56	764
SCHRDA			
Fred	Placer Virginia	62	665
SCHREDER			
Henry Y	Alameda Oakland	55	40
Wm	Yuba Long Bar	72	748
SCHREEBES			
Danl*	San Francisco San Francisco 1	68	854
SCHREIBE			
T	El Dorado Placerville	58	871
SCHREIBER			
Danl*	San Francisco San Francisco 1	68	854
Frederick	Yuba Marysville	72	858
Ida	San Francisco San Francisco 7	68	1325
Idi*	San Francisco San Francisco 7	68	1325
John	San Francisco San Francisco 10	67	217
SCHREIDER			
Eodocus	San Francisco San Francisco 8	68	1304
Frederick	San Francisco San Francisco 7	68	1419
Henry	San Francisco San Francisco 1	68	852
Herman*	San Francisco San Francisco 1	68	852
Jacob	San Francisco San Francisco 8	68	1306
SCHREINER			
Earnest*	Alameda Murray	55	225
SCHREM			
Henry	Shasta Shasta	66	674
SCHRER			
Chris	Sacramento Ward 1	63	43
SCHREUDER			
Henry*	San Francisco San Francisco 1	68	856
SCHREYER			
Morris	Yuba Marysville	72	900
SCHRICO			
E*	Shasta Shasta	66	665
SCHRIEFER			
D H	San Francisco San Francisco 10	67	209
SCHRIER			
Chris	Sacramento Ward 1	63	43
Daniel	San Francisco San Francisco 7	68	1417
SCHRIEVER			
E	Siskiyou Scott Va	69	51
SCHRIFRLY			
Christian*	Solano Vacaville	69	362
SCHRINDER			
John	Amador Twp 1	55	461
SCHRINDT			
E*	San Francisco San Francisco 5	67	491
SCHRINNON			
Albert*	Contra Costa Twp 3	57	589
SCHRINNOR			
Albert*	Contra Costa Twp 3	57	589
SCHRIPHEN			
C	Nevada Nevada	61	278
SCHRIPHERE			
C*	Nevada Nevada	61	278
SCHRIVER			
R	Shasta Shasta	66	665
SCHRIWIDEM			
Peter*	Stanislaus Emory	70	753
SCHRNTLER			
P*	Butte Kimshaw	56	570
SCHROAB			
Valentine*	Yuba Marysville	72	888
SCHROCK			
Edwin G	Calaveras Twp 4	57	329
Henry C	Calaveras Twp 6	57	153
Louis M*	Calaveras Twp 6	57	152
SCHRODER			
---	Sacramento Granite	63	255
Christopher	Yuba Marysville	72	864
Frederick	Yuba Marysville	72	924
G	Shasta Shasta	66	654
H	San Francisco San Francisco 1	68	853
Harod R	Sacramento Ward 4	63	563
J M	Amador Twp 5	55	344
Jas	Sacramento Ward 1	63	18
Louis	San Francisco San Francisco 3	67	67
Minnie	San Francisco San Francisco 8	68	1261
SCHROEBER			
Henry L*	Yuba New York	72	721
SCHROEDER			
A	San Francisco San Francisco 7	68	1435
A	San Francisco San Francisco 10	67	351
C F	San Francisco San Francisco 10	67	169
Caspar	Yuba Rose Bar	72	820
Casper	Yuba Rose Bar	72	820
Charles	Santa Clara Burnett	65	256
F	Shasta Shasta	66	674
Geo	San Francisco San Francisco 1	68	927
Henry	Sacramento Ward 1	63	42
Henry	San Francisco San Francisco 1	68	919
Henry L*	Yuba New York	72	721
J	Butte Oregon	56	642
Jack	Yuba Rose Bar	72	791
Jno D	Mendocino Arrana	60	857
John	Santa Clara San Jose	65	284
John	Siskiyou Yreka	69	138
John*	Yuba New York	72	721
Louid	Nevada Bloomfield	61	513
Louis	Nevada Bloomfield	61	513
Louis	San Francisco San Francisco 8	68	1318
Michael	Yuba Long Bar	72	742
Morgan	Santa Clara San Jose	65	330
Welth*	Siskiyou Yreka	69	139
SCHROEDOR			
Louis	San Francisco San Francisco 8	68	1318
SCHROELLBER			
Henry L	Yuba New York	72	721
SCHROGER			
Aaron	Marin San Rafael	60	765
SCHROLA			
Charles*	Calaveras Twp 5	57	218
SCHROLADO			
Jno	Sonoma Petaluma	69	550
SCHROLCE			
Charles H	Calaveras Twp 5	57	218
SCHRORORIS			
Henry*	Siskiyou Callahan	69	5
SCHROSS			
N J	San Francisco San Francisco 5	67	522
SCHROTE			
Charles H*	Calaveras Twp 5	57	218
SCHROTH			
Amelia	Sacramento Ward 1	63	24
Charles	San Francisco San Francisco 8	68	1313
Geo	Sacramento Ward 1	63	24
SCHROTT			
Henry	San Francisco San Francisco 7	68	1364
SCHROUDER			
---	San Francisco San Francisco 7	68	1355
SCHROVORIS			
Henry*	Siskiyou Callahan	69	5
SCHROWRIS			
Henry*	Siskiyou Callahan	69	5
SCHROWUR			
Henry	Siskiyou Callahan	69	5
SCHROYER			
Aaron	Marin San Rafael	60	765
SCHRSM			
Henry	Shasta Shasta	66	674
SCHRUDER			
Fritz	Del Norte Crescent	58	640
John	Alameda Brooklyn	55	143
SCHRUM			
Jacob	Tulara Visalia	71	30
SCHRUNK			
D	Siskiyou Klamath	69	96
SCHRUTZ			
Phillip	San Francisco San Francisco 2	67	776
SCHRVEISAN			
Ernest*	Marin Novato	60	736
SCHRVIR			
Frederick*	San Francisco San Francisco 3	67	80
	San Francisco		
SCHSAR			
Augusta*	Sacramento Ward 4	63	548
SCHSVAB			
Adolph*	San Francisco San Francisco 8	68	1316
SCHU			
---	Trinity Lewiston	70	957
SCHU?L			
Leonard	Sierra St Louis	66	815
SCHUAB			
Nicholas	Yuba Marysville	72	893
SCHUABACHER			
Louis	Placer Iona Hills	62	859
SCHUABEL			
F H*	Sacramento Ward 3	63	434
SCHUABLA			
Philip	Placer Ophirville	62	657
SCHUANNS			
H*	San Francisco San Francisco 9	68	1070
SCHUARG			
John*	Tuolumne Big Oak	71	139
SCHUATT			
S C*	Mariposa Twp 3	60	574
SCHUAUM			
H*	San Francisco San Francisco 9	68	1070
SCHUAWN			
H*	San Francisco San Francisco 9	68	1070
SCHUBAND			
Ernest	Calaveras Twp 7	57	23
SCHUBAR			
Martin	Marin Cortemad	60	756
SCHUBARDT			
John	Sonoma Salt Point	69	690
SCHUBER			
E	Sacramento Ward 1	63	10
George	Plumas Quincy	62	997
SCHUBERT			
Chas	San Francisco San Francisco 10	67	222
E	Sacramento Ward 1	63	10
Michael	Napa Napa	61	106
SCHUBILL			
L*	Nevada Washington	61	336
SCHUBUELL			
Simon	Humbolt Union	59	180
SCHUCHT			
Otto	Solano Fairfield	69	198
SCHUCK			
Geo	Santa Clara Santa Clara	65	481
Harman	Calaveras Twp 5	57	253
Harmon*	Calaveras Twp 5	57	253
Henry	Amador Twp 2	55	326
Lewis	Sacramento Ward 3	63	471
SCHUCTZE			
Edwd*	San Francisco San Francisco 2	67	685
SCHUDEL			
Christopher*	Yuba Marysville	72	958
SCHUDMACK			
Thos	San Francisco San Francisco 9	68	957
SCHUDWACK			
Thos	San Francisco San Francisco 9	68	957
SCHUEDER			
Herman*	San Francisco San Francisco 1	68	852
SCHUEDES			
Francis	Solano Benecia	69	317
SCHUEE			
Henry	Sierra Gibsonville	66	853
SCHUELL			
Joseph G	Mendocino Ukiah	60	801
SCHUENBERG			
W*	San Francisco San Francisco 1	68	825
SCHUESLER			
H*	Sutter Yuba	70	770
SCHUETZE			
Edwd*	San Francisco San Francisco 2	67	685
SCHUFRLY			
Christian	Solano Vacaville	69	362
SCHUGER			
Louis	Yuba Marysville	72	900

California 1860 Census Index

Name	County Locale	M653 Roll	Page
SCHUGLER			
N	Shasta Horsetown	66	688
SCHUHARDT			
John	Sonoma Salt Point	69	690
SCHULBY			
Patrick	Yuba Linda	72	984
SCHULCH			
Wm	Butte Oregon	56	614
SCHULDERS			
Jno	Sacramento Ward 4	63	553
SCHULE			
Jacob	San Joaquin Castoria	64	909
SCHULER			
Augustus	Amador Twp 2	55	310
Augustus	Amador Twp 2	55	312
F	Shasta Millvill	66	749
Frederick	San Francisco San Francisco 1	68	859
George	Contra Costa Twp 1	57	521
Hine	Yuba Long Bar	72	756
J	El Dorado Casumnes	58	1160
Jacob	Tuolumne Twp 2	71	387
Jas	Sacramento Ward 3	63	458
John	Shasta Shasta	66	662
John	Yuba Long Bar	72	750
Kline	Yuba Long Bar	72	755
SCHULF			
M	Siskiyou Callahan	69	10
SCHULG			
Fredk*	Tuolumne Big Oak	71	140
SCHULINBACK			
John	Placer Yankee J	62	761
SCHULL			
Leonard*	Sierra St Louis	66	815
SCHULLE			
S W*	Amador Twp 6	55	427
SCHULLENGO			
M	Amador Twp 6	55	427
SCHULLER			
Frank	Klamath Liberty	59	239
SCHULLIN			
John	Butte Ophir	56	781
SCHULLY			
Patrick	Yuba Suida	72	984
SCHULMERICK			
C	El Dorado Cold Spring	58	1100
SCHULMRICK			
C*	El Dorado Cold Spring	58	1100
SCHULMUCK			
C*	El Dorado Cold Spring	58	1100
SCHULTE			
S W*	Amador Twp 6	55	427
SCHULTHESS			
J F	San Francisco San Francisco 5	67	524
SCHULTHIER			
John	Alameda Brooklyn	55	212
SCHULTZ			
Acon	Tulara Twp 2	71	30
Alexander	Fresno Twp 3	59	12
Anna	Tuolumne Sonora	71	201
Anna	Tuolumne Chinese	71	493
C A	San Francisco San Francisco 6	67	460
Charles	San Francisco San Francisco 7	68	1372
Charles	San Francisco San Francisco 6	67	442
Charles	Solano Suisan	69	204
Chas	San Francisco San Francisco 1	68	926
Chas	Trinity Weaverville	70	1062
E	Sacramento Ward 1	63	80
E	San Francisco San Francisco 10	67	200
F	San Francisco San Francisco 5	67	500
Fred	Tuolumne Twp 2	71	410
G	El Dorado Placerville	58	838
Geo	San Francisco San Francisco 2	67	785
H	Trinity Weaverville	70	1066
Henry	Sacramento Franklin	63	332
Henry	San Diego Colorado	64	809
Henry	San Joaquin Stockton	64	1048
Henry	Solano Suisan	69	236
Isaac	San Joaquin Douglass	64	919
J	San Francisco San Francisco 9	68	1065
J	San Francisco San Francisco 5	67	491
Jacob	Tuolumne Big Oak	71	132
Jacob	Tuolumne Shawsfla	71	398
John	San Francisco San Francisco 4	68	1214
Joseph	Plumas Quincy	62	963
Joseph M C*	Fresno Twp 3	59	12
Lawrence	Sacramento Ward 3	63	433
Lewis	San Francisco San Francisco 1	68	928
Ludewick	San Francisco San Francisco 4	68	1163
M	Calaveras Twp 9	57	392
M	Nevada Eureka	61	393
Margaret	San Francisco San Francisco 6	67	400
Mary	San Francisco San Francisco 2	67	683
N H	Sacramento Ward 3	63	481
Peter	Solano Vallejo	69	259
R	Butte Kimshaw	56	579

Name	County Locale	M653 Roll	Page
SCHULTZ			
Sebastian	Yuba Marysville	72	876
Sebastran	Yuba Marysville	72	876
Theodore	Trinity New Rvr	70	1031
William	San Francisco San Francisco 7	68	1366
Wm	Sacramento Ward 3	63	486
Wm	Santa Clara San Jose	65	292
SCHULY			
Henry	Del Norte Crescent	58	642
SCHULZ			
Fredk	Tuolumne Twp 4	71	140
John	Tuolumne Big Oak	71	135
SCHUM			
M	Siskiyou Scott Va	69	22
SCHUMACHER			
Chas	San Francisco San Francisco 10 67		215
SCHUMACKER			
Adelbert*	Humbolt Union	59	180
Frederic	Humbolt Union	59	180
Gustave	Humbolt Union	59	182
SCHUMAKE			
N J	El Dorado Georgetown	58	703
SCHUMAKER			
Adelbert*	Humbolt Union	59	180
Augusta	Humbolt Union	59	179
D	San Francisco San Francisco 10 67		352
Ulrika	Humbolt Union	59	179
SCHUMAN			
Charles	Humbolt Union	59	180
Jacob	San Francisco San Francisco 3 67		71
Theresa*	Yuba Marysville	72	853
SCHUMELE			
---	Tulara Twp 2	71	35
SCHUMER			
Earnest*	Alameda Murray	55	225
Frank	San Francisco San Francisco 1	68	901
Jos*	Butte Oregon	56	638
SCHUN			
Fredrick*	Plumas Meadow Valley	62	933
SCHUNBEEN			
Thadeas*	Solano Benecia	69	309
SCHUNBEIN			
Thadeus*	Solano Benecia	69	309
SCHUNBUN			
Thadeas*	Solano Benecia	69	309
SCHUNDER			
George	Yuba Marysville	72	928
SCHUNG			
---	El Dorado Georgetown	58	747
SCHUNLIN			
George H*	Contra Costa Twp 2	57	561
SCHUNN			
---	El Dorado Georgetown	58	748
SCHUNT			
Margaret	Sierra Whiskey	66	849
Margsaret	Sierra Whiskey	66	849
SCHUNTER			
Werner	Placer Virginia	62	664
SCHUNTZ			
Rachael*	San Francisco San Francisco 7	68	1378
SCHUOLTS			
J	El Dorado Placerville	58	826
SCHUPERT			
Jas	Napa Napa	61	105
SCHUPF			
George	Yuba Marysville	72	943
SCHUR			
John	Tuolumne Columbia	71	296
William*	Sierra Port Win	66	795
SCHURBOUN			
Wm*	Mendocino Big Rvr	60	845
SCHURBOUW			
Wm*	Mendocino Big Rvr	60	845
SCHURBURN			
Wm*	Mendocino Big Rvr	60	845
SCHURFER			
Jos	San Francisco San Francisco 10 67		188
SCHURR			
Fredrick*	Plumas Meadow Valley	62	933
John*	San Francisco San Francisco 7	68	1404
William	Placer Michigan	62	810
SCHURTZ			
Chas	San Francisco San Francisco 2	67	649
John	San Francisco San Francisco 2	67	682
SCHUS			
John	Tuolumne Twp 2	71	296
SCHUSHER			
J	San Francisco San Francisco 5	67	519
SCHUSSLIN			
Frank	San Francisco San Francisco 2	67	671
SCHUSTER			
Frederick	Yuba Marysville	72	865
J S	San Francisco San Francisco 5	67	519

Name	County Locale	M653 Roll	Page
SCHUSTER			
John	Del Norte Happy Ca	58	670
SCHUSTIANO			
---	San Bernardino S Timate	64	692
SCHUTER			
Henry	San Francisco San Francisco 10 67		215
SCHUTILLAN			
---	Mendocino Big Rvr	60	855
SCHUTR			
E	Mariposa Twp 3	60	584
SCHUTT			
F	Sacramento Ward 1	63	34
SCHUTTE			
Christopher	San Francisco 11		101
	San Francisco 67		
S W	Amador Twp 6	55	427
SCHUTTLER			
Adelaide	San Francisco San Francisco 1	68	846
SCHUTTZ			
Ludewick	San Francisco San Francisco 4	68	1163
SCHUTYER			
S H	Calaveras Twp 9	57	382
T Y*	Calaveras Twp 9	57	382
SCHUTZ			
E	Mariposa Twp 3	60	584
E	Trinity Readings	70	996
John	Solano Benecia	69	284
SCHUTZER			
L H	Calaveras Twp 9	57	382
T H*	Calaveras Twp 9	57	382
SCHUYLER			
Jas	San Francisco San Francisco 10 67		188
SCHUZLER			
John	Trinity Weaverville	70	1065
N*	Shasta Horsetown	66	688
SCHWAB			
Adolph*	San Francisco San Francisco 8	68	1316
J M	Sacramento Ward 4	63	600
Nicholas	Yuba Marysville	72	893
SCHWABLE			
F H*	Sacramento Ward 3	63	434
SCHWABLY			
W F	San Francisco San Francisco 10 67		331
SCHWAK			
Conrad*	Calaveras Twp 6	57	113
SCHWAN			
Jacob	San Francisco San Francisco 8	68	1246
SCHWANG			
Hermann	San Francisco San Francisco 7	68	1365
SCHWANKEERR B			
Sanford	Sierra Poker Flats	66	837
SCHWARG			
John	Tuolumne Twp 4	71	139
SCHWART			
Charles W	Sierra Downieville	66	958
SCHWARTR			
Theo*	Nevada Rough &	61	413
SCHWARTS			
J	El Dorado Diamond	58	803
M*	Nevada Bridgeport	61	502
Wm*	Nevada Bridgeport	61	502
SCHWARTZ			
Barmar	San Francisco San Francisco 8	68	1290
Charles	Yuba Marysville	72	880
Chas	Sacramento Ward 3	63	434
Chas	Sacramento Ward 4	63	547
D	San Francisco San Francisco 1	68	810
Geo B	Sacramento Ward 1	63	84
Henry	San Francisco San Francisco 11		131
	San Francisco 67		
Isedore	Tuolumne Twp 4	71	135
Jno B	Sacramento Ward 1	63	84
John	San Francisco San Francisco 11		100
	San Francisco 67		
John S	San Francisco San Francisco 11		100
	San Francisco 67		
Joseph	Alameda Murray	55	219
Lewis	Santa Cruz Santa Cruz	66	614
Louis	Sacramento Ward 4	63	593
M*	Nevada Bridgeport	61	502
Peter	Butte Kimshaw	56	591
Reinhard	Sacramento Ward 1	63	34
Simon	Yuba Marysville	72	874
Theo	Nevada Rough &	61	413
Wm	Sacramento American	63	163
SCHWARTZBURG			
Johanna	San Francisco San Francisco 11		102
	San Francisco 67		
SCHWARTZBURY			
Johasma	San Francisco San Francisco 11		102
	San Francisco 67		
SCHWARTZERALTER			
Canada	Sierra Twp 7	66	907

California 1860 Census Index

Name	County Locale	M653 Roll	Page
SCHWARTZWALTER			
Canada	Sierra Twp 7	66	907
SCHWARZ			
F	San Francisco San Francisco 6	67	449
SCHWAT			
Cath	Sacramento Ward 4	63	531
SCHWATKA			
Andrew E	Siskiyou Yreka	69	153
Harry	Siskiyou Yreka	69	154
W F	Marin Tomales	60	719
SCHWATT			
D C	Mariposa Twp 3	60	574
SCHWATZER			
Frederik*	Sacramento Ward 4	63	581
SCHWEAR			
Charles	Yuba Long Bar	72	751
SCHWEE			
Matehes*	Mariposa Twp 3	60	573
SCHWEIDER			
Leopold	Klamath Klamath	59	228
SCHWEINEY			
John*	El Dorado Cold Spring	58	1101
SCHWEING			
John*	El Dorado Cold Spring	58	1101
SCHWEISANA			
Ernest	Marin Novato	60	736
SCHWEISOM			
Ernest*	Marin Novato	60	736
SCHWEITZER			
John	San Francisco San Francisco 10	67	227
SCHWENHEER			
R B	Sierra Poker Flats	66	837
SCHWENKA			
Chas	San Francisco San Francisco 9	68	1051
SCHWERIN			
Augustus	San Francisco San Francisco 7	68	1418
M	Sacramento Ward 4	63	506
Philip	Sacramento Ward 4	63	512
SCHWERINK			
Ernest	Sacramento Ward 4	63	508
SCHWERNEY			
John	El Dorado Cold Spring	58	1101
SCHWERT			
Elizabeth	San Francisco San Francisco 10	67	191
P	San Francisco San Francisco 10	67	191
SCHWERTZ			
Henry	San Francisco San Francisco 10	67	286
SCHWETSER			
T	El Dorado Coloma	58	1123
SCHWETSES			
T	El Dorado Coloma	58	1123
SCHWETZER			
Frederik*	Sacramento Ward 4	63	581
SCHWILK			
F	Tuolumne Shawsfla	71	383
SCHWIN			
John	Stanislaus Branch	70	700
John*	Stanislaus Oatvale	70	716
SCHWINN			
Jos	Butte Oregon	56	638
SCHWINS			
John	Tuolumne Don Pedro	71	538
SCHWITZER			
John	Nevada Bridgeport	61	450
SCHWOCRER			
Elizabeth*	Yuba Marysville	72	885
SCHWOERER			
Elizabeth*	Yuba Marysville	72	885
SCHWOK			
Louis M	Calaveras Twp 6	57	152
SCHWOND			
Peter	Trinity Rattle Snake	70	1029
SCHWORTS			
O	El Dorado Placerville	58	833
SCHWUNHEER			
R B	Sierra Poker Flats	66	837
SCHWUZ			
Jacob*	Sierra Downieville	66	972
SCHYLER			
Kline	Yuba Long Bar	72	754
SCHYLERMARIS			
Gerick	Alameda Brooklyn	55	184
SCHYNER			
Charles	Sacramento Franklin	63	310
SCIBNER			
Phillip	Calaveras Twp 5	57	199
SCIDMORE			
Richard	Tulara Visalia	71	2
W E	San Francisco San Francisco 6	67	454
SCIFFORD			
Andrew	Calaveras Twp 5	57	213
SCILLENBERGER			
Moses	Santa Clara San Jose	65	387
SCILLING			
A	Tuolumne Columbia	71	341
SCIMMERMAN			
Leo*	San Francisco San Francisco 2	67	700
SCIN			
Henry*	Sierra Twp 7	66	907
SCINE			
---*	Nevada Grass Valley	61	232
SCING			
---	Nevada Nevada	61	303
SCINO			
Pedro	Sierra Downieville	66	971
Prelro	Sierra Downieville	66	971
Pulro*	Sierra Downieville	66	971
SCINPER			
Samuel P	Yuba Marysville	72	872
SCIO			
---	Fresno Twp 1	59	80
SCIPIO			
Ferdinand	San Francisco San Francisco 8	68	1314
SCIPON			
A	Nevada Nevada	61	255
SCISSORS			
William	San Mateo Twp 1	65	67
SCITEL			
Henry	San Francisco San Francisco 2	67	786
SCITTLE			
Thomas	Mendocino Big Rvr	60	840
SCIVER			
M	Amador Twp 6	55	438
SCIWE			
Jose	Yuba Bear Rvr	72	1016
SCKINNER			
Elisha	San Francisco San Francisco 6	67	427
SCLARARI			
Bazilas	Calaveras Twp 6	57	162
SCLAVARI			
Bazilas*	Calaveras Twp 6	57	162
SCLAW			
Frank	Tulara Twp 2	71	23
SCLIN			
---*	Shasta Horsetown	66	705
SCLIOTT			
Conrad*	Sierra St Louis	66	817
SCLISELOT			
J	Yolo Washington	72	599
SCLMASBERRY			
Julius*	Placer Iona Hills	62	872
SCLOSSER			
Mike	Sonoma Petaluma	69	560
SCLUELLEN			
David*	Yuba Marysville	72	931
SCMIDT			
F*	Sacramento Sutter	63	290
SCNLLEY			
Pat	Yolo Putah	72	553
SCOBANK			
W H	Nevada Grass Valley	61	238
SCOBARA			
Jose	Tuolumne Twp 5	71	497
SCOBEL			
Henry	San Francisco San Francisco 2	67	786
SCOBES			
T	El Dorado Placerville	58	874
SCOBIE			
James	Tulara Keyesville	71	53
SCOBIL			
James	Tulara Twp 3	71	53
SCOBLE			
John	Nevada Bridgeport	61	478
Otis*	Marin Cortemad	60	787
Otto	Marin Cortemad	60	787
SCOBY			
Jos H	Placer Ophirville	62	653
SCOCK			
W S	Shasta Shasta	66	666
SCODE			
William	Tulara Petersburg	71	52
SCOFFIELD			
E	Nevada Nevada	61	244
J	Nevada Nevada	61	244
SCOFIELD			
Anson	Butte Kimshaw	56	602
Charles	San Joaquin Douglass	64	920
Charles	San Mateo Twp 3	65	109
E H	Siskiyou Scott Ri	69	73
George	Mariposa Twp 3	60	566
H A	San Mateo Twp 3	65	87
J	El Dorado Kelsey	58	1126
J	Nevada Grass Valley	61	150
Jno	Butte Kimshaw	56	578
Mark	Sierra Whiskey	66	846
Mary A	Mariposa Twp 3	60	568
Mary S	Mariposa Twp 3	60	568
Miles	Sierra Whiskey	66	845
Minor	San Joaquin Elkhorn	64	982
SCOFIELD			
R	El Dorado Georgetown	58	690
Richd	Sacramento Ward 1	63	46
Richd D	San Francisco San Francisco 2	67	704
Robert	Nevada Rough &	61	415
W H	Siskiyou Klamath	69	92
Wm	Sacramento San Joaquin	63	358
SCOGG			
J	Nevada Grass Valley	61	224
SCOGGIN			
Smith	Sierra Twp 5	66	920
W W	El Dorado Coloma	58	1086
SCOGGINS			
D F	Yolo Cache Crk	72	641
D G	Yolo Cache Crk	72	643
L*	Yolo Cache	72	643
SCOH			
---	Sacramento Centre	63	182
SCOIRLLE			
Jas*	Placer Dutch Fl	62	717
SCOIT			
Elizabeth*	Del Norte Crescent	58	627
SCOLBENGER			
Luther	San Mateo Twp 1	65	56
SCOLDEN			
John	Santa Clara San Jose	65	366
SCOLERY			
John	El Dorado Kelsey	58	1135
SCOLLAN			
Eugene	San Bernardino Santa Barbara	64	181
John	San Bernardino Santa Barbara	64	181
SCOLLINS			
J	Sacramento Cosumnes	63	399
SCOLUSKE			
R S	San Francisco San Francisco 9	68	963
SCOLUSKI			
R S	San Francisco San Francisco 9	68	963
SCOM			
J F C	Sacramento Ward 1	63	92
SCOMIN			
Aracar	Placer Auburn	62	585
SCON			
F S*	Mariposa Twp 3	60	575
SCONADO			
Barcelora	Alameda Brooklyn	55	208
SCONE			
---	Tulara Twp 2	71	36
SCONY			
Adolphus*	Marin Novato	60	736
SCOOFFY			
P M	San Francisco San Francisco 8	68	1264
SCOOFT			
Michael L*	Yuba Marysville	72	879
SCOOGER			
Charles*	Yuba Marysville	72	934
SCOOGERLAND			
O	Placer Todds Va	62	762
SCOON			
---*	Tulara Visalia	71	36
SCOONOVER			
David	Tuolumne Twp 4	71	125
SCOONS			
W C	San Francisco San Francisco 5	67	544
Wm	San Francisco San Francisco 1	68	915
SCOOTT			
Michael L*	Yuba Marysville	72	879
SCOPMITCH			
Gerolina*	Sacramento Ward 3	63	426
SCOPRACOR			
Paulin*	El Dorado Kelsey	58	1144
SCOPRACOS			
Paulin	El Dorado Kelsey	58	1144
SCORAL			
J	Nevada Grass Valley	61	218
SCORAY			
J	Nevada Grass Valley	61	149
SCOREING			
A*	Calaveras Twp 9	57	392
SCOREORY			
A*	Calaveras Twp 9	57	393
SCOREORZ			
A*	Calaveras Twp 9	57	393
SCOREY			
Adolphus*	Marin Novato	60	736
SCORLE			
N	Nevada Grass Valley	61	151
SCORLL			
N*	Nevada Grass Valley	61	151
SCORN			
Jesus*	Yuba Marysville	72	937
SCOROY			
Adolphus	Marin Novato	60	736
SCORQUIO			
J	Alameda Brooklyn	55	79
SCORRY			
D	Shasta Shasta	66	686

Name	County Locale	M653 Roll	Page
SCORY			
Adolphus*	Marin Novato	60	736
SCORYER			
---	Del Norte Klamath	58	654
SCOSSMITCH			
Gerolina*	Sacramento Ward 3	63	426
SCOT			
Jacob	Calaveras Twp 6	57	156
Wm	Marin Cortemad	60	785
SCOTCH			
Joseph	San Mateo Twp 1	65	63
Peter	San Mateo Twp 1	65	63
SCOTCHLER			
Jas	San Francisco San Francisco 10	287	67
John	San Francisco San Francisco 10	287	67
John	San Francisco San Francisco 3	67	49
John J	San Francisco San Francisco 3	67	49
Jos	San Francisco San Francisco 10	287	67
Mary	San Francisco San Francisco 10	287	67
SCOTLAND			
John R	San Francisco San Francisco 1	68	906
SCOTNA			
Eugene	Sierra Downieville	66	972
SCOTT			
A	Nevada Grass Valley	61	163
A	Nevada Grass Valley	61	174
A	Nevada Eureka	61	362
A	Sutter Sutter	70	810
A	Tehama Pasakent	70	855
A B	Placer Forest H	62	803
A G	Shasta Shasta	66	654
A H	Mariposa Coulterville	60	701
A L*	Sacramento Lee	63	216
A M	Nevada Eureka	61	360
A P	Nevada Red Dog	61	548
A S*	Sacramento Lee	63	216
A W	San Francisco San Francisco 9	681	054
Aaron	Santa Clara Gilroy	65	236
Abraham F	San Francisco San Francisco 9	681	008
Adam	San Francisco Placer Todds Va	62	784
Alex	Humbolt Union	59	183
Alexander F	San Francisco 11 San Francisco	95	67
Alfred	Sierra La Porte	66	772
Allen	Butte Chico	56	544
Allen	El Dorado Coloma	581	123
Amos L	Tuolumne Twp 5	71	500
Andrew	Sierra Poker Flats	66	838
Anthony	Santa Cruz Pajaro	66	557
Austin	Humbolt Union	59	193
B	El Dorado Placerville	58	865
B H	Mendocino Calpella	60	810
Benj W	Sonoma Santa Rosa	69	423
C C	Alameda Brooklyn	55	205
C L	Calaveras Twp 9	57	358
C L	Nevada Grass Valley	61	163
C L	Nevada Grass Valley	61	190
C L	Nevada Grass Valley	61	202
C S	Sacramento Ward 4	63	547
C W	El Dorado Diamond	58	766
Chals	El Dorado Georgetown	58	751
Charles	Marin San Rafael	60	764
Charles	San Francisco San Francisco 11	116	67
Charles R	Sierra Poker Flats	66	840
Chas	Santa Clara San Jose	65	345
Chas	Tuolumne Twp 4	71	140
Cyrus	Sacramento Ward 4	63	525
D	Butte Bidwell	56	714
D	El Dorado Diamond	58	793
David B	Yuba Marysville	72	906
Delia	Santa Cruz Watsonville	66	540
E	Amador Twp 7	55	413
E	Sacramento Lee	63	215
E A	Yuba Marysville	72	945
E G	Sacramento Ward 4	63	535
E M	Nevada Nevada	61	322
E S	Sacramento Brighton	63	195
Edmund	San Francisco San Francisco 2	67	668
Edward	El Dorado Mud Springs	58	991
Edward	Monterey Alisal	601	037
Edward	Nevada Little Y	61	531
Edwd	San Francisco San Francisco 2	67	691
Elizabeth	San Francisco San Francisco 10	245	67
Elizabeth*	Del Norte Crescent	58	627
Enoch	San Francisco San Francisco 10	226	67
Enoch	San Joaquin Castoria	64	904
F	Butte Kimshaw	56	585
F R	Napa Napa	61	71

Name	County Locale	M653 Roll	Page
SCOTT			
Felix	Del Norte Crescent	58	641
Finfield	San Luis Obispo San Luis Obispo	65	3
Frances H	Alameda Brooklyn	55	77
Frank	San Luis Obispo San Luis Obispo	65	37
Frank M	Calaveras Twp 10	57	277
Franklin	Santa Cruz Santa Cruz	66	626
Franklin	Santa Cruz Santa Cruz	66	628
Frankm	Calaveras Twp 10	57	277
Frederick	Solano Suisan	69	239
G	Nevada Grass Valley	61	177
G	Nevada Grass Valley	61	193
G	Sutter Sutter	70	810
G D	Nevada Grass Valley	61	222
G M	Tehama Red Bluff	70	919
G W	El Dorado Placerville	58	905
G W	Nevada Grass Valley	61	153
G W	Yolo Cottonwoood	72	650
Geo	Klamath S Fork	59	203
Geo	Nevada Nevada	61	289
Geo	San Francisco San Francisco 1	68	917
Geo A	San Francisco San Francisco 10	298	67
Geo W	Amador Twp 5	55	357
George	Amador Twp 5	55	343
George	El Dorado Georgetown	58	702
George	Placer Todds Va	62	764
George	San Francisco San Francisco 7	681	443
George	San Francisco San Francisco 2	67	731
George	Santa Cruz Santa Cruz	66	629
George	Tuolumne Twp 2	71	365
George	Yuba Marysville	72	878
George E	Santa Cruz Santa Cruz	66	627
H	Nevada Grass Valley	61	159
H	Shasta Millvill	66	755
H H	San Francisco San Francisco 5	67	525
H H	Yolo Putah	72	545
H J	Mariposa Coulterville	60	688
H L*	Calaveras Twp 9	57	358
H P	Mariposa Coulterville	60	688
Harry	Sierra Twp 7	66	863
Henry	Colusa Monroeville	57	443
Henry	Sacramento Franklin	63	313
Henry	Sierra St Louis	66	863
Henry	Sierra Twp 7	66	878
Henry P	Santa Cruz Santa Cruz	66	626
Henry P	Santa Cruz Santa Cruz	66	628
Hiram	Santa Cruz Santa Cruz	66	638
Isaac	Santa Clara Santa Clara	65	510
Isabella D	San Francisco San Francisco 6	67	414
Israel E	Plumas Quincy	62	968
J	Nevada Grass Valley	61	157
J	Nevada Grass Valley	61	190
J	Nevada Grass Valley	61	222
J	Nevada Grass Valley	61	223
J	Nevada Nevada	61	247
J	Nevada Nevada	61	288
J	Sacramento Cosummes	63	400
J	San Francisco San Francisco 9	681	033
J	San Francisco San Francisco 2	67	652
J	San Francisco San Francisco 1	68	923
J	Sutter Bear Rvr	70	825
J	Tehama Lassen	70	879
J	Tuolumne Jacksonville	71	172
J B	Nevada Grass Valley	61	163
J B	Nevada Grass Valley	61	218
J B	Nevada Grass Valley	61	222
J B	Sierra Grizzly	661	058
J C	Trinity Weaverville	701	051
J C	Tuolumne Columbia	71	319
J D	Santa Clara Santa Clara	65	475
J F	Nevada Eureka	61	379
J F	Shasta Shasta	66	666
J H	Sacramento American	63	166
J L	Santa Clara San Jose	65	341
J L	Santa Clara Alviso	65	413
J M	Nevada Bloomfield	61	511
J M	Nevada Bloomfield	61	512
J P	San Francisco San Francisco 2	67	656
J R	Nevada Grass Valley	61	207
J R	Nevada Eureka	61	378
J T	Nevada Eureka	61	379
J V	Amador Twp 4	55	242
J V	Santa Cruz Shasta	66	653
J W	Nevada Grass Valley	61	238
J W	Nevada Eureka	61	380
Jacob	Yolo Cache Crk	72	593
James	Amador Twp 2	55	317
James	Calaveras Twp 5	57	228
James	El Dorado Casumnes	581	173
James	Marin Cortemad	60	785
James	Mendocino Little L	60	836
James	Nevada Bridgeport	61	469
James	San Francisco San Francisco 9	681	082

Name	County Locale	M653 Roll	Page
SCOTT			
James	San Francisco San Francisco 11	121	67
James	San Mateo Twp 3	65	93
James	Santa Clara Santa Clara	65	512
James	Sierra St Louis	66	817
James	Solano Benecia	69	282
James	Trinity Mouth Ca	701	012
James	Tulara Twp 2	71	25
James M	Sierra Twp 7	66	893
James M	Yuba Bear Rvr	721	009
James W	Plumas Meadow Valley	62	928
Jane	San Francisco San Francisco 2	67	640
Jas	Butte Chico	56	563
Jas	Sacramento Ward 1	63	109
Jas	San Francisco San Francisco 1	68	913
Jas M	Butte Ophir	56	771
Jas N	Amador Twp 2	55	273
Jeff	Butte Kimshaw	56	607
Jefferson	Butte Kimshaw	56	598
Jno	Alameda Brooklyn	55	134
Jno	Alameda Oakland	55	33
Jno	Sacramento Ward 1	63	9
Jno S	Mendocino Calpella	60	810
Joeduthem	Sacramento Centre	63	179
Johathan R	Los Angeles Los Angeles	59	361
John	Alameda Brooklyn	55	171
John	Amador Twp 4	55	250
John	El Dorado Kelsey	581	152
John	El Dorado Placerville	58	903
John	Los Angeles Elmonte	59	250
John	Los Angeles Los Angeles	59	346
John	Los Angeles Los Angeles	59	369
John	Nevada Nevada	61	325
John	Placer Yankee J	62	759
John	Placer Forest H	62	791
John	Placer Iona Hills	62	876
John	Plumas Quincy	62	977
John	Sacramento Sutter	63	303
John	Sacramento Cosummes	63	399
John	San Francisco San Francisco 10	212	67
John	Siskiyou Callahan	69	18
John	Solano Benecia	69	290
John	Tuolumne Twp 1	71	215
John	Tuolumne Sonora	71	230
John	Tuolumne Columbia	71	314
John	Tuolumne Twp 2	71	322
John	Yuba Foster B	72	824
John B	Napa Napa	61	83
John C	Sonoma Mendocino	69	461
John E*	Contra Costa Twp 3	57	617
John G	El Dorado Placerville	58	915
John G	Los Angeles Los Angeles	59	293
John J	Siskiyou Yreka	69	131
John S	Trinity Indian C	70	988
John W	Yuba Marysville	72	929
Jonathan R	Los Angeles Los Angeles	59	361
Jos C	Sacramento Ward 3	63	431
Joseph	Calaveras Twp 5	57	251
Joseph	San Joaquin Stockton	641	010
Joseph	San Mateo Twp 3	65	103
Joseph	San Mateo Twp 3	65	88
Joseph	Siskiyou Callahan	69	18
Joseph	Sonoma Petaluma	69	562
Joseph	Tehama Lassen	70	879
Joseph	Yuba Marysville	72	908
Joseph E	Tulara Visalia	71	100
Juan	San Joaquin Castoria	64	900
Kemard	Tehama Lassen	70	869
L	Nevada Grass Valley	61	175
L C	Nevada Grass Valley	61	182
L M	Nevada Nevada	61	280
L S	Amador Twp 3	55	375
L V	Butte Chico	56	546
L W	Placer Forest H	62	797
Leonidius L	Calaveras Twp 5	57	16
Levi	Yuba Bear Rvr	721	012
Levin	Shasta Horsetown	66	696
Louisa	Tulara Visalia	71	99
Luther	Yuba Bear Rvr	721	012
M	El Dorado Georgetown	58	688
M	Nevada Nevada	61	247
M	San Francisco San Francisco 6	67	448
M A	Colusa Monroeville	57	441
M E	Sacramento Sutter	63	299
M E	Sacramento Alabama	63	413
M M	Placer Virginia	62	674
M S	Nevada Nevada	61	271
Mam*	Sacramento Ward 1	63	89
Manuel	San Bernardino Santa Barbara	64	180
Marlin	Calaveras Twp 9	57	375
Martin	Calaveras Twp 9	57	370
Martin	Calaveras Twp 9	57	375
Mary	Contra Costa Twp 3	57	589
Mary	Sacramento Ward 3	63	455

California 1860 Census Index

Name	County Locale	M653 RollPage
SCOTT		
Mary	Sacramento Ward 1	63 89
Mathew	Alameda Brooklyn	55 83
Matthew	Yuba Marysville	72 945
Michael	Santa Clara Santa Clara	65 523
Micheal	El Dorado Placerville	58 903
Milton	Santa Cruz Pajaro	66 559
Mont	Sierra Eureka	661049
N B	El Dorado Placerville	58 847
N B	San Francisco San Francisco 6	67 450
N F	Nevada Nevada	61 247
N T	Tuolumne Twp 3	71 459
Nancy	Yolo Cache Crk	72 633
Nelson	Siskiyou Callahan	69 18
O W	Mendocino Arrana	60 858
Oliver	El Dorado Kelsey	581145
Oliver J	Alameda Brooklyn	55 87
P W	Placer Iona Hills	62 860
Patrick	Sacramento Ward 1	63 24
Peter	Alameda Brooklyn	55 137
Peter	Mariposa Coulterville	60 685
R	El Dorado Placerville	58 859
R	Nevada Grass Valley	61 160
R C	Nevada Nevada	61 261
R C	Siskiyou Scott Ri	69 67
R F	Sacramento American	63 171
R H	Sacramento Ward 4	63 567
R R	Tuolumne Twp 1	71 198
Rebecca	Napa Hot Springs	61 17
Richard	San Francisco San Francisco 7	681339
Richard	San Joaquin Stockton	641079
Richard	Santa Cruz Pajaro	66 564
Richard J F	Santa Cruz Pajaro	66 533
Richd	Tuolumne Twp 1	71 249
Robert	El Dorado Georgetown	58 758
Robert	San Francisco San Francisco 11	162 65
Robert	Santa Clara San Jose	65 340
Robert	Santa Cruz Santa Cruz	66 603
Robert	Santa Cruz Pajaro	66 620
Robert	Yolo Cache Crk	72 591
Robert	Yolo Cache	72 633
Robert C	San Francisco San Francisco 4	681125
Robrt	San Francisco San Francisco 1	68 919
Robt	El Dorado Mud Springs	58 983
Robt	San Francisco San Francisco 1	68 910
Robt	Santa Clara San Jose	65 383
Robt	Sonoma Petaluma	69 579
Roobirth	Yolo Cache	72 591
Russell	Yuba Marysville	72 947
Ruth	San Francisco San Francisco 2	67 573
S	El Dorado Placerville	58 860
S	Nevada Grass Valley	61 163
S	Santa Clara San Jose	65 349
S B	El Dorado Mountain	581187
S D	Santa Clara Gilroy	65 237
S M	Sutter Sutter	70 810
S W	Tuolumne Jamestown	71 443
Sallie	San Francisco San Francisco 10	185 67
Sam	Merced Twp 2	60 916
Saml	Trinity Indian C	70 987
Samuel	Amador Twp 4	55 253
Samuel	Plumas Meadow Valley	62 908
Samuel	Siskiyou Scott Va	69 32
Sarah	Nevada Nevada	61 272
Stanmore	Plumas Quincy	62 982
Steve	Amador Twp 1	55 474
Sylvester	Sonoma Mendocino	69 467
T	Calaveras Twp 9	57 414
T S	Amador Twp 1	55 474
T W	Nevada Bridgeport	61 505
Thomas	Alameda Brooklyn	55 207
Thomas	San Bernardino Santa Barbara	64 180
Thomas	Sonoma Santa Rosa	69 423
Thomas	Tuolumne Twp 1	71 249
Thomas	Yuba Long Bar	72 755
Thomas	Yuba Long Bar	72 755
Thomas E	Yuba Suida	72 992
Thon*	Tuolumne Twp 1	71 249
Thos	Mariposa Coulterville	60 677
Thos	San Francisco San Francisco 1	68 872
Thos	San Francisco San Francisco 9	68 992
Thos	San Mateo Twp 3	65 93
Thos M*	Butte Oregon	56 625
Timothy F	Monterey Pajaro	601024
Tomothy F	Monterey Pajaro	601024
W	El Dorado Big Bar	58 742
W	Nevada Grass Valley	61 238
W	Nevada Eureka	61 377
W A	Amador Twp 2	55 265
W A	Shasta Shasta	66 654
W B	El Dorado Placerville	58 862
W C	Amador Twp 2	55 313
W D	San Joaquin Stockton	641038
W H	Santa Clara San Jose	65 332

Name	County Locale	M653 RollPage
SCOTT		
W M	Yolo Cache Crk	72 619
W P	El Dorado Diamond	58 774
W W	Nevada Grass Valley	61 171
W Y	Placer Dutch Fl	62 730
Wallace	Mendocino Calpella	60 821
Walter	Butte Kimshaw	56 594
Walter	Del Norte Crescent	58 659
Walter	Mendocino Calpella	60 821
Walter	San Francisco San Francisco 9	681036
Walter	San Francisco San Francisco 9	681064
Walter	Yuba New York	72 723
Walter A	Sierra Pine Grove	66 821
Walter S	San Joaquin Castoria	64 893
Watter A*	Sierra Pine Grove	66 821
Wiliam	Tulara Twp 3	71 62
William	Contra Costa Twp 2	57 541
William	Contra Costa Twp 3	57 593
William	El Dorado Salmon Falls	581045
William	Marin San Rafael	60 760
William	Marin Cortemad	60 788
William	Placer Michigan	62 837
William	Placer Michigan	62 838
William	San Francisco San Francisco 11	158 67
William	Shasta Horsetown	66 697
William	Sierra Poverty	66 799
William	Tulara Petersburg	71 52
William	Tulara Keyesvile	71 62
William	Yuba Long Bar	72 755
William F	Sierra Poker Flats	66 841
William J	Napa Hot Springs	61 12
Williiam	Sierra Poverty	66 799
Winfield	Sonoma Armally	69 508
Wm	Amador Twp 1	55 493
Wm	Butte Chico	56 566
Wm	Butte Bidwell	56 724
Wm	Butte Ophir	56 778
Wm	Marin Cortemad	60 785
Wm	Mendocino Ukiah	60 806
Wm	Nevada Nevada	61 274
Wm	Nevada Nevada	61 323
Wm	Sacramento Sutter	63 306
Wm	Sacramento Sutter	63 307
Wm	San Francisco San Francisco 3	67 70
Wm	Santa Clara San Jose	65 346
Wm	Santa Clara Santa Clara	65 512
Wm	Sonoma Vallejo	69 628
Wm	Yolo Slate Ra	72 707
Wm	Yuba Slate Ro	72 707
Wm A	San Francisco San Francisco 10	233 67
Wm G	Calaveras Twp 9	57 367
Wm G	San Francisco San Francisco 10	322 67
Wm H	Merced Monterey	60 940
Wm H	Monterey Monterey	60 940
Wm L	San Francisco San Francisco 1	68 807
Wm M	Klamath Klamath	59 225
Wm P	Mendocino Ukiah	60 806
Wm S	San Francisco San Francisco 2	67 716
Wm W	Alameda Brooklyn	55 154
SCOTTISH		
C	Nevada Grass Valley	61 186
SCOTTY		
E	Sacramento Ward 3	63 428
William	Calaveras Twp 7	57 6
SCOULLE		
Jas*	San Francisco San Francisco 2	67 612
SCOULLR		
Jas*	San Francisco San Francisco 2	67 612
Jos	San Francisco San Francisco 2	67 612
SCOUZY		
Gabriel N*	Yuba Marysville	72 911
SCOVAL		
Alfred	Marin Point Re	60 731
SCOVALL		
Herome B	Colusa Grand Island	57 474
R	Calaveras Twp 9	57 392
SCOVELL		
Geroge H	Tuolumne Twp 1	71 268
SCOVILL		
F W	Stanislaus Emory	70 756
George H	Tuolumne Twp 1	71 268
J S	El Dorado Georgetown	58 706
L C	Nevada Grass Valley	61 222
Thomas	El Dorado Georgetown	58 706
Wm J*	Calaveras Twp 9	57 347
SCOW		
---*	Tuolumne Chinese	71 525
Chong	Yuba Suida	72 991
Hana	Sierra Twp 5	66 920
Hance*	Sierra Twp 5	66 920
Harrce*	Sierra Twp 5	66 920
L	Nevada Grass Valley	61 217
SCOWALO		
Leo	Santa Clara San Jose	65 293

Name	County Locale	M653 RollPage
SCOX		
W*	Butte Oregon	56 638
Wm	Butte Oregon	56 638
SCOY		
---	Sacramento Ward 1	63 71
SCOYTT		
Michael L*	Yuba Marysville	72 879
SCPULRADA		
J D	Solano Suisan	69 228
SCPULVEDA		
Bartoto	Santa Clara Alviso	65 404
SCRADIGER		
John	San Francisco San Francisco 2	67 732
SCRAGGINS		
A	Nevada Eureka	61 372
Wm*	Nevada Nevada	61 330
SCRAGGIUS		
Wm*	Nevada Nevada	61 330
SCRAGGS		
John	Stanislaus Branch	70 712
SCRAGMAN		
John	Tuolumne Twp 1	71 257
SCRAHM		
Peter	El Dorado Eldorado	58 946
SCRAMBIA		
Peter	Calaveras Twp 9	57 348
SCRAMOS		
Jose	San Bernardino San Bernadino	64 638
SCRANLIN		
David	Los Angeles Los Angeles	59 512
SCRANTON		
A	Siskiyou Scott Va	69 35
A C	Siskiyou Scott Va	69 35
C	San Francisco San Francisco 5	67 498
Chas	Sacramento Ward 1	63 106
J B	Nevada Eureka	61 351
J S	Shasta Shasta	66 654
Joseph	San Bernardino San Bernadino	64 625
Joseph G	San Bernardino San Bernardino	64 625
R	Nevada Grass Valley	61 217
W M	Nevada Nevada	61 324
William	San Joaquin Douglass	64 921
Wm J	Nevada Nevada	61 330
SCRATE		
Francis	Klamath S Fork	59 203
SCRATZ		
J	Siskiyou Scott Va	69 53
SCRAVES		
G	Nevada Nevada	61 288
SCRAW		
---	Yuba Bear Rvr	721016
SCREBUER		
James B*	San Joaquin Elkhorn	64 993
SCREECH		
W	Tuolumne Twp 4	71 174
SCREWER		
Napoleon	Calaveras Twp 6	57 160
SCRHUP		
Eliza	San Francisco San Francisco 2	67 634
SCRIBER		
Christian	San Francisco San Francisco 10	170 67
Dick	Sierra Downieville	661011
SCRIBLER		
J P	Sierra Morristown	661054
SCRIBLING		
Alfred	Sacramento Cosummes	63 389
SCRIBNER		
C	Nevada Grass Valley	61 144
Daniel	Calaveras Twp 5	57 199
George W	Alameda Oakland	55 19
J	Nevada Grass Valley	61 217
J	Sacramento Sutter	63 293
Joel S	Monterey Pajaro	601018
N B	Tehama Pasakent	70 855
R	Nevada Grass Valley	61 217
S H	Shasta Shasta	66 729
SCRIGNI		
Fulgengio	San Francisco San Francisco 3	67 16
SCRIMGEOUR		
Jas	San Francisco San Francisco 10	329 67
SCRINGEOM		
D A	Sacramento Georgian	63 337
SCRITEN		
Dick	Sierra Downieville	661011
SCRIVAN		
Ed*	Solano Benecia	69 317
SCROGGINGS		
J W	Mariposa Twp 1	60 657
SCROGGINS		
A*	Nevada Eureka	61 372
John	Yuba Marysville	72 973
SCROGGINSON		
A S	Nevada Eureka	61 372

Name	County Locale	M653 RollPage
SCROGGS		
Alex	Sacramento Ward 4	63 514
SCROGWELL		
Wm	Nevada Nevada	61 314
SCROLL		
Jacob	Yuba Marysville	72 958
SCROYZS		
Gustuv R	Calaveras Twp 6	57 120
SCRUDER		
August	Tuolumne Twp 2	71 280
SCRUGGS		
Geo	Tuolumne Twp 1	71 252
W D	Stanislaus Branch	70 705
SCRUTCH		
Mitchell*	San Francisco San Francisco 3	67 41
SCRUZHAGEN		
Hans	San Francisco San Francisco 11	120 67
SCTRETT		
Conrad	Sierra St Louis	66 817
SCTT		
Louisa	Tulara Twp 1	71 99
SCTURARTZ		
Lewis	Santa Cruz Santa Cruz	66 614
SCUDAMORE		
Robt	Monterey S Antoni	60 973
SCUDDER		
Harry	San Francisco San Francisco 3	67 83
Jacob*	Plumas Quincy	62 918
Sarah	Sacramento Ward 1	63 102
Wm H	Amador Twp 2	55 263
SCUE		
Theodore*	Calaveras Twp 5	57 207
SCUGLEY		
Ira	Yuba Suida	72 988
SCUIGLEY		
Ira*	Yuba Linda	72 988
SCUL		
D E	Nevada Grass Valley	61 189
SCULL		
A C	Placer Dutch Fl	62 721
Joseph	Santa Clara San Jose	65 335
SCULLE		
Henry	Solano Benecia	69 292
John	Nevada Bloomfield	61 517
SCULLEN		
Henry	Solano Benecia	69 292
John	Placer Iona Hills	62 867
SCULLER		
Benjn	Sacramento Granite	63 234
SCULLEY		
Lawrence	Tulara Twp 3	71 52
Neill J	Tuolumne Springfield	71 370
Pat	Yolo Putah	72 553
SCULLIAN		
Margaret	Alameda Brooklyn	55 119
SCULLIN		
Austin S	Sierra Twp 7	66 910
SCULLION		
Sarah	Alameda Brooklyn	55 157
SCULLRIM		
Wm*	Butte Oro	56 677
SCULLUM		
Wm	Butte Oro	56 677
SCULLY		
Mary	San Francisco San Francisco 6	67 462
Michael	Mariposa Twp 3	60 597
Mychael	Mariposa Twp 3	60 597
Patrick	Alameda Brooklyn	55 101
Patrick	Los Angeles Los Angeles	59 365
Patrick	Tuolumne Twp 2	71 349
Peter	San Francisco San Francisco 12	362 67
Thomas	Los Angeles Santa Ana	59 447
Thomas J	Los Angeles Santa Ana	59 447
Thos	Sacramento Ward 1	63 61
SCULY		
Patrick	Yuba Marysville	72 912
SCUMSTOCK		
D	Sierra Downieville	661030
SCUN		
Theodore*	Calaveras Twp 5	57 207
SCURR		
Richard	Plumas Meadow Valley	62 902
Theodore*	Calaveras Twp 5	57 207
SCURRY		
D	Shasta Shasta	66 686
D	Shasta French G	66 722
SCURVY		
D*	Shasta French G	66 722
SCURWICK		
Henry	San Luis Obispo San Luis Obispo	65 32
SCUVIN		
David R	Yuba Suida	72 993
SCUZLER		
Chris	Trinity Trinity	70 974

Name	County Locale	M653 RollPage
SCVANK		
William	Yuba Marysville	72 907
SCWARTZ		
John R	Tuolumne Jamestown	71 444
SCYTHES		
Thomas	San Francisco San Francisco 3	67 43
SCYTHIS		
Thomas	San Francisco San Francisco 3	67 43
SDACRSTEIN		
Isaac*	Yuba Marysville	72 903
SDAM		
---	El Dorado Georgetown	58 756
SDAMO		
---	El Dorado Georgetown	58 761
SE CIM		
---	Mariposa Twp 3	60 613
SE HOY		
---	Sacramento Ward 1	63 60
SE VERSCHMAN		
Deofeild*	Amador Twp 4	55 245
SE WAK		
---	Mariposa Twp 3	60 608
SE		
---	Calaveras Twp 5	57 234
---	El Dorado Casumnes	581164
---	Nevada Nevada	61 309
---	Nevada Eureka	61 385
---	Sierra La Porte	66 774
---	Tuolumne Twp 5	71 512
Ang	Nevada Rough &	61 433
Chug	Nevada Bridgeport	61 491
Chung	Calaveras Twp 4	57 341
Chung*	Yuba Bear Rvr	721000
Cong	Butte Wyandotte	56 665
Din	Nevada Bridgeport	61 492
Gee	Nevada Bloomfield	61 521
Ham	Nevada Bridgeport	61 458
How	Calaveras Twp 4	57 334
Hoy	Sacramento Ward 1	63 60
Leo*	Butte Oregon	56 632
Long	Nevada Rough &	61 425
Lung	Nevada Rough &	61 398
Mang*	Calaveras Twp 6	57 182
Poy	Sacramento Ward 1	63 51
Quong	El Dorado Diamond	58 816
Ree	Yuba Marysville	72 925
Sam	Mariposa Twp 3	60 620
Say	Mariposa Twp 3	60 607
Sing	Mariposa Twp 3	60 613
Sing	Nevada Nevada	61 300
Tung	Calaveras Twp 10	57 295
Tuny	Calaveras Twp 10	57 295
Up	Placer Virginia	62 701
Wa	Mariposa Twp 3	60 579
Wau	Sacramento Natonia	63 283
Way	Shasta Shasta	66 668
SEA		
---	Amador Twp 2	55 326
---	Amador Twp 5	55 349
---	Calaveras Twp 10	57 285
---	Mariposa Twp 3	60 579
---	Mariposa Twp 1	60 651
---	Placer Auburn	62 575
---	Placer Auburn	62 576
---	Placer Auburn	62 582
---	Placer Virginia	62 666
---	Placer Illinois	62 742
---	Sierra Twp 5	66 932
---	Tuolumne Chinese	71 524
---	Tuolumne Twp 6	71 535
---*	Mariposa Twp 1	60 651
---	Placer Auburn	62 574
Huh	Nevada Grass Valley	61 227
Me	Placer Virginia	62 670
Sup	Nevada Grass Valley	61 227
T	San Francisco San Francisco 6	67 450
Yong	Placer Virginia	62 671
SEABAKER		
Charles	Tuolumne Montezuma	71 513
Henry	Tuolumne Twp 5	71 513
SEABALT		
S	San Francisco San Francisco 1	68 929
SEABAUGH		
A*	Sacramento Franklin	63 328
SEABERT		
Albert	Yuba Marysville	72 927
SEABINT		
Charles	San Francisco San Francisco 3	67 62
SEABIRRT		
Charles*	San Francisco San Francisco 3	67 62
SEABOUGH		
Chas B	Sacramento Ward 4	63 498
Samuel	Calaveras Twp 6	57 184
SEABROOK		
Geo	Sacramento Granite	63 252
SEABUM		
Mr*	Yolo Cottonwoood	72 646

Name	County Locale	M653 RollPage
SEABURR		
S S	Sierra La Porte	66 769
SEABURRG		
P G*	San Francisco San Francisco 3	67 49
SEABURRY		
P G*	San Francisco San Francisco 3	67 49
R G	San Francisco San Francisco 3	67 48
SEABURT		
Charles	San Francisco San Francisco 3	67 62
SEABURY		
S F	Sierra Gibsonville	66 860
S S	Sierra La Porte	66 769
SEACH		
Henderson	Contra Costa Twp 2	57 553
Joseph*	Amador Twp 4	55 254
S W*	Napa Napa	61 98
SEACHREST		
J C	Colusa Spring Valley	57 433
SEACOTT		
Frank	Amador Twp 2	55 264
Fred	Sonoma Bodega	69 537
Joseph	Sonoma Bodega	69 534
SEACY		
Ment*	Siskiyou Yreka	69 142
SEAD		
James*	Mariposa Twp 3	60 558
SEADS		
Miles*	Nevada Eureka	61 368
Niles*	Nevada Eureka	61 368
SEAGER		
Louis J F	San Diego Colorado	64 812
SEAGGIN		
W W	El Dorado Coloma	581086
SEAGHER		
John	San Francisco San Francisco 3	67 46
SEAGHIR		
John	San Francisco San Francisco 3	67 46
SEAGLE		
Jos	Sacramento Ward 4	63 508
SEAGRANE		
Curtis	Butte Oregon	56 628
Jno	Butte Oregon	56 628
SEAGRAVE		
Chapin M	San Francisco San Francisco 8	681267
SEAGRAVES		
C M	Santa Clara Santa Clara	65 465
SEAGREVE		
Saml	San Francisco San Francisco 1	68 858
SEAGUE		
Charles	Amador Twp 4	55 244
SEAH		
---	Mendocino Round Va	60 881
---	Yuba Long Bar	72 752
SEAHNY		
Joel	Yuba Slate Ro	72 688
SEAILS		
Niles*	Nevada Eureka	61 368
SEAIMS		
Wm*	Sonoma Petaluma	69 550
SEAK		
---*	Trinity Weaverville	701072
Carr W*	Calaveras Twp 9	57 360
SEAKELL		
W	Siskiyou Klamath	69 84
SEAKOUGH		
Samuel*	Calaveras Twp 5	57 185
SEAL		
Fred	San Joaquin Stockton	641091
J W	Amador Twp 6	55 447
James	Mariposa Twp 3	60 558
Neposum*	Yuba Marysville	72 917
Panils*	Mariposa Twp 3	60 558
Pareds*	Mariposa Twp 3	60 558
Parras	Mariposa Twp 3	60 558
Parris	Mariposa Twp 3	60 558
Pascas*	Mariposa Twp 3	60 558
SEALBURN		
M	Yolo Cottonwoood	72 646
SEALBURY		
W*	San Francisco San Francisco 10	250 67
Wm	San Francisco San Francisco 10	250 67
SEALE		
John*	Stanislaus Branch	70 705
SEALES		
A W	Sierra Scales D	66 800
W	San Francisco San Francisco 6	67 412
William M*	San Francisco San Francisco 8	681243
SEALEY		
J H	Napa Clear Lake	61 132
S	Sonoma Cloverdale	69 680
Thos	Sacramento Ward 1	63 109
W	El Dorado Placerville	58 824
Wm	El Dorado Kelsey	581154

California 1860 Census Index

Name	County Locale	M653 RollPage
SEALIGHT		
John	Yuba Timbucto	72 787
SEALMAR		
S	Calaveras Twp 9	57 391
SEALOHER		
P	Nevada Nevada	61 246
SEALRUN		
Mr*	Yolo Cottonwoood	72 646
SEALS		
Albert	Plumas Meadow Valley	62 908
Benjamin F	Yuba Marysville	72 906
Danl	San Francisco San Francisco 2	67 770
J	Mariposa Twp 3	60 583
John*	Stanislaus Branch	70 705
P	Mariposa Twp 3	60 583
R	San Francisco San Francisco 6	67 412
SEALUM		
M	Yolo Cache Crk	72 646
SEALY		
George	Sierra La Porte	66 770
Gerge	Sierra La Porte	66 770
M	El Dorado Casumnes	581171
Samuel T	Mariposa Twp 1	60 667
SEAM		
---	Sierra Twp 5	66 932
SEAMAN		
---	San Francisco San Francisco 2	67 667
Bradford	Napa Napa	61 101
C H	San Francisco San Francisco 7	681437
Charles	Plumas Quincy	62 986
Charles H	San Francisco San Francisco 7	681422
Clark	San Francisco San Francisco 4	681223
F A	Napa Napa	61 100
J	San Francisco San Francisco 2	67 695
J F	Sonoma Mendocino	69 466
J H	Trinity Weaverville	701069
John	Placer Nicolaus	62 691
Joseph	Contra Costa Twp 2	57 569
Manal	Sacramento Ward 4	63 534
O	Shasta Shasta	66 728
Porter	Shasta Shasta	66 732
Robert	Solano Vacaville	69 328
Robt B	Fresno Twp 3	59 22
Seth	San Francisco San Francisco 2	67 646
Seth	San Francisco San Francisco 1	68 932
Vernon	San Francisco San Francisco 9	681008
W H	Placer Todds Va	62 784
SEAMANS		
Jas	San Francisco San Francisco 2	67 701
Mitchell	Yuba Marysville	72 919
Mitchells	Yuba Marysville	72 919
SEAMMAN		
Benj*	Stanislaus Emory	70 754
SEAMMER		
S A	Calaveras Twp 9	57 386
SEAMMON		
Danl	Calaveras Twp 8	57 85
George	Calaveras Twp 7	57 39
SEAMON		
F*	Tuolumne Shawsfla	71 403
Henry	Solano Vacaville	69 360
SEAMONS		
T*	San Mateo Twp 1	65 62
SEAMORE		
F*	Tuolumne Shawsfla	71 403
John	Napa Napa	61 100
Peter	Tuolumne Twp 2	71 403
SEAMS		
John	Tuolumne Chinese	71 496
SEAMUN		
E	San Francisco San Francisco 3	67 74
SEAMWER		
S A*	Calaveras Twp 9	57 386
SEAN		
---	Amador Twp 5	55 352
---	Calaveras Twp 10	57 269
---	Placer Dutch Fl	62 737
---	Placer Illinois	62 753
Yat	San Francisco San Francisco 1	68 925
SEANAN		
John	Mariposa Twp 3	60 617
S A	El Dorado Placerville	58 827
SEANIER		
Mary*	Placer Goods	62 695
SEANN		
---	Placer Dutch Fl	62 729
SEANNELL		
Jacob	Santa Clara Redwood	65 456
SEANNY		
W F	Amador Twp 6	55 439
SEANY		
---	Calaveras Twp 5	57 209
---	Calaveras Twp 10	57 286
Jno*	Butte Oregon	56 610
SEAP		
---	Tuolumne Don Pedro	71 536
SEAR		
Croger*	Mariposa Twp 1	60 647
Crozir	Mariposa Twp 1	60 647
D V	Amador Twp 5	55 339
Grozer	Mariposa Twp 1	60 647
Joseph	San Diego Colorado	64 808
Wm*	Nevada Grass Valley	61 169
SEARCH		
P	San Joaquin Stockton	641049
SEARCUS		
Frank	Amador Twp 3	55 374
SEARCY		
James	Siskiyou Scott Va	69 22
Otis	San Francisco San Francisco 10	357 67
SEARE		
Peter	Sierra Downieville	661018
SEARES		
Jacob	Tulara Keyesville	71 58
SEAREY		
James	Siskiyou Scott Va	69 22
Ment*	Siskiyou Yreka	69 142
SEARING		
Matthias	San Francisco San Francisco 10	303 67
SEARINS		
Wm*	Sonoma Petaluma	69 550
SEARL		
G	Tehama Tehama	70 939
Geo	Tuolumne Twp 4	71 128
Henrick	Santa Cruz Watsonville	66 540
Henrieta	Santa Cruz Watsonville	66 540
Henrietta	Santa Cruz Watsonville	66 540
SEARLAN		
Bridget	San Francisco San Francisco 4	681214
SEARLE		
A T	San Francisco San Francisco 10	261 67
John	San Francisco San Francisco 12	375 67
SEARLEO		
Manuel	Calaveras Twp 9	57 376
SEARLER		
William	Monterey Alisal	601039
SEARLES		
---	Colusa Mansville	57 438
A C	El Dorado Placerville	58 823
A F	San Francisco San Francisco 6	67 412
Anson	Sacramento Ward 1	63 86
Bud*	Butte Chico	56 557
Buel	Butte Chico	56 557
David	El Dorado Mud Springs	58 959
James	Humbolt Eureka	59 164
Jno	Sacramento Ward 4	63 599
John	El Dorado White Oaks	581019
John	Santa Clara Santa Clara	65 497
SEARLEY		
E P	Butte Oregon	56 623
SEARLIS		
Anson*	Sacramento Ward 1	63 86
SEARLS		
A C	El Dorado Placerville	58 828
E	Sacramento Cosumnes	63 385
F D	Nevada Bridgeport	61 451
Fideas	Sonoma Vallejo	69 624
Harvey	Santa Cruz Pajaro	66 564
Ira	San Francisco San Francisco 2	67 687
J A	Trinity Redding	70 985
Jas	Sacramento Sutter	63 307
Jas	Sacramento Sutter	63 308
Jno	Tehama Red Bluff	70 905
Miles*	Nevada Eureka	61 368
Niles*	Nevada Eureka	61 368
Robert	Sierra Downieville	66 995
SEARLY		
B B	Sacramento Ward 4	63 517
Fideas	Sonoma Vallejo	69 624
SEARMAN		
John	Placer Sacramento	62 643
SEARNEY		
Philip*	Napa Yount	61 42
SEARRING		
W S	Alameda Brooklyn	55 120
SEARS		
A J	Shasta Horsetown	66 703
Alden	Tuolumne Columbia	71 316
C	El Dorado Placerville	58 934
C D	Sonoma Petaluma	69 599
C L	Santa Clara Redwood	65 453
Chauncy C	Sacramento Granite	63 248
Chauney C	Sacramento Granite	63 248
Conrad	Alameda Brooklyn	55 81
Edward	San Francisco San Francisco 11	155 67
Frances A	Colusa Colusi	57 419
George	Trinity Rearings	70 990
SEARS		
H W	Nevada Bridgeport	61 454
Henry	Tulara Twp 2	71 23
J	Sutter Bear Rvr	70 819
Jacob	Tulara Twp 3	71 58
James	Sacramento Ward 1	63 84
Johhn	San Joaquin Castoria	64 905
John	Amador Twp 5	55 339
John	Placer Rattle Snake	62 600
John B Jr	San Joaquin Castoria	64 877
John B Sr	San Joaquin Castoria	64 877
Joseph	Colusa Colusi	57 425
M*	Calaveras Twp 9	57 405
Mary	El Dorado Spanish	581125
Spencer	Sonoma Sonoma	69 661
T	Sacramento Ward 1	63 101
Theodore*	Calaveras Twp 5	57 207
Thos	Amador Twp 3	55 403
W	Sacramento Granite	63 227
W T	Shasta Horsetown	66 702
William	Yuba Marysville	72 854
William	Yuba Marysville	72 859
SEARTEO		
Manuel	Calaveras Twp 9	57 376
SEARWOOD		
Owen*	Calaveras Twp 9	57 384
SEARY		
Jas*	San Francisco San Francisco 2	67 560
Jno*	Butte Oregon	56 610
Jno*	Butte Eureka	56 650
Michael	Butte Kimshaw	56 607
W*	San Francisco San Francisco 9	681074
SEAS		
M	Shasta Horsetown	66 702
SEASILL		
John	Los Angeles Elmonte	59 269
SEAT		
---	El Dorado Placerville	58 830
---	Siskiyou Klamath	69 80
SEATE		
John	Tuolumne Twp 2	71 314
Saml	Tuolumne Twp 3	71 446
SEATER		
Tisbzallen*	Tulara Twp 1	71 79
SEATH		
A*	Tuolumne Big Oak	71 145
H J	Mariposa Coulterville	60 688
Wm	San Francisco San Francisco 3	67 78
SEATHERN		
C	Trinity Steiner	701000
SEATMAN		
L	Calaveras Twp 9	57 391
T	Calaveras Twp 9	57 391
SEATON		
G W	Amador Twp 5	55 336
Joseph	Tulara Visalia	71 7
W H	El Dorado Kelsey	581148
Wm	Butte Ophir	56 758
Wm	El Dorado White Oaks	581014
Wm	Sacramento Ward 1	63 43
SEATONE		
Joseph*	Tulara Twp 2	71 7
SEATORE		
John	Alameda Brooklyn	55 202
SEATT		
Saml	Tuolumne Jamestown	71 446
SEATTER		
Mary	San Joaquin Stockton	641064
SEAVER		
C H	Tuolumne Columbia	71 366
Charles*	Yuba Marysville	72 892
Margaret	Marin Bolinas	60 740
Thomas	Calaveras Twp 4	57 340
Wm H	San Francisco San Francisco 10	307 67
SEAVERLEY		
Edward	Santa Clara Gilroy	65 230
SEAVERS		
C M*	Sacramento Granite	63 242
John	Siskiyou Scott Va	69 28
SEAVERY		
John A	Nevada Rough &	61 422
SEAVEY		
C T	Mariposa Twp 3	60 557
Elisha P	Yuba Rose Bar	72 803
Elizabeth	San Francisco San Francisco 11	131 67
Ment*	Siskiyou Yreka	69 142
Oliver*	Humbolt Table Bl	59 141
SEAVITT		
George	Calaveras Twp 6	57 155
SEAVOIT		
George	Calaveras Twp 6	57 113
SEAVY		
A D	Tuolumne Twp 2	71 374
Anderson	Yuba Marysville	72 907

California 1860 Census Index

Name	County Locale	M653 Roll	Page
SEAVY			
David	Tuolumne Big Oak	71	125
David	Tuolumne Twp 4	71	127
F	Tuolumne Big Oak	71	125
George*	Amador Twp 4	55	254
Jas	San Francisco San Francisco 2	67	560
Napoleon	Tuolumne Big Oak	71	136
Robt	Sonoma Petaluma	69	547
SEAW			
---	Amador Twp 5	55	355
---	Amador Twp 5	55	364
SEAWARD			
James B*	Yuba Marysville	72	847
Thomas	Yuba Marysville	72	890
SEAWELE			
Abraham	Napa Napa	61	88
SEAWELL			
Abraham	Napa Napa	61	88
Henry S	Contra Costa Twp 2	57	561
John H	Napa Napa	61	90
John L*	Sonoma Sonoma	69	650
Matilda	Napa Napa	61	85
W A*	Napa Napa	61	68
W N	Napa Napa	61	68
Wm	Sonoma Russian	69	429
SEAWOOD			
Geo	Klamath S Fork	59	203
Owen*	Calaveras Twp 9	57	384
SEAY			
A G	Tuolumne Twp 1	71	264
SEBARIANO			
J	Tuolumne Sonora	71	481
SEBASABLE			
B	Shasta Millvill	66	747
SEBASCABLE			
B	Shasta Millvill	66	747
SEBASHAMT			
M*	El Dorado Georgetown	58	699
SEBASTANO			
Terta*	Placer Michigan	62	832
SEBASTEAN			
---	San Bernardino Santa Barbara	64	197
SEBASTER			
T Q	Tehama Antelope	70	886
SEBASTIAN			
---	San Bernardino Santa Inez	64	138
Corles	El Dorado Greenwood	58	718
George	El Dorado Greenwood	58	730
George	Shasta Shasta	66	681
J	El Dorado Kelsey	58	1156
John	Placer Forest H	62	773
N	Shasta Shasta	66	678
Weaver	Shasta French G	66	719
SEBASTION			
George	Shasta Shasta	66	681
SEBAUGH			
Mr	Sonoma Sonoma	69	643
SEBBERS			
Joseph	San Francisco San Francisco 4	68	1157
SEBBETT			
Edward F	Yuba Suida	72	990
SEBBEY			
W H	Nevada Eureka	61	376
SEBBRE			
Conrad	Sacramento American	63	161
SEBEGUTH			
Geo	Trinity Mouth Ca	70	1013
SEBEREANA			
---	Monterey Monterey	60	953
SEBERER			
Lorenzo	Alameda Brooklyn	55	82
SEBERINO			
Julien	Tuolumne Twp 5	71	499
SEBERRY			
Henry*	Mariposa Coulterville	60	702
SEBICE			
Cora	Contra Costa Twp 1	57	505
David	Contra Costa Twp 1	57	505
SEBLANCE			
E F	Siskiyou Klamath	69	92
SEBLEY			
Henry	San Francisco San Francisco 3	67	69
SEBO			
Joel*	Napa Clear Lake	61	121
SEBOLD			
D C	Trinity Lewiston	70	964
Sebastian	Sacramento Ward 4	63	507
Thoms*	El Dorado Georgetown	58	706
SEBON			
John	Amador Twp 4	55	244
SEBRAEN			
Clotilda	Alameda Oakland	55	58
SEBRALA			
John	Los Angeles Los Angeles	59	504
SEBREAN			
Pablo	Alameda Oakland	55	58

Name	County Locale	M653 Roll	Page
SEBRING			
Cyrus	Tehama Pasakent	70	855
Thomas*	Sonoma Armally	69	502
SEBSTER			
Albert*	San Joaquin O'Neal	64	1006
SEBY			
Joshua	Napa Yount	61	36
Samael W	Yuba Marysville	72	850
SEC TUCK			
---	Sacramento Ward 1	63	70
SEC			
---	Tuolumne Twp 5	71	512
J R*	Trinity Honest B	70	1043
SECE			
---	Amador Twp 5	55	331
SECERD			
Luke	Placer Lisbon	62	733
SECH			
Sing*	Mariposa Twp 3	60	579
SECHAL			
M	Nevada Eureka	61	392
SECHAN			
---	Sierra La Porte	66	780
SECHIL			
M	Nevada Eureka	61	392
SECHINE			
Andrew	San Francisco San Francisco 4	68	1215
SECHIVER			
Frederick*	San Francisco 3	67	80
	San Francisco		
SECHLER			
Antis*	Humbolt Table Bl	59	139
SECHRIST			
Adaline	Solano Vacaville	69	342
SECHRVIR			
Frederick*	San Francisco 3	67	80
	San Francisco		
SECK			
---	Calaveras Twp 4	57	341
---	El Dorado Salmon Hills	58	1054
SECKEL			
Geo	Tuolumne Twp 1	71	482
SECKLER			
A	Solano Vacaville	69	332
Antis*	Humbolt Table Bl	59	139
SECKOROP			
---	Fresno Twp 2	59	60
SECKSLEY			
Andrew*	Alameda Brooklyn	55	146
SECLERC			
Louis S*	Calaveras Twp 4	57	339
SECMERS			
Y*	San Mateo Twp 1	65	62
SECNTO			
Stephen*	Calaveras Twp 5	57	225
SECO			
Frank	Sierra Pine Grove	66	827
SECOMEA			
---	Fresno Twp 2	59	91
SECOMPLE			
John*	Yuba Marysville	72	903
SECORE			
Henry	Santa Clara San Jose	65	338
SECRE			
Saphen*	Calaveras Twp 5	57	225
SECREST			
Fred	Siskiyou Yreka	69	124
SECRET			
Saphen*	Calaveras Twp 5	57	225
SECRETAN			
Victoria	San Francisco San Francisco 10	67	182
SECRETEN			
August*	Nevada Bloomfield	61	520
SECRETEU			
August*	Nevada Bloomfield	61	520
SECRISH			
Joseph	Siskiyou Scott Va	69	42
SECRIST			
Joseph	Siskiyou Scott Va	69	42
Joseph C	Siskiyou Scott Va	69	42
May J	Solano Vacaville	69	341
SECROX			
Juan	Los Angeles Los Angeles	59	504
SECRTE			
Sophen*	Calaveras Twp 5	57	225
SECU			
Ferdinand	Calaveras Twp 6	57	153
SECULE			
John	Monterey San Juan	60	976
SECULIVICH			
P	San Francisco San Francisco 5	67	476
SECULOOICH			
P	San Francisco San Francisco 5	67	476
SECURE			
---*	Tulara Twp 2	71	4

Name	County Locale	M653 Roll	Page
SEDA			
Jose A	Santa Clara Santa Clara	65	495
SEDAY			
Soni*	San Francisco San Francisco 10	67	179
SEDDRELL			
R	Solano Vacaville	69	331
SEDDULL			
R	Solano Vacaville	69	331
SEDEILLAN			
Victorine	San Francisco San Francisco 10	67	249
SEDERGUST			
John C*	Placer Virginia	62	682
SEDERQUST			
John C*	Placer Virginia	62	682
SEDFORD			
T	San Francisco San Francisco 5	67	489
SEDGLEY			
Eliza	Solano Vallejo	69	248
John	Solano Vallejo	69	248
SEDGNICK			
M	San Francisco San Francisco 9	68	1074
SEDGREY			
Jos	San Francisco San Francisco 10	67	320
SEDGUICK			
Math	Alameda Brooklyn	55	90
SEDGURCK			
Charles	San Joaquin Douglass	64	920
Mathew	Alameda Brooklyn	55	83
SEDGWICK			
John	Tuolumne Sonora	71	202
Marshall	San Francisco San Francisco 2	67	646
Math	Alameda Brooklyn	55	90
Mathew	Alameda Brooklyn	55	83
SEDIKAR			
Thos F*	Stanislaus Oatvale	70	718
SEDILLO			
Juan	Santa Clara Gilroy	65	224
SEDLINGER			
Joseph*	Siskiyou Yreka	69	153
SEDMAN			
G F	Sonoma Mendocino	69	466
SEDON			
Dophiel*	Amador Twp 4	55	245
SEDORE			
Alvin	Amador Twp 1	55	473
SEDORS			
Dophiel*	Amador Twp 4	55	245
SEDRE			
Jose	Santa Cruz Santa Cruz	66	623
SEDRO			
---	San Bernardino S Timate	64	749
Jose*	Santa Cruz Santa Cruz	66	623
SEDWELL			
J M	Solano Montezuma	69	370
SEE CHOW			
---	Nevada Nevada	61	310
---*	Nevada Nevada	61	307
SEE CHUNA			
---	Tuolumne Jacksonville	71	516
SEE CONN			
---*	Nevada Nevada	61	304
SEE CUM			
---	Mariposa Twp 3	60	613
---	Tuolumne Sonora	71	476
SEE CUN			
Ah	Tuolumne Twp 2	71	346
SEE HAIN			
---	Nevada Nevada	61	302
SEE HOP			
---	Solano Suisan	69	205
SEE HOW			
---*	Nevada Nevada	61	302
SEE KONG			
---	Sacramento Ward 1	63	69
SEE KOW			
---	Sacramento Ward 1	63	71
---*	Mariposa Twp 3	60	599
SEE LE			
---	Mariposa Twp 3	60	613
SEE LIAUS			
---*	Mariposa Twp 3	60	608
SEE LO			
---	Mariposa Twp 3	60	608
SEE NE WAH			
---	Sacramento Ward 1	63	59
SEE NUN			
---	Mariposa Twp 3	60	607
SEE PU FOY			
---	Sacramento Ward 1	63	52
SEE PU TOY			
---*	Sacramento Ward 1	63	52
SEE QUA			
---	Mariposa Twp 3	60	609

California 1860 Census Index

Name	County Locale	M653 Roll	Page
SEE QUE			
---	Mariposa Twp 3	60	608
SEE SAN			
---	Mariposa Twp 3	60	612
---	Nevada Washington	61	339
SEE SEE			
---*	Nevada Nevada	61	308
SEE SHIN			
---	Nevada Washington	61	339
SEE SON			
---	Nevada Nevada	61	303
SEE SOU LA			
---	Mariposa Twp 3	60	607
SEE TOY			
---	Nevada Nevada	61	310
---*	Nevada Nevada	61	307
SEE TUCK			
---	Sacramento Ward 1	63	68
SEE TUP			
---*	Nevada Nevada	61	304
SEE WAN			
---	Sacramento Ward 1	63	68
SEE YOU			
---*	Nevada Nevada	61	305
SEE YOW			
Coung*	Mariposa Twp 1	60	627
SEE YU			
---	Nevada Nevada	61	304
SEE YUP			
---	Nevada Nevada	61	302
---	Nevada Nevada	61	303
---	Nevada Nevada	61	305
---	Nevada Nevada	61	308
---	Nevada Nevada	61	309
---	Nevada Washington	61	339
---	Nevada Washington	61	340
---	Nevada Washington	61	341
---*	Nevada Nevada	61	304
---*	Nevada Nevada	61	305
SEE			
---	Alameda Oakland	55	63
---	Amador Twp 4	55	233
---	Amador Twp 4	55	247
---	Amador Twp 4	55	251
---	Amador Twp 4	55	256
---	Amador Twp 2	55	281
---	Amador Twp 2	55	311
---	Amador Twp 2	55	315
---	Amador Twp 2	55	316
---	Amador Twp 2	55	327
---	Amador Twp 2	55	328
---	Amador Twp 5	55	331
---	Amador Twp 4	55	332
---	Amador Twp 5	55	336
---	Amador Twp 5	55	338
---	Amador Twp 5	55	341
---	Amador Twp 5	55	345
---	Amador Twp 5	55	349
---	Amador Twp 5	55	353
---	Amador Twp 5	55	359
---	Amador Twp 5	55	364
---	Amador Twp 3	55	402
---	Amador Twp 7	55	415
---	Amador Twp 6	55	422
---	Amador Twp 1	55	477
---	Amador Twp 1	55	492
---	Amador Twp 1	55	496
---	Amador Twp 1	55	497
---	Amador Twp 1	55	501
---	Amador Twp 1	55	502
---	Amador Twp 1	55	503
---	Amador Twp 1	55	510
---	Amador Twp 1	55	511
---	Butte Kimshaw	56	578
---	Butte Kimshaw	56	600
---	Butte Eureka	56	652
---	Butte Ophir	56	804
---	Butte Ophir	56	810
---	Calaveras Twp 8	57	107
---	Calaveras Twp 6	57	141
---	Calaveras Twp 6	57	149
---	Calaveras Twp 6	57	150
---	Calaveras Twp 6	57	158
---	Calaveras Twp 6	57	159
---	Calaveras Twp 6	57	164
---	Calaveras Twp 6	57	165
---	Calaveras Twp 6	57	167
---	Calaveras Twp 6	57	176
---	Calaveras Twp 6	57	181
---	Calaveras Twp 6	57	182
---	Calaveras Twp 5	57	192
---	Calaveras Twp 5	57	201
---	Calaveras Twp 5	57	205
---	Calaveras Twp 5	57	214
---	Calaveras Twp 5	57	219
---	Calaveras Twp 5	57	225
SEE			
---	Calaveras Twp 5	57	232
---	Calaveras Twp 5	57	234
---	Calaveras Twp 5	57	236
---	Calaveras Twp 5	57	241
---	Calaveras Twp 5	57	245
---	Calaveras Twp 5	57	251
---	Calaveras Twp 5	57	252
---	Calaveras Twp 5	57	256
---	Calaveras Twp 10	57	259
---	Calaveras Twp 10	57	261
---	Calaveras Twp 10	57	269
---	Calaveras Twp 10	57	271
---	Calaveras Twp 10	57	273
---	Calaveras Twp 10	57	280
---	Calaveras Twp 10	57	286
---	Calaveras Twp 10	57	296
---	Calaveras Twp 10	57	297
---	Calaveras Twp 4	57	315
---	Calaveras Twp 4	57	316
---	Calaveras Twp 4	57	326
---	Calaveras Twp 4	57	328
---	Calaveras Twp 7	57	37
---	Calaveras Twp 7	57	82
---	El Dorado White Oaks	58	1011
---	El Dorado Coloma	58	1075
---	El Dorado Coloma	58	1077
---	El Dorado Coloma	58	1078
---	El Dorado Coloma	58	1085
---	El Dorado Union	58	1089
---	El Dorado Georgetown	58	688
---	El Dorado Georgetown	58	692
---	El Dorado Georgetown	58	702
---	El Dorado Diamond	58	805
---	El Dorado Diamond	58	806
---	El Dorado Placerville	58	823
---	El Dorado Placerville	58	829
---	El Dorado Placerville	58	835
---	El Dorado Placerville	58	841
---	El Dorado Placerville	58	843
---	El Dorado Mud Springs	58	964
---	El Dorado Mud Springs	58	965
---	El Dorado Mud Springs	58	970
---	El Dorado Mud Springs	58	971
---	El Dorado Mud Springs	58	972
---	El Dorado Mud Springs	58	977
---	El Dorado Mud Springs	58	985
---	El Dorado Mud Springs	58	986
---	El Dorado Mud Springs	58	987
---	El Dorado Mud Springs	58	992
---	Mariposa Twp 3	60	581
---	Mariposa Twp 3	60	609
---	Mariposa Twp 3	60	618
---	Mariposa Twp 1	60	626
---	Mariposa Twp 1	60	627
---	Mariposa Twp 1	60	637
---	Mariposa Twp 1	60	641
---	Mariposa Twp 1	60	643
---	Mariposa Twp 1	60	648
---	Mariposa Twp 1	60	650
---	Mariposa Twp 1	60	661
---	Mariposa Twp 1	60	663
---	Mariposa Twp 1	60	666
---	Mariposa Twp 1	60	673
---	Mariposa Coulterville	60	692
---	Nevada Grass Valley	61	228
---	Nevada Grass Valley	61	230
---	Nevada Grass Valley	61	233
---	Nevada Grass Valley	61	234
---	Nevada Nevada	61	300
---	Nevada Nevada	61	302
---	Nevada Nevada	61	306
---	Nevada Nevada	61	308
---	Nevada Nevada	61	309
---	Nevada Washington	61	339
---	Nevada Washington	61	341
---	Nevada Eureka	61	385
---	Nevada Eureka	61	386
---	Nevada Rough &	61	425
---	Nevada Rough &	61	433
---	Nevada Rough &	61	436
---	Nevada Bridgeport	61	439
---	Nevada Bridgeport	61	454
---	Placer Auburn	62	573
---	Placer Virginia	62	681
---	Placer Virginia	62	687
---	Placer Illinois	62	749
---	Placer Iona Hills	62	889
---	Plumas Meadow Valley	62	909
---	Plumas Meadow Valley	62	913
---	Plumas Meadow Valley	62	914
---	Sacramento Granite	63	264
---	Sacramento Granite	63	268
---	Sacramento Natonia	63	283
---	Sacramento Cosumnes	63	397
---	Sacramento Cosumnes	63	398
SEE			
---	Sacramento Ward 3	63	491
---	Sacramento Ward 1	63	51
---	Sacramento Ward 1	63	52
---	Sacramento Ward 1	63	53
---	Sacramento Ward 1	63	54
---	Sacramento Ward 1	63	56
---	Sacramento Ward 4	63	610
---	San Francisco San Francisco	9	681087
---	San Francisco San Francisco	9	681088
---	San Francisco San Francisco	9	681092
---	San Francisco San Francisco	9	681095
---	San Francisco San Francisco	4	681174
---	San Francisco San Francisco	4	681180
---	San Francisco San Francisco	4	681187
---	San Francisco San Francisco	4	681189
---	San Francisco San Francisco	4	681193
---	San Francisco San Francisco	4	681196
---	San Francisco San Francisco	4	681197
---	San Francisco San Francisco	4	681209
---	San Francisco San Francisco	4	681210
---	San Francisco San Francisco	4	681212
---	San Francisco San Francisco	11	145
			67
---	Shasta French G	66	720
---	Sierra Downieville	66	1004
---	Sierra Downieville	66	1009
---	Sierra Downieville	66	1014
---	Sierra Twp 5	66	932
---	Sierra Downieville	66	985
---	Sierra Downieville	66	995
---	Sierra Downieville	66	996
---	Trinity Big Flat	70	1041
---	Tuolumne Big Oak	71	147
---	Tuolumne Don Pedro	71	163
---	Tuolumne Springfield	71	369
---	Tuolumne Shawsfla	71	385
---	Tuolumne Twp 2	71	398
---	Tuolumne Jamestown	71	421
---	Tuolumne Twp 3	71	422
---	Tuolumne Twp 3	71	433
---	Tuolumne Twp 3	71	438
---	Tuolumne Jamestown	71	440
---	Tuolumne Jamestown	71	442
---	Tuolumne Twp 3	71	459
---	Tuolumne Twp 3	71	460
---	Tuolumne Twp 3	71	467
---	Tuolumne Twp 3	71	469
---	Tuolumne Twp 2	71	474
---	Tuolumne Twp 1	71	478
---	Tuolumne Twp 1	71	485
---	Tuolumne Twp 5	71	510
---	Tuolumne Twp 5	71	512
---	Tuolumne Montezuma	71	513
---	Tuolumne Chinese	71	525
---	Tuolumne Twp 5	71	526
---	Tuolumne Don Pedro	71	536
---	Yolo Slate Ra	72	711
---	Yolo Slate Ra	72	712
---	Yuba Slate Ro	72	711
---	Yuba Slate Ro	72	712
---	Yuba Fosters	72	826
---	Yuba Marysville	72	894
---	Yuba Marysville	72	895
---	Yuba Marysville	72	920
---	Yuba Marysville	72	925
---	Yuba Linda	72	990
---*	Amador Twp 4	55	252
---*	Calaveras Twp 5	57	236
---*	Calaveras Twp 5	57	237
---*	Calaveras Twp 10	57	297
---*	El Dorado Coloma	58	1078
---*	El Dorado Georgetown	58	700
---*	Nevada Nevada	61	305
---*	Nevada Rough &	61	432
---*	Sacramento Centre	63	181
---*	Sacramento Centre	63	182
---*	Sacramento Mississipi	63	190
---*	Sacramento Ward 1	63	51
---*	Sacramento Ward 1	63	53
---*	Sacramento Ward 1	63	54
---*	Sacramento Ward 1	63	59
---*	Tuolumne Twp 3	71	457
---*	Tuolumne Twp 3	71	460
---*	Yuba Foster B	72	826
---*	Yuba Marysville	72	917
A W*	Mariposa Twp 3	60	577
Adam	Yolo Cottonwoood	72	556
Ah	Butte Mountain	56	735
Ah	Tuolumne Twp 4	71	147
Ah	Tuolumne Twp 4	71	159
Ah	Tuolumne Twp 4	71	163
Ah	Tuolumne Twp 4	71	179
Ah	Tuolumne Twp 2	71	346

California 1860 Census Index

Name	County Locale	M653 RollPage
SEE		
Ah	Tuolumne Twp 2	71 369
Ah	Tuolumne Twp 2	71 396
Ah	Yuba Suida	72 990
Amen*	El Dorado Georgetown	58 704
App	Nevada Nevada	61 300
As	Tuolumne Twp 4	71 169
Bang	Placer Forest H	62 773
Bung	San Francisco San Francisco 4	681 183
Cam	Tuolumne Columbia	71 347
Can	Mariposa Twp 3	60 580
Can	Nevada Grass Valley	61 232
Can*	Mariposa Twp 3	60 580
Cau*	Mariposa Twp 3	60 580
Chan	Nevada Grass Valley	61 233
Chenn*	Mariposa Twp 3	60 582
Chin	Nevada Rough &	61 425
Ching	Amador Twp 2	55 311
Ching	Mariposa Twp 3	60 553
Ching	Nevada Nevada	61 299
Chiry	Amador Twp 2	55 311
Chon	Nevada Washington	61 339
Chow	Nevada Nevada	61 307
Chow	Nevada Nevada	61 310
Chow	Nevada Eureka	61 385
Chow	San Francisco San Francisco 4	681 210
Choy	Nevada Nevada	61 301
Chum	Mariposa Twp 3	60 582
Chun	Mariposa Twp 3	60 572
Chun	Nevada Grass Valley	61 233
Chuw	Nevada Grass Valley	61 233
Cim*	Mariposa Twp 3	60 613
Con	Nevada Grass Valley	61 232
Conn	Nevada Nevada	61 304
Conne	Sierra Downieville	66 995
Cow	Nevada Nevada	61 302
Cow	Nevada Nevada	61 305
Cow	Nevada Washington	61 342
Cow*	Butte Oro	56 687
Coy	Nevada Washington	61 342
Cug	Mariposa Twp 3	60 553
Cumg	Plumas Quincy	621 009
David*	Placer Forest H	62 803
Faw	Yuba Long Bar	72 770
Fing	Amador Twp 2	55 312
Flea	Butte Oro	56 687
Fong	Plumas Quincy	62 948
Foo	Butte Bidwell	56 708
Foo	Nevada Grass Valley	61 233
Foot	Nevada Bridgeport	61 464
Fow	Nevada Grass Valley	61 228
Foy	San Francisco San Francisco 5	671 205
Fun	Nevada Grass Valley	61 228
H M	Yolo Cottonwood	72 559
Hain	Nevada Nevada	61 302
Ham	Mariposa Twp 3	60 581
Han	Mariposa Twp 3	60 581
Han*	Mariposa Twp 3	60 580
Hannah*	Napa Napa	61 104
Hau*	Mariposa Twp 3	60 581
Hay	Nevada Grass Valley	61 230
Hay	Nevada Nevada	61 300
Hay	Nevada Nevada	61 301
Hee	Nevada Nevada	61 301
Hen	Mariposa Twp 3	60 596
Hing	San Francisco San Francisco 9	681 096
Hon	Mariposa Twp 3	60 569
Hon	Nevada Nevada	61 299
Hon	Nevada Nevada	61 301
Hop	Mariposa Twp 3	60 543
Hop	Nevada Grass Valley	61 229
Hop	Solano Suisan	69 205
Hou	Mariposa Twp 3	60 588
How	Mariposa Twp 3	60 588
How	Nevada Nevada	61 299
How	Nevada Nevada	61 302
How*	San Francisco San Francisco 9	681 095
Hoy	Nevada Grass Valley	61 230
Hoy	Nevada Nevada	61 301
Hung	San Francisco San Francisco 9	681 096
Hup	Nevada Nevada	61 301
In*	Mariposa Twp 3	60 578
J R*	Trinity Honest B	701 043
Jny	Nevada Nevada	61 301
John	Sacramento Ward 1	63 64
John C*	Napa Napa	61 107
John*	Sacramento Centre	63 173
Jon	Mariposa Twp 3	60 569
Juan*	Mariposa Twp 3	60 580
Kam	Mariposa Twp 3	60 572
Kan	Mariposa Twp 3	60 582
Kau	Mariposa Twp 3	60 582
Kay	Nevada Nevada	61 300
Kee	Mariposa Twp 3	60 576
Kee	Mariposa Twp 3	60 581
King	Mariposa Twp 3	60 543
SEE		
King	Mariposa Twp 3	60 560
King	Mariposa Twp 3	60 569
Kon	Mariposa Twp 3	60 580
Kon*	Mariposa Twp 3	60 581
Kon*	Mariposa Twp 3	60 580
Kong	Sacramento Ward 1	63 69
Koo	Mariposa Twp 3	60 620
Kou	Mariposa Twp 3	60 576
Kou	Mariposa Twp 3	60 578
Kou	Mariposa Twp 3	60 580
Kou	Mariposa Twp 3	60 582
Kou*	Mariposa Twp 3	60 576
Kou*	Mariposa Twp 3	60 582
Kow	Mariposa Twp 3	60 553
Kow	Mariposa Twp 3	60 564
Kow	Mariposa Twp 3	60 576
Kow Yen	El Dorado Big Bar	58 734
La	Mariposa Twp 3	60 582
Lan	Mariposa Twp 3	60 581
Lang	Mariposa Twp 3	60 552
Lang*	Placer Illinois	62 748
Law	Mariposa Twp 3	60 544
Law	Sacramento Ward 3	63 492
Lay	Mariposa Twp 3	60 564
Le	Mariposa Twp 3	60 562
Le	Mariposa Twp 3	60 613
Leah	San Bernardino San Bernadino	64 644
Leay	Yuba Long Bar	72 764
Lee	Mariposa Twp 3	60 569
Lee	Mariposa Twp 3	60 572
Lee	Mariposa Twp 3	60 576
Lei	Yuba Long Bar	72 764
Ling	Sacramento Granite	63 259
Ling*	Butte Oro	56 687
Liry	Amador Twp 3	55 401
Lon	El Dorado Greenwood	58 731
Lon	Mariposa Twp 3	60 576
Lon*	Mariposa Twp 3	60 613
Long	Placer Illinois	62 704
Loo	Mariposa Twp 3	60 560
Lou	Mariposa Twp 3	60 564
Lou	Mariposa Twp 3	60 576
Low	Mariposa Twp 3	60 572
Low	Nevada Grass Valley	61 228
Low	Nevada Rough &	61 397
Low	San Francisco San Francisco 4	681 187
Lum	Mariposa Twp 3	60 575
Lum	Mariposa Twp 3	60 576
Lum*	Mariposa Twp 3	60 575
Lum*	Mariposa Twp 3	60 576
Lung	Placer Iona Hills	62 897
Luw*	Nevada Eureka	61 385
M M	Yolo Cottonwood	72 559
Man	Mariposa Twp 3	60 588
Man*	Mariposa Twp 3	60 580
Men	Mariposa Twp 3	60 620
Min	Nevada Nevada	61 299
Mon	Amador Twp 2	55 327
Moon	Mariposa Twp 3	60 588
My	Mariposa Twp 3	60 563
My	Nevada Nevada	61 301
Nancy A*	Sacramento Centre	63 178
Ne Wah*	Sacramento Ward 1	63 59
Nom*	Mariposa Twp 3	60 580
Non*	Mariposa Twp 3	60 576
Now	Mariposa Twp 3	60 576
Now	Mariposa Twp 3	60 576
Now	Mariposa Twp 3	60 580
One	Yuba Fosters	72 834
Ong	Yuba Long Bar	72 765
Onn	Yuba Long Bar	72 765
Poo	Amador Twp 2	55 312
Pu Toy*	Sacramento Ward 1	63 52
Qen*	Mariposa Twp 3	60 578
Qeui	Mariposa Twp 3	60 563
Qin*	Mariposa Twp 3	60 578
Qua	Mariposa Twp 3	60 569
Qua*	Mariposa Twp 3	60 575
Quan*	Mariposa Twp 3	60 580
Qui	Mariposa Twp 3	60 551
Qui	Mariposa Twp 3	60 571
Qui	Mariposa Twp 3	60 588
Qui*	Mariposa Twp 3	60 564
Quou	Mariposa Twp 3	60 563
Quy	Mariposa Twp 3	60 545
Quy	Mariposa Twp 3	60 546
Quy	Mariposa Twp 3	60 551
R N*	Sacramento Centre	63 177
Row	San Francisco San Francisco 4	681 196
Sam	Mariposa Twp 3	60 613
Sam	Sacramento Centre	63 181
San	Mariposa Twp 3	60 612
San	Mariposa Twp 3	60 613
San	Mariposa Twp 3	60 614
San	Mariposa Twp 3	60 620
SEE		
Sang	Mariposa Twp 3	60 613
Sang	Mariposa Twp 3	60 619
Sang	Yuba Long Bar	72 767
See	Mariposa Twp 3	60 553
See	Nevada Nevada	61 308
Sen	Mariposa Twp 3	60 619
Seu	El Dorado Georgetown	58 755
Shin	Nevada Nevada	61 307
Shing	Mariposa Twp 1	60 658
Sing	Amador Twp 6	55 423
Sing	Nevada Grass Valley	61 234
Sing	Nevada Nevada	61 307
Sing*	Mariposa Twp 1	60 641
Son*	Mariposa Twp 3	60 613
Suiy*	Yuba Bear Rvr	721 000
Sung	Mariposa Twp 1	60 641
Suw*	Nevada Eureka	61 385
Tan	Amador Twp 2	55 292
Thedore	Sacramento Ward 1	63 8
Thon	San Francisco San Francisco 9	681 096
Thow	San Francisco San Francisco 9	681 096
Ton	Nevada Grass Valley	61 228
Ton	Nevada Grass Valley	61 233
Ton	Nevada Nevada	61 299
Ton	Nevada Nevada	61 303
Ton	Yuba Long Bar	72 770
Ton Jo	San Francisco San Francisco 4	681 190
Tou	Nevada Grass Valley	61 233
Tow	Nevada Nevada	61 299
Tow	Nevada Nevada	61 300
Tow	Nevada Nevada	61 299
Toy	Nevada Nevada	61 307
Toy	Nevada Nevada	61 310
Toy	Nevada Washington	61 342
Tuck	Sacramento Ward 1	63 68
Tuck	Sacramento Ward 1	63 70
Tup*	Nevada Nevada	61 304
Tuz*	Tuolumne Twp 4	71 147
Uck	Del Norte Crescent	58 640
Ung	Calaveras Twp 5	57 257
Uny	Calaveras Twp 5	57 257
Wa	Mariposa Twp 3	60 553
Wa	Mariposa Twp 3	60 569
Wa	Sacramento Granite	63 268
Wah	Tuolumne Twp 6	71 528
Wan	Placer Iona Hills	62 897
Wan	El Dorado Georgetown	58 703
Way	Mariposa Twp 3	60 544
William	Yuba Rose Bar	72 802
Wo	San Francisco San Francisco 4	681 183
Wow	Yuba Fosters	72 827
Woy	Mariposa Twp 3	60 576
Wum*	El Dorado Georgetown	58 703
Wup	Nevada Washington	61 341
Yang	Nevada Nevada	61 301
Yap	Mariposa Twp 3	60 543
Yap	Nevada Nevada	61 299
Ye	Nevada Rough &	61 399
Yick*	Yuba Bear Rvr	721 000
Yin	Nevada Nevada	61 300
Yina	Placer Iona Hills	62 889
Yomp	Placer Illinois	62 742
Yon	San Francisco San Francisco 9	681 095
Yong	Nevada Nevada	61 301
You	Mariposa Twp 1	60 662
You	Nevada Nevada	61 305
You Loung	Mariposa Twp 1	60 627
Youn	Mariposa Twp 1	60 651
Youpe	Placer Auburn	62 581
Yow	Placer Auburn	62 582
Yow Coung*	Mariposa Twp 1	60 627
Yu	Nevada Nevada	61 300
Yu	Nevada Nevada	61 304
Yuh	Nevada Grass Valley	61 227
Yup	Nevada Grass Valley	61 227
Yup	Nevada Grass Valley	61 229
Yup	Nevada Grass Valley	61 231
Yup	Nevada Grass Valley	61 232
Yup	Nevada Grass Valley	61 233
Yup	Nevada Grass Valley	61 234
Yup	Nevada Nevada	61 299
Yup	Nevada Nevada	61 300
Yup	Nevada Nevada	61 301
Yup	Nevada Nevada	61 302
Yup	Nevada Nevada	61 303
Yup	Nevada Nevada	61 304
Yup	Nevada Nevada	61 305
Yup	Nevada Nevada	61 308
Yup	Nevada Nevada	61 309
Yup	Nevada Nevada	61 310
Yup	Nevada Washington	61 339
Yup	Nevada Washington	61 340
Yup	Nevada Washington	61 341
Yup	Nevada Washington	61 342
Yup	Nevada Eureka	61 383

California 1860 Census Index

Name	County Locale	M653 RollPage
SEE		
Yup	Nevada Eureka	61 384
Yup	Nevada Eureka	61 385
Yup	Placer Illinois	62 748
Yup*	Nevada Nevada	61 304
Yut	Nevada Grass Valley	61 230
Yut	Nevada Eureka	61 383
SEE'N		
---	Mariposa Twp 3	60 619
SEEA		
Sin	Butte Cascade	56 700
SEEAHANG		
---	Shasta French G	66 713
SEEBE		
Seth G	Alameda Brooklyn	55 191
SEEBER		
Jacob	Yuba Bear Rvr	721009
SEEBLIZIA		
John*	San Francisco San Francisco 3	67 53
SEEBRICHT		
C M*	San Francisco San Francisco 5	67 491
SEECE		
J*	Nevada Eureka	61 348
SEECHING		
---	Shasta French G	66 713
SEECKER		
Henrich*	San Francisco San Francisco 3	67 72
SEECOMPLE		
John*	Yuba Marysville	72 903
SEED		
---	Sierra Downieville	66 983
J W	Sierra Twp 7	66 875
SEEDER		
Geo M	Butte Chico	56 563
SEEDS		
Perry	San Joaquin Elliott	64 947
SEEDWICK		
John*	Yuba Marysville	72 926
SEEFUS		
Wm	Placer Rattle Snake	62 626
SEEGARD		
Julius	Tuolumne Montezuma	71 511
SEEGARS		
Julius	Tuolumne Twp 5	71 511
SEEGER		
Frederica	San Francisco San Francisco 8	681235
SEEGOOD		
John Y	Nevada Nevada	61 323
SEEHA		
---*	San Francisco San Francisco 9	68 964
SEEHEVIR		
Frederick	San Francisco San Francisco 3	67 80
SEEHEVIT		
P*	Merced Twp 1	60 912
SEEHOLTS		
W H	Solano Vallejo	69 271
SEEING		
---*	Mariposa Twp 3	60 569
SEEJMAN		
L E*	Nevada Little Y	61 535
SEEK		
---	Amador Twp 5	55 365
SEEKAMP		
Fred	San Francisco San Francisco 2	67 640
SEEKINS		
C H	Siskiyou Scott Va	69 51
SEELEY		
A C	Sacramento Cosumnes	63 383
D B	Sacramento Granite	63 228
David*	Sonoma Armally	69 509
G F	Butte Cascade	56 691
Geo	Butte Cascade	56 704
James	Marin Point Re	60 729
Joseph	Siskiyou Klamath	69 87
S L	Butte Cascade	56 692
Sarah J	Santa Clara Redwood	65 453
W G	Yolo Cache Crk	72 607
W G	Yolo Cache	72 608
Wm	Butte Ophir	56 751
Wm	Butte Ophir	56 799
SEELIG		
S	Shasta Shasta	66 658
SEELINGSON		
W	San Francisco San Francisco 2	67 700
SEELKEN		
B*	Mariposa Twp 3	60 577
SEELON		
Mateo*	San Francisco San Francisco 4	681133
SEELS		
George	Calaveras Twp 7	57 30
Wm	San Francisco San Francisco 2	67 603
SEELSEY		
M	Nevada Eureka	61 368
SEELY		
Charles	Sierra La Porte	66 776
Charles R	Solano Vacaville	69 348
SEELY		
David	San Bernardino San Bernadino	64 620
David*	Sonoma Armally	69 509
G	Shasta Shasta	66 654
G W	Solano Vacaville	69 347
George B	Yuba Marysville	72 873
George R	Los Angeles Los Angeles	59 405
Henry	Butte Chico	56 559
J G	Trinity E Weaver	701058
J U	Nevada Bridgeport	61 473
John*	Santa Cruz Santa Cruz	66 619
Orrene	Yolo Slate Ra	72 695
S	Shasta Shasta	66 658
S M	Sacramento Granite	63 227
Thomas W	Los Angeles Los Angeles	59 369
Thos W	San Francisco San Francisco 1	68 921
SEEMAN		
H S*	Butte Eureka	56 650
Joshua	Yolo Washington	72 599
L E	Nevada Little Y	61 535
Martin	Shasta Shasta	66 676
SEEMAS		
John	Placer Ophir	62 651
SEEMMERMAN		
Leo*	San Francisco San Francisco 2	67 700
SEEMONS		
William	San Joaquin Elkhorn	64 997
SEEN		
---	Amador Twp 2	55 294
---	Calaveras Twp 5	57 211
---	Calaveras Twp 4	57 315
---	Mariposa Twp 3	60 563
---	Mariposa Twp 3	60 619
---	Nevada Bloomfield	61 507
---	Plumas Quincy	62 920
---	San Francisco San Francisco 11	160 67
---	Tuolumne Montezuma	71 507
---	Tuolumne Green Springs	71 517
---*	Calaveras Twp 5	57 249
May	Mariposa Twp 3	60 619
Sang	San Francisco San Francisco 5	67 507
SEENS		
Seth*	San Francisco San Francisco 1	68 907
SEEOM		
---	Amador Twp 1	55 510
SEEP		
---	Amador Twp 5	55 333
---	Amador Twp 6	55 422
---	Amador Twp 6	55 423
---	Butte Kimshaw	56 608
---	Butte Oregon	56 632
Ah	Butte Oregon	56 632
SEEPER		
Robert*	Calaveras Twp 8	57 106
SEER		
---	Calaveras Twp 10	57 291
Derastns*	Contra Costa Twp 1	57 489
Oliver*	El Dorado Georgetown	58 675
Samuel	Contra Costa Twp 1	57 528
SEERS		
Lewis	Placer Todds Va	62 764
SEERY		
Bridget	San Francisco San Francisco 8	681320
SEESE		
Wm	Trinity Hay Fork	70 991
SEESS		
Abram*	Yuba Marysville	72 871
SEET		
---*	Yuba Bear Rvr	721000
Almon	Sacramento Ward 3	63 471
William*	Placer Michigan	62 808
SEETA		
---	Sierra Downieville	66 986
SEETE		
---	Yuba Linda	72 991
SEETEVIT		
P*	Merced Twp 1	60 912
SEETZ		
John*	Santa Cruz Santa Cruz	66 606
SEEU		
---	Calaveras Twp 5	57 211
SEEVERS		
T*	San Mateo Twp 1	65 62
SEEVILLE		
Wm J*	Calaveras Twp 9	57 347
SEEVY		
Thos*	El Dorado Georgetown	58 704
SEEW		
---	Calaveras Twp 4	57 310
SEEWE		
Jose*	Yuba Bear Rvr	721016
SEEWI		
Jose*	Yuba Bear Rvr	721016
SEF		
---	San Francisco San Francisco 4	681187
SEF		
---	San Francisco San Francisco 4	681188
SEFEBE		
Leon*	Calaveras Twp 10	57 296
SEFEBU		
Antoine*	Calaveras Twp 5	57 179
SEFER		
William	San Francisco San Francisco 9	68 945
SEFERS		
William	San Francisco San Francisco 9	68 945
SEFERT		
Wm	Santa Clara Santa Clara	65 481
SEFETRE		
Seon	Calaveras Twp 10	57 296
SEFEURE		
Antoine*	Calaveras Twp 6	57 179
SEFEVRE		
Josefa	San Bernardino Santa Barbara	64 152
SEFFE		
Thomas	El Dorado Kelsey	581135
SEFFERS		
Deaderick	San Francisco San Francisco 9	68 974
SEFFINS		
Chas	Placer Dutch Fl	62 709
SEFFT		
Wilkins	Yuba Bear Rvr	72 997
SEFIELD		
Charles*	Calaveras Twp 7	57 41
SEFRY		
Joseph*	Shasta Shasta	66 671
SEFTON		
Stephen	Solano Montezuma	69 371
Wm	Sacramento Ward 1	63 154
Wm*	Sacramento Ward 3	63 459
SEFUIN		
M	Calaveras Twp 9	57 413
SEFVERE		
Mack	Sierra Scales D	66 801
SEG		
---	Siskiyou Cottonwoood	69 101
SEGAFF		
John*	Calaveras Twp 4	57 339
SEGAL		
Albert	San Francisco San Francisco 2	67 613
SEGALA		
Paul*	Calaveras Twp 9	57 359
SEGALICA		
Louis*	Calaveras Twp 8	57 93
SEGAN		
---	Tulara Twp 3	71 47
A	Tuolumne Twp 4	71 151
SEGAR		
F May	San Bernardino San Bernadino	64 675
George	San Francisco San Francisco 11	127 67
Henry	San Francisco San Francisco 1	68 929
J M*	Nevada Red Dog	61 546
SEGARD		
A	San Francisco San Francisco 5	67 506
SEGEET		
Jas	Butte Ophir	56 791
SEGEL		
Marks	San Francisco San Francisco 2	67 613
SEGELEN		
Deitrick	Alameda Brooklyn	55 152
SEGELL		
George	San Francisco San Francisco 7	681392
SEGERHOLM		
John	Santa Cruz Santa Cruz	66 632
SEGERSON		
David	Solano Vallejo	69 276
SEGG		
T	Nevada Eureka	61 380
SEGH		
---	Trinity Weaverville	701072
SEGHLLE		
George*	Calaveras Twp 10	57 278
SEGIN		
John	Trinity Taylor'S	701036
Wah	Butte Cascade	56 699
SEGLEM		
John	San Francisco San Francisco 1	68 864
SEGMOUR		
A	Shasta Millvill	66 748
SEGNET		
Sarah	San Francisco San Francisco 2	67 706
SEGNI		
James*	Yuba Marysville	72 891
SEGNST		
Sarah*	San Francisco San Francisco 2	67 706
SEGO		
---	Sierra Twp 7	66 898
SEGON		
---	Calaveras Twp 10	57 268
SEGONIA		
Paul	El Dorado Georgetown	58 701

Name	County Locale	M653 Roll	Page
SEGOR			
John*	Calaveras Twp 5	57	230
SEGOUIN			
Zulo	Los Angeles Los Angeles	59	341
SEGOUNG			
---	Calaveras Twp 5	57	203
SEGOURNEY			
William	Placer Michigan	62	807
SEGOVIA			
Rosas	Tuolumne Montezuma	71	506
SEGOVIO			
Santas	Santa Clara Almaden	65	267
SEGRAMALL			
John	Mariposa Coulterville	60	678
SEGRAND			
A	Siskiyou Scott Va	69	49
SEGRANE			
Emory	Amador Twp 1	55	459
SEGRASS			
Joseph	Marin Bolinas	60	745
SEGRENDE			
E	Amador Twp 1	55	461
SEGRET			
H	Tuolumne Twp 1	71	221
SEGU			
---	Nevada Nevada	61	306
SEGUFF			
John*	Calaveras Twp 4	57	339
SEGUI			
James*	Yuba Marysville	72	891
Joseph	Contra Costa Twp 1	57	532
SEGUNDA			
---*	San Mateo Twp 2	65	111
Juanna	San Bernardino Santa Barbara	64	175
SEGUNDO			
Paype	Butte Chico	56	550
SEGUNTE			
Mara*	Amador Twp 2	55	323
SEGUR			
John	Sacramento Ward 1	63	75
S B	Sacramento Dry Crk	63	369
SEGURA			
Edwardo	Santa Clara Almaden	65	266
SEGURE			
George*	Contra Costa Twp 3	57	613
SEGWALT			
John*	Nevada Red Dog	61	546
SEH			
---	Calaveras Twp 4	57	328
---	Shasta Horsetown	66	698
---	Sierra St Louis	66	805
SEHALL			
Leonard	Sierra St Louis	66	815
SEHEIPLOUEH			
John*	San Francisco San Francisco 3	67	86
SEHEN			
Henry*	San Francisco San Francisco 7	68	1377
SEHENTY			
J P*	Yolo Cottonwoood	72	649
SEHEOG			
Ming	El Dorado Big Bar	58	738
SEHER			
Daviel*	Marin Cortemad	60	780
SEHERT			
Albert	El Dorado Mud Springs	58	957
SEHIBIA			
Nicholas**	Los Angeles Los Angeles	59	491
SEHILIO			
Chas	El Dorado Greenwood	58	710
SEHILY			
E*	El Dorado Placerville	58	853
SEHLE			
Geo*	Sacramento Mississipi	63	185
SEHLENK			
George*	El Dorado Georgetown	58	708
SEHLEY			
Matilda	Tuolumne Twp 3	71	451
SEHLINK			
George*	El Dorado Greenwood	58	708
SEHMAN			
Benj	Siskiyou Scott Ri	69	62
SEHMANS			
Benj*	Siskiyou Scott Ri	69	62
SEHOVIK			
John*	Sierra Scales D	66	802
SEHPHERD			
Charles	Tuolumne Springfield	71	367
Isaac G	Yuba Marysville	72	945
SEHRADER			
John	El Dorado Mud Springs	58	980
SEHRAM			
Jacob*	Napa Napa	61	108
SEHRUNK			
D*	Siskiyou Klamath	69	96
SEI			
---	Calaveras Twp 6	57	126
SEI			
---	Calaveras Twp 10	57	297
---	Calaveras Twp 4	57	327
---	El Dorado Greenwood	58	728
---	Mariposa Twp 1	60	648
---	Nevada Rough &	61	432
---	Placer Michigan	62	834
---	Tuolumne Twp 3	71	460
---*	Butte Kimshaw	56	598
---*	Nevada Rough &	61	432
David*	Placer Forest H	62	803
Dua*	Mariposa Twp 3	60	575
Fow	Calaveras Twp 10	57	278
How	Nevada Nevada	61	299
Wang	El Dorado Georgetown	58	703
SEIA			
---	Calaveras Twp 8	57	60
SEIBBERND			
John	Trinity Weaverville	70	1065
SEIBE			
G	San Francisco San Francisco 6	67	436
SEIBEGUTH			
Geo	Trinity Mouth Ca	70	1013
SEIBEN			
Jacob	Yuba Bear Rvr	72	1009
SEIBERG			
Rudolph	Sierra Downieville	66	977
SEIBERT			
A	Trinity Weaverville	70	1066
J	Nevada Eureka	61	358
S	Nevada Nevada	61	245
SEIBRICHT			
C H A	San Francisco San Francisco 5	67	491
C M*	San Francisco San Francisco 5	67	491
SEIBYH			
A*	Shasta Shasta	66	683
SEICER			
Franklin*	San Joaquin Stockton	64	1034
SEICHS			
Samuel*	San Francisco San Francisco 4	68	1159
SEICILY			
Amy*	Yuba Marysville	72	899
SEIDEN			
F	Nevada Bridgeport	61	454
SEIDENSTRIKER			
Frederic	San Francisco San Francisco 11	67	109
SEIFER			
John	Placer Todds Va	62	762
SEIFORT			
Alex	Placer Forest H	62	791
SEIG			
---	Shasta Shasta	66	680
F*	El Dorado Placerville	58	874
SEIGAR			
David	El Dorado Coloma	58	1080
SEIGEL			
Leuis	San Francisco San Francisco 2	67	606
Lewis	San Francisco San Francisco 2	67	606
SEIGH			
Cornelius*	Sacramento Granite	63	247
W W	El Dorado White Oaks	58	1010
SEIGHTON			
Joseph	Calaveras Twp 6	57	154
N	Placer Lisbon	62	735
SEIGIE			
Fred*	Sierra Downieville	66	994
SEIGLE			
Joseph	San Joaquin Stockton	64	1043
SEIGLEMAN			
L	San Francisco San Francisco 2	67	775
SEIGLER			
James	San Francisco San Francisco 6	67	440
SEIGN			
---	Placer Rattle Snake	62	637
SEIGNER			
A	San Francisco San Francisco 10	67	310
SEIKAMP			
Fred	San Francisco San Francisco 2	67	640
SEIKMAN			
Henry	Calaveras Twp 4	57	299
SEIKSLEY			
Andrew*	Alameda Brooklyn	55	146
SEILER			
John	Yuba Long Bar	72	755
Sophia	Trinity Weaverville	70	1066
SEILK			
J	El Dorado Diamond	58	808
SEILNACHT			
T*	San Joaquin Stockton	64	1040
SEILY			
John S	Humbolt Union	59	186
Joseph	Humbolt Union	59	181
SEIM			
---	Butte Oregon	56	627
SEIM			
---	Sierra Downieville	66	973
John H	San Francisco San Francisco 3	67	2
SEIMBACK			
Herman*	Sacramento San Joaquin	63	348
SEIMMAL			
J P*	Siskiyou Scott Va	69	48
SEIMMERMAN			
Leo*	San Francisco San Francisco 2	67	700
SEIMPO			
---*	Fresno Twp 2	59	18
SEIN			
---	Mariposa Twp 3	60	619
---	Nevada Rough &	61	431
Henry*	Sierra Twp 7	66	907
Peter	San Francisco San Francisco 3	67	50
Philip*	Trinity North Fo	70	1026
SEINAEDE			
Marcell*	Contra Costa Twp 1	57	515
SEINAN			
Chas	Calaveras Twp 6	57	113
SEINAW			
Jas	Butte Kimshaw	56	581
SEINBURGHER			
H	Sacramento Ward 1	63	116
SEINCHEIMER			
Simon	Klamath Salmon	59	208
SEING			
---	Amador Twp 1	55	497
---	Calaveras Twp 6	57	145
---	Placer Virginia	62	671
---	Plumas Quincy	62	949
SEINO			
Jesus*	Yuba Marysville	72	938
Pulvo*	Sierra Downieville	66	971
SEINOR			
Amile	Sierra Eureka	66	1049
SEINSEE			
---	El Dorado Georgetown	58	686
SEIP			
---	Amador Twp 5	55	333
---*	Butte Kimshaw	56	608
Ah	Butte Eureka	56	651
SEIPP			
John	Los Angeles Santa Ana	59	443
John	Sonoma Sonoma	69	656
SEIR			
---	Calaveras Twp 10	57	295
---	Yuba Marysville	72	874
Mary	Sacramento Centre	63	173
SEIRIS			
Richmond	Mariposa Twp 1	60	649
SEIS			
Jose M	San Francisco San Francisco 2	67	707
Juan B	Los Angeles Santa Ana	59	444
Rafal	Yuba Marysville	72	860
Rafeal*	Yuba Marysville	72	858
Ramon	Calaveras Twp 6	57	179
SEISDORFF			
Peter	Calaveras Twp 6	57	120
SEISEN			
John	Yuba New York	72	731
SEISENOUGH			
A	El Dorado Kelsey	58	1126
SEISHAN			
Edward	Calaveras Twp 5	57	223
SEISM			
Jacob	Sierra Pine Grove	66	819
SEITA			
Plulal	San Francisco San Francisco 2	67	791
SEITER			
Anna	Placer Yankee J	62	782
SEITYH			
A*	Shasta Shasta	66	683
SEITZ			
Frank	Sierra Downieville	66	969
SEITZEL			
George	Amador Twp 2	55	296
SEIUMINT			
James S	Calaveras Twp 5	57	216
SEIVA			
Esteban*	Monterey San Juan	60	997
SEIVALL			
D	San Francisco San Francisco 1	68	838
SEIVALPHA			
B	San Joaquin Stockton	64	1085
SEIVER			
Frank	Calaveras Twp 5	57	188
SEIVERS			
Harmon	Tuolumne Twp 2	71	407
Henry	Tuolumne Shawsfla	71	407
SEIVIS			
J*	Nevada Nevada	61	294
Richmond*	Mariposa Twp 1	60	649
SEIX			
Wm	San Francisco San Francisco 2	67	799

Name	County Locale	M653 Roll	Page
SEIZ			
Albert	San Francisco San Francisco 3	67	15
SEIZE			
---	Shasta Shasta	66	680
SEJ			
---	Amador Twp 3	55	402
SEJEHAM			
Herman	San Francisco San Francisco 2	67	726
SEKEIRE			
Fela	San Francisco San Francisco 2	67	777
SEKEIRO			
Fela	San Francisco San Francisco 2	67	777
SEKEL			
---	Tulara Visalia	71	114
SEKELY			
John	Yuba Marysville	72	922
SEKRUNK			
D*	Siskiyou Klamath	69	96
SELA			
M	El Dorado Placerville	58	874
SELABNRNO			
---	Mendocino Calpella	60	825
SELABURNO			
---	Mendocino Calpella	60	825
SELAHO			
Jose*	San Bernardino Santa Barbara	64	158
SELAHON			
Jose	Los Angeles San Jose	59	292
SELAJAR			
Mary	El Dorado Greenwood	58	717
SELAJO			
Jose*	San Bernardino Santa Barbara	64	158
SELAN			
G	San Francisco San Francisco 4	68	1170
John*	San Luis Obispo San Luis Obispo	65	27
Louis	Yuba Fosters	72	835
SELANDER			
D	Trinity Rearings	70	990
SELANDJ			
John	Nevada Little Y	61	532
SELARAN			
Geo W	Trinity Weaverville	70	1070
SELAYA			
Jose	Los Angeles Santa Ana	59	454
Juan	Los Angeles Los Nieto	59	435
SELBEN			
John	Santa Clara Santa Clara	65	507
SELBENIS			
F	El Dorado Placerville	58	899
SELBEY			
W H	El Dorado Kelsey	58	1137
SELBY			
Geo	Alameda Brooklyn	55	212
Geo W	Sacramento American	63	159
Hattie S	Sacramento American	63	172
John	Santa Clara San Jose	65	384
John M	Yuba Marysville	72	946
John U	Yuba Marysville	72	946
Levine	Sacramento Ward 1	63	146
Richard	Yuba Suida	72	989
Robert	San Joaquin Oneal	64	938
Samuel W	Yuba Marysville	72	850
Thos H	San Francisco San Francisco 10	67	354
Wm	Tehama Moons	70	853
SELDBLOCK			
Henry	Sierra Twp 5	66	920
SELDEN			
B	El Dorado Placerville	58	933
E C	Sacramento Ward 1	63	41
J R	Sacramento Ward 1	63	45
Jno N	Sacramento Ward 1	63	586
Wm	Yuba Rose Bar	72	815
SELDO			
Dephriano	Fresno Twp 1	59	81
Sephriano	Fresno Twp 1	59	81
SELDON			
Wm*	Yuba Rose Bar	72	815
SELE			
Daniel	Sonoma Armally	69	482
SELEAS			
Sacramento*	Mariposa Twp 1	60	629
SELEBART			
Lewis	Calaveras Twp 10	57	296
SELEMO			
Joseph*	Placer Michigan	62	850
SELENIE			
L	Nevada Nevada	61	252
SELENTS			
James	Yolo Washington	72	565
SELEOS			
Sacramento	Mariposa Twp 1	60	629
SELEPINGOR			
Lingish	Santa Clara San Jose	65	290
SELERS			
Mary	El Dorado Spanish	58	1125
SELERY			
Charles	El Dorado Placerville	58	917
M*	Tuolumne Big Oak	71	145
SELEUIE			
L	Nevada Nevada	61	252
SELEUTS			
James	Yolo Washington	72	565
SELEY			
Timothy	Napa Napa	61	71
SELF			
A M	El Dorado Mountain	58	1178
Frederick	Yuba New York	72	734
William	Calaveras Twp 4	57	342
SELFREDGE			
Jams M	Alameda Brooklyn	55	201
SELFRIDGE			
W O*	Sierra Twp 5	66	926
Wm*	Sierra Twp 5	66	926
SELFVERDALE			
J A	Tuolumne Big Oak	71	145
SELGA			
Joseph	Alameda Brooklyn	55	87
SELGADO			
Augus	Mariposa Twp 3	60	570
SELIAMKEN			
---	Mendocino Big Rvr	60	853
SELIAR			
Margt	San Francisco San Francisco 9	68	979
SELIBY			
Henry*	Sacramento Granite	63	242
SELIG			
Max*	Del Norte Crescent	58	626
R F	Del Norte Crescent	58	627
SELIGMAN			
---	Del Norte Crescent	58	626
Henry	San Francisco San Francisco 2	67	660
Leopold	San Francisco San Francisco 7	68	1351
SELIGMANN			
Frank	San Francisco San Francisco 8	68	1279
SELIM			
Joseph	Tuolumne Twp 3	71	469
SELINA			
Jose	Fresno Twp 1	59	81
SELING			
A	Sierra Downieville	66	974
SELINGER			
Daniel	El Dorado Mud Springs	58	966
SELINGHER			
George	San Joaquin Oneal	64	912
SELIRAN			
Thomas*	Calaveras Twp 8	57	82
SELIRAR			
Ferdinand	Alameda Brooklyn	55	212
SELIRELL			
Ellis*	Yuba Slate Ro	72	697
SELISGON			
Marx	San Francisco San Francisco 7	68	1392
SELITO			
Francisco	San Joaquin Stockton	64	1069
SELIVEN			
John	Sierra Downieville	66	1006
SELIX			
John	Alameda Brooklyn	55	99
SELK			
---	Sierra Downieville	66	990
SELKER			
Danie*	Calaveras Twp 8	57	94
SELKERK			
James	Nevada Bridgeport	61	467
SELKIRK			
James*	Nevada Bridgeport	61	467
W A	Placer Iona Hills	62	886
SELKO			
---	Sierra Downieville	66	990
SELL			
---	Monterey Monterey	60	965
---	Yolo No E Twp	72	681
Adam	Siskiyou Scott Va	69	50
Charles	Tuolumne Sonora	71	197
Daniel	Sonoma Armally	69	482
David	Sierra Downieville	66	956
Jacob	El Dorado Kelsey	58	1147
John	Tuolumne Twp 5	71	488
William	Tuolumne Sonora	71	190
SELLA			
J L	San Francisco San Francisco 2	67	682
SELLALA			
Rafael	Marin Cortemad	60	781
SELLAN			
Louis	Yuba Foster B	72	835
SELLAR			
John	San Francisco San Francisco 2	67	796
Laventhal	San Francisco San Francisco 2	67	796
SELLARS			
James	Sierra Scales D	66	801
Jariah	Santa Clara San Jose	65	357
SELLCRS			
Robert*	Solano Vacaville	69	342
SELLECK			
Silas	San Francisco San Francisco 8	68	1266
SELLED			
C	Alameda Oakland	55	71
SELLENBURY			
B	Tehama Red Bluff	70	910
SELLER			
Esta	Alameda Brooklyn	55	108
J	Sutter Nicolaus	70	841
Jno	Mendocino Calpella	60	819
Joseph	San Francisco San Francisco 9	68	971
SELLERS			
Frank	Butte Oregon	56	614
J E	Sacramento Georgian	63	340
James	Placer Yankee J	62	758
L	Mariposa Twp 3	60	554
M L	Sacramento Georgian	63	339
Marim	Yolo Cache Crk	72	607
Marrion	Yolo Cache	72	608
Michael	Sacramento Georgian	63	340
Reuben	Sacramento Mississipi	63	183
Robert	Solano Vacaville	69	342
S	Mariposa Twp 3	60	554
Samuel	Mariposa Twp 1	60	672
W H	Trinity Lewiston	70	966
SELLES			
J D	Nevada Grass Valley	61	222
SELLEY			
M S	Placer Virginia	62	700
Thomas	Calaveras Twp 8	57	79
Thomas	Sierra Twp 5	66	932
Thomas	Sierra Twp 5	66	933
Thomas	Tuolumne Jamestown	71	441
SELLHORN			
T J*	Napa Napa	61	57
SELLICK			
Henry	Tuolumne Twp 2	71	310
Joseph E	San Mateo Twp 2	65	121
Samuel	Solano Benecia	69	284
Sarah A	Butte Kimshaw	56	586
Silas	San Francisco San Francisco 8	68	1266
SELLIE			
W H*	Napa Napa	61	114
SELLIN			
Arther	Alameda Oakland	55	13
SELLING			
Benjamin	Yuba Long Bar	72	772
Isaac	Tuolumne Twp 1	71	200
John*	San Francisco San Francisco 2	67	654
Philip	Contra Costa Twp 3	57	612
SELLINGER			
Chas	Sacramento Ward 4	63	498
J	Nevada Eureka	61	367
SELLIS			
Frank*	Sacramento Ward 1	63	13
SELLOR			
Lewis	Calaveras Twp 4	57	323
SELLORTHORN			
Willim H*	San Francisco San Francisco 2	67	736
SELLS			
David	Mendocino Little L	60	836
Francis C	Siskiyou Yreka	69	142
H	Sacramento Alabama	63	414
Henry R	Siskiyou Yreka	69	137
R M	Nevada Grass Valley	61	222
SELLY			
Francis	Yuba Marysville	72	936
W R	Nevada Grass Valley	61	238
William	Sierra La Porte	66	786
SELLZER			
Henry	Sierra Forest C	66	909
SELMAN			
Daniel	Alameda Brooklyn	55	191
SELMIR			
Louis	El Dorado Placerville	58	921
SELN			
Yi	Sacramento Granite	63	269
SELNA			
Angelo	Mariposa Twp 1	60	631
G	San Joaquin Stockton	64	1042
Whaldo*	San Joaquin Stockton	64	1041
SELNER			
August	San Francisco San Francisco 2	67	708
SELOERSTEIR			
Isaac*	Yuba Marysville	72	903
SELON			
Antone*	Tuolumne Twp 2	71	284
Joseph	Yolo Washington	72	573
SELONG			
John	San Francisco San Francisco 1	68	930
SELOVAN			
Saml	Placer Stewart	62	606
SELOWTHORN			
Willim H*	San Francisco San Francisco 2	67	736

Name	County Locale	M653 Roll	Page
SELRES			
Wm*	Sierra Downieville	66	986
SELRIENES			
Frances*	Calaveras Twp 6	57	137
SELRIG			
Kate	San Francisco San Francisco 4	68	1112
SELRN			
John*	San Luis Obispo San Luis Obispo	65	27
SELSBURRY			
Clara	San Francisco San Francisco 4	68	1123
SELSBY			
Henry*	Sacramento Granite	63	242
SELSCUM			
Milton*	El Dorado Mud Springs	58	996
SELSER			
David	Shasta Shasta	66	660
Johanna*	San Francisco San Francisco 2	67	690
SELSULBIDS			
Jesus	Monterey San Juan	60	999
SELTAY			
---	Butte Chico	56	551
SELTER			
Aaron	Solano Suisan	69	226
SELTNER			
Saml	Sacramento Ward 3	63	427
SELTZER			
Jacob	Sacramento Ward 4	63	513
Wm	Sacramento Ward 1	63	12
SELUDIS			
Christian	Calaveras Twp 6	57	143
SELUNG			
---	Nevada Bloomfield	61	521
SELURIO			
Joseph	Calaveras Twp 10	57	260
SELURRO			
Joseph	Calaveras Twp 10	57	260
SELVA			
J	Tuolumne Twp 4	71	146
James	Sierra Downieville	66	1031
SELVAIN			
T*	Calaveras Twp 9	57	401
SELVAYE			
John	Humbolt Bucksport	59	155
SELVER			
James L	Mariposa Twp 3	60	546
Manuel	Yolo Washington	72	574
Peter	Tuolumne Sonora	71	484
SELVERSTEIR			
Isaac*	Yuba Marysville	72	903
SELVEY			
Robert	San Francisco San Francisco 2	67	632
SELVIA			
Antonia	San Francisco San Francisco 5	67	479
SELWYN			
George	San Bernardino San Bernadino	64	686
SEM			
---	Calaveras Twp 6	57	168
---	El Dorado Georgetown	58	680
---	El Dorado Georgetown	58	691
---	El Dorado Greenwood	58	731
---	Plumas Quincy	62	1008
---	Plumas Quincy	62	920
---	Trinity Weaverville	70	1074
---	Tuolumne Columbia	71	307
---	Tuolumne Columbia	71	346
---	Tuolumne Shawsfla	71	396
---	Tuolumne Shawsfla	71	397
---	Tuolumne Twp 2	71	407
---	Tuolumne Jamestown	71	421
---	Tuolumne Twp 3	71	440
---	Tuolumne Twp 3	71	442
Ah	Tuolumne Twp 2	71	307
Ah	Tuolumne Twp 2	71	346
Foo	Plumas Quincy	62	964
Sing*	Plumas Quincy	62	950
SEMA			
---	El Dorado Coloma	58	1078
---*	Butte Chico	56	566
Pedro*	Monterey San Juan	60	1001
SEMACO			
---	Butte Chico	56	550
SEMAINE			
Wancois	Los Angeles Los Angeles	59	301
SEMAN			
Paul	Yuba Marysville	72	932
SEMANTADO			
Sotario	Sacramento Ward 1	63	7
SEMANTRADO			
Sotario	Sacramento Ward 1	63	7
SEMASTI			
R B	El Dorado Georgetown	58	703
SEMBRIANO			
Jose Ma**	Marin Cortemad	60	783
SEMDERLEN			
Isaac*	Calaveras Twp 6	57	143
SEME			
---	San Francisco San Francisco 2	67	754
SEMEGA			
Gregona	Monterey Monterey	60	950
SEMELIRORDA			
---	Mendocino Twp 1	60	887
SEMENAKE			
---	Fresno Twp 2	59	104
SEMENOLE			
---	Fresno Twp 2	59	108
SEMEONE			
---	Fresno Twp 3	59	22
SEMER			
Ah	Butte Eureka	56	651
SEMERO			
---*	Fresno Twp 2	59	50
SEMHART			
A*	Trinity E Weaver	70	1061
SEMIA			
Peter*	Del Norte Crescent	58	642
SEMINI			
---*	San Francisco San Francisco 4	68	1223
SEMINNS			
Areoval*	Calaveras Twp 6	57	178
SEMINNT			
Aroval*	Calaveras Twp 5	57	178
SEMINO			
---	Butte Chico	56	550
SEMIRILE			
G B	Merced Twp 1	60	896
SEMITE			
Petere	Alameda Oakland	55	61
SEMIUUS			
Areoval*	Calaveras Twp 6	57	178
Arroval*	Calaveras Twp 6	57	178
SEMIYER			
Mad*	Nevada Nevada	61	270
SEMLA			
Antonio*	Alameda Murray	55	229
SEMLER			
---	San Francisco San Francisco 3	67	67
SEMM			
---	Plumas Quincy	62	926
SEMMAY			
F D*	Siskiyou Klamath	69	91
SEMMES			
Manuel	Alameda Brooklyn	55	117
SEMMIEAL			
Fanres*	Siskiyou Callahan	69	4
SEMMON			
Robert	Los Angeles Los Angeles	59	396
SEMMONS			
Orin*	Alameda Oakland	55	56
SEMNON			
C H*	Nevada Nevada	61	250
SEMO			
---	El Dorado Georgetown	58	675
James*	Tuolumne Green Springs	71	519
SEMON			
John B	Solano Fairfield	69	197
Paul*	Yuba Marysville	72	932
SEMONA			
A	El Dorado Diamond	58	802
SEMONE			
Peter	Alameda Brooklyn	55	97
SEMONS			
Peter	Alameda Brooklyn	55	97
SEMONSIEN			
Francois	Plumas Meadow Valley	62	933
SEMORAK			
---	Fresno Twp 2	59	47
SEMORALLO			
Joseph*	San Francisco San Francisco 3	67	16
SEMORE			
Andrew	Tuolumne Twp 2	71	473
James L	Tuolumne Twp 1	71	215
SEMOROE			
---	Fresno Twp 2	59	104
SEMOTSEMER			
---	Mendocino Twp 1	60	890
SEMPLE			
Ann*	San Francisco San Francisco 10	67	355
C D*	Colusa Colusi	57	423
George	Tulara Twp 2	71	1
John	Sonoma Bodega	69	540
Joseph	Sonoma Petaluma	69	561
Sarah	Sonoma Vallejo	69	611
Wiley	Colusa Spring Valley	57	436
SEMPLETON			
Jos	San Francisco San Francisco 9	68	1060
Mile L*	Solano Vacaville	69	354
SEMPONA			
---	Fresno Twp 3	59	99
SEMPS			
Joseph	San Francisco San Francisco 9	68	1082
SEMS			
Martin	Alameda Brooklyn	55	80
SEMU			
---*	Butte Eureka	56	651
SEN YOU SEE			
---	San Francisco San Francisco 6	67	453
SEN YOU			
See	San Francisco San Francisco 6	67	453
SEN YUW			
---	Calaveras Twp 10	57	268
SEN			
---	Amador Twp 2	55	315
---	Amador Twp 2	55	316
---	Amador Twp 1	55	502
---	Calaveras Twp 5	57	147
---	Calaveras Twp 6	57	165
---	Calaveras Twp 6	57	166
---	Calaveras Twp 5	57	232
---	Calaveras Twp 5	57	244
---	Calaveras Twp 5	57	252
---	Calaveras Twp 5	57	257
---	Calaveras Twp 10	57	259
---	Calaveras Twp 10	57	297
---	Calaveras Twp 4	57	333
---	Del Norte Crescent	58	630
---	El Dorado Coloma	58	1085
---	El Dorado Placerville	58	840
---	El Dorado Mud Springs	58	988
---	Mariposa Twp 3	60	546
---	Mariposa Twp 3	60	564
---	Nevada Nevada	61	303
---	Trinity East For	70	1025
---	Tuolumne Shawsfla	71	385
---	Tuolumne Shawsfla	71	390
---	Tuolumne Twp 3	71	442
---	Tuolumne Montezuma	71	512
---	Tuolumne Twp 1	71	529
---	Tuolumne Don Pedro	71	535
---	Yolo No E Twp	72	675
---	Yolo No E Twp	72	681
---*	Calaveras Twp 5	57	252
---	Sacramento Cosumnes	63	397
Ah	Yuba Suida	72	990
Ah*	Butte Oro	56	687
An	Del Norte Crescent	58	630
An	Sacramento Natonia	63	286
Benj Berry	Colusa Grand Island	57	482
Foy	Sacramento Granite	63	232
Fray Ho	San Francisco San Francisco 9	68	1094
Hee	Yuba Marysville	72	925
Hen	Yuba Marysville	72	921
Hong	Yuba Marysville	72	920
Kee*	Mariposa Twp 3	60	581
See	El Dorado Georgetown	58	700
Soy	Calaveras Twp 10	57	272
Toy	Calaveras Twp 4	57	300
Toy	Del Norte Crescent	58	631
Tuck	Calaveras Twp 10	57	272
Way Ho	San Francisco San Francisco 9	68	1094
Yar	Sacramento Natonia	63	280
Yen	Tuolumne Big Oak	71	149
You See	San Francisco San Francisco 6	67	453
Yow	Calaveras Twp 10	57	268
Yow	Trinity Weaverville	70	1072
SEN'N			
---	Mariposa Twp 3	60	609
SENA			
---	Fresno Twp 1	59	86
Jose M	Los Angeles Los Angeles	59	325
SENAFINA			
---	San Bernardino S Timate	64	755
SENAG			
---	Sacramento Ward 1	63	58
SENAHAN			
John	Trinity E Weaver	70	1061
SENAL			
---	Mendocino Calpella	60	822
SENAMON			
J	Calaveras Twp 9	57	410
SENAN			
Antonio	Calaveras Twp 9	57	376
SENARO			
Antonio	San Francisco San Francisco 3	67	83
SENATE			
Frank	Nevada Little Y	61	532
Jas	Butte Oregon	56	611
W	Nevada Grass Valley	61	219
William	El Dorado Kelsey	58	1139
SENAWD			
Marcella	Contra Costa Twp 1	57	494
SENCE			
H B*	Siskiyou Klamath	69	80
SENCELS			
Ellon	Monterey Monterey	60	950
SENCO			
---	Fresno Twp 2	59	104
SENDAMORE			
Robt*	Monterey S Antoni	60	973

Name	County Locale	M653 RollPage
SENDDER		
Harry	San Francisco San Francisco 3	67 83
SENDEN		
G D Von*	San Francisco San Francisco 10	315 67
SENDMAN		
Frank	Alameda Oakland	55 38
SENDRE		
Antonio	Calaveras Twp 9	57 376
SENDYKE		
Andrew	Placer Dutch Fl	62 722
SENE		
---	El Dorado Salmon Hills	581067
---	El Dorado Coloma	581122
Ah	Calaveras Twp 7	57 16
Ah	Tuolumne Twp 4	71 147
Henry	Sierra Twp 7	66 907
SENEAL		
A	Amador Twp 1	55 460
SENECAL		
Polile*	Sacramento Ward 4	63 550
Polite*	Sacramento Ward 4	63 550
Potile*	Sacramento Ward 4	63 550
SENEET		
Kew	Butte Cascade	56 690
SENEINUS		
Areoval*	Calaveras Twp 6	57 178
Arroval*	Calaveras Twp 6	57 178
SENELL		
Nicholas	Siskiyou Scott Ri	69 65
S G	Yolo Slate Ra	72 698
SENERADER		
---	Fresno Twp 2	59 58
SENERO		
Antonia*	San Francisco San Francisco 2	67 699
SENES		
Juan M	Monterey San Juan	60 991
SENETH		
John P*	Yuba Marysville	72 867
SENETS		
Robt*	El Dorado Greenwood	58 720
SENETT		
Sigh	Butte Bidwell	56 719
SENETTE		
John P*	Yuba Marysville	72 867
SENFANO		
Palandro*	Placer Michigan	62 832
SENFERT		
George A	San Joaquin Douglass	64 916
SENFIELD		
James	Sierra Downieville	66 975
SENFIELDS		
James	Sierra Downieville	66 975
SENFT		
Chas	San Francisco San Francisco 2	67 795
SENG		
---	Alameda Oakland	55 24
---	Amador Twp 5	55 329
---	Amador Twp 6	55 435
---	El Dorado Greenwood	58 731
---	Fresno Twp 2	59 112
---	Mariposa Twp 3	60 572
---	Mariposa Twp 1	60 648
---	Placer Auburn	62 591
---	Sacramento Ward 1	63 65
---	Trinity Mouth Ca	701011
---	Trinity East For	701025
---	Trinity Taylor'S	701033
---	Trinity Cox'S Bar	701037
---	Trinity Big Flat	701041
---	Trinity Big Flat	701042
---	Trinity Honest B	701043
---	Trinity Trinidad Rvr	701044
---	Trinity Trininidad Rvr	701045
---	Trinity Weaverville	701052
---	Trinity Weaverville	701053
---	Trinity Weaverville	701056
---	Trinity Weaverville	701074
---	Trinity Lewiston	70 955
---	Tuolumne Big Oak	71 128
---	Tuolumne Shawsfla	71 408
---	Tuolumne Twp 2	71 409
---	Tuolumne Twp 3	71 467
---	Yuba Bear Rvr	721000
---*	Trinity Trininidad Rvr	701048
Ar	Trinity Sturdiva	701007
Hew	Butte Mountain	56 743
Teir	San Francisco San Francisco 1	68 925
Tin*	Sacramento Ward 1	63 156
SENGAN		
Patrick	Contra Costa Twp 1	57 501
SENGERFETTER		
Rufus*	Calaveras Twp 4	57 341
SENGH		
---	Sierra Downieville	66 974
SENIACAL		
J	Sutter Vernon	70 847

Name	County Locale	M653 RollPage
SENIDER		
George	Tuolumne Jamestown	71 426
SENIL		
George	San Francisco San Francisco 4	681170
SENILA		
Manuel*	Alameda Brooklyn	55 124
SENING		
A	Calaveras Twp 9	57 407
SENINGLE		
Thomas*	El Dorado Salmon Falls	581050
SENIOR		
J	Calaveras Twp 9	57 391
Michael*	Santa Clara Santa Clara	65 486
SENIS		
J*	Nevada Nevada	61 294
SENITE		
F	Santa Clara Santa Clara	65 473
SENIVAFA		
---	San Bernardino S Timate	64 716
SENIVATRA		
---	San Bernardino S Timate	64 755
SENJER		
John	Santa Clara Alviso	65 410
SENK		
---	Del Norte Crescent	58 631
Fon	Del Norte Crescent	58 631
SENKINSON		
H H	Nevada Nevada	61 276
SENL		
---	Tuolumne Big Oak	71 147
SENLE		
James	Shasta Horsetown	66 697
SENLLEY		
John	Yolo Washington	72 564
SENLY		
S S	Nevada Nevada	61 242
SENMAN		
J	Siskiyou Scott Va	69 49
SENMANOH		
F*	El Dorado Mud Springs	58 996
SENMAR		
Christian*	Yuba Fosters	72 832
SENN		
---	Tuolumne Big Oak	71 147
Ah*	Calaveras Twp 7	57 16
Sing	Mariposa Twp 3	60 613
SENNA		
Peter*	Del Norte Crescent	58 642
SENNAN		
John	Solano Benecia	69 307
SENNANT		
Rich	Santa Clara San Jose	65 359
SENNEL		
Sam*	Yuba New York	72 734
SENNENG		
Adolph*	Mariposa Coulterville	60 694
SENNER		
S B*	Nevada Nevada T	61 327
SENNET		
J	San Francisco San Francisco 5	67 527
SENNG		
---	Trinity W Weaver	701054
SENNIDER		
George	Tuolumne Twp 3	71 426
SENNIEAL		
Fanres	Siskiyou Callahan	69 3
Fanres*	Siskiyou Callahan	69 4
SENNINA		
---	San Bernardino San Bernadino	64 667
SENNON		
P H	Napa Hot Springs	61 6
SENNOR		
Francis	Calaveras Twp 10	57 261
John	Nevada Nevada	61 250
SENNORE		
Francis	Calaveras Twp 10	57 261
SENNOTO		
Mathew*	Sacramento Granite	63 245
Nathen	Sacramento Granite	63 245
SENNOTT		
Mathew*	Sacramento Granite	63 245
SENNOX		
Andrew	Calaveras Twp 5	57 251
SENNYER		
Mad*	Nevada Nevada	61 270
SENOCK		
Henry	Butte Kimshaw	56 585
SENOLA		
Antonio*	Alameda Murray	55 229
Narcissa*	Alameda Murray	55 229
SENOLE		
Soringo	Contra Costa Twp 3	57 601
SENON		
Wm	San Francisco San Francisco 6	67 458
SENOR		
Michael*	Santa Clara Santa Clara	65 486

Name	County Locale	M653 RollPage
SENOR		
Samuel	Colusa Muion	57 461
SENORA		
B	El Dorado Placerville	58 833
SENORD		
Joseph*	Calaveras Twp 9	57 370
SENORDA		
Nicholasa	Calaveras Twp 10	57 260
SENORDU		
Nicholasa	Calaveras Twp 10	57 260
SENOUNLLY		
James*	Yuba New York	72 735
SENOYAUL		
Francis P*	Calaveras Twp 6	57 156
SENPACIZA		
Antone	Sonoma Petaluma	69 569
SENPER		
Mary	Calaveras Twp 9	57 414
SENRLAN		
Archebald*	San Francisco San Francisco 3	67 86
SENSEBAUGH		
John	Sonoma Russian	69 436
SENSER		
Geo	Butte Ophir	56 786
SENT		
---*	Calaveras Twp 5	57 204
Allice*	San Mateo Twp 3	65 88
Chrostopher*	Plumas Quincy	62 942
Kim	El Dorado Big Bar	58 734
SENTA		
Juan M*	Monterey San Juan	601002
SENTCLUE		
Henry	Butte Ophir	56 797
SENTE		
Don Juan	Tehama Tehama	70 940
SENTEA		
Eno	Amador Twp 5	55 336
SENTELL		
James	Alameda Oakland	55 15
S E	Nevada Bloomfield	61 520
SENTER		
L	Calaveras Twp 9	57 404
Relz*	Calaveras Twp 9	57 368
Rily*	Calaveras Twp 9	57 368
Rilz*	Calaveras Twp 9	57 368
Ritz	Calaveras Twp 9	57 368
SENTIA		
Eno	Amador Twp 5	55 336
SENTINS		
John*	Tuolumne Columbia	71 295
SENTON		
Martin	Calaveras Twp 10	57 280
T	Sutter Yuba	70 760
SENTONS		
J	Tuolumne Garrote	71 174
John*	Tuolumne Columbia	71 295
SENTOR		
Enoch*	Butte Chico	56 533
SENTRA		
Juan M*	Monterey San Juan	601002
SENTURIS		
Gubutta*	Calaveras Twp 8	57 102
SENTZ		
Herman	Tuolumne Twp 2	71 282
SENUS		
Wm P*	Calaveras Twp 9	57 367
SENUSHARD		
G*	El Dorado Placerville	58 825
SENWELL		
John L	Sonoma Sonoma	69 650
W M*	Tulara Big Oak	71 153
SENY		
---	Amador Twp 2	55 323
---	Calaveras Twp 5	57 149
---	Calaveras Twp 10	57 296
---*	Amador Twp 5	55 349
A	Sacramento Granite	63 251
Louix	Calaveras Twp 4	57 308
Wong	Sacramento Granite	63 259
SEO		
---	Amador Twp 2	55 327
---	Amador Twp 5	55 342
---	Calaveras Twp 5	57 139
---	Placer Virginia	62 670
Chey	Calaveras Twp 4	57 299
Chey	Calaveras Twp 4	57 300
Ellen*	Napa Napa	61 71
How	Nevada Nevada	61 299
SEOCHE		
John	El Dorado Kelsey	581142
SEOERANCE		
T Benton	Calaveras Twp 6	57 130
SEOGUG		
Joseph*	Shasta Shasta	66 655
SEOHR		
F	Nevada Eureka	61 379

California 1860 Census Index

Name	County Locale	M653 Roll	Page
SEOHR			
John	Nevada Eureka	61	379
SEOIRS			
Francis	San Francisco San Francisco 2	67	639
SEOKEY			
Mary I*	Calaveras Twp 6	57	120
SEON			
---	Amador Twp 5	55	353
---	El Dorado Greenwood	58	728
Guadalupe	Los Angeles Los Angeles	59	305
Jamesj	Amador Twp 4	55	233
Placentim	Los Angeles Los Angeles	59	300
SEONAN			
Matilda	Calaveras Twp 5	57	179
SEONG			
---	Amador Twp 1	55	479
---	Calaveras Twp 5	57	251
---	Calaveras Twp 5	57	254
---	Calaveras Twp 10	57	273
---	El Dorado Salmon Falls	58	1059
---	El Dorado Salmon Falls	58	1060
---	El Dorado Placerville	58	832
---	Mariposa Twp 1	60	663
---	Placer Rattle Snake	62	636
---	Trinity Trinindad Rvr	70	1047
---	Trinity Weaverville	70	1074
---*	Calaveras Twp 5	57	245
---*	El Dorado Salmon Falls	58	1064
---*	Placer Auburn	62	572
Pei	San Francisco San Francisco 5	67	507
See	San Francisco San Francisco 5	67	508
Zoo	San Francisco San Francisco 5	67	510
SEONY			
---	Amador Twp 3	55	410
---	Calaveras Twp 5	57	245
---	Calaveras Twp 10	57	286
---	El Dorado Greenwood	58	727
SEOOGER			
Charles*	Yuba Marysville	72	934
SEOR			
---	Calaveras Twp 4	57	306
SEORGEANT			
A	Nevada Bridgeport	61	501
SEORGIE			
William*	Sierra Port Win	66	798
SEORTE			
Saphen*	Calaveras Twp 5	57	225
SEORY			
---	Amador Twp 5	55	352
---	Amador Twp 5	55	356
SEOT			
Jacob	Calaveras Twp 6	57	156
SEOTTY			
William*	Calaveras Twp 7	57	6
SEOVILL			
Wm J	Calaveras Twp 9	57	347
SEOVOR			
Gilfred*	Santa Clara Santa Clara	65	477
SEOW			
---	Amador Twp 1	55	502
---	Calaveras Twp 4	57	310
Gin	Del Norte Crescent	58	631
SEOY			
---	San Francisco San Francisco 4	68	1189
SEOYNG			
Joseph*	Shasta Shasta	66	655
SEP			
---	Amador Twp 6	55	432
---	Butte Mountain	56	741
---	Butte Mountain	56	743
---	Merced Twp 1	60	914
---	Nevada Nevada	61	300
---	Plumas Meadow Valley	62	914
---	Sacramento Centre	63	182
---	Sacramento Cosummes	63	397
---	Sacramento Ward 1	63	71
---	Tuolumne Don Pedro	71	537
---*	Nevada Bridgeport	61	450
---*	Yuba Linda	72	990
Ah	Yuba Suida	72	990
SEPARRY			
C*	Shasta Horsetown	66	700
SEPATH			
Jose	Fresno Twp 1	59	81
SEPATI			
Jose	Fresno Twp 1	59	81
SEPAW			
---	Amador Twp 4	55	251
SEPEDA			
Jose	Santa Clara San Jose	65	364
SEPEON			
John	Napa Napa	61	99
SEPER			
Robert	Siskiyou Shasta Valley	69	120
SEPERRY			
C	Shasta Horsetown	66	700

Name	County Locale	M653 Roll	Page
SEPHARD			
George	Nevada Rough &	61	418
SEPHEN			
Jacob	Tuolumne Twp 5	71	506
SEPHENS			
J P	Yolo Washington	72	561
SEPHULADA			
Demisio	Santa Clara San Jose	65	329
SEPHUR			
J	Sierra Twp 7	66	888
SEPIR			
John	Placer Virginia	62	668
SEPLEY			
Samuel	Amador Twp 4	55	253
SEPLVULA			
Juan	Los Angeles Los Angeles	59	378
SEPORIA			
Juan	San Diego Temecula	64	788
SEPPY			
---	Fresno Twp 2	59	105
SEPTEMBRE			
Antonio	Tehama Red Bluff	70	920
SEPTON			
Charles	Yuba Marysville	72	936
SEPULBIDA			
Jose C	San Diego Agua Caliente	64	820
SEPULBIDO			
Jesus*	Monterey San Juan	60	999
SEPULDA			
John*	Sacramento Ward 1	63	153
Manuel	Sacramento Ward 1	63	110
SEPULIEDA			
Demcia*	Sacramento Ward 1	63	149
SEPULOIDA			
Matea	Los Angeles Los Angeles	59	324
SEPULORIDA			
Patricinio	Los Angeles Los Angeles	59	302
SEPULOULA			
Carjetano	Los Angeles Los Angeles	59	371
SEPULRADA			
J D	Solano Suisan	69	228
SEPULREDA			
Demcia	Sacramento Ward 1	63	149
SEPULSEDA			
Patricio	San Bernardino Santa Barbara	64	159
SEPULTATE			
Justo	Los Angeles San Juan	59	476
SEPULVEDA			
Demcia*	Sacramento Ward 1	63	149
Diego*	Los Angeles San Pedro	59	484
Dolores	Los Angeles Los Angeles	59	508
Dolores	Marin Cortemad	60	786
Juan	Marin Cortemad	60	787
Mauricio	Merced Monterey	60	936
Mauricis*	Monterey Monterey	60	936
Teresa B	Los Angeles Los Angeles	59	381
SEPULVERA			
Juan	San Luis Obispo San Luis Obispo	65	30
SEPULVIDA			
Cayetano	Los Angeles Los Angeles	59	371
Diego	Los Angeles San Pedro	59	484
Estefana	Los Angeles Los Angeles	59	296
Jesus	Los Angeles Santa Ana	59	453
Joaquin	Los Angeles San Juan	59	460
Jose	Los Angeles Los Angeles	59	307
Jose	Los Angeles San Pedro	59	482
Juan	Los Angeles San Pedro	59	482
Juan Ma*	Los Angeles Los Angeles	59	508
Ramona G	Los Angeles Los Angeles	59	508
Serbul	Los Angeles Santa Ana	59	453
Teresa B	Los Angeles Los Angeles	59	381
SEPULVILA			
Maria	Los Angeles Los Angeles	59	320
SEPY			
Joseph*	Shasta Shasta	66	671
SEQUE			
James	Yuba Marysville	72	891
SEQUI			
Baltasar*	San Francisco San Francisco 1	68	893
SEQUIN			
Chas	Santa Clara San Jose	65	357
SEQUIRAS			
J	Merced Twp 1	60	911
SEQUIRE			
Juan	San Diego Colorado	64	809
SEQUNTE			
Mara*	Amador Twp 2	55	323
SEQUUTE			
Mane	Amador Twp 2	55	323
SER			
---	Calaveras Twp 5	57	219
---	Calaveras Twp 10	57	268
---	Calaveras Twp 10	57	285
---	Calaveras Twp 10	57	296
---	Calaveras Twp 4	57	306
---	Calaveras Twp 4	57	327

Name	County Locale	M653 Roll	Page
SER			
---	Mariposa Twp 1	60	641
---	Mariposa Twp 1	60	648
---	Mariposa Twp 1	60	664
---	Nevada Rough &	61	433
---	Sierra Downieville	66	991
App	Nevada Nevada	61	300
Harg	Calaveras Twp 9	57	406
Hob	Santa Clara San Jose	65	374
Ing	San Francisco San Francisco 3	67	3
Isaac	Santa Clara San Jose	65	317
Ma	Sacramento Granite	63	269
Ou	Sierra Twp 7	66	876
Sung	Mariposa Twp 1	60	641
Sung	Nevada Bridgeport	61	466
We	Sacramento Natonia	63	280
SERA			
---	Calaveras Twp 5	57	211
SERADA			
J	Nevada Eureka	61	348
SERAFINA			
---	San Bernardino San Bernadino	64	678
---	San Bernardino S Timate	64	723
---	San Bernardino S Timate	64	740
---	San Bernardino S Timate	64	744
SERAG			
Antone	Placer Forest H	62	773
SERAGMAN			
John	Tuolumne Twp 1	71	257
SERAIMO			
Gregory	Sacramento Ward 1	63	104
SERAMB			
Michael*	Sacramento Ward 1	63	82
SERAMBIA			
Peter	Calaveras Twp 9	57	348
SERAMER			
Francisco	Calaveras Twp 5	57	188
Manwill	Calaveras Twp 5	57	188
SERAMLEN			
Warren	Sierra Gibsonville	66	851
SERAMLON			
Warren*	Sierra Gibsonville	66	851
SERANAH			
Manuella	Los Angeles Azuza	59	277
Salilina	Los Angeles Azuza	59	277
SERANLIN			
David	Los Angeles Los Angeles	59	512
SERANO			
Eulalia*	San Francisco San Francisco 2	67	695
Jno	Merced Twp 1	60	912
Lorenzo	Tuolumne Twp 3	71	459
M	Merced Twp 1	60	912
Manuel	San Bernardino Santa Ba	64	213
Maria J	San Bernardino San Bernadino	64	668
SERANTON			
---*	San Francisco San Francisco 7	68	1376
J B	Nevada Eureka	61	351
SERAPINA			
---	San Bernardino San Bernadino	64	679
SERARD			
Gustavas	Tulara Twp 1	71	100
SERARINO			
Gregory*	Sacramento Ward 1	63	104
SERARY			
C B	Nevada Grass Valley	61	163
SERATIOS			
Ada	San Francisco San Francisco 9	68	967
SERAWER			
Franciso	Calaveras Twp 5	57	188
SERBAT			
Yopterb	Sierra Downieville	66	1023
SERBOT			
Gofeterb*	Sierra Downieville	66	1023
SERBOTT			
J W	El Dorado Georgetown	58	699
SERBROUGH			
Milton	Placer Rattle Snake	62	627
SERBS			
Henry*	San Francisco San Francisco 1	68	810
SERCY			
Bessy	Colusa Colusi	57	426
SERE			
---	Tuolumne Twp 6	71	540
Jose Ma	San Francisco San Francisco 2	67	763
Jose Ma	San Francisco San Francisco 2	67	763
SERELL			
---*	San Francisco San Francisco 7	68	1361
SERENE			
John	Amador Twp 4	55	243
SERENGE			
Thomas	Contra Costa Twp 1	57	496
SERER			
Jose	San Francisco San Francisco 3	67	64
SERERSON			
George*	Fresno Millerto	59	1
SEREVAFA			
---	San Bernardino S Timate	64	710

California 1860 Census Index

Name	County Locale	M653 Roll	Page
SEREVSON			
George	Fresno Millerto	59	1
SERF			
Jules	San Francisco San Francisco 10	67	351
SERGANT			
Charles	Sierra Whiskey	66	844
SERGEANT			
George	Trinity Lewiston	70	953
SERGEART			
A*	Nevada Bridgeport	61	501
SERHUP			
Eliza	San Francisco San Francisco 2	67	634
SERIAS			
John*	Siskiyou Yreka	69	192
SERIES			
Jasper*	Siskiyou Yreka	69	192
Lajarus	Calaveras Twp 7	57	46
SERIFEE			
Browner	El Dorado Mud Springs	58	964
SERIGHT			
Jnoes	Sonoma Cloverdale	69	683
Jones	Sonoma Cloverdale	69	683
SERIL			
Delon	Los Angeles Los Angeles	59	320
SERIMGON ER			
Jas*	San Mateo Twp 3	65	85
SERIN			
Ah	Butte Oregon	56	627
SERINAN			
Ed*	Solano Benecia	69	317
SERINELL			
R H W	El Dorado Eldorado	58	945
SERINON			
W*	San Francisco San Francisco 9	68	1058
SERIVA			
---	San Bernardino San Bernadino	64	679
SERIVATRA			
---*	San Bernardino S Timate	64	727
---*	San Bernardino S Timate	64	742
SERIZ			
B	San Francisco San Francisco 3	67	78
SERLE			
A S	San Francisco San Francisco 6	67	465
SERLES			
Henry*	San Francisco San Francisco 1	68	810
SERLEY			
Daniel	Placer Virginia	62	673
SERLOCH			
P*	Sacramento Cosummes	63	410
SERLOCK			
P*	Sacramento Cosummes	63	410
SERM			
---	Amador Twp 5	55	360
SERMAN			
Augus N*	Sacramento Ward 1	63	34
Augus V*	Sacramento Ward 1	63	34
Peter	San Francisco San Francisco 3	67	65
SERMOUND			
V	San Francisco San Francisco 4	68	1216
SERN			
---	Calaveras Twp 10	57	291
---	Trinity E Weaver	70	1059
SERNA			
---	Butte Chico	56	566
Pedro*	Monterey San Juan	60	1001
SERNARD			
A V	Nevada Eureka	61	352
SERNDINS			
H	Calaveras Twp 9	57	416
SERNEGA			
Maria*	Monterey Monterey	60	965
SERNEY			
James	Alameda Oakland	55	8
SERNGE			
Amso	Santa Clara San Jose	65	359
SERNON			
Levi	San Francisco San Francisco 2	67	610
SERNS			
Martin	Alameda Brooklyn	55	80
SERNSTOPOL			
L	Yuba Slate Ro	72	688
SERO			
---	Sierra Twp 5	66	931
SEROANDRI			
---*	Nevada Bridgeport	61	484
SEROCHE			
John*	El Dorado Kelsey	58	1142
SEROCKE			
John*	El Dorado Kelsey	58	1142
SEROGGINGS			
J W*	Mariposa Twp 1	60	657
SEROIS			
J	El Dorado Georgetown	58	683
SERON			
Louis*	Sierra Downieville	66	969

Name	County Locale	M653 Roll	Page
SERON			
Manuel	Calaveras Twp 6	57	124
SEROT			
Josephine	San Francisco San Francisco 10	67	182
SEROW			
Louis	Sierra Downieville	66	969
SERPENTINE			
J	El Dorado Placerville	58	933
SERPON			
Jno	Butte Oregon	56	624
SERPP			
John	Sonoma Sonoma	69	656
SERPRINA			
---	San Bernardino San Bernadino	64	684
SERRA			
Jose*	Los Angeles Los Angeles	59	334
SERRANCE			
Paul	Sierra Poker Flats	66	840
SERRAND			
Paul*	Sierra Poker Flats	66	840
SERRANDIE			
---*	Nevada Bridgeport	61	484
SERRANDRI			
---*	Nevada Bridgeport	61	484
SERRANE			
Florencio	Merced Monterey	60	943
Florencio	Monterey Monterey	60	943
SERRANO			
Cisco	Los Angeles San Juan	59	466
Domingo	Los Angeles San Gabriel	59	416
Fernando	Los Angeles San Gabriel	59	421
Francisco	Los Angeles San Juan	59	474
Horencio*	Monterey Monterey	60	943
Jesus	San Bernardino Santa Barbara	64	197
Joaquin	Los Angeles San Juan	59	460
Jose	Los Angeles Santa Ana	59	446
Jose A	Los Angeles Los Nieto	59	427
Jose A	Los Angeles San Juan	59	460
Juan P	Los Angeles San Juan	59	473
Korencio*	Monterey Monterey	60	943
Maria De Los A	Santa Ana Los Angeles	59	446
Maria J	Los Angeles San Juan	59	474
Pedro	Los Angeles San Juan	59	473
Ramon	Los Angeles San Pedro	59	478
Refugio	Los Angeles Los Angeles	59	301
Wancisco	Los Angeles Los Angeles	59	348
SERRANT			
Alphonse*	San Francisco 2 San Francisco	67	696
SERRARD			
Geo	Trinity New Rvr	70	1030
SERRAVO			
Francisca	Los Angeles Los Nieto	59	432
SERREC			
John	Yuba Parks Ba	72	779
SERREE			
John	Yuba Parks Ba	72	779
SERREL			
Clinton P	San Francisco San Francisco 2	67	643
John	Yuba Rose Bar	72	808
SERRENO			
Lorenzo	Tuolumne Chinese	71	499
SERRETLER			
Nelson*	Calaveras Twp 5	57	240
SERRIE			
Frank	Alameda Brooklyn	55	91
SERRIN			
Chas	Calaveras Twp 10	57	291
Jabez	Plumas Quincy	62	938
N	Butte Kimshaw	56	603
W*	Butte Kimshaw	56	603
SERRINE			
Parley	San Bernardino San Salvador	64	653
SERRIT			
Jonathan	San Joaquin Elkhorn	64	995
SERRITTE			
Baptiste	Tuolumne Twp 4	71	140
SERRONO			
Jose A	Los Angeles Los Nieto	59	427
SERRUE			
Jose	San Francisco San Francisco 3	67	2
SERRY			
---	Nevada Grass Valley	61	228
SERS			
J W*	Calaveras Twp 9	57	392
SERSENON			
Michael	Yuba Long Bar	72	752
SERSONON			
Michael	Yuba Long Bar	72	752
SERTEJES			
Francisco*	Alameda Brooklyn	55	191
SERTHLE			
John	Placer Dutch Fl	62	718
SERTON			
John*	Shasta Shasta	66	675

Name	County Locale	M653 Roll	Page
SERTZH			
A	Shasta Shasta	66	683
SERULA			
Antonio*	Alameda Murray	55	229
SERUSTOPOL			
L*	Yolo Slate Ra	72	688
SERUTH			
Michael*	Alameda Oakland	55	72
SERUTZER			
Alonzo J	San Francisco San Francisco 3	67	80
SERVA			
Esteban*	Monterey San Juan	60	997
SERVAL			
Jean	San Francisco San Francisco 6	67	445
SERVANO			
Miguel	San Luis Obispo San Luis Obispo	65	22
SERVANT			
Alphonse*	San Francisco 2 San Francisco	67	696
SERVANTES			
Macidonea	Tuolumne Twp 5	71	490
Polita	Los Angeles Azuza	59	277
SERVENTA			
J	Tuolumne Twp 4	71	161
SERVEY			
---	Sacramento Centre	63	182
SERVIN			
Vecente	San Bernardino Santa Barbara	64	193
SERVIR			
Percophia	San Luis Obispo San Luis Obispo	65	45
SERVIS			
Jno*	Butte Oregon	56	614
Richmond	Mariposa Twp 1	60	949
SERWICH			
George	Tuolumne Twp 1	71	255
Geroge	Tuolumne Twp 1	71	255
SERWIN			
Friolen	Marin Cortemad	60	785
Frolen*	Marin Cortemad	60	785
SERY			
---	Amador Twp 2	55	328
---	Amador Twp 5	55	329
---	Tuolumne Twp 2	71	408
Foo	Amador Twp 2	55	312
SES			
---	El Dorado Georgetown	58	691
Ellen*	Napa Napa	61	71
SESANO			
Benino	Santa Clara Burnett	65	258
SESAVINO			
Isaac	San Francisco San Francisco 1	68	819
SESCTON			
Saml G	Tuolumne Sonora	71	479
SESDER			
---	El Dorado Greenwood	58	727
SESEDO			
---	Mendocino Calpella	60	823
SESIDO			
---	Mendocino Calpella	60	823
SESIRIA			
Maria	Santa Clara San Jose	65	361
SESLIA			
James*	Santa Cruz Santa Cruz	66	609
SESLIO			
J	Nevada Nevada	61	240
SESNEGA			
Maria	Monterey Monterey	60	965
SESNEY			
Richd*	San Francisco San Francisco 9	68	1077
SESSANCE			
Paul*	Sierra Poker Flats	66	840
SESSAY			
Armand	Calaveras Twp 5	57	173
SESSCHANSKY			
A*	Shasta Shasta	66	655
SESSEAIN			
Victor S*	Yuba Linda	72	990
SESSELBIN			
H	San Francisco San Francisco 5	67	513
SESSER			
Joseph	Sacramento American	63	162
Peter	San Francisco San Francisco 7	68	1343
SESSIER			
Jaques	Plumas Meadow Valley	62	934
SESSIONS			
Josiah	San Francisco San Francisco 6	67	424
W P	San Francisco San Francisco 6	67	422
SESSOR			
J S	El Dorado Placerville	58	849
SESSULDA			
John*	Sacramento Ward 1	63	153
SESSUY			
Armand*	Calaveras Twp 6	57	173
SESSY			
Joseph*	Shasta Shasta	66	671

Name	County Locale	M653 Roll	Page
SESTA			
---	Los Angeles San Pedro	59	486
SESTEBEN			
---	San Bernardino S Timate	64	752
SESTO			
---	Los Angeles San Pedro	59	486
SESTON			
Geiron	Fresno Twp 2	59	49
Patrick	Yuba Marysville	72	965
Wm M*	Alameda Brooklyn	55	154
SESTRAI			
Peter*	Calaveras Twp 6	57	167
SESTRAIS			
Peter*	Calaveras Twp 6	57	167
SESTRIE			
James	Santa Cruz Santa Cruz	66	609
SESURE			
L*	Nevada Washington	61	337
SET SING			
---	Nevada Rough &	61	436
SET			
---	Del Norte Crescent	58	643
---	El Dorado Coloma	58	1077
---	Napa Napa	61	89
---	Plumas Quincy	62	1008
---	San Francisco San Francisco 4	68	1190
---	Sierra St Louis	66	805
---	Trinity China Bar	70	959
---*	Mariposa Twp 3	60	581
---*	Nevada Bridgeport	61	450
Ching	Plumas Quincy	62	1008
Kou	Mariposa Twp 3	60	579
Sing	Nevada Rough &	61	436
SETCHFIELD			
Samuel	Yuba Bear Rvr	72	1003
SETCHIN			
Ellen	Calaveras Twp 5	57	233
SETE			
---	Amador Twp 1	55	496
SETER			
Lohar	Yolo Cache	72	642
SETH G			
Bradbury	Tuolumne Twp 1	71	201
SETH			
---	Sierra St Louis	66	805
James*	Alameda Brooklyn	55	100
SETHAR			
Saml	Trinity Ferry	70	977
SETHLEY			
Martin	San Francisco San Francisco 10		301
		67	
SETI			
J J	Colusa Monroeville	57	447
SETIENBUZER			
George	Marin San Rafael	60	765
SETIENKURZER			
George	Marin San Rafael	60	765
SETIGAR			
Charles*	Calaveras Twp 6	57	167
SETIGUS			
Charles*	Calaveras Twp 6	57	167
SETIM			
John*	Placer Dutch Fl	62	729
SETIYUS			
Charles*	Calaveras Twp 6	57	167
SETLERSON			
Sacel*	Yuba Marysville	72	950
SETLLE			
Clar	Sacramento Ward 1	63	67
SETOA			
Jascentho*	Santa Cruz Santa Cruz	66	612
Jascintho*	Santa Cruz Santa Cruz	66	612
Jasciutho*	Santa Cruz Santa Cruz	66	612
SETON			
A L*	Nevada Grass Valley	61	196
SETRAS			
Jose	San Bernardino Santa Barbara	64	185
SETRIENES			
Frances*	Calaveras Twp 6	57	137
SETRO			
Francisco	Amador Twp 4	55	241
SETROW			
Morris*	San Francisco San Francisco 3	67	27
SETRUNI			
Francis	Calaveras Twp 6	57	137
SETSHIDE			
James	Tuolumne Sonora	71	206
SETSOUE			
---	San Joaquin Stockton	64	1083
SETT			
Eloleto	Sierra La Porte	66	784
SETTER			
Jacob*	Los Angeles Los Angeles	59	321
James	El Dorado Placerville	58	933
SETTERLEN			
Antoine*	San Francisco San Francisco 2	67	687

Name	County Locale	M653 Roll	Page
SETTERS			
Levy	Shasta Millvill	66	740
SETTERSON			
Sacel*	Yuba Marysville	72	950
Saml	Yuba Marysville	72	950
Wm E	San Francisco San Francisco 2	67	621
SETTISH			
Antonio	Contra Costa Twp 1	57	510
SETTLE			
L B	Sacramento Ward 4	63	524
Lanford	Calaveras Twp 5	57	182
Lydia F*	Trinity Weaverville	70	1071
SETTLEJOHN			
James	Yuba Marysville	72	965
SETTLER			
J	El Dorado Placerville	58	890
SETUN			
John*	Placer Dutch Fl	62	729
SETUNG			
---	Trinity Trinindad Rvr	70	1049
SEU			
---	Amador Twp 4	55	251
---	Calaveras Twp 6	57	165
---	Calaveras Twp 5	57	232
---	Calaveras Twp 5	57	257
---	Calaveras Twp 10	57	259
---*	Calaveras Twp 5	57	252
Kee	Mariposa Twp 3	60	581
Ku*	Mariposa Twp 3	60	581
SEUCK			
K*	Amador Twp 4	55	239
SEUG			
---	Yuba Marysville	72	896
SEUGH			
---*	Sierra Downieville	66	974
SEUING			
---	Calaveras Twp 5	57	235
SEULER			
Jacob	Calaveras Twp 10	57	263
SEUM			
---	Shasta Shasta	66	680
---*	Butte Eureka	56	651
SEUMAN			
J	Siskiyou Scott Va	69	49
SEUN			
---	Calaveras Twp 10	57	269
Lee	El Dorado Georgetown	58	686
SEUNDO			
Joseph	Calaveras Twp 5	57	203
SEUNE			
---	Shasta Shasta	66	680
SEUNG			
---	Calaveras Twp 6	57	145
---	Calaveras Twp 5	57	209
---	Calaveras Twp 5	57	235
---	Calaveras Twp 5	57	254
---	Calaveras Twp 10	57	273
---	Calaveras Twp 10	57	286
---	Calaveras Twp 10	57	291
---	Calaveras Twp 4	57	306
---	Calaveras Twp 4	57	327
---	Plumas Meadow Valley	62	914
---*	Mariposa Twp 1	60	648
SEUNON			
W*	San Francisco San Francisco 9	68	1058
SEUNY			
---	Calaveras Twp 10	57	291
---	Calaveras Twp 4	57	306
SEUR			
Richard	El Dorado Eldorado	58	942
SEURLA			
Narcissa*	Alameda Murray	55	229
SEURLEY			
E P*	Butte Oregon	56	623
SEURT			
Nathan	Calaveras Twp 4	57	318
SEUT			
---	Calaveras Twp 4	57	299
---*	Siskiyou Klamath	69	80
Christopher*	Plumas Quincy	62	942
SEUTOR			
Enoch*	Butte Chico	56	533
SEUVEN			
Michael*	Yuba Marysville	72	904
SEUWELL			
John L*	Sonoma Sonoma	69	650
SEV			
---	Amador Twp 5	55	335
---	Calaveras Twp 6	57	139
Fox	Calaveras Twp 4	57	299
SEVAIN			
Thomas S	Tuolumne Twp 2	71	323
SEVAL			
Antonio	Tuolumne Twp 4	71	140
SEVALL			
Alexander*	Santa Cruz Pajaro	66	554

Name	County Locale	M653 Roll	Page
SEVALLA			
John	Amador Twp 2	55	319
SEVANO			
Eulalia*	San Francisco San Francisco 2	67	695
SEVAPEASE			
Hippolite	Plumas Meadow Valley	62	907
SEVAR			
Frank	Trinity Indian C	70	986
SEVARD			
Gustavus*	Tulara Visalia	71	100
SEVARIO			
Francis	Tuolumne Jamestown	71	425
SEVARO			
---	San Luis Obispo San Luis Obispo	65	32
Thomas	Tuolumne Chinese	71	495
SEVARONI			
Andrew	Calaveras Twp 5	57	220
SEVARTS			
G W	San Francisco San Francisco 5	67	553
SEVASTRA			
Antone*	Placer Iona Hills	62	891
SEVATIOS			
Ada*	San Francisco San Francisco 9	68	967
SEVE			
---	El Dorado Eldorado	58	947
SEVEEAQ			
Charles*	Yuba Marysville	72	846
SEVEEUQ			
Charles*	Yuba Marysville	72	846
SEVEINING			
Henry	Tuolumne Columbia	71	338
SEVELIA			
---	Calaveras Twp 9	57	378
SEVELL			
M	Nevada Eureka	61	373
SEVELLE			
G D	Nevada Grass Valley	61	236
SEVELT			
Jos H*	Sacramento Ward 1	63	87
SEVEN			
---	El Dorado Greenwood	58	728
John	Tuolumne Jamestown	71	435
SEVENARY			
Clara*	Yuba Marysville	72	917
SEVENICH			
Ewone*	Calaveras Twp 5	57	230
SEVENTS			
Daniel	Calaveras Twp 6	57	144
SEVENUSH			
Erorne*	Calaveras Twp 5	57	230
SEVERAGE			
Wm	Marin Cortemad	60	783
SEVERAH			
Jesus	Mariposa Twp 1	60	641
SEVERAN			
Dolores	Mariposa Twp 1	60	641
SEVERANCE			
C C P	Tuolumne Sonora	71	195
Haskell	Mendocino Big Rvr	60	848
J G	Amador Twp 1	55	463
James	Mendocino Big Rvr	60	851
Joseph	Sierra Twp 7	66	913
William W*	Calaveras Twp 6	57	157
SEVERAR			
Dolores	Mariposa Twp 1	60	641
Jesus	Mariposa Twp 1	60	641
SEVERE			
John	El Dorado Coloma	58	1080
Louis	Tuolumne Twp 1	71	269
Mary	Tuolumne Columbia	71	334
W D*	Sacramento Franklin	63	328
SEVERIANO			
Nobla	Los Angeles Tejon	59	540
SEVERINE			
Theodore	San Francisco San Francisco 2	67	701
SEVERINO			
Gozmon	San Francisco San Francisco 3	67	80
Gozvnon*	San Francisco San Francisco 3	67	80
SEVERLIA			
---	Calaveras Twp 9	57	378
SEVERLY			
R R	Butte Oregon	56	624
SEVERMORE			
Albert*	San Francisco San Francisco 4	68	1132
SEVERNEY			
C	Sacramento Cosumnes	63	409
SEVERNS			
Geo	Sonoma Mendocino	69	457
Geo W	Sonoma Mendocino	69	457
Henry H	Humbolt Eel Rvr	59	145
SEVERO			
Louis	Tuolumne Twp 1	71	269
SEVERS			
Francis	San Francisco San Francisco 2	67	639
SEVERSAGE			
Wm	Marin Cortemad	60	783

Name	County Locale	M653 RollPage
SEVERSON		
W	Siskiyou Klamath	69 96
SEVERTHS		
Layarus*	Calaveras Twp 7	57 6
SEVERTS		
John*	San Francisco San Francisco 3	67 40
SEVERTY		
John	Sonoma Sonoma	69 633
SEVERWALL		
Haskett*	Mendocino Big Rvr	60 848
SEVES		
Jasper*	Siskiyou Yreka	69 192
John*	Siskiyou Yreka	69 192
SEVESARIA		
William*	Calaveras Twp 6	57 157
SEVETTE		
John*	Yuba Marysville	72 867
O A	Shasta Shasta	66 734
SEVEY		
G W	Yolo Washington	72 561
Gillman	Sierra St Louis	66 807
William	Plumas Quincy	62 995
SEVIAR		
William	Contra Costa Twp 3	57 593
SEVICKEY		
Fred*	Siskiyou Yreka	69 157
SEVIER		
Coffee	Tulara Visalia	71 99
F	San Francisco San Francisco 5	67 535
Frank	San Francisco San Francisco 11	139 67
SEVIERS		
F	San Francisco San Francisco 6	67 466
SEVIESS		
Gordon	Butte Bidwell	56 705
SEVILE		
Manuell	Calaveras Twp 5	57 194
SEVILLE		
John	Placer Iona Hills	62 860
Manuell	Calaveras Twp 5	57 194
Peter K*	Amador Twp 4	55 235
SEVIMILLY		
John*	Calaveras Twp 10	57 288
SEVIN		
Danl F	San Francisco San Francisco 2	67 708
David R	Yuba Linda	72 993
Henry*	Calaveras Twp 5	57 174
Jacob	Placer Michigan	62 808
SEVING		
Newton	Trinity Steiner	70 999
SEVINILLY		
John*	Calaveras Twp 10	57 288
SEVINSON		
John	Calaveras Twp 5	57 240
Levin*	Calaveras Twp 5	57 240
Pierre	Calaveras Twp 5	57 240
Rurnow	Calaveras Twp 5	57 189
SEVINULLY		
John	Calaveras Twp 10	57 288
SEVIRAN		
Dolores	Mariposa Twp 1	60 641
SEVIRN		
Davis K	Calaveras Twp 5	57 207
SEVISON		
Meliam	Calaveras Twp 5	57 188
William*	Calaveras Twp 5	57 188
SEVITT		
Patrick	Contra Costa Twp 1	57 516
SEVO		
---	El Dorado Mud Springs	58 971
SEVOGANT		
Francis P*	Calaveras Twp 6	57 156
SEVORE		
Mary	Tuolumne Twp 2	71 334
SEVORTZ		
George	Calaveras Twp 5	57 241
Phillip	Calaveras Twp 5	57 185
SEVOUGH		
---	Mendocino Twp 1	60 887
SEVOY		
Jacob*	San Francisco San Francisco 12	393 67
SEVPHILS		
R	El Dorado Georgetown	58 690
SEVR		
Charles	Tulara Visalia	71 100
SEVRE		
Francisco	Amador Twp 5	55 361
SEVTO		
Richard	San Francisco San Francisco 7	681339
SEVTON		
John*	Shasta Shasta	66 675
SEVTT		
Allen	El Dorado Coloma	581123
SEVUNK		
Daniel*	Calaveras Twp 6	57 144

Name	County Locale	M653 RollPage
SEVURE		
Morny*	Alameda Oakland	55 61
SEVVY		
Jacob*	San Francisco San Francisco 12	393 67
SEVY		
Michael	Sacramento Ward 1	63 25
Pat	Sacramento American	63 167
S A*	Sacramento Ward 1	63 19
SEW		
---	Amador Twp 4	55 252
---	Amador Twp 5	55 289
---	Amador Twp 5	55 331
---	Amador Twp 6	55 332
---	Amador Twp 6	55 423
---	El Dorado Coloma	581123
---	El Dorado Diamond	58 798
---	El Dorado Placerville	58 886
---	El Dorado Mud Springs	58 952
---	El Dorado Mud Springs	58 972
---	El Dorado Mud Springs	58 985
---	El Dorado Mud Springs	58 986
---	El Dorado Mud Springs	58 988
---	Sacramento Cosumnes	63 391
---	Sierra Twp 5	66 934
---	Tuolumne Knights	71 529
---	Tuolumne Twp 6	71 536
---	Tuolumne Twp 6	71 537
---	Tuolumne Twp 6	71 542
---	Yolo Slate Ra	72 706
---*	Calaveras Twp 5	57 247
---*	Tuolumne Don Pedro	71 536
---*	Tuolumne Don Pedro	71 540
Byron N	Sierra Whiskey	66 850
Frank*	Sierra Pine Grove	66 827
George	Sierra Downieville	66 955
Ger*	El Dorado Georgetown	58 684
Tong	Sacramento Granite	63 232
You	Nevada Bloomfield	61 528
SEWA		
---	El Dorado Coloma	581082
---	El Dorado Coloma	581108
SEWAL		
Henry C	Yuba Marysville	72 922
Henry D	Yuba Marysville	72 922
SEWALL		
Delwell	El Dorado Georgetown	58 694
Harins*	San Francisco San Francisco 3	67 79
Harius*	San Francisco San Francisco 3	67 79
John*	Yuba Long Bar	72 770
SEWAND		
Paul*	Sierra Poker Flats	66 840
SEWANTT		
E	San Francisco San Francisco 9	681080
SEWARD		
Anson	Sonoma Mendocino	69 462
Ansor	Sonoma Mendocino	69 462
H L	Siskiyou Yreka	69 188
John S	Sonoma Russian	69 438
Juad	Tulara Twp 2	71 1
Juard	Tulara Visalia	71 1
S S	San Francisco San Francisco 2	67 803
W	El Dorado Diamond	58 786
William	Calaveras Twp 10	57 294
SEWART		
B W	Tehama Cottonwoood	70 901
J S	Sonoma Bodega	69 540
Wm	Butte Bidwell	56 715
SEWARTSON		
R R*	El Dorado Placerville	58 862
SEWAUTT		
E*	San Francisco San Francisco 9	681080
SEWAY		
---	Shasta Shasta	66 668
SEWEL		
John	Marin Cortemad	60 752
SEWELL		
A D	El Dorado Kelsey	581149
Alonzo	El Dorado Kelsey	581151
Andrew J*	Sierra St Louis	66 807
C	Trinity Weaverville	701064
Charles*	Santa Cruz Pescadero	66 649
Frank	Plumas Quincy	62 961
George	Plumas Meadow Valley	62 899
Jno	Sacramento Brighton	63 198
L G	Yuba Slate Ro	72 698
M	Nevada Eureka	61 373
N F	Placer Yankee J	62 761
S B	Shasta Horsetown	66 692
Sam*	Yuba New York	72 734
Thomas	El Dorado Salmon Falls	581059
W R	Sacramento Granite	63 222
Wm	Plumas Meadow Valley	62 903
SEWEN		
---	Napa Napa	61 89
SEWER		
---	Mendocino Round Va	60 886

Name	County Locale	M653 RollPage
SEWERS		
A J	Siskiyou Scott Va	69 28
Jno*	Sacramento Ward 1	63 31
SEWERT		
Wm	Butte Bidwell	56 717
SEWETT		
John	Siskiyou Yreka	69 126
SEWEY		
---	Del Norte Happy Ca	58 663
W	Nevada Eureka	61 378
SEWILL		
Wm J	Calaveras Twp 9	57 347
SEWIS		
J	Nevada Nevada	61 242
James C	Calaveras Twp 5	57 209
SEWITTE		
Baptiste	Tuolumne Big Oak	71 140
SEWKIRK		
Eldridge*	Amador Twp 4	55 244
SEWLL		
Jacob*	Yuba Marysville	72 958
SEWO		
---	Amador Twp 4	55 247
SEWPLE		
Mary B	Colusa Colusi	57 426
SEWTELLE		
A W*	Butte Oregon	56 611
SEWY		
Ah	Sacramento Granite	63 232
SEWYER		
Charles*	El Dorado White Oaks	581032
SEXANER		
Fred	Sacramento Ward 4	63 505
SEXELL		
Peter	Siskiyou Scott Ri	69 66
SEXEY		
Charles E	Yuba Long Bar	72 748
SEXTON		
Chas	Sacramento Cosumnes	63 383
Daniel	Marin Tomales	60 726
Danl	San Bernardino San Bernardino	64 668
Geo	Sonoma Petaluma	69 554
Geo W	El Dorado Coloma	581080
Haden	Los Angeles San Gabriel	59 411
Indania	Los Angeles Los Angeles	59 326
James	Sierra St Louis	66 810
John	Marin Bolinas	60 742
John	Yolo Cache Crk	72 595
Margaret	Placer Rattle Snake	62 601
Mary	Siskiyou Scott Va	69 46
Michael	Tulara Twp 3	71 46
Patrick	Yuba Marysville	72 965
Peter	Calaveras Twp 6	57 146
Phillip	Klamath Klamath	59 228
R R	Amador Twp 2	55 263
Soledad	Los Angeles Los Angeles	59 326
Terrence	San Francisco San Francisco 7	681387
Thos	San Francisco San Francisco 10	254 67
W	El Dorado Grizzly	581182
W T	Butte Ophir	56 789
Wm	Placer Rattle Snake	62 599
Wm	Yuba Rose Bar	72 816
SEXTOR		
John	Yolo Cache	72 595
SEY KEE		
---	Mariposa Twp 3	60 607
SEY		
---	Calaveras Twp 10	57 270
---	Mariposa Twp 3	60 586
---	Plumas Meadow Valley	62 913
---	Plumas Quincy	62 949
---*	Mariposa Twp 3	60 586
Jes*	Amador Twp 4	55 332
Jus*	Amador Twp 4	55 332
Ke	Mariposa Twp 3	60 576
Kee*	Mariposa Twp 3	60 543
Kee*	Mariposa Twp 3	60 586
Mon	El Dorado Georgetown	58 700
Yom	Placer Auburn	62 572
SEYAN		
John G	Calaveras Twp 10	57 281
SEYANS		
L*	Sierra Downieville	66 957
SEYAR		
John G*	Calaveras Twp 10	57 281
John*	Calaveras Twp 5	57 230
SEYARDO		
Paul	Calaveras Twp 5	57 224
Poul*	Calaveras Twp 5	57 224
SEYASDO		
Pond	Calaveras Twp 5	57 224
SEYAUS		
L*	Sierra Downieville	66 957
SEYDEN		
Peter	Calaveras Twp 6	57 157

California 1860 Census Index

Name	County Locale	M653 RollPage
SEYDER		
Peter*	Calaveras Twp 6	57 157
SEYEP		
---	Trinity Trinindad Rvr	701050
SEYER		
Edward	Contra Costa Twp 2	57 546
SEYERS		
H	Butte Cascade	56 693
Harry	Sonoma Vallejo	69 628
SEYHLLE		
George*	Calaveras Twp 10	57 278
SEYHTLE		
George*	Calaveras Twp 10	57 278
SEYLAEA		
Diego*	Alameda Murray	55 227
SEYLAIA		
Gaudalupe*	Alameda Murray	55 227
SEYLAIO		
Guadalupe*	Alameda Murray	55 227
SEYLARA		
Diego*	Alameda Murray	55 227
SEYLEA		
Jesus	Alameda Murray	55 227
SEYMANS		
Mary	Mariposa Twp 3	60 587
SEYMEUR		
J C	Butte Wyandotte	56 659
SEYMOAR		
Jesse	Yuba Marysville	72 974
SEYMOINE		
J Y*	Nevada Nevada	61 330
SEYMON		
E	Butte Kimshaw	56 598
SEYMOND		
A E	Nevada Nevada	61 250
SEYMOR		
J C	Sutter Yuba	70 762
SEYMORE		
A L	El Dorado Placerville	58 820
E	Butte Kimshaw	56 598
H	Sacramento Alabama	63 413
J G	Sacramento Granite	63 228
J N	Sacramento Granite	63 228
W	El Dorado Placerville	58 882
Warren	El Dorado Mud Springs	58 962
SEYMORN		
C B	Shasta Horsetown	66 698
C H*	Nevada Nevada	61 250
SEYMOUR		
A	Shasta Millvill	66 748
Andrew	San Francisco San Francisco 9	681037
B N	Yolo Slate Ra	72 696
C	San Francisco San Francisco 5	67 524
C B	Shasta Horsetown	66 698
C H*	Nevada Nevada	61 250
Emmery P*	San Francisco San Francisco 4	681220
	San Francisco	
H	San Francisco San Francisco 3	67 43
Harry	Butte Bidwell	56 730
Henry	Calaveras Twp 7	57 17
Henry O	Placer Nicolaus	62 691
J C	Butte Wyandotte	56 659
J S*	Sacramento Ward 4	63 515
J W	Sutter Nicolaus	70 827
J Y	Nevada Nevada	61 330
Jas	Placer Dutch Fl	62 718
Jas	Sacramento Granite	63 251
John	Los Angeles Azuza	59 272
Louis	San Francisco San Francisco 2	67 709
Lucy	Solano Benecia	69 295
Margaret	San Francisco San Francisco 4	681128
Mary	Mariposa Twp 3	60 587
R N	Yuba Slate Ro	72 696
Sm L	Sonoma Mendocino	69 457
Wilas	Calaveras Twp 5	57 241
Wilbur	Calaveras Twp 5	57 241
Wm	San Francisco San Francisco 7	681343
Wm L	Sonoma Mendocino	69 457
SEYMOURE		
J Y	Nevada Nevada	61 330
SEYNETZ		
Joseph*	Calaveras Twp 10	57 278
SEYNIN		
Baptise	Calaveras Twp 4	57 312
SEYNITZ		
Joseph	Calaveras Twp 10	57 278
SEYOMORE		
R	Yolo Merritt	72 581
SEYON		
---	Calaveras Twp 10	57 268
I M*	Nevada Red Dog	61 546
SEYONDA		
---	San Mateo Twp 2	65 111
SEYONG		
O	Placer Virginia	62 665
SEYOR		
John	Calaveras Twp 5	57 230

Name	County Locale	M653 RollPage
SEYTON		
John*	Yuba New York	72 728
SEYUFF		
John*	Calaveras Twp 4	57 339
SEYUIN		
Baptist	Calaveras Twp 4	57 312
SEZAR		
Jaber	Sierra Downieville	66 968
SEZARINKNOW		
R	San Francisco San Francisco 2	67 699
SEZAV		
Jaber*	Sierra Downieville	66 968
SEZROLS		
Daniel	Yolo Merritt	72 580
SFALEE		
N*	Nevada Nevada	61 246
SFALER		
N*	Nevada Nevada	61 246
SFALU		
N*	Nevada Nevada	61 246
SFITH		
Owen	Yuba Rose Bar	72 800
SFRANSHOR		
Charley*	Mariposa Coulterville	60 698
SFRAUSHAN		
Charley*	Mariposa Coulterville	60 698
SFROAT		
Joseph*	Mariposa Twp 3	60 609
SG HEN		
---	El Dorado Georgetown	58 693
SG		
Lin*	El Dorado Georgetown	58 703
Loney*	El Dorado Georgetown	58 693
Rim*	El Dorado Georgetown	58 702
Wen	El Dorado Georgetown	58 693
Yong*	El Dorado Georgetown	58 702
SGHANFILE		
Lewis	Sierra Twp 7	66 867
SGINOR		
E G*	San Francisco San Francisco 3	67 81
SGNACIO		
---	Mariposa Twp 3	60 616
SGNG		
---	El Dorado Georgetown	58 702
SGU		
Hung	San Francisco San Francisco 4	681212
SGUING		
---	El Dorado Georgetown	58 701
SGURE		
John B*	Yuba Marysville	72 877
SGUREO		
Henry	Mariposa Twp 1	60 663
SH CHOO		
---*	Yuba Long Bar	72 763
SH I CI		
---	Sierra Twp 5	66 939
SH LOW		
---*	Yuba Long Bar	72 763
SH LOY		
---*	Yuba Long Bar	72 764
SH		
Choo*	Yuba Long Bar	72 763
Low*	Yuba Long Bar	72 763
Loy*	Yuba Long Bar	72 764
Oua*	Mariposa Twp 3	60 560
SHA		
---	San Francisco San Francisco 9	681087
Ah	Calaveras Twp 7	57 31
Ling	Yuba Long Bar	72 762
M A*	Nevada Grass Valley	61 143
Michael	Placer Auburn	62 566
Shi	Yuba Long Bar	72 755
SHA?ESPEARE		
Joseph*	San Francisco San Francisco 2	67 556
SHAB		
Bee	Yuba Long Bar	72 765
SHABBY		
Wm	San Francisco San Francisco 2	67 686
SHABE		
J	San Francisco San Francisco 5	67 551
SHABEN		
August	San Francisco San Francisco 7	681416
SHABER		
B M	Calaveras Twp 8	57 80
Jacob	San Francisco San Francisco 4	681149
Wm R	San Francisco San Francisco 3	67 18
SHABOR		
Joseph J	Sierra Scales D	66 800
SHACHA		
Martin	Santa Cruz Pajaro	66 566
SHACK		
---	Tulara Twp 2	71 33
---	Yolo No E Twp	72 684
---*	Tulara Visalia	71 37
SHACKELFORD		
Maria	San Francisco San Francisco 4	681226

Name	County Locale	M653 RollPage
SHACKELFORD		
Richard	Santa Cruz Pajaro	66 563
Richard M	Yuba Marysville	72 949
SHACKELO		
---*	Tulara Visalia	71 34
SHACKELY		
R	Amador Twp 2	55 306
SHACKENDOR		
---	Mendocino Round Va	60 878
SHACKER		
Thos W	Sonoma Russian	69 438
SHACKEY		
Wm	Butte Wyandotte	56 664
SHACKFORD		
Georgiana	San Joaquin Castoria	64 895
Luther CSan Bernardino San Bernadino		64 675
SHACKILFAT		
Maria	San Francisco San Francisco 4	681226
SHACKILFORD		
Richard	Santa Cruz Pajaro	66 563
SHACKLE FOOT		
---	Tulara Twp 2	71 34
SHACKLEFORD		
J M	Tehama Antelope	70 886
Thomas	Tulara Visalia	71 102
SHACKLET		
George W	Calaveras Twp 7	57 8
Thomas	Calaveras Twp 7	57 30
SHACKLETON		
William	San Francisco San Francisco 9	68 996
SHACKLY		
Johnson*	El Dorado Georgetown	58 705
SHACKNERY		
---*	Mendocino Calpella	60 822
SHACKO		
---	Tulara Twp 2	71 37
---	Tulara Twp 2	71 40
---*	Tulara Visalia	71 33
---*	Tulara Visalia	71 40
SHAD		
---	Mariposa Coulterville	60 681
E K*	Shasta Shasta	66 667
Geo	Sacramento Ward 4	63 525
SHADBOLT		
James	Mariposa Twp 1	60 624
SHADDEN		
Anderson	Placer Nicolaus	62 691
Jos	Placer Nicolaus	62 691
SHADE		
Angeline	Alameda Brooklyn	55 128
Geo W	Alameda Brooklyn	55 135
Geo W	Alameda Brooklyn	55 136
Gilbert	Tuolumne Twp 5	71 504
Oscar	Tuolumne Twp 2	71 338
SHADEN		
T T	El Dorado Casumnes	581173
SHADER		
John	Nevada Bloomfield	61 523
Stephen R*	Sierra Morristown	661053
SHADRICK		
Samuel	San Francisco San Francisco 11	137 67
SHADTOWN		
Moses	Trinity Trinity	70 971
SHADWICK		
Henry	San Joaquin Stockton	641031
SHAE		
Michael	Sierra Poker Flats	66 842
SHAEFFER		
David	El Dorado Mountain	581185
Geo	San Francisco San Francisco 10	277 67
Henry	Los Angeles Los Angeles	59 328
SHAEP		
J*	Nevada Eureka	61 382
SHAFE		
O	Nevada Eureka	61 388
SHAFER		
Adam	Sonoma Petaluma	69 550
Dan	Amador Twp 2	55 411
F	San Francisco San Francisco 8	681245
Fred	Butte Hamilton	56 522
George	Sonoma Armally	69 492
J	Butte Oro	56 674
J	El Dorado Diamond	58 809
J	El Dorado Diamond	58 810
J J	Nevada Bridgeport	61 472
J V	Tehama Red Bluff	70 916
Jacob	Marin Tomales	60 721
James	El Dorado Georgetown	58 674
John	Nevada Bridgeport	61 489
John	San Francisco San Francisco 4	681217
John	San Francisco San Francisco 4	681228
John	San Joaquin Stockton	641017
John	Shasta Shasta	66 672
John	Sierra Downieville	661029

California 1860 Census Index

Name	County Locale	M653 Roll	Page
SHAFER			
John	Yolo Cache Crk	72	597
John H	San Francisco San Francisco 8	681	262
Joseph J	Sierra Scales D	66	800
Josiah	Contra Costa Twp 2	57	550
P	Solano Vallejo	69	280
Phillip	Sierra Gibsonville	66	858
Robert	Santa Clara San Jose	65	385
S	Nevada Eureka	61	375
T J*	Nevada Bridgeport	61	472
SHAFF			
D D	Calaveras Twp 8	57	76
Sherman W	Tuolumne Sonora	71	189
SHAFFER			
A	Calaveras Twp 9	57	408
Adam	Calaveras Twp 8	57	78
Caroline	Calaveras Twp 8	57	79
Daniel	Calaveras Twp 8	57	107
David	El Dorado Mountain	581	185
F	Siskiyou Scott Ri	69	78
Fremont	Sacramento Franklin	63	310
George	Sonoma Armally	69	493
Godluch	Amador Twp 3	55	377
H	Nevada Eureka	61	361
J	Nevada Eureka	61	368
J	Sacramento Ward 1	63	68
J J	San Francisco San Francisco 8	681	152
J M	San Francisco San Francisco 3	67	10
J W	San Francisco San Francisco 3	67	10
John	Butte Mountain	56	741
John	Napa Napa	61	88
John	San Mateo Twp 1	65	66
John	Sierra Downieville	66	987
John	Siskiyou Callahan	69	12
L	Nevada Eureka	61	368
L	San Francisco San Francisco 5	67	548
M	Nevada Nevada	61	253
M E	Nevada Nevada	61	241
Ms	Siskiyou Callahan	69	12
N	Nevada Nevada	61	253
Peter	Placer Iona Hills	62	880
Richard	Los Angeles Los Angeles	59	336
Richard	Los Angeles Los Angeles	59	396
S	Nevada Eureka	61	368
S	Santa Clara Santa Clara	65	485
Samuel	Plumas Quincy	62	972
Uriah	Plumas Quincy	62	972
William	Calaveras Twp 10	57	266
SHAFFIN			
H H	Sierra Twp 5	66	941
SHAFFLETON			
C D*	Shasta Shasta	66	657
SHAFFNER			
M*	San Mateo Twp 1	65	67
SHAFLER			
Genievieva	San Francisco San Francisco 8	681	249
SHAFORT			
Seaman*	Humbolt Pacific	59	134
SHAFT			
Henry	El Dorado Kelsey	581	142
Kate	El Dorado Placerville	58	907
O	Siskiyou Cottonwoood	69	107
SHAFTER			
Frank	San Francisco San Francisco 9	681	059
Fred	Tuolumne Twp 1	71	245
Genievieva	San Francisco San Francisco 8	681	249
Geo	Butte Chico	56	559
J D	Marin Point Re	60	729
J McM	San Francisco San Francisco 6	67	409
M	Shasta Horsetown	66	699
SHAGE			
---	Amador No 6	55	433
SHAGFORD			
Jas	San Francisco San Francisco 1	68	907
SHAGISON			
Hanse	Tuolumne Montezuma	71	506
SHAGOIN			
M	El Dorado Kelsey	581	139
SHAGORN			
M	El Dorado Kelsey	581	139
SHAH			
---	Tehama Red Bluff	70	932
SHAHAM			
Michiel*	Nevada Red Dog	61	548
SHAHEN			
George H	Sierra Eureka	661	046
SHAHL			
W*	Nevada Eureka	61	343
SHAHWA			
---	Tulara Twp 1	71	116
SHAIFF			
E*	Nevada Nevada	61	253
SHAIN			
Warren*	Placer Michigan	62	807
SHAINER			
John*	Mariposa Coulterville	60	679
SHAKE			
J B	Butte Kimshaw	56	590
SHAKELMENNUE			
---	Tulara Twp 2	71	38
SHAKER			
---	Fresno Twp 2	59	111
T	Nevada Grass Valley	61	188
SHAKESPEARE			
Joseph	San Francisco San Francisco 2	67	556
SHAKESPERE			
W	El Dorado White Oaks	581	017
SHAKLEFORD			
T	Nevada Nevada	61	294
SHAKLIFORD			
T	Nevada Nevada	61	294
SHAKLY			
Alex	Amador Twp 2	55	269
SHAKSPEARE			
Charles	San Francisco San Francisco 11	67	157
O P	Colusa Butte Crk	57	466
SHAKSPERE			
Tiberius*	Calaveras Twp 6	57	114
SHAKUM			
Michiel*	Nevada Red Dog	61	548
SHALALDON			
Louis	Amador Twp 1	55	459
SHALDON			
Bishop	San Francisco San Francisco 7	681	327
SHALE			
Timothy	San Francisco San Francisco 10	67	172
SHALHOUSER			
P	El Dorado Diamond	58	808
SHALL			
C	Yolo Cottonwoood	72	650
Charles	Plumas Meadow Valley	62	932
Lewis	Placer Dutch Fl	62	720
Samuel P	Sierra Pine Grove	66	832
W W	Butte Kimshaw	56	595
Wallace	Yuba Marysville	72	941
SHALLAND			
Edwin	Los Angeles Tejon	59	526
SHALLAX			
August	Sierra Downieville	661	001
SHALLEY			
David	Tuolumne Jamestown	71	470
Davis	Tuolumne Twp 3	71	470
SHALLON			
Patrick	Amador Twp 2	55	303
SHALLOW			
David*	Nevada Bridgeport	61	442
Patrick*	Amador Twp 2	55	303
SHALLUCK			
Elisebeth*	Sacramento Ward 4	63	577
SHAM			
---	Calaveras Twp 8	57	106
---	Calaveras Twp 6	57	158
---	Calaveras Twp 7	57	37
---	Calaveras Twp 8	57	65
--- *	Calaveras Twp 8	57	83
---	Calaveras Twp 8	57	101
Ah	Calaveras Twp 7	57	34
B Neil*	El Dorado Georgetown	58	752
Geo	Alameda Brooklyn	55	101
Hee	San Francisco San Francisco 11	67	159
R New*	El Dorado Georgetown	58	752
Timothy*	Mariposa Coulterville	60	695
SHAMA			
John*	Mariposa Coulterville	60	679
SHAMADKE			
Richard*	Sierra Downieville	661	028
SHAMAELKE			
Richard*	Sierra Downieville	661	028
SHAMAKER			
J B	Siskiyou Scott Va	69	32
SHAMAN			
John L*	Siskiyou Yreka	69	179
Newell	Siskiyou Scott Va	69	23
SHAMAS			
Stephen*	Stanislaus Empire	70	732
SHAMBING			
H*	Nevada Eureka	61	352
SHAMBIUG			
H*	Nevada Eureka	61	352
SHAMBO			
A L	Sonoma Washington	69	678
Peter O	Sonoma Washington	69	678
SHAMBUIG			
H*	Nevada Eureka	61	352
SHAMBURG			
H	Nevada Eureka	61	352
SHAMEL			
B	El Dorado Coloma	581	108
SHAMER			
John*	Mariposa Coulterville	60	679
SHAMESSY			
William	San Francisco San Francisco 7	681	358
SHAMFILTER			
F*	Nevada Grass Valley	61	174
SHAMLIN			
M D	San Francisco San Francisco 5	67	485
SHAMP			
C	Nevada Grass Valley	61	146
J T*	Nevada Nevada	61	279
SHAMPLIN			
J F	Calaveras Twp 9	57	413
SHAMTON			
J R*	Nevada Grass Valley	61	189
SHAMUN			
Thomas*	Los Angeles San Pedro	59	480
SHAN			
---	Alameda Oakland	55	57
---	Calaveras Twp 4	57	305
---	El Dorado Coloma	581	084
---	El Dorado Coloma	581	086
---	El Dorado Cold Spring	581	099
---	El Dorado Kelsey	581	132
---	Nevada Bloomfield	61	530
---	Shasta Horsetown	66	711
---	Yuba Linda	72	991
--- *	San Francisco San Francisco 11	67	145
C J	Yolo Cottonwoood	72	650
E M	San Francisco San Francisco 9	68	954
George	Shasta Shasta	66	759
Gra	Stanislaus Branch	70	715
Hah	El Dorado Georgetown	58	748
James*	Mendocino Little L	60	837
John	Sacramento Ward 4	63	516
John*	Monterey Monterey	60	959
Key	El Dorado Big Bar	58	738
Marshal	San Francisco San Francisco 3	67	54
Pleasant	Yuba Fosters	72	840
Saml	Sacramento Ward 4	63	519
T W	Tehama Tehama	70	947
Thr*	San Francisco San Francisco 10	67	356
SHANABRUCK			
J L	Mendocino Anderson	60	868
SHANAGALL			
Geo	San Francisco San Francisco 3	67	76
SHANAHAN			
Ebenezor	Contra Costa Twp 3	57	606
John	Humbolt Bucksport	59	159
William	Sierra La Porte	66	789
William	Solano Vallejo	69	243
SHANAHEM			
William S	Sierra La Porte	66	789
SHANAL			
Henry	San Francisco San Francisco 4	681	217
SHANB			
Peter*	Siskiyou Yreka	69	168
SHANCEY			
Eleja*	Yuba Marysville	72	944
Elza*	Yuba Marysville	72	944
SHANCHAN			
C	Trinity Weaverville	701	056
SHANCK			
A J	Sierra Twp 7	66	866
SHANCY			
C	El Dorado Placerville	58	854
P	Siskiyou Scott Ri	69	69
SHAND			
G M	Nevada Eureka	61	347
J*	Nevada Eureka	61	347
SHANDER			
Eliiz	Yolo Cache Crk	72	589
Elija	Yolo Cache	72	589
Mary*	Sacramento Ward 3	63	459
SHANDLE			
John	Calaveras Twp 6	57	146
SHANDRANN			
Francis	Mendocino Little L	60	830
SHANDRINN			
Francis*	Mendocino Little L	60	830
SHANDROAN			
Francis*	Mendocino Little L	60	830
SHANE			
---	Placer Rattle Snake	62	630
Adam	Sonoma Santa Rosa	69	394
Carlos W	Humbolt Union	59	192
E	Placer Dutch Fl	62	719
Eliza	Santa Clara Fremont	65	439
Fredk	Amador Twp 3	55	370
G M*	Nevada Eureka	61	347
Geoge	Tuolumne Twp 3	71	464
J M	Tuolumne Twp 4	71	176
J*	Nevada Eureka	61	347
James*	Mendocino Little L	60	837

Name	County Locale	M653 Roll	Page
SHANE			
John	Calaveras Twp 10	57	276
Mac*	El Dorado Georgetown	58	703
Marshal	San Francisco San Francisco 3	67	54
Mary	Santa Clara Fremont	65	439
Nicholas	Calaveras Twp 5	57	194
Susan A*	Sonoma Sonoma	69	654
Timothy	Mariposa Coulterville	60	695
Valentine	Amador Twp 3	55	370
SHANEL			
Carp	San Bernardino San Bernardino	64	673
G M*	Nevada Eureka	61	347
J*	Nevada Eureka	61	347
SHANEMAN			
Fred*	El Dorado Georgetown	58	703
SHANENY			
Louis	San Francisco San Francisco 4	681	171
SHANER			
Henry	Tuolumne Twp 1	71	482
Heny	Tuolumne Sonora	71	482
SHANEY			
Johnson	El Dorado Georgetown	58	705
P*	Siskiyou Scott Ri	69	69
SHANG			
---	Alameda Oakland	55	24
---	Calaveras Twp 8	57	107
---	Calaveras Twp 10	57	273
---	Calaveras Twp 10	57	276
---	Calaveras Twp 10	57	281
---	Calaveras Twp 4	57	320
---	Calaveras Twp 4	57	321
---	Calaveras Twp 8	57	60
---	El Dorado Georgetown	58	703
---	El Dorado Mud Springs	58	961
---	Mariposa Twp 1	60	648
---	Mariposa Twp 1	60	657
---	Mariposa Twp 1	60	658
---	Trinity Big Flat	70	1042
---	Trinity Lewiston	70	956
Ah	Calaveras Twp 7	57	30
Ah*	Calaveras Twp 7	57	8
How	Yuba Marysville	72	868
SHANGE			
Hale*	Calaveras Twp 8	57	59
SHANGHERESSY			
James	Sierra Pine Grove	66	826
SHANGHI			
----	Amador Twp 5	55	363
SHANGHNESSEY			
William	Calaveras Twp 8	57	54
SHANGHNESSY			
Larry*	Sacramento Ward 1	63	76
SHANGIES			
Ecaimentia*	Twp 1	57	496
	Contra Costa		
SHANGLES			
William	Del Norte Crescent	58	630
SHANGLNESSY			
Ed*	Santa Clara Fremont	65	438
SHANION			
Thomas*	Los Angeles San Pedro	59	480
SHANK			
---	Sierra Port Win	66	794
A J	Sierra Twp 7	66	866
Georg	Nevada Bridgeport	61	501
James M	San Joaquin Elkhorn	64	997
John S	Marin Cortemad	60	781
Maggie	Yuba Slate Ro	72	698
Peter*	El Dorado Georgetown	58	697
SHANKE			
Hirann G	Tuolumne Twp 1	71	187
Peter	El Dorado Georgetown	58	697
SHANKEY			
Robt	Trinity E Weaver	70	1060
SHANKK			
Charles	El Dorado Mud Springs	58	990
SHANKLAND			
Robt	San Francisco San Francisco 10		197
		67	
SHANKLIM			
L S*	Nevada Eureka	61	380
SHANKLIN			
Frederick	Sierra Twp 7	66	872
J	Tuolumne Twp 1	71	187
J W	Tuolumne Sonora	71	187
L S*	Nevada Eureka	61	380
T B	Nevada Bloomfield	61	523
Y B	Nevada Bloomfield	61	523
SHANKLUN			
L S*	Nevada Eureka	61	380
SHANKLY			
L	Nevada Grass Valley	61	153
SHANKS			
C C	Trinity Trinity	70	974
Chas	Calaveras Twp 9	57	349
J	Trinity Trinity	70	970

Name	County Locale	M653 Roll	Page
SHANKS			
John	Placer Michigan	62	811
SHANLEY			
Eliza	San Francisco San Francisco 2	67	772
James	San Francisco San Francisco 4	681	125
Jas	Placer Twp 2	62	660
John P	Los Angeles Los Angeles	59	366
Pat	Placer Auburn	62	588
Wm	San Francisco San Francisco 2	67	772
SHANLT			
Peter*	El Dorado Georgetown	58	697
SHANLY			
J*	Sacramento Ward 4	63	606
SHANMLY			
Peter	Sierra Cox'S Bar	66	952
SHANNAHAN			
John	San Francisco San Francisco 1	68	835
SHANNAN			
Jas	Calaveras Twp 9	57	357
L*	Mariposa Twp 3	60	585
Mary	Sacramento Ward 3	63	442
SHANNANN			
Kraus	Tuolumne Columbia	71	474
SHANNBUSH			
S*	Amador Twp 2	55	318
SHANNER			
John*	Sacramento Granite	63	261
SHANNESY			
James	San Francisco San Francisco 1	68	840
SHANNO			
John	Yuba Parks Ba	72	779
SHANNON			
A	Tuolumne Twp 1	71	258
Alfred E	Calaveras Twp 8	57	56
Ann	San Francisco San Francisco 1	68	816
Bridget	San Francisco San Francisco 2	67	584
Catharine	San Francisco San Francisco 10		176
		67	
Dennis	Klamath S Fork	59	202
George	Nevada Red Dog	61	547
Giles	Tuolumne Twp 4	71	126
J	Nevada Grass Valley	61	187
J	Santa Clara Redwood	65	444
J	Yolo Putah	72	553
J W	Mendocino Round Va	60	878
James	Calaveras Twp 8	57	80
James	Tuolumne Twp 3	71	468
Jefferson M	Fresno Twp 2	59	3
Jno	Butte Chico	56	559
John	Contra Costa Twp 3	57	607
John	Humbolt Table Bl	59	139
John	Sacramento San Joaquin	63	367
John	San Bernardino San Bernadino	64	670
John	San Francisco San Francisco 9	681	048
John	Solano Benecia	69	316
John	Tulara Twp 1	71	102
Jos	Klamath Trinidad	59	219
Jos	San Francisco San Francisco 2	67	642
L	Nevada Grass Valley	61	176
M S	Sacramento San Joaquin	63	367
Mary	Calaveras Twp 8	57	66
Mary	San Francisco San Francisco 8	681	252
Michael	San Francisco San Francisco 9	68	990
Michl	San Francisco San Francisco 9	681	076
Patrick	Del Norte Klamath	58	653
Patrick	San Bernardino San Bernadino	64	670
Patrick	Solano Benecia	69	315
Robt	Napa Hot Springs	61	2
Saml W	Contra Costa Twp 2	57	558
Stephen	Sierra Whiskey	66	845
Thomas	Los Angeles Los Angeles	59	364
Thomas	Los Angeles San Pedro	59	480
Thomas	Placer Iona Hills	62	882
Thomas	Tuolumne Jamestown	71	441
Thomas	Yuba Marysville	72	892
Thomas B	Plumas Meadow Valley	62	899
W	Yolo Putah	72	585
William	Calaveras Twp 5	57	207
William J	Los Angeles Los Angeles	59	353
SHANNY			
Eliza	Yuba Marysville	72	944
SHANOCK			
Andrew	Placer Todds Va	62	787
SHANON			
Andrew	Amador Twp 2	55	303
D P	El Dorado Diamond	58	809
Lewis	Placer Rattle Snake	62	628
Lewis W*	Placer Rattle Snake	62	628
Patrick	Placer Michigan	62	833
SHANOY			
Thos*	Yolo Merritt	72	584
SHANROW			
N L	Marin San Rafael	60	761
SHANS			
Eliza Jane*	Sonoma Petaluma	69	618
SHANSLY			
Peter*	Sierra Cox'S Bar	66	952

Name	County Locale	M653 Roll	Page
SHANTON			
Thomas	Tuolumne Twp 2	71	304
SHANVVY			
Thos	Yolo Merritt	72	584
SHANY			
---	Calaveras Twp 10	57	270
---	Calaveras Twp 10	57	276
---	Calaveras Twp 10	57	278
---	Calaveras Twp 10	57	281
---	Calaveras Twp 4	57	321
H T	Amador Twp 7	55	416
SHANYR			
J B*	Calaveras Twp 6	57	114
SHAO			
---	Mariposa Coulterville	60	681
SHAOER			
John P	Calaveras Twp 5	57	210
SHAOLIN			
Pat	Butte Bidwell	56	707
SHAPELL			
Louie*	Amador Twp 4	55	244
Louis*	Amador Twp 4	55	244
SHAPEN			
A*	Calaveras Twp 9	57	396
SHAPER			
A	Calaveras Twp 9	57	396
James	Tehama Antelope	70	894
SHAPERA			
James	Mariposa Twp 3	60	621
SHAPLAY			
Williaj	Tuolumne Twp 5	71	497
SHAPLEY			
F	Alameda Oakland	55	43
SHAPLY			
David	Sonoma Petaluma	69	583
Sarah	Sonoma Petaluma	69	583
SHAPPELL			
L	Nevada Eureka	61	353
S	Nevada Eureka	61	353
SHAPPINE			
F*	Shasta French G	66	718
SHAPPINO			
F	Shasta French G	66	718
SHAR			
---	El Dorado Diamond	58	806
SHARAR			
Jeremiah	San Joaquin Oneal	64	939
SHARATT			
John S*	Siskiyou Yreka	69	178
John W	Siskiyou Yreka	69	178
SHARBARA			
Bastolme	Tuolumne Twp 5	71	499
SHARBAYMEN			
---	Mendocino Round Va	60	883
SHARCK			
Ah	Sacramento Mississipi	63	188
SHARD			
John	Fresno Twp 3	59	6
Wm J	Mendocino Round Va	60	877
SHARDINO			
Irdin*	Mariposa Twp 1	60	647
SHARDINOR			
John	Mariposa Twp 1	60	647
SHARE			
H J	Amador Twp 1	55	480
Henry	Tulara Twp 3	71	45
James*	Mendocino Little L	60	837
John*	Monterey Monterey	60	959
SHAREAS			
Augustus	Santa Clara San Jose	65	323
SHAREN			
---	San Francisco San Francisco 9	681	104
SHARER			
John	Mariposa Twp 3	60	573
John	San Joaquin Elkhorn	64	1000
Manwell*	Mariposa Twp 1	60	651
W D	El Dorado Kelsey	58	1126
SHARERAFT			
Wessen	El Dorado Greenwood	58	721
SHARES			
H M*	Tehama Red Bluff	70	905
John	El Dorado Mud Springs	58	953
John	Mariposa Twp 3	60	573
W D	El Dorado Kelsey	58	1126
SHAREUN			
Peter	Calaveras Twp 10	57	260
SHARFF			
E	Nevada Nevada	61	253
SHARIS			
B	El Dorado Mud Springs	58	953
SHARK			
H W	Siskiyou Callahan	69	7
Henry	Alameda Brooklyn	55	152
Jno	Sacramento Ward 3	63	451
John S	Marin Cortemad	60	781
Martin*	Calaveras Twp 8	57	108

California 1860 Census Index

Name	County Locale	M653 Roll	Page
SHARK			
Mich*	Sacramento Ward 4	63	553
Robert	Tulara Keyesville	71	59
Urich*	Sacramento Ward 4	63	553
William	San Francisco San Francisco 9	68	1100
SHARKE			
Joseph	Nevada Rough &	61	408
SHARKEREY			
Andrew	Alameda Brooklyn	55	156
SHARKEY			
Ann	Sacramento Sutter	63	297
Anne*	Sacramento Ward 4	63	544
Barney	Nevada Bloomfield	61	518
Barney	Nevada Bloomfield	61	529
Danl	Trinity Indian C	70	989
Dennis	Alameda Oakland	55	44
J P	Sacramento Ward 1	63	21
James	Sierra Twp 7	66	915
Jas*	San Francisco San Francisco 9	68	1047
W*	Butte Oregon	56	636
Wm	Butte Chico	56	560
Wm	Butte Oregon	56	636
Wm	San Francisco San Francisco 1	68	917
SHARKLEY			
Jane	San Francisco San Francisco 2	67	590
June	San Francisco San Francisco 2	67	590
Thomas	Yuba Marysville	72	960
SHARKLY			
Johnson*	El Dorado Georgetown	58	705
SHARKNESS			
Mary	San Francisco San Francisco 7	68	1398
SHARLENKER			
Jacob	San Francisco San Francisco 4	68	1147
SHARLEY			
J	Sutter Vernon	70	842
SHARO			
T A*	Mendocino Big Rock	60	872
SHARON			
Wm	San Francisco San Francisco 10	67	292
Zack	Placer Forest H	62	767
SHAROOAL			
A M*	Nevada Nevada	61	283
SHARP			
A	Sacramento Ward 3	63	424
A N*	Siskiyou Callahan	69	7
A W	Siskiyou Callahan	69	7
Anne	San Francisco San Francisco 2	67	618
Ben	Tuolumne Twp 3	71	430
C	El Dorado Georgetown	58	675
C D	Napa Hot Springs	61	25
C S	El Dorado Mud Springs	58	982
Charles	Nevada Bridgeport	61	505
Chas N	Sacramento Ward 3	63	467
D W H	El Dorado Placerville	58	828
D*	Sacramento Alabama	63	418
David	Los Angeles Los Angeles	59	351
David	Los Angeles Los Angeles	59	365
Elias	Humbolt Union	59	185
Ellen	Del Norte Crescent	58	649
F	Nevada Nevada	61	276
Frank	San Joaquin Castoria	64	898
Fred	San Francisco San Francisco 2	67	689
G	Nevada Grass Valley	61	196
Geo	Amador Twp 1	55	463
Geo	Butte Chico	56	533
George	Yuba Parks Ba	72	780
George F	San Francisco San Francisco 8	68	1309
Geroge F	San Francisco San Francisco 8	68	1309
H	Sacramento Lee	63	217
Henry	San Francisco San Francisco 7	68	1367
Henry	Yuba New York	72	737
Henry W	Calaveras Twp 5	57	209
J	El Dorado Diamond	58	788
J	Nevada Eureka	61	375
J	Nevada Eureka	61	382
J H	El Dorado Placerville	58	855
J H	Sacramento Georgian	63	337
J H	Yuba Long Bar	72	773
J W	Yuba Rose Bar	72	788
J*	Nevada Eureka	61	382
James	El Dorado Placerville	58	924
James	Placer Yankee J	62	759
James	San Joaquin Elkhorn	64	997
James	Siskiyou Scott Va	69	53
Jane	San Francisco San Francisco 2	67	656
Jasiah	Marin S Antoni	60	706
Jno	Sacramento Ward 4	63	608
John	Amador Twp 2	55	277
John	Merced Twp 1	60	907
John	Sierra Twp 5	66	937
John	Yuba New York	72	739
John	Yuba Long Bar	72	741
John W	Calaveras Twp 5	57	208
Joseph	El Dorado Casumnes	58	1177
Josiah	Marin S Antoni	60	706

Name	County Locale	M653 Roll	Page
SHARP			
L	Amador Twp 3	55	377
Louis	Mariposa Twp 3	60	567
M	Tuolumne Columbia	71	332
M G	Nevada Grass Valley	61	223
Marcia A *	Sacramento Ward 3	63	468
Maria A*	Sacramento Ward 3	63	468
Mary Ann	Butte Ophir	56	755
Mary C	Mendocino Ukiah	60	804
Mary P	Mendocino Ukiah	60	804
P F	Siskiyou Scott Va	69	41
Peter	San Joaquin Castoria	64	889
R B	Nevada Grass Valley	61	143
Rachel	San Bernardino San Bernadino	64	632
Saml	Placer Dutch Fl	62	721
Samuel	Contra Costa Twp 1	57	536
Simon	El Dorado Placerville	58	877
T B	Amador Twp 6	55	433
Thomas	Sierra Twp 5	66	926
Thomas	Tulara Twp 3	71	58
Tom	Sacramento Georgian	63	345
W	Siskiyou Cottonwood	69	107
W	Siskiyou Cottonwoood	69	108
W H	Sacramento Georgian	63	341
W H	Siskiyou Scott Va	69	22
W M	Siskiyou Cottonwoood	69	104
W R	Tehama Tehama	70	941
Wesley	Nevada Bloomfield	61	530
Wesly	Nevada Bridgeport	61	473
William	Amador Twp 1	55	456
William	Mendocino Little L	60	837
William H	San Francisco San Francisco 8	68	1273
Willm	Sacramento Lee	63	217
Wm	Nevada Eureka	61	345
Wm	Sacramento Ward 4	63	507
Wm	San Francisco San Francisco 2	67	753
Wm	Sonoma Santa Rosa	69	398
SHARPE			
Abraham	San Francisco San Francisco 11	67	131
Augusta	San Francisco San Francisco 11	67	132
Henry A	Alameda Brooklyn	55	77
James	Plumas Meadow Valley	62	901
Laura B	Plumas Quincy	62	917
S R	Alameda Brooklyn	55	127
William	San Francisco San Francisco 11	67	135
SHARPER			
Henry	Sacramento Centre	63	173
John	Placer Forest H	62	771
Robert	Nevada Rough &	61	432
SHARPLERS			
Benj	Alameda Oakland	55	53
SHARPLESS			
P	Siskiyou Scott Va	69	52
SHARPNACK			
G	Yolo Cache	72	621
SHARPS			
Louis	Mariposa Twp 3	60	567
William	Mendocino Little L	60	837
SHARPTON			
Geo	Merced Twp 2	60	921
William	Siskiyou Yreka	69	154
SHARRETT			
John	Siskiyou Yreka	69	179
SHARRIN			
Pat	Napa Hot Springs	61	20
SHARRON			
Andrew*	Amador Twp 2	55	303
Henry	Amador Twp 1	55	486
John	Sonoma Armally	69	488
N L	Marin San Rafael	60	761
P	Amador Twp 6	55	423
SHARROTT			
James	San Joaquin Stockton	64	1047
SHARROTTS			
John B	Siskiyou Yreka	69	144
SHARROY			
Thos*	Yolo Merritt	72	584
SHARSEY			
---	Sierra Twp 5	66	927
SHARTIS			
Saml	Butte Kimshaw	56	606
SHARTZER			
Hiram	Santa Clara Santa Clara	65	517
SHARY			
Daniel*	Siskiyou Callahan	69	8
John	Yolo Putah	72	551
Levi*	Stanislaus Oatvale	70	716
SHARZ			
Daniel	Siskiyou Callahan	69	8
SHASE			
John	El Dorado Kelsey	58	1130
SHASES			
H M*	Tehama Red Bluff	70	905

Name	County Locale	M653 Roll	Page
SHASES			
John*	Mariposa Twp 3	60	573
SHASH			
Martin*	Calaveras Twp 8	57	108
SHASPO			
---	Mendocino Round Va	60	883
SHASRIN			
Pat*	Napa Hot Springs	61	20
SHASVIN			
Pat*	Napa Hot Springs	61	20
SHAT			
Jacob	Tuolumne Twp 1	71	193
M B*	Colusa Monroeville	57	440
Song	San Francisco San Francisco 11	67	160
Tow	San Francisco San Francisco 11	67	160
SHATENKIRK			
John	El Dorado Mud Springs	58	983
SHATER			
Wm	Sacramento Ward 1	63	43
SHATERY			
J*	Nevada Grass Valley	61	215
Z	Nevada Grass Valley	61	215
SHATH			
John	San Francisco San Francisco 7	68	1395
SHATHICK			
Elisebeth*	Sacramento Ward 4	63	577
SHATHOCK			
John L*	San Francisco San Francisco 3	67	80
SHATIRY			
J*	Nevada Grass Valley	61	215
Z	Nevada Grass Valley	61	215
SHATLAUS			
Conrad	Placer Dutch Fl	62	724
SHATLUCH			
Marrison	Sonoma Santa Rosa	69	407
SHATLUCK			
Chas F	Sacramento Ward 1	63	39
Frank W	Sonoma Santa Rosa	69	387
SHATON			
Jas	San Francisco San Francisco 2	67	763
Jos	San Francisco San Francisco 2	67	763
SHATRUCK			
Chas W	Sacramento Ward 4	63	503
SHATS			
E W	Sutter Bear Rvr	70	821
SHATTACK			
Phebe J*	Alameda Brooklyn	55	87
SHATTEN			
Henry L	Colusa Muion	57	458
SHATTER			
Martin*	Mariposa Twp 3	60	621
SHATTERCK			
Phebe J*	Alameda Brooklyn	55	87
SHATTERIK			
Mary A	Alameda Oakland	55	15
SHATTICK			
D	Calaveras Twp 9	57	401
SHATTON			
John	Santa Cruz Pescadero	66	645
T H	Yuba New York	72	729
SHATTROCK			
John L*	San Francisco San Francisco 3	67	80
SHATTU			
Martin*	Mariposa Twp 3	60	621
SHATTUCK			
Chas F	Sacramento Ward 1	63	39
Chas F	San Francisco San Francisco 8	68	1292
Chas W	Sacramento Ward 3	63	430
D	Calaveras Twp 9	57	401
David	Sonoma Sonoma	69	645
David O	San Francisco San Francisco 11	67	100
Elisebeth*	Sacramento Ward 4	63	577
F D	Alameda Oakland	55	9
Frank W	Sonoma Santa Rosa	69	387
H C	Solano Suisan	69	237
Harrison	Sonoma Santa Rosa	69	407
J	Nevada Grass Valley	61	225
J W	Sonoma Santa Rosa	69	387
Munroe	Monterey Pajaro	60	1020
Orville J*	Sierra Pine Grove	66	826
Phebe J	Alameda Brooklyn	55	87
Thomas	Solano Vallejo	69	257
Wm	Sacramento Ward 4	63	504
SHATTWICK			
Thomas*	Solano Vallejo	69	257
SHATWELL			
S W	Tuolumne Twp 2	71	326
SHATWILL			
Benj	Amador Twp 6	55	437
SHATZELL			
W H	Siskiyou Scott Va	69	41
SHAU			

Name	County Locale	M653 Roll Page
SHAU		
---*	San Francisco San Francisco 11	145 67
SHAUAHAN		
D W	Colusa Colusi	57 420
SHAUB		
Peter	Siskiyou Yreka	69 168
SHAUCY		
P*	Siskiyou Scott Ri	69 69
SHAUD		
G M*	Nevada Eureka	61 347
J*	Nevada Eureka	61 347
SHAUG		
---*	Calaveras Twp 10	57 278
SHAUGHNEPY		
Michael San Francisco San Francisco 10		238 67
SHAUGHNESSY		
Kate O San Francisco San Francisco 10		247 67
Larry	Sacramento Ward 1	63 76
Michael San Francisco San Francisco 10		238 67
SHAUKLIM		
L S*	Nevada Eureka	61 380
S*	Nevada Eureka	61 380
SHAUKLUN		
L S*	Nevada Eureka	61 380
SHAUL		
Jams	Placer Iona Hills	62 864
Peter San Francisco San Francisco 1		68 918
SHAULDING		
J	Tuolumne Twp 2	71 407
Luther San Joaquin Elkhorn		64 996
SHAULT		
Peter*	El Dorado Georgetown	58 697
SHAULY		
J*	Sacramento Ward 4	63 606
SHAUM		
John	Sacramento Granite	63 261
SHAUN		
---	Amador Twp 6	55 428
Joseph	El Dorado White Oaks	581018
See San Francisco San Francisco 11		159 67
SHAUNBUSH		
S*	Amador Twp 2	55 318
SHAUNGH		
Phillip J*	El Dorado Georgetown	58 707
SHAUNN		
John*	Sacramento Granite	63 261
SHAUOAL		
A M*	Nevada Nevada	61 283
SHAUR		
B New*	El Dorado Georgetown	58 752
George	Tuolumne Twp 3	71 464
SHAUSLY		
Peter*	Sierra Cox'S Bar	66 952
SHAUWN		
Michl San Francisco San Francisco 9		681076
SHAUY		
---*	Calaveras Twp 10	57 278
SHAVE		
J M	Tuolumne Garrote	71 176
Nicholas	Calaveras Twp 5	57 194
SHAVEN		
Morgan	San Joaquin Castoria	64 892
SHAVER		
Abram	Calaveras Twp 6	57 187
H J	Tuolumne Twp 2	71 382
Henry San Francisco San Francisco 12		363 67
John P	Calaveras Twp 5	57 210
N	Sacramento Brighton	63 206
Stephen R*	Sierra Morristown	661053
SHAVERS		
John*	Mariposa Twp 3	60 573
SHAVFER		
Hain*	Calaveras Twp 5	57 187
SHAVIN		
Bridget San Francisco San Francisco 7		681385
SHAVLIN		
Pat	Butte Bidwell	56 707
SHAW		
---	Amador Twp 7	55 414
---	Amador Twp 6	55 430
---	Calaveras Twp 4	57 305
---	Calaveras Twp 4	57 307
---	Calaveras Twp 9	57 375
---	Del Norte Klamath	58 655
---	El Dorado Kelsey	581133
---	Fresno Twp 1	59 25
---	Mariposa Twp 1	60 659
---	Mariposa Coulterville	60 681
---	Shasta Horsetown	66 711
---	Sierra Downieville	66 998

Name	County Locale	M653 Roll Page
SHAW		
A	Sacramento Dry Crk	63 375
A	San Mateo Twp 3	65 92
A M	Nevada Grass Valley	61 214
A S	Butte Oro	56 680
Ah	Yuba Suida	72 991
Albert	Mariposa Twp 3	60 575
Albert B San Joaquin Elliott		64 941
Alex	Butte Chico	56 559
Alex	Klamath S Fork	59 205
Alfred	Yuba Marysville	72 970
Allen	Marin Cortemad	60 754
Andrew	El Dorado White Oaks	581017
Andrew M*	Tuolumne Twp 5	71 512
Arthur	Calaveras Twp 9	57 402
B F	Napa Clear Lake	61 125
Benj J	Tuolumne Green Springs	71 527
Benjh J	Tuolumne Twp 5	71 527
C	San Francisco San Francisco 5	67 493
Charles	Contra Costa Twp 1	57 510
Charles	Tuolumne Twp 5	71 500
Charles	Yuba Bear Rvr	72 998
Clara B	Klamath Salmon	59 209
D B	Sonoma Santa Rosa	69 424
D H	Siskiyou Callahan	69 16
D W	Sacramento Dry Crk	63 375
D W	Tuolumne Twp 4	71 141
Daniel	Plumas Quincy	62 953
Danl	Sonoma Vallejo	69 618
Danl	Tuolumne Twp 2	71 285
Danl	Tuolumne Twp 2	71 288
E A	Placer Christia	62 736
E M*	San Francisco San Francisco 9	68 954
E W	Tuolumne Twp 2	71 345
Ed*	Sacramento Cosummes	63 383
Edwin	Siskiyou Scott Va	69 25
Edwin	Yuba New York	72 724
Eliza	Sacramento Ward 1	63 93
Eliza	San Francisco San Francisco 9	681003
Eliza	San Francisco San Francisco 6	67 428
Eliza S	San Francisco San Francisco 6	67 428
Ellen	San Francisco San Francisco 6	67 424
F	Calaveras Twp 9	57 409
F	Santa Clara San Jose	65 386
Frances A	Napa Napa	61 74
Francis A	Napa Napa	61 74
Frank	Contra Costa Twp 3	57 593
Frederick San Francisco San Francisco 7		681427
G	Nevada Grass Valley	61 169
G	Shasta Horsetown	66 704
G E	Sierra Downieville	66 965
G W	Butte Cascade	56 694
G W	Butte Bidwell	56 715
Gabriel	Amador Twp 2	55 291
Geo	Alameda Brooklyn	55 101
Geo	Trinity Trinity	70 973
Geo G	El Dorado Eldorado	58 935
Geo M	Alameda Oakland	55 19
Geo W	Butte Mountain	56 740
George	Shasta Shasta	66 759
George	Yuba Marysville	72 978
H	Nevada Grass Valley	61 190
Harry	San Mateo Twp 3	65 86
Henry	Alameda Oakland	55 10
Henry	El Dorado Coloma	581084
Henry	Placer Michigan	62 827
Isaac	San Mateo Twp 3	65 111
Isaac	Yuba Marysville	72 893
Isaiah	Santa Clara Gilroy	65 232
J	Nevada Grass Valley	61 214
J	Sacramento Ward 1	63 9
J A	Sonoma Santa Rosa	69 401
J C	Tuolumne Twp 2	71 394
J E	Trinity Rush Crk	70 965
J K	Sonoma Washington	69 668
J L	Butte Cascade	56 700
J M	Tehama Cottonwood	70 901
J W	San Francisco San Francisco 5	67 551
J W*	Placer Forest H	62 806
Jacob	Butte Hamilton	56 518
Jacob	Colusa Spring Valley	57 434
James	Calaveras Twp 5	57 238
James	Sacramento Dry Crk	63 370
James	Sonoma Santa Rosa	69 400
James	Tuolumne Twp 1	71 186
James B San Bernardino Santa Barbara		64 202
James J	Sierra Twp 7	66 881
James R	Plumas Meadow Valley	62 911
James S	Tuolumne Columbia	71 305
James*	Mendocino Little L	60 837
Jno N	Sacramento Natonia	63 279
John	Butte Ophir	56 755
John	Fresno Twp 1	59 5
John	Monterey Monterey	60 959
John	Nevada Washington	61 331
John	Nevada Washington	61 341

Name	County Locale	M653 Roll Page
SHAW		
John	Sacramento San Joaquin	63 363
John	San Francisco San Francisco 6	67 424
John	Solano Vacaville	69 323
John	Tehama Lassen	70 874
John	Tuolumne Twp 1	71 201
John O	Santa Clara San Jose	65 295
John R	Yolo Putah	72 586
Jos	San Francisco San Francisco 1	68 899
Joseph	Los Angeles Los Angeles	59 366
L B	Merced Twp 1	60 896
L C	San Francisco San Francisco 4	681109
L W	Trinity Bates	70 967
Levi*	Stanislaus Oatvale	70 716
Levy C	Placer Stewart	62 606
Luke	Placer Virginia	62 677
M	Sacramento Brighton	63 206
Margaret	San Joaquin Stockton	641017
Matthew	Amador Twp 1	55 474
Michael	Siskiyou Scott Va	69 37
Moses	San Francisco San Francisco 11	143 67
N R	Sonoma Bodega	69 520
Oliver P	Monterey Alisal	601026
Oliver W	Calaveras Twp 5	57 229
Phillip	Santa Clara Santa Clara	65 495
R	El Dorado Placerville	58 884
R	Santa Clara Redwood	65 456
R W	Calaveras Twp 8	57 80
Rich	Butte Kimshaw	56 581
Richard	El Dorado Big Bar	58 744
Richard	Placer Forest H	62 798
Robert	Nevada Eureka	61 357
Robt	Santa Clara Santa Clara	65 522
Robt	Trinity Hay Fork	70 993
S B	Merced Twp 1	60 896
S B	Tehama Lassen	70 877
S C	San Francisco San Francisco 4	681109
S C	San Francisco San Francisco 6	67 442
S U	San Francisco San Francisco 9	68 983
S W	Trinity Bates	70 967
Saml J	Solano Vallejo	69 257
Semansha	Butte Mountain	56 740
Semantha	Butte Mountain	56 740
Seth L	Humbolt Pacific	59 136
Solomon San Francisco San Francisco 4		681154
Stephen	Santa Clara San Jose	65 340
Susan A	Sonoma Sonoma	69 654
Sylvester	San Joaquin Douglass	64 919
T A*	Mendocino Big Rock	60 872
T W	Tuolumne Big Oak	71 141
Thomas	Marin San Rafael	60 762
Thos D	Tuolumne Sonora	71 483
Thos Ogg San Francisco San Francisco 10		337 67
Thos T	San Mateo Twp 3	65 78
W	El Dorado Placerville	58 884
W M	Sacramento Ward 4	63 548
W M	Siskiyou Callahan	69 16
William	Placer Iona Hills	62 872
William	Plumas Quincy	62 953
William P San Joaquin Stockton		641068
Wm	San Francisco San Francisco 2	67 618
Wm	Santa Clara San Jose	65 379
Wm	Tuolumne Big Oak	71 141
Wm A	Humbolt Mattole	59 123
Wm H	Santa Clara Gilroy	65 226
Wm J	San Francisco San Francisco 3	67 18
SHAWAY		
Ellis	Sonoma Mendocino	69 456
SHAWBURG		
H	Nevada Eureka	61 352
SHAWDER		
Mary*	Sacramento Ward 3	63 459
SHAWEL		
---*	Mendocino Round Va	60 883
SHAWIL		
---*	Mendocino Round Va	60 883
SHAWKLIN		
John	Sonoma Bodega	69 537
SHAWL		
Manuel	Placer Forest H	62 803
SHAWNBUSH		
S	Amador Twp 2	55 318
SHAWNESS		
J H	Sierra Excelsior	661033
SHAWOAL		
A M*	Nevada Nevada	61 283
SHAWP		
J T	Nevada Nevada	61 279
SHAWS		
Andrew	San Joaquin Douglass	64 924
Eliza Jane*	Sonoma Petaluma	69 618
Susan A*	Sonoma Sonoma	69 654
SHAWSEN		
J	Siskiyou Scott Ri	69 78

California 1860 Census Index

Name	County Locale	M653 Roll	Page
SHAXESPEARE			
Joseph*	San Francisco San Francisco 2	67	556
SHAY			
---	Calaveras Twp 4	57	299
Augustus	Placer Iona Hills	62	885
D	Nevada Grass Valley	61	156
Danl W	Placer Dutch Fl	62	714
J	Nevada Eureka	61	389
James	San Francisco San Francisco 3	67	32
John	San Francisco San Francisco 3	67	35
John	San Francisco San Francisco 3	67	75
John	Sierra Downieville	66	1024
John*	San Francisco San Francisco 3	67	19
Margt	San Francisco San Francisco 9	68	1000
Mary	San Francisco San Francisco 3	67	76
P O	San Francisco San Francisco 5	67	537
Patrick	Calaveras Twp 7	57	42
Peter	Sacramento Ward 4	63	532
Thos C	Shasta Shasta	66	653
Walter	San Bernardino San Salvador	64	649
Wm	Sonoma Petaluma	69	598
SHAYE			
---*	Amador Twp 6	55	433
SHAYER			
E L	Calaveras Twp 8	57	55
SHAYMAN			
Bernard	Placer Iona Hills	62	864
SHAYNOLDS			
G	Mariposa Twp 3	60	606
SHAYOCK			
S*	Yolo Putah	72	588
SHAYS			
M	San Francisco San Francisco 5	67	523
SHAYTHE			
Chas	Del Norte Happy Ca	58	670
Edwd	Del Norte Happy Ca	58	670
SHAYTOP			
---	Mendocino Round Va	60	883
SHCILL			
Christian	Sierra Twp 5	66	943
SHCNEIBOUY			
Danl*	Plumas Quincy	62	984
SHE CONG			
---	San Joaquin Stockton	64	1087
SHE			
---	Amador Twp 2	55	311
---	Amador Twp 1	55	490
---	Butte Oregon	56	638
---	Calaveras Twp 6	57	164
---	Calaveras Twp 10	57	284
---	Sierra Downieville	66	998
---	Tuolumne Big Oak	71	147
---*	Sacramento Cosumnes	63	407
Ah	Tuolumne Twp 4	71	147
Chick	Yuba Long Bar	72	760
Co	Sierra Twp 5	66	939
Fling	Yuba Parks Ba	72	780
Lee	Butte Ophir	56	801
Lie	Sierra Downieville	66	1014
Lio	Sierra Downieville	66	1014
Loo	Yuba Long Bar	72	763
Ming	Amador Twp 2	55	311
Miny	Amador Twp 2	55	311
Num	Amador Twp 2	55	311
Ong	Yuba Long Bar	72	759
Ti	Calaveras Twp 5	57	245
SHE?ON			
Eugen	Shasta Horsetown	66	692
SHEA			
---	Amador Twp 5	55	331
Ann	San Francisco San Francisco 10	67	219
Edward	Trinity E Weaver	70	1060
Ellen	Sacramento Ward 3	63	438
Eugine	Los Angeles Tejon	59	522
Frank	Klamath Liberty	59	231
James	San Francisco San Francisco 5	67	543
Jas	Placer Auburn	62	587
Jas M	Sacramento Ward 1	63	23
John	Calaveras Twp 8	57	72
John	Shasta French G	66	719
John A	Tuolumne Twp 2	71	334
Joseph	Solano Vallejo	69	270
M	Shasta French G	66	716
Mary	Placer Folsom	62	647
Mary	San Francisco San Francisco 10	67	232
Mary	San Francisco San Francisco 1	68	876
Michael	San Francisco San Francisco 1	68	835
Michael	Solano Suisan	69	229
P O	Nevada Grass Valley	61	225
Patrick	Colusa Spring Valley	57	430
Patrick	San Francisco San Francisco 10	67	219
Patrick*	Placer Yankee J	62	780
Peter	Sacramento Ward 1	63	64
SHEA			
Peter M	Placer Auburn	62	593
Roland H	Sacramento Ward 1	63	21
Thorntin	Sacramento Granite	63	259
Thos O	Butte Ophir	56	777
William G	San Luis Obispo San Luis Obispo	65	8
SHEABIN			
B F*	Stanislaus Empire	70	730
SHEACH			
Nick	Sierra Downieville	66	1011
SHEAD			
Vincent*	Yuba Fosters	72	835
SHEADIE			
Nicholas*	Yolo Cottonwoood	72	658
SHEAH			
T*	El Dorado Georgetown	58	675
SHEALER			
B F	Amador Twp 7	55	419
J H	Amador Twp 7	55	418
James	Amador Twp 7	55	417
SHEALY			
George	Calaveras Twp 9	57	366
O Myers*	Calaveras Twp 9	57	366
O Myons	Calaveras Twp 9	57	366
SHEAN			
Danl	Amador Twp 3	55	397
Geo	Butte Wyandotte	56	672
Hang*	San Francisco San Francisco 11	67	145
J	Nevada Grass Valley	61	213
J	Nevada Eureka	61	363
Johanna	San Joaquin Castoria	64	873
SHEANER			
F A	Siskiyou Scott Ri	69	71
T J*	Calaveras Twp 9	57	393
SHEANG			
---	Marin Cortemad	60	791
SHEAR			
---	El Dorado Coloma	58	1105
Abraham M	San Francisco San Francisco 11	67	151
Abram	Calaveras Twp 6	57	122
Charles H	San Joaquin Elkhorn	64	986
Conrad	San Francisco San Francisco 1	68	843
E E	Sacramento Casumnes	63	381
Feet	Amador Twp 5	55	362
J B	Siskiyou Scott Va	69	29
J B	Siskiyou Scott Va	69	55
John	Calaveras Twp 9	57	389
Jos N	Klamath Klamath	59	225
M*	San Francisco San Francisco 9	68	1062
Richard B	San Francisco San Francisco 7	68	1338
Robt	San Francisco San Francisco 9	68	1032
Waldon	San Francisco San Francisco 8	68	1324
Waldon	San Francisco San Francisco 7	68	1352
SHEARAKER			
Andrew	Calaveras Twp 6	57	144
SHEARE			
Patrick	Calaveras Twp 5	57	195
Thomasx	Calaveras Twp 5	57	195
SHEARER			
Albert	San Joaquin Oneal	64	930
Charles	San Joaquin Elkhorn	64	993
Edwin	Siskiyou Yreka	69	171
H M	El Dorado Placerville	58	850
Jas	Amador Twp 1	55	484
John	Plumas Quincy	62	980
Lewis	San Francisco San Francisco 2	67	659
M K	El Dorado Placerville	58	850
M M	El Dorado Diamond	58	795
Menick*	Marin Tomales	60	714
Merick*	Marin Tomales	60	714
Merrick	Marin Tomales	60	714
Robert	Siskiyou Yreka	69	130
T J*	Calaveras Twp 9	57	393
Tho	Siskiyou Cottonwoood	69	107
Thod	Siskiyou Cottonwoood	69	107
Volmey	Calaveras Twp 9	57	366
Volmez*	Calaveras Twp 9	57	366
Volmoy*	Calaveras Twp 9	57	366
Volney*	Calaveras Twp 9	57	366
Wm	Butte Ophir	56	747
Wm	Solano Vallejo	69	257
SHEARES			
Jno	Alameda Brooklyn	55	107
W	Nevada Nevada	61	319
SHEAREST			
Robert	Siskiyou Yreka	69	130
Tho*	Siskiyou Cottonwoood	69	107
SHEARHEN			
Edmond	Butte Ophir	56	782
Edmund	Butte Ophir	56	781
SHEARIN			
T J*	Calaveras Twp 9	57	393
SHEARMAN			
Freeman	Sierra Twp 5	66	925
SHEARN			
Owen	Calaveras Twp 5	57	178
P	El Dorado Diamond	58	775
Thomas	Calaveras Twp 5	57	195
SHEARNEY			
H	Merced Twp 2	60	920
SHEARS			
Edward	Placer Auburn	62	559
Frederick	Solano Suisan	69	239
J	Calaveras Twp 9	57	387
Jo	Calaveras Twp 9	57	387
William	San Francisco San Francisco 11	67	123
Wm*	Sonoma Petaluma	69	598
SHEARWOOD			
D W	Tehama Tehama	70	941
SHEATER			
Jackson	Amador Twp 7	55	418
SHEATHERS			
Henri	Placer Dutch Fl	62	724
SHEAVER			
Wm*	Solano Vallejo	69	257
SHEAVES			
A D	San Francisco San Francisco 9	68	1086
SHEAY			
Thomas	Los Angeles Los Angeles	59	365
Wm	Sonoma Petaluma	69	598
SHEBANK			
L*	Nevada Grass Valley	61	150
SHEBATE			
---	Mendocino Round Va	60	882
SHEBBER			
---	Sierra La Porte	66	782
SHEBEL			
George	San Francisco San Francisco 4	68	1158
SHEBERT			
A	San Francisco San Francisco 9	68	1085
SHEBLER			
J C	Sierra Downieville	66	961
SHEBLEY			
Joseph*	Nevada Red Dog	61	541
SHEBNMIAH			
---*	Mendocino Twp 1	60	888
SHEBUMIAH			
---*	Mendocino Twp 1	60	888
SHEBY			
W	San Francisco San Francisco 1	68	926
SHECAL			
---*	Mendocino Round Va	60	881
SHECHAN			
Bernistino	San Bernardino Santa Barbara	64	204
Ellen	San Joaquin Castoria	64	874
SHECHEY			
John	Santa Cruz Pajaro	66	525
SHECK			
Christ	Siskiyou Yreka	69	135
SHECKELLS			
James	Amador Twp 2	55	325
John	Amador Twp 2	55	321
SHECKELS			
Hezakiah	Calaveras Twp 4	57	311
SHECKITTON			
J	Nevada Nevada	61	287
SHECKY			
George	San Francisco San Francisco 7	68	1399
SHECY			
Jeremiah	Santa Cruz Pajaro	66	525
SHED			
Alvin	San Joaquin Castoria	64	877
Charles	San Francisco San Francisco 8	68	1302
Chas	Sacramento Granite	63	230
E K	Shasta Shasta	66	667
George	San Francisco San Francisco 2	67	672
George H	San Joaquin Oneal	64	940
Macks	Santa Clara San Jose	65	339
Roland H*	Sacramento Ward 1	63	21
SHEDAN			
Thomas	Yuba Fosters	72	824
SHEDBACK			
William	Sierra Pine Grove	66	826
SHEDBUCK			
William*	Sierra Pine Grove	66	826
SHEDD			
Chas	San Francisco San Francisco 1	68	918
Edwd D	San Francisco San Francisco 6	67	432
John H	Tuolumne Twp 2	71	312
SHEDE			
George	Sacramento Ward 4	63	554
SHEDEL			
Geo	San Francisco San Francisco 9	68	960
SHEDO			
---	Calaveras Twp 10	57	278
SHEDON			
J P	San Francisco San Francisco 9	68	1062
R H	Sonoma Armally	69	486

Copyright 1999 by Heritage Quest, a division of AGLL, Inc., Bountiful, UT 84011. All rights reserved

Name	County Locale	M653 RollPage
SHEDWICK		
Fred	Tuolumne Jamestown	71 441
SHEE		
---	Plumas Meadow Valley	62 913
---	San Francisco San Francisco 9	681093
---	San Joaquin Elliott	641103
---	Tuolumne Columbia	71 307
---	Tuolumne Twp 3	71 466
---	Tuolumne Twp 5	71 523
---	Tuolumne Twp 6	71 541
---	Yolo No E Twp	72 675
---	Yolo No E Twp	72 683
---	Yolo Slate Ra	72 706
---	Yolo Slate Ra	72 713
---	Yuba Slate Ro	72 713
Ah	Tuolumne Twp 2	71 307
Arthur*	San Mateo Twp 1	65 48
Ging	Yuba Marysville	72 916
Gueg	Yuba Marysville	72 916
Ling	Yuba Long Bar	72 762
Show	El Dorado Placerville	58 831
SHEEBARN		
Michael A	Yuba Marysville	72 868
SHEECK		
Christ*	Siskiyou Yreka	69 135
SHEEHAN		
B*	Napa Hot Springs	61 6
Cashann*	Napa Hot Springs	61 6
Charles	San Diego Colorado	64 807
Margaret	Sierra Downieville	66 966
Patrick	Santa Clara San Jose	65 333
Timothy	Sierra Twp 7	66 907
Timothy	Yuba Marysville	72 954
SHEEHEY		
Dennis	Siskiyou Shasta Valley	69 119
SHEEHY		
Timothy	Santa Cruz Pajaro	66 559
SHEEKEY		
Dennis*	Siskiyou Shasta Valley	69 119
SHEEL		
Charles*	San Francisco San Francisco 8	681302
SHEELER		
Julia	Amador Twp 6	55 424
Saml	Amador Twp 3	55 388
SHEELESIDES		
Alexander	Yuba Bear Rvr	72 997
SHEEMAKE		
A M*	Nevada Grass Valley	61 188
SHEEMAN		
Thomas	Sierra Downieville	661016
SHEEN		
---	Amador Twp 5	55 365
---	San Francisco San Francisco 11	145 67
SHEENAN		
Daniel	San Joaquin Castoria	64 874
SHEENEN		
Patrick	Marin Novato	60 737
SHEENING		
Caleb*	Sierra Downieville	661003
SHEEP		
---	Amador Twp 7	55 412
SHEER		
Antonio	Plumas Quincy	62 938
Michael*	Stanislaus Buena Village	70 724
W*	San Francisco San Francisco 5	67 498
SHEERD		
Vincent*	Yuba Fosters	72 835
SHEERE		
Christian	Alameda Brooklyn	55 148
SHEERIDAN		
Peter	San Francisco San Francisco 9	68 974
SHEERIN		
Danl	Sonoma Santa Rosa	69 400
SHEERLY		
William	Shasta Millvill	66 749
SHEET		
H C	Shasta Shasta	66 664
SHEETAN		
Daniel	San Francisco San Francisco 9	68 937
SHEETHAMBE		
A M*	Tuolumne Twp 2	71 281
SHEETS		
Andrew*	Santa Cruz Pescadero	66 648
Brewer	El Dorado Placerville	58 895
D	Solano Suisan	69 212
T F	Nevada Bridgeport	61 497
SHEEVER		
Wm S	Sierra Downieville	66 960
SHEEVEY		
Andias*	Tuolumne Twp 1	71 227
Audias*	Tuolumne Twp 1	71 227
SHEFEHIRD		
Jas T	Butte Kimshaw	56 578
SHEFF		
Michael*	Yuba Linda	72 987

Name	County Locale	M653 RollPage
SHEFFEL		
Chas	Sonoma Sonoma	69 638
SHEFFIELD		
Edward	San Francisco San Francisco 8	681320
Jno	San Francisco San Francisco 10	331 67
John	Los Angeles Los Angeles	59 328
S H	Nevada Rough &	61 422
S R	Klamath Liberty	59 233
Thomas	Plumas Quincy	62 983
W E	Sutter Butte	70 794
SHEFFIL		
Chas	Sonoma Sonoma	69 638
SHEFFLE		
S F	Calaveras Twp 9	57 369
SHEFTER		
Fred	Tuolumne Twp 1	71 245
SHEGAN		
Timothy	San Francisco San Francisco 7	681377
SHEHAN		
Dennis	Calaveras Twp 5	57 195
Jas	Sacramento Ward 1	63 14
Jas	Sacramento Ward 1	63 43
Micheil	Nevada Little Y	61 531
Morris	Nevada Rough &	61 400
Thomas*	Yuba Foster B	72 824
Wm	Sacramento Ward 1	63 117
SHEHE		
Krobt	Napa Napa	61 73
Robt	Napa Napa	61 73
SHEHEN		
Hensy	El Dorado Big Bar	58 738
SHEHERD		
Benj F*	Napa Yount	61 41
SHEHLEHEN		
Fred	Placer Ophir	62 652
SHEHON		
Ellen*	Yuba New York	72 724
SHEHUN		
Micheil	Nevada Little Y	61 531
SHEI		
---	Yuba Slate Ro	72 706
SHEICT		
John*	Alameda Oakland	55 58
SHEIDEN		
J*	Nevada Eureka	61 375
SHEIDER		
Chas	Butte Oregon	56 626
SHEIDS		
J C	Shasta Shasta	66 687
SHEIER		
Jas P	Calaveras Twp 6	57 122
SHEIK		
---	Tulara Twp 2	71 36
Michael	Plumas Quincy	62 924
SHEIKE		
---*	Tulara Visalia	71 36
SHEIL		
Catherine	Sacramento Sutter	63 294
SHEILDS		
John	San Joaquin Douglass	64 915
SHEILS		
A	Shasta Millvill	66 751
SHEIM		
John*	Santa Cruz Pescadero	66 646
SHEIMAN		
Jas	Butte Cascade	56 697
SHEIN		
Louis	Placer Iona Hills	62 889
SHEIT		
August	Shasta French G	66 719
SHEITT		
August*	Sierra St Louis	66 806
SHEIVER		
Wm S*	Sierra Downieville	66 960
SHEIVIN		
L H*	Merced Twp 1	60 905
SHEK		
---	Tuolumne Twp 6	71 537
SHEKASE		
Mary	San Joaquin Stockton	641066
SHEKEL		
Stephen R	Sacramento American	63 159
SHEKON		
Ellen	Yuba New York	72 724
Eugen*	Shasta Horsetown	66 692
SHEKUN		
Dennis	Calaveras Twp 5	57 195
SHELADEN		
F	Yolo Cache Crk	72 610
SHELAN		
Dem*	Sacramento Natonia	63 286
Den	Sacramento Natonia	63 286
Dene*	Sacramento Natonia	63 286
Dern*	Sacramento Natonia	63 286
SHELBURN		
M E	Amador Twp 1	55 481

Name	County Locale	M653 RollPage
SHELBURN		
Thos	Amador Twp 1	55 481
SHELBY		
Francis T	Mendocino Calpella	60 819
Henry	San Francisco San Francisco 2	67 707
J T	Klamath Trinidad	59 221
John	Solano Montezuma	69 373
L	Stanislaus Branch	70 697
Margaret	Sonoma Santa Rosa	69 395
Ranvill	Santa Cruz Santa Cruz	66 618
Ranwill	Santa Cruz Santa Cruz	66 618
Wm N	San Francisco San Francisco 2	67 630
Wm*	Amador Twp 2	55 320
SHELDAN		
James	Siskiyou Callahan	69 7
SHELDEN		
Barney	Mendocino Ukiah	60 806
David M	Siskiyou Shasta Valley	69 117
Frank	Placer Virginia	62 673
Henry B	Sierra Downieville	66 966
J G	Sacramento Franklin	63 313
James	Sierra Downieville	66 964
James	Siskiyou Callahan	69 7
Jas	San Francisco San Francisco 2	67 746
N	Tuolumne Twp 1	71 260
N P	Sierra Downieville	661023
Philo C	Sacramento Natonia	63 274
W P	Sierra Downieville	661023
SHELDER		
Johna	Yuba Marysville	72 967
Joshua	Yuba Marysville	72 967
SHELDIN		
John M	Santa Clara Redwood	65 454
SHELDON		
A	Alameda Murray	55 225
A C	Napa Hot Springs	61 4
B A	San Francisco San Francisco 5	67 493
B N	Solano Suisan	69 221
Barney	Mendocino Ukiah	60 806
Benj F	Plumas Meadow Valley	62 930
Catharine	San Francisco San Francisco 7	681410
Charles	Placer Michigan	62 828
Cyrus	Placer Mountain	62 707
David S	Calaveras Twp 5	57 141
E	El Dorado Placerville	58 883
F	Sonoma Salt Point	69 694
Gilbirt	Butte Ophir	56 799
Green	Yolo No E Twp	72 673
Green	Yuba North Ea	72 673
H	Sacramento Ward 1	63 77
H B	Solano Suisan	69 208
Hiram A	San Francisco San Francisco 10	247 67
J S	Solano Suisan	69 214
James	Siskiyou Callahan	69 7
Jas A	Placer Virginia	62 675
John	Placer Folsom	62 647
Jos W	Calaveras Twp 5	57 248
Joseh	Calaveras Twp 5	57 205
Joseph	Calaveras Twp 5	57 205
Joseph	Nevada Little Y	61 535
Josw	Calaveras Twp 5	57 248
Letetia*	Sierra Pine Grove	66 824
Letitia	Sierra Pine Grove	66 824
Luis	Monterey San Juan	60 993
M A	San Francisco San Francisco 7	681332
N	Tuolumne Twp 1	71 260
N P	Sacramento Ward 3	63 429
Norman	Sierra Pine Grove	66 822
R B	Shasta Shasta	66 761
R N	Solano Suisan	69 221
R O	San Francisco San Francisco 3	67 85
Ramford O	San Francisco San Francisco 8	681233
Rawley	Los Angeles Tejon	59 537
Sitita	Sierra Pine Grove	66 824
Thomas	Placer Iona Hills	62 891
Wb	Solano Suisan	69 208
Wm	Sacramento Lee	63 215
Wm H	Placer Folsom	62 639
Z S	El Dorado Mud Springs	58 956
SHELDONI		
Henry B	Sierra Downieville	66 966
SHELDORE		
Joseph	Plumas Meadow Valley	62 907
SHELFAD		
M*	Nevada Eureka	61 387
SHELFORD		
E	Nevada Eureka	61 387
J	Nevada Eureka	61 387
M*	Nevada Eureka	61 387
P	Nevada Eureka	61 387
SHELFRITZ		
John	Nevada Bridgeport	61 470
SHELFUD		
M*	Nevada Eureka	61 387

California 1860 Census Index

Name	County Locale	M653 Roll	Page
SHELILLA			
Alex	Sierra Twp 7	66	911
SHELL			
Alfred	Contra Costa Twp 1	57	522
Boney	Mariposa Twp 3	60	593
Israel	Sonoma Santa Rosa	69	417
Philip	Yolo Washington	72	566
Wm	Alameda Brooklyn	55	211
SHELLA			
Theodore*	Santa Cruz Pajaro	66	554
SHELLAC			
---	Butte Chico	56	566
SHELLBACK			
William	Sierra Pine Grove	66	826
SHELLCROP			
Wm D	Sacramento Ward 1	63	144
SHELLCROSS			
Wm D*	Sacramento Ward 1	63	144
SHELLEN			
John*	Sacramento Granite	63	251
SHELLENBERG			
Henry	Sierra Downieville	66	966
SHELLENBERGER			
Amos	Yuba Marysville	72	848
SHELLENBURGERS			
Amos	Yuba Marysville	72	848
SHELLERS			
John	Sacramento Granite	63	251
SHELLEY			
A J	Nevada Nevada	61	280
Edwd	San Francisco San Francisco 1	68	856
F	Siskiyou Callahan	69	2
Jas	Placer Nicolaus	62	691
John	Solano Montezuma	69	375
John	Tuolumne Columbia	71	366
Joseph	Siskiyou Yreka	69	156
Kw D	Siskiyou Scott Va	69	35
P	San Francisco San Francisco 5	67	528
W D	Siskiyou Scott Va	69	35
William	Tulara Visalia	71	6
Wm*	Amador Twp 2	55	320
SHELLHIMER			
Hesnal	Yolo Cache	72	634
SHELLHINMA			
Ellina S	Yolo Cache	72	633
SHELLHINNE			
Ellina S	Yolo Cache Crk	72	633
SHELLHINNER			
Usual*	Yolo Cache Crk	72	634
SHELLHIRMAN			
D	Yolo Cache Crk	72	646
SHELLHOINEN			
D*	Yolo Cottonwood	72	646
SHELLHORIN			
C*	Amador Twp 6	55	441
SHELLHORM			
C*	Amador Twp 6	55	441
SHELLHORN			
C*	Amador Twp 6	55	441
D	Yolo Cottonwood	72	646
SHELLING			
Frank	San Francisco San Francisco 11		154 67
John	Amador Twp 2	55	279
Levi	San Francisco San Francisco 9	68	964
SHELLINGBERGER			
Isaac	Amador Twp 2	55	262
SHELLKY			
J	Nevada Nevada	61	248
SHELLURBERG			
Henry*	Sierra Downieville	66	966
SHELLY			
Francis T	Mendocino Calpella	60	819
J*	Nevada Nevada	61	248
James	Tulara Keyesville	71	53
Jhn	San Francisco San Francisco 2	67	766
John	Plumas Quincy	62	922
John	San Francisco San Francisco 2	67	766
John	San Joaquin Elliott	64	941
John	Santa Cruz Pajaro	66	557
John	Tulara Visalia	71	7
L	San Mateo Twp 1	65	65
Lewis	Nevada Bridgeport	61	495
Margaret	San Francisco San Francisco 3	67	81
Percy B	Tuolumne Sonora	71	215
Thomas R	Yuba Marysville	72	951
William	Yuba Suida	72	980
Wm	Marin Cortemad	60	781
SHELOCK			
---	Mendocino Round Va	60	877
SHELOLLA			
Alexr	Sierra Twp 7	66	911
SHELON			
Helen	Butte Oro	56	679
SHELPITZ			
John*	Nevada Bridgeport	61	470

Name	County Locale	M653 Roll	Page
SHELPRITZ			
John*	Nevada Bridgeport	61	470
SHELSES			
David*	Humbolt Eel Rvr	59	154
SHELT			
Henry	Siskiyou Yreka	69	173
William O	Solano Vacaville	69	353
SHELTEN			
Elizabeth	Sonoma Armally	69	482
SHELTES			
David*	Humbolt Eel Rvr	59	154
SHELTON			
A W	Sacramento Ward 1	63	35
A W	Sacramento Ward 1	63	60
Elizabeth	Sonoma Armally	69	482
Geo	San Francisco San Francisco 6	67	438
H A	Colusa Colusi	57	420
H W	Nevada Nevada	61	322
Henry	Sacramento Ward 1	63	50
Henry	San Joaquin Douglass	64	917
Henry A	Calaveras Twp 5	57	199
J G	Colusa Colusi	57	420
James	Colusa Monroeville	57	443
James	Los Angeles Elmonte	59	257
James	Yuba Marysville	72	869
Jno	Mendocino Ukiah	60	795
John	Tulara Visalia	71	78
L	Siskiyou Scott Va	69	21
Martin	Mendocino Ukiah	60	796
W	Sutter Butte	70	781
William	Mendocino Ukiah	60	795
Wm	Sierra Twp 7	66	873
Wm F	Klamath Klamath	59	227
SHEM			
---	Sacramento Ward 1	63	65
---	Tuolumne Columbia	71	346
---	Tuolumne Shawsfla	71	390
---	Tuolumne Shawsfla	71	392
---	Tuolumne Shawsfla	71	394
---	Tuolumne Twp 2	71	414
---	Tuolumne Twp 3	71	436
---	Tuolumne Twp 3	71	458
---	Tuolumne Twp 3	71	469
---	Tuolumne Twp 5	71	522
---	Tuolumne Twp 6	71	533
---	Tuolumne Don Pedro	71	537
Ah	Tuolumne Twp 2	71	346
Ah	Tuolumne Twp 2	71	394
Frederick	Tuolumne Jamestown	71	469
SHEMAE			
A	Merced Twp 1	60	898
SHEMAN			
---	Yuba Parks Ba	72	779
Jhn	Shasta Shasta	66	672
SHEMAR			
B	Nevada Nevada	61	281
SHEMBORN			
A	Sacramento Sutter	63	301
SHEMDON			
James	Yuba Linda Twp	72	984
SHEMER			
Francis H	Siskiyou Yreka	69	167
SHEMTOOLHEM			
---	Mendocino Big Rvr	60	855
SHEMUG			
J	Placer Dutch Fl	62	726
SHEMUP			
---	Fresno Twp 3	59	21
SHEMUT			
---	Tulara Twp 1	71	114
SHEN			
---	El Dorado Coloma	58	1078
---	El Dorado Kelsey	58	1128
---	Sierra Twp 5	66	944
---	Yuba Marysville	72	925
Cam	Yuba Marysville	72	920
Hee	El Dorado Georgetown	58	755
Soen	Yuba Marysville	72	920
SHENADOKA			
---	Mendocino Twp 1	60	887
SHENAKER			
Andrew*	Calaveras Twp 5	57	144
Mathew M	Sierra Twp 7	66	888
SHENALE			
Jas	Placer Dutch Fl	62	717
SHENAN			
J	Nevada Grass Valley	61	219
SHENCK			
---	Calaveras Twp 10	57	273
SHENE			
Ah	Tuolumne Twp 2	71	390
Andrew W	San Diego Colorado	64	810
Mie	El Dorado Georgetown	58	703
SHENETS			
Phillip	Sierra Downieville	66	975
SHENG			
---	Calaveras Twp 8	57	94

Name	County Locale	M653 Roll	Page
SHENG			
---	Trinity Weaverville	70	1053
---	Trinity Lewiston	70	957
Peter	Mariposa Coulterville	60	685
SHENIBACK			
Peter T	San Francisco San Francisco 10		170 67
SHENIDEN			
Rose	San Francisco San Francisco 2	67	629
SHENIDER			
Rose	San Francisco San Francisco 2	67	629
SHENIN			
Jacob	Yolo Cache Crk	72	641
SHENING			
---	Sacramento Mississipi	63	190
SHENK			
---	Trinity Weaverville	70	1072
August	Sacramento Ward 3	63	437
SHENN			
---	Tuolumne Columbia	71	346
---	Tuolumne Shawsfla	71	385
SHENNAN			
C A*	Sierra Downieville	66	988
D	Nevada Eureka	61	376
J*	Nevada Eureka	61	372
Wm*	Nevada Eureka	61	372
SHENNEPY			
Kate*	San Francisco San Francisco 4	68	1227
SHENOTS			
Phillip*	Sierra Downieville	66	975
SHENOW			
Peter	Placer Goods	62	695
SHENTLER			
John	Colusa Spring Valley	57	434
SHENWAY			
James	Sierra Downieville	66	1001
SHENY			
L	Yolo Washington	72	601
SHEOFISHISE			
John	Tulara Visalia	71	102
SHEON			
---	Amador Twp 6	55	428
SHEONG			
---	El Dorado Union	58	1091
---	El Dorado Coloma	58	1111
Neer	San Francisco San Francisco 10		356 67
SHEOPAN			
B	Tehama Red Bluff	70	930
SHEORY			
---	Amador Twp 5	55	353
SHEP YE			
---	Tuolumne Montezuma	71	504
SHEP			
---	Placer Illinois	62	704
E A	Tehama Cottonwood	70	898
SHEPARD			
A J	San Francisco San Francisco 2	67	589
Edward A	Yuba Suida	72	982
Frank	Shasta Shasta	66	681
George	Placer Iona Hills	62	859
George	Placer Iona Hills	62	872
H B	Butte Wyandotte	56	670
J A	El Dorado Placerville	58	873
J H	Tuolumne Columbia	71	344
James	Stanislaus Emory	70	746
Mark	Contra Costa Twp 1	57	537
Milton	Contra Costa Twp 3	57	608
Nathaniel B	Placer Rattle Snake	62	632
Richard	Placer Michigan	62	826
Rodolphus	Contra Costa Twp 2	57	582
Thos	Butte Bidwell	56	705
W E	El Dorado Diamond	58	774
W F	El Dorado Placerville	58	855
W W	Butte Ophir	56	799
William	El Dorado Diamond	58	764
William*	El Dorado Greenwood	58	721
SHEPARDSON			
Dudley	Colusa Colusi	57	419
M D	Tehama Antelope	70	897
SHEPER			
I H*	San Francisco San Francisco 3	67	1
J H*	San Francisco San Francisco 3	67	1
SHEPERD			
Benj F	Plumas Meadow Valley	62	934
SHEPHARD			
Alfred	San Francisco San Francisco 2	67	667
Ann	San Francisco San Francisco 2	67	558
Frank	San Francisco San Francisco 9	68	994
G	Tehama Red Bluff	70	929
Geo	San Francisco San Francisco 1	68	893
Jas*	San Francisco San Francisco 1	68	836
Joseph	Mendocino Big Rvr	60	848
Joseph	Solano Benecia	69	314
Julius	San Joaquin Castoria	64	884
M	Marin Bolinas	60	727

Name	County Locale	M653 Roll	Page
SHEPHARD			
Mary	San Francisco San Francisco 2	67	602
Mary	San Francisco San Francisco 2	67	686
Mary E	Marin Cortemad	60	753
Sarah	San Francisco San Francisco 9	68	968
William	Siskiyou Klamath	69	87
Wm	San Francisco San Francisco 1	68	890
SHEPHER			
T*	Sacramento Ward 4	63	581
SHEPHERD			
A	Nevada Grass Valley	61	212
A	Sonoma Russian	69	440
A	Trinity Weaverville	70	1077
A L	San Francisco San Francisco 10	230 67	
Abel	San Francisco San Francisco 8	681	316
Adam	San Joaquin Elliott	64	947
B A	Shasta Horsetown	66	693
Benjamin	San Joaquin Tulare	64	870
Carlos	San Bernardino San Bernardino	64	643
Charles	Tuolumne Twp 2	71	367
E L	Yolo No E Twp	72	668
G A	Sierra Scales D	66	804
Geo	Sacramento Ward 4	63	590
George D	San Joaquin Castoria	64	874
H T	Siskiyou Yreka	69	181
Irvin	Siskiyou Yreka	69	189
Isaac	Alameda Brooklyn	55	107
Isaac G	Yuba Marysville	72	945
J C	Amador Twp 1	55	493
J G	Marin Cortemad	60	752
James	El Dorado Grizzly	58	1182
James	San Joaquin Castoria	64	873
James	Sierra Gibsonville	66	851
Jas S	Butte Kimshaw	56	578
John	Siskiyou Yreka	69	150
John R	Solano Green Valley	69	241
Jos	Sacramento Ward 3	63	435
Joseph	El Dorado Placerville	58	915
L	El Dorado Placerville	58	918
M	Napa Clear Lake	61	131
N H	Sutter Nicolaus	70	840
P E	El Dorado Greenwood	58	711
P W	San Francisco San Francisco 12	371 67	
Saml	San Bernardino San Bernadino	64	645
Samuel	Contra Costa Twp 1	57	514
William	Siskiyou Yreka	69	185
Wm	Siskiyou Scott Va	69	53
Wm*	Alameda Brooklyn	55	139
SHEPHERDS			
W H	Napa Clear Lake	61	129
SHEPHERDSON			
Elijah	San Francisco San Francisco 3	67	76
SHEPHERS			
Wm	Siskiyou Scott Va	69	53
SHEPHERSON			
J T	Nevada Grass Valley	61	218
W M	Nevada Grass Valley	61	218
SHEPHONSON			
C W	Mendocino Little L	60	837
SHEPLER			
L	Sacramento Franklin	63	308
SHEPLEY			
John	Marin Bolinas	60	741
Robert	Tuolumne Chinese	71	520
William	Tuolumne Chinese	71	497
Wm	Nevada Eureka	61	351
SHEPP			
Michael	Yuba Suida	72	987
SHEPPARD			
Arther	San Joaquin Stockton	64	1083
Benj	El Dorado Georgetown	58	674
Bradley	Del Norte Crescent	58	624
Calvin	Sierra Twp 7	66	879
David	Calaveras Twp 9	57	365
E G	San Joaquin Stockton	64	1048
F A	Sacramento Natonia	63	279
F A	Santa Clara Redwood	65	445
Henry	San Francisco San Francisco 2	67	558
J	Calaveras Twp 9	57	388
J B	Mariposa Twp 3	60	547
J S	Mariposa Twp 3	60	597
Joel	Mariposa Coulterville	60	693
John	San Francisco San Francisco 4	681	122
John C	Sierra Downieville	661	017
Joseph	Mendocino Arrana	60	858
Joseph	Santa Clara Redwood	65	447
Joseph	Solano Benecia	69	314
Lemuel	Tulara Yule Rvr	71	23
Levi	Tulara Visalia	71	105
Mary	Amador Twp 2	55	276
Miguel	Los Angeles San Gabriel	59	413
N H	Nevada Rough &	61	428
R C	Nevada Rough &	61	400
Samuel	Calaveras Twp 5	57	187

Name	County Locale	M653 Roll	Page
SHEPPARD			
Semuel	Tulara Twp 2	71	23
Sninl	Calaveras Twp 6	57	132
Summerfield	Tulara Visalia	71	111
William*	El Dorado Greenwood	58	721
Wm	San Francisco San Francisco 9	68	964
SHEPPARDSON			
Lewis	Calaveras Twp 4	57	337
Nathaniel*	Calaveras Twp 5	57	230
SHEPPARRD			
Levi	Tulara Visalia	71	105
SHEPPERD			
H	El Dorado Greenwood	58	724
John	El Dorado Placerville	58	933
Saml	San Bernardino San Salvador	64	645
Wm W	Monterey San Juan	60	975
SHEPPERDSON			
E H	Solano Benecia	69	293
Elijah	San Francisco San Francisco 3	67	76
SHEPPERSON			
Otis	Calaveras Twp 5	57	218
SHEPPORD			
David	Calaveras Twp 9	57	365
SHEPPORDSEN			
Nathaniel*	Calaveras Twp 5	57	230
SHEPPORDSON			
Mishanul*	Calaveras Twp 5	57	230
Nathanel	Calaveras Twp 5	57	230
SHER			
---	Mariposa Twp 1	60	666
---	Placer Iona Hills	62	896
Sap*	Mariposa Twp 1	60	641
SHERALIER			
Michael	Mariposa Twp 1	60	656
SHERAN			
Henry	Sierra Port Win	66	793
SHERBACK			
Owin	Monterey San Juan	60	976
SHERBAIN			
A*	Nevada Eureka	61	375
O*	Nevada Eureka	61	375
SHERBAND			
Chas A	Sacramento Granite	63	263
SHERBARN			
Michael A	Yuba Marysville	72	868
SHERBONARNI			
Job	El Dorado Greenwood	58	713
SHERBONDER			
John	El Dorado Casumnes	581	164
SHERBORN			
Richard	Sacramento Sutter	63	301
SHERBORNE			
G W*	Alameda Brooklyn	55	141
SHERBOUDEE			
John*	El Dorado Casumnes	581	164
SHERBOUDER			
John*	El Dorado Casumnes	581	164
SHERBUM			
D	San Francisco San Francisco 5	67	554
SHERBURN			
D*	San Francisco San Francisco 5	67	554
David	Tuolumne Twp 2	71	370
J	Nevada Eureka	61	375
O	Nevada Eureka	61	375
SHERBURNE			
Albert	Alameda Brooklyn	55	158
George	Trinity Grass Valley	70	962
S B	San Francisco San Francisco 10	312 67	
SHERCH			
John*	Alameda Oakland	55	58
SHERDAN			
Daniel	Placer Virginia	62	673
James	Sonoma Mendocino	69	457
James	Sonoma Salt Point	69	694
SHERDEN			
Danl	Butte Bidwell	56	729
H	Nevada Eureka	61	375
J	Nevada Eureka	61	375
SHERDON			
Danl	Butte Bidwell	56	729
M	Shasta Shasta	66	687
W R	Butte Ophir	56	799
SHERE			
Geo C	San Francisco San Francisco 9	681	015
SHEREDAN			
John	Trinity Sturdiva	701	006
SHEREE			
---	Sierra Twp 7	66	881
SHEREMONTZ			
Santhas*	San Mateo Twp 2	65	113
SHEREN			
Thomas	El Dorado Diamond	58	809
SHERER			
Edward	Calaveras Twp 9	57	361
Geo	Amador Twp 3	55	376

Name	County Locale	M653 Roll	Page
SHERER			
Henry R	San Francisco San Francisco 9	681	050
Louisa	San Francisco San Francisco 9	681	043
SHERERICK			
W	El Dorado Placerville	58	862
SHERES			
Wm	Colusa Spring Valley	57	432
SHERGER			
Jesse	Sierra Twp 7	66	907
SHERHOLD			
Hannon	Marin S Antoni	60	712
Harmon	Marin S Antoni	60	712
SHERIDAN			
A H	Santa Clara Alviso	65	410
Bernard	Calaveras Twp 6	57	112
E	Shasta Horsetown	66	709
Frank	Placer Iona Hills	62	882
G W	Shasta Millvill	66	744
George	Placer Iona Hills	62	862
Herbert	Nevada Rough &	61	423
J	Nevada Grass Valley	61	205
J E	Sacramento Franklin	63	323
James	San Francisco San Francisco 3	67	26
James	Yuba Rose Bar	72	797
Jas	San Francisco San Francisco 9	681	003
John	Sacramento Mississipi	63	185
John	Sierra Downieville	66	976
John	Solano Vallejo	69	274
Jos	San Francisco San Francisco 9	681	073
Martin	Calaveras Twp 6	57	145
Mary	San Francisco San Francisco 8	681	277
Mary	Santa Clara Santa Clara	65	472
Parick T	San Francisco San Francisco 1	68	856
Pat	Amador Twp 2	55	302
Peter	San Francisco San Francisco 9	68	974
Robert	Santa Clara Alviso	65	411
Sarah	San Francisco San Francisco 4	681	160
Thos A	Santa Clara Santa Clara	65	491
Wm	Butte Ophir	56	823
SHERIDAR			
Herbert*	Nevada Rough &	61	423
SHERIDEN			
A	Nevada Grass Valley	61	156
Henry	San Francisco San Francisco 2	67	786
Michael	Calaveras Twp 6	57	129
Thos	Amador Twp 4	55	259
SHERIE			
---	Sierra Twp 7	66	881
SHERIELDA			
Mary T	Butte Ophir	56	764
SHERIFF			
Alfred R	Yuba Marysville	72	880
Geo	Sacramento Brighton	63	192
SHERIIDAN			
Frank	San Joaquin Elkhorn	641	000
SHERINGTON			
Samuel	Colusa Spring Valley	57	433
SHERIR			
R H	Santa Clara Burnett	65	256
SHERITT			
William*	Placer Iona Hills	62	865
SHERK			
George	San Francisco San Francisco 7	681	335
Louis	San Francisco San Francisco 7	681	328
SHERKLAND			
Hugh	Yolo Slate Ra	72	687
SHERLAND			
Chas R	Sacramento Granite	63	263
E D	Sacramento Granite	63	242
E L*	Sacramento Granite	63	242
SHERLERGER			
Louisa*	San Francisco San Francisco 2	67	659
SHERLEY			
James M	Tuolumne Jamestown	71	432
Jane	San Joaquin Castoria	64	907
Mary	San Joaquin Castoria	64	906
William	Contra Costa Twp 3	57	597
SHERLOCK			
James	Santa Cruz Santa Cruz	66	626
Jno	Butte Eureka	56	653
John	Santa Cruz Santa Cruz	66	611
John	Yuba Marysville	72	883
Robert B	Sierra Twp 7	66	875
S W	San Francisco San Francisco 3	67	1
SHERLY			
C B	Tuolumne Twp 2	71	343
Wm	Sacramento Natonia	63	281
SHERMAKER			
Danl	Sierra Twp 5	66	925
SHERMAN			
---	Mendocino Little L	60	839
---	San Francisco San Francisco 3	67	54
---	Yuba Parks Ba	72	779
A	Sacramento Ward 1	63	17
A	Tehama Red Bluff	70	916
A	Tehama Red Bluff	70	925

California 1860 Census Index

Name	County Locale	M653 Roll	Page
SHERMAN			
A J	Nevada Nevada	61	284
Albert	Calaveras Twp 7	57	24
Albert G	San Francisco San Francisco 12	67	377
Andrew	Calaveras Twp 6	57	138
B	Tuolumne Twp 1	71	256
B*	Nevada Nevada	61	281
C	Shasta Horsetown	66	693
C	Shasta Horsetown	66	700
C A	Sierra Downieville	66	988
Caleb	Sonoma Armally	69	514
Catherine	San Joaquin Elkhorn	64	959
Charles	Sierra Downieville	66	1021
Chas	Sonoma Bodega	69	519
Christopher	Sierra Twp 5	66	938
Christopher	Yuba Marysville	72	881
D	Amador Twp 3	55	380
D D	Sacramento Ward 1	63	141
David	Tuolumne Chinese	71	520
David B	San Francisco San Francisco 9	68	1042
Dexter	Contra Costa Twp 1	57	594
E	Amador Twp 3	55	371
Edmund A	Los Angeles Los Angeles	59	328
Edward W	Placer Virginia	62	662
Elliott	San Joaquin Elliott	64	1101
Erin	Calaveras Twp 10	57	289
F A	San Francisco San Francisco 2	67	715
Francis	San Francisco San Francisco 10	67	291
Geo	Amador Twp 2	55	287
Geo	Sacramento Centre	63	173
Geo	San Francisco San Francisco 10	67	330
George	San Francisco San Francisco 9	68	1052
George	Yuba Bear Rvr	72	1011
George W	San Francisco San Francisco 3	67	56
Harriett	Yolo Merritt	72	580
Henry	Placer Michigan	62	834
Henry	San Joaquin Douglass	64	920
Henry	Sierra Port Win	66	793
Hiram	Marin Point Re	60	731
Isaac	Tuolumne Columbia	71	345
Isaac	Yuba Marysville	72	890
J	Nevada Eureka	61	372
J	Sacramento Ward 3	63	433
J N	Butte Bidwell	56	729
J S	San Francisco San Francisco 3	67	36
J T	Santa Clara Alviso	65	400
J*	Nevada Eureka	61	372
James	Tuolumne Twp 1	71	261
James H	San Francisco San Francisco 7	68	1403
Jas	Butte Cascade	56	697
Jesse	Siskiyou Yreka	69	153
Jim	Tehama Red Bluff	70	922
Jno	Mendocino Big Rvr	60	843
Jno	Nevada Eureka	61	372
John	Butte Ophir	56	783
John	Calaveras Twp 8	57	77
John	Colusa Monroeville	57	142
John	Colusa Monroeville	57	442
John	Placer Rattle Snake	62	604
John	Sacramento Centre	63	174
John	Sacramento San Joaquin	63	364
John	Shasta Shasta	66	672
John	Tehama Tehama	70	935
John	Trinity Trinity	70	971
John	Tuolumne Columbia	71	339
John*	Mariposa Coulterville	60	679
Joseph	San Francisco San Francisco 11	67	148
L	Sacramento Ward 4	63	533
Lapoor A	Placer Rattle Snake	62	625
Leonard	Plumas Quincy	62	940
M O	Colusa Colusi	57	419
Marshal B	San Mateo Twp 1	65	55
Marshall	Tuolumne Chinese	71	496
Mathew	Placer Auburn	62	566
Milton	Sacramento Ward 4	63	600
Otis	Amador Twp 2	55	276
Phelip	San Francisco San Francisco 2	67	761
Philep	San Francisco San Francisco 2	67	761
Sarah B	Calaveras Twp 4	57	336
Thaddeus	Placer Michigan	62	828
Thoams	Yolo Slate Ra	72	717
Thomas	Placer Yankee J	62	781
Thomas	Yuba Slate Ro	72	717
Thos	Placer Auburn	62	570
Valentine	San Francisco San Francisco 7	68	1342
Walter	Calaveras Twp 10	57	289
Washington	Solano Vallejo	69	276
Wm	Butte Cascade	56	690
Wm	Butte Ophir	56	824
Wm	Nevada Eureka	61	372
Wm	Sacramento Ward 4	63	517
Wm G	Alameda Brooklyn	55	187

Name	County Locale	M653 Roll	Page
SHERMAN			
Wm H	Napa Napa	61	62
Wm*	Nevada Eureka	61	372
SHERMANHOFF			
John	Amador Twp 1	55	511
SHERMANTINE			
James	Santa Clara Santa Clara	65	490
SHERMAR			
B*	Nevada Nevada	61	281
Wm	Sacramento Franklin	63	324
SHERMEN			
Andrew	Calaveras Twp 6	57	138
SHERMER			
Andrew	Calaveras Twp 5	57	138
SHERMIN			
J M	Sutter Yuba	70	761
SHERMPF			
Anlis*	Sierra Downieville	66	956
Aulis	Sierra Downieville	66	956
SHERN			
---	Sacramento Ward 1	63	65
Ah	Tuolumne Twp 2	71	385
SHERNE			
J	Siskiyou Klamath	69	88
SHERNING			
Caleb*	Sierra Downieville	66	1003
SHERNON			
John*	Tulara Visalia	71	102
SHERNSPF			
Anlis*	Sierra Downieville	66	956
SHEROCK			
Jo*	Mariposa Coulterville	60	685
SHEROOITES			
A	Calaveras Twp 9	57	378
SHEROY			
Francis*	El Dorado Kelsey	58	1135
SHERR			
W*	San Francisco San Francisco 5	67	498
SHERRALE			
Charles	Contra Costa Twp 1	57	507
SHERRAN			
Jacob	San Bernardino San Bernadino	64	668
SHERRELL			
Caroline	Siskiyou Shasta Valley	69	121
SHERREN			
J M	Mariposa Twp 3	60	599
J W	Mariposa Twp 3	60	599
SHERRET			
E	Butte Oregon	56	640
SHERRETT			
Thomas	San Francisco San Francisco 8	68	1239
SHERRIDAN			
Catherine	San Francisco San Francisco 7	68	1384
Patrick	Sierra Pine Grove	66	823
Peter	Nevada Rough &	61	421
SHERRIDEN			
E	Nevada Grass Valley	61	151
SHERRILL			
Wiliam	Plumas Quincy	62	938
SHERRIN			
Geo*	El Dorado Diamond	58	792
John	San Francisco San Francisco 9	68	1002
W	Mariposa Twp 3	60	556
SHERRITT			
Danl*	Sacramento Ward 1	63	80
Julia*	Sacramento Ward 1	63	80
SHERROCK			
James	Santa Cruz Santa Cruz	66	626
SHERRY			
David	Santa Clara Redwood	65	443
John	Placer Secret R	62	621
John A	San Joaquin Stockton	64	1086
L	Yolo Washington	72	601
Mich	Sacramento Ward 4	63	554
Michael	Placer Secret R	62	621
Peter	Calaveras Twp 5	57	228
Thomas	Alameda Oakland	55	45
Wm	Mariposa Twp 1	60	636
SHERT			
Joshua	Shasta Shasta	66	674
SHERTAS			
Henry*	San Francisco San Francisco 9	68	999
SHERUAN			
A L	Colusa Butte Crk	57	467
SHERUELDA			
Mary T	Butte Ophir	56	764
SHERVAN			
H*	San Francisco San Francisco 3	67	56
SHERVARR			
H	San Francisco San Francisco 3	67	56
SHERVIN			
L H*	Merced Twp 1	60	905
SHERWELL			
W S	Calaveras Twp 9	57	401
SHERWETER			
A	Calaveras Twp 9	57	378

Name	County Locale	M653 Roll	Page
SHERWIN			
Henry	Alameda Brooklyn	55	96
Jas L	Plumas Quincy	62	925
John	Plumas Meadow Valley	62	906
W W	Tuolumne Twp 1	71	256
William	Plumas Quincy	62	1005
SHERWOD			
S G	Butte Hamilton	56	519
SHERWOOD			
Alfred	Solano Vallejo	69	259
Alfred E	Mendocino Little L	60	839
B F	San Francisco San Francisco 2	67	804
Benj	San Joaquin Stockton	64	1013
C C	Sacramento Franklin	63	326
C H	Nevada Eureka	61	393
C S	Calaveras Twp 9	57	362
C T	Calaveras Twp 9	57	362
Chas	Sacramento Ward 3	63	434
D	Shasta Shasta	66	735
David	San Francisco San Francisco 7	68	1390
Elijah	San Francisco San Francisco 11	67	111
Eugene	Monterey S Antoni	60	973
Geo	San Francisco San Francisco 2	67	741
Henry G	San Bernardino San Bernadino	64	616
Henry H	Santa Clara Gilroy	65	246
J A	Sacramento Cosumnes	63	383
J C	El Dorado Mountain	58	1186
J O	Sacramento Cosumnes	63	401
James F	San Joaquin Douglass	64	924
John	Tuolumne Don Pedro	71	538
John C	Yuba Parks Ba	72	775
L	Yuba New York	72	732
M	San Mateo Twp 3	65	106
R	Nevada Eureka	61	347
Robt	San Francisco San Francisco 10	67	340
S	Yuba New York	72	732
S D	San Francisco San Francisco 9	68	1067
S G	Butte Hamilton	56	519
Saml	Klamath Trinidad	59	220
Thomas	Calaveras Twp 4	57	315
Thomas J	Yuba Marysville	72	910
Torrey	Calaveras Twp 6	57	166
W C	Amador Twp 2	55	303
W S	San Francisco San Francisco 5	67	485
William	Yuba Marysville	72	950
Wm	Nevada Eureka	61	346
Wm	Plumas Quincy	62	915
Wm	Sacramento San Joaquin	63	363
SHERY			
Andrew*	Nevada Rough &	61	400
SHES			
---	El Dorado Big Bar	58	738
SHESSHER			
T*	Sacramento Ward 4	63	581
SHET			
---	Amador Twp 3	55	401
SHETAT			
---	Calaveras Twp 10	57	278
SHETLAGE			
F	Siskiyou Scott Va	69	31
SHETLAND			
David	Calaveras Twp 5	57	239
David W	Calaveras Twp 5	57	239
SHETLEROWE			
Joseh	Marin Bolinas	60	747
SHETNEY			
C	El Dorado Placerville	58	854
SHETON			
Jos D	San Francisco San Francisco 2	67	606
Josse	San Francisco San Francisco 2	67	606
SHETREN			
Eugen*	Shasta Horsetown	66	692
SHETRON			
Eugen	Shasta Horsetown	66	692
SHETRY			
J	Sacramento Ward 1	63	78
SHETSY			
J	Sacramento Ward 1	63	78
SHETTAGE			
F*	Siskiyou Scott Va	69	31
SHETTLE			
Edward	Amador Twp 1	55	451
Ernest	El Dorado Greenwood	58	708
SHETTLUAN			
A	Colusa Muion	57	462
SHETTON			
James*	Yuba Marysville	72	869
SHETTROWE			
Joseph	Marin Bolinas	60	747
SHEUCK			
---	Calaveras Twp 10	57	273
SHEUM			
---	Placer Virginia	62	684
SHEURBORN			
A	Sacramento Sutter	63	301

Name	County Locale	M653 RollPage
SHEURN		
Patrick	Calaveras Twp 5	57 195
SHEVALIER		
Michael	Mariposa Twp 1	60 656
SHEVALU		
Meshell	Mariposa Twp 1	60 654
Meshill	Mariposa Twp 1	60 654
SHEVAN		
Fred K	Calaveras Twp 5	57 180
SHEVAR		
Fredk	Calaveras Twp 6	57 180
SHEVEAR		
August	Sierra Downieville	661002
SHEVENS		
Bridget A*	San Mateo Twp 1	65 48
SHEVER		
Geo	Butte Oro	56 687
SHEVOCK		
Jo	Mariposa Coulterville	60 685
SHEVRITT		
Danl*	Sacramento Ward 1	63 80
SHEW		
---	Butte Chico	56 562
---	Calaveras Twp 5	57 171
---	Calaveras Twp 4	57 325
---	Del Norte Crescent	58 640
---	Del Norte Happy Ca	58 664
---	El Dorado Diamond	58 776
---	El Dorado Diamond	58 787
---	El Dorado Diamond	58 816
---	El Dorado Placerville	58 829
---	El Dorado Placerville	58 834
---	El Dorado Mud Springs	58 978
---	Mariposa Twp 1	60 658
---	Sierra Twp 5	66 944
---	Tehama Red Bluff	70 934
---	Yolo No E Twp	72 684
Fah	Tehama Red Bluff	70 934
Hah	Tehama Red Bluff	70 934
Jacob	Sacramento Ward 1	63 37
L M*	Sacramento Ward 1	63 5
S M	Sacramento Ward 1	63 5
SHEWAN		
H*	San Francisco San Francisco 3	67 56
SHEWIG		
S L*	Nevada Grass Valley	61 168
SHEWIN		
L H*	Merced Twp 1	60 905
SHEWIY		
S L*	Nevada Grass Valley	61 168
SHEWTER		
A	San Francisco San Francisco 3	67 12
SHEWY		
Francis*	El Dorado Kelsey	581135
SHEY		
---	Amador Twp 5	55 356
---	Yuba Long Bar	72 770
A	San Francisco San Francisco 5	67 503
Adolph	Yuba Marysville	72 894
Adolpph	Yuba Marysville	72 894
W S	Tuolumne Twp 1	71 276
SHI		
---	Amador Twp 5	55 355
---	Calaveras Twp 7	57 37
---	Calaveras Twp 7	57 44
---	Calaveras Twp 8	57 94
---	Placer Secret R	62 622
---	Yuba Marysville	72 916
Chick	Yuba Long Bar	72 760
Ha*	Yuba Long Bar	72 755
Num	Amador Twp 2	55 311
Ong	Yuba Long Bar	72 759
Yut	El Dorado Georgetown	58 692
SHIA		
Eugine	Los Angeles Tejon	59 522
SHIAD		
N B*	Calaveras Twp 9	57 396
SHIADELDO		
Ewd*	Mariposa Coulterville	60 703
SHIAM		
Fred*	Placer Todds Va	62 787
SHIANE		
Fred*	Placer Todds Va	62 787
SHIANG		
---	Marin Cortemad	60 791
SHIARER		
T J	Calaveras Twp 9	57 393
SHIBBARD		
John	San Francisco San Francisco 12	393 67
SHIBBS		
Jssie*	San Francisco San Francisco 1	68 915
SHIBEL		
George	San Francisco San Francisco 4	681158
SHIBITER		
---	San Bernardino San Bernardino	64 678

Name	County Locale	M653 RollPage
SHIBLER		
Albert H*	Placer Secret R	62 609
J C	Sierra Downieville	66 961
SHIBLES		
Albert H*	Placer Secret R	62 609
SHICALHOKER		
---	Mendocino Twp 1	60 887
SHICK		
---	El Dorado Placerville	58 839
Pherl L	Sierra Twp 7	66 890
Phil L	Sierra Twp 7	66 890
Phillip	Sierra Twp 7	66 885
SHIDATO		
---	Mendocino Twp 1	60 887
SHIDD		
Edwd D	San Francisco San Francisco 6	67 432
SHIDEL		
Geo*	San Francisco San Francisco 9	68 960
SHIDLER		
Joseph	San Francisco San Francisco 11	89 67
SHIDUME		
---	Tulara Twp 2	71 36
SHIE		
---	Sierra Twp 5	66 948
SHIEAL		
Michael	Butte Ophir	56 779
SHIEB		
Andrew	Yuba Marysville	72 896
SHIEBILL		
L*	Nevada Washington	61 336
SHIECK		
Michael	Plumas Quincy	62 998
SHIEDS		
J C	Shasta Shasta	66 687
John*	Yolo Slate Ra	72 693
SHIEHAN		
Timothy*	Sierra Twp 7	66 907
SHIEL		
Ambrose	Yuba Marysville	72 896
SHIELAS		
Francis*	El Dorado Georgetown	58 758
SHIELD		
Augustus	Calaveras Twp 7	57 44
Elezebet*	San Francisco San Francisco 8	681272
Frank	Santa Clara Burnett	65 256
J	San Francisco San Francisco 1	68 813
Jands	El Dorado Coloma	581123
Thomas	San Francisco San Francisco 3	67 52
Wm	Sacramento American	63 167
SHIELDING		
John W*	Yuba Marysville	72 887
SHIELDS		
Andrew M	Yuba Marysville	72 904
Caleb L	Los Angeles San Pedro	59 481
Chas	Klamath Liberty	59 240
Daniel	Yuba Marysville	72 904
Danl	Butte Bidwell	56 729
Delia	Sacramento Ward 3	63 422
Dulcina	Mendocino Anderson	60 866
Edward	Sierra Downieville	661028
Eliza	Sacramento Ward 3	63 461
Elizabeth	San Francisco San Francisco 8	681255
Elizabeth	Yuba Marysville	72 999
F M	Sacramento Ward 4	63 529
Francis*	El Dorado Georgetown	58 758
Frank	San Mateo Twp 3	65 107
Frank B	Yuba Marysville	72 940
George	Humbolt Eel Rvr	59 145
J	San Francisco San Francisco 9	681079
J	Yolo Putah	72 615
J W	San Francisco San Francisco 9	681086
J W	San Francisco San Francisco 6	67 449
Jame	El Dorado Kelsey	581153
James	Alameda Brooklyn	55 135
James	Amador Twp 4	55 240
James	El Dorado Coloma	581123
James	Nevada Eureka	61 356
James	San Bernardino San Bernadino	64 635
James	San Francisco San Francisco 2	67 393
Jas	Butte Bidwell	56 712
Jas M	Butte Cascade	56 691
Jerme	El Dorado Kelsey	581153
Jno	Sacramento Brighton	63 196
Jno A	Butte Eureka	56 655
John	Amador Twp 4	55 242
John	El Dorado Mud Springs	58 953
John	Solano Suisan	69 210
John	Trinity Eastman	70 960
John	Yuba Slate Ro	72 693
John	Yuba Rose Bar	72 794
John F	San Bernardino San Salvador	64 655
M	El Dorado White Oaks	581016
M	Nevada Eureka	61 392
M	Sacramento Ward 4	63 613
Margaret	Sierra Pine Grove	66 822

Name	County Locale	M653 RollPage
SHIELDS		
Mary	San Francisco San Francisco 8	681298
Mary W	San Francisco San Francisco 2	67 568
Mary*	San Francisco San Francisco 8	681298
N	Sacramento Cosummes	63 398
Peter	Solano Montezuma	69 368
R H	Sutter Sutter	70 814
Robert	San Francisco San Francisco 10	217 67
Robt	San Francisco San Francisco 12	394 67
Robt	Trinity E Weaver	701058
Stephen	Sacramento Ward 1	63 94
Stephen W	Sacramento Ward 1	63 94
Thomas	Amador Twp 4	55 240
Thos	Butte Oregon	56 636
Thos	Sacramento Centre	63 176
Timothy	San Francisco San Francisco 9	68 945
W	Calaveras Twp 9	57 411
William	Placer Forest H	62 797
William	San Francisco San Francisco 7	681418
Wm	Amador Twp 2	55 321
Wm	Amador Twp 3	55 373
Wm	Santa Clara Santa Clara	65 471
SHIELE		
Elezebet*	San Francisco San Francisco 8	681272
SHIELS		
James	Yuba New York	72 737
SHIELTS		
Arin*	Mariposa Twp 3	60 609
SHIELTZ		
Arn	Mariposa Twp 3	60 609
SHIENHEINS		
G	Yolo Putah	72 587
SHIERDAN		
Peter*	Yuba Marysville	72 874
SHIERS		
James	Plumas Meadow Valley	62 934
SHIES		
A	El Dorado Placerville	58 867
Otto*	Shasta Shasta	66 655
SHIETS		
Frank	Nevada Bridgeport	61 473
SHIFF		
P	El Dorado Diamond	58 770
SHIFFFINS		
Thoms*	El Dorado Georgetown	58 752
SHIFFHAM		
John	El Dorado White Oaks	581030
SHIFFLE		
Edwd	San Francisco San Francisco 10	254 67
S F	Calaveras Twp 9	57 369
SHIFLET		
Permelia	Placer Stewart	62 607
SHIFT		
W C*	Yolo Cache Crk	72 632
SHIG		
---	Calaveras Twp 8	57 62
SHIGALL		
J	Sutter Butte	70 793
SHIGNIS		
Leuis	Nevada Rough &	61 418
SHIGRIES		
Lewis	Nevada Rough &	61 418
SHIGRIS		
Lewis	Nevada Rough &	61 418
SHIHAN		
B*	Napa Hot Springs	61 5
John	Plumas Quincy	621002
Pat*	Napa Hot Springs	61 8
SHIHERD		
Beng F*	Napa Yount	61 41
Benj F*	Napa Yount	61 41
SHIHUN		
B*	Napa Hot Springs	61 5
SHIK		
---	Calaveras Twp 10	57 278
SHIKARD		
Richd*	Mariposa Twp 3	60 557
SHIKEN		
G	Nevada Bridgeport	61 502
SHIKUD		
Benj F*	Napa Yount	61 41
SHILADAY		
John	Butte Bidwell	56 707
SHILD		
Wm	El Dorado Georgetown	58 691
SHILDEN		
M R	El Dorado Diamond	58 789
SHILDERS		
L	Nevada Grass Valley	61 213
SHILENGER		
Lewis*	Nevada Red Dog	61 542
SHILING		
Arreton	Mariposa Twp 1	60 631

Name	County Locale	M653 RollPage
SHILL		
John M	Santa Clara Gilroy	65 248
Saml	Santa Clara Redwood	65 453
SHILLAC		
---	Butte Chico	56 566
SHILLAND		
Benjm	San Francisco San Francisco 1	68 877
SHILLDS		
Mary*	San Francisco San Francisco 8	681298
SHILLEY		
Henry	Placer Dutch Fl	62 731
J J	Nevada Nevada	61 280
SHILLIGER		
James	El Dorado Georgetown	58 760
SHILLING		
A W	El Dorado Coloma	581082
Henry	El Dorado Coloma	581106
Isaiah	Siskiyou Yreka	69 124
J*	Calaveras Twp 9	57 405
Jsaiah*	Siskiyou Yreka	69 124
Louis	San Francisco San Francisco 9	681065
SHILLINGSBURG		
Wm	Solano Vallejo	69 257
SHILLITE		
John A	Nevada Rough &	61 416
SHILLITS		
John A*	Nevada Rough &	61 416
SHILLY		
Percy B	Tuolumne Sonora	71 212
SHILONGER		
Lewis*	Nevada Red Dog	61 542
SHILRUD		
Benj F*	Napa Yount	61 41
SHILTEAS		
M A*	Yuba Marysville	72 927
SHIM		
---	Calaveras Twp 4	57 304
---	Calaveras Twp 8	57 93
---	El Dorado Diamond	58 797
---	Sierra Downieville	661015
---	Tuolumne Shawsfla	71 385
---	Tuolumne Twp 3	71 461
---	Yuba Long Bar	72 766
Ah	Tuolumne Twp 2	71 392
Chas	Butte Mountain	56 734
Eliza	San Francisco San Francisco 9	681106
Michael	Shasta Shasta	66 760
SHIMAE		
A	Merced Twp 1	60 898
SHIMAN		
John L*	Alameda Brooklyn	55 133
SHIMER		
D B	Calaveras Twp 9	57 374
David	Mariposa Coulterville	60 699
Jacob*	Mariposa Coulterville	60 698
James*	Mariposa Coulterville	60 677
N L	Tehama Pasakent	70 860
SHIMMAL		
Peter	San Mateo Twp 3	65 106
SHIMMER		
George	El Dorado Greenwood	58 726
SHIMMERFUNNY		
Fred	Alameda Brooklyn	55 163
SHIMMIMAN		
Margt	San Francisco San Francisco 2	67 752
SHIMMINS		
Charles	Contra Costa Twp 1	57 520
SHIMPSON		
M M	Yolo Cache	72 609
SHIN		
---	Amador Twp 2	55 291
---	Amador Twp 2	55 312
---	Amador Twp 5	55 352
---	Amador Twp 6	55 449
---	Butte Ophir	56 810
---	Calaveras Twp 10	57 278
---	Del Norte Crescent	58 641
---	El Dorado White Oaks	581032
---	El Dorado Coloma	581122
---	San Francisco San Francisco 4	681204
---	Shasta Shasta	66 669
---	Shasta Shasta	66 670
---	Shasta Horsetown	66 703
---	Shasta Horsetown	66 704
---	Yuba Marysville	72 925
---*	El Dorado Georgetown	58 701
---*	Sierra Twp 5	66 945
A H	Mariposa Twp 3	60 600
Gim	El Dorado Georgetown	58 700
J M	Shasta Shasta	66 667
James	Mendocino Little L	60 837
James H	Shasta Shasta	66 673
Joseph	Shasta Shasta	66 673
Lam	Amador Twp 5	55 366
Loo	Amador Twp 2	55 311
Low	Stanislaus Branch	70 714

Name	County Locale	M653 RollPage
SHIN		
Michael	Shasta Shasta	66 760
Tin	El Dorado Greenwood	58 713
Ton*	Stanislaus Branch	70 713
Tow*	Stanislaus Branch	70 713
W	Calaveras Twp 9	57 395
W*	San Francisco San Francisco 5	67 498
We	Calaveras Twp 10	57 269
SHINDAN		
B K	Placer Yankee J	62 757
James	Yuba Rose Bar	72 797
SHINDLER		
Jacob	Placer Iona Hills	62 877
SHINE		
---	El Dorado Eldorado	58 946
---	Sierra Twp 5	66 945
---	Tuolumne Shawsfla	71 394
---*	Sierra Twp 5	66 945
Ah	Tuolumne Twp 2	71 394
Daniel	San Francisco San Francisco 9	68 992
Eliza	San Francisco San Francisco 9	681056
Eliza	San Francisco San Francisco 9	681106
F	San Francisco San Francisco 9	67 506
Jeremiah	Yuba Slate Ro	72 709
Joseph	San Francisco San Francisco 9	68 950
M T	San Mateo Twp 3	65 92
Margaret	San Francisco San Francisco 8	681292
Mary	San Francisco San Francisco 8	681283
Patrick	Tuolumne Columbia	71 359
Thomas	Tuolumne Columbia	71 346
William	Tuolumne Columbia	71 329
Wm	Butte Ophir	56 776
Wm	Sierra Twp 5	66 943
SHINELS		
C*	Sacramento Ward 1	63 27
SHINER		
J	Siskiyou Klamath	69 79
Jacob	Yolo Cache	72 641
John B	Yolo Slate Ra	72 705
John B	Yuba Slate Ro	72 705
SHINEWOLF		
William	Shasta Shasta	66 732
SHING		
---	Amador Twp 1	55 501
---	Butte Oregon	56 638
---	Butte Oregon	56 640
---	Calaveras Twp 4	57 314
---	Calaveras Twp 4	57 339
---	Calaveras Twp 7	57 45
---	Calaveras Twp 7	57 47
---	Calaveras Twp 8	57 74
---	Calaveras Twp 8	57 76
---	Calaveras Twp 8	57 79
---	El Dorado White Oaks	581022
---	El Dorado White Oaks	581023
---	El Dorado White Oaks	581024
---	El Dorado Salmon Falls	581040
---	El Dorado Salmon Falls	581054
---	El Dorado Salmon Falls	581064
---	El Dorado Coloma	581077
---	El Dorado Coloma	581105
---	El Dorado Kelsey	581134
---	El Dorado Kelsey	581135
---	El Dorado Mountain	581183
---	El Dorado Mountain	581189
---	El Dorado Big Bar	58 736
---	El Dorado Eldorado	58 939
---	El Dorado Eldorado	58 941
---	El Dorado Mud Springs	58 952
---	El Dorado Mud Springs	58 954
---	El Dorado Mud Springs	58 977
---	El Dorado Mud Springs	58 980
---	El Dorado Mud Springs	58 985
---	El Dorado Mud Springs	58 998
---	Marin Cortemad	60 782
---	Placer Auburn	62 596
---	Placer Iona Hills	62 892
---	Sacramento Granite	63 245
---	San Francisco San Francisco 9	681086
---	San Francisco San Francisco 4	681189
---	San Francisco San Francisco 4	681190
---	San Francisco San Francisco 4	681191
---	San Francisco San Francisco 4	681195
---	San Francisco San Francisco 4	681208
---	Shasta Shasta	66 677
---	Shasta Horsetown	66 704
---	Sierra St Louis	66 805
---	Tehama Tehama	70 944
---	Tuolumne Montezuma	71 508
---	Tuolumne Chinese	71 525
---	Yuba New York	72 739
---	Yuba Long Bar	72 758
---	Yuba Long Bar	72 759
---	Yuba Long Bar	72 761
---	Yuba Timbucto	72 787

Name	County Locale	M653 RollPage
SHING		
---	Yuba Marysville	72 868
---	Yuba Marysville	72 925
---*	Calaveras Twp 4	57 339
---*	Sacramento Granite	63 245
---*	Yuba Timbucto	72 787
Ah	Butte Oregon	56 638
Ah	Butte Oregon	56 640
Clen	Del Norte Crescent	58 631
Foe	El Dorado Placerville	58 829
Koy	San Francisco San Francisco 4	681191
Tu	Placer Michigan	62 837
Wa	Merced Twp 1	60 914
SHINGELLOIS		
John	Butte Cascade	56 695
SHINGLE		
Jacob	Placer Iona Hills	62 876
P	Nevada Nevada	61 277
Peter	San Francisco San Francisco 11	67 119
SHINGLETON		
P	Nevada Nevada	61 268
Samuel	Solano Vacaville	69 320
SHINIA		
J*	Nevada Eureka	61 367
SHINICK		
John*	Shasta Horsetown	66 692
SHINIER		
H	Butte Eureka	56 655
SHINISH		
John	Shasta Horsetown	66 692
SHINISK		
John*	Shasta Horsetown	66 692
SHINK		
Samuel	Calaveras Twp 7	57 44
SHINKEL		
Charles	Yuba Marysville	72 955
SHINLAR		
John	Amador Twp 2	55 328
SHINLEY		
John	Yolo Cache	72 591
SHINM		
---*	Calaveras Twp 8	57 59
SHINN		
---	Calaveras Twp 4	57 304
Cynthia	Sonoma Russian	69 438
James	Alameda Brooklyn	55 204
John L	Napa Clear Lake	61 124
John O	Sonoma Russian	69 438
John R	San Joaquin Elkhorn	64 979
John T	Napa Clear Lake	61 124
Moses	Placer Ophirville	62 655
S M	Sonoma Russian	69 439
Thomas	Tuolumne Columbia	71 298
Wm	Sonoma Armally	69 482
SHINNEN		
D*	Mariposa Twp 3	60 585
SHINNEPY		
Kate	San Francisco San Francisco 4	681227
SHINNER		
F H	San Francisco San Francisco 1	68 920
Jacob*	Mariposa Coulterville	60 698
James*	Mariposa Coulterville	60 677
Joseph	Yolo Cache	72 630
SHINNIPY		
Kate*	San Francisco San Francisco 4	681227
SHINNON		
P	Sutter Bear Rvr	70 819
SHINNUE		
---	San Joaquin Stockton	641037
SHINO		
---	El Dorado Placerville	58 923
SHINS		
---*	Yuba Marysville	72 895
Jeremiah	Yolo Slate Ra	72 709
SHINSER		
Richard*	El Dorado Coloma	581117
SHINSON		
Benj*	Placer Virginia	62 661
SHINY		
---	Calaveras Twp 10	57 283
---	Calaveras Twp 4	57 314
---	El Dorado Greenwood	58 728
---	Tuolumne Twp 6	71 533
---*	Calaveras Twp 4	57 339
---*	Sacramento Granite	63 245
SHIP		
---	El Dorado Salmon Falls	581041
---	El Dorado Salmon Falls	581043
---	El Dorado Placerville	58 884
---	San Francisco San Francisco 9	681096
---	San Francisco San Francisco 4	681200
Ah	Calaveras Twp 7	57 16
Forr	San Francisco San Francisco 5	671206
George	Tulara Twp 2	71 20
J M	Siskiyou Klamath	69 88

Name	County Locale	M653 Roll	Page
SHIP			
Yet	El Dorado Placerville	58	829
SHIPAND			
James	Stanislaus Emory	70	757
SHIPARD			
G G	Placer Iona Hills	62	873
George	Placer Todds Va	62	764
SHIPBERG			
Frank	San Francisco San Francisco 3	67	44
SHIPBIRG			
Frank	San Francisco San Francisco 3	67	44
SHIPER			
Coryden*	Napa Clear Lake	61	132
I H*	San Francisco San Francisco 3	67	1
J H*	San Francisco San Francisco 3	67	1
Kate	San Francisco San Francisco 9	681	085
Morris*	Napa Clear Lake	61	132
SHIPHERD			
J G	Marin Cortemad	60	752
M	Napa Clear Lake	61	131
SHIPIR			
Morris	Napa Clear Lake	61	132
SHIPLAY			
Richd	Butte Oregon	56	620
SHIPLEY			
Aaron	Plumas Quincy	621	006
Adam	Plumas Quincy	62	978
Andrew J	San Francisco San Francisco 7	681	441
B M	Stanislaus Empire	70	729
C L	Tehama Lassen	70	868
David	Amador Twp 6	55	442
E	Trinity Mouth Ca	701	010
Emeline	Yolo Cache	72	644
Falbutj E	Calaveras Twp 5	57	199
H W	Yolo Putah	72	614
James L	Calaveras Twp 7	57	13
Kate	San Francisco San Francisco 4	681	228
Perry L	Placer Virginia	62	670
R G	Sonoma Russian	69	429
Richd	Butte Oregon	56	620
Robert	Tuolumne Twp 5	71	520
S	Butte Cascade	56	695
Talbert	Calaveras Twp 5	57	199
Talbut E	Calaveras Twp 5	57	199
W M	El Dorado Placerville	58	922
W V	El Dorado Placerville	58	865
Wm*	Nevada Eureka	61	351
SHIPMAN			
Chas G	Sonoma Santa Rosa	69	388
George	Sierra Downieville	661	021
H	Sierra La Porte	66	783
J C	Amador Twp 1	55	457
John	Sonoma Russian	69	437
Sines	Sierra La Porte	66	783
SHIPP			
Forr	San Francisco San Francisco 5	671	206
J	Sutter Nicolaus	70	830
SHIPPANE			
Samuel*	Calaveras Twp 5	57	187
SHIPPARD			
Miguel	Los Angeles San Gabriel	59	413
SHIPPAVEL			
Samuel*	Calaveras Twp 5	57	187
SHIPPER			
L W	San Joaquin Stockton	641	058
SHIPPEY			
Burton	Marin Bolinas	60	733
Henry	Solano Vallejo	69	276
SHIPPLE			
Lonard D	El Dorado Georgetown	58	698
SHIPPOY			
Burton*	Marin Bolinas	60	733
SHIPPY			
J	El Dorado Grizzly	581	182
SHIPSTON			
John A	San Francisco San Francisco 11	67	152
SHIPTON			
M	Sacramento Sutter	63	294
SHIR			
---	Calaveras Twp 6	57	121
SHIRA			
Jacob	El Dorado Placerville	58	930
SHIRBEY			
Ed	Sacramento Cosumnes	63	382
SHIRE			
Dolores*	Los Angeles Los Angeles	59	363
Philip	Siskiyou Callahan	69	17
SHIRELAND			
Wm	Nevada Nevada	61	260
SHIRELY			
Craven	Plumas Quincy	62	920
SHIREN			
Mary	Marin San Rafael	60	769
SHIRER			
J M	Alameda Oakland	55	50

Name	County Locale	M653 Roll	Page
SHIRES			
J A*	Calaveras Twp 9	57	406
SHIRIDAN			
Sarah	San Francisco San Francisco 4	681	160
SHIRIDEN			
T	El Dorado Diamond	58	812
SHIRIFF			
Thos	Sonoma Sonoma	69	637
SHIRILT			
William*	Placer Iona Hills	62	865
SHIRINGLER			
William*	Del Norte Crescent	58	630
SHIRITT			
William*	Placer Iona Hills	62	865
SHIRLAND			
Frank	Placer Virginia	62	662
Mary	Alameda Oakland	55	5
SHIRLEY			
Adam	Nevada Rough &	61	396
Chas W	Placer Secret R	62	610
Francis	San Francisco San Francisco 1	68	909
Franklin	San Francisco San Francisco 9	681	034
George	San Mateo Twp 3	65	81
J H	Sacramento Ward 1	63	101
J H	Sacramento Ward 1	63	36
J L	Butte Kimshaw	56	596
J M	Calaveras Twp 8	57	80
James M	Tuolumne Twp 3	71	432
John	Butte Ophir	56	747
John	San Francisco San Francisco 4	681	127
John	Sierra Cox'S Bar	66	950
Lewis	Plumas Quincy	62	985
Lucy J	Colusa Monroeville	57	450
Madison	San Joaquin Castoria	64	882
Moses	Sierra Twp 5	66	938
Paul	Solano Benecia	69	295
S	San Joaquin Stockton	641	009
W D	El Dorado Mud Springs	58	979
William	San Joaquin Castoria	64	907
Wm	Sacramento Natonia	63	281
Wm H	Los Angeles Elmonte	59	257
Wm H	Los Angeles Elmonte	59	262
SHIRLING			
William	San Francisco San Francisco 7	681	374
SHIRLOCK			
S W*	San Francisco San Francisco 3	67	1
SHIRLY			
Agnes	San Francisco San Francisco 2	67	759
Benj	San Francisco San Francisco 2	67	646
Theodore	Placer Yankee J	62	775
SHIRMAN			
Edward	Yuba Marysville	72	865
Isaac T	Contra Costa Twp 2	57	549
Manuel*	Contra Costa Twp 3	57	614
SHIRT			
A	El Dorado Diamond	58	797
August	Shasta French G	66	719
J	Nevada Eureka	61	376
Joseua	Shasta Shasta	66	674
Lawrence	Butte Oregon	56	614
M B*	Colusa Monroeville	57	440
Thomas	Sierra Cox'S Bar	66	951
SHIRTAS			
Henry*	San Francisco San Francisco 9	68	999
SHIRTER			
William*	Siskiyou Scott Ri	69	82
SHIRTS			
Henry	Amador Twp 3	55	370
John H	Sierra Twp 7	66	900
SHIRWOOD			
John	Placer Yankee J	62	776
SHIRY			
---	Amador Twp 2	55	314
Chee	Amador Twp 5	55	333
Lee	Amador Twp 2	55	291
SHISE			
Philip*	Siskiyou Callahan	69	17
SHISEMAN			
Chas*	Nevada Bridgeport	61	469
SHISEY			
David*	Sacramento Ward 1	63	93
SHISLER			
Ernst	San Francisco San Francisco 1	68	834
SHISLEY			
W B	Stanislaus Emory	70	756
SHISS			
---	Amador Twp 1	55	496
SHISSLER			
John	Placer Michigan	62	821
SHISSMAN			
O	San Francisco San Francisco 3	67	21
SHISST			
Wm	Placer Stewart	62	607
SHISTER			
Henry	San Francisco San Francisco 8	681	307
SHISTLER			
George*	Yuba New York	72	736

Name	County Locale	M653 Roll	Page
SHISTONSON			
E J*	El Dorado Greenwood	58	712
SHIT			
---	Sierra Downieville	66	998
---*	Amador Twp 3	55	401
SHITE			
H	Nevada Grass Valley	61	236
Nicholas	El Dorado Salmon Falls	581	055
Wm	Merced Twp 2	60	917
SHITLING			
J	Calaveras Twp 9	57	405
SHIVALL			
Louis*	San Mateo Twp 3	65	106
SHIVARA			
R*	Mariposa Twp 3	60	592
SHIVELY			
V H	Tehama Red Bluff	70	903
W R	Trinity Weaverville	701	055
Wm B	Humbolt Pacific	59	131
SHIVER			
Orrin	Calaveras Twp 6	57	149
W	El Dorado Placerville	58	915
SHIVERS			
Wm P	Sierra Scales D	66	803
SHIVERSANT			
John	San Joaquin Oneal	64	937
SHIZA			
Conrad*	San Francisco San Francisco 7	681	333
SHIZIE			
---	El Dorado Eldorado	58	940
SHLEE			
A*	Nevada Eureka	61	353
SHLEGTHER			
Louis	San Francisco San Francisco 11	67	149
SHLESINGER			
Morris	Los Angeles Los Angeles	59	327
SHLETT			
Charles*	Plumas Quincy	62	967
SHLINGHEIDO			
Henry	San Francisco San Francisco 7	681	354
SHLINGRHYAN			
Augusts	San Francisco San Francisco 7	681	399
SHLISHAMS			
Ha	San Francisco San Francisco 10	67	330
SHLLON			
Thos	Sonoma Vallejo	69	626
SHLOSS			
M	San Francisco San Francisco 2	67	792
SHLOTLERBELT			
Frederick	San Francisco San Francisco 10	67	265
SHLOTTERBEK			
Frederick	San Francisco San Francisco 10	67	265
SHLUND			
S	Trinity Indian C	70	987
SHMILL			
Jno*	Butte Kimshaw	56	603
SHMITZ			
Annald	Placer Dutch Fl	62	724
SHN			
---	Calaveras Twp 10	57	295
---*	Tuolumne Montezuma	71	512
SHNEIDER			
Chas*	Butte Oregon	56	626
SHNIMER			
Christian*	Nevada Bloomfield	61	519
SHNISER			
Richard*	El Dorado Coloma	581	117
SHNPIT			
Shnpit	Tulara Twp 1	71	113
SHNTI			
Joseph*	Calaveras Twp 7	57	36
SHO			
---	Alameda Oakland	55	63
SHOABEATTEN			
Cheis*	Mariposa Twp 3	60	558
SHOAHEATON			
Ceheis	Mariposa Twp 3	60	558
SHOAHEATSON			
Ceheis*	Mariposa Twp 3	60	558
SHOAHEATTE			
Csheis*	Mariposa Twp 3	60	558
SHOAHIATTE			
Chas*	Mariposa Twp 3	60	558
SHOAL			
Joseph	Siskiyou Scott Va	69	23
SHOALWATER			
John	San Joaquin Stockton	641	064
SHOART			
H	Trinity Turner'S	70	997
Wm*	Alameda Oakland	55	11
SHOAT			
John	Tehama Pasakent	70	860

California 1860 Census Index

Name	County Locale	M653 Roll	Page
SHOATS			
Fred	Calaveras Twp 9	57	355
SHOBE			
A J	Sacramento Ward 4	63	515
Suther	Contra Costa Twp 2	57	547
SHOBRIDGE			
S A*	Sacramento Ward 1	63	132
SHOCH			
---	Mariposa Twp 1	60	664
SHOCK			
---	Mariposa Twp 1	60	664
Edward	Contra Costa Twp 3	57	590
John	Sacramento Ward 1	63	67
SHOCKER			
J*	Shasta Horsetown	66	708
SHOCKLESS			
Patrick	Plumas Quincy	62	957
SHOCKLEY			
Florroy*	San Francisco San Francisco 9	68	1003
Melinda	Yuba Marysville	72	968
William	San Francisco San Francisco 4	68	1147
SHOCKTON			
Antoine	Calaveras Twp 5	57	187
SHODES			
H	Nevada Grass Valley	61	236
SHODGEN			
Nathaniel	San Joaquin Castoria	64	911
SHODI			
John H*	Tuolumne Twp 1	71	483
SHODRON			
H	Amador Twp 7	55	417
SHODSON			
H*	Amador Twp 7	55	417
SHOEBRGS			
Louis*	El Dorado Georgetown	58	686
SHOEBRIDGE			
Frederick	San Francisco San Francisco 11	67	139
SHOEMAK			
Henry	San Francisco San Francisco 4	68	1124
SHOEMAKE			
Henry	San Francisco San Francisco 4	68	1124
John	Mendocino Arrana	60	858
Luther	Tuolumne Green Springs	71	527
William	Mendocino Arrana	60	857
SHOEMAKER			
Almis	Contra Costa Twp 2	57	545
C	Nevada Grass Valley	61	188
C	San Francisco San Francisco 2	67	674
C	Shasta Shasta	66	656
Chas	Amador Twp 1	55	493
Conrad	Sonoma Petaluma	69	580
D	Nevada Grass Valley	61	202
Danl	Sierra Twp 5	66	925
David W	San Joaquin Oneal	64	913
E	Klamath Liberty	59	234
E M	Sutter Yuba	70	773
F D	San Joaquin Douglass	64	914
Francis M	Calaveras Twp 4	57	333
Geo	Klamath Klamath	59	226
Geo	Klamath Liberty	59	234
George	Sierra Gibsonville	66	853
H	Shasta Millvill	66	744
H	Sutter Yuba	70	766
Henry	Placer Secret R	62	610
I S	Amador Twp 2	55	302
J A	Placer Mealsburg	62	702
J F	Nevada Bloomfield	61	509
James	Stanislaus Emory	70	753
Jno	Klamath Liberty	59	243
John	El Dorado Casumnes	58	1176
John	El Dorado Georgetown	58	699
John	Humbolt Pacific	59	130
John W	Colusa Grand Island	57	471
L S	Amador Twp 2	55	302
Luther	Tuolumne Twp 5	71	527
M	Shasta Horsetown	66	698
Michael	Tuolumne Big Oak	71	129
N	Mariposa Twp 3	60	575
Peter	Butte Ophir	56	773
T	El Dorado Placerville	58	847
T T	El Dorado Placerville	58	931
W B	Santa Clara San Jose	65	317
W S	Alameda Brooklyn	55	84
William D	Sierra Gibsonville	66	853
Wm	Tuolumne Big Oak	71	129
SHOEN			
Bastana	Santa Clara San Jose	65	290
SHOENBERG			
Saml	Tuolumne Twp 1	71	206
SHOENBIGS			
Louis*	El Dorado Georgetown	58	686
SHOENBOGS			
Louis*	El Dorado Georgetown	58	686
SHOENBORG			
John	Solano Montezuma	69	371
SHOENBRIGS			
Louis	El Dorado Georgetown	58	686
SHOENEMMAN			
Atto	San Francisco San Francisco 2	67	705
Otto	San Francisco San Francisco 2	67	705
SHOENHUTE			
M Aug	Santa Clara San Jose	65	335
SHOENS			
Louis	San Francisco San Francisco 3	67	31
SHOERDLIN			
Jno M	Sacramento Ward 4	63	531
SHOEST			
John*	Tuolumne Green Springs	71	527
SHOEWBRGS			
Louis*	El Dorado Georgetown	58	686
SHOEY			
---	Trinity Trininad Rvr	70	1047
SHOFEN			
L N*	El Dorado Georgetown	58	757
SHOFER			
Mary	Sacramento Ward 1	63	112
SHOFF			
Josiah	Sacramento Natonia	63	282
SHOFFER			
John	San Francisco San Francisco 4	68	1115
L	Nevada Eureka	61	368
SHOFFORD			
James H	Nevada Rough &	61	417
SHOH			
---	Alameda Oakland	55	24
SHOHR			
John	Alameda Brooklyn	55	140
SHOITS			
Peter	Solano Fremont	69	381
SHOIY			
Fink	El Dorado Greenwood	58	719
SHOK			
---	Calaveras Twp 10	57	278
SHOKA			
Madin	San Francisco San Francisco 4	68	1224
SHOLD			
Peter	San Mateo Twp 2	65	120
SHOLDS			
J	Sutter Sutter	70	813
SHOLEEY			
J	Nevada Grass Valley	61	215
SHOLES			
Charles L	Sierra Downieville	66	963
SHOLL			
Morris	Sierra Scales D	66	800
Peter	Del Norte Happy Ca	58	668
SHOLLA			
Lonie	Contra Costa Twp 1	57	521
SHOLLAND			
Kralt J*	Yuba Marysville	72	906
SHOLSON			
James	Yolo No E Twp	72	673
SHOLTZ			
Jno	Sacramento Granite	63	266
SHOMA			
Blaise	San Francisco San Francisco 10	67	248
SHOMACKER			
Albert	San Francisco San Francisco 2	67	674
SHOMAKE			
Peator	Amador Twp 2	55	286
SHOMAKET			
William	Klamath S Fork	59	197
SHOMBURY			
John	Solano Montezuma	69	371
SHOMDS			
Charles A*	San Francisco 3	67	83
SHOMMSHE			
Wm	Butte Ophir	56	774
SHOMPRA			
Jas	Sacramento Ward 4	63	514
SHOMS			
Oliver	Sierra Twp 7	66	910
SHON			
---	El Dorado Kelsey	58	1144
---	San Francisco San Francisco 4	68	1176
---	San Francisco San Francisco 7	68	1335
---	Shasta Shasta	66	677
---	Shasta Horsetown	66	703
---	Siskiyou Scott Va	69	22
---*	San Francisco San Francisco 9	68	1088
---*	San Francisco San Francisco 9	68	1092
Ah	Butte Bidwell	56	720
Ah*	Siskiyou Scott Va	69	22
Buck*	Yuba Bear Rvr	72	1000
SHONA			
---	El Dorado Casumnes	58	1164
SHONART			
George	Amador Twp 4	55	246
SHONE			
---	El Dorado Eldorado	58	939
SHONE			
---	El Dorado Mud Springs	58	975
A	Siskiyou Scott Va	69	25
John	Tehama Tehama	70	942
M G	El Dorado Placerville	58	893
Peter	San Francisco San Francisco 1	68	914
SHONEBURG			
E	Solano Benecia	69	309
SHONEMAN			
Fred*	El Dorado Georgetown	58	703
SHONERS			
Wm	Trinity Weaverville	70	1078
SHONES			
Frances	San Francisco San Francisco 1	68	856
SHONG			
---	Alameda Oakland	55	34
---	Amador Township	55	465
---	Calaveras Twp 6	57	122
---	Calaveras Twp 5	57	252
---	Calaveras Twp 5	57	255
---	Calaveras Twp 4	57	342
---	Calaveras Twp 8	57	62
---	Calaveras Twp 8	57	83
---	Del Norte Happy Ca	58	667
---	El Dorado White Oaks	58	1016
---	El Dorado Coloma	58	1086
---	El Dorado Coloma	58	1105
---	El Dorado Coloma	58	1108
---	El Dorado Placerville	58	929
---	El Dorado Mud Springs	58	966
---	Mariposa Twp 1	60	651
---	San Francisco San Francisco 9	68	1093
---	Tuolumne Twp 3	71	457
---	Yuba Long Bar	72	763
---*	Calaveras Twp 5	57	252
---*	Sacramento Granite	63	245
SHONIDS			
Charles A*	San Francisco 3	67	83
SHONLAR			
John*	Amador Twp 2	55	328
SHONLTZ			
F W*	Napa Napa	61	99
SHONS			
James A	Mendocino Ukiah	60	803
SHONSON			
J	Nevada Nevada	61	277
SHONST			
John*	Tuolumne Twp 5	71	527
SHONT			
W T	Tehama Tehama	70	942
Wm	San Francisco San Francisco 1	68	926
SHONTULBEYGAN			
---*	Nevada Eureka	61	365
SHONWASSER			
Saml	San Francisco San Francisco 2	67	639
SHONY			
---	Calaveras Twp 5	57	255
---	El Dorado Coloma	58	1108
---	El Dorado Greenwood	58	728
---	Plumas Meadow Valley	62	910
SHOO			
---	Amador Twp 4	55	332
---	Calaveras Twp 8	57	68
---	Del Norte Crescent	58	659
---	Tuolumne Jamestown	71	469
---*	Calaveras Twp 7	57	46
SHOOA			
---	El Dorado Union	58	1090
SHOOHTON			
Antoine*	Calaveras Twp 5	57	187
SHOOK			
---	Butte Oro	56	675
Henry	San Francisco San Francisco 1	68	861
John	Trinity Weaverville	70	1073
Peter	Placer Virginia	62	677
Thos	Placer Virginia	62	677
SHOOLER			
---	Amador Twp 5	55	343
SHOON			
---	El Dorado Coloma	58	1085
---	El Dorado Diamond	58	795
SHOONER			
Simon	San Francisco San Francisco 9	68	952
Wm*	San Francisco San Francisco 2	67	647
SHOOP			
John	Yuba New York	72	731
SHOOSTER			
Elizabeth	Sonoma Mendocino	69	461
Wm	Sonoma Mendocino	69	461
SHOP			
---	El Dorado Diamond	58	797
Ye	Tuolumne Twp 5	71	504
SHOPEN			
John	Yolo Cache	72	597
L N*	El Dorado Georgetown	58	757

California 1860 Census Index

Name	County Locale	M653 Roll Page
SHOPMAN		
A	Sonoma Washington	69 666
R	Sonoma Washington	69 666
SHOR		
---	Alameda Oakland	55 53
SHORA		
Ignalio	Los Angeles Azuza	59 275
SHORAN		
Fred	Sonoma Sonoma	69 659
SHORBURNE		
George	Trinity Grass Valley	70 962
SHORD		
C*	Nevada Grass Valley	61 195
SHORDON		
Thomas	San Francisco San Francisco 7	681387
SHORE		
Charles	Alameda Oakland	55 75
Delores	Los Angeles Los Angeles	59 363
Dolores*	Los Angeles Los Angeles	59 363
Ed*	Sacramento Cosumnes	63 383
Edward	Plumas Quincy	62 915
J M*	Shasta Shasta	66 667
James	San Joaquin Douglass	64 922
John W	Los Angeles Los Angeles	59 348
Robert	Santa Cruz Pescadero	66 645
Thomas	Santa Cruz Pescadero	66 645
Thos	Santa Clara Fremont	65 437
Thos P	Santa Clara Fremont	65 437
Wm	Santa Clara San Jose	65 384
SHOREAN		
Peter	Calaveras Twp 10	57 260
SHOREL		
C*	Nevada Grass Valley	61 195
SHORER		
J P	Colusa Grand Island	57 471
SHORERSON		
J*	San Francisco San Francisco 9	681058
SHORES		
F	Butte Kimshaw	56 589
J C	Siskiyou Scott Va	69 30
James	Siskiyou Scott Va	69 42
James A	Mendocino Ukiah	60 803
John	Napa Yount	61 46
William	Siskiyou Scott Va	69 42
SHORET		
C*	Nevada Grass Valley	61 195
SHOREY		
Samuel	Solano Suisan	69 209
SHORG		
---*	Calaveras Twp 5	57 252
SHORK		
George A	Calaveras Twp 8	57 80
SHORKER		
Jas	San Francisco San Francisco 1	68 864
SHORKLEY		
Tho	Nevada Eureka	61 356
Thos	Nevada Eureka	61 356
SHORLER		
William*	Siskiyou Scott Ri	69 82
SHORLIN		
Peter	Shasta Shasta	66 687
SHORMO		
---	Mendocino Calpella	60 823
SHORMUKER		
Francis M	Calaveras Twp 4	57 333
SHORMUKERS		
Francis M	Calaveras Twp 4	57 333
SHORN		
John	Shasta Millvill	66 752
SHORNMICK		
James*	Calaveras Twp 8	57 78
SHORNNICK		
James*	Calaveras Twp 8	57 78
SHOROCKS		
Thomas*	Placer Michigan	62 856
SHORPSHIRE		
John	Tulara Visalia	71 102
SHORST		
John*	Tuolumne Green Springs	71 527
SHORT LEGS		
---	Tulara Twp 2	71 38
SHORT		
A W	Klamath S Fork	59 198
Alex	Siskiyou Scott Va	69 43
Alex	Tehama Antelope	70 894
Andrew	Shasta Horsetown	66 706
B F	Klamath S Fork	59 197
Blake	Marin San Rafael	60 773
C	El Dorado Placerville	58 882
David	Sacramento Dry Crk	63 369
E S	Sutter Yuba	70 763
Elaine	Yuba Marysville	72 975
Elam	Yuba Marysville	72 975
F	Shasta Millvill	66 745
Geo	Mariposa Twp 1	60 641
H	Shasta Millvill	66 745
SHORT		
Harrison	Santa Clara Santa Clara	65 518
Henry	San Francisco San Francisco 8	681262
J	Marin San Rafael	60 760
J	Nevada Eureka	61 376
J	Siskiyou Scott Va	69 56
J L*	Sacramento Alabama	63 417
J M*	Shasta Shasta	66 667
J S*	Sacramento Alabama	63 417
James M	Humbolt Union	59 191
Jas	San Francisco San Francisco 1	68 872
Jno R	Mendocino Ukiah	60 798
Jno W	Mendocino Ukiah	60 798
John	San Francisco San Francisco 4	681114
John	San Francisco San Francisco 2	67 672
John	San Francisco San Francisco 1	68 828
John	Sierra Monte Crk	661038
John	Sierra Poker Flats	66 839
John	Tehama Moons	70 852
John	Tulara Sinks Te	71 43
L	Calaveras Twp 9	57 394
L R	Trinity Lewiston	70 953
Lewis	Yolo Washington	72 599
Morgan	Shasta Horsetown	66 705
Peter	San Francisco San Francisco 11	147
		67
R H	Mariposa Twp 3	60 615
Rufas	Santa Clara Santa Clara	65 506
S R	Trinity Lewiston	70 953
Sophie*	Shasta Horsetown	66 706
Sophio	Shasta Horsetown	66 706
Stephen	Santa Cruz Millvall	66 553
T	Calaveras Twp 9	57 394
Tho*	Trinity Taylor'S	701036
Thomas	Calaveras Twp 9	57 353
Thos	Trinity Taylor'S	701036
W C	Tehama Red Bluff	70 911
W H	Santa Clara Fremont	65 433
William	Siskiyou Yreka	69 190
William	Siskiyou Scott Va	69 43
Wm	Santa Clara Fremont	65 439
Wm H	Trinity Taylor'S	701036
Wm H	Humbolt Bucksport	59 162
Wm M	Sierra Eureka	661048
Young	San Francisco San Francisco 4	681161
SHORTALL		
M	Nevada Red Dog	61 556
Martin	Nevada Little Y	61 531
Robt	San Francisco San Francisco 10	167
		67
SHORTELL		
P*	Nevada Eureka	61 347
SHORTEN		
Jas	Sacramento Ward 4	63 538
Mary	San Francisco San Francisco 2	67 629
SHORTER		
Richard	Santa Clara San Jose	65 318
William*	Siskiyou Scott Ri	69 82
P	Nevada Eureka	61 347
SHORTILL		
P	Nevada Eureka	61 347
SHORTIN		
Peter	Shasta Shasta	66 687
SHORTLY		
A M	Nevada Grass Valley	61 189
SHORTOLL		
Martin	Nevada Little Y	61 531
SHORTON		
James	San Francisco San Francisco 9	68 952
SHORTRY		
S B*	El Dorado Mountain	581185
SHORTS		
Martin	Siskiyou Yreka	69 124
Peter	Solano Fremont	69 381
SHORTY		
---	Fresno Twp 2	59 110
---	Mendocino Big Rock	60 876
---	Placer Dutch Fl	62 731
S B	El Dorado Mountain	581185
SHORY		
Andrew	Nevada Rough &	61 400
John	Yolo Putah	72 551
SHORYER		
James*	Marin Cortemad	60 789
SHOSEY		
Samuel*	Solano Suisan	69 209
SHOSHOTE		
---	Mendocino Big Rvr	60 853
SHOSN		
John*	Shasta Millvill	66 752
SHOSTER		
John	Nevada Rough &	61 403
SHOT		
Jacob	Tuolumne Sonora	71 193
SHOTE		
John	Tehama Tehama	70 939
Marie S	San Francisco San Francisco 7	681412
SHOTERELL		
Benj*	Amador Twp 6	55 437
SHOTEULL		
Benj*	Amador Twp 6	55 437
SHOTIE		
R	San Francisco San Francisco 7	681332
SHOTRIDGE		
O F	Amador Twp 2	55 316
Samuel	Nevada Rough &	61 403
SHOTSWORTH		
Mary	San Francisco San Francisco 9	681034
SHOTWELL		
Benj*	Amador Twp 6	55 437
Isaac	Tuolumne Columbia	71 326
S W*	Tuolumne Columbia	71 326
SHOU		
---	El Dorado Georgetown	58 745
---	San Joaquin Stockton	641088
SHOUA		
---*	El Dorado Casumnes	581164
SHOUCK		
A	San Francisco San Francisco 5	67 491
SHOUET		
Hamond	Calaveras Twp 4	57 314
SHOULAR		
John*	Amador Twp 2	55 328
SHOULDER		
Frederick	San Diego Agua Caliente	64 855
SHOULTS		
Jas	San Mateo Twp 3	65 92
SHOULTZ		
F W	Napa Napa	61 99
SHOUNG		
---*	Calaveras Twp 5	57 246
SHOURDS		
Benjn	San Francisco San Francisco 9	68 990
Charles A*	San Francisco 3	67 83
	San Francisco	
SHOUSDS		
Charles A	San Francisco San Francisco 3	67 83
SHOUSE		
Benj	Napa Napa	61 75
Berry	Napa Napa	61 75
J	Shasta Millvill	66 745
SHOUT		
John	Sacramento Franklin	63 334
SHOUTRILBEYGAN		
---*	Nevada Eureka	61 365
SHOUTULBEYGAN		
---	Nevada Eureka	61 365
SHOUYR		
J B*	Calaveras Twp 6	57 114
SHOVEL		
J F	Tuolumne Twp 2	71 340
SHOVERSON		
J*	San Francisco San Francisco 9	681058
SHOVERZ		
James	Tuolumne Big Oak	71 137
SHOVES		
May	Mariposa Twp 3	60 546
Muny	Mariposa Twp 3	60 546
SHOVETT		
John	Sierra Scales D	66 802
SHOW		
---	Calaveras Twp 6	57 158
---	Calaveras Twp 10	57 275
---	Calaveras Twp 10	57 295
---	Calaveras Twp 4	57 307
---	Calaveras Twp 4	57 313
---	El Dorado Georgetown	58 745
---	El Dorado Mud Springs	58 951
---	Mariposa Twp 1	60 643
---	Mariposa Twp 1	60 659
---	San Francisco San Francisco 9	681088
---	San Francisco San Francisco 9	681092
---	Siskiyou Scott Ri	69 73
---*	San Francisco San Francisco 9	681092
Ah*	Siskiyou Scott Va	69 22
Buck	Yuba Bear Rvr	721000
Chas	San Francisco San Francisco 10	247
		67
Teresa	San Francisco San Francisco 10	247
		67
Wong*	Mariposa Twp 1	60 626
SHOWEE		
---	Alameda Oakland	55 63
SHOWER		
Chas	Placer Dutch Fl	62 724
Jacob	Placer Iona Hills	62 876
Lawrence	Placer Iona Hills	62 876
SHOWERS		
Jacob O	Humbolt Eel Rvr	59 147
James	Tuolumne Twp 4	71 137
Xavier	Los Angeles Los Angeles	59 314
SHOWHAN		
---	Mendocino Big Rvr	60 855

California 1860 Census Index

Name	County Locale	M653 RollPage
SHOWLER		
Thos	Sacramento Ward 1	63 27
SHOWLWATER		
Dan	Mariposa Twp 1	60 670
SHOWMAKER		
C	Shasta Shasta	66 656
George	Sierra Gibsonville	66 853
SHOWMAN		
Peter	San Francisco San Francisco 2	67 775
SHOWWALTERS		
John*	Calaveras Twp 6	57 187
Thos	Calaveras Twp 5	57 187
SHOY		
---	Amador Twp 3	55 410
---	Calaveras Twp 4	57 300
---	El Dorado Eldorado	58 940
---	San Francisco San Francisco 4	681178
---	San Francisco San Francisco 4	681187
---	Tuolumne Twp 1	71 476
David	Yuba Long Bar	72 756
Thos C	Santa Cruz Pescadero	66 653
Yon*	San Francisco San Francisco 4	681175
You	San Francisco San Francisco 4	681175
Yow*	San Francisco San Francisco 4	681175
SHOYOCK		
S*	Yolo Putah	72 588
SHPER		
Joseph	Sierra Scales D	66 800
SHQUAG		
---	Mariposa Coulterville	60 681
SHQUAY		
---	Mariposa Coulterville	60 681
SHR		
---	Calaveras Twp 6	57 164
---	Trinity Weaverville	701074
SHRAD		
T	Calaveras Twp 9	57 396
SHRADER		
Charles	Yolo Washington	72 572
F	Yolo Merritt	72 584
H	Yolo Merritt	72 584
Henry J	San Francisco San Francisco 10	247 67
John	Nevada Bloomfield	61 523
John	Yuba Suida	72 994
Nicholas	Yolo Cottonwoood	72 658
Wm A*	Napa Napa	61 110
Wm H	Napa Napa	61 110
SHRADIE		
Nicholas*	Yolo Cottonwoood	72 658
SHRAM		
John	Plumas Quincy	621005
SHRANK		
John	Yuba Bear Rvr	72 999
SHRANKS		
David	El Dorado Big Bar	58 741
SHRANT		
Peter	Santa Clara San Jose	65 283
SHRAP		
James	El Dorado Greenwood	58 718
SHRASER		
Joseph	Placer Forest H	62 765
SHREAL		
Andrew	Calaveras Twp 10	57 283
SHREEVE		
Benjamin*	Contra Costa Twp 2	57 544
SHREIRE		
A D	San Joaquin Oneal	64 930
SHREKEN		
Cornelius*	Santa Clara Fremont	65 439
SHRENK		
Peter	El Dorado Greenwood	58 708
SHREO		
---*	Calaveras Twp 6	57 150
SHRERK		
Peter*	El Dorado Georgetown	58 708
SHRESK		
Peter*	El Dorado Georgetown	58 708
SHRESLOCK		
Jno*	Butte Eureka	56 653
SHRETTS		
Andrew*	Santa Cruz Pescadero	66 648
SHREV		
---*	Calaveras Twp 6	57 150
SHREVE		
Benjamin F	Tuolumne Twp 5	71 500
Eorge W	Tuolumne Twp 5	71 500
George W	Tuolumne Chinese	71 500
John	Calaveras Twp 8	57 108
SHREVES		
Cristopher	Mariposa Twp 3	60 614
SHREWSBURY		
L M	El Dorado Mud Springs	58 965
N S	San Bernardino San Bernadino	64 626
SHRIBER		
Capist	Tuolumne Twp 5	71 513
SHRICK		
Augt	Sonoma Petaluma	69 596
SHRIES		
J A	Calaveras Twp 9	57 406
SHRILDS		
Jno A*	Butte Eureka	56 655
SHRIN		
---	Sierra La Porte	66 790
SHRINER		
A T*	Mariposa Twp 3	60 575
H	Butte Eureka	56 655
SHRING		
---	El Dorado Salmon Hills	581064
SHRINKEIMS		
G	Yolo Putah	72 587
SHRITE		
---	San Francisco San Francisco 4	681223
SHRITETON		
James*	El Dorado Georgetown	58 751
SHRIUN		
John D*	Nevada Rough &	61 405
SHRIVER		
C W	Mariposa Twp 3	60 575
J B	Sierra Downieville	66 995
John	Sierra Twp 5	66 936
SHRIVIR		
J B*	Sierra Downieville	66 995
SHRNIMEN		
Faier	El Dorado Georgetown	58 703
SHROBE		
John*	Sierra La Porte	66 779
SHROCK		
E	Mariposa Coulterville	60 697
SHROCKS		
Thomas*	Placer Michigan	62 856
SHRODER		
Henry	Plumas Quincy	621005
John D	San Francisco San Francisco 7	681376
M	Sutter Yuba	70 774
SHROLEY		
D J	Solano Fremont	69 381
SHRONE		
Louis H	Yolo Slate Ra	72 709
SHROON		
F J	Sacramento Ward 1	63 111
SHROPSHIRE		
James	Yolo Slate Ra	72 705
James	Yuba Slate Ro	72 705
Lemuel	Sonoma Mendocino	69 451
SHRUD		
Joseph	Tuolumne Twp 2	71 284
SHRUE		
A*	Siskiyou Scott Va	69 25
SHRUEL		
Joseph	Tuolumne Twp 2	71 284
SHRUESTER		
I T*	Nevada Red Dog	61 546
SHRULL		
Jno	Butte Kimshaw	56 603
SHRUM		
John D	Nevada Rough &	61 405
Joseph*	Yolo Cache Crk	72 630
SHRUVE		
Benjamin	Contra Costa Twp 2	57 544
SHRYOCK		
S	Yolo Putah	72 588
SHSHMORE		
J	Amador Twp 5	55 350
SHTIN		
Col C	El Dorado Greenwood	58 725
SHTTON		
Thos*	Sonoma Vallejo	69 626
SHU		
---	Amador Twp 5	55 356
---	Placer Iona Hills	62 869
---	Placer Iona Hills	62 894
---	Sierra St Louis	66 815
---	Trinity Weaverville	701074
---	Tuolumne Jamestown	71 421
---	Tuolumne Twp 3	71 466
---	Tuolumne Sonora	71 485
---	Yolo Slate Ra	72 715
---	Yuba Slate Ro	72 715
Hin	Yuba Long Bar	72 757
Hon	Yuba Long Bar	72 757
Lee	Shasta Horsetown	66 701
Lung	Placer Iona Hills	62 869
Su	Shasta Horsetown	66 701
Wang	Placer Iona Hills	62 869
Yng	Tuolumne Twp 6	71 533
SHUA		
---	Mendocino Calpella	60 824
---	Placer Secret R	62 621
Gim	El Dorado Mud Springs	58 961
SHUAN		
David	Tuolumne Sonora	71 237
SHUAN		
Davin	Tuolumne Twp 1	71 237
SHUAP		
J T	El Dorado Placerville	58 843
SHUART		
J S B	Santa Clara Alviso	65 403
SHUBACK		
Owin	Monterey San Juan	60 976
SHUBBUCK		
A L	Sierra Downieville	66 953
SHUBERT		
Albert	Los Angeles Los Angeles	59 340
Henry	San Francisco San Francisco 2	67 689
SHUBLE		
F	Butte Kimshaw	56 606
SHUBRICK		
Jacob	Sierra Pine Grove	66 824
SHUBUICK		
Jacob	Sierra Pine Grove	66 824
SHUCK		
---	Mariposa Twp 1	60 673
---	Shasta French G	66 712
Christ	Siskiyou Yreka	69 135
F	Sacramento Cosumnes	63 406
Frank	Los Angeles Tejon	59 537
J Z	Sierra Downieville	66 969
SHUCKELFORD		
John	San Joaquin Oneal	64 913
SHUCKERNY		
---	Mendocino Calpella	60 822
SHUCKINSON		
W	Tuolumne Twp 2	71 336
SHUCKIS		
Antonio	Santa Clara San Jose	65 323
SHUCKMAN		
Augustus	Colusa Colusi	57 423
SHUCKS		
Mary	San Francisco San Francisco 9	681017
SHUD		
Whitten*	Placer Michigan	62 852
SHUDDLY		
A B	Placer Virginia	62 673
SHUE		
---	Nevada Bridgeport	61 495
---	Shasta Horsetown	66 711
P J	Calaveras Twp 9	57 394
S	Calaveras Twp 9	57 394
SHUEBERT		
E	San Francisco San Francisco 5	67 518
SHUEN		
Chas*	Mariposa Twp 3	60 596
SHUETZ		
Chas*	San Francisco San Francisco 1	68 926
SHUEY		
Josephus	Contra Costa Twp 2	57 555
Martin	Alameda Brooklyn	55 91
Saml D	Alameda Brooklyn	55 91
William	Contra Costa Twp 2	57 556
SHUFFENER		
Jno	Tehama Red Bluff	70 922
SHUFFER		
J K	San Joaquin Stockton	641089
SHUFFLER		
Reuben	Tulara Visalia	71 1
SHUFFLETIN		
H	Shasta Horsetown	66 695
SHUFFLETON		
C D	Shasta Shasta	66 657
H	Shasta Horsetown	66 707
H*	Shasta Horsetown	66 695
SHUFFORD		
James	Siskiyou Scott Ri	69 83
SHUFORD		
A M	Trinity Weaverville	701063
SHUG		
---	Amador Twp 2	55 291
SHUGG		
James	Los Angeles San Gabriel	59 408
SHUGGLER		
Reuben	Tulara Twp 2	71 1
SHUGORER		
H	El Dorado Placerville	58 821
SHUGUINN		
Danl*	Tuolumne Twp 2	71 401
SHUHAM		
Andrew	Del Norte Klamath	58 654
SHUHAN		
B*	Napa Hot Springs	61 6
Cashanni*	Napa Hot Springs	61 6
Margaret	Sierra Downieville	66 966
Timothy	Yuba Marysville	72 904
Timothy*	Sierra Twp 7	66 907
SHUHY		
Timothy	Santa Cruz Pajaro	66 559
SHUILD		
William M*	Solano Montezuma	69 373

Name	County Locale	M653 Roll	Page
SHUILEO			
William M*	Solano Montezuma	69	373
SHUIMER			
Christian*	Nevada Bloomfield	61	519
SHUINER			
Christan	Nevada Bloomfield	61	519
SHUK			
---	El Dorado Georgetown	58	682
SHULAS			
William	Placer Iona Hills	62	878
SHULBY			
Jas*	Sacramento Granite	63	264
SHULEE			
---	Mariposa Twp 3	60	612
SHULER			
F	San Francisco San Francisco 7	681	383
Frank	San Francisco San Francisco 1	68	927
Geo S	Calaveras Twp 6	57	154
Jacob	Tuolumne Shawsfla	71	387
John	Nevada Bridgeport	61	478
Peter	Santa Clara Redwood	65	456
Wm H	Yuba Slate Ro	72	702
Wm M	Yolo Slate Ra	72	702
SHULES			
Geo S	Calaveras Twp 6	57	154
SHULEY			
John	San Francisco San Francisco 4	681	127
SHULL			
August	Sierra St Louis	66	806
John	Placer Forest H	62	796
W W*	Tuolumne Sonora	71	481
W W*	Butte Kimshaw	56	595
SHULLER			
Gultavus	Sierra La Porte	66	783
Gusturns	Sierra La Porte	66	783
Otto*	Contra Costa Twp 3	57	604
SHULLORD			
David	Nevada Bridgeport	61	442
SHULLOW			
David*	Nevada Bridgeport	61	442
SHULLY			
John	Sonoma Vallejo	69	626
John F*	Sierra Whiskey	66	850
SHULP			
D*	Sacramento Alabama	63	418
SHULSTINE			
Mary	San Francisco San Francisco 11	147 67	
SHULT			
John	Placer Secret R	62	612
SHULTER			
Albert*	Yolo Washington	72	564
SHULTERS			
G M	Nevada Grass Valley	61	202
SHULTG			
Adam*	Sierra Cold Can	66	836
SHULTIS			
Albert	Yolo Washington	72	564
SHULTS			
H	El Dorado Diamond	58	803
Henry	Sierra Twp 5	66	920
SHULTY			
Adam*	Sierra Cold Can	66	836
Jas	Sacramento Granite	63	264
SHULTZ			
A	Santa Clara Redwood	65	445
A*	Mariposa Twp 3	60	592
Absalom	Sonoma Santa Rosa	69	405
Adam	Sierra Cold Can	66	836
Alexander	Fresno Twp 2	59	17
Charles	San Francisco San Francisco 8	681	245
Chas	Amador Twp 2	55	284
Chris	Tuolumne Twp 1	71	215
Chs A	Los Angeles Tejon	59	539
D J	Sonoma Santa Rosa	69	393
F	El Dorado Diamond	58	799
Ferdinand	San Francisco San Francisco 8	681	305
Fred	Sonoma Petaluma	69	565
Fred	Tuolumne Columbia	71	474
Frederick	Tuolumne Twp 1	71	483
Frid	Tuolumne Twp 2	71	474
G S	San Francisco San Francisco 5	67	521
G W	Sierra La Porte	66	771
H C	Tuolumne Twp 1	71	259
Hans	Placer Virginia	62	667
Henry	Placer Dutch Fl	62	727
Henry	Tuolumne Jamestown	71	438
Henry	Yuba Suida	72	993
J	Sutter Sutter	70	815
J J	Butte Chico	56	531
J L	Sacramento Brighton	63	206
Jacob	El Dorado Salmon Falls	581	035
John	Mendocino Ukiah	60	799
John	Shasta Cottonwoood	66	736
John	Sierra Downieville	661	006
John	Solano Vallejo	69	244
SHULTZE			
Andrew W	Los Angeles Los Angeles	59	342
SHULTZI			
Godfry*	Placer Auburn	62	574
Godfy*	Placer Auburn	62	574
SHULTZS			
M	Calaveras Twp 9	57	392
SHULZ			
John	San Francisco San Francisco 7	681	431
SHUM			
---	Calaveras Twp 6	57	134
---	Calaveras Twp 8	57	62
---	San Francisco San Francisco 4	681	212
---	San Francisco San Francisco 5	67	510
---	Tuolumne Twp 3	71	461
Ah	Calaveras Twp 7	57	36
Ah	Tuolumne Twp 2	71	346
Chas	Butte Mountain	56	734
SHUMACHER			
John	Los Angeles Los Angeles	59	351
SHUMAKER			
A	San Francisco San Francisco 1	68	813
J B	Siskiyou Scott Va	69	32
John	San Francisco San Francisco 6	67	426
William	Stanislaus Empire	70	736
Wm	San Francisco San Francisco 1	68	813
SHUMAN			
---	San Joaquin Stockton	641	058
John L	Siskiyou Yreka	69	179
Newell	Siskiyou Scott Va	69	23
Valentine	San Francisco San Francisco 7	681	342
SHUMAR			
Henry	Solano Suisan	69	219
Louis	Tuolumne Chinese	71	494
SHUMER			
Fred	Contra Costa Twp 3	57	586
SHUMERAY			
Benj	Plumas Quincy	62	982
SHUMP			
T J	Sacramento Ward 1	63	144
SHUMWAY			
Paul	Amador Twp 1	55	473
S	Santa Clara Fremont	65	424
SHUN			
---	Butte Ophir	56	790
---	El Dorado Greenwood	58	730
---	Placer Auburn	62	596
---	San Francisco San Francisco 4	681	212
---	San Francisco San Francisco 5	67	509
James*	Santa Cruz Santa Cruz	66	612
SHUNAN			
L*	Mariposa Twp 3	60	585
SHUNBAR			
J	San Francisco San Francisco 1	68	846
SHUNCK			
Henry	Amador Twp 3	55	397
SHUNFIELD			
L E	Mariposa Twp 3	60	586
SHUNG			
---	Butte Oregon	56	633
---	Calaveras Twp 6	57	122
---	Calaveras Twp 6	57	131
---	Calaveras Twp 5	57	250
---	Calaveras Twp 5	57	254
---	Calaveras Twp 10	57	283
---	Calaveras Twp 10	57	284
---	Calaveras Twp 10	57	295
---	Calaveras Twp 4	57	320
---	Calaveras Twp 8	57	83
---	Fresno Twp 2	59	49
---	Mariposa Twp 1	60	671
---	Nevada Washington	61	339
---	Placer Virginia	62	684
---	Placer Illinois	62	738
---	Sacramento Mississipi	63	188
---	Stanislaus Branch	70	713
---	Stanislaus Branch	70	715
---	Tuolumne Twp 5	71	523
---	Tuolumne Don Pedro	71	533
---	Tuolumne Don Pedro	71	537
---	Tuolumne Don Pedro	71	541
---	Yolo Slate Ra	72	713
---	Yuba Slate Ro	72	713
---	Yuba New York	72	739
Ah	Calaveras Twp 7	57	32
Ah	Calaveras Twp 7	57	36
Fong	Placer Virginia	62	676
SHUNG			
Ho	Siskiyou Yreka	69	194
See	Calaveras Twp 5	57	223
SHUNING			
Caleb*	Sierra Downieville	661	003
SHUNK			
James M*	San Joaquin Elkhorn	64	997
SHUNKLIN			
Fredrick	Sierra Twp 7	66	872
SHUNNGH			
Phillip I*	El Dorado Georgetown	58	707
SHUNNON			
D*	Mariposa Twp 3	60	585
SHUNOMAR			
Edward	San Francisco San Francisco 4	681	158
SHUNT			
Edward	Placer Dutch Fl	62	726
SHUNTS			
Hiram	Yolo Slate Ra	72	714
SHUNY			
---	Calaveras Twp 5	57	254
---	Calaveras Twp 10	57	270
---	Calaveras Twp 10	57	295
---	Shasta Horsetown	66	711
---*	Tuolumne Don Pedro	71	533
SHUO			
---	El Dorado Mud Springs	58	998
SHUOCALPA			
---	Mendocino Big Rvr	60	853
SHUPART			
F	Mariposa Twp 1	60	630
SHUPE			
C	Nevada Nevada	61	260
SHUPIT			
---	Tulara Visalia	71	113
SHUQUINN			
Danl	Tuolumne Shawsfla	71	401
SHUR			
---*	Sierra Twp 5	66	945
C*	Calaveras Twp 9	57	395
SHURBEIN			
David*	Contra Costa Twp 2	57	571
SHURBURN			
David*	Contra Costa Twp 2	57	571
SHUREDAN			
B	Sacramento Ward 4	63	603
SHURELL			
A	Nevada Eureka	61	388
SHURELS			
C*	Sacramento Ward 1	63	27
SHURILL			
A*	Nevada Eureka	61	388
SHURIN			
Danl	Sonoma Santa Rosa	69	400
SHURKER			
C	Butte Mountain	56	738
SHURLER			
William M	Solano Montezuma	69	373
SHURLIFF			
John	Yolo Cache Crk	72	591
Sullivan	Alameda Brooklyn	55	126
SHURLL			
Barbara	San Francisco San Francisco 2	67	730
SHURMAN			
Harriett	Yolo Merritt	72	580
John	Napa Yount	61	34
L*	Mariposa Twp 3	60	585
Wm	Napa Napa	61	83
SHURPER			
Robert	Nevada Rough &	61	432
SHURT			
Alex	Siskiyou Scott Va	69	43
SHURTHER			
C*	Butte Mountain	56	738
SHURTLEFF			
B	Shasta Shasta	66	663
H J	Shasta Shasta	66	661
SHURTLIFF			
George	San Joaquin Stockton	641	024
George A	San Joaquin Stockton	641	024
SHURTTER			
C*	Butte Mountain	56	738
SHURY			
---*	Tuolumne Don Pedro	71	533
SHUS			
Ming	El Dorado Mud Springs	58	958
Thomas	Santa Clara Almaden	65	274
SHUSTER			
Michael M	Yuba Marysville	72	902
SHUT			
---	Placer Iona Hills	62	894
Edwin	Nevada Bridgeport	61	451
G V	Nevada Bridgeport	61	454
S S	Amador Twp 7	55	420
SHUTE			
---	San Francisco San Francisco 4	681	223

California 1860 Census Index

Name	County Locale	M653 RollPage
SHUTE		
Charles	San Francisco San Francisco	4 681 160
Daniel S	San Francisco San Francisco	8 681 323
G H	Siskiyou Callahan	69 15
Henry A	Sierra Poker Flats	66 837
Henry H	Sierra Poker Flats	66 837
N	Calaveras Twp 9	57 394
SHUTER		
Carl	Los Angeles Los Angeles	59 342
SHUTERS		
Francis	Alameda Brooklyn	55 164
SHUTERSHUT		
---	Tulara Twp 1	71 117
SHUTH		
A J	Napa Napa	61 109
SHUTIS		
J	El Dorado Placerville	58 848
SHUTLER		
George	Yuba New York	72 736
SHUTMAN		
Moses	Sacramento Natonia	63 281
SHUTS		
---*	Placer Dutch Fl	62 733
D*	Solano Suisan	69 212
SHUTT		
August	Sierra St Louis	66 806
Charles	Calaveras Twp 9	57 350
Henry	San Francisco San Francisco	11 116 67
Mary	San Francisco San Francisco	8 681 321
SHUTTER		
John	San Mateo Twp 1	65 68
Otto*	Contra Costa Twp 3	57 604
SHUTTES		
Fred	Sonoma Armally	69 504
SHUTTRUK		
Orville J*	Sierra Pine Grove	66 826
SHUTTS		
Andrew*	Santa Cruz Pescadero	66 648
Mark	Santa Cruz Santa Cruz	66 634
SHUTTTWIK		
Orville J	Sierra Pine Grove	66 826
SHUTTUCK		
Orville J	Sierra Pine Grove	66 826
SHUTTY		
D J	Sonoma Santa Rosa	69 393
John	Sonoma Vallejo	69 626
SHUTTZ		
Jefferson	San Francisco San Francisco	2 67 751
Levi S	San Francisco San Francisco	9 68 941
SHUTZ		
Frederick	Colusa Spring Valley	57 431
Mary	San Francisco San Francisco	7 681 406
William	San Francisco San Francisco	9 681 019
SHUVEY		
Andeas	Tuolumne Sonora	71 227
SHUVILL		
A	Nevada Eureka	61 388
SHVEN		
Chas*	Mariposa Twp 3	60 596
SHWARTZ		
Philip	Tuolumne Twp 2	71 328
SHWARTZKOPH		
Louis	Sacramento Ward 3	63 458
SHWESTER		
J T*	Nevada Red Dog	61 546
SHWITZER		
Jacob	Sacramento Franklin	63 325
SHY		
---	Calaveras Twp 8	57 101
---	Calaveras Twp 8	57 106
SHYKEY		
Robt	Butte Chico	56 533
SHYLER		
J*	Shasta Shasta	66 668
SHYPE		
C	Nevada Nevada	61 260
SHYRACH		
Jacob V	San Francisco San Francisco	7 681 359
SHYROCK		
W J	Butte Kimshaw	56 572
W J	Butte Kimshaw	56 573
SHYRUCH		
W J	Butte Kimshaw	56 572
SI CHAN		
---	Nevada Rough &	61 433
SI CHOW		
---	Nevada Bridgeport	61 466
SI CUM		
---	Tuolumne Columbia	71 307
Ah	Tuolumne Twp 2	71 307
SI E		
---	El Dorado Georgetown	58 701
SI WAPP		
---*	Nevada Nevada	61 303
SI YAY		
---	El Dorado Georgetown	58 693
SI		
---	Amador Twp 5	55 335
---	Calaveras Twp 5	57 234
---	Calaveras Twp 5	57 256
---	Calaveras Twp 5	57 257
---	Calaveras Twp 10	57 272
---	Calaveras Twp 4	57 328
---	Calaveras Twp 8	57 83
---	Del Norte Crescent	58 643
---	Mariposa Twp 1	60 662
---	Mariposa Coulterville	60 682
---	Nevada Rough &	61 396
---	Sacramento Ward 1	63 60
---	Sierra Downieville	661 008
---	Sierra Downieville	661 027
---	Solano Vallejo	69 256
---	Tulara Visalia	71 96
---	Tuolumne Shawsfla	71 407
---	Tuolumne Don Pedro	71 533
---	Tuolumne Don Pedro	71 537
---	Yuba Long Bar	72 759
---*	Nevada Nevada	61 305
Ah	Tuolumne Twp 2	71 346
Am	Nevada Bridgeport	61 492
Chan	Nevada Rough &	61 433
Chang*	El Dorado Georgetown	58 700
Chaw	Nevada Bridgeport	61 466
Ching	San Francisco San Francisco	4 681 198
Chung	San Francisco San Francisco	4 681 198
Coon	Amador Twp 2	55 312
Corn	Siskiyou Yreka	69 194
Fooa	Shasta French G	66 713
Hay	Del Norte Happy Ca	58 663
Hing	Nevada Bridgeport	61 491
Hu	San Francisco San Francisco	4 681 198
Kum	El Dorado Georgetown	58 692
Lang	El Dorado Georgetown	58 680
Lee	San Francisco San Francisco	4 681 198
Ling	Nevada Bridgeport	61 491
Long	Butte Bidwell	56 708
Looa	Shasta French G	66 713
Lu	San Francisco San Francisco	4 681 198
Sang	Mariposa Twp 3	60 579
Sing	Mariposa Twp 3	60 579
Wa	Mariposa Twp 3	60 579
Yang	Calaveras Twp 5	57 254
Yang	El Dorado Georgetown	58 701
Yany	Calaveras Twp 5	57 254
Yon	Amador Twp 5	55 354
You	El Dorado Georgetown	58 680
Yoy	El Dorado Georgetown	58 693
SI?		
---	Mendocino Round Va	60 882
SIA		
---	Calaveras Twp 8	57 60
SIADIS		
Sarah	Sonoma Petaluma	69 550
SIAGH		
Cornelius*	Sacramento Granite	63 247
SIAH		
---	Sacramento Ward 1	63 53
SIAM		
---	Sierra Twp 5	66 933
SIAMA		
---	Mendocino Twp 1	60 889
SIAMON		
William*	Placer Michigan	62 835
SIANA		
Roja	Monterey Pajaro	601 011
SIARAIG		
T T	Placer Todds Va	62 786
SIARCH		
John*	Stanislaus Empire	70 736
SIARING		
S D*	Placer Todds Va	62 786
SIAS		
J	Yolo Washington	72 604
James	Yolo Slate Ra	72 688
Juan*	Monterey San Juan	601 002
SIAVA		
Juan Antonio	Los Nieto Los Angeles	59 436
SIB		
---	El Dorado Placerville	58 842
SIBART		
J	El Dorado Placerville	58 850
SIBASTEIN		
Juan	Santa Clara Santa Clara	65 496
SIBASTIAN		
---	Los Angeles Tejon	59 529
SIBBALD		
Wm	Placer Auburn	62 585
SIBBERT		
J	San Francisco San Francisco	8 681 286
SIBBLER		
H C	Siskiyou Scott Va	69 38
SIBEAN		
A*	Sacramento Sutter	63 300
SIBECK		
Charles	El Dorado Placerville	58 898
SIBEL		
Peter	San Francisco San Francisco	2 67 795
SIBERT		
Anton	Tuolumne Twp 2	71 333
Anton	Tuolumne Twp 2	71 339
Henry	Amador Twp 3	55 405
Jackson	Placer Iona Hills	62 891
SIBIA		
Rafel	Los Angeles Los Angeles	59 493
SIBINGSTON		
Chas	Butte Bidwell	56 705
SIBIRANO		
Neibia	Contra Costa Twp 3	57 585
Ygnacio	Contra Costa Twp 3	57 584
SIBLAY		
---	San Francisco San Francisco	4 681 219
SIBLE		
Charles	Los Angeles Los Angeles	59 354
SIBLEY		
Ann	San Francisco San Francisco	4 681 157
F M	Butte Eureka	56 648
Henry	Sierra Pine Grove	66 822
Hinry	Sierra Pine Grove	66 822
J	Sacramento Granite	63 226
Levi	Placer Michigan	62 820
P H	Placer Iona Hills	62 861
W	Trinity Redding	70 985
William E	Calaveras Twp 6	57 158
William F	Calaveras Twp 6	57 158
SIBLIS		
Eugene	Sierra Poker Flats	66 840
SIBLY		
Newton	Placer Forest H	62 803
SIBO		
Ivil	Napa Clear Lake	61 121
Joel	Napa Clear Lake	61 123
Joel*	Napa Clear Lake	61 121
SIBOBAN		
Chalres	Los Angeles Los Angeles	59 513
Charles	Los Angeles Los Angeles	59 513
SIBRALA		
John	Los Angeles Los Angeles	59 504
SIBRIAN		
Rosa P	Contra Costa Twp 3	57 584
SIBRIANA		
Jose B	Contra Costa Twp 2	57 554
SIBRIANO		
Francisco	Contra Costa Twp 3	57 591
SIBS		
John	Placer Auburn	62 574
SIBSON		
Wm*	Napa Napa	61 77
SIBUNG		
Chas	San Francisco San Francisco	2 67 693
SIC		
---	Calaveras Twp 4	57 302
---	Tuolumne Twp 5	71 514
---*	Shasta Shasta	66 670
SICARROS		
Santos	Yuba Marysville	72 933
SICAUS		
Bernardo	Contra Costa Twp 3	57 599
SICCARD		
Clestine	Colusa Muion	57 461
SICEEL		
Saml*	Placer Secret R	62 610
SICEL		
John	Siskiyou Shasta Rvr	69 115
SICH		
Yu	Sacramento Natonia	63 283
SICHAN		
George	El Dorado Georgetown	58 760
SICHBLAN		
G	Trinity Price'S	701 019
SICHE		
John	Yuba Long Bar	72 769
SICHEL		
C	Nevada Eureka	61 352
Julius	Los Angeles Los Angeles	59 339
Julius	Los Angeles Los Angeles	59 369
M	Nevada Eureka	61 352
M C*	San Francisco San Francisco	3 67 86
Mateo	Los Angeles Los Angeles	59 339
Phillip	Los Angeles Los Angeles	59 339
SICHLOR		
George	Los Angeles Tejon	59 521
SICHRIST		
Chas N	Sonoma Santa Rosa	69 389
SICILY		
John	Placer Michigan	62 824
SICK		
---	Calaveras Twp 5	57 192

Name	County Locale	M653 Roll	Page
SICK			
---	Calaveras Twp 5	57	257
---	Calaveras Twp 4	57	308
---	Calaveras Twp 4	57	341
---	Merced Twp 1	60	914
---	Placer Rattle Snake	62	637
---	Placer Forest H	62	771
---	Sacramento Mississipi	63	190
---	Tuolumne Jacksonville	71	516
---*	Amador Twp 5	55	353
Bur	Butte Cascade	56	699
Hop	Butte Ophir	56	802
John	Sierra Downieville	66	1010
SICKALS			
Joseph	Contra Costa Twp 1	57	534
SICKAS			
John	Sacramento Granite	63	267
SICKE			
---	Plumas Quincy	62	949
SICKECHUCK			
---	Fresno Twp 3	59	96
SICKELS			
Daniel	Placer Virginia	62	676
SICKES			
John	Sacramento Granite	63	267
SICKFOE			
---	Mendocino Round Va	60	881
SICKLER			
A	Solano Vacaville	69	332
C H	San Francisco San Francisco 5	67	491
SICKLES			
Florence	Contra Costa Twp 1	57	537
George	Nevada Rough &	61	438
James	Amador Twp 2	55	305
John L	San Francisco San Francisco 9	68	1085
SICKS			
---	Calaveras Twp 5	57	192
SICKY			
Anne	San Francisco San Francisco 10	184 67	
Mary	San Francisco San Francisco 10	183 67	
SICN			
Ferdinand	Calaveras Twp 6	57	153
SICNEDAH			
---	Mendocino Twp 1	60	888
SICO			
Carlos	Sierra Downieville	66	1018
Charles	San Francisco San Francisco 7	68	1409
SICONDINA			
Antonio	Los Angeles Los Angeles	59	493
SICORD			
Beirrie*	Stanislaus Branch	70	701
William	Stanislaus Branch	70	697
SICRE			
Rosalie	Sacramento Ward 4	63	535
S	Sacramento Ward 1	63	14
SICTODA			
---	Mendocino Round Va	60	882
SICTSOIT			
P*	Merced Twp 1	60	912
SICUR			
John L	Santa Clara San Jose	65	306
SIDANCE			
Joseph*	Tuolumne Twp 1	71	253
SIDAR			
---	Nevada Bridgeport	61	460
SIDAS			
---*	Nevada Bridgeport	61	460
SIDAUSE			
Joseph	Tuolumne Twp 1	71	253
SIDDON			
W M	Sacramento Ward 1	63	10
SIDDONS			
Jas H	Sonoma Petaluma	69	585
SIDEBOTHAM			
C H	Del Norte Crescent	58	641
SIDEL			
Chris	Sacramento Ward 3	63	488
SIDELINGER			
George*	Yuba Fosters	72	840
SIDELL			
John M	Santa Cruz Santa Cruz	66	615
John W	Santa Cruz Santa Cruz	66	615
R A	Santa Clara Santa Clara	65	471
Sam	Sacramento Ward 1	63	146
SIDENBERY			
John	Placer Iona Hills	62	892
SIDENSPARDER			
Miles	Yolo No E Twp	72	669
SIDENSPARKER			
Miles	Yolo No E Twp	72	669
Miles	Yuba North Ea	72	669
SIDER			
Charles	Siskiyou Yreka	69	186
SIDERMANN			
George	San Francisco San Francisco 7	68	1424
SIDERS			
A	Calaveras Twp 9	57	411
SIDES			
A	Calaveras Twp 9	57	412
E H	Tuolumne Twp 2	71	392
Fuirds	Colusa Monroeville	57	456
H C	Tehama Red Bluff	70	934
Thos	Sacramento Franklin	63	326
SIDGNICK			
M*	San Francisco San Francisco 9	68	1074
SIDGURICH			
Thomas	San Joaquin Douglass	64	914
SIDGWICK			
John	Tuolumne Twp 1	71	202
Thomas	Plumas Quincy	62	945
SIDINS			
A	Calaveras Twp 9	57	411
SIDLE			
David	Contra Costa Twp 1	57	486
Frederick	Contra Costa Twp 1	57	489
Theophilers	San Joaquin Castoria	64	907
Thomas	Calaveras Twp 5	57	195
William	Contra Costa Twp 1	57	489
SIDLER			
Lewis	Tulara Visalia	71	76
Louis	Tulara Twp 1	71	76
SIDMORE			
Josiah	Tuolumne Twp 1	71	186
SIDNEY			
Wm	Butte Cascade	56	694
SIDNI			
---	San Bernardino S Timate	64	704
SIDNO			
---	San Bernardino S Timate	64	702
SIDON			
Jas	Sacramento Natonia	63	283
SIDRO			
---	San Bernardino S Timate	64	712
---	San Bernardino S Timate	64	723
---	San Bernardino S Timate	64	725
---	San Bernardino S Timate	64	726
---	San Bernardino S Timate	64	731
---	San Bernardino S Timate	64	734
---	San Bernardino S Timate	64	755
Sethro*	Plumas Meadow Valley	62	908
SIDWAY			
J	Tuolumne Big Oak	71	146
SIDWELL			
J M*	Solano Montezuma	69	370
John*	Siskiyou Scott Va	69	32
SIE SON			
---	Sacramento Ward 1	63	70
SIE			
---	Amador Twp 4	55	247
---	Calaveras Twp 5	57	205
---	Calaveras Twp 4	57	303
---	Calaveras Twp 4	57	315
---	Calaveras Twp 4	57	328
---	El Dorado Kelsey	58	1136
---	El Dorado Mud Springs	58	964
---	Mariposa Twp 1	60	637
---	Nevada Nevada	61	305
---	Nevada Bridgeport	61	439
---	Placer Virginia	62	681
---	Sacramento Ward 1	63	54
---	Sacramento Ward 1	63	71
---	Sierra Downieville	66	1014
---*	El Dorado Coloma	58	1084
---*	Placer Auburn	62	572
---*	Sacramento Ward 1	63	53
Ah	Tuolumne Twp 4	71	161
Feng	Placer Folsom	62	648
How	Mariposa Twp 3	60	562
Nou	Mariposa Twp 3	60	562
Son	Sacramento Ward 1	63	70
Youn	Mariposa Twp 1	60	651
SIEB			
Jos*	Amador Twp 2	55	265
SIEBE			
---	San Francisco San Francisco 2	67	623
J	San Francisco San Francisco 2	67	623
SIEBEL			
Phillip	San Francisco San Francisco 7	68	1339
SIEBERSMEYER			
Conrad	Los Angeles Los Angeles	59	390
SIEBERT			
Fred	Placer Michigan	62	817
Henry	San Francisco San Francisco 11	108 67	
L	Nevada Nevada	61	245
SIECK			
---	Sierra Downieville	66	996
SIEDENBURG			
J F	Trinity Raabs Ba	70	1020
SIEDERBURG			
H	San Francisco San Francisco 2	67	780
SIEG			
F	El Dorado Placerville	58	856
SIEGFRIED			
Phillip	San Francisco San Francisco 7	68	1407
SIEGIE			
Fred*	Sierra Downieville	66	994
SIELIRAN			
Thomas	Calaveras Twp 8	57	82
SIELLA			
Refupa	Mariposa Twp 3	60	595
SIELRENTHETER			
P	Amador Twp 3	55	398
SIEN			
---	Amador Twp 5	55	335
---	Calaveras Twp 7	57	36
SIENAZA			
Anastacia	San Francisco San Francisco 2	67	701
SIENEGA			
M	San Francisco San Francisco 2	67	709
SIENIGA			
M	San Francisco San Francisco 2	67	709
SIEP			
Henry	Yuba Marysville	72	934
SIEPOUL			
Andrew	Calaveras Twp 5	57	221
SIER			
Spooner	Sierra Gibsonville	66	852
SIERA			
George*	San Francisco San Francisco 11	92 67	
SIERGE			
Leopold*	Monterey Alisal	60	1028
SIERGO			
Leopold	Monterey Alisal	60	1028
SIEROS			
Timothy	Los Angeles Los Angeles	59	309
SIERRA			
---	Fresno Twp 1	59	77
SIERRES			
Encamarcion*	Los Angeles	59	350
	Los Angeles		
Encamarcun	Los Angeles	59	350
	Los Angeles		
Eucamarcion*	Los Angeles	59	350
	Los Angeles		
SIERRO			
Carpo	Tuolumne Columbia	71	318
Edwardo	Tuolumne Twp 2	71	318
SIERY			
Bridget*	San Francisco San Francisco 8	68	1320
SIES			
Jose M	San Francisco San Francisco 2	67	707
SIESINOW			
A	El Dorado Kelsey	58	1130
SIESS			
Fredrick*	Plumas Meadow Valley	62	933
SIESTA			
Fernand	Calaveras Twp 9	57	359
SIET			
Samuel	Placer Michigan	62	807
SIEVER			
Frank	Sierra St Louis	66	816
SIEVERS			
Harmon	Tuolumne Shawsfla	71	407
William	Mendocino Big Rvr	60	845
SIEZE			
---	Shasta Shasta	66	680
SIF			
Se	Placer Illinois	62	745
SIFENER			
John	El Dorado Mud Springs	58	964
SIFERT			
Fredrica	San Francisco San Francisco 7	68	1417
William	San Francisco San Francisco 7	68	1353
SIFFENSTIEN			
Wm	Nevada Eureka	61	374
SIFFERD			
W M	Nevada Rough &	61	425
SIFFERT			
Addam	Tuolumne Twp 5	71	509
Mary	San Francisco San Francisco 8	68	1258
SIFFORD			
Henry	Nevada Rough &	61	402
John D	Santa Clara Santa Clara	65	489
W A	Santa Clara Santa Clara	65	489
SIFFRON			
John	El Dorado Mud Springs	58	966
SIFIELD			
John*	Sacramento Dry Crk	63	372
SIFTON			
Stephen	San Francisco San Francisco 2	67	685
SIG			
---	Placer Dutch Fl	62	737
---	Shasta Horsetown	66	704
---	Sierra Twp 5	66	927
SIGAN			
A	Tuolumne Big Oak	71	151

Name	County Locale	M653 RollPage
SIGARNA		
Antonia	Los Angeles San Jose	59 291
SIGARST		
John*	Humbolt Mattole	59 126
SIGARTSON		
Jas	San Francisco San Francisco 1	68 892
SIGEARA		
Rufus Y*	El Dorado Georgetown	58 705
SIGEKER		
Henry*	El Dorado Mud Springs	58 993
SIGERET		
Maria*	Sacramento Ward 1	63 43
SIGERO		
Louisa*	El Dorado Georgetown	58 685
SIGGIN		
A L	Yolo Cache Crk	72 643
SIGGINS		
Isaac	Plumas Quincy	62 943
SIGH		
---*	Sierra Downieville	66 979
---*	Butte Ophir	56 807
Ah	Tuolumne Twp 4	71 182
Ling	Butte Bidwell	56 731
Long	Butte Cascade	56 702
Long	Butte Mountain	56 735
Sing	Butte Ophir	56 815
William	Contra Costa Twp 1	57 489
Yong	Butte Bidwell	56 731
SIGHHUR		
T	Sutter Butte	70 796
SIGHN		
Geo	Napa Clear Lake	61 127
SIGHS		
Long	Butte Bidwell	56 711
SIGHT		
---	Trinity Weaverville	701074
SIGHTER		
George	Alameda Brooklyn	55 102
SIGHTMAN		
Geo	Klamath S Fork	59 199
SIGHTNEE		
Fred	Trinity North Fo	701023
SIGHTNER		
C W	Sacramento Ward 1	63 3
SIGIER		
John*	Sierra Port Win	66 795
SIGINARIO		
Cicero	Tuolumne Twp 3	71 459
SIGINORIO		
Cicero	Tuolumne Twp 3	71 459
SIGLER		
Frederick	Yuba Marysville	72 960
James R	Calaveras Twp 7	57 33
Thomas	Yuba New York	72 747
Uriah	Yuba Marysville	72 934
SIGLERS		
Uriah	Yuba Marysville	72 934
SIGLON		
Geo*	Napa Clear Lake	61 127
SIGMAN		
David	Napa Hot Springs	61 13
John	Mariposa Twp 3	60 606
SIGME		
John	Shasta French G	66 717
SIGN		
Sinn	Butte Ophir	56 803
SIGNAL		
Geo	Butte Oregon	56 612
SIGNAR		
Lucien	Butte Chico	56 542
SIGNENANA		
Henry	Nevada Bridgeport	61 456
SIGNERIANA		
Henry*	Nevada Bridgeport	61 456
SIGNEUANA		
Henry*	Nevada Bridgeport	61 456
SIGNIT		
J	Calaveras Twp 9	57 406
SIGNO		
---	San Bernardino San Bernadino	64 667
SIGNOR		
Geo	Santa Clara San Jose	65 388
SIGNORANA		
Henry*	Nevada Bridgeport	61 456
SIGNORE		
Theodore*	Sacramento Franklin	63 311
SIGNORET		
Rosa	Los Angeles Los Angeles	59 344
SIGNORETT		
Felix	Los Angeles Los Angeles	59 344
SIGO		
---	Sierra Twp 7	66 898
SIGOND		
Julle*	Sierra Port Win	66 798
SIGONEL		
Julle*	Sierra Port Win	66 798

Name	County Locale	M653 RollPage
SIGONS		
Julle*	Sierra Scales D	66 804
SIGOUS		
Julle*	Sierra Scales D	66 804
SIGOVIA		
Paul*	El Dorado Georgetown	58 701
SIGRINE		
Louis	Sierra Twp 7	66 913
SIGRIST		
J J	San Francisco San Francisco 5	67 513
SIGRONE		
Louis	Sierra Twp 7	66 913
SIGUARA		
Rufus Y*	El Dorado Georgetown	58 705
SIGUIN		
John J	Los Angeles Los Angeles	59 512
SIGURST		
Fred*	Napa Napa	61 61
SIGUVRA		
Paul*	El Dorado Georgetown	58 701
SIGVAISNY		
Thomas*	El Dorado Georgetown	58 705
SIGVANENG		
Thomas*	El Dorado Georgetown	58 705
SIGVANENY		
Thomas*	El Dorado Georgetown	58 705
SIGWALT		
John*	Nevada Red Dog	61 546
SIHAM		
Christer	Butte Ophir	56 759
Chuster*	Butte Ophir	56 759
SIHEILINE		
Nathaniel	Sierra Gibsonville	66 854
SIHLE		
Geo*	Sacramento Mississipi	63 185
SIHLUKA		
John	San Joaquin Stockton	641083
SIHOUL		
---	Tulara Twp 2	71 40
SIHOVICK		
John*	Sierra Scales D	66 802
SIHOW		
---*	Tulara Twp 2	71 34
SIHULL		
Leonard	Sierra St Louis	66 815
SIJERO		
Louisa*	El Dorado Georgetown	58 685
SIJES		
Louisa	El Dorado Georgetown	58 685
SIJJAN		
Andrew	Marin San Rafael	60 771
SIJORN		
Rufus Y	El Dorado Georgetown	58 705
SIJVUIONY		
Thomas*	El Dorado Georgetown	58 705
SIK		
---	Calaveras Twp 5	57 242
---	Sierra Downieville	661008
---	Yuba Long Bar	72 758
SIKEN		
C D	Sierra Downieville	66 965
SIKERS		
Saml A*	Mariposa Coulterville	60 679
SIKES		
Chas	Santa Clara Fremont	65 420
G	Santa Clara Fremont	65 420
Henry	Placer Todds Va	62 783
J A	Solano Fremont	69 376
L W	Santa Clara Redwood	65 451
SIKLER		
George	Tulara Keeneysburg	71 47
SIKONLINE		
---	Tulara Twp 2	71 40
SIKONY		
---	Tulara Twp 2	71 39
SIKOUL		
---*	Tulara Visalia	71 40
SIKSTELLER		
John	San Diego Colorado	64 807
SIKUM		
---	Shasta Shasta	66 680
SIL		
---	El Dorado Georgetown	58 678
SILA		
Jas	Butte Oregon	56 636
SILAER		
Frank*	Alameda Brooklyn	55 125
W P	Placer Iona Hills	62 871
SILAS		
Andrew	El Dorado Greenwood	58 708
Manuel	Mariposa Twp 3	60 617
SILBER		
Antonio	Mariposa Twp 3	60 604
Joseph	Santa Clara San Jose	65 314
SILBERBURG		
M	El Dorado Placerville	58 839

Name	County Locale	M653 RollPage
SILBERSTINO		
S	El Dorado Placerville	58 839
SILBEST		
Martha	El Dorado Mud Springs	58 972
SILBETRE		
---	San Bernardino S Timate	64 711
SILBEY		
W H	El Dorado Kelsey	581137
SILBURY		
Clara	San Francisco San Francisco 4	681123
SILCER		
---	Alameda Brooklyn	55 125
SILE		
---	Sierra Downieville	66 992
Fred*	Sacramento Ward 3	63 486
SILEE		
Andrew*	El Dorado Georgetown	58 708
SILENT		
Charles	Amador Twp 5	55 330
Charlles	Amador Twp 5	55 330
SILER		
Andrew*	El Dorado Georgetown	58 708
Wm P	Alameda Brooklyn	55 105
SILERE		
R	Sutter Nicolaus	70 834
SILERY		
M*	Tuolumne Big Oak	71 145
SILEY		
A	Amador Twp 3	55 383
SILF		
Jackson	Plumas Meadow Valley	62 927
SILGA		
Joseph	Alameda Brooklyn	55 87
SILGIN		
Josephine*	Alameda Brooklyn	55 179
SILHAS		
Manuel*	Mariposa Twp 3	60 602
SILHESTRE		
---	San Bernardino S Timate	64 697
SILIA		
Antonio	Contra Costa Twp 1	57 493
SILIAR		
Margt	San Francisco San Francisco 9	68 979
SILIG		
Moses	San Francisco San Francisco 7	681430
SILIGMAN		
Leopold	San Francisco San Francisco 7	681351
SILIM		
Joseph	Tuolumne Jamestown	71 469
SILISEER		
Ignatio	Alameda Brooklyn	55 191
SILIVEN		
John	Sierra Downieville	661006
SILK		
J	Nevada Grass Valley	61 191
James	San Joaquin Castoria	64 904
James	Sierra La Porte	66 787
Jas W	San Francisco San Francisco 2	67 623
John	Colusa Muion	57 459
John	Tulara Visalia	71 81
Jos W	San Francisco San Francisco 2	67 623
Patrick	Alameda Brooklyn	55 177
SILKIRK		
Wm	Sierra Twp 5	66 924
SILKS		
William	Yuba Marysville	72 968
SILKWOOD		
O S	Amador Twp 5	55 357
SILL		
---	Sierra Downieville	661008
---	Sierra Downieville	66 982
Charles	Tuolumne Twp 1	71 197
D	Tehama Lassen	70 881
D Jr	Tehama Lassen	70 881
David	Sierra Downieville	66 956
F R	Tuolumne Twp 2	71 286
Fred*	Sacramento Ward 3	63 486
G E	Yolo Cottonwoood	72 651
George	Placer Stewart	62 607
George	Placer Secret R	62 608
Henry	Sacramento Ward 4	63 514
Joseph	Tuolumne Twp 2	71 284
Mary*	Sacramento Sutter	63 229
Mill	Butte Bidwell	56 708
Wm C ?	Mariposa Twp 3	60 584
SILLAND		
William	Sierra La Porte	66 783
SILLANDER		
Wm	San Francisco San Francisco 2	67 672
SILLANIL		
William	Sierra La Porte	66 783
SILLANS		
J	Stanislaus Emory	70 740
SILLARD		
G	Siskiyou Scott Ri	69 66
SILLARS		
David	Santa Clara Gilroy	65 235

California 1860 Census Index

Name	County Locale	M653 RollPage
SILLCOX		
R	Trinity Indian C	70 986
SILLEARD		
John	Monterey San Juan	60 976
SILLERS		
Robert*	Solano Vacaville	69 342
SILLESKIE		
David	El Dorado Georgetown	58 691
SILLEY		
Louis	El Dorado Coloma	581079
Thomas	Sierra Twp 5	66 933
SILLIA		
Chris	El Dorado Mud Springs	58 986
SILLICK		
L	El Dorado Placerville	58 877
SILLICROP		
T H	Sierra Twp 7	66 872
SILLIETT		
Alfred	Contra Costa Twp 1	57 511
SILLIMAN		
H N	Calaveras Twp 8	57 53
SILLING		
John*	San Francisco San Francisco 2	67 654
SILLINGER		
John	Placer Iona Hills	62 876
SILLIP		
B*	Butte Kimshaw	56 598
SILLIRAN		
Thomas*	Calaveras Twp 8	57 82
SILLIS		
A*	Nevada Washington	61 333
Frank*	Sacramento Ward 1	63 13
Fromk	Sacramento Ward 1	63 13
SILLIVAN		
A	Nevada Eureka	61 373
John	Marin Novato	60 738
SILLLEY		
Maria*	San Joaquin Stockton	641012
SILLMAN		
Frank*	San Francisco San Francisco 2	67 588
Geo	San Francisco San Francisco 1	68 916
SILLOW		
George	Sierra Twp 5	66 926
SILLRA		
Antonio	Mariposa Twp 3	60 617
SILLS		
B B	Sacramento Lee	63 216
David*	Sacramento Cosummes	63 403
Henry Clay	Sacramento Cosummes	63 403
James	San Francisco San Francisco 2	67 676
SILLSBY		
George B	San Francisco San Francisco 4	681123
SILLSON		
James	Mariposa Twp 3	60 603
SILLWARD		
A	Nevada Eureka	61 373
SILLY		
B*	Butte Kimshaw	56 598
George B*	Calaveras Twp 4	57 344
James	Tulara Twp 3	71 49
SILMA		
Joseph	Alameda Brooklyn	55 162
SILMAN		
H	San Joaquin Stockton	641093
J T	Tuolumne Shawsfla	71 406
L	Tuolumne Sonora	71 185
Peter	San Francisco San Francisco 12	377 67
S M*	Tuolumne Big Oak	71 145
SILMORE		
Ann	San Francisco San Francisco 4	681166
SILNER		
Morris	Amador Twp 1	55 455
SILNERS		
Joseph*	Mariposa Twp 3	60 622
SILNERTRA		
---	San Bernardino S Timate	64 691
SILNESTRA		
---*	San Bernardino S Timate	64 694
SILNESTRE		
---	San Bernardino San Bernadino	64 669
---	San Bernardino San Bernadino	64 681
SILOCE		
Frank*	Los Angeles San Pedro	59 481
SILON		
Frank	Calaveras Twp 10	57 269
John	Tuolumne Columbia	71 293
Manuel*	Tuolumne Columbia	71 321
SILORA		
John	Calaveras Twp 4	57 335
SILOS		
Charles	Tehama Tehama	70 950
SILOTRO		
Manuel	Placer Michigan	62 850
SILOTZ		
R	Shasta Millvill	66 747

Name	County Locale	M653 RollPage
SILOZO		
Cecilio	San Bernardino Santa Barbara	64 173
SILPAS		
Manuel*	Mariposa Twp 3	60 602
SILRA		
James	San Francisco San Francisco 9	681073
Manuel*	Monterey Pajaro	601018
SILRAN		
Lewis	Butte Kimshaw	56 582
SILRANG		
Herman*	San Francisco San Francisco 4	681134
SILRANZ		
Herman	San Francisco San Francisco 4	681134
SILRARY		
Herman*	San Francisco San Francisco 4	681134
SILRAS		
Antonio	San Bernardino Santa Ba	64 215
SILRIS		
Wm*	Sierra Downieville	66 986
SILSBEE		
Jacob B	Siskiyou Yreka	69 170
John W	Siskiyou Yreka	69 184
SILSBURY		
Thos	Butte Kimshaw	56 586
SILSBY		
W H	Butte Chico	56 549
SILSER		
Johanna*	San Francisco San Francisco 2	67 690
SILTON		
Wm	Sonoma Petaluma	69 552
SILTRU		
Antonio	Mariposa Twp 3	60 617
SILTS		
Peter	Santa Cruz Pajaro	66 573
SILTZER		
Henry	Sierra Twp 7	66 909
SILVA		
A	Sacramento Franklin	63 311
Antoniedoris	Placer Rattle Snake	62 633
Antonio	Placer Rattle Snake	62 602
Apalina	Calaveras Twp 10	57 292
Apalino	Calaveras Twp 10	57 292
August	Butte Oregon	56 635
Austin	Placer Ophirville	62 654
Chapo	San Diego Colorado	64 812
Chas M	Placer Rattle Snake	62 601
Custodia	Monterey San Juan	60 985
Faust	Sacramento Natonia	63 273
Fernando	Los Angeles San Pedro	59 486
Francis	Santa Clara Redwood	65 445
Francis*	Sacramento Granite	63 246
Frank	Monterey Monterey	60 925
Frank	Placer Michigan	62 850
Frank	Sacramento Granite	63 254
J	San Francisco San Francisco 5	67 517
J	San Francisco San Francisco 5	67 540
J	San Francisco San Francisco 1	68 865
James	Sacramento Granite	63 243
James	Sacramento Granite	63 246
James	San Francisco San Francisco 9	681073
Jascintho*	Santa Cruz Santa Cruz	66 612
Joaquin	Alameda Oakland	55 7
Joeph	Placer Iona Hills	62 895
John	Placer Stewart	62 607
John	Sacramento Granite	63 246
John	Sacramento Franklin	63 312
John*	Placer Rattle Snake	62 603
John*	Sacramento Granite	63 246
Joseph	Monterey Monterey	60 925
Joseph	Placer Rattle Snake	62 634
Joseph	San Francisco San Francisco 2	67 663
Joseph	San Francisco San Francisco 1	68 852
Joseph*	Sacramento Granite	63 254
Mannel	San Francisco San Francisco 3	67 85
Mannel*	Butte Oregon	56 636
Manuel	Alameda Brooklyn	55 124
Manuel	Butte Oregon	56 636
Manuel	Monterey Pajaro	601018
Manuel	Monterey Monterey	60 925
Manuel	Placer Rattle Snake	62 603
Manuel	Placer Rattle Snake	62 633
Manuel	Placer Rattle Snake	62 634
Manuel	Placer Rattle Snake	62 636
Manuel 3d	Butte Oregon	56 636
Manuel*	Butte Oregon	56 636
Manuel*	Monterey Pajaro	601018
Manuel*	Sacramento Granite	63 254
Manull*	Sacramento Granite	63 254
Marcelina	San Francisco San Francisco 2	67 790
Marcelinn	San Francisco San Francisco 2	67 790
N	Merced Twp 1	60 900
Peter	Tuolumne Twp 3	71 458
SILVAIN		
T	Calaveras Twp 9	57 401
SILVAL		
Pedro*	Calaveras Twp 5	57 183

Name	County Locale	M653 RollPage
SILVAN		
Louis	Butte Kimshaw	56 582
SILVANA		
Maria	Los Angeles San Juan	59 474
SILVAS		
A	Merced Twp 1	60 902
Antenia	San Bernardino San Bernadino	64 685
Antonio	San Bernardino S Buenav	64 215
Francisco	San Diego Agua Caliente	64 847
Jeronano	San Salvador	64 639
Jeronimo	San Bernardino	
	San Bernardino	64 639
Pedro	San Bernardino	
	Calaveras Twp 6	57 183
Romon	Santa Clara Almaden	65 267
SILVAT		
Pedro*	Calaveras Twp 5	57 183
SILVCE		
Frank*	Los Angeles San Pedro	59 481
SILVEA		
John	Calaveras Twp 4	57 335
SILVER		
A	Nevada Washington	61 332
A	Trinity Dead Wood	70 958
Antimi*	Alameda Murray	55 223
Antoine	Placer Rattle Snake	62 635
Anton	Nevada Rough &	61 424
Anton	Tuolumne Twp 2	71 284
Antone	Klamath Liberty	59 236
Antone	Mariposa Coulterville	60 691
Antone	Sierra St Louis	66 817
Antone	Trinity State Ba	701001
Antone	Trinity Indian C	70 986
Antone	Trinity Indian C	70 989
Antone	Tuolumne Twp 2	71 284
Antone	Yolo Merritt	72 578
Antonie	Alameda Brooklyn	55 104
Antonio	Alameda Brooklyn	55 100
Antonio	Alameda Brooklyn	55 104
Antonio	Alameda Brooklyn	55 125
Antonio	Alameda Brooklyn	55 165
Antonio	Alameda Brooklyn	55 94
Antonio	San Francisco San Francisco 2	67 787
Antonio	Tuolumne Twp 4	71 140
Antonio*	Alameda Murray	55 223
Antonio*	Mariposa Twp 3	60 617
Auton	Tuolumne Twp 2	71 284
Charles	Alameda Brooklyn	55 103
Charlie	Alameda Brooklyn	55 103
Emanuel	Trinity Rush Crk	70 965
Emanuel	Trinity Indian C	70 983
Emanuel	Trinity Indian C	70 989
Faust*	Sacramento Natonia	63 273
Floro	Alameda Brooklyn	55 124
Francis	Sacramento Granite	63 246
Frank	Amador Twp 5	55 337
Frank	Calaveras Twp 8	57 95
Frank	Klamath Salmon	59 209
Frank	Los Angeles San Pedro	59 481
Frank	Marin Bolinas	60 748
Frank	Sacramento Granite	63 254
Frank	Trinity Indian C	70 986
Frank	Tuolumne Shawsfla	71 389
Frank	Tuolumne Shawsfla	71 393
Frank M	Alameda Brooklyn	55 124
Frank*	Alameda Brooklyn	55 125
G F	Yolo Washington	72 574
Geo F	El Dorado Salmon Falls	581050
George	Nevada Rough &	61 424
George	Siskiyou Yreka	69 136
Henry	Sierra St Louis	66 816
Hosea	Alameda Brooklyn	55 165
J	Nevada Washington	61 332
J M	Siskiyou Callahan	69 19
James	Sacramento Granite	63 243
James	Sacramento Granite	63 246
Jas	Trinity Texas Ba	70 981
Jas	Yolo Cottonwoood	72 556
Jno	Trinity Lewiston	70 957
Joaquin	Tuolumne Twp 2	71 389
John	Alameda Brooklyn	55 116
John	Alameda Washington	55 170
John	Alameda Brooklyn	55 97
John	Calaveras Twp 6	57 124
John	Placer Rattle Snake	62 634
John	Placer Rattle Snake	62 636
John	Sacramento Granite	63 246
John	Shasta Shasta	66 671
John	Trinity Texas Ba	70 981
John	Trinity Indian C	70 986
John	Tuolumne Shawsfla	71 389
John	Tuolumne Columbia	71 473
John*	Alameda Brooklyn	55 97
John*	Placer Rattle Snake	62 603
John*	Sacramento Granite	63 246
John*	Tuolumne Twp 2	71 293

California 1860 Census Index

Name	County Locale	M653 Roll	Page
SILVER			
Johntius	Fresno Twp 1	59	81
Jonatius	Fresno Twp 1	59	81
Jos	Butte Kimshaw	56	591
Jos	Butte Kimshaw	56	606
Jos	Klamath Salmon	59	209
Jos	Klamath Liberty	59	236
Jos	Placer Rattle Snake	62	636
Jos Thos	Alameda Murray	55	217
Jose	Sacramento Granite	63	254
Jose	Tuolumne Jamestown	71	422
Joseh	Alameda Brooklyn	55	86
Joseh	Trinity Rush Crk	70	965
Joseph	Alameda Brooklyn	55	113
Joseph	Alameda Brooklyn	55	86
Joseph	El Dorado Salmon Falls	58	1051
Joseph	El Dorado Salmon Falls	58	1055
Joseph	Nevada Rough &	61	424
Joseph	Placer Rattle Snake	62	634
Joseph	Sacramento Granite	63	254
Joseph	Sierra St Louis	66	816
Joseph	Stanislaus Emory	70	754
Joseph	Trinity Dead Wood	70	958
Joseph	Trinity Rush Crk	70	965
Joseph	Tuolumne Columbia	71	307
Joseph*	Sacramento Granite	63	254
Julian	Alameda Brooklyn	55	93
Leorrer*	Tuolumne Twp 2	71	284
Lneia	Yolo Cottonwoood	72	558
M	Trinity Dead Wood	70	958
Manel	Tuolumne Shawsfla	71	379
Manual	Tehama Tehama	70	941
Manuel	Alameda Brooklyn	55	100
Manuel	Alameda Brooklyn	55	104
Manuel	Alameda Brooklyn	55	125
Manuel	Alameda Oakland	55	49
Manuel	Klamath Liberty	59	235
Manuel	Klamath Liberty	59	236
Manuel	Sacramento Granite	63	254
Manuel	San Francisco San Francisco 3	67	85
Manuel	Sierra St Louis	66	817
Manuel	Tuolumne Twp 2	71	321
Manuel	Tuolumne Twp 2	71	379
Manuel	Tuolumne Shawsfla	71	391
Manuel	Yolo Washington	72	574
Manuel*	Tuolumne Columbia	71	321
Manuell	Amador Twp 5	55	339
Manwell	Amador Twp 5	55	339
Martin	Mariposa Twp 1	60	651
Mary	Alameda Oakland	55	16
Moneil	Yolo Washington	72	574
Morreil*	Yolo Washington	72	574
Morris	Amador Twp 1	55	455
Oliver	El Dorado Salmon Falls	58	1051
P	Nevada Washington	61	331
P	Nevada Washington	61	341
P C	Tuolumne Twp 2	71	284
P C	Tuolumne Twp 2	71	284
P*	Nevada Washington	61	331
Pasel D	Sierra La Porte	66	770
Pasel L	Sierra La Porte	66	770
Peter	Tuolumne Sonora	71	479
Peter	Tuolumne Twp 1	71	484
Phillip	Alameda Brooklyn	55	118
Sevrrers*	Tuolumne Twp 2	71	284
Thojmas	Calaveras Twp 5	57	199
Thomas	Calaveras Twp 5	57	199
Thos	Amador Twp 5	55	337
Trinidad	Nevada Red Dog	61	539
W J	Butte Ophir	56	766
Wm	Amador Twp 5	55	352
SILVERA			
---	Los Angeles San Juan	59	464
Manuel	Alameda Brooklyn	55	116
SILVERBERG			
S	San Francisco San Francisco 7	68	1361
SILVERDALE			
J S	Tuolumne Twp 4	71	145
SILVERHORN			
Charles	El Dorado Salmon Falls	58	1036
SILVERMAN			
G	San Francisco San Francisco 5	67	483
John T	Placer Auburn	62	595
O	El Dorado Placerville	58	835
P	El Dorado Placerville	58	855
S	San Francisco San Francisco 6	67	400
SILVERO			
John	Tuolumne Twp 3	71	459
SILVERS			
Antonio P	Contra Costa Twp 1	57	520
Cose	Marin Cortemad	60	755
Frank	Trinity Indian C	70	989
Jno	Trinity Lewiston	70	953
John	Del Norte Crescent	58	623
Joseph	Marin S Antoni	60	707
Joseph	Mariposa Twp 3	60	622
SILVERS			
Josepph	Marin S Antoni	60	707
SILVERSMITH			
G	San Francisco San Francisco 4	68	1150
SILVERSON			
Hulway	Alameda Brooklyn	55	113
Manuel	Alameda Brooklyn	55	105
SILVERSTEIN			
Betsy	Sacramento Ward 1	63	36
H	Sacramento Ward 1	63	36
Isaac	Yuba Marysville	72	903
SILVERSTIN			
Harris	Sonoma Vallejo	69	620
SILVERSTINE			
H*	Sacramento Ward 1	63	96
SILVERSTONE			
H	Sacramento Ward 1	63	96
Solomon	San Francisco San Francisco 4	68	1135
SILVERSTUM			
William*	Placer Forest H	62	803
SILVERT			
John	Calaveras Twp 6	57	131
SILVERTEN			
Henry	San Francisco San Francisco 2	67	582
SILVERTERN			
W	Shasta Shasta	66	759
SILVERTHORN			
Rodin	Napa Napa	61	85
S	El Dorado Placerville	58	817
W	Shasta Shasta	66	759
SILVERTHORNE			
Willim H*	San Francisco San Francisco 2	67	736
SILVERWOOD			
John	Sierra Downieville	66	1010
SILVERY			
M	Tuolumne Twp 4	71	145
Thos	Amador Twp 5	55	359
SILVES			
Antoni	Mariposa Twp 3	60	617
Antonio*	Mariposa Twp 3	60	617
P*	Nevada Washington	61	331
Wm	San Francisco San Francisco 2	67	759
Wm*	Sierra Downieville	66	986
SILVESTEN			
Henry	San Francisco San Francisco 2	67	582
SILVESTER			
---	San Bernardino S Timate	64	710
Geo	San Francisco San Francisco 5	67	498
H	San Francisco San Francisco 2	67	462
Jno	Butte Oregon	56	636
SILVESTOR			
Thos	Santa Clara San Jose	65	345
SILVESTRA			
---	San Bernardino S Timate	64	698
---	San Bernardino S Timate	64	725
---	San Bernardino S Timate	64	738
---*	San Bernardino Sanbernr	64	694
SILVESTRE			
---	San Bernardino S Timate	64	695
---	San Bernardino S Timate	64	699
---	San Bernardino S Timate	64	714
---	San Bernardino S Timate	64	725
Louis	San Francisco San Francisco 2	67	647
SILVESTRO			
---	San Bernardino S Timate	64	703
---	San Bernardino S Timate	64	722
---	San Bernardino S Timate	64	735
SILVESTYNE			
Geo	San Francisco San Francisco 1	68	928
SILVETRA			
Peter*	Placer Michigan	62	850
SILVEY			
Albt	Butte Kimshaw	56	581
Elisha	Solano Vacaville	69	349
Frank	Marin Bolinas	60	748
Geo	Sonoma Salt Point	69	691
George R	Solano Vacaville	69	349
J B	Butte Chico	56	567
Jos	Butte Kimshaw	56	601
Kate	San Francisco San Francisco 4	68	1112
Robert	San Francisco San Francisco 2	67	632
SILVIA			
Antoni	Contra Costa Twp 1	57	523
Antonia	Butte Bidwell	56	728
Antonia	San Francisco San Francisco 5	67	479
Antonie	Butte Cascade	56	694
Chasen	Contra Costa Twp 2	57	556
Cipriand	Contra Costa Twp 1	57	496
Crotu	Calaveras Twp 6	57	123
Francis	Calaveras Twp 5	57	212
Frank	Butte Oro	56	678
Frank	Contra Costa Twp 1	57	508
Frank	Contra Costa Twp 1	57	519
Gochan	Fresno Twp 1	59	26
Jos	Butte Cascade	56	694
Jose	Contra Costa Twp 1	57	494
SILVIA			
Jose	Contra Costa Twp 1	57	518
Jose M	Contra Costa Twp 1	57	517
Joseph	Placer Rattle Snake	62	601
Manuel	Los Angeles San Pedro	59	483
Manuela	Contra Costa Twp 3	57	600
Mike	Butte Oro	56	678
Necucio	Contra Costa Twp 3	57	600
Untonia	San Francisco San Francisco 5	67	479
Wm	Butte Oro	56	686
Wm	Butte Bidwell	56	731
SILVID			
Francis	Calaveras Twp 5	57	212
SILVIRR			
John*	Tuolumne Twp 3	71	459
SILVIS			
Antome*	Butte Cascade	56	694
Antone*	Butte Cascade	56	694
Joaquin	Tuolumne Shawsfla	71	389
SILVISA			
Morghilo	Calaveras Twp 5	57	201
SILVIVO			
Anton	Tuolumne Sonora	71	189
SILVR			
Wm	Sierra Downieville	66	986
SILVRA			
John	Calaveras Twp 4	57	335
SILVRIVA			
Anton	Tuolumne Twp 1	71	189
SIM MAW			
---*	Nevada Nevada	61	306
SIM SHE			
---	Tuolumne Columbia	71	346
Ah	Tuolumne Twp 2	71	346
SIM			
---	Amador Twp 2	55	314
---	Amador Twp 2	55	328
---	Amador Twp 5	55	335
---	Amador Twp 5	55	340
---	Butte Kimshaw	56	589
---	Butte Kimshaw	56	598
---	Butte Wyandotte	56	672
---	Butte Cascade	56	690
---	Butte Cascade	56	704
---	Butte Bidwell	56	707
---	Butte Bidwell	56	713
---	Butte Bidwell	56	714
---	Butte Bidwell	56	715
---	Butte Bidwell	56	725
---	Butte Bidwell	56	726
---	Butte Bidwell	56	727
---	Butte Bidwell	56	728
---	Butte Ophir	56	783
---	Calaveras Twp 10	57	285
---	Calaveras Twp 4	57	302
---	Calaveras Twp 4	57	306
---	El Dorado Salmon Falls	58	1058
---	El Dorado Mountain	58	1189
---	El Dorado Georgetown	58	700
---	El Dorado Greenwood	58	719
---	El Dorado Greenwood	58	720
---	El Dorado Greenwood	58	727
---	El Dorado Greenwood	58	728
---	El Dorado Diamond	58	794
---	El Dorado Placerville	58	924
---	El Dorado Mud Springs	58	972
---	Fresno Twp 2	59	42
---	Fresno Twp 1	59	77
---	Mariposa Twp 3	60	581
---	Mariposa Twp 3	60	609
---	Mariposa Twp 3	60	613
---	Mariposa Twp 1	60	637
---	Nevada Rough &	61	396
---	Nevada Rough &	61	399
---	Nevada Rough &	61	432
---	Nevada Rough &	61	433
---	Nevada Bridgeport	61	462
---	Nevada Bridgeport	61	506
---	Nevada Red Dog	61	538
---	Placer Auburn	62	572
---	Placer Auburn	62	581
---	Placer Illinois	62	742
---	Placer Illinois	62	746
---	Placer Illinois	62	753
---	Placer Illinois	62	754
---	Plumas Quincy	62	920
---	Sacramento Cosumnes	63	392
---	Sacramento Ward 3	63	492
---	Sacramento Ward 1	63	70
---	San Francisco San Francisco 4	68	1176
---	Sierra Downieville	66	1009
---	Sierra Downieville	66	1014
---	Sierra Downieville	66	1029
---	Sierra Downieville	66	1030
---	Sierra La Porte	66	780
---	Sierra St Louis	66	861

Name	County Locale	M653 Roll	Page
SIM			
---	Sierra Twp 5	66	947
---	Sierra Downieville	66	954
---	Sierra Downieville	66	973
---	Sierra Downieville	66	979
---	Sierra Downieville	66	983
---	Sierra Downieville	66	999
---	Siskiyou Scott Va	69	32
---	Siskiyou Klamath	69	79
---	Trinity E Weaver	70	1059
---	Tuolumne Twp 2	71	397
---	Tuolumne Twp 3	71	421
---	Tuolumne Chinese	71	510
---*	El Dorado Salmon Falls	58	1053
---*	Nevada Rough &	61	432
---*	Sierra Downieville	66	999
Ah	Amador Twp 2	55	314
Ah	Butte Cascade	56	690
Ah	Butte Bidwell	56	725
Ah	Butte Bidwell	56	727
Ah	Siskiyou Klamath	69	79
Ah	Tuolumne Twp 2	71	396
Charley	Placer Auburn	62	573
Chin	Calaveras Twp 8	57	76
Chow	Butte Cascade	56	692
Chow	Tehama Red Bluff	70	932
Fim	Plumas Quincy	62	965
Fin*	Shasta Horsetown	66	701
Foo Law	Yuba Long Bar	72	763
Fook	Butte Kimshaw	56	582
George	San Francisco San Francisco 3	67	72
Hoy	Yuba North Ea	72	676
James	Sierra Pine Grove	66	820
Juk	El Dorado Big Bar	58	738
Lee	Butte Cascade	56	692
Lee	Placer Illinois	62	752
Ling	Butte Bidwell	56	723
Lung	Plumas Quincy	62	1009
Poo	Plumas Quincy	62	948
Sam	Butte Bidwell	56	725
Sick	Butte Kimshaw	56	586
Slu	Butte Oro	56	687
Sue	El Dorado Georgetown	58	746
Wa*	Nevada Nevada	61	304
Wm	Alameda Brooklyn	55	204
Wo	San Francisco San Francisco 11	67	145
Ye	Placer Illinois	62	752
Yea	Placer Auburn	62	575
Yup	Nevada Grass Valley	61	232
SIMAN			
Amos	Sierra Eureka	66	1049
Jacob*	Placer Ophir	62	652
Luie	Sonoma Sonoma	69	649
SIMANFIELD			
J	San Francisco San Francisco 3	67	71
SIMAS			
Manuel	El Dorado Mud Springs	58	986
SIMBLEUND			
John*	Placer Todds Va	62	762
SIMBLEY			
Henry	San Joaquin Stockton	64	1067
SIMBLUNA			
John*	Placer Todds Va	62	762
SIMBLUNN			
John*	Placer Todds Va	62	762
SIMBROCHER			
Peter	Placer Iona Hills	62	862
SIMCE			
M	Trinity Weaverville	70	1063
SIMDERHAUN			
Joseph*	Mariposa Twp 3	60	573
SIMDESHAUN			
Joseph*	Mariposa Twp 3	60	573
SIMDL			
Henry*	Sierra Downieville	66	1029
SIME			
---	Butte Oregon	56	632
---	Butte Oregon	56	642
---	Nevada Grass Valley	61	232
---	Placer Auburn	62	575
---	Placer Illinois	62	752
---	Sacramento Mississipi	63	186
Ah	Butte Oregon	56	632
Siny	Shasta Horsetown	66	701
SIMEA			
---	Fresno Twp 2	59	59
SIMEAH			
---	Tulara Twp 2	71	40
SIMENTAR			
Josefa*	San Francisco San Francisco 2	67	752
SIMEON H			
Brock	Sierra Gibsonville	66	852
SIMEON			
Jose	San Bernardino San Bernadino	64	684
L	San Joaquin Stockton	64	1097

Name	County Locale	M653 Roll	Page
SIMEON			
Peter	San Francisco San Francisco 7	68	1396
Rosina	San Francisco San Francisco 2	67	613
SIMER			
M	San Francisco San Francisco 2	67	709
SIMEREL			
Louis*	Alameda Brooklyn	55	139
SIMERITAR			
Josefa*	San Francisco San Francisco 2	67	752
SIMERS			
F	San Francisco San Francisco 2	67	743
SIMES			
Christopher	Marin Tomales	60	724
SIMEY			
Chas	Butte Oregon	56	635
SIMFFINS			
W S	Mendocino Ukiah	60	805
SIMG			
Fien*	Sacramento Ward 1	63	59
Tien	Sacramento Ward 1	63	59
SIMGE			
---	Sacramento Ward 1	63	68
SIMGLEY			
Resse R	Mendocino Ukiah	60	798
SIMINE			
---	San Francisco San Francisco 4	68	1223
SIMINER			
Jas*	Butte Chico	56	559
SIMINSON			
John	Butte Ophir	56	751
SIMINTON			
J H*	Sacramento Ward 1	63	73
SIMIRILE			
G B	Merced Twp 1	60	896
SIMISON			
S G	Siskiyou Cottonwoood	69	98
SIMKEL			
Frederick	Alameda Oakland	55	68
SIMKINS			
Charles	Placer Iona Hills	62	893
Chas	Sacramento Granite	63	265
SIMLER			
---	San Francisco San Francisco 3	67	67
SIMLUSKY			
H	Siskiyou Scott Ri	69	69
J	Siskiyou Scott Ri	69	69
SIMM			
---	Butte Wyandotte	56	672
---	Placer Horseshoe	62	650
Dora T*	San Francisco San Francisco 8	68	1294
Frank	Sierra Twp 5	66	943
SIMMCOUY			
F E*	Tuolumne Jamestown	71	470
SIMMENS			
Geore*	Siskiyou Yreka	69	145
SIMMERHER			
C*	Yolo Cottonwoood	72	559
SIMMERKER			
C*	Yolo Cottonwoood	72	559
SIMMERMAN			
George	San Francisco San Francisco 11	67	137
Henry	Contra Costa Twp 3	57	591
John	San Francisco San Francisco 11	67	139
Nable E*	Tuolumne Twp 3	71	452
SIMMERS			
Thaddus	Sierra St Louis	66	864
SIMMES			
Henry*	El Dorado Placerville	58	905
Herman	San Francisco San Francisco 3	67	82
Oliver C*	Alameda Brooklyn	55	215
SIMMILER			
Jacob	San Luis Obispo San Luis Obispo	65	23
SIMMINS			
A F*	Butte Cascade	56	692
Eliza A	Sacramento Franklin	63	325
James S	Calaveras Twp 5	57	216
T A	Calaveras Twp 9	57	417
SIMMON			
Alonzo R	San Francisco San Francisco 3	67	60
David	Sacramento Brighton	63	197
Frank	San Francisco San Francisco 2	67	747
Frederick	San Francisco San Francisco 4	68	1172
Joseph	Calaveras Twp 7	57	27
SIMMOND			
Jay	Monterey San Juan	60	989
SIMMONDS			
A	Butte Bidwell	56	712
A H	El Dorado Placerville	58	919
A*	Butte Bidwell	56	712
J H	Butte Ophir	56	762
John	Amador Twp 5	55	352
John	Napa Yount	61	48
John	Napa Napa	61	91
John Fitz	Santa Clara San Jose	65	356

Name	County Locale	M653 Roll	Page
SIMMONDS			
S G	Yolo Cache Crk	72	606
W C	Mendocino Little L	60	836
SIMMONDY			
John	Napa Napa	61	91
SIMMONER			
John	Alameda Oakland	55	48
SIMMONS			
---	San Francisco San Francisco 7	68	1343
A	San Mateo Twp 2	65	121
A D	El Dorado Kelsey	58	1148
A F	Butte Cascade	56	692
A J	Butte Kimshaw	56	595
Aaron	Butte Chico	56	539
Albert	Butte Ophir	56	783
Andrew	Alameda Brooklyn	55	188
Andrew J	Calaveras Twp 8	57	104
Antony	Marin Cortemad	60	785
Benjamin J	Sierra Scales D	66	804
Bertha	Sacramento Ward 1	63	90
C	Amador Twp 2	55	274
C B	Tehama Red Bluff	70	922
C C	Butte Kimshaw	56	599
C L	San Francisco San Francisco 2	67	598
C T	San Francisco San Francisco 2	67	598
Charles	Contra Costa Twp 1	57	532
Charles	San Francisco San Francisco 1	68	916
Charles	San Mateo Twp 1	65	57
Charles C*	Yuba Marysville	72	891
Charles D	Yuba Marysville	72	891
Chas	Butte Oregon	56	622
Clara	El Dorado Coloma	58	1079
Cordelia	El Dorado Kelsey	58	1140
D R	Sacramento Dry Crk	63	378
Daniel F	Colusa Grand Island	57	474
David	Alameda Brooklyn	55	102
E	San Francisco San Francisco 9	68	962
E J	San Francisco San Francisco 2	67	736
Edwin	Sacramento Ward 1	63	126
Elizabeth	Los Angeles Los Angeles	59	355
Elizabeth	Sonoma Mendocino	69	459
Ellen	Siskiyou Scott Ri	69	62
Emma	Los Angeles San Pedro	59	481
Frank	Tehama Red Bluff	70	922
Frank	Yuba Marysville	72	858
Frank	Yuba Marysville	72	860
G L	Sacramento Ward 1	63	25
G L	Sacramento Ward 1	63	36
Geo	El Dorado Mud Springs	58	956
Geo	San Francisco San Francisco 2	67	621
Geo	Sonoma Sonoma	69	642
George	Siskiyou Yreka	69	145
George A	San Francisco San Francisco 8	68	1320
George*	Siskiyou Yreka	69	145
Gregory	Santa Clara Redwood	65	456
Gubling	Siskiyou Callahan	69	3
H T	Sacramento Ward 1	63	35
Henry	El Dorado Casumnes	58	1176
Henry	San Mateo Twp 1	65	57
I C	San Francisco San Francisco 5	67	500
Isaac H	El Dorado Greenwood	58	724
J	El Dorado Coloma	58	1103
J	Nevada Grass Valley	61	236
J	San Joaquin Stockton	64	1099
J	Solano Vacaville	69	364
J	Sutter Butte	70	789
J A	Sacramento San Joaquin	63	351
J A	San Francisco San Francisco 2	67	736
J B	Nevada Nevada	61	320
J C	Santa Clara Santa Clara	65	494
J D	Sacramento Sutter	63	294
J D	Sacramento Sutter	63	300
J D	Sacramento Sutter	63	300
J E	Butte Chico	56	533
J E	El Dorado Eldorado	58	941
J L	Sutter Yuba	70	772
J M	Shasta Shasta	66	677
J P	Nevada Eureka	61	348
J P	Tuolumne Twp 2	71	388
J R	San Francisco San Francisco 1	68	924
J W	Mariposa Twp 3	60	587
J W*	Yuba Slate Ro	72	702
James	El Dorado Placerville	58	913
James	Mariposa Twp 3	60	610
James	Tuolumne Twp 2	71	288
James Fitz	Calaveras Twp 5	57	184
James S	Calaveras Twp 5	57	216
James*	Mariposa Twp 3	60	610
Jane	Amador Twp 5	55	346
Jas	San Francisco San Francisco 1	68	901
Jay	Monterey San Juan	60	989
Jno	Nevada Nevada	61	298
Jno	Sonoma Sonoma	69	642
John	Amador Twp 5	55	357
John	Amador Twp 5	55	358
John	Amador Twp 1	55	473

California 1860 Census Index

Name	County Locale	M653 Roll/Page
SIMMONS		
John	Butte Ophir	56 771
John	Nevada Bloomfield	61 514
John	Sacramento San Joaquin	63 365
John	San Francisco San Francisco 6	67 420
John	San Francisco San Francisco 2	67 692
John	San Mateo Twp 1	65 55
John	Tehama Lassen	70 879
John	Tuolumne Twp 1	71 253
John	Tuolumne Twp 3	71 468
John J	Tuolumne Twp 3	71 468
John R	Sonoma Mendocino	69 459
Jos S	San Francisco San Francisco 2	67 585
Joseph	El Dorado Placerville	58 917
Joseph	Solano Vallejo	69 269
Julaia A	San Francisco San Francisco 4	681131
L	Shasta Shasta	66 732
L D	San Francisco San Francisco 9	681011
L H	Solano Suisan	69 232
L W	Sierra Twp 7	66 913
Levi	Colusa Grand Island	57 470
M	El Dorado Kelsey	581154
M	Sacramento Ward 3	63 482
Margaret*	Nevada Red Dog	61 546
Marriet M	Los Angeles Los Angeles	59 356
Nable E	Tuolumne Jamestown	71 452
Nathan D	Sierra La Porte	66 769
Nicholas	Alameda Oakland	55 60
O	Butte Ophir	56 791
Orin*	Alameda Oakland	55 56
Owen	Butte Hamilton	56 519
Pat	Siskiyou Callahan	69 4
Pate	Siskiyou Callahan	69 3
Percilko	Amador Twp 2	55 313
Percilla	Amador Twp 2	55 313
Perimer*	Nevada Rough &	61 431
Peter	San Francisco San Francisco 9	681076
R C	Napa Yount	61 38
Riley	El Dorado Greenwood	58 726
Robert	San Francisco San Francisco 11	150 67
Robert	Santa Cruz Pajaro	66 577
Rosalie	Yuba Marysville	72 898
Rosalie	Yuba Marysville	72 899
S	Butte Oregon	56 622
S	Shasta Millvill	66 753
S	Tehama Red Bluff	70 916
S D	San Francisco San Francisco 6	67 449
Samuel	Monterey San Juan	60 988
Sarah	Colusa Grand Island	57 474
Seth	San Francisco San Francisco 7	681399
Simon	San Francisco San Francisco 2	67 604
T	Tehama Red Bluff	70 930
T D	Sacramento Sutter	63 294
Thomas	Siskiyou Callahan	69 6
Thomas	Tuolumne Sonora	71 223
Thoms	El Dorado Placerville	58 913
W	El Dorado Newtown	58 779
W C	Sutter Butte	70 781
W H	Sacramento Ward 4	63 613
W W	Tuolumne Jamestown	71 452
William	Calaveras Twp 6	57 112
William	San Francisco San Francisco 7	681363
William	Shasta Shasta	66 730
William	Solano Suisan	69 226
William	Tulara Keeneysburg	71 46
William	Tuolumne Springfield	71 373
Wm	Nevada Eureka	61 351
Wm	Tuolumne Twp 2	71 274
Wm H	Humbolt Eel Rvr	59 150
Wm H	Mariposa Twp 1	60 671
SIMMORICH		
Nicholas	San Francisco San Francisco 3	67 51
SIMMORKER		
C	Yolo Cottonwoood	72 559
SIMMP		
Henry	Butte Cascade	56 703
SIMMS		
A	Nevada Grass Valley	61 146
Aaron	El Dorado White Oaks	581019
Ansel	Tuolumne Twp 3	71 463
David	Alameda Oakland	55 64
Edwin	Alameda Oakland	55 60
Eliza	Marin San Rafael	60 760
Ellen	San Francisco San Francisco 6	67 447
George	San Joaquin Elkhorn	64 965
J	El Dorado Placerville	58 818
James D	Napa Yount	61 37
Jno	Mendocino Big Rvr	60 844
Joel	El Dorado Greenwood	58 726
John	Marin Cortemad	60 752
M	Klamath Orleans	59 217
N	Calaveras Twp 9	57 396
Oliver	Alameda Brooklyn	55 209
P	El Dorado Placerville	58 843
R N	Napa Yount	61 37

Name	County Locale	M653 Roll/Page
SIMMS		
R T	Mendocino Little L	60 830
T	Nevada Grass Valley	61 156
Thomas*	Placer Michigan	62 807
Wm	Napa Clear Lake	61 132
SIMMTON		
J H*	Sacramento Ward 1	63 73
SIMMUS		
J N*	Sacramento Granite	63 269
SIMN		
---	El Dorado Greenwood	58 720
SIMNS		
Henry	Placer Dutch Fl	62 717
SIMOMFELD		
Julius*	Del Norte Crescent	58 621
SIMON		
---	Los Angeles Santa Ana	59 456
---	Los Angeles San Juan	59 462
---	Los Angeles San Juan	59 467
---	Marin S Antoni	60 712
---	Mendocino Round Va	60 885
---	San Diego S Luis R	64 783
---	San Diego Agua Caliente	64 827
---	San Diego Agua Caliente	64 860
---	Tulara Twp 2	71 38
Alexander	Contra Costa Twp 2	57 564
Anne	San Francisco San Francisco 11	94 67
Atliff	Santa Clara Gilroy	65 238
August	Butte Bidwell	56 731
Bello	Santa Clara Alviso	65 415
Benhard	San Francisco San Francisco 1	68 828
Benjamin	San Francisco San Francisco 7	681367
Corsigluci	Calaveras Twp 6	57 115
Frank	Calaveras Twp 5	57 223
Frank	Sierra Twp 5	66 943
Henry	Del Norte Crescent	58 629
J	Sacramento Ward 4	63 503
J	San Francisco San Francisco 2	67 769
Jacob*	Placer Ophir	62 652
John	Contra Costa Twp 1	57 519
John	Monterey S Antoni	60 973
John	Nevada Red Dog	61 538
John	Sierra Gibsonville	66 851
Joseh	Alameda Brooklyn	55 91
Joseph*	Alameda Brooklyn	55 91
Julius	Calaveras Twp 10	57 295
Juluis	Calaveras Twp 10	57 295
Levi	San Francisco San Francisco 2	67 610
Louisa	San Francisco San Francisco 11	133 67
M	San Francisco San Francisco 6	67 428
N	San Francisco San Francisco 4	681138
Pascalra*	Alameda Brooklyn	55 151
Pascatra*	Alameda Brooklyn	55 151
Paul*	Yuba Marysville	72 932
Qujis	Calaveras Twp 6	57 179
Quju*	Calaveras Twp 5	57 179
Rosena	San Francisco San Francisco 2	67 613
S	Sacramento Ward 4	63 507
S	San Francisco San Francisco 1	68 828
Sigmund	San Francisco San Francisco 8	681288
Susan	San Francisco San Francisco 2	67 781
Trinidad	Los Angeles San Juan	59 466
W	Sacramento Ward 4	63 502
Walter	Sierra Twp 7	66 899
SIMONA		
---	San Bernardino San Bernadino	64 682
Maria	San Diego San Diego	64 776
SIMONAS		
James H	Tuolumne Twp 2	71 285
SIMOND		
E	San Francisco San Francisco 5	67 520
J	Tuolumne Garrote	71 173
SIMONDE		
Victoria*	San Francisco San Francisco 4	681145
SIMONDI		
Victoria	San Francisco San Francisco 4	681145
SIMONDS		
America	San Joaquin O'Neal	641004
C B	Yuba Rose Bar	72 792
Edward D	Tuolumne Twp 1	71 205
Henry	Yuba New York	72 726
Hiram C	San Francisco San Francisco 11	98 67
James G	Yuba Slate Ro	72 702
L	San Francisco San Francisco 10	307 67
M	Trinity Taylor'S	701036
Nathan	Sonoma Sonoma	69 647
T B	Trinity Trinity	70 974
SIMONEAN		
Jules	Santa Cruz Pajaro	66 574
SIMONEAU		
Jules	Santa Cruz Pajaro	66 574
SIMONEFELD		
Julius*	Del Norte Crescent	58 621

Name	County Locale	M653 Roll/Page
SIMONEH		
James G	Yolo Slate Ra	72 702
SIMONI		
Guiseppe	San Francisco San Francisco 3	67 25
SIMONIFELD		
Julius*	Del Norte Crescent	58 621
SIMONNTO		
Amanda	San Francisco San Francisco 6	67 459
SIMONOVICH		
Nicholas	San Francisco San Francisco 3	67 51
SIMONS		
A	Trinity Cox'S Bar	701038
A A	El Dorado Placerville	58 862
Alex	Santa Clara Fremont	65 424
Amanda	Butte Ophir	56 772
Archibald	San Francisco San Francisco 1	68 808
C W	Placer Iona Hills	62 881
Chas	Sacramento Georgian	63 344
Clark	Contra Costa Twp 1	57 526
E J	Merced Twp 1	60 895
Edward D	Tuolumne Sonora	71 205
Eider	San Joaquin Stockton	641044
H	El Dorado Placerville	58 855
H	Placer Dutch Fl	62 710
Henry	Marin Novato	60 736
J	Sutter Nicolaus	70 839
J C	Sutter Vernon	70 844
J G	El Dorado Placerville	58 852
J R	Trinity Price'S	701019
Jasper	Butte Ophir	56 760
John	San Joaquin Elliott	64 946
John	Tuolumne Twp 1	71 253
John Y	Tuolumne Twp 1	71 480
Joseph	Placer Iona Hills	62 891
Louis	San Francisco San Francisco 1	68 877
M J	Sacramento Granite	63 237
N P	Sacramento Sutter	63 296
N T	Sacramento Ward 1	63 151
Nathan	Sonoma Sonoma	69 647
R	Sacramento Granite	63 237
S	El Dorado Diamond	58 799
S	Siskiyou Scott Ri	69 72
S J*	Stanislaus Branch	70 699
Samuel	San Francisco San Francisco 3	67 30
Samuel	San Joaquin Castoria	64 887
Solomon	Stanislaus Branch	70 699
Solon S	Santa Clara Alviso	65 413
Stephen	Sacramento Sutter	63 295
SIMONSEN		
David	San Francisco San Francisco 2	67 799
SIMONSON		
Chas	San Francisco San Francisco 1	68 890
F E	Tuolumne Twp 3	71 470
SIMONTON		
Aug	Tuolumne Columbia	71 344
George W	San Joaquin Oneal	64 937
George W	Solano Suisan	69 235
J N	San Francisco San Francisco 5	67 547
J W	San Francisco San Francisco 5	67 547
M M	Tuolumne Twp 2	71 318
N M	San Francisco San Francisco 10	190 67
Robert G*	Humbolt Bucksport	59 159
SIMONY		
John	Siskiyou Yreka	69 157
SIMOONAY		
James H	Tuolumne Twp 2	71 285
SIMORALLO		
Joseph*	San Francisco San Francisco 3	67 16
SIMP		
---	Sierra Downieville	661014
SIMPER		
Samuel P	Yuba Marysville	72 872
SIMPERS		
George	Placer Iona Hills	62 894
SIMPES		
C	Amador Twp 6	55 425
SIMPIN		
Benja C	Calaveras Twp 5	57 208
SIMPKINS		
C	Yolo Cache	72 630
Charles H	Yuba Marysville	72 854
Charles H*	Yuba Marysville	72 859
Chas	Sacramento Granite	63 238
William	Yuba Marysville	72 941
SIMPLE		
Ann	San Francisco San Francisco 10	355 67
SIMPLER		
Mary Jane	San Francisco San Francisco 2	67 608
SIMPLICEA		
---	Monterey San Juan	60 991
SIMPS		
Jno	Alameda Brooklyn	55 97
Jose	Alameda Brooklyn	55 97

California 1860 Census Index

Name	County Locale	M653 RollPage
SIMPSIN		
Louis	Calaveras Twp 5	57 208
SIMPSON		
---	Tuolumne Twp 3	71 463
A	Butte Eureka	56 653
A	El Dorado Placerville	58 841
A	San Joaquin Stockton	641036
A G	Butte Ophir	56 763
A H	Shasta Cottonwood	66 737
A K	Shasta Cottonwoood	66 737
A O	Shasta Shasta	66 735
Alex	Alameda Murray	55 221
Allexander	Calaveras Twp 9	57 360
Andrew	San Francisco San Francisco 9	681044
Andrew	Tuolumne Jamestown	71 446
B C	Siskiyou Klamath	69 85
Bailey	Siskiyou Yreka	69 183
Ben	Humbolt Eureka	59 166
Benj	Plumas Quincy	62 987
Benj	San Francisco San Francisco 1	68 833
Benja C	Calaveras Twp 5	57 208
Benjamin	San Francisco San Francisco 7	681415
Benjamin	Yuba Fosters	72 837
Benjamin	Yuba Fosters	72 838
C	San Francisco San Francisco 5	67 477
C	San Francisco San Francisco 7	67 535
Calvin	Tuolumne Twp 2	71 285
Charles D	Tulara Twp 1	71 100
Chas	Butte Hamilton	56 515
Chas	San Francisco San Francisco 1	68 887
Cornelius	Calaveras Twp 7	57 19
Cyrus H	San Francisco San Francisco 7	681348
David	San Mateo Twp 3	65 108
E	Mariposa Twp 3	60 557
E C	Amador Twp 6	55 427
E E	San Francisco San Francisco 9	681086
E M	Amador Twp 6	55 422
E S	Siskiyou Scott Va	69 36
Ebin*	Placer Virginia	62 668
Edwd	Del Norte Klamath	58 654
Ellen	Yuba Marysville	72 933
Francis	Tulara Visalia	71 83
Frank	Placer Virginia	62 672
G B	Shasta Millvill	66 744
Geo	Alameda Brooklyn	55 190
Geo	Tehama Red Bluff	70 910
George	Calaveras Twp 5	57 196
George	Contra Costa Twp 2	57 563
George	Humbolt Eel Rvr	59 148
George	Tuolumne Twp 3	71 463
H	Trinity Lewiston	70 963
Hannah	San Diego San Diego	64 767
Harry S	Calaveras Twp 10	57 280
Harvey S	Calaveras Twp 10	57 280
Henry	Amador Twp 1	55 484
Henry	Sacramento San Joaquin	63 348
Henry	Santa Cruz Pescadero	66 646
Henry M	San Francisco San Francisco 4	681224
Hugh	Sierra Pine Grove	66 834
J	El Dorado Georgetown	58 697
J	El Dorado Placerville	58 866
J C	Amador Twp 4	55 257
J E	Placer Lisbon	62 735
J F	Siskiyou Callahan	69 6
J G E	Tehama Tehama	70 938
J H	El Dorado Mud Springs	58 962
J R	Butte Oregon	56 612
J W	San Francisco San Francisco 5	67 542
J W	Siskiyou Klamath	69 94
Jacob	Sierra St Louis	66 805
James	Alameda Brooklyn	55 133
James	Calaveras Twp 5	57 315
James	Mariposa Twp 3	60 543
James	Mendocino Little L	60 838
James	Santa Cruz Soguel	66 599
James	Yolo No E Twp	72 670
James	Yuba North Ea	72 670
James	Yuba Rose Bar	72 793
James	Yuba Marysville	72 956
Jas	San Francisco San Francisco 1	68 841
Jesse	San Joaquin Elkhorn	64 957
Jno	Sacramento Ward 1	63 114
Jno P	Mendocino Little L	60 838
Jo*	Mariposa Coulterville	60 685
John	Alameda Brooklyn	55 145
John	El Dorado Salmon Falls	581034
John	El Dorado Georgetown	58 677
John	El Dorado Mud Springs	58 989
John	Plumas Quincy	62 990
John	San Diego San Diego	64 767
John	San Francisco San Francisco 3	67 61
John	Sierra Whiskey	66 846
John	Tehama Tehama	70 947
John	Tuolumne Columbia	71 356
John	Yolo No E Twp	72 679
John	Yuba North Ea	72 679
John	Yuba Marysville	72 952
John A	San Joaquin Elkhorn	64 987
John G	Fresno Twp 2	59 48
John J	San Francisco San Francisco 2	67 771
John K	San Joaquin Elkhorn	64 957
John M	Sierra Poker Flats	66 841
Joseph	Marin Cortemad	60 779
Joseph	Shasta Shasta	66 734
L A	Amador Twp 1	55 489
Loius	Calaveras Twp 5	57 208
Luke	Plumas Quincy	62 941
M	San Joaquin Stockton	641093
M D	Siskiyou Scott Va	69 48
M H	Siskiyou Scott Va	69 41
M M	Siskiyou Scott Va	69 41
Margaret E	Yuba Linda	72 983
Mark	San Francisco San Francisco 7	681401
Martin	Solano Vallejo	69 279
Mary	Tuolumne Shawsfla	71 395
Mary	Yolo Washington	72 567
Melzi	Stanislaus Emory	70 748
Noah	Colusa Monroeville	57 441
P	Calaveras Twp 9	57 418
R C	Amador Twp 3	55 379
R L	Solano Vacaville	69 341
Robenia	Tehama Tehama	70 935
Robert	Contra Costa Twp 2	57 558
Robert	Mariposa Twp 1	60 652
Robert	Placer Forest H	62 767
Robert	Placer Michigan	62 821
Robert	San Francisco San Francisco 8	681239
Robert	San Francisco San Francisco 8	681286
Robert	Solano Vacaville	69 324
Robert	Solano Vacaville	69 328
Robert	Yuba New York	72 734
Robert R	Yuba Bear Rvr	721008
S	Butte Cascade	56 696
S	El Dorado Placerville	58 898
S	Tehama Red Bluff	70 910
S M	Alameda Murray	55 229
S T*	El Dorado Georgetown	58 757
Saml V	Butte Chico	56 554
Samuel	Placer Iona Hills	62 873
Samuel	Placer Iona Hills	62 874
Selim	Plumas Quincy	62 940
T B	Yuba Rose Bar	72 810
T C	Siskiyou Scott Va	69 34
T J	Merced Twp 1	60 911
T M	El Dorado Casumnes	581176
T*	Sacramento Ward 1	63 20
Tho J	Siskiyou Callahan	69 6
Thomas	Sierra Whiskey	66 847
Thos	Butte Kimshaw	56 569
Thos	Shasta Millvill	66 742
V S	Amador Twp 6	55 425
Volsery	San Luis Obispo San Luis Obispo	65 31
W	El Dorado Diamond	58 775
W	Sonoma Petaluma	69 596
Wiliam	Placer Yankee J	62 760
William	Placer Iona Hills	62 862
William	San Joaquin Elkhorn	64 966
William	San Joaquin Elkhorn	64 980
William	Tulara Yule Rvr	71 24
William	Tuolumne Twp 1	71 247
William H	Contra Costa Twp 2	57 577
Wm	Butte Bidwell	56 716
Wm	Calaveras Twp 9	57 361
Wm	Mariposa Twp 3	60 571
Wm	Tehama Lassen	70 868
Wm	Yuba Rose Bar	72 797
Wm H	Humbolt Mattole	59 128
Z	Sacramento Ward 1	63 20
SIMPSONS		
J W*	Siskiyou Klamath	69 94
SIMPTON		
G	Marin San Rafael	60 758
Geo	San Francisco San Francisco 1	68 880
S T*	El Dorado Georgetown	58 757
SIMS		
---	Placer Virginia	62 672
A H	Butte Ophir	56 786
Charles	San Francisco San Francisco 6	67 423
Chas	Placer Rattle Snake	62 599
Chs	Napa Napa	61 79
Columbus	Los Angeles Los Angeles	59 389
Elizabeth	Contra Costa Twp 1	57 531
Gabriel	Yuba Marysville	72 900
George	San Francisco San Francisco 7	681430
Isaac	San Mateo Twp 2	65 125
J	Nevada Grass Valley	61 150
J R	Sacramento Franklin	63 331
James	Contra Costa Twp 2	57 540
Jas	Los Angeles Tejon	59 536
John	Alameda Washington	55 214
John	Alameda Brooklyn	55 93
John	Colusa Spring Valley	57 431
John	El Dorado Placerville	58 844
John	Placer Auburn	62 595
John	Sacramento Franklin	63 331
John	San Francisco San Francisco 2	67 794
John	Sierra Port Win	66 794
John R	San Francisco San Francisco 4	681120
John S	Plumas Meadow Valley	62 929
Jos	Sacramento Ward 3	63 476
Lepoins	Butte Ophir	56 768
Lepoius*	Butte Ophir	56 768
Levi M	Los Angeles Los Angeles	59 405
Mary	Santa Cruz Santa Cruz	66 628
Mathew	San Mateo Twp 2	65 124
Morton	Plumas Quincy	62 999
Ornin*	Yuba Rose Bar	72 796
Orrim*	Yuba Rose Bar	72 796
Orrin*	Yuba Rose Bar	72 796
Orwin	Yuba Rose Par	72 796
Owin*	Yuba Rose Bar	72 796
Robert	San Francisco San Francisco 7	681327
Robt*	Placer Rattle Snake	62 630
Samuel	Sacramento Franklin	63 314
T J	Butte Bidwell	56 727
Thomas	Sierra Twp 7	66 887
William	Contra Costa Twp 1	57 528
William	Placer Iona Hills	62 865
William	Santa Cruz Santa Cruz	66 628
William	Santa Cruz Santa Cruz	66 630
William	Sierra La Porte	66 781
Wm	Sacramento Granite	63 255
SIMSON		
Henry M	San Francisco San Francisco 9	681099
Hery M*	San Francisco San Francisco 9	681099
Thomas	Sierra Twp 7	66 916
Thomas	Tuolumne Twp 1	71 185
William	Nevada Bridgeport	61 468
Wm	Sacramento Granite	63 222
SIMSPON		
James	Sutter Vernon	70 846
SIMT		
Nathan*	Calaveras Twp 4	57 318
SIMTMULLER		
Lewis*	Alameda Brooklyn	55 139
SIMU		
---	Placer Folsom	62 649
SIMYON		
N*	El Dorado Georgetown	58 754
SIN A SIN		
--*	Amador Twp 5	55 335
SIN CLAIR		
G W	Nevada Bridgeport	61 496
SIN FOY		
---	Sacramento Ward 1	63 71
SIN JON		
---	Sierra Twp 7	66 898
SIN K		
A E	Sutter Sutter	70 813
SIN KEE		
---	Sacramento Ward 1	63 68
SIN KINN		
---	Sacramento Ward 1	63 55
SIN LUNG		
---	Sacramento Ward 1	63 52
SIN OU		
---	Sierra Twp 7	66 876
SIN QUA		
---*	Mariposa Twp 1	60 668
SIN QUI		
---	Sacramento Ward 1	63 71
SIN QUOY		
---	Sacramento Ward 1	63 52
SIN SANG		
---	Sierra Twp 7	66 876
SIN SUNG		
---	Sacramento Ward 1	63 70
SIN TUCK		
---	Sacramento Ward 1	63 69
SIN WA		
---	Nevada Nevada	61 303
---	Nevada Nevada	61 304
SIN WE		
---	El Dorado Georgetown	58 693
SIN YET		
---	Butte Kimshaw	56 588
SIN YETT		
Ah	Butte Cascade	56 699
SIN YOUN		
---	Sierra Twp 5	66 927
SIN		
---	Amador Twp 4	55 256
---	Amador Twp 2	55 280
---	Amador Twp 2	55 288
---	Amador Twp 2	55 291
---	Amador Twp 2	55 308

California 1860 Census Index

Name	County Locale	M653 Roll	Page
SIN			
---	Amador Twp 2	55	312
---	Amador Twp 2	55	327
---	Amador Twp 5	55	359
---	Amador Twp 7	55	417
---	Amador Twp 6	55	424
---	Amador Twp 6	55	430
---	Amador Twp 6	55	436
---	Amador Twp 1	55	458
---	Amador Twp 1	55	476
---	Butte Kimshaw	56	578
---	Butte Oregon	56	644
---	Butte Oro	56	675
---	Butte Oro	56	677
---	Butte Oro	56	687
---	Butte Cascade	56	700
---	Butte Cascade	56	702
---	Butte Bidwell	56	708
---	Butte Bidwell	56	709
---	Butte Bidwell	56	728
---	Butte Ophir	56	750
---	Butte Ophir	56	780
---	Butte Ophir	56	788
---	Calaveras Twp 6	57	122
---	Calaveras Twp 6	57	151
---	Calaveras Twp 6	57	168
---	Calaveras Twp 5	57	173
---	Calaveras Twp 5	57	179
---	Calaveras Twp 5	57	182
---	Calaveras Twp 5	57	193
---	Calaveras Twp 5	57	205
---	Calaveras Twp 5	57	213
---	Calaveras Twp 5	57	218
---	Calaveras Twp 5	57	234
---	Calaveras Twp 5	57	235
---	Calaveras Twp 5	57	236
---	Calaveras Twp 5	57	239
---	Calaveras Twp 5	57	242
---	Calaveras Twp 5	57	244
---	Calaveras Twp 5	57	246
---	Calaveras Twp 5	57	257
---	Calaveras Twp 10	57	259
---	Calaveras Twp 10	57	269
---	Calaveras Twp 10	57	271
---	Calaveras Twp 10	57	272
---	Calaveras Twp 10	57	276
---	Calaveras Twp 10	57	284
---	Calaveras Twp 10	57	290
---	Calaveras Twp 10	57	295
---	Calaveras Twp 10	57	297
---	Calaveras Twp 4	57	300
---	Calaveras Twp 4	57	300
---	Calaveras Twp 4	57	303
---	Calaveras Twp 4	57	304
---	Calaveras Twp 4	57	306
---	Calaveras Twp 4	57	314
---	Calaveras Twp 4	57	315
---	Calaveras Twp 4	57	323
---	Calaveras Twp 4	57	324
---	Calaveras Twp 4	57	327
---	Calaveras Twp 4	57	333
---	Calaveras Twp 4	57	334
---	Calaveras Twp 4	57	342
---	Calaveras Twp 8	57	83
---	Calaveras Twp 8	57	84
---	Calaveras Twp 8	57	87
---	Del Norte Crescent	58	631
---	Del Norte Crescent	58	640
---	Del Norte Crescent	58	643
---	Del Norte Happy Ca	58	668
---	El Dorado White Oaks	58	1011
---	El Dorado Salmon Falls	58	1047
---	El Dorado Salmon Falls	58	1053
---	El Dorado Salmon Hills	58	1055
---	El Dorado Salmon Hills	58	1065
---	El Dorado Coloma	58	1076
---	El Dorado Coloma	58	1077
---	El Dorado Coloma	58	1084
---	El Dorado Coloma	58	1107
---	El Dorado Kelsey	58	1131
---	El Dorado Kelsey	58	1139
---	El Dorado Casumnes	58	1160
---	El Dorado Georgetown	58	692
---	El Dorado Georgetown	58	700
---	El Dorado Greenwood	58	714
---	El Dorado Georgetown	58	748
---	El Dorado Georgetown	58	756
---	El Dorado Diamond	58	785
---	El Dorado Diamond	58	800
---	El Dorado Diamond	58	816
---	El Dorado Placerville	58	823
---	El Dorado Placerville	58	841
---	El Dorado Placerville	58	843
---	El Dorado Placerville	58	844
---	El Dorado Placerville	58	906
SIN			
---	El Dorado Placerville	58	932
---	El Dorado Eldorado	58	940
---	El Dorado Eldorado	58	942
---	El Dorado Mud Springs	58	958
---	El Dorado Mud Springs	58	960
---	El Dorado Mud Springs	58	964
---	El Dorado Mud Springs	58	981
---	El Dorado Mud Springs	58	986
---	El Dorado Mud Springs	58	987
---	Fresno Twp 1	59	25
---	Marin Cortemad	60	782
---	Mariposa Twp 3	60	550
---	Mariposa Twp 3	60	589
---	Mariposa Twp 3	60	598
---	Mariposa Twp 3	60	613
---	Mariposa Twp 1	60	651
---	Mariposa Twp 1	60	665
---	Mariposa Coulterville	60	687
---	Mariposa Coulterville	60	689
---	Nevada Grass Valley	61	227
---	Nevada Bridgeport	61	462
---	Placer Auburn	62	572
---	Placer Auburn	62	573
---	Placer Auburn	62	581
---	Placer Auburn	62	583
---	Placer Secret R	62	623
---	Placer Folsom	62	647
---	Placer Virginia	62	665
---	Placer Dutch Fl	62	737
---	Placer Illinois	62	742
---	Placer Illinois	62	753
---	Plumas Quincy	62	1008
---	Plumas Quincy	62	920
---	Sacramento Granite	63	259
---	Sacramento Ward 1	63	52
---	Sacramento Ward 1	63	65
---	San Francisco San Francisco 1	68	885
---	San Francisco San Francisco 11	92	
		67	
---	Sierra Downieville	66	1000
---	Sierra Downieville	66	1004
---	Sierra Downieville	66	1007
---	Sierra Downieville	66	1014
---	Sierra Downieville	66	1020
---	Sierra Downieville	66	1025
---	Sierra Downieville	66	1027
---	Sierra Gibsonville	66	855
---	Sierra St Louis	66	861
---	Sierra Twp 5	66	944
---	Sierra Cox'S Bar	66	951
---	Sierra Downieville	66	983
---	Sierra Downieville	66	984
---	Sierra Downieville	66	985
---	Sierra Downieville	66	991
---	Sierra Downieville	66	997
---	Sierra Downieville	66	998
---	Sierra Downieville	66	999
---	Tuolumne Big Oak	71	149
---	Tuolumne Jacksonville	71	168
---	Tuolumne Columbia	71	350
---	Tuolumne Springfield	71	369
---	Tuolumne Shawsfla	71	386
---	Tuolumne Shawsfla	71	392
---	Tuolumne Twp 2	71	407
---	Tuolumne Twp 2	71	409
---	Tuolumne Twp 2	71	416
---	Tuolumne Twp 3	71	421
---	Tuolumne Twp 3	71	439
---	Tuolumne Twp 3	71	440
---	Tuolumne Twp 3	71	467
---	Tuolumne Twp 1	71	476
---	Tuolumne Jacksonville	71	514
---	Tuolumne Twp 5	71	517
---	Tuolumne Twp 6	71	529
---	Tuolumne Twp 6	71	531
---	Tuolumne Twp 6	71	533
---	Tuolumne Don Pedro	71	535
---	Tuolumne Don Pedro	71	537
---	Yuba Bear Rvr	72	1000
---*	Amador Twp 2	55	308
---*	Calaveras Twp 8	57	105
---*	Calaveras Twp 6	57	182
---*	Calaveras Twp 10	57	233
---*	Calaveras Twp 4	57	342
---*	Calaveras Twp 8	57	63
---*	El Dorado Casumnes	58	1160
---*	El Dorado Georgetown	58	700
---*	Sacramento Cosummes	63	392
---*	Sierra St Louis	66	861
A	Tuolumne Twp 2	71	386
Ah	Butte Cascade	56	700
Ah	Butte Cascade	56	702
Ah	Butte Cascade	56	704
Ah	Butte Bidwell	56	707
Ah	Butte Bidwell	56	709
SIN			
Ah	Butte Bidwell	56	713
Ah	Butte Bidwell	56	720
Ah	Tuolumne Twp 4	71	168
Ah	Tuolumne Twp 2	71	350
Ah	Tuolumne Twp 2	71	369
Ah	Tuolumne Twp 2	71	385
Ah	Tuolumne Twp 2	71	390
Ah	Tuolumne Twp 2	71	392
An	Del Norte Crescent	58	631
Ar	Sierra Downieville	66	984
Cheong	San Francisco San Francisco 5	67	508
Chi	Amador Twp 2	55	311
Chin	Butte Ophir	56	809
Chin	Placer Dutch Fl	62	737
Chon	Calaveras Twp 4	57	307
Chong*	Trinity Weaverville	70	1073
Chop	Calaveras Twp 4	57	308
Choss	Calaveras Twp 4	57	308
Chou	Butte Ophir	56	811
Chou	Siskiyou Yreka	69	195
Chow	Butte Ophir	56	788
Chow	Calaveras Twp 4	57	334
Choy	Butte Ophir	56	801
Choy	Butte Ophir	56	810
Choy	Butte Ophir	56	815
Choy	Butte Ophir	56	818
Coo	Butte Cascade	56	699
Coo	Butte Bidwell	56	709
Coy	Butte Bidwell	56	711
Coy	Butte Ophir	56	803
Coy	Butte Ophir	56	819
Dock	Nevada Bridgeport	61	506
Fee	Placer Illinois	62	753
Fi'At	Mariposa Twp 3	60	582
Fing	Butte Ophir	56	804
Foo	San Francisco San Francisco 5	67	507
Foy	Sacramento Ward 1	63	71
Gin	Shasta Horsetown	66	711
Goa	Butte Cascade	56	702
Hop	Butte Mountain	56	736
How	Butte Ophir	56	801
How	Butte Ophir	56	805
Hye	Butte Oro	56	675
Jim	Calaveras Twp 4	57	334
Kee	Amador Twp 2	55	275
Kee	Sacramento Ward 1	63	68
Kinn	Butte Ophir	56	812
Kinn	Sacramento Ward 1	63	55
Kop	Placer Dutch Fl	62	737
Lane	El Dorado Georgetown	58	756
Le	Tuolumne Twp 4	71	149
Lee	Butte Cascade	56	704
Lee	El Dorado Big Bar	58	736
Lee	Placer Iona Hills	62	898
Lee	Plumas Quincy	62	1008
Len	Butte Cascade	56	699
Let	Plumas Quincy	62	1008
Lin	Butte Ophir	56	817
Long	Butte Cascade	56	704
Long	Plumas Quincy	62	948
Lop	Butte Ophir	56	805
Low	Butte Ophir	56	788
Lue	Butte Ophir	56	820
Lung*	Sacramento Ward 1	63	52
Lynes	Butte Bidwell	56	715
Nha	Butte Oro	56	675
On	El Dorado Kelsey	58	1141
Pee	Placer Illinois	62	753
Pen	Calaveras Twp 5	57	220
Peu	Calaveras Twp 5	57	220
Qua	Mariposa Twp 1	60	668
Qui	Sacramento Ward 1	63	71
Sang	Sierra Twp 7	66	876
Se	Mariposa Twp 3	60	619
Seea	Butte Cascade	56	700
Sey	Butte Ophir	56	814
Sey	Butte Ophir	56	819
Sharo*	San Francisco San Francisco 4	68	1223
Shom*	El Dorado Georgetown	58	700
Sin	Butte Mountain	56	744
Sing	Butte Bidwell	56	709
Sing	Butte Bidwell	56	723
Sing	Butte Bidwell	56	726
Sing	El Dorado Big Bar	58	736
Sing	Sierra St Louis	66	861
Song	Calaveras Twp 10	57	272
Sony	Calaveras Twp 10	57	272
Sow	Sierra Downieville	66	992
Sung*	Sacramento Ward 1	63	70
Tan	Amador Twp 2	55	274
Ton	Amador Twp 2	55	312
Tony	Calaveras Twp 5	57	226
Tuce*	Placer Auburn	62	573
Tuck	Calaveras Twp 10	57	272
Tuck	Sacramento Ward 1	63	69

Name	County Locale	M653 RollPage
SIN		
Wack	Butte Cascade	56 699
Wag	Butte Cascade	56 700
Wah	Butte Cascade	56 698
Wah	Butte Cascade	56 700
Wha	Butte Oro	56 675
William	Tulara Twp 3	71 42
Yet	Butte Kimshaw	56 588
Yett	Butte Cascade	56 699
Yett	Butte Cascade	56 700
Yett	Butte Ophir	56 813
Yett	Butte Ophir	56 817
Yett	Butte Ophir	56 818
You	Sacramento Natonia	63 283
You	Siskiyou Yreka	69 194
Youp	Placer Dutch Fl	62 737
Yow	Calaveras Twp 10	57 286
Yow	Placer Rattle Snake	62 603
Zee	Butte Cascade	56 700
SIN'G		
Sam	Mariposa Twp 3	60 613
SINAITT		
John	Placer Folsom	62 639
SINAKA		
---	Fresno Twp 2	59 91
SINAMON		
J	Calaveras Twp 9	57 410
SINAN		
Jones G	San Francisco San Francisco 7	681338
Pat	Nevada Bridgeport	61 489
SINAR		
---	Sierra Cox'S Bar	66 951
SINATT		
John	Santa Clara Alviso	65 396
SINCALN		
J	El Dorado Placerville	58 851
SINCH		
Patrick	Yuba Suida	72 985
SINCHO		
Ah	Butte Eureka	56 653
SINCHOCK		
L*	Sutter Bear Rvr	70 826
SINCHOUME		
---	Tulara Twp 2	71 35
SINCILT		
Paul	Los Angeles Los Angeles	59 515
SINCLAIR		
A F	Placer Yankee J	62 756
Adam O	Sacramento Ward 3	63 438
Adam O	Sacramento Ward 1	63 46
Alex	Solano Vallejo	69 248
Collins	San Francisco San Francisco 2	67 725
Cy	Sacramento Ward 1	63 151
Cy	Sacramento Ward 1	63 77
Cyrus	Humbolt Eureka	59 176
David	Tulara Twp 1	71 97
Duncan	San Joaquin Douglass	64 924
George	San Joaquin Stockton	641068
George H	San Francisco San Francisco 7	681363
J A	Siskiyou Yreka	69 153
James	Alameda Brooklyn	55 170
James	Calaveras Twp 5	57 252
James	San Francisco San Francisco 7	681419
James	Shasta French G	66 715
Jas	Sacramento Granite	63 248
Jas	Sacramento Natonia	63 281
Jas*	Sacramento Granite	63 248
John	Calaveras Twp 10	57 288
John	San Francisco San Francisco 6	67 427
John M	Sacramento Centre	63 180
L P	Nevada Red Dog	61 540
L P	Nevada Red Dog	61 552
Mary	Siskiyou Yreka	69 183
Mary A	San Francisco San Francisco 10	357 67
P	Sacramento Ward 1	63 153
Prewit	Santa Cruz Pajaro	66 558
Sam	Nevada Bridgeport	61 447
Sam	Nevada Bridgeport	61 450
Saml F	Tuolumne Twp 2	71 362
T	San Francisco San Francisco 5	67 531
T	Sonoma Washington	69 679
Wade H	Contra Costa Twp 3	57 597
William	Calaveras Twp 10	57 293
Wm	Sacramento Ward 3	63 429
Wm H	Sacramento Ward 1	63 34
SINCON		
---	El Dorado Kelsey	581130
SIND		
---	Butte Kimshaw	56 588
---	El Dorado Big Bar	58 734
A L*	Sierra Twp 5	66 943
C	Nevada Eureka	61 377
SINDAMANN		
Aaron	Tuolumne Twp 1	71 209
SINDDLE		
Robt	El Dorado Kelsey	581138

Name	County Locale	M653 RollPage
SINDE		
Jacob	Placer Goods	62 694
SINDELL		
Chas	Placer Stewart	62 607
SINDER		
Henry	Placer Virginia	62 690
J	Sutter Sutter	70 814
SINDERMAN		
George	Plumas Meadow Valley	62 908
SINDERS		
Wm	Santa Clara San Jose	65 288
SINDILEY		
Horace*	Calaveras Twp 6	57 127
Hosacr*	Calaveras Twp 6	57 127
SINDILL		
M	Sutter Nicolaus	70 839
SINDLEY		
Nancy	Sacramento Ward 3	63 422
T M	Sacramento Ward 3	63 422
SINDMAN		
William*	San Francisco San Francisco 9	681077
SINDNER		
William	Los Angeles Los Angeles	59 333
SINDOIN		
John	Calaveras Twp 10	57 288
William	Calaveras Twp 10	57 293
SINDSAY		
John M	San Francisco San Francisco 11	98 67
SINDSEY		
R	Nevada Eureka	61 349
SINDUIR		
James	Calaveras Twp 5	57 252
SINE		
---	Butte Bidwell	56 709
---	Placer Illinois	62 754
---	Plumas Quincy	62 947
---	Sacramento Granite	63 232
Edward	Trinity Cox'S Bar	701038
John	Trinity Cox'S Bar	701037
Too	Amador Twp 2	55 293
SINEBERY		
Andy	Sacramento American	63 171
SINEBURGER		
Louis	Contra Costa Twp 2	57 582
SINEHAN		
John	Solano Fairfield	69 200
SINELAN		
Archibald*	San Francisco 3	67 86
	San Francisco	
SINEM		
---	Butte Wyandotte	56 672
SINEON		
John P	Fresno Twp 3	59 6
SINER		
James	El Dorado Mud Springs	58 996
SINERCE		
Camelleto*	Calaveras Twp 9	57 378
SINEREI		
Camelleto	Calaveras Twp 9	57 378
SINERGA		
Mural*	Sierra La Porte	66 790
SINERO		
Antonia*	San Francisco San Francisco 2	67 699
SINES		
Juan M	Monterey San Juan	60 991
S I	El Dorado White Oaks	581010
SINET		
---	Butte Oro	56 675
SINFAREN		
Maria	Alameda Brooklyn	55 173
SINFORASIO		
---	San Bernardino San Bernadino	64 669
SINFOREN		
Maria	Alameda Washington	55 173
SINFT		
S	El Dorado Salmon Falls	581063
SING CHOW		
---	Nevada Nevada	61 307
---	Sacramento Ward 1	63 52
SING CHOY		
---	Sacramento Ward 1	63 70
SING CUM		
Cum Su	Tuolumne Twp 3	71 433
SING FICK		
---	Sacramento Ward 1	63 68
SING GEA		
---*	Mariposa Coulterville	60 684
SING HO		
---	Solano Suisan	69 205
SING KE		
---	Mariposa Twp 3	60 607
SING LEE		
---	Mariposa Twp 1	60 667
---	Mariposa Twp 1	60 670
---	Mariposa Coulterville	60 691

Name	County Locale	M653 RollPage
SING LING		
---	Mariposa Twp 3	60 613
SING LUM		
---	Mariposa Twp 3	60 607
SING POO		
---	Plumas Quincy	62 969
---	Tuolumne Chinese	71 525
SING SANG		
---	Nevada Nevada	61 303
SING SING		
---	Butte Kimshaw	56 588
---	Mariposa Twp 3	60 612
---	Mariposa Twp 3	60 613
---*	Nevada Rough &	61 435
---*	Yuba Long Bar	72 756
SING SUM		
---	Mariposa Twp 3	60 613
SING TANG		
Lee Tee*	Yuba Rose Bar	72 800
SING TOO		
---	Butte Oregon	56 611
SING TOW		
---	Butte Oregon	56 613
---	Nevada Nevada	61 306
SING TOY		
---	Nevada Rough &	61 434
SING WA		
---	Nevada Nevada	61 310
SING WUH		
---	El Dorado Georgetown	58 693
SING YA		
---*	Nevada Nevada	61 302
SING YAH		
---	Sacramento Ward 1	63 65
SING		
---	Alameda Oakland	55 52
---	Alameda Oakland	55 53
---	Alameda Oakland	55 64
---	Amador Twp 4	55 252
---	Amador Twp 2	55 283
---	Amador Twp 2	55 288
---	Amador Twp 2	55 291
---	Amador Twp 2	55 308
---	Amador Twp 2	55 311
---	Amador Twp 2	55 314
---	Amador Twp 2	55 318
---	Amador Twp 2	55 323
---	Amador Twp 2	55 327
---	Amador Twp 2	55 328
---	Amador Twp 5	55 333
---	Amador Twp 5	55 334
---	Amador Twp 5	55 335
---	Amador Twp 5	55 345
---	Amador Twp 3	55 403
---	Amador Twp 7	55 412
---	Amador Twp 6	55 433
---	Amador Twp 6	55 434
---	Amador Twp 6	55 435
---	Amador Twp 6	55 439
---	Amador Twp 6	55 447
---	Amador Twp 1	55 479
---	Amador Twp 1	55 492
---	Amador Twp 1	55 500
---	Amador Twp 1	55 501
---	Amador Twp 1	55 504
---	Butte Hamilton	56 528
---	Butte Hamilton	56 530
---	Butte Chico	56 568
---	Butte Kimshaw	56 577
---	Butte Kimshaw	56 582
---	Butte Kimshaw	56 586
---	Butte Kimshaw	56 587
---	Butte Kimshaw	56 588
---	Butte Kimshaw	56 589
---	Butte Kimshaw	56 596
---	Butte Kimshaw	56 600
---	Butte Kimshaw	56 605
---	Butte Oregon	56 612
---	Butte Oregon	56 613
---	Butte Oregon	56 625
---	Butte Eureka	56 649
---	Butte Eureka	56 653
---	Butte Wyandotte	56 666
---	Butte Wyandotte	56 667
---	Butte Wyandotte	56 671
---	Butte Oro	56 686
---	Butte Oro	56 687
---	Butte Oro	56 688
---	Butte Cascade	56 691
---	Butte Cascade	56 692
---	Butte Cascade	56 698
---	Butte Cascade	56 699
---	Butte Cascade	56 702
---	Butte Bidwell	56 707
---	Butte Bidwell	56 708
---	Butte Bidwell	56 709

California 1860 Census Index

Name	County Locale	M653 RollPage	Name	County Locale	M653 RollPage	Name	County Locale	M653 RollPage
SING			**SING**			**SING**		
---	Butte Bidwell	56 711	---	Calaveras Twp 7	57 41	---	Mariposa Twp 1	60 665
---	Butte Bidwell	56 714	---	Calaveras Twp 8	57 79	---	Mariposa Twp 1	60 667
---	Butte Bidwell	56 715	---	Calaveras Twp 8	57 83	---	Mariposa Twp 1	60 670
---	Butte Bidwell	56 716	---	Calaveras Twp 8	57 87	---	Mariposa Coulterville	60 682
---	Butte Bidwell	56 717	---	Del Norte Crescent	58 641	---	Mariposa Coulterville	60 684
---	Butte Bidwell	56 719	---	Del Norte Crescent	58 651	---	Mariposa Coulterville	60 685
---	Butte Bidwell	56 720	---	Del Norte Crescent	58 659	---	Mariposa Coulterville	60 687
---	Butte Bidwell	56 723	---	Del Norte Happy Ca	58 667	---	Mariposa Coulterville	60 689
---	Butte Bidwell	56 724	---	Del Norte Happy Ca	58 669	---	Mariposa Coulterville	60 690
---	Butte Bidwell	56 725	---	El Dorado White Oaks	581011	---	Mariposa Coulterville	60 692
---	Butte Bidwell	56 726	---	El Dorado White Oaks	581023	---	Mariposa Coulterville	60 697
---	Butte Bidwell	56 727	---	El Dorado White Oaks	581025	---	Mariposa Coulterville	60 698
---	Butte Bidwell	56 728	---	El Dorado White Oaks	581033	---	Mariposa Coulterville	60 700
---	Butte Bidwell	56 731	---	El Dorado Salmon Falls	581040	---	Napa Napa	61 79
---	Butte Mountain	56 735	---	El Dorado Salmon Falls	581042	---	Napa Napa	61 98
---	Butte Mountain	56 741	---	El Dorado Salmon Falls	581046	---	Nevada Grass Valley	61 227
---	Butte Mountain	56 742	---	El Dorado Salmon Falls	581059	---	Nevada Grass Valley	61 228
---	Butte Mountain	56 743	---	El Dorado Salmon Hills	581060	---	Nevada Grass Valley	61 229
---	Butte Ophir	56 760	---	El Dorado Salmon Hills	581064	---	Nevada Grass Valley	61 230
---	Butte Ophir	56 762	---	El Dorado Salmon Falls	581066	---	Nevada Grass Valley	61 231
---	Butte Ophir	56 763	---	El Dorado Salmon Falls	581067	---	Nevada Grass Valley	61 232
---	Butte Ophir	56 766	---	El Dorado Coloma	581084	---	Nevada Grass Valley	61 233
---	Butte Ophir	56 776	---	El Dorado Union	581089	---	Nevada Grass Valley	61 234
---	Butte Ophir	56 777	---	El Dorado Union	581093	---	Nevada Nevada	61 299
---	Butte Ophir	56 782	---	El Dorado Cold Spring	581101	---	Nevada Nevada	61 300
---	Butte Ophir	56 796	---	El Dorado Coloma	581105	---	Nevada Nevada	61 301
---	Butte Ophir	56 801	---	El Dorado Coloma	581107	---	Nevada Nevada	61 303
---	Butte Ophir	56 802	---	El Dorado Coloma	581109	---	Nevada Nevada	61 304
---	Butte Ophir	56 803	---	El Dorado Coloma	581111	---	Nevada Nevada	61 305
---	Butte Ophir	56 804	---	El Dorado Kelsey	581133	---	Nevada Nevada	61 306
---	Butte Ophir	56 809	---	El Dorado Kelsey	581134	---	Nevada Nevada	61 307
---	Butte Ophir	56 813	---	El Dorado Casumnes	581163	---	Nevada Nevada	61 308
---	Butte Ophir	56 816	---	El Dorado Casumnes	581174	---	Nevada Nevada	61 309
---	Butte Ophir	56 817	---	El Dorado Mountain	581178	---	Nevada Nevada	61 310
---	Butte Ophir	56 818	---	El Dorado Mountain	581188	---	Nevada Washington	61 339
---	Butte Ophir	56 819	---	El Dorado Mountain	581189	---	Nevada Washington	61 340
---	Butte Ophir	56 820	---	El Dorado Mountain	581190	---	Nevada Washington	61 341
---	Calaveras Twp 8	57 100	---	El Dorado Georgetown	58 680	---	Nevada Washington	61 342
---	Calaveras Twp 8	57 105	---	El Dorado Georgetown	58 682	---	Nevada Eureka	61 383
---	Calaveras Twp 6	57 118	---	El Dorado Georgetown	58 684	---	Nevada Eureka	61 384
---	Calaveras Twp 6	57 134	---	El Dorado Georgetown	58 686	---	Nevada Eureka	61 385
---	Calaveras Twp 6	57 147	---	El Dorado Georgetown	58 692	---	Nevada Eureka	61 386
---	Calaveras Twp 6	57 148	---	El Dorado Georgetown	58 703	---	Nevada Rough &	61 397
---	Calaveras Twp 6	57 149	---	El Dorado Greenwood	58 720	---	Nevada Rough &	61 434
---	Calaveras Twp 6	57 151	---	El Dorado Greenwood	58 727	---	Nevada Bridgeport	61 457
---	Calaveras Twp 6	57 170	---	El Dorado Greenwood	58 728	---	Nevada Bridgeport	61 459
---	Calaveras Twp 6	57 175	---	El Dorado Greenwood	58 729	---	Nevada Bridgeport	61 462
---	Calaveras Twp 6	57 176	---	El Dorado Big Bar	58 733	---	Nevada Bridgeport	61 486
---	Calaveras Twp 5	57 181	---	El Dorado Big Bar	58 736	---	Nevada Bridgeport	61 493
---	Calaveras Twp 5	57 192	---	El Dorado Georgetown	58 755	---	Nevada Bridgeport	61 506
---	Calaveras Twp 5	57 202	---	El Dorado Georgetown	58 756	---	Nevada Bloomfield	61 507
---	Calaveras Twp 5	57 205	---	El Dorado Georgetown	58 761	---	Nevada Bloomfield	61 521
---	Calaveras Twp 5	57 208	---	El Dorado Diamond	58 802	---	Nevada Bloomfield	61 528
---	Calaveras Twp 5	57 211	---	El Dorado Diamond	58 804	---	Nevada Red Dog	61 541
---	Calaveras Twp 5	57 213	---	El Dorado Diamond	58 806	---	Nevada Red Dog	61 549
---	Calaveras Twp 5	57 223	---	El Dorado Diamond	58 815	---	Placer Auburn	62 570
---	Calaveras Twp 5	57 225	---	El Dorado Placerville	58 825	---	Placer Auburn	62 572
---	Calaveras Twp 5	57 234	---	El Dorado Placerville	58 831	---	Placer Auburn	62 575
---	Calaveras Twp 5	57 235	---	El Dorado Placerville	58 832	---	Placer Auburn	62 581
---	Calaveras Twp 5	57 237	---	El Dorado Placerville	58 839	---	Placer Auburn	62 591
---	Calaveras Twp 5	57 243	---	El Dorado Placerville	58 841	---	Placer Auburn	62 592
---	Calaveras Twp 5	57 244	---	El Dorado Placerville	58 842	---	Placer Rattle Snake	62 603
---	Calaveras Twp 5	57 246	---	El Dorado Placerville	58 843	---	Placer Stewart	62 606
---	Calaveras Twp 5	57 247	---	El Dorado Placerville	58 886	---	Placer Secret R	62 621
---	Calaveras Twp 5	57 248	---	El Dorado Placerville	58 923	---	Placer Secret R	62 623
---	Calaveras Twp 5	57 249	---	El Dorado Placerville	58 925	---	Placer Rattle Snake	62 626
---	Calaveras Twp 5	57 252	---	El Dorado Placerville	58 929	---	Placer Rattle Snake	62 637
---	Calaveras Twp 5	57 257	---	El Dorado Placerville	58 932	---	Placer Folsom	62 648
---	Calaveras Twp 10	57 259	---	El Dorado Eldorado	58 940	---	Placer Folsom	62 649
---	Calaveras Twp 10	57 267	---	El Dorado Mud Springs	58 959	---	Placer Ophirville	62 654
---	Calaveras Twp 10	57 270	---	El Dorado Mud Springs	58 961	---	Placer Virginia	62 669
---	Calaveras Twp 10	57 271	---	El Dorado Mud Springs	58 963	---	Placer Virginia	62 671
---	Calaveras Twp 10	57 272	---	El Dorado Mud Springs	58 966	---	Placer Virginia	62 672
---	Calaveras Twp 10	57 273	---	El Dorado Mud Springs	58 970	---	Placer Virginia	62 674
---	Calaveras Twp 10	57 274	---	El Dorado Mud Springs	58 971	---	Placer Virginia	62 676
---	Calaveras Twp 10	57 276	---	El Dorado Mud Springs	58 975	---	Placer Virginia	62 678
---	Calaveras Twp 10	57 281	---	El Dorado Mud Springs	58 977	---	Placer Virginia	62 679
---	Calaveras Twp 10	57 283	---	El Dorado Mud Springs	58 987	---	Placer Virginia	62 680
---	Calaveras Twp 10	57 284	---	El Dorado Mud Springs	58 992	---	Placer Virginia	62 681
---	Calaveras Twp 10	57 287	---	Fresno Twp 2	59 18	---	Placer Virginia	62 682
---	Calaveras Twp 10	57 290	---	Klamath Liberty	59 234	---	Placer Virginia	62 684
---	Calaveras Twp 10	57 291	---	Mariposa Twp 3	60 543	---	Placer Virginia	62 687
---	Calaveras Twp 10	57 297	---	Mariposa Twp 3	60 550	---	Placer Virginia	62 701
---	Calaveras Twp 4	57 300	---	Mariposa Twp 3	60 551	---	Placer Dutch Fl	62 732
---	Calaveras Twp 4	57 302	---	Mariposa Twp 3	60 572	---	Placer Christia	62 736
---	Calaveras Twp 4	57 304	---	Mariposa Twp 3	60 580	---	Placer Dutch Fl	62 737
---	Calaveras Twp 4	57 306	---	Mariposa Twp 3	60 588	---	Placer Illinois	62 738
---	Calaveras Twp 4	57 307	---	Mariposa Twp 3	60 608	---	Placer Illinois	62 739
---	Calaveras Twp 4	57 314	---	Mariposa Twp 1	60 640	---	Placer Illinois	62 740
---	Calaveras Twp 4	57 320	---	Mariposa Twp 1	60 641	---	Placer Illinois	62 741
---	Calaveras Twp 4	57 321	---	Mariposa Twp 1	60 644	---	Placer Illinois	62 742
---	Calaveras Twp 4	57 332	---	Mariposa Twp 1	60 645	---	Placer Illinois	62 745
---	Calaveras Twp 4	57 334	---	Mariposa Twp 1	60 653	---	Placer Illinois	62 747
---	Calaveras Twp 9	57 349	---	Mariposa Twp 1	60 656	---	Placer Illinois	62 748
---	Calaveras Twp 9	57 375	---	Mariposa Twp 1	60 657	---	Placer Illinois	62 749

California 1860 Census Index

Name	County Locale	M653 Roll	Page
SING			
---	Placer Illinois	62	750
---	Placer Illinois	62	752
---	Placer Illinois	62	753
---	Placer Illinois	62	754
---	Placer Yankee J	62	756
---	Placer Forest H	62	771
---	Placer Forest H	62	773
---	Placer Yankee J	62	779
---	Placer Forest H	62	794
---	Placer Iona Hills	62	896
---	Plumas Meadow Valley	62	910
---	Plumas Meadow Valley	62	914
---	Plumas Quincy	62	920
---	Sacramento Centre	63	181
---	Sacramento Centre	63	182
---	Sacramento Granite	63	250
---	Sacramento Granite	63	268
---	Sacramento Natonia	63	280
---	Sacramento Sutter	63	301
---	Sacramento Sutter	63	306
---	Sacramento Sutter	63	307
---	Sacramento Sutter	63	308
---	Sacramento Cosummes	63	388
---	Sacramento Cosummes	63	397
---	Sacramento Ward 3	63	424
---	Sacramento Ward 3	63	487
---	Sacramento Ward 3	63	491
---	Sacramento Ward 1	63	53
---	Sacramento Ward 1	63	54
---	Sacramento Ward 1	63	55
---	Sacramento Ward 1	63	56
---	Sacramento Ward 4	63	572
---	Sacramento Ward 1	63	58
---	Sacramento Ward 4	63	609
---	Sacramento Ward 1	63	60
---	Sacramento Ward 4	63	610
---	Sacramento Ward 4	63	612
---	Sacramento Ward 1	63	61
---	Sacramento Ward 1	63	65
---	Sacramento Ward 1	63	66
---	Sacramento Ward 1	63	67
---	Sacramento Ward 1	63	68
---	Sacramento Ward 1	63	72
---	Sacramento Ward 1	63	84
---	Sacramento Ward 1	63	8
---	Sacramento Ward 1	63	9
---	San Francisco San Francisco 9	68	1092
---	San Francisco San Francisco 4	68	1159
---	San Francisco San Francisco 4	68	1176
---	San Francisco San Francisco 4	68	1184
---	San Francisco San Francisco 4	68	1187
---	San Francisco San Francisco 4	68	1188
---	San Francisco San Francisco 4	68	1190
---	San Francisco San Francisco 4	68	1197
---	San Francisco San Francisco 4	68	1209
---	San Francisco San Francisco 4	68	1210
---	San Francisco San Francisco 4	68	1211
---	San Francisco San Francisco 4	68	1212
---	San Francisco San Francisco 10	67	314
---	San Francisco San Francisco 5	67	507
---	San Francisco San Francisco 3	67	79
---	San Joaquin Stockton	64	1039
---	San Joaquin Stockton	64	1087
---	Shasta Shasta	66	669
---	Shasta Shasta	66	668
---	Shasta Horsetown	66	701
---	Shasta Horsetown	66	704
---	Shasta Horsetown	66	711
---	Shasta French G	66	712
---	Shasta French G	66	713
---	Shasta French G	66	720
---	Sierra Downieville	66	1004
---	Sierra Downieville	66	1005
---	Sierra Downieville	66	1006
---	Sierra Downieville	66	1007
---	Sierra Downieville	66	1014
---	Sierra Downieville	66	1020
---	Sierra Downieville	66	1024
---	Sierra Downieville	66	1025
---	Sierra Downieville	66	1030
---	Sierra Downieville	66	1032
---	Sierra La Porte	66	774
---	Sierra La Porte	66	782
---	Sierra St Louis	66	805
---	Sierra St Louis	66	806
---	Sierra St Louis	66	813
---	Sierra Whiskey	66	849
---	Sierra St Louis	66	862
---	Sierra Twp 7	66	881
---	Sierra Twp 7	66	886
---	Sierra Twp 5	66	926
---	Sierra Twp 5	66	930
---	Sierra Twp 5	66	932
---	Sierra Twp 5	66	947
SING			
---	Sierra Cox'S Bar	66	949
---	Sierra Downieville	66	962
---	Sierra Downieville	66	973
---	Sierra Downieville	66	974
---	Sierra Downieville	66	979
---	Sierra Downieville	66	982
---	Sierra Downieville	66	983
---	Sierra Downieville	66	985
---	Sierra Downieville	66	990
---	Sierra Downieville	66	991
---	Sierra Downieville	66	996
---	Sierra Downieville	66	998
---	Sierra Downieville	66	999
---	Siskiyou Cottonwoood	69	109
---	Siskiyou Scott Va	69	46
---	Siskiyou Klamath	69	80
---	Siskiyou Scott Ri	69	82
---	Stanislaus Buena Village	70	724
---	Trinity Evans Ba	70	1003
---	Trinity Mouth Ca	70	1016
---	Trinity Mouth Ca	70	1017
---	Trinity Mouth Ca	70	1018
---	Trinity Taylor'S	70	1033
---	Trinity Taylor'S	70	1034
---	Trinity Taylor'S	70	1035
---	Trinity Cox'S Bar	70	1037
---	Trinity Trinindad Rvr	70	1044
---	Trinity Trinindad Rvr	70	1046
---	Trinity Trinindad Rvr	70	1050
---	Trinity Weaverville	70	1055
---	Trinity E Weaver	70	1059
---	Trinity Weaverville	70	1072
---	Trinity Weaverville	70	1074
---	Trinity Lewiston	70	954
---	Trinity Lewiston	70	956
---	Trinity Lewiston	70	957
---	Trinity Eastman	70	960
---	Trinity Lewiston	70	964
---	Tuolumne Jacksonville	71	166
---	Tuolumne Columbia	71	347
---	Tuolumne Shawsfla	71	386
---	Tuolumne Shawsfla	71	394
---	Tuolumne Twp 2	71	404
---	Tuolumne Twp 2	71	408
---	Tuolumne Twp 2	71	409
---	Tuolumne Twp 2	71	412
---	Tuolumne Twp 2	71	416
---	Tuolumne Twp 3	71	433
---	Tuolumne Twp 3	71	435
---	Tuolumne Twp 3	71	440
---	Tuolumne Twp 3	71	453
---	Tuolumne Twp 3	71	457
---	Tuolumne Twp 3	71	458
---	Tuolumne Twp 3	71	466
---	Tuolumne Twp 3	71	467
---	Tuolumne Jamestown	71	469
---	Tuolumne Columbia	71	474
---	Tuolumne Sonora	71	476
---	Tuolumne Sonora	71	478
---	Tuolumne Twp 1	71	485
---	Tuolumne Montezuma	71	503
---	Tuolumne Twp 5	71	507
---	Tuolumne Jacksonville	71	514
---	Tuolumne Jacksonville	71	515
---	Tuolumne Twp 5	71	516
---	Tuolumne Twp 5	71	517
---	Tuolumne Chinese	71	521
---	Tuolumne Twp 5	71	521
---	Yolo No E Twp	72	676
---	Yolo No E Twp	72	679
---	Yolo No E Twp	72	680
---	Yolo No E Twp	72	682
---	Yolo Slate Ra	72	712
---	Yolo Slate Ra	72	713
---	Yolo Slate Ra	72	719
---	Yuba North Ea	72	676
---	Yuba North Ea	72	680
---	Yuba North Ea	72	682
---	Yuba Slate Ro	72	712
---	Yuba Slate Ro	72	713
---	Yuba New York	72	735
---	Yuba New York	72	739
---	Yuba New York	72	740
---	Yuba Long Bar	72	757
---	Yuba Long Bar	72	763
---	Yuba Rose Bar	72	820
---	Yuba Fosters	72	826
---	Yuba Fosters	72	827
---	Yuba Fosters	72	834
---	Yuba Fosters	72	841
---	Yuba Fosters	72	842
---	Yuba Fosters	72	843
---	Yuba Marysville	72	896
---	Yuba Marysville	72	921
---	Yuba Marysville	72	925
SING			
---*	Butte Hamilton	56	530
---*	Calaveras Twp 5	57	223
---*	Calaveras Twp 5	57	235
---*	Calaveras Twp 8	57	63
---*	El Dorado Salmon Falls	58	1064
---*	Fresno Twp 1	59	28
---*	Mariposa Twp 3	60	550
---*	Nevada Nevada	61	301
---*	Nevada Washington	61	339
---*	Nevada Washington	61	341
---*	Nevada Red Dog	61	549
---*	Placer Auburn	62	565
---*	Placer Auburn	62	570
---*	Sacramento Cosummes	63	388
---*	Sacramento Cosummes	63	392
---*	Shasta French G	66	713
---*	Trinity McGillev	70	1021
---*	Trinity Weaverville	70	1074
---*	Yuba Rose Bar	72	820
---*	Yuba Foster B	72	826
---*	Yuba Foster B	72	827
---*	Yuba Foster B	72	834
---*	Yuba Fosters	72	841
---*	Yuba Fosters	72	842
---*	Yuba Fosters	72	843
A	Sacramento Granite	63	250
Adam*	Contra Costa Twp 2	57	574
Ah	Butte Oregon	56	625
Ah	Butte Eureka	56	649
Ah	Butte Oro	56	688
Ah	Butte Cascade	56	691
Ah	Butte Cascade	56	692
Ah	Butte Cascade	56	698
Ah	Butte Cascade	56	699
Ah	Butte Cascade	56	702
Ah	Butte Bidwell	56	707
Ah	Butte Bidwell	56	708
Ah	Butte Bidwell	56	709
Ah	Butte Bidwell	56	711
Ah	Butte Bidwell	56	714
Ah	Butte Bidwell	56	716
Ah	Butte Bidwell	56	717
Ah	Butte Bidwell	56	719
Ah	Butte Bidwell	56	720
Ah	Butte Bidwell	56	723
Ah	Butte Bidwell	56	725
Ah	Butte Bidwell	56	727
Ah	Butte Bidwell	56	731
Ah	Butte Mountain	56	735
Ah	Calaveras Twp 7	57	34
Ah	Calaveras Twp 7	57	36
Ah	Placer Forest H	62	771
Ah	Sacramento Ward 3	63	437
Ah	Sacramento Ward 1	63	8
Ah	Sacramento Ward 1	63	9
Ah	Siskiyou Scott Ri	69	80
Ah	Tuolumne Twp 4	71	166
Ah	Tuolumne Twp 2	71	307
Ah	Tuolumne Twp 2	71	347
Ah	Tuolumne Twp 2	71	386
Ah	Tuolumne Twp 2	71	394
Ah	Yuba Bear Rvr	72	1000
Ah Chung	Tuolumne Twp 2	71	407
Ah*	Butte Oro	56	687
Am	Sierra Downieville	66	990
Asper Mi	Placer Ophirville	62	654
Aung	Yuba Long Bar	72	760
Bay	Butte Bidwell	56	723
Boy	Nevada Washington	61	341
Cam	Amador Twp 2	55	280
Can	Calaveras Twp 9	57	360
Car	Calaveras Twp 9	57	360
Cen	Butte Ophir	56	812
Cham	Yuba Long Bar	72	764
Charlie	Yolo Slate Ra	72	706
Chaw	El Dorado Mud Springs	58	951
Chee	Yuba Fosters	72	830
Chen	Butte Ophir	56	808
Chen	Yuba Long Bar	72	764
Cheong	San Francisco San Francisco 2	67	687
Chew	Butte Ophir	56	801
Chew	Butte Ophir	56	806
Chew	Butte Ophir	56	810
Chew	Yuba Long Bar	72	764
Chi	Amador Twp 2	55	311
Chi	Amador Twp 2	55	312
Chin	Butte Ophir	56	808
Ching	Amador Twp 2	55	327
Ching	Butte Bidwell	56	728
Ching	Yuba Long Bar	72	760
Choe	Calaveras Twp 6	57	165
Choi	Calaveras Twp 5	57	193
Choir	Calaveras Twp 5	57	193
Choo	Plumas Quincy	62	946
Chow	Butte Bidwell	56	711

California 1860 Census Index

Name	County Locale	M653 Roll	Page
SING			
Chow	Butte Ophir	56	783
Chow	Butte Ophir	56	803
Chow	Butte Ophir	56	818
Chow	Nevada Grass Valley	61	229
Chow	Nevada Nevada	61	304
Chow	Nevada Nevada	61	307
Chow	Yuba Long Bar	72	756
Chow	Yuba Long Bar	72	759
Chow*	Sacramento Ward 1	63	52
Choy	Butte Ophir	56	787
Choy	Butte Ophir	56	804
Chu	Fresno Twp 2	59	4
Chung	Calaveras Twp 4	57	320
Chung	Plumas Quincy	62	946
Chung	Sacramento Mississipi	63	190
Chuny	Calaveras Twp 4	57	320
Come	El Dorado Coloma	58	1077
Con	Butte Bidwell	56	731
Con	Butte Mountain	56	744
Con	Mariposa Coulterville	60	681
Cone	Del Norte Crescent	58	633
Coop	Butte Bidwell	56	714
Cope	Butte Bidwell	56	731
Cow	Butte Ophir	56	801
Cow	Butte Ophir	56	802
Coy	Butte Ophir	56	709
Coy	Butte Bidwell	56	728
Cum	Tuolumne Jamestown	71	433
Dennis	Calaveras Twp 10	57	274
Due	Yuba Long Bar	72	770
Fan	Mariposa Twp 3	60	561
Fan	Nevada Grass Valley	61	228
Fany	Yuba Long Bar	72	758
Fey	Butte Ophir	56	808
Flin*	Butte Ophir	56	816
Fon	Plumas Meadow Valley	62	910
Fon	Plumas Meadow Valley	62	914
Foo	Amador Twp 2	55	288
Foo	Amador Twp 2	55	310
Foo	Butte Mountain	56	742
Foo	Butte Mountain	56	743
Foo	Butte Ophir	56	808
Foo	Butte Ophir	56	816
Foo	El Dorado Eldorado	58	948
Foo	Placer Michigan	62	858
Foo	Plumas Quincy	62	1008
Foo	Plumas Meadow Valley	62	909
Foo	Plumas Quincy	62	945
Foo	Plumas Quincy	62	946
Foo	Plumas Quincy	62	950
Foo	Yuba Long Bar	72	765
Foo Kee	Yuba Long Bar	72	760
Foo Ker	Yuba Long Bar	72	760
Foo La	Yuba Long Bar	72	762
Foo Loo	Yuba Long Bar	72	756
Fook*	Yuba Marysville	72	898
Fop	Butte Mountain	56	736
Fop	Butte Ophir	56	787
Fow	Nevada Grass Valley	61	227
Fow	Nevada Nevada	61	306
Fow	Placer Iona Hills	62	898
Fow	Yuba Parks Ba	72	780
Foy	Butte Mountain	56	743
Foy	Yuba Long Bar	72	767
Free	Mariposa Twp 3	60	582
Fun	Plumas Quincy	62	946
Fup	Nevada Grass Valley	61	231
Fy	San Francisco San Francisco 10	67	356
G	Mariposa Twp 3	60	551
Gea	Mariposa Coulterville	60	684
Gee	Mariposa Twp 1	60	667
Gee	Mariposa Twp 1	60	670
Gee	Mariposa Coulterville	60	682
Gee	Nevada Bridgeport	61	491
Geo W*	Siskiyou Cottonwoood	69	101
George	San Francisco San Francisco 7	68	1335
Gin	Butte Cascade	56	702
Gin*	Nevada Washington	61	342
Gru	Nevada Washington	61	342
Gu	Sacramento Natonia	63	286
Gue	Nevada Washington	61	342
H A*	Mariposa Twp 1	60	626
Hay	El Dorado Eldorado	58	941
He	Yuba Marysville	72	917
Hee	Yolo No E Twp	72	676
Hen	Yuba Fosters	72	826
Hi	Amador Twp 2	55	312
Hi	Solano Suisan	69	205
High	Butte Bidwell	56	726
High	Butte Ophir	56	804
High	Mariposa Twp 3	60	543
Hik	Sacramento Ward 4	63	609
Hip	Sacramento Mississipi	63	190
SING			
Ho	San Francisco San Francisco 11	159	67
Hoh	Butte Ophir	56	779
Hon	Butte Bidwell	56	720
Hon	Yuba Long Bar	72	760
Hong	El Dorado Eldorado	58	942
Hoop	Butte Mountain	56	735
Hoop	Butte Mountain	56	735
Hop	Butte Ophir	56	805
Hop	Butte Ophir	56	809
Hop	San Francisco San Francisco 4	681	210
Hop	San Francisco San Francisco 5	67	527
Hot*	Butte Ophir	56	779
Hoy	Butte Mountain	56	742
Hoy	Yuba Long Bar	72	767
Hue	Yuba Fosters	72	830
Hung	Sacramento Ward 4	63	610
J*	Nevada Red Dog	61	549
Jacob	Nevada Bridgeport	61	444
James	Siskiyou Yreka	69	185
Jat*	Mariposa Twp 3	60	579
Jim	Butte Bidwell	56	713
Jo	Stanislaus Branch	70	713
John	Yolo No E Twp	72	675
John	Yolo No E Twp	72	685
John	Yolo Slate Ra	72	706
John	Yolo Slate Ra	72	707
John	Yolo Slate Ra	72	708
John	Yuba New York	72	740
John	Yuba Fosters	72	824
John*	Nevada Bridgeport	61	462
John*	Sacramento Cosummes	63	396
John*	Yuba Slate Ro	72	707
John*	Yuba Long Bar	72	753
John*	Yuba Long Bar	72	764
Jom	Yuba Foster B	72	830
Jop	Butte Mountain	56	735
Jos	Butte Mountain	56	740
K	Nevada Grass Valley	61	231
Kee	Amador Twp 2	55	275
Kee	Butte Ophir	56	817
Kee	Yuba Rose Bar	72	800
Kew	El Dorado Mountain	581	187
Kin	El Dorado Greenwood	58	719
King	Butte Mountain	56	735
Kong	San Francisco San Francisco 5	671	205
Kong	Yuba Long Bar	72	755
Koop	Placer Illinois	62	742
Lan*	Mariposa Twp 3	60	607
Lang	Sierra La Porte	66	782
Law	Butte Bidwell	56	720
Le	Mariposa Twp 1	60	665
Le	Nevada Bridgeport	61	491
Lee	Alameda Oakland	55	14
Lee	Amador Twp 5	55	335
Lee	Butte Bidwell	56	726
Lee	Butte Mountain	56	741
Lee	Butte Ophir	56	750
Lee	Butte Ophir	56	803
Lee	Butte Ophir	56	805
Lee	Butte Ophir	56	807
Lee	Butte Ophir	56	816
Lee	Butte Ophir	56	819
Lee	Calaveras Twp 9	57	362
Lee	El Dorado Georgetown	58	756
Lee	Mariposa Twp 1	60	657
Lee	Mariposa Twp 1	60	661
Lee	Mariposa Twp 1	60	666
Lee	Mariposa Twp 1	60	667
Lee	Mariposa Twp 1	60	670
Lee	Mariposa Coulterville	60	691
Lee	Plumas Quincy	621	008
Lee	Sacramento Granite	63	250
Lee	Sacramento Granite	63	269
Lee	Yuba Marysville	72	947
Len	Yuba Long Bar	72	759
Lep	Shasta Horsetown	66	701
Lew	Butte Ophir	56	820
Li	Nevada Bridgeport	61	491
Lin	Placer Rattle Snake	62	631
Ling	Butte Ophir	56	817
Lon	Butte Ophir	56	819
Long	Butte Bidwell	56	717
Long	Sacramento Sutter	63	307
Loo	Amador Twp 2	55	294
Loo	Yuba Long Bar	72	756
Loo	Yuba Long Bar	72	757
Loo	Yuba Long Bar	72	767
Lou	Butte Ophir	56	806
Low	Amador Twp 2	55	311
Low	Butte Cascade	56	700
Low	Butte Bidwell	56	713
Low	Butte Bidwell	56	716
Low	Butte Bidwell	56	720
Low	Butte Bidwell	56	726
SING			
Low	Butte Bidwell	56	731
Low	Butte Ophir	56	814
Low*	Butte Ophir	56	816
Low*	Butte Ophir	56	819
Lu	Butte Ophir	56	772
Luk	El Dorado Big Bar	58	737
Lum	Placer Auburn	62	581
Mene	Butte Ophir	56	783
Mew	Butte Ophir	56	813
Min	Butte Ophir	56	813
Min	Butte Ophir	56	815
Min	Mariposa Coulterville	60	682
Ming	Del Norte Crescent	58	633
Minig*	Del Norte Crescent	58	633
Mores	Calaveras Twp 10	57	279
Mow	Butte Bidwell	56	707
Mow	Butte Mountain	56	735
Mow	Butte Ophir	56	802
Mru*	San Francisco San Francisco 4	681	178
Mue*	San Francisco San Francisco 4	681	178
Pat*	Mariposa Twp 3	60	579
Poo	Butte Bidwell	56	717
Poo	Tuolumne Twp 5	71	525
R	Sierra Twp 7	66	908
Sam	Butte Oregon	56	644
Sam	Siskiyou Scott Ri	69	66
Sam	Trinity E Weaver	701	059
Sam*	Nevada Washington	61	339
Sam*	Tulara Visalia	71	105
San*	Mariposa Twp 3	60	608
Sang	Calaveras Twp 6	57	148
Sang	San Francisco San Francisco 11	67	92
See	Mariposa Twp 1	60	655
See	Mariposa Coulterville	60	682
Sep	Shasta Horsetown	66	701
Ser	Mariposa Twp 1	60	664
Sew*	Butte Ophir	56	819
Sim	Mariposa Twp 3	60	613
Sin	Butte Bidwell	56	709
Sin	Butte Bidwell	56	723
Sin	Butte Bidwell	56	726
Sin	Sacramento Mississipi	63	185
Sing	Butte Kimshaw	56	588
Sing	Butte Ophir	56	787
Sing	Butte Ophir	56	803
Sing	Mariposa Twp 3	60	612
Sing	Mariposa Twp 3	60	613
Sing	Nevada Eureka	61	386
Sing	Nevada Rough &	61	435
Sing	Placer Rattle Snake	62	601
Sing	Sacramento Ward 1	63	37
Sing	Sacramento Ward 4	63	609
Sing*	Yuba Long Bar	72	756
Son	Nevada Grass Valley	61	228
Song	Calaveras Twp 5	57	237
Sonn	Mariposa Twp 3	60	580
Soy	Butte Bidwell	56	709
Su	Placer Forest H	62	771
Sun	Mariposa Coulterville	60	682
Sung	Calaveras Twp 6	57	148
Tang	Yuba Long Bar	72	758
Tang Lee Tee	Yuba Rose Bar	72	800
Tee	Placer Illinois	62	752
Thee	San Francisco San Francisco 4	681	178
To	Alameda Oakland	55	64
Tom	Yolo Slate Ra	72	698
Tom	Yuba Fosters	72	842
Tom*	Yuba Slate Ro	72	698
Tom*	Yuba New York	72	740
Ton	Butte Kimshaw	56	582
Too	Amador Twp 2	55	275
Too	Butte Oregon	56	611
Tou	Butte Kimshaw	56	582
Tow	Butte Oregon	56	613
Toy	Nevada Washington	61	341
Toy	Nevada Rough &	61	434
Tum	Amador Twp 2	55	327
Ty	San Francisco San Francisco 10	67	356
Tye	Butte Ophir	56	810
Tye	Butte Ophir	56	811
Up	Butte Mountain	56	742
W	Sacramento Sutter	63	290
W A	Sacramento Sutter	63	290
Wa	Nevada Nevada	61	310
Wa	Nevada Washington	61	341
Wa	Nevada Eureka	61	384
Wa	Nevada Eureka	61	386
Wah	Butte Bidwell	56	708
Wah	Butte Bidwell	56	711
Wah	Butte Mountain	56	735
Wah	El Dorado Georgetown	58	693
Wan	Fresno Twp 2	59	19
Wan	Yuba Marysville	72	868

Name	County Locale	Roll	Page
SING			
Warr	Plumas Quincy	62	946
Way	Butte Bidwell	56	724
Wee	Butte Bidwell	56	714
Wee	Mariposa Twp 3	60	641
Wen	El Dorado Big Bar	58	733
Wing	Mariposa Twp 1	60	641
Won	San Joaquin Stockton	64	1053
Wonp	Placer Iona Hills	62	896
Wow	Sacramento Ward 1	63	156
Ya	Nevada Nevada	61	302
Yah	Sacramento Ward 1	63	65
Yan	Sacramento Granite	63	269
Yaw	San Francisco San Francisco 4	68	1210
Yee	San Francisco San Francisco 4	68	1192
Yeng	Sacramento Natonia	63	283
Yie	Nevada Bridgeport	61	491
Yin La	El Dorado Georgetown	58	746
Yon	El Dorado Placerville	58	831
Yon	Yuba Marysville	72	898
Yon	Yuba Marysville	72	916
Yong	Plumas Meadow Valley	62	910
You	Mariposa Twp 1	60	627
You	Nevada Grass Valley	61	228
You	Nevada Grass Valley	61	230
You	San Francisco San Francisco 4	68	1210
You	Yuba Marysville	72	898
You	Yuba Marysville	72	916
Young	Butte Ophir	56	813
Yow	Nevada Grass Valley	61	227
Yow	Yuba Long Bar	72	764
Yow*	Mariposa Twp 1	60	627
Yu	San Francisco San Francisco 4	68	1210
Yuh	Nevada Grass Valley	61	227
Yuh	Nevada Grass Valley	61	228
Yup	Nevada Grass Valley	61	227
Yup	Nevada Grass Valley	61	230
Yup	Nevada Grass Valley	61	232
Yut	Nevada Grass Valley	61	228
SINGA			
---	Butte Cascade	56	699
Ah	Butte Cascade	56	699
SINGANE			
Hannah	San Francisco San Francisco 10	67	222
SINGAR			
N*	El Dorado Georgetown	58	754
SINGE			
---	El Dorado Georgetown	58	703
SINGED			
---	Shasta Shasta	66	684
SINGELER			
Francis*	Calaveras Twp 6	57	112
SINGER			
---	Placer Ophirville	62	659
A N	Butte Bidwell	56	726
Andrew	Mariposa Twp 3	60	560
August	El Dorado Greenwood	58	710
Conrad	Mariposa Twp 3	60	560
David	El Dorado Placerville	58	915
E J	San Francisco San Francisco 2	67	712
Frank	Nevada Bloomfield	61	523
Geo	Sacramento Ward 1	63	25
J	Shasta Cottonwood	66	737
J W	Nevada Nevada	61	250
Jacob B	San Francisco San Francisco 11	67	153
John M	Marin Cortemad	60	782
Peter	Placer Goods	62	695
Stan	Mariposa Twp 3	60	560
Thos	Butte Ophir	56	775
W E	Butte Bidwell	56	706
William	Yuba Marysville	72	936
William	Yuba Marysville	72	936
SINGERFETTER			
Rufus*	Calaveras Twp 4	57	341
SINGETT			
---	Butte Bidwell	56	708
Ah	Butte Bidwell	56	708
Ah	Butte Bidwell	56	711
Ker	Butte Cascade	56	702
SINGH			
---	Sierra Downieville	66	974
Cornelius*	Sacramento Granite	63	247
SINGHTON			
W R	Butte Ophir	56	755
SINGLE			
G M*	Yolo Putah	72	550
John	Nevada Rough &	61	418
Joseph	Butte Mountain	56	736
Joseph	Placer Michigan	62	852
Wm	Sierra Twp 7	66	913
SINGLETANY			
E C	Colusa Butte Crk	57	465
SINGLETOM			
C F	Colusa Monroeville	57	455

Name	County Locale	Roll	Page
SINGLETON			
Francis	Sacramento Ward 1	63	26
George	Plumas Meadow Valley	62	930
H	Siskiyou Scott Va	69	30
J A	Tehama Red Bluff	70	910
James	Santa Clara San Jose	65	344
James	Sierra Downieville	66	988
James B	Tehama Lewiston	70	961
James B	Trinity Lewiston	70	961
Jas	Sacramento Ward 3	63	476
Jas	San Bernardino San Bernardino	64	643
Jno	Sacramento Ward 4	63	524
John	Butte Ophir	56	776
John	Santa Clara Fremont	65	422
Jos	Sacramento Ward 1	63	154
M	Siskiyou Scott Va	69	30
M A	Sierra Twp 7	66	868
Robert	Los Angeles Elmonte	59	265
W A	Sierra Twp 7	66	868
W R	Butte Ophir	56	755
Wm	Sacramento Ward 1	63	115
Wm	Sacramento Ward 1	63	147
SINGLEY			
D H	Sutter Butte	70	790
Geo H*	Humbolt Table Bl	59	140
Jas	Sonoma Vallejo	69	610
Nicholas*	Humbolt Pacific	59	129
Resso R*	Mendocino Ukiah	60	798
SINGMAN			
Jno*	Sacramento Ward 3	63	443
SINGO			
Geo W*	Sacramento Alabama	63	411
SINGON			
N*	El Dorado Georgetown	58	754
SINGREFOS			
Juan	Placer Forest H	62	791
SINGULAR			
R*	Solano Vacaville	69	333
SINI			
---	El Dorado Greenwood	58	728
SINIENTAR			
Josefa*	San Francisco San Francisco 2	67	752
SINIFROM			
W W	Amador Twp 5	55	343
SINIG			
---	San Joaquin Stockton	64	1083
SINIM			
---	Butte Wyandotte	56	672
SINIMONS			
N C	Tuolumne Twp 2	71	312
W C	Tuolumne Columbia	71	312
SINIMUS			
J N*	Sacramento Granite	63	269
SININERS			
J W	Sacramento Granite	63	269
SININNS			
J N*	Sacramento Granite	63	269
SINISTER			
Jacob	Sierra Eureka	66	1048
SINIT			
---	Butte Oro	56	675
Nathan*	Calaveras Twp 4	57	318
SINITH			
S*	El Dorado Newtown	58	779
SINITT			
Low	Butte Bidwell	56	708
SINITTI			
James	San Luis Obispo San Luis Obispo	65	17
SINITY			
Thomas*	Calaveras Twp 4	57	321
SINK			
---	Shasta French G	66	713
---	Sierra Downieville	66	985
---*	Tulara Twp 2	71	4
Daniel	Sonoma Cloverdale	69	684
Joseph	Amador Twp 2	55	263
SINKA			
Harmon*	Santa Clara San Jose	65	288
SINKER			
Jas S	San Mateo Twp 1	65	58
SINKEY			
---	Tulara Twp 2	71	4
SINKLER			
A	Sutter Vernon	70	844
SINKNIP			
---*	Mendocino Round Va	60	883
SINKS			
Daniel A*	Siskiyou Yreka	69	144
SINKUIP			
---*	Mendocino Round Va	60	883
SINLEY			
Eli H*	Humbolt Eel Rvr	59	147
Levi*	Humbolt Eel Rvr	59	153
SINN			
---	Butte Kimshaw	56	589
---	Mariposa Twp 3	60	613

Name	County Locale	Roll	Page
SINN			
---	Placer Virginia	62	670
---	Placer Illinois	62	741
---	Sacramento Mississipi	63	190
---*	Butte Kimshaw	56	589
---*	Mariposa Coulterville	60	681
Choy	Butte Ophir	56	805
George*	San Francisco San Francisco 11	67	92
Jacob*	Sacramento Ward 1	63	88
James*	Sierra Pine Grove	66	820
Joseph N	Tuolumne Green Springs	71	518
Long	Butte Bidwell	56	727
Lung	Placer Iona Hills	62	869
Muck	Placer Iona Hills	62	897
Puck	Placer Iona Hills	62	898
Robert	Placer Forest H	62	767
Sick	Placer Forest H	62	772
Wack	Placer Iona Hills	62	897
Walter C*	Fresno Twp 3	59	8
William	Tulara Sinks Te	71	42
Wm*	Santa Clara Fremont	65	421
SINNA			
Peter*	Del Norte Crescent	58	642
SINNE			
Bob	Nevada Nevada	61	240
SINNER			
B*	Mariposa Twp 3	60	547
George	Sierra Downieville	66	964
Lewis	San Francisco San Francisco 2	67	714
SINNERTON			
J H*	Sacramento Ward 1	63	73
SINNETHO			
Ellen	San Joaquin Stockton	64	1013
SINNETT			
J	San Francisco San Francisco 5	67	527
SINNEY			
Chas	Butte Oregon	56	635
SINNG			
---*	Mariposa Twp 1	60	648
---*	Nevada Red Dog	61	539
SINNILLER			
Azro	Butte Ophir	56	793
SINNINBAUM			
Benj	Trinity Soldiers	70	1005
SINNK			
Dick*	Placer Auburn	62	588
SINNORY			
A C	Sutter Butte	70	792
SINNOT			
Pat	Placer Virginia	62	673
Wm	San Francisco San Francisco 2	67	746
SINNOTT			
Wm	San Francisco San Francisco 2	67	746
SINNP			
Henry	Butte Cascade	56	703
SINNS			
Wm*	Sacramento Granite	63	264
SINNY			
---	Placer Virginia	62	678
SINO			
---	Fresno Twp 3	59	31
SINOCK			
Henry*	Butte Kimshaw	56	585
SINOLL			
S E	Santa Clara San Jose	65	370
SINOMONDS			
A*	Butte Bidwell	56	712
SINON			
---	San Diego Agua Caliente	64	844
Trinidad	Los Angeles San Juan	59	466
W	San Francisco San Francisco 6	67	463
Wm	San Francisco San Francisco 6	67	458
SINOR			
Tun	Butte Cascade	56	704
SINOT			
Joseph*	Calaveras Twp 9	57	367
SINOTE			
P	Nevada Grass Valley	61	226
SINOTI			
---	Los Angeles Los Angeles	59	516
SINOTT			
Michael	Sierra Poker Flats	66	838
SINP			
---	Placer Illinois	62	754
SINPLICIA			
---	Monterey San Juan	60	991
SINRYETT			
Jas	Butte Bidwell	56	724
SINS			
Robert F	Humbolt Pacific	59	137
SINSEE			
---	Shasta Shasta	66	670
SINSHIEMER			
Simon	Humbolt Union	59	179
SINSMORE			
George	Sierra Twp 5	66	928

California 1860 Census Index

Name	County Locale	M653 Roll	Page
SINSON			
J C	Sierra St Louis	66	809
N C	Placer Dutch Fl	62	714
SINT			
Kate	San Joaquin Stockton	64	1076
SINTA ANNA			
---*	San Diego San Diego	64	771
SINTIN			
L	Calaveras Twp 9	57	404
SINTOCK			
George M*	Sierra Scales D	66	803
SINTON			
C B*	Sacramento American	63	172
Richd H	San Francisco San Francisco 2	67	673
Saml G	Tuolumne Twp 1	71	479
SINTONS			
S	Tuolumne Twp 4	71	174
SINTOUS			
Francisco*	Calaveras Twp 8	57	102
SINTRAS			
Hiram	Butte Cascade	56	703
SINTZER			
Andrew	Placer Lisbon	62	735
Samuel C*	Alameda Brooklyn	55	78
SINUBLEY			
John	Siskiyou Klamath	69	93
SINUERITAR			
Josefa*	San Francisco San Francisco 2	67	752
SINUS			
Thomas*	Placer Michigan	62	807
Wm*	Sacramento Granite	63	264
SINX			
Jose*	Tulara Twp 3	71	68
SINY			
---	Amador Twp 5	55	333
---	Amador Twp 5	55	341
---	Amador Twp 5	55	345
---	Amador Twp 5	55	351
---	Amador Twp 5	55	360
---	Amador Twp 6	55	428
---	Amador Twp 6	55	432
---	Calaveras Twp 5	57	192
---	Calaveras Twp 10	57	259
---	Calaveras Twp 10	57	270
---	Calaveras Twp 10	57	271
---	Calaveras Twp 10	57	272
---	Calaveras Twp 10	57	274
---	Calaveras Twp 10	57	281
---	Calaveras Twp 10	57	283
---	Calaveras Twp 10	57	287
---	Calaveras Twp 10	57	290
---	Calaveras Twp 4	57	300
---	Calaveras Twp 4	57	302
---	Calaveras Twp 4	57	306
---	Calaveras Twp 4	57	307
---	Mariposa Twp 1	60	664
---*	Calaveras Twp 4	57	223
A	Sacramento Granite	63	268
A	Sacramento Natonia	63	268
Adam*	Contra Costa Twp 2	57	574
Choy*	Butte Ophir	56	815
Gu	Sacramento Granite	63	269
N	Sacramento Granite	63	268
Tan	Amador Twp 5	55	352
SINYETT			
Jas	Butte Bidwell	56	724
SIODZER			
Samuel C*	Alameda Brooklyn	55	78
SIOIM			
David K*	Calaveras Twp 5	57	207
SIOM			
---	Sierra St Louis	66	812
SION			
Yot	San Francisco San Francisco 4	68	1178
SIONG			
---	Calaveras Twp 5	57	248
---	Placer Illinois	62	741
SIONNLEY			
Wm F*	Sacramento Ward 1	63	29
SIORGIE			
William*	Sierra Port Win	66	798
SIORTZER			
Samuel C	Alameda Brooklyn	55	78
SIOTO			
Manuel	Tuolumne Twp 2	71	295
SIP			
---	Amador Twp 3	55	387
---	Amador Twp 6	55	424
---	Butte Bidwell	56	717
---	Butte Mountain	56	741
---	Butte Ophir	56	802
---	Calaveras Twp 4	57	309
---	El Dorado Mud Springs	58	973
---	Mariposa Twp 1	60	662
---	Nevada Nevada	61	300
---	Placer Folsom	62	648

Name	County Locale	M653 Roll	Page
SIP			
---	Placer Virginia	62	671
---	Placer Virginia	62	672
---	Placer Illinois	62	745
---	Placer Illinois	62	748
---	Placer Illinois	62	749
---	Sacramento Granite	63	250
---	Sierra Downieville	66	1027
---	Tuolumne Twp 6	71	537
---*	Sacramento Mississipi	63	190
A	Sacramento Granite	63	250
Ah	Butte Bidwell	56	717
Gep*	Yuba Bear Rvr	72	1000
Ling	Placer Auburn	62	582
Lum	Placer Illinois	62	751
Lum	Placer Illinois	62	752
Sing	Placer Rattle Snake	62	603
Yum	Placer Auburn	62	581
SIPARA			
Jose*	Santa Cruz Watsonville	66	539
SIPE			
Hing	Butte Cascade	56	700
Luis	Santa Clara San Jose	65	322
SIPER			
John	San Joaquin Stockton	64	1073
Robert*	Siskiyou Shasta Valley	69	120
SIPES			
John	Butte Ophir	56	798
SIPEY			
---	Sacramento Mississipi	63	190
SIPIBUIDA			
Francisco	Santa Clara San Jose	65	303
SIPICLVEDA			
Lucia	Santa Clara San Jose	65	303
SIPIDO			
Pearo	Santa Clara San Jose	65	364
SIPINAN			
Solomon*	Sacramento Ward 1	63	119
SIPKER			
Henry	Amador Twp 4	55	251
SIPP			
Andrew	Sierra La Porte	66	784
SIPPETT			
A	Nevada Nevada	61	239
SIPPISA			
Fritz	Butte Ophir	56	764
SIPPLE			
Samuel	Solano Vallejo	69	266
Wm	Butte Oro	56	683
SIPPLER			
Mary Jane	San Francisco 2	67	608
---	San Francisco		
SIPPY			
---	Sacramento Centre	63	182
SIPSKY			
Fredk*	San Francisco San Francisco 2	67	640
SIPULBIDA			
Jose*	Santa Clara San Jose	65	329
SIPULVEDA			
Doloris	Los Angeles Los Angeles	59	508
SIPULVIDA			
Farnando	Los Angeles Los Angeles	59	492
Jose S	Santa Clara San Jose	65	365
Jose*	Santa Clara San Jose	65	329
Juan Ma	Los Angeles Los Angeles	59	508
Rimona G	Los Angeles Los Angeles	59	508
SIPULVIERA			
Luisa	Santa Clara San Jose	65	330
SIQUIES			
Geronimo*	Los Angeles Los Angeles	59	500
SIQUIRS			
Geronimo	Los Angeles Los Angeles	59	500
SIQUIST			
F??D*	Napa Napa	61	61
Fred	Napa Napa	61	61
SIR			
---	Calaveras Twp 6	57	158
---	Calaveras Twp 6	57	164
---	Calaveras Twp 5	57	201
---	Calaveras Twp 5	57	219
---	Calaveras Twp 5	57	233
---	Calaveras Twp 5	57	244
---	Calaveras Twp 10	57	285
---	Calaveras Twp 10	57	286
---	Calaveras Twp 10	57	295
---	Calaveras Twp 10	57	296
---	Calaveras Twp 10	57	297
---	Calaveras Twp 4	57	326
---	Mariposa Twp 1	60	643
---	Mariposa Twp 1	60	650
King	El Dorado Georgetown	58	701
SIRACES			
Frank	Sierra Twp 5	66	926
SIRANHISGERD			
John	El Dorado Greenwood	58	716
SIRASTRA			
Antone*	Placer Iona Hills	62	891

Name	County Locale	M653 Roll	Page
SIRATE			
Francis*	Klamath S Fork	59	203
SIRE			
---*	Placer Auburn	62	572
Paul	Nevada Bridgeport	61	472
SIREHILITA			
Tomas*	San Bernardino San Bernadino	64	665
SIRELY			
P	Trinity Eastman	70	960
SIRENO			
Lorenzo	Tuolumne Twp 3	71	459
SIREPIELD			
---	Sonoma Petaluma	69	543
SIRES			
John	Siskiyou Yreka	69	154
SIREY			
James	Tulara Twp 3	71	62
SIREYETT			
---	Butte Bidwell	56	711
SIRFEE			
R	Amador Twp 6	55	445
SIRHEL			
M C*	San Francisco San Francisco 3	67	86
SIRHER			
W N*	Nevada Nevada T	61	327
SIRILDO			
---	Los Angeles San Juan	59	474
SIRILL			
---*	San Francisco San Francisco 7	68	1361
Juan	Los Angeles Los Angeles	59	304
SIRIVAPA			
---	San Bernardino S Timate	64	718
SIRIZ			
B*	San Francisco San Francisco 3	67	78
SIRKER			
W N*	Nevada Nevada	61	327
SIRLAN			
Joseph	Yolo Slate Ra	72	698
SIRLOTT			
Geo	Amador Twp 2	55	265
SIRM			
High	Mariposa Twp 3	60	620
SIRMANTES			
Moranto	San Bernardino S Timate	64	688
SIRMERS			
John T*	Butte Ophir	56	756
SIRMEY			
Chas*	Butte Oregon	56	635
SIRMIR			
Josh	San Luis Obispo San Luis Obispo	65	8
SIRN			
---	Amador Twp 5	55	333
---	Butte Bidwell	56	720
SIRNDESHAUSR			
Joseph*	Mariposa Twp 3	60	573
SIROMS			
N	Calaveras Twp 9	57	396
SIRONG			
---	Sacramento Ward 1	63	61
SIRRA			
Tomas	Los Angeles Los Angeles	59	334
SIRRAN			
Jones G*	San Francisco San Francisco 7	68	1338
SIRRO			
M	Sacramento Ward 1	63	15
SIRRU			
George*	San Francisco San Francisco 11	67	92
SIRS			
J L	Calaveras Twp 9	57	392
SIRSA			
Geo*	Siskiyou Scott Va	69	48
SIRULA			
Manuel*	Alameda Brooklyn	55	124
SIRUT			
---*	Butte Oro	56	675
SIRY			
---	Amador Twp 2	55	308
---	Amador Twp 2	55	315
---	Amador Twp 2	55	327
---	Amador Twp 5	55	335
---	Amador Twp 5	55	354
---	Amador Twp 7	55	412
---	Amador Twp 6	55	428
---	Amador Twp 6	55	432
---	Amador Twp 6	55	439
---	Amador Twp 6	55	447
Liro	Amador Twp 2	55	311
Mi	Amador Twp 5	55	333
SIRZLES			
C	Yolo Cache Crk	72	644
SIS			
---	Calaveras Twp 5	57	233
---	Calaveras Twp 10	57	296
---	Nevada Rough &	61	437

Name	County Locale	M653 Roll	Page
SIS			
Ellen*	Napa Napa	61	71
SISBON			
Isaac	El Dorado Big Bar	58	735
SISCHS			
N N	El Dorado White Oaks	58	1009
SISCTON			
Saml G*	Tuolumne Sonora	71	479
SISE			
Lonencer*	Mariposa Twp 1	60	628
Lorencer	Mariposa Twp 1	60	628
Lorenza*	Mariposa Twp 1	60	628
SISEHA			
Thos	Santa Clara San Jose	65	388
SISEMORRE			
A	Siskiyou Scott Ri	69	83
SISEMOURE			
A	Siskiyou Scott Ri	69	83
SISENA			
Napaleon*	Calaveras Twp 6	57	160
SISENARO			
Jose C	Los Angeles Los Angeles	59	305
SISENER			
Napaleon*	Calaveras Twp 6	57	160
SISER			
Martin*	Sacramento Mississipi	63	188
SISES			
John*	Siskiyou Yreka	69	154
SISETON			
John M*	Tuolumne Twp 1	71	479
SISEUER			
Napaleon*	Calaveras Twp 6	57	160
SISIWASEKE			
Robt	Sonoma Petaluma	69	605
SISIWAZEKE			
Robt	Sonoma Petaluma	69	605
SISK			
John	San Joaquin Elkhorn	64	971
R	Sutter Butte	70	779
Richard	El Dorado Greenwood	58	720
Richard	Placer Auburn	62	594
Stephen	Siskiyou Yreka	69	147
T J	Sacramento Ward 1	63	18
Thos	Nevada Nevada	61	278
Wm	Sacramento Ward 4	63	523
SISKE			
E E	Sacramento Ward 1	63	81
SISMA			
Jesus	Santa Clara Almaden	65	273
SISNEROS			
Jose M	Monterey San Juan	60	982
SISON			
Charles	Tuolumne Twp 2	71	285
Nicholas	Tuolumne Twp 2	71	364
SISSAK			
Adolphus H	San Francisco 10		240
	San Francisco	67	
SISSLER			
J	Siskiyou Scott Va	69	47
SISSO			
M*	Sacramento Ward 1	63	15
SISSON			
Alfred	Nevada Red Dog	61	551
Arnold B	Tuolumne Twp 2	71	396
Danl A	Tuolumne Twp 2	71	396
Samuel*	Placer Michigan	62	839
Warren	Tuolumne Shawsfla	71	393
SISTER			
Samuel*	Plumas Quincy	62	997
SISTETA			
Louis	Amador Twp 2	55	295
SISUM			
M B	Butte Ophir	56	746
SIT TE			
---	Tulara Twp 1	71	116
SIT			
---	Calaveras Twp 4	57	315
---	El Dorado Georgetown	58	678
---	Placer Secret R	62	621
---*	Mariposa Twp 1	60	581
Kear	Butte Mountain	56	743
Ker	Butte Oro	56	688
Kin	Butte Cascade	56	702
Sem	Sierra Downieville	66	1004
Sun	Sierra Downieville	66	1004
SITAHES			
William N	San Francisco San Francisco 8	68	1288
SITASH			
Vanburton	Sierra Scales D	66	804
SITATES			
William N*	San Francisco 8	68	1288
	San Francisco		
SITATIES			
William N*	San Francisco 8	68	1288
	San Francisco		
SITCHFIELD			
Samuel	Yuba Bear Rvr	72	1003

Name	County Locale	M653 Roll	Page
SITCOMB			
John	Marin Tomales	60	713
SITE			
---	Butte Oregon	56	631
---	Butte Oregon	56	644
Ah	Butte Oregon	56	644
Eli	Siskiyou Klamath	69	86
SITES			
John	Colusa Colusi	57	427
SITH			
Patrick	Tuolumne Twp 2	71	472
SITIYUR			
Charles*	Calaveras Twp 6	57	167
SITLER			
Geo*	El Dorado Kelsey	58	1154
W P*	Siskiyou Scott Ri	69	74
SITNO			
S	Calaveras Twp 9	57	415
SITOA			
Jasciutho*	Santa Cruz Santa Cruz	66	612
Jascuitho*	Santa Cruz Santa Cruz	66	612
SITROW			
Morris*	San Francisco San Francisco 3	67	27
SITTAN			
Spencer	Sonoma Petaluma	69	569
SITTEN			
John*	Solano Benecia	69	314
T B*	Siskiyou Scott Ri	69	63
SITTER			
W F*	Siskiyou Scott Ri	69	74
SITTERAL			
C G	Shasta Millvill	66	752
SITTERLEN			
Antoine*	San Francisco San Francisco 2	67	687
SITTICK			
John*	Sierra Pine Grove	66	822
SITTLE			
Bernard	Contra Costa Twp 1	57	516
Mrs D	San Francisco San Francisco 2	67	775
Wm B*	San Francisco San Francisco 10		314
		67	
SITTLEJOHN			
Abram	Calaveras Twp 4	57	302
SITTON			
T B	Siskiyou Scott Ri	69	63
T S	Siskiyou Scott Ri	69	63
SITTREE			
John	Solano Benecia	69	314
SITTS			
Peter*	Santa Cruz Pajaro	66	573
SIU			
---	Calaveras Twp 5	57	226
---	Calaveras Twp 5	57	256
---	Calaveras Twp 5	57	257
---	Calaveras Twp 10	57	269
---	Calaveras Twp 10	57	276
Ah	Butte Oregon	56	644
Tong	Calaveras Twp 5	57	226
SIUNG			
---*	Nevada Red Dog	61	539
SIUNK			
Dick*	Placer Auburn	62	588
SIUO			
---	Sierra Downieville	66	1005
SIV			
---	Calaveras Twp 5	57	242
SIVAN			
G W*	El Dorado Kelsey	58	1154
Lyman	Alameda Brooklyn	55	168
Robt	Butte Oregon	56	624
SIVELEY			
David	Butte Cascade	56	704
SIVENISH			
Eroone*	Calaveras Twp 5	57	230
SIVER			
Frank	Calaveras Twp 5	57	188
SIVERA			
---	Los Angeles San Juan	59	464
SIVERANCE			
C C P	Tuolumne Twp 1	71	195
SIVERCE			
Camelleto*	Calaveras Twp 9	57	378
SIVERICH			
Frank	Tuolumne Jamestown	71	454
SIVERICK			
Frank	Tuolumne Twp 3	71	454
SIVERMON			
James	Amador Twp 3	55	406
SIVERMORE			
James	Amador Twp 3	55	406
SIVERNICH			
Eroone*	Calaveras Twp 5	57	230
SIVERR			
Jose*	Tuolumne Twp 3	71	435
SIVERS			
S	Sonoma Washington	69	664

Name	County Locale	M653 Roll	Page
SIVERS			
William	Calaveras Twp 5	57	215
SIVERT			
C F	Sutter Sutter	70	810
SIVERTS			
John*	San Francisco San Francisco 3	67	40
SIVERWILE			
Eroone*	Calaveras Twp 5	57	230
Evorne*	Calaveras Twp 5	57	230
Ewone*	Calaveras Twp 5	57	230
SIVIER			
Fred	Alameda Brooklyn	55	143
SIVILS			
W	Butte Wyandotte	56	657
SIVIM			
David K*	Calaveras Twp 5	57	207
SIVINERTON			
James*	Plumas Quincy	62	922
SIVINGSTON			
James	Trinity Mouth Ca	70	1012
SIVINGTON			
L	San Francisco San Francisco 10		204
		67	
SIVISA			
J W*	Alameda Brooklyn	55	149
SIVISON			
William*	Calaveras Twp 6	57	188
SIVTHEWS			
Bapliste	Trinity Lewiston	70	964
SIVTO			
Manuel	Tuolumne Columbia	71	295
SIW			
---	Calaveras Twp 6	57	147
---	Calaveras Twp 4	57	302
---	Tuolumne Chinese	71	525
---*	Tuolumne Don Pedro	71	536
Cunn	Butte Ophir	56	805
SIWA			
---	Tuolumne Jacksonville	71	514
SIWER			
C F*	Sonoma Vallejo	69	627
SIX			
---*	Mendocino Round Va	60	882
SIY KEE			
---	Mariposa Twp 3	60	616
SIY			
---	Mariposa Coulterville	60	691
---	Nevada Nevada	61	307
---	Tuolumne Columbia	71	346
Sing	Placer Dutch Fl	62	737
SIYMORE			
R	Yolo Merritt	72	581
SIYN			
George	Yolo Putah	72	587
SIYNE			
---	Butte Bidwell	56	709
SIZA			
Mall M*	Sacramento Granite	63	244
SIZE			
Jno	Butte Chico	56	549
SIZER			
Mall M*	Sacramento Granite	63	244
Samuel	Sierra Downieville	66	1029
SIZLER			
C	Yolo Cache	72	644
SJITH			
S	Placer Dutch Fl	62	710
SKAGGS			
A A	Amador Twp 3	55	371
Alex	Sonoma Mendocino	69	447
C M*	Sacramento Ward 1	63	17
E M	Sacramento Ward 1	63	17
Ebon	Sonoma Armally	69	485
Elijah	Sonoma Mendocino	69	447
Eliza	Sonoma Mendocino	69	447
James W	Sonoma Mendocino	69	448
Jos	Amador Twp 3	55	395
William	Plumas Quincy	62	957
Wm	Sonoma Mendocino	69	454
Wm	Sonoma Mendocino	69	455
SKAHAN			
Mary*	San Francisco San Francisco 9	68	961
SKALL			
Bridget	Tuolumne Twp 2	71	334
SKAN			
James	Santa Cruz Santa Cruz	66	612
SKANCHEN			
Richard	Sierra Twp 7	66	865
SKANER			
Joshua*	Sierra Downieville	66	1021
SKANIR			
Jashman	Sierra Downieville	66	1021
SKANLAN			
Patrick	Sierra Downieville	66	1010
SKATES			
Thos	San Francisco San Francisco 9	68	1063

Name	County Locale	M653 Roll/Page
SKATZ		
Wm	Sacramento Ward 4	63 514
SKCCHAN		
James*	Tuolumne Twp 2	71 369
SKEEHAN		
James	Tuolumne Springfield	71 369
SKEEN		
---	San Francisco San Francisco 10	355 67
Elizabeth	Siskiyou Scott Va	69 27
Elizabeth S	Siskiyou Scott Va	69 27
Frank	Shasta Millvill	66 749
Franks	Shasta Millvill	66 749
James	Siskiyou Scott Va	69 41
Joseph	Siskiyou Scott Va	69 33
Wm E	Tehama Lassen	70 866
SKEFFINGTON		
Sarah J	San Francisco San Francisco 8	681244
SKEIN		
Coinelius	San Francisco San Francisco 7	681424
John	Tehama Lassen	70 868
SKELLEY		
W P	Trinity Lewiston	70 953
SKELLY		
Jeremiah	San Francisco San Francisco 1	68 857
Michael	San Francisco San Francisco 10	190 67
Michael	Tuolumne Big Oak	71 141
Pat*	Amador Twp 2	55 296
Wm	Amador Twp 2	55 297
SKELTER		
B H	Mariposa Twp 3	60 574
S S*	Mariposa Twp 3	60 574
S U*	Mariposa Twp 3	60 574
SKELTON		
B H	Mariposa Twp 3	60 574
Elip	Sacramento Ward 1	63 126
Eliss	Sacramento Ward 1	63 126
G H	Butte Hamilton	56 521
H A	Merced Twp 1	60 895
James	Marin Cortemad	60 789
John	Sacramento Ward 1	63 107
Joseph	Trinity Indian C	70 986
M A	Yuba Marysville	72 927
W M	Butte Ophir	56 746
Wm	Butte Hamilton	56 525
Wm	Sierra Twp 7	66 873
SKEMMING		
C	Sacramento Ward 1	63 12
SKENHAN		
Thomas	Sierra Downieville	661016
SKENHAW		
Thomas*	Sierra Downieville	661016
SKENIVER		
Wm	Mariposa Twp 3	60 597
SKENK		
G	Butte Chico	56 564
SKENNER		
J G	Tuolumne Jacksonville	71 169
SKENZG		
---*	El Dorado Georgetown	58 702
SKEORN		
Thomas	Calaveras Twp 5	57 195
SKERRITT		
Danl*	Sacramento Ward 1	63 80
E L	El Dorado Placerville	58 852
SKESIS		
K	Tulara Twp 3	71 56
SKEUK		
G	Butte Chico	56 564
SKEY		
Josiah	San Joaquin Elkhorn	64 990
SKIARING		
Robbert*	Mariposa Twp 1	60 669
SKIDMORE		
J E	Alameda Brooklyn	55 121
James	El Dorado Indian D	581158
Rush	Nevada Bloomfield	61 520
Susan	Alameda Brooklyn	55 149
W B	Yolo Cottonwood	72 662
W M	Siskiyou Scott Va	69 32
Walter A	Marin San Rafael	60 757
SKIEL		
Mary A	Sacramento Ward 1	63 22
SKIEMER		
Charles	San Joaquin Oneal	64 938
SKIFF		
Chas	El Dorado Greenwood	58 724
Ed	Nevada Bridgeport	61 476
SKIFFINGTON		
Sarah J	San Francisco San Francisco 8	681244
SKIFT		
Edwd	Nevada Bridgeport	61 467
SKILES		
Harvey	Los Angeles Elmonte	59 249
Oswell	Colusa Muion	57 462
SKILLEN		
Isaac	Sierra La Porte	66 790
John	Alameda Brooklyn	55 126
SKILLING		
John D	Humbolt Eureka	59 166
SKILLINGER		
Isaac	Sierra Eureka	661048
SKILLMAN		
A	Shasta Shasta	66 654
J H	Klamath Liberty	59 234
SKILLY		
David*	San Mateo Twp 3	65 95
SKILMAN		
Theo	Sonoma Petaluma	69 576
Theodore	Sonoma Petaluma	69 568
SKIM		
---	El Dorado Georgetown	58 748
SKIMINS		
J	Santa Clara San Jose	65 347
Wm	Santa Clara San Jose	65 347
SKIMMER		
James	El Dorado White Oaks	581016
SKIMMERHAM		
John	Santa Clara Alviso	65 398
SKIN		
Joseph	Shasta Shasta	66 673
SKINDON		
James	Yuba Suida	72 982
SKINER		
A	Sacramento Ward 1	63 17
Frank	El Dorado Kelsey	581126
J*	Siskiyou Klamath	69 79
James	Siskiyou Yreka	69 169
SKINES		
R B	Sonoma Petaluma	69 554
SKING		
---	San Francisco San Francisco 4	681189
SKINGG		
---	El Dorado Georgetown	58 702
SKINKER		
John	Sacramento Ward 1	63 133
John	San Bernardino San Bernadino	64 668
SKINKLE		
Andrew	Plumas Meadow Valley	62 905
SKINN		
Cynthia*	Sonoma Russian	69 438
Joseph*	Santa Cruz Santa Cruz	66 600
S M*	Sonoma Russian	69 439
Walter*	Merced Twp 2	60 917
Wm	Sonoma Armally	69 482
SKINNER		
A M	Nevada Nevada	61 285
A S	Santa Clara San Jose	65 281
Albert	Sonoma Vallejo	69 623
And	Sacramento Ward 3	63 433
Andrew	Yuba Fosters	72 832
Chas	Mariposa Twp 1	60 644
David E	Santa Clara San Jose	65 320
E	Butte Cascade	56 692
Edward	Tuolumne Twp 2	71 349
F S	Butte Ophir	56 824
Frank	Tulara Keeneysburg	71 45
H	El Dorado Placerville	58 895
Henry	Sacramento Ward 3	63 515
Henry	Sierra La Porte	66 789
Hubbard	Nevada Bridgeport	61 448
J D	El Dorado Kelsey	581137
J G	Tuolumne Twp 4	71 169
J M*	Yolo Cottonwoood	72 647
James	Siskiyou Yreka	69 174
James*	Mariposa Coulterville	60 677
John T	Amador Twp 4	55 242
L	San Francisco San Francisco 5	67 484
Lamira E	Sonoma Mendocino	69 466
Maria	Nevada Rough &	61 408
Martin	Sonoma Vallejo	69 622
Moat	Siskiyou Yreka	69 176
Ned	Mariposa Twp 1	60 668
Peter	Tuolumne Columbia	71 361
R	San Francisco San Francisco 5	67 496
R W	San Joaquin Stockton	641033
Silas	Nevada Red Dog	61 548
Thomas	Yuba Parks Ba	72 784
W C	Sonoma Mendocino	69 466
W F	Siskiyou Callahan	69 19
Willi	Yolo Cottonwoood	72 558
Wm C	Sonoma Washington	69 664
Wm J	Sacramento Ward 4	63 611
Wm W	Mendocino Little L	60 830
Wm*	Los Angeles Tejon	59 528
SKINNERR		
E	Butte Cascade	56 692
SKINNERS		
L*	Mariposa Twp 3	60 585
SKINNIR		
Wm*	Los Angeles Tejon	59 528
SKINNOR		
Wm W	Mendocino Little L	60 830
SKINZY		
---*	El Dorado Georgetown	58 702
SKIPPERD		
Wm N	Monterey San Juan	60 975
SKIPT		
Edwd*	Nevada Bridgeport	61 467
SKIRING		
Robbert	Mariposa Twp 1	60 669
SKIRM		
Joseph	Santa Cruz Santa Cruz	66 600
SKIRSFUNSKI		
Adelbert	San Francisco San Francisco 6	67 415
SKIRT		
Fred*	Alameda Brooklyn	55 122
SKIVING		
Robbert*	Mariposa Twp 1	60 669
SKOAJLE		
C	Shasta Millvill	66 755
SKOAL		
Joseph	Siskiyou Scott Va	69 23
SKOALS		
Edward E*	Plumas Quincy	62 964
SKOATS		
Edward E*	Plumas Quincy	62 964
SKOFRILD		
J	Calaveras Twp 9	57 417
SKONG		
---	El Dorado Eldorado	58 940
SKOONER		
Wm*	San Francisco San Francisco 2	67 647
SKOSTRAMITZ		
P	San Francisco San Francisco 9	681014
SKRENSON		
James	Sacramento Ward 1	63 26
SKU		
Bach	El Dorado Georgetown	58 691
SKUCHAN		
James	Tuolumne Twp 2	71 369
SKUCHINSON		
W	Tuolumne Columbia	71 336
SKUDDER		
C B	Alameda Brooklyn	55 150
SKUDEMAN		
E	Sacramento Ward 1	63 89
SKUDY		
Samuel	Placer Forest H	62 794
SKUH		
Jacob	Sacramento Ward 1	63 38
SKULL		
W W*	Butte Kimshaw	56 595
SKULLEY		
Peter	Tuolumne Shawsfla	71 399
SKULLY		
Owen	Sacramento Ward 1	63 10
SKUM		
Walter*	Merced Twp 2	60 917
SKUM?AN		
D	Mariposa Twp 3	60 585
SKUMMILLER		
Lewis*	Sacramento American	63 166
SKUN		
James*	Santa Cruz Santa Cruz	66 612
SKUNE		
Walter*	Merced Twp 2	60 917
SKUNG		
---	El Dorado Georgetown	58 703
SKUNMILLER		
Lewis*	Sacramento American	63 166
SKUSTER		
Michael M*	Yuba Marysville	72 902
SKUT		
C B	Solano Vacaville	69 353
SLA		
---	Shasta French G	66 712
SLABACK		
Sam	San Luis Obispo San Luis Obispo 65	6
SLACK		
A L	Nevada Rough &	61 418
A P Van*	Nevada Rough &	61 429
C	El Dorado Kelsey	581157
Charles*	Monterey Pajaro	601021
Henry	Alameda Brooklyn	55 147
Hy	San Francisco San Francisco 1	68 896
J R	Yolo Slate Ra	72 716
J R	Yuba Slate Ro	72 716
Joel	Santa Cruz Santa Cruz	66 633
O L	Trinity Mouth Ca	701013
O S	Trinity Mouth Ca	701013
Pembroke S	Yuba Rose Par	72 796
Sarah	Tuolumne Twp 2	71 393
SLACKMILLER		
Vincent	Mendocino Big Rvr	60 842
SLADE		

Name	County Locale	M653 Roll Page
SLADE		
Calvin	San Francisco San Francisco	10 229
		67
Chester L	Placer Auburn	62 590
Geo M	Tuolumne Twp 2	71 349
H	Sonoma Salt Point	69 689
Jno	Nevada Nevada	61 243
John	Sierra Downieville	661019
Mary E	San Francisco San Francisco	10 230
		67
R P	Tuolumne Sonora	71 192
Thos P	Placer Dutch Fl	62 709
William D	Siskiyou Yreka	69 169
SLADER		
J H	Sonoma Salt Point	69 690
SLAES		
William	Sierra Pine Grove	66 825
SLAFFETHACH		
C*	San Francisco San Francisco	9 681052
SLAFFORD		
C*	Calaveras Twp 9	57 375
SLAG		
---*	Shasta Shasta	66 678
SLAGETER		
F J	San Francisco San Francisco	5 67 488
SLAGLE		
J	Yolo Cache Crk	72 607
J	Yolo Cache	72 608
W	Yolo Cache Crk	72 607
SLAGUNS		
Theraca	El Dorado Placerville	58 900
SLAIER		
Louis	San Francisco San Francisco	7 681426
SLAIM		
Jas	Butte Wyandotte	56 658
SLAINE		
Thomas	Tuolumne Twp 5	71 506
SLAKER		
Wm	San Francisco San Francisco	1 68 842
SLALLAGAN		
G W*	El Dorado Casumnes	581177
SLAM		
---*	Calaveras Twp 8	57 101
J	San Francisco San Francisco	5 67 516
SLAMAS		
Refugio*	Plumas Quincy	62 988
SLAN		
Chas F	Mariposa Twp 3	60 548
SLANDT		
Reuben	Sierra Gibsonville	66 859
SLANE		
J F*	Sierra Twp 5	66 921
SLANES		
Angel*	Los Angeles Santa Ana	59 446
Antonio	Los Angeles Los Angeles	59 396
Antonio*	Los Angeles San Juan	59 461
Nicolasa	Los Angeles Los Angeles	59 385
SLANG		
---	Calaveras Twp 10	57 268
R	Shasta Millvill	66 752
SLANGER		
C	Calaveras Twp 9	57 393
George	Sierra Twp 7	66 916
SLANGHTERBACK		
John*	Siskiyou Yreka	69 141
SLANGHTERBECK		
John*	El Dorado Coloma	581103
SLANK		
Thomas	Yolo Putah	72 585
SLANKARD		
George	Contra Costa Twp 2	57 567
Harrison	Contra Costa Twp 2	57 558
SLANT		
A M	Nevada Nevada	61 249
SLANTER		
C	El Dorado Kelsey	581155
SLANTON		
Thomas	El Dorado Mud Springs	58 965
SLANWOOD		
Saml*	Sacramento Ward 1	63 73
SLANY		
---	Calaveras Twp 10	57 268
SLAP		
Chas*	Trinity New Rvr	701030
Herman*	Shasta Shasta	66 655
Hingh	Sacramento Mississipi	63 190
SLAPBACK		
John C	Sierra Downieville	66 971
SLAPER		
W O	Tuolumne Columbia	71 326
SLAPP		
Howard*	Yuba New York	72 738
SLAPPER		
---	Fresno Twp 3	59 99
SLAPPY		
Fred	Siskiyou Klamath	69 94

Name	County Locale	M653 Roll Page
SLAPT		
Christian	Placer Michigan	62 847
SLAQUGHTER		
Isaac	Tulara Twp 3	71 48
SLAREN		
P	El Dorado Placerville	58 850
SLARMARD		
J H*	Calaveras Twp 9	57 356
SLARP		
Henry	Yuba New York	72 737
SLARRIX		
Benj	Sonoma Santa Rosa	69 401
SLARTINGS		
A J	Siskiyou Yreka	69 188
SLASEON		
Frank*	Tuolumne Twp 1	71 253
SLASS		
George*	Santa Cruz Santa Cruz	66 635
Herman*	Shasta Shasta	66 655
SLATA		
S	Sacramento Sutter	63 304
SLATE		
George	Nevada Rough &	61 429
SLATELY		
Jacob	Placer Iona Hills	62 890
SLATEN		
Henry	Calaveras Twp 8	57 95
Nicholas	Santa Clara Santa Clara	65 519
SLATER		
Adaline	El Dorado Casumnes	581164
Antonia A	Los Angeles Los Angeles	59 334
B F	Sacramento Brighton	63 198
E W	Butte Oregon	56 638
F	El Dorado Placerville	58 846
George	Nevada Rough &	61 429
H S	Tuolumne Twp 2	71 386
Henrieta	San Francisco San Francisco	6 67 399
Henry	Mendocino Big Rvr	60 848
J	Nevada Grass Valley	61 201
J B	Sacramento Brighton	63 202
James	Siskiyou Yreka	69 151
James	Tulara Sinks Te	71 43
James H	Los Angeles Tejon	59 528
Jas	Butte Mountain	56 739
Jas E	Placer Goods	62 698
John	Nevada Little Y	61 531
John	San Francisco San Francisco	1 68 863
John A	Plumas Quincy	62 984
Michael	Placer Secret R	62 613
Mrs	Stanislaus Buena Village	70 721
N	Sacramento Dry Crk	63 372
N	Sutter Butte	70 789
Patrick	San Francisco San Francisco	1 68 807
Silas*	Nevada Red Dog	61 554
Thomas	El Dorado Placerville	58 926
William	Placer Todds Va	62 783
Wm	Napa Clear Lake	61 135
Wm	Sacramento Ward 1	63 43
SLATERS		
Jonathan E	Yuba Marysville	72 859
SLATES		
Adaline	El Dorado Casumnes	581164
Geo	El Dorado Placerville	58 930
SLATHER		
John	Amador Twp 4	55 256
SLATMILLER		
Jacob*	Siskiyou Yreka	69 141
SLATT		
B	Yuba Slate Ro	72 716
R	Yolo Slate Ra	72 716
SLATTER		
W	Siskiyou Scott Ri	69 68
SLATTERBRY		
J D	Yolo Cache	72 595
SLATTERBY		
J D	Yolo Cache Crk	72 595
SLATTERLY		
Jno	Butte Kimshaw	56 606
Margaret	Sacramento Ward 1	63 94
SLATTERY		
James	Yuba Marysville	72 913
John	Sonoma Santa Rosa	69 391
Patrick C	Yuba Marysville	72 913
Thos	Trinity Sturdiva	701007
SLATTING		
William	Yuba Marysville	72 871
SLAUGHTER		
E J	Tuolumne Twp 1	71 265
E W D	Sacramento Granite	63 223
F	San Bernardino San Bernadino	64 671
F R	Trinity Big Flat	701039
Francis R*	Humbolt Union	59 189
Isaac	Tulara Keenesyburg	71 48
Jas	Sacramento Ward 1	63 34
Jesse	Sacramento Ward 4	63 568
Jno Henry	Alameda Brooklyn	55 79

Name	County Locale	M653 Roll Page
SLAUGHTER		
Joel	Tulara Twp 3	71 59
John	Amador Twp 6	55 438
John	Placer Iona Hills	62 875
Joseph H	San Joaquin Elkhorn	64 972
L M*	Sacramento Granite	63 223
S	Butte Bidwell	56 725
S M*	Sacramento Granite	63 223
Thomas H	San Luis Obispo	65 35
	San Luis Obispo	
W L	Sierra Twp 7	66 865
Wm	Plumas Quincy	62 916
SLAUGHTERBACK		
John*	Siskiyou Yreka	69 141
SLAUM		
Daniel*	El Dorado Placerville	58 929
SLAUTER		
C*	El Dorado Kelsey	581155
SLAVEN		
A G	Sacramento Dry Crk	63 372
Ann E	San Francisco San Francisco	10 231
		67
David	El Dorado Placerville	58 894
J W	El Dorado Diamond	58 812
Jas	Sonoma Petaluma	69 587
John	San Luis Obispo San Luis Obispo	65 17
M	El Dorado Placerville	58 932
Mary H	San Francisco San Francisco	10 231
		67
Patrick	San Francisco San Francisco	10 332
		67
Rosanna	San Francisco San Francisco	1 68 832
SLAVIN		
John G	Calaveras Twp 6	57 134
Stewart	San Luis Obispo San Luis Obispo	65 16
SLAVON		
P	Yolo Washington	72 599
SLAY		
---	Shasta Horsetown	66 702
---	Sierra Twp 5	66 928
SLAYBACK		
Antoine	Solano Fremont	69 380
Antoino	Solano Fremont	69 380
SLAYSON		
W	San Francisco San Francisco	5 67 496
SLAZ		
---*	Shasta Shasta	66 678
SLDERSON		
R	El Dorado Placerville	58 827
SLE		
A	Sacramento Granite	63 268
SLEADMAN		
Wm	San Francisco San Francisco	5 67 511
SLEAM		
---	Shasta Horsetown	66 711
SLEAP		
Chas*	Trinity New Rvr	701030
SLEBE		
M*	San Francisco San Francisco	5 67 506
SLECER		
Dorsey	Yuba Marysville	72 914
SLECPER		
S L	Siskiyou Callahan	69 14
SLED		
Carolina	Marin Bolinas	60 733
SLEDE		
H	Nevada Nevada	61 262
SLEDGER		
James G	Sonoma Mendocino	69 457
SLEE		
---	Shasta Horsetown	66 704
Edmund	Sierra Twp 7	66 894
Edward	Sierra Twp 7	66 894
Hop*	Sacramento Granite	63 243
Wm	Sierra Twp 7	66 896
SLEEN		
James*	Shasta Shasta	66 668
SLEENY		
Ah	Yuba Bear Rvr	721000
SLEEPER		
Coryden*	Napa Clear Lake	61 132
Frank	Santa Clara Fremont	65 439
G W	Siskiyou Klamath	69 96
J	Calaveras Twp 9	57 414
M	Siskiyou Callahan	69 14
Morris*	Napa Clear Lake	61 132
S L	Siskiyou Callahan	69 14
SLEET		
Henry	Butte Oro	56 683
SLEETS		
Charles*	Yuba Marysville	72 865
SLEGEMAN		
William*	Sierra Poker Flats	66 837
Willilam	Sierra Poker Flats	66 837
SLEHASE		
John	Calaveras Twp 5	57 228

California 1860 Census Index

Name	County Locale	M653 Roll	Page
SLEIDMORE			
Walter A	Marin San Rafael	60	757
SLEIFER			
Adam*	Placer Michigan	62	824
SLEIGH			
J S	Tehama Red Bluff	70	922
SLEIGHT			
Jno	Klamath Orleans	59	217
Thos	Butte Oregon	56	636
SLEIKARD			
Richd*	Mariposa Twp 3	60	557
SLEIN			
Ferdinand	San Francisco San Francisco 1	68	811
SLEINECK			
Jno	San Francisco San Francisco 9	68	1084
SLEIT			
Juan*	San Bernardino S Buenav	64	219
SLEIVARA			
R*	Mariposa Twp 3	60	592
SLEMONAM			
E	Amador Twp 3	55	409
SLENDEMAN			
E*	Sacramento Ward 1	63	89
SLENDER			
M C	Tuolumne Twp 4	71	156
SLENION			
Louis	Contra Costa Twp 1	57	528
SLERADER			
Frederick*	Yuba Marysville	72	924
SLERLAING			
George	Sierra Downieville	66	1002
SLEROP			
Paul	San Joaquin Castoria	64	874
SLERT			
Juan*	San Bernardino Santa Ba	64	218
Juan*	San Bernardino S Buenav	64	219
SLETCER			
Godlif	Calaveras Twp 6	57	160
Godlip*	Calaveras Twp 6	57	160
Godliss*	Calaveras Twp 6	57	160
SLETSON			
Geo*	Amador Twp 2	55	325
James*	Plumas Quincy	62	982
SLETTER			
Charles*	Yuba Marysville	72	874
SLETTICK			
M	San Francisco San Francisco 5	67	528
SLEUDEMAN			
E*	Sacramento Ward 1	63	89
SLEUN			
John*	Tehama Red Bluff	70	905
SLEVENSON			
H	Tuolumne Twp 4	71	145
SLEY			
Philip	Yuba Marysville	72	894
SLHAIN			
S*	Butte Bidwell	56	715
SLHAROIN			
S*	Butte Bidwell	56	714
SLHARVIN			
S*	Butte Bidwell	56	714
SLHAWIN			
S*	Butte Bidwell	56	714
SLIBBINS			
F	Butte Wyandotte	56	662
SLICER			
Dorsey	Yuba Marysville	72	914
SLICK			
---	Butte Chico	56	558
Emanuel	Colusa Grand Island	57	468
Jacob	Amador Twp 5	55	362
Jacob	San Francisco San Francisco 4	68	1157
S	Sutter Yuba	70	777
SLICKMUINE			
---*	Tulara Visalia	71	35
SLICKMUNE			
---	Tulara Twp 2	71	35
SLIE			
---	Siskiyou Scott Ri	69	76
SLIETER			
A*	San Francisco San Francisco 5	67	534
SLIFE			
Saml	Shasta Millvill	66	748
SLIFER			
Henry	San Francisco San Francisco 7	68	1326
SLIGER			
Emberson	Butte Hamilton	56	516
Jos	Butte Hamilton	56	516
Mary	Butte Hamilton	56	522
SLIGES			
Mary*	Butte Hamilton	56	522
SLIGGER			
Adam	Sierra Downieville	66	1032
SLIGHT			
E T*	Sacramento American	63	158
SLIH			
Lok	El Dorado Big Bar	58	740
SLIHN			
Frederick*	Santa Cruz Soguel	66	600
SLIKL			
---	Calaveras Twp 8	57	60
SLIM			
My*	El Dorado Greenwood	58	729
SLIMAN			
Franci*	El Dorado Georgetown	58	684
SLIMER			
Jacob*	Placer Grizzly	62	755
SLIN			
---	Shasta Horsetown	66	711
SLINAN			
James*	Mariposa Twp 3	60	575
SLINEY			
J*	Nevada Grass Valley	61	226
SLING			
---	Amador Twp 2	55	314
---	Calaveras Twp 7	57	48
---	Yolo Slate Ra	72	711
---	Yuba Slate Ro	72	711
George*	Calaveras Twp 8	57	79
Sluna	El Dorado Greenwood	58	719
SLINGAR			
Saml	Butte Chico	56	551
SLINGER			
W	Nevada Eureka	61	378
SLINGERLAND			
James	Yuba Slate Ro	72	688
T	Marin Novato	60	738
SLINGHEAD			
Arnold	Sacramento Granite	63	255
Harry	Sacramento Granite	63	255
Henry	Sacramento Granite	63	255
SLINGIE			
W	Nevada Eureka	61	378
SLINGLER			
Merner	Santa Cruz Santa Cruz	66	613
SLINGSLY			
William	Yuba Long Bar	72	753
William	Yuba Long Bar	72	755
SLINKAN			
James*	Mariposa Twp 3	60	575
SLINKANL			
Solomon	Los Angeles Los Angeles	59	356
SLINKARD			
James	Mariposa Twp 3	60	575
Jno	Fresno Twp 3	59	14
Richd*	Mariposa Twp 3	60	557
Solomon	Los Angeles Los Angeles	59	356
SLINKOW			
James*	Mariposa Twp 3	60	575
SLINNIS			
Joseph*	Nevada Rough &	61	420
SLINT			
Fred*	Alameda Brooklyn	55	122
SLIPPER			
M M	Sacramento Ward 1	63	62
SLIRK			
Jacob	San Francisco San Francisco 4	68	1157
SLIRKARD			
Richd*	Mariposa Twp 3	60	557
SLIRTEN			
A	San Francisco San Francisco 5	67	534
SLISK			
Martin	Solano Vallejo	69	247
SLISSMAN			
Jno	Butte Kimshaw	56	576
SLITER			
Joel	San Bernardino S Timate	64	688
Joel	Tulara Twp 3	71	47
SLITES			
A*	Siskiyou Cottonwoood	69	107
Wills	Tehama Lassen	70	873
SLITLE			
Isaac H*	Yuba Marysville	72	862
SLITLGEN			
Wm*	Butte Chico	56	551
SLITTGEN			
Wm*	Butte Chico	56	551
SLITZ			
John	Contra Costa Twp 2	57	553
SLIVERS			
D A*	San Francisco San Francisco 12	67	376
SLIYA			
James	El Dorado Big Bar	58	736
SLIYY			
J	Nevada Nevada	61	259
SLLEMING			
F T	San Joaquin Stockton	64	1046
SLMILL			
Jno	Butte Kimshaw	56	603
SLNIGO			
James	El Dorado Greenwood	58	726
SLO			
Sine	Butte Oro	56	687
SLOA			
---	Mariposa Twp 1	60	662
SLOAIN			
John	Tuolumne Sonora	71	233
SLOAN			
A D	Siskiyou Cottonwood	69	102
Alexn	Del Norte Crescent	58	645
Barny	Sonoma Vallejo	69	630
Chas*	Trinity Weaverville	70	1077
Clara	Yuba Marysville	72	910
Elizabeth	Santa Cruz Soguel	66	589
H J	Sacramento Sutter	63	308
H T	Sacramento Sutter	63	307
Henry	Sierra Pine Grove	66	827
Hugh	Del Norte Crescent	58	633
Hugh	Del Norte Crescent	58	634
I C	Tuolumne Twp 2	71	377
J	Siskiyou Klamath	69	89
J A	Trinity Mouth Ca	70	1017
J R	Sacramento Dry Crk	63	373
J T	Amador Twp 1	55	504
Jacob	Sonoma Sonoma	69	636
James	Tuolumne Twp 1	71	251
James	Tuolumne Columbia	71	298
James*	Shasta Shasta	66	668
Jas	Sacramento San Joaquin	63	357
John	San Joaquin Stockton	64	1033
John S	San Francisco San Francisco 2	67	557
M G*	Butte Chico	56	557
M M	Siskiyou Yreka	69	191
Mathew C	Contra Costa Twp 3	57	604
N M	Siskiyou Scott Va	69	37
Newton A	Contra Costa Twp 2	57	565
Patrick	San Joaquin Tulare	64	869
Patrick	Yolo Washington	72	604
Peter	Del Norte Crescent	58	660
Robert	Calaveras Twp 9	57	353
Robert	Calaveras Twp 8	57	89
Robt	Tuolumne Twp 2	71	313
S H	Sacramento Cosumnes	63	385
T	Nevada Grass Valley	61	158
T	Yolo Washington	72	599
T J	Placer Dutch Fl	62	709
Thomas	Mendocino Round Va	60	879
Thomas	Tuolumne Columbia	71	298
W	Nevada Eureka	61	357
W N	El Dorado Diamond	58	804
Wm R	San Francisco San Francisco 10	67	257
Wm R	Tuolumne Big Oak	71	133
SLOANAKER			
Isaac	San Francisco San Francisco 7	68	1325
SLOAND			
John*	Tuolumne Twp 1	71	233
SLOANE			
David	Tulara Twp 2	71	27
Israel	Yolo Washington	72	601
James	Placer Auburn	62	561
Joshua	San Diego San Diego	64	762
SLOANI			
John	San Joaquin Castoria	64	902
SLOANM			
L D	Yolo Washington	72	563
SLOANS			
John*	Tuolumne Twp 1	71	233
SLOAT			
C A	El Dorado Casumnes	58	1175
Lewis*	El Dorado Kelsey	58	1152
M C	Sacramento San Joaquin	63	357
W	Tehama Lassen	70	884
SLOATE			
E D	Sierra Downieville	66	959
SLOCAM			
W*	Santa Cruz Santa Cruz	66	618
SLOCANE			
M	Santa Cruz Santa Cruz	66	618
SLOCINY			
H L	Nevada Grass Valley	61	155
SLOCIUN			
William	Santa Cruz Santa Cruz	66	617
SLOCK			
Charles*	Monterey Pajaro	60	1021
SLOCKBOWER			
Robert	Placer Forest H	62	794
SLOCOM			
Geo	Klamath Trinidad	59	221
R H	San Francisco San Francisco 6	67	440
SLOCOMB			
James	San Francisco San Francisco 6	67	414
R W	San Francisco San Francisco 6	67	414
Wm	Los Angeles Tejon	59	527
SLOCUM			
A S	Tuolumne Sonora	71	480
C C	Nevada Rough &	61	434
C M	Sacramento Ward 4	63	612
Geo S	Amador Twp 3	55	376

California 1860 Census Index

Name	County Locale	M653 Roll Page
SLOCUM		
H	Nevada Grass Valley	61 220
H	Nevada Eureka	61 368
J C	Tuolumne Twp 1	71 253
J D	Yolo Washington	72 563
J M	Butte Ophir	56 757
James	Plumas Quincy	62 954
John	Tuolumne Jamestown	71 450
S S	Tuolumne Twp 1	71 480
W	Nevada Eureka	61 368
W	Santa Cruz Santa Cruz	66 618
William	Santa Cruz Santa Cruz	66 617
SLOCUMB		
A B	Nevada Grass Valley	61 149
Asa	Napa Clear Lake	61 124
H G	Nevada Nevada	61 248
H L*	Nevada Grass Valley	61 155
SLOCUMS		
H L*	Nevada Grass Valley	61 155
SLOCUMT		
A B	Nevada Grass Valley	61 149
SLOE		
John	El Dorado Kelsey	581127
SLOEUM		
J M*	Butte Ophir	56 757
L*	Santa Clara Santa Clara	65 509
SLOIE		
Charles*	Siskiyou Yreka	69 140
SLOM		
---*	El Dorado Georgetown	58 701
SLOMAN		
W	Nevada Nevada	61 317
SLOMON		
Levi	San Diego Colorado	64 809
SLON		
---	Calaveras Twp 8	57 60
SLOND		
Wm	Sonoma Petaluma	69 543
SLONE		
C A*	Alameda Oakland	55 71
John	San Francisco San Francisco 4	681226
Wm	Tehama Lassen	70 869
SLONER		
William	Yuba Marysville	72 969
SLONEY		
R	Shasta Millvill	66 752
SLONIKER		
Francis	Siskiyou Yreka	69 144
Lou*	Tuolumne Twp 3	71 455
SLONIKOR		
Francis	Siskiyou Yreka	69 144
SLONN		
Elizabeth	Santa Cruz Soguel	66 589
SLONNE		
Israel	Yolo Washington	72 601
SLONSSEN		
C	Yolo Washington	72 562
SLOOMAN		
Andrew J	Yuba Linda Twp	72 984
SLOOP		
---*	Calaveras Twp 8	57 83
SLOOT		
---	Del Norte Crescent	58 640
SLOP		
Ferd A	Plumas Meadow Valley	62 912
SLOPER		
A	Sacramento San Joaquin	63 359
C	Sacramento Sutter	63 306
Flavilla	Trinity Weaverville	701078
William	Shasta Millvill	66 738
SLOPETUCK		
A	San Joaquin Stockton	641097
SLOPON		
S B	Tehama Tehama	70 950
SLOPPY		
William*	San Mateo Twp 1	65 65
SLORERICH		
M	Nevada Nevada	61 243
SLORN		
H*	Nevada Nevada	61 260
John	Yolo Slate Ra	72 688
John	Yuba Slate Ro	72 688
SLORSON		
Wm E*	Butte Wyandotte	56 657
SLORYH		
Jno*	Sacramento Natonia	63 281
SLOSS		
Gordon E	Calaveras Twp 5	57 189
Gorton E	Calaveras Twp 5	57 189
Henry*	Sacramento Cosummes	63 395
SLOSSEN		
Emmet*	Yuba Marysville	72 977
J W	Butte Wyandotte	56 660
SLOSSON		
J W	Butte Wyandotte	56 660
SLOTEN		
Samuel*	Yuba Marysville	72 866

Name	County Locale	M653 Roll Page
SLOTHER		
L	El Dorado Placerville	58 823
SLOTT		
Fred	Placer Todds Va	62 785
SLOTTERY		
Dennis	Yuba Marysville	72 961
SLOTTING		
Owens	Yuba Marysville	72 961
SLOUD		
John	Nevada Eureka	61 344
SLOUGH		
H	Tuolumne Twp 4	71 145
Jno*	Sacramento Natonia	63 281
SLOUGHERTY		
Wm	Yuba New York	72 734
SLOUGHTER		
J	Tehama Lassen	70 867
SLOUGHTOR		
William	Fresno Twp 2	59 4
SLOUIKER		
Lou	Tuolumne Jamestown	71 455
SLOVEN		
Henry	Sacramento Dry Crk	63 370
SLOVER		
Jas	Butte Cascade	56 701
SLOW		
---	Mariposa Twp 3	60 553
M	San Mateo Twp 3	65 88
Sing	Yuba Long Bar	72 770
SLOWEL		
E	Amador Twp 3	55 381
SLOWEY		
James	Tuolumne Chinese	71 501
SLOWMAN		
Andrew	Yuba Suida	72 982
SLOZSON		
Wm E*	Butte Wyandotte	56 657
SLRELL		
Boney*	Mariposa Twp 3	60 593
SLRIELLO		
M	Merced Twp 1	60 905
SLTEN		
Richard*	Mariposa Coulterville	60 685
SLU		
---	Placer Illinois	62 742
Ah	Butte Oregon	56 638
Hop*	Sacramento Granite	63 243
SLUB		
Richard D*	Yuba Marysville	72 915
SLUCK		
A L	Nevada Rough &	61 418
Pembroke S*	Yuba Rose Bar	72 796
SLUDARUS		
John*	Sacramento Brighton	63 195
SLUDE		
William D	Siskiyou Yreka	69 169
SLUDER		
William D*	Siskiyou Yreka	69 169
SLUDGE		
Alexr*	Sacramento Mississipi	63 187
SLUES		
---	El Dorado Georgetown	58 701
Levi	Sonoma Russian	69 429
SLUGHLIN		
John O	Sierra La Porte	66 766
SLUHER		
---	Mendocino Big Rock	60 875
SLUHUN		
John	Placer Christia	62 736
SLUICMAN		
Jno	Sacramento Ward 1	63 31
SLUICMARR		
Jno	Sacramento Ward 1	63 31
SLULEVILL		
H*	Nevada Bloomfield	61 509
SLUM		
---	El Dorado Georgetown	58 686
SLUMBO		
---	Sacramento Cosummes	63 406
SLUMP		
S P	Nevada Rough &	61 414
SLUN		
---	Shasta Horsetown	66 711
---*	Butte Ophir	56 816
---*	El Dorado Georgetown	58 701
SLUNDLESHANK		
---	Tulara Keyesville	71 56
SLUNG		
---	Calaveras Twp 8	57 69
Peter	Sierra Twp 7	66 878
SLUNGER		
Clark	Sacramento Granite	63 230
SLUNKER		
Chas	Nevada Little Y	61 535
SLUPER		
Coryden*	Napa Clear Lake	61 132

Name	County Locale	M653 Roll Page
SLUPER		
Morris*	Napa Clear Lake	61 132
W O	Tuolumne Twp 2	71 326
SLUPIR		
Corydin	Napa Clear Lake	61 132
SLURE		
---	Sierra Twp 5	66 934
SLUREY		
J*	Nevada Grass Valley	61 226
SLURN		
John*	Tehama Red Bluff	70 905
SLURR		
---	El Dorado Georgetown	58 686
SLURTEVANT		
A*	San Francisco San Francisco 5	67 554
SLURTEVAROT		
A*	San Francisco San Francisco 5	67 554
SLUSEL		
Paul	Sonoma Santa Rosa	69 405
SLUSEON		
Frank*	Tuolumne Twp 1	71 253
SLUSEY		
David*	Sacramento Ward 1	63 93
SLUSHER		
D	Butte Ophir	56 778
Jacob	Contra Costa Twp 2	57 555
S	Nevada Nevada T	61 325
SLUSSER		
John	Sonoma Russian	69 429
Levi	Sonoma Russian	69 429
SLUSTER		
Shamhow	Placer Dutch Fl	62 722
SLUTE		
Wendell*	Placer Michigan	62 847
SLUTER		
A*	San Francisco San Francisco 5	67 534
Wm*	Napa Clear Lake	61 135
SLUTEVILL		
H*	Nevada Bloomfield	61 509
SLUTIR		
Wm	Napa Clear Lake	61 135
SLUTRU		
Henri*	Placer Dutch Fl	62 724
SLVARTZ		
August*	Alameda Brooklyn	55 150
SLVEYN		
Jno	Sacramento Natonia	63 281
SLY		
Abram	Yuba Bear Rvr	721007
James	Yuba Linda Twp	72 984
Louis	San Francisco San Francisco 7	681411
SLYE		
Nathan J	Sierra Whiskey	66 844
SLYEBENEZAR		
Vannon	San Joaquin O'Neal	641001
SLYER		
Charles	Siskiyou Yreka	69 194
SLYGER		
S	Butte Bidwell	56 716
SLYMOUR		
J	San Francisco San Francisco 3	67 43
SLYNN		
Mary E	Monterey Monterey	60 953
SLYNTZE		
Samuel	Siskiyou Yreka	69 130
SLYOR		
Charles*	Siskiyou Yreka	69 194
SM		
---	Calaveras Twp 5	57 219
SMACH		
George*	Tuolumne Big Oak	71 144
SMACK		
George	Tuolumne Twp 4	71 144
S	Nevada Grass Valley	61 187
SMACKENEMU		
---	Tulara Twp 2	71 35
SMADER		
Robert	Alameda Brooklyn	55 95
SMAIL		
R*	San Francisco San Francisco 5	67 547
SMAILE		
Geo	Butte Bidwell	56 713
SMAILS		
B B	Santa Clara Redwood	65 455
SMAIT		
H*	Nevada Grass Valley	61 193
J*	Nevada Grass Valley	61 172
P	Nevada Grass Valley	61 148
SMALEY		
David	Alameda Brooklyn	55 120
SMALL		
A G	Sierra Twp 5	66 920
Barlow	Santa Clara San Jose	65 360
Barton	Colusa Monroeville	57 445
C J	Mendocino Calpella	60 817
Casapein	El Dorado Greenwood	58 717

California 1860 Census Index

Name	County Locale	M653 Roll	Page
SMALL			
Catharine	San Francisco San Francisco	12	377
			67
Catherine	Santa Clara Fremont	65	428
Charles	Shasta French G	66	719
Daniel	Contra Costa Twp 2	57	551
Delwell	El Dorado Georgetown	58	694
E G	Sacramento Brighton	63	203
Frank	Alameda Oakland	55	48
George	Yuba Bear Rvr	72	1001
H	Butte Chico	56	548
H F	Nevada Eureka	61	379
H T	Nevada Eureka	61	379
J	Alameda Brooklyn	55	186
J	San Francisco San Francisco	5 67	536
J H	Yolo Cache Crk	72	619
J K	Calaveras Twp 9	57	408
J M	Yolo Cache	72	619
Jacob	Calaveras Twp 7	57	42
Jacob	Sierra St Louis	66	807
James	El Dorado Kelsey	58	1150
James	Shasta Millvill	66	739
John	San Joaquin Stockton	64	1073
John	San Mateo Twp 1	65	48
John	Yuba Long Bar	72	770
John G	Plumas Quincy	62	957
Joseph	Colusa Colusi	57	422
Joseph	El Dorado Mud Springs	58	1000
Joseph	Sierra Twp 7	66	912
Josiah	Sierra Twp 5	66	938
L W	Calaveras Twp 9	57	408
M A	Sacramento Cosumnes	63	410
N	El Dorado Georgetown	58	687
Nathan	Alameda Brooklyn	55	135
R H	San Mateo Twp 3	65	109
Robert	Tuolumne Big Oak	71	134
Robt	Placer Folsom	62	641
S H	Shasta Millvill	66	745
Thos	Trinity E Weaver	70	1060
William E	Los Angeles Los Angeles	59	373
Wm	Calaveras Twp 9	57	381
Wm	Santa Clara San Jose	65	359
Wm	Santa Clara San Jose	65	386
Wm	Sonoma Vallejo	69	609
SMALLEY			
Elijah	Calaveras Twp 7	57	26
G M	Calaveras Twp 7	57	18
H	Sacramento Brighton	63	208
James	Mendocino Anderson	60	868
P L	Nevada Nevada	61	286
Wm L	Sacramento Sutter	63	307
Wm L	Sacramento Sutter	63	308
SMALLFIELD			
A	Amador Twp 2	55	309
SMALLFRAGE			
Saml*	Del Norte Klamath	58	654
SMALLFRAZE			
Saml*	Del Norte Klamath	58	654
SMALLHAGE			
Saml*	Del Norte Klamath	58	654
SMALLING			
Isaac	San Joaquin Castoria	64	878
SMALLWOD			
P B	Mariposa Twp 1	60	623
SMALLWOOD			
Amos	Sierra Twp 5	66	923
J C	El Dorado Georgetown	58	676
J P	El Dorado Georgetown	58	676
James	El Dorado Georgetown	58	686
Joseph	El Dorado Coloma	58	1069
Martin	Sierra Downieville	66	1012
P B	Mariposa Twp 1	60	623
Townsend	Klamath Trinidad	59	220
William	Calaveras Twp 5	57	174
SMALTON			
James	Sacramento Granite	63	263
SMAN			
August*	Amador Twp 1	55	497
SMART			
Charles H	San Joaquin Oneal	64	938
Danl G	Calaveras Twp 5	57	183
H*	Nevada Grass Valley	61	193
Henry	Calaveras Twp 7	57	43
J	Nevada Grass Valley	61	172
J	Tuolumne Twp 4	71	166
J B	Nevada Eureka	61	360
J W	Placer Folsom	62	641
James	Contra Costa Twp 2	57	564
James	Sacramento Ward 1	63	48
Jas	Sacramento Natonia	63	281
Jas B	Sacramento Franklin	63	311
Jesse	Sacramento Ward 3	63	484
Jno	Butte Hamilton	56	516
John	Calaveras Twp 7	57	2
John	Santa Clara Gilroy	65	248
John	Sierra Twp 7	66	865
SMART			
John	Yuba Bear Rvr	72	1005
John H	Contra Costa Twp 3	57	617
Joseph	Tuolumne Twp 2	71	298
L	Sacramento Granite	63	237
L A	Shasta Cottonwood	66	736
P	Nevada Grass Valley	61	148
P	Nevada Grass Valley	61	188
Richard	Sierra Pine Grove	66	823
S	Mariposa Twp 3	60	621
Selor	Santa Clara San Jose	65	349
Tho J	Siskiyou Scott Va	69	33
Thos	Sacramento Brighton	63	194
Thos	Sacramento Sutter	63	299
W S	Tuolumne Jacksonville	71	166
William	Los Angeles Los Angeles	59	364
William F	San Joaquin Elkhorn	64	958
Winnie	Los Angeles Los Angeles	59	364
Wm H	Sacramento Franklin	63	311
SMARTICA			
D	San Francisco San Francisco	1 68	810
SMARTIEA			
D*	San Francisco San Francisco	1 68	810
SMARTON			
John	Butte Wyandotte	56	670
SMARTS			
P	Napa Hot Springs	61	26
SMARTYE			
B	Amador Twp 1	55	500
SMASEY			
L T*	Sacramento Ward 1	63	141
S T*	Sacramento Ward 1	63	141
SMATEN			
E E	Butte Bidwell	56	726
SMATON			
E E	Butte Bidwell	56	726
SMATY			
A	El Dorado Greenwood	58	725
SMATYLN			
Godfrey*	Placer Iona Hills	62	893
SMAWLEY			
J H	Nevada Nevada	61	322
SMBERS			
Grief*	San Bernardino San Bernadino	64	635
SMCKINZIE			
John	Sierra Pine Grove	66	828
SMDEN			
George	Shasta Shasta	66	758
SMEAD			
H D	Butte Ophir	56	761
SMEARENGIN			
B*	Del Norte Happy Ca	58	662
SMEATHMAN			
Henry	Sonoma Petaluma	69	602
SMEDDLEY			
---	Sierra Pine Grove	66	824
Jacob	Sierra Pine Grove	66	824
SMEDES			
R M	Butte Oregon	56	617
SMEDGER			
---	San Francisco San Francisco	3 67	46
SMEDGOR			
---	San Francisco San Francisco	3 67	46
SMEDLEY			
Tho	Siskiyou Scott Va	69	59
William	Contra Costa Twp 1	57	535
SMEDT			
Charles W	Yuba Rose Bar	72	819
SMEE			
R R	Shasta Shasta	66	663
SMEED			
Geo	El Dorado Coloma	58	1073
John W	Yuba Parks Ba	72	780
S J	El Dorado Georgetown	58	686
SMEFFER			
Charles	El Dorado Coloma	58	1069
SMEGDIER			
Thos*	El Dorado Georgetown	58	694
SMELL			
Jno A	Butte Hamilton	56	521
SMELSER			
Isaiah	Siskiyou Yreka	69	131
SMERGA			
Mural	Sierra La Porte	66	790
SMERGE			
John*	Santa Cruz Pajaro	66	568
SMETH			
James*	Yuba Bear Rvr	72	1013
SMETIAS			
Duncan*	Stanislaus Emory	70	746
SMETTE			
Henry*	Yuba Bear Rvr	72	1009
James*	Yuba Bear Rvr	72	1009
SMEYER			
C	Siskiyou Scott Ri	69	78
SMFITH			
Charlotte	Solano Benecia	69	307
SMFITH			
John	Solano Suisan	69	222
John	Solano Vallejo	69	248
SMGHRY			
Jesse	Siskiyou Scott Va	69	55
SMICH			
Peter*	Plumas Meadow Valley	62	912
SMIDDY			
John*	Sacramento Ward 1	63	123
SMIDS			
Geo	San Francisco San Francisco	1 68	825
SMIDT			
Adam	Placer Rattle Snake	62	598
Antonio	Tuolumne Jamestown	71	452
Charles	Tuolumne Jamestown	71	469
Emma	San Francisco San Francisco	7 68	1339
G*	Sacramento Alabama	63	412
SMIESKELTE			
Gates*	Nevada Bridgeport	61	480
SMIESKETTE			
Gates*	Nevada Bridgeport	61	480
Gortes*	Nevada Bridgeport	61	480
SMIESKITTI			
Gates*	Nevada Bridgeport	61	480
SMIFFINS			
L S*	Mendocino Ukiah	60	805
SMIFFIT			
John*	El Dorado Placerville	58	922
SMIFTON			
	Placer Dutch Fl	62	731
SMIGLETIN			
M	Siskiyou Scott Va	69	30
SMIGTH			
J C	Tuolumne Twp 4	71	147
SMILER			
Frederick	San Francisco San Francisco	3 67	67
Fredrick*	San Francisco San Francisco	3 67	67
SMILEY			
A S	Nevada Grass Valley	61	197
Charles	Placer Michigan	62	817
Edward	El Dorado Mountain	58	1184
Foster	Sierra Twp 5	66	928
G W	San Francisco San Francisco	5 67	511
H	Nevada Grass Valley	61	166
James C	Humbolt Eureka	59	165
Jas	Sacramento Sutter	63	291
Jas	San Francisco San Francisco	2 67	703
John	Placer Iona Hills	62	876
O	Trinity Trinity	70	970
P	Nevada Grass Valley	61	157
P L	Nevada Nevada	61	269
Patrick	Plumas Quincy	62	1002
Saml	Tuolumne Big Oak	71	134
Thomas	Solano Fremont	69	380
W	Siskiyou Scott Va	69	24
W P	San Joaquin Stockton	64	1023
SMILLEY			
Nicholas	San Joaquin Elkhorn	64	956
SMILLINGER			
F	Sacramento American	63	171
SMILSER			
Isaiah*	Siskiyou Yreka	69	131
SMILT			
Martin*	El Dorado Kelsey	58	1150
SMINEY			
G W*	Butte Ophir	56	766
SMIRGE			
John*	Santa Cruz Pajaro	66	568
SMISH			
Benjamin*	Calaveras Twp 7	57	41
SMIT			
Horatio	Tuolumne Twp 1	71	254
Stephen D	Calaveras Twp 8	57	78
SMITAKER			
S	San Joaquin Stockton	64	1033
SMITH DICKEN			
Henn*	El Dorado Georgetown	58	706
SMITH JNIDER			
M*	Nevada Nevada	61	249
SMITH			
---	Napa Napa	61	79
---	San Mateo Twp 3	65	100
---	Tulara Visalia	71	110
---	Tuolumne Twp 2	71	284
---*	Mariposa Twp 3	60	605
?U?lan	Calaveras Twp 6	57	160
A	Calaveras Twp 9	57	376
A	El Dorado Kelsey	58	1156
A	El Dorado Diamond	58	771
A	El Dorado Placerville	58	889
A	Los Angeles Tejon	59	525
A	Nevada Washington	61	333
A	Sacramento Ward 1	63	31
A	Sacramento Ward 4	63	548
A	San Francisco San Francisco	4 68	1231
A	San Francisco San Francisco	5 67	538

California 1860 Census Index

Name	County Locale	M653 Roll	Page
SMITH			
A	San Francisco San Francisco 1	68	921
A	San Mateo Twp 3	65	94
A	Santa Clara Santa Clara	65	473
A	Shasta Shasta	66	660
A	Sierra La Porte	66	786
A	Sierra Pine Grove	66	827
A A	Butte Oregon	56	617
A A	Nevada Rough &	61	397
A A	Nevada Rough &	61	408
A A	Placer Auburn	62	566
A A	Tehama Lassen	70	877
A B	Los Angeles Azuza	59	274
A B	Placer Todds Va	62	789
A B	Placer Michigan	62	814
A B	Sacramento Ward 4	63	527
A B	San Francisco San Francisco 2	67	605
A B	Santa Clara Santa Clara	65	490
A B	Sierra Eureka	661	045
A C	Mariposa Twp 3	60	616
A C	San Francisco San Francisco 5	67	500
A C	Santa Clara Burnett	65	257
A F	Sacramento Franklin	63	319
A G	San Francisco San Francisco 5	67	521
A H	Nevada Eureka	61	344
A H	Solano Montezuma	69	372
A J	Amador Twp 2	55	265
A J	El Dorado Georgetown	58	695
A J	Napa Napa	61	109
A J	Sacramento Ward 4	63	501
A J	Sacramento Ward 4	63	549
A J	San Francisco San Francisco 1	68	853
A J	San Joaquin Stockton	641	095
A J	Shasta Shasta	66	732
A J	Sierra Twp 7	66	900
A J	Sonoma Armally	69	498
A J	Tuolumne Springfield	71	375
A L	Nevada Bridgeport	61	465
A M	Nevada Eureka	61	370
A M	Sonoma Bodega	69	533
A P	Sacramento Sutter	63	290
A R	Butte Ophir	56	790
A R	Tuolumne Shawsfla	71	383
A W	Napa Napa	61	94
A W	Santa Clara San Jose	65	311
A W	Tehama Lassen	70	879
A*	Nevada Washington	61	333
Aaron	San Francisco San Francisco 9	681	089
Aaron	Yuba Marysville	72	860
Aaron	Yuba Marysville	72	915
Aaron W	Yuba Marysville	72	858
Abba	El Dorado Mud Springs	58	983
Abrahm	Sierra Twp 7	66	883
Abram	San Bernardino Santa Inez	64	136
Abram	San Francisco San Francisco 7	681	417
Acon	Placer Dutch Fl	62	712
Adam	Alameda Oakland	55	67
Adam	Amador Twp 1	55	498
Adam	Placer Iona Hills	62	868
Adam	Yolo Merritt	72	583
Adam	Yuba Marysville	72	885
Addison	Siskiyou Scott Va	69	31
Adonijah	Tulara Visalia	71	99
Adrian*	Calaveras Twp 6	57	160
Alanson	Shasta Cottonwood	66	736
Alanson	Sierra Downieville	66	965
Albert	Sierra Pine Grove	66	826
Albert	Solano Benecia	69	294
Albert	Tehama Red Bluff	70	922
Albert	Yolo Slate Ra	72	697
Albert	Yuba Slate Ro	72	697
Albert B	San Diego San Diego	64	759
Albert H	Sierra Pine Grove	66	826
Albert T	Plumas Quincy	621	000
Alex	San Francisco San Francisco 2	67	687
Alex	Tehama Lassen	70	875
Alexander	Placer Michigan	62	811
Alexander	San Francisco San Francisco 3	67	69
Alexander	Solano Vacaville	69	367
Alexander	Sonoma Russian	69	444
Alexander	Tulara Visalia	71	13
Alexander	Tuolumne Jacksonville	71	516
Alexander W	Monterey Pajaro	601	012
Alexr	San Francisco San Francisco 10	239	
		67	
Alexr	Sierra Downieville	66	960
Alfald	Siskiyou Yreka	69	186
Alfred	Calaveras Twp 5	57	172
Alfred	Calaveras Twp 9	57	367
Alfred	Calaveras Twp 8	57	51
Alfred	Marin Tomales	60	778
Alfred	Plumas Meadow Valley	62	901
Alfred	San Francisco San Francisco 3	67	81
Alfred	Shasta French G	66	714
Alfred	Siskiyou Shasta Rvr	69	112
Alfred	Tuolumne Twp 1	71	190
Alfried	Calaveras Twp 6	57	172
Algerine	San Francisco San Francisco 6	67	441
Algernon	San Francisco San Francisco 8	681	324
Algomon*	San Francisco 8	681	324
Allen	San Francisco		
Allen	Butte Ophir	56	745
Alson S	Butte Chico	56	535
Alvid O	Tuolumne Twp 2	71	298
Alvin	Tuolumne Twp 1	71	265
Amason	Placer Yankee J	62	759
Amlira*	Placer Dutch Fl	62	727
Amos	Placer Michigan	62	824
Amos T	Trinity North Fo	701	024
Andrew	Los Angeles Azuza	59	277
Andrew	Marin Tomales	60	774
Andrew	Nevada Rough &	61	423
Andrew	Placer Yankee J	62	776
Andrew	Placer Forest H	62	797
Andrew	Placer Michigan	62	821
Andrew	Placer Michigan	62	843
Andrew	Sacramento Granite	63	266
Andrew	San Francisco San Francisco 9	681	065
Andrew	San Francisco San Francisco 10	227	
		67	
Andrew	San Francisco San Francisco 3	67	56
Andrew	San Francisco San Francisco 3	67	75
Andrew	Sierra Poker Flats	66	839
Andrew	Sierra Twp 7	66	882
Andrew	Sierra Twp 5	66	939
Andrew	Sonoma Bodega	69	524
Andrew	Yolo No E Twp	72	669
Andrew J	Contra Costa Twp 2	57	560
Andrew V	San Francisco San Francisco 3	67	56
Andw	Sonoma Sonoma	69	659
Andy	Placer Michigan	62	837
Angel	San Diego San Diego	64	759
Angus B	Alameda Brooklyn	55	136
Ann	Placer Lisbon	62	735
Ann	San Francisco San Francisco 4	681	143
Ann	San Francisco San Francisco 7	681	407
Ann	San Francisco San Francisco 6	67	450
Ann	Shasta Shasta	66	657
Ann T	Sonoma Russian	69	431
Anna	Santa Clara Santa Clara	65	479
Anna E	Yuba Marysville	72	957
Annie	Sacramento Ward 4	63	601
Annie	San Mateo Twp 1	65	56
Annie E	Alameda Oakland	55	2
Anson	Monterey Monterey	60	957
Anthony	El Dorado Mud Springs	58	983
Antoine	Calaveras Twp 5	57	200
Antone	Amador Twp 1	55	480
Antone	El Dorado Salmon Falls	581	049
Antone	Yolo Merritt	72	583
Antony	Yuba Rose Bar	72	805
Arabella	Santa Cruz Soguel	66	579
Arrabella	Santa Cruz Soguel	66	579
Arthur	Calaveras Twp 9	57	377
Artron	Calaveras Twp 9	57	377
Asa	Tuolumne Twp 2	71	299
Aug	Nevada Bridgeport	61	448
August	Amador Twp 5	55	357
August	Sierra Downieville	66	956
Augustus	San Francisco San Francisco 1	68	915
Austin	Monterey Alisal	601	033
Austin	Tuolumne Columbia	71	334
Aziah	Yuba Marysville	72	976
B	Butte Hamilton	56	530
B	El Dorado White Oaks	581	002
B	El Dorado Union	581	087
B	Nevada Grass Valley	61	195
B	San Francisco San Francisco 5	67	500
B	San Francisco San Francisco 5	67	547
B	Trinity Redding	70	985
B A	Tuolumne Twp 1	71	194
B D	Klamath Liberty	59	238
B F	Butte Hamilton	56	523
B F	Siskiyou Scott Va	69	51
B F	Tuolumne Shawsfla	71	420
B G	Siskiyou Cottonwoood	69	105
B L	Tuolumne Twp 1	71	246
B T	Alameda Hamilton	55	523
B T	Siskiyou Scott Va	69	51
B T	Tuolumne Twp 2	71	342
Banj F	Placer Rattle Snake	62	630
Barbara	San Francisco San Francisco 11	120	
		67	
Barney	Calaveras Twp 9	57	372
Barney	El Dorado White Oaks	581	014
Barnhart	El Dorado White Oaks	581	023
Baxter	San Joaquin Elkhorn	64	991
Bay	Sierra Twp 7	66	878
Ben	Sacramento Ward 4	63	517
Benj	Sacramento Ward 3	63	433
Benj	Sierra Twp 7	66	878
Benj C	Plumas Quincy	62	994
Benj J	Tuolumne Twp 1	71	277
Benjamin	Humbolt Mattole	59	126
Benjamin	Monterey Monterey	60	956
Benjamin*	Calaveras Twp 7	57	41
Bennett	Tehama Lassen	70	868
Bernard	Nevada Bridgeport	61	481
Bernard	San Francisco San Francisco 5	67	546
Bernard	Sierra La Porte	66	790
Betty	Sutter Sutter	70	817
Bridget	Marin Cortemad	60	757
Byard	Sierra Twp 7	66	866
C	Amador Twp 1	55	509
C	Calaveras Twp 7	57	38
C	Calaveras Twp 8	57	54
C	El Dorado Diamond	58	791
C	El Dorado Placerville	58	846
C	El Dorado Placerville	58	891
C	Nevada Grass Valley	61	161
C	Nevada Grass Valley	61	181
C	Nevada Nevada	61	291
C	Nevada Nevada	61	313
C	Nevada Washington	61	333
C	Sacramento Ward 1	63	149
C	Sacramento Lee	63	216
C	San Francisco San Francisco 5	67	520
C	San Francisco San Francisco 5	67	535
C	San Francisco San Francisco 5	67	549
C	San Francisco San Francisco 2	67	639
C	San Francisco San Francisco 1	68	921
C	Santa Clara Burnett	65	260
C	Siskiyou Callahan	69	19
C	Siskiyou Scott Ri	69	71
C	Sutter Yuba	70	775
C	Tehama Lassen	70	881
C A	Placer Illinois	62	703
C B	Calaveras Twp 9	57	407
C Barr	Siskiyou Shasta Rvr	69	116
C C	Butte Ophir	56	770
C C	Nevada Grass Valley	61	201
C C	Nevada Nevada	61	251
C C	Sonoma Healdsbu	69	471
C D	Siskiyou Klamath	69	87
C F	Del Norte Crescent	58	641
C F	Nevada Grass Valley	61	143
C F	San Francisco San Francisco 5	67	526
C H	Placer Forest H	62	802
C H	San Francisco San Francisco 1	68	837
C J	Mariposa Twp 1	60	670
C J	Nevada Grass Valley	61	218
C J	San Francisco San Francisco 5	67	483
C J	San Francisco San Francisco 5	67	547
C L	Mariposa Twp 3	60	602
C L	Nevada Bridgeport	61	474
C L	San Francisco San Francisco 6	67	474
C M	Marin Tomales	60	726
C M	Sacramento Ward 4	63	547
C M	Tuolumne Shawsfla	71	384
C N	Siskiyou Scott Ri	69	81
C P	Amador Twp 1	55	472
C S	Sacramento Cosumnes	63	382
C W	Calaveras Twp 9	57	366
C W	Mariposa Twp 1	60	643
C W	Mariposa Coulterville	60	701
C W	Sacramento Ward 1	63	43
C W	San Francisco San Francisco 3	67	69
C W	Tuolumne Twp 1	71	480
Cal	Sacramento Ward 3	63	470
Caleb	El Dorado Georgetown	58	708
Calim	Butte Ophir	56	752
Calirn*	Butte Ophir	56	752
Calvin	Amador Twp 6	55	438
Calvin	Sacramento Ward 3	63	469
Calvin	Siskiyou Yreka	69	131
Carl A	Yuba Marysville	72	862
Carl G	Alameda Brooklyn	55	126
Carl O	Tuolumne Twp 5	71	494
Carl W	Tuolumne Chinese	71	494
Caroline	Alameda Oakland	55	23
Caroline	Sacramento Ward 3	63	449
Caroline	Sacramento Ward 4	63	495
Caroline	San Francisco San Francisco 9	681	105
Caroline	San Francisco San Francisco 4	681	142
Caroline	Santa Clara Santa Clara	65	508
Caroline	Tehama Red Bluff	70	916
Carrey J	Calaveras Twp 9	57	348
Carrie	Alameda Oakland	55	59
Cas	El Dorado Greenwood	58	716
Casper	Calaveras Twp 6	57	175
Casper	Contra Costa Twp 3	57	598
Cateman D	Sonoma Sonoma	69	655
Cath E	Sacramento Ward 3	63	489
Catharine	San Francisco San Francisco 8	681	267
Celia P	San Francisco San Francisco 7	681	426
Cha W	San Francisco San Francisco 2	67	561

California 1860 Census Index

Name	County Locale	M653 Roll Page
SMITH		
Chals	El Dorado Georgetown	58 683
Charles	Amador Twp 4	55 244
Charles	Calaveras Twp 6	57 131
Charles	Calaveras Twp 4	57 311
Charles	Calaveras Twp 8	57 90
Charles	Contra Costa Twp 3	57 596
Charles	El Dorado Salmon Hills	581052
Charles	El Dorado Kelsey	581145
Charles	Marin Cortemad	60 756
Charles	Marin Cortemad	60 784
Charles	Marin Cortemad	60 786
Charles	Marin Cortemad	60 790
Charles	Mariposa Coulterville	60 699
Charles	Monterey San Juan	60 976
Charles	Placer Forest H	62 767
Charles	Placer Iona Hills	62 865
Charles	Plumas Quincy	62 960
Charles	Plumas Quincy	62 980
Charles	Sacramento Ward 1	63 48
Charles	San Diego Agua Caliente	64 846
Charles	San Francisco San Francisco 4	681163
Charles	San Francisco San Francisco 7	681444
Charles	San Francisco San Francisco 3	67 4
Charles	San Francisco San Francisco 3	67 70
Charles	San Joaquin O'Neal	641004
Charles	San Joaquin Douglass	64 926
Charles	San Joaquin Elliott	64 941
Charles	San Joaquin Elkhorn	64 978
Charles	San Mateo Twp 3	65 79
Charles	Santa Clara Gilroy	65 242
Charles	Sierra La Porte	66 789
Charles	Siskiyou Scott Va	69 39
Charles	Solano Green Valley	69 241
Charles	Solano Benecia	69 313
Charles	Solano Fremont	69 381
Charles	Solano Fremont	69 385
Charles	Sutter Bear Rvr	70 820
Charles	Tulara Visalia	71 106
Charles	Tuolumne Columbia	71 339
Charles	Tuolumne Shawsfla	71 388
Charles	Tuolumne Jamestown	71 451
Charles	Yolo Merritt	72 581
Charles	Yuba Parks Ba	72 780
Charles	Yuba Fosters	72 837
Charles G	Contra Costa Twp 2	57 561
Charles H	Sierra Whiskey	66 843
Charles J	Tuolumne Big Oak	71 178
Charles M	Solano Suisan	69 205
Charles P	Yuba Marysville	72 942
Charles R	Sierra Downieville	661006
Charles S	Sonoma Russian	69 431
Charles W	San Francisco 4 (San Francisco)	681152
Charles W	San Francisco 7 (San Francisco)	681427
Charlotte	Calaveras Twp 4	57 305
Charlotte	Solano Benecia	69 307
Charlotte E	San Francisco 2 (San Francisco)	67 562
Charly	Tuolumne Twp 3	71 451
Chas	Amador Twp 5	55 345
Chas	Butte Kimshaw	56 594
Chas	Butte Oregon	56 612
Chas	Calaveras Twp 9	57 379
Chas	El Dorado Georgetown	58 694
Chas	El Dorado Greenwood	58 720
Chas	El Dorado Greenwood	58 724
Chas	Nevada Red Dog	61 548
Chas	Placer Horseshoe	62 650
Chas	Sacramento San Joaquin	63 349
Chas	Sacramento Cosummes	63 382
Chas	Sacramento Ward 3	63 437
Chas	Sacramento Ward 3	63 470
Chas	Sacramento Ward 4	63 526
Chas	San Bernardino San Salvador	64 654
Chas	San Francisco San Francisco 9	681034
Chas	San Francisco San Francisco 9	681049
Chas	San Francisco San Francisco 9	681065
Chas	San Francisco San Francisco 12	387 67
Chas	San Francisco San Francisco 1	68 869
Chas	San Francisco San Francisco 1	68 873
Chas	San Francisco San Francisco 1	68 892
Chas	San Francisco San Francisco 1	68 906
Chas	San Francisco San Francisco 1	68 907
Chas	San Francisco San Francisco 1	68 909
Chas	San Francisco San Francisco 1	68 920
Chas	San Francisco San Francisco 9	68 960
Chas	San Francisco San Francisco 9	68 968
Chas	Santa Clara San Jose	65 378
Chas	Santa Clara Alviso	65 410
Chas	Santa Clara Fremont	65 433
Chas	Santa Clara Fremont	65 434
Chas	Santa Cruz Santa Cruz	66 631
Chas	Santa Cruz Pescadero	66 647

Name	County Locale	M653 Roll Page
SMITH		
Chas	Sonoma Petaluma	69 563
Chas	Trinity Mouth Ca	701013
Chas	Tuolumne Big Oak	71 137
Chas A	Sonoma Petaluma	69 567
Chas E	Amador Twp 1	55 475
Chas E	Plumas Quincy	62 996
Chas H	El Dorado Big Bar	58 739
Chas M	Sacramento Ward 3	63 482
Chas W	San Francisco San Francisco 2	67 561
Chats*	El Dorado Georgetown	58 683
Chauls	Placer Forest H	62 769
Chauncey	Sacramento Ward 4	63 520
Chin*	El Dorado Mud Springs	58 979
Chots	El Dorado Georgetown	58 683
Chris H	San Francisco San Francisco 10	210 67
Chrisor H	San Francisco San Francisco 10	210
Christian	Sacramento Ward 3	63 487
Christopher	Alameda Oakland	55 74
Christopher	Sonoma Armally	69 511
Christopher C	Tuolumne Big Oak	71 133
Clara	Contra Costa Twp 1	57 511
Clark	Stanislaus Emory	70 751
Clemens	Del Norte Klamath	58 654
Columbus	Santa Cruz Pajaro	66 527
Connall	Calaveras Twp 9	57 370
Conrad	Alameda Brooklyn	55 90
Cooper	El Dorado Cold Spring	581100
Cornelias	Calaveras Twp 9	57 390
Cornelius	San Francisco San Francisco 1	68 849
Cornelius	Yuba Rose Bar	72 818
Cornelius*	San Francisco 3 (San Francisco)	67 77
Cornell	Calaveras Twp 9	57 370
Cornelus	San Francisco San Francisco 3	67 77
Cornleus	Yuba Rose Bar	72 818
Corrall	Calaveras Twp 9	57 370
Cristopher	Plumas Quincy	62 937
Crowson	Calaveras Twp 7	57 21
Cyrus	El Dorado Salmon Falls	581040
Cyrus	Siskiyou Shasta Rvr	69 111
Cyrus	Stanislaus Empire	70 735
Cyrus M	San Joaquin Elkhorn	64 962
Cyrus M	San Joaquin Elkhorn	64 999
D	Nevada Nevada	61 268
D B	Sacramento Natonia	63 286
D C	Butte Kimshaw	56 583
D C	Shasta Horsetown	66 695
D E	Mariposa Twp 1	60 642
D L	Marin S Antoni	60 705
D N	San Bernardino San Bernadino	64 620
D S	El Dorado Placerville	58 875
D T	Sierra Twp 7	66 893
D T	Tehama Cottonwoood	70 902
D W	Merced Twp 1	60 903
D W	San Francisco San Francisco 6	67 461
D W	Tuolumne Sonora	71 233
Dan	Amador Twp 2	55 273
Dan	El Dorado Greenwood	58 708
Daniel	Alameda Oakland	55 4
Daniel	Contra Costa Twp 2	57 555
Daniel	Marin S Antoni	60 709
Daniel	Tuolumne Green Springs	71 527
Daniel	Tuolumne Twp 6	71 538
Daniel S	Yuba Marysville	72 878
Danl	Yolo Merritt	72 578
Danl F	Calaveras Twp 4	57 316
David	Butte Oregon	56 639
David	El Dorado Coloma	581116
David	El Dorado Georgetown	58 685
David	Klamath Liberty	59 240
David	Nevada Rough &	61 413
David	Placer Lisbon	62 735
David	San Joaquin Oneal	64 932
David	Tuolumne Shawsfla	71 397
David	Tuolumne Jamestown	71 455
David A	Contra Costa Twp 2	57 569
David H	Mendocino Ukiah	60 793
David K	Contra Costa Twp 1	57 485
David P	Contra Costa Twp 2	57 562
David W	Mendocino Ukiah	60 793
David W	San Francisco San Francisco 4	681109
Delia	San Francisco San Francisco 12	364 67
Delia	Tuolumne Sonora	71 209
Done*	Butte Kimshaw	56 599
Dorman	El Dorado Coloma	581104
Dow*	Butte Kimshaw	56 599
Dulcinea A	Sonoma Healdsbu	69 471
Dulcinea H	Sonoma Healdsbu	69 471
E	Butte Oro	56 683
E	Calaveras Twp 9	57 414
E	El Dorado Mud Springs	58 999
E	Nevada Grass Valley	61 155

Name	County Locale	M653 Roll Page
SMITH		
E	Nevada Nevada	61 259
E	Nevada Eureka	61 370
E	Nevada Eureka	61 377
E	Santa Clara Santa Clara	65 471
E	Shasta French G	66 717
E	Shasta Millvill	66 752
E	Siskiyou Callahan	69 18
E	Sutter Butte	70 794
E	Tehama Red Bluff	70 916
E	Trinity Bates	70 967
E A	Amador Twp 3	55 393
E A	Sacramento Ward 3	63 431
E A	San Francisco San Francisco 9	68 939
E B	Sierra Twp 7	66 911
E C	Sierra La Porte	66 781
E D	Merced Twp 1	60 897
E D	San Francisco San Francisco 9	681029
E H	El Dorado Salmon Falls	581035
E H	El Dorado Placerville	58 887
E H	Mariposa Coulterville	60 677
E J	Mariposa Twp 1	60 670
E J	San Joaquin Stockton	641014
E J	Tuolumne Sonora	71 186
E Jane	Butte Mountain	56 740
E L	Merced Twp 1	60 906
E L	Sacramento Ward 1	63 109
E L	Sacramento Ward 4	63 528
E M	Amador Twp 1	55 470
E M	Tuolumne Springfield	71 370
E R	Siskiyou Callahan	69 6
E R	Trinity Trinity	70 973
E R	Trinity Douglas	70 978
E R	Yolo Cache	72 612
E S	Merced Twp 1	60 906
E W	Calaveras Twp 8	57 67
E W	Nevada Nevada	61 242
E W*	Mariposa Coulterville	60 701
Easper*	Calaveras Twp 5	57 175
Ebenezer	Mendocino Ukiah	60 798
Ebenezer	San Francisco San Francisco 11	119 67
Ed	El Dorado Mud Springs	58 996
Ed	Sacramento Ward 4	63 529
Ed	Tuolumne Twp 1	71 273
Edmond	Butte Bidwell	56 720
Edmund	Humbolt Eel Rvr	59 149
Edmund	Nevada Rough &	61 398
Edward	Alameda Brooklyn	55 199
Edward	Alameda Oakland	55 72
Edward	Mendocino Round Va	60 879
Edward	San Francisco San Francisco 7	681440
Edward	San Francisco San Francisco 3	67 47
Edward	San Francisco San Francisco 3	67 48
Edward	San Francisco San Francisco 2	67 798
Edward	San Joaquin Douglass	64 928
Edward	Santa Cruz Pescadero	66 641
Edward	Tuolumne Twp 1	71 268
Edward	Tuolumne Columbia	71 301
Edward	Yuba Marysville	72 899
Edward A	Mendocino Round Va	60 879
Edward D	Yuba Bear Rvr	721006
Edwd	Del Norte Crescent	58 635
Edwd	San Francisco San Francisco 9	681101
Edwd	San Francisco San Francisco 1	68 854
Edwin	Butte Ophir	56 800
Edwin A	Tuolumne Shawsfla	71 381
Edwin G	Placer Auburn	62 577
Edwrd	San Francisco San Francisco 1	68 899
Eiljah	San Joaquin Elliott	64 947
Elecha*	Sacramento Ward 4	63 510
Elehn	El Dorado Georgetown	58 677
Elerta*	Sacramento Ward 4	63 510
Eli	Mendocino Ukiah	60 793
Eli	Merced Twp 1	60 902
Eli P	San Bernardino S Timate	64 688
Elias	Humbolt Eel Rvr	59 148
Elias	Siskiyou Scott Va	69 39
Elihas C*	Calaveras Twp 6	57 158
Elihu*	El Dorado Georgetown	58 677
Elijah	Tulara Twp 1	71 78
Elijah*	Mariposa Coulterville	60 693
Elijoh	Mariposa Coulterville	60 693
Elisha	Calaveras Twp 6	57 188
Elisho	Calaveras Twp 5	57 188
Elizabe	San Francisco San Francisco 9	68 948
Elizabeth	Alameda Oakland	55 6
Elizabeth	Butte Wyandotte	56 662
Elizabeth	Marin Cortemad	60 756
Elizabeth	Napa Clear Lake	61 119
Elizabeth	San Francisco San Francisco 9	681039
Elizabeth	San Francisco San Francisco 9	681105
Elizabeth	San Francisco San Francisco 8	681284
Elizabeth	San Francisco San Francisco 9	68 948
Elizabeth	Santa Clara Alviso	65 411

California 1860 Census Index

Name	County Locale	M653 Roll Page
SMITH		
Elizabeth H	San Francisco 1	68 893
	San Francisco	
Ella	Sacramento Ward 1	63 127
Ellen	Sacramento Ward 1	63 115
Ellen	San Francisco San Francisco 2	67 616
Ellen	San Francisco San Francisco 9	68 956
Ellen	Santa Clara San Jose	65 298
Ellen	Solano Benecia	69 292
Ely	Mendocino Ukiah	60 793
Emaline	Sonoma Sonoma	69 634
Emanuel	Sacramento Ward 1	63 110
Emelia	San Francisco San Francisco 6	67 461
Emily	Sacramento Ward 1	63 105
Emily	San Francisco San Francisco 9	68 973
Emily J	Del Norte Crescent	58 623
Emma	Calaveras Twp 5	57 191
Erastus	Butte Hamilton	56 528
Erastus	Plumas Quincy	62 968
Erastus*	Butte Hamilton	56 528
Ernsno*	Calaveras Twp 5	57 191
Erzea D*	Calaveras Twp 5	57 205
Erzra D*	Calaveras Twp 5	57 205
Esther	San Francisco San Francisco 6	67 429
Evan	Yuba Marysville	72 952
Evelene	Sonoma Sonoma	69 655
Ezra	Alameda Brooklyn	55 187
Ezra	Alameda Brooklyn	55 201
Ezra D	Calaveras Twp 5	57 205
F	Alameda Oakland	55 34
F	Butte Kimshaw	56 585
F	Butte Wyandotte	56 663
F	El Dorado Placerville	58 820
F	El Dorado Placerville	58 827
F	Nevada Grass Valley	61 237
F	Nevada Eureka	61 367
F	Sacramento Granite	63 233
F	Santa Clara Redwood	65 454
F	Shasta Shasta	66 674
F	Sierra Port Win	66 791
F A	San Francisco San Francisco 1	68 878
F A	San Mateo Twp 1	65 58
F A	Siskiyou Yreka	69 187
F A	Sutter Vernon	70 844
F E	Butte Chico	56 531
F F	El Dorado Mountain	581185
F G	Calaveras Twp 8	57 53
F H	Sierra Twp 7	66 879
F J	Siskiyou Scott Va	69 21
F K	Nevada Red Dog	61 545
F L	El Dorado Placerville	58 864
F L P	Nevada Eureka	61 380
F M	Butte Ophir	56 792
F O	Sierra Forest C	66 909
F S	Sacramento Dry Crk	63 372
F W	El Dorado Placerville	58 918
F W	Sacramento Granite	63 257
F W	Trinity New Rvr	701030
Fanny	Nevada Grass Valley	61 172
Federick	San Francisco San Francisco 7	681444
Fidel	El Dorado Cold Spring	581101
Fomase*	Marin San Rafael	60 766
Forrents	Nevada Bloomfield	61 517
Foster	Nevada Red Dog	61 553
Frances	Sierra Gibsonville	66 857
Francis	Butte Kimshaw	56 602
Francis	Butte Oregon	56 625
Francis	Nevada Bridgeport	61 470
Francis	San Francisco San Francisco 7	681417
Francis	San Joaquin Elliott	64 941
Francis	Sierra Gibsonville	66 857
Francis	Sierra Twp 7	66 868
Francis H	San Francisco San Francisco 7	681445
Francis L	San Francisco San Francisco 2	67 584
Francis M	Yuba Marysville	72 967
Frank	Alameda Brooklyn	55 83
Frank	Amador Twp 2	55 263
Frank	Calaveras Twp 6	57 187
Frank	El Dorado Diamond	58 771
Frank	El Dorado Placerville	58 914
Frank	Placer Rattle Snake	62 635
Frank	Sacramento Ward 1	63 10
Frank	San Francisco San Francisco 1	68 901
Frank	Santa Cruz Santa Cruz	66 605
Frank	Sonoma Sonoma	69 633
Frank	Stanislaus Empire	70 726
Frank	Tuolumne Jamestown	71 454
Franklin	El Dorado Mud Springs	58 998
Fred	Amador Twp 6	55 448
Fred	El Dorado Placerville	58 912
Fred	Sacramento Ward 4	63 603
Fred	Santa Clara Fremont	65 424
Fred	Trinity Weaverville	701062
Fred	Trinity Indian C	70 989
Fred	Yolo Cache	72 623
Fred A*	Colusa Grand Island	57 482

Name	County Locale	M653 Roll Page
SMITH		
Fred G	Calaveras Twp 6	57 166
Frederick	El Dorado Greenwood	58 718
Frederick	San Francisco San Francisco 4	681121
Frederick	San Joaquin Elliott	641103
Frederick	Tulara Visalia	71 111
Frederick	Tuolumne Columbia	71 344
Frederick	Yuba Rose Bar	72 794
Frederick N	San Francisco 4	681121
	San Francisco	
Frederika	Sacramento Ward 1	63 82
Fredk	San Francisco San Francisco 10	244
		67
Fredk	San Francisco San Francisco 2	67 566
Fredk	San Francisco San Francisco 2	67 672
Fredk	San Francisco San Francisco 2	67 787
Fredrick	El Dorado Placerville	58 913
Fredrick	Plumas Quincy	62 999
Freeman	Solano Vallejo	69 259
Fs F	El Dorado Diamond	58 767
G	Nevada Eureka	61 365
G	Sacramento Brighton	63 203
G	San Francisco San Francisco 5	67 524
G	Sierra Port Win	66 791
G	Sutter Butte	70 795
G B	El Dorado Salmon Falls	581065
G Camying*	Mendocino Ukiah	60 801
G Canning*	Mendocino Ukiah	60 801
G F	San Francisco San Francisco 12	393
		67
G F	San Francisco San Francisco 1	68 905
G H	Colusa Monroeville	57 444
G K	Shasta Horsetown	66 700
G L	Amador Twp 1	55 456
G N	San Joaquin Stockton	641040
G N	Sutter Bear Rvr	70 821
G P	Tehama Pasakent	70 858
G R	Amador Twp 3	55 402
G S	Amador Twp 1	55 456
G W	Calaveras Twp 9	57 403
G W	El Dorado Georgetown	58 753
G W	San Francisco San Francisco 1	68 841
G W	Santa Clara Burnett	65 260
G W	Sonoma Bodega	69 532
G W	Stanislaus Branch	70 707
G W A	Tuolumne Twp 1	71 256
Ganet	Tulara Visalia	71 30
Garret*	Tulara Visalia	71 30
Gel	Monterey Monterey	60 954
Geo	Butte Kimshaw	56 581
Geo	Butte Kimshaw	56 608
Geo	El Dorado Eldorado	58 936
Geo	El Dorado Mud Springs	58 994
Geo	Napa Napa	61 76
Geo	Placer Goods	62 696
Geo	Sacramento Natonia	63 280
Geo	Sacramento Franklin	63 310
Geo	Sacramento Ward 3	63 433
Geo	Sacramento Ward 1	63 43
Geo	Sacramento Ward 3	63 484
Geo	Sacramento Ward 1	63 57
Geo	Sacramento Ward 4	63 580
Geo	Sacramento Ward 4	63 588
Geo	Sacramento Ward 1	63 96
Geo	San Francisco San Francisco 12	384
		67
Geo	San Francisco San Francisco 2	67 602
Geo	San Francisco San Francisco 1	68 880
Geo	San Francisco San Francisco 1	68 918
Geo	Santa Clara Alviso	65 414
Geo	Santa Clara Redwood	65 457
Geo	Siskiyou Callahan	69 19
Geo	Siskiyou Scott Ri	69 77
Geo	Solano Benecia	69 310
Geo	Stanislaus Emory	70 742
Geo	Stanislaus Emory	70 743
Geo	Yolo Cache	72 631
Geo A	Butte Chico	56 552
Geo E	Butte Ophir	56 765
Geo E	Placer Dutch Fl	62 718
Geo F L	Trinity Texas Ba	70 981
Geo L	San Joaquin Stockton	641056
Geo M	Mendocino Big Rvr	60 850
Geo P	Amador Twp 1	55 475
Geo W	Calaveras Twp 6	57 131
Geo W	Klamath Orleans	59 215
George	Alameda Oakland	55 42
George	Calaveras Twp 8	57 86
George	Contra Costa Twp 2	57 577
George	Contra Costa Twp 2	57 578
George	Los Angeles Los Angeles	59 367
George	Nevada Red Dog	61 544
George	Placer Michigan	62 851
George	Placer Iona Hills	62 867
George	Sacramento Franklin	63 334
George	San Bernardino Santa Inez	64 136

Name	County Locale	M653 Roll Page
SMITH		
George	San Diego San Diego	64 759
George	San Francisco San Francisco 9	681099
George	San Francisco San Francisco 9	681102
George	San Francisco San Francisco 4	681227
George	San Francisco San Francisco 7	681377
George	Santa Clara Almaden	65 266
George	Shasta Shasta	66 728
George	Sierra St Louis	66 809
George	Solano Vallejo	69 243
George	Solano Vallejo	69 264
George	Solano Vallejo	69 267
George	Solano Benecia	69 286
George	Solano Montezuma	69 375
George	Tuolumne Sonora	71 192
George	Tuolumne Twp 1	71 254
George	Yuba Fosters	72 829
George	Yuba Marysville	72 849
George	Yuba Marysville	72 966
George E	Sierra Gibsonville	66 856
George L	Los Angeles Los Angeles	59 359
George L	San Francisco San Francisco 7	681340
George L	Siskiyou Shasta Rvr	69 113
George N	San Joaquin Stockton	641026
George R	Trinity Browns C	70 984
George W	San Francisco San Francisco 7	681424
George W	San Joaquin Castoria	64 876
George W	San Joaquin Castoria	64 903
George W	Sierra St Louis	66 818
George W*	San Francisco 7	681424
	San Francisco	
Gerand	San Francisco San Francisco 2	67 577
Gerrill*	Butte Bidwell	56 730
Gerritt	Butte Bidwell	56 730
Gewitt*	Butte Bidwell	56 730
Gheridan P	Calaveras Twp 5	57 212
Gil	Merced Monterey	60 937
Gil	Monterey Monterey	60 937
Gilbert B	Sacramento Natonia	63 276
Gilbert S	Sacramento Ward 4	63 500
Gilmon	Sonoma Russian	69 440
Gilmon M	Sonoma Russian	69 440
Gilmore	El Dorado White Oaks	581011
Godfrey	San Joaquin Castoria	64 875
Guane	Marin Bolinas	60 747
Guano	Marin Bolinas	60 747
Gustavus S	Calaveras Twp 10	57 276
Gustuvus S	Calaveras Twp 10	57 276
Guy B	Humbolt Bucksport	59 162
H	Butte Wyandotte	56 669
H	Calaveras Twp 7	57 5
H	El Dorado Kelsey	581156
H	El Dorado Georgetown	58 690
H	El Dorado Placerville	58 882
H	Nevada Grass Valley	61 201
H	San Francisco San Francisco 5	67 536
H	San Joaquin Stockton	641062
H	Sutter Yuba	70 761
H	Sutter Vernon	70 845
H	Tuolumne Jacksonville	71 169
H A	Butte Chico	56 547
H B	Butte Eureka	56 645
H B	Sutter Yuba	70 774
H C	San Francisco San Francisco 9	681056
H D	Butte Eureka	56 653
H E	Siskiyou Scott Ri	69 76
H F	Klamath Trinidad	59 220
H F	Siskiyou Scott Va	69 50
H G	Sacramento Ward 1	63 132
H G	Sierra Downieville	661021
H H	Sierra Downieville	661021
H H	Siskiyou Callahan	69 15
H L	Mariposa Coulterville	60 695
H R	Sacramento Ward 1	63 17
H S	Butte Chico	56 540
H S	Santa Clara San Jose	65 374
H W	Butte Mountain	56 740
H W	El Dorado Kelsey	581129
Han	Yuba North Ea	72 679
Hando	Sacramento Ward 1	63 64
Hanna	San Francisco San Francisco 7	681441
Harriet	San Francisco San Francisco 9	681040
Harry	El Dorado Kelsey	581138
Harry J	Calaveras Twp 9	57 348
Hart	Sacramento Georgian	63 342
Harvey	Contra Costa Twp 1	57 527
Harvey	Placer Goods	62 693
Head	Nevada Nevada	61 313
Henrietta	Los Angeles Los Angeles	59 315
Henry	Alameda Brooklyn	55 207
Henry	Amador Twp 1	55 461
Henry	Butte Ophir	56 797
Henry	Butte Ophir	56 800
Henry	Calaveras Twp 5	57 183
Henry	Calaveras Twp 5	57 186

California 1860 Census Index

Name	County Locale	M653 Roll	Page
SMITH			
Henry	Contra Costa Twp 1	57	515
Henry	Del Norte Crescent	58	621
Henry	Del Norte Crescent	58	648
Henry	El Dorado Coloma	58	1108
Henry	El Dorado Kelsey	58	1147
Henry	Humbolt Union	59	181
Henry	Marin Bolinas	60	749
Henry	Mendocino Calpella	60	812
Henry	Mendocino Big Rvr	60	841
Henry	Nevada Rough &	61	418
Henry	Placer Auburn	62	586
Henry	Placer Auburn	62	596
Henry	Placer Secret R	62	621
Henry	Placer Iona Hills	62	878
Henry	Plumas Quincy	62	1004
Henry	Sacramento Natonia	63	273
Henry	Sacramento Natonia	63	280
Henry	Sacramento Georgian	63	344
Henry	Sacramento Ward 4	63	500
Henry	Sacramento Ward 4	63	571
Henry	San Francisco San Francisco 9	68	1063
Henry	San Francisco San Francisco 4	68	1153
Henry	San Francisco San Francisco 11		162 67
Henry	San Francisco San Francisco 3	67	42
Henry	San Francisco San Francisco 1	68	889
Henry	San Francisco San Francisco 1	68	913 67
Henry	San Joaquin Castoria	64	879
Henry	San Mateo Twp 1	65	59
Henry	Santa Clara Gilroy	65	239
Henry	Santa Clara Burnett	65	256
Henry	Santa Clara San Jose	65	287
Henry	Shasta Millvill	66	739
Henry	Sierra Eureka	66	1050
Henry	Sierra Twp 5	66	941
Henry	Sierra Cox'S Bar	66	951
Henry	Siskiyou Klamath	69	90
Henry	Solano Suisan	69	228
Henry	Tehama Lassen	70	874
Henry	Tehama Red Bluff	70	908
Henry	Trinity Whites Crk	70	1028
Henry	Tuolumne Twp 1	71	273
Henry	Tuolumne Columbia	71	345
Henry	Yolo Merritt	72	577
Henry	Yuba Bear Rvr	72	1009
Henry	Yuba New York	72	731
Henry	Yuba Fosters	72	837
Henry	Yuba Fosters	72	838
Henry A	Santa Clara San Jose	65	370
Henry C	Alameda Brooklyn	55	193
Henry E	Plumas Quincy	62	955
Henry H	Contra Costa Twp 3	57	594
Henry J	Siskiyou Yreka	69	124
Henry K	Sierra Pine Grove	66	835
Henry M	Butte Ophir	56	763
Henry P	Yuba Marysville	72	942
Henry S	Alameda Brooklyn	55	125
Henry*	Plumas Quincy	62	971
Henry*	Yuba Bear Rvr	72	1009
Herman	San Francisco San Francisco 10		293 67
Hernan	San Francisco San Francisco 11		130 67
Herran	Sutter Bear Rvr	70	824
Herry	Sacramento Natonia	63	273
Hesakiah	Placer Secret R	62	618
Hiram	Butte Kimshaw	56	581
Hiram	Butte Kimshaw	56	583
Hiram	Contra Costa Twp 2	57	561
Hiram W	Mendocino Calpella	60	810
Horace	Butte Oregon	56	631
Horace	Tuolumne Twp 1	71	248
Horace	Yuba Bear Rvr	72	1004
Horace	Yuba Marysville	72	959
Horatio	Tuolumne Twp 1	71	254
Horrace	Placer Auburn	62	562
Horrace	Yuba Bear Rvr	72	1004
Hugh	El Dorado Salmon Falls	58	1059
Hugh	El Dorado Placerville	58	924
Hugh	Tuolumne Columbia	71	301
Hughpayton	El Dorado Placerville	58	924
Huh	Tuolumne Twp 2	71	301
Hurbert	Los Angeles Los Angeles	59	350
Hyman	Yuba Marysville	72	940
Hyram	Yuba Marysville	72	940
I	Sacramento Granite	63	260
I B	Amador Twp 7	55	416
I F*	Siskiyou Callahan	69	17
I M	Amador Twp 4	55	316
I M	El Dorado Newtown	58	776
I*	Sacramento Ward 1	63	85
Indian*	Sacramento Centre	63	181
Ira H	Tuolumne Sonora	71	201
Isaac	El Dorado Greenwood	58	726
SMITH			
Isaac	Nevada Rough &	61	420
Isaac	San Francisco San Francisco 11		123 67
Isaac	San Francisco San Francisco 3	67	18
Isaac	San Francisco San Francisco 3	67	71
Isaac	Sonoma Russian	69	429
Isaac G	San Francisco San Francisco 12		380 67
Isaac M	San Francisco San Francisco 7	68	1402
Isaac P	Butte Hamilton	56	529
Isaac P	Sonoma Russian	69	429
Isaac P*	Butte Hamilton	56	529
Isaac S	San Joaquin Douglass	64	914
Isaac W	San Bernardino San Bernadino	64	675
Isac	Mariposa Twp 3	60	584
J	Calaveras Twp 9	57	407
J	El Dorado Diamond	58	790
J	El Dorado Placerville	58	831
J	El Dorado Placerville	58	856
J	El Dorado Placerville	58	896
J	Mariposa Twp 3	60	600
J	Nevada Grass Valley	61	149
J	Nevada Grass Valley	61	160
J	Nevada Grass Valley	61	170
J	Nevada Nevada	61	246
J	Nevada Eureka	61	362
J	Nevada Eureka	61	367
J	Sacramento Centre	63	179
J	Sacramento Brighton	63	200
J	Sacramento Lee	63	212
J	Sacramento Granite	63	260
J	Sacramento Dry Crk	63	369
J	San Bernardino Santa Barbara	64	179
J	San Francisco San Francisco 9	68	1061
J	San Francisco San Francisco 5	67	491
J	San Francisco San Francisco 5	67	529
J	San Francisco San Francisco 5	67	534
J	San Francisco San Francisco 5	67	539
J	San Francisco San Francisco 5	67	541
J	San Francisco San Francisco 5	67	542
J	San Francisco San Francisco 5	67	545
J	San Francisco San Francisco 5	67	548
J	San Francisco San Francisco 5	67	554
J	San Francisco San Francisco 3	67	71
J	San Francisco San Francisco 2	67	796
J	San Joaquin Stockton	64	1093
J	San Mateo Twp 3	65	110
J	Siskiyou Scott Ri	69	73
J	Solano Vacaville	69	327
J	Sonoma Santa Rosa	69	391
J	Sonoma Healdsbu	69	474
J	Stanislaus Emory	70	740
J	Sutter Butte	70	787
J	Sutter Sutter	70	817
J	Sutter Bear Rvr	70	826
J	Sutter Nicolaus	70	831
J	Tuolumne Twp 4	71	154
J	Tuolumne Twp 4	71	165
J	Tuolumne Twp 4	71	169
J	Yuba New York	72	725
J A	Butte Kimshaw	56	597
J B	Butte Chico	56	545
J B	Placer Christia	62	784
J B	Sacramento Granite	63	250
J B	San Francisco San Francisco 7	68	1436
J B	Siskiyou Scott Va	69	48
J B	Solano Benecia	69	285
J B	Sutter Sutter	70	801
J B	Tuolumne Big Oak	71	155
J B	Yolo Cache	72	637
J B	Yolo Cottonwoood	72	658
J B M	Butte Ophir	56	765
J Broom	Napa Napa	61	112
J C	Mendocino Arrana	60	862
J C	Nevada Grass Valley	61	210
J C	Nevada Grass Valley	61	212
J C	Sacramento Ward 3	63	430
J C	San Francisco San Francisco 5	67	524
J C	Santa Clara Redwood	65	450
J C	Shasta Shasta	66	678
J C	Sonoma Washington	69	667
J C	Tuolumne Shawsfla	71	381
J C	Yolo Cache	72	643
J Clark	Sacramento Ward 1	63	129
J D	Mariposa Twp 3	60	615
J D	Shasta Shasta	66	654
J D	Yolo Slate Ra	72	717
J D	Yuba Slate Ro	72	709
J D	Yuba Slate Ro	72	717
J E	Los Angeles Tejon	59	525
J E	San Francisco San Francisco 1	68	904
J E	Shasta French G	66	722
J E	Siskiyou Yreka	69	183
J F	Placer Todds Va	62	787
J F	San Francisco San Francisco 9	68	1079
SMITH			
J F	San Francisco San Francisco 5	67	532
J F	San Francisco San Francisco 5	67	543
J F	Siskiyou Callahan	69	17
J F*	Stanislaus Empire	70	732
J F*	Siskiyou Callahan	69	17
J G	Sacramento Ward 3	63	427
J G	Sacramento Ward 4	63	503
J G	Shasta French G	66	722
J G	Trinity Taylor'S	70	1034
J H	El Dorado Casumnes	58	1174
J H	El Dorado Georgetown	58	752
J H	Napa Napa	61	112
J H	Sacramento Granite	63	229
J H	Tehama Red Bluff	70	922
J H	Tuolumne Springfield	71	372
J H W	Butte Eureka	56	656
J J	Sacramento Ward 1	63	16
J J	San Joaquin Stockton	64	1099
J J	Sutter Butte	70	788
J K	Sonoma Bodega	69	532
J K	Yuba Rose Bar	72	791
J L	Colusa Grand Island	57	470
J L	El Dorado Placerville	58	860
J L	Placer Virginia	62	675
J L	San Francisco San Francisco 4	68	1165
J L P	Nevada Eureka	61	380
J M	Amador Twp 2	55	316
J M	Butte Ophir	56	790
J M	Nevada Eureka	61	346
J M	Placer Iona Hills	62	885
J M	Santa Clara Redwood	65	447
J M	Siskiyou Callahan	69	17
J M	Siskiyou Scott Va	69	43
J M	Sonoma Armally	69	483
J M	Sonoma Bodega	69	539
J M	Sutter Sutter	70	806
J M	Tuolumne Big Oak	71	136
J M	Tuolumne Springfield	71	370
J Mc Kinstry*	Butte Eureka	56	653
J N	Butte Kimshaw	56	597
J N	San Francisco San Francisco 5	67	477
J O	Shasta Shasta	66	678
J O	Sonoma Petaluma	69	608
J P	Butte Hamilton	56	513
J P	Sutter Sutter	70	805
J P	Tehama Red Bluff	70	916
J P	Yolo Cache Crk	72	637
J Plummer	Mendocino Big Rvr	60	852
J Q	Sacramento Brighton	63	200
J R	Butte Eureka	56	653
J R	El Dorado Casumnes	58	1168
J R	Shasta Millvill	66	725
J R	Shasta Millvill	66	751
J R	Yolo Cache Crk	72	639
J R	Yuba Rose Bar	72	791
J S	Sacramento Cosumnes	63	403
J S	Siskiyou Callahan	69	8
J S	Sutter Yuba	70	771
J W	Nevada Grass Valley	61	161
J W	Nevada Grass Valley	61	201
J W	Nevada Nevada	61	313
J W	Sacramento Granite	63	267
J W	Sacramento Sutter	63	304
J W	Sacramento Ward 3	63	486
J W	San Francisco San Francisco 5	67	477
J*	Sacramento Ward 1	63	85
J*	Siskiyou Callahan	69	17
Jabez	Tulara Twp 2	71	25
Jack W	Napa Hot Springs	61	3
Jacob	Butte Chico	56	547
Jacob	Butte Kimshaw	56	590
Jacob	Butte Kimshaw	56	601
Jacob	Butte Ophir	56	773
Jacob	El Dorado Casumnes	58	1161
Jacob	El Dorado Placerville	58	922
Jacob	Placer Virginia	62	666
Jacob	Placer Iona Hills	62	888
Jacob	Sacramento Alabama	63	411
Jacob	San Diego San Diego	64	770
Jacob	San Francisco San Francisco 9	68	1106
Jacob	San Francisco San Francisco 12		393 67
Jacob	San Francisco San Francisco 2	67	683
Jacob	Sierra Monte Crk	66	1037
Jacob	Sierra Gibsonville	66	855
Jacob	Siskiyou Yreka	69	143
Jacob	Trinity Mouth Ca	70	1012
Jacob	Yolo Putah	72	614
Jacob A	San Francisco San Francisco 1	68	834
Jacob G	Alameda Oakland	55	21
Jamas G	Los Angeles Tejon	59	523
James	Alameda Brooklyn	55	158
James	Alameda Brooklyn	55	195
James	Amador Twp 3	55	397
James	Calaveras Twp 8	57	70

California 1860 Census Index

Name	County Locale	M653 Roll Page
SMITH		
James	Colusa Spring Valley	57 429
James	Contra Costa Twp 1	57 501
James	Contra Costa Twp 1	57 511
James	Contra Costa Twp 1	57 523
James	Contra Costa Twp 2	57 549
James	Del Norte Crescent	58 623
James	Del Norte Happy Ca	58 670
James	El Dorado Coloma	581118
James	El Dorado Mountain	581185
James	El Dorado Georgetown	58 680
James	El Dorado Georgetown	58 706
James	El Dorado Big Bar	58 743
James	Humbolt Pacific	59 134
James	Klamath Trinidad	59 221
James	Marin Cortemad	60 787
James	Marin Cortemad	60 791
James	Mendocino Little L	60 831
James	Mendocino Big Rvr	60 851
James	Napa Yount	61 36
James	Nevada Rough &	61 430
James	Placer Grizzly	62 755
James	Placer Damascus	62 846
James	Placer Michigan	62 858
James	Plumas Quincy	62 940
James	Plumas Quincy	62 944
James	Plumas Quincy	62 954
James	Sacramento Ward 1	63 36
James	San Bernardino Santa Inez	64 142
James	San Francisco San Francisco 9	681021
James	San Francisco San Francisco 4	681117
James	San Francisco San Francisco 4	681148
James	San Francisco San Francisco 7	681368
James	San Francisco San Francisco 11	148 67
James	San Francisco San Francisco 3	67 31
James	San Francisco San Francisco 3	67 62
James	San Francisco San Francisco 3	67 67
James	San Joaquin Castoria	64 873
James	San Joaquin Castoria	64 877
James	San Joaquin Elkhorn	64 951
James	San Joaquin Elkhorn	64 994
James	San Mateo Twp 3	65 101
James	San Mateo Twp 2	65 126
James	Santa Clara San Jose	65 284
James	Santa Clara San Jose	65 359
James	Santa Clara Santa Clara	65 521
James	Santa Cruz Pajaro	66 552
James	Shasta Millvill	66 754
James	Shasta Shasta	66 759
James	Sierra Eureka	661045
James	Siskiyou Klamath	69 84
James	Solano Benecia	69 293
James	Solano Vacaville	69 349
James	Sonoma Sonoma	69 655
James	Stanislaus Branch	70 709
James	Tehama Tehama	70 947
James	Tulara Visalia	71 109
James	Tulara Petersburg	71 51
James	Tulara Twp 1	71 92
James	Tuolumne Sonora	71 243
James	Tuolumne Twp 1	71 260
James	Tuolumne Twp 2	71 360
James	Tuolumne Twp 3	71 436
James	Tuolumne Visalia	71 92
James	Yuba Bear Rvr	721009
James	Yuba Bear Rvr	721013
James	Yuba New York	72 734
James	Yuba New York	72 735
James A	Del Norte Happy Ca	58 661
James A	Yolo No E Twp	72 678
James A	Yuba North Ea	72 678
James A	Yuba Long Bar	72 748
James B	Monterey San Juan	601006
James B	Plumas Quincy	62 990
James B	Tuolumne Green Springs	71 518
James C	Calaveras Twp 10	57 292
James C	Los Angeles San Gabriel	59 412
James C	San Francisco San Francisco 3	67 36
James C	San Joaquin Elkhorn	64 998
James G	Los Angeles Tejon	59 523
James H	Mendocino Big Rock	60 873
James H	San Joaquin Elkhorn	64 955
James H	Sonoma Healdsbu	69 476
James H	Yuba Marysville	72 979
James N	Sonoma Santa Rosa	69 392
James R	Alameda Brooklyn	55 82
James S	Contra Costa Twp 2	57 570
James W	Santa Clara San Jose	65 339
James*	Yuba Bear Rvr	721009
James*	Yuba Bear Rvr	721013
Jane	Alameda Brooklyn	55 87
Jane	Sacramento Ward 1	63 140
Jane	San Bernardino San Bernadino	64 625
Jane	San Francisco San Francisco 2	67 703
Jane	San Francisco San Francisco 2	67 755
SMITH		
Jane A*	San Francisco San Francisco 2	67 755
Jas	Butte Hamilton	56 515
Jas	Butte Kimshaw	56 596
Jas	Butte Oregon	56 609
Jas	Calaveras Twp 9	57 369
Jas	Fresno Twp 3	59 16
Jas	Napa Napa	61 85
Jas	Sacramento Ward 1	63 151
Jas	Sacramento Granite	63 230
Jas	Sacramento Ward 1	63 28
Jas	Sacramento Sutter	63 300
Jas	Sacramento Ward 1	63 31
Jas	Sacramento Ward 3	63 431
Jas	Sacramento Ward 4	63 526
Jas	San Francisco San Francisco 10	242 67
Jas	San Francisco San Francisco 2	67 611
Jas	San Francisco San Francisco 1	68 872
Jas	San Francisco San Francisco 1	68 895
Jas	San Francisco San Francisco 1	68 906
Jas	Trinity Douglas	70 979
Jas	Yolo Washington	72 602
Jas A	San Bernardino San Bernardino	64 670
Jas B	Butte Oregon	56 634
Jas C	Butte Oregon	56 628
Jas C	Placer Virginia	62 661
Jas E	Butte Ophir	56 755
Jas H	Butte Kimshaw	56 573
Jas H	Del Norte Crescent	58 627
Jas L	Napa Napa	61 114
Jas M	Sacramento Ward 1	63 10
Jas R L	Napa Clear Lake	61 139
Jas R S	Napa Clear Lake	61 139
Jas Roger	San Francisco San Francisco 10	174 67
Jas T	Napa Napa	61 114
Jas W	Placer Rattle Snake	62 625
Jas W*	Napa Napa	61 109
Jason	San Joaquin Elkhorn	64 965
Jason	Tuolumne Columbia	71 299
Jason E	Butte Kimshaw	56 599
Jasper F	San Francisco San Francisco 6	67 401
Jasper N	Los Angeles Elmonte	59 246
Jeff	Butte Oregon	56 626
Jehiel	Sonoma Santa Rosa	69 421
Jennell	Butte Ophir	56 794
Jennie	Sacramento Ward 1	63 81
Jepe R	San Francisco San Francisco 10	203 67
Jeremiah	San Mateo Twp 1	65 58
Jeremiah J	Placer Secret R	62 615
Jerry K	Calaveras Twp 9	57 361
Jesse	Tulara Twp 2	71 5
Jesse N	Alameda Brooklyn	55 125
Jesse R*	San Francisco San Francisco 10	203 67
Jessee	Tulara Visalia	71 5
Jessie	San Francisco San Francisco 1	68 862
Jessie	Santa Cruz Watsonville	66 538
Jms	Klamath Liberty	59 238
Jno	Alameda Brooklyn	55 134
Jno	Alameda Oakland	55 69
Jno	Butte Hamilton	56 524
Jno	Butte Hamilton	56 526
Jno	Butte Kimshaw	56 576
Jno	Butte Oregon	56 639
Jno	Mendocino Big Rvr	60 852
Jno	Merced Twp 1	60 910
Jno	Nevada Nevada	61 243
Jno	Nevada Nevada	61 280
Jno	Sacramento American	63 171
Jno	Sacramento Brighton	63 197
Jno	Sacramento Ward 3	63 433
Jno	Sacramento Ward 4	63 522
Jno	Sacramento Ward 4	63 589
Jno	Sacramento Ward 1	63 76
Jno	Sacramento Ward 1	63 78
Jno	San Francisco San Francisco 9	681068
Jno	San Francisco San Francisco 9	681075
Jno	San Francisco San Francisco 9	681077
Jno	San Francisco San Francisco 8	681312
Jno	Sonoma Petaluma	69 557
Jno	Sonoma Sonoma	69 637
Jno A	Sacramento Ward 3	63 479
Jno Cole	Sacramento Ward 4	63 540
Jno F	San Francisco San Francisco 9	68 987
Jno F	Trinity Price'S	701019
Jno G	Klamath S Fork	59 202
Jno G	Nevada Nevada	61 273
Jno H	Sacramento American	63 157
Jno L	Klamath Liberty	59 235
Jno P	Sonoma Sonoma	69 655
Jno W	Napa Napa	61 109
Jno W	Trinity Douglas	70 978
Jno W*	Napa Napa	61 109
SMITH		
Jo	San Joaquin Stockton	641052
Joe	Tehama Red Bluff	70 928
Joe	Trinity Weaverville	701064
Joe	Yolo No E Twp	72 670
Joe	Yuba North Ea	72 670
Joel	Alameda Brooklyn	55 183
Joel	Mariposa Twp 1	60 650
Joel	Sacramento Ward 1	63 154
Joel	Sacramento Ward 1	63 20
Joseph E	Plumas Quincy	62 956
Joh	Solano Suisan	69 223
Joh	Solano Green Valley	69 242
Johiel	Sonoma Santa Rosa	69 421
John	Alameda Brooklyn	55 132
John	Alameda Oakland	55 73
John	Amador Twp 2	55 321
John	Amador Twp 5	55 336
John	Amador Twp 5	55 337
John	Amador Twp 6	55 427
John	Amador Twp 6	55 441
John	Amador Twp 1	55 467
John	Amador Twp 1	55 486
John	Butte Wyandotte	56 659
John	Butte Wyandotte	56 669
John	Butte Oro	56 673
John	Butte Cascade	56 701
John	Butte Bidwell	56 711
John	Butte Bidwell	56 721
John	Butte Mountain	56 736
John	Butte Ophir	56 751
John	Butte Ophir	56 766
John	Butte Ophir	56 769
John	Butte Ophir	56 784
John	Butte Ophir	56 791
John	Calaveras Twp 6	57 143
John	Calaveras Twp 6	57 161
John	Calaveras Twp 5	57 172
John	Calaveras Twp 5	57 227
John	Calaveras Twp 10	57 283
John	Calaveras Twp 4	57 328
John	Calaveras Twp 7	57 43
John	Calaveras Twp 8	57 83
John	Colusa Monroeville	57 456
John	Contra Costa Twp 1	57 505
John	Contra Costa Twp 1	57 513
John	Contra Costa Twp 2	57 571
John	Contra Costa Twp 2	57 580
John	Contra Costa Twp 3	57 589
John	Contra Costa Twp 3	57 596
John	El Dorado Kelsey	581146
John	El Dorado Grizzly	581181
John	El Dorado Grizzly	581182
John	El Dorado Greenwood	58 722
John	El Dorado Georgetown	58 754
John	El Dorado Placerville	58 877
John	El Dorado Placerville	58 891
John	Humbolt Pacific	59 133
John	Humbolt Eureka	59 174
John	Humbolt Union	59 192
John	Los Angeles Elmonte	59 245
John	Los Angeles Azuza	59 278
John	Marin Cortemad	60 757
John	Marin Cortemad	60 781
John	Monterey Alisal	601033
John	Napa Napa	61 74
John	Napa Napa	61 79
John	Napa Napa	61 87
John	Nevada Grass Valley	61 148
John	Nevada Nevada	61 240
John	Nevada Rough &	61 413
John	Nevada Rough &	61 420
John	Nevada Rough &	61 421
John	Nevada Rough &	61 425
John	Nevada Rough &	61 430
John	Nevada Bloomfield	61 527
John	Nevada Red Dog	61 550
John	Placer Ophirville	62 658
John	Placer Ophirville	62 659
John	Placer Dutch Fl	62 710
John	Placer Yankee J	62 758
John	Placer Forest H	62 800
John	Placer Michigan	62 842
John	Placer Michigan	62 850
John	Placer Iona Hills	62 866
John	Placer Iona Hills	62 897
John	Plumas Meadow Valley	62 900
John	Plumas Meadow Valley	62 901
John	Plumas Quincy	62 938
John	Plumas Quincy	62 942
John	Plumas Quincy	62 955
John	Sacramento Ward 1	63 107
John	Sacramento Ward 1	63 131
John	Sacramento Sutter	63 304
John	Sacramento Franklin	63 330

California 1860 Census Index

Name	County Locale	M653 Roll	Page
SMITH			
John	Sacramento Casumnes	63	381
John	Sacramento Ward 3	63	428
John	Sacramento Ward 1	63	51
John	San Bernardino S Timate	64	689
John	San Diego Colorado	64	808
John	San Francisco San Francisco 9	681064	
John	San Francisco San Francisco 4	681114	
John	San Francisco San Francisco 11	122 67	
John	San Francisco San Francisco 11	129 67	
John	San Francisco San Francisco 7	681384	
John	San Francisco San Francisco 7	681440	
John	San Francisco San Francisco 7	681444	
John	San Francisco San Francisco 11	148 67	
John	San Francisco San Francisco 12	369 67	
John	San Francisco San Francisco 12	385 67	
John	San Francisco San Francisco 6	67 456	
John	San Francisco San Francisco 5	67 477	
John	San Francisco San Francisco 5	67 491	
John	San Francisco San Francisco 2	67 558	
John	San Francisco San Francisco 3	67 55	
John	San Francisco San Francisco 2	67 571	
John	San Francisco San Francisco 2	67 617	
John	San Francisco San Francisco 3	67 67	
John	San Francisco San Francisco 1	68 850	
John	San Francisco San Francisco 1	68 853	
John	San Francisco San Francisco 1	68 890	
John	San Francisco San Francisco 1	68 895	
John	San Francisco San Francisco 1	68 916	
John	San Francisco San Francisco 1	68 930	
John	San Joaquin Castoria	64	899
John	San Joaquin Castoria	64	904
John	San Joaquin Castoria	64	909
John	San Mateo Twp 3	65	104
John	San Mateo Twp 1	65	69
John	Santa Clara San Jose	65	282
John	Santa Clara San Jose	65	372
John	Santa Clara Fremont	65	434
John	Santa Cruz Pajaro	66	561
John	Santa Cruz Santa Cruz	66	609
John	Santa Cruz Pescadero	66	645
John	Santa Cruz Pescadero	66	646
John	Shasta Shasta	66	666
John	Shasta Shasta	66	682
John	Sierra Grizzly	661058	
John	Sierra Poverty	66	799
John	Sierra St Louis	66	818
John	Sierra Pine Grove	66	819
John	Sierra Pine Grove	66	822
John	Sierra Poker Flats	66	840
John	Sierra Twp 5	66	923
John	Sierra Downieville	66	997
John	Siskiyou Yreka	69	124
John	Siskiyou Callahan	69	16
John	Siskiyou Yreka	69	180
John	Siskiyou Scott Va	69	33
John	Siskiyou Scott Va	69	43
John	Solano Suisan	69	222
John	Solano Suisan	69	223
John	Solano Suisan	69	229
John	Solano Suisan	69	232
John	Solano Green Valley	69	242
John	Solano Vallejo	69	248
John	Solano Vacaville	69	362
John	Solano Fremont	69	381
John	Sonoma Santa Rosa	69	417
John	Sonoma Armally	69	516
John	Tehama Tehama	70	946
John	Trinity State Ba	701001	
John	Trinity East For	701027	
John	Trinity Minersville	70	969
John	Trinity Indian C	70	986
John	Trinity Indian C	70	989
John	Tulara Twp 1	71	94
John	Tuolumne Big Oak	71	178
John	Tuolumne Twp 1	71	275
John	Tuolumne Twp 2	71	299
John	Tuolumne Twp 2	71	338
John	Tuolumne Twp 2	71	399
John	Tuolumne Twp 2	71	410
John	Tuolumne Twp 5	71	503
John	Tuolumne Visalia	71	94
John	Yolo Putah	72	553
John	Yolo Washington	72	572
John	Yolo Cache	72	610
John	Yolo Cottonwood	72	646
John	Yolo Cottonwood	72	651
John	Yolo No E Twp	72	669
John	Yolo No E Twp	72	672
John	Yolo No E Twp	72	679
John	Yuba North Ea	72	669
SMITH			
John	Yuba North Ea	72	672
John	Yuba Marysville	72	889
John	Yuba Marysville	72	940
John	Yuba Marysville	72	942
John	Yuba Marysville	72	964
John	Yuba Suida	72	989
John A	Amador Twp 1	55	457
John A	Sierra Poker Flats	66	842
John B	Tuolumne Sonora	71	222
John C	Placer Dutch Fl	62	727
John C	Plumas Meadow Valley	62	930
John C	Solano Suisan	69	210
John C	Sonoma Mendocino	69	462
John C	Tuolumne Sonora	71	191
John C	Tuolumne Columbia	71	315
John C	Calaveras Twp 10	57	278
John D	Santa Cruz Soguel	66	596
John E	Tuolumne Twp 2	71	280
John E	Tuolumne Twp 2	71	399
John F	Mariposa Coulterville	60	696
John F	Napa Napa	61	64
John F	San Bernardino Santa Barbara	64	162
John F	San Francisco San Francisco 4	681168	
John F	San Francisco San Francisco 2	67 598	
John F S	Contra Costa Twp 3	57	591
John G	El Dorado Georgetown	58	699
John H	Colusa Grand Island	57	468
John H	Nevada Rough &	61	421
John H	San Francisco San Francisco 1	68 895	
John H	San Joaquin Castoria	64	877
John H	Siskiyou Callahan	69	6
John H	El Dorado Salmon Falls	581034	
John L	San Francisco San Francisco 8	681276	
John L	Santa Clara San Jose	65	328
John M	Amador Twp 4	55	257
John M	Monterey Pajaro	601021	
John M	Sierra Eureka	661044	
John O	Santa Cruz Soguel	66	596
John P	Mendocino Ukiah	60	794
John P	Nevada Red Dog	61	556
John P	Siskiyou Shasta Valley	69	121
John P	Siskiyou Yreka	69	188
John P	Yuba Marysville	72	867
John P	Yuba Marysville	72	922
John P*	Mendocino Ukiah	60	794
John R	Trinity Cox'S Bar	701037	
John R S	Contra Costa Twp 2	57	539
John R*	Mendocino Ukiah	60	794
John S	Butte Oro	56	688
John S	Los Angeles Los Angeles	59	301
John S	Santa Cruz Santa Cruz	66	631
John S*	Butte Oro	56	688
John T	Sierra Pine Grove	66	829
John T	Tuolumne Twp 2	71	287
John U	San Francisco San Francisco 8	681295	
John W	San Joaquin Elliott	64	948
John W	Siskiyou Yreka	69	171
John W	Yuba Bear Rvr	72	999
John*	Calaveras Twp 5	57	172
John*	Napa Yount	61	32
John*	Sacramento Ward 1	63	131
Johnthan	Calaveras Twp 5	57	221
Johnthun	Calaveras Twp 5	57	221
Jonathan	Calaveras Twp 5	57	221
Jonathan	Mendocino Big Rvr	60	841
Jonathan	Tulara Twp 2	71	22
Jonathan W	Mendocino Big Rvr	60	841
Jos	Alameda Brooklyn	55	158
Jos	Amador Twp 3	55	404
Jos	Amador Twp 1	55	493
Jos	Butte Chico	56	551
Jos	Butte Kimshaw	56	577
Jos	Butte Oregon	56	636
Jos	Placer Rattle Snake	62	636
Jos	San Francisco San Francisco 10	242 67	
Jos	San Francisco San Francisco 10	246 67	
Jos	San Francisco San Francisco 2	67 611	
Jos	Tehama Red Bluff	70	910
Jos B	Butte Oregon	56	634
Jos J	Sacramento Ward 1	63	88
Jos J	Trinity Indian C	70	986
Jos L	San Francisco San Francisco 10	282 67	
Jos W	Amador Twp 2	55	279
Jos W	Klamath Liberty	59	235
Josep	Mariposa Twp 1	60	672
Joseph	Alameda Brooklyn	55	123
Joseph	Alameda Brooklyn	55	125
Joseph	Alameda Oakland	55	42
Joseph	Calaveras Twp 5	57	246
Joseph	Calaveras Twp 7	57	26
Joseph	Calaveras Twp 9	57	374
Joseph	Calaveras Twp 9	57	384
SMITH			
Joseph	Calaveras Twp 8	57	98
Joseph	El Dorado Salmon Hills	581059	
Joseph	Humbolt Bucksport	59	162
Joseph	Los Angeles Los Angeles	59	380
Joseph	Mendocino Big Rvr	60	852
Joseph	Napa Clear Lake	61	138
Joseph	Placer Rattle Snake	62	602
Joseph	Placer Ophirville	62	658
Joseph	Placer Todds Va	62	763
Joseph	Plumas Quincy	621007	
Joseph	San Diego Agua Caliente	64	834
Joseph	San Francisco San Francisco 4	681134	
Joseph	San Francisco San Francisco 4	681139	
Joseph	San Francisco San Francisco 7	681353	
Joseph	San Francisco San Francisco 3	67 56	
Joseph	San Francisco San Francisco 3	67 62	
Joseph	San Francisco San Francisco 1	68 807	
Joseph	San Joaquin Elkhorn	64	950
Joseph	San Mateo Twp 1	65	56
Joseph	Santa Clara Redwood	65	453
Joseph	Shasta Millvill	66	738
Joseph	Siskiyou Yreka	69	154
Joseph	Siskiyou Cottonwood	69	98
Joseph	Solano Benecia	69	315
Joseph	Sonoma Armally	69	503
Joseph	Yuba New York	72	726
Joseph A	Tuolumne Columbia	71	341
Joseph H	Siskiyou Yreka	69	124
Joseph L	San Francisco San Francisco 1	68 807	
Joseph M	Los Angeles Los Angeles	59	301
Joseph S	Sierra Downieville	661000	
Joseph T	San Joaquin Elkhorn	64	993
Joseph T	Yuba Marysville	72	850
Josephine	Monterey San Juan	60	997
Josephine	Tuolumne Twp 1	71	196
Joshua	Humbolt Union	59	180
Joshua	San Francisco San Francisco 2	67 631	
Joshua	Tuolumne Twp 5	71	489
Joshua F	Calaveras Twp 4	57	335
Josiah	Napa Clear Lake	61	138
Josiah J	Los Angeles Los Angeles	59	341
Jsaac P*	Butte Hamilton	56	529
Julia	San Francisco San Francisco 12	392 67	
Julia	San Joaquin Elkhorn	64	977
Julia B	Sonoma Russian	69	439
Julian*	Calaveras Twp 6	57	160
Julius	San Francisco San Francisco 8	681321	
Julius	Solano Vacaville	69	362
Jw	Nevada Nevada	61	313
K F	El Dorado Placerville	58	899
Kate	San Francisco San Francisco 6	67 445	
Kate	Yuba Marysville	72	898
L	Sacramento Granite	63	222
L	Sacramento Sutter	63	292
L	San Mateo Twp 1	65	61
L	Siskiyou Cottonwoood	69	103
L	Sonoma Washington	69	671
L	Trinity North Fo	701023	
L	Tuolumne Twp 4	71	154
L	Yolo Putah	72	553
L C	Merced Twp 1	60	899
L E	Sacramento Ward 4	63	528
L F	Sutter Nicolaus	70	830
L H P	Mariposa Twp 3	60	596
L L	Nevada Eureka	61	380
L P	Butte Oro	56	683
L P	El Dorado Diamond	58	771
L P	Sacramento Ward 4	63	527
L P	Siskiyou Callahan	69	5
L P*	Butte Oro	56	683
L R	Siskiyou Callahan	69	5
L*	Sacramento Ward 1	63	85
Landra	Sonoma Sonoma	69	637
Lane	San Joaquin Elkhorn	64	976
Lauranee	San Francisco San Francisco 2	67 764	
Lawrance	San Francisco San Francisco 2	67 764	
Lawson	San Joaquin Oneal	64	930
Lebby	Siskiyou Scott Va	69	33
Lenord F	Sacramento Ward 4	63	507
Leonard W	Sierra Pine Grove	66	829
Leretta	Calaveras Twp 5	57	206
Levi	Butte Chico	56	542
Levi	Contra Costa Twp 2	57	580
Levi	Marin Tomales	60	776
Levi	Sonoma Russian	69	444
Levi Junr	Sonoma Russian	69	444
Levi S	San Bernardino San Bernadino	64	621
Levi Senr	Sonoma Russian	69	444
Levi W	Sierra Poverty	66	799
Levy	El Dorado Salmon Falls	581035	
Lewis	Butte Ophir	56	796
Lewis	Marin San Rafael	60	765
Lewis	San Francisco San Francisco 12	384 67	

California 1860 Census Index

Name	County Locale	M653 Roll	Page	Name	County Locale	M653 Roll	Page	Name	County Locale	M653 Roll	Page
SMITH				**SMITH**				**SMITH**			
Lewis	Santa Clara Fremont	65	418	Mary	San Francisco San Francisco 4	681	223	Natl	Mendocino Big Rvr	60	846
Lewis C	Alameda Brooklyn	55	154	Mary	San Francisco San Francisco 10		182	Navton	Mariposa Twp 1	60	646
Lewis G	Placer Secret R	62	612			67		Ned	Butte Kimshaw	56	581
Liberty	Marin San Rafael	60	763	Mary	San Francisco San Francisco 10		183	Nelson	Sierra Gibsonville	66	852
Lizzie M	Sacramento Ward 3	63	462			67		Nelson	Sonoma Armally	69	483
Lonis	Mendocino Big Rvr	60	847	Mary	San Francisco San Francisco 6	67	407	Nelson	Tuolumne Twp 2	71	379
Lorenzo D	San Bernadino	64	674	Mary	San Francisco San Francisco 6	67	469	Nervton	Mariposa Twp 1	60	646
	San Bernardino			Mary	San Francisco San Francisco 2	67	573	Newton	Mariposa Twp 1	60	646
Lori A	Alameda Brooklyn	55	183	Mary	San Francisco San Francisco 2	67	632	Nicholas	Del Norte Happy Ca	58	669
Lorrenzo	Calaveras Twp 8	57	86	Mary	San Francisco San Francisco 1	68	846	Nicholas	Los Angeles Elmonte	59	263
Louis	Calaveras Twp 8	57	94	Mary	San Francisco San Francisco 1	68	852	Nicholas	San Francisco San Francisco 11		116
Louis	Mendocino Big Rvr	60	847	Mary	San Joaquin Douglass	64	925			67	
Louis	Sacramento Ward 4	63	520	Mary	Sierra La Porte	66	773	Nicholas	San Francisco San Francisco 12		368
Louisa	Napa Napa	61	102	Mary	Solano Vallejo	69	272			67	
Louisa	San Francisco San Francisco 4	681	171	Mary	Solano Vacaville	69	354	Nicholas	Siskiyou Yreka	69	185
Loyd	Alameda Brooklyn	55	209	Mary A	San Francisco San Francisco 2	67	798	Nicholas	Tuolumne Jamestown	71	448
Loyd T	Alameda Brooklyn	55	186	Mary A	Sonoma Armally	69	479	Nicholas	Yolo Cottonwoood	72	649
Lucey	Marin Bolinas	60	733	Mary B	San Francisco San Francisco 4	681	138	Nickolas	Plumas Quincy	621	007
Lucretia	Trinity Trinity	70	973	Mary E	San Francisco San Francisco 9	68	988	Nicola*	Shasta Shasta	66	673
Lucy	Marin Bolinas	60	733	Mary H	San Mateo Twp 1	65	58	Nicolos	Shasta Shasta	66	673
Luke	Alameda Murray	55	225	Mary J	Sacramento Natonia	63	276	Norman	Calaveras Twp 8	57	58
Lydery*	Tuolumne Twp 1	71	256	Mary J	San Francisco San Francisco 2	67	803	Norman	Trinity New Rvr	701	031
Lydia	El Dorado Greenwood	58	708	Mary O	Solano Vallejo	69	272	O	Calaveras Twp 8	57	71
Lyman	San Francisco San Francisco 11		147	Mary P	Yuba Marysville	72	942	O	El Dorado Placerville	58	869
		67		Mary Y	San Francisco San Francisco 2	67	803	O	Tuolumne Twp 2	71	284
Lyman A	Los Angeles Los Angeles	59	305	Mary*	San Francisco San Francisco 2	67	573	O A	Sacramento Ward 1	63	48
Lyman R	Yuba New York	72	721	Mathew	Placer Iona Hills	62	893	O H P	Butte Hamilton	56	525
M	Amador Twp 6	55	447	Mathew	Sacramento Ward 3	63	478	O J	Siskiyou Cottonwood	69	107
M	Calaveras Twp 9	57	379	Mathew	San Francisco San Francisco 2	67	633	O J	Siskiyou Cottonwoood	69	108
M	El Dorado Diamond	58	770	Mathew	San Francisco San Francisco 1	68	895	O L	Nevada Grass Valley	61	194
M	El Dorado Newtown	58	777	Mathew	Yuba Rose Bar	72	793	O M	Nevada Rough &	61	402
M	El Dorado Placerville	58	824	Matt	San Mateo Twp 3	65	93	O N	Siskiyou Scott Ri	69	81
M	El Dorado Placerville	58	881	Matthew	Sacramento Ward 4	63	519	O W	Solano Vacaville	69	347
M	Nevada Grass Valley	61	143	May J	Sacramento Natonia	63	276	O*	Nevada Washington	61	333
M	Nevada Nevada	61	298	Mc Duffy*	Humbolt Pacific	59	137	Ohio C	Sacramento Ward 3	63	474
M	Nevada Eureka	61	371	Medad D	Plumas Meadow Valley	62	905	Oliver	El Dorado Coloma	581	120
M	Sacramento Granite	63	223	Meguil*	San Bernardino Santa Inez	64	137	Oliver	San Francisco San Francisco 1	68	889
M	Sacramento Sutter	63	308	Michael	Calaveras Twp 7	57	25	Onen*	Yuba Rose Bar	72	800
M	Sacramento Georgian	63	342	Michael	Calaveras Twp 9	57	369	Orange A	Tuolumne Twp 3	71	431
M	San Francisco San Francisco 2	67	726	Michael	Calaveras Twp 8	57	77	Orca*	Napa Clear Lake	61	137
M	Siskiyou Cottonwoood	69	105	Michael	Placer Iona Hills	62	888	Oren	Napa Clear Lake	61	137
M	Siskiyou Callahan	69	16	Michael	San Francisco San Francisco 9	68	949	Orlando	Sacramento Ward 1	63	64
M	Sonoma Bodega	69	535	Michael	San Joaquin Stockton	641	078	Orrin	Napa Clear Lake	61	127
M	Sonoma Vallejo	69	622	Michael	Sierra Downieville	661	001	Orson K	Tulara Twp 1	71	94
M	Stanislaus Oatvale	70	718	Michael	Sierra La Porte	66	769	Orson K	Tuolumne Visalia	71	94
M	Trinity Weaverville	701	080	Michael	Tuolumne Columbia	71	355	Oscar	Los Angeles Los Angeles	59	363
M A	Siskiyou Scott Va	69	41	Michael	Yuba Rose Bar	72	793	Oscar	Los Angeles Los Angeles	59	367
M C	San Francisco San Francisco 9	68	948	Michal	San Francisco San Francisco 1	68	886	Oscar	Solano Fairfield	69	202
M J	Nevada Rough &	61	411	Micheal	Calaveras Twp 9	57	369	Otis	Mariposa Coulterville	60	684
M L	Calaveras Twp 8	57	69	Michl	San Francisco San Francisco 1	68	917	Owen	Yuba Rose Bar	72	800
M L C	Humbolt Bucksport	59	155	Miguel*	San Bernardino Santa Inez	64	137	P	Napa Clear Lake	61	119
M P	Monterey Mont	60	961	Mike	Amador Twp 5	55	335	P	Nevada Grass Valley	61	185
M S	San Francisco San Francisco 4	681	228	Mike	Santa Clara Santa Clara	65	487	P	San Francisco San Francisco 9	681	059
M V	Del Norte Happy Ca	58	669	Minor	Alameda Brooklyn	55	126	P	San Francisco San Francisco 10		348
M W	Colusa Colusi	57	428	Miss	Sierra La Porte	66	771			67	
M*	Mendocino Big Rvr	60	842	Mo*	Mendocino Big Rvr	60	842	P	San Francisco San Francisco 5	67	541
Mabert	Los Angeles Los Angeles	59	350	Morris	Butte Oregon	56	618	P	San Joaquin Stockton	641	099
Malcomb	Sierra Gibsonville	66	860	Morris	Placer Yankee J	62	761	P	Santa Clara San Jose	65	363
Malomb	Sierra Gibsonville	66	860	Morris	Placer Forest H	62	801	P B	El Dorado Georgetown	58	701
Marg A	San Francisco San Francisco 2	67	798	Morris	Plumas Meadow Valley	62	901	P B	Tuolumne Jamestown	71	437
Marg*	San Francisco San Francisco 2	67	573	Mortimer J	San Francisco 9	681	083	P C	Butte Cascade	56	700
Margaret	San Francisco San Francisco 3	67	28		San Francisco			P F	Trinity Trinity	70	973
Maria K	San Francisco San Francisco 5	67	546	Moses	Sacramento Ward 3	63	449	P H	Butte Chico	56	552
Marietta	San Francisco San Francisco 10		336	Moses	Sacramento Ward 1	63	9	P R	Mariposa Twp 3	60	615
		67		Moses J	Siskiyou Shasta Valley	69	120	P T	San Francisco San Francisco 7	681	420
Mark	Santa Cruz Santa Cruz	66	631	Mr	San Francisco San Francisco 10		311	P W	Nevada Washington	61	336
Mark P	San Francisco San Francisco 11		152			67		P W	San Francisco San Francisco 8	681	237
		67		Mr	Sonoma Vallejo	69	622	Panet C*	Stanislaus Emory	70	756
Marshall	El Dorado Casumnes	581	164	Mr*	Mendocino Big Rvr	60	842	Pat	Marin Bolinas	60	748
Mart T	Mendocino Arrana	60	861	Mrs	Mariposa Twp 3	60	548	Pat	Sonoma Sonoma	69	637
Martha	Contra Costa Twp 1	57	511	Mrs	Nevada Nevada	61	296	Pat	Yolo No E Twp	72	670
Martha	San Francisco San Francisco 3	67	77	Mrs	Solano Benecia	69	313	Pat	Yuba North Ea	72	670
Martha A	San Francisco San Francisco 10		228	Mughill*	San Francisco San Francisco 6	67	399	Pater	Santa Clara Alviso	65	410
		67		Mychael*	Mariposa Twp 3	60	563	Patr	Marin Bolinas	60	748
Martha A	Santa Clara Santa Clara	65	488	Myron	Sacramento Ward 3	63	431	Patrick	Calaveras Twp 7	57	34
Martha J	Sacramento Ward 4	63	531	N	Nevada Grass Valley	61	149	Patrick	Mendocino Ukiah	60	806
Martin	Placer Dutch Fl	62	728	N	Placer Dutch Fl	62	726	Patrick	Tuolumne Columbia	71	355
Martin	Plumas Meadow Valley	62	906	N	Sacramento Sutter	63	293	Patrick	Tuolumne Columbia	71	472
Martin	Sacramento Granite	63	259	N	San Francisco San Francisco 9	68	946	Patrick	Yolo Slate Ro	72	689
Martin	Sierra Eureka	661	048	N	Shasta Millvill	66	745	Patrick	Yuba Slate Ro	72	689
Martin	Sierra Morristown	661	054	N	Sutter Yuba	70	762	Paulina	Sonoma Healdsbu	69	476
Martin	Solano Benecia	69	287	N A	Sacramento Sutter	63	293	Peasant	Solano Suisan	69	214
Martin	Yuba Fosters	72	826	N H	Sutter Bear Rvr	70	825	Pete	Sonoma Sonoma	69	636
Martin L	Sacramento Granite	63	260	N L	Trinity Douglas	70	978	Peter	Alameda Brooklyn	55	147
Martina	Contra Costa Twp 1	57	528	N M	Sutter Sutter	70	815	Peter	Alameda Brooklyn	55	204
Marty	Trinity Weaverville	701	080	N S	El Dorado Georgetown	58	691	Peter	Amador Twp 2	55	321
Mary	Butte Mountain	56	734	N T	Placer Iona Hills	62	862	Peter	Amador Twp 1	55	459
Mary	Contra Costa Twp 1	57	491	N W	Napa Napa	61	64	Peter	Butte Wyandotte	56	665
Mary	Marin Bolinas	60	747	Nancy	Santa Clara San Jose	65	384	Peter	Calaveras Twp 7	57	72
Mary	Napa Napa	61	102	Napoleon B	Twp 1	57	485	Peter	Calaveras Twp 8	57	85
Mary	Nevada Red Dog	61	546		Contra Costa			Peter	El Dorado White Oaks	581	010
Mary	Sacramento Ward 3	63	438	Nate	Mendocino Big Rvr	60	846	Peter	El Dorado Coloma	581	073
Mary	San Francisco San Francisco 9	681	066	Nathan	San Francisco San Francisco 2	67	783	Peter	Marin Novato	60	737
Mary	San Francisco San Francisco 9	681	106	Nathaniel	Santa Clara Fremont	65	433	Peter	Nevada Nevada	61	298
Mary	San Francisco San Francisco 4	681	170	Nathl	San Francisco San Francisco 9	68	975	Peter	Placer Michigan	62	832

California 1860 Census Index

Name	County Locale	M653 Roll	Page
SMITH			
Peter	Plumas Quincy	62	1001
Peter	Plumas Quincy	62	1003
Peter	Plumas Meadow Valley	62	931
Peter	Plumas Quincy	62	952
Peter	Plumas Quincy	62	994
Peter	Sacramento Granite	63	266
Peter	Sacramento Ward 1	63	37
Peter	Sacramento Ward 4	63	603
Peter	San Francisco San Francisco 9	68	1061
Peter	San Francisco San Francisco 9	68	1064
Peter	San Francisco San Francisco 4	68	1159
Peter	San Francisco San Francisco 11	67	137
Peter	San Francisco San Francisco 11	67	155
Peter	San Francisco San Francisco 1	68	909
Peter	San Joaquin Castoria	64	877
Peter	Santa Clara Santa Clara	65	490
Peter	Santa Clara Santa Clara	65	513
Peter	Sierra Scales D	66	803
Peter	Siskiyou Callahan	69	15
Peter	Tulara Twp 1	71	92
Peter	Tuolumne Shawsfla	71	415
Peter	Tuolumne Visalia	71	92
Peter	Yuba Marysville	72	938
Peter B	Humbolt Mattole	59	125
Peter F	Sierra La Porte	66	786
Peter M	Sierra St Louis	66	815
Peter*	Plumas Meadow Valley	62	912
Petie	Calaveras Twp 8	57	95
Pheobe	San Francisco San Francisco 9	68	960
Phil W	Alameda Brooklyn	55	138
Philip	Alameda Brooklyn	55	201
Philip	Placer Goods	62	695
Philip	San Francisco San Francisco 3	67	51
Philip R	San Francisco San Francisco 3	67	52
Phillip	Humbolt Bucksport	59	156
Phillip	San Francisco San Francisco 7	68	1372
Phillip	Sierra Twp 7	66	901
Phillip N	San Francisco San Francisco 2	67	740
Phillips	Sierra Twp 7	66	901
Philo	Solano Vacaville	69	336
Phoebe	San Francisco San Francisco 9	68	960
Plulo	Solano Vacaville	69	336
Prentiss	Butte Eureka	56	651
Q R	El Dorado Casumnes	58	1176
Quinn	Yolo Merritt	72	579
R	Nevada Grass Valley	61	145
R	Nevada Eureka	61	380
R	Placer Lisbon	62	733
R	San Francisco San Francisco 1	68	923
R	San Mateo Twp 3	65	96
R	Santa Clara San Jose	65	292
R A	Nevada Rough &	61	408
R A	Sacramento Cosummes	63	394
R B	Stanislaus Empire	70	734
R C	Tuolumne Columbia	71	302
R D	Tuolumne Shawsfla	71	389
R G	San Francisco San Francisco 4	68	1138
R H	Klamath S Fork	59	199
R J	San Francisco San Francisco 5	67	538
R L*	Tuolumne Twp 1	71	246
R M	Nevada Bridgeport	61	486
R M	Sonoma Bodega	69	526
R P	Butte Cascade	56	700
R S	Sacramento Ward 4	63	582
R Ss	El Dorado Big Bar	58	743
Ralph	Marin Tomales	60	724
Raymond	El Dorado Greenwood	58	720
Reasant	Solano Suisan	69	214
Reuben	Los Angeles Los Angeles	59	387
Richard	Marin Tomales	60	720
Richard	Plumas Quincy	62	959
Richard	Santa Cruz Pajaro	66	568
Richard	Siskiyou Cottonwoood	69	101
Richard	Stanislaus Emory	70	742
Richard	Tuolumne Don Pedro	71	538
Richd	San Francisco San Francisco 10	67	260
Richd	Sonoma Petaluma	69	566
Rob	El Dorado Placerville	58	907
Robert	Calaveras Twp 6	57	156
Robert	Calaveras Twp 5	57	233
Robert	Mendocino Big Rvr	60	848
Robert	Nevada Bloomfield	61	512
Robert	Plumas Meadow Valley	62	901
Robert	Plumas Quincy	62	917
Robert	Sacramento Georgian	63	341
Robert	San Francisco San Francisco 8	68	1262
Robert	San Francisco San Francisco 8	68	1323
Robert	San Francisco San Francisco 2	67	605
Robert	San Francisco San Francisco 3	67	70
Robert	San Joaquin Tulare	64	870
Robert	Solano Vallejo	69	276
Robert	Tulara Twp 1	71	94
SMITH			
Robert	Tuolumne Visalia	71	94
Robert	Yuba Rose Bar	72	789
Robert A	Nevada Rough &	61	438
Robert M	Santa Cruz Pajaro	66	531
Robert S	Mendocino Little L	60	831
Robert W	Los Angeles Los Angeles	59	293
Robertson L	San Francisco 8	68	1293
Robt	Butte Cascade	56	702
Robt	El Dorado Mud Springs	58	996
Robt	San Francisco San Francisco 9	68	1068
Robt	San Francisco San Francisco 1	68	905
Robt D	Plumas Quincy	62	979
Robt E	Sonoma Santa Rosa	69	416
Robt O	Napa Clear Lake	61	127
Rodriguez	San Francisco San Francisco 7	68	1359
Rollen	Trinity Mouth Ca	70	1017
Rosann	San Francisco San Francisco 10	67	183
Rosanna	San Francisco San Francisco 10	67	183
Rufus	Los Angeles Los Angeles	59	503
Rufus	Mariposa Coulterville	60	695
Rufus C	Sierra Downieville	66	1012
Rufus*	Mariposa Coulterville	60	695
Rugas	Placer Virginia	62	661
Runnell	San Francisco San Francisco 7	68	1398
S	El Dorado Placerville	58	890
S	Nevada Little Y	61	535
S	Sacramento Ward 1	63	85
S	Siskiyou Scott Ri	69	73
S	Sonoma Sonoma	69	643
S	Tuolumne Big Oak	71	154
S B	Sierra Downieville	66	978
S C	El Dorado Kelsey	58	1134
S C	Mariposa Twp 3	60	616
S D	Sacramento Ward 3	63	485
S E	Trinity Redding	70	985
S F	El Dorado Mountain	58	1185
S F	El Dorado Greenwood	58	723
S F	Sacramento Alabama	63	412
S F	San Francisco San Francisco 10	67	297
S G	Amador Twp 4	55	244
S H	El Dorado Casumnes	58	1174
S H	San Francisco San Francisco 9	68	1053
S J	Del Norte Crescent	58	646
S L	Sacramento Ward 1	63	109
S M	Nevada Grass Valley	61	164
S M	Nevada Eureka	61	367
S M	Tuolumne Sonora	71	222
S N	Siskiyou Scott Ri	69	68
S N	Tuolumne Twp 1	71	222
S P	Sierra Downieville	66	1021
S R	Yolo Cache Crk	72	607
S R	Yolo Cache	72	608
S S	San Bernardino San Bernadino	64	628
S W	Amador Twp 3	55	406
S W	Nevada Eureka	61	367
S W	San Mateo Twp 1	65	68
S*	Sacramento Ward 1	63	85
Sally J	San Francisco San Francisco 2	67	587
Sam	Bloomfield	61	527
Sam	Sacramento Ward 1	63	68
Sam	Sonoma Petaluma	69	573
Sam	Sonoma Petaluma	69	576
Saml	Amador Twp 1	55	484
Saml	Butte Oregon	56	643
Saml	Nevada Bridgeport	61	445
Saml	Sacramento Ward 1	63	28
Saml	Sacramento Franklin	63	328
Saml	San Francisco San Francisco 2	67	561
Saml	San Francisco San Francisco 2	67	693
Saml	Shasta Horsetown	66	702
Saml	Sonoma Petaluma	69	572
Saml	Stanislaus Emory	70	743
Saml	Trinity Point Ba	70	976
Saml	Tuolumne Twp 2	71	368
Saml	Yolo Merritt	72	578
Saml A	San Francisco San Francisco 2	67	794
Saml E	San Francisco San Francisco 9	68	1054
Saml G	Tuolumne Twp 3	71	468
Saml J	Tuolumne Twp 1	71	250
Saml P	San Bernardino San Bernadino	64	671
Samluel	Sierra Downieville	66	1017
Sampon	Siskiyou Yreka	69	156
Sampson	Solano Suisan	69	232
Samuel	Alameda Oakland	55	58
Samuel	El Dorado Salmon Hills	58	1065
Samuel	El Dorado Kelsey	58	1126
Samuel	El Dorado Georgetown	58	683
Samuel	El Dorado Greenwood	58	724
Samuel	Humbolt Mattole	59	121
Samuel	Marin Sauciieto	60	750
Samuel	Mendocino Ukiah	60	798
SMITH			
Samuel	Nevada Nevada	61	317
Samuel	Sacramento Ward 1	63	9
Samuel	San Francisco San Francisco 11	67	154
Samuel	San Francisco San Francisco 2	67	750
Samuel	San Francisco San Francisco 11	67	90
Samuel	San Joaquin Castoria	64	906
Samuel	Sierra Downieville	66	1017
Samuel	Solano Vacaville	69	367
Samuel	Yolo No E Twp	72	667
Samuel	Yuba Marysville	72	957
Samuel B	Yuba Marysville	72	889
Samuel P	Solano Benecia	69	316
Samul	Sonoma Russian	69	432
Sandy	Mariposa Twp 1	60	668
Sanl A	San Francisco San Francisco 2	67	794
Sarah	Sonoma Petaluma	69	565
Sarah C	Sonoma Russian	69	429
Saul	Tuolumne Springfield	71	368
Seretta*	Calaveras Twp 5	57	206
Shas	San Francisco San Francisco 9	68	968
Shelly	Butte Chico	56	531
Sheridan P	Calaveras Twp 5	57	212
Sidney	Sacramento Sutter	63	290
Sidney	San Francisco San Francisco 3	67	14
Sidney	Shasta Shasta	66	674
Sidney	Sierra Twp 7	66	897
Silas C*	Calaveras Twp 6	57	158
Silus C*	Calaveras Twp 6	57	158
Silus*	Calaveras Twp 6	57	158
Simon	San Francisco San Francisco 9	68	1089
Sophey	Napa Napa	61	106
Sophia	San Francisco San Francisco 6	67	404
Sow*	Butte Kimshaw	56	599
Stepheb	Mendocino Round Va	60	879
Stephen	Colusa Colusi	57	422
Stephen	Placer Yankee J	62	775
Stephen	Placer Iona Hills	62	872
Stephen	San Francisco San Francisco 5	67	481
Stephen	San Francisco San Francisco 2	67	805
Stephen H	San Francisco San Francisco 7	68	1430
Stephen M	San Francisco San Francisco 7	68	1348
Stephen M	Sonoma Bodega	69	524
Stephen R	San Francisco San Francisco 9	68	1084
Steven	Tuolumne Twp 6	71	538
Stewart	San Francisco San Francisco 4	68	1119
Susan	San Francisco San Francisco 8	68	1314
Susan	San Francisco San Francisco 1	68	972
Susan	Sierra Whiskey	66	849
Swaney	Yolo Slate Ra	72	718
Swaney*	Yuba New York	72	718
Swight	Sierra Grizzly	66	1057
Sydney	Plumas Meadow Valley	62	913
Sydny	Tuolumne Twp 1	71	256
Sylus	Napa Napa	61	77
Sylvester	Sierra Eureka	66	1046
Sylvester	Sonoma Healdsbu	69	473
T	El Dorado Placerville	58	840
T	Nevada Grass Valley	61	161
T	Nevada Eureka	61	367
T	Nevada Eureka	61	391
T	San Francisco San Francisco 5	67	549
T	Sutter Yuba	70	759
T	Sutter Bear Rvr	70	826
T B	Amador Twp 7	55	416
T D	Sutter Yuba	70	778
T D	Yolo Slate Ra	72	709
T H	El Dorado Placerville	58	888
T J	Sonoma Santa Rosa	69	392
T J	Tuolumne Columbia	71	303
T L	Nevada Grass Valley	61	148
T L*	Nevada Nevada	61	316
T O	Sierra Downieville	66	997
T P	Amador Twp 1	55	470
T R	Placer Dutch Fl	62	723
T S	Nevada Nevada	61	316
T T	El Dorado Mountain	58	1185
Terance	Nevada Bloomfield	61	509
Terence	Nevada Bloomfield	61	509
Teresa	Napa Napa	61	90
Teretta*	Calaveras Twp 5	57	206
Theodore E	San Francisco San Francisco 7	68	1364
Thes	Sacramento Ward 1	63	49
Tho	Siskiyou Scott Va	69	53
Thomas	Alameda Oakland	55	18
Thomas	Calaveras Twp 5	57	172
Thomas	Calaveras Twp 5	57	230
Thomas	Calaveras Twp 4	57	308
Thomas	Calaveras Twp 4	57	319
Thomas	Calaveras Twp 8	57	54
Thomas	Contra Costa Twp 1	57	493

California 1860 Census Index

Name	County Locale	M653 Roll	Page
SMITH			
Thomas	Los Angeles Tejon	59	529
Thomas	Marin San Rafael	60	766
Thomas	Marin Cortemad	60	785
Thomas	Mendocino Ukiah	60	802
Thomas	Mendocino Little L	60	834
Thomas	Mendocino Little L	60	838
Thomas	Plumas Quincy	62	1001
Thomas	San Diego San Diego	64	757
Thomas	San Francisco San Francisco 12		393
		67	
Thomas	San Luis Obispo San Luis Obispo 65		3
Thomas	Santa Clara Burnett	65	260
Thomas	Santa Clara Fremont	65	438
Thomas	Santa Cruz Pajaro	66	543
Thomas	Sierra Morristown	66	1054
Thomas	Sierra La Porte	66	784
Thomas	Sierra Pine Grove	66	830
Thomas	Siskiyou Scott Va	69	26
Thomas	Sonoma Armally	69	490
Thomas	Sonoma Bodega	69	519
Thomas	Tulara Visalia	71	14
Thomas	Tulara Visalia	71	82
Thomas	Tuolumne Columbia	71	332
Thomas	Tuolumne Chinese	71	495
Thomas	Tuolumne Montezuma	71	503
Thomas	Yolo Slate Ra	72	688
Thomas	Yuba Slate Ro	72	688
Thomas	Yuba Fosters	72	839
Thomas A	Yuba Marysville	72	874
Thomas B	Tuolumne Jamestown	71	430
Thomas F	San Joaquin Oneal	64	940
Thomas K	Sierra Downieville	66	976
Thomas R	Tuolumne Twp 3	71	430
Thomas R	Yolo No E Twp	72	669
Thomas V	San Francisco 7	68	1361
	San Francisco		
Thos	Amador Twp 6	55	439
Thos	Los Angeles Tejon	59	537
Thos	Napa Napa	61	101
Thos	Nevada Bloomfield	61	514
Thos	Sacramento Georgian	63	338
Thos	Sacramento Ward 1	63	49
Thos	San Francisco San Francisco 9	68	1064
Thos	San Francisco San Francisco 12		387
		67	
Thos	San Francisco San Francisco 2	67	629
Thos	San Francisco San Francisco 1	68	872
Thos	Santa Clara Santa Clara	65	513
Thos	Santa Clara Santa Clara	65	517
Thos	Sonoma Santa Rosa	69	417
Thos A	Alameda Oakland	55	71
Thos C	Sacramento Cosumnes	63	398
Thos D	Shasta Horsetown	66	698
Thos H	Amador Twp 2	55	262
Thos J	Fresno Twp 3	59	14
Thos J	Mariposa Twp 3	60	570
Thos L	Santa Clara San Jose	65	383
Thos M	Sacramento San Joaquin	63	356
Thos N	San Francisco San Francisco 7	68	1333
Ths	Tuolumne Twp 5	71	495
Tim	Sierra Twp 7	66	875
Tim G	Nevada Bridgeport	61	483
Timothy R	Tuolumne Twp 6	71	543
Tip*	Humbolt Mattole	59	128
Tiss*	Humbolt Mattole	59	128
Tom	Sierra Twp 7	66	875
Tridk*	San Francisco San Francisco 2	67	566
Triez	San Bernardino Santa Barbara	64	186
Uriah	Calaveras Twp 9	57	353
Uriah	Sonoma Armally	69	495
Uriat*	Calaveras Twp 9	57	353
V C	Tuolumne Sonora	71	208
V J	Calaveras Twp 8	57	57
Van B	Sacramento Franklin	63	316
Vincent	Plumas Quincy	62	922
Vincent E	Plumas Quincy	62	944
Vincent G	Calaveras Twp 5	57	188
Volney	Amador Twp 1	55	451
W	Butte Cascade	56	701
W	Calaveras Twp 9	57	415
W	El Dorado Kelsey	58	1157
W	El Dorado Georgetown	58	699
W	El Dorado Diamond	58	807
W	Mariposa Twp 1	60	668
W	Nevada Washington	61	331
W	Nevada Washington	61	341
W	Placer Dutch Fl	62	728
W	San Francisco San Francisco 5	67	523
W	San Joaquin Stockton	64	1090
W	Shasta Horsetown	66	689
W	Shasta Millvill	66	751
W	Solano Vacaville	69	322
W	Sonoma Salt Point	69	694
W	Tehama Lassen	70	867
W	Yolo Washington	72	602

Name	County Locale	M653 Roll	Page
SMITH			
W A	Stanislaus Oatvale	70	716
W A	Yolo Cache Crk	72	663
W B	Nevada Red Dog	61	538
W B	Placer Auburn	62	564
W B	San Francisco San Francisco 1	68	904
W B	Sonoma Armally	69	505
W B	Yolo Putah	72	549
W C	Nevada Grass Valley	61	235
W C	Placer Forest H	62	793
W C Caly*	Nevada Bridgeport	61	474
W C R	San Mateo Twp 3	65	90
W D	Marin Bolinas	60	745
W D	San Francisco San Francisco 6	67	456
W E	Shasta Cottonwoood	66	723
W E	Yolo Cache Crk	72	643
W F	Trinity Rearings	70	990
W G	Marin Tomales	60	775
W H	Amador Twp 2	55	308
W H	El Dorado Placerville	58	834
W H	El Dorado Placerville	58	847
W H	Nevada Nevada	61	242
W H	Nevada Eureka	61	377
W H	Nevada Rough &	61	421
W H	Sacramento San Joaquin	63	351
W H	San Francisco San Francisco 9	68	961
W H	San Mateo Twp 3	65	85
W H	Siskiyou Cottonwoood	69	102
W H	Tehama Lassen	70	875
W H	Trinity E Weaver	70	1058
W H	Tuolumne Twp 3	71	464
W J	El Dorado Georgetown	58	691
W J	San Francisco San Francisco 5	67	536
W J	Solano Vacaville	69	355
W J	Tuolumne Twp 1	71	252
W L	Mariposa Coulterville	60	695
W L	Santa Clara San Jose	65	308
W L*	Sacramento Brighton	63	199
W M	Amador Twp 7	55	417
W M	El Dorado Cold Spring	58	1101
W M	El Dorado Placerville	58	826
W M	Tuolumne Twp 1	71	261
W N*	Butte Wyandotte	56	666
W O	San Francisco San Francisco 6	67	474
W O F	San Francisco San Francisco 5	67	522
W P	El Dorado Coloma	58	1119
W P	Marin Bolinas	60	742
W P	Sutter Sutter	70	805
W P	Tuolumne Springfield	71	372
W R	Butte Ophir	56	773
W R	Butte Ophir	56	784
W R	Calaveras Twp 8	57	77
W R	Mariposa Twp 1	60	649
W R	Mariposa Twp 1	60	949
W R	Santa Clara Santa Clara	65	474
W S	Nevada Red Dog	61	544
W S	Sutter Butte	70	798
W S*	Sacramento Brighton	63	199
W T	Solano Benecia	69	291
W W	Butte Wyandotte	56	666
W W	Napa Hot Springs	61	12
W W	Shasta Millvill	66	743
W W	Sierra Twp 7	66	874
W*	Butte Kimshaw	56	604
Walker	Humbolt Eel Rvr	59	150
Walker	Santa Clara Fremont	65	430
Walter	Alameda Oakland	55	11
Walter	Trinity Trinity	70	973
Warren	Sacramento Franklin	63	330
Warren	Sacramento San Joaquin	63	357
Warren C	Yuba Marysville	72	959
Warren H	San Francisco San Francisco 9	68	981
Washington	El Dorado Kelsey	58	1138
Welhelm	Monterey Alisal	60	1032
Wesley	San Bernardino S Timate	64	689
Wiliam	Calaveras Twp 5	57	210
Wiliam	San Joaquin Elkhorn	64	988
Willard M	San Francisco San Francisco 8	68	1297
William	Alameda Oakland	55	48
William	Amador Twp 2	55	279
William	Calaveras Twp 5	57	195
William	Calaveras Twp 5	57	210
William	Calaveras Twp 10	57	275
William	Calaveras Twp 4	57	335
William	Calaveras Twp 9	57	371
William	Calaveras Twp 8	57	70
William	Calaveras Twp 7	57	8
William	Contra Costa Twp 2	57	581
William	Contra Costa Twp 3	57	585
William	El Dorado White Oaks	58	1029
William	El Dorado Salmon Falls	58	1055
William	El Dorado Kelsey	58	1136
William	El Dorado Kelsey	58	1140
William	Klamath Klamath	59	226
William	Los Angeles Los Angeles	59	349
William	Marin Novato	60	736

Name	County Locale	M653 Roll	Page
SMITH			
William	Marin Tomales	60	776
William	Marin Cortemad	60	779
William	Mendocino Big Rvr	60	845
William	Mendocino Arrana	60	862
William	Monterey Pajaro	60	1022
William	Monterey Monterey	60	966
William	Nevada Rough &	61	412
William	Nevada Rough &	61	436
William	Nevada Bloomfield	61	513
William	Nevada Red Dog	61	555
William	Placer Michigan	62	832
William	Placer Michigan	62	839
William	Placer Michigan	62	842
William	Placer Michigan	62	849
William	Plumas Quincy	62	1001
William	Plumas Meadow Valley	62	902
William	Plumas Meadow Valley	62	928
William	Plumas Quincy	62	956
William	Plumas Quincy	62	962
William	San Bernardino Santa Barbara	64	199
William	San Diego San Diego	64	768
William	San Francisco San Francisco 9	68	1099
William	San Francisco San Francisco 4	68	1224
William	San Francisco San Francisco 8	68	1247
William	San Francisco San Francisco 8	68	1248
William	San Francisco San Francisco 7	68	1354
William	San Francisco San Francisco 7	68	1359
William	San Francisco San Francisco 7	68	1377
William	San Francisco San Francisco 7	68	1423
William	San Francisco San Francisco 7	68	1430
William	San Francisco San Francisco 12		387
		67	
William	San Francisco San Francisco 3	67	6
William	San Joaquin O'Neal	64	1007
William	San Joaquin Castoria	64	908
William	San Mateo Twp 3	65	85
William	San Mateo Twp 3	65	93
William	Santa Cruz Pajaro	66	527
William	Shasta French G	66	716
William	Sierra Poverty	66	799
William	Siskiyou Yreka	69	125
William	Solano Suisan	69	236
William	Solano Benecia	69	298
William	Tulara Yule Rvr	71	22
William	Tulara Keeneysburg	71	46
William	Tulara Petersburg	71	51
William	Tuolumne Twp 1	71	187
William	Tuolumne Columbia	71	293
William	Tuolumne Shawsfla	71	397
William	Tuolumne Shawsfla	71	399
William	Tuolumne Shawsfla	71	413
William	Tuolumne Jamestown	71	455
William	Tuolumne Twp 3	71	466
William	Yolo Cache	72	595
William	Yuba Fosters	72	823
William	Yuba Marysville	72	863
William	Yuba Marysville	72	975
William G	Tuolumne Chinese	71	501
William H	Contra Costa Twp 3	57	604
William H	San Francisco San Francisco 11	68	116
		67	
William H	San Francisco San Francisco 8	68	1315
William J	San Francisco San Francisco 7	68	1326
William P	San Francisco San Francisco 8	68	1276
William S	Contra Costa Twp 2	57	568
William S	San Francisco San Francisco 4	68	1167
William T	Solano Vacaville	69	354
William W	San Joaquin Elkhorn	64	975
William*	Placer Michigan	62	857
Willian*	Calaveras Twp 6	57	160
Willie A	San Joaquin Elkhorn	64	967
Wilson	Calaveras Twp 6	57	154
Wilson	El Dorado Mud Springs	58	996
Wilson	Sonoma Armally	69	483
Winsor F	San Francisco San Francisco 10	68	237
		67	
Wm	Alameda Brooklyn	55	132
Wm	Alameda Brooklyn	55	149
Wm	Amador Twp 2	55	268
Wm	Amador Twp 2	55	272
Wm	Amador Twp 2	55	283
Wm	Butte Kimshaw	56	604
Wm	Butte Oregon	56	620
Wm	Butte Bidwell	56	706
Wm	Butte Ophir	56	763
Wm	Calaveras Twp 6	57	155
Wm	Calaveras Twp 10	57	283
Wm	Calaveras Twp 9	57	385
Wm	Calaveras Twp 9	57	386
Wm	Calaveras Twp 9	57	388
Wm	Colusa Spring Valley	57	435
Wm	El Dorado Greenwood	58	708
Wm	Marin Cortemad	60	755
Wm	Marin Cortemad	60	781
Wm	Mariposa Twp 1	60	668

Name	County Locale	M653 Roll	Page
SMITH			
Wm	Merced Twp 1	60	901
Wm	Napa Napa	61	100
Wm	Napa Napa	61	91
Wm	Nevada Nevada	61	280
Wm	Nevada Nevada	61	296
Wm	Nevada Eureka	61	350
Wm	Placer Rattle Snake	62	631
Wm	Placer Rattle Snake	62	633
Wm	Placer Ophirville	62	654
Wm	Placer Virginia	62	685
Wm	Placer Dutch Fl	62	734
Wm	Plumas Meadow Valley	62	905
Wm	Sacramento Ward 1	63	110
Wm	Sacramento Ward 1	63	116
Wm	Sacramento Ward 1	63	132
Wm	Sacramento Ward 1	63	13
Wm	Sacramento American	63	171
Wm	Sacramento Ward 1	63	17
Wm	Sacramento Granite	63	253
Wm	Sacramento Ward 3	63	478
Wm	Sacramento Ward 4	63	505
Wm	San Francisco San Francisco 3	67	19
Wm	San Francisco San Francisco 10	67	227
Wm	San Francisco San Francisco 10	67	252
Wm	San Francisco San Francisco 10	67	270
Wm	San Francisco San Francisco 3	67	32
Wm	San Francisco San Francisco 3	67	70
Wm	San Francisco San Francisco 2	67	757
Wm	San Francisco San Francisco 2	67	792
Wm	San Francisco San Francisco 1	68	906
Wm	San Francisco San Francisco 1	68	919
Wm	San Francisco San Francisco 1	68	920
Wm	San Francisco San Francisco 1	68	923
Wm	Sierra Excelsior	66	1034
Wm	Sonoma Santa Rosa	69	394
Wm	Sonoma Russian	69	435
Wm	Sonoma Mendocino	69	464
Wm	Sonoma Armally	69	517
Wm	Sonoma Bodega	69	527
Wm	Tehama Lassen	70	866
Wm	Tehama Lassen	70	878
Wm	Trinity Texas Ba	70	981
Wm	Tuolumne Big Oak	71	130
Wm	Yolo No E Twp	72	675
Wm	Yolo No E Twp	72	684
Wm	Yolo Slate Ra	72	687
Wm	Yuba North Ea	72	675
Wm	Yuba Slate Ro	72	684
Wm	Yuba North Ea	72	687
Wm	Yuba Long Bar	72	765
Wm A	Sacramento Ward 4	63	599
Wm A	San Bernardino San Bernardino	64	616
Wm A	San Francisco San Francisco 2	67	563
Wm A	Santa Clara San Jose	65	306
Wm B	Calaveras Twp 10	57	294
Wm B	Mariposa Coulterville	60	679
Wm B	San Francisco San Francisco 1	68	832
Wm B	San Francisco San Francisco 1	68	834
Wm C S	Napa Napa	61	64
Wm D	Calaveras Twp 4	57	319
Wm D	Placer Dutch Fl	62	731
Wm D	Santa Clara Gilroy	65	251
Wm F	Alameda Brooklyn	55	199
Wm F	San Francisco San Francisco 3	67	37
Wm F	Yolo Slate Ra	72	703
Wm Fonte*	Alameda Oakland	55	2
Wm Foute*	Alameda Oakland	55	2
Wm Fowl	Alameda Oakland	55	2
Wm G	Nevada Nevada	61	273
Wm H	Humbolt Mattole	59	125
Wm H	Sacramento Ward 3	63	457
Wm H	Sonoma Petaluma	69	553
Wm H	Tuolumne Twp 1	71	216
Wm J	Humbolt Union	59	188
Wm J	Los Angeles Los Angeles	59	511
Wm J	San Francisco San Francisco 10	67	304
Wm J	San Francisco San Francisco 10	67	335
Wm J	Sierra Twp 5	66	941
Wm J	Sonoma Petaluma	69	565
Wm L	Sacramento Granite	63	260
Wm L	Tuolumne Twp 1	71	232
Wm M	Amador Twp 6	55	443
Wm M	Sacramento Ward 1	63	28
Wm M	San Francisco San Francisco 1	68	919
Wm N	Monterey Monterey	60	964
Wm O	Nevada Nevada	61	298
Wm R	Sonoma Santa Rosa	69	394
Wm S	Amador Twp 4	55	241
Wm S	Sierra Twp 5	66	941
SMITH			
Wm T	Yuba Slate Ro	72	703
Wm*	Butte Kimshaw	56	604
Zerelda	Yolo Cottonwood	72	650
Zirelda	Yolo Cottonwoood	72	650
SMITHE			
Andrew	Placer Yankee J	62	776
Eliza	San Francisco San Francisco 1	68	808
SMITHEMSEY			
Guster	El Dorado Greenwood	58	715
SMITHER			
John	Solano Suisan	69	218
SMITHERAM			
Harry	Stanislaus Empire	70	732
SMITHERS			
A	Sonoma Salt Point	69	690
E	Yolo Fremont	72	605
James	San Francisco San Francisco 8	68	1270
John	Plumas Quincy	62	973
William	Calaveras Twp 7	57	31
SMITHEY			
Jerry	Yuba Slate Ro	72	700
SMITHHENT			
Louis*	Calaveras Twp 4	57	334
SMITHLAND			
Louis	Calaveras Twp 4	57	334
SMITHLANT			
Louis*	Calaveras Twp 4	57	334
SMITHLEY			
P	Nevada Grass Valley	61	167
SMITHLING			
Jno	Nevada Nevada	61	278
SMITHRIGHT			
Robert	San Mateo Twp 3	65	97
SMITHS			
Edmond	Butte Bidwell	56	720
H	Butte Wyandotte	56	669
J M	Butte Ophir	56	753
John S*	Butte Oro	56	688
Jonathan	San Mateo Twp 2	65	122
S P	Butte Ophir	56	824
Wm	Butte Ophir	56	763
SMITHSNIDER			
M*	Nevada Nevada	61	249
SMITHSOM			
W L	Santa Clara San Jose	65	356
SMITHSON			
J	Santa Clara San Jose	65	389
M	El Dorado Kelsey	58	1135
SMITHTING			
Jno*	Nevada Nevada	61	278
SMITHWICK			
Edward	Placer Michigan	62	847
Ellen	San Francisco San Francisco 3	67	41
SMITHWORTH			
Hiram	Sierra Twp 7	66	879
W S	Shasta Shasta	66	731
SMITHZNIDER			
M*	Nevada Nevada	61	249
SMITT			
Antonio*	Tuolumne Twp 3	71	452
Charles	Tuolumne Twp 3	71	469
Elijah*	Mariposa Coulterville	60	693
Martin*	El Dorado Kelsey	58	1150
Nicola*	Shasta Shasta	66	673
Rufus*	Mariposa Coulterville	60	695
SMITTE			
Ananias	Sacramento Ward 4	63	555
SMITTEY			
George	Contra Costa Twp 2	57	556
SMITTLE			
John	Napa Yount	61	32
SMITTLETON			
Martin	Nevada Rough &	61	408
SMITTLY			
P	Sacramento Sutter	63	304
SMITY			
---	Shasta Shasta	66	670
SMITZER			
Frank	Placer Iona Hills	62	879
Henry	Placer Iona Hills	62	879
John	Placer Virginia	62	690
Joseph	Del Norte Crescent	58	637
SMMERS			
James W	Tuolumne Twp 1	71	250
SMO			
Gru	Nevada Washington	61	342
SMOATS			
Geo	Siskiyou Scott Va	69	27
SMOCKER			
---	Klamath Klamath	59	226
SMODGRASS			
Alyada	Yolo Cache Crk	72	592
SMOKE			
Samuel	Tuolumne Sonora	71	188
SMOKER			
---	Fresno Twp 2	59	109
SMOKKE			
Jacob	Alameda Oakland	55	73
SMOLLEN			
James	Sonoma Russian	69	436
SMOLLEY			
Jacob*	San Joaquin Stockton	64	1030
W	El Dorado Diamond	58	809
SMOMUDIO			
Clara	San Francisco San Francisco 6	67	440
SMONS			
John	Placer Yankee J	62	759
SMOOT			
John	Monterey San Juan	60	994
John*	Calaveras Twp 7	57	2
M	San Mateo Twp 3	65	79
Samuel	Fresno Twp 3	59	11
William	Fresno Twp 3	59	11
SMOOTH			
Charles	Yuba Rose Bar	72	808
SMOOTHLY			
Philip	San Francisco San Francisco 11	67	116
SMOOTS			
Geo	Siskiyou Scott Va	69	27
SMOOTZ			
Antone	Mendocino Round Va	60	879
SMOPE			
L*	Sacramento Granite	63	259
SMORT			
John	Monterey San Juan	60	994
SMOTHERS			
Thos	Placer Illinois	62	703
SMOUT			
Geo	Santa Clara San Jose	65	363
SMOW			
Levin	Alameda Brooklyn	55	125
SMTH			
John M	San Francisco San Francisco 7	68	1379
Stephen	Sonoma Bodega	69	525
SMTHWORTH			
Hiram*	Sierra Twp 7	66	879
SMTIH			
J	Tuolumne Big Oak	71	154
William	San Diego Agua Caliente	64	835
Wm	Amador Twp 2	55	281
SMUCKA			
---	Fresno Twp 2	59	114
SMUDDY			
John*	Sacramento Ward 1	63	123
SMULL			
George W	San Joaquin Elkhorn	64	986
SMURRW			
William	San Joaquin Elkhorn	64	951
SMUSH			
John D	Calaveras Twp 10	57	278
SMUT			
Joseph*	Calaveras Twp 9	57	367
SMUTHERS			
E	Yolo Fremont	72	605
SMUTT			
R W H	El Dorado Eldorado	58	937
SMUTYLN			
Godfrey*	Placer Iona Hills	62	893
SMUTZLU			
Charles*	Placer Forest H	62	799
SMYDER			
F V	Sierra Eureka	66	1044
SMYDTZ			
Carol	Los Angeles Tejon	59	525
SMYJTH			
Jerry	Calaveras Twp 9	57	401
SMYTH			
Alice A	San Francisco San Francisco 10	67	217
Henry	Alameda Brooklyn	55	134
J C	Tuolumne Big Oak	71	147
Jacob	Yolo Putah	72	614
James	Solano Vacaville	69	352
Jerry	Calaveras Twp 9	57	401
John F	Fresno Twp 1	59	33
John O	Shasta Shasta	66	674
Mathias	Solano Vacaville	69	352
Mychael*	Mariposa Twp 3	60	563
Peter	Del Norte Crescent	58	649
Rolenda	Tehama Lassen	70	869
Tho	Siskiyou Scott Ri	69	74
Wm	Tehama Red Bluff	70	923
SMYTHE			
H	Los Angeles Tejon	59	525
H	Nevada Washington	61	333
John	Solano Vacaville	69	334
John B	Del Norte Crescent	58	635
Kpatrick	Del Norte Crescent	58	633
Michard	Del Norte Crescent	58	635
Patrick	Del Norte Crescent	58	634
SMYTHY			
Mychael*	Mariposa Twp 3	60	563

California 1860 Census Index

Name	County Locale	M653 RollPage
SNABACHO		
---	Mendocino Calpella	60 825
SNADABAL		
Cruz	Santa Clara Almaden	65 269
SNADEN		
Jas*	Butte Chico	56 555
SNADER		
Allen	Sierra Excelsior	661033
SNADEW		
Jas*	Butte Chico	56 555
SNADON		
Jas	Butte Chico	56 555
SNAGGLE TOOTH		
---	Tulara Twp 2	71 36
SNAGGLE		
---	Fresno Twp 2	59 18
SNAGGLEWAUN		
---*	Tulara Visalia	71 35
SNAILE		
Geo*	Butte Bidwell	56 713
SNAIN		
John G*	Sierra Gibsonville	66 855
SNAKE EYE		
---	Tulara Twp 2	71 35
SNAKE		
Rattle	Tulara Twp 1	71 116
SNAKELMENNUE		
---*	Tulara Visalia	71 38
SNANE		
John	San Joaquin Stockton	641079
SNANG		
Wm L	Placer Dutch Fl	62 726
SNANN		
Joseph*	Yuba Fosters	72 837
Joseph*	Yuba Fosters	72 838
SNANSON		
Jo	Mariposa Coulterville	60 703
SNAP		
Joseph	Colusa Monroeville	57 454
SNAPP		
David W	San Joaquin Elkhorn	64 995
John*	Siskiyou Scott Ri	69 83
Rufus L	San Joaquin Elkhorn	64 995
SNAPPER		
Saml	San Francisco San Francisco 6	67 415
SNAREG		
Jose	San Francisco San Francisco 3	67 64
SNARLES		
William*	San Francisco San Francisco 8	681248
SNARO		
Feremine	Tuolumne Twp 5	71 498
SNASEY		
Charlott	San Francisco San Francisco 2	67 605
SNATCHER		
Louis	Santa Cruz Soguel	66 579
SNAVELY		
W J	Siskiyou Scott Va	69 21
SNAWN		
Charley	Sierra Twp 7	66 894
SNAY		
George*	Sacramento Brighton	63 197
SNDON		
Andw	Sonoma Petaluma	69 597
SNE		
---	Sacramento Ward 1	63 69
Lu	El Dorado Georgetown	58 701
SNEAD		
Geo	Mendocino Big Rvr	60 848
Jefferson	Sonoma Sonoma	69 637
John	Yuba Marysville	72 941
Samuel	Solano Fremont	69 382
W G	Yolo Slate Ra	72 718
W G	Yuba New York	72 718
SNEADS		
Jefferson	Sonoma Sonoma	69 637
SNEAK		
---	Tulara Twp 2	71 35
SNEANG		
Michael	Placer Virginia	62 673
SNEANKR		
Henry	Amador Twp 2	55 325
SNEASH		
F	Butte Mountain	56 734
SNEATH		
F	Butte Mountain	56 734
Henry	Sacramento Ward 4	63 538
L C	Nevada Nevada	61 323
R G	San Francisco San Francisco 10	223 67
SNEBALL		
J W	Yolo Cache Crk	72 607
SNEBLET		
Thos*	Nevada Rough &	61 430
SNED		
Samuel A	Yuba Slate Ro	72 698
SNEDDEN		
Samuel	Tulara Twp 3	71 51

Name	County Locale	M653 RollPage
SNEDDEN		
Samuel*	Tulara Petersburg	71 51
SNEDEKER		
H	Tehama Red Bluff	70 910
SNEDEKES		
H E	Amador Twp 2	55 314
SNEDEN		
Seth G	Tuolumne Sonora	71 201
SNEDER		
S*	Nevada Grass Valley	61 193
SNEDIKEN		
Thomas	Placer Michigan	62 845
SNEDIKER		
J L	Mariposa Twp 3	60 574
Sarah E*	San Francisco San Francisco 2	67 561
Sarah K	San Francisco San Francisco 2	67 561
Thomas	Contra Costa Twp 1	57 537
SNEDIKES		
H E	Amador Twp 2	55 314
SNEDIXER		
Sarah E	San Francisco San Francisco 2	67 561
SNEDLEY		
Tho*	Siskiyou Scott Va	69 59
SNEDRER		
Louis	Los Angeles Azuza	59 278
SNEE		
W*	Siskiyou Klamath	69 80
SNEED		
G	Nevada Nevada	61 277
Giles	Tuolumne Sonora	71 217
Gillmore	Yuba Bear Rvr	721001
H A	Yolo Cottonwoood	72 654
J S	El Dorado Coloma	581119
Jno	Nevada Nevada	61 294
M A	Yolo Cottonwoood	72 654
Samuel A	Yolo Slate Ra	72 698
Wiley	Napa Napa	61 68
Wm J	Yolo No E Twp	72 674
Wm J	Yuba North Ea	72 674
SNEEL		
Nicholas	Calaveras Twp 8	57 70
SNEENEY		
F	Calaveras Twp 8	57 66
SNEENY		
M*	San Joaquin Stockton	641100
M*	San Joaquin Stockton	641099
SNEET		
John D	San Luis Obispo San Luis Obispo	65 5
SNEETZER		
P	San Joaquin Stockton	641099
SNEIDER		
George	Tuolumne Sonora	71 239
J T	El Dorado Placerville	58 915
John	San Francisco San Francisco 2	67 637
Wm	Placer Auburn	62 588
SNELD		
Frank	Nevada Little Y	61 536
SNELL		
A	Nevada Nevada	61 297
Albert	Sierra Twp 7	66 875
Alfred	Placer Rattle Snake	62 626
B F	Nevada Grass Valley	61 199
Benjamin T	San Joaquin Castoria	64 897
Charles	Siskiyou Klamath	69 97
Geo W	San Francisco San Francisco 10	234 67
George	Napa Clear Lake	61 141
George	Nevada Rough &	61 436
Henry	Sierra Eureka	661049
Henry	Tuolumne Chinese	71 523
Hiram	Napa Clear Lake	61 141
I*	Shasta Shasta	66 660
J	Shasta Shasta	66 660
Jane*	San Francisco San Francisco 2	67 694
Jno	Butte Hamilton	56 521
Jno A*	Butte Hamilton	56 521
John*	Nevada Rough &	61 397
Johnhn*	Nevada Rough &	61 397
Johnthn*	Nevada Rough &	61 397
Lambert	Yuba Rose Bar	72 816
Perez	Tuolumne Twp 1	71 195
Robert	San Joaquin Stockton	641089
William	Nevada Red Dog	61 544
SNELLEN		
John	El Dorado Greenwood	58 717
SNELLENBERGER		
Thos	Stanislaus Empire	70 734
SNELLER		
Jacob*	Placer Michigan	62 840
SNELLING		
A S	Siskiyou Scott Va	69 28
J S	Klamath Liberty	59 243
J S	Siskiyou Scott Va	69 28
Julia	Tuolumne Twp 1	71 237
Wm	Tuolumne Big Oak	71 128
SNELSER		
Aeren	Tuolumne Green Springs	71 519

Name	County Locale	M653 RollPage
SNELSON		
W M	El Dorado Casumnes	581172
SNEN		
Ah*	Sacramento Ward 1	63 152
SNENER		
A	San Francisco San Francisco 4	681164
SNENY		
M	Sutter Yuba	70 760
SNEP		
Long	Butte Bidwell	56 708
SNERGE		
John*	Santa Cruz Pajaro	66 568
SNERTCOPE		
John	Trinity Hay Fork	70 991
SNETHERS		
Henry	El Dorado Coloma	581116
SNETON		
Lenia	Contra Costa Twp 1	57 525
SNEW		
Ah*	Sacramento Ward 1	63 152
SNEY		
---	Trinity Trinindad Rvr	701046
---*	Trinity Trinindad Rvr	701045
SNEYGERT		
Adam	San Francisco San Francisco 7	681410
SNG		
Lee	Mariposa Twp 1	60 667
SNI CLAW		
G W	Nevada Bridgeport	61 496
SNI		
---	El Dorado Greenwood	58 727
Kim	El Dorado Greenwood	58 727
SNIBBLY		
William	El Dorado Spanish	581125
SNIBBS		
J	Calaveras Twp 9	57 417
SNIBERS		
Grief*	San Bernardino San Bernadino	64 635
SNICLER		
Samuel	Sierra Gibsonville	66 859
SNIDDER		
Samuel*	Tulara Petersburg	71 51
SNIDDIN		
Joseph*	Del Norte Ferry P O	58 666
SNIDDIR		
Joseph*	Del Norte Ferry P O	58 666
SNIDDUS		
Joseph*	Del Norte Ferry P O	58 666
SNIDEN		
Gott*	Nevada Bridgeport	61 502
SNIDER		
---	Nevada Bridgeport	61 467
A	Tehama Red Bluff	70 916
A A	Nevada Little Y	61 531
Andrew	Del Norte Klamath	58 653
Andrew J	Siskiyou Yreka	69 124
Andrrewj	Siskiyou Yreka	69 124
Asa	Tehama Tehama	70 936
C	Sutter Yuba	70 764
Charles	Mariposa Twp 1	60 653
Charles C	Sonoma Washington	69 669
Ezbulon*	Los Angeles Los Angeles	59 492
Frank	Los Angeles Tejon	59 526
Fredrick*	San Francisco San Francisco 3	67 67
Gott	Nevada Bridgeport	61 502
H	Nevada Grass Valley	61 197
H	Sutter Sutter	70 813
H	Sutter Nicolaus	70 831
Henry	Sierra Twp 7	66 877
J	Siskiyou Yreka	69 193
J	Sutter Yuba	70 763
J D	Calaveras Twp 9	57 411
J D	Tehama Tehama	70 946
J W	El Dorado Casumnes	581174
Jacob	Nevada Bloomfield	61 523
Jacob	Tuolumne Twp 2	71 389
Jacob	Tuolumne Twp 2	71 414
Jeremiah M	Siskiyou Shasta Rvr	69 111
Jno	San Francisco San Francisco 12	386 67
L	Calaveras Twp 9	57 406
L N	Tehama Red Bluff	70 910
M Smith*	Nevada Nevada	61 249
N	El Dorado Kelsey	581156
P	Nevada Nevada	61 279
P	Nevada Nevada	61 280
Peter	Placer Stewart	62 606
Peter	Tuolumne Twp 3	71 443
Phillip	Nevada Bridgeport	61 498
S	Nevada Red Dog	61 540
S S	Tehama Red Bluff	70 930
S*	Nevada Grass Valley	61 193
Samuel	Sierra Gibsonville	66 859
Sopare	Mariposa Coulterville	60 675
Wm	Nevada Nevada	61 280
SNIDGRASS		
Geo	Yolo Cache	72 621

California 1860 Census Index

Name	County Locale	M653 RollPage
SNIDIR		
John	Los Angeles Los Angeles	59 511
SNIDOR		
Frank	Los Angeles Tejon	59 526
SNIED		
S J	El Dorado Georgetown	58 686
SNIEDER		
George*	Tuolumne Twp 1	71 239
SNIERL		
L P*	Butte Oro	56 683
SNIFT		
Houston	Butte Cascade	56 704
SNIG		
---	Sacramento Ward 1	63 56
---	San Joaquin Oneal	64 939
SNIGER		
Frank	Nevada Bloomfield	61 523
SNIGHRY		
Jesse*	Siskiyou Scott Va	69 55
SNIGHTON		
William	Placer Todds Va	62 764
SNIJLETON		
Robt*	San Bernardino San Bernadino	64 636
SNIKE		
William*	El Dorado Placerville	58 934
SNILD		
Frank	Nevada Little Y	61 536
SNILIERS		
Grief*	San Bernardino San Bernadino	64 635
SNINGLE		
G H*	Yolo Putah	72 550
SNIOELEY		
Daniel*	Napa Yount	61 29
SNIPLETON		
Robt*	San Bernardino San Bernadino	64 636
SNIRELY		
J H	Marin San Rafael	60 758
SNIRFF		
C H	Sacramento Ward 1	63 89
SNIROP		
---*	Del Norte Ferry P O	58 665
SNIRTGEN		
Henry*	Placer Sacramento	62 645
SNISH		
Wm	Sacramento Granite	63 235
SNISWOOD		
John M	Santa Clara San Jose	65 287
SNIT		
Jos	Butte Chico	56 564
SNITER		
John*	Yuba Timbucto	72 787
SNITH		
George W*	San Francisco 7	681424
	San Francisco	
John*	Sacramento Ward 1	63 131
Mary	Butte Mountain	56 734
W B	Butte Ophir	56 750
SNITHWORTH		
Hiram*	Sierra Twp 7	66 879
SNITS		
Jos	Butte Chico	56 546
SNITTERRIS		
Santiago	Contra Costa Twp 1	57 502
SNIVELEY		
Daniel*	Napa Yount	61 29
SNIVILEY		
Daniel	Napa Yount	61 29
SNLIVENT		
John	Yolo Merritt	72 577
SNNG		
---	El Dorado Salmon Hills	581059
SNOBALL		
J W	Yolo Cache	72 608
Norman	Yolo Cache	72 608
SNOCKS		
Wm	Mariposa Twp 3	60 567
SNODDY		
B A	Sonoma Sonoma	69 652
SNODE		
William*	San Francisco San Francisco 9	681028
SNODGRAP		
Thomas	Santa Cruz Watsonville	66 540
SNODGRASS		
---	Yolo Cottonwood	72 658
Andrew	Placer Michigan	62 830
Andrew	Yolo Cache Crk	72 623
Geo	Yolo Cache Crk	72 621
Geo	Yolo Cottonwood	72 658
Harvey W	Siskiyou Shasta Rvr	69 115
James	Calaveras Twp 10	57 261
James	Santa Clara Fremont	65 418
John	Sierra Pine Grove	66 832
John	Sonoma Armally	69 493
Thomas	Mariposa Twp 1	60 656
Thomas	Santa Cruz Watsonville	66 540
Thomas*	Mariposa Twp 1	60 656

Name	County Locale	M653 RollPage
SNODGRASS		
Thomas*	Santa Cruz Watsonville	66 540
Wm	Sierra Pine Grove	66 832
SNODGROP		
Jefferson	San Joaquin Elkhorn	64 952
SNODGSASS		
Thomas	Mariposa Twp 1	60 656
SNODYROSS		
James	Calaveras Twp 10	57 261
SNOGGLEWAUN		
---	Tulara Twp 2	71 35
SNOGRASS		
Andrew	Yolo Cache	72 623
SNOIFT		
W H	Siskiyou Scott Ri	69 72
SNOLL		
Thos E	Santa Clara San Jose	65 363
SNOMAN		
P	Yolo Putah	72 550
SNON		
---	Butte Bidwell	56 720
SNONGES		
Manuel*	Calaveras Twp 5	57 226
SNONGUS		
Manuel*	Calaveras Twp 5	57 226
SNONOUDT		
F	El Dorado Diamond	58 775
SNOOK		
Edward	San Francisco San Francisco 2	67 644
Geo W	San Francisco San Francisco 10	280 67
Henry	San Francisco San Francisco 3	67 12
S C	Siskiyou Scott Ri	69 67
Wm	San Francisco San Francisco 1	68 883
Wm S	San Francisco San Francisco 2	67 628
SNOOKS		
L	Merced Twp 2	60 916
Wm	Mariposa Twp 3	60 567
Wm P	Sonoma Mendocino	69 461
Wm*	Mariposa Twp 3	60 567
SNOPE		
H K	Butte Chico	56 531
SNOSSE		
H K*	Butte Chico	56 531
J C*	Tuolumne Springfield	71 371
SNOW		
A	Tuolumne Garrote	71 173
A C	Siskiyou Scott Ri	69 71
A R	Los Angeles Los Angeles	59 491
Abram	Nevada Rough &	61 430
Ancel*	San Francisco San Francisco 9	681067
Andrew	El Dorado Georgetown	58 679
Andrew	Sierra Pine Grove	66 828
Aucel*	San Francisco San Francisco 9	681067
Benjamin	San Joaquin Douglass	64 926
Benjamin	Yuba Marysville	72 953
Charles	San Francisco San Francisco 2	67 731
Chas	Santa Clara San Jose	65 386
Chester J	San Francisco San Francisco 8	681283
Cyrus	Santa Cruz Santa Cruz	66 638
Danl	Nevada Red Dog	61 546
David	Nevada Bridgeport	61 446
David	Solano Vallejo	69 258
Eliza F	Napa Napa	61 62
Eliza F	San Francisco San Francisco 2	67 678
F	Sacramento Brighton	63 203
Fanny	Calaveras Twp 4	57 337
Frank	Placer Folsom	62 639
Frank C	San Francisco San Francisco 3	67 21
G F	Marin Sauciteto	60 750
Geo	Calaveras Twp 9	57 411
Geo	Sacramento Ward 4	63 587
George	Sacramento Ward 4	63 554
H	Nevada Grass Valley	61 161
H	Sutter Butte	70 783
Isaac	Yuba New York	72 737
J	Butte Wyandotte	56 669
J C	Tuolumne Twp 2	71 371
J D	Santa Clara Almaden	65 275
J L	San Mateo Twp 3	65 103
James	Calaveras Twp 8	57 97
James	Yuba Marysville	72 906
James O	Trinity Weaverville	701081
Joel G	Napa Napa	61 92
John D	Napa Clear Lake	61 136
Jos	Sonoma Vallejo	69 611
L S	Tuolumne Twp 3	71 448
Lucius A	Butte Oregon	56 619
M M	Tuolumne Twp 2	71 278
Mary L	Napa Yount	61 37
N E	Santa Clara Santa Clara	65 521
Nick	Sonoma Armally	69 509
P W	Tuolumne Twp 2	71 286
R	Santa Clara Alviso	65 401
Reuben	Sonoma Vallejo	69 611
Rucel	San Francisco San Francisco 9	681067

Name	County Locale	M653 RollPage
SNOW		
S	El Dorado Diamond	58 803
Samuel B	Napa Yount	61 37
Thos	Alameda Brooklyn	55 117
Thos	Alameda Brooklyn	55 193
W N	Yuba New York	72 728
William	Stanislaus Emory	70 750
Yev	Calaveras Twp 9	57 411
SNOWBALL		
J W	Tuolumne Big Oak	71 138
SNOWBITE		
Hernard	Yuba Marysville	72 880
SNOWDEN		
C B*	Mariposa Twp 3	60 615
J D	Nevada Eureka	61 354
John	El Dorado Placerville	58 925
O B	Mariposa Twp 3	60 615
Robert	El Dorado Greenwood	58 709
Wm	Tuolumne Shawsfla	71 412
SNOWDON		
Q H*	Calaveras Twp 9	57 416
SNOWE		
A	San Francisco San Francisco 9	68 945
J C*	Tuolumne Springfield	71 371
SNOWEY		
J	Sacramento Ward 4	63 606
SNOWGRASS		
Isaac*	Stanislaus Emory	70 751
SNOWHITE		
Herman	Yuba Marysville	72 880
SNOWORTH		
W	Trinity Douglas	70 978
SNOWOUDT		
F*	El Dorado Diamond	58 775
SNSCOW		
Joseph*	Sierra Downieville	66 962
SNT		
---*	El Dorado Georgetown	58 692
SNTRO		
James	San Francisco San Francisco 3	67 62
SNUBLE		
Thos	Calaveras Twp 6	57 120
SNUD		
Giles*	Tuolumne Twp 1	71 217
SNUDDY		
John*	Sacramento Ward 1	63 123
SNUDER		
John	San Francisco San Francisco 2	67 637
SNUET		
Joseph*	Calaveras Twp 9	57 367
SNUFFINS		
L S*	Mendocino Ukiah	60 805
SNUFISON		
Jno*	Sacramento Ward 1	63 114
SNUG		
---	El Dorado Salmon Falls	581059
SNUNEY		
G W*	Butte Ophir	56 766
SNUYTHE		
James	San Joaquin Oneal	64 912
SNY		
---	El Dorado Greenwood	58 727
SNYAN		
Charles	Tuolumne Twp 2	71 332
SNYAROL		
C	Nevada Eureka	61 359
SNYDAM		
Geo	Sacramento Ward 1	63 35
J N	Colusa Colusi	57 420
Theo*	Sacramento Ward 1	63 62
SNYDAR		
Theo*	Sacramento Ward 1	63 62
SNYDAUR		
Geo*	Sacramento Ward 1	63 35
Theo*	Sacramento Ward 1	63 62
SNYDEN		
Egerton	San Bernardino San Bernardino	64 627
SNYDER		
A A	San Francisco San Francisco 6	67 451
A D	San Francisco San Francisco 4	681141
Abraham	San Francisco San Francisco 7	681444
Alex	Los Angeles Tejon	59 539
Andrew	Colusa Colusi	57 421
Andrew J	Yuba Marysville	72 909
August	Contra Costa Twp 3	57 590
Benjamin	San Francisco San Francisco 2	681341
Bernard	Plumas Meadow Valley	62 899
C M	Sacramento Franklin	63 320
Charles	Amador Twp 1	55 491
Charles	Siskiyou Klamath	69 97
Charles	Tuolumne Columbia	71 332
Chas	Klamath S Fork	59 199
Chas	Sacramento Franklin	63 319
Clara	Los Angeles Los Angeles	59 366
Clara	Los Angeles Los Angeles	59 36
D	Trinity North Fo	701024

Name	County Locale	M653 Roll	Page
SNYDER			
D H	Humbolt Union	59	191
Danl	Napa Napa	61	67
E H	Placer Michigan	62	851
E W	Shasta Horsetown	66	689
Egerton	San Bernardino San Bernadino	64	627
Emma G	Alameda Oakland	55	72
F C	Stanislaus Buena Village	70	720
F V	Sierra Eureka	66	1044
Fanny	Sacramento Ward 4	63	530
Frank	Butte Mountain	56	737
G M	San Francisco San Francisco 6	67	459
Geo	Amador Twp 2	55	321
Geo	Placer Dutch Fl	62	720
Geo	San Francisco San Francisco 9	68	1061
Geo	San Francisco San Francisco 2	67	626
Geo W	San Francisco San Francisco 9	68	1089
George	Calaveras Twp 4	57	312
George	Shasta Shasta	66	758
George	Solano Benecia	69	298
Henry	Tuolumne Sonora	71	242
J	Butte Chico	56	546
J	Nevada Washington	61	333
J B	Siskiyou Scott Va	69	30
J D	San Francisco San Francisco 2	67	562
J H	Colusa Butte Crk	57	464
J H	San Francisco San Francisco 5	67	505
J W	Siskiyou Scott Ri	69	72
Jacob	Plumas Meadow Valley	62	911
Jacob	San Francisco San Francisco 12	67	389
Jacob	Solano Vallejo	69	260
Jacob R	San Francisco San Francisco 2	67	572
James	San Mateo Twp 3	65	83
James	Sierra Scales D	66	800
James	Siskiyou Scott Va	69	29
Jeremiah	Yuba Marysville	72	881
Jermiah	Yuba Marysville	72	881
Jno	Mendocino Anderson	60	867
Jno N	Sacramento Natonia	63	272
John	Butte Cascade	56	690
John	Calaveras Twp 4	57	302
John	El Dorado Mud Springs	58	964
John	Placer Yankee J	62	759
John	San Francisco San Francisco 9	68	1089
John	San Francisco San Francisco 3	67	11
John	San Francisco San Francisco 3	67	20
John	Santa Clara Fremont	65	426
John	Sierra St Louis	66	815
John	Sierra Whiskey	66	850
John	Siskiyou Yreka	69	140
John	Siskiyou Scott Va	69	40
John	Sonoma Washington	69	679
John	Yolo No E Twp	72	667
John D	San Francisco San Francisco 3	67	67
John D	Sonoma Mendocino	69	460
John J	San Francisco San Francisco 7	68	1442
John P	Nevada Rough &	61	410
Joseph	Siskiyou Scott Va	69	25
L	Shasta Shasta	66	655
L*	El Dorado Placerville	58	914
Louis	San Francisco San Francisco 3	67	32
M H	San Francisco San Francisco 3	67	81
M W	Nevada Nevada	61	271
Maria	San Francisco San Francisco 4	68	1157
Mary	Humbolt Bucksport	59	155
Merritt	Yuba Fosters	72	840
Michael	Plumas Meadow Valley	62	933
Michael	Plumas Quincy	62	955
N*	El Dorado Georgetown	58	757
Nelson W	Sierra Whiskey	66	843
O	Sacramento Georgian	63	337
O	San Francisco San Francisco 5	67	518
O	San Joaquin Stockton	64	1031
P	Shasta French G	66	722
Paul	Solano Fremont	69	382
Peter	Calaveras Twp 5	57	247
Peter	Plumas Meadow Valley	62	907
Peter	Santa Clara Santa Clara	65	498
Phillip	Butte Bidwell	56	730
Phillip	San Francisco San Francisco 2	67	656
R	Butte Oregon	56	630
Ravinia	Los Angeles Los Angeles	59	314
Samuel	Colusa Colusi	57	419
T	San Francisco San Francisco 9	68	1060
T A	Butte Cascade	56	703
Thos	El Dorado Georgetown	58	694
Thos	Mariposa Twp 3	60	573
Thos J	Sacramento Ward 4	63	550
W	El Dorado Georgetown	58	683
W	San Francisco San Francisco 1	68	923
W	Siskiyou Scott Va	69	45
W H	Klamath Salmon	59	208
William	Amador Twp 4	55	243
William	San Mateo Twp 1	65	72
Wm	Butte Oro	56	681

Name	County Locale	M653 Roll	Page
SNYDER			
Wm	Nevada Nevada	61	319
Wm	Siskiyou Scott Va	69	45
Wm R	Nevada Eureka	61	369
Z	San Francisco San Francisco 6	67	409
SNYENLAND			
Henry	El Dorado Big Bar	58	741
SNYETER			
John	Sierra St Louis	66	815
SNYLLIR			
N*	El Dorado Georgetown	58	757
SNYTEY			
Mychael*	Mariposa Twp 3	60	563
SO BEGIO			
Ange*	Amador Twp 4	55	245
SO KI SEI MUN			
---*	Plumas Quincy	62	969
SO LON			
---	Sierra Twp 5	66	930
SO QUI			
---	Mariposa Twp 3	60	608
SO SAY			
---	Sierra Twp 5	66	931
SO SNOY			
---	Sacramento Ward 1	63	52
SO SONG			
---*	San Francisco San Francisco 11	67	159
Ah*	San Francisco San Francisco 11	67	159
SO TOW			
---	Sacramento Ward 1	63	55
SO TUCK			
---	Sacramento Ward 1	63	68
SO			
---	Alameda Oakland	55	35
---	Amador Twp 2	55	275
---	Calaveras Twp 6	57	166
---	Calaveras Twp 5	57	236
---	Calaveras Twp 5	57	242
---	Calaveras Twp 5	57	256
---	El Dorado Georgetown	58	680
---	Monterey Monterey	60	965
---	Nevada Bridgeport	61	462
---	Sacramento Ward 1	63	53
---	San Francisco San Francisco 4	68	1081
---	San Francisco San Francisco 4	68	1212
---	Sierra Downieville	66	1005
---	Tehama Red Bluff	70	934
---	Tuolumne Green Springs	71	517
---*	Sierra Downieville	66	1008
Chee*	Calaveras Twp 5	57	234
Chu*	Calaveras Twp 5	57	234
Chun	Mariposa Twp 3	60	620
Con	Nevada Grass Valley	61	229
Eulalia	Tuolumne Sonora	71	481
Fong	Tehama Red Bluff	70	934
Gue	Sierra Downieville	66	984
John	Mariposa Twp 3	60	561
Lan	Sierra Twp 5	66	930
Long	Sierra Downieville	66	979
Meen	Mariposa Twp 3	60	620
Mu	Calaveras Twp 5	57	244
Mung*	Butte Oregon	56	625
Say	Sierra Twp 5	66	931
Show	Calaveras Twp 9	57	375
Song Ah*	San Francisco San Francisco 11	67	159
Tuck	Sacramento Ward 1	63	68
Ty	Butte Oregon	56	625
Up	Butte Kimshaw	56	586
Ya	Tuolumne Big Oak	71	150
SOA			
---	Yuba Marysville	72	921
Hong	Yuba Marysville	72	920
SOAG			
---	Trinity East For	70	1025
---	Trinity Big Flat	70	1042
---	Trinity Trinindad Rvr	70	1048
---	Trinity Trinindad Rvr	70	1050
---*	Trinity Taylor'S	70	1033
---*	Trinity Cox'S Bar	70	1037
---*	Trinity Big Flat	70	1041
SOAGUIN			
Eamet	Alameda Oakland	55	13
SOAK			
Mary Ayester	El Dorado Georgetown	58	698
SOAL			
James	Sierra Twp 7	66	886
SOAMIRCE			
Tedobisa*	Solano Vacaville	69	359
SOAMIRE			
Tedobisa*	Solano Vacaville	69	359
SOANE			
Henry S	Solano Vallejo	69	263
SOANES			
Henry	Solano Benecia	69	311

Name	County Locale	M653 Roll	Page
SOANES			
Henry S	Solano Benecia	69	311
Joseph	Solano Benecia	69	311
SOAP			
Henry	Shasta Shasta	66	681
SOARN			
---*	Mariposa Twp 3	60	580
SOATH			
A	Tuolumne Twp 4	71	145
SOB			
Ambrosio*	Los Angeles San Juan	59	466
SOBECK			
Alexander	Contra Costa Twp 1	57	514
SOBER SIDE			
---*	Tulara Visalia	71	32
SOBER			
Antonie	Nevada Eureka	61	348
SOBERAMES			
Isabela	Monterey Monterey	60	950
SOBERANES			
Feliciano	Merced Monterey	60	934
Feliciano	Monterey Monterey	60	934
Francisco	Monterey S Antoni	60	967
Guadalupe	Merced Monterey	60	935
Guadalupe	Monterey Monterey	60	935
Iyakel*	Monterey S Antoni	60	968
Jose M	Monterey Monterey	60	934
Jose M*	Merced Monterey	60	934
Jyakel*	Monterey S Antoni	60	968
Maria De Los	Los Angeles	59	388
Mariano	Monterey S Antoni	60	967
Marians	Monterey Monterey	60	946
Mateo	Monterey S Antoni	60	971
Matro	Monterey S Antoni	60	971
Pamfilo*	Monterey Monterey	60	931
Panifilo*	Monterey Monterey	60	931
Ramanda	Monterey S Antoni	60	968
Rosano	Los Angeles Los Angeles	59	350
Rusanrio	Los Angeles Los Angeles	59	350
Victor	Monterey S Antoni	60	968
SOBERANO			
Jose A	Santa Cruz Soguel	66	583
SOBERAUES			
Paunfilo	Merced Monterey	60	931
SOBERBY			
C*	Nevada Grass Valley	61	194
SOBERLEY			
C*	Nevada Grass Valley	61	194
SOBERLINE			
---	San Joaquin Stockton	64	1099
SOBEROMES			
Isabela	Monterey Monterey	60	950
Iyakel*	Monterey S Antoni	60	968
Izakel*	Monterey S Antoni	60	968
Jyakel*	Monterey S Antoni	60	968
Ramanda*	Monterey S Antoni	60	968
SOBERORNES			
Isabela	Monterey Monterey	60	950
SOBITTA			
Camillo	San Francisco San Francisco 3	67	85
Cermillo	San Francisco San Francisco 3	67	85
SOBLET			
John	San Francisco San Francisco 3	67	63
SOBO			
Jesus	Monterey Monterey	60	931
SOBORANES			
Mariano	Monterey S Antoni	60	967
SOBORNE			
John	Yuba Bear Rvr	72	1003
SOBRE			
---	Tulara Twp 1	71	113
SOBREANAS			
G G	Napa Hot Springs	61	2
SOBRENO			
John	Santa Cruz Soguel	66	599
SOBVERS			
John	San Francisco San Francisco 9	68	1097
SOCARAS			
---	Mendocino Calpella	60	824
SOCARUS			
---	Mendocino Calpella	60	824
SOCETA			
---	Fresno Twp 3	59	97
SOCHER			
Jas*	Butte Oregon	56	613
SOCHERDNO			
August*	Sierra Downieville	66	977
SOCHRA			
Rosilia	Los Angeles Los Angeles	59	496
SOCK			
---	Butte Kimshaw	56	600
---	Nevada Bridgeport	61	491
---	Placer Iona Hills	62	894
---*	Amador Twp 4	55	233
---*	Calaveras Twp 5	57	234

California 1860 Census Index

Name	County Locale	M653 Roll/Page
SOCK		
---*	Placer Auburn	62 571
---*	Tulara Visalia	71 34
---*	Tulara Visalia	71 38
Benja	Calaveras Twp 5	57 207
Benje	Calaveras Twp 5	57 207
Geo*	Siskiyou Scott Va	69 50
Jonah*	Sacramento Mississipi	63 183
Jonathan*	Napa Clear Lake	61 124
SOCKER		
John W	San Mateo Twp 3	65 95
SOCKEY		
Daniel	Calaveras Twp 6	57 166
SOCKHEART		
Wm	Nevada Nevada	61 271
SOCKLAND		
Wm*	Calaveras Twp 9	57 368
SOCKO		
---	Tulara Twp 2	71 34
---	Tulara Twp 2	71 38
SOCKS		
Richard	Plumas Meadow Valley	62 908
SOCKWOOD		
Charles	Sierra Twp 7	66 866
H*	Trinity Weaverville	701066
Picket*	Calaveras Twp 4	57 319
SOCLERA		
Francis*	Calaveras Twp 6	57 144
SOCO		
---	Fresno Twp 2	59 104
SOCTON		
Benjamin E	Placer Secret R	62 609
SOCY		
---*	Yuba Linda	72 992
SODD		
Moore	San Francisco San Francisco 9	68 959
SODERES		
J N	Tuolumne Twp 2	71 314
SODLINGER		
Joseph*	Siskiyou Yreka	69 153
SODS		
C F*	Sacramento Ward 3	63 460
SOE MANG		
---*	Yuba Long Bar	72 756
SOE		
---	El Dorado Placerville	58 832
Ho	San Francisco San Francisco 4	681198
Hoo	San Francisco San Francisco 4	681198
Mang*	Yuba Long Bar	72 756
Wm*	Butte Kimshaw	56 597
SOEN		
---	San Francisco San Francisco 4	681174
SOES		
---	Calaveras Twp 5	57 211
SOET		
Mack	Nevada Rough &	61 410
SOEY LA		
---	Sacramento Ward 3	63 491
SOEY		
---	San Francisco San Francisco 9	681087
SOF		
---	Placer Illinois	62 745
SOFE		
Charles	El Dorado Big Bar	58 743
SOFER		
Chas	San Francisco San Francisco 2	67 618
SOFETECO		
Allen	Calaveras Twp 10	57 290
SOFFA		
Chas	San Francisco San Francisco 2	67 660
SOFFROTH		
Henry	Placer Forest H	62 767
SOFINIA		
M	Yolo Cottonwood	72 649
SOFTHENO		
Wm	Colusa Monroeville	57 446
SOFTY		
Jas	San Francisco San Francisco 1	68 858
SOG		
---	Nevada Washington	61 342
SOGAN		
---	Sierra Twp 5	66 926
J	Sutter Sutter	70 804
J*	Nevada Nevada	61 240
SOGGS		
John	Nevada Nevada	61 298
R*	Nevada Grass Valley	61 165
SOGH		
---	Mariposa Twp 3	60 543
SOGLE		
Geo*	Napa Napa	61 88
SOH		
---	Calaveras Twp 4	57 301
---	Sacramento Ward 3	63 489
---	San Francisco San Francisco 11	144 67
SOH		
Leow	Butte Ophir	56 788
SOHEDAR		
Antonio	San Bernardino San Bernadino	64 675
SOHILL		
William	El Dorado Georgetown	58 759
SOHIST		
Thos*	Alameda Oakland	55 67
SOHLKE		
J A	Sonoma Petaluma	69 580
SOHLOFFS		
Ernest	Tuolumne Twp 5	71 490
SOHLYAR		
Francis*	Calaveras Twp 6	57 147
SOHLYAS		
Francis	Calaveras Twp 6	57 147
SOHM		
John	Trinity Trinity	70 971
SOHMAN		
G C	Siskiyou Klamath	69 90
J B	Siskiyou Scott Va	69 27
SOHO SON		
---	Mendocino Big Rvr	60 854
SOHO		
---	Tulara Twp 2	71 4
SOHOE		
---	Fresno Twp 3	59 31
SOHSA		
Louis	Sacramento Ward 4	63 498
SOHSE		
Theadore	Sierra St Louis	66 807
SOHU		
John*	Calaveras Twp 6	57 138
SOHUSTT		
S C*	Mariposa Twp 3	60 574
SOHWINT		
John	Tuolumne Twp 6	71 538
SOI		
---	Calaveras Twp 4	57 334
---	Calaveras Twp 7	57 41
---	Mariposa Twp 3	60 580
---	Tuolumne Don Pedro	71 540
SOIELITY		
Matthew*	Tuolumne Twp 1	71 265
SOILA		
---	Los Angeles San Pedro	59 478
SOILE		
A P*	Sacramento Ward 1	63 151
SOILLOT		
A	San Francisco San Francisco 2	67 705
SOIMAKEN		
---	Tulara Twp 1	71 118
SOIMTEM		
A	San Francisco San Francisco 5	67 527
SOIREZ		
Miguel	Santa Cruz Santa Cruz	66 632
SOJ		
Lee	Mariposa Twp 3	60 575
SOK		
---	El Dorado Georgetown	58 756
---	San Francisco San Francisco 4	681197
SOKA		
---	Fresno Twp 2	59 91
SOKE		
---	Amador Twp 1	55 507
---	Calaveras Twp 4	57 334
SOKEN		
---	Calaveras Twp 10	57 284
SOKILL		
William*	El Dorado Georgetown	58 759
SOKKE BRAVE		
---	Fresno Twp 3	59 24
SOKKEL		
John	Tuolumne Twp 1	71 236
SOKLEY		
R*	Nevada Grass Valley	61 198
SOKO		
---	Calaveras Twp 4	57 308
SOL		
---	Placer Illinois	62 745
Ambrosio	Los Angeles San Juan	59 466
Ho	San Francisco San Francisco 4	681198
Hoo	San Francisco San Francisco 4	681198
Ken	San Francisco San Francisco 4	681199
SOLA YERMER		
---	Tulara Twp 2	71 32
SOLA		
A*	Nevada Grass Valley	61 144
SOLADAR		
---	Mendocino Twp 1	60 892
SOLAMAN		
A*	Nevada Grass Valley	61 174
SOLAMONSON		
G	Napa Napa	61 106
SOLAMOUSON		
G*	Napa Napa	61 106
SOLAN		
H	Butte Oregon	56 635
Jno C	San Francisco San Francisco 10	259 67
Louis	San Mateo Twp 3	65 104
Mary Ann	San Francisco San Francisco 10	207 67
SOLANA		
Augustus	Alameda Oakland	55 10
SOLANDS		
Kale	Sacramento Ward 1	63 82
SOLANE		
Joseph	San Francisco San Francisco 2	67 762
SOLANO		
Alejandro	Los Angeles Los Angeles	59 399
Bayello	Alameda Brooklyn	55 180
Joseph*	San Francisco San Francisco 2	67 762
Luan	San Francisco San Francisco 2	67 762
Miguel	Alameda Brooklyn	55 98
SOLANS		
Narcisso*	Los Angeles Tejon	59 536
SOLAR		
F B	Mariposa Twp 3	60 606
Felipp	El Dorado Georgetown	58 674
Geacomb	Tuolumne Twp 4	71 160
Joseph	Calaveras Twp 7	57 39
Micke	Calaveras Twp 7	57 5
SOLARAY		
Jno*	Sacramento Cosumnes	63 402
SOLARE		
G	San Joaquin Stockton	641097
SOLARES		
Augustin	San Bernardino S Buenav	64 207
SOLARI		
Frank	Tuolumne Jamestown	71 456
SOLAS		
Nicolas	Mariposa Twp 3	60 602
SOLASEDO		
Ramon	San Diego Temecula	64 785
SOLASON		
Amitio	Tuolumne Twp 1	71 235
SOLAVAY		
Jno*	Sacramento Cosumnes	63 402
SOLAWAY		
Thomas	Yuba Marysville	72 914
SOLBERRY		
Geo M	Nevada Nevada	61 273
SOLBEXTER		
John*	El Dorado Casumnes	581161
SOLBOTT		
J*	Calaveras Twp 9	57 366
SOLDADO		
Capt	San Diego Agua Caliente	64 857
SOLDATE		
Frank	Tulara Visalia	71 105
SOLDBLOCK		
Henry	Sierra Twp 5	66 920
SOLDDER		
Jane S	Santa Cruz Watsonville	66 537
SOLDMANN		
Anson	San Francisco San Francisco 7	681437
SOLDNEY		
John	San Francisco San Francisco 7	681420
SOLDOM		
Petros*	Calaveras Twp 8	57 95
SOLE		
---	Sacramento Ward 1	63 70
---	Yolo No E Twp	72 677
---	Yuba North Ea	72 677
C	Trinity Douglas	70 980
Elviras	Trinity Texas Ba	70 981
Gustavus	Nevada Rough &	61 413
W L	Siskiyou Scott Va	69 34
SOLECER		
Nesoia*	Mariposa Twp 1	60 624
Nesria*	Mariposa Twp 1	60 624
Nessia*	Mariposa Twp 1	60 624
SOLEDAD		
---	San Bernardino Santa Inez	64 138
SOLEER SIDES		
---	Tulara Twp 2	71 32
SOLEIDONT		
Wm	El Dorado Georgetown	58 707
SOLEOBY		
Samuel	San Francisco San Francisco 11	106 67
SOLEON		
David	Calaveras Twp 10	57 292
SOLER		
Albert	Merced Monterey	60 931
SOLERAY		
---	Sierra Downieville	66 973
SOLES		
Albert	Monterey Monterey	60 931
Andrew	Siskiyou Yreka	69 125
Antonia*	Monterey San Juan	60 999

Name	County Locale	M653 Roll	Page
SOLES			
Arnold	Tulara Visalia	71	106
J A	Placer Virginia	62	670
SOLEY			
Edwin	Sierra Downieville	66	1017
Marianna	San Francisco San Francisco 2	67	662
William*	San Francisco San Francisco 3	67	18
SOLEZ			
Timothy*	Yuba New York	72	722
SOLF			
F D*	Stanislaus Empire	70	734
SOLFRIDGE			
W A	Sierra Twp 5	66	926
W O*	Sierra Twp 5	66	926
Wm	Sierra Twp 5	66	926
SOLICA			
---	San Mateo Twp 2	65	112
SOLICAN			
Salvador	Los Angeles Santa Ana	59	452
SOLICE			
Caroline*	Sacramento Ward 1	63	77
Feliciona	Tuolumne Sonora	71	219
Filiciona	Tuolumne Twp 1	71	219
SOLIDA			
Nicholas	Fresno Twp 1	59	81
SOLIDAD			
---	Mendocino Calpella	60	825
---	San Bernardino San Bernadino	64	682
---	San Bernardino S Timate	64	714
---	San Bernardino S Timate	64	717
---	San Bernardino S Timate	64	727
---	San Bernardino S Timate	64	730
---	San Bernardino S Timate	64	739
---	San Bernardino S Timate	64	744
---	San Bernardino S Timate	64	745
---	San Bernardino S Timate	64	751
---	San Bernardino S Timate	64	753
SOLIER			
Caroline	Sacramento Ward 1	63	77
Cawhire	Sacramento Ward 1	63	77
SOLIKA			
Nicholas	Fresno Twp 1	59	81
SOLIN			
---	Shasta Horsetown	66	705
SOLING			
---	Sierra Downieville	66	974
---	Sierra Downieville	66	979
SOLINSKY			
Christian	Tuolumne Twp 5	71	487
SOLIR			
Benigra	San Luis Obispo San Luis Obispo	65	42
SOLIS			
Antonia	Monterey San Juan	60	999
H*	San Francisco San Francisco 4	68	1155
Jesus	Trinity North Fo	70	1023
Ranugio	San Francisco San Francisco 2	67	698
SOLISE			
Theadore*	Sierra St Louis	66	807
SOLITE			
N	Amador Twp 2	55	280
SOLIUS			
Otto	Los Angeles Santa Ana	59	440
SOLKELD			
W J	El Dorado Greenwood	58	715
SOLL			
---	El Dorado Georgetown	58	748
Gustavus	Nevada Rough &	61	413
SOLLA			
Mike	Alameda Brooklyn	55	99
SOLLAR			
Mike	Alameda Brooklyn	55	99
SOLLARS			
H	Amador Twp 2	55	297
SOLLER			
Esta	Alameda Brooklyn	55	108
Pat	Sacramento Natonia	63	276
SOLLES			
Jas R*	Sacramento Ward 4	63	506
SOLLING			
Geo M	Nevada Nevada	61	273
SOLLIS			
John	Napa Napa	61	85
SOLLY			
Anderson*	Calaveras Twp 9	57	351
William*	San Francisco San Francisco 3	67	18
SOLMAN			
Danson	Santa Cruz Pajaro	66	543
SOLMER			
Hugh	Sierra Twp 5	66	924
SOLMIDS			
Julius	San Francisco San Francisco 1	68	825
SOLMON			
A	San Francisco San Francisco 6	67	470
Daniel	Alameda Brooklyn	55	199
SOLMS			

Name	County Locale	M653 Roll	Page
SOLMS			
Eleanora	San Francisco San Francisco 12		387 67
Otto	Los Angeles Santa Ana	59	440
SOLMY			
Joseph	Shasta Shasta	66	671
SOLNEY			
Joseph*	Shasta Shasta	66	671
SOLNIER			
J	Calaveras Twp 9	57	393
SOLO			
Huliam	Los Angeles Azuza	59	274
SOLOMA			
Guslata*	Alameda Oakland	55	61
SOLOMAN			
Benj*	Butte Kimshaw	56	591
David	Los Angeles Los Angeles	59	319
Jas	Placer Rattle Snake	62	638
Louis	Placer Iona Hills	62	859
Pedro	Tuolumne Twp 4	71	131
Pemj*	Butte Kimshaw	56	591
Perry	Butte Kimshaw	56	591
SOLOMN			
Guslato*	Alameda Oakland	55	61
SOLOMON			
---	Los Angeles San Gabriel	59	410
---	San Bernardino S Timate	64	695
---	San Bernardino S Timate	64	697
---	San Bernardino S Timate	64	701
---	San Bernardino S Timate	64	720
---	San Bernardino S Timate	64	722
---	San Bernardino S Timate	64	723
---	San Bernardino S Timate	64	724
---	San Bernardino S Timate	64	727
---	San Bernardino S Timate	64	731
---	San Bernardino S Timate	64	732
---	San Bernardino S Timate	64	737
---	Tulara Twp 1	71	118
A	San Francisco San Francisco 4	68	1218
A T	San Joaquin Stockton	64	1009
Abraham	El Dorado Coloma	58	1069
Danl	San Francisco San Francisco 1	68	854
Ephraim	Tulara Twp 1	71	82
G	San Francisco San Francisco 5	67	521
H	Nevada Grass Valley	61	180
H	Sacramento Ward 1	63	29
H	San Francisco San Francisco 5	67	504
Hep	San Francisco San Francisco 4	68	1150
Hess	San Francisco San Francisco 4	68	1150
Isreal	San Francisco San Francisco 4	68	1132
Jacob	San Francisco San Francisco 3	67	27
Jacob	San Francisco San Francisco 3	67	63
Jno	San Francisco San Francisco 12		392 67
Joseph	San Francisco San Francisco 4	68	1141
Joshua	San Francisco San Francisco 2	67	706
L	Marin San Rafael	60	758
L	Yuba Fosters	72	822
Louis	San Francisco San Francisco 5	67	476
M	San Francisco San Francisco 6	67	464
Max	San Bernardino S Timate	64	688
May	Tehama Lassen	70	863
N	Amador Twp 2	55	270
Nelson	Los Angeles Los Angeles	59	365
P	Nevada Grass Valley	61	149
P L	San Francisco San Francisco 9	68	1105
Robt	Tuolumne Sonora	71	242
Rotet*	Tuolumne Twp 1	71	242
S	Marin San Rafael	60	758
S	San Francisco San Francisco 5	67	476
S	Tuolumne Twp 4	71	129
S	Tuolumne Twp 4	71	134
Sarah	San Francisco San Francisco 4	68	1153
Simon	San Francisco San Francisco 2	67	704
SOLON			
Peter	Tuolumne Sonora	71	208
SOLONSKY			
August	Tuolumne Columbia	71	356
SOLOSANA			
Antonio	Marin Bolinas	60	743
SOLOUSKY			
August	Tuolumne Twp 2	71	356
SOLOY			
Patrick*	Sierra Twp 7	66	911
SOLOZO			
Francisco	Santa Barbara San Bernardino	64	196
SOLPH			
Frederick*	Yuba Long Bar	72	750
SOLRONY			
---	Mendocino Twp 1	60	888
SOLSCER			
Nosoia	Mariposa Twp 1	60	624
SOLTEREVASSER			
Louisa*	Alameda Oakland	55	72
SOLTEVERASSER			
Louisa*	Alameda Oakland	55	72

Name	County Locale	M653 Roll	Page
SOLTMARNER			
Frederick	San Francisco San Francisco 7	68	1419
SOLUDAD			
Wm*	El Dorado Georgetown	58	707
SOLUMONSON			
G*	Napa Napa	61	106
SOLUMOUSON			
G*	Napa Napa	61	106
SOLUS			
James*	El Dorado Georgetown	58	745
SOLVA			
Manuel	Alameda Brooklyn	55	100
SOLVATHIO			
Julian	El Dorado Georgetown	58	677
SOLVATRIA			
Julian*	El Dorado Georgetown	58	677
SOM KE			
---	Mariposa Twp 3	60	609
SOM SACRE			
---*	Mariposa Twp 3	60	601
SOM			
---	Amador Twp 5	55	368
---	Calaveras Twp 6	57	166
---	Calaveras Twp 4	57	307
---	Calaveras Twp 4	57	322
---	El Dorado White Oaks	58	1009
---	El Dorado White Oaks	58	1011
---	El Dorado Salmon Falls	58	1042
---	El Dorado Salmon Hills	58	1054
---	El Dorado Salmon Falls	58	1060
---	El Dorado Salmon Hills	58	1062
---	El Dorado Salmon Hills	58	1063
---	El Dorado Salmon Falls	58	1064
---	El Dorado Salmon Falls	58	1067
---	El Dorado Coloma	58	1078
---	El Dorado Coloma	58	1084
---	El Dorado Union	58	1088
---	El Dorado Coloma	58	1102
---	El Dorado Coloma	58	1103
---	El Dorado Coloma	58	1105
---	El Dorado Kelsey	58	1141
---	El Dorado Casumnes	58	1160
---	El Dorado Casumnes	58	1174
---	El Dorado Casumnes	58	1175
---	El Dorado Georgetown	58	688
---	El Dorado Diamond	58	784
---	El Dorado Diamond	58	795
---	El Dorado Diamond	58	797
---	El Dorado Diamond	58	800
---	El Dorado Diamond	58	803
---	El Dorado Placerville	58	832
---	El Dorado Placerville	58	906
---	El Dorado Eldorado	58	940
---	El Dorado Mud Springs	58	958
---	El Dorado Mud Springs	58	962
---	El Dorado Mud Springs	58	964
---	El Dorado Mud Springs	58	970
---	El Dorado Mud Springs	58	971
---	El Dorado Mud Springs	58	976
---	El Dorado Mud Springs	58	985
---	El Dorado Mud Springs	58	986
---	El Dorado Mud Springs	58	987
---	Mariposa Twp 3	60	563
---	Mariposa Twp 3	60	588
---	Mariposa Twp 3	60	598
---	Mariposa Twp 3	60	607
---	Mariposa Twp 3	60	609
---	Mariposa Twp 3	60	612
---	Plumas Quincy	62	947
---	Plumas Quincy	62	949
---	Sacramento Cosumnes	63	392
---	Sacramento Ward 3	63	493
---	Sierra Downieville	66	1008
---	Sierra Downieville	66	1014
---	Sierra Cox'S Bar	66	950
---	Sierra Downieville	66	984
---	Sierra Downieville	66	985
---	Sierra Downieville	66	992
---	Sierra Downieville	66	999
---	Tuolumne Big Oak	71	148
---	Tuolumne Jacksonville	71	166
---	Tuolumne Jacksonville	71	167
---	Tuolumne Jacksonville	71	514
---	Yuba Slate Ro	72	712
---*	El Dorado Salmon Falls	58	1054
---*	El Dorado Salmon Falls	58	1067
---*	El Dorado Casumnes	58	1175
---*	Mariposa Twp 3	60	588
---*	Mariposa Twp 3	60	607
Ah	Tuolumne Twp 4	71	166
Chow	Yolo No E Twp	72	667
Jos	Sonoma Petaluma	69	546
Kat	El Dorado Georgetown	58	700
Lan	Shasta Horsetown	66	710
Toke	El Dorado Placerville	58	825
Yet	El Dorado Coloma	58	1084

California 1860 Census Index

Name	County Locale	M653 Roll	Page
SOM			
Yet	El Dorado Mud Springs	58	958
Yup	Nevada Nevada	61	305
SOMAN			
Geo	Nevada Nevada	61	268
SOMARIA			
Laurcerci*	San Luis Obispo	65	41
	San Luis Obispo		
SOMBANDI			
John	Calaveras Twp 5	57	217
SOMBANLI			
John	Calaveras Twp 5	57	217
SOMBARD			
Sevonia*	Butte Ophir	56	766
SOMBARDER			
Willm	Sacramento Centre	63	179
SOMBARDI			
John	Calaveras Twp 5	57	217
SOMBERGEN			
Dherman*	El Dorado Big Bar	58	744
SOMBERJEN			
Herman*	El Dorado Big Bar	58	744
SOMBORDI			
John	Calaveras Twp 5	57	216
SOMBRINO			
Ignacios*	Calaveras Twp 5	57	248
SOMBRIRRO			
Ignacius*	Calaveras Twp 5	57	248
SOMBROSA			
Victor	Placer Michigan	62	814
SOME			
---	El Dorado Placerville	58	933
---	Placer Rattle Snake	62	637
---	Tuolumne Big Oak	71	147
---*	Sierra Twp 5	66	934
A*	Sierra Twp 5	66	934
Ah	Tuolumne Twp 4	71	147
SOMERFIELD			
F	Yolo Merritt	72	584
Jas	Sacramento Ward 1	63	43
S	San Francisco San Francisco 2	67	684
SOMERFORD			
J H	Mariposa Twp 1	60	667
SOMERIN DYKE			
W S	Shasta Shasta	66	682
SOMERINDYKE			
Geo W	San Francisco San Francisco 2	67	625
SOMERMAN			
F W	El Dorado Mud Springs	58	985
SOMERS			
C	San Francisco San Francisco 10	67	330
Carlos D	San Francisco San Francisco 10	67	329
D B	Sacramento Dry Crk	63	374
Daniel	San Francisco San Francisco 3	67	56
Frank	Fresno Twp 3	59	16
G	Nevada Grass Valley	61	161
G	Nevada Nevada	61	321
G A	Nevada Grass Valley	61	183
H	San Francisco San Francisco 10	67	330
H C	San Francisco San Francisco 9	68	976
H L	Sacramento Granite	63	221
Henry	Alameda Oakland	55	18
Jas	Butte Ophir	56	791
Jas	Sacramento Natonia	63	272
John	Los Angeles Los Angeles	59	359
John	Los Angeles San Pedro	59	480
John C	Siskiyou Yreka	69	137
John C	Siskiyou Yreka	69	138
Louis	Tuolumne Twp 5	71	493
Peer	Butte Bidwell	56	712
Philip	San Francisco San Francisco 10	67	292
R	Nevada Grass Valley	61	149
Robert*	Siskiyou Yreka	69	137
S	Nevada Grass Valley	61	190
Sameul	San Joaquin Elkhorn	64	970
Saml	Stanislaus Branch	70	707
W J	San Francisco San Francisco 5	67	492
SOMERSET			
Robert	Alameda Brooklyn	55	159
T	San Francisco San Francisco 6	67	413
SOMERSETT			
R	Nevada Grass Valley	61	197
SOMERVILLE			
Mary	Sacramento Ward 1	63	45
W D	Colusa Colusi	57	423
SOMERY			
S	Nevada Grass Valley	61	155
SOMES			
Geo A	Klamath Orleans	59	215
SOMKIN			
Lysiveus*	Calaveras Twp 5	57	248
SOMMER			
J	Butte Kimshaw	56	586

Name	County Locale	M653 Roll	Page
SOMMER			
John	Marin Novato	60	736
SOMMERS			
A	San Francisco San Francisco 5	67	522
F A	San Joaquin O'Neal	64	1002
George	Los Angeles Los Angeles	59	365
Henry	San Francisco San Francisco 3	67	33
Herman	San Francisco San Francisco 3	67	65
SOMMERVILLE			
Peter	San Francisco San Francisco 2	67	627
SOMMONDS			
W C	Mendocino Little L	60	836
SOMNER			
Charles	San Francisco San Francisco 3	67	3
SOMON			
Juan	Monterey San Juan	60	1002
SOMONNTO			
Amanda	San Francisco San Francisco 6	67	459
SOMORA			
Juan	Tuolumne Twp 5	71	511
SOMOREL			
Louis*	Alameda Brooklyn	55	139
SOMORER			
Martin	Mariposa Twp 1	60	645
SOMOZA			
Agustin	Los Angeles Los Angeles	59	331
SOMTAS			
---	Monterey Monterey	60	957
SOMTRINO			
Ignacius*	Calaveras Twp 5	57	248
SOMULA			
---	Yuba Bear Rvr	72	1014
---	Yuba Bear Rvr	72	1015
SON DUES			
---*	Mariposa Twp 3	60	609
SON G			
Ah	Tuolumne Twp 2	71	306
SON LEE			
---	Mariposa Twp 3	60	608
SON			
---	Amador Twp 4	55	247
---	Amador Twp 3	55	397
---	Amador Twp 7	55	414
---	Amador Twp 6	55	435
---	Butte Oregon	56	638
---	Calaveras Twp 6	57	148
---	Calaveras Twp 6	57	165
---	Calaveras Twp 5	57	193
---	Calaveras Twp 5	57	214
---	Calaveras Twp 5	57	215
---	Calaveras Twp 5	57	230
---	Calaveras Twp 5	57	242
---	Calaveras Twp 10	57	261
---	Calaveras Twp 10	57	285
---	Calaveras Twp 10	57	287
---	Calaveras Twp 9	57	349
---	El Dorado White Oaks	58	1001
---	El Dorado White Oaks	58	1009
---	El Dorado Salmon Hills	58	1061
---	El Dorado Coloma	58	1085
---	El Dorado Union	58	1089
---	El Dorado Coloma	58	1106
---	El Dorado Coloma	58	1107
---	El Dorado Coloma	58	1120
---	El Dorado Coloma	58	1121
---	El Dorado Coloma	58	1122
---	El Dorado Coloma	58	1123
---	El Dorado Casumnes	58	1162
---	El Dorado Georgetown	58	697
---	El Dorado Diamond	58	784
---	El Dorado Diamond	58	796
---	El Dorado Diamond	58	797
---	El Dorado Diamond	58	803
---	El Dorado Placerville	58	830
---	El Dorado Placerville	58	839
---	El Dorado Mud Springs	58	958
---	El Dorado Mud Springs	58	964
---	El Dorado Mud Springs	58	971
---	El Dorado Mud Springs	58	972
---	El Dorado Mud Springs	58	978
---	El Dorado Mud Springs	58	985
---	Mariposa Twp 3	60	560
---	Mariposa Twp 3	60	564
---	Mariposa Twp 3	60	569
---	Mariposa Twp 3	60	588
---	Mariposa Twp 3	60	590
---	Mariposa Twp 3	60	608
---	Mariposa Twp 3	60	618
---	Mariposa Twp 3	60	620
---	Mariposa Twp 1	60	639
---	Mariposa Twp 1	60	657
---	Mariposa Twp 1	60	668
---	Mariposa Coulterville	60	681
---	Nevada Bridgeport	61	466
---	Placer Rattle Snake	62	625
---	Placer Virginia	62	665

Name	County Locale	M653 Roll	Page
SON			
---	Placer Virginia	62	670
---	Placer Virginia	62	677
---	Placer Virginia	62	681
---	Plumas Quincy	62	949
---	Sacramento Granite	63	232
---	Sacramento Granite	63	259
---	Sacramento Casumnes	63	381
---	Sacramento Cosumnes	63	396
---	Sacramento Cosumnes	63	409
---	Sacramento Ward 1	63	66
---	San Francisco San Francisco 4	68	1173
---	San Francisco San Francisco 4	68	1177
---	San Francisco San Francisco 4	68	1180
---	San Francisco San Francisco 4	68	1185
---	San Francisco San Francisco 4	68	1209
---	San Francisco San Francisco 4	68	1211
---	Shasta Horsetown	66	701
---	Shasta French G	66	712
---	Sierra Downieville	66	1015
---	Sierra Twp 5	66	932
---	Sierra Downieville	66	985
---	Sierra Downieville	66	992
---	Trinity Trinindad Rvr	70	1044
---	Trinity Trinindad Rvr	70	1045
---	Trinity Eastman	70	960
---	Tulara Twp 2	71	3
---	Tuolumne Big Oak	71	148
---	Tuolumne Big Oak	71	149
---	Tuolumne Big Oak	71	150
---	Tuolumne Don Pedro	71	163
---	Tuolumne Green Springs	71	517
---	Tuolumne Twp 6	71	536
---	Yolo Washington	72	562
---	Yolo No E Twp	72	681
---	Yolo No E Twp	72	685
---	Yolo Slate Ra	72	715
---	Yuba Fosters	72	841
---*	El Dorado Salmon Falls	58	1061
---*	El Dorado Casumnes	58	1162
---*	Mariposa Twp 3	60	576
---*	Mariposa Twp 3	60	580
---*	Nevada Nevada	61	305
---*	Sacramento Ward 1	63	66
---*	Yuba Fosters	72	841
Adolphus	San Francisco San Francisco 7	68	1407
Ah	Butte Oregon	56	638
Ah	Sacramento Cosumnes	63	380
Ah	Sacramento Cosumnes	63	381
Ah	Yolo Washington	72	562
At	Mariposa Twp 3	60	620
Ce	Mariposa Twp 3	60	618
Chung	Sacramento Granite	63	232
Con*	Mariposa Twp 3	60	581
Cou	Calaveras Twp 10	57	259
Ee	Tuolumne Big Oak	71	150
Fiat*	Mariposa Twp 3	60	582
Goo	Placer Illinois	62	753
Hei	Calaveras Twp 5	57	193
Kee	Mariposa Twp 3	60	580
Kin	Calaveras Twp 5	57	257
Kon	Mariposa Twp 3	60	580
Lee	Mariposa Twp 3	60	612
Low	Mariposa Twp 3	60	569
Mann	Yuba Marysville	72	895
Michael	Sierra Twp 7	66	870
Mow	Calaveras Twp 9	57	375
Peter	Trinity North Fo	70	1024
Sam	Nevada Rough &	61	437
Say*	Mariposa Twp 3	60	582
See	Mariposa Twp 3	60	613
Si	Butte Oro	56	677
Sin	Sierra Downieville	66	985
Sing	Mariposa Twp 3	60	578
Song	Mariposa Twp 1	60	667
Soy	Mariposa Twp 3	60	582
Yen	Sierra La Porte	66	790
Young*	Mariposa Twp 3	60	578
SONA			
---	El Dorado Salmon Hills	58	1064
---	El Dorado Union	58	1091
---	El Dorado Coloma	58	1112
---	El Dorado Casumnes	58	1176
---	El Dorado Diamond	58	806
---	El Dorado Placerville	58	842
---	El Dorado Mud Springs	58	991
---*	El Dorado Salmon Falls	58	1064
SONAMU			
---	Fresno Twp 2	59	52
SONAPP			
John*	Siskiyou Scott Ri	69	83
SONARD			
Alfred	Yuba Foster B	72	828
SONBERG			
Jos	San Francisco San Francisco 6	67	429
SONCAGE			
G*	San Francisco San Francisco 1	68	841

Name	County Locale	M653 Roll Page
SONCE		
Peter*	Butte Hamilton	56 525
SONCHAL		
A M	Butte Oregon	56 633
SONCI		
Paul	Butte Chico	56 553
Paul*	Butte Chico	56 555
SONCY		
Peter P*	Tuolumne Twp 3	71 458
SOND		
---	El Dorado Diamond	58 806
SONDAL		
Maria	Los Angeles Santa Ana	59 454
Rosa	Los Angeles Santa Ana	59 454
SONDBAND		
Jesse	Sonoma Petaluma	69 584
SONDECHER		
L*	San Francisco San Francisco 10	331 67
SONDEN		
Eugene	El Dorado Greenwood	58 715
SONDERS		
J	Shasta Horsetown	66 696
John	Alameda Brooklyn	55 132
SONDHEIMOR		
Emanuel	Sonoma Healdsbu	69 477
SONDORS		
William	Mendocino Ukiah	60 796
SONDS		
James	El Dorado Georgetown	58 696
SONE		
---	Calaveras Twp 4	57 307
---	El Dorado Salmon Hills	581060
---	El Dorado Salmon Falls	581067
---	El Dorado Coloma	581107
---	El Dorado Kelsey	581143
---	El Dorado Mountain	581188
---	El Dorado Placerville	58 839
---	El Dorado Placerville	58 843
---	El Dorado Mud Springs	58 964
---	Mariposa Twp 3	60 618
---	Placer Illinois	62 754
---	Sierra Downieville	661005
---	Sierra Downieville	661009
---	Sierra Twp 5	66 931
---	Sierra Downieville	66 983
---	Tuolumne Chinese	71 510
Poe	El Dorado Placerville	58 823
W	Shasta Shasta	66 732
SONENY		
Louis	El Dorado Greenwood	58 715
SONER		
C	El Dorado Placerville	58 845
Wiliam	Placer Yankee J	62 756
SONERS		
Peter	Butte Bidwell	56 712
SONEY		
---	Trinity Trininad Rvr	701044
L B	Butte Ophir	56 750
SONF		
Geo	Sacramento Ward 1	63 27
SONG AH PONG		
---	Marin Cortemad	60 780
SONG COW		
---	Tuolumne Jacksonville	71 516
SONG HUN		
---	Sacramento Ward 1	63 69
SONG ME		
---*	San Francisco San Francisco 4	681197
SONG TIE		
---	Sacramento Ward 1	63 69
SONG TUCK		
---	Sacramento Ward 1	63 69
SONG		
---	Alameda Oakland	55 24
---	Amador Twp 4	55 248
---	Amador Twp 2	55 274
---	Amador Twp 2	55 294
---	Amador Twp 4	55 332
---	Amador No 6	55 423
---	Amador Twp 1	55 501
---	Butte Hamilton	56 529
---	Butte Kimshaw	56 578
---	Calaveras Twp 8	57 109
---	Calaveras Twp 6	57 149
---	Calaveras Twp 6	57 164
---	Calaveras Twp 5	57 212
---	Calaveras Twp 5	57 231
---	Calaveras Twp 5	57 234
---	Calaveras Twp 5	57 243
---	Calaveras Twp 5	57 246
---	Calaveras Twp 5	57 252
---	Calaveras Twp 5	57 254
---	Calaveras Twp 5	57 256
---	Calaveras Twp 10	57 275
---	Calaveras Twp 4	57 299
SONG		
---	Calaveras Twp 4	57 331
---	Del Norte Crescent	58 641
---	El Dorado Salmon Falls	581061
---	El Dorado Salmon Falls	581063
---	El Dorado Coloma	581075
---	El Dorado Greenwood	58 728
---	El Dorado Diamond	58 801
---	El Dorado Diamond	58 814
---	El Dorado Diamond	58 816
---	El Dorado Mud Springs	58 981
---	El Dorado Mud Springs	58 988
---	Fresno Twp 2	59 17
---	Fresno Twp 2	59 20
---	Mariposa Twp 3	60 543
---	Mariposa Twp 3	60 544
---	Mariposa Twp 3	60 564
---	Mariposa Twp 3	60 572
---	Mariposa Twp 3	60 582
---	Mariposa Twp 1	60 640
---	Mariposa Twp 1	60 643
---	Mariposa Twp 1	60 648
---	Mariposa Twp 1	60 657
---	Mariposa Twp 1	60 658
---	Mariposa Twp 1	60 661
---	Mariposa Twp 1	60 662
---	Mariposa Twp 1	60 663
---	Mariposa Twp 1	60 668
---	Mariposa Coulterville	60 682
---	Mariposa Coulterville	60 687
---	Mariposa Coulterville	60 692
---	Nevada Grass Valley	61 234
---	Nevada Nevada	61 299
---	Nevada Nevada	61 301
---	Nevada Nevada	61 303
---	Nevada Nevada	61 305
---	Nevada Nevada	61 309
---	Nevada Bridgeport	61 462
---	Placer Rattle Snake	62 629
---	Placer Virginia	62 663
---	Placer Virginia	62 667
---	Placer Illinois	62 746
---	Sacramento Granite	63 231
---	Sacramento Granite	63 245
---	Sacramento Ward 4	63 535
---	Sacramento Ward 1	63 54
---	Sacramento Ward 1	63 59
---	Sacramento Ward 1	63 60
---	Sacramento Ward 1	63 69
---	Sacramento Ward 1	63 71
---	San Francisco San Francisco 4	681188
---	San Francisco San Francisco 4	681188
---	San Francisco San Francisco 4	681190
---	San Francisco San Francisco 4	681195
---	San Francisco San Francisco 4	681197
---	San Francisco San Francisco 4	681198
---	San Francisco San Francisco 4	681201
---	San Francisco San Francisco 4	681202
---	San Francisco San Francisco 11	145 67
---	San Francisco San Francisco 1	68 924
---	Shasta Horsetown	66 709
---	Sierra St Louis	66 862
---	Sierra Twp 7	66 876
---	Sierra Twp 5	66 923
---	Sierra Twp 5	66 930
---	Sierra Twp 5	66 932
---	Sierra Downieville	66 953
---	Trinity Trinindad Rvr	701046
---	Trinity Trinindad Rvr	701047
---	Trinity Lewiston	70 955
---	Tuolumne Twp 2	71 410
---	Tuolumne Twp 2	71 416
---	Tuolumne Twp 3	71 434
---	Tuolumne Twp 3	71 439
---	Tuolumne Twp 3	71 468
---	Tuolumne Twp 1	71 475
---	Tuolumne Twp 5	71 514
---	Tuolumne Twp 5	71 515
---	Tuolumne Don Pedro	71 533
---	Yolo No E Twp	72 676
---	Yolo No E Twp	72 677
---	Yolo No E Twp	72 681
---	Yolo No E Twp	72 684
---	Yolo Slate Ra	72 715
---	Yuba North Ea	72 677
---	Yuba Long Bar	72 758
---	Yuba Long Bar	72 761
---	Yuba Long Bar	72 762
---	Yuba Fosters	72 834
---	Yuba Fosters	72 841
---	Yuba Fosters	72 843
---	Yuba Marysville	72 924
---*	Amador Twp 5	55 349
---*	Calaveras Twp 4	57 339
---*	Calaveras Twp 4	57 341
SONG		
---*	El Dorado Coloma	581084
---*	El Dorado Georgetown	58 700
---*	Mariposa Twp 3	60 590
---*	Nevada Nevada	61 302
---*	Nevada Nevada	61 305
---*	Nevada Nevada	61 309
---*	Sacramento Cosumnes	63 391
---*	Shasta Shasta	66 669
---*	Trinity Cox'S Bar	701037
---*	Yuba Foster B	72 827
---*	Yuba Fosters	72 842
---*	Yuba Linda	72 992
A	Calaveras Twp 4	57 331
A	Klamath Klamath	59 229
Alex D	Trinity Whites Crk	701028
Chan	Nevada Grass Valley	61 234
Chew*	Butte Ophir	56 806
Ching	San Francisco San Francisco 2	67 770
Chong	San Francisco San Francisco 2	67 770
Chow	Calaveras Twp 5	57 246
Choy	Butte Ophir	56 805
Cow	Tuolumne Twp 5	71 516
Fee	Mariposa Twp 3	60 582
Fie	Mariposa Twp 3	60 581
Francis	Placer Iona Hills	62 883
Fui	San Francisco San Francisco 11	159 67
Fun	Del Norte Crescent	58 631
Fung	Trinity Texas Ba	70 981
Hen	Butte Mountain	56 743
Henry	Yuba Long Bar	72 745
Hi	San Francisco San Francisco 5	671205
High	Butte Bidwell	56 724
How*	Butte Mountain	56 743
Hun*	Sacramento Ward 1	63 69
J	Nevada Eureka	61 372
Jeremiah*	Trinity Weaverville	701077
Jos*	Sacramento Ward 1	63 154
Kee	San Francisco San Francisco 2	67 556
La	San Francisco San Francisco 5	671205
Li	San Francisco San Francisco 4	681201
Lon*	Mariposa Twp 1	60 627
Loo*	Yuba Bear Rvr	721000
M D	Nevada Eureka	61 343
Me	San Francisco San Francisco 4	681197
Mow	Butte Bidwell	56 731
Naw	Calaveras Twp 5	57 149
Num	Calaveras Twp 6	57 149
Pie	Mariposa Twp 3	60 581
S	Nevada Eureka	61 373
S	San Francisco San Francisco 2	67 610
Salmon*	Yuba Marysville	72 908
Sam	Sacramento Ward 1	63 152
Si	Yuba Marysville	72 916
Sing	Calaveras Twp 4	57 307
Sinn	Butte Bidwell	56 727
Tat	Mariposa Twp 3	60 579
Tom	Calaveras Twp 5	57 237
Tuck	Sacramento Centre	63 182
W D	Tuolumne Shawsfla	71 410
Yon*	Yuba Bear Rvr	721000
You	Yuba Bear Rvr	721000
SONGABAUGH		
Jno*	Sacramento American	63 163
SONGABOUGH		
Jno*	Sacramento American	63 163
SONGEE		
---	San Francisco San Francisco 11	159 67
SONGHY		
W J*	Butte Kimshaw	56 596
SONGLEY		
A L*	Placer Forest H	62 806
A S*	Placer Forest H	62 806
F H	Siskiyou Scott Ri	69 61
W J*	Butte Kimshaw	56 596
William	Placer Forest H	62 805
SONGMASTER		
Benja*	Calaveras Twp 4	57 340
SONGONG		
---	Plumas Quincy	62 969
SONGTIN		
Lewis	Amador Twp 4	55 245
SONI		
---	Placer Secret R	62 622
---	Placer Rattle Snake	62 638
SONIBAN		
Sevonia W*	Butte Ophir	56 766
SONICK		
R B*	Solano Montezuma	69 372
SONIN		
Robert*	Placer Dutch Fl	62 731
SONIO		
Lafucio	Los Angeles Elmonte	59 264
SONITH		
Ralph	Marin Tomales	60 724

Name	County Locale	M653 Roll	Page
SONITT			
Saml*	San Francisco San Francisco 1	68	916
SONJ			
---*	Mariposa Twp 3	60	564
SONK			
---	Trinity Raabs Ba	70	1020
SONKINP			
---*	Mendocino Round Va	60	883
SONLATT			
Fogustia	Sierra Twp 7	66	912
SONLE			
James*	Shasta Horsetown	66	697
SONLES			
G W*	Sacramento American	63	164
SONMEILLAN			
John*	Los Angeles Los Angeles	59	366
SONN			
---	Butte Mountain	56	741
---*	Mariposa Twp 3	60	608
---*	Mariposa Twp 3	60	607
---*	Mariposa Twp 3	60	608
SONNAN			
David	Solano Benecia	69	307
John*	Solano Benecia	69	307
SONNENBERG			
L B	San Francisco San Francisco 10		177
		67	
SONNETT			
Mitchell	Butte Chico	56	534
SONNEY			
P L J	Butte Mountain	56	740
SONNG			
---	Mariposa Twp 1	60	648
SONNICHSEN			
James	San Francisco San Francisco 8	68	1310
SONNON			
Ferdinand*	Nevada Bridgeport	61	502
Ferdinond*	Nevada Bridgeport	61	502
SONNS			
Jno	Butte Oregon	56	635
SONO			
How	El Dorado Mud Springs	58	959
SONOMA			
---	Mendocino Calpella	60	827
SONONO			
---	San Diego Agua Caliente	64	854
SONORA			
Ramone	Los Angeles San Jose	59	288
SONORENCA			
Victor	Monterey Monterey	60	962
SONOVIO			
Pelar	Los Angeles Los Angeles	59	512
SONOWAR			
H	San Francisco San Francisco 4	68	1166
SONREL			
Juan	Los Angeles Los Angeles	59	501
SONRIL			
Juan	Los Angeles Los Angeles	59	501
SONRION			
Ferdinond*	Nevada Bridgeport	61	502
SONRY			
George	Trinity Eastman	70	960
SONS			
Charles	Mendocino Ukiah	60	796
John*	San Francisco San Francisco 2	67	794
SONSALA			
B N	Tuolumne Big Oak	71	156
SONSEMBER			
Charles*	San Francisco San Francisco 8	68	1322
SONSEUR			
Joseph*	Amador Twp 4	55	245
SONSURE			
Joseph*	Amador Twp 4	55	245
SONT			
Jacob*	Yuba Marysville	72	898
SONTA			
Eve Joseph*	Calaveras Twp 6	57	163
SONTAANNA			
---	Mariposa Twp 1	60	653
SONTAG			
Henry A	San Francisco San Francisco 11		117
		67	
Hillar	Plumas Meadow Valley	62	933
Julius H	San Francisco San Francisco 2	67	615
Richard	San Francisco San Francisco 1	68	836
SONTEANES			
Francisco	Monterey San Juan	60	1001
SONTER			
Eve Joseph*	Calaveras Twp 6	57	163
John*	Shasta French G	66	717
SONTHER			
John	Calaveras Twp 8	57	81
SONTHERS			
M	Calaveras Twp 9	57	395
SONTHING			
Saml	Tuolumne Shawsfla	71	412
SONTHWOOD			
G B*	Mendocino Ukiah	60	795
SONTOTO			
---	Butte Chico	56	550
SONTTON			
G M	Yolo Cache	72	618
SONTU			
Eve Joseph	Calaveras Twp 6	57	163
SONW QUE			
---	Sierra Twp 7	66	898
SONX			
Cath	San Francisco San Francisco 10		278
		67	
SONY			
---	Calaveras Twp 6	57	164
---	Calaveras Twp 5	57	193
---	Calaveras Twp 5	57	212
---	Calaveras Twp 5	57	231
---	Calaveras Twp 5	57	237
---	Calaveras Twp 5	57	246
---	Calaveras Twp 5	57	256
---	Calaveras Twp 5	57	257
---	Calaveras Twp 10	57	270
---	Calaveras Twp 10	57	275
---	Calaveras Twp 4	57	300
---	Calaveras Twp 4	57	304
---	El Dorado Georgetown	58	688
---	Mariposa Twp 1	60	648
---*	El Dorado Georgetown	58	700
Dennis	Calaveras Twp 10	57	274
Moses	Calaveras Twp 10	57	279
Sing	Calaveras Twp 4	57	307
SONYET			
---	Trinity Trinindad Rvr	70	1044
SOO LOO			
---	Mariposa Twp 3	60	613
SOO TONG			
---	Tuolumne Sonora	71	476
SOO			
---	Amador Twp 4	55	256
---	Amador Twp 5	55	335
---	Amador Twp 1	55	497
---	Butte Hamilton	56	530
---	Butte Oregon	56	629
---	Butte Eureka	56	652
---	Calaveras Twp 6	57	147
---	Calaveras Twp 5	57	201
---	Calaveras Twp 5	57	223
---	Calaveras Twp 10	57	271
---	Calaveras Twp 10	57	272
---	Calaveras Twp 7	57	41
---	Calaveras Twp 8	57	74
---	El Dorado White Oaks	58	1011
---	El Dorado Salmon Hills	58	1064
---	El Dorado Kelsey	58	1131
---	El Dorado Diamond	58	803
---	El Dorado Diamond	58	805
---	El Dorado Diamond	58	808
---	El Dorado Placerville	58	841
---	El Dorado Placerville	58	842
---	El Dorado Placerville	58	905
---	El Dorado Placerville	58	934
---	El Dorado Mud Springs	58	957
---	El Dorado Mud Springs	58	961
---	Mariposa Twp 3	60	590
---	Nevada Rough &	61	399
---	Plumas Quincy	62	926
---	Sacramento Ward 1	63	53
---	San Francisco San Francisco 4	68	1180
---	San Francisco San Francisco 4	68	1189
---	San Francisco San Francisco 4	68	1200
---	San Joaquin Oneal	64	940
---	Tulara Twp 2	71	37
---	Tuolumne Jamestown	71	455
---	Tuolumne Twp 3	71	460
---	Tuolumne Twp 3	71	468
---	Tuolumne Twp 5	71	512
---	Yuba Marysville	72	925
---	Yuba Linda	72	992
---*	Calaveras Twp 5	57	232
---*	Nevada Rough &	61	399
---*	Tuolumne Big Oak	71	182
---*	Yuba Fosters	72	841
Ah	Butte Oregon	56	629
Ah	Butte Eureka	56	652
Ah	Tuolumne Twp 4	71	182
Ah	Yuba Suida	72	992
How	Yuba Marysville	72	917
J*	Nevada Rough &	61	399
John	Yolo No E Twp	72	675
Lee	Yuba Long Bar	72	764
Loo	Mariposa Twp 3	60	613
Mang	Yuba Long Bar	72	756
O*	Nevada Rough &	61	399
Quong	Yuba Parks Ba	72	782
Ran	Yuba Fosters	72	826
SOO			
Tim	Tuolumne Twp 4	71	150
Up	Butte Kimshaw	56	577
Ya	Amador Twp 5	55	355
Yak	Tuolumne Twp 5	71	526
SOOA			
---	El Dorado Mountain	58	1188
SOODAEGIE			
L	Tuolumne Twp 4	71	157
SOODRIP			
Ramon*	Calaveras Twp 5	57	206
SOODS			
J*	San Francisco San Francisco 5	67	487
James	Tuolumne Twp 3	71	425
SOOETT			
P B	Sutter Butte	70	792
SOOEY			
---	Yuba Fosters	72	827
SOOH			
Pah	San Francisco San Francisco 5	67	528
SOOK			
---	Amador Twp 4	55	256
---	Calaveras Twp 5	57	192
---	Calaveras Twp 10	57	285
---	Calaveras Twp 4	57	299
---	Calaveras Twp 4	57	300
---	Calaveras Twp 4	57	300
---	Calaveras Twp 4	57	303
---	Calaveras Twp 4	57	307
---	Placer Auburn	62	581
---	Tuolumne Twp 5	71	526
SOOLF			
Michael	Siskiyou Yreka	69	148
SOOLIN			
Charles*	Santa Cruz Watsonville	66	539
SOOLS			
Isial*	Calaveras Twp 9	57	356
SOOM			
---	Amador Twp 1	55	502
---	Mariposa Twp 3	60	608
SOOMAS			
S D	Mariposa Twp 1	60	642
SOON CRU			
---*	Mariposa Twp 3	60	607
SOON			
---	Amador Twp 1	55	492
---	Calaveras Twp 4	57	322
---	Calaveras Twp 8	57	87
---	Del Norte Crescent	58	641
---	El Dorado Salmon Falls	58	1053
---	El Dorado Salmon Hills	58	1060
---	El Dorado Coloma	58	1085
---	El Dorado Coloma	58	1086
---	El Dorado Union	58	1089
---	El Dorado Diamond	58	786
---	El Dorado Placerville	58	841
---	El Dorado Placerville	58	842
---	El Dorado Eldorado	58	943
---	Nevada Rough &	61	409
---	Nevada Bridgeport	61	456
---	Nevada Bridgeport	61	485
---	Nevada Bridgeport	61	493
---	Trinity Weaverville	70	1052
---	Trinity Lewiston	70	956
---	Tuolumne Twp 3	71	452
---	Tuolumne Twp 3	71	455
---	Tuolumne Twp 3	71	460
---	Tuolumne Twp 6	71	536
---	Yuba Long Bar	72	767
---	Yuba Linda	72	991
---*	Butte Hamilton	56	529
Ah	Yuba Suida	72	991
F T	Calaveras Twp 9	57	403
Gey	Shasta Horsetown	66	701
Gon	Mariposa Twp 3	60	614
Ten	Shasta Horsetown	66	710
Tone	Shasta Horsetown	66	701
SOONE			
M	Nevada Eureka	61	346
SOONG			
---	Amador Twp 1	55	492
SOOP			
---*	Butte Hamilton	56	529
Pak	San Francisco San Francisco 5	67	528
SOOPER			
S	Sutter Butte	70	796
SOORRIGHT			
W	Merced Twp 1	60	901
SOOS			
Philip*	Plumas Quincy	62	940
SOOT			
---	Butte Eureka	56	654
---	Calaveras Twp 4	57	299
---	Calaveras Twp 4	57	300
---	El Dorado Diamond	58	802
Ah	Butte Eureka	56	654

Name	County Locale	M653 Roll Page
SOOT		
James	Sierra Twp 7	66 886
SOOTS		
I*	Trinity Weaverville	70 1063
SOOW		
---*	Tuolumne Green Springs	71 531
SOOY		
---*	Yuba North Ea	72 676
D	Yuba New York	72 731
Elleanor	Yuba New York	72 733
Thomas	Plumas Quincy	62 961
SOP		
---	Butte Kimshaw	56 604
---	Calaveras Twp 10	57 285
---	Del Norte Crescent	58 651
---	Mariposa Twp 3	60 641
---	Sacramento Granite	63 231
---	Sacramento Cosumnes	63 394
---*	Yuba Linda	72 990
Lee	San Francisco San Francisco 4	68 1176
Lin	Butte Ophir	56 817
Sing	Calaveras Twp 10	57 272
Son	San Francisco San Francisco 4	68 1176
Sou	San Francisco San Francisco 4	68 1176
To	Fresno Twp 2	59 19
SOPA		
John	Placer Auburn	62 570
SOPE		
---	Calaveras Twp 5	57 256
SOPER		
Alfred C	Mariposa Twp 3	60 561
Fred	Contra Costa Twp 2	57 564
J W	Sierra Twp 7	66 888
John	Santa Cruz Santa Cruz	66 618
Samuel	El Dorado Mud Springs	58 965
SOPEY		
Appelonia	Contra Costa Twp 1	57 533
SOPEZ		
Anna	San Francisco San Francisco 2	67 767
Antonio*	Plumas Quincy	62 988
Francisa	Calaveras Twp 10	57 260
Francisco	Mariposa Twp 1	60 646
Samcramente	Calaveras Twp 5	57 248
Teresa	Los Angeles Los Angeles	59 301
Thomnas	Contra Costa Twp 1	57 491
SOPH		
Andrew	Sierra La Porte	66 784
SOPHIA		
Barbra	Napa Hot Springs	61 21
SOPHINO		
Angel	San Joaquin Stockton	64 1081
SOPHY		
---	Mendocino Calpella	60 827
SOPI		
---	Calaveras Twp 5	57 256
SOPIA		
Vallentine	Contra Costa Twp 1	57 493
SOPIO		
Francisco	Los Angeles Los Angeles	59 500
SOPIS		
Apordina	Los Angeles Los Angeles	59 511
Cyro	Los Angeles Los Angeles	59 498
Jose C	Los Angeles Los Angeles	59 508
Jose D	Los Angeles Los Angeles	59 503
Luterio*	Los Angeles Los Angeles	59 489
SOPIY		
Franco*	Mariposa Twp 1	60 646
SOPONA		
---*	Fresno Millerto	59 2
SOPP		
---	Yolo Slate Ra	72 715
SOPPINGTON		
Pias	Contra Costa Twp 3	57 601
SOPRENO		
Louisa	San Joaquin Castoria	64 878
SOR		
---	Calaveras Twp 4	57 306
---	Calaveras Twp 4	57 326
---	El Dorado Greenwood	58 731
---*	Sierra Downieville	66 991
Chim	El Dorado Big Bar	58 740
Sg	El Dorado Georgetown	58 693
SORA		
---*	Tuolumne Twp 4	71 161
SORACES		
Frank*	Sierra Twp 5	66 926
SORAIN		
Thomas	Los Angeles Los Angeles	59 512
SORAISS		
Manuel*	Los Angeles Los Angeles	59 496
SORANCE		
Joshua*	Humbolt Eel Rvr	59 147
SORAND		
Lorenzo	Tuolumne Jamestown	71 447
SORANO		
Lorenzo	Tuolumne Twp 3	71 447

Name	County Locale	M653 Roll Page
SORANSA		
Gerome	Monterey San Juan	60 974
SORANSEN		
S*	Amador Twp 2	55 309
SORANSON		
Rob*	Amador Twp 2	55 309
SORANX		
F	Nevada Eureka	61 365
SORASIN		
---*	Siskiyou Callahan	69 2
SORATIS		
Emma E	El Dorado Greenwood	58 712
SORAUBEIA		
Jno V*	San Francisco San Francisco 9	68 1027
SORAUX		
F	Nevada Eureka	61 365
SORBIN		
Mat	El Dorado Big Bar	58 733
SORBOTH		
J W*	El Dorado Georgetown	58 699
SORCE		
Maria	San Francisco San Francisco 10	281 67
SORCH		
Fredrich	Tuolumne Montezuma	71 513
SORD		
J C	Nevada Eureka	61 376
Jonathan*	Siskiyou Scott Va	69 53
SORDA		
Peter	San Joaquin Stockton	64 1065
SORDE		
John*	San Francisco San Francisco 9	68 1078
SORE		
---	Calaveras Twp 5	57 211
A	Trinity Weaverville	70 1077
SOREAD		
B	Amador Twp 1	55 460
SOREL		
H C*	Tehama Red Bluff	70 905
Louis	Santa Cruz Santa Cruz	66 608
SORELL		
Saml	Napa Hot Springs	61 17
SORELS		
Saml	Napa Hot Springs	61 17
SORENAN		
John*	Solano Benecia	69 307
SORENSEN		
Henry R	Sierra Twp 5	66 943
SORENSON		
Henry R	Sierra Twp 5	66 943
Theodore	Yuba Marysville	72 882
SORENZ		
Henry	Trinity E Weaver	70 1061
SORENZANA		
Juventius	Los Angeles Los Angeles	59 345
SORENZO		
---	Monterey S Antoni	60 970
---	Monterey S Antoni	60 972
SORER		
J H*	El Dorado Coloma	58 1082
SORETA		
Manuel	Calaveras Twp 9	57 390
SOREZZO		
Joseph	Solano Benecia	69 300
SORFIELD		
F	Butte Bidwell	56 716
SORGA		
Joseph	Calaveras Twp 5	57 221
SORGAN		
---	Sierra Twp 5	66 926
SORGE		
Robert	Solano Benecia	69 317
SORGOMARCIA		
Joseph	Calaveras Twp 6	57 164
SORGOMARCIN		
Joseph*	Calaveras Twp 6	57 164
SORGUET		
Paul*	San Francisco San Francisco 10	266 67
SORIA		
Manuel	Santa Cruz Soquel	66 592
SORIER		
Jose	Santa Cruz Santa Cruz	66 624
Jose	Santa Cruz Santa Cruz	66 626
SORIET		
Peter*	Mariposa Coulterville	60 679
Petes*	Mariposa Coulterville	60 679
Retes*	Mariposa Coulterville	60 679
SORIETS		
Robt*	El Dorado Greenwood	58 720
SORING		
Wm A*	Amador Twp 4	55 237
SORINIMGER		
Edward N	Santa Cruz Pajaro	66 533
SORIOVIO		
Pelar	Los Angeles Los Angeles	59 512

Name	County Locale	M653 Roll Page
SORITTUR		
Fred*	San Francisco San Francisco 3	67 69
SORK		
Alfred*	Plumas Quincy	62 982
William	Plumas Quincy	62 920
SORLANOS		
---	Mariposa Twp 1	60 625
SORLEY		
William W	San Francisco San Francisco 11	90 67
Wm	Sacramento Ward 3	63 434
SORMAN		
James*	Nevada Bridgeport	61 448
SORME		
Hugh M*	Sacramento American	63 172
SORMON		
---	Sierra Twp 5	66 934
SORMTEM		
A*	San Francisco San Francisco 5	67 527
SORMULA		
Wm	Yuba Bear Rvr	72 1015
SORN		
---	Amador Twp 5	55 363
---	Amador Twp 6	55 432
---	El Dorado Coloma	58 1084
---	El Dorado Coloma	58 1105
---	El Dorado Mud Springs	58 972
---	Sierra St Louis	66 812
Fin*	Shasta Horsetown	66 701
Gey	Shasta Horsetown	66 701
Heung	San Francisco San Francisco 5	67 510
SORNAR		
Mercedes*	Sacramento Ward 1	63 104
SORNESS		
Manuel	Los Angeles Los Angeles	59 496
SORNG		
Krigh	Mariposa Twp 3	60 619
SORNSEN		
Henry	Los Angeles Los Angeles	59 361
Wilson	Butte Kimshaw	56 578
SORNSER		
Wilson*	Butte Kimshaw	56 578
SORO		
Jose M	Santa Cruz Watsonville	66 536
Juliano*	Santa Cruz Watsonville	66 536
SOROE		
Stephen*	Calaveras Twp 6	57 164
SORON		
Jno	Alameda Oakland	55 15
SORR		
---	San Francisco San Francisco 5	67 508
---*	Calaveras Twp 5	57 211
D	Sacramento Cosumnes	63 385
SORRAUD		
Gismani*	Plumas Meadow Valley	62 927
SORREL		
Mary	San Bernardino Santa Barbara	64 153
SORRELL		
D F	Siskiyou Yreka	69 169
Dr F*	Siskiyou Yreka	69 169
F Dr*	Siskiyou Yreka	69 169
SORRELS		
Victor	Tulara Twp 1	71 111
SORRENSEN		
Charles E	San Francisco San Francisco 3	67 44
SORRENSON		
Charles E*	San Francisco	67 44
SORRINSON		
Charles E*	San Francisco San Francisco 3	67 44
SORROH		
W W	Sonoma Mendocino	69 448
SORRY		
F N	Sacramento Granite	63 260
F W	Sacramento Granite	63 260
SORSANA		
Juana	Los Angeles San Gabriel	59 409
SORTEL		
John	Napa Yount	61 34
SORTELL		
G S	Tuolumne Twp 2	71 279
W H	Tuolumne Twp 2	71 284
SORTON		
J T*	Butte Chico	56 540
SORTONI		
Joseph	Calaveras Twp 6	57 142
SORTONIS		
Joseph*	Calaveras Twp 6	57 142
SORTOTT		
J W*	El Dorado Georgetown	58 699
SORUD		
G	Nevada Nevada	61 277
SORUE		
Stephen*	Calaveras Twp 6	57 164
SORUN		
John	Calaveras Twp 4	57 340

Name	County Locale	M653 RollPage
SORUSER		
Wilson*	Butte Kimshaw	56 578
SORVE		
Stephen*	Calaveras Twp 6	57 164
SORY		
---	Amador Twp 5	55 333
---	Amador Twp 5	55 335
---	Amador Twp 5	55 336
---*	Amador Twp 6	55 423
D N	Mendocino Big Rvr	60 848
L N	Mendocino Big Rvr	60 848
SORYDON		
James*	El Dorado Georgetown	58 758
SORYOMORCEAUS		
John*	Calaveras Twp 5	57 228
SORYOMORCENS		
John*	Calaveras Twp 5	57 228
SOS		
Sow	Butte Ophir	56 805
SOSA		
Sonis	Contra Costa Twp 1	57 486
SOSANO		
Carlos	Plumas Quincy	62 988
SOSER		
Anthony*	Amador Twp 4	55 255
SOSIA		
Luis*	Calaveras Twp 6	57 178
SOSSEN		
Edward	Yuba Marysville	72 977
SOSSER		
A A	Nevada Bridgeport	61 487
SOSSIER		
Noisine*	Yuba Parke Ba	72 783
Norsine*	Yuba Parks Ba	72 783
SOSSING		
Peter	Calaveras Twp 6	57 168
SOSSONA		
---*	Fresno Millerto	59 2
SOSTANOS		
---	Mariposa Twp 1	60 625
SOSTEAN		
---	San Diego Temecula	64 789
SOSTINAS		
Antonio*	Los Angeles Los Angeles	59 378
SOSU		
---	Calaveras Twp 5	57 193
SOT		
---	Sacramento Cosummes	63 395
---	Sacramento Ward 1	63 59
---*	El Dorado Georgetown	58 702
Ken	San Francisco San Francisco 4	681199
Sing	Nevada Bridgeport	61 460
SOTA		
Andress	Monterey Alisal	601027
Antonio	San Bernardino Santa Barbara	64 176
Antonio	San Bernardino Santa Barbara	64 189
Antonio	Tulara Twp 3	71 55
Esmal	San Bernardino S Buenav	64 221
Francisco	Siskiyou Scott Ri	69 63
Jose	Santa Clara Fremont	65 432
Juan	Monterey San Juan	60 976
M	El Dorado Placerville	58 897
Matias	Los Angeles Los Angeles	59 373
Miguel*	San Bernardino Santa Inez	64 141
Rufina	Monterey San Juan	60 985
Ydurica	Monterey Alisal	601035
SOTAS		
John	Calaveras Twp 9	57 385
SOTCHAWA		
---	Del Norte Klamath	58 655
SOTCHU		
F	Stanislaus Oatvale	70 716
SOTDO		
Frank*	El Dorado Georgetown	58 699
SOTE		
---	Del Norte Klamath	58 655
Antone	Alameda Brooklyn	55 93
Jaim*	Mariposa Twp 3	60 543
Jesus	Merced Monterey	60 931
Macidonia	Mariposa Twp 1	60 652
SOTELLO		
Candelario	Los Angeles Los Angeles	59 302
Jose	Los Angeles Los Angeles	59 302
SOTELO		
Jose	San Bernardino San Bernadino	64 640
SOTER		
John	Mariposa Coulterville	60 698
Macdonia*	Mariposa Twp 1	60 652
Macidonia	Mariposa Twp 1	60 652
Wm	Sacramento Ward 1	63 43
SOTEREA		
---	San Bernardino Cecelio	64 136
SOTH		
Joseph*	El Dorado Georgetown	58 704
SOTHER		
Goss	Mariposa Twp 1	60 651

Name	County Locale	M653 RollPage
SOTHERLAND		
George W	Mariposa Coulterville	60 674
SOTHILL		
John*	San Francisco San Francisco 2	67 588
SOTILA		
Refugio	Monterey San Juan	60 999
SOTILO		
Clodio	Monterey San Juan	60 999
SOTMAN		
Jeremy R*	Yuba Marysville	72 884
SOTMON		
Danl	Alameda Brooklyn	55 199
SOTNE		
Lysander	Colusa Monroeville	57 440
SOTO MAJOR		
Vicente*	San Francisco San Francisco 1	68 814
SOTO		
---	Sierra Twp 7	66 898
??Idera*	Santa Clara Fremont	65 437
Andreas	Santa Cruz Santa Cruz	66 617
Antonia	Santa Cruz Soguel	66 587
Antonio	San Francisco San Francisco 9	681072
Antonio	Santa Cruz Soguel	66 587
Artemisa	Monterey San Juan	60 976
Avil	Santa Cruz Pajaro	66 561
B	Merced Twp 1	60 899
Bantisto	Monterey Monterey	60 948
Benillo	Contra Costa Twp 3	57 615
Betilla	Los Angeles Los Angeles	59 513
Bicento	Los Angeles Los Angeles	59 506
Botilla	Los Angeles Los Angeles	59 513
Cameto	Santa Cruz Pajaro	66 541
Camito	Santa Cruz Pajaro	66 541
Carmen C	Monterey Monterey	60 951
Cins*	Contra Costa Twp 1	57 497
Comito	Santa Cruz Pajaro	66 541
Domacio	Contra Costa Twp 3	57 600
Fernando	Santa Clara Santa Clara	65 495
Ffransita	Tuolumne Twp 4	71 137
Filieltas*	Santa Clara Gilroy	65 233
Francia*	Alameda Brooklyn	55 125
Francis	Sacramento Ward 1	63 145
Francis	Santa Cruz Santa Cruz	66 632
Francis A*	Alameda Brooklyn	55 125
Francisca	Plumas Quincy	62 995
Francisco	Contra Costa Twp 3	57 609
Francisco	Santa Cruz Pajaro	66 552
Franciser	Santa Cruz Pajaro	66 552
Gaudeloupe	Los Angeles Los Angeles	59 509
Gaudilaupo	Los Angeles Los Angeles	59 509
Guadalupu	Contra Costa Twp 3	57 610
Ignacio	Contra Costa Twp 3	57 589
Ignacio	Mariposa Twp 3	60 611
Ignacio	San Luis Obispo San Luis Obispo	65 30
Inez	Los Angeles Santa Ana	59 459
J	Calaveras Twp 9	57 387
James	Tuolumne Twp 1	71 460
Jana*	Mariposa Twp 3	60 543
Jann*	Mariposa Twp 3	60 545
Jann*	Mariposa Twp 3	60 547
Jaun*	Mariposa Twp 3	60 545
Jaun*	Mariposa Twp 3	60 547
Jesus	El Dorado Placerville	58 821
Jesus	Mariposa Twp 3	60 611
Jesus	Monterey San Juan	60 997
Jnon*	Mariposa Twp 3	60 611
Joaquina	Los Angeles Los Angeles	59 394
Joaquinca	Los Angeles Los Angeles	59 394
Jose	Contra Costa Twp 3	57 614
Jose	Los Angeles Tejon	59 522
Jose	Monterey Pajaro	601012
Jose	Santa Cruz Pajaro	66 576
Jose	Santa Cruz Santa Cruz	66 628
Jose B	Monterey Monterey	60 965
Jose M	Monterey Pajaro	601014
Jose M	Monterey Alisal	601026
Jose M	Santa Cruz Watsonville	66 536
Jose M	Santa Cruz Santa Cruz	66 617
Joseph*	El Dorado Georgetown	58 704
Juan	Los Angeles Los Nieto	59 429
Juan	Mariposa Twp 3	60 611
Juan	San Bernardino Santa Inez	64 141
Juan	Santa Cruz Santa Cruz	66 615
Juan H	Yuba Marysville	72 936
Juana	Monterey San Juan	601010
Juliano	Santa Cruz Watsonville	66 536
Leonicio	Los Angeles San Juan	59 477
Loratos	Yuba Marysville	72 936
Lorenzo	Los Angeles Santa Ana	59 449
Lorenzo	Los Angeles Santa Ana	59 455
Lorenzo	Monterey Pajaro	601011
Macedonia	Mariposa Twp 1	60 652
Magil	Los Angeles Los Angeles	59 497
Magila	Los Angeles Los Angeles	59 495
Malicia	Monterey San Juan	60 994
Manuel	Los Angeles Santa Ana	59 458

Name	County Locale	M653 RollPage
SOTO		
Manuel	Los Angeles Los Angeles	59 504
Manuel	Tuolumne Twp 2	71 306
Maria	Alameda Brooklyn	55 199
Mariano	Los Angeles Los Nieto	59 425
Martiniam	Los Angeles Los Angeles	59 400
Martiniano	Los Angeles Los Angeles	59 400
Max	Tuolumne Twp 1	71 234
Meguil*	Calaveras Twp 9	57 364
Miguel	Calaveras Twp 9	57 364
Miguel	Los Angeles Los Angeles	59 378
Miguel	Los Angeles Tejon	59 539
Miguel	Monterey S Antoni	60 968
Miguel	Yuba Marysville	72 936
Miguil*	Calaveras Twp 9	57 364
Miquel	Los Angeles Los Angeles	59 378
Nicolas	Monterey Alisal	601040
Padra	Santa Cruz Soguel	66 584
Padre	Santa Cruz Soguel	66 584
Palinera	Tuolumne Twp 1	71 261
Palinira	Tuolumne Twp 1	71 261
Pasguel	Santa Cruz Pajaro	66 565
Pasquel	Santa Cruz Pajaro	66 565
Phillip	Calaveras Twp 7	57 24
Racys*	Santa Cruz Pajaro	66 555
Raeys	Santa Cruz Pajaro	66 555
Ramon	Marin Cortemad	60 780
Ramon	San Luis Obispo San Luis Obispo	65 43
Ramon	Santa Cruz Pescadero	66 645
Raphael	Santa Cruz Pajaro	66 560
Refugia	San Francisco San Francisco 10	183 67
Rosalio	San Luis Obispo San Luis Obispo	65 13
Sancha	Tuolumne Twp 2	71 319
Sanche	Tuolumne Columbia	71 319
Sgnalio*	Mariposa Twp 3	60 611
Silvario	Contra Costa Twp 3	57 609
Transita	Tuolumne Big Oak	71 137
Z Sidera*	Santa Clara Fremont	65 437
SOTOMIRA		
A	Tuolumne Twp 2	71 283
SOTOMISA		
A	Tuolumne Twp 2	71 283
SOTOS		
John	Calaveras Twp 9	57 385
SOTOW		
---	Trinity Weaverville	701076
SOTRY		
Jacob*	Yuba Marysville	72 935
SOTS		
Isacc H	Yuba Marysville	72 936
Mark	Tuolumne Sonora	71 234
Miguel	Yuba Marysville	72 937
SOTT		
Eboleto*	Sierra La Porte	66 784
Eloleto*	Sierra La Porte	66 784
SOTTERLAND		
George W*	Mariposa Coulterville	60 674
SOTTERS		
Anthany	Sonoma Petaluma	69 551
SOTTIE		
Charles	Sierra Eureka	661043
SOTTO		
Francisco	Calaveras Twp 5	57 177
Francisco	Calaveras Twp 4	57 328
Francisco*	Calaveras Twp 6	57 177
SOTTS		
Andrew	San Francisco San Francisco 3	67 85
SOTZPINCH		
W	Sutter Yuba	70 763
SOU E SEE		
---	Mariposa Twp 3	60 613
SOU KAU		
---	Mariposa Twp 3	60 608
SOU KE		
---	Mariposa Twp 3	60 607
---	Mariposa Twp 3	60 609
SOU KEE		
---	Mariposa Twp 3	60 613
SOU LEE		
---	Mariposa Twp 3	60 612
SOU LOO		
---	Mariposa Twp 3	60 612
SOU SEE		
---	Mariposa Twp 3	60 613
SOU		
---	Calaveras Twp 5	57 148
---	Calaveras Twp 6	57 165
---	Calaveras Twp 5	57 231
---	Calaveras Twp 5	57 257
---	Calaveras Twp 10	57 272
---	Calaveras Twp 10	57 286
---	Calaveras Twp 7	57 36
---	El Dorado Salmon Falls	581061
---	Mariposa Twp 3	60 569
---	Mariposa Twp 3	60 576

California 1860 Census Index

Name	County Locale	M653 Roll Page
SOU		
---	Mariposa Twp 3	60 581
---	Mariposa Twp 3	60 613
---	Mariposa Twp 1	60 668
---	San Francisco San Francisco 4	681180
---	San Francisco San Francisco 4	681184
---	San Francisco San Francisco 4	681185
---	San Francisco San Francisco 4	681188
---	San Francisco San Francisco 4	681190
---	San Francisco San Francisco 4	681194
---	San Francisco San Francisco 4	681195
---	San Francisco San Francisco 4	681196
---	San Francisco San Francisco 4	681198
---	San Francisco San Francisco 4	681200
---	San Francisco San Francisco 4	681211
---	Tuolumne Don Pedro	71 535
---	Tuolumne Don Pedro	71 536
---*	Mariposa Twp 3	60 576
--- E*	Mariposa Twp 3	60 580
---*	Mariposa Twp 3	60 581
---*	Mariposa Twp 3	60 590
---*	Nevada Nevada	61 305
Ah	Calaveras Twp 7	57 15
Ah	Calaveras Twp 7	57 32
Ah	Tuolumne Twp 4	71 150
Cou*	Mariposa Twp 3	60 581
Ka	Mariposa Twp 3	60 620
Ke	Mariposa Twp 3	60 620
Kee	Mariposa Twp 3	60 576
Kee	Mariposa Twp 3	60 613
Kee	Mariposa Twp 3	60 619
Kee	Mariposa Twp 3	60 620
Kin	Butte Ophir	56 803
Kow*	Mariposa Twp 3	60 580
Lan	Mariposa Twp 3	60 578
Lou	Mariposa Twp 3	60 581
Mu	San Francisco San Francisco 4	681201
Se	Siskiyou Yreka	69 194
Sing	Mariposa Twp 3	60 588
Yonng	Mariposa Twp 3	60 578
You*	Sacramento Granite	63 259
SOUA		
---	El Dorado Mud Springs	58 998
---*	Tuolumne Twp 4	71 161
SOUARD		
Alfred	Yuba Fosters	72 828
SOUBILTZ		
August	San Francisco San Francisco 8	681275
SOUCAGE		
G*	San Francisco San Francisco 1	68 841
SOUCE		
Peter*	Butte Hamilton	56 525
SOUCHAL		
A M*	Butte Oregon	56 633
SOUCI		
Paul	Butte Chico	56 555
Peter*	Butte Hamilton	56 525
SOUD		
---*	Tuolumne Twp 4	71 161
F	Nevada Eureka	61 382
SOUDECHER		
L*	San Francisco San Francisco 10	331 67
SOUDERS		
J*	Shasta Horsetown	66 696
SOUDHEIMER		
Israel	Sonoma Salt Point	69 693
SOUDRY		
J G	Tuolumne Twp 2	71 320
SOUE		
---	El Dorado Mud Springs	58 998
---	Sierra Downieville	661009
SOUER		
---	El Dorado Mud Springs	58 955
SOUG		
---	Mariposa Twp 1	60 662
---	Nevada Nevada	61 300
Li	San Francisco San Francisco 4	681201
SOUGE		
L M*	Nevada Nevada	61 327
SOUGER		
Jacob	Calaveras Twp 7	57 5
SOUGHLAN		
Michael	Calaveras Twp 5	57 195
SOUGHRY		
Jesse*	Siskiyou Scott Va	69 55
SOUGHY		
W J*	Butte Kimshaw	56 596
SOUGLA		
---	Trinity Lewiston	70 961
SOUGN		
Bernice S	Calaveras Twp 6	57 129
SOUH		
James*	El Dorado Georgetown	58 696
SOUIDICK		
Peter*	Calaveras Twp 5	57 230

Name	County Locale	M653 Roll Page
SOUIDIDE		
Peter	Calaveras Twp 5	57 230
SOUIDIDO		
Peter*	Calaveras Twp 5	57 230
SOUIJE		
Gherring*	Calaveras Twp 7	57 8
SOUIR		
Nole	Contra Costa Twp 1	57 528
SOUIS		
Manuel*	Placer Yankee J	62 758
Saul	Nevada Nevada	61 242
SOUL		
A	El Dorado Big Bar	58 744
Ah	Calaveras Twp 7	57 32
Albert	El Dorado White Oaks	581005
Ap	Tuolumne Twp 4	71 150
B*	El Dorado Casumnes	581177
Charles	El Dorado White Oaks	581005
E R	El Dorado Placerville	58 866
M E*	Sacramento Lee	63 219
Obisco*	Sacramento Lee	63 219
SOULE		
A P*	Sacramento Ward 1	63 151
Artema*	Yuba Marysville	72 858
Artemas G	Yuba Marysville	72 853
Ben C	Sonoma Mendocino	69 464
Bertram	Tuolumne Jamestown	71 469
Charles	Sacramento Ward 1	63 97
Chas	Butte Oregon	56 620
Cyrus S	Sonoma Mendocino	69 448
Elizabeth	San Francisco San Francisco 4	681125
Eugene	Sacramento Ward 3	63 457
Francis*	Nevada Bridgeport	61 457
Frank	San Francisco San Francisco 12	368 67
H	Mariposa Twp 3	60 621
Hanniball S	Humbolt Pacific	59 135
Hiram	Butte Oregon	56 620
Hiram	Butte Oregon	56 638
James*	El Dorado Georgetown	58 696
James*	Shasta Horsetown	66 697
John	San Francisco San Francisco 1	68 855
John	Tuolumne Twp 3	71 466
Joseph	Tulara Visalia	71 30
Julian	Calaveras Twp 9	57 382
Martin	Nevada Bridgeport	61 452
Selden	Tuolumne Twp 2	71 344
Wm	Sonoma Bodega	69 525
Wm	Yuba New York	72 735
SOULES		
G W*	Sacramento American	63 164
George	Contra Costa Twp 2	57 551
J E	Sacramento Ward 4	63 522
Stephen	Sonoma Mendocino	69 451
SOULI		
Martin*	Nevada Bridgeport	61 452
SOULIS		
I	El Dorado Georgetown	58 759
SOULL		
Francis	Nevada Bridgeport	61 457
SOULS		
Henry	Sacramento Ward 3	63 467
SOULSBY		
Geroge	Tuolumne Twp 1	71 264
Matthew	Tuolumne Twp 1	71 265
SOULSLY		
Edw	Amador Twp 6	55 447
SOULTER		
Wm	Alameda Oakland	55 65
SOULTRY		
James*	Amador Twp 4	55 244
SOULTT		
J*	Nevada Grass Valley	61 157
SOUM		
---	Mariposa Twp 3	60 580
SOUMEILLAN		
John*	Los Angeles Los Angeles	59 366
SOUMERLLAN		
John*	Los Angeles Los Angeles	59 366
SOUMMALLAN		
John*	Los Angeles Los Angeles	59 366
SOUN		
---	Fresno Twp 2	59 20
J	San Francisco San Francisco 9	681058
Qring*	Mariposa Twp 3	60 580
SOUNG		
---	Tuolumne Big Oak	71 150
SOUNLIN		
George H*	Contra Costa Twp 2	57 561
SOUNTAG		
A M	Placer Dutch Fl	62 723
SOUOWAR		
H	San Francisco San Francisco 4	681166
SOUP		
---	Calaveras Twp 5	57 215
---	Tuolumne Chinese	71 525

Name	County Locale	M653 Roll Page
SOUP		
Dick Bean*	Sonoma Sonoma	69 649
SOUPER		
---*	Del Norte Klamath	58 657
SOUR		
---	Sierra Twp 5	66 932
SOURDAY		
J G*	Tuolumne Twp 2	71 320
SOURDRY		
J G	Tuolumne Columbia	71 320
SOURIPIAN		
Cristina	Santa Clara San Jose	65 280
SOURN		
---*	Mariposa Twp 3	60 580
SOURREN		
L*	Tuolumne Columbia	71 304
SOURRES		
L	Tuolumne Twp 2	71 357
SOURS		
Jno	Butte Oregon	56 635
John	San Francisco San Francisco 1	68 852
SOUSA		
J W*	Alameda Brooklyn	55 149
SOUSE		
---	Mariposa Twp 3	60 612
SOUSEMBER		
Charles	San Francisco San Francisco 8	681322
SOUSO		
---*	Nevada Nevada	61 304
SOUSOMBER		
Charles	San Francisco San Francisco 8	681322
SOUSS		
Manuel*	Placer Yankee J	62 758
SOUTE		
O P	El Dorado Georgetown	58 684
SOUTER		
John	Shasta French G	66 717
SOUTH		
Faster*	Sacramento Granite	63 255
Forster*	Sacramento Granite	63 255
Foster	Sacramento Granite	63 255
Jackson	Yolo New York	72 720
Jackson	Yuba New York	72 720
O P	El Dorado Georgetown	58 684
Samul	Sonoma Russian	69 432
William	San Joaquin Stockton	641014
SOUTHALL		
J	Nevada Nevada	61 315
Saml	Tuolumne Twp 2	71 412
SOUTHARD		
C C	San Francisco San Francisco 5	67 487
Edwin P	Humbolt Union	59 183
J B	Sonoma Petaluma	69 601
Jno W	Klamath Salmon	59 213
S	El Dorado Diamond	58 800
William	Contra Costa Twp 2	57 553
Wm H	Alameda Brooklyn	55 105
SOUTHART		
W	Calaveras Twp 9	57 391
SOUTHEN		
H B*	Sacramento Ward 1	63 27
J T	Nevada Nevada	61 261
SOUTHENS		
M*	Calaveras Twp 9	57 395
SOUTHER		
Asa F	Tuolumne Twp 3	71 448
C N*	Napa Napa	61 95
C W	Napa Napa	61 95
E G	Sierra St Louis	66 813
Elizabeth	Napa Napa	61 96
Fred	San Francisco San Francisco 3	67 69
J	San Francisco San Francisco 5	67 489
J W	San Francisco San Francisco 5	67 525
SOUTHERBY		
Thos	Nevada Rough &	61 398
SOUTHERLAND		
A	Nevada Grass Valley	61 183
A	Shasta Horsetown	66 696
A G	San Francisco San Francisco 9	681073
Edward	San Francisco San Francisco 4	681114
Geo	Siskiyou Klamath	69 90
H L	Nevada Washington	61 335
Hector	Solano Vacaville	69 343
J	El Dorado Diamond	58 809
J	Nevada Nevada	61 321
Jno	Fresno Twp 3	59 15
John	Sonoma Bodega	69 536
L*	Nevada Grass Valley	61 183
Saml	Santa Clara Fremont	65 429
W	Yolo Washington	72 601
William	San Joaquin Elliott	64 943
SOUTHERLANDS		
Jas	Butte Mountain	56 739
SOUTHERLY		
Thos	Nevada Rough &	61 398
SOUTHERN		
Robt	Trinity Rattle Snake	701029

Name	County Locale	M653 Roll	Page
SOUTHERN			
S S	Shasta Shasta	66	761
SOUTHERS			
H B	Sacramento Ward 1	63	27
M*	Calaveras Twp 9	57	395
SOUTHING			
Saml	Tuolumne Twp 2	71	412
SOUTHLAND			
W	Nevada Nevada	61	330
SOUTHMEAD			
John L	Humbolt Mattole	59	128
SOUTHMOND			
J A	Sacramento Ward 4	63	518
SOUTHNORTH			
P T	Santa Clara Santa Clara	65	513
SOUTHOVICK			
J B*	Nevada Eureka	61	344
SOUTHREN			
B S	Nevada Rough &	61	398
SOUTHRICH			
Benj	Sacramento Sutter	63	306
SOUTHTIN			
John W*	Placer Rattle Snake	62	630
SOUTHTRIN			
John W*	Placer Rattle Snake	62	630
SOUTHULAND			
Jas	Butte Mountain	56	739
SOUTHVOICK			
J B*	Nevada Eureka	61	344
SOUTHWALL			
John	San Francisco San Francisco 7	681	384
SOUTHWELL			
A C	San Francisco San Francisco 7	681	363
George H	San Francisco San Francisco 3	67	36
Jno	San Francisco San Francisco 2	67	699
John J	Sacramento Granite	63	229
O P	Napa Napa	61	63
SOUTHWICH			
Benj	Sacramento Sutter	63	306
SOUTHWICK			
E M	Nevada Nevada	61	269
Ellen	Napa Napa	61	62
H	El Dorado Newtown	58	781
H	El Dorado Diamond	58	793
J A	Sacramento Ward 3	63	486
J B	Nevada Eureka	61	344
L H	Nevada Bridgeport	61	466
P H*	Nevada Bridgeport	61	466
S H*	Nevada Bridgeport	61	466
S M	Nevada Grass Valley	61	164
Samuel	Yuba Marysville	72	904
W	Calaveras Twp 9	57	393
Willet	San Francisco San Francisco 10	337 67	
Wm	Trinity Weaverville	701	070
SOUTHWILL			
O P*	Napa Napa	61	63
SOUTHWITH			
Henry	San Joaquin Stockton	641	058
SOUTHWOOD			
G B	Mendocino Ukiah	60	795
S T	Nevada Rough &	61	438
SOUTHWORTH			
---	Del Norte Crescent	58	628
A B	San Francisco San Francisco 2	67	805
A P	Butte Ophir	56	759
Chas	Sacramento Ward 4	63	511
E C	San Francisco San Francisco 10	235 67	
James	Placer Iona Hills	62	881
James	Plumas Quincy	62	987
John	Santa Clara San Jose	65	279
L S	Sacramento Ward 1	63	107
S S	Sacramento Ward 1	63	107
Samuel	Yuba Marysville	72	904
W S	Shasta Shasta	66	731
SOUTHWORTHS			
A P	Butte Ophir	56	759
SOUTHY			
Wm	Nevada Nevada	61	257
SOUTSINHIGER			
J	Amador Twp 4	55	257
SOUTTE			
J*	Nevada Grass Valley	61	157
SOUX			
Cath*	San Francisco San Francisco 10	278 67	
SOUY			
Ping	San Francisco San Francisco 5	67	510
SOUYER			
Jacob	Calaveras Twp 7	57	5
SOUZO			
Antonio	Sacramento Ward 3	63	435
SOVARONIS			
Andrew	Calaveras Twp 5	57	220
SOVE			
Allen	Calaveras Twp 5	57	174

Name	County Locale	M653 Roll	Page
SOVE			
H H	Napa Clear Lake	61	128
SOVELL			
Hiram	Tuolumne Twp 2	71	288
James Q	Yuba Suida	72	982
SOVENS			
George	Mariposa Twp 1	60	631
SOVENT			
Chas	Mariposa Twp 1	60	644
SOVEPY			
Henry	Alameda Brooklyn	55	94
SOVERIT			
Chas*	Mariposa Twp 1	60	644
SOVERONIO			
Antonio*	Mariposa Coulterville	60	691
SOVERY			
Antonio	Mariposa Coulterville	60	691
Benj L	San Francisco San Francisco 10	320 67	
SOVETT			
P	Sutter Butte	70	792
SOVEY			
Samuel	Nevada Eureka	61	347
SOVH			
---	Calaveras Twp 4	57	300
SOVIDICK			
Peter*	Calaveras Twp 5	57	230
SOVIET			
Peter*	Mariposa Coulterville	60	679
Petes*	Mariposa Coulterville	60	679
SOVIRIT			
Chas	Mariposa Twp 1	60	644
SOVISTEANO			
---	San Diego Agua Caliente	64	862
SOVISTEONIO			
---	San Diego Temecula	64	788
SOVIT			
John P	Trinity Mouth Ca	701	012
SOVREL			
Patrick	Calaveras Twp 5	57	240
SOW			
---	Amador Twp 4	55	252
---	Amador Twp 2	55	280
---	Amador Twp 7	55	412
---	Amador Twp 1	55	479
---	Calaveras Twp 6	57	122
---	Calaveras Twp 6	57	165
---	Calaveras Twp 6	57	176
---	Calaveras Twp 5	57	202
---	Calaveras Twp 5	57	214
---	Calaveras Twp 5	57	215
---	Calaveras Twp 5	57	231
---	Calaveras Twp 5	57	234
---	Calaveras Twp 5	57	236
---	Calaveras Twp 5	57	237
---	Calaveras Twp 5	57	239
---	Calaveras Twp 5	57	249
---	Calaveras Twp 5	57	251
---	Calaveras Twp 5	57	257
---	Calaveras Twp 10	57	259
---	Calaveras Twp 10	57	260
---	Calaveras Twp 10	57	261
---	Calaveras Twp 10	57	267
---	Calaveras Twp 10	57	272
---	Calaveras Twp 10	57	273
---	Calaveras Twp 10	57	275
---	Calaveras Twp 10	57	284
---	Calaveras Twp 10	57	285
---	Calaveras Twp 10	57	286
---	Calaveras Twp 10	57	287
---	Calaveras Twp 4	57	302
---	Calaveras Twp 4	57	305
---	Calaveras Twp 4	57	306
---	Calaveras Twp 4	57	326
---	Calaveras Twp 4	57	337
---	Calaveras Twp 9	57	349
---	Calaveras Twp 8	57	66
---	Calaveras Twp 8	57	79
---	El Dorado Salmon Hills	581	067
---	El Dorado Diamond	58	796
---	Klamath Klamath	59	229
---	Mariposa Twp 3	60	552
---	Mariposa Twp 3	60	564
---	Mariposa Twp 3	60	569
---	Mariposa Twp 3	60	581
---	Mariposa Twp 3	60	588
---	Mariposa Twp 1	60	640
---	Mariposa Coulterville	60	685
---	Mariposa Coulterville	60	700
---	Nevada Nevada	61	304
---	Nevada Nevada	61	305
---	Nevada Rough &	61	398
---	Nevada Rough &	61	399
---	Nevada Rough &	61	409
---	Placer Auburn	62	573
---	Placer Auburn	62	582

Name	County Locale	M653 Roll	Page
SOW			
---	Placer Folsom	62	648
---	Placer Horseshoe	62	650
---	Placer Illinois	62	751
---	Sacramento Centre	63	182
---	Sacramento Mississipi	63	186
---	Sacramento Granite	63	232
---	Sacramento Granite	63	259
---	Sacramento Cosumnes	63	391
---	Sacramento Ward 1	63	55
---	Sacramento Ward 1	63	60
---	Sacramento Ward 1	63	66
---	San Francisco San Francisco 4	681	177
---	San Francisco San Francisco 4	681	194
---	San Francisco San Francisco 4	681	195
---	San Francisco San Francisco 4	681	196
---	San Francisco San Francisco 4	681	198
---	San Francisco San Francisco 4	681	200
---	Sierra Downieville	661	000
---	Sierra Downieville	661	004
---	Sierra Downieville	661	007
---	Sierra Downieville	661	008
---	Sierra Downieville	661	009
---	Sierra Downieville	661	020
---	Sierra Downieville	661	027
---	Sierra Downieville	661	030
---	Sierra Downieville	661	031
---	Sierra Twp 5	66	931
---	Sierra Twp 5	66	932
---	Sierra Twp 5	66	948
---	Sierra Cox'S Bar	66	949
---	Sierra Cox'S Bar	66	951
---	Sierra Downieville	66	980
---	Sierra Downieville	66	985
---	Sierra Downieville	66	990
---	Trinity Big Flat	701	041
---	Trinity Trinindad Rvr	701	046
---	Trinity Trinindad Rvr	701	049
---	Trinity Weaverville	701	053
---	Trinity Weaverville	701	076
---	Trinity Weaverville	701	079
---	Tuolumne Chinese	71	510
---	Tuolumne Twp 5	71	512
---	Tuolumne Jacksonville	71	515
---	Tuolumne Twp 5	71	517
---	Tuolumne Twp 5	71	524
---	Tuolumne Twp 5	71	525
---	Tuolumne Twp 6	71	531
---	Tuolumne Green Springs	71	532
---	Tuolumne Twp 6	71	536
---	Tuolumne Don Pedro	71	537
---	Yuba Marysville	72	868
---*	Amador Twp 4	55	233
---*	Calaveras Twp 5	57	237
---*	Calaveras Twp 4	57	337
---*	Calaveras Twp 4	57	343
---*	El Dorado Salmon Falls	581	067
---*	Nevada Nevada	61	305
---*	Nevada Rough &	61	396
---*	Sacramento Ward 1	63	66
---*	Sierra Twp 5	66	931
---*	Sierra Downieville	66	980
---*	Tuolumne Big Oak	71	182
---*	Tuolumne Green Springs	71	531
Ah	Tuolumne Twp 4	71	148
Ah	Tuolumne Twp 4	71	182
As	Tuolumne Twp 4	71	168
Chin	Calaveras Twp 6	57	168
Choo	Calaveras Twp 10	57	297
Chow	Calaveras Twp 5	57	257
Ciring	Butte Cascade	56	691
Cow*	San Francisco San Francisco 5	67	523
D	Butte Oregon	56	631
Foo	Amador Twp 4	55	256
He	Sacramento Granite	63	268
John	Yolo Cache	72	642
Kee	Mariposa Twp 3	60	576
Kin	Calaveras Twp 5	57	257
Kow	Mariposa Twp 3	60	580
Low	Mariposa Twp 3	60	553
Mee	San Francisco San Francisco 4	681	201
Que	Sierra Twp 7	66	898
Qui	Calaveras Twp 4	57	337
Sing	Mariposa Twp 3	60	588
Sow	Sierra Downieville	66	992
SOWARD			
H	Sonoma Santa Rosa	69	426
SOWDER			
John	San Francisco San Francisco 3	67	67
SOWDERS			
J*	Shasta Horsetown	66	696
SOWE			
---	Placer Auburn	62	581
---	Shasta Horsetown	66	702
James*	Amador Twp 4	55	244
Stephen*	Calaveras Twp 6	57	164

Name	County Locale	M653 Roll Page
SOWELL		
Andrew J*	Sierra St Louis	66 807
G H	Nevada Eureka	61 373
Wm H	Nevada Nevada	61 250
SOWEN		
Patrick*	Calaveras Twp 5	57 196
SOWER		
Daniel	Tuolumne Twp 6	71 539
M	El Dorado Placerville	58 850
SOWERS		
Emma*	Sacramento Ward 3	63 452
J	Nevada Grass Valley	61 161
Orlando	Butte Kimshaw	56 590
R*	Nevada Grass Valley	61 149
SOWERY		
K	Nevada Eureka	61 380
SOWES		
Daniel*	Tuolumne Twp 6	71 539
SOWLE		
Ann L	Alameda Brooklyn	55 184
James*	Shasta Horsetown	66 697
SOWN		
---	Nevada Grass Valley	61 228
SOWNSLEY		
Alaxander*	Napa Yount	61 43
SOWORER		
Martin*	Mariposa Twp 1	60 645
Martino*	Mariposa Twp 1	60 645
Martius*	Mariposa Twp 1	60 645
SOWPER		
---*	Del Norte Klamath	58 657
SOWRREN		
L*	Tuolumne Columbia	71 304
SOWY		
---	Mariposa Twp 1	60 648
---	Sacramento Mississipi	63 188
---	Shasta Horsetown	66 710
SOX		
---	Sierra Cox'S Bar	66 949
SOY SE		
---	Mariposa Twp 3	60 607
SOY		
---	Amador Twp 4	55 251
---	Amador Twp 6	55 431
---	Amador Twp 1	55 510
---	Calaveras Twp 5	57 173
---	Calaveras Twp 5	57 193
---	Calaveras Twp 5	57 242
---	Calaveras Twp 5	57 255
---	Calaveras Twp 10	57 268
---	Calaveras Twp 10	57 269
---	Calaveras Twp 10	57 270
---	Calaveras Twp 10	57 284
---	Calaveras Twp 10	57 296
---	Calaveras Twp 4	57 299
---	Calaveras Twp 4	57 300
---	Calaveras Twp 4	57 300
---	Calaveras Twp 4	57 315
---	Calaveras Twp 4	57 341
---	El Dorado Georgetown	58 705
---	El Dorado Placerville	58 930
---	Fresno Twp 3	59 32
---	Mariposa Twp 3	60 576
---	Mariposa Twp 1	60 648
---	Mariposa Twp 1	60 651
---	Mariposa Coulterville	60 691
---	Nevada Nevada	61 299
---	Nevada Nevada	61 302
---	Nevada Nevada	61 305
---	Nevada Nevada	61 307
---	Nevada Washington	61 342
---	Nevada Bridgeport	61 439
---	Placer Iona Hills	62 896
---	Plumas Meadow Valley	62 909
---	Plumas Meadow Valley	62 913
---	Plumas Quincy	62 947
---	Plumas Quincy	62 949
---	Sacramento Ward 3	63 489
---	Sacramento Ward 3	63 492
---	Sacramento Ward 1	63 53
---	Sacramento Ward 1	63 59
---	San Francisco San Francisco 4	681 195
---	San Francisco San Francisco 4	681 209
---	San Francisco San Francisco 11	146 67
---	Trinity Cox'S Bar	701 037
---	Trinity Big Flat	701 042
---	Tuolumne Columbia	71 346
---	Tuolumne Twp 5	71 514
---	Tuolumne Twp 5	71 516
---	Tuolumne Green Springs	71 531
---	Tuolumne Twp 6	71 532
---	Tuolumne Twp 6	71 533
---	Yolo Slate Ra	72 710
---	Yolo Slate Ra	72 711
---	Yolo Slate Ra	72 712

Name	County Locale	M653 Roll Page
SOY		
---	Yolo Slate Ra	72 715
---	Yuba Slate Ro	72 710
---	Yuba Slate Ro	72 711
---	Yuba Slate Ro	72 712
---	Yuba Slate Ro	72 713
---*	Calaveras Twp 4	57 341
---*	El Dorado Georgetown	58 705
---*	Fresno Twp 1	59 30
---*	Nevada Nevada	61 302
---*	Nevada Nevada	61 305
---*	Nevada Nevada	61 306
---*	San Francisco San Francisco 9	681 087
---*	San Francisco San Francisco 5	67 510
Ah	Tuolumne Twp 2	71 346
Chow	San Francisco San Francisco 4	681 174
Hay	Mariposa Twp 3	60 562
Hin	El Dorado Greenwood	58 719
John	Yolo Slate Ra	72 711
John	Yolo Slate Ra	72 713
John*	Yuba Slate Ro	72 710
John*	Yuba Slate Ro	72 713
Joj Muir	El Dorado Big Bar	58 733
Ke	Mariposa Twp 3	60 576
Kee	Mariposa Twp 3	60 576
Kee	Mariposa Twp 3	60 582
La	Mariposa Twp 3	60 582
Lan	Mariposa Twp 3	60 580
Lau	Mariposa Twp 3	60 580
Lee	Mariposa Twp 3	60 575
Loo	Mariposa Twp 3	60 582
M	Nevada Nevada	61 313
Re	Mariposa Twp 3	60 576
Sing	Butte Bidwell	56 709
To	San Francisco San Francisco 5	671 205
Wang*	Yuba Bear Rvr	721 000
You	Yuba Fosters	72 841
SOYAT		
Ah*	Siskiyou Klamath	69 79
SOYD		
---	Trinity Big Flat	701 042
SOYE		
---	Sacramento Ward 1	63 50
---	Sacramento Ward 1	63 60
John	Tuolumne Big Oak	71 182
SOYER		
Theodore	Calaveras Twp 5	57 228
SOYI		
John	Tuolumne Twp 4	71 182
SOYLAN		
Tabina	San Francisco San Francisco 6	67 408
SOYOMAN		
John	Calaveras Twp 5	57 203
SOYOY		
---	Sierra Downieville	661 015
SOYRS		
Theodore	Calaveras Twp 5	57 228
SOYUS		
---	Butte Chico	56 550
SOZA		
Pedro*	Yuba Marysville	72 947
SOZO		
Cynlo	San Bernardino Santa Barbara	64 187
SP		
Yo	Placer Illinois	62 745
SPACHER		
J	Sacramento Ward 1	63 6
Peter	San Francisco San Francisco 4	681 217
SPACKELO		
---	Tulara Twp 2	71 34
SPACKS		
Henry*	Butte Cascade	56 704
SPAD		
Andrew*	Placer Rattle Snake	62 604
SPADONIA		
Moris	Santa Cruz Watsonville	66 536
SPAEENA		
Mahiry	Mariposa Twp 3	60 559
SPAFFORD		
J C	El Dorado Coloma	581 116
Thos	Placer Goods	62 697
SPAGNOLI		
D	Amador Twp 1	55 486
SPAGUE		
Eugene	Sonoma Vallejo	69 622
SPAHN		
Joseph	Sierra Whiskey	66 843
M	Siskiyou Scott Va	69 52
Wm	Sacramento Ward 3	63 433
SPAIF		
---	Sierra Downieville	66 984
SPAIKS		
Edward*	Butte Ophir	56 824
SPAILING		
Jos*	Butte Cascade	56 693
W*	Butte Cascade	56 701

Name	County Locale	M653 Roll Page
SPAIN		
Alonzo A	Placer Virginia	62 677
Henry C	Contra Costa Twp 3	57 597
Thomas D*	Tulara Keeneysburg	71 49
Thomas*	Mendocino Anderson	60 867
Thos	Butte Cascade	56 697
SPAINER		
Joseph	Yuba Marysville	72 883
SPALDEN		
William	Siskiyou Scott Va	69 31
SPALDING		
A C*	San Francisco San Francisco 7	681 431
Alexander	Siskiyou Yreka	69 125
Alexander	Siskiyou Yreka	69 143
Caroline	San Francisco San Francisco 12	369 67
Charles	Colusa Colusi	57 421
David	Sacramento Ward 4	63 511
E M	Butte Kimshaw	56 598
Frances M	Sierra Gibsonville	66 853
Francis M	Sierra Gibsonville	66 853
Frank	Colusa Colusi	57 421
G W	El Dorado Casumnes	581 175
George	Placer Forest H	62 796
Harriet N	Sacramento Ward 3	63 476
Henry	Sierra Twp 7	66 893
John	Siskiyou Yreka	69 144
John	Siskiyou Yreka	69 144
John B	Siskiyou Yreka	69 152
Samuel	Sierra Gibsonville	66 857
Thomas	El Dorado Casumnes	581 166
U A*	San Francisco San Francisco 7	681 431
Wm	Butte Wyandotte	56 661
SPALDON		
William	Siskiyou Scott Va	69 31
SPALENI		
Patrick*	San Francisco San Francisco 4	681 214
SPALGERING		
R N	Sierra St Louis	66 818
SPALGING		
R N	Sierra St Louis	66 818
SPALINE		
Patrick	San Francisco San Francisco 4	681 214
SPALLING		
Alexander	Siskiyou Yreka	69 143
SPAM		
Thomas*	Mendocino Anderson	60 867
SPAMIN		
H	El Dorado Placerville	58 821
SPAMIR		
Joeph*	Yuba Marysville	72 883
SPAN		
James	Colusa Muion	57 461
M M	Amador Twp 6	55 425
SPANAGALL		
Geo	San Francisco San Francisco 3	67 76
SPANCAIY		
Kirk*	Shasta Cottonwood	66 723
SPANCARY		
Kirk*	Shasta Cottonwoood	66 723
SPANCE		
Henry	Sierra Morristown	661 051
SPANCILT		
Jacob*	El Dorado Placerville	58 906
SPANEAIY		
Kirk*	Shasta Cottonwoood	66 723
SPANEDING		
A*	Calaveras Twp 9	57 410
SPANG		
Jos S	San Joaquin Stockton	641 047
SPANGLE		
Frederick	Amador Twp 7	55 416
G*	Sacramento Cosumnes	63 401
Wm	Amador Twp 6	55 438
SPANGLER		
D	Placer Todds Va	62 785
Daniel	Sierra Twp 7	66 913
Daniel	Tulara Twp 1	71 74
Fred	Siskiyou Klamath	69 94
J H	Placer Michigan	62 852
J S	Trinity Trinity	70 971
John*	San Joaquin Stockton	641 050
Joseph	Tuolumne Don Pedro	71 539
SPANGLR		
Daniel*	Sierra Twp 7	66 913
SPANGLS		
Daniel*	Sierra Twp 7	66 913
SPANGURBERG		
E M	San Francisco San Francisco 6	67 436
SPANIARD		
---	Marin Novato	60 734
---	Marin Novato	60 738
---	Marin Bolinas	60 740
---	Marin San Rafael	60 768
SPANISH JOE		
---	Nevada Little Y	61 535

Name	County Locale	M653 Roll Page
SPANISH		
Joe*	Nevada Little Y	61 535
SPANK		
Maggie	Yolo Slate Ra	72 698
SPANKER		
Jas	San Joaquin Elkhorn	64 989
SPANLDING		
A*	Calaveras Twp 9	57 410
J R	El Dorado Georgetown	58 697
SPANLEY		
James	San Francisco San Francisco 4	681 125
SPANN		
John W	Placer Virginia	62 663
SPANT		
Martin*	El Dorado Georgetown	58 752
SPAR		
Elizabeth	San Francisco San Francisco 2	67 680
SPAREGA		
---	Mendocino Little L	60 839
SPAREGG		
---	Mendocino Little L	60 839
SPAREN		
---	San Francisco San Francisco 9	681 104
SPARGH		
Frederick	Amador Twp 7	55 416
SPARGO		
P	Nevada Grass Valley	61 210
SPARGUR		
Henry	Plumas Quincy	62 916
SPARHAWK		
J S	Placer Iona Hills	62 864
SPARK		
Edward J	Placer Goods	62 695
J F	San Francisco San Francisco 9	681 067
Quartus S	San Bernadino	64 623
	San Bernardino	
Robert	Tulara Twp 3	71 59
S P	Sierra Downieville	66 953
SPARKES		
Joseph	Marin Novato	60 737
M	El Dorado Diamond	58 799
SPARKIS		
John	El Dorado Placerville	58 931
SPARKS		
Alex	Placer Virginia	62 666
B	Santa Clara Redwood	65 455
E B	Sacramento Georgian	63 342
E J	Sutter Nicolaus	70 831
E M	Butte Eureka	56 653
Edward*	Butte Ophir	56 824
Flora	San Francisco San Francisco 8	681 249
G W	El Dorado Placerville	58 868
Genge W	San Salvador	64 651
	San Bernardino	
Gresmns*	Yuba New York	72 738
Grosmus	Yuba New York	72 738
Henry	Butte Cascade	56 704
Isaac	Colusa Monroeville	57 453
J J	San Bernardino Santa Barbara	64 155
James	Placer Iona Hills	62 870
Jas	Sacramento Granite	63 247
Jesse	San Joaquin Castoria	64 907
John	Placer Michigan	62 838
John	Sierra Twp 7	66 883
John M	Plumas Meadow Valley	62 908
Joseph	Marin Novato	60 737
Louisa	Tulara Visalia	71 80
M N	Sutter Bear Rvr	70 820
Mathew	Colusa Monroeville	57 441
Patrick	Contra Costa Twp 2	57 581
Quartus S	San Bernadino	64 623
	San Bernardino	
Richard	Placer Michigan	62 849
Sally	San Bernardino Santa Barbara	64 155
Samuel	El Dorado White Oaks	581 008
Samuel S	San Diego Colorado	64 809
Thomas	Calaveras Twp 4	57 320
Thomas	Plumas Meadow Valley	62 908
Thomas	Tulara Twp 1	71 111
Thos J	Santa Clara Fremont	65 424
W J	Butte Ophir	56 772
Wesley C	Calaveras Twp 4	57 300
Westly	Shasta Shasta	66 679
Wirley C	Calaveras Twp 4	57 299
Wm	Butte Ophir	56 798
Wm	Mariposa Twp 1	60 631
SPARLIN		
P	El Dorado Placerville	58 864
SPARLING		
Jos	Butte Cascade	56 693
W	Butte Cascade	56 701
SPARNIR		
Wensin G	El Dorado Greenwood	58 723
SPARO		
Peter*	Alameda Oakland	55 73
SPAROW		
Joseph	Contra Costa Twp 2	57 553

Name	County Locale	M653 Roll Page
SPARRIE		
Louis*	Mariposa Twp 3	60 615
SPARROK HAWK		
---	Fresno Twp 1	59 55
SPARROW		
---	Tulara Twp 2	71 31
Arny*	Placer Iona Hills	62 867
F	Amador Twp 3	55 386
J F	Tuolumne Twp 4	71 173
Jas	Sacramento Sutter	63 308
John	Amador Twp 1	55 509
John	San Francisco San Francisco 11	132 67
Jos	San Francisco San Francisco 9	681 042
M	San Mateo Twp 3	65 109
Mary	San Francisco San Francisco 11	152 67
Morris F	San Joaquin Tulare	64 871
Sanders J	Yuba Marysville	72 870
William E	Klamath Orleans	59 216
Wm	Sacramento Franklin	63 320
SPARROWS		
Isaac	San Francisco San Francisco 1	68 864
SPARRY		
Henry*	Mariposa Twp 3	60 615
SPART		
Geo	El Dorado Kelsey	581 154
SPASE HAWKE		
---	Tulara Twp 2	71 31
SPATEE		
N E	Sacramento Ward 1	63 28
SPATEO		
N E*	Sacramento Ward 1	63 28
SPATES		
Seth	Placer Grizzly	62 755
SPATRY		
Frederick*	Yuba Marysville	72 935
SPATSY		
Frederick	Yuba Marysville	72 935
SPATZ		
H	Shasta Shasta	66 664
SPAUGH		
A	Sacramento Ward 4	63 607
SPAUGLE		
G*	Sacramento Cosummes	63 401
SPAUGLEY		
Wm	Butte Wyandotte	56 670
SPAULDIN		
M C	Tehama Tehama	70 948
SPAULDING		
---	Siskiyou Cottonwoood	69 105
A	Calaveras Twp 9	57 410
A	Tuolumne Twp 2	71 310
A S	Napa Napa	61 95
A T	Napa Napa	61 95
A*	Calaveras Twp 9	57 410
Alexander	San Francisco San Francisco 7	681 345
Alonzo P	Yuba Marysville	72 874
Berford*	Placer Virginia	62 690
C	Stanislaus Emory	70 738
Dennis	Sierra Whiskey	66 846
E R	Sacramento Sutter	63 308
Elinore	Sacramento Ward 1	63 116
Elmor	Sacramento Ward 1	63 116
Franklin	Sonoma Petaluma	69 549
G N	Tuolumne Twp 2	71 331
G W	Marin Tomales	60 724
G W	Tuolumne Columbia	71 331
Geo	San Francisco San Francisco 1	68 905
George S	Sierra Gibsonville	66 853
H E	El Dorado Georgetown	58 697
Hattie	Sonoma Petaluma	69 574
J	Siskiyou Scott Va	69 55
J	Tuolumne Shawsfla	71 407
J D	Solano Vacaville	69 333
J R	El Dorado Georgetown	58 697
J T G	Sacramento American	63 160
James	San Joaquin Stockton	641 032
Jas	Napa Napa	61 75
John	Napa Napa	61 104
John	Siskiyou Scott Va	69 41
John A	San Francisco San Francisco 6	67 402
Kirk	Shasta Cottonwood	66 723
L K	Trinity Minersville	70 968
L W	Sacramento Ward 4	63 559
Lucy	Trinity Lewiston	70 953
Madison	Alameda Brooklyn	55 149
Madison	Tuolumne Shawsfla	71 405
N H	Tuolumne Columbia	71 361
N W	Sacramento Ward 1	63 32
Otis	Sonoma Petaluma	69 549
Philip	San Francisco San Francisco 3	67 59
T V	Butte Bidwell	56 729
T Y	Butte Bidwell	56 729
W	Marin S Antoni	60 706
W H	Sacramento Ward 1	63 41

Name	County Locale	M653 Roll Page
SPAULDING		
Wallace	Alameda Brooklyn	55 116
Zetos N	Plumas Quincy	62 983
SPAULDUN		
Joseph*	San Mateo Twp 3	65 105
SPAWLDING		
R	San Mateo Twp 3	65 105
SPAWLDWIN		
Joseph*	San Mateo Twp 3	65 81
Rodger*	San Mateo Twp 3	65 81
SPAYNE		
Smytick	Sacramento American	63 164
SPEAD		
J H**	Nevada Nevada	61 319
SPEADY		
Mary	Alameda Brooklyn	55 84
SPEAK		
Jacob	Napa Hot Springs	61 11
L P*	Napa Hot Springs	61 10
SPEAKE		
Richard	Placer Dutch Fl	62 715
SPEAKMAN		
John	Sierra St Louis	66 807
SPEAKS		
C	San Joaquin Stockton	641 095
SPEALDIN		
Martin	Sacramento Ward 3	63 423
SPEALER		
Thomas	Contra Costa Twp 3	57 590
SPEAM		
A	Calaveras Twp 9	57 413
SPEAR HAWK		
---*	Tulara Yule Rvr	71 31
SPEAR		
Andrew P	Yuba Marysville	72 863
Arthur	Amador Twp 1	55 489
Benjamin H	Yuba Marysville	72 861
Charles	San Francisco San Francisco 3	67 78
Christian	Calaveras Twp 9	57 384
David	Placer Michigan	62 826
E	San Francisco San Francisco 5	67 479
F A	Tuolumne Sonora	71 228
I L	Amador Twp 7	55 413
Isaac	Yolo Slate Ra	72 691
Isaac*	Yuba Slate Ro	72 691
J	Nevada Grass Valley	61 192
J	San Joaquin Stockton	641 094
J L	Amador Twp 7	55 413
Jacob	Tuolumne Twp 2	71 289
Jas	San Francisco San Francisco 9	681 081
Jason	Sonoma Russian	69 591
John	Plumas Quincy	62 995
John J Jr	El Dorado Georgetown	58 686
Jos	San Francisco San Francisco 9	681 081
Joseh	Sacramento Natonia	63 273
Joseph	Sacramento Natonia	63 273
Joseph	Tuolumne Columbia	71 316
Leander	Calaveras Twp 6	57 142
Leonder	Calaveras Twp 6	57 142
Madison	Sonoma Russian	69 443
Noah	Sierra St Louis	66 805
Rutherford	Sierra Twp 7	66 914
S G	San Francisco San Francisco 5	67 550
T G	San Francisco San Francisco 6	67 459
Thomas G	San Francisco San Francisco 3	67 17
Walter	Butte Bidwell	56 712
Watter*	Butte Bidwell	56 712
Wm	San Francisco San Francisco 1	68 879
Wm H	Tuolumne Sonora	71 481
Wm N	Alameda Brooklyn	55 123
SPEARIN		
R	Yuba Rose Par	72 795
SPEARKY		
Joseph	Sierra Whiskey	66 845
Joseph	Sierra Whiskey	66 845
SPEARS		
Arnold C	Humbolt Eureka	59 177
Egbert	Humbolt Eel Rvr	59 144
George	Humbolt Eureka	59 177
Hugh	San Francisco San Francisco 3	67 51
James	Los Angeles San Gabriel	59 422
Jas	Placer Auburn	62 597
Jas	Placer Rattle Snake	62 598
John	Calaveras Twp 10	57 281
S K	Merced Twp 2	60 915
Saml	San Francisco San Francisco 1	68 879
SPEASMAR		
A T	Calaveras Twp 9	57 415
SPECE		
Jas M	Butte Bidwell	56 732
T	Butte Bidwell	56 711
SPECHT		
Jacob	San Francisco San Francisco 2	67 681
SPECIS		
Thomas	Sierra St Louis	66 805

Name	County Locale	M653 Roll	Page
SPECK			
Andrew	Shasta Shasta	66	728
Hanah	Napa Napa	61	79
J	Sutter Vernon	70	843
Jacob	Napa Hot Springs	61	11
L P*	Napa Hot Springs	61	10
SPECKELS			
Hezekiah*	Calaveras Twp 4	57	311
SPECKINS			
Vick	Santa Clara Santa Clara	65	469
SPECKLES			
Wm A	San Francisco San Francisco 6 67		424
SPECKMAN			
Henry	San Joaquin Stockton	64	1017
SPEEC			
William	Sierra La Porte	66	779
SPEED			
C J	Butte Chico	56	536
George	Siskiyou Shasta Rvr	69	112
George*	Calaveras Twp 8	57	69
L	Butte Kimshaw	56	597
Louis	Butte Oregon	56	609
W	Solano Vacaville	69	331
SPEEDY			
David	Del Norte Crescent	58	642
SPEER			
Hugh	San Francisco San Francisco 10		354
		67	
John D	El Dorado Greenwood	58	723
Willis	Tehama Lassen	70	864
SPEERS			
W	Siskiyou Scott Ri	69	74
SPEICKERMAN			
Henry	Sierra Downieville	66	1028
SPEIGHT			
Christian San Francisco San Francisco 7 68			1325
SPEIGLES			
Jasper	Butte Chico	56	546
Martin	Butte Chico	56	547
SPEIGLEZ			
Jasper*	Butte Chico	56	546
Martin*	Butte Chico	56	547
SPEIL			
Peter	Sacramento Ward 1	63	63
SPEILMAN			
Louisa	San Francisco San Francisco 10		195
		67	
SPEINY			
Julius	San Joaquin Elkhorn	64	995
SPELL			
George	Sierra Whiskey	66	846
John	Marin Cortemad	60	752
Thomas	Sierra Whiskey	66	846
Walter	Sierra Whiskey	66	846
SPELLENBERG			
George	Sierra Twp 7	66	864
SPELLER			
E P*	Butte Kimshaw	56	601
F	Napa Yount	61	49
R D	Butte Hamilton	56	524
SPELLMAN			
H	San Francisco San Francisco 9 68		1086
Henry	Santa Clara Santa Clara	65	499
M M	El Dorado Kelsey	58	1149
N M	El Dorado Kelsey	58	1149
Thos	Calaveras Twp 6	57	118
William	Calaveras Twp 8	57	61
SPELLS			
Alex*	Nevada Nevada	61	325
SPELLUN			
John	Placer Virginia	62	667
SPELLY			
Michael	Tuolumne Twp 4	71	141
SPELMAN			
A P	Sutter Sutter	70	811
Catherine	Santa Clara San Jose	65	315
SPELTEST			
Jacob	Butte Bidwell	56	716
SPEM			
J M*	Yolo Cottonwoood	72	647
SPEMPH			
Jacob	San Francisco San Francisco 2 67		782
SPEMS			
Orlendo*	Yolo Washington	72	562
SPEN??			
J C	Yolo Cottonwoood	72	654
SPENA			
Robt*	Sonoma Sonoma	69	643
Wylie*	Sonoma Sonoma	69	642
SPENABLE			
A C	Sierra Twp 7	66	899
SPENCE			
A H	El Dorado Placerville	58	856
Christopher	San Francisco 4 68		1224
	San Francisco		

Name	County Locale	M653 Roll	Page
SPENCE			
Christopher	San Francisco 3 67		53
	San Francisco		
Christopher*	San Francisco 9 68		1099
	San Francisco		
Christopher*	San Francisco 4 68		1224
	San Francisco		
Christophir	San Francisco 3 67		53
	San Francisco		
David	Butte Cascade	56	694
David	Monterey Monterey	60	939
E F	Nevada Nevada	61	241
E T	Nevada Nevada	61	241
Henry	Monterey S Antoni	60	973
Hugh	Butte Kimshaw	56	571
J	Merced Twp 1	60	896
J	San Francisco San Francisco 5 67		539
J	Santa Clara San Jose	65	376
J F	Sonoma Armally	69	502
Jacob	Yolo Cache Crk	72	642
James	Mariposa Coulterville	60	703
Jas	Butte Hamilton	56	523
Jas M	Butte Bidwell	56	732
John	Solano Vallejo	69	273
John*	Mariposa Coulterville	60	703
Joseph	Mariposa Coulterville	60	696
Joseph	Trinity Indian C	70	989
Mary	Solano Vallejo	69	270
Mary	Yuba Marysville	72	923
Morgan	Sacramento Sutter	63	300
Patk	Klamath Liberty	59	239
Robt	Sonoma Sonoma	69	643
S C	El Dorado Placerville	58	849
Sambo	Butte Ophir	56	799
T	Butte Bidwell	56	711
W	Calaveras Twp 9	57	418
W H	Butte Wyandotte	56	659
William A	San Francisco San Francisco 4 68		1216
Wylie	Sonoma Sonoma	69	642
SPENCER			
A	Sacramento Franklin	63	310
A B	Yuba Fosters	72	825
A J	Shasta Horsetown	66	705
A O	San Francisco San Francisco 1 68		921
A S	Santa Clara San Jose	65	316
Albron	Santa Cruz Santa Cruz	66	623
Alex	Sacramento Ward 3	63	489
Alex	Siskiyou Scott Va	69	58
Alexander	Los Angeles Los Angeles	59	369
C	Nevada Washington	61	334
C	Shasta Horsetown	66	692
C P	Tuolumne Twp 2	71	410
Channcy	Mariposa Twp 1	60	644
Charles	Amador Twp 1	55	505
Charles	San Joaquin Oneal	64	929
Charles	Sierra Grizzly	66	1058
Charles R	Sierra Gibsonville	66	853
Chas	San Francisco San Francisco 10		334
		67	
Chauncy	Mariposa Twp 1	60	644
Christopher	San Francisco 9 68		1099
	San Francisco		
Christopher	Solano Benecia	69	304
Christopher*	San Francisco 4 68		1224
	San Francisco		
D	San Francisco San Francisco 9 68		1073
D A	Sonoma Armally	69	504
Daniel	Contra Costa Twp 2	57	580
David	Merced Monterey	60	939
David	San Francisco San Francisco 9 68		1035
Dwyt	Napa Napa	61	70
E G	El Dorado Georgetown	58	673
E G	Placer Iona Hills	62	874
Ebenezer	Placer Iona Hills	62	874
Ed	Sacramento Dry Crk	63	372
Eduard	Yuba Long Bar	72	749
Edwin	Tuolumne Montezuma	71	512
Eliza	Sacramento Ward 3	63	489
Ephram	Plumas Quincy	62	979
F N	El Dorado Placerville	58	881
Ferdinand	Los Angeles Los Angeles	59	400
Frances	San Luis Obispo San Luis Obispo	65	4
G A	Butte Ophir	56	786
Geo	San Francisco San Francisco 10		210
		67	
Geo	San Francisco San Francisco 1 68		894
George	Alameda Oakland	55	11
George	Humbolt Eureka	59	177
George	Santa Clara Almaden	65	278
George	Shasta Horsetown	66	699
George W	Alameda Oakland	55	32
George W	Nevada Little Y	61	533
H S	El Dorado Casumnes	58	1175
Henry	Butte Ophir	56	751
Henry	Butte Ophir	56	773
Henry	Trinity Mouth Ca	70	1012

Name	County Locale	M653 Roll	Page
SPENCER			
Hiram	Yolo Cache Crk	72	597
Isaac	Tuolumne Shawsfla	71	387
Isaac	Yuba Marysville	72	909
Isaac	Yuba Marysville	72	915
Isaih	Butte Kimshaw	56	604
J	El Dorado Newtown	58	781
J C	Calaveras Twp 9	57	374
J C	Calaveras Twp 8	57	86
J C	Sacramento Ward 1	63	30
J C	Shasta Horsetown	66	690
J C	Yolo Cottonwoood	72	654
J M	El Dorado Newtown	58	779
J R	Shasta Millvill	66	743
J R	Siskiyou Cottonwoood	69	106
J*	San Francisco San Francisco 2 67		665
Jacob	Sacramento Dry Crk	63	370
James	Calaveras Twp 7	57	10
James	Colusa Butte Crk	57	466
James	Santa Cruz Santa Cruz	66	621
James	Santa Cruz Santa Cruz	66	622
James C	Mendocino Calpella	60	821
James C	Santa Clara San Jose	65	355
Jas	Napa Napa	61	71
Jas	Placer Lisbon	62	735
Jasper	Yuba Long Bar	72	772
Jepe	Shasta Shasta	66	731
Jesse	Shasta Shasta	66	731
Jno	Sacramento Ward 1	63	136
Jno	Sacramento Ward 3	63	434
Jno C	Sacramento Ward 4	63	560
John	Colusa Grand Island	57	468
John	Nevada Nevada	61	247
John	Nevada Bridgeport	61	443
John	Santa Cruz Santa Cruz	66	631
John	Siskiyou Scott Ri	69	67
John	Sonoma Bodega	69	522
John C	Butte Ophir	56	768
John D	Calaveras Twp 10	57	279
John D	San Francisco San Francisco 6 67		425
John S	Nevada Bridgeport	61	443
Joseph	Plumas Quincy	62	960
Joseph	Sierra Gibsonville	66	853
Joseph*	Tuolumne Twp 3	71	469
L	El Dorado Diamond	58	809
L	El Dorado Placerville	58	881
Luther	Plumas Quincy	62	980
Martin	Los Angeles Los Angeles	59	399
Mary	Solano Vallejo	69	270
Mary C	Sonoma Mendocino	69	466
Mary P	Sacramento Ward 3	63	489
Melissa	Butte Kimshaw	56	605
Michael	Butte Ophir	56	797
Michael	Humbolt Eel Rvr	59	148
Nathan	Alameda Oakland	55	49
Noah	Contra Costa Twp 2	57	567
O C	Mendocino Big Rvr	60	840
O J	Placer Iona Hills	62	874
Oliver	Tuolumne Twp 1	71	250
Peter	Sacramento Ward 3	63	483
R A	Nevada Grass Valley	61	216
R T	El Dorado White Oaks	58	1003
Rebecca	Sacramento Ward 4	63	566
Robert	Calaveras Twp 4	57	318
Robert W	Contra Costa Twp 3	57	597
Robirt	Calaveras Twp 4	57	318
Robt W	Shasta Horsetown	66	690
S	Sutter Butte	70	790
Saml	San Francisco San Francisco 10		220
		67	
Saml S	Santa Clara San Jose	65	352
Samuel	Alameda Oakland	55	61
Samuel	Tuolumne Jamestown	71	469
Samuel C	Santa Clara San Jose	65	355
Samuel*	Tuolumne Twp 3	71	469
Sarah	Yuba Marysville	72	928
Sasper	Yuba Long Bar	72	772
Simeon	Tuolumne Twp 1	71	276
Stephen	Yolo Slate Ra	72	689
Stephen	Yuba Slate Ro	72	689
T	San Francisco San Francisco 3 67		45
Thos	San Joaquin Elkhorn	64	991
Thos	Sonoma Mendocino	69	466
Thos	Trinity Mouth Ca	70	1010
W	Mariposa Twp 1	60	629
W A	Mariposa Twp 1	60	629
W C	Santa Clara San Jose	65	352
W H	Nevada Grass Valley	61	189
Wade H	Calaveras Twp 10	57	279
William	San Francisco San Francisco 7 68		1335
William	Solano Montezuma	69	367
William	Tuolumne Twp 3	71	449
William H	San Francisco San Francisco 7 68		1335
Wm	Amador Twp 5	55	342
Wm	Sonoma Vallejo	69	626
Wm	Trinity Eastman	70	960

Name	County Locale	M653 RollPage
SPENCER		
Wm B	Butte Ophir	56 797
Wm L	Tuolumne Jamestown	71 450
SPENCY		
William	Yuba Bear Rvr	721007
SPEND		
James	Mariposa Coulterville	60 703
SPENDLER		
Peter	Yuba Marysville	72 958
SPENEIL		
Loyed	Butte Ophir	56 785
SPENER		
William A*	San Francisco 4 681216	
	San Francisco	
SPENG		
Peter	Mariposa Coulterville	60 685
SPENGLER		
S	El Dorado Placerville	58 853
SPENIY		
William*	Yuba Bear Rvr	721007
SPENKINS		
T S	Sutter Bear Rvr	70 819
SPENN		
J M*	Yolo Cottonwood	72 647
Orlendo*	Yolo Washington	72 562
SPENNETO		
Angelo	San Francisco San Francisco 2 67 570	
SPENNY		
Hiram	San Francisco San Francisco 3 67 13	
SPENOSA		
Mavis*	Amador Twp 4	55 242
Navis*	Amador Twp 4	55 242
Tavis*	Amador Twp 4	55 242
SPENSEN		
H	San Francisco San Francisco 9 681103	
SPENSER		
David	San Francisco San Francisco 9 681081	
Richard OSan Francisco San Francisco 3 67 1		
SPENSOR		
Henry	San Mateo Twp 1	65 49
SPEORD		
Joseph	Mariposa Twp 3	60 585
SPERE		
Obudock*	Calaveras Twp 5	57 187
Ohidoch	Calaveras Twp 6	57 187
SPEREIR		
T	San Francisco San Francisco 3 67 45	
SPERGER		
Jesse	Sierra Twp 7	66 907
SPERIFF		
Thos	Sonoma Sonoma	69 637
SPERLMAN		
Souisa	San Francisco San Francisco 10 195	
		67
SPERMAN		
Geo	El Dorado Kelsey	581145
SPERN		
Orlendo	Yolo Washington	72 562
SPERNDLI		
John	Siskiyou Klamath	69 93
SPERNER		
James	El Dorado Mud Springs	58 966
SPERR		
F	Siskiyou Klamath	69 84
SPERREN		
A M*	Napa Napa	61 106
SPERRIE		
Louis	Mariposa Twp 3	60 615
SPERRIER		
Joseph	Tuolumne Jamestown	71 469
SPERRINGER		
John	Tulara Twp 2	71 30
SPERRMAN		
Geo	El Dorado Kelsey	581145
SPERRO		
Peter*	Alameda Oakland	55 73
SPERRY		
Addison	Yuba Rose Bar	72 820
Alvord	San Joaquin Castoria	64 902
Austin	San Joaquin Stockton	641061
B W	San Joaquin Stockton	641061
Benj	Placer Secret R	62 612
Charles	San Joaquin Elkhorn	64 970
Charles C	San Joaquin Elkhorn	64 972
Elij N	San Joaquin Castoria	64 903
Elijah	Calaveras Twp 5	57 189
F P	Nevada Nevada	61 245
George S	Calaveras Twp 5	57 189
Giddion	Placer Michigan	62 851
Henry*	Mariposa Twp 3	60 615
Jas L	Calaveras Twp 5	57 355
John H C	Sacramento Ward 4	63 552
L W	San Joaquin Stockton	641009
Lorenzo	Calaveras Twp 10	57 282
Sheldia	Shasta Shasta	66 734
Sheldon	Shasta Shasta	66 734

Name	County Locale	M653 RollPage
SPERRY		
Willia	Tuolumne Twp 2	71 393
William D	San Joaquin Castoria	64 890
Willis	Tuolumne Shawsfla	71 393
Wm	Sacramento Ward 4	63 567
SPERSON		
Jacob	Yuba Bear Rvr	721000
SPERSUR		
Joseph	Tuolumne Twp 3	71 469
SPERTO		
Antonio	Tuolumne Twp 1	71 254
SPERU		
Otridoch*	Calaveras Twp 5	57 187
SPES		
Cathrine San Francisco San Francisco 2 67 732		
SPESKS		
J T	El Dorado Greenwood	58 716
SPEUSER		
David*	San Francisco San Francisco 9 681081	
SPEVER		
Frank*	San Joaquin Stockton	641034
SPEVET		
J W*	Nevada Nevada	61 319
SPEWER		
Joseph*	Mariposa Coulterville	60 696
SPEXLEY		
S W	Sierra Twp 7	66 886
SPEZZIA		
Novatus San Francisco San Francisco 11 121		
		67
SPHEN		
David A*	Marin San Rafael	60 773
SPHENG		
Joseph	Mariposa Twp 1	60 623
SPHERE		
David A	Marin San Rafael	60 773
SPHERNENAR		
Jo*	Mariposa Coulterville	60 688
SPHINK		
M E	Sutter Sutter	70 814
SPI		
---	Placer Illinois	62 742
SPIARS		
A	Sutter Yuba	70 764
SPICEN		
M A	Nevada Bloomfield	61 524
SPICER		
Austin	Placer Michigan	62 853
E R	Solano Vacaville	69 367
Edward	Yuba Long Bar	72 749
Henry	Sacramento Franklin	63 330
J H	Colusa Grand Island	57 478
John	El Dorado Placerville	58 914
M A	Nevada Bloomfield	61 524
Marsha M	Los Angeles Elmonte	59 265
Samuel B	Sierra Pine Grove	66 823
Thomas	Calaveras Twp 8	57 78
SPICOR		
J H	Colusa Grand Island	57 478
SPIDLE		
Abner	Klamath S Fork	59 198
Mathew	Placer Dutch Fl	62 732
SPIEGEL		
D	San Francisco San Francisco 10 165	
		67
SPIEGLE		
Jacob	Santa Cruz Santa Cruz	66 628
SPIEGLER		
Charles	Calaveras Twp 7	57 22
SPIEIR		
Francis*	Del Norte Klamath	58 654
SPIER		
Francis*	Del Norte Klamath	58 654
M	San Francisco San Francisco 4 681220	
Samuel B	Sierra Pine Grove	66 823
SPIERLING		
H	El Dorado Placerville	58 820
SPIERS		
And	Sacramento Ward 3	63 485
Chas	Fresno Millerto	59 1
Saml*	Napa Hot Springs	61 16
Sarul	Napa Hot Springs	61 16
T*	Sutter Nicolaus	70 829
SPIES		
Frederick San Francisco San Francisco 7 681431		
J W*	Del Norte Happy Ca	58 669
M*	San Francisco San Francisco 4 681220	
SPIFFARD		
Leander*	Alameda Brooklyn	55 139
SPIFFER		
Benjamin	San Diego Colorado	64 809
SPIFFINS		
Thoms*	El Dorado Georgetown	58 752
SPIGE		
M	Butte Wyandotte	56 669
SPIGNASA		
Sebastian	Los Angeles Los Angeles	59 343

Name	County Locale	M653 RollPage
SPIKER		
John	Sierra Gibsonville	66 858
W S	Butte Ophir	56 760
SPIKINE		
Jas	Butte Bidwell	56 729
SPILE		
Jacob	Siskiyou Klamath	69 94
SPILIR		
Francis*	Del Norte Klamath	58 654
SPILL		
Jacob*	Siskiyou Klamath	69 94
SPILLAN		
Mike	Klamath Liberty	59 233
SPILLENBERG		
George	Sierra St Louis	66 864
SPILLER		
E P	Butte Kimshaw	56 601
SPILLERS		
Samuel	Contra Costa Twp 3	57 597
SPILLIN		
Corneilus	Sacramento Sutter	63 297
SPILLMAN		
---	San Francisco San Francisco 7 681339	
H	San Francisco San Francisco 9 681086	
J E P	Sacramento Ward 1	63 21
John D	Butte Ophir	56 769
Joseph	San Francisco San Francisco 7 681348	
SPILMAN		
B R	Yolo No E Twp	72 669
B R	Yuba North Ea	72 669
Calvin	Yuba North Ea	72 673
Geo	Butte Bidwell	56 732
Michael	Sierra Downieville	66 963
SPILMON		
Calvin	Yolo No E Twp	72 673
SPILTY		
Frederick San Francisco San Francisco 7 681400		
SPIM		
J M*	Yolo Cottonwoood	72 647
SPIN		
M*	San Francisco San Francisco 4 681220	
SPINA		
Robt*	Sonoma Sonoma	69 643
Wylie*	Sonoma Sonoma	69 642
SPINAR		
Henry	Yolo Merritt	72 580
SPINBACK		
A S	El Dorado Grizzly	581180
SPINCE		
Christopher*	San Francisco 9 681099	
	San Francisco	
J	San Francisco San Francisco 5 67 539	
Robt	Butte Ophir	56 767
SPINCER		
Chauncy	Mariposa Twp 1	60 644
J*	San Francisco San Francisco 2 67 665	
SPINCINHAM		
Peck	Butte Cascade	56 703
SPINDLER		
Peter	Yuba Marysville	72 958
SPINDTHROP		
A T	Yolo Cache Crk	72 664
SPINENBURGH		
Alfred	Sierra Downieville	661022
SPINER		
A	Siskiyou Cottonwoood	69 98
John	Placer Iona Hills	62 871
Joseph*	Mariposa Coulterville	60 696
Robt*	Sonoma Sonoma	69 643
Samuel	Placer Iona Hills	62 888
William A*	San Francisco 4 681216	
	San Francisco	
Wylie*	Sonoma Sonoma	69 642
SPINES		
A	Siskiyou Cottonwoood	69 98
SPING		
---*	Yuba Timbucto	72 787
SPINGER		
John	Sierra Twp 5	66 935
R	Nevada Eureka	61 344
SPINGLE		
Stephen	Calaveras Twp 8	57 56
SPINGLER		
John*	San Joaquin Stockton	641050
SPINGLESTEIN		
Josiah	San Joaquin Castoria	64 890
SPINGR		
B*	Mariposa Twp 3	60 547
SPINIS		
A**	El Dorado Georgetown	58 753
SPINISA		
Francis*	El Dorado Georgetown	58 684
SPINK		
B	Nevada Eureka	61 393
Eizeikal*	Calaveras Twp 5	57 210

Name	County Locale	M653 RollPage
SPINK		
Eliza	San Francisco San Francisco 11	132
		67
Eszeikal*	Calaveras Twp 5	57 210
Ezeikal*	Calaveras Twp 5	57 210
Ezeikul*	Calaveras Twp 5	57 210
Ezekiel*	Calaveras Twp 5	57 210
Job W	Butte Kimshaw	56 575
SPINKLER		
August	Butte Bidwell	56 731
SPINKS		
R	Sacramento Granite	63 227
SPINLOCK		
William	San Mateo Twp 3	65 103
SPINNER		
John	Nevada Bridgeport	61 445
Sam	Butte Ophir	56 760
Thomas J	San Joaquin Elkhorn	64 958
SPINNETO		
Angelo	San Francisco San Francisco 2	67 570
SPINNEY		
Waldron S	San Francisco San Francisco 11	143
		67
SPINNGER		
Mary	Amador Twp 2	55 297
SPINNING		
Francis M	San Joaquin Elliott	64 948
SPINNY		
Hiram*	San Francisco San Francisco 3	67 13
SPINOBE		
Jooquin*	Calaveras Twp 6	57 162
SPINOLA		
Joaquin*	Calaveras Twp 6	57 162
Joaquin	Calaveras Twp 6	57 162
Jooquin*	Calaveras Twp 6	57 162
SPINOLER		
Joaquin*	Calaveras Twp 6	57 162
SPINONI		
Joseph	Santa Cruz Pajaro	66 531
SPINOZA		
J M	Tuolumne Sonora	71 239
SPINS		
Chas D	Calaveras Twp 6	57 154
SPINSER		
Richard O*	San Francisco 3	67 1
	San Francisco	
SPINWALL		
Tho A	Siskiyou Scott Va	69 58
SPIOZEN		
Martha*	San Francisco San Francisco 4	681171
SPIRE		
Jas	Napa Napa	61 109
SPIRES		
Charles W	Plumas Quincy	62 957
Chas D	Calaveras Twp 6	57 154
George W	Plumas Quincy	62 962
Henry T	Plumas Quincy	62 962
Saml*	Napa Hot Springs	61 16
Sarah	Butte Ophir	56 785
SPIRRITE		
Manuel	Tuolumne Jamestown	71 424
SPIRRITO		
Manuel	Tuolumne Twp 3	71 424
SPIRT		
Fred*	Alameda Brooklyn	55 122
Thomas	Sierra Cox'S Bar	66 951
SPIRUSA		
Francis	El Dorado Georgetown	58 684
SPITS		
Albert	Monterey San Juan	60 991
SPITZER		
John	Butte Bidwell	56 721
John	Butte Bidwell	56 730
W S	Butte Ophir	56 760
SPIUS		
Saml*	Napa Hot Springs	61 16
SPIVA		
Johnn	Butte Ophir	56 745
Johrn*	Butte Ophir	56 745
SPIVET		
J W*	Nevada Nevada	61 319
SPIZER		
Jacob	Butte Ophir	56 785
SPLAANA		
Mohay*	Mariposa Twp 3	60 559
SPLAEENA		
Mohay*	Mariposa Twp 3	60 559
SPLAIF		
P F	Sierra Downieville	661016
SPLAIN		
Morris	Calaveras Twp 7	57 6
SPLAMM		
John	Solano Vallejo	69 243
SPLAN		
Dennis	Placer Secret R	62 614
SPLANE		
P F	Sierra Downieville	661016

Name	County Locale	M653 RollPage
SPLANGLER		
Daniel	Sierra St Louis	66 864
SPLANUM		
John	Solano Vallejo	69 243
SPLAUGLER		
Daniel	Sierra Twp 7	66 864
SPLAUNA		
Makery*	Mariposa Twp 3	60 559
SPLINETT		
Charles	El Dorado Mud Springs	58 966
SPLIVALO		
Augustu D	San Francisco 8	681292
	San Francisco	
Augustus D	San Francisco 8	681292
	San Francisco	
S*	Santa Clara Santa Clara	65 498
SPOAGER		
H C	Trinity Taylor'S	701036
SPOCK		
Joseph	San Francisco San Francisco 5	67 546
SPOEN		
Peter*	Yuba Marysville	72 913
SPOERER		
Charles	Alameda Brooklyn	55 130
SPOFFOND		
J L	San Francisco San Francisco 5	67 515
SPOFFORD		
A P K	San Francisco San Francisco 7	681360
James H	Nevada Rough &	61 417
Josiah	Yuba Marysville	72 971
SPOHER		
Peter	Sacramento Ward 4	63 532
SPOHN		
G	Amador Twp 3	55 377
SPOLDING		
Henry	Sierra Twp 7	66 893
SPOLITO		
Rosario	Los Angeles Santa Ana	59 453
SPOLLS		
Alex*	Nevada Nevada	61 325
SPOMY		
M*	Calaveras Twp 9	57 396
SPONABLE		
A C	Sierra Twp 7	66 899
SPONDLA		
Danl	Sacramento Ward 3	63 437
SPONEY		
M*	Calaveras Twp 9	57 396
SPONG		
John	Yuba New York	72 730
SPONNER		
Joseph	San Francisco San Francisco 3	67 56
SPONOGLE		
James	Solano Vacaville	69 359
SPONSLER		
J	El Dorado Placerville	58 868
SPOOK		
---	Fresno Twp 3	59 96
SPOOLS		
Joseph	El Dorado Georgetown	58 704
SPOON		
---	Del Norte Happy Ca	58 667
J M*	Yolo Cottonwoood	72 647
Joseph	San Francisco San Francisco 3	67 57
SPOONER		
Alfred	Placer Iona Hills	62 895
Ann	San Francisco San Francisco 10	215
		67
D	Calaveras Twp 9	57 396
G A	Amador Twp 1	55 455
George	Sierra Gibsonville	66 852
Gergamin F	San Joaquin Stockton	641073
James	Calaveras Twp 7	57 27
John	Calaveras Twp 7	57 1
John	El Dorado Eldorado	58 946
O P	Sierra Chappare	661040
Pardon*	Calaveras Twp 7	57 16
Parolon*	Calaveras Twp 7	57 16
Peter	Calaveras Twp 10	57 288
Simon	San Francisco San Francisco 9	68 952
Thos	San Francisco San Francisco 10	213
		67
Wyman	El Dorado Kelsey	581138
SPOONINAPER		
G*	Butte Oregon	56 609
SPOONMAKER		
G	Butte Oregon	56 609
SPOONMAPER		
G	Butte Oregon	56 609
SPOOR		
George	Sierra La Porte	66 769
H C	Nevada Rough &	61 413
James	Tuolumne Big Oak	71 141
SPORE		
N P*	Stanislaus Branch	70 702
SPORI		
Lewis	San Francisco San Francisco 2	67 681

Name	County Locale	M653 RollPage
SPORNDLEY		
Jacob	Sierra Twp 7	66 890
SPORNDLI		
John	Siskiyou Klamath	69 93
SPORRY		
Henry*	Mariposa Twp 3	60 615
SPORTA		
---	Mendocino Little L	60 839
Antonio	Tuolumne Twp 1	71 254
SPORTAL		
---	Mendocino Little L	60 839
SPORTAT		
---*	Mendocino Little L	60 839
SPORTHALE		
Jno	Sacramento Granite	63 225
SPOSATI		
N	San Joaquin Stockton	641040
SPOSETO		
George	Siskiyou Yreka	69 175
SPOSITO		
Paul	San Francisco San Francisco 3	67 26
SPOSITS		
Paul	Klamath Liberty	59 234
SPOTRY		
Frederick*	Yuba Marysville	72 935
SPOTSWOOD		
M	San Francisco San Francisco 5	67 497
SPOTTS		
Alex	Nevada Nevada	61 325
J	San Francisco San Francisco 2	67 788
SPOWER		
Joseph	Alameda Oakland	55 43
SPOWEY		
M*	Calaveras Twp 9	57 396
SPRAA		
Catharine	San Francisco San Francisco 9	68 948
SPRAG		
E D	El Dorado Kelsey	581151
SPRAGAR		
B H	Sierra Twp 5	66 929
E M	Nevada Eureka	61 393
SPRAGE		
E A	El Dorado Placerville	58 912
James	Tuolumne Shawsfla	71 386
Joseph	Tuolumne Chinese	71 489
SPRAGEE		
Lylle	Butte Cascade	56 698
SPRAGEN		
Harris*	Tuolumne Twp 2	71 286
John	Butte Oro	56 684
William L*	Calaveras Twp 7	57 14
SPRAGNE		
M C	Siskiyou Scott Va	69 48
SPRAGUC		
Leonard	Yolo Cache	72 629
SPRAGUE		
A	Monterey Monterey	60 956
A	Tuolumne Jamestown	71 470
B W	Sierra Twp 5	66 929
Charles	Placer Iona Hills	62 875
Charles*	Placer Iona Hills	62 864
Chs J	San Francisco San Francisco 6	67 403
D R	Yolo Putah	72 547
E	Monterey Monterey	60 956
E M	Nevada Eureka	61 393
E S	San Joaquin Stockton	641033
Elijah	Sonoma Petaluma	69 584
Eugene	Sonoma Vallejo	69 622
F A	Placer Goods	62 693
H C	Trinity Taylor'S	701036
Harris	Tuolumne Twp 2	71 286
Henry	Placer Forest H	62 803
J J	Sacramento Ward 1	63 17
J L	Sacramento Ward 4	63 608
J R	Yolo Putah	72 547
J S	Sacramento Ward 1	63 17
Jas	Butte Chico	56 562
John	Amador Twp 2	55 303
John	Butte Oro	56 684
John	Calaveras Twp 9	57 382
John	Yolo Cache Crk	72 630
L D*	Tuolumne Twp 1	71 247
Leonard	Yolo Cache Crk	72 629
Lowren	Sierra Poker Flats	66 842
Lowsin	Sierra Poker Flats	66 842
Lytle	Butte Cascade	56 698
M	Sacramento Sutter	63 293
M C	Siskiyou Scott Va	69 48
O S	Sacramento Granite	63 229
Peter	San Bernardino San Bernadino	64 615
R T	Nevada Grass Valley	61 194
R T	Shasta Shasta	66 659
Sampson	Tuolumne Jamestown	71 449
Samuel	El Dorado Salmon Falls	581049
Samuel S	San Francisco San Francisco 7	681373
T	Nevada Grass Valley	61 207

Name	County Locale	M653 RollPage
SPRAGUE		
T*	Nevada Grass Valley	61 190
W H	El Dorado Placerville	58 915
SPRAGUS		
A	Tuolumne Twp 3	71 470
SPRAIN		
C T	Amador Twp 6	55 431
SPRAIZER		
H M*	Tuolumne Twp 1	71 255
SPRAJEN		
William L*	Calaveras Twp 7	57 14
SPRAKER		
F	Nevada Eureka	61 379
SPRAN		
James	San Francisco San Francisco 4	681169
SPRANGE		
H	El Dorado Placerville	58 858
R W*	Nevada Nevada	61 312
SPRANGER		
H U*	Tuolumne Twp 1	71 255
SPRANGS		
L D*	Tuolumne Twp 1	71 247
SPRANSHAN		
Charley	Mariposa Coulterville	60 698
SPRANT		
J T	El Dorado Casumnes	581172
SPRAT		
Bertram	Placer Secret R	62 613
SPRATE		
Elizabeth	Placer Michigan	62 858
SPRATT		
John	Yolo Cache	72 591
Jos	San Francisco San Francisco 10	251 67
Robt	Tuolumne Twp 4	71 139
Thomas	Placer Forest H	62 805
Veneble	San Joaquin Elkhorn	64 988
SPRAUAR		
R A	Nevada Nevada	61 271
SPRAUGE		
L D	Tuolumne Twp 1	71 247
R A	Nevada Nevada	61 271
R D	Nevada Nevada	61 273
R T	Nevada Nevada	61 273
R W	Nevada Nevada	61 312
SPRAUGER		
H U*	Tuolumne Twp 1	71 255
SPRAUGUE		
Sowren	Sierra Poker Flats	66 842
SPRAUL		
Jus	El Dorado Casumnes	581172
SPRAWL		
Andrew	San Francisco San Francisco 9	681053
SPRAY		
---	Nevada Bridgeport	61 467
Wm	Amador Twp 2	55 300
SPRECHER		
Jacob	Amador Twp 7	55 414
Jacob	Amador No 3	55 415
SPRECHIR		
Jacob*	Amador Twp 7	55 414
SPRECHIT		
Charles	Yuba Marysville	72 880
SPRECKELS		
Diederich	San Francisco San Francisco 10	272 67
SPRECKLES		
C	San Francisco San Francisco 10	272 67
SPREGGINS		
J W*	Napa Napa	61 69
SPRICHT		
Charlie	Yuba Marysville	72 880
SPRIDGINS		
Jas*	Merced Twp 1	60 906
SPRIDGIUS		
Jas	Merced Twp 1	60 906
SPRIENBURG		
Smith	Sierra Downieville	661022
SPRIGG		
Zach	El Dorado Eldorado	58 939
SPRIGGING		
J W*	Napa Napa	61 69
SPRIGGS		
Ephraim	Tuolumne Don Pedro	71 541
J M	Yolo Cache Crk	72 619
John	San Mateo Twp 2	65 128
SPRIGS		
Ephraim	Tuolumne Twp 6	71 541
SPRINEBURG		
Smith	Sierra Downieville	661022
SPRINEN		
Sam	Butte Ophir	56 760
SPRINER		
H M	Nevada Eureka	61 344
SPRING		
A	Sonoma Bodega	69 530

Name	County Locale	M653 RollPage
SPRING		
F M	El Dorado Diamond	58 782
Gardner	Tuolumne Don Pedro	71 541
Geo	El Dorado White Oaks	581024
Geo	El Dorado Placerville	58 888
James S	Nevada Red Dog	61 550
Jas L*	Calaveras Twp 9	57 355
John	Yuba Marysville	72 858
John	Yuba Marysville	72 859
Louisa	San Francisco San Francisco 7	681354
Mary	Alameda Oakland	55 47
William	San Francisco San Francisco 4	681138
William	Yuba Bear Rvr	721007
SPRINGAMETER		
Benja*	Calaveras Twp 4	57 340
SPRINGER		
A	Calaveras Twp 9	57 405
A B	Nevada Bridgeport	61 482
A C	Sacramento Ward 1	63 75
B	Sacramento Sutter	63 301
Barney	Tulara Twp 1	71 110
Chas	Sacramento Dry Crk	63 374
E	El Dorado Diamond	58 810
E	Yolo Washington	72 564
E C	El Dorado Diamond	58 767
Elias	Santa Clara Fremont	65 437
Elias D	Plumas Quincy	62 965
F J	Solano Vallejo	69 263
Gariett*	Butte Ophir	56 758
Garrett	Butte Ophir	56 758
H I	Amador Twp 2	55 325
H J	Amador Twp 2	55 325
Henry	Amador Twp 2	55 307
Henry	Tulara Twp 3	71 59
Henry*	Amador Twp 2	55 307
Isabel	El Dorado Coloma	581124
J L	Sonoma Bodega	69 522
J R	El Dorado Mountain	581184
Jas	Butte Ophir	56 760
Jason	Butte Oro	56 687
John	Santa Clara Fremont	65 439
John	Yolo Cache	72 630
Louisanna	Sacramento Ward 4	63 605
Mary	Amador Twp 1	55 453
N	Yolo Cache	72 629
R	El Dorado Mountain	581184
R	Nevada Eureka	61 344
R	Yolo Slate Ra	72 707
R	Yuba Slate Ro	72 707
Samuel	Calaveras Twp 5	57 199
Samuel	El Dorado Mud Springs	58 990
Samuel W*	San Mateo Twp 2	65 122
Sarah	Nevada Rough &	61 418
Sarah C	Butte Cascade	56 689
T A	Amador Twp 1	55 453
Theodore T	Sacramento Ward 4	63 606
W	Nevada Grass Valley	61 213
Wilson	Sacramento Ward 4	63 606
Wilson	Santa Clara San Jose	65 351
Wilson	Santa Clara San Jose	65 354
SPRINGES		
Isabel	El Dorado Coloma	581124
SPRINGLER		
Frederick	Colusa Spring Valley	57 429
William*	Del Norte Crescent	58 630
William*	Placer Michigan	62 836
SPRINGLES		
William*	Placer Michigan	62 836
SPRINGOO		
Henry*	Amador Twp 2	55 307
SPRINGOR		
J P	Santa Clara Redwood	65 446
SPRINGS		
John	San Francisco San Francisco 4	681225
SPRINGSTEAD		
H	Yolo Putah	72 548
SPRINGSTEAL		
S W	Tehama Red Bluff	70 920
SPRINGSTED		
H	Yolo Putah	72 548
Wm	Del Norte Happy Ca	58 670
Wm	Placer Goods	62 699
SPRINGSTEEN		
Moses*	Sierra Twp 5	66 928
SPRINGSTEIN		
Benj	Sierra Twp 7	66 893
Benjn	Sierra Twp 7	66 893
Laurence	Sierra Twp 7	66 892
Moses	Sierra Twp 5	66 928
SPRINGSTER		
W E	Butte Bidwell	56 727
SPRINGSTIEN		
Laurence	Sierra Twp 7	66 892
SPRINGSTON		
Wm	Napa Clear Lake	61 137
SPRINGTON		
S B	Butte Oregon	56 640

Name	County Locale	M653 RollPage
SPRINKEY		
Wm	Butte Ophir	56 799
SPRINKLE		
J C	Amador Twp 6	55 445
SPRINKLES		
Geo	Mendocino Anderson	60 871
Philip	Placer Michigan	62 838
SPRIR		
F R*	San Francisco San Francisco 4	681156
SPRIY		
Peter*	Colusa Butte Crk	57 466
SPRIZER		
Jos	Butte Ophir	56 800
SPRN		
F R*	San Francisco San Francisco 4	681156
SPROAL		
Mary M	Butte Chico	56 542
Oliver	Butte Chico	56 542
S M	Butte Chico	56 542
SPROAT		
G T	San Francisco San Francisco 12	389 67
Joseph	Mariposa Twp 3	60 609
Saml	Butte Chico	56 541
SPROIT		
John	Santa Clara San Jose	65 286
SPROLE		
James	Tuolumne Twp 4	71 143
Joseph*	El Dorado Georgetown	58 704
SPROLES		
Elizabeth	Merced Twp 1	60 895
SPROLL		
Joseph*	El Dorado Georgetown	58 704
SPRONA		
James*	Nevada Bridgeport	61 478
SPRONCE		
James*	Nevada Bridgeport	61 478
SPRONE		
James	Nevada Bridgeport	61 478
SPRONER		
James*	Nevada Bridgeport	61 478
SPRONG		
John*	Yuba New York	72 730
SPRONH		
James*	Placer Michigan	62 857
SPRONL		
J A	Sonoma Petaluma	69 543
SPRONLE		
James*	Placer Michigan	62 857
SPROONER		
Simon	Sierra Downieville	661030
SPRORE		
Joseph	Alameda Oakland	55 46
SPROUL		
Alonzo	Calaveras Twp 4	57 299
J A	Sonoma Petaluma	69 543
James	Siskiyou Callahan	69 1
M J	Solano Vacaville	69 339
Marion	San Francisco San Francisco 10	199 67
Robt	Trinity Texas Ba	70 982
W D	Solano Vacaville	69 339
SPROULE		
Jas	San Francisco San Francisco 10	173 67
Wm M G	Humbolt Union	59 192
SPROULL		
John	San Francisco San Francisco 11	129 67
SPROULS		
Andrew	Siskiyou Klamath	69 83
W	Siskiyou Klamath	69 83
SPROUT		
Ephraim	Humbolt Eel Rvr	59 149
F*	Nevada Grass Valley	61 168
G T	San Francisco San Francisco 2	67 669
John L	Nevada Nevada	61 327
T	Nevada Grass Valley	61 188
SPROW		
Frank	Tulara Visalia	71 112
SPROWL		
James	Trinity Weaverville	701078
John	Plumas Quincy	62 923
SPRUANCE		
John	Sacramento Granite	63 229
SPRUCE		
John	Solano Vallejo	69 273
Mary	Yuba Marysville	72 923
SPRUEL		
Morgan*	Sacramento Sutter	63 300
SPRUGEN		
W	Yolo Cache Crk	72 629
SPRUHAN		
Walter	San Francisco San Francisco 7	681349
SPRUY		
---*	Nevada Bridgeport	61 467

Name	County Locale	M653 RollPage
SPSNENBURGH		
Alfred	Sierra Downieville	66 1022
SPUCKLES		
Peter	Yuba Marysville	72 928
SPUDY		
James	El Dorado Georgetown	58 674
SPUGGING		
J W*	Napa Napa	61 69
SPUGGINS		
J W*	Napa Napa	61 69
SPUGH		
James L	Monterey Pajaro	60 1015
James S	Monterey Pajaro	60 1015
SPUIR		
Lucius*	El Dorado Georgetown	58 703
SPUIRT		
Lueius	El Dorado Georgetown	58 703
SPULVEDA		
Dolores	Marin Cortemad	60 786
SPULZ		
Soloman	Alameda Oakland	55 13
SPUN		
J M*	Yolo Cottonwoood	72 647
SPUNDLE SHANK		
---	Tulara Twp 3	71 56
SPUNGE		
John	Amador Twp 1	55 485
S W	El Dorado White Oaks	58 1011
SPUNGER		
John	Sierra Twp 5	66 935
SPUNLICK		
Jacob*	Yuba New York	72 730
SPUR		
F R	San Francisco San Francisco 4	68 1156
Hugh*	San Francisco San Francisco 10	354 67
M*	San Francisco San Francisco 4	68 1220
SPURBACK		
M	El Dorado Kelsey	58 1150
SPURGEE		
Jesse	Sierra Twp 7	66 903
SPURGER		
Jesse*	Sierra Twp 7	66 903
Joseph	San Joaquin Douglass	64 923
SPURGSON		
Charles	Mendocino Big Rock	60 874
SPURR		
John	Los Angeles Los Angeles	59 322
Wm	Sonoma Santa Rosa	69 401
SPURS		
T*	Sutter Nicolaus	70 829
SPURYER		
Jesse*	Sierra Twp 7	66 903
SPUS		
J W*	Del Norte Happy Ca	58 669
SPUTNOR		
Charles	San Francisco San Francisco 11	117 67
SPUY		
Jas L*	Calaveras Twp 9	57 355
SPUYLEBURG		
Henry	Trinity Trinity	70 975
SPUZEN		
Martha	San Francisco San Francisco 4	68 1171
SPYTH		
A	Nevada Grass Valley	61 213
SQINOR		
E G	San Francisco San Francisco 3	67 81
SQUACH		
Terrence	Yuba Marysville	72 928
SQUARES		
William	Sierra Gibsonville	66 860
SQUARZA		
---	San Francisco San Francisco 5	67 505
SQUAW		
---	Fresno Twp 2	59 42
---	Fresno Twp 2	59 64
SQUCH		
Hugh*	Yuba Marysville	72 957
Terrence	Yuba Marysville	72 928
SQUELL		
Richard	Yuba Marysville	72 913
SQUIBB		
L W	Tuolumne Twp 4	71 171
N L	Napa Yount	61 55
T W	Tuolumne Jacksonville	71 171
SQUIER		
John H	San Francisco San Francisco 11	92 67
William	Sierra Gibsonville	66 854
Zalman	Sierra Gibsonville	66 854
SQUIERS		
J B	Tehama Lassen	70 861
Morgan L	Alameda Oakland	55 29
P*	Tuolumne Twp 1	71 260
SQUIMINE		
---	Tulara Twp 2	71 34

Name	County Locale	M653 RollPage
SQUIOR		
E G*	San Francisco San Francisco 3	67 81
SQUIR		
Lucius*	El Dorado Georgetown	58 703
SQUIRE		
H C	San Francisco San Francisco 3	67 73
Henry C	San Francisco San Francisco 3	67 7
I E*	Nevada Red Dog	61 548
J E*	Nevada Red Dog	61 548
L H	Yuba Parks Ba	72 786
S	Calaveras Twp 9	57 413
S H	Yuba Parke Ba	72 786
Sonis	Placer Todds Va	62 784
SQUIRES		
Chas	Santa Clara Fremont	65 439
E W	Los Angeles Los Angeles	59 499
Elizabeth	Placer Folsom	62 640
F A	Tuolumne Sonora	71 212
G	San Francisco San Francisco 5	67 530
Geo	Butte Ophir	56 768
Geo	Placer Dutch Fl	62 723
George	San Joaquin Castoria	64 895
George W	Yuba Bear Rvr	72 999
H	Butte Ophir	56 797
H	Nevada Nevada	61 318
H T	Trinity Weaverville	70 1053
Henry	San Francisco San Francisco 4	68 1137
Horace	Calaveras Twp 5	57 251
J A	Napa Yount	61 51
J H	Napa Yount	61 51
Jas	Sonoma Petaluma	69 549
John	Sacramento Georgian	63 339
John	Santa Clara Santa Clara	65 476
John	Shasta Shasta	66 731
L	Sonoma Cloverdale	69 680
Moses P	Placer Folsom	62 640
O	El Dorado Placerville	58 871
P	Tuolumne Twp 1	71 260
S	San Francisco San Francisco 5	67 530
S	Santa Clara Santa Clara	65 506
Simon	Santa Clara Santa Clara	65 468
Sol	Stanislaus Branch	70 715
Stephen	Yuba Fosters	72 823
Stephen	Yuba Marysville	72 963
Thos	Sacramento Georgian	63 343
William K	Solano Montezuma	69 373
Wm	Humbolt Eureka	59 170
SQUIRIS		
F A	Tuolumne Twp 1	71 212
SQUIRS		
E W	Los Angeles Los Angeles	59 499
SQUQUER		
Jos	San Francisco San Francisco 9	68 1047
SQURES		
Henry	Mariposa Twp 1	60 663
SQURING		
---	Yolo No E Twp	72 685
SR		
Ham	Sierra Downieville	66 986
Sin	Sierra Downieville	66 979
Sing	Sierra Twp 5	66 947
SRABELL		
Peter	Siskiyou Klamath	69 84
SRAF		
Mary	Placer Forest H	62 768
SRAFIN		
John*	Marin Cortemad	60 755
SRAIS		
Manuela*	Yuba Marysville	72 951
SRAM		
Joseph	Nevada Rough &	61 424
SRAN		
Cum	Tuolumne Twp 5	71 525
SRANK		
Aimy*	Calaveras Twp 6	57 144
Jackson	Calaveras Twp 6	57 144
SRAY		
Homer	Tuolumne Twp 2	71 328
SRCHEL		
Liel	San Francisco San Francisco 3	67 86
M C	San Francisco San Francisco 3	67 86
SRCHOLS		
Peter	Butte Eureka	56 649
SRDLINGER		
Joseph*	Siskiyou Yreka	69 153
SREAMS		
Frank	San Joaquin Stockton	64 1021
SREARENGEN		
Mary*	Sacramento Ward 1	63 45
SREDMAN		
C	San Joaquin Stockton	64 1055
SREEM		
Mark*	Nevada Red Dog	61 538
SRELEA		
John*	Yuba New York	72 747
SREN		
---*	Calaveras Twp 5	57 211

Name	County Locale	M653 RollPage
SRENGIS		
Wm*	Butte Ophir	56 751
SRENIGO		
Adreas*	Santa Cruz Pajaro	66 543
SRENSDALE		
R M*	San Francisco San Francisco 6	67 435
SRENSEL		
B	San Francisco San Francisco 9	68 949
SREURENCE		
William	Calaveras Twp 6	57 146
SREUSDALE		
R M	San Francisco San Francisco 6	67 435
SREUSEL		
B*	San Francisco San Francisco 9	68 949
SREVER		
C F	Sonoma Vallejo	69 627
SRI		
---	Calaveras Twp 6	57 141
---	Calaveras Twp 6	57 149
SRIAIN		
John G*	Sierra Gibsonville	66 855
SRICE		
E	Merced Twp 1	60 913
SRICKLIFER		
John	Butte Bidwell	56 724
SRIET		
Peter*	Mariposa Coulterville	60 679
Petes*	Mariposa Coulterville	60 679
Retes*	Mariposa Coulterville	60 679
SRIFOLO		
Cruz*	Santa Clara Burnett	65 260
SRIGDER		
Chas	Santa Clara San Jose	65 338
SRIGGS		
John	Yolo Putah	72 546
SRILEY		
Kate	San Mateo Twp 1	65 49
SRINDGRUN		
Peter O*	San Francisco San Francisco 3	67 69
SRINE		
Cerile	Tuolumne Twp 5	71 498
SRING		
M	San Joaquin Stockton	64 1097
SRINGAMETER		
Benj*	Calaveras Twp 4	57 340
SRINGR		
B*	Mariposa Twp 3	60 547
SRINIGO		
Andrew	Santa Cruz Pajaro	66 543
SRIODGRASS		
Thomas*	Mariposa Twp 1	60 656
SRIOR		
S	Calaveras Twp 9	57 391
SRITRO		
James*	San Francisco San Francisco 3	67 62
SRIVELY		
C	Sacramento Cosumnes	63 394
SROA		
J	Sutter Butte	70 796
SROAGEY		
J S	El Dorado Greenwood	58 726
SROARMS		
William	Calaveras Twp 6	57 141
SROCENY		
Jas*	Sacramento Ward 1	63 29
SRODAGUTT		
H*	Yolo Putah	72 545
SROESSER		
Ono	Santa Cruz Watsonville	66 535
SROIM		
David K*	Calaveras Twp 5	57 207
SROIMLEY		
Wm F*	Sacramento Ward 1	63 29
SROLLO		
Joseph	Calaveras Twp 4	57 324
SRONFE		
B*	Sonoma Vallejo	69 628
SRONG		
C	Nevada Grass Valley	61 151
L W	Nevada Nevada	61 321
SRONTS		
John	San Joaquin Elkhorn	64 969
SROODDIOIRS		
W W*	Butte Cascade	56 703
SROPATH		
Edward*	Calaveras Twp 9	57 371
SROPE		
Geo F*	Sacramento Granite	63 248
Mr	Sonoma Sonoma	69 638
SROROVANT		
Nathan	Santa Cruz Watsonville	66 536
SROSSE		
Mr*	Sonoma Sonoma	69 638
SROTTER		
R	Shasta Shasta	66 677
SROU		
---*	Calaveras Twp 5	57 211

Name	County Locale	M653 RollPage
SROUF		
Adelia	Sonoma Petaluma	69 592
G W*	Sonoma Petaluma	69 593
Jno	Sonoma Petaluma	69 581
SROUFE		
B	Sonoma Vallejo	69 628
SROUSE		
D	Butte Kimshaw	56 586
S	Butte Kimshaw	56 586
SRRA		
---	Tuolumne Twp 5	71 514
SRUBODY		
Josiah*	Napa Yount	61 39
SRUCNEY		
Otto	Tuolumne Twp 3	71 438
SRUF		
Geo*	Sacramento Ward 1	63 27
SRUGULDR		
R*	Solano Vacaville	69 333
SRUINEY		
Otto*	Tuolumne Jamestown	71 438
SRUIRL		
L P*	Butte Oro	56 683
SRUM		
Joseph*	Nevada Rough &	61 424
SRUMP		
Jos	Butte Cascade	56 689
SRUS		
Robt*	Placer Rattle Snake	62 630
SRWDDIOIRS		
W W*	Butte Cascade	56 703
SRWER		
C F*	Sonoma Vallejo	69 627
SRY		
John N*	Trinity Weaverville	701078
SSCHUSTTZ		
Louis	San Francisco San Francisco 4	681161
SSEE		
---	Mariposa Twp 1	60 641
SSHALTIC		
Wm	Plumas Quincy	62 947
SSHILEWELL		
James P	Colusa Monroeville	57 457
SSING		
---	San Francisco San Francisco 2	67 754
---	Tuolumne Shawsfla	71 407
SSMITH		
Orange A	Tuolumne Jamestown	71 431
SSRECKLES		
Wm A	San Francisco San Francisco 6	67 424
SSRESLOCK		
Jno*	Butte Eureka	56 653
SSSTINKARD		
Arabella	Tulara Visalia	71 82
ST ANNA		
---	San Bernardino San Bernadino	64 677
Hosea	Alameda Brooklyn	55 156
ST CELAIR		
J	Nevada Grass Valley	61 143
ST CLAIR STEVEN		
D*	Sacramento Ward 4	63 558
ST CLAIR		
A	San Francisco San Francisco 2	67 671
A	Tuolumne Columbia	71 300
Abel	Plumas Quincy	62 973
Alonzo	Placer Secret R	62 611
Arthur	Alameda Brooklyn	55 204
Chas	San Francisco San Francisco 1	68 912
Henry	Sacramento Ward 1	63 12
J*	Nevada Grass Valley	61 174
Jno	Sonoma Petaluma	69 543
John	El Dorado Mountain	581187
John	San Francisco San Francisco 5	67 477
John	Solano Montezuma	69 372
Kate	Nevada Nevada	61 329
Peter	Sacramento American	63 166
Peter	Sierra La Porte	66 783
Robert	Solano Fremont	69 384
Saml	Sonoma Petaluma	69 596
Thos	Monterey Alisal	601035
Wm	El Dorado Mud Springs	58 979
ST CLAN		
Mary	Sierra Twp 7	66 901
ST CLARE		
Ann	Sierra Twp 7	66 915
John*	El Dorado Mountain	581187
Malvina	Placer Nicolaus	62 691
Mary	Sierra Twp 7	66 901
ST CYR		
Eugene	Tuolumne Sonora	71 242
Eugine*	Tuolumne Twp 1	71 242
ST DENNIS		
Peter	Stanislaus Branch	70 710
ST DINA		
---*	Mariposa Twp 3	60 570
ST DIVA		
---*	Mariposa Twp 3	60 570

Name	County Locale	M653 RollPage
ST FELIX		
Edward	Plumas Quincy	62 978
ST GEORGE		
John*	Nevada Bloomfield	61 516
ST GERMAN		
Eugene	Alameda Oakland	55 13
ST GIRD		
M	Sonoma Washington	69 666
ST JOHN		
C	Yolo Cottonwoood	72 555
Charles H	Tuolumne Twp 4	71 135
Charley	Colusa Monroeville	57 455
D B	Butte Ophir	56 823
David	Sacramento Ward 1	63 12
Ellen	Sierra Twp 7	66 894
F	Tuolumne Twp 4	71 149
Henry	Placer Todds Va	62 762
J*	El Dorado Kelsey	581149
Jeremiah	Tuolumne Big Oak	71 137
Louis	El Dorado White Oaks	581033
Nel	Butte Oregon	56 634
Patrick	Plumas Quincy	62 955
Pierce	Solano Vallejo	69 278
R	Butte Oregon	56 634
Reuben	El Dorado Salmon Falls	581035
W	El Dorado Salmon Falls	581056
W A	Placer Forest H	62 802
ST JOHNS		
Enos	Yuba Marysville	72 965
Jennie	Plumas Quincy	621005
Jennie	Sierra La Porte	66 771
S	Nevada Nevada	61 278
ST JOHNSON		
D	San Francisco San Francisco 10	194 67
ST LEWIS		
Oliver	Amador Twp 2	55 295
ST LOUIS		
C	Yolo Cache Crk	72 606
Charles	Nevada Bridgeport	61 474
Colbert	Yolo Cache Crk	72 624
E	Yolo Cache Crk	72 623
J	Yolo Cache Crk	72 624
Mary	San Francisco San Francisco 10	178 67
Wm	Alameda Brooklyn	55 83
ST MARIA		
Manuel	Placer Michigan	62 850
ST MARY		
Alexander	San Joaquin Castoria	64 886
Lewis	San Francisco San Francisco 3	67 72
Seasi	San Bernardino San Salvador	64 653
ST MASICO		
Manuel	Placer Michigan	62 850
ST MASSIE		
Louis	Siskiyou Callahan	69 3
ST PAUL		
Frank	Amador Twp 2	55 306
Jane	Alameda Brooklyn	55 127
John	Siskiyou Callahan	69 4
ST PERRE		
Perre	Contra Costa Twp 1	57 522
ST POHLKER		
J	San Francisco San Francisco 10	288 67
ST STONE		
W*	San Francisco San Francisco 6	67 414
ST SURE		
Chas	Butte Chico	56 533
ST TAYLOR		
W	San Francisco San Francisco 10	308 67
ST		
Diva*	Mariposa Twp 3	60 570
STAAK		
D	Los Angeles Tejon	59 526
STAANTON		
Michael P*	Calaveras Twp 4	57 318
STAARD		
C B	Nevada Nevada	61 279
STAATS		
Jos	San Francisco San Francisco 6	67 423
STABB		
Frederick	Yuba Marysville	72 939
STABBERD		
J L	Sonoma Armally	69 503
STABBINS		
Henry*	Tuolumne Columbia	71 326
STABBS		
D	Nevada Eureka	61 347
STABER		
L	El Dorado Placerville	58 858
STABLE		
Frederick	Yuba Marysville	72 865
Henry*	San Francisco San Francisco 2	67 763
Jolnez	El Dorado Greenwood	58 721

Name	County Locale	M653 RollPage
STABLE		
Walter	Santa Clara San Jose	65 387
STABLER		
S J	Sutter Yuba	70 771
STACEK		
George	Sierra Downieville	66 969
STACEY		
George	Sierra Downieville	66 969
Henry	San Francisco San Francisco 9	681074
M V B	Solano Suisan	69 210
W H	Nevada Bridgeport	61 449
STACFORD		
Charles*	Yuba Marysville	72 904
STACHLER		
F	Tuolumne Twp 4	71 153
STACIA		
---	San Bernardino S Timate	64 722
---	San Bernardino S Timate	64 730
STACK		
Edward H	Alameda Brooklyn	55 156
J	Shasta Horsetown	66 697
John	San Francisco San Francisco 1	68 854
John H	Yolo Putah	72 588
STACKABAL		
Geo	Trinity Whites Crk	701028
STACKER		
Augustus	Tuolumne Twp 1	71 268
STACKFORD		
Wm	San Francisco San Francisco 1	68 878
STACKHOUSE		
Adelaide	San Francisco San Francisco 1	68 824
George	Tehama Tehama	70 938
James	Placer Michigan	62 815
Sylvester*	Sacramento Centre	63 174
Thomas	Contra Costa Twp 3	57 586
STACKLER		
F	Tuolumne Big Oak	71 153
STACKMAN		
Henry*	Calaveras Twp 5	57 140
John	El Dorado Salmon Falls	581044
STACKMANHENRY		
Ginn	San Joaquin Stockton	641041
STACKMILLER		
Vincent	Mendocino Big Rvr	60 842
STACKPOLE		
C	Tuolumne Twp 2	71 273
Charles	Sierra Twp 5	66 920
Chas E*	Nevada Red Dog	61 545
STACKPOLI		
Chas E*	Nevada Red Dog	61 545
STACKPOLO		
Charles	Sierra Twp 5	66 920
STACKPORE		
J	El Dorado Mud Springs	58 967
STACKS		
Joseph	Plumas Meadow Valley	62 903
STACOM		
Maria	San Francisco San Francisco 2	67 649
STACR		
Wm*	Calaveras Twp 10	57 294
STACY		
Abram	Nevada Bridgeport	61 444
Ed	Tehama Tehama	70 939
Geo	Santa Clara Redwood	65 454
John	Santa Clara Santa Clara	65 490
William	Mendocino Big Rvr	60 850
STADANT		
John*	Stanislaus Emory	70 743
STADAO		
S*	El Dorado Placerville	58 892
STADDAM		
Wm	Santa Clara San Jose	65 288
STADE		
Frderick	Tuolumne Twp 4	71 144
Fred*	Calaveras Twp 6	57 117
Frederick*	Tuolumne Big Oak	71 144
L	Mariposa Twp 3	60 600
STADERMEN		
Chas	San Francisco San Francisco 3	67 86
STADLER		
Thos	Shasta Horsetown	66 699
STADMIRE		
Nelson	Sacramento Ward 1	63 114
STADS		
J	Sutter Sutter	70 817
STADZINSKY		
Benj	San Francisco San Francisco 7	681405
STAE		
George	Calaveras Twp 4	57 342
STAEL		
Rachard	Placer Dutch Fl	62 726
STAFAN		
Louisa	San Francisco San Francisco 9	68 979
STAFANY		
August	El Dorado Mud Springs	58 964
STAFF		
G P	Mariposa Twp 3	60 575

Name	County Locale	M653 Roll	Page
STAFF			
John	Calaveras Twp 4	57	340
John	Sacramento Ward 1	63	63
Mary T*	Mariposa Twp 3	60	575
Wilson	Tuolumne Twp 1	71	249
STAFFER			
F	El Dorado Georgetown	58	682
Jas	Sonoma Sonoma	69	646
P	El Dorado Diamond	58	811
STAFFERD			
G W*	Tehama Red Bluff	70	915
John	Butte Ophir	56	783
John	San Francisco San Francisco 9	68	944
STAFFERTON			
Andrew	San Diego Colorado	64	807
STAFFETHACH			
C*	San Francisco San Francisco 9	68	1052
STAFFIRD			
William	Colusa Grand Island	57	476
STAFFON			
A	El Dorado Diamond	58	804
STAFFOR			
Jas	Sonoma Sonoma	69	646
STAFFORCE			
Eugene	Calaveras Twp 7	57	4
STAFFORD			
A J	Shasta Horsetown	66	696
A K	Tuolumne Columbia	71	289
Ben	Amador Twp 3	55	403
C	Calaveras Twp 9	57	375
C N	Mariposa Twp 1	60	659
C W	Mariposa Twp 1	60	659
C*	Calaveras Twp 9	57	375
Charles	San Mateo Twp 3	65	85
Chas	Santa Clara Santa Clara	65	515
E F	San Joaquin Stockton	64	1079
E M	Nevada Eureka	61	362
Eugene	Calaveras Twp 7	57	4
G W*	Tehama Red Bluff	70	915
Geo	Trinity Minersville	70	968
Geo W	Calaveras Twp 4	57	309
George	San Mateo Twp 3	65	85
Henry	Los Angeles Los Angeles	59	373
Henry	San Diego Colorado	64	806
J A	Trinity Arkansas	70	1004
J B	Marin San Rafael	60	765
J C	El Dorado Coloma	58	1116
J E	Amador Twp 3	55	405
James	El Dorado Placerville	58	927
John	Butte Ophir	56	783
John	San Francisco San Francisco 9	68	944
John	Sierra Pine Grove	66	819
John A	Calaveras Twp 7	57	28
M	Calaveras Twp 9	57	396
M	San Francisco San Francisco 5	67	552
Margaret	Nevada Bridgeport	61	441
Mary	Sacramento Ward 4	63	509
Mary	Sonoma Petaluma	69	597
Mary	Yuba Fosters	72	829
Mary Frances	Solano Benecia	69	300
Mary V	Yuba Foster B	72	829
Mary*	Sonoma Petaluma	69	597
R S	Butte Oregon	56	623
Robert	Contra Costa Twp 1	57	514
Sarah	San Mateo Twp 3	65	85
Sidney J*	Calaveras Twp 8	57	79
Stephen	El Dorado Eldorado	58	938
Stephen	Mariposa Twp 1	60	644
Stephin	Mariposa Twp 1	60	644
T	Sacramento Ward 1	63	8
Theodore	San Mateo Twp 3	65	99
Thos	Sacramento Ward 3	63	452
Thos	Sacramento Ward 4	63	509
W	El Dorado Kelsey	58	1157
W	Nevada Grass Valley	61	201
W J	Butte Oregon	56	612
W Y	Butte Oregon	56	612
William	Solano Vallejo	69	269
William M	Tulara Visalia	71	96
Wilson*	Sonoma Petaluma	69	595
STAFFRY			
T	Nevada Nevada	61	316
STAFIN			
John	Marin Cortemad	60	755
STAFNEY			
C	El Dorado Kelsey	58	1135
STAFORD			
A H	Tuolumne Twp 2	71	289
Seaman*	Humbolt Pacific	59	134
STAGE			
Edward	Yuba Marysville	72	951
STAGEBUN			
B B	Sacramento Ward 4	63	530
STAGEMANN			
Jacob	Colusa Spring Valley	57	431
STAGER			
Henry	Placer Yankee J	62	782

Name	County Locale	M653 Roll	Page
STAGERD			
Geo	Butte Bidwell	56	721
STAGES			
Geo	El Dorado White Oaks	58	1031
John*	Mariposa Twp 3	60	586
STAGG			
Jacob	Santa Cruz Soquel	66	596
Thomas A	Yuba Marysville	72	931
Warner	Plumas Meadow Valley	62	912
Wm	Stanislaus Emory	70	740
STAGGER			
Ann	Santa Cruz Santa Cruz	66	621
STAGGI			
Joseph	Santa Clara Santa Clara	65	482
STAGGS			
Catherine	San Francisco San Francisco 4	68	1115
STAGLE			
Frank	San Francisco San Francisco 7	68	1339
John	El Dorado Placerville	58	898
STAGLICH			
August	Tuolumne Columbia	71	340
STAGMIRE			
Frederick	Yuba Marysville	72	977
STAGNEY			
Wm	Napa Clear Lake	61	136
STAGORD			
Geo	Butte Bidwell	56	721
STAGOREY			
C	El Dorado Kelsey	58	1135
STAGRELL			
J A	El Dorado Placerville	58	847
STAGS			
Edward	Yuba Marysville	72	951
STAGUIRE			
Frederick	Yuba Marysville	72	977
STAGUNO			
Francisco	El Dorado Placerville	58	900
STAHKER			
E W	Tuolumne Sonora	71	484
STAHL			
C G	San Francisco San Francisco 5	67	488
Christian G	San Francisco 10		260
	San Francisco	67	
E	San Francisco San Francisco 6	67	418
Frederick	Yuba Marysville	72	939
J G	Butte Oregon	56	627
James	Yuba Marysville	72	882
Jno	Sacramento Ward 1	63	33
John	El Dorado Kelsey	58	1134
John A	Sierra St Louis	66	814
Joseph	El Dorado Kelsey	58	1140
Solomon	Yuba Marysville	72	872
Thomas C	Yuba Marysville	72	910
STAHLE			
Henry	San Francisco San Francisco 2	67	763
Henry*	San Francisco San Francisco 2	67	763
Henry*	San Francisco San Francisco 2	67	764
STAHLHUTH			
G	Tuolumne Sonora	71	207
STAHLI			
Frank*	Alameda Brooklyn	55	152
STAIDIVANT			
A	Tuolumne Twp 2	71	285
STAIGER			
William U*	San Francisco 7	68	1419
	San Francisco		
STAIL			
G C	Tehama Red Bluff	70	917
STAIN			
J	Amador Twp 1	55	466
STAINE			
E*	Nevada Eureka	61	389
STAINLY			
Nicholas*	Plumas Quincy	62	972
STAIP			
Conrad	San Francisco San Francisco 7	68	1422
STAIR			
Alexander	Tuolumne Twp 5	71	489
STAIRGEL			
A C	Placer Virginia	62	667
STAKE			
Peter Jr	Colusa Spring Valley	57	431
STAKEMIN			
R	El Dorado Diamond	58	807
STAKER			
John W	Placer Ophirville	62	657
Mel??Thew*	Siskiyou Yreka	69	143
Melanthon*	Siskiyou Yreka	69	143
Melemathew*	Siskiyou Yreka	69	143
Melvinthon*	Siskiyou Yreka	69	143
STAKERMINE			
J	El Dorado Diamond	58	811
STAKES			
A G	Stanislaus Emory	70	748
Charles J*	Tuolumne Twp 3	71	431
G M	Siskiyou Scott Va	69	29

Name	County Locale	M653 Roll	Page
STAKES			
H*	El Dorado Kelsey	58	1155
J J	El Dorado Placerville	58	881
Jas R	Mariposa Twp 1	60	644
Jessee	Santa Clara Santa Clara	65	522
Jonathan	Santa Clara San Jose	65	382
Sarah A	Tuolumne Jamestown	71	431
William	El Dorado White Oaks	58	1024
STAKEUP			
Jeffe	Klamath S Fork	59	203
STAKEY			
J F	Sierra Downieville	66	961
STAKLE			
Elizabeth	San Francisco San Francisco 2	67	680
STAKLEY			
Jacob	Siskiyou Yreka	69	168
STALAIR			
A	Tuolumne Twp 1	71	278
STALCUP			
Sarah	Yuba Long Bar	72	746
Smith	Yuba Parke Ba	72	781
STALDEN			
H	El Dorado Coloma	58	1083
STALDER			
Joseph	Yuba Long Bar	72	751
STALE			
Abraham	San Francisco San Francisco 10		307
		67	
J T*	San Francisco San Francisco 6	67	412
STALEN			
Adonigah	Santa Clara Gilroy	65	225
Joseph	Santa Clara Gilroy	65	225
STALENP			
Sarah*	Yuba New York	72	746
STALES			
Geo	El Dorado Mud Springs	58	996
STALEY			
Angelina	Sonoma Santa Rosa	69	424
F	Nevada Eureka	61	375
F	Sonoma Washington	69	664
Isaac	Sonoma Washington	69	664
R	El Dorado Placerville	58	835
Thos	San Francisco San Francisco 9	68	1012
STALFORD			
Jacob	San Francisco San Francisco 2	67	622
STALHAN			
Henry	Mendocino Anderson	60	866
STALIS			
W	Yolo Putah	72	551
STALKER			
Daniel	Sierra Twp 7	66	895
Wm	Sacramento Ward 1	63	141
Wm	Sacramento Ward 1	63	62
STALKING			
G	San Joaquin Stockton	64	1099
STALKUM			
J	Nevada Eureka	61	364
STALL			
G F	San Francisco San Francisco 3	67	55
H	Yolo Cottonwoood	72	653
Isaac M*	San Francisco San Francisco 10		344
		67	
John	Sierra St Louis	66	816
Lewis*	Sonoma Petaluma	69	605
M	Nevada Nevada	61	254
William	Sierra St Louis	66	810
STALLAPEN			
E S*	El Dorado Placerville	58	909
STALLARD			
Thomas*	Siskiyou Yreka	69	126
STALLCUP			
Jesse	Klamath S Fork	59	203
STALLE			
Frederick*	Tuolumne Big Oak	71	144
STALLIGAN			
Kate Miss	San Francisco San Francisco 10		181
		67	
STALLMAN			
Christina	San Francisco San Francisco 7	68	1399
James S	San Francisco San Francisco 7	68	1431
STALLMIEL			
B	Siskiyou Scott Va	69	32
STALLO			
Theo D	Fresno Millerto	59	2
STALLRNIEL			
B*	Siskiyou Scott Va	69	32
STALLRY			
T*	Nevada Nevada	61	316
STALLS			
M*	Nevada Washington	61	333
STALMILLER			
Jacob	Siskiyou Yreka	69	141
STALTEZ			
Fred	Tuolumne Columbia	71	338
STALTS			
M*	Nevada Washington	61	333

Name	County Locale	M653 Roll	Page
STALTZ			
Fred	Tuolumne Twp 2	71	338
STALY			
???S*	Sonoma Washington	69	664
James*	Sonoma Washington	69	664
STAM			
Edward	Yolo No E Twp	72	668
STAMALL			
Barbara*	San Joaquin Stockton	641	051
STAMANR			
C	El Dorado Diamond	58	811
STAMBEAN			
Peter*	Butte Oregon	56	638
STAMBEAU			
Peter*	Butte Oregon	56	638
STAMBER			
Florence*	Alameda Brooklyn	55	132
STAMBEUU			
Peter	Butte Oregon	56	638
STAMBOW			
S*	San Mateo Twp 3	65	82
STAMD			
Thomas*	Sierra Downieville	661	006
STAME			
C W	Placer Illinois	62	706
STAMER			
John	San Francisco San Francisco 1	68	905
STAMES			
Samuel	Amador Twp 6	55	428
STAMFIELD			
Hetty*	Yuba Parks Ba	72	774
STAMFLY			
Nicholas*	Plumas Quincy	62	972
STAMFLYS			
Frank	Plumas Quincy	62	971
STAMFORD			
Charly	Tuolumne Twp 2	71	275
STAMFSER			
Mary	San Joaquin Castoria	64	908
STAMJERS			
Juan	Mariposa Twp 3	60	573
STAMMOJOCH			
Mary	San Francisco San Francisco 4	681	162
STAMNER			
William	Tuolumne Twp 1	71	193
STAMNS			
William	Tuolumne Sonora	71	193
STAMP			
Henry	San Francisco San Francisco 2	67	632
John	Alameda Brooklyn	55	143
STAMPE			
Auguste	San Francisco San Francisco 2	67	701
Henry	Placer Iona Hills	62	888
STAMPER			
Jas	San Francisco San Francisco 2	67	775
Jos	San Francisco San Francisco 2	67	775
Julius	San Francisco San Francisco 7	681	431
Michael	Tuolumne Big Oak	71	128
P	Tuolumne Twp 4	71	175
STAMPFT			
Franklin	San Francisco San Francisco 7	681	395
STAMPLEY			
Arville*	Santa Cruz Santa Cruz	66	619
Orville	Santa Cruz Santa Cruz	66	619
STAMPS			
C F	Sonoma Armally	69	499
John	Amador Twp 3	55	405
V G	Tuolumne Jamestown	71	470
STAMSLOWSKEY			
Gustus	Humbolt Union	59	182
STAMTER			
Florence*	Alameda Brooklyn	55	132
STAMTROW			
S*	San Mateo Twp 3	65	82
STAMTSON			
William B	San Joaquin Castoria	64	908
STAMYON			
Chs H	San Francisco San Francisco 9	68	961
STAN			
Nicolas	Sacramento Dry Crk	63	371
STANAKER			
---	Siskiyou Scott Va	69	38
STANARD			
D C	Calaveras Twp 7	57	15
STANARIAN			
Jofhn	El Dorado Placerville	58	932
STANAS			
Charles	Santa Clara Almaden	65	274
STANAWAY			
I	El Dorado Diamond	58	785
STANB			
Adolf	San Francisco San Francisco 7	681	037
STANBAUGH			
Walter	Plumas Quincy	62	954
STANBON			
Jno B*	Nevada Nevada	61	241

Name	County Locale	M653 Roll	Page
STANBRY			
H A	Mariposa Twp 1	60	637
H H	Mariposa Twp 1	60	637
STANBURN			
A H	Nevada Nevada	61	267
STANBURY			
James	Tuolumne Sonora	71	238
John	Santa Clara San Jose	65	382
STANCLIFF			
Reuben	Yuba Long Bar	72	754
STANCLIFFE			
Wm	Placer Rattle Snake	62	628
STAND			
A	Sutter Yuba	70	768
STANDAGE			
Hiram	Contra Costa Twp 2	57	546
John	Contra Costa Twp 3	57	587
STANDARD			
Geo	Sacramento Ward 3	63	458
James	Contra Costa Twp 2	57	574
John	Calaveras Twp 8	57	70
Richard C	Calaveras Twp 5	57	202
STANDARDS			
H G	Butte Wyandotte	56	660
STANDARED			
Richard C	Calaveras Twp 5	57	202
STANDEFORD			
J W	Napa Hot Springs	61	25
John*	Napa Hot Springs	61	25
Saml	Santa Clara Fremont	65	422
STANDER			
C	San Francisco San Francisco 2	67	629
Henry	Placer Yankee J	62	781
Richard	San Joaquin Oneal	64	938
STANDFORD			
Mary	Sacramento Ward 4	63	556
W W	El Dorado Mud Springs	58	949
William	El Dorado Salmon Falls	581	055
STANDIFEN			
William	Tulara Twp 3	71	49
STANDIFER			
William	Tulara Keeneysburg	71	49
STANDISH			
G W	Tuolumne Twp 1	71	273
G W	Tuolumne Twp 1	71	276
J I	El Dorado Diamond	58	764
Philande H	Contra Costa Twp 3	57	610
Tyranus	Contra Costa Twp 3	57	610
W G	Napa Napa	61	59
STANDIWICK			
Jas	San Francisco San Francisco 2	67	658
STANDLE			
George	Plumas Quincy	62	978
STANDLEY			
M	El Dorado Gold Hill	581	095
STANDLIR			
J*	Sutter Yuba	70	763
STANDON			
T	El Dorado Placerville	58	866
STANDORDS			
H G	Butte Wyandotte	56	660
STANDTSFORD			
Jacob	San Francisco San Francisco 2	67	626
STANDWOOD			
N D	Yolo Washington	72	565
STANE			
J F*	Sierra Twp 5	66	921
STANEDING			
H E	El Dorado Georgetown	58	697
STANELS			
Julia	San Francisco San Francisco 1	68	912
STANESH			
Charles*	Sierra Downieville	661	007
STANESLEA			
Samuel*	Alameda Oakland	55	70
STANESTEA			
Samuel*	Alameda Oakland	55	70
STANFENBERG			
Geo	Humbolt Eel Rvr	59	154
STANFERD			
Thos	Mariposa Twp 3	60	560
STANFFER			
Benedict	Yolo Cottonwoood	72	654
STANFIELD			
Ashley B	Sonoma Russian	69	432
Ellen	San Francisco San Francisco 10	183 67	
John	San Francisco San Francisco 5	67	546
Letty*	Yuba Parks Ba	72	774
Margaret	Stanislaus Emory	70	740
Martin	Nevada Rough &	61	398
Moses	Sacramento Ward 4	63	507
Phillip	San Francisco San Francisco 9	681	037
Robert	Siskiyou Yreka	69	156
STANFORD			
C	Nevada Grass Valley	61	155

Name	County Locale	M653 Roll	Page
STANFORD			
Charles	Marin Point Re	60	732
Charles	Tuolumne Twp 1	71	275
E V	El Dorado Placerville	58	931
Elijah*	Placer Michigan	62	818
Genl Jackson	Napa Clear Lake	61	136
John	San Francisco San Francisco 11	131 67	
Leland	Sacramento Ward 1	63	76
O P	Placer Michigan	62	836
Thos	Mariposa Twp 3	60	560
Thos	Napa Clear Lake	61	135
STANGER			
George	Sierra Twp 7	66	916
STANGHLER			
M S	Sierra St Louis	66	865
STANGHTERBECK			
John*	El Dorado Coloma	581	103
STANGROM			
Mathew	Placer Michigan	62	820
STANGROVON			
C W	Nevada Nevada	61	258
STANHAN			
Thos	El Dorado Georgetown	58	690
STANHOPE			
C	Trinity Douglas	70	978
F A	Yolo Cottonwoood	72	651
Fredk	Calaveras Twp 4	57	323
STANIELS			
Wm	San Francisco San Francisco 10	305 67	
STANISLADO			
---	Marin Cortemad	60	792
STANISLAUS S			
---	San Mateo Twp 1	65	63
STANISLAUS			
---	San Mateo Twp 1	65	60
STANISTACIS			
Mary Siste	Santa Clara San Jose	65	373
STANISTAN			
Jose	Santa Clara San Jose	65	323
STANLEY			
A	El Dorado Salmon Falls	581	057
Alere J	Calaveras Twp 10	57	277
Alex	Calaveras Twp 10	57	277
Andw	Sonoma Petaluma	69	553
Anne	Solano Suisan	69	217
Archalus	Sacramento Natonia	63	276
Asa	Plumas Quincy	621	006
Augustus	Nevada Red Dog	61	555
Benj	Alameda Brooklyn	55	126
C A	San Francisco San Francisco 6	67	416
C H	Siskiyou Yreka	69	153
Charles	Los Angeles Los Angeles	59	354
Chas	San Francisco San Francisco 1	68	920
Edward	San Francisco San Francisco 7	681	439
Elizabeth	Sonoma Petaluma	69	545
Elzoda	Sonoma Petaluma	69	553
F	Siskiyou Cottonwoood	69	98
F B	Butte Bidwell	56	711
Frank	San Francisco San Francisco 9	681	073
Franklin	Contra Costa Twp 2	57	544
Frederick	Yuba Marysville	72	945
Geo	Alameda Brooklyn	55	186
George A	Calaveras Twp 10	57	266
H M	Siskiyou Scott Ri	69	71
Harrey	Marin S Antoni	60	711
Harrison	Mendocino Ukiah	60	793
Henry	Alameda Brooklyn	55	86
Isac	Mariposa Twp 3	60	574
J	Nevada Eureka	61	353
J J	Sonoma Mendocino	69	466
J N	San Joaquin Stockton	641	099
J R	Sacramento Cosumnes	63	380
J R	Sacramento Casumnes	63	381
J R A	Tuolumne Springfield	71	370
J S*	El Dorado Diamond	58	775
James	El Dorado Greenwood	58	713
James	Nevada Little Y	61	532
Jas	Amador Twp 1	55	455
Jno R	Alameda Brooklyn	55	93
John	Amador Twp 3	55	405
John	Colusa Monroeville	57	447
John	El Dorado White Oaks	581	010
John	Los Angeles Tejon	59	522
John	Mendocino Ukiah	60	799
John	Placer Rattle Snake	62	635
John	San Joaquin Elkhorn	64	997
John	Santa Clara Redwood	65	456
John	Siskiyou Scott Va	69	32
John C	Sierra Downieville	66	964
John P	Amador Twp 6	55	441
John W	Sonoma Mendocino	69	449
Joseph	Mendocino Calpella	60	820
Josiah	Marin Tomales	60	721
L	Sacramento Ward 3	63	458

California 1860 Census Index

Name	County Locale	M653 RollPage
STANLEY		
Lonas R*	Mendocino Ukiah	60 796
Lonis R	Mendocino Ukiah	60 796
Malrida J	Sacramento Ward 3	63 468
Margaret	Calaveras Twp 6	57 129
N	Colusa Monroeville	57 446
O H	Siskiyou Yreka	69 153
O P	Shasta Shasta	66 663
R	Siskiyou Cottonwoood	69 98
R D	El Dorado Placerville	58 863
Saml L	San Francisco San Francisco 9	681078
Sarah	Sonoma Petaluma	69 553
Sol	Sonoma Mendocino	69 448
Thomas	Calaveras Twp 6	57 148
Thos	Alameda Brooklyn	55 90
Thos	Sonoma Mendocino	69 448
Thos B	Alameda Brooklyn	55 186
Wesley	Sacramento Natonia	63 277
Wesly	Sacramento Natonia	63 277
William	Siskiyou Scott Va	69 30
William	Tuolumne Twp 3	71 453
William B	Sierra Pine Grove	66 820
Wm	Sacramento Natonia	63 288
Wm	Sacramento Sutter	63 303
Wm S	Sonoma Mendocino	69 448
STANLON		
L	Nevada Nevada	61 288
STANLY		
---	Shasta Shasta	66 668
G W	Sonoma Petaluma	69 602
Harvey	Marin S Antoni	60 711
Henry	El Dorado Georgetown	58 706
Mitchell*	Mariposa Twp 3	60 575
S K	Mariposa Twp 3	60 575
Samuel	Plumas Meadow Valley	62 928
Sk	Mariposa Twp 3	60 575
STANMIER		
Frederick W	Yuba Marysville	72 943
STANMITZ		
Jacob	Amador Twp 4	55 236
STANNARD		
E	San Francisco San Francisco 5	67 542
STANNEDY		
William	Shasta Shasta	66 761
STANNEL		
Horatiow	Yuba Marysville	72 885
STANNEN		
Geo	El Dorado Kelsey	581134
STANNSCE		
Frederick W*	Yuba Marysville	72 943
STANNTON		
Michael P*	Calaveras Twp 4	57 318
STANNTOR		
Jams	Alameda Brooklyn	55 103
STANNTOS		
James	Alameda Brooklyn	55 103
STANS		
David	El Dorado Casumnes	581166
STANSBERRY		
Geo	Siskiyou Scott Ri	69 78
STANSBOROIGH		
Jas L*	San Francisco San Francisco 1	68 916
STANSBORORIGH		
Js L*	San Francisco San Francisco 1	68 916
STANSBURY		
David	El Dorado Mud Springs	58 982
Francis	Humbolt Pacific	59 133
Geo	Siskiyou Scott Ri	69 78
Jno S	Sacramento Ward 4	63 594
STANSEL		
Ervin	Tulara Twp 3	71 45
STANSEN		
Kate*	Sacramento Ward 4	63 545
STANSH		
Charles	Sierra Downieville	661007
STANSLEN		
D D	Sutter Butte	70 796
STANSON		
Antonio	San Francisco San Francisco 1	68 906
Joshua	Placer Forest H	62 794
STANT		
John	Amador Twp 3	55 381
STANTEN		
E*	Alameda Brooklyn	55 93
Wm	Butte Bidwell	56 730
STANTIN		
Jno B*	Nevada Nevada	61 241
L	Nevada Nevada	61 288
STANTLEY		
Tyne	San Joaquin Elkhorn	64 996
STANTON		
Alford	El Dorado Georgetown	58 687
Alfred	El Dorado Georgetown	58 687
Alonzo P	Calaveras Twp 6	57 156
Andrew P	San Francisco San Francisco 12	379 67

Name	County Locale	M653 RollPage
STANTON		
Benj	Sacramento Franklin	63 314
Bridget	San Francisco San Francisco 8	681249
Bridwell Clion	Yuba Marysville	72 898
Charles	Sacramento Ward 1	63 123
Charles	Sierra Twp 7	66 912
Chas	San Francisco San Francisco 9	681089
Danl	San Francisco San Francisco 1	68 838
E	Alameda Brooklyn	55 93
Edwd	Sacramento Brighton	63 192
F	Tuolumne Twp 1	71 230
Frederick	Sierra Downieville	66 976
G W	Amador Twp 4	55 254
George	San Francisco San Francisco 5	67 522
George W	Yuba Marysville	72 863
J	Sutter Nicolaus	70 830
J E	El Dorado Georgetown	58 687
James	San Francisco San Francisco 11	114 67
James	San Francisco San Francisco 4	681229
James	San Francisco San Francisco 8	681269
James	San Francisco San Francisco 3	67 81
James	Sierra Eureka	661043
John	Nevada Rough &	61 407
John	San Francisco San Francisco 4	681157
John	San Francisco San Francisco 1	68 855
John	Yolo Washington	72 605
Margaret	Yuba Marysville	72 881
Patk	Sacramento Mississipi	63 188
Patrick*	El Dorado Kelsey	581142
Perrin	Sacramento Ward 4	63 566
T E	El Dorado Georgetown	58 687
Thomas	Alameda Oakland	55 16
Thomas	Santa Cruz Santa Cruz	66 618
Thomas	Santa Cruz Santa Cruz	66 619
Thos	San Francisco San Francisco 1	68 906
William	Nevada Rough &	61 407
STANULAUS		
---	San Bernardino Santa Ba	64 214
STANWELL		
Thos	San Francisco San Francisco 1	68 904
STANWOOD		
D	Trinity Trinity	70 975
Edwin C	Humbolt Pacific	59 137
K P	Placer Forest H	62 799
N D	Yolo Washington	72 565
Richard	Yuba Marysville	72 850
Richard G*	Yuba Marysville	72 850
Saml	Nevada Nevada	61 241
Saml	Sacramento Ward 4	63 524
Saml	Sacramento Ward 1	63 73
Saml*	Nevada Nevada	61 241
W	San Francisco San Francisco 6	67 446
Wm	Sacramento Ward 1	63 107
STANYON		
Chs H*	San Francisco San Francisco 9	68 961
STANYOW		
Chs H*	San Francisco San Francisco 9	68 961
STAPBACK		
John C	Sierra Downieville	66 971
STAPE		
John A	Sierra St Louis	66 814
STAPELS		
Daniel	Calaveras Twp 5	57 240
STAPETON		
John	San Francisco San Francisco 10	334 67
STAPHI		
M	El Dorado Placerville	58 822
STAPLE		
Jacob	San Francisco San Francisco 1	68 916
STAPLEN		
Jno*	Sacramento Mississipi	63 188
STAPLER		
Charles	El Dorado Casumnes	581174
Samuel	Mendocino Big Rvr	60 840
STAPLES		
A F	Calaveras Twp 9	57 376
A J	Marin Bolinas	60 727
Alley P	Alameda Oakland	55 61
Alpheus	Alameda Oakland	55 60
C	Tuolumne Twp 2	71 345
Chas	Amador Twp 3	55 399
Chas	Merced Twp 1	60 915
Daniel	Calaveras Twp 5	57 240
David J	San Joaquin Elkhorn	64 987
E O	Calaveras Twp 9	57 391
Ellen E	San Francisco San Francisco 7	681414
F	El Dorado Georgetown	58 682
F O	San Francisco San Francisco 3	67 16
Frank F	Calaveras Twp 6	57 157
Frederick	San Joaquin Elkhorn	64 987
Geo W	San Francisco San Francisco 10	280 67
Isabella	San Joaquin Stockton	641089
J A	San Francisco San Francisco 5	67 535

Name	County Locale	M653 RollPage
STAPLES		
J N	Sutter Nicolaus	70 841
Joseph	El Dorado Coloma	581082
L	Shasta Shasta	66 735
Mariah	Sonoma Petaluma	69 565
Marshall	Placer Virginia	62 664
Samuel	Mendocino Big Rvr	60 840
Seth	Marin S Antoni	60 705
Solomon	Solano Vacaville	69 346
Thomas	Nevada Bloomfield	61 519
W B	San Francisco San Francisco 5	67 535
STAPLETON		
Alex	El Dorado Eldorado	58 937
Harrison	Plumas Quincy	62 977
Henry	Yuba Marysville	72 869
Patrick	San Joaquin Douglass	64 923
Ros	Santa Clara San Jose	65 333
T	El Dorado Diamond	58 793
Wm	Tehama Antelope	70 885
STAPLIN		
Jno*	Sacramento Mississipi	63 188
STAPP		
Andrew	Nevada Rough &	61 420
D*	Nevada Bridgeport	61 477
G P*	Mariposa Twp 3	60 575
Howard*	Yuba New York	72 738
Isaac N	Sonoma Mendocino	69 455
Martha E	Sonoma Mendocino	69 455
Mary T*	Mariposa Twp 3	60 575
Wm	Los Angeles Los Angeles	59 490
Wm	Placer Auburn	62 589
STAPPARD		
Moses	Mendocino Little L	60 834
STAPPE		
Howard	Yuba New York	72 738
STAPPIRBECK		
E	Tuolumne Sonora	71 192
STAPPORBICK		
E	Tuolumne Twp 1	71 192
STAR		
Eben	Nevada Rough &	61 395
Even	Nevada Rough &	61 395
Monrow	El Dorado Mud Springs	58 969
STARAR		
Jacob	Humbolt Eel Rvr	59 154
STARBIRD		
R J	Tuolumne Columbia	71 318
STARBROCK		
Jacob	Sierra Twp 7	66 902
STARBUCK		
Geo	San Francisco San Francisco 10	168 67
John B	Placer Mealsburg	62 702
S	San Joaquin Stockton	641035
STARCENGGEN		
G*	Tuolumne Columbia	71 333
STARCENGGER		
G	Tuolumne Twp 2	71 333
STARCHIN		
---	Mendocino Big Rock	60 874
STARD		
Paul*	Mariposa Twp 3	60 560
STARDE		
Edward*	Calaveras Twp 6	57 128
STARE		
Alexander	Tuolumne Chinese	71 489
Jerry	Sierra Poker Flats	66 842
Samuel	El Dorado Grizzly	581180
STAREN		
Charles**	Yuba Marysville	72 893
STARFON		
L B	El Dorado Placerville	58 835
STARGES		
James H	El Dorado Salmon Falls	581047
STARHITE		
Geo	Butte Hamilton	56 515
STARING		
Edwin	Tuolumne Twp 2	71 321
Edwin	Tuolumne Twp 2	71 331
STARK		
A B	Nevada Bridgeport	61 451
A D	Solano Vacaville	69 343
A M	Yuba Rose Bar	72 817
Alexander	San Francisco San Francisco 11	90 67
C K	El Dorado Placerville	58 880
C S	Placer Virginia	62 673
Charles	San Francisco San Francisco 7	681416
Isaac	Butte Chico	56 561
Isham	Tuolumne Twp 1	71 484
J	El Dorado Placerville	58 865
J	Tehama Red Bluff	70 913
J J C	Tuolumne Shawsfla	71 384
J S	Napa Napa	61 87
Jas	Sacramento Granite	63 244
Jas*	Santa Clara San Jose	65 321

California 1860 Census Index

Name	County Locale	M653 Roll	Page
STARK			
Jno W	San Francisco San Francisco	10	179 67
John	Yuba Rose Bar	72	789
John	Yuba Rose Bar	72	792
John H*	Yolo Putah	72	588
Lewis	Tulara Visalia	71	103
Michael	Yuba New York	72	734
Mick*	Sacramento Ward 4	63	553
R R	Amador Twp 2	55	318
R W	Sutter Yuba	70	764
Richard	Calaveras Twp 6	57	162
Robert	Tulara Sinks Te	71	43
Thomas	Plumas Quincy	62	963
Thos	Nevada Rough &	61	410
Urich*	Sacramento Ward 4	63	553
W R	Butte Wyandotte	56	662
Wm	Santa Clara San Jose	65	391
STARKARATHIN			
James*	Placer Michigan	62	838
STARKARTHER			
Alfred	San Joaquin Elkhorn	64	971
STARKASATHIN			
James*	Placer Michigan	62	838
STARKE			
Amy	Sonoma Petaluma	69	590
Fred	Sonoma Petaluma	69	559
Joseph	Alameda Brooklyn	55	197
STARKENGTHER			
Eugene*	Placer Michigan	62	838
STARKER			
Charles	Tuolumne Shawsfla	71	403
STARKES			
Charles J	Tuolumne Jamestown	71	431
J A	El Dorado Newtown	58	779
W H	El Dorado Newtown	58	779
STARKEY			
A T	Alameda Brooklyn	55	168
Anna	San Francisco San Francisco 8	68	1318
Isaiah	Mendocino Calpella	60	814
Isniah*	Mendocino Calpella	60	814
J	San Francisco San Francisco 2	67	805
Robert	San Francisco San Francisco 1	68	884
Singleton	Sonoma Petaluma	69	556
Thomas	Plumas Quincy	62	955
STARKLEY			
John	El Dorado Mud Springs	58	954
M*	Yolo Putah	72	552
Morgan	El Dorado Casumnes	58	1168
Thomas	Yuba Marysville	72	960
STARKMAN			
James	El Dorado Georgetown	58	704
STARKS			
---	Amador Twp 2	55	307
A D	Solano Vacaville	69	343
George W	Sierra Scales D	66	801
Hu A	Tuolumne Big Oak	71	145
Jesse	Los Angeles Tejon	59	522
Mary	Mariposa Twp 3	60	588
Robert	Tulara Twp 3	71	43
Thos	Amador Twp 6	55	426
STARLING			
F	El Dorado Placerville	58	893
STARMAH			
---	Del Norte Klamath	58	657
STARMAN			
J H	Calaveras Twp 9	57	356
Jno	Butte Hamilton	56	516
STARMARD			
J H*	Calaveras Twp 9	57	356
STARN			
Edward*	Yolo No E Twp	72	668
STARNES			
Samuel	Amador Twp 6	55	428
Thos C	Amador Twp 6	55	428
STARNS			
R	Trinity Taylor'S	70	1036
STARP			
Conrad	San Francisco San Francisco 7	68	1422
STARR			
A C	Yuba Marysville	72	952
A D	Yuba Marysville	72	952
A W	Sacramento Ward 3	63	429
Abram	Siskiyou Scott Ri	69	65
Anderson	Napa Napa	61	58
Anderson C	Napa Napa	61	58
Augustus	Santa Clara Santa Clara	65	519
Augustus	Trinity North Fo	70	1024
C A	Merced Twp 2	60	918
David	Siskiyou Scott Va	69	58
E J	Santa Clara Santa Clara	65	474
Edward	Butte Ophir	56	792
Edward	San Francisco San Francisco 7	68	1412
Facund	Tuolumne Twp 2	71	380
G	Sutter Sutter	70	808
Henry	Nevada Nevada	61	241

Name	County Locale	M653 Roll	Page
STARR			
Henry	Nevada Bridgeport	61	494
Henry	Nevada Red Dog	61	539
Henry	Sacramento Ward 4	63	543
J	San Francisco San Francisco 6	67	448
Jacob	San Francisco San Francisco 6	67	448
Jerry	Sierra Poker Flats	66	842
Jno	Butte Hamilton	56	515
John	Calaveras Twp 8	57	100
John	Calaveras Twp 8	57	64
John	Del Norte Crescent	58	642
John	Siskiyou Scott Ri	69	65
John	Tuolumne Twp 3	71	431
John M	Sierra Twp 7	66	904
John W	Sierra Twp 7	66	904
Jose	Tuolumne Jamestown	71	431
Josiah	Butte Oregon	56	638
L	Calaveras Twp 9	57	401
L	Sierra La Porte	66	776
Michael	Yuba Bear Rvr	72	1005
S	Sierra La Porte	66	776
Saml H	Napa Napa	61	95
T B	San Joaquin Stockton	64	1089
Thomas	Sierra La Porte	66	788
Thos A*	Alameda Oakland	55	25
Thos N*	Alameda Oakland	55	25
W	San Francisco San Francisco 3	67	72
William	San Francisco San Francisco 11	150 67	
William	Tulara Petersburg	71	51
William H	Sierra Gibsonville	66	860
William W	Siskiyou Yreka	69	139
Wm	San Francisco San Francisco 10	209 67	
STARRBON			
Jno B*	Nevada Nevada	61	241
STARRES			
Thos	San Francisco San Francisco 6	67	424
STARRGROOM			
C M	Nevada Nevada	61	258
STARRIX			
Benj	Sonoma Santa Rosa	69	401
STARROP			
John	San Francisco San Francisco 10	302 67	
STARRS			
P*	El Dorado Coloma	58	1070
STARRSEN			
Kate*	Sacramento Ward 4	63	545
STARRWOOD			
Richard G*	Yuba Marysville	72	850
Saml*	Nevada Nevada	61	241
STARSKS			
H A	Tuolumne Twp 4	71	145
START			
Michael*	Yuba Bear Rvr	72	1005
Thos	San Francisco San Francisco 1	68	906
STARTE			
Edward	Calaveras Twp 6	57	128
STARTERANT			
Geo	Butte Kimshaw	56	602
STARTK			
J J	Tuolumne Twp 2	71	384
STARTSMAN			
T	El Dorado Placerville	58	896
STARWOOD			
Ase A	El Dorado Greenwood	58	711
STARY			
W R	Amador Twp 3	55	372
STASEL			
Geo	Amador Twp 1	55	499
STASMAN			
J H*	Calaveras Twp 9	57	356
STASSERMAN			
Solomon	Santa Cruz Santa Cruz	66	605
STATBURY			
Jno	Alameda Brooklyn	55	197
STATE			
David	Nevada Rough &	61	429
George	San Francisco San Francisco 2	67	652
STATELOR			
John*	Del Norte Crescent	58	620
STATEN			
Cath	Sacramento Ward 3	63	473
Francis M	Yuba Bear Rvr	72	1005
Jeremiah	Siskiyou Callahan	69	15
Jno	Sacramento Ward 1	63	46
Joseph	Monterey San Juan	60	975
Osmea	Alameda Brooklyn	55	167
STATER			
Henry	Mendocino Big Rvr	60	848
Robert	San Joaquin Elkhorn	64	968
STATES			
Jonathan E	Yuba Marysville	72	858
STATEVILL			
H	Nevada Bloomfield	61	509

Name	County Locale	M653 Roll	Page
STATFORD			
Jacob	San Francisco San Francisco 2	67	622
STATHAM			
Albert H	Fresno Twp 2	59	5
STATHRY			
T*	Nevada Nevada	61	316
STATIS			
W	Yolo Putah	72	551
STATKUM			
J	Nevada Eureka	61	364
STATLAN			
John W	Alameda Brooklyn	55	128
STATLAR			
Jonah	Santa Clara Santa Clara	65	490
STATLER			
J W	Sierra Twp 7	66	912
John C*	Plumas Quincy	62	1004
STATMAN			
Fritz	Sacramento Franklin	63	326
STATMILLEN			
Frank*	Calaveras Twp 4	57	310
STATMILLER			
Frank	Calaveras Twp 4	57	310
Jacob*	Siskiyou Yreka	69	141
STATON			
Geo W	Placer Nicolaus	62	692
John F	San Joaquin Elkhorn	64	996
Joseph	Sacramento Georgian	63	341
Robert	Santa Clara Gilroy	65	234
STATS			
M	Nevada Washington	61	333
STATSON			
M*	Yuba Long Bar	72	749
STATT			
D H	Nevada Nevada	61	251
Franklin	Placer Forest H	62	805
STATTAPEN			
E S*	El Dorado Placerville	58	909
STATTARD			
S	Calaveras Twp 9	57	417
Thomas	Siskiyou Yreka	69	126
STATTEL			
S W	Sierra Twp 7	66	912
STATTON			
John	Sierra Twp 7	66	864
STATTS			
D	Nevada Eureka	61	347
D H	Nevada Nevada	61	251
M	Nevada Washington	61	333
S D	Nevada Nevada	61	262
STATTUCK			
John H	Santa Clara San Jose	65	360
STATZRNAGGER			
Ann Cath*	Alameda Oakland	55	1
STAUB			
Adolf	San Francisco San Francisco 7	68	1325
STAUDEFORD			
J W*	Napa Hot Springs	61	25
John*	Napa Hot Springs	61	25
STAUFF			
Josiah	Tuolumne Twp 3	71	438
STAUFFER			
Benedict	Yolo Cottonwoood	72	654
STAUGHTER			
E J	Tuolumne Twp 1	71	265
STAUNARD			
E*	San Francisco San Francisco 5	67	542
STAUNTON			
Michael P*	Calaveras Twp 4	57	318
STAUR			
S F	Sierra Twp 5	66	921
STAURI			
Leopold*	Sierra Whiskey	66	847
STAURPLEY			
Orville*	Santa Cruz Santa Cruz	66	619
STAURSH			
Charles*	Sierra Downieville	66	1007
STAUTIN			
Joseph B	Colusa Grand Island	57	469
STAVAS			
John	Mendocino Calpella	60	829
STAVE			
Charles	Calaveras Twp 6	57	172
STAVER			
---	Tulara Twp 3	71	57
STAVIN			
John	Tuolumne Columbia	71	326
STAWKER			
E W	Tuolumne Twp 1	71	484
STAY			
Heon	Nevada Nevada	61	301
STAYBACK			
A J	Yuba Marysville	72	966
STAZLE			
John	Placer Virginia	62	665
STAZNICHDL			
William*	Calaveras Twp 4	57	343

Name	County Locale	M653 Roll	Page
STCH			
Louis*	Nevada Bridgeport	61	465
STCLAIR			
John	Del Norte Ferry P O	58	665
John	Solano Montezuma	69	372
Mary	Colusa Monroeville	57	457
Robert	Solano Fremont	69	384
STEAD			
John*	Placer Goods	62	696
Margt	San Francisco San Francisco 9	68	974
S C	Placer Dutch Fl	62	729
W	Nevada Nevada	61	317
STEADEMAN			
Amy*	Sacramento Ward 4	63	551
STEADLER			
John	Sonoma Petaluma	69	559
STEADMAN			
A	Santa Clara San Jose	65	376
Amos	Sonoma Russian	69	429
D	Calaveras Twp 9	57	405
D P	El Dorado Georgetown	58	679
E C	Butte Hamilton	56	526
H L	El Dorado Newtown	58	780
Seymoor	Marin S Antoni	60	711
Seymor	Marin S Antoni	60	711
STEADSON			
F	Yolo Cache Crk	72	642
T	Yolo Cache	72	642
STEADWELL			
Josiah	Yolo Slate Ra	72	694
Josiah	Yuba Slate Ro	72	694
STEAEHLE			
Jacob*	Tuolumne Chinese	71	493
STEAFO			
Antoine*	Yuba Marysville	72	941
STEAHAN			
Joseph	Yuba New York	72	734
STEAKY			
Stephen	El Dorado White Oaks	58	1030
STEALEY			
Thos	San Francisco San Francisco 10	67	225
STEALY			
John	San Francisco San Francisco 10	67	226
STEAMES			
Oscar*	Amador Twp 2	55	309
STEAMPFLY			
Theodore	San Francisco San Francisco 7	68	1325
STEAMS			
Abel	Los Angeles Los Angeles	59	345
Geo*	San Joaquin O'Neal	64	1006
Leonard*	Tulara Visalia	71	102
STEAN			
Charles	San Francisco San Francisco 7	68	1335
Christopher	Santa Clara Santa Clara	65	498
Joseph*	Santa Cruz Santa Cruz	66	614
STEANDMAN			
J M	El Dorado Newtown	58	780
STEANPELS			
A	El Dorado Georgetown	58	694
STEANS			
L A	Santa Clara San Jose	65	346
STEAP			
Antoine	Yuba Marysville	72	941
Catharine*	Yuba Marysville	72	942
Catherine	Yuba Marysville	72	942
STEAQDMAN			
F	El Dorado Placerville	58	896
STEAREY			
Syman	Tuolumne Twp 2	71	285
STEARLIN			
D	Amador Twp 1	55	468
STEARM			
J W	Tuolumne Shawsfla	71	390
STEARNE			
Able	San Francisco San Francisco 5	67	494
STEARNES			
Joseph	Solano Benecia	69	292
M A	San Francisco San Francisco 10	67	330
Oscar*	Amador Twp 2	55	309
STEARNS			
Caroline	Santa Cruz Soguel	66	579
Charles	Santa Cruz Santa Cruz	66	604
Edward	Santa Cruz Pescadero	66	647
G G	Butte Oregon	56	623
Isaac	Calaveras Twp 7	57	22
J H	San Francisco San Francisco 5	67	505
J W	Tuolumne Twp 2	71	390
John	Santa Cruz Soguel	66	580
John	Santa Cruz Santa Cruz	66	621
Leonard	Tulara Visalia	71	102
Marshall S	Sonoma Mendocino	69	463
R	Trinity Taylor'S	70	1036
Robert	Santa Cruz Pescadero	66	646

Name	County Locale	M653 Roll	Page
STEARNS			
W H	Sierra Downieville	66	976
W R	San Francisco San Francisco 12	67	390
William H	San Joaquin Elkhorn	64	996
STEARNY			
Lyman	Tuolumne Twp 2	71	285
STEARUS			
Caroline	Santa Cruz Soguel	66	579
Charles*	Santa Cruz Santa Cruz	66	604
John	Santa Cruz Soguel	66	580
John	Santa Cruz Santa Cruz	66	621
STEATS			
John	Placer Lisbon	62	733
STEAUB			
Edward*	Sierra St Louis	66	808
STEAUBS			
Edward*	Sierra St Louis	66	808
STEAVEN			
Peter	Yuba Bear Rvr	72	996
STEAVER			
Peter	Yuba Bear Rvr	72	996
STEAVES			
S	Santa Clara San Jose	65	290
STEAVNS			
Leonard*	Tulara Visalia	71	102
T	Amador Twp 1	55	459
STEBBEN			
Charles*	Yuba Marysville	72	958
James*	San Francisco San Francisco 4	68	1115
STEBBENS			
Charles	Yuba Marysville	72	958
Geo*	Placer Secret R	62	610
H N	San Francisco San Francisco 6	67	474
Henry	Tuolumne Twp 2	71	326
Isaac T	Alameda Oakland	55	73
Lilly	San Francisco San Francisco 9	68	1025
S G	El Dorado Kelsey	58	1148
W P C	San Francisco San Francisco 6	67	430
William	Tuolumne Chinese	71	489
Willliam	Tuolumne Twp 5	71	489
STEBE			
M*	San Francisco San Francisco 5	67	506
STEBINS			
D	El Dorado Kelsey	58	1134
STEBY			
Fred	El Dorado Placerville	58	898
STECH			
T C	Yolo Putah	72	552
STECIA			
---	San Bernardino San Bernadino	64	677
STECK			
Phillip	Tulara Twp 3	71	53
STECKER			
Henry*	San Francisco San Francisco 10	67	292
STECKFLETH			
Peter	San Francisco San Francisco 8	68	1265
STECKLAND			
R*	Nevada Grass Valley	61	158
STECKLE			
Wm	Amador Twp 1	55	469
STECKLER			
Chas	Amador Twp 1	55	455
STECNMANN			
Jacob*	Yuba Marysville	72	902
STED			
Henry	Mariposa Twp 3	60	563
John	Humbolt Pacific	59	138
STEDHAM			
Charles	Amador Twp 6	55	425
Chaules*	Amador Twp 6	55	425
Thos	Amador Twp 6	55	425
W	Shasta Horsetown	66	695
STEDLAN			
Andrew*	Placer Michigan	62	840
STEDMAN			
Chas J*	Calaveras Twp 4	57	329
Eliza	San Francisco San Francisco 8	68	1295
Francis A P	Siskiyou Yreka	69	129
Henry	Sierra Twp 7	66	893
Jane	San Francisco San Francisco 2	67	800
Jas	San Francisco San Francisco 1	68	872
Jas	San Francisco San Francisco 1	68	883
Mary A	Calaveras Twp 4	57	329
Nilcorn J*	Calaveras Twp 4	57	329
P	El Dorado Newtown	58	776
Sheldon	Tuolumne Don Pedro	71	540
Thecorer J*	Calaveras Twp 4	57	329
Thecorn*	Calaveras Twp 4	57	329
Wilcom J*	Calaveras Twp 4	57	329
Wilcorn J	Calaveras Twp 4	57	329
STEDMUN			
Chas J*	Calaveras Twp 4	57	329
Mary A*	Calaveras Twp 4	57	329

Name	County Locale	M653 Roll	Page
STEDMUN			
Wilcom J*	Calaveras Twp 4	57	329
STEDNEY			
Jno B	Alameda Brooklyn	55	81
STEDORDS			
Sheldon	Tuolumne Twp 6	71	540
STEECE			
Fredrich	Nevada Rough &	61	404
STEED			
A C	Sonoma Salt Point	69	693
STEEDEN			
J Tum*	San Francisco San Francisco 5	67	530
STEEDMAN			
Henry*	Alameda Brooklyn	55	150
J	Tuolumne Twp 4	71	164
STEEG			
Rebecca	San Francisco San Francisco 2	67	734
STEEGEN			
John*	Sierra Twp 7	66	870
STEEGER			
Alexander	San Francisco San Francisco 7	68	1354
STEEKLER			
Chas	Amador Twp 1	55	455
STEEL			
Andrew	Yolo Slate Ra	72	691
Andrew*	Yuba Slate Ro	72	691
C C	El Dorado Mud Springs	58	968
Charles	Placer Michigan	62	831
Cornelia	Alameda Oakland	55	18
Cornelia	San Francisco San Francisco 2	67	641
Daniel	San Mateo Twp 1	65	56
David	Butte Oro	56	686
David W*	Sierra St Louis	66	810
E	Siskiyou Yreka	69	185
E W	Marin Point Re	60	729
F	El Dorado Newtown	58	780
F R	Nevada Red Dog	61	552
Frank	Colusa Muion	57	462
Franklin	Marin San Rafael	60	771
Huett	Contra Costa Twp 2	57	545
I C*	Yolo Putah	72	552
J	Solano Suisan	69	230
J	Yolo Washington	72	602
J A	Sonoma Armally	69	501
J C	Marin Point Re	60	729
J C*	Yolo Putah	72	552
J N	El Dorado Kelsey	58	1143
J P	El Dorado Diamond	58	799
J W	El Dorado Kelsey	58	1143
James	Placer Michigan	62	811
James	Sierra La Porte	66	789
James	Tulara Visalia	71	91
Jefferson	Tuolumne Chinese	71	500
John	Placer Forest H	62	805
John	Plumas Meadow Valley	62	902
John	San Francisco San Francisco 9	68	1097
John	Sonoma Santa Rosa	69	414
John H	Calaveras Twp 5	57	206
John H	Sierra La Porte	66	772
John M	Sierra Whiskey	66	850
Joseph	El Dorado Mud Springs	58	983
Joseph	Siskiyou Callahan	69	18
Marshall	Sonoma Santa Rosa	69	414
Michael	Placer Iona Hills	62	890
N	Siskiyou Cottonwoood	69	98
Nat	El Dorado Eldorado	58	939
P*	Siskiyou Klamath	69	95
Patrick	Mariposa Twp 3	60	570
R	Calaveras Twp 9	57	376
R E	Marin Point Re	60	729
S B	Nevada Grass Valley	61	149
S R	Placer Auburn	62	585
Saml*	Nevada Grass Valley	61	166
Samuel	Sierra Downieville	66	961
T H	Siskiyou Scott Va	69	52
T*	Siskiyou Klamath	69	95
Thomas	Sierra St Louis	66	814
Thomas	Yuba New York	72	723
Thomas W	Sierra Gibsonville	66	856
Thomas W	Sierra Downieville	66	971
Thomas*	Yuba New York	72	723
William	Calaveras Twp 4	57	313
William	Sierra Poker Flats	66	842
William	Siskiyou Yreka	69	130
William*	Sierra St Louis	66	810
Z	Solano Suisan	69	230
Zina	El Dorado Coloma	58	1116
STEELE			
A	San Francisco San Francisco 9	68	1081
D H	Napa Yount	61	52
H	San Francisco San Francisco 5	67	499
Henry	San Francisco San Francisco 9	68	1054
Henry	Sierra Gibsonville	66	853
Isaac	Sonoma Petaluma	69	607
John	Alameda Brooklyn	55	92
John	Calaveras Twp 7	57	17

Name	County Locale	M653 Roll Page
STEELE		
John	Sacramento Alabama	63 415
John	Sonoma Santa Rosa	69 414
John A	Yuba Marysville	72 900
John M	Colusa Colusi	57 426
Marshall	Sonoma Santa Rosa	69 414
O R	Placer Iona Hills	62 891
R J	Placer Forest H	62 791
Richard D	Yuba Marysville	72 915
S G	Nevada Red Dog	61 547
S G	Trinity Prices B	701 019
S H	Santa Clara San Jose	65 381
S J*	El Dorado Georgetown	58 676
Thos	Sacramento Alabama	63 415
Wm	San Francisco San Francisco 2	67 571
STEELEY		
J W	El Dorado Coloma	581 070
STEELL		
Jacob	El Dorado Coloma	581 114
Wm	Amador Twp 2	55 308
Wm	Yuba Rose Bar	72 806
STEELS		
Charles	Yuba Marysville	72 865
STEELY		
B F*	El Dorado Placerville	58 891
John	Yuba Suida	72 980
STEEMER		
Premig*	San Francisco San Francisco 7	681 355
STEEN		
Alolph	El Dorado Coloma	581 120
Conrad	San Francisco San Francisco 10	205 67
J F	San Francisco San Francisco 12	374 67
Jacob	Santa Cruz Pajaro	66 534
James*	Shasta Shasta	66 668
Robert	Siskiyou Shasta Valley	69 120
Thomas	Siskiyou Yreka	69 189
William	San Mateo Twp 3	65 109
STEENMITZ		
Henry	San Francisco San Francisco 4	681 222
STEENY		
---	Yuba Bear Rvr	721 000
STEER		
John	San Mateo Twp 3	65 100
STEERE		
J	Siskiyou Scott Va	69 55
J	Tuolumne Garrote	71 173
STEEREEN		
Charles*	Yuba Marysville	72 893
STEEREN		
Charles*	Yuba Marysville	72 893
STEERMAN		
Wm	Mariposa Twp 1	60 641
STEERS		
Richd*	Napa Clear Lake	61 137
STEEVE		
Henry*	Calaveras Twp 6	57 162
Wm	Alameda Brooklyn	55 82
STEEVENS		
B F	San Mateo Twp 2	65 127
Bridget A*	San Mateo Twp 1	65 48
STEFFANE		
Camillo	Yuba Suida	72 981
STEFFANI		
Camillo*	Yuba Linda Twp	72 981
STEFFEN		
Jacob	Sacramento Ward 4	63 555
Peter	El Dorado Gold Hill	581 096
STEFFENS		
John H	Yuba Suida	72 989
STEFFINS		
C	San Francisco San Francisco 5	67 531
John H*	Yuba Linda	72 989
Peter	San Francisco San Francisco 3	67 63
STEFFLER		
C	Yolo Putah	72 585
William	Calaveras Twp 5	57 229
STEFPHENS		
John	Calaveras Twp 5	57 171
STEGE		
Geo	San Francisco San Francisco 9	681 070
J G*	San Francisco San Francisco 2	67 674
STEGEMAN		
William*	Sierra Poker Flats	66 837
STEGER		
G	Trinity Redding	70 985
John J	Butte Bidwell	56 730
Oscar S	Tuolumne Twp 1	71 187
STEGES		
Oscar S	Tuolumne Sonora	71 187
STEGMAN		
C H	Mariposa Twp 1	60 623
Henry	Mariposa Twp 1	60 634
STEH		
Louis*	Nevada Bridgeport	61 465

Name	County Locale	M653 Roll Page
STEHENS		
Matthew	Tuolumne Twp 2	71 289
STEHISON		
Thos*	Merced Twp 2	60 915
STEHLING		
Catharine*	Placer Auburn	62 591
STEHNSA		
C S*	Mariposa Twp 3	60 573
STEHR		
Charles	Siskiyou Klamath	69 94
STEIB		
W*	El Dorado Placerville	58 912
STEICH		
Julius	San Francisco San Francisco 2	67 763
STEICHLER		
Henry	San Francisco San Francisco 10	351 67
STEID		
Henry	Sonoma Armally	69 503
STEIDMAN		
Henry	Yuba Marysville	72 868
Henry*	Alameda Brooklyn	55 150
STEIGER		
Alex	San Francisco San Francisco 9	68 961
Chas	San Francisco San Francisco 9	68 969
S	San Francisco San Francisco 6	67 466
STEIGLEMAN		
George	San Francisco San Francisco 7	681 398
STEIHL		
Wm F	Placer Stewart	62 606
STEIL		
W*	El Dorado Placerville	58 912
STEILES		
James*	Placer Michigan	62 857
STEILL		
Wm	Amador Twp 2	55 308
STEIMAN		
Henry	Calaveras Twp 5	57 203
STEIME		
Meehlat*	Santa Clara Alviso	65 415
STEIMEGGER		
Henry	San Francisco San Francisco 8	681 312
STEIMER		
T H*	Sacramento Ward 4	63 505
STEIMMAN		
Fredoline	Tulara Visalia	71 79
Peter	Tulara Twp 1	71 76
STEIMPKE		
Carl*	San Francisco San Francisco 9	681 084
STEIN		
A	Nevada Grass Valley	61 202
Abbott	San Francisco San Francisco 1	68 856
Anw	Calaveras Twp 6	57 127
Charles	San Francisco San Francisco 6	67 435
Chs*	San Francisco San Francisco 5	67 480
Coinelius	San Francisco San Francisco 7	681 424
Conrad	San Francisco San Francisco 10	205 67
Conrad	San Francisco San Francisco 10	227 67
David	San Francisco San Francisco 5	67 475
Edwd F	San Francisco San Francisco 5	67 545
Georel	Trinity East For	701 025
Jacob	San Francisco San Francisco 7	681 394
Jacob	San Francisco San Francisco 2	67 710
Kjo	El Dorado Georgetown	58 679
L H	Marin Tomales	60 716
Lorenzo	San Francisco San Francisco 7	681 352
Martin	San Francisco San Francisco 5	67 544
Meyer	San Francisco San Francisco 3	67 2
Miyer	San Francisco San Francisco 3	67 2
Nicholas	Calaveras Twp 5	57 194
William F	Calaveras Twp 5	57 191
Wm	Placer Dutch Fl	62 725
Wm J	Mendocino Anderson	60 866
STEINARD		
R*	Mariposa Twp 3	60 592
STEINBACK		
John	Contra Costa Twp 1	57 487
Oscas	Napa Napa	61 114
STEINBARK		
Oscas*	Napa Napa	61 114
STEINBECK		
William	Marin Cortemad	60 753
Wm	Marin San Rafael	60 759
STEINBECKER		
John	Tuolumne Big Oak	71 132
STEINBERG		
Lawrence	Marin Novato	60 739
STEINBERGER		
G	Merced Twp 1	60 904
Rosa	San Francisco San Francisco 2	67 622
STEINBOOK		
J	El Dorado Coloma	581 070
STEINBRICK		
Geo	San Francisco San Francisco 2	67 767

Name	County Locale	M653 Roll Page
STEINBULLER		
William	San Francisco San Francisco 7	681 348
STEINBURG		
M	El Dorado Placerville	58 854
STEINBURGHER		
Saml	Calaveras Twp 4	57 324
STEINDORF		
J	Butte Oregon	56 615
STEINECK		
Jno	San Francisco San Francisco 9	681 084
STEINER		
A	Sacramento Ward 1	63 17
Adam	Yolo Cache	72 631
B	Trinity Steiner	701 000
Edwd	San Francisco San Francisco 2	67 649
H	San Francisco San Francisco 5	67 513
Jacob	Yuba Marysville	72 972
John	Calaveras Twp 7	57 7
Joohn	Yuba Marysville	72 972
William	San Joaquin Castoria	64 873
STEINERS		
A G	El Dorado Georgetown	58 753
John	Yuba Marysville	72 972
STEINES		
Elira A	Mariposa Twp 3	60 587
Eliza A	Mariposa Twp 3	60 587
STEINFELT		
Charles	Placer Auburn	62 565
STEINFIELD		
L E	Mariposa Twp 3	60 586
Martin	Nevada Rough &	61 398
STEINGOOD		
Robert	Calaveras Twp 10	57 267
STEINGRANT		
L	Solano Benecia	69 284
STEINGRAUT		
L	Solano Benecia	69 284
STEINHART		
Wm	San Francisco San Francisco 10	265 67
STEINHEIMER		
H W	Sonoma Santa Rosa	69 392
STEINHEISON		
Solomon	San Francisco San Francisco 10	198 67
STEINHOFF		
Levi	Tulara Visalia	71 107
STEINIEGGER		
Henry*	San Francisco San Francisco 8	681 312
STEINIGKE		
William*	San Francisco San Francisco 7	681 400
STEINKAMP		
John P*	Yuba Linda	72 990
STEINLE		
B	San Francisco San Francisco 7	681 373
STEINLER		
Geo*	Amador Twp 2	55 309
STEINLRENGHER		
Luml*	Calaveras Twp 4	57 324
STEINMAN		
Fredoline*	Tulara Twp 1	71 79
Henry	Klamath Liberty	59 241
STEINMEITZ		
Martin	Sacramento Ward 4	63 529
STEINMETZ		
Henry	San Francisco San Francisco 4	681 222
STEINMILLER		
John	Sacramento American	63 171
S S	Sacramento American	63 171
STEINNIETZ		
George	San Joaquin Tulare	64 870
STEINPKE		
Carl	San Francisco San Francisco 9	681 084
STEINRACUP		
John P	Yuba Suida	72 990
STEINTRINYHEN		
Luml*	Calaveras Twp 4	57 324
STEINUGGER		
Henry*	San Francisco San Francisco 8	681 312
STEINWIG		
Chas	San Francisco San Francisco 10	261 67
STEIRE		
J	Tuolumne Twp 4	71 173
STEITPAPER		
Augustus	Sacramento Ward 4	63 512
STEITZ		
William	Marin Cortemad	60 788
STEIVARA		
R*	Mariposa Twp 3	60 592
STEIVARS		
A B	Mariposa Twp 3	60 601
STEIVE		
Wm*	Alameda Brooklyn	55 82
STEJADE		
Juan	San Luis Obispo San Luis Obispo	65 42

Name	County Locale	M653 Roll	Page
STELELURA			
E	Santa Clara San Jose	65	354
STELENT			
Andrew*	Yuba Bear Rvr	72	1008
STELER			
W	El Dorado Kelsey	58	1141
STELES			
B	El Dorado Mud Springs	58	977
Wm C	Nevada Nevada	61	280
STELFRITE			
Fred	Nevada Bloomfield	61	530
STELFROTR			
Fred*	Nevada Bloomfield	61	530
STELL			
Isaah	Yuba Rose Bar	72	806
Valentine	Contra Costa Twp 1	57	503
STELLA			
Christopher	Santa Clara Fremont	65	425
STELLE			
Dewitt*	Plumas Quincy	62	916
Geo	Sacramento Cosumnes	63	389
Saml	Sacramento Sutter	63	299
STELLER			
Charles*	Yuba Marysville	72	874
John	San Francisco San Francisco 1	68	907
STELLEY			
P	Nevada Grass Valley	61	223
STELLICK			
M	San Francisco San Francisco 5	67	528
STELLING			
John*	San Francisco San Francisco 3	67	5
Peter	San Francisco San Francisco 11	67	92
William	Yuba Marysville	72	871
STELLINGER			
Mary*	Sacramento Ward 3	63	444
STELLO			
---	Tulara Keyesville	71	67
---	Tulara Keyesville	71	70
STELLWAGON			
B M	Tuolumne Twp 1	71	250
STELLWELL			
R S	Tuolumne Sonora	71	245
STELLY			
Charles	Siskiyou Klamath	69	93
H C*	Nevada Nevada	61	316
Richard*	San Francisco San Francisco 1	68	849
STELTZ			
Charles	Siskiyou Klamath	69	93
STELURD			
Andrew*	Yuba Bear Rvr	72	1008
STELZER			
H	San Francisco San Francisco 5	67	476
STEM			
Anne	San Francisco San Francisco 2	67	792
Patric	Calaveras Twp 9	57	369
STEMAR			
Manuel	Tuolumne Twp 2	71	282
STEMAS			
Manuel	Tuolumne Twp 2	71	282
STEMBERG			
John	Tuolumne Twp 1	71	222
STEME			
W*	El Dorado Georgetown	58	685
STEMERMAN			
Henry*	San Francisco San Francisco 9	68	1051
STEMGRANT			
Sonis	Contra Costa Twp 1	57	483
STEMHEISON			
Solomon	San Francisco San Francisco 10	67	198
STEMIPKE			
Carl*	San Francisco San Francisco 9	68	1084
STEMLEY			
Jno	Sonoma Petaluma	69	550
STEMMAN			
Jac	Sacramento Ward 1	63	46
STEMMAU			
Jac*	Sacramento Ward 1	63	46
STEMME			
William	Siskiyou Yreka	69	142
STEMMEL			
P	Tuolumne Big Oak	71	153
STEMMENS			
Ann	Siskiyou Yreka	69	172
STEMMER			
P*	Tulara Big Oak	71	153
STEMMERMAN			
Christ	Sacramento Ward 4	63	600
Geo W*	Sacramento Ward 4	63	600
Mary	Santa Clara Gilroy	65	240
STEMMET			
P	Tuolumne Twp 4	71	153
STEMMETY			
C*	Nevada Washington	61	335
STEMMITY			
C*	Nevada Washington	61	335

Name	County Locale	M653 Roll	Page
STEMNER			
John	Humbolt Table Bl	59	141
STEMNING			
A*	Butte Ophir	56	794
STEMPLE			
H M	Marin Tomales	60	723
STEMWOOD			
M A	San Francisco San Francisco 9	68	1031
STENAN			
Wm B*	San Francisco San Francisco 9	68	1078
STENBENS			
Alex*	Sacramento Georgian	63	347
STENBER			
Wm	Sacramento Ward 4	63	552
STENCHFIELD			
Moses	Nevada Red Dog	61	555
STENDEMAN			
Amy*	Sacramento Ward 4	63	551
E*	Sacramento Ward 1	63	89
Julius	Placer Goods	62	697
STENDERO			
J H	Nevada Nevada	61	239
STENDMAN			
Charles	Sierra La Porte	66	770
STENE			
Martin	El Dorado Big Bar	58	737
STENEBURG			
Wm*	Nevada Nevada T	61	327
STENER			
J	Amador Twp 3	55	394
STENGEE			
John	El Dorado Casumnes	58	1174
STENGER			
Charles W	Solano Benecia	69	316
Chas W	San Bernardino San Bernardino	64	671
Frederick	Yuba Marysville	72	901
J	Sacramento Alabama	63	414
J B	Santa Clara San Jose	65	380
John	El Dorado Casumnes	58	1174
STENGIS			
Wm	Butte Ophir	56	751
STENHAM			
Thos	El Dorado Georgetown	58	690
STENIE			
W*	El Dorado Georgetown	58	685
STENINS			
James	Calaveras Twp 9	57	370
STENLEN			
William N*	Tulara Visalia	71	100
STENLON			
William N*	Tulara Visalia	71	100
STENMAM			
John	San Francisco San Francisco 1	68	902
STENMAN			
Jacob	Yuba Marysville	72	902
STENN			
A Y	Sierra Downieville	66	997
STENNER			
Joe*	Sacramento Ward 4	63	505
STENNET			
Thomas	Marin Cortemad	60	788
STENNS			
M*	San Francisco San Francisco 4	68	1154
STENNUITY			
C*	Nevada Washington	61	335
STENSEBOUGH			
J B*	San Joaquin Stockton	64	1051
STENSEN			
Mary	Sacramento Granite	63	222
STENSHOW			
Edward	Klamath Dillins	59	214
STENSLING			
F C*	Tehama Red Bluff	70	933
STENSON			
G C	Tuolumne Columbia	71	297
Joseph	Sierra Morristown	66	1055
Louisa	San Francisco San Francisco 2	67	706
Perry*	San Francisco San Francisco 2	67	675
Thomas	San Francisco San Francisco 4	68	1146
STENSTROM			
P L*	Placer Michigan	62	839
STENT			
John*	Mariposa Twp 3	60	606
STENTE			
Charles	San Francisco San Francisco 4	68	1160
STENTON			
Patrick	El Dorado Kelsey	58	1142
STENTOSH			
Milo Ma*	Yuba Marysville	72	940
STENTSON			
B T	Santa Clara Santa Clara	65	487
STEO			
Josiah	Fresno Twp 1	59	81
STEOFFI			
Petrus	San Francisco San Francisco 11	67	121

Name	County Locale	M653 Roll	Page
STEOMSIN			
Jas*	Butte Wyandotte	56	668
STEORNS			
Milton	Calaveras Twp 5	57	222
STEP			
James C	Colusa Grand Island	57	482
S G	Sacramento Ward 1	63	63
STEPENS			
S H	Mariposa Coulterville	60	686
STEPENSON			
Jos	Placer Virginia	62	664
Mary E	Siskiyou Yreka	69	181
S	Sutter Butte	70	783
STEPHAN			
Nancy	Mariposa Coulterville	60	686
STEPHANSEON			
J C	Shasta Millvill	66	739
STEPHANSON			
S	Shasta Millvill	66	740
STEPHEN			
---	Siskiyou Scott Va	69	23
Carana	Calaveras Twp 7	57	12
Cerf	Contra Costa Twp 3	57	612
Chas	Placer Stewart	62	605
D S	Siskiyou Scott Va	69	46
Demingo	Tuolumne Twp 1	71	190
H L	Placer Virginia	62	675
J	Siskiyou Klamath	69	93
Jacob	Sierra Poker Flats	66	840
James	Siskiyou Klamath	69	93
John	Placer Virginia	62	676
John	Tuolumne Sonora	71	241
Jonathan	Yolo Cottonwoood	72	559
Lincoln	Santa Cruz Santa Cruz	66	633
Mary E	Marin Cortemad	60	753
Nancy	Mariposa Coulterville	60	686
Nathan	Sierra Eureka	66	1043
Peter	Sierra Poker Flats	66	840
Wm	El Dorado Georgetown	58	706
STEPHENS			
A	Siskiyou Scott Va	69	40
A	Tehama Antelope	70	893
A L	Santa Clara San Jose	65	317
Adolph	San Francisco San Francisco 7	68	1384
Alfred	Plumas Quincy	62	960
B T	San Joaquin Stockton	64	1031
B W	Yolo Cottonwoood	72	647
Benjamin	Los Angeles Elmonte	59	263
Bradford	Plumas Quincy	62	1002
C	Nevada Grass Valley	61	153
C	Nevada Grass Valley	61	178
C P	Tuolumne Twp 2	71	373
Caroline	Los Angeles Elmonte	59	256
Catharne	Sacramento San Joaquin	63	367
Charles	Contra Costa Twp 1	57	505
Charles	Placer Todds Va	62	763
Charles O	Contra Costa Twp 2	57	572
Chas	Placer Auburn	62	567
Chas	Sonoma Santa Rosa	69	405
Chas W	San Francisco San Francisco 10	67	174
Daniel	Placer Sacramento	62	645
Danl	Amador Twp 3	55	405
Danl	Sonoma Mendocino	69	459
Dewit C	Siskiyou Shasta Valley	69	118
E J	Mariposa Twp 3	60	567
Edward	Marin Saucileto	60	750
F	Nevada Eureka	61	366
F	Sutter Yuba	70	767
F P*	San Francisco San Francisco 9	68	1099
Fefferson	Mendocino Ukiah	60	802
Frances	Amador Twp 6	55	435
Frank	Sacramento American	63	165
G	Nevada Grass Valley	61	147
G	Nevada Bridgeport	61	453
G W	Marin Novato	60	738
G W	San Francisco San Francisco 5	67	521
Gabriel	Sierra La Porte	66	788
George	Solano Suisan	69	237
George	Tuolumne Twp 2	71	411
George H	Placer Auburn	62	565
H	Siskiyou Klamath	69	85
Henry	Calaveras Twp 6	57	112
Henry	Calaveras Twp 5	57	171
Henry	Fresno Twp 1	59	76
Henry	Mendocino Big Rvr	60	846
Henry	Plumas Quincy	62	953
Henry	Santa Clara Santa Clara	65	495
Henry	Siskiyou Scott Va	69	36
Henry	Yuba Suida	72	989
Henry D	San Francisco San Francisco 7	68	1408
Henry N	Mendocino Arrana	60	859
Hester	El Dorado Placerville	58	929
Howard	San Joaquin Elkhorn	64	970
Ira	Santa Clara Gilroy	65	249
Isaac	Yuba Marysville	72	936

California 1860 Census Index

Name	County Locale	M653 Roll	Page
STEPHENS			
Isaac A	Tuolumne Sonora	71	201
Isabella	Placer Lisbon	62	735
J	San Francisco San Francisco 5	67	518
J	Shasta French G	66	717
J	Siskiyou Klamath	69	78
J	Sutter Sutter	70	808
J E	Calaveras Twp 9	57	412
J E	Sutter Yuba	70	769
J F	Sutter Butte	70	780
J J	Yolo Cottonwoood	72	659
J L P	Yolo Cache Crk	72	597
J M	El Dorado Placerville	58	864
J M	Sonoma Armally	69	494
J P	Napa Clear Lake	61	125
J P	Yolo Cottonwood	72	559
J R	Placer Auburn	62	584
James	Calaveras Twp 4	57	313
James	El Dorado Placerville	58	932
James	Placer Folsom	62	639
James	Yolo Merritt	72	577
Janet	Santa Clara San Jose	65	382
Jas	San Francisco San Francisco 1	68	917
Jas H	Amador Twp 2	55	277
Jesse	Yolo Merritt	72	577
Jno	Mendocino Arrana	60	864
John	Alameda Brooklyn	55	209
John	Calaveras Twp 6	57	171
John	San Francisco San Francisco 1	68	887
John	Sierra Whiskey	66	844
John D	Yolo Cottonwood	72	654
John F	Los Angeles Los Angeles	59	398
John L	Mariposa Twp 3	60	593
John N	Calaveras Twp 6	57	137
John Q	Placer Secret R	62	609
Joseph	Calaveras Twp 10	57	289
Joseph	San Luis Obispo San Luis Obispo	65	17
Joseph	Tulara Twp 1	71	95
Joseph	Tuolumne Visalia	71	95
Joseph G	El Dorado Placerville	58	920
Julien	San Francisco San Francisco 7	681	444
L	Siskiyou Klamath	69	94
L A	Tehama Red Bluff	70	899
L*	Siskiyou Klamath	69	94
Lanford	El Dorado Kelsey	581	140
Lorenzo D	San Joaquin Tulare	64	870
Louis	San Francisco San Francisco 3	67	79
M L	Santa Clara Alviso	65	401
Maggie	Yuba Marysville	72	962
Marshall	Siskiyou Shasta Valley	69	118
Mary	Humbolt Eel Rvr	59	147
Mary	Sonoma Armally	69	500
Mathew	Yuba Rose Bar	72	793
Matthew	Tuolumne Columbia	71	289
O N	Tuolumne Twp 2	71	392
O W	Tuolumne Shawsfla	71	392
Othoiel	Siskiyou Yreka	69	193
P	Shasta Horsetown	66	690
P S	Trinity Weaverville	701	055
Peter	Napa Clear Lake	61	124
Peter	Tuolumne Twp 1	71	270
Price	Shasta Millvill	66	756
Priere	Shasta Millvill	66	756
R W	Yolo Cache Crk	72	647
Ricd	Tuolumne Springfield	71	372
Richard	Yuba Marysville	72	905
Robert	San Francisco San Francisco 1	68	880
Robert H	Calaveras Twp 6	57	174
S	Nevada Nevada	61	271
S	San Joaquin Stockton	641	040
S	Sutter Bear Rvr	70	819
S C*	Sacramento Granite	63	242
S H	Mariposa Coulterville	60	686
S*	Siskiyou Klamath	69	94
Saml	San Francisco San Francisco 6	67	422
Samuel	Mendocino Anderson	60	870
Sanford	El Dorado Kelsey	581	140
Savant	Yolo Cottonwood	72	662
Scott	Nevada Nevada	61	250
Solace M	Placer Auburn	62	597
Stephen	Nevada Nevada	61	271
T C	Sacramento Granite	63	242
T P	San Francisco San Francisco 9	681	099
Thomas	El Dorado Placerville	58	932
Thomas	Plumas Quincy	621	006
Thomas	Siskiyou Shasta Valley	69	118
Thomas	Siskiyou Callahan	69	12
Thos	Sacramento Natonia	63	279
Thos	Santa Clara Almaden	65	275
Thos E	Placer Auburn	62	577
W	San Francisco San Francisco 1	68	927
W J	Tuolumne Jamestown	71	450
William	Mendocino Ukiah	60	807
William	Plumas Quincy	62	963
William	Siskiyou Scott Va	69	31
Wm	Los Angeles Los Angeles	59	501
STEPHENS			
Wm	Solano Vallejo	69	243
Wm	Tehama Red Bluff	70	905
Wm	Tuolumne Columbia	71	298
Wm H	Amador Twp 2	55	263
Wm W	San Francisco San Francisco 10		213 67
STEPHENSEN			
D C	Shasta Millvill	66	739
R	Shasta Shasta	66	660
STEPHENSON			
A J	San Francisco San Francisco 7	681	356
C W	Mendocino Little L	60	837
D	Sonoma Bodega	69	520
David	Sonoma Bodega	69	523
E W	Siskiyou Klamath	69	79
Edward	Calaveras Twp 5	57	235
Edward S	Calaveras Twp 5	57	235
G	Yolo Putah	72	549
Henry	Marin Novato	60	737
J	Shasta Horsetown	66	708
J D	San Francisco San Francisco 6	67	431
James	Santa Clara San Jose	65	392
James	Yuba Marysville	72	960
Jas	San Francisco San Francisco 1	68	889
Jno A	Mendocino Ukiah	60	797
John	Calaveras Twp 6	57	155
John	Contra Costa Twp 1	57	537
John	Placer Sacramento	62	646
John	Placer Michigan	62	825
John	San Francisco San Francisco 7	681	326
John	San Francisco San Francisco 1	68	855
John	Sierra St Louis	66	809
John	Sonoma Mendocino	69	464
John	Tuolumne Twp 1	71	194
Joseph	Yuba Marysville	72	861
L	Shasta Millvill	66	740
Lewis	Sonoma Bodega	69	523
M	Nevada Grass Valley	61	193
Mary C	San Francisco San Francisco 8	681	268
Mat	Plumas Meadow Valley	62	908
R	Amador Twp 1	55	485
T S	Shasta French G	66	720
Thomas	Calaveras Twp 5	57	144
Thos	Sacramento Natonia	63	279
W	San Francisco San Francisco 6	67	468
W A	Mendocino Ukiah	60	797
W H	Nevada Grass Valley	61	193
Wm	Santa Clara Redwood	65	460
Wm M	Sonoma Santa Rosa	69	397
STEPHERD			
L C	Sutter Butte	70	783
STEPHIN			
Donango	Tuolumne Sonora	71	190
STEPHINE			
D	Tehama Antelope	70	893
STEPHINS			
G	Nevada Grass Valley	61	147
J Jp	Napa Clear Lake	61	125
James	Stanislaus Branch	70	710
Peter	Napa Clear Lake	61	124
William	Fresno Twp 1	59	81
STEPHMSON			
G*	Yolo Putah	72	549
STEPHONS			
Jefferson	Mendocino Ukiah	60	802
STEPL			
David	San Francisco San Francisco 3	67	7
STEPLES			
Robt	El Dorado Casumnes	581	175
STEPLOR			
William	Siskiyou Cottonwoood	69	107
STEPNEY			
R	San Francisco San Francisco 6	67	450
STEPNEZ			
K	Tehama Tehama	70	940
STEPP			
Henry	Nevada Nevada	61	328
STEPPACHER			
M	San Francisco San Francisco 2	67	609
STEPPEN			
Joseph	El Dorado Georgetown	58	699
STEPPENBECK			
Christophe	Los Angeles Santa Ana	59	443
STEPPER			
Chas	Placer Virginia	62	686
STEPPERFIELD			
J F	Tuolumne Sonora	71	223
STEPPERMAN			
J H	Stanislaus Oatvale	70	720
STEPPERSON			
Otis	Calaveras Twp 5	57	218
STEPPICK			
M	Shasta Shasta	66	674
STEPPINS			
Geo*	Placer Secret R	62	610
STEPPLEN			
Peter*	El Dorado Georgetown	58	752
STEPPLER			
Peter*	El Dorado Georgetown	58	752
STEPPSEN			
Joseph	El Dorado Georgetown	58	699
STEPSON			
A M	Siskiyou Klamath	69	85
STEPTON			
Chas*	Nevada Red Dog	61	540
STERBURGS			
D*	Napa Hot Springs	61	3
STERD			
John L*	Placer Virginia	62	675
STERDEVANT			
J C	Tuolumne Twp 2	71	396
Jas	Butte Oregon	56	641
Seth	Tuolumne Shawsfla	71	395
STEREFORD			
B H*	Sacramento Lee	63	211
STERENS			
T	San Francisco San Francisco 3	67	83
STERENSON			
George*	Tulara Visalia	71	100
STERESON			
J A	Trinity Mouth Ca	701	011
STERGEE			
Manuel A	El Dorado Georgetown	58	687
STERGEN			
Jeromah	Contra Costa Twp 2	57	569
STERGENAGER			
John*	Napa Hot Springs	61	25
STERGER			
A	Butte Kimshaw	56	605
STERGERVA			
H	Santa Clara San Jose	65	359
STERGILL			
Manuel A	El Dorado Georgetown	58	687
STERGSON			
Reuben	San Joaquin Elliott	64	945
STERH			
Charles	Siskiyou Yreka	69	193
STERINGS			
D*	Napa Hot Springs	61	3
STERITT			
J	Tehama Cottonwoood	70	901
STERK			
Julia	Colusa Monroeville	57	457
STERKEY			
Eugene	San Bernardino Santa Barbara	64	149
STERKSBURG			
John*	San Francisco San Francisco 1	68	885
STERLINE			
Susan M	Humbolt Union	59	187
STERLING			
A W	Yuba Marysville	72	952
F	Trinity Prices B	701	019
F C*	Tehama Red Bluff	70	933
George	Placer Forest H	62	796
George	Tehama Red Bluff	70	914
H	Nevada Washington	61	334
H	San Joaquin Stockton	641	099
Htomas	Siskiyou Yreka	69	125
J	Tuolumne Twp 4	71	152
J W	Sierra Twp 7	66	895
Jacob	Placer Auburn	62	591
James	Napa Hot Springs	61	21
James	Yuba Suida	72	987
Jeanna	San Francisco San Francisco 10		224 67
Jno F	San Francisco San Francisco 9	681	039
Joanna	San Francisco San Francisco 10		224 67
John	Trinity Douglas	70	978
Joseph*	Tuolumne Green Springs	71	518
M M	San Francisco San Francisco 6	67	415
M W	Butte Oro	56	684
Miner	Yuba Marysville	72	873
Philep W	Alameda Oakland	55	33
R H	Napa Napa	61	95
Richard	Amador Twp 4	55	257
Robt	Nevada Bridgeport	61	443
Robt	Sacramento Sutter	63	306
Robt	Sacramento Sutter	63	307
Thad	Shasta Shasta	66	735
Windsor	Plumas Quincy	62	943
STERMES			
B	Tuolumne Sonora	71	243
STERMS			
F B	Amador Twp 3	55	389
M	San Francisco San Francisco 4	681	154
P R*	San Mateo Twp 3	65	109
STERN			
Adam	Yolo Cache Crk	72	631
Anne*	San Francisco San Francisco 2	67	792
Chs	San Francisco San Francisco 5	67	476

California 1860 Census Index

Name	County Locale	M653 RollPage
STERN		
David	San Francisco San Francisco	8 681301
Henry	Humbolt Union	59 179
Leopold	San Francisco San Francisco	8 681307
Martin	San Francisco San Francisco	8 681307
P	Amador Twp 1	55 455
Palre*	Calaveras Twp 9	57 369
Tolamy	Placer Iona Hills	62 863
STERNBERG		
J	Nevada Grass Valley	61 184
STERNBERN		
George	Shasta Horsetown	66 695
STERNE		
Chas	Santa Clara Santa Clara	65 479
STERNES		
Walter	Sacramento Natonia	63 271
William	El Dorado Union	581094
STERNFELDT		
Saml	Sacramento Ward 4	63 495
STERNFELS		
A	El Dorado Georgetown	58 694
STERNFILS		
A	El Dorado Georgetown	58 676
STERNHEIM		
H	San Francisco San Francisco	5 67 520
STERNNIERMAN		
Christ*	Sacramento Ward 4	63 600
Geo W*	Sacramento Ward 4	63 600
STERNOX		
T*	Sutter Yuba	70 767
STERNS		
A B	San Francisco San Francisco	12 387 67
C E	San Francisco San Francisco	12 387 67
Calvin D	Sierra La Porte	66 788
E J	Mariposa Twp 3	60 549
J A	El Dorado Eldorado	58 935
John	Tulara Keeneysburg	71 45
Nelson	Humbolt Pacific	59 133
Oliver	Los Angeles Los Angeles	59 495
William	San Joaquin Elkhorn	641000
STERR		
Moses	El Dorado Greenwood	58 709
STERRAN		
Wm B*	San Francisco San Francisco	9 681078
STERRANGTON		
Sam*	San Joaquin Stockton	641037
STERRETT		
Joseph A*	Marin Cortemad	60 784
STERRILL		
Anderson	San Joaquin Elkhorn	64 966
STERRIT		
W E	El Dorado Placerville	58 885
STERRITT		
Willard	San Joaquin Elkhorn	64 966
STERTING		
Thomas*	Siskiyou Yreka	69 125
STERTLEY		
Wm	Tehama Tehama	70 943
STERTOCK		
James	Santa Cruz Santa Cruz	66 628
STERVANT		
S	Tehama Red Bluff	70 914
STERZENAGER		
John	Napa Hot Springs	61 25
STESH		
Charles	Siskiyou Yreka	69 193
STETCER		
Godlip*	Calaveras Twp 6	57 160
STETCHENS		
C C*	Nevada Grass Valley	61 164
STETHENS		
C C*	Nevada Grass Valley	61 164
S*	Nevada Grass Valley	61 174
STETLE		
Dewitt*	Plumas Quincy	62 916
STETRO		
John	Alameda Brooklyn	55 182
STETSEN		
Geo	Amador Twp 2	55 325
STETSON		
A L	Trinity Price'S	701019
A M	San Francisco San Francisco	5 67 518
A S	Trinity Prices B	701019
Chas J	Sacramento Ward 1	63 131
Chs	Stanislaus Emory	70 747
Francis H	San Francisco San Francisco	10 336 67
Geo*	Amador Twp 2	55 325
George W	Sierra Twp 7	66 869
James*	Plumas Quincy	62 982
Jas B	San Francisco San Francisco	10 217 67
Jos B	San Francisco San Francisco	10 217 67

Name	County Locale	M653 RollPage
STETSON		
Josiah	Placer Yankee J	62 780
Lewis	Stanislaus Branch	70 711
M	San Francisco San Francisco	5 67 548
M	Yuba Long Bar	72 749
William W	Los Angeles Los Angeles	59 333
STETTEN		
Ellen	Sacramento Ward 4	63 608
STETTER		
Charles*	Yuba Marysville	72 874
Clarles*	Yuba Marysville	72 874
STETTERAN		
Patrick*	Sierra Downieville	66 978
STETTIVAN		
Patrick*	Sierra Downieville	66 978
STETTNER		
S*	Nevada Grass Valley	61 177
STEUART		
Samuel	Solano Vallejo	69 280
Wm	San Francisco San Francisco	1 68 815
Wm M	Placer Illinois	62 706
STEUBEN		
L*	Nevada Grass Valley	61 182
STEUBENS		
Alex*	Sacramento Georgian	63 347
STEUDEMAN		
E*	Sacramento Ward 1	63 89
STEUDMAN		
Charles	Sierra La Porte	66 770
STEUITZER		
Chas*	Sacramento Sutter	63 291
STEULEN		
William N*	Tulara Twp 1	71 100
STEUN		
A Y*	Sierra Downieville	66 997
STEUNGH		
Phillip J*	El Dorado Georgetown	58 707
STEUNNAN		
Jac*	Sacramento Ward 1	63 46
STEURERMAN		
Henry*	San Francisco San Francisco	9 681051
STEURNEY		
Phillip J	El Dorado Georgetown	58 707
STEUT		
John*	Mariposa Twp 3	60 606
STEVAN		
R	Sacramento Sutter	63 307
STEVANS		
Henry	El Dorado Casumnes	581166
Samuel	Sierra Pine Grove	66 834
Wm W*	Butte Chico	56 537
STEVART		
J B*	San Francisco San Francisco	5 67 550
STEVEES		
James*	Santa Cruz Soguel	66 582
STEVEKBAN		
Louis	San Francisco San Francisco	4 681158
STEVEN S		
G G	Butte Oregon	56 623
Geo	Tuolumne Twp 4	71 164
STEVEN		
G D*	El Dorado Georgetown	58 677
James*	Santa Cruz Soguel	66 582
W	El Dorado Placerville	58 817
STEVENES		
P J*	Calaveras Twp 9	57 408
STEVENS		
---	Nevada Bridgeport	61 465
A	Sacramento Dry Crk	63 369
A H	Calaveras Twp 9	57 367
A H	Calaveras Twp 9	57 389
A M	San Francisco San Francisco	2 67 711
A*	Napa Yount	61 45
Albert	San Francisco San Francisco	9 681050
And	Sacramento Ward 4	63 566
Andrew	Sacramento San Joaquin	63 352
Andrew	San Francisco San Francisco	9 68 940
B F	Butte Ophir	56 757
B R	Butte Ophir	56 773
Bartentt	Santa Cruz Santa Cruz	66 614
Bartin H	Santa Cruz Santa Cruz	66 614
Barton H	Santa Cruz Santa Cruz	66 614
Bartoutt*	Santa Cruz Santa Cruz	66 614
C	Butte Mountain	56 738
C	San Francisco San Francisco	5 67 535
C	Shasta Millvill	66 752
C A	Sierra Twp 7	66 905
C B	Siskiyou Scott Va	69 28
C E	Sacramento Granite	63 267
C P	Nevada Red Dog	61 548
Cahns J	Alameda Brooklyn	55 198
Calvin P	Sacramento Ward 4	63 560
Caroline C	San Francisco	2 67 736
	San Francisco	
Cath	Sacramento Ward 3	63 471
Charles	Contra Costa Twp 2	57 555

Name	County Locale	M653 RollPage
STEVENS		
Charles	Sierra Twp 7	66 913
Charles	Yolo Slate Ra	72 695
Charles	Yuba Slate Ro	72 695
Charles	Yuba Marysville	72 910
Chas H	Sacramento Natonia	63 282
Colman	San Francisco San Francisco	11 150 67
D H	Nevada Bridgeport	61 465
D S Claire*	Sacramento Ward 4	63 558
D St Clair*	Sacramento Ward 4	63 558
E	Santa Clara Fremont	65 442
E A	Nevada Bridgeport	61 505
E M	Nevada Red Dog	61 548
E M	Siskiyou Yreka	69 183
E S	Butte Chico	56 537
E S	Butte Ophir	56 757
Edward C	San Diego Colorado	64 806
Edwd	Santa Clara Fremont	65 441
Elija	Yolo Washington	72 561
Ellen E	San Francisco San Francisco	2 67 659
Eloja	Yolo Washington	72 561
F	Sacramento Georgian	63 345
F F	Sacramento Ward 3	63 488
Fanny	Santa Cruz Pajaro	66 574
Fenny*	Santa Cruz Pajaro	66 574
Ferdinand	Calaveras Twp 5	57 190
Fesdimund	Calaveras Twp 5	57 190
Frank	Trinity E Weaver	701060
Frederick	Calaveras Twp 4	57 303
G H	Butte Ophir	56 800
G P	Placer Forest H	62 797
G S	Amador Twp 1	55 462
Garry	Sierra Twp 7	66 897
Geo	Butte Oregon	56 613
Geo	Sacramento Ward 1	63 5
Geo	San Francisco San Francisco	9 681000
Geo	San Francisco San Francisco	1 68 891
Geo	Tuolumne Jacksonville	71 164
Geo W	San Francisco San Francisco	7 681383
George	Santa Cruz Santa Cruz	66 615
George	Sierra St Louis	66 814
George	Yuba Fosters	72 837
George	Yuba Fosters	72 838
George F	San Francisco San Francisco	11 111 67
Gilbert L	Yuba Foster B	72 833
H A	San Francisco San Francisco	10 260 67
H S	Nevada Bridgeport	61 486
Ham	Sacramento Ward 4	63 538
Hany	Sierra Twp 7	66 897
Henry	Butte Chico	56 560
Henry	Butte Bidwell	56 712
Henry	Butte Bidwell	56 729
Henry	Calaveras Twp 8	57 66
Henry	Santa Cruz Pajaro	66 574
Henry	Sierra Excelsior	661033
Henry	Sierra Monte Crk	661038
Henry	Yuba Long Bar	72 749
Henry F	Los Angeles Los Angeles	59 353
Henry L	Santa Clara San Jose	65 343
Hezekiah W	San Salvador	64 652
	San Bernardino	
Isaac	Amador Twp 2	55 278
Isaac	Yolo Slate Ra	72 718
Isaac	Yuba New York	72 718
Isaac N	Humbolt Mattole	59 128
J	El Dorado Placerville	58 876
J	Nevada Eureka	61 374
J	Nevada Eureka	61 378
J	Sacramento Granite	63 222
J	Sacramento Alabama	63 416
J B	Placer Iona Hills	62 883
J B	Sierra Monte Crk	661038
J B	Sierra Twp 7	66 884
J D	Butte Chico	56 564
J F	Sierra Twp 5	66 935
J H	El Dorado Placerville	58 868
J H	Nevada Bridgeport	61 478
J S	Butte Ophir	56 745
Jabez	Sacramento Ward 1	63 24
James	Santa Cruz Pajaro	66 572
James	Yolo No E Twp	72 670
James	Yuba North Ea	72 670
James ?*	Calaveras Twp 9	57 370
James B	Tulara Twp 1	71 83
James G*	Calaveras Twp 9	57 370
James L	San Joaquin Elliott	641101
James*	Santa Cruz Soguel	66 582
Jas	Butte Chico	56 537
Jas	Sacramento Natonia	63 281
Jas	Sacramento Ward 3	63 470
Jas	Sacramento Ward 4	63 520
Jas	Santa Clara Santa Clara	65 512
Jeff N	Yuba Slate Ro	72 704

California 1860 Census Index

Name	County Locale	M653 Roll	Page
STEVENS			
John	Alameda Brooklyn	55	90
John	Placer Mealsburg	62	702
John	Placer Forest H	62	768
John	Sacramento Ward 1	63	143
John	San Bernardino San Salvador	64	651
John	San Francisco San Francisco 8	68	1294
John	Sierra La Porte	66	777
John	Yuba Long Bar	72	741
John A	Yuba Rose Bar	72	800
John B	Alameda Brooklyn	55	91
John F	Butte Ophir	56	745
John N	Napa Yount	61	45
John T	Sierra Twp 5	66	922
Joseph	Placer Michigan	62	824
Joseph	Santa Clara Alviso	65	402
Joseph	Yolo Slate Ra	72	691
Joseph	Yolo Slate Ra	72	694
Joseph	Yuba Slate Ro	72	691
K	Sacramento Ward 1	63	32
L A	Calaveras Twp 7	57	3
L E	Sacramento Ward 3	63	458
L H	Del Norte Happy Ca	58	664
L*	Sacramento Brighton	63	194
Leonard A	San Francisco San Francisco 11	67	116
Levi	San Francisco San Francisco 9	68	954
Louis V	Butte Eureka	56	654
Louise	Amador Twp 2	55	262
M	Tehama Red Bluff	70	927
M A	Sacramento Sutter	63	300
M J	Nevada Nevada	61	290
Milton	Calaveras Twp 5	57	222
Mortimer	Sierra Downieville	66	987
N H	Sutter Butte	70	795
N V	San Francisco San Francisco 7	68	1431
N W	Sierra Twp 5	66	924
N*	Sacramento Brighton	63	194
Nicolas	Sacramento Ward 1	63	34
O C	Sutter Butte	70	788
Oliver	Sierra Forest C	66	910
P	Sierra Downieville	66	1011
P M	Yuba Bear Rvr	72	1011
Pergenia	Santa Clara Santa Clara	65	476
Peter	Siskiyou Scott Va	69	24
Philip	San Francisco San Francisco 3	67	43
R	San Joaquin Stockton	64	1088
R	Santa Clara San Jose	65	354
R I*	San Francisco San Francisco 2	67	735
R J	San Francisco San Francisco 2	67	735
R K	Sutter Butte	70	788
Robt	Santa Clara Santa Clara	65	475
Romelus R	Calaveras Twp 7	57	19
Rosa	Yuba Foster B	72	829
Rupel	Sierra St Louis	66	818
Russel	Sierra St Louis	66	818
S	Sutter Yuba	70	770
S R	Sierra Downieville	66	988
S*	Sacramento Brighton	63	194
Saml	Sacramento American	63	169
Saml	San Francisco San Francisco 9	68	1018
Saml B	Calaveras Twp 5	57	189
Samuel	San Francisco San Francisco 7	68	1347
Samuel	San Francisco San Francisco 7	68	1402
Samuel	Sierra Twp 5	66	936
Simon	Alameda Brooklyn	55	205
Susan	Sacramento Granite	63	221
Sylvester	Sacramento Ward 4	63	509
T	El Dorado Placerville	58	849
Theodore N	Napa Yount	61	47
Thomas	El Dorado Kelsey	58	1138
Thomas	Fresno Twp 1	59	75
Thomas	Monterey Pajaro	60	1022
Thomas	Placer Michigan	62	844
Thomas	Sierra Poker Flats	66	842
Thomas	Yuba Rose Bar	72	810
Thos	Nevada Red Dog	61	543
Thos	Sacramento Ward 4	63	553
Thos	Trinity E Weaver	70	1057
Thos S	Napa Hot Springs	61	27
Truman*	Placer Iona Hills	62	861
W	Butte Kimshaw	56	598
W	Sutter Nicolaus	70	832
W H	Butte Ophir	56	768
W M	Butte Kimshaw	56	607
W R	Sierra Eureka	66	1045
W T	Klamath Orleans	59	217
Welton	Sierra Downieville	66	1007
William	Tuolumne Montezuma	71	502
William	Calaveras Twp 8	57	73
William	El Dorado Placerville	58	900
William	Placer Michigan	62	830
William	San Francisco San Francisco 7	68	1336
William	San Francisco San Francisco 3	67	70
William	Santa Cruz Pescadero	66	641
William	Sierra La Porte	66	766
STEVENS			
William	Tuolumne Twp 5	71	502
William	Tuolumne Montezuma	71	505
William F	Santa Cruz Pajaro	66	569
William G	Santa Cruz Pajaro	66	569
William H	San Francisco San Francisco 4	68	1115
William L	Santa Cruz Pajaro	66	569
William*	San Luis Obispo San Luis Obispo	65	41
Wilton	Sierra Downieville	66	1007
Wm	Butte Chico	56	560
Wm	Butte Kimshaw	56	598
Wm	Sonoma Cloverdale	69	683
Wm	Yolo Slate Ra	72	694
Wm H	Nevada Nevada	61	260
Wm W	Butte Chico	56	537
Wm*	Yuba Slate Ro	72	694
STEVENSEN			
Jacob*	Placer Michigan	62	827
Robert	Tulara Twp 1	71	91
Saml	Sacramento Granite	63	243
Thos J	Trinity Weaverville	70	1070
STEVENSON			
A	Butte Ophir	56	762
A	Merced Twp 1	60	907
A J	San Francisco San Francisco 5	67	482
A M	Amador Twp 3	55	369
A M	Solano Vacaville	69	362
Agnes	San Francisco San Francisco 11	67	147
Alex	Sacramento Ward 3	63	453
Alexander	Alameda Oakland	55	1
Andrew	Alameda Oakland	55	67
C H	Solano Vacaville	69	329
Charles A	Yuba Rose Par	72	796
Charlotte F	Sacramento Ward 4	63	515
Colman	San Francisco San Francisco 11	67	147
D	Sacramento Ward 4	63	515
David	San Francisco San Francisco 1	68	932
David	Sierra Twp 7	66	895
E A	Tehama Lassen	70	861
E F	San Francisco San Francisco 9	68	954
Elizabeth	Tulara Visalia	71	104
Ernest	San Francisco San Francisco 9	68	974
Eva	Sacramento Sutter	63	299
G B	Solano Vacaville	69	362
G C	Placer Forest H	62	794
George	Santa Cruz Santa Cruz	66	620
George	Tulara Twp 1	71	100
H	San Francisco San Francisco 4	68	1168
H	Tuolumne Big Oak	71	145
Hampton	Yuba Fosters	72	839
J	Sacramento Ward 3	63	428
J A	Trinity Mouth Ca	70	1011
J J	Merced Twp 1	60	908
Jacob*	Placer Michigan	62	827
James	Sacramento Ward 1	63	26
James H	Yuba Marysville	72	926
Jas	Butte Wyandotte	56	668
Jerome	Yuba Rose Bar	72	811
John	Contra Costa Twp 1	57	492
John S	Butte Cascade	56	693
John T	Sierra Gibsonville	66	859
Jos	San Francisco San Francisco 2	67	716
L C	Yuba Rose Par	72	796
L R	Yuba North Ea	72	844
Mariah	Solano Vacaville	69	362
Merr*	Santa Cruz Santa Cruz	66	615
Merv*	Santa Cruz Santa Cruz	66	615
Morr*	Santa Cruz Santa Cruz	66	615
Non*	Santa Cruz Santa Cruz	66	615
Nori	Santa Cruz Santa Cruz	66	615
Norr*	Santa Cruz Santa Cruz	66	615
Preston	Tulara Twp 1	71	91
Preston	Tuolumne Visalia	71	91
Robert	Tuolumne Visalia	71	91
S F	San Francisco San Francisco 9	68	954
Samuel	Calaveras Twp 9	57	372
Samuel	Sierra La Porte	66	790
Samuel C	San Francisco San Francisco 3	67	14
T P	Butte Chico	56	546
Thomas	El Dorado Placerville	58	913
Thos	Sacramento Ward 4	63	518
V	El Dorado Placerville	58	841
Virgil	Amador Twp 6	55	446
W H C	Sacramento Ward 1	63	135
William	Sierra Gibsonville	66	859
William	Solano Vacaville	69	362
Wlfc	Sacramento Ward 1	63	135
Wm	San Francisco San Francisco 1	68	830
Wm	Yolo Slate Ra	72	695
Wm	Yolo Slate Ra	72	697
Wm	Yolo Slate Ra	72	705
Wm	Yuba Slate Ro	72	695
Wm	Yuba Slate Ro	72	697
STEVENSON			
Wm	Yuba Slate Ro	72	705
STEVEO			
L R*	Shasta Shasta	66	664
STEVER			
Wm*	Nevada Nevada	61	324
STEVERS			
A	Napa Yount	61	45
James*	Santa Cruz Soguel	66	582
STEVES			
Joshua	Stanislaus Emory	70	750
Saml*	Stanislaus Emory	70	750
STEVICH			
John	Amador Twp 1	55	490
STEVIE			
W*	El Dorado Georgetown	58	685
STEVINS			
D J	Butte Chico	56	564
Milton	Calaveras Twp 5	57	222
Saml B	Calaveras Twp 5	57	189
STEVINSON			
A	Butte Ophir	56	762
STEVISON			
William	Tuolumne Twp 6	71	542
STEVITZER			
Chas*	Sacramento Sutter	63	291
STEVNAN			
Jno*	San Francisco San Francisco 10	67	314
STEVNIES			
P J*	Calaveras Twp 9	57	408
STEVNIS			
Walter*	Sacramento Natonia	63	271
STEVNUS			
J*	Calaveras Twp 9	57	408
STEVSKSBURY			
Richd*	San Francisco San Francisco 1	68	886
STEVVENS			
John	Placer Iona Hills	62	875
STEWARD			
---	Mariposa Twp 3	60	600
A H	San Francisco San Francisco 9	68	955
Andrew J	Sierra La Porte	66	771
Charly	Mariposa Twp 1	60	626
F H	Nevada Eureka	61	343
F W	Nevada Eureka	61	343
H	El Dorado Georgetown	58	706
H	San Francisco San Francisco 4	68	1167
Hugh	San Francisco San Francisco 1	68	836
Isaac	Sierra Twp 7	66	915
J M*	Mariposa Twp 1	60	656
John	San Mateo Twp 3	65	99
John	Siskiyou Scott Va	69	44
Jose M*	Plumas Quincy	62	941
Joseph	Alameda Brooklyn	55	117
Joseph	Tuolumne Twp 5	71	504
L S	Yolo Washington	72	568
Nicholas	San Mateo Twp 3	65	86
Oliver	Sierra Whiskey	66	844
P C*	Siskiyou Cottonwoood	69	99
Philander	Humbolt Eureka	59	173
R	El Dorado Kelsey	58	1135
R M G	Butte Oregon	56	622
Richard	Plumas Meadow Valley	62	906
Robert	Alameda Brooklyn	55	125
Robert	San Francisco San Francisco 1	68	862
Saml	Monterey Alisal	60	1036
Samuel	Siskiyou Scott Va	69	37
Samuel	Siskiyou Scott Va	69	40
T C*	Siskiyou Cottonwoood	69	99
Thomas	Siskiyou Callahan	69	7
W E*	San Francisco San Francisco 9	68	941
Wilber	San Joaquin Castoria	64	877
William	Solano Vallejo	69	279
Wm W	Alameda Brooklyn	55	199
STEWAREL			
Charly	Mariposa Twp 1	60	626
STEWART			
---	San Francisco San Francisco 9	68	997
---	Sonoma Salt Point	69	692
---	Stanislaus Oatvale	70	717
A	Butte Bidwell	56	706
A	El Dorado Placerville	58	825
A	El Dorado Placerville	58	854
A	El Dorado Placerville	58	877
A	El Dorado Mud Springs	58	997
A	Nevada Nevada	61	295
A	Santa Clara Burnett	65	257
A	Sutter Butte	70	791
A	Tehama Red Bluff	70	929
A	Yuba Rose Bar	72	789
A B	Mariposa Twp 3	60	601
A D	Yuba New York	72	731
A J	El Dorado Diamond	58	767
A L	El Dorado White Oaks	58	1017
A M	Colusa Mansville	57	438

California 1860 Census Index

STEWART

Name	County Locale	M653 Roll Page
Alex	Sacramento Mississipi	63 188
Alexander	Marin Bolinas	60 747
Alexander	San Francisco San Francisco 3	67 40
Alexander	Yuba Marysville	72 874
Alice	Sacramento Ward 1	63 16
Allen	San Joaquin Elkhorn	64 974
Andrew	San Francisco San Francisco 11	132 67
Andrew J	Sierra La Porte	66 771
Archd	San Francisco San Francisco 2	67 738
B R*	El Dorado Placerville	58 883
Belle	Shasta Shasta	66 660
Benj	Sacramento Ward 4	63 523
C	San Joaquin Stockton	64 1091
C C	El Dorado Cold Spring	58 1101
C H	El Dorado Casumnes	58 1175
C H	Yolo Cottonwoood	72 656
C K	San Francisco San Francisco 9	68 1103
C W	Yolo Cottonwoood	72 656
Cas	Napa Napa	61 111
Cassius C	Monterey Pajaro	60 1020
Catharine	Napa Clear Lake	61 120
Catharine	San Francisco San Francisco 2	67 573
Catherine	San Francisco San Francisco 3	67 8
Charles	Alameda Oakland	55 3
Charles	Marin Novato	60 739
Charles	Placer Michigan	62 851
Charles	San Francisco San Francisco 2	67 603
Charles	Solano Vallejo	69 277
Charles	Sonoma Armally	69 513
Charles	Tuolumne Columbia	71 326
Charles	Yuba Marysville	72 897
Charles B	San Francisco San Francisco 11	117 67
Charles H	Yuba Bear Rvr	72 999
Chas C	Napa Clear Lake	61 119
Conright	Butte Ophir	56 747
Cornelius	Fresno Twp 2	59 49
Cowright*	Butte Ophir	56 747
D B	Sacramento Ward 3	63 436
D D	Sutter Yuba	70 771
Daniel	Alameda Oakland	55 13
Danl	Amador Twp 2	55 271
Danl	Tuolumne Columbia	71 360
David	El Dorado Kelsey	58 1142
David	Plumas Quincy	62 953
David	Yolo Slate Ra	72 700
David	Yuba Slate Ro	72 700
Deborah	Sacramento Ward 3	63 489
Donald	El Dorado Coloma	58 1103
Duncan	El Dorado Placerville	58 910
E	Nevada Eureka	61 369
E	Sacramento Ward 3	63 436
E	Sonoma Salt Point	69 689
E G	San Francisco San Francisco 3	67 14
E J	Santa Clara San Jose	65 348
Ebben	Alameda Brooklyn	55 212
Edward	El Dorado Casumnes	58 1168
Elijah	Solano Benecia	69 295
Erum	Amador Twp 5	55 345
Esther N	San Francisco San Francisco 1	68 931
F	Nevada Eureka	61 357
Frank	San Joaquin Stockton	64 1086
Frank	Yolo Cache	72 590
Frank	Yuba Marysville	72 910
G	Sacramento Sutter	63 301
G A	El Dorado Placerville	58 821
G W	Nevada Nevada	61 247
G W	Santa Clara Santa Clara	65 492
G W	Tehama Lassen	70 878
Geo	Mariposa Twp 3	60 594
Geo	Mendocino Big Rvr	60 847
Geo	Sacramento Granite	63 234
Geo B	Napa Clear Lake	61 140
Geo W	Sacramento Ward 3	63 424
George	Sacramento Franklin	63 330
George	Santa Cruz Pajaro	66 564
George	Yuba Rose Bar	72 802
George R	Sacramento Ward 1	63 104
H	San Joaquin Stockton	64 1049
H B	Sutter Butte	70 799
H G	Tuolumne Shawsfla	71 401
H L	Trinity Ferry	70 977
H W	Butte Kimshaw	56 594
Hamilton	Yolo Slate Ra	72 717
Hamilton	Yuba Slate Ro	72 717
Harcus	Santa Cruz Pajaro	66 564
Henry	Alameda Brooklyn	55 213
Henry	El Dorado Placerville	58 916
Henry	San Francisco San Francisco 10	221 67
Henry	San Francisco San Francisco 3	67 36
Henry	San Mateo Twp 3	65 86
Henry	Tuolumne Shawsfla	71 420
Henry L	Plumas Quincy	62 957

STEWART

Name	County Locale	M653 Roll Page
Henry S	Siskiyou Shasta Valley	69 121
Horatio	Yuba Marysville	72 885
I*	Nevada Nevada	61 322
Isaac T	Sierra La Porte	66 766
J	El Dorado Diamond	58 791
J	Nevada Nevada	61 322
J	Nevada Eureka	61 378
J	Sacramento Ward 1	63 3
J	San Francisco San Francisco 1	68 922
J	Shasta Shasta	66 729
J	Sutter Yuba	70 777
J	Sutter Sutter	70 811
J	Sutter Nicolaus	70 828
J	Trinity Indian C	70 983
J A	Sacramento Ward 4	63 506
J B	Merced Twp 1	60 895
J B	Shasta French G	66 716
J B	Tuolumne Twp 1	71 266
J B*	San Francisco San Francisco 5	67 550
J G	Yolo Cache Crk	72 625
J H	Butte Hamilton	56 517
J H	Sacramento Ward 4	63 529
J J	Butte Oregon	56 637
J M	El Dorado Casumnes	58 1169
J M	El Dorado Placerville	58 913
J M	Mariposa Twp 1	60 656
J R	San Francisco San Francisco 10	347 67
J S	Sacramento Cosummes	63 409
J S	Solano Montezuma	69 374
J T	Sutter Bear Rvr	70 825
J W	Tuolumne Jamestown	71 431
J*	Nevada Nevada	61 322
J*	Sonoma Salt Point	69 689
Jacob	Placer Michigan	62 838
Jacob W	Plumas Quincy	62 1065
James	El Dorado Georgetown	58 762
James	El Dorado Placerville	58 933
James	Marin Saucileto	60 749
James	San Francisco San Francisco 3	67 51
James	Sierra Scales D	66 800
James	Sierra Twp 5	66 935
James	Solano Benecia	69 301
James	Tuolumne Sonora	71 190
James	Yuba Bear Rvr	72 1012
James	Yuba New York	72 730
James	Yuba Fosters	72 832
James C	Yuba Rose Bar	72 796
James D	Yuba Marysville	72 911
James M	Tuolumne Twp 3	71 459
Jas	Amador Twp 7	55 414
Jas	Napa Napa	61 94
Jas	Placer Secret R	62 609
Jas	San Bernardino San Bernadino	64 630
Jas	San Francisco San Francisco 10	175 67
Jas H	Amador Twp 2	55 272
Jas T	Placer Virginia	62 686
Jeft*	Mariposa Twp 1	60 656
Jesse	Sacramento Ward 1	63 346
Jno	Amador Twp 5	55 333
Jno	Butte Chico	56 558
Jno	Mendocino Big Rock	60 872
Jno F	Sacramento Centre	63 175
Jno L	Mendocino Arrana	60 862
John	Amador Twp 7	55 414
John	Amador Twp 1	55 470
John	Colusa Monroeville	57 441
John	Contra Costa Twp 2	57 555
John	Marin Cortemad	60 785
John	Monterey Pajaro	60 1022
John	Placer Ophirville	62 653
John	Placer Forest H	62 747
John	Plumas Quincy	62 990
John	Sacramento Franklin	63 326
John	San Francisco San Francisco 7	68 1403
John	San Francisco San Francisco 7	68 1438
John	San Francisco San Francisco 1	68 910
John	Santa Clara Redwood	65 452
John	Shasta French G	66 715
John	Tuolumne Twp 1	71 272
John	Tuolumne Springfield	71 373
John	Tuolumne Twp 3	71 461
John	Yolo No E Twp	72 667
John	Yolo Slate Ra	72 696
John	Yuba Slate Ro	72 696
John B	Plumas Quincy	62 984
John B	Sacramento Ward 3	63 442
John H	Calaveras Twp 8	57 58
John M	San Bernardino S Timate	64 687
John R	Santa Clara Fremont	65 439
Jos	San Francisco San Francisco 9	68 1073
Joseph	Calaveras Twp 6	57 164
Joseph	Placer Michigan	62 826
Joseph	Plumas Quincy	62 916

STEWART

Name	County Locale	M653 Roll Page
Joseph	Sierra Whiskey	66 844
Joseph	Solano Vallejo	69 280
Joseph	Tuolumne Sonora	71 198
Joseph H	Yuba Marysville	72 906
K	Nevada Little Y	61 536
L	Alameda Oakland	55 50
L L	Marin Point Re	60 732
Lambert	Los Angeles Los Angeles	59 390
Lucretia	Santa Cruz Pajaro	66 564
Lunran	San Joaquin Castoria	64 901
M	Sutter Yuba	70 768
M	Trinity Steiner	70 1000
M A	Tuolumne Sonora	71 232
M W	Trinity Trinity	70 974
Marcus	Santa Cruz Pajaro	66 564
Mary	Sacramento Ward 1	63 23
Mary	Tuolumne Twp 2	71 284
Mary E	Santa Clara Santa Clara	65 476
Mary L*	Sacramento Ward 4	63 546
Mary S*	Sacramento Ward 4	63 546
Morris	Nevada Red Dog	61 544
N E	Tuolumne Twp 3	71 457
Nancy	Solano Vallejo	69 270
Nelson	Amador Twp 1	55 484
Newton B	Placer Auburn	62 595
Norman	Sacramento San Joaquin	63 350
Norris	Tuolumne Twp 1	71 260
O	Trinity Ferry	70 977
Olive	Tehama Red Bluff	70 927
Oliver	Sierra Whiskey	66 844
Orrim*	Yuba Parke Ba	72 781
Orwin	Yuba Parks Ba	72 781
Oscar	Plumas Quincy	62 917
P	Sacramento Ward 3	63 435
P J	San Francisco San Francisco 3	67 44
Peter	Placer Rattle Snake	62 634
Peter	Sonoma Armally	69 479
Peter	Tuolumne Twp 2	71 367
R	Butte Ophir	56 795
R	Sacramento Brighton	63 202
R	Sutter Butte	70 787
R	Sutter Butte	70 788
R G	Trinity Weaverville	70 1076
R J	San Francisco San Francisco 3	67 44
R S	Sacramento Cosummes	63 385
Richard	Sacramento Ward 4	63 604
Rob	Stanislaus Buena Village	70 721
Robert	Alameda Brooklyn	55 101
Robert	Amador Twp 1	55 462
Robert	Butte Kimshaw	56 607
Robert	Mendocino Big Rvr	60 843
Robert	Yolo Washington	72 563
Robt	Alameda Brooklyn	55 104
Robt	Sacramento Sutter	63 306
Robt	Sacramento Sutter	63 307
Robt	Sacramento Ward 1	63 74
Robt	Sacramento Ward 1	63 89
Robt	Santa Clara Redwood	65 445
S	Sonoma Salt Point	69 692
S B	Tuolumne Twp 1	71 278
S B	Tuolumne Columbia	71 342
S C	Sierra Twp 5	66 936
S C	Sonoma Salt Point	69 691
S L	El Dorado Union	58 1088
S P	Sacramento Casumnes	63 380
S S	Tuolumne Jamestown	71 432
Sak*	El Dorado Placerville	58 926
Saml H	Tuolumne Columbia	71 317
Samuel	Nevada Rough &	61 408
Samuel	Plumas Quincy	62 955
Samuel	Sierra Twp 7	66 877
Samuel	Solano Vallejo	69 280
Samuel	Solano Montezuma	69 367
Samuel J	Siskiyou Yreka	69 139
Silas	Monterey Pajaro	60 1020
Smith	Sacramento Lee	63 210
T	Mendocino Arrana	60 857
T	Sacramento Cosummes	63 390
T G	Sacramento San Joaquin	63 368
Teresa	San Francisco San Francisco 10	273 67
Thomas	Calaveras Twp 5	57 174
Thomas	Contra Costa Twp 3	57 597
Thomas	El Dorado Union	58 1089
Thomas	San Francisco San Francisco 3	67 36
Thomas	Siskiyou Callahan	69 7
Thomas E	Solano Montezuma	69 367
Thos	San Francisco San Francisco 10	351 67
Thos G	Placer Secret R	62 609
Truman	Calaveras Twp 9	57 371
Truman A	Calaveras Twp 9	57 371
Trumary	Calaveras Twp 9	57 371
Usance	Sierra La Porte	66 766
W	El Dorado Georgetown	58 706

Name	County Locale	M653 RollPage
STEWART		
W	Sacramento Sutter	63 301
W	Sutter Sutter	70 811
W B	Tuolumne Columbia	71 358
W C	Tuolumne Twp 4	71 175
W E	San Francisco San Francisco 10	234 67
W F	Santa Clara San Jose	65 372
W H	Nevada Rough &	61 414
W M	Tuolumne Twp 2	71 385
W W	El Dorado Diamond	58 797
Wallace	Mendocino Big Rvr	60 846
Walter	Butte Ophir	56 766
Warren A	San Francisco San Francisco 2	67 637
Well	Tuolumne Shawsfla	71 385
William	El Dorado Placerville	58 910
William	Placer Yankee J	62 760
William	San Francisco San Francisco 3	67 23
William	San Joaquin Elkhorn	64 976
William	Shasta Horsetown	66 708
William	Sierra Scales D	66 801
William	Sierra St Louis	66 805
William	Sierra Pine Grove	66 835
William	Siskiyou Yreka	69 179
William	Solano Vacaville	69 352
William	Yuba Rose Bar	72 789
William B	Yuba Fosters	72 837
William B	Yuba Fosters	72 838
Wm	Alameda Brooklyn	55 158
Wm	Amador Twp 2	55 323
Wm	Butte Chico	56 533
Wm	Colusa Colusi	57 427
Wm	Napa Napa	61 77
Wm	Sacramento Franklin	63 315
Wm	San Francisco San Francisco 10	313 67
Wm	San Francisco San Francisco 1	68 815
Wm	Sierra Twp 7	66 890
Wm	Yolo No E Twp	72 667
Wm	Yolo Slate Ra	72 694
Wm	Yuba Slate Ro	72 694
Wm A	Colusa Butte Crk	57 467
Wm E	Sonoma Armally	69 512
Wm E	Stanislaus Emory	70 739
Wm E	Tuolumne Columbia	71 311
Wm F	San Francisco San Francisco 1	68 931
Wm H	Del Norte Crescent	58 623
Wm M	Sierra Downieville	66 978
Wm R	Tuolumne Columbia	71 317
Wm W	Placer Auburn	62 567
Woodford	Siskiyou Shasta Rvr	69 111
STEWARTR		
Jack	San Joaquin Castoria	64 889
Samuel	San Joaquin Castoria	64 893
STEWARTS		
Horatcoa*	Yuba Marysville	72 885
Horatio*	Yuba Marysville	72 885
STEWELL		
M B	San Francisco San Francisco 4	681222
Otis W*	Sierra Pine Grove	66 823
Ratiot*	Sierra Downieville	66 969
STEWELLCE		
Charles	Sierra Gibsonville	66 858
STEWELLEE		
Charles*	Sierra Gibsonville	66 858
STEWERT		
H P	San Joaquin Stockton	641034
STEWETT		
Joseph A	Marin Cortemad	60 784
Otis W	Sierra Pine Grove	66 823
STEWIE		
W*	El Dorado Georgetown	58 685
STEWITT		
Otis W	Sierra Pine Grove	66 823
STEWQART		
James	Colusa Grand Island	57 476
STEWSKSBURY		
Richd*	San Francisco San Francisco 1	68 886
STHAR		
John*	Mariposa Twp 1	60 638
Wm	Mariposa Twp 1	60 638
STHERLAND		
William	Sierra Whiskey	66 849
STHERNEINER		
Jo*	Mariposa Coulterville	60 688
STHILL		
John	Plumas Meadow Valley	62 907
STHR		
John	Mariposa Twp 1	60 638
STHRALA		
Paul	San Francisco San Francisco 7	681395
STHROBE		
John*	Sierra La Porte	66 779
STIAN		
Joseph*	Santa Cruz Santa Cruz	66 614
STIAUB		
Edward*	Sierra St Louis	66 808
STIAUBS		
Edward*	Sierra St Louis	66 808
STIBBENS		
James	San Francisco San Francisco 4	681115
STIBBINS		
F	Butte Wyandotte	56 662
Jno	Alameda Brooklyn	55 196
STICE		
Abraham	Napa Yount	61 43
Moses	Napa Yount	61 54
Rebeca	Napa Yount	61 43
Richmond	Solano Vacaville	69 336
STICH		
John	San Francisco San Francisco 10	301 67
Wm	Sierra Downieville	66 968
STICHER		
Frederick	Calaveras Twp 7	57 18
STICHNEY		
Isaac*	Tuolumne Jacksonville	71 516
STICK		
Henry	Placer Auburn	62 583
Philip	Placer Forest H	62 795
Wm	Sierra Downieville	66 968
STICKAN		
Andrew	Santa Clara San Jose	65 363
STICKDALE		
R S	El Dorado Georgetown	58 699
STICKEEN		
Bridget*	Yuba Marysville	72 857
STICKEIN		
Bridget*	Yuba Marysville	72 852
STICKEL		
David	Yuba Marysville	72 914
Henry	Amador Twp 1	55 469
STICKEM		
Bridget*	Yuba Marysville	72 857
STICKENE		
Bridget*	Yuba Marysville	72 852
STICKENGER		
J	Siskiyou Scott Ri	69 70
STICKER		
Henry	San Francisco San Francisco 10	292 67
Jacob	Yuba Marysville	72 958
Michael*	Santa Cruz Santa Cruz	66 626
STICKET		
David	Yuba Marysville	72 914
STICKLAND		
Benjn	Sierra Twp 7	66 884
Geo	San Francisco San Francisco 10	312 67
Joseph	Sierra Twp 7	66 895
M L	Placer Dutch Fl	62 709
STICKLE		
Edmund	Calaveras Twp 8	57 51
George	Calaveras Twp 8	57 51
STICKLER		
Martin	Amador Twp 5	55 362
STICKLES		
Lilas A	Calaveras Twp 5	57 210
Lilas H	Calaveras Twp 5	57 210
Silas H	Calaveras Twp 5	57 210
STICKLEY		
Gabe	Yuba New York	72 728
STICKLITZ		
Hermand L	Siskiyou Yreka	69 137
STICKMAN		
Wm H	Sacramento Ward 4	63 515
STICKNER		
H	Tuolumne Twp 2	71 296
STICKNES		
H P	Tuolumne Columbia	71 296
STICKNEY		
Antony*	Placer Michigan	62 814
Charles	Sierra Eureka	661047
Jno B	Alameda Brooklyn	55 81
John	Sacramento Ward 1	63 17
Joseph	El Dorado Coloma	581108
Saml	San Francisco San Francisco 10	269 67
STICKNOTH		
Henry	Calaveras Twp 10	57 289
STICKSON		
Mathew	Yuba Rose Bar	72 818
STICKTOR		
John	Napa Yount	61 36
STIEBING		
John	Los Angeles Los Angeles	59 371
STIEBRING		
John*	Los Angeles Los Angeles	59 371
STIEBURG		
John*	Los Angeles Los Angeles	59 371
STIEEN		
Joseph	Santa Cruz Santa Cruz	66 614
STIEFEE		
Golbet	Solano Benecia	69 317
STIEFEE		
L*	San Francisco San Francisco 10	267 67
STIEFEL		
Gotlib	Solano Benecia	69 317
L	San Francisco San Francisco 10	267 67
STIEGER		
William	Calaveras Twp 7	57 25
STIEKTON		
Isaac N*	Siskiyou Yreka	69 129
STIEL		
David W*	Sierra St Louis	66 810
STIEMER		
Premig	San Francisco San Francisco 7	681355
STIEN		
C B	Sacramento Ward 1	63 19
Isaac*	El Dorado Georgetown	58 679
STIENBERGER		
S	Mariposa Twp 3	60 605
STIENER		
John	Calaveras Twp 7	57 6
John	Calaveras Twp 7	57 7
STIENFORD		
Frederick	Marin Cortemad	60 755
STIENHOFF		
Clarissa	Humbolt Bucksport	59 156
STIENIGER		
A	El Dorado Placerville	58 849
STIER		
Henry	San Joaquin Stockton	641077
STIERLING		
F	Trinity Price'S	701019
STIEVE		
Henry*	Calaveras Twp 6	57 162
STIEVENS		
Bridget*	San Mateo Twp 1	65 48
STIEVES		
Henry*	Calaveras Twp 6	57 162
STIFEL		
Peter	El Dorado Coloma	581116
STIFFE		
Charles	Calaveras Twp 7	57 9
STIFFENHAGEN		
Henry	San Diego Colorado	64 807
STIFFENS		
Peter*	San Francisco San Francisco 3	67 63
STIFFINS		
John H*	Yuba Linda	72 989
Peter*	San Francisco San Francisco 3	67 63
STIFFLER		
C	Yolo Putah	72 585
William	Calaveras Twp 5	57 229
STIFFY		
Margaret	Santa Clara Gilroy	65 251
STIGALL		
H	El Dorado Georgetown	58 675
STIGE		
J G*	San Francisco San Francisco 2	67 674
STIGEMAN		
William	Sierra Poker Flats	66 837
STIGER		
Christian	Del Norte Crescent	58 637
STIGGER		
O P	Nevada Bridgeport	61 470
STIGHT		
E T*	Sacramento American	63 158
STIGMAN		
Lewis	Santa Clara Santa Clara	65 463
STIGNER		
Geo	Tuolumne Columbia	71 331
STIKES		
John	Sacramento Ward 4	63 516
STILBONE		
W	Sutter Vernon	70 845
STILE		
Charles	El Dorado Placerville	58 895
Frederick	Contra Costa Twp 1	57 505
Henry	El Dorado Casumnes	581163
STILES		
A	San Bernardino San Bernadino	64 615
A G	San Francisco San Francisco 10	232 67
A H*	Sonoma Russian	69 437
A L	Solano Benecia	69 281
B L*	Sacramento Brighton	63 204
B S*	Sacramento Brighton	63 204
C	Shasta Millvill	66 751
C D	Shasta Millvill	66 751
C W	Mendocino Ukiah	60 801
Catharine	Trinity E Weaver	701061
Henry	Nevada Bridgeport	61 450
J	Nevada Nevada	61 287
John	San Francisco San Francisco 10	225 67
L	Butte Ophir	56 783

Name	County Locale	M653 RollPage
STILES		
Lyman C	Plumas Quincy	62 972
M W	El Dorado Kelsey	581143
N A	Shasta Millvill	66 726
Oscar E	Colusa Monroeville	57 447
S	Nevada Washington	61 336
S	Nevada Eureka	61 365
S P	Nevada Nevada	61 281
S*	Nevada Washington	61 336
W W	Mendocino Ukiah	60 803
William	Placer Iona Hills	62 864
Wm A	Nevada Nevada	61 261
STILESMCK		
Elias	San Bernardino Santa Barbara	64 170
STILL		
Alonzo D	Calaveras Twp 4	57 328
Charles L	Sierra Downieville	66 964
J	San Joaquin Stockton	641099
John H	San Francisco San Francisco 8	681143
Joseph S	San Joaquin Elkhorn	64 949
Samuel	San Francisco San Francisco 6	67 411
Sarah	San Francisco San Francisco 6	67 431
Sarah C	San Francisco San Francisco 6	67 431
William G	Los Angeles Los Angeles	59 343
Wm C*	Mariposa Twp 3	60 584
STILLAGAN		
G W	El Dorado Casumnes	581177
STILLBORN		
Wm	Sacramento Ward 3	63 424
STILLE		
Chris	Santa Clara San Jose	65 289
STILLENGER		
James	El Dorado Casumnes	581178
STILLER		
A A	Trinity Evans Ba	701003
F	El Dorado Placerville	58 880
STILLERAN		
Patrick*	Sierra Downieville	66 978
STILLES		
B L*	Sacramento Cosumnes	63 399
R L*	Sacramento Cosumnes	63 399
STILLHIE		
Alfred*	Sacramento Natonia	63 277
STILLHN		
Alfred*	Sacramento Natonia	63 277
STILLING		
John	San Francisco San Francisco 3	67 5
STILLINGER		
E D	Siskiyou Klamath	69 85
Mary*	Sacramento Ward 3	63 444
STILLMAN		
Ausin	Amador Twp 5	55 362
E	San Francisco San Francisco 5	67 549
E D	Siskiyou Klamath	69 85
Giles	Butte Chico	56 545
Giles	Butte Chico	56 564
J A	El Dorado Diamond	58 795
J B	Sacramento Ward 3	63 424
J B	Sacramento Ward 4	63 496
J D	Sacramento Ward 4	63 566
James	Sonoma Salt Point	69 695
Julia	San Francisco San Francisco 2	67 728
Richman	Sierra Twp 7	66 894
Tho	Siskiyou Klamath	69 89
STILLS		
Geo	Siskiyou Klamath	69 88
John	Solano Suisan	69 240
STILLUAGGON		
W W*	Napa Napa	61 88
STILLUC		
Alfred	Sacramento Natonia	63 277
STILLWAGGON		
W W	Napa Napa	61 88
STILLWAY		
George	Shasta Shasta	66 660
STILLWELL		
D	Merced Twp 1	60 911
Joseph	Sacramento Ward 4	63 588
Joseph	Santa Clara San Jose	65 312
R S	Tuolumne Twp 1	71 245
Robt	Trinity Indian C	70 983
T	Sacramento Ward 4	63 606
Wm	Trinity Trinity	70 975
STILMAN		
J A	El Dorado Diamond	58 791
STILSON		
David	Santa Clara Gilroy	65 245
Kiram	Santa Clara Gilroy	65 245
STILT		
Robert	San Francisco San Francisco 10	271
		67
Samuel*	Napa Yount	61 41
STILTEVAN		
Patrick*	Sierra Downieville	66 978
STILTIRAN		
Patrick*	Sierra Downieville	66 978

Name	County Locale	M653 RollPage
STILTMAN		
James	Sonoma Salt Point	69 695
STILTS		
Geo*	Siskiyou Klamath	69 88
STILWELL		
A	Sierra Twp 7	66 911
Charles	Stanislaus Emory	70 754
George A	Sierra Twp 7	66 878
George W	Sierra Twp 7	66 878
Henry*	El Dorado Kelsey	581156
Mariah	Sonoma Armally	69 513
S M	El Dorado Eldorado	58 935
STILWILL		
Henry*	El Dorado Kelsey	581156
STILY		
Ebenezer	Placer Iona Hills	62 877
STILZ		
Lewis*	Alameda Brooklyn	55 129
STIM		
Ton	El Dorado Diamond	58 769
STIMARN		
J S*	El Dorado Georgetown	58 759
STIMBERG		
Lawrence	Marin Novato	60 739
STIMER		
E*	Sutter Yuba	70 766
Jacob*	Placer Grizzly	62 755
M	Sutter Yuba	70 774
STIMLER		
Geo*	Amador Twp 2	55 309
STIMMELL		
H E	Siskiyou Yreka	69 173
STIMONAM		
E	Amador Twp 3	55 409
STIMPSON		
Charles M	San Joaquin Stockton	641026
John W	Placer Stewart	62 606
STINARD		
August	Siskiyou Scott Va	69 28
J	Siskiyou Klamath	69 95
STINCEN		
Margar A*	Sacramento Ward 1	63 97
Margaret S	Sacramento Ward 1	63 97
Margaret*	Sacramento Ward 1	63 97
STINCHACAM		
George	Yuba Fosters	72 828
STINCHACUM		
George	Yuba Foster B	72 828
STINCHFIELD		
George	Colusa Grand Island	57 477
J	Tuolumne Twp 2	71 302
Jos	Klamath Salmon	59 208
STINCHICAM		
Samuel*	Yuba Long Bar	72 768
STINDERO		
J H	Nevada Nevada	61 239
STINE		
Charles	Siskiyou Yreka	69 170
Edwin	Siskiyou Shasta Rvr	69 116
Elias*	Siskiyou Shasta Rvr	69 116
Frederick*	Siskiyou Shasta Valley	69 118
G W*	Siskiyou Klamath	69 92
Henry*	Trinity Big Flat	701040
J D	Sonoma Armally	69 514
John	Siskiyou Yreka	69 170
Joseph	Contra Costa Twp 2	57 573
L	El Dorado Salmon Hills	581057
Phillip	Tulara Visalia	71 89
Robert*	Siskiyou Klamath	69 92
Rochez	Monterey San Juan	60 990
S M*	Siskiyou Klamath	69 92
STINEHOUSE		
N	Nevada Eureka	61 388
STINER		
Jacob	Klamath Liberty	59 235
Leopold	Placer Rattle Snake	62 600
S	Sutter Yuba	70 766
Thos*	Mariposa Twp 3	60 609
STINES		
John F	Plumas Quincy	62 925
STING		
Chas	Nevada Nevada	61 239
Geo W	Siskiyou Callahan	69 10
John*	El Dorado Georgetown	58 680
STINGEEN		
Alse*	Amador Twp 2	55 325
STINGER		
A	Nevada Eureka	61 363
A*	Sacramento Dry Crk	63 376
Joseph B	Yuba New York	72 748
M	Nevada Eureka	61 363
STINGES		
John	Los Angeles San Pedro	59 479
STINGLE		
C	Sonoma Salt Point	69 691
Jacob	Napa Napa	61 103

Name	County Locale	M653 RollPage
STINGLEY		
B S	Mendocino Ukiah	60 796
Wm	Santa Clara Gilroy	65 236
STINGTZELL		
John	Contra Costa Twp 1	57 485
STINHESKENS		
F	El Dorado Greenwood	58 714
STINKHAM		
Alvin	Santa Cruz Santa Cruz	66 602
STINNBACK		
John	Contra Costa Twp 1	57 487
STINNER		
Henry	Sacramento Cosumnes	63 390
William*	San Luis Obispo	65 41
	San Luis Obispo	
STINNMETE		
George	Tuolumne Twp 1	71 209
STINNS		
Jacob	Colusa Grand Island	57 472
STINO		
Henry*	Trinity Big Flat	701040
STINOR		
Jacob	Amador Twp 3	55 398
STINRELL		
Chas*	Alameda Brooklyn	55 126
STINSCOCKER		
G H*	El Dorado Georgetown	58 698
STINSELL		
Chas*	Alameda Brooklyn	55 126
STINSEN		
James	Mendocino Big Rvr	60 843
Saul	Amador Twp 5	55 342
STINSHELL		
Wm	Alameda Brooklyn	55 126
STINSMAN		
J S*	El Dorado Georgetown	58 759
STINSON		
Abner	Placer Sacramento	62 644
Alfred	El Dorado Casumnes	581168
Ann	San Francisco San Francisco 6	67 418
G C	Tuolumne Twp 2	71 297
J W	Yuba Long Bar	72 772
James	Mendocino Big Rvr	60 843
James	Stanislaus Emory	70 740
James	Stanislaus Emory	70 751
John	Alameda Brooklyn	55 185
Jonas B	Monterey Alisal	601031
Lewis J	Plumas Quincy	62 919
Lucy J	San Francisco San Francisco 8	681263
Michael	Santa Cruz Santa Cruz	66 629
Perry*	San Francisco San Francisco 2	67 675
R	Nevada Nevada	61 272
Samuel	Plumas Quincy	62 919
Wm	Trinity Big Flat	701039
STINT		
C*	Calaveras Twp 9	57 398
STINTA		
Joseph	Calaveras Twp 8	57 90
STINTER		
Velncy	El Dorado Greenwood	58 729
STINTISE		
W	San Francisco San Francisco 1	68 927
STINTON		
P F	Nevada Grass Valley	61 199
R	Nevada Grass Valley	61 169
STIONIS		
Walter*	Sacramento Natonia	63 271
STIPHINA		
---	Los Angeles Tejon	59 529
STIPL		
David	San Francisco San Francisco 3	67 7
STIPLAND		
S	Sutter Nicolaus	70 833
STIPLAW		
J	Sutter Nicolaus	70 833
STIPP		
D*	Nevada Bridgeport	61 477
STIPPICK		
M*	Shasta Shasta	66 674
STIPSEY		
Wm	Butte Ophir	56 747
STIRE		
V	Santa Clara Santa Clara	65 462
STIRER		
Jacob	Yuba Parks Ba	72 778
Timothy B	Solano Benecia	69 310
STIRLEY		
William	Solano Vallejo	69 249
STIRLING		
Pedro	San Francisco San Francisco 6	67 445
STIRLY		
James*	Placer Michigan	62 857
STIRNFILS		
A*	El Dorado Georgetown	58 676
STIRNS		
Oliver*	Los Angeles Los Angeles	59 495

Name	County Locale	M653 RollPage
STIRRIT		
Jas	Sonoma Bodega	69 537
STIRWAY		
A*	Shasta Millvill	66 751
STISS		
Henry	El Dorado Big Bar	58 737
STISSLER		
T W	El Dorado Georgetown	58 696
STISSLOR		
T N	El Dorado Georgetown	58 696
STITCH		
Alexander	San Joaquin Douglass	64 926
STITES		
A	Siskiyou Cottonwoood	69 107
A H	Sonoma Russian	69 437
A*	Siskiyou Cottonwoood	69 107
Alexander	Sonoma Healdsbu	69 472
Henry	Siskiyou Cottonwoood	69 107
Henry	Siskiyou Cottonwoood	69 108
John	Yuba Bear Rvr	72 998
Wm A	Nevada Nevada	61 261
STITH		
Isaac H	Yuba Marysville	72 862
STITLE		
Isaac H*	Yuba Marysville	72 862
STITLERAN		
Patrick*	Sierra Downieville	66 978
STITSHINBOUR		
J	El Dorado Newtown	58 776
STITSMAN		
Stephen	Nevada Little Y	61 534
STITSON		
William P	San Joaquin Stockton	641032
STITT		
A J	Trinity Minersville	70 968
Samuel*	Napa Yount	61 41
Samul*	Napa Yount	61 41
Thos	Tuolumne Big Oak	71 126
Thos	Tuolumne Twp 4	71 128
STITTE		
Isaac H*	Yuba Marysville	72 862
STITTON		
Thos*	Sonoma Vallejo	69 626
STITWELL		
A	Sierra Twp 7	66 911
STITZBURGER		
A C	Butte Kimshaw	56 590
STIVENS		
Lafayette*	San Francisco 2	67 566
	San Francisco	
STIVER		
Christ	San Francisco San Francisco 2	67 562
David	Napa Yount	61 44
John E	Sierra Poker Flats	66 842
Thos*	Mariposa Twp 3	60 609
STIVERS		
D A*	San Francisco San Francisco 12	376 67
Jas	Calaveras Twp 9	57 380
Lafayette*	San Francisco 2	67 566
	San Francisco	
STIVNIES		
J*	Calaveras Twp 9	57 408
STIX		
Robert*	Santa Cruz Santa Cruz	66 630
Thadeus*	Santa Cruz Santa Cruz	66 630
STJOHN		
A C	Colusa Monroeville	57 455
STKINSON		
J	El Dorado Georgetown	58 684
STLELAIR		
A*	Tuolumne Twp 2	71 300
STLEYR		
Eugine*	Tuolumne Twp 1	71 242
STOAG		
William*	Santa Cruz Pescadero	66 645
STOAK		
D*	Los Angeles Tejon	59 526
Seduardo	San Mateo Twp 2	65 132
STOAKS		
Alfredo	San Mateo Twp 2	65 132
STOAN		
A	Nevada Nevada	61 260
M G	Butte Chico	56 557
STOANAKER		
Saml	Tuolumne Twp 1	71 208
STOANAKES		
Saml	Tuolumne Sonora	71 208
STOAS		
George*	Yuba Marysville	72 872
STOBAUGH		
C C	Sierra Twp 7	66 866
STOBEL		
Jules	Alameda Brooklyn	55 101
STOBER		
L	El Dorado Placerville	58 871

Name	County Locale	M653 RollPage
STOBLER		
John	Santa Clara Santa Clara	65 490
STOBLETZILL		
Harmon S	Yuba Marysville	72 870
STOBZ		
Eliza*	Sacramento Granite	63 252
STOCCONI		
August*	Tuolumne Columbia	71 357
STOCE		
Clement*	Sacramento American	63 158
Clinton	Nevada Red Dog	61 543
STOCEOM		
August	Tuolumne Twp 2	71 357
STOCEONI		
August*	Tuolumne Columbia	71 357
STOCERN		
L*	Sacramento Brighton	63 200
S*	Sacramento Brighton	63 200
STOCEY		
Henry*	San Francisco San Francisco 9	681074
STOCK		
Albert	Sierra Twp 7	66 900
Charles	Monterey Pajaro	601021
Charles	Solano Benecia	69 316
Chas	San Bernardino San Bernadino	64 671
Edward	Siskiyou Scott Va	69 31
Francis	Santa Clara San Jose	65 280
H	San Francisco San Francisco 5	67 542
Jacob	San Francisco San Francisco 4	681153
Jas*	Santa Clara San Jose	65 321
John	Calaveras Twp 6	57 146
John	Contra Costa Twp 3	57 606
John	San Francisco San Francisco 3	67 16
Robert	San Francisco San Francisco 4	681139
Winsel	El Dorado Union	581088
STOCKARD		
J T	Merced Twp 1	60 907
STOCKDALE		
D F	El Dorado Diamond	58 799
Hugh	Sonoma Armally	69 493
Jas	San Francisco San Francisco 1	68 884
Robt	El Dorado Coloma	581082
STOCKDALL		
J	Nevada Grass Valley	61 192
STOCKDLE		
Jas	San Francisco San Francisco 1	68 833
STOCKDON		
H C	Tehama Red Bluff	70 911
STOCKELAGER		
Fred	Siskiyou Yreka	69 171
STOCKELY		
J M	Sacramento Ward 1	63 151
STOCKEN		
W	San Francisco San Francisco 1	68 819
STOCKENOERLD		
L	San Francisco San Francisco 4	681231
STOCKENVERLD		
L*	San Francisco San Francisco 4	681231
STOCKER		
Ann J	San Francisco San Francisco 3	67 17
J F*	Marin San Rafael	60 758
Joseph	Calaveras Twp 5	57 240
STOCKEY CONDEY		
M*	El Dorado Diamond	58 802
STOCKEY		
Oliver	Sierra St Louis	66 810
STOCKFLETH		
Peter*	San Francisco San Francisco 8	681265
STOCKFLITH		
Peter*	San Francisco San Francisco 8	681265
STOCKHAM		
Henry	Plumas Quincy	621003
Thos	San Francisco San Francisco 1	68 898
STOCKING		
Clark B	Humbolt Eel Rvr	59 146
J C	Sonoma Armally	69 512
N	Colusa Grand Island	57 475
STOCKLE		
Gop*	San Joaquin Stockton	641040
S	San Francisco San Francisco 1	68 855
STOCKLIN		
Jams M*	Mariposa Coulterville	60 683
Janes M*	Mariposa Coulterville	60 683
STOCKLY		
G	San Francisco San Francisco 1	68 811
STOCKMAN		
F	Amador Twp 5	55 343
Geo	Siskiyou Scott Ri	69 81
Henry	Calaveras Twp 6	57 140
STOCKMON		
D E	Solano Suisan	69 208
STOCKPOLE		
Jacob E	Calaveras Twp 10	57 291
STOCKS		
John	Calaveras Twp 5	57 146
John	Yolo Cache Crk	72 626

Name	County Locale	M653 RollPage
STOCKSLAGER		
Fred	Siskiyou Yreka	69 171
STOCKSTEIN		
David	Yolo Slate Ra	72 697
STOCKSTILL		
James	Tuolumne Twp 1	71 258
STOCKSTINN		
Daniel	Yuba Slate Ro	72 697
STOCKTON		
B G	Alameda Brooklyn	55 168
Ella	Shasta Horsetown	66 694
Gabriel	Sonoma Petaluma	69 555
George	Yuba Marysville	72 894
Isaac	Sonoma Petaluma	69 552
James	El Dorado Georgetown	58 704
James	Los Angeles Elmonte	59 248
James M	Mariposa Coulterville	60 683
Jno E	Butte Hamilton	56 528
John	Tulara Visalia	71 10
Mary A E	Yuba Marysville	72 942
Rafael	San Diego Agua Caliente	64 855
S	Napa Napa	61 61
S W	Marin Tomales	60 774
William M	Los Angeles San Gabriel	59 408
Wm B	Santa Clara Santa Clara	65 464
STOCKTUN		
Joseph	Sacramento Franklin	63 314
STOCKWELL		
Alvin W	San Francisco San Francisco 8	681300
E R	San Joaquin Stockton	641011
Eben S	Sonoma Mendocino	69 451
Elbridge	Calaveras Twp 4	57 337
Ellridge*	Calaveras Twp 4	57 337
J M	Napa Napa	61 112
J P	San Joaquin Stockton	641023
John D	Placer Auburn	62 593
Maremaid	Sonoma Petaluma	69 560
S S	Sierra Twp 7	66 910
Sylvan	Sonoma Petaluma	69 563
W	San Joaquin Stockton	641100
Will	San Joaquin Stockton	641027
STOCKWILL		
Eldridge	Calaveras Twp 4	57 337
STOCO		
Jacob	Calaveras Twp 9	57 379
STOCTDON		
W S	Mariposa Twp 1	60 647
STOCTETON		
W S*	Mariposa Twp 1	60 647
STOCTITON		
W S	Mariposa Twp 1	60 647
STOCTON		
Nathaniel	Santa Cruz Santa Cruz	66 620
W D	El Dorado Casumnes	581165
STOCUM		
Chas	Placer Folsom	62 641
STOCUMANN		
Jacob*	Yuba Marysville	72 902
STOCUMB		
Asa	Napa Clear Lake	61 124
STOD		
Peter	Nevada Nevada	61 241
STODARD		
Cyrus	Yuba Bear Rvr	721000
W	Sutter Sutter	70 817
STODDANT		
C*	Nevada Nevada	61 289
O*	Nevada Nevada	61 289
STODDARD		
A	Nevada Grass Valley	61 158
A	Nevada Eureka	61 346
C	San Joaquin Elkhorn	64 983
D H	Placer Iona Hills	62 891
E M	Calaveras Twp 8	57 85
H S	Alameda Brooklyn	55 155
J	Nevada Eureka	61 391
James	San Francisco San Francisco 9	681010
James	Santa Clara Gilroy	65 245
Joel	Yuba Bear Rvr	721000
John	Calaveras Twp 8	57 89
John	El Dorado Greenwood	58 715
John	Placer Michigan	62 845
L	Yolo Cottonwoood	72 650
N K	San Francisco San Francisco 5	67 492
O	Nevada Nevada	61 289
Relin	San Bernardino San Salvador	64 659
Robert	Siskiyou Yreka	69 140
Russel R	Yuba Marysville	72 883
S	Nevada Eureka	61 391
S B	San Francisco San Francisco 4	681121
Sheldon	San Bernardino San Salvador	64 658
T A	Yolo Cache	72 609
Thomas	El Dorado Placerville	58 917
Thos R	Tuolumne Twp 1	71 210
W B	Shasta French G	66 717
W C	Sutter Sutter	70 816

California 1860 Census Index

Name	County Locale	M653 RollPage
STODDARD		
W J	Amador Twp 6	55 439
W M	Merced Twp 1	60 899
W W	Merced Twp 1	60 899
William	Santa Clara San Jose	65 318
Wm	Nevada Eureka	61 391
STODDART		
David	San Francisco San Francisco 10	221 67
Wm M	Sacramento Ward 1	63 115
STODDER		
Edwin	San Joaquin Stockton	641052
Geo	San Francisco San Francisco 6	67 438
STODELAND		
T A	Yolo Cache Crk	72 609
STODLOF		
Diedreck	Los Angeles Santa Ana	59 444
STOEBLIN		
H	San Francisco San Francisco 9	681106
STOEGH		
A	San Joaquin Stockton	641056
STOEKEVELL		
Alvin W	San Francisco San Francisco 8	681300
STOEL		
Peter*	Nevada Nevada	61 241
STOEMER		
August	Los Angeles Los Angeles	59 328
STOEO		
Jacob	Calaveras Twp 9	57 379
STOEP		
George W	Plumas Quincy	62 941
STOESSER		
Ono	Santa Cruz Watsonville	66 535
STOEVE		
Edwin P	Yuba Marysville	72 914
STOFELS		
Nicholas	El Dorado Union	581093
STOFER		
Andrew	El Dorado Georgetown	58 694
STOFFARD		
James	Santa Clara Gilroy	65 226
STOFFER		
F B	Trinity Lewiston	70 963
Jacob	Placer Todds Va	62 762
T B	Trinity Lewiston	70 963
STOFFERS		
Thos	San Francisco San Francisco 9	681037
STOFFIN		
Julian	San Francisco San Francisco 9	681106
STOFFORD		
Mary Frances	Solano Benecia	69 300
STOFLITZELL		
Harmon S*	Yuba Marysville	72 870
STOGDELL		
James	Nevada Bloomfield	61 513
STOGELL		
S B	Butte Mountain	56 733
Thos	Butte Oro	56 684
STOGLER		
J	El Dorado Union	581092
STOH		
E A	Sierra Pine Grove	66 831
George	Sierra Pine Grove	66 831
STOHINSOR		
C S*	Mariposa Twp 3	60 573
STOHL		
Jules*	Alameda Brooklyn	55 101
Mike	San Joaquin Stockton	641033
STOHR		
Matilda	San Francisco San Francisco 10	165 67
STOIE		
Charles	Siskiyou Yreka	69 140
STOKE		
Jno	Butte Chico	56 560
STOKELY		
James	Tehama Lassen	70 881
William	Los Angeles Elmonte	59 262
STOKER		
Clun	Placer Todds Va	62 785
Fichd	Tuolumne Twp 2	71 414
J R	Tuolumne Shawsfla	71 404
Jacob	El Dorado Placerville	58 916
Richd	Tuolumne Shawsfla	71 414
STOKES		
Adolpho	San Diego S Luis R	64 779
Alfredo	Los Angeles San Juan	59 476
Anabella	Calaveras Twp 4	57 309
Anabelle	Calaveras Twp 4	57 309
B F	Nevada Nevada	61 265
Brice M	Humbolt Union	59 184
Charles J*	Tuolumne Twp 3	71 431
David	Sierra Twp 7	66 867
Frank	Colusa Grand Island	57 476
G M	Siskiyou Scott Va	69 29
Gancy	Tulara Twp 1	71 77

Name	County Locale	M653 RollPage
STOKES		
Geo	San Francisco San Francisco 10	272 67
H	El Dorado Kelsey	581155
J	Nevada Eureka	61 363
James	Monterey Alisal	601038
James K	Alameda Brooklyn	55 198
Jas R	Mariposa Twp 1	60 644
John	Yuba Marysville	72 906
John W	Tulara Twp 1	71 82
Johnson	Butte Kimshaw	56 587
Mary	San Francisco San Francisco 2	67 601
Mary A	Sacramento Ward 4	63 571
R	Butte Bidwell	56 717
Richard	Alameda Oakland	55 46
Richd	Trinity North Fo	701023
Sarah A	Tuolumne Twp 3	71 431
Thos	Sacramento Ward 1	63 19
W P	Marin Point Re	60 731
William C	Yuba Marysville	72 904
Wm	Tuolumne Columbia	71 359
Yancy	Tulara Visalia	71 77
STOKEY		
Mary I*	Calaveras Twp 6	57 120
Oliver	Sierra St Louis	66 810
STOKIM		
Jake	Tuolumne Twp 2	71 284
STOLDDER		
Anthony	Santa Cruz Watsonville	66 537
Jane	Santa Cruz Watsonville	66 537
STOLE		
John	Sacramento Ward 3	63 426
STOLEL		
Jules*	Alameda Brooklyn	55 101
STOLEMAN		
H	Sutter Butte	70 791
STOLES		
Samuel	Nevada Rough &	61 404
STOLEY		
L	El Dorado Placerville	58 852
STOLL		
Henry	Tulara Visalia	71 98
Wm*	Sacramento Ward 1	63 49
STOLLINGS		
Saml W	Calaveras Twp 10	57 293
STOLLIS		
John	Alameda Oakland	55 14
STOLLSTIMER		
Fred	Tuolumne Sonora	71 201
STOLOM		
---	Mendocino Round Va	60 883
STOLSS		
William R	San Joaquin Elkhorn	64 969
STOLTEN		
Julius	San Francisco San Francisco 2	67 696
STOLTON		
Samuel	Yolo No E Twp	72 670
Samuel	Yuba North Ea	72 670
STOLTZ		
Augustus	Marin Cortemad	60 783
STOLZ		
A	San Francisco San Francisco 10	249 67
Eliza	Sacramento Granite	63 252
STOM		
A	El Dorado Diamond	58 808
STOMANS		
H S	Sacramento Ward 1	63 91
STOMBACK		
J	Yolo Cottonwoood	72 646
STOMBAL		
Nicholas	Alameda Oakland	55 73
STOMBALL		
Henry	Santa Clara Gilroy	65 240
STOMBS		
T A	San Joaquin Stockton	641052
STOMFIELD		
Hetty*	Yuba Parks Ba	72 774
STOMME		
William*	Siskiyou Yreka	69 142
STON		
---	Nevada Bridgeport	61 466
Larres	Calaveras Twp 9	57 380
Whitney W	San Francisco 8 San Francisco	681287
STONAH		
William*	San Francisco San Francisco 9	68 985
STONBRY		
Peter	Yolo Slate Ra	72 716
Peter	Yuba Slate Ro	72 716
STONBURGH		
Nelson F	Yuba New York	72 737
Wilson F	Yuba New York	72 737
STONCOM		
Fred	El Dorado Union	581092
STOND		
Henry	Mendocino Big Rvr	60 848

Name	County Locale	M653 RollPage
STOND		
Paul*	Mariposa Twp 3	60 560
STONDO		
Miguel	Santa Clara San Jose	65 309
STONE		
A	Nevada Grass Valley	61 199
A	Nevada Nevada	61 317
A A	Tehama Antelope	70 893
A B	Yolo Slate Ra	72 711
A B	Yuba Slate Ro	72 711
Abraham	Yuba Marysville	72 896
Ah	Sacramento Brighton	63 208
Albert	Contra Costa Twp 2	57 578
Alexander	Tuolumne Big Oak	71 134
Angy	Solano Suisan	69 211
B H	Calaveras Twp 9	57 369
Benj	El Dorado Salmon Falls	581045
C	Nevada Grass Valley	61 153
C A *	Alameda Oakland	55 71
C E	Yuba Long Bar	72 748
Catharine	Butte Ophir	56 778
Charles	Humbolt Bucksport	59 157
Charles	Sutter Nicolaus	70 840
Charles	Yuba Marysville	72 867
Charles*	Santa Cruz Soguel	66 597
Chas	Nevada Nevada	61 274
Chas	San Francisco San Francisco 3	67 19
Chas	Tuolumne Twp 3	71 430
Chas L	Tuolumne Jamestown	71 430
Clement	Sacramento American	63 172
Cudley C*	Yuba Marysville	72 859
Cyrus	San Francisco San Francisco 2	67 750
D	El Dorado Placerville	58 867
D	Sacramento Brighton	63 203
Dudley C	Yuba Marysville	72 854
Dudley C*	Yuba Marysville	72 859
E E	Sonoma Bodega	69 538
E F	San Francisco San Francisco 5	67 500
E H	Butte Cascade	56 690
E L	Stanislaus Emory	70 742
E P	Trinity Mouth Ca	701012
Ebinezor	Contra Costa Twp 3	57 609
Edward	Sierra Gibsonville	66 856
Edwin	Siskiyou Shasta Rvr	69 116
Edwin	Tuolumne Twp 5	71 510
Edwin P*	Yuba Marysville	72 914
Elias	Alameda Brooklyn	55 163
Elias	Contra Costa Twp 2	57 582
Elias	Siskiyou Shasta Rvr	69 116
Elias C	Tuolumne Columbia	71 345
Elias*	Siskiyou Shasta Rvr	69 116
Erastus	Yolo Putah	72 547
Erwin	Los Angeles Los Angeles	59 293
F	Calaveras Twp 9	57 394
F	Santa Clara San Jose	65 393
F M	Sacramento Franklin	63 318
F N	Trinity E Weaver	701058
Francis	San Diego Agua Caliente	64 847
Frank	El Dorado Georgetown	58 707
Franklin	San Joaquin Douglass	64 927
Frederick	Contra Costa Twp 2	57 545
Frederick*	Siskiyou Shasta Valley	69 118
Fria C	Stanislaus Empire	70 726
G	Butte Kimshaw	56 589
G	El Dorado Placerville	58 866
G	Nevada Grass Valley	61 161
G	Siskiyou Klamath	69 92
G W	Butte Kimshaw	56 589
G W	Sacramento Ward 1	63 1
G W	Siskiyou Klamath	69 92
Geo	El Dorado Placerville	58 866
Geo	Nevada Nevada	61 266
Geo	San Bernardino Santa Ba	64 207
George	Contra Costa Twp 2	57 580
George	Nevada Bridgeport	61 466
George	Placer Forest H	62 793
George	Santa Clara Santa Clara	65 509
George S	San Joaquin Elkhorn	64 950
H K	El Dorado Union	581092
H M	Sacramento Ward 3	63 447
H M	Tehama Tehama	70 945
H S	Sutter Sutter	70 813
Harris*	Calaveras Twp 9	57 380
Henry	Del Norte Crescent	58 650
Henry	Mendocino Big Rvr	60 848
Henry	Placer Auburn	62 569
Henry	Tuolumne Jamestown	71 429
Henry F	Yuba Bear Rvr	721003
Henry L	Plumas Quincy	62 961
Henry S	Tuolumne Sonora	71 199
Horac*	Stanislaus Emory	70 755
Horatio	Contra Costa Twp 2	57 548
I A *	Nevada Red Dog	61 544
I A *	Nevada Red Dog	61 555
Isaac	Sacramento American	63 170
J	Nevada Grass Valley	61 146

Name	County Locale	M653 RollPage
STONE		
J	Santa Clara San Jose	65 387
J	Sutter Yuba	70 767
J	Sutter Bear Rvr	70 820
J	Sutter Nicolaus	70 839
J	Sutter Vernon	70 843
J A*	Nevada Red Dog	61 544
J A*	Nevada Red Dog	61 555
J C	Solano Benecia	69 284
J C	Sonoma Vallejo	69 619
J H	Placer Dutch Fl	62 723
J L	Tehama Antelope	70 886
J N	Klamath S Fork	59 199
J P	Nevada Grass Valley	61 171
J P	Solano Benecia	69 284
J S	Tehama Red Bluff	70 920
J*	Siskiyou Scott Va	69 55
Jacob	Marin Cortemad	60 792
Jacob L	Marin Cortemad	60 792
James	Contra Costa Twp 2	57 582
James	Siskiyou Klamath	69 92
James	Solano Benecia	69 284
James	Sonoma Bodega	69 538
James L	Calaveras Twp 8	57 78
James P	Yuba Marysville	72 900
James*	Siskiyou Klamath	69 92
Jehnat*	El Dorado Greenwood	58 714
Jerome D	Contra Costa Twp 2	57 582
John	El Dorado Placerville	58 925
John	Nevada Bloomfield	61 517
John	Sacramento Ward 4	63 524
John	San Francisco San Francisco 1	68 898
John	San Joaquin Castoria	64 906
John	Solano Benecia	69 299
John	Yolo No E Twp	72 669
John A	San Joaquin Castoria	64 875
John D	Colusa Monroeville	57 453
John H	San Joaquin Oneal	64 939
Johnson	Sonoma Bodega	69 538
Joseph	El Dorado Kelsey	581148
Joseph	Klamath Klamath	59 225
Joseph	San Joaquin Castoria	64 911
Joseph	Tulara Visalia	71 12
Joseph M	Sacramento Ward 4	63 571
Joseph*	San Francisco San Francisco 10	235 67
Joshua	Shasta Shasta	66 731
L P	Marin Cortemad	60 784
Leonard	Alameda Brooklyn	55 128
Lewis	El Dorado Cold Spring	581101
Lewis	Humbolt Eel Rvr	59 151
Lucy A	San Francisco San Francisco 2	67 559
M D	Solano Suisan	69 219
M H	Sierra Twp 7	66 867
M S	Tuolumne Twp 2	71 387
Maria	Plumas Quincy	62 984
Martha	Napa Napa	61 110
Mathias	Amador Twp 2	55 296
Medred	San Joaquin Stockton	641068
N	San Francisco San Francisco 6	67 472
N J	Tehama Lassen	70 877
Nathan	Sonoma Sonoma	69 636
Nathan	Tuolumne Twp 1	71 222
O	Nevada Grass Valley	61 192
O B	Santa Clara San Jose	65 312
Oliver	Humbolt Mattole	59 126
Orrin	Placer Forest H	62 796
Oscar J	Klamath Orleans	59 215
P	Napa Napa	61 100
P	Sacramento Dry Crk	63 376
Patrick	San Francisco San Francisco 2	67 593
Paul	Mariposa Twp 3	60 560
Peter	El Dorado Gold Hill	581098
Phillip	Tulara Twp 1	71 89
R	Sacramento Ward 4	63 575
R D	Siskiyou Callahan	69 16
R M	Trinity North Fo	701024
R N	Nevada Nevada	61 246
R S	Tuolumne Twp 1	71 255
R S	Tuolumne Twp 3	71 448
R S	Tuolumne Twp 3	71 449
R W	Nevada Nevada	61 246
Robert	Los Angeles Los Angeles	59 354
Robert	Siskiyou Klamath	69 92
Rochez	Monterey San Juan	60 990
S	Butte Cascade	56 701
S	Sutter Butte	70 783
S A	San Francisco San Francisco 10	222 67
S B	Butte Chico	56 557
S D	Tehama Tehama	70 935
S L	Sierra St Louis	66 809
S M	Siskiyou Klamath	69 92
S P	Placer Iona Hills	62 883
S S	Tehama Tehama	70 948
Samuel	Yolo No E Twp	72 668

Name	County Locale	M653 RollPage
STONE		
Sherrod	San Francisco San Francisco 10	326 67
Silas	Contra Costa Twp 2	57 579
Silas A	San Francisco San Francisco 7	681440
T	Santa Clara Alviso	65 404
Timothy	Santa Clara San Jose	65 333
Toney	Sacramento Ward 3	63 448
Trarris*	Calaveras Twp 9	57 380
Travies*	Calaveras Twp 9	57 380
W	El Dorado Georgetown	58 707
W	Nevada Grass Valley	61 211
W	Sacramento Cosummes	63 410
W	San Francisco San Francisco 7	681423
W	Shasta Shasta	66 732
W B	Yuba Rose Bar	72 820
W D	Butte Cascade	56 690
W H	El Dorado Salmon Falls	581048
W H	Trinity Rush Crk	70 965
W St*	San Francisco San Francisco 6	67 414
W W	Siskiyou Klamath	69 80
Warris*	Calaveras Twp 9	57 380
Wiliam	Sierra Pine Grove	66 829
Willard	Siskiyou Shasta Rvr	69 116
William	Calaveras Twp 8	57 97
William	Contra Costa Twp 2	57 579
William	Del Norte Crescent	58 621
William	Napa Hot Springs	61 27
William	San Joaquin Elkhorn	64 985
William	Sierra Pine Grove	66 829
Willm	Sacramento Granite	63 228
Wm	Napa Yount	61 54
Wm	Napa Napa	61 85
Wm	Nevada Nevada	61 315
Wm	Sacramento Sutter	63 306
Wm	Sacramento Sutter	63 307
Wm	Sacramento Franklin	63 331
Wm	San Bernardino San Salvador	64 647
Wm	San Francisco San Francisco 7	681423
Wm	San Francisco San Francisco 10	262 67
Wm	San Francisco San Francisco 1	68 926
Wm	Santa Clara San Jose	65 282
Wm	Santa Clara San Jose	65 384
Wm	Tehama Lassen	70 870
Wm H	El Dorado Georgetown	58 687
Wm H	Monterey San Juan	60 974
Wm H	Sacramento Ward 4	63 495
Wm H	Yolo Slate Ra	72 718
Wm H	Yuba New York	72 718
Wm*	Yuba Slate Ro	72 694
Ws	Tuolumne Shawsfla	71 387
STONEALL		
Danl*	Napa Napa	61 108
STONEAN		
A	San Francisco San Francisco 5	67 550
STONEBACK		
J	Yolo Cache Crk	72 646
STONEBRAKER		
John	El Dorado Casumnes	581161
STONEBREAKER		
Wm	Napa Clear Lake	61 124
STONEBRIDE		
L	Nevada Grass Valley	61 144
STONEBRIDS		
L*	Nevada Grass Valley	61 144
STONEBRIDZ		
L*	Nevada Grass Valley	61 144
STONEBROKER		
Fred	El Dorado Kelsey	581142
STONEBURG		
Wm	Nevada Nevada	61 327
STONECIPHER		
G G	Amador Twp 4	55 257
STONEE		
J*	Siskiyou Scott Va	69 55
STONEHILL		
E B	Nevada Grass Valley	61 168
STONEHOUSE		
Thomas	Los Angeles Los Angeles	59 338
STONEKING		
E	Tuolumne Jamestown	71 421
STONELL		
Chas*	San Francisco San Francisco 1	68 918
STONEMAN		
Finis	Tulara Visalia	71 76
James	Tulara Twp 1	71 76
STONER		
A	Sacramento Ward 4	63 527
Christian C	Yuba Suida	72 981
Christian D	Yuba Linda Twp	72 981
L	Yuba Long Bar	72 754
L*	Yuba Long Bar	72 756
Lander J	Yuba Long Bar	72 755
Philip	Placer Auburn	62 565
William	Yuba Marysville	72 969

Name	County Locale	M653 RollPage
STONEROAD		
N B	Merced Twp 2	60 920
STONES		
Chas H	Sacramento Natonia	63 282
J*	Siskiyou Scott Va	69 55
STONESIPER		
Isaac	Placer Virginia	62 663
STONEY		
Thos P	Napa Napa	61 97
STONG		
David	Tulara Visalia	71 81
Geo S	Humbolt Bucksport	59 161
Horatio	El Dorado Coloma	581068
Michael	Tulara Visalia	71 81
STONGER		
C	Calaveras Twp 9	57 393
Dominick	Calaveras Twp 4	57 340
STONIGER		
C	Sutter Sutter	70 813
STONINGER		
Andrew	Placer Rattle Snake	62 630
Franklin*	San Francisco San Francisco 7	681335
STONJ		
Randolph T*	Yuba Long Bar	72 769
STONKS		
John	San Mateo Twp 3	65 82
STONLMAN		
W H	Yolo Slate Ra	72 716
W H	Yuba Slate Ro	72 716
STONLY		
Peter*	Napa Hot Springs	61 11
STONNE		
O V*	Nevada Washington	61 335
STONNES		
Jacob	Solano Vacaville	69 340
STONS		
George	Mendocino Ukiah	60 800
Isaac	Contra Costa Twp 2	57 567
M	Sacramento Dry Crk	63 373
William	Sierra La Porte	66 779
STONT		
STONTENBOROUGH		
John H	San Francisco San Francisco 8	681282
STONY		
C	Nevada Grass Valley	61 166
Leonard	Marin Saucileto	60 750
STONYER		
Dominick*	Calaveras Twp 4	57 340
STOOG		
James*	Shasta Horsetown	66 707
STOOLFOULT		
Adam	Sacramento Ward 4	63 517
STOOPS		
Andrew J	Sonoma Healdsbu	69 472
Philip	Yuba Marysville	72 890
Robert	Yuba Marysville	72 890
Thos	San Francisco San Francisco 10	258 67
STOOTHOFF		
W H	Sutter Vernon	70 844
STOOTS		
Frederick	Amador Twp 1	55 505
William	Monterey Pajaro	601014
STOPER		
C	Sacramento Sutter	63 306
STOPHER		
W H	Klamath Trinidad	59 220
STOPLE		
Chas	Amador Twp 3	55 407
STOPLER		
Charles	El Dorado Casumnes	581174
STOPLES		
A F	Calaveras Twp 9	57 376
A P	Calaveras Twp 9	57 376
Thomas*	Nevada Bloomfield	61 519
STOPP		
D*	Nevada Bridgeport	61 477
STOPPARD		
Moses	Mendocino Little L	60 834
STOPPEL		
Henry	Plumas Quincy	62 957
STOPR		
Geo F	Sacramento Granite	63 248
STOPUCH		
Bayillis	Calaveras Twp 7	57 5
STORADER		
Frederick*	Yuba Marysville	72 924
STORCH		
Peter	Solano Fremont	69 385
STORCROSS		
D C	Sacramento Sutter	63 300
STORE		
Charles*	Siskiyou Yreka	69 140
Clement*	Sacramento American	63 158
STOREE		
Charles*	Santa Cruz Soguel	66 597

Name	County Locale	M653 Roll	Page
STOREMEYER			
Fredrick*	Plumas Quincy	62	999
STORER			
Charles	Santa Cruz Soquel	66	597
Chas P	San Francisco San Francisco 9	68	996
Henry W	Placer Virginia	62	661
I F	Mariposa Twp 1	60	642
J F	Mariposa Twp 1	60	642
Silas	Yuba Fosters	72	840
Teinoltz B	Solano Benecia	69	310
STORES			
C H	Yolo Cache	72	619
Domince*	Calaveras Twp 5	57	226
STOREY			
Mathew*	Placer Todds Va	62	786
Wm N	Plumas Meadow Valley	62	913
STORFF			
Antonio*	Plumas Quincy	62	976
STORG			
James*	Shasta Horsetown	66	707
STORGES			
Chris	Mariposa Twp 3	60	583
STORK			
Jas*	Santa Clara San Jose	65	321
STORKES			
A J	Sutter Sutter	70	810
STORKS			
John	Butte Oro	56	684
Thomas	San Francisco San Francisco 3	67	54
STORLI			
Domince*	Calaveras Twp 5	57	226
STORM			
---	Butte Chico	56	566
Charles	Siskiyou Scott Va	69	60
Jos	San Mateo Twp 3	65	108
Peter	Siskiyou Klamath	69	91
STORMANT			
J B	Siskiyou Scott Va	69	59
STORMES			
A V*	Nevada Washington	61	335
O V*	Nevada Washington	61	335
STORMS			
A	Nevada Grass Valley	61	174
C	San Francisco San Francisco 6	67	421
J	San Francisco San Francisco 2	67	763
J	San Francisco San Francisco 2	67	763
John	Los Angeles Elmonte	59	250
S H	San Francisco San Francisco 7	681	342
Simon P	Mendocino Round Va	60	877
Thos A	San Francisco San Francisco 9	681	008
W T	Sonoma Petaluma	69	583
STORN			
Charles	Siskiyou Scott Va	69	60
John	Trinity Whites Crk	701	028
STORNLY			
James	Yolo Slate Ra	72	707
STORPEN			
Peter N	Tuolumne Sonora	71	199
STORRD			
E*	Marin San Rafael	60	769
STORRE			
J	San Francisco San Francisco 2	67	671
Josephine	San Francisco San Francisco 6	67	441
STORREL			
E*	Marin San Rafael	60	769
STORRS			
P	El Dorado Coloma	581	070
STORRY			
John	San Francisco San Francisco 5	67	494
STORT			
Michael*	Yuba Bear Rvr	721	005
STORTE			
Benj	San Bernardino S Timate	64	687
STORTING			
Thomas*	Siskiyou Yreka	69	125
STORTON			
John	San Diego Colorado	64	807
STORTS			
John	Butte Oro	56	684
STORTZ			
John	San Francisco San Francisco 7	681	377
STORVE			
Josephers*	San Francisco 3	67	60
	San Francisco		
STORY			
Albert	Sacramento Brighton	63	191
C D	Sierra Port Win	66	793
Charles	Yuba Marysville	72	927
Chas A	Sacramento Ward 4	63	567
Chas P	Amador Twp 4	55	254
Christ	Nevada Bloomfield	61	511
D W C	El Dorado Placerville	58	918
Franklin	San Francisco San Francisco 7	681	335
Geo	Nevada Nevada	61	290
Geo	Sonoma Mendocino	69	449
Geo	Trinity Trinity	70	974

Name	County Locale	M653 Roll	Page
STORY			
Geo F	San Francisco San Francisco 10	234 67	
Geo W	Amador Twp 3	55	405
George	San Mateo Twp 3	65	107
J S	Butte Chico	56	559
J W	Butte Chico	56	552
James	El Dorado Salmon Falls	581	038
James	El Dorado Mud Springs	58	997
James	Shasta Horsetown	66	707
Jno T	Butte Oregon	56	617
John	Calaveras Twp 4	57	315
John	Sacramento Centre	63	179
John L	Solano Vacaville	69	341
John W	Fresno Twp 3	59	12
Jonathan	Sierra Poverty	66	799
Joseph	San Francisco San Francisco 3	67	54
Joseph	San Francisco San Francisco 2	67	748
Joseph	Tulara Keyesville	71	55
Julias	Tulara Twp 2	71	5
Laurann	Santa Clara San Jose	65	350
Lewis	Solano Suisan	69	218
Luis	Solano Suisan	69	218
Mary	San Francisco San Francisco 2	67	748
Mathew*	Placer Todds Va	62	786
O W	Sierra Port Win	66	793
Phillip	Sierra St Louis	66	818
R A	Santa Clara Santa Clara	65	521
Stepen C	San Francisco San Francisco 10	257 67	
T C	Sacramento Ward 3	63	486
Thos H	San Francisco San Francisco 1	68	837
W	Napa Hot Springs	61	15
William	Napa Clear Lake	61	139
William	Solano Vacaville	69	354
Wm	Humbolt Pacific	59	130
STORYTON			
Moses	Tulara Twp 1	71	76
STOSS			
Gorton E*	Calaveras Twp 5	57	189
STOSSEN			
Wm E	Butte Wyandotte	56	657
STOSSER			
Emmet*	Yuba Marysville	72	977
STOTEN			
James	Calaveras Twp 6	57	125
Samuel	Yuba Marysville	72	866
STOTENBRAG			
Abrah	Yolo Washington	72	561
STOTER			
J H	El Dorado Coloma	581	071
T H	El Dorado Coloma	581	071
STOTHER			
John	Nevada Bridgeport	61	465
STOTLYE			
F	Tuolumne Columbia	71	344
STOTT			
A	San Mateo Twp 3	65	74
Thomas C	Yuba Marysville	72	910
Wm	Sacramento Ward 1	63	49
STOTTS			
Charles	San Francisco San Francisco 2	67	570
Eliza	Sacramento Granite	63	230
STOTTYE			
F	Tuolumne Twp 2	71	344
STOTUNBREG			
Abrah*	Yolo Washington	72	561
STOTWNBREG			
Abrah*	Yolo Washington	72	561
STOUAH			
William	San Francisco San Francisco 9	68	985
STOUB			
E	San Francisco San Francisco 6	67	474
STOUCH			
Peter	Solano Fremont	69	385
STOUCKING			
E	Tuolumne Twp 3	71	421
STOUD			
Betty	Yuba Linda	72	984
STOUGH			
Geo	El Dorado Coloma	581	104
STOUGHER			
John	Tehama Lassen	70	866
STOUKS			
Randolph T*	Yuba Long Bar	72	769
STOULENBROUGH			
J	Shasta Shasta	66	676
STOULEY			
Henry	Alameda Brooklyn	55	86
STOUMEYER			
Fredrick*	Plumas Quincy	62	999
STOUNE			
Peter*	Napa Hot Springs	61	11
STOUR			
David	El Dorado Casumnes	581	166
STOUT			
A H	Tehama Red Bluff	70	916

Name	County Locale	M653 Roll	Page
STOUT			
A W	Nevada Eureka	61	344
Abner	Amador Twp 3	55	405
B	Siskiyou Klamath	69	86
C	Nevada Grass Valley	61	153
Cynthia	San Francisco San Francisco 11	127 67	
G W	El Dorado Placerville	58	882
Geo W	Sacramento Ward 4	63	550
J	Nevada Grass Valley	61	190
J B	Nevada Eureka	61	344
J C	El Dorado Georgetown	58	676
J T	El Dorado Georgetown	58	676
Jacob	Solano Vacaville	69	340
John	Siskiyou Yreka	69	189
L M	Nevada Grass Valley	61	188
M	Nevada Grass Valley	61	183
Moses	Sacramento Ward 3	63	489
N B	San Francisco San Francisco 4	681	159
Robert	Plumas Quincy	62	966
S L	Nevada Nevada	61	249
S S	Nevada Nevada	61	249
Sarah	Tehama Red Bluff	70	917
Seth	Monterey Alisal	601	039
Susan	San Francisco San Francisco 7	681	426
Thomas B	San Joaquin Douglass	64	917
William	San Joaquin Douglass	64	916
Wm	Sacramento Ward 3	63	461
STOUTENBOROUGH			
John H	San Francisco San Francisco 8	681	282
STOUTENBROUGH			
J*	Shasta Shasta	66	676
STOUTLEY			
Jno	Butte Kimshaw	56	596
STOUTON			
J	Nevada Grass Valley	61	226
STOUTOR			
J	Nevada Grass Valley	61	226
STOUTZ			
R A De	San Francisco San Francisco 8	681	294
STOVAL			
Jesse C	Colusa Spring Valley	57	433
Patter	Santa Cruz Santa Cruz	66	615
Patters	Santa Cruz Santa Cruz	66	615
STOVALL			
W W	Sacramento Ward 3	63	441
STOVCAB			
A	Sutter Butte	70	796
STOVE			
Abraham*	Yuba Marysville	72	896
Edwin P*	Yuba Marysville	72	914
James P*	Yuba Marysville	72	900
Martha	Napa Napa	61	110
STOVEALE			
Danl	Napa Napa	61	108
STOVEALL			
Danl*	Napa Napa	61	108
STOVER			
Captain	Yolo Slate Ra	72	694
Captain	Yuba Slate Ro	72	694
Chas	San Francisco San Francisco 12	388 67	
Chas P	San Francisco San Francisco 9	68	996
Flora	Yolo Cache Crk	72	592
H	Santa Clara San Jose	65	282
J	Butte Kimshaw	56	597
James	Trinity Price'S	701	019
Jas	Butte Cascade	56	701
Johnson	Yolo Slate Ra	72	694
Johnson	Yuba Slate Ro	72	694
Jonathan	Tuolumne Twp 3	71	459
L R	Shasta Shasta	66	664
Peter	Nevada Bridgeport	61	456
R A	Klamath S Fork	59	198
Silas	Yuba Fosters	72	840
William	El Dorado Placerville	58	895
William	Yuba Marysville	72	975
Wm*	Nevada Nevada	61	324
Wm*	Yolo Slate Ra	72	694
STOVES			
Wm*	Nevada Nevada	61	324
STOVESON			
Alfred	El Dorado Big Bar	58	742
STOW			
Chancy	Yolo Cache Crk	72	636
G	Sacramento Ward 4	63	604
Oliver B	Sonoma Sonoma	69	654
Wm J	Butte Oro	56	686
STOWALL			
Nathan	Alameda Oakland	55	11
STOWB			
E	San Francisco San Francisco 6	67	474
STOWBRIDGE			
Aaron*	Sacramento American	63	159
G*	Nevada Grass Valley	61	216
John	Yuba Rose Bar	72	797

Name	County Locale	M653 Roll	Page
STOWBRIDGE			
S*	Nevada Grass Valley	61	216
Y*	Nevada Grass Valley	61	216
STOWD			
E*	Marin San Rafael	60	769
STOWE			
Beecher	Santa Clara Santa Clara	65	483
Danl	San Francisco San Francisco 9	681091	
Elizabeth*	San Francisco	10	349
	San Francisco	67	
George	Sierra La Porte	66	768
J	Siskiyou Scott Va	69	55
Joseph	San Francisco San Francisco 10	235	
		67	
Josephine	San Francisco San Francisco 6	67	441
Josephus	San Francisco San Francisco 3	67	60
Wm	Sierra Twp 7	66	911
STOWEL			
E	Marin San Rafael	60	769
Gabiel	Sierra Downieville	66	969
Geo	El Dorado Placerville	58	888
STOWELL			
Ablert H	San Francisco San Francisco 12		385
		67	
Elias	Placer Folsom	62	639
Frank	Contra Costa Twp 1	57	519
George	Placer Forest H	62	771
H	Nevada Grass Valley	61	211
Lydia	Tuolumne Sonora	71	205
Ratiob*	Sierra Downieville	66	969
Ratiot*	Sierra Downieville	66	969
Richard	Sacramento Granite	63	255
W	San Francisco San Francisco 6	67	471
W S	San Francisco San Francisco 4	681223	
Wm	San Bernardino San Bernadino	64	684
STOWELO			
J H	Tehama Antelope	70	889
STOWER			
John	Butte Bidwell	56	730
STOWERS			
Henry	Amador Twp 1	55	505
STOWS			
Jas A	Amador Twp 2	55	268
STOWTLEY			
Jno	Butte Kimshaw	56	596
STOWWELL			
Robt	Tuolumne Twp 2	71	357
STOY			
Ling	San Francisco San Francisco 5	67	509
STOYELL			
S B	Butte Mountain	56	733
Thos	Butte Oro	56	684
STOYRE			
Frederick	Contra Costa Twp 1	57	506
STOYY			
J	Nevada Nevada	61	259
STOZSON			
Wm E*	Butte Wyandotte	56	657
STPEHENS			
Jas B	Yolo Cache	72	597
STPHENS			
D G	El Dorado Greenwood	58	728
STRAANS			
Henretta	San Francisco San Francisco 2	67	573
STRAAT			
John H	Amador Twp 7	55	412
STRAAUS			
Henretta*	San Francisco San Francisco 2	67	573
STRABOM			
Philip*	Tuolumne Columbia	71	321
STRABONI			
Philip	Tuolumne Twp 2	71	321
STRACHAN			
Abram	Sacramento Ward 1	63	148
STRACHM			
Jas	San Francisco San Francisco 10		350
		67	
STRACKEY			
Wm*	Butte Wyandotte	56	664
STRACY			
Thomas	Nevada Bridgeport	61	440
STRADDARD			
A A	El Dorado Greenwood	58	720
STRADE			
George	Tuolumne Twp 4	71	178
J L	Tehama Cottonwoood	70	900
L	Mariposa Twp 3	60	600
Peter	Siskiyou Yreka	69	136
STRADER			
S S	Nevada Bloomfield	61	511
STRADMAN			
D P	El Dorado Georgetown	58	679
STRADS			
George	Tuolumne Big Oak	71	178
STRAEHLE			
Jacob	Tuolumne Twp 5	71	493

Name	County Locale	M653 Roll	Page
STRAEHLE			
Teresa	Tuolumne Chinese	71	496
STRAERP			
Louis*	San Francisco San Francisco 4	681136	
STRAFF			
John	Sacramento Ward 1	63	63
STRAFFAN			
J	Sutter Butte	70	791
STRAFFORD			
T	Sacramento Ward 1	63	8
STRAG			
William*	Santa Cruz Pescadero	66	645
STRAGGINS			
Wm*	Nevada Nevada	61	330
STRAHAN			
John	San Francisco San Francisco 9	68	949
Joseph	Yuba New York	72	734
Wm	Sierra Twp 7	66	892
STRAHBIN			
Jacob	Trinity North Fo	701026	
STRAHL			
Charles	San Francisco San Francisco 7	681414	
Jac	Sacramento Ward 1	63	33
Jacob	San Francisco San Francisco 3	67	14
W	Nevada Eureka	61	343
STRAHLAIN			
Antone*	Nevada Bridgeport	61	446
STRAHLE			
Paul	San Francisco San Francisco 8	681320	
STRAHT			
J	Nevada Eureka	61	343
W	Nevada Eureka	61	343
STRAID			
Charles*	Tulara Petersburg	71	52
STRAIDO			
Charles	Tulara Twp 3	71	52
STRAIER			
Isaac*	Yuba Marysville	72	974
STRAIN			
Henry	Marin Bolinas	60	741
Isaac*	Yuba Marysville	72	974
J E	Sutter Vernon	70	846
J M	Tuolumne Columbia	71	334
John	Butte Ophir	56	795
John	Marin Bolinas	60	741
John S	Del Norte Klamath	58	654
Robert	Marin Bolinas	60	742
Robert	San Francisco San Francisco 7	681339	
STRAINEY			
A*	Shasta Millvill	66	751
STRAINGER			
L	El Dorado Kelsey	581154	
STRAINS			
Nathanul	Monterey San Juan	60	987
STRAINY			
Amelia	San Francisco San Francisco 9	68	974
STRAIRAY			
A*	Shasta Millvill	66	751
STRAIRS			
Amelia*	San Francisco San Francisco 9	68	974
T*	San Francisco San Francisco 3	67	78
STRAIT			
B B	El Dorado Eldorado	58	935
STRALEY			
Jacob	Sacramento Ward 3	63	458
STRALKER			
Wm	Sacramento Ward 1	63	62
STRALRAN			
John*	San Francisco San Francisco 9	68	949
STRAMA			
Joseph	Sonoma Petaluma	69	556
STRAMDAHL			
A W*	Shasta French G	66	716
STRAMLER			
William	Tulara Visalia	71	74
STRAMMER			
W*	Butte Kimshaw	56	599
STRAMP			
Clemer	Sonoma Sonoma	69	658
STRAMPO			
F	San Francisco San Francisco 5	67	500
STRAMS			
Geo*	San Joaquin O'Neal	641006	
Nathaniel	Monterey San Juan	60	987
STRAN			
John S	San Francisco San Francisco 2	67	557
STRANAHAN			
---	Tuolumne Twp 3	71	430
Mary	Tuolumne Twp 2	71	411
STRANBURY			
C M	Butte Bidwell	56	727
STRAND			
Charles	Del Norte Crescent	58	627
Fredk	Del Norte Crescent	58	631
Wm	San Francisco San Francisco 1	68	850
STRANDAHL			
A W*	Shasta French G	66	716

Name	County Locale	M653 Roll	Page
STRANDER			
A	Sacramento Ward 4	63	537
STRANE			
David*	San Francisco San Francisco 1	68	879
STRANEA			
B O	Calaveras Twp 7	57	20
STRANER			
Francis*	San Francisco San Francisco 3	67	70
STRANES			
Abram*	Calaveras Twp 6	57	136
STRANFS			
Mark	Del Norte Crescent	58	621
STRANG			
J	Nevada Eureka	61	368
J*	Nevada Grass Valley	61	148
Lyman	Tuolumne Twp 3	71	468
P	Nevada Grass Valley	61	197
STRANGE			
Benj	Nevada Rough &	61	406
E M	Calaveras Twp 9	57	368
Henry	Sierra Downieville	66	986
Robt	Butte Ophir	56	782
Wm	Calaveras Twp 9	57	370
STRANGER			
C	Calaveras Twp 9	57	394
Wm	Placer Folsom	62	639
STRANGMAN			
John	Tuolumne Twp 3	71	429
STRANHNA			
J*	Sonoma Bodega	69	539
STRANHND			
J*	Sonoma Bodega	69	539
STRANIGER			
C*	Calaveras Twp 9	57	394
STRANLOW			
M	Tuolumne Twp 3	71	427
STRANMER			
J R*	Butte Kimshaw	56	599
STRANNACH			
A	El Dorado White Oaks	581031	
STRANNOR			
Garrett	Sonoma Sonoma	69	656
STRANS			
E L	Trinity Weaverville	701068	
T	San Francisco San Francisco 3	67	78
STRANSBURG			
Robert	San Diego Colorado	64	809
STRANSS			
B	Calaveras Twp 8	57	52
Fredrick	San Bernardino Santa Barbara	64	151
STRANSSER			
H	San Francisco San Francisco 2	67	756
STRANT			
N	Tuolumne Twp 2	71	372
STRANTER			
Ascus	Calaveras Twp 8	57	73
STRANTON			
Alonzo P*	Calaveras Twp 6	57	156
Chas	Sacramento Ward 1	63	151
Wm J*	Nevada Nevada	61	330
STRANTZ			
Alrord*	San Francisco San Francisco 11		94
		67	
Alvord*	San Francisco San Francisco 11		94
		67	
STRANUACH			
A*	El Dorado White Oaks	581031	
STRANY			
J	Nevada Grass Valley	61	148
STRAP			
Henry	Tuolumne Sonora	71	209
STRAPER			
Adam	Trinity Douglas	70	978
STRAPLAIN			
Antone*	Nevada Bridgeport	61	446
STRASGICLY			
P	Amador Twp 1	55	490
STRASS			
Henry*	Tuolumne Twp 1	71	209
Sophia	San Francisco San Francisco 9	681041	
STRASSER			
Adam	Placer Goods	62	696
Geo	San Francisco San Francisco 2	67	655
STRASSMAN			
Charles	Placer Iona Hills	62	859
STRASY			
Chas*	Sacramento Ward 3	63	425
STRASYS			
Chas*	Sacramento Ward 3	63	425
STRATEN			
Jno	Sacramento Ward 1	63	46
STRATER			
Salon*	Placer Michigan	62	851
STRATFOOT			
Adam	Sacramento Ward 4	63	505
STRATFORD			
Richard	Marin Bolinas	60	742

Name	County Locale	M653 Roll Page
STRATHER		
A	El Dorado Placerville	58 859
STRATMAN		
John	San Francisco San Francisco 3	67 87
STRATON		
P D	Calaveras Twp 9	57 392
STRATOR		
P D	Calaveras Twp 9	57 393
STRATT		
Nicolas	San Joaquin Stockton	641066
STRATTAN		
William	Calaveras Twp 8	57 82
STRATTEN		
F*	Napa Hot Springs	61 5
John*	Calaveras Twp 8	57 90
Walter	Alameda Brooklyn	55 120
STRATTER		
Martin	Mariposa Twp 3	60 621
STRATTIN		
Thomas	Sierra Twp 5	66 924
STRATTMAN		
Ann	San Francisco San Francisco 2	67 562
STRATTMEISTER		
R	San Francisco San Francisco 2	67 800
STRATTON		
A	Nevada Nevada	61 316
Alfred	Santa Cruz Pescadero	66 648
C M	Trinity Indian C	70 988
Cornelius A	Yuba Marysville	72 864
D F	Sonoma Armally	69 515
E W	Mariposa Twp 3	60 585
G M	Butte Chico	56 548
Henry	Nevada Rough &	61 426
J H	Alameda Oakland	55 11
J H	Tuolumne Twp 2	71 383
J L*	Sacramento Cosummes	63 387
J M	Placer Forest H	62 792
J S*	Sacramento Cosummes	63 387
James	San Francisco San Francisco 9	68 946
Joseph	Alameda Brooklyn	55 95
Mary F	Sacramento Ward 4	63 525
Richd S	San Francisco San Francisco 2	67 583
S A	San Francisco San Francisco 6	67 461
S C	Sacramento San Joaquin	63 363
Samuel	Sacramento Sutter	63 299
T H	Yuba New York	72 729
Thomas	Sierra Twp 5	66 924
W	El Dorado Kelsey	581164
W C	Sacramento Ward 3	63 437
Wm A G	San Joaquin O'Neal	641001
STRATTOR		
E W	Mariposa Twp 3	60 585
E W C	Mariposa Twp 3	60 585
STRATTWIK		
John L	San Francisco San Francisco 3	67 80
STRAUAHAN		
S N	Tuolumne Twp 2	71 411
STRAUB		
Gaper	Trinity Whites Crk	701028
Geo A	Del Norte Crescent	58 627
STRAUBERGER		
L	Butte Ophir	56 772
STRAUER		
Francis*	San Francisco San Francisco 3	67 70
STRAUES		
Abram	Calaveras Twp 5	57 136
STRAUFS		
S*	Sacramento Ward 1	63 32
STRAUMER		
J R*	Butte Kimshaw	56 599
STRAUP		
Geo*	Sacramento Ward 1	63 152
Louis*	San Francisco San Francisco 4	681136
STRAUPS		
S*	Sacramento Ward 1	63 32
STRAUS		
Gottlieb*	Plumas Quincy	62 971
Rose	San Francisco San Francisco 2	67 756
T	San Francisco San Francisco 3	67 78
STRAUSE		
Leopold	Sierra Whiskey	66 847
S J*	San Francisco San Francisco 10	174 67
Sulian	Sierra Twp 7	66 906
STRAUSS		
A	Sierra Downieville	66 961
Adam	Calaveras Twp 6	57 136
Bermhardt	San Francisco	San Francisco 8 681300
Bernhardt	San Francisco San Francisco 8	681300
Caroline	San Francisco San Francisco 2	67 659
Daniel	Placer Michigan	62 810
Geo*	Sacramento Ward 1	63 152
Jacob	San Francisco San Francisco 8	681294
John	Tulara Twp 2	71 28
Julius	Sierra Twp 7	66 906
STRAUSS		
L	Sacramento Ward 1	63 32
L	Sacramento Ward 3	63 424
Lonis	Los Angeles Los Angeles	59 321
M	San Francisco San Francisco 5	67 475
M	San Francisco San Francisco 5	67 520
Richd	Sacramento Cosummes	63 394
Rosalia	San Francisco San Francisco 7	681380
S N	San Francisco San Francisco 5	67 520
STRAUSSER		
H	San Francisco San Francisco 2	67 756
L	San Francisco San Francisco 5	67 503
STRAUT		
N*	Tuolumne Springfield	71 372
STRAUTERGER		
L*	Butte Ophir	56 772
STRAUTZ		
Alvord*	San Francisco San Francisco 11	94 67
STRAVAHAN		
S N	Tuolumne Shawsfla	71 411
STRAVER		
Isaac	Yuba Marysville	72 974
STRAW		
Chas*	Trinity Weaverville	701077
W	Santa Clara Fremont	65 441
STRAWBRIDGE		
Geo	Klamath Trinidad	59 221
Geo E	Klamath Liberty	59 235
STRAWDAHL		
A W*	Shasta French G	66 716
STRAWS		
Amelia*	San Francisco San Francisco 9	68 974
STRAY		
L W	Nevada Grass Valley	61 217
STRAYER		
S E	Sierra Twp 7	66 903
S J	Sierra Twp 7	66 903
STREACH		
Lewis	Sierra Downieville	661011
STREAM		
Fred	Placer Michigan	62 842
STREANTON		
Alonzo P*	Calaveras Twp 6	57 156
STREAR		
Isaac*	Yuba Slate Ro	72 691
STREARER		
Arthur	Santa Clara San Jose	65 284
STREBE		
Catherine	San Francisco San Francisco 3	67 4
STREBECH		
Henry	Sacramento Ward 4	63 496
STREBL		
Catherine*	San Francisco 3	67 4
	San Francisco	
STREBLING		
Chas	Plumas Quincy	62 925
STRECH		
Isaac A	San Joaquin Elliott	641101
STRECHER		
Charles	San Francisco San Francisco 7	681406
STRECKLER		
J E	San Francisco San Francisco 5	67 522
STREDES		
Billy*	Tehama Red Bluff	70 916
STREEF		
Garrett	Tulara Visalia	71 80
STREEITYS		
J	San Francisco San Francisco 6	67 471
STREEKER		
Henry	Placer Auburn	62 585
STREELMAN		
H*	Nevada Eureka	61 353
STREEN		
Christian	El Dorado White Oaks	581014
Joseph	Santa Cruz Santa Cruz	66 614
STREENT		
Vincent*	Yuba Fosters	72 835
STREET		
Chas*	Sacramento Natonia	63 285
G D	Marin San Rafael	60 770
Geor	Nevada Grass Valley	61 165
H C	Shasta Shasta	66 664
H L	Tuolumne Twp 1	71 199
James	Colusa Monroeville	57 442
James H	Yuba Rose Bar	72 818
Jas	San Francisco San Francisco 10	215 67
Jessee	Solano Benecia	69 315
John	Shasta Shasta	66 735
Jos	San Francisco San Francisco 10	215 67
L*	Sacramento Brighton	63 198
P P	Siskiyou Scott Va	69 46
S*	Sacramento Brighton	63 198
Thomas	Sacramento Ward 1	63 45
STREET		
Thos	Butte Cascade	56 696
William	Fresno Twp 2	59 114
William	Napa Hot Springs	61 4
STREETER		
A C*	Sonoma Sonoma	69 657
Allen C	Tuolumne Twp 1	71 268
D B	San Bernardino Santa Barbara	64 152
Henry	San Mateo Twp 2	65 131
Leuden	Monterey Pajaro	601021
Linden A*	Monterey Pajaro	601021
P	Siskiyou Scott Ri	69 62
Sylvester	Amador Twp 2	55 269
Wm A	San Bernardino Santa Barbara	64 150
STREETON		
William	Marin S Antoni	60 708
STREETS		
Sunim*	Amador Twp 3	55 405
Sunion	Amador Twp 3	55 405
Suuim*	Amador Twp 3	55 405
STREEUL		
Vincent*	Yuba Fosters	72 835
STREGE		
Martin*	Shasta Shasta	66 676
STREIP		
Saml	Trinity Browns C	70 984
STREITBERGER		
Christoph	San Francisco San Francisco 12	392 67
STREIVER		
Eustus*	San Francisco San Francisco 6	67 430
STREKER		
J F	Marin San Rafael	60 758
STREKTIN		
Isaac N*	Siskiyou Yreka	69 129
STREKTON		
Isaac V	Siskiyou Yreka	69 129
STREL		
Jaes	Colusa Monroeville	57 142
STREMING		
C	Sacramento Ward 1	63 12
STRENAN		
Wm B	San Francisco San Francisco 9	681078
STRENFORD		
Geo*	Santa Clara Fremont	65 418
STRENIGKE		
William*	San Francisco San Francisco 7	681400
STRENTZELL		
Henry	Contra Costa Twp 1	57 485
STRERORAY		
A*	Shasta Millvill	66 751
STRESHLEY		
Orlando	Plumas Quincy	62 985
STRETCHER		
Louis	San Joaquin Stockton	641035
STRETT		
C L	Tuolumne Twp 1	71 199
STRETTS		
Andrew*	Santa Cruz Pescadero	66 648
STREUNTON		
Alonzo P*	Calaveras Twp 6	57 156
STREWBECK		
John	San Francisco San Francisco 1	68 921
STREWE		
H G A*	Amador Twp 1	55 452
STRFEA		
Anelaus*	El Dorado Georgetown	58 694
STRIBBING		
Richd*	Sacramento Ward 4	63 557
STRIBBS		
Jepe	San Francisco San Francisco 10	274 67
STRIBING		
Henry	Sacramento Ward 1	63 62
STRIBLING		
Richd*	Sacramento Ward 4	63 557
STRICK		
H	Nevada Eureka	61 376
STRICKER		
Henry	Mariposa Twp 1	60 660
STRICKLAND		
Alex	Sacramento Ward 4	63 519
B	Merced Twp 1	60 896
Benjn	Sierra Twp 7	66 884
David	Sacramento Ward 4	63 557
David	Sacramento Ward 1	63 67
Emesiah	Marin Cortemad	60 789
G A	Sutter Butte	70 785
G P	Siskiyou Scott Va	69 27
Jacob	Colusa Spring Valley	57 430
John	Napa Napa	61 109
Joseph	Sierra Twp 7	66 895
Osrcle W	Colusa Muion	57 461
P	Merced Twp 1	60 896
Peter	Calaveras Twp 7	57 25
Wm	Sacramento Ward 1	63 73

Name	County Locale	M653 Roll	Page
STRICKLANE			
N	Tuolumne Twp 4	71	162
STRICKLER			
Henry	Plumas Quincy	62	980
Jacob	Plumas Quincy	62	957
STRICKLIFER			
John	Butte Bidwell	56	724
STRICKLY			
G T	Sutter Nicolaus	70	841
STRICKMIRE			
John	Nevada Bloomfield	61	525
STRICKS			
H	Nevada Eureka	61	376
STRIDDANT			
H*	El Dorado Georgetown	58	758
STRIDLEY			
E	San Francisco San Francisco 5	67	501
STRIEB			
Mary A*	Sacramento Ward 1	63	22
STRIEDLE			
M	San Bernardino Santa Barbara	64	151
STRIEFF			
Jno M	Sacramento Ward 4	63	605
STRIEL			
Mary A*	Sacramento Ward 1	63	22
STRIGHES			
John C	San Joaquin Douglass	64	914
STRIKDALE			
R S*	El Dorado Georgetown	58	699
STRIKDALL			
R S*	El Dorado Georgetown	58	699
STRIKE			
J	Sutter Bear Rvr	70	820
STRIKEN			
G	Nevada Bridgeport	61	502
STRIKER			
B F	Butte Oregon	56	644
F R	Butte Kimshaw	56	580
F S	Sacramento Ward 4	63	539
STRIKES			
B F	Butte Oregon	56	644
STRILEY			
William	Solano Vallejo	69	249
STRILL			
Henry*	Mariposa Twp 1	60	638
STRIM			
J M*	Yolo Cottonwood	72	647
STRIMP			
J H*	Sacramento American	63	165
STRING			
Geo W	Siskiyou Callahan	69	10
Martin	Alameda Brooklyn	55	128
Martin*	Alameda Brooklyn	55	129
STRINGER			
A*	Sacramento Dry Crk	63	376
Joseph	San Francisco San Francisco 7	68	1415
Wm	San Francisco San Francisco 10		316
		67	
STRINGFELLOW			
Jno	Sacramento Ward 1	63	81
STRINGFIELD			
Levier*	Humbolt Eel Rvr	59	151
Sevier*	Humbolt Eel Rvr	59	151
STRINGFULTON			
J A	Santa Clara San Jose	65	384
STRINGHONBURY			
R T	Butte Bidwell	56	716
STRINGURN			
C	Tehama Pasakent	70	858
STRIOE			
T*	Sutter Yuba	70	765
STRIPLAND			
S	Sutter Nicolaus	70	833
STRIPLING			
Eligah	Tuolumne Don Pedro	71	538
STRIPPLER			
Henry	San Francisco San Francisco 10		275
		67	
STRISBOW			
Harmon	Marin Cortemad	60	756
STRIVA			
Johnn*	Butte Ophir	56	745
STRIVUS			
John	Trinity Rattle Snake	70	1029
STROAD			
Nancy	Yuba Marysville	72	848
STROART			
Wm*	Alameda Oakland	55	11
STROB			
R*	Butte Oregon	56	623
STROBE			
Thomas*	Placer Yankee J	62	761
STROBEL			
Man	Mariposa Twp 3	60	554
Max	Mariposa Twp 3	60	554
STROBLE			
Chas	Sacramento Ward 1	63	76

Name	County Locale	M653 Roll	Page
STROBLE			
John	Sierra La Porte	66	779
Thomas*	Placer Yankee J	62	761
STROBRIDGE			
J S	Sacramento Granite	63	233
M	Nevada Eureka	61	392
S A	Sacramento Ward 1	63	132
STROBRIDZE			
M*	Nevada Eureka	61	392
STROBRIDZO			
M*	Nevada Eureka	61	392
STROCKBRIDGE			
George	Santa Cruz Pajaro	66	532
STROCKER			
William	San Francisco San Francisco 3	67	51
Williammm	San Francisco San Francisco 3	67	51
STROCKLAND			
Benjamin	Sierra Twp 5	66	938
STROCKLNAD			
Benjamin	Sierra Twp 5	66	938
STROCKTON			
H	Sutter Vernon	70	842
STRODE			
Albert G	Solano Vacaville	69	347
Charles E	Contra Costa Twp 3	57	596
Francis	San Joaquin Stockton	64	1010
George	Solano Vacaville	69	349
Isaac E	Solano Vacaville	69	350
John H	Tuolumne Sonora	71	483
John S	Solano Vacaville	69	350
Lorenzo	Fresno Twp 2	59	114
Saml E	Napa Clear Lake	61	125
STRODER			
Henry	Butte Cascade	56	702
James	Contra Costa Twp 2	57	565
STRODH			
C	Trinity Evans Ba	70	1002
STRODI			
James*	Stanislaus Oatvale	70	717
STRODO			
Saml E*	Napa Clear Lake	61	125
STRODS			
J	Tehama Red Bluff	70	899
STROE			
John	El Dorado Coloma	58	1114
STROEDER			
John	Siskiyou Yreka	69	153
STROEDIN			
Henry	San Francisco San Francisco 8	68	1276
STROFER			
Geo F*	Sacramento Granite	63	248
STROH			
R*	Butte Oregon	56	623
STROHAO			
Amandas	Placer Todds Va	62	763
STROHL			
J	San Joaquin Stockton	64	1059
STROKER			
D W	Tuolumne Twp 1	71	199
J F*	Marin San Rafael	60	758
STROKES			
D W	Tuolumne Sonora	71	199
W P*	Marin Point Re	60	731
STROLBURGH			
H	Butte Bidwell	56	708
STROLBURGHS			
H	Butte Bidwell	56	708
STROLIN			
E F	San Francisco San Francisco 3	67	9
STROLL			
Benjamin F	San Luis Obispo	65	44
	San Luis Obispo		
STROLUN			
Philip	San Joaquin Oneal	64	932
STROMBACK			
Theodore	Fresno Twp 2	59	19
STROME			
Peter	Klamath Liberty	59	235
STROMEYER			
Joseph	San Francisco San Francisco 7	68	1422
STROMP			
Henry	El Dorado Placerville	58	921
L T	El Dorado Salmon Falls	58	1039
M M	El Dorado Placerville	58	878
STRONBRIDGE			
John*	Yuba Rose Bar	72	797
STRONCH			
David*	Sacramento American	63	164
STROND			
Fredk	Del Norte Crescent	58	632
Ira	Fresno Twp 2	59	48
Irza J	Fresno Twp 2	59	48
STRONG			
---	Mariposa Twp 1	60	651
Absolum	Tuolumne Twp 2	71	286

Name	County Locale	M653 Roll	Page
STRONG			
Al	Tehama Tehama	70	936
Alfred	Sonoma Russian	69	443
Alonso	Colusa Grand Island	57	477
Alonzo	Tulara Twp 1	71	101
Apperton W	San Francisco 8	68	1310
	San Francisco		
C	Nevada Grass Valley	61	151
C	Nevada Grass Valley	61	197
C B	Yuba Long Bar	72	771
Charles	Tulara Visalia	71	104
Charlotte	San Francisco San Francisco 11		106
		67	
Chas	Sacramento Franklin	63	328
Chas E	Alameda Brooklyn	55	151
David	Tulara Twp 1	71	81
E Y	San Francisco San Francisco 6	67	437
Frank	Plumas Quincy	62	976
G W	Nevada Nevada	61	321
Geo	San Francisco San Francisco 9	68	958
Geo D*	San Francisco San Francisco 9	68	1045
Henry	Fresno Twp 1	59	34
Horatio	El Dorado Coloma	58	1068
J	Nevada Eureka	61	371
J*	San Francisco San Francisco 1	68	921
James	Klamath Liberty	59	239
James	Tulara Visalia	71	5
James H	Tuolumne Twp 3	71	458
James M	Sonoma Russian	69	431
Jas	Butte Chico	56	559
Jas	Sacramento Lee	63	211
Jas D	Alameda Oakland	55	52
Job	Plumas Meadow Valley	62	906
John	Contra Costa Twp 1	57	535
John	Sacramento Georgian	63	345
John	Shasta Horsetown	66	703
John	Tehama Tehama	70	937
John	Tuolumne Jamestown	71	444
John P	Santa Clara Fremont	65	430
Justin E	Yuba Marysville	72	875
L	Yuba Marysville	72	931
L W	Nevada Nevada	61	321
Leir*	Butte Ophir	56	768
Leo	San Francisco San Francisco 9	68	958
Levi	Butte Ophir	56	768
M	Santa Clara Alviso	65	400
Mary	Sacramento Cosummes	63	401
Mary J	San Francisco San Francisco 8	68	1298
Nathaniel	Plumas Quincy	62	995
S	Yuba Marysville	72	931
Samuel	El Dorado Indian D	58	1157
Samuel	Humbolt Eel Rvr	59	145
Sarah	Santa Clara Fremont	65	430
Thoedore F	San Luis Obispo	65	4
	San Luis Obispo		
Thomas	Plumas Quincy	62	973
Thomas	Tuolumne Springfield	71	373
W	Shasta Millvill	66	745
W C	Nevada Nevada	61	330
Wm R	Sacramento Ward 4	63	566
STRONGBURGH			
Annitt	Butte Bidwell	56	707
STRONGBURGHS			
Annett	Butte Bidwell	56	707
STRONGER			
Dominick	Calaveras Twp 4	57	340
STRONGHILL			
Marchell	San Francisco San Francisco 1	68	914
STRONL			
James*	Siskiyou Callahan	69	1
STRONSE			
S J*	San Francisco San Francisco 10		174
		67	
STROOP			
John*	Yuba New York	72	731
STROOWELL			
H*	Nevada Grass Valley	61	215
STROPE			
D B	San Francisco San Francisco 7	68	1436
Geo F*	Sacramento Granite	63	248
STROPI			
Geo F*	Sacramento Granite	63	248
STROPLE			
Charles	Placer Michigan	62	814
STRORA			
Demetro*	Calaveras Twp 9	57	354
STROS			
George	Yuba Marysville	72	872
STROSE			
Denise	Sacramento Ward 4	63	531
STROSS			
Henerretta	San Francisco 1	68	932
	San Francisco		
STROTES			
Maithinas*	El Dorado Placerville	58	917
STROTH			
Julia C	San Francisco San Francisco 9	68	1019

California 1860 Census Index

Name	County Locale	M653 RollPage
STROTHE		
R T	Merced Twp 2	60 923
STROTHER		
Danl F	Sonoma Petaluma	69 544
STROTHMAN		
C	San Francisco San Francisco 2	67 686
STROTHN		
Danl F	Sonoma Petaluma	69 544
STROTHUR		
R T	Merced Twp 2	60 923
STROTRIDGE		
O F*	Amador Twp 2	55 316
STROTTS		
Agustus*	Mariposa Twp 3	60 598
STROUCE		
John W*	Napa Yount	61 39
STROUCH		
David*	Sacramento American	63 164
STROUD		
Betty	Yuba Suida	72 984
Daniel	Yuba Linda	72 985
J	Shasta Shasta	66 671
Jacob	San Joaquin Oneal	64 940
John W	Napa Yount	61 39
Nancy	Yuba Marysville	72 848
Robert	Yuba Fosters	72 836
Saml	Shasta Millvill	66 739
Samuel	Calaveras Twp 6	57 155
Thomas H	Yuba Parks Ba	72 783
STROUEL		
Robert*	Yuba Fosters	72 836
STROUP		
A	Tehama Red Bluff	70 924
Abraham	Calaveras Twp 4	57 309
C	Sacramento Ward 4	63 502
L	El Dorado Casumnes	581172
STROUS		
Agustus	Mariposa Twp 3	60 598
Chas	Butte Mountain	56 737
STROUSE		
Barbara	San Francisco San Francisco 10	351 67
STROUSER		
L*	San Francisco San Francisco 2	67 763
S	San Francisco San Francisco 2	67 763
S*	San Francisco San Francisco 2	67 763
STROUSS		
Abraham	Calaveras Twp 2	57 123
Abraham	Calaveras Twp 4	57 309
Emanuel	Calaveras Twp 4	57 303
L*	El Dorado Casumnes	581172
M	San Francisco San Francisco 10	204 67
STROUT		
Andrew	San Joaquin Oneal	64 936
E M	El Dorado Diamond	58 766
Jacob	Sonoma Armally	69 497
STROUTT		
T S	San Joaquin Stockton	641045
STROVA		
Dametro*	Calaveras Twp 9	57 354
Damotro*	Calaveras Twp 9	57 354
Domotro*	Calaveras Twp 9	57 354
STROVEL		
J F	Tuolumne Columbia	71 340
STROW		
James	Placer Iona Hills	62 877
STROWBIN		
Edward	Sierra Twp 5	66 930
STROWBRIDGE		
A M	Nevada Bridgeport	61 490
Aaron*	Sacramento American	63 159
Addison	San Francisco San Francisco 7	681439
Geo	Sacramento American	63 172
J	San Francisco San Francisco 1	68 820
J H	Sacramento American	63 159
J M	San Francisco San Francisco 7	681439
John*	Yuba Rose Bar	72 797
STROWE		
J*	Sutter Yuba	70 766
STROWL		
Elliot G	Calaveras Twp 4	57 303
Nathaniel	Calaveras Twp 4	57 303
STROY		
John	Tuolumne Twp 3	71 444
STROYKES		
John	Santa Cruz Pescadero	66 641
STRPP		
D*	Nevada Bridgeport	61 477
STRUB		
Mary A*	Sacramento Ward 1	63 22
STRUBBE		
A	San Francisco San Francisco 5	67 524
STRUBBLE		
Chas	Sacramento Ward 1	63 12
STRUBE		
Carl	San Francisco San Francisco 6	67 400

Name	County Locale	M653 RollPage
STRUBEN		
Wm	Tuolumne Twp 4	71 144
STRUBERS		
Wm*	Tuolumne Big Oak	71 144
STRUBIN		
Harmon	Marin Cortemad	60 756
STRUCK		
Antone	Los Angeles Santa Ana	59 440
John	Amador Twp 1	55 478
STRUCY		
Thomas*	Nevada Bridgeport	61 440
STRUDTE		
F	San Francisco San Francisco 5	67 485
STRUGELL		
James	San Joaquin Elkhorn	64 995
STRUKLAND		
John	Napa Napa	61 109
John	Santa Clara San Jose	65 318
STRULEN		
William N*	Tulara Twp 1	71 100
STRULMAN		
H*	Nevada Eureka	61 353
STRUMMER		
W*	Butte Kimshaw	56 599
STRUMNER		
W*	Butte Kimshaw	56 599
STRUMP		
F	Sutter Yuba	70 763
Jos*	Butte Cascade	56 689
STRUNA		
Geo R*	Santa Cruz Soguel	66 584
STRUNCKE		
Chas P	San Francisco San Francisco 1	68 829
STRUNING		
A	Shasta Millvill	66 751
STRUNK		
John	Los Angeles Azuza	59 272
STRUSE		
John	Calaveras Twp 9	57 360
STRUT		
C	Calaveras Twp 9	57 389
C*	Calaveras Twp 9	57 398
Chas*	Sacramento Natonia	63 285
Chris*	Santa Cruz Pescadero	66 645
Edwin	Nevada Bridgeport	61 451
J	Sutter Butte	70 780
STRUTENHOUSE		
Albert	San Francisco San Francisco 7	681428
STRUTER		
A C	Sonoma Sonoma	69 657
STRUTNALER		
John	El Dorado Kelsey	581127
STRUTS		
Samuel	San Joaquin Douglass	64 928
STRUTWATER		
John	El Dorado Kelsey	581127
STRUTZ		
Julius	Sacramento Ward 3	63 428
STRUVE		
H G A	Amador Twp 1	55 452
STRUVER		
Eustus	San Francisco San Francisco 6	67 430
STRUWE		
Henry	Tuolumne Twp 1	71 192
STRYKER		
Charles	Sonoma Healdsbu	69 478
Francis	Sacramento Ward 1	63 32
STRYLER		
George	San Joaquin Castoria	64 880
STRYPE		
A*	Nevada Nevada	61 246
J	Nevada Nevada	61 246
STSULER		
John	Solano Suisan	69 211
STSUTER		
John	Solano Suisan	69 211
STTARNENUS		
Jo*	Mariposa Coulterville	60 688
STTERNEIRAR		
---	Mariposa Coulterville	60 688
STTERNEIRAS		
Jo*	Mariposa Coulterville	60 688
STTEVENS		
Traman	Placer Iona Hills	62 861
STTINEHOUSE		
N	Nevada Eureka	61 388
STTIR		
John*	Mariposa Twp 1	60 638
STUARART		
W C	Tuolumne Garrote	71 175
STUARD		
C B	Nevada Nevada	61 279
STUART		
A	Yolo Washington	72 605
Abel	El Dorado Georgetown	58 704
Abell	Sonoma Petaluma	69 548

Name	County Locale	M653 RollPage
STUART		
Agnes	San Francisco San Francisco 7	681351
Alexdr	San Francisco San Francisco 8	681241
C	Nevada Grass Valley	61 216
C A	Nevada Grass Valley	61 220
C K	San Francisco San Francisco 9	681103
Charles H	San Francisco San Francisco 8	681233
Charles H	Yuba Bear Rvr	72 999
Chas	Sonoma Sonoma	69 647
David	Sonoma Vallejo	69 628
George	El Dorado Big Bar	58 740
George	San Francisco San Francisco 7	681421
H	San Francisco San Francisco 9	681102
H	San Francisco San Francisco 9	681103
I M*	Trinity E Weaver	701060
J F	San Francisco San Francisco 6	67 438
J H	Santa Clara Alviso	65 400
James	Contra Costa Twp 1	57 491
James	Santa Clara Alviso	65 405
Jane	San Francisco San Francisco 10	338 67
Jas	San Francisco San Francisco 1	68 900
Jas	Sonoma Petaluma	69 602
Jno	Klamath Liberty	59 240
Jno	Sonoma Sonoma	69 644
John	Calaveras Twp 7	57 30
John	Calaveras Twp 7	57 32
John	El Dorado Greenwood	58 721
John	Sonoma Petaluma	69 557
John C	San Diego San Diego	64 757
Joseph	El Dorado Greenwood	58 719
K F	El Dorado Big Bar	58 743
Leo	Tuolumne Big Oak	71 177
M	Nevada Grass Valley	61 185
M	Nevada Grass Valley	61 216
Maria A	San Francisco San Francisco 10	325 67
Mary	Alameda Brooklyn	55 134
Mary	San Francisco San Francisco 6	67 428
Mary	Sonoma Vallejo	69 624
Orrin	Yuba Parks Ba	72 781
P R	Calaveras Twp 7	57 3
Philip	Santa Cruz Soguel	66 581
Robert	Calaveras Twp 7	57 2
Robert	Tulara Twp 3	71 53
S R	Calaveras Twp 7	57 3
Thos	Sonoma Petaluma	69 546
W H	Sacramento Georgian	63 337
William	Calaveras Twp 6	57 133
Wm	San Bernardino San Salvador	64 648
Wm	Sonoma Bodega	69 521
STUARTS		
Samuel	Yuba New York	72 740
STUATZ		
Wm	Nevada Eureka	61 391
STUBB		
John	Amador Twp 3	55 389
STUBBLEBRAN		
Jacob*	Calaveras Twp 4	57 343
STUBBLEFIELD		
A	Napa Hot Springs	61 15
Beverly	San Joaquin Castoria	64 897
STUBBLEHAM		
Jacob	Calaveras Twp 4	57 343
STUBBLEHAN		
Jacob	Calaveras Twp 4	57 343
STUBBS		
Chas	Napa Clear Lake	61 135
Frank	El Dorado Georgetown	58 699
Jesse	San Francisco San Francisco 10	274 67
Jos	Butte Kimshaw	56 598
Moses R	Humbolt Eel Rvr	59 148
STUBER		
Guadalupe	Mendocino Big Rvr	60 848
M	San Francisco San Francisco 5	67 490
Moritz	San Francisco San Francisco 10	311 67
Wm	Sacramento Natonia	63 279
STUBING		
Henry*	Sacramento Ward 1	63 62
STUBLEY		
Charles	Plumas Quincy	621007
STUBYMAN		
C G*	Shasta Horsetown	66 692
STUCE		
Fredrich*	Nevada Rough &	61 404
W	El Dorado Diamond	58 797
STUCHMAN		
John	Placer Nicolaus	62 692
STUCK		
J*	Shasta Horsetown	66 697
John	Calaveras Twp 6	57 146
STUCKER		
A J	Tehama Antelope	70 893
Jacob	Yuba Marysville	72 958

California 1860 Census Index

Name	County Locale	M653 Roll	Page
STUCKER			
Joseph	Calaveras Twp 5	57	240
STUCKMAN			
Henry	Calaveras Twp 6	57	140
STUCKWORTH			
Nicholls	Sierra Twp 7	66	880
STUCSAWER			
S T*	Nevada Bridgeport	61	470
STUCTENBERRY			
J W	Yolo Cache	72	596
STUDARUS			
John*	Sacramento Brighton	63	195
STUDDARD			
Mike	Sonoma Petaluma	69	599
STUDELY			
Smith S	San Francisco San Francisco 11	67	125
STUDEN			
J Tum	San Francisco San Francisco 5	67	530
STUDENBURY			
J H*	Yolo Cache Crk	72	596
STUDER			
Christian	Trinity North Fo	70	1026
STUDERMEN			
Chas	San Francisco San Francisco 3	67	86
STUDES			
Billy*	Tehama Red Bluff	70	916
STUDESSERS			
Jas*	Amador Twp 6	55	437
STUDESSNS			
Jas*	Amador Twp 6	55	437
STUDESSUS			
Jas	Amador Twp 6	55	437
STUDGE			
Alexr*	Sacramento Mississipi	63	187
STUDL EY			
Warren	San Francisco San Francisco 3	67	54
STUDLEY			
B F	Siskiyou Yreka	69	153
E*	San Francisco San Francisco 5	67	501
Smith	San Francisco San Francisco 8	681	245
Thomas	El Dorado Salmon Falls	581	059
Warren	San Francisco San Francisco 3	67	54
STUDMAN			
H*	Nevada Eureka	61	353
L	Sacramento Ward 3	63	421
T*	Sacramento Ward 3	63	421
STUDMARE			
H*	Nevada Eureka	61	353
STUDSON			
W N	San Francisco San Francisco 5	67	512
STUEBE			
Eliza	San Francisco San Francisco 10	67	323
STUEBER			
Jno	Sacramento Sutter	63	292
STUEGIS			
Wm	Butte Ophir	56	751
STUEKPOLE			
Jacob E*	Calaveras Twp 10	57	291
STUELMAN			
H*	Nevada Eureka	61	353
STUERNE			
Prosper	San Francisco San Francisco 10	67	251
STUERR			
Wh*	Nevada Grass Valley	61	200
STUF			
---	Del Norte Klamath	58	657
STUFF			
John	Calaveras Twp 4	57	340
STUFFORD			
Mary*	Sonoma Petaluma	69	597
Nelson	Sonoma Petaluma	69	595
Ushon*	Sonoma Petaluma	69	595
STUGAN			
John	Sierra Twp 7	66	870
STUGDER			
Louis	Fresno Twp 3	59	16
STUGEN			
John*	Sierra Twp 7	66	870
STUGERMAN			
John	Solano Vacaville	69	350
STUGES			
Jacob	El Dorado Grizzly	581	182
STUGSAWER			
S T*	Nevada Bridgeport	61	470
STUILTZ			
Louize	Sacramento Ward 4	63	500
STUIR			
Amuel	Placer Dutch Fl	62	716
STUIVE			
Henry	Tuolumne Sonora	71	192
STUKEY			
J F	Sierra Downieville	66	961
STULCE			
John	San Francisco San Francisco 3	67	4

Name	County Locale	M653 Roll	Page
STULCEY			
Constance	San Francisco 2	67	711
	San Francisco		
STULE			
John	San Francisco San Francisco 2	67	670
John A*	Yuba Marysville	72	900
Wm	San Francisco San Francisco 2	67	669
STULEVILL			
H*	Nevada Bloomfield	61	509
STULING			
R H*	Napa Napa	61	95
STULL			
Geo	Sacramento Ward 4	63	603
Henry	Mariposa Twp 1	60	638
Robert	Contra Costa Twp 2	57	540
STULLA			
Ginoma*	Calaveras Twp 7	57	11
John	Calaveras Twp 7	57	11
STULLBARK			
Gustavos*	Placer Michigan	62	853
STULLE			
Augustin	San Francisco San Francisco 2	67	687
STULLINGS			
Faml W	Calaveras Twp 10	57	293
STULLY			
Margaret	San Francisco San Francisco 3	67	81
STULP			
T	Sutter Nicolaus	70	839
STULTS			
Samuel*	Monterey Pajaro	601	021
STULTZ			
---	San Francisco San Francisco 7	681	368
Abraham*	San Francisco 7	681	434
	San Francisco		
Geo W	Sacramento Ward 4	63	498
L	San Francisco San Francisco 1	68	930
STULUON			
Joseph	Calaveras Twp 5	57	205
STULZMAN			
C G	Shasta Horsetown	66	692
STUMBE			
J C*	Sonoma Bodega	69	523
STUMBERG			
Harman	Marin Cortemad	60	782
Herman	Marin Cortemad	60	782
STUMHOPR			
Fredk	Calaveras Twp 4	57	323
STUMMOYICH			
Mary	San Francisco San Francisco 4	681	162
STUMNING			
A*	Butte Ophir	56	794
STUMP			
C P	El Dorado Placerville	58	849
Chas	Sacramento Granite	63	230
E	El Dorado Placerville	58	887
Henry	Sonoma Bodega	69	528
J H*	Sacramento American	63	165
Jacob	Sierra Downieville	66	993
Jacob K	Los Angeles Los Angeles	59	500
Jas	Napa Napa	61	99
John	Sacramento Ward 1	63	67
John	Sierra Downieville	66	993
Jos*	Butte Cascade	56	689
S P	Nevada Rough &	61	414
T J	Sacramento Ward 1	63	144
Terrance	Butte Kimshaw	56	581
Thos	Butte Oro	56	674
STUMPE			
J C*	Sonoma Bodega	69	523
STUMPF			
Hippolye	San Francisco San Francisco 12	67	395
STUN			
Isaac*	El Dorado Georgetown	58	679
T H	El Dorado Placerville	58	873
STUNBERGER			
G	Merced Twp 1	60	904
STUNCT			
John*	Solano Fremont	69	383
STUNE			
Jacob	Placer Dutch Fl	62	725
STUNG			
Martin*	Alameda Brooklyn	55	129
STUNGES			
John	Calaveras Twp 4	57	343
STUNGHONBURY			
R T*	Butte Bidwell	56	716
STUNGNER			
W	El Dorado Diamond	58	791
STUNIGKE			
William*	San Francisco San Francisco 7	681	400
STUNKY			
Mary E	Sonoma Petaluma	69	596
STUNLEY			
George A*	Calaveras Twp 10	57	266
Mary E	Sonoma Petaluma	69	596

Name	County Locale	M653 Roll	Page
STUNLEY			
William B	Sierra Pine Grove	66	820
STUNOP			
Terrance	Butte Kimshaw	56	581
STUNTER			
Geo	Amador Twp 2	55	309
STUOGO			
Julius*	Mendocino Calpella	60	829
STUOWELL			
H*	Nevada Grass Valley	61	215
STUPMAN			
J	Sacramento Dry Crk	63	371
STUPP			
Mary	San Francisco San Francisco 4	681	136
STUPPALKANP			
A H	San Francisco San Francisco 2	67	715
STUPPALKAUP			
A H	San Francisco San Francisco 2	67	715
STUPPLER			
Henry	San Francisco San Francisco 10	67	275
STURDENANT			
L*	San Francisco San Francisco 5	67	505
STURDERANT			
Jas*	Butte Oregon	56	641
STURDERVANT			
L*	San Francisco San Francisco 5	67	505
STURDEVANT			
George H	Contra Costa Twp 3	57	616
Jas*	Butte Oregon	56	641
STURDINAN			
B F	El Dorado Mud Springs	58	981
STURDISANT			
W	Shasta Shasta	66	760
STURDIVANT			
G W	Siskiyou Scott Va	69	51
Hiram*	Nevada Bloomfield	61	508
Horam*	Nevada Bloomfield	61	508
J A	Trinity Sturdiva	701	007
M	Shasta Shasta	66	760
STURDIVEN			
Hiram	Nevada Bloomfield	61	508
STURE			
---	Sierra Twp 5	66	934
STURENBURG			
F	San Francisco San Francisco 2	67	787
STURESENT			
M A*	El Dorado Georgetown	58	748
STURGE			
Franklin	Stanislaus Branch	70	710
STURGEEN			
Alse*	Amador Twp 2	55	325
F M	Amador Twp 7	55	411
STURGEM			
Samuel R T	Los Angeles Los Angeles	59	321
STURGEN			
Henry	Butte Bidwell	56	712
STURGEON			
Alse	Amador Twp 2	55	325
Edward	Contra Costa Twp 2	57	571
F M	Amador Twp 7	55	411
STURGEP			
Thos W	San Francisco San Francisco 10	67	231
STURGES			
Henry	Calaveras Twp 4	57	309
Henry M	Calaveras Twp 6	57	137
John	Calaveras Twp 4	57	343
Josiah*	Contra Costa Twp 1	57	531
STURGESS			
Thos W*	San Francisco San Francisco 10	67	231
STURGIS			
John	Solano Montezuma	69	371
Josiah*	Contra Costa Twp 1	57	531
Wm*	Butte Ophir	56	751
STURGO			
Julius*	Mendocino Little L	60	829
STURGON			
E B	San Francisco San Francisco 1	68	931
Henry	Butte Bidwell	56	712
Jas M	Butte Ophir	56	797
STURKE			
Wm	San Francisco San Francisco 10	67	297
STURLI			
Domince	Calaveras Twp 5	57	226
STURLING			
Dominick	Amador Twp 1	55	466
STURLS			
Dominos	Calaveras Twp 5	57	226
STURM			
John*	San Joaquin Stockton	641	023
STURMAN			
Isaac	Yuba Marysville	72	890
J	Amador Twp 3	55	378

Name	County Locale	M653 Roll	Page
STURMAN			
Manuel*	Contra Costa Twp 3	57	614
S	San Francisco San Francisco 5	67	517
STURN			
John	Contra Costa Twp 2	57	580
STURR			
D R	Sacramento Cosumnes	63	382
STURS			
Chris*	Santa Cruz Pescadero	66	645
Richd	Napa Clear Lake	61	137
STURT			
Chris*	Santa Cruz Pescadero	66	645
STURTERANT			
Ablert*	Yuba Fosters	72	838
Albert	Yuba Fosters	72	837
Albert*	Yuba Fosters	72	838
STURTEVANT			
A*	San Francisco San Francisco 5	67	554
Geo*	Butte Kimshaw	56	602
James	Mendocino Anderson	60	867
STURTIVANT			
R O	San Francisco San Francisco 10	67	285
STURTOSH			
Milo Ma*	Yuba Marysville	72	940
STURVESENT			
M A*	El Dorado Georgetown	58	748
STURYES			
Henry M	Calaveras Twp 6	57	137
John*	Calaveras Twp 4	57	343
STUSEY			
David	Sacramento Ward 1	63	93
STUTE			
Wendell*	Placer Michigan	62	847
STUTESMAN			
Joseph L	Los Angeles Elmonte	59	257
STUTEVILL			
H*	Nevada Bloomfield	61	509
STUTLZ			
Abraham*	San Francisco 7	681	434
	San Francisco		
STUTON			
J	Calaveras Twp 9	57	396
STUTRMAN			
Silas*	Placer Folsom	62	640
STUTSMAN			
David	Yuba Rose Bar	72	799
STUTSON			
Danl	Amador Twp 3	55	393
John	San Francisco San Francisco 1	68	916
STUTT			
George	Placer Michigan	62	835
William	Contra Costa Twp 1	57	527
STUTTBARK			
Gustavos*	Placer Michigan	62	853
STUTTMEISTER			
R	San Francisco San Francisco 2	67	800
STUTTS			
Samuel	Monterey Pajaro	60	1021
STUTTZ			
Abraham*	San Francisco 7	681	434
	San Francisco		
STUTZENAGGER			
Ann Cath*	Alameda Oakland	55	1
STUTZMAN			
Saml	Tuolumne Sonora	71	207
STUTZMANN			
Saml	Tuolumne Twp 1	71	207
STUTZRNAGGER			
Ann Cath*	Alameda Oakland	55	1
STUUNTON			
Michael P*	Calaveras Twp 4	57	318
STUUT			
Moses*	Sacramento Ward 3	63	489
STUVE			
Henry	Calaveras Twp 6	57	162
STUZA			
Conrad	San Francisco San Francisco 7	681	333
STUZENCHALL			
William	Calaveras Twp 4	57	343
STUZENCHEL			
William*	Calaveras Twp 4	57	343
STUZNICHDL			
William*	Calaveras Twp 4	57	343
STUZNICHEL			
William*	Calaveras Twp 4	57	343
STUZNICHELL			
William*	Calaveras Twp 4	57	343
STUZRUCHDL			
William*	Calaveras Twp 4	57	343
STUZSAWER			
S T*	Nevada Bridgeport	61	470
STVEKPOLE			
Jacob E*	Calaveras Twp 10	57	291
STVUT			
Moses*	Sacramento Ward 3	63	489

Name	County Locale	M653 Roll	Page
STWAND			
P*	Nevada Eureka	61	390
STWARD			
Charles	Humbolt Pacific	59	135
STWART			
J B	San Francisco San Francisco 5	67	550
STWINS			
William H	San Francisco San Francisco 4	681	115
STWITZER			
Chas	Sacramento Sutter	63	291
STWOGO			
Julius*	Mendocino Little L	60	829
STWOWELL			
H*	Nevada Grass Valley	61	215
STYCE			
B	Napa Napa	61	66
STYKER			
Paul	Santa Clara Fremont	65	419
STYLE			
H	San Francisco San Francisco 1	68	928
John	Marin Cortemad	60	779
Juan	San Bernardino Santa Barbara	64	183
STYLES			
---	Amador Twp 3	55	401
E B	Amador Twp 5	55	363
G H	Nevada Rough &	61	428
G N	Nevada Rough &	61	428
Geo W	Amador Twp 7	55	419
George	Nevada Bridgeport	61	489
Henry	San Francisco San Francisco 2	67	587
James	Tehama Lassen	70	877
John	Marin Cortemad	60	779
Mistes	Amador Twp 3	55	395
R D	Amador Twp 1	55	454
Seymour	Yuba Marysville	72	856
Seymour	Yuba Marysville	72	861
STYMAST			
Wm	Klamath Liberty	59	235
SU CON			
---*	Nevada Nevada	61	305
SU FOOT			
---	Nevada Bridgeport	61	464
SU FUN			
---*	Nevada Nevada	61	307
SU M			
---	Calaveras Twp 5	57	237
SU POY			
Choy	San Francisco San Francisco 2	67	673
SU SING			
---	Mariposa Twp 1	60	669
---	Nevada Nevada	61	307
SU SUNG			
---	Nevada Bridgeport	61	466
SU YOU			
---	Nevada Nevada	61	305
SU YUP			
---	Nevada Nevada	61	307
---	Nevada Washington	61	339
---*	Nevada Nevada	61	302
---	Nevada Nevada	61	310
SU			
---	Butte Kimshaw	56	582
---	Calaveras Twp 6	57	164
---	Calaveras Twp 6	57	165
---	Calaveras Twp 6	57	167
---	Calaveras Twp 6	57	168
---	Calaveras Twp 5	57	176
---	Calaveras Twp 5	57	181
---	Calaveras Twp 5	57	182
---	Calaveras Twp 5	57	205
---	Calaveras Twp 5	57	214
---	Calaveras Twp 5	57	219
---	Calaveras Twp 5	57	232
---	Calaveras Twp 5	57	233
---	Calaveras Twp 5	57	234
---	Calaveras Twp 5	57	235
---	Calaveras Twp 5	57	236
---	Calaveras Twp 5	57	237
---	Calaveras Twp 5	57	241
---	Calaveras Twp 5	57	244
---	Calaveras Twp 5	57	245
---	Calaveras Twp 5	57	251
---	Calaveras Twp 5	57	252
---	Calaveras Twp 5	57	256
---	Calaveras Twp 10	57	259
---	Calaveras Twp 10	57	261
---	Calaveras Twp 10	57	268
---	Calaveras Twp 10	57	269
---	Calaveras Twp 10	57	271
---	Calaveras Twp 10	57	273
---	Calaveras Twp 10	57	280
---	El Dorado Big Bar	58	737
---	El Dorado Diamond	58	806
---	Mariposa Twp 1	60	652
---	Mariposa Coulterville	60	681
---	Mariposa Coulterville	60	682

Name	County Locale	M653 Roll	Page
SU			
---	Mariposa Coulterville	60	690
---	Nevada Nevada	61	305
---	Nevada Rough &	61	425
---	Nevada Bridgeport	61	462
---	Placer Dutch Fl	62	737
---	Placer Iona Hills	62	896
---	Plumas Meadow Valley	62	914
---	Sacramento Granite	63	268
---	Sacramento Ward 1	63	59
---	San Francisco San Francisco 4	681	174
---	San Francisco San Francisco 4	681	177
---	San Francisco San Francisco 4	681	178
---	San Francisco San Francisco 4	681	180
---	San Francisco San Francisco 4	681	186
---	San Francisco San Francisco 4	681	189
---	San Francisco San Francisco 4	681	193
---	San Francisco San Francisco 4	681	194
---	San Francisco San Francisco 4	681	196
---	San Francisco San Francisco 4	681	197
---	San Francisco San Francisco 4	681	209
---	San Francisco San Francisco 4	681	210
---	San Francisco San Francisco 4	681	212
---	San Francisco San Francisco 2	67	688
---	Tuolumne Columbia	71	346
---	Tuolumne Shawsfla	71	396
---	Tuolumne Twp 2	71	408
---	Tuolumne Shawsfla	71	409
---	Tuolumne Twp 3	71	421
---	Tuolumne Jamestown	71	433
---	Tuolumne Twp 3	71	436
---	Tuolumne Jamestown	71	438
---	Tuolumne Twp 3	71	440
---	Tuolumne Twp 3	71	459
---	Tuolumne Twp 5	71	525
---	Yuba Marysville	72	917
---	Yuba Marysville	72	921
---*	Calaveras Twp 5	57	233
---*	Calaveras Twp 5	57	236
---*	Calaveras Twp 5	57	237
---*	Calaveras Twp 10	57	297
---*	Calaveras Twp 4	57	326
---*	El Dorado Coloma	581	084
---*	Sacramento Ward 1	63	51
---*	Sacramento Ward 1	63	59
---*	Tuolumne Twp 3	71	460
Ah	Butte Eureka	56	652
Ah	Calaveras Twp 7	57	16
Avnon	El Dorado Georgetown	58	703
Ching	Placer Dutch Fl	62	737
Chon	Placer Illinois	62	738
Chung	Placer Dutch Fl	62	737
Cow*	Nevada Washington	61	342
Cunn	Tuolumne Shawsfla	71	396
Ing	San Francisco San Francisco 3	67	3
Ip	Butte Ophir	56	787
Kee	Mariposa Twp 3	60	582
Kee	San Francisco San Francisco 4	681	202
King*	El Dorado Georgetown	58	701
Ku	San Francisco San Francisco 4	681	202
Lang	Yuba Long Bar	72	767
Lang*	Placer Illinois	62	748
Leong	El Dorado Georgetown	58	703
Lou	San Francisco San Francisco 4	681	187
Luck	Butte Kimshaw	56	578
Mong	El Dorado Georgetown	58	702
Mong	Sacramento Ward 3	63	494
Mu	Sacramento Granite	63	268
Ong	Calaveras Twp 5	57	235
Ping	Sierra Downieville	66	986
Poy	Tuolumne Twp 5	71	524
Sing	Tehama Red Bluff	70	932
Son	Siskiyou Yreka	69	194
Song	Butte Oro	56	688
Ting	Sierra Downieville	66	986
Tong	Plumas Quincy	62	925
Tye	Mariposa Twp 1	60	664
Tyr	Mariposa Twp 1	60	664
Wan	San Francisco San Francisco 6	67	470
Wum*	El Dorado Georgetown	58	703
Young*	Tuolumne Columbia	71	346
Yow	Nevada Nevada	61	305
Yu	Sacramento Granite	63	268
Yup	Nevada Nevada	61	307
Yup	Nevada Washington	61	339
Yup	Nevada Eureka	61	385
Yup	Nevada Washington	61	339
Yup*	Nevada Washington	61	340
Yup*	Nevada Washington	61	341
Yup*	Placer Michigan	62	843
SUA			
---	Butte Ophir	56	818
---	Placer Illinois	62	739
Ahu	Fresno Twp 2	59	4
SUADA			
Antone*	Placer Michigan	62	850

Name	County Locale	M653 Roll	Page
SUADA			
Frank M*	El Dorado Georgetown	58	699
SUAEL			
Francisco*	Calaveras Twp 6	57	162
SUAIN			
Charles	Yuba Fosters	72	838
SUAL			
Benvenuto	Los Angeles Los Angeles	59	385
Benvuunto	Los Angeles Los Angeles	59	385
SUALL			
Francisco*	Calaveras Twp 6	57	162
SUAM			
Charles*	Placer Michigan	62	821
SUAN			
---	Calaveras Twp 10	57	273
---	Santa Clara San Jose	65	374
Benj T*	Mariposa Twp 3	60	590
Thomas M	Solano Suisan	69	217
SUANET			
Charles	San Francisco San Francisco 8	68	1312
SUANEY			
A M	Mariposa Twp 3	60	589
SUANGG			
S*	El Dorado Georgetown	58	697
SUANL			
Dolores	Santa Clara San Jose	65	332
SUANN			
Joseph*	Yuba Fosters	72	838
SUAP			
Henry*	Shasta Shasta	66	681
SUAREZ			
Jose	San Francisco San Francisco 3	67	64
SUARI			
Benj T*	Mariposa Twp 3	60	590
SUARO			
Ledro Mello	Calaveras Twp 5	57	187
Pedro Mello*	Calaveras Twp 6	57	187
SUARTZ			
B*	El Dorado Kelsey	58	1152
L	San Francisco San Francisco 1	68	929
SUAS			
Jos Venita*	Mariposa Twp 3	60	548
SUASEY			
Samuel	Solano Benecia	69	291
SUATCHER			
Louis*	Santa Cruz Soguel	66	579
SUATZ			
Wm	Nevada Eureka	61	391
SUAW			
---	Amador Twp 7	55	415
SUAWN			
Charley*	Sierra Twp 7	66	894
SUAY			
---	Shasta Horsetown	66	701
George*	Sacramento Brighton	63	197
SUAYNE			
Mary Dominica S	Solano Benecia	69	300
SUAYNO			
A C*	Shasta Shasta	66	681
SUAZNO			
A C*	Shasta Shasta	66	681
SUBANDER			
Leonard	Calaveras Twp 4	57	324
SUBB			
John	Fresno Twp 1	59	82
SUBBLEFIEKD			
Robert	Tuolumne Twp 6	71	543
SUBBLEFIELD			
Robert	Tuolumne Twp 6	71	543
SUBBT			
Wm H*	Nevada Nevada	61	268
SUBCAPT			
Joaquin*	Tulara Keyesville	71	55
SUBE			
G	San Francisco San Francisco 6	67	436
SUBECK			
D W*	Placer Auburn	62	565
SUBER			
Danl	Tuolumne Sonora	71	218
J	Sutter Yuba	70	775
SUBERAN			
Dolores	Santa Clara Burnett	65	257
SUBERG			
Rodolph	Sierra Downieville	66	977
SUBERT			
Jno	Nevada Nevada	61	284
Mary S	Solano Benecia	69	313
SUBIG			
T	Calaveras Twp 9	57	395
SUBIO			
Manuel	Santa Clara San Jose	65	394
SUBLED			
J	Siskiyou Scott Va	69	50
SUBLER			
Henry	Calaveras Twp 4	57	299
SUBLETT			
Willis	Solano Vacaville	69	319
SUBLETT			
Wm H*	Nevada Nevada	61	268
SUBLIEN			
John	Trinity Rattle Snake	70	1029
SUBLIN			
---	Mendocino Big Rvr	60	855
SUBLITT			
Wm H	Nevada Nevada	61	268
SUBLIZIA			
John	San Francisco San Francisco 3	67	53
SUBRAND			
M	San Francisco San Francisco 2	67	725
SUBRIEL			
---*	San Francisco San Francisco 12	67	395
SUBUSH			
Lorin	Contra Costa Twp 1	57	533
SUC			
---	Tuolumne Twp 5	71	516
SUCACIS			
Lucra	Calaveras Twp 6	57	147
SUCASSON			
Lucas	Trinity Evans Ba	70	1003
SUCAWBRELL			
Martin	Siskiyou Scott Va	69	50
SUCE			
---	Monterey San Juan	60	977
Henry	Calaveras Twp 4	57	338
Henry*	Calaveras Twp 4	57	339
Henry*	Calaveras Twp 4	57	339
J	Nevada Eureka	61	348
Jumis J	Calaveras Twp 5	57	189
Luther J*	Calaveras Twp 4	57	339
Luther S	Calaveras Twp 4	57	339
SUCEN			
Jose M*	Los Angeles Los Nieto	59	436
SUCHER			
Jas*	Butte Oregon	56	613
SUCHERLIN			
W D*	Trinity Weaverville	70	1053
SUCHET			
---	Mendocino Big Rvr	60	854
SUCHO			
---	Butte Eureka	56	653
SUCHRE			
Joseph	Sacramento Ward 4	63	583
SUCI			
---*	Calaveras Twp 6	57	149
SUCIA			
John	Placer Yankee J	62	757
SUCIT			
Les B*	Amador Twp 2	55	302
SUCITLES			
B*	Amador Twp 2	55	302
SUCK			
---	Amador Twp 4	55	332
---	Calaveras Twp 5	57	234
---	Calaveras Twp 5	57	236
---	Calaveras Twp 4	57	300
---	Sacramento Centre	63	182
---	Sierra Downieville	66	974
---	Sierra Downieville	66	979
---	Sierra Downieville	66	996
Francis S	Contra Costa Twp 3	57	592
SUCKA FAH LEE			
---	Plumas Quincy	62	970
SUCKE			
---*	Tulara Visalia	71	37
SUCKEE			
Henry*	Sacramento American	63	171
SUCKER			
Henrich*	San Francisco San Francisco 3	67	72
Henry*	Sacramento American	63	171
SUCKERT			
Lou	San Francisco San Francisco 7	68	1385
SUCKETT			
A W Dye	Calaveras Twp 9	57	410
A W*	Tuolumne Twp 1	71	204
John	Yuba New York	72	723
SUCKLOW			
---*	Tulara Visalia	71	36
SUCKO			
---	Tulara Twp 2	71	39
SUCLERA			
Francis*	Calaveras Twp 5	57	144
SUCO			
Jesus	Merced Twp 1	60	906
SUCOMBERA			
William	Sierra Scales D	66	801
SUCR			
Luther S	Calaveras Twp 4	57	338
SUCRAMIENTO			
---	Tulara Twp 3	71	67
SUCRE			
David	Sonoma Santa Rosa	69	408
SUCTO			
---	Fresno Twp 2	59	107
SUCUM			
---	Tuolumne Columbia	71	346
SUCUS			
John*	Mariposa Twp 1	60	640
SUCUT			
John*	Mariposa Twp 1	60	640
SUD			
---	Sacramento Ward 1	63	54
---	Sierra Downieville	66	983
SUDBERRY			
Thomas	Tuolumne Jamestown	71	429
SUDDIN			
Robt	San Francisco San Francisco 9	68	1009
SUDE			
---*	Yolo No E Twp	72	685
SUDEL			
Francisco*	Calaveras Twp 6	57	162
SUDGATE			
Robt	Amador Twp 2	55	264
SUDITH			
Henry*	Plumas Quincy	62	997
SUDLAM			
Fitch R	San Francisco San Francisco 10	67	258
SUDLINGER			
Joseph*	Siskiyou Yreka	69	153
SUDLUM			
Anthony*	San Francisco San Francisco 10	67	218
SUDRA			
Joseph	Alameda Brooklyn	55	116
SUDRO			
---	Fresno Twp 3	59	96
SUDRON			
John	Sierra Twp 7	66	894
SUDROW			
Welsey	Yuba Marysville	72	966
SUDSON			
J C*	Sonoma Petaluma	69	595
SUDWIG			
S W	Trinity Weaverville	70	1062
SUE HE			
---	Tuolumne Chinese	71	524
SUE			
---	Amador Twp 4	55	256
---	Amador Twp 1	55	495
---	Butte Ophir	56	788
---	Butte Ophir	56	811
---	El Dorado Big Bar	58	736
---	El Dorado Georgetown	58	756
---	Fresno Twp 2	59	72
---	Mariposa Twp 1	60	648
---	Mariposa Coulterville	60	682
---	Sacramento Mississipi	63	186
---	Sacramento Cosummes	63	407
---	Sacramento Ward 1	63	65
---	Shasta Shasta	66	669
---	Shasta Shasta	66	678
---	Shasta Horsetown	66	711
---	Sierra Downieville	66	1004
---	Sierra Downieville	66	1009
---	Sierra Morristown	66	1055
---	Sierra La Porte	66	785
---	Sierra Pine Grove	66	827
---	Sierra Downieville	66	983
---	Sierra Downieville	66	985
---	Sierra Downieville	66	996
---	Sierra Downieville	66	998
---	Trinity Price'S	70	1019
---	Trinity Weaverville	70	1072
---	Trinity Weaverville	70	1074
---	Tuolumne Twp 3	71	466
---	Tuolumne Montezuma	71	512
---	Tuolumne Jacksonville	71	516
---	Yuba Bear Rvr	72	1000
---	Yuba Marysville	72	916
---*	Shasta Shasta	66	671
---*	Yuba Marysville	72	916
Ah	Yuba Bear Rvr	72	1000
Faw	Amador Twp 2	55	292
Fee	Butte Wyandotte	56	666
Kim	San Francisco San Francisco 2	67	689
Ling	El Dorado Georgetown	58	748
Yin	El Dorado Big Bar	58	736
Yun	El Dorado Greenwood	58	719
Yup	Nevada Washington	61	342
SUEANKR			
Henry*	Amador Twp 2	55	325
SUEAUKS			
Henry*	Amador Twp 2	55	325
SUEBLET			
Thos	Nevada Rough &	61	430
SUEENEY			
Catharine*	San Francisco 8	68	1285
	San Francisco		
D M	San Francisco San Francisco 7	68	1422

Name	County Locale	M653 Roll Page
SUEENEY		
Timothy	San Francisco San Francisco	8 681288
W*	San Francisco San Francisco	5 67 529
SUEI		
---*	Calaveras Twp 5	57 149
SUEITZER		
Frank	Amador Twp 5	55 345
SUEK		
---	Sierra Downieville	661004
SUEL		
---	Butte Hamilton	56 529
---	Butte Kimshaw	56 606
Jno	Nevada Nevada	61 298
SUELL		
Frank	San Joaquin Elkhorn	64 980
Jane	San Francisco San Francisco	2 67 694
SUEN		
---	El Dorado Georgetown	58 680
---*	Mariposa Twp 3	60 590
---*	Trinity Trinindad Rvr	701045
---*	Yuba Linda	72 990
Hee	San Francisco San Francisco	10 356 67
SUER		
---	El Dorado Georgetown	58 705
---*	Yuba Linda	72 990
SUERES		
Manuel*	Contra Costa Twp 1	57 515
SUERGERT		
Casper*	Napa Clear Lake	61 129
SUERIN		
Patrick	Yuba Foster B	72 833
SUERIX		
Patrick	Yuba Fosters	72 833
SUERRIS		
Francisco	Contra Costa Twp 1	57 497
SUESE		
Frenedar*	Mariposa Twp 1	60 632
Frinedar	Mariposa Twp 1	60 632
SUESMAN		
Earnest*	San Francisco San Francisco	11 136 67
SUET		
Mack	Nevada Rough &	61 410
SUETH		
John	Yuba Linda	72 989
SUETSER		
James T	Yuba New York	72 733
SUETT		
Charles*	Nevada Bridgeport	61 449
SUETZE		
Frank	San Francisco San Francisco	1 68 811
SUETZO		
Frank*	San Francisco San Francisco	1 68 811
SUEUS		
Mand	Calaveras Twp 6	57 142
SUEY		
---	Del Norte Crescent	58 641
---	Mariposa Coulterville	60 689
---	Shasta Horsetown	66 701
---	Trinity Trinindad Rvr	701048
---*	Mariposa Coulterville	60 689
SUEZ		
---	Trinity Lewiston	70 954
SUFEBER		
John*	Calaveras Twp 10	57 288
SUFEY		
Charley	Calaveras Twp 4	57 341
SUFFERD		
C P	Placer Virginia	62 668
SUFFEREL		
Wm	Yuba Fosters	72 839
SUFFY		
Hannah	Placer Ophirville	62 655
SUFIELD		
C W	El Dorado Diamond	58 806
SUFITRCO		
Allen	Calaveras Twp 10	57 290
SUFRINS		
A*	Butte Oro	56 684
SUFTINS		
A	Butte Oro	56 684
SUG		
---	Placer Virginia	62 667
---	Yuba Marysville	72 921
SUGAIN		
Swiny*	El Dorado Georgetown	58 705
SUGAROL		
C	Nevada Eureka	61 359
SUGDON		
R	Los Angeles Tejon	59 525
SUGENDORF		
E	Calaveras Twp 9	57 406
SUGERS		
Charles	Solano Fremont	69 385
SUGG		
---	Tuolumne Jamestown	71 469
SUGG		
Chritine	San Francisco San Francisco	2 67 622
Margaret	San Francisco San Francisco	7 681438
Margaret	San Francisco San Francisco	2 67 622
SUGGS		
William	Tuolumne Twp 3	71 470
Wm	Tuolumne Twp 1	71 237
SUGHE		
John	Calaveras Twp 6	57 161
SUGIE		
Fred	Sierra Downieville	66 994
SUGIN		
---	Sierra Downieville	661015
SUGLEY		
R B	Calaveras Twp 9	57 396
SUGO		
Bicenta*	Los Angeles Los Angeles	59 496
Breenta	Los Angeles Los Angeles	59 496
Felipe	Los Angeles Los Angeles	59 494
Filipi*	Los Angeles Los Angeles	59 494
Francisco	Los Angeles Los Angeles	59 494
Jose	San Bernardino Santa Inez	64 141
Jose Ma*	Los Angeles Los Angeles	59 494
Juan	San Bernardino Santa Inez	64 144
Maria	Los Angeles Los Angeles	59 496
Maria	Los Angeles Los Angeles	59 498
Maria*	Los Angeles Los Angeles	59 496
Maria*	Los Angeles Los Angeles	59 498
Modesta	Los Angeles Los Angeles	59 496
Pilar	Los Angeles Los Angeles	59 367
Santiago	Los Angeles Los Angeles	59 494
Saturnino	Santa Barbara	64 158
	San Bernardino	
Vincent	Los Angeles Los Angeles	59 496
SUGODON		
Tho*	Siskiyou Scott Ri	69 81
SUGOLDSBY		
John*	San Francisco San Francisco	11 104 67
SUGRO		
Wm*	Amador Twp 2	55 299
SUGUE		
Muidad	Los Angeles Los Angeles	59 307
SUH		
B	San Francisco San Francisco	12 395 67
SUHER		
W ?	Nevada Nevada	61 327
W N*	Nevada Nevada	61 327
SUHIE		
John	Calaveras Twp 5	57 138
SUHL		
Christian	Tuolumne Twp 2	71 369
Henry*	Tuolumne Twp 1	71 272
SUHOLTS		
Harriet	Solano Vallejo	69 271
SUHOW		
---*	Tulara Twp 2	71 34
SUI		
---	Fresno Twp 3	59 31
---	Tuolumne Twp 3	71 466
Ah	Yuba Bear Rvr	721000
An	Del Norte Crescent	58 631
Wan	Yuba Linda	72 993
Yet	Plumas Quincy	62 948
SUICK		
---	Del Norte Happy Ca	58 669
SUIG WA		
---	Sacramento Ward 1	63 66
SUIG		
---	El Dorado Mountain	581187
---	Sacramento Granite	63 232
---	Sierra Downieville	661004
---	Sierra Downieville	661030
See	Yuba Bear Rvr	721000
SUIN		
---	Calaveras Twp 5	57 191
---	Calaveras Twp 5	57 243
---	Calaveras Twp 5	57 247
---	Calaveras Twp 10	57 274
---	Calaveras Twp 10	57 283
---	Calaveras Twp 10	57 296
---	Calaveras Twp 4	57 306
---	Mariposa Twp 3	60 590
---	Sierra Downieville	661004
Tu	San Francisco San Francisco	5 67 508
SUINARD		
A	Siskiyou Klamath	69 97
SUING		
---	El Dorado Greenwood	58 732
J	Calaveras Twp 9	57 404
SUINGLE		
G M*	Yolo Putah	72 550
SUION		
Nicholine	Sierra Whiskey	66 843
Nicholini	Sierra Whiskey	66 843
SUIR		
Jospeh	Calaveras Twp 10	57 268
SUIS		
---	Monterey Monterey	60 954
Bonificio	Los Angeles Los Angeles	59 511
SUISA		
---	Monterey San Juan	60 991
SUISEN		
John	Yuba New York	72 731
SUIT		
Jno	Sacramento Ward 4	63 523
SUITER		
John	Yuba Timbucto	72 787
SUITI		
Frank*	Placer Rattle Snake	62 601
SUITOR		
O	San Francisco San Francisco	7 681347
SUITS		
Jos	Butte Chico	56 546
Jos	Butte Chico	56 552
SUITZER		
Henry	Solano Suisan	69 233
Julia A	Solano Suisan	69 233
SUIY		
See*	Yuba Bear Rvr	721000
SUIZE		
Joseph	Amador Twp 4	55 245
SUIZIER		
Wm	Amador Twp 1	55 471
SUJAIN		
Louis*	El Dorado Georgetown	58 705
Swing*	El Dorado Georgetown	58 705
SUJAN		
Jesus	Los Angeles Los Angeles	59 294
SUJITON		
Plato	El Dorado Greenwood	58 717
SUJJAW		
Andrew*	Marin San Rafael	60 771
SUJO COW		
---	Tuolumne Green Springs	71 517
SUJO		
Francisco	Santa Inez	64 141
	San Bernardino	
SUK		
---	Sacramento Ward 4	63 613
---	Sacramento Ward 1	63 68
Ku	Placer Iona Hills	62 869
Pu	El Dorado Georgetown	58 756
Se	El Dorado Georgetown	58 755
SUKAL		
Ralph	Sacramento Alabama	63 411
SUKE		
---	Calaveras Twp 5	57 254
---	Fresno Twp 2	59 43
Chee	Yuba Foster B	72 834
Edwin F	Calaveras Twp 5	57 236
SUKEN		
Jos F*	Sacramento Ward 4	63 554
SUKES		
Christian	Contra Costa Twp 1	57 512
SUKEY		
---	Del Norte Klamath	58 656
---	Mendocino Big Rock	60 875
SUKI		
---	Calaveras Twp 5	57 256
SUKOW		
---*	Tulara Twp 2	71 34
SUL DO		
Gidro*	Los Angeles Los Angeles	59 350
SULARN		
Jacob*	Calaveras Twp 5	57 221
SULAS		
Gidrp	Los Angeles Los Angeles	59 350
SULASE		
John	Calaveras Twp 5	57 216
SULASHA		
---	Mendocino Round Va	60 882
SULBY		
John	San Francisco San Francisco	7 681435
SULE		
---	El Dorado Georgetown	58 686
Adam*	Siskiyou Callahan	69 7
James*	Placer Michigan	62 815
John*	Placer Michigan	62 818
SULECT		
C B	Siskiyou Scott Va	69 57
SULEEN		
---	Trinity Trinindad Rvr	701046
---	Trinity Weaverville	701073
SULEIN		
David	Yuba Slate Ro	72 698
SULEN		
Henry W	Calaveras Twp 5	57 171
SULENGER		
William*	Napa Yount	61 34
SULER		
Henry W	Calaveras Twp 6	57 171

Name	County Locale	M653 Roll	Page
SULES			
Wm*	Sacramento Natonia	63	275
SULEY			
---*	Sierra Twp 5	66	942
Geo	Stanislaus Emory	70	745
Hannah	Butte Ophir	56	785
SULI			
---	El Dorado Georgetown	58	686
SULIAMENTO			
Marnea	Calaveras Twp 6	57	132
SULING			
Rank	Placer Grizzly	62	755
SULINGIR			
William	Napa Yount	61	34
SULIO			
Josephine	Calaveras Twp 4	57	330
SULISCER			
Isaac	Tehama Red Bluff	70	910
SULIVAN			
C W	El Dorado Placerville	58	889
Cornelius	Calaveras Twp 8	57	53
Cornelius	Nevada Bridgeport	61	488
D	Mariposa Twp 1	60	637
Daniel	Calaveras Twp 8	57	93
Denis	Nevada Rough &	61	396
Dennis H	Placer Rattle Snake	62	632
Dun	Placer Auburn	62	594
Frederick	Calaveras Twp 7	57	9
Geo O*	Placer Rattle Snake	62	626
James	Nevada Rough &	61	433
James	Siskiyou Callahan	69	9
Jno	Alameda Brooklyn	55	202
John	Calaveras Twp 6	57	156
John	Nevada Bridgeport	61	489
John	Nevada Bridgeport	61	499
Owen	Nevada Bridgeport	61	471
Peter	Calaveras Twp 7	57	25
S	Mariposa Twp 3	60	587
Thos	Placer Virginia	62	673
Timothy	Nevada Bloomfield	61	529
W	Stanislaus Emory	70	745
William H	Placer Auburn	62	563
SULIVANT			
John	Yolo Merritt	72	577
SULIZAR			
Joseph*	Calaveras Twp 5	57	206
SULKEN			
B*	Mariposa Twp 3	60	577
SULL			
---	Yuba Fosters	72	841
SULLAN			
John	Stanislaus Branch	70	702
SULLAWAY			
Charles	Siskiyou Shasta Rvr	69	113
George H	Siskiyou Shasta Rvr	69	112
William	Siskiyou Shasta Rvr	69	112
SULLEBURY			
John B	Los Angeles Los Angeles	59	510
SULLENGER			
John C*	Napa Yount	61	35
Madison	Sonoma Russian	69	437
SULLER			
Fredrick	Sierra Gibsonville	66	860
Michael	San Francisco San Francisco 8	68	1305
SULLERO			
Jose V	Tuolumne Montezuma	71	513
SULLERS			
Jose V	Tuolumne Twp 5	71	513
SULLEY			
J*	Nevada Eureka	61	344
Mary	Placer Secret R	62	611
Wm	El Dorado Coloma	58	1103
SULLIBURY			
John B*	Los Angeles Los Angeles	59	510
SULLINGAN			
John C*	Napa Yount	61	35
SULLINGER			
John C*	Napa Yount	61	35
Lawrence	San Francisco San Francisco 1	68	820
S J	Sutter Butte	70	789
SULLINS			
James	Calaveras Twp 10	57	280
SULLIRHUFF			
Ben	Nevada Bloomfield	61	520
Vien*	Nevada Bloomfield	61	520
SULLISAN			
Mary	Sacramento Ward 1	63	128
SULLIVAN			
---	Calaveras Twp 9	57	389
A	Nevada Eureka	61	373
Abby	San Francisco San Francisco 8	68	1295
Abram	Calaveras Twp 10	57	288
Alfred	San Joaquin Douglass	64	918
Andrew	Sonoma Petaluma	69	597
Andrew	Tuolumne Jamestown	71	450
Ann	Sacramento Ward 1	63	88
SULLIVAN			
Ann A	Solano Vacaville	69	336
Anna	San Joaquin Elkhorn	64	969
Bartlet B	Calaveras Twp 10	57	280
Burton	El Dorado Mud Springs	58	970
C	Nevada Grass Valley	61	158
C	Nevada Grass Valley	61	165
C	Nevada Grass Valley	61	212
C	Nevada Grass Valley	61	225
C	Nevada Eureka	61	359
C	Sacramento Ward 4	63	534
C J	Tuolumne Big Oak	71	148
C	Placer Forest H	62	792
C N	Butte Eureka	56	651
Catharine	San Francisco San Francisco 10	67	167
Catharine	San Francisco San Francisco 9	68	961
Catharine	Yuba Marysville	72	903
Catherine	Santa Clara San Jose	65	281
Catherine	Solano Vallejo	69	264
Catherine	Yuba Marysville	72	952
Catherine E	Yuba Marysville	72	884
Charles	El Dorado Coloma	58	1071
Charles	Marin Cortemad	60	782
Charles	Santa Cruz Pajaro	66	562
Charles	Santa Cruz Santa Cruz	66	640
Conelius	Tuolumne Twp 1	71	271
Cor	San Francisco San Francisco 2	67	786
Cori	San Francisco San Francisco 2	67	786
Corn	Sacramento Ward 1	63	46
Cornelius	Calaveras Twp 9	57	351
Cornelius	Placer Forest H	62	766
Cornelius	Placer Iona Hills	62	877
Cornelius	San Francisco San Francisco 10	67	359
Cornelius	Tuolumne Twp 2	71	271
Cornelius O*	San Francisco San Francisco 8	68	1250
Cors	Sacramento Ward 3	63	427
D	Butte Kimshaw	56	590
D	Nevada Grass Valley	61	143
D	Nevada Grass Valley	61	161
D	Nevada Grass Valley	61	179
D	Nevada Grass Valley	61	192
D	Nevada Grass Valley	61	212
D	Nevada Grass Valley	61	225
D	Nevada Nevada	61	263
D	Sacramento Ward 4	63	525
D	Sacramento Ward 4	63	606
D	Siskiyou Cottonwoood	69	101
D	Trinity Trinity	70	972
D	Tuolumne Twp 4	71	148
D M	Sonoma Petaluma	69	603
Dan	Calaveras Twp 9	57	379
Daniel	Mendocino Little L	60	839
Daniel	Placer Iona Hills	62	877
Daniel	San Diego Colorado	64	807
Daniel	San Francisco San Francisco 7	68	1330
Daniel	San Francisco San Francisco 3	67	15
Daniel	Sierra St Louis	66	806
Daniel	Solano Fremont	69	376
Daniel	Tuolumne Twp 4	71	132
Danl	San Francisco San Francisco 9	68	1026
Danl	San Francisco San Francisco 9	68	999
Danl B	Calaveras Twp 6	57	157
David	Butte Kimshaw	56	601
Dennis	Alameda Brooklyn	55	111
Dennis	Alameda Oakland	55	71
Dennis	Calaveras Twp 6	57	141
Dennis	Plumas Meadow Valley	62	904
Dennis	Sacramento Ward 1	63	26
Dennis	San Francisco San Francisco 7	68	1334
Dennis W	Yuba Marysville	72	857
Dennis W	Yuba Marysville	72	862
Don	Sonoma Petaluma	69	603
E	Nevada Grass Valley	61	156
E	San Joaquin Stockton	64	1091
Edward	El Dorado White Oaks	58	1027
Edward	El Dorado Coloma	58	1112
Edwd	Sonoma Petaluma	69	605
Elizabeth E	San Francisco San Francisco 10	67	174
Ellen	Sacramento Ward 1	63	105
Eugene	El Dorado White Oaks	58	1013
Eugene	Sierra Twp 7	66	867
F L	Amador Twp 6	55	438
F R	Tehama Moons	70	854
Florintine	Santa Clara Santa Clara	65	481
Francis	Alameda Brooklyn	55	113
Frederick	San Joaquin Elkhorn	64	987
G P	Amador Twp 3	55	380
H	Nevada Grass Valley	61	155
Hanna	San Francisco San Francisco 8	68	1260
Hannah	San Francisco San Francisco 2	67	652
Hannover	Butte Kimshaw	56	587
Harvey	Colusa Spring Valley	57	431
SULLIVAN			
Henry	Fresno Millerto	59	1
Honora	San Francisco San Francisco 7	68	1346
Honora	San Francisco San Francisco 6	67	439
I*	Butte Kimshaw	56	590
J	Nevada Grass Valley	61	156
J	Nevada Grass Valley	61	157
J	Nevada Grass Valley	61	204
J	Nevada Grass Valley	61	205
J	Nevada Grass Valley	61	212
J	Nevada Grass Valley	61	225
J	Nevada Washington	61	333
J	San Francisco San Francisco 5	67	531
J	Siskiyou Scott Ri	69	81
J M	Tuolumne Twp 2	71	407
J R	Sacramento Granite	63	237
J S	Tuolumne Columbia	71	359
J W	Calaveras Twp 8	57	108
J W	San Francisco San Francisco 2	67	586
J W	Sonoma Armally	69	496
James	Colusa Monroeville	57	443
James	Klamath Liberty	59	233
James	Placer Iona Hills	62	878
James	San Francisco San Francisco 9	68	1034
James	San Francisco San Francisco 4	68	1150
James	San Francisco San Francisco 7	68	1377
James	San Francisco San Francisco 7	68	1387
James	San Francisco San Francisco 3	67	24
James	San Francisco San Francisco 3	67	54
James	San Francisco San Francisco 9	68	977
James	San Joaquin Stockton	64	1025
James	Santa Clara Santa Clara	65	478
James	Tuolumne Twp 1	71	278
James A	Calaveras Twp 6	57	157
James H	Calaveras Twp 6	57	157
James O	Tuolumne Sonora	71	200
James*	Yuba Rose Bar	72	795
Jane	San Francisco San Francisco 8	68	1250
Jannah	San Francisco San Francisco 11	67	120
Jas	Sacramento Ward 1	63	14
Jas	Sacramento Ward 3	63	428
Jas	San Francisco San Francisco 2	67	612
Jas B	San Francisco San Francisco 2	67	589
Jas M	Calaveras Twp 9	57	370
Jas O	Sonoma Petaluma	69	603
Jas*	Sacramento Ward 1	63	78
Jas*	San Francisco San Francisco 9	68	1044
Jeremiah	San Francisco San Francisco 10	67	196
Jerh W	San Francisco San Francisco 2	67	585
Jerry	Alameda Brooklyn	55	127
Jerry	Sacramento Ward 4	63	526
Jerry	Sacramento Ward 4	63	562
Jerry	Sierra Twp 5	66	935
Jesse	San Francisco San Francisco 2	67	672
Jno	Klamath Liberty	59	237
Jno	Nevada Eureka	61	345
Jno	San Francisco San Francisco 9	68	950
Joanna	San Francisco San Francisco 6	67	418
Joanna	San Francisco San Francisco 6	67	434
Joh	Sonoma Petaluma	69	566
John	Alameda Brooklyn	55	100
John	Amador Twp 3	55	381
John	Amador Twp 3	55	486
John	Butte Cascade	56	694
John	Calaveras Twp 6	57	156
John	El Dorado Cold Spring	58	1101
John	Marin Novato	60	738
John	Sacramento American	63	170
John	Sacramento Granite	63	263
John	San Francisco San Francisco 9	68	1002
John	San Francisco San Francisco 8	68	1277
John	San Francisco San Francisco 12	67	375
John	San Mateo Twp 1	65	71
John	San Mateo Twp 3	65	98
John	Shasta Horsetown	66	689
John	Sierra Port Win	66	794
John	Siskiyou Cottonwoood	69	101
John	Solano Vallejo	69	274
John	Solano Benecia	69	317
John	Tuolumne Columbia	71	327
John	Yolo No E Twp	72	672
John	Yuba Bear Rvr	72	1001
John	Yuba North Ea	72	672
John	Yuba New York	72	723
John D	Calaveras Twp 6	57	180
John D	Sacramento Sutter	63	306
John H	Santa Clara Redwood	65	453
Jos	San Francisco San Francisco 2	67	612
Jos B	San Francisco San Francisco 2	67	589
Josep	Solano Vallejo	69	245
Joseph	Solano Vallejo	69	245
Josephine	San Francisco San Francisco 1	68	824
Julia	Nevada Eureka	61	388

California 1860 Census Index

Name	County Locale	M653 Roll	Page
SULLIVAN			
Julia	San Francisco San Francisco 10		181
		67	
Julia	San Francisco San Francisco 10		321
		67	
Julia	Solano Benecia	69	295
Kate	San Francisco San Francisco 10		324
		67	
L	Nevada Grass Valley	61	206
L	Sacramento Ward 1	63	79
L	San Francisco San Francisco 5	67	499
Laurens	Calaveras Twp 5	57	249
Lawrence	San Francisco San Francisco 7	68	1334
Lewis S	Colusa Spring Valley	57	435
Lizzie	San Francisco San Francisco 4	68	1172
M	Calaveras Twp 9	57	411
M	Nevada Grass Valley	61	156
M	Nevada Grass Valley	61	158
M	Nevada Grass Valley	61	206
M	Nevada Grass Valley	61	212
M	Nevada Grass Valley	61	213
M	Nevada Grass Valley	61	225
M	Nevada Nevada	61	270
M	Nevada Washington	61	331
M	Nevada Washington	61	335
M	Nevada Washington	61	341
M	Nevada Eureka	61	368
M	Nevada Eureka	61	388
M	Sacramento San Joaquin	63	360
M	San Francisco San Francisco 2	67	672
M A	San Francisco San Francisco 9	68	1057
M B	Sacramento Ward 1	63	151
M L	Colusa Grand Island	57	470
M S	Butte Ophir	56	790
Manely*	Sacramento Georgian	63	340
Margaret	Monterey Alisal	60	1028
Margaret	San Francisco San Francisco 8	68	1239
Margaret	Santa Clara Almaden	65	263
Mary	Alameda Oakland	55	27
Mary	Napa Napa	61	104
Mary	Sacramento Ward 1	63	103
Mary	San Francisco San Francisco 8	68	1261
Mary	San Francisco San Francisco 10		185
		67	
Mary	San Francisco San Francisco 6	67	472
Mary	San Francisco San Francisco 2	67	745
Mary O	San Mateo Twp 1	65	71
Mich	Alameda Brooklyn	55	97
Michael	Alameda Brooklyn	55	139
Michael	Alameda Brooklyn	55	82
Michael	Calaveras Twp 5	57	196
Michael	Placer Ophirville	62	655
Michael	Sacramento Ward 3	63	440
Michael	San Francisco San Francisco 7	68	1409
Michael	San Francisco San Francisco 10		268
		67	
Michael	San Mateo Twp 1	65	50
Michael	Santa Clara San Jose	65	377
Michael	Sierra La Porte	66	783
Michael	Solano Vallejo	69	255
Michael	Tuolumne Jamestown	71	451
Michael	Yuba Rose Bar	72	809
Morris	Sacramento Ward 1	63	145
Morris	San Francisco San Francisco 10		295
		67	
Morris	Yuba Marysville	72	906
Morty	San Francisco San Francisco 1	68	835
Munely*	Sacramento Georgian	63	340
N C	Calaveras Twp 9	57	385
Owen	San Francisco San Francisco 1	68	864
P	Calaveras Twp 9	57	411
P	Nevada Eureka	61	359
P	Shasta Shasta	66	687
P H	Tuolumne Twp 1	71	259
P S	Sacramento Ward 4	63	600
Pat	San Francisco San Francisco 9	68	960
Patk	Klamath Liberty	59	230
Patrick	Calaveras Twp 10	57	289
Patrick	Santa Clara San Jose	65	377
Patrick	Santa Cruz Pajaro	66	573
Patrick	Sierra Downieville	66	978
Patrick	Siskiyou Yreka	69	191
Patrick	Siskiyou Yreka	69	192
Peter	Napa Hot Springs	61	8
Peter	San Francisco San Francisco 9	68	1032
Peter	San Francisco San Francisco 10		285
		67	
Phillip	Sierra Pine Grove	66	829
Robert	Santa Clara Santa Clara	65	472
Roger	Trinity North Fo	70	1023
S	Mariposa Twp 3	60	587
Simon O*	Yuba Rose Bar	72	808
Stephen	San Francisco San Francisco 2	67	744
Sylvester	San Francisco San Francisco 11		116
		67	
T	Nevada Grass Valley	61	205

Name	County Locale	M653 Roll	Page
SULLIVAN			
T	Nevada Grass Valley	61	215
T	Sacramento Ward 1	63	79
T	San Francisco San Francisco 5	67	555
T	Solano Vallejo	69	255
T J	El Dorado Coloma	58	1120
T J	San Francisco San Francisco 5	67	490
T O	Nevada Eureka	61	367
T*	Butte Kimshaw	56	590
T*	Calaveras Twp 9	57	411
Thomas	Calaveras Twp 6	57	127
Thomas	El Dorado Coloma	58	1072
Thomas	Placer Iona Hills	62	876
Thomas	Sierra La Porte	66	788
Thomas	Sierra La Porte	66	789
Thomas	Siskiyou Yreka	69	123
Thomas	Yuba Marysville	72	856
Thomas	Yuba Marysville	72	861
Thomas J	Siskiyou Yreka	69	123
Thos	Napa Napa	61	113
Thos	Sacramento Ward 3	63	488
Thos	Sacramento Ward 1	63	67
Thos	San Francisco San Francisco 1	68	825
Thos	San Francisco San Francisco 1	68	832
Thos	San Francisco San Francisco 1	68	835
Thos	San Francisco San Francisco 1	68	921
Thos	San Francisco San Francisco 1	68	922
Thos	Solano Benecia	69	306
Timothy	Klamath Liberty	59	240
Timothy	Sacramento Granite	63	246
Timothy	San Francisco San Francisco 9	68	1032
Timothy	Tuolumne Twp 1	71	217
Timothy	Yuba Rose Bar	72	804
Timothy	Yuba Rose Bar	72	814
Timothy J	San Francisco San Francisco 7	68	1435
Timothy T	Alameda Oakland	55	72
W	San Francisco San Francisco 6	67	440
W	San Francisco San Francisco 7	67	546
W C	Siskiyou Scott Va	69	33
W C	Siskiyou Scott Va	69	37
William	San Francisco San Francisco 4	68	1133
Wm	Merced Twp 1	60	911
Wm	Napa Napa	61	70
Wm	Nevada Grass Valley	61	158
Wm	Nevada Eureka	61	361
Wm	Sacramento Ward 4	63	554
Wm	San Francisco San Francisco 12		382
		67	
Wm	San Francisco San Francisco 1	68	835
Wm	Santa Clara Redwood	65	451
Wm	Solano Vallejo	69	277
Wm	Tehama Antelope	70	890
Wm	Tehama Red Bluff	70	908
Wm	Tehama Red Bluff	70	925
Wm	Yuba Rose Bar	72	802
Wm D	Solano Vallejo	69	277
SULLIVANE			
Dan	Trinity Trinity	70	972
SULLIVANT			
H M	Yolo Cache Crk	72	637
John	Yolo Washington	72	570
P	Yolo Putah	72	551
P	Yolo Putah	72	553
SULLIVEE			
Cornelius*	Sacramento Natonia	63	271
SULLIVEN			
Cornelius	Sacramento Natonia	63	271
Dennis	Sacramento Natonia	63	276
James	Yuba Rose Par	72	795
Lewis	Sacramento Natonia	63	276
SULLIVER			
Cornelius*	Sacramento Natonia	63	271
SULLIVHUFF			
Vien*	Nevada Bloomfield	61	520
SULLIVIN			
John	Sacramento Granite	63	263
SULLUYHEN			
James	Calaveras Twp 6	57	157
SULLWAN			
John	Alameda Brooklyn	55	100
Patrick	Santa Cruz Pajaro	66	573
SULLWANT			
P	Yolo Putah	72	553
SULLY			
H C*	Nevada Nevada	61	316
J*	Nevada Eureka	61	354
SULO			
Wm	Trinity Sturdiva	70	1006
SULONE			
James	Santa Cruz Santa Cruz	66	605
SULPUTA			
---	Fresno Twp 2	59	57
SULSAR			
J W	Nevada Bridgeport	61	502
SULSER			
J W	Nevada Bridgeport	61	502

Name	County Locale	M653 Roll	Page
SULSETHER			
Amparro	Mariposa Twp 1	60	653
SULTAN			
Alexander	Solano Vallejo	69	275
SULTEN			
Jas*	Sacramento Franklin	63	330
Lewis	Sacramento Franklin	63	309
SULTER			
J D*	Mariposa Twp 3	60	598
SULTIFF			
S*	San Francisco San Francisco 5	67	538
SULTON			
J L*	Sacramento Franklin	63	317
James*	Plumas Quincy	62	938
SULTZEBERGER			
S	Sutter Butte	70	795
SULUEE			
Michael	Calaveras Twp 5	57	220
SULUM			
Jocob*	Calaveras Twp 5	57	221
Jacob	Calaveras Twp 1	57	221
SULURN			
Jacob	Calaveras Twp 5	57	221
SULURR			
Michael	Calaveras Twp 5	57	220
SULUSCI			
Jacob*	Calaveras Twp 5	57	221
SULUSCR			
Jacob*	Calaveras Twp 5	57	221
SULUSR			
John	Calaveras Twp 5	57	216
SULUTA			
James	Santa Clara Santa Clara	65	511
SULVAIN			
T*	Calaveras Twp 9	57	401
SULVIA			
James*	Santa Cruz Santa Cruz	66	605
SULVIN			
James*	Santa Cruz Santa Cruz	66	605
SULVISA			
Morghilo	Calaveras Twp 5	57	201
SULVO			
Gidro*	Los Angeles Los Angeles	59	350
SULY			
P*	Sacramento Brighton	63	194
SULZE			
Francis*	Calaveras Twp 6	57	112
SULZER			
John	San Francisco San Francisco 3	67	44
SULZOR			
John*	San Francisco San Francisco 3	67	44
SUM CEN			
---	Sacramento Ward 1	63	70
SUM CHUCK			
---	San Joaquin Stockton		64 1063
SUM HI			
---	Sacramento Ward 1	63	69
SUM KING			
---	Mariposa Twp 3	60	616
SUM LAT			
---	Butte Kimshaw	56	588
SUM SING			
---	Santa Clara San Jose	65	372
SUM WA			
---	Nevada Nevada	61	308
---*	Nevada Nevada	61	304
SUM YUP			
---	Nevada Nevada	61	307
SUM			
---	Amador Twp 4	55	252
---	Amador Twp 2	55	293
---	Amador Twp 2	55	326
---	Amador Twp 5	55	335
---	Amador Twp 3	55	402
---	Amador Twp 5	55	445
---	Butte Kimshaw	56	580
---	Butte Kimshaw	56	589
---	Calaveras Twp 6	57	147
---	Calaveras Twp 6	57	149
---	Calaveras Twp 6	57	181
---	Calaveras Twp 5	57	191
---	Calaveras Twp 5	57	192
---	Calaveras Twp 5	57	193
---	Calaveras Twp 5	57	195
---	Calaveras Twp 5	57	201
---	Calaveras Twp 5	57	219
---	Calaveras Twp 5	57	222
---	Calaveras Twp 5	57	225
---	Calaveras Twp 5	57	237
---	Calaveras Twp 5	57	243
---	Calaveras Twp 5	57	244
---	Calaveras Twp 5	57	247
---	Calaveras Twp 5	57	257
---	Calaveras Twp 5	57	258
---	Calaveras Twp 10	57	259
---	Calaveras Twp 10	57	268
---	Calaveras Twp 10	57	274

Name	County Locale	M653 Roll	Page
SUM			
---	Calaveras Twp 10	57	275
---	Calaveras Twp 10	57	276
---	Calaveras Twp 10	57	283
---	Calaveras Twp 10	57	284
---	Calaveras Twp 10	57	286
---	Calaveras Twp 10	57	294
---	Calaveras Twp 4	57	300
---	Calaveras Twp 4	57	304
---	Calaveras Twp 4	57	306
---	Calaveras Twp 4	57	315
---	Calaveras Twp 4	57	321
---	Calaveras Twp 4	57	327
---	Calaveras Twp 4	57	332
---	Calaveras Twp 4	57	343
---	Calaveras Twp 8	57	84
---	Del Norte Happy Ca	58	663
---	El Dorado Union	58	1091
---	El Dorado Casumnes	58	1160
---	El Dorado Georgetown	58	691
---	El Dorado Georgetown	58	703
---	El Dorado Diamond	58	798
---	El Dorado Mud Springs	58	985
---	Fresno Twp 2	59	18
---	Fresno Twp 3	59	32
---	Marin Cortemad	60	785
---	Mariposa Twp 3	60	574
---	Mariposa Twp 3	60	578
---	Mariposa Twp 3	60	589
---	Mariposa Twp 3	60	612
---	Mariposa Twp 3	60	613
---	Mariposa Twp 1	60	661
---	Mariposa Coulterville	60	683
---	Mariposa Coulterville	60	691
---	Mariposa Coulterville	60	697
---	Mariposa Coulterville	60	700
---	Nevada Washington	61	342
---	Nevada Rough &	61	434
---	Nevada Bridgeport	61	460
---	Nevada Bridgeport	61	466
---	Placer Auburn	62	572
---	Placer Auburn	62	576
---	Placer Virginia	62	671
---	Placer Virginia	62	679
---	Placer Virginia	62	687
---	Placer Illinois	62	740
---	Placer Illinois	62	751
---	Placer Michigan	62	821
---	Sacramento Ward 1	63	54
---	Sacramento Ward 1	63	56
---	Sacramento Ward 4	63	612
---	Sacramento Ward 1	63	65
---	Sacramento Ward 1	63	70
---	San Francisco San Francisco 4	68	1187
---	San Francisco San Francisco 4	68	1188
---	San Francisco San Francisco 4	68	1203
---	Sierra Downieville	66	1020
---	Sierra St Louis	66	813
---	Sierra Downieville	66	973
---	Sierra Downieville	66	982
---	Sierra Downieville	66	984
---	Sierra Downieville	66	991
---	Sierra Downieville	66	996
---	Sierra Downieville	66	997
---	Siskiyou Callahan	69	12
---	Siskiyou Scott Va	69	46
---	Trinity Big Flat	70	1042
---	Tuolumne Jamestown	71	434
---	Tuolumne Sonora	71	485
---	Tuolumne Jacksonville	71	516
---	Tuolumne Chinese	71	523
---	Yolo Slate Ra	72	710
---	Yuba Slate Ro	72	710
---*	Butte Kimshaw	56	589
---*	Fresno Twp 1	59	26
---*	Mariposa Twp 3	60	582
---*	Sacramento Cosumnes	63	390
Ah	Tuolumne Twp 2	71	369
Cen	Sacramento Ward 1	63	70
Choo	Butte Kimshaw	56	582
Fo	Butte Kimshaw	56	576
Fook	Butte Kimshaw	56	582
Frank	Sacramento Ward 1	63	146
Hi	Sacramento Ward 1	63	69
Hing	San Francisco San Francisco 5	67	508
Lee	Butte Kimshaw	56	584
Lee	Mariposa Twp 3	60	619
Ler	Butte Kimshaw	56	584
Ne	El Dorado Georgetown	58	701
Neno	Fresno Twp 2	59	19
Que*	Sierra Downieville	66	1025
Sing	Placer Auburn	62	572
Ton	Butte Kimshaw	56	588
Ton	Nevada Nevada	61	307
Voe	Placer Illinois	62	754
Wa	Nevada Nevada	61	304
SUM			
Wa	Nevada Nevada	61	308
Wo	San Francisco San Francisco 5	67	507
Ye	Placer Illinois	62	754
SUMAN			
Frederick	San Francisco San Francisco 4	68	1172
L E*	Nevada Little Y	61	535
SUMBARD			
Peter*	Sierra Downieville	66	957
SUMBECK			
Wm*	Siskiyou Callahan	69	12
SUMBER			
Chas*	Sacramento Ward 1	63	144
SUMBIE			
Fay*	Nevada Eureka	61	365
SUMDESHAUS			
Joseph*	Mariposa Twp 3	60	573
SUMELLE			
Joseph	Calaveras Twp 4	57	313
SUMEN			
Bart	Mendocino Calpella	60	823
SUMENA			
Hiram	Calaveras Twp 6	57	155
Saml M	Calaveras Twp 6	57	155
SUMER			
Chas	Placer Auburn	62	575
Jacob	Butte Kimshaw	56	580
L B*	Nevada Nevada	61	327
S B*	Nevada Nevada T	61	327
SUMERKRUP			
Henry	San Bernardino San Bernadino	64	625
SUMERS			
Christopher	Los Angeles Azuza	59	271
H B	Sierra Downieville	66	955
James	Amador Twp 2	55	293
John T	Butte Ophir	56	756
Robert	Siskiyou Yreka	69	138
Robert*	Siskiyou Yreka	69	137
Sidney	Sierra St Louis	66	818
SUMES			
George*	Sierra Downieville	66	964
SUMFERD			
J H L*	Shasta Shasta	66	673
SUMFORD			
J H L*	Shasta Shasta	66	673
SUMG			
---*	Nevada Red Dog	61	539
SUMGA			
Rafael	San Luis Obispo San Luis Obispo	65	14
SUMHER			
Chas*	Sacramento Ward 1	63	144
SUMI			
---	El Dorado Big Bar	58	734
SUMKER			
John	Contra Costa Twp 2	57	574
SUMLER			
J W	Santa Clara Alviso	65	410
SUMLEY			
John	Trinity Oregon G	70	1008
SUMM			
---	Del Norte Crescent	58	651
Ah	Tuolumne Twp 4	71	147
Hellen*	San Francisco San Francisco 2	67	737
SUMMA			
Henry	El Dorado Placerville	58	905
Lewis	Sierra Downieville	66	1017
SUMMACE			
N R*	Nevada Nevada	61	321
SUMMANY			
Joel	Shasta Millvill	66	756
SUMMARS			
R	El Dorado Indian D	58	1158
SUMME			
G R*	Nevada Nevada	61	321
Michiel*	Nevada Little Y	61	534
SUMMEN			
James	Tuolumne Twp 2	71	301
SUMMER			
Charles*	El Dorado Placerville	58	877
Daniel	El Dorado Big Bar	58	740
J	Tuolumne Jacksonville	71	170
Jacob	Tehama Red Bluff	70	921
Jno	Butte Kimshaw	56	582
John	Butte Oro	56	686
John	Contra Costa Twp 3	57	593
Marry	Sacramento Ward 1	63	24
Michiel	Nevada Little Y	61	534
Saml	Santa Clara Redwood	65	453
Stephen	San Joaquin Douglass	64	918
W S	Santa Clara Santa Clara	65	476
Wm	Santa Clara San Jose	65	292
SUMMERCAMP			
William	Siskiyou Shasta Valley	69	118
William F	Siskiyou Shasta Valley	69	118
SUMMERFIELD			
A A	Nevada Eureka	61	379
SUMMERFIELD			
Jas W	Sacramento Mississipi	63	188
S*	Nevada Eureka	61	379
SUMMERLAND			
F	Yuba North Ea	72	670
J	Yolo No E Twp	72	670
SUMMERLY			
Samuel	Yuba Marysville	72	968
SUMMERS			
A P	El Dorado Kelsey	58	1148
C A	San Francisco San Francisco 5	67	477
Celia Ann	Calaveras Twp 10	57	265
Chas	Calaveras Twp 6	57	168
Chas	Placer Mealsburg	62	702
Chas	Sacramento Ward 1	63	79
David	Tuolumne Columbia	71	302
E	Mariposa Twp 3	60	605
E A	Tuolumne Twp 1	71	250
Francis	Contra Costa Twp 3	57	595
Fred	Mariposa Coulterville	60	693
G W	Tuolumne Twp 1	71	252
George	Plumas Quincy	62	921
George	Tuolumne Twp 1	71	240
George W	Plumas Meadow Valley	62	899
H B*	Sierra Downieville	66	978
J	El Dorado Kelsey	58	1155
J	Tuolumne Twp 4	71	170
James	Del Norte Happy Ca	58	662
James	El Dorado Salmon Falls	58	1049
James	Nevada Bridgeport	61	503
James	San Bernardino Santa Barbara	64	150
James	Tuolumne Columbia	71	301
James W	Tuolumne Twp 1	71	250
Jessee	Tulara Visalia	71	9
John	Napa Napa	61	103
John	Napa Napa	61	69
John	Tuolumne Twp 1	71	243
John	Tuolumne Twp 1	71	250
John	Yuba Long Bar	72	742
John A	Butte Ophir	56	798
Joseph	Solano Benecia	69	286
Joseph P	Tuolumne Sonora	71	236
L W	Nevada Nevada	61	312
Mc Mullen	Mariposa Twp 3	60	605
Raymond	San Francisco San Francisco 3	67	43
Richd	Sacramento American	63	171
S W	Nevada Nevada	61	312
Thaddius	Sierra Twp 7	66	864
Theodore	Calaveras Twp 4	57	311
Thomas	Calaveras Twp 10	57	265
Thomas	San Francisco San Francisco 3	67	73
Thomas	Tuolumne Twp 2	71	354
Thomas*	San Francisco San Francisco 3	67	73
William	San Joaquin Stockton	64	1030
Wm F	Sonoma Vallejo	69	630
Wm T	Sacramento Ward 1	63	151
SUMMERVILLA			
Wm	Mariposa Twp 3	60	565
SUMMERVILLE			
F	Nevada Nevada	61	317
Stuart	Sonoma Petaluma	69	577
Wm	Mariposa Twp 3	60	565
SUMMERY			
David*	Tuolumne Twp 2	71	302
SUMMES			
David	Alameda Brooklyn	55	96
Joseph	Solano Benecia	69	286
SUMMEX			
H B*	Sierra Downieville	66	978
SUMMEY			
H B*	Sierra Downieville	66	978
John	Napa Napa	61	103
SUMMIER			
Charles*	El Dorado Placerville	58	877
SUMMINS			
Raymond	San Francisco San Francisco 3	67	43
SUMMON			
Chas*	Calaveras Twp 6	57	168
H B*	Sierra Downieville	66	978
SUMMONS			
Edwin	Sacramento Ward 1	63	126
Nicholas	Tuolumne Twp 3	71	441
S D	San Francisco San Francisco 6	67	449
Wm	Mariposa Twp 1	60	642
Wm	Tuolumne Jamestown	71	441
SUMMORS			
Chas*	Calaveras Twp 6	57	168
SUMMOUS			
Wm	Tuolumne Twp 3	71	441
SUMMY			
Joel*	Shasta Millvill	66	756
SUMNER			
C	Sonoma Russian	69	442
C H	Tehama Red Bluff	70	911
Charles*	Placer Michigan	62	850
Chas	San Francisco San Francisco 2	67	594

California 1860 Census Index

Name	County Locale	M653 Roll Page
SUMNER		
Chas*	Sacramento Ward 1	63 144
Ellen	San Francisco San Francisco 7	681374
Franklin	Monterey Alisal	601044
Jake	Tehama Red Bluff	70 928
James T	Tulara Twp 1	71 78
Jas	Butte Chico	56 552
Jas	Butte Chico	56 559
Jas	Butte Kimshaw	56 582
John	Marin Cortemad	60 791
Mary	Sacramento Ward 1	63 24
Robert	Tulara Keyesville	71 60
W A	San Francisco San Francisco 12	374 67
W R*	Nevada Nevada	61 321
SUMNERS		
George	San Joaquin Tulare	64 871
J W	Yolo Slate Ra	72 702
SUMNEY		
John	Butte Oro	56 677
SUMON		
L E	Nevada Little Y	61 535
SUMOND		
G R*	Nevada Nevada	61 321
SUMONT		
Sylvina	Sonoma Mendocino	69 455
SUMPSON		
Thomas	Shasta Millvill	66 727
SUMPTER		
Julius	Los Angeles Los Angeles	59 321
SUMPTION		
Joseph	Humbolt Union	59 188
Wesley	Humbolt Union	59 188
SUMPTOR		
C	El Dorado Mud Springs	58 985
SUMTIER		
Chas*	Sacramento Ward 1	63 144
SUMTUR		
Chas*	Sacramento Ward 1	63 144
SUMTZLU		
Charles*	Placer Forest H	62 799
SUMUT		
---	Tulara Twp 1	71 114
SUMYEK		
---	Trinity Trinindad Rvr	701048
---	Trinity Weaverville	701076
SUN CHOW		
---*	Nevada Nevada	61 310
SUN G		
---	El Dorado Greenwood	58 728
SUN KEE		
---	Mariposa Twp 3	60 608
---	Mariposa Twp 3	60 609
SUN PAN		
---	Tuolumne Montezuma	71 511
SUN SICK		
---*	Butte Kimshaw	56 586
SUN SING		
---	Mariposa Twp 3	60 607
---	Nevada Nevada	61 306
SUN TON		
---*	Nevada Nevada	61 307
SUN TOY		
---	Nevada Washington	61 339
SUN WA		
---	Nevada Nevada	61 304
SUN		
---	Amador Twp 4	55 246
---	Amador Twp 5	55 331
---	Amador Twp 5	55 353
---	Amador Twp 5	55 356
---	Amador Twp 6	55 445
---	Amador Twp 6	55 450
---	Amador Twp 5	55 502
---	Butte Ophir	56 817
---	Calaveras Twp 6	57 127
---	Calaveras Twp 5	57 176
---	Calaveras Twp 5	57 181
---	Calaveras Twp 5	57 182
---	Calaveras Twp 5	57 205
---	Calaveras Twp 5	57 208
---	Calaveras Twp 5	57 215
---	Calaveras Twp 5	57 225
---	Calaveras Twp 5	57 230
---	Calaveras Twp 5	57 237
---	Calaveras Twp 5	57 245
---	Calaveras Twp 5	57 247
---	Calaveras Twp 5	57 257
---	Calaveras Twp 5	57 258
---	Calaveras Twp 10	57 261
---	Calaveras Twp 10	57 269
---	Calaveras Twp 10	57 270
---	Calaveras Twp 10	57 275
---	Calaveras Twp 10	57 284
---	Calaveras Twp 10	57 286
---	Calaveras Twp 10	57 296

Name	County Locale	M653 Roll Page
SUN		
---	Calaveras Twp 4	57 304
---	Calaveras Twp 4	57 310
---	Calaveras Twp 4	57 315
---	Calaveras Twp 4	57 324
---	Calaveras Twp 4	57 325
---	Calaveras Twp 4	57 327
---	Calaveras Twp 4	57 328
---	Calaveras Twp 4	57 338
---	Calaveras Twp 4	57 343
---	Calaveras Twp 7	57 44
---	Calaveras Twp 8	57 69
---	Calaveras Twp 8	57 74
---	Calaveras Twp 8	57 95
---	El Dorado Georgetown	58 692
---	El Dorado Big Bar	58 740
---	El Dorado Georgetown	58 747
---	El Dorado Georgetown	58 750
---	El Dorado Georgetown	58 756
---	El Dorado Placerville	58 906
---	Mariposa Twp 3	60 574
---	Mariposa Twp 3	60 619
---	Mariposa Twp 1	60 641
---	Mariposa Twp 1	60 651
---	Mariposa Twp 1	60 659
---	Mariposa Twp 1	60 661
---	Mariposa Coulterville	60 682
---	Mariposa Coulterville	60 700
---	Nevada Nevada	61 306
---	Nevada Rough &	61 396
---	Nevada Rough &	61 434
---	Nevada Bridgeport	61 460
---	Nevada Bridgeport	61 485
---	Placer Rattle Snake	62 629
---	Placer Virginia	62 670
---	Placer Virginia	62 682
---	Placer Illinois	62 704
---	Placer Illinois	62 742
---	Sacramento Centre	63 182
---	Sacramento Cosumnes	63 392
---	Sacramento Cosumnes	63 400
---	Sacramento Ward 1	63 56
---	Sacramento Ward 4	63 612
---	Sacramento Ward 1	63 65
---	San Francisco San Francisco 4	681184
---	San Francisco San Francisco 4	681185
---	San Francisco San Francisco 4	681186
---	San Francisco San Francisco 4	681187
---	San Francisco San Francisco 4	681197
---	San Francisco San Francisco 4	681203
---	San Francisco San Francisco 4	681204
---	San Francisco San Francisco 11	161 67
---	Sierra Downieville	661004
---	Sierra Downieville	661005
---	Sierra Downieville	661008
---	Sierra Downieville	661015
---	Sierra Downieville	661025
---	Sierra St Louis	66 806
---	Sierra St Louis	66 813
---	Sierra St Louis	66 816
---	Sierra Downieville	66 973
---	Sierra Downieville	66 979
---	Sierra Downieville	66 980
---	Sierra Downieville	66 981
---	Sierra Downieville	66 983
---	Sierra Downieville	66 984
---	Sierra Downieville	66 985
---	Sierra Downieville	66 999
---	Siskiyou Yreka	69 195
---	Trinity Dead Wood	70 958
---	Tuolumne Don Pedro	71 162
---	Tuolumne Twp 3	71 460
---	Tuolumne Twp 5	71 517
---*	Calaveras Twp 5	57 249
---*	Nevada Rough &	61 432
---*	Sierra St Louis	66 816
Ah	Calaveras Twp 7	57 15
Ah	Calaveras Twp 7	57 36
Angeline	San Francisco San Francisco 2	67 773
At*	Mariposa Twp 1	60 651
Ching	Mariposa Coulterville	60 682
Chow	Nevada Washington	61 342
Choy	Placer Iona Hills	62 897
Choy	Siskiyou Yreka	69 195
Fee	San Francisco San Francisco 4	681202
Fu	San Francisco San Francisco 4	681202
Fuk	San Francisco San Francisco 4	681202
Gu	El Dorado Georgetown	58 747
Hop	Placer Auburn	62 582
Hung	San Francisco San Francisco 5	671206
Ki	Mariposa Twp 1	60 651
Lee	Sacramento Natonia	63 281
Lee	Shasta Shasta	66 670
Qui	Calaveras Twp 5	57 246
Se*	Mariposa Twp 3	60 612

Name	County Locale	M653 Roll Page
SUN		
Tin	Calaveras Twp 4	57 300
Tin	Calaveras Twp 4	57 300
Toy	Nevada Washington	61 339
Wa*	Nevada Nevada	61 304
Wee	El Dorado Georgetown	58 700
Yow	San Francisco San Francisco 4	681201
SUNA		
Norberto	Monterey Pajaro	601013
Sanlos	Contra Costa Twp 1	57 486
SUNAGER		
Pauline*	Placer Auburn	62 561
SUNAGIN		
Brian	Alameda Brooklyn	55 179
SUNALLIS		
Niconali	Santa Cruz Watsonville	66 540
SUNARD		
J*	Nevada Nevada	61 316
SUNBORN		
Abram	Sonoma Santa Rosa	69 407
SUNCHIST		
Charles	San Mateo Twp 1	65 57
SUNDAM		
F T*	Sacramento Ward 1	63 28
SUNDAY		
James	Los Angeles Tejon	59 526
SUNDBURY		
Edward	Alameda Brooklyn	55 199
SUNDECKER		
Geo	Butte Kimshaw	56 577
SUNDERHAUSE		
John	Sierra Twp 5	66 936
SUNDERLAND		
D	El Dorado Placerville	58 849
F	Butte Kimshaw	56 591
Nancy	Shasta Cottonwoood	66 737
Thos	Napa Napa	61 86
SUNDERLAUD		
Thos	Napa Napa	61 86
SUNDGREEN		
Peter O*	San Francisco San Francisco 3	67 69
SUNDGRUN		
Peter O*	San Francisco San Francisco 3	67 69
SUNDICKER		
Geo	Butte Kimshaw	56 577
SUNDIE		
Margaret	San Francisco San Francisco 6	67 414
SUNDINO		
Aolis	Santa Clara San Jose	65 386
SUNDLIN		
Wm*	Sonoma Petaluma	69 608
SUNE		
---	Amador Twp 2	55 292
---	Amador Twp 5	55 353
---	Amador Twp 6	55 450
---	Amador Twp 1	55 458
---*	Nevada Grass Valley	61 232
Cerilo	Tuolumne Chinese	71 498
King	Shasta Horsetown	66 701
SUNEGA		
Chela	Merced Monterey	60 943
Chela	Monterey Monterey	60 943
Gregoria	Monterey Monterey	60 950
SUNEGE		
Jacinto	Tuolumne Chinese	71 498
SUNER		
---*	Sierra Downieville	66 991
Chas	Butte Wyandotte	56 669
SUNERKRUP		
Henry*	San Bernardino San Bernardino	64 625
SUNG CHENG		
---	Mariposa Twp 3	60 613
SUNG CHOW		
---	San Joaquin Stockton	641063
SUNG TIEN		
---	Sacramento Ward 1	63 59
SUNG YE		
---	Sacramento Ward 1	63 60
SUNG		
---	Amador Twp 2	55 280
---	Amador Twp 2	55 293
---	Amador Twp 1	55 502
---	Butte Hamilton	56 528
---	Butte Hamilton	56 530
---	Calaveras Twp 6	57 131
---	Calaveras Twp 6	57 134
---	Calaveras Twp 6	57 136
---	Calaveras Twp 6	57 147
---	Calaveras Twp 6	57 168
---	Calaveras Twp 6	57 173
---	Calaveras Twp 6	57 181
---	Calaveras Twp 6	57 195
---	Calaveras Twp 5	57 208
---	Calaveras Twp 5	57 219
---	Calaveras Twp 5	57 222
---	Calaveras Twp 5	57 223

California 1860 Census Index

Name	County Locale	M653 RollPage
SUNG		
---	Calaveras Twp 5	57 232
---	Calaveras Twp 5	57 233
---	Calaveras Twp 5	57 235
---	Calaveras Twp 5	57 242
---	Calaveras Twp 5	57 247
---	Calaveras Twp 5	57 251
---	Calaveras Twp 5	57 255
---	Calaveras Twp 10	57 268
---	Calaveras Twp 10	57 269
---	Calaveras Twp 10	57 271
---	Calaveras Twp 10	57 276
---	Calaveras Twp 10	57 280
---	Calaveras Twp 10	57 283
---	Calaveras Twp 10	57 285
---	Calaveras Twp 10	57 286
---	Calaveras Twp 8	57 74
---	El Dorado Kelsey	581141
---	El Dorado Diamond	58 797
---	Fresno Twp 3	59 32
---	Mariposa Twp 1	60 644
---	Mariposa Twp 1	60 653
---	Mariposa Twp 1	60 661
---	Mariposa Twp 1	60 663
---	Mariposa Twp 1	60 664
---	Mariposa Twp 1	60 665
---	Mariposa Twp 1	60 673
---	Mariposa Coulterville	60 700
---	Nevada Nevada	61 302
---	Nevada Washington	61 340
---	Nevada Rough &	61 433
---	Placer Rattle Snake	62 629
---	Placer Folsom	62 648
---	Placer Dutch Fl	62 737
---	Placer Illinois	62 752
---	Placer Iona Hills	62 893
---	Placer Iona Hills	62 894
---	Sacramento Centre	63 182
---	Sacramento Mississipi	63 187
---	Sacramento Mississipi	63 190
---	Sacramento Granite	63 245
---	Sacramento Granite	63 251
---	Sacramento Cosummes	63 392
---	Sacramento Ward 3	63 490
---	Sacramento Ward 3	63 493
---	Sacramento Ward 1	63 59
---	Sacramento Ward 1	63 60
---	Sacramento Ward 1	63 67
---	Sacramento Ward 1	63 68
---	Sacramento Ward 1	63 69
---	Sacramento Ward 1	63 71
---	San Francisco San Francisco 4	681178
---	San Francisco San Francisco 4	681182
---	San Francisco San Francisco 4	681187
---	San Francisco San Francisco 4	681188
---	San Francisco San Francisco 4	681189
---	San Francisco San Francisco 4	681195
---	San Francisco San Francisco 4	681208
---	San Francisco San Francisco 5	67 527
---	San Francisco San Francisco 2	67 754
---	Sierra Downieville	661015
---	Sierra La Porte	66 785
---	Trinity Cox'S Bar	701037
---	Trinity Big Flat	701041
---	Trinity Big Flat	701042
---	Trinity Trinidad Rvr	701044
---	Trinity Trinidad Rvr	701048
---	Trinity Trinidad Rvr	701049
---	Tuolumne Columbia	71 306
---	Tuolumne Columbia	71 307
---	Tuolumne Columbia	71 347
---	Tuolumne Shawsfla	71 409
---	Tuolumne Twp 2	71 416
---	Tuolumne Twp 3	71 433
---	Tuolumne Twp 3	71 439
---	Tuolumne Twp 3	71 442
---	Tuolumne Twp 3	71 446
---	Tuolumne Twp 3	71 457
---	Tuolumne Twp 3	71 467
---	Tuolumne Twp 3	71 468
---	Tuolumne Sonora	71 478
---	Tuolumne Jacksonville	71 514
---	Tuolumne Twp 6	71 540
---*	Butte Hamilton	56 530
---*	Calaveras Twp 6	57 161
---*	Calaveras Twp 5	57 247
---*	Fresno Twp 1	59 26
---*	Nevada Washington	61 340
---*	Sacramento Mississipi	63 190
---*	Sacramento Cosummes	63 391
---*	Sacramento Cosummes	63 392
---*	Sacramento Cosummes	63 397
---*	Sacramento Ward 1	63 69
---*	Stanislaus Buena Village	70 724
---*	Yuba Foster B	72 826
A	Sacramento Granite	63 221

Name	County Locale	M653 RollPage
SUNG		
Ah	Sacramento Ward 1	63 156
Ah	Sacramento Mississipi	63 187
Ah	Tuolumne Twp 4	71 174
Ah	Tuolumne Twp 2	71 347
---	Tuolumne Columbia	71 347
---	Tuolumne Shawsfla	71 409
---	Tuolumne Twp 2	71 416
---	Tuolumne Twp 3	71 433
---	Tuolumne Twp 3	71 439
---	Tuolumne Twp 3	71 442
---	Tuolumne Twp 3	71 446
---	Tuolumne Twp 3	71 457
---	Tuolumne Twp 3	71 467
---	Tuolumne Twp 3	71 468
---	Tuolumne Sonora	71 478
---	Tuolumne Jacksonville	71 514
---	Tuolumne Twp 6	71 540
---*	Butte Hamilton	56 530
---*	Calaveras Twp 6	57 161
---*	Calaveras Twp 5	57 247
---*	Fresno Twp 1	59 26
---*	Nevada Washington	61 340
---*	Sacramento Mississipi	63 190
---*	Sacramento Cosummes	63 391
---*	Sacramento Cosummes	63 392
---*	Sacramento Cosummes	63 397
---*	Sacramento Ward 1	63 69
---*	Stanislaus Buena Village	70 724
---*	Yuba Foster B	72 826
A	Sacramento Granite	63 221
Ah	Sacramento Ward 1	63 156
Ah	Sacramento Mississipi	63 187
Ah	Tuolumne Twp 4	71 174
Ah	Tuolumne Twp 2	71 347
Ching	Mariposa Twp 3	60 613
Choy	Sacramento Ward 1	63 70
Hi	Placer Forest H	62 771
Him	Mariposa Twp 3	60 581
Pee	Mariposa Twp 3	60 620
Sam	Fresno Twp 1	59 28
Sam	Fresno Twp 2	59 4
Sam	Humbolt Union	59 183
Say	El Dorado Georgetown	58 692
See	Placer Forest H	62 773
See*	Mariposa Twp 1	60 641
Sung	Calaveras Twp 4	57 302
Thos	El Dorado Georgetown	58 704
Tin*	Sacramento Ward 1	63 156
Tong	Sacramento Granite	63 232
Tong	Sacramento Cosummes	63 389
Wah	Placer Todds Va	62 786
Wee	Mariposa Twp 3	60 641
Wu	Del Norte Crescent	58 630
Ye	Sacramento Ward 1	63 60
Youk	Yuba Marysville	72 845
SUNGLEN		
Charles	Siskiyou Scott Va	69 47
SUNGLET		
E G*	Napa Clear Lake	61 121
E N	Napa Clear Lake	61 121
SUNGLIT		
E G*	Napa Clear Lake	61 121
SUNGNS		
Lewis*	Yolo Cache	72 618
SUNGUINATI		
Santela	Calaveras Twp 4	57 340
SUNGUNETTI		
John	Calaveras Twp 5	57 216
SUNGUS		
Lewis*	Yolo Cache	72 618
SUNHILL		
Charles	Siskiyou Yreka	69 184
SUNI		
---	Calaveras Twp 5	57 201
---	Calaveras Twpenwood	57 225
SUNNEFRANK		
Ah	El Dorado Greenwood	58 709
SUNNER		
J*	San Francisco San Francisco 1	68 921
SUNNERLY		
Samuel	Yuba Marysville	72 968
SUNNEWILL		
Joseph*	El Dorado Placerville	58 918
SUNNEY		
Thomas*	Calaveras Twp 6	57 160
SUNNG		
---	Butte Kimshaw	56 606
Peter	Butte Oro	56 688
SUNNIPARK		
Case	El Dorado Greenwood	58 709
SUNNY		
---	Placer Rattle Snake	62 629
Bridget	Solano Vallejo	69 250
John J*	San Francisco San Francisco 9	68 954
SUNO		
---	Tulara Twp 1	71 115

Name	County Locale	M653 RollPage
SUNO		
John*	Napa Napa	61 85
SUNOX		
Stephen	Placer Dutch Fl	62 729
SUNP		
---	Sierra Downieville	661014
SUNS		
Seth	San Francisco San Francisco 1	68 907
SUNSFORD		
Ruben*	Napa Napa	61 70
SUNSL		
Miguel	Los Angeles Los Angeles	59 293
SUNT		
Moses H*	Amador Twp 4	55 258
SUNTFELT		
---	Trinity Trinidad Rvr	701050
SUNTHEY		
Jerry	Yolo Slate Ra	72 700
SUNTI		
---	Calaveras Twp 10	57 273
SUNTMULLER		
Lewis*	Alameda Brooklyn	55 139
SUNTON		
P*	Nevada Grass Valley	61 179
SUNTOS BEYA		
Joseph	Calaveras Twp 4	57 333
SUNWA		
J	Amador Twp 1	55 483
SUNY		
---	Amador Twp 5	55 340
---	Calaveras Twp 6	57 161
---	Calaveras Twp 5	57 208
---	Calaveras Twp 5	57 213
---	Calaveras Twp 5	57 219
---	Calaveras Twp 5	57 222
---	Calaveras Twp 5	57 223
---	Calaveras Twp 5	57 226
---	Calaveras Twp 5	57 233
---	Calaveras Twp 5	57 255
---	Calaveras Twp 10	57 259
---	Calaveras Twp 10	57 268
---	Calaveras Twp 10	57 269
---	Calaveras Twp 10	57 276
---	Calaveras Twp 10	57 280
---	Calaveras Twp 10	57 283
---	Calaveras Twp 10	57 285
---	Calaveras Twp 10	57 296
---*	Calaveras Twp 6	57 161
Suny	Calaveras Twp 4	57 302
SUNYLEY		
Keil*	Calaveras Twp 6	57 160
SUO		
---	Calaveras Twp 6	57 166
---	Calaveras Twp 5	57 249
---	Calaveras Twp 10	57 269
SUOCK		
---	Sierra Twp 7	66 898
SUODE		
William	San Francisco San Francisco 9	681028
SUOH		
---	Calaveras Twp 4	57 300
SUOILL		
George	Tuolumne Twp 1	71 202
SUON		
---	Mariposa Twp 3	60 608
SUONG		
---	Sacramento Ward 1	63 61
SUONGES		
Manuel*	Calaveras Twp 5	57 226
SUONGUS		
Manuel*	Calaveras Twp 5	57 226
SUONYES		
Manuel*	Calaveras Twp 5	57 226
SUONYOS		
Manuel*	Calaveras Twp 5	57 226
SUONYUS		
Manuel*	Calaveras Twp 5	57 226
SUOORT		
Julius*	Calaveras Twp 4	57 324
SUOORZ		
Julius*	Calaveras Twp 4	57 324
SUOP		
Henry*	Shasta Shasta	66 681
SUOR		
---*	Placer Auburn	62 581
SUOUTZ		
A*	Mariposa Twp 3	60 592
SUOY		
---	Sacramento Ward 1	63 51
---	Sacramento Ward 4	63 612
SUOZNO		
A C*	Shasta Shasta	66 681
SUP		
---	Butte Hamilton	56 528
---	Butte Kimshaw	56 600
---	Butte Eureka	56 651

Name	County Locale	M653 Roll	Page
SUP			
---	Calaveras Twp 5	57	242
---	Mariposa Coulterville	60	691
---	Mariposa Coulterville	60	700
---	Placer Auburn	62	572
---	Placer Virginia	62	665
---	Placer Illinois	62	751
---	Placer Michigan	62	835
---	Sacramento Granite	63	250
---	Sacramento Granite	63	259
---	Sacramento Granite	63	268
---	Sacramento Ward 1	63	51
---	Sacramento Ward 1	63	56
---	Sacramento Ward 1	63	70
---	Tuolumne Don Pedro	71	163
---	Tuolumne Don Pedro	71	535
---	Yuba Marysville	72	895
---*	Butte Ophir	56	818
---*	Mariposa Coulterville	60	697
A	Sacramento Granite	63	250
Kee	Butte Ophir	56	812
Kin	Butte Ophir	56	820
Lum	Placer Illinois	62	751
You	Placer Auburn	62	571
Yu	Sacramento Granite	63	269
Yum	Placer Auburn	62	572
SUPAN			
Mathias*	Humbolt Mattole	59	125
SUPE			
---	Calaveras Twp 10	57	284
C	Amador Twp 3	55	395
SUPER			
Jacob	Amador Twp 1	55	463
Jacob*	Amador Twp 4	55	237
SUPERVILLE			
Peter	Tuolumne Twp 1	71	213
Poter	Tuolumne Sonora	71	213
SUPH			
Clara	San Francisco San Francisco 4	681	155
SUPHENIS			
Thomas	Sierra Twp 7	66	900
SUPI			
---	Sacramento Ward 1	63	70
SUPN			
---	Calaveras Twp 10	57	284
SUPONL			
Andrew	Calaveras Twp 5	57	221
SUPOUL			
Andrew	Calaveras Twp 5	57	221
SUPPEAH			
---*	Tulara Visalia	71	39
SUPPEAHE			
---	Tulara Twp 2	71	39
SUPPEL			
David	San Francisco San Francisco 3	67	41
SUPPEX			
---	Tulara Twp 2	71	38
SUPRAM			
Ordeas	Amador Twp 5	55	332
SUPRESS			
F	Siskiyou Scott Va	69	46
SUPULVARY			
Mary	Marin San Rafael	60	759
SUPULVIA			
Rosa	Amador Twp 1	55	469
SUR			
---	Calaveras Twp 5	57	211
---	Calaveras Twp 5	57	225
---	Calaveras Twp 5	57	245
---	Mariposa Coulterville	60	682
---	Sierra Twp 5	66	945
---	Sierra Downieville	66	981
Charles	Tulara Twp 1	71	100
Jung	Yuba Marysville	72	916
Lon	San Francisco San Francisco 3	67	37
Oliver	El Dorado Georgetown	58	675
SURA			
Goo*	Sacramento Granite	63	243
SURALL			
Robert	Tuolumne Twp 4	71	134
SURARTHY			
James*	Santa Cruz Pajaro	66	546
SURBER			
J B	Tehama Red Bluff	70	925
SURBLED			
Francois	San Francisco San Francisco 10	67	358
SURCENY			
Jas*	Sacramento Ward 1	63	29
SURCOULT			
L*	Sacramento Brighton	63	210
S*	Sacramento Brighton	63	210
SURDAM			
Royce G	Plumas Quincy	62	957
SURDAN			
Truman	Contra Costa Twp 1	57	519

Name	County Locale	M653 Roll	Page
SUREN			
Francisco	Calaveras Twp 4	57	331
J J	San Francisco San Francisco 6	67	453
SURENDIN			
Peter	Calaveras Twp 10	57	287
SURENEY			
Bridget*	Calaveras Twp 6	57	160
SURENK			
Daniel*	Calaveras Twp 5	57	144
SURERKRUP			
Henry*	San Bernardino San Bernadino	64	625
SURETLER			
Nelson*	Calaveras Twp 5	57	240
SUREY			
Eli	Placer Yankee J	62	778
SURFACE			
Almira	Amador Twp 2	55	279
James	Amador Twp 2	55	267
John	Amador Twp 2	55	268
SURGAR			
Emille	San Francisco San Francisco 2	67	784
SURGER			
Emille	San Francisco San Francisco 2	67	784
SURGU			
John	Calaveras Twp 5	57	221
SURHETE			
Mary A O*	Yuba Marysville	72	924
SURI			
---	Calaveras Twp 6	57	149
SURIAGA			
Joaquin	Santa Clara Almaden	65	264
SURIG			
---	Placer Horseshoe	62	650
SURING			
John*	Calaveras Twp 5	57	148
SURITA			
Wm F*	Sacramento Ward 1	63	29
Feorrin	San Bernardino Santa Barbara	64	201
Jose	Merced Twp 1	60	900
Rafail	San Bernardino Santa Inez	64	139
Ramon	San Bernardino Santa Inez	64	139
SURK			
---	Calaveras Twp 5	57	232
SURMAN			
J*	Yolo Putah	72	550
Joseph	Contra Costa Twp 2	57	539
SURN			
---	San Francisco San Francisco 4	681	188
SURPIN			
Hamilton*	Napa Yount	61	29
Wm*	Placer Secret R	62	618
SURRA			
Carlos*	San Bernardino Santa Inez	64	145
SURREY			
Lorenzo	Placer Forest H	62	791
SURRING			
John	Calaveras Twp 6	57	148
SURRNEY			
Bridget*	Calaveras Twp 6	57	160
Fridget	Calaveras Twp 6	57	160
Thomas*	Calaveras Twp 6	57	160
SURRNY			
John	Calaveras Twp 6	57	148
SURRO			
Carps	Tuolumne Twp 2	71	318
Michel*	Calaveras Twp 4	57	340
SURRS			
M*	Calaveras Twp 9	57	405
SURRTLES			
Nelson*	Calaveras Twp 5	57	240
SURRUY			
John*	Calaveras Twp 5	57	148
SURT			
D	Tuolumne Jacksonville	71	172
SURTAH			
---	Mendocino Twp 1	60	889
SURTAN			
John*	Calaveras Twp 5	57	187
SURY			
---	Amador Twp 5	55	336
---	Amador Twp 5	55	343
---	Amador Twp 5	55	353
---	Sierra Twp 7	66	881
Eliza	San Mateo Twp 1	65	68
Teo	Amador Twp 5	55	333
SUS			
---	Calaveras Twp 5	57	211
SUSA			
---	Mariposa Twp 1	60	626
---	Mendocino Calpella	60	826
Antonio	El Dorado Greenwood	58	716
Manuel*	Placer Michigan	62	850
SUSAN INDIAN			
---*	Sonoma Sonoma	69	662
SUSAN			
---	Del Norte Klamath	58	658

Name	County Locale	M653 Roll	Page
SUSAN			
---	Fresno Twp 1	59	80
---	Mendocino Calpella	60	820
---	Mendocino Calpella	60	821
---	Mendocino Calpella	60	825
---	Mendocino Calpella	60	826
---	Mendocino Big Rock	60	874
---	Mendocino Twp 1	60	889
---	Sacramento Cosumnes	63	406
---	Shasta Shasta	66	670
---	Siskiyou Shasta Rvr	69	111
Indian*	Sonoma Sonoma	69	662
Jabez S	Alameda Oakland	55	27
SUSANA			
---	Los Angeles Los Angeles	59	376
---	Marin San Rafael	60	769
---	Monterey S Antoni	60	972
---	San Bernardino S Timate	64	737
---	San Bernardino S Timate	64	738
---	San Bernardino S Timate	64	750
---	Tulara Twp 1	71	113
SUSANAH			
---	Santa Cruz Santa Cruz	66	640
---	Tulara Twp 1	71	120
SUSANBITH			
John C	Tuolumne Twp 2	71	356
SUSANER			
---	Mariposa Twp 1	60	628
SUSANNA			
---	San Bernardino San Bernadino	64	678
---	San Bernardino San Bernadino	64	681
---	San Bernardino San Bernadino	64	682
---	San Bernardino S Timate	64	703
---	San Bernardino S Timate	64	708
---	San Bernardino S Timate	64	712
---	San Bernardino S Timate	64	713
---	San Bernardino S Timate	64	715
---	San Bernardino S Timate	64	716
---	San Bernardino S Timate	64	719
---	San Bernardino S Timate	64	722
---	San Bernardino S Timate	64	723
---	San Bernardino S Timate	64	725
---	San Bernardino S Timate	64	726
---	San Bernardino S Timate	64	727
---	San Bernardino S Timate	64	731
---	San Bernardino S Timate	64	733
---	San Bernardino S Timate	64	736
---	San Bernardino S Timate	64	741
---	San Bernardino S Timate	64	742
---	San Bernardino S Timate	64	744
---	San Bernardino S Timate	64	745
---	San Bernardino S Timate	64	746
---	San Bernardino S Timate	64	751
---	San Bernardino S Timate	64	752
---	San Bernardino S Timate	64	754
---	San Bernardino S Timate	64	755
Manin	San Bernardino San Bernadino	64	682
SUSANNAH			
---	Mendocino Calpella	60	821
---	Mendocino Calpella	60	827
---	Mendocino Big Rvr	60	855
---	Mendocino Big Rock	60	876
---	Mendocino Twp 1	60	888
---	Mendocino Twp 1	60	892
SUSARA			
Manuel*	Santa Cruz Santa Cruz	66	602
SUSARE			
Juan	Santa Cruz Pajaro	66	571
SUSARIO			
Francisco	Contra Costa Twp 2	57	577
SUSCAS			
E	Nevada Eureka	61	377
SUSE			
---	Yuba Bear Rvr	721	015
Ballentus	Mariposa Twp 1	60	632
SUSEN			
---*	Mariposa Twp 1	60	626
Manwell*	Mariposa Twp 1	60	672
SUSENBECK			
J C	Tuolumne Columbia	71	338
SUSER			
Manwell	Mariposa Twp 1	60	672
SUSGEATHE			
Louis*	Yuba New York	72	729
SUSI			
---	El Dorado Georgetown	58	692
SUSIA			
Miguela	Yuba Marysville	72	954
SUSIE			
---	Amador Twp 5	55	354
SUSIGNAN			
Theodore	Calaveras Twp 7	57	25
SUSISTRA			
Jose	Fresno Twp 1	59	76
SUSJI			
---*	El Dorado Georgetown	58	745

Name	County Locale	M653 RollPage
SUSK		
Chaes W*	El Dorado Georgetown	58 698
Joseph*	San Francisco San Francisco 3	67 72
SUSKELL		
Warren*	Sacramento Granite	63 246
SUSN		
---	Calaveras Twp 4	57 299
SUSNRO		
---	Tulara Twp 2	71 39
SUSOUX		
John	Calaveras Twp 4	57 326
SUSRETIA		
Sister	Santa Clara San Jose	65 373
SUSS		
Abram*	Yuba Marysville	72 871
Fredrick*	Plumas Meadow Valley	62 933
SUSSAN		
Mathias*	Humbolt Mattole	59 125
SUSSELLI		
John	Calaveras Twp 5	57 217
SUSSET		
Margaret	Contra Costa Twp 1	57 536
SUSTAR		
John	Calaveras Twp 5	57 187
SUSTOR		
Theodore	El Dorado Georgetown	58 696
SUSTRER		
Wm	Amador Twp 2	55 308
SUSU		
---	Calaveras Twp 5	57 192
---	Calaveras Twp 5	57 193
---	Mariposa Twp 1	60 626
SUSUMA		
---	Fresno Twp 2	59 57
SUSVITCH		
Mara	Butte Ophir	56 766
SUT HO		
---	Sacramento Ward 1	63 69
SUT		
---	Placer Secret R	62 623
---	Sacramento Mississipi	63 190
---	Sacramento Ward 3	63 494
---	Sacramento Ward 4	63 612
---	Sacramento Ward 1	63 69
---	Tuolumne Chinese	71 510
---*	Calaveras Twp 4	57 326
Ho	Sacramento Ward 1	63 69
Keen	Tuolumne Twp 6	71 529
William*	Placer Michigan	62 808
SUTAM		
---	Nevada Bridgeport	61 464
SUTCHARD		
Richard W*	Yuba Slate Ro	72 699
SUTCHENFAL		
Gottlitch	San Mateo Twp 1	65 48
SUTCLIFFE		
James*	Plumas Quincy	62 961
SUTE		
---	El Dorado Georgetown	58 680
Sam	El Dorado Greenwood	58 719
SUTEN		
Thenda	Placer Virginia	62 675
W O	Amador Twp 7	55 412
SUTENCE		
F*	Sacramento Sutter	63 293
SUTENEE		
F*	Sacramento Sutter	63 293
SUTENIE		
F	Sacramento Sutter	63 293
SUTEO		
James*	San Francisco San Francisco 3	67 62
SUTER		
Frank	Siskiyou Yreka	69 191
Levi	Siskiyou Scott Va	69 46
Peter	Sierra St Louis	66 811
SUTERMAN		
Fred	Calaveras Twp 9	57 357
SUTES		
S P	Colusa Colusi	57 423
SUTGEN		
Henry	San Joaquin Stockton	641063
SUTH		
John*	Alameda Brooklyn	55 82
Joseph	El Dorado Georgetown	58 704
SUTHAN		
Thomas F	Calaveras Twp 10	57 294
SUTHER		
Charles	Siskiyou Yreka	69 150
Martin	Santa Clara Santa Clara	65 472
SUTHERLAND		
---	Calaveras Twp 6	57 132
Agus	Mendocino Big Rvr	60 841
Alex	Sonoma Bodega	69 528
Ann	Sacramento Ward 4	63 539
Anna Ma*	San Francisco 1	68 874
	San Francisco	

Name	County Locale	M653 RollPage
SUTHERLAND		
August	San Francisco San Francisco 1	68 864
Chals	El Dorado Georgetown	58 754
Charles	Calaveras Twp 4	57 340
Chas	Del Norte Crescent	58 640
D A	Colusa Monroeville	57 445
Danl	Tuolumne Twp 2	71 315
David	Solano Vallejo	69 255
David	Tuolumne Sonora	71 197
E	San Francisco San Francisco 7	681435
Ed	Sacramento Ward 3	63 529
Edwin	San Francisco San Francisco 1	68 873
G	Nevada Eureka	61 369
G W	Stanislaus Empire	70 734
George	Yuba Rose Bar	72 819
Isabella	San Francisco San Francisco 8	681318
J A	Tuolumne Twp 1	71 192
J J	San Francisco San Francisco 6	67 441
J M	Nevada Grass Valley	61 238
James	San Francisco San Francisco 7	681398
Jas	Fresno Twp 3	59 14
Jno	Sacramento Ward 4	63 554
John	Calaveras Twp 6	57 134
John	Colusa Mansville	57 437
John	El Dorado Kelsey	581153
John	Nevada Bridgeport	61 443
John	San Mateo Twp 2	65 122
John	Trinity Weaverville	701068
M	El Dorado Georgetown	58 706
Peter	Plumas Meadow Valley	62 901
Robert	San Francisco San Francisco 7	681352
Robert	Sierra La Porte	66 778
Robert	Sierra Whiskey	66 843
Robet*	Plumas Quincy	621000
Robt*	Plumas Quincy	621000
Roderick	Butte Chico	56 548
S	El Dorado Casumnes	581167
S	San Mateo Twp 3	65 85
Sam	Mendocino Big Rvr	60 841
Simon	San Mateo Twp 3	65 79
Thomas	Calaveras Twp 6	57 133
W	Sacramento Ward 1	63 78
W H	Sacramento Ward 4	63 530
William	San Joaquin Stockton	641080
William	San Mateo Twp 3	65 93
William	Sierra Whiskey	66 849
SUTHERLIN		
W	Butte Chico	56 567
W D*	Trinity Weaverville	701053
SUTHERLUND		
Charles	Calaveras Twp 4	57 340
SUTHERMAN		
William	Calaveras Twp 5	57 203
SUTHERTONE		
W	Tehama Lassen	70 880
SUTHFEN		
Rich	Sacramento Granite	63 266
SUTHFERE		
Rich*	Sacramento Granite	63 266
SUTHIAN		
Josephine	Sonoma Petaluma	69 552
SUTHOARO		
Andw*	Sonoma Petaluma	69 597
SUTHVARO		
Andw*	Sonoma Petaluma	69 597
SUTI		
---	Nevada Bridgeport	61 485
SUTIMTA		
---	Mendocino Calpella	60 825
SUTINOIS		
Arsenino*	Calaveras Twp 4	57 313
SUTLIFF		
Henry	San Francisco San Francisco 3	67 10
Jobe	Trinity Weaverville	701079
John*	Nevada Red Dog	61 547
Patrick*	Santa Clara Santa Clara	65 463
S	San Francisco San Francisco 5	67 538
William	Placer Michigan	62 843
SUTO		
---	Sierra Twp 7	66 898
SUTREEN		
B J*	Mariposa Twp 3	60 586
SUTREIN		
B J*	Mariposa Twp 3	60 586
SUTRELL		
James L*	Alameda Brooklyn	55 90
John*	Alameda Brooklyn	55 91
SUTRO		
Gustave	San Francisco San Francisco 8	681288
SUTRUN		
B J*	Mariposa Twp 3	60 586
SUTSETHER		
Amparro	Mariposa Twp 1	60 653
SUTSINGER		
Robert	Trinity Mouth Ca	701010
SUTSOIT		
P*	Merced Twp 1	60 912

Name	County Locale	M653 RollPage
SUTT		
---	Nevada Bridgeport	61 463
SUTTAGO		
And*	Nevada Eureka	61 372
SUTTAN		
F	Nevada Nevada	61 265
SUTTE		
P	Nevada Nevada	61 260
SUTTEL		
Francisco*	Calaveras Twp 6	57 162
SUTTEN		
Jas*	Sacramento Franklin	63 330
Lewis*	Sacramento Sutter	63 309
Robert	Contra Costa Twp 2	57 570
Wm	Sacramento Natonia	63 276
SUTTER		
Aaron	Sacramento Sutter	63 300
B	Tuolumne Twp 4	71 162
Charles	San Francisco San Francisco 3	67 11
Charles Jr	San Francisco San Francisco 3	67 20
D R	Yolo Cache Crk	72 612
Daniel	San Francisco San Francisco 8	681325
E W	Sutter Sutter	70 813
Geo J A	Sutter Sutter	70 813
Henry	El Dorado Indian D	581158
J D	Mariposa Twp 3	60 598
J S*	Mariposa Twp 3	60 598
John*	Yuba Rose Bar	72 791
Lewis*	Sacramento Sutter	63 309
Rosa	Siskiyou Yreka	69 186
S	Trinity North Fo	701026
Saml	San Francisco San Francisco 2	67 573
Samuel	El Dorado Indian D	581158
Samuel	El Dorado Casumnes	581176
Wm	Los Angeles Los Angeles	59 491
SUTTERAN		
Perry	Sierra Twp 5	66 935
SUTTERFIELD		
C	Butte Hamilton	56 515
SUTTERMAN		
William	Calaveras Twp 5	57 203
SUTTGHES		
Gustavus*	Sierra Port Win	66 795
SUTTIFF		
L B	El Dorado Diamond	58 812
S*	San Francisco San Francisco 5	67 538
SUTTIMER		
Wm H	Calaveras Twp 5	57 194
SUTTIVAN		
James	Marin San Rafael	60 763
SUTTLE		
E	Nevada Nevada	61 282
G S*	Siskiyou Scott Va	69 51
William	San Mateo Twp 1	65 58
SUTTLIFF		
Patrick	Santa Clara Santa Clara	65 463
SUTTNEY		
Srthur	Colusa Grand Island	57 475
SUTTON		
A	Siskiyou Scott Ri	69 71
Andrew	Contra Costa Twp 2	57 580
Campbell	Santa Clara San Jose	65 369
Chas	San Francisco San Francisco 9	68 980
Chas	San Joaquin Elkhorn	64 991
Henry	Amador Twp 1	55 473
J	Nevada Grass Valley	61 213
J M	Calaveras Twp 7	57 23
J M	Yolo Cache Crk	72 618
James	Placer Michigan	62 835
James*	Plumas Quincy	62 938
Jas	Calaveras Twp 9	57 403
Jas	Sonoma Sonoma	69 652
Jas L	San Mateo Twp 1	65 69
Jepe	San Francisco San Francisco 3	67 74
Jesse	San Francisco San Francisco 3	67 74
John	Mariposa Twp 1	60 644
John	San Francisco San Francisco 2	67 592
John	Santa Clara Fremont	65 417
John	Tuolumne Jamestown	71 430
John	Yuba Foster B	72 824
John C	Tuolumne Twp 3	71 430
Joseph	Sacramento Sutter	63 295
Joseph	San Francisco San Francisco 9	681028
Kjas	Calaveras Twp 9	57 403
Levi	Butte Chico	56 565
Mary	Sonoma Santa Rosa	69 388
Morris	Santa Clara Santa Clara	65 522
N	Trinity Weaverville	701052
N B	Placer Todds Va	62 764
O P Sr	San Francisco San Francisco 2	67 664
R	Calaveras Twp 9	57 407
Smith	Yuba Fosters	72 824
Thomas	Solano Vacaville	69 351
Thos	Santa Clara San Jose	65 293
W	Nevada Grass Valley	61 200
W	Nevada Grass Valley	61 213

California 1860 Census Index

Name	County Locale	M653 Roll	Page
SUTTON			
W T	San Mateo Twp 1	65	69
William	Santa Cruz Pajaro	66	549
Wm	Sacramento Sutter	63	300
Wm	Santa Clara San Jose	65	298
Wm	Santa Clara San Jose	65	310
SUTTOR			
Charles	San Francisco San Francisco 3	67	11
SUTTRELL			
J R*	Siskiyou Scott Va	69	28
SUTUM			
---	Nevada Bridgeport	61	464
SUTZ			
John*	Santa Cruz Santa Cruz	66	606
Mary	Sacramento Natonia	63	281
SUTZBERGER			
F	Sutter Yuba	70	759
SUTZEUAN			
Herman	Santa Cruz Soguel	66	587
SUU			
---	Mariposa Twp 3	60	569
Ku	Mariposa Twp 3	60	620
SUV			
---	Sierra Downieville	66	1008
SUVA			
Clara	Los Angeles Los Angeles	59	515
Enos*	Yuba Marysville	72	946
SUVANRUNIS			
Andrew*	Calaveras Twp 5	57	220
SUVIDO			
Clande	San Diego Agua Caliente	64	821
SUVITTI			
Andrew	San Luis Obispo San Luis Obispo	65	33
SUVORZ			
Julius*	Calaveras Twp 4	57	324
SUW			
---	Calaveras Twp 6	57	126
---	Calaveras Twp 6	57	127
---	Calaveras Twp 5	57	195
---	Calaveras Twp 5	57	215
---	Calaveras Twp 5	57	237
---	Calaveras Twp 10	57	268
---	Calaveras Twp 10	57	285
---	Mariposa Twp 3	60	619
---	Sacramento Ward 1	63	66
---	Sierra Downieville	66	1025
---	Sierra Downieville	66	1027
SUWG			
---	Tuolumne Twp 2	71	409
SUY CUM			
---	Tuolumne Chinese	71	525
SUY			
---	Calaveras Twp 6	57	166
---	El Dorado Greenwood	58	719
---	El Dorado Georgetown	58	756
---	Mariposa Twp 1	60	669
---	Mariposa Twp 1	60	673
---	Mariposa Coulterville	60	685
---*	Shasta Shasta	66	680
Kee	Mariposa Twp 3	60	618
Lee	El Dorado Georgetown	58	756
Lu	Sacramento Granite	63	259
SUYALEZ			
Lewis	San Luis Obispo San Luis Obispo	65	33
SUYDAIN			
Theo*	Sacramento Ward 1	63	62
SUYDAM			
C W	San Francisco San Francisco 5	67	511
F T*	Sacramento Ward 1	63	28
Geo*	Sacramento Ward 1	63	35
Theo*	Sacramento Ward 1	63	62
SUYELER			
Francis*	Calaveras Twp 6	57	112
SUYERS			
John T	Mariposa Twp 1	60	638
SUYLETON			
Robt*	San Bernardino San Bernadino	64	636
SUYNAN			
Lanl*	Calaveras Twp 4	57	324
SUYO			
Jose Mn*	Los Angeles Los Angeles	59	494
Santiago	Los Angeles Los Angeles	59	494
SUYONG			
---	Calaveras Twp 6	57	159
SUZ			
Indian*	Sacramento Centre	63	181
SUZARO			
Aloino	Yuba Marysville	72	925
Olivia*	Yuba Marysville	72	925
SUZNJ			
Joseph*	Shasta Shasta	66	655
SUZOR			
Joseph	Tuolumne Twp 2	71	284
Joseph	Tuolumne Twp 2	71	284
SVARTWONT			
James*	Placer Iona Hills	62	867

Name	County Locale	M653 Roll	Page
SVENSEL			
B*	San Francisco San Francisco 9	68	949
SVERSON			
Inger*	Alameda Brooklyn	55	113
SVEUSEL			
B*	San Francisco San Francisco 9	68	949
SWA?EY			
John	Sacramento Ward 1	63	39
SWAAY			
Charles	Yuba Marysville	72	846
SWAD			
John*	Yuba Marysville	72	941
SWADLEY			
W W	Tuolumne Twp 1	71	261
SWADY			
H	Nevada Grass Valley	61	155
SWAGERT			
Casper*	Napa Clear Lake	61	129
SWAGG			
Joseph	El Dorado Greenwood	58	721
SWAGGARD			
Wm	Sacramento San Joaquin	63	351
SWAGGER			
Jno H	Sonoma Mendocino	69	457
SWAIF			
George	Sierra Gibsonville	66	852
John G	Sierra Gibsonville	66	855
SWAILE			
Geo*	Butte Bidwell	56	713
SWAILS			
Thomas	Humbolt Pacific	59	129
SWAIMGER			
Peter*	Nevada Bloomfield	61	512
SWAIMGOR			
Peter	Nevada Bloomfield	61	512
SWAIN			
A	Nevada Nevada	61	292
A E	Butte Wyandotte	56	662
Abigail	San Francisco San Francisco 12	67	391
Albert	Humbolt Bucksport	59	156
Charles	Santa Cruz Pajaro	66	526
Charles M	Siskiyou Yreka	69	150
Charles*	Contra Costa Twp 3	57	594
Cornelius	San Joaquin Elkhorn	64	969
Elisha	Siskiyou Callahan	69	19
Frederick	Contra Costa Twp 1	57	536
Frederick	San Francisco San Francisco 3	67	79
Gardner	San Francisco San Francisco 2	67	555
George	Sierra Gibsonville	66	852
George A	Contra Costa Twp 3	57	600
H C	Sacramento Dry Crk	63	377
H C	Siskiyou Callahan	69	19
H F	Napa Napa	61	98
Henry	Mariposa Twp 1	60	667
Henry	San Francisco San Francisco 3	67	79
Hugh	San Francisco San Francisco 9	68	1106
Isaac	San Francisco San Francisco 4	68	1136
J G	Butte Oregon	56	614
J T	Trinity Taylor'S	70	1034
James	Contra Costa Twp 3	57	604
James M	Contra Costa Twp 2	57	551
Jane	San Francisco San Francisco 7	68	1350
Jas H	San Francisco San Francisco 2	67	668
John	Tuolumne Sonora	71	236
Josiah C	Los Angeles Los Angeles	59	351
Josiah H	San Francisco San Francisco 2	67	644
Mimas	Colusa Colusi	57	422
O C	Siskiyou Callahan	69	19
P B	Nevada Eureka	61	367
P S	Nevada Eureka	61	367
R B	San Francisco San Francisco 10	67	331
Robt	Sonoma Petaluma	69	566
Sarah C	San Francisco San Francisco 2	67	640
Seth M	Contra Costa Twp 1	57	533
Stephen	San Francisco San Francisco 6	67	415
Sylvenus	Contra Costa Twp 1	57	532
T S	Sacramento Cosumnes	63	400
T S*	Sacramento Cosumnes	63	394
Thomas	Santa Cruz Santa Cruz	66	640
Thomas S	Tuolumne Columbia	71	323
Thoms	Santa Cruz Santa Cruz	66	640
Thos	Santa Clara Redwood	65	455
W H	Butte Wyandotte	56	659
William C	Yuba Marysville	72	874
Wm B	San Francisco San Francisco 2	67	617
Wm C	Sonoma Petaluma	69	566
SWAINEGER			
Peter*	Nevada Bloomfield	61	512
SWAINS			
Charles H	San Francisco San Francisco 4	68	1125
SWAIONS			
S J*	Stanislaus Branch	70	699
SWALB			
John*	Yuba Slate Ro	72	710

Name	County Locale	M653 Roll	Page
SWALLEN			
Apgh*	Yuba Marysville	72	846
SWALLOW			
Henry	Sierra Downieville	66	988
SWAM			
Charles*	Contra Costa Twp 3	57	594
Henry	San Francisco San Francisco 3	67	79
SWAMA			
---	Santa Clara Gilroy	65	224
SWAMB			
Michael*	Sacramento Ward 1	63	82
SWAMTLY			
C H	Santa Clara Gilroy	65	237
SWAN			
Albert	San Francisco San Francisco 7	68	1371
Allice	Sonoma Bodega	69	526
August	Amador Township	55	497
B B	Siskiyou Scott Ri	69	81
Benj T	Mariposa Twp 3	60	590
Chas	Sacramento Mississipi	63	188
Douglas	Klamath S Fork	59	207
Edwd S	San Francisco San Francisco 10	67	346
Franklin	Sierra Pine Grove	66	834
G W	El Dorado Kelsey	58	1154
G W	El Dorado Placerville	58	872
G W*	El Dorado Kelsey	58	1154
George	San Francisco San Francisco 3	67	28
George	San Francisco San Francisco 3	67	49
H W	Calaveras Twp 7	57	3
Hugh	Klamath Orleans	59	215
Isaac N	Amador Twp 1	55	473
J	Siskiyou Scott Ri	69	71
J	Siskiyou Scott Ri	69	73
J	Sonoma Armally	69	515
J G	Sierra Downieville	66	1023
Jno	Butte Kimshaw	56	575
John	Placer Iona Hills	62	889
L	Nevada Grass Valley	61	195
Lyman P	Alameda Brooklyn	55	169
Moses	San Joaquin Castoria	64	899
N P	Sonoma Mendocino	69	462
P G	Sierra Downieville	66	1023
Peter	Santa Cruz Santa Cruz	66	633
Robt	Butte Oregon	56	624
S	Siskiyou Scott Ri	69	73
Sebastian	El Dorado Greenwood	58	722
T S*	Sacramento Cosummes	63	394
W H	El Dorado Kelsey	58	1152
SWANDERULT			
F	El Dorado Diamond	58	790
SWANE			
Frederick	San Francisco San Francisco 9	68	1097
James	Yolo Cottonwoood	72	648
SWANEY			
Daniel	Tuolumne Montezuma	71	503
Danl	Tuolumne Columbia	71	298
Edwd	San Francisco San Francisco 9	68	1063
Hugh	Santa Cruz Santa Cruz	66	626
John	San Francisco San Francisco 7	68	1388
John	Tuolumne Chinese	71	501
John*	Sacramento Ward 1	63	39
Morrigan	San Francisco San Francisco 7	68	1396
Owens	Mendocino Ukiah	60	807
Thos	Santa Cruz Santa Cruz	66	628
SWANG			
J M	Santa Clara Redwood	65	454
SWANGER			
J C	Colusa Muion	57	458
SWANIB			
Michael*	Sacramento Ward 1	63	82
SWANK			
Daniel*	Calaveras Twp 6	57	144
Jackson	Calaveras Twp 6	57	144
James	Contra Costa Twp 2	57	549
Philip	Tuolumne Twp 2	71	372
William	Yuba Marysville	72	907
SWANN			
David	Merced Twp 2	60	923
James	Contra Costa Twp 3	57	597
James*	Yolo Cottonwoood	72	648
SWANS			
Chas	Sonoma Petaluma	69	547
SWANSA			
Gerome	Monterey San Juan	60	974
SWANSEE			
---	Fresno Twp 3	59	16
SWANSEN			
Fred	Siskiyou Scott Ri	69	70
SWANSON			
Andrew	Sonoma Petaluma	69	603
C	Shasta Horsetown	66	708
Fred	Siskiyou Scott Ri	69	70
Geo	Mariposa Twp 1	60	663
Hiliner	El Dorado Salmon Falls	58	1044
J*	El Dorado Georgetown	58	759

Name	County Locale	M653 Roll	Page
SWANSON			
Jo	Mariposa Coulterville	60	703
John	El Dorado Georgetown	58	702
John	San Francisco San Francisco 3	67	61
John	San Joaquin Douglass	64	928
John	Tulara Visalia	71	3
Joseph	Contra Costa Twp 1	57	534
Saml	Stanislaus Emory	70	746
William	San Francisco San Francisco 9	68	981
Williams	San Francisco San Francisco 9	68	981
SWANSTON			
Tobert	Santa Clara Almaden	65	264
SWANSTREN			
Jacob	Tuolumne Twp 2	71	296
SWANTHEN			
Jacob	Tuolumne Columbia	71	296
SWANTON			
---*	San Francisco San Francisco 7	68	1376
Charles	Santa Cruz Soguel	66	579
SWAP			
William	Santa Cruz Pescadero	66	645
SWARDSTOM			
J	San Francisco San Francisco 2	67	670
SWAREEN			
Henry*	San Mateo Twp 1	65	72
SWARFORD			
Presley	Napa Yount	61	44
Risley*	Napa Yount	61	44
SWARMS			
William	Calaveras Twp 5	57	141
SWARNES			
William*	Calaveras Twp 6	57	141
SWARRER			
William*	Tuolumne Twp 2	71	402
SWARRIS			
William	Tuolumne Shawsfla	71	402
SWART			
A T	San Mateo Twp 2	65	121
Danl	Sacramento Brighton	63	194
Danl	Sacramento Sutter	63	299
H	Nevada Eureka	61	379
J A	Nevada Eureka	61	379
Kindle	El Dorado Placerville	58	872
Lizzie	Santa Clara Fremont	65	421
SWARTGASTS			
W H	Butte Bidwell	56	727
SWARTHON			
Nathan San Bernardino San Bernadino		64	644
SWARTHONT			
Nathan San Bernardino San Salvador		64	644
SWARTS			
George H	Napa Hot Springs	61	26
P*	Napa Hot Springs	61	26
SWARTWELL			
C	Nevada Bloomfield	61	507
O	Nevada Bloomfield	61	507
SWARTZ			
A*	Mariposa Twp 3	60	592
August*	Alameda Brooklyn	55	150
C	San Francisco San Francisco 10	67	247
Chas	Calaveras Twp 5	57	213
Estano	Santa Cruz Pescadero	66	645
Frederick	Contra Costa Twp 1	57	522
Frederick	San Francisco San Francisco 3	67	28
G T	San Francisco San Francisco 7	68	1444
Geo	Colusa Grand Island	57	475
Hennan*	Mendocino Anderson	60	867
Henry	Plumas Quincy	62	993
Henry	Santa Clara Redwood	65	449
Herman*	Mendocino Anderson	60	867
J	El Dorado Georgetown	58	760
Jacob	Colusa Butte Crk	57	464
John	Sacramento San Joaquin	63	349
John	San Mateo Twp 3	65	106
John	Sierra Twp 5	66	928
Joseph	Alameda Brooklyn	55	160
Locies	Tuolumne Columbia	71	344
Loeiss	Tuolumne Twp 2	71	344
Phillip	Calaveras Twp 5	57	185
Rich?	Butte Oregon	56	626
Richd	Butte Oregon	56	626
Russell	San Bernardino Santa Inez	64	136
Samuel	San Francisco San Francisco 3	67	23
Simon	Contra Costa Twp 1	57	528
Victor	San Francisco San Francisco 3	67	70
William	Contra Costa Twp 1	57	504
SWARTZA			
Jacob	Calaveras Twp 4	57	303
SWARTZAN			
Jacob	Calaveras Twp 4	57	303
SWASEY			
B	Shasta Shasta	66	674
Charlotte San Francisco San Francisco 2		67	605
John*	Sacramento Ward 1	63	39
S T	Sacramento Ward 1	63	141

Name	County Locale	M653 Roll	Page
SWASEY			
Samuel	Solano Benecia	69	291
SWASSE			
Gustave San Francisco San Francisco 11		67	126
SWASSEY			
John	Sacramento Ward 1	63	39
SWAT			
F L	Tuolumne Twp 3	71	452
P	Sacramento Cosumnes	63	395
SWATT			
J A	Nevada Eureka	61	379
SWATTMAN			
John	San Francisco San Francisco 2	67	651
SWATTS			
E	Nevada Grass Valley	61	168
SWATZEL			
James	Shasta Shasta	66	732
SWATZER			
S	Siskiyou Scott Ri	69	67
SWAUBEIA			
Jno V* San Francisco San Francisco 9		68	1027
SWAY			
---	Nevada Rough &	61	437
---	San Francisco San Francisco 4	68	1193
SWAYNE			
A W	Shasta Millvill	66	725
Frank	San Joaquin Castoria	64	900
Mary Dominica SSolano Benecia		69	300
SWAYNEY			
Timothy	Tuolumne Twp 2	71	349
SWAZEY			
Wm	Napa Napa	61	78
SWEAD			
Jacob	Siskiyou Yreka	69	131
SWEAR			
John*	Yolo Cottonwooood	72	651
SWEAREGEN			
Wm	Amador Twp 2	55	267
SWEARENGEN			
G K*	Sacramento Ward 1	63	45
SWEAREY			
Lucy*	Alameda Oakland	55	74
SWEARNGEN			
And	Humbolt Eureka	59	175
SWEASEY			
Lucy*	Alameda Oakland	55	74
Wm	Humbolt Eel Rvr	59	149
SWEAT			
G W	Sacramento Cosumnes	63	394
Jacob	Siskiyou Yreka	69	131
William	Plumas Quincy	62	951
William	Plumas Quincy	62	962
SWEATZEN			
Saml	Napa Napa	61	113
SWEBLET			
Thos*	Nevada Rough &	61	430
SWECNEY			
Bernard*	Calaveras Twp 4	57	312
SWEDEN			
Chas	San Francisco San Francisco 3	67	83
SWEDENSTIEM			
Margaret B	San Francisco 10	67	228
	San Francisco		
SWEDINSHIMAN			
Margaret San Francisco San Francisco 10		67	228
SWEDINSTIEMA			
Margaret San Francisco San Francisco 10		67	228
SWEDSNSTIEMA			
Margaret San Francisco San Francisco 10		67	228
SWEED			
Charles S	Yuba Bear Rvr	72	1001
SWEEDE			
Albert	Placer Rattle Snake	62	632
SWEEDLE			
Richd	Alameda Brooklyn	55	132
SWEELER			
Lucy*	Yuba Marysville	72	945
SWEENER			
J T	Calaveras Twp 7	57	3
SWEENEY			
A J*	Mariposa Twp 3	60	599
Ann	San Francisco San Francisco 8	68	1283
Barth*	San Francisco San Francisco 10	67	187
Barthw	San Francisco San Francisco 10	67	187
Bernard	Calaveras Twp 4	57	312
Catharine San Francisco San Francisco 8		68	1285
Chas	Sacramento Ward 4	63	513
D L	Nevada Bridgeport	61	457
D M*	San Francisco San Francisco 7	68	1422

Name	County Locale	M653 Roll	Page
SWEENEY			
Danl	San Francisco San Francisco 10	67	242
Danl	San Francisco San Francisco 10	67	342
Edward	Humbolt Bucksport	59	158
Edward	San Francisco San Francisco 11	67	149
Edward	San Mateo Twp 1	65	53
Ellen	San Francisco San Francisco 9	68	1017
F	Butte Oregon	56	624
Geo	San Francisco San Francisco 10	67	335
Geo	San Francisco San Francisco 1	68	862
Goolsby*	Mendocino Calpella	60	811
Henry M	Santa Clara San Jose	65	332
J F	Butte Oregon	56	609
J P	San Francisco San Francisco 10	67	330
James	Placer Michigan	62	810
James	Sacramento Ward 1	63	106
James W	Santa Cruz Watsonville	66	535
Jane	San Francisco San Francisco 8	68	1303
Jane	San Francisco San Francisco 10	67	214
Jeremiah	Solano Suisan	69	221
Jno	San Francisco San Francisco 5	67	553
John	Calaveras Twp 7	57	6
John	San Francisco San Francisco 1	68	857
John O P	Solano Benecia	69	314
Joseph	Nevada Rough &	61	421
Julia	San Francisco San Francisco 6	67	408
L W	Amador Twp 6	55	446
M	Yolo Putah	72	550
M	Yolo Putah	72	598
Mary	Nevada Nevada	61	330
Maty	Nevada Nevada	61	330
Pat	Solano Fremont	69	384
Richrd San Francisco San Francisco 1		68	899
Robert	Tulara Visalia	71	19
Thomas W Humbolt Eel Rvr		59	146
Timothy San Francisco San Francisco 8		68	1288
Tomas* San Francisco San Francisco 11		67	147
Wm	Sierra Twp 5	66	936
SWEENTY			
Thomas San Francisco San Francisco 11		67	150
SWEENY			
A P	Yuba New York	72	736
A R	Yuba New York	72	736
A W	Sonoma Sonoma	69	657
Charles	Yuba Marysville	72	862
Clara	San Francisco San Francisco 6	67	461
D	Shasta Horsetown	66	691
Francis	Sierra Twp 5	66	941
Francis	Yuba Bear Rvr	72	999
Goolsby	Mendocino Calpella	60	811
H	Shasta Shasta	66	677
James	Solano Vacaville	69	365
James G	Solano Vacaville	69	365
Jas*	Sacramento Ward 1	63	29
John	San Mateo Twp 3	65	78
John	Solano Vacaville	69	366
Kate	Yuba Marysville	72	847
M*	San Joaquin Stockton	64	1099
Mary	San Francisco San Francisco 4	68	1122
Mary	Yuba Marysville	72	852
Mary	Yuba Marysville	72	857
Micael San Francisco San Francisco 7		68	1430
Michael San Francisco San Francisco 11		67	132
Michael	Siskiyou Yreka	69	149
Miles	Yolo No E Twp	72	672
Miles	Yuba North Ea	72	672
P	Siskiyou Klamath	69	84
Pat	Sonoma Petaluma	69	565
Paul	San Francisco San Francisco 5	67	480
T A E	Siskiyou Scott Va	69	41
Thos	Solano Benecia	69	304
William	Solano Vacaville	69	365
SWEESEY			
Oscar	Sonoma Petaluma	69	585
SWEESY			
C F	Sonoma Vallejo	69	629
G F	Sonoma Vallejo	69	629
SWEET			
---	Amador Twp 2	55	263
Abert* San Francisco San Francisco 9		68	1075
Al P	Alameda Brooklyn	55	130
Alphonzo	Nevada Red Dog	61	548
C B	Siskiyou Callahan	69	1
C B	Siskiyou Scott Va	69	57
C L	Siskiyou Scott Ri	69	75
Calow	Merced Monterey	60	932
Calvin	Merced Monterey	60	941

California 1860 Census Index

Name	County Locale	M653 Roll	Page
SWEET			
Calvin	Monterey Monterey	60	932
Calvin	Monterey Monterey	60	941
E	Siskiyou Scott Va	69	57
E	Siskiyou Scott Ri	69	75
E P	San Francisco San Francisco 4	681	129
F S	Tuolumne Jamestown	71	452
G F	Siskiyou Scott Va	69	34
H A	Shasta French G	66	719
J F	Siskiyou Scott Va	69	34
Jack	Nevada Red Dog	61	547
Jasyoh	Calaveras Twp 9	57	367
Jno	San Francisco San Francisco 10	231 67	
Jon	San Francisco San Francisco 11	144 67	
Joseph*	Calaveras Twp 9	57	367
L D	Butte Wyandotte	56	667
Lulu	Siskiyou Scott Ri	69	75
M A	San Francisco San Francisco 9	68	978
Mara T*	Sonoma Bodega	69	533
Rob M	Sacramento Granite	63	248
Rufus	Sierra La Porte	66	778
Saml S	Placer Rattle Snake	62	628
Solomon	Tulara Visalia	71	103
Thos	Amador Twp 1	55	486
Thos	Placer Secret R	62	620
Zara*	Sonoma Bodega	69	533
SWEETAND			
O S	Sonoma Petaluma	69	602
SWEETAPPLE			
Henry	Napa Napa	61	109
SWEETEN			
Wm	Colusa Spring Valley	57	430
SWEETLAND			
B R	Sacramento Ward 1	63	42
H P	Nevada Bridgeport	61	444
James	Sierra Twp 5	66	919
SWEETMAN			
C H	Siskiyou Scott Va	69	35
SWEETSEN			
G*	San Francisco San Francisco 4	681	154
SWEETSER			
Andrew	San Francisco San Francisco 10	313 67	
John	Nevada Bridgeport	61	446
SWEETSIDER			
H	San Francisco San Francisco 9	68	976
SWEETT			
Merit	Placer Yankee J	62	775
SWEETY			
William	Santa Cruz Santa Cruz	66	632
SWEETYES			
E F	Yolo Merritt	72	580
SWEEWER			
J T	Calaveras Twp 7	57	3
SWEEY			
Michael	Sierra Gibsonville	66	858
SWEGAQN			
J M*	San Francisco San Francisco 9	68	945
SWEI			
---	Sierra Downieville	66	981
SWEIGERT			
Joseph	San Francisco San Francisco 3	67	15
SWEINEY			
James	Contra Costa Twp 1	57	532
SWEITZER			
---	Sonoma Cloverdale	69	683
SWELL			
Jane*	San Francisco San Francisco 2	67	694
Jno A*	Butte Hamilton	56	521
Wm	Sierra Twp 5	66	936
SWELLAR			
George	Amador Twp 4	55	243
SWELT			
Joseph M*	Nevada Bridgeport	61	448
SWENDSY			
A	San Joaquin Stockton	641	067
SWENE			
Felix	San Francisco San Francisco 12	385 67	
SWENEY			
A J	Mariposa Twp 3	60	599
D M*	San Francisco San Francisco 7	681	422
G W	Sacramento Brighton	63	194
Geo	Nevada Nevada	61	254
James	El Dorado Coloma	581	103
Jeremiah	Solano Suisan	69	221
Owens	Mendocino Ukiah	60	807
W*	San Francisco San Francisco 5	67	529
SWENGH			
Thos	Sacramento Granite	63	266
SWENICTE			
James	Sierra Twp 7	66	915
SWENNY			
John	Contra Costa Twp 3	57	586

Name	County Locale	M653 Roll	Page
SWENSON			
C	Shasta Horsetown	66	708
Carshu*	Placer Michigan	62	811
Charles	Placer Iona Hills	62	892
J G	Sierra Downieville	661	032
SWENULL			
Lorenzo	Calaveras Twp 5	57	209
SWENY			
Charles H	Tuolumne Twp 5	71	510
Lewis	Sonoma Petaluma	69	593
SWEONEY			
M	Yolo Putah	72	598
SWERBLE			
Henry*	Sacramento Natonia	63	280
Herry*	Sacramento Natonia	63	280
SWERGERLY			
John	San Francisco San Francisco 6	67	436
SWERGERT			
Casper	Napa Clear Lake	61	129
SWERGRE			
At	Placer Rattle Snake	62	631
SWERINGER			
Jno	Butte Chico	56	542
SWERLEY			
Benj	Tuolumne Twp 1	71	261
SWERNETE			
James*	Sierra Twp 7	66	915
SWERRER			
John	Tuolumne Twp 2	71	402
William*	Tuolumne Twp 2	71	402
SWERRES			
John	Tuolumne Shawsfla	71	402
SWERRINGER			
Isabella	San Francisco San Francisco 8	681	318
Isabella V	San Francisco San Francisco 8	681	318
SWERS			
Charles	Sierra La Porte	66	771
SWERT			
Albert	San Francisco San Francisco 9	681	075
Alert*	San Francisco San Francisco 9	681	075
SWERUETE			
James*	Sierra Twp 7	66	915
SWETH			
John	Yuba Marysville	72	964
William	Yuba Marysville	72	975
SWETSER			
A C	Sacramento Ward 3	63	461
SWETT			
A W	Alameda Brooklyn	55	83
Charles	Nevada Bridgeport	61	449
Geo	San Francisco San Francisco 10	186 67	
Lorenzo	San Francisco San Francisco 6	67	404
Nathan P	San Francisco San Francisco 8	681	255
Orlo F	San Francisco San Francisco 11	152 67	
SWETZEL			
Abbie	Sacramento Ward 4	63	510
Jacob	Sacramento Ward 4	63	509
SWEV			
---	Sierra Downieville	66	981
SWEYNEE			
J D*	Sacramento Franklin	63	324
SWEYNER			
J D*	Sacramento Franklin	63	324
SWIAILE			
Geo*	Butte Bidwell	56	713
SWIBRICK			
J	Siskiyou Klamath	69	94
SWICKEY			
Fred	Siskiyou Yreka	69	157
SWIET			
E P	San Francisco San Francisco 4	681	129
SWIFERLTON			
Henry	Sacramento Sutter	63	299
SWIFIELD			
Mr	Sonoma Petaluma	69	543
SWIFT			
---	San Francisco San Francisco 3	67	58
---	Yuba Bear Rvr	721	009
Alex	Mariposa Twp 3	60	617
Alfred J	Yuba Marysville	72	931
Berry	Colusa Spring Valley	57	433
C	Sacramento Ward 1	63	91
C B	Amador Twp 2	55	265
C H	Nevada Grass Valley	61	238
C H	Sacramento Ward 1	63	89
C S	El Dorado Georgetown	58	677
C Ths	Mariposa Twp 3	60	617
Chas	Amador Twp 4	55	339
D B	El Dorado Georgetown	58	751
E	Sacramento Ward 1	63	91
E	Shasta Millvill	66	748
E	Sonoma Petaluma	69	589
E	Sutter Butte	70	790
Edward D	Calaveras Twp 5	57	236

Name	County Locale	M653 Roll	Page
SWIFT			
Francis	Contra Costa Twp 1	57	499
Frank	Sacramento Ward 4	63	570
G P	Sonoma Sonoma	69	633
Geo	Butte Ophir	56	797
Geo	Siskiyou Scott Ri	69	74
H	Nevada Nevada	61	271
Hallett	San Francisco San Francisco 8	681	238
Henry N	Yolo No E Twp	72	667
Houston	Butte Cascade	56	704
J	El Dorado Greenwood	58	716
J	Tehama Tehama	70	936
James F	San Francisco San Francisco 3	67	25
Jas	Sacramento Ward 4	63	558
John	Solano Green Valley	69	242
John F	San Francisco San Francisco 8	681	281
Joseph	Amador Twp 4	55	240
Joseph	San Francisco San Francisco 4	681	139
L*	El Dorado Salmon Hills	581	063
Melessee	Sierra Whiskey	66	843
Michael L	Yuba Marysville	72	879
Miles	San Mateo Twp 3	65	75
Milissee	Sierra Whiskey	66	843
P A	Sacramento Ward 4	63	509
Richard	Napa Hot Springs	61	19
S*	El Dorado Salmon Hills	581	063
Solomon	Sierra Pine Grove	66	835
Thos	Calaveras Twp 9	57	391
Thos	San Mateo Twp 3	65	75
W A	Siskiyou Scott Ri	69	72
W C	Yolo Cache	72	632
W H	Siskiyou Scott Ri	69	72
William	Calaveras Twp 5	57	228
SWIGANT			
Francis	Calaveras Twp 6	57	156
SWIGART			
Jonar	Tuolumne Sonora	71	192
SWIGG			
Timothy	Santa Clara San Jose	65	282
SWIGGEN			
John	Santa Clara Fremont	65	420
SWIGURT			
Jonas	Tuolumne Twp 1	71	192
SWILER			
Jo	Tehama Red Bluff	70	933
SWILLER			
John	Colusa Grand Island	57	481
SWIM			
Isaac	Sierra Downieville	661	018
Shepherd	Napa Napa	61	62
SWIME			
John	Yolo Putah	72	586
SWIMEY			
Margaret	San Joaquin Stockton	641	072
SWIMLEY			
Wm F	Sacramento Ward 1	63	29
SWIN			
Andrew	El Dorado Diamond	58	765
J*	El Dorado Diamond	58	765
Jno	Mendocino Anderson	60	865
SWINARD			
A	Siskiyou Cottonwoood	69	97
SWINBANK			
Thomas	Sierra Twp 7	66	896
SWINBURN			
William	Santa Clara San Jose	65	326
SWINDEL			
John	Tuolumne Twp 1	71	259
SWINDELLS			
John	Tuolumne Twp 1	71	259
SWINDLEHURST			
Thomas	Calaveras Twp 7	57	19
SWINE			
John	Yolo Putah	72	586
Louise	Sacramento Ward 1	63	75
Maria	San Francisco San Francisco 10	315 67	
SWINEHART			
Jas	Sacramento Georgian	63	342
Samuel	Siskiyou Yreka	69	139
SWINERTON			
Henry	Sierra Gibsonville	66	852
J W	Sacramento Ward 4	63	565
James*	Plumas Quincy	62	922
W R	Sacramento Ward 3	63	448
SWINESTON			
Jos	Sacramento Ward 4	63	526
SWINEY			
Jhn	Calaveras Twp 6	57	148
John	Calaveras Twp 5	57	148
Thomas	Tuolumne Twp 3	71	447
SWINFORD			
Geo*	Santa Clara Fremont	65	418
John M	Santa Clara Fremont	65	418
SWING			
Bartola	San Luis Obispo San Luis Obispo	65	40

Name	County Locale	M653 RollPage
SWING		
Emoline*	Tehama Red Bluff	70 917
J	Calaveras Twp 9	57 404
Sugain	El Dorado Georgetown	58 705
SWINGDALE		
Jacob A	Calaveras Twp 7	57 14
SWINGLER		
M M	Sacramento Ward 4	63 534
SWINGSTON		
James	Trinity Mouth Ca	701012
John H	Contra Costa Twp 1	57 537
Robert	Contra Costa Twp 2	57 580
SWINIE		
Osavia	Tehama Tehama	70 949
SWINK		
A J	Tehama Antelope	70 886
SWINNEY		
Daniel	Napa Yount	61 33
S	Tehama Red Bluff	70 929
Sallie	Tehama Red Bluff	70 923
Thomas A*	San Joaquin Tulare	64 870
SWINNY		
Morgan	Contra Costa Twp 1	57 501
SWINSON		
Frank	Placer Rattle Snake	62 632
Samuel	Placer Michigan	62 841
SWINSTON		
H	Mendocino Big Rvr	60 840
SWIRES		
J W	Trinity North Fo	701024
SWIRIS		
Richmond*	Mariposa Twp 1	60 649
SWIRNAN		
Joseph*	Contra Costa Twp 2	57 539
SWIROP		
---*	Del Norte Ferry P O	58 665
SWIRTY		
A	El Dorado Georgetown	58 707
SWISS		
Henery	Los Angeles Tejon	59 526
Henry*	Los Angeles Tejon	59 526
Hinny*	Los Angeles Tejon	59 526
SWISTLE		
Fred A*	Colusa Grand Island	57 482
SWITCHELL		
Ed	Sacramento Ward 1	63 38
SWITCHILLE		
Theodore	Yuba Marysville	72 938
SWITT		
Charles*	Nevada Bridgeport	61 449
D	San Francisco San Francisco 5	67 492
SWITTE		
B O	Colusa Monroeville	57 454
SWITZELER		
A	Sutter Nicolaus	70 839
SWITZEN		
John	Calaveras Twp 8	57 105
Peter	Sacramento Georgian	63 340
SWITZER		
Comodore P	Los Angeles Los Angeles	59 327
Henry	San Joaquin Elkhorn	64 963
Henry	Solano Suisan	69 233
J B	Marin Novato	60 738
John	Nevada Bridgeport	61 446
Joseph*	Del Norte Crescent	58 637
Lany*	Mendocino Big Rvr	60 853
Larry*	Mendocino Big Rvr	60 853
Lowrey	Contra Costa Twp 1	57 485
N C	Shasta Shasta	66 674
Nicodemus*	Mendocino Big Rvr	60 853
Nicodenns	Mendocino Big Rvr	60 853
Nn C	Shasta Shasta	66 674
Robt	Napa Napa	61 56
William	Plumas Quincy	62 964
Wm	Sacramento Ward 3	63 458
SWIZE		
Mary	Amador Twp 4	55 245
SWIZER		
Julia	San Francisco San Francisco 9	68 968
SWOBB		
George	Nevada Red Dog	61 548
SWODGERS		
Alyada	Yolo Cache	72 592
SWODOWSKY		
Martin	Santa Cruz Pajaro	66 532
SWOFFER		
Isaac	Santa Clara Santa Clara	65 490
SWOILL		
George	Tuolumne Sonora	71 202
SWON		
---	El Dorado Georgetown	58 701
SWOOK		
---	Sierra St Louis	66 812
SWOOVT		
Julias*	Calaveras Twp 4	57 324

Name	County Locale	M653 RollPage
SWOP		
Micholas	Placer Iona Hills	62 888
SWOPE		
Elias	Napa Yount	61 55
G M	Stanislaus Empire	70 734
L	Sacramento Granite	63 259
T	Butte Kimshaw	56 576
SWORD		
Antone*	Trinity North Fo	701026
Henry	Marin S Antoni	60 706
Robert G	San Joaquin Oneal	64 938
SWORDS		
Thos	San Francisco San Francisco 10	233 67
SWORSS		
Thos	San Francisco San Francisco 10	233 67
SWORTZ		
A	El Dorado Georgetown	58 707
Chas	Calaveras Twp 5	57 213
Davis	El Dorado Georgetown	58 685
Phillip	Calaveras Twp 5	57 185
William	Los Angeles Los Angeles	59 322
SWSITE		
J	Colusa Muion	57 459
SWUGIS		
Wm*	Butte Ophir	56 751
SWUILLY		
John	Yuba Long Bar	72 751
SWUING		
John	Shasta Shasta	66 757
SWUNEY		
G W	Butte Ophir	56 766
SWUNK		
Daniel*	Calaveras Twp 5	57 144
SWURGH		
Thos	Sacramento Granite	63 266
SWUTSEN		
G	San Francisco San Francisco 4	681154
SWUTZER		
Alonzo J	San Francisco San Francisco 3	67 80
SWVAIL		
R*	San Francisco San Francisco 5	67 547
SWW		
---	Yuba Rose Bar	72 794
SWYCAFFER		
Joseph	San Diego San Diego	64 764
SWYER		
James F	Mendocino Calpella	60 820
SWYERS		
John T	Mariposa Twp 1	60 638
SWYNG		
John	Shasta Shasta	66 757
Joseph*	Shasta Shasta	66 655
SXISSIN		
A*	Nevada Nevada	61 255
SXRAVES		
G*	Nevada Nevada	61 288
SY CUN		
---	Mariposa Twp 3	60 607
SY YING		
---	El Dorado Georgetown	58 702
SY		
---	Amador Twp 5	55 367
---	Amador Twp 1	55 501
---	Amador Twp 1	55 511
---	Calaveras Twp 4	57 304
---	El Dorado Greenwood	58 715
---	Nevada Bridgeport	61 460
Han	El Dorado Georgetown	58 693
Hong*	El Dorado Georgetown	58 702
Ing	El Dorado Georgetown	58 701
Kee	Mariposa Twp 3	60 582
Lin	El Dorado Georgetown	58 703
Louey	El Dorado Georgetown	58 693
Minsy	El Dorado Georgetown	58 755
Quay	Mariposa Twp 3	60 545
Wen	El Dorado Georgetown	58 693
SYANS		
Samuel	Nevada Eureka	61 346
SYAO		
Andrew	Los Angeles Los Angeles	59 519
SYBALT		
Auguste	Plumas Quincy	621001
SYBERT		
Jno	Klamath S Fork	59 203
Robert	San Diego San Diego	64 762
SYBLE		
John	Calaveras Twp 9	57 355
SYDDAS		
Gilbert*	Alameda Oakland	55 62
SYDEDALE		
Richd*	Mendocino Anderson	60 866
SYDNER		
Wm	Humbolt Table Bl	59 140
SYDNEY		
F	Sacramento Brighton	63 199

Name	County Locale	M653 RollPage
SYDNEY		
Paul	San Francisco San Francisco 7	681428
SYDNOR		
John B	Contra Costa Twp 2	57 581
SYDORLING		
Gilbert	Sierra Gibsonville	66 857
SYDUES		
R B*	Colusa Monroeville	57 451
SYE		
---	Sacramento Ward 1	63 69
Choy	Butte Ophir	56 801
Sing	Butte Ophir	56 802
SYELTHS		
Antonio*	Butte Bidwell	56 732
SYENI		
---	El Dorado Big Bar	58 736
SYEPHER		
A	Butte Cascade	56 696
SYERCH		
William*	Calaveras Twp 10	57 281
SYERO		
Louisa*	El Dorado Georgetown	58 685
SYEROX		
Louisa*	El Dorado Georgetown	58 685
SYERS		
Andrew	Butte Bidwell	56 729
SYETHS		
Antonio	Butte Bidwell	56 732
SYETTHS		
Antonio*	Butte Bidwell	56 732
SYFORD		
John	San Francisco San Francisco 6	67 412
SYING		
Sy	El Dorado Big Bar	58 733
SYIVER		
Eleakim*	Sierra Gibsonville	66 857
SYKES		
Charles	Solano Benecia	69 289
E R	Trinity Trinity	70 974
John	Placer Virginia	62 673
Mary	San Francisco San Francisco 8	681242
Mary C	San Francisco San Francisco 8	681242
Noah	Placer Michigan	62 851
Peater	Amador Twp 2	55 319
Peates*	Amador Twp 2	55 319
W J	Butte Chico	56 556
Wm	Humbolt Eureka	59 178
SYLAS		
Clara M	Yuba Marysville	72 950
SYLIA		
Muell*	San Francisco San Francisco 9	681098
Nenel*	San Francisco San Francisco 9	681098
Nerrel*	San Francisco San Francisco 9	681098
SYLIN		
---	Humbolt Eureka	59 174
SYLINGER		
Frank	Santa Cruz Soguel	66 583
SYLIVAN		
Frank	Santa Cruz Soguel	66 583
SYLLACA		
Jesus	San Luis Obispo San Luis Obispo 65	11
SYLLIBRIDGE		
D M	Butte Eureka	56 653
SYLLIBRIDGER		
D M	Butte Eureka	56 653
SYLMAN		
Frank	Santa Cruz Soguel	66 583
SYLOA		
Jo*	Sacramento Natonia	63 273
M	Tuolumne Twp 4	71 146
Sopata	Tuolumne Jamestown	71 424
SYLOER		
Jo*	Sacramento Natonia	63 273
SYLONE		
Joseph	Santa Cruz Soguel	66 590
SYLOR		
Clara M	Yuba Marysville	72 950
SYLORA		
Frank*	Alameda Brooklyn	55 118
SYLRA		
Jose*	Yuba Parke Ba	72 786
Joseph	Yuba Long Bar	72 744
SYLSER		
John	Calaveras Twp 7	57 44
SYLVA		
Antonio	Yuba Parks Ba	72 785
Frank	Yuba Fosters	72 823
Jacinto	Yuba Foster B	72 821
John	Yuba New York	72 728
John	Yuba Parks Ba	72 783
John	Yuba Parks Ba	72 785
Jose	Monterey Alisal	601033
Jose	Yuba Parks Ba	72 785
Jose	Yuba Parks Ba	72 786
Joseph	Monterey Alisal	601028
Lopata	Tuolumne Twp 3	71 424

California 1860 Census Index

Name	County Locale	M653 RollPage
SYLVA		
Manuel	Placer Auburn	62 563
Manuel	Yuba Parke Ba	72 785
Manuel	Yuba Fosters	72 821
V*	Tuolumne Big Oak	71 146
Vu*	Tuolumne Big Oak	71 146
SYLVAD		
Maria A	Merced Monterey	60 933
SYLVANDER		
August	San Francisco San Francisco 1 68 890	
SYLVANIA		
---	Los Angeles San Juan	59 467
SYLVAS		
Epipheno	Los Angeles Tejon	59 539
Eugenio	Los Angeles Los Angeles	59 318
Jose	Los Angeles Los Nieto	59 424
Jose	Marin Cortemad	60 789
Manuel	Los Angeles Los Angeles	59 335
Maria A	Monterey Monterey	60 933
Maria De Los A	San Juan	59 472
	Los Angeles	
Maria De Los A*	San Juan	59 472
	Los Angeles	
Pascual	Los Angeles Santa Ana	59 456
Petra	Los Angeles Los Angeles	59 388
Pio	Los Angeles Los Angeles	59 324
Wancisca	Los Angeles Los Angeles	59 306
SYLVASTER		
Lorean	Klamath Liberty	59 236
Manuel	Klamath Liberty	59 235
SYLVEN		
John	Sonoma Vallejo	69 625
SYLVER		
Jo	Sacramento Natonia	63 273
SYLVERO		
V	Tuolumne Columbia	71 471
SYLVERS		
John	Sonoma Vallejo	69 625
SYLVESTER		
Adolphus	Los Angeles Los Angeles	59 322
Azel	Plumas Quincy	62 976
Chas	Butte Cascade	56 703
Daniel	San Francisco San Francisco 7 681364	
Danl	Stanislaus Buena Village	70 722
E	Sutter Bear Rvr	70 818
Ellen A	Tuolumne Springfield	71 371
Frank	Merced Monterey	60 938
Frank	Monterey Monterey	60 938
George	San Joaquin Tulare	64 869
H	Nevada Grass Valley	61 174
Heinchman	Placer Iona Hills	62 878
Issac	Calaveras Twp 8	57 92
J E	Yuba Bear Rvr	721937
Jas H	Plumas Quincy	62 937
Jas M	Butte Ophir	56 751
John	Calaveras Twp 7	57 35
John	Calaveras Twp 8	57 70
John	Placer Rattle Snake	62 635
John J	San Joaquin Castoria	64 878
Jos	San Francisco San Francisco 5 67 480	
Jos	Trinity Big Flat	701040
L	San Francisco San Francisco 4 681152	
Martin	San Joaquin Castoria	64 900
N	Tuolumne Twp 1	71 207
Saml F	Santa Cruz Pajaro	66 531
Stephen	Calaveras Twp 10	57 291
Theo	San Francisco San Francisco 1 68 914	
Thos	San Francisco San Francisco 9 681081	
W	Sacramento Granite	63 221
W G	Sacramento Granite	63 247
Wm	Amador Twp 6	55 428
Wm	Amador Twp 1	55 512
SYLVESTRE		
---	San Diego S Luis R	64 783
---	San Diego Agua Caliente	64 837
---	San Diego Agua Caliente	64 839
Maria	Los Angeles San Juan	59 464
Maria J	Los Angeles San Juan	59 464
SYLVIA		
Charles	Santa Cruz Pajaro	66 549
Francisco	Contra Costa Twp 1	57 495
Frank	Contra Costa Twp 1	57 515
Frank	Yuba Parks Ba	72 783
Frank	Yuba Parks Ba	72 784
Frenk*	Yuba Parke Ba	72 783
Gabriel	Contra Costa Twp 1	57 520
James	Santa Cruz Santa Cruz	66 605
Jose	Yuba New York	72 730
Jose	Yuba New York	72 734
Joseph	San Francisco San Francisco 1 68 857	
Joseph	Santa Cruz Soguel	66 590
Manuel	Contra Costa Twp 1	57 508
Manuel	Contra Costa Twp 1	57 515
Miller	Butte Bidwell	56 732
SYLVIRO		
V	Tuolumne Twp 2	71 471

Name	County Locale	M653 RollPage
SYLVUS		
Jas	Sacramento Natonia	63 281
SYM		
---	Sierra Downieville	66 982
Tog	El Dorado Georgetown	58 746
SYME		
John B*	Yuba Marysville	72 877
John C*	Calaveras Twp 4	57 336
Reharles	Tuolumne Twp 3	71 468
SYMES		
J W	Tuolumne Twp 1	71 211
SYMMES		
Cath	Alameda Brooklyn	55 97
David	Alameda Brooklyn	55 96
James	Tuolumne Sonora	71 480
John W	Alameda Oakland	55 35
SYMMS		
Charles	San Francisco San Francisco 7 681325	
Daniel	Tuolumne Twp 3	71 459
James	Tuolumne Twp 1	71 480
SYMONDE		
Augustus	Tuolumne Columbia	71 323
SYMONDS		
C H	Siskiyou Klamath	69 85
SYMONS		
P	Solano Vacaville	69 362
William	Solano Benecia	69 288
SYMOUR		
Z	Santa Clara Fremont	65 435
SYMPSON		
J	Sutter Yuba	70 765
SYMPTON		
C J	Marin Cortemad	60 752
SYMS		
John	Butte Ophir	56 786
SYNAT		
---	Fresno Twp 3	59 7
SYNCH		
J	Nevada Eureka	61 347
James	San Francisco San Francisco 6 67 457	
P	Mariposa Twp 1	60 663
P	Nevada Eureka	61 376
Peter*	Contra Costa Twp 1	57 503
SYNDE		
W C	Sacramento Ward 1	63 84
SYNDENOUTH		
P H*	Placer Iona Hills	62 871
SYNDER		
A	San Francisco San Francisco 5 67 517	
Charles	San Joaquin Stockton	641051
George	Calaveras Twp 4	57 312
P	Calaveras Twp 9	57 385
T J	Nevada Eureka	61 376
SYNDMOUTH		
P H*	Placer Iona Hills	62 871
SYNDON		
James N	Yuba Marysville	72 963
SYNDRE		
Wiliam	Contra Costa Twp 2	57 569
SYNE		
Frank	Trinity Weaverville	701056
SYNEK		
Peter*	Contra Costa Twp 1	57 503
SYNELL		
Low	Butte Bidwell	56 708
SYNER		
A*	Mariposa Twp 3	60 614
SYNES		
Sin	Butte Bidwell	56 714
SYNG		
---	El Dorado Georgetown	58 702
Wy	Merced Twp 2	60 916
SYOE		
---*	Sierra Downieville	66 983
SYOI		
---*	Sierra Downieville	66 983
SYONS		
Frederick	Tuolumne Chinese	71 523
G T	Nevada Eureka	61 347
J	Nevada Eureka	61 346
M	Nevada Eureka	61 378
Martin	Contra Costa Twp 1	57 525
S	Nevada Eureka	61 350
SYPAYO		
Pepiano	Sacramento Ward 1	63 110
Pipiano	Sacramento Ward 1	63 110
SYPES		
E	Butte Mountain	56 740
SYPHAL		
Fidin	Calaveras Twp 9	57 361
SYPHAT		
Feden*	Calaveras Twp 9	57 361
Fiden*	Calaveras Twp 9	57 361
Fider*	Calaveras Twp 9	57 361
SYPHERS		
John	Mariposa Coulterville	60 702

Name	County Locale	M653 RollPage
SYPRESS		
F	Siskiyou Scott Va	69 46
SYRNL		
Jas	Sacramento Ward 1	63 79
SYRO		
Andrew	Los Angeles Los Angeles	59 519
SYRUP		
Fredk W	San Francisco San Francisco 8 681255	
SYSAULT		
William*	San Francisco San Francisco 7 681427	
SYSHE		
Alexander	Yuba Marysville	72 963
SYSON		
Daniel	Siskiyou Yreka	69 131
SYSPIT		
Antonio	Butte Bidwell	56 731
SYSTER		
Frederick	San Francisco San Francisco 3 67 45	
W S*	San Francisco San Francisco 3 67 86	
SYTER		
Levi	Siskiyou Scott Va	69 46
SYTHE		
John	Butte Cascade	56 703
SYTHER		
Richard*	Napa Yount	61 39
SYTHES		
Julius	San Francisco San Francisco 7 681334	
SYTON		
J	Tuolumne Twp 4	71 147
SYTTON		
Descon S	Tuolumne Jamestown	71 445
Discon S	Tuolumne Twp 3	71 445
SYU		
---	Sierra Twp 5	66 932
SYVA		
Jacinto	Yuba Fosters	72 821
SYVERTO		
Moyano	Tuolumne Twp 1	71 239
SYVERTS		
Moyano	Tuolumne Sonora	71 239
SYVIA		
James	Santa Cruz Santa Cruz	66 605
SYWER		
Eleakim*	Sierra Gibsonville	66 857
SZAWASH		
Somo T	Los Angeles Santa Ana	59 440
SZOLLOSY		
J B Louis	Sacramento Ward 1	63 46
J Blouis	Sacramento Ward 1	63 46
T LOO		
Qah*	Tuolumne Chinese	71 526
T SOO		
Yah*	Tuolumne Chinese	71 526
T		
Ow	Nevada Bridgeport	61 461
Son	Amador Twp 6	55 422
T???TIR		
J???	Mariposa Twp 3	60 601
TA		
---	Alameda Oakland	55 53
---	Alameda Oakland	55 64
---	Amador Twp 4	55 252
---	Amador Twp 5	55 335
---	Amador Twp 5	55 490
---	Nevada Nevada	61 301
Cha Lee	Yuba Long Bar	72 757
Chow	San Francisco San Francisco 5 67 509	
Cog*	Calaveras Twp 5	57 254
Cring	San Francisco San Francisco 5 67 509	
Foo	Yuba Long Bar	72 756
Por	Plumas Quincy	62 965
Shee	San Francisco San Francisco 11 160	
		67
Thie	San Francisco San Francisco 5 671206	
Thu	San Francisco San Francisco 5 671206	
Ue	Mariposa Twp 3	60 618
Yang	San Francisco San Francisco 5 671206	
TAA		
---*	Calaveras Twp 6	57 175
TAAE		
B	Tuolumne Twp 4	71 174
TAANATY		
H	Trinity Hay Fork	70 994
TAB		
---	Butte Oregon	56 626
---	Calaveras Twp 5	57 181
Ah	Butte Oregon	56 626
TABACHA		
Juan	Los Angeles San Juan	59 476
TABARDINE		
John	Amador Twp 1	55 491
TABAT		
Henry	Mariposa Twp 3	60 566
TABBETS		
Jeremiah	Calaveras Twp 5	57 146
TABBLER		
Daniel	Siskiyou Scott Va	69 22

California 1860 Census Index

Name	County Locale	M653 RollPage
TABBLER		
Daniels	Siskiyou Scott Va	69 22
TABBLET		
Daniel	Siskiyou Scott Va	69 22
TABE		
Fred	Placer Forest H	62 766
TABEN		
Richd	Amador Twp 5	55 344
TABENAUGH		
Thos*	Sacramento San Joaquin	63 349
TABER		
A G	Yolo Putah	72 549
C	El Dorado Diamond	58 809
Charles	San Francisco San Francisco 3	67 21
Chas	Nevada Bloomfield	61 512
Chas A	San Francisco San Francisco 10	273 67
Frederick	Sacramento Granite	63 261
G T	Tuolumne Columbia	71 348
Geo*	San Joaquin Stockton	641046
Henry	Sacramento Ward 4	63 553
Henry*	Yuba Marysville	72 883
Isaac	San Francisco San Francisco 8	681283
Jeremiah	Solano Vacaville	69 353
Lorenzo	Sacramento Granite	63 262
R T	Butte Oregon	56 617
Wm L	Sonoma Armally	69 502
TABERMAN		
J R	Sacramento Ward 1	63 39
TABERSY		
Julias	Nevada Little Y	61 533
TABERY		
C F*	Tuolumne Twp 2	71 303
TABET		
F	Tuolumne Twp 4	71 157
TABETT		
John	Amador Twp 3	55 380
TABILLION		
Stephen	Santa Clara Almaden	65 277
TABIN		
H	Tuolumne Columbia	71 472
TABINO		
Dominico*	Sierra Whiskey	66 849
TABIR		
A G*	Yolo Putah	72 549
TABLE		
Albert	Nevada Bloomfield	61 509
Patrick	San Diego Colorado	64 806
TABLER		
Joseph	San Francisco San Francisco 9	681085
TABLET		
Jeremiah	Calaveras Twp 6	57 146
TABLIO		
John	Tuolumne Columbia	71 322
TABOAS		
Donisu*	Merced Monterey	60 937
Manims*	Monterey Monterey	60 942
Maxims*	Monterey Monterey	60 942
TABON		
Josh*	San Francisco San Francisco 1	68 915
TABOR		
A G	Colusa Monroeville	57 447
Charles W	San Francisco San Francisco 8	681254
Frederick	San Joaquin Elliott	64 945
Gilbert	Calaveras Twp 5	57 141
J C	Nevada Nevada	61 330
Jacob S	Humbolt Union	59 181
James	Contra Costa Twp 3	57 591
James	Sonoma Mendocino	69 456
James H	Yuba Marysville	72 928
John M	Contra Costa Twp 3	57 591
Josh*	San Francisco San Francisco 1	68 915
R T	Butte Oregon	56 617
William	San Joaquin Castoria	64 872
William H	San Francisco San Francisco 8	681254
Wm	Sacramento Ward 1	63 39
Wm	Sonoma Mendocino	69 456
TABOSMEA		
---	Fresno Twp 2	59 57
TABOT		
Henry*	Mariposa Twp 3	60 566
TABOUR		
John	Calaveras Twp 10	57 273
TABOX		
Saml H	Solano Benecia	69 282
TABRISKIE		
Policarpui	Santa Barbara San Bernardino	64 203
TABY		
Edward	Amador Twp 1	55 470
TACAR		
---	Amador Twp 1	55 499
TACE		
---	Tuolumne Twp 3	71 468
TACH		
---	Yuba North Ea	72 677

Name	County Locale	M653 RollPage
TACHEE		
Augustus	Butte Ophir	56 777
TACILA		
---	Los Angeles Los Angeles	59 495
TACK		
---	Amador Twp 5	55 344
---	Amador Twp 5	55 360
---	Amador Twp 1	55 496
---	Calaveras Twp 8	57 106
---	Calaveras Twp 10	57 274
---	Calaveras Twp 8	57 61
---	Calaveras Twp 8	57 62
---	El Dorado Salmon Falls	581042
---	El Dorado Salmon Falls	581045
---	El Dorado Salmon Falls	581046
---	El Dorado Salmon Hills	581058
---	Mariposa Twp 1	60 651
---	Yolo No E Twp	72 677
Geo W	Del Norte Crescent	58 623
Marian	Del Norte Crescent	58 623
Nicholas	Del Norte Crescent	58 622
TACKABERRY		
W	El Dorado Placerville	58 861
TACKEL		
Christ	Alameda Brooklyn	55 179
TACKER		
W R	San Francisco San Francisco 5	67 512
TACKET		
A I*	Nevada Bridgeport	61 504
A J	Nevada Bridgeport	61 504
TACKETT		
B R	Solano Vacaville	69 359
Kirk*	Napa Napa	61 56
TACKHOFF		
W	El Dorado Mountain	581184
TACKMIRE		
F	El Dorado Placerville	58 820
TACKNEY		
H*	Napa Napa	61 78
J W*	Napa Yount	61 36
Wm*	Sacramento Ward 3	63 427
TACLA		
---	Monterey Monterey	60 937
TACOMASENA		
Felep	Mariposa Twp 1	60 625
Felix*	Mariposa Twp 1	60 625
TACT		
---	Sacramento Ward 4	63 610
TAD		
---	Amador Twp 2	55 280
---	Calaveras Twp 10	57 297
TADDIE		
Louis	Calaveras Twp 7	57 29
Peter	Calaveras Twp 7	57 29
TADIS		
---	Monterey San Juan	60 992
TADLOCK		
J C	Yolo Cache	72 632
M	Yolo Cottonwoood	72 647
T E	Merced Twp 2	60 923
TAE		
---	Calaveras Twp 5	57 205
TAEN		
---	Mariposa Twp 3	60 551
TAES		
Wilson	Tuolumne Big Oak	71 136
TAESERE		
Josa	Amador Twp 5	55 332
TAESTRO		
Pedro	Tuolumne Montezuma	71 507
TAFA		
L	Siskiyou Callahan	69 5
Miguil	Santa Clara Burnett	65 259
TAFF		
C*	Sutter Yuba	70 778
TAFFA		
Theodor	Santa Cruz Santa Cruz	66 636
TAFFARO		
Jose J	San Francisco San Francisco 2	67 581
TAFFE		
Wm	San Francisco San Francisco 2	67 569
TAFFEN		
Ellen	San Francisco San Francisco 9	68 995
TAFFERTY		
Frances	Amador Twp 3	55 373
TAFFESS		
Thos*	Nevada Bridgeport	61 478
TAFFIA		
Peter	Calaveras Twp 5	57 135
TAFFLE		
Lawrence	San Francisco San Francisco 7	681372
TAFFS		
Joseph	Calaveras Twp 8	57 57
TAFFT		
Dexter	San Francisco San Francisco 7	681435
TAFFTS		
Hanson	Plumas Quincy	62 992

Name	County Locale	M653 RollPage
TAFFUSS		
Thos	Nevada Bridgeport	61 478
TAFIA		
Auselino*	Los Angeles Santa Ana	59 455
Guadalupe*	Los Angeles Los Nieto	59 435
Margarita*	Los Angeles Los Nieto	59 435
TAFMATER		
T C	Del Norte Happy Ca	58 667
TAFORTA		
Mitchel*	Calaveras Twp 6	57 167
TAFT		
Axcy	San Francisco San Francisco 10	176 67
Axoy	San Francisco San Francisco 10	176 67
Benj	San Francisco San Francisco 2	67 755
C C	Nevada Nevada	61 266
C J	Yuba Marysville	72 876
D H	Sacramento Granite	63 245
Danl M	San Bernardino San Bernadino	64 615
E	Shasta Shasta	66 761
E H	Sacramento Ward 3	63 434
Hiram	San Francisco San Francisco 11	122 67
Jno H	Sacramento Natonia	63 271
John P	San Francisco San Francisco 9	681071
P M	El Dorado Placerville	58 909
Walter	Placer Michigan	62 834
William	Shasta Millvill	66 746
Wm*	Nevada Nevada	61 323
TAFTE		
Harley	Los Angeles Los Angeles	59 322
TAG		
---	Mariposa Twp 1	60 651
TAGARD		
John	El Dorado Kelsey	581148
TAGART		
A J	Stanislaus Oatvale	70 716
M M	Nevada Bridgeport	61 488
TAGEMIYER		
F	El Dorado Placerville	58 839
TAGER		
Alfred	El Dorado Georgetown	58 690
John*	El Dorado Georgetown	58 685
TAGERT		
C*	Calaveras Twp 9	57 392
TAGG		
Joseph	San Joaquin Oneal	64 930
TAGGARD		
E W	El Dorado Placerville	58 868
J A	El Dorado Placerville	58 877
Lucius L	San Francisco San Francisco 3	67 49
Lucius L*	San Francisco San Francisco 3	67 48
TAGGART		
A	Nevada Nevada	61 316
Isaac J	Tuolumne Twp 5	71 489
J T	Nevada Nevada	61 267
Jacob	Tuolumne Twp 5	71 503
Jno	Butte Oregon	56 632
Patk	San Francisco San Francisco 10	342 67
R R	Butte Oregon	56 640
Wm	Sacramento Ward 1	63 63
TAGGERT		
Geo	Klamath Klamath	59 225
Rosanna	San Francisco San Francisco 8	681250
TAGGET		
John M	Tuolumne Shawsfla	71 406
TAGGETT		
J	Nevada Grass Valley	61 149
Jno L	San Francisco San Francisco 9	681030
TAGGORT		
T G	Shasta Horsetown	66 711
TAGLOR		
O R	Butte Ophir	56 750
TAGRRETT		
Thomas	Sierra St Louis	66 813
TAGRUE		
Ed	Sacramento Franklin	63 328
TAGUE		
F M	El Dorado White Oaks	581008
Jno	Klamath S Fork	59 205
T*	Nevada Grass Valley	61 161
TAGURRIE		
J	Nevada Grass Valley	61 148
TAH CHAH		
---	Tuolumne Jacksonville	71 515
TAH		
---	Calaveras Twp 8	57 105
---	Calaveras Twp 8	57 61
---	Tuolumne Big Oak	71 147
Ah	Tuolumne Twp 4	71 147
Chah	Tuolumne Twp 5	71 515
TAHE		
---*	Yuba Slate Ro	72 712
---*	Amador Twp 7	55 415

Name	County Locale	M653 Roll	Page
TAHILER			
Edmund	San Francisco San Francisco 2	67	653
TAHIS			
G T	Tuolumne Twp 2	71	348
TAHLOTE			
Henry	Amador Twp 6	55	443
TAHSAL			
Rafaega	Mariposa Twp 3	60	547
Rafalga	Mariposa Twp 3	60	547
TAHTOTIN			
Bob	Del Norte Klamath	58	658
TAHY			
Marty	Amador Twp 2	55	293
Patrick*	Amador Twp 4	55	244
TAI			
---	Calaveras Twp 6	57	149
TAIDEE			
---	Tulara Twp 1	71	117
---	Tulara Twp 1	71	118
TAILIER			
John*	Nevada Nevada	61	327
TAILIES			
John	Nevada Nevada	61	327
TAILOR			
Jules	San Francisco San Francisco 2	67	700
Nicholas	Yuba New York	72	730
TAILTAR			
James D*	Colusa Monroeville	57	442
TAILTON			
James D*	Colusa Monroeville	57	442
TAIN			
---	Del Norte Happy Ca	58	663
---	Sierra Downieville	66	1005
Foo	Yuba Long Bar	72	760
Low	Sierra Downieville	66	1004
See	Nevada Nevada	61	300
TAINCOSEN			
Adolphus	Yuba Marysville	72	918
Carmen*	Yuba Marysville	72	918
TAINSBURY			
James*	Sacramento Ward 1	63	39
TAINTER			
A*	Napa Hot Springs	61	4
Oscar	Nevada Rough &	61	405
Wm H*	Mendocino Big Rvr	60	844
TAINTES			
A*	Napa Hot Springs	61	4
TAINTOR			
Samuel	Los Angeles Los Angeles	59	337
TAIP			
---	El Dorado Diamond	58	787
TAIR			
William*	El Dorado Georgetown	58	693
TAIS			
Casue	Mariposa Twp 1	60	637
TAIT			
David	Calaveras Twp 5	57	224
George	Tuolumne Jamestown	71	449
James A	Calaveras Twp 5	57	251
Julius A	Calaveras Twp 5	57	251
TAITE			
William	Siskiyou Yreka	69	167
TAJ			
Yup	Nevada Grass Valley	61	234
TAJRY			
---	El Dorado Georgetown	58	756
TAK			
---	Amador Twp 6	55	431
---	Shasta Shasta	66	669
---	Yolo Slate Ra	72	712
---	Yolo Slate Ra	72	713
---	Yuba Slate Ro	72	712
W W	Yuba Slate Ro	72	713
	Sacramento Ward 1	63	63
TAKAR			
---	Fresno Twp 1	59	29
TAKE			
---	Amador Twp 2	55	319
---	Amador Twp 5	55	341
---	Amador Twp 3	55	398
---	Amador Twp 7	55	415
---	Amador Twp 6	55	449
---	Amador Twp 6	55	450
---	Amador Twp 1	55	490
---	Amador Twp 1	55	494
---	Calaveras Twp 5	57	251
---	Calaveras Twp 10	57	276
---	Calaveras Twp 10	57	286
---	Calaveras Twp 4	57	302
---	Plumas Quincy	62	950
---	Tuolumne Twp 6	71	529
---	Yolo Slate Ra	72	712
---	Yolo Slate Ra	72	713
---*	Amador Twp 7	55	415
Geo	San Francisco San Francisco 9	68	1084
J W	Amador Twp 3	55	371
TAKE			
Sam	Amador Twp 3	55	386
TAKHELDER			
W H	Trinity Weaverville	70	1070
TAKI			
---	Calaveras Twp 10	57	276
TAKOKI			
---	Stanislaus Oatvale	70	720
TAKOR			
Joseph*	Santa Clara Alviso	65	399
TALAMADGE			
C V	Sacramento Franklin	63	332
TALAMANKIS			
Antonis	Marin S Antoni	60	709
TALAMANTA			
Antonio	Tuolumne Twp 5	71	497
TALAMANTEN			
Antonio*	Marin S Antoni	60	709
TALAMANTER			
Antonio	Tuolumne Chinese	71	497
Semona	Marin S Antoni	60	708
TALAMANTES			
Elenor M	Los Angeles San Pedro	59	485
Leonardo	Los Angeles San Pedro	59	478
TALAMANTEUS			
Antonio*	Marin S Antoni	60	709
TALAMANTUS			
Antonio*	Marin S Antoni	60	709
Semona*	Marin S Antoni	60	708
TALAMENTES			
Jose*	Los Angeles Los Angeles	59	507
Pedro*	Los Angeles Los Angeles	59	505
TALAMENTIS			
Jesus	Los Angeles Los Angeles	59	505
Jose D	Los Angeles Los Angeles	59	507
Pedro*	Los Angeles Los Angeles	59	505
Solida	Los Angeles Los Angeles	59	507
TALAMENTUS			
Tomas	Los Angeles Los Angeles	59	506
TALAMINTIS			
Jesus	Los Angeles Los Angeles	59	505
Pedro*	Los Angeles Los Angeles	59	505
Tomas	Los Angeles Los Angeles	59	506
TALAN			
H H	El Dorado Casumnes	58	1173
TALAND			
Neal	Amador Twp 2	55	286
TALAX			
J	Nevada Eureka	61	390
Q	Nevada Eureka	61	390
TALBER			
Justine	Tuolumne Columbia	71	473
TALBERT			
George	Calaveras Twp 7	57	5
J H	Solano Vacaville	69	365
James F	Calaveras Twp 10	57	266
John	Sacramento Ward 1	63	23
Josph	Napa Yount	61	46
Mathew	Sacramento Cosummes	63	387
R	San Mateo Twp 3	65	101
S H	Sacramento Granite	63	226
T A	Sacramento Ward 1	63	16
Virginia	Solano Vacaville	69	365
W L	Yuba Parks Ba	72	784
TALBETT			
Treeman	Tulara Twp 3	71	52
TALBOT			
A	Butte Ophir	56	749
Boules	Sonoma Santa Rosa	69	409
Chas	Plumas Meadow Valley	62	903
Coleman	Sonoma Santa Rosa	69	409
Eliza	Sonoma Santa Rosa	69	409
Isaac	Sonoma Armally	69	514
J	Calaveras Twp 9	57	407
J A	Calaveras Twp 9	57	411
James	Sacramento American	63	170
James R	Colusa Mansville	57	437
James W	Yuba Marysville	72	890
Joseph	Napa Yount	61	46
Nathan	Tulara Twp 3	71	6
Patrick	San Joaquin Oneal	64	913
Q A	Calaveras Twp 9	57	411
R	Tehama Red Bluff	70	917
S	Nevada Grass Valley	61	189
Sarah	San Francisco San Francisco 4	68	1132
Simean B	Colusa Monroeville	57	453
Thomas J	Colusa Mansville	57	437
W L	Yuba Parke Ba	72	784
TALBOTE			
Thomas	Tuolumne Twp 1	71	245
TALBOTT			
Albert G	Yuba Marysville	72	891
Freeman	Tulara Petersburg	71	52
George	Tulara Twp 3	71	60
H R	Butte Kimshaw	56	590
Hiram	Yuba Marysville	72	905
TALBOTT			
Hiram E	Yuba Marysville	72	905
J	Calaveras Twp 9	57	366
Martin S	Yuba Marysville	72	905
Nathan	Tuolumne Columbia	71	365
Thomas	Tulara Keyesville	71	58
Thomas	Tuolumne Sonora	71	245
William	Yuba Marysville	72	866
TALBOX			
Saml A*	Solano Benecia	69	282
TALBRANGH			
R*	Tehama Tehama	70	949
TALBUT			
James F	Calaveras Twp 10	57	266
TALCOT			
George	San Mateo Twp 3	65	106
TALCOTT			
H W	Sonoma Petaluma	69	605
W A	Sacramento Ward 3	63	487
TALDAR			
Chas*	Sacramento Ward 4	63	553
TALDOT			
Charles P	Tuolumne Columbia	71	353
TALE			
Benj*	Tehama Red Bluff	70	915
Geo	Sonoma Sonoma	69	640
TALEAFERRO			
A W	Marin San Rafael	60	768
TALEMINTIS			
Jose*	Los Angeles Los Angeles	59	507
TALEN			
John	El Dorado Kelsey	58	1146
TALENTE			
Vincent	Tuolumne Twp 3	71	454
TALEOTT			
H W	Sonoma Petaluma	69	605
TALEY			
---	Mendocino Round Va	60	885
TALIAFERN			
H	Marin Cortemad	60	752
TALIER			
Fred	El Dorado Salmon Falls	58	1039
TALIFAERRO			
Mary	San Francisco San Francisco 2	67	775
T W	San Francisco San Francisco 2	67	775
TALIMANI			
Angel	Calaveras Twp 7	57	35
TALIMENTES			
Jose	Los Angeles Los Angeles	59	507
TALIMIA			
Angel*	Calaveras Twp 8	57	87
TALINIA			
Angel*	Calaveras Twp 8	57	87
TALINIO			
Angel	Calaveras Twp 7	57	34
TALJAMB			
Henry	Siskiyou Scott Ri	69	66
TALK			
Harrison*	Mariposa Twp 3	60	605
TALKINGTON			
John	Plumas Quincy	62	962
TALKNER			
Jas	Butte Ophir	56	823
TALL			
G A	Tuolumne Twp 2	71	289
H H	El Dorado Placerville	58	871
J W	Tuolumne Twp 2	71	284
Jas	Yolo Washington	72	574
R S	Santa Clara Santa Clara	65	498
TALLA			
Juan*	Amador Twp 7	55	412
TALLAHAN			
Hannah	San Francisco San Francisco 2	67	600
TALLANCE			
John	San Joaquin Douglass	64	914
TALLANT			
Nathan	Siskiyou Scott Ri	69	66
TALLANTS			
Wm H	San Francisco San Francisco 3	67	80
TALLEMAN			
Etiruns	Calaveras Twp 6	57	164
TALLEMAND			
Etieune*	Calaveras Twp 6	57	164
TALLEMEET			
John*	Yuba Marysville	72	874
TALLENT			
Michael	Yuba Bear Rvr	72	1006
N W	San Francisco San Francisco 5	67	550
W W	San Francisco San Francisco 5	67	550
TALLEO			
---	Sierra Downieville	66	1005
TALLER			
C H	Nevada Little Y	61	531
TALLERNAND			
Etirune*	Calaveras Twp 6	57	164
TALLERNUT			
John*	Yuba Marysville	72	874

California 1860 Census Index

Name	County Locale	M653 RollPage
TALLES		
Caslton*	Yuba Marysville	72 926
TALLETT		
Lyman	Tuolumne Columbia	71 354
TALLEY		
A B	Tuolumne Twp 3	71 464
Arminta	Solano Vacaville	69 344
Armistead	Solano Vacaville	69 344
J W	Butte Oro	56 683
John	Tulara Twp 2	71 6
John	Tuolumne Sonora	71 482
M	Nevada Eureka	61 350
S R	Nevada Grass Valley	61 222
William	Nevada Bridgeport	61 502
TALLEYRAND		
T A	Amador Twp 3	55 369
TALLICK		
Saml	Tuolumne Twp 1	71 188
TALLIMIER		
Alexr	Sierra Downieville	661022
TALLISON		
W*	Mariposa Twp 3	60 585
TALLIVER		
Jas*	San Francisco San Francisco 9	681090
TALLMADGE		
George E	Sierra Downieville	66 958
Jgeorge E	Sierra Downieville	66 958
TALLMAN		
F C	Tuolumne Twp 1	71 208
G W	Nevada Washington	61 333
H	Nevada Nevada	61 311
James	Shasta Horsetown	66 693
R S	Nevada Nevada	61 260
Samuel	Sierra Twp 5	66 923
Wm	Nevada Eureka	61 371
TALLMARE		
John	Tuolumne Twp 1	71 253
TALLMRE		
M*	Nevada Eureka	61 389
TALLNUE		
M*	Nevada Eureka	61 389
TALLOCK		
Wm	Butte Ophir	56 779
TALLON		
J	Nevada Eureka	61 350
T	Nevada Eureka	61 373
TALLONRE		
M*	Nevada Eureka	61 389
TALLOW		
Thomas	Los Angeles Tejon	59 524
TALLY		
---	Tuolumne Twp 5	71 511
France	Sacramento Natonia	63 273
J B	Nevada Grass Valley	61 222
J M	Nevada Grass Valley	61 146
Jerry	Sacramento Granite	63 263
John*	Amador Twp 2	55 268
Kj B	Nevada Grass Valley	61 222
O B*	Nevada Grass Valley	61 189
TALLYMAN		
J W	Nevada Eureka	61 388
TALMADGE		
Frank L	Los Angeles Elmonte	59 249
Harriet	Sacramento Franklin	63 333
J*	Sacramento Brighton	63 207
T*	Sacramento Brighton	63 207
TALMAGE		
Charles	Calaveras Twp 7	57 47
E L	Tehama Red Bluff	70 910
TALMANS		
Wm	Calaveras Twp 9	57 381
TALMAR		
Wm	Calaveras Twp 9	57 381
TALMASS		
John	Tuolumne Twp 1	71 253
TALMON		
George	Tuolumne Twp 2	71 284
TALOR		
George*	Mariposa Coulterville	60 688
James H	Yuba Marysville	72 928
Robt H	Sierra Downieville	66 967
William	Siskiyou Yreka	69 167
TALORER		
C Jp	Nevada Nevada	61 275
C P	Nevada Nevada	61 275
TALRUCK		
J	Yolo Cache Crk	72 622
TALSARTY		
Thos	Nevada Bloomfield	61 530
TALTETT		
Lym An	Tuolumne Twp 2	71 354
TALTEY		
William	Nevada Bridgeport	61 502
TALUS		
Henry	Siskiyou Scott Ri	69 62
TALY		
Astur*	Calaveras Twp 6	57 164

Name	County Locale	M653 RollPage
TAM DI		
---	Calaveras Twp 5	57 255
TAM		
---	Amador Twp 5	55 330
---	Amador Twp 5	55 350
---	Amador Twp 5	55 353
---	Amador Twp 3	55 386
---	Amador Twp 6	55 423
---	Amador Twp 1	55 479
---	Calaveras Twp 8	57 106
---	Calaveras Twp 5	57 223
---	Calaveras Twp 5	57 236
---	Calaveras Twp 10	57 272
---	El Dorado Casumnes	581163
---	Nevada Washington	61 341
---	Sierra Downieville	661005
---	Tuolumne Twp 5	71 521
---	Tuolumne Twp 5	71 525
---	Tuolumne Twp 6	71 536
---*	Calaveras Twp 5	57 223
---*	Calaveras Twp 10	57 299
Chow	Nevada Grass Valley	61 232
Foo	Yuba Long Bar	72 760
Joseph	San Joaquin Elkhorn	64 974
Lin	Sierra Downieville	661004
See	Nevada Nevada	61 300
Sh	Tuolumne Big Oak	71 181
TAMADO		
George*	El Dorado Georgetown	58 701
TAMAN		
Patrick	Alameda Oakland	55 18
TAMANLES		
Carlos	San Joaquin Stockton	641072
TAMARANS		
Pablo	El Dorado Placerville	58 918
TAMARICO		
---	San Diego Agua Caliente	64 830
TAMARONO		
Pablo*	El Dorado Placerville	58 918
TAMASA		
---	San Diego Agua Caliente	64 864
TAMBELAS		
---	El Dorado Diamond	58 805
TAMBERT		
Fred	Tuolumne Twp 1	71 201
TAMBOLIN		
John	Los Angeles Los Angeles	59 329
TAMBORINE		
S M	Tuolumne Twp 1	71 261
Soll	Tuolumne Twp 1	71 261
TAMBROECK		
J*	Sacramento Ward 1	63 19
TAMBS		
Wm H*	Mendocino Big Rvr	60 844
TAMCOSA		
Carmea*	Yuba Marysville	72 918
Carmen*	Yuba Marysville	72 918
TAMEDON		
H C	Amador Twp 2	55 265
TAMEL		
Peter*	San Francisco San Francisco 1	68 812
TAMEMAN		
James*	El Dorado Georgetown	58 698
TAMEN		
John*	Mariposa Twp 3	60 604
TAMERON		
M H	Nevada Grass Valley	61 235
TAMEROR		
M H	Nevada Grass Valley	61 235
TAMILPO		
---	Tulara Keyesville	71 67
TAMISTA		
---	San Francisco San Francisco 4	681219
TAMLER		
Wm H*	Mendocino Big Rvr	60 844
TAMLIN		
J C	Nevada Nevada	61 320
TAMMEL		
Fields	Mendocino Little L	60 830
TAMMING		
John H	Nevada Bridgeport	61 477
TAMP		
William*	El Dorado Georgetown	58 693
TAMPKIMS		
G	Shasta Millvill	66 751
TAMPOSA		
---	Mariposa Twp 1	60 625
TAMQUI		
Agustin*	Los Angeles San Juan	59 476
Sefarnio*	Los Angeles San Juan	59 474
TAMS		
Sampson	Calaveras Twp 7	57 23
TAMTER		
Wm H*	Mendocino Big Rvr	60 844
TAMUR		
George	El Dorado Kelsey	581126

Name	County Locale	M653 RollPage
TAMUS		
John	Tuolumne Twp 1	71 241
TAMY		
Joel*	Shasta Horsetown	66 708
TAN ??CK		
Jacob*	San Francisco San Francisco 7	681352
TAN EYCK		
Jacob*	San Francisco San Francisco 7	681352
TAN		
---	Amador Twp 2	55 289
---	Amador Twp 2	55 291
---	Amador Twp 2	55 312
---	Amador Twp 5	55 338
---	Amador Twp 5	55 342
---	Amador Twp 5	55 353
---	Amador Twp 5	55 355
---	Amador Twp 3	55 398
---	Amador Twp 3	55 410
---	Amador Twp 6	55 431
---	Amador Twp 6	55 437
---	Amador Twp 1	55 479
---	Amador Twp 1	55 492
---	Calaveras Twp 8	57 101
---	Calaveras Twp 6	57 149
---	Calaveras Twp 6	57 151
---	Calaveras Twp 6	57 176
---	Calaveras Twp 5	57 236
---	Calaveras Twp 5	57 237
---	Calaveras Twp 5	57 254
---	Calaveras Twp 10	57 260
---	Calaveras Twp 10	57 267
---	Calaveras Twp 10	57 268
---	Calaveras Twp 4	57 306
---	Calaveras Twp 4	57 320
---	Calaveras Twp 4	57 324
---	Calaveras Twp 4	57 332
---	Calaveras Twp 8	57 63
---	Calaveras Twp 8	57 84
---	El Dorado White Oaks	581023
---	El Dorado Kelsey	581128
---	El Dorado Georgetown	58 678
---	El Dorado Georgetown	58 756
---	El Dorado Diamond	58 787
---	El Dorado Diamond	58 805
---	El Dorado Diamond	58 807
---	El Dorado Diamond	58 814
---	El Dorado Mud Springs	58 958
---	El Dorado Mud Springs	58 964
---	El Dorado Mud Springs	58 973
---	El Dorado Mud Springs	58 987
---	El Dorado Mud Springs	58 988
---	Nevada Grass Valley	61 227
---	Nevada Grass Valley	61 229
---	Nevada Grass Valley	61 230
---	Nevada Grass Valley	61 231
---	Nevada Grass Valley	61 232
---	Nevada Grass Valley	61 234
---	Nevada Nevada	61 305
---	Nevada Rough &	61 399
---	Nevada Rough &	61 424
---	Nevada Bridgeport	61 464
---	Sacramento Ward 1	63 53
---	Sierra Downieville	661005
---	Sierra Pine Grove	66 827
---	Sierra Downieville	66 980
---*	Nevada Washington	61 339
---*	Tuolumne Jacksonville	71 167
Chan	Nevada Grass Valley	61 232
Chi	San Francisco San Francisco 5	671207
Chow	Nevada Grass Valley	61 232
Gee	Plumas Quincy	62 948
Hae	San Francisco San Francisco 11	67 146
John	Yolo No E Twp	72 675
Kong	El Dorado Georgetown	58 680
Sing	Mariposa Twp 3	60 561
Wa	Nevada Nevada	61 300
Ya	Nevada Nevada	61 300
Yeen*	San Francisco San Francisco 11	67 144
You	Nevada Rough &	61 399
Yow	Nevada Rough &	61 399
Yup	Nevada Eureka	61 384
TANAN		
Catherine*	Calaveras Twp 4	57 344
TANASUALED		
Peabody*	Mariposa Twp 3	60 596
TANBILL		
Diego	El Dorado Greenwood	58 718
TANBLEY		
A	El Dorado Placerville	58 837
TANCOT		
Richard	Mariposa Coulterville	60 700
TANDEE		
I*	Nevada Grass Valley	61 181
TANDEN		
A	Trinity Mouth Ca	701010

Name	County Locale	M653 Roll	Page
TANDER			
I*	Nevada Grass Valley	61	181
TANDLER			
A	San Francisco San Francisco 2	67	714
TANDLOR			
A	San Francisco San Francisco 2	67	714
TANE			
---	Nevada Washington	61	339
---	Tuolumne Chinese	71	510
---	Tuolumne Twp 5	71	526
---	Tuolumne Green Springs	71	531
Charley*	Amador Twp 2	55	270
See*	Placer Todds Va	62	786
Su*	Placer Todds Va	62	786
TANEAN			
Mary	San Francisco San Francisco 2	67	585
TANELLI			
Louis G	Calaveras Twp 6	57	162
TANEQUI			
Agustin*	Los Angeles San Juan	59	476
Jose B	Los Angeles San Juan	59	474
Sefanio*	Los Angeles San Juan	59	474
TANERY			
T	Mariposa Twp 3	60	584
TANES			
Chas	Mariposa Twp 3	60	597
TANESLADO			
Jose M	Los Angeles Los Nieto	59	438
TANESON			
W T	Amador Twp 6	55	431
TANET			
Daniel*	Sierra Twp 7	66	866
TANETT			
H B	San Francisco San Francisco 5	67	546
TANEY			
Joseph	San Francisco San Francisco 9	68	978
Thos	Nevada Little Y	61	535
TANFER			
Elizabeth	San Francisco San Francisco 2	67	714
TANFIELD			
James W	Tuolumne Twp 5	71	493
TANG			
---	Amador Twp 3	55	379
---	Calaveras Twp 5	57	234
---	Calaveras Twp 5	57	247
---	Calaveras Twp 5	57	255
---	Calaveras Twp 4	57	307
---	Calaveras Twp 4	57	323
---	Calaveras Twp 4	57	338
---	Calaveras Twp 8	57	84
---	El Dorado Salmon Hills	58	1055
---	El Dorado Coloma	58	1120
---	El Dorado Georgetown	58	691
---	El Dorado Georgetown	58	692
---	El Dorado Georgetown	58	746
---	El Dorado Georgetown	58	748
---	El Dorado Placerville	58	888
---	Mariposa Twp 1	60	670
---	Nevada Grass Valley	61	229
---	Nevada Nevada	61	300
---	Nevada Nevada	61	304
---	Nevada Rough &	61	434
---	Nevada Red Dog	61	549
---	Sacramento Ward 4	63	610
---	Sacramento Ward 1	63	66
---	San Francisco San Francisco 11	67	146
---	Sierra Downieville	66	1025
---	Tuolumne Columbia	71	347
---	Tuolumne Twp 2	71	410
---	Tuolumne Twp 2	71	416
---	Tuolumne Jamestown	71	439
---	Tuolumne Jamestown	71	440
---	Tuolumne Twp 3	71	468
---	Yolo No E Twp	72	681
---	Yuba Long Bar	72	761
---	Yuba Fosters	72	836
---	Yuba Marysville	72	895
---*	Calaveras Twp 5	57	232
---*	Yuba Fosters	72	843
How	Nevada Grass Valley	61	229
Jel	Yuba Bear Rvr	72	1000
Wa	Nevada Nevada	61	304
Woah	Yuba Marysville	72	928
Yuw	Calaveras Twp 10	57	278
TANGAMITA			
Benja*	Calaveras Twp 4	57	340
TANGAMITER			
Benja*	Calaveras Twp 4	57	340
TANGARL			
John	Santa Cruz Santa Cruz	66	603
TANGERMAN			
John	San Joaquin Douglass	64	928
TANGERSON			
C	El Dorado White Oaks	58	1031
TANGHON			
---	Nevada Grass Valley	61	228
TANGO			
Laura	Yuba Marysville	72	876
TANH			
---	Tuolumne Twp 3	71	468
TANIGUI			
Sefarino*	Los Angeles San Juan	59	474
TANINGS			
Joseph*	Sutter Yuba	70	766
TANIQUI			
Sefarino*	Los Angeles San Juan	59	474
TANISIER			
Adolph	San Francisco San Francisco 10	67	318
TANK			
---	Amador Twp 5	55	342
---	Amador Twp 6	55	437
---	Yuba Long Bar	72	760
G B	Nevada Grass Valley	61	196
J*	Nevada Nevada	61	314
TANKAR			
---	Fresno Twp 2	59	102
TANKE			
---	Amador Twp 2	55	285
TANKSLY			
William	San Joaquin O'Neal	64	1006
TANN			
---	Klamath Salmon	59	213
---	Klamath Liberty	59	232
---	Yuba North Ea	72	676
Catharin	Sonoma Petaluma	69	573
James*	Marin San Rafael	60	773
TANNA			
---	Tulara Visalia	71	113
---	Tulara Visalia	71	98
C	Nevada Nevada	61	319
H	Nevada Grass Valley	61	220
Hk	Nevada Grass Valley	61	220
T	Nevada Grass Valley	61	220
TANNAHILL			
George J	Sierra Downieville	66	992
TANNCHILL			
J*	Tuolumne Garrote	71	175
TANNE			
Manuel*	Alameda Oakland	55	51
TANNEBAAM			
P	San Francisco San Francisco 10	67	266
TANNEBAUM			
P*	San Francisco San Francisco 10	67	266
TANNEHILL			
J	Tuolumne Twp 4	71	175
TANNER			
Albert	Santa Cruz Pajaro	66	558
Conrad	San Diego Agua Caliente	64	846
Cornelia	San Francisco San Francisco 6	67	445
D	Santa Clara San Jose	65	378
Edmund	Sacramento Cosumnes	63	388
F M	Amador Twp 3	55	382
George	El Dorado Kelsey	58	1126
J S	Amador Twp 4	55	131
Jacob*	Tuolumne Twp 1	71	258
Jno P	Klamath Liberty	59	239
John	Placer Secret R	62	612
John	Placer Michigan	62	853
Louis*	San Francisco San Francisco 3	67	27
Mark A	Yuba Linda	72	992
Pat	San Joaquin O'Neal	64	1005
Richard B	San Francisco San Francisco 1	68	821
Robert	Tuolumne Twp 3	71	445
Thomas	Los Angeles Los Angeles	59	316
Walter	Amador Twp 4	55	255
Walter	Amador Twp 2	55	286
Wesley	Santa Clara San Jose	65	312
Wm	Sacramento Ward 3	63	456
Wm	Solano Suisan	69	225
TANNERMAN			
Martin	Calaveras Twp 5	57	190
TANNERNAN			
Antonio*	Amador Twp 2	55	310
TANNESS			
D C	Nevada Bridgeport	61	457
TANNEYHILL			
M H	Los Angeles Elmonte	59	257
TANNIERE			
Elsinnie*	San Francisco San Francisco 3	67	2
TANNIESE			
Elsennie*	San Francisco San Francisco 3	67	2
TANNNER			
S W	Santa Clara Alviso	65	399
TANNOCK			
David*	San Francisco San Francisco 2	67	697
TANO			
---	Fresno Twp 3	59	31
TANONI			
Guitan*	Calaveras Twp 5	57	217
TANONIS			
Guitan	Calaveras Twp 5	57	217
TANOUI			
Guitan*	Calaveras Twp 5	57	217
TANPLER			
Thomas J*	Placer Auburn	62	584
TANPOSA			
---	Mariposa Twp 1	60	625
TANS			
Sains	Butte Cascade	56	700
TANSCH			
C F	San Francisco San Francisco 1	68	898
TANSEY			
A K*	Napa Napa	61	81
Bridget	Tuolumne Columbia	71	302
Patrick	Tuolumne Columbia	71	295
TANSMAN			
Henry*	Sacramento Ward 4	63	607
John*	Sacramento Ward 4	63	607
TANSON			
William*	San Francisco San Francisco 9	68	1058
TANSTUCKEN			
---*	Mendocino Big Rvr	60	853
TANSWORTH			
John F*	El Dorado Georgetown	58	759
John T*	El Dorado Georgetown	58	759
TANT			
---	Amador Twp 2	55	292
---	Sierra Downieville	66	996
---	Yuba Fosters	72	831
TANTAN			
Mathew	Santa Clara Santa Clara	65	489
TANTFAS			
Peter	Yuba Marysville	72	931
TANTIGUA			
---*	Tulara Twp 3	71	63
TANTION			
Simon	Sierra Downieville	66	1031
TANTITS			
---	Tulara Visalia	71	113
TANTO			
Joseph	Calaveras Twp 6	57	153
TANTON			
Edwd	San Francisco San Francisco 9	68	1090
TANTOON			
Mafrasio*	Mariposa Twp 3	60	558
Mapresio*	Mariposa Twp 3	60	558
Massdrio	Mariposa Twp 3	60	558
Massino*	Mariposa Twp 3	60	558
Nuafrino*	Mariposa Twp 3	60	558
Nuapano*	Mariposa Twp 3	60	558
Wuapano*	Mariposa Twp 3	60	558
TANTOTONY			
Mary*	Del Norte Crescent	58	623
TANTURUIRN			
Louis*	Calaveras Twp 10	57	296
TANTY			
S H	Nevada Grass Valley	61	222
TANY			
---	Calaveras Twp 5	57	255
---	Calaveras Twp 4	57	304
---	Calaveras Twp 4	57	307
---	Calaveras Twp 4	57	323
---	Calaveras Twp 4	57	338
---	Nevada Grass Valley	61	228
---	Nevada Grass Valley	61	229
---	Sacramento Ward 1	63	66
---	Yuba North Ea	72	681
---	Yuba Long Bar	72	760
How	Nevada Grass Valley	61	229
Hugh*	Placer Virginia	62	690
J*	Nevada Eureka	61	366
Yow	Calaveras Twp 10	57	278
TAO			
---	Trinity Mouth Ca	70	1011
---	Trinity Mouth Ca	70	1014
TAOING			
---	El Dorado Salmon Falls	58	1054
TAONG			
---	El Dorado Salmon Hills	58	1054
---	El Dorado Coloma	58	1107
TAOO			
---	Trinity Mouth Ca	70	1011
TAOS			
Ernst	Tuolumne Twp 2	71	296
TAPE			
---	Calaveras Twp 4	57	300
---	Marin Cortemad	60	787
E H*	Nevada Nevada	61	312
Geo	Sonoma Salt Point	69	693
TAPEA			
Antonio	Monterey Pajaro	60	1014
John	Calaveras Twp 10	57	283
TAPEAN			
Fred	Trinity East For	70	1025
TAPER			
---	Calaveras Twp 4	57	299

California 1860 Census Index

Name	County Locale	M653 Roll/Page
TAPETE		
Jesus	Monterey San Juan	60 998
TAPHAN		
Wm	San Francisco San Francisco 9	681077
TAPIA		
Anselino*	Los Angeles Santa Ana	59 455
Anselmo*	Los Angeles Santa Ana	59 455
Antonia	Los Angeles Los Angeles	59 308
Antonio	Los Angeles Los Angeles	59 313
Antonio	Monterey Pajaro	601014
Crindo*	San Francisco San Francisco 2	67 663
Felix	Tuolumne Knights	71 528
Francisco*	Los Angeles Los Angeles	59 337
Gertrudes	Tuolumne Big Oak	71 131
Guadalupe	Los Angeles Los Nieto	59 435
Jooseph	San Mateo Twp 2	65 115
Jose	Monterey San Juan	60 977
Jose C	Los Angeles Los Nieto	59 438
Jose M	Los Angeles Los Nieto	59 426
Jose*	Santa Cruz Soguel	66 587
Juan	Los Angeles Santa Ana	59 455
Leveado	Tuolumne Twp 1	71 225
Liviado	Tuolumne Sonora	71 225
Margarita	Los Angeles Los Nieto	59 435
Paula	Tuolumne Sonora	71 225
Ramon	Calaveras Twp 5	57 212
Ramon	Los Angeles Los Angeles	59 324
Remonda*	Santa Cruz Watsonville	66 538
Wancisco	Los Angeles Los Angeles	59 308
Wancisco*	Los Angeles Los Angeles	59 337
TAPIE		
Remonde	Santa Cruz Watsonville	66 538
Romondo	Santa Cruz Watsonville	66 538
TAPIER		
Tanato*	Calaveras Twp 4	57 308
Tancita	Calaveras Twp 4	57 308
TAPIN		
Depphine	Calaveras Twp 10	57 287
Desphine	Calaveras Twp 10	57 287
Felix	Tuolumne Twp 6	71 528
Frasdo	Calaveras Twp 4	57 314
John	Calaveras Twp 10	57 283
Ruyman	Calaveras Twp 10	57 288
Trusde*	Calaveras Twp 4	57 314
TAPING		
Bennett	Yuba Bear Rvr	721011
TAPISY		
---	Del Norte Klamath	58 656
TAPLETZ		
Lewis	San Francisco San Francisco 10	193 67
TAPLEY		
Wm	Nevada Nevada	61 324
TAPLIN		
D W	San Francisco San Francisco 5	67 552
F	Butte Chico	56 545
John O	San Francisco San Francisco 11	129 67
TAPLITZ		
Louis	San Francisco San Francisco 10	258 67
TAPOO		
---	Plumas Quincy	62 969
Law	Plumas Quincy	62 965
TAPP		
Ah	Calaveras Twp 7	57 16
TAPPAN		
F B	Sacramento Granite	63 240
Isabella*	Calaveras Twp 8	57 56
Jaems	Mendocino Calpella	60 821
TAPPESNE		
Jos	Klamath Liberty	59 230
TAPPEY		
---	Tulara Keyesville	71 55
TAPPIE		
A	Shasta French G	66 713
William	Yuba Marysville	72 962
TAPPIER		
Jaun	Mariposa Coulterville	60 699
TAPPIN		
Benjamin	San Francisco San Francisco 3	67 15
Hamdton	Tuolumne Shawsfla	71 407
Hamelton	Tuolumne Twp 2	71 407
Phineas	Tuolumne Green Springs	71 527
TAPPING		
Benjamin	Yuba Bear Rvr	721004
J	San Francisco San Francisco 10	331 67
TAPUM		
D	Amador Twp 5	55 344
TAQIER		
T H	Tuolumne Twp 1	71 276
TAQW		
---	Amador Twp 2	55 289
TAR HEAD		
---	Fresno Twp 2	59 20
TAR HEAD		
---	Tulara Twp 3	71 56
TAR		
---	Amador Twp 4	55 256
---	Amador Twp 2	55 328
---	Amador Twp 1	55 458
---	Calaveras Twp 6	57 139
---	Calaveras Twp 5	57 205
---	Calaveras Twp 5	57 214
---	Sierra Twp 5	66 944
Ah	Tehama Tehama	70 950
Lo	Tehama Tehama	70 950
TARABIE		
A L	Santa Clara San Jose	65 382
TARACCO		
Jas*	Amador Twp 3	55 384
TARALSON		
W	Siskiyou Scott Va	69 49
TARBET		
Alexander	Calaveras Twp 8	57 61
TARBLE		
D C	Placer Todds Va	62 788
TARBOLT		
James	Santa Cruz Pajaro	66 577
TARBOX		
A T	San Francisco San Francisco 9	68 955
E T	San Francisco San Francisco 5	67 481
Henry	Tulara Visalia	71 100
Saml A*	Solano Benecia	69 282
TARBUSH		
P F*	Shasta Horsetown	66 690
TARCE		
Francisco*	Monterey Monterey	60 935
Trancisco	Merced Monterey	60 935
Trancisco*	Monterey Monterey	60 935
TARCHO		
Cumtuck	Solano Benecia	69 283
TARCOVICH		
Lucha*	San Francisco San Francisco 3	67 53
Luctia*	San Francisco San Francisco 3	67 53
TARDIFS		
Wm D	San Francisco San Francisco 9	68 986
TARDISS		
Wm D	San Francisco San Francisco 9	68 986
TARDY		
H F	Siskiyou Yreka	69 183
TAREL		
Sylvester	Tuolumne Twp 5	71 526
TARER		
G*	Sacramento Brighton	63 200
TAREVAN		
Felix	Alameda Brooklyn	55 91
TAREWATER		
John	Amador Twp 4	55 254
TAREY		
James W	Mariposa Twp 3	60 586
TARFAS		
Johanna*	San Francisco San Francisco 2	67 753
TARFREY		
Wm	Sacramento Ward 1	63 147
TARGAR		
Johanna*	San Francisco San Francisco 2	67 753
TARGATE		
Urial	Shasta Cottonwoood	66 737
TARGE		
Wm	Alameda Brooklyn	55 88
TARGIS		
T	Siskiyou Scott Va	69 28
TARGISH		
Peater	Amador Twp 1	55 465
TARHEAD		
---	Tulara Keyesville	71 56
TARIK		
---	Amador Twp 5	55 356
TARIN		
Isabel*	San Francisco San Francisco 2	67 655
TARINA		
C*	Nevada Nevada	61 319
TARINAHILL		
George J*	Sierra Downieville	66 992
TARK		
---	Amador Twp 1	55 510
---	Trinity McGillev	701021
John	San Francisco San Francisco 1	68 922
TARKELSON		
C	Napa Hot Springs	61 4
TARKIE		
---	Trinity Lewiston	70 961
TARKS		
W	Nevada Eureka	61 376
TARLENTI		
Louis	Tuolumne Jamestown	71 454
TARLETON		
H T	El Dorado Georgetown	58 704
John	Calaveras Twp 5	57 238
Wm S	San Bernardino San Bernadino	64 625
TARLEY		
William	Yuba Marysville	72 854
William	Yuba Marysville	72 859
William*	Yuba Marysville	72 854
TARLGAR		
Johanna*	San Francisco San Francisco 2	67 753
TARLO		
Martinan*	Calaveras Twp 5	57 211
TARLON		
Nicholas	Yuba New York	72 730
TARLOR		
Henry	Solano Fremont	69 385
TARLTEN		
Thos S	Sacramento Natonia	63 280
TARLTIN		
G W	Colusa Monroeville	57 457
TARLTON		
Fulton	San Francisco San Francisco 9	681018
James D	Colusa Monroeville	57 142
James M	Alameda Oakland	55 74
M G	Tehama Lassen	70 884
P	Nevada Grass Valley	61 156
TARMAN		
Truman	Santa Clara Gilroy	65 238
TARN		
---*	Calaveras Twp 5	57 223
Heey	San Francisco San Francisco 5	67 508
TARNEL		
Peter*	San Francisco San Francisco 1	68 812
TARNELL		
Edward*	San Francisco San Francisco 1	68 869
TARNER		
Addison A*	Yuba Marysville	72 859
Robert	Tuolumne Jamestown	71 445
TARNTER		
Oscar*	Nevada Rough &	61 405
TARO		
Santiago	Amador Twp 1	55 495
TAROLARA		
Jas*	San Francisco San Francisco 2	67 713
TARON		
James	Mariposa Twp 3	60 568
TARP		
---	Trinity Weaverville	701052
TARPEN		
Mary J	Tuolumne Twp 1	71 215
TARPEY		
Wm	Sacramento Ward 1	63 147
TARPING		
J N	El Dorado Union	581090
TARPLEY		
H J	Trinity Mouth Ca	701016
Lindsey B	Alameda Oakland	55 5
TARPO		
Francisco	Tuolumne Columbia	71 319
TARPY		
Matthew	Monterey Pajaro	601024
TARR		
J H	Butte Hamilton	56 525
J L	Butte Ophir	56 795
Jeffers	Amador Twp 3	55 393
Joseph L	Plumas Meadow Valley	62 901
Michael	San Francisco San Francisco 5	67 477
Philip	San Joaquin Douglass	64 927
Warren	San Bernardino Santa Barbara	64 168
Warrington	Amador Twp 3	55 393
William*	El Dorado Georgetown	58 693
TARRAN		
Chas J*	San Francisco San Francisco 9	68 995
TARRANT		
Henry F	Yuba Marysville	72 865
TARRAW		
Chas J*	San Francisco San Francisco 9	68 995
TARRE		
Isaac*	Tuolumne Twp 3	71 437
TARREL		
William	Calaveras Twp 4	57 300
TARRELL		
O C	Siskiyou Scott Va	69 35
TARREN		
Louis	Amador Twp 6	55 426
TARRENSON		
Fred*	Amador Twp 2	55 325
Jno*	Amador Twp 2	55 325
TARRENTS		
Peater	Amador Twp 1	55 452
TARRETT		
H B*	San Francisco San Francisco 5	67 546
TARREY		
Joseph*	San Francisco San Francisco 9	68 978
TARRIN		
Thos*	San Francisco San Francisco 9	68 995
TARRINGTON		
B	San Francisco San Francisco 9	681065
TARRIS		
Farbey W	Tulara Twp 1	71 110

Name	County Locale	M653 Roll	Page
TARRITO			
Manel	Tuolumne Twp 3	71	459
TARRNESS			
D C*	Nevada Bridgeport	61	457
TARROL			
I A	El Dorado Placerville	58	861
TARRY			
Adam	Amador Twp 3	55	397
J*	Nevada Eureka	61	366
TARSIO			
Joseph	El Dorado Georgetown	58	696
TARSON			
Andreas	Amador Twp 1	55	468
Peter	El Dorado Mud Springs	58	966
TART			
---	Amador Twp 2	55	286
---	Amador Twp 1	55	497
---	Amador Twp 1	55	501
TARTARAN			
A	Trinity Weaverville	70	1062
TARTE			
J M	Sierra Downieville	66	1028
William	Siskiyou Yreka	69	167
TARTIN			
W J*	Solano Benecia	69	309
TARTOUT			
Etienne	Amador Twp 1	55	469
TARTT			
John A	Sacramento Ward 1	63	139
TARTWELL			
Mary*	Yuba Marysville	72	862
TARUER			
Addison A*	Yuba Marysville	72	859
TARVIS			
Catherine	Santa Clara San Jose	65	376
TARWATER			
Gabriel	Contra Costa Twp 3	57	590
Robert	Mendocino Anderson	60	868
TARWELL			
Chas*	Nevada Rough &	61	395
TARY			
---	Amador Twp 5	55	340
---	Nevada Grass Valley	61	231
Hon	Nevada Grass Valley	61	228
TAS SETH			
---	Mendocino Calpella	60	828
TAS SILL			
---	Mendocino Calpella	60	828
TASAR			
A	Amador Twp 1	55	491
TASCHER			
Elkiah	Yuba Marysville	72	934
TASCO			
Wm J	Solano Suisan	69	210
TASCOE			
E S	Nevada Grass Valley	61	193
TASE			
W H	Calaveras Twp 9	57	413
TASER			
Frank	El Dorado Greenwood	58	711
TASEY			
Louis	Calaveras Twp 4	57	340
TASGOOD			
G S W*	Yolo No E Twp	72	671
TASH			
Hiram	Yuba New York	72	740
J M	Amador Twp 7	55	419
James	El Dorado Placerville	58	931
TASHER			
---	Mariposa Twp 3	60	605
Henry*	Mariposa Twp 3	60	605
TASINER			
Robert	Calaveras Twp 10	57	282
TASK			
H	Butte Wyandotte	56	663
Harrison*	Mariposa Twp 3	60	605
TASKELL			
Benjn	Mendocino Big Rvr	60	851
TASKER			
Byron	Stanislaus Emory	70	756
Byron	Tuolumne Twp 2	71	289
C	El Dorado Placerville	58	819
W H	Nevada Bridgeport	61	441
TASKS			
Theo	Mariposa Twp 3	60	557
TASLINTO			
Louis	Tuolumne Twp 3	71	454
TASNEY			
John	San Francisco San Francisco 10	247	67
TASPER			
Mary	Tuolumne Sonora	71	215
TASPO			
Francisco	Tuolumne Twp 2	71	319
TASS			
---	Nevada Rough &	61	426

Name	County Locale	M653 Roll	Page
TASS			
John Van	San Francisco San Francisco 4	681	164
TASSA			
Bara	San Francisco San Francisco 3	67	3
Basa	San Francisco San Francisco 3	67	3
TASSAWAY			
Charles*	Nevada Rough &	61	401
TASSET			
Henry	Marin San Rafael	60	763
Jean	San Francisco San Francisco 2	67	598
TASSETE			
Jesus*	Monterey San Juan	60	998
TASSHAN			
Wm*	San Francisco San Francisco 9	681	077
TASSIE			
R	Nevada Grass Valley	61	150
TASSO			
Eugene	Calaveras Twp 5	57	138
TASSON			
A*	Nevada Nevada	61	327
TASSOU			
A*	Nevada Nevada	61	327
TASSURO			
Thomas	Calaveras Twp 6	57	174
TASSY			
Louis*	Calaveras Twp 4	57	340
TASTIE			
C W*	Nevada Nevada	61	312
TASTIN			
W J*	Solano Benecia	69	309
TASTOR			
William	Nevada Bridgeport	61	470
TASWELL			
Chas	Nevada Rough &	61	395
TAT			
---	Amador Twp 3	55	409
---	Calaveras Twp 5	57	237
---	Calaveras Twp 10	57	269
---	Calaveras Twp 10	57	284
---	Calaveras Twp 10	57	297
---	Calaveras Twp 4	57	320
---	Calaveras Twp 4	57	333
---	El Dorado Georgetown	58	682
---	El Dorado Georgetown	58	684
---	El Dorado Georgetown	58	702
---	El Dorado Mud Springs	58	977
---	Nevada Rough &	61	396
---	Placer Auburn	62	582
---	Sacramento Ward 1	63	66
---	San Francisco San Francisco 2	67	688
---	Tuolumne Jacksonville	71	516
---	Tuolumne Twp 5	71	517
Ah	Sacramento Ward 3	63	487
Mare	El Dorado Georgetown	58	700
TATAM			
---	Amador Twp 5	55	350
TATAT			
Henry*	Mariposa Twp 3	60	566
TATCHLAFF			
L	El Dorado Georgetown	58	698
TATE			
---	Tuolumne Jacksonville	71	515
---	Tuolumne Don Pedro	71	537
Alexr R	Plumas Quincy	62	924
Benj*	Tehama Red Bluff	70	915
Catharine	San Francisco San Francisco 10	245	67
D M	Klamath S Fork	59	206
Edward	Mendocino Big Rock	60	872
George	Contra Costa Twp 3	57	612
George*	Calaveras Twp 4	57	342
H	San Francisco San Francisco 9	681	059
J D	Sacramento Ward 1	63	8
Jadge R*	Siskiyou Yreka	69	126
James	Sonoma Bodega	69	521
Jefferson	Colusa Muion	57	462
John	Los Angeles Azuza	59	271
John	Tulara Twp 2	71	3
Judge R	Siskiyou Yreka	69	126
L R	Nevada Rough &	61	397
Marcus	Calaveras Twp 4	57	302
Moses	Marin Cortemad	60	786
Narcus	Calaveras Twp 4	57	302
Roberson*	Tuolumne Twp 6	71	538
Saml E	Plumas Quincy	62	924
Thomas	Santa Cruz Pajaro	66	526
W	Sacramento Granite	63	229
W W	Sacramento Ward 1	63	63
TATER			
George	Mariposa Coulterville	60	688
W G	Trinity Red Bar	70	998
TATERBURGER			
Geo*	Butte Kimshaw	56	590
TATERELL			
Antony	Plumas Quincy	62	962
TATHAM			
J	Butte Kimshaw	56	600

Name	County Locale	M653 Roll	Page
TATHAM			
Jno	Butte Chico	56	555
Jno	Butte Chico	56	567
Jno	Butte Kimshaw	56	603
Jno*	Butte Chico	56	555
TATHEM			
Jno	Butte Chico	56	567
TATMAN			
Andrew	Sacramento Franklin	63	313
Lezzie	Tuolumne Visalia	71	93
Lizzie	Tulara Twp 1	71	93
Mary A	Sacramento Cosummes	63	385
TATPIN			
Phineas	Tuolumne Twp 5	71	527
TATSON			
J H	Calaveras Twp 9	57	407
TATT			
E M	Sierra Downieville	66	1011
TATTE			
William	El Dorado Placerville	58	898
TATTEN			
A W	Mariposa Twp 3	60	562
T	Siskiyou Scott Va	69	33
TATTERSON			
Jacob	Santa Clara San Jose	65	295
TATTLE			
Hiram S	Santa Cruz Santa Cruz	66	611
TATTMAN			
G W	San Francisco San Francisco 10	274	67
TATTON			
T	Siskiyou Scott Va	69	33
TATUM			
Silas	Placer Virginia	62	683
Wm	Tehama Antelope	70	888
TAU			
---	Amador Twp 5	55	338
---	Calaveras Twp 5	57	236
---	Calaveras Twp 10	57	267
---	Calaveras Twp 10	57	268
---	Nevada Grass Valley	61	232
E M	Nevada Nevada	61	296
Ya	Nevada Nevada	61	300
Yeen*	San Francisco San Francisco 11	144	67
TAUBERT			
F A	Tuolumne Sonora	71	201
TAUBROCK			
John	Amador Twp 6	55	429
TAUDER			
I*	Nevada Grass Valley	61	181
TAUFER			
John	San Joaquin Stockton	64	1025
TAUFFE			
Geo O	Alameda Oakland	55	36
TAUFIELD			
Archer	Calaveras Twp 6	57	167
TAUGARL			
John*	Santa Cruz Santa Cruz	66	603
TAUGHEA			
Talmento	Amador Twp 5	55	332
TAUGHNAN			
John M	Tuolumne Twp 1	71	217
TAUHEART			
John	Los Angeles Los Angeles	59	517
TAUK			
J*	Nevada Nevada	61	314
TAULE			
Wm	Sacramento Ward 3	63	480
TAULHALDER			
Antonio	San Francisco San Francisco 8	681	276
TAUN			
---	Calaveras Twp 5	57	223
---	El Dorado Mud Springs	58	978
TAUNEBAAM			
P*	San Francisco San Francisco 10	266	67
TAUNEBAUM			
P*	San Francisco San Francisco 10	266	67
TAUNTAIN			
Thomas	Tuolumne Twp 1	71	247
TAUNTON			
W C	Amador Twp 1	55	470
TAUP			
Her	San Francisco San Francisco 10	356	67
TAUR			
---*	Calaveras Twp 10	57	299
TAUSIP			
Wm*	Amador Twp 6	55	443
TAUSMAN			
Henry*	Sacramento Ward 4	63	607
John*	Sacramento Ward 4	63	607
TAUSON			
William*	San Francisco San Francisco 9	681	058

California 1860 Census Index

Name	County Locale	M653 Roll	Page
TAUT			
---	Amador Twp 2	55	326
---*	Yuba Foster B	72	831
TAUTFAS			
Jacob*	Santa Clara Alviso	65	405
TAUTOON			
Mafredio*	Mariposa Twp 3	60	558
TAVANIAS			
Marcial	Los Angeles Los Angeles	59	348
TAVARRA			
Angel	Contra Costa Twp 1	57	488
TAVARSORD			
Antonio*	Tuolumne Big Oak	71	140
TAVED			
Jonatio	Fresno Twp 1	59	75
TAVER			
G*	Sacramento Brighton	63	200
TAVERNETTI			
B	El Dorado Diamond	58	798
TAVERS			
A R	Nevada Grass Valley	61	147
TAVERSY			
Julias	Nevada Little Y	61	533
TAVERY			
T	Mariposa Twp 3	60	584
TAVES			
Chas*	Mariposa Twp 3	60	597
TAVIN			
Isabel*	San Francisco San Francisco 2	67	655
TAW			
---	Amador Twp 2	55	285
---	Amador Twp 2	55	286
---	Amador Twp 2	55	289
---	Amador Twp 2	55	292
---	Amador Twp 2	55	327
---	Amador Twp 2	55	328
---	Amador Twp 6	55	428
---	Amador Twp 6	55	431
---	Calaveras Twp 5	57	239
---	Calaveras Twp 5	57	254
---	Calaveras Twp 10	57	285
---	Calaveras Twp 4	57	299
---	Calaveras Twp 4	57	306
---	El Dorado White Oaks	58	1023
---	El Dorado White Oaks	58	1033
---	El Dorado Coloma	58	1077
---	El Dorado Coloma	58	1105
---	El Dorado Kelsey	58	1131
---	Nevada Bridgeport	61	492
---	Nevada Bloomfield	61	521
---	Tuolumne Twp 4	71	416
---	Tuolumne Jamestown	71	440
---	Tuolumne Twp 3	71	468
---	Tuolumne Twp 1	71	475
---	Tuolumne Twp 5	71	521
---	Yuba North Ea	72	680
Ah*	Sacramento Cosumnes	63	382
E M	Nevada Nevada	61	296
Haw	Amador Twp 2	55	291
TAWAGATE			
T J	Butte Ophir	56	775
TAWAN			
---	Tehama Tehama	70	944
TAWATER			
David	Sacramento Ward 1	63	55
TAWEY			
---	El Dorado Coloma	58	1086
TAWLE			
Robt H	Tuolumne Twp 2	71	357
TAWN			
---	Calaveras Twp 10	57	272
Mau	Siskiyou Yreka	69	194
TAWNE			
Manuel*	Alameda Oakland	55	51
TAWNS			
J J	Tuolumne Twp 1	71	482
TAXILA			
---*	Los Angeles Los Angeles	59	495
TAY			
---	Amador Twp 2	55	292
---	Amador Twp 2	55	318
---	Amador Twp 2	55	320
---	Amador Twp 2	55	327
---	Amador Twp 5	55	340
---	Amador Twp 5	55	342
---	Amador Twp 5	55	349
---	Amador Twp 5	55	353
---	Amador Twp 5	55	354
---	Amador Twp 5	55	355
---	Amador Twp 5	55	356
---	Amador Twp 5	55	360
---	Amador Twp 3	55	402
---	Amador Twp 6	55	428
---	Amador Twp 1	55	502
---	Amador Twp 1	55	510
---	Butte Kimshaw	56	589
TAY			
---	Butte Kimshaw	56	604
---	Calaveras Twp 5	57	237
---	Calaveras Twp 10	57	272
---	Calaveras Twp 10	57	285
---	Calaveras Twp 10	57	297
---	Calaveras Twp 8	57	68
---	El Dorado Coloma	58	1078
---	El Dorado Mud Springs	58	962
---	Nevada Grass Valley	61	228
---	Nevada Grass Valley	61	229
---	Nevada Grass Valley	61	230
---	Nevada Grass Valley	61	232
---	Nevada Rough &	61	435
---	Nevada Bridgeport	61	459
---	Nevada Bridgeport	61	463
---	Nevada Bridgeport	61	493
---	Sacramento Granite	63	259
---	San Joaquin Stockton	64	1096
---	Shasta French G	66	712
---	Sierra Downieville	66	1027
---	Siskiyou Yreka	69	194
---	Tuolumne Twp 3	71	457
---	Yolo No E Twp	72	680
---*	El Dorado Union	58	1089
---*	Nevada Bloomfield	61	522
---*	Sacramento Granite	63	245
D	Tuolumne Twp 4	71	146
E A*	Amador Twp 2	55	288
Fah	El Dorado Big Bar	58	740
Fan	Amador Twp 2	55	292
Geo	San Francisco San Francisco 10	67	329
George	Tulara Visalia	71	32
Jesse	Yolo Slate Ra	72	717
John	San Francisco San Francisco 5	67	549
Michael	San Francisco San Francisco 10	67	204
Walter	Sierra Morristown	66	1051
TAYASON			
Mary A	San Francisco San Francisco 10	67	181
TAYATE			
Urial	Shasta Cottonwoood	66	737
TAYEN			
John*	El Dorado Georgetown	58	685
TAYER			
John*	El Dorado Georgetown	58	685
TAYERS			
Camuel*	Tuolumne Twp 5	71	522
TAYETT			
Sarah	Placer Iona Hills	62	895
TAYGORT			
T G	Shasta Horsetown	66	711
TAYLAR			
C W*	Shasta Shasta	66	682
TAYLE			
---*	Mendocino Twp 1	60	891
TAYLER			
---*	Mendocino Twp 1	60	891
Albert E	Alameda Brooklyn	55	185
Augustus C	San Francisco San Francisco 3	67	4
C H	Sacramento Granite	63	252
C W	Shasta Shasta	66	682
Danl	San Francisco San Francisco 10	67	315
G W	Solano Vacaville	69	325
Geo	El Dorado White Oaks	58	1016
Geo L	San Francisco San Francisco 10	67	316
George*	Alameda Oakland	55	3
H	Sacramento Ward 4	63	512
H D	San Francisco San Francisco 10	67	202
Henry*	Napa Clear Lake	61	133
John	Sacramento Granite	63	251
John D	Siskiyou Yreka	69	133
John S	Siskiyou Yreka	69	148
John*	Alameda Oakland	55	2
M	San Mateo Twp 3	65	88
Margaret*	Fresno Twp 1	59	33
Matthew	Siskiyou Yreka	69	149
O R*	Butte Ophir	56	750
S H	Colusa Grand Island	57	469
Samuel	Siskiyou Yreka	69	148
Scott	El Dorado Big Bar	58	742
Thos	Amador Twp 2	55	324
William B*	Fresno Twp 1	59	33
Wm	Nevada Nevada	61	259
Wm	Sacramento Granite	63	248
TAYLERR			
John	Placer Iona Hills	62	897
TAYLOR			
---	San Francisco San Francisco 9	68	1020
---	Siskiyou Callahan	69	15
TAYLOR			
A	Amador Twp 3	55	372
A	Butte Chico	56	536
A	Butte Bidwell	56	722
A	Butte Ophir	56	783
A	El Dorado Mud Springs	58	1000
A	Mariposa Twp 3	60	567
A	Nevada Nevada	61	272
A	San Mateo Twp 3	65	101
A	Siskiyou Callahan	69	15
A	Sonoma Santa Rosa	69	402
A	Sonoma Cloverdale	69	682
A	Tuolumne Sonora	71	210
A A	Trinity Douglas	70	980
A C	Shasta Shasta	66	678
A E	Nevada Bridgeport	61	496
A M	El Dorado Kelsey	58	1149
A T	El Dorado Placerville	58	848
A W	Marin San Rafael	60	772
Agnes H	San Francisco San Francisco 4	68	1113
Albert	San Francisco San Francisco 5	67	479
Alex	San Francisco San Francisco 10	67	202
Alex	San Francisco San Francisco 5	67	480
Alexander	Monterey Monterey	60	927
Alexander	Santa Cruz Pajaro	66	560
Alexr	San Francisco San Francisco 10	67	202
Alfeed	San Joaquin Stockton	64	1017
Alfred	Placer Forest H	62	797
Allen	Calaveras Twp 9	57	350
Amanda	Santa Clara Santa Clara	65	465
Ambrose	Los Angeles San Gabriel	59	415
Ames*	Sacramento Natonia	63	274
Amos	Sacramento Natonia	63	274
Amos	Santa Cruz Pajaro	66	561
Andrew	Butte Chico	56	355
Andrew	Santa Clara San Jose	65	355
Andrew J	San Joaquin O'Neal	64	1002
Ann	Amador Twp 2	55	301
Ann	Butte Chico	56	547
Ann	Santa Clara San Jose	65	359
Anos*	Sacramento Natonia	63	274
Anson	San Joaquin Elkhorn	64	971
Archibald	Amador Twp 4	55	236
Asa	Trinity Oregon G	70	1009
Asher S	Sacramento Ward 3	63	427
August C	San Francisco San Francisco 3	67	4
Augustus	San Francisco San Francisco 3	67	4
B E	Napa Yount	61	48
Bardin	Tulara Visalia	71	106
Benj	Sonoma Armally	69	483
Benj F	San Bernardino San Bernardino	64	619
Benjamin	Contra Costa Twp 3	57	597
Biras	Nevada Rough &	61	421
Boone	Yuba Rose Bar	72	802
C	El Dorado Diamond	58	810
C	Sacramento Ward 1	63	86
C D	Sacramento Ward 4	63	528
C F	El Dorado Mountain	58	1184
C H	Sacramento Granite	63	252
C J	Yolo Washington	72	565
C L	San Francisco San Francisco 6	67	459
C N	Siskiyou Scott Va	69	41
C W	Mariposa Twp 1	60	635
C W	San Francisco San Francisco 10	67	236
C W	Yuba Parks Ba	72	774
Calvin	San Francisco San Francisco 7	68	1337
Catherine	Butte Hamilton	56	520
Charles	Los Angeles Los Angeles	59	329
Charles	Nevada Rough &	61	433
Charles E	Yolo Washington	72	561
Chas	Sacramento Lee	63	212
Chas	San Francisco San Francisco 9	68	1065
Chas	San Francisco San Francisco 9	68	1071
Chas	Sonoma Petaluma	69	566
Chas	Trinity Big Flat	70	1040
Chas C	Mendocino Ukiah	60	793
Chas F Jr	San Francisco San Francisco 1	68	931
Chas R	Sacramento Ward 1	63	116
Clark	Butte Kimshaw	56	587
Clavin	Santa Clara San Jose	65	384
Clay	Nevada Nevada	61	252
D	El Dorado Diamond	58	764
D	El Dorado Diamond	58	775
D	Los Angeles Tejon	59	522
D	Placer Illinois	62	705
D F	Siskiyou Scott Va	69	37
D G	Trinity Hay Fork	70	992
Daniel	Marin San Rafael	60	758
Daniel	Solano Suisan	69	224
Daniel	Tuolumne Twp 2	71	282
Danl	Nevada Rough &	61	405

California 1860 Census Index

Name	County Locale	Roll	Page
TAYLOR			
Danl	San Francisco San Francisco 10	67	315
David	Klamath Klamath	59	224
David	Nevada Rough &	61	405
David	Sacramento Brighton	63	197
David	Sacramento Ward 4	63	524
David	Sonoma Armally	69	484
David	Trinity Weaverville	70	1056
Dry	Monterey Pajaro	60	1020
Dyer T	Sonoma Mendocino	69	453
Dzer L	Sonoma Mendocino	69	453
E	Nevada Washington	61	337
E	Nevada Eureka	61	394
E	Sacramento Ward 1	63	86
E	San Bernardino San Bernadino	64	635
E A	San Francisco San Francisco 3	67	76
E C	Yolo Washington	72	561
E F	El Dorado Casumnes	58	1165
E H	Yolo Slate Ra	72	697
E H	Yuba Slate Ro	72	697
E L	Butte Kimshaw	56	599
E M	Sacramento Lee	63	212
E N	San Mateo Twp 1	65	64
E O	Calaveras Twp 9	57	397
E T	Sacramento Ward 1	63	101
E W	San Francisco San Francisco 2	67	804
E W	Sonoma Bodega	69	537
Edmond G	Butte Ophir	56	782
Edward	Siskiyou Yreka	69	153
Edward	Siskiyou Yreka	69	155
Edward	Tulara Twp 1	71	90
Edward	Tuolumne Twp 3	71	445
Edward*	San Francisco San Francisco 4	68	1116
Edward*	Tulara Visalia	71	90
Edwd	Butte Hamilton	56	520
Edwin*	Calaveras Twp 6	57	155
Eliza	Yolo Washington	72	565
Ellen	San Francisco San Francisco 6	67	460
Ellen	San Francisco San Francisco 1	68	931
F A	San Joaquin Stockton	64	1086
F B	Calaveras Twp 9	57	411
F F	Sacramento Ward 3	63	431
Floyd D	Yuba Rose Bar	72	812
Frances	Sonoma Mendocino	69	456
Francis	San Francisco San Francisco 10	67	321
Francis	Sonoma Mendocino	69	456
Frank	Marin Cortemad	60	780
Frank	Placer Todds Va	62	785
Frank	Sierra Twp 7	66	878
Frederick	Calaveras Twp 8	57	96
Frederick	San Francisco San Francisco 7	68	1326
G	Sacramento Ward 1	63	19
G	Sierra Pine Grove	66	826
G	Sutter Sutter	70	816
G	Yuba Rose Bar	72	802
G F	Tuolumne Twp 4	71	170
G M	Placer Iona Hills	62	874
G T	Tuolumne Jacksonville	71	170
G W	Solano Suisan	69	238
Geo	Klamath Trinidad	59	221
Geo	Nevada Nevada	61	243
Geo	Sacramento Lee	63	214
Geo	San Francisco San Francisco 10	67	236
Geo	San Francisco San Francisco 2	67	638
Geo	Trinity Lewiston	70	953
Geo D	Placer Folsom	62	641
Geo L	San Francisco San Francisco 10	67	316
Geo W	Plumas Meadow Valley	62	904
Geoge*	El Dorado Georgetown	58	689
George	Calaveras Twp 9	57	367
George	El Dorado Georgetown	58	678
George	El Dorado Georgetown	58	689
George	Marin Cortemad	60	783
George	Monterey Monterey	60	960
George	San Diego Agua Caliente	64	814
George	San Francisco San Francisco 7	68	1370
George	San Francisco San Francisco 6	67	456
George	Shasta Shasta	66	759
George	Sierra Twp 5	66	935
George	Yuba Marysville	72	978
George B	Yuba Marysville	72	858
George B	Yuba Marysville	72	859
George T	San Francisco San Francisco 7	68	1340
George W	Sierra Pine Grove	66	820
George*	Alameda Oakland	55	3
George*	El Dorado Georgetown	58	689
Gilbert	San Francisco San Francisco 9	68	991
Godfrey	Yuba Marysville	72	941
Grennburg B	San Luis Obispo San Luis Obispo	65	8
H	Amador Twp 6	55	428
H	Butte Cascade	56	692
H	Butte Cascade	56	694
H	El Dorado Diamond	58	774
H	Sacramento Lee	63	214
H	Sacramento Ward 1	63	4
H	San Joaquin Stockton	64	1095
H	Solano Vacaville	69	321
H	Yolo Cottonwood	72	656
H B	El Dorado White Oaks	58	1009
H B	El Dorado Kelsey	58	1155
H B	Nevada Bloomfield	61	515
H B	Santa Clara San Jose	65	282
H D	San Francisco San Francisco 10	67	202
H F	Tuolumne Twp 2	71	288
H M	Nevada Eureka	61	351
H P	Sacramento Ward 1	63	137
H T	Klamath Liberty	59	235
H*	Yolo Cottonwood	72	656
Hall	Shasta Shasta	66	659
Harriet P	Tuolumne Twp 2	71	284
Harry	Butte Ophir	56	786
Harvey	Placer Michigan	62	853
Henry	Butte Ophir	56	823
Henry	Napa Clear Lake	61	133
Henry	Sacramento Ward 1	63	15
Henry	Santa Clara Redwood	65	461
Henry	Siskiyou Cottonwood	69	100
Henry	Trinity Lewiston	70	964
Henry	Tulara Visalia	71	18
Henry	Tuolumne Big Oak	71	129
Henry M	Sonoma Santa Rosa	69	420
Henry S	Yuba Marysville	72	967
Henry*	Napa Clear Lake	61	133
Hiram	Colusa Spring Valley	57	435
Horace	Amador Twp 6	55	424
Hugh	El Dorado Kelsey	58	1150
I	San Mateo Twp 3	65	106
I C	Nevada Nevada	61	319
I T	Sacramento Ward 1	63	101
I*	El Dorado Kelsey	58	1154
Ira	San Joaquin Castoria	64	875
Isabel	Santa Clara Alviso	65	415
Isaiah	Yuba Marysville	72	962
J	Butte Oro	56	680
J	Calaveras Twp 9	57	400
J	El Dorado Kelsey	58	1154
J	Nevada Grass Valley	61	219
J	Nevada Eureka	61	380
J	Sacramento Lee	63	213
J	San Joaquin Stockton	64	1086
J	Sutter Butte	70	796
J A	Calaveras Twp 9	57	399
J B	Nevada Eureka	61	378
J B	Placer Virginia	62	682
J B	Placer Christia	62	736
J B	Sacramento Brighton	63	197
J B	Sonoma Cloverdale	69	682
J C	Nevada Nevada	61	243
J C	Nevada Nevada	61	319
J C	Yolo Washington	72	603
J D	Sierra Twp 7	66	905
J E	Siskiyou Scott Va	69	32
J F	Nevada Bridgeport	61	454
J H	Siskiyou Klamath	69	79
J L	Marin Tomales	60	717
J L	Siskiyou Klamath	69	89
J N	Yuba Rose Bar	72	810
J P L	Tuolumne Twp 1	71	479
J R	Nevada Eureka	61	394
J S	Trinity Minersville	70	969
J W	Santa Clara Gilroy	65	239
J W	Yolo Cache Crk	72	621
J*	El Dorado Kelsey	58	1154
Jackson	Santa Clara San Jose	65	344
James	Alameda Brooklyn	55	126
James	Amador Twp 4	55	252
James	Calaveras Twp 4	57	344
James	El Dorado Casumnes	58	1162
James	Marin Point Re	60	730
James	Marin Cortemad	60	787
James	Mariposa Twp 3	60	600
James	Mendocino Calpella	60	818
James	Monterey S Antoni	60	973
James	Plumas Quincy	62	988
James	San Francisco San Francisco 9	68	1034
James	San Francisco San Francisco 4	68	1229
James	San Francisco San Francisco 3	67	56
James	San Francisco San Francisco 9	68	978
James	San Joaquin O'Neal	64	1004
James	San Joaquin Oneal	64	932
James	San Joaquin Elkhorn	64	975
James	Santa Clara Fremont	65	426
James	Santa Clara Redwood	65	454
James	Santa Cruz Pescadero	66	645
James	Sierra Port Win	66	791
James	Trinity Soldiers	70	1005
James	Tuolumne Columbia	71	290
James H	Marin Cortemad	60	791
James S	San Francisco San Francisco 8	68	1321
Jane	Napa Napa	61	104
Jane	San Francisco San Francisco 4	68	1143
Jane	San Francisco San Francisco 8	68	1261
Jas	Butte Chico	56	559
Jas	Butte Cascade	56	695
Jas	San Joaquin Elkhorn	64	990
Jas	Sonoma Vallejo	69	623
Jas	Yolo Washington	72	572
Jas	Yolo Merritt	72	578
Jas B	Amador Twp 2	55	264
Jas G	Sacramento Ward 4	63	499
Jas M	Placer Secret R	62	611
Jas M	San Francisco San Francisco 9	68	1044
Jerry	San Mateo Twp 3	65	90
Jno	Sacramento Ward 4	63	520
Jno F	Amador Twp 6	55	424
Jno F	San Francisco San Francisco 9	68	1048
Job T	Plumas Quincy	62	978
John	Alameda Brooklyn	55	209
John	Alameda Oakland	55	2
John	Alameda Brooklyn	55	88
John	Amador Twp 3	55	374
John	Butte Ophir	56	799
John	Contra Costa Twp 1	57	536
John	Contra Costa Twp 2	57	546
John	El Dorado Kelsey	58	1152
John	El Dorado Placerville	58	903
John	Humbolt Bucksport	59	161
John	Nevada Rough &	61	416
John	Placer Iona Hills	62	890
John	Sacramento Centre	63	179
John	Sacramento Granite	63	251
John	Sacramento Sutter	63	295
John	Sacramento Ward 1	63	40
John	Sacramento Ward 1	63	86
John	San Francisco San Francisco 3	67	75
John	San Francisco San Francisco 2	67	793
John	San Mateo Twp 3	65	109
John	San Mateo Twp 1	65	54
John	San Mateo Twp 3	65	78
John	Santa Clara Burnett	65	255
John	Santa Clara Santa Clara	65	472
John	Shasta Millvill	66	756
John	Sierra Twp 7	66	911
John	Siskiyou Callahan	69	5
John	Solano Suisan	69	226
John	Solano Suisan	69	232
John	Trinity Lewiston	70	957
John	Tuolumne Chinese	71	522
John	Yolo Putah	72	585
John	Yolo Putah	72	587
John	Yuba Marysville	72	950
John B	San Francisco San Francisco 9	68	1002
John D	Siskiyou Yreka	69	133
John K	San Francisco San Francisco 4	68	1227
John M	Sierra Twp 5	66	938
John O	Siskiyou Yreka	69	190
John R	San Francisco San Francisco 4	68	1227
John S	Siskiyou Yreka	69	148
John*	Alameda Oakland	55	2
Jos	Butte Mountain	56	733
Jos H	Alameda Brooklyn	55	127
Jos W	Sacramento Ward 1	63	8
Joseph	El Dorado Salmon Falls	58	1037
Joseph	Placer Michigan	62	814
Joseph	San Francisco San Francisco 2	67	590
Joseph	Sierra Pine Grove	66	832
Joseph P	Contra Costa Twp 2	57	561
Joseph W	Yuba Rose Bar	72	811
Josephina	Santa Clara San Jose	65	328
Josph P	Sonoma Healdsbu	69	474
Julia A	Sacramento Ward 1	63	101
Kinney	Colusa Monroeville	57	457
L	Nevada Grass Valley	61	147
L D	Alameda Oakland	55	9
L H	Sacramento Cosumnes	63	389
L K	Santa Clara Gilroy	65	249
L S	Sacramento Ward 4	63	564
L W	Nevada Grass Valley	61	235
Latricia	Butte Ophir	56	778
Lemuel R	San Joaquin Douglass	64	916
Levi	Siskiyou Scott Va	69	52
Levi W	Yuba Marysville	72	859
Levi W	Yuba Marysville	72	860
Llewis	Santa Clara Fremont	65	426
Lucretia	Sacramento Ward 4	63	559
Luther	Sonoma Petaluma	69	576
M	El Dorado Greenwood	58	723
M	El Dorado Placerville	58	839
M	Nevada Grass Valley	61	147
M	Nevada Nevada	61	245

California 1860 Census Index

Name	County Locale	M653 Roll	Page
TAYLOR			
M	Nevada Nevada	61	294
M	San Francisco San Francisco 1	68	921
M	San Francisco San Francisco 1	68	922
M	Siskiyou Scott Va	69	53
M	Yuba Fosters	72	828
M P	El Dorado White Oaks	58	1026
M P	Sacramento Ward 1	63	111
Magar	Nevada Bridgeport	61	453
Majar*	Nevada Bridgeport	61	453
Malilda*	San Francisco San Francisco 2	67	803
Mannum	Humbolt Eel Rvr	59	150
Margaret	San Francisco San Francisco 6	67	474
Margaret*	Fresno Twp 1	59	33
Margarett	Yolo Cottonwood	72	649
Marion	Los Angeles Elmonte	59	252
Martin	Placer Michigan	62	852
Martin	San Bernardino San Bernadino	64	616
Mary	Amador Twp 5	55	358
Mary	Sacramento Lee	63	211
Mary	San Francisco San Francisco 3	67	13
Mary	San Francisco San Francisco 2	67	779
Mary	San Francisco San Francisco 9	68	945
Mary	Tuolumne Twp 4	71	170
Mary J	San Francisco San Francisco 8	68	1302
Mary J	San Francisco San Francisco 2	67	779
Matilda	San Francisco San Francisco 2	67	803
Matthew	Siskiyou Yreka	69	149
Milo	Klamath Klamath	59	226
Monroe	Del Norte Crescent	58	626
N	Santa Clara Fremont	65	421
N S R	Siskiyou Yreka	69	176
Nath	Klamath S Fork	59	199
Nathl	Los Angeles Tejon To	59	535
Nellie	San Joaquin Stockton	64	1022
Nelson	Monterey Monterey	60	927
Nelson	Santa Cruz Santa Cruz	66	601
Newton	Tuolumne Twp 1	71	270
O	Butte Oro	56	685
O	El Dorado Cold Spring	58	1101
O F	El Dorado Mountain	58	1184
O M	El Dorado Placerville	58	885
O R	Butte Ophir	56	750
O*	El Dorado Cold Spring	58	1101
Obediah Jr	San Francisco San Francisco 3	67	24
Oliver H	San Francisco San Francisco 7	68	1325
Oscar	San Francisco San Francisco 9	68	1071
Over*	Calaveras Twp 8	57	72
Ovir E*	Calaveras Twp 8	57	72
P W	Sacramento Ward 3	63	425
Pascheil*	Plumas Quincy	62	985
Peter	Sonoma Bodega	69	530
Philip	Solano Fremont	69	382
Putnam	Sonoma Russian	69	431
R	Tuolumne Twp 4	71	167
R B	Monterey San Juan	60	1007
R J	El Dorado Placerville	58	887
R L	San Francisco San Francisco 3	67	76
R T	Nevada Grass Valley	61	235
Richard	El Dorado Salmon Falls	58	1038
Richard	San Francisco San Francisco 11	67	148
Richd	Santa Clara Gilroy	65	229
Riley	Santa Cruz Pajaro	66	560
Robert	Alameda Brooklyn	55	187
Robert	Plumas Quincy	62	945
Robert	Sierra Downieville	66	1028
Robet	Plumas Quincy	62	944
Robt	Butte Cascade	56	698
Robt	Klamath Liberty	59	240
Robt	Sacramento Ward 1	63	95
Robt H	Sierra Downieville	66	967
Rosmon	Tulara Visalia	71	30
S	Mariposa Twp 3	60	567
S	San Bernardino San Bernadino	64	635
S	Sutter Bear Rvr	70	820
S F	Solano Suisan	69	206
S H	Los Angeles Tejon To	59	535
S N	Mendocino Ukiah	60	793
S P	El Dorado Indian D	58	1157
S P	Santa Clara Fremont	65	425
S W	Alameda Oakland	55	10
S W	Solano Montezuma	69	374
Sacio	Contra Costa Twp 2	57	575
Sam	El Dorado Georgetown	58	673
Saml	Santa Clara San Jose	65	363
Saml	Tuolumne Columbia	71	313
Saml P	San Francisco San Francisco 1	68	876
Samuel	Nevada Bloomfield	61	523
Samuel	Placer Forest H	62	797
Samuel	Sierra Twp 5	66	925
Samuel	Siskiyou Yreka	69	148
Samuel H	Los Angeles Tejon	59	522
Samuel*	Sierra Twp 5	66	925
Sanford	Alameda Brooklyn	55	153
TAYLOR			
Sarah	Sonoma Armally	69	494
Sarah A	San Francisco San Francisco 10	67	271
Seth	Tuolumne Twp 2	71	395
Seth E	Tuolumne Twp 2	71	384
Silas	Sacramento Lee	63	212
Simon	Placer Virginia	62	673
Simon	Sonoma Petaluma	69	562
Simon	Stanislaus Buena Village	70	723
Simon	Tulara Visalia	71	73
Solomon M	Tuolumne Twp 1	71	205
Sophia	San Francisco San Francisco 6	67	447
Steward	San Francisco San Francisco 7	68	1403
Susan	Sacramento Ward 3	63	456
T	El Dorado Placerville	58	879
T	Nevada Grass Valley	61	195
T	Sutter Bear Rvr	70	824
T B	Calaveras Twp 9	57	407
T D	Yolo Washington	72	601
T E	Tuolumne Columbia	71	318
T George	Santa Cruz Watsonville	66	535
T H	Nevada Nevada	61	329
Tabitha	San Francisco San Francisco 8	68	1282
Tabitha N	San Francisco San Francisco 8	68	1282
Terry	Santa Clara Gilroy	65	232
Thom	El Dorado Georgetown	58	707
Thoma	San Francisco San Francisco 6	67	436
Thomas	Amador Twp 4	55	250
Thomas	Los Angeles Los Angeles	59	378
Thomas	Los Angeles Tejon	59	525
Thomas	Sacramento Centre	63	179
Thomas	San Francisco San Francisco 4	68	1134
Thomas	San Francisco San Francisco 6	67	436
Thomas	Sierra La Porte	66	768
Thomas	Tulara Visalia	71	100
Thomas	Tulara Visalia	71	14
Thomas	Yuba Marysville	72	867
Thomas J	Yuba Marysville	72	847
Thomas W	Sierra Morristown	66	1054
Thornton	El Dorado Mud Springs	58	949
Thos	Amador Twp 2	55	324
Thos	Butte Kimshaw	56	576
Thos	Sacramento Centre	63	178
Thos	San Francisco San Francisco 2	67	624
Thos	Yolo Washington	72	573
Thos L	Sacramento Ward 4	63	495
Tom	Plumas Quincy	62	970
Truman	Nevada Bloomfield	61	509
W	Merced Twp 1	60	910
W	Nevada Nevada	61	320
W	Sacramento Cosumnes	63	405
W	San Francisco San Francisco 5	67	488
W	San Francisco San Francisco 5	67	547
W	Sierra La Porte	66	781
W	Sonoma Bodega	69	527
W	Yolo Putah	72	551
W A	Marin San Rafael	60	765
W A	Sacramento Ward 1	63	112
W B	Sierra Twp 7	66	872
W C	Sacramento Ward 1	63	101
W E	Napa Hot Springs	61	6
W H	El Dorado Coloma	58	1070
W H	El Dorado Kelsey	58	1153
W H	Sacramento Lee	63	214
W H	San Francisco San Francisco 10	67	308
W M	Nevada Washington	61	336
W R	Butte Eureka	56	647
W S R	Siskiyou Yreka	69	176
W V	Nevada Nevada	61	320
W*	San Francisco San Francisco 10	67	308
Warren G	Placer Ophirville	62	653
Welt	El Dorado Georgetown	58	685
Wesley	Tuolumne Twp 1	71	191
West	El Dorado Georgetown	58	685
Wiliam	Placer Todds Va	62	784
William	El Dorado Grizzly	58	1179
William	Napa Clear Lake	61	136
William	Napa Hot Springs	61	9
William	Nevada Rough &	61	414
William	Nevada Bridgeport	61	484
William	Placer Forest H	62	797
William	Placer Michigan	62	856
William	Plumas Meadow Valley	62	930
William	Plumas Quincy	62	976
William	San Francisco San Francisco 7	68	1426
William	San Joaquin Elkhorn	64	985
William	Siskiyou Yreka	69	167
William	Siskiyou Yreka	69	194
William B*	Fresno Twp 1	59	33
William Bz*	Tuolumne Twp 6	71	534
William H	Solano Fremont	69	376
Wm	Alameda Brooklyn	55	138
Wm	Alameda Brooklyn	55	200
TAYLOR			
Wm	Butte Bidwell	56	722
Wm	Butte Ophir	56	793
Wm	El Dorado Georgetown	58	757
Wm	Humbolt Eel Rvr	59	153
Wm	Humbolt Eureka	59	178
Wm	Marin Cortemad	60	791
Wm	Nevada Nevada	61	243
Wm	Nevada Nevada	61	245
Wm	Nevada Nevada	61	259
Wm	Nevada Nevada	61	325
Wm	Nevada Eureka	61	364
Wm	Sacramento Granite	63	248
Wm	Sacramento Sutter	63	297
Wm	Sacramento Ward 4	63	506
Wm	Sacramento Ward 1	63	99
Wm	San Francisco San Francisco 3	67	49
Wm	San Francisco San Francisco 3	67	69
Wm	San Francisco San Francisco 1	68	824
Wm	San Joaquin Stockton	64	1040
Wm	Solano Suisan	69	205
Wm	Solano Suisan	69	236
Wm	Solano Vallejo	69	266
Wm	Trinity New Rvr	70	1030
Wm	Yuba Rose Bar	72	811
Wm A	Sacramento Ward 1	63	117
Wm C*	Del Norte Happy Ca	58	661
Wm H	Butte Ophir	56	759
Wm H	Sacramento Ward 1	63	151
Wm*	Marin Cortemad	60	791
Wm*	Solano Suisan	69	236
Zachary	San Francisco San Francisco 1	68	839
TAYLORD			
Wm C	Del Norte Happy Ca	58	661
TAYLY			
John	Amador Twp 3	55	397
TAYNC			
Francois L	San Francisco San Francisco 7	68	1400
TAYO			
---	Amador Twp 2	55	318
TAYON			
Dolphin*	Del Norte Crescent	58	644
TAYOR			
---	Calaveras Twp 5	57	226
TAYPUNE			
Joe	Amador Twp 1	55	451
TAYRELL			
Thomas	Sierra St Louis	66	813
TAYRO			
John	Solano Suisan	69	215
TAYSO			
John	Solano Suisan	69	215
TAYTLOR			
William	Nevada Rough &	61	414
TAYTOR			
James	San Francisco San Francisco 9	68	978
Samuel*	Nevada Bloomfield	61	523
TAYTUM			
I*	San Francisco San Francisco 2	67	748
J*	San Francisco San Francisco 2	67	748
TAYTY			
---*	Mendocino Twp 1	60	891
TAYWEN			
---	Shasta Shasta	66	669
TAZE			
Wak	Tuolumne Twp 6	71	531
TAZER			
Alfred	El Dorado Georgetown	58	690
C A*	Shasta Shasta	66	656
TAZIER			
L H	Tuolumne Twp 2	71	276
Saml	Tuolumne Twp 2	71	289
TBEURLD			
L*	Solano Vacaville	69	330
TCARTOR			
Josa	Amador Twp 5	55	354
TCHING			
---	San Francisco San Francisco 2	67	754
TCHNEAR			
Charles*	Yuba Long Bar	72	751
TE FOI			
---*	Tuolumne Don Pedro	71	537
TE LAD HA MA			
---	Mendocino Calpella	60	823
TE SAM			
---	Tuolumne Chinese	71	521
TE SAN			
---	Tuolumne Chinese	71	521
TE SING			
---	Tuolumne Chinese	71	521
TE			
---	Calaveras Twp 5	57	246
---	Calaveras Twp 10	57	269
---	Mariposa Coulterville	60	690
---	Plumas Quincy	62	920
---	San Francisco San Francisco 4	68	1194

Name	County Locale	M653 Roll	Page
TE			
---	Sierra Downieville	66	984
Chan	El Dorado Placerville	58	869
Cong	El Dorado Mud Springs	58	981
Foi	Tuolumne Twp 6	71	537
Hang	El Dorado Mud Springs	58	972
La	Butte Kimshaw	56	588
Lu Ah	Yuba Long Bar	72	766
Min	San Francisco San Francisco 11	92 67	
Ming	Calaveras Twp 4	57	320
Ott	Calaveras Twp 10	57	272
Pi	Amador Twp 2	55	312
Ro	San Francisco San Francisco 3	67	50
Sing	Alameda Oakland	55	38
Sing	Tuolumne Twp 5	71	521
Soo	El Dorado Mud Springs	58	950
Yong	Amador Twp 2	55	285
TEA			
---	Amador Twp 2	55	326
---	Amador Twp 5	55	352
---	Amador Twp 5	55	354
---	Amador Twp 6	55	436
---	Calaveras Twp 10	57	276
---	Calaveras Twp 4	57	333
---	Calaveras Twp 4	57	343
---	El Dorado Georgetown	58	708
---	El Dorado Placerville	58	831
---	Mariposa Twp 1	60	648
---	Mariposa Twp 1	60	652
---	Mariposa Twp 1	60	655
---	Mariposa Twp 1	60	656
---	Mariposa Twp 1	60	657
---	Mariposa Twp 1	60	662
---	Mariposa Twp 1	60	666
---	Mariposa Twp 1	60	667
---	Mariposa Twp 1	60	669
---	Mariposa Twp 1	60	670
---	Mariposa Twp 1	60	672
---	Mariposa Coulterville	60	681
---	Mariposa Coulterville	60	684
---	Mariposa Coulterville	60	685
---	Mariposa Coulterville	60	689
---	Mariposa Coulterville	60	690
---	Mariposa Coulterville	60	691
---	Mariposa Coulterville	60	700
---	Sierra Downieville	66	1032
---*	Mariposa Coulterville	60	684
Geo	Amador Twp 2	55	318
Han	Amador Twp 5	55	352
Yon	Amador Twp 5	55	356
TEABEAN			
Thos	Butte Oregon	56	631
TEABROCK			
George*	Yuba Marysville	72	926
TEACHER			
D	Yolo Washington	72	572
TEACK			
---	Nevada Rough &	61	432
TEADEN			
August	Calaveras Twp 7	57	19
TEADOCIO			
---	San Bernardino S Timate	64	721
TEADORIO			
---	San Bernardino S Timate	64	731
---	San Bernardino S Timate	64	736
TEADORO			
---	San Bernardino S Timate	64	716
---	San Bernardino S Timate	64	721
---	San Bernardino S Timate	64	731
---	San Bernardino S Timate	64	732
---	San Bernardino S Timate	64	734
---	San Bernardino S Timate	64	740
---	San Bernardino S Timate	64	742
---	San Bernardino S Timate	64	746
---	San Bernardino S Timate	64	747
---	San Bernardino S Timate	64	753
TEADSELL			
James W*	Tuolumne Twp 5	71	512
TEAFORO			
---	San Bernardino S Timate	64	724
TEAG			
A	San Mateo Twp 3	65	96
TEAGRA			
---*	Yuba Bear Rvr	72	1014
TEAGUE			
William	Tuolumne Twp 1	71	264
TEAHAN			
William	Contra Costa Twp 2	57	569
TEAHTAN			
H J	El Dorado Georgetown	58	704
TEAINER			
John*	San Francisco San Francisco 7	68	1428
TEAKEN			
---*	Yuba Bear Rvr	72	1014
TEAKINS			
Wm	Solano Fairfield	69	199
TEAL			
---	Tuolumne Don Pedro	71	163
Chales*	Nevada Red Dog	61	545
H	Nevada Nevada	61	296
H J	Nevada Eureka	61	345
H J	Nevada Eureka	61	361
Hiram H	Amador Twp 4	55	252
John W	Placer Dutch Fl	62	727
Leow	San Joaquin Castoria	64	886
Louis	Sacramento Ward 1	63	19
Peter	Napa Hot Springs	61	20
Sanl	Nevada Grass Valley	61	153
TEALL			
Wm E	Tuolumne Big Oak	71	125
Wm E	Tuolumne Twp 4	71	127
TEALNITE			
M	San Joaquin Stockton	64	1091
TEALY			
J W	San Francisco San Francisco 3	67	50
TEAM			
John	San Mateo Twp 3	65	106
TEAMAH			
Juan	San Joaquin Stockton	64	1070
TEAMIY			
Patrick	San Francisco San Francisco 1	68	908
TEAN			
---	Amador Twp 1	55	497
Nathaniel	Yuba Parke Ba	72	782
TEANEP			
Millery	San Francisco San Francisco 7	68	1347
TEANER			
San	El Dorado Placerville	58	821
TEANESS			
Mellery*	San Francisco San Francisco 7	68	1347
Mellory*	San Francisco San Francisco 7	68	1347
TEANGE			
C	Shasta Millvill	66	726
TEAR			
James	Calaveras Twp 7	57	5
TEARCE			
James*	San Joaquin Stockton	64	1012
TEARE			
Thomas	Tuolumne Shawsfla	71	417
Wm	Tuolumne Twp 2	71	417
TEARLEY			
B B	Yolo Putah	72	587
TEARNEY			
Michael	San Mateo Twp 1	65	53
Patrick	San Francisco San Francisco 3	67	37
Thomas	San Francisco San Francisco 9	68	956
Thos	Klamath Liberty	59	241
TEARSEAN			
Jean	San Francisco San Francisco 2	67	802
TEAS			
Henry	Amador Twp 3	55	395
Henry	Amador Twp 3	55	401
TEASALL			
Wm B*	Mariposa Coulterville	60	680
TEASDALE			
Thomas	El Dorado Mountain	58	1187
TEASDALL			
T	El Dorado Newtown	58	779
TEASE			
E A*	Nevada Rough &	61	434
TEASLEY			
B B	Yolo Putah	72	587
TEASS			
E A	Nevada Rough &	61	434
TEAT			
D W	El Dorado Placerville	58	821
TEAVERS			
C M*	Sacramento Granite	63	242
TEAVETT			
J*	Nevada Grass Valley	61	147
TEAVITT			
J*	Nevada Grass Valley	61	147
TEAW			
---	Klamath Liberty	59	232
Nathaniel	Yuba Parks Ba	72	782
Wing Fong	San Francisco San Francisco 5	67	510
---	San Francisco		
TEAY			
Chas*	Sonoma Salt Point	69	692
TEAZAR			
William	Tuolumne Twp 1	71	264
TEAZEWELL			
S	Sacramento Cosumnes	63	394
TEBANE			
---	Butte Chico	56	551
TEBAS			
---	Fresno Twp 1	59	86
TEBBE			
H	Trinity Soldiers	70	1005
TEBBETTS			
George P	San Diego S Luis R	64	781
Rufus B	San Diego San Diego	64	757
TEBBS			
M	El Dorado Eldorado	58	937
TEBOS			
Sharmb	Butte Ophir	56	745
TEBURCIO			
---	Monterey S Antoni	60	972
TECH			
---	Yuba Fosters	72	841
TECHENCO			
Francisco	San Joaquin Elkhorn	64	970
TECHENOR			
Stephen	San Francisco San Francisco 10	259 67	
TECHMAKER			
H F	San Francisco San Francisco 5	67	499
TECK MENG			
---	Tuolumne Jacksonville	71	515
TECK			
---	El Dorado Salmon Falls	58	1042
---	El Dorado Salmon Falls	58	1054
---	El Dorado Salmon Falls	58	1060
---	El Dorado Salmon Hills	58	1067
---	El Dorado Union	58	1091
---	El Dorado Coloma	58	1108
---	El Dorado Coloma	58	1109
---	El Dorado Coloma	58	1115
---	El Dorado Coloma	58	1120
---	El Dorado Diamond	58	806
---	Placer Auburn	62	582
---	Yuba Fosters	72	827
K C*	San Francisco San Francisco 3	67	79
Meng	Tuolumne Twp 5	71	515
R C*	San Francisco San Francisco 3	67	79
Sem	Calaveras Twp 7	57	47
TECTMAN			
A C*	San Francisco San Francisco 3	67	50
TEDADO			
---	San Diego Agua Caliente	64	835
TEDALE			
Maria H	San Francisco San Francisco 10	285 67	
TEDAM			
William	Calaveras Twp 4	57	310
TEDBALL			
Joseph	Yuba Marysville	72	872
TEDDING			
Thos	San Francisco San Francisco 9	68	1075
TEDDY			
Mary	Mariposa Twp 3	60	563
Ricard	Tuolumne Twp 1	71	188
Richd	Tuolumne Twp 1	71	262
Thos	Mariposa Twp 3	60	563
TEDDYFORD			
?	Yuba Rose Bar	72	802
J	Yuba Rose Bar	72	802
L*	Yuba Rose Bar	72	802
TEDFORD			
A C	Yuba Rose Bar	72	803
J N	Sonoma Bodega	69	522
Josiah C	Yuba Marysville	72	870
R B	Tuolumne Twp 4	71	126
TEDORA			
---	Tulara Keyesville	71	55
TEDORS			
Damingo	Mariposa Coulterville	60	698
TEDORT			
Domingo*	Mariposa Coulterville	60	698
TEDRO			
Joseph	Los Angeles Elmonte	59	270
TEE			
---	Alameda Oakland	55	64
---	Amador Twp 2	55	289
---	Amador Twp 2	55	292
---	Amador Twp 1	55	480
---	Amador Twp 1	55	503
---	Butte Hamilton	56	530
---	Calaveras Twp 5	57	237
---	Calaveras Twp 10	57	270
---	Calaveras Twp 10	57	274
---	El Dorado Salmon Hills	58	1061
---	Fresno Twp 2	59	18
---	Fresno Twp 2	59	20
---	Mariposa Twp 1	60	627
---	Mariposa Twp 1	60	646
---	Mariposa Twp 1	60	665
---	Nevada Nevada	61	300
---	Nevada Nevada	61	302
---	Nevada Rough &	61	398
---	Nevada Bridgeport	61	462
---	Nevada Bridgeport	61	463
---	Placer Iona Hills	62	889
---	San Francisco San Francisco 9	68	1095
---	San Francisco San Francisco 4	68	1193
---	San Francisco San Francisco 4	68	1212
---	Sierra Downieville	66	1000
---	Sierra Downieville	66	1014

Name	County Locale	M653 RollPage
TEE		
---	Sierra Downieville	661015
---	Sierra Downieville	661026
---	Sierra Twp 5	66 931
---	Sierra Downieville	66 990
---	Sierra Downieville	66 995
---	Sierra Downieville	66 996
---	Siskiyou Scott Ri	69 82
---	Tuolumne Twp 3	71 460
---	Tuolumne Montezuma	71 512
---	Tuolumne Twp 5	71 523
---	Yolo Slate Ra	72 715
---	Yuba Long Bar	72 758
---*	Fresno Twp 1	59 26
---*	Nevada Rough &	61 398
---*	San Francisco San Francisco 11	161
		67
---*	Trinity Weaverville	701053
---*	Yuba Slate Ro	72 715
---*	Yuba Long Bar	72 753
Ah	Sacramento Cosumnes	63 386
Boy	San Francisco San Francisco 4	681175
Charles	Amador Twp 3	55 393
James	Amador Twp 6	55 436
Ott	Calaveras Twp 10	57 272
Pe	Yolo No E Twp	72 675
San	San Francisco San Francisco 4	681180
Sim	Plumas Quincy	621009
Wo	San Francisco San Francisco 4	681184
Ya	Amador Twp 2	55 291
TEECUN		
---	Fresno Twp 2	59 20
TEED		
Harvey W	Yuba Marysville	72 867
Henry	San Francisco San Francisco 6	67 403
TEEGARDEN		
Eli	Yuba Marysville	72 952
TEEGEN		
Frederick	Marin San Rafael	60 766
TEEHAN		
John*	San Francisco San Francisco 9	68 982
TEEK		
---	Amador Twp 7	55 412
---	Calaveras Twp 8	57 68
---	El Dorado Union	581091
---	El Dorado Mud Springs	58 981
TEEL		
Jas	Merced Twp 1	60 913
TEELY		
John	Santa Cruz Santa Cruz	66 619
TEEM		
---	Plumas Meadow Valley	62 910
TEEN		
---	Amador Twp 2	55 294
---	Amador Twp 5	55 335
---	Calaveras Twp 8	57 84
---	Mariposa Twp 1	60 660
---	San Francisco San Francisco 4	681212
Chok	San Francisco San Francisco 11	146
		67
Han	San Francisco San Francisco 11	146
		67
Moon	San Francisco San Francisco 5	67 507
TEENMER		
George	Sierra Downieville	66 977
TEENY		
Patrick	El Dorado Coloma	581121
TEEPEL		
D C*	Nevada Eureka	61 379
M	Nevada Eureka	61 379
TEEPIL		
D C	Nevada Eureka	61 379
TEERNEY		
J*	Tuolumne Big Oak	71 179
TEESE		
Howard	Trinity Redding	70 985
Latham*	Mendocino Big Rvr	60 849
Lewis	San Francisco San Francisco 7	681420
Louis*	San Francisco San Francisco 3	67 82
TEET		
---	Butte Kimshaw	56 600
TEETERS		
Jas L	Butte Hamilton	56 526
TEETH		
Thadions	Amador Twp 7	55 418
Thadious	Amador Twp 7	55 418
TEETMAN		
A C*	San Francisco San Francisco 3	67 50
TEEUMER		
George*	Sierra Downieville	66 977
TEFFCOAT		
Jno	Sacramento Sutter	63 294
TEFFT		
Lander*	Plumas Quincy	62 994
Leander*	Plumas Quincy	62 994
Wilkins*	Yuba Bear Rvr	72 997

Name	County Locale	M653 RollPage
TEFIOQUANO		
A	Stanislaus Branch	70 701
TEFONSO		
---	Monterey Monterey	60 953
TEFT		
Perry G	Calaveras Twp 5	57 189
Samuel O	Yuba Marysville	72 977
Samuel V	Yuba Marysville	72 977
Tabor	Calaveras Twp 5	57 194
TEGAN		
Patrick T*	Solano Benecia	69 298
TEGARD		
C	Butte Bidwell	56 715
TEGHIR		
Edmond	El Dorado Greenwood	58 723
TEGHLMAN		
T H*	San Francisco San Francisco 5	67 504
TEGLISOW		
Thos	Butte Ophir	56 753
TEHARA		
Michael	San Francisco San Francisco 2	67 802
Mighael	San Francisco San Francisco 2	67 802
TEHATOS		
Peter	Contra Costa Twp 1	57 509
TEHENET		
Louis	Sierra Downieville	661022
TEHERA		
Jeses	San Joaquin Stockton	641071
TEHEUET		
Lewis*	Sierra Downieville	661022
TEHNEAR		
Charles*	Yuba Long Bar	72 751
TEHOY		
---	Sacramento Ward 3	63 493
TEI		
---	Calaveras Twp 6	57 150
---	Calaveras Twp 5	57 215
---	Calaveras Twp 10	57 270
---	Calaveras Twp 10	57 274
---	El Dorado Georgetown	58 703
---	El Dorado Mud Springs	58 957
---	San Francisco San Francisco 11	144
		67
---*	Yuba Slate Ro	72 717
Ah	San Francisco San Francisco 3	67 37
Wo	San Francisco San Francisco 4	681184
TEIAEL		
T	Amador Twp 1	55 491
TEICE		
---	Mendocino Big Rock	60 875
TEIDEAN		
Eliza	Yuba Bear Rvr	721002
TEIDMAN		
John*	Placer Michigan	62 847
TEIGE		
Frederick	San Joaquin Castoria	64 900
TEIGENBAUM		
Joseph	Humbolt Bucksport	59 158
TEIGER		
Peter	Siskiyou Cottonwood	69 99
TEILLIS		
S B	Siskiyou Cottonwoood	69 100
TEILZ		
Warren	Amador Twp 2	55 261
TEIN		
---	Calaveras Twp 10	57 285
---	Calaveras Twp 8	57 59
---	El Dorado Union	581090
---	San Francisco San Francisco 4	681182
---	San Francisco San Francisco 7	681343
TEINDLER		
J S*	Sacramento Georgian	63 346
TEINE		
---	Fresno Twp 3	59 31
TEINER		
Henry	Sacramento Brighton	63 207
TEINTAMANN		
Wm	San Francisco San Francisco 2	67 564
TEINTURNIRN		
Louis*	Calaveras Twp 10	57 296
TEINTURURIN		
Louis*	Calaveras Twp 10	57 296
TEIO		
---	Sierra Twp 7	66 876
TEIPLE		
Warren	Tuolumne Twp 2	71 402
TEIR		
William*	El Dorado Georgetown	58 693
TEIRMEY		
Winiford	Marin Cortemad	60 754
TEIRNEY		
Wineford	Marin Cortemad	60 754
TEIRTAMANN		
Wm*	San Francisco San Francisco 2	67 564
TEISE		
Louis*	San Francisco San Francisco 3	67 82

Name	County Locale	M653 RollPage
TEISER		
K	El Dorado Salmon Falls	581040
TEISO		
Louis	San Francisco San Francisco 3	67 82
TEITFEN		
H	San Francisco San Francisco 6	67 458
TEITZ		
Adam	San Francisco San Francisco 2	67 704
TEJONNA		
Nicanor	San Francisco San Francisco 8	681320
TEK		
---	San Francisco San Francisco 4	681174
---	San Francisco San Francisco 11	146
		67
---	Yolo No E Twp	72 680
---	Yuba North Ea	72 680
Jon	El Dorado Greenwood	58 713
TEKLOTE		
Henry	Amador Twp 6	55 443
TELA		
---	Sierra Downieville	66 985
TELATONE		
Maria	Monterey Monterey	60 943
TELBER		
Jno	Tehama Red Bluff	70 925
TELBOT		
Alexander*	San Francisco San Francisco 3	67 37
TELDEN		
M C*	Sacramento Ward 1	63 39
TELEGRAPH		
---	Fresno Twp 2	59 70
TELESITOR		
Arismendis	Amador Twp 1	55 459
TELFORD		
Frank	San Francisco San Francisco 3	67 14
TELIAN		
Charles	Tuolumne Twp 3	71 448
TELICATA		
---	Monterey S Antoni	60 972
TELICIANO		
---	Monterey Monterey	60 957
TELINN		
Robt*	Sacramento Franklin	63 329
TELIO		
August	Calaveras Twp 8	57 96
TELIUN		
Robt*	Sacramento Franklin	63 329
TELL		
---	Nevada Bridgeport	61 463
---	Sierra St Louis	66 813
---	Tuolumne Columbia	71 474
---	Yuba North Ea	72 681
C*	Siskiyou Callahan	69 3
J	San Joaquin Stockton	641040
Jas	Butte Oregon	56 629
Jon Le	Tehama Lassen	70 872
Jos*	Butte Oregon	56 629
Wm	San Francisco San Francisco 2	67 665
TELLA		
Placitus	San Francisco San Francisco 8	681322
TELLAR		
Isaac	San Francisco San Francisco 2	67 740
Rosa*	San Francisco San Francisco 2	67 567
Rose	San Francisco San Francisco 2	67 567
TELLARO		
La???Rd*	Calaveras Twp 10	57 292
Laocandi*	Calaveras Twp 10	57 292
Laonard*	Calaveras Twp 10	57 292
TELLATT		
W	San Francisco San Francisco 5	67 521
TELLEIR		
Louis	Amador Twp 1	55 453
TELLER		
J D B	San Francisco San Francisco 10	218
		67
Joseph*	Tuolumne Twp 2	71 293
TELLERY		
Joseph	Tuolumne Columbia	71 473
TELLES		
Joseph*	Tuolumne Columbia	71 293
TELLESARIO		
---	San Diego Temecula	64 798
TELLEY		
Edward	Sierra Downieville	661018
Henry	Tuolumne Twp 3	71 450
John	El Dorado Casumnes	581175
TELLIER		
Louis	Amador Twp 1	55 453
TELLIS		
Joseph*	Tuolumne Twp 2	71 293
TELLITE		
Frank	Amador Twp 5	55 361
TELLS		
S	Calaveras Twp 9	57 392
TELLY		
W R	Nevada Grass Valley	61 238

Name	County Locale	M653 Roll	Page
TELMAN			
Henry*	San Francisco San Francisco	7 681	373
TELONE			
Babtirna*	Tuolumne Twp 2	71	302
TELOYD			
Wm B	Mariposa Twp 1	60	665
TELSCUM			
Milton*	El Dorado Mud Springs	58	996
TELSOUR			
Sarah J	Yuba Marysville	72	924
TELTERS			
Chris*	Mariposa Twp 3	60	560
TELTON			
J L	Butte Oregon	56	626
Wm*	Sacramento Ward 1	63	154
TEM			
---	Amador Twp 6	55	424
---	Butte Wyandotte	56	666
---	El Dorado Union	581	090
---	Tuolumne Jamestown	71	442
---	Tuolumne Twp 3	71	457
---	Tuolumne Twp 3	71	467
---	Tuolumne Twp 1	71	477
---	Tuolumne Twp 5	71	514
---*	San Francisco San Francisco	4 681	182
Nelson*	Sierra Pine Grove	66	828
Yow	Placer Illinois	62	752
TEMAN			
James W	Mendocino Little L	60	832
TEMDLER			
J S*	Sacramento Georgian	63	346
TEMEF			
Randolph*	San Francisco San Francisco	9 681	106
TEMEL			
Dirk	Tuolumne Montezuma	71	513
Geo W*	Del Norte Klamath	58	652
TEMIRN			
E D	Amador Twp 5	55	330
TEMLER			
Fred	El Dorado Cold Spring	581	100
TEMLEY			
J	Siskiyou Cottonwoood	69	107
TEMMAR			
Christian*	Yuba Fosters	72	832
TEMOIN			
E D*	Amador Twp 5	55	330
TEMOLINASON			
John*	Calaveras Twp 9	57	372
TEMOP			
I*	Mariposa Twp 1	60	667
TEMPANY			
John	San Francisco San Francisco	2 67	631
TEMPLAR			
J	Nevada Eureka	61	381
J C	Nevada Eureka	61	381
TEMPLE			
C D*	Colusa Colusi	57	423
Daniel	Sonoma Vallejo	69	622
David	Sonoma Vallejo	69	622
David	Tulara Yule Rvr	71	8
David	Yuba Rose Bar	72	794
Edward P	Yuba Marysville	72	959
F P F	Los Angeles Elmonte	59	260
Geo B	Del Norte Crescent	58	642
George	Yuba Bear Rvr	721	001
Isaac J	San Francisco San Francisco	2 67	659
Jackson	Sonoma Santa Rosa	69	393
Jas A	Solano Suisan	69	210
John	Los Angeles Los Angeles	59	335
John	Mariposa Twp 3	60	591
John	San Francisco San Francisco	2 67	663
John	Sierra Gibsonville	66	856
John*	Mariposa Twp 3	60	591
Jos A	Solano Suisan	69	210
Richard A	El Dorado Salmon Falls	581	035
Saml	Tuolumne Twp 3	71	442
Stubbs	San Joaquin Elkhorn	64	966
Thomas	San Joaquin Elkhorn	64	964
Tull*	Placer Michigan	62	834
W	Sonoma Salt Point	69	690
W B A	El Dorado Mud Springs	58	974
TEMPLES			
E E	Tuolumne Jamestown	71	470
TEMPLETON			
B S	Trinity Hay Fork	70	993
Carolin A	Yolo Cottonwoood	72	651
Caroline A	Yolo Cottonwoood	72	651
Geo	Napa Yount	61	40
H	San Mateo Twp 3	65	105
John	Sacramento Ward 1	63	14
Mile L	Solano Vacaville	69	354
S	Calaveras Twp 9	57	391
S H	San Francisco San Francisco	3 67	74
TEMPLIN			
S P	Sierra Twp 7	66	874

Name	County Locale	M653 Roll	Page
TEMPLIN			
Wm	Mariposa Coulterville	60	689
TEMPLING			
F	San Francisco San Francisco	5 67	549
TEMPLO			
---	Tulara Twp 3	71	68
---	Tulara Twp 3	71	71
TEN BROECK			
John M	Sacramento Ward 3	63	468
TEN EYCH			
Saml	San Francisco San Francisco	5 67	478
TEN EYCK			
George*	Placer Iona Hills	62	871
Theodore M	Tulara Visalia	71	105
TEN			
---	Amador Twp 4	55	251
---	Amador Twp 4	55	256
---	Amador Twp 2	55	290
---	Amador Twp 2	55	326
---	Amador Twp 5	55	342
---	Amador Twp 5	55	364
---	Amador Twp 7	55	415
---	Amador Twp 1	55	490
---	Amador Twp 1	55	510
---	Calaveras Twp 6	57	150
---	Calaveras Twp 6	57	166
---	Calaveras Twp 4	57	333
---	Calaveras Twp 8	57	60
---	El Dorado Mud Springs	58	972
---	Mariposa Twp 1	60	646
---	Mariposa Twp 1	60	651
---	Shasta Horsetown	66	702
---	Trinity Weaverville	701	052
---	Trinity Lewiston	70	961
---	Tuolumne Green Springs	71	521
---	Tuolumne Twp 6	71	529
---	Tuolumne Twp 6	71	530
---	Tuolumne Don Pedro	71	533
---	Yuba Long Bar	72	759
---*	Yuba Foster B	72	826
Ah	Yuba Bear Rvr	721	000
Hing	El Dorado Georgetown	58	684
Pow	Yuba Marysville	72	921
Tong	El Dorado Placerville	58	828
TENACK			
N	Nevada Eureka	61	360
TENAGRANT			
Nathan	Colusa Muion	57	458
TENAIS			
Eliza*	Yuba Marysville	72	977
Elynia	Yuba Marysville	72	977
TENANT			
Elizabeth	Sonoma Santa Rosa	69	411
James	Nevada Bridgeport	61	483
William	Placer Michigan	62	819
William	San Francisco San Francisco	7 681	367
TENARRI			
Angelli*	Mariposa Twp 3	60	600
TENARY			
E L*	Butte Chico	56	567
TENAX			
W G	Sutter Nicolaus	70	840
TENBROCK			
George*	Yuba Marysville	72	926
TENBROECK			
J*	Sacramento Ward 1	63	19
TENCE			
A	San Francisco San Francisco	6 67	473
C*	San Francisco San Francisco	5 67	486
TENCH			
Noah	San Joaquin Douglass	64	918
TENCHA			
Leola	Amador Twp 5	55	360
TENCHAM			
Wallace*	San Joaquin Stockton	641	018
TENCKHAM			
H C	Tuolumne Columbia	71	289
TENDER			
D	Nevada Eureka	61	390
E	Sacramento Ward 1	63	149
TENDERBERRY			
Jos	San Mateo Twp 2	65	119
TENE			
---	Plumas Meadow Valley	62	913
---	Plumas Quincy	62	949
Victorine	San Francisco San Francisco	7 681	370
TENEE			
Jas*	Sacramento Georgian	63	337
TENENY			
Martina	Marin Saucileto	60	751
TENER			
Jas*	Sacramento Georgian	63	337
TENERICK			
T C	Shasta Shasta	66	684
TENESA			
---	San Bernardino S Timate	64	716

Name	County Locale	M653 Roll	Page
TENEY			
E*	Tuolumne Big Oak	71	154
Michel	Nevada Rough &	61	412
TENEYCK			
Theodore M	Tulara Visalia	71	105
TENG			
---	Amador Twp 2	55	311
---	Amador Twp 2	55	327
---	Butte Kimshaw	56	603
---	Nevada Grass Valley	61	233
---	Nevada Rough &	61	432
---	Trinity Arkansas	701	004
---	Trinity Mouth Ca	701	012
---	Trinity Mouth Ca	701	016
---	Trinity Mouth Ca	701	017
---	Trinity East For	701	025
---	Trinity Taylor'S	701	033
---	Trinity Taylor'S	701	034
---	Trinity Taylor'S	701	036
---	Trinity Cox'S Bar	701	037
---	Trinity Big Flat	701	041
---	Trinity Big Flat	701	042
---	Trinity Honest B	701	043
---	Trinity Trinindad Rvr	701	044
---	Trinity Trinindad Rvr	701	045
---	Trinity Trinindad Rvr	701	046
---	Trinity Weaverville	701	052
---	Trinity Weaverville	701	056
---	Trinity E Weaver	701	061
---	Trinity Weaverville	701	072
---	Trinity Weaverville	701	074
---	Trinity Lewiston	70	957
---	Tuolumne Twp 2	71	408
---	Tuolumne Twp 3	71	440
---	Tuolumne Twp 3	71	467
---*	Trinity Taylor'S	701	036
Ah	Sacramento Mississipi	63	190
Ah	Tuolumne Twp 2	71	347
Chow	Tehama Red Bluff	70	932
TENI			
---	Nevada Rough &	61	399
TENIGUE			
George	San Francisco San Francisco	2 67	671
TENILL			
Geo W*	Del Norte Klamath	58	652
H F	Tuolumne Twp 1	71	208
TENISER			
Harvey	Sierra Downieville	66	995
TENKATE			
Gradus*	Placer Ophirville	62	659
TENKHAM			
M M*	Tuolumne Twp 2	71	345
TENKINS			
Wm E	Mariposa Twp 1	60	623
TENKSBURY			
James D*	Humbolt Pacific	59	131
TENKUM			
Z B*	Tuolumne Columbia	71	326
TENKUN			
Z B	Tuolumne Twp 2	71	326
TENLEY			
L	Nevada Nevada	61	290
TENLOSKY			
Joseph*	Yuba Parke Ba	72	785
TENN			
---	Mariposa Twp 1	60	665
---	Tuolumne Don Pedro	71	163
Ah	Calaveras Twp 7	57	16
E D	El Dorado Greenwood	58	726
TENNANT			
E W	Nevada Nevada	61	326
J D	Los Angeles Tejon	59	536
John	Contra Costa Twp 1	57	529
Maria	Contra Costa Twp 1	57	529
Saml J	Contra Costa Twp 1	57	514
Wm	Santa Clara Gilroy	65	243
TENNCAT			
John H*	Yuba Marysville	72	863
TENNCUT			
John H*	Yuba Marysville	72	863
TENNE			
G*	San Francisco San Francisco	4 681	216
Patrick*	Alameda Oakland	55	62
TENNEAT			
John H*	Yuba Marysville	72	863
TENNEBER			
Paul*	San Francisco San Francisco	9 681	106
TENNELL			
James*	Mariposa Coulterville	60	690
Janes	Mariposa Coulterville	60	690
Thos H*	Mariposa Twp 3	60	560
TENNELY			
R C	Nevada Eureka	61	349
TENNENG			
Adolph*	Mariposa Coulterville	60	694
TENNENT			
John H	Yuba Marysville	72	863

Name	County Locale	M653 RollPage
TENNENT		
T P	San Francisco San Francisco 6	67 433
W P	Sierra Downieville	66 975
TENNER		
B	Sutter Vernon	70 844
Jacob*	Tuolumne Twp 1	71 258
Lewis*	San Francisco San Francisco 1	68 893
TENNERSON		
Joseph*	El Dorado Casumnes	581172
TENNESON		
J A	Amador Twp 3	55 371
TENNESSY		
Catherine	Yuba Marysville	72 871
TENNEST		
James	Mariposa Twp 3	60 600
TENNEY		
Augustus	Placer Iona Hills	62 891
Francis	Tuolumne Twp 5	71 518
Geo	Nevada Eureka	61 349
Isaac B	Calaveras Twp 6	57 154
John	Placer Secret R	62 614
John	Sierra Downieville	66 995
Patrick	San Francisco San Francisco 1	68 856
Wm S	Tuolumne Twp 2	71 471
TENNG		
---*	Trinity Trinindad Rvr	701050
TENNICE		
H	El Dorado Placerville	58 892
TENNIE		
R	Nevada Nevada	61 261
TENNIENST		
John	Santa Clara San Jose	65 359
TENNING		
Wm*	San Francisco San Francisco 1	68 835
TENNIS		
Elynia	Yuba Marysville	72 977
Hance	El Dorado Coloma	581111
Rose	Butte Wyandotte	56 657
S L*	San Francisco San Francisco 5	67 506
Tennis	El Dorado Coloma	581111
TENNISON		
Abraham	Plumas Quincy	62 976
F	Nevada Eureka	61 344
Jno	San Francisco San Francisco 5	67 480
TENNISONL		
F*	Nevada Eureka	61 344
TENNISORD		
F*	Nevada Eureka	61 344
TENNOR		
John*	Nevada Nevada	61 250
TENNY		
Daniel	Siskiyou Scott Va	69 31
E L	Butte Chico	56 567
Joel*	Shasta Horsetown	66 708
John S	San Joaquin Stockton	641042
Pryer	Sierra Gibsonville	66 859
TENNYSON		
Hugh	Calaveras Twp 10	57 277
Joseph J	Calaveras Twp 10	57 277
Joseph L	Calaveras Twp 10	57 277
TENOIN		
E D*	Amador Twp 5	55 330
TENOLER		
Hermann*	San Francisco 3	67 36
	San Francisco	
TENOY		
Antone*	Yolo Merritt	72 583
TENROY		
Pryer*	Sierra Gibsonville	66 859
TENRY		
---	Amador Twp 5	55 363
TENSA		
Chris	Nevada Bridgeport	61 497
TENSLCK		
Joseph*	Yuba New York	72 729
TENT		
---	Calaveras Twp 5	57 204
W H	Klamath Liberty	59 242
TENTAHS		
Gattaf*	Siskiyou Yreka	69 136
Gattafs*	Siskiyou Yreka	69 136
TENTE		
Patrick*	San Francisco San Francisco 3	67 81
TENTEBARK		
Frederick	San Francisco San Francisco 8	681237
TENTERMACHER		
Martin	San Francisco San Francisco 8	681311
TENTHOW		
Mary*	San Francisco San Francisco 2	67 647
TENTS		
Wm	Sonoma Sonoma	69 634
TENUF		
Randolph*	San Francisco 9	681106
	San Francisco	
TENUNT		
James	Nevada Bridgeport	61 483
TENVIRE		
Enock	Sierra Twp 7	66 882
TENWIS		
Rose	Butte Wyandotte	56 657
TENWY		
Daniel*	Siskiyou Scott Va	69 31
TENY		
---	Amador Twp 2	55 281
---	Amador Twp 2	55 289
Chuy	Amador Twp 2	55 281
J W*	Nevada Eureka	61 371
TEO		
---	Calaveras Twp 6	57 168
---	Mariposa Coulterville	60 681
---	Placer Virginia	62 678
---	Placer Virginia	62 680
---	Trinity Lewiston	70 954
Josiah S*	Fresno Twp 1	59 81
Yuny	Calaveras Twp 10	57 299
TEODACIO		
---	San Bernardino S Timate	64 719
TEODOCIO		
---	San Bernardino S Timate	64 700
---	San Bernardino S Timate	64 704
TEODORA S		
---	Monterey San Juan	60 991
TEODORA		
---	San Bernardino S Timate	64 700
Desedario	Contra Costa Twp 1	57 509
TEODORE		
---	San Bernardino S Timate	64 698
---	San Bernardino S Timate	64 700
---	San Bernardino S Timate	64 702
---	San Bernardino S Timate	64 711
---	San Bernardino S Timate	64 712
---	San Bernardino S Timate	64 713
---	San Bernardino S Timate	64 718
TEODORO		
---	Monterey Alisal	601028
---	San Bernardino S Timate	64 697
---	San Bernardino S Timate	64 703
---	San Bernardino S Timate	64 709
---	San Bernardino S Timate	64 718
---	San Bernardino S Timate	64 749
---	San Bernardino S Timate	64 752
---	San Bernardino S Timate	64 754
TEODROE		
---	San Bernardino S Timate	64 719
TEOFILA		
Maria	Los Angeles San Juan	59 465
TEOFILO		
---	Fresno Twp 1	59 87
TEOIARO		
W	Amador Twp 3	55 379
TEON		
---	Plumas Meadow Valley	62 910
---	Sierra Twp 7	66 877
TEONE		
---	Amador Twp 1	55 507
TEONEY		
Margaret*	Napa Napa	61 82
TEONG		
---	Amador Twp 4	55 255
---	El Dorado Coloma	581111
---*	San Francisco San Francisco 2	67 754
Yat	San Francisco San Francisco 1	68 925
TEONY		
---	Amador Twp 7	55 417
---	Amador Twp 6	55 450
---	San Francisco San Francisco 2	67 754
TEORANITZ		
Onto*	San Francisco San Francisco 9	681076
TEORY		
---	San Francisco San Francisco 2	67 754
A T*	Yuba Long Bar	72 752
TEOY		
---	Mariposa Coulterville	60 687
TEP		
---	El Dorado Placerville	58 906
---	Trinity McGillev	701021
Wy	Sacramento Natonia	63 283
TEPES		
Antonie	Mariposa Twp 3	60 617
TEPHEN		
William S	Fresno Twp 1	59 81
TEPHENS		
John	Sierra Whiskey	66 844
TEPKINS		
Nocholos	Calaveras Twp 4	57 318
TEPP		
M*	Siskiyou Scott Ri	69 71
TEPPEL		
Jacob	Tuolumne Sonora	71 228
TEPPEN		
Edward	San Francisco San Francisco 2	67 610
TEPPING		
James A	San Joaquin Oneal	64 930
TER		
---	Calaveras Twp 5	57 244
---	Sierra Twp 7	66 898
TERACE		
Angel	Merced Twp 1	60 899
TERADOWELL		
Oscar	Calaveras Twp 7	57 13
TERAIR		
Mareo	Yuba Slate Ro	72 711
TERALE		
Juan	San Joaquin Stockton	641071
TERAN		
Angel	Merced Twp 1	60 899
Jesus	Los Angeles Los Angeles	59 316
TERASAZ		
Manuel	Monterey Pajaro	601012
TERAUTER		
J*	El Dorado Georgetown	58 676
TERAVILLIGER		
E B*	El Dorado Georgetown	58 674
TERBOUQUE		
Bernard	San Francisco San Francisco 2	67 700
TERBUSH		
P F*	Shasta Horsetown	66 690
TERCACS		
Eliza*	Yuba Marysville	72 977
TERCE		
Dirk*	Tuolumne Twp 5	71 513
TERCEC		
Francois*	Sierra Downieville	66 963
TERCEE		
Francois*	Sierra Downieville	66 963
TERCHELBERGER		
George*	San Joaquin Oneal	64 930
TERCOTT		
James	Yuba Marysville	72 927
TERELL		
John*	Yuba Slate Ro	72 704
TERES		
Francisco*	Mariposa Twp 3	60 617
Franciseo	Mariposa Twp 3	60 617
Theodore*	Tuolumne Columbia	71 337
TERESA		
---	Fresno Twp 1	59 88
---	Los Angeles San Gabriel	59 420
---	San Bernardino S Timate	64 722
---	San Bernardino S Timate	64 730
---	San Bernardino S Timate	64 739
---	San Bernardino S Timate	64 744
---	San Bernardino S Timate	64 746
---	San Bernardino S Timate	64 751
---	San Bernardino S Timate	64 752
---	San Bernardino S Timate	64 754
---	San Bernardino S Timate	64 755
W	San Joaquin Stockton	641100
TERGO		
Eugew	Sierra Downieville	661007
TERGUSEN		
Pat*	Amador Twp 7	55 412
TERGUSON		
E*	Tuolumne Twp 1	71 256
TERHORN		
George*	Placer Michigan	62 822
TERI		
---	Amador Twp 2	55 290
TERIE		
M	Nevada Grass Valley	61 224
TERIENY		
Martin	Marin Saucileto	60 751
TERILL		
Oliver L*	Sacramento Georgian	63 346
Oliver S*	Sacramento Georgian	63 346
Paul	Siskiyou Yreka	69 156
TERIS		
Theodore	Tuolumne Twp 2	71 337
TERK		
K C	San Francisco San Francisco 3	67 79
TERKINS		
C H*	San Francisco San Francisco 3	67 83
E S	San Francisco San Francisco 3	67 83
TERKNIS		
C H*	San Francisco San Francisco 3	67 83
TERL		
M	Sutter Sutter	70 805
Rachel	Klamath S Fork	59 207
TERLELOV		
Alexder*	Shasta Shasta	66 654
TERLETON		
Alexder	Shasta Shasta	66 654
TERM		
---	Butte Bidwell	56 709
Jeovany*	San Mateo Twp 1	65 65
TERME		
Louis	San Francisco San Francisco 3	67 7
TERMENT		
John	Butte Ophir	56 786

Name	County Locale	M653 RollPage
TERMONT		
S A	Mariposa Twp 3	60 601
TERMOUT		
T A*	Mariposa Twp 3	60 601
TERN		
---	Fresno Twp 2	59 19
Sing	Butte Bidwell	56 709
TERNAN		
J*	Nevada Grass Valley	61 226
Nicholas*	Calaveras Twp 6	57 160
TERNBERGT		
John	Placer Dutch Fl	62 724
TERNE		
---	Fresno Twp 1	59 28
TERNELE		
Michael*	San Francisco San Francisco 1	68 886
TERNER		
Sola*	Tulara Visalia	71 32
TERNEY		
John	Solano Benecia	69 316
William	El Dorado Kelsey	581131
TERNG		
---	Fresno Twp 1	59 26
TERNMERMAN		
Peter*	Yuba Marysville	72 846
TERNN		
Louis*	San Francisco San Francisco 3	67 7
TERNO		
John	Del Norte Crescent	58 635
TERNSLER		
Fred	Amador Twp 5	55 330
TERNVAULT		
J	Sacramento Lee	63 215
TERNY		
Edward	Placer Iona Hills	62 891
TERNZATE		
H B*	Los Angeles Tejon	59 537
TERO		
Geo W*	Sonoma Petaluma	69 602
TERONE		
Frederick*	San Francisco 7	681384
	San Francisco	
TERONGLIT		
J*	Colusa Butte Crk	57 466
TEROS		
---	Fresno Twp 3	59 95
TERR		
Geo W	Sonoma Petaluma	69 602
George*	San Francisco San Francisco 3	67 72
TERRAIR		
Marco	Yolo Slate Ra	72 711
TERRAIS		
Mareo*	Yuba Slate Ro	72 711
TERRAN		
Antonio	Los Angeles Los Angeles	59 317
Luciano	Los Angeles Los Angeles	59 316
TERRE		
John*	Mariposa Coulterville	60 689
TERREL		
Christofeo J	Monterey Monterey	60 958
TERRELE		
Michael*	San Francisco San Francisco 1	68 886
TERRELL		
Bridget	San Francisco San Francisco 10	189 67
Edward	San Francisco San Francisco 4	681170
Francis	Tuolumne Jamestown	71 424
J E	San Francisco San Francisco 1	68 899
Jeremiah	Alameda Oakland	55 33
John	Yolo Slate Ra	72 704
L	Nevada Grass Valley	61 199
Martin	Amador Twp 3	55 377
S*	Calaveras Twp 8	57 88
Wm*	Sacramento Lee	63 212
TERREY		
Daniel*	Butte Oregon	56 621
E	Tuolumne Twp 4	71 154
Wm	Mariposa Twp 1	60 666
TERRIE		
Frank	Alameda Brooklyn	55 91
Hosea M	Alameda Brooklyn	55 131
M*	Nevada Grass Valley	61 224
TERRIL		
J	Nevada Grass Valley	61 215
TERRILE		
Francis	Tuolumne Twp 3	71 424
TERRILL		
Ann	San Francisco San Francisco 8	681270
Benj	Alameda Brooklyn	55 184
E*	Trinity E Weaver	701057
Edward*	San Francisco San Francisco 4	681170
Francisco	Contra Costa Twp 1	57 490
Francisco	Contra Costa Twp 1	57 491
G	Siskiyou Cottonwoood	69 101
Hais*	Sacramento Natonia	63 281
Has	Sacramento Natonia	63 281

Name	County Locale	M653 RollPage
TERRILL		
Hens*	Sacramento Natonia	63 281
M	Sacramento Natonia	63 278
Michael	San Joaquin Stockton	641067
Peter	San Francisco San Francisco 1	68 918
R A	Los Angeles Tejon	59 525
W	Nevada Grass Valley	61 191
W L	San Francisco San Francisco 4	681231
Wm*	Sacramento Lee	63 212
TERRIS		
Jno	San Francisco San Francisco 9	68 956
TERRLMAN		
Wm C	Butte Eureka	56 655
TERRNELL		
Thos H*	Mariposa Twp 3	60 560
TERRO		
Claus	Alameda Brooklyn	55 140
TERRONEY		
John	Sierra Poverty	66 799
TERROY		
Antone*	Yolo Merritt	72 583
TERRY		
---	Sacramento Granite	63 250
C C*	Solano Benecia	69 301
C H	San Francisco San Francisco 10	188 67
Constant	Amador Twp 2	55 290
D E	San Francisco San Francisco 5	67 530
David S*	Calaveras Twp 6	57 165
E S	Mariposa Twp 3	60 587
Ellen	San Francisco San Francisco 7	681349
Eugene	Amador Twp 3	55 375
G W	Trinity Hay Fork	70 994
George*	Placer Iona Hills	62 886
H W	Tuolumne Twp 1	71 187
Hiram	Tuolumne Springfield	71 369
J H	Mendocino Ukiah	60 800
J W	Sacramento Cosummes	63 391
J W*	Nevada Eureka	61 371
John	San Francisco San Francisco 8	681321
John	San Francisco San Francisco 3	67 32
John H	Nevada Bridgeport	61 496
Joseph	San Joaquin Stockton	641025
Kw D	Nevada Nevada	61 248
Louis	Shasta Shasta	66 672
Mathew	El Dorado Placerville	58 903
Orcn	Tuolumne Columbia	71 315
Oren	Tuolumne Twp 2	71 315
Stephen	Merced Twp 1	60 912
Thomas	Plumas Quincy	62 920
Thomas	Plumas Meadow Valley	62 930
Truman	Sonoma Russian	69 433
W D	Nevada Nevada	61 248
W E	Sacramento Ward 1	63 104
W H	Tuolumne Sonora	71 187
W T	Trinity Hay Fork	70 994
William	Nevada Bloomfield	61 513
William	Nevada Bloomfield	61 527
William	Tuolumne Twp 1	71 232
Wm	Mariposa Twp 1	60 666
TERS		
---	Calaveras Twp 5	57 244
TERSERRO		
George*	Sierra Port Win	66 798
TERSERRS		
George*	Sierra Port Win	66 798
TERSEY		
Daniel*	Butte Oregon	56 621
TERSHER		
Henry*	Mariposa Twp 3	60 605
TERSON		
Paul*	Sacramento Franklin	63 313
TERSTEGGE		
Frank	Yuba Long Bar	72 750
TERSTIGG		
Frank	Yuba Long Bar	72 750
TERSY		
Isaieh	El Dorado Greenwood	58 723
TERT		
Lawrence*	Plumas Quincy	62 990
TERTRAND		
Cornelius T*	Yuba Marysville	72 868
TERTRANO		
Cornelius T	Yuba Marysville	72 868
TERUS		
Arsimendis	Amador Twp 1	55 459
TERUSA		
E Sandro*	Mariposa Twp 1	60 625
TERUSER		
E Sadro	Mariposa Twp 1	60 625
E Sandro*	Mariposa Twp 1	60 625
TERUSON		
Bales*	Mariposa Coulterville	60 675
TERV		
George*	San Francisco San Francisco 3	67 72
TERVEY		
Danl	Butte Kimshaw	56 579

Name	County Locale	M653 RollPage
TERVILLEGER		
Jasper	Amador Twp 5	55 348
TERWILEGER		
David	Butte Chico	56 536
TERWILLEGER		
Amos*	Plumas Quincy	621002
TERWILLIGEE		
Amos*	Plumas Quincy	621002
TERWILLIGER		
Lorenzo	Calaveras Twp 7	57 33
Sydney	Siskiyou Yreka	69 129
TERY		
---	Amador Twp 2	55 311
---	Amador Twp 2	55 327
---	Amador Twp 3	55 402
---*	Amador Twp 5	55 330
E S*	Mariposa Twp 3	60 587
TESARIE		
Ange	Mariposa Twp 3	60 556
TESDALE		
Geo	Alameda Brooklyn	55 94
TESENBACHER		
J	El Dorado Georgetown	58 698
TESERO		
Susan	Solano Vallejo	69 274
TESESO		
David	Solano Vallejo	69 274
TESH		
D S*	Trinity Weaverville	701077
Daniel	Siskiyou Yreka	69 171
John	Plumas Quincy	62 953
Wm	Trinity Mouth Ca	701014
TESKE		
Henry	Butte Bidwell	56 716
TESKELSON		
P	Siskiyou Klamath	69 93
TESLER		
E	Butte Wyandotte	56 659
TESMAN		
Victor T	Yuba Suida	72 990
TESNOTT		
W D	El Dorado Greenwood	58 722
TESON		
Rolette	Marin San Rafael	60 761
Roletto	Marin San Rafael	60 761
TESONG		
---	Fresno Twp 1	59 28
TESRENS		
Howard*	Yuba Marysville	72 907
TESS		
Perry G	Calaveras Twp 5	57 189
TESSA		
Amady	Calaveras Twp 8	57 54
TESSARIND		
F*	San Francisco San Francisco 2	67 690
TESSEAIN		
Victor S*	Yuba Linda	72 990
TESSENDAN		
John M P*	San Mateo Twp 3	65 87
TESSENDEN		
Alen	El Dorado Georgetown	58 702
TESTA		
M	San Francisco San Francisco 5	67 540
TESTER		
M*	San Francisco San Francisco 5	67 540
TESTRAM		
Samuel	San Francisco San Francisco 11	132 67
TESTROY		
W	Nevada Grass Valley	61 209
TESTUM		
Corbiere*	San Francisco San Francisco 5	67 540
TET		
---	Amador Twp 1	55 499
---	Amador Twp 1	55 511
---	Mariposa Twp 1	60 658
---	Tuolumne Don Pedro	71 537
TETCHHEIMER		
Charles	Tulara Visalia	71 106
TETER		
Oasas	Amador Twp 2	55 317
TETERS		
Louis	San Francisco San Francisco 3	67 86
TETERSON		
Wm	Plumas Quincy	62 924
TETES		
Oasas	Amador Twp 2	55 317
TETESITOR		
Arismendis	Amador Twp 1	55 459
TETINA		
---*	Stanislaus Empire	70 735
TETLERY		
---	Mariposa Twp 3	60 552
TETMAN		
Nicholas	Calaveras Twp 6	57 160
TETRO		
A	Sutter Yuba	70 759

California 1860 Census Index

Name	County Locale	M653 Roll Page
TETT		
---	Yolo No E Twp	72 684
---*	Yuba Bear Rvr	72 1000
TETTEL		
Charles*	San Francisco San Francisco 7	68 1391
TETTERS		
Chris	Mariposa Twp 3	60 560
TETTSON		
Thomas*	San Francisco San Francisco 7	68 1440
TETUS		
S J	El Dorado Kelsey	58 1130
TEU SAM		
---	Sierra Twp 7	66 876
TEU		
---	Calaveras Twp 6	57 166
---	Calaveras Twp 10	57 259
---	Calaveras Twp 10	57 276
---	Tuolumne Twp 5	71 512
---	Tuolumne Twp 6	71 533
TEUBNER		
H*	San Francisco San Francisco 6	67 464
TEUBNIR		
H	San Francisco San Francisco 6	67 464
TEUBROCK		
John	Amador Twp 6	55 429
TEUBUIR		
H*	San Francisco San Francisco 6	67 464
TEUGH		
---	Calaveras Twp 4	57 306
TEULOSKY		
Joseph*	Yuba Parke Ba	72 785
TEUNG		
---	Trinity Taylor'S	70 1033
---	Trinity Trininad Rvr	70 1050
---	Trinity Weaverville	70 1056
---*	Trinity Trininad Rvr	70 1050
TEURBON		
Simon	Sierra La Porte	66 784
TEUSIER		
Louis	San Francisco San Francisco 1	68 932
TEUTE		
Patrick*	San Francisco San Francisco 3	67 81
TEUTEBARK		
Frederick	San Francisco San Francisco 8	68 1237
TEUY		
J W*	Nevada Eureka	61 371
TEVALAN		
James	Trinity Lewiston	70 964
TEVARA		
A	Amador Twp 6	55 427
As	Amador Twp 6	55 427
TEVEAN		
Clara	Yuba Marysville	72 917
TEVECLY		
James	Sierra Scales D	66 803
TEVEED		
John*	San Francisco San Francisco 4	68 1229
TEVEL		
Frederick	San Francisco San Francisco 8	68 1256
TEVENS		
Elizabeth*	Mariposa Twp 3	60 602
Mary*	Mariposa Twp 3	60 602
TEVERBAUGH		
John	Sacramento Ward 4	63 539
TEVIED		
John*	San Francisco San Francisco 4	68 1229
TEVIER		
John H	Tuolumne Columbia	71 473
TEVIEY		
Daniel	Butte Oregon	56 621
TEVING		
James*	Plumas Meadow Valley	62 929
TEVINGE		
Joseph*	Calaveras Twp 5	57 172
TEVIS		
Lloyd	San Francisco San Francisco 4	68 1131
Willis	San Francisco San Francisco 2	67 777
TEVLETOV		
Alexder*	Shasta Shasta	66 654
TEVOLEY		
M	Nevada Eureka	61 366
TEVON		
William	Santa Clara San Jose	65 292
TEVRENS		
Howard*	Yuba Marysville	72 907
TEVY		
Thomas De	Sierra St Louis	66 809
TEW		
---	Calaveras Twp 10	57 285
---	El Dorado Diamond	58 787
---	Sierra Downieville	66 1003
---	Sierra Downieville	66 983
---	Sierra Downieville	66 998
---	Tuolumne Twp 5	71 514
A L	San Francisco San Francisco 5	67 544
A T	Stanislaus Emory	70 755

Name	County Locale	M653 Roll Page
TEW		
Kee	Sierra Downieville	66 973
Sam	Sierra Twp 7	66 876
TEWELL		
J B	Siskiyou Scott Va	69 57
TEWELPE		
---	Butte Chico	56 550
TEWERY		
W	Sonoma Bodega	69 540
TEWES		
Fred	Siskiyou Yreka	69 148
TEWEY		
Peter	El Dorado Coloma	58 1112
TEWKSBURY		
James D*	Humbolt Pacific	59 131
John	Humbolt Eel Rvr	59 152
M R	San Francisco San Francisco 7	68 1360
TEWKSHERY		
M R	San Francisco San Francisco 10	323 67
TEWNS		
Palmer A*	Alameda Oakland	55 60
TEWO		
---	Del Norte Crescent	58 631
An	Del Norte Crescent	58 631
TEXAS		
Maria	San Diego Agua Caliente	64 850
TEY		
---	Amador Twp 2	55 294
---	Amador Twp 5	55 336
---	Amador Twp 1	55 497
---	Mariposa Twp 1	60 642
---	Sacramento Granite	63 250
A	Sacramento Granite	63 250
Kee	Mariposa Twp 3	60 586
Kee*	Mariposa Twp 3	60 543
TEYLER		
Wm	Sacramento Ward 1	63 27
TGEL		
Ludwig	San Francisco San Francisco 10	282 67
TGGART		
M M*	Nevada Bridgeport	61 486
TH		
Foo	Yuba Foster B	72 827
THACERUS		
Martinel	Santa Cruz Pajaro	66 554
THACHER		
J L	Tuolumne Twp 2	71 318
Thomas	Sierra Twp 5	66 941
Tyler	Yuba Marysville	72 968
THACK		
---	Yuba Slate Ro	72 684
THACKER		
Edward	Yuba Marysville	72 926
Harvey M	Humbolt Pacific	59 135
Henry H	Sonoma Russian	69 439
Hiram	Humbolt Pacific	59 136
Joel	Sonoma Petaluma	69 554
Robert	Yuba Marysville	72 930
Robet*	Yuba Marysville	72 930
THACKERUS		
Martinel	Santa Cruz Pajaro	66 554
THACKERY		
Elizabeth	Solano Benecia	69 313
THACKHAM		
James	Yuba Linda	72 989
THACKNER		
J	El Dorado Placerville	58 826
THADFORD		
Gershon	Humbolt Eureka	59 173
THAGISON		
Hanse	Tuolumne Twp 5	71 506
THAID		
August	San Francisco San Francisco 11	149 67
THAIM		
L	Sonoma Salt Point	69 691
THAIYER		
Robert H*	Yuba Rose Bar	72 790
THALEAR		
Mary E	El Dorado Placerville	58 912
THALEAS		
Mary E*	El Dorado Placerville	58 912
THALEC		
John	Tuolumne Twp 5	71 506
THALEE		
John	Tuolumne Montezuma	71 506
THALER		
Anton	Sacramento Ward 1	63 99
THALGOVE		
Geo	Nevada Nevada	61 330
THALK		
---	San Francisco San Francisco 11	144 67
THAM		
---*	Calaveras Twp 8	57 94

Name	County Locale	M653 Roll Page
THAM		
G	Nevada Grass Valley	61 235
THAMB		
J*	Nevada Grass Valley	61 143
THAMCO		
Peter O*	Sonoma Washington	69 678
THAME		
Jas	Amador Twp 1	55 491
THAMEY		
Philip*	Yuba Rose Bar	72 793
THAMH		
J*	Nevada Grass Valley	61 143
THAMHILL		
C	Nevada Grass Valley	61 238
THAMPSON		
J	Nevada Grass Valley	61 235
THAN		
---	Amador Twp 6	55 450
---	Mariposa Twp 3	60 618
---	Placer Forest H	62 806
Nong	San Francisco San Francisco 11	159 67
THANAS		
William*	Siskiyou Scott Va	69 43
THANE		
Edwind M	Monterey San Juan	60 987
Fred	Nevada Bloomfield	61 529
John	Calaveras Twp 10	57 276
THANPSON		
Mary	Siskiyou Callahan	69 9
THAOSS		
William	San Francisco San Francisco 11	153 67
THARBER		
Henry	Siskiyou Scott Va	69 57
THARE		
Dagoer	Mariposa Twp 1	60 660
THARGER		
A W*	Shasta Shasta	66 684
THARJER		
A W	Shasta Shasta	66 684
THARNEY		
Philip	Yuba Rose Bar	72 793
THARO		
Dagoer	Mariposa Twp 1	60 660
THARP		
H L	Stanislaus Emory	70 741
Hale	Tulara Twp 2	71 29
James W	Colusa Monroeville	57 449
T B	Amador Twp 2	55 262
Thos*	Placer Nicolaus	62 692
THARRIETA		
Francisco*	Calaveras Twp 4	57 341
THARTEY		
A B*	Nevada Nevada	61 284
THARTHY		
A B*	Nevada Nevada	61 284
THARTY		
A B*	Nevada Nevada	61 284
THARYER		
Robert H*	Yuba Rose Bar	72 790
THASE		
John*	El Dorado Kelsey	58 1130
THASES		
John*	Mariposa Twp 3	60 573
THASHER		
A	El Dorado Eldorado	58 944
THATCHER		
A	Butte Wyandotte	56 670
A M	El Dorado Placerville	58 850
Caroline	Los Angeles Los Angeles	59 334
Charles R	San Mateo Twp 3	65 88
David	Napa Napa	61 103
E F	Shasta Cottonwood	66 724
E T	Shasta Cottonwoood	66 724
George	Los Angeles Los Angeles	59 333
H P	Sierra Downieville	66 1017
Hugh	Tehama Tehama	70 940
J	Sacramento Cosumnes	63 410
Jacob	Sierra Cox'S Bar	66 949
Jefferson	Sierra Downieville	66 1000
John	Nevada Rough &	61 410
L B	Sierra Twp 5	66 941
Peter	Sierra Monte Crk	66 1035
Prentice	Monterey Alisal	60 1035
Scot	Sierra Cox'S Bar	66 949
T A	Sierra La Porte	66 787
W	El Dorado Placerville	58 898
W W	Sacramento Lee	63 214
William	Amador Twp 4	55 244
William	Yuba Marysville	72 922
Wm*	Butte Wyandotte	56 657
THATCHN		
Wm	Butte Wyandotte	56 657
THATIKER		
David	Napa Napa	61 103

Name	County Locale	M653 Roll Page
THATTEN		
J A	San Francisco San Francisco	2 67 676
THATTER		
Martin*	Mariposa Twp 3	60 621
THAUNG		
---	Fresno Twp 3	59 31
THAVIOR		
G D*	El Dorado Georgetown	58 677
THAW		
---	Amador Twp 2	55 286
G	Nevada Grass Valley	61 235
THAYER		
A W	Shasta Shasta	66 684
Andrew	Siskiyou Scott Va	69 34
Andrew E	San Francisco San Francisco	1 68 884
B B	San Francisco San Francisco	10 165 67
Charles	Yuba Rose Bar	72 796
Charles A	Yuba Rose Bar	72 798
Charles R	San Francisco San Francisco	7 681340
D V	Sonoma Santa Rosa	69 421
David N	Butte Bidwell	56 729
E F	Trinity Ferry	70 977
Edwd	San Francisco San Francisco	2 67 755
Emilens	Yuba Fosters	72 840
Emilius	Yuba Fosters	72 840
Enseliene*	San Francisco San Francisco	9 68 978
	San Francisco	
Enselime*	San Francisco San Francisco	9 68 978
Eugene	Tuolumne Sonora	71 201
Eusebine*	San Francisco San Francisco	9 68 978
Euselune*	San Francisco San Francisco	9 68 978
Henry	San Francisco San Francisco	10 274 67
James	Marin Cortemad	60 789
Jas P	Butte Oregon	56 609
Jno	San Francisco San Francisco	12 379 67
John	Calaveras Twp 5	57 228
John	Plumas Quincy	62 985
John S	Nevada Rough &	61 416
Julia D	Sacramento Ward 1	63 91
L	Nevada Grass Valley	61 222
L C	Nevada Nevada	61 320
Leonard	Sonoma Santa Rosa	69 421
Lewis	Sacramento Ward 4	63 504
M C	Sacramento Ward 4	63 547
N*	Tuolumne Twp 1	71 201
Noah	Santa Cruz Pajaro	66 528
O	Butte Bidwell	56 708
R M	Nevada Nevada	61 269
Robert H	Yuba Rose Bar	72 790
S	Nevada Grass Valley	61 222
S	Sacramento Ward 4	63 536
S E C	San Francisco San Francisco	7 681332
S J	Butte Ophir	56 783
T	Sacramento Ward 4	63 547
T	San Francisco San Francisco	6 67 438
Wales	Yuba Marysville	72 872
William	San Francisco San Francisco	9 681045
William K	Yuba Marysville	72 867
Wm G	Nevada Nevada	61 327
THAYNE		
Geo*	Butte Kimshaw	56 599
H T*	Butte Chico	56 560
THAYRE		
Geo	Butte Kimshaw	56 599
Geo T	Butte Hamilton	56 527
Geo*	Butte Kimshaw	56 599
H F	Butte Chico	56 560
H T*	Butte Chico	56 560
Louis	Butte Kimshaw	56 570
THE		
---*	Nevada Bridgeport	61 462
---*	Sacramento Cosummes	63 407
Loo	Yuba Long Bar	72 763
THEA		
Peter	Sacramento Ward 1	63 64
THEABIN		
B F*	Stanislaus Empire	70 730
THEADORA		
Catherine	Napa Napa	61 84
THEADORE		
Jesus	Napa Napa	61 84
THEALL		
George A	Sierra Twp 7	66 905
George C	Sierra Twp 7	66 905
Hiram W	Yuba Marysville	72 870
THEARER		
Jno	Alameda Brooklyn	55 107
THEASEN		
Chas	San Francisco San Francisco	9 681064
THEBANK		
L	Nevada Grass Valley	61 150
THEBARD		
Petar	Tuolumne Big Oak	71 137

Name	County Locale	M653 Roll Page
THEBARD		
Peter*	Tuolumne Twp 4	71 137
THEBARNI		
P E	Santa Clara San Jose	65 296
THEBOLT		
Frankf	Contra Costa Twp 3	57 595
THEDFORD		
Morgan	Sierra Scales D	66 804
THEDO		
Gustavis	Trinity Weaverville	701072
THEDORE		
Frinin*	Mariposa Coulterville	60 699
Frmin*	Mariposa Coulterville	60 699
Odoul	San Francisco San Francisco	11 140 67
THEE		
---	San Francisco San Francisco	4 681175
---	San Francisco San Francisco	4 681208
---	Yuba North Ea	72 675
Now	San Francisco San Francisco	11 160 67
THEEL		
I H	Amador Twp 2	55 324
THEEN		
Tee	San Francisco San Francisco	11 160 67
THEERING		
Mad	San Francisco San Francisco	10 328 67
THEERY		
Forn*	Mariposa Twp 3	60 555
Horn*	Mariposa Twp 3	60 555
THEES		
Mihola	Solano Benecia	69 298
Nicholas	Solano Benecia	69 298
THEHAN		
Thomas*	Yuba Foster B	72 824
THEHER		
Julia	San Francisco San Francisco	2 67 582
Michael	Santa Cruz Santa Cruz	66 628
THEHON		
Ellen*	Yuba New York	72 724
THEIDEL		
Louis	Siskiyou Klamath	69 88
THEIL		
Catherine	Sacramento Sutter	63 294
THEILE		
F H	San Francisco San Francisco	2 67 784
THEILERCKEN		
Fred*	Del Norte Crescent	58 626
THEILERCKER		
Fred*	Del Norte Crescent	58 626
THEIM		
John	Santa Cruz Pescadero	66 646
THEIME		
E	Nevada Nevada	61 278
THEIN		
Nicholas	San Bernardino San Salvador	64 659
THEING		
John	San Francisco San Francisco	4 681163
THEINKE		
Edward	Tuolumne Montezuma	71 513
THEIR		
Henry	Butte Oregon	56 630
John*	Placer Dutch Fl	62 713
THEIRE		
Stephen	Santa Clara San Jose	65 366
THEIS		
Jacob	Mariposa Coulterville	60 674
THEISHER		
Phillip	El Dorado Coloma	581069
THEISON		
John*	El Dorado Eldorado	58 938
THEISS		
Charles	El Dorado Mud Springs	58 981
THELINGER		
John	El Dorado Mud Springs	58 987
THELLA		
Theodore	Santa Cruz Pajaro	66 554
THELLER		
Anne	San Francisco San Francisco	11 152 67
THELRELL		
James	Santa Cruz Soguel	66 583
THELUE		
Mathias	El Dorado Placerville	58 917
THEM		
---	Tuolumne Columbia	71 346
Ah	Tuolumne Twp 2	71 346
THEMDYKE		
David W*	Placer Dutch Fl	62 717
THEMTON		
Joseph	Colusa Muion	57 459
THEN		
---	Sierra Downieville	661015
---	Yuba Slate Ro	72 684

Name	County Locale	M653 Roll Page
THENCKAUF		
T*	El Dorado Georgetown	58 746
THENCY		
William*	San Francisco San Francisco	9 681056
THENG		
---	Calaveras Twp 10	57 271
THENGATE		
Wm	Sacramento Natonia	63 273
THENICKUFF		
F*	Santa Clara Santa Clara	65 489
THENING		
Louis	San Francisco San Francisco	2 67 636
THENISH		
John	Amador Twp 1	55 460
THENLWELL		
J*	Nevada Eureka	61 344
THENLWILL		
J*	Nevada Eureka	61 344
THENNEKUFF		
F*	Santa Clara Santa Clara	65 489
THENON		
George	Los Angeles Los Angeles	59 343
THENY		
Peter	Calaveras Twp 5	57 228
THEOBALD		
John	San Francisco San Francisco	2 67 723
THEOBAULT		
Henry T	Sacramento San Joaquin	63 360
William	Contra Costa Twp 1	57 530
THEODNER		
Geo	Sacramento Granite	63 260
THEODORA		
Machanita*	Placer Michigan	62 840
THEODORE		
---	Calaveras Twp 8	57 86
---	Fresno Twp 2	59 101
Dennis	Trinity Weaverville	701080
Geo	Sacramento Granite	63 260
J	San Francisco San Francisco	5 67 490
J	San Joaquin Stockton	641089
John	Tuolumne Twp 2	71 414
Jose	Tuolumne Shawsfla	71 414
Thoring	Santa Clara San Jose	65 334
THEODRA		
Farncisco*	Amador Twp 2	55 316
THEODRN		
Francisco*	Amador Twp 2	55 316
THEODRU		
Francisca	Amador Twp 2	55 316
THEODULAS		
B	San Francisco San Francisco	6 67 441
THEOLINA		
Thomas	Santa Cruz Pajaro	66 547
THEOMAN		
John	Calaveras Twp 4	57 309
THEOMB		
Amias*	San Francisco San Francisco	1 68 807
THEOPHIO		
Hubert	Sierra Downieville	661022
THEOPLUS		
Hubert	Sierra Downieville	661022
THEORAKAUF		
T*	El Dorado Georgetown	58 746
THER		
---	Yuba Slate Ro	72 683
F F*	San Francisco San Francisco	1 68 929
THERBER		
Albert E	San Francisco San Francisco	7 681338
Benja F*	Calaveras Twp 5	57 243
THERCEAR		
Julius	San Francisco San Francisco	2 67 797
THERCOFF		
Anthony	Sonoma Sonoma	69 642
Frank*	Sonoma Sonoma	69 642
THEREOFF		
Frank*	Sonoma Sonoma	69 642
THERESA		
Maria	Yuba Long Bar	72 744
THERESE		
Marcelino	Calaveras Twp 7	57 27
Sister	Yuba Marysville	72 961
THERFULL		
Jas	Alameda Brooklyn	55 177
THERLER		
Benja F*	Calaveras Twp 5	57 243
THERMAN		
Saml	Tuolumne Twp 2	71 286
THERMIER		
Henry	Mariposa Twp 3	60 603
THERNDYKE		
David W*	Placer Dutch Fl	62 717
THERNE		
J	Siskiyou Klamath	69 88
THESCOFF		
Anthony	Sonoma Sonoma	69 642
Frank	Sonoma Sonoma	69 642

Name	County Locale	M653 Roll/Page
THESMAN		
Saml	Tuolumne Twp 2	71 286
THESSER		
O S	El Dorado White Oaks	581007
THESUP		
Benfa F	Calaveras Twp 5	57 243
THETARD		
Julius	Solano Benecia	69 315
THEUR		
Joaquin*	Mariposa Twp 1	60 641
THEURY		
William*	San Francisco San Francisco 9	681056
THEVENIN		
Julius	Siskiyou Yreka	69 188
THEVING		
Bill*	Tulara Visalia	71 116
J G*	San Francisco San Francisco 8	681298
THEY		
Thay*	San Francisco San Francisco 4	681151
THEYIS		
M M*	Napa Hot Springs	61 16
THI		
---	Sierra St Louis	66 813
Lee*	Butte Ophir	56 815
THIAN WANG		
---*	Mariposa Coulterville	60 683
THIBBETS		
John	Mariposa Coulterville	60 679
THIBOD		
Eugene	Yuba Marysville	72 875
THICKEY		
Julia*	Yuba Marysville	72 858
THICKLEY		
Willaim	San Francisco San Francisco 4	681167
William	San Francisco San Francisco 4	681167
THICLE		
Henry	Sacramento Ward 4	63 593
THIDMAN		
Wm	Mariposa Coulterville	60 686
THIE		
Pow	San Francisco San Francisco 4	681196
To	San Francisco San Francisco 4	681201
THIEBEAN		
Jos B	Sonoma Healdsbu	69 477
Mary Ann	Sonoma Healdsbu	69 477
THIEE		
J F*	Amador Twp 2	55 324
THIEL		
J F*	Amador Twp 2	55 324
THIELBAR		
Henry	Sacramento Ward 1	63 83
THIELE		
Henry J	Sacramento Ward 1	63 135
Juilius	San Francisco San Francisco 2	67 640
Robert	San Francisco San Francisco 8	681271
THIELHARER		
A	Amador Twp 7	55 412
N	Amador Twp 7	55 412
THIELO		
Elezebet*	San Francisco San Francisco 8	681272
Elizebet	San Francisco San Francisco 8	681272
THIELTRE		
M*	San Francisco San Francisco 5	67 552
THIER		
Henry*	Butte Oregon	56 630
THIERE		
Wilfred	Santa Clara San Jose	65 289
THIERING BILL		
---*	Tulara Twp 1	71 116
THIEROY		
J B	Sacramento Ward 1	63 42
THIERRY		
J B	Sacramento Ward 1	63 42
THIES		
Otto	Shasta Shasta	66 655
THIESON		
Charles	San Francisco San Francisco 9	681098
John*	El Dorado Eldorado	58 938
THIEVING BILL		
---*	Tulara Twp 1	71 116
THIEVING		
Bill*	Tulara Visalia	71 116
THIHI		
---	Calaveras Twp 8	57 59
THIHN		
Louis	Santa Cruz Santa Cruz	66 600
THIKEL		
---	Tulara Twp 1	71 115
THILANTE		
F J	San Francisco San Francisco 4	681112
THILANTT		
F J	San Francisco San Francisco 4	681112
THILL		
Theodore	Santa Cruz Pajaro	66 554
THILODENAUX		
Oliver T	Yuba Long Bar	72 743

Name	County Locale	M653 Roll/Page
THILODEOUX		
Oliver*	Yuba New York	72 743
THILRELL		
James	Santa Cruz Soguel	66 583
THIM		
---	Sierra Downieville	661015
Joaquin*	Mariposa Twp 1	60 641
THIMAS		
Harry*	Butte Ophir	56 824
Jas	Butte Chico	56 566
O P	Butte Chico	56 561
THIME		
Geo	El Dorado Salmon Falls	581034
THIMFIELD		
L E*	Mariposa Twp 3	60 586
THIMLET		
John	Placer Grizzly	62 755
THIMPOON		
Nathaniel	Sierra Twp 7	66 875
THIMPSEN		
Wm	Butte Wyandotte	56 668
THIMPSON		
D	Butte Wyandotte	56 667
E H	Sierra Twp 7	66 904
James W	Sierra Twp 7	66 887
N	Butte Wyandotte	56 670
Wm*	Butte Wyandotte	56 668
THIMSON		
James*	Sierra Twp 7	66 884
THIN		
---	San Francisco San Francisco 4	681209
Chow	Nevada Washington	61 341
Hee	San Francisco San Francisco 4	681201
Hu	San Francisco San Francisco 4	681201
Loo*	Amador Twp 2	55 311
Sou	El Dorado Greenwood	58 713
Yup	Nevada Eureka	61 384
THINAGER		
George	San Francisco San Francisco 7	681382
THINELS		
C*	Sacramento Ward 1	63 27
THING		
---	Calaveras Twp 10	57 271
---	Calaveras Twp 8	57 76
---	Sacramento Ward 1	63 54
A	Sonoma Salt Point	69 692
Mrs	Sonoma Salt Point	69 692
THINGLEBERGER		
F*	El Dorado Diamond	58 763
THINGNELLEA		
Iniallis	Calaveras Twp 7	57 1
Quiallis*	Calaveras Twp 7	57 1
THINK		
Hiram	Yuba Slate Ro	72 714
THINKER		
L H	Butte Chico	56 539
THINKLE		
Soloman	El Dorado Mud Springs	58 967
THINKLOULD		
Hugh*	Yuba North Ea	72 687
THINNER		
Andrew*	Yuba Foster B	72 832
THINR		
Joaguris*	Mariposa Twp 1	60 641
Joaquin*	Mariposa Twp 1	60 641
Joaquino*	Mariposa Twp 1	60 641
THINY		
---	Calaveras Twp 5	57 219
---*	Calaveras Twp 5	57 205
THIORY		
Fora*	Mariposa Twp 3	60 555
Forn*	Mariposa Twp 3	60 555
THIPHERD		
Isaac	Alameda Brooklyn	55 107
THIRBLEHOM		
J C*	Nevada Nevada	61 296
THIRKLOULD		
Hugh*	Yuba North Ea	72 687
THIRLE		
Otto	Placer Goods	62 696
THIRMAN		
Edward*	Yuba Marysville	72 865
THIRNUS		
David	Sacramento Natonia	63 271
Joseph	Nevada Bridgeport	61 472
THIRST		
Pat	Tehama Antelope	70 885
THIRSTRUM		
Joseph*	Contra Costa Twp 2	57 562
THIRSTUM		
Joseph*	Contra Costa Twp 2	57 562
THISELL		
George W	Solano Vacaville	69 359
THISEN		
Benj	El Dorado Eldorado	58 936
THISLE		
Watson	Solano Vacaville	69 362

Name	County Locale	M653 Roll/Page
THISTHELAND		
John	Placer Illinois	62 704
THIT		
---	San Francisco San Francisco 9	681094
---	San Francisco San Francisco 10	356 67
THITICKER		
Charles*	Placer Auburn	62 566
THITICKS		
Charles*	Placer Auburn	62 566
THITNEY		
Henry	San Francisco San Francisco 7	681338
THITTIES		
John F*	Siskiyou Yreka	69 124
THIURMAN		
Leech B*	Napa Clear Lake	61 130
Seech B*	Napa Clear Lake	61 130
THIVING		
J G*	San Francisco San Francisco 8	681298
THLESSMAN		
Geo	Siskiyou Scott Ri	69 61
THM		
---*	El Dorado Georgetown	58 701
THMPSON		
J	Tuolumne Twp 1	71 255
THO		
---	San Francisco San Francisco 4	681180
---	San Francisco San Francisco 12	392 67
THOADS		
Thomas F	Tuolumne Twp 5	71 508
Wm P	Sierra St Louis	66 863
THOAMS		
John	Siskiyou Callahan	69 2
THOBURN		
H T	San Francisco San Francisco 4	681224
THOCKER		
J	Shasta Horsetown	66 708
THODE		
H	San Francisco San Francisco 1	68 891
THODEHALD		
---	Nevada Bloomfield	61 511
THODES		
James	Stanislaus Emory	70 756
Thomas	San Francisco San Francisco 7	681409
THOIN		
Benj K	Calaveras Twp 5	57 189
THOLAY		
---	Nevada Bridgeport	61 458
THOLMAS		
John	Yuba Linda	72 985
THOM		
---	Siskiyou Scott Va	69 30
---	Siskiyou Scott Va	69 32
---*	Fresno Twp 1	59 118
A H	San Joaquin Elkhorn	64 989
Alexander	Sierra Twp 7	66 894
C W*	Nevada Grass Valley	61 196
Cameron E	Los Angeles Los Angeles	59 336
Chas	San Francisco San Francisco 1	68 920
H W*	Nevada Grass Valley	61 196
J*	Nevada Grass Valley	61 151
James*	Solano Vallejo	69 271
Joseph F	Mariposa Twp 1	60 641
L C*	Nevada Grass Valley	61 198
M S	San Francisco San Francisco 4	681127
N	Nevada Nevada	61 312
Richard	Yolo Cache Crk	72 663
S	Nevada Grass Valley	61 190
S G*	Napa Grass Valley	61 146
S G*	Nevada Grass Valley	61 146
Solomon*	Marin Cortemad	60 779
Wm	Monterey Pajaro	601020
Wm*	Nevada Eureka	61 349
THOMAN		
John*	Los Angeles Los Angeles	59 36
THOMAS		
---	Calaveras Twp 9	57 358
---	Del Norte Klamath	58 655
---	Del Norte Klamath	58 658
---	Mendocino Calpella	60 819
---	Mendocino Calpella	60 821
---	Mendocino Round Va	60 878
---	Mendocino Round Va	60 885
---	San Bernardino Santa Inez	64 137
---	San Bernardino San Bernadino	64 677
---	San Bernardino S Timate	64 696
---	San Francisco San Francisco 12	392 67
---	San Mateo Twp 3	65 106
---	Santa Cruz Santa Cruz	66 623
---	Siskiyou Yreka	69 128
---	Siskiyou Yreka	69 156
---	Tulara Twp 3	71 55
---	Yuba Parks Ba	72 779
A	Amador Twp 2	55 272

California 1860 Census Index

Name	County Locale	M653 Roll	Page
THOMAS			
A	Napa Napa	61	92
A	Nevada Grass Valley	61	165
A	Nevada Grass Valley	61	195
A	Nevada Grass Valley	61	207
A	Shasta Millvill	66	756
A D	Sacramento Ward 1	63	125
A J	San Francisco San Francisco 6	67	427
A L	Sacramento Ward 1	63	125
A M	Sacramento Ward 1	63	145
A T	Butte Ophir	56	780
Abel	El Dorado Mud Springs	58	978
Abraham S	San Joaquin Castoria	64	911
Alexander	Nevada Eureka	61	361
Alexander	Nevada Red Dog	61	543
Allen	Amador Twp 4	55	235
Alvis	Calaveras Twp 5	57	185
Angelina	Sonoma Petaluma	69	587
Ann	Nevada Bridgeport	61	445
Anna	Sacramento Ward 1	63	83
Anna	Yuba Marysville	72	869
Antoine	San Francisco San Francisco 3	67	79
Antonio	San Francisco San Francisco 3	67	79
Arthur	Butte Oregon	56	640
B	Amador Twp 1	55	496
B	Klamath S Fork	59	198
B	Siskiyou Yreka	69	140
Barney	El Dorado Georgetown	58	747
Benj	Amador Twp 1	55	493
Benjamin	Tulara Twp 2	71	21
Bob	San Francisco San Francisco 11	67	138
Bradley A	Alameda Brooklyn	55	192
Brash	Placer Damascus	62	846
C	Nevada Grass Valley	61	150
C J*	Nevada Grass Valley	61	182
C R	Tuolumne Twp 1	71	202
C S	Yolo Cache	72	607
Charles	Mendocino Big Rvr	60	848
Charles	Sierra Twp 7	66	897
Charles	Sierra Twp 5	66	946
Charles	Siskiyou Scott Va	69	39
Charles L	Yuba Marysville	72	869
Chas	Placer Dutch Fl	62	709
Chas	San Bernardino San Bernadino	64	668
Chas	San Francisco San Francisco 9	68	1076
Chas	Trinity Weaverville	70	1068
Chas G	Santa Clara San Jose	65	389
Chester	Sacramento Ward 1	63	76
Cornelius	Nevada Bridgeport	61	477
Cyrus	Siskiyou Yreka	69	158
Cyrus	Siskiyou Yreka	69	165
D	El Dorado Coloma	58	1082
D	Nevada Nevada	61	296
D	Nevada Eureka	61	371
D C	Trinity Raabs Ba	70	1020
Dan	Siskiyou Klamath	69	85
Dan J	Sacramento Ward 1	63	58
Daniel	San Joaquin Castoria	64	907
Danl	Del Norte Happy Ca	58	668
David	El Dorado Coloma	58	1122
David	Nevada Bridgeport	61	453
David	Placer Iona Hills	62	878
David	Sacramento Natonia	63	271
David	San Francisco San Francisco 1	68	862
David	Sierra Port Win	66	796
David	Siskiyou Scott Va	69	55
David	Tuolumne Shawsfla	71	412
David W	Sierra Chappare	66	1040
Dawson	San Francisco San Francisco 7	68	1367
Dunham	Sierra Downieville	66	963
E H	Mariposa Coulterville	60	696
E H	Tuolumne Twp 4	71	166
E M	Calaveras Twp 8	57	98
Eben K	Siskiyou Yreka	69	136
Ebenezer	Sierra Monte Crk	66	1038
Ed	Sacramento Natonia	63	282
Edw H	San Bernardino San Salvador	64	652
Edward	Amador Twp 4	55	246
Edward	Placer Dutch Fl	62	723
Edward	San Francisco San Francisco 2	67	563
Edward	Yolo Cache Crk	72	641
Eleazer	San Francisco San Francisco 6	67	410
Eliazer	Placer Michigan	62	807
Eliazer	Placer Michigan	62	823
Elis	Sacramento Ward 4	63	574
Elisab Eth	Sierra Eureka	66	1046
Elizabeth	Placer Sacramento	62	642
Elizabeth	San Francisco San Francisco 2	67	565
Ellen*	Sacramento Ward 1	63	97
Ellis	Calaveras Twp 8	57	56
Ephraim	Placer Dutch Fl	62	721
Evan	San Francisco San Francisco 7	68	1444
Evan	San Francisco San Francisco 3	67	62
F	Los Angeles Tejon	59	526
F C	Butte Eureka	56	648

Name	County Locale	M653 Roll	Page
THOMAS			
F M	Sierra Twp 5	66	920
Finlay	Monterey San Juan	60	974
Francis	Mariposa Twp 1	60	672
Francis	Plumas Quincy	62	942
Francis	Sierra Monte Crk	66	1039
Francis	Yolo Slate Ra	72	707
Francis	Yuba Slate Ro	72	707
Frank	Placer Virginia	62	689
Frank	Plumas Quincy	62	943
Frank	Plumas Quincy	62	981
Frank	Sierra Downieville	66	1001
Frederick	Calaveras Twp 6	57	444
Frederick	Contra Costa Twp 1	57	524
G	Nevada Grass Valley	61	165
G	Nevada Grass Valley	61	190
G	Shasta Millvill	66	756
G	Siskiyou Scott Ri	69	74
G R	Butte Oregon	56	633
Geo	Butte Ophir	56	783
Geo	Nevada Grass Valley	61	223
Geo	Nevada Eureka	61	349
Geo	Nevada Eureka	61	370
Geo	Placer Rattle Snake	62	634
Geo	Sacramento Sutter	63	306
Geo	San Francisco San Francisco 1	68	908
Geo F	Sacramento Ward 1	63	108
Geo T	Sacramento Ward 1	63	108
Geo W	San Francisco San Francisco 6	67	465
George	Mendocino Calpella	60	810
George	Nevada Bloomfield	61	521
George	Sierra Twp 5	66	947
George	Solano Suisan	69	231
George	Tuolumne Twp 1	71	264
George	Tuolumne Shawsfla	71	388
George A	Los Angeles Los Angeles	59	386
Geroge	Tuolumne Twp 1	71	264
Giles	Yuba Marysville	72	977
Godshall	Sierra Whiskey	66	850
Granville	Tulara Visalia	71	76
Grumville	Tulara Twp 1	71	76
H	Butte Cascade	56	692
H	Calaveras Twp 9	57	414
H	Los Angeles Tejon	59	526
H	Nevada Grass Valley	61	184
H	Nevada Grass Valley	61	187
H	Shasta Horsetown	66	697
H	Sonoma Washington	69	675
H A	Sacramento Ward 4	63	605
H H	Nevada Grass Valley	61	207
H J	El Dorado Placerville	58	821
H J	Nevada Bridgeport	61	440
H M	Placer Iona Hills	62	883
H R	Butte Eureka	56	654
H R	Butte Ophir	56	795
Hennreietta F	San Francisco San Francisco 7	68	1351
Henrietta F	San Francisco San Francisco 7	68	1351
Henry	Los Angeles San Jose	59	281
Henry	Plumas Quincy	62	996
Henry	San Francisco San Francisco 10	67	271
Henry	Sierra Twp 5	66	939
Henry F	Sonoma Russian	69	440
Hermon	Butte Bidwell	56	730
Hiram	Del Norte Happy Ca	58	670
Hirum	Butte Bidwell	56	730
Hobson	Sacramento Ward 1	63	33
Howel	Nevada Bridgeport	61	440
Howel P	Nevada Bridgeport	61	470
Hugh	San Joaquin Elkhorn	64	972
Hugh	Tuolumne Shawsfla	71	412
I M*	Nevada Red Dog	61	554
Ingraham	Placer Iona Hills	62	894
Isaac	Santa Clara San Jose	65	312
Isac C*	Calaveras Twp 9	57	352
Isac P	Calaveras Twp 9	57	352
Ishmael	Nevada Red Dog	61	550
Isiah	Sonoma Armally	69	498
Israel	Santa Clara Thomas	65	443
J	Butte Oregon	56	648
J	El Dorado Coloma	58	1121
J	El Dorado Diamond	58	774
J	Nevada Grass Valley	61	151
J	Nevada Grass Valley	61	189
J	Nevada Grass Valley	61	190
J	Nevada Grass Valley	61	201
J	Nevada Grass Valley	61	209
J	Nevada Grass Valley	61	220
J	Nevada Grass Valley	61	224
J	Nevada Grass Valley	61	236
J	Nevada Nevada	61	315
J	Nevada Nevada	61	326
J	Nevada Washington	61	336
J	Nevada Eureka	61	367

Name	County Locale	M653 Roll	Page
THOMAS			
J	Sacramento Brighton	63	201
J	Sacramento Brighton	63	204
J	Shasta Millvill	66	745
J	Sutter Yuba	70	764
J B	San Francisco San Francisco 6	67	405
J F	Nevada Nevada	61	327
J H	Nevada Nevada	61	312
J J	Sutter Yuba	70	778
J M	Sierra Twp 5	66	920
J M*	Nevada Red Dog	61	554
J N	San Francisco San Francisco 5	67	502
J S	Alameda Brooklyn	55	165
J S	Nevada Grass Valley	61	217
J T	El Dorado Big Bar	58	741
J T M	Mariposa Twp 3	60	584
J W	Placer Dutch Fl	62	716
Jacob	El Dorado Salmon Falls	58	1051
Jacob	Nevada Red Dog	61	554
James	Calaveras Twp 7	57	48
James	Contra Costa Twp 2	57	565
James	Mariposa Coulterville	60	677
James	Mendocino Ukiah	60	793
James	San Francisco San Francisco 9	68	982
James	Santa Cruz Pajaro	66	526
James	Siskiyou Scott Va	69	31
James	Tuolumne Sonora	71	233
James	Yuba Long Bar	72	747
James A	Tuolumne Twp 1	71	254
James E	Siskiyou Scott Va	69	24
James F	Tuolumne Twp 2	71	378
James H	Mendocino Round Va	60	880
James H	Sierra Twp 7	66	879
James*	Yuba New York	72	747
Jane	San Francisco San Francisco 4	68	1149
Jas	Butte Chico	56	543
Jas	Butte Chico	56	566
Jas	Butte Bidwell	56	721
Jas	Napa Napa	61	74
Jas	Placer Virginia	62	685
Jas	Sacramento Natonia	63	271
Jas	San Francisco San Francisco 2	67	805
Jas	Trinity Texas Ba	70	981
Jas E	Butte Ophir	56	755
Jeremiah	Sacramento Natonia	63	271
Jeremimiah	Colusa Muion	57	461
Jessee	San Francisco San Francisco 9	68	1083
Jessie	San Francisco San Francisco 9	68	1083
Jjohn	Del Norte Happy Ca	58	669
Jno	Butte Oregon	56	635
Jno	Monterey Monterey	60	963
Jno	Nevada Nevada	61	321
Jno	Nevada Nevada	61	324
Jno	Nevada Eureka	61	349
Jno	Sacramento Ward 4	63	559
Jno E	Klamath S Fork	59	197
John	Alameda Brooklyn	55	107
John	Alameda Brooklyn	55	196
John	Amador Twp 2	55	299
John	Amador Twp 1	55	456
John	Butte Wyandotte	56	664
John	Calaveras Twp 6	57	163
John	Calaveras Twp 5	57	200
John	Calaveras Twp 4	57	317
John	El Dorado Greenwood	58	729
John	Humbolt Eureka	59	176
John	Marin Bolinas	60	728
John	Mariposa Twp 3	60	591
John	Mariposa Twp 1	60	668
John	Mariposa Coulterville	60	679
John	Nevada Grass Valley	61	235
John	Nevada Nevada	61	326
John	Nevada Rough &	61	411
John	Placer Folsom	62	640
John	Placer Dutch Fl	62	711
John	Placer Forest H	62	767
John	Placer Iona Hills	62	869
John	Placer Iona Hills	62	874
John	Placer Iona Hills	62	878
John	Placer Iona Hills	62	880
John	Plumas Meadow Valley	62	899
John	Plumas Quincy	62	952
John	San Bernardino San Salvador	64	655
John	San Francisco San Francisco 10	67	310
John	San Francisco San Francisco 2	67	676
John	San Francisco San Francisco 1	68	914
John	San Mateo Twp 1	65	48
John	San Mateo Twp 3	65	79
John	Santa Clara San Jose	65	390
John	Sierra La Porte	66	784
John	Sierra Twp 7	66	895
John	Siskiyou Callahan	69	2
John	Solano Vallejo	69	245
John	Sonoma Petaluma	69	599

California 1860 Census Index

Name	County	Locale	M653 Roll	Page
THOMAS				
John	Tehama	Lassen	70	871
John	Trinity	Rattle Snake	70	1029
John	Tuolumne	Twp 2	71	282
John	Tuolumne	Sonora	71	484
John	Yolo	Washington	72	572
John	Yolo	No E Twp	72	667
John	Yuba	Marysville	72	972
John	Yuba	Suida	72	985
John A	San Francisco	San Francisco 2	67	774
John S	Placer	Iona Hills	62	874
John W	Sierra	Twp 7	66	877
Jon	Solano	Vallejo	69	245
Jos	Calaveras	Twp 4	57	317
Jos	Sacramento	Ward 3	63	432
Jos	San Francisco	San Francisco 2	67	805
Joseph	El Dorado	Salmon Hills	58	1052
Joseph	Nevada	Rough &	61	431
Joseph	Nevada	Bridgeport	61	472
Joseph	Nevada	Bloomfield	61	507
Joseph	Plumas	Quincy	62	1000
Joseph	Tulara	Visalia	71	104
Joseph	Tuolumne	Twp 1	71	185
Joseph A	Siskiyou	Shasta Valley	69	120
Joseph N	Tulara	Visalia	71	104
Josephine	San Francisco	San Francisco 10	67	181
Js	Calaveras	Twp 4	57	317
Julia A	Sacramento	Ward 1	63	104
Julius	Plumas	Quincy	62	941
Kemma	Sacramento	Ward 1	63	83
L	Butte	Ophir	56	745
L	Nevada	Grass Valley	61	146
L	Nevada	Grass Valley	61	150
L	Nevada	Grass Valley	61	160
L	Nevada	Grass Valley	61	224
L	Santa Clara	Redwood	65	456
L	Shasta	Millvill	66	746
L H	Tehama	Antelope	70	890
Laurant	San Joaquin	Stockton	64	1033
Lewis B	Tuolumne	Shawsfla	71	411
Louis	San Francisco	San Francisco 11	67	151
Lucius W	Yuba	Suida	72	985
M	Butte	Ophir	56	748
M	Nevada	Grass Valley	61	157
M	Nevada	Washington	61	334
M F	Trinity	Lewiston	70	954
M G	Yolo	Slate Ra	72	703
M K	Siskiyou	Scott Ri	69	71
M S	Yuba	Slate Ro	72	703
M W	Siskiyou	Callahan	69	8
Major W	San Joaquin	Castoria	64	896
Manday*	Sierra	Downieville	66	963
Margt	San Francisco	San Francisco 2	67	673
Marshall	Nevada	Red Dog	61	549
Mary	Plumas	Quincy	62	936
Mary	San Francisco	San Francisco 3	67	43
Mary	San Francisco	San Francisco 2	67	781
Mary Ann	San Bernardino	San Salvador	64	653
Massey	Santa Clara	Gilroy	65	250
McHls	Butte	Hamilton	56	514
Me*	Mariposa	Twp 1	60	653
Morgan	Calaveras	Twp 5	57	241
N	Yolo	Washington	72	602
N C	Shasta	Shasta	66	760
N F	Yolo	Slate Ra	72	704
N F	Yuba	Slate Ro	72	704
N J	Nevada	Bridgeport	61	440
N P	Tuolumne	Twp 2	71	378
Nathan C	Siskiyou	Shasta Valley	69	120
Nathan H	Trinity	Raabs Ba	70	1020
Neland	Sierra	Downieville	66	963
Netty	Sacramento	Ward 4	63	572
Nichols	Sacramento	Ward 4	63	537
Nulace*	Calaveras	Twp 6	57	163
O P	Butte	Chico	56	561
Onorene	San Francisco	San Francisco 2	67	763
Onorene*	San Francisco	San Francisco 2	67	763
Owen	Sierra	Eureka	66	1043
Owen	Sierra	Cold Can	66	836
P	Stanislaus	Branch	70	703
Patrick	San Francisco	San Francisco 2	67	597
Pausmus	El Dorado	Georgetown	58	691
Peter	Nevada	Bloomfield	61	510
Peter	San Francisco	San Francisco 9	68	1090
Philip	Trinity	Turner'S	70	997
Philip W	Placer	Auburn	62	559
Platt	San Francisco	San Francisco 3	67	23
Pleas	Sierra	La Porte	66	781
R	Nevada	Grass Valley	61	157
R	San Francisco	San Francisco 5	67	553
R	Sutter	Bear Rvr	70	826
R A	Nevada	Grass Valley	61	198
R A	Trinity	Weaverville	70	1062

Name	County	Locale	M653 Roll	Page
THOMAS				
R S	Trinity	New Rvr	70	1031
Ricd L	Tuolumne	Twp 2	71	412
Richard	Klamath	Klamath	59	226
Richard	Placer	Michigan	62	829
Richard	Placer	Michigan	62	830
Richard F	Yuba	Suida	72	985
Richford	Placer	Damascus	62	846
Robert	Sierra	Pine Grove	66	821
Robert T	Humbolt	Eureka	59	166
Robson*	Sacramento	Ward 1	63	33
Robt	Sonoma	Petaluma	69	563
Robt	Trinity	E Weaver	70	1058
S	Butte	Ophir	56	745
S	Nevada	Grass Valley	61	150
S	Nevada	Grass Valley	61	190
S	Santa Clara	Redwood	65	455
S	Tuolumne	Big Oak	71	150
S A	Sutter	Yuba	70	763
S C	Santa Clara	San Jose	65	306
S G	Calaveras	Twp 9	57	373
S J	Sutter	Bear Rvr	70	826
S M	Nevada	Grass Valley	61	191
S P	Calaveras	Twp 9	57	373
S P	Sacramento	Ward 1	63	50
S S	Tehama	Red Bluff	70	926
Sam	Solano	Fremont	69	380
Saml	Butte	Ophir	56	758
Saml	Calaveras	Twp 6	57	157
Saml	Mariposa	Twp 3	60	577
Samuel	Placer	Yankee J	62	775
Samuel P	Placer	Auburn	62	562
Sarah	Alameda	Oakland	55	27
Sarah	Amador	Twp 1	55	455
Sarah	Mariposa	Twp 3	60	577
Sarah	Tuolumne	Twp 2	71	355
Sercius W*	Yuba	Linda	72	985
Shepherd	Alameda	Oakland	55	69
Silas	Sierra	La Porte	66	781
Summma	Sierra	Downieville	66	1017
Sylvester	Butte	Cascade	56	703
Sylvester	Plumas	Quincy	62	935
T A	San Mateo	Twp 3	65	100
T B	Sierra	Twp 7	66	897
T G	Placer	Todds Va	62	764
T H	Sutter	Nicolaus	70	830
Teranic*	Placer	Todds Va	62	787
Thomas	El Dorado	Mud Springs	58	994
Thomas	Sacramento	Ward 1	63	99
Thomas	San Francisco	San Francisco 2	67	598
Thomas	Sierra	Downieville	66	1016
Thomas	Sierra	Monte Crk	66	1038
Thomas E	San Joaquin	Elkhorn	64	1000
Thornton	Siskiyou	Callahan	69	2
Thos	Amador	Twp 1	55	509
Thos	Butte	Hamilton	56	527
Thos	Butte	Chico	56	557
Thos	Butte	Oregon	56	639
Victor H	Yuba	New York	72	730
Victor H	Yuba	New York	72	734
W	Nevada	Grass Valley	61	212
W	Nevada	Grass Valley	61	215
W	Nevada	Eureka	61	387
W	San Francisco	San Francisco 5	67	530
W	San Joaquin	Stockton	64	1091
W	Tehama	Lassen	70	879
W C	Stanislaus	Buena Village	70	721
W E	Sacramento	Centre	63	174
W F	Trinity	Lewiston	70	954
W F	Tuolumne	Twp 1	71	254
W H	Sacramento	Ward 1	63	18
W H	Siskiyou	Klamath	69	89
W H R	Butte	Oregon	56	616
W J	Nevada	Grass Valley	61	210
W L	El Dorado	Georgetown	58	674
W L	Tehama	Lassen	70	873
W M	Sierra	Excelsior	66	1034
W P	Sierra	Downieville	66	1003
W P	Tuolumne	Shawsfla	71	378
W W	Yolo	Cache	72	630
Walace	Calaveras	Twp 6	57	163
Walter F	Tulara	Twp 1	71	76
Warren	Alameda	Oakland	55	11
William	Alameda	Brooklyn	55	102
William	Contra Costa	Twp 1	57	524
William	El Dorado	White Oaks	58	1018
William	El Dorado	Greenwood	58	720
William	Klamath	Dillins	59	214
William	Nevada	Rough &	61	413
William	Nevada	Bridgeport	61	440
William	Nevada	Bloomfield	61	516
William	Placer	Michigan	62	828
William	Placer	Michigan	62	852
William	Placer	Iona Hills	62	870
William	San Francisco	San Francisco 7	68	1333
William	San Francisco	San Francisco 7	68	1426

Name	County	Locale	M653 Roll	Page
THOMAS				
William	Sierra	Pine Grove	66	834
William	Siskiyou	Scott Va	69	43
William	Tulara	Twp 2	71	10
William	Yuba	Rose Bar	72	807
William D	San Francisco	San Francisco 11	67	126
William G	Yolo	Merritt	72	578
William J	Siskiyou	Shasta Valley	69	120
William L	Yolo	Merritt	72	578
William M	Siskiyou	Yreka	69	146
William*	Siskiyou	Scott Va	69	43
Willilam D	Calaveras	Twp 8	57	58
Wm	Calaveras	Twp 9	57	359
Wm	Klamath	Klamath	59	224
Wm	Marin	Bolinas	60	743
Wm	Nevada	Grass Valley	61	159
Wm	Nevada	Eureka	61	366
Wm	Nevada	Eureka	61	373
Wm	Sacramento	Ward 1	63	74
Wm	San Francisco	San Francisco 2	67	763
Wm	San Francisco	San Francisco 2	67	763
Wm	Sierra	Monte Crk	66	1036
Wm	Sierra	Downieville	66	961
Wm	Sonoma	Petaluma	69	585
Wm	Yolo	Slate Ra	72	687
Wm	Yolo	Slate Ra	72	702
Wm	Yuba	North Ea	72	687
Wm	Yuba	Slate Ro	72	702
Wm	Yuba	Parks Ba	72	779
Wm A	San Bernardino	S Timate	64	688
Wm G	El Dorado	Greenwood	58	729
Zephrin	Sierra	Poker Flats	66	839
THOMASITA				
---	San Bernardino	San Bernadino	64	677
THOMASON				
Jno	Sacramento	Ward 4	63	529
O	San Francisco	San Francisco 1	68	864
Vanse	Calaveras	Twp 9	57	371
THOMASS				
John*	Los Angeles	Los Angeles	59	36
THOMASSON				
Thos	Butte	Hamilton	56	526
W H	Butte	Chico	56	565
THOMB				
J	Nevada	Grass Valley	61	143
THOMBERRY				
C N	Siskiyou	Scott Va	69	28
THOMBO				
Peter O*	Sonoma	Washington	69	678
THOMBROOK				
M	Nevada	Grass Valley	61	167
THOMBY				
T	Marin	Tomales	60	713
THOME				
H*	Nevada	Nevada	61	324
THOMES				
Jacob	Mariposa	Coulterville	60	698
THOMET				
Chas	San Francisco	San Francisco 2	67	710
N	San Francisco	San Francisco 6	67	472
THOMFELDT				
Dettow	Calaveras	Twp 5	57	229
THOMFORD				
Henry	San Francisco	San Francisco 10	67	165
THOMGHAMSON				
Sanford	Shasta	Millvill	66	748
THOMH				
J*	Nevada	Grass Valley	61	143
THOMHILL				
C	Nevada	Grass Valley	61	188
J	Nevada	Eureka	61	371
S	Nevada	Grass Valley	61	195
THOMKINS				
D B	Tehama	Tehama	70	937
THOMLEW				
L	Butte	Eureka	56	648
THOMLEY				
Ben	Trinity	Trinity	70	973
THOMNER				
J F	San Bernardino	San Bernadino	64	627
THOMPA				
Archibald	Calaveras	Twp 6	57	155
David	Mariposa	Twp 3	60	622
THOMPAON				
Wm	San Francisco	San Francisco 10	67	357
THOMPAR				
Orin	Sacramento	Natonia	63	278
THOMPEN				
J H	Sacramento	Sutter	63	308
James*	Calaveras	Twp 4	57	335
THOMPHSON				
Geo	Butte	Eureka	56	653
THOMPIN				
Daniel	Calaveras	Twp 6	57	128

California 1860 Census Index

Name	County Locale	M653 RollPage
THOMPIN		
David	Calaveras Twp 6	57 128
James*	Calaveras Twp 4	57 335
THOMPKIN		
H C	Siskiyou Klamath	69 90
John	Siskiyou Scott Va	69 47
THOMPKINS		
G	Sierra La Porte	66 773
H C	Siskiyou Klamath	69 90
J M	Siskiyou Scott Va	69 42
J M	Siskiyou Scott Va	69 43
Jas R	Butte Oregon	56 634
John	Siskiyou Callahan	69 18
Lambert	El Dorado Greenwood	58 729
Louis A	Siskiyou Scott Va	69 43
M M	Sacramento Ward 4	63 608
Silas	Siskiyou Scott Ri	69 65
W B	Siskiyou Scott Va	69 27
THOMPN		
David*	Mariposa Twp 3	60 622
THOMPO		
Wm*	Mariposa Coulterville	60 677
THOMPON		
Alexander	Calaveras Twp 6	57 128
Alexander	Sierra Pine Grove	66 825
Benja F	Calaveras Twp 10	57 277
J H	Sacramento Sutter	63 307
James	Calaveras Twp 4	57 335
Jesse*	Calaveras Twp 4	57 337
John*	Calaveras Twp 9	57 399
Lynch	Placer Auburn	62 596
R L	Butte Hamilton	56 519
THOMPSEN		
Alex	Amador Twp 2	55 300
D H	San Francisco San Francisco 3	67 45
David	Mariposa Twp 3	60 622
Ed	Sacramento Natonia	63 285
Elias	Sacramento Granite	63 248
George H	Monterey Monterey	60 958
Jno M	Sacramento Natonia	63 274
John	Amador Twp 2	55 306
Lewis H	Sacramento Ward 4	63 496
Paul	Sacramento Sutter	63 305
THOMPSO		
Wm*	Mariposa Coulterville	60 677
THOMPSOLN		
David	Siskiyou Yreka	69 128
THOMPSON		
---	Amador Twp 3	55 381
---	Nevada Bridgeport	61 451
---	Siskiyou Shasta Valley	69 118
---	Yuba Marysville	72 941
---*	San Joaquin Douglass	64 920
A	Butte Cascade	56 700
A	El Dorado Georgetown	58 684
A	Nevada Grass Valley	61 235
A	Nevada Washington	61 332
A	Nevada Eureka	61 381
A	San Francisco San Francisco 5	67 548
A	Tehama Lassen	70 882
A	Tehama Antelope	70 894
A A*	Solano Fremont	69 376
A B	San Bernardino Santa Barbara	64 150
A C	Nevada Eureka	61 359
A E	San Joaquin Stockton	641094
A G	Nevada Nevada	61 262
A G	Siskiyou Scott Va	69 38
A H	El Dorado White Oaks	581013
A H	Sacramento Granite	63 262
A J	Butte Oregon	56 632
A J	Sacramento Ward 1	63 47
A J	Trinity Trinity	70 973
A L	Siskiyou Klamath	69 80
A M	Santa Clara Santa Clara	65 523
A P	El Dorado Coloma	581123
A W	Sonoma Petaluma	69 583
Aaron	Tulara Visalia	71 32
Abram	Nevada Bridgeport	61 494
Alex	Alameda Brooklyn	55 120
Alex	Amador Twp 2	55 319
Alex	Calaveras Twp 6	57 122
Alex	Humbolt Bucksport	59 157
Alex	Nevada Rough &	61 433
Alex	San Francisco San Francisco 10	292 67
Alexander	Calaveras Twp 6	57 128
Alexander	Sierra Pine Grove	66 825
Alexander	Yuba New York	72 733
Allen B	Santa Cruz Pescadero	66 647
Amanda	Nevada Little Y	61 536
Amasa	Plumas Meadow Valley	62 903
Andrew	Del Norte Happy Ca	58 668
Andrew	El Dorado Georgetown	58 759
Andrew	Marin Novato	60 736
Andrew	San Francisco San Francisco 11	134 67

Name	County Locale	M653 RollPage
THOMPSON		
Andrew	San Francisco San Francisco 10	349 67
Andrew	San Francisco San Francisco 3	67 53
Andrew	Santa Cruz Pescadero	66 641
Andrew	Santa Cruz Pescadero	66 647
Andrew J	San Joaquin Elliott	64 944
Andrew V	Placer Sacramento	62 646
Andw	Sacramento Lee	63 215
Anee	El Dorado Salmon Falls	581035
Anna	Tuolumne Twp 1	71 219
Aos	Placer Forest H	62 773
Archibald	Calaveras Twp 6	57 155
Asa	Del Norte Crescent	58 620
Asa	Plumas Quincy	621005
B	Amador Twp 1	55 489
B	El Dorado Mud Springs	58 954
B	Santa Clara Redwood	65 444
B B	Yuba Fosters	72 839
B D	Klamath Liberty	59 235
B F	El Dorado Kelsey	581126
B F	Sacramento Cosumnes	63 394
B R	Nevada Nevada	61 284
Barton	Santa Clara San Jose	65 344
Benja F	Calaveras Twp 10	57 277
Bernard	El Dorado Placerville	58 920
Bernard	San Joaquin Castoria	64 885
Bridget	Calaveras Twp 8	57 52
C	Nevada Nevada	61 270
C	Nevada Nevada	61 280
C	Nevada Washington	61 332
C	San Francisco San Francisco 9	681059
C	San Francisco San Francisco 5	67 529
C	San Francisco San Francisco 5	67 541
C	Siskiyou Cottonwood	69 99
C	Trinity Honest B	701043
C	Tuolumne Twp 3	71 459
C E	San Francisco San Francisco 4	681225
C F	Amador Twp 6	55 438
C L	Tuolumne Shawsfla	71 415
C M	Sutter Sutter	70 802
C R	Tehama Red Bluff	70 905
C S	Sacramento Granite	63 241
Cail*	Butte Chico	56 554
Capt	Placer Secret R	62 611
Carl	Butte Chico	56 554
Catharine	San Francisco San Francisco 2	67 655
Charles	Calaveras Twp 7	57 1
Charles	Calaveras Twp 7	57 6
Charles	Marin Cortemad	60 779
Charles	Monterey San Juan	601007
Charles	Placer Forest H	62 766
Charles	Plumas Meadow Valley	62 913
Charles	San Francisco San Francisco 2	67 712
Charles	San Joaquin Elliott	64 942
Charles	Solano Vallejo	69 244
Charles	Yuba Linda	72 984
Charles C	Calaveras Twp 7	57 1
Charles S	San Joaquin Elkhorn	64 980
Chas	Amador Twp 1	55 473
Chas	Amador Twp 1	55 488
Chas	Amador Twp 1	55 505
Chas	Butte Ophir	56 762
Chas	Calaveras Twp 10	57 298
Chas	Del Norte Happy Ca	58 669
Chas	Mariposa Twp 3	60 616
Chas	Placer Stewart	62 607
Chas	Sacramento Centre	63 174
Chas	Sacramento Cosumnes	63 382
Chas	Sacramento Ward 3	63 427
Chas	San Francisco San Francisco 3	67 70
Chauncy	Plumas Meadow Valley	62 934
Chs	Sonoma Petaluma	69 597
Cirl W	Tuolumne Chinese	71 494
Clara	Sierra La Porte	66 772
Clarck	El Dorado Placerville	58 925
Clinton	San Diego Colorado	64 811
D	Amador Twp 1	55 505
D	Butte Wyandotte	56 667
D	Calaveras Twp 9	57 417
D B	Tuolumne Twp 4	71 167
D E	Solano Fremont	69 381
D H	San Francisco San Francisco 3	67 45
D V	Solano Vacaville	69 324
D W	San Bernardino Santa Barbara	64 149
D W C	San Francisco San Francisco 10	201 67
Daniel	Calaveras Twp 10	57 293
Daniel	Calaveras Twp 7	57 3
Daniel	Santa Cruz Santa Cruz	66 614
Daniel	Solano Fremont	69 376
David	Marin Cortemad	60 791
David	Nevada Bloomfield	61 520
David	San Mateo Twp 2	65 126
David	Siskiyou Yreka	69 128
David	Tulara Twp 2	71 5

Name	County Locale	M653 RollPage
THOMPSON		
Decater	Sierra La Porte	66 777
Decator	Sierra La Porte	66 777
Dominic	Amador Twp 4	55 242
E	Sacramento Ward 1	63 41
E	Sacramento Ward 4	63 514
E H	Sierra Twp 7	66 904
E O	San Francisco San Francisco 5	67 550
Ed	Sacramento Natonia	63 285
Ediora R	San Joaquin Elliott	64 948
Edward	Calaveras Twp 7	57 14
Edward	El Dorado White Oaks	581004
Edward	Yuba Marysville	72 944
Edward	Yuba Bear Rvr	72 998
Edwd	San Francisco San Francisco 1	68 847
Edwin	Sierra Downieville	661013
Elias	Sacramento Granite	63 248
Elisha	Tuolumne Twp 1	71 264
Eliza	Sonoma Mendocino	69 462
Ellen	San Francisco San Francisco 4	681228
Emma	San Francisco San Francisco 4	681112
F	Amador Twp 1	55 453
F H	Yuba New York	72 736
F W	San Bernardino Santa Barbara	64 150
Fane	Colusa Grand Island	57 470
Fayette	Sierra Downieville	661013
Feorge W	Colusa Muion	57 460
Fernando	Sierra La Porte	66 777
Field W	Klamath Klamath	59 228
Fleming	Yuba New York	72 721
Francis	Alameda Brooklyn	55 199
Francis	Siskiyou Callahan	69 9
Frank	Marin Cortemad	60 779
Frank	San Francisco San Francisco 8	681306
Frank	Siskiyou Scott Va	69 39
Frank	Tehama Lassen	70 884
Franklin	San Francisco San Francisco 9	68 975
Fred	Mariposa Twp 1	60 670
Fred	Placer Forest H	62 769
Fred	San Francisco San Francisco 9	681055
Fred	San Francisco San Francisco 3	67 70
Fred	Tuolumne Twp 2	71 360
G	Nevada Grass Valley	61 196
G	San Francisco San Francisco 9	681060
G	San Joaquin Stockton	641099
G	Shasta Cottonwood	66 736
G B	Sonoma Cloverdale	69 680
G Deon	Tuolumne Twp 5	71 516
G H	El Dorado Placerville	58 889
G W	Butte Kimshaw	56 585
G W	Mariposa Coulterville	60 703
G W	Shasta Shasta	66 686
Geo	Butte Eureka	56 653
Geo	Butte Ophir	56 754
Geo	El Dorado Coloma	581079
Geo	Nevada Washington	61 338
Geo	Placer Auburn	62 585
Geo	Sacramento Ward 4	63 587
Geo	San Francisco San Francisco 9	681072
Geo	San Francisco San Francisco 9	681076
Geo	San Francisco San Francisco 9	681089
Geo	San Francisco San Francisco 6	67 446
Geo	Yolo Merritt	72 582
Geo C	San Francisco San Francisco 2	67 726
Geo E	San Francisco San Francisco 1	68 854
Geo W	Alameda Brooklyn	55 93
Geo W	Tuolumne Twp 1	71 252
George	Placer Michigan	62 856
George	Plumas Quincy	62 966
George	San Diego Colorado	64 809
George	San Joaquin Elliott	64 941
George	Tuolumne Twp 5	71 494
George H	Monterey Monterey	60 958
George W	Yuba Marysville	72 864
Georgiana	San Joaquin Stockton	641057
Geroge	Tuolumne Chinese	71 494
Gideon	Tuolumne Jacksonville	71 516
Gilber	Sonoma Vallejo	69 627
Gilber L	Sonoma Vallejo	69 627
Gilbert	Sonoma Petaluma	69 546
H	Amador Twp 5	55 345
H	El Dorado Georgetown	58 684
H	Nevada Nevada	61 279
H	Nevada Eureka	61 381
H	Sacramento Ward 4	63 515
H	San Francisco San Francisco 9	681059
H	San Francisco San Francisco 5	67 544
H	Shasta Shasta	66 666
H C	San Francisco San Francisco 4	681229
H D	Butte Oregon	56 618
H F	Tuolumne Twp 2	71 400
H J*	Nevada Nevada	61 316
H L	Nevada Nevada	61 316
H L	Solano Benecia	69 307
H L	Yolo Cottonwood	72 661
H P	El Dorado Coloma	581123

California 1860 Census Index

THOMPSON

Name	County Locale	M653 Roll	Page
H W	Butte Oregon	56	616
Hanah	Contra Costa Twp 1	57	536
Hannah	San Francisco San Francisco 11	67	107
Hannah	San Francisco San Francisco 10	67	223
Hannah	Sonoma Petaluma	69	586
Hans	San Francisco San Francisco 2	67	572
Hartwell C	Yuba Marysville	72	958
Harvey P	San Joaquin Elkhorn	64	951
Haus*	San Francisco San Francisco 2	67	572
Henry	Amador Twp 1	55	474
Henry	El Dorado Kelsey	58	1139
Henry	Marin Cortemad	60	785
Henry	Napa Hot Springs	61	20
Henry	Placer Folsom	62	639
Henry	Placer Todds Va	62	763
Henry	Plumas Quincy	62	956
Henry	San Francisco San Francisco 3	67	65
Henry	Sierra Twp 5	66	939
Henry	Siskiyou Yreka	69	155
Henry	Sonoma Washington	69	672
Henry	Tuolumne Twp 2	71	403
Henry C	Placer Sacramento	62	643
Henry J	Calaveras Twp 10	57	264
Hiram	Los Angeles Los Angeles	59	322
Hiram	Tuolumne Twp 2	71	401
I	El Dorado Georgetown	58	760
I P	Mariposa Twp 3	60	594
Ira	Los Angeles Elmonte	59	269
Isaac	El Dorado Big Bar	58	741
Isaac	San Francisco San Francisco 1	68	918
Isaac	Yuba Bear Rvr	72	1006
Isaac N	Santa Clara Santa Clara	65	483
J	El Dorado Georgetown	58	703
J	Nevada Grass Valley	61	235
J	San Francisco San Francisco 9	68	1058
J	San Francisco San Francisco 9	68	1060
J	San Francisco San Francisco 4	68	1231
J	Shasta Cottonwood	66	736
J	Sutter Yuba	70	774
J	Sutter Bear Rvr	70	826
J	Tuolumne Twp 1	71	255
J A	Nevada Eureka	61	378
J A	Tuolumne Twp 2	71	279
J B	Nevada Nevada	61	320
J B	Sonoma Armally	69	495
J B	Amador Twp 3	55	405
J C	Calaveras Twp 8	57	69
J C	Sonoma Armally	69	495
J C	Sutter Yuba	70	769
J D	Butte Chico	56	543
J D	Sacramento Ward 4	63	544
J D	Siskiyou Scott Va	69	39
J D	Siskiyou Scott Ri	69	78
J E	Nevada Bloomfield	61	516
J G	Mariposa Coulterville	60	698
J H	Butte Cascade	56	691
J H	Mariposa Coulterville	60	679
J H	Nevada Eureka	61	378
J H	Tuolumne Sonora	71	217
J H	Yolo Washington	72	600
J J	Santa Clara Santa Clara	65	493
J J	Tuolumne Garrote	71	176
J K	Sutter Butte	70	792
J L	Nevada Grass Valley	61	168
J M	Placer Forest H	62	805
J M	Sacramento Ward 4	63	529
J M	San Joaquin Stockton	64	1097
J N	Calaveras Twp 9	57	370
J O	Nevada Nevada	61	250
J P	Mariposa Twp 3	60	594
J S	Klamath S Fork	59	197
J S	Nevada Nevada	61	320
J T	Napa Clear Lake	61	139
J U	Solano Fairfield	69	201
J W	Colusa Spring Valley	57	431
J W	El Dorado Placerville	58	868
J W	Sacramento Ward 4	63	528
J W	San Francisco San Francisco 7	68	1406
J W	Siskiyou Callahan	69	9
J W	Yolo Washington	72	600
Jackson	Placer Michigan	62	845
Jacob	Placer Damascus	62	846
Jacob	San Francisco San Francisco 9	68	1097
Jacob	San Francisco San Francisco 4	68	1145
James	Amador Twp 3	55	382
James	Amador Twp 3	55	385
James	Calaveras Twp 10	57	292
James	Calaveras Twp 4	57	335
James	Contra Costa Twp 1	57	501
James	Contra Costa Twp 2	57	578
James	El Dorado Kelsey	58	1140
James	El Dorado Big Bar	58	736
James	Humbolt Bucksport	59	160
James	Klamath Klamath	59	228
James	Los Angeles Los Angeles	59	510
James	Monterey Alisal	60	1039
James	Plumas Quincy	62	943
James	Plumas Quincy	62	978
James	Sacramento Ward 1	63	144
James	San Francisco San Francisco 11	67	115
James	San Francisco San Francisco 3	67	20
James	San Francisco San Francisco 3	67	69
James	San Francisco San Francisco 3	67	81
James	Santa Clara Fremont	65	417
James	Tuolumne Twp 1	71	483
James	Yuba Marysville	72	903
James A	San Francisco San Francisco 3	67	1
James B	Siskiyou Shasta Valley	69	119
James F	Yuba Bear Rvr	72	1003
James H	Santa Cruz Watsonville	66	538
James H	Sonoma Mendocino	69	462
James H*	Fresno Twp 3	59	10
James M	Calaveras Twp 10	57	280
James W	Sierra Twp 7	66	887
Jane	Sacramento Sutter	63	305
Jas	Butte Chico	56	554
Jas	Calaveras Twp 9	57	381
Jas	Napa Clear Lake	61	123
Jas	Sacramento Ward 4	63	517
Jas	San Francisco San Francisco 9	68	1072
Jas	San Francisco San Francisco 5	67	482
Jas	San Francisco San Francisco 2	67	572
Jas	San Francisco San Francisco 2	67	698
Jas F	Napa Clear Lake	61	123
Jas J	Sacramento Ward 4	63	505
Jas P	San Francisco San Francisco 7	68	1428
Jas S	San Francisco San Francisco 2	67	697
Jefferson	Sonoma Sonoma	69	645
Jesse	Calaveras Twp 4	57	337
Jno	Amador Twp 5	55	357
Jno	Butte Chico	56	553
Jno	Butte Oregon	56	615
Jno	Mendocino Big Rvr	60	840
Jno	San Francisco San Francisco 9	68	1084
Jno	San Francisco San Francisco 9	68	1089
Jno	Tehama Cottonwoood	70	898
Jno B	Sacramento Ward 1	63	148
Jno D	Sonoma Russian	69	435
Jno M	Sacramento Natonia	63	274
Jno S	Klamath Orleans	59	215
Jofsr*	Calaveras Twp 4	57	337
John	Alameda Brooklyn	55	141
John	Alameda Brooklyn	55	192
John	Amador Twp 2	55	320
John	Butte Ophir	56	791
John	Calaveras Twp 4	57	303
John	Calaveras Twp 9	57	368
John	Calaveras Twp 9	57	399
John	El Dorado White Oaks	58	1010
John	El Dorado Gold Hill	58	1096
John	El Dorado Georgetown	58	754
John	Fresno Twp 3	59	8
John	Nevada Bridgeport	61	440
John	Nevada Bridgeport	61	450
John	Placer Michigan	62	823
John	Placer Michigan	62	842
John	Plumas Quincy	62	922
John	Plumas Quincy	62	956
John	Sacramento Ward 1	63	14
John	Sacramento Sutter	63	304
John	San Francisco San Francisco 11	67	114
John	San Francisco San Francisco 2	67	565
John	San Francisco San Francisco 2	67	619
John	San Francisco San Francisco 1	68	842
John	San Francisco San Francisco 1	68	872
John	San Francisco San Francisco 1	68	895
John	San Francisco San Francisco 1	68	910
John	San Joaquin Elliott	64	1104
John	San Joaquin Elkhorn	64	994
John	San Mateo Twp 3	65	99
John	Santa Clara Santa Clara	65	499
John	Santa Cruz Pajaro	66	525
John	Santa Cruz Pajaro	66	528
John	Santa Cruz Pajaro	66	559
John	Santa Cruz Soguel	66	600
John	Siskiyou Yreka	69	137
John	Siskiyou Yreka	69	138
John	Solano Suisan	69	220
John	Sonoma Bodega	69	527
John	Sonoma Vallejo	69	627
John	Sonoma Sonoma	69	636
John	Stanislaus Emory	70	750
John	Tehama Red Bluff	70	912
John	Trinity S Fork	70	1032
John	Trinity Weaverville	70	1080
John	Trinity China Bar	70	959
John	Tulara Visalia	71	15
John	Tulara Twp 1	71	95
John	Tuolumne Shawsfla	71	403
John	Tuolumne Jamestown	71	451
John	Tuolumne Visalia	71	95
John A	Yolo Putah	72	614
John D	San Luis Obispo San Luis Obispo	65	16
John L	San Joaquin Elkhorn	64	981
John M	El Dorado Union	58	1092
John M	Yuba Bear Rvr	72	1000
John W	San Francisco San Francisco 8	68	1323
John W	Siskiyou Shasta Valley	69	120
John W	Yuba Marysville	72	864
John*	Amador Twp 2	55	306
John*	Calaveras Twp 9	57	399
Jon	Stanislaus Emory	70	751
Jos	Amador Twp 2	55	301
Jos	San Francisco San Francisco 2	67	572
Jos	Stanislaus Branch	70	706
Jos A	Klamath Orleans	59	215
Joseph	Alameda Brooklyn	55	193
Joseph	Fresno Twp 3	59	31
Joseph	Marin Cortemad	60	790
Joseph	Mariposa Twp 3	60	610
Joseph	Napa Napa	61	81
Joseph	Plumas Meadow Valley	62	931
Joseph	Sierra Downieville	66	995
Joseph	Siskiyou Cottonwoood	69	98
Joseph	Tuolumne Twp 4	71	177
Joseph	Yuba Rose Bar	72	808
Josse*	Calaveras Twp 4	57	337
June	San Francisco San Francisco 2	67	582
L	Butte Kimshaw	56	570
L	San Francisco San Francisco 9	68	1058
L	Sierra Morristown	66	1053
L	Sonoma Vallejo	69	621
L H	Yuba New York	72	736
Lamuel L	Los Angeles Elmonte	59	246
Landin	San Francisco San Francisco 8	68	1324
Landin	San Francisco San Francisco 3	67	87
Larry	Tuolumne Columbia	71	313
Laudin*	San Francisco San Francisco 8	68	1324
Laura	Solano Vallejo	69	278
Levisa*	Napa Napa	61	86
Lewis	San Francisco San Francisco 9	68	1058
Lewis	San Francisco San Francisco 4	68	1224
Loranzo	Sierra Morristown	66	1052
Louis B	Calaveras Twp 5	57	208
Lucinda	Butte Chico	56	553
M	Butte Bidwell	56	727
M	El Dorado Placerville	58	849
M	San Francisco San Francisco 6	67	445
M	Sonoma Washington	69	665
M	Sutter Bear Rvr	70	826
M A	Tuolumne Twp 2	71	384
M E	San Francisco San Francisco 10	67	173
M M	Yolo Cache Crk	72	609
M S	San Francisco San Francisco 4	68	1228
M S	Siskiyou Klamath	69	79
Malcolm	Placer Iona Hills	62	861
Malcom	Humbolt Pacific	59	137
Manly	Plumas Quincy	62	975
Marcus	Sonoma Russian	69	432
Marcus L	Sonoma Russian	69	432
Margaret	Calaveras Twp 5	57	189
Margaret	Calaveras Twp 8	57	52
Margarett	Placer Iona Hills	62	878
Maria	San Francisco San Francisco 6	67	416
Mary	Sacramento American	63	164
Mary	San Francisco San Francisco 2	67	713
Mary	Siskiyou Callahan	69	9
Mary B	Sacramento Ward 1	63	150
Mary D	Sacramento Ward 4	63	564
Mary E	San Francisco San Francisco 2	67	665
Mathew	Yuba Parks Ba	72	780
Mc G	Napa Clear Lake	61	138
Michael	San Francisco San Francisco 10	67	172
Michael	Santa Cruz Pajaro	66	573
Michal	San Francisco San Francisco 1	68	904
Minton	Nevada Bridgeport	61	449
Miron	Solano Benecia	69	292
Miror*	Solano Benecia	69	292
Mr	Sonoma Sonoma	69	642
Munroe	Sierra Downieville	66	954
N	Butte Wyandotte	56	670
N	Klamath Trinidad	59	220
N	Tehama Red Bluff	70	933
N G	El Dorado Placerville	58	856
N G*	Alameda Oakland	55	3
N J	Alameda Oakland	55	3
N N	Stanislaus Emory	70	754
Nancy G	Monterey Pajaro	60	1015
Nathan	Siskiyou Yreka	69	142

Name	County Locale	M653 Roll Page
THOMPSON		
Nathaniel	El Dorado Placerville	58 904
Nathaniel	Sierra Twp 7	66 875
Neil	Placer Iona Hills	62 878
Nelson	Butte Chico	56 553
Ole	Sierra Twp 5	66 947
Ole	Solano Fremont	69 376
P	Nevada Eureka	61 367
P	Placer Mountain	62 708
P	San Francisco San Francisco 9	681060
P	Tuolumne Twp 3	71 464
Patrick	Santa Clara Santa Clara	65 480
Peter	Amador Twp 1	55 488
Peter	Butte Kimshaw	56 584
Peter	Calaveras Twp 6	57 120
Peter	Contra Costa Twp 2	57 546
Peter	El Dorado White Oaks	581018
Peter	El Dorado Salmon Falls	581034
Peter	Marin Cortemad	60 786
Peter	Mendocino Big Rvr	60 843
Peter	Placer Mountain	62 708
Peter	Placer Dutch Fl	62 732
Peter	Placer Michigan	62 842
Peter	San Francisco San Francisco 11	131 67
Peter	San Francisco San Francisco 1	68 854
Peter	San Francisco San Francisco 1	68 904
Peter	Sierra Downieville	661002
Peter	Tuolumne Twp 1	71 244
Peter	Yolo No E Twp	72 683
Peter	Yuba Slate Ro	72 683
Peter R	Sonoma Russian	69 442
Phil R	Sonoma Vallejo	69 618
Pleasant	Monterey Monterey	60 966
Q D*	Siskiyou Scott Va	69 39
R	Nevada Grass Valley	61 186
R	Nevada Washington	61 331
R	Nevada Washington	61 341
R	San Francisco San Francisco 5	67 486
R	San Francisco San Francisco 5	67 541
R	San Francisco San Francisco 9	68 976
R	Trinity Weaverville	701055
R A	San Francisco San Francisco 5	67 511
R Aug	San Francisco San Francisco 2	67 636
R E	Stanislaus Emory	70 747
R F	Siskiyou Cottonwoood	69 106
R H	Sonoma Santa Rosa	69 387
R S	Napa Napa	61 61
R T	Butte Hamilton	56 519
R T	Sacramento Dry Crk	63 373
R W	San Francisco San Francisco 6	67 416
Rebecca	San Francisco San Francisco 2	67 602
Rich D	Placer Rattle Snake	62 630
Richard	Plumas Meadow Valley	62 900
Richard	Plumas Quincy	62 968
Richard	San Francisco San Francisco 7	681440
Richard	Solano Vallejo	69 257
Richd	San Francisco San Francisco 1	68 889
Robert	Calaveras Twp 6	57 116
Robert	Del Norte Crescent	58 625
Robert	San Francisco San Francisco 7	681443
Robert	Siskiyou Scott Va	69 25
Robert	Tulara Visalia	71 102
Robert	Yuba Marysville	72 866
Robert P	Santa Clara San Jose	65 340
Robt	Calaveras Twp 5	57 247
Robt	El Dorado Kelsey	581134
Robt	Santa Clara San Jose	65 344
Robt	Trinity Douglas	70 979
Robt	Tuolumne Twp 4	71 143
Rufus S	San Joaquin Elkhorn	64 967
S	Yolo Putah	72 547
S B	Nevada Bloomfield	61 513
S C	Del Norte Crescent	58 645
S D	Marin Cortemad	60 781
S G	San Francisco San Francisco 7	681388
S S	Tehama Red Bluff	70 923
S S	Tehama Tehama	70 939
Sam	Sacramento Ward 1	63 153
Saml	Del Norte Crescent	58 647
Saml	Placer Dutch Fl	62 730
Saml	San Francisco San Francisco 2	67 681
Saml	San Francisco San Francisco 1	68 851
Saml	San Francisco San Francisco 1	68 855
Saml	Stanislaus Branch	70 701
Saml	Tehama Antelope	70 892
Saml F	Mendocino Round Va	60 879
Samuel	Santa Cruz Santa Cruz	66 632
Samuel	Sierra Eureka	661042
Samuel	Sierra Poker Flats	66 842
Samuel	Siskiyou Scott Va	69 29
Samuel	Siskiyou Scott Va	69 59
Samuel L	Sierra Poker Flats	66 842
Samuel S	San Francisco San Francisco 11	124 67
THOMPSON		
Sarah	San Francisco San Francisco 11	150 67
Sarah	Tuolumne Jamestown	71 453
Sarah C	San Francisco San Francisco 11	127 67
Scott	San Joaquin Stockton	641092
Sevisa	Napa Napa	61 86
Simon	Santa Cruz Santa Cruz	66 629
Simpson	Napa Napa	61 75
Steven	Placer Michigan	62 842
Syrous	Placer Folsom	62 640
T	Nevada Grass Valley	61 198
T	Sacramento Ward 3	63 423
T	San Francisco San Francisco 6	67 457
T	Tuolumne Twp 1	71 203
T D	Siskiyou Scott Va	69 39
T J	Sacramento Ward 1	63 47
T K	Mendocino Ukiah	60 798
T O	Nevada Nevada	61 250
T O	Sonoma Healdsbu	69 477
Theodore	Plumas Quincy	62 959
Thomas	Alameda Brooklyn	55 155
Thomas	Placer Michigan	62 853
Thomas	Tuolumne Twp 5	71 504
Thos	Butte Mountain	56 735
Thos	Nevada Eureka	61 390
Thos	Sacramento San Joaquin	63 360
Thos	San Francisco San Francisco 10	178 67
Thos	Santa Clara Santa Clara	65 512
Tipton	Sonoma Russian	69 439
Uriah	Santa Cruz Soguel	66 592
V	Tehama Antelope	70 889
Vance	Calaveras Twp 9	57 371
Vanpes	Calaveras Twp 9	57 371
W	El Dorado Casumnes	581175
W	El Dorado Georgetown	58 705
W	El Dorado Placerville	58 864
W	El Dorado Placerville	58 869
W	Nevada Washington	61 333
W	San Francisco San Francisco 6	67 432
W	San Francisco San Francisco 2	67 700
W	San Mateo Twp 3	65 90
W	Sonoma Washington	69 665
W	Yolo Cottonwoood	72 646
W B	Merced Twp 1	60 911
W G	Mariposa Coulterville	60 674
W H	San Francisco San Francisco 3	67 83
W H	Siskiyou Yreka	69 183
W H	Yolo Washington	72 574
W J	El Dorado Big Bar	58 744
W J	Sonoma Petaluma	69 572
W Jr	San Francisco San Francisco 5	67 487
W L	Mariposa Coulterville	60 674
W M	Siskiyou Yreka	69 183
W R	San Francisco San Francisco 6	67 417
W T	Amador Twp 7	55 411
W W	Sierra Downieville	66 961
Wilder*	San Francisco San Francisco 8	681264
Wildes	San Francisco San Francisco 8	681264
William	Amador Ward 4	55 257
William	Calaveras Twp 5	57 194
William	Calaveras Twp 5	57 200
William	Contra Costa Twp 1	57 504
William	Contra Costa Twp 1	57 505
William	Contra Costa Twp 1	57 522
William	Los Angeles Los Angeles	59 344
William	Placer Forest H	62 791
William	Placer Michigan	62 825
William	Placer Michigan	62 842
William	Plumas Quincy	62 956
William	San Diego Agua Caliente	64 821
William	San Francisco San Francisco 9	681025
William	San Francisco San Francisco 7	681444
William	San Francisco San Francisco 11	150 67
William	San Francisco San Francisco 9	68 938
William	San Joaquin Stockton	641058
William	Shasta Shasta	66 682
William	Siskiyou Yreka	69 147
William	Siskiyou Scott Va	69 36
William	Tulara Keeneysburg	71 41
William	Tulara Twp 1	71 81
William	Yuba Long Bar	72 771
William	Yuba Marysville	72 941
William A	Calaveras Twp 7	57 16
William A	San Francisco San Francisco 11	119 67
William B	San Diego San Diego	64 766
William B	San Francisco San Francisco 11	158 67
William G	San Joaquin Castoria	64 885
William G	Fresno Twp 1	59 81
William P	Yuba Marysville	72 884
Williams	Tulara Twp 3	71 41
THOMPSON		
Willis	Nevada Red Dog	61 554
Willm	Los Angeles Tejon	59 536
Winton*	Nevada Bridgeport	61 449
Wm	Amador Twp 1	55 480
Wm	Butte Wyandotte	56 668
Wm	Calaveras Twp 6	57 155
Wm	El Dorado Mud Springs	58 987
Wm	Mariposa Twp 3	60 602
Wm	Napa Napa	61 109
Wm	Nevada Nevada	61 326
Wm	Sacramento Granite	63 237
Wm	Sacramento Sutter	63 294
Wm	Sacramento Cosummes	63 396
Wm	Sacramento Ward 4	63 539
Wm	Sacramento Ward 1	63 7
Wm	San Francisco San Francisco 10	324 67
Wm	San Francisco San Francisco 10	357 67
Wm	San Francisco San Francisco 2	67 620
Wm	San Francisco San Francisco 2	67 672
Wm	San Francisco San Francisco 3	67 71
Wm	San Francisco San Francisco 1	68 874
Wm	San Francisco San Francisco 1	68 915
Wm	San Francisco San Francisco 1	68 922
Wm	San Francisco San Francisco 9	68 940
Wm	Sonoma Vallejo	69 628
Wm	Tehama Lassen	70 866
Wm	Tehama Lassen	70 874
Wm	Yuba New York	72 735
Wm	Yuba Foster B	72 829
Wm C	Amador Twp 2	55 296
Wm F	San Francisco San Francisco 4	681227
Wm G	Amador Twp 1	55 453
Wm H	Alameda Brooklyn	55 188
Wm H	El Dorado Greenwood	58 726
Wm J	Sacramento Ward 1	63 35
Wm L	Placer Rattle Snake	62 627
Wm L	Solano Benecia	69 295
Wm Meily	San Francisco 10	245 67
Wm Neily	San Francisco San Francisco 10	245 67
Wm T	Nevada Nevada	61 326
Wm*	Mariposa Coulterville	60 677
Y	Tehama Lassen	70 865
Y B	Sonoma Cloverdale	69 680
Zac	Monterey Alisal	601044
THOMPWICK		
J	Nevada Grass Valley	61 206
THOMS		
Amos O	Tulara Visalia	71 103
Harriet	San Joaquin Elkhorn	64 963
R H	Tehama Tehama	70 950
THOMSAS		
---	San Mateo Twp 3	65 82
THOMSEN		
George	Sierra Pine Grove	66 828
THOMSILL		
J*	Nevada Eureka	61 371
THOMSLOE		
Henry	San Joaquin Douglass	64 925
THOMSN		
Christian	Sierra Whiskey	66 850
THOMSON		
C	Tuolumne Jacksonville	71 169
Edward D	Sierra La Porte	66 770
George	Sierra Pine Grove	66 828
George W	San Francisco San Francisco 4	681225
J E	San Joaquin Stockton	641087
James	Sierra Poker Flats	66 841
James*	Sierra Twp 7	66 884
Jamjes	Sierra Poker Flats	66 841
Jane	Santa Cruz Pajaro	66 559
Jno	Alameda Oakland	55 20
John	Humbolt Union	59 186
Moses	Sierra Whiskey	66 846
Moses M	Sierra Whiskey	66 844
P	San Francisco San Francisco 5	67 497
T	San Francisco San Francisco 5	67 499
William	Santa Cruz Pajaro	66 562
Wm S	San Francisco San Francisco 10	253 67
THOMSOR		
George W	San Francisco San Francisco 4	681225
THOMSPN		
W W	Sierra Downieville	66 961
THOMTON		
G	Nevada Grass Valley	61 150
G	Nevada Grass Valley	61 221
J R*	Nevada Grass Valley	61 189
Leward	Sacramento Ward 3	63 488
M	Calaveras Twp 9	57 417
M P	Sierra Downieville	66 989
S K	Monterey Monterey	60 958

Name	County Locale	M653 RollPage
THOMTON		
Seward	Sacramento Ward 3	63 488
Wm	Del Norte Crescent	58 645
THON		
---	San Francisco San Francisco 4	681180
Ching	Yuba Foster B	72 826
L V	Butte Hamilton	56 517
THON???		
J F*	San Bernardino San Bernadino	64 627
THONBROUGH		
W	Sutter Butte	70 797
THONE		
---	El Dorado Placerville	58 906
THONG		
---	El Dorado Mud Springs	58 961
---	San Francisco San Francisco 4	681176
---	San Francisco San Francisco 4	681212
---	Siskiyou Klamath	69 79
Ah	Siskiyou Klamath	69 79
Thomas	Tuolumne Twp 2	71 373
THONO		
---*	Fresno Twp 1	59 118
THONS		
---*	San Francisco San Francisco 9	68 963
THONSNER		
J F*	San Bernardino San Bernadino	64 627
THONSOW		
James*	Sierra Twp 7	66 884
THONTON		
Jos	Butte Chico	56 540
THONWALTERS		
John	Calaveras Twp 5	57 187
THONY		
---	San Francisco San Francisco 4	681176
THOOMPSON		
Hartwell C	Yuba Marysville	72 958
Jos W	San Mateo Twp 2	65 120
THOON		
Wm*	Nevada Eureka	61 349
THOONBO		
Peter O*	Sonoma Washington	69 678
THOOR		
J W	Butte Chico	56 558
THOPKINS		
G	El Dorado Placerville	58 927
THOR		
Carl	Butte Oregon	56 615
Cavl	Butte Oregon	56 615
L T	Butte Oregon	56 629
L V*	Butte Hamilton	56 517
THORABEOGE		
Morgan R	Placer Goods	62 695
THORAS		
Brichare*	San Mateo Twp 1	65 62
THORBUS		
Ed	Sacramento Ward 4	63 507
THORBUSH		
Catharine	Amador Twp 2	55 318
THORELL		
Andrew	Placer Forest H	62 796
THORES		
Ivan	Mariposa Twp 1	60 646
Juan	Mariposa Twp 1	60 646
THORIENG		
John	San Francisco San Francisco 2	67 796
THORIN		
C*	Tehama Red Bluff	70 912
THORK		
W C	Nevada Grass Valley	61 235
THORLING		
Augustus	Humbolt Union	59 182
THORMAN		
John	Los Angeles Los Angeles	59 366
Thomas	El Dorado Coloma	581082
THORN		
A W	Santa Clara Alviso	65 411
Benj K	Calaveras Twp 5	57 189
Benji K	Calaveras Twp 5	57 198
E B	San Francisco San Francisco 9	681072
Eliza	Placer Iona Hills	62 880
Era John*	Nevada Bridgeport	61 502
F	Yolo Cache Crk	72 637
F J	San Francisco San Francisco 7	681444
G A	Nevada Eureka	61 351
Geo	San Francisco San Francisco 10	241 67
George	Contra Costa Twp 2	57 561
Hiram	Contra Costa Twp 5	57 555
J	El Dorado Placerville	58 837
J	Nevada Grass Valley	61 151
Jackson A	Fresno Twp 1	59 12
James	Contra Costa Twp 1	57 516
James	Solano Vallejo	69 271
John	San Joaquin Stockton	641011
John M	Contra Costa Twp 3	57 617
Joseph	Nevada Bridgeport	61 502

Name	County Locale	M653 RollPage
THORN		
Joseph	San Bernardino San Bernadino	64 630
Joseph C	S Timate	64 756
	San Bernardino	
Joseph F	Mariposa Twp 1	60 641
Lydia	Butte Oro	56 681
M D	Butte Oro	56 682
M S	San Francisco San Francisco 4	681127
Nathaniel	Napa Napa	61 80
Nathanuo*	Napa Napa	61 80
Philip	Alameda Brooklyn	55 196
R O	Nevada Eureka	61 362
Richard	Yolo Cache Crk	72 663
S G*	Nevada Grass Valley	61 146
S R	El Dorado Placerville	58 885
Solomon	Marin Cortemad	60 779
Thas	Santa Clara Santa Clara	65 471
Thos	Monterey Alisal	601033
William	Monterey San Juan	601005
Willis	Butte Chico	56 556
Wm	Nevada Eureka	61 349
THORNAIKE		
A	Stanislaus Emory	70 740
THORNAR		
James*	Yuba New York	72 747
THORNAS		
John	Mariposa Twp 1	60 668
Mik*	El Dorado White Oaks	581017
THORNBERG		
Wm B	Santa Clara Santa Clara	65 511
THORNBERGER		
John	Placer Virginia	62 677
THORNBERRY		
C N	Siskiyou Scott Va	69 28
THORNBURG		
J M	Sonoma Washington	69 675
Wm	Santa Clara San Jose	65 366
THORNBY		
T	Marin Tomales	60 713
THORNDALE		
E P	San Francisco San Francisco 2	67 678
THORNDIKE		
Eliza H	San Francisco San Francisco 6	67 423
THORNDYKE		
E O	Tuolumne Columbia	71 335
S	Shasta Shasta	66 758
THORNE		
A I	Mariposa Twp 1	60 650
Charles M	Alameda Oakland	55 57
Ezeikel	Plumas Quincy	62 976
Fred	Nevada Bloomfield	61 529
H I	Mariposa Twp 1	60 650
H J	Mariposa Twp 1	60 650
Isaac N	San Francisco San Francisco 10	319 67
Isreal	Tuolumne Twp 3	71 470
Nathaniel	San Francisco San Francisco 2	67 658
THORNHILL		
J	Nevada Eureka	61 371
Joseph	San Francisco San Francisco 4	681157
L	Nevada Nevada	61 312
THORNIL		
Caroline	Placer Ophirville	62 653
THORNLY		
Henry	Sonoma Sonoma	69 651
Wm	Tuolumne Twp 3	71 421
THORNPO		
Wm	Mariposa Coulterville	60 677
THORNSBERRY		
S B C	Mariposa Twp 1	60 654
THORNSDALL		
G L*	El Dorado Georgetown	58 753
THORNSTON		
Frances	Solano Vallejo	69 261
THORNTON		
A	Nevada Eureka	61 363
Abel	Napa Napa	61 74
Arthur	San Luis Obispo San Luis Obispo	65 8
David	El Dorado Eldorado	58 938
De Witt M	Fresno Twp 2	59 3
E H	Santa Clara Fremont	65 439
Edward	San Mateo Twp 1	65 69
Emery C	Yuba Marysville	72 859
Frances	Solano Vallejo	69 261
G*	Nevada Grass Valley	61 150
H I	Sierra Downieville	66 958
H J	Sierra Downieville	66 958
Harry J	Alameda Oakland	55 34
J	Nevada Grass Valley	61 221
J D	El Dorado Big Bar	58 735
James	Yolo Slate Ra	72 689
James	Yuba Slate Ro	72 689
Jas D	San Francisco San Francisco 2	67 776
Jessey	Los Angeles Los Angeles	59 489
John	Sacramento Ward 1	63 107
John	San Joaquin Douglass	64 924

Name	County Locale	M653 RollPage
THORNTON		
Jos D	San Francisco San Francisco 2	67 776
Jos*	Butte Chico	56 540
Joseph	Yuba Parks Ba	72 775
M	Sutter Nicolaus	70 834
M P	Sierra Downieville	66 989
Matilda	San Francisco San Francisco 1	68 846
Michl	Butte Chico	56 536
Mike	Butte Chico	56 538
Percy	Yolo No E Twp	72 679
Percy	Yuba North Ea	72 679
R S	San Mateo Twp 1	65 57
Ruth	San Francisco San Francisco 10	195 67
Sam	Merced Twp 1	60 899
Saml	Trinity Hay Fork	70 991
Sarah	San Francisco San Francisco 11	109 67
Thomas	Solano Vallejo	69 261
Thomas	Tuolumne Sonora	71 237
Thomas G	Sierra Downieville	661013
William	Marin Novato	60 735
William	San Francisco San Francisco 4	681152
William	Santa Cruz Pajaro	66 562
Wm	Amador Twp 2	55 305
Wm	Nevada Nevada	61 320
THORONGHMAN		
Jno*	Butte Chico	56 540
THOROUGHMAN		
Jno	Butte Chico	56 540
THORP		
A	Sutter Butte	70 791
David	El Dorado Eldorado	58 948
David	Placer Iona Hills	62 860
Edward	San Joaquin Elkhorn	64 990
G	Nevada Washington	61 334
Geo	El Dorado Placerville	58 921
James H	San Joaquin Elliott	64 941
Maces	Calaveras Twp 5	57 222
Moses	Calaveras Twp 5	57 222
Mr*	Napa Napa	61 101
Oscar	Butte Oregon	56 617
S H	Nevada Nevada	61 321
S W	Nevada Nevada	61 321
T	Nevada Grass Valley	61 195
T V	Butte Kimshaw	56 588
Thomas	Colusa Colusi	57 420
Thomas	Sierra Downieville	661024
Thos	Placer Ophirville	62 654
Thos*	Placer Nicolaus	62 692
W M	Butte Chico	56 546
Wm	Napa Napa	61 101
THORPE		
Eli	Plumas Quincy	621005
Jas M	Sacramento Ward 1	63 63
John	San Mateo Twp 1	65 71
Joseph	Tuolumne Montezuma	71 505
William	Tuolumne Don Pedro	71 542
Wm	Nevada Washington	61 336
THORPS		
Thos	Stanislaus Branch	70 712
THORR		
Wm	Butte Chico	56 558
THORREL		
John	Placer Yankee J	62 775
THORSE		
S*	Nevada Grass Valley	61 197
THORSEN		
John	Siskiyou Cottonwoood	69 98
THORSS		
Maces*	Calaveras Twp 5	57 222
Mares*	Calaveras Twp 5	57 222
THORT		
Thos*	Trinity Taylor'S	701036
THORTON		
J J	Yolo Cache	72 618
James	San Joaquin Stockton	641071
THORTZ		
S B*	El Dorado Mountain	581185
THORYER		
James*	Marin Cortemad	60 789
THOS		
---	San Mateo Twp 3	65 100
---	San Mateo Twp 3	65 109
Albt	Butte Chico	56 532
Burlingham	Butte Bidwell	56 719
Canton*	Amador Twp 5	55 333
Carter	Butte Bidwell	56 719
Eaton	San Mateo Twp 1	65 51
L T*	Butte Oregon	56 629
THOSMER		
Chester	Tuolumne Twp 5	71 519
THOSS		
---	El Dorado Diamond	58 767
W H	El Dorado Diamond	58 767
THOU		
---	San Francisco San Francisco 4	681180

Name	County Locale	M653 Roll/Page
THOU		
---	San Francisco San Francisco	4 681 186
THOUR		
L C*	Nevada Grass Valley	61 198
THOUS		
---	San Francisco San Francisco	9 68 963
THOUVENIN		
Otas*	Plumas Meadow Valley	62 927
THOW		
---	San Francisco San Francisco	4 681 186
THOWFILTF		
G W*	El Dorado Placerville	58 880
THOWLER		
Thos	Sacramento Ward 1	63 27
THOWLILT		
G W*	El Dorado Placerville	58 880
THOWN		
F	Yolo Cache	72 637
THOY		
---	San Francisco San Francisco	4 681 209
Yoru	San Francisco San Francisco	4 681 175
You	San Francisco San Francisco	4 681 175
THOYMUT		
---	Tulara Twp 1	71 116
THOYSNNT		
Thoysnnt	Tulara Twp 1	71 116
THOYTS		
I	Calaveras Twp 9	57 389
J	Calaveras Twp 9	57 398
THRALE		
S C	San Francisco San Francisco	10 245 67
THRALL		
Charles	Calaveras Twp 6	57 132
Cleris*	San Francisco San Francisco	9 681 019
H H	San Francisco San Francisco	6 67 440
Hiram W	Yuba Marysville	72 870
S C	San Francisco San Francisco	10 245 67
THRAP		
J B	Sonoma Armally	69 507
THRASHER		
A F	Yuba Rose Bar	72 816
C	Sutter Yuba	70 766
J	Nevada Grass Valley	61 214
James	Napa Hot Springs	61 6
John	Yuba New York	72 725
W	Nevada Eureka	61 378
W	Yuba Long Bar	72 748
Willis	Colusa Colusi	57 423
THREATUM		
---	Tulara Twp 1	71 116
THREEAS		
Dolores	San Mateo Twp 2	65 113
THREFALL		
Wm	Alameda Brooklyn	55 185
THREHKELL		
A D*	Siskiyou Scott Va	69 50
THRELFALL		
John	Alameda Brooklyn	55 183
THRELHELL		
A D	Siskiyou Scott Va	69 50
THRELKELD		
Joseph T	Monterey Monterey	60 963
THRELKELL		
A D*	Siskiyou Scott Va	69 50
C A	Siskiyou Scott Va	69 55
THRELKILL		
Geo W	Placer Auburn	62 597
THRELSHELL		
C A	Siskiyou Scott Va	69 55
THRENSHAW		
William*	Santa Cruz Santa Cruz	66 635
THRENTHAR		
William*	Santa Cruz Santa Cruz	66 635
THREPER		
A	Siskiyou Scott Ri	69 66
THRESH		
George W	Yuba Rose Bar	72 803
George*	Yuba Rose Bar	72 803
THRESHAR		
Valentine	Tuolumne Twp 1	71 258
THRESHER		
M L	San Joaquin Stockton	641 056
N	Sacramento San Joaquin	63 367
S P	Butte Hamilton	56 515
W	Yuba New York	72 748
THRESKELL		
A D	Siskiyou Scott Va	69 50
THREUTHAN		
William*	Santa Cruz Santa Cruz	66 635
THRIENG		
John	San Francisco San Francisco	2 67 796
THRIFT		
E	Mariposa Twp 1	60 635
Elmira	Sacramento Ward 4	63 530
THRIFT		
James	Santa Cruz Pajaro	66 569
Lewellen	Santa Cruz Watsonville	66 535
Thomas	Solano Vacaville	69 358
THRINSTON		
W	Sutter Butte	70 798
THRISH		
George W*	Yuba Rose Bar	72 803
THROCKMORTON		
L R	San Francisco San Francisco	10 259 67
S R	San Francisco San Francisco	10 259 67
THROMAN		
Wm*	Mariposa Coulterville	60 686
THRONE		
Charley	Alameda Brooklyn	55 145
THRONEL		
S	San Mateo Twp 1	65 47
THRONST		
S	San Mateo Twp 1	65 47
THROP		
David	El Dorado Eldorado	58 945
John*	Sonoma Russian	69 435
Jon	Sonoma Russian	69 435
THROSS		
John*	Sonoma Russian	69 435
THROUGHMAN		
Sanford	Shasta Millvill	66 748
THRUELS		
C*	Sacramento Ward 1	63 27
THRUSH		
Chas	Sacramento Granite	63 260
G	Sacramento Cosummes	63 408
Richard	Sacramento Granite	63 258
THRUSHER		
A F*	Yuba Rose Bar	72 816
THRUSTLE		
Henry	Siskiyou Klamath	69 87
THU		
---	San Francisco San Francisco	4 681 175
---	San Francisco San Francisco	4 681 208
Ah	Calaveras Twp 7	57 16
Pou	San Francisco San Francisco	4 681 196
To	San Francisco San Francisco	4 681 201
THUA		
---	Mendocino Calpella	60 824
THUBLEHORN		
J C	Nevada Nevada	61 296
THUDWELL		
J*	Nevada Eureka	61 344
THUFFLETON		
H*	Shasta Horsetown	66 695
THUG		
Thay*	San Francisco San Francisco	4 681 151
THUGH		
---	Fresno Twp 1	59 25
THUING		
J G	San Francisco San Francisco	8 681 298
THUIRMAN		
Leech B*	Napa Clear Lake	61 130
THUIRMANB		
Seech B*	Napa Clear Lake	61 130
THUKLENBARY		
Hans	Sierra Twp 7	66 872
THUKLENBURY		
Hans	Sierra Twp 7	66 872
THULE		
William	San Francisco San Francisco	9 681 054
THULFALL		
Walton*	Santa Cruz Pajaro	66 526
THULIN		
N L	El Dorado Union	581 094
THULTRE		
M	San Francisco San Francisco	5 67 552
THUM		
Martin	Yolo Cache	72 642
THUMAN		
Wm	Mariposa Coulterville	60 686
THUMBROOKE		
A	El Dorado Georgetown	58 685
THUMPAS		
Orin	Sacramento Natonia	63 278
THUMPSO		
Wm*	Mariposa Coulterville	60 677
THUN		
---	San Francisco San Francisco	4 681 182
Alexander	Sierra Twp 7	66 894
Feng	San Francisco San Francisco	4 681 185
Martin	Yolo Cache Crk	72 642
THUNDER		
---	Tulara Keyesville	71 56
THUNFIELD		
L E*	Mariposa Twp 3	60 586
THUNG		
---	San Francisco San Francisco	9 681 086
THUNG		
---	San Francisco San Francisco	4 681 182
John*	San Francisco San Francisco	4 681 163
THUNMPER		
Christian	Sierra La Porte	66 768
THUNNIPON		
Christian	Sierra La Porte	66 768
THUR		
Joaquin*	Mariposa Twp 1	60 641
THURBER		
E R	Solano Vacaville	69 357
Henry	Siskiyou Scott Va	69 57
J Q A	San Mateo Twp 3	65 86
Leander	San Francisco San Francisco	11 153 67
THURBERS		
Isaac	San Francisco San Francisco	11 162 67
THURBUS		
Edward	Sacramento Ward 4	63 511
THURDALL		
Julius	El Dorado Georgetown	58 754
THURELS		
C*	Sacramento Ward 1	63 27
THURGOOD		
Margarite G	Sonoma Healdsbu	69 471
Wm S	Sonoma Healdsbu	69 471
THURGTESON		
Samuel	Solano Vacaville	69 320
THURLBART		
John W	Los Angeles Los Angeles	59 322
THURLEM		
S*	Butte Eureka	56 648
THURLEUR		
S*	Butte Eureka	56 648
THURLEW		
S*	Butte Eureka	56 648
THURLEY		
L	Siskiyou Scott Ri	69 74
THURLOW		
Simon	Calaveras Twp 7	57 31
THURLWELL		
J*	Nevada Eureka	61 344
THURMAN		
Eli	Mariposa Twp 1	60 634
Frank	Solano Suisan	69 218
Henry	Butte Oregon	56 609
Jerry	Marin Cortemad	60 782
John	Tehama Tehama	70 941
John B	Mariposa Twp 3	60 555
John*	Napa Yount	61 34
Leech B	Napa Clear Lake	61 130
Seech B*	Napa Clear Lake	61 130
Thos	Butte Kimshaw	56 592
Wm	Napa Napa	61 83
Wm*	Mariposa Coulterville	60 686
THURMON		
James	Solano Suisan	69 235
THURNBULL		
S*	Nevada Nevada	61 312
THURNNAUER		
Wm	San Francisco San Francisco	5 67 475
THURNSTON		
Henry	El Dorado Georgetown	58 706
THURRELS		
C*	Sacramento Ward 1	63 27
THURRIETA		
Francisco*	Calaveras Twp 4	57 341
THURRIRTA		
Francisco*	Calaveras Twp 4	57 341
THURRY		
M	El Dorado Placerville	58 877
THURSBY		
W E	Stanislaus Branch	70 698
THURSITRU		
Francisco	Calaveras Twp 4	57 341
THURST		
Arnold	Mariposa Twp 3	60 615
THURSTON		
Daniel	Placer Todds Va	62 786
E	Trinity New Rvr	701 031
Ed	Sacramento Ward 1	63 129
Ella	Amador Twp 3	55 393
George	Solano Fremont	69 384
George A	San Francisco San Francisco	8 681 316
H H	San Joaquin Oneal	64 940
Hannibal	Sonoma Armally	69 492
Henry	El Dorado Georgetown	58 706
Henry	Tuolumne Shawsfla	71 384
J L*	Sacramento Alabama	63 417
J M	Sonoma Bodega	69 540
J P	Amador Twp 3	55 395
J S*	Sacramento Alabama	63 417
Jas	Sacramento Dry Crk	63 369
John	El Dorado Georgetown	58 679
M C	Sierra St Louis	66 815

Name	County Locale	M653 Roll	Page
THURSTON			
M J	Tuolumne Twp 2	71	285
Nathaniel	San Francisco San Francisco 7	681	410
S W	Siskiyou Scott Va	69	28
Samuel H	Yuba New York	72	723
T	Calaveras Twp 9	57	409
Thomas	Calaveras Twp 5	57	209
THURY			
Ford*	Mariposa Twp 3	60	555
Forn*	Mariposa Twp 3	60	555
Horn*	Mariposa Twp 3	60	555
THUSAN			
Benj	El Dorado Eldorado	58	947
THUSDALL			
Julius*	El Dorado Georgetown	58	754
THUSES			
John	Mariposa Twp 3	60	573
THUSHAS			
Valentine*	Tuolumne Twp 1	71	258
THUSTON			
A C*	Siskiyou Klamath	69	96
THUTLY			
A B	Nevada Nevada	61	284
THUY THUY			
---	Tulara Twp 1	71	118
THUY			
---	Calaveras Twp 5	57	223
Thay	San Francisco San Francisco 4	681	151
Thuy	Tulara Twp 1	71	118
THUYSHE			
---	Tulara Twp 1	71	118
THWING			
J G*	San Francisco San Francisco 8	681	298
THY			
---	Butte Ophir	56	812
THYE			
Michael	San Francisco San Francisco 10		289
		67	
THYER			
Michael*	Santa Cruz Santa Cruz	66	633
THYLER			
J	Shasta Shasta	66	668
THYUPPE			
---	Tulara Visalia	71	117
TI CHUNG			
---	Sacramento Ward 1	63	70
TI FU			
---*	Tuolumne Don Pedro	71	533
TI HE			
---	Nevada Bridgeport	61	462
TI HO			
---*	Yuba Marysville	72	921
TI MOORS			
---	Sacramento Ward 1	63	52
TI			
---	Amador Twp 5	55	335
---	Amador Twp 5	55	336
---	Calaveras Twp 5	57	144
---	Calaveras Twp 5	57	149
---	Calaveras Twp 6	57	151
---	Calaveras Twp 6	57	164
---	Calaveras Twp 6	57	165
---	Calaveras Twp 6	57	168
---	Calaveras Twp 6	57	170
---	Calaveras Twp 6	57	171
---	Calaveras Twp 6	57	173
---	Calaveras Twp 6	57	176
---	Calaveras Twp 5	57	202
---	Calaveras Twp 5	57	205
---	Calaveras Twp 5	57	226
---	Calaveras Twp 5	57	236
---	Calaveras Twp 5	57	245
---	Calaveras Twp 5	57	246
---	Calaveras Twp 5	57	247
---	Calaveras Twp 5	57	252
---	Calaveras Twp 5	57	254
---	Calaveras Twp 5	57	255
---	Calaveras Twp 10	57	260
---	Calaveras Twp 10	57	268
---	Calaveras Twp 10	57	269
---	Calaveras Twp 10	57	270
---	Calaveras Twp 10	57	271
---	Calaveras Twp 10	57	273
---	Calaveras Twp 10	57	276
---	Calaveras Twp 10	57	278
---	Calaveras Twp 10	57	281
---	Calaveras Twp 10	57	286
---	Calaveras Twp 10	57	291
---	Calaveras Twp 10	57	294
---	Calaveras Twp 10	57	295
---	Calaveras Twp 4	57	302
---	Calaveras Twp 4	57	307
---	Calaveras Twp 4	57	309
---	Mariposa Twp 1	60	625
---	Mariposa Twp 1	60	626
---	Mariposa Twp 1	60	658

Name	County Locale	M653 Roll	Page
TI			
---	Mariposa Coulterville	60	681
---	Mariposa Coulterville	60	687
---	Mariposa Coulterville	60	697
---	Mariposa Coulterville	60	700
---	Nevada Nevada	61	299
---	Nevada Nevada	61	301
---	Nevada Nevada	61	305
---	Placer Iona Hills	62	893
---	Sacramento Cosumnes	63	400
---	San Francisco San Francisco 9	681	094
---	San Francisco San Francisco 9	681	096
---	Stanislaus Emory	70	753
---	Tulara Twp 1	71	96
---	Tuolumne Columbia	71	350
---	Tuolumne Twp 2	71	409
---	Tuolumne Twp 3	71	433
---	Tuolumne Twp 3	71	446
---	Tuolumne Twp 3	71	468
---	Tuolumne Twp 1	71	477
---	Tuolumne Twp 5	71	515
---	Tuolumne Twp 5	71	521
---	Tuolumne Don Pedro	71	538
---	Tuolumne Twp 6	71	539
---	Tuolumne Don Pedro	71	540
---	Yuba Long Bar	72	754
---*	Mariposa Twp 1	60	626
---*	Nevada Nevada	61	305
Ah	Sacramento Cosumnes	63	391
Ah	Tuolumne Twp 2	71	350
Ah*	Amador Twp 4	55	332
Attu	Placer Iona Hills	62	898
Bang*	Placer Michigan	62	843
Bran	Mariposa Coulterville	60	682
Chu	Calaveras Twp 5	57	254
Chung	Sacramento Ward 1	63	70
Coe	Tuolumne Don Pedro	71	538
Coe	Tuolumne Twp 6	71	539
Con	Tuolumne Don Pedro	71	537
Cow	Calaveras Twp 4	57	308
Cum	Yuba Marysville	72	920
Cun	Siskiyou Yreka	69	195
Fow	Calaveras Twp 4	57	334
Fu*	Tuolumne Don Pedro	71	533
He	Nevada Bridgeport	61	462
Hea	Calaveras Twp 4	57	334
Hee	Calaveras Twp 4	57	334
Ho*	Yuba Marysville	72	921
How	Calaveras Twp 4	57	334
Hu	Nevada Bloomfield	61	528
Lee*	San Francisco San Francisco 9	681	094
Long	Sacramento Cosumnes	63	400
Lu	Alameda Oakland	55	38
Lu	San Francisco San Francisco 9	681	094
Lu*	Placer Michigan	62	843
Lu*	San Francisco San Francisco 9	681	094
Luck	Placer Iona Hills	62	897
Mo	San Francisco San Francisco 11		161
		67	
Mooy	Sacramento Ward 1	63	52
Nie	Nevada Bloomfield	61	528
Oon	Placer Michigan	62	858
Row	Sacramento Granite	63	231
Sang	Calaveras Twp 4	57	304
Sang	Placer Yankee J	62	760
Sany	Calaveras Twp 4	57	304
Sing	Placer Forest H	62	771
Sing	Siskiyou Yreka	69	194
Son	Calaveras Twp 5	57	256
Sou	Calaveras Twp 4	57	300
Sou	Calaveras Twp 4	57	300
Sun	Mariposa Coulterville	60	682
Tong	Nevada Rough &	61	436
Tow	Calaveras Twp 4	57	334
Wack	Placer Iona Hills	62	897
Wan	Placer Iona Hills	62	869
Wang	Placer Iona Hills	62	869
Wapp	Nevada Nevada	61	303
Woh	Calaveras Twp 4	57	302
Yon	Amador Twp 5	55	335
Yon	Calaveras Twp 4	57	304
You	Calaveras Twp 4	57	304
You	Siskiyou Yreka	69	194
Yung	Sacramento Granite	63	232
TIA			
---	Mariposa Twp 1	60	627
TIAL			
Charles*	Nevada Red Dog	61	545
TIALOR			
Wm	Mariposa Twp 3	60	601
TIANLY			
Pat*	Nevada Bloomfield	61	529
TIAP			
S D	Sierra Twp 7	66	908
TIAVERS			
C M*	Sacramento Granite	63	242

Name	County Locale	M653 Roll	Page
TIB			
---	Sacramento Cosumnes	63	407
TIBAN			
Alex	Sacramento Ward 4	63	603
TIBARDO			
Robello	San Diego Agua Caliente	64	847
TIBBATTS			
A J	Stanislaus Buena Village	70	724
TIBBELT			
Edward*	Amador Twp 2	55	307
TIBBELTS			
Chas*	Sacramento Ward 1	63	49
TIBBERT			
George	Mariposa Twp 3	60	566
TIBBETES			
J S*	Tuolumne Columbia	71	350
TIBBETS			
Benj	Sacramento Sutter	63	298
Bery*	Sacramento Sutter	63	298
David	Calaveras Twp 5	57	199
David	Sonoma Armally	69	514
Ralph A	San Francisco San Francisco 11		103
		67	
Samuel W	Sierra La Porte	66	774
TIBBETT			
Edward	Amador Twp 2	55	307
Edward	Los Angeles Los Angeles	59	375
Edward*	Amador Twp 2	55	307
Saml	Alameda Brooklyn	55	175
TIBBETTS			
Calvin	Santa Clara Santa Clara	65	496
Chas	Sacramento Ward 1	63	49
G	Nevada Grass Valley	61	153
Henry	Plumas Meadow Valley	62	907
Henry	San Diego Colorado	64	806
J B	Mendocino Big Rock	60	873
John	Colusa Mansville	57	438
John L	Tuolumne Springfield	71	369
Mary	Sacramento Sutter	63	299
Nathan H	Tuolumne Columbia	71	355
Richard M	San Joaquin Castoria	64	892
T	Nevada Grass Valley	61	206
W	San Francisco San Francisco 5	67	549
William	Calaveras Twp 5	57	227
Wm	Monterey Monterey	60	956
Wm	Sonoma Petaluma	69	572
TIBBETY			
J S*	Tuolumne Columbia	71	350
TIBBEY			
Mary A	San Francisco San Francisco 2	67	706
TIBBITS			
Grancis	Amador Twp 4	55	234
J P	Placer Iona Hills	62	863
James	Santa Cruz Santa Cruz	66	640
Samuel	Sierra La Porte	66	774
TIBBITTEN			
Joseph	Sonoma Santa Rosa	69	393
TIBBITTS			
J S	Tuolumne Twp 2	71	350
Jonathan	Los Angeles Elmonte	59	250
Nathan H	Tuolumne Twp 2	71	355
William	Calaveras Twp 5	57	227
Wm	Monterey Monterey	60	956
TIBBLES			
Sam	Nevada Rough &	61	424
TIBBORBESN			
Mary	Colusa Monroeville	57	448
TIBBOTTS			
Jeremiah	Contra Costa Twp 3	57	590
TIBBRTS			
David	Calaveras Twp 5	57	199
TIBBS			
---	Siskiyou Shasta Rvr	69	116
B F	Yolo Cache Crk	72	641
G C	Yolo Cache	72	638
Geo W	Sacramento Georgian	63	336
William F	Sierra St Louis	66	807
TIBBY			
Samuel	Santa Cruz Soguel	66	579
TIBE			
Jno A	Klamath Liberty	59	240
TIBEAN			
A*	Sacramento Sutter	63	300
TIBER LYON			
Pons*	Contra Costa Twp 3	57	612
TIBIN			
Rich	San Francisco San Francisco 2	67	601
TIBINCIO			
---	Monterey S Antoni	60	972
TIBOUT			
N	Sacramento Ward 1	63	61
TIBTITS			
G M	Amador Twp 5	55	351
TIBURACIA			
Maria*	Los Angeles San Juan	59	465
TIBURCIA			
---	Monterey S Antoni	60	972

California 1860 Census Index

Name	County Locale	M653 Roll Page
TIBURCIA		
Maria	Los Angeles San Juan	59 465
TIBURCIO		
---	Los Angeles Los Angeles	59 401
---	Los Angeles Los Angeles	59 402
TICE		
Alanson	San Francisco San Francisco	4 681 160
Alfred	Sacramento Ward 4	63 603
Harver	San Francisco San Francisco	8 681 308
Harves*	San Francisco San Francisco	8 681 308
Henry M	San Francisco San Francisco	7 681 433
James	Contra Costa Twp 2	57 550
James M	Contra Costa Twp 2	57 550
TICHE		
---	Fresno Twp 2	59 20
John	Yuba Long Bar	72 769
TICHENOR		
A	Tuolumne Big Oak	71 152
E	Calaveras Twp 9	57 410
H B	San Francisco San Francisco	9 681 090
M B	San Francisco San Francisco	9 681 090
Stephen	San Francisco San Francisco	10 259 67
TICHER		
Daniel*	El Dorado Coloma	581 082
TICHFELDER		
William	San Diego San Diego	64 758
TICHLER		
Himan	Los Angeles Los Angeles	59 374
Himaro	Los Angeles Los Angeles	59 374
TICHMIRE		
T	El Dorado Placerville	58 924
TICHNER		
Henry	San Francisco San Francisco	2 67 743
Henry	Siskiyou Yreka	69 136
Saml	San Francisco San Francisco	2 67 612
TICHNOR		
Louis	San Francisco San Francisco	8 681 303
TICHOSTER		
James	Yolo Washington	72 565
TICHTOR		
M	Trinity McGillev	701 021
TICK		
---	Butte Hamilton	56 530
---	Calaveras Twp 5	57 234
---	Calaveras Twp 10	57 270
---	Calaveras Twp 10	57 283
---	Calaveras Twp 4	57 303
---	Del Norte Crescent	58 634
---	El Dorado White Oaks	581 021
---	El Dorado White Oaks	581 023
---	El Dorado Salmon Falls	581 047
---	El Dorado Salmon Falls	581 066
---	El Dorado Union	581 091
---	El Dorado Coloma	581 106
---	El Dorado Coloma	581 111
---	El Dorado Coloma	581 123
---	El Dorado Casumnes	581 177
---	El Dorado Placerville	58 884
---	El Dorado Placerville	58 902
---	El Dorado Placerville	58 923
---	El Dorado Placerville	58 932
Yaw	Solano Benecia	69 283
TICKEN		
W G	Sutter Sutter	70 806
TICKER		
Daniel*	El Dorado Coloma	581 082
TICKLE		
John*	Siskiyou Callahan	69 18
TICKNER		
B	Mariposa Coulterville	60 699
H C	Siskiyou Scott Ri	69 75
John	San Francisco San Francisco	9 681 002
TICKNOR		
Henry H	Humbolt Bucksport	59 155
TICKSHAW		
---	Shasta Shasta	66 680
TICKSHEW		
---	Shasta Shasta	66 680
TICO		
Fernando	S Buenav San Bernardino	64 208
Jouquin	San Bernardino Santa Barbara	64 172
Madelina	San Bernardino Santa Ba	64 218
Madelina	San Bernardino S Buenav	64 219
TICOHAN		
Edward	Calaveras Twp 5	57 210
TICSE		
Frederick*	San Francisco San Francisco	3 67 30
TICUNE		
---*	Yuba Marysville	72 920
TID		
Jas*	Merced Twp 1	60 913
TIDALL		

Name	County Locale	M653 Roll Page
TIDALL		
Maria A	San Francisco San Francisco	10 285 67
TIDAMA		
C	San Francisco San Francisco	2 67 793
TIDBALL		
Alexander S	Yuba Marysville	72 879
Joseph	Yuba Marysville	72 872
Thomas	Santa Cruz Soguel	66 590
TIDD		
Danl	San Francisco San Francisco	1 68 905
I M*	Placer Iona Hills	62 875
J A	Yolo Cottonwoood	72 652
Peter	Nevada Rough &	61 420
Wm	Solano Suisan	69 220
TIDDING		
Thos	San Francisco San Francisco	9 681 075
TIDDLER		
L D	Los Angeles Tejon	59 536
TIDEMAN		
F	Butte Bidwell	56 716
TIDMIR		
Kate	San Francisco San Francisco	2 67 734
TIDSALL		
James	Shasta Millvill	66 742
TIDSON		
Jno	San Joaquin Stockton	641 094
TIDWEL		
Thos H*	Nevada Rough &	61 395
TIDWELL		
Thos F*	Nevada Rough &	61 395
Thos H	Nevada Rough &	61 395
TIE COW		
---	Sacramento Ward 1	63 71
TIE LEE		
---	Sacramento Ward 1	63 65
TIE PING		
---	Sacramento Ward 1	63 70
TIE		
---	Amador Twp 2	55 328
---	Butte Kimshaw	56 598
---	Calaveras Twp 5	57 215
---	Calaveras Twp 8	57 87
---	El Dorado White Oaks	581 008
---	El Dorado White Oaks	581 011
---	El Dorado Salmon Falls	581 040
---	El Dorado Salmon Falls	581 052
---	El Dorado Salmon Falls	581 057
---	El Dorado Coloma	581 084
---	El Dorado Union	581 089
---	El Dorado Union	581 091
---	El Dorado Coloma	581 109
---	El Dorado Coloma	581 121
---	El Dorado Coloma	581 122
---	El Dorado Kelsey	581 136
---	El Dorado Kelsey	581 141
---	El Dorado Kelsey	581 143
---	El Dorado Casumnes	581 162
---	El Dorado Mud Springs	58 976
---	El Dorado Mud Springs	58 978
---	El Dorado Mud Springs	58 982
---	Mariposa Twp 1	60 665
---	Mariposa Coulterville	60 681
---	Nevada Rough &	61 398
---	Nevada Rough &	61 434
---	Nevada Rough &	61 437
---	Nevada Bridgeport	61 463
---	Nevada Bridgeport	61 466
---	Nevada Bridgeport	61 485
---	Nevada Bloomfield	61 507
---	Sacramento Ward 1	63 53
---	Sacramento Ward 1	63 56
---	Sacramento Ward 1	63 61
---	Sacramento Ward 1	63 69
---	San Francisco San Francisco	4 681 177
---	San Francisco San Francisco	4 681 188
---	San Francisco San Francisco	5 671 205
---	San Francisco San Francisco	4 681 210
---	San Francisco San Francisco	1 68 926
---	Trinity Mouth Ca	701 015
---*	Butte Kimshaw	56 606
---*	El Dorado Coloma	581 084
---*	Sacramento Ward 1	63 56
---*	Trinity E Weaver	701 061
Cow	Sacramento Ward 1	63 71
Fo	San Francisco San Francisco	4 681 180
Fow	Calaveras Twp 4	57 334
Fu	San Francisco San Francisco	4 681 190
Gow	El Dorado Coloma	581 075
Hae	El Dorado Coloma	581 075
Hei	San Francisco San Francisco	4 681 203
Ho	San Francisco San Francisco	4 681 189
Ko	San Francisco San Francisco	4 681 204
Lee	Sacramento Ward 1	63 65
Pung*	Sacramento Ward 1	63 70
Ring*	Sacramento Ward 1	63 70

Name	County Locale	M653 Roll Page
TIE		
Soe	San Francisco San Francisco	4 681 204
Yu	San Francisco San Francisco	4 681 209
TIEDMAN		
John*	Placer Michigan	62 847
TIEH		
---	El Dorado Union	581 091
TIEHER		
Daniel*	El Dorado Coloma	581 082
TIEK		
---	El Dorado Mud Springs	58 962
---	El Dorado Mud Springs	58 976
TIEL		
H W	Amador Twp 1	55 453
Jas*	Merced Twp 1	60 913
TIELUR		
Henrietta	Mariposa Twp 1	60 623
TIEMAN		
Henry	San Francisco San Francisco	7 681 384
TIEMPO		
---	Fresno Twp 1	59 119
TIEN		
---	Amador Twp 2	55 289
---	Calaveras Twp 6	57 168
---	Sacramento Ward 1	63 67
TIENCHER		
D	San Francisco San Francisco	6 67 434
TIENCKER		
D*	San Francisco San Francisco	6 67 434
TIERECKER		
D*	San Francisco San Francisco	6 67 434
TIERMAN		
Charles R	Fresno Twp 2	59 48
Henry	Tuolumne Columbia	71 294
J P	Trinity Douglas	70 978
TIERNAG		
E P	El Dorado Greenwood	58 721
TIERNAN		
Ann	San Francisco San Francisco	6 67 445
Michael*	Sacramento Ward 4	63 606
R*	San Francisco San Francisco	7 681 420
TIERNAY		
Dennis	San Diego Colorado	64 806
William	Alameda Oakland	55 46
TIERNEY		
Edward	Humbolt Pacific	59 133
J	San Francisco San Francisco	5 67 512
J*	Tuolumne Big Oak	71 179
Jas	San Francisco San Francisco	1 68 887
M A	Nevada Grass Valley	61 170
Mary	San Francisco San Francisco	8 681 241
Patrick	Siskiyou Scott Va	69 39
Thomas	Tuolumne Columbia	71 299
Wm	Sacramento Ward 4	63 575
Wm	Sacramento Ward 4	63 612
TIERNY		
Thos	San Francisco San Francisco	10 208 67
TIEROFF		
Augustus*	San Francisco San Francisco	1 68 818
TIESE		
Frederick*	San Francisco San Francisco	3 67 30
TIESON		
---	Shasta French G	66 713
TIETER		
Sophie*	San Francisco San Francisco	2 67 762
TIETZ		
L*	Sacramento Ward 4	63 586
TIEU		
---	San Francisco San Francisco	11 161 67
TIEVNAN		
Jno	San Francisco San Francisco	10 314 67
TIF		
---	Sacramento Cosumnes	63 409
Hon	Yuba Fosters	72 842
TIFANY		
Homer	El Dorado Casumnes	581 166
Horner	El Dorado Casumnes	581 166
TIFF		
J M*	Placer Iona Hills	62 875
TIFFAMY		
R J*	San Francisco San Francisco	6 67 424
TIFFANEY		
R J*	San Francisco San Francisco	6 67 424
TIFFANY		
Joseph C	Sierra Gibsonville	66 859
Owen	San Francisco San Francisco	12 374 67
R	Santa Clara Alviso	65 398
R J*	San Francisco San Francisco	6 67 424
W H	San Francisco San Francisco	5 67 498
TIFFEE		
John R	Colusa Mansville	57 438

Name	County Locale	M653 RollPage
TIFFERD		
W M*	Nevada Rough &	61 425
TIFFIN		
J E	Shasta Shasta	66 684
TIFFNEY		
Joseph	Sierra Pine Grove	66 830
TIFFON		
D G	Sutter Sutter	70 810
TIFFT		
Lucinda	San Francisco San Francisco 9	68 954
TIFFTIS		
Andrew	Amador Twp 6	55 426
TIFT		
W	San Francisco San Francisco 5	67 544
W H	Mendocino Anderson	60 871
TIFTNER		
H	San Francisco San Francisco 5	67 502
TIG		
---	Nevada Bridgeport	61 464
TIGARON		
Jose	Tuolumne Twp 3	71 435
TIGE		
---	Placer Virginia	62 680
TIGER		
Peter	Klamath Liberty	59 240
TIGERLY		
James	Sierra Downieville	661018
TIGERTY		
James*	Sierra Downieville	661018
TIGGARD		
James	El Dorado Placerville	58 933
TIGHE		
Jno	Klamath Liberty	59 231
P*	San Francisco San Francisco 9	681082
TIGHLMAN		
T H*	San Francisco San Francisco 5	67 504
TIGHTMAN		
Sophia	San Francisco San Francisco 1	68 807
TIGRE		
---	Placer Virginia	62 680
TIGUEROA		
Jesus*	Monterey San Juan	60 997
TIGUTY		
James*	Sierra Downieville	661018
TII		
---	El Dorado Placerville	58 830
TIK		
---	San Francisco San Francisco 9	681088
---	San Francisco San Francisco 11	145 67
---	Tuolumne Twp 6	71 537
Feu	San Francisco San Francisco 11	161 67
Fo	San Francisco San Francisco 11	159 67
Heen	San Francisco San Francisco 11	161 67
TIKE		
---	Sierra Downieville	66 998
TIKO		
---	Tulara Twp 1	71 115
TIL		
Hoid	Stanislaus Emory	70 752
TILAERTON		
---	San Francisco San Francisco 7	681337
TILBALL		
Thomas	Alameda Brooklyn	55 98
TILBOT		
Alexander*	San Francisco / San Francisco 3	67 37
Wm	El Dorado Mud Springs	58 982
TILCOMB		
John S	Calaveras Twp 6	57 137
TILDAFF		
Martin	Sierra Scales D	66 803
TILDEN		
Aaron	Calaveras Twp 9	57 401
Alphonso	Los Angeles Los Angeles	59 334
Ann	San Francisco San Francisco 8	681303
B F	Mariposa Coulterville	60 689
B T*	Mariposa Coulterville	60 689
Edward C	San Francisco San Francisco 7	681341
H S	Sutter Butte	70 785
Heber N	San Francisco San Francisco 10	198 67
Huriman J	Calaveras Twp 6	57 132
J B	Sacramento Ward 3	63 423
J W	San Francisco San Francisco 5	67 511
Level	Sacramento Natonia	63 271
Levid	Sacramento Natonia	63 271
M C	Sacramento Ward 1	63 39
Peter E	Yuba Rose Bar	72 799
Peter G	Yuba Rose Bar	72 799
Robert L	Siskiyou Yreka	69 181
Rosalie	Sacramento Ward 3	63 424
T J	Butte Eureka	56 650

Name	County Locale	M653 RollPage
TILDEN		
Thos W	Butte Chico	56 564
W P	Butte Chico	56 541
TILDON		
Aaron	Calaveras Twp 9	57 401
Ann	San Francisco San Francisco 8	681303
Edward C	San Francisco San Francisco 7	681341
Heber N	San Francisco San Francisco 10	198 67
TILEE		
Marten	Santa Clara Santa Clara	65 469
TILER		
---	El Dorado Placerville	58 865
TILESTON		
Edward	San Francisco San Francisco 7	681421
TILGHAM		
Charity	Tuolumne Twp 2	71 329
TILGHMAN		
Fench	Sacramento Ward 4	63 538
Geo	San Joaquin Stockton	641036
Thos H	San Francisco San Francisco 3	67 87
TILGHURAN		
T*	Sacramento Ward 4	63 602
TILGLURRAN		
T*	Sacramento Ward 4	63 602
TILGNER		
Francis	San Francisco San Francisco 2	67 740
TILIGAM		
Patrick	Santa Clara San Jose	65 282
TILIS		
John	Los Angeles Los Angeles	59 512
TILL		
---	Tuolumne Twp 2	71 474
---*	Nevada Bridgeport	61 463
Alfred	Fresno Twp 2	59 89
An	Del Norte Crescent	58 631
Mary	Sacramento Sutter	63 299
TILLA		
Placitus*	San Francisco San Francisco 8	681322
TILLAPANGH		
Will*	Yuba Rose Bar	72 795
TILLAPAUGH		
Will	Yuba Rose Par	72 795
TILLAR		
Rosa*	San Francisco San Francisco 2	67 567
TILLBURG		
P J	Tehama Red Bluff	70 911
TILLBROWN		
Henry	Tulara Twp 1	71 110
TILLEE		
Thomas*	Santa Cruz Pescadero	66 644
TILLEMAN		
Henry*	Nevada Bridgeport	61 465
TILLER		
Fred	Yolo Cache	72 634
J J	Butte Eureka	56 656
Thomas	Santa Cruz Pescadero	66 644
TILLET		
J S*	Mariposa Twp 3	60 598
M	Mariposa Coulterville	60 688
TILLETTS		
Albert	Yuba Long Bar	72 756
TILLEY		
B V*	Sutter Yuba	70 760
C P	Trinity Lewiston	70 953
David G	Calaveras Twp 4	57 322
Edward	Placer Auburn	62 566
G H	Sierra Twp 5	66 929
Geo H	Sacramento Sutter	63 298
Henry	Tuolumne Jamestown	71 450
J W	Nevada Nevada	61 322
John	Tuolumne Twp 1	71 260
John	Yolo Cache Crk	72 634
Joseph	Tuolumne Twp 2	71 473
M J	Nevada Nevada	61 241
Peter S	Calaveras Twp 6	57 156
R W	Nevada Nevada	61 241
S C	Nevada Nevada	61 241
W C	Nevada Nevada	61 241
W J	Sacramento Sutter	63 298
TILLFORD		
James	Calaveras Twp 10	57 288
TILLHORN		
T J	Napa Napa	61 57
TILLIMAN		
Henry*	Nevada Bridgeport	61 465
TILLINGHART		
Albert	Solano Vallejo	69 246
TILLINGHAST		
W H	San Francisco San Francisco 6	67 420
TILLMAN		
A	San Francisco San Francisco 5	67 525
Devit	Sonoma Bodega	69 525
Frank*	San Francisco San Francisco 2	67 588
Henry	Nevada Bridgeport	61 465
John	San Francisco San Francisco 8	681313

Name	County Locale	M653 RollPage
TILLMAN		
John I	San Francisco San Francisco 7	681406
John J	San Francisco San Francisco 8	681323
M	Calaveras Twp 9	57 416
R	El Dorado Diamond	58 807
Wm	Santa Clara Redwood	65 451
Wm	Sonoma Petaluma	69 614
TILLMANN		
Fredck	San Francisco San Francisco 7	681434
TILLON		
Andrew	Calaveras Twp 10	57 267
TILLOTSON		
H	Sutter Yuba	70 774
Henry	Yuba Marysville	72 919
Isaac	Mendocino Round Va	60 878
Mary	Yuba Marysville	72 919
TILLS		
David*	Sacramento Cosummes	63 403
TILLSON		
Josiah	Contra Costa Twp 3	57 598
TILLUM		
Thos	Tehama Cottonwoood	70 902
TILLY		
George H	Humbolt Union	59 182
H A*	Yuba Slate Ro	72 712
H H	Sacramento Brighton	63 193
Isac H*	Mariposa Coulterville	60 676
Thomas	Mariposa Twp 1	60 638
TILMAN		
Henry*	San Francisco San Francisco 7	681373
T	Tehama Antelope	70 888
TILNS		
N J	Colusa Grand Island	57 476
TILOREO		
Juan	Mariposa Twp 3	60 611
TILSEEN		
Horace	Sacramento Ward 4	63 514
TILSON		
D H	El Dorado Greenwood	58 709
J D	Amador Twp 2	55 302
Josiah	Santa Clara San Jose	65 283
TILTEE		
Thomas*	Santa Cruz Pescadero	66 644
TILTIN		
C E	San Francisco San Francisco 5	67 533
I	Calaveras Twp 9	57 396
TILTON		
Andrew	Calaveras Twp 10	57 267
B F	Sonoma Armally	69 494
C A*	Nevada Bloomfield	61 520
C E	San Francisco San Francisco 5	67 533
Charles H	San Mateo Twp 1	65 67
Clement	San Joaquin O'Neal	641008
F C	Nevada Nevada	61 296
G	San Mateo Twp 1	65 67
Hasin	Humbolt Eureka	59 177
J	Calaveras Twp 9	57 396
J A	San Mateo Twp 1	65 69
J L	Butte Oregon	56 626
J R	Sacramento American	63 166
Jane	Calaveras Twp 5	57 238
John	El Dorado Mud Springs	58 990
John	Sacramento American	63 167
John G	Contra Costa Twp 3	57 607
Ledic	Calaveras Twp 6	57 174
N N	San Joaquin Elkhorn	64 977
Richmond	Plumas Quincy	62 959
S J	Nevada Red Dog	61 548
S S	San Francisco San Francisco 12	391 67
Thos	Yolo Washington	72 572
Valentine	Plumas Quincy	62 925
Wm*	Sacramento Ward 1	63 154
TILTOW		
F C	Nevada Nevada	61 296
TILTS		
Harry	Calaveras Twp 10	57 294
Harvy	Calaveras Twp 10	57 294
TILUM		
J	Tuolumne Twp 4	71 146
TIM MAN		
---*	Nevada Nevada	61 306
TIM WANG		
---	Nevada Bridgeport	61 463
TIM		
---	Amador Twp 4	55 256
---	Amador Twp 2	55 285
---	Amador Twp 2	55 290
---	Amador Twp 5	55 330
---	Amador Twp 5	55 336
---	Amador Twp 5	55 344
---	Amador Twp 5	55 354
---	Amador Twp 5	55 355
---	Amador Twp 5	55 356
---	Amador Twp 5	55 360
---	Amador Twp 7	55 415

California 1860 Census Index

Name	County Locale	M653 RollPage
TIM		
---	Amador Twp 6	55 425
---	Amador Twp 6	55 432
---	Amador Twp 6	55 445
---	Butte Chico	56 556
---	Butte Chico	56 558
---	Butte Wyandotte	56 666
---	Butte Ophir	56 773
---	Calaveras Twp 5	57 214
---	Calaveras Twp 5	57 219
---	Calaveras Twp 4	57 299
---	Calaveras Twp 4	57 338
---	Del Norte Crescent	58 651
---	Del Norte Happy Ca	58 667
---	El Dorado Salmon Falls	581047
---	El Dorado Salmon Falls	581058
---	El Dorado Salmon Hills	581061
---	El Dorado Union	581091
---	El Dorado Greenwood	58 728
---	El Dorado Placerville	58 934
---	El Dorado Mud Springs	58 958
---	Mariposa Coulterville	60 682
---	Nevada Grass Valley	61 231
---	Nevada Rough &	61 399
---	Nevada Rough &	61 432
---	Nevada Bridgeport	61 439
---	Nevada Bridgeport	61 462
---	Nevada Bridgeport	61 485
---	Nevada Bloomfield	61 528
---	Sacramento Cosumnes	63 386
---	Sacramento Ward 3	63 492
---	Sacramento Ward 3	63 493
---	Sacramento Ward 1	63 55
---	Sacramento Ward 1	63 69
---	San Francisco San Francisco 2	67 754
---	Shasta French G	66 713
---	Sierra Downieville	661004
---	Sierra Downieville	661015
---	Sierra Twp 5	66 931
---	Sierra Twp 5	66 947
---	Sierra Cox'S Bar	66 949
---	Sierra Cox'S Bar	66 951
---	Sierra Downieville	66 981
---	Tuolumne Big Oak	71 149
---	Tuolumne Twp 3	71 442
---	Tuolumne Twp 3	71 457
---*	Amador Twp 5	55 336
---*	Butte Wyandotte	56 666
---*	El Dorado Salmon Falls	581053
---*	El Dorado Georgetown	58 700
---*	Mariposa Twp 3	60 589
---*	Nevada Bridgeport	61 459
---*	Tuolumne Big Oak	71 179
Ah	Tehama Tehama	70 950
Chow	Nevada Grass Valley	61 231
Kee*	San Francisco San Francisco 5	67 493
Lee	Plumas Quincy	621009
Long	Amador Twp 2	55 326
Lory*	Amador Twp 2	55 326
Man	Nevada Nevada	61 306
Phat	El Dorado Georgetown	58 674
Sam	Mariposa Twp 1	60 637
Samuel	Sierra Twp 5	66 939
Sein	Plumas Quincy	62 949
TIMANTES		
Ricante*	Sacramento Ward 1	63 57
TIMATHY		
N M	Yolo Cache	72 629
TIMBALL		
Robt*	Fresno Millerto	59 2
TIMBERLAKE		
Henry	Tuolumne Twp 2	71 283
Warren	Tuolumne Twp 2	71 283
TIMBERMAN		
A G	Klamath Liberty	59 238
TIMBERS		
William	Calaveras Twp 8	57 97
TIMBULL		
Robt*	Fresno Millerto	59 2
TIME		
---	Butte Hamilton	56 530
---	Butte Eureka	56 651
---	Calaveras Twp 5	57 192
---	Sacramento Cosumnes	63 407
---*	Butte Hamilton	56 530
---*	Placer Auburn	62 576
Paul*	San Francisco San Francisco 8	681317
TIMENY		
Leonor	Calaveras Twp 4	57 332
Leonos*	Calaveras Twp 4	57 332
Leouor*	Calaveras Twp 4	57 332
TIMERMAN		
John	Placer Forest H	62 794
TIMERTY		
Thos	San Francisco San Francisco 2	67 642
TIMG		
---*	Mariposa Coulterville	60 679

Name	County Locale	M653 RollPage
TIMGS		
Charles A*	Yuba Slate Ro	72 699
TIMIGA		
Manuel*	Monterey Monterey	60 930
TIMIRETY		
Thos*	San Francisco San Francisco 2	67 642
TIMISCO		
---*	San Diego Agua Caliente	64 860
TIMLER		
Fred	El Dorado Cold Spring	581100
Thumelda	San Francisco San Francisco 2	67 606
TIMLEY		
Michael*	Placer Auburn	62 585
TIMLIN		
James*	San Francisco San Francisco 8	681255
TIMMANS		
Stephen*	Nevada Nevada	61 251
TIMMEL		
Louis	Los Angeles Santa Ana	59 443
TIMMER		
John S	Yuba Marysville	72 867
Tom	San Mateo Twp 2	65 131
TIMMERMAN		
A	Trinity Weaverville	701056
Chas W	Trinity Weaverville	701076
Henry	San Francisco San Francisco 11	92
		67
J	El Dorado Casumnes	581169
Jos	Amador Twp 5	55 345
Louisa	San Francisco San Francisco 6	67 435
M*	San Francisco San Francisco 2	67 799
Wm	Merced Monterey	60 938
Wm	Monterey Monterey	60 938
TIMMERNAU		
Antonie*	Amador Twp 2	55 310
TIMMERSON		
E*	El Dorado Casumnes	581171
TIMMIONS		
Saml	Mariposa Twp 1	60 645
TIMMONS		
Anthony	Sonoma Petaluma	69 564
E	El Dorado Placerville	58 847
J	Butte Kimshaw	56 572
J	El Dorado Placerville	58 860
J	San Francisco San Francisco 5	67 493
James	Marin Cortemad	60 781
John	Nevada Red Dog	61 546
L	El Dorado Placerville	58 862
Owen	Butte Hamilton	56 519
Saml	Mariposa Twp 1	60 645
William	Shasta Shasta	66 730
TIMMRNAN		
Antoine*	Amador Twp 2	55 310
TIMMS		
Jaochin	Tuolumne Sonora	71 216
Jaochine	Tuolumne Twp 1	71 216
TIMMUMAN		
M	San Francisco San Francisco 2	67 799
TIMMUNS		
Steplhen	Nevada Nevada	61 251
TIMON		
J W*	El Dorado Placerville	58 839
Jno	San Francisco San Francisco 9	681071
TIMORS		
Jno F	Fresno Twp 2	59 3
TIMOTEO		
Cono	Los Angeles Tejon	59 540
TIMOTHY		
John	Solano Vallejo	69 277
Joseph	Sierra Twp 7	66 877
Marchini	Sierra Poker Flats	66 839
W M	Yolo Cache Crk	72 629
TIMOTO		
---*	Mendocino Calpella	60 824
TIMPER		
C	Amador Twp 6	55 425
TIMPKINS		
C H	Siskiyou Scott Va	69 47
TIMPLER		
Emily*	Placer Auburn	62 584
Emly*	Placer Auburn	62 584
Thomas J	Placer Auburn	62 584
TIMPLETON		
Geo	Napa Yount	61 40
TIMPLIN		
S P	Sierra Twp 7	66 874
TIMS		
Augustus W	San Pedro Los Angeles	59 483
John	Yuba Rose Bar	72 789
TIMSON		
R P	Sierra Twp 7	66 893
TIMUS		
Levardo	Calaveras Twp 5	57 226
TIN A TIN		
---*	Amador Twp 5	55 335

Name	County Locale	M653 RollPage
TIN COY		
---	Tuolumne Chinese	71 524
TIN IN NO		
	Mendocino Calpella	60 823
TIN SON		
	Marin Cortemad	60 790
TIN		
---	Alameda Oakland	55 33
---	Amador Twp 4	55 247
---	Amador Twp 2	55 289
---	Amador Twp 2	55 311
---	Amador Twp 2	55 312
---	Amador Twp 2	55 315
---	Amador Twp 2	55 316
---	Amador Twp 2	55 319
---	Amador Twp 5	55 341
---	Amador Twp 5	55 342
---	Amador Twp 5	55 350
---	Amador Twp 5	55 352
---	Amador Twp 5	55 353
---	Amador Twp 5	55 355
---	Amador Twp 3	55 379
---	Amador Twp 3	55 398
---	Amador Twp 7	55 414
---	Amador Twp 6	55 434
---	Amador Twp 1	55 472
---	Amador Twp 1	55 477
---	Amador Twp 1	55 492
---	Calaveras Twp 5	57 182
---	Calaveras Twp 5	57 198
---	Calaveras Twp 5	57 212
---	Calaveras Twp 5	57 214
---	Calaveras Twp 5	57 215
---	Calaveras Twp 5	57 219
---	Calaveras Twp 5	57 226
---	Calaveras Twp 5	57 233
---	Calaveras Twp 5	57 235
---	Calaveras Twp 5	57 236
---	Calaveras Twp 5	57 244
---	Calaveras Twp 5	57 245
---	Calaveras Twp 5	57 247
---	Calaveras Twp 5	57 256
---	Calaveras Twp 5	57 257
---	Calaveras Twp 5	57 258
---	Calaveras Twp 10	57 260
---	Calaveras Twp 10	57 267
---	Calaveras Twp 10	57 268
---	Calaveras Twp 10	57 269
---	Calaveras Twp 10	57 270
---	Calaveras Twp 10	57 271
---	Calaveras Twp 10	57 272
---	Calaveras Twp 10	57 274
---	Calaveras Twp 10	57 276
---	Calaveras Twp 10	57 284
---	Calaveras Twp 10	57 286
---	Calaveras Twp 10	57 295
---	Calaveras Twp 4	57 301
---	Calaveras Twp 4	57 302
---	Calaveras Twp 4	57 315
---	Calaveras Twp 4	57 328
---	Calaveras Twp 4	57 332
---	Calaveras Twp 4	57 338
---	Calaveras Twp 8	57 60
---	Calaveras Twp 8	57 63
---	Del Norte Crescent	58 640
---	El Dorado Salmon Falls	581062
---	El Dorado Coloma	581075
---	El Dorado Coloma	581077
---	El Dorado Coloma	581084
---	El Dorado Coloma	581086
---	El Dorado Coloma	581102
---	El Dorado Coloma	581106
---	El Dorado Coloma	581111
---	El Dorado Coloma	581114
---	El Dorado Coloma	581116
---	El Dorado Coloma	581120
---	El Dorado Coloma	581121
---	El Dorado Kelsey	581141
---	El Dorado Diamond	58 794
---	El Dorado Placerville	58 905
---	El Dorado Placerville	58 906
---	El Dorado Eldorado	58 946
---	El Dorado Mud Springs	58 971
---	El Dorado Mud Springs	58 987
---	Mariposa Twp 1	60 646
---	Mariposa Twp 1	60 648
---	Mariposa Coulterville	60 681
---	Mariposa Coulterville	60 683
---	Mariposa Coulterville	60 692
---	Nevada Grass Valley	61 231
---	Placer Illinois	62 753
---	Sacramento Granite	63 268
---	Sacramento Ward 3	63 489
---	Sacramento Ward 4	63 609
---	Sacramento Ward 1	63 65
---	Sacramento Ward 1	63 69

Name	County Locale	M653 RollPage	Name	County Locale	M653 RollPage	Name	County Locale	M653 RollPage
TIN			**TINDALL**			**TING**		
---	San Francisco San Francisco 2	67 786	Thomas H	Siskiyou Yreka	69 134	---	Tulara Visalia	71 106
---	Shasta Horsetown	66 704	**TINDER**			---	Tuolumne Columbia	71 350
---	Shasta Horsetown	66 710	L B	Yolo No E Twp	72 674	---	Tuolumne Shawsfla	71 386
---	Sierra Downieville	661000	L B*	Yuba North Ea	72 674	---	Tuolumne Shawsfla	71 408
---	Sierra Downieville	661003	William	Tuolumne Sonora	71 197	---	Tuolumne Twp 2	71 409
---	Sierra Downieville	661008	**TINDLEY**			---	Tuolumne Twp 2	71 416
---	Sierra Downieville	661009	Wm*	Butte Kimshaw	56 599	---	Tuolumne Twp 3	71 422
---	Sierra Downieville	661025	**TINE**			---	Tuolumne Twp 3	71 433
---	Sierra Downieville	661030	---	Calaveras Twp 5	57 237	---	Tuolumne Jamestown	71 440
---	Sierra Twp 7	66 915	---	Sacramento Ward 1	63 67	---	Tuolumne Twp 3	71 467
---	Sierra Downieville	66 973	---	Shasta Shasta	66 669	---	Tuolumne Twp 3	71 468
---	Sierra Downieville	66 980	---	Sierra Downieville	661027	---	Tuolumne Sonora	71 476
---	Sierra Downieville	66 982	---	Sierra Twp 7	66 886	---	Tuolumne Sonora	71 477
---	Sierra Downieville	66 996	---	Trinity Lewiston	70 956	---	Tuolumne Sonora	71 478
---	Tuolumne Don Pedro	71 163	Ah	Butte Eureka	56 651	---	Tuolumne Twp 5	71 521
---	Tuolumne Twp 1	71 477	B C	Siskiyou Scott Ri	69 67	---	Yolo No E Twp	72 684
---	Tuolumne Twp 5	71 521	**TINEO**			---	Yuba North Ea	72 679
---	Tuolumne Twp 6	71 537	Frank	Amador Twp 1	55 486	---	Yuba Slate Ro	72 683
---	Yolo No E Twp	72 680	**TINER**			---	Yuba Slate Ro	72 684
---	Yuba Long Bar	72 758	J L	Tehama Red Bluff	70 914	---*	Amador Twp 6	55 430
---*	Sacramento Granite	63 268	**TINES**			---*	Mariposa Coulterville	60 679
---*	Sacramento Ward 1	63 55	George	Sierra La Porte	66 788	---*	Sacramento Cosumms	63 388
A	Sacramento Granite	63 268	**TINESDALE**			---*	Trinity Taylor'S	701036
A Tin*	Amador Twp 5	55 335	W	Yuba North Ea	72 671	---*	Tuolumne Big Oak	71 181
Bong	Calaveras Twp 5	57 257	**TINEY**			Ah	Calaveras Twp 7	57 35
Bony	Calaveras Twp 5	57 257	---	Calaveras Twp 5	57 192	Ah	Sacramento Cosumms	63 384
Can*	Placer Auburn	62 579	---	Nevada Grass Valley	61 229	Ah	Tuolumne Twp 2	71 350
Cee*	Calaveras Twp 5	57 205	Albert*	Sierra Twp 7	66 912	Ah	Tuolumne Twp 2	71 386
Chat	El Dorado Georgetown	58 674	**TING**			Ah*	Butte Oregon	56 640
Che	Calaveras Twp 10	57 272	---	Alameda Oakland	55 63	Ar	Trinity Mouth Ca	701015
Chin	Butte Ophir	56 811	---	Amador Twp 2	55 289	Ching	Siskiyou Yreka	69 195
Ching	Nevada Rough &	61 435	---	Amador Twp 2	55 326	Choi	Calaveras Twp 5	57 193
Chon	San Francisco San Francisco 4	681179	---	Amador Twp 3	55 407	Chow	Nevada Grass Valley	61 233
Chong	San Francisco San Francisco 5	67 508	---	Amador Twp 3	55 410	Chu	Calaveras Twp 10	57 278
Chou	San Francisco San Francisco 4	681179	---	Amador Twp 1	55 477	Fos	Yuba Slate Ro	72 707
Choy	Butte Ophir	56 787	---	Amador Twp 1	55 478	Hoy	Butte Bidwell	56 727
Choy	Butte Ophir	56 819	---	Butte Kimshaw	56 588	Leck*	Yuba Long Bar	72 766
Cke	Calaveras Twp 5	57 205	---	Butte Oregon	56 640	Leek*	Yuba Long Bar	72 766
Cle	Calaveras Twp 5	57 205	---	Calaveras Twp 6	57 149	Low	Yuba Long Bar	72 766
Coy	Tuolumne Twp 5	71 524	---	Calaveras Twp 6	57 151	Sam	Trinity Trinity	70 975
Fok	Calaveras Twp 6	57 165	---	Calaveras Twp 5	57 219	Shin	Mariposa Coulterville	60 681
Foo	El Dorado Mud Springs	58 988	---	Calaveras Twp 5	57 222	Tching*	Plumas Quincy	62 946
Hew	Yuba Marysville	72 921	---	Calaveras Twp 5	57 235	Wa	San Francisco San Francisco 5	67 507
Hi	Stanislaus Emory	70 748	---	Calaveras Twp 10	57 286	You	Yuba Long Bar	72 766
Hin	Butte Ophir	56 817	---	Calaveras Twp 4	57 300	**TINGLER**		
Hoe	Butte Ophir	56 820	---	Calaveras Twp 4	57 307	John	Tuolumne Chinese	71 523
Hoo	Butte Ophir	56 819	---	Calaveras Twp 4	57 320	S	El Dorado Placerville	58 897
Kar	El Dorado Mud Springs	58 953	---	Calaveras Twp 4	57 322	**TINGLEY**		
Kin	Butte Ophir	56 812	---	Calaveras Twp 4	57 333	Byron	San Francisco San Francisco 8	681315
Kum	Butte Ophir	56 817	---	Calaveras Twp 4	57 339	George B	San Francisco San Francisco 8	681315
Lean*	Butte Ophir	56 809	---	Calaveras Twp 8	57 50	James	El Dorado Cold Spring	581100
Lim	Del Norte Crescent	58 643	---	Calaveras Twp 8	57 66	Jas	Butte Kimshaw	56 599
Long	Butte Bidwell	56 725	---	Calaveras Twp 8	57 84	O	Sutter Sutter	70 815
Meh	Calaveras Twp 4	57 300	---	Del Norte Crescent	58 630	S	El Dorado Newtown	58 781
Mik	Calaveras Twp 4	57 300	---	Del Norte Crescent	58 641	Saml	Sacramento Dry Crk	63 373
Mu	Calaveras Twp 10	57 272	---	Del Norte Crescent	58 659	**TINGMAN**		
Nah	Butte Ophir	56 806	---	Del Norte Happy Ca	58 667	Jno*	Sacramento Ward 3	63 443
Roo	Calaveras Twp 6	57 136	---	El Dorado Coloma	581115	**TINGUA**		
San	Sacramento Ward 1	63 70	---	El Dorado Georgetown	58 747	---	Sierra Twp 5	66 933
Sin	El Dorado Diamond	58 801	---	El Dorado Diamond	58 789	**TINI**		
Sing	Butte Wyandotte	56 666	---	El Dorado Diamond	58 815	---	San Joaquin Stockton	641063
Sing	Butte Ophir	56 815	---	El Dorado Placerville	58 830	**TINILL**		
So	Sierra Morristown	661055	---	El Dorado Placerville	58 890	Geo W*	Del Norte Klamath	58 652
Son	Marin Cortemad	60 790	---	El Dorado Placerville	58 894	**TINK**		
Ton	Sierra Twp 5	66 933	---	El Dorado Mud Springs	58 975	Ah	Siskiyou Klamath	69 79
Un	Calaveras Twp 5	57 246	---	El Dorado Mud Springs	58 991	John P*	San Joaquin Castoria	64 905
Wa	Nevada Nevada	61 304	---	Mariposa Coulterville	60 679	**TINKAM**		
Wah	Butte Ophir	56 787	---	Mariposa Coulterville	60 683	Gilbert*	Nevada Rough &	61 421
Wah	Butte Ophir	56 809	---	Mariposa Coulterville	60 685	**TINKARA**		
Wah	Butte Ophir	56 813	---	Mariposa Coulterville	60 691	Gilbert*	Nevada Rough &	61 421
Wah	Butte Ophir	56 818	---	Nevada Grass Valley	61 233	**TINKASA**		
Wahs	Butte Ophir	56 809	---	Nevada Nevada	61 300	Gilbert	Nevada Rough &	61 421
Wing	Calaveras Twp 4	57 308	---	Nevada Nevada	61 304	**TINKELL**		
Yee	Butte Cascade	56 702	---	Nevada Bridgeport	61 439	Coonrod	Trinity Grass Valley	70 962
Yon	San Francisco San Francisco 4	681175	---	Nevada Bridgeport	61 459	Counrod	Trinity Grass Valley	70 962
TINAMAN			---	Nevada Bridgeport	61 460	**TINKENAR**		
Robt	El Dorado Salmon Falls	581038	---	Nevada Bridgeport	61 463	Gilbert*	Nevada Rough &	61 421
TINBATH			---	Nevada Bridgeport	61 506	**TINKER**		
Wm	Santa Clara Almaden	65 276	---	Nevada Bloomfield	61 530	Henry H	Plumas Quincy	62 987
TINBY			---	Nevada Red Dog	61 556	Joseh	Nevada Rough &	61 428
William	Tuolumne Twp 1	71 251	---	Placer Auburn	62 576	Joseph	Nevada Rough &	61 428
William	Tuolumne Twp 1	71 251	---	Placer Virginia	62 701	Robert*	San Bernardino Santa Barbara	64 199
TINCE			---	Placer Michigan	62 858	Saml	San Francisco San Francisco 1	68 847
A	San Francisco San Francisco 6	67 473	---	Placer Iona Hills	62 898	**TINKERM**		
C*	San Francisco San Francisco 5	67 486	---	Plumas Quincy	62 926	Gilbert*	Nevada Rough &	61 421
M*	Nevada Nevada	61 290	---	Sacramento Mississipi	63 190	**TINKEY**		
TINCHE			---	Sacramento Granite	63 231	David	Solano Suisan	69 240
---	Tulara Visalia	71 114	---	Sacramento Sutter	63 308	**TINKHAM**		
TIND			---	Sacramento Cosumms	63 392	A	Del Norte Ferry P O	58 665
---	Fresno Twp 3	59 31	---	Sierra Downieville	661004	C P	Yolo Putah	72 553
TINDA			---	Sierra Downieville	661025	M M	Tuolumne Columbia	71 345
A T*	Yuba Rose Bar	72 791	---	Sierra Downieville	661026	P N	Trinity Trinity	70 970
TINDAL			---	Sierra Twp 5	66 927	Wm B	San Francisco San Francisco 5	67 545
Thomas H*	Siskiyou Yreka	69 134	---	Sierra Downieville	66 982	**TINKLE**		
TINDALL			---	Trinity Mouth Ca	701015	Robert B	Humbolt Eel Rvr	59 149
Benj	Yolo Cache Crk	72 665						

Name	County Locale	M653 Roll Page
TINKLER		
Jno	Butte Oregon	56 620
TINKMN		
J*	Yolo Putah	72 553
TINKNON		
J*	Yolo Putah	72 553
TINKSFORD		
Jas	Butte Bidwell	56 720
TINKSWALLE		
Benjamin*	Calaveras Twp 8	57 103
TINKUM		
Charles	Contra Costa Twp 3	57 604
Jas*	San Francisco San Francisco 10	212 67
Jos	San Francisco San Francisco 10	212 67
Z B*	Tuolumne Columbia	71 326
TINKURN		
Jas*	San Francisco San Francisco 10	212 67
TINLEY		
E*	Nevada Nevada	61 297
James	El Dorado Mud Springs	58 976
John*	Los Angeles Tejon	59 537
L	Nevada Nevada	61 290
TINLK		
---*	Mariposa Twp 1	60 626
TINLY		
Jame*	Nevada Bridgeport	61 496
TINMENS		
J	Butte Kimshaw	56 572
TINMPLER		
Janbury	Yolo Washington	72 573
TINN		
---	Sierra Downieville	66 990
---*	Nevada Eureka	61 386
Kim	Butte Bidwell	56 719
TINNAN		
T	El Dorado Diamond	58 799
TINNANT		
Wm	Santa Clara Burnett	65 254
TINNE		
---	El Dorado Placerville	58 906
G*	San Francisco San Francisco 4	681 216
TINNEBER		
Paul*	San Francisco San Francisco 9	681 106
TINNELEY		
C S*	Butte Hamilton	56 522
TINNELL		
Wm	Stanislaus Emory	70 739
TINNEN		
W J	Trinity Weaverville	701 062
W W	Trinity Weaverville	701 062
TINNER		
Lewis*	San Francisco San Francisco 1	68 893
TINNERMAN		
Antonie	Amador Twp 2	55 312
TINNERSON		
Joseph*	El Dorado Casumnes	581 172
TINNERT		
W P	Sierra Downieville	66 975
TINNERTY		
Thos*	San Francisco San Francisco 2	67 642
TINNERY		
J	San Francisco San Francisco 1	68 860
TINNEY		
A	El Dorado Coloma	581 104
Francis*	Tuolumne Green Springs	71 518
George W	San Diego Colorado	64 809
John	Sierra Downieville	66 995
William	San Joaquin Oneal	64 931
TINNIER		
A C*	Yuba Rose Bar	72 812
TINNIN		
A C*	Yuba Rose Bar	72 812
W J	Yuba Rose Bar	72 812
TINNING		
Wm*	San Francisco San Francisco 1	68 835
TINNINGS		
Matilda I*	Stanislaus Empire	70 734
TINNISON		
F*	Nevada Eureka	61 344
TINNISORD		
F*	Nevada Eureka	61 344
TINNSEND		
G	Butte Cascade	56 696
TINNURNAN		
Antonie*	Amador Twp 2	55 310
TINOLER		
Hermann*	San Francisco 3 67	36
	San Francisco	
TINON		
---	Calaveras Twp 4	57 328
Jno	Sacramento Franklin	63 311
TINONS		
J W*	San Francisco San Francisco 9	681 080
TINPIN		
William	San Joaquin Stockton	641 060
TINRIAS		
Sanil	Amador Twp 5	55 343
TINSBY		
J	El Dorado Diamond	58 802
TINSEL		
---	Fresno Twp 1	59 118
TINSIMGER		
D W*	Tuolumne Twp 1	71 258
TINSINGER		
D W	Tuolumne Twp 1	71 258
TINSLEY		
James A	Trinity S Fork	701 032
Richard	Placer Forest H	62 804
TINSMERMAN		
L	Trinity Trinity	701 022
TINSSELL		
A	Monterey Monterey	60 964
TINTERMACHER		
Martin*	San Francisco San Francisco 8	681 311
TINTHOW		
Mary*	San Francisco San Francisco 2	67 647
TINUS		
Levardo	Calaveras Twp 5	57 226
TINVIES		
Enock*	Sierra Twp 7	66 882
TINY		
---	Amador Twp 2	55 326
---	Amador Twp 5	55 341
---	Amador Twp 5	55 347
---	Amador Twp 5	55 364
---	Amador Twp 3	55 398
---	Amador Twp 5	55 408
---	Calaveras Twp 5	57 149
---	Calaveras Twp 5	57 219
---	Calaveras Twp 5	57 222
---	Calaveras Twp 10	57 286
---	Calaveras Twp 4	57 307
---	Calaveras Twp 4	57 314
---	Calaveras Twp 4	57 322
---	Calaveras Twp 4	57 333
Chu	Calaveras Twp 10	57 278
Quiny	Calaveras Twp 10	57 285
Yon	Yuba Long Bar	72 766
TIO		
---	El Dorado Coloma	581 084
Ho	San Francisco San Francisco 4	681 202
TIOBALL		
Robt	Trinity Rearings	70 990
TIOES		
Benado	San Bernardino Santa Inez	64 142
TIOOS		
Francisco	Yuba Marysville	72 946
TIOT		
James M	Tulara Visalia	71 103
TIOUGIE		
Amile*	Mariposa Coulterville	60 680
TIP		
---	El Dorado Kelsey	581 135
---	Placer Illinois	62 751
---	Placer Forest H	62 772
---	Sacramento Cosumnes	63 407
---	San Francisco San Francisco 4	681 182
---	San Francisco San Francisco 5	67 507
---	Sierra Twp 7	66 876
---	Trinity Mouth Ca	701 018
---*	Yuba Long Bar	72 767
Ah	Yuba Long Bar	72 767
TIPARA		
Jose*	Santa Cruz Watsonville	66 539
TIPIT		
John	Placer Dutch Fl	62 728
TIPKIS		
Nicholas	Calaveras Twp 4	57 318
TIPLER		
Isaac	Placer Ophirville	62 657
TIPLON		
M*	Sacramento Granite	63 226
TIPP		
---	Tulara Twp 3	71 48
TIPPAN		
James	Mendocino Calpella	60 821
TIPPEL		
Jacob	Tuolumne Twp 1	71 228
Wm	Tuolumne Sonora	71 228
TIPPELT		
S L T*	Santa Clara Santa Clara	65 490
TIPPEN		
Edward	San Francisco San Francisco 2	67 610
TIPPET		
Randolph	Humbolt Union	59 186
TIPPETT		
S L T*	Santa Clara Santa Clara	65 490
TIPPINGGER		
N	San Francisco San Francisco 5	67 528
TIPPLE		
F E	El Dorado Salmon Falls	581 035
Solomon	Sierra La Porte	66 783
William	Sierra La Porte	66 770
TIPSWOREL		
Albert	El Dorado Placerville	58 925
TIPTAN		
John*	Stanislaus Buena Village	70 725
TIPTON		
J C	Tehama Red Bluff	70 928
J L	El Dorado White Oaks	581 022
James	San Francisco San Francisco 3	67 38
M	El Dorado Kelsey	581 148
M*	Sacramento Granite	63 226
TIR		
---	Amador Twp 2	55 328
---	Calaveras Twp 10	57 268
---	Mariposa Twp 1	60 658
---	San Francisco San Francisco 4	681 189
TIRAMBLY		
Chas W	Trinity McGillev	701 021
TIRAND		
Eugene	San Bernardino Santa Barbara	64 151
TIRDG		
Jame*	Nevada Bridgeport	61 496
TIRE		
---	Tuolumne Twp 6	71 532
TIRES		
Francisco*	Mariposa Twp 3	60 617
W H*	El Dorado Placerville	58 911
TIRET		
Huburt	Calaveras Twp 10	57 261
TIRIDO		
Benito	Los Angeles Tejon	59 521
TIRIST		
J P*	Nevada Bridgeport	61 455
TIRLE		
John*	Siskiyou Yreka	69 137
TIRM		
---	Amador Twp 6	55 450
---	Mariposa Twp 1	60 643
TIRN		
---	Amador Twp 5	55 330
---	Nevada Bridgeport	61 459
---*	Amador Twp 5	55 336
TIRNON		
J W*	El Dorado Placerville	58 839
TIRNY		
C F	Placer Iona Hills	62 891
TIROFF		
Augustus	San Francisco San Francisco 1	68 818
TIRPING		
Menton	El Dorado Coloma	581 081
TIRPLETT		
John	Sierra Downieville	66 963
TIRPRING		
Newton	El Dorado Coloma	581 081
TIRR		
A	Sacramento Granite	63 250
TIRRELL		
Geo	Sacramento Ward 1	63 15
Richard	Santa Cruz Pescadero	66 642
S	Calaveras Twp 8	57 88
TIRREY		
Albert*	Sierra Twp 7	66 912
TIRRILL		
M	Sacramento Natonia	63 278
TIRRONS		
J W*	San Francisco San Francisco 9	681 080
TIRROUS		
J W*	San Francisco San Francisco 9	681 080
TIRROY		
Michell	Amador Twp 5	55 362
TIRSH		
Francis	Santa Clara Burnett	65 256
TIRSO		
Keroota*	Santa Cruz Pajaro	66 561
Kiroota	Santa Cruz Pajaro	66 561
Kroota*	Santa Cruz Pajaro	66 561
TIRSONS		
J W	San Francisco San Francisco 9	681 080
TIRTZ		
Adam*	San Francisco San Francisco 2	67 704
TIRU		
Lee	Amador Twp 5	55 366
TIRVILL		
E A	San Joaquin Elliott	64 945
TIRVRY		
Danl*	Butte Kimshaw	56 579
TIRY		
---	Amador Twp 5	55 335
---	Amador Twp 5	55 360
---	Amador Twp 3	55 407
---	Amador Twp 3	55 410
A	Sacramento Granite	63 245
TIS		
---	Calaveras Twp 6	57 126

Name	County Locale	M653 RollPage
TIS		
---	Calaveras Twp 6	57 134
---	Calaveras Twp 6	57 165
---	Calaveras Twp 5	57 226
---	Calaveras Twp 10	57 260
---	Calaveras Twp 10	57 270
---	Calaveras Twp 10	57 271
TISBY		
J B	Sutter Sutter	70 803
TISCONIA		
Antonia	Mariposa Twp 1	60 636
TISCONICA		
Antonia	Mariposa Twp 1	60 636
TISDAH		
J J*	Yolo No E Twp	72 670
TISDAL		
A J	Shasta Millvill	66 740
Thos R*	Calaveras Twp 9	57 353
TISDALE		
A J	Shasta Millvill	66 740
Geo	Alameda Brooklyn	55 94
H	Tuolumne Columbia	71 338
H D	Solano Suisan	69 220
J J	Yuba North Ea	72 670
J W	Colusa Monroeville	57 448
Margaret	San Bernardino Santa Barbara	64 154
T R	Calaveras Twp 8	57 83
Wm	Tuolumne Big Oak	71 135
Wm I*	Nevada Eureka	61 392
Wm J	Nevada Eureka	61 392
TISDALL		
James	Shasta Millvill	66 742
TISDELL		
M	El Dorado Diamond	58 793
TISDORE		
Johm*	Santa Cruz Soguel	66 595
John	Santa Cruz Soguel	66 595
Johne*	Santa Cruz Soguel	66 595
TISE		
---	Fresno Twp 1	59 25
Richard	Solano Suisan	69 230
William	El Dorado Big Bar	58 738
TISEN		
C	El Dorado Diamond	58 816
TISER		
Martin*	Sacramento Mississipi	63 188
N	El Dorado Diamond	58 811
TISH		
Ah	Butte Bidwell	56 717
Oliver*	Mariposa Coulterville	60 686
Russel H*	Calaveras Twp 6	57 168
TISHORN		
George*	Placer Michigan	62 822
TISK		
A	Tuolumne Columbia	71 318
R F	Sacramento Granite	63 221
TISKE		
A	Tuolumne Twp 2	71 318
TISLIN		
George	Placer Iona Hills	62 871
TISLOW		
Thomas J	Humbolt Union	59 188
TISNIDE		
Alexandria	Tuolumne Sonora	71 215
TISON		
E H	Mariposa Twp 1	60 660
E N	Mariposa Twp 1	60 660
N	El Dorado Diamond	58 783
TISSARIND		
F*	San Francisco San Francisco 2	67 690
TISSEN		
A	Sacramento Franklin	63 308
TISSIER		
Derrick	Sierra Port Win	66 797
TISSON		
A	Sacramento Sutter	63 308
TISSOT		
Jean	San Francisco San Francisco 2	67 782
Paul	San Francisco San Francisco 11	127 67
TISSRO		
---*	San Bernardino S Timate	64 733
TISTGOR		
Fred	El Dorado Kelsey	581148
TISTN		
---	San Bernardino San Bernadino	64 681
TISWODE		
Alescudria*	Tuolumne Twp 1	71 215
TISYEAR		
Peter	Nevada Bridgeport	61 456
TISYEUR		
Peter*	Nevada Bridgeport	61 456
TIT		
---	Calaveras Twp 5	57 232
---	Calaveras Twp 5	57 252
---	El Dorado Coloma	581103

Name	County Locale	M653 RollPage
TIT		
---	El Dorado Placerville	58 905
TITAS		
Lana A	Calaveras Twp 6	57 111
W	Amador Twp 2	55 302
TITBALL		
Thomas	Solano Vacaville	69 337
TITCHUELLE		
William H	Contra Costa Twp 1	57 490
TITCOM		
Isaac	Siskiyou Scott Va	69 60
TITCOMB		
Amos	San Francisco San Francisco 1	68 807
John	Marin Tomales	60 713
John H	San Francisco San Francisco 4	681128
R	San Francisco San Francisco 3	67 72
TITCOMD		
Mary A*	Placer Secret R	62 615
TITCOURD		
Mary A*	Placer Secret R	62 615
TITGRAVES		
Wm	Sacramento Ward 4	63 578
TITLER		
Geo	El Dorado Kelsey	581154
TITMAN		
E A	San Francisco San Francisco 3	67 84
TITMAR		
Charles	Los Angeles Los Angeles	59 344
TITO		
---	Fresno Twp 1	59 87
TITORS		
J M	Tehama Lassen	70 862
TITTEE		
Thomas*	Santa Cruz Pescadero	66 644
TITTEL		
Charles C C	San Francisco 7	681396
	San Francisco	
Charles*	San Francisco San Francisco 7	681391
Ernst*	San Francisco San Francisco 7	681396
T G A*	San Francisco San Francisco 7	681396
T G W	San Francisco San Francisco 7	681396
TITTEMORE		
Chas	Sonoma Armally	69 512
TITTER		
Sophie*	San Francisco San Francisco 2	67 762
TITTLE		
Augustus	San Francisco San Francisco 7	681394
Chas	San Francisco San Francisco 1	68 926
Chas	San Francisco San Francisco 1	68 930
Conrad	San Francisco San Francisco 7	681396
David	Mariposa Coulterville	60 686
E M*	Yolo Washington	72 568
Jone	Mariposa Twp 3	60 566
TITTLER		
John	El Dorado Kelsey	581146
TITTOW		
Thomas	Del Norte Klamath	58 655
TITTSON		
Thomas	San Francisco San Francisco 7	681440
TITTUL		
Frederick*	San Francisco 7	681396
	San Francisco	
TITTUS		
Jesse	Sierra Pine Grove	66 822
TITUS		
Abner S	Plumas Quincy	62 918
Albert E	Tehama Lassen	70 863
D	Shasta Horsetown	66 693
D M	Trinity Trinity	70 970
F J	Tehama Lassen	70 864
F J	Tuolumne Twp 1	71 276
Geo	Siskiyou Scott Ri	69 67
George	Calaveras Twp 6	57 172
Gilbert	Trinity New Rvr	701030
Henry	Yolo Washington	72 571
J H	Butte Bidwell	56 718
J H	Sacramento Ward 1	63 104
J W	Nevada Nevada	61 323
Jesse	Sierra Pine Grove	66 822
John	Contra Costa Twp 1	57 510
John	Del Norte Ferry P O	58 665
Joseph	San Francisco San Francisco 7	681373
Louis	San Francisco San Francisco 3	67 86
M	Siskiyou Scott Ri	69 75
Nathan J	San Bernardino San Bernardino	64 637
S	El Dorado Placerville	58 827
S J	El Dorado Kelsey	581130
Samuel	El Dorado Placerville	58 913
T	Butte Cascade	56 695
William	Contra Costa Twp 2	57 539
TITZEIMMONS		
Bridget	San Francisco San Francisco 8	681283
TITZER		
Christopher C	Yuba Bear Rvr	721000
TIU		
---	Calaveras Twp 5	57 215

Name	County Locale	M653 RollPage
TIU		
---	El Dorado Mud Springs	58 954
---	Mariposa Twp 1	60 648
---	San Francisco San Francisco 4	681194
TIUK		
---	Siskiyou Klamath	69 79
TIULEY		
John*	Los Angeles Tejon	59 537
TIULK		
---	Mariposa Twp 1	60 626
TIUONS		
J W*	San Francisco San Francisco 9	681080
TIV		
Luke	Yuba Foster B	72 830
TIVE		
Hee	San Francisco San Francisco 4	681202
TIVIS		
Louis*	San Francisco San Francisco 4	681219
TIVIST		
J P	Nevada Bridgeport	61 455
TIVLE		
John*	Siskiyou Yreka	69 137
TIVO		
---	El Dorado Coloma	581083
TIVOLI		
Pierre	Yuba Fosters	72 833
TIVOMLEY		
Charles	San Francisco San Francisco 4	681146
TIW		
---	Calaveras Twp 5	57 234
TIXCALLA		
S	Amador Twp 3	55 394
TIY		
---	Nevada Bridgeport	61 464
TIYAH		
---	Mendocino Twp 1	60 887
TIYH		
Kelly	Sonoma Petaluma	69 599
TIZE		
---	Sacramento Cosummes	63 406
TIZRAN		
---	Trinity Taylor'S	701034
TLAJI		
Barno*	Mariposa Twp 3	60 600
TLANBY		
Pat*	Nevada Bloomfield	61 529
TLANLY		
Pat*	Nevada Bloomfield	61 529
TLARITY		
Bridget*	Nevada Rough &	61 435
TLENON		
P*	Nevada Grass Valley	61 170
TLL		
---	Yuba Slate Ro	72 712
TLOMER		
John*	Amador Twp 2	55 321
TLORENT		
Emile	Amador Twp 5	55 336
TLUO		
---	Calaveras Twp 5	57 247
TMINS		
Sarah & Edwd	Butte Oro	56 687
TMITT		
Martin*	El Dorado Kelsey	581150
TNA FORO		
---*	Mariposa Twp 3	60 611
TNCLIN		
A W	Yolo Cache	72 593
TNI		
---*	Sacramento Granite	63 268
TNTHILL		
Franklin*	San Francisco San Francisco 2	67 734
TNYITT		
---	Tulara Twp 1	71 116
TO KIWA		
---	Butte Chico	56 550
TO LA		
---	Butte Kimshaw	56 588
TO LONG		
---	Nevada Bridgeport	61 463
TO SEE		
---*	Yuba Long Bar	72 758
TO WING		
---	Mariposa Twp 3	60 607
TO		
---	Amador Twp 5	55 340
---	Amador Twp 6	55 431
---	Del Norte Crescent	58 633
---	Fresno Twp 1	59 27
---	Mariposa Twp 1	60 667
---	Mariposa Coulterville	60 683
---	Mariposa Coulterville	60 687
---	Mariposa Coulterville	60 692
---	Sacramento Granite	63 259
---	San Francisco San Francisco 9	681096
---	San Francisco San Francisco 1	68 925

California 1860 Census Index

Name	County Locale	M653 Roll	Page
TO			
---	Sierra Downieville	66	1005
---	Sierra Twp 5	66	930
---	Sierra Twp 5	66	931
---	Sierra Twp 5	66	945
---	Sierra Downieville	66	984
---	Tehama Red Bluff	70	934
---	Yolo No E Twp	72	675
---	Yuba North Ea	72	675
Choy	San Francisco San Francisco 4	681	192
Co Poo La	Plumas Quincy	62	965
Cone	Tuolumne Chinese	71	526
Kee	San Francisco San Francisco 9	681	093
Kewa	Butte Chico	56	550
Ku*	San Francisco San Francisco 9	681	093
Latt	Yuba Long Bar	72	756
Long	Nevada Bridgeport	61	463
Lung*	Fresno Twp 2	59	19
Mong	San Francisco San Francisco 11	160	67
Mow	Calaveras Twp 5	57	237
Mung	Butte Kimshaw	56	600
On	Butte Kimshaw	56	585
Ou	Butte Kimshaw	56	585
Per	San Francisco San Francisco 4	681	175
See*	Yuba Long Bar	72	758
Shuen*	San Francisco San Francisco 11	160	67
Too	Tehama Red Bluff	70	932
Tow	Calaveras Twp 4	57	334
Yu	El Dorado Georgetown	58	691
TOA			
---	El Dorado Salmon Hills	581	060
TOABEE			
Raymond*	Yuba Marysville	72	869
TOABIE			
Raymond	Yuba Marysville	72	869
TOAGRA			
---*	Yuba Bear Rvr	721	014
TOAH			
Ah	Butte Oregon	56	627
TOAK			
---	Mariposa Twp 3	60	579
TOAL			
Rosanna	San Francisco San Francisco 10	165	67
TOAMINE			
Tedobisa	Solano Vacaville	69	359
TOAN			
---	El Dorado Georgetown	58	756
---	Placer Illinois	62	753
TOB			
---	Calaveras Twp 6	57	181
TOBA			
Edwd	Sonoma Petaluma	69	581
TOBACA			
Ignacio	San Luis Obispo San Luis Obispo 65		36
TOBANY			
Sopha	El Dorado Gold Hill	581	095
TOBART			
C M	Nevada Nevada	61	319
Lones*	Alameda Brooklyn	55	153
Louis*	Alameda Brooklyn	55	153
TOBAS			
Elia	El Dorado Kelsey	581	135
TOBBIN			
T	Calaveras Twp 9	57	397
TOBEN			
James	Siskiyou Yreka	69	147
Richd	San Francisco San Francisco 2	67	601
TOBENER			
Charles	El Dorado Coloma	581	103
TOBEO			
---	Fresno Twp 1	59	54
TOBERNER			
William	El Dorado Gold Hill	581	098
TOBERTS			
William	Monterey Pajaro	601	023
TOBEY			
B	Sutter Sutter	70	811
James	El Dorado Salmon Falls	581	037
Leander	Tuolumne Twp 2	71	362
N G*	Tuolumne Columbia	71	303
W H	Sacramento Ward 1	63	35
TOBIAS			
A J	San Francisco San Francisco 6	67	408
Albert J	San Francisco San Francisco 10	240	67
Chas	Butte Kimshaw	56	575
Jas	Butte Kimshaw	56	599
John T	Nevada Little Y	61	537
M	Nevada Grass Valley	61	235
M*	Solano Benecia	69	283
N C	Solano Benecia	69	283
S	Calaveras Twp 9	57	393
TOBIN			
E	Sutter Sutter	70	815

Name	County Locale	M653 Roll	Page
TOBIN			
Frank	Butte Mountain	56	737
G R	Nevada Grass Valley	61	186
Haurice	San Francisco San Francisco 2	67	724
Henry	Sonoma Armally	69	504
J	Nevada Grass Valley	61	218
James	Solano Vallejo	69	269
James F	Solano Vallejo	69	251
James G	Mendocino Big Rvr	60	841
Jk*	Nevada Grass Valley	61	218
John	San Francisco San Francisco 1	68	897
L	Sacramento Ward 4	63	607
M	San Francisco San Francisco 9	681	053
Mark	San Francisco San Francisco 11	119	67
Maurice	San Francisco San Francisco 2	67	724
Michael	Sacramento Ward 4	63	553
Pat	Butte Oregon	56	620
Pat	San Francisco San Francisco 9	681	072
Patk	San Francisco San Francisco 10	172	67
Philip*	Napa Napa	61	61
Richard	San Francisco San Francisco 2	67	654
Richd	San Francisco San Francisco 2	67	601
Robert	San Francisco San Francisco 1	68	845
Saml	Butte Ophir	56	768
T	San Francisco San Francisco 5	67	525
T D	Sacramento Ward 4	63	587
Wiliam	Placer Iona Hills	62	879
Willam H	San Joaquin Oneal	64	939
Wm	Butte Kimshaw	56	571
TOBINO			
Dominico	Sierra Whiskey	66	849
TOBINY			
James G	Mendocino Big Rvr	60	841
TOBIUS			
Jas*	Butte Kimshaw	56	599
TOBLIN			
T	Calaveras Twp 9	57	397
TOBLINHAMER			
P	Amador Twp 1	55	490
TOBLUS			
Jose	Mariposa Twp 1	60	643
TOBMAN			
Wm	Calaveras Twp 4	57	344
TOBOTS			
C	Sutter Sutter	70	816
TOBY			
---	Siskiyou Shasta Rvr	69	111
Astien*	Calaveras Twp 6	57	164
Astun*	Calaveras Twp 6	57	164
G	Tuolumne Twp 2	71	303
Henry	Stanislaus Empire	70	731
James L	Calaveras Twp 10	57	282
James S	Calaveras Twp 10	57	282
Jesse	Merced Twp 1	60	906
M	Nevada Grass Valley	61	223
N G*	Tuolumne Columbia	71	303
TOCALL			
---	Tulara Twp 2	71	4
TOCCHIN			
---	Trinity Weaverville	701	072
TOCHAE			
Fred	San Joaquin Stockton	641	061
TOCHINS			
Stephen	Alameda Brooklyn	55	188
TOCK			
---	Amador Twp 1	55	511
---	Calaveras Twp 6	57	333
---	Del Norte Crescent	58	651
---	Del Norte Happy Ca	58	664
---	El Dorado White Oaks	581	022
---	El Dorado White Oaks	581	023
---	El Dorado Salmon Falls	581	040
---	El Dorado Salmon Falls	581	064
---	El Dorado Salmon Falls	581	067
---	El Dorado Coloma	581	084
---	El Dorado Coloma	581	105
---	El Dorado Placerville	58	894
---	Fresno Twp 1	59	25
---*	Trinity Raabs Ba	701	020
Chong*	El Dorado Indian D	581	159
Quan	Butte Ophir	56	805
TOCRUSE			
Edwldro*	Mariposa Twp 1	60	625
TOCTO			
---	San Bernardino San Bernadino	64	678
TOD			
Joseph	Plumas Quincy	62	963
Sing	Butte Kimshaw	56	595
TODA			
L	Sutter Butte	70	779
TODAULT			
Benj	Siskiyou Scott Va	69	37
TODD			
A	Siskiyou Klamath	69	95

Name	County Locale	M653 Roll	Page
TODD			
A N	Amador Twp 2	55	315
Aaron	Sierra Twp 7	66	896
Alexander	San Francisco San Francisco 9	681	066
Alvin	San Francisco San Francisco 3	67	49
C B	Nevada Grass Valley	61	224
C W	Nevada Grass Valley	61	216
Caroline	Sonoma Mendocino	69	453
Caroline	Sonoma Mendocino	69	465
David	San Francisco San Francisco 10	290	67
David	San Mateo Twp 1	65	68
E F	San Francisco San Francisco 9	68	982
E J	San Francisco San Francisco 9	68	982
Edward	San Francisco San Francisco 5	67	476
Edwin	Plumas Quincy	62	923
Ezra	Sacramento Franklin	63	328
Francis	Placer Todds Va	62	786
Frank	Nevada Bloomfield	61	525
G	Nevada Grass Valley	61	206
G O	Nevada Grass Valley	61	163
Geo	Placer Folsom	62	649
George	Yuba Slate Ro	72	691
George	Yuba Fosters	72	832
Geroge	Yolo Slate Ra	72	691
H	Nevada Grass Valley	61	215
H W	Nevada Eureka	61	352
Henry	Nevada Red Dog	61	557
Henry	Santa Clara Redwood	65	456
J	El Dorado Diamond	58	801
J	El Dorado Placerville	58	823
J	El Dorado Placerville	58	828
J	Nevada Grass Valley	61	215
J H	Sacramento Mississipi	63	188
J W	Nevada Nevada	61	328
James	Marin Cortemad	60	788
Jas	Sacramento Ward 1	63	46
Jas	Sacramento Ward 4	63	507
Jas J	Amador Twp 6	55	441
Jno	Sacramento Ward 1	63	84
Jno	San Joaquin Stockton	641	093
Jno A*	Sacramento Ward 4	63	547
John	Calaveras Twp 6	57	116
John	El Dorado Kelsey	581	145
John	Nevada Nevada	61	330
John	Placer Folsom	62	641
John	Placer Michigan	62	826
John	San Francisco San Francisco 9	681	007
John	Yuba Marysville	72	874
Joohn	El Dorado Kelsey	581	145
Jos	Nevada Nevada	61	264
Joseph	El Dorado Georgetown	58	678
Joseph	Sierra Port Win	66	798
Josiah*	El Dorado Georgetown	58	678
L	Nevada Grass Valley	61	224
L M	Nevada Grass Valley	61	144
L M	Solano Suisan	69	209
L S	Calaveras Twp 9	57	382
M V	Sutter Yuba	70	776
Mary L	Placer Horseshoe	62	650
N J	Santa Clara Fremont	65	436
N L	Yolo Cache	72	628
Nelson	Yuba Marysville	72	962
O	Sacramento Sutter	63	295
R M	Butte Eureka	56	647
Robert	Alameda Brooklyn	55	202
Rodney	Sonoma Mendocino	69	465
Rodney A	Sonoma Mendocino	69	453
S M	Nevada Grass Valley	61	144
S S	Sonoma Santa Rosa	69	393
S T	Sonoma Santa Rosa	69	393
S*	Nevada Grass Valley	61	165
Samuel	Plumas Quincy	62	987
Samuel	San Francisco San Francisco 7	681	330
Samuel	Tuolumne Sonora	71	483
T D	San Joaquin Stockton	641	035
Thomas	Los Angeles Elmonte	59	249
W H	Nevada Grass Valley	61	238
W H	San Joaquin Stockton	641	038
W L	Yolo Cache Crk	72	628
William	Tuolumne Twp 6	71	530
William	Tuolumne Knights	71	530
William	Yolo Fremont	72	605
Wm	Klamath Liberty	59	240
Wm	Nevada Eureka	61	349
Wm	Sacramento Ward 3	63	464
Wm	Sacramento Ward 4	63	574
Wm	San Joaquin Stockton	641	023
Wm	Sierra Downieville	661	018
Wm	Trinity Weaverville	701	051
TODDDS			
E L*	Nevada Grass Valley	61	144
TODDILS			
E L*	Nevada Grass Valley	61	144
TODDMAN			
C E	Tuolumne Twp 1	71	250

California 1860 Census Index

Name	County Locale	M653 RollPage
TODDY		
---	Fresno Twp 2	59 110
TODEY		
James	San Francisco San Francisco 9	681082
TODHUNTER		
W	Yolo Washington	72 562
TODKIT		
James*	Nevada Red Dog	61 542
TODOTE NE		
---*	Butte Chico	56 551
TODOTE		
Ne*	Butte Chico	56 551
TOE BEE PAH		
---	Sacramento Ward 1	63 71
TOE		
---	El Dorado Salmon Falls	581061
---	El Dorado Coloma	581119
---	Mariposa Twp 1	60 664
---	Sacramento Ward 1	63 53
---	Tuolumne Jacksonville	71 167
---*	Sacramento Cosumnes	63 390
---*	Tuolumne Twp 6	71 535
Ah	Tuolumne Twp 4	71 167
Bee Pah	Sacramento Ward 1	63 71
Choy	San Francisco San Francisco 4	681192
Cuow*	Butte Ophir	56 817
Hie	Fresno Twp 3	59 31
Sing	Yuba Parks Ba	72 775
TOEK		
---	El Dorado Mud Springs	58 976
TOELL		
Andrew	Amador Township	55 465
TOENNIES		
Aug*	Nevada Bridgeport	61 443
TOEPEY		
Patrick	San Mateo Twp 1	65 52
TOEY		
---	Plumas Meadow Valley	62 910
---	San Francisco San Francisco 4	681178
---	San Francisco San Francisco 4	681194
---*	San Francisco San Francisco 4	681189
TOFIAS		
Albert J	San Francisco San Francisco 10	240 67
TOFO		
Chas*	San Francisco San Francisco 1	68 869
TOFPIA		
Petro*	Calaveras Twp 6	57 135
TOFT		
Albert	Calaveras Twp 6	57 111
Andrew	Calaveras Twp 6	57 111
TOG		
---	Butte Wyandotte	56 666
---	El Dorado Georgetown	58 678
---	El Dorado Diamond	58 789
---	Yuba Marysville	72 868
TOGAN		
R	Nevada Grass Valley	61 166
TOGART		
H E	Nevada Grass Valley	61 215
J	Nevada Grass Valley	61 215
TOGE		
James	El Dorado Kelsey	581139
TOGEL		
Joseph	Yuba Linda Twp	72 983
TOGER		
H M	San Francisco San Francisco 10	200 67
TOGERS		
Antoina	Calaveras Twp 6	57 135
TOGGARTY		
Kate	San Francisco San Francisco 2	67 747
Luey	San Francisco San Francisco 2	67 747
TOGH		
---*	Mariposa Twp 3	60 579
TOGIN		
---	Tulara Twp 1	71 113
TOGLER		
Martin	Placer Iona Hills	62 880
TOGLESON		
Thos	Butte Ophir	56 753
TOGNAGGINE		
Mausoveto	Sierra Poker Flats	66 839
TOGNAZZINE		
Marrsoveto*	Sierra Poker Flats	66 839
Mausoveto*	Sierra Poker Flats	66 839
TOGO		
Peter F	San Francisco San Francisco 7	681440
TOGT		
Herman D	Alameda Brooklyn	55 144
TOH		
---	Alameda Oakland	55 63
---	Sacramento Ward 3	63 490
TOHEIRT		
Frederick*	Calaveras Twp 6	57 127
TOHEY		
Jere	Sacramento Centre	63 174
TOHILL		
J*	Nevada Grass Valley	61 205
Joseph	San Francisco San Francisco 7	681362
TOHLITZ		
Louis	San Francisco San Francisco 9	68 953
TOHM		
James G*	Mendocino Big Rvr	60 841
TOHN		
Chow	Nevada Grass Valley	61 234
TOI		
---	Amador Twp 1	55 478
---	Calaveras Twp 6	57 149
---	Sierra St Louis	66 813
Choy	San Francisco San Francisco 4	681192
Sin	El Dorado Georgetown	58 687
TOIE		
G L	Calaveras Twp 9	57 378
TOILES		
M	El Dorado Placerville	58 870
TOILL		
Saml*	Yolo Putah	72 587
TOIRELLA		
Augustina	Contra Costa Twp 3	57 612
TOIREN		
James*	Calaveras Twp 5	57 183
TOIS		
---	Calaveras Twp 6	57 159
---	Calaveras Twp 6	57 173
---	Sierra Twp 5	66 947
TOIY		
---*	Plumas Quincy	62 969
TOJAS		
Francisco	Yuba Marysville	72 946
TOK		
---	Amador Twp 5	55 342
---	Sacramento Ward 1	63 68
---	San Francisco San Francisco 11	159 67
TOKA		
Ramoon	San Mateo Twp 2	65 118
TOKE		
---	Calaveras Twp 5	57 245
---	El Dorado Diamond	58 788
---	Sacramento Ward 1	63 51
---	Sacramento Ward 1	63 53
---	Sacramento Ward 1	63 56
---	Shasta Horsetown	66 697
---	Tuolumne Twp 6	71 531
TOKES		
---	Calaveras Twp 10	57 287
TOKLEY		
R*	Nevada Grass Valley	61 198
TOLACIN		
Fremcisa*	El Dorado Mud Springs	58 982
TOLAK		
---*	Mendocino Big Rvr	60 855
TOLAN		
Eugene	Sacramento Ward 4	63 589
TOLAND		
H H*	San Francisco San Francisco 4	681137
Hugh	Sierra Morristown	661052
James	San Francisco San Francisco 9	681082
Joh N	San Francisco San Francisco 1	68 892
John	Butte Cascade	56 695
John	Plumas Quincy	62 961
John	San Francisco San Francisco 9	681073
Joseph	Santa Clara San Jose	65 318
N	Amador Twp 2	55 283
Stephen	Butte Ophir	56 798
Wm	Solano Suisan	69 224
Wm	Sonoma Vallejo	69 631
Wm*	Solano Suisan	69 224
TOLANDE		
J	San Francisco San Francisco 9	681061
TOLAR		
George	Sacramento Ward 1	63 120
TOLBERT		
---	San Francisco San Francisco 2	67 566
James	Nevada Bridgeport	61 501
Richard	Sierra St Louis	66 813
Robert	Nevada Little Y	61 531
Samuel	San Mateo Twp 3	65 101
William C	San Francisco San Francisco 9	681011
TOLBOS		
Jomas	Nevada Bridgeport	61 501
TOLBOT		
Sam C	San Francisco San Francisco 9	681021
TOLBOTT		
J S	Calaveras Twp 9	57 366
J*	Calaveras Twp 9	57 366
TOLBY		
Anderson	Calaveras Twp 9	57 351
TOLE		
Manuel*	Alameda Brooklyn	55 93
R H	San Francisco San Francisco 4	681148
TOLEDO		
---	Butte Chico	56 566
TOLEDO		
Ambrose	Calaveras Twp 10	57 259
Facindo	Tuolumne Montezuma	71 502
Facundo	Tuolumne Twp 5	71 502
Jose	Monterey San Juan	601002
TOLER		
Christoph	Sonoma Santa Rosa	69 419
Wm N	Alameda Brooklyn	55 106
TOLES		
E W	Nevada Nevada	61 284
TOLEY		
Danl	Trinity Whites Crk	701028
Danl B*	San Francisco San Francisco 10	189 67
Edwin	Sierra Downieville	661017
N	Nevada Nevada	61 287
W	Nevada Nevada	61 287
TOLFMAN		
L	Nevada Grass Valley	61 202
TOLIN		
Isaac	Humbolt Union	59 185
TOLK		
---	Sierra Morristown	661056
Goo	El Dorado Greenwood	58 719
TOLL		
C B	Placer Iona Hills	62 862
Charley	Sacramento Ward 4	63 528
E B	El Dorado Placerville	58 920
E H	Nevada Nevada	61 272
E W	Nevada Nevada	61 272
Edward	Sacramento Ward 4	63 527
Emmet	Siskiyou Callahan	69 3
Geo	Butte Oregon	56 613
Jas T	Butte Hamilton	56 517
Mary	Sacramento Brighton	63 194
Nelson	Sacramento Ward 4	63 528
R A	Alameda Brooklyn	55 108
Silas	Sacramento Brighton	63 208
Thos	Alameda Brooklyn	55 96
Thos	Sacramento Ward 1	63 122
Wm	El Dorado Georgetown	58 696
Wm	Placer Auburn	62 571
Wm R	Sacramento Ward 4	63 528
TOLLAND		
C	Sutter Yuba	70 767
TOLLAR		
Patrick	Alameda Brooklyn	55 102
TOLLE		
Christopher	San Francisco San Francisco 2	67 588
P T	San Francisco San Francisco 5	67 528
TOLLENAM		
John	Placer Iona Hills	62 866
Rufus	Placer Iona Hills	62 866
TOLLES		
Abram	Yuba Marysville	72 970
James S	Yuba Marysville	72 971
Jas R*	Sacramento Ward 4	63 506
TOLLEY		
Benjamin	Alameda Brooklyn	55 103
W H	Trinity Minersville	70 969
TOLLIDAY		
Isaac	Contra Costa Twp 3	57 589
John	Contra Costa Twp 3	57 608
TOLLIER		
---	Mendocino Twp 1	60 890
TOLLINS		
R J	Tuolumne Twp 1	71 266
TOLLIR		
Thomas	Plumas Quincy	62 947
TOLLIVER		
Jas*	San Francisco San Francisco 9	681090
Jos	San Francisco San Francisco 9	681090
TOLLL		
J W	Tuolumne Twp 2	71 284
TOLLMAN		
F C	Tuolumne Sonora	71 208
H	Nevada Grass Valley	61 150
TOLLS		
J B	Shasta Shasta	66 684
TOLLUS		
---	Del Norte Klamath	58 656
TOLLY		
Anderson*	Calaveras Twp 9	57 351
Cornelius	San Francisco San Francisco 9	68 989
TOLMAN		
A	Sonoma Washington	69 667
Dancan	Santa Cruz Pajaro	66 543
Danson	Santa Cruz Pajaro	66 543
G B	San Francisco San Francisco 2	67 684
Isaac	Santa Cruz Pajaro	66 557
Jacob	El Dorado Placerville	58 903
John L	Nevada Eureka	61 394
Plase	San Luis Obispo San Luis Obispo	65 4
TOLO		
Manuel	Alameda Washington	55 214

Name	County Locale	M653 RollPage
TOLO		
Manuel*	Alameda Brooklyn	55 93
TOLON		
S	Calaveras Twp 9	57 396
TOLOR		
George	Mariposa Coulterville	60 688
TOLSARTY		
Thos*	Nevada Bloomfield	61 530
TOLSOM		
Thomas S	Tuolumne Jacksonville	71 515
TOLT		
---	Nevada Rough &	61 396
TOLTON		
A W*	Mariposa Twp 3	60 562
TOLY		
Astur*	Calaveras Twp 6	57 164
TOM & JERRY		
---	Fresno Twp 2	59 110
TOM BUNN		
---*	Plumas Quincy	62 970
TOM CHOW		
---	Nevada Nevada	61 306
TOM KIL SHON		
---*	San Francisco San Francisco 9	681062
TOM SING		
---*	Nevada Nevada	61 307
TOM WA		
---	Nevada Nevada	61 303
TOM YUP		
---	Nevada Nevada	61 305
TOM		
---	Amador Twp 4	55 233
---	Amador Twp 5	55 340
---	Amador Twp 5	55 341
---	Amador Twp 5	55 343
---	Amador Twp 3	55 409
---	Butte Chico	56 558
---	Butte Chico	56 563
---	Butte Chico	56 566
---	Calaveras Twp 5	57 237
---	Calaveras Twp 10	57 269
---	Calaveras Twp 4	57 322
---	Del Norte Crescent	58 631
---	El Dorado White Oaks	581023
---	El Dorado Coloma	581086
---	El Dorado Union	581089
---	El Dorado Coloma	581120
---	El Dorado Mountain	581189
---	El Dorado Placerville	58 832
---	Fresno Twp 1	59 53
---	Fresno Twp 2	59 89
---	Klamath S Fork	59 206
---	Klamath Salmon	59 213
---	Klamath Liberty	59 241
---	Klamath Liberty	59 242
---	Mariposa Twp 3	60 574
---	Mendocino Calpella	60 822
---	Mendocino Big Rock	60 876
---	Mendocino Round Va	60 880
---	Mendocino Twp 1	60 889
---	Nevada Nevada	61 307
---	Nevada Eureka	61 384
---	Placer Rattle Snake	62 635
---	Placer Rattle Snake	62 637
---	Sacramento Cosumnes	63 406
---	Sacramento Cosumnes	63 407
---	Sacramento Ward 4	63 608
---	San Francisco San Francisco 12	392 67
---	San Francisco San Francisco 2	67 754
---	Sierra La Porte	66 782
---	Sierra St Louis	66 813
---	Sierra Twp 5	66 931
---	Sierra Downieville	66 981
---	Sierra Downieville	66 983
---	Tulara Twp 2	71 27
---	Tuolumne Twp 5	71 514
---	Yolo No E Twp	72 677
---	Yolo No E Twp	72 682
---	Yuba Bear Rvr	721014
---	Yuba North Ea	72 677
---	Yuba North Ea	72 682
---	Yuba North Ea	72 685
---*	Butte Chico	56 558
---*	El Dorado Coloma	581122
---*	El Dorado Casumnes	581175
---*	Nevada Nevada	61 307
Ah	Sacramento Ward 3	63 432
Ah	Sacramento Ward 3	63 467
An	Del Norte Crescent	58 631
Chano*	Butte Chico	56 550
Chin*	Yuba Long Bar	72 756
Ching	Yuba Slate Ro	72 684
Chow	Nevada Grass Valley	61 234
Chow	Nevada Nevada	61 306
Chow	Nevada Nevada	61 308
TOM		
Chow	Nevada Eureka	61 384
Hee*	Yuba Slate Ro	72 708
Hike*	Yuba New York	72 740
Hing	Yuba Slate Ro	72 713
Hong	Yuba Long Bar	72 753
Kossuth*	Yuba Parks Ba	72 777
Ling	Nevada Grass Valley	61 230
Ling	Yuba New York	72 735
Ling	Yuba New York	72 740
Ling	Yuba Long Bar	72 753
Loo	Yuba New York	72 718
Lung	Yuba New York	72 718
Rufer*	Butte Chico	56 550
See	Nevada Eureka	61 373
Sifn	El Dorado Placerville	58 934
Sing	Mariposa Twp 3	60 561
Sing	Mariposa Twp 3	60 581
Sing	Nevada Nevada	61 307
Sing	Yuba New York	72 735
Sing	Yuba Fosters	72 830
Sing	Yuba Fosters	72 842
Sing*	Yuba New York	72 740
Sinor	Butte Cascade	56 704
Wa	Nevada Nevada	61 303
TOMA S		
---	San Bernardino S Timate	64 692
TOMACEA		
Peter	El Dorado Placerville	58 926
TOMADE		
George*	El Dorado Georgetown	58 701
TOMAGO		
Laguiane*	Alameda Brooklyn	55 152
TOMAKO		
---	Fresno Twp 2	59 101
TOMALES		
Felipe	San Bernardino Santa Barbara	64 190
TOMALO		
Frances	Sonoma Santa Rosa	69 401
TOMAN		
James M	Mendocino Little L	60 832
James W*	Mendocino Little L	60 832
M S	Tuolumne Twp 2	71 284
TOMANCE		
I	Yolo Putah	72 549
TOMANLO		
Francis*	Sonoma Santa Rosa	69 401
TOMAR		
Wm*	San Francisco San Francisco 1	68 889
TOMAS		
---	Los Angeles Los Angeles	59 398
---	Los Angeles Los Angeles	59 402
---	Los Angeles San Gabriel	59 411
---	Los Angeles San Juan	59 460
---	Los Angeles San Juan	59 470
---	Los Angeles Tejon	59 529
---	Mendocino Calpella	60 826
---	Nevada Bridgeport	61 464
---	San Bernardino Santa Barbara	64 202
---	San Bernardino Santa Ba	64 219
---	San Bernardino S Buenav	64 220
---	San Bernardino San Bernadino	64 681
---	San Bernardino S Timate	64 695
---	San Bernardino S Timate	64 698
---	San Bernardino S Timate	64 701
---	San Bernardino S Timate	64 702
---	San Bernardino S Timate	64 704
---	San Bernardino S Timate	64 705
---	San Bernardino S Timate	64 706
---	San Bernardino S Timate	64 707
---	San Bernardino S Timate	64 708
---	San Bernardino S Timate	64 709
---	San Bernardino S Timate	64 711
---	San Bernardino S Timate	64 713
---	San Bernardino S Timate	64 718
---	San Bernardino S Timate	64 721
---	San Bernardino S Timate	64 726
---	San Bernardino S Timate	64 729
---	San Bernardino S Timate	64 731
---	San Bernardino S Timate	64 732
---	San Bernardino S Timate	64 733
---	San Bernardino S Timate	64 735
---	San Bernardino S Timate	64 738
---	San Bernardino S Timate	64 740
---	San Bernardino S Timate	64 741
---	San Bernardino S Timate	64 744
---	San Bernardino S Timate	64 746
---	San Bernardino S Timate	64 748
---	San Bernardino S Timate	64 750
---	San Bernardino S Timate	64 752
---	San Diego San Diego	64 771
---	San Diego San Diego	64 776
---	San Diego Temecula	64 784
---	San Diego Temecula	64 803
---	San Diego Colorado	64 813
---	San Diego Agua Caliente	64 824
TOMAS		
---	San Diego Agua Caliente	64 840
---	San Diego Agua Caliente	64 847
---	Tulara Keyesville	71 63
---	Tulara Keyesville	71 66
---	Tulara Twp 3	71 67
---	Tulara Twp 3	71 70
---	Tulara Twp 3	71 72
Andres*	San Francisco San Francisco 2	67 701
H*	Siskiyou Scott Va	69 45
Metal	San Diego Agua Caliente	64 851
Pablo	Mariposa Twp 1	60 625
W H	Nevada Grass Valley	61 209
TOMASA		
---	Los Angeles Santa Ana	59 453
---	Monterey San Juan	60 991
---	San Bernardino Santa Inez	64 138
---	San Bernardino Santa Barbara	64 202
---	San Bernardino S Timate	64 691
---	San Bernardino S Timate	64 693
---	San Bernardino S Timate	64 698
---	San Bernardino S Timate	64 719
---	San Bernardino S Timate	64 720
---	San Bernardino S Timate	64 730
---	San Bernardino S Timate	64 732
---	San Bernardino S Timate	64 740
---	San Bernardino S Timate	64 746
---	San Bernardino S Timate	64 752
---	San Bernardino S Timate	64 756
TOMASITO		
---	San Bernardino S Timate	64 720
TOMASS		
Charles	San Luis Obispo San Luis Obispo	65 7
TOMATO		
Antoine	Calaveras Twp 4	57 330
Antonine	Calaveras Twp 4	57 330
TOMAYAH		
---	Butte Chico	56 550
TOMAYO		
Laguiano*	Alameda Brooklyn	55 152
TOMB		
Alex	Trinity Lewiston	70 961
Benjamin	Yuba Marysville	72 878
TOMBER		
S P*	Nevada Nevada	61 320
TOMBERLIN		
E G L	Tuolumne Twp 4	71 141
Elizabeth	Tuolumne Twp 4	71 142
TOMBES		
L P	Nevada Nevada	61 320
TOMBLY		
J	Nevada Grass Valley	61 147
TOMBO		
Ferninande	Calaveras Twp 7	57 23
TOMBOHM		
Maltee L	Humbolt Bucksport	59 156
TOMBORENO		
---	Fresno Twp 2	59 91
TOMBS		
Harry	Butte Ophir	56 750
W*	El Dorado Placerville	58 893
Wm	Santa Clara Gilroy	65 251
TOME		
J	Amador Twp 1	55 483
TOMEKA		
---	Fresno Twp 2	59 58
TOMEKO		
---	Fresno Twp 2	59 65
TOMEO		
---	Fresno Twp 3	59 23
TOMER		
Chals	El Dorado Georgetown	58 686
H S	Trinity Sturdiva	701006
TOMERO		
Andelino	Santa Clara Gilroy	65 234
Phillip	San Francisco San Francisco 9	681072
TOMEY		
---	Amador Twp 5	55 350
---*	Calaveras Twp 5	57 198
Barney	Sierra Twp 7	66 911
TOMFORD		
Henry	Tuolumne Jamestown	71 453
TOMILPO		
---	Tulara Keyesville	71 70
TOMILSOM		
S*	El Dorado Georgetown	58 688
TOMILSON		
John D	Siskiyou Yreka	69 132
John W	Siskiyou Yreka	69 132
S	El Dorado Georgetown	58 688
TOMILSORN		
S*	El Dorado Georgetown	58 688
TOMISA		
---	San Bernardino S Timate	64 710
TOMKINS		
Charles	El Dorado Coloma	581103

Name	County Locale	M653 RollPage
TOMKINSON		
Jas	San Francisco San Francisco 10	233 67
TOMLIN		
F	Calaveras Twp 9	57 416
F	Merced Twp 2	60 919
Lafayette	Sacramento Ward 4	63 564
William	El Dorado Spanish	581125
TOMLINS		
G	El Dorado Diamond	58 807
TOMLINSEN		
Lewis	Sacramento Granite	63 267
TOMLINSON		
A A	Trinity Whites Crk	701028
Archibald	Calaveras Twp 10	57 274
Benjn*	Calaveras Twp 10	57 290
Beray*	Calaveras Twp 10	57 290
C M	Nevada Nevada	61 287
Chas A	San Francisco San Francisco 7	681340
Edwin	Humbolt Eureka	59 163
Geo	Placer Rattle Snake	62 632
J H	Nevada Nevada	61 322
John	Sierra Gibsonville	66 856
John J	Los Angeles San Pedro	59 483
Lewis	Sacramento Granite	63 267
M	Sacramento Granite	63 227
O M	Nevada Nevada	61 287
R I	Klamath Liberty	59 230
William	Siskiyou Cottonwoood	69 101
TOMLISTON		
Richard	Klamath Trinidad	59 222
TOMLO		
Pierre	Yuba Parks Ba	72 785
TOMMER		
Hock*	Plumas Quincy	62 970
Pah*	Plumas Quincy	62 970
TOMO		
---	Amador Twp 5	55 340
TOMOS		
---	Fresno Twp 1	59 78
Pablo	Mariposa Twp 1	60 625
TOMOTH		
P	Trinity Redding	70 985
TOMPHKINS		
A*	Butte Oregon	56 622
TOMPKIN		
A R	Santa Clara Santa Clara	65 468
TOMPKINS		
A J	Calaveras Twp 7	57 28
A*	Butte Oregon	56 622
Benj	Nevada Little Y	61 533
Buck	El Dorado Georgetown	58 702
Burck	El Dorado Georgetown	58 702
C	Nevada Grass Valley	61 210
C H	Shasta Millvill	66 751
C H	Siskiyou Scott Va	69 47
Chas E	Butte Oregon	56 623
E A	Nevada Eureka	61 377
E O	Nevada Eureka	61 377
Elisha B	San Francisco San Francisco 3	67 26
G W	Sierra La Porte	66 773
Geo W	Humbolt Eel Rvr	59 145
H	Butte Oregon	56 622
H	El Dorado Kelsey	581151
Harriet	Yuba Marysville	72 892
Ira	Sacramento Ward 3	63 474
John	San Francisco San Francisco 11	110 67
John	Santa Clara San Jose	65 358
John	Santa Clara Fremont	65 440
John	Tuolumne Twp 2	71 419
L	Siskiyou Klamath	69 95
M	Santa Clara Santa Clara	65 485
Nick	Humbolt Table Bl	59 139
R A	Nevada Grass Valley	61 186
Samuel B	Sierra Twp 5	66 924
Sceylen C	Yuba Marysville	72 877
Sciyler C*	Yuba Marysville	72 877
T B	San Francisco San Francisco 6	67 466
Thos	San Bernardino San Bernardino	64 637
William	San Luis Obispo San Luis Obispo	65 31
William	Sierra Scales D	66 801
Wm	Sonoma Petaluma	69 615
Wm R	San Bernardino Santa Barbara	64 202
TOMPKINSON		
Jos	San Francisco San Francisco 10	233 67
Joseph	San Francisco San Francisco 1	68 831
TOMPLINS		
John	Tuolumne Shawsfla	71 419
TOMPSKINS		
C H	Shasta Millvill	66 751
TOMPSON		
G	Shasta Millvill	66 751
H	El Dorado Placerville	58 883
Joseph A	Tuolumne Twp 6	71 534

Name	County Locale	M653 RollPage
TOMPSON		
Louis	Amador Twp 6	55 439
Peter	Sacramento Ward 1	63 154
Ralph	Tuolumne Montezuma	71 512
Thomas	Sierra Whiskey	66 847
TOMPULAS		
---	Mendocino Big Rvr	60 855
TOMS		
Frank	Calaveras Twp 4	57 323
George	Tuolumne Twp 1	71 251
J M	Tuolumne Twp 2	71 306
TOMSON		
T	Calaveras Twp 9	57 396
Wm	Tuolumne Big Oak	71 146
TOMY		
Thomas*	Placer Forest H	62 767
TON WA		
---	Nevada Washington	61 340
TON WAY		
---	Sacramento Ward 1	63 59
TON		
---	Amador Twp 4	55 248
---	Amador Twp 2	55 293
---	Amador Twp 2	55 294
---	Amador Twp 5	55 346
---	Amador Twp 5	55 350
---	Amador Twp 5	55 351
---	Amador Twp 3	55 394
---	Amador Twp 6	55 430
---	Amador Twp 6	55 435
---	Amador Twp 6	55 437
---	Butte Kimshaw	56 582
---	Calaveras Twp 5	57 214
---	Calaveras Twp 5	57 237
---	Calaveras Twp 5	57 244
---	Calaveras Twp 5	57 250
---	Calaveras Twp 10	57 261
---	Calaveras Twp 10	57 296
---	Calaveras Twp 4	57 307
---	Calaveras Twp 7	57 36
---	Calaveras Twp 8	57 60
---	Del Norte Crescent	58 643
---	Del Norte Happy Ca	58 668
---	El Dorado Salmon Hills	581055
---	El Dorado Salmon Falls	581061
---	El Dorado Coloma	581076
---	El Dorado Kelsey	581141
---	El Dorado Placerville	58 841
---	El Dorado Placerville	58 900
---	El Dorado Placerville	58 904
---	El Dorado Mud Springs	58 949
---	El Dorado Mud Springs	58 954
---	El Dorado Mud Springs	58 978
---	Fresno Twp 2	59 17
---	Fresno Twp 2	59 19
---	Mariposa Twp 1	60 663
---	Mariposa Coulterville	60 689
---	Mariposa Coulterville	60 690
---	Mariposa Coulterville	60 700
---	Nevada Grass Valley	61 227
---	Nevada Grass Valley	61 228
---	Nevada Grass Valley	61 232
---	Nevada Rough &	61 432
---	Placer Secret R	62 623
---	Placer Virginia	62 679
---	Sacramento Granite	63 268
---	Sacramento Cosummes	63 397
---	San Francisco San Francisco 9	681094
---	Sierra Downieville	661009
---	Sierra Downieville	661027
---	Sierra St Louis	66 813
---	Sierra Downieville	66 983
---	Sierra Downieville	66 996
---	Tuolumne Don Pedro	71 538
---	Tuolumne Twp 6	71 539
---	Yolo No E Twp	72 675
---	Yuba Bear Rvr	721015
---	Yuba North Ea	72 675
---	Yuba Slate Ro	72 685
---*	Calaveras Twp 5	57 159
---*	Calaveras Twp 4	57 326
---*	El Dorado Salmon Falls	581055
---*	El Dorado Coloma	581076
---*	Nevada Nevada	61 306
---*	San Francisco San Francisco 9	681094
Ack	Yuba Long Bar	72 767
Ah	Butte Oregon	56 644
Ah*	Amador Twp 4	55 332
Chew	Calaveras Twp 4	57 300
Cog*	Calaveras Twp 5	57 254
Fak	Shasta Shasta	66 670
Fay	Plumas Quincy	62 949
Fuk	Shasta Shasta	66 670
King*	Mariposa Twp 3	60 580
Le	El Dorado Georgetown	58 704
Ling	Nevada Grass Valley	61 230

Name	County Locale	M653 RollPage
TON		
R	Sutter Butte	70 800
Seow	Calaveras Twp 4	57 300
Seow	Calaveras Twp 4	57 300
Shung	Calaveras Twp 4	57 322
Sing*	Mariposa Twp 3	60 578
Song	Mariposa Twp 1	60 627
Tee	San Francisco San Francisco 4	681192
Thos	San Mateo Twp 3	65 94
Too	Nevada Bridgeport	61 505
Tor*	Nevada Bridgeport	61 505
Tu	San Francisco San Francisco 4	681192
Wa	Nevada Washington	61 340
Way*	Sacramento Ward 1	63 59
Yup	Nevada Eureka	61 384
TONAELSON		
Jule	San Francisco San Francisco 2	67 607
TONAILSON		
Jule	San Francisco San Francisco 2	67 607
TONAMA		
---	Fresno Twp 2	59 107
TONAR		
H C	Nevada Bridgeport	61 493
TONBER		
G H	Sutter Yuba	70 762
TONBIE		
Raymond*	Yuba Marysville	72 869
TONCHARD		
Gustar	San Francisco San Francisco 2	67 573
Gustav*	San Francisco San Francisco 2	67 573
TONCHETT		
Jasper H*	Monterey San Juan	60 977
Sanford L*	Monterey San Juan	60 977
TONCHO		
---	Mendocino Twp 1	60 889
TONDO		
J B*	Marin Novato	60 735
TONE		
---	Amador Twp 4	55 246
---	El Dorado Salmon Falls	581042
---	El Dorado Salmon Falls	581054
---	El Dorado Salmon Hills	581066
---	El Dorado Salmon Hills	581067
---	El Dorado Coloma	581086
---	El Dorado Coloma	581107
---	El Dorado Coloma	581109
---	El Dorado Coloma	581115
---	El Dorado Mountain	581178
---	El Dorado Mountain	581189
---	El Dorado Greenwood	58 732
---	El Dorado Diamond	58 775
---	El Dorado Diamond	58 785
---	El Dorado Diamond	58 806
---	El Dorado Placerville	58 898
---	El Dorado Mud Springs	58 962
---	El Dorado Mud Springs	58 991
---	Fresno Twp 3	59 31
---	Klamath Liberty	59 232
---	Plumas Meadow Valley	62 914
---	Plumas Quincy	62 949
---	Sacramento Granite	63 231
---	Shasta Shasta	66 669
---	Shasta French G	66 720
---	Sierra Twp 7	66 886
---	Sierra Downieville	66 983
---	Tuolumne Green Springs	71 517
---	Tuolumne Chinese	71 521
Thos	Amador Twp 2	55 324
Wm*	Sacramento Ward 1	63 62
TONEL		
Christofeo J	Monterey Monterey	60 958
TONELL		
L	Nevada Grass Valley	61 224
TONELLE		
Louis	Yuba New York	72 731
TONELY		
Michael*	Humbolt Pacific	59 130
TONENALD		
L	El Dorado Placerville	58 827
TONER		
Henry	San Francisco San Francisco 1	68 892
Margaret	San Francisco San Francisco 8	681312
Mary	San Francisco San Francisco 2	67 716
Peter	Sierra Downieville	66 995
Phillip*	Mariposa Twp 1	60 625
TONERSS		
Joseph	Santa Clara San Jose	65 343
TONES		
Francisco*	Mariposa Twp 3	60 603
TONEY		
Bartholemew	Calaveras Twp 5	57 191
C W	Nevada Nevada	61 319
George*	Calaveras Twp 5	57 189
John	Amador Twp 2	55 262
Thos*	Nevada Little Y	61 535
TONFILED		
Archer*	Calaveras Twp 6	57 167

Name	County Locale	M653 RollPage
TONFOY		
---	Trinity Trinindad Rvr	701046
TONG COW		
---	Nevada Rough &	61 434
TONG FOO		
---	Yuba Slate Ro	72 707
TONG GIVE		
---*	Nevada Rough &	61 433
TONG GORD		
---*	Nevada Red Dog	61 539
TONG GWE		
---*	Nevada Rough &	61 433
TONG MUN		
---	Tuolumne Chinese	71 525
TONG SEEN		
---*	Nevada Rough &	61 438
TONG SUNG		
---	Sacramento Ward 1	63 69
TONG WA		
---	Nevada Nevada	61 304
TONG		
---	Alameda Oakland	55 34
---	Alameda Oakland	55 52
---	Amador Twp 4	55 252
---	Amador Twp 2	55 285
---	Amador Twp 2	55 293
---	Amador Twp 2	55 294
---	Amador Twp 5	55 330
---	Amador Twp 3	55 410
---	Amador Twp 7	55 415
---	Amador Twp 1	55 477
---	Amador Twp 1	55 490
---	Butte Kimshaw	56 579
---	Butte Kimshaw	56 604
---	Butte Oregon	56 613
---	Butte Oregon	56 618
---	Calaveras Twp 8	57 106
---	Calaveras Twp 6	57 126
---	Calaveras Twp 6	57 166
---	Calaveras Twp 5	57 213
---	Calaveras Twp 5	57 232
---	Calaveras Twp 5	57 235
---	Calaveras Twp 5	57 247
---	Calaveras Twp 5	57 248
---	Calaveras Twp 5	57 256
---	Calaveras Twp 10	57 269
---	Calaveras Twp 10	57 273
---	Calaveras Twp 10	57 276
---	Calaveras Twp 4	57 300
---	Calaveras Twp 4	57 301
---	Calaveras Twp 4	57 327
---	Calaveras Twp 4	57 339
---	Calaveras Twp 7	57 37
---	Calaveras Twp 7	57 39
---	Calaveras Twp 8	57 60
---	Calaveras Twp 8	57 62
---	Calaveras Twp 8	57 65
---	Calaveras Twp 8	57 76
---	Calaveras Twp 8	57 93
---	Del Norte Crescent	58 630
---	El Dorado Salmon Falls	581056
---	El Dorado Salmon Falls	581058
---	El Dorado Coloma	581077
---	El Dorado Coloma	581084
---	El Dorado Coloma	581086
---	El Dorado Coloma	581106
---	El Dorado Coloma	581107
---	El Dorado Coloma	581110
---	El Dorado Coloma	581119
---	El Dorado Kelsey	581129
---	El Dorado Kelsey	581134
---	El Dorado Kelsey	581135
---	El Dorado Kelsey	581141
---	El Dorado Kelsey	581144
---	El Dorado Indian D	581159
---	El Dorado Casumnes	581162
---	El Dorado Casumnes	581164
---	El Dorado Mountain	581189
---	El Dorado Georgetown	58 691
---	El Dorado Georgetown	58 692
---	El Dorado Greenwood	58 708
---	El Dorado Greenwood	58 711
---	El Dorado Diamond	58 787
---	El Dorado Diamond	58 801
---	El Dorado Placerville	58 834
---	El Dorado Placerville	58 886
---	El Dorado Placerville	58 917
---	El Dorado Placerville	58 923
---	El Dorado Mud Springs	58 952
---	El Dorado Mud Springs	58 957
---	El Dorado Mud Springs	58 959
---	El Dorado Mud Springs	58 964
---	El Dorado Mud Springs	58 972
---	El Dorado Mud Springs	58 975
---	Klamath Klamath	59 229
---	Klamath Liberty	59 232

Name	County Locale	M653 RollPage
TONG		
---	Mariposa Twp 1	60 626
---	Mariposa Twp 1	60 643
---	Mariposa Twp 1	60 648
---	Mariposa Twp 1	60 661
---	Mariposa Twp 1	60 670
---	Mariposa Twp 1	60 673
---	Mariposa Coulterville	60 692
---	Merced Twp 2	60 916
---	Nevada Nevada	61 300
---	Nevada Nevada	61 302
---	Nevada Rough &	61 432
---	Nevada Bridgeport	61 459
---	Nevada Bridgeport	61 461
---	Placer Illinois	62 739
---	Placer Illinois	62 742
---	Placer Michigan	62 834
---	Plumas Quincy	62 920
---	Plumas Quincy	62 926
---	Plumas Quincy	62 950
---	Plumas Quincy	62 969
---	Sacramento Granite	63 231
---	Sacramento Cosummes	63 386
---	Sacramento Cosummes	63 390
---	Sacramento Cosummes	63 400
---	Sacramento Ward 3	63 424
---	Sacramento Ward 4	63 613
---	San Francisco San Francisco 4	681179
---	San Francisco San Francisco 4	681180
---	San Francisco San Francisco 4	681195
---	San Francisco San Francisco 4	681196
---	San Francisco San Francisco 11	146 67
---	San Francisco San Francisco 11	147 67
---	San Francisco San Francisco 11	162 67
---	San Francisco San Francisco 2	67 688
---	San Francisco San Francisco 2	67 754
---	Shasta Horsetown	66 701
---	Shasta Horsetown	66 705
---	Sierra Downieville	661004
---	Sierra Downieville	661005
---	Sierra Downieville	661009
---	Sierra Downieville	66 982
---	Siskiyou Scott Va	69 47
---	Tehama Red Bluff	70 932
---	Tehama Tehama	70 944
---	Trinity Price'S	701019
---	Trinity McGillev	701021
---	Trinity Taylor'S	701033
---	Trinity Big Flat	701041
---	Trinity Trinindad Rvr	701044
---	Trinity Trinindad Rvr	701046
---	Trinity Trinindad Rvr	701047
---	Trinity Trinindad Rvr	701049
---	Trinity Trinindad Rvr	701050
---	Trinity Weaverville	701052
---	Trinity Weaverville	701055
---	Trinity Weaverville	701074
---	Trinity Lewiston	70 956
---	Tulara Visalia	71 106
---	Yolo No E Twp	72 683
---	Yolo No E Twp	72 684
---	Yolo No E Twp	72 685
---	Yolo Slate Ra	72 708
---	Yolo Slate Ra	72 712
---	Yolo Slate Ra	72 715
---	Yuba Slate Ro	72 683
---	Yuba Slate Ro	72 684
---	Yuba Slate Ro	72 708
---	Yuba Slate Ro	72 715
---	Yuba Long Bar	72 757
---	Yuba Long Bar	72 758
---	Yuba Long Bar	72 759
---	Yuba Long Bar	72 760
---	Yuba Long Bar	72 768
---	Yuba Parks Ba	72 774
---	Yuba Linda	72 991
---*	Amador Twp 5	55 330
---*	Calaveras Twp 4	57 341
---*	El Dorado Coloma	581084
---*	El Dorado Georgetown	58 703
---*	El Dorado Georgetown	58 708
---*	Placer Virginia	62 680
---*	Placer Dutch Fl	62 714
---*	Sacramento Cosummes	63 391
Achick	Plumas Quincy	62 946
Ah	Butte Oregon	56 618
Ah	Calaveras Twp 7	57 11
Ah	Calaveras Twp 7	57 16
Ah	Calaveras Twp 7	57 34
Ah	Sacramento Cosummes	63 397
Ah	Trinity Mouth Ca	701014
Andrew C	Mendocino Ukiah	60 802
Ark	Yolo No E Twp	72 668

Name	County Locale	M653 RollPage
TONG		
Cow	Nevada Rough &	61 434
Ein	Tuolumne Big Oak	71 181
Fee	San Francisco San Francisco 11	159 67
Fong	San Francisco San Francisco 5	67 510
Gwe	Nevada Rough &	61 433
H	El Dorado White Oaks	581007
Ho	San Francisco San Francisco 11	161 67
Hong	Plumas Quincy	62 946
John	Nevada Rough &	61 425
Kee	Plumas Quincy	62 945
Kee	Plumas Quincy	62 948
King	El Dorado Mud Springs	58 982
Kong	San Francisco San Francisco 11	158 67
Lar Lee	Yuba Marysville	72 920
Lay	Plumas Quincy	62 950
Lee	Plumas Quincy	621008
Lee	Yuba Marysville	72 895
Lee Lee	Yuba Marysville	72 920
Lee*	Yuba Marysville	72 895
Lees	Yuba Marysville	72 882
Len	Yuba Long Bar	72 759
Loo	Tuolumne Twp 2	71 347
Mee	San Francisco San Francisco 11	162 67
Mun	Tuolumne Twp 5	71 525
Nyo	San Francisco San Francisco 11	159 67
Samuel	El Dorado White Oaks	581007
Sang	San Francisco San Francisco 11	162 67
See	Plumas Quincy	621008
See*	Yuba Marysville	72 895
Seen	Nevada Rough &	61 438
Shee	Yuba Long Bar	72 766
Sing	Nevada Rough &	61 425
Sing	Plumas Quincy	62 946
Soe	San Francisco San Francisco 1	68 926
Sun	Siskiyou Yreka	69 194
Sung	Sacramento Ward 1	63 69
Tching*	Plumas Quincy	62 946
Tee	Plumas Quincy	62 948
Thon	Plumas Quincy	62 948
Thum	Plumas Quincy	621009
Ti	San Francisco San Francisco 11	161 67
Ting	Sacramento Cosummes	63 386
Wa	Nevada Nevada	61 304
Way	El Dorado Salmon Falls	581054
Willian Yon*	Santa Cruz Santa Cruz	66 612
Woah	Yuba Marysville	72 928
Won	San Francisco San Francisco 11	147 67
Won*	Sacramento Ward 1	63 65
Woo*	Sacramento Ward 1	63 65
Yang	San Francisco San Francisco 11	159 67
Yong	San Francisco San Francisco 3	67 73
Young	Plumas Quincy	62 948
TONGAMBO		
James*	Sierra Twp 5	66 940
TONGATE		
Elias	Monterey S Antoni	60 969
TONGE		
---	Mariposa Twp 1	60 640
---	Mariposa Twp 1	60 643
TONGET		
James	Yuba Linda Twp	72 984
William	Calaveras Twp 7	57 26
TONGFEN		
Henry	Tuolumne Jamestown	71 437
TONGFOO		
---	Trinity Trinindad Rvr	701047
TONGLA		
---	Trinity Weaverville	701075
TONGLONE		
---	Shasta Shasta	66 670
TONGO		
---	Mariposa Twp 1	60 643
TONGS		
---*	Tehama Red Bluff	70 934
TONGTONG		
Fred	Nevada Bloomfield	61 510
TONH		
Madaline	Mariposa Twp 3	60 622
TONI		
---	Amador Twp 5	55 351
F	El Dorado Placerville	58 905
TONICK		
Andrew	San Francisco San Francisco 8	681265
TONID		
Quong	Placer Auburn	62 572
TONIDI		
George	El Dorado Georgetown	58 701

California 1860 Census Index

Name	County Locale	M653 Roll	Page
TONIHUE			
Benj	El Dorado Gold Hill	58	1096
TONING			
---	Calaveras Twp 5	57	198
TONK			
---	El Dorado Greenwood	58	731
---	Yolo Slate Ra	72	686
TONKIN			
W S	Nevada Grass Valley	61	200
Wm	Nevada Grass Valley	61	158
TONLINSON			
Wm	Butte Bidwell	56	711
TONLOUME			
---*	Tulara Visalia	71	38
TONLOUMNE			
---*	Tulara Visalia	71	36
TONLUVE			
---	Fresno Twp 3	59	31
TONN			
Andrew C*	Mendocino Ukiah	60	802
Kessath*	Yuba Parks Ba	72	777
TONNAD			
Solomon	Placer Virginia	62	675
TONNER			
D	Nevada Nevada	61	294
H	Alameda Brooklyn	55	198
Jacob	Tuolumne Twp 1	71	258
Lewis*	San Francisco San Francisco 1	68	893
Louis*	San Francisco San Francisco 3	67	27
TONNIEY			
Dennis*	Sacramento Ward 1	63	83
TONNO			
M	Calaveras Twp 9	57	396
TONNSEND			
G	Butte Cascade	56	696
TONNY			
Thomas*	Placer Forest H	62	767
TONO			
---	Fresno Twp 1	59	54
---	Fresno Twp 3	59	7
TONOUESA			
Jose	Fresno Twp 1	59	75
TONSANG			
Nuno	Mariposa Twp 3	60	574
TONSANY			
Muno	Mariposa Twp 3	60	574
TONSELL			
Robt	Nevada Rough &	61	435
TONSEN			
William	Solano Vacaville	69	337
TONSHARD			
Edmond	Marin San Rafael	60	764
Edmund	Marin San Rafael	60	764
TONSIG			
Edward	San Francisco San Francisco 2	67	791
TONSO			
---	Sierra Twp 7	66	898
TONSON			
O	Sacramento Sutter	63	300
W R	Nevada Bridgeport	61	439
TONSSANT			
Wm*	San Francisco San Francisco 10	67	267
TONSWORTH			
Dennia	San Francisco San Francisco 9	68	998
L S B	Mariposa Coulterville	60	676
TONT			
---	Sierra Downieville	66	983
TONTON			
Theophile	Sierra La Porte	66	772
TONUY			
---*	Calaveras Twp 5	57	198
TONY WON			
---	Sacramento Ward 1	63	65
TONY			
---	Amador Twp 2	55	287
---	Amador Twp 5	55	347
---	Amador Twp 5	55	348
---	Amador Twp 5	55	350
---	Amador Twp 7	55	413
---	Calaveras Twp 5	57	139
---	Calaveras Twp 5	57	213
---	Calaveras Twp 5	57	222
---	Calaveras Twp 5	57	226
---	Calaveras Twp 5	57	232
---	Calaveras Twp 5	57	256
---	Calaveras Twp 10	57	260
---	Calaveras Twp 10	57	269
---	Calaveras Twp 10	57	273
---	Calaveras Twp 10	57	276
---	Calaveras Twp 10	57	291
---	Calaveras Twp 4	57	300
---	Calaveras Twp 4	57	323
---	Calaveras Twp 4	57	327
---	Calaveras Twp 4	57	339
---	Mariposa Twp 1	60	648
TONY			
---	Nevada Grass Valley	61	228
---	Nevada Nevada	61	301
---	Nevada Nevada	61	305
---	Plumas Quincy	62	949
---	San Francisco San Francisco 2	67	754
---	Tuolumne Knights	71	529
Andrew C*	Mendocino Ukiah	60	802
Gilbert	El Dorado White Oaks	58	1006
J A	Sutter Sutter	70	812
James N	Contra Costa Twp 3	57	612
Lip	Calaveras Twp 4	57	313
R	Nevada Grass Valley	61	149
Seth	Mendocino Little L	60	838
Sip	Calaveras Twp 4	57	313
TONYLON			
John	Siskiyou Yreka	69	184
TOO CHONG			
---	Butte Oregon	56	614
TOO QUONG			
Be*	Sacramento Ward 1	63	152
TOO			
---	Amador Twp 4	55	255
---	Amador Twp 4	55	256
---	Amador Twp 2	55	312
---	Amador Twp 5	55	335
---	Amador Twp 5	55	350
---	Amador Twp 5	55	353
---	Amador Twp 5	55	367
---	Amador Twp 6	55	436
---	Butte Kimshaw	56	578
---	Butte Oregon	56	613
---	Butte Eureka	56	653
---	Calaveras Twp 5	57	176
---	Calaveras Twp 5	57	202
---	Calaveras Twp 5	57	214
---	Calaveras Twp 5	57	235
---	Calaveras Twp 5	57	237
---	Calaveras Twp 5	57	241
---	Calaveras Twp 5	57	242
---	Calaveras Twp 5	57	249
---	Calaveras Twp 5	57	252
---	Calaveras Twp 10	57	271
---	Calaveras Twp 4	57	301
---	El Dorado Mountain	58	1189
---	El Dorado Georgetown	58	682
---	El Dorado Placerville	58	832
---	Nevada Rough &	61	409
---	Placer Auburn	62	579
---	Sacramento Cosumnes	63	388
---	San Francisco San Francisco 4	68	1180
---	Shasta Horsetown	66	705
---	Tehama Red Bluff	70	934
---	Tuolumne Twp 3	71	434
---	Tuolumne Twp 3	71	440
---	Tuolumne Twp 3	71	467
---	Tuolumne Twp 3	71	468
---	Tuolumne Twp 1	71	476
---	Tuolumne Twp 5	71	522
---	Yolo No E Twp	72	675
---	Yuba North Ea	72	675
---	Yuba Long Bar	72	758
---	Yuba Marysville	72	920
---	Yuba Marysville	72	925
---*	Amador Twp 2	55	311
---*	Sacramento Ward 4	63	610
Ah	Butte Eureka	56	653
Chas	Plumas Quincy	62	949
Chong	Butte Oregon	56	614
Fue	Yuba Long Bar	72	761
Gou	Nevada Rough &	61	397
Ling	Butte Bidwell	56	717
Louy*	San Francisco San Francisco 4	68	1191
Souy	San Francisco San Francisco 4	68	1191
Suck	Plumas Quincy	62	1009
Too	Tehama Red Bluff	70	934
Tor*	Nevada Bridgeport	61	505
Tow	Tehama Red Bluff	70	932
Wam	Plumas Quincy	62	1009
Yi	Calaveras Twp 5	57	249
TOOA			
---	Calaveras Twp 4	57	325
TOOBAH			
A*	Mariposa Twp 3	60	622
TOOD			
Aaron	Sierra Twp 7	66	896
Thas	Calaveras Twp 9	57	391
TOOFAH			
A*	Mariposa Twp 3	60	622
TOOFRAH			
A	Mariposa Twp 3	60	622
TOOFUH			
A*	Mariposa Twp 3	60	622
TOOH			
---*	Butte Oregon	56	627
TOOHER			
Thomas	Yolo No E Twp	72	672
TOOHER			
Thomas*	Yuba North Ea	72	672
TOOHY			
James	Solano Benecia	69	299
TOOING			
Wm	Mariposa Twp 3	60	567
TOOK			
---	Amador Twp 3	55	410
---	Amador Twp 6	55	400

Name	County Locale	M653 Roll	Page
TOO			
---	Yuba Long Bar	72	758
---	Yuba Marysville	72	920
---	Yuba Marysville	72	925
---*	Amador Twp 2	55	311
---*	Sacramento Ward 4	63	610
Ah	Butte Eureka	56	653
Chas	Plumas Quincy	62	949
Chong	Butte Oregon	56	614
Fue	Yuba Long Bar	72	761
Gou	Nevada Rough &	61	397
Ling	Butte Bidwell	56	717
Louy*	San Francisco San Francisco 4	68	1191
Souy	San Francisco San Francisco 4	68	1191
Suck	Plumas Quincy	62	1009
Too	Tehama Red Bluff	70	934
Tor*	Nevada Bridgeport	61	505
Tow	Tehama Red Bluff	70	932
Wam	Plumas Quincy	62	1009
Yi	Calaveras Twp 5	57	249
TOOA			
---	Calaveras Twp 4	57	325
TOOBAH			
A*	Mariposa Twp 3	60	622
TOOD			
Aaron	Sierra Twp 7	66	896
Thas	Calaveras Twp 9	57	391
TOOFAH			
A*	Mariposa Twp 3	60	622
TOOFRAH			
A	Mariposa Twp 3	60	622
TOOFUH			
A*	Mariposa Twp 3	60	622
TOOH			
---*	Butte Oregon	56	627
TOOHER			
Thomas	Yolo No E Twp	72	672
Thomas*	Yuba North Ea	72	672
TOOHY			
James	Solano Benecia	69	299
TOOING			
Wm	Mariposa Twp 3	60	567

Name	County Locale	M653 Roll	Page
TOOK			
---	Amador Twp 3	55	410
---	Amador Twp 7	55	413
---	Amador Twp 7	55	414
---	Amador Twp 6	55	450
---	Butte Oregon	56	613
---	Calaveras Twp 4	57	327
---	Mariposa Twp 3	60	590
---	Nevada Bridgeport	61	464
---	Placer Iona Hills	62	893
---	San Francisco San Francisco 9	68	1094
---	Tuolumne Twp 3	71	468
---	Tuolumne Sonora	71	478
Hom*	Butte Ophir	56	748
Long	Butte Bidwell	56	728
Robert	Alameda Oakland	55	71
Wor	Placer Illinois	62	738
TOOKE			
---	Placer Secret R	62	624
---	Placer Illinois	62	738
TOOKER			
Thomas*	Yuba North Ea	72	672
Wallace	Nevada Bloomfield	61	509
TOOKUH			
S*	Mariposa Twp 3	60	622
TOOKY			
Jas	Butte Oregon	56	619
TOOL			
James	San Francisco San Francisco 2	67	609
John	Placer Michigan	62	833
John O	Sierra Eureka	66	1042
Patrick*	Siskiyou Yreka	69	155
Peter	Nevada Rough &	61	430
Peter	Placer Michigan	62	843
Peter	Sierra Cox'S Bar	66	950
Peter	Trinity Weaverville	70	1053
TOOLAND			
F	Sacramento Granite	63	223
TOOLANE			
Andrew	San Joaquin Stockton	64	1076
TOOMBS			
G W	Stanislaus Emory	70	738
G*	Nevada Eureka	61	343
Henry C	Sonoma Mendocino	69	452
L	Nevada Grass Valley	61	196

		M653	
Name	County Locale	Roll	Page

TOOMBS
R A	Nevada Grass Valley	61	197
Thomas L Los Angeles San Pedro	59	479
W*	Nevada Grass Valley	61	189
Wm H	Sonoma Mendocino	69	451

TOOMBY
| W | Nevada Washington | 61 | 338 |

TOOMES
| A G | Tehama Tehama | 70 | 940 |
| John | Tulara Twp 1 | 71 | 85 |

TOOMEY
Ambrose M	Twp 2	57	548
	Contra Costa		
Daniel	San Francisco San Francisco 3	67	66
Dennis	Sacramento Ward 1	63	83
H	San Francisco San Francisco 5	67	500
Jno	San Francisco San Francisco 10	294
		67	
John	Solano Vallejo	69	244
Margaret San Francisco San Francisco 11	107
		67	
William	San Joaquin Tulare	64	870
Wm	Mariposa Twp 3	60	567

TOOMS
| Jas | Sonoma Petaluma | 69 | 605 |

TOOMY
| Henry | San Francisco San Francisco 6 | 67 | 452 |

TOON
---	Amador Twp 2	55	323
---	Amador Twp 7	55	414
---	Calaveras Twp 5	57	241
---	Klamath Liberty	59	238
---	Placer Rattle Snake	62	598
---	Shasta French G	66	712
---	Sierra Morristown	661056
---	Yuba Marysville	72	882
---*	Butte Hamilton	56	529
Ling	Mariposa Twp 3	60	581

TOONCK
| Lee | Plumas Quincy | 621009 |

TOONEY
Bartholemeu Calaveras Twp 5	57	191
Bartholemew Calaveras Twp 5	57	191
Ellen	San Francisco San Francisco 10	286
		67	
J B	Nevada Grass Valley	61	149
Mary A	Sacramento Ward 4	63	571

TOONG
| ---* | Amador Twp 6 | 55 | 430 |

TOONIBS
| Peter | Los Angeles Tejon | 59 | 525 |

TOONY
| ---* | Amador Twp 6 | 55 | 430 |
| L* | Nevada Grass Valley | 61 | 167 |

TOOP
---	Butte Hamilton	56	529
---*	Butte Oregon	56	627
J H	Sutter Butte	70	781
M C	Sutter Butte	70	797

TOOR
| --- | Del Norte Happy Ca | 58 | 668 |

TOORA
| John | Tuolumne Twp 1 | 71 | 226 |

TOORE
| --- | Sierra Morristown | 661056 |

TOORMAN
| H W | El Dorado Diamond | 58 | 799 |

TOORRY
| T* | San Francisco San Francisco 4 681231 |

TOOSE
| --- | Butte Kimshaw | 56 | 587 |

TOOTER
| Kitty* | Del Norte Klamath | 58 | 655 |

TOOTHACHEE
| L H* | Nevada Grass Valley | 61 | 151 |

TOOTHACHER
| L H | Nevada Grass Valley | 61 | 151 |
| Luther | Calaveras Twp 6 | 57 | 123 |

TOOTHAKER
| H P | Solano Vallejo | 69 | 266 |

TOOTHASKER
| E | Shasta Horsetown | 66 | 690 |

TOOTOO
| Kitty* | Del Norte Klamath | 58 | 655 |

TOOTS
| George K* | Yuba Marysville | 72 | 924 |

TOOW
| --- | Yolo No E Twp | 72 | 667 |

TOOXY
| --- | Del Norte Klamath | 58 | 658 |

TOOYOTO
| --- | Tulara Twp 1 | 71 | 115 |

TOP
---	Butte Kimshaw	56	587
---	Fresno Twp 3	59	31
---	Yuba Long Bar	72	758

TOP
Hang	Butte Ophir	56	812
Kim	Butte Ophir	56	812
Ling	Butte Ophir	56	813
Won	Calaveras Twp 4	57	313

TOPATH
| Edward* | Calaveras Twp 9 | 57 | 371 |

TOPE
| William | Nevada Rough & | 61 | 437 |

TOPEA
| Hosa | El Dorado Mud Springs | 58 | 974 |

TOPEMOK
| --- | Fresno Twp 2 | 59 | 116 |

TOPER
| Wadpole | Amador Twp 5 | 55 | 332 |

TOPETAS
| Jose San Bernardino Santa Inez | 64 | 140 |

TOPETT
| Thos | Trinity Minersville | 70 | 968 |

TOPHAM
| Geo | Amador Twp 3 | 55 | 388 |

TOPIER
| Delarus | Mariposa Twp 1 | 60 | 637 |
| Delorus | Mariposa Twp 1 | 60 | 637 |

TOPIM
| John | Butte Wyandotte | 56 | 671 |

TOPIMA
| --- | Mendocino Calpella | 60 | 824 |

TOPIN
John	Butte Wyandotte	56	671
R J	Solano Benecia	69	312
Raymon	Calaveras Twp 10	57	288
Trusdr*	Calaveras Twp 4	57	314

TOPITZ
| ---* | Tulara Visalia | 71 | 37 |

TOPKINS
| Henry San Francisco San Francisco 3 | 67 | 40 |

TOPLASS
| Margaret San Francisco San Francisco 6 | 67 | 436 |

TOPLEY
| James | Solano Vallejo | 69 | 266 |

TOPLITZ
F	San Francisco San Francisco 5	67	514
Lousi	San Francisco San Francisco 9	68	953
Rosa	San Francisco San Francisco 9	68	953

TOPPER
Charles	Calaveras Twp 10	57	277
Petler	Calaveras Twp 6	57	140
Petter	Calaveras Twp 6	57	140

TOPPEY
| Cahs | Sonoma Sonoma | 69 | 633 |

TOPPIA
| Peter* | Calaveras Twp 6 | 57 | 135 |

TOPPING
Benjamin	Yuba Foster B	72	829
Bennett	Yuba Bear Rvr	721011
James	Sierra Twp 5	66	938

TOPPMAN
| Conrad San Francisco San Francisco 8 681295 |

TOPPY
---	Fresno Twp 3	59	100
---	Fresno Twp 2	59	110
Chas	Sonoma Sonoma	69	633

TOPRER
| Delorus* | Mariposa Twp 1 | 60 | 637 |

TOPRINA
| --- | Mendocino Calpella | 60 | 824 |

TOPSER
| Delorus* | Mariposa Twp 1 | 60 | 637 |

TOR SING
| --- | Tuolumne Jacksonville | 71 | 515 |

TOR
| --- | Sierra Twp 5 | 66 | 944 |

TORA
| Gile | Mariposa Twp 3 | 60 | 550 |

TORACK
| Wm San Francisco San Francisco 1 | 68 | 908 |

TORAGUSTUS
| E A | Yolo Cottonwoood | 72 | 556 |

TORAMUS
| H | El Dorado Placerville | 58 | 870 |

TORANGCAUD
| Gudovis* | Calaveras Twp 6 | 57 | 145 |

TORARGEAND
| Gudavus* | Calaveras Twp 5 | 57 | 145 |

TORAS
| Clamentin | El Dorado Mud Springs | 58 | 974 |
| Manuel | Sonoma Bodega | 69 | 524 |

TORASES
| Alega | Yuba Marysville | 72 | 948 |
| Alejas | Yuba Marysville | 72 | 948 |

TORATER
| Antonio* | Amador Twp 2 | 55 | 288 |

TORAUTMAN
| R B | Nevada Nevada | 61 | 273 |

TORBOT
| Saml | Sacramento Granite | 63 | 225 |

TORBUT
| William | Yolo Cottonwood | 72 | 650 |

TORD
| Barnard | Humbolt Union | 59 | 184 |
| Geo* | El Dorado Casumnes | 581176 |

TORDIAN
| L P* | Trinity Cox'S Bar | 701038 |

TORE
---	San Bernardino S Timate	64	699
F*	Nevada Nevada	61	324
Ma Arismondis Amador Twp 1	55	459
T	Nevada Nevada	61	324

TOREENS
| James* | Calaveras Twp 6 | 57 | 183 |

TORELLO
| Pedro | Solano Benecia | 69 | 309 |

TORES
Alfred	Marin Saucileto	60	751
Calarenar	Mariposa Twp 1	60	624
Calarinar	Mariposa Twp 1	60	624
Catherine	Yuba Marysville	72	938
Dolores	Plumas Meadow Valley	62	908
Guadaloupe	Yuba Marysville	72	934
Guadeloupe	Yuba Marysville	72	934
Inan*	Mariposa Twp 3	60	611
Jose	Monterey San Juan	601002
Juan	Mariposa Twp 3	60	611
Manuel San Bernardino Santa Barbara	64	190
Manuel	Yuba Marysville	72	946
Vivierno	San Luis Obispo	65	19
	San Luis Obispo		

TORETTI
| David | Tuolumne Jamestown | 71 | 425 |

TOREY
| --- | Calaveras Twp 4 | 57 | 327 |
| James W | Mariposa Twp 3 | 60 | 586 |

TOREZ
| Antonia | Monterey San Juan | 601002 |

TORGUET
| Paul San Francisco San Francisco 10 | 266 |
| | | 67 | |

TORI
| --- | Calaveras Twp 6 | 57 | 138 |

TORIAC
| John | Tuolumne Sonora | 71 | 235 |

TORIAS
| Mary | Tuolumne Columbia | 71 | 321 |

TORIES
| Frances | Napa Napa | 61 | 84 |
| Francis | Napa Napa | 61 | 84 |

TORIG
| --- | El Dorado Kelsey | 581144 |

TORING
| Fred* | Sacramento Ward 4 | 63 | 605 |
| Taylor | Yuba New York | 72 | 726 |

TORIOS
| Mary | Tuolumne Twp 2 | 71 | 321 |

TORIP
| --- | Del Norte Klamath | 58 | 656 |
| John | Del Norte Klamath | 58 | 657 |

TORISSANT
| Wm San Francisco San Francisco 10 | 267 |
| | | 67 | |

TORKO
| --- | San Francisco San Francisco 11 | 145 |
| | | 67 | |

TORMAN
| A | Butte Bidwell | 56 | 707 |

TORMENT
| John* | Butte Ophir | 56 | 786 |

TORMEY
| John | Solano Vallejo | 69 | 244 |
| Patrick | Solano Suisan | 69 | 231 |

TORMSEND
| Wm | Monterey San Juan | 60 | 976 |

TORN
| ---* | Butte Chico | 56 | 558 |
| Lon G | Tulara Twp 1 | 71 | 114 |

TORNAN
| M S | Tuolumne Twp 2 | 71 | 284 |

TORNAR
| Mercedes* Sacramento Ward 1 | 63 | 104 |

TORNAS
| H | Siskiyou Scott Va | 69 | 45 |

TORNE
| --- | Mariposa Twp 1 | 60 | 643 |

TORNEY
| Christopher Calaveras Twp 5 | 57 | 196 |
| G W San Francisco San Francisco 3 | 67 | 59 |
| James San Francisco San Francisco 8 681320 |
| M Green | Butte Chico | 56 | 534 |

TORNILEI
| Madis | Calaveras Twp 8 | 57 | 73 |

TORNILSA
| Janies | Mariposa Coulterville | 60 | 696 |

TORNJEKINS
| Chas E* | Butte Oregon | 56 | 623 |

Name	County Locale	M653 RollPage
TORNLO		
Pierre*	Yuba Parke Ba	72 785
TORO		
---	San Bernardino S Timate	64 697
---	Tulara Keyesville	71 71
Cepriano*	Calaveras Twp 4	57 341
J*	Tuolumne Big Oak	71 150
Juan	Los Angeles Los Angeles	59 294
TOROLE		
G W*	Santa Clara Santa Clara	65 483
TOROLI		
W J	Butte Oregon	56 609
TOROS		
---	Fresno Twp 1	59 54
TOROW		
Matthew	Calaveras Twp 6	57 149
TOROYTON		
W T	Sierra Downieville	66 961
TORPERY		
Francis	Nevada Rough &	61 431
TORPEY		
Ellen	San Francisco San Francisco 2	67 697
TORPY		
Michael*	San Francisco San Francisco 9	68 962
TORQUAY		
Francisco	Calaveras Twp 9	57 362
TORQUET		
Paul	San Francisco San Francisco 10	266 67
TORR		
---	San Francisco San Francisco 1	68 926
J H*	Butte Hamilton	56 525
TORRANCE		
Geo	San Francisco San Francisco 6	67 440
S H	Sonoma Armally	69 508
TORRAR		
Geo	Sonoma Vallejo	69 629
TORRAS		
Geo	Sonoma Vallejo	69 629
TORRCAS		
Charles*	Yuba Marysville	72 975
TORRE		
James M	San Francisco San Francisco 6	67 455
Peter	Butte Kimshaw	56 582
TORREAS		
Charles	Yuba Marysville	72 975
TORRELKERN		
James*	Mariposa Twp 3	60 567
TORRENCE		
Milton	Placer Michigan	62 857
Robert	Marin S Antoni	60 707
Rpbert	Marin S Antoni	60 707
TORRENS		
Charles*	Yuba Marysville	72 975
Howard	Yuba Marysville	72 907
James*	Calaveras Twp 6	57 183
TORRENTE		
Andrez	San Bernardino S Buenav	64 215
TORRES		
Adelaida	San Bernardino Santa Barbara	64 166
Concha	San Francisco San Francisco 2	67 683
Felipe	San Francisco San Francisco 2	67 702
Francisco	Mariposa Twp 3	60 603
Ignacio	Santa Clara Almaden	65 278
Jeronimo*	Marin Cortemad	60 786
John	Los Angeles Los Angeles	59 299
Jose M	Los Angeles Los Angeles	59 317
Leonada	San Bernardino Santa Barbara	64 147
Manuel	Alameda Brooklyn	55 121
Manuel	Santa Cruz Pajaro	66 576
Manuel	Yolo Slate Ra	72 688
Maria	Santa Clara San Jose	65 309
Maria*	Monterey Monterey	60 932
Mejorio	Santa Clara Almaden	65 263
Peromino	Marin Cortemad	60 786
Peronimo*	Marin Cortemad	60 786
Rebocindo	Plumas Quincy	62 941
Reducida	Plumas Quincy	62 941
Rosaina	San Francisco San Francisco 2	67 663
Soler	Alameda Oakland	55 31
Teodore	San Bernardino San Bernadino	64 664
TORRESO		
Juana	San Francisco San Francisco 2	67 683
TORREY		
Abner W	Yuba Marysville	72 875
Abuen W*	Yuba Marysville	72 875
Chas H	Calaveras Twp 8	57 104
E N	San Francisco San Francisco 6	67 454
George	Calaveras Twp 5	57 189
Lyman	Calaveras Twp 6	57 166
Middian	Sacramento Ward 1	63 98
Middran	Sacramento Ward 1	63 98
Obrien W*	Yuba Marysville	72 875
TORREZ		
Manuel	Monterey S Antoni	60 971
TORRIAS		
Andres*	San Francisco San Francisco 2	67 701

Name	County Locale	M653 RollPage
John	San Francisco San Francisco 2	67 741
TORRIS		
Antone	Siskiyou Yreka	69 139
Manuel	Contra Costa Twp 1	57 507
Manuel	Yuba Slate Ro	72 688
TORRITY		
Rosa	San Francisco San Francisco 9	68 991
TORRO		
Andrew	Calaveras Twp 5	57 203
Peter	Butte Kimshaw	56 582
TORRSWORTH		
L S B*	Mariposa Coulterville	60 676
TORRY		
Jas	Butte Chico	56 553
Michael*	Placer Michigan	62 851
Willim	Nevada Bloomfield	61 513
Winnifred	Yuba Marysville	72 961
TORRYTON		
W T	Sierra Downieville	66 961
TORSELKERN		
James*	Mariposa Twp 3	60 567
TORSELKEROR		
James*	Mariposa Twp 3	60 567
TORSHEY		
J H*	El Dorado Indian D	581157
TORSSY		
Michael*	San Francisco San Francisco 9	68 962
TORSYTHE		
William	Nevada Little Y	61 531
TORTON		
Opelin*	Mariposa Twp 3	60 616
Phelin*	Mariposa Twp 3	60 616
Phelisi*	Mariposa Twp 3	60 616
TORUS		
Antonia	Mariposa Twp 1	60 636
Trinada	Mariposa Twp 1	60 656
TORUSS		
---	Del Norte Klamath	58 657
TORY		
---	Amador Twp 5	55 341
---	Amador Twp 5	55 344
---	Amador Twp 5	55 359
---	Amador Twp 5	55 364
---	Amador Twp 3	55 410
---	Amador Twp 7	55 415
---	Amador Twp 6	55 432
---	Amador Twp 6	55 434
---	San Francisco San Francisco 4	681194
---*	San Francisco San Francisco 4	681178
Joseph	Calaveras Twp 6	57 170
Lone	Shasta Shasta	66 670
TORZER		
W*	Shasta Shasta	66 655
TOS		
---	Calaveras Twp 4	57 333
TOSAND		
Wm*	Solano Suisan	69 224
TOSCARO		
---	Fresno Twp 1	59 86
TOSEN		
Cliris	Amador Twp 1	55 468
TOSH		
John	Marin Cortemad	60 782
TOSHACH		
McGarvin	San Francisco San Francisco 2	67 670
TOSIMET		
August	Calaveras Twp 4	57 325
TOSINET		
August	Calaveras Twp 4	57 325
TOSKY		
John*	Amador Twp 2	55 278
TOSMAN		
Pedro*	Yuba Marysville	72 917
TOSOW		
---	Calaveras Twp 4	57 322
TOSRIAS		
Jose M	Solano Vacaville	69 359
TOSS		
Louis*	San Joaquin Stockton	641042
Won	Calaveras Twp 4	57 313
TOSSAR		
Richd	San Francisco San Francisco 1	68 814
TOSSIE		
R P*	San Mateo Twp 3	65 81
TOSSIN		
R J*	Solano Benecia	69 312
TOSSIO		
Joseph	El Dorado Georgetown	58 696
TOSSY		
Louis	Calaveras Twp 4	57 340
TOSTER		
Mrs	Amador Twp 5	55 359
TOT		
---	Calaveras Twp 5	57 232
---	Calaveras Twp 10	57 267

Name	County Locale	M653 RollPage
TOT		
---	Calaveras Twp 10	57 297
---	Del Norte Crescent	58 651
---	Sierra Downieville	661008
---	Tuolumne Twp 6	71 537
---	Yuba Long Bar	72 756
Antoni	Contra Costa Twp 1	57 513
Sung	Nevada Bridgeport	61 458
Yufs	Sacramento Granite	63 250
TOTHAM		
H M*	Sacramento Cosumnes	63 387
TOTHILL		
John	San Francisco San Francisco 2	67 588
TOTMAN		
A	Butte Bidwell	56 707
Andw	Napa Napa	61 69
Jeremy R	Yuba Marysville	72 884
Wm	Calaveras Twp 4	57 344
TOTON		
Thos	Trinity Oregon G	701008
TOTS		
---	Calaveras Twp 5	57 149
TOTT		
---	Yuba Long Bar	72 757
E M	Sierra Downieville	661011
TOTTEN		
A W	Mariposa Twp 3	60 562
Jefferson	Tulara Twp 3	71 49
TOTTHAMER		
Louis*	Sacramento Ward 4	63 549
TOU YUP		
---	Nevada Nevada	61 305
TOU		
---	Amador Twp 2	55 319
---	Butte Kimshaw	56 582
---	Calaveras Twp 5	57 235
---	Calaveras Twp 8	57 92
---	El Dorado Coloma	581076
---	El Dorado Kelsey	581141
---	El Dorado Georgetown	58 690
---	Mariposa Twp 1	60 662
---	Mariposa Coulterville	60 683
---	Mariposa Coulterville	60 690
---	Nevada Grass Valley	61 227
---	Nevada Grass Valley	61 233
---	San Francisco San Francisco 4	681192
---	San Francisco San Francisco 4	681197
---	San Francisco San Francisco 4	681209
---*	El Dorado Salmon Falls	581055
---*	El Dorado Coloma	581076
Ah	Calaveras Twp 7	57 16
Gow	Nevada Rough &	61 397
King	Mariposa Twp 3	60 580
Me	San Francisco San Francisco 4	681191
Sing*	Mariposa Twp 3	60 578
Song	San Francisco San Francisco 11	160 67
TOUCH		
---	Calaveras Twp 6	57 168
TOUCHARD		
Gustar*	San Francisco San Francisco 2	67 573
TOUCK		
---	Calaveras Twp 6	57 168
TOUDO		
J B*	Marin Novato	60 735
TOUDY		
Julius C	San Francisco San Francisco 3	67 14
TOUEDEW		
H	Butte Chico	56 563
TOUEY		
C W*	Nevada Nevada	61 319
TOUG		
---	Nevada Nevada	61 301
TOUGERE		
Colett*	Mariposa Coulterville	60 679
Colette*	Mariposa Coulterville	60 679
E	Mariposa Coulterville	60 679
TOUGET		
James	Yuba Suida	72 982
TOUIHUE		
Benj*	El Dorado Gold Hill	581096
TOUING		
Taylor*	Yuba New York	72 726
TOUK		
---	Sierra Downieville	661015
---*	Trinity Big Flat	701041
TOULE		
E F	San Joaquin Stockton	641035
W A	Sacramento Alabama	63 413
TOULKS		
Thomas D	Yuba Slate Ro	72 701
TOULOUME		
---	Tulara Twp 2	71 38
TOULOUMUE		
---	Tulara Twp 2	71 36
TOULUME		
---	Tulara Twp 2	71 39

Name	County Locale	M653 Roll	Page
TOULUME			
---	Tulara Twp 2	71	40
TOULUMME			
---	Tulara Twp 2	71	4
TOUNG			
---	Calaveras Twp 5	57	198
---	Yuba Long Bar	72	743
Ah	Tuolumne Twp 4	71	150
Fred*	Sacramento Ward 4	63	605
TOUNGE			
Wm H	Mariposa Twp 1	60	635
TOUNK			
---	Sierra Downieville	66	1015
TOUNRENDS			
John	Mariposa Coulterville	60	700
TOUNSEND			
Dennis	Amador Twp 6	55	443
J W	San Francisco San Francisco 5	67	528
John B	Sierra Twp 7	66	863
W A	Shasta Horsetown	66	689
TOUNTAIN			
Thomas	Tuolumne Twp 1	71	247
TOUO			
---	Calaveras Twp 10	57	261
TOUP			
---	Tuolumne Twp 5	71	525
TOUR			
---	Sierra Downieville	66	999
Wm	Sacramento Ward 1	63	62
TOURE			
---	San Francisco San Francisco 9	68	963
TOURNBULL			
Belle	San Francisco San Francisco 9	68	1105
TOURNEY			
Justh	San Francisco San Francisco 6	67	402
Richard	Placer Stewart	62	605
TOURNS			
Peter	Yuba New York	72	726
TOURS			
J T	Santa Clara San Jose	65	289
TOURTELLOT			
H J	Solano Vacaville	69	358
TOUSANG			
Nuno*	Mariposa Twp 3	60	574
TOUSDELL			
C*	Tuolumne Jacksonville	71	168
TOUSE			
---	Nevada Nevada	61	304
---	San Francisco San Francisco 9	68	963
---*	Nevada Nevada	61	304
TOUSEN			
William*	Solano Vacaville	69	337
TOUSSANT			
Wm	San Francisco San Francisco 10	67	267
TOUT			
---	Sierra Downieville	66	983
Jacob	Amador Twp 2	55	294
Jacob	Plumas Meadow Valley	62	901
Joseph	San Francisco San Francisco 3	67	62
TOUX			
Cath*	San Francisco San Francisco 10	67	278
TOUY			
Eugene*	Mariposa Twp 1	60	636
TOUYON			
---*	San Francisco San Francisco 9	68	963
TOV			
---	El Dorado Georgetown	58	690
TOVAL			
Joseph	Calaveras Twp 10	57	286
TOVEY			
Patrick	San Francisco San Francisco 1	68	880
TOVING			
James*	Plumas Meadow Valley	62	929
TOVINGER			
Geo*	Butte Kimshaw	56	601
TOVO			
Cepriano*	Calaveras Twp 4	57	341
Ceprineno*	Calaveras Twp 4	57	341
TOVOLEY			
M*	Nevada Eureka	61	366
TOW KEE			
---	Sacramento Ward 3	63	490
TOW LO			
---	Sacramento Ward 1	63	53
TOW ZOW			
---	Nevada Nevada	61	301
TOW			
---	Amador Twp 5	55	336
---	Butte Kimshaw	56	600
---	Butte Kimshaw	56	605
---	Butte Oregon	56	613
---	Butte Oregon	56	625
---	Butte Oregon	56	636
---	Butte Oregon	56	643

Name	County Locale	M653 Roll	Page
TOW			
---	Butte Oregon	56	644
---	Butte Eureka	56	655
---	Calaveras Twp 5	57	138
---	Calaveras Twp 6	57	159
---	Calaveras Twp 5	57	211
---	Calaveras Twp 5	57	215
---	Calaveras Twp 5	57	219
---	Calaveras Twp 5	57	234
---	Calaveras Twp 5	57	235
---	Calaveras Twp 5	57	244
---	Calaveras Twp 5	57	257
---	Calaveras Twp 10	57	259
---	Calaveras Twp 10	57	267
---	Calaveras Twp 10	57	268
---	Calaveras Twp 10	57	270
---	Calaveras Twp 10	57	273
---	Calaveras Twp 10	57	276
---	Calaveras Twp 10	57	286
---	Calaveras Twp 10	57	287
---	Calaveras Twp 10	57	294
---	Calaveras Twp 10	57	295
---	Calaveras Twp 10	57	296
---	Calaveras Twp 4	57	299
---	Calaveras Twp 4	57	300
---	Calaveras Twp 4	57	320
---	Calaveras Twp 4	57	334
---	Calaveras Twp 8	57	59
---	Del Norte Crescent	58	651
---	El Dorado White Oaks	58	1021
---	El Dorado Coloma	58	1076
---	El Dorado Coloma	58	1085
---	El Dorado Coloma	58	1086
---	El Dorado Union	58	1090
---	El Dorado Coloma	58	1105
---	El Dorado Casumnes	58	1164
---	El Dorado Greenwood	58	727
---	El Dorado Diamond	58	815
---	El Dorado Placerville	58	886
---	El Dorado Mud Springs	58	949
---	El Dorado Mud Springs	58	955
---	Mariposa Twp 3	60	564
---	Mariposa Twp 1	60	626
---	Mariposa Twp 1	60	658
---	Mariposa Twp 1	60	659
---	Mariposa Twp 1	60	662
---	Mariposa Twp 1	60	663
---	Mariposa Twp 1	60	667
---	Mariposa Coulterville	60	683
---	Nevada Grass Valley	61	227
---	Nevada Grass Valley	61	233
---	Nevada Nevada	61	300
---	Nevada Nevada	61	301
---	Nevada Nevada	61	303
---	Nevada Nevada	61	304
---	Nevada Nevada	61	305
---	Nevada Nevada	61	306
---	Nevada Nevada	61	308
---	Nevada Eureka	61	384
---	Nevada Rough &	61	396
---	Nevada Rough &	61	423
---	Nevada Bridgeport	61	461
---	Nevada Bridgeport	61	464
---	Nevada Bridgeport	61	492
---	Placer Illinois	62	752
---	Plumas Meadow Valley	62	914
---	Sacramento Cosumnes	63	400
---	Sacramento Ward 1	63	51
---	San Francisco San Francisco 9	68	1094
---	San Francisco San Francisco 4	68	1192
---	San Francisco San Francisco 4	68	1197
---	San Francisco San Francisco 4	68	1209
---	Shasta Shasta	66	670
---	Shasta Horsetown	66	703
---	Sierra Downieville	66	1003
---	Sierra Downieville	66	1004
---	Sierra Downieville	66	1005
---	Sierra Downieville	66	1009
---	Sierra Downieville	66	1025
---	Sierra Downieville	66	1029
---	Sierra Twp 5	66	931
---	Sierra Twp 5	66	932
---	Sierra Twp 5	66	945
---	Sierra Downieville	66	980
---	Sierra Downieville	66	983
---	Sierra Downieville	66	990
---	Tuolumne Shawsfla	71	416
---	Tuolumne Twp 3	71	434
---	Tuolumne Sonora	71	475
---	Tuolumne Montezuma	71	504
---	Tuolumne Twp 5	71	515
---	Tuolumne Twp 5	71	525
---	Tuolumne Knights	71	528
---	Tuolumne Knights	71	529
---	Tuolumne Twp 6	71	533
---	Tuolumne Twp 6	71	541

Name	County Locale	M653 Roll	Page
TOW			
---	Yolo No E Twp	72	667
---	Yolo No E Twp	72	681
---	Yuba North Ea	72	677
---	Yuba North Ea	72	681
---	Yuba Fosters	72	831
---	Yuba Marysville	72	868
---*	Calaveras Twp 6	57	159
---*	Nevada Nevada	61	303
---*	San Francisco San Francisco 9	68	1094
---*	Tuolumne Big Oak	71	181
---*	Yuba Foster B	72	831
A	Sacramento Granite	63	268
Ah	Butte Oregon	56	625
Ah	Butte Oregon	56	643
Ah*	Butte Oregon	56	636
C	Shasta Shasta	66	759
Chow	Butte Ophir	56	812
F*	Nevada Nevada	61	324
King*	Mariposa Twp 3	60	580
Le	Sacramento Ward 1	63	53
Low	Sacramento Cosummes	63	385
Me	San Francisco San Francisco 4	68	1191
Pin	Tuolumne Big Oak	71	147
Pou	Nevada Grass Valley	61	234
Pow	Nevada Grass Valley	61	234
Sam	Nevada Washington	61	340
Sam*	Yuba Rose Bar	72	790
Sang	Yuba Rose Bar	72	790
Shung	Calaveras Twp 4	57	322
Sing	Tuolumne Twp 5	71	515
Song	Sacramento Cosummes	63	385
Yong	Yolo Washington	72	562
You	Nevada Nevada	61	301
Yup	Nevada Nevada	61	305
TOWAT			
---	Fresno Twp 2	59	18
TOWBRIDGE			
L B	Siskiyou Cottonwood	69	107
TOWE			
---	El Dorado Eldorado	58	947
---	Fresno Twp 3	59	31
Thomas	Tuolumne Twp 2	71	287
TOWEE			
---	Fresno Twp 1	59	25
TOWEL			
O	Tuolumne Big Oak	71	152
TOWELL			
Azman G	Alameda Brooklyn	55	194
Jas	Butte Hamilton	56	530
TOWELS			
R H*	Tuolumne Columbia	71	327
TOWEN			
David*	Placer Iona Hills	62	870
Henry	Placer Iona Hills	62	881
TOWER			
A D	Nevada Nevada	61	256
Alrasn	Calaveras Twp 10	57	263
C M	Nevada Grass Valley	61	144
Chas	San Francisco San Francisco 10	67	299
G W	Sonoma Armally	69	508
George	Santa Cruz Pajaro	66	563
George M	Plumas Quincy	62	997
J	Sutter Sutter	70	816
J*	Nevada Grass Valley	61	216
Jacob S	Calaveras Twp 10	57	263
Jessee	San Diego San Diego	64	765
L H	Shasta Horsetown	66	711
Levi	Calaveras Twp 6	57	142
Lewis	Humbolt Bucksport	59	157
M	Nevada Grass Valley	61	216
Phinny*	Calaveras Twp 10	57	263
Richard	Calaveras Twp 8	57	54
TOWERS			
Geo	Klamath Salmon	59	213
George	Del Norte Ferry P O	58	665
J ?*	Los Angeles Tejon	59	526
J F	Los Angeles Tejon	59	526
J G*	Los Angeles Tejon	59	526
J*	Nevada Grass Valley	61	161
TOWES			
Deonicio*	San Mateo Twp 2	65	131
Maria	Merced Monterey	60	932
TOWHENY			
Carl	Sacramento Natonia	63	276
TOWHERY			
Coml*	Sacramento Natonia	63	276
Conel*	Sacramento Natonia	63	276
TOWHEY			
Jeremiah	Sacramento Ward 1	63	48
TOWKIN			
---	Sacramento Ward 1	63	55
TOWL			
B G	San Francisco San Francisco 5	67	552
B H	San Francisco San Francisco 5	67	552

California 1860 Census Index

Name	County Locale	M653 Roll	Page
TOWLE			
Calvin S*	Santa Clara Alviso	65	405
G W	Napa Napa	61	100
G W*	Santa Clara Santa Clara	65	483
H D	Nevada Bridgeport	61	453
Hiram L	Plumas Quincy	62	956
James	San Francisco San Francisco 8	68	1319
R H	Tuolumne Twp 2	71	327
Robt H*	Tuolumne Columbia	71	357
Thos	Butte Kimshaw	56	593
Thos F	Butte Oregon	56	609
Thos*	Butte Kimshaw	56	593
W J	Butte Oregon	56	609
William*	Placer Auburn	62	566
TOWLER			
James*	San Francisco San Francisco 8	68	1319
TOWLES			
Betsy*	Siskiyou Yreka	69	123
James*	San Francisco San Francisco 8	68	1319
TOWLEY			
Michael*	Humbolt Pacific	59	130
TOWLREY			
Jeremiah*	Sacramento Ward 1	63	48
TOWLS			
Robt H*	Tuolumne Columbia	71	357
TOWMAN			
G	Nevada Little Y	61	535
TOWN			
---	Calaveras Twp 4	57	322
A E	Sonoma Santa Rosa	69	399
Benj	Monterey S Antoni	60	967
Edward	Sonoma Armally	69	516
Franklin	El Dorado Kelsey	58	1155
George	Nevada Bloomfield	61	523
J W	Sonoma Santa Rosa	69	399
James	Marin San Rafael	60	773
James	Santa Cruz Pescadero	66	645
Jas	Sacramento Lee	63	214
John	Santa Cruz Santa Cruz	66	612
Matthew	Calaveras Twp 6	57	149
Peter	San Mateo Twp 3	65	76
Stephen	San Francisco San Francisco 2	67	560
William	San Joaquin Elkhorn	64	950
TOWNE			
Asa B	Alameda Oakland	55	6
C H	San Francisco San Francisco 6	67	474
G	Butte Oregon	56	641
S D	Sacramento Ward 1	63	90
S D	Sonoma Petaluma	69	588
Thomas	El Dorado Greenwood	58	726
TOWNER			
Abraham	San Joaquin Oneal	64	940
TOWNES			
J J	Tuolumne Sonora	71	482
S H	San Mateo Twp 3	65	107
TOWNESEND			
C C	Nevada Grass Valley	61	194
L	Nevada Grass Valley	61	144
TOWNEY			
Michael	Alameda Brooklyn	55	187
TOWNI			
G	Butte Oregon	56	641
TOWNNY			
Michael*	San Mateo Twp 1	65	58
TOWNS			
Doctor	Yuba New York	72	726
Palmer A*	Alameda Oakland	55	60
William	Santa Cruz Santa Cruz	66	638
TOWNSAND			
E M	Shasta Millvill	66	747
H L	Shasta Millvill	66	749
Henry	Sacramento Natonia	63	278
W A	Shasta Horsetown	66	689
TOWNSEAD			
Saml	Napa Napa	61	66
TOWNSEN			
Ashland	Sacramento Natonia	63	271
TOWNSEND			
A	Tehama Pasakent	70	856
A B	Nevada Eureka	61	360
A C	Shasta Millvill	66	752
A D	Nevada Grass Valley	61	182
A G	Sacramento Sutter	63	289
Ashland*	Sacramento Natonia	63	271
B	Yuba Long Bar	72	747
B M	Napa Napa	61	95
Benj	Yolo Merritt	72	580
C H	El Dorado Placerville	58	868
Charles	Yuba New York	72	733
Chas	Butte Bidwell	56	716
Dennis	Amador Twp 6	55	443
E	Yolo Washington	72	599
E L	Sonoma Petaluma	69	569
E M	Shasta Millvill	66	747
Edward	San Francisco San Francisco 2	67	580
Elijah	Yuba Suida	72	986

Name	County Locale	M653 Roll	Page
TOWNSEND			
Elisabeth	Yuba New York	72	733
Emery*	Napa Clear Lake	61	129
Emory*	Napa Clear Lake	61	129
Evi S	Humbolt Eureka	59	177
F O	Solano Montezuma	69	369
G P	Butte Kimshaw	56	597
Geo	Siskiyou Scott Va	69	29
George G	Marin Cortemad	60	789
H	Sacramento San Joaquin	63	348
H L	Shasta Millvill	66	749
Hiram	San Joaquin Elkhorn	64	997
Homer C	Tulara Visalia	71	103
J	Nevada Grass Valley	61	161
J	Nevada Grass Valley	61	169
J	San Francisco San Francisco 9	68	1060
J S	Siskiyou Scott Ri	69	75
J W	San Francisco San Francisco 5	67	528
Ja	San Francisco San Francisco 1	68	923
James	Mendocino Big Rvr	60	850
James	San Francisco San Francisco 2	67	730
John	Mariposa Coulterville	60	700
Jos	Butte Ophir	56	753
Jos	San Francisco San Francisco 12	67	381
L R	San Francisco San Francisco 6	67	439
Martin	San Francisco San Francisco 10	67	176
N A	Shasta Shasta	66	758
Norcesi	Placer Secret R	62	610
Plander A	Placer Rattle Snake	62	633
S S	Yolo Slate Ro	72	717
S S	Yuba Slate Ro	72	717
Saml	Napa Napa	61	66
T S	Yuba New York	72	730
Thos B	Napa Hot Springs	61	9
Timothy	Alameda Brooklyn	55	92
W	San Francisco San Francisco 5	67	549
W H	Mendocino Anderson	60	867
William	Siskiyou Shasta Valley	69	119
Wm	Nevada Eureka	61	366
Wm	Sacramento Ward 1	63	153
Wm	Sonoma Sonoma	69	634
Wm H	Sacramento San Joaquin	63	348
Wm L	Del Norte Crescent	58	631
Wm M A	Sonoma Sonoma	69	635
Wm S	Del Norte Crescent	58	632
Wm*	Monterey San Juan	60	976
TOWNSENT			
Ashland*	Sacramento Natonia	63	271
TOWNSHIP			
Martinez	Santa Clara San Jose	65	297
TOWNSILL			
Chas	Plumas Quincy	62	919
TOWNSLEY			
Alaxander	Napa Yount	61	43
TOWNSLY			
W	Shasta Millvill	66	749
TOWNTER			
Oscar*	Nevada Rough &	61	405
TOWODE			
William	Solano Montezuma	69	375
TOWREY			
George*	Calaveras Twp 5	57	189
Jas E*	Butte Chico	56	533
TOWSEN			
---	Trinity Mouth Ca	70	1011
Andresin*	El Dorado Georgetown	58	749
TOWSEND			
W C	El Dorado Placerville	58	931
TOWSON			
O	Sacramento Sutter	63	300
S P	Sierra Eureka	66	1044
TOX			
Gin	Calaveras Twp 4	57	313
TOY			
---	Amador Twp 2	55	283
---	Amador Twp 5	55	335
---	Amador Twp 5	55	336
---	Amador Twp 5	55	340
---	Butte Hamilton	56	530
---	Butte Kimshaw	56	607
---	Butte Eureka	56	652
---	Butte Wyandotte	56	666
---	Butte Ophir	56	770
---	Calaveras Twp 8	57	109
---	Calaveras Twp 5	57	256
---	Calaveras Twp 10	57	259
---	Calaveras Twp 10	57	284
---	Calaveras Twp 4	57	307
---	Calaveras Twp 8	57	51
---	Calaveras Twp 8	57	76
---	Calaveras Twp 8	57	83
---	Del Norte Crescent	58	631
---	Del Norte Happy Ca	58	668
---	El Dorado Salmon Falls	58	1040

Name	County Locale	M653 Roll	Page
TOY			
---	El Dorado Salmon Falls	58	1054
---	El Dorado Salmon Falls	58	1060
---	El Dorado Coloma	58	1084
---	El Dorado Union	58	1089
---	El Dorado Kelsey	58	1129
---	El Dorado Kelsey	58	1130
---	El Dorado Casumnes	58	1164
---	El Dorado Georgetown	58	678
---	El Dorado Diamond	58	805
---	El Dorado Diamond	58	813
---	El Dorado Placerville	58	865
---	El Dorado Eldorado	58	948
---	Fresno Twp 3	59	31
---	Mariposa Twp 1	60	669
---	Mariposa Twp 1	60	670
---	Mariposa Coulterville	60	687
---	Mariposa Coulterville	60	691
---	Mariposa Coulterville	60	692
---	Nevada Grass Valley	61	228
---	Nevada Grass Valley	61	229
---	Nevada Grass Valley	61	230
---	Nevada Grass Valley	61	231
---	Nevada Nevada	61	299
---	Nevada Nevada	61	300
---	Nevada Nevada	61	301
---	Nevada Nevada	61	302
---	Nevada Nevada	61	305
---	Nevada Nevada	61	306
---	Nevada Nevada	61	307
---	Nevada Nevada	61	308
---	Nevada Nevada	61	309
---	Nevada Nevada	61	310
---	Nevada Washington	61	339
---	Nevada Washington	61	340
---	Nevada Washington	61	341
---	Nevada Washington	61	342
---	Nevada Eureka	61	383
---	Nevada Eureka	61	384
---	Nevada Eureka	61	385
---	Nevada Eureka	61	386
---	Nevada Rough &	61	435
---	Placer Rattle Snake	62	627
---	Placer Iona Hills	62	894
---	San Francisco San Francisco 11	67	145
---	San Francisco San Francisco 2	67	673
---	San Francisco San Francisco 2	67	688
---	San Francisco San Francisco 2	67	689
---	San Francisco San Francisco 1	68	892
---	Shasta Shasta	66	671
---	Shasta Horsetown	66	704
---	Shasta Horsetown	66	710
---	Sierra Downieville	66	1006
---	Sierra Twp 5	66	927
---	Sierra Twp 5	66	932
---	Siskiyou Yreka	69	194
---	Siskiyou Yreka	69	195
---	Stanislaus Branch	70	713
---	Trinity Mouth Ca	70	1016
---	Trinity Big Flat	70	1042
---	Trinity Trininadad Rvr	70	1044
---	Trinity Trininadad Rvr	70	1045
---	Trinity Trininadad Rvr	70	1046
---	Trinity Trininadad Rvr	70	1047
---	Trinity Trininadad Rvr	70	1048
---	Trinity Trininadad Rvr	70	1049
---	Trinity Lewiston	70	954
---	Tuolumne Shawsfla	71	409
---	Tuolumne Twp 3	71	433
---	Tuolumne Twp 3	71	440
---	Tuolumne Twp 3	71	457
---	Tuolumne Twp 3	71	467
---	Tuolumne Twp 3	71	468
---	Tuolumne Twp 1	71	478
---	Tuolumne Montezuma	71	509
---	Tuolumne Chinese	71	523
---	Tuolumne Chinese	71	524
---	Tuolumne Don Pedro	71	533
---	Yolo No E Twp	72	677
---	Yolo No E Twp	72	684
---	Yolo Slate Ra	72	711
---	Yolo Slate Ra	72	712
---	Yuba North Ea	72	677
---	Yuba North Ea	72	680
---	Yuba Slate Ro	72	684
---	Yuba Long Bar	72	767
---*	El Dorado Union	58	1089
---*	Fresno Twp 1	59	26
---*	Nevada Nevada	61	300
---*	Nevada Nevada	61	305
---*	Nevada Nevada	61	307
---*	Nevada Nevada	61	308
---*	Nevada Washington	61	339
---*	Nevada Washington	61	341
---*	Nevada Washington	61	342

Name	County Locale	M653 Roll	Page
TOY			
---*	Trinity Taylor'S	70	1035
Ah	Butte Eureka	56	652
Ah	Calaveras Twp 7	57	36
Al	Yuba Marysville	72	867
An	Del Norte Crescent	58	631
C	Butte Chico	56	537
Catharine	San Francisco San Francisco 8	68	1303
Chas F*	San Francisco San Francisco 9	68	969
Choy	San Francisco San Francisco 4	68	1197
Chung	El Dorado Greenwood	58	729
Cout	Shasta Shasta	66	670
Daniel	San Francisco San Francisco 8	68	1280
Fon	El Dorado Coloma	58	1114
Jno*	San Francisco San Francisco 9	68	1076
John	Yolo No E Twp	72	684
John*	San Francisco San Francisco 9	68	1073
Ne	San Francisco San Francisco 4	68	1201
Qui	Calaveras Twp 10	57	296
Sam	Nevada Washington	61	339
Sam	Nevada Washington	61	340
Sam*	Nevada Washington	61	339
Sam*	Nevada Washington	61	340
Sam*	Nevada Washington	61	341
She	Amador Twp 1	55	490
Sin	Del Norte Crescent	58	631
Sou	Plumas Quincy	62	1009
TOYAN			
Joseph*	Siskiyou Yreka	69	133
TOYE			
---	El Dorado Coloma	58	1114
---	Sierra Hill 5	66	944
Frank	Sacramento Ward 4	63	561
TOYEE			
---	Fresno Twp 3	59	31
TOYIER			
H*	Shasta Horsetown	66	689
TOYNINE			
Batista*	Trinity North Fo	70	1026
TOYON			
---	Tulara Visalia	71	113
Dennis	Del Norte Crescent	58	647
TOYRINE			
Batista*	Trinity North Fo	70	1026
TOYWON			
---	Shasta Shasta	66	669
TOZ			
---*	Trinity Taylor'S	70	1035
TOZEO			
W*	Shasta Shasta	66	655
TOZER			
C H	Sacramento Ward 3	63	451
H M*	San Francisco San Francisco 10	200	67
W*	Shasta Shasta	66	655
TOZIER			
Elijah	Stanislaus Emory	70	756
Geo*	Sacramento Cosumnes	63	405
H	Shasta Horsetown	66	689
Jack	Santa Clara San Jose	65	334
Saml	Tuolumne Columbia	71	289
TP			
---	Amador Twp 5	55	351
TR			
---	Calaveras Twp 6	57	165
TRAA			
---	Tulara Twp 1	71	121
TRABAJO			
---*	Tulara Twp 1	71	121
TRABAP			
---*	Tulara Twp 1	71	121
TRABBES			
Mananna	Mariposa Twp 1	60	652
TRABECO			
Torniry*	Mariposa Twp 3	60	545
Tornirz*	Mariposa Twp 3	60	545
TRABITTY			
N	Tuolumne Twp 1	71	269
TRABLUS			
Marianna	Mariposa Twp 1	60	652
TRABOUT			
John	Tuolumne Sonora	71	209
TRABTTY			
N	Tuolumne Twp 1	71	269
TRABUCK			
Louis	Mariposa Twp 3	60	545
Louise	Mariposa Twp 3	60	545
TRACE			
D*	Yolo Cottonwoood	72	656
TRACEY			
C C	San Francisco San Francisco 2	67	669
Edward	San Francisco San Francisco 11	92	67
H F	El Dorado Mud Springs	58	963
I	San Francisco San Francisco 1	68	911
TRACEY			
John	San Francisco San Francisco 11	162	67
John	San Francisco San Francisco 1	68	911
O A B	San Joaquin Elkhorn	64	977
Philip	San Francisco San Francisco 3	67	52
T F	El Dorado Placerville	58	831
Talrick	Yuba Parks Ba	72	684
William	San Francisco San Francisco 11	136	67
TRACK			
G	Nevada Grass Valley	61	153
Miller	Tuolumne Twp 2	71	312
TRACKER			
---	Fresno Twp 1	59	118
TRACON			
Hosa	El Dorado Coloma	58	1118
TRACY			
A	Sonoma Bodega	69	525
Anna	San Bernardino Santa Barbara	64	203
C	Nevada Grass Valley	61	160
Clara	Sacramento Brighton	63	202
E P	Sutter Bear Rvr	70	818
Edward	Amador Twp 1	55	509
Edward	Placer Iona Hills	62	886
Edwd	San Francisco San Francisco 10	335	67
F	Butte Ophir	56	795
F	San Francisco San Francisco 5	67	492
F Jr*	Shasta Shasta	66	657
Francis	Contra Costa Twp 3	57	600
Fredk P	San Francisco San Francisco 10	271	67
G A*	San Francisco San Francisco 9	68	1099
Geo	Sacramento Cosumnes	63	389
H	Sacramento Brighton	63	200
Hiram	Sacramento Centre	63	174
J	El Dorado Placerville	58	822
James	Placer Forest H	62	805
Jas	San Francisco San Francisco 2	67	595
Jas	Yolo Cache	72	591
Jas L	San Francisco San Francisco 10	255	67
Jno	Sonoma Petaluma	69	550
Jno C	Sacramento Ward 3	63	448
John	Placer Yankee J	62	775
Jon L	San Francisco San Francisco 10	255	67
Jonathan	Calaveras Twp 6	57	164
Jonathan	Calaveras Twp 6	57	164
Joseph	Humbolt Eel Rvr	59	148
Levi	Sacramento Franklin	63	319
Margaret	Santa Cruz Soquel	66	596
Margret	Santa Cruz Pajaro	66	535
Margt	San Francisco San Francisco 7	68	1354
Mary	Sacramento Ward 4	63	561
P	San Francisco San Francisco 3	67	1
P L*	Placer Michigan	62	849
P S	Placer Michigan	62	849
Patrick	Santa Cruz Santa Cruz	66	608
Patrick	Yuba Parks Ba	72	684
Patrick*	Sierra Pine Grove	66	831
Peter	Tuolumne Twp 1	71	248
Philip	San Francisco San Francisco 1	68	892
Scoazy L	Yuba Suida	72	986
Silas J	San Francisco San Francisco 12	386	67
Thomas	San Francisco San Francisco 9	68	981
Thos	Sacramento Brighton	63	196
Thos	Sacramento Ward 4	63	519
Verrict	San Joaquin Elkhorn	64	955
William	Calaveras Twp 7	57	43
Wm	Mariposa Coulterville	60	691
Wm	Sacramento Natonia	63	286
Wm	Sacramento Ward 4	63	601
Wm N	Sierra Downieville	66	961
Wm*	Mariposa Coulterville	60	691
TRACZ			
F Jr*	Shasta Shasta	66	657
TRADE			
Lydia*	San Francisco San Francisco 1	68	815
TRADEAN			
Chas	Butte Oregon	56	611
TRADER			
S S S*	Nevada Bloomfield	61	511
TRADLEY			
James	San Joaquin Tulare	64	869
TRADORO			
---	San Bernardino Santa Inez	64	138
TRAEY			
G A*	San Francisco San Francisco 9	68	1099
TRAFATT			
L W	Nevada Grass Valley	61	223
TRAFFORD			
Hannah	San Joaquin Stockton	64	1062
TRAFORT			
C*	Calaveras Twp 9	57	392
TRAFT			
Chas	Sacramento Ward 4	63	500
TRAFTEN			
Charles	Monterey Pajaro	60	1019
George A	Monterey Pajaro	60	1019
John E	Monterey Pajaro	60	1019
Mary E	Monterey Pajaro	60	1019
TRAFTER			
John E	Monterey Pajaro	60	1019
TRAFTIN			
Charles*	Placer Yankee J	62	781
TRAFTON			
A	Sacramento San Joaquin	63	355
Charles	Plumas Quincy	62	938
Charles*	Placer Yankee J	62	781
W B	Nevada Grass Valley	61	171
Wm	Sacramento Ward 1	63	62
TRAGENZE			
Thos	Sacramento San Joaquin	63	359
TRAGERT			
C*	Calaveras Twp 9	57	392
TRAGG			
L E*	Nevada Grass Valley	61	217
TRAGON			
Charles W*	Sierra Scales D	66	802
TRAGUIRE			
M	Nevada Grass Valley	61	144
TRAHAM			
Wm	Tuolumne Twp 2	71	299
TRAHEIM			
Samuel B	San Joaquin Stockton	64	1074
TRAHEM			
Washington*	Castoria San Joaquin	64	878
TRAHEN			
Wm	Tuolumne Columbia	71	299
TRAHLEY			
Pat*	El Dorado Big Bar	58	735
TRAHOON			
John	Placer Forest H	62	774
TRAHOUSE			
J	Sutter Sutter	70	813
TRAHOUT			
John	Tuolumne Twp 1	71	209
TRAHVERS			
R H*	Mariposa Coulterville	60	694
TRAIL			
E H	Nevada Rough &	61	426
F M	Nevada Rough &	61	405
TRAILSON			
Crist*	Tuolumne Columbia	71	332
TRAIMER			
Hester	Butte Oregon	56	639
TRAIN			
---	Calaveras Twp 4	57	307
Edward*	Siskiyou Scott Ri	69	68
M R	Siskiyou Scott Va	69	37
TRAINER			
Francis	Calaveras Twp 5	57	212
Geo K	Butte Kimshaw	56	605
H	Sacramento Ward 4	63	525
J A	Tuolumne Columbia	71	349
J O	Nevada Bridgeport	61	503
J P	Nevada Little Y	61	532
James	Solano Suisan	69	210
James	Tuolumne Columbia	71	311
John	San Francisco San Francisco 8	68	1250
John	San Francisco San Francisco 5	67	478
John	San Francisco San Francisco 2	67	598
John W	San Francisco San Francisco 10	284	67
John*	San Francisco San Francisco 7	68	1428
Luke*	Sacramento Granite	63	264
Owen	Solano Suisan	69	225
TRAINOR			
Frank*	Yuba Linda Twp	72	983
Freemon	Calaveras Twp 5	57	199
Heenono*	Calaveras Twp 5	57	199
Hester	Butte Oregon	56	639
James	Calaveras Twp 5	57	145
James	Solano Suisan	69	210
Jas	Butte Oregon	56	629
Jaseph	Calaveras Twp 8	57	82
John	San Francisco San Francisco 8	68	1250
John	San Francisco San Francisco 5	67	478
John	San Francisco San Francisco 2	67	747
John*	Sacramento Sutter	63	306
Joseph	Calaveras Twp 8	57	82
Mary	Santa Clara San Jose	65	384
Peter	Sacramento Ward 4	63	531
Tremono	Calaveras Twp 5	57	199
TRAISE			
Frances	Calaveras Twp 5	57	212
Francis	Calaveras Twp 5	57	212
TRAITOR			
---	Tulara Keyesville	71	56

Name	County Locale	M653 Roll	Page
TRAKEN			
---	Yuba Bear Rvr	72	1015
TRAKLEY			
Pat*	El Dorado Big Bar	58	735
TRALISE			
W	Nevada Nevada	61	317
TRALOR			
Louis	San Joaquin Castoria	64	875
Wm	Mariposa Twp 3	60	601
TRAMA			
Stephin D*	Mariposa Coulterville	60	677
TRAMAD			
James	Del Norte Crescent	58	624
TRAMBLY			
Julian	Yuba Marysville	72	914
TRAMELL			
Lee	Napa Yount	61	46
TRAMER			
Luke*	Sacramento Granite	63	264
Patrick	Santa Clara San Jose	65	384
Stephin D*	Mariposa Coulterville	60	677
TRAMERO			
Solida	Fresno Twp 1	59	84
TRAMONE			
---	Mariposa Twp 1	60	628
TRAMOR			
Frank*	Yuba Linda Twp	72	983
J O*	Butte Chico	56	543
TRAMP			
Isaac	San Francisco San Francisco 2	67	802
TRAN EY			
Henry	Yolo Putah	72	585
TRAN KINTHALL			
S*	El Dorado Georgetown	58	686
TRAN KINWALL			
S*	El Dorado Georgetown	58	686
TRANANES			
Andrew	Sierra Downieville	66	1012
TRANBERTH			
L	Nevada Grass Valley	61	151
TRANCE			
T	Yolo Washington	72	573
TRANCES			
Emanwel	Nevada Rough &	61	424
TRANCHARD			
Chas	Napa Napa	61	75
TRANCHURD			
Chas*	Napa Napa	61	75
TRANCIS			
G	El Dorado Placerville	58	837
TRANDONE			
A*	San Francisco San Francisco 1	68	929
TRANDORE			
A	San Francisco San Francisco 1	68	929
TRANER			
Hamell	El Dorado Gold Hill	58	1095
P L*	Calaveras Twp 9	57	383
TRANEY			
Henry	Yolo Putah	72	585
TRANGLERY			
Coro	San Joaquin Stockton	64	1083
TRANIBLE			
Isaac	Marin Bolinas	60	727
TRANJEN			
G W	El Dorado Greenwood	58	720
TRANKIS			
Jessie	Amador Twp 3	55	406
TRANKMAN			
H A	Nevada Nevada	61	293
TRANOR			
Philip*	San Mateo Twp 1	65	70
Thos*	San Mateo Twp 1	65	70
TRANS			
Marc*	Yuba Fosters	72	833
TRANSDALE			
Wm B*	Calaveras Twp 9	57	373
TRANSEN			
Jacob*	Sacramento Cosumnes	63	385
TRANSFIELD			
Albeon	San Francisco San Francisco 11	67	105
Delia	San Francisco San Francisco 11	67	104
Delia	San Francisco San Francisco 8	68	1233
TRANSON			
James*	Sacramento Granite	63	258
TRANSUE			
Jacob	Amador Twp 5	55	358
Jacob*	Sacramento Cosumnes	63	385
TRANT			
L	Nevada Grass Valley	61	146
TRANTER			
Jacob	Mariposa Twp 3	60	566
TRANTMAN			
C G	Nevada Grass Valley	61	238
H A*	Nevada Nevada	61	293
TRANTRETS			
A	San Francisco San Francisco 2	67	800
TRANTRETTI			
A*	San Francisco San Francisco 2	67	800
TRANTSETTI			
A*	San Francisco San Francisco 2	67	800
TRANTVETTI			
A*	San Francisco San Francisco 2	67	800
TRANTZ			
C	San Francisco San Francisco 2	67	784
TRANVERSE			
Jas	Sacramento Ward 1	63	14
TRANYER			
D S	Sonoma Armally	69	490
TRAOES			
Charles*	Yuba Marysville	72	875
TRAPHAJEN			
N R	Placer Iona Hills	62	865
TRAPP			
Alfonso	Butte Chico	56	542
Ariah S	Amador Twp 4	55	249
Barbury	Sonoma Petaluma	69	574
Jno	San Francisco San Francisco 2	67	699
Louis	San Francisco San Francisco 11	67	113
TRAPPER			
---	Tulara Twp 1	71	121
TRARES			
Marc*	Yuba Fosters	72	833
TRARESICK			
Daniel	Yuba Fosters	72	825
TRARILLIAN			
James	El Dorado Mud Springs	58	963
TRART			
E	El Dorado Placerville	58	833
TRARY			
T W	San Francisco San Francisco 3	67	84
TRASE			
Michael	Yuba Marysville	72	969
TRASER			
James	Nevada Bridgeport	61	489
TRASERY			
Jas	Yolo Cache	72	592
TRASEY			
Jas	Yolo Cache Crk	72	592
TRASH			
Y S	Siskiyou Scott Va	69	47
TRASHER			
Edward	Sonoma Armally	69	508
TRASHOUR			
Elizabeth	San Joaquin Elkhorn	64	961
TRASK			
A	Sacramento Ward 1	63	2
A	San Francisco San Francisco 12	67	394
B F	Trinity Douglas	70	978
C O*	Placer Iona Hills	62	877
E	Trinity Weaverville	70	1077
E T	Placer Forest H	62	796
Edward B	El Dorado Placerville	58	928
Freeman	San Francisco San Francisco 7	68	1442
Glosswell	Placer Yankee J	62	760
J A	Placer Todds Va	62	787
J B	San Francisco San Francisco 5	67	483
J R	Tuolumne Columbia	71	343
Jas L	San Francisco San Francisco 2	67	626
Joseph W	Calaveras Twp 9	57	371
John*	San Francisco San Francisco 9	68	1050
Jos L	San Francisco San Francisco 2	67	626
Joseph W*	Calaveras Twp 9	57	371
Mary	Placer Iona Hills	62	886
R E	El Dorado Diamond	58	765
S B	Nevada Grass Valley	61	218
V	Butte Ophir	56	793
W W	El Dorado Placerville	58	928
Y S*	Siskiyou Scott Va	69	47
TRASKE			
J R	Tuolumne Twp 2	71	343
TRASPELL			
William	San Francisco San Francisco 7	68	1355
TRASQUILLO			
Reyes	Los Angeles Los Angeles	59	400
TRASSON			
Z	San Joaquin Stockton	64	1047
TRAST			
J	Nevada Eureka	61	367
TRASTE			
Wm	Placer Secret R	62	610
TRASUM			
William	Placer Iona Hills	62	877
TRASY			
Ed	Placer Iona Hills	62	879
TRATKIUS			
Cyrus*	Placer Michigan	62	847
TRAUGH			
Lemuel G	Plumas Quincy	62	987
TRAUSDALE			
Wm B*	Calaveras Twp 9	57	373
TRAUT			
J A S	Tuolumne Twp 2	71	391
TRAUTMAN			
H A*	Nevada Nevada	61	293
N A*	Sacramento Ward 1	63	61
TRAVED			
Charles	Yolo Cache	72	590
TRAVEDICK			
S J	Nevada Nevada	61	292
TRAVEL			
V	Santa Clara San Jose	65	302
TRAVELLI			
Charles	Siskiyou Scott Ri	69	69
TRAVELSTED			
Abagail	San Joaquin Castoria	64	896
TRAVEN			
Albt	Butte Oregon	56	641
TRAVER			
Charles	Yolo Cache Crk	72	590
P L*	Calaveras Twp 9	57	383
TRAVERS			
Aaron*	Mendocino Calpella	60	813
C M	Sacramento Granite	63	242
Geo W	San Francisco San Francisco 1	68	870
J	Nevada Grass Valley	61	224
Jas K	San Francisco San Francisco 1	68	807
Jos K	San Francisco San Francisco 1	68	807
L	Nevada Grass Valley	61	224
M	Nevada Grass Valley	61	206
N	Yolo No E Twp	72	673
N	Yuba North Ea	72	673
Oscar E	San Diego Colorado	64	811
R	Nevada Grass Valley	61	160
S	Nevada Grass Valley	61	224
TRAVERSE			
M H	Sacramento Ward 1	63	85
Mary	San Francisco San Francisco 10	67	182
Thos	Sacramento San Joaquin	63	363
TRAVERSY			
James	Nevada Little Y	61	533
TRAVES			
Charles	Yuba Marysville	72	875
TRAVESA			
Joseph	San Francisco San Francisco 2	67	686
TRAVESSO			
Sanetus	Santa Clara Santa Clara	65	481
TRAVEY			
T W	San Francisco San Francisco 3	67	84
TRAVIAS			
---	San Luis Obispo San Luis Obispo	65	32
TRAVIDICK			
S J	Nevada Nevada	61	292
TRAVIER			
Charles	El Dorado Placerville	58	918
TRAVIS			
B B	Tuolumne Twp 2	71	315
B C	Tuolumne Twp 2	71	324
Danile	Contra Costa Twp 1	57	484
E	Napa Yount	61	53
E D	Siskiyou Scott Va	69	39
Edwin	San Joaquin Elkhorn	64	994
Francis	Santa Clara Santa Clara	65	465
Frank	Merced Twp 2	60	924
Geo	Solano Vacaville	69	335
J B	Sierra Downieville	66	987
Jacob	San Francisco San Francisco 4	68	1163
James	Contra Costa Twp 1	57	484
Jos E	Alameda Oakland	55	30
Joseph	Nevada Red Dog	61	542
Joseph D	Tulara Visalia	71	100
Susan	Contra Costa Twp 3	57	606
Theodore	Sonoma Bodega	69	532
W D	Santa Clara San Jose	65	294
W S	Butte Oro	56	687
Whiteley	Sonoma Armally	69	493
TRAVISE			
S B	Nevada Bridgeport	61	496
S R	Nevada Bridgeport	61	496
TRAW			
John	Alameda Oakland	55	20
TRAXEL			
William	San Francisco San Francisco 7	68	1352
TRAXLER			
Wm	Marin S Antoni	60	711
TRAXTER			
Jacob*	Mariposa Twp 3	60	566
TRAY			
---	Sacramento Mississipi	63	187
D	Santa Clara Fremont	65	429
Franas*	Sacramento Dry Crk	63	370
Martin*	San Francisco San Francisco 7	68	1436
S	Sacramento Dry Crk	63	371
Tranas*	Sacramento Dry Crk	63	370

California 1860 Census Index

Name	County Locale	M653 Roll	Page
TRAY			
Z	Nevada Grass Valley	61	157
TRAYG			
J*	Nevada Grass Valley	61	217
L E*	Nevada Grass Valley	61	217
TRAYLER			
C P	Amador Twp 2	55	320
W W	Tuolumne Sonora	71	204
TRAYMAS			
W	Yolo Cache	72	639
TRAYMOS			
M	Sierra St Louis	66	818
TRAYNER			
B	Sierra St Louis	66	817
TRAYNOR			
B	Sierra St Louis	66	817
M	Sierra St Louis	66	818
Wm	Butte Eureka	56	654
TRAYRE			
G	Nevada Grass Valley	61	158
TRAYY			
L E*	Nevada Grass Valley	61	217
TRAZEE			
Carman	Los Angeles San Gabriel	59	411
TRE			
---	Calaveras Twp 6	57	168
TREADING			
Emmon	Sonoma Santa Rosa	69	396
TREADUELL			
L S	San Francisco San Francisco 5	67	525
TREADWAY			
Fredrick	Sierra Pine Grove	66	822
George	Sonoma Santa Rosa	69	396
Griffin	Sonoma Santa Rosa	69	396
J A	Mendocino Little L	60	839
James P	Calaveras Twp 4	57	318
Sylvester	San Joaquin Elkhorn	64	975
TREADWELL			
Hannah	San Francisco San Francisco 9	68	982
TREAGER			
J*	Nevada Grass Valley	61	158
Jno*	San Francisco San Francisco 9	681074	
TREAGLE			
John	Sacramento Mississipi	63	186
TREAMER			
R	Amador Twp 1	55	468
TREANIR			
G M	Nevada Bridgeport	61	451
TREANOR			
Alex B	San Francisco San Francisco 2	67	718
G M*	Nevada Bridgeport	61	451
Jas	San Francisco San Francisco 2	67	717
Marcilles	Sacramento Ward 4	63	594
TREAON			
H W	Tuolumne Big Oak	71	149
TREARNE			
Christian*	Calaveras Twp 4	57	323
TREARRIE			
Christian*	Calaveras Twp 4	57	323
TREARY			
Michl*	Sacramento Ward 1	63	94
TREASER			
John	San Francisco San Francisco 2	67	576
TREAT			
Chas	Santa Clara Santa Clara	65	498
Ira	El Dorado Georgetown	58	708
J	Nevada Grass Valley	61	218
J D	Sacramento Ward 1	63	37
J Franklin	Calaveras Twp 5	57	185
J W	Sacramento Ward 1	63	37
John	Calaveras Twp 4	57	334
S	Sacramento San Joaquin	63	362
W W	El Dorado Placerville	58	853
TREAVER			
F	Yuba Marysville	72	905
TREAYER			
J	Nevada Grass Valley	61	158
TREBELCOCK			
John	Sierra Twp 7	66	879
TREBLE			
George	Placer Yankee J	62	761
TREBLECOT			
W	Trinity E Weaver	701057	
TREBRE			
Thomas*	Trinity E Weaver	701059	
TREDENWICK			
J*	Trinity E Weaver	701057	
TREDON			
Louis*	San Francisco San Francisco 3	67	80
TREE			
Fred	Alameda Oakland	55	59
Michael	San Francisco San Francisco 3	67	70
TREEBLOOD			
Elison	Tehama Red Bluff	70	903
TREECE			
John*	San Francisco San Francisco 9	681018	
TREED			
Augustin	Napa Hot Springs	61	21
TREEGO			
Laura*	Yuba Marysville	72	876
TREEGON			
Charles W*	Sierra Scales D	66	802
TREELY			
B F*	El Dorado Placerville	58	891
TREEMA			
Stephen D*	Mariposa Coulterville	60	677
TREEMAN			
J C	Sierra Eureka	661044	
Stephen D*	Mariposa Coulterville	60	677
TREENLOFER			
Paul*	San Francisco San Francisco 7	681342	
TREES			
Dan L	San Francisco San Francisco 9	68	976
Thomas J	Sierra Twp 5	66	919
TREETON			
J P*	Nevada Grass Valley	61	186
TREEWHOFER			
Paul*	San Francisco San Francisco 7	681342	
TREFF			
D O S*	Sacramento Mississipi	63	183
TREFITO			
Henacio	Fresno Twp 1	59	84
TREFROY			
Benj*	Placer Goods	62	698
TREFRY			
James A	Alameda Brooklyn	55	182
TREFSER			
Burge	Butte Cascade	56	693
TREFUTHEREN			
B*	Tuolumne Jacksonville	71	171
TREGAN			
J	Nevada Grass Valley	61	220
TREGASKES			
Thomas	Sierra La Porte	66	765
TREGASKIS			
Richard	Sierra La Porte	66	780
TREGAY			
James	Trinity Weaverville	701056	
Jane	Tuolumne Twp 1	71	250
TREGO			
---	Fresno Twp 2	59	93
TREHNER			
David*	Contra Costa Twp 1	57	523
TREICHLER			
Peter*	Sacramento Ward 1	63	154
TREID			
Moses*	Contra Costa Twp 1	57	531
TREIDERNE			
Christian*	Calaveras Twp 4	57	323
TREINAN			
Mich*	Sacramento Ward 1	63	83
Peter*	Sacramento Ward 1	63	12
TREINER			
A H	Mariposa Twp 3	60	556
TREIPOLGER			
---	San Francisco San Francisco 10	67	175
TRELAIG			
J	Nevada Grass Valley	61	222
TRELAUR			
Samuel	Sierra Twp 7	66	871
TRELBY			
Thos*	San Francisco San Francisco 9	68	986
TRELFALL			
Richd	Alameda Brooklyn	55	186
TRELJENS			
Peter	Sacramento Ward 1	63	42
TRELLEASE			
Ricard	Tuolumne Columbia	71	472
TRELLY			
Thos	San Francisco San Francisco 9	68	986
TRELMAN			
Christlan	Sonoma Petaluma	69	583
TRELOR			
Benjamine	Sierra Twp 7	66	873
TRELOW			
Thomas	Trinity E Weaver	701059	
TRELTON			
J P*	Nevada Grass Valley	61	186
TREMAN			
Mich	Sacramento Ward 1	63	83
Peter	Sacramento Ward 1	63	12
TREMBLE			
Francis M	San Joaquin Elkhorn	64	986
Isaac	Marin Bolinas	60	727
James	Siskiyou Yreka	69	143
Jno	Alameda Brooklyn	55	177
Jno*	Alameda Brooklyn	55	159
Thomas G	Monterey Pajaro	601021	
Thomas J	Siskiyou Yreka	69	141
W	Sonoma Washington	69	670
Y B	Amador Twp 1	55	504
TREMER			
Joseph	Nevada Rough &	61	413
TREMLEICKE			
Vincent*	Tulara Petersburg	71	51
TREMLEICKI			
Vincent*	Tulara Petersburg	71	51
TREMSON			
James*	Sacramento Granite	63	258
TRENAN			
James	Santa Cruz Pajaro	66	528
TRENARD			
Edwd T	Sacramento Mississipi	63	187
TRENB			
Henry	Amador Twp 1	55	461
TRENBERTH			
J*	Nevada Grass Valley	61	172
TRENCH			
Asa	Tulara Visalia	71	17
Baron Fred*	Sacramento Ward 4	63	561
Cerfind*	Sacramento Ward 4	63	595
TRENDALL			
Mathew*	Solano Benecia	69	316
TRENEL			
Antoni	El Dorado Coloma	581086	
Antonio	El Dorado Coloma	581086	
TRENEN			
D*	Yolo Cache Crk	72	591
John	Sonoma Sonoma	69	650
TRENGRAVE			
Jas	Sacramento Natonia	63	273
TRENGROVE			
Jas	Sacramento Natonia	63	273
Wm	Tuolumne Twp 1	71	234
TRENHOLM			
Abijah	Tuolumne Chinese	71	510
TRENHOLTZ			
E	El Dorado Mud Springs	58	989
TRENISE			
Jean	San Francisco San Francisco 2	67	783
TRENITA			
---	Sierra La Porte	66	773
TRENKLE			
J	San Francisco San Francisco 10	67	346
TRENLER			
V*	Sacramento Ward 1	63	120
TRENNIES			
Aug*	Nevada Bridgeport	61	443
TRENOLDE			
Joseph	Yuba New York	72	729
TRENRNE			
Christian*	Calaveras Twp 4	57	323
TRENS			
Wm H*	Alameda Oakland	55	68
TRENT			
F Franklin*	Calaveras Twp 5	57	185
Franklin J	Calaveras Twp 5	57	185
G M	Nevada Grass Valley	61	144
Henry	Amador Twp 1	55	461
Horman	Tuolumne Twp 2	71	405
J	Calaveras Twp 9	57	403
J Franklin	Calaveras Twp 6	57	185
John	Calaveras Twp 4	57	334
TRENTYMAN			
John	Del Norte Happy Ca	58	670
TRENY			
---	Calaveras Twp 10	57	275
TREOT			
John	Calaveras Twp 4	57	334
TREPLETT			
Z A*	Siskiyou Callahan	69	1
TRER			
Wm F	Tuolumne Twp 1	71	475
Yung	Calaveras Twp 4	57	299
TRERCH			
Cerfind*	Sacramento Ward 4	63	595
TRERNAN			
Mich*	Sacramento Ward 1	63	83
TRERSLER			
V	Sacramento Ward 1	63	120
TRES			
Francisco*	Mariposa Twp 3	60	617
Wilson	Tuolumne Twp 4	71	136
TRESASE			
E*	Nevada Grass Valley	61	207
TRESCOTT			
E H	Mariposa Twp 1	60	630
G	Yolo Merritt	72	583
J C	El Dorado Coloma	581083	
Jas	Yolo Merritt	72	583
Wm	Sonoma Salt Point	69	691
TRESHANY			
James	Calaveras Twp 4	57	317
TRESHWAY			
James	Calaveras Twp 4	57	317
TRESIGER			
Harriet F	Calaveras Twp 4	57	319

Name	County Locale	M653 RollPage
TRESIZE		
Harriet F	Calaveras Twp 4	57 319
TRESSE		
H	El Dorado Diamond	58 765
TRESSER		
Burge	Butte Cascade	56 693
TRESTEAL		
Geo	Trinity Arkansas	701004
TRETHEREN		
B	Tuolumne Twp 4	71 171
TRETHILL		
Franklin*	San Francisco San Francisco 2	67 734
TRETJONS		
Peter*	Sacramento Ward 1	63 42
TRETKET		
---	Tulara Twp 1	71 121
TRETON		
Geo*	Mariposa Twp 3	60 596
TRETT		
A	Nevada Nevada	61 319
J	Nevada Grass Valley	61 222
TRETTON		
J P*	Nevada Grass Valley	61 186
TREUDALL		
Mathew*	Solano Benecia	69 316
TREUS		
Wm H*	Alameda Oakland	55 68
TREVER		
Frank	Sonoma Armally	69 494
TREVIER		
J	Nevada Grass Valley	61 150
Wm	Siskiyou Scott Va	69 55
TREVIR		
Wm	Siskiyou Scott Va	69 55
TREVOR		
George G	Sonoma Armally	69 479
TREWELLA		
H	Nevada Grass Valley	61 159
TREWELLER		
H*	Nevada Grass Valley	61 159
TREWEN		
Robert	Santa Cruz Pajaro	66 534
TREWET		
Jas	Sacramento Ward 1	63 12
TREWETT		
J C*	Butte Oro	56 684
Levi C	Yuba Marysville	72 867
TREWGNE		
W D	Sonoma Petaluma	69 575
TREWIT		
Jas*	Sacramento Ward 1	63 12
TREWITT		
Charles	Sierra La Porte	66 768
J C*	Butte Oro	56 684
TREWNIES		
Aug*	Nevada Bridgeport	61 443
TREWS		
Wm H*	Alameda Oakland	55 68
TREYASKIS		
Thomas	Sierra La Porte	66 765
TRGONTELLA		
---	Mariposa Twp 1	60 628
TRHAIN		
Charles*	Contra Costa Twp 2	57 539
TRI		
---	Sacramento Granite	63 268
---	Sacramento Ward 1	63 53
TRIBBLE		
Newton	Tuolumne Twp 3	71 461
TRIBBS		
C M	Yolo Washington	72 569
G C	Yolo Cache Crk	72 638
TRIBLE		
Jno	Sacramento Ward 3	63 458
TRIBLIES		
Marianna*	Mariposa Twp 1	60 652
TRIBUCA		
Andrea	Calaveras Twp 7	57 33
TRIBUE		
B	El Dorado Kelsey	581143
TRICER		
F	Siskiyou Callahan	69 10
TRICHETT		
Jasper H*	Monterey San Juan	60 977
Sanford L*	Monterey San Juan	60 977
TRICK		
---	Calaveras Twp 10	57 284
Henry*	Sacramento Franklin	63 312
W J	Tehama Red Bluff	70 912
TRICKEEM		
---	Tulara Twp 2	71 36
TRICKEL		
J	Siskiyou Scott Ri	69 83
John	Siskiyou Klamath	69 83
TRICKERBURY		
F*	Los Angeles Tejon	59 527

Name	County Locale	M653 RollPage
TRICKSWELL		
C	Butte Bidwell	56 721
TRICKWELL		
C	Butte Bidwell	56 721
TRICOT		
Louis	El Dorado Mud Springs	58 954
TRIDELL		
John B	Los Angeles Los Angeles	59 339
TRIDEN		
Lewis	San Francisco San Francisco 2	67 737
TRIDFETTER		
Andrew*	Siskiyou Shasta Valley	69 121
TRIE		
---*	Sacramento Granite	63 268
TRIEBER		
Conrad	San Francisco San Francisco 3	67 33
TRIECHLER		
Peter*	Sacramento Ward 1	63 154
TRIEFLECH		
Geo*	Alameda Oakland	55 46
TRIEGH		
Cornelius*	Sacramento Granite	63 247
TRIEGON		
Charles W*	Sierra Scales D	66 802
TRIEK		
Ca	Mariposa Twp 1	60 653
TRIENS		
Peter	Nevada Bridgeport	61 465
TRIERGE		
John*	Santa Cruz Pajaro	66 568
TRIESLEN		
Frank	Sacramento Ward 4	63 526
TRIEWHOFER		
Paul*	San Francisco San Francisco 7	681342
TRIFF		
A G*	Nevada Bridgeport	61 451
TRIFO		
Vel*	Sacramento Centre	63 182
Vet*	Sacramento Centre	63 182
TRIFT		
P	San Joaquin Stockton	641033
TRIGE		
A	Tehama Antelope	70 889
TRIGENES		
Jeratudes	San Bernadino	64 666
	San Bernardino	
TRIGG		
Stephen	Tuolumne Shawsfla	71 386
TRIGGS		
Geo	San Francisco San Francisco 1	68 901
TRIGH		
Cornelous	Sacramento Granite	63 247
TRIGILLO		
Dorotio	San Bernardino San Bernardino	64 664
Polonia*	Los Angeles Los Angeles	59 360
TRIGLE		
J*	Nevada Eureka	61 387
TRIGLONE		
John	Alameda Oakland	55 47
TRIGONT		
Francis	Yuba Foster B	72 822
TRIHNER		
David*	Contra Costa Twp 1	57 523
TRIJILLO		
Inbian	San Bernardino San Bernardino	64 664
Iscipilo	San Bernardino San Bernardino	64 664
Lorenzo	San Bernardino San Bernardino	64 665
TRIJOLES		
---*	Tulara Twp 1	71 121
TRIKS		
W	Nevada Eureka	61 376
TRILAING		
M	Nevada Grass Valley	61 222
TRILBY		
Thos*	San Francisco San Francisco 9	68 986
TRILD		
Josiah*	El Dorado Georgetown	58 678
TRILLEASE		
Ricard	Tuolumne Twp 2	71 472
TRILLEY		
John	Yolo Cache	72 634
TRILLY		
John	Sacramento Ward 1	63 122
TRIM		
---*	Nevada Red Dog	61 556
TRIMANE		
R*	Nevada Grass Valley	61 223
TRIMAYER		
Wm	Tuolumne Twp 1	71 259
TRIMBALL		
John*	El Dorado Big Bar	58 744
TRIMBEL		
James	Siskiyou Scott Va	69 34
TRIMBELL		
Charles F*	Los Angeles Los Angeles	59 365
Charles W	Los Angeles Los Angeles	59 365

Name	County Locale	M653 RollPage
TRIMBLE		
Alexander	San Joaquin Castoria	64 906
Allen	Yuba Bear Rvr	721004
Geo A	El Dorado Coloma	581082
J J	Amador Twp 1	55 473
James	Siskiyou Scott Va	69 34
John	Santa Clara San Jose	65 393
Martha J	Sonoma Mendocino	69 455
Mary C	Yuba Bear Rvr	721005
Thomas J	Siskiyou Yreka	69 141
William H	San Francisco San Francisco 8	681272
Wm H	Sonoma Mendocino	69 455
TRIMBY		
Jacob	El Dorado Casumnes	581164
TRIMDAD		
Maira	San Bernardino San Bernadino	64 684
TRIMDOU		
Joseph*	Calaveras Twp 10	57 288
TRIME		
P R*	Nevada Nevada	61 239
TRIMINE		
R	Nevada Grass Valley	61 223
TRIMINGHAM		
James	Alameda Washington	55 175
TRIMLEICKE		
Vincent	Tulara Twp 3	71 51
TRIMM		
John	Tuolumne Columbia	71 310
TRIMMER		
Martin	San Diego Agua Caliente	64 855
TRIMMINS		
John	Sacramento Ward 1	63 110
TRIMPLE		
Geo	El Dorado Coloma	581081
---	Mariposa Twp 3	60 596
---	Mariposa Coulterville	60 682
Ah	Tuolumne Twp 4	71 149
Nelson*	Sierra Pine Grove	66 828
TRINADAR		
---	Mariposa Twp 1	60 628
TRINANT		
Wm	Santa Clara Santa Clara	65 504
TRINBAL		
J	Sutter Bear Rvr	70 823
TRINEDAD		
Jesus	Calaveras Twp 5	57 185
TRINEN		
J	El Dorado Diamond	58 799
TRING		
---	San Francisco San Francisco 4	681174
TRINIDAD		
---	Los Angeles San Juan	59 466
---	Los Angeles San Juan	59 477
---	Los Angeles Tejon	59 529
---	San Diego San Diego	64 772
---	San Diego San Diego	64 774
---	Yuba Linda Twp	72 984
Jesus	Calaveras Twp 5	57 185
Johnson	Santa Clara Fremont	65 428
Joseph	Calaveras Twp 10	57 288
Sanchez	San Francisco San Francisco 11	148 67
TRINILY		
T	San Joaquin Stockton	641094
TRINK		
Andrew	Sierra St Louis	66 809
Marie*	El Dorado Georgetown	58 677
TRINKARD		
Willm*	Sacramento Mississipi	63 188
TRINKER		
Robert*	San Bernardino Santa Barbara	64 199
TRINMER		
Iscar	Butte Ophir	56 790
TRINNIGAN		
Dan*	Sacramento Ward 1	63 74
TRINSCHEL		
A	Amador Twp 1	55 460
TRINX		
---	Calaveras Twp 10	57 284
TRINY		
---	Calaveras Twp 5	57 205
TRIOIN		
Thomas*	Sierra Poker Flats	66 838
TRION		
H W	Tuolumne Twp 4	71 149
S*	Calaveras Twp 9	57 391
TRIOR		
S	Calaveras Twp 9	57 391
TRIP		
---	Amador Twp 5	55 365
Danl E	Sacramento Ward 1	63 107
Isaac	Tehama Red Bluff	70 910
John	Amador Twp 2	55 313
L	Butte Cascade	56 696
R O	San Mateo Twp 3	65 82

595

California 1860 Census Index

Name	County Locale	M653 Roll	Page
TRIP			
William	Siskiyou Yreka	69	127
William	Siskiyou Yreka	69	130
TRIPARA			
Jose	Santa Cruz Watsonville	66	539
TRIPE			
Jose Ma	San Francisco San Francisco 2	67	684
TRIPLE			
Miguel	San Luis Obispo San Luis Obispo	65	33
T	San Joaquin Stockton	64	1086
Warren	Tuolumne Shawsfla	71	402
TRIPLET			
Frank	Sierra Downieville	66	1010
J F	El Dorado Placerville	58	860
L P M	El Dorado Coloma	58	1117
Remus	Santa Clara Santa Clara	65	501
Warren	Santa Clara Redwood	65	460
Wm	Santa Clara Santa Clara	65	501
TRIPLETT			
Alex	Nevada Red Dog	61	555
B	San Joaquin O'Neal	64	1006
Dan	Amador Twp 1	55	463
H O	Mendocino Calpella	60	810
James	Alameda Brooklyn	55	95
John	Sierra Downieville	66	963
Peter	Sierra Downieville	66	1011
T	Nevada Eureka	61	356
TRIPP			
A G	Nevada Bridgeport	61	451
A G	Placer Michigan	62	854
A G*	Nevada Bridgeport	61	451
A S	Nevada Bridgeport	61	448
Byron	Amador Twp 4	55	249
D T	San Mateo Twp 2	65	126
G C	Solano Suisan	69	225
Garner C	Napa Hot Springs	61	22
Geo	Amador Twp 2	55	279
Geo F	Amador Twp 2	55	279
George	Placer Michigan	62	842
Gideon F	Yuba Marysville	72	862
H	El Dorado Placerville	58	890
H F	Yolo Merritt	72	579
Henry	San Francisco San Francisco 10	67	217
Howard F	Contra Costa Twp 3	57	617
Isaac	Amador Twp 1	55	469
James C	San Francisco San Francisco 8	68	1259
John L	Napa Napa	61	112
John S	Napa Napa	61	112
Latan	Tulara Visalia	71	32
Philander	San Francisco San Francisco 10	67	273
Phillip	El Dorado Mud Springs	58	978
Russell B	Monterey Pajaro	60	1020
S R	El Dorado Placerville	58	887
Saml	Nevada Bridgeport	61	451
Samuel	Los Angeles San Jose	59	281
Samuel V	Los Angeles Los Angeles	59	404
Satan	Tulara Twp 2	71	32
Silas	San Francisco San Francisco 4	68	1158
Steven	San Mateo Twp 3	65	107
W O	Tuolumne Sonora	71	202
William A	Klamath Orleans	59	217
Wm F*	Butte Kimshaw	56	585
TRIPPS			
W F*	Butte Kimshaw	56	585
Wm F	Butte Kimshaw	56	585
TRIS CONEY			
Alberto*	Monterey Alisal	60	1029
TRISCONEY			
Alberto	Monterey Alisal	60	1029
TRISDORE			
John	Santa Cruz Soguel	66	595
TRISELAER			
Julius	Amador Twp 4	55	246
TRISH			
Gonzkry*	San Mateo Twp 3	65	94
TRISK			
Frank*	San Francisco San Francisco 3	67	21
TRISTE			
---	Tulara Keyesville	71	63
TRISTER			
Charles	San Francisco San Francisco 2	67	693
TRISTO			
---	Tulara Twp 3	71	63
---	Tulara Keyesville	71	64
TRISTZ			
Joseph	San Francisco San Francisco 2	67	721
TRITT			
H E	Yolo Cottonwoood	72	661
TRITTON			
Thomas	Placer Todds Va	62	785
Thomas	Placer Todds Va	62	788
TRITWASH			
---	Tulara Twp 1	71	119
TRIVERS			
Henry	El Dorado Kelsey	58	1134
TRIWDOD			
Joseph*	Calaveras Twp 10	57	288
TRIYIS			
Celestino*	Monterey Monterey	60	947
TRIYVER			
Peter*	San Francisco San Francisco 9	68	1099
TRIZISA			
Henry	Tuolumne Chinese	71	496
TRIZZLE			
R	Nevada Eureka	61	374
TRNAN			
H*	El Dorado Kelsey	58	1153
TRNEBODDIE			
John*	San Francisco San Francisco 4	68	1114
TROANLT			
Benj*	Siskiyou Scott Va	69	37
TROAULT			
Benj*	Siskiyou Scott Va	69	37
TROBBIS			
Marianna*	Mariposa Twp 1	60	652
TROBETY			
E	Trinity Texas Ba	70	981
TROBLUS			
Marianna*	Mariposa Twp 1	60	652
TROBOCK			
Nicholas	San Francisco San Francisco 3	67	42
TROBRIDGE			
J S	Amador Twp 1	55	493
Jas	Sacramento Granite	63	235
Lyman	Siskiyou Yreka	69	147
TROCO			
Magel	El Dorado Placerville	58	921
TRODEN			
Thomas	Calaveras Twp 4	57	319
TRODOCHO			
John	Calaveras Twp 5	57	218
TRODOCIO			
John	Calaveras Twp 5	57	218
TRODOCKS			
John	Calaveras Twp 5	57	218
TROE			
---	Alameda Oakland	55	24
TROECTS			
---	Tulara Twp 1	71	116
TROETS			
---	Tulara Twp 1	71	118
TROFATHER			
George L	San Francisco San Francisco 8	68	1280
TROFIC			
Peter*	Sacramento Ward 4	63	544
TROFIE			
Peter*	Sacramento Ward 4	63	544
TROGON			
W	Butte Ophir	56	766
TROGUE			
T	San Francisco San Francisco 6	67	474
TROHAN			
August	Solano Benecia	69	317
TROHEO			
Thos	Amador Twp 6	55	426
TROHES			
Thos	Amador Twp 6	55	426
TROHLING			
John	Los Angeles Los Angeles	59	404
TROILLIGER			
John	Amador Twp 2	55	279
TROIS			
Jose M	Yuba Marysville	72	938
TROITCHELL			
Theodore W	Yuba Marysville	72	938
TROITEN			
Thomas	Calaveras Twp 4	57	319
TROJAL			
Jose M	Yuba Marysville	72	922
TROKEN			
---*	Yuba Bear Rvr	72	1014
TROLA			
Stephan	Sierra Downieville	66	1014
TROLE			
Ramio	Alameda Brooklyn	55	175
TROLET			
Benj*	San Francisco San Francisco 2	67	671
TROLL			
Joseph	Alameda Brooklyn	55	164
TROLLINGER			
Henry	San Joaquin Castoria	64	880
TROLLOPE			
David	Colusa Monroeville	57	446
TROLOLT			
Dorain*	Nevada Bloomfield	61	526
Doran*	Nevada Bloomfield	61	526
TROM			
---*	Nevada Red Dog	61	556
TROMBS			
W*	El Dorado Placerville	58	893
TROME			
P	Yuba Foster B	72	822
TROMLY			
Peter	Santa Clara Gilroy	65	227
TRON			
---	Sierra Twp 5	66	932
---	Siskiyou Yreka	69	146
TRONAE			
---*	Fresno Twp 2	59	18
TRONAN			
H*	El Dorado Kelsey	58	1153
TRONBADOUR			
---	Amador Twp 1	55	484
TRONBRIDGE			
J D*	Yuba Rose Bar	72	791
TRONCIN			
John*	San Francisco San Francisco 11	67	139
TRONCIU			
John*	San Francisco San Francisco 11	67	139
TRONER			
D*	Mariposa Twp 3	60	609
TRONEY			
Dennis	Alameda Oakland	55	21
Margaret	Napa Napa	61	82
TRONG			
---*	Calaveras Twp 6	57	169
TRONGHSON			
Jas	Butte Bidwell	56	710
TRONGHTON			
S	Sutter Sutter	70	808
TRONRE			
P	Yuba Fosters	72	822
TRONSCHEL			
A	Amador Twp 1	55	460
TRONSDALE			
John*	Mariposa Coulterville	60	697
M*	Calaveras Twp 9	57	404
TRONSDELL			
C*	Tuolumne Jacksonville	71	168
TRONSEN			
John*	San Francisco San Francisco 11	67	139
TRONSON			
Christopher	Sierra Gibsonville	66	852
TRONT			
George	Yolo Washington	72	599
TRONY			
---	Calaveras Twp 10	57	284
TROO			
---	Tuolumne Twp 5	71	524
TROOKEY			
John*	Sierra La Porte	66	789
TROOKS			
---	Klamath Liberty	59	234
TROOLIE			
Victor*	Yuba Fosters	72	835
TROOMEN			
Geo	Sacramento Natonia	63	271
TROPATH			
Edward*	Calaveras Twp 9	57	371
TROPE			
Alex*	Sacramento Ward 4	63	589
John*	El Dorado White Oaks	58	1015
Peter*	Sacramento Ward 4	63	544
TROPHRIA			
Maria	Siskiyou Yreka	69	175
TROPMAN			
George	Sierra Twp 7	66	870
TROPP			
William	Tuolumne Twp 1	71	261
William	Tuolumne Twp 1	71	261
TROQUE			
T	San Francisco San Francisco 6	67	474
TRORARTHY			
James*	Santa Cruz Pajaro	66	546
TRORY			
Joseph	Tuolumne Green Springs	71	519
TROSDELL			
C	Tuolumne Twp 4	71	168
TROSPES			
S L	Sonoma Bodega	69	534
TROSSE			
Alex*	Sacramento Ward 4	63	589
Peter*	Sacramento Ward 4	63	544
TROTH			
Geo*	Alameda Brooklyn	55	212
TROTHER			
Lucy	San Francisco San Francisco 2	67	747
TROTMAN			
John*	El Dorado Mud Springs	58	1000
TROTT			
Saml	Placer Rattle Snake	62	628
TROTTER			
A W	Amador Twp 3	55	376
Jas	Mariposa Twp 1	60	664
Jas	San Francisco San Francisco 1	68	930

California 1860 Census Index

Name	County Locale	M653 Roll	Page
TROTTER			
R	Shasta Shasta	66	677
W	El Dorado Diamond	58	790
Wm*	Trinity Weaverville	70	1066
TROTTIR			
Jas	Mariposa Twp 1	60	664
TROTY			
John	Yolo Washington	72	569
TROUBADOR			
---*	Amador Twp 1	55	484
TROUBEMEKE			
---*	Tulara Visalia	71	35
TROUBRIDGE			
J D*	Yuba Rose Bar	72	791
TROUGHTON			
Jas	Butte Bidwell	56	710
TROULEMEKE			
---	Tulara Twp 2	71	35
TROUNDEL			
A	El Dorado Placerville	58	819
TROUP			
William	El Dorado Georgetown	58	693
TROUPE			
C	Merced Twp 1	60	896
TROURE			
P*	Yuba Fosters	72	822
TROURLSEN			
Edward*	Calaveras Twp 5	57	183
TROURLSON			
Edward*	Calaveras Twp 6	57	183
TROUSDALE			
John*	Mariposa Coulterville	60	697
M	Calaveras Twp 9	57	404
TROUSDELL			
C*	Tuolumne Jacksonville	71	168
TROUSE			
J S	Nevada Nevada	61	320
TROUSSEAN			
Louis	Tuolumne Green Springs	71	527
TROUSSEAU			
Louis	Tuolumne Twp 5	71	527
TROUST			
Chas	San Francisco San Francisco 2	67	783
TROUT			
Chas	Sacramento Ward 4	63	572
J A S	Tuolumne Shawsfla	71	391
TROUTEN			
Wm	Los Angeles Tejon	59	526
TROUTMAN			
A	Sacramento Ward 3	63	432
C G	Nevada Grass Valley	61	238
Henry	Sacramento Ward 3	63	458
TROUTON			
Wm	Los Angeles Tejon	59	526
TROVER			
D*	Mariposa Twp 3	60	609
TROVERS			
Edwin	Mendocino Calpella	60	813
TROVETT			
Charles W	Sierra La Porte	66	768
TROVINGER			
Geo	Butte Kimshaw	56	601
TROWAE			
---*	Fresno Twp 2	59	18
TROWBRIDGE			
J D*	Yuba Rose Bar	72	791
L B*	Siskiyou Cottonwood	69	107
L B*	Siskiyou Cottonwoood	69	108
TROWELSON			
Edward*	Calaveras Twp 6	57	183
Edwerd*	Calaveras Twp 6	57	183
Edwud*	Calaveras Twp 6	57	183
TROWILLE			
Jaques	El Dorado Greenwood	58	715
Justin	El Dorado Greenwood	58	715
TROWILSEN			
Edward*	Calaveras Twp 5	57	183
TROWLRIDGE			
J D*	Yuba Rose Bar	72	791
TROWSKY			
Mary	Sonoma Santa Rosa	69	391
Mary O	Sonoma Santa Rosa	69	391
TROXEL			
Henry	Sierra Twp 5	66	917
TROXELL			
B B	Yolo Slate Ra	72	705
TROY			
---	Yolo No E Twp	72	681
---	Yuba North Ea	72	681
Daniel	Sonoma Armally	69	500
John H	Contra Costa Twp 3	57	612
Lucy*	Calaveras Twp 10	57	246
Mary	San Francisco San Francisco 12	67	379
Pat	Siskiyou Scott Va	69	56
Patrick	Contra Costa Twp 3	57	617
TROY			
Sam*	San Francisco San Francisco 11	67	146
Thomas	Tuolumne Springfield	71	370
Thomas D	Sierra St Louis	66	809
William H	San Francisco San Francisco 3	67	61
TRPARO			
Jose	Santa Cruz Watsonville	66	539
TRU			
---	Amador Twp 5	55	346
A	Sacramento Granite	63	259
D B*	Nevada Nevada	61	245
Wa	Nevada Nevada	61	300
TRUAN			
H A	Nevada Grass Valley	61	216
TRUAZOGY			
S*	El Dorado Georgetown	58	697
TRUBECK			
Herman	Alameda Brooklyn	55	134
TRUBERG			
Francisco	San Bernardino Santa Ba	64	218
TRUBODY			
Josiah	Napa Yount	61	39
Josiah S	Napa Yount	61	40
Josiah*	Napa Yount	61	39
TRUBROECK			
J*	Sacramento Ward 1	63	19
TRUCHUR			
Carl	San Francisco San Francisco 4	68	1154
TRUCKEE			
---	Tulara Twp 2	71	35
---	Tulara Twp 2	71	37
---*	Tulara Visalia	71	35
---*	Tulara Visalia	71	37
TRUCKER			
August*	San Francisco San Francisco 1	68	812
TRUCKMENENE			
---	Tulara Twp 2	71	35
TRUCKNENENE			
---*	Tulara Visalia	71	35
TRUCKS			
Michael M	Calaveras Twp 6	57	147
Nicholas	Plumas Quincy	62	961
Theodore A	Calaveras Twp 6	57	147
TRUCKSFORD			
James	Plumas Meadow Valley	62	905
TRUDELL			
Joseph	Placer Iona Hills	62	892
TRUDELLE			
Leander	Amador Twp 5	55	362
TRUDER			
E	Sacramento Ward 1	63	149
TRUDFETTER			
Andrew*	Siskiyou Shasta Valley	69	121
TRUE			
---	Sacramento Granite	63	245
A	Sacramento Ward 1	63	89
A P	Tuolumne Columbia	71	335
C F	Amador Twp 3	55	393
Elijah	Napa Napa	61	94
Elyah	Napa Napa	61	94
G L	Calaveras Twp 9	57	378
James M*	Amador Twp 4	55	131
Nelson	Sierra Pine Grove	66	828
S H	Mariposa Twp 3	60	621
T	Sacramento Ward 1	63	89
Thomas	Plumas Quincy	62	923
Wm	Mariposa Twp 3	60	618
TRUEBODDIE			
John	San Francisco San Francisco 4	68	1114
TRUEDELL			
Eugene	Amador Twp 5	55	361
TRUEDEN			
H	Butte Chico	56	563
TRUEED			
W*	Yolo Cottonwoood	72	556
TRUEL			
A	San Joaquin Stockton	64	1089
TRUELOVE			
Chs C	Napa Napa	61	75
Sarah	Tulara Twp 1	71	108
TRUELSON			
Crist*	Tuolumne Columbia	71	332
T	Tuolumne Twp 2	71	273
TRUELT			
Neil*	Alameda Brooklyn	55	114
TRUEMAN			
---	Fresno Twp 2	59	111
A*	Sutter Butte	70	780
Jno	Alameda Brooklyn	55	157
L A	El Dorado Placerville	58	889
TRUEPLAR			
J	Nevada Eureka	61	381
TRUER			
Edward	San Joaquin Elkhorn	64	985
TRUES			
Felipe	San Diego Colorado	64	811
TRUESDALE			
S V	San Francisco San Francisco 5	67	485
TRUESDALL			
Geo	Placer Folsom	62	647
TRUESDELL			
Jesser*	Placer Secret R	62	615
Levi	Placer Secret R	62	615
O P	San Francisco San Francisco 5	67	506
TRUET			
Mary J	Santa Clara Santa Clara	65	505
TRUETT			
H B	San Francisco San Francisco 5	67	546
Isaac	Butte Chico	56	531
Meyers	Calaveras Twp 8	57	70
Miles T	San Francisco San Francisco 3	67	41
Neil*	Alameda Brooklyn	55	114
O	Solano Vacaville	69	321
Pamier*	Solano Vacaville	69	340
Panner*	Solano Vacaville	69	340
Wm	Sacramento Ward 1	63	32
TRUETTE			
J	Siskiyou Klamath	69	87
John	Tuolumne Twp 2	71	321
TRUEWORT			
C	San Francisco San Francisco 5	67	553
TRUEWORTH			
C	San Francisco San Francisco 5	67	553
TRUEWRATHE			
James	Tuolumne Twp 1	71	262
TRUEX			
J C	Placer Virginia	62	672
TRUEY			
Patrick	Sierra Pine Grove	66	831
TRUFANT			
P	Trinity Weaverville	70	1079
TRUFF			
Francis	Santa Clara Santa Clara	65	482
TRUFLECH			
Geo*	Alameda Oakland	55	46
TRUGADA			
Juan	San Bernardino Santa Barbara	64	190
TRUGAMBO			
James*	Sierra Twp 5	66	940
TRUGHMAN			
John M	Tuolumne Sonora	71	217
TRUGO			
Laura*	Yuba Marysville	72	876
TRUGON			
Charles W*	Sierra Scales D	66	802
TRUILSON			
Crest	Tuolumne Twp 2	71	332
TRUIT			
Daniel*	Sierra Twp 7	66	866
TRUITFETTER			
Andrew*	Siskiyou Shasta Valley	69	121
TRUITT			
John R	Sonoma Healdsbu	69	476
M K	Sonoma Washington	69	672
TRUIY			
Patrick*	Sierra Pine Grove	66	831
TRUJILLO			
Jose	Monterey San Juan	60	1002
TRUJIO			
Celestino	Monterey Monterey	60	947
Guadalupe	Monterey Monterey	60	947
TRULL			
John	Tuolumne Twp 4	71	129
TRULLOCH			
James	Amador Twp 3	55	387
TRULY			
Geo*	Monterey Monterey	60	963
TRUMAN			
A J	Los Angeles Tejon	59	538
B A	Nevada Grass Valley	61	222
C W	El Dorado Placerville	58	871
Elizabeth	San Francisco San Francisco 12	67	362
G C	El Dorado Georgetown	58	759
G W	El Dorado Placerville	58	866
Geo	Sacramento Natonia	63	271
J R	El Dorado Placerville	58	864
Jacob	Placer Iona Hills	62	898
James M	Mendocino Big Rock	60	874
John	Butte Cascade	56	695
John	Placer Iona Hills	62	898
Louis*	Alameda Brooklyn	55	135
Michael*	Sacramento Ward 4	63	606
P	Nevada Grass Valley	61	218
Samuel*	Tulara Twp 1	71	96
Stephen D*	Mariposa Coulterville	60	677
Wm	El Dorado Greenwood	58	708
Wm	Nevada Eureka	61	348
TRUMBALL			
Richard B*	Yuba Marysville	72	969

Name	County Locale	M653 RollPage
TRUMBER		
Chas	San Francisco San Francisco	9 681086
TRUMBILL		
James	Yuba New York	72 729
TRUMBLEY		
Wm H*	San Francisco San Francisco	1 68 847
TRUMBLY		
Julian	Yuba Marysville	72 914
TRUMBULL		
David	Mariposa Coulterville	60 695
Dvid	Mariposa Coulterville	60 695
George	Plumas Quincy	62 966
James	Yuba New York	72 729
John	Placer Michigan	62 830
Luther	Placer Michigan	62 827
Peter	San Joaquin Stockton	641042
Richard B	Yuba Marysville	72 969
S B	Nevada Grass Valley	61 166
TRUMIAN		
Wm*	Nevada Eureka	61 348
TRUMONT		
James	Monterey San Juan	60 990
TRUMP		
Wm	San Francisco San Francisco	2 67 692
TRUMPLE		
George	Yuba Bear Rvr	721001
TRUMPLER		
J C	Tehama Pasakent	70 858
Janbury	Yolo Washington	72 573
John	Tehama Pasakent	70 858
TRUMPS		
Henry	San Francisco San Francisco	9 681019
TRUNBACK		
Christian	El Dorado White Oaks	581022
TRUNBALL		
John*	El Dorado Big Bar	58 744
TRUNER		
Thomas*	El Dorado Salmon Falls	581052
TRUNEY		
Isaac B*	Calaveras Twp 6	57 154
TRUNK		
J*	Sutter Yuba	70 772
TRUNMAN		
Jos*	Butte Ophir	56 817
TRUNNAN		
Wm*	Nevada Eureka	61 348
TRUO		
---	El Dorado Union	581090
A P	Tuolumne Columbia	71 338
TRUOWGY		
S*	El Dorado Georgetown	58 697
TRUR		
---*	Sacramento Granite	63 245
Nelson*	Sierra Pine Grove	66 828
TRURAN		
John	Amador Twp 4	55 238
TRUREST		
Fredreck*	Mariposa Coulterville	60 700
TRURGOUR		
Wm	Tuolumne Twp 1	71 242
TRUROY		
Leonard	Yolo Slate Ra	72 709
TRURY		
Patrick*	Sierra Pine Grove	66 831
TRUSCOT		
Fredreck	Mariposa Coulterville	60 700
TRUSDALE		
Andrew	Santa Cruz Pescadero	66 646
TRUSE		
C*	Nevada Grass Valley	61 166
Michael	Yuba Marysville	72 969
TRUSGOVE		
Wm	Tuolumne Sonora	71 242
TRUSH		
Geo	Sacramento Cosumnes	63 404
TRUSIP		
Wm*	Amador Twp 6	55 443
TRUSSEL		
Alfonzo	Monterey Alisal	601028
W	Sacramento San Joaquin	63 359
TRUSSELL		
H G	San Bernardino Santa Barbara	64 186
Wm	Sacramento Dry Crk	63 378
TRUST		
Anderno	Santa Cruz Santa Cruz	66 614
Andrew	Santa Cruz Santa Cruz	66 614
Andruo	Santa Cruz Santa Cruz	66 614
Jacob	Santa Cruz Santa Cruz	66 613
TRUSTAY		
B	San Francisco San Francisco	1 68 930
TRUSTIN		
Chambers	Sonoma Petaluma	69 544
TRUTH		
A	El Dorado Coloma	581117
Conrad	Santa Clara Gilroy	65 224
Geo*	Alameda Brooklyn	55 212
TRUTMAN		
N W	Sacramento Ward 1	63 61
TRUTTE		
Alfred H	San Luis Obispo	65 8
	San Luis Obispo	
TRUULDE		
Thomas*	Calaveras Twp 6	57 161
TRUVETT		
J C*	Butte Oro	56 684
TRUWELL		
Isaac	Tehama Moons	70 852
TRUXELL		
B B	Yuba Slate Ro	72 705
TRUXILLO		
---*	San Diego Agua Caliente	64 849
TRUY		
J W*	Nevada Eureka	61 371
TRUZLOFF		
William	Calaveras Twp 4	57 308
TRVEED		
W*	Yolo Cottonwoood	72 556
TRWAY		
---	Fresno Twp 1	59 30
TRWIN		
Thomas*	Sierra Poker Flats	66 838
W H*	San Francisco San Francisco	10 222 67
TRY		
---	Amador Twp 5	55 356
R F	Amador Twp 3	55 369
TRYAN		
E	Siskiyou Yreka	69 153
George	Calaveras Twp 8	57 64
Joseph*	Siskiyou Yreka	69 133
TRYCE		
James	San Bernardino Santa Barbara	64 169
TRYE		
---	Placer Virginia	62 677
TRYK		
Kellie	Sonoma Petaluma	69 599
TRYLOR		
George	Monterey Monterey	60 960
TRYMAN		
Wm	Yolo Slate Ra	72 692
TRYON		
A G	Sacramento Ward 3	63 422
Albert	Sacramento Ward 4	63 574
Dolphin*	Del Norte Crescent	58 644
Ezra	Yolo Putah	72 548
Jas	Napa Clear Lake	61 138
Julia	San Francisco San Francisco	7 681433
Linos	Sacramento Ward 3	63 449
Philo	Sacramento Ward 3	63 456
Syl	Sacramento Ward 3	63 456
TRYOU		
Dolphin*	Del Norte Crescent	58 644
TRYVER		
Peter*	San Francisco San Francisco	9 681099
TSAN		
---	Amador Twp 2	55 274
TSEMAN		
Jonathan*	Sierra Scales D	66 803
TSING		
---	El Dorado Greenwood	58 732
TSN		
Jih*	El Dorado Georgetown	58 692
Lee	El Dorado Georgetown	58 747
TSOO		
Towo	Tuolumne Twp 5	71 526
TSU		
---*	El Dorado Greenwood	58 729
Jih*	El Dorado Georgetown	58 692
Stu	El Dorado Georgetown	58 748
TSUENG		
---	Fresno Twp 2	59 4
TSUNN		
Kee	San Francisco San Francisco	6 67 474
TTOM		
Chin	Yuba Long Bar	72 756
TU		
---	Calaveras Twp 6	57 168
---	Calaveras Twp 10	57 276
---	Calaveras Twp 8	57 94
---	El Dorado Union	581089
---	El Dorado Georgetown	58 692
---	El Dorado Georgetown	58 703
---	El Dorado Georgetown	58 762
---	Mariposa Twp 1	60 658
---	Mariposa Coulterville	60 681
---	Mariposa Coulterville	60 690
---	Sacramento Granite	63 232
---	Sacramento Cosumnes	63 386
---	San Francisco San Francisco	4 681187
---	San Francisco San Francisco	4 681188
---	San Francisco San Francisco	4 681193
---	San Francisco San Francisco	5 671205
TU		
---	San Francisco San Francisco	4 681210
---	San Francisco San Francisco	4 681212
---	Sierra Downieville	661032
---	Sierra Downieville	66 980
---	Yolo No E Twp	72 682
---	Yuba North Ea	72 682
---	Yuba Fosters	72 843
---*	Calaveras Twp 10	57 270
---*	Shasta Shasta	66 670
---*	Trinity Weaverville	701053
A	Sacramento Granite	63 268
Ah	Nevada Nevada	61 300
Boy	San Francisco San Francisco	4 681175
Cory	Calaveras Twp 5	57 254
Coy*	Calaveras Twp 5	57 254
Fo	San Francisco San Francisco	4 681180
Fu	San Francisco San Francisco	4 681190
Goey	San Francisco San Francisco	4 681187
Goey	San Francisco San Francisco	4 681188
Ho	San Francisco San Francisco	4 681189
Ho	San Francisco San Francisco	4 681202
Hoo	San Francisco San Francisco	5 67 490
Hu	San Francisco San Francisco	4 681203
Ko	San Francisco San Francisco	4 681204
Loey	San Francisco San Francisco	4 681188
Loi	San Francisco San Francisco	4 681204
Pan	El Dorado Diamond	58 783
Po	Amador Twp 2	55 327
Poo	San Francisco San Francisco	5 67 510
San	El Dorado Coloma	581078
San	San Francisco San Francisco	4 681180
Sang	San Francisco San Francisco	11 159 67
Song	Plumas Quincy	621009
Suny	Calaveras Twp 10	57 271
TUA		
---	Calaveras Twp 5	57 175
---	Sierra Downieville	66 986
---*	Calaveras Twp 6	57 175
TUADO		
Victor	Tehama Tehama	70 936
TUAM		
---	Sierra Downieville	66 982
TUAN		
---	Sierra Downieville	66 982
---*	Sierra Twp 7	66 899
TUANG		
---	Plumas Quincy	62 926
TUARTZ		
B*	El Dorado Kelsey	581152
TUAS		
Jos Venita	Mariposa Twp 3	60 548
TUAW		
---*	Sierra Twp 7	66 899
TUBB		
William H	Tuolumne Twp 5	71 507
TUBBERT		
A	Amador Twp 1	55 459
TUBBEY		
Isaac	Amador Twp 2	55 297
TUBBS		
Agnus	Tuolumne Twp 1	71 217
Alfred	Alameda Brooklyn	55 111
C M*	Yolo Washington	72 569
Catharine	San Francisco San Francisco	8 681263
Edward	Butte Oro	56 680
Hiram	Alameda Brooklyn	55 111
Hiram	Los Angeles Los Angeles	59 369
Israel	Santa Clara Gilroy	65 231
J	Nevada Grass Valley	61 148
J C*	Sacramento Lee	63 210
J S	Alameda Oakland	55 57
John	San Mateo Twp 3	65 88
Mical	Alameda Brooklyn	55 112
O H	Sacramento Ward 1	63 111
S C*	Sacramento Lee	63 210
TUBBY		
Agnes	Tuolumne Sonora	71 217
Jaems	Tuolumne Twp 2	71 285
James	Tuolumne Twp 2	71 285
TUBLES		
Martin	Placer Yankee J	62 780
TUC		
---	Calaveras Twp 8	57 101
---	Sacramento Ward 1	63 51
---	Stanislaus Branch	70 714
---	Tuolumne Twp 5	71 512
TUCHS		
Adana*	Sacramento Ward 1	63 74
TUCHUR		
Carl*	San Francisco San Francisco	4 681154
TUCIN		
Lahg	Sierra Twp 7	66 877
TUCIUS		
John	Amador Twp 1	55 478

Name	County Locale	M653 Roll	Page
TUCK YE			
---	Sacramento Ward 1	63	72
TUCK			
---	Alameda Oakland	55	41
---	Amador Twp 2	55	280
---	Amador Twp 2	55	315
---	Amador Twp 2	55	326
---	Amador Twp 2	55	327
---	Amador Twp 5	55	350
---	Amador Twp 5	55	351
---	Amador Twp 5	55	352
---	Amador Twp 5	55	355
---	Amador Twp 5	55	356
---	Amador Twp 5	55	365
---	Amador Twp 5	55	368
---	Amador Twp 1	55	477
---	Amador Twp 1	55	478
---	Amador Twp 1	55	479
---	Amador Twp 1	55	489
---	Amador Twp 1	55	500
---	Amador Twp 1	55	511
---	Butte Hamilton	56	530
---	Butte Kimshaw	56	577
---	Butte Kimshaw	56	582
---	Butte Kimshaw	56	587
---	Butte Kimshaw	56	599
---	Butte Oregon	56	630
---	Calaveras Twp 8	57	109
---	Calaveras Twp 6	57	171
---	Calaveras Twp 5	57	191
---	Calaveras Twp 5	57	192
---	Calaveras Twp 5	57	203
---	Calaveras Twp 5	57	205
---	Calaveras Twp 5	57	215
---	Calaveras Twp 5	57	222
---	Calaveras Twp 5	57	234
---	Calaveras Twp 5	57	247
---	Calaveras Twp 5	57	249
---	Calaveras Twp 5	57	250
---	Calaveras Twp 5	57	251
---	Calaveras Twp 5	57	254
---	Calaveras Twp 5	57	257
---	Calaveras Twp 10	57	271
---	Calaveras Twp 10	57	272
---	Calaveras Twp 10	57	274
---	Calaveras Twp 10	57	284
---	Calaveras Twp 10	57	295
---	Calaveras Twp 4	57	320
---	Calaveras Twp 4	57	322
---	Calaveras Twp 4	57	323
---	Calaveras Twp 4	57	333
---	Calaveras Twp 4	57	343
---	Calaveras Twp 8	57	68
---	El Dorado Salmon Falls	58	1058
---	El Dorado Casumnes	58	1177
---	Mariposa Coulterville	60	683
---	Nevada Rough &	61	398
---	Nevada Rough &	61	399
---	Nevada Rough &	61	432
---	Nevada Red Dog	61	549
---	Plumas Quincy	62	926
---	Sacramento Cosummes	63	388
---	Sacramento Ward 1	63	50
---	Sacramento Ward 4	63	612
---	Sacramento Ward 1	63	68
---	Trinity Weaverville	70	1072
---	Trinity Lewiston	70	956
---	Tuolumne Columbia	71	347
---	Tuolumne Columbia	71	350
---	Tuolumne Twp 2	71	409
---	Tuolumne Twp 2	71	410
---	Tuolumne Twp 2	71	416
---	Tuolumne Twp 3	71	433
---	Tuolumne Twp 3	71	434
---	Tuolumne Twp 3	71	439
---	Tuolumne Twp 3	71	468
---	Tuolumne Twp 1	71	475
---	Tuolumne Twp 1	71	476
---	Yuba Long Bar	72	759
---	Yuba Marysville	72	969
Ah	Butte Oregon	56	630
Ah	Sacramento Ward 1	63	156
Ah	Tuolumne Twp 4	71	159
Ah	Tuolumne Twp 2	71	347
Ah	Tuolumne Twp 2	71	350
Ah	Yuba Marysville	72	969
Ca	Mariposa Twp 1	60	653
Cheng	Yuba Marysville	72	895
Chouy	Yuba Marysville	72	895
Cloo	Plumas Quincy	62	1008
Cueu	Calaveras Twp 5	57	202
Cum	Calaveras Twp 5	57	202
Ha*	Yuba Long Bar	72	755
J	Solano Vacaville	69	324
J C	Alameda Brooklyn	55	179
Jeremiah	Solano Vacaville	69	345
TUCK			
John	San Francisco San Francisco 10		224 / 67
Lein	Calaveras Twp 8	57	109
Lou	Plumas Quincy	62	1009
Mow	Calaveras Twp 5	57	246
Pete	Sacramento Ward 1	63	156
Saml	Sacramento Granite	63	222
See	Calaveras Twp 6	57	168
Set	Sacramento Ward 3	63	492
Song	Sacramento Ward 3	63	491
Ua	Mariposa Coulterville	60	682
Wa	Mariposa Coulterville	60	682
Woo	Plumas Quincy	62	1008
Woo	Plumas Meadow Valley	62	910
Woo	Plumas Quincy	62	950
Ye	Sacramento Ward 1	63	72
Yo	Sacramento Ward 3	63	493
TUCKAHANA			
---	El Dorado Kelsey	58	1132
TUCKAND			
Edward	Calaveras Twp 5	57	231
TUCKE			
---	Calaveras Twp 5	57	205
TUCKEE			
---	Tulara Twp 2	71	37
TUCKEMEA			
---	Fresno Twp 2	59	48
TUCKER			
---	Mendocino Twp 1	60	886
? F*	Nevada Eureka	61	357
A	Nevada Eureka	61	361
A W	Los Angeles Tejon	59	522
A W	Yolo Cache Crk	72	593
Alfred	Santa Clara Gilroy	65	232
Alfred J	Calaveras Twp 5	57	210
Alfred L	Calaveras Twp 5	57	210
Alfred S	Calaveras Twp 5	57	210
Allen	Nevada Little Y	61	533
Almond	Calaveras Twp 9	57	370
Ben F	Sonoma Healdsbu	69	472
Benjm	Mendocino Little L	60	834
Benjn	Mendocino Little L	60	834
C	San Francisco San Francisco 5	67	530
Celestian	Tuolumne Big Oak	71	177
Chester	Sonoma Sonoma	69	652
Chestir	Sonoma Sonoma	69	652
D	Yuba Marysville	72	943
D F*	Nevada Eureka	61	357
E	El Dorado Placerville	58	888
E	Tuolumne Big Oak	71	144
Edward	Contra Costa Twp 1	57	522
Edward	Placer Michigan	62	826
Eliza	Napa Clear Lake	61	139
Erastus	Sacramento Ward 4	63	513
Eugene	San Luis Obispo San Luis Obispo	65	28
F L	Tuolumne Sonora	71	484
F M	Calaveras Twp 9	57	373
F S	Nevada Eureka	61	343
Francis M	San Joaquin Oneal	64	937
G O	Nevada Grass Valley	61	189
G W	El Dorado Placerville	58	852
G W	San Joaquin Oneal	64	939
George	Colusa Monroeville	57	450
George	Napa Hot Springs	61	10
H	Sacramento San Joaquin	63	368
H	Siskiyou Callahan	69	9
Henry	Sacramento Ward 3	63	453
Henry	Siskiyou Yreka	69	154
Hiram	Butte Chico	56	536
Hosea	Yuba Marysville	72	917
J C	San Francisco San Francisco 10		287 / 67
J H	Calaveras Twp 9	57	370
J H	San Joaquin Stockton	64	1048
J M	Siskiyou Scott Ri	69	70
J W	Los Angeles Los Angeles	59	519
J W	Merced Twp 1	60	912
J W	San Francisco San Francisco 9	68	1104
Jacob	Tuolumne Twp 2	71	370
James	Los Angeles Los Angeles	59	507
James	Tuolumne Visalia	71	92
James T	Tulara Twp 1	71	84
Jas	Los Angeles Tejon	59	538
Jefferson	Tuolumne Montezuma	71	503
Johana	San Francisco San Francisco 3	67	31
John	Colusa Colusi	57	424
John	Contra Costa Twp 1	57	529
John	Napa Hot Springs	61	10
John	Plumas Meadow Valley	62	905
John	Plumas Quincy	62	976
John	San Francisco San Francisco 3	67	31
John	Yuba Marysville	72	971
John F	Yuba Rose Bar	72	814
John J	Yuba Marysville	72	967
Joseph	Yolo Slate Ra	72	707
TUCKER			
Joseph	Yuba Marysville	72	859
Joseph	Yuba Marysville	72	860
Joseph W	El Dorado Spanish	58	1125
Joseph W	Los Angeles Los Angeles	59	365
L*	Sacramento Brighton	63	204
Lawrence	Tulara Twp 2	71	33
Leonard	Sierra St Louis	66	812
Leonard B	Sierra St Louis	66	812
Levi	Placer Secret R	62	615
Lewis	Siskiyou Scott Va	69	27
M	Nevada Eureka	61	356
Maria K*	Mariposa Twp 3	60	604
Martin	Amador Twp 4	55	332
Mary	Yuba Marysville	72	933
Matilda	Calaveras Twp 5	57	246
Mikasa	Tulara Yule Rvr	71	23
Morgan G	Del Norte Klamath	58	652
N M	Sacramento Alabama	63	414
Nion	San Francisco San Francisco 7	68	1429
Orson	Yuba Marysville	72	968
Phillip	Fresno Twp 1	59	75
R F	Butte Chico	56	553
R P	Napa Hot Springs	61	10
Richard	Fresno Twp 1	59	75
Robert	Colusa Butte Crk	57	466
Rosina	San Francisco San Francisco 1	68	812
S	Calaveras Twp 9	57	403
S	Nevada Grass Valley	61	187
S F	Nevada Eureka	61	357
S G	Calaveras Twp 9	57	403
S N	Butte Cascade	56	697
S S	Napa Napa	61	107
S*	Sacramento Brighton	63	204
Saml	San Francisco San Francisco 2	67	739
Samuel	Marin S Antoni	60	710
Sarah	San Francisco San Francisco 2	67	739
Stephen	Napa Clear Lake	61	121
Tho	Siskiyou Scott Va	69	41
Thos J	Napa Yount	61	42
Truston H	Sierra Pine Grove	66	834
W H	San Joaquin Stockton	64	1097
W W	Butte Cascade	56	693
Warren	Tuolumne Sonora	71	191
Washington	San Joaquin Oneal	64	939
William	Placer Iona Hills	62	867
William	San Joaquin Castoria	64	899
William	Tuolumne Columbia	71	365
William R	Tuolumne Chinese	71	497
TUCKERK			
Maria*	Mariposa Twp 3	60	604
TUCKERMAN			
Mathew	Calaveras Twp 5	57	204
TUCKERT			
Charles	El Dorado Mud Springs	58	962
TUCKES			
Warren	Tuolumne Twp 1	71	191
TUCKET			
Carl	San Francisco San Francisco 4	68	1154
TUCKEY			
F	Sacramento Sutter	63	307
Jas	San Francisco San Francisco 1	68	915
Z M	El Dorado Diamond	58	769
TUCKFIELD			
Joseph	Tuolumne Twp 2	71	290
TUCKIN			
John	Sierra Excelsior	66	1034
TUCKIR			
G	Calaveras Twp 9	57	414
TUCKMAYER			
Stephen A	San Luis Obispo	65	40
	San Luis Obispo		
TUCKS			
---	Amador Twp 5	55	347
TUCKSFORD			
W	Shasta Shasta	66	731
TUCKSON			
Lena*	Alameda Brooklyn	55	136
TUCKY			
John	Amador Twp 5	55	360
TUDE			
---	Yolo Slate Ra	72	712
TUDELL			
F	Sacramento Granite	63	235
TUDIAN			
Eliza*	Yuba Bear Rvr	72	1002
TUDLES			
Wm	Sacramento Lee	63	217
TUDON			
Benja F	Calaveras Twp 10	57	266
Benjo F	Calaveras Twp 10	57	266
Louis*	San Francisco San Francisco 3	67	80
TUDOR			
Abram	Amador Twp 1	55	474
Wm	Amador Twp 1	55	511
TUDSBURY			
W S	El Dorado Union	58	1090

Name	County Locale	M653 Roll	Page
TUDSBURY			
W T	El Dorado Union	58	1090
TUDY			
Adam	Amador Twp 5	55	339
TUE			
---	Amador Twp 4	55	246
---	El Dorado Georgetown	58	693
---	Sacramento Granite	63	259
---	Sierra Twp 5	66	931
---	Sierra Downieville	66	980
---	Sierra Downieville	66	981
---	Sierra Downieville	66	983
An	Del Norte Crescent	58	630
TUECKY			
Saul*	Sierra Twp 5	66	920
TUEDY			
William*	Placer Michigan	62	850
TUEG			
---*	Plumas Quincy	62	1008
TUEK			
---	El Dorado Mud Springs	58	985
Quan	Butte Ophir	56	812
TUELEY			
William H	San Joaquin Castoria	64	899
TUERSON			
Thos	Sonoma Petaluma	69	557
TUES			
Wm	Amador Twp 3	55	369
TUEY			
---*	Mariposa Coulterville	60	687
---*	Trinity Honest B	70	1043
TUFFELL			
Homey	San Joaquin Stockton	64	1074
TUFFIELD			
Jacques	San Francisco San Francisco 11	67	151
TUFFLY			
George	Sierra Scales D	66	802
TUFFMAN			
Charles M	Sierra La Porte	66	774
TUFFS			
L	Marin Cortemad	60	752
TUFFY			
George	Sierra Scales D	66	802
TUFKIN			
I G	Amador Twp 2	55	313
J G*	Amador Twp 2	55	313
TUFORTA			
Mitchel	Calaveras Twp 6	57	167
TUFT			
Maggie	San Francisco San Francisco 11	67	133
TUFTO			
A D	Sacramento Ward 3	63	431
TUFTS			
A L	Sacramento Ward 4	63	497
C H	Nevada Bridgeport	61	450
John	Sierra Twp 7	66	892
Joshua	Solano Fremont	69	376
O H	Nevada Bridgeport	61	450
Saml	San Francisco San Francisco 10	67	193
TUFY			
Mary	El Dorado Diamond	58	764
TUG			
---	Amador Twp 2	55	291
---	Amador Twp 2	55	293
---	El Dorado Placerville	58	919
TUGASKIS			
George	Sierra Eureka	66	1045
TUGENHEIN			
Johanna*	San Francisco San Francisco 9	68	972
TUGG			
S*	Nevada Grass Valley	61	195
TUGMAN			
Wm	Sierra Downieville	66	994
TUHAIN			
Charles*	Contra Costa Twp 2	57	539
TUHMAN			
H	Siskiyou Yreka	69	187
TUI			
---	Amador Twp 2	55	291
---	Mariposa Coulterville	60	692
---	Sierra Downieville	66	982
---*	Mariposa Twp 3	60	589
Fas	Calaveras Twp 5	57	193
Wah*	Butte Ophir	56	809
TUICHEL			
A P*	Nevada Red Dog	61	548
TUILLALY			
Joseph*	San Bernardino San Bernadino	64	635
TUILY			
Geo*	Monterey Monterey	60	963
TUIN			
---	Nevada Nevada	61	303
Ann	Shasta Millvill	66	750

Name	County Locale	M653 Roll	Page
TUINGA			
Manuel	Merced Monterey	60	930
Manuel*	Monterey Monterey	60	930
TUIR			
---	Sierra Downieville	66	981
TUIRS			
A*	El Dorado Diamond	58	795
TUIS			
---	Sierra Twp 5	66	947
TUISIH			
Wm*	Amador Twp 6	55	443
TUISIP			
Wm*	Amador Twp 6	55	443
TUITE			
John	San Francisco San Francisco 5	67	544
Michael	San Francisco San Francisco 2	67	629
TUITX			
John*	San Francisco San Francisco 5	67	544
TUJY			
---*	Calaveras Twp 8	57	109
TUK SAM			
---	Tuolumne Chinese	71	523
TUK			
---	San Francisco San Francisco 10	67	355
---	Shasta French G	66	712
Lom	Tuolumne Twp 6	71	537
Moon	Tuolumne Knights	71	529
San	Tuolumne Twp 5	71	523
TUKCER			
? F	Nevada Eureka	61	357
TUKE			
---	Butte Kimshaw	56	606
---	Yuba Slate Ro	72	712
---	Yuba Slate Ro	72	713
TUKEY			
F	Sacramento Sutter	63	306
Francis	Sacramento Ward 1	63	46
TUL			
---	Sierra Downieville	66	980
Jas*	Merced Twp 1	60	913
TULA			
---	San Diego San Diego	64	771
TULAMAN			
---	Butte Chico	56	550
TULAR			
Wm	Nevada Nevada	61	246
TULBI			
Justine	Tuolumne Twp 2	71	473
TULCEN			
Frank	Sacramento Granite	63	240
TULE			
---	Fresno Twp 1	59	118
---	Tulara Twp 2	71	37
---	Tulara Twp 2	71	40
TULEY			
---*	Sierra Twp 5	66	942
John*	Placer Rattle Snake	62	632
Samuel	Klamath Klamath	59	226
Theodore	Trinity Weaverville	70	1053
TULIO			
Josephine*	Calaveras Twp 4	57	330
TULKEY			
Elizabeth	San Francisco San Francisco 9	68	1008
TULKINGTON			
Warner	Plumas Quincy	62	957
TULKS			
A*	San Mateo Twp 3	65	88
TULL			
C C	San Joaquin Douglass	64	921
J W	Shasta Shasta	66	662
John R	Plumas Quincy	62	991
John W	Contra Costa Twp 2	57	557
L R	Trinity Lewiston	70	953
Nichols	San Joaquin Douglass	64	921
S F*	Shasta Shasta	66	662
S R	Trinity Lewiston	70	953
Stephen	Klamath Salmon	59	213
Virgil	Sierra Pine Grove	66	823
Wm	El Dorado Georgetown	58	696
TULLAR			
A H	El Dorado Salmon Falls	58	1034
TULLE			
Henry A	San Francisco San Francisco 8	68	1265
TULLER			
C H	Nevada Little Y	61	531
S L	Nevada Rough &	61	405
T A	Tuolumne Twp 4	71	147
TULLES			
David A	San Joaquin Castoria	64	901
TULLEY			
J	Nevada Eureka	61	344
L	Siskiyou Scott Va	69	51
TULLIS			
R	El Dorado Mountain	58	1190
TULLOCK			
D W	Stanislaus Emory	70	737

Name	County Locale	M653 Roll	Page
TULLOCK			
Wm	Trinity Douglas	70	980
TULLY			
Daniel	Solano Benecia	69	316
David	Napa Clear Lake	61	140
E C	Santa Clara Gilroy	65	250
J	Nevada Eureka	61	354
J	San Francisco San Francisco 1	68	836
J*	Nevada Eureka	61	354
James	Tuolumne Columbia	71	300
John	Sacramento Ward 1	63	122
John	San Francisco San Francisco 1	68	849
John*	Santa Clara San Jose	65	355
Julia	San Joaquin Stockton	64	1016
Leoinda*	Contra Costa Twp 1	57	535
Leonard	Napa Hot Springs	61	27
Margaret	San Francisco San Francisco 2	67	745
Marjaret	San Francisco San Francisco 2	67	745
O N	Santa Clara San Jose	65	355
P B	Santa Clara Gilroy	65	254
Rosanna	Placer Todds Va	62	786
Teoinda*	Contra Costa Twp 1	57	535
Thos	San Francisco San Francisco 9	68	986
W P	Nevada Nevada	61	314
Wm	San Francisco San Francisco 1	68	931
TULO			
---	Los Angeles Los Nieto	59	439
TULSIFHER			
O	Sacramento Ward 4	63	527
TULTON			
J L*	Sacramento Franklin	63	317
Samuel*	Tulara Twp 1	71	89
TULTZ			
M	Siskiyou Cottonwoood	69	107
TULUCE			
---	Mendocino Twp 1	60	890
TULVERT			
G H	San Joaquin Oneal	64	937
TULY			
John M	Calaveras Twp 5	57	212
TUM STEEDEN			
J	San Francisco San Francisco 5	67	530
TUM			
---	Amador Twp 2	55	291
---	Amador Twp 2	55	323
---	Amador Twp 5	55	342
---	Amador Twp 6	55	434
---	Amador Twp 6	55	450
---	Amador Twp 1	55	457
---	Amador Twp 1	55	458
---	Amador Twp 1	55	477
---	Calaveras Twp 8	57	101
---	Calaveras Twp 5	57	225
---	Mariposa Twp 3	60	579
---	Mariposa Twp 3	60	588
---	Mariposa Twp 1	60	643
---	Nevada Grass Valley	61	229
---	Nevada Grass Valley	61	233
---	Nevada Washington	61	342
---	Placer Virginia	62	680
---	Sacramento Cosumnes	63	387
---*	Mariposa Twp 3	60	579
---*	Nevada Rough &	61	399
Chow*	Nevada Washington	61	342
Hi	Calaveras Twp 8	57	84
Tung*	Butte Kimshaw	56	586
TUMAN			
Mich*	Sacramento Ward 1	63	83
TUMBALL			
John*	El Dorado Big Bar	58	744
TUME			
P R*	Nevada Nevada	61	239
TUMER			
Albrige	Nevada Rough &	61	415
J N	Nevada Nevada	61	325
James	San Joaquin Elkhorn	64	949
John	San Joaquin Elkhorn	64	971
TUMERS			
G	Calaveras Twp 9	57	403
TUMERY			
D	Sacramento Sutter	63	308
TUMEY			
Mary*	San Francisco San Francisco 1	68	887
S D	Sierra Twp 7	66	912
TUMF			
Randolph*	San Francisco 9	68	1106
	San Francisco		
TUMFRUS			
F S	Santa Clara San Jose	65	301
TUMINS			
G	Calaveras Twp 9	57	403
TUMIPSEE			
T	Sutter Sutter	70	811
TUMIS			
James	Yolo Cache Crk	72	641
TUMISON			
F*	Nevada Eureka	61	344

Name	County Locale	M653 Roll/Page
TUMISONL		
F*	Nevada Eureka	61 344
TUMMERMAN		
J	El Dorado Casumnes	581169
Peter	Yuba Marysville	72 846
TUMMERTON		
Jno*	Sacramento Ward 4	63 547
TUMMONS		
Saml*	Mariposa Twp 1	60 645
TUMPLE		
Geo*	El Dorado Coloma	581081
TUMSEND		
John B	Sierra St Louis	66 863
TUMSHEE		
---	Tulara Twp 1	71 117
TUMWALT		
M	Sacramento Alabama	63 413
TUN CHOW		
---*	Nevada Nevada	61 307
TUN		
---	Amador Twp 2	55 323
---	Amador Twp 2	55 326
---	Amador Twp 5	55 342
---	Amador Twp 5	55 355
---	Butte Kimshaw	56 582
---	Calaveras Twp 5	57 249
---	Calaveras Twp 10	57 260
---	Calaveras Twp 10	57 269
---	Calaveras Twp 10	57 285
---	Calaveras Twp 4	57 302
---	Calaveras Twp 4	57 306
---	Calaveras Twp 4	57 324
---	Calaveras Twp 4	57 326
---	Calaveras Twp 4	57 332
---	El Dorado Salmon Hills	581058
---	Fresno Twp 1	59 30
---	Mariposa Twp 1	60 660
---	Nevada Grass Valley	61 229
---	Nevada Grass Valley	61 232
---	Nevada Nevada	61 308
---	Nevada Nevada	61 309
---	Nevada Washington	61 339
---	Nevada Washington	61 340
---	Nevada Bridgeport	61 462
---	Nevada Bridgeport	61 485
---	Sacramento Ward 1	63 59
---	San Francisco San Francisco 4	681212
---	Shasta Shasta	66 680
---	Sierra Downieville	661004
---	Sierra Downieville	661005
---	Sierra Downieville	661015
---	Sierra Downieville	661027
---	Sierra Downieville	66 981
---	Sierra Downieville	66 982
---	Stanislaus Emory	70 747
---	Trinity Weaverville	701053
---*	Nevada Washington	61 339
---*	Nevada Washington	61 340
---*	Nevada Bridgeport	61 459
---*	Sacramento Cosumnes	63 396
---*	Sacramento Cosumnes	63 398
---*	Sacramento Ward 1	63 59
---*	San Francisco San Francisco 4	681182
---*	Tuolumne Garrote	71 174
Chow	Nevada Nevada	61 308
Coy*	Calaveras Twp 5	57 254
Daniel R	San Francisco San Francisco 3	67 10
Qui	Calaveras Twp 5	57 246
TUNBO		
J F	Amador Twp 3	55 383
TUNCOR		
John	Calaveras Twp 8	57 109
TUNDERLAND		
Nancy	Shasta Cottonwoood	66 737
TUNE		
---	Butte Eureka	56 655
---	Calaveras Twp 5	57 192
---	El Dorado Coloma	581083
---	Mariposa Twp 1	60 643
---	Monterey Monterey	60 965
---	Nevada Rough &	61 426
---	Sierra Downieville	661027
---	Tuolumne Chinese	71 524
---*	Butte Hamilton	56 530
A	Sierra Twp 7	66 878
John	El Dorado Salmon Falls	581034
Paul*	San Francisco San Francisco 8	681317
TUNEG		
---*	Amador Twp 2	55 315
TUNER		
Amanda	El Dorado Georgetown	58 681
Thos H	El Dorado Big Bar	58 738
Wm	Amador Twp 6	55 449
TUNERY		
T	Mariposa Twp 3	60 584
TUNES		
Thomas*	Contra Costa Twp 3	57 601

Name	County Locale	M653 Roll/Page
TUNESDALE		
W	Yolo No E Twp	72 671
TUNEY		
---	Amador Twp 2	55 315
TUNG CHOW		
---	Nevada Nevada	61 302
TUNG FOY		
---	Sacramento Ward 1	63 59
TUNG HUNG		
---	Sacramento Ward 1	63 68
TUNG KIE		
---	Sacramento Ward 1	63 65
TUNG SING		
---	Sacramento Ward 1	63 68
TUNG TIE		
---	Nevada Bridgeport	61 458
TUNG		
---	Amador No 6	55 430
---	Amador Twp 1	55 458
---	Amador Twp 1	55 479
---	Amador Twp 1	55 480
---	Amador Twp 1	55 497
---	Amador Twp 1	55 508
---	Butte Kimshaw	56 603
---	Calaveras Twp 8	57 105
---	Calaveras Twp 6	57 131
---	Calaveras Twp 5	57 136
---	Calaveras Twp 5	57 147
---	Calaveras Twp 6	57 168
---	Calaveras Twp 6	57 169
---	Calaveras Twp 6	57 171
---	Calaveras Twp 6	57 173
---	Calaveras Twp 6	57 181
---	Calaveras Twp 5	57 205
---	Calaveras Twp 5	57 219
---	Calaveras Twp 5	57 230
---	Calaveras Twp 5	57 233
---	Calaveras Twp 5	57 255
---	Calaveras Twp 10	57 267
---	Calaveras Twp 10	57 276
---	Calaveras Twp 10	57 284
---	Calaveras Twp 10	57 291
---	Calaveras Twp 4	57 323
---	Calaveras Twp 4	57 333
---	Del Norte Crescent	58 651
---	Fresno Twp 2	59 18
---	Fresno Twp 1	59 26
---	Mariposa Twp 1	60 658
---	Mariposa Twp 1	60 661
---	Mariposa Coulterville	60 679
---	Monterey Monterey	60 965
---	Nevada Nevada	61 302
---	Nevada Red Dog	61 556
---	Placer Rattle Snake	62 601
---	Placer Horseshoe	62 650
---	Placer Virginia	62 676
---	Placer Virginia	62 678
---	Placer Virginia	62 681
---	Placer Forest H	62 771
---	Placer Forest H	62 791
---	Plumas Quincy	62 926
---	Sacramento Granite	63 233
---	Sacramento Ward 3	63 492
---	Sacramento Ward 1	63 54
---	Sacramento Ward 1	63 58
---	Sacramento Ward 1	63 59
---	Sacramento Ward 1	63 60
---	Sacramento Ward 1	63 68
---	San Francisco San Francisco 9	681093
---	San Francisco San Francisco 2	67 688
---	Shasta Horsetown	66 708
---	Sierra Downieville	661029
---	Sierra St Louis	66 816
---	Trinity Mouth Ca	701017
---	Trinity Mouth Ca	701018
---	Trinity Taylor'S	701033
---	Trinity Big Flat	701042
---	Trinity Trininad Rvr	701047
---	Trinity Weaverville	701076
---	Trinity Lewiston	70 964
---	Trinity Steiner	70 999
---	Tuolumne Columbia	71 347
---	Tuolumne Twp 3	71 439
---	Tuolumne Twp 3	71 440
---	Tuolumne Sonora	71 475
---	Tuolumne Twp 6	71 531
---	Tuolumne Twp 6	71 536
---	Tuolumne Don Pedro	71 538
---	Tuolumne Twp 6	71 539
---	Yolo No E Twp	72 679
---	Yolo No E Twp	72 683
---	Yuba Slate Ro	72 713
---	Yuba Long Bar	72 758
---	Yuba Long Bar	72 760
---	Yuba Long Bar	72 770
---	Yuba Fosters	72 841

Name	County Locale	M653 Roll/Page
TUNG		
---	Yuba Marysville	72 916
---*	Butte Kimshaw	56 586
---*	El Dorado Georgetown	58 703
---*	Fresno Twp 1	59 28
---*	Placer Auburn	62 571
---*	Sacramento Mississipi	63 190
---*	Sacramento Cosumnes	63 391
---*	Trinity Big Flat	701042
---*	Yuba Foster B	72 836
---*	Yuba Marysville	72 916
A*	Tuolumne Twp 2	71 386
Ah	Sacramento Cosumnes	63 387
Ah	Tuolumne Twp 2	71 347
Chow	Nevada Nevada	61 302
Foo Chou	Yuba Long Bar	72 760
Foy*	Sacramento Ward 1	63 59
Hing	Sacramento Ward 1	63 68
Ho	Calaveras Twp 4	57 338
Hop	San Francisco San Francisco 9	681093
Kie	Sacramento Ward 1	63 65
Koo	Plumas Quincy	62 945
Mop	San Francisco San Francisco 9	681093
Nyo	San Francisco San Francisco 11	67 160
Shin	Mariposa Coulterville	60 681
Sing	Sacramento Ward 1	63 68
Tong	Sacramento Cosumnes	63 401
Won	Sacramento Cosumnes	63 389
TUNGATE		
G W	Tehama Tehama	70 936
John	Mariposa Twp 3	60 599
TUNGE		
---	Fresno Twp 1	59 27
TUNGOEY		
---	Trinity Lewiston	70 954
TUNIERIE		
Antonio*	Los Angeles Los Angeles	59 503
TUNIGA		
Manuel*	Monterey Monterey	60 930
TUNIN		
Patrick	Alameda Brooklyn	55 93
TUNIS		
Cath*	El Dorado Georgetown	58 750
Richard	San Joaquin Stockton	641053
TUNISON		
R	El Dorado Coloma	581071
TUNLIN		
James*	San Francisco San Francisco 8	681255
TUNMANS		
Stephen*	Nevada Nevada	61 251
TUNMER		
George*	Sierra Downieville	66 977
TUNMONS		
Michael	Humbolt Eureka	59 168
TUNNAN		
Patrick	Calaveras Twp 7	57 37
TUNNCEOMAN		
Peter*	Yuba Marysville	72 846
TUNNELL		
M F*	Sacramento Franklin	63 331
TUNNER		
Jard	El Dorado Georgetown	58 686
TUNNERSON		
T O	Sacramento Granite	63 237
TUNNOCK		
David	San Francisco San Francisco 2	67 697
TUNSEY		
A K*	Napa Napa	61 81
TUNSORO		
Andrew*	San Francisco San Francisco 3	67 16
TUNSTUCKEN		
---*	Mendocino Big Rvr	60 853
TUNURIE		
Antonio	Los Angeles Los Angeles	59 503
TUNY		
---	Amador Twp 5	55 364
---	Amador Twp 6	55 430
---	Calaveras Twp 5	57 205
---	Calaveras Twp 5	57 219
---	Calaveras Twp 5	57 230
---	Calaveras Twp 5	57 255
---	Calaveras Twp 10	57 267
---	Calaveras Twp 10	57 271
---	Calaveras Twp 10	57 284
---	Calaveras Twp 10	57 296
---	Calaveras Twp 4	57 320
---	Calaveras Twp 4	57 333
---	San Francisco San Francisco 4	681174
---	Tuolumne Twp 5	71 521
Chas	Placer Secret R	62 615
I M M*	El Dorado Georgetown	58 750
TUNZATE		
H B*	Los Angeles Tejon	59 537
TUO		
---	Sacramento Ward 1	63 51

TUO

Name	County Locale	Roll	Page
Lou	Stanislaus Emory	70	753
Wa	Nevada Nevada	61	303
Yen	Shasta Horsetown	66	711
TUOHEY			
Bridget	San Francisco San Francisco 2	67	669
TUOKY			
John*	San Joaquin Castoria	64	881
TUOLIE			
Victor	Yuba Foster B	72	835
TUORT			
James*	Sierra Downieville	66	1028
TUP LEE			
Lee**	Yuba Foster B	72	827
TUP			
---	El Dorado Georgetown	58	761
---	Nevada Grass Valley	61	231
---	Nevada Eureka	61	383
---	Stanislaus Emory	70	745
Lee Lee*	Yuba Foster B	72	827
Lu	El Dorado Georgetown	58	761
TUPIA			
F	Siskiyou Scott Ri	69	63
TUPIV			
Jiran*	Calaveras Twp 8	57	105
TUPKIN			
J G*	Amador Twp 2	55	313
TUPLETT			
Samuel	Solano Vacaville	69	341
TUPLEY			
Euvendich J*	Calaveras Twp 6	57	152
TUPPER			
Charles	Tuolumne Twp 1	71	240
Charles A	Contra Costa Twp 3	57	611
Charly	Tuolumne Sonora	71	240
G A	Sonoma Santa Rosa	69	413
G R	Sacramento Alabama	63	412
Harris	Alameda Brooklyn	55	87
J B	Sonoma Armally	69	500
Lemuel	Yuba Rose Bar	72	802
Maria	Alameda Brooklyn	55	87
Roswell	Humbolt Eureka	59	171
TUPPIN			
John H	Sonoma Vallejo	69	613
TUPPLE			
H D	San Francisco San Francisco 1	68	818
TUPPSE			
Jacob	Plumas Quincy	62	967
TUPPTE			
H D*	San Francisco San Francisco 1	68	818
TUQUE			
Simon*	Mariposa Twp 1	60	625
TUR			
---	Alameda Oakland	55	22
---	Amador Twp 3	55	402
---	Sierra Downieville	66	996
A	Sacramento Granite	63	268
Daniel R	San Francisco San Francisco 3	67	10
Lune	Sierra Twp 7	66	898
TURA			
Juan*	Amador Twp 2	55	288
TURAMBLY			
Chas W	Trinity McGillev	70	1021
TURARTHRY			
James	Santa Cruz Pajaro	66	546
TURARTHY			
James	Santa Cruz Pajaro	66	546
TURBIT			
Elln A	Sonoma Petaluma	69	574
TURBOLOTTE			
J H	Trinity Bates	70	967
TURCHEL			
A P*	Nevada Red Dog	61	548
TURCK			
James M	Shasta Shasta	66	653
Thomas M	Shasta Shasta	66	653
W M	Shasta Shasta	66	653
TURCKY			
Saml	Sierra Twp 5	66	920
Saul*	Sierra Twp 5	66	920
TURCONOVICH			
Georgi	San Francisco San Francisco 3	67	39
TURCOT			
P	Amador Twp 2	55	295
TUREK			
Alexander	Santa Cruz Pajaro	66	532
TUREN			
Antonia	Napa Yount	61	53
TURENO			
Manuel	San Luis Obispo San Luis Obispo	65	36
TURES			
John	Mariposa Coulterville	60	690
TURETA			
Electo	Calaveras Twp 6	57	130
TURF			
J P	San Francisco San Francisco 9	68	1069

TURFFREY

Name	County Locale	Roll	Page
Luke	Yuba Parks Ba	72	775
TURFLER			
Christina*	San Francisco San Francisco 8	68	1263
TURG			
---	Amador Twp 3	55	410
TURHERY			
John	Sierra La Porte	66	789
TURIC			
---	Tuolumne Twp 5	71	524
TURING			
John*	Plumas Quincy	62	974
TURK			
Benj	Sacramento Ward 4	63	570
Benj*	Sacramento Ward 3	63	427
David	Sonoma Sonoma	69	650
Edward E	Humbolt Table Bl	59	143
F	Siskiyou Scott Va	69	41
J B	Siskiyou Scott Va	69	45
Jno	San Francisco San Francisco 9	68	1071
Joe	Tehama Pasakent	70	856
TURKINGTON			
W	San Francisco San Francisco 5	67	489
TURKMAN			
D P	Sonoma Armally	69	507
Wm C	Butte Eureka	56	655
TURKS			
John	San Francisco San Francisco 9	68	1104
TURLETT			
Wm	Yuba Foster B	72	825
TURLEY			
David	Solano Vacaville	69	361
William*	Yuba Marysville	72	854
TURLY			
Jame*	Nevada Bridgeport	61	496
TURMAN			
Ben	Sonoma Petaluma	69	568
Benj	Sonoma Petaluma	69	576
H W*	El Dorado Placerville	58	862
Isaac	Sonoma Petaluma	69	619
L A	El Dorado Placerville	58	880
P	Nevada Grass Valley	61	218
TURMELELES			
August	San Bernardino Santa Barbara	64	190
TURMEM			
Louis*	Alameda Brooklyn	55	135
TURMEN			
John	Placer Auburn	62	590
TURN			
---	Amador Twp 5	55	352
---	Calaveras Twp 8	57	106
---	Calaveras Twp 8	57	62
---	Mariposa Twp 3	60	579
---*			
Ah	Tuolumne Twp 4	71	174
Chow	Nevada Nevada	61	307
TURNALT			
Anton	Amador Twp 1	55	478
TURNAR			
Wm*	San Francisco San Francisco 1	68	889
TURNBAKER			
A	Butte Chico	56	536
TURNBILL			
John	Amador Twp 2	55	319
TURNBULL			
Belle	San Francisco San Francisco 9	68	1105
John	Amador Twp 2	55	319
Nichol	Santa Clara Gilroy	65	225
R H	Siskiyou Yreka	69	191
Robert	Fresno Twp 2	59	48
Robert	San Joaquin Elkhorn	64	982
Robt	Tuolumne Columbia	71	307
TURNE			
W H	Butte Chico	56	551
TURNEE			
H*	Nevada Grass Valley	61	220
TURNELL			
M F*	Sacramento Franklin	63	331
TURNEN			
Robert M	Yuba Suida	72	984
TURNER			
* R*	Yuba Slate Ro	72	691
A	San Francisco San Francisco 5	67	490
A C	Butte Oregon	56	609
A C	Colusa Spring Valley	57	432
A G	San Francisco San Francisco 8	68	1254
A M	Marin Tomales	60	717
Abraham	Calaveras Twp 7	57	21
Abram	Sacramento Dry Crk	63	377
Ada	El Dorado Georgetown	58	686
Addison A	Yuba Marysville	72	860
Albrige	Nevada Rough &	61	415
Alx	Napa Napa	61	56
Amanda	El Dorado Georgetown	58	681
Andrew	Nevada Bridgeport	61	449
Andrew	San Francisco San Francisco 9	68	997
Archibald W	Yuba Linda	72	988

TURNER

Name	County Locale	Roll	Page
Archibold W	Yuba Suida	72	988
August	San Francisco San Francisco 11		90
			67
B F	Butte Chico	56	532
Barkit	Nevada Bridgeport	61	452
Benj	Sacramento Ward 3	63	434
Benjamin	Tuolumne Twp 6	71	541
Benjamin	Yuba Marysville	72	882
Benjamine	Tuolumne Don Pedro	71	541
C	San Joaquin Elkhorn	64	992
C	Sutter Butte	70	783
C H	Sacramento Cosumnes	63	381
C H	Solano Vacaville	69	321
C J	Tuolumne Twp 1	71	248
Cephas	San Francisco San Francisco 6	67	427
Ceplias	San Francisco San Francisco 6	67	427
Charles	San Francisco San Francisco 3	67	56
Chas	Butte Ophir	56	781
Chas	Sacramento Lee	63	217
Chas M	El Dorado Big Bar	58	738
Cornelius	San Francisco San Francisco 2	67	721
D	Mariposa Twp 3	60	609
D A	El Dorado Casumnes	58	1173
D S	San Francisco San Francisco 12		381
			67
Daniel	Placer Secret R	62	612
Daniel	Solano Vallejo	69	278
David	Alameda Brooklyn	55	175
David	Solano Vallejo	69	278
David	Tuolumne Twp 2	71	373
E	El Dorado Diamond	58	792
E	Sutter Butte	70	789
E	Sutter Sutter	70	806
E C	Marin Tomales	60	716
E D	Yolo Slate Ra	72	698
E D	Yolo Slate Ra	72	702
E D	Yuba Slate Ro	72	698
E D	Yuba Slate Ro	72	702
E J	Santa Clara San Jose	65	279
E J	Santa Clara San Jose	65	338
Elmond	Tuolumne Twp 2	71	283
Ephraim	Humbolt Union	59	188
Ezekiel	Yuba Slate Ro	72	696
Ezra	El Dorado Placerville	58	914
F	San Francisco San Francisco 5	67	526
F	Yuba Marysville	72	905
Frank	San Joaquin Elkhorn	64	999
Frank	Sierra Chappare	66	1040
Frank A	Colusa Spring Valley	57	433
Freeman	Yolo Slate Ra	72	694
Freeman	Yuba Slate Ro	72	694
G E	Nevada Nevada	61	261
Geo	Butte Kimshaw	56	569
Geo	Merced Twp 1	60	896
Geo	Nevada Eureka	61	394
Geo A	Tuolumne Twp 2	71	388
Geo F	Butte Kimshaw	56	596
Geo N	Tuolumne Shawsfla	71	388
Geo T	Butte Kimshaw	56	596
George	Alameda Oakland	55	67
George	Alameda Oakland	55	70
George	Mendocino Little L	60	831
George	San Francisco San Francisco 2	67	644
George	Santa Clara San Jose	65	314
George	Yuba Foster B	72	829
George	Yuba Marysville	72	959
George R	Sierra Twp 5	66	929
George*	Yuba Marysville	72	959
Georgre	Tuolumne Twp 1	71	249
Gustavus	San Francisco San Francisco 8	68	1308
H	Nevada Grass Valley	61	220
H K	Nevada Little Y	61	532
H*	Nevada Grass Valley	61	220
Hannah	Sacramento Ward 3	63	447
Harriet	Sacramento Ward 1	63	100
Harvey	Plumas Meadow Valley	62	931
Harvey	Sierra Downieville	66	995
Henry	San Joaquin Douglass	64	919
Hugh	Del Norte Crescent	58	640
I H*	Nevada Red Dog	61	547
I N	Nevada Nevada	61	325
Irs	Amador Twp 7	55	414
J	El Dorado Kelsey	58	1152
J	Nevada Grass Valley	61	225
J	Sutter Sutter	70	802
J	Tuolumne Twp 4	71	156
J Foots	Amador Twp 2	55	273
J H	Sutter Bear Rvr	70	823
J H	Tuolumne Twp 1	71	185
J H	Tuolumne Twp 2	71	352
J H*	Nevada Red Dog	61	547
J L	Merced Twp 2	60	923
J L	Tuolumne Twp 2	71	318
J M	El Dorado Casumnes	58	1173
J N	Sutter Bear Rvr	70	820

Name	County Locale	M653 RollPage
TURNER		
J N*	Nevada Nevada	61 325
J S	Nevada Grass Valley	61 221
J W	San Mateo Twp 3	65 88
Jacob	El Dorado Mud Springs	58 963
Jacob	Tuolumne Twp 5	71 508
James	El Dorado Georgetown	58 754
James	San Joaquin Castoria	64 887
James	Tuolumne Twp 1	71 249
Jard*	El Dorado Georgetown	58 686
Jaris*	El Dorado Georgetown	58 686
Jas	Placer Virginia	62 690
Jas	Sacramento Franklin	63 329
Jas	San Francisco San Francisco 1	68 859
Jim Osborn*	Humbolt Union	59 179
Jno	San Francisco San Francisco 10	208 67
Jno	Trinity Hay Fork	70 995
Joel	Amador Twp 1	55 487
John	Amador Twp 3	55 369
John	Colusa Spring Valley	57 435
John	El Dorado Greenwood	58 721
John	Los Angeles Los Angeles	59 331
John	Nevada Nevada	61 240
John	Nevada Nevada T	61 326
John	Nevada Bloomfield	61 525
John	Placer Michigan	62 829
John	Placer Iona Hills	62 890
John	San Francisco San Francisco 8	681300
John	San Francisco San Francisco 5	67 554
John	San Joaquin Stockton	641035
John	San Joaquin Castoria	64 887
John	San Joaquin Elkhorn	64 950
John	Sierra Monte Crk	661036
John	Tuolumne Sonora	71 241
John	Yuba Suida	72 987
John J	Placer Auburn	62 593
Johni	Yuba Linda	72 987
Jonas	Sonoma Armally	69 485
Jos	Amador Twp 7	55 414
Jos	Butte Chico	56 542
Joseph	Placer Secret R	62 611
Joseph	Sierra Poverty	66 799
Joseph	Yuba New York	72 724
Joshua N	Tulara Visalia	71 97
L	Tuolumne Twp 4	71 156
Leomidan	Solano Green Valley	69 242
Leonard	Yuba Fosters	72 837
Leonidas	Solano Green Valley	69 242
Louy	Mariposa Twp 1	60 668
Luben	Alameda Brooklyn	55 177
Luch D	San Francisco San Francisco 2	67 597
Lucy D	San Francisco San Francisco 2	67 597
M	Calaveras Twp 2	57 21
M	Nevada Grass Valley	61 224
M	Siskiyou Scott Va	69 38
M V	Yolo Slate Ra	72 692
M V	Yuba Slate Ro	72 692
Maria	San Francisco San Francisco 8	681284
Marion	Shasta Shasta	66 760
Mary	Siskiyou Yreka	69 183
Mary T	San Francisco San Francisco 10	184 67
Michael	Santa Cruz Pajaro	66 532
Milo H	Amador Twp 2	55 271
N	Merced Twp 2	60 923
Nathan	Sierra Downieville	661017
Nathl	Plumas Quincy	621003
Nicholas	Tuolumne Twp 2	71 292
Norman W	Santa Clara Fremont	65 430
O W	Marin Tomales	60 717
Oakes	Tuolumne Shawsfla	71 398
Patrick	San Francisco San Francisco 1	68 917
Peter	Butte Hamilton	56 521
R	Nevada Grass Valley	61 187
R J	El Dorado Gold Hill	581097
Randolph	Sonoma Petaluma	69 546
Rhoda	Monterey Pajaro	601023
Richrd	San Francisco San Francisco 1	68 897
Robert	Calaveras Twp 10	57 282
Robert	Placer Michigan	62 809
Robert	San Francisco San Francisco 9	681089
Robert M	Yuba Linda	72 984
Robt	Butte Hamilton	56 514
Ruffer	Tulara Visalia	71 19
S	Calaveras Twp 9	57 406
S	Nevada Eureka	61 357
S	Tuolumne Big Oak	71 156
S B	Trinity Trinity	70 972
S K	Trinity Weaverville	701077
S L*	San Francisco San Francisco 5	67 506
S M	Amador Twp 4	55 249
S M	Tuolumne Sonora	71 481
S R	El Dorado Mud Springs	58 974
Sam	Sonoma Bodega	69 540
Samuel B	Yolo Slate Ra	72 698

Name	County Locale	M653 RollPage
TURNER		
Samuel P	Siskiyou Yreka	69 170
Samuel S	Tuolumne Twp 1	71 475
Samul B*	Yuba Slate Ro	72 698
Samul P	Siskiyou Yreka	69 170
Sarah	Yuba Linda	72 984
Sett	Tuolumne Twp 1	71 481
Silian*	Yuba Marysville	72 960
Simon	Tulara Yule Rvr	71 8
Sophia	San Francisco San Francisco 8	681247
Sophia	San Francisco San Francisco 2	67 657
Stephen	Placer Auburn	62 569
T	Calaveras Twp 9	57 392
T	Nevada Grass Valley	61 198
T S	Sacramento Ward 4	63 579
T*	Nevada Eureka	61 357
Theodore	Santa Clara Santa Clara	65 491
Thomas	San Joaquin Tulare	64 869
Thomas	Shasta Shasta	66 735
Thomas A	Plumas Quincy	621003
Thomas E	Del Norte Klamath	58 653
Thomas J*	Plumas Quincy	62 971
Thomas*	El Dorado Salmon Falls	581052
Thos	Butte Chico	56 534
Thos	Butte Cascade	56 697
V R	Yolo Slate Ra	72 691
W	El Dorado Placerville	58 860
W	El Dorado Placerville	58 877
W	Merced Twp 2	60 923
W	Nevada Grass Valley	61 210
W	Nevada Grass Valley	61 212
W	Merced Twp 1	60 908
W G	Amador Twp 2	55 273
W H	Butte Chico	56 551
W H	El Dorado Placerville	58 881
W L	Butte Bidwell	56 729
W R	Klamath Trinidad	59 220
W R	Sonoma Santa Rosa	69 408
W R	Trinity E Weaver	701058
William	Sonoma Armally	69 487
William	Calaveras Twp 7	57 21
William	Marin Tomales	60 776
William	Marin Cortemad	60 780
William	San Joaquin Stockton	641042
William	Solano Vacaville	69 343
William	Stanislaus Branch	70 706
William	Tulara Visalia	71 17
William M	Klamath Orleans	59 215
Wm	Nevada Eureka	61 354
Wm	Placer Auburn	62 587
Wm	Placer Auburn	62 589
Wm	Sacramento Franklin	63 322
Wm	Sonoma Vallejo	69 616
Wm E	Amador Twp 2	55 272
Wm F	Tuolumne Sonora	71 475
Wm H	Solano Suisan	69 230
Wm M	Tuolumne Twp 2	71 352
Y	Amador Twp 1	55 471
Y	Nevada Eureka	61 357
TURNESSEY		
Catherine*	Yuba Marysville	72 871
TURNESSY		
Catherine*	Yuba Marysville	72 871
TURNET		
Peter	Santa Cruz Pajaro	66 565
TURNEY		
E P	San Francisco San Francisco 8	681263
Isaac	Tuolumne Twp 1	71 259
J K*	San Francisco San Francisco 9	681102
Jno L	Sacramento Ward 4	63 606
John	Sierra Downieville	66 995
Lucy	Placer Forest H	72 791
Mary*	San Francisco San Francisco 1	68 887
S B	Nevada Bridgeport	61 498
S D*	Sierra Twp 7	66 912
Tho	Siskiyou Callahan	69 2
Thomas	Tuolumne Jamestown	71 447
TURNG		
John*	Plumas Quincy	62 974
TURNGREVE		
Geo	Sacramento Natonia	63 281
TURNHAM		
Wm R	Nevada Eureka	61 365
TURNIA		
Frank	Amador Twp 2	55 299
TURNIER		
Joseph	Yuba New York	72 724
TURNING		
A*	San Francisco San Francisco 1	68 830
TURNIS		
James	Yolo Cache	72 641
Nickolas	Tuolumne Columbia	71 292
TURNLEY		
John*	Napa Napa	61 67
TURNLY		
John	Sonoma Santa Rosa	69 418

Name	County Locale	M653 RollPage
TURNS		
Elizabeth San Francisco San Francisco 2		67 735
TURNY		
Jno	Butte Oregon	56 636
TUROFF		
Augustus*	San Francisco 1	68 818
	San Francisco	
TURPIN		
Fred	Sacramento Ward 1	63 3
Hamilton*	Napa Yount	61 29
Jno N	Sacramento Ward 1	63 11
Jonathan	Tuolumne Montezuma	71 504
R	Tehama Red Bluff	70 910
R S	Tehama Red Bluff	70 933
Solomon	Stanislaus Empire	70 730
Wm	Sacramento Ward 4	63 579
Wm*	Placer Secret R	62 618
TURPING		
J N	El Dorado Union	581090
TURRE		
Paul*	San Francisco San Francisco 8	681317
Robt*	El Dorado Eldorado	58 937
TURRITO		
Manel	Tuolumne Twp 3	71 459
TURRY		
John*	Solano Suisan	69 215
Sury	Amador Twp 5	55 366
Wm	Sierra Monte Crk	661036
TURSE		
Kiroota	Santa Cruz Pajaro	66 561
TURSORO		
Andrew* San Francisco San Francisco 3		67 16
TURTH		
Danl	Nevada Bridgeport	61 469
TURTHAM		
Mary W* San Francisco San Francisco 9		681009
TURTIN		
Columbus	Sonoma Petaluma	69 543
Isaac	Sonoma Petaluma	69 550
Saml	Sonoma Petaluma	69 571
TURTLE DOVE		
---	Tulara Twp 2	71 35
TURTLE EYE		
---	Tulara Twp 2	71 4
TURTLE SNAKE		
---	Tulara Twp 2	71 34
TURTLE		
Danl*	Nevada Bridgeport	61 469
TURTOLOTTE		
J H	Trinity Bates	70 967
TURTS		
Gilbert	Tehama Red Bluff	70 909
TURVER		
Adam	Butte Oregon	56 629
TURVIES		
Enock*	Sierra Twp 7	66 882
TURY		
---	Amador Twp 5	55 350
---	Amador Twp 5	55 352
---	Amador Twp 5	55 354
---	Amador Twp 5	55 355
---	Amador Twp 5	55 356
TURYMAN		
Anthony*	Nevada Eureka	61 359
TUSCALL		
T	Nevada Eureka	61 366
TUSCHER		
Fred	Amador Twp 3	55 384
TUSCOE		
Jeptha	Tulara Twp 3	71 41
TUSE		
Latham*	Mendocino Big Rvr	60 849
TUSEN		
---*	Fresno Twp 1	59 27
TUSH		
---	Nevada Nevada	61 300
TUSHER		
William San Luis Obispo San Luis Obispo 65		26
TUSK		
Chals W*	El Dorado Georgetown	58 698
Christian	Contra Costa Twp 1	57 509
F	Siskiyou Scott Va	69 41
Frank*	San Francisco San Francisco 3	67 21
TUSKER		
August	Butte Bidwell	56 730
TUSLIN		
Allen	Solano Vallejo	69 280
TUSON		
James	Calaveras Twp 6	57 145
TUSOR		
Hery	Calaveras Twp 9	57 388
James	Calaveras Twp 5	57 145
TUSSAE		
---	Butte Chico	56 566
TUSSDELL		
Jesser*	Placer Secret R	62 615

California 1860 Census Index

Name	County Locale	M653 RollPage
TUSSELL		
G	Butte Cascade	56 697
TUSSO		
Eujeur	Calaveras Twp 6	57 138
TUSTIN		
Allen	Solano Vallejo	69 280
Alvira	Sonoma Petaluma	69 561
John	Sonoma Petaluma	69 561
TUT		
---	Amador Twp 5	55 356
---	Butte Kimshaw	56 608
---	Calaveras Twp 5	57 251
---	Calaveras Twp 10	57 260
---	Calaveras Twp 10	57 266
---	Calaveras Twp 10	57 273
---	El Dorado Salmon Hills	581053
---	Sacramento Ward 1	63 52
---	Sierra Downieville	661008
---	Tuolumne Twp 5	71 517
---	Tuolumne Twp 5	71 524
---	Tuolumne Twp 5	71 526
---	Tuolumne Don Pedro	71 540
Lawrence*	Plumas Quincy	62 990
TUTCHEN		
Yans	Alameda Brooklyn	55 138
TUTHILL		
David	Los Angeles Los Angeles	59 363
Franklin	San Francisco San Francisco 2	67 734
William	Tuolumne Twp 1	71 234
TUTILE		
John*	San Bernardino San Bernadino	64 636
TUTJONS		
Peter*	Sacramento Ward 1	63 42
TUTKERSON		
John	Sonoma Santa Rosa	69 402
Trib	Sonoma Santa Rosa	69 402
TUTLE		
Edgar*	Sacramento Franklin	63 313
Henry A	San Francisco San Francisco 8	681265
TUTMAN		
A C*	San Francisco San Francisco 3	67 50
TUTT		
Benjn	Sierra Monte Crk	661039
Chs	Tehama Moons	70 854
J A	Tehama Lassen	70 884
John A	Sacramento Ward 1	63 139
W L	Yolo Cottonwoood	72 653
TUTTAN		
Harman	Plumas Quincy	62 954
TUTTE		
Edgar*	Sacramento Franklin	63 313
TUTTERR		
Mrs	Alameda Brooklyn	55 92
TUTTLE		
A	San Francisco San Francisco 9	681064
A A H	Sacramento Ward 4	63 530
A C	Yuba Slate Ro	72 697
Albert	Marin San Rafael	60 771
Amos	Tuolumne Shawsfla	71 387
Amos S	Tuolumne Twp 2	71 387
B F	Sonoma Petaluma	69 583
B F	Tuolumne Jamestown	71 448
Billy*	Sacramento Centre	63 176
Bully*	Sacramento Centre	63 176
C M	Mendocino Big Rvr	60 844
Caroline	Los Angeles Tejon	59 526
Cephas*	Plumas Quincy	62 974
Charles A	Placer Auburn	62 562
D	Nevada Grass Valley	61 201
D W	Amador Twp 3	55 384
Daniel	Santa Cruz Pajaro	66 559
Danl*	Nevada Bridgeport	61 469
David	Mendocino Little L	60 835
Dexter	Sierra Grizzly	661058
E	Shasta Shasta	66 731
E T	Nevada Grass Valley	61 189
E W	Mendocino Big Rvr	60 844
Edmund	Calaveras Twp 5	57 227
Fanny	Sierra Downieville	66 955
Franch*	Shasta Horsetown	66 706
Frank	Shasta Horsetown	66 706
Frank S	Del Norte Crescent	58 650
French*	Shasta Horsetown	66 706
G H	Sierra Downieville	66 955
Geo N	Napa Napa	61 97
Hiram	Sacramento Ward 1	63 142
Hiram	Santa Cruz Santa Cruz	66 611
Hiram S*	Santa Cruz Santa Cruz	66 611
J W	Siskiyou Scott Va	69 29
James	San Joaquin Castoria	64 877
James*	Placer Auburn	62 565
John	Sacramento Centre	63 177
John G	Alameda Oakland	55 41
John W	Tuolumne Twp 2	71 355
Joseph	Solano Benecia	69 286
Like	Sierra St Louis	66 863

Name	County Locale	M653 RollPage
TUTTLE		
Luke	Sierra Twp 7	66 863
M E	Los Angeles Tejon	59 526
Minen G	San Bernardino San Bernadino	64 673
Mrs	Alameda Brooklyn	55 92
O W	Siskiyou Scott Va	69 47
S	Yuba Linda	72 986
Sam	Nevada Bridgeport	61 468
Smith	Sacramento Ward 1	63 41
Thomas J	Shasta Millvill	66 755
W	Siskiyou Scott Ri	69 64
W G	El Dorado Gold Hill	581096
W H	Mariposa Twp 1	60 655
W J	Sacramento Cosumnes	63 382
W S	San Francisco San Francisco 5	67 480
Wealthy	Sacramento Ward 4	63 509
William	Monterey San Juan	60 976
Wm	San Francisco San Francisco 1	68 845
Wm J	Sacramento Ward 1	63 2
Wm S	Sacramento Ward 1	63 2
TUTTLIE		
James*	Placer Auburn	62 565
TUU		
---	Amador Twp 5	55 367
TUUMER		
George*	Sierra Downieville	66 977
TUVER		
---	Fresno Twp 2	59 41
TUW		
---	Calaveras Twp 10	57 285
---	Calaveras Twp 4	57 302
---*	Nevada Washington	61 339
---*	Nevada Eureka	61 385
---*	Nevada Eureka	61 386
Hom*	Yuba Long Bar	72 753
Latham*	Mendocino Big Rvr	60 849
TUY		
---	Amador Twp 2	55 328
---	Amador Twp 5	55 351
---	Nevada Nevada	61 299
---*	Sacramento Granite	63 245
Ah	Sacramento Ward 1	63 156
TUYASON		
Mary A*	San Francisco San Francisco 10	181 67
TUYKITS		
---	Tulara Twp 1	71 116
TUYMAN		
R	Amador Twp 5	55 343
TUYMON		
Wm	Yuba Slate Ro	72 692
TUYTUM		
J	San Francisco San Francisco 2	67 748
TUZEP		
---	Trinity Lewiston	70 954
TVILL		
Saml*	Yolo Putah	72 587
TWADELL		
E L	Butte Kimshaw	56 572
TWADY		
H	Nevada Grass Valley	61 155
TWAGIE		
Amile	Mariposa Coulterville	60 680
TWAITES		
W	San Francisco San Francisco 5	67 484
TWALLES		
Moses	Nevada Rough &	61 397
TWAMBLEY		
R	Colusa Monroeville	57 448
TWAMPLY		
J H L	Siskiyou Scott Va	69 34
TWAN		
---	Sierra Downieville	66 982
---	Sierra Downieville	66 983
TWAULT		
Benj	Siskiyou Scott Va	69 37
TWAY		
John	Placer Forest H	62 793
TWEDY		
Samuel	Tuolumne Twp 5	71 508
William*	Placer Michigan	62 850
TWEED		
Charles	Yolo Washington	72 605
Gillmore	Yuba Bear Rvr	721001
Hiram	Yuba Bear Rvr	721005
James	Los Angeles Los Angeles	59 343
John	San Francisco San Francisco 4	681229
TWEEDY		
James	Sierra Scales D	66 803
Robert	Los Angeles Elmonte	59 269
Samuel	Tuolumne Montezuma	71 508
TWEEN		
D	Yolo Cottonwoood	72 556
TWEENEY		
John	Humbolt Eureka	59 174
TWEK		
Ca	Mariposa Twp 1	60 653

Name	County Locale	M653 RollPage
TWEKER		
Henry A	Placer Ophirville	62 655
TWELT		
Joseph M	Nevada Bridgeport	61 448
TWENDLE		
Julia*	Alameda Brooklyn	55 123
TWENER		
M	Siskiyou Scott Va	69 38
TWENULL		
Lorenzo*	Calaveras Twp 5	57 209
TWERLAD		
T S	Sierra Twp 7	66 868
TWERLAID		
F S	Sierra Twp 7	66 868
TWI		
Hu	San Francisco San Francisco 4	681202
TWIAN		
Johnson	Sierra Twp 7	66 873
TWICE		
Isac D	Mariposa Twp 1	60 624
TWICHELL		
Claudins C	Los Angeles San Gabriel	59 417
Claudius C	Los Angeles San Gabriel	59 417
Jasper R	Monterey San Juan	60 977
TWICHELLS		
Sanford L	Monterey San Juan	60 977
TWIGG		
C A	Nevada Grass Valley	61 221
E G	Nevada Grass Valley	61 221
Richard	Shasta Shasta	66 730
TWIGGS		
Thos*	Los Angeles Tejon	59 538
Wm F	Los Angeles Los Angeles	59 510
TWIGLEY		
Ira*	Yuba Linda	72 988
TWILGAR		
E Man*	El Dorado Georgetown	58 751
TWILLEN		
Richd	Napa Clear Lake	61 123
TWIMAN		
W*	Sierra Twp 7	66 864
TWIMBLEY		
Wm H*	San Francisco San Francisco 1	68 847
TWIN		
---	San Francisco San Francisco 4	681190
TWINAN		
W	Sierra St Louis	66 864
TWINEN		
John	Sonoma Sonoma	69 650
TWING		
---	Fresno Twp 2	59 20
Daniel I	San Francisco San Francisco 11	129 67
Stephen	San Francisco San Francisco 7	681328
TWINGROVE		
Geo*	Sacramento Natonia	63 281
TWINS		
Elizabeth*	Mariposa Twp 3	60 602
Mary*	Mariposa Twp 3	60 602
TWIST		
Eli	Tuolumne Sonora	71 245
TWITCHEL		
Joshua	Monterey San Juan	60 983
TWITCHELL		
Sidney	Sierra Chappare	661040
TWITHAM		
Mary W*	San Francisco San Francisco 9	681009
TWITT		
A G	Nevada Grass Valley	61 238
U G	Nevada Grass Valley	61 238
TWIZZS		
Thos*	Los Angeles Tejon	59 538
TWLAY		
---*	Nevada Bridgeport	61 458
TWO		
---	El Dorado White Oaks	581025
---	El Dorado Coloma	581083
---	El Dorado Casumnes	581163
---	El Dorado Mountain	581189
---	El Dorado Diamond	58 786
---	El Dorado Placerville	58 897
---	Tuolumne Sonora	71 477
TWOGOOD		
G S W	Yuba North Ea	72 671
TWOKEY		
John*	Sierra La Porte	66 789
TWONG		
Fee	San Francisco San Francisco 4	681202
Fu	San Francisco San Francisco 4	681202
TWUNAN		
W*	Sierra Twp 7	66 864
TWYASON		
Mary A*	San Francisco San Francisco 10	181 67
TWZ		
See*	Tuolumne Big Oak	71 147

Name	County Locale	M653 Roll	Page
TY COON			
---	Sacramento Ward 1	63	59
TY LEE			
---*	Yuba Long Bar	72	767
TY SAN			
---	Sacramento Ward 1	63	70
TY SING			
---	Butte Kimshaw	56	589
TY			
---	Amador Twp 2	55	280
---	Amador Twp 2	55	283
---	Amador Twp 2	55	312
---	Amador Twp 2	55	314
---	Amador Twp 2	55	320
---	Amador Twp 2	55	328
---	Amador Twp 4	55	332
---	Amador Twp 5	55	343
---	Amador Twp 5	55	351
---	Amador Twp 5	55	353
---	Amador Twp 5	55	356
---	Amador Twp 3	55	394
---	Amador Twp 3	55	398
---	Amador Twp 3	55	410
---	Amador Twp 6	55	428
---	Amador Twp 6	55	432
---	Amador Twp 6	55	433
---	Amador Twp 6	55	449
---	Amador Twp 1	55	501
---	Amador Twp 1	55	502
---	Butte Hamilton	56	529
---	Butte Kimshaw	56	579
---	Butte Oregon	56	613
---	Butte Eureka	56	649
---	Del Norte Crescent	58	631
---	Del Norte Happy Ca	58	663
---	Del Norte Happy Ca	58	669
---	El Dorado Georgetown	58	695
---	Sacramento Granite	63	250
---	Sacramento Granite	63	259
---	Shasta Shasta	66	670
---	Shasta Horsetown	66	697
---	Shasta Horsetown	66	705
A	Sacramento Granite	63	250
A	Sacramento Granite	63	259
An	Del Norte Crescent	58	630
An	Del Norte Crescent	58	631
Coon	Sacramento Ward 1	63	59
Dew	Sacramento Cosumnes	63	385
Kee	Calaveras Twp 4	57	334
Lee	El Dorado Georgetown	58	756
Lee	Yuba Long Bar	72	767
Low	Amador Twp 2	55	311
Pi	Amador Twp 2	55	312
Si	Amador Twp 2	55	328
Sing	Butte Kimshaw	56	589
Yaw	Placer Dutch Fl	62	720
TYALL			
Ambrose	Tulara Visalia	71	74
TYAN			
Catharine	San Francisco San Francisco 9	68	983
James	Amador Twp 6	55	426
TYCHAN			
---	Mendocino Calpella	60	823
TYDER			
E B	Yolo Slate Ra	72	710
TYE			
---	Amador Twp 4	55	246
---	Amador Twp 2	55	320
---	Butte Bidwell	56	725
---	Butte Bidwell	56	727
---	Butte Mountain	56	735
---	Butte Mountain	56	742
---	Butte Ophir	56	762
---	Butte Ophir	56	770
---	Butte Ophir	56	804
---	Butte Ophir	56	805
---	Butte Ophir	56	808
---	Butte Ophir	56	811
---	Butte Ophir	56	819
---	Butte Ophir	56	820
---	Placer Virginia	62	679
---	Placer Virginia	62	681
---	Sacramento Ward 1	63	61
---	San Francisco San Francisco 2	67	754
---	San Joaquin Stockton	641	087
---	Trinity Weaverville	701	052
Ah	Butte Bidwell	56	727
Ah	Butte Mountain	56	735
Along	San Joaquin Stockton	641	083
Bridget	San Francisco San Francisco 9	681	003
Chas	San Francisco San Francisco 2	67	742
Lee	Butte Ophir	56	801
Ling	Butte Ophir	56	808
Ling	Butte Ophir	56	817
Lu	Mariposa Twp 1	60	664
Michael	San Francisco San Francisco 2	67	671

Name	County Locale	M653 Roll	Page
TYE			
Michael	San Francisco San Francisco 1	68	840
Patrick	San Joaquin Stockton	641	079
Sing	Butte Ophir	56	803
Sing	Butte Ophir	56	812
Sing	Butte Ophir	56	813
Thos	San Francisco San Francisco 2	67	759
Yee	Butte Bidwell	56	726
TYECK			
William	Tuolumne Springfield	71	372
TYEJ			
Chas	San Francisco San Francisco 2	67	742
TYELR			
Wm B	Sierra Twp 5	66	917
TYER			
---	Yuba Fosters	72	843
Hiram	Calaveras Twp 10	57	289
John A	San Joaquin Castoria	64	891
TYERIND			
F	Amador Twp 1	55	495
TYERING			
---	Butte Bidwell	56	708
TYEWALL			
James	Sierra Twp 7	66	909
TYGART			
M M*	Nevada Bridgeport	61	486
TYHA			
---	Placer Secret R	62	621
TYI			
---	Amador Twp 2	55	320
TYIN			
---	Amador Twp 6	55	428
TYLAN			
Frank	Yuba Fosters	72	823
TYLCK			
William	Tuolumne Twp 2	71	372
TYLER			
A A	Siskiyou Cottonwoood	69	99
Andrew	Alameda Brooklyn	55	171
Augustus C	Siskiyou Shasta Rvr	69	112
B	Sacramento Cosumnes	63	408
C	Sacramento Sutter	63	300
Charles	San Bernardino San Bernardino	64	615
Charles	Tulara Twp 1	71	88
Charles	Yuba Bear Rvr	721	005
Charles W	San Francisco 4	681	116
Charls	San Bernardino San Bernardino	64	615
Cyrus	Placer Yankee J	62	775
D G	Trinity Indian C	70	988
D S	El Dorado Casumnes	581	170
E B	Los Angeles Tejon	59	538
E B	Sierra St Louis	66	818
Ed	Sacramento Ward 1	63	42
Edward	Placer Michigan	62	808
Edward*	San Francisco San Francisco 4	681	116
Edwin	Calaveras Twp 6	57	155
Frances*	Plumas Quincy	62	977
Geo W	San Francisco San Francisco 1	68	819
George	Nevada Rough &	61	421
Harmon	Plumas Quincy	62	987
Heal	Solano Fairfield	69	201
Henry	Plumas Quincy	62	961
J	Sonoma Petaluma	69	587
J C	Tehama Tehama	70	942
James	Sierra Pine Grove	66	819
James	Tuolumne Twp 1	71	193
James	Yuba Marysville	72	927
James A	Plumas Quincy	62	953
James W	Calaveras Twp 10	57	283
Jas	Butte Hamilton	56	513
Jas	Napa Napa	61	77
Jennie	San Francisco San Francisco 6	67	441
Jerimiah*	Plumas Quincy	62	977
Jesse	Siskiyou Yreka	69	149
John	Calaveras Twp 8	57	80
John	San Joaquin Castoria	64	902
John	San Mateo Twp 3	65	89
John	Yuba Marysville	72	883
John W	Calaveras Twp 6	57	184
John W	Sierra Downieville	66	997
John*	Yuba Parke Ba	72	783
L	San Francisco San Francisco 10	215 / 67	
L C*	Sacramento Georgian	63	338
Louiza	Sierra Downieville	66	969
M W*	Nevada Bridgeport	61	486
Mathew	Los Angeles Tejon	59	537
Montgomery	Los Angeles Elmonte	59	251
N	El Dorado Casumnes	581	170
Nath A	Humbolt Eureka	59	177
O B	Sierra Downieville	66	975
O C	San Francisco San Francisco 10	258 / 67	
Orin	Sonoma Petaluma	69	605

Name	County Locale	M653 Roll	Page
TYLER			
Peter	San Mateo Twp 3	65	89
Presley	Sonoma Petaluma	69	549
S C*	Sacramento Georgian	63	338
S H	San Francisco San Francisco 12	382 / 67	
Saml	Mariposa Coulterville	60	694
Saml	Sacramento Sutter	63	300
Saml	Sacramento Sutter	63	300
Samuel	El Dorado Placerville	58	928
Saxton G	Solano Vacaville	69	353
Simeon	San Francisco San Francisco 3	67	59
Smith	San Diego Colorado	64	806
U	Nevada Grass Valley	61	219
Wm	Sierra Twp 7	66	895
Wm	Tehama Lassen	70	884
Wm B	Sierra Twp 5	66	917
Wm S	Tuolumne Twp 1	71	212
TYLOR			
Edward	San Francisco San Francisco 4	681	116
Edward	Tuolumne Jamestown	71	445
Edward*	San Francisco San Francisco 4	681	116
Edwin*	Calaveras Twp 6	57	155
Frank	Yuba Foster B	72	823
Joseph*	Yuba Foster B	72	821
O	Tuolumne Twp 4	71	146
O T	San Mateo Twp 1	65	64
TYLVA			
Joseph*	Yuba Foster B	72	821
TYMAN			
James	Calaveras Twp 10	57	281
Patrick	San Francisco San Francisco 10	294 / 67	
TYMEE			
---	San Diego Agua Caliente	64	856
TYMESSON			
A M	San Francisco San Francisco 5	67	521
TYMUN			
James*	Calaveras Twp 6	57	117
TYN			
---	Amador Twp 2	55	289
---	Amador Twp 2	55	320
---	Amador Twp 5	55	352
TYN???			
James	Calaveras Twp 6	57	117
TYNACIA			
Maria	San Diego Agua Caliente	64	856
TYNAN			
James	Calaveras Twp 10	57	281
M	Amador Twp 2	55	324
Richard	Amador Twp 2	55	306
Thomas	Tuolumne Columbia	71	357
TYNE			
C	San Joaquin Stockton	641	061
Doan	Amador Twp 2	55	323
TYNELL			
Richard	Yuba Marysville	72	913
TYNER			
Aaron	Tuolumne Twp 2	71	299
Henry	San Joaquin Castoria	64	891
TYNES			
A	Mariposa Twp 3	60	614
TYO			
---	Amador Twp 2	55	280
Wm	Trinity Evans Ba	701	002
TYOCOTO			
---	Tulara Twp 1	71	116
TYON			
---	Amador Twp 6	55	428
David	Yolo Putah	72	548
TYR			
---	San Francisco San Francisco 10	356 / 67	
TYRE			
---	Placer Rattle Snake	62	635
---	Placer Rattle Snake	62	636
---	Placer Horseshoe	62	650
E H	Nevada Nevada	61	312
TYREE			
Thomas K	Los Angeles Los Angeles	59	365
TYREL			
Elisabeth	Stanislaus Branch	70	707
Mary	San Francisco San Francisco 8	681	253
TYRELL			
A H	San Francisco San Francisco 10	170 / 67	
Bernard	Alameda Brooklyn	55	208
Bernard	San Francisco San Francisco 1	68	836
Bonny	Tuolumne Twp 3	71	449
Fred	Sacramento Ward 4	63	579
Joseph	San Francisco San Francisco 1	68	836
TYRIEL			
Jas*	Sacramento Ward 1	63	79
TYRRELL			
Grove	Yuba Marysville	72	976
Henry	Yuba Marysville	72	975

California 1860 Census Index

Name	County Locale	M653 RollPage
TYRRELL		
James	Yuba Marysville	72 926
Jas	San Francisco San Francisco 10	302 67
TYRRIL		
Jas*	Sacramento Ward 1	63 79
TYRSIL		
Jas*	Sacramento Ward 1	63 79
TYSON		
Andrew	Siskiyou Scott Va	69 50
Anna	Yuba Marysville	72 905
Daniel*	Siskiyou Yreka	69 131
Isaac	San Francisco San Francisco 8	681245
Jacob	San Francisco San Francisco 8	681241
Jacob	San Mateo Twp 1	65 48
James	Calaveras Twp 8	57 79
Jno	Sacramento Ward 4	63 531
Joseph	Calaveras Twp 4	57 333
Joseph	Siskiyou Yreka	69 193
R	Nevada Grass Valley	61 145
R	Nevada Grass Valley	61 223
William A	Tuolumne Twp 5	71 509
Wm	Alameda Brooklyn	55 205
TYSRILL		
W C	Mariposa Twp 1	60 669
TYTHER		
Richard*	Napa Yount	61 39
TYUPPE		
---	Tulara Twp 1	71 121
TYWICKER		
John*	Sacramento Ward 1	63 33
TZENOBITCH		
P*	Sacramento Ward 1	63 84
TZROX		
---	Fresno Twp 1	59 56
U		
---	Sierra Downieville	661005
Euck	Sierra Downieville	661009
U???TT		
J K	Mariposa Coulterville	60 680
UA		
---	Calaveras Twp 4	57 299
UAN		
J	San Bernardino San Bernadino	64 679
UANG		
Chum	Mariposa Coulterville	60 680
UAOTON		
William J	Solano Fairfield	69 202
UAPAUSA		
---	Plumas Quincy	62 970
UAR		
---	Sierra Cox'S Bar	66 951
UATEMAN		
R U	Solano Fairfield	69 198
UBACH		
Anthony	Monterey San Juan	60 986
UBACK		
Anthony	Monterey San Juan	60 986
UBARRA		
Josefa	Los Angeles Los Angeles	59 350
UBBERA		
Pedro	Calaveras Twp 6	57 131
UBEL		
L	San Francisco San Francisco 5	67 513
UBELL		
H	Calaveras Twp 9	57 363
UBER		
Peter	Plumas Quincy	62 944
UBHOFF		
Henry	Napa Napa	61 57
UBICH		
A	San Francisco San Francisco 6	67 470
UBLEDINE		
Wm	El Dorado Casumnes	581164
UBRICK		
Charles	Amador Twp 3	55 371
UCADES		
Patra	Yuba Marysville	72 946
Santiago	Yuba Marysville	72 946
UCHELE		
Bernardo*	Los Angeles Elmonte	59 267
UCHILLE		
Grange	Los Angeles San Gabriel	59 408
UDALE		
Jas	Butte Hamilton	56 524
UDDLE		
William	Placer Iona Hills	62 895
UDE		
Anna	Amador Twp 1	55 494
UDELL		
C P	Placer Michigan	62 811
Henry	Solano Vacaville	69 363
O C	Solano Vacaville	69 364
UDER		
G A*	Sacramento Lee	63 211
J A*	Sacramento Lee	63 211

Name	County Locale	M653 RollPage
UDILL		
Henry	Solano Vacaville	69 363
UDOLPH		
Vincent	Calaveras Twp 9	57 381
UDONS		
Dolores*	San Francisco San Francisco 2	67 790
UDSTON		
William M	Yuba Marysville	72 960
UDY		
Thomas	Sierra Twp 7	66 888
Wm	Sierra Twp 7	66 888
UE		
---*	Sierra Twp 5	66 927
UEA		
M*	Tuolumne Big Oak	71 146
UEEMECKSON		
Ueeing	Calaveras Twp 4	57 328
UEENZAY		
Ueensy	Calaveras Twp 4	57 329
UEHELE		
Bernardo*	Los Angeles Elmonte	59 267
UEIN		
Augusten	Tehama Red Bluff	70 926
UEIP		
John*	Sacramento Ward 1	63 14
UELLINSONS		
C	Yolo Merritt	72 581
UELLNER		
Casper*	Mariposa Twp 1	60 647
UEN		
---	Calaveras Twp 4	57 322
Cheany	Calaveras Twp 4	57 333
UENHAUSER		
Henry*	San Francisco San Francisco 11	157 67
UENLS		
Owen*	Sonoma Petaluma	69 595
UENS		
J*	Nevada Eureka	61 352
UENUTEACT		
H S	Nevada Nevada	61 268
UENZ		
J*	Nevada Eureka	61 352
UERAH		
Jose F	Los Angeles Azuza	59 276
UERTNER		
Jane E*	San Francisco San Francisco 10	242 67
UESSEY		
Wm*	Nevada Eureka	61 370
UGALUN		
Parti	Alameda Oakland	55 14
UGENIO		
---	Monterey S Antoni	60 972
UGH		
---	Mariposa Twp 1	60 664
UGNACIA		
Maria	Los Angeles Los Angeles	59 400
UGUR		
---	San Francisco San Francisco 11	146 67
UH		
---	Mariposa Twp 1	60 653
Fonz	San Francisco San Francisco 11	146 67
UHANIS		
Peater	Amador Twp 1	55 468
UHE		
Frank X	San Francisco San Francisco 10	191 67
UHERG		
C H*	Sacramento Ward 3	63 488
UHIEG		
C H*	Sacramento Ward 3	63 488
UHL		
Adam*	San Francisco San Francisco 10	287 67
Geo	Sacramento Ward 4	63 579
Valentine	Placer Iona Hills	62 892
UHLENCAMP		
C	El Dorado White Oaks	581029
Martin	El Dorado White Oaks	581029
W L	Sacramento Ward 1	63 24
UHLEY		
Frederick	San Francisco San Francisco 4	681125
UHLRICH		
Julia	Sacramento Ward 4	63 577
UHLY		
Frederick*	San Francisco San Francisco 4	681125
UHO		
Mow	Calaveras Twp 5	57 252
UHOLT		
Geo*	San Francisco San Francisco 9	681090
UHRBAECK		
Henry*	Santa Clara Santa Clara	65 463

Name	County Locale	M653 RollPage
UHRIG		
C A	San Francisco San Francisco 10	334 67
UHS		
---	Siskiyou Yreka	69 195
UHTER		
Chas	San Francisco San Francisco 2	67 693
UHTIR		
Chas*	San Francisco San Francisco 2	67 693
UI		
---*	Mariposa Twp 3	60 581
UIELL		
John*	Placer Forest H	62 805
UIN		
John	Santa Cruz Santa Cruz	66 633
K*	Mariposa Twp 3	60 553
UINNABB		
Margarat*	Los Angeles Tejon	59 523
UINS		
J	Nevada Eureka	61 352
UIT		
---	El Dorado Mud Springs	58 958
UIXOM		
J C	Solano Fairfield	69 199
UJAH		
Concepeion	Los Angeles San Jose	59 285
Fatruis	Los Angeles San Jose	59 285
Francisco	Los Angeles San Jose	59 288
Juan	Los Angeles Azuza	59 273
Pablo	Los Angeles San Jose	59 287
UK		
---	Sacramento Ward 4	63 609
UKE		
Adam	San Francisco San Francisco 10	287 67
UKER		
---	Siskiyou Yreka	69 146
UKIT		
---*	Trinity Weaverville	701075
---*	Trinity Trinindad Rvr	701047
UKLY		
Fredrick*	San Francisco San Francisco 4	681125
John*	El Dorado Georgetown	58 750
ULA		
B	Tehama Red Bluff	70 916
ULAITH		
Lewis*	Sonoma Petaluma	69 602
ULARIA		
---	Monterey San Juan	60 985
ULDON		
Mary	Tehama Red Bluff	70 930
ULDRICK		
Henry	San Francisco San Francisco 7	681405
ULEE		
---	Shasta Shasta	66 669
ULES		
John	Napa Napa	61 70
M H*	Sacramento Brighton	63 208
ULESWELL		
Thadeus*	Santa Clara Fremont	65 418
ULFELDER		
Saml	San Francisco San Francisco 2	67 659
ULHEELER		
L S*	Sonoma Petaluma	69 597
ULIMIGIN		
F	Calaveras Twp 9	57 404
ULINFIELD		
David	Sonoma Petaluma	69 594
ULIS		
T W	El Dorado Big Bar	58 737
ULIZA		
Eugene	Santa Clara San Jose	65 327
ULLERY		
Jno	Butte Hamilton	56 524
ULLMAN		
Bertha	Siskiyou Yreka	69 169
Daniel	San Francisco San Francisco 10	195 67
J	San Francisco San Francisco 2	67 786
ULLOA		
Domingo	Tuolumne Big Oak	71 141
ULLON		
Espiridion	Calaveras Twp 6	57 129
ULMAN		
James	Siskiyou Yreka	69 168
ULMER		
Charles	Calaveras Twp 10	57 289
E	San Francisco San Francisco 9	68 943
M	San Francisco San Francisco 6	67 470
ULMFICH		
Daniel*	Sonoma Petaluma	69 594
ULMFICK		
Daniel*	Sonoma Petaluma	69 594
ULRIC		
James	Mariposa Twp 3	60 596
ULRICH		
Antony	Solano Vacaville	69 365

California 1860 Census Index

Name	County Locale	M653 Roll	Page
ULRICH			
Antorry*	Solano Vacaville	69	365
ULRICK			
Catharine	San Francisco San Francisco 7	68	1411
ULRIGHT			
Geo	Tehama Red Bluff	70	923
ULRIO			
James*	Mariposa Twp 3	60	596
ULROLLERY			
Joseph*	Sierra Excelsior	66	1034
ULSOFFER			
George	San Francisco San Francisco 11	67	154
ULT			
Hiram*	Plumas Quincy	62	981
ULTZ			
Adam*	Placer Iona Hills	62	893
ULYARD			
Augustus	Los Angeles Los Angeles	59	358
ULYN			
Ellicue	Placer Secret R	62	614
UM			
---	Tuolumne Don Pedro	71	535
Ba	Butte Oro	56	686
Bay	Butte Ophir	56	811
Bon	Calaveras Twp 5	57	240
Brow	Stanislaus Branch	70	713
Hay	Butte Wyandotte	56	665
J	Nevada Rough &	61	437
Sip	Placer Virginia	62	671
UMBARDS			
Castino	Tuolumne Twp 1	71	257
UMBARFIELD			
George	Shasta French G	66	721
UMBARGER			
David	Santa Clara San Jose	65	361
UMBER			
Charles	Siskiyou Yreka	69	165
Charles P	Siskiyou Yreka	69	166
UMBERSON			
George*	El Dorado Georgetown	58	755
UMBORFIELD			
George	Shasta French G	66	721
UMBSELM			
Henry	Tuolumne Twp 2	71	393
UMBSUR			
Harry	Tuolumne Twp 2	71	381
UMG			
---	Tuolumne Chinese	71	526
UMISCO			
Frank*	San Francisco San Francisco 11	67	122
UMLAUF			
Minney	San Joaquin Stockton	64	1029
Philip	San Joaquin Stockton	64	1029
UMLAUFF			
D	San Joaquin Stockton	64	1041
Henry*	San Joaquin O'Neal	64	1003
UMLESUR			
Harry*	Tuolumne Shawsfla	71	381
UMP			
---	Mariposa Twp 3	60	569
UMPK			
---	Mariposa Twp 3	60	553
UMPKENSTOCK			
M	Trinity North Fo	70	1024
UMPKINAH			
---	Mendocino Twp 1	60	887
UMSTEAD			
H S	Nevada Nevada	61	268
R H	El Dorado Placerville	58	920
UN			
---	Calaveras Twp 4	57	300
---	El Dorado Salmon Hills	58	1058
---	Mariposa Coulterville	60	684
---	Nevada Bridgeport	61	463
---	Sierra Morristown	66	1034
---	Tuolumne Twp 5	71	516
De	Tuolumne Big Oak	71	150
Doe	Tuolumne Twp 6	71	537
Gee	El Dorado Placerville	58	830
Gee	El Dorado Placerville	58	834
Gee	Shasta Horsetown	66	705
Geu	Calaveras Twp 5	57	205
Gin	Shasta Horsetown	66	706
Git	Calaveras Twp 5	57	251
Git	Calaveras Twp 10	57	276
June	Calaveras Twp 5	57	240
Pow	Calaveras Twp 5	57	209
Row	Calaveras Twp 5	57	209
San	Fresno Twp 2	59	19
Say	Calaveras Twp 10	57	278
Sing	Placer Auburn	62	573
Wan	Calaveras Twp 10	57	278
You	Calaveras Twp 5	57	236
Yow	Calaveras Twp 5	57	202

Name	County Locale	M653 Roll	Page
UNA			
---	Tuolumne Montezuma	71	513
Sal	Placer Forest H	62	801
UNAIGAN			
P A*	Calaveras Twp 9	57	409
UNARDO			
---	San Diego Agua Caliente	64	822
UNATHER			
John	Amador Twp 3	55	372
UNCUM			
Wm	Sonoma Petaluma	69	546
UNDENHAMER			
Alex*	Sacramento Ward 1	63	91
UNDENHAUM			
Alex*	Sacramento Ward 1	63	91
UNDERBRUMMER			
John	Tuolumne Twp 5	71	506
UNDERCOUPLE			
F	Tehama Red Bluff	70	909
UNDERCRAFF			
F	Tehama Red Bluff	70	928
UNDERE			
Petre*	Alameda Oakland	55	46
UNDERHILL			
---	Sierra Pine Grove	66	832
Alphias	San Mateo Twp 3	65	91
Gidney	Sierra La Porte	66	778
Henry B	San Joaquin Stockton	64	1016
Howard	Siskiyou Yreka	69	166
Jacob	San Francisco San Francisco 7	68	1435
John	Sonoma Santa Rosa	69	406
Sidney	Sierra La Porte	66	778
W A	San Francisco San Francisco 2	67	632
William*	Sierra Pine Grove	66	832
UNDERLAND			
S	El Dorado Placerville	58	835
UNDERMAND			
Charles	San Mateo Twp 3	65	73
UNDERO			
Petre*	Alameda Oakland	55	46
UNDERRIDGE			
J	Calaveras Twp 9	57	408
UNDERSHOT			
Marcus	Placer Forest H	62	773
UNDERSHOTT			
William	Placer Michigan	62	853
UNDERSOOD			
Alvah	Calaveras Twp 4	57	301
UNDERWEDDER			
Emily A	Sonoma Mendocino	69	462
Jno	Sonoma Mendocino	69	462
UNDERWERT			
Joseph	Tulara Twp 2	71	23
UNDERWEST			
Joseph	Tulara Yule Rvr	71	23
UNDERWOOD			
Abner	San Francisco San Francisco 1	68	903
Alvah	Calaveras Twp 4	57	301
Benj	Alameda Brooklyn	55	81
C C	Tehama Cottonwood	70	901
Captain	Klamath Klamath	59	227
Chas F*	Napa Napa	61	108
Chs F	Napa Napa	61	108
Gane H*	Nevada Nevada	61	239
Garrett	Nevada Nevada	61	239
Geo	San Francisco San Francisco 1	68	820
George B	Marin Cortemad	60	788
George S	Calaveras Twp 4	57	300
George S	Calaveras Twp 4	57	300
Ira J*	Placer Virginia	62	664
Isaac	Sonoma Vallejo	69	624
J	Butte Chico	56	560
J	San Mateo Twp 3	65	92
J B	Siskiyou Scott Ri	69	72
J H	Klamath Trinidad	59	220
J K	Tuolumne Garrote	71	173
J W	Siskiyou Klamath	69	96
James	Plumas Quincy	62	944
John	San Francisco San Francisco 1	68	904
John	San Joaquin Oneal	64	935
M	Sacramento Ward 1	63	106
M	San Joaquin Stockton	64	1041
M	Santa Clara Santa Clara	65	513
M*	Siskiyou Callahan	69	13
M*	Sacramento Ward 1	63	106
N G	Alameda Brooklyn	55	140
N I	Sacramento Ward 4	63	559
N V*	Sacramento Ward 1	63	106
Norman	Humbolt Mattole	59	124
Peter	Butte Wyandotte	56	668
R Q	Colusa Spring Valley	57	435
Sephrony	Humbolt Union	59	184
Thomas	San Francisco San Francisco 8	68	1238
Wesley	Humbolt Eel Rvr	59	153
Wieden	San Joaquin Oneal	64	936
Wm	Klamath Trinidad	59	220

Name	County Locale	M653 Roll	Page
UNDEWEDDER			
Jno	Sonoma Mendocino	69	462
UNDIA			
---	Mendocino Big Rvr	60	855
UNDISUDGE			
J*	Calaveras Twp 9	57	408
UNDORN			
---	Trinity Lewiston	70	954
UNDRIGHT			
Mary	Alameda Murray	55	225
UNE			
---	Amador Twp 1	55	503
---	El Dorado Mud Springs	58	977
---	El Dorado Mud Springs	58	985
---	El Dorado Mud Springs	58	987
---	El Dorado Mud Springs	58	988
---	Yuba Fosters	72	831
Sin	Amador Twp 2	55	292
UNETOQUE			
---	Fresno Twp 3	59	23
UNFIELD			
Abraham	Siskiyou Scott Va	69	35
UNG GAH			
---	Tuolumne Jacksonville	71	516
UNG GARE			
---	Tuolumne Montezuma	71	505
UNG GEE			
---	Tuolumne Jacksonville	71	516
UNG YE			
---	Tuolumne Chinese	71	510
UNG			
---	Calaveras Twp 5	57	219
---	Calaveras Twp 5	57	241
---	Calaveras Twp 10	57	267
---	Calaveras Twp 10	57	296
---	Calaveras Twp 4	57	306
---	El Dorado Georgetown	58	695
---	El Dorado Diamond	58	784
---	Placer Rattle Snake	62	636
---	Sacramento Cosumnes	63	387
---	Trinity Price'S	70	1019
---	Tuolumne Montezuma	71	503
---	Tuolumne Twp 5	71	512
---	Tuolumne Twp 5	71	514
---	Tuolumne Twp 5	71	524
---	Tuolumne Chinese	71	525
---	Tuolumne Twp 6	71	533
---	Tuolumne Don Pedro	71	535
---	Tuolumne Don Pedro	71	536
Chi	San Francisco San Francisco 2	67	691
Chow	Tuolumne Twp 6	71	528
Foo	Tuolumne Don Pedro	71	535
Gah	Tuolumne Twp 5	71	516
Game	Yuba Long Bar	72	757
Gare	Tuolumne Twp 5	71	505
Gaw	Yuba Long Bar	72	760
Gee	Tuolumne Twp 5	71	516
Gee	Tuolumne Don Pedro	71	537
Gee	Yuba Long Bar	72	766
Gen	Yuba Long Bar	72	760
Gon	Tuolumne Don Pedro	71	536
Gow	Tuolumne Don Pedro	71	537
Gow	Yuba Long Bar	72	760
He	Fresno Twp 3	59	31
Nun	Tuolumne Don Pedro	71	536
Ye	Tuolumne Twp 5	71	510
Yon	Yuba Long Bar	72	770
UNGALD			
Minna*	San Francisco San Francisco 7	68	1392
UNGER			
Adolphus	San Francisco San Francisco 8	68	1289
Elias*	Nevada Bridgeport	61	443
Hardin*	San Bernardino San Bernadino	64	634
Herman	San Francisco San Francisco 6	67	441
Hery	El Dorado Coloma	58	1086
John	El Dorado Gold Hill	58	1097
UNKNOWN			
George	Marin Bolinas	60	748
Name*	Siskiyou Cottonwoood	69	102
Name*	Siskiyou Yreka	69	156
UNKRECK			
Philip	Trinity Trinity	70	1022
UNLAPHER			
John*	Mariposa Coulterville	60	679
UNO			
---	Tuolumne Twp 5	71	513
UNORO			
---	Sierra Twp 7	66	898
UNPHAM			
James	Yuba New York	72	733
UNRIDE			
John*	San Francisco San Francisco 8	68	1235
UNSTS			
S Z*	Calaveras Twp 9	57	405
UNTHIRE			
---*	Napa Napa	61	63

Name	County Locale	M653 Roll Page
UNTLEY		
Gustavus*	Marin Novato	60 737
UNUCKFESS		
T T	Marin Saucileto	60 749
UNY		
---	Calaveras Twp 5	57 218
---	Calaveras Twp 5	57 219
---	Calaveras Twp 10	57 267
---	Calaveras Twp 10	57 296
---	Calaveras Twp 4	57 306
UNYEE		
---	Amador Twp 1	55 496
UONLAPHER		
John*	Mariposa Coulterville	60 679
UONTANDEN		
Wm*	Sacramento Ward 4	63 552
UOON		
---	Tuolumne Twp 5	71 515
UORET		
Joseph*	Mariposa Twp 1	60 648
UP HOY		
---	Sierra La Porte	66 780
UP SI		
---	Mariposa Twp 1	60 669
UP SIGH		
---	Mariposa Twp 1	60 667
UP		
---	Calaveras Twp 5	57 205
---	Calaveras Twp 5	57 236
---	Mariposa Twp 1	60 661
Boon	Del Norte Crescent	58 659
Ha	Mariposa Twp 1	60 658
Hang	Butte Ophir	56 788
Hang	Butte Ophir	56 801
Hang	Butte Ophir	56 815
Hang	Butte Ophir	56 817
Haug	Butte Ophir	56 802
Hoe	Butte Ophir	56 802
Hoy	Sierra La Porte	66 780
Hung	Butte Ophir	56 812
Hung	Monterey Monterey	60 965
Kenn*	Butte Ophir	56 788
Kum	Butte Ophir	56 788
Ling	San Francisco San Francisco 5	671206
Lon	Butte Ophir	56 820
Pait*	Butte Ophir	56 820
Si	Mariposa Twp 1	60 669
Sigh	Mariposa Twp 1	60 667
Sing	San Francisco San Francisco 5	671206
UPCHURCH		
Richard B	Napa Yount	61 43
UPDIKE		
Herman	Alameda Oakland	55 64
Hugh	El Dorado Gold Hill	581095
UPDYKE		
George	Yuba North Ea	72 670
Geroge	Yolo No E Twp	72 670
Jas	Amador Twp 1	55 479
UPENNY		
Joseph	El Dorado Kelsey	581132
UPERGRAFF		
J	Tehama Lassen	70 870
UPHAM		
Emery	Del Norte Crescent	58 620
Frank K	Yuba Marysville	72 904
J M	San Francisco San Francisco 3	67 74
James	Yuba New York	72 733
Johln	Siskiyou Yreka	69 147
John*	Siskiyou Yreka	69 147
T	El Dorado Placerville	58 876
UPLTAUG		
---*	Butte Ophir	56 812
UPMAN		
M	San Francisco San Francisco 4	681159
UPON		
L	Sacramento Sutter	63 298
UPP		
Adam	Mendocino Little L	60 829
Peter	Mendocino Calpella	60 829
UPPER		
Benj	Yolo Putah	72 585
Nelson	Yolo Putah	72 585
UPPINGHAM		
Morris	Sonoma Vallejo	69 613
UPPMYHAM		
Morris	Sonoma Petaluma	69 613
UPSON		
Cornelia	Sacramento Ward 3	63 439
L A	El Dorado Placerville	58 862
UPT		
---	San Francisco San Francisco 4	681173
UPTEGROVE		
Charles W	San Joaquin Elkhorn	64 966
UPTIN		
Robt	Napa Clear Lake	61 129
UPTON		
B	Calaveras Twp 9	57 391

Name	County Locale	M653 Roll Page
UPTON		
Chs D	San Francisco San Francisco 6	67 415
D L	Sacramento Franklin	63 323
David	Sierra Twp 7	66 903
Eugene A	San Francisco San Francisco 10	229 67
Frank	Amador Twp 1	55 512
John W	Del Norte Crescent	58 640
M G	Sacramento Ward 1	63 91
Robt	Napa Clear Lake	61 129
S	El Dorado Placerville	58 821
S B	Merced Twp 1	60 911
W W	Sacramento Sutter	63 289
Wiliam	Placer Yankee J	62 776
Wm	Sacramento Ward 3	63 444
UPTOR		
B*	Calaveras Twp 9	57 391
UR DIE		
---	Sierra Twp 7	66 915
UR		
---	Sierra Twp 7	66 898
Die	Sierra Twp 7	66 915
Kee	Sierra Twp 5	66 945
Seng	Sierra Downieville	66 973
Sing	Sierra Twp 5	66 926
Sing	Sierra Downieville	66 973
URAIGAN		
P A*	Calaveras Twp 9	57 409
URAN		
John	Tuolumne Sonora	71 188
URANO		
Francisco*	Santa Cruz Watsonville	66 540
URAP		
---*	Mariposa Twp 3	60 569
URATERHALDER		
Charles*	Santa Cruz Santa Cruz	66 618
URBAIN		
---	Mariposa Twp 1	60 655
URBAIS		
John	San Francisco San Francisco 2	67 615
URBAN		
F	Sacramento Sutter	63 293
George	Sierra Downieville	661016
URBANA		
---	Tulara Keyesville	71 55
URBAND		
D H	San Francisco San Francisco 10	289 67
URBANO		
---	Los Angeles Santa Ana	59 456
URBARR		
Joseph	San Francisco San Francisco 7	681416
URCAR		
Felisano	Contra Costa Twp 1	57 488
URE		
Michael	Solano Vacaville	69 361
UREA		
James	San Joaquin Castoria	64 884
UREAGA		
Marie	Monterey Monterey	60 959
UREAS		
Felesano	Calaveras Twp 1	57 488
Felisano*	Contra Costa Twp 1	57 488
UREBER		
John*	Stanislaus Oatvale	70 720
UREBO		
Paulo	Tuolumne Chinese	71 499
UREMADIN		
---*	Mendocino Round Va	60 882
UREN		
Chas	Trinity E Weaver	701059
John B	Placer Dutch Fl	62 728
Nickolas A	Monterey Pajaro	601022
Thomas	Sierra Twp 7	66 906
Wm	Placer Dutch Fl	62 720
URENDELL		
Michael	Siskiyou Shasta Valley	69 118
URETAR		
Juana N	Calaveras Twp 5	57 136
URETARIO		
---	Calaveras Twp 9	57 376
UREW		
Nickolas A*	Monterey Pajaro	601022
UREY		
C M	Butte Mountain	56 737
URGAHART		
James S*	Yuba Marysville	72 871
URGE		
---	Sierra Downieville	66 983
URGGINZ		
William*	Monterey San Juan	60 986
URGGNIZ		
William*	Monterey San Juan	60 986
URGNAHART		
Jas F	Fresno Twp 2	59 4
URGO		
---	Sierra Downieville	66 954

Name	County Locale	M653 Roll Page
URGUEN		
Enacio*	Yuba Marysville	72 948
URGUHART		
James S	Yuba Marysville	72 871
URGUIDES		
Jose M	Los Angeles Los Angeles	59 368
Maria De J*	San Gabriel	59 418
	Los Angeles	
URGUIN		
Enacio	Yuba Marysville	72 948
URGUNHURST		
Charles	Calaveras Twp 4	57 332
URIA		
George	Santa Clara San Jose	65 350
Nicholas*	Los Angeles Los Angeles	59 490
URIBES		
Juana M	Los Angeles San Pedro	59 484
URICH		
J H	Sacramento Cosumnes	63 393
Wm	Tuolumne Big Oak	71 125
Wm	Tuolumne Twp 4	71 127
URIE		
Jackson	Plumas Quincy	62 956
James S	San Francisco San Francisco 2	67 569
URIETERHALDER		
Theodore	Santa Cruz Santa Cruz	66 617
URIETERHELDER		
Charles*	Santa Cruz Santa Cruz	66 618
URIETERLEALDER		
Theodor	Santa Cruz Santa Cruz	66 617
URIG		
---	Tuolumne Twp 5	71 512
---*	Mariposa Twp 3	60 561
Joel	El Dorado Georgetown	58 691
URIGAHEART		
Daniel*	Placer Michigan	62 829
URIN		
Clement	Placer Dutch Fl	62 723
Marco*	Sacramento Ward 1	63 34
URIRE		
Andrus	Monterey San Juan	60 985
Jose	Monterey San Juan	60 985
URITIA		
Francisco*	San Mateo Twp 2	65 131
URIVES		
Jose M	Los Angeles Santa Ana	59 439
Juana M*	Los Angeles San Pedro	59 484
URJNANAY		
A*	San Francisco San Francisco 5	67 529
URK		
---	Sierra Twp 5	66 932
---	Sierra Twp 5	66 933
URKHART		
A	Tuolumne Twp 1	71 247
URKIDES		
Isabel	Monterey Pajaro	601015
URLAIS		
John	San Francisco San Francisco 2	67 615
URLEY		
William*	Santa Cruz Santa Cruz	66 612
URLORY		
J M*	Nevada Eureka	61 373
URMY		
Wm S	San Francisco San Francisco 6	67 410
URNANS		
Steph J	Sacramento Ward 1	63 14
URNE		
Andres	Monterey San Juan	60 985
URNES		
H	El Dorado Diamond	58 806
URNGHAM		
Saml*	Sacramento Ward 1	63 10
URNP		
---*	Mariposa Twp 3	60 569
URNS		
J*	Nevada Eureka	61 352
URPHY		
Jas	Calaveras Twp 9	57 380
URQUAHUNT		
Charles	Calaveras Twp 4	57 332
URQUIDES		
Josefa	Los Angeles Los Angeles	59 385
Maria De J*	San Gabriel	59 418
	Los Angeles	
William	Los Angeles Los Angeles	59 380
URQUIN		
Felez	Yuba Marysville	72 948
URQUNHARST		
Charles	Calaveras Twp 4	57 332
URRAH		
William*	Calaveras Twp 6	57 112
URRAVRUK		
Geo	Amador Twp 5	55 362
URSE		
Preston*	Santa Cruz Pajaro	66 574
URSEINAN		
Geo*	Sacramento Ward 1	63 1

California 1860 Census Index

Name	County Locale	M653 Roll	Page
URSERY			
G M*	Merced Twp 1	60	909
URSIMAN			
Geo*	Sacramento Ward 1	63	1
URSIRY			
G M	Merced Twp 1	60	909
URSON			
W J	Butte Bidwell	56	717
URSULA			
---	San Bernardino Santa Inez	64	142
URSUY			
G M*	Merced Twp 1	60	909
URTAR			
Francisco*	Marin Bolinas	60	728
URTAS			
Francisco*	Marin Bolinas	60	728
URTE			
---	Sierra Twp 5	66	944
URTHINGTON			
Henry*	Santa Cruz Santa Cruz	66	612
URTON			
W J	Butte Bidwell	56	717
W L	San Francisco San Francisco 12	60	380
		67	
URUNUELA			
Pedro	Los Angeles San Pedro	59	485
URUYHART			
J W*	Siskiyou Scott Ri	69	76
URUZ			
J*	Nevada Eureka	61	352
URY			
Felix	Alameda Brooklyn	55	120
Jeremiah	Del Norte Crescent	58	633
Jeremiah	Del Norte Crescent	58	634
USA			
M*	Tuolumne Big Oak	71	146
USABIA			
Jose Rios	Tulara Twp 3	71	43
USALLO UYAL			
---*	Mendocino Calpella	60	825
USAN			
Maragot	Mariposa Twp 1	60	654
Moragot*	Mariposa Twp 1	60	654
USAWHER			
Whaner	Mariposa Coulterville	60	702
USBAN			
F	Sacramento Sutter	63	293
USCHINSKI			
John	Tuolumne Twp 4	71	133
USE			
---	Stanislaus Empire	70	733
USEENAN			
V*	Butte Kimshaw	56	585
USERA			
Maguil	Contra Costa Twp 1	57	537
USEREO			
---	Monterey S Antoni	60	970
USHER			
Elizabeth	Santa Clara Santa Clara	65	506
G F	Siskiyou Scott Ri	69	64
Gilman*	Tuolumne Columbia	71	306
Gilmari*	Tuolumne Columbia	71	306
Gimar	Tuolumne Twp 2	71	306
Jas	Yolo Cache	72	617
Joseph	Amador Twp 4	55	239
Mary	Sacramento Alabama	63	411
Wm	Butte Kimshaw	56	570
Wm	Del Norte Crescent	58	634
Wm*	Del Norte Crescent	58	633
USILL			
John*	Yolo Cottonwood	72	647
USIREO			
---	Monterey S Antoni	60	970
USIT			
Chas	Mariposa Twp 1	60	647
USIVIE			
Juan	Los Angeles Los Angeles	59	513
USLAR			
Francis	Tuolumne Twp 5	71	520
USN			
---	Calaveras Twp 4	57	321
USON			
Pablo	Monterey San Juan	60	981
USONO			
Volonio	Yuba Linda Twp	72	980
USOODUIN			
Albert J	Solano Fairfield	69	200
USOUD			
Valonio	Yuba Suida	72	980
USSELS			
Matilda*	Yuba Bear Rvr	72	1004
USSEY			
Wm	Nevada Eureka	61	370
USSWE			
---	Nevada Bridgeport	61	491
USTERSAITIGO			
Pablo*	San Bernardino S Buenav	64	212

Name	County Locale	M653 Roll	Page
USTERSARTIGO			
Pablo	San Bernardino Santa Ba	64	212
USTICK			
W L	Sacramento Ward 1	63	80
USUNAN			
V*	Butte Kimshaw	56	585
USUNAW			
A*	Butte Kimshaw	56	585
USUYHART			
J W*	Siskiyou Scott Ri	69	76
UT			
---	Sierra Twp 7	66	898
UTAY			
John	Sierra Pine Grove	66	820
UTBY			
O	Shasta Cottonwood	66	737
UTBZ			
C*	Shasta Cottonwoood	66	737
UTDOSSOLA			
Rosa	San Francisco San Francisco 2	67	615
UTERICH			
John	San Francisco San Francisco 1	68	911
UTERO			
Jose Maria	Fresno Twp 1	59	75
UTES			
M H*	Sacramento Brighton	63	208
UTHOFF			
Henry	Yuba Marysville	72	867
UTLEY			
George	Yuba New York	72	729
John	Calaveras Twp 4	57	325
Merret*	Sierra Scales D	66	801
Merrit*	Sierra Scales D	66	801
William	Solano Suisan	69	229
UTT			
Hiram*	Plumas Quincy	62	981
Lysander*	Placer Auburn	62	595
Wm	Butte Chico	56	563
UTTER			
Isaac	Sonoma Washington	69	664
John	Solano Fremont	69	381
William H	Tuolumne Chinese	71	496
William*	Placer Michigan	62	814
UTTEZ			
C*	Shasta Cottonwoood	66	737
UTTIN			
Geo*	Placer Folsom	62	648
UTTU			
Joseph*	Placer Michigan	62	807
UTY			
Lytto	El Dorado Mud Springs	58	959
UUA			
---*	Sierra Twp 5	66	933
UUESON			
A	San Joaquin Stockton	64	1092
UVEMADIN			
---*	Mendocino Round Va	60	882
UVISA			
Juan*	El Dorado Georgetown	58	747
UXINN			
J R*	Nevada Eureka	61	357
UXUM			
J R	Nevada Eureka	61	357
UY			
---	Mariposa Coulterville	60	684
---	Placer Secret R	62	623
UYAH			
Francisco	Los Angeles Elmonte	59	261
UYETA			
Louis	San Francisco San Francisco 6	67	446
UYNANAY			
A	San Francisco San Francisco 5	67	529
UYNEZ			
---	Mendocino Calpella	60	826
UZETA			
Louis	San Francisco San Francisco 6	67	446
Maricia	San Francisco San Francisco 2	67	612
UZNAY			
Chas	San Francisco San Francisco 10	67	229
VA			
---	Yuba Marysville	72	894
VAANDICK			
Boney*	Sierra Port Win	66	791
VABNEY			
James*	Placer Iona Hills	62	873
VACA			
Antonio	Los Angeles Los Angeles	59	365
D	Solano Fremont	69	383
Escupula	San Luis Obispo	65	22
	San Luis Obispo		
Hosea	Solano Fremont	69	378
Jase C	Santa Clara Gilroy	65	224
Jesus	San Bernardino San Bernadino	64	664
Jesus	Solano Fremont	69	377
Jose	Solano Fremont	69	377

Name	County Locale	M653 Roll	Page
VACA			
Jose	Solano Fremont	69	380
Louis	Calaveras Twp 7	57	39
Louis	Calaveras Twp 8	57	92
Louis	San Francisco San Francisco 5	67	477
Pablo	Santa Clara Gilroy	65	224
Pedro	San Luis Obispo San Luis Obispo	65	34
R	Merced Twp 2	60	919
Rumaldo	Santa Clara Gilroy	65	224
T	Solano Fremont	69	383
VACARAYA			
Antonio	Calaveras Twp 8	57	105
VACARO			
August	San Francisco San Francisco 2	67	731
VACCA			
---	Tulara Twp 1	71	118
Jacob*	Contra Costa Twp 3	57	596
VACHAN			
Jos	Trinity New Rvr	70	1030
VACHE			
Tefila	Monterey San Juan	60	974
VACHT			
C*	Napa Napa	61	61
VACILIOS			
Oliver	Santa Cruz Pescadero	66	642
VACIOS			
Francisco	Santa Cruz Watsonville	66	540
VACLA			
Pedro	San Bernardino Santa Inez	64	135
VACTOR			
Sarah	Sacramento Ward 1	63	99
VADA			
Marie	San Francisco San Francisco 3	67	84
Marri*	San Francisco San Francisco 3	67	84
VADE			
Ellen	San Francisco San Francisco 9	68	940
Patrick	San Francisco San Francisco 9	68	940
VADER			
Harvey	Del Norte Crescent	58	644
VADESEY			
Candie	Colusa Monroeville	57	453
VADO			
Gonicio	Sacramento Ward 1	63	110
Gornicio	Sacramento Ward 1	63	110
VADOR			
Charles	Humbolt Pacific	59	138
VADURA			
Christien	San Francisco San Francisco 6	67	463
Christion	San Francisco San Francisco 6	67	463
VAGATHER			
Jose	Amador Township	55	466
VAGATHIR			
Jose	Amador Twp 1	55	466
VAGEL			
John	Tuolumne Twp 2	71	329
VAGENER			
Eleezer*	San Francisco San Francisco 8	68	1239
Eleizer	San Francisco San Francisco 8	68	1239
VAGES			
Laduas	El Dorado Coloma	58	1118
VAGINA			
N*	Amador Twp 6	55	428
VAGINIA			
N*	Amador Twp 6	55	428
VAGUIDER			
Rafael	San Joaquin Stockton	64	1073
VAHANT			
Joseph	Alameda Brooklyn	55	111
VAHE			
Z	San Francisco San Francisco 2	67	698
VAHER			
H	Amador Twp 3	55	379
VAHLE			
F*	Sutter Nicolaus	70	838
VAICURT			
Nathan	Placer Iona Hills	62	870
VAIGAS			
Juan	Santa Clara Santa Clara	65	513
VAIGH			
Wesley	Calaveras Twp 9	57	368
VAIL			
Augustus	Placer Secret R	62	619
Chas H	San Francisco San Francisco 10	67	285
Edward J	Humbolt Eureka	59	163
Hatt	Calaveras Twp 5	57	230
Jno	Sacramento Ward 4	63	604
John	Placer Yankee J	62	778
Joseph	Santa Cruz Soguel	66	589
L B	Tehama Red Bluff	70	918
M	Calaveras Twp 9	57	391
Milton	Contra Costa Twp 3	57	591
Otto	Yolo Slate Ra	72	696
Otto	Yuba Slate Ro	72	696
Platt	Calaveras Twp 5	57	230

Name	County Locale	M653 RollPage
VAIL		
R S	Sonoma Santa Rosa	69 393
Valentine	Yolo Putah	72 586
Valintine	Yolo Putah	72 586
VAILES		
J	San Joaquin Stockton	641097
John E F	San Francisco San Francisco 3	67 77
VAILLALAS		
John Thingo*	Yuba Parke Ba	72 785
VAILLARD		
Constant	Tuolumne Twp 3	71 465
VAILS		
J E F	San Joaquin Stockton	641096
VAIME		
Wm	Placer Auburn	62 590
VAIMORITE		
S	San Francisco San Francisco 9	68 945
VAINA		
Anton	Tuolumne Columbia	71 473
VAINEY		
A*	Nevada Nevada	61 326
J*	Nevada Nevada T	61 326
Thomas	El Dorado Mud Springs	58 973
VAIRKIN		
Martin*	Placer Auburn	62 584
VAIT		
M	Calaveras Twp 9	57 391
VAITTINE		
Ashley A*	San Francisco 9	681103
	San Francisco	
VAKER		
H	Tuolumne Jacksonville	71 164
VAKLE		
F*	Sutter Nicolaus	70 838
J	Sutter Nicolaus	70 838
VAKOICH		
Lewis W	Tuolumne Twp 1	71 191
VALACE		
M B	Shasta French G	66 722
VALADE		
Juan	San Mateo Twp 2	65 131
VALAFSA		
Loretta	Los Angeles San Jose	59 286
VALAGO		
Luce*	Napa Napa	61 78
VALAHOGO		
Batola	El Dorado Placerville	58 926
VALAIDA		
Ramon*	Los Angeles San Jose	59 281
VALAIR		
J	El Dorado Placerville	58 827
VALAJO		
Luce*	Napa Napa	61 78
VALANDE		
Pablo	San Bernardino San Bernadino	64 663
VALARIO		
Jose	Sacramento Ward 1	63 57
VALASCIS		
Lesavell	Los Angeles San Jose	59 285
VALASCUS		
Robert	Placer Auburn	62 568
VALASE		
M B	Shasta French G	66 722
VALASQUEZ		
Gregorio	Los Angeles Los Angeles	59 384
VALATRA		
J	Tuolumne Columbia	71 291
VALAYO		
Luce*	Napa Napa	61 78
VALBEEERDA		
Francis	Santa Clara San Jose	65 296
VALCIRO		
Jose	Sacramento Ward 1	63 57
VALDANS		
P	San Joaquin Stockton	641071
VALDARES		
Nocenta	Los Angeles San Jose	59 282
VALDAS		
Alcario	Contra Costa Twp 2	57 549
VALDENOSA		
Ricardina	San Francisco San Francisco 2	67 683
VALDENUR		
Hosea	Alameda Oakland	55 55
VALDER		
S	Merced Twp 2	60 924
VALDES		
A	Merced Twp 1	60 900
Antonio	Los Angeles Los Angeles	59 510
Antonio	San Francisco San Francisco 2	67 798
Dolores	Merced Twp 1	60 901
F	Merced Twp 1	60 900
Francisco	Yuba Marysville	72 936
Francisco	Yuba Marysville	72 937
Ignacio	San Diego San Diego	64 769
Jose	Santa Clara Almaden	65 277
L	Merced Twp 1	60 900
VALDES		
M J	Merced Twp 1	60 900
S	Merced Twp 2	60 924
VALDESS		
Manuel	Colusa Mansville	57 439
VALDETARO		
Charles	Yuba Marysville	72 929
VALDEZ		
Albino	San Diego Agua Caliente	64 862
Antonio	Calaveras Twp 5	57 250
Antonio	San Francisco San Francisco 2	67 798
Brusir	San Luis Obispo San Luis Obispo	65 27
Bueno	San Luis Obispo San Luis Obispo	65 42
Carmel	Los Angeles San Gabriel	59 418
Cornelis	San Bernardino San Bernadino	64 615
Eduardo	Los Angeles Los Angeles	59 382
Edwardo	Los Angeles Los Angeles	59 382
Francisco	Santa Inez	64 141
	San Bernardino	
Jesus	San Francisco San Francisco 2	67 782
Jose	Los Angeles Los Angeles	59 301
Jose	San Bernardino Santa Barbara	64 175
Jose	San Bernardino San Bernadino	64 663
Jose Maria	San Bernadino	64 635
Juan	Marin Cortemad	60 783
Juan	San Bernardino San Bernadino	64 639
Julian	Los Angeles Los Angeles	59 382
Leandn	San Francisco San Francisco 2	67 569
Leandro	San Francisco San Francisco 2	67 569
Louis	San Bernardino San Bernadino	64 619
Manuel	Calaveras Twp 5	57 250
Manuel	San Bernardino Santa Barbara	64 194
Manuel	San Luis Obispo San Luis Obispo	65 44
Maria	Los Angeles Los Angeles	59 379
Maria L A	Los Angeles Los Angeles	59 363
Maria M	San Bernardino San Bernadino	64 664
Pantalion	Los Angeles Los Angeles	59 312
Pedro	San Francisco San Francisco 11	151
		67
Pedro	San Mateo Twp 2	65 131
Peter	Calaveras Twp 4	57 336
Petra	Calaveras Twp 4	57 336
Petri	Calaveras Twp 4	57 336
Rafiel	San Bernardino Santa Barbara	64 154
Ramon	San Luis Obispo San Luis Obispo	65 44
Romon	San Bernardino Santa Ba	64 211
Selso	San Francisco San Francisco 11	153
		67
Wancisca	Los Angeles Los Angeles	59 328
VALDIS		
Antonio	Los Angeles Los Angeles	59 510
Bonito	Los Angeles Los Angeles	59 509
Doloris	Los Angeles Los Angeles	59 509
Jose	Los Angeles Los Angeles	59 509
VALDUCE		
F	El Dorado Diamond	58 813
VALE		
D	San Francisco San Francisco 9	681086
John	Yuba Foster B	72 833
Richd	Sonoma Vallejo	69 612
Wm	Sonoma Vallejo	69 619
VALECINO		
Juan	Plumas Quincy	62 938
VALEJO		
Joanno	Yuba Marysville	72 919
VALENACIA		
C	San Mateo Twp 1	65 60
VALENAN		
Carlos*	Monterey Monterey	60 936
VALENCHES		
M	Nevada Washington	61 332
VALENCIA		
---	San Diego Agua Caliente	64 839
Alejo	Santa Clara Fremont	65 431
Antonia	Sierra Downieville	66 963
Antonio	Calaveras Twp 7	57 29
Benanda	Marin San Rafael	60 759
Bencinda*	Marin San Rafael	60 759
Benito	San Bernardino Santa Barbara	64 162
Candelario	Santa Clara Almaden	65 277
Dolone*	Calaveras Twp 5	57 211
Doloni	Calaveras Twp 5	57 211
Dolores	Calaveras Twp 5	57 211
Dolory*	Calaveras Twp 5	57 211
Eligio	Marin San Rafael	60 760
Francisca	Santa Barbara	64 147
	San Bernardino	
Guadaloupe	Santa Barbara	64 168
	San Bernardino	
Jacinto	Marin Cortemad	60 790
Jesus	Los Angeles Los Angeles	59 386
Jesus	Merced Marysville	60 938
Jesus	Monterey Monterey	60 938
Jesus M	Yuba Marysville	72 960
Jose	San Bernardino S Buenav	64 212
VALENCIA		
Jose	Tuolumne Chinese	71 501
Jose M	Los Angeles Los Angeles	59 387
Juan	San Bernardino Santa Barbara	64 163
Juan	San Diego Colorado	64 810
Juan	San Luis Obispo San Luis Obispo	65 25
Juan B	Los Angeles Los Angeles	59 386
Julio	Santa Clara Alviso	65 414
Letha	San Mateo Twp 2	65 111
Loreta	Los Angeles Los Angeles	59 294
M	San Francisco San Francisco 2	67 672
Manuel	Santa Clara Alviso	65 413
Maria J	Los Angeles San Gabriel	59 419
Maria R	Los Angeles Los Nieto	59 425
Marial*	Marin Tomales	60 774
Miguil	San Bernardino Santa Barbara	64 171
Nicolas	Santa Cruz Soguel	66 593
Pablo	San Bernardino Santa Barbara	64 163
Pablo	San Bernardino Santa Barbara	64 195
Pablo	Yuba Marysville	72 919
Pedro	San Bernardino S Buenav	64 220
Petro	San Bernardino Santa Ba	64 219
Pulgaria	San Luis Obispo San Luis Obispo	65 26
Rafaid	San Bernardino Santa Inez	64 139
Ramon	Los Angeles Los Angeles	59 329
Rita	Los Angeles San Pedro	59 479
Sacramento	Los Angeles Los Angeles	59 387
Segunda*	San Mateo Twp 2	65 111
Sgnatra*	Calaveras Twp 7	57 26
Tefara	Calaveras Twp 10	57 281
Trinedad	Calaveras Twp 6	57 136
Trinidad	Calaveras Twp 5	57 136
Trinidad	Los Angeles Los Angeles	59 376
Viceate	San Bernardino S Buenav	64 210
Vicente	San Bernardino Santa Ba	64 210
Waloop	San Mateo Twp 3	65 99
VALENCIANA		
Francisco	San Francisco San Francisco 2	67 694
VALENCIN		
Antonio	Calaveras Twp 6	57 134
Timidad	Calaveras Twp 6	57 136
VALENCIO		
Antonio	San Bernardino S Buenav	64 222
Doloni	Calaveras Twp 5	57 211
Trefara	Calaveras Twp 10	57 281
VALENEIA		
Mariah	Marin Tomales	60 774
VALENEY		
James*	Placer Iona Hills	62 873
VALENGERELA		
Desedani*	San Luis Obispo	65 29
	San Luis Obispo	
VALENGUELLA		
Teodore	San Luis Obispo	65 41
	San Luis Obispo	
VALENGUILA		
Slata	Santa Clara San Jose	65 328
VALENIER		
Francisco*	Santa Clara Santa Clara	65 513
VALENNZALA		
Jose*	Yuba Linda Twp	72 980
VALENQUELLA		
Dolores	Santa Clara Almaden	65 269
VALENS		
Justaque	Alameda Oakland	55 58
VALENSNEL		
Isabel	San Francisco San Francisco 2	67 593
VALENSSULLA		
Carnelita	Yolo Slate Ra	72 700
VALENSUALA		
Jose Ma	San Bernardino Santa Ba	64 218
Jose Ma*	S Buenav	64 219
	San Bernardino	
VALENSUALIR		
Jose	San Bernardino San Bernadino	64 665
VALENSUDA		
Francisco	Santa Barbara	64 185
	San Bernardino	
VALENSUELA		
Augustin	San Bernardino Santa Barbara	64 167
Cleodo	San Bernardino Santa Barbara	64 200
Felipe	San Bernardino Santa Barbara	64 160
Jesus	San Bernardino Santa Barbara	64 193
Jose Ma	San Bernardino Santa Barbara	64 157
Juan	San Bernardino Santa Barbara	64 194
Juan Y	San Bernardino Santa Barbara	64 194
Lasira	Los Angeles Azuza	59 279
Maria	San Bernardino Santa Barbara	64 175
VALENSUOLA		
Jose M	San Bernardino S Buenav	64 222
VALENTAE		
Henry*	Nevada Bloomfield	61 518
VALENTIA		
Condille	San Francisco San Francisco 11	127
		67
Cusinta	San Francisco San Francisco 2	67 763

California 1860 Census Index

Name	County Locale	M653 Roll Page
VALENTIA		
Cusinta*	San Francisco San Francisco	2 67 763
Lauteno	Los Angeles Los Angeles	59 353
Lauterio	Los Angeles Los Angeles	59 353
Marion	Sierra Downieville	66 987
Raymond	San Francisco San Francisco	11 128 67
Rumoni	Los Angeles Azuza	59 279
Salvador	Butte Oregon	56 614
VALENTIN		
Antonia	Los Angeles Los Angeles	59 382
Marion	Sierra Downieville	66 987
VALENTINA		
---	Los Angeles San Juan	59 465
VALENTINE		
---	Mariposa Twp 1	60 641
---	San Diego Agua Caliente	64 858
---	San Mateo Twp 3	65 108
Alex	San Francisco San Francisco	6 67 446
Augustine	Calaveras Twp 5	57 177
C B	Sacramento San Joaquin	63 351
Charles	Santa Cruz Soquel	66 598
Chas	Mariposa Twp 3	60 603
D	Butte Bidwell	56 721
E	Shasta Horsetown	66 691
E H	El Dorado Mud Springs	58 956
Edward B	San Joaquin Oneal	64 938
Harrison	Sonoma Armally	69 504
Henry	Nevada Bloomfield	61 529
Henry	Yuba Rose Bar	72 816
Henry*	Nevada Bloomfield	61 518
Isaac	Nevada Bridgeport	61 470
Isaac	Nevada Bridgeport	61 478
J	El Dorado Eldorado	58 947
J	San Francisco San Francisco	5 67 551
J J	El Dorado Eldorado	58 937
James	Yuba New York	72 733
Jas	San Francisco San Francisco	5 67 554
Jno	San Francisco San Francisco	9 681086
John	Sacramento Cosummes	63 382
John	San Francisco San Francisco	11 99 67
John G	Del Norte Crescent	58 641
M	San Francisco San Francisco	3 67 50
Manny	San Francisco San Francisco	10 244 67
Manry*	San Francisco San Francisco	10 244 67
Martin	San Francisco San Francisco	11 132 67
Mary A	San Francisco San Francisco	11 133 67
Michael	Santa Cruz Watsonville	66 535
Mr	Sonoma Sonoma	69 651
Pedre	Santa Cruz Santa Cruz	66 622
Saml	Sacramento Ward 1	63 62
W H	El Dorado Coloma	581105
VALENTINO		
---	Monterey Pajaro	601011
---	San Diego Agua Caliente	64 833
Alex	San Francisco San Francisco	6 67 446
Margaret	Calaveras Twp 6	57 177
Pedro	Santa Cruz Santa Cruz	66 621
Thos B	San Francisco San Francisco	3 67 201
William	Plumas Meadow Valley	62 931
VALENTIRE		
Henry*	Nevada Bloomfield	61 518
VALENZALA		
Jose	Yuba Suida	72 980
VALENZUALE		
Ramon*	Alameda Murray	55 228
VALENZUALO		
Ramon*	Alameda Murray	55 228
VALENZUELA		
Bonifacio	Los Angeles Los Angeles	59 365
Candelario	Santa Clara Almaden	65 274
Claudio	Los Angeles Los Nieto	59 434
Desedano*	San Luis Obispo	65 29
	San Luis Obispo	
Desiderio	Los Angeles Los Angeles	59 397
Disiderio	Los Angeles Shaffer	59 397
Dolores	Los Angeles Los Angeles	59 363
Dolores	Santa Clara San Jose	65 300
Eduardo*	Yuba Marysville	72 937
Francisco	Los Angeles Santa Ana	59 453
Gertrudes	Los Angeles Los Angeles	59 305
Ignacio	Los Angeles San Juan	59 462
J	Monterey Monterey	60 947
Jesus	San Luis Obispo San Luis Obispo	65 31
Joquin	Los Angeles Los Angeles	59 490
Jose D	Los Angeles Los Angeles	59 367
Jose L	Los Angeles San Juan	59 467
Jose M	Los Angeles Santa Ana	59 442
Jose M	Marin Cortemad	60 785
Jose Ma*	Marin Cortemad	60 786
Juan	San Francisco San Francisco	2 67 698
VALENZUELA		
Juan	Santa Clara Alviso	65 404
Juan A	Marin Cortemad	60 780
Luis	Los Angeles Los Angeles	59 502
Manuela	Los Angeles Los Angeles	59 301
Maria	Los Angeles Los Angeles	59 311
Maria S	Los Angeles Los Angeles	59 498
Maria T	Los Angeles Los Angeles	59 381
Pedro	Los Angeles San Juan	59 475
Ramon	Los Angeles Los Angeles	59 383
Ramon	Los Angeles Los Nieto	59 430
Romaldo	Los Angeles Los Nieto	59 435
Sacramento	Los Angeles Los Angeles	59 386
Sicondino	Los Angeles Los Angeles	59 498
Texano	Los Angeles Los Angeles	59 500
Tomasa	Los Angeles Los Angeles	59 498
Ylaia	Los Angeles Los Nieto	59 426
Ylaria	Los Angeles Los Nieto	59 426
VALENZUELAL		
Ignacio	Los Angeles San Juan	59 462
VALENZUELAS		
F	Napa Napa	61 114
VALENZUELLA		
Jesus	Mariposa Twp 1	60 639
VALENZUILA		
Dolores	Los Angeles Los Angeles	59 504
Francisco	Los Angeles Los Angeles	59 503
Luis	Los Angeles Los Angeles	59 503
Maria S	Los Angeles Los Angeles	59 498
Pedro	Los Angeles Los Angeles	59 515
Sicondino	Los Angeles Los Angeles	59 498
Tixano	Los Angeles Los Angeles	59 500
Tomasa	Los Angeles Los Angeles	59 498
VALENZUITA		
Hypolita*	Santa Clara Burnett	65 259
VALENZULDA		
Reginaldo	San Francisco San Francisco	2 67 643
VALEQUES		
Victonia	Napa Napa	61 115
VALEREGALDA		
Reginaldo	San Francisco San Francisco	2 67 643
VALES		
Leander	Plumas Quincy	62 966
VALESCER		
Frederick*	Santa Cruz Pajaro	66 549
VALESQUES		
Isaak	Sierra Downieville	661031
Victonia	Napa Napa	61 115
VALETINE		
Fred	San Joaquin Stockton	641087
VALETTA		
Ceprian	Yuba Marysville	72 881
Cipian	Yuba Marysville	72 881
Louis	Yuba Marysville	72 902
VALEUAN		
Carlos*	Monterey Monterey	60 936
VALEYWELLA		
Jesno*	Mariposa Twp 1	60 639
VALEZUELLA		
Jesus	Mariposa Twp 1	60 639
VALFIN		
Gabriel	Siskiyou Callahan	69 5
VALFREY		
Rachel	Alameda Brooklyn	55 190
VALGO		
Andrew	Contra Costa Twp 1	57 502
VALIANT		
Peter	San Francisco San Francisco	7 681443
Peter	San Francisco San Francisco	1 68 917
VALICA		
Varcuniles*	Calaveras Twp 5	57 211
VALICE		
Varciendes*	Calaveras Twp 5	57 211
Varcunde	Calaveras Twp 5	57 211
Varcunile	Calaveras Twp 5	57 211
VALICS		
Vascunile	Calaveras Twp 5	57 211
VALINDE		
Juan	Del Norte Crescent	58 626
VALINDO		
Nichols	Sierra Downieville	661012
Nicholas	Sierra Downieville	661012
VALINSSULL		
Carmelita*	Yuba Slate Ro	72 700
VALINTINE		
D	Butte Bidwell	56 721
VALINTIO		
Manuel	Tuolumne Twp 3	71 463
VALIPPI		
John	Calaveras Twp 8	57 108
VALISA		
Maria	Santa Cruz Pajaro	66 546
Thomas	Santa Cruz Pajaro	66 546
VALISCA		
Frederick	Santa Cruz Pajaro	66 549
VALISCO		
Frederick*	Santa Cruz Pajaro	66 549
VALISE		
James	Santa Clara San Jose	65 294
VALK		
Henry	San Francisco San Francisco	3 67 64
VALL		
J N	El Dorado Casumnes	581163
VALLA		
Jose Ant	San Bernardino Santa Barbara	64 181
VALLADO		
Jose	Mendocino Big Rvr	60 846
VALLANSWELLA		
Jose	Colusa Colusi	57 426
VALLANT		
Jules	San Francisco San Francisco	4 681145
Julius A	Sacramento Granite	63 244
VALLARD		
Anthony	Del Norte Crescent	58 628
Virginia	Del Norte Crescent	58 637
VALLAY		
Amelia	Sierra Pine Grove	66 819
VALLAYELUS		
Augustus	El Dorado Salmon Falls	581054
VALLE		
Antono	Mariposa Twp 1	60 623
Benito	Los Angeles Los Angeles	59 300
Celene	San Francisco San Francisco	10 181 67
Cllene*	San Francisco San Francisco	10 181 67
Frinidar	Monterey Monterey	60 964
Gubriclla*	Calaveras Twp 4	57 332
Gutriclla	Calaveras Twp 4	57 332
Leon	Tuolumne Sonora	71 227
M	Yuba Rose Bar	72 792
Pierre	Yuba New York	72 722
Pierri	Yuba New York	72 722
Rachael	Sonoma Santa Rosa	69 395
Thomas	San Bernardino Santa Barbara	64 153
Trinidad	Monterey Monterey	60 964
W	Yuba Rose Bar	72 792
VALLEAN		
Buttes	Amador Twp 3	55 385
VALLEE		
C M	Trinity Trinity	70 972
VALLEGO		
---	Tulara Keyesville	71 65
VALLEJO		
---	Tulara Twp 3	71 67
---	Tulara Keyesville	71 69
---	Tulara Keyesville	71 70
Gaudelupe	Santa Barbara	64 156
	San Bernardino	
Joveta	San Francisco San Francisco	8 681249
VALLELEC		
Edwd*	San Francisco San Francisco	1 68 808
VALLELEE		
Edwd	San Francisco San Francisco	1 68 808
VALLELY		
Rose	San Francisco San Francisco	10 232 67
VALLENCIA		
---	San Diego Agua Caliente	64 816
Antonio	Plumas Quincy	62 924
Antonio	San Diego S Luis R	64 780
Brino	Contra Costa Twp 1	57 488
Bruno*	Contra Costa Twp 1	57 488
Buno*	Contra Costa Twp 1	57 488
Christoval	Calaveras Twp 6	57 168
Meguil	Contra Costa Twp 1	57 488
Miguel	Contra Costa Twp 1	57 488
Vicente	Contra Costa Twp 3	57 588
VALLENCIAS		
Joseph	Calaveras Twp 6	57 170
VALLENCIUS		
Joseph	Calaveras Twp 5	57 170
VALLENCIVILLA		
John	Calaveras Twp 4	57 328
VALLENCWELLA		
John	Calaveras Twp 4	57 328
VALLENGULA		
Sancus	Contra Costa Twp 3	57 600
VALLENS		
Constant	Tuolumne Twp 3	71 465
VALLENSTINE		
H	Sutter Sutter	70 805
VALLENSUELO		
Jose	San Diego Colorado	64 810
Sacramento	San Diego San Diego	64 760
VALLENSWELLER		
J*	Mariposa Twp 1	60 634
VALLENSWELLO		
Trafel	Mariposa Twp 1	60 634
VALLER		
J N	Yolo Merritt	72 581
J R	Yolo Merritt	72 581
VALLERY		
Peter	Yuba Slate Ro	72 710

Name	County Locale	M653 Roll Page
VALLES		
---	Fresno Twp 1	59 86
Francisco	Los Angeles Los Nieto	59 435
VALLET		
J C	San Francisco San Francisco 10	358 67
Laves	Santa Clara San Jose	65 302
R	San Joaquin Stockton	641096
VALLETER		
E*	Tuolumne Twp 1	71 206
VALLETLE		
E	Tuolumne Sonora	71 206
VALLEX		
Legar	San Francisco San Francisco 2 67 673
VALLEY		
J B	Siskiyou Yreka	69 190
John	Placer Todds Va	62 763
VALLEYCATT		
J	Tuolumne Twp 1	71 265
VALLIE		
L B	Nevada Nevada	61 321
VALLIJO		
Andronnco	Sonoma Sonoma	69 653
Androunce	Sonoma Sonoma	69 653
M G	Sonoma Sonoma	69 653
VALLIO		
L B	Nevada Nevada	61 321
VALLLERY		
Peter	Yolo Slate Ra	72 710
VALLOIS		
Julios*	Calaveras Twp 5	57 198
Juluos*	Calaveras Twp 5	57 198
VALLON		
J R	Tuolumne Twp 1	71 211
VALLOO		
Charles	San Francisco San Francisco 4 681217
VALLORLY		
John	Mendocino Little L	60 837
VALLORY		
John	Mendocino Little L	60 837
VALLOU		
Charles	San Francisco San Francisco 4 681217
VALLOYELUS		
Augustus	El Dorado Salmon Hills	581054
VALLUE		
Thos P	Alameda Brooklyn	55 164
VALLUER		
Constant	Tuolumne Twp 3	71 465
VALNENSUELA		
Estavan	Yuba Marysville	72 936
VALNITUE		
Henry	Nevada Bloomfield	61 518
VALNOIS		
Gutier	San Francisco San Francisco 2 67 803
Gutrer*	San Francisco San Francisco 2 67 803
Gutur*	San Francisco San Francisco 2 67 803
VALNOK		
John*	Sierra Cox'S Bar	66 952
VALPENA		
Jno	Tuolumne Twp 4	71 144
VALPEY		
A*	Stanislaus Emory	70 744
VALPILLAR		
Stephen	Tuolumne Sonora	71 206
VALPILLAS		
Stephen	Tuolumne Twp 1	71 206
VALPONA		
Jno	Tuolumne Big Oak	71 144
VALPY		
O S	Santa Clara Santa Clara	65 521
VALSO		
Santo	Amador Twp 5	55 337
VALUE		
Henry	Butte Ophir	56 748
VALUENZALA		
Jose*	Yuba Linda Twp	72 980
VALUICIA		
Osans	El Dorado Coloma	581119
VALUOK		
John*	Sierra Cox'S Bar	66 952
VALUSKE		
Peter*	Alameda Brooklyn	55 139
VALUSKI		
Peter*	Alameda Brooklyn	55 139
VALVACA		
James	Tuolumne Jamestown	71 455
VALVANADE		
Jose	Sierra Downieville	66 963
VALVANEDA		
Maria	Los Angeles San Gabriel	59 420
VALVERD		
D D*	Nevada Grass Valley	61 181
VALVERDE		
Amauel*	Tuolumne Twp 1	71 213
VALVIRDE		
Amanil*	Tuolumne Sonora	71 213

Name	County Locale	M653 Roll Page
VAM		
Joseph*	Sonoma Sonoma	69 643
VAMANT		
Nicolas*	Sierra Twp 5	66 941
VAMBURGH		
J H	Butte Ophir	56 800
VAME		
H	El Dorado Placerville	58 875
VAMER		
James	San Joaquin Elkhorn	64 954
VAMESVALL		
C*	Alameda Brooklyn	55 139
VAMEY		
A*	Nevada Nevada	61 326
Libias H	San Francisco San Francisco 8 681283
VAMISIER		
Adolph	San Francisco San Francisco 10 358 67
VAMO		
Jacob*	Mendocino Calpella	60 814
Ritt W*	Mendocino Calpella	60 814
Robt W*	Mendocino Calpella	60 814
Wm H	Mendocino Calpella	60 814
VAMORI		
A S	Shasta French G	66 722
VAMORO		
A I*	Shasta French G	66 722
VAMP		
Edward	Yuba Long Bar	72 765
VAN ACLAN		
James	Santa Clara Santa Clara	65 481
VAN AERNAM		
John	Humbolt Table Bl	59 142
VAN AIKIN		
Oree*	Shasta Millvill	66 740
Orie*	Shasta Millvill	66 740
VAN ALDT		
John G	San Diego San Diego	64 760
VAN ALEN		
W K	San Francisco San Francisco 2 67 637
VAN ALETEN		
Alonzo*	San Francisco San Francisco 3 67 31
VAN ALLEN		
L C	San Joaquin Stockton	641045
Mary	San Francisco San Francisco 2 67 803
Susan E	Contra Costa Twp 2	57 553
VAN ALSTEIN		
Maria	Sonoma Mendocino	69 450
VAN ALSTEN		
L	El Dorado Placerville	58 851
VAN ALSTINE		
C	El Dorado Placerville	58 848
E*	El Dorado Placerville	58 868
J	Sacramento Ward 4	63 541
Oscar	Sacramento Ward 4	63 546
VAN ALSTONE		
Harrison	Sierra St Louis	66 861
VAN AMBERG		
David	San Francisco San Francisco 7 681339
VAN AMEN		
James*	Placer Iona Hills	62 898
VAN AMONS		
Reirain*	Placer Michigan	62 811
VAN ANKIN		
M*	San Francisco San Francisco 5 67 552
VAN ANTWERP		
Anne	San Francisco San Francisco 12 364 67
Jacob	San Francisco San Francisco 10 332 67
VAN ARDALE		
Jno G	Alameda Brooklyn	55 150
VAN AREN		
George	Placer Forest H	62 796
VAN ASTINE		
Harrison	Sierra St Louis	66 861
VAN AUDIN		
John*	Placer Forest H	62 799
VAN AUKEN		
M	San Francisco San Francisco 5 67 552
VAN AUREN		
James*	Placer Iona Hills	62 898
VAN AWKIN		
---	Yuba Bear Rvr	721007
VAN BERGEN		
John*	San Francisco San Francisco 2 67 762
Nicholas	San Francisco San Francisco 2 67 762
Nicholas*	San Francisco San Francisco 2 67 762
VAN BERGER		
H	San Francisco San Francisco 1 68 928
M*	Nevada Grass Valley	61 171
VAN BERJAR		
Nicholas*	San Francisco San Francisco 2 67 762
VAN BERJEN		
Jas O	San Francisco San Francisco 10 214 67

Name	County Locale	M653 Roll Page
VAN BERJEN		
John	San Francisco San Francisco 2 67 762
VAN BERTRAM		
Charles	Solano Benecia	69 298
VAN BEUNRUN		
Mita*	Calaveras Twp 9	57 354
VAN BIBBEN		
A	Amador Twp 7	55 414
N	Amador Twp 7	55 414
VAN BIONRON		
Mila*	Calaveras Twp 9	57 354
VAN BIOURON		
Mila*	Calaveras Twp 9	57 354
Mita*	Calaveras Twp 9	57 354
VAN BLAKE		
John	Siskiyou Yreka	69 134
VAN BLAM		
Jacob	Nevada Rough &	61 411
VAN BLAUR		
Jacob*	Nevada Rough &	61 411
VAN BOKELEN		
Geo A	San Francisco San Francisco 10 256 67
VAN BOSKINK		
William*	Plumas Quincy	62 972
VAN BRONIAR		
Meta*	Calaveras Twp 9	57 354
VAN BRUKE		
John	Placer Yankee J	62 759
VAN BRYEN		
Jos O	San Francisco San Francisco 10 214 67
VAN BUR SCHOTEN		
J W	Stanislaus Empire	70 734
VAN BUREN		
Edward	San Bernardino San Salvador	64 657
Geo	Sacramento Ward 1	63 34
Josiah	Yuba Rose Bar	72 807
Peter	San Joaquin Oneal	64 933
VAN BUSHERK		
Reuben	Calaveras Twp 6	57 119
VAN CADEN		
G	Butte Oregon	56 618
VAN CAMP		
L	Butte Chico	56 552
Wm	Butte Kimshaw	56 597
VAN CAMPEN		
Ira	Mariposa Twp 1	60 638
W R	Mariposa Twp 1	60 647
VAN CAMPIN		
W R	Mariposa Twp 1	60 647
VAN CERT		
Wm*	San Francisco San Francisco 7 681411
VAN CIRT		
Wm*	San Francisco San Francisco 7 681411
VAN CLINE		
Maria V	San Francisco San Francisco 9 681104
VAN COLLEN		
Jno*	Mendocino Big Rvr	60 846
VAN COLLIN		
Jno	Mendocino Big Rvr	60 846
VAN COLLON		
Jno*	Mendocino Big Rvr	60 846
VAN COMPEN		
Josiphine*	Stanislaus Emory	70 753
VAN CORN		
A V	San Francisco San Francisco 10 242 67
VAN COTT		
J F	Sacramento Ward 1	63 21
J*	Sacramento Ward 1	63 20
VAN COYKE		
Stephen	Yuba Marysville	72 948
VAN CROMBRUGHE		
Alfred	San Francisco San Francisco 10 274 67
VAN DALLER		
Henry*	Calaveras Twp 6	57 143
VAN DAME		
H	San Francisco San Francisco 6 67 461
VAN DANSON		
Wm	Mariposa Coulterville	60 684
VAN DE BURCH		
W	Stanislaus Empire	70 734
VAN DE CASTEL		
---*	San Francisco San Francisco 8 681323
VAN DEALEN		
Charles	Santa Cruz Watsonville	66 536
VAN DEALER		
Charles	Santa Cruz Watsonville	66 536
VAN DEGRIFT		
Geo W	Humbolt Pacific	59 137
VAN DENHOFF		
E B	Nevada Eureka	61 368
VAN DENSEN		
Mary*	Sacramento Ward 3	63 443

Name	County Locale	M653 RollPage
VAN DER CLIFT		
---*	Mariposa Twp 3	60 583
VAN DER HOFF		
William	Placer Iona Hills	62 870
VAN DERENTHERE		
Michl	San Bernardino San Bernadino	64 674
VAN DEURSEN		
Hubert	San Francisco San Francisco 11	154 67
VAN DEUSEN		
Mary*	Sacramento Ward 3	63 443
VAN DINE		
Wm H	Butte Wyandotte	56 668
VAN DOREN		
Joseph	Sonoma Petaluma	69 585
W L	Sonoma Petaluma	69 593
VAN DORIS		
George	Yuba Marysville	72 888
VAN DROTHFELS		
George	Yuba Fosters	72 835
VAN DUSEN		
Chas	Sacramento Granite	63 248
Cornelia	San Francisco San Francisco 8	681236
Edward	Los Angeles Los Angeles	59 353
H	Butte Kimshaw	56 572
J	Amador Twp 2	55 267
L	Butte Kimshaw	56 592
L	Nevada Eureka	61 364
S	Stanislaus Emory	70 743
Thomas	Placer Michigan	62 852
VAN DWEN		
John	Placer Iona Hills	62 883
VAN DYKE		
Jas	San Francisco San Francisco 2	67 765
Jos	San Francisco San Francisco 2	67 765
Joseph	San Francisco San Francisco 8	681306
Ruben	El Dorado Mud Springs	58 950
Stephen	Yuba Marysville	72 948
Walter	Humbolt Eureka	59 172
VAN EATON		
J D	El Dorado Placerville	58 861
VAN EMON		
?*	Placer Michigan	62 808
VAN EVERY		
H	Sacramento Ward 1	63 103
VAN FORSON		
Levy	El Dorado Mud Springs	58 949
VAN FOSON		
Wm	El Dorado Placerville	58 922
VAN GEEON		
John*	Siskiyou Scott Va	69 33
VAN GEERN		
John	Siskiyou Scott Va	69 33
VAN GEISEN		
Henry	Placer Mealsburg	62 702
VAN GEISON		
George	Placer Virginia	62 700
John	Placer Virginia	62 700
VAN GERGEN		
M*	Nevada Grass Valley	61 171
VAN GERNELY		
Jacob	Sierra La Porte	66 787
VAN GESON		
John	Siskiyou Scott Va	69 33
VAN GIERSON		
A	Sacramento Brighton	63 206
VAN GILDER		
A A	El Dorado Coloma	581083
VAN GLAHN		
F	Sacramento Sutter	63 306
VAN GORDON		
Asa	Tulara Twp 2	71 29
Charles	San Francisco San Francisco 4	681147
Ira	Tulara Visalia	71 29
VAN GULPHEN		
Charles*	San Francisco San Francisco 7	681441
VAN GULPHUR		
Charles*	San Francisco San Francisco 7	681441
VAN GUNCLY		
Jacob	Sierra La Porte	66 787
VAN GUNDY		
Wm	Santa Clara Gilroy	65 226
VAN HADEN		
John	San Francisco San Francisco 2	67 622
VAN HAGAN		
A*	Calaveras Twp 9	57 391
J P	Sacramento Ward 3	63 427
Jas B	Nevada Nevada	61 255
VAN HAGAR		
A	Calaveras Twp 9	57 391
VAN HAGEN		
John	Yolo Slate Ra	72 690
John	Yuba Slate Ro	72 690
VAN HARAN		
Albert*	San Francisco San Francisco 10	354 67

Name	County Locale	M653 RollPage
VAN HARD		
S V	Amador Twp 7	55 420
VAN HARN		
A C	Klamath S Fork	59 198
VAN HASS		
C	San Francisco San Francisco 3	67 78
VAN HEART		
J H	Butte Eureka	56 655
VAN HEERAN		
Albert*	San Francisco San Francisco 10	354 67
VAN HEES		
C	San Francisco San Francisco 1	68 880
VAN HENSEN		
J K	Sacramento Ward 3	63 447
VAN HERT		
J H	Butte Eureka	56 655
VAN HEUSEN		
Henry	Sacramento Ward 4	63 564
VAN HOLLAMS		
Henry	Sonoma Petaluma	69 565
VAN HONTLIN		
W	Sonoma Petaluma	69 584
VAN HOOKER		
Jno*	Sacramento Ward 1	63 85
VAN HORN		
A	Nevada Eureka	61 363
Franklin	Tulara Visalia	71 33
G W	Trinity Weaverville	701073
Jeremah	Sonoma Petaluma	69 570
M	Mariposa Twp 1	60 642
Theodore	Tulara Visalia	71 14
VAN HOUTON		
G*	Nevada Nevada	61 280
VAN HOWLAN		
G*	Nevada Nevada	61 280
VAN HOWLANL		
G*	Nevada Nevada	61 280
VAN HOWON		
G*	Nevada Nevada	61 280
VAN HOY		
Simon*	Siskiyou Klamath	69 96
VAN HYMNG		
W A*	Alameda Brooklyn	55 127
VAN HYNING		
W A*	Alameda Brooklyn	55 127
VAN JOON		
Henry	Yuba Marysville	72 965
VAN JOOSE		
Henry	Yuba Marysville	72 965
VAN KINWALL		
S*	El Dorado Georgetown	58 686
VAN LAKE		
Albert	Plumas Quincy	62 938
VAN LEAR		
B B	Tuolumne Twp 4	71 152
VAN LEEOM		
S W*	Yuba Marysville	72 970
VAN LEMBROUCK		
Louis	Sacramento Ward 1	63 125
VAN LEUREN		
Gerson	San Bernardino San Bernadino	64 671
Hannah	San Bernardino San Salvador	64 651
Hiram	San Bernardino San Bernadino	64 686
VAN LEURON		
Frederick	San Bernardino	64 686
VAN LEVIN		
S M	Yuba Marysville	72 970
VAN LINDA		
A	El Dorado White Oaks	581013
VAN LOAK		
L	San Francisco San Francisco 5	67 531
VAN LOON		
Luther	Yolo Slate Ra	72 689
Luther	Yuba Slate Ro	72 689
VAN LORN		
M	Mariposa Twp 1	60 642
VAN MAKER		
William	Nevada Rough &	61 426
VAN MATEE		
J W*	Sacramento Ward 3	63 429
VAN MATER		
J W*	Sacramento Ward 3	63 429
Otis	San Francisco San Francisco 1	68 920
VAN MATHENESSE		
Francis	Tuolumne Chinese	71 487
VAN MATHENFAST		
Francis	Tuolumne Twp 5	71 487
VAN MATRE		
Peter	Trinity Lewiston	70 966
VAN MATRO		
Peter	Trinity Lewiston	70 966
VAN MDELEWORTH		
Andrew	Sierra St Louis	66 814
VAN MEDLEWORTH		
Andrew*	Sierra St Louis	66 814

Name	County Locale	M653 RollPage
VAN MIDDLEWORTH		
P	Shasta Millvill	66 756
VAN MIDLEWOJTH		
Andrew*	Sierra St Louis	66 814
VAN MITER		
---	Monterey San Juan	601004
VAN MULLER		
Ernest	Yuba Marysville	72 864
VAN NAGER		
Underhill*	San Francisco San Francisco 1	68 931
VAN NASTRANES		
D*	San Francisco San Francisco 9	681102
VAN NEAR		
Jas	Butte Chico	56 555
VAN NEFS		
Cornelius	San Francisco San Francisco 7	681427
VAN NEIR		
Edwrd*	San Francisco San Francisco 1	68 915
VAN NERY		
Cornel	Sacramento Natonia	63 279
VAN NESS		
Cornelius	San Francisco San Francisco 7	681427
E	El Dorado Kelsey	581146
Henry	San Francisco San Francisco 2	67 633
J P	San Francisco San Francisco 6	67 454
Jeff	Butte Kimshaw	56 584
Jos	Butte Kimshaw	56 584
VAN NEST		
Barrant	Humbolt Eureka	59 164
Peter	Colusa Spring Valley	57 430
Wm A	Colusa Spring Valley	57 429
VAN NETT		
James	San Francisco San Francisco 11	108 67
VAN NHATTIE		
G*	Nevada Eureka	61 369
VAN NORDEN		
Robt T	Sacramento Ward 3	63 451
VAN NORVEW		
Seth	Butte Chico	56 559
VAN NOSHANT		
Geo*	El Dorado White Oaks	581001
VAN NOSTRANES		
D*	San Francisco San Francisco 9	681102
VAN NOSTROM		
Isaac*	San Diego Colorado	64 811
VAN NOWEN		
Seth	Butte Chico	56 559
VAN OLINDA		
E A	Amador Twp 2	55 262
VAN ORDEN		
G	Butte Oregon	56 618
Jno*	Sacramento Ward 4	63 598
L*	Butte Ophir	56 767
T A	Butte Kimshaw	56 573
W B*	Butte Cascade	56 694
VAN ORDERS		
Jno*	Sacramento Ward 4	63 598
VAN ORDIN		
D T	San Francisco San Francisco 6	67 457
VAN ORDSEN		
W B	Butte Cascade	56 694
VAN ORDSER		
W B*	Butte Cascade	56 694
VAN ORMAN		
M	Amador Twp 2	55 287
VAN PAN		
Henry*	Placer Iona Hills	62 867
VAN PATTEN		
David	Contra Costa Twp 2	57 565
VAN PAW		
Henry*	Placer Iona Hills	62 867
VAN PELT		
D F	San Francisco San Francisco 4	681142
George	Calaveras Twp 10	57 265
John	Calaveras Twp 6	57 120
P	San Francisco San Francisco 5	67 520
VAN PRAAG		
Sam	Sacramento Ward 1	63 64
Saml	Tuolumne Twp 1	71 207
VAN QUITZON		
Albert	Los Angeles Santa Ana	59 440
VAN RAN?ATER		
J B*	Nevada Nevada	61 330
VAN RANSALIER		
Wm	San Francisco San Francisco 3	67 9
VAN RANSATER		
J B*	Nevada Nevada	61 330
VAN RANSELIER		
M	Nevada Grass Valley	61 163
VAN RANSILLER		
Robert	Placer Forest H	62 803
VAN RAU?ATER		
J B*	Nevada Nevada	61 330
VAN RAUSALIER		
Wm*	San Francisco San Francisco 3	67 9

California 1860 Census Index

Name	County Locale	M653 RollPage
VAN RAUSATER		
J B*	Nevada Nevada	61 330
VAN REID		
F L	San Francisco San Francisco 2	67 573
VAN RELT		
Jas	Sacramento Sutter	63 307
VAN RENSLER		
Jerry	San Francisco San Francisco 2	67 584
VAN REUSLER		
Jerry*	San Francisco San Francisco 2	67 584
VAN REYNEGONE		
Anne*	San Francisco San Francisco 12	379 67
VAN RIGAN		
H*	San Francisco San Francisco 3	67 68
VAN RIGM		
H*	San Francisco San Francisco 3	67 68
VAN RIGON		
H	San Francisco San Francisco 3	67 68
VAN RIPEN		
James	San Francisco San Francisco 4	681110
VAN RIPON		
C	Los Angeles Tejon	59 525
VAN RIPOR		
C	Los Angeles Tejon	59 525
VAN RYN		
John M	Los Angeles Los Angeles	59 333
VAN SANN		
J H	Sacramento Ward 1	63 129
VAN SANT		
Joshua	Humbolt Eureka	59 174
VAN SHATTIE		
G	Nevada Eureka	61 369
VAN SICLEN		
George	Humbolt Eureka	59 177
VAN SIEN		
John	Placer Forest H	62 769
VAN SLACK		
A P	Nevada Rough &	61 429
VAN SLUCK		
A P*	Nevada Rough &	61 429
VAN SLYKE		
J	Nevada Grass Valley	61 143
VAN SORN		
Isaac	San Francisco San Francisco 6	67 409
VAN STRAATON		
B E	San Francisco San Francisco 5	67 522
VAN SYCKLE		
Almira	Sacramento Ward 3	63 476
VAN SYCLE		
Geo	Sacramento Sutter	63 296
R W	Sacramento Ward 1	63 133
R W	Sacramento Ward 1	63 86
VAN TANSEL		
Jno*	Sacramento Georgian	63 340
VAN TASS		
John	San Francisco San Francisco 4	681164
VAN TASSELL		
T	San Francisco San Francisco 5	67 485
VAN TERIL		
Wm W*	Butte Kimshaw	56 594
VAN TILBURY		
Virg*	Yolo Slate Ra	72 716
Viry*	Yuba Slate Ro	72 716
VAN TINE		
Wm W	Butte Kimshaw	56 594
VAN TRIES		
J H	Sacramento Ward 3	63 481
VAN TUNSEL		
Jno*	Sacramento Georgian	63 340
VAN ULICK		
H	El Dorado Placerville	58 873
VAN URANKEN		
Eber	Yuba Marysville	72 972
VAN VACTOR		
William	Placer Iona Hills	62 860
VAN VALEN		
Jeremiah	Yuba Marysville	72 966
VAN VALKENBAUGH		
Lauren	Calaveras Twp 6	57 143
VAN VALKENBERG		
Edgar	San Diego San Diego	64 757
Garrett	San Joaquin Castoria	64 893
VAN VALKENBURG		
Lamen	Calaveras Twp 5	57 143
Noah*	Sonoma Vallejo	69 611
VAN VALKENBURGH		
Henry	San Francisco San Francisco 2	67 568
VAN VALKENBURY		
Lauren	Calaveras Twp 6	57 143
VAN VALKENHAIGH		
Lauren	Calaveras Twp 6	57 143
VAN VALKINBURG		
Noah*	Sonoma Vallejo	69 611
VAN VALKINBURY		
Noah	Sonoma Vallejo	69 611

Name	County Locale	M653 RollPage
VAN VAULKENBERG		
Ephrai	Tulara Twp 2	71 14
VAN VEANS		
John*	Mariposa Twp 3	60 594
VAN VECHLIN		
Temio*	Sacramento Centre	63 180
VAN VECHTIN		
Temio*	Sacramento Centre	63 180
VAN VICTON		
D	Tuolumne Columbia	71 351
VAN VICTOR		
D	Tuolumne Twp 2	71 351
VAN VLEAN		
George	San Luis Obispo San Luis Obispo 65	2
VAN VLECK		
H B	San Francisco San Francisco 5	67 479
J W	San Francisco San Francisco 6	67 469
VAN VLICK		
A	El Dorado Placerville	58 889
H B	San Francisco San Francisco 5	67 479
J W	San Francisco San Francisco 6	67 469
VAN VORHIES		
Wm	Alameda Brooklyn	55 123
VAN VORIES		
George	Yuba Marysville	72 888
VAN VRANKIN		
C B	Nevada Eureka	61 382
Hester	Sacramento Ward 1	63 133
VAN VRAUKIS		
B*	Placer Forest H	62 792
VAN WAGENER		
James	San Francisco San Francisco 7	681344
VAN WAGENOR		
V	El Dorado Kelsey	581149
VAN WAGINOR		
James*	San Francisco San Francisco 7	681344
VAN WAGMOR		
James*	San Francisco San Francisco 7	681344
VAN WAGNER		
C	Nevada Eureka	61 356
Edgar	Yuba New York	72 730
VAN WAGONER		
V	El Dorado Kelsey	581149
VAN WANKIN		
C B*	Nevada Eureka	61 382
VAN WART		
Wm	San Francisco San Francisco 12	363 67
Wm	San Francisco San Francisco 1	68 922
Wm*	San Francisco San Francisco 12	363 67
VAN WATTIE		
G*	Nevada Eureka	61 369
VAN WERT		
Danl	Butte Chico	56 552
Wm	Butte Chico	56 552
VAN WEST		
S D	Butte Chico	56 533
VAN WIC		
A	Shasta Shasta	66 665
VAN WINKEL		
Mathew	Sierra St Louis	66 811
VAN WINKLE		
---	Sierra Pine Grove	66 822
A J	San Francisco San Francisco 7	681408
Henry	Sierra St Louis	66 807
John	Sierra Pine Grove	66 824
Margaret	Sierra Pine Grove	66 822
Mathew	Sierra St Louis	66 811
R W	El Dorado White Oaks	581010
Th	Sonoma Vallejo	69 612
Thos	Sonoma Petaluma	69 556
VAN WYCK		
Albert	San Francisco San Francisco 2	67 792
VAN WYKE		
H D*	Siskiyou Scott Va	69 25
VAN ZANDT		
J W	San Francisco San Francisco 3	67 61
VAN ZANT		
Julia	San Francisco San Francisco 6	67 412
VAN		
---	El Dorado Placerville	58 898
Charley	Trinity Eastman	70 960
John	Merced Monterey	60 941
Sow	Sierra Twp 7	66 907
VAN??RATTER		
G	Nevada Eureka	61 369
VAN?ANK??		
Hurman*	Napa Yount	61 39
VANACHER		
Eugene*	Santa Cruz Santa Cruz	66 608
VANADAL		
Valentine	Calaveras Twp 5	57 248
Valentino	Calaveras Twp 5	57 248
VANAERMOAH		
Alonzo*	Calaveras Twp 8	57 69

Name	County Locale	M653 RollPage
VANAKEN		
A J	Sierra Eureka	661046
Paul	Tuolumne Twp 2	71 402
VANAKER		
Jas B*	Alameda Oakland	55 38
VANALCHA		
Eugene*	Santa Cruz Santa Cruz	66 608
VANALLEN		
John	Marin San Rafael	60 767
P C	Santa Clara Santa Clara	65 521
VANALLSER		
David	Sacramento Sutter	63 303
VANALLSON		
David	Sacramento Sutter	63 303
VANALLSTINE		
Wm	Mariposa Twp 1	60 673
VANALSTINE		
Dav	Sacramento Ward 4	63 524
George	Placer Forest H	62 774
Robt*	Stanislaus Emory	70 746
VANALSTON		
D	Sacramento Alabama	63 417
VANANDE		
Lewis	San Francisco San Francisco 10	205 67
VANANDER		
Wm	Mendocino Calpella	60 815
VANANSWALER		
Jose	Los Angeles Azuza	59 275
VANARKIN		
Owen	Shasta Millvill	66 740
VANARSDALL		
Mary	Santa Clara San Jose	65 367
VANARSDEN		
A	Yolo Putah	72 550
VANASCHA		
Eugene	Santa Cruz Santa Cruz	66 608
VANASCHER		
Eugene*	Santa Cruz Santa Cruz	66 608
VANASCHEV		
Eugene*	Santa Cruz Santa Cruz	66 608
VANASTINE		
Emma	Sacramento Ward 4	63 538
VANATTEN		
William*	Tulara Twp 3	71 54
VANATTER		
William	Tulara Keyesville	71 54
VANAUSDALL		
C	Tuolumne Twp 2	71 391
VANAVERY		
A J	Marin Tomales	60 713
VANBAUN		
Edwin V*	Alameda Murray	55 223
VANBERBER		
Thos	Alameda Brooklyn	55 185
VANBERGEN		
A H	San Francisco San Francisco 5	67 500
Christina	San Francisco San Francisco 1	68 873
VANBIBBIR		
Henry	Alameda Brooklyn	55 182
VANBLOCK		
Henry	Tuolumne Twp 2	71 370
VANBOSKIRK		
H H*	Napa Hot Springs	61 27
H K*	Napa Hot Springs	61 27
VANBOSKISK		
H K*	Napa Hot Springs	61 27
VANBRAKER		
Augustus	Sacramento Ward 4	63 514
VANBROWN		
Edward	Sacramento Ward 4	63 512
VANBURAN		
Cornelius	Marin Bolinas	60 745
VANBURG		
Phenius	Tulara Sinks Te	71 43
Thomas	Tulara Twp 3	71 43
VANBURGAN		
T	Siskiyou Klamath	69 90
VANBURGANS		
P	Siskiyou Klamath	69 90
VANBUSKIRK		
R H	Butte Chico	56 565
VANCAMPEN		
Ira	Mariposa Twp 1	60 638
VANCAN		
Fielding	Amador Twp 2	55 321
VANCE		
Alex	Placer Virginia	62 662
Alexander	San Diego Agua Caliente	64 821
Andrew	Butte Hamilton	56 525
Andrew	Butte Kimshaw	56 581
Edwin	Humbolt Eureka	59 176
Eliphalet	Plumas Quincy	62 945
Geo	El Dorado Placerville	58 913
George	Humbolt Eureka	59 171
H	Butte Kimshaw	56 584

Name	County Locale	M653 RollPage
VANCE		
H	El Dorado Newtown	58 780
H C	Sutter Sutter	70 802
Horrace	Santa Clara Santa Clara	65 502
Hugh	Amador Twp 3	55 398
J	El Dorado Placerville	58 873
J	San Francisco San Francisco 5	67 522
J	Trinity Taylor'S	701034
J M*	Butte Oregon	56 610
J W	Butte Oregon	56 610
J W	Nevada Eureka	61 370
James	San Joaquin Elliott	64 944
James R	Yuba Marysville	72 905
Jas	Placer Dutch Fl	62 724
John	Humbolt Eureka	59 172
John	Placer Rattle Snake	62 634
John	San Joaquin Stockton	641053
Joseph	Marin Cortemad	60 791
Joseph H	Amador Twp 2	55 265
Joseph*	Marin Cortemad	60 791
Lucinda	Tulara Twp 1	71 82
M	Nevada Eureka	61 381
Milt	Sacramento Ward 4	63 516
R	Nevada Eureka	61 381
R H	San Francisco San Francisco 5	67 498
Richd	Amador Twp 3	55 375
Robert	San Joaquin Elkhorn	64 988
Robert	Yolo Putah	72 614
S	Sacramento Ward 1	63 48
Sam	Sacramento Ward 1	63 29
T H	Calaveras Twp 9	57 374
Thos	Santa Clara Redwood	65 445
W L	Trinity Douglas	70 980
William	Placer Yankee J	62 781
William	San Francisco San Francisco 8	681258
Wm	Humbolt Eel Rvr	59 146
Wm	Santa Clara Fremont	65 434
Z Taylor	San Joaquin Douglass	64 917
VANCES		
T H	Calaveras Twp 9	57 374
VANCHEIS		
Rhoda A	Siskiyou Yreka	69 175
VANCHRIS		
Rhoda A	Siskiyou Yreka	69 175
VANCI		
Joseph*	Marin Cortemad	60 791
VANCLEAVE		
N V	Sonoma Cloverdale	69 679
VANCLIEF		
Peter	Sierra Downieville	66 955
VANCOREN		
J	Sierra Downieville	661020
VANCOURT		
John M	Santa Clara Fremont	65 426
VANCTSAE		
Andrews A*	Placer Auburn	62 566
VANCUBURG		
Mary*	Santa Cruz Pajaro	66 571
VANCUREN		
J	Sierra Downieville	661020
VAND		
Martin	Fresno Twp 1	59 75
VANDALL		
B	Amador Twp 3	55 407
VANDALLEN		
Henry	Calaveras Twp 5	57 143
VANDANSON		
Paris*	Mariposa Coulterville	60 696
Wm	Mariposa Coulterville	60 684
VANDEBERG		
Charles	Tuolumne Columbia	71 298
VANDEBURG		
Mary*	Santa Cruz Pajaro	66 571
William*	Santa Cruz Pajaro	66 571
VANDECAN		
E*	Calaveras Twp 9	57 401
VANDECAR		
Elind*	Sierra Downieville	661016
Israel	Sierra Downieville	661016
VANDEFRIFT		
G B W	Mariposa Twp 1	60 949
VANDEGRIF		
John	Napa Napa	61 99
VANDEGRIFF		
G B W	Mariposa Twp 1	60 649
VANDEGRIFFE		
John	Plumas Quincy	62 962
VANDEGRIFT		
G B W*	Mariposa Twp 1	60 649
VANDEGRITT		
G B W	Mariposa Twp 1	60 649
VANDEINENT		
Jacob*	Amador Twp 3	55 400
VANDEL		
P	El Dorado Diamond	58 802
VANDELIP		
Edward	Sierra Port Win	66 792

Name	County Locale	M653 RollPage
VANDEM		
Chas D	Sacramento Granite	63 266
VANDEMAN		
Chas D	Sacramento Ward 3	63 488
E P	Amador Twp 3	55 388
VANDEMARK		
S J*	Amador Twp 2	55 276
VANDEME		
Theresa	San Francisco San Francisco 2	67 729
VANDEMENT		
Jacob*	Amador Twp 3	55 400
VANDENBERG		
Ed L	Sacramento Ward 4	63 575
L B	Sacramento Ward 4	63 495
VANDENBRUEL		
L	Shasta French G	66 713
VANDENBURG		
C	Tuolumne Sonora	71 484
F G	Los Angeles Los Angeles	59 519
John P B	Santa Clara San Jose	65 295
VANDENE		
Peter	Nevada Little Y	61 531
VANDENHOFF		
E B	Nevada Eureka	61 368
VANDER SCHEER		
G M	San Francisco San Francisco 2	67 691
VANDERAN		
Geo	Placer Auburn	62 591
VANDERANCE		
Joseph	Sierra Downieville	661020
VANDERBACKER		
Andy*	Sacramento San Joaquin	63 354
VANDERBECK		
Henry	San Francisco San Francisco 8	681290
VANDERBERG		
William*	Calaveras Twp 4	57 335
VANDERBILT		
Ann	San Francisco San Francisco 6	67 408
J	Tuolumne Twp 2	71 330
J H	El Dorado Placerville	58 846
K	El Dorado Placerville	58 846
W H	San Francisco San Francisco 9	681070
William	Marin Tomales	60 719
VANDERBITT		
J	Tuolumne Columbia	71 330
VANDERBRICK		
Franklin	Calaveras Twp 5	57 188
VANDERBRUCK		
Franklin	Calaveras Twp 5	57 188
VANDERBUCK		
Jrunkli*	Calaveras Twp 5	57 188
VANDERBURG		
F G	Los Angeles Los Angeles	59 519
William	Calaveras Twp 4	57 335
VANDERCEIPT		
---*	Mariposa Twp 3	60 583
VANDERCOOK		
Ferederick*	Yuba Long Bar	72 753
Frederick	Yuba Long Bar	72 753
VANDEREAR		
E H*	Placer Auburn	62 560
VANDERER		
G W	Nevada Nevada	61 270
VANDERFORD		
N V	Sutter Yuba	70 775
VANDERGUFT		
G	El Dorado Mud Springs	58 954
VANDERHAR		
Ann	Sierra Cox'S Bar	66 952
Hun	Sierra Cox'S Bar	66 952
VANDERHOEF		
Edgar	San Francisco San Francisco 10	220 67
VANDERHOF		
Jno H	Trinity Redding	70 985
VANDERHOFF		
John	Butte Oro	56 684
VANDERHOOF		
Sarah	Alameda Brooklyn	55 161
VANDERHOOT		
F	Calaveras Twp 9	57 388
VANDERHURST		
William	Santa Cruz Watsonville	66 538
VANDERHUSY		
C	Tuolumne Twp 1	71 484
VANDERIAR		
F P*	Shasta Shasta	66 684
VANDERLACKER		
Andy*	Sacramento San Joaquin	63 354
VANDERLIP		
Catharine	Sierra La Porte	66 783
Martland	Merced Monterey	60 942
Martland	Monterey Monterey	60 942
VANDERMARK		
Abram	Yuba Marysville	72 861
L	El Dorado Kelsey	581137

Name	County Locale	M653 RollPage
VANDERMASH		
L	El Dorado Kelsey	581137
VANDERMICH		
J	San Francisco San Francisco 2	67 699
VANDERNARK		
S J*	Amador Twp 2	55 276
VANDERNATIN		
James	Placer Forest H	62 802
VANDEROFT		
John	San Mateo Twp 3	65 87
VANDERPOOL		
Antony	Plumas Quincy	62 936
D	Tuolumne Columbia	71 330
George	Marin Cortemad	60 782
Jacob	San Francisco San Francisco 9	681003
Jno C	San Francisco San Francisco 9	681009
Peter	San Joaquin Oneal	64 933
Sw	Colusa Grand Island	57 470
W R	Tuolumne Columbia	71 332
VANDERPOOLE		
W B	Tuolumne Twp 2	71 332
VANDERPOOT		
D	Tuolumne Twp 2	71 330
VANDERS		
W B*	Amador Twp 1	55 465
VANDERSLICE		
Wm K	San Francisco San Francisco 3	67 17
VANDERTRUCK		
Frankli	Calaveras Twp 6	57 188
VANDERVAKE		
A K*	Sierra Downieville	661012
VANDERVAL		
Jno D	San Francisco San Francisco 9	681008
VANDERVILLE		
A	Tuolumne Columbia	71 294
VANDERVOORT		
Jas A	Del Norte Crescent	58 620
VANDERVOOT		
G J*	Yuba Marysville	72 979
VANDERVORT		
G J	Yuba Marysville	72 979
VANDERWATEN		
William H	San Francisco San Francisco 8	681290
VANDERWATER		
William	San Francisco San Francisco 8	681290
VANDERWOOD		
Joseph	Mendocino Little L	60 834
VANDEVENTES		
Frank	Contra Costa Twp 2	57 562
VANDEVER		
Jas	San Francisco San Francisco 10	333 67
VANDEVIAR		
F P*	Shasta Shasta	66 684
VANDEVIER		
F P	Shasta Shasta	66 684
J P*	Shasta Shasta	66 684
VANDEVILLE		
John H	San Francisco San Francisco 3	67 33
VANDEVORE		
Henry	Colusa Grand Island	57 476
VANDEVORT		
G J*	Yuba Marysville	72 979
VANDEWAKE		
A K	Sierra Downieville	661012
VANDEWATER		
John	San Francisco San Francisco 3	67 19
R J	San Francisco San Francisco 4	681120
VANDEWOK		
Frederick*	Yuba Long Bar	72 753
VANDICAN		
E	Calaveras Twp 9	57 401
VANDICAR		
Israel	Sierra Downieville	661016
Silas H	Tuolumne Twp 4	71 177
VANDICK		
Kanillier	Sierra Twp 5	66 926
Rancellin	Sierra Twp 5	66 926
VANDIKE		
J M	Mariposa Twp 3	60 574
VANDIM		
Edwin*	Calaveras Twp 4	57 309
VANDINAN		
Isaac*	Siskiyou Yreka	69 131
VANDINE		
Ebben	Santa Clara Redwood	65 444
James	Sierra Excelsior	661034
VANDINGER		
E C*	Nevada Red Dog	61 540
VANDIRER		
W	Nevada Nevada	61 244
VANDIVER		
W*	Nevada Nevada	61 244
VANDIZER		
B G	Sutter Butte	70 795
VANDLAN		
D	Sacramento Brighton	63 202

California 1860 Census Index

Name	County Locale	M653 Roll Page
VANDLSTINE		
Robt*	Stanislaus Emory	70 746
VANDMAN		
Isaac	Siskiyou Yreka	69 131
VANDOLSAN		
Henry	Santa Clara San Jose	65 318
VANDORAN		
Danl	Napa Napa	61 88
VANDOREN		
V J	Napa Napa	61 93
VANDOUSAN		
P H	San Joaquin Stockton	641092
VANDRIN		
Edwin	Calaveras Twp 4	57 309
VANDROTTFELS		
George*	Yuba Foster B	72 835
VANDUGEN		
James	Contra Costa Twp 2	57 560
VANDUN		
Edwin*	Calaveras Twp 4	57 309
VANDURANCE		
Joseph	Sierra Downieville	661020
VANDURER		
? K	Sacramento Ward 1	63 32
VANDUSEN		
Arthur	El Dorado Placerville	58 929
Chas	Sacramento Granite	63 248
H	Butte Kimshaw	56 572
VANDUSER		
James	Santa Cruz Santa Cruz	66 602
VANDUZAN		
Martin	Marin Bolinas	60 741
VANDUZART		
Martin	Marin Bolinas	60 741
VANDUZEN		
A P	Siskiyou Scott Va	69 37
John J	Contra Costa Twp 2	57 554
VANDVILL		
Alfred	Sierra Scales D	66 803
VANDVILT		
Alfred	Sierra Scales D	66 803
VANDWAR		
? K	Sacramento Ward 1	63 32
VANDWEER		
C K	Sacramento Ward 1	63 32
VANDWIER		
? K	Sacramento Ward 1	63 32
VANDWUR		
? K	Sacramento Ward 1	63 32
VANDYKE		
Benj	Placer Stewart	62 607
C	Siskiyou Klamath	69 89
H D	Siskiyou Scott Va	69 25
J M	Mariposa Twp 3	60 574
John	Siskiyou Klamath	69 89
VANE		
Jno	Klamath S Fork	59 199
Joseph	Sonoma Sonoma	69 643
Peter	Mariposa Twp 3	60 594
VANEE		
E	Alameda Oakland	55 64
VANEGAS		
Bernidina	San Bernardino Santa Ba	64 215
Casmes*	San Bernardino Santa Inez	64 139
Crisofono*	San Bernardino Santa Inez	64 139
Damaso	San Bernardino Santa Inez	64 140
Maria	Los Angeles San Juan	59 466
Pedro	San Bernardino Santa Barbara	64 199
VANEIR		
John	San Francisco San Francisco	2 67 712
VANELA		
Cenela	El Dorado Casumnes	581170
Cinela*	El Dorado Casumnes	581170
VANELIANE		
Malicom	Santa Clara San Jose	65 353
VANENBURG		
William	Santa Cruz Pajaro	66 571
VANENGO		
Juan	Alameda Washington	55 171
VANEORE		
A W*	Shasta French G	66 722
VANERTA		
Antonio	Alameda Brooklyn	55 116
VANES		
Joseph	Solano Benecia	69 304
VANEST		
George B	Santa Clara San Jose	65 286
Sidney	San Francisco San Francisco	2 67 662
VANETING		
Geo	Santa Clara San Jose	65 370
VANETRAE		
Andrews A*	Placer Auburn	62 566
VANETRIE		
Andrew*	Yuba Rose Bar	72 798

Name	County Locale	M653 Roll Page
VANEVOOCT		
Ann*	San Francisco San Francisco	4 681149
VANEVOOET		
Ann*	San Francisco San Francisco	4 681149
VANEVOVET		
Ann*	San Francisco San Francisco	4 681149
VANEVRIE		
Andrew	Yuba Rose Bar	72 798
VANEZUELA		
Dolores	Alameda Brooklyn	55 151
VANFOPEN		
W M	Trinity Trinity	70 971
VANFOSSON		
Jane	El Dorado Diamond	58 773
VANFRANKIN		
E	Tehama Antelope	70 890
VANG		
---	Calaveras Twp 6	57 169
---	El Dorado Georgetown	58 692
---	Placer Folsom	62 648
VANGANT		
A	Amador Twp 3	55 404
J B*	Placer Michigan	62 856
VANGDDER		
John*	Napa Napa	61 80
VANGEISAN		
John*	Placer Auburn	62 595
VANGHAN		
C S V	Sutter Sutter	70 804
G H	El Dorado Georgetown	58 694
George	Yolo Merritt	72 579
J	Sutter Sutter	70 801
J O	Nevada Nevada	61 312
Walter*	Calaveras Twp 6	57 180
VANGHIN		
Levi S	Sierra La Porte	66 770
VANGHN		
W W	Calaveras Twp 9	57 405
VANGILDER		
John	Napa Napa	61 78
John	Napa Napa	61 80
VANGISEN		
A	Calaveras Twp 9	57 391
VANGLAHN		
F	Sacramento Sutter	63 306
VANGLEN		
John*	San Francisco San Francisco	7 681419
VANGORDEN		
William	Calaveras Twp 4	57 300
VANGORDER		
William	Calaveras Twp 4	57 300
VANGOTH		
M	Calaveras Twp 9	57 392
VANGOTT		
M	Calaveras Twp 9	57 392
VANGRANDY		
G	Santa Clara Redwood	65 452
VANGUE		
John	Placer Rattle Snake	62 636
VANHAGAN		
A	Calaveras Twp 9	57 391
James*	Tuolumne Twp 2	71 384
VANHANE		
D O*	Nevada Eureka	61 372
VANHARD		
S V	Amador Twp 7	55 420
VANHATTER		
Jas	Amador Twp 5	55 334
VANHAVE		
D A*	Nevada Eureka	61 372
VANHEERAN		
Albert	San Francisco San Francisco	10 354 67
VANHEMACETT		
John*	Sierra Downieville	661016
VANHOLINGER		
John	Tuolumne Sonora	71 214
VANHOLLAND		
Anna M	Marin Novato	60 737
G F	Marin Novato	60 736
VANHOM		
William	Siskiyou Shasta Rvr	69 112
VANHOOKER		
Jos*	Sacramento Ward 1	63 85
VANHORN		
Edwin	Calaveras Twp 8	57 86
F D*	Sacramento Ward 4	63 574
F W	Yolo Putah	72 588
H C	Butte Mountain	56 739
H J	Shasta Shasta	66 675
John	Sierra Gibsonville	66 858
P H	Tehama Lassen	70 881
S	El Dorado Diamond	58 773
William	Siskiyou Shasta Rvr	69 112
VANHOUSEN		

Name	County Locale	M653 Roll Page
VANHOUSEN		
Wm	San Francisco San Francisco	10 330 67
VANHOVE		
Bernard	San Francisco San Francisco	3 67 8
VANHUTER		
James	Sacramento Ward 4	63 508
VANIBALDI		
Jno*	San Francisco San Francisco	2 67 749
VANICA		
Chas	Butte Ophir	56 792
VANICE		
Cornelius	Sacramento Granite	63 255
Cornelius	Sacramento Granite	63 255
V	Santa Clara Alviso	65 409
VANIL		
Charles M	Yolo Slate Ra	72 696
J H	Yolo Slate Ra	72 696
VANIMOR		
P	Sutter Butte	70 780
VANJEAN		
D	Mariposa Twp 3	60 573
VANJILDER		
John*	Napa Hot Springs	61 80
VANKAGEN		
James*	Tuolumne Twp 2	71 384
VANKERSAN		
Cornelius*	Marin Bolinas	60 745
VANKINKLE		
Peter W	Alameda Oakland	55 38
VANKS		
Albert	San Francisco San Francisco	3 67 79
VANKUSAN		
Cornelius*	Marin Bolinas	60 745
VANLEAR		
M H	Santa Clara Santa Clara	65 466
VANLECOM		
S W*	Yuba Marysville	72 970
VANLEMBRONEK		
Louis*	Sacramento Ward 1	63 125
VANLEMBROUCK		
Louis*	Sacramento Ward 1	63 125
VANLENZUELA		
Joquin	Los Angeles Los Angeles	59 490
VANLEUREN		
Benj	San Bernardino San Bernadino	64 671
VANLEUWEN		
Setti	Colusa Monroeville	57 454
VANLIND		
John G	Sacramento Ward 4	63 509
VANMAKEN		
R*	El Dorado Placerville	58 889
VANMAKER		
R*	El Dorado Placerville	58 889
VANMAKU		
R*	El Dorado Placerville	58 889
VANMARKEN		
Eben	Yuba Marysville	72 972
VANMATER		
John M*	Placer Auburn	62 577
Wm	Placer Sacramento	62 646
VANMATLER		
Isaac*	Placer Dutch Fl	62 712
VANN		
Abram	Calaveras Twp 6	57 175
Edward	Sonoma Armally	69 483
Pett W*	Mendocino Calpella	60 814
R L	Napa Clear Lake	61 118
Smith J	Napa Yount	61 32
Thos A	Napa Napa	61 113
Wm H	Napa Yount	61 34
Wm N*	Napa Yount	61 34
VANNALKENBERG		
John	Sacramento Franklin	63 311
VANNAMIS		
H M*	El Dorado Georgetown	58 758
VANNAMU		
H M*	El Dorado Georgetown	58 758
VANNATTO		
G P	El Dorado Placerville	58 880
VANNE		
Albert	Sacramento Ward 1	63 95
VANNEA		
Blasco	Colusa Monroeville	57 440
VANNEANS		
John*	Mariposa Twp 3	60 594
VANNEL		
Albert	Sacramento Ward 1	63 46
VANNERBECK		
Peter	Trinity Point Ba	70 976
VANNESS		
H*	Merced Twp 2	60 919
H*	San Francisco San Francisco	9 681060
James	San Francisco San Francisco	11 108 67
S D	San Francisco San Francisco	1 68 894

California 1860 Census Index

Name	County Locale	M653 RollPage
VANNESS		
W	Santa Clara Redwood	65 447
VANNEST		
James A	Colusa Colusi	57 421
N	Trinity E Weaver	701059
VANNETT		
J	Sacramento Granite	63 229
VANNIMOR		
A*	Sutter Butte	70 779
VANNINOR		
A*	Sutter Butte	70 779
VANNIPER		
Munson	Tuolumne Jacksonville	71 516
VANNISS		
H*	Merced Twp 2	60 919
Jeff	Butte Kimshaw	56 584
VANNOLEN		
John	El Dorado Kelsey	581126
VANNOSTRAND		
G W	El Dorado Placerville	58 882
VANOCHEN		
Gilbert	Sierra St Louis	66 815
VANOIS		
V	San Joaquin Stockton	641092
VANOLEET		
D C*	Yolo Cottonwood	72 656
Eli J	Alameda Brooklyn	55 102
VANOLEN		
John	El Dorado Kelsey	581126
VANOLUT		
D C	Yolo Cottonwood	72 656
VANON		
Augustus*	Solano Benecia	69 286
VANOR		
John	Tuolumne Sonora	71 190
VANORANKEA		
Harman*	Napa Yount	61 39
VANORAUKUA		
Harman*	Napa Yount	61 39
VANORDEN		
G B	Butte Hamilton	56 525
T A	Butte Kimshaw	56 573
VANORHEN		
Gilbert*	Sierra St Louis	66 815
VANORHIES		
A A	El Dorado Placerville	58 851
VANORMAN		
Nathaniel	Sierra Poker Flats	66 842
VANORY		
Augustus	Solano Benecia	69 286
VANPELT		
Chas*	Napa Napa	61 109
Chs*	Napa Napa	61 109
Jas	Sacramento Ward 4	63 512
VANPER		
Maria	Santa Clara Santa Clara	65 467
VANPRAAG		
Joseph	Tuolumne Twp 1	71 220
Saml	Tuolumne Twp 1	71 207
VANPREE		
Eliza	Santa Clara Santa Clara	65 467
VANRACTER		
J B	Yuba Rose Bar	72 788
J W*	Yuba Rose Bar	72 788
VANRARARION		
Peter*	Sacramento Centre	63 177
VANRAVARION		
Peter*	Sacramento Centre	63 177
VANREED		
J H	San Francisco San Francisco 10	337 67
VANRIPER		
Munson	Tuolumne Twp 5	71 516
VANROSSUM		
H C	Klamath Liberty	59 234
VANS		
H A	Calaveras Twp 9	57 394
VANSALSTINE		
Oren	Sacramento Ward 4	63 538
VANSANT		
Guctar Rico*	Calaveras Twp 6	57 173
Guitar Rico	Calaveras Twp 5	57 173
Gurtar Rico*	Calaveras Twp 6	57 173
Gurtav Rico*	Calaveras Twp 6	57 173
Gustar Rico*	Calaveras Twp 6	57 173
Gustav Rico*	Calaveras Twp 6	57 173
John W	Alameda Brooklyn	55 108
VANSAUT		
Gustar Rico*	Calaveras Twp 6	57 173
Gustav Rico*	Calaveras Twp 6	57 173
John W*	Alameda Brooklyn	55 108
VANSCHAICK		
H D	Santa Clara Gilroy	65 227
J	Shasta Shasta	66 665
John	Trinity Big Flat	701040
Wm	Trinity North Fo	701023

Name	County Locale	M653 RollPage
VANSCOCK		
J	San Joaquin Elkhorn	64 977
VANSEL		
Lewis	El Dorado Kelsey	581132
VANSICKLE		
Thos	Amador Twp 2	55 314
VANSICKLEN		
W H*	San Francisco San Francisco 7	681439
VANSICLE		
William	Solano Vacaville	69 346
VANSLYKE		
Wm	Santa Clara Santa Clara	65 463
VANSON		
Gustil	Nevada Bridgeport	61 467
VANSOS		
Esta	Amador Twp 2	55 290
VANSOX		
Simen	Siskiyou Klamath	69 96
VANSTADANT		
Catharine	San Francisco San Francisco 3 67	55
VANSTAN		
Thomas*	San Francisco San Francisco 3 67	38
VANSTAVOREN		
C	Santa Clara Redwood	65 451
VANSTEEN		
Thomas*	San Francisco San Francisco 3 67	38
VANSTIN		
Frank*	Placer Auburn	62 568
VANSTRANTEN		
J H	Calaveras Twp 8	57 51
VANSYCKLER		
Henry	Colusa Mansville	57 439
VANSYCLE		
R W	Sacramento Ward 1	63 133
R W	Sacramento Ward 1	63 86
VANSYKE		
Peter	Placer Dutch Fl	62 731
VANT		
Ephraim	Tuolumne Twp 1	71 259
Thomas	Sierra Pine Grove	66 833
VANTA		
George	Nevada Bloomfield	61 510
VANTAGE		
L W	Santa Clara Gilroy	65 232
VANTAPEL		
H B	Tehama Lassen	70 860
Lewis	Tehama Lassen	70 860
M	Tehama Lassen	70 860
VANTASSEL		
Alex	San Francisco San Francisco 10	220 67
Caroline	Contra Costa Twp 2	57 562
H B	Shasta Shasta	66 657
VANTHATTER		
G*	Nevada Eureka	61 369
VANTHATTIE		
G*	Nevada Eureka	61 369
VANTHROP		
Charles	San Francisco San Francisco 4	681125
VANTILT		
George	Calaveras Twp 10	57 265
VANTINE		
Chas	Butte Eureka	56 646
J	El Dorado Placerville	58 851
James	Nevada Nevada	61 286
James	San Francisco San Francisco 5 67	495
W D*	Butte Mountain	56 740
VANTLING		
A	Calaveras Twp 9	57 380
VANTRAN		
H J*	Shasta Shasta	66 675
VANTREMACETT		
John	Sierra Downieville	661016
VANTRESS		
B F	Los Angeles Los Angeles	59 512
VANTRIES		
Daniel	Placer Sacramento	62 646
VANTRISS		
B F	Los Angeles Los Angeles	59 512
VANTUIE		
Chas*	Butte Eureka	56 646
VANTURA		
---	Marin San Rafael	60 772
VANUNSWATER		
Aloho	Mariposa Twp 1	60 653
VANUSVALL		
C*	Alameda Brooklyn	55 139
VANVACTER		
J B*	Yuba Rose Bar	72 788
J W*	Yuba Rose Bar	72 788
VANVALKENBURG		
John A	Fresno Twp 2	59 114
VANVALKENBURGH		
Henry	San Francisco San Francisco 2 67	568
VANVALKERING		
Jno	Sacramento Cosumnes	63 386

Name	County Locale	M653 RollPage
VANVAPERBURG		
Samuel	Santa Cruz Santa Cruz	66 634
VANVAULKENBERG		
Ephraim	Tulara Visalia	71 14
VANVEANS		
John	Mariposa Twp 3	60 594
VANVELSER		
John H	San Francisco San Francisco 3 67	8
VANVETER		
John	Sierra Gibsonville	66 856
Johyn	Sierra Gibsonville	66 856
VANVILSER		
John H	San Francisco San Francisco 3 67	8
VANVLACK		
John	Tuolumne Twp 1	71 268
VANVLEET		
Eli J	Alameda Brooklyn	55 102
VANVLICK		
Erma	El Dorado Placerville	58 890
Newton	Colusa Butte Crk	57 466
VANVORHUS		
B J*	El Dorado Diamond	58 768
VANVRANKEN		
Harman*	Napa Yount	61 39
Hester	Sacramento Ward 1	63 133
VANVRANKIN		
C B	Nevada Eureka	61 382
VANWAGNER		
C	Shasta Millvill	66 725
Cornelius	Contra Costa Twp 2	57 564
VANWARBECK		
Martin	Sacramento Ward 4	63 525
VANWIE		
A	Shasta Shasta	66 665
A W*	Shasta French G	66 722
VANWINKLE		
A J	San Mateo Twp 1	65 56
Elanor	San Francisco San Francisco 2 67	589
Peter	San Mateo Twp 3	65 73
S F	Amador Twp 6	55 445
VANWOOD		
Ann	San Francisco San Francisco 4	681149
VANWOOET		
Ann*	San Francisco San Francisco 4	681149
VANWYKE		
H D	Siskiyou Scott Va	69 25
VANZANT		
J B*	Placer Michigan	62 856
VANZEISON		
John*	Placer Auburn	62 595
G	Nevada Nevada	61 248
VAPEL		
Juan M	Monterey San Juan	60 974
VAR DER HADEN		
J C	El Dorado Coloma	581070
VAR		
---	Calaveras Twp 6	57 159
John C	Placer Auburn	62 595
VARA		
Ignacio	Santa Cruz Santa Cruz	66 610
Iguach*	Santa Cruz Santa Cruz	66 610
Iguach*	Santa Cruz Santa Cruz	66 610
VARACAN		
Thos	Yolo Putah	72 614
VARAGO		
Jara	Amador Twp 5	55 331
Jera	Amador Twp 5	55 331
VARALES		
Enis	Alameda Brooklyn	55 152
VARATH		
William	Marin Cortemad	60 789
VARB		
P J*	Butte Eureka	56 653
VARBAGELOT		
Jas	Amador Twp 4	55 245
VARBAJAL		
Nicholas	San Francisco San Francisco 2 67	688
VARCICE		
Wm D	Colusa Mansville	57 439
VARCIGOS		
Jessee	Contra Costa Twp 3	57 596
VARDESHADEN		
J C	El Dorado Coloma	581070
VARDING		
Isabell	Santa Cruz Soguel	66 597
VARDMAIN		
James	Siskiyou Yreka	69 124
VARDNEY		
Isabell	Santa Cruz Soguel	66 597
VARED		
Edward	Sierra Scales D	66 804
VAREL		
Mary	Alameda Brooklyn	55 177
VARELA		
Tgnacio	San Bernardino Santa Barbara	64 169

Name	County Locale	M653 RollPage
VARELAS		
Jose D	Los Angeles Los Angeles	59 395
VARELY		
Richd	San Bernardino San Salvador	64 646
VARENDY		
Eliza D	Sierra Twp 7	66 866
VARENISS		
H*	Merced Twp 2	60 919
VARENNE		
Mary	Tuolumne Twp 6	71 538
VARES		
Antonio	El Dorado Salmon Falls	581051
VARETINE		
W D*	Butte Mountain	56 740
VAREURAUD		
Frank*	Tuolumne Twp 3	71 437
VARGALES		
Manuel*	Placer Michigan	62 850
VARGARA		
Jose	Amador Twp 1	55 469
VARGAS		
Cerjio	Monterey San Juan	601010
Cerju*	Monterey San Juan	601010
E	San Francisco San Francisco 2	67 801
Matias	Monterey Monterey	60 951
Thos	Sacramento Ward 1	63 20
VARGAZ		
Conforosa	Monterey Monterey	60 960
VARGERY		
Jesus	San Luis Obispo San Luis Obispo	65 6
VARGES		
Manuel	Alameda Brooklyn	55 107
VARGISA		
Rafael	San Joaquin Stockton	641066
VARGOES		
John	Sacramento Natonia	63 273
VARGONEZ		
Leonardo	San Francisco San Francisco 2	67 571
VARGOS		
Joseph	Calaveras Twp 5	57 227
VARGSIA		
Josa Maria	San Joaquin Stockton	641066
VARHORN		
J W	Tehama Tehama	70 948
VARHOW		
Oliver*	Calaveras Twp 6	57 147
VARIAN		
Wm H	Klamath Orleans	59 216
VARIARA		
Charles	San Luis Obispo San Luis Obispo	65 30
VARIAS		
Sterano	Alameda Brooklyn	55 143
VARIEL		
Edward	Sierra Scales D	66 804
VARIET		
Charles M	Yuba Slate Ro	72 696
VARILLO		
Joseph	Plumas Quincy	62 920
VARIN		
P W	Sonoma Washington	69 668
VARIOS		
Manuel	San Bernardino S Buenav	64 214
VARIS		
Charles	El Dorado Kelsey	581132
Pomona	Napa Napa	61 115
Romono	Napa Napa	61 115
VARKIN		
Thos	San Francisco San Francisco 10	293 67
VARLETT		
F S	Sonoma Petaluma	69 607
VARLEY		
John	Sierra La Porte	66 789
VARMA TINIA		
---*	Mendocino Calpella	60 824
VARNENN		
Loring*	Siskiyou Scott Va	69 21
Loving*	Siskiyou Scott Va	69 21
VARNER		
Ezra L	Plumas Quincy	62 980
J	Yolo Putah	72 586
James	Santa Clara Redwood	65 456
Robert D	Plumas Quincy	62 964
W	Nevada Rough &	61 397
VARNEY		
A*	Nevada Nevada	61 326
B F	Siskiyou Scott Ri	69 74
George	Tuolumne Twp 2	71 324
J	San Francisco San Francisco 5	67 553
J*	Nevada Nevada T	61 326
Jake	Trinity Weaverville	701073
Josh	Yolo Slate Ra	72 718
Josh	Yuba New York	72 718
Libias H*	San Francisco San Francisco 8	681283
Robt	Sonoma Petaluma	69 607
Seth	Trinity Sturdiva	701007

Name	County Locale	M653 RollPage
VARNEY		
T	El Dorado Kelsey	581145
VARNGNAT		
Peter*	Calaveras Twp 5	57 142
VARNHAM		
F W	San Francisco San Francisco 10	220 67
VARNUM		
Loring*	Siskiyou Scott Va	69 21
Loving*	Siskiyou Scott Va	69 21
VARNUNN		
Living*	Siskiyou Scott Va	69 21
VARQUES		
J P	Sonoma Sonoma	69 657
VARQUEZ		
Antonio M	Monterey Monterey	60 964
Carlos	San Francisco San Francisco 2	67 713
Jose C	San Francisco San Francisco 2	67 713
VARR		
Jno*	Klamath S Fork	59 197
VARRA		
Vicente	Contra Costa Twp 1	57 494
VARRAGRARDS		
Ed	Stanislaus Branch	70 699
VARREL		
Francisco	Calaveras Twp 4	57 314
VARRESY		
Asuza	Los Angeles San Jose	59 281
VARRILLAS		
Marcamis	Calaveras Twp 10	57 289
Mascanuis	Calaveras Twp 10	57 289
VARRO		
Manuel	Calaveras Twp 6	57 161
VARSE		
Michael	Sierra Gibsonville	66 858
VARSIPULCH		
Louis	Calaveras Twp 4	57 329
VARSRENCE		
David	Sierra Port Win	66 797
VART		
J	San Francisco San Francisco 2	67 773
VARTTINE		
Ashley A	San Francisco San Francisco 9	681103
VARURAND		
Frank	Tuolumne Jamestown	71 437
VARWIG		
Herman	Sacramento Ward 4	63 591
VARY		
Chas R	Sacramento Natonia	63 278
VARYOS		
Joseph*	Calaveras Twp 5	57 227
VAS NASTRAMEL		
William	Sierra Pine Grove	66 832
William*	Sierra Pine Grove	66 832
VAS NASTRAMIL		
William*	Sierra Pine Grove	66 832
VAS NASTRANUL		
William*	Sierra Pine Grove	66 832
VAS		
---	Calaveras Twp 6	57 159
William	El Dorado Mountain	581184
VASA		
Rafael	Los Angeles Elmonte	59 259
VASAJA		
Antonio	Santa Clara Fremont	65 434
VASAN		
L	San Francisco San Francisco 1	68 811
Leno	San Francisco San Francisco 2	67 768
VASARIA		
Louis	Sacramento Ward 3	63 441
VASATH		
William*	Marin Cortemad	60 789
VASBURG		
Walter	Nevada Bridgeport	61 444
VASBURY		
Walter	Nevada Bridgeport	61 444
VASCHER		
Emale	Los Angeles Los Angeles	59 375
Emile	Los Angeles Los Angeles	59 375
VASCONCELLOS		
J J	Tuolumne Big Oak	71 125
VASCOWCELLOS		
J J	Tuolumne Twp 4	71 127
VASCUEZ		
Pablo	San Bernardino Santa Barbara	64 187
Ramon	San Mateo Twp 2	65 134
VASE		
John	El Dorado Casumnes	581175
Juan	San Bernardino Santa Barbara	64 203
Reuben	Colusa Grand Island	57 473
Richd	San Francisco San Francisco 10	276 67
VASEMAN		
John	Calaveras Twp 6	57 161
VASER		
George	Plumas Quincy	62 936

Name	County Locale	M653 RollPage
VASFA		
Peter	Tuolumne Twp 5	71 512
VASGUES		
Charlotte	Yuba Marysville	72 954
VASHA		
Adolf	Monterey San Juan	60 977
VASHAW		
Oliver*	Calaveras Twp 6	57 147
Olvier	Calaveras Twp 6	57 147
VASHON		
Oliver	Calaveras Twp 5	57 147
VASILIO		
Jose	Los Angeles Los Angeles	59 393
VASLETT		
F S*	Sonoma Petaluma	69 607
VASMER		
J F	Sacramento Sutter	63 304
VASNEY		
D B	Tuolumne Twp 2	71 284
D B	Tuolumne Twp 2	71 284
VASO		
Cerila	Monterey San Juan	60 977
VASORS		
Christopher	Fresno Twp 1	59 75
VASQES		
Guliana	Monterey Alisal	601028
VASQUE		
Vicente	Tuolumne Montezuma	71 513
Vicento	Tuolumne Twp 5	71 513
VASQUES		
Antonio M	Monterey Monterey	60 964
Domingo	Monterey Monterey	60 963
J P	Sonoma Sonoma	69 657
Jessie	San Francisco San Francisco 4	681133
Jose	Yuba Parks Ba	72 786
Jose Maria	San Mateo Twp 2	65 118
Juan*	Monterey Monterey	60 926
Margt	San Francisco San Francisco 2	67 768
Pedro	Monterey Alisal	601027
Theodosia*	Monterey Monterey	60 925
Tobacia*	San Mateo Twp 2	65 117
VASQUEZ		
Bernardino	Monterey Monterey	60 942
Brinardino	Merced Monterey	60 942
Carlos	San Francisco San Francisco 2	67 797
Charlotte	Yuba Marysville	72 954
Clandir	Monterey Monterey	60 964
Claudio	Monterey Monterey	60 964
Dolores	Merced Monterey	60 939
Dolores	Monterey Monterey	60 939
Guillermo	Monterey Monterey	60 940
Guliana	Monterey Alisal	601028
Juan	Monterey Alisal	601040
Marcos	Merced Monterey	60 930
Marcos	Monterey Monterey	60 930
Pedro	Monterey Alisal	601027
Petra	Santa Clara San Jose	65 301
Ramon	Monterey Monterey	60 960
Theodoria*	Monterey Monterey	60 925
VASS		
---	El Dorado Coloma	581123
Alexander	Sierra Pine Grove	66 826
VASSA		
Peter	Tuolumne Montezuma	71 512
VASSALL		
J	El Dorado Diamond	58 802
VASSALLO		
Frank	Tuolumne Twp 4	71 126
VASSAN		
E Santo*	San Francisco San Francisco 2	67 768
VASSANLT		
F*	Siskiyou Scott Va	69 52
Harmon*	Siskiyou Scott Va	69 40
J F*	Siskiyou Scott Va	69 34
VASSANTT		
J F*	Siskiyou Scott Va	69 34
VASSAR		
C	Butte Hamilton	56 524
Ed W	Butte Chico	56 541
Jos	Butte Chico	56 549
VASSAULT		
F	San Francisco San Francisco 2	67 776
F	Siskiyou Scott Va	69 52
Harmon	Siskiyou Scott Va	69 40
J F*	Siskiyou Scott Va	69 34
VASSCAR		
Alexcander	Tuolumne Twp 3	71 465
VASSELIN		
Hym	San Francisco San Francisco 3	67 77
Hyra*	San Francisco San Francisco 3	67 77
VASSELYN		
Hapolite	San Francisco San Francisco 7	681392
VASSIER		
Theophile	San Francisco San Francisco 7	681396
VASTAQUE		
Joseph	San Joaquin Castoria	64 875

Name	County Locale	M653 Roll Page
VASTING		
John	Placer Iona Hills	62 888
VASTPHOIL		
Fred	Siskiyou Scott Va	69 49
VASURA		
Jose	San Bernardino San Salvador	64 638
VASYOS		
Joseph*	Calaveras Twp 5	57 227
VAT		
---	Calaveras Twp 6	57 134
VATAM		
Lilas*	El Dorado Casumnes	581170
Silas	El Dorado Casumnes	581170
VATARO		
P	Merced Twp 1	60 909
VATAW		
Lilas*	El Dorado Casumnes	581170
VATES		
Solomon	Mendocino Little L	60 831
VATILLA		
Louis*	Yuba Marysville	72 902
VATISEO		
---	San Diego Agua Caliente	64 831
VATISETT		
John	Sierra Port Win	66 794
VATISOTT		
John	Sierra Port Win	66 794
VATOIA		
B T	Amador Twp 7	55 417
VATORA		
B T	Amador Twp 7	55 417
VATTANE		
Joseph	San Joaquin Stockton	641070
VATTS		
Mary	Los Angeles Los Angeles	59 315
VATVER		
A G	Sierra St Louis	66 809
VAUBL		
C	Siskiyou Scott Va	69 49
VAUCAN		
Fielding*	Amador Twp 2	55 321
VAUCE		
J W*	Nevada Eureka	61 370
VAUDECAR		
Silas H	Tuolumne Big Oak	71 177
VAUGANT		
A	Amador Twp 3	55 404
VAUGH		
John	Placer Iona Hills	62 883
VAUGHAM		
Walter*	Calaveras Twp 6	57 180
VAUGHAN		
---	San Joaquin Elkhorn	64 999
D E	Sierra Twp 7	66 914
E P	Amador Twp 2	55 302
G H	El Dorado Georgetown	58 694
George	Colusa Muion	57 463
J F	Nevada Nevada	61 312
J W	Sierra St Louis	66 863
James H	San Bernardino San Bernadino	64 617
James M	Sonoma Mendocino	69 454
Jas	Placer Virginia	62 661
Jas	San Francisco San Francisco 9	681068
John	El Dorado Georgetown	58 693
Jos	Amador Twp 1	55 512
Louisa J	Sonoma Mendocino	69 460
Thos	Placer Secret R	62 615
Thos H	Sonoma Mendocino	69 460
Walter*	Calaveras Twp 6	57 180
William	San Francisco San Francisco 8	681244
Wm F	Klamath Orleans	59 217
Wm P	Sacramento Ward 1	63 14
VAUGHLIN		
Fred	Placer Virginia	62 701
VAUGHN		
A H	Butte Ophir	56 797
Alexander	Placer Iona Hills	62 869
Andrew	Placer Michigan	62 847
Bill	Mariposa Coulterville	60 678
Colburn	Sonoma Petaluma	69 556
D E	Sierra Twp 7	66 914
Danl	Sonoma Santa Rosa	69 412
Edward	Sacramento Ward 3	63 442
Elizabeth	Sacramento Ward 3	63 443
Francis	Tulara Twp 1	71 88
Frank	Yuba New York	72 738
Fred	Klamath S Fork	59 197
Fredrick	Los Angeles Tejon	59 525
Frink*	Yuba New York	72 738
G J	Butte Ophir	56 772
Geo	El Dorado Mud Springs	58 969
Geo	Siskiyou Scott Ri	69 69
George	Sierra Port Win	66 796
George	Tulara Visalia	71 9
Glendown M	Calaveras Twp 6	57 134
H S	Solano Vallejo	69 247

Name	County Locale	M653 Roll Page
VAUGHN		
Henry	San Francisco San Francisco 9	68 976
Henry	Siskiyou Scott Ri	69 78
James	Tulara Visalia	71 9
John S	Plumas Quincy	62 915
Levi L	Sierra La Porte	66 770
Leviny	Tulara Yule Rvr	71 31
Mary	San Francisco San Francisco 10	316 67
Michael	San Francisco San Francisco 1	68 851
R	Amador Twp 2	55 269
Sengtetin	Solano Benecia	69 314
Seth	Sacramento Ward 1	63 17
Singleton*	Solano Benecia	69 314
Stephen	Calaveras Twp 7	57 5
Sterling	Tulara Twp 2	71 15
Thomas	Tulara Twp 1	71 88
W	Nevada Grass Valley	61 179
W P	Sacramento Brighton	63 202
W W	Calaveras Twp 9	57 405
Wm	Butte Chico	56 541
Wm	Mariposa Coulterville	60 700
Wm	Sonoma Santa Rosa	69 396
VAUGHTON		
A M*	Napa Napa	61 56
VAUGHTT		
Teinperana	Contra Costa Twp 2	57 581
VAUGHUN		
Walter	Calaveras Twp 5	57 180
VAUGLEN		
John*	San Francisco San Francisco 7	681419
VAUGN		
Anson	Calaveras Twp 9	57 405
Lucy	Calaveras Twp 9	57 405
VAUHAGIN		
James	Tuolumne Shawsfla	71 384
VAUHL		
Jacob	Sierra Gibsonville	66 858
VAUMATER		
John M*	Placer Auburn	62 577
VAUN		
Abram*	Calaveras Twp 5	57 175
Adam	Solano Vacaville	69 360
Mathur*	Napa Hot Springs	61 1
VAUNBURG		
J H	Butte Wyandotte	56 671
VAUNDECK		
Boney	Sierra Port Win	66 791
VAUNDICK		
Boney*	Sierra Port Win	66 791
VAUNESS		
H*	Merced Twp 2	60 919
VAUNEY		
Cernel	Sacramento Natonia	63 279
VAUNISS		
H	Merced Twp 2	60 919
VAURANT		
Nicolas	Sierra Twp 5	66 941
VAUSANT		
Nicolas*	Sierra Twp 5	66 941
VAUSICKLEN		
W H*	San Francisco San Francisco 7	681439
VAUSTIN		
Frank*	Placer Auburn	62 568
VAUT		
Ephraim*	Tuolumne Twp 1	71 259
VAUTINE		
Chas*	Butte Eureka	56 646
W D*	Butte Mountain	56 740
VAUWIAKEE		
W H	San Joaquin Castoria	64 906
VAUX		
Ellen	San Francisco San Francisco 10	219 67
VAW		
Charley	Trinity Eastman	70 960
VAWCH		
Lizzie	San Francisco San Francisco 4	681138
VAWCURREN		
Ferd	Sierra Downieville	66 955
VAWENRREN		
Ford	Sierra Downieville	66 955
VAWRACTER		
J W*	Yuba Rose Bar	72 788
VAY		
C D	Nevada Nevada	61 259
C D S*	Nevada Nevada	61 259
John	Monterey Monterey	60 941
VAYARD		
Danl	Butte Oregon	56 631
VAYNE		
Thos	Mariposa Twp 3	60 599
VBARNETT		
Thomas	Yuba Slate Ro	72 702
VEA		
Casa*	Alameda Oakland	55 58

Name	County Locale	M653 Roll Page
VEA		
M	Tuolumne Twp 4	71 146
VEABROCK		
Henrey*	Yuba Linda	72 986
Henry	Yuba Suida	72 986
VEACH		
E T	El Dorado Kelsey	581129
Elisha	Butte Chico	56 554
J E	San Joaquin Elkhorn	64 995
Jacob*	Contra Costa Twp 3	57 596
L M	Siskiyou Yreka	69 182
Margt	San Francisco San Francisco 2	67 711
S M	Siskiyou Yreka	69 182
VEACIS		
Traffel*	Mariposa Twp 1	60 624
VEADIRO		
Damaso	San Francisco San Francisco 3	67 6
VEAEIO		
Traffel	Mariposa Twp 1	60 624
VEAEIR		
Traffel*	Mariposa Twp 1	60 624
VEAL		
Aime Mad	San Francisco San Francisco 10	274 67
J	Butte Oregon	56 637
Mad Aime	San Francisco San Francisco 10	274 67
Martha*	Mendocino Calpella	60 815
Peter	Yuba Marysville	72 936
Peter	Yuba Marysville	72 937
Wm	Sacramento Ward 3	63 437
VEALICH		
Peter	Amador Twp 2	55 306
VEAN		
---	Placer Auburn	62 592
VEAND		
D*	San Francisco San Francisco 5	67 486
VEARRY		
William	Calaveras Twp 4	57 323
VEARY		
Oscar	Fresno Twp 1	59 35
VEASER		
Henry	Santa Clara San Jose	65 380
VEASEY		
Horace M	Alameda Brooklyn	55 168
Wm	Alameda Brooklyn	55 120
VEASSEY		
John	El Dorado Mountain	581185
VEATCH		
Andrew	Napa Clear Lake	61 135
J J	Alameda Oakland	55 24
VEATE		
Wm	Sonoma Petaluma	69 612
VEATG		
D J	San Francisco San Francisco 3	67 74
VEATLATA		
Antonio*	Alameda Brooklyn	55 155
VEAUX		
Isidore*	Yuba Parke Ba	72 781
VECENTA		
---	San Bernardino S Timate	64 704
VECK		
William S	Los Angeles Los Angeles	59 364
VECKER		
A V	Trinity Cox'S Bar	701037
VECTOR		
Sarah	Sacramento Ward 1	63 99
VEDA		
Peter	Napa Napa	61 110
VEDAL		
Esteran	San Francisco San Francisco 3	67 6
VEDAR		
Paul	San Francisco San Francisco 11	119 67
VEDARD		
Nottie	San Francisco San Francisco 4	681155
VEDDER		
Albert	Siskiyou Klamath	69 96
Daniel	Tuolumne Chinese	71 489
Lucinda	Sacramento Ward 1	63 93
VEDELER		
Daniel	Tuolumne Twp 5	71 489
VEDELI		
Maria*	San Francisco San Francisco 2	67 685
VEDIE		
Jule	Alameda Brooklyn	55 91
VEE		
Scow*	Tuolumne Chinese	71 525
VEEDER		
Chas H	Mendocino Calpella	60 816
VEEN		
---*	Fresno Twp 2	59 17
VEETH		
John	Santa Clara San Jose	65 336
VEETLY		
John F*	Calaveras Twp 6	57 111

California 1860 Census Index

Name	County Locale	M653 RollPage
VEGA		
Ignacio	Los Angeles Los Angeles	59 490
Jesus	Sierra Pine Grove	66 820
Jose*	Los Angeles Los Angeles	59 489
VEGARO		
L	El Dorado Placerville	58 836
VEGAS		
Cecelio	Santa Clara Santa Clara	65 482
VEGO		
Jose M	Fresno Twp 1	59 75
VEGOLD		
Francis	Sierra Twp 7	66 868
VEGONREUX		
Geo*	San Francisco San Francisco 2	67 693
VEGOOD		
Joseph	Yuba Marysville	72 864
VEGORD		
Joseph*	Yuba Marysville	72 864
VEGUEDES		
Guadaloupe*	Yuba Marysville	72 933
VEHA		
Catrudas	Los Angeles Elmonte	59 255
VEHELE		
Bernardo*	Los Angeles Elmonte	59 267
Bicenta	Los Angeles Elmonte	59 268
VEHOFF		
Henry	Plumas Meadow Valley	62 907
VEHOHORAY		
Rachael	Los Angeles San Jose	59 282
VEHOM		
James*	Marin Cortemad	60 790
VEHORN		
James	Marin Cortemad	60 790
VEIGER		
L	El Dorado Casumnes	581163
VEILLALAS		
John Thingo*	Yuba Parke Ba	72 785
VEIN		
George*	Siskiyou Yreka	69 134
Wan	Fresno Twp 2	59 19
VEINEY		
William	Calaveras Twp 4	57 323
VEINGE		
Vincent O Revd	Solano Benecia	69 314
VEINGES		
Vincent Revd	Solano Benecia	69 314
VEINX		
Louis	Yuba New York	72 725
VEIOOICK		
Sam*	Butte Ophir	56 765
VEIRECK		
W	San Francisco San Francisco 6	67 474
VEISAN		
Peter	Santa Clara Santa Clara	65 509
VEITCH		
John	Calaveras Twp 5	57 209
John	Sierra Twp 7	66 912
Joseph	Sierra Twp 7	66 914
VEITIERS		
Thomas	San Luis Obispo San Luis Obispo	65 31
VEJAL		
Louis	Los Angeles Los Angeles	59 320
VEJAR		
Manuel J	Los Angeles Los Angeles	59 352
Maria D A	Los Angeles Los Angeles	59 351
Maria P*	Los Angeles Los Angeles	59 388
Miguel	Los Angeles Santa Ana	59 452
Ymigdio*	Los Angeles San Juan	59 466
Yneigdio*	Los Angeles San Juan	59 466
Ynugdio*	Los Angeles San Juan	59 466
Yruigdio*	Los Angeles San Juan	59 466
VELADE		
Henrigues	San Mateo Twp 2	65 131
Ignacio	San Mateo Twp 2	65 131
Juan	San Bernardino Santa Barbara	64 163
Ygnacio	San Bernardino Santa Barbara	64 165
VELANTE		
Andrea	Los Angeles Los Angeles	59 305
VELAR		
Ascencion	Santa Barbara	64 197
	San Bernardino	
VELARDE		
---	Los Angeles San Gabriel	59 413
Andrea	Los Angeles Los Angeles	59 313
Estefana	Los Angeles Los Angeles	59 389
Jese M	Los Angeles Los Angeles	59 403
Jose M	Los Angeles Los Angeles	59 403
Tomas	Los Angeles Los Angeles	59 403
VELARDES		
Sireaio	Alameda Brooklyn	55 201
VELARDS		
Jose	Santa Clara Almaden	65 275
VELASCO		
Jesus	San Diego Agua Caliente	64 854
VELASGUES		
VELASGUES		
Gaudalupe	San Francisco 2	67 768
	San Francisco	
VELASQUES		
B	San Francisco San Francisco 5	67 542
Gaudalupe	San Francisco 2	67 768
	San Francisco	
VELASQUEZ		
Antonio	Los Angeles San Juan	59 475
Fracisco	Santa Clara San Jose	65 281
Maria D	Los Angeles San Juan	59 472
Romuald	Santa Clara Almaden	65 266
Salvador	Los Angeles San Juan	59 477
VELASQUIS		
E	San Francisco San Francisco 5	67 542
VELASSA		
Francisca	San Francisco San Francisco 2	67 771
VELBET		
John	Marin Tomales	60 720
VELDIOPRT		
Jesus	Calaveras Twp 6	57 131
VELENCHES		
M	Nevada Washington	61 332
VELENSUELA		
Salvador	San Bernardino Santa Barbara	64 159
VELERA		
Veneta	El Dorado Gold Hill	581096
VELEY		
Jasper	Amador Twp 1	55 465
VELIA		
Alex	Plumas Quincy	62 921
VELKEE		
Marks	San Francisco San Francisco 2	67 704
VELLAGRANO		
Diago	Monterey San Juan	601004
VELLARASA		
Francis Sado	Solano Benecia	69 314
VELLELU		
Gietano*	Plumas Quincy	62 995
VELLELUS		
Gietano*	Plumas Quincy	62 995
VELLEMEUD		
J J*	San Francisco San Francisco 3	67 17
VELLES		
F	San Francisco San Francisco 5	67 496
VELOSA		
D	San Francisco San Francisco 2	67 798
VELSENSHALL		
P*	El Dorado Georgetown	58 686
VEM		
---	Amador Twp 1	55 501
VEMAL		
---*	San Francisco San Francisco 7	681437
VEMGNAT		
Peter	Calaveras Twp 6	57 142
VEMGUAT		
Peter*	Calaveras Twp 6	57 142
VEMQUAT		
Peter*	Calaveras Twp 6	57 142
VEMYARD		
James R*	Los Angeles Tejon	59 528
VEN IS NO		
---	Mendocino Calpella	60 823
VENA		
---	San Bernardino S Timate	64 708
Jemona	Fresno Twp 1	59 75
VENABLE		
Geo A	Butte Chico	56 543
H	Butte Chico	56 543
Joseph W	Contra Costa Twp 2	57 546
VENABLES		
G	El Dorado Diamond	58 771
VENACEA		
Emille	San Francisco San Francisco 2	67 616
VENACHER		
Louis	Calaveras Twp 5	57 200
VENACKER		
Louis	Calaveras Twp 5	57 200
VENAGAS		
Puebla	Monterey San Juan	60 981
VENALLEN		
Leopoldo*	San Mateo Twp 2	65 134
VENAMON		
William	Nevada Bridgeport	61 440
VENAMOW		
William*	Nevada Bridgeport	61 440
VENANA		
---	San Diego Agua Caliente	64 827
VENANCIO		
---	San Diego Temecula	64 805
VENARD		
J	San Francisco San Francisco 7	681379
Stephen	Nevada Nevada	61 242
VENBERRY		
Benjamin	Yuba Slate Ro	72 697
Henry	Yuba Slate Ro	72 697
VENCEL		
Lewis*	San Francisco San Francisco 1	68 877
VENCEN		
John B	Amador Twp 4	55 245
VENCENTE		
---	San Bernardino Santa Inez	64 137
VENCHUREN		
S O R	Yolo Washington	72 562
VEND		
Agustus*	Santa Cruz Pescadero	66 644
Augustus*	Santa Cruz Pescadero	66 644
VENDE		
Monte*	San Francisco San Francisco 8	681284
VENDECK		
J S	Sierra Downieville	66 961
VENDEGES		
Francisco	Santa Ba	64 214
	San Bernardino	
VENDER		
A	El Dorado Placerville	58 868
VENDHUZEN		
S V R	Yolo Washington	72 562
VENDNE		
W	El Dorado Diamond	58 800
VENDO		
Monte	San Francisco San Francisco 8	681284
VENEBLE		
Henry	Santa Cruz Pescadero	66 642
VENEDRO		
Jose	San Bernardino Santa Barbara	64 200
VENEGA		
Jose	Santa Clara Alviso	65 413
VENEGAS		
Mariano	San Diego Agua Caliente	64 861
Pedro	Monterey San Juan	60 997
Rosario	Yuba Marysville	72 944
Ternando	San Francisco San Francisco 2	67 768
VENEGOS		
Fernando	San Francisco San Francisco 2	67 768
VENENER		
Ann*	Sacramento Ward 1	63 95
VENER		
Perry	Tehama Red Bluff	70 933
W	Tehama Red Bluff	70 920
VENERABLE		
Arnold	San Francisco San Francisco 1	68 855
VENESE		
Yourer*	San Francisco San Francisco 9	681052
VENEYARD		
James R*	Los Angeles Tejon	59 528
VENFEST		
Nancy E	San Francisco San Francisco 10	288 67
VENG		
Ar	Trinity Point Ba	70 976
VENGER		
Jno	Klamath Salmon	59 213
VENGERTY		
Edward	Humbolt Mattole	59 126
VENGIN		
---	Placer Auburn	62 596
VENGNEY		
D De*	San Francisco San Francisco 10	358 67
VENGON		
August	Tuolumne Twp 3	71 461
Aupurt	Tuolumne Twp 3	71 461
VENICK		
William*	San Francisco San Francisco 8	681305
VENIEL		
L	Nevada Grass Valley	61 154
VENING		
A	Calaveras Twp 9	57 407
L	Calaveras Twp 9	57 406
VENKER		
E F	San Francisco San Francisco 10	275 67
VENLAIN		
Louis*	Calaveras Twp 5	57 179
VENN		
Thos	San Francisco San Francisco 2	67 637
VENNABLE		
Margarat	Los Angeles Tejon	59 523
VENNINGO		
Antonio*	Calaveras Twp 10	57 249
VENNINGS		
Antonio*	Calaveras Twp 5	57 249
VENNINYO		
Antonio*	Calaveras Twp 10	57 249
VENNMAN		
H	Santa Clara Gilroy	65 224
VENOER		
J*	Butte Oro	56 675
VENOHAN		
Patrick*	Santa Cruz Santa Cruz	66 626
VENOLIV		
Ambrose	Calaveras Twp 8	57 96

Name	County Locale	M653 RollPage
VENOM		
O H	Santa Clara San Jose	65 379
VENON		
James	Sierra Twp 7	66 879
Jos*	Butte Oro	56 682
VENPIRO		
Simeon	Tuolumne Twp 1	71 257
VENRENT		
Frances*	San Francisco San Francisco 3 67	80
VENSON		
John	Yuba New York	72 734
Secul	Tuolumne Twp 3	71 452
VENT		
G D*	Calaveras Twp 8	57 103
Geo	Placer Lisbon	62 735
VENTCH		
Geo W	Sonoma Petaluma	69 583
VENTHOREY		
P	San Francisco San Francisco 10	358 67
VENTON		
A B	Napa Napa	61 95
Wm	Sacramento Ward 1	63 62
VENTRDA		
---	Marin San Rafael	60 768
VENTURA		
---	Los Angeles San Pedro	59 486
---	Marin Tomales	60 774
---	Mariposa Twp 1	60 640
---	Monterey San Juan	60 992
---	San Diego Agua Caliente	64 848
Janna	San Joaquin Stockton	641071
Manuel	San Diego Agua Caliente	64 854
Tomas	San Diego San Diego	64 769
VENTURO		
---	Los Angeles San Gabriel	59 420
---	Los Angeles San Pedro	59 478
---	San Diego Temecula	64 790
VENUL		
L*	Nevada Grass Valley	61 154
VENUM		
H	Butte Chico	56 560
VENUO		
John	Mariposa Twp 1	60 669
VENUS		
---	Trinity S Fork	701032
VENVE		
E S	Santa Clara San Jose	65 342
VENVER		
J*	Butte Oro	56 675
VENYARD		
G W	El Dorado Placerville	58 928
VEOGA		
Catrudo*	Calaveras Twp 6	57 183
Catruilu	Calaveras Twp 5	57 183
VEON		
George	Siskiyou Yreka	69 134
VEOT		
Eugene	San Francisco San Francisco 2 67	797
VEOTCH		
Andrew	Napa Clear Lake	61 135
VEPER		
R	San Francisco San Francisco 3 67	64
VEQUEDES		
Guadaloupe*	Yuba Marysville	72 933
VEQUETTE		
Benjamin	Tulara Twp 2	71 15
VEQUISA		
Guadaloupe	Yuba Marysville	72 933
VER MEHE		
John L*	San Francisco San Francisco 8	681249
VER MEHR		
John L	San Francisco San Francisco 8	681249
VER THEMBER		
Louis*	San Francisco San Francisco 8	681284
VERA		
Delphina	San Francisco San Francisco 2 67	601
Ellis	Solano Vallejo	69 249
Juan J	Los Angeles Los Angeles	59 368
Lullenta	Calaveras Twp 8	57 85
Manuel	Solano Vallejo	69 249
Marcus	Los Angeles Los Angeles	59 400
Ramon	San Diego Colorado	64 809
VERABAY		
Antone	Sierra Downieville	66 954
Antono	Sierra Downieville	66 954
VERALES		
Francisco	Alameda Brooklyn	55 152
VERALIS		
Manwill	Calaveras Twp 5	57 207
VERAMBAUM		
Jnle	Sacramento Ward 1	63 13
Jule	Sacramento Ward 1	63 13
VERARD		
Stephen*	Nevada Nevada	61 242
VERARD		
Thos	San Francisco San Francisco 10	190 67
VERAS		
Mary	Tuolumne Sonora	71 226
VERATH		
Henry	San Francisco San Francisco 8	681274
VERAVEN		
Joseph	Tuolumne Shawsfla	71 405
VERAVIN		
Joseph	Tuolumne Twp 2	71 405
VERBE		
A	San Francisco San Francisco 2 67	804
VERBIST		
Charles	Tuolumne Twp 2	71 282
VERDA		
Ignacia	Calaveras Twp 6	57 186
VERDEN		
Celest	Sacramento Ward 3	63 469
VERDENAL		
John B	San Francisco San Francisco 2 67	771
VERDENBARGH		
W T*	Santa Clara San Jose	65 294
VERDIEGO		
Jose A	Los Angeles Los Angeles	59 399
VERDIER		
Bernard	San Francisco San Francisco 7	681413
Emil	San Francisco San Francisco 4	681224
VERDIGO		
Domingo	Tuolumne Chinese	71 495
VERDILLAC		
C	San Francisco San Francisco 6 67	465
VERDLER		
Joseph	Calaveras Twp 5	57 238
VERDO		
Ignacio	Calaveras Twp 5	57 186
VERDON		
Ignacio*	Calaveras Twp 5	57 186
VERDRIR		
Emil	San Francisco San Francisco 4	681224
VERDUGIR		
Ramona	Los Angeles Los Angeles	59 325
VERDUGO		
Jose A	Los Angeles Los Angeles	59 399
Manuela	Los Angeles Los Nieto	59 432
Maria F	Los Angeles Los Angeles	59 394
Opedro	Los Angeles Los Nieto	59 428
Pedro	Los Angeles Los Nieto	59 428
Pedro	Los Angeles San Pedro	59 478
Rafael	Los Angeles Los Nieto	59 432
Wancisco	Los Angeles Los Angeles	59 309
VERDULING		
Chas*	Nevada Nevada	61 248
VERDULLING		
Chas	Nevada Nevada	61 248
VEREIR		
Louis*	Calaveras Twp 6	57 179
VERERIER		
Lascasin*	San Francisco San Francisco 3 67	82
Sascasier	San Francisco San Francisco 3 67	82
VERETT		
H	Tehama Tehama	70 943
VEREZ		
Aberto	San Francisco San Francisco 11	151 67
VERGA		
Juan	Santa Cruz Santa Cruz	66 634
VERGEUNE		
L P De	San Francisco San Francisco 6 67	464
L P De V	San Francisco San Francisco 6 67	464
VERGO		
Eugow	Sierra Downieville	661007
VERGON		
James	Del Norte Crescent	58 648
VERGRAT		
Paul	San Francisco San Francisco 11	141 67
VERGRET		
Francis	Santa Clara Santa Clara	65 481
VERGYNSKY		
M	San Francisco San Francisco 10	214 67
VERHAN		
A	Solano Benecia	69 291
VERHARE		
A*	Solano Benecia	69 291
VERHOOFF		
C	Tuolumne Columbia	71 294
VERHOVEN		
John	El Dorado Coloma	581122
VERIER		
Louis*	Calaveras Twp 6	57 179
VERILL		
S E	Placer Dutch Fl	62 734
VERINDES		
Geo	El Dorado Mud Springs	58 974
VERINER		
Lascasin*	San Francisco San Francisco 3 67	82
VERLANDER		
George	Contra Costa Twp 2	57 559
VERLANG		
L*	San Francisco San Francisco 5 67	504
VERLE		
B	San Francisco San Francisco 2 67	618
John O	Sierra St Louis	66 808
VERM		
Wm*	Sierra Monte Crk	661039
VERMAL		
Jose	Los Angeles Santa Ana	59 445
VERMANOURAGE		
C	Mariposa Coulterville	60 688
VERMEHREN		
T	San Francisco San Francisco 5 67	506
VERMELL		
Heriull	Sierra La Porte	66 775
VERMERS		
Peter	Sierra Twp 7	66 906
VERMETT		
Hereull	Sierra La Porte	66 775
VERMIEN		
Elizabeth	San Francisco San Francisco 8	681277
VERMIERE		
Elizabeth*	San Francisco San Francisco 8 / San Francisco	681277
VERMILLION		
Wm	El Dorado White Oaks	581031
VERMILLO		
Visalia	Colusa Colusi	57 420
VERMILZA		
Amelia*	San Francisco San Francisco 10	169 67
VERMINGO		
Antonio	Calaveras Twp 10	57 249
VERMINOURIGE		
C	Mariposa Coulterville	60 688
VERMINYO		
Antonio*	Calaveras Twp 5	57 249
VERMMOURZE		
C*	Mariposa Coulterville	60 688
VERMOREL		
Jules	San Francisco San Francisco 4	681153
VERMUDES		
Dolores	San Bernardino Santa Barbara	64 148
VERMUDEZ		
Casemir*	San Bernardino Santa Barbara	64 205
Casemor	San Bernardino S Buenav	64 218
Casomor	San Bernardino Santa Ba	64 217
Francisca	San Bernardino Santa Barbara	64 188
VERN HORN		
S*	El Dorado Diamond	58 810
VERNAL		
---*	San Francisco San Francisco 7	681437
Jose	Los Angeles Santa Ana	59 445
VERNAND		
Rosa	San Francisco San Francisco 8	681303
VERNARD		
S G	San Francisco San Francisco 7	681412
VERNENDY		
Eliza D	Sierra Twp 7	66 866
VERNENI		
Doi	El Dorado Georgetown	58 749
VERNEY		
Victor	San Francisco San Francisco 3 67	52
VERNIER		
H	Butte Ophir	56 766
VERNINOURZE		
C*	Mariposa Coulterville	60 688
VERNON		
Chs	San Francisco San Francisco 6 67	439
E	San Francisco San Francisco 5 67	498
George W	Yuba North Ea	72 678
Geroge W	Yolo No E Twp	72 678
James	Sierra Twp 7	66 879
Jos	Sacramento Ward 3	63 441
Jos V	San Francisco San Francisco 10	296 67
Louisa	San Francisco San Francisco 10	182 67
Reuben	Plumas Quincy	62 920
S	Calaveras Twp 9	57 394
S T	Calaveras Twp 9	57 393
W P	El Dorado Gold Hill	581095
William	Amador Twp 3	55 379
VERNULZA		
Amelia*	San Francisco San Francisco 10	169 67
VERNUN		
H	Butte Ophir	56 766
VERON		
Alexande	Sonoma Russian	69 432

Name	County Locale	M653 Roll	Page
VERON			
Alexander	Sonoma Russian	69	432
VERPLAND			
Joseph	Tuolumne Twp 3	71	469
VERPLANK			
Joseh	Tuolumne Twp 3	71	469
VERPONIS			
Jerome	Calaveras Twp 5	57	225
VERRETT			
William	San Joaquin Stockton	64	1047
VERRICK			
William	San Francisco San Francisco 8	68	1305
VERRIL			
Samuel K	Siskiyou Yreka	69	129
VERRILL			
Samuel K	Siskiyou Yreka	69	129
VERRILLA			
James	Amador Twp 4	55	242
VERRLEET			
Charles*	San Francisco San Francisco 11	67	103
VERRNUDEZ			
Casimir*	San Bernardino Lkbarbar	64	205
VERSCHMAN			
Doefield S*	Amador Twp 4	55	245
VERSECHOYLE			
Eugene	Sacramento Sacramento 4	63	535
VERSEPULCH			
Louis	Calaveras Twp 4	57	329
VERSHOPKY			
J	Nevada Nevada	61	252
VERSILA			
---	San Diego Agua Caliente	64	845
VERSON			
James	Tulara Twp 1	71	80
VERSTEEGEN			
Peter	Trinity Evans Ba	70	1002
VERSUCHOYLE			
Eugenie*	Sacramento Ward 4	63	535
VERSUY			
Victor*	San Francisco San Francisco 3 67	52	
VERTA			
Antonio	Alameda Brooklyn	55	129
VERTAL			
Solomon	Sonoma Petaluma	69	547
VERTERLEIN			
C	Siskiyou Klamath	69	90
VERTERTEM			
C	Siskiyou Klamath	69	90
VERTERVELT			
Louis	San Francisco San Francisco 7	68	1416
VERTEWELT			
William	San Francisco San Francisco 7	68	1416
VERTHEMBER			
Louis	San Francisco San Francisco 8	68	1284
VERTI			
Guiseppe	San Francisco San Francisco 11 67	154	
VERTICO			
---	San Diego Temecula	64	799
---	Tulara Twp 3	71	64
VERTIE			
A*	Tehama Red Bluff	70	915
VERTIMER			
P	Sacramento Ward 1	63	22
VERTMIER			
P*	Sacramento Ward 1	63	22
VERTNER			
Jane E	San Francisco San Francisco 10 67	242	
VERTO			
Rumaldo	Alameda Oakland	55	55
VERTON			
Louis	Butte Kimshaw	56	579
VERTRUS			
William	Nevada Bridgeport	61	472
VERUEJOS			
Manuel	San Luis Obispo San Luis Obispo 65	34	
VERUPOWYS			
Galpard*	Calaveras Twp 10	57	296
VERVA			
Leonora	Los Angeles San Jose	59	285
VERVLEET			
Charles*	San Francisco San Francisco 11 67	103	
Charley*	San Francisco San Francisco 11 67	103	
VERY			
David*	San Francisco San Francisco 10 67	217	
VERZOCHOYLE			
Eugenie*	Sacramento Ward 4	63	535
VESARIA			
Louise	Sacramento Ward 4	63	596
VESDEIR			
Louis*	Calaveras Twp 6	57	179

Name	County Locale	M653 Roll	Page
VESENA			
Robt	Nevada Bridgeport	61	455
VESEVA			
Robt*	Nevada Bridgeport	61	455
VESEY			
J	Yuba Long Bar	72	741
Parker	Butte Cascade	56	690
Perley	Sierra La Porte	66	776
VESFAL			
Henry	Tuolumne Chinese	71	496
VESH			
Rudolph	Solano Benecia	69	316
VESPER			
Fred*	Placer Iona Hills	62	888
VESPERS			
J	El Dorado Diamond	58	796
VESSAY			
William	Calaveras Twp 5	57	229
VESSELHOFT			
J	Stanislaus Emory	70	742
VESSER			
Benj	Marin S Antoni	60	710
S H	Marin S Antoni	60	710
VESSEY			
David D	Calaveras Twp 6	57	185
William	Calaveras Twp 5	57	229
VESSY			
Pearley*	Plumas Quincy	62	982
VEST			
Jasper	Tulara Keyesville	71	53
John	Yuba Marysville	72	948
M M	Sutter Nicolaus	70	834
VESTAL			
A	Santa Clara San Jose	65	387
B E	Del Norte Crescent	58	647
M S*	Nevada Washington	61	337
N S	Nevada Washington	61	337
Richard	Santa Cruz Santa Cruz	66	611
VESTEC			
Alphonse*	San Francisco 2 67	696	
	San Francisco		
VESTER			
Andrew	San Francisco San Francisco 6 67	435	
VESTIE			
A*	Tehama Red Bluff	70	915
VESTING			
Paul	San Francisco San Francisco 2 67	596	
VESTO			
Henry	Fresno Twp 1	59	81
VESTOR			
Henry	Fresno Twp 1	59	81
VETARIA			
Joseph	El Dorado Placerville	58	906
VETASCO			
Jesus	San Diego Agua Caliente	64	855
VETASO			
---	San Diego Agua Caliente	64	822
VETEWAL			
L*	Siskiyou Cottonwood	69	102
S*	Siskiyou Cottonwoood	69	102
VETH			
Rudolph	Solano Benecia	69	316
VETINN			
Geo	Nevada Nevada	61	252
VETOR			
---*	Siskiyou Scott Va	69	40
Mal*	Siskiyou Callahan	69	3
VETSTIN			
Wm	San Francisco San Francisco 4	68	1221
VETTMAR			
Henry*	San Francisco San Francisco 7	68	1423
VEUD			
Augustus*	Santa Cruz Pescadero	66	644
VEUN			
---*	Placer Auburn	62	575
VEUTHOREY			
P*	San Francisco San Francisco 10 67	358	
VEUX			
Pierre*	Yuba New York	72	725
VEVANS			
Samuel*	Sierra Cox'S Bar	66	950
VEVLE			
B*	San Francisco San Francisco 2 67	618	
VEWOICK			
Sam*	Butte Ophir	56	765
VEYA			
Jose	Los Angeles Tejon	59	528
VEZINA			
Charles*	San Francisco San Francisco 7	68	1427
VEZNOR			
S T	Calaveras Twp 9	57	393
VEZUELREAB			
Eugene*	San Joaquin Stockton	64	1053
VHIM			
Wm*	Sacramento Ward 1	63	93

Name	County Locale	M653 Roll	Page
VHL			
Frank K*	San Francisco San Francisco 10 67	191	
VI???TI			
Ba	Santa Cruz Pajaro	66	563
VIA			
Antonio	Los Angeles Los Angeles	59	516
Betra	Los Angeles Los Angeles	59	503
Casa*	Alameda Oakland	55	58
Concipcion	Los Angeles Los Angeles	59	518
Lorenzo	Merced Twp 1	60	900
Manuel	Los Angeles Los Angeles	59	516
Mariana	Los Angeles Los Angeles	59	502
Petra	Los Angeles Los Angeles	59	503
Tomasa	Los Angeles Los Angeles	59	293
VIACRUZ			
Jesus*	San Bernardino S Buenav	64	208
Jusus*	San Bernardino S Buenav	64	208
VIAGAS			
Francisco	Monterey San Juan	60	998
VIAL			
James	Klamath Liberty	59	232
VIALL			
Ransom M	Los Angeles Los Angeles	59	371
VIALOBAS			
Jose B	Los Angeles Shaffer	59	397
VIALOBO			
Albins*	Napa Napa	61	115
Alvino*	Napa Napa	61	115
Pedro	Los Angeles San Pedro	59	478
VIALOBOS			
Epifiano	Los Angeles Los Angeles	59	384
Jose B	Los Angeles Los Angeles	59	397
Jose M	Los Angeles Los Angeles	59	385
VIALOVO			
Albino	Napa Napa	61	115
Albins*	Napa Napa	61	115
Alvino*	Napa Napa	61	115
VIAND			
D*	San Francisco San Francisco 5	67	486
VIANEVA			
Dolores*	Los Angeles Santa Ana	59	442
VIAR			
Pablo	Calaveras Twp 4	57	331
VIARA			
Patrick	San Luis Obispo San Luis Obispo 65	29	
VIARD			
Mary*	El Dorado Georgetown	58	673
P	San Francisco San Francisco 6	67	448
VIARS			
Raphuel*	Calaveras Twp 5	57	175
VIATEN			
John	El Dorado Georgetown	58	706
VIATER			
John*	El Dorado Georgetown	58	706
VIATG			
D J*	San Francisco San Francisco 3	67	74
VIATZ			
D J*	San Francisco San Francisco 3	67	74
VIAUEVA			
Dolores*	Los Angeles Santa Ana	59	442
VIAULT			
Marie	Yuba Fosters	72	822
VIAUX			
Gidou	Yuba Parks Ba	72	781
Isidore	Yuba Parke Ba	72	781
VIBBETTS			
David	Butte Kimshaw	56	607
VIBERT			
N	Siskiyou Klamath	69	93
VICANX			
Rish	Yuba Parks Ba	72	781
VICAR			
James M*	Mendocino Big Rock	60	873
VICARS			
Michael	Solano Benecia	69	296
VICARTO			
Lucy	Sacramento Ward 1	63	97
VICCUZI			
Carlo*	San Francisco San Francisco 11 67	154	
VICE			
Carlos	San Francisco San Francisco 2	67	767
Carlotta	San Francisco San Francisco 2	67	767
Carlottee	San Francisco San Francisco 2	67	767
David	Placer Rattle Snake	62	632
Nathaniel	Los Angeles Elmonte	59	252
VICELLO			
Vencent	Mariposa Twp 3	60	605
Vincent	Mariposa Twp 3	60	605
VICENT			
Martin	Santa Cruz Pescadero	66	650
VICENTA			
---	San Bernardino San Bernadino	64	678
---	San Bernardino S Timate	64	706

California 1860 Census Index

Name	County Locale	M653 Roll	Page
VICENTA			
---	San Bernardino S Timate	64	708
---	San Bernardino S Timate	64	709
---	San Bernardino S Timate	64	712
---	San Bernardino S Timate	64	721
VICENTE			
---	Los Angeles San Juan	59	467
---	San Bernardino Santa Barbara	64	202
---	San Bernardino S Timate	64	706
---	San Diego Temecula	64	794
---	San Diego Temecula	64	795
---	San Diego Agua Caliente	64	829
---	San Diego Agua Caliente	64	864
Jose*	Napa Napa	61	115
VICENTO			
---	San Bernardino S Timate	64	697
Jose	Napa Napa	61	115
VICES			
Raphael*	Calaveras Twp 6	57	175
VICEUZI			
Carlo*	San Francisco San Francisco 11	67	154
VICHAR			
Edwd	San Francisco San Francisco 6	67	430
VICHER			
Edwd	San Francisco San Francisco 6	67	430
VICHIAM			
Micha	Tuolumne Sonora	71	210
VICHIARN			
Micha*	Tuolumne Twp 1	71	210
VICHINE			
D	Tuolumne Sonora	71	216
VICINCIO			
O	Tuolumne Twp 4	71	156
VICINI			
Anton	Tuolumne Columbia	71	293
VICINTA			
Arsamora	San Francisco San Francisco 2	67	694
VICINTE			
---	Monterey S Antoni	60	971
VICISA			
Francis	Tuolumne Twp 1	71	189
VICK			
---*	Tuolumne Twp 5	71	511
Joseph	Yuba Long Bar	72	771
R L	Sonoma Armally	69	494
VICKBENER			
J	Calaveras Twp 9	57	388
VICKER			
John	Tuolumne Springfield	71	371
VICKERBY			
Edward	Sierra Twp 5	66	918
VICKERS			
A J	Sacramento Granite	63	235
Charles	Calaveras Twp 5	57	227
James	Placer Michigan	62	845
James	Tehama Red Bluff	70	920
Robert	El Dorado Placerville	58	925
Wm	Tuolumne Twp 1	71	258
VICKERY			
A G	Nevada Bridgeport	61	466
I D	Mariposa Twp 3	60	591
I F*	Mariposa Twp 3	60	591
John	Calaveras Twp 10	57	278
VICKES			
John	Tuolumne Twp 2	71	371
VICKING			
A G	Nevada Bridgeport	61	466
VICKOICH			
Lewis W	Tuolumne Sonora	71	191
VICKREY			
J F	Mariposa Twp 3	60	552
J G	Mariposa Twp 3	60	552
VICKRY			
Robert	Calaveras Twp 10	57	277
VICONDA			
John	Tuolumne Twp 1	71	270
VICONS			
Joseph	Mariposa Coulterville	60	688
VICORS			
Michael	Solano Benecia	69	285
VICOTR			
John A	Tuolumne Twp 2	71	284
VICOUS			
Joseph	Mariposa Coulterville	60	688
VICRS			
Raphael*	Calaveras Twp 6	57	175
VICTIN			
Negett*	El Dorado Georgetown	58	749
VICTOR			
---	Los Angeles San Juan	59	470
---	San Bernardino S Timate	64	693
---	San Joaquin Stockton	64	1099
Aaron	San Francisco San Francisco 9	68	991
Berlee*	Mariposa Twp 1	60	636
Berlie	Mariposa Twp 1	60	636

Name	County Locale	M653 Roll	Page
VICTOR			
Buron	San Francisco San Francisco 2	67	559
C	San Francisco San Francisco 6	67	449
C W	Napa Napa	61	92
Cenier	Calaveras Twp 5	57	142
Cerrier	Calaveras Twp 6	57	142
Charlier	Alameda Brooklyn	55	98
Charlies	Alameda Brooklyn	55	98
Cimes	Calaveras Twp 6	57	142
D	Nevada Grass Valley	61	174
D	Tuolumne Columbia	71	351
Emile	Yuba Marysville	72	902
Francis	Sacramento Ward 4	63	542
Fretizny	San Francisco San Francisco 8	68	1265
Harriett	Siskiyou Callahan	69	4
Henry	El Dorado Kelsey	58	1130
Honbill*	Siskiyou Callahan	69	4
Honvill*	Siskiyou Callahan	69	4
J	San Francisco San Francisco 2	67	591
John	Shasta Shasta	66	671
John A	Tuolumne Twp 2	71	284
John J	Contra Costa Twp 2	57	552
Jose	San Bernardino S Timate	64	690
Jose	San Bernardino S Timate	64	694
Jose	Santa Cruz Santa Cruz	66	622
Jose	Santa Cruz Santa Cruz	66	624
Julia	Butte Kimshaw	56	574
Larala	San Mateo Twp 1	65	48
Lavala	San Mateo Twp 1	65	48
Louis	San Francisco San Francisco 5	67	480
Louis	Tuolumne Twp 3	71	431
M	El Dorado Diamond	58	814
Mal	Siskiyou Callahan	69	3
Nande*	Del Norte Crescent	58	641
Peigem	Siskiyou Callahan	69	3
Pierre	Tuolumne Twp 3	71	431
Thomas	San Francisco San Francisco 5	67	478
VICTORIA			
---	San Bernardino San Bernadino	64	682
---	San Bernardino S Timate	64	695
---	San Bernardino S Timate	64	756
Francisco	Tehama Antelope	70	885
John De	Santa Clara San Jose	65	330
Millie	Sacramento Ward 1	63	146
Rosaleo	San Joaquin Stockton	64	1065
Sister	Yuba Marysville	72	961
VICTORIANE			
---	Monterey San Juan	60	977
VICTORIANO			
---	San Diego Temecula	64	801
VICTORY			
John	Yuba Rose Bar	72	793
VIDAL			
Francisco	Santa Barbara	64	177
Juanna	San Bernardino, San Bernardino Santa Barbara	64	177
VIDCAN			
Ramon*	Yuba Marysville	72	968
VIDEACE			
Henry	Yuba Marysville	72	897
VIDEAN			
Henry	Yuba Marysville	72	897
Ramon*	Yuba Marysville	72	968
Rasscon	Yuba Marysville	72	968
VIDEAU			
Henry*	Yuba Marysville	72	897
VIDELA			
Enamecia	San Francisco San Francisco 2	67	601
VIDELI			
Maria*	San Francisco San Francisco 2	67	685
VIDON			
P	El Dorado Placerville	58	820
VIDORIANE			
---	Monterey San Juan	60	977
VIEAD			
Mary	El Dorado Georgetown	58	673
VIEAUX			
Rish*	Yuba Parke Ba	72	781
Risli*	Yuba Parks Ba	72	781
VIED			
Jacob	Shasta Shasta	66	663
VIEDCOCK			
Charles	Yuba Marysville	72	878
VIEDE			
Deaderick	San Francisco San Francisco 7	68	1337
VIEDROCK			
Charles	Yuba Marysville	72	878
VIEGAS			
Francisco	Monterey San Juan	60	998
VIEGO			
Lucinna*	Monterey Monterey	60	961
VIEIRA			
Anthony	Klamath Liberty	59	236
VIELA			
Felipe	Los Angeles Los Angeles	59	391
VIELLALAS			
John Thingo*	Yuba Parks Ba	72	785

Name	County Locale	M653 Roll	Page
VIELLEY			
T M	El Dorado Diamond	58	809
VIEN			
---*	Fresno Twp 2	59	17
VIENNA			
M	San Francisco San Francisco 5	67	532
VIENT			
Joh N	San Francisco San Francisco 3	67	50
VIENTE			
---	San Diego Agua Caliente	64	842
VIEONT			
John*	San Francisco San Francisco 3	67	50
VIER			
Caji*	Placer Yankee J	62	778
Mibly	Amador Twp 3	55	392
VIERCE			
R H	Tehama Red Bluff	70	916
VIERECK			
Geo*	San Francisco San Francisco 9	68	1075
VIETCH			
John*	Sierra Twp 7	66	912
VIETOR			
Thomas	San Francisco San Francisco 5	67	478
Ira	Tehama Red Bluff	70	928
VIEUX			
Louis	Yuba New York	72	725
VIGA			
Jesus*	Sierra Pine Grove	66	820
VIGAND			
Amile	San Francisco San Francisco 2	67	679
VIGAR			
A C	Sacramento Natonia	63	286
VIGAS			
R	Calaveras Twp 8	57	80
VIGGER			
---	Fresno Twp 2	59	69
VIGI			
Saml	San Francisco San Francisco 2	67	795
VIGIL			
Julian	Los Angeles Los Angeles	59	346
VIGINER			
Saml	Shasta French G	66	718
VIGLEY			
Emael	Tuolumne Sonora	71	222
Email*	Tuolumne Twp 1	71	222
VIGNET			
Vital F	Los Angeles Los Angeles	59	392
VIGNOLA			
Angelo*	Tuolumne Big Oak	71	141
VIGNOLEE			
Angelo	Tuolumne Twp 4	71	141
VIGNOY			
Frank	Amador Twp 1	55	492
VIGO			
Antonio	Los Angeles Los Angeles	59	509
Jose*	Los Angeles Los Angeles	59	489
VIGONREUX			
Geo*	San Francisco San Francisco 2	67	693
VIGOREUX			
A W	San Francisco San Francisco 10	67	263
Peter	San Francisco San Francisco 9	68	1004
VIGUE			
Louis	Los Angeles Los Angeles	59	376
VIGUES			
John M	Los Angeles Los Angeles	59	322
VIGUET			
Vital F	Los Angeles Los Angeles	59	392
VIGUS			
John	Amador Twp 6	55	439
Thos P	Sacramento American	63	167
VIKICH			
Saml	Tuolumne Twp 1	71	255
VILA			
F*	San Mateo Twp 1	65	63
VILACEGUE			
Eugene	San Francisco San Francisco 2	67	616
VILACEQUE			
Eugene	San Francisco San Francisco 2	67	616
VILAND			
Christophe*	Yuba Fosters	72	831
Christopher	Yuba Foster B	72	831
VILASQUE			
Guardiano	Santa Clara Burnett	65	261
VILASSA			
Francisco	San Francisco San Francisco 2	67	771
VILBROK			
David*	Placer Dutch Fl	62	724
VILDERMED			
John T*	Mariposa Twp 3	60	609
VILDOSSOLA			
Rosa	San Francisco San Francisco 2	67	615
VILHAC			
L	San Joaquin Stockton	64	1033
VILKEE			
Marks	San Francisco San Francisco 2	67	704

Name	County Locale	M653 RollPage
VILLA		
Antonio	San Luis Obispo San Luis Obispo	65 26
Antonio Ma	Santa Inez	64 140
	San Bernardino	
Buenna Ventura*	Tulara Twp 3	71 43
Buennaventura*	Tulara Sinks Te	71 43
Camen	Mariposa Twp 1	60 624
Carlos	San Luis Obispo San Luis Obispo	65 41
Catarina	San Mateo Twp 2	65 134
Emile	San Francisco San Francisco 2	67 687
Estevan	Los Angeles Los Angeles	59 362
Francisco	Los Angeles Santa Ana	59 444
Francisco	San Luis Obispo	65 43
	San Luis Obispo	
Gregonia	Los Angeles San Gabriel	59 419
Gregoria	Los Angeles San Gabriel	59 419
Jaime	San Bernardino Santa Barbara	64 203
Jesus	Los Angeles Los Angeles	59 315
Jose	Santa Clara Almaden	65 276
Jose A	Los Angeles Santa Ana	59 455
Jose Antonio	San Jose	65 390
	Santa Clara	
Josefa	San Bernardino Santa Ba	64 218
Josefa	San Bernardino S Buenav	64 219
Maria T	San Bernardino S Buenav	64 211
Maria Y	San Bernardino Santa Ba	64 211
Mariano	Los Angeles Los Angeles	59 392
Napomuclluo*	Santa Ana	59 443
	Los Angeles	
Nepomuceno	Santa Ana	59 443
	Los Angeles	
Rafael	San Luis Obispo San Luis Obispo	65 18
Rafael	San Luis Obispo San Luis Obispo	65 33
Raminda*	San Luis Obispo	65 42
	San Luis Obispo	
Ramonda*	San Luis Obispo	65 42
	San Luis Obispo	
Rieard	Santa Clara Almaden	65 276
Robert	San Luis Obispo San Luis Obispo	65 18
Timotea	Los Angeles Los Angeles	59 380
Timotia	Los Angeles Los Angeles	59 380
Uginio	Los Angeles Los Angeles	59 400
Yginio*	Los Angeles Los Angeles	59 400
VILLAESCUSA		
Jesus	Los Angeles Los Angeles	59 294
VILLAGIANCE		
Earrisda	Contra Costa Twp 3	57 615
VILLAGRANA		
Sepriano*	Monterey San Juan	60 998
Sipriano	Monterey San Juan	60 998
VILLAGROMCO		
Sepriano*	Monterey San Juan	60 998
VILLALAS		
John Thingo*	Yuba Parks Ba	72 785
VILLANO		
Hilario	Tuolumne Twp 3	71 424
VILLARA		
Roman	San Bernardino Santa Barbara	64 169
VILLARASA		
Francis Sado	Solano Benecia	69 314
VILLARDI		
Jose C	San Luis Obispo San Luis Obispo	65 45
VILLARENA		
Marina	San Diego San Diego	64 757
VILLARET		
Hypolite	San Francisco San Francisco 3	67 20
VILLARSON		
Oscar De	San Francisco San Francisco 10	277 67
VILLAS		
Miguel	Santa Clara Almaden	65 273
VILLAZERON		
Juan	Tehama Red Bluff	70 932
VILLE		
Fortinato	Calaveras Twp 10	57 288
Fortinuto	Calaveras Twp 10	57 288
VILLEGOS		
Manuel	Plumas Meadow Valley	62 927
VILLEGUEZ		
Domingo	Marin Cortemad	60 791
VILLEMEAU		
J J*	San Francisco San Francisco 3	67 17
VILLEMEUD		
J J*	San Francisco San Francisco 3	67 17
VILLEMURA		
Trinidad*	Yuba Marysville	72 858
VILLENGER		
Geo*	Tehama Red Bluff	70 929
Seon	San Joaquin Elkhorn	64 968
VILLENNOOS		
Trinidad*	Yuba Marysville	72 858
VILLENNZES		
Geo*	Tehama Red Bluff	70 929
VILLEQUEZ		
Domingo	Marin Cortemad	60 791
VILLERLY		
John*	Mendocino Little L	60 837

Name	County Locale	M653 RollPage
VILLERMOS		
Amanuela	San Francisco San Francisco 2	67 683
VILLERO		
C	Santa Clara San Jose	65 335
VILLERS		
Carlote	Marin San Rafael	60 757
Desserede*	Sierra Port Win	66 794
Dessereile*	Sierra Port Win	66 794
Desserele	Sierra Port Win	66 794
VILLES		
Frederick	San Francisco San Francisco 5	67 552
VILLIAN		
Jean	Shasta Shasta	66 671
VILLIARD		
C	Stanislaus Branch	70 698
VILLIER		
Jim	Shasta Shasta	66 671
VILLIRE		
Emili	San Francisco San Francisco 5	67 476
VILLIS		
A H	Tuolumne Columbia	71 309
VILLMAN		
John	Placer Iona Hills	62 888
VILLROK		
David*	Placer Dutch Fl	62 724
VILLURA		
Rafail	San Bernardino Santa Barbara	64 196
VILLURE		
Emih*	San Francisco San Francisco 5	67 476
Emili*	San Francisco San Francisco 5	67 476
VILM		
Frank ?	Calaveras Twp 6	57 180
Frank X	Calaveras Twp 5	57 180
VILONT		
John*	San Francisco San Francisco 3	67 50
VILPANDO		
Gabriel	Los Angeles Los Angeles	59 358
VILSINSKI		
Tobias	San Francisco San Francisco 3	67 30
VILTA		
F*	San Francisco San Francisco 2	67 672
VIM		
---	El Dorado Casumnes	581160
VIMAL		
Lewis	Sierra Downieville	661006
VIN		
---	Butte Kimshaw	56 598
---	Butte Kimshaw	56 608
---	Butte Oregon	56 629
---	Butte Eureka	56 651
---	El Dorado Mountain	581183
---	Yuba North Ea	72 680
---*	Butte Kimshaw	56 598
---*	Placer Christia	62 736
Ah	Butte Oregon	56 629
Augustus	Calaveras Twp 6	57 163
VINA		
A	San Joaquin Stockton	641096
B	Sutter Butte	70 800
Chas	Sonoma Petaluma	69 588
VINACCA		
Emille*	San Francisco San Francisco 2	67 616
VINACEA		
Emile*	San Francisco San Francisco 2	67 616
VINAGA		
Adolfo	Santa Clara Almaden	65 265
VINAL		
Roland	Yuba Long Bar	72 772
VINCEL		
Lewis*	San Francisco San Francisco 1	68 877
VINCENERS		
Jno	Sacramento Granite	63 266
VINCENEU		
Joseph	Calaveras Twp 7	57 34
VINCENIO		
Joseph	Calaveras Twp 8	57 82
VINCENNS		
Jno*	Sacramento Granite	63 266
VINCENT		
A	Yuba Marysville	72 918
A D	San Joaquin Elkhorn	64 999
Albt	Sonoma Petaluma	69 599
Bell	El Dorado Coloma	581075
Berthan	Santa Cruz Watsonville	66 539
Bos	Alameda Brooklyn	55 96
Burton	San Joaquin Castoria	64 908
Charles	Los Angeles Los Angeles	59 361
Charles D	Yuba Suida	72 990
David	Yolo Cottonwoood	72 648
Dow	Tehama Red Bluff	70 920
E	San Joaquin Stockton	641083
Elias	Tehama Red Bluff	70 920
Ellen E	Colusa Colusi	57 419
Frances	San Francisco San Francisco 3	67 80
Frank O	Colusa Colusi	57 419
Geo	San Joaquin Stockton	641039

Name	County Locale	M653 RollPage
VINCENT		
George	San Bernardino San Bernadino	64 635
Henry	Santa Cruz Santa Cruz	66 599
J	Nevada Grass Valley	61 207
J	Sutter Yuba	70 759
James	Trinity E Weaver	701057
Jerry	Tulara Sinks Te	71 42
John	Placer Forest H	62 773
John	Plumas Quincy	62 922
Joseph	Calaveras Twp 7	57 32
Joseph	Tuolumne Shawsfla	71 412
Josiah	Tuolumne Twp 1	71 251
Louis	Yuba New York	72 747
Martin	Santa Cruz Soguel	66 589
Martin	Santa Cruz Pescadero	66 650
Micholas	Placer Iona Hills	62 863
Nicholas*	Placer Forest H	62 806
Oscar	Santa Clara Alviso	65 407
Warren	Yuba Rose Bar	72 816
William	Colusa Colusi	57 419
William*	El Dorado Placerville	58 898
VINCENTA		
---	San Bernardino S Timate	64 710
---	San Bernardino S Timate	64 748
VINCENTE		
Sanchez	Los Angeles Los Angeles	59 368
VINCENTER		
Olisme	Sierra La Porte	66 768
VINCENTES		
Olisme	Sierra La Porte	66 768
VINCENUS		
Jno*	Sacramento Granite	63 266
VINCIENT		
Bell	El Dorado Coloma	581075
VINCINESLY		
Steccino*	Butte Ophir	56 766
VINCINISLY		
Steccino	Butte Ophir	56 766
VINCINO		
Wm	San Francisco San Francisco 2	67 722
VINDE		
Monte*	San Francisco San Francisco 8	681284
VINDECK		
J S	Sierra Downieville	66 961
VINDICUS		
Fred	Tuolumne Twp 2	71 280
VINE		
James	Sierra Twp 7	66 883
VINEEN		
Jos	Klamath Liberty	59 236
VINEGARHOLTZ		
Jno G	Mendocino Arrana	60 856
VINEGRIS		
Fernando*	Marin Cortemad	60 782
Fernands	Marin Cortemad	60 782
VINEN		
James	Sierra Twp 7	66 873
James	Sierra Twp 7	66 884
VINENER		
Ann	Sacramento Ward 1	63 95
VINER		
John H	San Francisco San Francisco 2	67 650
VINES		
Bartlett	Napa Yount	61 36
Danl B	San Francisco San Francisco 10	204 67
W H	Mariposa Twp 3	60 547
VINESE		
Yourer*	San Francisco San Francisco 9	681052
VINEY		
J A	Sierra Excelsior	661033
VINEYARD		
J R	Nevada Nevada	61 286
John F*	Yuba Rose Bar	72 818
John T	Yuba Rose Bar	72 818
Wm B	Yuba Rose Bar	72 817
VING		
---	Alameda Oakland	55 24
---	Placer Illinois	62 749
VINGENT		
Chas*	San Francisco San Francisco 2	67 559
VINGESON		
A*	Nevada Eureka	61 371
VINGNEER		
Amee	San Francisco San Francisco 6	67 458
VINGNIER		
Amie	San Francisco San Francisco 6	67 458
VINGOLT		
Peter*	El Dorado Salmon Falls	581056
VINGOTT		
Peter	El Dorado Salmon Hills	581056
VINIAL		
Lewis	Sierra Downieville	661006
VINICH		
Saml	Tuolumne Twp 1	71 255
VINING		
L	Calaveras Twp 9	57 406

Name	County Locale	M653 Roll	Page
VINING			
Robert	Solano Vallejo	69	248
VINIS			
Danl B	San Francisco San Francisco 10		204 67
VINKLE			
Peter	Alameda Brooklyn	55	146
VINMAN			
D G	Sutter Bear Rvr	70	818
VINNIORE			
Peter*	Sierra Twp 7	66	906
VINO			
---	El Dorado Salmon Falls		581052
VINOL			
J D	Marin San Rafael	60	767
VINPIRE			
Simron	Tuolumne Twp 1	71	257
VINSON			
Davis G	Tuolumne Twp 2	71	332
Margt	San Francisco San Francisco 9		681004
Theodore	Sacramento San Joaquin	63	368
Thomas	Tuolumne Chinese	71	488
Wm	Placer Ophir	62	651
VINTON			
Geo	Butte Oregon	56	631
John	Shasta French G	66	722
Wm	Sacramento Ward 1	63	62
VINYARD			
Elida A	Yuba Parks Ba	72	777
James	Nevada Bloomfield	61	509
John	Shasta Shasta	66	676
VINZENT			
Chas	San Francisco San Francisco 2	67	559
VINZINNI			
Alexr	Plumas Meadow Valley	62	931
VIO			
S D G	Tuolumne Twp 1	71	254
VIOGA			
Catrudo*	Calaveras Twp 6	57	183
VIOGT			
Mary	San Mateo Twp 3	65	93
VIOLET			
J	Butte Ophir	56	795
VIOLETT			
James	San Joaquin Elliott	64	942
VIOLIN			
John	Tuolumne Twp 3	71	459
VIOLINE			
Sargent*	Amador Twp 3	55	407
VION			
John	Yuba Long Bar	72	749
Thon	Yuba Long Bar	72	751
Thor*	Yuba Long Bar	72	751
VIOT			
Eugene	San Francisco San Francisco 2	67	797
VIOULT			
Marie	Yuba Foster B	72	822
VIOUS			
Chas	Calaveras Twp 5	57	212
VIOVIAN			
Nathan	Calaveras Twp 4	57	319
VIPARD			
Arthur	Santa Clara San Jose	65	308
VIPRRY			
James C*	Nevada Bloomfield	61	510
VIRAD			
Mary*	El Dorado Georgetown	58	673
VIRAIDA			
Mariquita	San Francisco San Francisco 2	67	768
VIRAINE			
Louis	Tehama Lassen	70	874
VIRALTO			
Farnando	Marin Sauciloto	60	751
VIRATH			
Henry	San Francisco San Francisco 8		681274
VIRATTO			
Fernando	Marin Sauciloto	60	751
VIRBAIN			
---	Mariposa Twp 1	60	655
VIRBE			
X	San Francisco San Francisco 12		364 67
VIRBIST			
Charles	Tuolumne Twp 2	71	282
VIRCLUS			
Nicole*	Placer Iona Hills	62	892
VIRDIER			
A	Sacramento Brighton	63	195
VIRERTA			
Jesus	San Francisco San Francisco 2	67	644
VIREZ			
Rafael	Santa Clara Santa Clara	65	494
VIRGIL			
P S	Butte Chico	56	553
VIRGIN			
Danl	Sacramento Ward 3	63	435
VIRGIN			
E F	Siskiyou Callahan	69	20
Jesse	Siskiyou Scott Va	69	35
VIRGINIA			
A*	Stanislaus Buena Village	70	721
Spencer	Yuba Rose Bar	72	791
VIRGO			
I	Nevada Nevada	61	319
J	Nevada Nevada	61	319
Jos H	Sacramento Ward 4	63	608
VIRIAN			
Geo*	Merced Twp 1	60	904
VIRINA			
Francis*	Tuolumne Sonora	71	189
VIRM			
---	Amador Twp 2	55	328
VIRNAN			
Claude	Stanislaus Branch	70	700
VIRON			
A	Nevada Eureka	61	358
VIRORTA			
Jesus	San Francisco San Francisco 2	67	644
VIRPLANK			
J B	Tuolumne Twp 1	71	251
VIRPLUNK			
J B	Tuolumne Twp 1	71	251
VIRRAIN			
E*	Stanislaus Empire	70	727
VIRRICK			
William*	San Francisco San Francisco 8		681305
VIRTRESE			
Alfred	Tulara Visalia	71	9
VIRUPEUX			
Gaspard	Calaveras Twp 10	57	296
VIRZA			
A	San Francisco San Francisco 5	67	539
VISCHER			
G N	San Joaquin Stockton		641009
VISE			
Ah	Butte Eureka	56	651
Jacob	Calaveras Twp 4	57	324
John	Monterey San Juan		601006
VISENTE			
Smith	San Bernardino Santa Barbara	64	155
VISERD			
Patrick*	Tuolumne Don Pedro	71	538
VISHAN			
William	San Francisco San Francisco 4		681146
VISHER			
Sebastian	San Joaquin Castoria	64	889
VISITARIS			
Francisco	Los Angeles San Jose	59	290
VISORD			
Patrick	Tuolumne Twp 6	71	540
VISTA			
---	Tulara Twp 3	71	44
VISTAL			
W	Sutter Nicolaus	70	832
VISTEC			
Alphonse*	San Francisco San Francisco 2	67	696
VISTORIA			
---	San Bernardino S Timate	64	693
VISULES			
Manwell	Calaveras Twp 5	57	207
VISULIS			
Manwell	Calaveras Twp 5	57	207
VITA			
F*	San Mateo Twp 1	65	63
VITE			
John	Solano Vacaville	69	327
VITMAN			
Geo	San Francisco San Francisco 2	67	797
VITNAN			
Jno P*	Klamath S Fork	59	207
VITOLO			
---	San Diego Agua Caliente	64	844
VITRY			
Louis	Calaveras Twp 6	57	142
VITS			
C	El Dorado Newtown	58	781
VITSELL			
Harman	Santa Clara San Jose	65	286
VITTA			
F*	San Francisco San Francisco 2	67	672
VITTE			
Jules	Yuba Parks Ba	72	777
VITTENGER			
Geo*	Tehama Red Bluff	70	929
VITTIGER			
William	San Diego Agua Caliente	64	846
VITUM			
Geo	Nevada Nevada	61	252
VITZGISH			
James	Sierra Twp 5	66	930
VIUNARE			
Peter*	Sierra Twp 7	66	906
VIUR			
Rablo	Calaveras Twp 4	57	331
VIUS			
Mauel	Contra Costa Twp 1	57	497
VIV			
---*	Placer Christia	62	736
VIVANS			
Samuel	Sierra Cox'S Bar	66	950
VIVAS			
Chas	Calaveras Twp 5	57	212
VIVAUS			
Samuel*	Sierra Cox'S Bar	66	950
VIVEN			
Jno L	Sacramento Ward 1	63	77
VIVEY			
Perley	Sierra La Porte	66	776
VIVIAN			
F	Trinity E Weaver		701057
Geo	Merced Twp 1	60	904
George	Tuolumne Jamestown	71	445
J J	Yolo Cottonwoood	72	661
James	Sierra Twp 7	66	875
John	Stanislaus Empire	70	732
Johnson	Sierra Twp 7	66	873
R T	Amador Twp 1	55	472
T J	Yolo Cottonwoood	72	661
Wm	Sierra Twp 7	66	873
VIVIANA			
---	Monterey Monterey	60	961
August	Siskiyou Scott Va	69	46
VIVIER			
C	San Francisco San Francisco 6	67	474
VIVIN			
Jno L*	Sacramento Ward 1	63	77
VIVIY			
Claude	Stanislaus Branch	70	699
VIVOS			
Chas	Calaveras Twp 5	57	212
VIYA			
Jose	Amador Twp 2	55	282
VIZA			
A	San Francisco San Francisco 5	67	539
VIZARD			
Thos	San Francisco San Francisco 10		190 67
VIZINA			
Charles	San Francisco San Francisco 7		681427
VJAH			
Ramono	Los Angeles San Jose	59	286
Ricardo	Los Angeles San Jose	59	285
VLABLATA			
Antonio*	Alameda Brooklyn	55	155
VLENN			
Mary F	San Francisco San Francisco 2	67	638
VLESON			
Autroph*	Sierra Downieville	66	957
VLIUN			
Wm*	Sacramento Ward 1	63	93
VMES			
Solomon	Mendocino Anderson	60	865
VNFIELD			
Abraham	Siskiyou Scott Va	69	35
VNRESZAGT			
Andrew*	San Francisco San Francisco 2	67	697
VO			
Yon	Sierra Downieville	66	984
VOACE			
W T	San Mateo Twp 3	65	109
VOBBE			
Mitchel*	San Joaquin Stockton		641031
VOBBES			
A	San Joaquin Stockton		641037
VOCERA			
Lorianna	Los Angeles Elmonte	59	260
VOCHELET			
Maria	San Francisco San Francisco 2	67	693
VOCHT			
C	Napa Napa	61	61
VOD			
Harry	Trinity Rearings	70	990
VODERQUES			
Manuel	Santa Cruz Soguel	66	587
VODGE			
David	Contra Costa Twp 1	57	515
VODGES			
J R*	Trinity Weaverville		701051
VOELE			
Jason	San Joaquin Elkhorn	64	984
VOELLA			
Harman	Sonoma Petaluma	69	571
VOGAL			
Jos	San Francisco San Francisco 10		313 67
VOGALISIOF			
---	San Francisco San Francisco 3	67	12

Name	County Locale	M653 RollPage
VOGAN		
James L	Yuba New York	72 748
John	Amador Twp 1	55 504
VOGASINES		
Henry*	Calaveras Twp 5	57 252
VOGD		
Jos	Butte Oregon	56 619
VOGDIES		
Wm	Alameda Brooklyn	55 149
VOGEL		
Adam	Del Norte Crescent	58 628
Chas	Sacramento Ward 1	63 82
Ernest	Trinity Weaverville	701066
John	Sierra Gibsonville	66 859
VOGELGARONG		
George L*	Calaveras Twp 5	57 253
VOGELGASONG		
George L*	Calaveras Twp 5	57 253
VOGELGESANG		
Henry	Calaveras Twp 5	57 253
VOGELGESONG		
Henry*	Calaveras Twp 5	57 253
VOGELGESONY		
Henry*	Calaveras Twp 5	57 253
VOGELY		
John	Placer Iona Hills	62 862
VOGELYASONY		
George L*	Calaveras Twp 5	57 253
VOGH		
George	Yuba Bear Rvr	721002
VOGI		
Saml	San Francisco San Francisco 2	67 795
VOGIT		
J	Sutter Butte	70 782
VOGL		
Gurgi*	San Francisco San Francisco 3	67 42
VOGLE		
George*	Yuba Bear Rvr	721002
Maggy	Placer Todds Va	62 762
Vinick	Mendocino Calpella	60 821
VOGLO		
L	San Joaquin Stockton	641095
VOGM		
Wm*	San Francisco San Francisco 3	67 66
VOGNI		
Wm*	San Francisco San Francisco 3	67 66
VOGON		
James L*	Yuba Long Bar	72 748
VOGOSINES		
Henry	Calaveras Twp 5	57 252
VOGOSINIS		
Henry	Calaveras Twp 5	57 252
VOGT		
George	San Francisco San Francisco 3	67 42
J S	El Dorado Georgetown	58 753
VOGUE		
Wm*	San Francisco San Francisco 3	67 66
VOGUES		
Francisco	Yuba Marysville	72 946
VOH		
Manuel	San Luis Obispo San Luis Obispo	65 16
VOICE		
Charles	San Francisco San Francisco 4	681146
VOID		
---	Butte Kimshaw	56 600
---	Butte Eureka	56 651
Ah	Butte Eureka	56 651
J	Nevada Eureka	61 368
VOIGH		
Godfrey F*	Los Angeles San Juan	59 463
VOIGHT		
Augustus	Tuolumne Twp 4	71 132
Fred	Amador Twp 2	55 264
Gosche	San Francisco San Francisco 6	67 436
Gosetie	San Francisco San Francisco 6	67 436
VOIGIN		
Theodore	San Francisco San Francisco 10	249 67
VOIGT		
Augustus	Tuolumne Big Oak	71 132
Godfrey F	Los Angeles San Juan	59 463
VOIJELLE		
Antonie	Yuba Marysville	72 902
VOIT		
Frank*	Nevada Red Dog	61 548
VOJUEE		
Alex*	Calaveras Twp 4	57 312
VOLANT		
Christian	Placer Iona Hills	62 880
Louis	Plumas Meadow Valley	62 928
VOLARD		
Peter	Calaveras Twp 9	57 366
VOLATRA		
J*	Tuolumne Twp 2	71 291
VOLBERG		
VOLBERG		
Chas	San Francisco San Francisco 10	265 67
VOLDDER		
Jane S*	Santa Cruz Watsonville	66 537
VOLDEZ		
Ramon	San Bernardino S Buenav	64 211
VOLDIER		
Chas	San Francisco San Francisco 2	67 687
VOLEPKA		
John	Solano Suisan	69 236
VOLEZ		
Diego	San Bernardino Santa Barbara	64 200
VOLGSTADT		
Elizabeth	San Francisco San Francisco 9	681006
VOLGUIRE		
P	San Francisco San Francisco 2	67 801
VOLHER		
Margt*	San Francisco San Francisco 1	68 811
VOLKER		
G W	El Dorado Casumnes	581169
VOLL		
Christian	San Francisco San Francisco 4	681222
Wm	Tuolumne Big Oak	71 129
VOLLARS		
Lewis	Sonoma Armally	69 487
VOLLE		
Frederick	Sacramento Centre	63 173
VOLLEME		
D H*	San Francisco San Francisco 3	67 50
VOLLENGUELA		
Ignacio*	Contra Costa Twp 3	57 613
VOLLERS		
Henry	San Francisco San Francisco 7	681424
Henry	San Francisco San Francisco 10	346 67
Martin	San Francisco San Francisco 7	681423
VOLLIER		
Joseph*	Sierra Downieville	66 965
VOLLIME		
D H*	San Francisco San Francisco 3	67 50
VOLLIMI		
D G*	San Francisco San Francisco 3	67 50
VOLLIN		
Joseph	Sierra Downieville	66 965
VOLLMER		
Joseph	Sierra Twp 7	66 914
VOLLMERS		
Michael	Trinity Weaverville	701062
VOLLNER		
Margt	San Francisco San Francisco 1	68 811
VOLLS		
Christian	San Francisco San Francisco 4	681222
VOLLUM		
Douglas	San Francisco San Francisco 1	68 911
E P	Shasta Millvill	66 750
Geo N	San Francisco San Francisco 2	67 627
Geo W	San Francisco San Francisco 2	67 627
VOLMAR		
D	San Francisco San Francisco 10	339 67
VOLMER		
Margt	San Francisco San Francisco 1	68 811
VOLMERS		
Otto	Trinity Weaverville	701062
VOLNAS		
Sarah	Colusa Colusi	57 426
VOLNER		
J	San Joaquin Stockton	641096
John F	Tuolumne Chinese	71 501
VOLNOK		
John	Sierra Cox'S Bar	66 952
VOLOHA		
---*	Mendocino Big Rvr	60 854
VOLPHONE		
J	Tuolumne Twp 4	71 146
VOLSEY		
Jas B	Santa Clara Gilroy	65 229
VOLSRICK		
Augustus	El Dorado Greenwood	58 709
VOLT		
John	Yuba Fosters	72 833
VOLZURE		
P	San Francisco San Francisco 2	67 801
VOM HOOKER		
Jno*	Sacramento Ward 1	63 85
VOM		
---	Placer Illinois	62 752
VOMERA		
Navissa	Alameda Brooklyn	55 173
VON AHNEN		
Gertrude	San Francisco San Francisco 2	67 661
VON BASKIRK		
Howard	San Francisco San Francisco 10	211 67
VON DER CLIFT		
---*	Mariposa Twp 3	60 583
VON DIHSON		
Geo	San Francisco San Francisco 10	266 67
VON GILMAN		
Geo	San Francisco San Francisco 2	67 628
VON GLAHN		
C	San Francisco San Francisco 10	213 67
Jno	San Francisco San Francisco 10	202 67
VON HASS		
C	San Francisco San Francisco 3	67 78
VON HONSEN		
Henry	Yuba Slate Ro	72 688
VON KIHSON		
Geo	San Francisco San Francisco 10	266 67
VON MAKER		
William	Nevada Rough &	61 426
VON PILDORPE		
William*	San Diego Colorado	64 807
VON POLNITZ		
Wm	Nevada Nevada	61 242
VON RONM		
William*	Calaveras Twp 9	57 354
VON RORM		
William*	Calaveras Twp 9	57 354
VON ROUM		
William*	Calaveras Twp 9	57 354
VON SCHMIDT		
Julius H	Yuba Bear Rvr	721009
Wm*	San Francisco San Francisco 1	68 915
VON SENDEN		
G D	San Francisco San Francisco 10	315 67
VON		
---*	Sacramento Ward 1	63 50
VONACH		
Joseph	Tuolumne Sonora	71 222
VONAN		
Lewis*	Sierra Gibsonville	66 859
VONATH		
Andrew H	San Francisco San Francisco 7	681355
VONBRAN		
Jacob	San Francisco San Francisco 2	67 606
VONDANSON		
Par*	Mariposa Coulterville	60 696
VONDELL		
Dennis	Calaveras Twp 4	57 326
Epolit	Calaveras Twp 4	57 326
Henry	Calaveras Twp 6	57 144
VONDER MEDEN		
F E	San Francisco San Francisco 5	67 512
VONDERDAHT		
G*	San Francisco San Francisco 7	681394
VONDERLEIGHT		
John	San Francisco San Francisco 11	95 67
VONEGAS		
Pedro*	Monterey San Juan	60 997
VONEKA		
---	Mendocino Big Rvr	60 855
VONESTADEN		
John*	San Francisco San Francisco 3	67 37
VONG		
Hi	Del Norte Crescent	58 640
VONGHT		
G C	Sacramento Ward 1	63 63
VONGNIER		
Gorden*	Sierra Downieville	661001
VONGUEIR		
Gorden*	Sierra Downieville	661001
VONGUIER		
Gorden*	Sierra Downieville	661001
Gordin*	Sierra Downieville	661001
VONHADEN		
John	San Francisco San Francisco 2	67 622
VONHAN		
Jacob	San Francisco San Francisco 2	67 606
VONHOMAN		
John*	Mendocino Big Rvr	60 842
VONHONIAN		
John	Mendocino Big Rvr	60 842
VONICO		
Mary	San Francisco San Francisco 10	182 67
VONISTADEN		
John*	San Francisco San Francisco 3	67 37
VONLER		
Louis	Calaveras Twp 6	57 140
VONNER		
C H	Nevada Eureka	61 352
VONOCE		
Jas	Butte Ophir	56 792
VONPFISTER		
E H	Solano Benecia	69 293

Name	County Locale	M653 Roll	Page
VONSCHMIDT			
A W	San Francisco San Francisco	11 67	89
Julias H	San Francisco San Francisco	11 67	89
VONSEGGEN			
Henry	Tuolumne Sonora	71	194
VONSEGGERN			
H	San Francisco San Francisco	12 67	375
VONTHON			
William	Contra Costa Twp 1	57	498
VONTTINE			
Ashley A*	San Francisco San Francisco	9 681	103
VONTURA			
---	San Bernardino Santa Inez	64	139
VOOMAN			
H	Sutter Yuba	70	769
VOOR			
Edward	Placer Yankee J	62	775
VOORHES			
Wm	Amador Twp 5	55	331
VOORHIES			
J	Sacramento Ward 1	63	9
Jas	Sacramento Ward 1	63	19
Joseph A	San Francisco San Francisco	11 67	123
R	Solano Suisan	69	219
T	Nevada Eureka	61	372
VOORHIRS			
T	Nevada Eureka	61	372
VOORHUS			
T*	Nevada Eureka	61	372
VOORKES			
Catherine	San Joaquin Castoria	64	899
VOORMAN			
Henry	San Francisco San Francisco	2 67	761
VOORSYP			
Alexandre	San Francisco San Francisco	2 67	582
VOOSTER			
H*	El Dorado Georgetown	58	706
VOP			
L	Nevada Eureka	61	382
S*	Nevada Eureka	61	382
VORAT			
Richard	Placer Iona Hills	62	881
VORATH			
H C	Placer Forest H	62	768
VORBE			
Alphonse	San Francisco San Francisco	2 67	804
Joseph	San Francisco San Francisco	2 67	625
VORBECK			
Fritz	Alameda Brooklyn	55	148
VORBURG			
W	Tehama Red Bluff	70	910
VORCE			
Charles	San Francisco San Francisco	4 681	146
VORD			
Samuel	San Francisco San Francisco	2 67	559
VORE			
Chandler*	Sacramento Ward 1	63	57
VOREE			
Henry	Mariposa Coulterville	60	691
VORHEES			
William*	Placer Iona Hills	62	890
VORIX			
B	Nevada Nevada	61	293
VORLANDER			
Richd	Del Norte Crescent	58	629
VORNOR			
S	Calaveras Twp 9	57	394
VORRAND			
Vhsmani*	Plumas Meadow Valley	62	927
VORRATH			
Christian	San Francisco San Francisco	2 67	683
VORRAUD			
Gismani*	Plumas Meadow Valley	62	927
VORRHIRS			
T	Nevada Eureka	61	372
VORSOME			
Jas*	Calaveras Twp 9	57	387
VORSONIO			
Jas	Calaveras Twp 9	57	387
VORTON			
J W	Marin Tomales	60	721
VORTRESE			
Alfred	Tulara Twp 2	71	9
VORUJA			
E*	Sacramento Ward 1	63	5
VORZIN			
Theodore	San Francisco San Francisco	10 67	249
VOSBARG			
Fitz James	Yuba Marysville	72	878
Fitzjames	Yuba Marysville	72	878
VOSBURG			
Joseph	Placer Todds Va	62	788
Sonis	Placer Todds Va	62	788
VOSE			
C H	Trinity Trinity	70	970
Chandler	Sacramento Ward 1	63	57
Geo H	Sacramento Ward 4	63	578
Jno	Klamath S Fork	59	197
Richd	San Francisco San Francisco	10 67	276
Stephen	San Francisco San Francisco	10 67	349
Warren	Stanislaus Emory	70	756
VOSEMAN			
John	Calaveras Twp 6	57	161
VOSGOS			
Joseph	Calaveras Twp 5	57	227
VOSHAY			
Joseph	Trinity Indian C	70	987
VOSS			
Jacob	San Francisco San Francisco	7 681	373
James	San Joaquin Castoria	64	891
L*	Nevada Eureka	61	382
S*	Nevada Eureka	61	382
VOSSIEE			
Alex*	Calaveras Twp 4	57	312
VOTAR			
Francisco*	Marin Bolinas	60	728
VOTEPKA			
John	Solano Suisan	69	236
VOTORE			
T	Nevada Eureka	61	350
VOU			
---	Calaveras Twp 6	57	134
VOUAN			
Lewis*	Sierra Gibsonville	66	859
VOUCH			
Lizzie	San Francisco San Francisco	4 681	138
VOUCHE			
Augustine	San Francisco San Francisco	8 681	255
VOUDY			
George	Humbolt Pacific	59	138
VOUEE			
Alex*	Calaveras Twp 4	57	312
VOUGH			
Gifford	Amador Twp 7	55	414
VOUGHE			
Augustine	San Francisco San Francisco	8 681	255
VOUGLDRAW			
Christopher	San Joaquin Castoria	64	883
VOUGRIERS			
Gerden*	Sierra Downieville	661	1001
VOUGUIN			
Gordin*	Sierra Downieville	661	1001
VOUREAT			
Victorine*	San Francisco San Francisco	4 681	151
VOURMAN			
Edgar	Sacramento San Joaquin	63	356
VOUSEGGERN			
Henry	Tuolumne Twp 1	71	194
VOUTTINE			
Ashley A*	San Francisco San Francisco	9 681	103
VOUX			
B	Nevada Nevada	61	293
VOW			
---	El Dorado Casumnes	581	160
VOWET			
Claus	Nevada Rough &	61	430
VOY			
---	Butte Kimshaw	56	598
---*	Stanislaus Branch	70	713
VOYELYESONY			
Henry*	Calaveras Twp 5	57	253
VOYLE			
Louis	Stanislaus Buena Village	70	723
VOYT			
Henry	Sierra Twp 5	66	936
VRADFORD			
Robert	Tuolumne Twp 4	71	126
VRAMSON			
C A*	Siskiyou Scott Va	69	22
VRANES			
Meshildo	Contra Costa Twp 1	57	519
VRANEVA			
Dolores*	Los Angeles Santa Ana	59	442
VRAUEVA			
Dolores*	Los Angeles Santa Ana	59	442
VRAUKIS			
V Ban*	Placer Forest H	62	792
VREELAND			
S B	Sacramento Ward 1	63	24
VRENDEL			
Michael	Siskiyou Shasta Valley	69	118
VRENDELL			
Michael	Siskiyou Shasta Valley	69	118
VRERDENBARGH			
W T*	Santa Clara San Jose	65	294
VRICKENS			
Robert	El Dorado Placerville	58	922
VRIEDO			
Deaderick	San Francisco San Francisco	7 681	337
VRIGO			
Luciana	Monterey Monterey	60	961
VRITES			
Wm	Sacramento Ward 3	63	436
VRIVESZAGT			
Andrew*	San Francisco San Francisco	2 67	697
VROMAN			
Adam	Calaveras Twp 6	57	156
George	Calaveras Twp 6	57	156
Henry	Calaveras Twp 6	57	156
Peter	Calaveras Twp 6	57	156
Schooly D	Calaveras Twp 5	57	208
VROOM			
P L	San Francisco San Francisco	3 67	56
P Q	San Francisco San Francisco	3 67	56
VROOMAN			
Martin	Butte Ophir	56	792
T	Butte Hamilton	56	516
VROWN			
John	Los Angeles San Pedro	59	481
VUAVADA			
Angel	Santa Clara San Jose	65	331
VUE			
---	El Dorado Placerville	58	904
VUI			
---	El Dorado Placerville	58	906
VUILLENME			
A*	San Francisco San Francisco	6 67	452
VUILLEUME			
A	San Francisco San Francisco	6 67	452
VUINA			
Anton	Tuolumne Twp 2	71	473
VULLAGE			
L W*	El Dorado Diamond	58	782
VULLER			
John*	El Dorado Placerville	58	934
VULNER			
Chas	San Francisco San Francisco	2 67	660
VULTZ			
Martin	San Francisco San Francisco	1 68	927
VUMARE			
Peter*	Sierra Twp 7	66	906
VUN			
---	Amador Twp 4	55	247
VUNBASTEL			
Henry*	San Francisco San Francisco	7 681	428
VUNCIENT			
William*	El Dorado Placerville	58	898
VUNG			
See	Tuolumne Twp 6	71	528
VUNGHRO			
H S	Solano Vallejo	69	247
VUNHOOSEN			
Jerome	Plumas Quincy	62	988
VUONCARA			
Lora Amma*	Mariposa Twp 1	60	631
Loraanima*	Mariposa Twp 1	60	631
VUONCORA			
Lera Anima*	Mariposa Twp 1	60	631
VUONERTI			
Loraanna*	Mariposa Twp 1	60	631
VUP			
---	Tulara Twp 1	71	117
VURENER			
Ann*	Sacramento Ward 1	63	95
VURN			
---	Amador Twp 7	55	412
VUROHAN			
Patrick*	Santa Cruz Santa Cruz	66	626
VUSS			
Alexander*	Sierra Pine Grove	66	826
VUSTOT			
Philip	Yuba Marysville	72	975
VUT			
---	El Dorado Salmon Falls	581	1059
---	El Dorado Diamond	58	805
VUTLY			
John F*	Calaveras Twp 6	57	111
W E			
---	Sierra Downieville	661	1009
W TON			
---*	Nevada Nevada	61	305
W			
Sing	Nevada Nevada	61	300
Tin	Sierra Downieville	66	984
Yarcks	Yolo Cache	72	643
W'MULLING			
George*	Yuba Rose Bar	72	792
W'STON			
Whitney*	San Francisco San Francisco	8 681	287

California 1860 Census Index

Name	County Locale	M653 RollPage
WA CA TO		
---	Mendocino Calpella	60 824
WA CHOW		
---	Nevada Nevada	61 306
---	Nevada Nevada	61 309
---	Nevada Washington	61 340
WA COW		
---	Nevada Nevada	61 310
---	Nevada Washington	61 341
WA FUN		
---	Nevada Nevada	61 307
WA HA		
---	Nevada Washington	61 339
WA HING		
---	Sacramento Ward 1	63 69
WA KOW		
---	Mendocino Calpella	60 821
WA MUKA		
---	Plumas Quincy	62 970
WA SHA		
---	Mendocino Calpella	60 822
WA TANG		
---	Nevada Nevada	61 301
WA YOU		
---	Nevada Washington	61 339
WA YUP		
---	Nevada Nevada	61 307
---	Nevada Nevada	61 308
---	Nevada Nevada	61 310
---	Nevada Nevada	61 339
WA		
---	Amador Twp 5	55 359
---	Calaveras Twp 5	57 256
---	Calaveras Twp 10	57 261
---	Calaveras Twp 10	57 268
---	Calaveras Twp 10	57 287
---	Mariposa Twp 3	60 618
---	Mariposa Twp 1	60 666
---	Nevada Nevada	61 299
---	Nevada Nevada	61 300
---	Nevada Nevada	61 306
---	Nevada Nevada	61 309
---	Nevada Washington	61 341
---	Nevada Washington	61 342
---	Nevada Eureka	61 383
---	Nevada Eureka	61 385
---	Nevada Eureka	61 386
---	Nevada Red Dog	61 549
---	Placer Michigan	62 837
---	Sacramento Granite	63 268
---	Sacramento Ward 4	63 610
---	San Francisco San Francisco 4	681 202
---	Tuolumne Twp 5	71 524
---	Tuolumne Chinese	71 525
---	Tuolumne Twp 6	71 539
---*	Calaveras Twp 10	57 261
A	Sacramento Granite	63 268
Ah	Sierra St Louis	66 816
Ches	Tuolumne Twp 6	71 529
Chew	Tuolumne Knights	71 529
Ching	Butte Mountain	56 741
Ching	San Francisco San Francisco 4	681 192
Chow	Nevada Nevada	61 306
Chow	Nevada Nevada	61 309
Chow	Nevada Washington	61 340
Chow	Nevada Washington	61 342
Chow	Nevada Eureka	61 383
Chow	Nevada Eureka	61 384
Chow	Nevada Eureka	61 385
Chung	Tuolumne Twp 6	71 539
Cow	Nevada Nevada	61 310
Cow	Nevada Washington	61 341
Evey	Sacramento Granite	63 245
Fou	Nevada Grass Valley	61 232
Fun	Nevada Nevada	61 307
Ha	Nevada Washington	61 339
Hing	Sacramento Ward 1	63 69
Ho	Sacramento Granite	63 269
Hop	San Francisco San Francisco 5	67 529
How	San Francisco San Francisco 3	67 54
Hyang	San Francisco San Francisco 10	355 67
Kee	El Dorado Salmon Falls	581 048
Lee	Yuba Marysville	72 939
Lu	Sacramento Granite	63 268
Man	Nevada Eureka	61 385
Maw*	Nevada Eureka	61 385
Pow	Nevada Washington	61 341
Rong	San Francisco San Francisco 10	355 67
Sam	Nevada Eureka	61 383
Sam*	Nevada Washington	61 340
Sha*	Mendocino Calpella	60 822
Sing	Nevada Eureka	61 384
Sing	Nevada Eureka	61 385
Sing	Yuba Rose Bar	72 794
WA		
Tang	Nevada Nevada	61 301
Ti	Calaveras Twp 5	57 250
Yang	Butte Ophir	56 817
Yew	Tuolumne Knights	71 529
Yin	Nevada Eureka	61 383
Yon	Nevada Washington	61 339
Yon	Tuolumne Twp 6	71 537
You	Nevada Eureka	61 383
You	Tuolumne Don Pedro	71 537
Yup	Nevada Nevada	61 307
Yup	Nevada Nevada	61 308
Yup	Nevada Nevada	61 310
Yup	Nevada Washington	61 339
Yup	Nevada Washington	61 342
Yup	Nevada Eureka	61 384
Yup	Nevada Eureka	61 385
Yup	Nevada Eureka	61 386
WA??		
E S	Mariposa Coulterville	60 680
WAA KA SHAW		
---	Plumas Quincy	62 970
WAA		
---	Butte Kimshaw	56 600
WAAH		
Hesa	El Dorado Casumnes	581 176
WAAN		
---*	Calaveras Twp 9	57 349
WAATS		
Edward	Solano Fremont	69 384
WABB		
E	Sutter Yuba	70 773
WABL		
John C*	Yuba Marysville	72 849
WABLEN		
D*	Placer Virginia	62 661
WABRE		
Adelaide*	Santa Clara San Jose	65 389
WABREVEN		
C	Sacramento Mississipi	63 185
WAC K		
Chaw	El Dorado Newtown	58 781
WACCA		
Franklin	San Francisco San Francisco 5	67 512
WACE		
Hop	Yuba Marysville	72 876
J A*	Santa Clara Santa Clara	65 521
WACH		
Sin	Butte Cascade	56 699
Wm	Sonoma Sonoma	69 635
WACHANTERE		
Archy	Sierra Twp 7	66 881
WACHANTIRE		
Archy*	Sierra Twp 7	66 881
WACHENRENDER		
Klus*	San Francisco San Francisco 10	257 67
WACHENREUDER		
Klus*	San Francisco San Francisco 10	257 67
WACHENRINDER		
Klus	San Francisco San Francisco 10	257 67
WACHER		
Thos L*	San Mateo Twp 2	65 122
WACHILL		
S	Calaveras Twp 9	57 386
WACHLET		
J R*	Yuba Parks Ba	72 778
WACHNUTH		
J W	Sierra Twp 5	66 921
WACHORST		
Heren*	Sacramento Ward 1	63 16
Herin*	Sacramento Ward 1	63 16
Herom	Sacramento Ward 1	63 16
WACHSA		
---	Tulara Twp 2	71 39
WACHSAE		
---	Tulara Twp 2	71 39
WACHTEL		
J R	Yuba Parks Ba	72 778
WACHTET		
J R*	Yuba Parks Ba	72 778
WACK		
---	Nevada Rough &	61 410
---	Nevada Bridgeport	61 460
---	Nevada Bridgeport	61 492
WACKANTIN		
Archy*	Sierra Twp 7	66 881
WACKER		
Ersamus D	San Joaquin Elliott	641 101
WACKMAN		
Theeden	Sierra Downieville	66 958
WACKMANN		
Joseph	Sierra Downieville	66 958
WADAC		
H	Trinity Minersville	70 969
WADAMEAR		
H	Sutter Yuba	70 762
WADDAMS		
Caleb	Butte Chico	56 534
WADDELL		
B F	Amador Twp 1	55 505
John	Sonoma Sonoma	69 658
Rachael	Yuba Long Bar	72 771
W	San Francisco San Francisco 9	681 073
Wm	Solano Benecia	69 289
WADDEN		
---	Amador Twp 1	55 509
H M	Napa Yount	61 53
Joseph	Mariposa Twp 1	60 648
WADDILL		
Saml W	Tuolumne Twp 1	71 215
WADDIN		
Joseph	Mariposa Twp 1	60 648
WADDLE		
Alexandre	Sonoma Armally	69 511
Allen	Placer Illinois	62 703
David	Placer Forest H	62 806
John J	Contra Costa Twp 2	57 572
Joseph	Amador Twp 2	55 286
Saml	Amador Twp 2	55 322
WADDON		
Joseph*	Siskiyou Yreka	69 144
WADDOW		
Joseph	Siskiyou Yreka	69 144
WADDY		
Meansza*	Placer Auburn	62 559
Miansza*	Placer Auburn	62 559
WADE		
A	San Francisco San Francisco 5	67 526
A C	El Dorado Georgetown	58 699
A D	Marin Bolinas	60 742
A J	Sacramento Centre	63 180
Abel	San Francisco San Francisco 11	154 67
Abner	Sacramento Ward 3	63 453
Abram	Calaveras Twp 6	57 146
Adam	Plumas Quincy	621 006
Andrew	Nevada Bridgeport	61 484
Arch	Nevada Bridgeport	61 458
B	Sacramento Brighton	63 204
B B*	Shasta Horsetown	66 707
B F	Amador Twp 2	55 281
C	Amador Twp 1	55 488
C H	Trinity Trinity	70 970
Catherine	Solano Benecia	69 308
Chapman W	Fresno Twp 3	59 32
Chas	Santa Clara Alviso	65 411
Chas	Santa Clara Alviso	65 412
David	Sacramento Ward 4	63 505
David	San Francisco San Francisco 3	67 23
Eliza	San Francisco San Francisco 2	67 804
Francis	Tulara Keyesville	71 60
Francis F	San Francisco San Francisco 2	67 655
Fred	Alameda Brooklyn	55 203
G	El Dorado Diamond	58 773
G	El Dorado Diamond	58 810
G	Sutter Yuba	70 761
George W	Contra Costa Twp 2	57 570
H	San Francisco San Francisco 9	681 061
H A	Tuolumne Jamestown	71 423
H R	Tuolumne Shawsfla	71 383
Harden	Trinity Steiner	701 000
Harry	Santa Clara Alviso	65 411
Henry C	Mendocino Calpella	60 817
Hiram	Yolo Cottonwood	72 649
I L M*	El Dorado Georgetown	58 701
J	Shasta Shasta	66 730
J J	Los Angeles Azuza	59 278
James	El Dorado Placerville	58 925
James P	Calaveras Twp 6	57 122
Jas	San Francisco San Francisco 2	67 636
John	Calaveras Twp 9	57 357
John	Nevada Rough &	61 417
John	San Francisco San Francisco 8	681 244
John J	Yuba Suida	72 981
Jos N	San Francisco San Francisco 2	67 604
Joseph	Calaveras Twp 9	57 354
Lawrenc	El Dorado Georgetown	58 699
Lawrence	El Dorado Georgetown	58 699
Lydia	San Francisco San Francisco 1	68 815
Mary	El Dorado Diamond	58 773
Michael	Yuba Marysville	72 976
Nathan	Tuolumne Jamestown	71 456
Peter	Los Angeles Los Angeles	59 500
R B	Shasta Horsetown	66 707
R M	Siskiyou Yreka	69 188
Richard	Yolo Slate Ra	72 688
Richard	Yuba Slate Ro	72 688
S S	Shasta Shasta	66 656
Samuel	Placer Yankee J	62 778
Simon H	San Francisco San Francisco 7	681 361

Name	County Locale	M653 Roll Page
WADE		
T	Calaveras Twp 9	57 400
T B	El Dorado Placerville	58 855
T B	Sacramento Alabama	63 417
Thomas	San Francisco San Francisco 7	681351
Thomas	Solano Benecia	69 295
Thomas	Tulara Twp 1	71 95
Thomas	Tuolumne Visalia	71 95
Thomas B	Napa Hot Springs	61 22
W	San Francisco San Francisco 6	67 466
W L	Siskiyou Scott Ri	69 70
Warren	Los Angeles Azuza	59 278
William	Klamath S Fork	59 207
Wm	Santa Clara Fremont	65 437
Wm N	San Francisco San Francisco 2	67 645
WADELOVE		
H B	Sacramento Granite	63 223
WADER		
Alexander	Tuolumne Twp 4	71 133
Henry	Tuolumne Twp 3	71 466
WADES		
Hram	Yolo Cottonwoood	72 649
WADHAMS		
Collins	San Francisco San Francisco 12	368 67
L	San Francisco San Francisco 2	67 587
William	San Francisco San Francisco 4	681110
WADHOMS		
William	San Francisco San Francisco 4	681110
WADICADE		
Edward	Siskiyou Yreka	69 190
WADIE		
J T	Butte Oregon	56 616
WADIMER		
Charistopher*	Twp 1 San Mateo	65 72
WADISH		
Jas	Sacramento Ward 3	63 468
WADKING		
A	Nevada Grass Valley	61 237
WADKINS		
Amos	Butte Chico	56 563
J	Sierra Downieville	66 989
James	Amador Twp 2	55 320
Wm R	Marin Cortemad	60 791
WADLEIGH		
J	San Francisco San Francisco 5	67 547
J W	Sacramento Ward 1	63 136
John	Sacramento Georgian	63 337
WADLENGTHBY		
Mark	Butte Oregon	56 615
WADLENGTHLY		
Mark*	Butte Oregon	56 615
WADLEY		
A S	Nevada Bridgeport	61 468
Benjamin S	Placer Auburn	62 569
G L	Sierra La Porte	66 776
Mary A	El Dorado Salmon Falls	581047
WADLIEGH		
Gardener	Siskiyou Yreka	69 124
WADLOUP		
Fred	Amador Twp 1	55 486
WADLOW		
Joseph	Siskiyou Yreka	69 144
WADMIRE		
Nelson	Sacramento Ward 1	63 114
WADNAGE		
Anaolato*	Marin Cortemad	60 783
Anaslato	Marin Cortemad	60 783
WADO		
Thomas	San Francisco San Francisco 7	681351
WADONIAS		
Jaun	Mariposa Twp 1	60 638
WADONIOS		
Jaun	Mariposa Twp 1	60 638
WADPOLE		
Toper	Amador Twp 5	55 332
WADSNOVIN		
J	Nevada Eureka	61 365
WADSUOVIN		
J*	Nevada Eureka	61 365
WADSWORTH		
E	Siskiyou Yreka	69 177
Eden	Sacramento Ward 1	63 119
H W	San Francisco San Francisco 10	214 67
Isaac	Placer Dutch Fl	62 727
Jason	Yolo No E Twp	72 678
Jason	Yuba North Ea	72 678
Jno	San Francisco San Francisco 9	681076
Louise	Sacramento Ward 1	63 41
Robt	Amador Twp 1	55 482
T H	Del Norte Crescent	58 650
W	San Francisco San Francisco 6	67 459
William	Tuolumne Twp 5	71 511
WADWORTH		
W R	San Francisco San Francisco 6	67 442

Name	County Locale	M653 Roll Page
WADY		
Anthony	San Francisco San Francisco 2	67 592
WAE		
---	Placer Auburn	62 581
---	San Francisco San Francisco 11	161 67
Sae	San Francisco San Francisco 11	146 67
Young	El Dorado Salmon Hills	581062
WAEDE		
Frederick*	Alameda Brooklyn	55 140
WAEE		
J*	Nevada Eureka	61 391
WAEKS		
John*	Marin Cortemad	60 780
WAERATH		
A	San Francisco San Francisco 10	308 67
WAEVER		
Eli	Sierra Twp 7	66 867
WAFF		
Saml	Santa Clara San Jose	65 281
WAFFLE		
Parley G	Colusa Monroeville	57 455
WAFFORD		
J B	Calaveras Twp 9	57 406
Thomas	Los Angeles Los Angeles	59 337
WAFSE		
Nicholas H*	San Francisco 7 San Francisco	681435
WAG		
---	Butte Ophir	56 787
---	Shasta French G	66 712
W C	Butte Oro	56 685
W Z	Butte Oro	56 684
WAGAMAN		
Jac*	Sacramento Ward 1	63 34
Jao*	Sacramento Ward 1	63 34
WAGAMAW		
Jac*	Sacramento Ward 1	63 34
WAGATE		
C C*	Shasta Shasta	66 761
WAGEN		
L H	Amador Twp 2	55 317
WAGENBLAST		
Chris F	Sacramento Ward 4	63 572
WAGENER		
Henry	San Francisco San Francisco 2	67 631
WAGENHEIM		
Amuel	Calaveras Twp 4	57 336
Solomon	Calaveras Twp 10	57 294
WAGER		
Alonzo*	Placer Rattle Snake	62 625
Charles	Mendocino Round Va	60 877
D	Tehama Lassen	70 869
David	Humbolt Mattole	59 122
Elias*	Nevada Bridgeport	61 443
George	Tuolumne Twp 5	71 497
Geroge	Tuolumne Chinese	71 497
H	Sutter Sutter	70 815
Hiram	Humbolt Mattole	59 122
John	Humbolt Bucksport	59 155
John	Siskiyou Cottonwoood	69 103
Lynn	Yolo Cache Crk	72 637
Owen	Nevada Bridgeport	61 488
Pete	Nevada Rough &	61 411
Peter	Nevada Rough &	61 411
WAGERMANN		
E	Tuolumne Twp 3	71 469
WAGERNAR		
Elinse	San Joaquin Castoria	64 884
WAGES		
A	El Dorado Casumnes	581163
WAGEY		
Rufus	San Joaquin Elkhorn	64 961
WAGG		
Janr	Calaveras Twp 6	57 153
Jans	Calaveras Twp 6	57 153
Jas	Yolo Putah	72 551
Phillip*	Tulara Twp 3	71 53
WAGGEMAN		
E	Tuolumne Sonora	71 221
WAGGENER		
Philips	Amador Twp 5	55 340
WAGGENHALL		
W	Butte Hamilton	56 523
WAGGERMAN		
E	Tuolumne Twp 1	71 221
WAGGET		
Chas*	El Dorado Georgetown	58 678
WAGGINS		
Leapold	Nevada Bloomfield	61 526
WAGGNER		
Paul	Placer Michigan	62 836
WAGGNOR		
Phillip	Amador Twp 5	55 345

Name	County Locale	M653 Roll Page
WAGGONER		
---	Yuba Marysville	72 967
D M	Tuolumne Twp 2	71 288
G W	Amador Twp 1	55 484
Jacob	Tuolumne Columbia	71 343
Julius	Siskiyou Yreka	69 183
Max W	Siskiyou Yreka	69 151
Phillip	San Francisco San Francisco 2	67 705
R M	Sacramento Georgian	63 341
T	Merced Twp 2	60 916
Vencence	Siskiyou Yreka	69 186
WAGGORD		
Hammond	Calaveras Twp 9	57 388
WAGGOTT		
C L	Nevada Nevada	61 297
WAGGSTAFF		
John	Amador Twp 3	55 377
WAGGY		
Joseph	Sonoma Vallejo	69 621
WAGH		
---	El Dorado Diamond	58 798
---	Tuolumne Twp 6	71 532
---*	El Dorado Georgetown	58 700
Patrick	Butte Oregon	56 618
WAGHTER		
Hubert	Butte Wyandotte	56 665
WAGLEY		
William	Contra Costa Twp 2	57 540
WAGMAN		
Henry A	Sonoma Santa Rosa	69 407
Jacob	Sacramento Ward 4	63 519
WAGMER		
Jacob	Alameda Oakland	55 72
WAGMIER		
Peter	Alameda Brooklyn	55 172
WAGNER		
A	San Francisco San Francisco 4	681222
A	San Joaquin Stockton	641046
Aaron	Napa Clear Lake	61 138
Adam	San Francisco San Francisco 3	67 58
Adolp	San Francisco San Francisco 7	681325
Adolph	San Francisco San Francisco 7	681325
Alonzo*	Placer Rattle Snake	62 625
Andrew	El Dorado White Oaks	581027
Anthon	Sacramento Ward 3	63 444
Antone	El Dorado Union	581089
Arastus	Shasta Millvill	66 742
Augustus	Sierra Scales D	66 803
C	El Dorado Coloma	581068
C	Shasta Shasta	66 655
C Van*	Nevada Eureka	61 356
Charles	San Francisco San Francisco 3	67 81
Charles	Tuolumne Sonora	71 212
Chas	San Francisco San Francisco 9	681055
Chas	San Francisco San Francisco 9	681100
Dennis	San Francisco San Francisco 2	67 565
Edward	Alameda Brooklyn	55 147
Erastus	Shasta Millvill	66 742
F O	San Francisco San Francisco 5	67 512
Ferdenand	San Francisco 2 San Francisco	67 771
Frank	Butte Oro	56 679
Frank	Tuolumne Twp 4	71 138
Fred	Placer Michigan	62 825
Fred	Tuolumne Twp 2	71 345
Frederick	San Francisco San Francisco 7	681416
Fredrick	Sierra Scales D	66 803
George	Tuolumne Twp 5	71 489
H	San Francisco San Francisco 5	67 475
H H	El Dorado White Oaks	581003
Henry	Del Norte Happy Ca	58 661
Henry	El Dorado Coloma	581071
Henry	Sierra Twp 5	66 917
Henry	Yuba Marysville	72 876
Hiram	San Joaquin Stockton	641079
Horatis	El Dorado White Oaks	581003
J B	Siskiyou Scott Ri	69 62
Jacob	Sacramento Granite	63 266
Jacob	San Joaquin Stockton	641017
James*	Yolo Cache Crk	72 643
John	El Dorado Salmon Hills	581052
John	Plumas Quincy	621003
John	Plumas Quincy	62 960
John	Santa Cruz Santa Cruz	66 604
John	Trinity Weaverville	701079
John H	San Francisco San Francisco 6	67 432
John P	Humbolt Union	59 182
John W	Placer Dutch Fl	62 718
Joseph	Siskiyou Callahan	69 10
L	El Dorado Placerville	58 871
Louis	Plumas Meadow Valley	82 908
Max	San Joaquin Stockton	641040
Michael	Sacramento Ward 3	63 432
Michael	San Francisco San Francisco 7	681395
Michael	San Francisco San Francisco 1	68 813
Nette	El Dorado Georgetown	58 687

California 1860 Census Index

Name	County Locale	M653 Roll	Page
WAGNER			
O H	Nevada Bridgeport	61	450
Oliver	Siskiyou Callahan	69	18
P	San Francisco San Francisco 1	68	832
P B	San Joaquin Stockton	64	1041
Peter	San Francisco San Francisco 5	67	475
Phillip	El Dorado Coloma	58	1103
Sam	Nevada Bridgeport	61	486
T	Nevada Eureka	61	370
Tho	Siskiyou Callahan	69	18
To	Siskiyou Callahan	69	18
Van	Sierra Twp 7	66	875
W	San Francisco San Francisco 7	68	1421
William	El Dorado White Oaks	58	1017
William	Plumas Meadow Valley	62	903
William	Plumas Quincy	62	939
Wm	Yolo Slate Ra	72	700
Wm	Yuba Slate Ro	72	700
WAGNIN			
Jno*	Butte Chico	56	551
WAGNIS			
Charles	Tuolumne Twp 1	71	212
WAGNON			
Jno	Butte Chico	56	551
Jno	Butte Chico	56	562
Jno	Butte Oregon	56	636
Jno*	Butte Chico	56	551
WAGNOR			
Frank	Butte Oro	56	679
Jost	El Dorado Kelsey	58	1142
Peter	Butte Cascade	56	704
Post	El Dorado Kelsey	58	1142
WAGNR			
Wm	Yolo Slate Ra	72	698
Wm	Yuba Slate Ro	72	698
WAGON			
L H	Amador Twp 2	55	317
W A	San Francisco San Francisco 1	68	811
WAGONCRAFT			
Oliver	San Bernardino San Bernadino	64	625
WAGONER			
A	Nevada Nevada	61	321
Andrew	Contra Costa Twp 3	57	613
C	Sutter Nicolaus	70	835
E H	Solano Vacaville	69	323
Emile	Santa Clara Alviso	65	406
G	Nevada Grass Valley	61	197
Geo	El Dorado White Oaks	58	1008
George	Fresno Twp 1	59	34
J	Calaveras Twp 9	57	377
J	Trinity China Bar	70	959
J D	Amador Twp 6	55	434
J L	Amador Twp 6	55	434
J S	Yolo Putah	72	550
Jacob	Calaveras Twp 9	57	388
Jacob	El Dorado Placerville	58	878
James	Yolo Cache	72	643
John	Alameda Brooklyn	55	119
John	San Joaquin Castoria	64	892
John	Solano Suisan	69	225
Legis	Fresno Twp 3	59	15
N	Sutter Yuba	70	767
Peter	Alameda Washington	55	172
Peter	Santa Clara San Jose	65	308
Saml	Sonoma Petaluma	69	588
T	Nevada Nevada	61	244
William	Calaveras Twp 9	57	379
Wm*	Amador Twp 5	55	368
Wm*	Calaveras Twp 5	57	247
WAGONN			
Wm*	Calaveras Twp 5	57	247
WAGOS			
W	El Dorado Placerville	58	825
WAGSTAFF			
Geo	Amador Twp 1	55	463
Geo	Butte Hamilton	56	513
George	Amador Twp 4	55	244
Jas	Butte Hamilton	56	513
Jeremiah	Tuolumne Big Oak	71	138
WAGY			
Phillip	Tulara Keyesville	71	53
WAH CHU			
---	Fresno Twp 2	59	43
WAH HO			
---	Sacramento Ward 3	63	491
WAH KI CAN			
---	Colusa Monroeville	57	456
WAH KO			
---	Sacramento Ward 3	63	491
WAH LO			
---	Sacramento Ward 3	63	489
WAH			
---	Alameda Oakland	55	22
---	Amador Twp 5	55	365
---	Butte Cascade	56	702
---	Butte Cascade	56	704
WAH			
---	Butte Bidwell	56	708
---	Butte Bidwell	56	717
---	Butte Bidwell	56	723
---	Butte Bidwell	56	728
---	Butte Ophir	56	788
---	Butte Ophir	56	802
---	Butte Ophir	56	803
---	Butte Ophir	56	810
---	Butte Ophir	56	815
---	Butte Ophir	56	818
---	Calaveras Twp 10	57	271
---	Calaveras Twp 10	57	286
---	Calaveras Twp 10	57	291
---	Calaveras Twp 4	57	303
---	Calaveras Twp 4	57	305
---	Calaveras Twp 4	57	308
---	Calaveras Twp 4	57	315
---	Calaveras Twp 4	57	320
---	Calaveras Twp 4	57	322
---	Calaveras Twp 4	57	49
---	El Dorado Georgetown	58	680
---	El Dorado Georgetown	58	703
---	El Dorado Georgetown	58	748
---	El Dorado Mud Springs	58	982
---	Marin Cortemad	60	792
---	Placer Michigan	62	844
---	Sacramento Granite	63	232
---	Sacramento Casumnes	63	381
---	Sacramento Cosummes	63	392
---	Sacramento Cosummes	63	398
---	Sacramento Ward 1	63	59
---	Sacramento Ward 1	63	65
---	Shasta Shasta	66	669
---	Shasta Horsetown	66	698
---	Shasta Horsetown	66	701
---	Shasta Horsetown	66	704
---	Sierra La Porte	66	780
---	Trinity Mouth Ca	70	1015
---	Trinity Mouth Ca	70	1017
---	Tuolumne Big Oak	71	148
---	Tuolumne Twp 4	71	181
---	Tuolumne Jacksonville	71	515
---	Tuolumne Green Springs	71	521
---	Tuolumne Twp 5	71	524
---	Tuolumne Chinese	71	525
---	Tuolumne Twp 6	71	536
---*	Mariposa Twp 3	60	608
---*	Tuolumne Big Oak	71	181
Ah	Butte Cascade	56	702
Ah	Butte Cascade	56	704
Ah	Butte Bidwell	56	708
Ah	Butte Bidwell	56	723
Ah	Butte Bidwell	56	728
Ah	Placer Iona Hills	62	898
Ah	Sacramento Cosummes	63	380
Ah	Sacramento Cosummes	63	381
Ann	Santa Clara Santa Clara	65	516
Chas*	Mariposa Coulterville	60	694
Ching	Butte Bidwell	56	727
Chip	Butte Bidwell	56	724
Choy	Del Norte Happy Ca	58	663
Chu	Butte Cascade	56	701
Flinn	Butte Bidwell	56	708
Gee	El Dorado Georgetown	58	747
Hop	Placer Michigan	62	844
Hum	El Dorado Georgetown	58	745
Kim	Butte Bidwell	56	728
Lin	Butte Cascade	56	698
Ling	Butte Bidwell	56	723
Lo*	Sacramento Ward 3	63	489
Lu	El Dorado Georgetown	58	746
Mous	Tuolumne Twp 4	71	150
My	El Dorado Georgetown	58	702
San	Sacramento Granite	63	232
See	Plumas Quincy	62	949
Segin	Butte Cascade	56	699
Si	Placer Forest H	62	771
Sin	Butte Cascade	56	700
Sing	Butte Bidwell	56	708
Sing	Butte Bidwell	56	711
Sing	Butte Bidwell	56	724
Sing	Butte Mountain	56	735
Sing	Butte Mountain	56	743
Sing	Butte Ophir	56	801
Sing	Calaveras Twp 4	57	334
Song	Placer Michigan	62	858
Sung	Placer Forest H	62	773
Teen	Tuolumne Twp 4	71	148
Tu	Placer Michigan	62	844
Wee	Butte Cascade	56	698
Yung	Fresno Twp 2	59	19
Yung	Fresno Twp 3	59	32
WAHA			
James	El Dorado Kelsey	58	1132
WAHAM			
Jno	San Francisco San Francisco 9	68	1072
WAHBURN			
Lyrander*	Calaveras Twp 4	57	318
Lyrunder*	Calaveras Twp 4	57	318
WAHDEL			
Henry	San Francisco San Francisco 7	68	1422
WAHE			
---	Butte Bidwell	56	709
WAHEL			
Francis	Santa Clara San Jose	65	342
WAHEN			
William	Nevada Rough &	61	395
WAHINGTON			
George	Tuolumne Twp 5	71	501
WAHL			
Bridget	Yuba Marysville	72	955
Christian	Sonoma Russian	69	435
John C	Yuba Marysville	72	849
William	Plumas Quincy	62	951
WAHLEN			
Andrew	Yolo No E Twp	72	668
WAHLER			
Joseph	San Francisco San Francisco 4	68	1217
WAHLOWS			
Henry	Yuba Marysville	72	924
WAHMUCK			
---	Fresno Twp 1	59	53
WAHNOOT			
Henry*	Alameda Brooklyn	55	77
WAHON			
Jas	Sacramento Ward 1	63	55
WAHONER			
T	Nevada Nevada	61	244
WAHONG			
---	Trinity Lewiston	70	957
WAHOO			
---*	Fresno Twp 1	59	56
WAHR			
Wm F	Trinity Steiner	70	999
WAHROOT			
Henry	Alameda Brooklyn	55	77
WAHS			
---	Butte Ophir	56	819
Ching	Butte Bidwell	56	723
WAHSBURN			
C	Calaveras Twp 9	57	397
WAI			
---*	Mariposa Twp 3	60	578
WAIANS			
Stephen*	Yuba Marysville	72	885
WAID			
T	Tehama Lassen	70	866
WAIDE			
---	Tulara Keeneysburg	71	50
WAIDMAN			
H	Sonoma Bodega	69	520
W H	Sonoma Bodega	69	520
WAIDNER			
J	Nevada Eureka	61	350
WAIE			
Edwd*	Butte Hamilton	56	520
WAIF			
N H	Sacramento Ward 1	63	55
WAIGELL			
Joseph	Yuba Marysville	72	864
WAIGHT			
John	Amador Twp 3	55	382
WAIKNE			
Elias	Calaveras Twp 6	57	170
Elius	Calaveras Twp 5	57	170
WAILACE			
W F	Monterey San Juan	60	987
WAILE			
Geo	Sacramento Ward 3	63	481
WAILLEY			
G L	Sierra La Porte	66	776
WAILOR			
George*	Yuba Marysville	72	883
WAIMAN			
P	Siskiyou Cottonwoood	69	106
WAIMER			
Andrew*	El Dorado Eldorado	58	936
WAIMSUR			
B F*	El Dorado Eldorado	58	936
WAIN			
---	Placer Michigan	62	834
Albert T	Yuba Marysville	72	945
Thos	El Dorado Georgetown	58	678
WAINE			
---	Sierra Twp 7	66	876
WAINER			
E	Shasta French G	66	717
Henry	Sierra Downieville	66	1013
WAINRIGHT			
Amos	Calaveras Twp 9	57	382
Edward	San Francisco San Francisco 11	67	101

California 1860 Census Index

Name	County Locale	M653 RollPage
WAINSCOTT		
Francis	Sacramento Franklin	63 327
WAINT		
Louis	El Dorado Kelsey	581139
WAINWRIGHT		
Jas	San Francisco San Francisco 1	68 845
John	San Francisco San Francisco 7	681334
John	Tuolumne Sonora	71 187
William	San Francisco San Francisco 8	681290
WAIR		
Jas *	Sacramento Granite	63 261
Joseph *	Yuba Marysville	72 941
Levi *	Santa Cruz Santa Cruz	66 628
Sin	Placer Rattle Snake	62 629
WAIRDIOS		
---	Sierra Eureka	661042
WAIRFIELD		
R	Sutter Sutter	70 815
WAIRHAYE		
James	Sierra Twp 7	66 882
WAISAHO		
---	Tulara Twp 2	71 40
WAIT		
---	Placer Goods	62 694
Abraham	San Francisco San Francisco 7	681429
Alfred	San Francisco San Francisco 6	67 417
Burton L	Humbolt Humbolt	59 168
David	El Dorado Salmon Falls	581051
Edward	Del Norte Klamath	58 654
Harry	Shasta Millvill	66 739
Henry	Shasta Millvill	66 739
I	El Dorado Georgetown	58 760
John	El Dorado Coloma	581114
L	Nevada Eureka	61 357
L	Nevada Rough &	61 416
Lanselott	Mendocino Calpella	60 816
Leroy	Butte Kimshaw	56 603
Mary	Sacramento Sutter	63 307
Robt	Trinity Trinity	70 971
Samuel	Contra Costa Twp 1	57 501
W W	Nevada Rough &	61 423
Walter	Butte Ophir	56 791
WAITE		
C	San Francisco San Francisco 5	67 552
Daniel	Placer Michigan	62 815
E G	Nevada Eureka	61 368
Frank	San Francisco San Francisco 10	238 67
James A	Los Angeles Los Angeles	59 333
Jas M	San Francisco San Francisco 10	236 67
Jas S	San Bernardino San Bernadino	64 633
Jos M	San Francisco San Francisco 10	236 67
M N	San Francisco San Francisco 10	346 67
R H	Placer Michigan	62 839
Robert	El Dorado Georgetown	58 702
W	El Dorado Georgetown	58 707
Waters	Sierra La Porte	66 769
Waters N	Sierra La Porte	66 769
WAITERS		
John	Solano Suisan	69 216
WAITH		
Lewis *	Sonoma Petaluma	69 602
WAITOUR		
Anne M *	San Francisco San Francisco 10	176 67
WAITS		
G W	Nevada Nevada	61 249
John	Mariposa Twp 3	60 590
WAITT		
A	Amador Twp 5	55 333
James M	San Francisco San Francisco 11	140 67
Robert	San Francisco San Francisco 11	150 67
WAITTE		
Adolphus *	Amador Twp 4	55 255
WAJ		
---	Mariposa Twp 3	60 562
WAJGMER		
Julius	Siskiyou Yreka	69 183
WAJH		
---	El Dorado Georgetown	58 700
WAJIDA		
Josepha	Tuolumne Sonora	71 227
WAK KA-MEA		
---	Fresno Twp 2	59 47
WAK		
---	Butte Bidwell	56 728
---	Mariposa Twp 3	60 608
Sin	Butte Cascade	56 700
WAKE		
Ah	Butte Bidwell	56 709
James	El Dorado Georgetown	58 759

Name	County Locale	M653 RollPage
WAKE		
James F	San Francisco San Francisco 7	681398
W	Calaveras Twp 9	57 414
WAKEA		
Watee	Fresno Twp 2	59 92
WAKEFIELD		
Chape	Santa Clara San Jose	65 284
Geo W	Sacramento Franklin	63 320
George	Los Angeles Los Angeles	59 517
H	Butte Chico	56 534
H M	Alameda Brooklyn	55 195
H S	Del Norte Crescent	58 635
Ira	Alameda Brooklyn	55 188
J A	Trinity Mouth Ca	701012
J R	Stanislaus Branch	70 703
L	Butte Oregon	56 619
Levi S	San Francisco San Francisco 10	234 67
Loreanzo	Calaveras Twp 4	57 299
Lorenzo	Calaveras Twp 10	57 299
Mike D	San Joaquin Douglass	64 924
R B	El Dorado Georgetown	58 696
R L	El Dorado Mud Springs	58 997
Thomas	El Dorado Eldorado	58 938
W F	El Dorado Coloma	581114
William	Sierra Pine Grove	66 822
WAKELAND		
Jiles	Mariposa Coulterville	60 694
WAKELEE		
William P	San Francisco San Francisco 9	681078
WAKELER		
William P	San Francisco San Francisco 9	681078
WAKELEY		
T H	San Francisco San Francisco 7	681436
WAKELL		
---	Del Norte Klamath	58 656
WAKELY		
C H	San Francisco San Francisco 2	67 787
P	Amador Twp 6	55 446
Thos	San Francisco San Francisco 1	68 889
WAKEMAN		
--- *	San Francisco San Francisco 9	681001
A J	Sacramento San Joaquin	63 360
B	Nevada Eureka	61 354
Edgar	Alameda Brooklyn	55 85
F A	San Francisco San Francisco 9	681003
George	Placer Forest H	62 773
Martin	San Francisco San Francisco 3	67 1
Mary L	Alameda Brooklyn	55 85
WAKEN		
John	San Bernardino San Bernadino	64 673
John	Shasta Cottonwoood	66 736
WAKENONING		
Henry	Calaveras Twp 5	57 190
WAKER		
Jos	Butte Kimshaw	56 597
Sarah A	Tuolumne Sonora	71 199
WAKERMAN		
Michael	Plumas Meadow Valley	62 932
WAKERS		
James *	Santa Cruz Pajaro	66 553
WAKERSHAM		
Isaac	Sonoma Petaluma	69 544
WAKES		
Jno L *	Sacramento Ward 1	63 84
WAKETY		
P	Amador Twp 6	55 446
WAKEY		
Anna	Sierra Eureka	661044
WAKHAM		
Jas	Napa Napa	61 87
WAKIMAN		
Martin	San Francisco San Francisco 3	67 1
WAKIS		
Jno L *	Sacramento Ward 1	63 84
WAKLEY		
J W	Siskiyou Cottonwoood	69 99
WAKLUM		
Lysander	Calaveras Twp 4	57 318
WAKN		
Jno L *	Sacramento Ward 1	63 84
WAKOO		
--- *	Fresno Twp 1	59 56
WAKS		
Jackson	Monterey San Juan	60 989
Thomas	Santa Cruz Santa Cruz	66 621
WAKUNCUR		
Willet *	Placer Todds Va	62 788
WAL		
---	Mendocino Little L	60 839
WALAHAN		
Alexander	Sierra Cold Can	66 836
WALATON		
W H	El Dorado Placerville	58 890
WALBECK		
Martin	Sacramento Ward 1	63 38

Name	County Locale	M653 RollPage
WALBECK		
Martin	Sacramento Ward 4	63 533
WALBERT		
Martin	Contra Costa Twp 1	57 529
WALBERTON		
---	San Bernardino S Timate	64 700
WALBIDGE		
Elsa	Yuba North Ea	72 671
WALBINT		
T *	Calaveras Twp 9	57 395
WALBRIDGE		
Elesa	Yolo No E Twp	72 671
F	San Francisco San Francisco 5	67 548
L	Solano Vallejo	69 249
Samuel	Tulara Twp 3	71 41
WALBUT		
T *	Calaveras Twp 9	57 395
WALBY		
John *	Nevada Nevada	61 319
WALCH		
---	San Francisco San Francisco 1	68 862
Abby	San Francisco San Francisco 10	241 67
Edward	Del Norte Klamath	58 654
Hymas	Siskiyou Callahan	69 8
Ingold	San Francisco San Francisco 7	681399
James	Calaveras Twp 6	57 146
James	Del Norte Crescent	58 626
James	Placer Auburn	62 567
John	Napa Clear Lake	61 119
Julius	Placer Virginia	62 661
Margaret	Placer Virginia	62 689
Michael	El Dorado Casumnes	581168
Michael	San Mateo Twp 3	65 93
Michael	Yuba Rose Bar	72 799
Micheal	El Dorado Casumnes	581168
T	Calaveras Twp 9	57 411
Thomas	Siskiyou Callahan	69 8
William	San Francisco San Francisco 7	681430
WALCHER		
Chester *	Napa Napa	61 82
WALCK		
Michael *	Yuba Rose Bar	72 799
WALCOM		
Jacob	San Francisco San Francisco 10	235 67
John	Trinity Hay Fork	70 991
WALCOTT		
Aeo	San Francisco San Francisco 8	681291
Asa	San Francisco San Francisco 8	681291
B P	San Francisco San Francisco 5	67 477
C H	Tuolumne Big Oak	71 125
C H	Tuolumne Twp 4	71 127
John	San Joaquin Stockton	641055
Oliver	Tuolumne Twp 1	71 218
Syvanus	Yolo Slate Ra	72 694
WALCOU		
George *	Calaveras Twp 8	57 109
WALCURE		
Charles	Calaveras Twp 7	57 40
WALD		
F E	San Francisco San Francisco 4	681216
WALDE		
Peter	Placer Ophirville	62 657
WALDEGER		
Chas	Butte Oregon	56 623
WALDEGG		
Augustus	San Francisco San Francisco 12	384 67
WALDEN		
August	Siskiyou Scott Va	69 36
F	Siskiyou Scott Va	69 58
H	Sacramento Alabama	63 418
H L	Butte Oregon	56 626
H S	Butte Oregon	56 626
James	El Dorado Coloma	581075
John	Trinity Raabs Ba	701020
M F	Tuolumne Twp 2	71 284
S A	Colusa Grand Island	57 477
Thos E	Shasta Millvill	66 725
William	Solano Vacaville	69 337
Wm	Placer Secret R	62 611
Wm H	Butte Bidwell	56 732
WALDER		
August	Siskiyou Scott Va	69 36
Carson	Yolo Putah	72 587
Charles	Santa Cruz Pescadero	66 644
F	Butte Eureka	56 649
Jno	Nevada Nevada	61 322
John T	El Dorado Mud Springs	58 975
Sidney	Solano Suisan	69 220
Theodore	Napa Napa	61 61
WALDEYER		
Chas	Butte Oregon	56 623
WALDIN		
Henry	San Francisco San Francisco 7	681400

Name	County Locale	M653 Roll Page
WALDLENFILD		
A	Santa Clara San Jose	65 290
WALDMAN		
Abraham	Alameda Brooklyn	55 81
WALDO		
Anson	El Dorado Kelsey	581137
J W	Yolo Cache Crk	72 663
WALDOIN		
Foank	Mariposa Twp 1	60 653
WALDON		
J	San Francisco San Francisco 2	67 784
Thos	Napa Napa	61 113
William	Nevada Bloomfield	61 527
Wm H	Butte Bidwell	56 732
WALDORF		
Jacob	Trinity Weaverville	701051
WALDORN		
Frank	Mariposa Twp 1	60 653
WALDOTE		
---*	Butte Chico	56 550
WALDRADT		
Jacob	Sacramento Sutter	63 294
WALDREN		
A T	Tuolumne Twp 1	71 266
Wm	Sacramento Granite	63 260
WALDRICH		
Agustus	Yuba Long Bar	72 754
Isaac	Yuba New York	72 738
WALDRICK		
Agustus	Yuba Long Bar	72 754
WALDRIGE		
N S	Napa Yount	61 45
N T	Napa Yount	61 45
WALDRIM		
J J	San Francisco San Francisco 2	67 730
WALDRIN		
Frank	Mariposa Twp 1	60 653
WALDRIP		
Isaac	Yuba New York	72 740
WALDROM		
Jas M	Placer Folsom	62 647
Wm	Placer Virginia	62 660
WALDROME		
A*	Nevada Nevada	61 278
WALDRON		
A T	Tuolumne Twp 1	71 266
Geo B	San Francisco San Francisco 3	67 86
Henry	Butte Kimshaw	56 607
Henry	San Francisco San Francisco 7	681400
Henry	Yuba Rose Bar	72 805
J B	Napa Napa	61 88
John	Placer Stewart	62 606
Jos	Sacramento American	63 172
Wallace	Napa Napa	61 81
Warren	Sacramento Ward 1	63 147
Wm	Butte Cascade	56 695
Wm	Sacramento American	63 171
Wm	Sacramento Granite	63 260
WALDRONN		
A	Nevada Nevada	61 278
WALDROW		
Wallace*	Napa Napa	61 81
Wm Col	Marin Tomales	60 776
WALDS		
---	Amador Twp 3	55 377
Anson	El Dorado Kelsey	581137
WALDSIM		
J J	San Francisco San Francisco 2	67 730
WALDSON		
Henry*	Yuba Rose Bar	72 805
Wm	Butte Cascade	56 695
WALDSTEIN		
Abraham San Francisco San Francisco 8		681305
WALE		
M*	Siskiyou Cottonwoood	69 98
Martin	Contra Costa Twp 1	57 500
Thos*	San Francisco San Francisco 1	68 858
WALEE WALEE		
---	Fresno Twp 3	59 23
WALEEKUK		
---	Fresno Twp 3	59 38
WALENA		
J	El Dorado Diamond	58 803
WALENCE		
Thomas	Sacramento Granite	63 265
WALENSWALER		
Marcus	Los Angeles Azuza	59 274
WALER		
J	Nevada Grass Valley	61 207
WALERFORD		
Ann	San Francisco San Francisco 4	681130
WALERHOUSE		
Jesefot*	Napa Hot Springs	61 16
WALES		
Aa	Siskiyou Yreka	69 184
C H	San Francisco San Francisco 5	67 544

Name	County Locale	M653 Roll Page
WALES		
C P	El Dorado Placerville	58 867
Ed	Siskiyou Yreka	69 185
George	Alameda Oakland	55 47
H W	El Dorado Kelsey	581151
J D	San Francisco San Francisco 5	67 544
James	Sierra Twp 7	66 879
John	Colusa Muion	57 460
John	Mariposa Twp 3	60 572
John	Sierra Downieville	661028
John	Tuolumne Big Oak	71 141
Joseph	Los Angeles Los Angeles	59 369
Layd	Mariposa Twp 1	60 633
Loyd*	Mariposa Twp 1	60 633
P	El Dorado Diamond	58 799
P P	Tuolumne Twp 2	71 330
Peter	El Dorado Mountain	581189
T P	Tuolumne Columbia	71 330
Thomas	Sierra Twp 7	66 879
Warren	Sierra Port Win	66 791
Warren P	Sierra Port Win	66 791
Wm	Alameda Brooklyn	55 132
Wm	Alameda Brooklyn	55 190
WALEVER		
N C	Siskiyou Scott Ri	69 75
WALEY		
A	Sacramento Brighton	63 198
WALF		
George	Calaveras Twp 9	57 375
George	Tuolumne Twp 2	71 406
L	El Dorado Placerville	58 854
WALFING		
C	Tuolumne Shawsfla	71 383
WALFREM		
Adam	Santa Clara San Jose	65 298
WALFRERT		
John	Alameda Brooklyn	55 168
WALFSTEIN		
Andrew	Placer Goods	62 697
Henry*	Calaveras Twp 5	57 190
WALFSTEINE		
Jacob	Placer Dutch Fl	62 730
WALGAMOT		
J	Nevada Washington	61 334
WALGARNOT		
J*	Nevada Washington	61 334
WALGREEN		
Christian	Tulara Twp 3	71 52
Peter	Tulara Petersburg	71 52
WALGREN		
John	Santa Clara Alviso	65 410
WALHEN		
Anthony	Plumas Meadow Valley	62 933
WALHER		
J J	Siskiyou Callahan	69 14
M H	Siskiyou Scott Va	69 52
WALHERBY		
Nathaniel San Joaquin Oneal		64 933
WALHIER		
Wm	Placer Dutch Fl	62 716
WALHMER		
Henry San Francisco San Francisco 7		681378
WALIL		
John C*	Yuba Marysville	72 849
WALING		
I J*	Nevada Nevada	61 325
WALIS		
J D*	San Francisco San Francisco 5	67 544
WALK		
---	El Dorado White Oaks	581024
---	Yuba Long Bar	72 763
Anthony	El Dorado Mud Springs	58 991
Fred	El Dorado Mud Springs	58 996
M	El Dorado Diamond	58 770
WALKE		
N	Amador Twp 7	55 417
WALKEN		
Thos	Tehama Antelope	70 896
WALKENHEIM		
Lasser	San Francisco San Francisco 2	67 769
WALKER		
---	Mariposa Twp 3	60 570
---	Mendocino Twp 1	60 889
---	Stanislaus Empire	70 734
---	Tulara Twp 3	71 50
A	Butte Oro	56 683
A	Mariposa Twp 1	60 641
A B	Napa Napa	61 88
A H	Placer Iona Hills	62 893
A J	Sacramento Granite	63 249
A J	Solano Vallejo	69 277
A L	Napa Yount	61 36
A S	Sierra Eureka	661048
Abner J	Napa Napa	61 86
Adolphus	Yuba Marysville	72 865
Alexander	Siskiyou Yreka	69 149

Name	County Locale	M653 Roll Page
WALKER		
Alfred	Monterey San Juan	60 995
Alonzo	Sonoma Armally	69 517
Andrew	San Francisco San Francisco 2	67 600
Anna	San Francisco San Francisco 8	681310
Asa	Alameda Brooklyn	55 85
Augus	Alameda Oakland	55 8
August	Napa Hot Springs	61 11
Azeriah	San Joaquin Stockton	641010
B A	Amador Twp 2	55 324
B F	Amador Twp 2	55 324
B F	Calaveras Twp 9	57 382
B F	Placer Dutch Fl	62 710
B F	Placer Dutch Fl	62 714
Benjamin	Santa Cruz Pajaro	66 549
Benjamin	Tulara Twp 3	71 52
C	Siskiyou Klamath	69 80
C A	San Francisco San Francisco 3	67 48
C A	San Francisco San Francisco 3	67 49
C F	Trinity Raabs Ba	701020
C H	El Dorado White Oaks	581019
C H	El Dorado Placerville	58 927
Calvin	Tulara Twp 1	71 112
Carl	Alameda Oakland	55 38
Charels	Tuolumne Green Springs	71 519
Charles	Alameda Brooklyn	55 155
Charles	Contra Costa Twp 3	57 599
Charles	Humbolt Eureka	59 169
Charles	Marin Bolinas	60 733
Charles	Plumas Quincy	621006
Charles	Sierra Pine Grove	66 828
Charles	Tuolumne Twp 4	71 126
Charles	Tuolumne Twp 5	71 519
Charles F	Fresno Twp 2	59 18
Charles H Contra Costa Twp 2		57 576
Chas	Amador Twp 2	55 270
Chas	Sacramento Ward 1	63 45
Chas	Sonoma Petaluma	69 572
Chas	Sonoma Vallejo	69 628
Chs	Stanislaus Emory	70 738
Columbus San Francisco San Francisco 7		681344
D	El Dorado Placerville	58 856
D	El Dorado Placerville	58 892
Danl	Tuolumne Columbia	71 306
David	Mariposa Twp 3	60 593
David	Sacramento Dry Crk	63 378
David M	Placer Secret R	62 614
E G	Mariposa Twp 3	60 587
E G W	Mariposa Twp 3	60 587
E H	Alameda Brooklyn	55 199
E S	San Francisco San Francisco 1	68 888
Edward	Sacramento American	63 163
Edward	San Francisco San Francisco 1	68 843
Edward F	Calaveras Twp 5	57 211
Eliza	San Francisco San Francisco 8	681249
Eliza A	Monterey Pajaro	601015
Ellen C	Tuolumne Twp 1	71 194
Erastus	San Joaquin Elkhorn	64 982
F	Sutter Butte	70 781
Frank	Sonoma Mendocino	69 452
G	Sacramento Ward 4	63 590
G B	Amador Twp 5	55 348
G B	San Francisco San Francisco 5	67 547
Gandaloupe	Sonoma Armally	69 506
Geo	Siskiyou Scott Va	69 61
Geo	Sonoma Petaluma	69 580
Geo M	Alameda Brooklyn	55 176
Geo R	Amador Twp 4	55 234
George	Alameda Brooklyn	55 155
George	Alameda Oakland	55 50
George	Plumas Meadow Valley	62 902
George	Shasta Shasta	66 667
George	Tulara Twp 3	71 52
George	Tuolumne Twp 1	71 268
George	Tuolumne Jamestown	71 452
George	Yuba Fosters	72 839
George W	Yuba Marysville	72 945
Geroge	Tuolumne Twp 1	71 268
H	San Joaquin Elkhorn	64 992
H W	San Francisco San Francisco 2	67 725
Harrison K	Humbolt Eureka	59 167
Hartnell	Calaveras Twp 9	57 362
Hartwell	Calaveras Twp 9	57 362
Harvey	Mariposa Twp 3	60 570
Harvey	Placer Virginia	62 678
Henry	Humbolt Pacific	59 134
Howard	Alameda Brooklyn	55 181
Hugh	San Francisco San Francisco 9	681036
Isaac	Sacramento Cosumnes	63 383
J	Butte Cascade	56 695
J	El Dorado Placerville	58 892
J	Monterey Monterey	60 957
J	Sacramento Brighton	63 201
J	Sacramento Franklin	63 316
J	Santa Clara San Jose	65 343
J	Sonoma Armally	69 505

California 1860 Census Index

Name	County Locale	M653 Roll/Page
WALKER		
J A	Trinity New Rvr	701031
J B	San Francisco San Francisco 3	67 21
J C	Amador Twp 7	55 411
J C	Napa Clear Lake	61 134
J C	Nevada Nevada	61 291
J D	Siskiyou Callahan	69 14
J F	Tuolumne Twp 2	71 366
J J	Siskiyou Callahan	69 14
J L	Sonoma Armally	69 505
J M	Sierra Pine Grove	66 822
J M	Sonoma Armally	69 506
J M	Yolo Cache Crk	72 610
J S	Mendocino Ukiah	60 806
J S	Sutter Sutter	70 815
J W	Tuolumne Columbia	71 298
J W*	Siskiyou Scott Va	69 33
Jacob	El Dorado Big Bar	58 736
Jacob	Plumas Quincy	62 941
James	Alameda Oakland	55 69
James	El Dorado Georgetown	58 703
James	Klamath S Fork	59 207
James	Sacramento San Joaquin	63 365
James	Sierra Morristown	661051
James	Sierra La Porte	66 781
James	Sierra Gibsonville	66 858
James N	Fresno Twp 2	59 18
James T	Contra Costa Twp 3	57 608
Jared	Alameda Brooklyn	55 175
Jared T	Alameda Washington	55 175
Jas	Butte Chico	56 539
Jas	Butte Cascade	56 701
Jas	Butte Ophir	56 769
Jas	Sacramento Natonia	63 279
Jas	San Francisco San Francisco 1	68 910
Jefferson	Colusa Monroeville	57 440
Jeremiah R	Calaveras Twp 4	57 303
Jesse	Humbolt Mattole	59 121
Jestes	Merced Monterey	60 943
Jestes	Monterey Monterey	60 943
Jestus	Monterey Monterey	60 943
Jno	Butte Oregon	56 610
Jno	Nevada Nevada	61 265
Jno	Sacramento Ward 4	63 556
Jno B	Butte Chico	56 539
John	Alameda Brooklyn	55 108
John	Alameda Brooklyn	55 134
John	Calaveras Twp 7	57 2
John	Calaveras Twp 9	57 357
John	Del Norte Crescent	58 640
John	Humbolt Eel Rvr	59 149
John	Placer Michigan	62 855
John	San Joaquin Castoria	64 906
John	Sierra Twp 5	66 936
John	Solano Vacaville	69 342
John	Tuolumne Jamestown	71 452
John C	Fresno Twp 2	59 18
John Jr	Tuolumne Sonora	71 482
John K	Sonoma Russian	69 437
John W	Calaveras Twp 10	57 282
John W	Fresno Twp 1	59 76
John W	Tuolumne Sonora	71 233
Jos	Butte Ophir	56 793
Jos	Sacramento Natonia	63 279
Jos	Stanislaus Emory	70 746
Jos*	Butte Cascade	56 701
Jose	Tulara Keysville	71 53
Joseph	El Dorado Greenwood	58 713
Joseph	Sacramento Dry Crk	63 375
Joseph	San Francisco San Francisco 9	681097
Joseph	Sonoma Santa Rosa	69 393
Joseph	Yuba New York	72 735
L	Sacramento Franklin	63 324
L	Yuba New York	72 734
L F	Amador Twp 3	55 404
L J*	Napa Napa	61 107
L W	Marin S Antoni	60 708
Lewis	San Francisco San Francisco 7	681398
Lurry*	Alameda Oakland	55 32
Luther	San Joaquin Oneal	64 940
M	Sierra Pine Grove	66 822
M H	Siskiyou Scott Va	69 52
M J	Mariposa Twp 3	60 603
M J	Sierra Downieville	661013
M M	Los Angeles Tejon	59 524
M P	Mariposa Twp 3	60 603
M R	Sierra Twp 7	66 886
M*	Marin San Rafael	60 773
Margary	Alameda Brooklyn	55 203
Martha	Sacramento Ward 1	63 98
Martin A	Tuolumne Green Springs	71 518
Martin G	Placer Secret R	62 620
Mary E	Alameda Brooklyn	55 85
Matthew	Sonoma Santa Rosa	69 393
Michael	Solano Benecia	69 315
Michael T	San Francisco San Francisco 1	68 904
WALKER		
Mr	Marin San Rafael	60 773
Nathan	Tuolumne Montezuma	71 502
Nathaniel	Sonoma Russian	69 440
Nelsen*	Siskiyou Shasta Valley	69 121
Nelson	Siskiyou Shasta Valley	69 121
Nicholas	Tuolumne Shawsfla	71 400
O	Butte Chico	56 547
O	Siskiyou Klamath	69 80
O	Sutter Nicolaus	70 837
P*	Nevada Washington	61 334
Phillip	Santa Clara Santa Clara	65 497
R A	El Dorado Placerville	58 843
R C	Amador Twp 3	55 400
Robert	Alameda Oakland	55 69
Robert	Nevada Red Dog	61 538
Robert	San Joaquin Castoria	64 907
Robert	Sierra Pine Grove	66 831
Robert A	Sierra Twp 5	66 943
Robt J	Klamath Klamath	59 225
S	Sonoma Cloverdale	69 684
S	Yolo Cache Crk	72 612
S J	Napa Napa	61 107
S L	Nevada Rough &	61 412
S N	El Dorado Mud Springs	58 956
S T	San Mateo Twp 3	65 79
Saml	Butte Cascade	56 703
Saml	Del Norte Crescent	58 637
Saml M	Alameda Brooklyn	55 101
Samuel	Alameda Brooklyn	55 165
Samuel	Santa Cruz Pescadero	66 641
Samuel	Santa Cruz Pescadero	66 642
Samuel	Solano Green Valley	69 242
Samuel	Yuba Fosters	72 837
Samuell	Yuba Fosters	72 838
Samuell	Santa Cruz Pescadero	66 641
Sarah E	Santa Clara Gilroy	65 236
Sarah S	Tuolumne Twp 1	71 199
Sidney	Solano Suisan	69 220
Silas	Sonoma Washington	69 672
Solon	Sierra Pine Grove	66 835
Surry*	Alameda Oakland	55 32
T	San Francisco San Francisco 9	681075
T B	Butte Ophir	56 749
T C	Sacramento Georgian	63 338
T S	Amador Twp 1	55 492
Thas	Calaveras Twp 9	57 365
Theo	Calaveras Twp 9	57 370
Thomas	Calaveras Twp 4	57 300
Thomas	El Dorado White Oaks	581018
Thomas	Plumas Quincy	62 939
Thomas	San Mateo Twp 3	65 78
Thomas	Santa Cruz Pajaro	66 534
Thomas	Siskiyou Yreka	69 167
Thomas	Yuba New York	72 741
Thomas J*	Yuba Marysville	72 928
Thos	Calaveras Twp 9	57 365
Thos	San Francisco San Francisco 1	68 886
Thos R	Alameda Oakland	55 24
W	Nevada Eureka	61 363
W	San Francisco San Francisco 5	67 523
W B	Tehama Red Bluff	70 924
W B	Tehama Tehama	70 936
W C	San Francisco San Francisco 10	324 67
W D	Siskiyou Klamath	69 95
W D	Solano Vacaville	69 359
W J	Tuolumne Columbia	71 298
W R	Butte Ophir	56 751
W R	Sierra Twp 7	66 886
W W	Marin Tomales	60 774
Whitefield	Colusa Monroeville	57 440
William	Monterey San Juan	601007
William	San Bernardino Santa Barbara	64 185
William	San Francisco San Francisco 3	67 56
William	San Mateo Twp 3	65 78
William	Siskiyou Shasta Valley	69 111
William	Solano Vallejo	69 256
William	Solano Vallejo	69 261
William	Solano Vacaville	69 335
William	Tulara Twp 1	71 85
William	Yuba Bear Rvr	721017
Wm	Marin Cortemad	60 791
Wm	Placer Lisbon	62 733
Wm	Sacramento Ward 1	63 324
Wm	San Francisco San Francisco 10	310 67
Wm	Sierra Morristown	661052
Wm	Sierra Morristown	661055
Wm	Sonoma Armally	69 493
Wm	Trinity Rush Crk	70 965
Wm	Trinity Rearings	70 990
Wm B*	Placer Sacramento	62 642
Wm J	San Francisco San Francisco 2	67 604
Wm W	San Francisco San Francisco 2	67 567
Wm*	Monterey Alisal	601038
WALKERLEY		
William	Tuolumne Twp 5	71 487
WALKING		
W C*	Mariposa Coulterville	60 693
WALKINHAM		
Lassen	San Francisco San Francisco 2	67 769
WALKINS		
Andrew J	San Joaquin Castoria	64 893
Chas	Mariposa Twp 3	60 594
George	Yuba Marysville	72 975
Jas T	San Francisco San Francisco 10	242 67
John	Monterey San Juan	601004
Jos T	San Francisco San Francisco 10	242 67
Joseph E	Sierra Twp 7	66 904
Tedekink*	Calaveras Twp 6	57 161
William R	Napa Hot Springs	61 15
Wm	Sierra Twp 7	66 899
Zedekiah	Calaveras Twp 6	57 161
WALKINSHAW		
Franco	San Francisco San Francisco 8	681282
Robt	San Bernardino San Bernadino	64 627
Robt	San Bernardino San Bernadino	64 632
Robt F	San Bernardino San Bernadino	64 627
WALKINTON		
Geo	San Francisco San Francisco 2	67 559
WALKIWHAW		
Franco	San Francisco San Francisco 8	681282
WALKMANN		
Saml	San Francisco San Francisco 2	67 572
WALKON		
William	Nevada Bloomfield	61 527
WALKS		
Wliam	Tulara Twp 1	71 83
WALKUP		
Joseph	Placer Auburn	62 566
R W	Colusa Monroeville	57 449
WALL EYE		
---	Tulara Twp 2	71 4
WALL		
---	Calaveras Twp 5	57 192
---	San Francisco San Francisco 7	681336
A J	Nevada Rough &	61 412
Andrew	El Dorado Casumnes	581166
Arch	Nevada Rough &	61 412
Arternas	Contra Costa Twp 2	57 561
B	Nevada Grass Valley	61 171
B F	Amador Twp 6	55 427
Barney	Tuolumne Twp 3	71 423
C	Nevada Eureka	61 349
C	Tehama Red Bluff	70 930
C J	Tehama Red Bluff	70 920
Chas J	Sacramento Ward 1	63 107
Chas J	Sacramento Natonia	63 276
Chas*	Sonoma Petaluma	69 603
Couroyo	Contra Costa Twp 2	57 539
David	San Joaquin Stockton	641058
E G	Mariposa Twp 1	60 638
E G	Yolo Cache Crk	72 596
Ernest	Nevada Nevada	61 247
Ferdinand	Tuolumne Twp 2	71 403
G W	Nevada Nevada	61 318
Geo	Sacramento Ward 4	63 534
George	Calaveras Twp 9	57 375
George	Solano Benecia	69 312
Granvill	Placer Stewart	62 606
H	Nevada Grass Valley	61 216
H	Nevada Eureka	61 349
H A	Tuolumne Twp 2	71 281
H E	Nevada Nevada	61 247
H W	Nevada Grass Valley	61 216
Henry	San Francisco San Francisco 3	67 48
J	Nevada Grass Valley	61 207
J	Nevada Grass Valley	61 216
J H	Santa Clara San Jose	65 368
J S	Nevada Nevada	61 247
J S	Tuolumne Twp 1	71 484
J*	Nevada Eureka	61 391
James	Humbolt Pacific	59 130
James	Santa Cruz Pajaro	66 550
James	Sonoma Armally	69 508
James A	San Francisco San Francisco 8	681320
John	Alameda Brooklyn	55 147
John	Butte Oro	56 678
John	Butte Ophir	56 781
John	El Dorado Placerville	58 929
John	Los Angeles Elmonte	59 263
John	Sacramento Dry Crk	63 370
John	San Francisco San Francisco 8	681300
John	San Francisco San Francisco 1	68 822
John	Sierra Pine Grove	66 822
John	Yuba New York	72 736
John	Yuba Parks Ba	72 779
John K	Sierra St Louis	66 807
Joseph	Humbolt Eureka	59 164

California 1860 Census Index

WALL

Name	County Locale	M653 Roll	Page
Joseph G	Del Norte Crescent	58	619
Julia	Marin Tomales	60	724
Kate	San Francisco San Francisco 4	68	1110
L R*	Sacramento Lee	63	212
M	Amador Twp 4	55	254
Maggie	San Francisco San Francisco 4	68	1129
Maggie	Sonoma Petaluma	69	593
Margaret	Yuba Marysville	72	910
Marry Ann	Calaveras Twp 5	57	185
Mary	San Francisco San Francisco 6	67	455
Mary Ann	Calaveras Twp 5	57	185
Michael	San Francisco San Francisco 7	68	1353
Michael	Tuolumne Twp 2	71	353
Parwer	Colusa Muion	57	462
Peter	San Francisco San Francisco 6	67	418
Rufus	Sacramento Brighton	63	195
S R*	Sacramento Lee	63	212
Stewart	Merced Twp 2	60	920
Thomas	Alameda Oakland	55	32
Thomas	Solano Montezuma	69	373
Thos	Sacramento Ward 4	63	496
W	Shasta Millvill	66	751
W V	Tuolumne Columbia	71	327
William	Mendocino Ukiah	60	801
William	San Joaquin Stockton	64	1026
Wm H	Humbolt Union	59	180
Yan	Yuba Marysville	72	896

WALLA WAL

Name	County Locale	M653 Roll	Page
---	Mendocino Calpella	60	825

WALLA WALLA

Name	County Locale	M653 Roll	Page
---	Fresno Twp 2	59	94
---*	Fresno Twp 2	59	20

WALLA

Name	County Locale	M653 Roll	Page
---	Butte Chico	56	566
---	Fresno Twp 2	59	71
---	Sacramento Cosumnes	63	407
---	Sierra Twp 7	66	912
---	Tulara Twp 3	71	49
John	San Francisco San Francisco 11	67	142
Walla*	Fresno Twp 2	59	20

WALLAC

Name	County Locale	M653 Roll	Page
Sam	Amador Twp 2	55	262

WALLACE

Name	County Locale	M653 Roll	Page
---	Mendocino Big Rock	60	876
---	Tulara Twp 2	71	4
A	San Francisco San Francisco 4	68	1231
A C	Siskiyou Scott Ri	69	63
A M	Amador Twp 2	55	302
A M	Sonoma Santa Rosa	69	427
A*	Nevada Eureka	61	346
Albert O	Los Angeles Los Angeles	59	351
Alex	Amador Twp 2	55	299
Amanda	Los Angeles Los Angeles	59	293
Andrew	El Dorado Georgetown	58	746
Andrew	San Francisco San Francisco 3	67	75
Andrew H	Siskiyou Yreka	69	168
Ann	Placer Secret R	62	616
Annie	Los Angeles Los Angeles	59	339
Augustus	San Francisco San Francisco 4	68	1217
B F	Sacramento Casumnes	63	380
B M	San Bernardino San Salvador	64	647
Bartlett	Sierra Gibsonville	66	851
Bartlett C	Sierra Gibsonville	66	851
Ben F	Sonoma Santa Rosa	69	398
Benjamin	San Joaquin Elkhorn	64	999
C	Nevada Grass Valley	61	153
Charles	Calaveras Twp 10	57	279
Chas	Placer Dutch Fl	62	729
Chas F*	San Francisco San Francisco 2	67	717
Chas I*	San Francisco San Francisco 2	67	717
Chas J*	San Francisco San Francisco 2	67	717
Chas T	San Francisco San Francisco 2	67	717
D J C	Tuolumne Jamestown	71	436
David	Alameda Brooklyn	55	148
David	Mendocino Little L	60	834
David	Sacramento Granite	63	245
Edmmond	Calaveras Twp 7	57	11
Edward	Amador Twp 6	55	437
Edward	San Mateo Twp 2	65	124
Edward	San Mateo Twp 2	65	125
Edwin L	Humbolt Union	59	183
Elizabeth	San Francisco San Francisco 4	68	1147
Elizabeth	San Francisco San Francisco 8	68	1289
Elizabeth	San Francisco San Francisco 7	68	1408
F*	San Francisco San Francisco 5	67	537
Ferris	Calaveras Twp 5	57	249
Frank	Contra Costa Twp 1	57	520
G P	Sonoma Santa Rosa	69	427
G W	Butte Ophir	56	745
G W	El Dorado Mud Springs	58	996
G W	Nevada Nevada	61	244
G W	Sacramento Ward 4	63	543
Geo	Butte Chico	56	539
Geo	Mariposa Twp 3	60	598
Geo	Sacramento San Joaquin	63	362
Geo	San Francisco San Francisco 10	67	244
Geo	Santa Clara Alviso	65	412
Geo	Santa Clara Santa Clara	65	502
George	Santa Cruz Pajaro	66	558
George	Sonoma Washington	69	670
Henry	Plumas Quincy	62	976
Henry	Plumas Quincy	62	996
Henry	San Francisco San Francisco 2	67	585
Henry	San Joaquin Elkhorn	64	985
Henry	San Mateo Twp 1	65	58
Henry	Sonoma Santa Rosa	69	398
Hiram W	Sierra Pine Grove	66	825
Hiram*	Placer Michigan	62	842
Isaac	San Bernardino Santa Barbara	64	204
Isaac	Yuba Long Bar	72	753
J	Nevada Nevada	61	286
J	San Francisco San Francisco 5	67	514
J	Santa Clara Fremont	65	420
J	Tehama Red Bluff	70	930
J N	Siskiyou Cottonwoood	69	101
J R	Sacramento Brighton	63	198
J S	Sutter Nicolaus	70	833
James	Contra Costa Twp 1	57	492
James	Contra Costa Twp 1	57	507
James	Contra Costa Twp 3	57	591
James	Mendocino Anderson	60	868
James	Plumas Quincy	62	977
James	Siskiyou Cottonwoood	69	100
James	Siskiyou Yreka	69	190
James	Tuolumne Twp 4	71	137
Jas	Butte Hamilton	56	524
Jas	San Bernardino San Bernadino	64	675
Jas	San Francisco San Francisco 10	67	291
Jas	San Francisco San Francisco 2	67	619
Jeremiah	Santa Cruz Santa Cruz	66	618
Jermiah	Santa Cruz Santa Cruz	66	618
Jno	Nevada Nevada	61	322
Jno	Sonoma Sonoma	69	635
John	Alameda Oakland	55	11
John	Butte Cascade	56	698
John	Butte Cascade	56	702
John	Monterey Monterey	60	949
John	Nevada Bloomfield	61	520
John	Nevada Bloomfield	61	526
John	San Francisco San Francisco 1	68	858
John	San Francisco San Francisco 9	68	986
John	San Mateo Twp 1	65	58
John	Santa Clara San Jose	65	366
John	Santa Clara Fremont	65	442
John	Shasta Shasta	66	673
John	Sierra Twp 5	66	919
John	Tuolumne Twp 2	71	318
John A	Calaveras Twp 8	57	77
John C	Yuba Suida	72	982
John C	Yuba Linda Twp	72	983
John C	Yuba Linda	72	984
John H	Yuba Marysville	72	966
John K	Plumas Quincy	62	952
John*	Tuolumne Columbia	71	318
Jonathan	Tulara Twp 1	71	22
Jos	San Francisco San Francisco 9	68	1070
Jos	San Francisco San Francisco 10	67	291
Jos	San Francisco San Francisco 2	67	619
Joseph	Marin S Antoni	60	706
Joseph S	Santa Clara Fremont	65	429
L	Shasta Shasta	66	673
L*	Sacramento San Joaquin	63	357
Ld	San Mateo Twp 1	65	100
Lee	Calaveras Twp 5	57	228
Lee*	Napa Napa	61	82
Lorenzo A	Fresno Twp 3	59	32
Lu	Napa Napa	61	82
M H	Sacramento Franklin	63	314
M R	Solano Montezuma	69	370
Margt	Butte Hamilton	56	524
Marin L	Placer Stewart	62	605
Mary	Napa Napa	61	91
Mary	San Francisco San Francisco 4	68	1144
Mary	San Francisco San Francisco 1	68	883
Mary W	Napa Napa	61	91
Mathew	Placer Todds Va	62	790
Michael	Sierra Twp 5	66	919
N C*	Napa Napa	61	90
N O	Calaveras Twp 9	57	416
O W	Sacramento American	63	157
Oro	Sacramento American	63	157
P R	Napa Yount	61	37
Patrick	Colusa Grand Island	57	471
Patrick	San Francisco San Francisco 11	67	131
Patrick	San Francisco San Francisco 7	68	1435
Peter	Alameda Brooklyn	55	199
Peter	Butte Ophir	56	798
Peter	Santa Clara San Jose	65	392
Peter	Solano Benecia	69	294
R	Solano Suisan	69	211
R B	Nevada Red Dog	61	556
R B	San Francisco San Francisco 6	67	421
R L	Mendocino Anderson	60	868
R M	Tuolumne Twp 1	71	264
Rich B	Butte Kimshaw	56	595
Richard	Sacramento Dry Crk	63	373
Richard	Sierra Twp 5	66	919
Ritchard	Nevada Bridgeport	61	496
Robert	San Francisco San Francisco 2	67	732
Robert	Sierra Whiskey	66	849
Robt S	Placer Secret R	62	616
S	El Dorado Diamond	58	798
S B	El Dorado Placerville	58	855
S R	Del Norte Crescent	58	646
S*	Sacramento San Joaquin	63	357
Samuel	Sacramento Sutter	63	307
Samuel	Sacramento Sutter	63	308
Samuel	San Mateo Twp 1	65	59
Samuel	Solano Vallejo	69	254
Sei*	Calaveras Twp 5	57	228
Silas*	Napa Clear Lake	61	122
Silus	Napa Clear Lake	61	122
Simon	Shasta Shasta	66	673
Sri*	Calaveras Twp 5	57	228
Stephen	San Francisco San Francisco 3	67	58
Stephen T	San Francisco San Francisco 3	67	58
Su*	Napa Napa	61	82
T	San Francisco San Francisco 5	67	526
T W	Nevada Red Dog	61	543
Thomas	Contra Costa Twp 1	57	492
Thomas	Contra Costa Twp 1	57	504
Thomas	El Dorado White Oaks	58	1014
Thomas	Sacramento Granite	63	265
Thomas	San Francisco San Francisco 7	68	1352
Thomas	San Francisco San Francisco 7	68	1357
Thomas	Santa Cruz Pajaro	66	577
Thomas	Sierra Downieville	66	957
Thomas	Tuolumne Big Oak	71	135
Thomas	Tuolumne Twp 1	71	257
Thos	Placer Ophirville	62	657
Thos	San Francisco San Francisco 2	67	729
W	El Dorado Placerville	58	850
W	El Dorado Placerville	58	876
W	El Dorado Placerville	58	897
W	Nevada Grass Valley	61	158
W	Nevada Grass Valley	61	181
W	San Francisco San Francisco 9	68	1069
W C	Napa Napa	61	90
W F	Monterey San Juan	60	987
W H	Nevada Nevada	61	261
W H	Shasta Horsetown	66	699
W J	Mariposa Twp 3	60	554
W L	Butte Ophir	56	745
W L	Santa Clara San Jose	65	319
W P	San Mateo Twp 3	65	90
W W	Nevada Nevada	61	261
W*	Nevada Grass Valley	61	158
William	Amador Twp 4	55	240
William	Calaveras Twp 8	57	64
William	Contra Costa Twp 2	57	575
William	Los Angeles Azuza	59	272
William	Plumas Meadow Valley	62	901
William	San Francisco San Francisco 11	67	128
William	San Francisco San Francisco 7	68	1401
William	San Francisco San Francisco 9	68	949
William	Santa Cruz Santa Cruz	66	620
William	Sierra Scales D	66	803
William	Yuba Long Bar	72	743
William C	Contra Costa Twp 2	57	557
Wm	Amador Twp 2	55	299
Wm	Amador Twp 3	55	369
Wm	Amador Twp 3	55	394
Wm	Butte Bidwell	56	713
Wm	Butte Bidwell	56	717
Wm	Butte Bidwell	56	729
Wm	Butte Bidwell	56	732
Wm	Butte Ophir	56	760
Wm	Mariposa Twp 3	60	610
Wm	Nevada Eureka	61	357
Wm	Placer Rattle Snake	62	599
Wm	Santa Clara San Jose	65	286
Wm	Santa Clara Santa Clara	65	469
Wm	Sonoma Russian	69	430
Wm	Sonoma Mendocino	69	451
Wm	Tuolumne Twp 3	71	464
Wm H	Placer Illinois	62	705
Wm H	San Francisco San Francisco 9	68	1042
Wm M	Nevada Nevada	61	239

Name	County Locale	M653 Roll/Page
WALLACE		
Wm W	Sonoma Santa Rosa	69 404
Wm *	Mariposa Twp 3	60 610
WALLACI		
Sre *	Calaveras Twp 5	57 228
WALLACK		
F	San Francisco San Francisco 5	67 537
J H S	Nevada Nevada	61 274
WALLACO		
John *	Tuolumne Columbia	71 318
WALLACS		
W *	Nevada Grass Valley	61 158
WALLAGER		
P	Nevada Nevada	61 245
WALLALUPIA		
Mary	Butte Ophir	56 792
WALLAN		
A	Nevada Eureka	61 346
WALLAND		
C	Placer Iona Hills	62 877
WALLARD		
A	Nevada Eureka	61 346
WALLASE		
Hiram *	Placer Michigan	62 842
Wm *	Mariposa Twp 3	60 610
WALLASON		
George	Yuba Marysville	72 905
WALLAUL		
A *	Nevada Eureka	61 346
WALLAZ		
J M	Sutter Yuba	70 761
WALLCE		
John C	Yuba Suida	72 984
William *	Sierra Scales D	66 803
WALLCOT		
Theophilus	Los Angeles Azuza	59 278
WALLDRONN		
L	Nevada Nevada	61 278
WALLDROWN		
L	Nevada Nevada	61 278
WALLE CUTER		
---	Fresno Twp 1	59 51
WALLECK		
Elias	Plumas Quincy	62 945
WALLEJO		
---	Tulara Twp 3	71 70
WALLEMENUE		
---	Tulara Twp 2	71 35
WALLEN		
Andrew *	Monterey Monterey	60 965
C S	Santa Clara San Jose	65 357
Charles	San Joaquin Castoria	64 882
Charles	Yuba Suida	72 992
D *	Placer Virginia	62 661
George	Nevada Bridgeport	61 467
J R	Butte Chico	56 558
John	El Dorado White Oaks	581012
John	Tuolumne Twp 3	71 447
L	Nevada Grass Valley	61 235
Saml	Tuolumne Twp 1	71 268
WALLENBEY		
Geo	Amador Twp 2	55 279
WALLENCE		
---	Sierra Downieville	661028
WALLER		
Alfred	Napa Clear Lake	61 127
Andrew	Siskiyou Callahan	69 9
Chas *	Mariposa Twp 1	60 641
Davison	Solano Vacaville	69 343
Edward	San Joaquin Stockton	641048
F	Nevada Eureka	61 356
F	Trinity Weaverville	701073
Geo	San Francisco San Francisco 1	68 876
Georg *	Nevada Bloomfield	61 517
George	Plumas Quincy	62 924
Hengh	Yolo Cache	72 628
Hiram	Calaveras Twp 7	57 40
Hugh	Yolo Cache Crk	72 628
J W	Tuolumne Twp 2	71 298
James	Tuolumne Jamestown	71 442
Joe	Tehama Red Bluff	70 916
John	Tuolumne Twp 3	71 453
John J	Yuba New York	72 737
John W	Tuolumne Twp 3	71 447
Jos	Klamath Liberty	59 237
L P	Nevada Eureka	61 392
Louisa	Calaveras Twp 4	57 316
Nicholas	Tuolumne Twp 2	71 369
R *	Sacramento Cosumms	63 405
Royal H	Alameda Oakland	55 57
Stephen	Yolo Washington	72 568
Stephene *	Yolo Washington	72 568
Stephens *	Yolo Washington	72 568
Unam *	Calaveras Twp 8	57 108
WALLERMAN		
Solomon	Santa Cruz Santa Cruz	66 605

Name	County Locale	M653 Roll/Page
WALLES		
R *	Sacramento Cosumms	63 405
WALLESON		
James P	Mariposa Coulterville	60 701
WALLET		
Andrew *	Siskiyou Callahan	69 9
M	Sacramento Sutter	63 305
WALLETT		
W	Nevada Eureka	61 372
WALLETTS		
Fred	Amador Twp 4	55 246
WALLEY		
Alfred	San Francisco San Francisco 6	67 448
Charles	Siskiyou Scott Va	69 35
D	San Francisco San Francisco 5	67 505
Frank A	Contra Costa Twp 1	57 484
WALLIE		
William *	Sierra Scales D	66 803
WALLIN		
E H	El Dorado Mud Springs	58 994
Ezre	Amador Twp 2	55 288
Francis W	Alameda Brooklyn	55 164
WALLINBURG		
J	Amador Twp 1	55 458
WALLINBURY		
L	El Dorado Coloma	581120
WALLINE		
Henry	Placer Dutch Fl	62 725
WALLING		
C A	Nevada Nevada	61 323
C P	Tuolumne Twp 1	71 249
Christian	Tuolumne Shawsfla	71 410
E P	Tuolumne Twp 1	71 249
Horrace	San Joaquin Elkhorn	64 976
J	Nevada Eureka	61 348
J	Nevada Eureka	61 349
John Low *	Nevada Bridgeport	61 440
L A	Nevada Rough &	61 418
Lucinda	Merced Twp 1	60 897
Thomas	Klamath Klamath	59 226
W C	Mariposa Coulterville	60 693
WALLINGFORD		
E	San Francisco San Francisco 10	301 67
WALLINGURG		
J	Amador Twp 1	55 458
WALLIROD		
George *	San Francisco San Francisco 3	67 18
WALLIS		
B F	Stanislaus Branch	70 705
Benjamin	Tuolumne Visalia	71 94
E W	Trinity Weaverville	701065
Eirge	Sierra Twp 5	66 937
George	Sierra Twp 5	66 937
George	Tulara Visalia	71 110
Jacob	Sierra St Louis	66 863
John B	Calaveras Twp 6	57 174
Reese	Tulara Twp 1	71 112
Reeve *	Tulara Visalia	71 112
William A	Calaveras Twp 5	57 208
WALLISOU		
George *	San Francisco San Francisco 3	67 18
WALLISS		
James	Siskiyou Shasta Rvr	69 113
WALLMAKER		
Lewis	Santa Clara San Jose	65 319
WALLOCK		
Danl	Butte Ophir	56 766
WALLOIS		
Julius	Calaveras Twp 5	57 198
WALLON		
Frederick *	San Francisco 9	68 943
	San Francisco	
WALLOUPA		
---	Fresno Twp 1	59 85
WALLOWELL		
John *	Mariposa Coulterville	60 699
WALLS		
Benj	Solano Vallejo	69 249
Benjamin	San Francisco San Francisco 7	681344
D G	San Francisco San Francisco 7	681332
Daniel	Trinity Indian C	70 983
David	Sacramento Franklin	63 314
Edmund	Sacramento Franklin	63 324
Frances	San Francisco San Francisco 4	681155
Henry	Sonoma Mendocino	69 459
J B	Santa Clara San Jose	65 343
J C	Shasta Millvill	66 739
J O	Shasta Millvill	66 739
Jacob	Los Angeles Azuza	59 278
Jno	Nevada Nevada	61 243
M	Sacramento Ward 1	63 10
Phillip	Calaveras Twp 5	57 187
Richard	San Joaquin Douglass	64 921
S C *	Mariposa Twp 3	60 596
Thofmas	Solano Vallejo	69 280

Name	County Locale	M653 Roll/Page
WALLS		
Thos	Placer Rattle Snake	62 628
Thos	Sonoma Santa Rosa	69 404
V E	El Dorado Newtown	58 780
William	Nevada Bloomfield	61 509
Wm C	Colusa Monroeville	57 443
WALLSEN		
Mary *	Shasta Shasta	66 673
WALLSON		
Andrew	Monterey Monterey	60 965
Mary	Shasta Shasta	66 673
WALLUP		
Charles	Calaveras Twp 10	57 265
WALLWEE		
Augustus *	San Francisco 4	681217
	San Francisco	
WALLY		
Benjamin	Tulara Twp 1	71 94
John *	Nevada Nevada	61 319
WALMER		
J	San Francisco San Francisco 5	67 531
WALNERTON		
N L	Santa Clara Santa Clara	65 469
WALNUR		
J *	San Francisco San Francisco 5	67 531
WALPALE		
David	Santa Clara San Jose	65 363
WALPER		
John	San Francisco San Francisco 7	681414
WALPING		
C	Tuolumne Twp 2	71 383
WALPLING		
John	Tuolumne Twp 1	71 212
WALPOLE		
Thos	San Francisco San Francisco 9	681031
WALRAD		
J O	Sacramento Ward 4	63 534
J W	Sacramento Ward 4	63 534
WALRANN		
William	Plumas Meadow Valley	62 899
WALRAREN		
G W	Solano Suisan	69 216
WALRASEN		
G W	Solano Suisan	69 216
WALRATH		
A	San Francisco San Francisco 10	308 67
J L	Tehama Lassen	70 874
WALRAVEN		
Elias *	Plumas Quincy	621007
WALROTH		
W H	Sierra Downieville	66 953
WALSBER		
Riter	Butte Bidwell	56 729
WALSCH		
Martin	San Francisco San Francisco 10	179 67
WALSCOORTH		
Edward B *	Yuba Marysville	72 853
WALSCOURTH		
Edward B *	Yuba Marysville	72 853
WALSEN		
Jas R	Sacramento Georgian	63 335
WALSER		
Daniel	Tulara Visalia	71 85
F	Shasta Horsetown	66 708
Fred	Sacramento Ward 4	63 547
WALSEY		
H S	Santa Clara San Jose	65 382
Jacob	El Dorado White Oaks	581024
WALSH		
Aaron	San Francisco San Francisco 7	681339
Annis	San Francisco San Francisco 6	67 431
Annis J	San Francisco San Francisco 6	67 431
Anthony	San Francisco San Francisco 2	67 671
Antonio	Calaveras Twp 9	57 387
Benjamin	San Francisco San Francisco 7	681358
Catharine	San Francisco San Francisco 11	131 67
Christopher	Santa Clara Fremont	65 423
David	Santa Clara San Jose	65 379
Debra	San Francisco San Francisco 8	681271
Delra	San Francisco San Francisco 8	681271
Edward	San Diego San Diego	64 767
Edward	San Francisco San Francisco 8	681281
Edward	San Francisco San Francisco 7	681346
Edwd	San Francisco San Francisco 1	68 883
Ellen	San Francisco San Francisco 7	681386
Ellen	San Francisco San Francisco 7	681393
F	San Joaquin Stockton	641042
Frank	San Joaquin Elkhorn	64 968
G	Calaveras Twp 9	57 411
G	Nevada Washington	61 334
George	San Joaquin Castoria	64 908
Henry	Placer Iona Hills	62 859
Henry H	San Francisco San Francisco 8	681254

Name	County	Locale	M653 Roll	Page
WALSH				
Isaac	Plumas	Quincy	62	986
J H	San Francisco	San Francisco 7	68	1349
J M	Calaveras	Twp 8	57	54
J Walter	San Francisco	San Francisco 2	67	785
James	San Francisco	San Francisco 9	68	1043
James	San Francisco	San Francisco 11	67	137
James	Sierra	Twp 7	66	868
James	Sierra	Twp 7	66	904
James	Sierra	Twp 5	66	918
James	Tulara	Keyesville	71	59
James	Tuolumne	Big Oak	71	125
James	Tuolumne	Twp 4	71	127
James M	San Francisco	San Francisco 8	68	1282
Jas	Calaveras	Twp 9	57	353
Jas	Calaveras	Twp 9	57	363
Jas	Placer	Secret R	62	619
Jas	Sacramento	Ward 1	63	19
Jno	Mendocino	Round Va	60	879
Jno	Sacramento	Ward 1	63	141
John	Placer	Auburn	62	589
John	Placer	Rattle Snake	62	637
John	Sacramento	Ward 1	63	40
John	San Francisco	San Francisco 4	68	1112
John	San Francisco	San Francisco 8	68	1250
John	Solano	Benecia	69	284
John	Solano	Benecia	69	295
John	Trinity	East For	70	1027
John	Yuba	Marysville	72	864
Jos W	San Francisco	San Francisco 9	68	1030
Jos*	Placer	Secret R	62	619
Juan	San Bernardino	Santa Barbara	64	204
Kale*	Monterey	Alisal	60	1038
Kate	Monterey	Alisal	60	1038
Laurance	San Francisco	San Francisco 7	68	1332
Lausence	Solano	Vallejo	69	280
Lawrance	San Francisco	San Francisco 7	68	1332
Lawrence	Solano	Vallejo	69	280
M	Butte	Kimshaw	56	596
M	Nevada	Grass Valley	61	226
M J	San Joaquin	Stockton	64	1037
M*	Butte	Kimshaw	56	596
Maggey	Solano	Suisan	69	210
Martin	Klamath	Liberty	59	241
Mary	San Francisco	San Francisco 7	68	1345
Mary	San Francisco	San Francisco 9	68	942
Mary	San Joaquin	Stockton	64	1011
Mary Magdelen S	Solano	Benecia	69	300
Mich	Butte	Kimshaw	56	581
Mich	Sacramento	Ward 4	63	606
Michael	San Francisco	San Francisco 9	68	1071
Michael	San Francisco	San Francisco 3	67	27
Michael	San Francisco	San Francisco 1	68	812
Michel	Butte	Oregon	56	615
Michl	Butte	Oregon	56	615
Mike	Yuba	Rose Bar	72	801
Morris	Klamath	Liberty	59	241
Morris	Mendocino	Big Rvr	60	842
Morris	San Francisco	San Francisco 1	68	894
Nichols	San Joaquin	Douglass	64	920
O	Sutter	Nicolaus	70	841
P	Mariposa	Twp 3	60	549
P	Santa Clara	San Jose	65	289
P	Shasta	Millvill	66	751
P J	San Francisco	San Francisco 5	67	515
Patrick	San Francisco	San Francisco 11	67	130
Peter	San Francisco	San Francisco 3	67	80
R J	Colusa	Monroeville	57	456
Richard	Yuba	Marysville	72	894
Richd	Sacramento	Ward 1	63	131
Robert	San Francisco	San Francisco 7	68	1370
Robt	Trinity	E Weaver	70	1059
Sarah	San Francisco	San Francisco 8	68	1286
Simon T	San Francisco	San Francisco 10	67	335
T	Calaveras	Twp 9	57	415
T	San Joaquin	Stockton	64	1099
T	Sutter	Yuba	70	778
T J	Nevada	Grass Valley	61	210
T J	Nevada	Grass Valley	61	212
Thomas	Calaveras	Twp 7	57	2
Thomas	Humbolt	Eureka	59	163
Thomas	San Francisco	San Francisco 4	68	1126
Thomas	San Francisco	San Francisco 8	68	1240
Thos	Sacramento	Ward 1	63	153
Thos	San Francisco	San Francisco 1	68	849
Thos	San Joaquin	Stockton	64	1012
W	Butte	Kimshaw	56	590
W	San Francisco	San Francisco 9	68	1057
Walter	San Francisco	San Francisco 9	68	962
William	Klamath	Liberty	59	241
William	San Francisco	San Francisco 4	68	1158
William	Siskiyou	Scott Va	69	57
WALSH				
William	Solano	Vallejo	69	258
William	Tuolumne	Twp 6	71	534
Wm	Amador	Twp 3	55	396
Wm	Butte	Kimshaw	56	590
WALSHOM				
T H J	San Francisco	San Francisco 7	68	1360
WALSIE				
Jno	Butte	Kimshaw	56	585
WALSON				
David*	Siskiyou	Yreka	69	150
Jno C	Nevada	Nevada	61	292
Thomas	Sonoma	Santa Rosa	69	391
WALSTANSTHAD				
Sarafine	Sierra	Gibsonville	66	858
WALSTANSTHALL				
Larufine	Sierra	Gibsonville	66	858
WALSTEIN				
George	Calaveras	Twp 6	57	127
WALSTON				
Norton	San Francisco	San Francisco 8	68	1300
WALSWORTH				
Edward B	Yuba	Marysville	72	858
H T	Sonoma	Mendocino	69	455
WALT				
Julias*	El Dorado	White Oaks	58	1026
Leroy*	Butte	Kimshaw	56	603
Orrin	Tuolumne	Twp 5	71	520
WALTACE				
Henry*	San Francisco	San Francisco 2	67	585
WALTAM				
H P	El Dorado	Georgetown	58	761
WALTEN				
John	Sierra	Twp 7	66	900
N G	San Francisco	San Francisco 3	67	49
Samuel	Calaveras	Twp 5	57	201
William*	Siskiyou	Yreka	69	127
WALTENS				
Georg	Nevada	Bloomfield	61	517
W A	San Francisco	San Francisco 9	68	1075
WALTER				
---	Tulara	Keyesville	71	56
Albertino	Santa Clara	San Jose	65	387
C J	Sacramento	Sutter	63	305
Charles	Monterey	San Juan	60	1004
Charles	Yuba	Bear Rvr	72	1003
Chas	Sacramento	Dry Crk	63	373
Chas*	Mariposa	Twp 1	60	641
D N	San Francisco	San Francisco 5	67	475
D O	San Francisco	San Francisco 5	67	548
David	Nevada	Bloomfield	61	526
E	San Francisco	San Francisco 3	67	3
Emanuel	San Francisco	San Francisco 9	68	971
F*	Trinity	Weaverville	70	1073
Ferdinand	Calaveras	Twp 4	57	318
Francis	Siskiyou	Yreka	69	193
Frank	Contra Costa	Twp 1	57	521
Frank	Sonoma	Bodega	69	535
Geo	San Francisco	San Francisco 1	68	859
Geo	San Francisco	San Francisco 9	68	973
George	Los Angeles	Los Angeles	59	304
George F	San Francisco	San Francisco 8	68	1267
H	Shasta	Horsetown	66	699
Hans*	Sacramento	Mississipi	63	188
Jacob	Siskiyou	Yreka	69	144
Jas	Amador	Twp 6	55	425
Jesse*	Sierra	St Louis	66	805
Jno	Mendocino	Big Rvr	60	842
John	Calaveras	Twp 7	57	2
John	Nevada	Bridgeport	61	493
John	Trinity	Trinity	70	975
John*	Siskiyou	Yreka	69	155
Joseph	Sacramento	Ward 4	63	498
L	San Francisco	San Francisco 9	68	1081
Lewis	Santa Clara	San Jose	65	387
M	Sacramento	Sutter	63	305
M*	Mendocino	Big Rvr	60	842
Mar	Sacramento	Ward 1	63	13
Mary	Yuba	Marysville	72	890
Max*	Sacramento	Ward 1	63	13
Mo*	Mendocino	Big Rvr	60	842
Mr*	Mendocino	Big Rvr	60	842
P	Nevada	Washington	61	334
Peter	San Francisco	San Francisco 1	68	912
S W	San Francisco	San Francisco 9	68	1081
Samuel	Alameda	Brooklyn	55	182
Samuel	Calaveras	Twp 5	57	201
Thomas	Calaveras	Twp 4	57	299
Thomas J	Yuba	Marysville	72	928
W	Nevada	Eureka	61	377
William	Alameda	Oakland	55	54
William	Nevada	Bridgeport	61	448
William	Yolo	Cottonwoood	72	646
Wm	Sacramento	Ward 4	63	599
Wm	Sacramento	Ward 4	63	607
WALTERS				
Augustus	Klamath	S Fork	59	197
WALTERS				
Calvin	Tulara	Visalia	71	110
Cathrine	Napa	Yount	61	31
Chas	Butte	Bidwell	56	729
Chas	Calaveras	Twp 6	57	113
Chas	Nevada	Bloomfield	61	523
Chas	San Francisco	San Francisco 1	68	878
Chas*	Mariposa	Twp 3	60	595
D	Butte	Hamilton	56	515
David	Nevada	Bloomfield	61	526
David	Yuba	Suida	72	995
E	Santa Clara	Santa Clara	65	520
Ezekiel	Calaveras	Twp 6	57	154
Ezikiel	Calaveras	Twp 6	57	154
F	Butte	Chico	56	531
Geo	Santa Clara	Santa Clara	65	489
Georg*	Nevada	Bloomfield	61	517
George W	Napa	Yount	61	31
Henry	Plumas	Meadow Valley	62	933
Henry	Sierra	Gibsonville	66	852
Herman	Del Norte	Crescent	58	630
J	El Dorado	Placerville	58	848
J	Siskiyou	Scott Ri	69	77
J B	Siskiyou	Scott Va	69	50
J J	Napa	Yount	61	31
J W	Sonoma	Bodega	69	530
James W	Siskiyou	Shasta Rvr	69	113
Jas M	Butte	Bidwell	56	727
Jno	Sacramento	Ward 4	63	600
John	Calaveras	Twp 5	57	251
John	Del Norte	Crescent	58	629
John	Tulara	Twp 3	71	41
John	Tulara	Twp 3	71	47
John	Yuba	Linda	72	994
John Show*	Calaveras	Twp 6	57	187
Jonothon	Calaveras	Twp 5	57	187
Jos W H	San Francisco	San Francisco 9	68	1027
Joseph	Calaveras	Twp 7	57	1
Julia	San Francisco	San Francisco 2	67	626
Julius	Sierra	Gibsonville	66	852
Louisa	San Francisco	San Francisco 7	68	1384
Nathan	Tulara	Twp 2	71	33
P L	Merced	Twp 1	60	910
Patrick	Sierra	Cox'S Bar	66	951
R W	Sierra	Twp 7	66	875
Richard	Yuba	Suida	72	994
Russia	Sonoma	Mendocino	69	454
Saml	Amador	Twp 2	55	309
Solomon	Napa	Yount	61	29
Sylvester	Yolo	No E Twp	72	673
Sylvester	Yuba	North Ea	72	673
Thomas	Nevada	Bloomfield	61	516
W	Amador	Twp 3	55	373
W	Tuolumne	Twp 4	71	153
W A	San Francisco	San Francisco 9	68	1075
W B	Siskiyou	Cottonwoood	69	107
W B	Siskiyou	Cottonwoood	69	108
W*	Tulara	Big Oak	71	153
William H	Siskiyou	Yreka	69	146
Wm	Butte	Ophir	56	799
Wm	San Francisco	San Francisco 3	67	36
Wm	Sonoma	Mendocino	69	454
WALTERSON				
Elizabeth	San Francisco	San Francisco 9	68	941
WALTERSX				
David	Yuba	Linda	72	995
WALTHALE				
Madison	San Joaquin	Oneal	64	929
Madison*	San Joaquin	Douglass	64	928
WALTHER				
G W*	Stanislaus	Buena Village	70	721
WALTHOM				
D F	Sacramento	Ward 4	63	582
WALTIE				
---	Trinity	Taylor'S	70	1034
WALTIN				
E J	Butte	Hamilton	56	517
Edward R*	Siskiyou	Shasta Rvr	69	116
Silas	Siskiyou	Yreka	69	179
WALTIS				
John	Sacramento	Granite	63	263
William A*	Calaveras	Twp 5	57	208
WALTISON				
A*	Calaveras	Twp 9	57	410
WALTKINS				
Jason	Yolo	Cache	72	630
WALTMAN				
Samujel	San Joaquin	Stockton	64	1045
WALTN				
Maj A*	Nevada	Rough &	61	400
WALTON				
Catharin	Sonoma	Petaluma	69	575
Charles	Amador	Twp 3	55	381
Chas	San Francisco	San Francisco 2	67	692
D H	Sacramento	Ward 1	63	30
E J	Butte	Hamilton	56	517

California 1860 Census Index

Name	County Locale	M653 Roll	Page
WALTON			
Edward R	Siskiyou Shasta Rvr	69	116
Frederick	San Francisco San Francisco 9	68	943
G S	Sacramento Sutter	63	306
G S	Sacramento Sutter	63	307
Geo	Siskiyou Scott Va	69	36
Geo	Sutter Yuba	70	773
George	Del Norte Crescent	58	635
George W	Yuba Slate Ro	72	696
Geroge W	Yolo Slate Ra	72	696
Henry	Nevada Rough &	61	420
Henry G	San Francisco San Francisco 4	68	1109
Henry N	Tuolumne Twp 2	71	329
Isaac	San Francisco San Francisco 4	68	1145
J	Nevada Eureka	61	343
J H	Nevada Washington	61	334
J P	Stanislaus Empire	70	729
J W	Amador Twp 3	55	391
James	Yuba Bear Rvr	72	1000
James P	Calaveras Twp 5	57	249
Jas	San Francisco San Francisco 1	68	854
Jno C	Nevada Nevada	61	292
John	San Francisco San Francisco 2	67	664
Jonathan	Sierra Gibsonville	66	859
L L	Solano Vacaville	69	325
L L	Solano Vacaville	69	357
L W	Tuolumne Jamestown	71	446
Levi	Sonoma Petaluma	69	597
Maj A	Nevada Rough &	61	400
Margaret	Amador Twp 6	55	445
Margrey	San Francisco San Francisco 2	67	697
Marjaret	Amador Twp 6	55	445
Mart A	Stanislaus Empire	70	729
Mary	San Francisco San Francisco 1	68	860
Mary	Yuba Marysville	72	890
N C	Sonoma Petaluma	69	580
N G	San Francisco San Francisco 3	67	48
O	Sutter Sutter	70	808
Peter	Santa Clara San Jose	65	392
Samuel	Calaveras Twp 5	57	201
Sarah	Sonoma Sonoma	69	647
Silas	Siskiyou Yreka	69	179
Thomas	San Francisco San Francisco 3	67	81
Thomas	San Joaquin Castoria	64	897
Thomas D O	Yuba Slate Ro	72	696
Thomas H O	Yolo Slate Ra	72	696
Thomas*	San Francisco San Francisco 9	68	1098
Thos	Sacramento Ward 3	63	432
Tisdale	Placer Michigan	62	811
W	El Dorado Placerville	58	890
W	San Francisco San Francisco 3	67	72
W	Sutter Yuba	70	776
William	Siskiyou Yreka	69	127
William J	San Francisco San Francisco 7	68	1415
William*	Siskiyou Yreka	69	127
Wm	Alameda Brooklyn	55	182
Wm	Nevada Eureka	61	343
Wm	Sacramento Franklin	63	316
Wm	Trinity East For	70	1027
Wright	Placer Michigan	62	854
WALTREP			
Geo	Sonoma Sonoma	69	650
WALTRESS			
Geo	Sonoma Sonoma	69	650
WALTS			
J M*	Siskiyou Klamath	69	87
Walter*	Butte Ophir	56	797
William	Yolo Cache Crk	72	646
WALTSON			
S B*	San Francisco San Francisco 10	67	268
WALTY			
Nicholas	Siskiyou Yreka	69	173
WALTZ			
Daniel O	Tuolumne Chinese	71	491
WALTZAR			
Conrad	San Francisco San Francisco 10	67	227
WALTZE			
Chas	Placer Dutch Fl	62	728
WALUS			
John	Butte Ophir	56	746
WALVERGER			
Daniel*	Yuba Marysville	72	892
WALVERTON			
J	El Dorado Placerville	58	922
WALWORK			
Jas	Calaveras Twp 9	57	380
WALWORTH			
Ben T	Tuolumne Don Pedro	71	538
Ben T	Tuolumne Twp 6	71	540
Eugine	Tuolumne Shawsfla	71	418
WALWUR			
J*	San Francisco San Francisco 5	67	531
WALY			
Augustus	Placer Dutch Fl	62	709
WALZ			
Mary	San Francisco San Francisco 2	67	701
WAM CHOW			
---	Nevada Nevada	61	309
WAM			
---	El Dorado Georgetown	58	691
---	El Dorado Georgetown	58	746
---	El Dorado Georgetown	58	761
---	Yuba Long Bar	72	757
---*	Nevada Rough &	61	395
Chow	Nevada Nevada	61	309
Chow	Yuba Long Bar	72	769
Poo*	San Francisco San Francisco 5	67	514
WAMACK			
W	Nevada Grass Valley	61	194
WAMAE			
Simon*	Mariposa Twp 3	60	584
WAMAR			
Stryen*	Mariposa Twp 3	60	584
WAMAT			
Simon*	Mariposa Twp 3	60	584
WAMBLEDORFF			
Warren	Yuba Marysville	72	969
WAMBO			
---	Sacramento Cosumnes	63	408
WAMBOLD			
Henry	Amador Twp 6	55	442
WAMBURGH			
Geo	Butte Oro	56	675
WAME			
P	Calaveras Twp 9	57	418
WAMEHTO			
O H*	Nevada Eureka	61	374
WAMENELEAH			
---*	Tulara Visalia	71	37
WAMER			
A S	Butte Chico	56	551
Charles	El Dorado Greenwood	58	715
WAMERICLEAHE			
---	Tulara Twp 2	71	37
WAMGAR			
Timothy	San Francisco San Francisco 1	68	838
WAMKE			
Fred	Trinity E Weaver	70	1058
WAMMOW			
---*	Tulara Visalia	71	39
WAMNOU			
---	Tulara Twp 2	71	39
WAMOIGHT			
R*	Nevada Eureka	61	348
WAMP			
Isaac*	San Francisco San Francisco 2	67	802
WAMPECK			
Theodore	El Dorado Mud Springs	58	983
WAMPLER			
S S	Tuolumne Twp 1	71	256
Wm G	Plumas Meadow Valley	62	911
WAMS			
John*	Yolo Washington	72	573
WAMSER			
A*	Mariposa Twp 3	60	615
WAMSLEY			
Robt	Santa Clara Santa Clara	65	461
WAMSOTA			
---	Fresno Twp 2	59	106
WAMTOLD			
Henry	Amador Twp 6	55	442
WAN CHEY			
---*	Mariposa Twp 3	60	590
WAN CUM			
---	Tuolumne Chinese	71	525
WAN KEN			
---	Sacramento Ward 1	63	71
WAN MAX			
---	Fresno Twp 2	59	63
WAN			
---	Amador Twp 2	55	292
---	Amador Twp 2	55	328
---	Amador Twp 5	55	354
---	Amador Twp 5	55	360
---	Amador Twp 5	55	364
---	Amador Twp 1	55	477
---	Amador Twp 1	55	503
---	Butte Hamilton	56	529
---	Butte Hamilton	56	530
---	Butte Kimshaw	56	606
---	Butte Kimshaw	56	607
---	Butte Cascade	56	696
---	Calaveras Twp 6	57	164
---	Calaveras Twp 5	57	218
---	Calaveras Twp 5	57	251
---	Calaveras Twp 10	57	271
---	Calaveras Twp 10	57	272
---	Calaveras Twp 10	57	275
---	Calaveras Twp 10	57	278
---	Calaveras Twp 10	57	296
WAN			
---	Calaveras Twp 4	57	305
---	Calaveras Twp 4	57	315
---	El Dorado White Oaks	58	1033
---	El Dorado Salmon Falls	58	1043
---	El Dorado Salmon Falls	58	1046
---	El Dorado Salmon Falls	58	1054
---	El Dorado Salmon Falls	58	1067
---	El Dorado Coloma	58	1078
---	El Dorado Kelsey	58	1130
---	El Dorado Kelsey	58	1155
---	El Dorado Casumnes	58	1175
---	El Dorado Georgetown	58	680
---	El Dorado Diamond	58	785
---	El Dorado Diamond	58	815
---	El Dorado Placerville	58	821
---	El Dorado Placerville	58	830
---	El Dorado Placerville	58	869
---	El Dorado Placerville	58	870
---	El Dorado Placerville	58	886
---	El Dorado Eldorado	58	948
---	El Dorado Mud Springs	58	991
---	Fresno Twp 3	59	31
---	Mariposa Twp 3	60	546
---	Mariposa Twp 3	60	559
---	Mariposa Twp 3	60	569
---	Mariposa Twp 3	60	578
---	Mariposa Twp 3	60	582
---	Mariposa Twp 1	60	651
---	Mariposa Twp 1	60	655
---	Mariposa Twp 1	60	662
---	Mariposa Twp 1	60	673
---	Mariposa Coulterville	60	692
---	Mariposa Coulterville	60	693
---	Nevada Bridgeport	61	459
---	Nevada Bridgeport	61	461
---	Nevada Bridgeport	61	485
---	Placer Folsom	62	649
---	Placer Iona Hills	62	869
---	Placer Iona Hills	62	898
---	Sacramento Cosumnes	63	407
---	Sacramento Ward 3	63	488
---	Sacramento Ward 4	63	539
---	Sacramento Ward 1	63	55
---	Sacramento Ward 1	63	60
---	Sacramento Ward 4	63	613
---	Sacramento Ward 1	63	65
---	Shasta Shasta	66	669
---	Sierra Downieville	66	1003
---	Sierra St Louis	66	812
---	Sierra Twp 5	66	925
---	Sierra Downieville	66	973
---	Sierra Downieville	66	991
---	Trinity Mouth Ca	70	1014
---	Trinity Price'S	70	1019
---	Tuolumne Big Oak	71	147
---	Tuolumne Twp 5	71	522
---	Tuolumne Twp 5	71	524
---	Yuba New York	72	739
---	Yuba Long Bar	72	752
---	Yuba Long Bar	72	758
---	Yuba Parks Ba	72	774
---	Yuba Marysville	72	916
---	Yuba Linda	72	991
---*	Amador Twp 2	55	328
---*	Butte Hamilton	56	530
---*	Butte Kimshaw	56	602
---*	El Dorado Salmon Falls	58	1067
---*	Mariposa Twp 3	60	578
---*	Yuba Marysville	72	916
Ab	Yuba Marysville	72	914
Ah	Butte Eureka	56	652
Ah	Butte Cascade	56	696
Ah	Tehama Tehama	70	950
Ah	Tuolumne Twp 4	71	147
Ah	Yuba Suida	72	991
Chey	Mariposa Twp 3	60	590
Ching	Butte Bidwell	56	708
Ching*	Sacramento Ward 1	63	156
Chung*	Sacramento Ward 1	63	156
Con	Calaveras Twp 4	57	334
Cow	El Dorado Greenwood	58	710
Eye	Sierra St Louis	66	813
Fok	Calaveras Twp 10	57	278
Gan	Sierra Downieville	66	981
Gee	El Dorado Georgetown	58	748
Ha	Amador Twp 2	55	285
Hoan	Sacramento Ward 3	63	492
Hoen	Sacramento Ward 1	63	156
Hung	Sacramento Ward 3	63	494
J P	Sacramento Ward 3	63	487
J*	Nevada Eureka	61	391
Jacob*	El Dorado Placerville	58	898
James	San Francisco San Francisco 4	68	1124
John	Nevada Bloomfield	61	526
John	Tehama Tehama	70	935

Name	County Locale	M653 Roll	Page
WAN			
John*	Nevada Bloomfield	61	526
Kee	San Francisco San Francisco 11		146
			67
Kim	El Dorado Georgetown	58	703
King	Sierra La Porte	66	781
Kon	Sacramento Ward 1	63	71
Levi*	Santa Cruz Santa Cruz	66	628
Lin	Yuba Suida	72	993
Lu	Sacramento Natonia	63	283
Man	Amador Twp 5	55	354
Man	Amador Twp 5	55	364
Mie	El Dorado Mud Springs	58	984
Sam	Placer Todds Va	62	786
Sam*	Yuba New York	72	740
See*	Placer Todds Va	62	786
Song	San Francisco San Francisco 5	671	207
Su*	Placer Todds Va	62	786
Yan	Sierra Downieville	66	981
Yen	Sacramento Ward 3	63	491
WANA			
---*	Sacramento Ward 1	63	66
WANAAMAN			
Asa L	Sacramento Ward 1	63	97
WANADE			
W*	Siskiyou Scott Ri	69	64
WANAGHAN			
Thos	Butte Mountain	56	737
WANBLE			
J	El Dorado Newtown	58	778
WANCANOOT			
---	Fresno Twp 2	59	73
WANCE			
G	El Dorado Mountain	581	185
WANCISCO			
Joseph	Los Angeles Los Angeles	59	305
WANCO			
Adrian	Los Angeles Los Angeles	59	323
WAND			
August	Sacramento Ward 4	63	507
Hugh	El Dorado Georgetown	58	705
Jas	Calaveras Twp 9	57	365
John	San Francisco San Francisco 2	67	709
P H	Nevada Eureka	61	374
R H	Nevada Eureka	61	390
R H*	Nevada Eureka	61	374
S	San Francisco San Francisco 10		165
			67
WANDALL			
Ruth A	Santa Clara San Jose	65	379
WANDEL			
W F	Butte Oregon	56	625
W T	Butte Oregon	56	625
WANDELE			
S	El Dorado Placerville	58	817
WANDEN			
John*	San Francisco San Francisco 1	68	904
WANDERER			
H*	San Francisco San Francisco 3	67	12
WANDERES			
H*	San Francisco San Francisco 3	67	12
WANDERLY			
Henr	Sonoma Sonoma	69	654
Henry	Sonoma Sonoma	69	654
WANDERR			
Geo	Amador Twp 5	55	340
WANDLE			
James	Contra Costa Twp 1	57	504
WANDO			
Ramoris	Amador Twp 5	55	332
WANDORAN			
Len	Solano Montezuma	69	371
WANE			
---	El Dorado Mountain	581	188
E	Sutter Butte	70	789
James	San Bernardino S Timate	64	687
L	Tehama Antelope	70	893
Sam	Santa Clara San Jose	65	374
Stephen	Tuolumne Twp 4	71	142
WANEAH			
---*	Tulara Visalia	71	34
WANEAHE			
---	Tulara Twp 2	71	34
WANEAHO			
---	Tulara Twp 2	71	34
WANEG			
Geo	Alameda Brooklyn	55	93
WANEMAKER			
H	Siskiyou Scott Ri	69	76
WANEN			
Hugh G	Napa Yount	61	31
WANENAH			
---*	Tulara Visalia	71	38
WANENAHO			
---	Tulara Twp 2	71	38
WANER			
John	Mariposa Coulterville	60	703
WANERO			
Hosa	El Dorado Mud Springs	58	974
WANES			
J T*	Mariposa Twp 3	60	587
WANETTER			
Chas	Alameda Brooklyn	55	99
WANFIELD			
J J	Sierra Downieville	661	016
WANFLET			
W	Sutter Butte	70	789
WANG CHINN			
---*	Mariposa Coulterville	60	680
WANG YOU FOO			
---	Marin Cortemad	60	779
WANG			
---	Alameda Oakland	55	35
---	Alameda Oakland	55	52
---	Amador Twp 2	55	280
---	Amador Twp 2	55	289
---	Amador Twp 5	55	331
---	Amador Twp 1	55	478
---	Calaveras Twp 6	57	181
---	Calaveras Twp 5	57	211
---	Calaveras Twp 10	57	268
---	Calaveras Twp 7	57	47
---	Calaveras Twp 8	57	59
---	El Dorado White Oaks	581	021
---	El Dorado Salmon Falls	581	067
---	El Dorado Coloma	581	084
---	El Dorado Kelsey	581	130
---	El Dorado Casumnes	581	162
---	El Dorado Georgetown	58	696
---	El Dorado Georgetown	58	701
---	El Dorado Georgetown	58	761
---	El Dorado Placerville	58	923
---	El Dorado Mud Springs	58	962
---	El Dorado Mud Springs	58	966
---	Mariposa Twp 3	60	607
---	Mariposa Twp 1	60	626
---	Mariposa Twp 1	60	658
---	Mariposa Twp 1	60	668
---	Mariposa Coulterville	60	683
---	Nevada Rough &	61	432
---	Nevada Rough &	61	435
---	Nevada Bridgeport	61	459
---	Nevada Bridgeport	61	492
---	Nevada Bloomfield	61	521
---	Placer Auburn	62	573
---	Placer Dutch Fl	62	714
---	Placer Yankee J	62	760
---	Placer Forest H	62	798
---	Placer Iona Hills	62	897
---	Sacramento Ward 4	63	609
---	Sacramento Ward 4	63	612
---	Sacramento Ward 1	63	66
---	Sacramento Ward 1	63	68
---	Sacramento Ward 1	63	69
---	Sacramento Ward 1	63	70
---	Shasta Shasta	66	677
---	Shasta French G	66	712
---	Sierra St Louis	66	815
---	Sierra Poker Flats	66	840
---	Sierra Twp 5	66	934
---	Tuolumne Shawsfla	71	410
---	Tuolumne Chinese	71	525
---	Tuolumne Don Pedro	71	533
---	Yuba Long Bar	72	765
---	Yuba Long Bar	72	766
---	Yuba Long Bar	72	767
---	Yuba Long Bar	72	768
---*	Mariposa Twp 1	60	662
Ah	Calaveras Twp 7	57	14
Ah	Calaveras Twp 7	57	30
Benhart	Yuba Long Bar	72	754
Chee	Mariposa Coulterville	60	682
Choy	Placer Iona Hills	62	897
Chum	Mariposa Coulterville	60	680
Chunn	Mariposa Coulterville	60	680
Eah	Yolo Washington	72	563
Foo	Placer Michigan	62	858
K	Placer Iona Hills	62	897
Le	Sacramento Natonia	63	283
Pot	Sierra St Louis	66	815
R	El Dorado Georgetown	58	696
See	Tuolumne Don Pedro	71	537
Sie	Calaveras Twp 4	57	333
Soy	Yuba Bear Rvr	721	000
Sung	Placer Forest H	62	771
WANGAISSAN			
Asa L*	Sacramento Ward 1	63	97
WANGAMAN			
Asa L*	Sacramento Ward 1	63	97
John	Santa Cruz Watsonville	66	537
WANGAMEN			
John	Santa Cruz Watsonville	66	537
WANGANIAN			
Asa L*	Sacramento Ward 1	63	97
WANGENHEIN			
A L*	San Francisco San Francisco 10		276
			67
WANGERMAN			
Chas S	Alameda Oakland	55	23
WANGH			
---	Del Norte Crescent	58	633
---	El Dorado Diamond	58	802
---	El Dorado Mud Springs	58	949
James*	Shasta Shasta	66	673
Lorenzo	Sonoma Vallejo	69	621
S W	El Dorado Diamond	58	801
WANGLE			
J	El Dorado Diamond	58	816
WANGLER			
A	El Dorado Diamond	58	811
WANHANT			
Joshua	Alameda Brooklyn	55	213
WANHELL			
Jesse	Yolo Cache	72	613
WANHILOO			
Luisa	Santa Clara San Jose	65	322
WANIG			
Geo*	Alameda Washington	55	214
WANIN			
S	Calaveras Twp 9	57	412
WANING			
Jas*	Stanislaus Oatvale	70	716
Richard	Colusa Butte Crk	57	465
WANIPLER			
S S*	Tuolumne Twp 1	71	256
WANISSLER			
S S*	Tuolumne Twp 1	71	256
WANK			
---	Mariposa Coulterville	60	683
Wm	Calaveras Twp 9	57	387
WANKELL			
Samuel*	Santa Cruz Pajaro	66	575
WANKIN			
Samuel	Santa Cruz Pajaro	66	575
WANKLIN			
Marshal	Los Angeles San Pedro	59	479
WANMAKER			
Christ	San Francisco San Francisco 2	67	785
Peter	Sierra Cox'S Bar	66	950
WANN			
Ah	Tuolumne Twp 4	71	147
Chim*	Marin Bolinas	60	740
Chin*	Marin Bolinas	60	740
Enro	Tehama Red Bluff	70	916
Lee*	San Francisco San Francisco 1	68	892
WANNA			
---	Tulara Twp 2	71	34
WANNAH			
---*	Tulara Visalia	71	40
WANNAMAKER			
Richd	Sacramento Ward 1	63	48
WANNAME			
---	Tulara Twp 2	71	39
WANNANEAH			
---*	Tulara Visalia	71	40
WANNBALT			
David	Contra Costa Twp 1	57	524
WANNEAHA			
---	Tulara Twp 2	71	38
WANNENEAH			
---	Tulara Twp 2	71	40
WANNER			
George	Yuba Marysville	72	921
Jospeh	Siskiyou Shasta Valley	69	121
WANNES			
Joseph	Siskiyou Shasta Valley	69	121
WANNETA			
---	Tulara Twp 2	71	37
WANNICK			
J F	Siskiyou Scott Va	69	52
WANNIGAN			
Samuel*	Mendocino Calpella	60	821
WANNIY			
D*	Nevada Eureka	61	388
WANNUS			
Procntia	Amador Twp 7	55	412
Proventia	Amador Twp 7	55	412
WANOCK			
---	Del Norte Klamath	58	657
WANPELT			
Chs	Napa Napa	61	109
WANSANT			
A A	Amador Twp 2	55	324
WANSHAKER			
Christ	San Francisco San Francisco 2	67	785
WANSLEY			
W C	Sutter Yuba	70	778
WANSOCK			
Samuel	San Diego Agua Caliente	64	847
WANSONG			
Antonio	Trinity Lewiston	70	964

California 1860 Census Index

Name	County Locale	M653 Roll/Page
WANSSEY		
James N	Calaveras Twp 7	57 9
WANT		
Mary	San Francisco San Francisco 2	67 772
WANTE		
Porapel*	El Dorado Kelsey	581139
WANTEO		
Martin*	Sacramento Ward 1	63 149
WANTER		
Martin	Sacramento Ward 1	63 149
WANTLAND		
Theodore	Placer Todds Va	62 763
WANVOIGHT		
R*	Nevada Eureka	61 348
WANY		
---	Calaveras Twp 10	57 268
---	Sacramento Granite	63 250
---	Sierra Twp 5	66 934
Gui	Calaveras Twp 4	57 333
WAONN		
Samuel*	Yuba Marysville	72 952
WAOODIMISS		
Mary A*	Santa Clara Fremont	65 427
WAOTT		
---	Tulara Twp 1	71 115
WAOTTON		
J	Tuolumne Twp 4	71 179
WAOUR		
---*	Placer Auburn	62 581
WAOWR		
---*	Placer Auburn	62 581
WAPELL		
J E	San Joaquin Stockton	641061
WAPERMAN		
A	San Francisco San Francisco 7	681442
Elcan*	San Francisco San Francisco 7	681442
Elean*	San Francisco San Francisco 7	681442
WAPLER		
Adolph	San Francisco San Francisco 2	67 740
WAPLES		
Wm	Butte Mountain	56 737
WAPLEY		
B R	El Dorado Greenwood	58 717
WAPPLE		
Charles	Yuba Marysville	72 905
George	Yuba Marysville	72 905
Michael	Yuba Marysville	72 886
WAPTO		
---	Fresno Twp 2	59 36
WAPTON		
W	Sacramento Sutter	63 289
WAQNSEY		
A H	El Dorado Placerville	58 889
WAQTERS		
Thos	Nevada Bridgeport	61 487
WAR HORSE		
---	Fresno Twp 2	59 94
WAR		
---	Amador Twp 2	55 328
---	Amador Twp 5	55 342
---	Amador Twp 5	55 354
---	Amador Twp 3	55 402
---	Amador Twp 3	55 408
---	Amador Twp 6	55 449
---	Amador Twp 6	55 450
---	Amador Twp 1	55 477
---	Amador Twp 1	55 492
---	Amador Twp 1	55 511
---	Calaveras Twp 5	57 192
---	Calaveras Twp 4	57 305
---	El Dorado Salmon Falls	581040
---	El Dorado Salmon Falls	581055
---	El Dorado Coloma	581119
---	El Dorado Casumnes	581160
---	Mariposa Twp 3	60 559
---	Mariposa Twp 1	60 627
---	Mariposa Twp 1	60 641
---	Mariposa Twp 1	60 655
---	Mariposa Twp 1	60 666
---	Mariposa Twp 1	60 673
---	Mariposa Coulterville	60 687
---	Mariposa Coulterville	60 692
---	Mariposa Coulterville	60 700
---	Placer Auburn	62 572
---	Placer Auburn	62 579
---	Placer Auburn	62 581
---	Placer Auburn	62 583
---	Placer Rattle Snake	62 602
---	Placer Rattle Snake	62 629
---	Placer Rattle Snake	62 633
---	Placer Folsom	62 647
---	Placer Folsom	62 648
---	Placer Virginia	62 677
---	Placer Virginia	62 683
---	Placer Illinois	62 741
---	Sierra Twp 7	66 886

Name	County Locale	M653 Roll/Page
WAR		
---	Trinity Dead Wood	70 958
Ah	Trinity Point Ba	70 976
Chung	Placer Rattle Snake	62 631
Pun Can	Placer Folsom	62 648
WARA		
J*	Mariposa Twp 3	60 599
WARAMBOW		
Jluius*	Santa Clara Fremont	65 430
WARBERRY		
John	Sacramento Ward 1	63 33
WARBIN		
J C	Yolo Cache	72 591
WARBURTON		
H H	Santa Clara Santa Clara	65 468
John	San Francisco San Francisco 12	391
		67
WARCELLS		
Herman	Santa Clara San Jose	65 288
WARCISCO		
Jose	Santa Cruz Pajaro	66 525
WARCLEROLE		
William*	Sierra Port Win	66 798
WARD		
---	San Francisco San Francisco 7	681407
A	Marin S Antoni	60 705
A	Nevada Washington	61 336
A	Nevada Eureka	61 388
A	San Francisco San Francisco 5	67 532
A A	Butte Ophir	56 756
A J	Sonoma Washington	69 665
A*	Nevada Washington	61 338
Abram	Sonoma Petaluma	69 599
Affred	Calaveras Twp 5	57 214
Alesd H	San Francisco San Francisco 7	681327
Alexdr A	San Francisco San Francisco 7	681327
Alexr	Sierra Grizzly	661057
Alfred	Calaveras Twp 5	57 214
Alfred	Calaveras Twp 5	57 218
Alfred	Klamath Liberty	59 234
Alice	Monterey San Juan	60 983
Alice M	San Francisco San Francisco 10	229
		67
Alrah	Colusa Spring Valley	57 435
Alter M	San Francisco San Francisco 10	229
		67
Alvin G	San Joaquin Castoria	64 875
Amos N	Klamath Orleans	59 217
Andrew J W	Alameda Oakland	55 14
Arvin	Nevada Bloomfield	61 512
B	San Joaquin Stockton	641086
B H	Shasta Shasta	66 668
B J	Placer Iona Hills	62 875
B M	Sonoma Salt Point	69 689
Barney	Amador Twp 4	55 258
Barthal	Nevada Bridgeport	61 467
Barthol	Nevada Bridgeport	61 467
Benjamin	Yuba Marysville	72 866
Bennett	San Francisco San Francisco 1	68 867
Bridget	Placer Michigan	62 833
C	San Francisco San Francisco 2	67 804
C D	Butte Bidwell	56 711
C*	Nevada Washington	61 338
Caleb	Tuolumne Columbia	71 365
Calib	Tuolumne Twp 2	71 365
Calvin	Sierra La Porte	66 786
Calvin W	Sonoma Mendocino	69 467
Charles	Sierra Pine Grove	66 830
Charles	Yuba Bear Rvr	721011
Charles	Yuba Rose Bar	72 806
Chas	Trinity Trinity	70 972
Clayton	Santa Clara Santa Clara	65 509
Colin	San Francisco San Francisco 2	67 726
Conderion	Mendocino Calpella	60 818
Cordelia	San Francisco San Francisco 2	67 609
Daniel	El Dorado White Oaks	581031
Daniel	Yuba Long Bar	72 749
Danville	Tuolumne Twp 2	71 309
Davis	Yuba Bear Rvr	721008
E	Nevada Washington	61 338
E	Nevada Eureka	61 394
E B*	Sierra Gibsonville	66 860
E S	Mariposa Coulterville	60 680
Edward	San Diego Temecula	64 792
Edward	San Joaquin Castoria	64 901
Edwd	San Francisco San Francisco 1	68 856
Egbert	Siskiyou Yreka	69 166
Eli	Klamath Orleans	59 219
Elijah	Humbolt Pacific	59 132
F G	Siskiyou Klamath	69 91
F J	Alameda Brooklyn	55 149
F P	Solano Vacaville	69 325
Francis	Placer Virginia	62 673
Frank	Marin Cortemad	60 786
Frank	Mariposa Coulterville	60 690
Frank	Tuolumne Columbia	71 364

Name	County Locale	M653 Roll/Page
WARD		
G H	Nevada Grass Valley	61 178
G M	Sonoma Armally	69 498
G W	Merced Twp 2	60 917
G W	Trinity Weaverville	701076
Geo	Butte Kimshaw	56 576
Geo	San Francisco San Francisco 2	67 725
Geo R	San Francisco San Francisco 5	67 499
George	Placer Michigan	62 852
George	Placer Michigan	62 853
George	Placer Michigan	62 854
George	San Joaquin Castoria	64 877
George	Sierra St Louis	66 863
George	Siskiyou Shasta Rvr	69 111
George	Tuolumne Twp 3	71 448
George A	Sierra Twp 7	66 864
George J	Tuolumne Twp 2	71 335
H	El Dorado Newtown	58 781
H	Nevada Nevada T	61 326
H	Tehama Antelope	70 889
H C	Amador Twp 1	55 473
H C	Siskiyou Yreka	69 183
H E	Tuolumne Twp 4	71 172
H S	El Dorado Mud Springs	58 973
H*	Sierra La Porte	66 786
Harrison	Siskiyou Yreka	69 131
Henderson	Mendocino Calpella	60 818
Henry	El Dorado Mud Springs	58 975
Henry	Napa Hot Springs	61 17
Henry	Nevada Bridgeport	61 497
Henry	Sierra Twp 7	66 873
Hiram	Tuolumne Twp 2	71 312
Hiram P	San Francisco San Francisco 12	385
		67
Hubert	Yuba Rose Bar	72 808
Hugh*	El Dorado Georgetown	58 705
I M	Calaveras Twp 8	57 103
Isaac	Stanislaus Empire	70 733
Isaac M	San Francisco San Francisco 10	341
		67
Isabel	Calaveras Twp 5	57 194
J	Mariposa Twp 3	60 599
J	Sacramento Natonia	63 276
J	Yolo Putah	72 598
J D	Butte Ophir	56 765
J G	Santa Clara Gilroy	65 223
J J	El Dorado Placerville	58 928
J M	Butte Ophir	56 756
J M	Sonoma Washington	69 665
J M	Merced Twp 1	60 912
J N	Sacramento Ward 1	63 147
J W	Mariposa Twp 3	60 599
Jacob	Calaveras Twp 7	57 35
Jacob	San Joaquin Elliott	64 943
James	El Dorado White Oaks	581027
James	Los Angeles Los Angeles	59 361
James	Santa Cruz Pajaro	66 528
James	Tuolumne Twp 2	71 288
James	Tuolumne Columbia	71 362
James	Yuba New York	72 733
James	Yuba Fosters	72 836
James P	Sierra Morristown	661051
James W	Sierra Twp 7	66 913
Jane	San Francisco San Francisco 8	681313
Jas	Calaveras Twp 9	57 365
Jas	Placer Secret R	62 614
Jas	Placer Rattle Snake	62 636
Jas	San Francisco San Francisco 1	68 890
Jas	Santa Clara Fremont	65 433
Jas	Trinity Mouth Ca	701010
Jas*	Calaveras Twp 9	57 365
Jerry	San Joaquin Castoria	64 902
Jiobel	Calaveras Twp 5	57 194
Jno	Mendocino Arrana	60 859
Jno	Sacramento Ward 1	63 14
Jno	Sacramento Ward 4	63 561
Jno J	Klamath Orleans	59 217
Jno M	San Francisco San Francisco 9	681008
John	Calaveras Twp 8	57 103
John	El Dorado Big Bar	58 743
John	El Dorado Placerville	58 927
John	El Dorado Mud Springs	58 984
John	Los Angeles Los Angeles	59 386
John	Mariposa Twp 1	60 635
John	Mariposa Twp 1	60 638
John	Mendocino Big Rvr	60 841
John	Plumas Quincy	62 977
John	San Bernardino San Salvador	64 646
John	San Joaquin Elkhorn	64 994
John	Santa Clara Redwood	65 446
John	Sisklyou Yreka	69 185
John	Solano Vallejo	69 272
John	Solano Benecia	69 291
John	Sonoma Petaluma	69 608
John	Tuolumne Columbia	71 340
John	Tuolumne Columbia	71 348

California 1860 Census Index

Name	County Locale	M653 RollPage
WARD		
John	Tuolumne Montezuma	71 502
John	Yuba Marysville	72 943
John B	Alameda Brooklyn	55 123
John C	Sierra Gibsonville	66 854
John H	Sierra Gibsonville	66 855
John S	Plumas Quincy	62 983
John W	San Joaquin Elkhorn	64 988
John*	Mariposa Twp 1	60 638
Joseph	Placer Michigan	62 833
Joseph	Sonoma Vallejo	69 613
L A	Amador Twp 1	55 488
L D	San Francisco San Francisco 5	67 530
L G	Siskiyou Klamath	69 91
L M	Mariposa Coulterville	60 702
L N	Mariposa Coulterville	60 702
L P	Calaveras Twp 6	57 112
Liulel*	Calaveras Twp 5	57 194
Loomis	Tehama Tehama	70 945
M L	Tuolumne Shawsfla	71 379
M R	Trinity New Rvr	701031
Margaret	Humbolt Eureka	59 172
Martin E	Calaveras Twp 9	57 370
Mary	Siskiyou Scott Va	69 23
Mary K	Alameda Brooklyn	55 100
Matthew	Sacramento Ward 1	63 37
Michael	Plumas Quincy	62 999
Michael	San Francisco San Francisco 8	681303
Michael	San Francisco San Francisco 7	681438
Michael	San Francisco San Francisco 3	67 19
Michael	San Francisco San Francisco 5	67 546
Michael	Santa Cruz Santa Cruz	66 602
Michael	Tuolumne Twp 2	71 348
Michael	Tuolumne Twp 2	71 364
Mike	San Francisco San Francisco 3	67 82
Miko	San Francisco San Francisco 3	67 82
Mirhail	San Francisco San Francisco 5	67 546
Moses	Sacramento Ward 1	63 33
N J	Sonoma Washington	69 665
Nelson	San Joaquin Stockton	641093
Olin	Tuolumne Twp 2	71 309
Olin	Tuolumne Columbia	71 327
P	San Francisco San Francisco 5	67 519
P	Solano Vallejo	69 280
Patrick	San Francisco San Francisco 5	67 545
Patrick	San Joaquin Douglass	64 923
Patrick	San Mateo Twp 3	65 73
Patrick	Sierra Downieville	661001
Penelope	Merced Twp 2	60 920
Peter	Santa Clara San Jose	65 321
Peter	Santa Clara Redwood	65 453
Phillip J	Calaveras Twp 5	57 252
Phinea	San Joaquin Castoria	64 901
Porter	Marin S Antoni	60 706
Porter	Sacramento Natonia	63 272
R H	Merced Twp 1	60 903
Rebecca	Sonoma Mendocino	69 467
Ricd M	Sacramento San Joaquin	63 363
Rich R	Fresno Twp 3	59 16
Robert A	Siskiyou Scott Va	69 26
Rodney	Sierra Pine Grove	66 830
Rodney G*	Sierra Pine Grove	66 830
Rufus K	Mendocino Little L	60 837
Rufus M	Mendocino Little L	60 836
S J	Merced Twp 1	60 905
Sol	Sierra Downieville	66 993
Sylvester	Sonoma Petaluma	69 553
T	San Francisco San Francisco 5	67 532
T	Tehama Lassen	70 872
Tho'S	Mariposa Twp 3	60 605
Thomas	Monterey San Juan	60 982
Thomas	Santa Clara Fremont	65 433
Thos	San Bernardino San Bernadino	64 686
Thos*	Santa Clara Santa Clara	65 517
Thos	Solano Vallejo	69 243
Thos	Sonoma Petaluma	69 605
Thos M	San Francisco San Francisco 9	68 992
Timothy	Calaveras Twp 10	57 282
Trowbridge E	Plumas Quincy	62 968
V B	Sierra Twp 7	66 866
W	Sacramento Granite	63 221
W	San Joaquin Stockton	641092
W B	Merced Twp 1	60 910
W E	Shasta Shasta	66 679
William	Marin San Rafael	60 773
William	Nevada Bridgeport	61 471
William	Nevada Bridgeport	61 476
William	Placer Yankee J	62 757
William	San Francisco San Francisco 9	681055
William	San Francisco San Francisco 4	681218
William	San Joaquin Stockton	641089
William	Siskiyou Yreka	69 131
William	Yuba Bear Rvr	721004
William H	Plumas Quincy	62 941
William T	Plumas Quincy	62 968
Wilson	Tulara Keyesville	71 59
WARD		
Wm	Butte Wyandotte	56 670
Wm	San Francisco San Francisco 10	300
		67
Wm	San Francisco San Francisco 1	68 878
Wm	Sierra Twp 7	66 892
WARDE		
Alexander	Placer Auburn	62 585
WARDELL		
Catharine	Placer Secret R	62 616
Chas	Sacramento Granite	63 249
G W	Marin Cortemad	60 792
Isaac	Sacramento Cosummes	63 398
John	Santa Clara San Jose	65 284
John*	Placer Rattle Snake	62 634
Matilda	Santa Clara San Jose	65 312
Stephen	Placer Illinois	62 703
WARDEN		
A	Santa Clara Redwood	65 447
Asa*	Siskiyou Shasta Valley	69 118
D	Amador Twp 6	55 439
Ellen A	Klamath Liberty	59 243
George	Mariposa Coulterville	60 703
Henry	Merced Twp 1	60 903
Henry	Sacramento Ward 4	63 533
Henry	Siskiyou Scott Ri	69 75
Ira	Siskiyou Shasta Valley	69 118
James	Siskiyou Klamath	69 91
Jane	Sacramento Ward 1	63 22
John	San Francisco San Francisco 1	68 907
John B	San Francisco San Francisco 7	681402
John*	San Francisco San Francisco 1	68 904
L	Amador Twp 6	55 439
Levi M	Mendocino Twp 1	60 891
S M	Siskiyou Scott Va	69 39
Thomas	Tulara Twp 3	71 55
Windsor D	Klamath Liberty	59 243
WARDENBURK		
William	Siskiyou Scott Va	69 50
WARDENS		
K E	Santa Clara San Jose	65 360
WARDER		
Robt K	Sonoma Washington	69 664
WARDERLIN		
R	San Francisco San Francisco 6	67 471
WARDES		
Robt K	Sonoma Washington	69 664
WARDEVELL		
George T*	Marin Cortemad	60 784
WARDEW		
S H	Nevada Bloomfield	61 507
WARDLEY		
J	Butte Ophir	56 775
M	Amador Twp 5	55 367
WARDLOW		
Edwd	Sonoma Sonoma	69 656
WARDLY		
M L	Butte Ophir	56 794
WARDMAN		
James	Sierra Twp 7	66 894
WARDMILL		
A M	Calaveras Twp 8	57 81
WARDNER		
F H	Sacramento Ward 1	63 152
Frank	Sacramento Ward 1	63 27
J J	Yolo Slate Ra	72 693
T J*	Yuba Slate Ro	72 693
WARDNOCK		
Thm	Mariposa Coulterville	60 693
Thos	Mariposa Coulterville	60 693
WARDOCK		
Rubican	Siskiyou Scott Va	69 35
WARDON		
Dean W	Butte Ophir	56 774
WARDROBE		
D D	San Joaquin Elkhorn	64 984
E H	San Joaquin Elkhorn	64 983
R S	San Joaquin Elkhorn	64 983
WARDROCK		
Gideon	Santa Cruz Soguel	66 593
WARDROP		
D	Tuolumne Big Oak	71 147
WARDRUSS		
William*	Fresno Twp 2	59 49
WARDSON		
M J	Butte Kimshaw	56 603
WARDSURRIH		
Fred	San Francisco San Francisco 3	67 46
WARDSWORTH		
Fredk	San Francisco San Francisco 3	67 46
Henry	Klamath Klamath	59 225
WARDUSEN		
Wm S	San Bernardino S Timate	64 688
WARDWEA		
George*	Santa Cruz Pescadero	66 648
WARDWEER		
George*	Santa Cruz Pescadero	66 648
WARDWELL		
C O	San Francisco San Francisco 6	67 422
George	Marin Cortemad	60 784
Gideon	Santa Cruz Soguel	66 593
Henry	Butte Bidwell	56 730
J A	Butte Ophir	56 761
Jas	Butte Ophir	56 824
WARE		
---*	Nevada Rough &	61 395
E P	Yolo Slate Ra	72 690
Edward	Alameda Oakland	55 2
Edwd	Butte Hamilton	56 520
Elizabeth	Calaveras Twp 7	57 7
George W	Colusa Colusi	57 421
Harry C	Placer Auburn	62 562
Henry	Placer Todds Va	62 763
Henry	Sacramento Granite	63 252
Henry	Sierra Twp 7	66 873
Heny	Sacramento Granite	63 252
J A*	Santa Clara Santa Clara	65 521
J M	Marin Cortemad	60 752
J S	Tehama Red Bluff	70 920
James	San Francisco San Francisco 4	681124
Jno	Butte Kimshaw	56 571
John	Los Angeles Los Angeles	59 361
John H*	Sierra Gibsonville	66 855
Lim	Sacramento Natonia	63 280
M	Calaveras Twp 9	57 396
Nicholas	Sacramento Ward 1	63 146
Oscar	Napa Yount	61 33
Philip H	Contra Costa Twp 2	57 552
Saml C	Santa Clara Santa Clara	65 521
Stephen*	Tuolumne Big Oak	71 142
T J	Butte Hamilton	56 522
W	Tehama Red Bluff	70 920
W H	Santa Clara Santa Clara	65 501
William W	San Diego San Diego	64 757
Wm	Santa Clara Fremont	65 437
Wm	Trinity Weaverville	701055
Wm T	Sacramento Granite	63 263
WAREL		
H	Sierra La Porte	66 786
John C*	Sierra Gibsonville	66 854
Rodney G*	Sierra Pine Grove	66 830
Rodney J*	Sierra Pine Grove	66 830
WARELEROLE		
William*	Sierra Port Win	66 798
WAREMBERG		
August*	Tuolumne Columbia	71 308
WAREN		
Henry L	Alameda Brooklyn	55 95
Henry*	Trinity Trinity	70 973
Michael	El Dorado Coloma	581113
Micheal	El Dorado Coloma	581113
WARENA		
Romea	El Dorado Coloma	581119
WARENDORF		
Jas	Sacramento Ward 1	63 151
WARERER		
Wm*	Amador Twp 2	55 322
WARES		
Jno K	Alameda Brooklyn	55 194
WARETRAND		
Monston	San Joaquin Castoria	64 896
WARF		
A J	El Dorado Mud Springs	58 993
David*	Sonoma Vallejo	69 624
WARFEN		
Sylvert	San Francisco San Francisco 7	681347
WARFF		
Marten	Alameda Brooklyn	55 147
WARFIELD		
J	Alameda Brooklyn	55 181
J B	Nevada Bridgeport	61 467
J B	Sacramento Ward 1	63 50
J B	San Francisco San Francisco 3	67 19
James	Sonoma Armally	69 512
Robt	Trinity Douglas	70 979
WARFORD		
John	Tuolumne Twp 1	71 482
WARFORT		
Wm*	San Francisco San Francisco 1	68 913
WARFULL		
John	Placer Forest H	62 805
WARG		
---	Amador Twp 2	55 286
WARGAN		
A	El Dorado Placerville	58 877
P	San Francisco San Francisco 5	67 491
WARGAR		
Peter	Mariposa Twp 1	60 638
WARHLOTT		
J K*	Mariposa Coulterville	60 680
WARIEAH		
---*	Tulara Visalia	71 34
WARIFRILD		
L	Butte Oregon	56 619

Name	County Locale	M653 RollPage
WARIGH		
Geo	Alameda Brooklyn	55 104
WARING		
Amos	Yolo Washington	72 563
Stephen H	Solano Benecia	69 287
WARIS		
Joseph	Sierra St Louis	66 863
WARK		
---	Amador Twp 6	55 438
Al	Amador Twp 6	55 438
WARKE		
James M	San Francisco San Francisco 4	681151
WARKEN		
W D	Yuba New York	72 731
WARLACK		
J	Nevada Nevada	61 249
WARLOCK		
John	Sonoma Petaluma	69 543
WARLOON		
Bushwood	San Bernadino San Bernardino	64 672
WARM		
---	Nevada Bridgeport	61 462
Joseph	Tuolumne Jamestown	71 424
WARMACK		
J	Nevada Eureka	61 394
WARMAH		
---	Tulara Twp 2	71 37
WARMAHE		
---*	Tulara Visalia	71 37
WARMER		
A C*	Placer Virginia	62 677
C*	Placer Virginia	62 668
Richd	Sonoma Santa Rosa	69 390
WARMICK		
J F	Siskiyou Scott Va	69 52
WARMS		
C R	Tuolumne Twp 3	71 460
WARMSER		
Isaac	San Francisco San Francisco 10	259 67
Louis	San Francisco San Francisco 10	259 67
WARMSLEY		
Wm*	Sacramento Mississipi	63 187
WARN		
---	Placer Virginia	62 674
P	Sutter Yuba	70 766
William	El Dorado Salmon Falls	581048
WARNAGA		
H	Siskiyou Scott Va	69 58
WARNAGOR		
H	Siskiyou Scott Va	69 58
WARNAR		
Sim?On	Mariposa Twp 3	60 584
WARNBOLD		
Saml	Sacramento Brighton	63 192
WARNE		
G B	San Francisco San Francisco 9	681086
Jos	Trinity E Weaver	701057
WARNEER		
E J	Sierra La Porte	66 781
WARNER		
---	Marin San Rafael	60 772
A C*	Placer Virginia	62 677
A J	San Francisco San Francisco 2	67 662
A K	Alameda Brooklyn	55 86
A S	Butte Chico	56 551
Abraim	San Francisco San Francisco 2	67 632
Adam	Sacramento Franklin	63 326
Andrew	Plumas Meadow Valley	62 928
Andrew*	El Dorado Eldorado	58 936
B	El Dorado Kelsey	581153
Bery	Amador Twp 5	55 346
C	San Francisco San Francisco 5	67 516
C L	Sacramento San Joaquin	63 357
C M	San Francisco San Francisco 6	67 471
C R	Tuolumne Twp 3	71 460
Casius P	Placer Auburn	62 595
Charles	San Francisco San Francisco 7	681428
Chas	San Francisco San Francisco 10	329 67
Chas S	Sacramento Ward 4	63 552
Christopher	Sacramento Ward 3	63 483
D	Tehama Lassen	70 881
E	Nevada Grass Valley	61 180
E	Placer Dutch Fl	62 726
E	Shasta French G	66 717
E C	Butte Ophir	56 792
E J	Sierra La Porte	66 781
Eden	El Dorado Mud Springs	58 964
Eliza N	Sacramento Ward 4	63 508
Frank	Placer Grizzly	62 755
Franklin	Alameda Oakland	55 21
Frdk	San Joaquin Stockton	641042
G A	El Dorado Kelsey	581139

Name	County Locale	M653 RollPage
WARNER		
Garrett	Tulara Twp 1	71 101
Geo	Klamath Klamath	59 226
Geo	Sacramento Ward 3	63 441
George	San Francisco San Francisco 9	681072
Gustarus*	Tulara Keyesville	71 54
Gustavis	Tulara Twp 3	71 54
Gustavus*	Tulara Keyesville	71 54
Gustuvus	Sonoma Petaluma	69 545
Henry	Calaveras Twp 6	57 166
Henry	Plumas Quincy	62 986
Henry	Sacramento Ward 3	63 442
Henry	Shasta French G	66 717
Henry	Sierra Downieville	661013
Henry S	San Bernardino San Salvador	64 653
Hiram	Sacramento San Joaquin	63 353
Hiram	Sonoma Bodega	69 532
I	El Dorado Diamond	58 767
J	Solano Benecia	69 297
J A	Santa Clara Gilroy	65 230
J E	Del Norte Crescent	58 626
J M	Napa Napa	61 104
Jackson	Placer Iona Hills	62 889
James	San Francisco San Francisco 4	681111
James	Stanislaus Oatvale	70 717
Jane	San Francisco San Francisco 2	67 723
Jhn	Humbolt Eureka	59 174
Jno	San Francisco San Francisco 9	681079
John	Placer Forest H	62 804
John	Plumas Quincy	62 938
John	Solano Benecia	69 295
John	Solano Benecia	69 305
John J	Los Angeles Los Angeles	59 337
L	Sutter Nicolaus	70 834
L	Yolo Putah	72 586
Lilla	Solano Montezuma	69 367
M S	El Dorado Georgetown	58 757
Margaret E	Napa Napa	61 83
Miram	San Diego Agua Caliente	64 816
N	Nevada Nevada	61 274
N B	Del Norte Crescent	58 642
Noah	Placer Dutch Fl	62 727
Noh	Placer Iona Hills	62 889
Patrick	Placer Forest H	62 771
Peter	Calaveras Twp 9	57 387
Peter	Santa Cruz Soguel	66 598
Philemon	Sonoma Santa Rosa	69 404
R	Butte Kimshaw	56 608
R	El Dorado Kelsey	581153
Richd	Sonoma Santa Rosa	69 390
Saml M	Shasta Shasta	66 672
Sihil	San Bernardino San Bernardino	64 684
Suyan*	Mariposa Twp 3	60 584
Suyon*	Mariposa Twp 3	60 584
T M	San Francisco San Francisco 3	67 73
Thomas	El Dorado Kelsey	581152
Thomas	Tulara Twp 1	71 82
W	El Dorado Placerville	58 840
W	San Francisco San Francisco 3	67 72
W G	Yolo Putah	72 585
W H	Stanislaus Oatvale	70 717
W K	Yolo Putah	72 585
William	Nevada Bridgeport	61 444
William	San Francisco San Francisco 8	681307
William	Solano Fremont	69 376
William	Tuolumne Twp 2	71 412
Wlliam	Nevada Bridgeport	61 444
Wm	San Francisco San Francisco 2	67 672
Wm*	Amador Twp 2	55 322
WARNERFIELD		
H	Tuolumne Twp 4	71 173
WARNETTA		
---	Tulara Twp 2	71 39
WARNEY		
S	Santa Cruz Pescadero	66 653
WARNICK		
A M	El Dorado Placerville	58 933
Henry*	El Dorado Kelsey	581134
John	Yuba Rose Bar	72 804
Robert	Colusa Butte Crk	57 466
WARNIE		
T C	Placer Sacramento	62 644
WARNING		
Amio	Yolo Washington	72 563
WARNINGTON		
Hary	Sierra Twp 5	66 918
Heny*	Sierra Twp 5	66 918
Herry*	Sierra Twp 5	66 918
WARNIS		
William	Tuolumne Shawsfla	71 412
WARNKEY		
Frederick*	Santa Cruz Pescadero	66 641
WARNKKEY		
Frederick	Santa Cruz Pescadero	66 641
WARNOCK		
P	Sacramento Ward 1	63 31

Name	County Locale	M653 RollPage
WARNOCK		
W R	Sacramento Ward 4	63 542
William	San Diego San Diego	64 764
WARNS		
John	Yolo Washington	72 573
WARNSDELL		
Benjamin	Yuba Marysville	72 861
WARNSER		
A	Mariposa Twp 3	60 615
WARO		
B H	Shasta Shasta	66 668
WARP		
David	Sonoma Vallejo	69 624
Henry	Trinity E Weaver	701058
WARPER		
George	San Mateo Twp 3	65 92
WARR		
---	Siskiyou Yreka	69 195
Alice	Monterey San Juan	60 983
Charly	Nevada Bloomfield	61 526
John	Sacramento Ward 1	63 35
WARRAN		
Ed	Amador Twp 2	55 266
WARRATH		
Caroline	San Francisco San Francisco 9	681008
WARREE		
Mich*	Sacramento Natonia	63 277
WARREG		
Geo*	Alameda Washington	55 214
WARREN		
---	Amador Twp 2	55 307
---	San Francisco San Francisco 4	681229
---	San Francisco San Francisco 10	171 67
A C	Yolo New York	72 720
A C	Yuba New York	72 720
A E	Sacramento Alabama	63 417
A J	Butte Oregon	56 616
A S	Santa Clara San Jose	65 313
Alnois	San Bernardino San Salvador	64 653
Ann M*	Mariposa Coulterville	60 678
Aron	Sonoma Bodega	69 536
Asa	Sacramento Brighton	63 193
August	San Francisco San Francisco 10	319 67
Benjamin	Placer Iona Hills	62 864
Bessey	Yuba Marysville	72 881
C	Placer Dutch Fl	62 726
C A	El Dorado White Oaks	581003
C D	Trinity E Weaver	701058
C H	Trinity Weaverville	701079
Chas W	Placer Dutch Fl	62 730
David	Sacramento Granite	63 244
E D	Napa Hot Springs	61 5
E D	San Francisco San Francisco 9	68 980
E J	Napa Napa	61 99
Eugene	Santa Cruz Pescadero	66 645
F M	San Joaquin Stockton	641094
Francis	San Joaquin Elkhorn	64 950
Frank	Placer Secret R	62 608
Frank	Tulara Visalia	71 105
Frank E	Mendocino Big Rvr	60 843
Fred	Sierra La Porte	66 772
G	Placer Goods	62 669
G	San Joaquin Stockton	641100
G A	El Dorado Placerville	58 825
G A	Sacramento San Joaquin	63 357
G S	Siskiyou Scott Va	69 24
Geo	El Dorado White Oaks	581016
Geo	El Dorado Kelsey	581137
Geo	Sacramento Ward 3	63 464
Geo H	Sacramento Ward 4	63 515
George	Santa Clara San Jose	65 316
George R	San Mateo Twp 3	65 79
Gilbert	Sierra La Porte	66 768
H	El Dorado Salmon Falls	581052
H	Tuolumne Twp 4	71 169
H J	Butte Oregon	56 616
Hannah	San Francisco San Francisco 4	681127
Henry	Napa Clear Lake	61 137
Henry	Sierra La Porte	66 783
Henry	Siskiyou Scott Va	69 50
Henry	Tuolumne Shawsfla	71 395
Henry L	Alameda Brooklyn	55 95
Hera	Santa Clara San Jose	65 292
Hiram	San Francisco San Francisco 11	132 67
Hugh G	Napa Yount	61 31
J B	Nevada Nevada	61 272
J C	Mariposa Twp 3	60 546
J C	Sacramento Ward 3	63 428
J E	Amador Twp 3	55 408
J H	Nevada Nevada	61 261
J N	Nevada Nevada	61 261
J Q A	Sacramento Ward 4	63 550
J S	Nevada Nevada	61 272

Name	County Locale	M653 Roll	Page
WARREN			
J W	Butte Bidwell	56	718
J W	Siskiyou Scott Ri	69	62
James	Amador Twp 3	55	381
James	El Dorado Kelsey	58	1132
James	Nevada Bridgeport	61	505
James	Santa Cruz Pajaro	66	564
Jas	San Bernardino San Salvador	64	658
Jas	Tehama Antelope	70	889
John	Alameda Brooklyn	55	119
John	Los Angeles Los Angeles	59	359
John	San Francisco San Francisco 10	67	255
John	San Joaquin Elkhorn	64	970
John	San Mateo Twp 1	65	62
John	Siskiyou Cottonwoood	69	100
John	Tuolumne Columbia	71	308
John C	Sierra Eureka	66	1049
John K	San Francisco San Francisco 3	67	33
John P	Alameda Oakland	55	66
Jophn	San Mateo Twp 1	65	56
Joseph	Calaveras Twp 7	57	8
Joseph	Contra Costa Twp 1	57	531
Joseph	Siskiyou Callahan	69	12
Joseph	Siskiyou Yreka	69	192
Joseph	Trinity Lewiston	70	957
Josephus	Sacramento Ward 3	63	429
Leonard	Sacramento Franklin	63	325
Levi R	Siskiyou Yreka	69	158
Levi R	Siskiyou Yreka	69	165
M	Nevada Grass Valley	61	209
M	Sacramento Brighton	63	203
M	Sacramento Cosummes	63	394
M B	Los Angeles Elmonte	59	247
M P	Sacramento Ward 4	63	549
Manual	Yuba Marysville	72	910
Mark	Amador Twp 2	55	320
Mark	San Bernardino San Bernadino	64	623
Mary R	San Francisco San Francisco 8	68	1253
Mich	Sacramento Natonia	63	277
Moses	Sacramento Ward 1	63	95
Nathan	Tulara Twp 2	71	20
Newton	Los Angeles Azuza	59	278
O P	San Francisco San Francisco 10	67	253
P	Nevada Grass Valley	61	209
Peter	Sacramento Ward 1	63	154
Phillip	Calaveras Twp 9	57	364
R	Yuba Rose Bar	72	806
Robert	Calaveras Twp 7	57	9
Russel	San Francisco San Francisco 10	67	333
Russell	Yuba Rose Bar	72	811
S D	Santa Clara Gilroy	65	247
S M	El Dorado Casumnes	58	1176
Smith	Butte Ophir	56	784
Smith	Sacramento Ward 1	63	154
Stafford	Alameda Brooklyn	55	199
Thomas	Yolo No E Twp	72	670
Thomas	Yuba North Ea	72	670
Thos	Alameda Oakland	55	74
Thos	Sacramento Ward 1	63	89
V T*	Amador Twp 2	55	320
W	El Dorado Kelsey	58	1143
W	El Dorado Placerville	58	835
W	Sutter Nicolaus	70	827
W B	Trinity Mouth Ca	70	1014
W J*	Sacramento Ward 1	63	89
W P	Napa Hot Springs	61	22
W T	Sacramento Ward 1	63	89
W T*	Amador Twp 2	55	320
W W	Klamath Trinidad	59	220
W W	Tuolumne Sonora	71	484
West	Mariposa Coulterville	60	678
William	Calaveras Twp 7	57	21
William	Los Angeles Los Angeles	59	341
William	Plumas Quincy	62	985
William	Santa Cruz Santa Cruz	66	623
William	Santa Cruz Santa Cruz	66	625
William C	Los Angeles Los Angeles	59	337
William H	San Francisco San Francisco 7	68	1438
Wm	Amador Twp 2	55	322
Wm	El Dorado Kelsey	58	1143
Wm	Marin Bolinas	60	748
Wm	Mendocino Big Rvr	60	842
Wm	Placer Folsom	62	640
Wm H	Yuba Long Bar	72	773
Wm*	Amador Twp 2	55	322
Ws*	Amador Twp 2	55	320
Zephannah	San Salvador San Bernardino	64	652
WARRENDORF			
N	Sacramento Ward 1	63	5
WARRENGTON			
Adrian	Sonoma Santa Rosa	69	413
WARRES			
Joaquin	Santa Cruz Soguel	66	585
Louis	Santa Cruz Soguel	66	587
WARRICK			
Thos	Alameda Brooklyn	55	133
WARRIETTA			
---*	Tulara Visalia	71	39
WARRIG			
Geo*	Alameda Washington	55	214
WARRILL			
L M	Nevada Nevada	61	266
WARRIN			
Louis	Santa Cruz Soguel	66	587
WARRINER			
B S	Trinity North Fo	70	1024
WARRING			
Benj	Santa Clara San Jose	65	379
Jas*	Stanislaus Oatvale	70	716
S	Shasta Shasta	66	653
WARRINGTON			
Adrian	Sonoma Santa Rosa	69	413
Gno H	Mendocino Big Rvr	60	841
Jno	Mendocino Big Rvr	60	841
Jno H	Mendocino Big Rvr	60	841
Jos	Placer Dutch Fl	62	725
WARRIOR			
---	Fresno Twp 1	59	118
---	Fresno Twp 1	59	35
---	Fresno Twp 1	59	55
---	Fresno Twp 2	59	71
WARRIS			
Francis	Santa Cruz Pajaro	66	561
Joaquin	Santa Cruz Soguel	66	585
Louis	Santa Cruz Soguel	66	587
WARRN			
Mich*	Sacramento Natonia	63	277
WARRNICK			
J F*	Siskiyou Scott Va	69	52
WARRWICK			
J F*	Siskiyou Scott Va	69	52
WARSEN			
Catharine*	Monterey Monterey	60	966
Saml	Amador Twp 2	55	317
WARSEVITCH			
Nickolas	Plumas Quincy	62	1001
WARSEY			
Frank	Santa Clara San Jose	65	293
WARSHANSKI			
D	El Dorado Eldorado	58	983
WARSHAUR			
G	San Francisco San Francisco 3	67	50
WARSLY			
Alfred	Placer Iona Hills	62	896
WARSON			
Cadwell	El Dorado Union	58	1090
I	El Dorado Diamond	58	774
Saml	Amador Twp 2	55	317
Thos	San Francisco San Francisco 1	68	879
WARSWORTH			
M L	Tehama Cottonwood	70	898
WART			
---	Placer Rattle Snake	62	629
Ethan*	Humbolt Table Bl	59	142
F M	Alameda Brooklyn	55	159
John*	Mariposa Twp 1	60	638
L	Nevada Grass Valley	61	187
L	Nevada Eureka	61	357
Norton	Mendocino Ukiah	60	805
Wm Van*	San Francisco San Francisco 12	67	363
Wm Van*	San Francisco San Francisco 1	68	922
WARTEMBERG			
Simon	Mendocino Calpella	60	816
WARTENBAUM			
Adam*	Yuba Marysville	72	930
WARTENBURG			
Louis	Los Angeles Los Angeles	59	327
WARTENHU			
J W	El Dorado White Oaks	58	1017
WARTES			
N	El Dorado Placerville	58	821
WARTH			
Claiborne	Contra Costa Twp 1	57	486
Gidion	El Dorado Mud Springs	58	994
Lewis	Sonoma Petaluma	69	602
Louisana	Contra Costa Twp 1	57	487
Souisana*	Contra Costa Twp 1	57	487
Sowisana*	Contra Costa Twp 1	57	487
WARTHAN			
Peter	Sierra Downieville	66	1022
WARTHEN			
A	Santa Clara Gilroy	65	237
H W A	El Dorado Placerville	58	856
WARTHER			
William	Alameda Brooklyn	55	207
WARTHGRANE			
W*	Butte Kimshaw	56	568
WARTHGRAVE			
W*	Butte Kimshaw	56	568
WARTHING			
N	Butte Cascade	56	696
WARTHOP			
---	Mariposa Twp 1	60	629
WARTHOTT			
J K*	Mariposa Coulterville	60	680
WARTHOUSE			
Henry	San Francisco San Francisco 7	68	1405
WARTHY			
Joseph	El Dorado Kelsey	58	1154
WARTMAN			
Levi	Yolo Cache Crk	72	617
WARTNER			
F	El Dorado Placerville	58	853
John	Santa Cruz Soguel	66	583
WARTOKAS			
---	Fresno Twp 1	59	35
WARTON			
J H*	El Dorado Kelsey	58	1152
Jno	Sonoma Petaluma	69	584
John A*	Yuba Marysville	72	870
John*	Butte Mountain	56	734
Joseph	San Francisco San Francisco 2	67	558
WARTOW			
---	Sierra Downieville	66	985
WARTREN			
J W	Butte Bidwell	56	718
WARTS			
George	Nevada Bridgeport	61	454
WARTTON			
J*	Tuolumne Big Oak	71	179
WARTWORTH			
Wm	Butte Kimshaw	56	574
WARTZER			
J B	Siskiyou Scott Va	69	37
Peter	Siskiyou Scott Va	69	37
WARUE			
G B*	San Francisco San Francisco 9	68	1086
WARUN			
Phillip	Calaveras Twp 9	57	364
WARVOGAL			
Martin	Napa Clear Lake	61	135
WARWEDE			
Caroline	San Francisco San Francisco 6	67	417
WARWICH			
Wm	Butte Chico	56	556
WARWICK			
Austin	El Dorado White Oaks	58	1013
D	Nevada Eureka	61	390
Henry	El Dorado Kelsey	58	1134
J H	Sacramento Ward 1	63	102
John*	Yuba Rose Bar	72	804
Thos	Alameda Brooklyn	55	138
Wm*	Butte Chico	56	556
WARY			
---	Tuolumne Chinese	71	525
---	Tuolumne Twp 6	71	533
WAS TA			
---*	Mariposa Coulterville	60	692
WAS			
---	Calaveras Twp 5	57	249
Hoy	San Francisco San Francisco 4	68	1199
To	Mariposa Coulterville	60	692
WASACHA			
A	Stanislaus Branch	70	699
WASACUTA			
---	Fresno Twp 2	59	113
WASAM			
Miner	Stanislaus Empire	70	728
WASBURG			
J N	El Dorado Placerville	58	881
WASBURN			
Jane	San Francisco San Francisco 2	67	776
W M	Solano Montezuma	69	373
WASBURY			
B	Tehama Lassen	70	866
WASCHAWER			
M	Siskiyou Yreka	69	184
WASCHAWES			
M	Siskiyou Yreka	69	184
WASCO			
---	Sacramento Cosummes	63	408
WASCOWITCH			
Geo	San Francisco San Francisco 1	68	893
WASDON			
J	San Francisco San Francisco 2	67	784
WASE			
Edwd*	Butte Hamilton	56	520
WASEL			
Rodney G	Sierra Pine Grove	66	830
WASEN			
Milton*	Solano Vacaville	69	363
Owen	El Dorado Coloma	58	1108
WASENO			
Hasa*	Siskiyou Yreka	69	172

California 1860 Census Index

Name	County Locale	M653 Roll	Page
WASERTER			
Atinino	El Dorado Placerville	58	908
WASGATT			
Cornelius	Humbolt Eel Rvr	59	151
WASH			
---	Butte Bidwell	56	708
---	Calaveras Twp 5	57	222
---*	El Dorado Georgetown	58	700
Ah	Butte Bidwell	56	708
Chi	Amador Twp 5	55	335
George	Sierra La Porte	66	788
J	Siskiyou Scott Ri	69	77
John	San Joaquin Stockton	64	1073
Min	Amador Twp 5	55	335
Thomas	Plumas Quincy	62	991
WASHAMUA			
---*	Fresno Twp 2	59	45
WASHBANK			
C	Siskiyou Shasta Rvr	69	114
WASHBERG			
Wm	Placer Secret R	62	614
WASHBORN			
J J	Yolo Washington	72	565
WASHBOURN			
N	Shasta Shasta	66	733
WASHBOWN			
N*	Shasta Shasta	66	733
WASHBURN			
A	Sutter Butte	70	799
Alfred F*	Mariposa Twp 3	60	615
Alfred T*	Mariposa Twp 3	60	615
C	Calaveras Twp 9	57	397
C	El Dorado White Oaks	58	1021
E	Sacramento Ward 1	63	141
E C	San Francisco San Francisco 10	67	232
E P	Mariposa Twp 3	60	610
Edwin T	Alameda Oakland	55	74
Fredik	Plumas Meadow Valley	62	930
G M	Tuolumne Twp 3	71	369
G W	Tuolumne Springfield	71	369
George	Placer Todds Va	62	763
Jas M	San Francisco San Francisco 6	67	409
John	Marin Novato	60	738
John S	San Francisco San Francisco 3	67	77
Johnathan	Solano Benecia	69	317
Joseph F	Calaveras Twp 5	57	190
Joseph G	Calaveras Twp 5	57	190
L	Sacramento Ward 3	63	441
L	Sutter Yuba	70	759
L*	El Dorado Diamond	58	768
Mary A	San Francisco San Francisco 1	68	826
Nelson	Mendocino Anderson	60	871
P L	Yolo Slate Ro	72	716
P L	Yuba Slate Ro	72	716
Seymour*	San Francisco San Francisco 11	67	154
Silas	Tuolumne Twp 1	71	204
W	Alameda Brooklyn	55	128
W	El Dorado Diamond	58	808
W M	Solano Montezuma	69	373
WASHDILL			
B	Butte Oregon	56	635
WASHE			
----	Tulara Twp 1	71	115
WASHEIM			
Fred	Placer Michigan	62	807
WASHELER			
Charles	Sierra Grizzly	66	1058
WASHER			
Henry	Sonoma Santa Rosa	69	391
WASHHOLAN			
Wm	Sierra Downieville	66	1021
WASHING			
John	Santa Cruz Santa Cruz	66	622
John	Santa Cruz Santa Cruz	66	624
WASHINGTON			
---	Del Norte Klamath	58	656
A	Tuolumne Big Oak	71	150
Bej F	San Francisco San Francisco 10	67	241
Beverly	Sierra St Louis	66	812
C	San Francisco San Francisco 6	67	463
F A	San Francisco San Francisco 10	67	243
Francis	San Francisco San Francisco 2	67	711
G	Sutter Butte	70	783
G H	Nevada Bloomfield	61	508
Geo	San Francisco San Francisco 9	68	1076
George	San Francisco San Francisco 4	68	1122
George	San Francisco San Francisco 2	67	675
George	Tuolumne Chinese	71	501
H	Butte Eureka	56	646
Harriet	San Francisco San Francisco 2	67	646
Henry	Sierra St Louis	66	812
J	San Mateo Twp 3	65	103
WASHINGTON			
John	El Dorado Cold Spring	58	1101
O	Trinity E Weaver	70	1061
T	Sacramento Sutter	63	291
W	San Francisco San Francisco 9	68	1083
W C	Yolo Washington	72	569
Wm	San Francisco San Francisco 2	67	757
WASHKEN			
Alfred F*	Mariposa Twp 3	60	615
WASHKER			
Alfred F*	Mariposa Twp 3	60	615
WASHLAND			
Albert	Plumas Meadow Valley	62	899
WASHLON			
Benj	San Francisco San Francisco 9	68	1092
WASHMOTH			
Clifford	El Dorado Placerville	58	909
WASHTON			
Benj	San Francisco San Francisco 9	68	1092
WASHUEST			
Thomas	Santa Clara San Jose	65	315
WASK			
Cahs	Santa Clara Gilroy	65	234
John	San Francisco San Francisco 3	67	65
Joseph A	Los Angeles San Pedro	59	483
Joseph W*	Calaveras Twp 9	57	371
WASKAMUA			
---*	Fresno Twp 2	59	45
WASKER			
Wm*	Monterey Alisal	60	1038
WASKETA			
---	Fresno Twp 2	59	103
WASKISS			
Mary	San Francisco San Francisco 11	67	113
WASLACKIM			
---*	Tehama Tehama	70	940
WASLEY			
John	San Joaquin Douglass	64	914
Thomas	San Joaquin Douglass	64	914
WASLING			
H	Sutter Yuba	70	762
WASLY			
E J	El Dorado Georgetown	58	697
WASMER			
C	San Francisco San Francisco 5	67	518
Henry	Sacramento Ward 1	63	14
WASMUTHE			
Phillip W	Klamath Orleans	59	215
WASNER			
H	El Dorado Placerville	58	929
WASON			
James P	Solano Vacaville	69	363
Milton	Solano Vacaville	69	363
R H*	Butte Kimshaw	56	579
WASS			
Henry	San Francisco San Francisco 1	68	864
Henry J	San Francisco San Francisco 9	68	1097
Say	Tuolumne Jacksonville	71	167
WASSAL			
John H	Placer Dutch Fl	62	730
WASSAMA			
---	Marin Tomales	60	776
WASSAN			
J	Shasta Millvill	66	755
WASSE			
Nicholas H*	San Francisco San Francisco 7	68	1435
WASSEA			
Archibald	San Francisco San Francisco 11	67	105
Joseph	El Dorado Placerville	58	844
WASSEAN			
Shoes*	Sierra Scales D	66	804
WASSEN			
Andrew*	Monterey Monterey	60	965
Charles	Placer Yankee J	62	759
Henry	Placer Iona Hills	62	894
William	Placer Yankee J	62	759
WASSERDIALL			
Solomon	Santa Cruz Santa Cruz	66	605
WASSERMAM			
Augustus*	San Francisco San Francisco 8	68	1288
WASSERMAN			
Augustus	San Francisco San Francisco 8	68	1288
Elken	San Francisco San Francisco 7	68	1437
Henry	San Francisco San Francisco 9	68	1104
S	Sacramento Ward 3	63	425
Solomon	Santa Cruz Santa Cruz	66	605
WASSERMAUR			
Augustus*	San Francisco San Francisco 8	68	1288
WASSMAN			
G	San Francisco San Francisco 5	67	515
WASSNER			
Thos	San Francisco San Francisco 1	68	919
WASSON			
Archibald	San Francisco San Francisco 11	67	105
David	Nevada Bridgeport	61	447
David	Tuolumne Columbia	71	298
G H	El Dorado Diamond	58	774
G M	Trinity Bates	70	967
J R	El Dorado Diamond	58	774
Jas L	Butte Bidwell	56	717
John W	Trinity Eastman	70	960
John*	Butte Mountain	56	734
WASSREM			
Thos A*	Napa Yount	61	43
WASSUM			
John	Napa Yount	61	43
Thos A*	Napa Yount	61	43
WASSURA			
Thos	Napa Yount	61	43
WAST			
J J	Colusa Monroeville	57	451
WASTENBURG			
Henry	Los Angeles Los Angeles	59	327
WASTER			
I M	Amador Twp 2	55	322
J M*	Amador Twp 2	55	322
Marutte*	El Dorado Placerville	58	929
WASTES			
J M*	Amador Twp 2	55	322
WASTIN			
Fred	Placer Grizzly	62	755
WASTINS			
R M*	San Francisco San Francisco 5	67	533
WASTON			
J H	El Dorado Kelsey	58	1152
William	Solano Fremont	69	382
WAT			
---	Calaveras Twp 5	57	257
---	Calaveras Twp 4	57	299
---	Calaveras Twp 4	57	300
---	Fresno Twp 1	59	80
---	San Francisco San Francisco 4	68	1180
Che	Mariposa Twp 3	60	619
Emanuel	Trinity Indian C	70	989
L F	El Dorado Placerville	58	914
Lee	Merced Twp 1	60	914
M	El Dorado Placerville	58	857
William*	Santa Cruz Soguel	66	590
WATAIN			
John	Stanislaus Empire	70	734
WATCH			
Mary	San Francisco San Francisco 4	68	1141
WATCHENCHA			
---*	Mendocino Big Rock	60	875
WATCHIGON			
F	El Dorado Diamond	58	801
WATCHIM			
---	Del Norte Klamath	58	656
WATCHIN			
---	Mendocino Big Rock	60	875
WATCHINCHA			
---*	Mendocino Big Rock	60	875
WATCHOY			
---	Fresno Twp 2	59	18
WATDOTE			
---	Butte Chico	56	550
WATE			
---	Calaveras Twp 4	57	306
Mary	San Francisco San Francisco 10	67	233
WATEMATH			
J H	Sacramento Ward 1	63	120
WATEN			
Joseph*	Monterey San Juan	60	975
WATENBAUN			
R	Sacramento Granite	63	227
WATER			
E W*	Butte Oregon	56	638
Jas W	San Bernardino San Bernadino	64	674
Jno	Monterey Monterey	60	963
Jno	Sacramento Brighton	63	194
Simon*	San Joaquin Stockton	64	1050
WATERAN			
Adam	Yuba Marysville	72	930
WATERBAUM			
Jas	Yolo Merritt	72	582
WATERBURG			
Jas	Yolo Merritt	72	582
WATERBURY			
Ann	San Francisco San Francisco 4	68	1130
WATERFORD			
Chas	Sierra Scales D	66	803
Chas	Sierra Scales D	66	804
Columbus	Sacramento Ward 4	63	544
Jeseph*	Napa Hot Springs	61	16
Jesept*	Napa Hot Springs	61	16
WATERHOUSE			

Name	County Locale	M653 RollPage
WATERHOUSE		
John	San Joaquin Stockton	641083
Joseph*	Napa Hot Springs	61 16
L G	Sacramento Ward 3	63 438
Mark	Sierra La Porte	66 784
WATERMAN		
A	Butte Oro	56 688
Antony	Plumas Meadow Valley	62 932
B H	Shasta Millvill	66 744
C D	Tuolumne Twp 1	71 253
Charles	San Mateo Twp 3	65 105
Charles	Tuolumne Twp 6	71 530
E	Sacramento Natonia	63 286
Edwin R	San Francisco San Francisco 2	67 563
Elisha	Calaveras Twp 8	57 54
Eowen R	San Francisco San Francisco 2	67 563
Frances D*	Napa Hot Springs	61 23
Francis D	Napa Hot Springs	61 23
Frank	Sonoma Vallejo	69 621
G	San Francisco San Francisco 6	67 465
George	Solano Suisan	69 222
Hannan*	Calaveras Twp 6	57 160
Hanson	Solano Vacaville	69 336
Harman	Calaveras Twp 6	57 160
Harrison	Tulara Twp 2	71 9
Hasman*	Calaveras Twp 6	57 160
Henry L*	Humbolt Pacific	59 134
Henry S*	Humbolt Pacific	59 134
Hubert	Butte Oregon	56 624
J	Nevada Nevada	61 264
J H	Solano Fremont	69 384
J P	Stanislaus Emory	70 756
James	Shasta Shasta	66 666
Jas	Sacramento Ward 1	63 9
John	Nevada Bridgeport	61 470
John	San Francisco San Francisco 10	323 67
M	Solano Vacaville	69 331
Martin	San Francisco San Francisco 10	287 67
Moses	Yuba Marysville	72 850
R U	Solano Fairfield	69 198
S S	Sierra Twp 7	66 903
Samuel	Tulara Visalia	71 89
Sela	Tulara Visalia	71 9
W F	Sacramento Ward 1	63 10
W F	Tuolumne Twp 2	71 288
Walkr	Tuolumne Columbia	71 307
Walter	Tuolumne Twp 2	71 307
William	Placer Forest H	62 804
William	Santa Cruz Santa Cruz	66 627
Wm	Placer Auburn	62 566
Wm	Sacramento Ward 1	63 33
WATERMEN		
William	Santa Cruz Santa Cruz	66 625
WATERMYRE		
Henry	Trinity Douglas	70 979
WATERS		
Abraham	Placer Dutch Fl	62 717
Andr	Butte Oregon	56 621
Ann	Alameda Oakland	55 15
Ann	Sacramento Brighton	63 193
Arthur	San Francisco San Francisco 7	681401
Benj	Santa Cruz Pescadero	66 648
Charles	San Francisco San Francisco 6	67 442
E D	San Francisco San Francisco 9	681032
Edward	Yuba Marysville	72 906
Eliz L	Sacramento Ward 3	63 477
Elizabeth	El Dorado Mud Springs	58 993
F	Shasta Horsetown	66 703
Fj	Shasta Horsetown	66 703
Fred	Sacramento Ward 4	63 592
Frederick	San Bernadino	64 632
	San Bernardino	
G G	Sacramento San Joaquin	63 349
Geo	Butte Kimshaw	56 575
Geo	Mendocino Arrana	60 858
Geo L	Sacramento Ward 1	63 84
Henry	Amador Twp 2	55 300
Henry	Placer Dutch Fl	62 717
J	El Dorado Placerville	58 846
J	El Dorado Placerville	58 874
J	El Dorado Placerville	58 890
J	Nevada Grass Valley	61 148
James	Butte Ophir	56 767
James	Calaveras Twp 5	57 216
James	San Francisco San Francisco 3	67 32
James	Santa Cruz Pajaro	66 553
James A	Mendocino Ukiah	60 808
James N*	Shasta Shasta	66 684
James R	Mendocino Ukiah	60 808
James V	Shasta Shasta	66 684
James*	Calaveras Twp 5	57 216
James*	Santa Cruz Pajaro	66 553
Jane M	San Francisco San Francisco 12	379 67

Name	County Locale	M653 RollPage
WATERS		
Jas	San Francisco San Francisco 1	68 903
John	Butte Ophir	56 746
John	Placer Dutch Fl	62 717
John	Placer Iona Hills	62 881
John	Stanislaus Empire	70 734
Joseph	Placer Michigan	62 858
Joseph*	Placer Michigan	62 824
Lucinda	Sacramento Ward 1	63 116
Margaret	Placer Auburn	62 578
Maria	San Francisco San Francisco 7	681346
Mary Ann	Yuba Marysville	72 931
Michael	Placer Auburn	62 588
Patrick	Placer Auburn	62 585
R S	Nevada Nevada	61 288
Sarah	San Francisco San Francisco 9	68 978
T	Nevada Nevada	61 317
Thomas	Alameda Oakland	55 44
Thomas	Calaveras Twp 5	57 200
Thomas	San Francisco San Francisco 7	681391
Thomas	Solano Suisan	69 226
Thos	Sacramento Ward 4	63 559
Thos W	Nevada Bridgeport	61 487
W	Nevada Nevada	61 244
William	San Francisco San Francisco 9	681089
William	San Francisco San Francisco 11	119 67
William	San Francisco San Francisco 9	68 947
William	Tuolumne Jamestown	71 441
William P	San Francisco San Francisco 9	681089
Winified	San Francisco San Francisco 7	681349
Winifrid	San Francisco San Francisco 7	681349
Wm	Nevada Nevada	61 286
Wm	Placer Dutch Fl	62 718
Wm R	Sacramento Ward 1	63 136
Wm R	Sacramento Ward 3	63 476
WATERSON		
C	Tuolumne Columbia	71 313
J H	Napa Napa	61 108
WATERT		
James*	Calaveras Twp 5	57 216
WATERTON		
Peter	San Francisco San Francisco 9	681051
WATES		
Jno	Sacramento Ward 1	63 19
W	Nevada Nevada	61 244
WATH		
Chas*	Sonoma Petaluma	69 603
WATHEN		
J D	Tehama Lassen	70 866
William A	San Francisco San Francisco 8	681267
WATHERTY		
Simon	Santa Clara San Jose	65 366
WATHING		
John	Tulara Twp 3	71 62
WATHINSON		
Joseph L	San Joaquin Oneal	64 940
Mary*	Los Angeles Tejon	59 526
WATHON		
S*	Nevada Grass Valley	61 177
WATIS		
Charles E*	Yuba Marysville	72 904
WATISHOUSE		
L	Calaveras Twp 9	57 416
WATKINS		
Adison	Tulara Keyesville	71 58
Allen	Placer Goods	62 696
Ammon G	El Dorado Greenwood	58 727
B F	Santa Clara Santa Clara	65 492
C	Mariposa Twp 3	60 549
C	Shasta Millvill	66 741
Calvin	Sierra Downieville	661019
Camillas	Alameda Brooklyn	55 168
Charles	San Francisco San Francisco 7	681371
Charles	Siskiyou Callahan	69 2
Charles*	Butte Eureka	56 655
Charlie	Butte Chico	56 567
Chas*	Mariposa Twp 3	60 594
Cyras	Placer Michigan	62 807
Daniel	Santa Cruz Pescadero	66 648
David	El Dorado Mud Springs	58 995
David	San Francisco San Francisco 3	67 68
Ebinezer	Sierra Monte Crk	661037
Edmund	Sonoma Santa Rosa	69 425
Fanny	Santa Cruz Pescadero	66 646
Geo	El Dorado White Oaks	581007
Geo	Sacramento Ward 3	63 474
George	Solano Suisan	69 204
George W	Amador Twp 4	55 236
Henry	Napa Yount	61 54
Henry	San Francisco San Francisco 9	681009
Henry P	Yuba Marysville	72 884
Isaac	Tehama Lassen	70 876
Isaac	Yuba Marysville	72 922
J A	Trinity Lewiston	70 966

Name	County Locale	M653 RollPage
WATKINS		
J B	San Francisco San Francisco 10	207 67
J C	El Dorado Coloma	581108
J C	Santa Clara San Jose	65 352
J N	Yuba Parks Ba	72 786
J T	Napa Napa	61 60
J T	San Francisco San Francisco 9	681071
James	El Dorado Mud Springs	58 994
Jas	Yolo Cache Crk	72 645
Jason	Yolo Cache Crk	72 630
John	Sacramento Franklin	63 319
John	San Francisco San Francisco 8	681279
John	Sonoma Petaluma	69 575
John	Tulara Keyesville	71 62
Jos	San Francisco San Francisco 9	681044
Joseh	Sierra Port Win	66 798
Joseph	Sierra Port Win	66 798
Joseph E	Sierra Twp 7	66 904
Kjames F	Del Norte Crescent	58 641
M M	Tehama Moons	70 852
Peter	Plumas Quincy	62 920
Q N	Shasta Shasta	66 684
Reley	Monterey Alisal	601044
Riley	Monterey Alisal	601044
Sarah	Alameda Oakland	55 24
Sarah	Napa Yount	61 30
W	Nevada Nevada	61 287
W	Sacramento Granite	63 236
W F	Siskiyou Scott Va	69 41
Warren	Napa Yount	61 46
William	San Joaquin Castoria	64 894
William	Santa Cruz Pescadero	66 646
William	Siskiyou Yreka	69 174
William	Tulara Twp 1	71 94
William	Tuolumne Visalia	71 94
William	Yuba Rose Bar	72 817
William S	Yuba Rose Bar	72 817
Willis	Butte Chico	56 564
Wm	Nevada Nevada	61 275
Wm	Sacramento Cosummes	63 408
Wm	Sierra Twp 7	66 899
WATKINSON		
Mary	Los Angeles Tejon	59 526
WATLAND		
Joseph	Sacramento San Joaquin	63 362
WATLE		
Ar	Sierra Downieville	66 973
WATLING		
Elizabeth	San Francisco San Francisco 10	180 67
WATLLES		
C H	El Dorado Spanish	581125
WATMAN		
Josephine	Sacramento Ward 4	63 582
N	Shasta Horsetown	66 702
WATOCA		
---	Fresno Twp 3	59 8
WATON		
Nicholas	Placer Yankee J	62 760
WATRON		
M R*	Butte Oregon	56 626
W E*	Siskiyou Yreka	69 185
WATRONS		
Benjamine	Tuolumne Chinese	71 496
Fred*	Mendocino Big Rvr	60 850
WATROUS		
Benjamine	Tuolumne Twp 5	71 496
Fred*	Mendocino Big Rvr	60 850
WATRUMFS		
William*	Contra Costa Twp 2	57 553
WATRUMP		
William*	Contra Costa Twp 2	57 553
WATRUYO		
---	Tulara Twp 1	71 116
WATS		
C L	Shasta Shasta	66 680
WATSAG		
Augustus	Nevada Bridgeport	61 487
WATSEN		
Andrew	Monterey Monterey	60 965
Andrew	San Francisco San Francisco 3	67 75
Catharine*	Monterey Monterey	60 966
John R	Sacramento Granite	63 247
WATSENBORN		
H	Shasta Horsetown	66 699
WATSER		
Andrew*	San Francisco San Francisco 3	67 75
James	Mariposa Twp 3	60 622
WATSON		
---	Napa Napa	61 108
A	Nevada Eureka	61 344
A	San Francisco San Francisco 10	166 67
Alex	Santa Clara Gilroy	65 229
Alphonzo	San Joaquin Douglass	64 918

California 1860 Census Index

Name	County Locale	M653 RollPage
WATSON		
Amelia P	Sonoma Bodega	69 524
Andrew	Monterey Monterey	60 951
Andrew	Santa Cruz Pescadero	66 646
Ann Frances	Sonoma Santa Rosa	69 395
Archibald	Sierra Downieville	661021
B F	Sutter Yuba	70 773
Benjamin	Tuolumne Twp 5	71 517
Bridget	Marin Cortemad	60 753
C W	Tuolumne Twp 2	71 392
Charles	San Diego San Diego	64 765
Charles H	San Joaquin Douglass	64 914
Chas	Sacramento Granite	63 224
Chester*	Sacramento Ward 4	63 569
D D	Sierra Twp 7	66 910
D G	San Francisco San Francisco 5	67 548
Dan	Siskiyou Yreka	69 185
David	Placer Virginia	62 669
David	San Joaquin Castoria	64 881
David*	Siskiyou Yreka	69 150
E	Mariposa Twp 1	60 630
E H	El Dorado Georgetown	58 688
E S	Sierra Downieville	66 965
Edwin	Placer Iona Hills	62 897
Elijah	Tuolumne Columbia	71 301
Elizabeth	Contra Costa Twp 2	57 556
Ellen A	Yuba Suida	72 992
Emma	Contra Costa Twp 1	57 526
Enos	Colusa Muion	57 462
Eri	San Joaquin Stockton	641095
F	Sacramento Granite	63 223
F N	Yuba Rose Bar	72 790
Fadthen A	Sierra Whiskey	66 844
Fadthen H	Sierra Whiskey	66 844
Faidthen*	Sierra Whiskey	66 844
Francisco	Monterey Alisal	601040
G	San Francisco San Francisco 10	332 67
G	Sutter Yuba	70 764
G B	San Francisco San Francisco 1	68 884
G W	Calaveras Twp 9	57 403
Geo	San Francisco San Francisco 2	67 604
Geo W	Tuolumne Twp 4	71 132
Geo*	Sutter Yuba	70 773
George	Los Angeles Los Angeles	59 337
George	San Bernardino San Bernadino	64 635
George	San Francisco San Francisco 3	67 67
George	Solano Vallejo	69 243
George K	Siskiyou Shasta Rvr	69 114
H	Butte Hamilton	56 523
H	San Francisco San Francisco 1	68 923
H	San Francisco San Francisco 1	68 928
H E	Calaveras Twp 9	57 362
H L	Sutter Bear Rvr	70 826
Henry	Butte Cascade	56 697
Henry	Monterey San Juan	601010
Henry	Santa Cruz Pajaro	66 531
Henry	Santa Cruz Soguel	66 599
Henry	Sierra Downieville	661024
Henry	Tehama Red Bluff	70 916
Hiram	Alameda Oakland	55 28
Hiram	Colusa Monroeville	57 444
Hugh	Amador Twp 2	55 325
Isaac	Sacramento Ward 3	63 458
Isaac	Tuolumne Green Springs	71 532
J	Butte Cascade	56 700
J	El Dorado Kelsey	581153
J	San Francisco San Francisco 1	68 923
J G	Trinity Weaverville	701051
J H P	San Francisco San Francisco 1	68 924
J J	Sacramento Ward 1	63 8
J L	El Dorado Placerville	58 907
J N	Sutter Bear Rvr	70 826
J S	Butte Bidwell	56 729
J S	San Francisco San Francisco 9	681071
Jacob	Monterey San Juan	601009
Jacob	Plumas Quincy	62 986
James	El Dorado Kelsey	581146
James	Mariposa Twp 3	60 622
James	Monterey S Antoni	60 970
James	San Francisco San Francisco 9	681101
James	Siskiyou Scott Va	69 34
James	Solano Vacaville	69 245
James	Sonoma Bodega	69 520
James A	Monterey Monterey	60 925
James G	San Joaquin Castoria	64 873
Jane	Nevada Nevada	61 268
Jane	San Joaquin Elkhorn	64 954
Jas	Butte Mountain	56 736
Jas	San Francisco San Francisco 9	681090
Jas A	Butte Wyandotte	56 661
Jas H	Napa Napa	61 75
Jas L*	Butte Bidwell	56 717
Jeremiah	Santa Cruz Soguel	66 599
Jeseph	Mariposa Twp 3	60 615
Jno	Alameda Brooklyn	55 106
WATSON		
Jno	Klamath S Fork	59 207
Jno	Klamath Liberty	59 235
Jno	San Francisco San Francisco 9	681076
Jno	San Francisco San Francisco 9	681089
Jno B	Alameda Brooklyn	55 89
Jno S	Butte Chico	56 565
John	Butte Mtn Springs	56 734
John	Del Norte Crescent	58 641
John	Humbolt Eureka	59 177
John	Sacramento Ward 4	63 517
John	San Francisco San Francisco 9	681045
John	San Francisco San Francisco 1	68 890
John	San Francisco San Francisco 1	68 909
John	Siskiyou Klamath	69 90
John	Solano Vallejo	69 243
John	Sonoma Bodega	69 524
John	Trinity Taylor'S	701034
John	Tuolumne Twp 5	71 490
John	Yolo Fremont	72 603
John	Yolo Slate Ra	72 696
John	Yuba Slate Ro	72 696
John A	Trinity Weaverville	701073
John Jr	Sonoma Bodega	69 524
John M	Contra Costa Twp 2	57 556
John R	Sacramento Granite	63 247
John V	San Francisco San Francisco 6	67 431
John V	San Francisco San Francisco 5	67 482
Jon	Stanislaus Emory	70 751
Jos	San Francisco San Francisco 9	681095
Jos	San Francisco San Francisco 9	681090
Joseph	El Dorado Georgetown	58 699
Joseph	Mariposa Twp 3	60 615
Joseph	San Joaquin Stockton	641028
Joseph	Sierra Twp 7	66 908
King	El Dorado Georgetown	58 706
L S	Siskiyou Yreka	69 185
L S	Siskiyou Yreka	69 189
L T	Butte Chico	56 562
Lemuel	Sacramento Georgian	63 342
Leonard	Klamath Liberty	59 238
Leroy	Humbolt Union	59 191
Lorenza	Merced Monterey	60 931
Lorenza	Monterey Monterey	60 931
Lorenzo	Alameda Brooklyn	55 145
Louis	Mariposa Twp 3	60 570
Louisa	Mariposa Coulterville	60 684
M	San Francisco San Francisco 2	67 766
M A	Mariposa Coulterville	60 680
M B	Tuolumne Twp 2	71 368
M R	Butte Oregon	56 626
Marian	Sierra La Porte	66 769
Mary	Placer Michigan	62 828
Mary	Santa Clara San Jose	65 307
Matilda	Monterey Monterey	60 925
N A	Yolo Slate Ra	72 695
N A	Yuba Slate Ro	72 695
N N Jr	Yolo Cache Crk	72 610
Nancy J	Mendocino Ukiah	60 804
Nelson	Calaveras Twp 5	57 201
Phephen	Santa Cruz Pajaro	66 553
R A	Nevada Nevada	61 271
R D	Napa Yount	61 53
R H	El Dorado Coloma	581069
R H	El Dorado Gold Hill	581098
Richard	El Dorado Placerville	58 925
Richd	Trinity E Weaver	701057
Robert	San Francisco San Francisco 3	67 51
Robert	Sierra Twp 7	66 896
Robert	Solano Vacaville	69 333
Robert	Tulara Keyesville	71 59
Robt	Shasta Horsetown	66 688
Robt	Tuolumne Big Oak	71 130
Samuel	Sierra Downieville	661028
Sherman	Sacramento Dry Crk	63 375
Stephen	Santa Cruz Pajaro	66 553
Stephen	Trinity E Weaver	701061
Steve	Nevada Nevada	61 294
Stone	Nevada Nevada	61 294
Susan	Butte Chico	56 565
Susan	El Dorado Georgetown	58 688
T	Sutter Butte	70 782
T K	Marin Cortemad	60 752
Thomas	Merced Monterey	60 928
Thomas	Monterey Monterey	60 928
Thomas	Plumas Quincy	62 976
Thomas	Santa Cruz Santa Cruz	66 640
Thos	Butte Bidwell	56 719
Thos	San Mateo Twp 2	65 122
Thos	Santa Clara Santa Clara	65 502
Tomas	Monterey S Antoni	60 970
W	Butte Oro	56 682
W	Calaveras Twp 9	57 392
W	Calaveras Twp 9	57 393
W	Calaveras Twp 9	57 404
W	San Francisco San Francisco 1	68 921
WATSON		
W	Shasta Shasta	66 664
W B	Tuolumne Springfield	71 368
W E*	Siskiyou Yreka	69 185
W H	Butte Cascade	56 702
W H	Tuolumne Twp 1	71 200
W H Jr	Yolo Cache Crk	72 610
W R	Trinity E Weaver	701060
W S	Butte Cascade	56 700
W S	Butte Ophir	56 797
W S	Calaveras Twp 9	57 399
Wiley	Tulara Twp 1	71 97
William	Del Norte Crescent	58 644
William	Los Angeles Los Angeles	59 365
William	San Joaquin Castoria	64 881
William	Santa Cruz Santa Cruz	66 617
William	Solano Fremont	69 382
William	Tuolumne Twp 1	71 247
Wilson	Calaveras Twp 5	57 201
Wm	Butte Oro	56 686
Wm	Monterey Monterey	60 963
Wm	Sacramento Granite	63 252
Wm	San Francisco San Francisco 2	67 589
Wm G	Placer Auburn	62 593
Wm H	Sacramento Ward 1	63 137
Wm O	San Francisco San Francisco 2	67 657
Wm S	Calaveras Twp 9	57 399
WATSONBORN		
H*	Shasta Horsetown	66 699
WATSONS		
Wiley	Tulara Visalia	71 97
Wilson	Calaveras Twp 5	57 201
WATSOR		
Andrew*	San Francisco San Francisco 3	67 75
WATSWON		
William	Santa Cruz Santa Cruz	66 617
WATT		
---	Nevada Bridgeport	61 439
Chas	Sacramento San Joaquin	63 365
E S	Mariposa Coulterville	60 680
Geo	Sacramento Ward 1	63 26
Geo	Siskiyou Cottonwoood	69 106
George	San Luis Obispo San Luis Obispo	65 9
George	Tuolumne Shawsfla	71 404
George	Yolo Cottonwoood	72 660
Get	Sacramento Ward 1	63 26
James	Placer Todds Va	62 784
James	Shasta Shasta	66 685
James	Solano Vacaville	69 331
Jno	Sacramento Ward 1	63 149
Jno	Sacramento Ward 3	63 477
Julias*	El Dorado White Oaks	581026
Laura	Nevada Bridgeport	61 486
Leroy*	Butte Kimshaw	56 603
M	Sacramento Ward 4	63 506
Mary	San Francisco San Francisco 10	233 67
Mathew R	San Mateo Twp 3	65 90
Rosalia	Tuolumne Sonora	71 226
Susan	El Dorado Mud Springs	58 974
Thos	Amador Twp 1	55 494
WATTACE		
Henry*	San Francisco San Francisco 2	67 585
WATTAN		
Thomas*	San Francisco San Francisco 9	681098
WATTE		
---	Sierra Downieville	66 973
WATTEN		
Charles S	Placer Iona Hills	62 860
E N	Amador Twp 5	55 337
F S*	Napa Hot Springs	61 5
WATTER		
Jesse*	Sierra St Louis	66 805
John	Siskiyou Yreka	69 155
William M*	Nevada Rough &	61 421
WATTERMAN		
G	San Francisco San Francisco 4	681156
James	Contra Costa Twp 2	57 550
Oloynas*	Sacramento San Joaquin	63 349
Richd	San Francisco San Francisco 2	67 654
Solynas*	Sacramento San Joaquin	63 349
WATTERMOUTH		
S W	Trinity E Weaver	701061
WATTERNATH		
J H	Sacramento Ward 1	63 120
WATTERS		
Chas*	Mariposa Twp 3	60 595
Henry	Sierra Gibsonville	66 852
J J	Napa Yount	61 31
Jas M*	Butte Bidwell	56 727
John	Contra Costa Twp 1	57 492
John	Contra Costa Twp 2	57 550
Joseph	Calaveras Twp 7	57 1
Nathan	Tulara Visalia	71 33
Patrick*	Sierra Cox'S Bar	66 951
R W	Sierra Twp 7	66 875

Name	County Locale	M653 RollPage
WATTERS		
Saml*	Amador Twp 2	55 309
William	Solano Vacaville	69 356
WATTERSON		
Geo D	Sacramento Ward 3	63 472
WATTHER		
G W*	Stanislaus Buena Village	70 721
WATTIN		
W	San Francisco San Francisco 5	67 529
WATTING		
Elizabeth	San Francisco San Francisco 10	180 67
WATTINGTON		
Samuel	Placer Forest H	62 804
WATTINH		
W*	San Francisco San Francisco 5	67 529
WATTINS		
G	Calaveras Twp 9	57 416
W	Nevada Nevada	61 287
W*	San Francisco San Francisco 5	67 529
WATTISON		
A*	Calaveras Twp 9	57 410
WATTLERS		
John D	Sierra Downieville	661012
WATTLES		
C H	El Dorado Spanish	581125
WATTLESS		
John D	Sierra Downieville	661012
WATTLWORTH		
Charles	Tuolumne Twp 1	71 194
WATTMAN		
Jas	Amador Twp 3	55 383
WATTNEY		
Walter	Yuba New York	72 735
WATTO		
John*	Mariposa Coulterville	60 686
WATTON		
E W	Amador Twp 5	55 337
Geo	Siskiyou Scott Va	69 36
James S	San Francisco San Francisco 9	68 946
Thomas	San Francisco San Francisco 9	681098
WATTRAN		
S C*	San Francisco San Francisco 1	68 828
WATTRESS		
B C	Calaveras Twp 9	57 416
WATTRIDGE		
F W	Sierra Downieville	661032
WATTS		
Biddy	San Joaquin Stockton	641099
C B	Merced Twp 1	60 902
C L	Shasta Shasta	66 681
Clarinda	Shasta Shasta	66 681
Clarinda C	Shasta Shasta	66 681
David F	Calaveras Twp 5	57 206
Elizabeth	Sonoma Vallejo	69 627
Emerson	Calaveras Twp 9	57 363
Eran	Nevada Bridgeport	61 477
Evan*	Nevada Bridgeport	61 477
F	Sacramento Ward 4	63 506
George	Siskiyou Yreka	69 191
George W	Mariposa Twp 3	60 618
Irving	Tulara Twp 3	71 58
J	Mariposa Twp 3	60 622
J	Siskiyou Yreka	69 189
J A*	Mariposa Twp 3	60 588
J B	Tuolumne Twp 2	71 302
J H	Tuolumne Twp 4	71 173
J M*	Siskiyou Klamath	69 87
J S	Mariposa Twp 3	60 588
James	El Dorado Big Bar	58 738
James	Marin Cortemad	60 787
James	Nevada Red Dog	61 544
James	Nevada Red Dog	61 555
James M	Marin Cortemad	60 787
John	Butte Cascade	56 698
John	Calaveras Twp 8	57 53
John	Mariposa Coulterville	60 686
John	Mariposa Coulterville	60 702
John	Placer Forest H	62 805
John	San Francisco San Francisco 2	67 679
John	Tulara Twp 2	71 6
Joseph	Mendocino Little L	60 834
M S	Nevada Nevada	61 254
Nelson	El Dorado Georgetown	58 757
Owen	Tuolumne Chinese	71 520
Phillip	Calaveras Twp 8	57 63
Richd	Sonoma Vallejo	69 626
Ross	Calaveras Twp 8	57 65
S	Sutter Butte	70 783
S C	Mariposa Twp 3	60 596
S F	San Francisco San Francisco 3	67 74
Saml T	Del Norte Crescent	58 619
Shannon T	Yuba Marysville	72 885
Stannon T*	Yuba Marysville	72 885
Thomas	Tulara Visalia	71 30
Thos	Mariposa Coulterville	60 691

Name	County Locale	M653 RollPage
WATTS		
W E	Calaveras Twp 9	57 408
Walter	Butte Wyandotte	56 660
Walter	Butte Bidwell	56 720
Walter	Butte Ophir	56 797
William	Alameda Oakland	55 41
William	Calaveras Twp 4	57 338
William	Tulara Visalia	71 14
William A	San Francisco San Francisco 11	130 67
Wm	Calaveras Twp 9	57 387
Wm	Santa Clara Gilroy	65 230
WATTSON		
Henry	Alameda Brooklyn	55 192
L B	San Francisco San Francisco 10	268 67
T B*	San Francisco San Francisco 10	268 67
WATTY		
Nicholas	Siskiyou Yreka	69 173
WATZEN		
Henry	Sierra Twp 7	66 878
WATZKY		
Joseph	San Francisco San Francisco 8	681236
WATZOFF		
Maxx*	Del Norte Klamath	58 653
WAU		
---	Calaveras Twp 10	57 284
---	Nevada Nevada	61 304
---*	Amador Twp 2	55 328
WAUDLING		
Henry	Plumas Meadow Valley	62 933
WAUE		
John C*	Sierra Gibsonville	66 854
WAUGENHEIN		
A L*	San Francisco San Francisco 10	276 67
WAUGH		
---	Del Norte Crescent	58 633
---	Del Norte Happy Ca	58 663
---	Del Norte Happy Ca	58 664
---	El Dorado Diamond	58 785
---	El Dorado Eldorado	58 939
---	El Dorado Eldorado	58 940
---	El Dorado Eldorado	58 944
---	Placer Iona Hills	62 898
---	Sacramento Mississipi	63 187
---	Trinity Weaverville	701074
Geo	Alameda Brooklyn	55 104
Henry	Sonoma Petaluma	69 545
James	Shasta Shasta	66 673
James	Sierra Scales D	66 804
James*	Shasta Shasta	66 673
John	Sonoma Petaluma	69 565
Joseph	Shasta Shasta	66 728
Lorenzo	Sonoma Vallejo	69 621
Robert	Sierra Twp 7	66 871
S	El Dorado Newtown	58 776
Samuel	Sierra St Louis	66 809
WAUGHIHEIN		
A L*	San Francisco San Francisco 10	276 67
WAUGHTEL		
Wm	Trinity Lewiston	70 963
WAUGN		
Anson	Calaveras Twp 9	57 405
WAULDMANUN		
Geo	San Francisco San Francisco 7	681394
WAULUPA		
Jose	Los Angeles San Jose	59 287
WAUM		
---	Fresno Twp 1	59 27
WAUMEUM		
---*	Tulara Visalia	71 35
WAUMEUME		
---	Tulara Twp 2	71 35
WAUMSEN		
B F*	El Dorado Eldorado	58 936
WAUN		
---*	Tulara Visalia	71 37
WAUNAHO		
---	Tulara Twp 2	71 40
WAUNCASTLE		
Francis M	Contra Costa Twp 3	57 587
WAUNE		
---	Tulara Twp 2	71 37
WAUNI		
Aua	San Francisco San Francisco 5	67 543
WAUROIGHT		
R*	Nevada Eureka	61 348
WAVE		
Stephen*	Tuolumne Big Oak	71 142
WAVER		
Ford	Colusa Mansville	57 437
Jaes	El Dorado Georgetown	58 706
Saml	Nevada Little Y	61 535

Name	County Locale	M653 RollPage
WAVER		
Saul	Nevada Little Y	61 535
WAVES		
Mary E*	Plumas Quincy	62 968
WAVIS		
G W	Sierra Twp 5	66 947
WAW		
---	Butte Kimshaw	56 602
---	Calaveras Twp 5	57 222
---	Calaveras Twp 10	57 284
---	Calaveras Twp 10	57 286
---	Calaveras Twp 10	57 296
---	El Dorado Coloma	581078
---	Fresno Twp 3	59 32
---	Nevada Rough &	61 395
---	Nevada Bridgeport	61 439
---	Placer Christia	62 736
---	Sacramento Ward 1	63 65
---	Shasta Horsetown	66 711
---	Yolo No E Twp	72 680
---	Yuba North Ea	72 680
---	Yuba Long Bar	72 756
---	Yuba Long Bar	72 758
---	Yuba Long Bar	72 762
---	Yuba Linda	72 992
---*	Nevada Rough &	61 395
---*	Nevada Bridgeport	61 439
---*	Sacramento Ward 1	63 60
Ah	Yuba Suida	72 992
He	Yolo No E Twp	72 667
John*	Nevada Bloomfield	61 526
Mow	San Francisco San Francisco 5	671206
Wing	Fresno Twp 1	59 28
WAWN		
---	Butte Hamilton	56 530
WAX		
P	El Dorado Diamond	58 763
WAXEAH		
---*	Tulara Visalia	71 40
WAXMER		
Henry*	Sacramento Ward 1	63 14
WAXON		
Jos	Yolo Washington	72 574
WAY ANG		
---	Nevada Bridgeport	61 460
WAY		
---	Calaveras Twp 4	57 323
---	Del Norte Crescent	58 630
---	El Dorado Salmon Falls	581046
---	El Dorado Coloma	581111
---	El Dorado Kelsey	581139
---	El Dorado Mud Springs	58 978
---	Mariposa Twp 3	60 544
---	Mariposa Twp 3	60 564
---	Mariposa Twp 3	60 607
---	Mariposa Twp 3	60 613
---	Nevada Rough &	61 408
---	Nevada Rough &	61 431
---	Nevada Bridgeport	61 457
---	Nevada Bridgeport	61 491
---	Nevada Bloomfield	61 522
---	Placer Folsom	62 649
---	Placer Virginia	62 672
---	Placer Dutch Fl	62 732
---	Placer Iona Hills	62 895
---	Placer Iona Hills	62 897
---	Placer Iona Hills	62 898
---	Sacramento Mississipi	63 190
---	Sacramento Granite	63 250
---	Sacramento Granite	63 259
---	San Francisco San Francisco 4	681173
---	San Francisco San Francisco 2	67 754
---	Shasta Shasta	66 669
---	Shasta Shasta	66 678
---	Shasta French G	66 712
---	Sierra St Louis	66 815
---	Trinity Weaverville	701052
---	Yuba Long Bar	72 766
---	Yuba Marysville	72 925
A	Trinity Trinity	70 973
An	Del Norte Crescent	58 630
C S	San Francisco San Francisco 6	67 451
Che	Mariposa Twp 3	60 589
Chong	Tuolumne Big Oak	71 182
Danl E	San Francisco San Francisco 10	237 67
Frank	Tuolumne Columbia	71 289
George	Shasta Millvill	66 749
Henry	Tulara Twp 3	71 54
J	El Dorado Diamond	58 810
James*	Placer Iona Hills	62 866
Leas	Sacramento Granite	63 259
M W	Napa Clear Lake	61 130
Ma	Mariposa Twp 3	60 613
Matilda	San Francisco San Francisco 2	67 673
N H	Sacramento Ward 1	63 55

Name	County Locale	M653 RollPage
WAY		
Richard	Yuba Marysville	72 944
Robert	Humbolt Pacific	59 133
Seny	Sacramento Granite	63 259
Song*	El Dorado Georgetown	58 700
Ter*	Del Norte Klamath	58 657
Thos	Napa Clear Lake	61 130
Tong	El Dorado Salmon Hills	581054
Tong*	El Dorado Georgetown	58 700
Valentine	Napa Clear Lake	61 130
W	Napa Clear Lake	61 134
WAYAN		
Jacob	Sacramento Granite	63 266
WAYANG		
---	Nevada Bridgeport	61 460
WAYATE		
C C*	Shasta Shasta	66 761
WAYERLY		
Peter	Sierra La Porte	66 789
WAYERTY		
Peter	Sierra La Porte	66 789
WAYFIELD		
Andw	Sonoma Petaluma	69 572
WAYGOFF		
C S	Nevada Nevada	61 245
WAYLAND		
Albt	Butte Chico	56 552
Andrew	Nevada Eureka	61 362
Arnes	San Luis Obispo San Luis Obispo	65 7
C	Nevada Grass Valley	61 235
Franklin	San Luis Obispo San Luis Obispo	65 7
Geo B	Nevada Eureka	61 343
Geo S	Nevada Eureka	61 343
H	Nevada Grass Valley	61 215
Joseph	San Joaquin Castoria	64 911
Michiel	Nevada Rough &	61 408
William	Nevada Bridgeport	61 450
WAYLDEY		
John	Sacramento Ward 4	63 536
WAYLESETT		
August*	Yuba Suida	72 994
WAYLEY		
John	San Bernardino San Salvador	64 648
WAYMAN		
John	Solano Suisan	69 233
John H	Sierra Twp 7	66 908
Thomas	Sierra St Louis	66 864
Wm*	Calaveras Twp 5	57 247
WAYMER		
Geo	Nevada Nevada	61 313
WAYMIRE		
Nancy	Siskiyou Yreka	69 148
Samuel	Siskiyou Yreka	69 148
WAYMON		
Wm*	Nevada Nevada	61 314
WAYMOND		
Wm*	Nevada Nevada	61 314
WAYMOUTH		
John	Placer Michigan	62 824
WAYNE		
Ali	Amador Twp 3	55 386
B F	Amador Twp 2	55 267
George	Alameda Brooklyn	55 162
H S	Sacramento Alabama	63 415
James	Shasta Horsetown	66 696
James G	Shasta Horsetown	66 696
John	El Dorado White Oaks	581020
W	Siskiyou Callahan	69 2
Wm L	Sonoma Russian	69 430
WAYONN		
Wm*	Calaveras Twp 5	57 247
WE HAVE		
---	Mariposa Twp 3	60 612
WE HENG		
---	Sacramento Ward 1	63 70
WE SUNG		
---	Nevada Bridgeport	61 458
WE		
---	El Dorado Coloma	581107
---	El Dorado Georgetown	58 701
---	El Dorado Diamond	58 815
---	El Dorado Placerville	58 829
---	Mariposa Twp 3	60 569
---	Mariposa Twp 3	60 620
---	Mariposa Twp 1	60 661
---	Sacramento Cosumnes	63 390
---	Sacramento Cosumnes	63 392
---	San Francisco San Francisco 4	681199
---	Sierra Downieville	661003
---	Sierra Downieville	661027
---	Sierra Twp 7	66 898
---*	Trinity Weaverville	701074
Chin	Shasta French G	66 720
Ching	Butte Oro	56 686
Ching	Butte Bidwell	56 728
Chun	Calaveras Twp 5	57 215

Name	County Locale	M653 RollPage
WE		
Get	Nevada Bridgeport	61 492
Git	Nevada Bridgeport	61 459
Heng	Nevada Bridgeport	61 492
Heng	Sacramento Ward 1	63 70
Hoo	El Dorado Georgetown	58 691
Hoo	Shasta Horsetown	66 710
Hop	San Francisco San Francisco 4	681185
Jang	Butte Ophir	56 788
Kim	El Dorado Georgetown	58 700
Kum	El Dorado Georgetown	58 700
Lan	San Francisco San Francisco 9	681093
Law*	San Francisco San Francisco 9	681093
Lee	Butte Bidwell	56 711
Low	El Dorado Greenwood	58 730
Lupho	San Francisco San Francisco 10	276
		67
May	El Dorado Mud Springs	58 950
Moy	San Francisco San Francisco 9	681093
Ong	Nevada Bridgeport	61 492
Ong	Nevada Bloomfield	61 521
Puong	El Dorado Diamond	58 798
Sam	Yuba Foster B	72 830
Song	San Francisco San Francisco 4	681196
Tung	Nevada Bridgeport	61 458
Wa	Calaveras Twp 5	57 254
War	Mariposa Twp 1	60 673
WEA		
---	Amador Twp 5	55 350
---	Amador Twp 5	55 353
---	Mariposa Twp 1	60 659
---	Sierra Cox'S Bar	66 949
WEABAKA		
Frederic	Los Angeles Los Angeles	59 351
WEAD		
Welton	El Dorado Big Bar	58 737
WEADER		
Joseph*	Sierra Pine Grove	66 834
WEAKEIK		
---	Fresno Twp 3	59 98
WEAKFIELD		
Isaiah	Siskiyou Yreka	69 169
WEAKS		
Washington P	Yuba Marysville	72 850
WEAL		
J O*	Nevada Grass Valley	61 170
Jean	San Francisco San Francisco 2	67 797
William	Placer Michigan	62 821
WEALS		
Charles	Sierra Downieville	661017
WEALSH		
Geo	Placer Auburn	62 591
WEAM		
---	Sacramento Cosumnes	63 407
WEAMER		
Benj	El Dorado Coloma	581074
P L	El Dorado Coloma	581073
WEAN		
---	Placer Auburn	62 574
---	Placer Virginia	62 687
W L	Sierra Downieville	66 975
WEANER		
Duff G*	San Bernardino San Bernadino	64 676
William*	Napa Hot Springs	61 19
WEANS		
J W	Sonoma Russian	69 437
WEAPEN		
Wm	Calaveras Twp 9	57 374
WEAPLE		
Richard E*	Yuba Marysville	72 959
WEAR		
Alex	Sierra La Porte	66 783
E N	Sonoma Washington	69 666
John	Yolo Washington	72 570
Joseph	Yuba Marysville	72 881
Levi J	Yolo Merritt	72 582
W	El Dorado Placerville	58 858
WEARE		
Edward*	Sierra Twp 5	66 921
Levi J	Yolo Merritt	72 582
Saml	Placer Virginia	62 666
Theodore	Sierra Downieville	661030
WEARER		
Ogore	Yolo Putah	72 586
WEARES		
Samuel	El Dorado Placerville	58 910
WEARH		
Richard W*	Alameda Oakland	55 27
WEARING		
Peter	Sierra Downieville	66 977
WEARN		
Jno T*	Trinity Big Flat	701039
WEARNER		
P L*	El Dorado Coloma	581073
WEARON		
Jno T*	Trinity Big Flat	701039

Name	County Locale	M653 RollPage
WEARS		
Carson	Yolo Putah	72 587
WEARY		
Danl	Nevada Bridgeport	61 483
David	Nevada Rough &	61 438
R F*	Sierra Twp 5	66 923
WEASE		
Edward	Sierra Twp 5	66 921
John*	Nevada Red Dog	61 555
WEASES		
Samuel*	El Dorado Placerville	58 910
WEASK		
I H	Amador Twp 2	55 325
J H*	Amador Twp 2	55 325
WEAST		
Andrew	Colusa Grand Island	57 473
J K	Colusa Grand Island	57 473
WEASY		
David*	Nevada Rough &	61 438
WEATH		
Richard W*	Alameda Oakland	55 27
WEATHERBY		
Duncan C	Humbolt Eureka	59 177
J A	Sacramento American	63 165
WEATHERHEAD		
James	Plumas Quincy	621002
WEATHERS		
J H	Sacramento San Joaquin	63 356
Peter J	Sacramento Granite	63 263
Wm	Sacramento San Joaquin	63 357
WEATHERSPOON		
J H	Yolo Putah	72 615
J M	Yolo Putah	72 615
Robt	Plumas Quincy	62 955
WEATHERWAS		
J M B	El Dorado Eldorado	58 944
L	El Dorado Placerville	58 862
WEATHIMAN		
S C	Sutter Yuba	70 763
WEATON		
D	El Dorado Mud Springs	58 951
Wash	Sierra Twp 7	66 890
WEATS		
Elisha	Nevada Bridgeport	61 466
WEAU		
W L*	Sierra Downieville	66 975
WEAVE		
Peter	Sierra Downieville	661018
WEAVER		
---	Siskiyou Yreka	69 154
A	San Francisco San Francisco 5	67 483
A G	Nevada Eureka	61 366
Adam	Sacramento Sutter	63 292
Albert	Butte Ophir	56 795
Alfred	Santa Cruz Pescadero	66 641
Ann	Alameda Brooklyn	55 95
Anne	San Francisco San Francisco 2	67 637
B H	Nevada Eureka	61 354
C	Yuba Parks Ba	72 774
Catharine	Trinity S Fork	701032
Chas	Yolo Cache Crk	72 594
D S	Shasta Shasta	66 659
D T	San Francisco San Francisco 10	200
		67
Daniel C	San Francisco San Francisco 11	142
		67
Danl	Santa Clara Santa Clara	65 500
David	Butte Ophir	56 770
Duff G*	San Bernardino San Bernadino	64 676
Eli	Sierra Twp 7	66 867
Elias	Yolo Cache	72 594
Francis	Contra Costa Twp 1	57 485
Frank	Los Angeles Los Angeles	59 342
Fred	El Dorado Mud Springs	58 987
Frederick	Sacramento Franklin	63 314
G H	Sacramento Ward 4	63 528
G H	Yolo Cache Crk	72 645
Geo	Sacramento Ward 4	63 502
Henry	Amador Twp 2	55 318
Henry	Calaveras Twp 9	57 359
Henry	San Joaquin Stockton	641054
Henry	Sonoma Sonoma	69 637
Henry	Trinity Trinity	70 973
Henry E	Tulara Visalia	71 97
J E	Yolo Merritt	72 579
Jack	San Joaquin Elkhorn	64 987
Jacob	Colusa Colusi	57 421
Jacob	Santa Clara Santa Clara	65 481
Jacob	Yolo Cottonwoood	72 659
James*	El Dorado Georgetown	58 706
Jane	Yolo Cache Crk	72 594
Jesse	Tuolumne Sonora	71 480
John	Sacramento Centre	63 180
John	San Francisco San Francisco 7	681436
John	San Joaquin Elkhorn	64 973
John F	Placer Secret R	62 611

Name	County Locale	M653 RollPage
WEAVER		
John H	Contra Costa Twp 3	57 603
Jos	Butte Kimshaw	56 577
Jos	Butte Kimshaw	56 591
Joseph	Sierra Pine Grove	66 834
Leon M	Humbolt Eel Rvr	59 149
Leroy B	Humbolt Pacific	59 130
Lewis	San Francisco San Francisco 3	67 47
Lydia	Santa Cruz Pajaro	66 541
Mary E	Tulara Twp 1	71 97
Mr	San Francisco San Francisco 10	256 67
Nicholas	Los Angeles Los Angeles	59 389
Nicolas	Los Angeles Los Angeles	59 389
O W	Del Norte Crescent	58 648
Ogore	Yolo Putah	72 586
Paul	Sierra Poker Flats	66 842
Peter S	Humbolt Eureka	59 170
Robert	San Joaquin Elkhorn	64 985
S L	Shasta Millvill	66 752
W J	Trinity Arkansas	701004
William	San Francisco San Francisco 9	681090
William	San Mateo Twp 3	65 82
Wm	Calaveras Twp 9	57 374
Wm	Humbolt Pacific	59 143
Wm	Tehama Pasakent	70 859
WEAVERS		
Elizabeth	San Francisco San Francisco 2	67 658
WEAVOR		
Ann*	San Francisco San Francisco 2	67 751
WEAZK		
J H*	Amador Twp 2	55 325
WEB		
Elisha	Placer Secret R	62 610
WEBB		
A	Nevada Washington	61 334
A	Sacramento Brighton	63 196
A H	Tehama Red Bluff	70 924
Albert S	Yuba Parks Ba	72 782
Amelia	Calaveras Twp 5	57 201
Augusta	El Dorado Georgetown	58 706
Augustus	El Dorado Georgetown	58 706
B F	Amador Twp 2	55 267
Barnulus	Contra Costa Twp 2	57 561
C C	San Francisco San Francisco 5	67 545
C O	San Francisco San Francisco 5	67 545
Charles	Tulara Keeneysburg	71 46
Charles*	Amador Twp 2	55 322
Chas	Sacramento Natonia	63 276
Chas	Sacramento Cosummes	63 406
Chesles*	Amador Twp 2	55 322
Chester	Amador Twp 2	55 322
Christopher C	San Francisco 8	681251
	San Francisco	
D E	San Francisco San Francisco 6	67 422
D F	Amador Twp 1	55 487
E	Nevada Grass Valley	61 210
Eliza	Alameda Oakland	55 70
Elizabeth	Yuba Marysville	72 859
Elizabeth	Yuba Marysville	72 860
G B	El Dorado Placerville	58 846
Gabriel	San Francisco San Francisco 3	67 15
Geo W	Mendocino Little L	60 837
Handley N	Sonoma Mendocino	69 461
Henry	El Dorado Mud Springs	58 995
Henry	San Francisco San Francisco 8	681317
Henry	San Francisco San Francisco 10	275 67
Henry	Siskiyou Klamath	69 79
Hiram	Sierra Pine Grove	66 820
J P	Shasta Millvill	66 740
J R	Colusa Monroeville	57 447
J S	El Dorado Kelsey	581138
J S	Yolo Cache Crk	72 645
J W	Sierra Downieville	661031
Jacob	Sierra St Louis	66 815
James	El Dorado Georgetown	58 758
James	San Joaquin Castoria	64 902
James	Tulara Twp 1	71 98
James	Yuba Marysville	72 902
James Jr	Sacramento Franklin	63 314
Jas	Sacramento Ward 4	63 572
Jas F	San Francisco San Francisco 5	67 477
Jesse	San Joaquin Castoria	64 903
Jo	Tehama Red Bluff	70 919
John	El Dorado White Oaks	581019
John	El Dorado Kelsey	581143
John	Placer Auburn	62 566
John	Plumas Quincy	62 985
John	San Francisco San Francisco 3	67 15
John	Sierra St Louis	66 809
John	Tulara Twp 3	71 60
John	Tuolumne Shawsfla	71 375
John	Yolo Washington	72 563
John	Yuba Marysville	72 859
John	Yuba Marysville	72 860

Name	County Locale	M653 RollPage
WEBB		
John J	San Bernardino San Bernadino	64 618
John M	Alameda Oakland	55 59
John T	San Joaquin Douglass	64 923
Jos	Sacramento Ward 4	63 569
Jos F	San Francisco San Francisco 5	67 477
Joseph	Mariposa Twp 3	60 559
Joseph W	San Francisco San Francisco 9	68 951
K A	San Francisco San Francisco 3	67 86
L D	Butte Mountain	56 738
Lewis	Nevada Bridgeport	61 481
Louise	San Francisco San Francisco 8	681252
M	San Joaquin Elkhorn	64 992
Mabtin	El Dorado Georgetown	58 703
Mary	San Francisco San Francisco 4	681144
Monroe	Butte Kimshaw	56 588
N	Sutter Nicolaus	70 841
N L	Sierra Twp 7	66 916
Nathaniel	Tuolumne Columbia	71 360
Nelson	Merced Monterey	60 930
Nelson	Monterey Monterey	60 930
O	Nevada Washington	61 334
O	Santa Clara Redwood	65 458
Peter L	San Francisco San Francisco 9	68 953
Phillip	El Dorado Kelsey	581143
R A	San Francisco San Francisco 3	67 86
S W	Mariposa Twp 3	60 577
Samuel	San Joaquin Elliott	64 948
Sanfred	Fresno Twp 1	59 76
Sarah*	Trinity Weaverville	701071
Simon	Yuba Parke Ba	72 782
T M	Alameda Oakland	55 49
Thos	Sacramento Franklin	63 320
W S	Sutter Yuba	70 767
W W	El Dorado Grizzly	581180
Walker	Shasta Millvill	66 742
William	Plumas Quincy	62 917
William	San Joaquin Douglass	64 923
William	San Joaquin Douglass	64 927
William	Solano Suisan	69 206
William H	Yuba Marysville	72 969
Wm	Sacramento Ward 1	63 151
Wm	Sacramento Cosummes	63 395
Wm H	Nevada Nevada	61 260
WEBBER		
---	Amador Twp 2	55 289
---	Sierra La Porte	66 786
A	Nevada Washington	61 337
Adolph	Placer Todds Va	62 763
August	Sacramento Ward 4	63 551
Augustus	Sacramento Ward 4	63 496
C	San Francisco San Francisco 5	67 527
C	San Francisco San Francisco 2	67 734
C W	Alameda Brooklyn	55 120
Charles H	Contra Costa Twp 3	57 586
Charles*	El Dorado White Oaks	581301
Chas	Placer Twp 2	62 660
Chesley	Sacramento Brighton	63 209
D	Nevada Nevada	61 256
D	Nevada Nevada	61 275
D G	Sierra Downieville	661017
Daniel	Amador Twp 1	55 460
Elbridge G	Alameda Oakland	55 71
Frank	Alameda Brooklyn	55 140
Frederick	Yuba Linda	72 985
Fredrick	Plumas Quincy	62 978
G	San Joaquin Stockton	641037
George	Calaveras Twp 5	57 200
George	Calaveras Twp 5	57 247
George	Sierra Downieville	661017
H	Sacramento Ward 1	63 5
H C	Butte Ophir	56 754
Hannah	Sacramento Ward 4	63 583
Henry	San Francisco San Francisco 1	68 931
Henry	Solano Vacaville	69 361
Henry	Tuolumne Shawsfla	71 404
Isaac N	Placer Snowpoint	62 693
Issac*	Calaveras Twp 8	57 97
J	Sacramento Ward 4	63 607
J G	Butte Eureka	56 645
Jacob	Sacramento Ward 3	63 449
James	El Dorado Georgetown	58 706
John	Mariposa Twp 3	60 585
John	Nevada Nevada	61 241
John	Nevada Rough &	61 418
John	Plumas Meadow Valley	62 912
John*	Mariposa Twp 3	60 585
Jos	Sacramento Ward 3	63 444
Joseph	Sierra Gibsonville	66 856
L B	Sacramento Ward 4	63 597
Louis	Plumas Meadow Valley	62 899
Lowel	Marin Tomales	60 716
M N	Nevada Red Dog	61 541
Martin	San Francisco San Francisco 11	98 67
Matthew	San Diego Colorado	64 806

Name	County Locale	M653 RollPage
WEBBER		
O C	Nevada Nevada	61 325
O*	Nevada Washington	61 337
Paul	Yuba Marysville	72 936
Peter	Alameda Brooklyn	55 140
Peter	El Dorado Kelsey	581127
Robert	Nevada Bridgeport	61 473
Saml	San Francisco San Francisco 9	681079
Sarah	San Francisco San Francisco 3	67 46
Solomon M	Yuba Marysville	72 852
Solomon M	Yuba Marysville	72 857
Theodore	Santa Clara Gilroy	65 223
Thos	San Francisco San Francisco 1	68 896
William	Contra Costa Twp 1	57 528
William	San Francisco San Francisco 7	681377
Wm	Amador Twp 6	55 438
WEBBERD G		
Robinson	Sierra Downieville	661017
WEBBERS		
Pendleton	Santa Clara Fremont	65 435
WEBBLER		
Lowel	Marin Tomales	60 716
WEBBROCK		
Richard*	Yuba Long Bar	72 750
WEBBROOK		
Richard*	Yuba Long Bar	72 750
WEBBS		
John	Tehama Antelope	70 894
WEBBWICK		
Richard*	Yuba Long Bar	72 750
WEBELELL		
Henry	Placer Virginia	62 700
WEBELER		
William	Tuolumne Twp 1	71 202
WEBER		
C	San Francisco San Francisco 5	67 524
Charles	San Francisco San Francisco 7	681349
Charles	San Joaquin Stockton	641038
Charles M	San Joaquin Stockton	641025
D G	Sacramento Brighton	63 204
F R	Mariposa Twp 3	60 597
Frank	Alameda Brooklyn	55 150
Franklin	San Francisco San Francisco 7	681328
G R	Sonoma Salt Point	69 692
Henry E	San Francisco San Francisco 2	67 598
Jas A	Napa Napa	61 98
Joseph	San Joaquin Castoria	64 904
Julius	Sacramento Ward 4	63 507
Louis	Calaveras Twp 9	57 389
Rufus E	Calaveras Twp 6	57 122
W L	Butte Oregon	56 625
W S*	Butte Oregon	56 625
Wm	San Francisco San Francisco 1	68 825
WEBERMAN		
B H	Shasta Millvill	66 744
WEBIR		
W L*	Butte Oregon	56 625
WEBLER		
Nelson*	Placer Michigan	62 828
WEBLERD		
F	Sacramento Ward 4	63 606
WEBLIN		
George	Placer Yankee J	62 759
WEBSO		
W S*	Butte Oregon	56 625
WEBSTEE		
Geo*	Nevada Eureka	61 347
WEBSTER		
A B	Nevada Nevada	61 276
Albin B	Alameda Brooklyn	55 77
Alonzo	Contra Costa Twp 3	57 584
Alvin B	Alameda Brooklyn	55 77
Amos	Tuolumne Twp 1	71 253
Ann	San Bernardino San Salvador	64 654
Augustus	Trinity E Weaver	701060
B	El Dorado Placerville	58 860
C B	Solano Suisan	69 206
C F	San Francisco San Francisco 6	67 446
Charles	Solano Suisan	69 206
Charles A	Tulara Twp 1	71 99
Chas H	San Francisco San Francisco 10	350 67
Constant	Alameda Brooklyn	55 132
Daniel	El Dorado Georgetown	58 751
Daniel	Mariposa Twp 3	60 572
David	Siskiyou Yreka	69 141
Erastus W	Siskiyou Yreka	69 152
F W	Yuba Long Bar	72 772
Franklin	San Francisco San Francisco 9	681014
G R	Sacramento Ward 1	63 105
G W	Tuolumne Big Oak	71 128
Geo	Nevada Eureka	61 347
Geo	San Francisco San Francisco 2	67 685
Geo	San Joaquin Stockton	641036
Geo L	Butte Oregon	56 617
Geo*	Nevada Eureka	61 347

California 1860 Census Index

Name	County Locale	M653 Roll/Page
WEBSTER		
George	Contra Costa Twp 1	57 486
George	Placer Forest H	62 794
George	Sacramento Ward 4	63 549
George	Yuba Bear Rvr	721011
George C	Tuolumne Chinese	71 526
George S	Tuolumne Twp 1	71 214
George W	Contra Costa Twp 2	57 567
H	Nevada Nevada	61 280
H G	Butte Cascade	56 700
H H	Trinity Trinity	70 973
Horace	Alameda Oakland	55 64
Horace	Siskiyou Yreka	69 156
J	Nevada Grass Valley	61 201
J	Siskiyou Scott Va	69 39
J B	El Dorado Placerville	58 835
J B	San Joaquin Stockton	641056
J T	Nevada Grass Valley	61 210
J V	Alameda Brooklyn	55 108
Jacob E	Contra Costa Twp 2	57 563
Jas	Sonoma Sonoma	69 659
Jas K	San Francisco San Francisco 10	169 67
Jno	San Francisco San Francisco 5	67 553
Jno J W	San Francisco San Francisco 10	336 67
Jno L	San Francisco San Francisco 9	681009
John	Butte Cascade	56 703
John	Calaveras Twp 9	57 355
John	Shasta Horsetown	66 694
John	Sonoma Petaluma	69 549
John	Yolo Cottonwoood	72 659
John L	Yuba Marysville	72 884
John N	San Joaquin Stockton	641010
John R	San Bernardino San Salvador	64 644
John W	Alameda Oakland	55 75
Margt	San Francisco San Francisco 9	68 968
Mary	San Francisco San Francisco 6	67 427
Mary R	Alameda Oakland	55 31
Noah	Yuba Rose Bar	72 804
P	San Mateo Twp 2	65 112
Porter	San Francisco San Francisco 11	141 67
Preston R	Humbolt Union	59 181
R G	Mariposa Twp 3	60 597
Richd	San Francisco San Francisco 10	350 67
Robt	Napa Napa	61 97
S D	Siskiyou Callahan	69 10
S M	El Dorado Mountain	581187
Samuel	San Francisco San Francisco 7	681402
Samuel T	Yuba Marysville	72 873
Stephen R	Siskiyou Shasta Valley	69 119
T J	El Dorado Coloma	581123
T W	Yuba Long Bar	72 772
Thomas T	Sierra Downieville	66 953
W	Shasta Millvill	66 756
W P	Butte Eureka	56 652
Walernian	Tuolumne Big Oak	71 133
Waterman	Tuolumne Twp 4	71 133
William	Calaveras Twp 4	57 345
Wm J	Humbolt Pacific	59 130
WEBZA		
E B	Sacramento Granite	63 263
WEBZEL		
A	Shasta Shasta	66 759
WECH		
M	Nevada Grass Valley	61 213
WECHENA		
Florentina*	Sierra Downieville	66 970
WECHERA		
Florentinn	Sierra Downieville	66 970
WECHMAN		
Henry	Sierra Twp 5	66 945
WECK		
---	Trinity Trinindad Rvr	701048
Frank A	Humbolt Union	59 181
M	Nevada Grass Valley	61 213
WECKIHA		
Joseph	Siskiyou Callahan	69 12
WECKRHA		
Joseph	Siskiyou Callahan	69 12
WECKS		
John	Tuolumne Twp 2	71 394
WECNOR		
Ann*	San Francisco San Francisco 2	67 751
WECTMERE		
C M*	San Francisco San Francisco 5	67 514
WECTO		
James	Yuba Bear Rvr	721016
WEDD		
Lawnis*	El Dorado Georgetown	58 758
WEDDERSPON		
John	San Francisco San Francisco 2	67 745
WEDDING		
Jan	Solano Suisan	69 204

Name	County Locale	M653 Roll/Page
WEDDING		
Jane	Solano Suisan	69 204
John	Yuba Long Bar	72 755
John	Yuba Long Bar	72 755
Richd	Solano Suisan	69 212
WEDDLE		
Elizabeth	Napa Napa	61 81
Moses C	Napa Napa	61 69
William	Napa Napa	61 81
WEDDREIN		
Henry F*	Yuba Marysville	72 867
Henry*	Yuba Marysville	72 867
WEDDRIE		
George*	Alameda Oakland	55 54
WEDDWIN		
Henry*	Yuba Marysville	72 867
WEDE		
J L M*	El Dorado Georgetown	58 701
WEDEDRASS		
Lewis*	Yuba Long Bar	72 750
Louis	Yuba Long Bar	72 750
WEDEN		
Frederick	Siskiyou Yreka	69 151
WEDERIACO		
Jose	Los Angeles Los Angeles	59 323
WEDERICO		
Andres	Los Angeles Los Angeles	59 305
WEDERMOUTH		
John H	Calaveras Twp 4	57 335
WEDGER		
John	Butte Wyandotte	56 667
WEDGWOOD		
William	San Francisco San Francisco 8	681293
WEDHIGH		
Joseph*	El Dorado Georgetown	58 748
WEDIMER		
Henry	Humbolt Bucksport	59 160
WEDLOCK		
William	Tuolumne Twp 1	71 264
WEDMAN		
George	Placer Iona Hills	62 888
WEDSNY		
James*	Nevada Bridgeport	61 502
WEDTUGH		
Joseph*	El Dorado Georgetown	58 748
WEE		
---	Amador Twp 2	55 285
---	Amador Twp 5	55 353
---	Butte Oro	56 686
---	Butte Cascade	56 698
---	Butte Bidwell	56 708
---	Butte Bidwell	56 714
---	Calaveras Twp 5	57 220
---	Calaveras Twp 4	57 308
---	El Dorado Big Bar	58 734
---	El Dorado Big Bar	58 738
---	El Dorado Mud Springs	58 972
---	Mariposa Twp 1	60 661
---	Nevada Rough &	61 396
---	Placer Virginia	62 701
---	Placer Illinois	62 748
---	San Francisco San Francisco 4	681174
---	San Francisco San Francisco 4	681199
---	San Francisco San Francisco 11	145 67
---	Sierra Cox'S Bar	66 949
---	Trinity Grass Valley	70 962
---*	Nevada Red Dog	61 549
---*	San Francisco San Francisco 4	681199
---*	Shasta Shasta	66 669
Ah	Butte Cascade	56 698
Ah	Butte Bidwell	56 708
Che	San Francisco San Francisco 4	681189
Ching	Butte Bidwell	56 731
Fo	San Francisco San Francisco 11	159 67
Gaug	Butte Ophir	56 804
Ho	San Francisco San Francisco 4	681192
Hoy	San Francisco San Francisco 4	681203
Hung	San Francisco San Francisco 4	681167
Jaug	Butte Ophir	56 803
King	San Francisco San Francisco 11	161 67
Lee*	Butte Cascade	56 699
Low	San Francisco San Francisco 4	681189
Nah	Butte Cascade	56 698
Sing	Butte Bidwell	56 715
So	San Francisco San Francisco 4	681189
Sung*	Mariposa Twp 1	60 641
William	El Dorado Greenwood	58 727
Woi	San Francisco San Francisco 4	681189
Yang	Butte Ophir	56 805
Yup	Nevada Nevada	61 310
WEEAPLE		
Richard E	Yuba Marysville	72 959
WEED		
David R	Trinity North Fo	701023

Name	County Locale	M653 Roll/Page
WEED		
Deaderick	San Francisco San Francisco 7	681337
E E	Marin Novato	60 738
Edmond	Yolo Washington	72 602
Elizabeth	Nevada Rough &	61 396
Hampton	Napa Napa	61 97
Harriett	Solano Vacaville	69 337
Isaac L	Nevada Rough &	61 396
J H	San Francisco San Francisco 1	68 884
James	Sonoma Bodega	69 533
Joseph	San Francisco San Francisco 2	67 608
Louis	Sacramento Ward 4	63 512
O	Butte Chico	56 539
O E	El Dorado Kelsey	581138
William*	Placer Forest H	62 797
WEEDE		
John	Sierra Twp 5	66 942
WEEDEN		
Daniel	Sierra Downieville	661018
Doctor	Yolo Slate Ra	72 704
Richd	Stanislaus Emory	70 744
S E	Mariposa Twp 1	60 642
WEEDHAM		
Edwd	Sonoma Petaluma	69 553
WEEDIN		
Doctor	Yuba Slate Ro	72 704
S E	Mariposa Twp 1	60 642
WEEDLE		
William	Napa Hot Springs	61 81
WEEK		
Andrew R	Sierra Twp 5	66 947
J	Nevada Eureka	61 363
J W	Sierra Cox'S Bar	66 952
William H*	Yuba Marysville	72 893
WEEKERMAN		
John*	Butte Wyandotte	56 666
WEEKES		
Elva	San Joaquin Elkhorn	64 992
Saml	San Bernardino San Bernadino	64 634
WEEKFIELD		
Isaiah	Siskiyou Yreka	69 169
WEEKHAM		
Jas*	Napa Napa	61 87
WEEKLAND		
E P	Alameda Brooklyn	55 154
WEEKLY		
Mary*	Alameda Brooklyn	55 137
WEEKS		
Alfred	Alameda Washington	55 175
Branat	Santa Cruz Pescadero	66 643
Brauat*	Santa Cruz Pescadero	66 643
C J	San Francisco San Francisco 10	233 67
Chas	Tuolumne Jamestown	71 428
Daniel	Sierra La Porte	66 789
E J	San Francisco San Francisco 10	232 67
G P	San Francisco San Francisco 7	681337
George W	Sierra Twp 5	66 946
Henry	San Joaquin Elkhorn	64 976
J	Nevada Grass Valley	61 208
J E P	Sacramento Ward 4	63 583
J H	Nevada Grass Valley	61 208
J S	Butte Oregon	56 624
Jacob	Yolo Slate Ra	72 703
James	Santa Clara Burnett	65 255
John	Marin Cortemad	60 780
John	Tuolumne Shawsfla	71 394
John S	Trinity Red Bar	70 998
Mary	Santa Clara San Jose	65 313
Nelson	Tuolumne Twp 3	71 464
Parker	Sonoma Petaluma	69 584
R J	Klamath Orleans	59 217
R J	San Mateo Twp 2	65 126
Ruben	Siskiyou Yreka	69 135
Sumner	Marin Bolinas	60 748
Susan	San Bernardino San Salvador	64 652
T	San Francisco San Francisco 5	67 529
Thomas	Santa Cruz Santa Cruz	66 623
W C	Sonoma Petaluma	69 597
W H	Butte Cascade	56 692
W H	Sacramento Ward 1	63 38
W N	San Francisco San Francisco 10	218 67
W R	Butte Ophir	56 786
William	Los Angeles Los Angeles	59 379
William	Los Angeles Los Angeles	59 379
William	San Joaquin Stockton	641087
Wm H	Alameda Brooklyn	55 208
WEEL		
A	San Francisco San Francisco 5	67 476
Emile*	San Francisco San Francisco 2	67 670
Silvian	San Francisco San Francisco 5	67 479
WEELER		
J W*	Nevada Eureka	61 351
WEELEY		
Wm*	Amador Twp 2	55 281

Name	County Locale	M653 Roll	Page
WEELS			
J L M	El Dorado Georgetown	58	701
WEEMAN			
Henry	San Joaquin Elkhorn	64	953
WEEN			
La	Mariposa Twp 3	60	614
Lee	Butte Cascade	56	699
WEENER			
Wm	Santa Clara Santa Clara	65	466
WEER			
Jas*	San Francisco San Francisco 10 67		279
Lee*	Butte Cascade	56	699
WEERER			
Charles*	Yuba Fosters	72	829
WEESE			
James	Tulara Keeneysburg	71	45
WEESEG			
John	San Francisco San Francisco 2	67	782
WEESER			
Pete	Trinity Weaverville	70	1080
WEETMERE			
C M*	San Francisco San Francisco 5	67	514
WEETO			
James*	Yuba Bear Rvr	72	1016
WEEVER			
Charles	Yuba Foster B	72	829
WEFER			
Wm	Trinity Rearings	70	990
WEFF			
J	Sutter Bear Rvr	70	823
WEFLER			
John	Contra Costa Twp 1	57	492
WEFSELS			
Jno	Klamath Salmon	59	213
WEFSENBERG			
Peter F*	Marin Bolinas	60	745
WEGANSTINE			
G	El Dorado Placerville	58	834
WEGENER			
Christian San Francisco San Francisco 12 67			368
WEGER			
C	Sutter Sutter	70	813
WEGG			
Edwin	San Francisco San Francisco 7	68	1351
WEGGIN			
P*	Solano Vacaville	69	338
WEGGINGER			
Alart	Santa Clara Santa Clara	65	482
WEGGINS			
George W*	Calaveras Twp 7	57	1
P*	Solano Vacaville	69	338
WEH			
---	El Dorado Georgetown	58	680
WEHALE			
Jos	Butte Mountain	56	741
WEHARTER			
Leuis*	Mariposa Coulterville	60	677
WEHE			
Albert	Napa Napa	61	80
WEHEN			
---	Trinity Weaverville	70	1074
WEHER			
Charles F	Yuba Marysville	72	888
Jas A*	Napa Napa	61	98
WEHERGREN			
Frank L*	San Bernardino San Bernadino	64	634
WEHL			
Martin	El Dorado Georgetown	58	703
WEHLS			
John*	San Joaquin O'Neal	64	1003
WEHMALLER			
Wm	San Francisco San Francisco 10 67		339
WEHMAN			
Eli	San Bernardino S Timate	64	689
WEHN			
Henry	Siskiyou Yreka	69	143
WEHNER			
A W*	San Francisco San Francisco 10 67		294
WEHRING			
Chas	Nevada Bridgeport	61	468
WEHRTER			
John R*	San Bernardino San Bernadino	64	644
WEHS			
Harrt	Santa Cruz Santa Cruz	66	630
Harry*	Santa Cruz Santa Cruz	66	630
WEHUER			
A W*	San Francisco San Francisco 10 67		294
WEI			
---	Amador Twp 5	55	350
How	San Francisco San Francisco 3	67	54
WEIBER			
Alexander	Tuolumne Columbia	71	364
WEIBERT			
Cask	Alameda Brooklyn	55	79
Cath	Alameda Brooklyn	55	79
WEICHIL			
John*	Yuba Marysville	72	911
WEID			
Elizabeth*	Nevada Rough &	61	396
WEIDEMEYER			
Henry	Alameda Brooklyn	55	153
WEIDEMURS			
Louis	Tuolumne Shawsfla	71	379
WEIDENMILLER			
Fred	Alameda Brooklyn	55	141
WEIDENREICH			
Saml	San Francisco San Francisco 2	67	749
WEIDERHOLD			
Charles	San Francisco San Francisco 3	67	9
WEIDERSCHEIN			
August*	Yuba Marysville	72	902
WEIDERSCHWIN			
August*	Yuba Marysville	72	902
WEIDEUREICH			
Saml	San Francisco San Francisco 2	67	749
WEIDMAN			
Simon	Los Angeles San Juan	59	460
WEIF			
John	Sacramento Ward 1	63	14
WEIFFENBACH			
John	Siskiyou Yreka	69	135
Lydia	Siskiyou Yreka	69	136
WEIGEL			
E	Amador Twp 6	55	441
WEIGENER			
F O	San Francisco San Francisco 5	67	484
WEIGH			
H	San Francisco San Francisco 5	67	529
Mary J	Yolo Cache	72	594
WEIGHARD			
Chas	Calaveras Twp 9	57	364
WEIGHT			
George	El Dorado Greenwood	58	723
James	Tuolumne Montezuma	71	505
Wm	Santa Clara Fremont	65	441
WEIGHTMAN			
William E*	Yuba Marysville	72	880
WEIGLE			
Jacob	Yuba Marysville	72	958
WEIGLER			
Christ	Siskiyou Yreka	69	189
WEIGLESETT			
August*	Yuba Linda	72	994
WEIGNAL			
Samuel C	Calaveras Twp 9	57	368
WEIGRAL			
Samuel*	Calaveras Twp 9	57	368
WEIHER			
Mathias*	Sierra Scales D	66	802
WEIKER			
E*	Sierra Whiskey	66	844
WEIL			
A	San Francisco San Francisco 5	67	476
Abraham	Contra Costa Twp 2	57	546
David	Shasta Shasta	66	686
Emile*	San Francisco San Francisco 2	67	670
Henry	Nevada Bridgeport	61	470
Henry	Yuba Marysville	72	894
Jacob	Los Angeles Los Angeles	59	327
Jacob	Los Angeles Los Angeles	59	335
Jno	Sonoma Petaluma	69	607
John	Sierra Downieville	66	969
Joseph	San Bernardino Santa Barbara	64	155
L	Shasta Horsetown	66	689
M	Sonoma Petaluma	69	587
Marcus	San Bernardino Santa Barbara	64	155
Mary	Sonoma Petaluma	69	607
Meyer	Calaveras Twp 6	57	123
Morris	Siskiyou Yreka	69	186
S	Placer Auburn	62	564
Silvian	San Francisco San Francisco 5	67	479
W	El Dorado Placerville	58	860
W	Shasta Shasta	66	676
WEILD			
L	Calaveras Twp 6	57	119
WEILEGE			
Elisebeth	Sacramento Ward 4	63	555
WEILENIEUN			
Rebecca*	San Francisco San Francisco 8	68	1301
WEILENISUN			
Rebecca	San Francisco San Francisco 8	68	1301
WEILER			
Alexander	Tuolumne Twp 2	71	364
J W	Nevada Eureka	61	351
Jacob	Siskiyou Yreka	69	137
Lewis	San Francisco San Francisco 5	67	475
WEILEUISUN			
Rebecca*	San Francisco San Francisco 8	68	1301
WEILL			
Eli	San Francisco San Francisco 1	68	932
Henry	Tuolumne Columbia	71	337
Jacob	Tuolumne Shawsfla	71	397
Joseph	Tuolumne Columbia	71	321
R	San Francisco San Francisco 5	67	497
WEILLER			
L	San Francisco San Francisco 6	67	467
WEILLYE			
Ida	Alameda Brooklyn	55	154
WEILS			
E L	Nevada Bridgeport	61	469
J B	San Francisco San Francisco 1	68	929
WEILSDONE			
---	Mendocino Calpella	60	822
WEILSINEIM			
Rebecca*	San Francisco San Francisco 8	68	1301
WEIMAN			
L	Sacramento Ward 4	63	511
WEIMER			
Agnes	Sacramento Ward 3	63	425
Elijah	Fresno Twp 3	59	14
Frederick	Calaveras Twp 4	57	325
George	Tulara Visalia	71	111
Henry	Placer Auburn	62	561
John	San Luis Obispo San Luis Obispo	65	38
Joseph	El Dorado Coloma	58	1114
S	Amador Twp 5	55	368
WEIMERS			
Adelaide	San Joaquin Elliott	64	944
WEIMET			
David	Amador Twp 1	55	504
WEIMOLAND			
J P	Solano Vacaville	69	328
WEIN			
L	Solano Montezuma	69	368
WEINATE			
---	Mendocino Big Rvr	60	854
WEINBAGH			
Richard	Yuba Marysville	72	907
WEINBUSH			
Henry	Placer Yankee J	62	756
WEINER			
J	Sacramento American	63	170
Jacob	Sacramento Ward 4	63	541
John	Amador Twp 2	55	295
John	San Francisco San Francisco 10 67		311
Otto	San Francisco San Francisco 2	67	777
Phillip	Sierra Downieville	66	1012
WEINMAM			
F P*	Solano Benecia	69	281
WEINMAN			
F P*	Solano Benecia	69	281
WEINRICH			
Henry	Sacramento Ward 4	63	600
WEINSERANK			
Pauline*	San Francisco San Francisco 2	67	649
WEINSHENK			
Andrew	Los Angeles Los Angeles	59	366
WEINTERGIA			
George*	San Mateo Twp 1	65	48
WEINTRAUT			
Charles	San Francisco San Francisco 3	67	23
WEIP			
Frank	Tehama Red Bluff	70	921
John*	Sacramento Ward 1	63	14
WEIR			
Alexander	Tuolumne Twp 6	71	532
Benjamin	San Joaquin Douglass	64	928
Charles	Solano Suisan	69	215
Charles	Yuba Marysville	72	875
Eliza	Placer Todds Va	62	784
Ellen	San Francisco San Francisco 10 67		189
G D	Mariposa Twp 1	60	671
G P	Mariposa Twp 1	60	671
Geo W	Sonoma Washington	69	666
George	Placer Forest H	62	767
Hannie P	Marin San Rafael	60	767
Harriet P	Marin San Rafael	60	767
Hiram A	Sierra Poker Flats	66	841
Hiram H	Sierra Poker Flats	66	841
Jas	Sonoma Vallejo	69	630
Jas*	San Francisco San Francisco 10 67		279
John	Alameda Brooklyn	55	137
John	Sonoma Washington	69	677
John*	Placer Dutch Fl	62	713
Jos	Sacramento Ward 1	63	85
William	San Joaquin Elliott	64	941
William	Santa Cruz Soguel	66	590
William*	Santa Cruz Soguel	66	590
William*	Tulara Twp 3	71	51
Wm G	San Francisco San Francisco 10 67		194

California 1860 Census Index

Name	County Locale	M653 RollPage
WEIRD		
E	Alameda Oakland	55 42
WEIRNER		
Frederick	Calaveras Twp 4	57 325
Joseph	El Dorado Coloma	581114
WEIRS		
Charles	Yuba Marysville	72 875
Henry*	Sacramento Ward 4	63 588
Jesse E	Alameda Brooklyn	55 84
WEIRSRAMK		
A*	San Francisco San Francisco 2	67 648
WEIRTERGIA		
George*	San Mateo Twp 1	65 48
WEIS		
---	Fresno Twp 1	59 26
Eugene	Yuba Marysville	72 871
Geo	San Joaquin Stockton	641033
Jacob	Trinity Mouth Ca	701013
John	Plumas Quincy	62 920
Jos	Sacramento Ward 1	63 85
WEISBAUM		
Jacob*	Merced Twp 1	60 895
WEISE		
Auguste	Sacramento Ward 3	63 430
J	Tuolumne Don Pedro	71 163
Jon P	San Francisco San Francisco 7	681429
Joseph	Siskiyou Yreka	69 188
WEISEL		
Christopher	Sacramento Ward 4	63 536
Loyd	El Dorado Placerville	58 912
WEISELMAN		
Chas	Sacramento Ward 4	63 515
WEISENBORN		
F	San Francisco San Francisco 12	390 67
WEISENBURG		
Charles	Siskiyou Scott Va	69 48
WEISERMAN		
Diedrick*	Yuba Marysville	72 923
WEISMEYER		
James*	Placer Michigan	62 844
WEISMGER		
James*	Placer Michigan	62 844
WEISNOR		
---*	Mendocino Calpella	60 825
WEISS		
C L	Nevada Bridgeport	61 469
Charles	Sierra St Louis	66 863
H E	Butte Kimshaw	56 591
Henry	San Francisco San Francisco 11	117 67
Henry	San Francisco San Francisco 2	67 793
Henry*	Sacramento Ward 4	63 588
Louis	San Francisco San Francisco 7	681390
William	San Francisco San Francisco 7	681416
WEISSICH		
Wm O	Tuolumne Twp 4	71 137
Wm P	Tuolumne Big Oak	71 137
WEIST		
H E	Butte Kimshaw	56 591
R R	Tuolumne Twp 3	71 445
WEISTER		
Martin	Solano Fremont	69 380
WEISTKOFF		
Adam	Humbolt Bucksport	59 161
WEIT		
A*	El Dorado Placerville	58 871
WEITCH		
John	Calaveras Twp 5	57 209
WEITMAN		
William	San Francisco San Francisco 7	681397
WEIXEL		
Jacob	Los Angeles Los Angeles	59 334
WEIYEMAN		
Max*	San Francisco San Francisco 5	67 518
WEIZ		
Chas	San Francisco San Francisco 1	68 825
Joseph	Sierra Downieville	661031
WEIZEMAN		
Max*	San Francisco San Francisco 5	67 518
WEKEPER		
John	Solano Benecia	69 316
WEKES		
Henry M	San Bernardino San Bernadino	64 673
WEKS		
Nelson	Tuolumne Twp 3	71 464
WELAND		
C	San Francisco San Francisco 4	681218
John*	San Francisco San Francisco 10	227 67
WELB		
Jas	San Francisco San Francisco 1	68 838
WELBER		
Charles*	El Dorado White Oaks	581031
WELBERN		
David	Tuolumne Twp 2	71 407

Name	County Locale	M653 RollPage
WELBOWINE		
Delia*	Sacramento American	63 163
WELBRECH		
Hennan*	Siskiyou Yreka	69 148
Herman	Siskiyou Yreka	69 148
WELBUR		
W W	Sutter Butte	70 790
WELBWICK		
Richard*	Yuba Long Bar	72 750
WELBY		
D W	Sacramento Ward 1	63 134
James	Sacramento Ward 1	63 131
WELCH		
A	Sutter Yuba	70 771
Alexander	Yuba Fosters	72 839
Alfred	Santa Clara San Jose	65 319
Andrew	Sacramento Ward 3	63 438
Ann	San Francisco San Francisco 10	333 67
Ben	Sacramento Ward 1	63 139
C	Siskiyou Scott Ri	69 83
C H	Butte Hamilton	56 517
Charles	San Francisco San Francisco 2	67 569
Charles*	San Francisco San Francisco 7	681398
Chs	Stanislaus Empire	70 730
Crosby	Yolo Washington	72 563
Danl	San Francisco San Francisco 6	67 411
Danl J	Amador Twp 2	55 263
Delos	Tulara Twp 3	71 46
Delos	Tulara Twp 3	71 49
E	Sutter Butte	70 782
E M	Marin San Rafael	60 758
E W	Marin San Rafael	60 758
Edmund	San Francisco San Francisco 3	67 22
Edmund	San Francisco San Francisco 12	382 67
Edward	Sierra La Porte	66 784
Edward	Solano Vallejo	69 255
Edward	Solano Benecia	69 311
Edwd	San Francisco San Francisco 10	288 67
Elizabeth	Del Norte Crescent	58 631
Elizabeth	Del Norte Crescent	58 632
Ellen	San Francisco San Francisco 3	67 75
Ellen	San Francisco San Francisco 1	68 898
Ellen	Santa Clara San Jose	65 338
F W	Napa Hot Springs	61 1
Frank	Sonoma Sonoma	69 661
G C	San Bernardino Santa Ba	64 207
G W	Nevada Nevada	61 252
Geo	Sacramento Ward 3	63 432
Geo D	Sacramento Ward 1	63 139
H B	Sacramento Ward 3	63 431
Hanison	Solano Vallejo	69 245
Henry	Sacramento Granite	63 227
Henry	Siskiyou Yreka	69 156
Isaac	Santa Clara Santa Clara	65 497
J	Nevada Eureka	61 352
J	Sacramento Sutter	63 306
J	Sacramento Sutter	63 307
J C	Yolo Cache Crk	72 616
J J	Yolo Cache Crk	72 628
J M	San Francisco San Francisco 5	67 537
J W	Sutter Yuba	70 770
James	Calaveras Twp 5	57 146
James	El Dorado Coloma	581113
James	Plumas Quincy	62 989
James	Sacramento Ward 1	63 83
James	San Francisco San Francisco 9	681073
James	Sierra Twp 7	66 904
James	Yolo Putah	72 554
James C	Los Angeles Los Angeles	59 346
Jane	Yolo Cache	72 595
Jas	Placer Virginia	62 685
Jas	Sacramento Granite	63 264
Jas	San Bernardino San Bernadino	64 668
Jas	San Francisco San Francisco 10	337 67
Jas	Yolo Putah	72 549
Jno	Sacramento Ward 4	63 562
Jno	San Francisco San Francisco 10	194 67
John	Butte Ophir	56 792
John	Calaveras Twp 5	57 239
John	Calaveras Twp 4	57 312
John	Colusa Grand Island	57 470
John	Marin Cortemad	60 779
John	Napa Hot Springs	61 11
John	Sacramento Sutter	63 290
John	Sacramento Sutter	63 306
John	Sacramento Sutter	63 306
John	Sacramento Sutter	63 307
John	San Francisco San Francisco 3	67 22
John	San Francisco San Francisco 1	68 889
John	San Francisco San Francisco 1	68 900
John	Santa Clara Burnett	65 254

Name	County Locale	M653 RollPage
WELCH		
John	Santa Clara Redwood	65 451
John	Santa Cruz Pajaro	66 574
John	Sierra Downieville	661006
John	Sierra Forest C	66 909
John	Solano Vallejo	69 249
John	Solano Vallejo	69 264
John	Solano Benecia	69 292
John	Solano Benecia	69 314
John	Tehama Pasakent	70 858
John	Tuolumne Don Pedro	71 540
John	Yolo Cache Crk	72 665
John	Yuba New York	72 721
John	Yuba Rose Bar	72 818
John	Yuba Marysville	72 874
John C	San Francisco San Francisco 9	681035
John C	San Joaquin Elkhorn	64 956
John H*	Tulara Visalia	71 103
John*	Tuolumne Twp 6	71 540
Jos	Butte Bidwell	56 710
Julia	Nevada Rough &	61 407
Julia	San Francisco San Francisco 6	67 468
L	Tuolumne Twp 4	71 156
Laurence	Nevada Rough &	61 395
Lewis	Tuolumne Knights	71 529
M	Butte Kimshaw	56 577
M	Nevada Nevada	61 245
M	Nevada Washington	61 331
M	Nevada Washington	61 341
M	Sacramento Franklin	63 307
M	San Francisco San Francisco 2	67 663
M	Siskiyou Cottonwood	69 102
Margaret	Santa Clara San Jose	65 377
Maria	San Francisco San Francisco 2	67 704
Martin	Nevada Rough &	61 404
Martin	Sacramento Cosumnes	63 399
Mary	San Francisco San Francisco 10	277 67
Mary	San Francisco San Francisco 10	320 67
Mary	San Francisco San Francisco 12	381 67
Mary	Santa Clara San Jose	65 385
Matthew	San Francisco San Francisco 12	382 67
Medad	Siskiyou Shasta Rvr	69 112
Meelad*	Siskiyou Shasta Rvr	69 112
Michael	Amador Twp 3	55 378
Michael	Calaveras Twp 5	57 184
Michael	Sacramento Ward 3	63 479
Michael	San Francisco San Francisco 10	300 67
Michael	San Francisco San Francisco 10	353 67
Michael	Santa Clara San Jose	65 344
Michael	Sierra Twp 7	66 889
Nancy	Butte Chico	56 538
Nicholas	Calaveras Twp 5	57 215
P	Amador Twp 1	55 478
Patk	San Francisco San Francisco 10	342 67
Patrick	Del Norte Klamath	58 654
Peter	Sonoma Petaluma	69 562
Phillip	Solano Vallejo	69 264
R	San Francisco San Francisco 1	68 921
R E	Sutter Sutter	70 809
Richard	Colusa Monroeville	57 440
Richard	Marin Bolinas	60 740
Richard	Solano Vallejo	69 243
Robert	Sacramento Ward 1	63 130
Robert	Sacramento Ward 1	63 131
Robert	San Francisco San Francisco 3	67 31
Robert	Santa Clara San Jose	65 377
Robert	Sierra Twp 5	66 920
Robert	Siskiyou Scott Va	69 48
Robt	San Francisco San Francisco 12	382 67
Roceval C	Marin Bolinas	60 728
S	Tuolumne Big Oak	71 156
S D	Butte Oregon	56 625
Samuel	Yuba Long Bar	72 742
Samuel E*	Yuba Long Bar	72 742
Sarah	Nevada Washington	61 331
Sarah	Sacramento Ward 3	63 463
Stephen	Siskiyou Cottonwoood	69 97
T G	Sacramento Lee	63 210
Teresa	San Francisco San Francisco 2	67 792
Teresa	San Joaquin Castoria	64 905
Thomas	Tuolumne Twp 2	71 355
Thomas	Yuba Marysville	72 914
Thos	Butte Cascade	56 695
Thos	Butte Bidwell	56 732
Thos	Napa Hot Springs	61 8
Thos	Placer Secret R	62 615
Thos	Placer Virginia	62 673
W	Sacramento Sutter	63 308

Name	County Locale	M653 RollPage	Name	County Locale	M653 RollPage	Name	County Locale	M653 RollPage
WELCH			**WELKER**			**WELLIR**		
W	Sacramento Ward 4	63 607	J W	Siskiyou Scott Va	69 33	Silas*	Napa Yount	61 33
W	Yolo Cache Crk	72 616	Louis	Tuolumne Twp 5	71 513	**WELLIS**		
W	Yolo Cache Crk	72 618	Q P	Klamath Salmon	59 209	Richd	Butte Ophir	56 773
W J	Tehama Antelope	70 897	**WELKESON**			**WELLMAN**		
W P	Yolo Cache Crk	72 597	P C	San Francisco San Francisco 9	68 997	C	Siskiyou Scott Ri	69 81
William	San Luis Obispo San Luis Obispo	65 7	**WELKINS**			Daniel	Yuba Suida	72 995
William	Siskiyou Yreka	69 147	Chapman	Amador Twp 4	55 240	E	Butte Ophir	56 784
William	Tulara Twp 3	71 62	E G	El Dorado Georgetown	58 674	E	Siskiyou Scott Ri	69 81
Wm	Amador Twp 6	55 439	Wilkins	Tuolumne Twp 2	71 364	Henry	Calaveras Twp 10	57 263
Wm	Butte Ophir	56 781	**WELKS**			John	Sierra Twp 5	66 940
Wm	Sacramento Ward 1	63 131	William	Tulara Visalia	71 83	O J	Yuba Rose Bar	72 796
Wm	Sacramento Ward 4	63 516	**WELL**			**WELLNAME**		
Wm	Sacramento Ward 4	63 519	Andrew	Amador Twp 1	55 465	John	Solano Vacaville	69 345
Wm	Sacramento Ward 4	63 587	Henry H	Sacramento Granite	63 249	**WELLOR**		
Wm	Santa Clara Alviso	65 408	James	Tulara Visalia	71 98	John	Sierra Gibsonville	66 851
Wm	Sonoma Santa Rosa	69 391	John D	Yuba Slate Ro	72 705	Landro	San Francisco San Francisco 9	68 945
WELCHAEFF			L W	Mariposa Twp 3	60 547	Leaudn*	San Francisco San Francisco 9	68 945
F	Yuba Long Bar	72 752	Simon*	Yuba Parks Ba	72 782	P C*	Butte Kimshaw	56 592
WELCHE			**WELLAT**			**WELLS**		
G W	Nevada Nevada	61 252	Adam	Sierra Poker Flats	66 841	---*	Placer Auburn	62 569
WELCHELL			**WELLE**			A	Nevada Eureka	61 348
M*	Sacramento Mississipi	63 186	W*	Mendocino Anderson	60 867	A	Shasta Millvill	66 725
WELCHER			**WELLENAN**			A	Tehama Lassen	70 866
G	Siskiyou Scott Va	69 60	Daniel*	Yuba Linda	72 995	A F	Shasta Shasta	66 662
WELCKER			**WELLENDORF**			A F	Siskiyou Yreka	69 184
G*	Siskiyou Scott Va	69 60	Oscar	San Joaquin Stockton	641029	A G	Yolo No E Twp	72 672
WELCKES			**WELLER**			A G	Yuba North Ea	72 672
G*	Siskiyou Scott Va	69 60	A B	Nevada Eureka	61 372	A M	Nevada Eureka	61 344
WELCOB			Aaron	Siskiyou Scott Va	69 44	A V*	Nevada Eureka	61 356
Walter	San Joaquin Castoria	64 909	Charles	Amador Twp 1	55 461	Ab	Nevada Eureka	61 356
WELCON			Charles L	Alameda Brooklyn	55 93	Alex	Klamath Trinidad	59 223
James S	Tuolumne Sonora	71 484	Charles S*	Alameda Brooklyn	55 93	Alfred	Nevada Rough &	61 401
WELCOPE			Chas L*	San Francisco San Francisco 8	681313	B W	Tehama Red Bluff	70 909
John	San Francisco San Francisco 9	681105	E	El Dorado Coloma	581070	Benjamin H	Sierra Pine Grove	66 827
WELCOPS			Ebanezer*	Napa Napa	61 69	C	Butte Ophir	56 791
John*	San Francisco San Francisco 9	681105	Elias	Santa Clara Gilroy	65 237	C	Nevada Eureka	61 344
WELCOT			Frank	Tehama Red Bluff	70 921	C C	Placer Rattle Snake	62 634
Oscar	Placer Goods	62 699	Geo L	Trinity Trinity	70 971	Catherine	El Dorado Greenwood	58 709
WELCOX			George E	San Joaquin Stockton	641044	Charity	Siskiyou Yreka	69 184
Charles	Yuba Bear Rvr	721009	Gustane	Yuba Marysville	72 968	Charles	Marin Bolinas	60 740
WELD			H	Yuba Rose Bar	72 810	Charles	San Joaquin Elkhorn	64 972
Benjamin G	San Diego Colorado	64 812	H O	Santa Clara Alviso	65 405	Charles C	San Mateo Twp 2	65 120
Descartes	Placer Auburn	62 578	John	San Francisco San Francisco 1	68 918	Chas	Sacramento Ward 1	63 10
Edward*	Placer Christia	62 736	John	Sierra Gibsonville	66 851	Chas	Santa Clara Freemont	65 416
Edwin J F	Contra Costa Twp 1	57 531	John B	Alameda Brooklyn	55 93	Chas	Santa Clara Santa Clara	65 508
John	Tehama Moons	70 853	Lyman	Amador Twp 2	55 308	Chester	Plumas Meadow Valley	62 900
WELDEN			Nathan	Nevada Rough &	61 420	Chester W	San Francisco 2	67 587
A*	Calaveras Twp 9	57 414	Nathaniel	Nevada Rough &	61 420		San Francisco	
Albert*	Sacramento Cosummes	63 391	P C	Butte Kimshaw	56 592	Christopher	San Joaquin Elkhorn	64 982
Allen	Placer Yankee J	62 780	Peter W	San Francisco San Francisco 10	351	D	El Dorado Placerville	58 850
Allen J	Plumas Quincy	62 921			67	D S	Sonoma Petaluma	69 605
Chris	Sacramento Franklin	63 331	S E	Sacramento Ward 4	63 525	David	Calaveras Twp 4	57 342
W	El Dorado Diamond	58 796	Silas	Napa Yount	61 33	Dexter	San Francisco San Francisco 7	681427
William	Placer Yankee J	62 779	Wm	Butte Kimshaw	56 607	Dough	Nevada Little Y	61 534
WELDER			**WELLES**			E	Butte Kimshaw	56 595
John	San Francisco San Francisco 7	681394	Aaron*	Siskiyou Scott Va	69 44	E	Santa Clara Fremont	65 430
WELDES			**WELLIAR**			E J	El Dorado Georgetown	58 683
Allen	Tuolumne Shawsfla	71 393	Sallie*	Alameda Oakland	55 59	E L	Sonoma Petaluma	69 608
WELDON			**WELLICK**			E P	Sutter Sutter	70 801
David K	San Francisco San Francisco 11	155	Christina	San Francisco San Francisco 7	681398	E S	Sonoma Petaluma	69 605
		67	**WELLIE**			Ed R	Sacramento Ward 1	63 128
George	Calaveras Twp 5	57 172	Hannah	Yuba Marysville	72 892	Edgar*	Sacramento Ward 4	63 613
James	Humbolt Eureka	59 166	**WELLIMAN**			Edward	San Francisco San Francisco 2	67 777
Josep	Solano Vacaville	69 357	William	Colusa Colusi	57 422	Eli	Sacramento Brighton	63 194
Josip	Solano Vacaville	69 357	**WELLIN**			Elizabeth	Tuolumne Don Pedro	71 542
S	El Dorado Mud Springs	58 969	Silas*	Napa Yount	61 33	Ellen	San Bernardino San Salvador	64 657
Thofmas	Solano Benecia	69 318	**WELLING**			Evein	Santa Clara Almaden	65 270
Thomas	Solano Benecia	69 318	Charles G	San Francisco San Francisco 1	68 807	F	San Francisco San Francisco 4	681231
William	Tulara Twp 3	71 57	Jno W	San Francisco San Francisco 9	68 965	F	San Joaquin Stockton	641099
WELDY			**WELLINGHAM**			F H	San Francisco San Francisco 5	67 505
N L	Tuolumne Twp 1	71 229	Anderson	Tuolumne Knights	71 530	Franklin	Klamath Salmon	59 213
Wm	Los Angeles Tejon	59 527	Ellen	Tuolumne Twp 3	71 436	Franklin	Plumas Quincy	62 956
WELEH			Peter*	Nevada Red Dog	61 544	Genell	Tehama Cottonwood	70 902
William	Siskiyou Yreka	69 147	**WELLINGTON**			Geo	Sacramento Natonia	63 278
WELER			C	Tehama Red Bluff	70 927	Geo	Sacramento Georgian	63 340
Kendall	Calaveras Twp 7	57 41	Danl	Sacramento Granite	63 230	Geo H	Amador Twp 2	55 264
WELETEN			Edmond	Tuolumne Shawsfla	71 395	George	Contra Costa Twp 3	57 602
Smythe	San Joaquin Stockton	641017	Edwd	Nevada Rough &	61 427	George	San Joaquin Douglass	64 915
WELEY			Elijah	Yolo No E Twp	72 669	George	San Joaquin Oneal	64 933
George	Yuba Marysville	72 969	Fred	Placer Rattle Snake	62 626	George	Santa Clara Santa Clara	65 519
J R*	Sacramento Georgian	63 347	Herth*	San Francisco San Francisco 1	68 918	George	Sierra Twp 5	66 918
WELGONG			Hertt*	San Francisco San Francisco 1	68 918	H	Nevada Nevada	61 323
Peter	Los Angeles Los Angeles	59 342	J W	Tuolumne Twp 3	71 445	H H	Trinity Douglas	70 979
WELGRARE			James	Tulara Twp 2	71 28	H P	Nevada Eureka	61 373
Henry*	Napa Clear Lake	61 134	Jno	Butte Kimshaw	56 585	H T	Butte Oregon	56 614
WELGRAVE			John	Tuolumne Sonora	71 238	H W	Nevada Grass Valley	61 153
Henry*	Napa Clear Lake	61 134	John K	Tuolumne Twp 3	71 445	H*	Nevada Nevada	61 323
WELHELMI			M	Butte Kimshaw	56 585	H*	Nevada Eureka	61 372
Amelia*	San Francisco San Francisco 3	67 31	Newton	Los Angeles Elmonte	59 252	Hamilton	Napa Yount	61 41
WELHITE			W	Calaveras Twp 9	57 409	Hamitton	Napa Yount	61 41
E W	El Dorado Placerville	58 837	Wm A	Tuolumne Twp 2	71 383	Hannah	Nevada Grass Valley	61 168
WELICH			**WELLINSHAM**			Hannah	Nevada Nevada	61 239
Christina	El Dorado Coloma	581074	Anderson	Tuolumne Twp 6	71 530	Harriet	El Dorado Georgetown	58 682
WELKER			**WELLIOR**			Harriet	San Francisco San Francisco 6	67 440
G	Siskiyou Scott Va	69 60	J W	Mariposa Twp 3	60 547	Henry	Sierra Twp 5	66 918

California 1860 Census Index

Name	County Locale	M653 RollPage
WELLS		
Henry J	San Francisco San Francisco 4	681120
Hiram A	Sierra Twp 5	66 922
Howard	Tuolumne Chinese	71 523
Hudsin*	Siskiyou Shasta Rvr	69 114
Hudson	Siskiyou Shasta Rvr	69 114
Isadore*	Placer Auburn	62 594
J	Nevada Grass Valley	61 162
J	Santa Clara Alviso	65 401
J	Tehama Cottonwood	70 902
J C	Nevada Rough &	61 401
J S	Calaveras Twp 9	57 372
J T	Mariposa Twp 3	60 596
J W	Sacramento Ward 4	63 557
James	Mendocino Little L	60 831
James	San Francisco San Francisco 8	681288
James	San Francisco San Francisco 9	68 941
James	Santa Clara San Jose	65 345
James	Sierra Pine Grove	66 823
James	Tulara Twp 1	71 99
James A	San Bernardino Santa Barbara	64 204
James P	Trinity Trinity	70 970
James*	Tulara Visalia	71 99
Jas	Mariposa Twp 1	60 949
Jas	Sacramento Granite	63 261
Jeffrey	Yuba New York	72 723
Jeymour	Sacramento American	63 162
Jno N	Sacramento Granite	63 229
John	El Dorado White Oaks	581020
John	El Dorado Spanish	581125
John	El Dorado Kelsey	581140
John	Napa Hot Springs	61 13
John	Nevada Grass Valley	61 168
John	Placer Goods	62 699
John	Sacramento Franklin	63 324
John	San Francisco San Francisco 9	68 959
John	San Joaquin Elkhorn	64 969
John	San Joaquin Elkhorn	64 978
John	Sonoma Petaluma	69 600
John	Yolo Slate Ra	72 718
John	Yuba New York	72 718
John R	Butte Ophir	56 776
John S	San Joaquin Stockton	641024
John W	Sacramento Cosummes	63 380
John W	Trinity Weaverville	701080
John*	Alameda Brooklyn	55 141
Josiah	Tehama Red Bluff	70 907
Killy	Mariposa Twp 3	60 601
Kitty	Mariposa Twp 3	60 601
L H	Yuba Timbucto	72 787
L J	Sacramento Georgian	63 347
L*	Sacramento Ward 4	63 550
Leonard	Yuba Rose Bar	72 809
Levi	Humbolt Eureka	59 177
Lucinda	San Joaquin Elkhorn	64 982
Luther	Marin San Rafael	60 773
Lyman	San Francisco San Francisco 6	67 459
M	Nevada Eureka	61 371
M	Sacramento Alabama	63 411
M	Tehama Red Bluff	70 910
M H	Butte Oregon	56 609
M J	Mariposa Twp 1	60 649
Madison	Los Angeles Tejon	59 536
Milton	El Dorado Georgetown	58 700
Morgan	Tulara Visalia	71 18
N	Stanislaus Empire	70 728
N V	San Francisco San Francisco 6	67 442
Nancy	San Francisco San Francisco 7	681439
Oscar	Sierra La Porte	66 766
Oscar	Yuba Marysville	72 978
Oscur	Sierra La Porte	66 766
Otho	San Bernardino San Salvador	64 656
P	Nevada Eureka	61 348
P	Nevada Eureka	61 356
P	Nevada Eureka	61 374
P	Tehama Red Bluff	70 926
Peter	Amador Twp 4	55 256
R	Sacramento Cosummes	63 405
R B	Trinity W Weaver	701054
R W	Klamath Liberty	59 242
Robert	San Francisco San Francisco 9	681020
Robert	San Francisco San Francisco 7	681348
Russel	Sierra Twp 5	66 924
Russell	Sierra Twp 5	66 924
Russell	Yolo No E Twp	72 680
Russell	Yuba North Ea	72 680
S*	Sacramento Ward 4	63 550
Sam A	San Francisco San Francisco 3	67 85
Saml	Sacramento Sutter	63 305
Saml	Santa Clara Santa Clara	65 517
Saml P	Yuba Marysville	72 845
Samuel	San Joaquin Douglass	64 919
Sarah	Santa Clara San Jose	65 375
Seth	San Francisco San Francisco 9	68 988
Soloman	El Dorado Mud Springs	58 951
T	San Francisco San Francisco 4	681231
WELLS		
T	Tehama Red Bluff	70 906
Thomas	Calaveras Twp 10	57 282
Thomas	Humbolt Eureka	59 164
Thomas	Placer Auburn	62 594
Thomas*	Mendocino Big Rvr	60 853
Thos	Butte Ophir	56 763
Thos	Sacramento Lee	63 218
Thos	San Francisco San Francisco 9	681084
Thos D	Amador Twp 1	55 463
W	Sacramento Brighton	63 205
W	San Francisco San Francisco 1	68 921
W A	San Francisco San Francisco 7	681332
W R	Sonoma Petaluma	69 605
W W	Amador Twp 2	55 264
Walter	San Francisco San Francisco 1	68 865
Wen E*	Mariposa Twp 1	60 949
West	San Francisco San Francisco 4	681109
Willam	San Francisco San Francisco 5	67 546
William	Amador Twp 3	55 379
William	San Francisco San Francisco 9	681064
William	San Francisco San Francisco 5	67 546
William	Yuba Rose Par	72 795
William E	Yuba Marysville	72 904
William H	Contra Costa Twp 2	57 561
William H	Solano Vacaville	69 346
William P	Amador Twp 4	55 237
William S	Solano Fairfield	69 197
Williums	Calaveras Twp 6	57 114
Wm	San Francisco San Francisco 2	67 676
Wm	Sonoma Armally	69 504
Wm	Sonoma Sonoma	69 638
Wm E	Mariposa Twp 1	60 649
Wm H	Mariposa Twp 1	60 635
Wm W	Plumas Quincy	62 961
Won E	Mariposa Twp 1	60 649
WELLSA F		
Foote	Shasta Shasta	66 662
WELLSA		
Sallie*	Alameda Oakland	55 59
WELLSCOTT		
Theo	Sonoma Sonoma	69 654
WELLSLEY		
John	Yolo Cache	72 641
WELLSON		
H	Amador Twp 6	55 439
WELMARCUS		
J H	Tuolumne Twp 2	71 391
WELMOT		
S A*	Napa Clear Lake	61 119
WELNER		
Delorns	Contra Costa Twp 1	57 483
WELOST		
M	Nevada Grass Valley	61 154
WELPIDYS		
Martin	Calaveras Twp 10	57 290
WELSAE		
D	Butte Hamilton	56 517
WELSAN		
W T*	Mariposa Twp 3	60 621
WELSCH		
Jas	Sacramento Natonia	63 283
WELSEY		
Richard	Solano Vacaville	69 347
William	Solano Vacaville	69 363
WELSH		
A J	Sierra Grizzly	661058
Abram	Alameda Brooklyn	55 84
Andrew	Sierra Pine Grove	66 820
Annie	San Francisco San Francisco 4	681148
Bobert	Sierra La Porte	66 787
Chas	El Dorado Georgetown	58 696
Chris	El Dorado Georgetown	58 696
Daniel	Yuba Marysville	72 924
De Los	Yuba Marysville	72 935
Delos	Yuba Marysville	72 935
Dward	Yuba Marysville	72 924
Edward	Sierra La Porte	66 784
Edward	Yuba Marysville	72 924
Ellen	Tuolumne Big Oak	71 125
Ellen	Tuolumne Twp 4	71 127
Enrigue	Contra Costa Twp 2	57 549
Gillermo	Contra Costa Twp 3	57 585
Henry	Placer Forest H	62 803
Henry	Tuolumne Columbia	71 297
Henry J	San Francisco San Francisco 12	377 67
J	San Joaquin Stockton	641096
J O	Shasta Shasta	66 735
James	Alameda Oakland	55 15
James	Placer Iona Hills	62 869
James	Shasta Shasta	66 731
James	Sierra Twp 7	66 904
James	Yuba Marysville	72 851
James F	Placer Auburn	62 559
James W	Yuba Marysville	72 947
WELSH		
Jno	Butte Kimshaw	56 586
Joel	Humbolt Mattole	59 125
John	Contra Costa Twp 3	57 607
John	Los Angeles Los Angeles	59 328
John	Plumas Quincy	621002
John	San Francisco San Francisco 7	681373
John	San Francisco San Francisco 2	67 628
John	San Joaquin Douglass	64 923
John	Sierra Downieville	661006
John	Sierra La Porte	66 767
John	Solano Benecia	69 284
John	Yuba Marysville	72 874
John	Solano Vacaville	69 357
Joseph	San Francisco San Francisco 1	68 816
Joseph	Sonoma Armally	69 511
Juan	Contra Costa Twp 2	57 549
Julea	Yuba Marysville	72 859
Julia	Yuba Marysville	72 854
Julia	Yuba Marysville	72 857
Maggie	Alameda Oakland	55 18
Margt	San Francisco San Francisco 1	68 856
Michael	Placer Folsom	62 640
Michael	Shasta Shasta	66 683
Mike	Yuba Rose Bar	72 801
Morris	San Francisco San Francisco 1	68 842
Morris	Sierra La Porte	66 787
Nicholas	Placer Yankee J	62 758
Oliver	Placer Michigan	62 829
P	Calaveras Twp 8	57 75
P Y	Merced Twp 2	60 923
Patrick	Calaveras Twp 9	57 354
Patrick J	Yuba Marysville	72 893
Paul	San Francisco San Francisco 1	68 839
Richard	San Francisco San Francisco 9	681047
Richd	San Francisco San Francisco 1	68 816
Robert*	Sierra La Porte	66 787
Sam*	Mariposa Twp 3	60 566
Saml	San Francisco San Francisco 1	68 910
Spencer	Yuba Marysville	72 939
Stephen	Tuolumne Twp 1	71 214
T J	Butte Oregon	56 611
Thomas	Alameda Oakland	55 15
Thomas	Alameda Brooklyn	55 211
Thomas	Placer Forest H	62 769
Thomas	Placer Forest H	62 801
Thomas	Sierra La Porte	66 769
Thomas	Sierra Gibsonville	66 858
Thomas	Yuba Marysville	72 914
Thos	San Francisco San Francisco 2	67 655
Thos	San Francisco San Francisco 1	68 817
Walter	Contra Costa Twp 2	57 569
William	Placer Iona Hills	62 886
Wm	Butte Kimshaw	56 577
Wm	San Francisco San Francisco 2	67 568
WELSHER		
P	Butte Ophir	56 784
P	San Francisco San Francisco 5	67 521
WELSHIRE		
Henry	San Bernardino San Salvador	64 643
WELSLEY		
John	Yolo Cache Crk	72 641
WELSON		
A*	Calaveras Twp 9	57 414
Charly	Tuolumne Twp 2	71 403
Frances*	Alameda Brooklyn	55 100
Jonus	San Bernardino Santa Barbara	64 181
P A	San Francisco San Francisco 3	67 49
P H*	Alameda Oakland	55 8
T*	Nevada Eureka	61 348
Thomas	Tuolumne Twp 1	71 266
WELSOR		
Sam*	Mariposa Twp 3	60 566
WELSY		
J R*	Sacramento Georgian	63 347
WELTHCOTT		
Theo	Sonoma Sonoma	69 654
WELTHY		
E	El Dorado Placerville	58 854
WELTING		
Danl	Butte Chico	56 552
WELTON		
Bay	Sierra Downieville	66 995
E W	El Dorado Placerville	58 851
Fwilliam	El Dorado Georgetown	58 760
Isaac	Nevada Red Dog	61 553
J A	Nevada Bridgeport	61 486
John F	Del Norte Crescent	58 631
John F	Del Norte Crescent	58 632
John S	Del Norte Klamath	58 652
Merrit	San Francisco San Francisco 11	105 67
Wm	Sonoma Bodega	69 521
WELTORRULLE		
J R*	Napa Hot Springs	61 23
WELTORVULLE		
J R*	Napa Hot Springs	61 23

Name	County Locale	M653 Roll	Page
WELTSEY			
W	El Dorado Placerville	58	889
WELTY			
Amos	Butte Kimshaw	56	605
Andrew	Butte Ophir	56	780
D W	Sacramento Ward 1	63	134
Geo	Sacramento Ward 3	63	430
Jacob	Sacramento Ward 1	63	130
Jacob	Sacramento Ward 1	63	131
Jacob	Yolo Washington	72	571
John	El Dorado White Oaks	581006	
WELVANTON			
Lewis	Mariposa Coulterville	60	677
WELVARTOR			
Leuis*	Mariposa Coulterville	60	677
WELVERTON			
Lewis*	Mariposa Coulterville	60	677
WELVIN			
William*	El Dorado Cold Spring	581101	
WELZEN			
Anna*	San Francisco San Francisco 3	67	48
WELZER			
Ann	San Francisco San Francisco 3	67	48
WELZIN			
Anna*	San Francisco San Francisco 3	67	48
WEM			
---	El Dorado White Oaks	581033	
---*	Sacramento Ward 3	63	488
WEMER			
Andrew	Del Norte Crescent	58	636
WEMPH			
Henry	Humbolt Eureka	59	166
WEMPLE			
V	Nevada Eureka	61	382
WEMUK			
---	Fresno Twp 2	59	89
WEN			
---	El Dorado Salmon Falls	581046	
---	El Dorado Georgetown	58	762
---	Nevada Bridgeport	61	506
---	Tuolumne Chinese	71	510
---	Yolo No E Twp	72	680
---	Yuba North Ea	72	680
Jacob	Alameda Brooklyn	55	79
Jas	Sacramento Brighton	63	200
Shee	San Francisco San Francisco 10	67	356
Suj	El Dorado Big Bar	58	738
WENA			
---	San Bernardino S Timate	64	723
WENARS			
Henry	Tuolumne Columbia	71	334
WENBAN			
Simeon	Sierra Twp 7	66	892
WENBERY			
F	Butte Ophir	56	765
WENBESY			
F	Butte Ophir	56	765
WENCH			
Joseph*	San Francisco San Francisco 5	67	481
WENCHELL			
George*	Sierra Gibsonville	66	859
WENDAL			
Lewis	Humbolt Eureka	59	165
WENDALL			
August	San Francisco San Francisco 1	68	906
Charles	Calaveras Twp 6	57	174
John	Yuba Marysville	72	882
Thos	Yuba New York	72	741
WENDEL			
Peter	El Dorado Coloma	581108	
WENDELL			
James	San Francisco San Francisco 8	681305	
Lemina*	Del Norte Crescent	58	620
WENDER			
Angus	San Francisco San Francisco 7	681364	
WENDERLY			
J P*	El Dorado Greenwood	58	715
WENDHALLON			
Jacob	Nevada Rough &	61	413
WENDHALLOW			
Jacob	Nevada Rough &	61	413
WENDLER			
Dons*	Alameda Brooklyn	55	164
Doris*	Alameda Brooklyn	55	164
WENDT			
Herman	San Francisco San Francisco 10	67	211
John	San Francisco San Francisco 1	68	905
WENEE			
T M	El Dorado Greenwood	58	730
WENEGAR			
William	San Diego Colorado	64	810
WENG			
---	Mariposa Twp 3	60	607
---	Trinity Arkansas	701004	
WENG			
--- *	Trinity E Weaver	701060	
---*	Sacramento Ward 1	63	72
Ar	Trinity Mouth Ca	701014	
Orange	Yuba Bear Rvr	721012	
Sang*	Mariposa Twp 1	60	641
To	Mariposa Twp 3	60	607
WENGALE			
Jos	San Francisco San Francisco 10	67	315
WENGATE			
Jas*	San Francisco San Francisco 10	67	315
WENGER			
Jno	Klamath S Fork	59	197
WENHAUSER			
Henry*	San Francisco San Francisco 11	67	157
WENHUERTFS			
Nathan*	Placer Michigan	62	844
WENHUM			
Donald	Sierra La Porte	66	784
WENISEN			
Francis*	Amador Twp 4	55	245
WENK			
---	El Dorado Greenwood	58	732
Nickolos*	El Dorado Placerville	58	899
Thomas B	Tuolumne Sonora	71	216
WENKER			
Chas	Amador Twp 1	55	496
WENKFORD			
---	Sutter Yuba	70	778
WENN			
Tristram	Nevada Rough &	61	429
WENNERHOLD			
Christian	San Francisco San Francisco 10	67	323
WENNING			
B	El Dorado Placerville	58	899
WENOCAH			
---	Butte Chico	56	550
WENPLEY			
V	Nevada Eureka	61	382
WENROW			
Samuel*	San Francisco San Francisco 3	67	59
WENSELL			
A	Amador Twp 2	55	266
WENSINGER			
F S	San Francisco San Francisco 2	67	573
WENSON			
Jno	San Francisco San Francisco 9	681089	
WENSTANLEY			
Jno*	Alameda Washington	55	172
WENT			
Henry S	Sacramento Ward 1	63	45
John	Placer Secret R	62	619
Nickolos*	El Dorado Placerville	58	899
WENTAS			
Antonia	Mariposa Twp 1	60	654
WENTER			
Antoine	Butte Bidwell	56	713
Antone	Butte Bidwell	56	713
Daniel	Sacramento Ward 4	63	523
WENTERBURA			
A L*	Santa Clara San Jose	65	389
WENTERBURN			
A L*	Santa Clara San Jose	65	389
WENTERERA			
George	San Mateo Twp 1	65	48
WENTERGIA			
George*	San Mateo Twp 1	65	48
WENTERSMALL			
Antone*	El Dorado Coloma	581071	
WENTFORTH			
Chas	Amador Twp 2	55	319
WENTLEN			
M	Tuolumne Twp 2	71	394
WENTON			
Anitonia	Mariposa Twp 1	60	654
Crayton	Alameda Brooklyn	55	133
WENTRE			
Frankkin*	Siskiyou Yreka	69	125
Franklin*	Siskiyou Yreka	69	125
WENTWORSH			
G E*	Napa Napa	61	56
WENTWORTH			
Albert C	Mendocino Little L	60	833
Aleander	Sierra Whiskey	66	850
Andrew	Sierra La Porte	66	774
C	San Francisco San Francisco 6	67	469
Charles	Placer Michigan	62	820
Chas	Amador Twp 2	55	318
Chas W	San Francisco San Francisco 3	67	20
G E	Napa Napa	61	56
George*	San Mateo Twp 3	65	87
Henry	Tehama Red Bluff	70	914
WENTWORTH			
Ira	Plumas Meadow Valley	62	901
J E	Klamath Salmon	59	208
J E P	Nevada Nevada	61	291
J J H	San Francisco San Francisco 5	67	481
Jackson	Placer Michigan	62	811
John	Placer Folsom	62	647
John	Sierra St Louis	66	807
John	Siskiyou Callahan	69	13
John	Solano Vallejo	69	258
Kate	Sacramento Ward 1	63	101
L D	El Dorado Georgetown	58	759
Mo A	San Joaquin Stockton	641052	
Nathan	San Francisco San Francisco 10	67	238
Philip	Yuba Long Bar	72	747
Phillip	Yuba New York	72	747
R P	Butte Chico	56	531
S	Tuolumne Twp 2	71	352
T	Tuolumne Columbia	71	351
Warren	El Dorado Mud Springs	58	984
WENTY			
Geo W	Sacramento Ward 4	63	517
WENTZ			
A	El Dorado Diamond	58	775
Christian	Santa Clara Gilroy	65	246
Jeremiah	El Dorado White Oaks	581018	
John	Tuolumne Columbia	71	338
John D	San Francisco San Francisco 11	67	128
WENTZELL			
Gustus	San Francisco San Francisco 7	681433	
Gustus*	San Francisco San Francisco 3	67	39
WENY			
Conraad	Amador Twp 4	55	237
WENYUCK INDIAN			
---*	Sonoma Sonoma	69	662
WENYUCK			
Indian*	Sonoma Sonoma	69	662
WENZEL			
A	San Francisco San Francisco 10	67	165
Fred*	Calaveras Twp 6	57	117
Frederick	San Francisco San Francisco 7	681379	
Wm	San Francisco San Francisco 1	68	811
WENZELL			
D*	San Francisco San Francisco 3	67	22
Wm	San Francisco San Francisco 1	68	825
WEOBER			
F	San Francisco San Francisco 6	67	447
WEPPE			
J*	San Francisco San Francisco 3	67	48
WEPPLE			
Charles	Yuba Marysville	72	905
WER			
---	Sierra Twp 7	66	898
WERA			
---	San Bernardino S Timate	64	720
---	San Bernardino S Timate	64	724
---	San Bernardino S Timate	64	732
---	San Bernardino S Timate	64	735
---	San Bernardino S Timate	64	750
Barsola	Alameda Brooklyn	55	189
WERBER			
F*	San Francisco San Francisco 6	67	447
WERDEN			
G W	Napa Clear Lake	61	126
Kg W	Napa Clear Lake	61	126
WERDER			
Harman	Los Angeles Santa Ana	59	441
WERDERKIRK			
Augustus	Tuolumne Twp 1	71	189
WEREDEVATT			
Martin*	Mariposa Twp 3	60	559
WEREDWATT			
Martin	Mariposa Twp 3	60	559
WEREN			
Eliza	Tuolumne Sonora	71	240
WERETA			
---	San Bernardino S Timate	64	721
WERFAIT			
William	Alameda Brooklyn	55	148
WERG			
---	San Bernardino S Timate	64	695
WERGENEISE			
Frederick*	San Francisco San Francisco 7	681436	
WERGES			
William	Placer Iona Hills	62	893
WERGFORD			
Wm	Calaveras Twp 9	57	399
WERGRUEISE			
Frederick*	San Francisco San Francisco 7	681436	
WERH			
T	Mariposa Twp 1	60	642

California 1860 Census Index

Name	County Locale	M653 Roll	Page
WERICH			
Lawrance*	Alameda Brooklyn	55	129
Valentine	San Francisco San Francisco 8	68	1279
WERIGHT			
John	Amador Twp 2	55	262
WERIS			
Jose	San Bernardino Santa Ba	64	217
Jose*	San Bernardino S Buenav	64	218
WERISLOW			
S M T	Tuolumne Twp 4	71	137
WERK			
George W	Humbolt Union	59	183
T	Mariposa Twp 1	60	642
WERKER			
Deitrick	Alameda Brooklyn	55	139
WERKS			
Alfred	Santa Clara Almaden	65	278
WERLER			
J W*	Nevada Eureka	61	351
WERLEY			
F A	Placer Yankee J	62	761
Samuel	Shasta Shasta	66	757
WERLIN			
J G	San Francisco San Francisco 5	67	500
WERLING			
Henry*	Alameda Brooklyn	55	140
WERMER			
Frances	Alameda Brooklyn	55	143
WERMUTH			
Frederick M	San Joaquin Elkhorn	64	968
WERN			
---*	Sacramento Ward 3	63	488
WERNER			
Adam	Sacramento Ward 1	63	54
Benedict	Humbolt Eel Rvr	59	153
Chas	San Francisco San Francisco 10	67	204
Chrn	San Francisco San Francisco 10	67	204
Fred	Sacramento Ward 4	63	587
Fred	Sierra La Porte	66	773
Frederick	San Francisco San Francisco 7	68	1431
Frederick	Solano Fremont	69	379
George	Tulara Twp 1	71	111
Jacob	Sierra Gibsonville	66	851
Jacob	Solano Fremont	69	380
John	Santa Cruz Santa Cruz	66	614
Otto*	San Francisco San Francisco 2	67	777
P C	El Dorado Greenwood	58	722
Phillip	Sierra Downieville	66	1012
T	San Francisco San Francisco 3	67	78
Valentine	San Mateo Twp 3	65	82
Wm	Sierra Downieville	66	1012
WERNKIN			
Henry	Trinity Rearings	70	990
WERO			
---	San Bernardino S Timate	64	698
WEROZT			
Hervey	Sierra Downieville	66	1014
WERRE			
John	Tulara Twp 3	71	44
WERRELL			
William*	Placer Michigan	62	828
WERRY			
Conrad*	Amador Twp 4	55	237
WERSBUTH			
A*	Calaveras Twp 9	57	391
WERSFITH			
A*	Calaveras Twp 9	57	391
WERSIN			
H	Sutter Nicolaus	70	835
WERT			
Wm*	Sierra Twp 5	66	942
WERTDELL			
W N	Butte Ophir	56	759
WERTE			
Robert	El Dorado Georgetown	58	703
WERTH			
Chas	Sacramento Ward 1	63	34
Louis B*	San Francisco San Francisco 7	68	1416
WERTHAMES			
Michael	Contra Costa Twp 3	57	592
WERTHE			
Jacob	Tuolumne Twp 2	71	286
WERTHEIM			
B	Siskiyou Scott Va	69	51
WERTHEIMER			
Rudolph	San Francisco San Francisco 8	68	1319
WERTHERMER			
Aarow*	Contra Costa Twp 3	57	612
Rudolph	San Francisco San Francisco 8	68	1319
WERTHERN			
A*	Tehama Lassen	70	873
WERTHIMIER			
Sping	San Bernardino Santa Barbara	64	148
WERTHUM			
A*	Tehama Lassen	70	873
WERTNER			
Frederick	Solano Benecia	69	281
WERTS			
J	El Dorado Placerville	58	868
WERTSMITH			
Jno	San Francisco San Francisco 10	67	207
WERTTY			
Chas	Amador Twp 1	55	461
WERTY			
Rodolph	Sierra La Porte	66	779
WERTZ			
Constine	Trinity Taylor'S	70	1034
Francis	Sonoma Mendocino	69	465
Geo W	Sonoma Mendocino	69	465
Goe W	Sonoma Mendocino	69	465
Philip	Trinity Taylor'S	70	1034
WERVE			
John	Tulara Sinks Te	71	44
WERZBICKI			
F P	San Francisco San Francisco 6	67	468
WES			
---	Calaveras Twp 4	57	308
---	Calaveras Twp 4	57	333
Franklin	Butte Oro	56	678
Pasqua	San Luis Obispo San Luis Obispo	65	24
WESALL			
Eli W	Tuolumne Twp 1	71	481
WESBET			
James	Yuba Bear Rvr	72	1013
Thomas	Yuba Suida	72	988
WESCO			
Paulino	Fresno Twp 1	59	75
WESCOF			
Frank	Marin Bolinas	60	728
WESCOLT			
E*	Nevada Rough &	61	397
WESCOT			
Frank	Marin Bolinas	60	728
WESCOTT			
E	Nevada Grass Valley	61	161
E	Nevada Rough &	61	397
E G	El Dorado Union	58	1090
E*	Nevada Rough &	61	397
Edmond G	Calaveras Twp 5	57	147
Edmund G	Calaveras Twp 6	57	147
Edmund M	Calaveras Twp 6	57	147
Jas	Sacramento Georgian	63	345
O B	Yolo Cottonwood	72	558
Thos	San Francisco San Francisco 1	68	869
Thos*	Butte Oregon	56	625
WESDERHOLD			
Charles	San Francisco San Francisco 3	67	9
WESDLY			
A G	San Joaquin Stockton	64	1094
WESE			
James	Tulara Twp 3	71	45
WESEL			
John	Sonoma Sonoma	69	650
WESEMAN			
Rudolph*	Yuba Marysville	72	928
WESENGIR			
R M*	Calaveras Twp 9	57	392
WESGATE			
Joseph	Yuba Marysville	72	952
WESHBURN			
Lyrander*	Calaveras Twp 4	57	318
WESICK			
William	Yuba Bear Rvr	72	1013
WESING			
---	Trinity Weaverville	70	1075
WESJTEN			
Albert	El Dorado Greenwood	58	717
WESKER			
Wm*	San Francisco San Francisco 3	67	24
WESKIE			
Ed	Butte Chico	56	560
WESKIN			
Jas	Trinity Indian C	70	989
WESLEAN			
N B	Butte Ophir	56	792
WESLERBOLT			
Charles*	Mariposa Coulterville	60	698
WESLERTIDT			
Charles*	Mariposa Coulterville	60	698
WESLEY			
Chas	Sonoma Santa Rosa	69	393
Hardin	Sonoma Russian	69	439
John	El Dorado Greenwood	58	723
John	Santa Cruz Santa Cruz	66	635
John*	Yolo Putah	72	547
W	San Francisco San Francisco 9	68	1059
William	San Francisco San Francisco 9	68	952
WESLEYS			
John	Yolo Putah	72	547
WESLING			
Henry*	Alameda Brooklyn	55	140
WESLONY			
James*	Nevada Bridgeport	61	502
WESMAN			
Salomon*	Sonoma Petaluma	69	595
WESMOLUND			
J P	Solano Vacaville	69	328
WESMON			
Salomon*	Sonoma Petaluma	69	595
WESMUTH			
Alex	San Joaquin Elkhorn	64	973
WESNER			
Joaquin*	Calaveras Twp 10	57	276
WESSEG			
John	San Francisco San Francisco 2	67	782
WESSEL			
J	Tuolumne Twp 4	71	153
J C	Tuolumne Big Oak	71	153
Wm	Sacramento Georgian	63	338
WESSELL			
Wm	Amador Twp 6	55	441
WESSELS			
Fred	San Joaquin Stockton	64	1023
Samuel	Yuba Rose Bar	72	798
WESSENBERG			
Peter F*	Marin Bolinas	60	745
WESSIEL			
B	Sacramento Ward 4	63	607
WESSING			
William*	San Francisco San Francisco 9	68	1005
WESSON			
Geo	Butte Ophir	56	764
WESSPER			
Catharine*	Butte Oro	56	684
WESSPSE			
Catharine	Butte Oro	56	684
WEST HAAS			
T	San Francisco San Francisco 3	67	78
WEST			
---*	El Dorado Kelsey	58	1149
A	Solano Vacaville	69	352
A	Sutter Yuba	70	770
A	Sutter Butte	70	782
Alexander	Marin San Rafael	60	772
Amelia	Santa Clara San Jose	65	285
Andrew	Shasta Shasta	66	731
Annie	Butte Kimshaw	56	576
B R	Shasta French G	66	717
B W	Sonoma Santa Rosa	69	423
Benj L	San Francisco San Francisco 6	67	436
Benjamin	Del Norte Crescent	58	620
C	San Francisco San Francisco 5	67	536
C	Santa Clara San Jose	65	279
C H	Amador Twp 5	55	348
C H	Solano Vacaville	69	347
Charles	Marin Tomales	60	724
Charles	Sierra Twp 5	66	920
Charles	Tehama Lassen	70	880
Charles	Tuolumne Jamestown	71	445
Charles	Tuolumne Jacksonville	71	515
Charles B	San Joaquin Stockton	64	1053
Charles H	San Francisco San Francisco 11	67	94
Charles M	Los Angeles San Pedro	59	481
Charles M	San Diego Agua Caliente	64	835
Chas	San Francisco San Francisco 1	68	887
Chas	Santa Cruz Santa Cruz	66	634
Chas H	San Francisco San Francisco 7	68	1440
Chas O	San Francisco San Francisco 2	67	736
D J	Santa Clara Alviso	65	411
Daniel	Yuba Marysville	72	864
David J	Contra Costa Twp 3	57	584
E	Sutter Butte	70	791
E A	Sacramento Ward 1	63	67
E A	Sonoma Russian	69	438
E O	Sacramento Ward 3	63	463
Eduards	Amador Twp 2	55	324
Edward	Placer Todds Va	62	762
Edwards	Amador Twp 2	55	324
Edwd	Sonoma Vallejo	69	628
Edwin W	Sacramento Ward 3	63	464
Elliott	Placer Todds Va	62	764
Emperor Of The	Brooklyn Alameda	55	122
F	El Dorado Mud Springs	58	991
Fernando	Los Angeles Santa Ana	59	452
Francisco	San Diego Colorado	64	812
Frank	San Francisco San Francisco 1	68	923
Frederick	San Francisco San Francisco 7	68	1441
Frederick	San Mateo Twp 1	65	69
Geo	Butte Ophir	56	748
Geo	El Dorado Kelsey	58	1148
Geo	Nevada Nevada T	61	327
Geo	San Francisco San Francisco 9	68	1073
Geo L	Tuolumne Jamestown	71	445
George	El Dorado Georgetown	58	702
George	San Joaquin O'Neal	64	1004

Name	County Locale	M653 Roll	Page
WEST			
George	Santa Clara Almaden	65	265
George	Tuolumne Columbia	71	290
Guadalupe T	Sonoma Santa Rosa	69	422
Guadalupe T	Sonoma Santa Rosa	69	422
H	Butte Hamilton	56	514
H	Sutter Butte	70	793
H H	El Dorado Diamond	58	787
H K	Nevada Red Dog	61	551
Henry	Napa Clear Lake	61	124
Henry	Sacramento Ward 3	63	427
Henry	San Francisco San Francisco 8	681	258
Henry	Shasta Horsetown	66	689
Henry	Sierra Twp 7	66	870
Henry E	Calaveras Twp 8	57	97
Hermon	Sierra Downieville	661	028
Ira E	San Diego Colorado	64	806
Isaac	Sacramento Mississipi	63	185
Isham S	Plumas Quincy	62	964
J	El Dorado Newtown	58	779
J A	Los Angeles Tejon	59	526
J C*	El Dorado Casumnes	581	166
J D	Tehama Lassen	70	875
J L	Tehama Antelope	70	895
J S	San Joaquin Stockton	641	095
J W	Amador Twp 3	55	385
Jacob	Placer Iona Hills	62	878
James	San Bernardino San Salvador	64	650
James	Santa Cruz Watsonville	66	536
James	Siskiyou Klamath	69	96
James E	San Francisco San Francisco 8	681	264
James H	San Joaquin Douglass	64	914
James H	Sonoma Mendocino	69	453
James W	Sierra St Louis	66	807
Jane	Sonoma Santa Rosa	69	415
Jas	Butte Ophir	56	768
Jno	Alameda Brooklyn	55	168
John	Calaveras Twp 5	57	204
John	Placer Folsom	62	639
John	San Joaquin Elliott	64	993
John	Santa Clara Santa Clara	65	513
John	Sierra Whiskey	66	843
John	Solano Suisan	69	214
John	Sonoma Santa Rosa	69	423
John	Tuolumne Twp 1	71	262
John	Tuolumne Twp 3	71	455
John	Yuba Foster B	72	833
John L	Tuolumne Twp 2	71	290
John T	Sierra Twp 7	66	878
John*	El Dorado Kelsey	581	149
Johnathan	Tuolumne Twp 2	71	407
Jonathan	Santa Clara San Jose	65	294
Joseph	Plumas Meadow Valley	62	904
Joseph	Plumas Meadow Valley	62	908
Joseph	Siskiyou Yreka	69	190
Joseph	Tuolumne Twp 1	71	250
Joseph R	San Francisco San Francisco 8	681	251
K	Siskiyou Klamath	69	95
Lirsy*	Mariposa Coulterville	60	703
M B	Butte Eureka	56	650
M W	San Francisco San Francisco 6	67	450
Maria	San Francisco San Francisco 4	681	145
Mary*	San Joaquin Oneal	64	930
Mary*	Sonoma Petaluma	69	607
Mrs	Sacramento Ward 3	63	464
N	Siskiyou Klamath	69	95
N	Solano Vacaville	69	352
Parker	Alameda Oakland	55	74
Peter	Sierra St Louis	66	813
Philo	Sacramento Ward 4	63	539
R H	El Dorado Greenwood	58	724
Richard	Santa Cruz Soguel	66	582
Richard	Santa Cruz Santa Cruz	66	634
Rita	San Diego Colorado	64	812
Robert	Nevada Bridgeport	61	501
Robt H	Napa Napa	61	88
S H	Tuolumne Twp 4	71	141
Samuel M	San Francisco San Francisco 8	681	233
Sarah	Placer Rattle Snake	62	600
Sarah	Yuba Marysville	72	854
Sarah	Yuba Marysville	72	859
Sarah A	San Joaquin Castoria	64	898
Silvester	Tuolumne Sonora	71	233
Susan	San Francisco San Francisco 10	336	
		67	
Susanna	Siskiyou Yreka	69	190
T C	Mariposa Twp 1	60	631
Thomas	Sierra Downieville	66	963
W	San Francisco San Francisco 9	681	102
W	San Francisco San Francisco 5	67	548
W B	San Francisco San Francisco 5	67	554
W G	Shasta Shasta	66	654
W H	Butte Ophir	56	757
W J	Tehama Antelope	70	895
W W	Amador Twp 5	55	359
William	San Francisco San Francisco 3	67	69

Name	County Locale	M653 Roll	Page
WEST			
William	Tulara Twp 3	71	53
William	Tulara Twp 1	71	83
William	Tuolumne Twp 1	71	262
William A	Sierra Pine Grove	66	823
William B	Tuolumne Green Springs	71	518
William*	Santa Cruz Soguel	66	590
Wm	El Dorado Mud Springs	58	993
Wm	San Francisco San Francisco 10	297	
		67	
Wm A	Humbolt Bucksport	59	157
Wm A	Napa Yount	61	35
Wm J	Humbolt Mattole	59	123
Wm*	Sierra Twp 5	66	942
WESTADT			
Wm	San Francisco San Francisco 1	68	889
WESTAL			
Samuel	Sonoma Bodega	69	526
WESTALL			
Alfred	Sierra Poverty	66	799
Ann M	San Francisco San Francisco 7	681	424
WESTANHOMER			
P	Siskiyou Scott Va	69	42
WESTBROOK			
A G	El Dorado Georgetown	58	707
Henry	Del Norte Crescent	58	648
James	Del Norte Crescent	58	648
James	San Joaquin Elliott	64	943
James	Yuba Slate Ro	72	704
R L	Siskiyou Scott Va	69	34
WESTBROOKS			
James	Yolo Slate Ra	72	704
WESTBURY			
C	San Francisco San Francisco 4	681	231
WESTCOATT			
B R	Yuba Parks Ba	72	774
Jonas	Yuba Marysville	72	951
Nelson	Yuba Marysville	72	855
Nelson	Yuba Marysville	72	860
WESTCOTE			
S B	Shasta Shasta	66	662
WESTCOTT			
S B	Shasta Shasta	66	662
Varmem	Fresno Twp 2	59	49
Wm	Sierra Downieville	66	992
WESTCOUTT			
B R	Yuba Parks Ba	72	774
WESTDELL			
W N	Butte Ophir	56	759
WESTEL			
Henry	Butte Wyandotte	56	662
WESTELL			
Robinson	Yuba Long Bar	72	741
WESTEM			
J	Yuba Rose Par	72	795
WESTEMHOMER			
P	Siskiyou Scott Va	69	42
WESTEN			
Geo	Sacramento Natonia	63	281
J*	Shasta Shasta	66	685
William*	Calaveras Twp 6	57	179
WESTENHAVER			
Christophe	Yuba Linda Twp	72	982
M	Sonoma Cloverdale	69	686
M E	Sonoma Cloverdale	69	686
WESTENHOVER			
Christophe	Yuba Suida	72	982
WESTENMAN			
Henry	El Dorado Georgetown	58	691
WESTENUTON			
Frederick*	Calaveras Twp 4	57	321
WESTEON			
Sumner	Alameda Brooklyn	55	174
WESTER			
A	San Francisco San Francisco 5	67	535
George	Marin Cortemad	60	791
WESTERFIELD			
August	Humbolt Bucksport	59	161
Benjn	Calaveras Twp 10	57	275
Benjo	Calaveras Twp 10	57	275
W J	Nevada Bridgeport	61	439
W S	Nevada Bridgeport	61	439
William	Nevada Rough &	61	407
WESTERHELL			
Charles	Mariposa Coulterville	60	698
WESTERHOLT			
Charles*	Mariposa Coulterville	60	698
WESTERHOMER			
P*	Siskiyou Scott Va	69	42
WESTERMAN			
Alex	San Francisco San Francisco 3	67	39
Henry	El Dorado Georgetown	58	691
John	Sacramento Sutter	63	298
WESTERMANN			
J	Tuolumne Shawsfla	71	413
WESTERN			
Franklin*	San Francisco San Francisco 9	68	999

Name	County Locale	M653 Roll	Page
WESTERN			
H	San Francisco San Francisco 2	67	685
J	Yuba Rose Bar	72	795
John	Tuolumne Twp 2	71	472
Joseph	San Francisco San Francisco 9	68	977
Sumner*	Alameda Washington	55	174
WESTERO			
J	Shasta Shasta	66	685
WESTERU			
Joseph	San Francisco San Francisco 9	68	977
WESTERVELS			
T A	Colusa Colusi	57	423
WESTES			
Herman	San Diego Colorado	64	808
WESTFACE			
B C	Sonoma Santa Rosa	69	399
WESTFALE			
Crisman	Napa Yount	61	54
WESTFALL			
A P	Sacramento Franklin	63	311
B	Sacramento Georgian	63	338
B C	Sonoma Santa Rosa	69	399
Benj C	Sonoma Santa Rosa	69	413
H H	El Dorado Mountain	581	189
Jacob	Los Angeles Los Angeles	59	347
Jim	Sacramento Georgian	63	343
John	Amador Twp 1	55	485
John	Sonoma Petaluma	69	549
M J	Trinity Weaverville	701	066
Reuben	Sacramento Georgian	63	339
Samuel	Tulara Twp 3	71	60
WESTFALO			
Crisman*	Napa Yount	61	54
WESTFIELD			
Wm	Sierra Twp 5	66	937
WESTGALE			
Joseph	Marin Bolinas	60	728
WESTGATE			
A G	Solano Montezuma	69	371
Jos	Amador Twp 2	55	308
WESTHOUSE			
J	San Francisco San Francisco 2	67	792
WESTILL			
Palinson	Yuba New York	72	741
WESTIM			
Geo*	Sacramento Natonia	63	281
WESTIN			
Mary E*	Butte Wyandotte	56	661
William*	Calaveras Twp 6	57	179
WESTINDOR			
Frederick*	Calaveras Twp 4	57	321
WESTINFELT			
H	Placer Forest H	62	795
WESTINGHOUSE			
E	Tuolumne Twp 1	71	265
WESTLAKE			
E	San Joaquin Elkhorn	64	992
Geo	Sacramento Ward 1	63	129
WESTLEY			
H	Tuolumne Twp 1	71	264
J B	Sacramento Georgian	63	337
J C	San Joaquin Stockton	641	048
Thornton	Tuolumne Columbia	71	329
WESTMAN			
John	Marin Cortemad	60	780
WESTMORLAND			
Frederick*	Calaveras Twp 4	57	321
WESTMORLUND			
Frederick	Calaveras Twp 4	57	321
WESTOELL			
W N*	Butte Ophir	56	759
WESTON			
A	Napa Hot Springs	61	5
A	Shasta Shasta	66	656
Anna	San Francisco San Francisco 5	67	520
Benjamin S	Los Angeles San Pedro	59	481
C	El Dorado Placerville	58	888
C	Tuolumne Twp 2	71	343
Charles	Siskiyou Klamath	69	93
Charles	Yuba Marysville	72	959
D G	El Dorado Kelsey	581	145
Danl	Klamath S Fork	59	207
E	Sutter Bear Rvr	70	826
E S	Sacramento Franklin	63	323
Edward	Butte Mountain	56	740
F Q	Tehama Red Bluff	70	926
Fred	Sonoma Armally	69	482
G	Nevada Grass Valley	61	213
G G	Sacramento Dry Crk	63	371
George	Calaveras Twp 6	57	174
George	Tehama Lassen	70	863
H G	Sierra St Louis	66	810
H L	Sonoma Petaluma	69	588
Ira	Plumas Quincy	62	997
J	Nevada Grass Valley	61	213
J F	El Dorado Diamond	58	792

Name	County Locale	M653 Roll Page
WESTON		
J T	El Dorado Placerville	58 868
J*	Shasta Shasta	66 685
James	Tulara Twp 3	71 58
Jas	Sacramento Ward 3	63 447
Jos	Tehama Red Bluff	70 926
Jubal	Colusa Monroeville	57 457
L H	Tehama Pasakent	70 858
Leonard	Sierra Twp 7	66 908
Mary	Butte Wyandotte	56 661
Mary E*	Butte Wyandotte	56 661
O F	Sonoma Petaluma	69 561
R K	Tuolumne Twp 1	71 199
R S	Sierra Twp 7	66 893
Thomas	Tulara Visalia	71 105
W E	Tuolumne Twp 1	71 264
W H	San Francisco San Francisco 1	68 907
William R	Solano Vacaville	69 335
Wm	El Dorado Greenwood	58 717
Wm	Sacramento Ward 3	63 441
WESTOROUTH		
J R	Napa Hot Springs	61 23
WESTRO		
Amile	San Joaquin Stockton	641077
WESTRUN		
Axel	Santa Cruz Santa Cruz	66 637
WESTSELL		
W V	Butte Ophir	56 759
WESTSTALL		
Phebe	San Francisco San Francisco 1	68 827
WESTTEN		
John	Nevada Nevada	61 241
WESTUN		
Geo*	Sacramento Natonia	63 281
WET		
---	Nevada Rough &	61 435
---	San Francisco San Francisco 4	681189
Ah	Butte Oregon	56 640
Alfred	Calaveras Twp 5	57 173
WETBEL		
Cyrus	Sierra Pine Grove	66 826
WETCH		
Frank	Sonoma Vallejo	69 609
WETCHELL		
M*	Sacramento Mississipi	63 186
WETH		
Charles	Santa Clara San Jose	65 281
WETHELMI		
Amelia*	San Francisco San Francisco 3	67 31
WETHERALD		
M	Nevada Grass Valley	61 208
WETHERBEE		
Asa	Tulara Visalia	71 13
Calvin H	San Francisco San Francisco 8	681238
Charles	Contra Costa Twp 1	57 507
G W	El Dorado Casumnes	581172
WETHERBY		
Seth	San Francisco San Francisco 9	681027
WETHERD		
James S	San Francisco San Francisco 10	166 67
WETHERELL		
W	Tuolumne Twp 4	71 170
WETHERHOGG		
J	Nevada Grass Valley	61 235
WETHERILL		
Clayton	Tuolumne Twp 6	71 538
W	El Dorado Placerville	58 836
WETHERS		
John	Santa Clara San Jose	65 344
WETHERWAX		
Henry	Amador Twp 1	55 473
Wallace	Amador Twp 4	55 244
WETHERWILL		
W*	Trinity Weaverville	701053
WETHIOLUPA		
---	Marin Novato	60 735
WETLINGER		
Drice*	Napa Yount	61 54
Fred H*	Napa Yount	61 54
WETMON		
Henry G	Solano Suisan	69 222
WETMORE		
G S	Yuba New York	72 726
J L	San Francisco San Francisco 6	67 399
Reuben	Plumas Quincy	62 943
WETON		
John A	Yolo Cache Crk	72 620
WETSAG		
Augustus	Nevada Bridgeport	61 487
WETSELL		
W H	Trinity Indian C	70 987
WETSON		
Eliza*	Placer Virginia	62 701
WETTE		
Henry	Yuba Marysville	72 900

Name	County Locale	M653 Roll Page
WETTER		
John	Mariposa Coulterville	60 691
T L*	Calaveras Twp 9	57 357
WETTERGREN		
Frank L*	San Bernardino San Bernadino	64 634
WETTES		
John*	Mariposa Coulterville	60 691
WETTINBEN		
James	Placer Yankee J	62 781
WETTINGER		
Drice*	Napa Yount	61 54
WETTON		
Benj	Sierra Downieville	66 995
WETTS		
Henry F*	Yuba Marysville	72 900
WETTURRAY		
Benjamin	Sierra St Louis	66 811
WETWORTH		
John	Sierra St Louis	66 807
S L	Solano Montezuma	69 369
WETZ		
John	El Dorado Placerville	58 844
Peter	Marin Cortemad	60 783
WETZAR		
Martin	Solano Suisan	69 208
WETZEL		
Geo	Yolo Cache Crk	72 619
H	Nevada Nevada	61 254
John	Sacramento Ward 4	63 507
John	Sacramento Ward 4	63 508
Martin	Sacramento Ward 4	63 510
Peter	Sacramento Ward 4	63 216
Sheodon*	Calaveras Twp 8	57 61
Sicmond	Siskiyou Yreka	69 185
Theodon*	Calaveras Twp 8	57 62
Theodore	Calaveras Twp 8	57 105
Wm D	Calaveras Twp 4	57 317
WETZELL		
A	Siskiyou Yreka	69 186
E	El Dorado Georgetown	58 707
Jacob	Calaveras Twp 4	57 311
WETZLAR		
Fred	Sacramento Franklin	63 326
Gustaves	Sacramento Ward 4	63 558
Jacob	Sacramento Franklin	63 324
Julius	Sacramento Ward 4	63 558
WEUBAN		
Simeon*	Sierra Twp 7	66 892
WEUD		
William	El Dorado Mud Springs	58 998
WEUR		
Alex*	Sierra La Porte	66 783
WEUSE		
John*	Nevada Red Dog	61 555
WEVARINE		
A	Mariposa Twp 1	60 630
WEVARRINE		
A	Mariposa Twp 1	60 630
WEVELY		
M	Sierra Downieville	661017
WEVER		
Charles*	Yuba Fosters	72 829
Edward	Sierra La Porte	66 765
James	Nevada Bridgeport	61 489
WEVERS		
J K	Mariposa Twp 3	60 611
WEW		
---	Sierra Twp 5	66 934
WEXON		
Augustus*	San Francisco 1 San Francisco	68 837
WEXTER		
Andrew J	Sonoma Santa Rosa	69 392
John*	Contra Costa Twp 1	57 504
WEY		
---	Placer Iona Hills	62 898
---	Plumas Quincy	62 926
Fat	San Francisco San Francisco 5	67 508
WEYAND		
Gustavus	Colusa Spring Valley	57 431
Julilus	Colusa Spring Valley	57 431
Thos	Yolo Cache Crk	72 644
WEYARD		
Thos	Yolo Cache	72 644
WEYBARK		
James	San Mateo Twp 3	65 107
WEYBBOCK		
Peter*	Yuba Linda	72 990
WEYER		
Caroline*	Yuba Marysville	72 938
Christian*	Yuba Marysville	72 956
Fredrick	Tuolumne Twp 5	71 490
J C	Sutter Butte	70 785
Joseph*	Yuba Marysville	72 952
WEYHE		
William	Contra Costa Twp 1	57 498

Name	County Locale	M653 Roll Page
WEYL		
Edwd	San Francisco San Francisco 2	67 691
WEYLEBACK		
Peter	Yuba Suida	72 990
WEYMAN		
W	Sacramento Cosummes	63 395
WEYMER		
John	San Francisco San Francisco 3	67 1
Lewis	Sierra St Louis	66 808
Louis	Sierra St Louis	66 808
William	Nevada Bridgeport	61 471
WEYMETZA		
---	Mendocino Calpella	60 825
WEYMIR		
John	San Francisco San Francisco 3	67 1
WEYMITZA		
---	Mendocino Calpella	60 825
WEYMONTH		
Wm	Yolo New York	72 720
WEYMORE		
Wm	Nevada Nevada	61 314
WEYMOUTH		
Andrew	Sierra Twp 5	66 922
Charles	Placer Michigan	62 828
J L	El Dorado Placerville	58 820
S M	Tuolumne Twp 1	71 248
S W	Tuolumne Twp 1	71 248
Wm	Yuba New York	72 720
WEZBURN		
Saml	Amador Twp 2	55 284
WGER		
---*	Yuba Bear Rvr	721014
WHA		
---	Calaveras Twp 8	57 101
---	Mariposa Twp 1	60 653
---	Sacramento Cosummes	63 397
---	Stanislaus Buena Village	70 724
Ah	Butte Oregon	56 626
Nim	Butte Cascade	56 701
Ua	Mariposa Twp 3	60 560
WHAC		
---*	Calaveras Twp 8	57 62
WHACK		
---	Calaveras Twp 6	57 171
WHAH		
---	Calaveras Twp 8	57 101
WHAITENLEY		
J*	Nevada Nevada T	61 327
WHAITENLY		
J*	Nevada Nevada T	61 327
WHAITON		
Jno*	Butte Hamilton	56 513
R	Nevada Nevada	61 264
WHAKERMAN		
Theodore	Calaveras Twp 10	57 298
WHALE		
C F	San Joaquin Stockton	641089
Charles	Tulara Sinks Te	71 43
WHALEN		
Bridget	San Francisco San Francisco 9	68 977
Catharine	San Francisco San Francisco 7	681428
Charles	San Francisco San Francisco 4	681127
Dennis	San Francisco San Francisco 2	67 678
Ed	Trinity E Weaver	701061
Harney	Amador Twp 6	55 429
James	Alameda Brooklyn	55 160
James	Yuba Marysville	72 964
John	San Francisco San Francisco 12	365 67
John	San Francisco San Francisco 2	67 601
John	Yuba Rose Bar	72 805
M	Calaveras Twp 9	57 369
M	Tuolumne Twp 4	71 156
Mary	San Francisco San Francisco 8	681311
Murray	San Francisco San Francisco 2	67 639
N	Siskiyou Klamath	69 87
Patrick	San Francisco San Francisco 11	135 67
Richd	Sacramento Ward 4	63 524
Thoma	San Francisco San Francisco 10	318 67
Thomas	San Francisco San Francisco 10	318 67
Thos	Trinity Weaverville	701062
V	Siskiyou Klamath	69 87
WHALER		
Angeline	Placer Ophirville	62 659
Benjamin	Yuba Long Bar	72 755
G L	Sacramento San Joaquin	63 350
M M	Sutter Yuba	70 774
WHALES		
Patrick	Colusa Colusi	57 423
W	El Dorado Placerville	58 859
WHALEW		
Carney	Amador Twp 6	55 429
WHALEY		
C P	Sacramento Lee	63 216

Name	County Locale	M653 Roll	Page
WHALEY			
E	Nevada Eureka	61	349
F S	Tuolumne Columbia	71	473
H M	Sacramento Ward 3	63	429
Henry A	San Bernardino San Bernadino	64	623
Henry H	San Bernardino San Bernardino	64	623
J	Sacramento American	63	172
James H	Tuolumne Big Oak	71	177
John	Sonoma Santa Rosa	69	411
John A	Humbolt Union	59	183
Jon	Sonoma Santa Rosa	69	411
Margaret	San Francisco San Francisco 4	68	1216
Thos	San Francisco San Francisco 9	68	994
Wm	Trinity Douglas	70	978
WHALIN			
Rose	Mariposa Twp 3	60	545
WHALING			
Jas C	Butte Chico	56	554
Julia O	San Francisco San Francisco 8	68	1248
Matthew	Butte Oregon	56	614
S	El Dorado Placerville	58	882
WHALLEN			
J*	Nevada Grass Valley	61	179
WHALLER			
J*	Nevada Grass Valley	61	179
WHALLEY			
A	Nevada Eureka	61	348
D W	Siskiyou Klamath	69	94
Emily	San Francisco San Francisco 10	67	327
John W	Siskiyou Yreka	69	137
WHALLING			
L E	Tuolumne Big Oak	71	138
WHALON			
A	Mariposa Twp 3	60	591
Alexander	Yuba Marysville	72	963
John	Yuba Rose Bar	72	805
S	Mariposa Twp 3	60	591
WHALOND			
John	Butte Ophir	56	746
WHAN			
---	Calaveras Twp 9	57	349
---	Calaveras Twp 9	57	358
---	Calaveras Twp 9	57	363
---	El Dorado Greenwood	58	731
---	Sacramento Granite	63	268
---*	Stanislaus Buena Village	70	721
WHANAH			
Austice	Amador Twp 5	55	332
WHANG SOMI			
---	Sierra La Porte	66	785
WHANG			
---	Calaveras Twp 10	57	273
---	Yuba Fosters	72	830
Some	Sierra La Porte	66	785
WHANY			
---	Calaveras Twp 10	57	273
---*	Yuba Foster B	72	830
WHAO			
---	Placer Auburn	62	574
WHAR			
---	Amador Twp 5	55	356
---	Amador Twp 6	55	428
---	Amador Twp 1	55	465
---	Calaveras Twp 9	57	358
---	Mariposa Twp 1	60	655
James*	Sierra St Louis	66	817
WHARON			
R*	San Francisco San Francisco 9	68	1058
WHARS			
Robert	San Francisco San Francisco 1	68	918
WHARTA			
Maria	San Joaquin Stockton	64	1071
WHARTENBY			
J*	Nevada Nevada	61	327
WHARTENLEY			
J*	Nevada Nevada	61	327
WHARTENLY			
J*	Nevada Nevada T	61	327
WHARTENTY			
J*	Nevada Nevada	61	327
WHARTERRLEY			
J*	Nevada Nevada	61	327
WHARTIN			
R	Nevada Nevada	61	264
WHARTON			
F	Sutter Nicolaus	70	835
J P	Sierra Gibsonville	66	860
James*	Yuba Marysville	72	907
Jno*	Butte Hamilton	56	513
WHAS			
James	Sierra St Louis	66	817
WHASON			
R*	San Francisco San Francisco 9	68	1058
WHASSAR			
John*	San Mateo Twp 2	65	117

Name	County Locale	M653 Roll	Page
WHASSAY			
John*	San Mateo Twp 2	65	117
WHAT			
---	Sacramento Granite	63	268
---	Shasta French G	66	712
WHATELY			
R	San Francisco San Francisco 5	67	547
WHATES			
Robt	Santa Clara San Jose	65	351
WHATING			
P*	Nevada Washington	61	336
WHATKINS			
John	Butte Ophir	56	824
WHATLEY			
R H	San Francisco San Francisco 6	67	460
WHATNIG			
P*	Nevada Washington	61	336
WHATSELL			
T	Butte Wyandotte	56	665
WHATTON			
Abner	San Francisco San Francisco 4	68	1122
WHAU			
---*	Stanislaus Buena Village	70	721
WHAW			
O Co*	Mendocino Calpella	60	826
WHAY			
---	Mariposa Twp 3	60	559
---	Tuolumne Twp 3	71	457
Nough	Shasta Horsetown	66	701
WHAYLEN			
Andrew	Sierra Pine Grove	66	833
WHE			
---	Calaveras Twp 5	57	202
---	El Dorado Kelsey	58	1141
WHEA			
---	Calaveras Twp 8	57	106
---	Placer Virginia	62	670
WHEADON			
A	Sacramento Centre	63	174
Augustus	Sacramento Ward 3	63	469
Theo	Sacramento Centre	63	174
WHEALDON			
Jonathan	Yuba New York	72	726
WHEALDS			
Jonathan*	Yuba New York	72	726
WHEALER			
B F	Amador Twp 7	55	419
Noah	El Dorado Diamond	58	767
WHEALON			
C H	Tuolumne Twp 1	71	475
Julia	Santa Cruz Pajaro	66	551
WHEAT			
Alexander	Calaveras Twp 4	57	344
E M*	Nevada Red Dog	61	550
George	Plumas Quincy	62	1006
Jas	Yolo Merritt	72	581
Jas L	San Francisco San Francisco 2	67	557
Job	Merced Twp 1	60	896
William A	Yuba Marysville	72	972
WHEATER			
H B	Amador Twp 1	55	485
WHEATLEY			
E D	Sacramento Ward 1	63	130
E D	Sacramento Ward 1	63	131
James	Marin Cortemad	60	785
WHEATMAN			
Henry	Calaveras Twp 8	57	97
WHEATON			
Benjamin	San Francisco San Francisco 8	68	1246
C	Nevada Nevada	61	266
C H*	Tuolumne Sonora	71	475
E E	Tuolumne Twp 4	71	172
Edward	San Francisco San Francisco 7	68	1415
Henry S	Sierra Twp 7	66	892
Jedediah	San Bernardino San Salvador	64	655
John C	Tuolumne Twp 1	71	475
Jolen C	Tuolumne Sonora	71	475
M A	Solano Suisan	69	210
Olivill	San Francisco San Francisco 7	68	1415
Orvill*	San Francisco San Francisco 7	68	1415
Thos	San Mateo Twp 3	65	109
W	El Dorado Kelsey	58	1151
Walter W	San Joaquin Castoria	64	883
Warahm	Monterey San Juan	60	1008
WHEAZTON			
Wm	San Bernardino San Salvador	64	655
WHEDOCK			
R W*	Shasta Horsetown	66	696
WHEE			
---	Calaveras Twp 9	57	349
---	El Dorado Placerville	58	823
---*	Calaveras Twp 9	57	349
J*	Nevada Eureka	61	391
WHEEKEY			
John	Santa Cruz Soquel	66	583
WHEELAN			
Henry*	Marin Cortemad	60	780

Name	County Locale	M653 Roll	Page
WHEELAN			
Heny*	Marin Cortemad	60	780
James	Alameda Brooklyn	55	132
M	Merced Twp 1	60	914
Thomas	Solano Benecia	69	316
WHEELAND			
Michael	Placer Dutch Fl	62	728
Rosana	San Francisco San Francisco 4	68	1120
WHEELEHAM			
Patrick	San Mateo Twp 1	65	53
WHEELEM			
Wm*	Napa Napa	61	83
WHEELEN			
Ellen*	Calaveras Twp 6	57	129
Robert	Sierra St Louis	66	806
William	El Dorado Greenwood	58	725
Wm H	Amador Twp 1	55	456
Wm*	Napa Napa	61	83
WHEELENS			
Wm*	Napa Napa	61	83
WHEELER			
---	Mariposa Twp 3	60	555
---	San Francisco San Francisco 10	67	173
A	Sacramento Brighton	63	198
A	San Mateo Twp 1	65	70
A G	Siskiyou Scott Va	69	47
A R	Sacramento Granite	63	246
Alfred	San Francisco San Francisco 10	67	198
Alfred	San Francisco San Francisco 2	67	744
Alice	Tuolumne Twp 1	71	201
Alonzo	Napa Napa	61	61
Alonzo	Napa Napa	61	67
Amos	Sierra Downieville	66	971
Augustus	Napa Yount	61	46
Augustus	Plumas Quincy	62	996
Benjamin	Yuba Long Bar	72	755
C D	Nevada Bridgeport	61	490
C L	Sacramento Ward 4	63	502
C P	El Dorado Mountain	58	1189
C W	Tuolumne Twp 3	71	466
Charles	El Dorado Mountain	58	1185
Charles H	El Dorado Mountain	58	1184
Chas N*	Sacramento Granite	63	246
Chas W	Sacramento Granite	63	246
D	Santa Clara Santa Clara	65	509
Danl	San Francisco San Francisco 5	67	494
David	San Francisco San Francisco 12	67	364
David	Santa Clara San Jose	65	311
David	Solano Fremont	69	376
David	Yuba Bear Rvr	72	1003
Dudley E	Yuba Marysville	72	923
Dwight	Tuolumne Twp 1	71	268
E	Sacramento Granite	63	223
E	San Joaquin Elkhorn	64	997
E	Trinity Ferry	70	977
E A	Napa Napa	61	68
Edward	San Francisco San Francisco 7	68	1325
Edward	San Francisco San Francisco 2	67	608
Edward A	San Francisco San Francisco 7	68	1352
Edward D	Yuba Marysville	72	961
Eli N	Sierra Gibsonville	66	858
Ellen*	Calaveras Twp 6	57	129
F L	El Dorado Kelsey	58	1135
F W	Shasta French G	66	715
Francis	Plumas Quincy	62	952
Francis*	Mariposa Twp 3	60	587
Frank	Sacramento Granite	63	223
Frank	San Francisco San Francisco 10	67	168
Frank	Tuolumne Twp 1	71	258
Fredk	San Francisco San Francisco 2	67	791
Fredrick	Plumas Quincy	62	944
Fruman	Sacramento Ward 1	63	98
G	Nevada Eureka	61	387
G	Sacramento Ward 3	63	484
Geo	El Dorado Grizzly	58	1181
Geo	Mendocino Big Rvr	60	848
Geo	San Francisco San Francisco 1	68	910
George	Placer Iona Hills	62	870
George	Tuolumne Sonora	71	222
George M	Sierra Twp 7	66	863
George W	Sierra St Louis	66	863
Gilbert	Butte Oregon	56	627
Grany	Yolo Washington	72	572
Gruny	Yolo Washington	72	572
H	San Francisco San Francisco 5	67	512
H N	Nevada Nevada	61	249
Harman	Calaveras Twp 5	57	188
Harrison	Solano Vacaville	69	364
Henry	Santa Cruz Pescadero	66	641
Henry H	Siskiyou Shasta Rvr	69	113
Horace N	Sierra Pine Grove	66	825
Horaie N	Sierra Pine Grove	66	825

California 1860 Census Index

Name	County Locale	M653 Roll	Page
WHEELER			
Horuie N*	Sierra Pine Grove	66	825
Isaac	Plumas Quincy	62	925
Isabella	San Francisco San Francisco 10	67	222
J B	Tehama Red Bluff	70	916
J F	San Francisco San Francisco 5	67	551
J L*	Siskiyou Scott Ri	69	64
J S	Siskiyou Scott Ri	69	64
J T	Amador Twp 4	55	251
J W	Nevada Eureka	61	351
James	Alameda Brooklyn	55	86
James	Amador Twp 6	55	424
James	Nevada Rough &	61	431
James	Placer Iona Hills	62	863
James	Placer Iona Hills	62	885
James	Sacramento Dry Crk	63	371
James	Siskiyou Yreka	69	188
Jas	Butte Ophir	56	774
Jason D	Calaveras Twp 7	57	29
Jno F	Mendocino Big Rvr	60	844
Jno P	Mendocino Big Rvr	60	844
Joh S	Calaveras Twp 10	57	279
John	San Francisco San Francisco 8	68	1271
John	San Francisco San Francisco 7	68	1436
John	San Francisco San Francisco 1	68	904
John O	Los Angeles Los Angeles	59	350
John O	San Diego San Diego	64	769
John S	Calaveras Twp 10	57	279
Jos M	Plumas Quincy	62	938
Joseph	Nevada Bloomfield	61	528
Joseph	Sacramento Franklin	63	320
Josiah	Sonoma Armally	69	507
Judson	Placer Todds Va	62	762
Julia	Amador Twp 6	55	424
Julia	Calaveras Twp 4	57	318
L S	Sonoma Petaluma	69	597
Lander	Placer Secret R	62	622
Larinda	Sonoma Mendocino	69	463
Lenas	Mariposa Twp 1	60	663
Lenicia	Contra Costa Twp 1	57	536
Levy	El Dorado Mud Springs	58	968
M	Tehama Lassen	70	869
M P	Tuolumne Twp 2	71	331
Marcus	Contra Costa Twp 3	57	589
Mareus	Sierra Twp 5	66	935
Marshal	San Mateo Twp 3	65	76
Mary A	Butte Chico	56	533
Mary J	Sierra La Porte	66	775
Michael	San Francisco San Francisco 9	68	1013
Minna	San Francisco San Francisco 2	67	608
N A	Siskiyou Scott Va	69	31
N P	Trinity E Weaver	70	1058
Nathan	Calaveras Twp 4	57	317
Nathan	Calaveras Twp 9	57	382
O C	Sacramento Ward 3	63	455
R	El Dorado Placerville	58	882
R	El Dorado Placerville	58	885
R B P	Tuolumne Columbia	71	471
R D	Nevada Bloomfield	61	507
R H	Nevada Bloomfield	61	507
S	San Francisco San Francisco 5	67	511
S	San Francisco San Francisco 5	67	521
S	Tuolumne Twp 4	71	173
S C	Amador Twp 6	55	424
S S	El Dorado Placerville	58	890
S T	San Francisco San Francisco 1	68	878
Saml	San Francisco San Francisco 1	68	871
Saml S	Santa Clara Redwood	65	453
Samuel	Sierra Pine Grove	66	821
Simeon	Sierra Port Win	66	791
T J	Del Norte Crescent	58	630
T S	Del Norte Crescent	58	630
Thomas	San Francisco San Francisco 8	68	1242
Thomas	Santa Cruz Pajaro	66	577
Thos	Nevada Nevada	61	287
Thos	Santa Clara Gilroy	65	237
Thos	Stanislaus Emory	70	754
Truman	Sacramento Ward 1	63	98
W H	Santa Clara San Jose	65	366
W P	Tuolumne Columbia	71	331
W P	Tuolumne Twp 2	71	349
W P*	Stanislaus Branch	70	704
Warren	Tuolumne Twp 2	71	385
Wheeler	El Dorado White Oaks	58	1016
William	Plumas Meadow Valley	62	901
William	Plumas Quincy	62	951
Wm	Sonoma Bodega	69	521
Wm H	Amador Twp 1	55	456
Wm T	Marin Cortemad	60	780
Wright	San Francisco San Francisco 7	68	1336
WHEELERIGHT			
Joseph	Sacramento Sutter	63	295
WHEELES			
W	El Dorado Placerville	58	921
WHEELEY			
James	Nevada Rough &	61	427
WHEELEY			
Margaret	San Francisco San Francisco 4	68	1216
WHEELIN			
Peter	Shasta Shasta	66	730
William	Shasta Shasta	66	730
WHEELING			
John H	Tuolumne Sonora	71	217
Oliver	Yuba Marysville	72	882
Olivr	Yuba Marysville	72	882
William	Calaveras Twp 5	57	173
WHEELLERS			
John*	Santa Cruz Soguel	66	583
WHEELN			
Marcy*	Placer Iona Hills	62	863
WHEELOCK			
A	El Dorado Placerville	58	885
A	Nevada Washington	61	338
A	Nevada Eureka	61	358
Clara	Sacramento Ward 1	63	16
Falton	Marin Cortemad	60	787
Hamsen	San Francisco San Francisco 2	67	763
Henry	Plumas Quincy	62	935
Irvin	Sierra Twp 7	66	863
Johanna	San Francisco San Francisco 11	67	117
Joseph	Sacramento Ward 4	63	534
Luke	Tuolumne Sonora	71	197
O	Nevada Washington	61	338
O C	Siskiyou Scott Va	69	24
R W	Shasta Horsetown	66	696
T	Santa Clara Alviso	65	406
Thadeus	Monterey Pajaro	60	1015
WHEELRIGHT			
Geo	Trinity Big Flat	70	1039
WHEENEY			
John	Santa Cruz Soguel	66	583
WHEER			
James*	Sierra St Louis	66	817
WHEETESEDES			
Alexdar*	Yuba Bear Rvr	72	997
WHEETHROP			
William	Calaveras Twp 4	57	318
WHEETING			
Grove*	Yuba Linda	72	989
WHEETSEDIS			
Alexdar*	Yuba Bear Rvr	72	997
WHEIT			
Battolt*	Calaveras Twp 9	57	350
Battolte	Calaveras Twp 9	57	350
Battoth	Calaveras Twp 9	57	350
WHELAN			
Dennis	Nevada Bridgeport	61	502
Geo	Sacramento Mississipi	63	188
James	San Francisco San Francisco 3	67	30
John	San Francisco San Francisco 9	68	988
L	Sacramento Franklin	63	316
Miles	San Francisco San Francisco 3	67	49
Thos	Trinity Weaverville	70	1056
WHELDEN			
Isaac C	San Francisco San Francisco 10	67	315
WHELDME			
Chas C	Alameda Brooklyn	55	210
WHELEN			
Fred	Alameda Brooklyn	55	102
W	Trinity Big Flat	70	1040
WHELLEN			
Catharine	San Francisco San Francisco 10	67	315
WHELLER			
Charles	El Dorado Mountain	58	1185
David	Solano Fremont	69	376
WHELOCK			
A G	Marin San Rafael	60	771
WHELTEMORE			
William*	Alameda Oakland	55	74
WHELTIMORE			
William*	Alameda Oakland	55	74
WHELTON			
James	Trinity Oregon G	70	1008
P	Trinity Oregon G	70	1008
WHELY			
James	Nevada Rough &	61	429
WHENNEY			
S	Sonoma Washington	69	664
WHENSON			
Peter*	Tuolumne Twp 3	71	430
WHENTON			
William B	San Francisco San Francisco 4	68	1172
WHERBE			
Frank	Tuolumne Twp 1	71	258
WHERER			
Robert*	Tehama Lassen	70	871
WHERT			
Batto*	Calaveras Twp 9	57	350
WHESTONE			
Saml	Stanislaus Buena Village	70	722
WHETNER			
William	El Dorado Mud Springs	58	954
WHETSTONE			
Henry S	San Francisco San Francisco 3	67	49
Washington F	Calaveras Twp 4	57	335
William C	Calaveras Twp 4	57	335
WHETTIER			
Isaac	San Francisco San Francisco 1	68	906
WHETTON			
Angaline	Napa Napa	61	107
J W	Napa Napa	61	106
WHEY			
---	San Francisco San Francisco 2	67	754
Hough	Shasta Horsetown	66	701
WHIADOW			
Augustus	Sacramento Ward 4	63	515
WHIASKY			
---	Mendocino Calpella	60	828
WHIAT			
E M*	Nevada Red Dog	61	550
WHIBLEY			
David*	Tuolumne Twp 5	71	518
WHIBNEY			
Franklin	Sierra Pine Grove	66	830
WHICKER			
Harvey	Stanislaus Buena Village	70	724
WHICOMB			
W H	Napa Hot Springs	61	13
WHIDDEN			
J G	Tuolumne Twp 2	71	411
Wm	Alameda Brooklyn	55	201
WHIDDER			
J G	Tuolumne Shawsfla	71	411
WHIDING			
John H	Tuolumne Twp 1	71	217
WHIET			
Battolte*	Calaveras Twp 9	57	350
Battoth*	Calaveras Twp 9	57	350
WHIETER			
David*	San Francisco San Francisco 12	67	364
WHIGHT			
James	Sierra Morristown	66	1054
WHIHARDT			
John	Sacramento Ward 3	63	430
WHIKE			
---	Yuba Long Bar	72	764
WHILAMARE			
F G	Mariposa Coulterville	60	694
WHILAN			
John	San Francisco San Francisco 2	67	641
Miles	San Francisco San Francisco 3	67	49
WHILAND			
J	Calaveras Twp 9	57	397
WHILANE			
Thos	Santa Clara San Jose	65	294
WHILDING			
Evan	Nevada Bridgeport	61	488
WHILDRUG			
Eran*	Nevada Bridgeport	61	488
Evan*	Nevada Bridgeport	61	488
WHILEMAN			
Jas	San Francisco San Francisco 2	67	785
WHILFORD			
F*	Tuolumne Twp 4	71	143
Jas	San Francisco San Francisco 2	67	785
Jos	San Francisco San Francisco 2	67	785
WHILI			
M	Amador Twp 3	55	397
WHILING			
R L	San Francisco San Francisco 9	68	1081
WHILLEY			
H R*	Sutter Butte	70	789
WHILLIAMSON			
L	Nevada Eureka	61	378
WHILT			
David*	Butte Oregon	56	613
WHILTEN			
Lucy	Stanislaus Empire	70	735
WHILUS			
J A*	Calaveras Twp 9	57	392
WHIM			
J	Calaveras Twp 9	57	413
WHIMLY			
Wm M	Sierra Twp 7	66	886
WHIN			
Wm*	Sacramento Ward 1	63	93
WHINE			
---	El Dorado Greenwood	58	729
WHINEY			
W M	Sierra Downieville	66	1002
W W	Sierra Downieville	66	1002
WHINGALES			
J	Sacramento Ward 1	63	6
WHINGATES			
J*	Sacramento Ward 1	63	6

Name	County Locale	M653 RollPage
WHINNEY		
Henry	Santa Cruz Santa Cruz	66 619
S	Sonoma Washington	69 664
WHINNY		
G H	Yolo Cache Crk	72 621
WHINOJATES		
J*	Sacramento Ward 1	63 6
WHINY		
G F	Yolo Cache	72 621
WHIPKE		
Margaret	Calaveras Twp 6	57 119
WHIPLEY		
D H	Sacramento Ward 3	63 441
John	Los Angeles Los Angeles	59 298
Wm H	Sacramento Natonia	63 276
WHIPPERMAN		
Henry	Calaveras Twp 7	57 21
WHIPPEY		
Wm	Amador Twp 3	55 405
WHIPPLE		
A A	Tuolumne Twp 1	71 214
Benj	Calaveras Twp 9	57 385
Benjamin	Santa Cruz Pajaro	66 563
C B	Sacramento Ward 1	63 21
D W	Shasta Shasta	66 758
David	Butte Bidwell	56 718
David	Butte Bidwell	56 731
David	Butte Ophir	56 774
Edward	San Francisco San Francisco 8	681 314
Edwin	San Joaquin Elliott	641 104
Elsha	Humbolt Mattole	59 125
Enoch J	Mendocino Big Rvr	60 842
F A	Calaveras Twp 9	57 358
G A	San Francisco San Francisco 7	681 436
George	Calaveras Twp 7	57 23
H	San Francisco San Francisco 1	68 926
Henry	Sacramento Ward 4	63 519
J C	Sonoma Petaluma	69 589
J D	Sierra Downieville	66 975
John	Contra Costa Twp 1	57 503
Levi	Santa Clara Gilroy	65 244
Lf A	Calaveras Twp 9	57 358
Louis	San Francisco San Francisco 11	141
		67
Loward D*	El Dorado Georgetown	58 698
Lyman	Nevada Bridgeport	61 452
Orlanda	Calaveras Twp 9	57 373
Osborne	Colusa Muion	57 461
Phillip	Monterey Pajaro	601 021
S	Sacramento Ward 4	63 524
S C	Sierra Twp 7	66 872
S T	San Mateo Twp 1	65 67
Saml	Butte Oro	56 683
Sarah	Sonoma Petaluma	69 589
Simon	Nevada Bridgeport	61 448
Soward D*	El Dorado Georgetown	58 698
Stephen B	San Francisco San Francisco 8	681 296
Stephen G	Humbolt Union	59 181
William W	Yuba Marysville	72 926
Wm	Sonoma Petaluma	69 607
WHIPPLEGATE		
George	Sierra Port Win	66 793
WHIPPO		
Otto	Sacramento Ward 3	63 484
WHIPPS		
Samuel B	Los Angeles Tejon	59 521
WHIPS		
Peter	Los Angeles Los Angeles	59 364
WHIRITY		
James	Calaveras Twp 5	57 197
WHIRRILY		
James	Calaveras Twp 5	57 197
Peter	Calaveras Twp 5	57 198
WHIRRITY		
James	Calaveras Twp 5	57 197
Patrick	Calaveras Twp 5	57 195
Peter	Calaveras Twp 5	57 198
WHIRSITY		
Patrick*	Calaveras Twp 5	57 195
WHIRT		
Battolh*	Calaveras Twp 9	57 350
WHIRTIN		
John*	San Francisco San Francisco 3	67 45
WHIRTTER		
Thomas H*	Sierra Twp 7	66 890
WHISE		
H	Sacramento Lee	63 215
WHISELL		
John	Shasta Millvill	66 749
WHISETT		
John	Shasta Millvill	66 749
WHISHEY		
R	El Dorado White Oaks	581 007
WHISLER		
G	Sierra La Porte	66 787
WHISLOW		
E	Marin Tomales	60 776

Name	County Locale	M653 RollPage
WHISMAN		
Andrew	Santa Clara Fremont	65 427
John	Santa Clara Fremont	65 426
John W	Santa Clara Santa Clara	65 513
WHISMENT		
Thos	El Dorado Georgetown	58 689
WHISMONT		
Thos	El Dorado Georgetown	58 689
WHISNER		
Henry	Nevada Rough &	61 421
WHISSON		
E*	Butte Ophir	56 755
WHISTHA		
W G	El Dorado Greenwood	58 723
WHISTIN		
J F	El Dorado Big Bar	58 739
WHISTLER		
Michael	Los Angeles Elmonte	59 249
Thomas H	Sierra Twp 7	66 890
WHITACRE		
Thomas	Placer Todds Va	62 783
WHITADGE		
Edward F*	Calaveras Twp 5	57 146
WHITAKER		
C D	Nevada Eureka	61 357
Charlotte	San Francisco San Francisco 1	68 814
Frank	Tulara Twp 3	71 45
H	Sacramento Ward 1	63 103
Horace	Tulara Visalia	71 11
Horrace	Tulara Twp 2	71 11
J	Sacramento Alabama	63 413
J A	Butte Chico	56 549
J W	Amador Twp 6	55 436
J W	San Francisco San Francisco 6	67 456
Ja W	San Francisco San Francisco 6	67 456
James	Yuba Marysville	72 905
James F	Yuba Marysville	72 905
James R	Trinity Trinity	70 971
Jas	San Francisco San Francisco 5	67 518
John	Plumas Quincy	62 954
John	Trinity Bates	70 967
L	Yolo Cache Crk	72 620
Peter	Sonoma Petaluma	69 550
Robert	Amador Twp 3	55 384
Samuel	Tulara Visalia	71 14
T	San Francisco San Francisco 5	67 517
W	San Francisco San Francisco 6	67 446
W	Siskiyou Scott Va	69 38
William	Yuba Marysville	72 960
Wm P	Santa Clara Santa Clara	65 500
WHITALL		
James	Shasta Horsetown	66 692
WHITANSARS		
T G*	Mariposa Coulterville	60 694
WHITBACK		
William	Contra Costa Twp 1	57 520
WHITBECK		
D D	Sacramento Casumnes	63 381
G W	Sacramento Cosumnes	63 385
W H	El Dorado Placerville	58 915
Wm*	San Francisco San Francisco 5	67 554
WHITBICK		
Wm*	San Francisco San Francisco 5	67 554
WHITBY		
Ephraim	Monterey San Juan	601 004
F G*	Tuolumne Twp 2	71 379
R	San Joaquin Stockton	641 089
Wm	Santa Clara Gilroy	65 240
WHITCANB		
S F	Shasta Millvill	66 752
WHITCHAN		
J E	Alameda Oakland	55 8
WHITCHER		
Abner	Placer Folsom	62 639
Charles	Merced Monterey	60 943
Charles	Monterey Monterey	60 943
WHITCHILL		
Isaac	Sierra Downieville	661 018
P P	Nevada Eureka	61 390
WHITCHIVICH		
William	Siskiyou Scott Va	69 48
WHITCHOVICH		
William	Siskiyou Scott Va	69 48
WHITCHWICH		
---	Siskiyou Scott Va	69 48
William*	Siskiyou Scott Va	69 48
WHITCKER		
M M	Tehama Red Bluff	70 924
WHITCOMB		
A C	San Francisco San Francisco 5	67 484
A L	Placer Michigan	62 855
A W	Santa Clara Freemont	65 416
Byron	Yolo Slate Ra	72 688
Byron	Yuba Slate Ro	72 688
C G	Yolo Slate Ra	72 688
C G	Yuba Slate Ro	72 688

Name	County Locale	M653 RollPage
WHITCOMB		
Charles	Contra Costa Twp 2	57 540
Danl	San Francisco San Francisco 6	67 434
David	Yolo No E Twp	72 676
David	Yuba North Ea	72 676
Geo W*	Sacramento Franklin	63 316
J B	Sierra Twp 5	66 919
Jas	Sacramento Ward 4	63 519
John	Placer Michigan	62 858
Octavery	Tuolumne Twp 1	71 273
S H	Shasta Millvill	66 752
WHITCOMBE		
A H	Sacramento San Joaquin	63 348
Geo W*	Sacramento Franklin	63 316
WHITCOME		
H H	San Mateo Twp 2	65 128
Ogden	Siskiyou Yreka	69 150
WHITCONB		
Actavey	Tuolumne Twp 2	71 273
WHITCRAFT		
D H	Sonoma Washington	69 666
Josephine	Solano Fairfield	69 197
WHITCUMBE		
John	Colusa Muion	57 462
WHITE EYE		
---	Tulara Twp 2	71 32
WHITE L L		
L L	Colusa Grand Island	57 477
WHITE		
A	Nevada Nevada	61 282
A	San Francisco San Francisco 6	67 467
A	Stanislaus Branch	70 705
A	Sutter Butte	70 796
A A	San Francisco San Francisco 4	681 129
A C	San Francisco San Francisco 2	67 730
A C	Santa Clara Burnett	65 256
A F	Santa Clara Gilroy	65 240
A G	San Francisco San Francisco 5	67 554
A G	Tuolumne Twp 2	71 341
A S	Sonoma Washington	69 670
Aaron	Butte Oregon	56 617
Adam	El Dorado Spanish	581 125
Albert	San Francisco San Francisco 4	681 153
Albert	Yuba Marysville	72 939
Albert W	Alameda Oakland	55 22
Alexander	Contra Costa Twp 1	57 510
Alexander	Contra Costa Twp 1	57 519
Alexander	Yuba Marysville	72 971
Alfred J	Santa Clara San Jose	65 307
Amel	Santa Cruz Santa Cruz	66 615
Amos	Santa Clara San Jose	65 350
Andrew	Los Angeles Los Angeles	59 345
Ann	San Francisco San Francisco 3	67 76
Ansel	Santa Cruz Santa Cruz	66 615
Asa	Siskiyou Callahan	69 2
Asa	Solano Vacaville	69 359
Augusta	Santa Cruz Santa Cruz	66 608
Augusta	Santa Cruz Santa Cruz	66 613
B F	Napa Napa	61 75
Benj	Butte Kimshaw	56 569
Benj	Marin Tomales	60 718
Benj	Plumas Meadow Valley	62 904
Benj	Trinity Lewiston	70 953
Benj	Yolo Putah	72 548
Birta	Placer Dutch Fl	62 713
Bituma	Amador Twp 3	55 372
Burill	Yolo Slate Ra	72 704
Burrill	Yuba Slate Ro	72 704
Bynam	Sonoma Russian	69 431
C	Calaveras Twp 9	57 377
C	Marin Tomales	60 718
C B	Butte Hamilton	56 513
C B	Butte Bidwell	56 722
C C D	Colusa Monroeville	57 441
C E	Sacramento Centre	63 179
C J	Nevada Bloomfield	61 511
C S	San Francisco San Francisco 5	67 548
C S	Yolo Cache Crk	72 645
Cabel	El Dorado White Oaks	581 027
Caleb	Alameda Brooklyn	55 138
Calvin	Fresno Twp 3	59 9
Carlos E	San Francisco San Francisco 3	67 8
Cas	Napa Hot Springs	61 16
Catharine	San Francisco San Francisco 10	168
		67
Cecelia M	Solano Vallejo	69 249
Chamberlin	Sacramento Granite	63 245
Charles	Calaveras Twp 6	57 167
Charles	Humbolt Union	59 181
Charles	Marin San Rafael	60 761
Charles	Placer Michigan	62 827
Charles	Plumas Quincy	62 976
Charles	San Francisco San Francisco 3	67 75
Charles	San Joaquin Stockton	641 074
Charles	San Luis Obispo San Luis Obispo	65 16
Charles	Siskiyou Scott Va	69 50

California 1860 Census Index

Name	County Locale	Roll	Page
WHITE			
Charles	Tulara Keeneysburg	71	46
Charles	Tuolumne Twp 1	71	235
Charles B	Sierra La Porte	66	768
Charly	Tuolumne Sonora	71	235
Chas	Butte Ophir	56	824
Chas	Mariposa Twp 3	60	587
Chas	Napa Napa	61	104
Chas	Nevada Red Dog	61	544
Chas	Sacramento Ward 1	63	145
Chas	Sierra St Louis	66	815
Chas W	Calaveras Twp 9	57	369
Chas W	San Francisco San Francisco 2	67	686
Chas W	Sonoma Santa Rosa	69	389
Cleaveland	Plumas Meadow Valley	62	930
Cormelius	Calaveras Twp 5	57	202
Cornelia	Sacramento Ward 1	63	97
Cornelius G	Del Norte Crescent	58	649
Cornelius L	Calaveras Twp 5	57	202
D	Mariposa Twp 3	60	621
D	Sacramento Ward 1	63	6
D	Tehama Antelope	70	896
D C	Amador Twp 1	55	456
D I	Yolo Putah	72	586
D J	El Dorado Placerville	58	851
D L	Siskiyou Scott Va	69	37
D R	Del Norte Crescent	58	640
D S	Siskiyou Scott Va	69	37
D S	Yolo Putah	72	586
Dand	Alameda Brooklyn	55	114
Daniel	Colusa Monroeville	57	441
Daniel	Sierra Gibsonville	66	857
Daniel	Sierra Twp 7	66	867
Daniel	Yolo Washington	72	561
Daniel W	Siskiyou Shasta Valley	69	117
Danl	Santa Clara San Jose	65	386
Danl	Sonoma Vallejo	69	611
David	Butte Oregon	56	613
David	Contra Costa Twp 1	57	487
David	San Francisco San Francisco 7	68	1376
David	San Francisco San Francisco 10	67	357
David	Siskiyou Yreka	69	153
David	Yolo Washington	72	561
David*	Butte Oregon	56	613
Delores	Los Angeles Los Nieto	59	437
Dennis	San Francisco San Francisco 9	68	981
Dolores	Los Angeles Los Nieto	59	437
Dr M	El Dorado Diamond	58	772
E	Napa Napa	61	70
E	San Francisco San Francisco 5	67	544
E	Trinity Trinity	70	974
E B	Mendocino Big Rvr	60	840
E B	San Francisco San Francisco 9	68	1072
E E	Tuolumne Columbia	71	321
E J	Tuolumne Columbia	71	340
E J	Tuolumne Columbia	71	358
E Z	Sacramento Alabama	63	416
Edward	Calaveras Twp 7	57	18
Edward	Nevada Little Y	61	534
Edward	Plumas Quincy	62	1005
Edward	San Francisco San Francisco 4	68	1124
Edward	San Francisco San Francisco 3	67	62
Edwin B	Calaveras Twp 6	57	116
Edwin P	Alameda Brooklyn	55	100
Elija	San Francisco San Francisco 12	67	380
Eliz M	Sacramento Granite	63	253
Eliza	Butte Chico	56	557
Eliza J	Butte Chico	56	557
Elizabeth	San Francisco San Francisco 2	67	574
Elizabeth F	Sonoma Petaluma	69	604
Ellen	San Francisco San Francisco 12	67	381
Ellen	San Francisco San Francisco 3	67	40
Ellen	San Francisco San Francisco 3	67	82
Ellen	San Francisco San Francisco 1	68	836
Ellon	Nevada Bridgeport	61	447
Ester	San Francisco San Francisco 2	67	704
F	Butte Chico	56	538
F	Nevada Nevada	61	262
F	Nevada Washington	61	333
F B	Sacramento Ward 1	63	42
F E	Nevada Grass Valley	61	212
Francis	Sonoma Petaluma	69	564
Francis	Tuolumne Twp 2	71	277
Francis	Tuolumne Twp 2	71	387
Francis M	Yuba Bear Rvr	72	1001
Frank	Sacramento Ward 4	63	561
Frank	San Francisco San Francisco 2	67	714
Frank	Sonoma Petaluma	69	556
Frank	Yolo Slate Ra	72	709
Frank	Yuba Slate Ro	72	709
Fred	Sacramento Ward 3	63	475
Freeman	Butte Chico	56	538
G	Sutter Sutter	70	814
WHITE			
G C	El Dorado Newtown	58	776
G G	Sacramento Alabama	63	415
G H	Mariposa Coulterville	60	680
G K	Sacramento Ward 1	63	29
G V	Yuba New York	72	736
G W	Tehama Tehama	70	939
Geo	El Dorado Placerville	58	845
Geo	Mendocino Round Va	60	877
Geo	Placer Illinois	62	705
Geo	Sacramento Granite	63	234
Geo	San Francisco San Francisco 1	68	825
Geo	San Francisco San Francisco 1	68	853
Geo	San Francisco San Francisco 1	68	904
Geo	San Francisco San Francisco 1	68	917
Geo	Santa Clara Redwood	65	452
Geo	Santa Clara Santa Clara	65	498
Geo A	Klamath Klamath	59	226
George	Amador Twp 1	55	452
George	Marin San Rafael	60	773
George	Nevada Little Y	61	531
George	Sacramento San Joaquin	63	354
George	San Francisco San Francisco 9	68	1073
George	San Francisco San Francisco 9	68	1443
George	San Francisco San Francisco 3	67	40
George	San Francisco San Francisco 2	67	555
George	Santa Cruz Pajaro	66	551
George	Shasta Millvill	66	751
Gib S	Santa Cruz Santa Cruz	66	633
Giles	Santa Cruz Santa Cruz	66	633
H	Butte Kimshaw	56	593
H	Mariposa Twp 3	60	574
H	Nevada Grass Valley	61	236
H	Nevada Eureka	61	344
H	San Francisco San Francisco 9	68	1101
H	Shasta Horsetown	66	708
H	Sonoma Santa Rosa	69	422
H	Yolo Cache Crk	72	627
H H	Stanislaus Emory	70	740
H H	Sutter Sutter	70	807
H K	Siskiyou Yreka	69	188
H K	Tuolumne Twp 1	71	207
H L	Tehama Red Bluff	70	910
Hannah	Trinity Trinity	70	974
Harriette	Amador Twp 4	55	239
Harrison	Yuba Long Bar	72	765
Harvey	Calaveras Twp 5	57	202
Harvey	San Francisco San Francisco 7	68	1347
Harvey B	Calaveras Twp 5	57	202
Henry	Butte Chico	56	549
Henry	Butte Cascade	56	698
Henry	Butte Ophir	56	782
Henry	El Dorado Placerville	58	918
Henry	Klamath Liberty	59	231
Henry	Mendocino Big Rvr	60	841
Henry	Plumas Quincy	62	1006
Henry	San Francisco San Francisco 11	67	154
Henry	San Francisco San Francisco 10	67	192
Henry	San Francisco San Francisco 3	67	66
Henry	San Francisco San Francisco 1	68	891
Henry	San Mateo Twp 1	65	54
Henry	Santa Cruz Pajaro	66	531
Henry	Siskiyou Scott Va	69	23
Henry	Siskiyou Scott Ri	69	71
Henry	Sonoma Santa Rosa	69	425
Henry	Tuolumne Twp 1	71	234
Henry	Tuolumne Twp 1	71	481
Henry A	Colusa Monroeville	57	441
Hiram	Sonoma Mendocino	69	464
Horace	Butte Eureka	56	650
Huff	Tulara Yule Rvr	71	31
Isaac	Trinity Whites Crk	70	1028
Isaac K	San Francisco San Francisco 3	67	49
Israel	Plumas Meadow Valley	62	911
J	El Dorado Diamond	58	810
J	El Dorado Placerville	58	859
J	Nevada Grass Valley	61	208
J	Nevada Eureka	61	390
J	San Francisco San Francisco 5	67	550
J	San Francisco San Francisco 2	67	798
J	San Francisco San Francisco 1	68	923
J	Siskiyou Cottonwoood	69	100
J	Solano Vacaville	69	338
J	Tuolumne Jacksonville	71	170
J	Tuolumne Columbia	71	340
J A	Butte Oro	56	684
J B	Butte Oro	56	685
J B	El Dorado Placerville	58	909
J B	Sonoma Armally	69	485
J B	Tuolumne Twp 2	71	281
J C	Amador Twp 1	55	451
J C	San Joaquin Elkhorn	64	989
J C	Stanislaus Emory	70	738
J F	El Dorado Georgetown	58	683
WHITE			
J F	Marin Tomales	60	719
J F S	Marin Tomales	60	719
J H	Placer Todds Va	62	784
J H	Sacramento Ward 4	63	599
J H	San Francisco San Francisco 12	67	367
J I	Solano Vacaville	69	325
J J	Tuolumne Twp 1	71	273
J J	Tuolumne Springfield	71	371
J M	El Dorado Mud Springs	58	957
J P	Siskiyou Callahan	69	17
J Q	Yuba Long Bar	72	750
J S	Butte Bidwell	56	730
J S	Sacramento Dry Crk	63	368
J S	San Francisco San Francisco 5	67	511
J S	Solano Vacaville	69	325
J T	El Dorado Georgetown	58	683
J T	San Francisco San Francisco 9	68	1080
J V	Nevada Bridgeport	61	501
J W	Trinity Redding	70	985
J W	Solano Vacaville	69	338
J*	Del Norte Crescent	58	633
Jacob	Del Norte Crescent	58	634
Jacob	Sierra Twp 5	66	939
James	Alameda Brooklyn	55	128
James	El Dorado Eldorado	58	948
James	Klamath Liberty	59	242
James	Mariposa Twp 1	60	632
James	Mariposa Twp 1	60	657
James	Mendocino Ukiah	60	793
James	Nevada Washington	61	333
James	Nevada Eureka	61	355
James	Placer Illinois	62	738
James	Placer Iona Hills	62	864
James	Sacramento San Joaquin	63	364
James	San Francisco San Francisco 9	68	964
James	Santa Clara San Jose	65	342
James	Santa Clara Fremont	65	440
James	Santa Clara Santa Clara	65	514
James	Santa Cruz Santa Cruz	66	602
James	Trinity Cox'S Bar	70	1037
James	Tulara Yule Rvr	71	22
James	Tulara Keeneysburg	71	45
James	Tuolumne Columbia	71	323
James	Yolo Slate Ra	72	687
James	Yuba North Ea	72	687
James	Yuba Marysville	72	859
James	Yuba Marysville	72	860
James	Yuba Marysville	72	970
James A	San Francisco San Francisco 8	68	1302
James A	San Joaquin Castoria	64	872
James B	Los Angeles Los Angeles	59	510
James B	Plumas Quincy	62	940
James C	San Joaquin Tulare	64	870
James C	San Joaquin Oneal	64	929
James C	San Joaquin Oneal	64	930
James F	Santa Cruz Pajaro	66	574
James R	Mariposa Twp 1	60	632
James W	Calaveras Twp 5	57	202
James Y	Contra Costa Twp 1	57	520
Jane	Tuolumne Shawsfla	71	399
Jane	Tuolumne Twp 2	71	399
Jas	Amador Twp 1	55	473
Jas	Butte Bidwell	56	723
Jas	San Francisco San Francisco 12	67	380
Jas	Sonoma Vallejo	69	629
Jas	Tehama Lassen	70	884
Jas C	San Francisco San Francisco 2	67	716
Jas M	Butte Oregon	56	617
Jas M	San Francisco San Francisco 2	67	559
Jas W	San Francisco San Francisco 10	67	280
Jason	San Francisco San Francisco 11	67	162
Jennie	San Francisco San Francisco 10	67	183
Jhames	Nevada Eureka	61	355
Jno	Butte Oregon	56	611
Jno	Nevada Nevada	61	296
Jno	Nevada Eureka	61	356
Jno	San Francisco San Francisco 6	67	414
Jno C	San Francisco San Francisco 9	68	978
Job	Yolo Putah	72	585
John	Alameda Brooklyn	55	102
John	Alameda Brooklyn	55	150
John	Amador Twp 2	55	269
John	Amador Twp 3	55	372
John	Amador Twp 3	55	382
John	Butte Wyandotte	56	669
John	Butte Cascade	56	697
John	Butte Ophir	56	794
John	Calaveras Twp 6	57	133
John	Calaveras Twp 4	57	332
John	Del Norte Crescent	58	644

California 1860 Census Index

Name	County Locale	M653 Roll	Page
WHITE			
John	El Dorado Salmon Falls	58	1058
John	El Dorado Spanish	58	1124
John	El Dorado Kelsey	58	1144
John	El Dorado Casumnes	58	1166
John	El Dorado Georgetown	58	760
John	Marin Bolinas	60	748
John	Mariposa Coulterville	60	703
John	Placer Yankee J	62	761
John	Placer Michigan	62	847
John	Sacramento Granite	63	235
John	Sacramento Granite	63	239
John	Sacramento Ward 1	63	40
John	San Bernardino San Bernadino	64	635
John	San Diego Agua Caliente	64	814
John	San Francisco San Francisco 7	68	1432
John	San Francisco San Francisco 3	67	27
John	San Francisco San Francisco 12	67	394
John	San Francisco San Francisco 3	67	56
John	Santa Clara Alviso	65	405
John	Shasta Horsetown	66	689
John	Sierra Pine Grove	66	828
John	Sierra Twp 5	66	918
John	Solano Vallejo	69	257
John	Solano Vallejo	69	277
John	Sonoma Armally	69	516
John	Trinity Mouth Ca	70	1015
John	Trinity North Fo	70	1023
John	Trinity Ferry	70	977
John	Tulara Twp 2	71	14
John	Tuolumne Columbia	71	294
John	Tuolumne Columbia	71	325
John	Tuolumne Columbia	71	363
John	Yuba New York	72	734
John	Yuba Marysville	72	949
John A	Calaveras Twp 7	57	16
John B	Placer Secret R	62	612
John C	Calaveras Twp 7	57	15
John D	Santa Clara San Jose	65	350
John Esly*	Sonoma Santa Rosa	69	425
John H	Yuba Marysville	72	850
John M	San Joaquin Stockton	64	1021
John P	Shasta Horsetown	66	706
John R	Sierra Whiskey	66	845
John S	San Francisco San Francisco 3	67	79
Jos	Butte Cascade	56	697
Jos	Klamath Liberty	59	236
Jos	Tehama Lassen	70	873
Jos W	San Francisco San Francisco 10	67	280
Jose M	Los Angeles San Gabriel	59	409
Jose U	Los Angeles San Gabriel	59	409
Joseh	Mendocino Ukiah	60	797
Joseph	El Dorado Mud Springs	58	1000
Joseph	El Dorado White Oaks	58	1014
Joseph	El Dorado Gold Hill	58	1098
Joseph	El Dorado Mud Springs	58	994
Joseph	Mendocino Ukiah	60	797
Joseph	Placer Todds Va	62	786
Joseph	San Francisco San Francisco 8	68	1320
Joseph	San Francisco San Francisco 11	67	153
Joseph	San Francisco San Francisco 10	67	180
Joseph	San Mateo Twp 3	65	76
Joseph D	Placer Sacramento	62	644
Joseph Jr	Tuolumne Twp 2	71	386
Julius	Butte Oregon	56	618
Julius	Calaveras Twp 6	57	112
Kate	Colusa Colusi	57	421
L	El Dorado White Oaks	58	1015
L	El Dorado Placerville	58	826
L	Nevada Eureka	61	354
L	Tehama Lassen	70	866
L	Tehama Lassen	70	867
L E	Mendocino Arrana	60	864
Lambert W	Yuba Marysville	72	858
Laohaiah	Calaveras Twp 6	57	154
Lawrence	Amador Twp 3	55	399
Leonard	Del Norte Crescent	58	637
Lewis	Mariposa Coulterville	60	683
Lewis	San Francisco San Francisco 1	68	915
Loma*	Sonoma Petaluma	69	598
Lomia*	Sonoma Petaluma	69	598
Louis	Placer Michigan	62	808
Louis	Placer Michigan	62	811
Louis	Placer Michigan	62	814
Louisa	Sonoma Petaluma	69	598
Lovell	Nevada Bridgeport	61	447
Lucy	Santa Clara Burnett	65	256
M	Butte Wyandotte	56	659
M	Nevada Grass Valley	61	203
M	Nevada Washington	61	331
M	Nevada Washington	61	341
M C	Alameda Brooklyn	55	187
WHITE			
M F	Amador Twp 3	55	379
M H	Tuolumne Twp 2	71	316
M H	Tuolumne Twp 2	71	324
Margaret	San Francisco San Francisco 4	68	1141
Margaret	San Francisco San Francisco 2	67	574
Margtr	San Francisco San Francisco 6	67	409
Mariette	Sierra La Porte	66	782
Martin	San Francisco San Francisco 9	68	1091
Martin	San Francisco San Francisco 10	67	228
Mary	Sacramento Granite	63	234
Mary	San Francisco San Francisco 9	68	1041
Mary	San Francisco San Francisco 7	68	1403
Mary	Solano Vallejo	69	270
Mary A *	Alameda Brooklyn	55	100
Mary E	San Francisco San Francisco 9	68	987
Mary E	Santa Clara San Jose	65	375
Mary J	San Francisco San Francisco 2	67	798
Maryet*	Alameda Brooklyn	55	100
Mayet	Amador Twp 3	55	100
Michael	Los Angeles San Gabriel	59	408
Michael	Santa Clara Almaden	65	268
Michael	Tuolumne Sonora	71	218
Micheal T	Calaveras Twp 7	57	16
Nicholas	Santa Clara Burnett	65	257
Milton Jr	Amador Twp 3	55	406
Morris*	El Dorado Placerville	58	919
Moses	San Mateo Twp 3	65	108
Murray	Amador Twp 4	55	253
N	Siskiyou Scott Va	69	37
N	Yolo Cache	72	627
Neal	San Joaquin Stockton	64	1063
Nicholas	San Francisco San Francisco 11	67	101
Nicholas	Solano Vallejo	69	264
Nicholas E	Napa Napa	61	82
Nicholos	Solano Vallejo	69	264
O H P	Sacramento Ward 1	63	143
Oliver	San Mateo Twp 1	65	53
Oseould*	Calaveras Twp 6	57	145
Oswald	Calaveras Twp 6	57	145
P	Nevada Grass Valley	61	189
P	Nevada Eureka	61	367
P	Siskiyou Scott Va	69	50
P J	Sierra Downieville	66	957
P M	Butte Cascade	56	692
Pat	Nevada Rough &	61	430
Pat	Nevada Little Y	61	531
Pat	Sacramento Natonia	63	285
Patrick	El Dorado Salmon Falls	58	1058
Patrick	Santa Clara Santa Clara	65	466
Patrick	Sierra Twp 5	66	930
Patrick	Tuolumne Sonora	71	222
Peter	Calaveras Ward 5	57	200
Peter	El Dorado Salmon Hills	58	1058
Peter	Mariposa Twp 3	60	549
Peter	San Francisco San Francisco 1	68	915
Peter	Sierra Twp 5	66	935
Philo	San Francisco San Francisco 7	68	1437
R B	El Dorado Placerville	58	819
R B	Butte Ophir	56	824
R B	El Dorado Casumnes	58	1169
R B	El Dorado Diamond	58	793
R J	Solano Vallejo	69	252
R M	Nevada Nevada	61	256
Randh	Klamath Orleans	59	216
Reickn*	Nevada Nevada	61	295
Reuben	Nevada Nevada	61	295
Rich	Sacramento Dry Crk	63	374
Richard	San Francisco San Francisco 4	68	1165
Richard P	Contra Costa Twp 2	57	567
Richd	Butte Chico	56	551
Robert	Mendocino Little L	60	838
Robert	Sierra Twp 7	66	915
Robert	Tuolumne Twp 3	71	450
Robert W	Contra Costa Twp 2	57	564
S A	Butte Ophir	56	791
S C	San Francisco San Francisco 12	67	380
S C	Tuolumne Sonora	71	245
S E	Tuolumne Twp 1	71	245
S J	Solano Vacaville	69	327
S M	El Dorado Coloma	58	1118
S S	Nevada Bloomfield	61	527
S S	San Mateo Twp 1	65	54
S T	Tehama Red Bluff	70	899
S V	Yuba New York	72	736
Saml	Placer Dutch Fl	62	728
Saml	Sacramento Dry Crk	63	368
Saml	San Francisco San Francisco 9	68	1006
Saml	San Francisco San Francisco 10	67	345
Saml	Stanislaus Emory	70	747
Saml	Trinity Indian C	70	988
WHITE			
Samuel	Siskiyou Klamath	69	92
Samuel	Sonoma Russian	69	444
Samul	Siskiyou Klamath	69	92
Sarah	Alameda Brooklyn	55	199
Sarah	El Dorado White Oaks	58	1013
Sarah	San Francisco San Francisco 7	68	1341
Sarah	San Francisco San Francisco 2	67	630
Sarah	Yuba Marysville	72	966
Schyler	Sierra Whiskey	66	846
Silas	Yolo Slate Ra	72	696
Silas	Yuba Slate Ro	72	696
Solomon	Calaveras Twp 8	57	65
Spencer	Trinity S Fork	70	1032
Stephen	Calaveras Twp 10	57	281
Stephen	Plumas Quincy	62	985
Stephen	Santa Cruz Pescadero	66	647
Susan	San Francisco San Francisco 6	67	427
T	Butte Bidwell	56	721
T B	Tuolumne Columbia	71	352
T H	Sonoma Washington	69	669
T J	San Francisco San Francisco 7	68	1331
T J	Solano Fairfield	69	198
T M	El Dorado Coloma	58	1118
T W	Sacramento Ward 1	63	150
Thas S*	Calaveras Twp 9	57	381
Theodore	Del Norte Crescent	58	671
Thomas	Placer Iona Hills	62	888
Thomas	San Francisco San Francisco 11	67	114
Thomas	San Francisco San Francisco 3	67	50
Thomas	Sierra Eureka	66	1046
Thomas	Sierra Twp 7	66	894
Thomas	Solano Montezuma	69	368
Thomas	Solano Fremont	69	376
Thomas	Tuolumne Twp 5	71	495
Thomas	Yuba Long Bar	72	755
Thomas	Yuba Marysville	72	905
Thomas	Yuba Suida	72	983
Thomas J	Los Angeles Los Angeles	59	392
Thos	Alameda Oakland	55	70
Thos	Mariposa Coulterville	60	694
Thos	San Francisco San Francisco 10	67	258
Thos	Sonoma Bodega	69	523
Thos L	Calaveras Twp 9	57	381
Thos S*	Calaveras Twp 9	57	381
Timothy	Placer Michigan	62	835
V H	Butte Chico	56	566
Vincent	Mendocino Big Rvr	60	851
W	Butte Oregon	56	639
W	Calaveras Twp 9	57	413
W	Nevada Grass Valley	61	226
W	Santa Clara Redwood	65	453
W	Solano Vacaville	69	323
W A	El Dorado Placerville	58	877
W A	Placer Iona Hills	62	862
W B	Sacramento Ward 1	63	49
W B	Sonoma Vallejo	69	630
W F	Butte Wyandotte	56	668
W H	Placer Iona Hills	62	863
W H	Sonoma Armally	69	511
W J	El Dorado Placerville	58	839
W J	Klamath Trinidad	59	220
W P	Butte Chico	56	560
W S	El Dorado Kelsey	58	1137
W T	Sacramento Dry Crk	63	370
W W	Calaveras Twp 9	57	389
W W	Calaveras Twp 9	57	398
W W	Calaveras Twp 9	57	413
W W	San Joaquin Stockton	64	1038
W W	Trinity Douglas	70	979
Walter	Placer Michigan	62	845
Warren	El Dorado Kelsey	58	1138
Whilliam	Sierra Whiskey	66	843
Willard	Mendocino Big Rvr	60	847
William	Colusa Colusi	57	424
William	Del Norte Crescent	58	648
William	El Dorado Coloma	58	1105
William	El Dorado Placerville	58	898
William	Klamath Orleans	59	215
William	Mendocino Big Rvr	60	850
William	Merced Twp 2	60	917
William	Placer Iona Hills	62	889
William	Plumas Quincy	62	947
William	Plumas Quincy	62	976
William	San Francisco San Francisco 7	68	1440
William	San Francisco San Francisco 11	67	90
William	San Joaquin Elkhorn	64	988
William	Santa Cruz Soguel	66	591
William	Shasta Millvill	66	753
William	Siskiyou Shasta Rvr	69	112
William	Siskiyou Klamath	69	89
William	Siskiyou Klamath	69	92
William	Tuolumne Twp 1	71	261

California 1860 Census Index

Name	County Locale	M653 Roll	Page
WHITE			
William	Yuba Parks Ba	72	781
William F	Santa Cruz Pajaro	66	525
William N	San Francisco San Francisco 8	681	291
William W	San Francisco San Francisco 7	681	423
Wilson Y	Sonoma Russian	69	434
Wm	Colusa Colusi	57	426
Wm	Colusa Muion	57	458
Wm	Colusa Muion	57	461
Wm	Humbolt Eel Rvr	59	144
Wm	Napa Napa	61	90
Wm	Placer Auburn	62	567
Wm	Placer Dutch Fl	62	732
Wm	Sacramento American	63	163
Wm	Sacramento Sutter	63	298
Wm	Sacramento Ward 1	63	39
Wm	San Francisco San Francisco 1	68	812
Wm	Sierra Monte Crk	661	039
Wm	Sierra Grizzly	661	058
Wm	Sonoma Petaluma	69	575
Wm	Tehama Moons	70	852
Wm A	Sacramento Ward 1	63	96
Wm B	Calaveras Twp 4	57	299
Wm B	Solano Fairfield	69	201
Wm H	Mendocino Calpella	60	816
Wm H	Placer Mountain	62	707
Wm H	San Francisco San Francisco 10	67	331
Wm J	Mariposa Twp 1	60	671
Wm T	Mariposa Twp 1	60	671
Y*	Solano Vacaville	69	338
Zachaiah	Calaveras Twp 6	57	154
Zeno	Siskiyou Scott Va	69	52
WHITEACRE			
E	Nevada Little Y	61	534
WHITEBACK			
William	Contra Costa Twp 1	57	498
WHITEBELL			
Isaac	Yuba Marysville	72	863
WHITEBREAD			
Godford	Sierra St Louis	66	815
Godford	Sierra St Louis	66	815
Peter	Sierra St Louis	66	811
WHITEBREND			
Peter	Sierra St Louis	66	811
WHITECOMB			
Jas	Sacramento Ward 4	63	519
WHITEFIELD			
John	Placer Forest H	62	794
Peter	Mariposa Twp 3	60	597
WHITEHAM			
H D	Sacramento Granite	63	246
WHITEHARST			
Abram	Calaveras Twp 4	57	310
WHITEHEAD			
Austin	Sacramento Natonia	63	278
C	Calaveras Twp 9	57	414
Chas	Sacramento Ward 1	63	26
Chas	Sacramento Ward 4	63	523
I L	Amador Twp 7	55	414
J L	Amador Twp 7	55	414
J L	Sutter Nicolaus	70	827
Jarvis	Stanislaus Emory	70	750
John	San Francisco San Francisco 8	681	291
John	Sonoma Sonoma	69	647
Jos	Placer Rattle Snake	62	628
Pleasant	San Joaquin Castoria	64	883
Timothy	Sacramento Ward 4	63	588
W H	Amador Twp 3	55	409
W M	Sutter Nicolaus	70	827
William	Yuba Marysville	72	960
WHITEHILL			
Isaac	Sierra Downieville	661	018
Isaac	Yuba Marysville	72	863
J	El Dorado Placerville	58	819
R R*	Nevada Eureka	61	390
WHITEHORN			
Archy	Mendocino Little L	60	832
George	Los Angeles Los Angeles	59	354
Mary	Los Angeles Los Angeles	59	355
Richy	Mendocino Little L	60	832
WHITEHORSE			
David*	Calaveras Twp 5	57	183
WHITEHOUSE			
Chas	Sacramento Ward 3	63	449
Chas H	Sacramento Ward 4	63	499
David	Calaveras Twp 6	57	174
David	Calaveras Twp 6	57	183
Geo	Napa Hot Springs	61	20
M C	San Francisco San Francisco 12	67	392
WHITEHURST			
Abram*	Calaveras Twp 4	57	310
Abrum*	Calaveras Twp 4	57	310
WHITEKER			
David	El Dorado Mud Springs	58	997
WHITEKER			
Joseph	Sierra Whiskey	66	847
WHITELAN			
Jas G	Butte Oregon	56	630
WHITELATCH			
Henry	Calaveras Twp 10	57	262
WHITELAW			
Jas G	Butte Oregon	56	630
Sarah	Butte Oregon	56	630
WHITELY			
Jno	Butte Chico	56	563
Jno	Butte Chico	56	564
John	Sierra Downieville	661	010
Marshall	Del Norte Klamath	58	654
WHITEMAN			
Adam	Butte Eureka	56	647
Charles	Yolo Putah	72	548
G F	San Francisco San Francisco 10	67	264
Gideon	San Francisco San Francisco 7	681	443
H	Amador Twp 3	55	383
Jos	San Francisco San Francisco 2	67	785
Joseph R	San Francisco San Francisco 11	67	103
M	Butte Oregon	56	640
Nicholas	Calaveras Twp 4	57	316
S	Sacramento Ward 4	63	513
W E	Butte Oregon	56	632
WHITEMANBOY			
---	Mendocino Big Rock	60	875
WHITEMORE			
David	Butte Bidwell	56	730
John	El Dorado Placerville	58	919
WHITENBURG			
Fred	El Dorado White Oaks	581	001
WHITER			
D	Nevada Eureka	61	354
WHITERBY			
Oliver S	San Diego San Diego	64	765
WHITESAL			
J D	Calaveras Twp 7	57	6
Jas*	Nevada Grass Valley	61	180
WHITESEDIS			
Thos*	Amador Twp 3	55	406
WHITESELL			
William	Nevada Rough &	61	400
WHITESIDE			
Isaiah	Sacramento Ward 4	63	518
W B	Sacramento Brighton	63	191
WHITESIDER			
Joshua	Santa Clara Santa Clara	65	514
Nismun E	Yuba Parks Ba	72	777
WHITESIDES			
A	Sacramento Ward 1	63	50
A R	Butte Chico	56	547
C H	Sacramento Ward 1	63	24
Charles	Sacramento Ward 1	63	80
Chas	Sacramento Ward 1	63	152
Elisa	San Bernardino San Bernadino	64	618
Emma	Sacramento Ward 1	63	120
Ises	Sacramento Mississipi	63	188
J B	Butte Chico	56	547
Mary	Sacramento San Joaquin	63	351
Nimrin E*	Yuba Parks Ba	72	777
Ninnin E*	Yuba Parks Ba	72	777
P M	Tuolumne Springfield	71	370
Pete	Tuolumne Twp 2	71	370
Peter	Calaveras Twp 6	57	173
Pritchd	Sacramento Mississipi	63	188
Sam	Yolo Slate Ra	72	705
Sam	Yuba Slate Ro	72	705
Samuel	Yuba Parks Ba	72	777
Samuel A	Yuba Parks Ba	72	777
Thos*	Amador Twp 3	55	406
W H	Sonoma Petaluma	69	603
Whos	Santa Clara Alviso	65	409
Wm	Sacramento San Joaquin	63	351
WHITESTINS			
S	Nevada Nevada	61	251
WHITETIDES			
L	Nevada Grass Valley	61	208
WHITETON			
Jno	Sacramento Ward 4	63	520
WHITETREE			
Austie*	Sacramento Natonia	63	278
Austir*	Sacramento Natonia	63	278
WHITETREED			
Austir*	Sacramento Natonia	63	278
WHITEWOOD			
Allen	Butte Oregon	56	641
WHITEZEDES			
Thos	Amador Twp 3	55	406
WHITFIELD			
Bynam	Sacramento Natonia	63	270
Bynard	Sacramento Natonia	63	270
Chas G	Calaveras Twp 10	57	277
WHITFIELD			
J	Tuolumne Twp 2	71	371
J T	Trinity New Rvr	701	031
James	Tulara Twp 3	71	51
John	Placer Forest H	62	802
John W	Amador Twp 4	55	248
N	Shasta Shasta	66	760
Peter	Mariposa Twp 3	60	597
Robert	Sacramento Ward 1	63	123
W M	Solano Vallejo	69	253
WHITFORD			
Alfred	Siskiyou Shasta Rvr	69	111
Andrew	Sacramento Ward 1	63	28
D	Yolo Cache Crk	72	597
F	Tuolumne Big Oak	71	143
Hugh	Tuolumne Shawsfla	71	379
J O	Sacramento Granite	63	269
Richard	Tuolumne Jamestown	71	453
Thos G	Alameda Brooklyn	55	208
William	Tulara Visalia	71	21
WHITHAM			
E F	Santa Clara Gilroy	65	240
Jas E	San Francisco San Francisco 5	67	477
WHITHAN			
H D*	Sacramento Granite	63	246
WHITHEAD			
William	Yuba Long Bar	72	772
WHITHEN			
W J*	San Francisco San Francisco 4	681	146
WHITHEWSH			
Henry*	San Francisco San Francisco 9	68	946
WHITHUN			
H D*	Sacramento Granite	63	246
WHITHURST			
Henry	San Francisco San Francisco 9	68	946
L A	Santa Clara Redwood	65	453
WHITHY			
Winiard*	San Bernardino San Bernadino	64	633
WHITIE			
---*	Placer Auburn	62	591
WHITIES			
J A	Calaveras Twp 9	57	392
WHITIKER			
Nathl	San Francisco San Francisco 4	681	143
WHITINEY			
W R	El Dorado White Oaks	581	002
WHITING			
A	Butte Oregon	56	636
A	Butte Oro	56	685
A J	Shasta Shasta	66	680
B	Placer Dutch Fl	62	728
B F	Sacramento Ward 1	63	98
B G	San Francisco San Francisco 2	67	674
B J*	Sacramento Ward 1	63	98
Barnet	Alameda Oakland	55	31
C L	San Francisco San Francisco 10	67	316
Charles	Contra Costa Twp 3	57	598
Charles	Monterey San Juan	601	009
Cornelius S	San Francisco San Francisco 9	68	999
Danforth Thoma	Shasta Millvill	66	727
E H	Nevada Grass Valley	61	175
E W	Tehama Red Bluff	70	928
Elisha	Yuba Parks Ba	72	774
F	Nevada Grass Valley	61	220
F M	Shasta Shasta	66	678
Fenton B	Plumas Meadow Valley	62	899
Geo A	Tuolumne Twp 1	71	273
Geo W	San Francisco San Francisco 9	681	055
Grove	Yuba Suida	72	989
H	Sacramento Ward 3	63	456
Harry	El Dorado Kelsey	581	151
Henry	Tuolumne Sonora	71	484
Henry*	Placer Michigan	62	814
J	Calaveras Twp 9	57	387
J	Sutter Nicolaus	70	826
J D	Butte Cascade	56	689
J R	San Francisco San Francisco 7	681	438
James	Tuolumne Columbia	71	290
James W	Contra Costa Twp 2	57	553
James*	Placer Michigan	62	845
Jno	Mendocino Big Rvr	60	843
John	Contra Costa Twp 3	57	601
Joseph P	San Francisco San Francisco 4	681	165
L	El Dorado Kelsey	581	151
L C	Tuolumne Twp 2	71	368
L D	Amador Twp 3	55	386
L L	Nevada Grass Valley	61	194
L W	Placer Dutch Fl	62	731
Levi P	Plumas Quincy	62	954
Lewis	Alameda Brooklyn	55	80
Nois	Napa Napa	61	76
O S	Tuolumne Twp 2	71	320
Peter	Siskiyou Scott Ri	69	70
R L	San Francisco San Francisco 9	68	986

California 1860 Census Index

Name	County Locale	M653 Roll	Page
WHITING			
Robert*	Placer Michigan	62	847
Ruggles	San Joaquin Stockton	64	1019
S	Nevada Grass Valley	61	220
S C	Tuolumne Springfield	71	368
Samuel W	Siskiyou Yreka	69	173
Smith	San Joaquin Stockton	64	1018
Th A	Siskiyou Scott Va	69	59
Thos	Sacramento Ward 1	63	73
Timothy	Butte Kimshaw	56	584
Timothy A	Siskiyou Yreka	69	155
William J	San Francisco San Francisco 4	68	1133
WHITINY			
Joseph P	San Francisco San Francisco 4	68	1165
William J	San Francisco San Francisco 4	68	1133
WHITISUTY			
W H	Sonoma Petaluma	69	603
WHITLACK			
Danl*	Sacramento Cosumnes	63	393
WHITLAN			
Francis H*	Calaveras Twp 9	57	354
WHITLEY			
Charles L	San Joaquin Castoria	64	890
Cynthia	Tulara Visalia	71	108
D	Nevada Grass Valley	61	185
David	Tuolumne Twp 5	71	518
E	Siskiyou Scott Ri	69	81
Emma	Siskiyou Yreka	69	194
F G	Tuolumne Shawsfla	71	379
George T	Solano Suisan	69	211
Jonthan	San Bernardino S Timate	64	687
M	Sacramento Sutter	63	306
Thomas	Los Angeles San Pedro	59	481
Winiard	San Bernardino San Bernadino	64	633
WHITLOCH			
Chas	Tuolumne Big Oak	71	142
WHITLOCK			
Almy	San Bernardino San Salvador	64	653
Chaes*	El Dorado Georgetown	58	706
Chals*	El Dorado Georgetown	58	706
Charles*	Colusa Mansville	57	437
Chas	Trinity Douglas	70	980
D D	Sacramento Cosumnes	63	381
Danl*	Sacramento Cosumnes	63	393
Geo	Sacramento Ward 1	63	124
Geo W	Sacramento Ward 1	63	126
Harvey G San Bernardino	San Bernadino	64	629
J M	Butte Oregon	56	618
James H	Plumas Meadow Valley	62	901
Jason	Placer Michigan	62	807
Jason	Placer Michigan	62	811
Joseph	Colusa Mansville	57	438
Thos	Napa Yount	61	53
Welsey	San Mateo Twp 3	65	100
Wm	San Francisco San Francisco 5	67	554
WHITLON			
Francis H*	Calaveras Twp 9	57	354
WHITLOW			
Francis H*	Calaveras Twp 9	57	354
Joseph	Mendocino Ukiah	60	800
Wm	Tuolumne Twp 1	71	262
WHITLUCK			
J M*	Butte Oregon	56	618
WHITLY			
J M	Shasta Millvill	66	749
S V	Shasta Millvill	66	749
Samuel	San Joaquin Elkhorn	64	975
WHITMAN			
A	Nevada Eureka	61	361
A P	San Joaquin Stockton	64	1034
A P	Solano Benecia	69	284
Adam	Butte Eureka	56	647
Annie	Butte Kimshaw	56	597
B C	Solano Benecia	69	290
C J	Sonoma Russian	69	435
Charles B	Humbolt Eureka	59	177
Chas	Alameda Brooklyn	55	136
Chas	Calaveras Twp 5	57	198
Conrad	Butte Eureka	56	655
D K	Sacramento Natonia	63	281
David	Yuba Parke Ba	72	784
Flinly	Monterey Alisal	60	1039
Flinty	Monterey Alisal	60	1039
Francis B	Tuolumne Twp 1	71	275
G W	Nevada Nevada	61	256
Henry	Nevada Nevada	61	256
J	Nevada Grass Valley	61	199
J W	Sonoma Cloverdale	69	682
J*	Nevada Grass Valley	61	172
Jas A	Placer Ophir	62	652
John	Alameda Murray	55	218
John	Tuolumne Twp 2	71	294
Jos	Placer Dutch Fl	62	718
Luther P	San Joaquin Castoria	64	878
M	El Dorado Placerville	58	835

Name	County Locale	M653 Roll	Page
WHITMAN			
Marcy G	San Francisco San Francisco 6	67	441
Mercy G	San Francisco San Francisco 6	67	441
Monroe	Plumas Quincy	62	945
R P	Solano Benecia	69	290
Saml	Butte Kimshaw	56	593
Thomas	Calaveras Twp 9	57	359
W C	El Dorado Placerville	58	837
Wm	San Francisco San Francisco 2	67	722
WHITMAR			
Chas	Calaveras Twp 5	57	198
WHITMARSH			
P P*	Nevada Red Dog	61	552
S P*	Nevada Red Dog	61	552
Samuel	Placer Auburn	62	564
Susan E	Placer Auburn	62	564
WHITMER			
F L	Sacramento Ward 1	63	89
WHITMEY			
N	Nevada Eureka	61	354
WHITMIN			
George*	San Francisco San Francisco 2	67	576
WHITMINE			
J B*	San Francisco San Francisco 5	67	521
WHITMIRE			
George*	San Francisco San Francisco 2	67	576
R H	San Mateo Twp 2	65	123
Thomas	Siskiyou Shasta Valley	69	117
WHITMON			
George W	Sierra Twp 5	66	930
H M	San Francisco San Francisco 6	67	456
William	San Francisco San Francisco 7	68	1440
WHITMOR			
D S	Sacramento Ward 1	63	136
WHITMORE			
Adrien S	Placer Secret R	62	611
B F	Napa Hot Springs	61	20
B J	Napa Hot Springs	61	20
Charles	Alameda Brooklyn	55	130
Chas	Trinity Oregon G	70	1009
D K	Sacramento Natonia	63	281
D W	Sacramento Ward 1	63	20
Daniel	San Joaquin Elkhorn	64	970
David	Butte Bidwell	56	730
Dudly	Yolo Slate Ra	72	691
Dudly	Yuba Slate Ro	72	691
Efraim*	Yuba Parks Ba	72	781
Ephraim	Yuba Parks Ba	72	781
Epraim	Yuba Parke Ba	72	781
George	San Francisco San Francisco 3	67	53
George	San Francisco San Francisco 2	67	576
George W	Sierra Twp 5	66	930
H M	San Francisco San Francisco 6	67	456
H M	San Francisco San Francisco 6	67	468
H W	El Dorado Mud Springs	58	967
Hannibal	Calaveras Twp 6	57	138
Heennibral*	Calaveras Twp 5	57	138
Hunnibral*	Calaveras Twp 5	57	138
J B*	San Francisco San Francisco 5	67	521
J S	Trinity Sturdiva	70	1007
J W	El Dorado Cold Spring	58	1100
Jerre	Trinity Sturdiva	70	1006
John	Monterey Monterey	60	927
Joseph	Humbolt Eel Rvr	59	144
L O	Calaveras Twp 8	57	70
Mary	Calaveras Twp 8	57	98
Peter	San Bernardino Santa Barbara	64	180
Q A	Calaveras Twp 9	57	413
S P	San Francisco San Francisco 6	67	453
S S	Sacramento Ward 1	63	136
Saml	Butte Ophir	56	791
Samuel H	Contra Costa Twp 2	57	569
Tiler	El Dorado Casumnes	58	1168
Tiles	El Dorado Casumnes	58	1168
W	Napa Napa	61	75
William	Santa Cruz Pajaro	66	573
WHITNALL			
J L	San Francisco San Francisco 3	67	21
WHITNER			
Caroline	Napa Napa	61	94
WHITNERS			
A P	Sierra Morristown	66	1051
WHITNEY			
A	Sonoma Washington	69	667
A C	San Francisco San Francisco 6	67	437
A D	Sacramento Ward 1	63	74
A W	Stanislaus Emory	70	742
Albert	San Francisco San Francisco 9	68	1078
Alfred	Calaveras Twp 10	57	263
Almira*	Sacramento Ward 1	63	90
Alnire	Sacramento Ward 1	63	90
Alniux*	Sacramento Ward 1	63	90
Alonzo	Trinity Weaverville	70	1052
Alpren	Calaveras Twp 10	57	263
Anna	Napa Napa	61	103
Asa	Sonoma Washington	69	667

Name	County Locale	M653 Roll	Page
WHITNEY			
Asa	Yuba Foster B	72	825
B L	Sierra Downieville	66	997
C C	Tehama Red Bluff	70	910
C S	San Francisco San Francisco 5	67	522
Chas	San Francisco San Francisco 3	67	32
D G	Sacramento Ward 1	63	48
Danforth Thoma	Shasta Millvill	66	727
Danl	Santa Clara San Jose	65	335
Edward	Mendocino Big Rvr	60	842
Edward L	Humbolt Eureka	59	171
Edward W	Yuba Marysville	72	881
Elmera	San Francisco San Francisco 10	67	215
F L	Sacramento Ward 1	63	89
F S*	Sacramento Ward 1	63	89
Francis L*	Placer Secret R	62	618
Francis S*	Placer Secret R	62	618
Franklin	Sierra Pine Grove	66	830
Frederica	San Francisco San Francisco 10	67	182
Geo	Klamath Orleans	59	216
Geo	Placer Secret R	62	618
Geo O	San Francisco San Francisco 6	67	418
Geo W	Sacramento Ward 1	63	107
H A	San Francisco San Francisco 10	67	316
H L	Sierra Downieville	66	997
Harrison	Humbolt Eureka	59	170
Henry	San Francisco San Francisco 7	68	1338
Henry	Sierra Twp 5	66	917
Henry	Tuolumne Twp 1	71	484
Henry C	San Joaquin Castoria	64	875
Henry M	San Francisco San Francisco 10	67	352
Henry*	Placer Michigan	62	814
Isaac W	Santa Clara Gilroy	65	226
J B	Yolo Slate Ra	72	716
J B	Yuba Slate Ro	72	716
J D	Butte Cascade	56	689
J M	Siskiyou Scott Va	69	48
J R	Placer Virginia	62	675
J R	San Francisco San Francisco 10	67	316
Jacob	Sonoma Armally	69	507
James	San Francisco San Francisco 9	68	982
James	San Mateo Twp 3	65	75
James	Tuolumne Twp 2	71	290
James	Tuolumne Columbia	71	313
Jas	Sacramento Ward 4	63	524
Jesse	San Francisco San Francisco 1	68	843
Jno	Sacramento Ward 1	63	149
Jno O	Butte Kimshaw	56	575
John	Contra Costa Twp 1	57	535
John	Monterey San Juan	60	988
John	Tuolumne Springfield	71	368
Joseph	San Francisco San Francisco 9	68	1101
L	El Dorado Mud Springs	58	1000
Lewis	Alameda Brooklyn	55	80
Lyman	San Bernardino Santa Ba	64	211
Mary	El Dorado Salmon Falls	58	1037
N	Nevada Eureka	61	354
N C	Calaveras Twp 9	57	396
N*	Nevada Eureka	61	354
Norman H	Yuba Marysville	72	879
P M	San Francisco San Francisco 5	67	522
Robert*	Placer Michigan	62	847
S A	San Francisco San Francisco 5	67	522
S M	Siskiyou Scott Va	69	48
Samuel	Calaveras Twp 6	57	153
Sarah	Santa Clara San Jose	65	335
T W	Yolo Washington	72	570
Thomas	El Dorado Casumnes	58	1169
Thomas	Sacramento Ward 1	63	119
Thos	Yolo Putah	72	614
W	El Dorado Coloma	58	1102
W F	Sacramento Ward 3	63	458
W R	San Francisco San Francisco 4	68	1165
W*	Nevada Eureka	61	354
Walter	Placer Michigan	62	827
Walter	San Francisco San Francisco 8	68	1252
Warren	San Joaquin Elkhorn	64	953
Wdight	Santa Clara Gilroy	65	226
William	Calaveras Twp 6	57	131
William	Contra Costa Twp 3	57	586
William	San Francisco San Francisco 11	67	143
William	Tulara Sinks Te	71	43
William D	San Joaquin Castoria	64	875
Wm	Amador Twp 1	55	480
Wm	Nevada Nevada	61	244
Wm E	San Francisco San Francisco 7	68	1441
WHITNIN G			
Kate	San Francisco San Francisco 4	68	1121
WHITNING			
Kate	San Francisco San Francisco 4	68	1121

California 1860 Census Index

Name	County Locale	M653 Roll	Page
WHITNOTT			
K C*	Mariposa Twp 3	60	612
R C	Mariposa Twp 3	60	612
WHITNY			
Edward	Mendocino Big Rvr	60	842
James	San Francisco San Francisco 11	153	67
WHITON			
Wm	El Dorado Kelsey	58	1151
WHITREDGE			
Edward F*	Calaveras Twp 6	57	146
WHITRICK			
Henry	Placer Todds Va	62	762
WHITRIDGE			
Alfred	Santa Clara Redwood	65	455
James W	Sierra Downieville	66	970
WHITS			
G W	Nevada Nevada	61	249
WHITSEAD			
E	San Francisco San Francisco 6	67	448
WHITSEDGE			
Edward F*	Calaveras Twp 6	57	146
WHITSEL			
Wm C K	Humbolt Mattole	59	123
WHITSELL			
Elijah	Tuolumne Twp 1	71	268
J M	Butte Oregon	56	619
WHITSET			
William C	Siskiyou Yreka	69	126
WHITSHA			
Edward	Tuolumne Twp 2	71	329
WHITSIRON			
Nierinibral*	Calaveras Twp 6	57	138
WHITSON			
B F	Butte Kimshaw	56	598
David	Yolo Slate Ra	72	704
David	Yuba Slate Ro	72	704
E*	Butte Ophir	56	755
J E	Butte Ophir	56	755
WHITSTINO			
Jenry S	San Francisco San Francisco 3	67	48
WHITT			
Cecelia M*	Solano Vallejo	69	249
David*	Butte Oregon	56	613
WHITTAKER			
A	Sacramento Dry Crk	63	373
D	El Dorado Georgetown	58	690
Francis	Sacramento Georgian	63	337
J H	Butte Bidwell	56	716
J H	Butte Bidwell	56	722
James	San Joaquin Stockton	64	1052
Jno M	Sacramento Dry Crk	63	372
John	Calaveras Twp 8	57	83
John	Sacramento Ward 4	63	518
John	Tulara Twp 4	71	45
John R	Calaveras Twp 8	57	56
Joseph	Mendocino Ukiah	60	793
Ralph J	Sacramento American	63	169
Thos	Sacramento Georgian	63	337
Wm	Sacramento Ward 4	63	505
Wm	Sacramento Ward 4	63	556
WHITTALE			
W C	Amador Twp 3	55	382
WHITTAM			
Georege	El Dorado Greenwood	58	709
WHITTARDY			
John W	San Luis Obispo San Luis Obispo	65	15
WHITTELL			
James	San Francisco San Francisco 2	67	608
WHITTEM			
J M	Colusa Monroeville	57	454
WHITTEN			
Amos	Shasta Shasta	66	732
C A*	Placer Forest H	62	806
John	Tuolumne Jamestown	71	427
M	Sacramento Sutter	63	307
M	Siskiyou Scott Va	69	55
Oliver	San Francisco San Francisco 12	366	67
Samuel B	Humbolt Table Bl	59	141
Thomas Y	Contra Costa Twp 3	57	588
Wm L	Mariposa Twp 3	60	584
WHITTENBERG			
P	Marin Bolinas	60	727
WHITTER			
C C	Shasta Horsetown	66	698
WHITTERD			
Wm L	Mariposa Twp 3	60	584
WHITTETT			
James	San Francisco San Francisco 2	67	608
WHITTEY			
E	Siskiyou Scott Ri	69	81
Foster	Nevada Rough &	61	428
Tho	Siskiyou Scott Va	69	60
WHITTIEEN			
Amisor*	Alameda Brooklyn	55	126
WHITTIER			
A W	Solano Suisan	69	205
Alpheus	San Francisco San Francisco 7	68	1408
B	San Mateo Twp 3	65	105
C E	Santa Clara Burnett	65	258
D A	Marin Saucileto	60	751
Howard	Tuolumne Columbia	71	294
Isaac	San Francisco San Francisco 1	68	905
John F	Siskiyou Yreka	69	124
Louis	Sacramento Ward 4	63	564
Merrett	Butte Mountain	56	739
Merritt	Butte Mountain	56	739
Niles	San Francisco San Francisco 11	156	67
Philip	Placer Michigan	62	850
Roland	San Francisco San Francisco 2	67	738
W F	San Francisco San Francisco 10	200	67
Wilson*	Placer Yankee J	62	777
WHITTIKER			
D	El Dorado Georgetown	58	690
Jas P	Marin Tomales	60	721
WHITTIN			
Oliver	San Francisco San Francisco 12	366	67
WHITTING			
Thomas	Calaveras Twp 8	57	63
WHITTINGTON			
J H	Solano Suisan	69	221
WHITTIUN			
Amisor*	Alameda Brooklyn	55	126
WHITTLE			
Dennis	San Francisco San Francisco 7	68	1410
J C	Amador Twp 5	55	358
Jno	San Francisco San Francisco 10	309	67
John	Trinity S Fork	70	1032
Luther*	Colusa Monroeville	57	446
M W	Santa Clara Santa Clara	65	470
Robert	Siskiyou Yreka	69	143
Robert	Siskiyou Yreka	69	149
Thomas	Tuolumne Twp 1	71	251
Thos	San Mateo Twp 1	65	50
William	San Mateo Twp 3	65	87
Wm	El Dorado Greenwood	58	710
WHITTLER			
C C	Shasta Horsetown	66	698
WHITTLESEY			
J W	Tuolumne Twp 3	71	460
WHITTO			
Thomas	Tuolumne Shawsfla	71	412
WHITTOCK			
Charles	El Dorado Georgetown	58	706
Charles*	Colusa Mansville	57	437
Robert	Solano Fremont	69	384
Willard	Tuolumne Jamestown	71	422
WHITTOD			
Robert	Solano Fremont	69	384
WHITTON			
Abe	Shasta Shasta	66	730
C A*	Placer Forest H	62	806
Congrave J	Napa Yount	61	37
Daniel	Placer Forest H	62	765
Eligah	Napa Yount	61	37
Elijah	Napa Yount	61	37
Ephraim	Placer Forest H	62	802
Green	Napa Yount	61	34
J W*	Napa Napa	61	106
Morgan S	Napa Yount	61	37
R J	Napa Yount	61	35
W	Siskiyou Scott Va	69	55
WHITTREN			
W J*	San Francisco San Francisco 4	68	1146
WHITTRIS			
Wilson*	Placer Yankee J	62	777
WHITTY			
Jasher	San Joaquin Castoria	64	890
Wm	Sacramento Ward 1	63	79
WHITUDGE			
Edward F*	Calaveras Twp 5	57	146
WHITUDYR			
Edward F	Calaveras Twp 6	57	146
WHITWILL			
W H	Del Norte Happy Ca	58	668
WHITWORTH			
H	Tuolumne Jacksonville	71	164
Henry	Tuolumne Jacksonville	71	164
Henry	Tuolumne Twp 1	71	466
Jas	San Bernardino San Bernadino	64	645
Jas	Trinity Douglas	70	980
John	Placer Auburn	62	571
Samuel	El Dorado Placerville	58	895
WHL			
Frank K	San Francisco San Francisco 10	191	67
WHLAN			
---	Mendocino Round Va	60	885
WHLER			
Jas*	Sacramento Ward 1	63	97
WHLRAXTAR			
Leuis*	Mariposa Coulterville	60	677
WHLY			
Frederick*	San Francisco San Francisco 4	68	1125
WHO HU			
Ah	Sierra Whiskey	66	843
WHO			
---	Amador Twp 5	55	345
---	Amador Twp 6	55	430
---	Amador Twp 6	55	432
---	Butte Oregon	56	626
---	Calaveras Twp 10	57	261
---	Calaveras Twp 10	57	285
---	Calaveras Twp 10	57	286
---	Sacramento Ward 1	63	54
---	Sierra Poker Flats	66	839
Fimg	Butte Ophir	56	801
Ha	Sierra Pine Grove	66	825
Hu	Sierra Whiskey	66	843
WHOF			
Henry	Butte Mountain	56	740
WHOFF			
Wm H	Butte Ophir	56	795
WHOLCKE			
William	Sierra Whiskey	66	850
WHOLEMAN			
J R	Napa Clear Lake	61	127
WHOLER			
Richd*	San Francisco San Francisco 2	67	757
WHOLT			
Geo	San Francisco San Francisco 9	68	1090
WHON			
---	Placer Secret R	62	622
WHONG			
---	Calaveras Twp 5	57	236
---	San Francisco San Francisco 4	68	1204
---	Yuba Long Bar	72	766
Fing	San Francisco San Francisco 5	67	508
WHOO			
---	Amador Twp 6	55	447
WHOODHEAD			
Ed	Tuolumne Twp 3	71	464
WHOR			
---	Placer Auburn	62	573
WHORLEY			
Michael	San Francisco San Francisco 12	382	67
WHORTON			
John	San Francisco San Francisco 3	67	45
Robert	Contra Costa Twp 3	57	614
WHOSON			
Robert*	Nevada Bridgeport	61	496
WHOSTER			
L	Tehama Lassen	70	880
WHSON			
S	Sacramento Ward 3	63	431
WHTE			
L	Nevada Eureka	61	354
Milton Jr	Amador Twp 3	55	406
WHTTRIS			
Wilson*	Placer Yankee J	62	777
WHU			
---	Calaveras Twp 5	57	223
---	Calaveras Twp 10	57	261
---	Calaveras Twp 8	57	60
---	Calaveras Twp 8	57	92
---	Mariposa Twp 1	60	666
---*	Calaveras Twp 9	57	349
WHUCK			
Frank	Tuolumne Twp 1	71	255
WHUKERMAN			
Theodore*	Calaveras Twp 10	57	298
WHULEM			
Wm*	Napa Napa	61	83
WHULEN			
James	El Dorado Big Bar	58	735
M*	Tuolumne Big Oak	71	156
WHULER			
A R*	Sacramento Granite	63	246
Gilbert*	Butte Oregon	56	627
W P*	Stanislaus Branch	70	704
WHULLICK			
Hamsen	San Francisco San Francisco 2	67	763
WHULTE			
H F	Sutter Yuba	70	770
WHUMBER			
Peter	Santa Clara San Jose	65	295
WHUNLY			
Wm M*	Sierra Twp 7	66	886
WHUR			
James*	Sierra St Louis	66	817
WHUS			
Samuel*	Alameda Brooklyn	55	93

Name	County Locale	M653 Roll	Page
WHUSTEN			
A C*	Siskiyou Klamath	69	96
WHUTER			
David*	San Francisco San Francisco 12		364
			67
WHUTHAMBE			
A M*	Tuolumne Twp 2	71	281
WHUTHROP			
William*	Calaveras Twp 4	57	318
WHUTIR			
S	El Dorado Greenwood	58	723
WHY			
---	Calaveras Twp 5	57	223
---	Marin Cortemad	60	791
---	Mariposa Twp 1	60	627
---	Sacramento Granite	63	232
---	Sacramento Cosumnes	63	409
---	Stanislaus Branch	70	713
---	Yuba Fosters	72	843
Ah	Sacramento Mississipi	63	188
Ah	Sacramento Cosumnes	63	396
WHYERS			
John H	Santa Clara Santa Clara	65	499
WHYLAN			
M	San Francisco San Francisco 5	67	497
WHYLER			
E	Sutter Yuba	70	769
Elizabeth	Sutter Yuba	70	766
J	Sutter Yuba	70	769
Josephine	Yuba Marysville	72	845
WHYTE			
J P	San Francisco San Francisco 5	67	530
Richd J	Santa Clara Santa Clara	65	481
WI			
---	Amador Twp 1	55	511
---	Calaveras Twp 5	57	192
---	Calaveras Twp 4	57	333
Dee	El Dorado Diamond	58	797
Fou	Calaveras Twp 4	57	320
Get	Nevada Bridgeport	61	492
Kum	El Dorado Georgetown	58	747
Lic	Stanislaus Emory	70	752
Ling	San Francisco San Francisco 3	67	7
Ong	Nevada Bridgeport	61	492
Sam	Sacramento Ward 1	63	156
Sing	San Francisco San Francisco 3	67	7
Yang*	Fresno Twp 1	59	25
WIAH			
---	Fresno Twp 1	59	28
WIANER			
William*	Napa Hot Springs	61	19
WIARMOUTH			
Robt	Plumas Meadow Valley	62	903
WIATT			
E S B	Tuolumne Jamestown	71	422
WIBB			
S G	Calaveras Twp 9	57	415
Sarah*	Trinity Weaverville	70	1071
WIBBER			
J	El Dorado Diamond	58	786
Peter*	Calaveras Twp 7	57	18
WIBBERT			
Joseph	Calaveras Twp 7	57	18
WIBDEN			
Tayes	Mendocino Ukiah	60	798
WIBEOX			
S T	Butte Bidwell	56	719
WIBER			
Henry	Yolo Washington	72	566
John	San Francisco San Francisco 3	67	12
Louis*	Calaveras Twp 9	57	389
WIBERRG			
John	San Francisco San Francisco 3	67	69
WIBLE			
Elias	Amador Twp 2	55	261
WIBLER			
Peter*	Calaveras Twp 7	57	18
WIBLEY			
J	Sierra Twp 7	66	895
William	Placer Michigan	62	854
WIBLING			
Henry	Butte Hamilton	56	515
WIBOR			
Louis*	Calaveras Twp 9	57	389
WIBURG			
John	San Francisco San Francisco 3	67	69
WIBY			
John*	Shasta Shasta	66	667
WIBZ			
John*	Shasta Shasta	66	667
WIC CHAMONE			
---	Tulara Twp 2	71	31
WIC			
---	Tuolumne Twp 5	71	525
WICE			
J	El Dorado White Oaks	58	1025

Name	County Locale	M653 Roll	Page
WICE			
Martin	San Francisco San Francisco 7	681	392
Moses	San Francisco San Francisco 7	681	368
WICHELHAUSEN			
Herman*	Mendocino Calpella	60	816
Louis	San Francisco San Francisco 10		188
			67
WICHELL			
Franklin	Sacramento Natonia	63	273
WICHEN			
---	Mendocino Big Rock	60	875
Godfrid	Plumas Quincy	62	916
Thomas	Monterey Monterey	60	956
WICHENA			
Florentina*	Sierra Downieville	66	970
WICHER			
Johnson	Amador Twp 6	55	439
Matthews	Sierra Scales D	66	802
WICHERS			
Herman	Klamath Liberty	59	231
WICHEW			
Thomas	Monterey Monterey	60	956
WICHLOW			
Henry	Tuolumne Shawsfla	71	417
WICHMAN			
T	El Dorado Placerville	58	865
WICHS			
Moser	Alameda Brooklyn	55	126
WICHWAN			
Henry	Sierra Twp 5	66	945
WICK			
---	Nevada Bridgeport	61	439
A T	Solano Vacaville	69	339
Charles	Tulara Keyesville	71	57
J	Sierra Downieville	66	953
J R	Sierra Downieville	66	953
R K	Sacramento Ward 4	63	572
S B	Placer Michigan	62	808
WICKAFF			
D D*	Napa Clear Lake	61	137
WICKELIOT			
L W	Yolo Putah	72	549
WICKELIST			
S M	Yolo Putah	72	549
WICKEMUDGE			
Henry	Fresno Twp 2	59	48
WICKER			
C	El Dorado Newtown	58	776
Corbin	Tulara Sinks Te	71	42
I C	Amador Twp 2	55	306
J C	Amador Twp 2	55	306
Johnson*	Amador Twp 6	55	439
Marshal	Tehama Red Bluff	70	918
WICKERHAIN			
J	Tuolumne Twp 4	71	161
WICKERSHAM			
Wesley H*	Yuba Marysville	72	853
WICKERSHAW			
Wesley H	Yuba Marysville	72	858
Wesley H*	Yuba Marysville	72	853
WICKERSON			
James	Plumas Quincy	62	944
WICKHAM			
Daniel	Calaveras Twp 6	57	171
Danl C	Calaveras Twp 6	57	165
J	Siskiyou Scott Va	69	52
M	Trinity Weaverville	70	1065
S S	Nevada Rough &	61	420
Thomas H	Los Angeles Los Angeles	59	357
WICKHUM			
Dawniel	Calaveras Twp 5	57	171
WICKIE			
Jno	Butte Chico	56	534
WICKINTON			
David	Sonoma Armally	69	493
WICKITON			
Charles	Mendocino Big Rvr	60	840
WICKIVIN			
Hiram*	Marin Bolinas	60	746
WICKLAND			
Peter	Plumas Meadow Valley	62	902
WICKLE			
D L	Nevada Eureka	61	374
D S	Nevada Eureka	61	374
WICKLEFF			
D D*	Napa Clear Lake	61	137
WICKLER			
John	Yuba Marysville	72	872
WICKLEY			
Charles	Placer Forest H	62	772
WICKLIFF			
D D	Napa Clear Lake	61	137
Robt	Placer Virginia	62	686
WICKLIFFE			
Geo	Butte Kimshaw	56	597
WICKLOW			
Hanry	Tuolumne Twp 2	71	417

Name	County Locale	M653 Roll	Page
WICKLY			
Mary*	Alameda Brooklyn	55	137
WICKMAN			
John	Butte Mountain	56	734
WICKMIRE			
W T*	El Dorado Newtown	58	781
WICKNP			
Wicknp	Tulara Twp 1	71	114
WICKS			
A M	El Dorado Placerville	58	932
Chas	Tuolumne Twp 3	71	428
E	Siskiyou Scott Va	69	38
G C	Santa Clara Santa Clara	65	515
H H	Nevada Nevada	61	247
J	El Dorado Georgetown	58	754
L C	Nevada Nevada	61	247
Moses	Butte Eureka	56	645
P	Nevada Nevada	61	247
R	Mariposa Coulterville	60	699
S C	Nevada Nevada	61	247
Sarah	Siskiyou Klamath	69	87
Sumner*	Marin Bolinas	60	748
W N	San Francisco San Francisco 10		218
			67
Wiley	Trinity Lewiston	70	953
WICKSELL			
Thomas	Santa Clara Fremont	65	421
WICKSTON			
Charles	Mendocino Big Rvr	60	840
WICKUP			
---	Tulara Visalia	71	114
WICKURAN			
William*	San Francisco San Francisco 9	681	012
WICKWAN			
George C	San Francisco San Francisco 3	67	11
WICKWARE			
George C	San Francisco San Francisco 3	67	11
WICKWASE			
George C	San Francisco San Francisco 3	67	11
WICKWERE			
G	El Dorado Diamond	58	764
WIDDEMAN			
Chas	San Francisco San Francisco 2	67	746
WIDDES			
M	Siskiyou Scott Va	69	22
WIDDESS			
Jno	Siskiyou Scott Va	69	21
Tho	Siskiyou Scott Va	69	21
WIDDRIE			
George*	Alameda Oakland	55	54
WIDEMAN			
David	Santa Cruz Soguel	66	594
Frederick E	Yuba Marysville	72	936
Geo	Butte Chico	56	560
James	Santa Cruz Soguel	66	582
WIDENBAUGH			
F	Shasta Horsetown	66	699
WIDENER			
R	Nevada Eureka	61	357
WIDENNAM			
Charles	El Dorado Eldorado	58	938
WIDEOC			
Otto*	San Francisco San Francisco 8	681	315
WIDEOE			
Otto*	San Francisco San Francisco 8	681	315
WIDER			
Anna	Tuolumne Sonora	71	200
WIDERC			
Otto*	San Francisco San Francisco 8	681	315
WIDERHOLD			
John	Napa Napa	61	67
WIDGMEYER			
W G	Sacramento Ward 1	63	63
WIDGWORM			
Charles*	Placer Michigan	62	854
WIDGWORTH			
Charles*	Placer Michigan	62	854
WIDIANES			
W W*	Shasta Millvill	66	747
WIDIOC			
Otto*	San Francisco San Francisco 8	681	315
WIDLASS			
Isaac	Sacramento Cosumnes	63	394
WIDLER			
Jacob	Yolo Slate Ra	72	712
WIDLICH			
Antone	Klamath S Fork	59	206
WIDLNER			
John	Alameda Brooklyn	55	144
WIDMAN			
Adolf	San Francisco San Francisco 11		92
			67
WIDNER			
Anthony	Amador Twp 4	55	244
WIDNEY			
Thos	Santa Clara Santa Clara	65	468

Name	County Locale	M653 Roll	Page
WIDONS			
Jas	Yolo Cache Crk	72	591
WIDOWS			
Jas	Yolo Cache	72	591
WIDSEN			
Hayden	Sierra Downieville	66	1017
WIE			
---	Tuolumne Montezuma	71	509
---	Tuolumne Chinese	71	525
WIEDELL			
Augustus	Yuba Marysville	72	911
WIEDERHOLD			
W M	San Francisco San Francisco 10	67	190
WIEDERSHEIM			
S C	Sonoma Washington	69	668
WIEGANT			
John*	Yuba Marysville	72	972
WIEGHARD			
Chas*	Calaveras Twp 9	57	364
WIEGHSETT			
August*	Yuba Suida	72	994
WIEGLAND			
Henry	Plumas Meadow Valley	62	905
WIEHE			
Caroline	San Francisco San Francisco 10	67	286
WIEHER			
Mathias*	Sierra Scales D	66	802
WIEK			
J	El Dorado Placerville	58	858
WIEKE			
Caroline*	San Francisco San Francisco 10	67	286
WIEKENONING			
Henry	Calaveras Twp 5	57	190
WIEL			
---	Amador Twp 2	55	327
A*	Nevada Bridgeport	61	469
John*	Sierra Downieville	66	969
WIELAND			
Fred	San Francisco San Francisco 2	67	607
John	San Francisco San Francisco 10	67	227
WIELCKO			
Henry	San Francisco San Francisco 1	68	901
WIELE			
Michael	Calaveras Twp 5	57	136
WIELES			
Michael*	Calaveras Twp 6	57	136
WIELZEN			
Henry*	San Francisco San Francisco 3	67	48
WIEMERS			
M	San Francisco San Francisco 5	67	514
WIEN			
Jas*	Sacramento Granite	63	261
Louisa	San Francisco San Francisco 3	67	2
Margaret	San Francisco San Francisco 8	68	1321
WIENBECK			
Fredk	Tuolumne Twp 4	71	137
WIENE			
Hannah	Yuba Marysville	72	892
WIENEARS			
Peter*	Nevada Red Dog	61	552
WIENEKE			
George	San Joaquin Castoria	64	878
WIENER			
John	San Francisco San Francisco 10	67	311
Morrice	El Dorado Coloma	58	1069
WIENZELL			
Frederick	Yuba Marysville	72	880
WIER			
---	Yuba Long Bar	72	759
A	Calaveras Twp 9	57	394
J W	Shasta Millvill	66	756
James B	Tulara Visalia	71	89
Jno	San Francisco San Francisco 10	67	235
Joseph	Yuba Marysville	72	941
Nich	Alameda Brooklyn	55	143
William	Tulara Petersburg	71	51
William F	Tulara Visalia	71	80
WIERBECH			
Fredk	Tuolumne Big Oak	71	137
WIERDEN			
Daniel	Sierra Downieville	66	1018
WIEREL			
E B	Sierra Gibsonville	66	860
WIERS			
Andrew	Calaveras Twp 10	57	282
WIERZBICKE			
F P	San Francisco San Francisco 6	67	468
WIES			
Peter	Yuba Marysville	72	906
WIESE			
Henry	Tuolumne Columbia	71	294

Name	County Locale	M653 Roll	Page
WIESEN			
A*	Nevada Eureka	61	352
WIESER			
A*	Nevada Eureka	61	352
Fredk	San Francisco San Francisco 7	68	1429
William	Siskiyou Yreka	69	136
WIESINER			
Isaac	Shasta Millvill	66	742
WIESNER			
Geo	Sonoma Salt Point	69	689
WIESNN			
Constantine*	Yuba Long Bar	72	741
WIESNOR			
---	Mendocino Calpella	60	825
WIESON			
George*	Marin Cortemad	60	784
WIESS			
Charles*	Sierra Twp 7	66	863
E	Nevada Nevada	61	283
E H	San Francisco San Francisco 10	67	264
Ed	San Joaquin Stockton	64	1045
WIESSERSMITH			
J L*	Nevada Rough &	61	413
WIESTRAND			
George	Plumas Meadow Valley	62	902
WIETON			
Robert	Placer Iona Hills	62	874
WIETZEN			
Henry*	San Francisco San Francisco 3	67	48
WIF			
G	Calaveras Twp 8	57	107
WIFAR			
---	Napa Yount	61	45
WIFE			
---	Tulara Twp 1	71	121
Geo E	Butte Oregon	56	641
WIFFALL			
James H*	Mendocino Calpella	60	829
WIFLER			
Saml	Sonoma Mendocino	69	468
WIFLEY			
Ruth	Sonoma Mendocino	69	468
Saml	Sonoma Mendocino	69	468
WIFMAN			
B H	San Francisco San Francisco 9	68	1070
WIFS			
John*	Nevada Grass Valley	61	149
WIG			
---	Mariposa Twp 3	60	551
---	Sierra Twp 7	66	881
Un Hy	El Dorado Georgetown	58	748
WIGANT			
John	Yuba Marysville	72	972
WIGENHAM			
S	El Dorado Placerville	58	852
WIGENSTEIN			
Saml	Sierra Downieville	66	965
WIGER			
Wm*	Del Norte Happy Ca	58	670
WIGGANS			
Chas L	San Francisco San Francisco 9	68	980
WIGGARD			
Benjamin*	Amador Twp 4	55	245
WIGGERS			
George	San Joaquin Tulare	64	869
WIGGIN			
Ezra	Sierra Pine Grove	66	829
Ezra P	Sierra Pine Grove	66	829
John	Alameda Oakland	55	69
P	Solano Vacaville	69	338
Thomas	Plumas Quincy	62	923
WIGGINS			
---	Tulara Twp 3	71	56
Chase	Humbolt Bucksport	59	157
D S	San Francisco San Francisco 10	67	357
F M	Los Angeles Elmonte	59	247
Franklin	Tulara Visalia	71	33
Frederick	Sierra Pine Grove	66	830
Fredrick	Sierra Pine Grove	66	830
Geo	Yolo Putah	72	553
Geo W	Sacramento Ward 4	63	557
Hiram	Tulara Keyesville	71	58
James M	Mariposa Twp 1	60	646
James W	Mariposa Twp 1	60	646
John	Los Angeles Tejon	59	538
John	Napa Napa	61	77
John*	San Francisco San Francisco 1	68	880
Jos	Butte Chico	56	536
L C	Sierra Downieville	66	1012
Lyman	Nevada Rough &	61	410
Lyman C	Nevada Rough &	61	410
Rufu A	Calaveras Twp 7	57	11
Thomas J	Los Angeles Elmonte	59	246

Name	County Locale	M653 Roll	Page
WIGGINS			
W W	San Francisco San Francisco 10	67	233
Watson	Plumas Quincy	62	1006
William	Tulara Twp 3	71	60
Wm H	San Francisco San Francisco 10	67	211
Wm*	San Francisco San Francisco 1	68	922
WIGGITT			
H	El Dorado Placerville	58	874
WIGGLE			
D	Shasta Millvill	66	752
WIGGLER			
Sman	Sonoma Petaluma	69	548
Wm	Sonoma Petaluma	69	548
WIGGLERWORTH			
E S	Tuolumne Twp 1	71	254
WIGGLESWORTH			
E S	Tuolumne Twp 1	71	254
WIGGNIS			
William	Monterey San Juan	60	986
WIGGO			
Jas P	Amador Twp 2	55	288
WIGGONER			
C	El Dorado Placerville	58	827
WIGGS			
Charles A	Yuba Marysville	72	888
Walter R	Contra Costa Twp 2	57	551
WIGH			
E	Tehama Moons	70	851
Henry*	Yuba Marysville	72	902
WIGHAIR			
Danl*	Sacramento American	63	164
WIGHAM			
Danl*	Sacramento American	63	164
Mr	Marin Tomales	60	776
WIGHT			
A J	Yuba Long Bar	72	742
Daria	Solano Vallejo	69	261
David	Solano Vallejo	69	261
Edward	San Francisco San Francisco 9	68	1013
Edward	Yolo Fremont	72	605
George	Tuolumne Twp 2	71	297
Joe	Yuba Rose Bar	72	806
R A	Butte Mountain	56	738
Robert	Sierra Downieville	66	1010
William	San Francisco San Francisco 9	68	1013
William H	San Francisco San Francisco 9	68	1013
WIGHTMAN			
A C	San Francisco San Francisco 10	67	255
C	Yolo Fremont	72	604
Geo	Butte Kimshaw	56	604
J D	Solano Vacaville	69	325
Jno	San Francisco San Francisco 10	67	255
William E*	Yuba Marysville	72	880
WIGHTNIGALE			
Wm J*	San Francisco San Francisco 7	68	1443
WIGHTOUP			
Theodore	Placer Dutch Fl	62	709
WIGININ			
Spencer*	Yuba Rose Bar	72	791
WIGINSTEIN			
Saml	Sierra Downieville	66	965
WIGINSTINE			
C	El Dorado Placerville	58	872
WIGLER			
Peter	Butte Bidwell	56	721
WIGLEY			
C H	El Dorado Placerville	58	878
WIGMAN			
Louis	San Joaquin Stockton	64	1024
WIGMORE			
Athor	San Francisco San Francisco 9	68	997
Catharine	San Francisco San Francisco 9	68	990
WIGNALL			
Jas*	Calaveras Twp 9	57	399
Thos	Calaveras Twp 9	57	399
WIGONTON			
C	Siskiyou Klamath	69	89
G	Siskiyou Klamath	69	89
WIGRALL			
Jas	Calaveras Twp 9	57	399
Thos	Calaveras Twp 9	57	399
WIGSLEY			
H	Sacramento Brighton	63	207
WIGTON			
A J	Placer Iona Hills	62	886
WIH			
---	Sacramento Mississipi	63	188
WIHELY			
Saml	Tuolumne Twp 1	71	261
WIHER			
Math B*	Nevada Bridgeport	61	480
WIHEY			
E*	Tuolumne Twp 1	71	267

Name	County Locale	M653 Roll	Page
WIHEY			
Francis	Sonoma Petaluma	69	549
Henry*	Sonoma Petaluma	69	549
WIHLOWS			
Mary*	Yuba Marysville	72	924
WIHOY			
Henry*	Sonoma Petaluma	69	549
WIHRLY			
Saml	Tuolumne Twp 1	71	261
WIHUER			
A W	San Francisco San Francisco 10		294
		67	
WIK WUN			
---*	Tulara Visalia	71	98
WIK			
Wun*	Tulara Visalia	71	98
WIKE			
---	Yuba Long Bar	72	764
WIKEN			
---	Tulara Twp 1	71	117
WIKERLINE			
John	Shasta French G	66	714
WIKES			
Wm	Sonoma Santa Rosa	69	388
WIKEY			
E	Tuolumne Twp 1	71	267
WIKIANES			
W W*	Shasta Millvill	66	747
WIKINITS			
Martios*	San Bernardino San Bernadino	64	669
WIKINS			
J W	Tehama Red Bluff	70	917
WIKLEY			
John	Tehama Cottonwoood	70	900
WIKLKISIN			
William*	Siskiyou Yreka	69	126
WIL FA DUK			
---	Mendocino Calpella	60	823
WIL			
---	Yuba Marysville	72	916
WILABY			
Wm	El Dorado Kelsey	58	1150
WILAN			
Michael	San Francisco San Francisco 1	68	859
WILAR			
Ebanezer	Napa Napa	61	69
W	Sutter Sutter	70	816
WILARDA			
---	Mendocino Round Va	60	885
WILAS			
Ellen*	Napa Clear Lake	61	133
Ellin	Napa Clear Lake	61	133
WILAXON			
J	Yolo Fremont	72	604
WILBAR			
Augustus W	Yuba Marysville	72	876
E J	San Francisco San Francisco 4	68	1125
M	San Francisco San Francisco 10		345
		67	
W	Shasta Shasta	66	657
WILBARUS			
Jno	Butte Kimshaw	56	571
WILBASKEY			
Wm	Sacramento Ward 4	63	504
WILBECK			
Peter	San Francisco San Francisco 9	68	967
WILBELHAM			
John*	El Dorado Placerville	58	913
WILBER			
A P	Klamath Liberty	59	242
Dean	Butte Ophir	56	802
E	Sutter Butte	70	798
G W	Siskiyou Scott Va	69	36
Giles D*	Placer Virginia	62	662
J	Sutter Butte	70	788
James	San Francisco San Francisco 4	68	1142
John	Sonoma Cloverdale	69	679
L F	Butte Ophir	56	794
WILBERG			
A M*	Nevada Nevada	61	315
WILBERHAM			
John*	El Dorado Placerville	58	913
WILBERT			
Fred	Sacramento Ward 4	63	605
Harry	Alameda Brooklyn	55	198
J	Sierra Downieville	66	975
V	San Joaquin Stockton	64	1039
WILBERY			
A M*	Nevada Nevada	61	315
WILBOR			
J	San Joaquin Stockton	64	1096
W*	Shasta Shasta	66	657
WILBORN			
C B	Yolo Fremont	72	605
T C	Calaveras Twp 9	57	406
Tyle	Calaveras Twp 9	57	406
WILBORNE			
Saml	Contra Costa Twp 1	57	521
WILBOUN			
John*	Yuba Marysville	72	866
WILBOUR			
G B	San Francisco San Francisco 5	67	524
Hery*	Mendocino Big Rvr	60	850
John*	Yuba Marysville	72	866
WILBOURE			
John*	Yuba Marysville	72	866
WILBOURN			
James	Sonoma Bodega	69	539
John*	Yuba Marysville	72	866
WILBOWINE			
Delia*	Sacramento American	63	163
WILBUM			
J*	Nevada Rough &	61	407
WILBUN			
William	Tulara Twp 1	71	73
WILBUR			
George C	Plumas Meadow Valley	62	911
Jackson	Tehama Tehama	70	939
Jos	San Francisco San Francisco 6	67	433
P	Sutter Butte	70	790
Perry	Trinity Indian C	70	986
Seth	Placer Rattle Snake	62	632
WILBURN			
A L	Nevada Rough &	61	416
Anne	San Francisco San Francisco 2	67	609
C B	Yolo Fremont	72	605
Geo	San Francisco San Francisco 10		298
		67	
J	Nevada Rough &	61	407
J	Sacramento Dry Crk	63	370
J*	Nevada Rough &	61	407
Jas	Sacramento Granite	63	229
Leon	San Francisco San Francisco 2	67	623
M	San Mateo Twp 3	65	108
Maria Delos A	Los Angeles	59	349
	Los Angeles		
Mary F	Los Angeles Los Angeles	59	315
Roberto	Los Angeles Los Angeles	59	349
S H	Sacramento Ward 4	63	584
Thomas J	Monterey Pajaro	60	1017
Thomas*	Santa Cruz Pescadero	66	651
W	Sacramento Dry Crk	63	369
W S	Sacramento Cosummes	63	410
William	Tulara Visalia	71	73
WILBURNE			
E A	Sacramento Ward 1	63	125
WILBWINE			
E A*	Sacramento Ward 1	63	125
WILBY			
Edwd	San Francisco San Francisco 1	68	817
John*	Nevada Nevada	61	319
Kate	San Francisco San Francisco 1	68	821
Thomas	San Francisco San Francisco 11		140
		67	
Thomas G	Nevada Bridgeport	61	442
WILCAK			
Henry	Mariposa Twp 1	60	668
WILCASE			
G P	Tuolumne Twp 2	71	285
WILCET			
Valentine*	Sierra Scales D	66	801
WILCH			
Charles*	San Francisco San Francisco 7	68	1398
John H	Tulara Visalia	71	103
WILCOCKSON			
Allen	Tulara Visalia	71	108
Allen R	Tulara Twp 1	71	108
WILCOK			
Henry*	Mariposa Twp 1	60	668
WILCOM			
Seth	Nevada Rough &	61	423
WILCOPE			
John*	San Francisco San Francisco 9	68	1105
WILCOPS			
John*	San Francisco San Francisco 9	68	1105
WILCOSE			
Seth P	Tuolumne Sonora	71	479
WILCOT			
Alex	Mariposa Coulterville	60	696
George	Tuolumne Columbia	71	296
Jacklan	Santa Clara Alviso	65	405
Peter*	Solano Fremont	69	382
WILCOTT			
Edw	San Francisco San Francisco 9	68	994
Edwd	San Francisco San Francisco 9	68	994
J	Nevada Bloomfield	61	512
Joseph L	San Francisco San Francisco 11		113
		67	
WILCOX			
Alex	Calaveras Twp 5	57	248
Alfred	Tehama Lassen	70	867
Alfred	Tulara Yule Rvr	71	23
WILCOX			
Amelia	Sacramento American	63	157
Benj M	San Francisco San Francisco 8	68	1290
Benjn	San Francisco San Francisco 8	68	1290
Bruce	Amador Twp 3	55	388
C H	Santa Clara San Jose	65	279
Charles	Alameda Oakland	55	52
Charles	Yuba Bear Rvr	72	1009
Charles E	Sierra Downieville	66	972
Chas	Butte Bidwell	56	716
Chas	Butte Ophir	56	765
Chas	Santa Clara San Jose	65	294
Clayton	Yuba Marysville	72	851
Clayton E	Yuba Marysville	72	851
D C	Sacramento Natonia	63	279
D W	Butte Hamilton	56	524
E	Santa Clara Redwood	65	457
E J	Santa Clara San Jose	65	279
Edward	San Bernardino San Salvador	64	656
Elias	Tehama Lassen	70	867
F	Butte Mountain	56	741
Frank	Santa Clara Redwood	65	445
G P	Tuolumne Twp 2	71	285
Geo	Sacramento Natonia	63	275
Harvey	Solano Vacaville	69	351
Henry	Shasta Shasta	66	675
Hiram	Shasta Shasta	66	761
Isarah	Alameda Brooklyn	55	92
Iseah R	Calaveras Twp 4	57	316
Isiah R*	Calaveras Twp 4	57	316
J	El Dorado Coloma	58	1080
J H	Nevada Grass Valley	61	161
James	Calaveras Twp 5	57	171
James	Tulara Twp 2	71	31
James C	Plumas Quincy	62	921
James S	Tuolumne Twp 1	71	484
Jas	Sacramento Granite	63	243
Jas	Sacramento Natonia	63	277
Jeremiah	Plumas Quincy	62	954
Jerimiah	Plumas Quincy	62	978
Jno	Sacramento Natonia	63	281
John	Contra Costa Twp 1	57	516
John	Contra Costa Twp 1	57	519
John	Placer Michigan	62	858
John	Shasta Shasta	66	672
John	Siskiyou Shasta Valley	69	119
John	Tulara Twp 3	71	58
L	Sacramento Cosummes	63	405
La Jayell	Sacramento Ward 1	63	144
Lafayett*	Sacramento Ward 1	63	144
Lafayette*	Sacramento Ward 1	63	144
Leonard G	Calaveras Twp 5	57	209
Loonerdas	Placer Rattle Snake	62	631
Lyman	Solano Vallejo	69	255
M	Amador Twp 6	55	433
Mithan	Nevada Rough &	61	404
N	Sacramento Lee	63	220
Nathan	Nevada Rough &	61	404
Oliver	Monterey Pajaro	60	1020
Parker	Yolo Slate Ra	72	686
Parker	Yuba North Ea	72	686
R	Nevada Eureka	61	369
Rich	Sacramento Ward 3	63	424
Richd	Amador Twp 2	55	273
Robert	San Joaquin Tulare	64	870
S J	Butte Ophir	56	784
S T	Butte Bidwell	56	719
Saml	San Francisco San Francisco 1	68	924
Sarah*	Alameda Brooklyn	55	92
Sardos	Tulara Yule Rvr	71	23
Seth P	Tuolumne Twp 1	71	479
Silas	Stanislaus Branch	70	704
Solon	Yuba Marysville	72	877
Solow*	Yuba Marysville	72	877
T	El Dorado Placerville	58	880
T	Sacramento Ward 3	63	462
T J E	Merced Twp 2	60	923
T S	El Dorado Diamond	58	812
Thos	Butte Cascade	56	694
W	Butte Cascade	56	698
Walter	Nevada Bridgeport	61	487
William	Nevada Rough &	61	416
William	Shasta Cottonwoood	66	723
Wm	Sacramento Georgian	63	342
Wm	Santa Clara Santa Clara	65	504
Wm	Yuba New York	72	721
WILCOXON			
Jas	Yolo Fremont	72	605
Jefferson	Yolo Washington	72	570
WILCOXSON			
Benjamin F	Santa Cruz Pajaro	66	533
J	Yolo Washington	72	604
M A	Colusa Monroeville	57	446
Saml	Calaveras Twp 10	57	279
WILD			
B	Butte Ophir	56	754

California 1860 Census Index

Name	County Locale	M653 Roll	Page
WILD			
B	Calaveras Twp 9	57	412
Edward*	Placer Christia	62	736
George H	San Francisco San Francisco 7	68	1428
George W	Calaveras Twp 9	57	352
H	Solano Vacaville	69	342
H	Yolo Cache Crk	72	631
J	Nevada Grass Valley	61	152
J W	Nevada Grass Valley	61	187
John	Amador Twp 3	55	397
John	San Francisco San Francisco 1	68	919
Jonathan	Siskiyou Yreka	69	184
N	Yolo Cache	72	631
Peter	Solano Vallejo	69	255
R G	Nevada Grass Valley	61	187
S F	Nevada Nevada	61	276
Susan F	Yuba Marysville	72	860
Susan F*	Yuba Marysville	72	860
Wm	Sacramento Granite	63	256
WILDCAT			
---	Tulara Keyesville	71	56
WILDCUT			
---	Tulara Twp 3	71	56
WILDE			
Chas W	Sacramento Granite	63	255
David	San Francisco San Francisco 7	68	1374
J	Amador Twp 1	55	465
John R	San Francisco San Francisco 8	68	1292
John W	San Francisco San Francisco 8	68	1292
Louis	San Francisco San Francisco 8	68	1236
WILDEE			
Chas W	Sacramento Granite	63	255
WILDEN			
E	Nevada Nevada	61	274
William	Santa Cruz Pescadero	66	645
Yates*	Mendocino Ukiah	60	798
WILDENBING			
S H	Nevada Nevada	61	242
WILDENBURG			
S H	Nevada Nevada	61	242
WILDER			
Ann	Yuba Fosters	72	836
Benj W	Sacramento San Joaquin	63	353
C H	Sacramento Granite	63	255
Chas B	San Francisco San Francisco 1	68	906
Chesterfield	Humbolt Bucksport	59	155
D	Marin Bolinas	60	741
Daniel L*	Humbolt Mattole	59	127
Daniel S*	Humbolt Mattole	59	127
Danl	San Francisco San Francisco 9	68	1091
E	Sutter Butte	70	799
F A	Nevada Bridgeport	61	503
F S	Nevada Bridgeport	61	503
Frederick	Calaveras Twp 5	57	146
G	Nevada Washington	61	335
George	Yuba Marysville	72	930
H	San Francisco San Francisco 6	67	467
H G	Napa Napa	61	100
Henry	Klamath Orleans	59	217
Henry	Placer Forest H	62	772
Henry	Placer Yankee J	62	782
Henry	San Francisco San Francisco 10	67	202
Henry	San Francisco San Francisco 2	67	708
Henry	San Mateo Twp 1	65	54
J	El Dorado Placerville	58	918
J B	Tuolumne Columbia	71	331
James C	El Dorado Union	58	1092
L J	San Francisco San Francisco 1	68	844
Leoctt	Calaveras Twp 6	57	154
Leuis	Yuba Fosters	72	837
Levett	Calaveras Twp 6	57	154
Lewis	Yuba Fosters	72	837
Louis	San Francisco San Francisco 7	68	1368
N C	Tuolumne Twp 2	71	329
O	Yolo Washington	72	602
P C	Tehama Lassen	70	868
Peter	San Diego San Diego	64	759
S	Nevada Nevada	61	316
T	Sutter Butte	70	780
Thomas	Alameda Brooklyn	55	210
Thos	Nevada Nevada	61	328
William	Santa Cruz Pescadero	66	645
William P	San Francisco San Francisco 11	67	154
Wm	Sacramento San Joaquin	63	353
Wm	San Francisco San Francisco 2	67	681
WILDERMED			
John*	Mariposa Twp 3	60	609
WILDERMERT			
John	Mariposa Twp 3	60	609
WILDERMOUTH			
John H	Calaveras Twp 4	57	335
WILDES			
Allen	Tuolumne Twp 2	71	393
J H	San Francisco San Francisco 6	67	430
WILDIN			
O	Yolo Washington	72	602
WILDMAN			
William T	Amador Twp 4	55	237
Wilson	Sacramento Ward 4	63	528
WILDO			
John W	San Francisco San Francisco 8	68	1292
WILDON			
E H	Yolo Merritt	72	580
George	Fresno Twp 2	59	49
H D	Butte Bidwell	56	732
WILDRED			
Joseph	Sacramento Ward 1	63	154
WILDS			
A	Sacramento Cosummes	63	382
A E	Calaveras Twp 9	57	413
Albert	Contra Costa Twp 3	57	604
Ann	Yuba Fosters	72	836
E N	Santa Clara San Jose	65	279
Ellen*	Napa Clear Lake	61	133
Green	Sacramento Ward 4	63	608
H	Solano Vacaville	69	342
H D	Butte Cascade	56	695
Jane	Yuba New York	72	725
John	Nevada Eureka	61	389
M H	Sierra St Louis	66	818
S S	Santa Clara San Jose	65	313
Wm	Marin Cortemad	60	784
WILDWOOD			
W	El Dorado Placerville	58	898
WILDY			
N L	Tuolumne Sonora	71	229
Wm	Los Angeles Tejon	59	527
Wm	Los Angeles Tejon To	59	535
WILE			
A J	Nevada Grass Valley	61	143
WILEAK			
Henry*	Mariposa Twp 1	60	668
WILEAT			
George	Tuolumne Twp 2	71	296
WILECT			
Alex*	Mariposa Coulterville	60	696
WILELT			
Valentine*	Sierra Scales D	66	801
WILEN			
F	Yolo Putah	72	550
WILENS			
Alex	Tehama Lassen	70	867
WILER			
J D	Tehama Lassen	70	876
John	Tuolumne Green Springs	71	527
WILEREY			
B P	Sierra Morristown	66	1051
WILERORK			
Jas	Calaveras Twp 9	57	380
WILES			
A C	Nevada Nevada	61	329
A*	San Francisco San Francisco 9	68	1045
H O	Yolo Washington	72	565
J A	Sonoma Russian	69	438
Leott	Calaveras Twp 6	57	154
M O	Yolo Washington	72	565
R W	Tehama Moons	70	851
WILET			
Alen*	Mariposa Coulterville	60	696
WILETT			
Erastus	Monterey Alisal	60	1036
Valentine*	Sierra Scales D	66	801
WILEURITH			
Arlantis*	Nevada Bloomfield	61	510
WILEWS			
Philip	Yolo Washington	72	563
WILEY			
A E	Napa Hot Springs	61	15
Alex	El Dorado White Oaks	58	1007
Alexander	Siskiyou Yreka	69	153
Amasa	Butte Cascade	56	689
Austin	Humbolt Eureka	59	172
B F	Yuba Foster B	72	825
B T	Amador Twp 2	55	265
Beason*	Humbolt Eureka	59	163
C	San Francisco San Francisco 10	67	332
Cebren	Mendocino Calpella	60	809
Charles	San Joaquin Castoria	64	900
Chas	Placer Secret R	62	609
Danial*	Humbolt Eel Rvr	59	144
Daniel*	Humbolt Eel Rvr	59	144
E R	Sonoma Armally	69	506
Edwd	San Francisco San Francisco 5	67	546
Egbert	San Joaquin Castoria	64	889
Geo	Sacramento Ward 1	63	30
George	San Francisco San Francisco 11	67	113
George	Yuba Marysville	72	969
H Y	Los Angeles Los Angeles	59	514
Intrepid M	Yuba Marysville	72	858
Isaac N	Calaveras Twp 7	57	15
J	El Dorado Placerville	58	822
J B	Nevada Bridgeport	61	473
J C	Sacramento Ward 4	63	581
J R	Placer Todds Va	62	790
James	Contra Costa Twp 1	57	519
James	San Francisco San Francisco 9	68	1098
James	Tuolumne Twp 3	71	455
James R	Calaveras Twp 7	57	343
Janette	San Joaquin Castoria	64	911
Jas	Placer Virginia	62	675
John	Butte Oro	56	676
John	Mariposa Twp 3	60	604
John	San Francisco San Francisco 4	68	1227
John	San Joaquin Elliott	64	1102
John	Sonoma Armally	69	500
John	Yolo Merritt	72	583
John*	Mariposa Twp 3	60	604
John*	Shasta Shasta	66	667
Jos	Butte Bidwell	56	706
Joseph	San Joaquin O'Neal	64	1006
Joseph H	Amador Twp 1	55	463
Jutupid M	Yuba Marysville	72	859
L	Butte Bidwell	56	711
Lewis	Placer Auburn	62	579
Louis	Nevada Bridgeport	61	490
Merrel	Sierra Scales D	66	801
Nathan	Tuolumne Twp 1	71	223
P	Butte Kimshaw	56	603
P	Butte Eureka	56	654
Pat	Siskiyou Callahan	69	13
Reason*	Humbolt Eureka	59	163
Reuben	San Joaquin Castoria	64	883
Robert	Placer Todds Va	62	788
S	Butte Bidwell	56	711
Simeon	Napa Yount	61	35
Thomas	San Joaquin Elliott	64	1102
Thos	Yolo Cottonwoood	72	649
Wheeler	San Joaquin Elliott	64	1102
William	Del Norte Crescent	58	631
William	Del Norte Crescent	58	632
William	Santa Cruz Santa Cruz	66	612
Wilma	Yolo Cache Crk	72	666
Wm	Amador Twp 1	55	493
Wm	Los Angeles Los Angeles	59	491
WILEYS			
David*	Yolo Merritt	72	579
WILFORD			
John	Napa Yount	61	45
WILFRED			
John	Santa Clara San Jose	65	384
Joseph	Marin Cortemad	60	779
WILGER			
F*	Yolo Putah	72	550
WILGERS			
James	Yuba Marysville	72	870
John	San Francisco San Francisco 11	67	130
WILGN			
F*	Yolo Putah	72	550
I	Yolo Putah	72	552
WILGNS			
Aaron H	Sacramento Ward 1	63	7
WILGORS			
James*	Yuba Marysville	72	870
WILGRARE			
Henry	Napa Clear Lake	61	134
WILGUS			
Aaron H	Sacramento Ward 1	63	7
WILHALA			
---	Fresno Twp 2	59	110
WILHAMS			
Peter	Sierra Twp 7	66	899
WILHAMSON			
T H	El Dorado Placerville	58	864
WILHANS			
Simon*	El Dorado Georgetown	58	702
WILHARO			
---*	Mendocino Round Va	60	878
WILHART			
Louis	Los Angeles Los Angeles	59	330
WILHAW			
---*	Mendocino Round Va	60	878
WILHE			
C A	Sonoma Vallejo	69	612
WILHEAT			
F L	Mariposa Twp 3	60	593
WILHEIMER			
S	Santa Clara Fremont	65	423
Saml	Santa Clara Fremont	65	423
WILHELM			
G	Shasta Shasta	66	656
Gustus	San Joaquin Stockton	64	1035
N A	Sacramento Natonia	63	286

California 1860 Census Index

Name	County Locale	M653 Roll	Page
WILHELMING			
Emily	Alameda Oakland	55	27
WILHELMS			
Samul	Siskiyou Yreka	69	151
WILHENNER			
G A	San Francisco San Francisco 10	257 67	
WILHERSON			
Wm	Sonoma Mendocino	69	468
WILHILM			
W A	Sacramento Natonia	63	286
WILHILMEE			
W*	San Francisco San Francisco 6	67	466
WILHILMIE			
W	San Francisco San Francisco 6	67	466
WILHITE			
Elisha	San Francisco San Francisco 2	67	802
Jane	Sacramento Granite	63	239
WILHOIT			
Elizabeth	Sonoma Mendocino	69	459
R E	San Joaquin Stockton	641	037
Simeon G	Sonoma Mendocino	69	459
WILHOLM			
Francis R	San Joaquin Elkhorn	64	981
WILHOMENS			
Chrles*	San Francisco San Francisco 3	67	3
WILHOMINS			
Charles	San Francisco San Francisco 3	67	3
WILHOMMS			
Charles*	San Francisco San Francisco 3	67	3
WILHONS			
Hery*	Mendocino Big Rvr	60	850
WILHOUS			
Hery*	Mendocino Big Rvr	60	850
WILIAMS			
Calvin	Tuolumne Twp 1	71	267
Enoch	Tuolumne Twp 1	71	480
Joe	Placer Forest H	62	791
John	Placer Forest H	62	799
John	San Joaquin Elkhorn	64	970
Joseph	Placer Yankee J	62	758
WILIAMSON			
Michael	San Francisco San Francisco 2	67	555
WILICALAY			
---	Mendocino Round Va	60	884
WILIER			
Math B*	Nevada Bridgeport	61	480
WILIS			
Daniel	Placer Forest H	62	801
WILISTON			
Cary	San Francisco San Francisco 5	67	544
WILKAESON			
Peter	Santa Cruz Santa Cruz	66	611
WILKARSON			
Peter*	Santa Cruz Santa Cruz	66	611
WILKE			
Fredk E	San Francisco San Francisco 2	67	786
WILKEE			
C	San Francisco San Francisco 5	67	527
WILKENNY			
Henry*	Shasta Horsetown	66	702
WILKENRY			
Henry	Shasta Horsetown	66	702
WILKENS			
W W	Sonoma Vallejo	69	609
WILKENSON			
James	Santa Clara Santa Clara	65	522
P	Butte Oregon	56	640
Peter	Santa Cruz Santa Cruz	66	619
WILKER			
C	San Francisco San Francisco 5	67	527
Charles	Yuba Marysville	72	968
Francis	Yuba Marysville	72	903
Louis*	San Francisco San Francisco 7	681	416
WILKERLINE			
John	Shasta French G	66	714
WILKERSEN			
Jas	Butte Hamilton	56	520
WILKERSON			
A	Placer Yankee J	62	781
America	Sonoma Mendocino	69	468
E C	El Dorado Mud Springs	58	991
Francis B	Siskiyou Yreka	69	127
H	Tuolumne Twp 2	71	377
J H	Placer Dutch Fl	62	719
James	Tehama Red Bluff	70	917
Jas	Butte Hamilton	56	520
Mary	San Francisco San Francisco 6	67	435
P	Butte Oregon	56	640
Thomas	San Joaquin Elkhorn	64	976
W	El Dorado Placerville	58	855
W S	Butte Wyandotte	56	672
Wm	Sonoma Mendocino	69	468
WILKES			
Berryman	Butte Chico	56	554
Francis	Yuba Marysville	72	903

Name	County Locale	M653 Roll	Page
WILKES			
G*	Nevada Nevada	61	312
Louis*	San Francisco San Francisco 7	681	416
Lunsford	El Dorado Georgetown	58	702
Lunsjird*	El Dorado Georgetown	58	702
W	Siskiyou Scott Ri	69	80
William J*	Yuba Marysville	72	926
WILKESKY			
Harris*	Sacramento Ward 1	63	121
WILKESON			
William H	Siskiyou Yreka	69	126
WILKEY			
---	San Francisco San Francisco 10	301 67	
Edward	San Francisco San Francisco 11	106 67	
Wm	San Francisco San Francisco 10	317 67	
WILKIE			
D	Sutter Sutter	70	815
F	Siskiyou Scott Ri	69	81
F C	Siskiyou Scott Ri	69	72
Jas	San Francisco San Francisco 1	68	855
Jno	Butte Hamilton	56	525
WILKIM			
J W*	Mariposa Twp 3	60	567
James	Alameda Brooklyn	55	92
WILKIN			
Henry A	San Francisco San Francisco 7	681	326
James*	Mariposa Coulterville	60	676
WILKINBURG			
Fred	Placer Forest H	62	766
WILKINE			
James*	Alameda Brooklyn	55	92
James*	Sacramento Granite	63	260
WILKING			
George	Sierra Downieville	661	020
WILKINHOUSE			
Frederick	San Francisco San Francisco 7	681	391
WILKINS			
Annie	Colusa Grand Island	57	472
Antone	Yolo Cache Crk	72	624
Asa A	El Dorado Georgetown	58	747
Benjamin	San Francisco San Francisco 11	149 67	
C P	Sonoma Santa Rosa	69	387
Calvin	Sierra Downieville	661	019
Charles G	San Luis Obispo	65	36
Charles*	El Dorado Placerville	58	914
Charly	Tuolumne Sonora	71	201
E G	El Dorado Georgetown	58	674
Edward T	Yuba Marysville	72	973
Elijah	San Joaquin O'Neal	641	005
Frderick E	San Francisco San Francisco 7	681	326
Fred	Amador Twp 1	55	470
Frederick E	San Francisco San Francisco 7	681	326
Gardner R	Sierra Gibsonville	66	854
H Q	Shasta Millvill	66	742
Henry	San Francisco San Francisco 2	67	576
Henry A	San Francisco San Francisco 7	681	326
Herman	San Francisco San Francisco 1	68	929
Isaac	Tulara Keyesville	71	62
J	Calaveras Twp 9	57	391
J B	San Francisco San Francisco 3	67	83
J F	Colusa Grand Island	57	470
James*	Sacramento Granite	63	260
Jas	Sacramento Ward 1	63	28
John	El Dorado Mud Springs	58	965
John	San Joaquin Stockton	641	016
John	San Joaquin Oneal	64	930
John G	Amador Twp 1	55	470
John S	Calaveras Twp 6	57	154
Jos	San Joaquin Elkhorn	64	992
Lenard	Amador Twp 3	55	380
M D	Nevada Grass Valley	61	171
Mary J	San Bernardino Santa Barbara	64	156
Mathias	San Francisco San Francisco 10	266 67	
Matthias	San Francisco San Francisco 10	266 67	
Mr	Marin Bolinas	60	748
Peter	Butte Eureka	56	653
Peter	Santa Cruz Watsonville	66	536
Richard	Placer Secret R	62	613
Robert	San Francisco San Francisco 11	154 67	
Robert	Sierra Poker Flats	66	839
Thomas	Sierra Poker Flats	66	839
Violet	Colusa Grand Island	57	472
W W	Sonoma Sonoma	69	662
Wilkins	Tuolumne Columbia	71	364
Wm	Amador Twp 5	55	341
Wm P	Los Angeles Tejon	59	523
WILKINSAN			
V*	Los Angeles Los Angeles	59	491

Name	County Locale	M653 Roll	Page
WILKINSEN			
C D	Sacramento Ward 1	63	73
WILKINSER			
Wm C	Sacramento Natonia	63	274
WILKINSON			
Abel	Los Angeles Tejon	59	524
Abil	Los Angeles Tejon	59	524
Benj	El Dorado Placerville	58	927
C D	Sacramento Ward 1	63	73
F D	San Francisco San Francisco 9	681	100
Frank E	Santa Clara San Jose	65	350
Geo	San Francisco San Francisco 9	681	003
Geo	San Francisco San Francisco 12	392 67	
George	San Francisco San Francisco 7	681	351
George	San Mateo Twp 3	65	110
Green	Humbolt Eel Rvr	59	153
H N	Shasta Millvill	66	754
H T	Napa Hot Springs	61	2
H V	Shasta Millvill	66	754
J A	Sutter Butte	70	791
Jacob	Contra Costa Twp 1	57	531
James	Santa Clara Almaden	65	277
James E	San Joaquin Oneal	64	913
Jas	Napa Napa	61	65
Jas	Sacramento Ward 3	63	469
Jas	San Francisco San Francisco 10	197 67	
John	Placer Auburn	62	595
John	San Francisco San Francisco 11	96 67	
John	Sierra Pine Grove	66	829
John	Sierra Twp 7	66	868
John	Yolo Slate Ra	72	710
John	Yuba Slate Ro	72	710
Jos	Alameda Brooklyn	55	187
Laura	El Dorado Greenwood	58	708
Moses	Sierra Twp 7	66	864
Moses	Yolo Slate Ra	72	692
Moses	Yuba Slate Ro	72	692
Nathan	Nevada Red Dog	61	544
Peter	Santa Cruz Santa Cruz	66	611
Peter	Santa Cruz Santa Cruz	66	619
Peter	Sierra Pine Grove	66	829
Phillip	Calaveras Twp 4	57	329
Robert	Tulara Twp 3	71	59
S C	Yolo Putah	72	614
Samuel	Tulara Twp 3	71	59
Sarah	San Francisco San Francisco 7	681	439
Sprague	Colusa Monroeville	57	449
Thos S	Sacramento Ward 3	63	469
William	Contra Costa Twp 3	57	590
William	San Francisco San Francisco 11	107 67	
William H	Plumas Quincy	621	004
WILKISON			
Chas	Amador Twp 2	55	284
WILKOSKY			
Harris	Sacramento Ward 1	63	121
WILKOWSKY			
Conrad	Los Angeles Tejon	59	523
WILKRSKY			
Harris*	Sacramento Ward 1	63	121
WILKS			
Albert	Contra Costa Twp 2	57	577
Frank	Contra Costa Twp 1	57	500
G	Nevada Grass Valley	61	222
J	El Dorado Mud Springs	58	985
Jno	Klamath Klamath	59	228
P S	Amador Twp 7	55	417
Samuel	Calaveras Twp 7	57	25
WILKSAN			
C E	Butte Eureka	56	655
WILKSON			
H	Butte Oregon	56	636
Wm	Sierra Downieville	661	024
WILKUN			
J W*	Mariposa Twp 3	60	567
WILKURS			
James	Sacramento Granite	63	260
WILKUSON			
W S	Butte Wyandotte	56	672
WILKY			
Mary	San Francisco San Francisco 2	67	721
WILL			
---	Mariposa Twp 3	60	608
Chy	El Dorado Greenwood	58	731
F A	San Francisco San Francisco 4	681	221
F R	Tuolumne Twp 2	71	286
J	Nevada Eureka	61	393
John*	Yolo Cottonwood	72	647
Joseph	Stanislaus Buena Village	70	726
Mary E	San Francisco San Francisco 2	67	780
Saml	Yolo Putah	72	587
W N*	Merced Twp 1	60	898
WILLA			
Antonio	San Luis Obispo San Luis Obispo	65	19

Name	County Locale	M653 Roll/Page
WILLABY		
G W	El Dorado Casumnes	581176
WILLAIMS		
David	Sierra Port Win	66 794
J L	Shasta Millvill	66 744
WILLAIRE		
James	El Dorado Big Bar	58 733
WILLAMS		
A	Yuba New York	72 722
Saml	Placer Dutch Fl	62 731
Susan	Sierra Pine Grove	66 824
WILLARD		
---	Placer Virginia	62 663
? J*	Yolo Cottonwoood	72 646
A J	San Mateo Twp 1	65 59
A J	Yolo Cache Crk	72 646
Alex	Sacramento Franklin	63 320
Chas	Butte Kimshaw	56 580
Chris	Sacramento Georgian	63 339
Clara	Sierra Gibsonville	66 854
D E	Sierra La Porte	66 781
D E S	Sierra La Porte	66 781
E F	Sierra La Porte	66 770
E J*	Yolo Cottonwoood	72 646
E L	Sierra La Porte	66 770
Finneas	Butte Kimshaw	56 608
Finneus	Butte Kimshaw	56 608
Fred	El Dorado Placerville	58 904
G K	Shasta Horsetown	66 693
Geo	Butte Kimshaw	56 579
Geo	Napa Clear Lake	61 129
George	Tulara Twp 3	71 61
Gu	Butte Kimshaw	56 579
H A	Nevada Bridgeport	61 468
H A	Sonoma Washington	69 672
H P	Sacramento Sutter	63 299
Isaac	Sierra Monte Crk	661039
J P	Sacramento Mississipi	63 187
J W	Sacramento Ward 3	63 484
Jackson	Sacramento Franklin	63 320
Jacob	Sierra Twp 7	66 871
James	Amador Twp 3	55 402
Jas	San Francisco San Francisco 5	67 481
Joel	Napa Clear Lake	61 129
Joshua	Solano Benecia	69 294
M	Merced Twp 2	60 921
N J	Yolo Cottonwoood	72 646
Ninian	Napa Clear Lake	61 130
Ralph	Monterey Pajaro	601020
S K*	Shasta Horsetown	66 693
Theo	Sonoma Healdsbu	69 472
Thos	Sacramento Georgian	63 347
Thos S	Butte Eureka	56 655
W F	Siskiyou Scott Ri	69 63
Warren	Sonoma Armally	69 479
Wm	Alameda Brooklyn	55 145
Wm	San Francisco San Francisco 12	379 67
WILLARDURE		
W R	El Dorado Kelsey	581146
WILLARE		
Adelaide*	Santa Clara San Jose	65 389
Augustus*	San Francisco 4 / San Francisco	681217
WILLARET		
Warren	Sonoma Armally	69 479
WILLASON		
A	Butte Wyandotte	56 669
WILLBORN		
Josephine	Tuolumne Twp 4	71 169
WILLBURN		
Josephine	Tuolumne Jacksonville	71 169
WILLBY		
Edwd	San Francisco San Francisco 1	68 817
WILLCANY		
John	Napa Napa	61 101
WILLCOX		
Arn M	Mariposa Twp 3	60 547
Benjamen	Monterey San Juan	601005
Benjamin	Monterey San Juan	601005
J W	Mariposa Twp 3	60 547
R	El Dorado Union	581088
WILLCOXEN		
D*	Siskiyou Cottonwood	69 109
WILLE		
John*	Alameda Brooklyn	55 141
Joseph	Alameda Brooklyn	55 143
W*	Mendocino Anderson	60 867
WILLEAMS		
L	Shasta Shasta	66 679
WILLEBIND		
Henry	Alameda Oakland	55 30
WILLEM		
Wm	Butte Ophir	56 768
WILLER		
Adam*	Santa Clara Redwood	65 455
WILLER		
Chas L	San Francisco San Francisco 8	681313
Ebanezer*	Napa Napa	61 69
William J*	Yuba Marysville	72 926
WILLERS		
O F	San Francisco San Francisco 5	67 521
William	Sierra La Porte	66 779
William J*	Yuba Marysville	72 926
WILLERT		
Fred	Tuolumne Twp 2	71 471
WILLERTY		
Henry	Sonoma Armally	69 508
WILLES		
August	San Francisco San Francisco 9	681100
Chas	San Francisco San Francisco 10	306 67
G	Nevada Nevada	61 312
G*	Nevada Grass Valley	61 222
G*	Nevada Nevada	61 312
Richard	Calaveras Twp 6	57 185
William	El Dorado Spanish	581125
WILLESS		
John	San Francisco San Francisco 2	67 671
WILLET		
Allen	Calaveras Twp 10	57 297
Edward	Placer Michigan	62 831
Elijah J	Napa Napa	61 89
Fonda	Placer Rattle Snake	62 601
Henry*	Mendocino Ukiah	60 805
Peter*	Solano Fremont	69 382
S W	Amador Twp 5	55 363
WILLETS		
Andrew	Calaveras Twp 6	57 157
WILLETT		
A L	Sierra Twp 7	66 874
Eli	Yolo Cache Crk	72 606
Erastus	Monterey Alisal	601036
Hiram	Mendocino Little L	60 829
John	Placer Illinois	62 703
John	Santa Clara Fremont	65 421
Lewis	Plumas Quincy	62 958
Mary	Tulara Keeneysburg	71 45
Peter	Placer Michigan	62 827
Saml	Yolo Fremont	72 605
William F	Napa Yount	61 35
WILLETTS		
Eli	Yolo Cache	72 606
John	Yolo Washington	72 605
WILLEY		
Alex	Sonoma Bodega	69 528
Alexander	Calaveras Twp 5	57 185
Barney	Butte Oro	56 688
C J	San Francisco San Francisco 6	67 426
Chas	Sierra Port Win	66 798
D	Yolo Slate Ra	72 719
George	Yuba Marysville	72 970
Jno	Mendocino Big Rvr	60 848
John W	Alameda Oakland	55 22
L	El Dorado Mud Springs	58 974
Mno	Mendocino Big Rvr	60 848
Oliver C	Calaveras Twp 10	57 289
P	Siskiyou Callahan	69 14
Richard	Calaveras Twp 5	57 185
Stanly	Santa Clara San Jose	65 380
T B	San Francisco San Francisco 10	330 67
WILLFORD		
Jas	Butte Ophir	56 775
WILLHELMS		
W	Siskiyou Callahan	69 10
WILLHITE		
Benjamine	Sierra Cox'S Bar	66 951
WILLHONSEN		
Chas*	Sacramento American	63 170
WILLHOUSEN		
Chas*	Sacramento American	63 170
WILLIAM H		
Gardner	Amador Twp 4	55 238
WILLIAM LIDDEH		
Dayman	Santa Cruz Santa Cruz	66 630
WILLIAM S		
Daniel	Siskiyou Yreka	69 130
WILLIAM		
---	Calaveras Twp 6	57 182
---	El Dorado Salmon Falls	581062
---	Mendocino Calpella	60 820
---	Mendocino Twp 1	60 889
---	San Francisco San Francisco 9	681097
---	Siskiyou Yreka	69 154
---	Siskiyou Scott Va	69 46
---	Tulara Twp 3	71 48
---	Tulara Keeneysburg	71 49
---	Tulara Keyesville	71 53
---	Tulara Keyesville	71 55
---	Tulara Keyesville	71 57
---*	Tulara Keeneysburg	71 48
WILLIAM		
A	Butte Ophir	56 746
A H	Yolo Cottonwoood	72 660
Anthony	Amador Twp 1	55 462
Augustus*	San Francisco 4 / San Francisco	681217
Boyes	San Francisco San Francisco 8	681324
Cason	San Mateo Twp 1	65 51
Clark	Santa Cruz Santa Cruz	66 599
Crawford	San Mateo Twp 1	65 51
Daniel D	Siskiyou Yreka	69 180
Diety	Sierra Whiskey	66 850
Downey	San Mateo Twp 1	65 51
Dr	Siskiyou Scott Va	69 46
Evers	Sierra Whiskey	66 850
G W	Siskiyou Scott Ri	69 65
George	Marin Cortemad	60 781
George	Tulara Twp 3	71 61
George*	Marin Cortemad	60 781
Gotte*	Sierra Whiskey	66 850
H P	Sutter Sutter	70 807
Hix	Santa Cruz Santa Cruz	66 630
J	San Francisco San Francisco 2	67 784
J	Yolo Slate Ra	72 694
J	Yuba Slate Ro	72 694
J K	El Dorado Big Bar	58 735
J L	Shasta Millvill	66 744
Jas	Sacramento Ward 3	63 440
Jno	Butte Oregon	56 621
Jno	San Francisco San Francisco 10	253 67
Jno	Sonoma Mendocino	69 454
John	El Dorado Big Bar	58 735
John	San Joaquin Elliott	64 947
John	Yolo Slate Ra	72 694
John	Yuba Rose Bar	72 808
John H	San Francisco San Francisco 9	681105
John J	Sacramento Granite	63 259
Jos	Sonoma Mendocino	69 454
Jos	Trinity State Ba	701001
Joseph	Alameda Brooklyn	55 108
Joseph*	El Dorado Georgetown	58 674
Julian	San Francisco San Francisco 4	681226
King*	Santa Cruz Santa Cruz	66 630
Lhwalow	Calaveras Twp 7	57 38
Louis	Yuba Marysville	72 964
Lydia	Amador Twp 3	55 378
Margaret	El Dorado Georgetown	58 750
Mc Bride	El Dorado Coloma	581083
Moore	Amador Twp 4	55 238
Morton	Tuolumne Twp 5	71 534
Noah	Siskiyou Yreka	69 141
Noah	Siskiyou Yreka	69 173
Prince A	Alameda Brooklyn	55 105
R	Sutter Bear Rvr	70 821
Rudolph*	Yuba Marysville	72 928
S	El Dorado Georgetown	58 750
W	San Francisco San Francisco 9	681074
W	Shasta Shasta	66 682
Wilkins	Tuolumne Twp 1	71 201
William	Siskiyou Scott Va	69 57
William W	Tuolumne Twp 5	71 519
WILLIAMES		
J D	Amador Twp 6	55 436
Owens	Sierra Monte Crk	661035
WILLIAMS		
---	Monterey San Juan	601000
---	Nevada Eureka	61 354
---	San Francisco San Francisco 2	67 647
---	San Joaquin Stockton	641060
---	Sonoma Salt Point	69 692
A	Butte Ophir	56 746
A	El Dorado Coloma	581071
A	El Dorado Coloma	581086
A	Sacramento Ward 4	63 516
A	Shasta Millvill	66 754
A	Tehama Pasakent	70 857
A	Yuba New York	72 722
A D	Nevada Bridgeport	61 451
A D	Tehama Lassen	70 884
A G	Shasta Shasta	66 674
A H	Tuolumne Twp 2	71 274
A J	Del Norte Crescent	58 648
A J	San Bernardino Santa Barbara	64 190
A J C	Tuolumne Twp 1	71 274
A M	Sacramento Sutter	63 291
A P	Calaveras Twp 9	57 404
A P	Sierra Downieville	66 955
Aace	Yuba Parks Ba	72 775
Ace	Yuba Parks Ba	72 775
Albert	San Francisco San Francisco 6	67 444
Albert	Sierra Pine Grove	66 820
Albert	Sierra Pine Grove	66 826
Albert	Sonoma Bodega	69 529
Alex	Sacramento Sutter	63 297
Alex	Sacramento Dry Crk	63 369

WILLIAMS

Name	County Locale	M653 Roll	Page
Alexander	Santa Clara Gilroy	65	235
Alexr	Plumas Quincy	62	917
Alfred	Calaveras Twp 10	57	265
Alfred	Sierra Twp 7	66	895
Allen	Sonoma Petaluma	69	545
Alma	San Bernardino San Bernadino	64	628
Alonso	Napa Hot Springs	61	14
Alpheno F	Sierra St Louis	66	808
Alpheus F	Sierra St Louis	66	808
Amben	Mendocino Ukiah	60	797
Ambrose	Mendocino Arrana	60	856
Amon	Calaveras Twp 9	57	352
Amos	Sierra Twp 7	66	899
Andrew	Colusa Mansville	57	438
Andrew	Los Angeles San Gabriel	59	408
Andrew	San Francisco San Francisco 3	67	19
Andrew	San Mateo Twp 1	65	58
Andrew	Solano Benecia	69	306
Ann	Nevada Rough &	61	420
Anna	Placer Dutch Fl	62	711
Anthony	Plumas Quincy	62	1001
Antone	Sierra Whiskey	66	845
Antonio	Alameda Brooklyn	55	160
Antonio	Contra Costa Twp 1	57	520
Archibald	Butte Eureka	56	645
Augustus	El Dorado White Oaks	58	1006
Augustus	Placer Folsom	62	641
B	Mariposa Coulterville	60	686
B	San Francisco San Francisco 10	67	181
B	San Francisco San Francisco 3	67	722
B A	San Bernardino Santa Barbara	64	178
B B	San Francisco San Francisco 2	67	665
B F	Sonoma Armally	69	499
B H	Tuolumne Big Oak	71	153
B P	Nevada Rough &	61	397
B S	Amador Twp 2	55	282
B S E	Amador Twp 2	55	293
B Sister	San Francisco San Francisco 10	67	181
B T	Butte Wyandotte	56	669
B*	Mariposa Coulterville	60	686
Barnard M	Yuba Rose Bar	72	796
Barnett	Yuba Rose Bar	72	793
Barney	Yuba Rose Bar	72	797
Ben	Amador Twp 2	55	293
Benedict	Placer Iona Hills	62	893
Benj	Calaveras Twp 6	57	144
Benj	Contra Costa Twp 3	57	605
Benj	Merced Monterey	60	937
Benj	Plumas Meadow Valley	62	931
Benj	Santa Clara Gilroy	65	237
Benja	Calaveras Twp 6	57	144
Benjamin	San Luis Obispo San Luis Obispo	65	12
Benjamin	Santa Cruz Pajaro	66	564
Benjamin	Santa Cruz Pajaro	66	577
Benjn	Monterey Monterey	60	937
Berg	Alameda Brooklyn	55	197
Bill	Yuba Parks Ba	72	779
Byron	Placer Iona Hills	62	891
C	Butte Kimshaw	56	598
C	Del Norte Happy Ca	58	669
C	El Dorado Diamond	58	812
C	Mariposa Twp 1	60	654
C	San Francisco San Francisco 5	67	478
C	San Francisco San Francisco 5	67	493
C	San Francisco San Francisco 5	67	512
C	Shasta Shasta	66	732
C	Sutter Butte	70	786
C	Sutter Nicolaus	70	841
C	Tehama Red Bluff	70	909
C C	Butte Kimshaw	56	573
C C	Tehama Lassen	70	868
C D	Yolo Putah	72	586
C E	Trinity Weaverville	70	1066
C F	Tuolumne Twp 2	71	309
C H	El Dorado Casumnes	58	1161
C H	Shasta Shasta	66	722
C L	Shasta Shasta	66	681
C O F	San Francisco San Francisco 5	67	506
C S	Tehama Red Bluff	70	914
Caleb	Placer Virginia	62	683
Caleb O	Alameda Oakland	55	34
Calvin	Tuolumne Twp 1	71	267
Caroline	Alameda Oakland	55	41
Caswell S	Mendocino Ukiah	60	808
Cath	Sacramento Ward 4	63	557
Cath	San Francisco San Francisco 9	68	1052
Cath	San Francisco San Francisco 6	67	440
Catharine	Butte Ophir	56	758
Charles	Alameda Brooklyn	55	128
Charles	Calaveras Twp 5	57	199
Charles	El Dorado Coloma	58	1075
Charles	El Dorado Placerville	58	914

WILLIAMS

Name	County Locale	M653 Roll	Page
Charles	Placer Michigan	62	842
Charles	San Francisco San Francisco 9	68	1083
Charles	San Joaquin Elliott	64	1103
Charles	San Joaquin Douglass	64	916
Charles	San Luis Obispo San Luis Obispo	65	6
Charles	Santa Cruz Santa Cruz	66	620
Charles	Tuolumne Sonora	71	233
Charles	Tuolumne Twp 2	71	338
Charles	Tuolumne Twp 2	71	394
Charles H	Mariposa Twp 1	60	657
Charles H	San Francisco San Francisco 3	67	24
Chas	Butte Oregon	56	621
Chas	El Dorado Georgetown	58	696
Chas	Santa Clara San Jose	65	345
Chas	Trinity Lewiston	70	963
Chas C	Napa Yount	61	54
Chas E	Sacramento Georgian	63	337
Chs	Butte Oregon	56	621
Chs	San Francisco San Francisco 5	67	482
Chs	San Francisco San Francisco 5	67	494
Cordelia	Sonoma Mendocino	69	465
Cyrus	Tulara Keyesville	71	61
D	Butte Oregon	56	613
D	Del Norte Crescent	58	645
D E	Sierra Excelsior	66	1033
D H	Nevada Nevada	61	256
D H	Nevada Nevada	61	262
D M	Sacramento Dry Crk	63	373
D M	Tuolumne Columbia	71	319
D R	Nevada Bridgeport	61	440
Dan'El	Yuba New York	72	722
Daniel	Nevada Bridgeport	61	442
Daniel	Nevada Little Y	61	532
Daniel	Siskiyou Yreka	69	130
Daniel	Tulara Twp 3	71	52
Daniel	Tuolumne Jamestown	71	455
Daniel D	Siskiyou Yreka	69	180
Danl	Sonoma Petaluma	69	543
Danl	Sonoma Petaluma	69	544
David	Butte Kimshaw	56	592
David	Nevada Bridgeport	61	470
David	Nevada Bridgeport	61	483
David	Placer Auburn	62	588
David	San Francisco San Francisco 5	67	482
David	Santa Clara San Jose	65	321
David	Sierra Port Win	66	794
David	Siskiyou Yreka	69	171
David	Siskiyou Klamath	69	84
David	Stanislaus Emory	70	755
David	Tuolumne Twp 3	71	455
David	Yuba Slate Ro	72	701
David	Yuba New York	72	722
David H	Sierra Twp 7	66	900
David J	Sierra Pine Grove	66	830
David M	Colusa Butte Crk	57	465
David R	Siskiyou Yreka	69	126
Dennis	Plumas Quincy	62	1007
Dennis	Plumas Quincy	62	961
Dow	Los Angeles San Pedro	59	480
E	Del Norte Crescent	58	630
E	El Dorado Georgetown	58	694
E	Nevada Eureka	61	354
E	Nevada Eureka	61	377
E	San Francisco San Francisco 5	67	493
E	Siskiyou Cottonwood	69	102
E	Siskiyou Scott Va	69	38
E A	San Francisco San Francisco 9	68	1083
E B	San Bernardino Santa Barbara	64	155
E B	San Joaquin Stockton	64	1036
E H	Yuba Rose Bar	72	813
E J	Trinity Mouth Ca	70	1015
Ed	Sacramento Granite	63	243
Ederan*	Sierra Excelsior	66	1035
Edgar	Butte Kimshaw	56	590
Ediran*	Sierra Excelsior	66	1035
Edmin	Trinity Weaverville	70	1056
Edmund	San Joaquin Elkhorn	64	971
Edward	Humbolt Eureka	59	164
Edward	Nevada Bridgeport	61	495
Edward	Nevada Red Dog	61	541
Edward	Plumas Meadow Valley	62	911
Edward	Sonoma Mendocino	69	457
Edward	Tuolumne Sonora	71	188
Edward	Tuolumne Jamestown	71	445
Edward B	San Francisco San Francisco 7	68	1329
Edward T	Yuba Marysville	72	973
Edwaro	San Mateo Twp 1	65	52
Edwd	Nevada Bridgeport	61	469
Edwin	San Francisco San Francisco 6	67	453
Edwin	Santa Clara San Jose	65	389
Eleanor	Sonoma Mendocino	69	464
Eli	San Joaquin Elliott	64	1103
Elisha	Calaveras Twp 6	57	187
Elisha	Placer Michigan	62	843

WILLIAMS

Name	County Locale	M653 Roll	Page
Elisha	Sierra Twp 7	66	871
Eliza	San Francisco San Francisco 4	68	1165
Elizabeth	San Francisco San Francisco 4	68	1120
Elizabeth	San Francisco San Francisco 8	68	1262
Elizabeth	San Francisco San Francisco 10	67	291
Elizabeth	Solano Vallejo	69	279
Elizabeth	Sonoma Mendocino	69	455
Elizabeth	Tuolumne Twp 4	71	137
Ellah	Humbolt Bucksport	59	157
Ellen	San Francisco San Francisco 10	67	213
Ellen	Santa Cruz Santa Cruz	66	613
Enoch	Tuolumne Sonora	71	480
Ephraim	Tuolumne Twp 6	71	534
Eran	Nevada Bridgeport	61	477
Eugene B	San Francisco San Francisco 8	68	1261
Evan	Calaveras Twp 5	57	139
Evan	Placer Forest H	62	799
Evan	Sierra Monte Crk	66	1035
F	Calaveras Twp 9	57	402
F	Sacramento Franklin	63	318
F	San Francisco San Francisco 9	68	1059
F	Shasta Shasta	66	682
F	Shasta Shasta	66	683
F	Sonoma Bodega	69	533
F	Sutter Yuba	70	765
F	Sutter Butte	70	786
F	Sutter Bear Rvr	70	823
F	Yolo Washington	72	572
F L	Sonoma Petaluma	69	580
Farlow M	Nevada Bridgeport	61	447
Felix	Contra Costa Twp 2	57	566
Ferlen K	Calaveras Twp 10	57	264
Fesse	Plumas Quincy	62	985
Frances*	San Francisco San Francisco 2	67	740
Francis	San Francisco San Francisco 2	67	740
Francis	San Mateo Twp 1	65	52
Francis	Sierra St Louis	66	812
Francis A A	San Francisco San Francisco 2	67	623
Francis O A*	San Francisco San Francisco 2	67	623
Francisco	San Francisco San Francisco 2	67	677
Frank	Alameda Brooklyn	55	149
Frank	Alameda Brooklyn	55	150
Frank	Mariposa Twp 1	60	652
Frank	Nevada Nevada	61	282
Frank	Placer Stewart	62	607
Frank	Sacramento Ward 1	63	27
Frank	Sacramento Ward 1	63	96
Frank	San Francisco San Francisco 7	68	1415
Frank	San Francisco San Francisco 1	68	823
Frank	San Francisco San Francisco 3	67	83
Frank	San Mateo Twp 1	65	58
Frank	Santa Cruz Pajaro	66	549
Frank	Siskiyou Yreka	69	145
Frank	Solano Vacaville	69	344
Frank	Tuolumne Shawsfla	71	388
Frank	Tuolumne Shawsfla	71	391
Frank	Tuolumne Columbia	71	471
Frank	Yolo Merritt	72	583
Franklin	Calaveras Twp 10	57	282
Franklin	San Francisco San Francisco 3	67	26
Franklin	Solano Vacaville	69	320
Franklin	Tuolumne Twp 3	71	464
Frante	Mariposa Twp 1	60	652
Fred	Placer Auburn	62	568
Frederick	Calaveras Twp 10	57	264
Frederick	Monterey San Juan	60	989
Frederick	Sierra Downieville	66	991
Fredk	San Francisco San Francisco 9	68	1077
G	Calaveras Twp 9	57	408
G	El Dorado Diamond	58	807
G	Nevada Nevada	61	315
G	San Francisco San Francisco 5	67	534
G	Sutter Vernon	70	844
G B	Sonoma Petaluma	69	584
G B	Marin Cortemad	60	752
G S	El Dorado Casumnes	58	1171
G W	Butte Mountain	56	734
G W	Sacramento Ward 1	63	31
G W	Siskiyou Scott Va	69	56
G W	Siskiyou Scott Ri	69	65
G W	Tehama Red Bluff	70	925
Geo	Amador Twp 2	55	317
Geo	Amador Twp 3	55	396
Geo	Butte Oregon	56	615
Geo	Butte Cascade	56	702
Geo	Mariposa Twp 3	60	600
Geo	Mendocino Big Rvr	60	845
Geo	Nevada Grass Valley	61	185
Geo	Sacramento Ward 1	63	26
Geo	San Francisco San Francisco 10	67	196

California 1860 Census Index

WILLIAMS

Name	County Locale	M653 Roll/Page
Geo	San Francisco San Francisco 1	68 910
Geo	Trinity Weaverville	701 065
Geo M	San Francisco San Francisco 10	196 67
Geo M	San Francisco San Francisco 10	215 67
Geo W	Sacramento Ward 3	63 430
Geo W	San Francisco San Francisco 9	681 098
Geo*	Mendocino Big Rvr	60 845
George	Alameda Oakland	55 21
George	Alameda Oakland	55 33
George	Calaveras Twp 8	57 83
George	Contra Costa Twp 1	57 494
George	Contra Costa Twp 1	57 524
George	El Dorado Greenwood	58 726
George	Plumas Quincy	621 006
George	Plumas Quincy	62 998
George	Sacramento Ward 1	63 132
George	San Joaquin Elkhorn	64 965
George	San Mateo Twp 3	65 102
George	Santa Cruz Pajaro	66 549
George	Santa Cruz Pajaro	66 551
George	Shasta Millvill	66 749
George	Sierra Downieville	66 957
George	Solano Suisan	69 211
George	Trinity Trinity	70 970
George	Tulara Keyesville	71 61
George A	Alameda Oakland	55 41
George H	Nevada Rough &	61 412
George M	Tulara Visalia	71 105
George R F	San Francisco 11 San Francisco	148 67
George W	Sierra Twp 7	66 877
George W	Siskiyou Yreka	69 187
Gilliam	Marin Cortemad	60 784
Gillians	Marin Cortemad	60 784
Gor*	Mendocino Big Rvr	60 845
Griffith	Yolo Slate Ra	72 701
Griffith	Yuba Slate Ro	72 701
H	Butte Oregon	56 621
H	El Dorado Diamond	58 765
H	Nevada Grass Valley	61 158
H	Nevada Grass Valley	61 214
H	Nevada Nevada	61 282
H	Nevada Eureka	61 375
H	San Francisco San Francisco 5	67 517
H	Santa Clara Alviso	65 406
H C	San Joaquin Stockton	641 100
H F	San Francisco San Francisco 6	67 456
H F	Sierra Twp 5	66 923
H J	Sacramento Ward 1	63 44
H L	Nevada Eureka	61 375
H P	Calaveras Twp 9	57 407
H S	Placer Dutch Fl	62 732
H W	Tuolumne Twp 1	71 244
Hamp	Mariposa Twp 1	60 668
Hannah	Placer Iona Hills	62 869
Hannah	San Joaquin Stockton	641 076
Hannah B	Calaveras Twp 5	57 144
Hannah B	Calaveras Twp 6	57 144
Hannilla	Mariposa Twp 3	60 561
Harriet	San Francisco San Francisco 4	681 150
Harrison	Mendocino Calpella	60 811
Harry	Santa Cruz Pajaro	66 546
Harvey	Mariposa Twp 3	60 570
Harvey	Santa Clara San Jose	65 345
Hennrietta	San Francisco San Francisco 8	681 273
Henrietta	San Francisco San Francisco 8	681 273
Henry	Butte Cascade	56 698
Henry	Butte Ophir	56 749
Henry	Butte Ophir	56 767
Henry	Calaveras Twp 6	57 160
Henry	Colusa Mansville	57 438
Henry	El Dorado Georgetown	58 689
Henry	Marin Cortemad	60 789
Henry	Monterey San Juan	60 975
Henry	Placer Rattle Snake	62 628
Henry	Plumas Quincy	62 986
Henry	Sacramento Ward 1	63 122
Henry	San Francisco San Francisco 9	681 065
Henry	San Francisco San Francisco 9	681 100
Henry	San Francisco San Francisco 6	67 433
Henry	San Francisco San Francisco 1	68 922
Henry	Santa Cruz Pajaro	66 529
Henry	Sierra Downieville	66 971
Henry	Sonoma Petaluma	69 592
Henry	Trinity Whites Crk	701 028
Henry	Tuolumne Sonora	71 222
Henry	Tuolumne Sonora	71 242
Henry B	San Francisco San Francisco 6	67 433
Henry C	Humbolt Bucksport	59 162
Henry W	Butte Oro	56 688
Henry W	Tuolumne Twp 3	71 452
Heroy	Amador Twp 6	55 421

WILLIAMS

Name	County Locale	M653 Roll/Page
Herry	Santa Cruz Pajaro	66 546
Hewy	Amador Twp 6	55 421
Hiram	Placer Dutch Fl	62 727
Hiram	San Bernardino San Bernadino	64 676
Horner	Sierra Scales D	66 804
Hugh	Colusa Muion	57 462
Hugh	Yolo Cache	72 595
I	Tuolumne Columbia	71 329
I E P*	Nevada Red Dog	61 557
I K	Shasta Shasta	66 681
I M	Tuolumne Columbia	71 305
Inagaretto V*	Shasta Shasta	66 733
Inasjarette V	Shasta Shasta	66 733
Isaac	Sacramento Ward 1	63 119
Isaac	Santa Cruz Pajaro	66 529
Isaac	Tulara Petersburg	71 51
Isaac	Yolo Cache Crk	72 625
Isaac J	San Francisco San Francisco 3	67 52
Ismael	Monterey San Juan	60 981
Issac	San Francisco San Francisco 3	67 52
J	Calaveras Twp 9	57 405
J	El Dorado White Oaks	581 031
J	El Dorado Kelsey	581 138
J	El Dorado Georgetown	58 685
J	El Dorado Placerville	58 855
J	Nevada Grass Valley	61 158
J	Nevada Grass Valley	61 171
J	Nevada Grass Valley	61 185
J	Nevada Grass Valley	61 208
J	Nevada Grass Valley	61 209
J	Nevada Grass Valley	61 237
J	Nevada Grass Valley	61 238
J	Nevada Eureka	61 369
J	Nevada Eureka	61 373
J	Sacramento Granite	63 226
J	Sacramento Alabama	63 415
J	San Francisco San Francisco 1	681 058
J	San Francisco San Francisco 2	67 784
J A	El Dorado Placerville	58 883
J A	Marin Novato	60 737
J A	Tuolumne Shawsfla	71 391
J B	Colusa Monroeville	57 443
J B	Mariposa Twp 3	60 558
J B	Shasta Shasta	66 733
J B P	Mariposa Twp 3	60 558
J B*	Yolo Cottonwoood	72 661
J C	San Francisco San Francisco 3	67 18
J C	San Francisco San Francisco 5	67 521
J C	Tehama Red Bluff	70 924
J D	Amador Twp 6	55 436
J D	Nevada Grass Valley	61 223
J D	Stanislaus Empire	70 734
J D H	Sonoma Armally	69 493
J E P*	Nevada Red Dog	61 557
J H	Amador Twp 2	55 298
J H	El Dorado Casumnes	581 173
J H	El Dorado Placerville	58 856
J H	Trinity Weaverville	701 056
J H	Tuolumne Sonora	71 215
J H	Tuolumne Twp 2	71 288
J H	El Dorado Placerville	58 903
J J	San Francisco San Francisco 10	255 67
J J	Tuolumne Columbia	71 310
J J	Shasta Shasta	66 681
J K	Butte Kimshaw	56 603
J L	El Dorado Coloma	581 103
J L	Nevada Nevada	61 273
J L	Shasta Millvill	66 744
J L	Sonoma Santa Rosa	69 416
J M	Alameda Brooklyn	55 190
J M	Nevada Bridgeport	61 472
J M	Tuolumne Twp 2	71 305
J M*	Calaveras Twp 9	57 410
J M*	Nevada Bridgeport	61 472
J P	Sacramento Ward 3	63 438
J R	Calaveras Twp 9	57 375
J R	Sacramento Franklin	63 323
J R	Stanislaus Buena Village	70 725
J S	Calaveras Twp 8	57 85
J S	San Francisco San Francisco 2	67 667
J S	Siskiyou Klamath	69 84
J S	Siskiyou Klamath	69 88
J S	Sonoma Petaluma	69 583
J T	Calaveras Twp 8	57 67
J T	Santa Clara Fremont	65 441
J W	El Dorado Placerville	58 897
J W	Mariposa Twp 3	60 559
J W	Nevada Grass Valley	61 238
J W	San Francisco San Francisco 6	67 456
J W	Shasta Horsetown	66 697
J W	Tuolumne Twp 2	71 388
J W	Tuolumne Twp 3	71 444
J*	Sacramento Brighton	63 205
Jack	Sacramento Georgian	63 345

WILLIAMS

Name	County Locale	M653 Roll/Page
Jack	San Joaquin Castoria	64 874
Jackson	Los Angeles Tejon	59 539
Jacob	Contra Costa Twp 2	57 550
Jacob	Plumas Quincy	62 973
Jacob	San Francisco San Francisco 7	681 326
Jacob	San Francisco San Francisco 2	67 666
Jacob	Sierra Twp 7	66 865
Jacob	Tuolumne Twp 2	71 411
Jacob	Yuba Marysville	72 935
Jacom	El Dorado White Oaks	581 014
James	Butte Ophir	56 798
James	Contra Costa Twp 1	57 521
James	Contra Costa Twp 3	57 609
James	El Dorado Mud Springs	58 957
James	Fresno Twp 1	59 76
James	Marin San Rafael	60 763
James	Mariposa Twp 3	60 566
James	Plumas Meadow Valley	62 904
James	Plumas Meadow Valley	62 908
James	Plumas Quincy	62 983
James	Sacramento Ward 4	63 535
James	San Francisco San Francisco 4	681 123
James	San Francisco San Francisco 4	681 136
James	San Francisco San Francisco 11	153 67
James	San Joaquin Castoria	64 906
James	San Mateo Twp 3	65 84
James	Santa Cruz Santa Cruz	66 602
James	Santa Cruz Santa Cruz	66 635
James	Sierra Downieville	661 007
James	Sierra La Porte	66 768
James	Solano Benecia	69 289
James	Solano Fremont	69 385
James	Sonoma Mendocino	69 464
James	Tehama Lassen	70 868
James	Trinity East For	701 025
James	Tulara Twp 2	71 3
James	Tuolumne Big Oak	71 182
James	Tuolumne Twp 2	71 393
James	Yolo Washington	72 563
James	Yolo Cache Crk	72 665
James F	Contra Costa Twp 1	57 532
James F	Plumas Quincy	62 941
James F	Sierra Pine Grove	66 823
James K	Butte Ophir	56 800
James M	Sierra Pine Grove	66 824
James R	Colusa Monroeville	57 451
Jane	Butte Cascade	56 703
Jane	Colusa Muion	57 462
Jane	Sierra Monte Crk	661 036
Jas	Butte Oregon	56 611
Jas	Butte Oregon	56 613
Jas	Calaveras Twp 9	57 370
Jas	Mariposa Twp 1	60 642
Jas	Napa Hot Springs	61 27
Jas	Napa Napa	61 91
Jas	Placer Dutch Fl	62 718
Jas	San Francisco San Francisco 9	681 055
Jas	San Francisco San Francisco 1	68 838
Jas	San Mateo Twp 3	65 88
Jas	Trinity State Ba	701 001
Jas A	Butte Chico	56 531
Jas H	San Francisco San Francisco 2	67 671
Jasper	Sacramento Franklin	63 313
Jedediah	Solano Vacaville	69 320
Jeremiah	Los Angeles Los Angeles	59 338
Jeremiah	Nevada Bloomfield	61 517
Jeremiah	Sierra Downieville	661 019
Jeremiah	Sierra Downieville	66 960
Jesse	Shasta French G	66 714
Jesse	Sierra Twp 5	66 925
Jesse	Yuba Bear Rvr	721 005
Jessee H	Contra Costa Twp 2	57 552
Jhn	Nevada Bridgeport	61 470
Jilt	Santa Clara San Jose	65 285
Jno	Butte Kimshaw	56 571
Jno	Butte Oregon	56 636
Jno	Mendocino Big Rvr	60 845
Jno	Nevada Nevada	61 286
Jno	Nevada Nevada	61 296
Jno	Sacramento Granite	63 245
Jno	Sacramento Ward 1	63 49
Jno	San Francisco San Francisco 9	681 061
Jno	San Francisco San Francisco 10	222 67
Jno	Tehama Pasakent	70 859
Jno Q	Sonoma Vallejo	69 622
Jo	Mariposa Coulterville	60 692
Joanna	Sonoma Petaluma	69 585
Job	Amador Twp 5	55 334
Joe	Trinity Dead Wood	70 958
Joel	Trinity Dead Wood	70 958
John L	Los Angeles Los Angeles	59 371
Johln	Siskiyou Yreka	69 148
John	Alameda Brooklyn	55 142

California 1860 Census Index

WILLIAMS

Name	County Locale	M653 Roll/Page
John	Alameda Oakland	55 55
John	Alameda Oakland	55 75
John	Amador Twp 2	55 278
John	Amador Twp 3	55 408
John	Amador Twp 7	55 413
John	Amador Twp 1	55 461
John	Butte Wyandotte	56 657
John	Butte Ophir	56 758
John	Calaveras Twp 6	57 144
John	Calaveras Twp 7	57 19
John	Calaveras Twp 5	57 203
John	Calaveras Twp 5	57 224
John	Calaveras Twp 4	57 321
John	Calaveras Twp 9	57 399
John	Calaveras Twp 8	57 77
John	Calaveras Twp 8	57 86
John	Colusa Spring Valley	57 435
John	Colusa Monroeville	57 446
John	Contra Costa Twp 1	57 505
John	Del Norte Happy Ca	58 667
John	El Dorado White Oaks	581007
John	El Dorado Salmon Falls	581050
John	El Dorado Kelsey	581145
John	El Dorado Eldorado	58 941
John	El Dorado Mud Springs	58 977
John	Fresno Twp 2	59 18
John	Los Angeles Azuza	59 274
John	Los Angeles Los Angeles	59 321
John	Los Angeles San Gabriel	59 408
John	Los Angeles Tejon	59 522
John	Marin Bolinas	60 742
John	Marin Cortemad	60 781
John	Marin Cortemad	60 787
John	Mariposa Twp 3	60 573
John	Mariposa Coulterville	60 699
John	Monterey San Juan	60 994
John	Napa Napa	61 101
John	Nevada Bridgeport	61 470
John	Nevada Bridgeport	61 478
John	Nevada Bridgeport	61 495
John	Placer Auburn	62 590
John	Placer Rattle Snake	62 603
John	Placer Stewart	62 605
John	Placer Goods	62 694
John	Placer Dutch Fl	62 719
John	Placer Todds Va	62 786
John	Placer Michigan	62 811
John	Placer Michigan	62 824
John	Placer Michigan	62 832
John	Placer Michigan	62 847
John	Placer Michigan	62 855
John	Sacramento Sutter	63 300
John	San Diego San Diego	64 761
John	San Francisco San Francisco 7	681440
John	San Francisco San Francisco 3	67 36
John	San Francisco San Francisco 3	67 50
John	San Francisco San Francisco 2	67 610
John	San Francisco San Francisco 3	67 67
John	San Francisco San Francisco 3	67 69
John	San Francisco San Francisco 2	67 742
John	San Francisco San Francisco 1	68 812
John	San Francisco San Francisco 3	67 83
John	San Francisco San Francisco 1	68 854
John	San Francisco San Francisco 1	68 871
John	San Francisco San Francisco 1	68 889
John	San Francisco San Francisco 1	68 909
John	San Francisco San Francisco 1	68 931
John	San Mateo Twp 1	65 58
John	Santa Clara Fremont	65 417
John	Santa Clara Fremont	65 429
John	Santa Cruz Watsonville	66 539
John	Santa Cruz Soguel	66 587
John	Santa Cruz Santa Cruz	66 602
John	Santa Cruz Yuba	66 653
John	Shasta Shasta	66 653
John	Shasta Shasta	66 664
John	Sierra Downieville	661029
John	Sierra Monte Crk	661037
John	Sierra Monte Crk	661038
John	Sierra Monte Crk	661039
John	Sierra St Louis	66 816
John	Sierra Twp 7	66 868
John	Sierra Twp 7	66 877
John	Siskiyou Yreka	69 148
John	Siskiyou Yreka	69 193
John	Solano Suisan	69 221
John	Solano Suisan	69 231
John	Solano Benecia	69 298
John	Solano Benecia	69 299
John	Sonoma Santa Rosa	69 415
John	Sonoma Petaluma	69 553
John	Sonoma Petaluma	69 572
John	Stanislaus Buena Village	70 724
John	Tehama Antelope	70 893
John	Trinity State Ba	701001
John	Trinity Mouth Ca	701016
John	Trinity Weaverville	701063
John	Trinity Weaverville	701079
John	Tuolumne Twp 1	71 223
John	Tuolumne Twp 3	71 449
John	Yuba Slate Ro	72 694
John	Yuba Long Bar	72 744
John	Yuba Parks Ba	72 779
John	Yuba Rose Bar	72 808
John	Yuba Fosters	72 839
John	Yuba Marysville	72 851
John B	El Dorado Big Bar	58 736
John E	Sonoma Santa Rosa	69 415
John G	Sierra Twp 5	66 925
John G	Yuba Marysville	72 866
John H	Calaveras Twp 6	57 156
John H	San Francisco San Francisco 9	681105
John H	Tuolumne Jamestown	71 449
John H	Yolo Slate Ra	72 702
John H	Yuba Slate Ro	72 702
John J	Del Norte Crescent	58 649
John L	Los Angeles Los Angeles	59 371
John M	Monterey Pajaro	601018
John M	San Francisco San Francisco 9	68 996
John N	El Dorado Georgetown	58 680
John N	San Francisco San Francisco 3	67 34
John P	Sierra Twp 5	66 936
John P	Yuba Marysville	72 878
John R	Stanislaus Oatvale	70 720
John S	Placer Sacramento	62 645
John S	San Joaquin Stockton	641059
John S	Sonoma Healdsbu	69 475
John S	Stanislaus Branch	70 704
John W	Los Angeles Tejon	59 528
John W	Monterey S Antoni	60 967
John W	Plumas Quincy	62 953
John W	Solano Vallejo	69 260
John*	Santa Cruz Soguel	66 587
Johnson	Shasta Millvill	66 755
Johnson	Yuba Suida	72 986
Jonathan	San Francisco San Francisco 7	681415
Jonathon	Santa Cruz Pajaro	66 529
Jos	Butte Kimshaw	56 577
Jos	Butte Kimshaw	56 591
Jos	Butte Cascade	56 694
Jos	Butte Ophir	56 767
Jos	Merced Twp 1	60 896
Jos	Tehama Red Bluff	70 923
Jos M	San Francisco San Francisco 9	681052
Jose	Marin S Antoni	60 708
Josep	Shasta Shasta	66 682
Joseph	Alameda Brooklyn	55 108
Joseph	Alameda Brooklyn	55 124
Joseph	Amador Twp 1	55 456
Joseph	El Dorado Georgetown	58 674
Joseph	Mendocino Arrana	60 860
Joseph	Nevada Eureka	61 354
Joseph	Nevada Bridgeport	61 451
Joseph	Placer Rattle Snake	62 634
Joseph	San Francisco San Francisco 4	681117
Joseph	Santa Cruz Pajaro	66 552
Joseph	Shasta Shasta	66 682
Joseph	Shasta Horsetown	66 702
Joseph	Sierra Grizzly	661058
Joseph	Sonoma Sonoma	69 644
Joseph	Yuba Marysville	72 977
Josephine	San Francisco San Francisco 4	681150
Jrs	Amador Twp 5	55 334
Juah	Calaveras Twp 9	57 370
Juan	Yuba New York	72 726
Juaquin	Monterey Monterey	60 926
Julia	Sacramento Ward 4	63 545
Juoquin	Monterey Monterey	60 926
K	Sutter Yuba	70 778
Kate	Nevada Bridgeport	61 475
Kate	San Francisco San Francisco 4	681228
L	Amador Twp 1	55 480
L	El Dorado Mud Springs	58 967
L	Placer Dutch Fl	62 709
L	San Francisco San Francisco 6	67 449
L	Shasta Shasta	66 679
L	Siskiyou Cottonwood	69 99
L	Tehama Lassen	70 870
L B	San Bernardino Santa Barbara	64 179
L D	Nevada Little Y	61 532
L V	Amador Twp 3	55 392
L*	Sacramento Brighton	63 205
L*	Sacramento San Joaquin	63 361
Lang	Tuolumne Shawsfla	71 393
Leonard	Yuba Marysville	72 915
Lewellen	Sacramento Ward 3	63 440
Lewis	El Dorado Casumnes	581174
Lewis	Sierra Eureka	661042
Lewis J	Tuolumne Twp 6	71 530
Louis	San Francisco San Francisco 7	681382
Louisiana	Sacramento Ward 3	63 445
M	Nevada Grass Valley	61 185
M	Sutter Sutter	70 809
M A	Tuolumne Twp 1	71 215
M J	San Francisco San Francisco 9	681103
M L	Solano Vacaville	69 331
M W	Marin Cortemad	60 757
Manuel	Alameda Oakland	55 49
Manuel	Nevada Rough &	61 430
Manuel	Placer Michigan	62 850
Manuel*	Nevada Rough &	61 430
Manwel	Nevada Rough &	61 430
Marcus	Santa Clara San Jose	65 313
Margarette V	Shasta Shasta	66 733
Maria M	Los Angeles Los Angeles	59 352
Mark	San Joaquin Castoria	64 892
Marshal	Santa Cruz Pajaro	66 558
Martha	San Francisco San Francisco 4	681146
Martin	Sacramento Ward 1	63 149
Martin	Santa Clara Alviso	65 413
Mary	San Francisco San Francisco 1	68 873
Mary	Solano Vallejo	69 279
Mary	Tulara Twp 1	71 94
Mary	Tuolumne Visalia	71 94
Mary Ann	Alameda Oakland	55 13
Mary E	San Francisco San Francisco 2	67 625
Mary V	Placer Dutch Fl	62 711
Mason	Amador Twp 3	55 390
Mathew	Placer Dutch Fl	62 734
Michael	Solano Vallejo	69 245
Mike	Tehama Moons	70 853
Miles	San Joaquin O'Neal	641002
Miles	Yuba Linda	72 992
Miley	Calaveras Twp 6	57 129
Mimay	Sierra Twp 7	66 875
Mooris*	San Francisco San Francisco 9	68 963
Moril	Tuolumne Twp 2	71 365
Morris	San Francisco San Francisco 9	68 963
Morton	Tuolumne Don Pedro	71 534
Moses	Sierra Port Win	66 793
Mr	Sonoma Salt Point	69 692
Murray	Sierra Twp 7	66 875
N	Sacramento Ward 3	63 430
N D	Yolo Cache Crk	72 619
N J	Yuba New York	72 725
N P	Yolo Cache	72 619
N S	Yuba New York	72 725
Napol	Sonoma Petaluma	69 583
Nat	Trinity Indian C	70 989
Nat	Yolo No E Twp	72 680
Nat	Yuba North Ea	72 680
Nathan	Sonoma Petaluma	69 585
Nathaniel	Sacramento Franklin	63 324
Nicholas	Calaveras Twp 6	57 141
Noah	Siskiyou Yreka	69 137
Noah	Siskiyou Yreka	69 138
Noah	Siskiyou Yreka	69 141
Noah	Siskiyou Yreka	69 173
Norton	Colusa Colusi	57 423
O F	Tuolumne Columbia	71 309
O M*	Nevada Bridgeport	61 472
Oliver	Sonoma Vallejo	69 624
Oren	Placer Stewart	62 607
Owen	El Dorado White Oaks	581031
Owen	Nevada Bridgeport	61 441
P	Amador Twp 3	55 383
P	Nevada Eureka	61 380
P	Sacramento Granite	63 223
P B	Mariposa Twp 3	60 558
P F	Calaveras Twp 7	57 24
P T	El Dorado Cold Spring	581099
Parker	Placer Michigan	62 827
Paronema	Marin S Antoni	60 709
Parris	Solano Green Valley	69 242
Parsey L	Colusa Grand Island	57 475
Part Misor*	Placer Michigan	62 830
Patrick	Sacramento Ward 1	63 155
Paul	Yuba Marysville	72 966
Pena	San Francisco San Francisco 1	68 809
Perra*	San Francisco San Francisco 1	68 809
Perry	Solano Fairfield	69 197
Pesse	Sierra Twp 5	66 925
Peter	Amador Twp 1	55 490
Peter	Butte Bidwell	56 725
Peter	Butte Ophir	56 799
Peter	El Dorado Kelsey	581152
Peter	Placer Forest H	62 803
Peter	Placer Michigan	62 849
Peter	Sacramento Granite	63 252
Peter	San Francisco San Francisco 2	67 703
Peter	San Luis Obispo San Luis Obispo	65 40
Peter	Santa Clara Fremont	65 421
Peter	Sierra Twp 7	66 899
Peter	Tuolumne Twp 3	71 439
Peter	Tuolumne Jamestown	71 448

California 1860 Census Index

Name	County Locale	M653 Roll	Page
WILLIAMS			
Peter	Yuba Marysville	72	913
Phillip	Calaveras Twp 4	57	329
Phillip	Santa Clara Gilroy	65	237
Prince	Alameda Brooklyn	55	78
Prince A	Alameda Brooklyn	55	105
R	Amador Twp 2	55	317
R	El Dorado Georgetown	58	698
R	Nevada Nevada	61	282
R	Nevada Eureka	61	355
R	Nevada Grass Valley	61	220
R B	Nevada Grass Valley	61	220
R F	Mariposa Coulterville	60	689
R F	Mendocino Big Rvr	60	847
R I	Placer Forest H	62	767
R M	Mariposa Twp 3	60	596
R N	El Dorado Placerville	58	912
R S	Sacramento Franklin	63	320
R T	Mariposa Twp 3	60	547
R T	Mariposa Coulterville	60	689
R T	Placer Iona Hills	62	882
Ransom	Tuolumne Twp 3	71	462
Reace	Sierra Monte Crk	66	1035
Reice	Sierra Monte Crk	66	1035
Reuben	Mendocino Ukiah	60	797
Reuel	San Francisco San Francisco 7	68	1441
Richard	Placer Forest H	62	794
Richard	Sierra La Porte	66	776
Richard	Solano Vallejo	69	279
Richard	Yolo Slate Ra	72	701
Richard	Yuba Slate Ro	72	701
Richard N	Yolo Slate Ra	72	701
Richd	Amador Twp 5	55	342
Richd	Butte Ophir	56	799
Richd	Nevada Bridgeport	61	453
Roberati*	San Mateo Twp 1	65	52
Robert	Colusa Butte Crk	57	464
Robert	El Dorado Salmon Falls	58	1037
Robert	Sacramento Sutter	63	309
Robert	San Francisco San Francisco 9	68	1064
Robert	San Francisco San Francisco 3	67	69
Robert	Sierra Excelsior	66	1033
Robert	Solano Benecia	69	310
Robert	Tuolumne Twp 6	71	534
Robert M	Humbolt Bucksport	59	158
Robert N	Sierra St Louis	66	808
Robt	Calaveras Twp 6	57	120
Robt	Tuolumne Twp 1	71	261
Robt J	Trinity Mouth Ca	70	1013
Robt L	Klamath Klamath	59	224
Robt S	San Bernardino Santa Barbara	64	178
Rornes	Sierra Scales D	66	804
Ross	Sierra Downieville	66	957
Ross	Sierra Downieville	66	962
Rowdy H	Mendocino Anderson	60	871
Ruel	Yuba Marysville	72	966
S	Calaveras Twp 9	57	360
S	Nevada Grass Valley	61	237
S	Sacramento Ward 1	63	45
S	San Francisco San Francisco 9	68	1075
S	San Joaquin Stockton	64	1060
S	Shasta Millvill	66	725
S A	San Francisco San Francisco 10	67	177
S H	Del Norte Crescent	58	625
S S	Siskiyou Cottonwoood	69	105
S S	Tuolumne Twp 3	71	452
S W	Alameda Brooklyn	55	190
S W	Calaveras Twp 9	57	360
S*	Sacramento Brighton	63	205
S*	Sacramento San Joaquin	63	361
Sabina	San Francisco San Francisco 6	67	416
Saml	Amador Twp 2	55	298
Saml	Sacramento Ward 4	63	568
Saml	San Francisco San Francisco 1	68	838
Saml	San Francisco San Francisco 1	68	923
Saml	Shasta Shasta	66	734
Saml	Sierra Twp 7	66	903
Saml	Placer Virginia	62	684
Saml J	Sierra Twp 7	66	903
Samuel	Butte Kimshaw	56	607
Samuel	Plumas Quincy	62	986
Samuel	Solano Vallejo	69	251
Sanil	Amador Twp 5	55	366
Sarah	Del Norte Crescent	58	622
Sarah	Napa Clear Lake	61	133
Sarah	San Francisco San Francisco 8	68	1290
Sarah	San Francisco San Francisco 10	67	184
Sarah	Tuolumne Twp 4	71	163
Sarah Ann	Calaveras Twp 9	57	376
Schugle	Tulara Visalia	71	97
Selden	Sacramento Ward 1	63	45
Seth	Napa Napa	61	81
Simon	El Dorado Georgetown	58	702
Sister B*	San Francisco San Francisco 10	67	181

Name	County Locale	M653 Roll	Page
WILLIAMS			
Solomon	Placer Dutch Fl	62	727
Sophia	San Francisco San Francisco 8	68	1299
Sophie	San Francisco San Francisco 4	68	1152
Stepen	Sierra Cold Can	66	836
Stephen G	Yuba Marysville	72	911
Susan	Sierra Pine Grove	66	824
Susan	Yuba Marysville	72	898
T	Butte Chico	56	559
T	El Dorado Placerville	58	835
T	Mariposa Twp 3	60	615
T	Nevada Washington	61	337
T	San Francisco San Francisco 9	68	1081
T	Yolo Cache	72	621
T E	Siskiyou Scott Ri	69	83
T G	Sonoma Vallejo	69	619
T H	El Dorado Coloma	58	1073
T J	El Dorado Placerville	58	881
T J	Nevada Nevada	61	258
T S	El Dorado Casumnes	58	1172
Thadeus	Tehama Lassen	70	873
Tho	Siskiyou Scott Va	69	50
Tho	Sonoma Vallejo	69	612
Thomas	Calaveras Twp 6	57	161
Thomas	Calaveras Twp 5	57	231
Thomas	Calaveras Twp 7	57	48
Thomas	Colusa Monroeville	57	441
Thomas	Colusa Muion	57	462
Thomas	Contra Costa Twp 2	57	551
Thomas	El Dorado White Oaks	58	1018
Thomas	Marin Cortemad	60	787
Thomas	Placer Auburn	62	568
Thomas	Placer Michigan	62	830
Thomas	Plumas Quincy	62	944
Thomas	San Francisco San Francisco 7	68	1329
Thomas	San Francisco San Francisco 7	68	1440
Thomas	San Joaquin O'Neal	64	1001
Thomas	Sierra Downieville	66	1020
Thomas	Sierra Port Win	66	796
Thomas	Siskiyou Yreka	69	142
Thomas	Tuolumne Twp 3	71	439
Thomas	Yuba Parke Ba	72	785
Thomas H	Sierra Eureka	66	1042
Thomas L	Yuba Marysville	72	858
Thomas L	Yuba Marysville	72	859
Thos	Butte Chico	56	535
Thos	Butte Kimshaw	56	599
Thos	Butte Wyandotte	56	670
Thos	Butte Ophir	56	797
Thos	Nevada Bridgeport	61	470
Thos	Nevada Little Y	61	533
Thos	Placer Virginia	62	673
Thos	Sacramento Ward 1	63	62
Thos	San Francisco San Francisco 9	68	1054
Thos	San Francisco San Francisco 9	68	1060
Thos	San Francisco San Francisco 1	68	928
Thos	Santa Clara San Jose	65	321
Thos	Santa Clara Thomas	65	443
Thos	Shasta Horsetown	66	708
Thos	Tehama Moons	70	854
Thos	Trinity East For	70	1027
Thos	Trinity Eastman	70	960
Thos G	San Francisco San Francisco 2	67	735
Thos R	Nevada Bridgeport	61	444
Thos T	Los Angeles Tejon	59	536
U J	Amador Twp 3	55	409
Uriah	Humbolt Pacific	59	133
W	El Dorado Diamond	58	769
W	El Dorado Placerville	58	855
W	El Dorado Placerville	58	857
W	El Dorado Placerville	58	876
W	El Dorado Placerville	58	898
W	Mendocino Anderson	60	868
W	Nevada Nevada	61	282
W	Sacramento Granite	63	241
W	San Francisco San Francisco 5	67	518
W	Shasta Horsetown	66	697
W	Sierra Port Win	66	793
W	Siskiyou Cottonwoood	69	107
W	Sutter Nicolaus	70	835
W	Trinity Weaverville	70	1063
W A	Sacramento Granite	63	238
W B	Amador Twp 6	55	421
W B	Nevada Bridgeport	61	440
W F	Amador Twp 5	55	342
W F	Butte Bidwell	56	721
W H	Napa Clear Lake	61	140
W H	Nevada Grass Valley	61	238
W J	Trinity E Weaver	70	1058
W M	Napa Hot Springs	61	14
W M	Nevada Bridgeport	61	445
W R	Tehama Red Bluff	70	906
W W	Butte Cascade	56	702
W W	Butte Ophir	56	771
W W	Calaveras Twp 9	57	404
W W	Placer Goods	62	697

Name	County Locale	M653 Roll	Page
WILLIAMS			
Walter	Butte Ophir	56	754
Walter	Butte Ophir	56	760
Washington	Sonoma Mendocino	69	455
Water*	Plumas Quincy	62	996
Watkins	Sierra Monte Crk	66	1036
Wesley	Tulara Twp 3	71	58
Wiley	Santa Clara Gilroy	65	235
Wiliams	El Dorado Coloma	58	1080
Willam C	Tuolumne Twp 5	71	503
William	Calaveras Twp 10	57	294
William	El Dorado Salmon Falls	58	1049
William	El Dorado Coloma	58	1086
William	Marin Novato	60	738
William	Nevada Bridgeport	61	496
William	Nevada Bloomfield	61	510
William	Placer Forest H	62	767
William	Placer Michigan	62	830
William	San Diego Agua Caliente	64	863
William	San Francisco San Francisco 4	68	1134
William	San Francisco San Francisco 3	67	43
William	Sierra Cold Can	66	836
William	Siskiyou Scott Ri	69	71
William	Solano Montezuma	69	373
William	Tulara Twp 1	71	89
William	Tuolumne Twp 1	71	254
William	Tuolumne Twp 2	71	281
William	Yuba Rose Bar	72	796
William	Yuba Rose Bar	72	813
William C	Tuolumne Montezuma	71	503
William F	Nevada Bridgeport	61	496
William G	Contra Costa Twp 1	57	506
William H	San Francisco San Francisco 11		100
		67	
William H	Yuba Marysville	72	969
William H H	Yuba Marysville	72	969
William L	Yuba Marysville	72	861
William R	Nevada Bloomfield	61	525
William W	Tuolumne Green Springs	71	519
William*	Yuba Rose Bar	72	813
Williams	El Dorado Coloma	58	1080
Wm	Alameda Brooklyn	55	79
Wm	Butte Cascade	56	701
Wm	Butte Bidwell	56	726
Wm	Butte Ophir	56	776
Wm	Del Norte Crescent	58	625
Wm	Humbolt Pacific	59	137
Wm	Los Angeles Elmonte	59	252
Wm	Nevada Nevada	61	289
Wm	Nevada Nevada	61	317
Wm	Placer Auburn	62	585
Wm	Placer Dutch Fl	62	731
Wm	Sacramento Granite	63	246
Wm	Sacramento San Joaquin	63	363
Wm	Sacramento San Joaquin	63	366
Wm	Sacramento Cosumnes	63	380
Wm	Sacramento Casumnes	63	381
Wm	San Francisco San Francisco 1	68	841
Wm	Sierra Twp 7	66	869
Wm	Sierra Twp 7	66	888
Wm	Sierra Twp 7	66	911
Wm	Stanislaus Branch	70	706
Wm	Trinity Taylor'S	70	1034
Wm	Trinity Readings	70	996
Wm	Tuolumne Sonora	71	244
Wm	Solano Vallejo	69	276
Wm F	Calaveras Twp 4	57	307
Wm F	Tuolumne Twp 3	71	460
Wm F W	Tuolumne Twp 3	71	460
Wm H	Colusa Monroeville	57	142
Wm H	Colusa Spring Valley	57	430
Wm H	Colusa Monroeville	57	442
Wm H	Nevada Nevada	61	263
Wm H	Santa Clara Redwood	65	458
Wm O	Yolo Slate Ra	72	702
Wm O	Yuba Slate Ro	72	702
Wm P	Mendocino Arrana	60	861
Wm W	Sierra Chappare	66	1041
WILLIAMSEN			
Chas M	Sacramento Natonia	63	274
George	Sacramento Granite	63	254
George	Sacramento Granite	63	264
J H	Sacramento Granite	63	246
John	San Francisco San Francisco 10		357
		67	
John	San Francisco San Francisco 3	67	42
John J	Sacramento Granite	63	259
R M D	Shasta Shasta	66	680
Wm F	San Francisco San Francisco 3	67	51
WILLIAMSON			
Andw	Monterey Alisal	60	1044
Andw	San Francisco San Francisco 10		348
		67	
Archy	Solano Suisan	69	232
Augus	Solano Suisan	69	210
August	Solano Suisan	69	210

Name	County Locale	M653 RollPage
WILLIAMSON		
Bill	Colusa Muion	57 458
C V	Tuolumne Big Oak	71 129
Callins	Solano Vallejo	69 255
Charles	Contra Costa Twp 1	57 507
Charles	Yuba Marysville	72 903
Clara	Sacramento Ward 1	63 104
Claud	Contra Costa Twp 1	57 507
Collins	Solano Vallejo	69 255
D H	El Dorado Placerville	58 931
D J	San Francisco San Francisco 6	67 446
D L*	Sacramento Brighton	63 196
D S*	Sacramento Brighton	63 196
Daniel	Solano Vallejo	69 252
David	San Francisco San Francisco 2	67 805
Davide	San Joaquin Elkhorn	64 956
Duncan	San Francisco San Francisco 10	342 67
Duncan	Solano Suisan	69 204
E A	Santa Clara Fremont	65 419
Elias	Placer Michigan	62 855
Fanny	San Francisco San Francisco 6	67 443
G W	Shasta Millvill	66 740
Geo	Sacramento Ward 4	63 580
Geo D	Napa Napa	61 74
George	Sacramento Granite	63 254
George	Sacramento Granite	63 264
H	Sacramento Ward 1	63 147
Henry	Alameda Oakland	55 50
Henry	Plumas Quincy	62 998
Henry	Solano Suisan	69 232
Henry B	Yuba Marysville	72 947
Hiram B	Yuba Marysville	72 906
J	El Dorado Placerville	58 887
J F	Sacramento Ward 3	63 429
J H	El Dorado Placerville	58 902
J H	Sacramento Granite	63 246
J L	Yolo Cache Crk	72 646
J P	Calaveras Twp 9	57 376
J R	Butte Cascade	56 698
J R	Placer Michigan	62 837
J Y	El Dorado Placerville	58 882
Jackson	Yolo Cache Crk	72 665
James	Calaveras Twp 8	57 80
James	Santa Clara San Jose	65 279
James	Yuba Marysville	72 873
Jas H	Sacramento Mississipi	63 185
Jeremiah	Nevada Rough &	61 401
Jermiah	Nevada Rough &	61 401
Jno	Alameda Oakland	55 65
John	Alameda Oakland	55 11
John	San Bernardino San Bernadino	64 671
John	San Francisco San Francisco 10	357 67
John	San Francisco San Francisco 3	67 42
John	Santa Cruz Santa Cruz	66 631
John	Santa Cruz Santa Cruz	66 634
John	Sierra Downieville	661010
John	Solano Benecia	69 316
John	Tuolumne Twp 2	71 377
John	Yolo Fremont	72 605
John	Yuba Marysville	72 904
John S	San Joaquin Elkhorn	64 950
Joseph N	Santa Cruz Pajaro	66 531
L	Nevada Eureka	61 378
Lindley	Colusa Muion	57 458
Lizzie	Sacramento Ward 1	63 82
M	Butte Wyandotte	56 666
Martin	San Francisco San Francisco 9	681026
Mary	San Francisco San Francisco 6	67 442
Michael	San Francisco San Francisco 2	67 555
Nelson	Los Angeles Los Angeles	59 360
P	Tuolumne Columbia	71 337
P S	San Francisco San Francisco 6	67 459
Peter	San Francisco San Francisco 1	68 891
Peter	Tuolumne Shawsfla	71 375
Peter	Yolo Putah	72 586
R M D*	Shasta Shasta	66 680
R S	San Francisco San Francisco 7	681346
R S*	Sacramento Dry Crk	63 379
R T*	Sacramento Dry Crk	63 379
R W	El Dorado Coloma	581073
Robert	Amador Twp 4	55 241
S	Nevada Eureka	61 378
S	Tuolumne Twp 2	71 377
S C	Yolo Putah	72 614
Sarah	Tuolumne Twp 1	71 209
T	Solano Vacaville	69 329
T	Yolo Cache Crk	72 621
T P	San Joaquin Stockton	641074
Thomas	San Francisco San Francisco 4	681168
Thos	Sacramento Ward 1	63 64
Thos D	Sonoma Santa Rosa	69 393
Thos W	Sonoma Santa Rosa	69 393
W	El Dorado Placerville	58 884
W	Nevada Nevada	61 317

Name	County Locale	M653 RollPage
WILLIAMSON		
W M	Santa Clara San Jose	65 374
Warren	El Dorado Placerville	58 915
William	Marin Tomales	60 715
William	Siskiyou Yreka	69 152
Willm	Sacramento Mississipi	63 187
Wilson	Tulara Twp 3	71 51
Wm	Del Norte Happy Ca	58 662
Wm	El Dorado Placerville	58 844
Wm	Los Angeles Tejon	59 523
Wm	Mendocino Ukiah	60 806
Wm	Sierra Downieville	661010
Wm F	San Francisco San Francisco 3	67 51
Wm M	Sonoma Santa Rosa	69 393
WILLIAMSONS		
Duncan	Solano Suisan	69 204
WILLIAN		
Geo	Stanislaus Empire	70 728
WILLIANN		
William*	Yuba Rose Bar	72 813
WILLIANS		
Antone	Sierra Whiskey	66 845
WILLIANY		
Jas	Napa Napa	61 91
WILLIARD		
A H	Yolo Cottonwoood	72 660
Chester	Amador Twp 1	55 475
J G	Sierra Morristown	661051
John M	Placer Auburn	62 550
S S	Placer Todds Va	62 785
WILLIAS		
Jno	San Joaquin Stockton	641093
WILLIBEE		
N	Butte Ophir	56 798
WILLIDGE		
Elisebeth	Sacramento Ward 4	63 575
WILLIE		
---	Mariposa Twp 1	60 655
Abram	Amador Twp 4	55 234
C A	Sonoma Vallejo	69 612
Edmond	Calaveras Twp 7	57 13
Harry	San Francisco San Francisco 10	218 67
John	Placer Michigan	62 826
John	Santa Clara Santa Clara	65 509
Jos	Butte Ophir	56 755
L H	San Francisco San Francisco 10	217 67
Louis	Calaveras Twp 7	57 47
Mary	Yuba Foster B	72 823
Roft	El Dorado Mud Springs	58 997
S H	San Francisco San Francisco 10	217 67
W	Butte Kimshaw	56 587
WILLIFER		
J N	Mendocino Arrana	60 859
WILLIKEN		
Samuel	Santa Cruz Santa Cruz	66 628
WILLIMAN		
John*	Placer Yankee J	62 778
WILLIMAS		
W W	Shasta Millvill	66 747
WILLIMS		
John	Calaveras Twp 5	57 224
WILLIN		
L	El Dorado Salmon Falls	581038
WILLINAN		
Louis	Yuba Marysville	72 964
WILLINGHAM		
Peter*	Nevada Red Dog	61 544
WILLINGHBY		
C	Butte Oro	56 681
WILLINGTON		
E	Calaveras Twp 9	57 408
George	El Dorado Georgetown	58 680
John	Tuolumne Twp 1	71 238
W	Calaveras Twp 9	57 409
Wm	Sierra Excelsior	661033
WILLIS		
A M	Siskiyou Klamath	69 87
Andy	El Dorado White Oaks	581012
B	Butte Oregon	56 620
Benjamin	Tulara Visalia	71 78
C	El Dorado Greenwood	58 711
C J	Tuolumne Columbia	71 292
Calvin*	Siskiyou Yreka	69 143
Chas	San Francisco San Francisco 10	306 67
Chas	Sonoma Petaluma	69 568
Cyrus	Yuba Rose Bar	72 819
D L	Siskiyou Yreka	69 190
D M	Yolo Slate Ra	72 718
Daniel	Tulara Twp 1	71 85
David	Tulara Visalia	71 85
Debb*	Yuba New York	72 718
Delb*	Yuba New York	72 718

Name	County Locale	M653 RollPage
WILLIS		
E L	San Francisco San Francisco 4	681112
Edward	Calaveras Twp 7	57 6
Edward B	Butte Ophir	56 761
F M	Sonoma Sonoma	69 657
Fred	Sierra Downieville	66 960
Frederck J*	San Francisco 7	681428
G S	San Francisco Calaveras Twp 9	57 406
Geo	Sacramento Ward 4	63 534
Geo S	Mariposa Twp 3	60 591
George	Sacramento Georgian	63 342
George	Tulara Twp 1	71 108
George H	Yuba Rose Bar	72 802
Henry	Klamath S Fork	59 203
Henry	Siskiyou Yreka	69 143
Henry	Sonoma Vallejo	69 621
J	Siskiyou Klamath	69 87
J H	Yolo Cottonwoood	72 657
J J	Calaveras Twp 8	57 80
J L*	Sacramento Brighton	63 209
J N	Yolo Cottonwoood	72 657
J S	Sacramento Granite	63 221
J S	Sacramento Georgian	63 336
J S*	Sacramento Brighton	63 209
J T	Tuolumne Twp 1	71 247
J*	Siskiyou Klamath	69 87
Jas	Butte Oregon	56 629
Jas	Sacramento Granite	63 258
Jennie	Sacramento Ward 1	63 16
John	San Francisco San Francisco 2	67 635
John	San Francisco San Francisco 3	67 76
John	Shasta Millvill	66 751
John	Sonoma Armally	69 481
John F	San Francisco San Francisco 3	67 76
Jos	Butte Cascade	56 697
Lilas W	Yuba Suida	72 993
M	Nevada Grass Valley	61 237
M E	San Francisco San Francisco 5	67 545
M J	Nevada Nevada	61 320
Mareilla	San Francisco San Francisco 3	67 76
Martha	Nevada Nevada	61 297
Mary	Sacramento Granite	63 263
May	Sacramento Granite	63 263
N	Mariposa Twp 3	60 590
Otis W	Calaveras Twp 5	57 251
Philip	San Joaquin Elkhorn	641000
R	Shasta Shasta	66 657
R J*	Sacramento Ward 3	63 466
Robt	Sacramento Franklin	63 334
S R	El Dorado Kelsey	581144
Selos W*	Yuba Linda	72 993
Silas W*	Yuba Linda	72 993
T H	El Dorado Kelsey	581145
Thomas	Tuolumne Jamestown	71 444
Thomas M	Tuolumne Twp 2	71 418
Thoms M	Tuolumne Shawsfla	71 418
W	Calaveras Twp 9	57 414
W J	Tuolumne Twp 2	71 381
Walter	Placer Michigan	62 825
Willard	Butte Ophir	56 753
William	El Dorado Greenwood	58 725
William	Mendocino Big Rvr	60 849
William	Placer Michigan	62 835
William	San Francisco San Francisco 3	67 18
William	San Francisco San Francisco 3	67 25
Wilson C	Tuolumne Twp 2	71 285
Wm	Amador Twp 1	55 471
Wm	Sacramento Granite	63 243
Wm E	Mendocino Little L	60 833
WILLISM		
Henry	Klamath S Fork	59 203
WILLISTON		
Benj	San Francisco San Francisco 3	67 64
Bery	San Francisco San Francisco 3	67 64
Cary	San Francisco San Francisco 5	67 544
Edward B	San Diego San Diego	64 765
WILLISTOW		
C	Sutter Butte	70 785
WILLIT		
Henry	Mendocino Ukiah	60 805
WILLITS		
Stephen	El Dorado White Oaks	581016
W H	El Dorado White Oaks	581016
WILLITTS		
John	Yolo Fremont	72 605
WILLIUNS		
Ed*	Sacramento Granite	63 243
WILLLIAM		
---	San Francisco San Francisco 12	391 67
WILLMAN		
Bela	San Francisco San Francisco 3	67 48
Bela	San Francisco San Francisco 3	67 49
John	Sierra Twp 5	66 940
Lonis*	Placer Yankee J	62 778

California 1860 Census Index

Name	County Locale	M653 Roll	Page
WILLMANN			
Joseph	Alameda Oakland	55	1
WILLMART			
S N	Mariposa Twp 3	60	611
WILLMEN			
George	El Dorado Greenwood	58	724
Isaac	El Dorado Greenwood	58	724
WILLMENT			
George	Placer Auburn	62	559
WILLMONT			
S N*	Mariposa Twp 3	60	611
WILLMOT			
A	Shasta Millvill	66	754
D S	Los Angeles Los Angeles	59	519
WILLOCK			
Ann	San Francisco San Francisco 1	68	820
R C	Sierra Twp 7	66	884
Wm H	San Francisco San Francisco 1	68	869
WILLON			
Emma	Sierra Downieville	66	970
WILLONBY			
E	San Francisco San Francisco 10		184
			67
WILLONGHBY			
Chas*	Butte Eureka	56	656
WILLOR			
T*	Sutter Sutter	70	815
WILLOREBY			
E*	San Francisco San Francisco 10		184
			67
WILLOT			
Peter*	Solano Fremont	69	382
WILLOTT			
Fletcher	Sonoma Sonoma	69	656
WILLOUGHBY			
Andrew J	San Francisco San Francisco 11		141
			67
Chas*	Butte Eureka	56	656
E	San Francisco San Francisco 5	67	498
J R	San Francisco San Francisco 10		355
			67
Milton	Tulara Keeneysburg	71	41
WILLOW			
Elias	El Dorado Eldorado	58	936
Joseph	El Dorado White Oaks	581	006
Joseph	El Dorado White Oaks	581	016
Mathew	San Francisco San Francisco 9	681	019
Wm	San Francisco San Francisco 10		172
			67
WILLS			
A	Mariposa Twp 1	60	649
A	Mariposa Twp 1	60	949
A J	Tuolumne Jamestown	71	439
Agripha	Nevada Bridgeport	61	503
Agrippa	Nevada Bridgeport	61	503
Ben	Mariposa Twp 1	60	649
C	Calaveras Twp 9	57	392
Charles	Yolo Washington	72	572
Danl	Mariposa Twp 1	60	650
Geo	Sacramento Natonia	63	278
George	Tuolumne Jamestown	71	444
George	Yolo Washington	72	575
H	Nevada Eureka	61	372
Henry	Sonoma Vallejo	69	621
J A	El Dorado Kelsey	581	152
J H	Mariposa Twp 1	60	649
James	Calaveras Twp 8	57	80
James	Placer Michigan	62	823
James*	Tulara Visalia	71	99
Jas	Mariposa Twp 1	60	649
Jas	Sacramento Granite	63	261
Jas	San Mateo Twp 1	65	58
John	Nevada Red Dog	61	552
John	Placer Rattle Snake	62	632
John	San Francisco San Francisco 2	67	746
Joseph	Tuolumne Twp 1	71	190
M	Nevada Eureka	61	371
M N	Amador Twp 4	55	250
P	Nevada Eureka	61	374
Patk	Butte Bidwell	56	706
Richard	Santa Clara San Jose	65	283
Robt W	Klamath Orleans	59	215
Thadeus	San Francisco San Francisco 11		121
			67
Tho	Siskiyou Klamath	69	85
Thomas*	Mendocino Big Rvr	60	853
Thos	San Mateo Twp 1	65	58
W S	Shasta Shasta	66	661
Wm H	Mariposa Twp 1	60	635
WILLSHER			
Wm	Trinity Honest B	701	043
WILLSOM			
Chals*	El Dorado Georgetown	58	698
Chrls	El Dorado Georgetown	58	698
WILLSON			
Abram	Alameda Brooklyn	55	179

Name	County Locale	M653 Roll	Page
WILLSON			
B	Shasta Millvill	66	749
B F	Shasta Horsetown	66	700
Benjm	Tuolumne Twp 4	71	125
Capt	Mariposa Twp 3	60	610
Chaes*	El Dorado Georgetown	58	698
Charles	El Dorado Salmon Hills	581	060
Charles	Stanislaus Emory	70	739
Cyrus	Sonoma Bodega	69	537
George	Amador Twp 5	55	341
Gere	Mariposa Twp 3	60	615
H A	Shasta Horsetown	66	698
Henry	Stanislaus Emory	70	749
Henry M	Sonoma Mendocino	69	447
J	El Dorado Salmon Falls	581	038
J C	Shasta Shasta	66	671
Jacob	Stanislaus Emory	70	745
James	Los Angeles Elmonte	59	257
James	Mariposa Twp 3	60	558
James	Mariposa Twp 3	60	563
James	Tuolumne Big Oak	71	126
James	Tuolumne Twp 4	71	128
James R*	El Dorado Mountain	581	185
James W*	Marin Cortemad	60	782
James*	Mariposa Twp 3	60	603
Jasper	Los Angeles Azuza	59	275
John	Alameda Brooklyn	55	146
John	Alameda Washington	55	171
John	Amador Twp 6	55	426
John	Shasta Cottonwoood	66	737
John	Shasta Millvill	66	738
John	Stanislaus Emory	70	748
John	Tuolumne Montezuma	71	509
John T	Alameda Brooklyn	55	99
Joseph	El Dorado Kelsey	581	127
Nicholas	Alameda Brooklyn	55	135
Oran	Alameda Brooklyn	55	174
P	Tuolumne Jacksonville	71	164
P	Tuolumne Jacksonville	71	171
Pames	Mariposa Twp 3	60	558
Peter	El Dorado Kelsey	581	127
Richard	Los Angeles Azuza	59	276
Sam	Sacramento Ward 4	63	517
Samuel H	Alameda Oakland	55	49
Samuel*	Alameda Brooklyn	55	79
Thomas	Shasta Shasta	66	730
Thos	Mariposa Twp 3	60	610
Thos	Stanislaus Empire	70	734
W M	Mariposa Coulterville	60	688
W M C	Shasta Cottonwoood	66	736
W W C	Shasta Cottonwoood	66	736
William	Alameda Murray	55	224
Wm	Los Angeles Elmonte	59	257
WILLUM			
A L*	Nevada Rough &	61	416
WILLWINE			
E A*	Sacramento Ward 1	63	125
WILLY			
A*	Nevada Eureka	61	393
H	Nevada Grass Valley	61	215
John	Mariposa Coulterville	60	679
Michael	Calaveras Twp 5	57	196
Thomas G	Nevada Bridgeport	61	442
WILMAN			
---	Mariposa Twp 3	60	555
---	Mendocino Round Va	60	883
Henry	Plumas Meadow Valley	62	901
J S	Nevada Bloomfield	61	523
WILMANS			
Clemence	Solano Suisan	69	227
WILMAR			
---	Mariposa Twp 3	60	555
L	San Francisco San Francisco 5	67	504
WILMARTH			
Barton	Tuolumne Twp 3	71	460
J	Nevada Eureka	61	349
WILMEED			
John	Yuba Parks Ba	72	780
WILMER			
Myron	Plumas Quincy	62	982
Robert	Tuolumne Twp 4	71	125
WILMERDING			
J C	San Francisco San Francisco 5	67	512
WILMES			
T P	San Francisco San Francisco 7	681	439
WILMONE			
---	Tulara Twp 2	71	40
WILMONT			
Augustus	Alameda Oakland	55	43
WILMOT			
Carlo N	Calaveras Twp 7	57	11
Chas	San Francisco San Francisco 2	67	576
Geo	Sacramento Granite	63	241
John	Napa Yount	61	30
L A	Napa Clear Lake	61	119
M B	Sacramento Lee	63	211

Name	County Locale	M653 Roll	Page
WILMOT			
S A*	Napa Clear Lake	61	119
Silas	San Francisco San Francisco 11		100
			67
WILMOTT			
Eliza S	Butte Kimshaw	56	570
Jno	Butte Oregon	56	633
N	Yolo Washington	72	602
R	Yolo Washington	72	602
Valentine	Butte Kimshaw	56	570
W	El Dorado Placerville	58	874
WILMOUTH			
William	Plumas Quincy	621	000
William	Plumas Quincy	62	999
WILNON			
W	Yolo Cache Crk	72	593
WILNOW			
W	Yolo Cache	72	593
WILOHINE			
George T*	San Bernadino	64	645
	San Bernardino		
WILOLL			
Valentine	Sierra Scales D	66	801
WILOTT			
Valentine*	Sierra Scales D	66	801
WILOTUNES			
George T*	San Bernadino	64	645
	San Bernardino		
WILRIN			
Wm	Butte Ophir	56	823
WILS			
M A	Nevada Grass Valley	61	166
WILSAE			
D	Butte Hamilton	56	517
James*	El Dorado Georgetown	58	745
WILSALINN			
---	Mendocino Little L	60	839
WILSALUM			
---	Mendocino Little L	60	839
WILSEN			
Isaac M	Sacramento Natonia	63	274
J B*	Siskiyou Cottonwoood	69	109
John	Amador Twp 2	55	302
Joseph	Siskiyou Shasta Rvr	69	111
L*	Mendocino Arrana	60	863
William M*	Siskiyou Yreka	69	146
WILSER			
Nath B	Nevada Bridgeport	61	480
R G	Mendocino Round Va	60	881
WILSEY			
James M	Mendocino Round Va	60	880
L*	Mendocino Arrana	60	863
Owen	El Dorado Georgetown	58	698
Samuel	Tehama Lassen	70	875
Theodore	El Dorado Placerville	58	898
W A	San Mateo Twp 1	65	47
William*	Solano Vacaville	69	363
Wilsey A	Mendocino Round Va	60	880
WILSHIRE			
George T	San Salvador	64	645
	San Bernardino		
George W	Solano Suisan	69	238
Henry	San Bernardino San Bernadino	64	643
WILSHIRES			
George T	San Salvador	64	645
	San Bernardino		
WILSN			
Chas Y	San Francisco San Francisco 2	67	751
WILSON			
---	Nevada Bridgeport	61	467
A	Butte Chico	56	540
A	Nevada Washington	61	334
A	Sacramento Lee	63	220
A	San Francisco San Francisco 5	67	511
A	San Francisco San Francisco 5	67	531
A	Sierra Eureka	661	044
A	Sonoma Sonoma	69	638
A	Tehama Red Bluff	70	927
A	Trinity Indian C	70	986
A	Yuba Rose Par	72	797
A B	Los Angeles Los Angeles	59	491
A B	Sacramento Ward 3	63	430
A C	Sierra Twp 7	66	863
A H	Sacramento Ward 1	63	33
A J C	Tuolumne Shawsfla	71	386
A M	Siskiyou Scott Va	69	43
A T	Marin S Antoni	60	706
Abram	Tuolumne Twp 2	71	306
Addison	San Francisco San Francisco 6	67	410
Albert	Butte Ophir	56	793
Albert	Sacramento Ward 3	63	478
Albert	Santa Clara Gilroy	65	225
Albert	Sonoma Petaluma	69	578
Alex	Humbolt Eureka	59	176
Alex	Klamath Salmon	59	209
Alex	San Francisco San Francisco 9	68	965

Name	County Locale	M653 Roll Page
WILSON		
Alex A	Sonoma Russian	69 434
Alexander	San Joaquin Castoria	64 890
Alfred	Merced Twp 2	60 920
Alfred	San Francisco San Francisco 9	681034
Andrew	Alameda Brooklyn	55 82
Andrew	Alameda Brooklyn	55 83
Andrew	El Dorado White Oaks	581001
Andrew	San Mateo Twp 1	65 71
Andrew	Tuolumne Twp 1	71 209
Ann	San Francisco San Francisco 3	67 23
Anna	Amador Twp 4	55 258
Anna	El Dorado White Oaks	581011
Anne R	Humbolt Eel Rvr	59 149
Anthony	Contra Costa Twp 1	57 519
Anto Ma	Contra Costa Twp 1	57 488
Antoma*	Contra Costa Twp 1	57 488
Antonio	Fresno Twp 1	59 76
Archibuld	Calaveras Twp 4	57 317
August	Contra Costa Twp 3	57 617
Ayms	San Francisco San Francisco 9	681066
B	Sierra Downieville	661013
B	Sutter Bear Rvr	70 822
Benj	Placer Secret R	62 613
Benjamin	San Joaquin Castoria	64 891
Benjamin D	Los Angeles San Gabriel	59 412
C	El Dorado Georgetown	58 751
C	Sacramento Cosumnes	63 397
C	San Francisco San Francisco 3	67 69
C A	Nevada Eureka	61 378
C G	Trinity Trinity	70 971
C H	Marin Cortemad	60 790
C L	San Francisco San Francisco 7	681435
C W	Sonoma Armally	69 503
Cahs G	Plumas Meadow Valley	62 902
Carlton	Calaveras Twp 6	57 130
Casij	Tuolumne Twp 1	71 260
Catharine	Contra Costa Twp 3	57 599
Charles	Alameda Oakland	55 49
Charles	Amador Twp 4	55 247
Charles	Contra Costa Twp 1	57 507
Charles	El Dorado Mud Springs	58 966
Charles	El Dorado Mud Springs	58 970
Charles	Mendocino Big Rvr	60 843
Charles	Monterey San Juan	601003
Charles	Nevada Rough &	61 411
Charles	San Francisco San Francisco 4	681149
Charles	San Francisco San Francisco 3	67 30
Charles	San Francisco San Francisco 2	67 568
Charles	San Francisco San Francisco 3	67 62
Charles	San Francisco San Francisco 3	67 71
Charles	San Joaquin Elkhorn	64 959
Charles	Sierra Pine Grove	66 834
Charles	Siskiyou Callahan	69 8
Charles	Tuolumne Twp 1	71 238
Charles	Tuolumne Shawsfla	71 403
Charles	Yolo Cache Crk	72 666
Charles	Yuba Long Bar	72 755
Charles	Yuba Long Bar	72 756
Charles C	San Francisco San Francisco 8	681248
Charles C	Sierra Twp 5	66 942
Charles C*	Mendocino Big Rvr	60 843
Charles E	San Francisco San Francisco 7	681436
Charles M	Siskiyou Yreka	69 169
Charles*	Siskiyou Callahan	69 8
Charly	Tuolumne Sonora	71 238
Chas	Amador Twp 2	55 266
Chas	Klamath Orleans	59 215
Chas	Klamath Trinidad	59 221
Chas	Placer Rattle Snake	62 599
Chas	Sacramento Ward 1	63 13
Chas	Sacramento Ward 1	63 151
Chas	Sacramento Granite	63 254
Chas	Sacramento Franklin	63 333
Chas	Sacramento Cosumnes	63 394
Chas	San Francisco San Francisco 1	68 895
Chas	Santa Clara San Jose	65 321
Chas	Sonoma Santa Rosa	69 400
Chas B	Calaveras Twp 9	57 362
Chas D	Klamath Orleans	59 215
Chas T	San Francisco San Francisco 2	67 751
Chris	Tuolumne Twp 1	71 260
Chs	San Francisco San Francisco 6	67 441
Clah*	Yuba Fosters	72 829
Clark	Yuba Foster B	72 829
Curtis	Solano Suisan	69 237
Cyrus	San Francisco San Francisco 9	681066
Cyrus	Sonoma Bodega	69 541
D	El Dorado Mountain	581185
D	Sacramento Mississipi	63 186
D E	Butte Hamilton	56 527
D H	Sonoma Vallejo	69 609
D L	Amador Twp 6	55 438
D S	Sutter Yuba	70 777
Daniel	Monterey San Juan	60 983
Daniel	Sierra Whiskey	66 844

Name	County Locale	M653 Roll Page
WILSON		
Daniel A	Yuba Marysville	72 884
Daniel G	Calaveras Twp 10	57 282
Danl	Santa Clara San Jose	65 353
David	Placer Auburn	62 564
David	Placer Auburn	62 587
David	San Francisco San Francisco 3	67 70
David	Santa Clara Gilroy	65 223
Dennis	Plumas Quincy	62 957
Dorsin	Santa Clara Gilroy	65 229
E	Sacramento Lee	65 213
E	San Francisco San Francisco 9	681027
E	Sutter Sutter	70 807
E B	Solano Vacaville	69 339
E H	Nevada Nevada	61 249
E H	San Francisco San Francisco 5	67 502
E J	Solano Vallejo	69 270
Ed	Nevada Rough &	61 424
Edmd	Sonoma Petaluma	69 565
Edwad	San Francisco San Francisco 5	67 476
Edward	Placer Forest H	62 767
Edward	San Francisco San Francisco 10	198
		67
Edward	San Francisco San Francisco 5	67 476
Eli	Sonoma Armally	69 517
Eli	Sonoma Petaluma	69 547
Elijah	Yolo No E Twp	72 672
Elijah	Yuba North Ea	72 672
Eliz	Sacramento Ward 4	63 542
Eliza	San Francisco San Francisco 4	681155
Eliza	Yuba Marysville	72 898
Eliza A	Tuolumne Sonora	71 216
Elizabeth	Butte Cascade	56 690
Elizabeth	El Dorado Coloma	581076
Ellen	Klamath Klamath	59 227
Ellen	Sacramento Ward 1	63 2
Ellis R	Tuolumne Shawsfla	71 383
Emily	Solano Benecia	69 313
F	San Francisco San Francisco 3	67 48
F	Sonoma Cloverdale	69 683
F	Sutter Sutter	70 811
F E	El Dorado White Oaks	581031
F W	Del Norte Crescent	58 637
Faster	Siskiyou Callahan	69 10
Fastor*	Siskiyou Callahan	69 10
Foster	Siskiyou Callahan	69 10
Frances	Alameda Brooklyn	55 100
Francis	El Dorado Georgetown	58 687
Francis	Plumas Quincy	62 952
Francis	Tuolumne Twp 1	71 203
Francis M	Marin Cortemad	60 786
Francis W	Marin Cortemad	60 786
Francisco	Santa Cruz Santa Cruz	66 607
Frank	El Dorado Placerville	58 924
Frank	Yuba Marysville	72 881
Freccesa M	Calaveras Twp 7	57 48
Fred	Sierra Twp 5	66 923
Fred	Sonoma Petaluma	69 563
Fredk	Sierra Twp 5	66 923
G	El Dorado Eldorado	58 935
G	Nevada Grass Valley	61 162
G	San Francisco San Francisco 4	681231
G	Siskiyou Scott Ri	69 65
G L	El Dorado Mud Springs	58 996
G L	Sacramento Ward 4	63 513
G L	San Joaquin Stockton	641056
G T	San Francisco San Francisco 3	67 84
G W	Nevada Red Dog	61 542
Gabriel	El Dorado Kelsey	581129
Geo	Butte Ophir	56 793
Geo	El Dorado White Oaks	581032
Geo	Sacramento Brighton	63 207
Geo	Sacramento Dry Crk	63 368
Geo	Sacramento Ward 4	63 499
Geo	San Francisco San Francisco 9	681061
Geo A	Klamath Liberty	59 241
Geo H	Klamath Liberty	59 236
Geo O	San Francisco San Francisco 9	681033
Geo W	Butte Oregon	56 632
Geoge	Sierra La Porte	66 776
George	Calaveras Twp 6	57 150
George	Calaveras Twp 5	57 190
George	Calaveras Twp 7	57 27
George	Calaveras Twp 4	57 317
George	Calaveras Twp 4	57 318
George	Calaveras Twp 4	57 338
George	Calaveras Twp 4	57 339
George	Marin Cortemad	60 754
George	Marin Cortemad	60 784
George	Marin Cortemad	60 792
George	Placer Todds Va	62 763
George	Plumas Quincy	62 937
George	Plumas Quincy	62 940
George	Plumas Quincy	62 979
George	San Francisco San Francisco 3	67 26

Name	County Locale	M653 Roll Page
WILSON		
George	San Francisco San Francisco 3	67 41
George	San Joaquin Oneal	64 931
George	San Mateo Twp 3	65 101
George	Sierra La Porte	66 776
George	Sierra Twp 7	66 866
George	Sierra Downieville	66 995
George	Tulara Visalia	71 87
George	Yolo Washington	72 567
George D	Humbolt Eureka	59 173
George F	Calaveras Twp 9	57 375
George O	Los Angeles Los Angeles	59 407
George S	San Joaquin Stockton	641076
George W*	Yuba Marysville	72 917
George*	Marin Cortemad	60 784
Georgiana	San Francisco San Francisco 1	68 817
Giles	Contra Costa Twp 2	57 544
Graves	Santa Clara San Jose	65 387
H	Butte Hamilton	56 519
H	Sacramento Ward 4	63 524
H	Santa Clara San Jose	65 366
H	Yolo Cache Crk	72 644
H	Yuba Fosters	72 828
H A	Placer Virginia	62 661
H B	Sutter Nicolaus	70 830
H C	Tehama Tehama	70 937
H G	Sacramento Brighton	63 196
H I	Amador Twp 2	55 313
H J	Amador Twp 2	55 313
H L	Tehama Tehama	70 937
H N	Sierra Chappare	661040
H S	Siskiyou Cottonwoood	69 100
Harriett	Placer Todds Va	62 787
Henderson	Sonoma Santa Rosa	69 413
Henry	Amador Twp 6	55 427
Henry	Del Norte Happy Ca	58 670
Henry	Los Angeles Los Angeles	59 369
Henry	Plumas Quincy	62 982
Henry	Plumas Quincy	62 990
Henry	Sacramento Sutter	63 290
Henry	San Francisco San Francisco 9	681080
Henry	San Francisco San Francisco 11	151
		67
Henry	San Francisco San Francisco 5	67 494
Henry	San Francisco San Francisco 1	68 903
Henry	San Joaquin Castoria	64 884
Henry	San Joaquin Elkhorn	64 962
Henry	San Mateo Twp 3	65 93
Henry	Solano Vallejo	69 271
Henry	Solano Montezuma	69 375
Henry	Sonoma Russian	69 438
Henry	Tulara Twp 3	71 58
Henry	Tuolumne Twp 1	71 274
Henry	Tuolumne Twp 3	71 431
Henry	Tuolumne Columbia	71 471
Horatio	Calaveras Twp 6	57 131
Horrace	Santa Clara Gilroy	65 225
Hugh	Sierra Whiskey	66 850
Hugh H	Sacramento Ward 4	63 550
I	Amador Twp 5	55 344
I	Mariposa Twp 1	60 644
I C A	Napa Napa	61 58
Ira	Santa Clara Santa Clara	65 519
Ira	Sonoma Petaluma	69 613
Isaac	Contra Costa Twp 3	57 594
Isaac	Sacramento Granite	63 265
Isaac M	Sacramento Natonia	63 274
Isaac M	San Francisco San Francisco 2	67 760
Isabella	San Francisco San Francisco 3	67 10
Israel	Tulara Visalia	71 86
Israel C	Santa Cruz Santa Cruz	66 603
Israel O*	Santa Cruz Santa Cruz	66 603
J	Butte Chico	56 549
J	Butte Oregon	56 609
J	Butte Wyandotte	56 658
J	El Dorado Diamond	58 813
J	El Dorado Diamond	58 816
J	El Dorado Placerville	58 837
J	El Dorado Placerville	58 879
J	El Dorado Placerville	58 894
J	Mariposa Twp 1	60 624
J	Mariposa Twp 1	60 644
J	Nevada Grass Valley	61 173
J	Nevada Grass Valley	61 237
J	Nevada Nevada	61 240
J	Nevada Nevada	61 287
J	Nevada Eureka	61 380
J	Sacramento American	63 165
J	San Francisco San Francisco 5	67 484
J	San Francisco San Francisco 5	67 529
J	San Francisco San Francisco 5	67 536
J	San Francisco San Francisco 1	68 833
J	San Francisco San Francisco 1	68 923
J	Sonoma Sonoma	69 661
J	Sutter Butte	70 785
J	Sutter Bear Rvr	70 822

California 1860 Census Index

Name	County Locale	M653 Roll	Page
WILSON			
J	Trinity Mouth Ca	70	1011
J	Yolo Putah	72	554
J	Yolo Washington	72	568
J A	Tuolumne Twp 1	71	240
J B	Merced Twp 2	60	917
J B	Nevada Nevada	61	323
J B	Sacramento Ward 1	63	19
J B	Siskiyou Cottonwoood	69	109
J B	Tuolumne Sonora	71	187
J B	Yuba Fosters	72	834
J B*	Siskiyou Cottonwoood	69	109
J Burroughs	Sacramento Ward 1	63	127
J C	El Dorado Newtown	58	778
J C	Tuolumne Twp 2	71	284
J C A	Napa Napa	61	58
J C E	Tehama Red Bluff	70	925
J D	San Francisco San Francisco 9	68	1013
J E	San Francisco San Francisco 1	68	924
J G	Calaveras Twp 9	57	382
J H	Siskiyou Scott Va	69	45
J H	Sonoma Bodega	69	540
J H	Sonoma Petaluma	69	561
J J	Santa Clara Fremont	65	435
J J J	Sierra Twp 7	66	901
J M	Amador Twp 2	55	283
J M	Butte Wyandotte	56	658
J M	San Francisco San Francisco 4	68	1225
J P	Siskiyou Callahan	69	17
J P	Siskiyou Scott Va	69	34
J S	Siskiyou Klamath	69	92
J S	Sutter Nicolaus	70	829
J S	Tehama Red Bluff	70	906
J S	Tehama Tehama	70	938
J W	Nevada Nevada	61	297
J W	Trinity Douglas	70	980
J Y	Calaveras Twp 9	57	382
Jabe	Contra Costa Twp 3	57	598
Jack	Yolo No E Twp	72	680
Jack	Yuba North Ea	72	680
Jacob	San Joaquin Elkhorn	64	959
Jacob	Sonoma Petaluma	69	557
Jacob	Trinity Weaverville	70	1077
Jake	Trinity Oregon G	70	1008
James	Alameda Brooklyn	55	165
James	Alameda Oakland	55	24
James	Amador Twp 4	55	252
James	Amador Twp 7	55	411
James	Calaveras Twp 5	57	207
James	Contra Costa Twp 3	57	585
James	Contra Costa Twp 3	57	592
James	El Dorado Kelsey	58	1145
James	El Dorado Georgetown	58	745
James	Fresno Twp 2	59	17
James	Klamath Trinidad	59	222
James	Mariposa Twp 3	60	549
James	Mariposa Twp 3	60	558
James	Mariposa Coulterville	60	676
James	Mendocino Little L	60	833
James	Monterey Alisal	60	1039
James	Nevada Rough &	61	412
James	Nevada Bloomfield	61	511
James	Nevada Bloomfield	61	530
James	Placer Michigan	62	836
James	Placer Iona Hills	62	895
James	Plumas Quincy	62	954
James	San Francisco San Francisco 4	68	1133
James	San Francisco San Francisco 7	68	1435
James	San Francisco San Francisco 10	67	353
James	San Francisco San Francisco 12	67	364
James	San Luis Obispo San Luis Obispo	65	30
James	Santa Clara Gilroy	65	249
James	Santa Clara San Jose	65	386
James	Santa Clara Fremont	65	429
James	Santa Clara Santa Clara	65	515
James	Sierra Downieville	66	1017
James	Sierra Twp 5	66	939
James	Siskiyou Yreka	69	145
James	Siskiyou Callahan	69	8
James	Tehama Red Bluff	70	925
James	Tulara Visalia	71	30
James	Tuolumne Twp 1	71	248
James	Tuolumne Columbia	71	332
James	Yolo Cache	72	639
James	Yolo Cottonwoood	72	652
James	Yolo Slate Ra	72	689
James	Yuba Slate Ro	72	689
James	Yuba New York	72	723
James A	Monterey Pajaro	60	1022
James C	Colusa Monroeville	57	440
James C	Solano Montezuma	69	374
James C	Yuba Marysville	72	871
James D	Plumas Meadow Valley	62	928
James R	Monterey Pajaro	60	1022
WILSON			
James S	Sierra St Louis	66	806
James W	Marin Cortemad	60	782
Jas	Butte Cascade	56	690
Jas	Butte Cascade	56	696
Jas	Butte Ophir	56	824
Jas	Calaveras Twp 9	57	375
Jas	Sacramento Granite	63	255
Jas	Sacramento Ward 3	63	431
Jas	San Francisco San Francisco 9	68	1044
Jas	San Francisco San Francisco 2	67	709
Jas	San Francisco San Francisco 1	68	890
Jas	San Francisco San Francisco 1	68	904
Jas	Santa Clara San Jose	65	358
Jas	Tehama Lassen	70	873
Jas E	Santa Clara San Jose	65	381
Jas J	Sacramento Ward 1	63	30
Jas M	Napa Napa	61	82
Jas R	Butte Cascade	56	689
Jas W	San Bernardino San Bernadino	64	625
Jerry	Klamath Klamath	59	226
Jesse	Solano Vacaville	69	347
Jesse	Yuba Bear Rvr	72	1004
Jesse W	Yuba Marysville	72	931
Jim	Sacramento Georgian	63	340
Jms H*	Klamath S Fork	59	199
Jno	Nevada Nevada	61	240
Jno	Sacramento Ward 1	63	1
Jno	San Francisco San Francisco 9	68	1074
Jno	San Francisco San Francisco 9	68	1076
Jno	San Francisco San Francisco 9	68	1080
Jno	Sonoma Russian	69	609
Jno C	Sacramento Ward 4	63	554
Jno G	Fresno Twp 3	59	13
Jno G	Mendocino Little L	60	836
Jno L	Sacramento Sutter	63	294
Jno S	Sacramento Sutter	63	294
John	Amador Twp 2	55	302
John	Amador Twp 6	55	426
John	Butte Kimshaw	56	607
John	Butte Wyandotte	56	668
John	Butte Ophir	56	823
John	Contra Costa Twp 2	57	552
John	Del Norte Crescent	58	649
John	Del Norte Klamath	58	653
John	Del Norte Ferry P O	58	666
John	El Dorado Coloma	58	1076
John	El Dorado Kelsey	58	1129
John	El Dorado Casumnes	58	1171
John	El Dorado Greenwood	58	724
John	Fresno Twp 3	59	37
John	Humbolt Bucksport	59	161
John	Humbolt Eureka	59	171
John	Humbolt Union	59	190
John	Los Angeles Los Angeles	59	369
John	Marin Novato	60	738
John	Marin Cortemad	60	786
John	Napa Napa	61	61
John	Nevada Bridgeport	61	471
John	Placer Auburn	62	567
John	Placer Forest H	62	797
John	Placer Michigan	62	841
John	Placer Michigan	62	847
John	Placer Iona Hills	62	865
John	Placer Iona Hills	62	887
John	Plumas Quincy	62	1005
John	Plumas Meadow Valley	62	902
John	Plumas Quincy	62	938
John	Plumas Quincy	62	958
John	Plumas Quincy	62	966
John	Plumas Quincy	62	993
John	Sacramento American	63	162
John	Sacramento Sutter	63	306
John	Sacramento Ward 1	63	45
John	San Francisco San Francisco 9	68	1043
John	San Francisco San Francisco 9	68	1064
John	San Francisco San Francisco 4	68	1114
John	San Francisco San Francisco 4	68	1116
John	San Francisco San Francisco 7	68	1329
John	San Francisco San Francisco 10	67	178
John	San Francisco San Francisco 12	67	385
John	San Francisco San Francisco 6	67	429
John	San Francisco San Francisco 5	67	478
John	San Francisco San Francisco 5	67	548
John	San Francisco San Francisco 3	67	59
John	San Francisco San Francisco 3	67	74
John	San Francisco San Francisco 2	67	796
John	San Francisco San Francisco 1	68	854
John	San Francisco San Francisco 1	68	855
John	San Francisco San Francisco 9	68	968
John	San Joaquin Stockton	64	1024
John	San Joaquin Stockton	64	1086
John	San Joaquin Elkhorn	64	959
John	San Luis Obispo San Luis Obispo	65	26
WILSON			
John	San Mateo Twp 1	65	71
John	Santa Clara Gilroy	65	247
John	Santa Cruz Santa Cruz	66	601
John	Sierra Downieville	66	1013
John	Sierra Downieville	66	954
John	Siskiyou Callahan	69	1
John	Solano Green Valley	69	242
John	Solano Vallejo	69	249
John	Solano Fremont	69	380
John	Stanislaus Branch	70	706
John	Tulara Petersburg	71	52
John	Tulara Keyesville	71	62
John	Tulara Visalia	71	73
John	Tuolumne Twp 1	71	257
John	Yuba Parks Ba	72	774
John	Yuba Rose Bar	72	788
John	Yuba Rose Bar	72	792
John	Yuba Marysville	72	920
John A	Placer Ophirville	62	659
John A	Placer Dutch Fl	62	725
John A	Plumas Meadow Valley	62	932
John A	San Francisco San Francisco 7	68	1358
John B	El Dorado Mountain	58	1185
John B	Sonoma Santa Rosa	69	396
John B	Sonoma Russian	69	434
John C	Merced Monterey	60	944
John C	Monterey Monterey	60	944
John E	San Francisco San Francisco 10	67	240
John F	Placer Auburn	62	583
John F	Santa Clara Santa Clara	65	485
John G	San Francisco San Francisco 3	67	41
John G S	Colusa Monroeville	57	442
John I*	Fresno Twp 2	59	49
John J*	Fresno Twp 2	59	49
John M	Sierra Forest C	66	909
John N	San Francisco San Francisco 4	68	1121
John R	Butte Mountain	56	740
John R	Santa Clara San Jose	65	334
John R*	El Dorado Mountain	58	1185
John S	Colusa Monroeville	57	142
John S	San Francisco San Francisco 4	68	1220
John W	Sierra Twp 7	66	909
John Y	San Francisco San Francisco 7	68	1437
John*	Yuba Rose Bar	72	788
Johnson	Nevada Red Dog	61	552
Jon	Solano Green Valley	69	242
Jon	Yuba Marysville	72	920
Jonathan G	Mendocino Little L	60	836
Jos	Sacramento Ward 4	63	511
Jos	San Francisco San Francisco 9	68	1076
Jos	San Francisco San Francisco 2	67	672
Jos	San Francisco San Francisco 1	68	890
Jos	San Mateo Twp 2	65	124
Jos	San Mateo Twp 2	65	125
Jos	Tehama Red Bluff	70	915
Jos L	San Francisco San Francisco 12	67	376
Jose	Contra Costa Twp 1	57	483
Joseph	Contra Costa Twp 1	57	483
Joseph	Contra Costa Twp 2	57	574
Joseph	Del Norte Crescent	58	637
Joseph	Marin Tomales	60	713
Joseph	Placer Todds Va	62	785
Joseph	Sacramento Ward 4	63	599
Joseph	San Bernardino San Bernadino	64	672
Joseph	San Francisco San Francisco 9	68	1083
Joseph	Siskiyou Shasta Rvr	69	111
Joseph	Tuolumne Twp 1	71	483
Josiah W	Tulara Twp 1	71	98
Jra*	Sonoma Vallejo	69	613
L	Calaveras Twp 9	57	349
L	Sutter Vernon	70	843
L P	Merced Twp 2	60	915
L P	San Francisco San Francisco 3	67	41
L S	Siskiyou Callahan	69	17
Laedo*	Sacramento Granite	63	258
Laido	Sacramento Granite	63	258
Lawo*	Sacramento Granite	63	258
Leonard	Plumas Quincy	62	925
Levi	San Joaquin Castoria	64	894
Levi G	Sierra Whiskey	66	844
Levi J*	Plumas Quincy	62	997
Lewis	El Dorado Grizzly	58	1182
Lewis	Humbolt Mattole	59	126
Lewis	San Francisco San Francisco 3	67	71
Livena	Santa Clara Gilroy	65	225
Logan L	Napa Clear Lake	61	139
Lucy	San Francisco San Francisco 9	68	962
M	Amador Twp 6	55	427
M	Sacramento Ward 4	63	520
M	Yolo Cache	72	644
M	Yolo Slate Ra	72	707
M	Yuba Slate Ro	72	707
M A	Nevada Eureka	61	360

Name	County Locale	M653 Roll Page
WILSON		
M H	Sonoma Sonoma	69 661
M L C	Colusa Grand Island	57 468
M R	Sutter Vernon	70 844
M S	Marin Point Re	60 731
M S	Yolo Putah	72 585
Mac	Klamath Orleans	59 219
Manuel	San Mateo Twp 3	65 83
Marg	San Francisco San Francisco 7	681393
Mary	El Dorado Indian D	581159
Mary	San Francisco San Francisco 10	347 67
Mary A	San Francisco San Francisco 7	681351
Mary E	Sonoma Santa Rosa	69 410
Mason	Solano Vacaville	69 322
Mathew	Butte Chico	56 539
Mathew	Placer Forest H	62 774
May	Tuolumne Twp 3	71 431
Michael	Calaveras Twp 5	57 187
Michael	Santa Clara Alviso	65 397
Michael	Santa Cruz Watsonville	66 537
Michael	Tuolumne Chinese	71 493
Michal	Amador Twp 2	55 283
Miles	Calaveras Twp 5	57 211
Milton	San Joaquin Tulare	64 870
Miss C	Sonoma Santa Rosa	69 400
Moses	Contra Costa Twp 1	57 500
N C	Sonoma Russian	69 433
N G	Sutter Bear Rvr	70 822
N H	Calaveras Twp 9	57 374
N Irving	San Francisco San Francisco 9	681083
Nancy	Amador Twp 2	55 264
Nathaniel	Calaveras Twp 8	57 88
Noah	Sacramento Lee	63 212
Oliver	Contra Costa Twp 1	57 506
Oliver*	Plumas Quincy	621004
Oscar	Santa Cruz Pajaro	66 569
Oscar*	Alameda Washington	55 174
P	Butte Eureka	56 652
P	San Francisco San Francisco 4	681231
P A	San Francisco San Francisco 3	67 49
P A	Sierra Twp 7	66 877
P H*	Alameda Oakland	55 8
P L	Yolo Cache Crk	72 636
P S*	Sacramento Cosummes	63 391
Pablo	Yuba Fosters	72 835
Pat	Trinity Browns C	70 984
Peter	Alameda Murray	55 217
Peter	Butte Chico	56 568
Peter	Butte Kimshaw	56 577
Peter	Butte Kimshaw	56 583
Peter	Calaveras Twp 6	57 150
Peter	Calaveras Twp 8	57 95
Peter	El Dorado Kelsey	581126
Peter	El Dorado Georgetown	58 761
Peter	Los Angeles Los Angeles	59 327
Peter	Los Angeles Los Angeles	59 372
Peter	Marin Novato	60 739
Peter	Sacramento Dry Crk	63 373
Peter	San Francisco San Francisco 3	67 55
Peter	Tuolumne Twp 3	71 541
Peter F	Tuolumne Don Pedro	71 541
R	Calaveras Twp 9	57 407
R	Nevada Eureka	61 369
R	Sacramento Brighton	63 209
R	San Francisco San Francisco 9	681057
R	San Mateo Twp 3	65 106
R C	Butte Chico	56 540
R L*	Sacramento Dry Crk	63 375
R M	El Dorado Salmon Falls	581035
R M	Nevada Bridgeport	61 472
R W	Nevada Bridgeport	61 468
R W	Tehama Red Bluff	70 924
Raft	El Dorado Gold Hill	581097
Rebecca	Siskiyou Scott Ri	69 62
Rebecca	Sonoma Santa Rosa	69 396
Renshaw	Sonoma Armally	69 486
Richard	Monterey Pajaro	601018
Richd	San Francisco San Francisco 1	68 890
Robert	Alameda Brooklyn	55 150
Robert	Calaveras Twp 7	57 34
Robert	Calaveras Twp 8	57 86
Robert	Calaveras Twp 8	57 98
Robert	Los Angeles Tejon	59 528
Robert	Mendocino Big Rvr	60 842
Robert	Nevada Rough &	61 430
Robert	Sacramento Granite	63 259
Robert	San Francisco San Francisco 9	681049
Robert	San Francisco San Francisco 7	681441
Robert	San Francisco San Francisco 2	67 688
Robert	San Joaquin Elkhorn	64 989
Robt	Butte Chico	56 536
Robt	El Dorado Gold Hill	581097
Robt	Los Angeles Tejon To	59 535
Robt	San Francisco San Francisco 10	230 67
WILSON		
Robt	San Mateo Twp 3	65 105
Robt	Trinity Rattle Snake	701029
Rufus*	Sacramento Dry Crk	63 371
S	Amador Twp 5	55 368
S	Butte Cascade	56 698
S	El Dorado Placerville	58 837
S	El Dorado Placerville	58 863
S	San Francisco San Francisco 5	67 552
S	Solano Suisan	69 210
S	Tehama Pasakent	70 858
S B	Sutter Nicolaus	70 834
S C	San Francisco San Francisco 1	68 892
S E	Sierra Eureka	661043
S E*	Sacramento Alabama	63 415
S L	Sacramento Georgian	63 346
S M	San Francisco San Francisco 2	67 776
S R	Sutter Bear Rvr	70 822
S W	Nevada Nevada	61 281
S W	Sacramento Ward 1	63 144
Saml	Santa Clara Redwood	65 459
Saml	Santa Clara Santa Clara	65 496
Saml A	Santa Clara San Jose	65 353
Saml B	Del Norte Crescent	58 660
Saml B	Napa Napa	61 112
Saml E	Sacramento Ward 4	63 520
Saml M	Alameda Brooklyn	55 195
Saml U	Sonoma Mendocino	69 451
Samluel	Sierra Downieville	66 977
Samuel	Calaveras Twp 10	57 264
Samuel	Placer Michigan	62 835
Samuel	San Joaquin Castoria	64 888
Samuel	Sierra Downieville	66 977
Samuel S	El Dorado Eldorado	58 939
Sarah L	Siskiyou Scott Va	69 45
Sarah S	Siskiyou Scott Va	69 45
Sevi J*	Plumas Quincy	62 997
Spencer H	Los Angeles Los Angeles	59 403
Sugan L*	Napa Clear Lake	61 139
Sylvester	Sonoma Santa Rosa	69 396
T	Calaveras Twp 9	57 405
T	Nevada Grass Valley	61 174
T	San Francisco San Francisco 5	67 523
T B*	Nevada Grass Valley	61 173
T H	Nevada Washington	61 336
T I	San Francisco San Francisco 2	67 725
T J	San Francisco San Francisco 2	67 725
T J	Sierra Downieville	66 989
T K	Sonoma Petaluma	69 582
T*	Nevada Nevada	61 348
Tho	Siskiyou Scott Va	69 39
Thomas	Calaveras Twp 8	57 97
Thomas	Los Angeles Los Angeles	59 503
Thomas	Placer Iona Hills	62 874
Thomas	Plumas Quincy	621000
Thomas	Plumas Meadow Valley	62 903
Thomas	Plumas Quincy	62 920
Thomas	San Francisco San Francisco 11	148 67
Thomas	San Joaquin Castoria	64 872
Thomas	San Mateo Twp 3	65 101
Thomas	Sierra Whiskey	66 847
Thomas	Sierra Downieville	66 995
Thomas	Tuolumne Twp 1	71 266
Thomas	Tuolumne Don Pedro	71 534
Thomas	Yuba Rose Bar	72 806
Thomas C	Contra Costa Twp 3	57 594
Thomas E	Plumas Meadow Valley	62 931
Thomas J	Sierra Downieville	661013
Thoms J	Sierra Downieville	661013
Thos	Amador Twp 4	55 250
Thos	El Dorado Georgetown	58 746
Thos	Nevada Nevada	61 245
Thos	San Francisco San Francisco 10	173 67
Thos J	Santa Clara Alviso	65 411
Thos J	Santa Clara Fremont	65 432
Tilda	Nevada Little Y	61 532
V V	Trinity Weaverville	701071
Valentine	Plumas Meadow Valley	62 912
Valentine	Solano Suisan	69 210
W	El Dorado Placerville	58 869
W	Sacramento San Joaquin	63 350
W	San Francisco San Francisco 9	681069
W	San Francisco San Francisco 9	681070
W	San Francisco San Francisco 5	67 539
W	San Francisco San Francisco 2	67 626
W C	Merced Twp 1	60 904
W C	Santa Clara San Jose	65 336
W D	Sacramento Lee	63 213
W E A	Tuolumne Twp 3	71 446
W F	San Francisco San Francisco 6	67 467
W G	El Dorado Mud Springs	58 996
W H	Sacramento Ward 4	63 564
W H	Solano Montezuma	69 373
W H	Sonoma Armally	69 502
WILSON		
W H	Sonoma Vallejo	69 609
W J	Trinity Red Bar	70 998
W L	Sonoma Sonoma	69 651
W O	San Francisco San Francisco 2	67 635
Walker	Humbolt Union	59 181
Walter	Colusa Butte Crk	57 466
Walter F	Humbolt Eel Rvr	59 149
Washington A	Contra Costa Twp 3	57 611
Willam	Calaveras Twp 5	57 187
Willard	Klamath S Fork	59 203
William	Calaveras Twp 5	57 187
William	Calaveras Twp 10	57 288
William	Calaveras Twp 8	57 95
William	El Dorado White Oaks	581017
William	El Dorado Gold Hill	581096
William	Los Angeles Los Angeles	59 349
William	Los Angeles San Pedro	59 485
William	Mendocino Calpella	60 814
William	Mendocino Big Rvr	60 847
William	Mendocino Big Rvr	60 849
William	Monterey Alisal	601032
William	Napa Yount	61 38
William	Nevada Bridgeport	61 467
William	Plumas Quincy	621007
William	Plumas Quincy	62 926
William	Plumas Quincy	62 956
William	Plumas Quincy	62 957
William	San Francisco San Francisco 9	681084
William	San Francisco San Francisco 1	68 883
William	San Mateo Twp 3	65 82
William	Santa Cruz Watsonville	66 535
William	Santa Cruz Santa Cruz	66 637
William	Solano Vacaville	69 343
William	Tulara Keeneysburg	71 41
William	Tuolumne Sonora	71 201
William	Tuolumne Twp 3	71 431
William B	Placer Auburn	62 561
William J	San Francisco San Francisco 9	681050
William M	Siskiyou Yreka	69 146
William R	Plumas Quincy	62 944
William W	San Francisco San Francisco 9	681034
Williams	San Francisco El Dorado Salmon Falls	581054
Willsang	El Dorado Salmon Hills	581054
Wm	Butte Bidwell	56 727
Wm	Butte Ophir	56 791
Wm	Butte Ophir	56 798
Wm	Humbolt Pacific	59 130
Wm	Mariposa Twp 1	60 642
Wm	Mendocino Big Rvr	60 840
Wm	Merced Twp 1	60 906
Wm	Placer Secret R	62 608
Wm	Placer Ophir	62 651
Wm	Placer Dutch Fl	62 717
Wm	Placer Dutch Fl	62 718
Wm	Sacramento Sutter	63 308
Wm	Sacramento Ward 1	63 84
Wm	San Francisco San Francisco 10	285 67
Wm	San Francisco San Francisco 3	67 29
Wm	San Francisco San Francisco 2	67 578
Wm	San Francisco San Francisco 2	67 741
Wm	San Francisco San Francisco 2	67 769
Wm	San Francisco San Francisco 1	68 894
Wm	Sonoma Petaluma	69 613
Wm	Tehama Red Bluff	70 923
Wm	Trinity Indian C	70 989
Wm	Tuolumne Twp 1	71 238
Wm	Tuolumne Twp 2	71 351
Wm	Yuba Rose Bar	72 814
Wm E	Plumas Quincy	62 952
Wm H	Amador Twp 5	55 345
Wm H	Calaveras Twp 10	57 281
Wm J	Butte Kimshaw	56 599
Wm J	Placer Secret R	62 624
Wm M	Butte Oregon	56 623
Wm M	Sonoma Russian	69 438
Wm P	Plumas Quincy	62 956
Wm*	San Francisco San Francisco 9	681055
WILSONL		
J*	Nevada Nevada	61 240
Jno*	Nevada Nevada	61 240
WILSONT		
E H*	Nevada Nevada	61 249
WILSOON		
Gillermo	Contra Costa Twp 1	57 483
WILSSON		
John	San Joaquin Stockton	641076
WILST		
J C*	El Dorado Casumnes	581166
WILSTAD		
Catharine*	Trinity Weaverville	701063
WILT		
Edward*	Placer Iona Hills	62 892

California 1860 Census Index

Name	County Locale	M653 Roll	Page
WILT			
Enoch*	Placer Iona Hills	62	859
Henry C	Yuba Marysville	72	914
WILTEN			
J G	Nevada Eureka	61	378
WILTER			
Chester R	Calaveras Twp 8	57	80
WILTERS			
J*	Calaveras Twp 9	57	392
WILTES			
G*	Nevada Grass Valley	61	222
WILTHINGTON			
R H*	Amador Twp 2	55	277
WILTINGTON			
R H*	Amador Twp 2	55	277
WILTMAN			
Lonis*	Placer Yankee J	62	778
WILTMER			
William*	San Francisco San Francisco 11	67	108
WILTON			
Andrew B	Placer Dutch Fl	62	721
E	El Dorado Big Bar	58	743
George	Nevada Red Dog	61	556
J	Nevada Grass Valley	61	186
M W	Nevada Nevada	61	256
Thomas C	Colusa Muion	57	459
W	San Francisco San Francisco 5	67	543
WILTPUV			
---	Del Norte Klamath	58	655
WILTRINGTON			
R H*	Amador Twp 2	55	277
WILTS			
P	Nevada Eureka	61	343
Walter	Nevada Eureka	61	343
WILTSEE			
Charles*	Yuba Marysville	72	861
WILTSIE			
C G	Butte Chico	56	545
J	Butte Chico	56	545
WILTY			
William	Yuba Marysville	72	867
Wm	Humbolt Mattole	59	126
WILTYA			
John*	Shasta Horsetown	66	699
WILTZ			
John	Contra Costa Twp 2	57	555
WILTZA			
John*	Shasta Horsetown	66	699
WILTZER			
John	Shasta Horsetown	66	699
WILWATT			
Jno	Butte Oregon	56	633
WILWOT			
John	Colusa Colusi	57	421
WILY			
James	Sonoma Armally	69	508
John	Shasta Shasta	66	667
WILZEN			
F	San Francisco San Francisco 3	67	48
Henry	San Francisco San Francisco 3	67	48
WIM			
---	Amador Twp 5	55	365
---	Butte Wyandotte	56	666
---	El Dorado Salmon Falls	58	1041
---	El Dorado Georgetown	58	682
---	El Dorado Big Bar	58	733
---	El Dorado Mud Springs	58	958
Ah	Butte Cascade	56	699
Lee	Butte Oro	56	675
Lee	Butte Bidwell	56	723
Pae	El Dorado Mud Springs	58	985
Wan	Butte Oro	56	677
WIMAN			
John L	Tuolumne Columbia	71	294
Stephen*	Yuba Marysville	72	885
WIMANS			
Kate A	Sacramento Ward 3	63	447
WIMAS			
J W	Colusa Colusi	57	426
WIMBERBY			
Louis	El Dorado Mud Springs	58	961
WIMER			
A J	Siskiyou Scott Va	69	26
Geo	Mendocino Calpella	60	811
WIMGARDEN			
Danl*	Sonoma Sonoma	69	643
WIMGLETON			
Bernard*	San Francisco San Francisco 7	68	1325
WIMIENY			
Robert*	Calaveras Twp 4	57	343
WIMLEY			
Elias*	Sacramento Ward 3	63	479
WIMMER			
George	Contra Costa Twp 2	57	559
Jacob	San Francisco San Francisco 3	67	33

Name	County Locale	M653 Roll	Page
WIMMER			
Jacob	San Francisco San Francisco 5	67	482
L	San Francisco San Francisco 5	67	482
WIMPHY			
J*	Nevada Eureka	61	391
WIMPLE			
Joseph C	Plumas Quincy	62	978
Peter	El Dorado Diamond	58	769
WIMSTINE			
Mary*	San Francisco San Francisco 9	68	945
WIN HON			
---	El Dorado Georgetown	58	691
WIN			
---	Amador Twp 4	55	256
---	Butte Hamilton	56	530
---	Butte Oregon	56	629
---	Butte Wyandotte	56	666
---	El Dorado Salmon Falls	58	1046
---	El Dorado Salmon Falls	58	1053
---	El Dorado Salmon Falls	58	1056
---	El Dorado Coloma	58	1085
---	El Dorado Coloma	58	1109
---	El Dorado Kelsey	58	1128
---	El Dorado Georgetown	58	755
---	El Dorado Mud Springs	58	953
---	El Dorado Mud Springs	58	962
---	Mariposa Twp 3	60	599
---	Mariposa Twp 1	60	627
---	Mariposa Twp 1	60	663
---	Mariposa Twp 1	60	670
---	Nevada Bridgeport	61	459
---	Sacramento Cosumnes	63	392
---	San Francisco San Francisco 4	68	1177
---	San Francisco San Francisco 4	68	1185
---	Sierra Downieville	66	982
---	Sierra Downieville	66	983
---	Sierra Downieville	66	991
---	Siskiyou Yreka	69	195
---	Trinity Lewiston	70	957
---	Yuba Long Bar	72	752
---*	Mariposa Twp 3	60	599
---*	Nevada Bridgeport	61	459
Cin	Sierra Downieville	66	985
Folk	Butte Kimshaw	56	585
Jas	Sonoma Vallejo	69	630
Kow	San Francisco San Francisco 10	67	356
Lin	El Dorado Georgetown	58	748
Long	Tehama Red Bluff	70	934
Sim	El Dorado Greenwood	58	730
Sing	Butte Ophir	56	817
Sing	San Francisco San Francisco 3	67	60
Sing	San Francisco San Francisco 3	67	60
Siry	El Dorado Georgetown	58	747
Su	El Dorado Georgetown	58	747
Thomas	Solano Vacaville	69	335
Tim	El Dorado Placerville	58	907
Wareen*	Amador Twp 2	55	314
Warren*	Amador Twp 2	55	314
William	Tuolumne Columbia	71	296
Yow	Stanislaus Emory	70	744
WINAGARDEN			
Wm	Santa Clara San Jose	65	331
WINALL			
Stewart	San Francisco San Francisco 9	68	1039
WINAN			
D N	Marin San Rafael	60	766
Samuel	Santa Cruz Santa Cruz	66	607
WINANS			
Florence U	San Francisco San Francisco 10	67	222
J E	Nevada Bridgeport	61	450
Jno C	San Francisco San Francisco 10	67	222
Jos W	Sacramento Ward 3	63	464
Steph J*	Sacramento Ward 1	63	14
Stephen	Yuba Marysville	72	885
WINANT			
J J	San Francisco San Francisco 3	67	21
Saml	San Francisco San Francisco 10	67	304
WINARS			
J E	Nevada Bridgeport	61	450
WINBAL			
P	Sutter Bear Rvr	70	823
WINBERLY			
William A	Yuba Bear Rvr	72	1004
WINCAPAN			
A C F	Siskiyou Scott Va	69	59
J S	Siskiyou Scott Va	69	59
M F	Siskiyou Scott Va	69	59
WINCAPAW			
Robert W	Siskiyou Yreka	69	155
WINCH			
Charles	Merced Twp 2	60	918
Joseph*	San Francisco San Francisco 5	67	481
WINCHEIMEN			
Martin	Calaveras Twp 4	57	319

Name	County Locale	M653 Roll	Page
WINCHEL			
Darius*	Yolo Putah	72	546
Darwin	Yolo Putah	72	545
WINCHELL			
A W	Trinity Rush Crk	70	965
Charles	Calaveras Twp 5	57	174
E I	Sacramento Ward 1	63	85
Ed	Sacramento Ward 1	63	85
Elisha C	Fresno Twp 2	59	3
George	Sierra Gibsonville	66	859
Getchell	Amador Twp 5	55	333
H E	Sacramento Ward 4	63	524
H H	Santa Clara San Jose	65	391
L T	Butte Kimshaw	56	596
Laura C	Sacramento Ward 4	63	564
M G	Colusa Spring Valley	57	430
Mary	Solano Suisan	69	233
Theodon	Solano Suisan	69	214
Theodore	Solano Suisan	69	214
Wm H	Solano Suisan	69	213
Wm K	Del Norte Crescent	58	627
Woodson W	Calaveras Twp 4	57	312
WINCHESTER			
Chas	Napa Clear Lake	61	118
E B	Placer Goods	62	696
E H	San Francisco San Francisco 6	67	445
E W	Sacramento Ward 1	63	41
Frank	Tulara Twp 2	71	1
H	Napa Clear Lake	61	117
John	Colusa Spring Valley	57	434
L D	Amador Twp 1	55	452
L S	Nevada Rough &	61	425
M	Sutter Vernon	70	842
S L	Nevada Rough &	61	425
Susan	Sacramento Ward 1	63	98
Wiliam	Placer Yankee J	62	760
WINCHISTER			
Chas	Napa Clear Lake	61	118
H	Napa Clear Lake	61	117
WINCILIER			
J*	Napa Yount	61	35
WINCIS			
W	El Dorado Placerville	58	827
WINCKELMAN			
H	San Francisco San Francisco 5	67	492
WINCO			
---	Amador Twp 2	55	292
---	Sacramento Cosumnes	63	406
WINCUP			
A B	San Joaquin Stockton	64	1099
WINCUT			
William*	San Francisco San Francisco 9	68	993
WIND			
---	El Dorado Georgetown	58	701
WINDADE			
John*	Calaveras Twp 10	57	264
WINDALD			
Pauletto	Fresno Twp 1	59	75
WINDALE			
Elizabeth*	Nevada Red Dog	61	546
Harry	Siskiyou Cottonwoood	69	107
WINDALL			
Chris	Nevada Little Y	61	533
Elizabeth*	Nevada Red Dog	61	546
WINDAM			
Jesse	Humbolt Union	59	190
WINDATE			
Harry	Siskiyou Cottonwoood	69	107
WINDEBAM			
Henry	San Francisco San Francisco 9	68	982
WINDEBARN			
Henry*	San Francisco San Francisco 9	68	982
WINDEFF			
Jacob	Tuolumne Shawsfla	71	396
WINDELER			
John	Tuolumne Twp 2	71	281
WINDER			
Thomas	El Dorado Kelsey	58	1139
WINDERKING			
Augustus	Tuolumne Sonora	71	189
WINDESBY			
J P*	El Dorado Greenwood	58	715
WINDGER			
---	El Dorado Georgetown	58	702
WINDHAM			
Benj	Sonoma Armally	69	482
James	San Francisco San Francisco 6	67	439
Jno	Mendocino Little L	60	837
WINDITH			
W C	Calaveras Twp 9	57	408
WINDOICK			
A	Sacramento Sutter	63	294
WINDOPP			
Jacob	Tuolumne Twp 2	71	396
WINDRAP			
Saml	San Francisco San Francisco 3	67	66

Name	County Locale	M653 Roll/Page
WINDRICK		
A	Sacramento Sutter	63 294
WINDROW		
Joseph	San Francisco San Francisco	11 138 67
WINDSA		
Richard*	Monterey S Antoni	60 967
WINDSIR		
Richard*	Monterey S Antoni	60 967
WINDSOR		
J	Sonoma Washington	69 670
J N	Sonoma Washington	69 671
John	Santa Clara Alviso	65 396
John B*	Mariposa Twp 3	60 573
Richard	Monterey S Antoni	60 967
Win B*	Mariposa Twp 3	60 573
Wm	San Francisco San Francisco	10 323 67
Wm B	Mariposa Twp 3	60 573
WINDULL		
Charles*	Calaveras Twp 5	57 174
WINE		
---	El Dorado Salmon Hills	581054
---	San Francisco San Francisco	4 681177
---	Shasta French G	66 720
---	Sierra La Porte	66 780
Con	Shasta Horsetown	66 701
John	El Dorado Kelsey	581132
John	Tulara Twp 1	71 73
Thomas	Solano Vacaville	69 335
WINEAPAN		
J S	Siskiyou Scott Va	69 59
WINEBERRY		
James	Trinity Weaverville	701063
WINECOOP		
Charles	El Dorado White Oaks	581028
Edward	El Dorado Gold Hill	581095
WINEGAR		
A B	San Francisco San Francisco	6 67 414
Charles	Solano Benecia	69 310
E G	Siskiyou Scott Va	69 58
F	Shasta Millvill	66 739
Geo	Siskiyou Scott Va	69 58
James G	Siskiyou Callahan	69 12
WINEHEIMAN		
Martin	Calaveras Twp 4	57 319
WINELADE		
John	Calaveras Twp 10	57 264
WINELL		
John*	El Dorado Coloma	581115
WINEMILLER		
A J	Tehama Tehama	70 949
Daniel	Yuba Marysville	72 894
Jno	Sacramento Ward 4	63 570
WINER		
Frederick	San Francisco San Francisco	7 681395
M E*	Marin Bolinas	60 726
Margaret	Sonoma Petaluma	69 576
Richard H	Calaveras Twp 4	57 318
WINERS		
Benard	Tuolumne Columbia	71 366
WINES		
C	Trinity Lewiston	70 953
C B*	San Francisco San Francisco	5 67 545
C R	San Francisco San Francisco	5 67 545
Chas*	Napa Napa	61 109
Chs	Napa Napa	61 109
Henry*	Sacramento Ward 1	63 23
Jacob	El Dorado Union	581093
M E*	Marin Bolinas	60 726
Wm	Sierra Twp 5	66 921
Yellock	Amador Twp 3	55 397
WINESETT		
C	Shasta Shasta	66 664
WINESOTT		
C*	Shasta Shasta	66 664
WINESTINE		
Mary	San Francisco San Francisco	9 68 945
WINFIELD		
Danl	Sonoma Petaluma	69 615
George	San Joaquin Elkhorn	64 967
H	Calaveras Twp 9	57 403
J	El Dorado Newtown	58 779
Susan	San Francisco San Francisco	3 67 77
WINFREY		
Isaac	Sierra La Porte	66 779
J P	Sutter Butte	70 781
Richard W	Los Angeles Elmonte	59 267
WING CHING		
---	San Francisco San Francisco	7 681341
WING JONG		
---	El Dorado Georgetown	58 700
WING LENG		
---	Sacramento Ward 1	63 65
WING MOW		
---	Sacramento Ward 1	63 68
WING WA		
---	Tuolumne Chinese	71 523
WING		
---	Amador Twp 2	55 293
---	Amador Twp 2	55 315
---	Amador Twp 5	55 334
---	Amador No 6	55 435
---	Amador Twp 1	55 497
---	Amador Twp 1	55 499
---	Amador Twp 1	55 511
---	Butte Kimshaw	56 580
---	Butte Oro	56 688
---	Butte Cascade	56 691
---	Butte Cascade	56 700
---	Butte Cascade	56 702
---	Butte Bidwell	56 709
---	Butte Bidwell	56 725
---	Butte Bidwell	56 727
---	Butte Mountain	56 742
---	Butte Mountain	56 743
---	Butte Ophir	56 770
---	Butte Ophir	56 781
---	Butte Ophir	56 801
---	Butte Ophir	56 813
---	Butte Ophir	56 815
---	Butte Ophir	56 817
---	Butte Ophir	56 818
---	Calaveras Twp 6	57 165
---	Calaveras Twp 5	57 194
---	Calaveras Twp 5	57 240
---	Calaveras Twp 5	57 254
---	Calaveras Twp 4	57 301
---	Calaveras Twp 4	57 302
---	Calaveras Twp 4	57 305
---	Calaveras Twp 4	57 333
---	Calaveras Twp 4	57 339
---	Calaveras Twp 8	57 49
---	Calaveras Twp 8	57 79
---	Calaveras Twp 8	57 93
---	Del Norte Crescent	58 630
---	El Dorado White Oaks	581021
---	El Dorado White Oaks	581025
---	El Dorado White Oaks	581033
---	El Dorado Salmon Falls	581042
---	El Dorado Salmon Falls	581043
---	El Dorado Salmon Falls	581045
---	El Dorado Salmon Falls	581060
---	El Dorado Salmon Falls	581067
---	El Dorado Coloma	581077
---	El Dorado Coloma	581105
---	El Dorado Coloma	581120
---	El Dorado Coloma	581122
---	El Dorado Casumnes	581160
---	El Dorado Casumnes	581161
---	El Dorado Mountain	581178
---	El Dorado Mountain	581181
---	El Dorado Mountain	581188
---	El Dorado Georgetown	58 684
---	El Dorado Georgetown	58 695
---	El Dorado Georgetown	58 700
---	El Dorado Georgetown	58 705
---	El Dorado Greenwood	58 720
---	El Dorado Georgetown	58 761
---	El Dorado Diamond	58 787
---	El Dorado Placerville	58 831
---	El Dorado Placerville	58 899
---	El Dorado Placerville	58 905
---	El Dorado Placerville	58 923
---	El Dorado Placerville	58 925
---	El Dorado Placerville	58 933
---	El Dorado Eldorado	58 939
---	El Dorado Mud Springs	58 961
---	Fresno Twp 1	59 28
---	Fresno Twp 1	59 32
---	Mariposa Twp 3	60 607
---	Mariposa Twp 3	60 609
---	Mariposa Twp 1	60 626
---	Mariposa Twp 1	60 658
---	Napa Napa	61 89
---	Nevada Bridgeport	61 459
---	Nevada Bridgeport	61 459
---	Nevada Bridgeport	61 506
---	Nevada Bloomfield	61 522
---	Placer Rattle Snake	62 629
---	Placer Forest H	62 792
---	Placer Iona Hills	62 893
---	Placer Iona Hills	62 897
---	Sacramento Mississipi	63 188
---	Sacramento Granite	63 245
---	Sacramento Ward 1	63 59
---	Sacramento Ward 1	63 65
---	Sacramento Ward 1	63 67
---	San Francisco San Francisco	9 681086
---	San Francisco San Francisco	9 681088
---	San Francisco San Francisco	9 681092
---	San Francisco San Francisco	9 681095
WING		
---	San Francisco San Francisco	4 681173
---	San Francisco San Francisco	4 681179
---	San Francisco San Francisco	4 681180
---	San Francisco San Francisco	4 681181
---	San Francisco San Francisco	4 681183
---	San Francisco San Francisco	4 681188
---	San Francisco San Francisco	4 681190
---	San Francisco San Francisco	4 681204
---	San Francisco San Francisco	5 671206
---	San Francisco San Francisco	4 681209
---	Shasta Shasta	66 678
---	Shasta Shasta	66 680
---	Sierra Twp 5	66 944
---	Siskiyou Scott Va	69 46
---	Stanislaus Branch	70 714
---	Trinity Mouth Ca	701014
---	Trinity McGillev	701021
---	Tuolumne Shawsfla	71 410
---	Tuolumne Twp 1	71 478
---	Yolo No E Twp	72 681
---	Yuba North Ea	72 681
---	Yuba Fosters	72 831
---	Yuba Fosters	72 841
---	Yuba Marysville	72 868
---	Yuba Marysville	72 925
---	Yuba Marysville	72 927
---*	Amador Twp 5	55 354
---*	San Francisco San Francisco	4 681173
---*	Yuba Foster B	72 831
---*	Yuba Fosters	72 841
A	Sacramento Granite	63 245
A B	Sierra Twp 5	66 919
Ah	Butte Oro	56 688
Ah	Butte Cascade	56 691
Ah	Butte Cascade	56 702
Ah	Butte Bidwell	56 709
Ah	Butte Bidwell	56 725
Ah	Butte Bidwell	56 727
Ah	Sacramento Ward 1	63 152
Ah Ho	San Francisco San Francisco	5 671205
Ah*	San Francisco San Francisco	4 681173
Albert	Placer Iona Hills	62 876
At	San Francisco San Francisco	5 67 508
Ching	Nevada Bridgeport	61 459
Ching	San Francisco San Francisco	7 681341
Chong*	San Francisco San Francisco	2 67 691
Chu	San Francisco San Francisco	2 67 789
E	Butte Ophir	56 790
E	El Dorado White Oaks	581026
Emmeline	Yuba Bear Rvr	721012
Fat	San Francisco San Francisco	5 67 507
Fee	San Francisco San Francisco	5 671205
Fee	San Francisco San Francisco	1 68 925
Fee*	San Francisco San Francisco	1 68 924
Fing	San Francisco San Francisco	4 681210
Fing	San Francisco San Francisco	5 67 507
Fix	San Francisco San Francisco	5 67 508
Florence	Yuba Bear Rvr	721013
Fong	San Francisco San Francisco	5 671207
Fong	San Francisco San Francisco	11 160 67
Fong	San Francisco San Francisco	10 356 67
Fong	San Francisco San Francisco	5 67 507
Fong	San Francisco San Francisco	5 67 508
Fong	San Francisco San Francisco	5 67 509
Fong	San Francisco San Francisco	5 67 510
Foo	Butte Cascade	56 700
Fook	San Francisco San Francisco	5 67 507
Foy	San Francisco San Francisco	5 671205
Freg	San Francisco San Francisco	5 67 508
Fu	San Francisco San Francisco	5 671205
Fu	San Francisco San Francisco	1 68 924
Geo B	San Francisco San Francisco	12 387 67
Gu	El Dorado Georgetown	58 684
Harry	San Francisco San Francisco	11 96 67
Hee	San Francisco San Francisco	4 681202
Hing	San Francisco San Francisco	4 681211
Ho	San Francisco San Francisco	4 681194
Ho*	San Francisco San Francisco	5 671205
Hong	San Francisco San Francisco	4 681211
Hong	San Francisco San Francisco	5 67 506
Hong	San Francisco San Francisco	5 67 510
Hop	Sacramento Natonia	63 280
Hop	San Francisco San Francisco	5 671206
Hoy	San Francisco San Francisco	5 671205
Hu	San Francisco San Francisco	4 681202
James	El Dorado White Oaks	581018
Jane	San Francisco San Francisco	10 223 67
John	Placer Virginia	62 690
John	Tulara Visalia	71 73

California 1860 Census Index

Name	County Locale	M653 Roll	Page
WING			
Josiah	Solano Suisan	69	221
Kee	Butte Ophir	56	801
Kee	San Francisco San Francisco 4	68	1194
Kee	San Francisco San Francisco 4	68	1198
Kimker*	Butte Bidwell	56	706
Ko	San Francisco San Francisco 4	68	1197
Ko	San Francisco San Francisco 4	68	1198
Ko	San Francisco San Francisco 4	68	1201
Kong	San Francisco San Francisco 5	67	1205
Koy	San Francisco San Francisco 5	67	1205
Krinker	Butte Bidwell	56	706
Ku	San Francisco San Francisco 4	68	1194
Ku	San Francisco San Francisco 4	68	1198
Ku	San Francisco San Francisco 5	67	509
Kung	San Francisco San Francisco 5	67	510
Lee	Butte Cascade	56	700
Lee	Butte Ophir	56	810
Lee	Butte Ophir	56	819
Lee	El Dorado Georgetown	58	688
Lee	Nevada Bridgeport	61	492
Lee	Placer Iona Hills	62	896
Lee	San Francisco San Francisco 4	68	1175
Lee	San Francisco San Francisco 4	68	1193
Lee	San Francisco San Francisco 4	68	1211
Leng	Sacramento Ward 1	63	65
Leong	San Francisco San Francisco 4	68	1202
Ling	San Francisco San Francisco 5	67	507
Ling	Yuba Long Bar	72	769
Lo	Butte Oregon	56	644
Lo	San Francisco San Francisco 4	68	1193
Loe	San Francisco San Francisco 11	161 / 67	
Log	San Francisco San Francisco 4	68	1173
Loi	San Francisco San Francisco 5	67	1205
Los	San Francisco San Francisco 4	68	1202
Low	Butte Bidwell	56	709
Low	Butte Ophir	56	805
Loy	San Francisco San Francisco 5	67	510
Lu	San Francisco San Francisco 4	68	1211
Lu	San Francisco San Francisco 4	68	1211
M P	Mariposa Twp 3	60	596
Mary	Sierra Downieville	66	959
Mo	San Francisco San Francisco 4	68	1174
Mong	San Francisco San Francisco 4	68	1202
Mow	Sacramento Ward 1	63	68
Moy	San Francisco San Francisco 4	68	1203
Mung	San Francisco San Francisco 5	67	1205
O	San Francisco San Francisco 1	68	872
Orange	Yuba Bear Rvr	72	1012
Pie	Butte Ophir	56	788
Pie	Butte Ophir	56	802
Pie	Butte Ophir	56	803
Pie	Butte Ophir	56	815
Piu	Butte Ophir	56	810
Pow	Butte Ophir	56	802
Quaw	Yuba Long Bar	72	762
Rong	San Francisco San Francisco 1	68	924
Sae	San Francisco San Francisco 5	67	507
Se	San Francisco San Francisco 4	68	1202
See	San Francisco San Francisco 5	67	1205
Shung	San Francisco San Francisco 5	67	510
Sin	San Francisco San Francisco 5	67	507
Sing	Butte Wyandotte	56	665
Song	San Francisco San Francisco 4	68	1204
Song	San Francisco San Francisco 11	158 / 67	
Stephen	Tuolumne Columbia	71	329
Su	El Dorado Georgetown	58	703
Su	San Francisco San Francisco 5	67	1205
Su	San Francisco San Francisco 5	67	510
Sum	San Francisco San Francisco 5	67	507
Sung	San Francisco San Francisco 5	67	510
Thie	San Francisco San Francisco 4	68	1201
Thu	San Francisco San Francisco 4	68	1201
Ti	San Francisco San Francisco 11	161 / 67	
Tie	Mariposa Twp 3	60	581
Tie	San Francisco San Francisco 5	67	1206
Too	San Francisco San Francisco 4	68	1211
Tor	San Francisco San Francisco 4	68	1211
Tu	San Francisco San Francisco 5	67	1206
Tye	Butte Ophir	56	817
Wa	Tuolumne Twp 5	71	523
Wan	Yuba Marysville	72	895
Wh Chon	San Francisco San Francisco 4	68	1178
Wh Chou*	San Francisco San Francisco 4	68	1178
Wm	Butte Ophir	56	772
Wo	San Francisco San Francisco 4	68	1203
Wong	San Francisco San Francisco 4	68	1201
Woo Cheong	San Francisco San Francisco 5	67	507
	San Francisco		
Yan	Yuba Fosters	72	841
WINGALL			
A	Calaveras Twp 9	57	391
WINGARTEN			
John D	Los Angeles Los Angeles	59	401
WINGATE			
A*	Calaveras Twp 9	57	391
Alvin	Butte Chico	56	560
C E	Sacramento Ward 4	63	504
H S	Nevada Nevada	61	268
Helena	San Francisco San Francisco 6	67	433
Henry	Sacramento Ward 1	63	12
Herry	Sacramento Ward 1	63	12
Isaac T	Alameda Oakland	55	33
Jas*	San Francisco San Francisco 10	315 / 67	
John W	Calaveras Twp 10	57	263
O C	Shasta Shasta	66	761
WINGE			
T J*	Sierra Cox'S Bar	66	949
WINGER			
Jacob	Del Norte Crescent	58	626
WINGERT			
David	Yuba Parks Ba	72	783
WINGERTEN			
John D*	Los Angeles Los Angeles	59	401
WINGERTER			
Charles J	San Francisco San Francisco 7	68	1415
WINGFIELD			
Anaxiander	Tulara Twp 3	71	45
Anaxinander	Tulara Keeneysburg	71	45
WINGFORD			
W	Calaveras Twp 9	57	399
WINGHAM			
Saml	Sacramento Ward 1	63	10
Saml	Sacramento Ward 1	63	95
Saml*	Sacramento Ward 1	63	10
WINGINGTON			
Sarah A	Sacramento Georgian	63	341
WINGLETON			
Bernard*	San Francisco San Francisco 7	68	1325
WINGO			
J L	Amador Twp 2	55	309
T J	Sierra Cox'S Bar	66	949
W E	Tehama Lassen	70	877
William	Sonoma Russian	69	441
WINGOE			
J H	El Dorado Mud Springs	58	970
WINGOHIER			
Jacob	Nevada Bridgeport	61	497
WINGOTNER			
Jacob	Nevada Bridgeport	61	497
WINGSELL			
---	Butte Bidwell	56	709
Ah	Butte Bidwell	56	709
WINGULL			
A	Calaveras Twp 9	57	391
WINHAM			
M A	Nevada Bridgeport	61	482
William*	Nevada Bridgeport	61	487
Wm	Butte Bidwell	56	706
WINHAN			
William*	Nevada Bridgeport	61	487
WINICH			
William	El Dorado Mud Springs	58	1000
WINIGARDEN			
Danl	Sonoma Sonoma	69	643
WINIGER			
C O	Amador Twp 5	55	344
WININGER			
G W	Butte Ophir	56	762
WINIS			
C B*	San Francisco San Francisco 5	67	545
WINK			
Charles	San Francisco San Francisco 3	67	15
I	Calaveras Twp 9	57	389
WINKAM			
William	Nevada Bridgeport	61	487
WINKELFF			
John	Yuba Slate Ro	72	692
WINKELIFF			
John	Yolo Slate Ra	72	692
WINKELMAN			
Jacob	El Dorado Greenwood	58	712
WINKENBURG			
Henry	Tulara Twp 3	71	46
WINKER			
Adolp	Siskiyou Yreka	69	175
WINKERS			
Chas	Butte Bidwell	56	731
WINKLE			
August	Sacramento Ward 1	63	75
August	Trinity Turner'S	70	997
Henry	San Francisco San Francisco 1	68	889
Henry	Trinity Lewiston	70	963
John Van*	Sierra Pine Grove	66	824
John*	El Dorado Placerville	58	916
Van	Sierra Pine Grove	66	822
WINKLEMAN			
Fred	Sacramento San Joaquin	63	364
H	El Dorado Newtown	58	780
WINKLEMAN			
Peter	Sacramento San Joaquin	63	358
WINKLER			
Chas	San Francisco San Francisco 2	67	649
Claton	Sonoma Armally	69	499
G	San Francisco San Francisco 5	67	514
John	Yolo Slate Ra	72	691
John	Yuba Slate Ro	72	691
John	Yuba Marysville	72	872
L B	Mariposa Twp 1	60	635
Wm	San Francisco San Francisco 2	67	653
WINKLEY			
Philip W	Yuba Marysville	72	856
Philip W	Yuba Marysville	72	861
WINKLR			
Adolp*	Siskiyou Yreka	69	175
WINKS			
James	Calaveras Twp 4	57	307
James	Mariposa Twp 3	60	615
WINLEY			
Elias*	Sacramento Ward 3	63	479
H H	Amador Twp 6	55	438
WINMAN			
F P*	Solano Benecia	69	281
WINMEYER			
F	San Francisco San Francisco 6	67	458
WINN			
---	Butte Ophir	56	796
---	Butte Ophir	56	813
---	El Dorado Georgetown	58	682
---	Yuba Long Bar	72	759
A G	Sacramento Ward 1	63	10
Albert T	Yuba Marysville	72	945
Ann	San Francisco San Francisco 9	68	1001
Ann	San Francisco San Francisco 10	301 / 67	
Charles	San Francisco San Francisco 7	68	1356
Daniel	Solano Vallejo	69	273
Danl	San Francisco San Francisco 1	68	825
Dominque*	San Francisco San Francisco 1	68	825
	San Francisco		
Eliza N	Solano Suisan	69	222
Gustares*	Tulara Keyesville	71	61
Gustars*	Tulara Keyesville	71	61
Gustavis	Tulara Twp 3	71	61
H S	Sacramento Ward 3	63	489
J	Nevada Nevada	61	264
James*	Nevada Red Dog	61	544
Jas	Alameda Brooklyn	55	168
Jno P	San Francisco San Francisco 9	68	988
Joseh	Calaveras Twp 9	57	357
Joseph	Calaveras Twp 9	57	357
Loran	Stanislaus Branch	70	703
Margaret	Sonoma Petaluma	69	568
Mary	San Francisco San Francisco 10	238 / 67	
Pat	San Joaquin Stockton	64	1045
R	San Francisco San Francisco 6	67	449
Tristram	Nevada Rough &	61	429
William	San Francisco San Francisco 9	68	1026
William	San Francisco San Francisco 9	68	944
Willow	San Francisco San Francisco 9	68	1010
Wm	Mariposa Twp 3	60	601
WINNANS			
Stephen	Nevada Bridgeport	61	450
WINNAS			
Lewis	Amador Twp 2	55	278
WINNE			
D B	Butte Chico	56	566
Nathaniel	Sacramento Ward 4	63	538
Timothy	Tuolumne Twp 4	71	143
WINNEBUCK			
---	Fresno Twp 3	59	95
WINNEBUCO			
---	Fresno Twp 2	59	89
WINNEGAN			
Chris	Amador Twp 5	55	346
Samuel*	Mendocino Calpella	60	821
WINNEMUCK			
---	Fresno Twp 1	59	54
WINNENBERG			
W H	San Francisco San Francisco 10	287 / 67	
WINNER			
Geo*	Mendocino Calpella	60	811
Hank*	Tulara Twp 3	71	45
T	San Francisco San Francisco 3	67	78
WINNEY			
E G	Napa Napa	61	105
Jacob	San Francisco San Francisco 9	68	1011
John	Contra Costa Twp 2	57	542
WINNIGAN			
James*	Calaveras Twp 8	57	57
Samuel	Mendocino Calpella	60	821
WINNING			
Robert	Calaveras Twp 4	57	343

California 1860 Census Index

Name	County Locale	M653 Roll	Page
WINNO			
Antonino*	Sierra Downieville	66	972
WINNY			
James	Nevada Bridgeport	61	484
WINOGAR			
F	Shasta Millvill	66	739
WINONTS			
Agusta	Yuba Slate Ro	72	689
Agusta*	Yolo Slate Ra	72	689
WINORNTS			
Newell*	Yuba Slate Ro	72	689
WINP			
---*	Mariposa Twp 3	60	576
John	Colusa Grand Island	57	474
WINPURN			
M A	Nevada Bridgeport	61	482
WINR			
---*	San Francisco San Francisco 9	681086	
WINRING			
Robert*	Calaveras Twp 4	57	343
WINROW			
Mary	San Francisco San Francisco 3	67	60
Michael	Nevada Bridgeport	61	501
Samuel	San Francisco San Francisco 3	67	59
WINS			
---	Shasta French G	66	720
WINSDALL			
Edgar*	Yolo Merritt	72	584
WINSEL			
D A	Sierra Downieville	66	953
WINSET			
H	Sutter Bear Rvr	70	818
WINSGARDEN			
Danl*	Sonoma Sonoma	69	643
WINSHAFT			
Thomas	San Francisco San Francisco 9	681011	
WINSHAW			
Y	San Joaquin Elkhorn	64	990
WINSHELL			
Paul	Yuba Bear Rvr	721007	
WINSHIP			
C F	Sutter Butte	70	800
J	Sutter Butte	70	799
John	Siskiyou Klamath	69	91
Thos J	San Francisco San Francisco 1	68	916
W	San Francisco San Francisco 2	67	701
WINSLETT			
Jno W	Trinity S Fork	701032	
WINSLEW			
Frank H	Colusa Monroeville	57	440
WINSLOE			
Robert	Tulara Twp 3	71	60
WINSLON			
Jno M	Sacramento Sutter	63	299
WINSLOW			
Asel M	Tulara Visalia	71	103
B W	Santa Clara San Jose	65	341
Benj F	Marin Bolinas	60	727
Benjamin	San Francisco San Francisco 7	681364	
D H	Amador Twp 1	55	481
Daniel F	Santa Clara San Jose	65	321
Desin	Tuolumne Twp 2	71	372
Desire	Tuolumne Springfield	71	372
E	Marin Tomales	60	776
Edwd	San Francisco San Francisco 9	681078	
Ella	San Francisco San Francisco 10	213	
		67	
G	Merced Twp 2	60	920
Geo	San Francisco San Francisco 9	681067	
George H	San Francisco San Francisco 4	681145	
J T	Sacramento San Joaquin	63	358
John	El Dorado Georgetown	58	706
Robert	Tulara Twp 3	71	62
S N F	Tuolumne Big Oak	71	137
Thomas	Tulara Visalia	71	107
W	San Francisco San Francisco 9	681036	
William	San Joaquin Elkhorn	64	971
WINSMILLER			
Daniel*	Yuba Marysville	72	894
WINSON			
G D A	El Dorado Salmon Falls	581043	
Jno	San Francisco San Francisco 9	681089	
Samuel*	San Francisco San Francisco 3	67	59
WINSPIAR			
Robert	Placer Forest H	62	794
WINSTANLEY			
Jno	Alameda Washington	55	172
Jus	Alameda Brooklyn	55	172
WINSTATILY			
C*	El Dorado Placerville	58	894
WINSTON			
Banks	Tuolumne Twp 2	71	380
D A	Amador Twp 3	55	391
David	Trinity Weaverville	701064	
H A	Santa Clara San Jose	65	360
Henry	Tulara Keyesville	71	62

Name	County Locale	M653 Roll	Page
WINSTON			
James	Yuba Marysville	72	903
James B	Los Angeles Los Angeles	59	344
John	Sierra Twp 7	66	863
John	Tulara Keyesville	71	62
Joseph	Los Angeles Los Angeles	59	364
Joseph	Los Angeles Los Angeles	59	519
W B	Yolo Cache	72	637
William	Tulara Keyesville	71	62
WINSWORTH			
J	Sutter Bear Rvr	70	826
WINSZTON			
John	Sierra St Louis	66	863
WINTENBERG			
Adolph	San Francisco San Francisco 7	681380	
WINTER			
Albert	Sierra Twp 7	66	870
Augustus T	Calaveras Twp 8	57	101
B	Santa Clara San Jose	65	360
C	San Francisco San Francisco 5	67	478
Charles	San Francisco San Francisco 8	681294	
Charles	San Francisco San Francisco 7	681438	
Charles	San Joaquin O'Neal	641005	
Clinton	San Francisco San Francisco 7	681326	
Conrad	San Francisco San Francisco 2	67	782
Edmund C	Calaveras Twp 8	57	101
Edward	Solano Benecia	69	298
George	Tehama Tehama	70	945
H	Siskiyou Scott Ri	69	81
Henry	Tuolumne Twp 4	71	139
J A	Butte Cascade	56	692
J S	Siskiyou Scott Va	69	46
James W	Yuba Marysville	72	863
John	Butte Ophir	56	772
John	El Dorado Coloma	581102	
John	Sacramento Centre	63	173
John	San Francisco San Francisco 7	681424	
John	San Francisco San Francisco 1	68	928
Louis	Sacramento Ward 1	63	33
Marcus*	Yuba Marysville	72	894
Michael	San Francisco San Francisco 1	68	926
P	San Francisco San Francisco 8	681245	
R	Butte Ophir	56	790
Robert	Sierra St Louis	66	810
Saarah	San Francisco San Francisco 10	251	
		67	
Samuel	El Dorado Coloma	581069	
Sarah	San Francisco San Francisco 10	251	
		67	
William	San Francisco San Francisco 4	681218	
Z	Santa Clara Almaden	65	275
WINTERBIEN			
G H	Santa Clara San Jose	65	293
WINTERBUEN			
Frank	Santa Clara San Jose	65	293
WINTERBUM			
Joseph	San Francisco San Francisco 1	68	822
WINTERBURN			
Joseph	Santa Clara San Jose	65	314
WINTERHALDER			
Charles	Santa Cruz Santa Cruz	66	618
Theodore	Santa Cruz Santa Cruz	66	617
Theodore*	Santa Cruz Santa Cruz	66	617
WINTERHALTER			
George G	San Joaquin Elkhorn	64	949
WINTERHOLDER			
Theodore*	Santa Cruz Santa Cruz	66	617
WINTERLEALDER			
Theodore	Santa Cruz Santa Cruz	66	617
WINTERMAILL			
Antone	El Dorado Coloma	581071	
WINTERMANTTE			
Louis	El Dorado Coloma	581081	
WINTERN			
Banks	Tuolumne Shawsfla	71	380
WINTERS			
Andrew	Alameda Brooklyn	55	155
Aron	Yuba Fosters	72	839
C E	Tuolumne Twp 2	71	389
Charlotte	San Francisco San Francisco 10	184	
		67	
Chas	Butte Bidwell	56	731
Chas	Klamath S Fork	59	205
Chas	Sacramento Granite	63	251
Chas	Sacramento Ward 1	63	85
Chas	San Francisco San Francisco 3	67	71
Chs	Sacramento Granite	63	251
D W	Sierra Twp 7	66	869
Denis	San Mateo Twp 1	65	53
E	El Dorado Mud Springs	58	984
Elijah	Yolo Slate Ra	72	691
Elijah	Yuba Slate Ro	72	691
Eliza	San Francisco San Francisco 2	67	711
George	Nevada Red Dog	61	546
H	Siskiyou Scott Ri	69	81
H A	San Francisco San Francisco 6	67	456

Name	County Locale	M653 Roll	Page
WINTERS			
Hannah	San Francisco San Francisco 10	183	
		67	
Henry	Contra Costa Twp 2	57	565
Henry	Sacramento Ward 1	63	109
Henry*	Placer Michigan	62	856
Hinz*	Placer Michigan	62	856
J	Calaveras Twp 9	57	392
James	Plumas Quincy	62	954
Jane	San Francisco San Francisco 2	67	642
Jno	Sacramento Natonia	63	281
Jno	San Francisco San Francisco 12	383	
		67	
John	Placer Ophir	62	652
John D	San Joaquin Tulare	64	869
Joseph	Tuolumne Twp 1	71	249
M	Nevada Eureka	61	388
Michael	San Francisco San Francisco 8	681278	
Michael	San Francisco San Francisco 7	681353	
N	Nevada Grass Valley	61	169
Peter H	Placer Secret R	62	618
Phillip	Butte Ophir	56	797
Robert	San Joaquin Elkhorn	64	984
Stephen	Shasta Shasta	66	731
W	Nevada Eureka	61	388
W C	San Mateo Twp 1	65	53
W H	Napa Napa	61	57
William	San Francisco San Francisco 7	681340	
William	Tulara Twp 1	71	59
Wm	Sacramento Franklin	63	325
WINTERSMALL			
Antone*	El Dorado Coloma	581071	
WINTERSTEEN			
Charles	Placer Todds Va	62	790
WINTERTON			
John R	San Francisco San Francisco 8	681296	
WINTHROP			
James	Tehama Lassen	70	874
Thomas	Calaveras Twp 7	57	21
WINTICHEL			
J	Santa Clara San Jose	65	325
WINTON			
John	San Francisco San Francisco 4	681115	
N W	Tuolumne Sonora	71	485
Victor	Sierra Twp 5	66	921
WINTORY			
B	El Dorado White Oaks	581004	
WINTOUR			
Anne M	San Francisco San Francisco 10	176	
		67	
WINTRANT			
S	San Francisco San Francisco 3	67	59
WINTRAUB			
S	San Francisco San Francisco 3	67	59
WINTRELL			
Lewis*	Santa Clara Redwood	65	454
WINTROWTH			
Francis*	Siskiyou Yreka	69	134
WINTRY			
Jacob*	El Dorado Placerville	58	918
WINTWORHT			
Francis	Siskiyou Yreka	69	134
WINTWORTH			
Danl	Santa Clara San Jose	65	282
George*	San Mateo Twp 3	65	87
Louis	San Francisco San Francisco 4	681146	
S	Siskiyou Yreka	69	191
T	Tuolumne Twp 2	71	351
WINTZ			
Geo	Sacramento Ward 3	63	433
WINTZELL			
Gustus*	San Francisco San Francisco 3	67	39
WINTZER			
Charles	Mendocino Anderson	60	867
WINVING			
Robert*	Calaveras Twp 4	57	343
WINVINY			
Robert*	Calaveras Twp 4	57	343
WINY			
---	Calaveras Twp 5	57	254
---	Calaveras Twp 10	57	270
---	Calaveras Twp 4	57	300
---	Calaveras Twp 4	57	302
WINYARD			
Adam	San Francisco San Francisco 11	141	
		67	
WINZELL			
Joseph	Yuba Marysville	72	864
WINZILT			
D*	San Francisco San Francisco 3	67	22
WIOM			
Jane*	Sacramento Ward 1	63	86
WIONE			
Jane*	Sacramento Ward 1	63	86
WIOUR			
Jane*	Sacramento Ward 1	63	86

California 1860 Census Index

Name	County Locale	M653 RollPage
WIP		
---	Calaveras Twp 5	57 236
William*	Placer Folsom	62 639
WIPMAN		
F C*	San Joaquin Stockton	641063
WIPPE		
J	San Francisco San Francisco 3	67 48
WIPPERHOFF		
Charles*	Placer Michigan	62 847
WIR		
---	San Francisco San Francisco 4	681174
WIRDIMURS		
Louis	Tuolumne Twp 2	71 379
WIRE		
Henry	Calaveras Twp 4	57 315
William	Calaveras Twp 4	57 315
WIREINGER		
G W*	Butte Ophir	56 762
WIREN		
Charles	Tuolumne Jamestown	71 437
WIRGHS		
Fred*	Mariposa Twp 3	60 600
WIRICH		
Lawrance*	Alameda Brooklyn	55 129
WIRKS		
James	Calaveras Twp 4	57 307
WIRM		
James*	Nevada Red Dog	61 544
WIRME		
D B*	Butte Chico	56 566
WIRNER		
A J*	Siskiyou Scott Va	69 26
WIRNIR		
T*	San Francisco San Francisco 3	67 78
WIROZT		
Heivey*	Sierra Downieville	661014
WIRR		
---	San Francisco San Francisco 9	681086
John	Tuolumne Twp 5	71 491
WIRRY		
---	Amador Twp 2	55 315
WIRSEN		
A*	Nevada Eureka	61 352
WIRSON		
A*	Nevada Eureka	61 352
WIRSS		
Charles*	Sierra Twp 7	66 863
WIRT		
Robt*	Nevada Red Dog	61 542
WIRTLEY		
Gorstavus*	Marin Novato	60 737
WIRTRILL		
Lewis*	Santa Clara Redwood	65 454
WIRTSON		
Peter	Sierra Downieville	661001
WIRTY		
Rodolph	Sierra La Porte	66 779
WIRY		
---	Amador Twp 5	55 354
---*	Amador Twp 6	55 435
WIRZ		
John	Tuolumne Chinese	71 491
WIS		
---	Calaveras Twp 4	57 333
WISBURN		
Lewis	Plumas Meadow Valley	62 903
WISCH		
Harry	San Francisco San Francisco 10	194 67
WISCHUSEN		
D	San Francisco San Francisco 6	67 451
WISCO		
---	Sacramento Cosumnes	63 406
WISCOL		
E F*	Stanislaus Branch	70 703
WISCOM		
Nathan	San Bernardino San Bernadino	64 627
Reuben	San Bernardino San Salvador	64 637
WISCOTT		
Thos	Butte Oregon	56 625
WISCWELL		
Luther	Sacramento Ward 1	63 41
WISDEN		
James B	El Dorado Greenwood	58 718
WISDOM		
A T	Sierra Twp 7	66 874
WISE		
Abraham	Stanislaus Emory	70 754
Adam	Tuolumne Montezuma	71 508
Alex	Monterey San Juan	60 982
Alexr	Monterey San Juan	60 982
C N	Tuolumne Sonora	71 213
Charles	Solano Green Valley	69 242
Chas	Santa Cruz Santa Cruz	66 636
Christopher	Sonoma Sonoma	69 643
David	Napa Yount	61 34
WISE		
E N	Tuolumne Twp 1	71 213
Ed	Siskiyou Klamath	69 89
Edwd H	Monterey Alisal	601036
Elbert	Sonoma Petaluma	69 581
F W	Solano Vacaville	69 338
Francis	Placer Iona Hills	62 892
Frank	Tuolumne Twp 2	71 357
H	Sacramento Cosumnes	63 404
Henry	Solano Fremont	69 385
Henry	Sonoma Santa Rosa	69 388
J W	Sutter Butte	70 795
Jacob	Sacramento Ward 3	63 463
James	Alameda Oakland	55 37
James	Yolo Washington	72 563
James H	Yuba Suida	72 985
James M*	Yuba Linda	72 985
Jasper	Sacramento Georgian	63 336
Jno	Fresno Twp 3	59 16
John	Fresno Twp 2	59 49
John	Sacramento Granite	63 223
John	San Francisco San Francisco 4	681122
John	Solano Vallejo	69 269
John W	Napa Yount	61 37
Josep*	Sacramento Georgian	63 336
Joseph*	Sacramento Georgian	63 336
Leonard	Tuolumne Twp 1	71 241
M	Santa Clara San Jose	65 296
M	Sonoma Santa Rosa	69 391
Mary	Sacramento Ward 3	63 462
Orlando U	Humbolt Mattole	59 127
Peter	Nevada Rough &	61 412
Preston	Santa Cruz Watsonville	66 535
Preston	Santa Cruz Pajaro	66 574
Rich J	Placer Rattle Snake	62 630
Robt	Santa Clara Fremont	65 419
W H	San Francisco San Francisco 1	68 928
W W	Tuolumne Twp 2	71 272
William	Yuba Marysville	72 958
Wm	Sacramento Ward 3	63 478
WISEGARNED		
Frederick	Santa Clara Santa Clara	65 461
WISEIN		
Lewes	Butte Ophir	56 771
WISELL		
D	Calaveras Twp 9	57 376
WISEMAN		
---	Butte Ophir	56 824
A	Sutter Bear Rvr	70 824
D	San Francisco San Francisco 6	67 466
G	El Dorado Kelsey	581156
Geo	Sacramento Ward 1	63 1
George	Calaveras Twp 7	57 21
H M	Amador Twp 2	55 263
J	Sutter Bear Rvr	70 824
John	San Francisco San Francisco 7	681357
Jos	Sacramento Ward 1	63 119
Julia	San Francisco San Francisco 9	68 951
Mary	Sonoma Santa Rosa	69 426
Peter	Butte Cascade	56 692
Peter	Butte Ophir	56 786
Peter	Butte Ophir	56 824
R	San Francisco San Francisco 1	68 921
Rudolph*	Yuba Marysville	72 928
Thomas	Yuba Rose Bar	72 797
WISEMERE		
John	Butte Cascade	56 690
WISENBERG		
Henry	Sierra Downieville	66 977
WISENDOLPH		
M	San Francisco San Francisco 6	67 458
WISENOR		
Jos H*	Alameda Brooklyn	55 159
WISEO		
H A	Shasta Shasta	66 672
WISER		
Alex	San Francisco San Francisco 9	681072
Charles	El Dorado Salmon Falls	581038
Fred	Santa Clara Santa Clara	65 462
Fred	Santa Clara Santa Clara	65 469
H A	Shasta Shasta	66 672
John	Los Angeles Tejon	59 525
WISERMAN		
Dadrich*	Yuba Marysville	72 923
WISERNAN		
Julia	San Francisco San Francisco 9	68 951
WISEROLER		
P	Calaveras Twp 9	57 392
WISEWELL		
Luther	Sacramento Ward 1	63 41
WISHAW		
Jas	Placer Rattle Snake	62 604
WISHEART		
James	Amador Twp 7	55 419
WISHESTON		
Wm H	San Francisco San Francisco 9	681083
WISHIT		
William	El Dorado White Oaks	581001
WISHON		
James*	Santa Cruz Santa Cruz	66 634
WISKER		
Wm*	San Francisco San Francisco 3	67 24
WISLER		
Jacob	Yuba Slate Ro	72 712
William	Placer Iona Hills	62 864
William	Placer Iona Hills	62 867
WISLSON		
Charles*	San Francisco San Francisco 3	67 71
WISM		
James*	Nevada Red Dog	61 544
WISMAN		
Jonathan	El Dorado Mud Springs	58 993
WISNELL		
Ohirn	Nevada Nevada	61 241
Oluin*	Nevada Nevada	61 241
WISNER		
Constantine*	Yuba New York	72 741
J	Nevada Eureka	61 389
J	Sutter Sutter	70 802
John B	El Dorado Mud Springs	58 951
T*	Nevada Eureka	61 389
Wm	Sierra Downieville	661012
WISNEY		
John H	Santa Cruz Watsonville	66 537
WISON		
Richard	Monterey Pajaro	601018
S	El Dorado Placerville	58 847
WISS		
John	Nevada Grass Valley	61 149
William*	Placer Folsom	62 639
WISSELS		
W M	Siskiyou Scott Va	69 48
WISSICK		
Juleus	Butte Ophir	56 793
WISSING		
Jacob	San Francisco San Francisco 9	681027
William*	San Francisco San Francisco 9	681005
WISSINGER		
John W	San Francisco San Francisco 3	67 24
WISSMAN		
F C*	San Joaquin Stockton	641063
WISSOR		
George F	Calaveras Twp 9	57 375
WISSY		
Randolph	Butte Ophir	56 766
WIST HAAS		
T*	San Francisco San Francisco 3	67 78
WIST		
Henry	Napa Clear Lake	61 124
Robt*	Nevada Red Dog	61 542
WISTAN		
Saml	Santa Clara San Jose	65 376
WISTELHUM		
Jacob*	Placer Auburn	62 588
WISTER		
---	Mendocino Big Rock	60 875
WISTERMANN		
J	Tuolumne Twp 2	71 413
WISTIN		
William*	Calaveras Twp 6	57 179
WISTLE		
Lewis	Placer Folsom	62 640
WISTON		
Daniel	Sierra Eureka	661043
W H	Calaveras Twp 9	57 374
WISTPALL		
Chas	Santa Clara Santa Clara	65 463
WISTRCONTECK		
---	Mendocino Big Rvr	60 853
WISTS		
E P	Amador Twp 2	55 284
WISWELER		
J	Calaveras Twp 9	57 393
WISWELL		
Eda	Merced Twp 2	60 924
Eila	Merced Twp 2	60 924
H	Merced Twp 2	60 923
J	Merced Twp 2	60 922
N	Sonoma Vallejo	69 628
U	Sonoma Vallejo	69 628
WISWELT		
J	Merced Twp 2	60 922
WIT		
---	Butte Oregon	56 640
---	Nevada Rough &	61 435
---	Nevada Bridgeport	61 468
---	San Francisco San Francisco 4	681189
Michael De	San Francisco San Francisco 4	681164
	San Francisco	
WITCH		
John	El Dorado Placerville	58 923
WITCHIEF		
Martin	San Francisco San Francisco 1	68 889

California 1860 Census Index

Name	County Locale	M653 Roll	Page
WITCHMAN			
Jacob	Sierra Twp 7	66	877
WITCHUR			
James*	Placer Michigan	62	814
WITCOM			
Seth	Nevada Rough &	61	423
WITCOXON			
Jefferson	Yolo Washington	72	570
WITEY			
William	Solano Suisan	69	229
WITH			
Frederick	San Francisco San Francisco 3	67	15
Henry*	Yuba Marysville	72	900
Joseph	Los Angeles Los Angeles	59	344
WITHAM			
---	Mendocino Round Va	60	881
Charles	Tuolumne Columbia	71	345
G T	Yolo Washington	72	564
Jos E	San Francisco San Francisco 5	67	477
Josua D	San Francisco San Francisco 10	67	324
Otis H*	Calaveras Twp 8	57	107
William	San Francisco San Francisco 8	681	249
WITHARN			
Charles*	Tuolumne Twp 2	71	345
WITHBURG			
Mich	Sacramento Granite	63	254
WITHENNER			
G A	San Francisco San Francisco 10	67	257
WITHENS			
Isaac	Butte Hamilton	56	524
Peter E	Nevada Bloomfield	61	509
WITHERALD			
J	Siskiyou Klamath	69	86
WITHERALL			
R	Santa Clara San Jose	65	338
WITHERBEE			
Calvin H	San Francisco San Francisco 8	681	238
WITHERBY			
David S	San Francisco San Francisco 1	68	821
WITHERELL			
Alfred	Monterey Alisal	601	037
WITHERILL			
Abel	Siskiyou Yreka	69	171
C	Siskiyou Scott Va	69	46
WITHERLY			
Meriah	Marin Cortemad	60	756
WITHERM			
James	Mariposa Twp 3	60	566
WITHERN			
James	Mariposa Twp 3	60	566
WITHERON			
Cas	Napa Hot Springs	61	16
WITHEROW			
Cas	Napa Hot Springs	61	16
James	Plumas Meadow Valley	62	931
W W	Santa Clara Santa Clara	65	471
WITHERS			
Hiram*	Butte Kimshaw	56	583
Isaac	Butte Hamilton	56	524
J S	Yuba New York	72	737
J*	Calaveras Twp 9	57	392
James	Sonoma Cloverdale	69	686
Jas*	Butte Kimshaw	56	604
John*	San Francisco San Francisco 9	68	966
Peter E*	Nevada Bloomfield	61	509
Stephen A	Santa Clara Gilroy	65	240
Walter	Butte Kimshaw	56	607
William	Siskiyou Cottonwoood	69	98
Wm	Butte Kimshaw	56	606
WITHERTON			
Stephen B	Siskiyou Yreka	69	152
WITHERY			
Foster*	Nevada Rough &	61	428
Jas	Butte Kimshaw	56	604
WITHEY			
Foster	Nevada Rough &	61	428
WITHIM			
J W	Mariposa Twp 3	60	567
WITHING			
A	Sonoma Salt Point	69	692
WITHINGBONE			
G E	Nevada Nevada	61	263
WITHINGTON			
George	San Joaquin Elliott	64	942
Henry	Santa Cruz Santa Cruz	66	612
WITHISLEO			
B F	El Dorado Greenwood	58	716
WITHOWSHER			
Elias	Amador Twp 2	55	302
WITHOWSHIN			
Elias	Amador Twp 2	55	302
WITHRON			
A	Santa Clara Santa Clara	65	475
WITHROW			
Charles	Sonoma Washington	69	670
WITHROW			
J R	Tuolumne Columbia	71	300
WITHSOW			
J R	Tuolumne Twp 2	71	300
WITHUM			
Albion	Tuolumne Twp 2	71	362
Alleion	Tuolumne Columbia	71	362
WITHUS			
Hiram	Butte Kimshaw	56	583
WITHWELL			
W	Tuolumne Jacksonville	71	170
WITKIM			
J W	Mariposa Twp 3	60	567
WITKOSKY			
M	Sacramento Ward 1	63	74
WITLACH			
Walter	Los Angeles Los Angeles	59	406
WITLAR			
---	Mendocino Big Rock	60	875
WITLER			
Adam*	Santa Clara Redwood	65	455
WITLOF			
Eliza*	Yuba Marysville	72	874
WITMAN			
Henry	San Francisco San Francisco 9	68	988
Matilda	San Francisco San Francisco 10	67	289
WITMEN			
Jonis*	Siskiyou Cottonwoood	69	97
Louis	Siskiyou Klamath	69	97
WITMERE			
W N	San Francisco San Francisco 6	67	408
WITMORE			
Chancy E	Contra Costa Twp 3	57	605
Ed	Yuba New York	72	726
Hermann	San Francisco San Francisco 11	67	139
WITNER			
Henry	Alameda Murray	55	218
John	Nevada Eureka	61	369
W D	Nevada Eureka	61	369
WITNEY			
John H	Santa Cruz Watsonville	66	537
WITON			
Marcus B	El Dorado Greenwood	58	727
WITOWSKY			
Nathan	Los Angeles Los Angeles	59	335
WITRET			
Nicholas	Yolo No E Twp	72	675
Nicholas	Yuba North Ea	72	675
WITS			
Theodore	Placer Goods	62	698
WITSLERJOHN			
Galderon	Amador Twp 1	55	495
WITT			
A K	Butte Kimshaw	56	575
Caswell	Solano Suisan	69	230
Edward*	Placer Iona Hills	62	892
Enoch*	Placer Iona Hills	62	859
Geo	Siskiyou Cottonwoood	69	106
Hugh	Yuba Marysville	72	914
Joel	Nevada Rough &	61	430
John	El Dorado Eldorado	58	943
John	El Dorado Mud Springs	58	981
Joseph	Santa Cruz Pajaro	66	542
L D	El Dorado Eldorado	58	943
Nancy	Tuolumne Visalia	71	93
Napolion B	Fresno Twp 3	59	10
Nicholas	Marin Cortemad	60	756
P A	Mendocino Round Va	60	879
Theodore	El Dorado Georgetown	58	747
Thomas	Yuba Fosters	72	837
Thomas	Yuba Fosters	72	838
Thos	Butte Cascade	56	689
William	Yuba Linda	72	994
Wm L L*	Fresno Twp 3	59	10
Wm S S*	Fresno Twp 3	59	10
WITTACK			
G	Calaveras Twp 9	57	404
WITTAKER			
Jacob	Amador Twp 3	55	369
WITTE			
Henry	San Francisco San Francisco 3	67	12
Jno	Sacramento Ward 3	63	469
Wm	Tehama Tehama	70	946
WITTEINGTON			
G E	Nevada Nevada	61	263
WITTEL			
David	Sierra St Louis	66	810
WITTEN			
Ahria*	Sierra Downieville	66	972
Aliria	Sierra Downieville	66	972
Amos	Shasta Shasta	66	732
J G	Nevada Eureka	61	378
R	Calaveras Twp 9	57	409
W J	San Francisco San Francisco 4	681	146
WITTENBROOK			
Henry	Sacramento American	63	168
R	Sacramento American	63	168
WITTENMYER			
Louis	Contra Costa Twp 1	57	536
WITTER			
T L	Calaveras Twp 9	57	357
WITTERMAME			
August	San Francisco San Francisco 8	681	271
WITTERMANIO			
August*	San Francisco San Francisco 8	681	271
WITTERMANN			
August*	San Francisco San Francisco 8	681	271
WITTET			
Henry*	Mendocino Ukiah	60	805
WITTEY			
John*	Mariposa Coulterville	60	679
WITTHANSERS			
Chris*	Sacramento Ward 4	63	561
WITTHAUSAS			
Chris*	Sacramento Ward 4	63	561
WITTILLIN			
Rubare	Sierra La Porte	66	783
WITTINGTON			
Elizabeth	Amador Twp 2	55	313
Geo	Amador Twp 2	55	313
John	Placer Forest H	62	773
WITTLE			
Madoline	Yuba Marysville	72	923
WITTLINGER			
C	San Francisco San Francisco 5	67	512
WITTMAN			
Lewis*	Placer Yankee J	62	778
WITTMANN			
A	Tuolumne Twp 2	71	328
WITTMER			
William	San Francisco San Francisco 11	67	108
WITTOF			
Eliza	Yuba Marysville	72	874
WITTON			
Thomas	Del Norte Crescent	58	660
WITTOR			
S L*	Calaveras Twp 9	57	357
WITTRAM			
C	San Francisco San Francisco 5	67	499
WITTS			
John	Sonoma Petaluma	69	598
Walter	Nevada Eureka	61	343
Wm	San Francisco San Francisco 10	67	267
WITTSEE			
Charles	Yuba Marysville	72	861
WITTY			
John	Mariposa Coulterville	60	679
John A	San Joaquin Castoria	64	873
Nicolas	Mendocino Ukiah	60	801
William*	Yuba Marysville	72	867
WITZ			
Jos	San Francisco San Francisco 2	67	710
WITZEL			
Phillip	Sacramento Ward 1	63	37
WITZELL			
Adam S	Sierra Downieville	661	012
Henry	Sierra Downieville	661	012
T*	Siskiyou Klamath	69	94
WITZETT			
T	Siskiyou Klamath	69	94
WIU			
---*	Nevada Bridgeport	61	459
WIULLER			
William*	Alameda Brooklyn	55	142
WIV CONG			
---	San Joaquin Stockton	641	083
WIVE			
William*	Calaveras Twp 4	57	315
WIVES			
Jas	Sacramento Granite	63	261
WIXCOM			
Nathan	San Bernardino San Bernadino	64	627
WIXOM			
J C	Solano Fairfield	69	199
WIXON			
Augustus*	San Francisco San Francisco 1	68	837
J	Nevada Eureka	61	390
John	Napa Napa	61	61
John	Placer Secret R	62	624
WIZARD			
Geo	Butte Kimshaw	56	579
WIZENBURG			
John	Sierra Gibsonville	66	857
WIZENTNRY			
John*	Sierra Gibsonville	66	857
WIZER			
Jacob*	Klamath S Fork	59	198

California 1860 Census Index

Name	County Locale	M653 Roll	Page
WLAKER			
Sly	Colusa Monroeville	57	440
WLAL			
Margaret	Yuba Marysville	72	910
WLAOUE			
R C	Sierra Twp 7	66	875
WLDEN			
J D	El Dorado Greenwood	58	725
WLEUSH			
John*	Napa Yount	61	54
WLLIAMS			
Richd*	Nevada Bridgeport	61	453
WM M			
Lader	Santa Clara Fremont	65	434
WM			
Ah	Butte Oregon	56	629
Collins	Santa Cruz Santa Cruz	66	633
Thompsond	Santa Clara Alviso	65	406
Watson	Butte Bidwell	56	719
WMALGRAM			
Niles M	San Mateo Twp 3	65	95
WMITH			
Abraham	Sierra Twp 7	66	883
Edward	Tuolumne Twp 1	71	268
Jno	San Francisco San Francisco 9	681007	
John D	Santa Cruz Soguel	66	596
William	San Francisco San Francisco 8	681248	
WMSON			
J	Nevada Nevada	61	255
WMSSON			
J	Nevada Nevada	61	255
WNAK			
---	El Dorado Greenwood	58	730
WNENS			
David	San Mateo Twp 1	65	68
WNGER			
Elias*	Nevada Bridgeport	61	443
WNTONIO			
Jose	San Bernardino S Timate	64	692
WO KEE			
Hing	San Francisco San Francisco 4	681177	
WO			
---	Amador Twp 6	55	431
---	Butte Eureka	56	649
---	Calaveras Twp 5	57	195
---	Calaveras Twp 5	57	215
---	Calaveras Twp 5	57	237
---	Calaveras Twp 5	57	246
---	Calaveras Twp 10	57	287
---	Calaveras Twp 10	57	295
---	El Dorado Georgetown	58	678
---	El Dorado Georgetown	58	701
---	Mariposa Coulterville	60	694
---	Nevada Rough &	61	396
---	Nevada Bridgeport	61	463
---	Nevada Red Dog	61	556
---	Placer Illinois	62	748
---	Sacramento Ward 1	63	54
---	Sacramento Ward 1	63	56
---	Sacramento Ward 4	63	613
---	Sacramento Ward 1	63	70
---	San Francisco San Francisco 4	681177	
---	San Francisco San Francisco 4	681180	
---	San Francisco San Francisco 4	681186	
---	San Francisco San Francisco 4	681187	
---	San Francisco San Francisco 4	681209	
---	San Francisco San Francisco 11	67	145
---	San Francisco San Francisco 11	67	161
---	San Francisco San Francisco 5	67	510
---	Sierra Downieville	66	998
---	Stanislaus Branch	70	713
---	Tuolumne Chinese	71	524
Cheong	San Francisco San Francisco 4	681178	
Cheong	San Francisco San Francisco 4	681185	
Ching	San Francisco San Francisco 8	681255	
Chu	San Francisco San Francisco 4	681185	
Chung	San Francisco San Francisco 4	681181	
Hop	Butte Hamilton	56	530
Hop	San Francisco San Francisco 4	681180	
Kee	San Francisco San Francisco 4	681177	
Kin	Calaveras Twp 10	57	284
King	El Dorado Diamond	58	784
Ku	San Francisco San Francisco 9	681093	
Kung	San Francisco San Francisco 4	681210	
Lee	San Francisco San Francisco 4	681198	
Lee	San Francisco San Francisco 4	681199	
Lu	San Francisco San Francisco 4	681198	
Lu	San Francisco San Francisco 4	681199	
Man*	San Francisco San Francisco 11	67	160
Pu	San Francisco San Francisco 5	67	509
Quiny	Solano Suisan	69	221
See	San Francisco San Francisco 4	681203	
Sheap	San Francisco San Francisco 9	681093	

Name	County Locale	M653 Roll	Page
WO			
Su	San Francisco San Francisco 4	681203	
Tang	Fresno Twp 1	59	28
Tow	Sierra Downieville	66	985
Wa	Calaveras Twp 5	57	254
Yan	San Francisco San Francisco 9	681096	
Yang*	Fresno Twp 1	59	25
Yaw*	San Francisco San Francisco 9	681096	
Yung	San Francisco San Francisco 5	67	510
Zuen	San Francisco San Francisco 5	67	510
WOA			
---	Calaveras Twp 8	57	79
---	El Dorado Salmon Hills	581053	
WOAA			
---	El Dorado Mountain	581188	
WOADHENSE			
John	Placer Todds Va	62	763
WOAK			
J W	Butte Oregon	56	638
WOAL			
---	San Francisco San Francisco 6	67	470
WOATS			
Edward	Solano Fremont	69	384
WOAU			
---	Calaveras Twp 5	57	212
WOAY			
---	El Dorado Greenwood	58	728
WOB			
---	Calaveras Twp 4	57	306
WOBRINE			
George*	Yuba Rose Bar	72	820
WOCHARTZ			
Charles	San Francisco San Francisco 7	681421	
WOCHLER			
Ernest	Tuolumne Columbia	71	322
WOCHSA			
---*	Tulara Visalia	71	39
WOCK			
---	El Dorado Diamond	58	812
---	Trinity Weaverville	701076	
John	Trinity Mouth Ca	701010	
WOCY			
---	Shasta Shasta	66	669
WODDINGTON			
A	Del Norte Crescent	58	642
WODMAN			
Frederick	San Francisco San Francisco 7	681396	
WOE			
---	Amador Twp 3	55	386
---	San Francisco San Francisco 4	681173	
---*	Tuolumne Jacksonville	71	170
John	Sacramento Franklin	63	307
WOEMS			
W	San Francisco San Francisco 1	68	927
WOERNER			
David	San Francisco San Francisco 10	67	227
WOESSELLER			
E B	Tuolumne Columbia	71	322
WOESSNER			
C	El Dorado Coloma	581071	
WOEY			
---	Shasta Shasta	66	669
WOFF			
Walter	Shasta Millvill	66	742
William*	Monterey Pajaro	601024	
WOFFENDEN			
Richard M	Humbolt Table Bl	59	142
WOGAN			
Thos	Sacramento Ward 1	63	36
Thos	Sacramento Ward 1	63	38
Thos	Sacramento Ward 4	63	527
WOGE			
Chas	Trinity Weaverville	701069	
WOGES			
S W*	San Francisco San Francisco 5	67	547
WOGHFORD			
Harry	Calaveras Twp 10	57	289
WOGHT			
Henry	Solano Vallejo	69	252
WOH LA			
---	Sacramento Ward 3	63	490
WOH			
---	Alameda Oakland	55	22
---	Calaveras Twp 5	57	242
---	Calaveras Twp 5	57	252
---	Calaveras Twp 10	57	271
---	Calaveras Twp 10	57	291
---	Calaveras Twp 4	57	305
---	Calaveras Twp 4	57	308
---	Calaveras Twp 4	57	315
---	El Dorado Georgetown	58	680
---	El Dorado Georgetown	58	703
Chee	El Dorado Greenwood	58	728
Chug	Placer Dutch Fl	62	737
K	Calaveras Twp 10	57	291

Name	County Locale	M653 Roll	Page
WOH			
Sam*	Sacramento Ward 1	63	60
Sy	El Dorado Greenwood	58	714
WOHLEN			
Richd*	San Francisco San Francisco 2	67	757
WOHLER			
Anita C	Merced Monterey	60	944
Anita C	Monterey Monterey	60	944
Francis	Sacramento Ward 1	63	12
Valentine	Sacramento Centre	63	173
WOHLERS			
H	San Francisco San Francisco 10	67	289
Henry	Calaveras Twp 9	57	354
Herman	Monterey Monterey	60	944
Richd*	San Francisco San Francisco 2	67	757
WOHLFREM			
Ellas	Colusa Spring Valley	57	430
WOHLFROM			
Joseph	Colusa Spring Valley	57	430
WOHLFRON			
J W*	Solano Vacaville	69	342
WOHLFSON			
J W	Solano Vacaville	69	342
WOHN			
---	Tuolumne Twp 6	71	529
WOHOTER			
H	Nevada Grass Valley	61	185
WOI			
---	El Dorado Salmon Falls	581047	
---	Yuba Marysville	72	921
WOIGNER			
Christopher	Los Angeles Los Angeles	59	376
WOIL			
David*	Shasta Shasta	66	686
L*	Shasta Horsetown	66	689
WOING			
---	El Dorado Georgetown	58	697
WOJESCIZOWELL			
And P*	San Francisco San Francisco 3	67	12
Aud P*	San Francisco San Francisco 3	67	12
WOK			
---	Calaveras Twp 5	57	233
WOKEE			
John	San Joaquin Stockton	641038	
WOKOMEA			
---*	Fresno Twp 1	59	51
WOKON			
Mr	Plumas Quincy	62	965
Wm*	Plumas Quincy	62	965
WOL			
---	San Francisco San Francisco 4	681173	
WOLAIS			
David	El Dorado Eldorado	58	943
WOLAMAR			
Fred	San Joaquin Stockton	641038	
WOLAMER			
Henry	San Joaquin Stockton	641038	
WOLB			
Hiram S*	Sierra Pine Grove	66	820
WOLBERTO			
---	San Bernardino S Timate	64	707
WOLBRLGEMURTH			
Max*	Napa Clear Lake	61	129
WOLBRLGEMUTH			
Mox*	Napa Clear Lake	61	129
WOLCH			
Cathrine	San Mateo Twp 3	65	80
WOLCHEDIE			
Josephine	San Francisco San Francisco 8	681243	
WOLCHODICE			
Benedict	San Francisco San Francisco 8	681242	
WOLCOB			
Chas	Mariposa Twp 1	60	663
WOLCOM			
William	Sierra Twp 7	66	882
WOLCOT			
B*	El Dorado Coloma	581103	
C P	Tuolumne Twp 2	71	284
Chas	Mariposa Twp 1	60	663
R M*	El Dorado Union	581088	
WOLCOTT			
C P	Tuolumne Twp 2	71	284
J N	Sierra Twp 5	66	938
O J	Placer Michigan	62	832
R	Butte Cascade	56	694
R	Butte Mountain	56	738
Ransome	Alameda Brooklyn	55	172
Russel	Tuolumne Sonora	71	231
S N	Sierra Twp 5	66	938
Sylvanus	Yuba Slate Ro	72	694
W S	Placer Iona Hills	62	886
WOLCOX			
B	El Dorado Coloma	581103	
B M*	El Dorado Union	581088	
B*	El Dorado Coloma	581103	

Name	County Locale	M653 Roll Page
WOLCOX		
R M*	El Dorado Union	581088
WOLCUT		
Chas	Mariposa Twp 1	60 663
WOLD		
R S	Placer Stewart	62 607
Susan F*	Yuba Marysville	72 860
WOLDENBERG		
D	Sacramento Granite	63 242
WOLDRICH		
Chas	Butte Kimshaw	56 582
WOLDRIDGE		
W	Butte Chico	56 551
WOLENBERG		
J	Tuolumne Big Oak	71 146
WOLER		
Geo	El Dorado Salmon Falls	581035
WOLF		
A H	Calaveras Twp 9	57 386
A H	Shasta Shasta	66 663
A*	San Francisco San Francisco 2	67 659
Andrew	San Joaquin Stockton	641030
Auspach	Tuolumne Twp 2	71 334
Auspack	Tuolumne Columbia	71 334
B	San Francisco San Francisco 4	681219
C H	Sacramento Ward 3	63 434
Catherine	Calaveras Twp 5	57 194
Charles	Calaveras Twp 6	57 152
Charles	Calaveras Twp 7	57 37
Charles	Calaveras Twp 8	57 91
Charles W	San Francisco San Francisco 4	681121
Chas	Sonoma Petaluma	69 547
Christian	Amador Twp 5	55 344
Clemence	San Francisco San Francisco 2	67 622
Crosby	San Francisco San Francisco 8	681289
D	San Francisco San Francisco 4	681227
David	San Francisco San Francisco 9	681007
Elizabeth	San Francisco San Francisco 8	681285
Elizabeth	San Francisco San Francisco 1	68 833
Fred	Butte Oregon	56 634
Fred	Sacramento Ward 4	63 531
Frederick	Contra Costa Twp 1	57 505
G	Sutter Yuba	70 771
G L	Butte Kimshaw	56 570
G W	San Joaquin Stockton	641052
Geo	El Dorado Coloma	581103
Geo	Sacramento Ward 1	63 29
Geo	Sacramento Ward 4	63 594
Geo	Santa Clara Gilroy	65 231
Geo	Sonoma Petaluma	69 547
Geo	Trinity Mouth Ca	701010
Geo	Tuolumne Garrote	71 175
George	Solano Benecia	69 299
George	Tuolumne Shawsfla	71 406
H	Butte Hamilton	56 514
H	Butte Oro	56 684
Hans	San Francisco San Francisco 3	67 64
Harris	San Francisco San Francisco 2	67 758
Harry	San Francisco San Francisco 2	67 576
Henry	Calaveras Twp 5	57 252
Henry	El Dorado White Oaks	581029
Hermon	Tuolumne Twp 2	71 343
Hiram S	Sierra Pine Grove	66 820
Hirmon	Tuolumne Columbia	71 343
Hyman	San Francisco San Francisco 2	67 660
Isaac	Yuba Rose Bar	72 819
J	Nevada Eureka	61 370
J	San Francisco San Francisco 1	68 850
Jacob	Santa Clara Gilroy	65 250
Jacob	Sierra St Louis	66 815
Jacob*	Butte Oregon	56 641
James	Tulara Twp 1	71 79
James E	San Francisco San Francisco 8	681256
Jno F	Napa Hot Springs	61 6
John	Calaveras Twp 6	57 149
John	San Joaquin Elkhorn	64 994
John	Sierra St Louis	66 809
John	Sonoma Petaluma	69 573
John	Yolo Putah	72 550
John	Yuba Marysville	72 927
John	Yuba Suida	72 984
John D	Yolo Slate Ra	72 705
Joseph	Sacramento Dry Crk	63 369
Joseph M	Tuolumne Twp 2	71 370
Josephine	Siskiyou Yreka	69 176
L	Siskiyou Scott Ri	69 68
L D	Calaveras Twp 9	57 391
Louis	San Francisco San Francisco 10	334 67
Louis	San Joaquin Stockton	641040
M	San Francisco San Francisco 2	67 731
M*	San Francisco San Francisco 4	681166
Marcus	Tuolumne Columbia	71 356
Margaret	Calaveras Twp 4	57 344

Name	County Locale	M653 Roll Page
WOLF		
Mark	San Francisco San Francisco 10	189 67
Marks	San Francisco San Francisco 10	189 67
Maurice	Sierra Port Win	66 792
Morris	Sierra La Porte	66 783
N	Amador Twp 1	55 493
O T	El Dorado Georgetown	58 757
Peter	Amador Twp 2	55 284
Peter	Napa Napa	61 86
Peter	Tuolumne Twp 1	71 259
Philip	Tuolumne Twp 1	71 206
Phillip	Calaveras Twp 5	57 253
Phillip	El Dorado Kelsey	581135
S	San Francisco San Francisco 5	67 475
S A*	Siskiyou Scott Va	69 59
S J	Siskiyou Scott Va	69 59
Sebastian	San Francisco San Francisco 10	166 67
Simon	Calaveras Twp 6	57 131
Simon	Contra Costa Twp 2	57 564
Stephen De*	Siskiyou Yreka	69 174
Theodore	Santa Cruz Soguel	66 582
Thos	Sacramento Sutter	63 290
Thos	San Francisco San Francisco 10	219 67
W	San Francisco San Francisco 2	67 784
Walserga	Tuolumne Twp 5	71 522
William	Mendocino Calpella	60 814
William	San Francisco San Francisco 9	681085
WOLFAND		
John H	San Francisco San Francisco 4	681145
WOLFE		
Barard	San Francisco San Francisco 2	67 659
Benjamin B	Yuba Marysville	72 924
Christine	Plumas Quincy	621000
Fred	San Francisco San Francisco 1	68 929
George	Sonoma Armally	69 516
J H	Yuba Long Bar	72 755
J H	Yuba Long Bar	72 755
J*	Nevada Nevada	61 318
Jackson	Sierra Eureka	661047
Jas	San Francisco San Francisco 2	67 635
Jno	Sacramento Ward 4	63 496
John	Napa Hot Springs	61 20
John	Sierra Twp 7	66 880
Jos	San Francisco San Francisco 2	67 635
Joseph	Del Norte Crescent	58 671
Joseph	Los Angeles Los Angeles	59 340
Louis	San Diego Temecula	64 785
Maurice	Los Angeles Los Angeles	59 340
Michael	San Mateo Twp 2	65 127
Peter	San Francisco San Francisco 11	111 67
Peter	San Francisco San Francisco 1	68 912
Saml	San Francisco San Francisco 2	67 623
T	Nevada Nevada	61 253
W	San Francisco San Francisco 2	67 756
W	San Francisco San Francisco 1	68 861
Walserga	Tuolumne Chinese	71 522
WOLFF		
Charles	San Francisco San Francisco 7	681355
Fred	El Dorado Salmon Falls	581055
George	Yuba Marysville	72 878
Joseph	Yuba Marysville	72 936
Joseph	Yuba Marysville	72 937
S W	Nevada Nevada	61 254
Segismund	Yuba Marysville	72 873
Sigismund	Yuba Marysville	72 873
U	El Dorado Placerville	58 839
William	Siskiyou Yreka	69 145
WOLFFE		
Matilda	San Bernardino San Bernadino	64 623
WOLFINDER		
Margaret	San Francisco San Francisco 7	681395
WOLFINGER		
P	Napa Napa	61 110
WOLFLEN		
A F	San Francisco San Francisco 2	67 637
WOLFLENN		
A F	San Francisco San Francisco 2	67 637
WOLFLING		
John	Tuolumne Sonora	71 212
WOLFNAM		
K	San Francisco San Francisco 3	67 78
WOLFO		
J*	Nevada Nevada	61 318
WOLFOCK		
Rebecca*	Sacramento Ward 1	63 101
WOLFOHUNUR		
Chas*	Butte Kimshaw	56 578
WOLFORD		
G W	Siskiyou Callahan	69 11
Geo	Klamath S Fork	59 198
George	Sierra Downieville	661019

Name	County Locale	M653 Roll Page
WOLFORD		
J W	Siskiyou Callahan	69 11
WOLFORK		
Rebecca*	Sacramento Ward 1	63 101
WOLFRAM		
J	San Francisco San Francisco 5	67 526
WOLFRIDES		
D	Sonoma Bodega	69 534
WOLFRIDGE		
Wm*	Sierra Twp 5	66 926
WOLFROT		
Hary	Alameda Brooklyn	55 197
WOLFS		
J*	Nevada Nevada	61 318
WOLFSBERG		
Nicholas*	Placer Michigan	62 836
Y	San Francisco San Francisco 3	67 73
WOLFSHIMER		
F	Butte Chico	56 568
WOLFSHIMIER		
Chas*	Butte Kimshaw	56 578
WOLFSHINNER		
Chas*	Butte Kimshaw	56 578
WOLFSKILL		
John R	Solano Vacaville	69 360
Mathew	Solano Vacaville	69 360
Milton	Solano Vacaville	69 359
William	Los Angeles Los Angeles	59 401
WOLFSON		
J	San Francisco San Francisco 5	67 501
WOLFSTEIN		
Henry	Calaveras Twp 5	57 190
WOLFSTIEN		
John	Calaveras Twp 9	57 402
WOLFSTUN		
John	Calaveras Twp 9	57 402
WOLFTEIN		
Henry*	Calaveras Twp 5	57 190
WOLGAMOT		
David	Yolo Cache Crk	72 593
J	Yolo Cache Crk	72 593
Jno	Klamath S Fork	59 197
WOLGAMUTH		
Henry	Trinity East For	701027
WOLGUMOT		
David	Yolo Cache	72 593
WOLGWNOT		
J	Yolo Cache	72 593
WOLINA		
C	El Dorado Placerville	58 860
WOLKER		
Robt	El Dorado Kelsey	581129
WOLKINS		
Wm	Sierra Twp 5	66 928
WOLLER		
Hans*	Sacramento Mississipi	63 188
WOLLERLGEMURT		
Mox*	Napa Clear Lake	61 129
WOLLERLGEMUTH		
Mox*	Napa Clear Lake	61 129
WOLLERLGERNURT		
Mox*	Napa Clear Lake	61 129
WOLLESON		
James P	Mariposa Coulterville	60 701
WOLLET		
Chas	Sacramento Ward 3	63 455
WOLLEY		
Henry	Sacramento Granite	63 244
WOLLIME		
D H	San Francisco San Francisco 3	67 50
WOLLIVER		
P C	Butte Kimshaw	56 571
WOLLOCK		
Rebecca*	Sacramento Ward 1	63 101
WOLLORK		
Rebecca*	Sacramento Ward 1	63 101
WOLNEY		
Joseph	Placer Forest H	62 800
WOLOWER		
John	Marin Tomales	60 722
WOLPE		
John	Sierra Twp 7	66 880
WOLRIDGE		
Saml	Butte Chico	56 551
WOLRINE		
George*	Yuba Rose Bar	72 820
WOLSBURG		
John	San Francisco San Francisco 1	68 900
WOLSCH		
Deaderick	San Francisco San Francisco 8	681242
WOLSET		
B	Nevada Eureka	61 377
WOLSEY		
J	El Dorado Placerville	58 866
J L	Sonoma Armally	69 508
T	El Dorado Placerville	58 819

California 1860 Census Index

Name	County Locale	M653 Roll	Page
WOLSEY			
William	San Joaquin Douglass	64	919
WOLSH			
Antonio*	Calaveras Twp 9	57	387
Thomas	Calaveras Twp 7	57	2
WOLSINGSON			
W	Sierra Twp 7	66	884
WOLSKEY			
Chris	Trinity Mouth Ca	70	1013
WOLSKY			
Chris	Trinity Mouth Ca	70	1013
WOLSON			
John	Yuba Parks Ba	72	774
WOLSTEIN			
F	Trinity Honest B	70	1043
WOLSTER			
Robt	Butte Bidwell	56	729
WOLTEE			
Josefa	Monterey Monterey	60	957
WOLTER			
Josefa	Monterey Monterey	60	957
WOLTERS			
John	San Francisco San Francisco 10		300
			67
WOLTZ			
Frederick	Yuba Marysville	72	901
WOLVERTON			
Alfred	Humbolt Eel Rvr	59	147
M	Sonoma Salt Point	69	690
WOLVINE			
George*	Yuba Rose Bar	72	820
WOLWORDGONNERY			
George*	Yuba Marysville	72	915
WOLWORTH			
Morgan	Placer Forest H	62	806
S L	Nevada Grass Valley	61	162
WOM			
---	Butte Cascade	56	699
---	Nevada Bridgeport	61	459
---	Placer Virginia	62	671
---*	El Dorado Salmon Falls	58	1067
Ah	Butte Cascade	56	699
WOMACK			
C S	Calaveras Twp 9	57	416
WOMAN			
China*	Siskiyou Yreka	69	157
WOMAS			
Cheeko	San Mateo Twp 3	65	99
WOMBA			
---	Plumas Quincy	62	926
WOMBACH			
M	Trinity Mouth Ca	70	1013
WOMBACK			
M	Trinity Mouth Ca	70	1013
WOMBLE			
G N	Tuolumne Twp 2	71	327
G W	Tuolumne Columbia	71	327
J R	Sacramento Ward 1	63	78
WOMEN			
Nichols	San Joaquin Elkhorn	64	970
WOMMACK			
P G	Nevada Rough &	61	402
WOMSER			
M	Alameda Brooklyn	55	122
WON			
---	Amador Twp 2	55	293
---	Amador Twp 5	55	331
---	Amador Twp 6	55	447
---	Calaveras Twp 6	57	168
---	Calaveras Twp 5	57	179
---	Calaveras Twp 5	57	192
---	Calaveras Twp 5	57	218
---	Calaveras Twp 5	57	222
---	Calaveras Twp 5	57	236
---	Calaveras Twp 5	57	250
---	Calaveras Twp 5	57	255
---	Calaveras Twp 10	57	269
---	Calaveras Twp 10	57	271
---	Calaveras Twp 10	57	290
---	Calaveras Twp 4	57	309
---	Del Norte Happy Ca	58	667
---	El Dorado Salmon Falls	58	1043
---	El Dorado Salmon Falls	58	1053
---	El Dorado Salmon Falls	58	1061
---	El Dorado Salmon Falls	58	1065
---	El Dorado Salmon Falls	58	1066
---	El Dorado Coloma	58	1078
---	El Dorado Coloma	58	1083
---	El Dorado Union	58	1091
---	El Dorado Coloma	58	1122
---	El Dorado Kelsey	58	1133
---	El Dorado Mountain	58	1189
---	El Dorado Georgetown	58	680
---	El Dorado Greenwood	58	728
---	El Dorado Big Bar	58	737
---	El Dorado Diamond	58	789

Name	County Locale	M653 Roll	Page
WON			
---	El Dorado Eldorado	58	939
---	El Dorado Mud Springs	58	955
---	El Dorado Mud Springs	58	964
---	El Dorado Mud Springs	58	973
---	Fresno Twp 2	59	17
---	Mariposa Twp 1	60	673
---	Nevada Bridgeport	61	461
---	Placer Auburn	62	581
---	Placer Iona Hills	62	889
---	Sacramento Granite	63	231
---	San Francisco San Francisco 4		681174
---	San Francisco San Francisco 4		681182
---	San Francisco San Francisco 4		681208
---	San Francisco San Francisco 11		146
			67
---	San Francisco San Francisco 3	67	7
---	Sierra Twp 5	66	945
---	Tuolumne Chinese	71	521
---	Yuba Fosters	72	843
---	Yuba Marysville	72	925
---*	Calaveras Twp 5	57	250
---*	Yuba Fosters	72	843
Ah	Sacramento Cosumnes	63	391
Chee*	San Francisco San Francisco 4		681173
Chow	Nevada Washington	61	342
Chu	San Francisco San Francisco 4		681173
Chu	San Francisco San Francisco 4		681185
Chu*	San Francisco San Francisco 4		681173
Fong	Tehama Red Bluff	70	934
How	El Dorado Diamond	58	784
Kee	San Francisco San Francisco 4		681194
Ku	San Francisco San Francisco 4		681194
Long	Yuba Long Bar	72	759
Lung	San Francisco San Francisco 4		681181
Put	San Francisco San Francisco 4		681201
Win	Sierra Downieville	66	986
WONA			
---	El Dorado Placerville	58	919
WONANS			
Jno C	San Francisco San Francisco 10		222
			67
Steph J*	Sacramento Ward 1	63	14
WOND			
Hugh*	El Dorado Georgetown	58	705
WONDER			
George	Marin San Rafael	60	767
Gerrge	Marin San Rafael	60	767
Louisa	Sacramento Granite	63	223
WONDERLY			
A	El Dorado Placerville	58	883
WONE			
---	El Dorado White Oaks	58	1033
---	El Dorado Salmon Falls	58	1054
---	El Dorado Kelsey	58	1143
---	El Dorado Diamond	58	787
---	San Francisco San Francisco 4		681186
Cen	Shasta Horsetown	66	701
WONELL			
Jno	Nevada Nevada	61	266
WONER			
Abinia	San Francisco San Francisco 10		289
			67
WONES			
John	Mariposa Coulterville	60	703
WONG CHOY			
---	Sacramento Ward 1	63	69
WONG YON CONG			
---	San Francisco San Francisco 2	67	801
WONG			
---	Alameda Oakland	55	23
---	Amador Twp 6	55	427
---	Amador Twp 6	55	447
---	Butte Oregon	56	643
---	Calaveras Twp 8	57	100
---	Calaveras Twp 8	57	102
---	Calaveras Twp 8	57	109
---	Calaveras Twp 8	57	49
---	Calaveras Twp 8	57	65
---	Calaveras Twp 8	57	83
---	Calaveras Twp 8	57	94
---	Del Norte Crescent	58	633
---	El Dorado White Oaks	58	1023
---	El Dorado Salmon Falls	58	1041
---	El Dorado Salmon Falls	58	1047
---	El Dorado Salmon Falls	58	1063
---	El Dorado Coloma	58	1102
---	El Dorado Casumnes	58	1160
---	El Dorado Georgetown	58	700
---	El Dorado Georgetown	58	701
---	El Dorado Georgetown	58	708
---	El Dorado Big Bar	58	733
---	El Dorado Diamond	58	806
---	El Dorado Placerville	58	830
---	El Dorado Placerville	58	842
---	El Dorado Placerville	58	931

Name	County Locale	M653 Roll	Page
WONG			
---	El Dorado Eldorado	58	939
---	El Dorado Eldorado	58	946
---	El Dorado Mud Springs	58	975
---	Mariposa Twp 1	60	658
---	Mariposa Twp 1	60	673
---	Nevada Bridgeport	61	463
---	Nevada Bridgeport	61	472
---	Nevada Bridgeport	61	492
---	Nevada Bloomfield	61	513
---	Placer Rattle Snake	62	629
---	Placer Rattle Snake	62	637
---	Placer Folsom	62	648
---	Placer Folsom	62	649
---	Placer Virginia	62	663
---	Placer Virginia	62	671
---	Placer Virginia	62	681
---	Placer Virginia	62	682
---	Placer Illinois	62	704
---	Placer Dutch Fl	62	737
---	Placer Illinois	62	738
---	Placer Illinois	62	739
---	Placer Illinois	62	748
---	Placer Illinois	62	749
---	Placer Forest H	62	773
---	Sacramento Cosumnes	63	395
---	Sacramento Ward 3	63	493
---	Sacramento Ward 1	63	72
---	San Francisco San Francisco 9		681093
---	San Francisco San Francisco 9		681096
---	San Francisco San Francisco 4		681178
---	San Francisco San Francisco 4		681181
---	San Francisco San Francisco 4		681185
---	San Francisco San Francisco 4		681187
---	San Francisco San Francisco 4		681188
---	San Francisco San Francisco 4		681193
---	San Francisco San Francisco 4		681194
---	San Francisco San Francisco 4		681195
---	San Francisco San Francisco 4		681196
---	San Francisco San Francisco 4		681198
---	San Francisco San Francisco 4		681199
---	San Francisco San Francisco 4		681202
---	San Francisco San Francisco 4		681208
---	San Francisco San Francisco 4		681210
---	San Francisco San Francisco 4		681211
---	San Francisco San Francisco 5	67	507
---	San Francisco San Francisco 5	67	508
---	Shasta French G	66	712
---	Siskiyou Scott Va	69	46
---	Trinity Honest B	70	1043
---	Trinity Lewiston	70	966
---	Tuolumne Sonora	71	478
---	Tuolumne Twp 5	71	510
---	Tuolumne Twp 6	71	533
---	Tuolumne Twp 6	71	541
---	Yuba Long Bar	72	752
---	Yuba Fosters	72	827
---	Yuba Fosters	72	842
---	Yuba Marysville	72	895
---	Yuba Marysville	72	896
---*	Butte Oregon	56	613
---*	Mariposa Twp 1	60	667
---*	Sacramento Ward 1	63	72
---*	Shasta Shasta	66	670
---*	Yuba Fosters	72	842
Ah	Butte Oregon	56	643
Ah	Sacramento Ward 1	63	152
Ah	Sacramento Mississipi	63	188
Ching	Nevada Bridgeport	61	459
Ching	Nevada Bloomfield	61	521
Cho	San Francisco San Francisco 5	67	1207
Chow	Placer Dutch Fl	62	737
Chow*	Mariposa Twp 1	60	626
Choy	Sacramento Ward 1	63	69
Chung	San Francisco San Francisco 4		681199
Fa	San Francisco San Francisco 4		681203
Fee	San Francisco San Francisco 10		356
			67
Feng	San Francisco San Francisco 5	67	509
Fol	San Francisco San Francisco 5	67	509
Fong	San Francisco San Francisco 4		681183
Fong	San Francisco San Francisco 4		681203
Fook	San Francisco San Francisco 4		681203
Fook	San Francisco San Francisco 5	67	1207
Foy	El Dorado Eldorado	58	948
Fuk	San Francisco San Francisco 4		681189
Fung	San Francisco San Francisco 4		681102
Fung	San Francisco San Francisco 5	67	507
Fuo	San Francisco San Francisco 4		681184
Hee	San Francisco San Francisco 4		681185
Hei	San Francisco San Francisco 4		681185
Hing	San Francisco San Francisco 4		681184
Hing	San Francisco San Francisco 4		681188
Hing	San Francisco San Francisco 4		681201
Kou	San Francisco San Francisco 4		681181

Name	County Locale	M653 Roll	Page
WONG			
Kung	San Francisco San Francisco 4	68	1182
Lee	El Dorado Georgetown	58	756
Lee	San Francisco San Francisco 4	68	1203
Lee	San Francisco San Francisco 5	67	1207
Long	San Francisco San Francisco 4	68	1197
Long	San Francisco San Francisco 5	67	1207
Lou	San Francisco San Francisco 11	67	145
Lu	Sacramento Natonia	63	286
Lu	San Francisco San Francisco 4	68	1196
Lu	San Francisco San Francisco 4	68	1203
Lu	San Francisco San Francisco 5	67	1207
Mae	Placer Illinois	62	704
Ming	San Francisco San Francisco 6	67	466
Mong	San Francisco San Francisco 1	68	926
Mow	San Francisco San Francisco 10	67	355
Moy	San Francisco San Francisco 4	68	1210
Ning	San Francisco San Francisco 1	68	925
Pah	Yuba Long Bar	72	757
Quong	San Francisco San Francisco 4	68	1203
Quoy	San Francisco San Francisco 4	68	1181
Rung	San Francisco San Francisco 4	68	1182
S	San Francisco San Francisco 4	68	1210
Sam	El Dorado Placerville	58	843
Se	San Francisco San Francisco 4	68	1201
See	San Francisco San Francisco 4	68	1196
See	San Francisco San Francisco 4	68	1203
See	San Francisco San Francisco 4	68	1210
Sen	San Francisco San Francisco 4	68	1203
Seong	San Francisco San Francisco 5	67	508
Shing	San Francisco San Francisco 10	67	355
Si	San Francisco San Francisco 4	68	1201
Song	San Francisco San Francisco 4	68	1202
Song	San Francisco San Francisco 1	68	925
Tane	El Dorado Mud Springs	58	958
Thing	San Francisco San Francisco 4	68	1192
Tong	Sacramento Cosummes	63	384
Tue	Placer Auburn	62	577
Tuo	San Francisco San Francisco 4	68	1184
Waf*	San Francisco San Francisco 9	68	1093
Wo	San Francisco San Francisco 4	68	1181
Wof*	San Francisco San Francisco 9	68	1093
Wok	San Francisco San Francisco 4	68	1204
Yo	San Francisco San Francisco 4	68	1179
Yon Cong	San Francisco San Francisco 2	67	801
WONGANS			
Phillip G*	San Francisco San Francisco 9	68	946
WONGLON			
---*	Shasta Shasta	66	670
Fred	Placer Virginia	62	661
WONGLOU			
---*	Shasta Shasta	66	670
WONILL			
Jno	Nevada Nevada	61	266
WONJLOW			
---	Shasta Shasta	66	670
WONK			
---	Mariposa Coulterville	60	683
WONNER			
P*	Nevada Washington	61	331
WONNES			
P*	Nevada Washington	61	331
WONNG			
---	Butte Ophir	56	787
WONNWOOD			
H C	Nevada Bridgeport	61	488
WONSEY			
Henry	Nevada Bridgeport	61	473
WONTHEIM			
B	Siskiyou Scott Va	69	51
WONTOUR			
Anne M*	San Francisco San Francisco 10	67	176
WONY			
---	Calaveras Twp 4	57	305
WOO CONG			
---	San Joaquin Stockton	64	1087
WOO LEE			
---	San Francisco San Francisco 8	68	1268
WOO			
---	Calaveras Twp 6	57	149
---	Calaveras Twp 10	57	291
---	Calaveras Twp 8	57	68
---	Calaveras Twp 8	57	74
---	El Dorado White Oaks	58	1021
---	El Dorado White Oaks	58	1025
---	El Dorado Kelsey	58	1128
---	El Dorado Casumnes	58	1160
---	El Dorado Placerville	58	823
---	El Dorado Mud Springs	58	955
---	Fresno Twp 1	59	28
---	Fresno Twp 2	59	4
---	San Francisco San Francisco 4	68	1177
---	San Francisco San Francisco 4	68	1180
---	San Francisco San Francisco 4	68	1197
---	San Joaquin Stockton	64	1037
---	Siskiyou Scott Va	69	32
---	Tuolumne Don Pedro	71	536
---	Yuba Fosters	72	843
---	Yuba Marysville	72	921
---*	Yuba Fosters	72	843
Chung	Yuba Long Bar	72	756
Ee	Yuba Long Bar	72	765
Hii	San Francisco San Francisco 4	68	1193
Hu	San Francisco San Francisco 4	68	1193
Lee	San Francisco San Francisco 8	68	1268
Lee	San Francisco San Francisco 11	67	160
Lon	San Joaquin Stockton	64	1053
Long	San Joaquin Stockton	64	1039
Nong	Yuba Long Bar	72	768
Nony	Yuba Long Bar	72	768
Ong	Yuba Long Bar	72	766
Ony	Yuba Long Bar	72	766
WOOA			
---	El Dorado Salmon Falls	58	1064
---	El Dorado Coloma	58	1085
---	El Dorado Casumnes	58	1160
---	El Dorado Mountain	58	1188
WOOBERY			
Silas	Yolo Putah	72	549
WOOD CHUCK			
---	Tulara Twp 2	71	32
WOOD			
---	Mariposa Coulterville	60	674
---	Monterey San Juan	60	1007
---	Yuba Marysville	72	925
A	Nevada Eureka	61	371
A	San Francisco San Francisco 5	67	501
A	San Joaquin Stockton	64	1047
A	Sierra Downieville	66	989
A	Yolo Cache Crk	72	617
A A	Nevada Grass Valley	61	169
A B	Amador Twp 1	55	460
A C	Santa Clara Gilroy	65	236
A G	San Francisco San Francisco 6	67	412
A N	El Dorado Greenwood	58	726
A P	Amador Twp 6	55	433
A W	El Dorado Mud Springs	58	968
Aaron	San Joaquin Douglass	64	921
Aaron	Yuba Marysville	72	866
Abel	Sacramento Ward 4	63	584
Albert	Nevada Eureka	61	394
Alen	Tehama Tehama	70	939
Alerck	Sacramento Georgian	63	343
Alfred	Santa Clara Gilroy	65	241
Alice	Sacramento Ward 3	63	454
Allen	Plumas Quincy	62	942
Allen J	Plumas Meadow Valley	62	929
Alx	Nevada Eureka	61	362
Amos P	San Francisco San Francisco 7	68	1443
Amos P	San Francisco San Francisco 10	67	176
Andrew	San Francisco San Francisco 4	68	1166
Andrew	San Joaquin Elkhorn	64	954
Andrew A	Nevada Bloomfield	61	529
Andrew J	Plumas Meadow Valley	62	900
Archibald	Yuba Marysville	72	905
Archibold*	Yuba Marysville	72	905
Augustus	Shasta Millvill	66	742
B	El Dorado Kelsey	58	1148
Benj	Nevada Bridgeport	61	450
Benj	Nevada Bridgeport	61	472
Benjamin	Del Norte Crescent	58	624
Benjamin	Tulara Keeneysburg	71	47
Bridget	San Francisco San Francisco 2	67	676
C	Sacramento Ward 1	63	31
C	Trinity Lewiston	70	963
C L	San Francisco San Francisco 5	67	533
Charles	Calaveras Twp 7	57	9
Charles	San Francisco San Francisco 7	68	1349
Charles	San Francisco San Francisco 7	68	1420
Charles	San Francisco San Francisco 3	67	68
Charles	San Joaquin Tulare	64	869
Charles	Shasta Millvill	66	727
Charles	Yuba New York	72	733
Charles	Yuba Marysville	72	854
Charles	Yuba Marysville	72	859
Charles S	San Francisco San Francisco 7	68	1349
Charles S	Yuba Bear Rvr	72	1001
Charless	Yuba New York	72	733
Charley	Sacramento Georgian	63	343
Charley	Yuba New York	72	735
Chas W	Mendocino Ukiah	60	803
Clement L*	Alameda Murray	55	220
Clement S*	Alameda Murray	55	220
Clemet	Alameda Oakland	55	26
D	Tehama Tehama	70	947
D J	Nevada Bridgeport	61	439
Daniel	Amador Twp 7	55	420
Danl	Merced Twp 2	60	923
Danl W	San Francisco San Francisco 9	68	1048
E A	Sierra Twp 7	66	869
E D	Tehama Tehama	70	944
E H	Tuolumne Twp 3	71	425
E W	San Francisco San Francisco 5	67	544
Ebenzer	San Joaquin Castoria	64	911
Eduard*	San Francisco San Francisco 1	68	922
Edward*	San Francisco San Francisco 1	68	922
Edwd P	San Francisco San Francisco 1	68	861
Eisha B	Butte Oregon	56	621
Elisha	Butte Oregon	56	612
Elisha B	Butte Oregon	56	621
Ellen	Sonoma Russian	69	443
Emma	El Dorado Greenwood	58	709
Enis P	San Joaquin Stockton	64	1064
Epraim	Marin Point Re	60	729
Ezra R	San Francisco San Francisco 2	67	589
F	Siskiyou Callahan	69	2
F	Trinity New Rvr	70	1030
F F Ellen*	Nevada Red Dog	61	542
F L	Sierra Downieville	66	954
F L*	Siskiyou Scott Ri	69	77
F R*	Sacramento Franklin	63	334
Fanny	San Francisco San Francisco 1	68	817
Francis	Marin San Rafael	60	769
Francis	Tuolumne Twp 2	71	401
Frank	Alameda Washington	55	171
Frank	Nevada Bridgeport	61	443
Franklin	Tuolumne Twp 5	71	499
G H	Amador Twp 4	55	254
G W	Sutter Yuba	70	764
G W	Trinity Lewiston	70	964
Gabriel	Humbolt Eureka	59	172
Geo	Butte Chico	56	549
Geo	Nevada Eureka	61	371
Geo	San Francisco San Francisco 10	67	304
Geo A	Tuolumne Twp 1	71	244
Geo W	Siskiyou Scott Ri	69	61
George	Santa Clara Gilroy	65	245
George	Santa Clara San Jose	65	378
George	Shasta Shasta	66	760
George	Siskiyou Yreka	69	140
George L	Humbolt Eel Rvr	59	149
George M	San Francisco San Francisco 8	68	1298
George W	Yuba Marysville	72	879
George W	Yuba Marysville	72	944
H	El Dorado Greenwood	58	709
H B	Nevada Bloomfield	61	507
H F	Sierra Downieville	66	1010
H H	El Dorado Cold Spring	58	1099
H W	Nevada Rough &	61	417
Hamilton J	Humbolt Eureka	59	171
Harriet	San Francisco San Francisco 10	67	282
Harris	San Francisco San Francisco 10	67	220
Harrison	Amador Twp 4	55	239
Harry	San Francisco San Francisco 2	67	705
Has H	Napa Napa	61	112
Henry	Butte Oregon	56	612
Henry	Napa Napa	61	78
Henry	Nevada Rough &	61	419
Henry	San Francisco San Francisco 9	68	1061
Henry	San Francisco San Francisco 7	68	1351
Henry	San Joaquin Castoria	64	878
Henry	Yuba Marysville	72	880
I C	Trinity Weaverville	70	1063
Ira H	Fresno Twp 3	59	13
Ira J	Tuolumne Twp 1	71	191
Isaiah H	Sonoma Mendocino	69	450
J	Butte Cascade	56	695
J	Nevada Grass Valley	61	165
J	Nevada Eureka	61	394
J	Sacramento Granite	63	233
J	San Francisco San Francisco 1	68	911
J A	Siskiyou Cottonwoood	69	108
J C	Merced Twp 1	60	899
J C	Tehama Antelope	70	887
J D	Sonoma Russian	69	443
J H	Tehama Antelope	70	885
J Hop	Colusa Colusi	57	422
J J	Nevada Grass Valley	61	202
J J	Stanislaus Buena Village	70	724
J K	San Francisco San Francisco 9	68	1081
J P	Siskiyou Scott Va	69	29
J S	El Dorado Mountain	58	1185
J W	Tuolumne Twp 4	71	174
Jabe	Yolo Merritt	72	580
James	Colusa Monroeville	57	448
James	Contra Costa Twp 1	57	522
James	Los Angeles San Jose	59	281

Name	County Locale	M653 RollPage
WOOD		
James	Monterey Alisal	601035
James	Nevada Rough &	61 398
James	Nevada Rough &	61 417
James	San Francisco San Francisco 3	67 70
James	San Joaquin Elkhorn	64 971
James	San Mateo Twp 2	65 127
James	San Mateo Twp 1	65 53
James	Shasta Shasta	66 681
James	Sierra Twp 7	66 899
James	Siskiyou Callahan	69 20
James	Sonoma Washington	69 671
James J	Yuba Marysville	72 939
James W	Nevada Bridgeport	61 443
Jane	Shasta Millvill	66 742
Jas	Butte Cascade	56 691
Jas	Butte Cascade	56 694
Jas	San Francisco San Francisco 1	68 905
Jas H	Napa Napa	61 112
Jed	Sierra Downieville	66 978
Jennette	San Francisco San Francisco 2	67 637
Jeremiah	Nevada Bloomfield	61 509
Jesse	Siskiyou Scott Va	69 33
Jno	Butte Chico	56 548
Jno	Sacramento Ward 1	63 122
Jno	Sacramento Lee	63 217
Jno B	Sonoma Petaluma	69 607
Jobe	Yolo Merritt	72 580
Joel	Sierra Downieville	66 978
Joel	Yolo Cottonwoood	72 656
John	Alameda Brooklyn	55 129
John	El Dorado Georgetown	58 752
John	El Dorado Mud Springs	58 996
John	Humbolt Mattole	59 128
John	Marin Tomales	60 726
John	Sacramento San Joaquin	63 348
John	San Bernardino San Salvador	64 654
John	San Francisco San Francisco 3	67 50
John	San Francisco San Francisco 2	67 715
John	San Francisco San Francisco 3	67 81
John	San Joaquin Stockton	641085
John	San Mateo Twp 1	65 66
John	Sonoma Santa Rosa	69 391
John	Sonoma Santa Rosa	69 411
John	Sonoma Mendocino	69 450
John	Sonoma Petaluma	69 604
John	Sonoma Salt Point	69 693
John	Trinity New Rvr	701031
John	Yuba New York	72 737
John	Yuba Rose Bar	72 814
John	Yuba Marysville	72 943
John B	Shasta Shasta	66 680
John D	San Joaquin Stockton	641064
John F	Stanislaus Emory	70 753
John O	Butte Ophir	56 752
John S	Solano Benecia	69 299
John W	Siskiyou Yreka	69 193
Jonathan	Sierra Downieville	66 964
Jos	San Francisco San Francisco 6	67 412
Jos H	Sacramento Ward 4	63 515
Joseph	El Dorado Mud Springs	58 966
Joseph	Shasta Horsetown	66 703
Joseph	Sonoma Bodega	69 537
Joseph	Yuba Foster B	72 825
Josepine A *	Placer Auburn	62 564
Josipine A *	Placer Auburn	62 564
Josshua *	Placer Auburn	62 596
Jozhua *	Placer Auburn	62 596
L	Shasta Horsetown	66 705
L H	El Dorado Kelsey	581152
L P	Marin Bolinas	60 732
Lewis K	Humbolt Union	59 187
M C	Sacramento Lee	63 217
Mary	Sacramento Ward 4	63 501
Mary	San Francisco San Francisco 9	681105
Mary A	Sacramento Ward 3	63 454
Mary C	Trinity New Rvr	701031
Michael	Nevada Bridgeport	61 495
Mickey	San Joaquin Elliott	641102
N B *	Sonoma Petaluma	69 602
N C	San Mateo Twp 1	65 66
N G	Mariposa Coulterville	60 675
N T *	Mariposa Coulterville	60 675
N *	Calaveras Twp 8	57 95
Oliver	Yuba Marysville	72 877
Orange G	Humbolt Eureka	59 170
Orlo	Alameda Brooklyn	55 137
Orlo B	Alameda Brooklyn	55 117
P P	Del Norte Crescent	58 640
Peter	Plumas Quincy	621001
Plummer P	San Francisco San Francisco 1	68 847
R H	San Francisco San Mateo Twp 2	65 112
Rich	Sacramento Ward 4	63 504
Richard	Marin Cortemad	60 792
Robt	El Dorado Union	581091

Name	County Locale	M653 RollPage
WOOD		
Roxwell J	Contra Costa Twp 3	57 585
S	Nevada Nevada	61 297
S A	San Francisco San Francisco 6	67 451
S Austin	San Francisco San Francisco 7	681361
S D	Alameda Brooklyn	55 189
S D	Sierra Forest C	66 909
S H	Butte Ophir	56 797
S N *	San Joaquin O'Neal	641001
S W	Tuolumne Twp 2	71 400
Saml	San Francisco San Francisco 10	291
		67
Saml S	Sacramento Alabama	63 411
Saml T	Napa Yount	61 53
Samuel	Nevada Nevada	61 291
Samuel	Sierra La Porte	66 778
Samuel	Sonoma Mendocino	69 447
Samuel	Tuolumne Montezuma	71 508
Samuel W	Humbolt Eel Rvr	59 144
Sarah	Nevada Bridgeport	61 483
Sarah	San Francisco San Francisco 2	67 623
Sarah C	San Francisco San Francisco 2	67 607
Silas	Placer Virginia	62 661
Silus	San Mateo Twp 3	65 109
Solomon	Sierra Downieville	66 964
Stehen	Nevada Bridgeport	61 445
Stephen	Nevada Bridgeport	61 445
T M	Nevada Grass Valley	61 179
T P	Marin Bolinas	60 732
T R *	Sacramento Franklin	63 334
Thadius	San Francisco San Francisco 2	67 608
Theodore S	Yuba Marysville	72 859
Thomas	Placer Auburn	62 569
Thomas G	San Joaquin Stockton	641009
U B	Sonoma Petaluma	69 602
W	Santa Clara San Jose	65 288
W B	Merced Twp 1	60 910
W B	Shasta Horsetown	66 703
W B	Yolo Fremont	72 605
W C	Yolo Putah	72 550
W E	Shasta Shasta	66 679
W G	Mariposa Coulterville	60 675
W H	San Francisco San Francisco 10	215
		67
W H *	Siskiyou Scott Ri	69 68
W T	Calaveras Twp 9	57 397
W W	Nevada Rough &	61 401
Warner	Tehama Antelope	70 893
Wesley	Sonoma Santa Rosa	69 408
William	Calaveras Twp 5	57 141
William	Contra Costa Twp 1	57 522
William	El Dorado Kelsey	581127
William	San Mateo Twp 1	65 66
William	Sierra La Porte	66 787
William	Siskiyou Klamath	69 80
William	Tuolumne Sonora	71 186
William	Yolo Washington	72 561
William	Yuba Marysville	72 910
William	Yuba Marysville	72 914
William A	San Francisco San Francisco 8	681308
William *	Nevada Red Dog	61 550
Wm	Colusa Spring Valley	57 435
Wm	Humbolt Union	59 192
Wm	San Francisco San Francisco 2	67 763
Wm	San Francisco San Francisco 2	67 763
Wm	Solano Suisan	69 221
Wm	Tehama Antelope	70 890
Wm	Tuolumne Twp 4	71 157
Wm B	San Francisco San Francisco 10	195
		67
Wm F	Solano Benecia	69 299
Wm G	San Francisco San Francisco 12	387
		67
Wm W	Sacramento Granite	63 254
Wm W	Sierra Morristown	661051
Y T	San Mateo Twp 1	65 66
WOODALL		
G C	Shasta Millvill	66 746
J	Butte Hamilton	56 518
William	Shasta Millvill	66 746
Wm	Yuba Long Bar	72 741
WOODAN		
Geo	El Dorado Mud Springs	58 996
WOODANELL		
T	El Dorado White Oaks	581032
WOODARD		
---	Monterey S Antoni	60 967
A	El Dorado Kelsey	581157
Abel G	San Francisco San Francisco 10	258
		67
D B	Yolo Cache	72 592
Ezra	Solano Vacaville	69 359
Frances	Sierra Twp 7	66 875
G W	Yolo Cache Crk	72 589
J A	Sierra Twp 5	66 921
J B	Yolo Cache Crk	72 592

Name	County Locale	M653 RollPage
WOODARD		
J E	Nevada Bloomfield	61 518
Jas	Napa Clear Lake	61 134
Jno	Sonoma Sonoma	69 656
John	Tuolumne Twp 3	71 449
Joseph	Marin Bolinas	60 727
Newton	Yolo Washington	72 565
Nuton	Yolo Washington	72 565
Untmown *	Monterey S Antoni	60 967
W	Yolo Washington	72 566
W	Yolo Cache Crk	72 589
W R	San Francisco San Francisco 5	67 511
William	El Dorado White Oaks	581005
Witmown *	Monterey S Antoni	60 967
WOODBECK		
Norman	Sacramento San Joaquin	63 352
WOODBERG		
P *	Nevada Grass Valley	61 180
WOODBERRY		
G W	Tuolumne Twp 4	71 176
Geo	Santa Clara San Jose	65 352
J	Trinity Weaverville	701056
R F	Calaveras Twp 7	57 16
Wm H	Del Norte Crescent	58 623
WOODBERY		
P *	Nevada Grass Valley	61 180
WOODBRIDGE		
Albert S	San Joaquin Stockton	641010
Mary E	Solano Benecia	69 313
S Jr	Solano Benecia	69 300
W	Solano Vacaville	69 323
WOODBUM		
John *	Amador Twp 2	55 316
WOODBURG		
Jno	Sonoma Sonoma	69 645
WOODBURN		
Aurelius	Placer Yankee J	62 761
J B	El Dorado Indian D	581157
J F	Colusa Butte Crk	57 467
James	Amador Twp 3	55 369
John	Amador Twp 2	55 316
S	Tehama Lassen	70 864
William	Sierra Poker Flats	66 837
WOODBURRY		
George	Calaveras Twp 6	57 157
WOODBURY		
Calvin	San Francisco San Francisco 12	374
		67
Chas	Santa Clara San Jose	65 383
George	Calaveras Twp 6	57 157
J M	El Dorado Coloma	581080
Jno	Sonoma Sonoma	69 645
John C	Tuolumne Shawsfla	71 389
N	El Dorado Salmon Falls	581044
P	El Dorado Placerville	58 852
P *	Nevada Grass Valley	61 180
R R	El Dorado White Oaks	581018
Thomas	San Francisco San Francisco 3	67 57
WOODCOCK		
G	El Dorado Georgetown	58 754
Geo	Placer Rattle Snake	62 638
Hartwell	Sierra Downieville	661020
Joseph	Calaveras Twp 6	57 163
Joseph	Placer Michigan	62 835
N	Yolo Cache	72 633
Robert	Santa Cruz Santa Cruz	66 621
Robert	Santa Cruz Santa Cruz	66 623
T T	Tehama Red Bluff	70 899
WOODEN		
Albert H *	Placer Auburn	62 561
George	San Mateo Twp 3	65 91
John	Napa Yount	61 46
John	Napa Yount	61 52
Stephen B *	Placer Auburn	62 561
Wm	Solano Vallejo	69 280
Wm	Tuolumne Columbia	71 309
WOODER		
J B	Tehama Red Bluff	70 909
WOODERARD		
Susan	San Francisco San Francisco 2	67 626
WOODERY		
Frances	Sacramento Franklin	63 315
WOODES		
Maria *	San Francisco San Francisco 6	67 401
William	Plumas Quincy	62 973
Wm	Calaveras Twp 10	57 294
WOODEY		
James	San Luis Obispo San Luis Obispo	65 28
Spanel	Tulara Visalia	71 18
Taswell	Tulara Visalia	71 18
W H	El Dorado Union	581091
WOODFERD		
W *	Sacramento Granite	63 242
WOODFIELD		
H	Nevada Grass Valley	61 210
J	Nevada Grass Valley	61 210

Name	County Locale	M653 Roll	Page
WOODFIN			
John	Tuolumne Twp 3	71	456
WOODFORD			
A *	Siskiyou Cottonwoood	69	104
C F	Siskiyou Cottonwoood	69	106
Clinton	Klamath Orleans	59	217
Elias	El Dorado Kelsey	58	1137
Hiram N	Calaveras Twp 6	57	162
Noah N	Contra Costa Twp 3	57	613
W	Sacramento Granite	63	242
WOODHALL			
J	Calaveras Twp 9	57	389
J	Calaveras Twp 9	57	398
J	Sutter Butte	70	783
Jerry	Sierra Pine Grove	66	833
WOODHAMER			
O	Calaveras Twp 9	57	383
WOODHAMS			
Joseph	Santa Clara Santa Clara	65	483
WOODHEAD			
George	San Francisco San Francisco 7	68	1369
Thos M	San Mateo Twp 3	65	89
WOODHOUSE			
George	Los Angeles Tejon	59	525
John D	Sierra Poker Flats	66	837
WOODIN			
Albert H *	Placer Auburn	62	561
Jos	Sonoma Petaluma	69	549
Stephen B *	Placer Auburn	62	561
WOODIS			
Maria *	San Francisco San Francisco 6	67	401
WOODISON			
G	El Dorado Salmon Falls	58	1060
WOODIUM			
John *	Sierra Downieville	66	989
WOODLAND			
C	Sonoma Bodega	69	526
H	El Dorado Placerville	58	838
Jane	Sacramento Ward 1	63	133
T W	San Francisco San Francisco 6	67	439
WOODLEAF			
Henry	San Francisco San Francisco 10	277	67
WOODLEE			
H	Trinity Indian C	70	989
WOODLEY			
G	El Dorado Placerville	58	822
John	Solano Vacaville	69	346
WOODLIFF			
Anna	Nevada Bridgeport	61	475
WOODLOCK			
P	Butte Oro	56	677
WOODLUF			
Thos	Sacramento Granite	63	242
WOODLY			
Lewis *	Nevada Red Dog	61	557
WOODMAN			
A	San Francisco San Francisco 5	67	544
A S	Alameda Brooklyn	55	165
B B	Tuolumne Twp 2	71	331
B R	Tuolumne Columbia	71	331
C T	Butte Oregon	56	614
D C	Shasta Millvill	66	756
David	Yolo Washington	72	571
David R	Mendocino Little L	60	829
E	El Dorado Placerville	58	916
E W	Colusa Colusi	57	425
Edward	Butte Ophir	56	785
Ellen	San Mateo Twp 1	65	71
Geo H	Mendocino Little L	60	836
H E	Tuolumne Twp 2	71	289
Henry	Solano Suisan	69	216
J F	Sierra Downieville	66	1023
J L	San Joaquin Stockton	64	1043
J W	Butte Mountain	56	733
Jno B	Sacramento Ward 1	63	25
L C	Shasta Millvill	66	756
Michael	San Mateo Twp 1	65	71
Moses L	Placer Illinois	62	703
O P	Shasta Shasta	66	673
R P	Trinity Big Flat	70	1039
Richard	El Dorado Salmon Falls	58	1038
T	Butte Oregon	56	614
T J	Butte Ophir	56	786
Thos	Butte Cascade	56	692
W	Yuba Rose Bar	72	806
W C	Tuolumne Columbia	71	297
W W	Sierra Morristown	66	1051
WOODMANCY			
Elias	El Dorado Placerville	58	922
WOODMASTER			
Charles D	San Joaquin Douglass	64	925
WOODNARD			
Geo	El Dorado Placerville	58	933
M J *	San Francisco San Francisco 5	67	533
WOODNARK			
Gardener	El Dorado Mud Springs	58	956

Name	County Locale	M653 Roll	Page
WOODNEFF			
H	Solano Vallejo	69	280
WOODPECKER			
---	Mendocino Calpella	60	823
WOODRAHAN			
Thomas *	Yuba Bear Rvr	72	1009
WOODRALEAN			
Thomas *	Yuba Bear Rvr	72	1009
WOODRAN			
Henry	Solano Suisan	69	216
WOODRID			
Edwd	Sonoma Petaluma	69	606
WOODRIDE			
J	Nevada Eureka	61	394
WOODRIDGE			
David K	San Joaquin Stockton	64	1010
WOODRIFF			
H	Solano Vallejo	69	280
WOODRILL			
Geo	Amador Twp 5	55	358
WOODROCK			
W *	Mariposa Twp 3	60	595
WOODRODE			
D L	El Dorado Placerville	58	880
WOODROW			
Edgar	Yuba Marysville	72	882
John	Napa Hot Springs	61	17
WOODRUF			
Charles G	Yuba Marysville	72	952
WOODRUFF			
A L	Nevada Bloomfield	61	507
Albert	Nevada Bloomfield	61	508
Alburt *	Placer Goods	62	693
Alpha	Siskiyou Yreka	69	143
Charles	San Mateo Twp 3	65	108
Charles	Yuba Bear Rvr	72	1003
Charles G	Yuba Marysville	72	952
Cyrino	Solano Vacaville	69	360
Daniel	San Francisco San Francisco 7	68	1368
E	San Francisco San Francisco 6	67	408
E	Sierra Downieville	66	988
Edwards	Yuba Marysville	72	863
Erastus	El Dorado Coloma	58	1081
Ernstus	El Dorado Coloma	58	1081
Grow	Del Norte Crescent	58	645
H L	Nevada Bloomfield	61	507
Harvey *	Placer Michigan	62	821
Henry	Butte Oro	56	676
Henry *	Placer Michigan	62	821
Hiram	Butte Hamilton	56	521
Isam	El Dorado Georgetown	58	761
J	Sacramento Sutter	63	306
J	Sacramento Sutter	63	307
J G	Shasta Horsetown	66	696
J H	Sierra Twp 7	66	874
Jno	Tuolumne Big Oak	71	138
John	San Joaquin Elkhorn	64	952
M	Nevada Washington	61	334
M	San Francisco San Francisco 5	67	520
M	San Francisco San Francisco 5	67	549
Martin	Yuba Marysville	72	976
Mary	Siskiyou Yreka	69	142
S	San Francisco San Francisco 5	67	521
Samuel	San Joaquin Elkhorn	64	967
Simon	Contra Costa Twp 3	57	594
Simon	Sierra Downieville	66	955
W	Tehama Pasakent	70	855
William	Siskiyou Yreka	69	143
Wm	Sacramento Ward 4	63	549
Wm	Santa Clara Redwood	65	449
Wm	Yolo No E Twp	72	683
Wm	Yuba Slate Ro	72	683
WOODRUFFE			
George	Plumas Quincy	62	920
WOODS			
A	Sacramento Ward 1	63	16
A	Sacramento Ward 1	63	329
A R	Sutter Butte	70	780
Albert	Yuba New York	72	736
Albert S	Sacramento American	63	161
Alph	El Dorado Greenwood	58	713
Ann	San Joaquin Stockton	64	1064
Archibald	Sacramento Franklin	63	324
Arthur	Tulara Visalia	71	29
Benj	Plumas Quincy	62	995
Benj	Sacramento Granite	63	251
Bridget	Sacramento Ward 1	63	79
C	San Francisco San Francisco 5	67	539
C D	Nevada Nevada	61	279
C S	Sutter Bear Rvr	70	818
Chas H	Sacramento Ward 4	63	568
Christ	Alameda Brooklyn	55	100
D H	Sacramento Ward 1	63	18
David	Sacramento Ward 4	63	570
David	Sierra Port Win	66	791
David	Tulara Twp 1	71	77

Name	County Locale	M653 Roll	Page
WOODS			
David M	Colusa Grand Island	57	472
E	El Dorado Diamond	58	807
E	Tuolumne Jamestown	71	421
E R	Napa Napa	61	86
E *	Tuolumne Twp 3	71	421
Edward	Fresno Twp 1	59	34
Edward	Yuba Marysville	72	950
Edward J	Plumas Quincy	62	974
Elizabeth L	San Francisco 10	283	67
	San Francisco		67
Emma	San Francisco San Francisco 5	67	496
F	Sutter Bear Rvr	70	823
F H	San Francisco San Francisco 6	67	421
F W	Marin S Antoni	60	712
Francis H	Napa Yount	61	34
Franklin	Tuolumne Chinese	71	499
Geo W	Del Norte Happy Ca	58	670
George	Placer Iona Hills	62	864
George	Santa Cruz Santa Cruz	66	629
Guy M	Marin Tomales	60	723
H W	Sacramento Natonia	63	288
Harris	San Francisco San Francisco 10	220	67
			67
Henry W	Los Angeles San Gabriel	59	411
Horace	Sacramento American	63	164
Hugh P	Solano Vallejo	69	257
I M	Amador Twp 7	55	420
Isaac W	Yolo No E Twp	72	670
Isaac W	Yuba North Ea	72	670
J	Merced Twp 1	60	898
J	Nevada Washington	61	333
J	Nevada Eureka	61	369
J	Sacramento Ward 1	63	114
J	Solano Montezuma	69	373
J A	Amador Twp 5	55	362
J G	Sacramento American	63	160
J K	San Francisco San Francisco 9	68	1073
J L	Yolo Washington	72	566
J M	Amador Twp 7	55	420
J M	Stanislaus Emory	70	756
J W	El Dorado Kelsey	58	1143
James	El Dorado Coloma	58	1108
James	Placer Michigan	62	847
James	Santa Cruz Pajaro	66	576
James	Tulara Visalia	71	10
James	Tuolumne Jamestown	71	425
James C	Solano Benecia	69	283
James P	Solano Benecia	69	283
Jas	Amador Twp 2	55	307
Jas	Sacramento Cosumnes	63	410
Jas C	Fresno Millerto	59	1
Jeremiah H	San Joaquin Elkhorn	64	977
Jerry	Yuba Marysville	72	931
Jesse	Yuba Long Bar	72	772
John	Placer Virginia	62	672
John	Placer Forest H	62	802
John	Santa Cruz Soguel	66	598
John	Sierra Pine Grove	66	835
John	Tulara Twp 2	71	27
John	Tulara Twp 3	71	62
John	Tuolumne Big Oak	71	129
John B	Napa Yount	61	49
John L L *	Fresno Twp 3	59	8
John N	San Joaquin Elkhorn	64	977
John S S *	Fresno Twp 3	59	8
John W	Fresno Twp 3	59	5
Jos	San Mateo Twp 2	65	120
Joseph	Tulara Visalia	71	30
Joseph C	Yuba Bear Rvr	72	999
Joseph J	Del Norte Crescent	58	633
Joseph J	Del Norte Crescent	58	634
Kate V	Yolo Cottonwoood	72	654
L	Calaveras Twp 9	57	377
L	Nevada Washington	61	334
L A	Sacramento Ward 1	63	112
L A	Sacramento Franklin	63	324
L A *	Sacramento Ward 1	63	112
Lemuel	Amador Twp 3	55	387
Lewis	Sierra Eureka	66	1047
Louis	San Francisco San Francisco 10	258	67
			67
Louisa M	Yuba Bear Rvr	72	999
M	Amador Twp 1	55	506
M A	Yolo Cottonwoood	72	654
M C	Sutter Yuba	70	778
Martin	El Dorado Salmon Falls	58	1041
Martin	Sierra Pine Grove	66	835
Mary	Alameda Brooklyn	55	172
Mary	Amador Twp 1	55	484
Mary	Contra Costa Twp 1	57	535
Mary	Marin Tomales	60	723
Mary	Yuba Marysville	72	898
Mathew	Los Angeles Los Angeles	59	519
Matthew	Yuba Parks Ba	72	777
Matthew	Yuba Marysville	72	851

Name	County Locale	M653 Roll	Page
WOODS			
Michael	Los Angeles Los Angeles	59	364
Munroe	Sacramento Franklin	63	333
O F	Napa Yount	61	50
Owen	Yuba Bear Rvr	72	999
P	El Dorado Placerville	58	843
Paul	Amador Twp 2	55	284
Peter	San Francisco San Francisco 12	67	385
Peter	Siskiyou Callahan	69	4
R	Nevada Eureka	61	367
R M	Tehama Tehama	70	948
Rabecca	Marin Tomales	60	723
Richard	Sacramento Franklin	63	319
Richmond	Sacramento Ward 4	63	547
Robt	Napa Yount	61	46
S	Nevada Nevada	61	297
S A*	Sacramento Ward 1	63	112
S D	Sierra Twp 7	66	909
S E	El Dorado Mud Springs	58	983
Saml	Plumas Quincy	62	975
Saml	Sierra Eureka	66	1049
Samuel M	San Joaquin Elkhorn	64	997
Stephen	Stanislaus Branch	70	703
T	Calaveras Twp 9	57	377
T B	Tuolumne Twp 2	71	368
T H	El Dorado White Oaks	58	1003
T W	Marin S Antoni	60	712
Thoas	Monterey Pajaro	60	1015
Thomas	Mendocino Little L	60	830
Thomas	Monterey Pajaro	60	1015
Thomas P	Solano Vallejo	69	275
Thos	Nevada Bridgeport	61	469
Thos	Solano Vallejo	69	243
Tupply	Tehama Tehama	70	942
W B	Sonoma Armally	69	513
W F	Butte Wyandotte	56	657
W H R	Sacramento Ward 1	63	91
W J	Yuba Parks Ba	72	782
W P	El Dorado White Oaks	58	1016
W V	Sutter Nicolaus	70	827
William	Calaveras Twp 6	57	141
William	Placer Iona Hills	62	870
William	Tulara Twp 3	71	52
Wm	Calaveras Twp 10	57	294
Wm	Mariposa Twp 1	60	660
Wm	Nevada Eureka	61	389
WOODSACK			
C	Sacramento Ward 1	63	85
WOODSASK			
W*	Mariposa Twp 3	60	595
WOODSEDE			
A	San Joaquin Stockton	64	1095
WOODSIDE			
A	Nevada Washington	61	335
E G*	San Francisco San Francisco 7	68	1406
James	Yuba Marysville	72	969
John	Trinity China Bar	70	959
John	Yuba Parks Ba	72	778
Preston	Monterey Monterey	60	948
Preston K	Monterey Monterey	60	948
WOODSIDES			
H A	Mariposa Twp 3	60	552
J P	Mariposa Twp 3	60	549
WOODSMON			
John	Sierra Downieville	66	989
WOODSOCK			
W*	Mariposa Twp 3	60	595
WOODSON			
A B	Siskiyou Scott Ri	69	70
A C	Yolo New York	72	720
A C	Yuba New York	72	720
Achy	San Joaquin Elkhorn	64	979
Benjamin	San Joaquin Elkhorn	64	954
Chester	Sacramento Ward 1	63	49
Chester S	Sacramento Ward 1	63	49
Edgar*	Yuba Marysville	72	882
G	Sonoma Armally	69	510
J	Sonoma Santa Rosa	69	396
J A	Sonoma Santa Rosa	69	396
John	Napa Hot Springs	61	17
Oliver A	Yolo New York	72	720
Oliver R	Yuba New York	72	720
P?S	Sacramento Ward 1	63	64
Pphillip J	Plumas Quincy	62	989
Pres*	Sacramento Ward 1	63	64
Prs	Sacramento Ward 1	63	64
Stephen	Santa Clara Redwood	65	459
William	San Francisco San Francisco 7	68	1341
WOODSTOD			
John R	San Joaquin Castoria	64	898
WOODSUM			
John*	Sierra Downieville	66	989
WOODSWORK			
W*	Mariposa Twp 3	60	595
WOODTHOP			
Georgiana	San Francisco San Francisco 2	67	731

Name	County Locale	M653 Roll	Page
WOODTHORP			
John W	San Francisco San Francisco 2	67	675
WOODWAN			
H S	Amador Twp 2	55	262
WOODWARD			
A	Stanislaus Buena Village	70	722
A A	Nevada Bridgeport	61	493
Abram	Sacramento San Joaquin	63	367
Benjamin	Placer Michigan	62	844
Charles	Mariposa Coulterville	60	677
Chesley	Humbolt Union	59	183
D F	Napa Napa	61	96
E F	Tehama Tehama	70	946
Edgar	Placer Todds Va	62	790
Elias	Sierra Poker Flats	66	837
Elijah	Marin Cortemad	60	785
Fanny	San Francisco San Francisco 10	67	190
Francis	Sierra Twp 7	66	875
Francis	Tuolumne Columbia	71	296
Francis M	Yolo Slate Ra	72	691
Fred	Sacramento Ward 3	63	474
G B	Trinity Rearings	70	990
G C	Tehama Red Bluff	70	929
Geo	Del Norte Crescent	58	645
George	Plumas Quincy	62	997
Gideon	Yuba Marysville	72	877
J	Sacramento Centre	63	179
J	Sacramento Granite	63	235
J	Tuolumne Twp 1	71	251
J E	Placer Todds Va	62	785
James	Humbolt Pacific	59	130
James	Sierra Twp 7	66	885
James B	San Bernardino San Bernadino	64	619
Jesse	Plumas Quincy	62	915
John	Placer Ophir	62	652
John	Sacramento Granite	63	222
John	Santa Clara Redwood	65	455
John	Shasta Cottonwoood	66	736
John	Sierra Twp 7	66	871
John	Yuba Rose Bar	72	795
Joseph	Plumas Quincy	62	991
Joseph	Sacramento Natonia	63	271
Joseph	San Mateo Twp 1	65	70
L	Mendocino Big Rvr	60	844
M	Nevada Eureka	61	358
M J	San Francisco San Francisco 5	67	533
Mary	Yuba Marysville	72	962
Milton	San Francisco San Francisco 12	67	385
Milton	San Francisco San Francisco 2	67	785
Myron	Tuolumne Twp 6	71	528
P	Sacramento San Joaquin	63	367
P A	Placer Yankee J	62	781
P J	Merced Twp 2	60	917
R B	San Francisco San Francisco 10	67	244
R H	Sacramento Ward 1	63	37
R J	Merced Twp 2	60	917
S	San Joaquin Stockton	64	1099
S A	Del Norte Happy Ca	58	667
S P	Alameda Brooklyn	55	130
T F	Sacramento Dry Crk	63	371
Thos	Nevada Rough &	61	434
W	Tuolumne Twp 4	71	167
W A	San Francisco San Francisco 5	67	481
William	San Francisco San Francisco 9	68	1011
William	San Francisco San Francisco 4	68	1153
Z	Merced Twp 1	60	915
WOODWIN			
A S	Sierra Twp 7	66	902
WOODWORD			
Thomas M	Yuba Slate Ro	72	691
WOODWORT			
Joseph	Alameda Oakland	55	27
WOODWORTH			
Abijah	Marin Tomales	60	726
Abiyah	Marin Tomales	60	726
Alonzo	Monterey San Juan	60	983
B A	Sacramento Ward 3	63	147
Byron	Santa Cruz Watsonville	66	535
C	Calaveras Twp 9	57	408
Charles	Colusa Muion	57	459
D W	Tuolumne Twp 4	71	144
Darius	Sonoma Armally	69	487
E	El Dorado Placerville	58	867
E	Sutter Yuba	70	768
F A	San Francisco San Francisco 10	67	231
H	Sutter Butte	70	793
H F	Sacramento Dry Crk	63	371
H H	Tuolumne Jacksonville	71	166
Hiram	Colusa Muion	57	459
Homer	Butte Ophir	56	767
Isra	San Joaquin Douglass	64	914
James	Tuolumne Twp 2	71	284

Name	County Locale	M653 Roll	Page
WOODWORTH			
James*	Tuolumne Twp 2	71	284
John	Placer Rattle Snake	62	637
John D	Los Angeles Los Angeles	59	336
Jos M	Siskiyou Klamath	69	97
Laurin H	Fresno Twp 3	59	37
Lucien	San Bernardino San Bernadino	64	621
Lydia	San Francisco San Francisco 10	67	232
Lyman	Yolo Cache Crk	72	609
Martin	Mariposa Twp 3	60	559
Merrick	Los Angeles Azuza	59	272
P	Butte Chico	56	553
P M	Sonoma Armally	69	486
Peter	Sierra St Louis	66	810
R	Butte Chico	56	553
R	Sacramento Ward 1	63	3
R M	Sacramento Ward 1	63	3
Rachael	Marin Sauciletto	60	750
Rowland S	Sierra Gibsonville	66	853
S J	Sonoma Armally	69	487
Selim E	San Francisco San Francisco 10	67	232
Silas E	Sierra St Louis	66	810
Thos	Butte Cascade	56	694
V	Amador Twp 1	55	452
W	Marin Tomales	60	726
W M	Sutter Butte	70	793
Walace	Los Angeles Los Angeles	59	390
Wallace	Los Angeles Los Angeles	59	390
Wm R	San Francisco San Francisco 10	67	232
WOODWORTHS			
Thos	Butte Cascade	56	694
WOODY			
E R	Napa Napa	61	86
J	Sutter Butte	70	785
James	Los Angeles Los Angeles	59	403
James G	Calaveras Twp 10	57	263
John	Solano Suisan	69	233
Lumes G	Calaveras Twp 10	57	263
M	Sierra Downieville	66	1017
Marcus L	Monterey Pajaro	60	1024
William	Solano Suisan	69	218
WOODYARD			
H W	San Francisco San Francisco 6	67	437
Jno	Sacramento Ward 4	63	527
WOOE			
---	Calaveras Twp 5	57	212
---	Fresno Twp 2	59	20
WOOELREY			
Schryler*	Mendocino Ukiah	60	807
WOOFNAKER			
C	El Dorado Newtown	58	778
WOOFORD			
J	Nevada Grass Valley	61	185
WOOKE			
M*	San Francisco San Francisco 5	67	552
WOOKEY			
F	Butte Kimshaw	56	569
WOOL			
Francis	Solano Suisan	69	231
James*	San Francisco San Francisco 3	67	70
Jerome	Sacramento Alabama	63	411
John	San Francisco San Francisco 7	68	1435
John	Yuba Marysville	72	954
Thomas	Solano Suisan	69	231
WOOLAOT			
N	Shasta Shasta	66	731
WOOLARER			
John	Solano Green Valley	69	241
WOOLBRIDGE			
H	Tuolumne Twp 4	71	164
WOOLCOY			
Silas*	Yolo Putah	72	549
WOOLDIRDGE			
Chas*	Butte Kimshaw	56	586
WOOLDRIDGE			
Chas	Butte Kimshaw	56	586
WOOLEHAN			
Thomas	Sacramento Georgian	63	344
WOOLEREY			
Schuyler	Mendocino Ukiah	60	807
WOOLERY			
James W	Mendocino Ukiah	60	802
L	Sacramento Cosummes	63	394
Silas	Yolo Putah	72	549
WOOLEY			
A G	Colusa Monroeville	57	454
Alfred	Santa Cruz Pajaro	66	563
E	Sutter Yuba	70	772
E B	Amador Twp 3	55	374
George	San Joaquin Elkhorn	64	950
H	Tuolumne Twp 1	71	262
Henry	Tuolumne Twp 1	71	264

Name	County Locale	M653 Roll	Page
WOOLEY			
Henry J	San Francisco San Francisco 10	240	
		67	
J	San Francisco San Francisco 5	67	506
J S	Shasta Shasta	66	731
James	Nevada Eureka	61	355
James	Sacramento Granite	63	244
John	Yuba Marysville	72	860
John F	Sacramento Franklin	63	329
Jon	Yuba Marysville	72	858
Joseph	El Dorado Casumnes	581	161
Joseph	Shasta Shasta	66	757
Norman	Siskiyou Yreka	69	150
T	Sacramento Ward 1	63	19
William	El Dorado Kelsey	581	139
WOOLF			
---	San Francisco San Francisco 4	681	220
---*	Mendocino Round Va	60	885
A	Sacramento Granite	63	242
August	Siskiyou Yreka	69	177
G W	Yolo Cache Crk	72	606
J W	Yolo Cottonwoood	72	653
John	Sacramento Ward 1	63	47
Martin	Sacramento Granite	63	248
Michael	Siskiyou Yreka	69	148
Peter	Santa Clara Santa Clara	65	492
WOOLFE			
J	Trinity Readings	70	996
WOOLFORD			
G	Nevada Grass Valley	61	195
Jacob	Monterey San Juan	60	987
Wm	Amador Twp 3	55	403
WOOLFORK			
C G	Amador Twp 3	55	406
Chas	Amador Twp 3	55	403
Wm	Amador Twp 3	55	403
WOOLINGTON			
W	Sacramento Sutter	63	292
WOOLLEY			
---	Tulara Twp 3	71	56
Abram S	Calaveras Twp 4	57	315
E S	San Francisco San Francisco 2	67	705
L H	San Francisco San Francisco 10	279	
		67	
William	Calaveras Twp 10	57	288
WOOLLY			
William	Calaveras Twp 10	57	288
WOOLNER			
Benj	Solano Suisan	69	221
WOOLOOT			
N	Shasta Shasta	66	731
WOOLRIDGE			
Saml	Plumas Meadow Valley	62	912
WOOLS			
George	San Diego Colorado	64	808
WOOLSEN			
E	Sacramento Natonia	63	282
WOOLSEY			
Elijah	Santa Cruz Pajaro	66	533
G	Amador Twp 2	55	305
James	Yuba Suida	72	982
James	Yuba Linda Twp	72	984
Luther S	San Francisco San Francisco 9	68	995
William	Contra Costa Twp 3	57	589
WOOLSHEAD			
J	San Francisco San Francisco 5	67	535
WOOLSON			
Jas	Sacramento Brighton	63	194
WOOLSTEAD			
J	San Francisco San Francisco 5	67	535
WOOLT			
---*	Mendocino Round Va	60	885
WOOLVERSON			
John	Sierra Forest C	66	910
WOOLY			
Elizabeth	San Francisco San Francisco 2	67	746
Mary	San Francisco San Francisco 2	67	643
WOON			
---	Amador Twp 1	55	508
---	El Dorado Salmon Falls	581	066
---	El Dorado Coloma	581	105
---	El Dorado Kelsey	581	144
---	El Dorado Georgetown	58	756
---	El Dorado Mud Springs	58	969
---	Placer Illinois	62	741
---	Placer Michigan	62	835
---	Placer Iona Hills	62	889
---	Yuba Linda	72	991
James*	Nevada Rough &	61	412
Lu	El Dorado Greenwood	58	731
WOONER			
Leo	San Francisco San Francisco 4	681	176
Luo	San Francisco San Francisco 4	681	176
WOORMER			
Philip*	San Francisco San Francisco 11	123	
		67	

Name	County Locale	M653 Roll	Page
WOOSEMAN			
Ardos	Yuba Slate Ro	72	714
Santos	Yolo Slate Ra	72	714
Santos	Yuba Slate Ro	72	714
WOOSHAN			
Joseph	Yuba Marysville	72	897
WOOSLER			
Marshall	Amador Twp 3	55	404
WOOSLEY			
William	Tulara Keyesville	71	62
WOOSTER			
A J	Nevada Bridgeport	61	456
Abby	Sacramento Ward 4	63	552
B	Sacramento Ward 4	63	431
C T	San Joaquin Stockton	641	033
D	Sacramento Ward 4	63	502
David	San Francisco San Francisco 8	681	247
Eli	Sonoma Sonoma	69	661
George	Plumas Quincy	62	942
Henry	San Francisco San Francisco 7	681	397
J M	Tuolumne Sonora	71	483
J Marshall	Amador Twp 3	55	404
Jeremiah	Plumas Quincy	621	000
Jno	Sonoma Vallejo	69	609
S L	San Francisco San Francisco 5	67	549
Seanard	Shasta Horsetown	66	700
Seaward	Shasta Horsetown	66	700
Wm	Butte Chico	56	559
WOOSWICK			
Chas R*	Sacramento Granite	63	245
Chris R	Sacramento Granite	63	245
WOOTEN			
John	Tuolumne Jamestown	71	450
Levi	Tuolumne Twp 2	71	306
Vincent	Tuolumne Twp 3	71	423
William	Fresno Twp 3	59	11
WOOTERS			
John	Tuolumne Jamestown	71	441
John	Tuolumne Twp 3	71	450
WOOWOOMUCT			
---	Tulara Twp 1	71	122
WOPPNER			
Henry	Marin Cortemad	60	789
WOR			
---	Calaveras Twp 5	57	222
---	San Francisco San Francisco 4	681	202
WORCESTER			
Horace	Del Norte Crescent	58	633
Horace	Del Norte Crescent	58	634
Mary	Sacramento Ward 1	63	101
Olive	Santa Cruz Pescadero	66	648
Saml	Tuolumne Twp 3	71	462
William	Tulara Twp 3	71	42
WORCHING			
Sam	Placer Auburn	62	576
WORD			
B F	Tuolumne Shawsfla	71	408
Benj	Nevada Bridgeport	61	472
C	Sacramento Ward 1	63	31
D J*	Nevada Bridgeport	61	439
F L*	Siskiyou Scott Ri	69	81
Fanny	San Francisco San Francisco 1	68	817
Francis	Tuolumne Shawsfla	71	401
Geo	Placer Virginia	62	668
James C	Del Norte Ferry P O	58	665
John	El Dorado Big Bar	58	743
John H	Calaveras Twp 5	57	227
Phillip J*	Calaveras Twp 10	57	252
W H	Siskiyou Scott Ri	69	68
William	San Francisco San Francisco 9	681	010
William	Siskiyou Klamath	69	79
William*	Nevada Red Dog	61	550
Wm C*	Placer Virginia	62	676
Wm O*	Placer Virginia	62	676
WORDBY			
Elizabeth	San Francisco San Francisco 9	681	005
WORDELL			
Abram	San Francisco San Francisco 10	295	
		67	
Abram	San Francisco San Francisco 9	68	993
WORDEN			
A	Nevada Bridgeport	61	483
Casey	Alameda Brooklyn	55	188
Charles	Los Angeles Elmonte	59	263
Chas	Butte Hamilton	56	525
Cylvester V	Napa Hot Springs	61	20
Cylvestor V	Napa Hot Springs	61	20
G B	Tuolumne Twp 4	71	165
G R*	Tuolumne Jacksonville	71	165
George	Mariposa Coulterville	60	703
J D	Butte Oro	56	683
Thomas H	Humbolt Union	59	188
P	Tuolumne Twp 4	71	157
WORDFORD			
A*	Siskiyou Cottonwood	69	104

Name	County Locale	M653 Roll	Page
WORDIN			
C	San Francisco San Francisco 5	67	513
WORDLE			
Robert	Placer Yankee J	62	778
WORDLY			
Lewis*	Nevada Red Dog	61	557
WORDMAN			
W C*	Tuolumne Twp 2	71	297
WORDON			
Edwin	Contra Costa Twp 3	57	609
WORDS			
E*	Tuolumne Twp 3	71	421
J*	San Francisco San Francisco 5	67	487
WORDSON			
H	Butte Oregon	56	642
M J	Butte Kimshaw	56	603
WORDWARD			
A A	Nevada Bridgeport	61	493
WORDWELL			
W	San Francisco San Francisco 10	312	
		67	
Wallace	San Francisco San Francisco 10	312	
		67	
WORDWORTH			
B A	Sacramento Ward 1	63	147
James*	Tuolumne Twp 2	71	284
Jos M	Siskiyou Cottonwood	69	97
WORDY			
Marcus L**	Monterey Pajaro	601	024
WORECESTER			
Saml	Tuolumne Twp 3	71	462
WORED			
Wm	Butte Wyandotte	56	670
WOREL			
John H*	Calaveras Twp 5	57	227
WORES			
Joseph*	San Francisco San Francisco 3	67	14
WORETHN			
Luois*	Siskiyou Yreka	69	155
WORFSHINNER			
F	Butte Chico	56	568
WORGEL			
John	Alameda Brooklyn	55	81
WORHAM			
William*	Calaveras Twp 6	57	164
WORIE			
John*	Yuba Marysville	72	904
WORIMER			
Philip*	San Francisco San Francisco 11	123	
		67	
WORINGTON			
Charles	Santa Cruz Soguel	66	590
WORITOUR			
Anne M*	San Francisco San Francisco 10	176	
		67	
WORK			
Chas	Placer Lisbon	62	733
David*	Sonoma Petaluma	69	591
Fleming	Tulara Visalia	71	20
Frances	Sacramento Lee	63	213
Hopkins	Tulara Visalia	71	20
J W	San Francisco San Francisco 8	681	234
Jane	Santa Cruz Pajaro	66	535
Jas	Sacramento Lee	63	211
Jeff	Nevada Nevada	61	255
Jefferson	Sierra Twp 7	66	901
John	Tuolumne Don Pedro	71	541
Mitchell	Tulara Visalia	71	20
W	Siskiyou Scott Va	69	55
WORKE			
Fleming*	Tulara Twp 2	71	20
Hopkins*	Tulara Twp 2	71	20
M	San Francisco San Francisco 5	67	552
Mitchell*	Tulara Twp 2	71	20
WORKHIEM			
Morris	Tuolumne Sonora	71	200
WORKINS			
John	Napa Napa	61	87
WORKINY			
John	Napa Napa	61	87
WORKMAN			
Bridget	Sacramento American	63	168
Geo	Trinity Mouth Ca	701	015
James	San Joaquin Elliott	64	942
Nancy	Los Angeles Los Angeles	59	335
Thomas H	Los Angeles San Pedro	59	480
Thomas M	Los Angeles San Pedro	59	480
William	Los Angeles Elmonte	59	268
WORKOVER			
Thos	Napa Hot Springs	61	25
WORKS			
Hiram	Yolo Slate Ra	72	704
Hiram	Yuba Slate Ro	72	704
Thomas	Yolo Slate Ra	72	707
Thomas	Yuba Slate Ro	72	707
WORL			
James*	San Francisco San Francisco 3	67	70

California 1860 Census Index

Name	County Locale	M653 Roll	Page
WORLAN			
C R*	Calaveras Twp 9	57	407
WORLAND			
Charles	Tulara Twp 3	71	45
WORLARE			
C R*	Calaveras Twp 9	57	407
WORLE			
James*	San Francisco San Francisco 3	67	70
WORLEY			
George W	Sierra La Porte	66	772
James	Shasta Horsetown	66	703
Nathan	Amador Twp 1	55	488
Silas J	San Joaquin Castoria	64	906
Stephen	Amador Twp 3	55	370
Stephen*	Nevada Rough &	61	412
WORLINGER			
Babbit*	San Francisco San Francisco 7	68	1365
WORLMAN			
Wm*	Alameda Brooklyn	55	153
WORLSEY			
Ebrim*	Alameda Oakland	55	17
Ebrun*	Alameda Oakland	55	17
Luther	San Francisco San Francisco 9	68	995
Wm	Alameda Brooklyn	55	208
WORLY			
Joseph	Shasta Shasta	66	757
WORM			
August W	Plumas Quincy	62	982
John	San Diego Agua Caliente	64	855
W	Nevada Grass Valley	61	156
WORMAGETER			
Jos	Placer Dutch Fl	62	717
WORMAN			
Geo	Alameda Brooklyn	55	88
WORMEL			
R A	Trinity Weaverville	70	1070
WORMELL			
Nathaniel*	San Joaquin Stockton	64	1013
WORMER			
C*	Placer Virginia	62	668
WORMOTH			
Charles	Sierra La Porte	66	770
WORMS			
Solomon	San Francisco San Francisco 7	68	1390
W*	San Francisco San Francisco 1	68	927
WORMSER			
I	Sacramento Ward 1	63	35
J	Sacramento Ward 1	63	35
S	Sacramento Ward 1	63	36
WORMSLEY			
Wm	San Francisco San Francisco 2	67	787
Wm*	Sacramento Mississipi	63	187
WORMWOOD			
C	Yolo Cache Crk	72	627
H C	Nevada Bridgeport	61	488
WORMWORTH			
Charles	Sierra La Porte	66	771
WORN			
George A	San Francisco San Francisco 8	68	1268
Harriet	San Francisco San Francisco 8	68	1268
Mary A	San Francisco San Francisco 8	68	1268
WORNER			
L P	Yolo Cache Crk	72	626
Stephen*	Calaveras Twp 6	57	125
WORNES			
Julius*	Yuba Marysville	72	899
WORNN			
Stephen*	Calaveras Twp 6	57	125
WORNSLEY			
Solomon	San Diego Agua Caliente	64	816
WORRALL			
Joseph	Tuolumne Twp 2	71	287
WORRELL			
Chas	San Francisco San Francisco 2	67	571
WORREN			
J M*	Siskiyou Scott Ri	69	62
J W	Siskiyou Scott Ri	69	62
WORRILL			
Chas*	San Francisco San Francisco 2	67	571
WORRINGTON			
John	Mariposa Twp 3	60	621
WORRY			
David*	Nevada Rough &	61	410
WORSHAN			
Frank	Nevada Bloomfield	61	512
WORSHAU			
Frank	Nevada Bloomfield	61	512
WORSLER			
Joseph	Sacramento Granite	63	222
WORSLEY			
Ann	Placer Dutch Fl	62	734
John	Placer Auburn	62	569
WORSTER			
J M	Tuolumne Twp 1	71	483
WORTEL			
Jacob	San Francisco San Francisco 3	67	69

Name	County Locale	M653 Roll	Page
WORTELL			
Frederick*	Yuba Bear Rvr	72	998
WORTEMAN			
D	San Francisco San Francisco 7	68	1363
WORTH			
Aaron S	San Diego Agua Caliente	64	820
C	San Francisco San Francisco 6	67	444
Chas A	San Francisco San Francisco 10	279	67
Geo	Butte Eureka	56	647
Geo B	El Dorado Mud Springs	58	994
George F	Contra Costa Twp 1	57	483
George*	Yuba Marysville	72	870
Henry	Tuolumne Twp 2	71	367
Henry C	San Francisco San Francisco 12	381	67
Jack	Humbolt Eureka	59	178
James	El Dorado Mud Springs	58	996
John	Solano Vallejo	69	247
Martin	Nevada Bridgeport	61	476
Thomas J	Humbolt Eureka	59	178
William	San Francisco San Francisco 9	68	990
WORTHEIMER			
Manuel	San Francisco San Francisco 8	68	1309
WORTHELL			
Antonio	Tuolumne Twp 1	71	228
WORTHEN			
B N	Sacramento Ward 1	63	130
B N	Sacramento Ward 1	63	131
WORTHGLEE			
Henry	Butte Oro	56	675
WORTHING			
J	San Francisco San Francisco 6	67	473
N	Butte Cascade	56	696
WORTHINGTON			
A	Sacramento Ward 3	63	469
A*	Napa Yount	61	33
C H	Santa Clara Santa Clara	65	487
Chas	Santa Clara Fremont	65	421
Elijah	Yuba Marysville	72	866
H	San Francisco San Francisco 5	67	500
Henry	Santa Cruz Santa Cruz	66	612
J G	Sacramento Ward 1	63	141
James	Amador Twp 3	55	388
James	Colusa Monroeville	57	444
James	Humbolt Eureka	59	178
Joseph L	Humbolt Eureka	59	175
Lewis N	Santa Clara Gilroy	65	236
R	Mariposa Twp 3	60	599
Saml	Placer Christia	62	736
Simeon	Tulara Twp 2	71	26
T H	Yuba New York	72	737
Wm	Sacramento San Joaquin	63	350
Wm	San Francisco San Francisco 3	67	11
Wm	Tehama Lassen	70	873
Wm R	Humbolt Table Bl	59	140
WORTHLEY			
Henry	Yuba New York	72	724
Mary	Monterey Alisal	60	1036
William	San Francisco San Francisco 9	68	980
WORTHLY			
Henry	Yuba New York	72	724
WORTHN			
Luois*	Siskiyou Yreka	69	155
WORTHOUSE			
Henry	El Dorado Casumnes	58	1161
WORTHSOHETSOKER			
Carl*	Tuolumne Jacksonville	71	169
WORTHSOHITSOKER			
Carl	Tuolumne Twp 4	71	169
WORTHWORTH			
N C	El Dorado Kelsey	58	1137
WORTHY			
H Lang*	Stanislaus Buena Village	70	725
Joseph	Yuba New York	72	737
William	Yolo Putah	72	615
WORTIMHAM			
Reuben	Sacramento San Joaquin	63	355
WORTLO			
John	Mariposa Coulterville	60	686
WORTLY			
Joseph	Yuba New York	72	737
WORTMAN			
Aaron	Alameda Oakland	55	26
George*	Sonoma Armally	69	516
Joseph	Calaveras Twp 5	57	210
William*	Calaveras Twp 5	57	210
Wm*	Alameda Brooklyn	55	153
WORTON			
Chas*	San Francisco San Francisco 9	68	1046
Danl*	Placer Goods	62	695
Frank	Calaveras Twp 5	57	199
Peter	Nevada Rough &	61	432
WORTRRAN			
George*	Sonoma Armally	69	516
WORVEL			
W*	Nevada Grass Valley	61	158

Name	County Locale	M653 Roll	Page
WORY			
---	Amador Twp 5	55	334
---	Amador Twp 5	55	354
WOS			
John	Yuba New York	72	737
WOSELEY			
Albert	El Dorado Union	58	1094
Albert P	El Dorado Union	58	1094
WOSHBURN			
George S	Calaveras Twp 5	57	189
WOSHNAN			
Joseph	Calaveras Twp 5	57	210
WOSK			
Henry J	Yuba Marysville	72	976
WOSTER			
H*	El Dorado Georgetown	58	706
WOSTMAN			
Joseph*	Calaveras Twp 5	57	210
WOSTRUIAN			
Joseph*	Calaveras Twp 5	57	210
WOT			
---	Calaveras Twp 5	57	204
---	Calaveras Twp 5	57	257
---	El Dorado Georgetown	58	702
WOTHAM			
William*	Calaveras Twp 6	57	164
WOTHEL			
Peter*	Yuba Marysville	72	904
WOTONG			
---	Fresno Millerto	59	2
WOTSON			
Chester*	Sacramento Ward 4	63	569
WOTT			
Jas	Amador Twp 2	55	264
WOTTING			
J	Trinity Taylor'S	70	1036
WOU KEE			
---	Mariposa Twp 3	60	607
WOU			
---	Amador Twp 6	55	447
---	El Dorado Salmon Falls	58	1043
---	Mariposa Twp 3	60	582
---	Nevada Rough &	61	399
---	San Francisco San Francisco 4	68	1186
Fok	Calaveras Twp 10	57	278
Mou	San Francisco San Francisco 5	67	1206
Sti	San Francisco San Francisco 11	160	67
WOUGH			
---	Sacramento Mississipi	63	190
R G	Trinity Weaverville	70	1063
WOUK			
---	Mariposa Coulterville	60	683
WOUL			
---	El Dorado Georgetown	58	761
WOULD			
Chas D*	Del Norte Crescent	58	636
WOULES			
Jesus*	Yuba Marysville	72	937
WOULFE			
John W	San Francisco San Francisco 12	385	67
Wm	Yuba Long Bar	72	749
WOUNG			
---	El Dorado Mud Springs	58	969
---	Placer Virginia	62	671
Saug	Nevada Nevada	61	300
WOUREA			
W*	El Dorado Placerville	58	847
WOUSHAN			
Joseph	Yuba Marysville	72	897
WOUU			
---	Calaveras Twp 5	57	212
WOUWIVMNET			
---	Tulara Twp 1	71	122
WOVEN			
J H	Sierra Twp 7	66	890
WOW			
---	Calaveras Twp 5	57	211
---	Calaveras Twp 5	57	215
---	Calaveras Twp 5	57	222
---	El Dorado Union	58	1091
---	El Dorado Kelsey	58	1135
---	Placer Secret R	62	623
---	Placer Folsom	62	648
---	Placer Horseshoe	62	650
---	Placer Ophirvile	62	656
---	Placer Virginia	62	672
---	Placer Illinois	62	741
---	San Francisco San Francisco 11	161	67
---	Sierra Downieville	66	1003
---	Sierra Twp 7	66	876
---	Tuolumne Twp 5	71	521
---	Yolo Slate Ra	72	710
---	Yuba Slate Ro	72	710

Name	County Locale	Roll	Page
WOW			
---*	Mariposa Twp 1	60	651
Chung	Placer Dutch Fl	62	737
Hog	El Dorado Greenwood	58	719
Lee	Yuba Foster B	72	827
Tong	Sacramento Cosumnes	63	398
WOWEN			
J M*	Siskiyou Scott Ri	69	62
WOWLAND			
S S	Tehama Tehama	70	938
WOY			
---	Butte Cascade	56	704
---	Calaveras Twp 4	57	323
---	El Dorado Casumnes	58	1160
---	El Dorado Big Bar	58	734
---	Sacramento Granite	63	250
---	San Francisco San Francisco 4	68	1173
---	San Francisco San Francisco 4	68	1174
---	San Francisco San Francisco 4	68	1176
---	San Francisco San Francisco 4	68	1177
---	San Francisco San Francisco 4	68	1178
---	San Francisco San Francisco 4	68	1184
---	Yuba Marysville	72	895
---	Yuba Linda	72	991
Ah	Butte Cascade	56	702
Ah	Butte Cascade	56	704
Che*	Mariposa Twp 3	60	589
Fee	San Francisco San Francisco 4	68	1207
Fong	San Francisco San Francisco 4	68	1207
Foo	San Francisco San Francisco 4	68	1207
Fu	San Francisco San Francisco 4	68	1207
Fuy	San Francisco San Francisco 4	68	1181
Hue	San Francisco San Francisco 4	68	1194
Hui	San Francisco San Francisco 4	68	1194
Ku	San Francisco San Francisco 9	68	1093
See	San Francisco San Francisco 4	68	1201
Su	San Francisco San Francisco 4	68	1201
Teoy	San Francisco San Francisco 4	68	1202
Tuk	San Francisco San Francisco 4	68	1203
WOYOCTENA			
---*	Butte Chico	56	551
WOYOCTINA			
---*	Butte Chico	56	551
WOZEMAN			
Henry	Calaveras Twp 4	57	340
WOZEMAR			
Henry*	Calaveras Twp 4	57	340
WOZENCRAFT			
Oliner	San Bernardino San Bernadino	64	625
WQUIRE			
Mack	Sierra Twp 5	66	948
WRAH			
William*	Calaveras Twp 6	57	112
WRAMTH			
Newell*	Yolo Slate Ra	72	689
WRANTLAND			
Kinsey	Sacramento Franklin	63	328
WRAY			
C B	Marin Bolinas	60	742
James	Mariposa Twp 1	60	638
John	Tuolumne Twp 2	71	284
Joseph W	Sierra Chappare	66	1041
Philip	Marin Cortemad	60	754
WREDE			
C	San Francisco San Francisco 5	67	524
WREED			
Deaderick	San Francisco San Francisco 7	68	1337
WREN			
Eliza	Tuolumne Twp 1	71	240
J	Sacramento Mississipi	63	184
L	Stanislaus Emory	70	741
Samson	Calaveras Twp 8	57	57
Thomas	Sierra Twp 7	66	906
Thos	El Dorado Georgetown	58	678
W C	Siskiyou Klamath	69	84
WREND			
Jos	Butte Kimshaw	56	600
WRENN			
George	Amador Twp 4	55	248
WRENPHY			
W H	Butte Mountain	56	739
WREST			
Thos*	San Francisco San Francisco 1	68	905
WRETENS			
L	Amador Twp 1	55	507
WRETTI			
George	Colusa Mansville	57	437
WREZESIERSKY			
Ester*	Sacramento Ward 4	63	598
WREZESUISKY			
Ester*	Sacramento Ward 4	63	598
WRIEDKIND			
A	San Francisco San Francisco 5	67	548
WRIG			
---	Shasta Shasta	66	680
WRIGGLES			
Henry	Nevada Bridgeport	61	478

Name	County Locale	Roll	Page
WRIGH			
J	Sutter Butte	70	800
WRIGHS			
J A	Butte Cascade	56	701
WRIGHT			
---	Monterey San Juan	60	1004
---	Stanislaus Emory	70	751
A	Calaveras Twp 9	57	407
A	Sacramento Franklin	63	329
A	San Francisco San Francisco 5	67	514
A	San Francisco San Francisco 5	67	547
A	San Joaquin Stockton	64	1055
A C	Siskiyou Scott Ri	69	67
A S	San Francisco San Francisco 10	67	257
Albert	Alameda Murray	55	222
Albert	Sacramento Ward 3	63	435
Alexander	Yolo No E Twp	72	684
Alexander	Yuba Slate Ro	72	684
Alvin	San Francisco San Francisco 7	68	1412
Alx	Stanislaus Branch	70	697
Andrew	Humbolt Eel Rvr	59	153
Ann	San Francisco San Francisco 2	67	569
Ann	San Francisco San Francisco 9	68	989
Anna	Santa Clara Alviso	65	411
Anson	Sacramento Ward 1	63	128
Anthony	Amador Twp 2	55	303
Augusteen	Tuolumne Twp 5	71	506
B P	Shasta Shasta	66	734
Benj	Mendocino Calpella	60	817
Benjn	Sierra Monte Crk	66	1039
Berry	Mendocino Calpella	60	817
Byron	Stanislaus Emory	70	738
C	Butte Oregon	56	635
C	El Dorado Placerville	58	865
C	Sonoma Washington	69	674
C	Sutter Vernon	70	844
C B	El Dorado Mud Springs	58	949
C B	Sacramento Brighton	63	202
C H	Siskiyou Scott Va	69	34
Carmina	Yolo Cache	72	635
Charles	San Mateo Twp 1	65	54
Charles	Sierra Eureka	66	1046
Charles	Sonoma Cloverdale	69	682
Charles	Tehama Lassen	70	876
Chas	Alameda Brooklyn	55	192
Chas	Sacramento Ward 4	63	513
Chas	Santa Clara San Jose	65	321
Chas M	Amador Twp 1	55	484
Chs J	San Francisco San Francisco 6	67	416
D H	Sonoma Armally	69	502
D I W*	Tuolumne Twp 2	71	471
Daniel T	San Francisco San Francisco 7	68	1339
David	El Dorado White Oaks	58	1001
David	Placer Secret R	62	611
David	San Joaquin Oneal	64	929
Delno	Tuolumne Columbia	71	471
Drucilla	Nevada Bloomfield	61	509
E	Sacramento Franklin	63	329
E	Sutter Butte	70	785
E A	Mariposa Twp 3	60	549
E B	Sierra Downieville	66	960
E G	Tuolumne Twp 3	71	460
E J	San Francisco San Francisco 9	68	998
E J	Tuolumne Columbia	71	289
Edward	Yolo Washington	72	605
Edward A	San Francisco San Francisco 11	67	130
Edward G	Placer Secret R	62	621
Edward M	Yuba Marysville	72	944
Edwd	Sonoma Petaluma	69	557
Elisha	San Joaquin Elkhorn	64	988
Elisha	Santa Cruz Pajaro	66	555
Emily	San Francisco San Francisco 2	67	634
F	Mariposa Twp 3	60	555
Fred	Mariposa Twp 3	60	600
G A	Amador Twp 1	55	451
G H	San Francisco San Francisco 5	67	523
Geo	Mendocino Arrana	60	858
Geo	Nevada Eureka	61	359
Geo	San Francisco San Francisco 12	67	385
Geo	San Francisco San Francisco 1	68	912
Geo S	San Francisco San Francisco 2	67	804
Geo W	Placer Secret R	62	624
George	Marin Cortemad	60	779
George	Tuolumne Twp 1	71	208
H	Nevada Eureka	61	378
H	Sutter Butte	70	798
H	Tehama Tehama	70	942
H C	San Francisco San Francisco 6	67	430
H D	Siskiyou Scott Va	69	32
H J	El Dorado Diamond	58	810
H J	Tuolumne Twp 2	71	400
H N	San Francisco San Francisco 2	67	804
Harrison	San Joaquin Elliott	64	941

Name	County Locale	Roll	Page
WRIGHT			
Henry	Marin San Rafael	60	764
Henry	Mariposa Coulterville	60	700
Henry	Placer Forest H	62	804
Henry	San Francisco San Francisco 2	67	605
Henry	Sierra Gibsonville	66	851
Henry	Siskiyou Yreka	69	184
Henry	Solano Suisan	69	207
Henry E	San Joaquin Oneal	64	929
Henry W	Marin Cortemad	60	785
Henry W	Yuba Bear Rvr	72	1002
Herry	Solano Vallejo	69	255
Irwin	Mendocino Calpella	60	813
Isaac J	Sonoma Petaluma	69	560
Isaac N	Tuolumne Twp 1	71	208
J	Siskiyou Scott Ri	69	71
J	Solano Vacaville	69	327
J	Sutter Yuba	70	776
J ?	Mariposa Twp 1	60	637
J A	Butte Cascade	56	701
J B	Nevada Eureka	61	358
J D	Placer Virginia	62	675
J F	Mariposa Twp 1	60	637
J H	Napa Hot Springs	61	18
J K	Butte Mountain	56	739
J T	Nevada Bloomfield	61	509
J Y	Nevada Bloomfield	61	509
J Z	Mariposa Twp 1	60	637
Jack	Sonoma Santa Rosa	69	410
James	El Dorado Mud Springs	58	959
James	San Francisco San Francisco 4	68	1147
James	Tehama Lassen	70	865
James	Tehama Lassen	70	866
James	Tuolumne Twp 1	71	251
James	Tuolumne Shawsfla	71	417
James	Tuolumne Twp 5	71	505
James	Yolo Slate Ra	72	713
James	Yuba Slate Ro	72	713
James K	Calaveras Twp 10	57	282
James R	Calaveras Twp 10	57	282
Jas	San Francisco San Francisco 10	67	194
Jas	Tehama Lassen	70	867
Jas A	San Francisco San Francisco 9	68	1005
Jas K	San Francisco San Francisco 10	67	316
Jenny	Sacramento Ward 1	63	111
Jhn	Plumas Meadow Valley	62	901
Jno	Sacramento Cosumnes	63	403
Jno	Sacramento Ward 4	63	529
Jno E	Sacramento Ward 1	63	113
Johanna	San Francisco San Francisco 2	67	773
John	Amador Twp 3	55	406
John	Butte Ophir	56	749
John	Marin Tomales	60	774
John	Placer Todds Va	62	790
John	Sacramento Ward 1	63	100
John	Sacramento Franklin	63	312
John	Sacramento Franklin	63	317
John	San Joaquin Stockton	64	1047
John	Santa Clara Alviso	65	408
John	Santa Cruz Santa Cruz	66	601
John	Santa Cruz Santa Cruz	66	603
John	Sierra La Porte	66	789
John C	Amador Twp 3	55	387
John C	Plumas Quincy	62	978
John C	Siskiyou Yreka	69	145
John H	Yuba Marysville	72	897
John J	Solano Vallejo	69	258
John P	Trinity E Weaver	70	1059
John R	Napa Hot Springs	61	18
John T	San Francisco San Francisco 2	67	638
John T	Santa Cruz Santa Cruz	66	601
Johnathon	Mariposa Twp 3	60	554
Jonas	San Joaquin Oneal	64	936
Jonathan	Napa Clear Lake	61	138
Jonathon	Mariposa Twp 3	60	554
Jos	San Francisco San Francisco 10	67	194
Jos K	San Francisco San Francisco 10	67	316
Joseph	Sonoma Santa Rosa	69	414
Julia Ann	Butte Ophir	56	760
Justice A	Yuba Marysville	72	944
Justin A	Yuba Marysville	72	944
L	Sacramento Ward 4	63	529
L	Tehama Red Bluff	70	911
L F	El Dorado Diamond	58	790
L H	Nevada Grass Valley	61	186
L R	Sonoma Russian	69	437
Leman*	Humbolt Eel Rvr	59	150
Letitia	San Francisco San Francisco 8	68	1248
Lucian	Humbolt Mattole	59	122
Lucien G	Plumas Meadow Valley	62	905
Luther	Solano Benecia	69	287
Margaret	Santa Clara Redwood	65	445

California 1860 Census Index

Name	County Locale	M653 RollPage
WRIGHT		
Maria	Santa Clara San Jose	65 306
Martin	Solano Vallejo	69 248
Mary	San Francisco San Francisco 9	681104
Mary	San Francisco San Francisco 4	681148
N P	Amador Twp 7	55 412
Nathl K	Plumas Quincy	62 940
Nelson	Sacramento Ward 1	63 11
Norman K	Plumas Meadow Valley	62 902
O F*	Placer Michigan	62 839
O P	Yolo Slate Ra	72 688
O P	Yuba Slate Ro	72 688
Oren*	Solano Vacaville	69 320
Orrin	Butte Eureka	56 648
Oscar	Sacramento Lee	63 218
Owen	Alameda Brooklyn	55 102
Owen	San Francisco San Francisco 9	681035
Owen	Solano Vacaville	69 320
Patrick	Siskiyou Shasta Valley	69 118
Peter S	Tuolumne Chinese	71 488
R	Butte Ophir	56 783
R	El Dorado Placerville	58 915
R S	Trinity Mouth Ca	701013
Randolph	Contra Costa Twp 3	57 594
Reuben	Sacramento Dry Crk	63 373
Robert*	Sierra Downieville	661010
S	El Dorado Placerville	58 885
S D	Nevada Grass Valley	61 181
S H	Santa Clara Santa Clara	65 481
S M	Sutter Sutter	70 801
S S	San Francisco San Francisco 6	67 428
S W	Butte Oregon	56 633
S W	Nevada Bridgeport	61 482
Sam	Butte Wyandotte	56 661
Saml	San Francisco San Francisco 1	68 928
Saml	Yolo Cache	72 611
Saml L	San Francisco San Francisco 9	681024
Sampson	Sonoma Santa Rosa	69 417
Samuel	Colusa Grand Island	57 478
Samuel	Santa Clara Gilroy	65 234
Sedgwick C	Siskiyou Shasta Rvr	69 111
Seman*	Humbolt Eel Rvr	59 150
Stephen	San Joaquin Oneal	64 929
Stephen P	Del Norte Crescent	58 626
Theo L	Siskiyou Yreka	69 137
Tho G	Siskiyou Scott Va	69 31
Thomas	Amador Twp 4	55 235
Thomas	Calaveras Twp 9	57 370
Thomas	Contra Costa Twp 1	57 506
Thomas	Santa Cruz Santa Cruz	66 612
Thomas	Santa Cruz Santa Cruz	66 618
Thomas	Sierra Twp 7	66 908
Thomas A	San Francisco 7	681354
	San Francisco	
Thos	San Francisco San Francisco 1	68 900
Thos A	Placer Ophirville	62 655
Thos G	Siskiyou Scott Va	69 31
Thos S	Butte Chico	56 564
W	Calaveras Twp 9	57 399
W	Nevada Grass Valley	61 185
W	Sacramento Brighton	63 207
W	San Francisco San Francisco 9	681074
W	San Joaquin Stockton	641043
W	Shasta French G	66 718
W	Siskiyou Scott Va	69 54
W B	Butte Oro	56 685
W C	Yolo Cache Crk	72 634
W G	Amador Twp 2	55 319
W H	Placer Damascus	62 846
W H	Santa Clara Alviso	65 406
W H	Sierra Downieville	66 966
W H	Tuolumne Springfield	71 374
W J	Nevada Rough &	61 414
W M	Sonoma Santa Rosa	69 410
W P	Amador Twp 7	55 412
W P	Butte Chico	56 564
W R	Butte Wyandotte	56 663
W S M	Sonoma Santa Rosa	69 410
W W	El Dorado Placerville	58 913
Wash	Amador Twp 1	55 462
Wilber	Santa Clara San Jose	65 296
William	Calaveras Twp 6	57 116
William	Calaveras Twp 5	57 187
William	Fresno Twp 3	59 10
William	Nevada Red Dog	61 545
William	San Joaquin Douglass	64 920
William	San Joaquin Elkhorn	64 970
William A	San Joaquin Elkhorn	64 964
William C	San Francisco San Francisco 7	681333
William S	Solano Fairfield	69 197
Willis	Sacramento Dry Crk	63 372
Wm	Butte Kimshaw	56 581
Wm	Calaveras Twp 9	57 399
Wm	El Dorado Eldorado	58 938
Wm	Los Angeles Los Angeles	59 501
Wm	Placer Dutch Fl	62 709

Name	County Locale	M653 RollPage
WRIGHT		
Wm	Sacramento Franklin	63 308
Wm	Sacramento Cosummes	63 404
Wm	San Francisco San Francisco 9	681074
Wm	San Francisco San Francisco 1	68 880
Wm	Sonoma Salt Point	69 693
Wm	Tehama Red Bluff	70 928
Wm C	Butte Chico	56 538
Wm C	Colusa Muion	57 458
Wm Henry	Alameda Brooklyn	55 85
Wm*	San Francisco San Francisco 9	681074
WRIGHTINGTON		
Juanita	San Diego San Diego	64 759
WRIGHTMAN		
C	Yolo Washington	72 604
William E	Yuba Marysville	72 880
WRIGHTSEMAN		
David	San Joaquin Elkhorn	64 986
WRIGHTSLEY		
John	Siskiyou Yreka	69 133
WRIGHTSON		
Henry	Shasta Millvill	66 727
WRIGLESETT		
August*	Yuba Linda	72 994
WRIGLEY		
Joseph	San Francisco San Francisco 11	111 67
WRIKER		
E	Sierra Whiskey	66 844
WRIN		
Thomas D	San Joaquin Stockton	641057
WRING		
---	Mariposa Twp 1	60 659
WRINKLE		
August	Sacramento Ward 1	63 75
WRINKLER		
James J	Colusa Muion	57 459
WRIPPLE		
David	Butte Bidwell	56 731
WRIST		
Thos*	San Francisco San Francisco 1	68 905
WRIT		
Mary	Sacramento Sutter	63 307
WRITERHOLD		
Frank*	Calaveras Twp 7	57 25
WRITHERALD		
J*	Siskiyou Klamath	69 86
WRONERT		
Charles*	Sierra Downieville	66 960
WRONEST		
Charles	Sierra Downieville	66 960
WROSTER		
Martin*	Plumas Quincy	62 993
WRTHINGTON		
Henry*	Santa Cruz Santa Cruz	66 612
WRYCK		
Haston	Yuba Suida	72 987
Maston*	Yuba Linda	72 987
WRYHT		
W	Shasta French G	66 718
WRYHTON		
Thomas*	Del Norte Happy Ca	58 664
WU YUP		
---*	Nevada Nevada	61 310
WU		
---	Calaveras Twp 5	57 257
---	Calaveras Twp 10	57 259
---	Nevada Bridgeport	61 463
---	Sacramento Natonia	63 283
---*	San Francisco San Francisco 4	681199
Che	San Francisco San Francisco 4	681189
Ho	San Francisco San Francisco 4	681192
Hoy	San Francisco San Francisco 4	681203
Hung	San Francisco San Francisco 4	681187
Kou*	San Francisco San Francisco 4	681196
Lou	San Francisco San Francisco 4	681189
Sing	Del Norte Crescent	58 630
So	San Francisco San Francisco 4	681189
Woi	San Francisco San Francisco 4	681189
WUAR		
---*	Calaveras Twp 9	57 349
WUAULL		
---	El Dorado Georgetown	58 756
WUAY		
---	Yuba Long Bar	72 761
WUBBEN		
George H	San Francisco San Francisco 7	681347
WUDENHAMER		
Alex*	Sacramento Ward 1	63 91
WUDENWOOD		
J S	Sacramento San Joaquin	63 363
WUG		
---*	Sacramento Ward 1	63 61
---*	Shasta French G	66 712
WUGER		
Elias*	Nevada Bridgeport	61 443

Name	County Locale	M653 RollPage
WUGGINS		
Ambrose*	Placer Yankee J	62 759
WUHLER		
Andrew*	Yolo No E Twp	72 668
WUI		
Sim	El Dorado Big Bar	58 733
WUIN		
Bridget	Alameda Brooklyn	55 87
WUIRSTINE		
Mary*	San Francisco San Francisco 9	68 945
WUITHWORTH		
R*	El Dorado Mountain	581187
WUJELLO		
Pedro	Los Angeles Los Angeles	59 346
WUK		
Andrew R*	Sierra Twp 5	66 947
WUKENONING		
Henry	Calaveras Twp 5	57 190
WUKERMAN		
John*	Butte Wyandotte	56 666
WUKHAM		
Jas	Napa Napa	61 87
WUL		
Emile*	San Francisco San Francisco 2	67 670
WULAPHER		
John*	Mariposa Coulterville	60 679
WULER		
Anna	Tuolumne Twp 1	71 200
J W*	Nevada Eureka	61 351
WULF		
August	Nevada Bloomfield	61 530
L D	Calaveras Twp 9	57 391
WULLERM		
Alice	San Francisco San Francisco 4	681119
WULLING		
John Low*	Nevada Bridgeport	61 440
WULLY		
Michael*	Calaveras Twp 5	57 196
WULSEY		
James	Tehama Antelope	70 893
WULTER		
---	Tulara Twp 3	71 56
WUM		
---	El Dorado Georgetown	58 746
---	Yuba Long Bar	72 757
---	Yuba Long Bar	72 759
Chow	Yuba Long Bar	72 769
WUMA		
Geo R*	Santa Cruz Soguel	66 584
WUMBER		
Chas*	San Francisco San Francisco 9	681086
WUMEE		
Geo R*	Santa Cruz Soguel	66 584
WUMP		
---*	Mariposa Twp 3	60 582
WUN		
---	El Dorado Georgetown	58 756
---	Placer Rattle Snake	62 636
---	San Francisco San Francisco 4	681178
---*	Nevada Nevada	61 305
Chow	Nevada Washington	61 342
Kim	El Dorado Georgetown	58 682
Kino	El Dorado Georgetown	58 682
Sing	Yuba Long Bar	72 759
William*	Tuolumne Twp 2	71 296
WUNBER		
William	Tuolumne Sonora	71 200
WUNCH		
Jacob	San Francisco San Francisco 10	287 67
WUNER		
Otto*	San Francisco San Francisco 2	67 777
WUNG LEE		
Sy	El Dorado Greenwood	58 730
WUNG		
---	Merced Twp 2	60 916
---	Placer Horseshoe	62 650
---	Sacramento Cosummes	63 396
---	Sacramento Ward 1	63 65
---	San Joaquin Stockton	641088
---	Stanislaus Branch	70 714
An	Del Norte Crescent	58 630
Ling	Yuba Long Bar	72 769
Pie	Butte Ophir	56 805
Quaw	Yuba Long Bar	72 762
WUNIN		
A*	Stanislaus Buena Village	70 723
WUNLEY		
H H	Amador Twp 6	55 438
WUNN		
---	San Francisco San Francisco 4	681176
WUNNENBERG		
W H	San Francisco San Francisco 10	287 67
WUNP		
---*	Mariposa Twp 3	60 552

Name	County Locale	M653 Roll	Page
WUNPLE			
V*	Nevada Eureka	61	382
WUNSTINE			
Mary*	San Francisco San Francisco 9	68	945
WUR			
---	San Francisco San Francisco 4	681	186
WURE			
E P	Yuba Slate Ro	72	690
WUREL			
E B*	Sierra Gibsonville	66	860
WUREMBERG			
August*	Tuolumne Columbia	71	308
WURM			
Joseph	Tuolumne Twp 3	71	424
WURND			
Geo R*	Santa Cruz Soguel	66	584
WURRY			
George*	San Mateo Twp 1	65	71
William*	San Mateo Twp 1	65	71
WURSSER			
Charles*	Solano Fairfield	69	203
WURTEMLING			
Simon*	Mendocino Calpella	60	816
WURTHLIN			
James*	El Dorado Georgetown	58	755
WURTHNORTH			
R	El Dorado Mountain	581	187
WURTHWORTH			
R*	El Dorado Mountain	581	187
WURTY			
Casper	Sierra La Porte	66	770
WURTZ			
Casper	Sierra La Porte	66	770
WUSBAUM			
Jacob*	Merced Twp 1	60	895
WUSBAURN			
Jacob	Merced Twp 1	60	895
WUSEN			
A*	Nevada Eureka	61	352
WUSNOR			
---*	Mendocino Calpella	60	825
WUSSEAN			
Shoes*	Sierra Scales D	66	804
WUSSIAN			
Shoes*	Sierra Scales D	66	663
WUST			
---	El Dorado Georgetown	58	684
WUSTACKIN			
---*	Tehama Tehama	70	940
WUSTAKE			
H	El Dorado Placerville	58	870
WUSTEFELD			
H	San Francisco San Francisco 5	67	527
WUT			
---	Calaveras Twp 6	57	167
Wm	Sierra Twp 5	66	942
WUTERHOLD			
Frank*	Calaveras Twp 7	57	25
WUTH			
Louis B*	San Francisco San Francisco 7	681	416
WUTTER			
Jesse*	Sierra St Louis	66	805
Richard*	Calaveras Twp 10	57	274
WUY			
---*	Shasta French G	66	712
WWIST			
R R	Tuolumne Jamestown	71	445
WWNGANS			
Phillip*	San Francisco San Francisco 9	68	946
WWOODFORD			
Hiram N	Calaveras Twp 6	57	162
WY			
---	Amador Twp 2	55	301
---	Amador Twp 3	55	394
---	Amador Twp 1	55	457
---	Amador Twp 1	55	501
---	Butte Kimshaw	56	600
---	Butte Kimshaw	56	605
---	Butte Oregon	56	626
---	Butte Oregon	56	642
---	Butte Ophir	56	805
---	Calaveras Twp 5	57	233
---	Calaveras Twp 7	57	44
---	Calaveras Twp 8	57	69
---	Del Norte Happy Ca	58	663
---	Del Norte Happy Ca	58	669
---	Mariposa Twp 1	60	673
---	Mariposa Coulterville	60	681
---	Mariposa Coulterville	60	694
---	Mariposa Coulterville	60	700
---	Merced Twp 2	60	915
---	Sacramento Ward 1	63	51
---	Sacramento Ward 1	63	60
---	Shasta French G	66	713
---	Trinity Lewiston	70	964
---	Yolo No E Twp	72	685

Name	County Locale	M653 Roll	Page
WY			
---	Yuba North Ea	72	685
---	Yuba Long Bar	72	764
---	Yuba Fosters	72	842
Ching	Nevada Bridgeport	61	492
Gee	El Dorado Placerville	58	832
Hee	El Dorado Georgetown	58	704
Lee*	Yuba Long Bar	72	761
Lei	Yuba Long Bar	72	761
Sack	Yuba New York	72	721
Sigh	Butte Ophir	56	802
Yup	Stanislaus Empire	70	734
WYAH			
---	Fresno Twp 1	59	27
WYALL			
Albert	Tuolumne Shawsfla	71	398
W	Sacramento Dry Crk	63	378
WYAMT			
E M*	Siskiyou Cottonwoood	69	98
WYAND			
L	El Dorado Diamond	58	784
WYANET			
E M*	Siskiyou Cottonwoood	69	98
WYARD			
Robert	San Mateo Twp 3	65	100
WYARNT			
E M*	Siskiyou Cottonwoood	69	98
WYAT			
A	El Dorado Placerville	58	866
W G	El Dorado Placerville	58	886
WYATT			
Alen	El Dorado Georgetown	58	673
Andrew	Shasta Shasta	66	659
Black	Mariposa Twp 1	60	671
Buford B	Yuba Suida	72	982
Buford B	Yuba Linda Twp	72	984
Edward	Tuolumne Twp 1	71	186
G L	Nevada Nevada	61	315
George H	San Joaquin Oneal	64	913
J K	Nevada Grass Valley	61	201
James	Napa Hot Springs	61	20
Jno*	Sacramento Natonia	63	284
John	Sacramento Ward 1	63	34
Ju*	Sacramento Natonia	63	284
Lemericus*	Plumas Quincy	62	979
Mark	Mariposa Twp 1	60	671
Mark A	Mariposa Twp 3	60	562
O P	Santa Clara Gilroy	65	237
Oliver	Monterey San Juan	60	974
Olivre	Monterey San Juan	60	974
R C	Nevada Bridgeport	61	505
S W	Nevada Eureka	61	344
Semericus*	Plumas Quincy	62	979
Thos A	Napa Yount	61	32
William	Contra Costa Twp 3	57	595
Wm	El Dorado Georgetown	58	703
WYATTE			
E E	Marin Bolinas	60	727
WYBBOCK			
Pepter*	Yuba Linda	72	990
WYBLE			
Joseph	Los Angeles Los Angeles	59	381
WYBURN			
T	Nevada Eureka	61	357
WYCHIK			
B F	El Dorado Mud Springs	58	951
WYCHOFF			
A F	Sierra Morristown	661	051
WYCKMAN			
Wm	Sacramento Sutter	63	300
WYCKOFF			
D	El Dorado Kelsey	581	156
George	San Francisco San Francisco 3	67	33
Gertrud	Amador Twp 1	55	500
Henry	Yolo Cache	72	594
J J S	Yolo Cache	72	590
N	Yolo Cache Crk	72	589
W	Yolo Cache	72	589
Wm	Tuolumne Twp 1	71	203
WYCOFF			
Chas	Butte Bidwell	56	718
Geo	Sacramento Granite	63	264
Henry	Sacramento Granite	63	266
J P	San Francisco San Francisco 5	67	502
WYDER			
John	Siskiyou Yreka	69	187
WYDICK			
Isaac	Butte Chico	56	537
WYE			
---	Amador Twp 5	55	354
---	Amador Twp 6	55	437
---	El Dorado Salmon Falls	581	036
---	El Dorado Salmon Falls	581	040
---	El Dorado Salmon Falls	581	042
---	El Dorado Salmon Falls	581	067
---	El Dorado Coloma	581	083

Name	County Locale	M653 Roll	Page
WYE			
---	El Dorado Coloma	581	122
---	El Dorado Kelsey	581	141
---	El Dorado Casumnes	581	176
---	El Dorado Diamond	58	784
---	El Dorado Diamond	58	787
---	El Dorado Placerville	58	922
---	Sacramento Ward 3	63	491
---	Sacramento Ward 3	63	493
---	San Francisco San Francisco 11		145
			67
Hyram*	San Francisco San Francisco 9	681	049
Jordon	El Dorado Coloma	581	083
Newton	San Joaquin Stockton	641	064
Sing	El Dorado Salmon Falls	581	042
WYEKOFF			
D	El Dorado Kelsey	581	156
WYEN			
---	Yuba Bear Rvr	721	015
WYER			
---*	Yuba Bear Rvr	721	014
Antoomo	Contra Costa Twp 1	57	493
WYERS			
Henry*	Mariposa Coulterville	60	684
William	San Joaquin Stockton	641	077
WYFS			
Martin	Klamath Klamath	59	224
WYGALE			
Warren	Los Angeles Elmonte	59	245
WYGANT			
Jos F	Sacramento Ward 4	63	612
WYKOFF			
J P	San Francisco San Francisco 7	681	438
Jonathan	Solano Vacaville	69	342
WYLANDER			
Wm	Tuolumne Big Oak	71	133
WYLE			
S K	San Francisco San Francisco 4	681	127
S R	San Francisco San Francisco 4	681	127
WYLER			
Geo	Sacramento Ward 1	63	80
WYLEY			
Joe	Siskiyou Yreka	69	177
Joseph	Contra Costa Twp 2	57	574
Robt	El Dorado Casumnes	581	166
Robt	El Dorado Casumnes	581	174
WYLIA			
James*	El Dorado Diamond	58	775
WYLIE			
Geo	Sacramento Ward 1	63	80
James*	El Dorado Diamond	58	775
WYLIR			
Geo*	Sacramento Ward 1	63	80
WYLLIE			
James	Sierra Twp 7	66	872
WYMAN			
A	Nevada Washington	61	336
A A	Butte Ophir	56	769
A D	Yuba Rose Bar	72	791
A N	Tuolumne Twp 2	71	324
A P	Tuolumne Twp 2	71	330
Abram	Yuba Rose Bar	72	802
Alfred P	Nevada Rough &	61	416
B F	Tuolumne Columbia	71	342
B H	San Francisco San Francisco 9	681	070
B Henry	San Francisco San Francisco 3	67	19
Benjamin	Humbolt Union	59	182
Chas C	Nevada Nevada	61	245
D F	Del Norte Crescent	58	631
D F	Del Norte Crescent	58	632
F L	Tuolumne Columbia	71	321
G D	San Francisco San Francisco 5	67	496
G F	Marin Cortemad	60	789
G H	El Dorado Casumnes	581	170
George	San Mateo Twp 2	65	123
George	Tulara Keyesville	71	53
Henry A	San Francisco San Francisco 7	681	390
J	Nevada Eureka	61	358
J	Nevada Eureka	61	363
J	Sacramento Ward 3	63	468
J	San Francisco San Francisco 6	67	448
J D	Butte Hamilton	56	514
Jacob	Yolo Slate Ra	72	703
Jacob	Yuba Slate Ro	72	703
John	Yuba Marysville	72	948
Justus E	Humbolt Union	59	182
Levy	Alameda Washington	55	172
Lizzie	Alameda Brooklyn	55	188
Oliver	San Francisco San Francisco 7	681	338
Saml	Placer Virginia	62	668
Saml*	Tuolumne Twp 2	71	400
Susan	Butte Chico	56	542
Thomas*	Placer Michigan	62	858
W S	Nevada Rough &	61	408
Wm	Butte Wyandotte	56	663
WYMANB			
L D	Colusa Muion	57	458

California 1860 Census Index

Name	County Locale	M653 Roll	Page
WYMANS			
J R	El Dorado Cold Spring	58	1101
Jno	Butte Chico	56	559
WYMOTTE			
Wm	San Francisco San Francisco 1	68	837
WYNAM			
James*	Marin Bolinas	60	733
WYNAN			
Saml	Tuolumne Shawsfla	71	400
WYNANS			
Jacob*	Sierra Twp 5	66	938
James	Marin Bolinas	60	733
WYNANTS			
P A	Tuolumne Twp 4	71	176
WYNAUS			
Jacob*	Sierra Twp 5	66	938
WYND			
Robt B	San Francisco San Francisco 10	330 67	
WYNDHAM			
Jas C	San Francisco San Francisco 2	67	567
Jos C	San Francisco San Francisco 2	67	567
WYNE			
---	El Dorado Diamond	58	805
WYNES			
J	Sutter Yuba	70	761
WYNN			
Jesse	Humbolt Table Bl	59	141
John B	Monterey Alisal	60	1028
WYNNE			
Nicholas	San Francisco San Francisco 8	68	1312
Ptk	San Francisco San Francisco 10	292 67	
WYNOTTE			
John	San Francisco San Francisco 1	68	837
WYO			
---	San Francisco San Francisco 4	68	1212
WYOTT			
Geo	Nevada Nevada	61	268
WYR			
---	Amador Twp 5	55	331
---	San Francisco San Francisco 4	68	1212
WYRICK			
Horace A	Humbolt Eel Rvr	59	146
Jacob	Humbolt Eureka	59	169
WYSE			
Alexr	San Francisco San Francisco 10	317 67	
E J	Butte Wyandotte	56	664
John	Solano Benecia	69	284
Julius G	Los Angeles Los Angeles	59	381
Louis	San Francisco San Francisco 10	283 67	
WYTE			
---	El Dorado Diamond	58	785
WYUANS			
Jacob*	Sierra Twp 5	66	938
WYUANTS			
R A	Tuolumne Garrote	71	176
Y			
---	Calaveras Twp 9	57	348
---	Calaveras Twp 9	57	362
---	Sierra Downieville	66	1007
---	Sierra Cox'S Bar	66	950
---	Sierra Downieville	66	998
Aw	Nevada Nevada	61	299
Chow*	Nevada Nevada	61	308
Is*	Calaveras Twp 5	57	242
YA WYUP			
---*	Nevada Nevada	61	309
YA			
---	Amador Twp 1	55	501
---	Butte Cascade	56	699
---	San Francisco San Francisco 9	68	1088
Ah	Butte Cascade	56	699
Can	Nevada Bridgeport	61	458
Ching	Butte Ophir	56	811
Ching	Butte Ophir	56	816
Ching	Butte Ophir	56	818
Chung	Butte Ophir	56	806
Ling	Butte Cascade	56	700
Lo	Tuolumne Twp 4	71	150
Tong	El Dorado Placerville	58	825
Wan	Yuba Marysville	72	916
You*	Sacramento Granite	63	259
YAAKINI			
Samuel*	Santa Cruz Pajaro	66	560
YAAOUT			
---	Tulara Twp 1	71	117
YAB			
---	Sacramento Natonia	63	283
YABEZ			
Jose	Butte Oregon	56	614
YABLE			
Julius	Amador Township	55	464
YABLONSKY			
Myer	San Francisco San Francisco 2	67	647
YACE			
Hog*	Tulara Yule Rvr	71	31
YACELLAS			
Nicholas*	Mariposa Twp 1	60	669
YACH			
---*	Yuba Fosters	72	843
YACK			
---	Fresno Twp 2	59	17
---	Mariposa Twp 1	60	664
---	Mariposa Coulterville	60	688
---	Nevada Bridgeport	61	457
---	Yuba Long Bar	72	755
---	Yuba Fosters	72	843
Sam	Sacramento Ward 4	63	610
YACKA			
Maguil*	Napa Napa	61	84
YACKS			
---	Calaveras Twp 5	57	192
YACO			
---	Fresno Twp 1	59	54
YAD			
---	Tuolumne Jacksonville	71	516
YADALPHO			
John B	Calaveras Twp 5	57	217
YAE			
---	Nevada Rough &	61	424
YAGAMMAH			
---	Butte Chico	56	551
YAGEL			
Thomas	Calaveras Twp 10	57	262
YAGEN			
Peater*	Amador Twp 5	55	330
YAGER			
Adam	Sacramento Ward 3	63	481
Anna	El Dorado Casumnes	58	1175
Christian	San Francisco San Francisco 1	68	926
Christopher	San Francisco San Francisco 4	68	1171
Cornelius	Contra Costa Twp 3	57	616
F	Butte Kimshaw	56	576
Henry	Santa Clara San Jose	65	382
Henry*	El Dorado Salmon Falls	58	1044
Jo	Amador Twp 2	55	323
John	Amador Twp 1	55	485
John	Contra Costa Twp 3	57	616
John	Sacramento Franklin	63	324
John	Tuolumne Twp 1	71	237
John*	El Dorado Georgetown	58	685
L	Sacramento Ward 3	63	445
Lawrence	Sacramento Ward 4	63	587
Mary	El Dorado Casumnes	58	1174
Michel	Amador Twp 5	55	330
P	Sacramento Ward 4	63	600
Peater*	Amador Twp 5	55	330
Peter	San Francisco San Francisco 4	68	1228
Phillip	Amador Twp 5	55	358
Phillip*	Butte Cascade	56	690
R P	Sierra Twp 7	66	884
Rodolph	Solano Benecia	69	281
So	Amador Twp 2	55	323
T J	Amador Twp 1	55	487
YAGES			
John	Tuolumne Sonora	71	237
YAGINIA			
N	Amador Twp 6	55	428
YAGO			
Anastaico	Amador Twp 2	55	282
YAGON			
Peater	Amador Twp 5	55	330
YAH LAH			
---	Santa Clara San Jose	65	374
YAH LAM			
---	Sierra La Porte	66	774
YAH			
---	Alameda Oakland	55	57
---	Calaveras Twp 10	57	285
---	Calaveras Twp 5	57	299
---	Del Norte Crescent	58	659
---	Tuolumne Twp 5	71	516
---	Yuba Long Bar	72	758
Ching	San Francisco San Francisco 5	67	1207
Cum	Fresno Twp 2	59	19
Le	Tuolumne Twp 4	71	179
Thou*	San Francisco San Francisco 5	67	1207
Thow	San Francisco San Francisco 5	67	1207
YAHAMMAH			
---	Butte Chico	56	551
YAHMER			
Samuel*	Placer Auburn	62	567
YAHNER			
Sanwell*	Placer Auburn	62	567
YAHTS			
N H	San Francisco San Francisco 1	68	918
YAILL			
Jas A	Santa Clara San Jose	65	280
YAINT			
Elizabeth*	San Francisco San Francisco 8	68	1249
YAIR			
---	Amador Twp 5	55	364
YAISB			
Joel*	Plumas Meadow Valley	62	904
YAJES			
John	El Dorado Georgetown	58	685
YAK			
---	El Dorado Georgetown	58	747
---	Sierra La Porte	66	780
---	Yolo No E Twp	72	681
---	Yuba Long Bar	72	758
---	Yuba Fosters	72	842
YAKE			
---	Tuolumne Twp 5	71	509
---	Tuolumne Green Springs	71	518
---	Yuba Long Bar	72	761
---	Yuba Long Bar	72	764
---	Yuba Fosters	72	826
---	Yuba Fosters	72	827
---*	Yuba Foster B	72	826
Benj*	Sierra Downieville	66	1029
YAKES			
John L	San Francisco San Francisco 7	68	1426
YAKET			
---	Yuba Bear Rvr	72	1015
Sam*	Yuba Bear Rvr	72	1014
YALE			
A	Trinity Rearings	70	990
Geo	San Francisco San Francisco 10	245 67	
George	Plumas Quincy	62	998
Jerry	Yuba Marysville	72	845
John	Sierra Twp 7	66	902
Miles H	Trinity Mouth Ca	70	1014
YALENCIA			
Juan	Alameda Brooklyn	55	200
YALES			
Solomon	Mendocino Little L	60	831
YALLEP			
Honea C	Alameda Brooklyn	55	178
YALLEY			
John	Tulara Visalia	71	6
YALLO			
Martin	San Francisco San Francisco 1	68	911
YALOK			
---	Sacramento Ward 1	63	54
YALPY			
Geo W	Alameda Brooklyn	55	190
YAM KIM			
---	Plumas Quincy	62	970
YAM			
---	Amador Twp 2	55	327
---	Amador Twp 1	55	497
---	Amador Twp 1	55	502
---	Calaveras Twp 8	57	68
---	Calaveras Twp 8	57	92
---	Del Norte Happy Ca	58	667
---	El Dorado White Oaks	58	1023
---	El Dorado Salmon Falls	58	1041
---	El Dorado Union	58	1091
---	El Dorado Coloma	58	1103
---	El Dorado Kelsey	58	1131
---	El Dorado Kelsey	58	1135
---	El Dorado Mountain	58	1189
---	El Dorado Diamond	58	790
---	El Dorado Placerville	58	923
---	Mariposa Twp 3	60	607
---	Placer Rattle Snake	62	629
---	Tuolumne Jamestown	71	433
---	Tuolumne Jamestown	71	442
---	Yuba New York	72	740
---*	Amador Twp 2	55	289
---*	Placer Auburn	62	583
---*	Tuolumne Big Oak	71	178
Ah	Tuolumne Twp 4	71	178
Chon	Nevada Grass Valley	61	234
Chow	Nevada Grass Valley	61	232
See	San Francisco San Francisco 11	159 67	
YAMATA			
---	Mendocino Round Va	60	885
YAMEL			
Bennet	Marin Cortemad	60	753
YAMFOO			
---	Trinity Trinindad Rvr	70	1050
YAMG			
---	Mariposa Twp 3	60	544
YAMMEITE			
John A	San Francisco San Francisco 5	67	504
YAMOLD			
Richard	El Dorado Kelsey	58	1147
YAMON			
---	Trinity Mouth Ca	70	1011
YAMPA			
---	Sacramento Granite	63	269
YAN			
---	Amador Twp 2	55	285

California 1860 Census Index

Name	County Locale	M653 RollPage	Name	County Locale	M653 RollPage	Name	County Locale	M653 RollPage
YAN			**YAN**			**YANG**		
---	Amador Twp 2	55 291	Po	Sacramento Granite	63 268	---	Yuba Fosters	72 842
---	Amador Twp 2	55 292	Quoy	San Francisco San Francisco 4	681204	---	Yuba Fosters	72 843
---	Amador Twp 2	55 319	So	San Francisco San Francisco 5	671207	---	Yuba Marysville	72 921
---	Amador Twp 2	55 320	Soo	Yuba Fosters	72 827	Ah	Sacramento Ward 1	63 152
---	Amador Twp 5	55 334	Thomas*	Placer Iona Hills	62 879	Chung	Plumas Quincy	62 946
---	Amador Twp 5	55 350	Thung	San Francisco San Francisco 5	671206	Fan	Mariposa Twp 1	60 665
---	Amador Twp 5	55 354	Wall	Yuba Marysville	72 896	Fun	Plumas Quincy	62 946
---	Amador Twp 5	55 355	Wing	Yuba Fosters	72 841	Hi	Sacramento Granite	63 268
---	Amador Twp 6	55 422	**YANABRANT**			Kom Lon G	Tuolumne Twp 4	71 181
---	Amador Twp 6	55 432	Jesse	Plumas Meadow Valley	62 899	Kom Long	Tuolumne Big Oak	71 181
---	Amador Twp 1	55 477	**YANAE**			Lee	Nevada Bridgeport	61 439
---	Amador Twp 1	55 479	---	San Diego Agua Caliente	64 863	See	Tuolumne Knights	71 528
---	Amador Twp 1	55 496	**YANAHAH**			Te	Alameda Oakland	55 34
---	Amador Twp 1	55 503	---*	Butte Chico	56 550	Tou	Mariposa Twp 1	60 665
---	Amador Twp 1	55 504	**YANAKER**			Wan	Yuba Long Bar	72 756
---	Amador Twp 1	55 511	Jas B*	Alameda Oakland	55 38	Waw	Yuba Long Bar	72 756
---	Calaveras Twp 5	57 246	**YANBON**			**YANGER**		
---	Calaveras Twp 9	57 360	Lawrence	Calaveras Twp 7	57 17	E	Sacramento San Joaquin	63 359
---	Calaveras Twp 9	57 363	**YANCE**			**YANGO**		
---	Calaveras Twp 9	57 375	Frederick*	Contra Costa Twp 3	57 598	D	Amador Twp 2	55 294
---	Calaveras Twp 8	57 62	J W	Butte Cascade	56 701	**YANI WO**		
---	Del Norte Happy Ca	58 663	John	Butte Bidwell	56 707	---	Fresno Twp 2	59 69
---	El Dorado Salmon Falls	581041	**YANCEY**			**YANI**		
---	El Dorado Salmon Falls	581046	Charles A	Fresno Twp 1	59 33	---	Nevada Grass Valley	61 227
---	El Dorado Salmon Falls	581058	E C	Trinity Douglas	70 979	Louis	Tuolumne Jamestown	71 431
---	El Dorado Salmon Falls	581060	Frederick	San Francisco San Francisco 7	681443	**YANK**		
---	El Dorado Coloma	581077	H	Nevada Washington	61 338	---	Amador Twp 2	55 289
---	El Dorado Union	581091	H I	El Dorado Placerville	58 907	---	Sierra Downieville	661026
---	El Dorado Coloma	581107	H J	El Dorado Placerville	58 907	Charles	Placer Iona Hills	62 893
---	El Dorado Coloma	581110	James	Santa Cruz Pajaro	66 570	**YANKE**		
---	El Dorado Coloma	581111	Thomas	El Dorado Placerville	58 908	John	Los Angeles Elmonte	59 263
---	El Dorado Coloma	581120	W K	Trinity Weaverville	701062	**YANKENER**		
---	El Dorado Kelsey	581129	William R	Solano Suisan	69 235	J M	Siskiyou Scott Va	69 49
---	El Dorado Kelsey	581131	**YANCH**			**YANLIS**		
---	El Dorado Kelsey	581136	Martin	Nevada Bridgeport	61 497	Henry	Sacramento Ward 1	63 135
---	El Dorado Diamond	58 796	**YANCY**			**YANN**		
---	El Dorado Diamond	58 797	Fred	San Francisco San Francisco 5	67 494	---	Calaveras Twp 10	57 274
---	El Dorado Placerville	58 823	I P	Tuolumne Twp 3	71 453	**YANNNA**		
---	El Dorado Placerville	58 832	John	Tuolumne Twp 1	71 198	Mary*	San Francisco San Francisco 4	681160
---	El Dorado Placerville	58 933	Marshall	Siskiyou Shasta Valley	69 121	**YANO**		
---	El Dorado Mud Springs	58 985	T	San Francisco San Francisco 6	67 431	---*	Amador Twp 2	55 289
---	El Dorado Mud Springs	58 990	William	Contra Costa Twp 3	57 594	**YANONIS**		
---	Mariposa Twp 1	60 658	**YANDENER**			Guilan	Calaveras Twp 5	57 217
---	Mariposa Twp 1	60 662	J M*	Siskiyou Scott Va	69 49	**YANOVA**		
---	Nevada Grass Valley	61 227	**YANDLE**			Jno A	San Francisco San Francisco 10	67 219
---	Nevada Bridgeport	61 457	J M	Yolo Cache	72 609			
---	Placer Rattle Snake	62 629	**YANE**			Jon A	San Francisco San Francisco 10	67 219
---	Placer Rattle Snake	62 633	---	Amador Twp 2	55 280			
---	Placer Rattle Snake	62 638	---	Placer Secret R	62 621	**YANPA**		
---	Placer Folsom	62 640	Sam*	Stanislaus Buena Village	70 722	---	Sacramento Granite	63 269
---	Sacramento Granite	63 245	**YANER**			**YANS**		
---	Sacramento Granite	63 269	Shal*	Mariposa Twp 1	60 640	Edmund	Los Angeles Los Angeles	59 405
---	Sacramento Ward 4	63 558	**YANES**			**YANSEN**		
---	San Francisco San Francisco 4	681194	Letrii?Tina*	Tuolumne Sonora	71 224	Frank	San Francisco San Francisco 11	67 97
---	San Francisco San Francisco 10	67 356	Letristina	Tuolumne Twp 1	71 224			
---	Shasta Horsetown	66 710	Ramon	San Diego San Diego	64 772	**YANSEY**		
---	Sierra Downieville	661006	**YANETTER**			F	El Dorado Placerville	58 872
---	Sierra Downieville	661007	Chas	Alameda Brooklyn	55 99	**YANSH**		
---	Sierra Downieville	661015	**YANEY**			Bernard	Calaveras Twp 7	57 1
---	Sierra Morristown	661056	I P	Tuolumne Jamestown	71 453	**YANSON**		
---	Sierra Downieville	66 981	John	Tuolumne Sonora	71 198	Peter	Alameda Brooklyn	55 136
---	Sierra Downieville	66 985	**YANEZ**			**YANT**		
---	Siskiyou Scott Ri	69 76	Antonio	Los Angeles San Pedro	59 479	G W	Nevada Nevada	61 284
---	Stanislaus Emory	70 744	Eliza	Tuolumne Sonora	71 224	**YANTE**		
---	Tuolumne Don Pedro	71 163	Francisco	Santa Ba	64 221	---	Placer Dutch Fl	62 714
---	Yuba Long Bar	72 761		San Bernardino		**YANTER**		
---	Yuba Fosters	72 842	Louis	Tuolumne Twp 1	71 227	M	Shasta Millvill	66 727
---	Yuba Linda	72 993	Louis*	Tuolumne Twp 3	71 431	**YANTZ**		
---*	Nevada Bridgeport	61 463	**YANG LEE**			Bernard	Calaveras Twp 8	57 86
---*	San Francisco San Francisco 9	681095	---	Nevada Bridgeport	61 439	**YANY**		
---*	Tuolumne Jacksonville	71 169	**YANG**			---	Calaveras Twp 10	57 259
---*	Yuba Foster B	72 826	---	Calaveras Twp 5	57 136	Almond*	Nevada Bloomfield	61 519
Ah	Tuolumne Twp 4	71 163	---	Calaveras Twp 6	57 172	Gir	Sacramento Natonia	63 286
Ah	Tuolumne Twp 4	71 169	---	Calaveras Twp 10	57 259	J	Nevada Eureka	61 366
Choi	Calaveras Twp 8	57 87	---	Calaveras Twp 10	57 271	**YANZ**		
Choy	San Francisco San Francisco 4	681210	---	El Dorado Mountain	581187	Louis*	Tuolumne Twp 3	71 431
Die	Butte Ophir	56 813	---	El Dorado Mountain	581188	**YAP**		
Die	Butte Ophir	56 818	---	El Dorado Mountain	581189	---	Butte Kimshaw	56 586
Edward*	Alameda Oakland	55 2	---	El Dorado Big Bar	58 738	---	Butte Kimshaw	56 587
Fe	San Francisco San Francisco 9	681093	---	El Dorado Eldorado	58 939	---	Sierra La Porte	66 780
Fi	Mariposa Twp 3	60 579	---	Mariposa Twp 3	60 544	---*	Butte Kimshaw	56 586
Fri	Mariposa Twp 3	60 579	---	Mariposa Twp 3	60 576	Kae	San Francisco San Francisco 10	67 356
Gee	Sacramento Granite	63 269	---	Mariposa Twp 1	60 626			
Hu	San Francisco San Francisco 1	68 925	---	Mariposa Twp 1	60 658	Lau	Sacramento Granite	63 268
J*	Nevada Bridgeport	61 457	---	Mariposa Twp 1	60 666	**YAPIA**		
Kee	El Dorado Coloma	581078	---	Nevada Grass Valley	61 233	Jose	Santa Cruz Soguel	66 587
Kien	Butte Oro	56 680	---	Nevada Grass Valley	61 234	**YAPLE**		
King	San Francisco San Francisco 4	681204	---	Placer Secret R	62 623	H B	Tuolumne Twp 2	71 374
Ku	San Francisco San Francisco 4	681185	---	Placer Rattle Snake	62 637	Perry	San Joaquin Stockton	641050
L L*	Stanislaus Branch	70 711	---	Placer Virginia	62 682	**YAR**		
Lan	Amador Twp 2	55 292	---	San Francisco San Francisco 4	681197	---	Amador Twp 1	55 502
Lawey	San Francisco San Francisco 4	681204	---	Yolo No E Twp	72 682	---	Calaveras Twp 5	57 245
Lon	Yuba Bear Rvr	721000	---	Yolo Slate Ra	72 688	---	Mariposa Twp 1	60 651
Pah	Stanislaus Emory	70 752	---	Yuba Long Bar	72 754	---	Mariposa Coulterville	60 692
			---	Yuba Long Bar	72 758			

California 1860 Census Index

Name	County Locale	M653 Roll	Page
YAR			
---	Sacramento Granite	63	262
Par*	Mariposa Twp 1	60	651
Sing	Sacramento Natonia	63	283
YARABULDI			
Stephen*	Calaveras Twp 10	57	260
YARAR			
Carlota	Sacramento Ward 1	63	17
YARBER			
Chas	Mendocino Round Va	60	877
YARBOROUGH			
Absolem	Fresno Twp 2	59	48
Albert	Fresno Twp 2	59	48
Shadrack N	Calaveras Twp 6	57	166
Thadruck N*	Calaveras Twp 6	57	166
YARBRO			
---	Tulara Keyesville	71	68
David C	Sonoma Mendocino	69	458
John*	Tulara Keeneysburg	71	49
YARBROUGH			
John	Tulara Visalia	71	106
W H	Sonoma Russian	69	438
YARCK			
W*	Yolo Cache	72	643
YARD			
Charles D	San Francisco San Francisco 8	681	308
Geo M	Alameda Oakland	55	31
YARDLEY			
Jas	Yolo Cache Crk	72	609
YARER			
Shab	Mariposa Twp 1	60	640
Shal	Mariposa Twp 1	60	640
YARG			
---	Amador Twp 2	55	314
YARGEN			
Patrick	San Francisco San Francisco 1	68	858
YARGUES			
Anton	Tuolumne Twp 2	71	320
YARICKS			
H	Yolo Cache Crk	72	643
YARIGER			
P C	Tuolumne Twp 2	71	332
YARINGTON			
William*	Placer Michigan	62	823
YARISH			
Bernard*	Calaveras Twp 7	57	1
YARLO			
Martinan	Calaveras Twp 5	57	211
Martinas*	Calaveras Twp 5	57	211
YARMAN			
Loren	Calaveras Twp 9	57	352
Lorenzo	Calaveras Twp 9	57	352
YARMY			
Pasco	Calaveras Twp 7	57	1
YARN			
---	Amador Twp 2	55	280
Mannuilda	Calaveras Twp 8	57	86
YARNEL			
Bennet	Marin Cortemad	60	753
YARNELB			
Geo*	Sacramento Ward 1	63	32
YARNELL			
Geo	Sacramento Ward 1	63	32
YARNET			
Bennet	Marin San Rafael	60	766
YARNOLD			
R	El Dorado Placerville	58	884
YAROLD			
John*	Plumas Meadow Valley	62	904
YAROTEY			
J	San Joaquin Stockton	64	1059
YARRENGLEN			
Henry	Sacramento Granite	63	229
YARROW			
Henry	Los Angeles Los Angeles	59	342
YARRY			
Joseph	Mariposa Twp 3	60	570
YAS			
---	Calaveras Twp 5	57	245
YASS			
F E	Butte Oregon	56	637
YASSEM			
Y	El Dorado Georgetown	58	707
YAST			
J H*	Sacramento Alabama	63	413
YAT			
---	Alameda Oakland	55	71
---	Amador Twp 3	55	410
---	Amador Twp 6	55	446
---	Calaveras Twp 5	57	176
---	Calaveras Twp 5	57	215
---	Calaveras Twp 10	57	269
---	Calaveras Twp 10	57	296
---	Calaveras Twp 10	57	297
---	Calaveras Twp 4	57	299
---	Calaveras Twp 4	57	300
YAT			
---	Del Norte Crescent	58	641
---	El Dorado Coloma	58	1077
---	El Dorado Placerville	58	832
---	Mariposa Coulterville	60	680
---	Mendocino Big Rvr	60	852
---	Nevada Bridgeport	61	458
---	Placer Virginia	62	684
---	Sacramento Ward 1	63	56
---	Sacramento Ward 1	63	63
---	San Francisco San Francisco 4	681	178
---	San Francisco San Francisco 4	681	187
---	San Francisco San Francisco 4	681	190
---	San Francisco San Francisco 11	144 67	
---	San Francisco San Francisco 2	67	754
---	Tuolumne Twp 4	71	169
---	Tuolumne Jacksonville	71	516
---	Tuolumne Green Springs	71	517
---	Yuba Long Bar	72	761
---*	Sacramento Granite	63	245
---*	Tuolumne Jacksonville	71	168
---*	Tuolumne Jacksonville	71	169
---*	Tuolumne Twp 4	71	168
Ah Ching	San Francisco San Francisco 5	671	207
Goo	Sacramento Granite	63	269
Thou*	San Francisco San Francisco 5	671	207
YATE			
Ann E	Contra Costa Twp 2	57	543
Jadge R*	Siskiyou Yreka	69	126
YATES			
Adam	Merced Twp 1	60	895
Alfred	San Joaquin Stockton	64	1064
Charles	Yuba Foster B	72	824
Chas	Sacramento Ward 1	63	105
Chas	San Francisco San Francisco 1	68	922
Chester	Amador Twp 2	55	281
David M	Butte Oregon	56	626
Douss	Monterey Alisal	60	1035
Edward	Amador Twp 6	55	431
Edward	Tuolumne Twp 1	71	234
Edwd	San Francisco San Francisco 6	67	440
Ellen*	San Francisco San Francisco 10	188 67	
G E	Nevada Bridgeport	61	487
H H	Sonoma Russian	69	434
James	Los Angeles Azuza	59	272
James	Solano Suisan	59	210
James J	San Francisco San Francisco 7	681	332
Jno	Nevada Nevada	61	258
Joel S	Tuolumne Columbia	71	294
John	San Joaquin Elkhorn	64	969
John	Shasta Cottonwood	66	737
John	Solano Benecia	69	302
John A	Amador Township	55	465
John D	Los Angeles Los Angeles	59	329
John E	Mariposa Twp 3	60	561
John J	Amador Twp 1	55	465
John L*	San Francisco San Francisco 7	681	426
John W	Sonoma Russian	69	434
John*	El Dorado Georgetown	58	678
Jonathan L	Sierra Whiskey	66	843
Jonathan L*	Sierra Whiskey	66	843
Joseph	Mendocino Ukiah	60	805
Joseph	San Francisco San Francisco 10	188 67	
Joshua	Calaveras Twp 6	57	171
Lewis	Santa Clara Santa Clara	65	520
Matilda H	San Francisco San Francisco 2	67	803
Moses	El Dorado Georgetown	58	707
Oscar	El Dorado Casumnes	58	1175
Qameo	Colusa Colusi	57	424
Robt	San Francisco San Francisco 1	68	918
Thomas	Santa Cruz Santa Cruz	66	611
Thos	Siskiyou Cottonwood	69	99
W J	Sutter Bear Rvr	70	826
Washington	Nevada Rough &	61	398
William H	San Diego Agua Caliente	64	814
William H	San Francisco San Francisco 4	681	214
William H	San Francisco San Francisco 3	67	63
Wm	Nevada Nevada	61	261
Wm	San Francisco San Francisco 1	68	860
YATLOR			
A M	El Dorado Kelsey	58	1149
YATYES			
Ellen	San Francisco San Francisco 10	188 67	
YATZ			
Danl	Santa Clara San Jose	65	363
YAU			
---	Calaveras Twp 5	57	246
A	Sacramento Granite	63	269
Fong	San Francisco San Francisco 11	160 67	
Kong	San Francisco San Francisco 11	160 67	
YAU			
Lin	Butte Ophir	56	815
Ming	San Francisco San Francisco 11	160 67	
Sing	San Francisco San Francisco 11	160 67	
Yee	San Francisco San Francisco 11	159 67	
YAUDING			
Henry	El Dorado Mud Springs	58	987
YAUM			
Lip	Placer Rattle Snake	62	631
YAUN			
---	Tuolumne Jacksonville	71	167
---	Tuolumne Twp 3	71	457
Ah	Tuolumne Twp 4	71	167
YAUNEME			
---	Tulara Twp 2	71	36
YAUNNA			
Mary	San Francisco San Francisco 4	681	160
YAUSEN			
Frank*	San Francisco San Francisco 11	97 67	
YAVEL			
A De*	San Francisco San Francisco 7	681	426
YAVUT			
---*	Tulara Twp 1	71	119
YAW O			
Ow	Yuba Marysville	72	895
YAW			
---	Amador Twp 2	55	280
---	Amador Twp 6	55	430
---	Calaveras Twp 5	57	192
---	Calaveras Twp 10	57	268
---	Calaveras Twp 9	57	360
---	Calaveras Twp 9	57	375
---	Calaveras Twp 8	57	84
---	El Dorado Salmon Hills	58	1059
---	El Dorado Kelsey	58	1132
---	Fresno Twp 1	59	28
---	Nevada Bridgeport	61	459
---	Placer Dutch Fl	62	722
---	Sacramento Mississipi	63	184
---	Yolo Slate Ra	72	715
---	Yuba Slate Ro	72	715
---	Yuba Long Bar	72	763
---*	San Francisco San Francisco 9	681	095
---*	Tuolumne Big Oak	71	182
---*	Yuba Foster B	72	831
---*	Yuba Fosters	72	842
Ah	Butte Oro	56	687
Ah	Tuolumne Twp 4	71	182
Ku	San Francisco San Francisco 4	681	185
Leon*	Calaveras Twp 9	57	361
Thung	San Francisco San Francisco 5	671	206
Tung	Amador Twp 2	55	285
Ya	Sacramento Granite	63	259
YAWGER			
P C	Tuolumne Columbia	71	332
YAY			
---	Mariposa Twp 3	60	552
---*	Nevada Bloomfield	61	522
YAYTON			
John*	Mariposa Twp 1	60	663
YAYTOR			
Samuel*	Nevada Bloomfield	61	523
YAZER			
Joseph	San Francisco San Francisco 1	68	807
YAZTON			
John*	Mariposa Twp 1	60	663
YBARA			
Manuel	San Bernardino Santa Inez	64	140
YBARRA			
Andreas	San Diego S Luis R	64	777
Celestino	Los Angeles Los Angeles	59	389
Felipe	San Diego S Luis R	64	777
Filomeno	Los Angeles Los Angeles	59	305
Filonieno	Los Angeles Los Angeles	59	313
Geronimo	Los Angeles Los Angeles	59	304
Guadalupe R	Los Angeles Los Angeles	59	324
Jose	Los Angeles Los Angeles	59	325
Jose	San Diego S Luis R	64	778
Josefa	Los Angeles Los Angeles	59	350
Maria	Los Angeles Los Angeles	59	319
Maria	Los Angeles Los Angeles	59	338
Maria C	San Diego S Luis R	64	777
Miguel	San Diego S Luis R	64	777
Ramon	Los Angeles Los Angeles	59	331
Sautos	Los Angeles Los Angeles	59	304
YBASETA			
Juan Dios*	Sacramento Franklin	63	322
YCHICK			
Isaac	Amador Twp 2	55	287
YCHOSS			
---	Humbolt Eureka	59	172

Name	County Locale	M653 Roll	Page
YDALGO			
Agapeto	Monterey S Antoni	60	968
YE A			
---	Yuba Long Bar	72	757
YE CHOY			
---	Tuolumne Chinese	71	524
YE LEON			
---	Tuolumne Chinese	71	524
YE ONG			
---	Sacramento Ward 1	63	66
YE SE FA			
---*	San Francisco San Francisco 9	681	062
YE WA			
---	Tuolumne Chinese	71	524
YE WAH			
---	Tuolumne Chinese	71	524
YE			
---	Amador Twp 6	55	422
---	Amador Twp 1	55	481
---	Calaveras Twp 6	57	164
---	Calaveras Twp 6	57	165
---	Calaveras Twp 6	57	176
---	Calaveras Twp 5	57	233
---	Calaveras Twp 5	57	234
---	Calaveras Twp 5	57	249
---	Calaveras Twp 10	57	276
---	Calaveras Twp 10	57	295
---	Del Norte Crescent	58	643
---	El Dorado White Oaks	581	009
---	El Dorado White Oaks	581	023
---	El Dorado Salmon Falls	581	053
---	El Dorado Coloma	581	077
---	El Dorado Kelsey	581	144
---	El Dorado Indian D	581	159
---	El Dorado Casumnes	581	160
---	El Dorado Casumnes	581	162
---	El Dorado Mountain	581	183
---	El Dorado Mountain	581	190
---	El Dorado Diamond	58	790
---	El Dorado Diamond	58	806
---	El Dorado Placerville	58	832
---	El Dorado Placerville	58	834
---	El Dorado Placerville	58	871
---	El Dorado Placerville	58	886
---	El Dorado Placerville	58	919
---	El Dorado Mud Springs	58	960
---	El Dorado Mud Springs	58	961
---	El Dorado Mud Springs	58	971
---	El Dorado Mud Springs	58	985
---	Mariposa Coulterville	60	700
---	Nevada Rough &	61	398
---	Nevada Bridgeport	61	457
---	Placer Auburn	62	596
---	Placer Illinois	62	746
---	Sacramento Cosumnes	63	387
---	Sacramento Ward 1	63	56
---	Sierra La Porte	66	780
---	Sierra Twp 5	66	945
---	Sierra Cox'S Bar	66	951
---	Trinity Lewiston	70	956
---	Tulara Twp 1	71	96
---	Tuolumne Chinese	71	510
---	Tuolumne Twp 5	71	514
---	Tuolumne Twp 5	71	524
---	Tuolumne Chinese	71	525
---	Tuolumne Don Pedro	71	535
---	Tuolumne Twp 6	71	536
---	Yuba Long Bar	72	757
A	Sacramento Ward 1	63	56
Ah Sam*	Plumas Meadow Valley	62	909
Chang	Sacramento Ward 1	63	59
Chee*	Butte Ophir	56	804
Ching	Mariposa Coulterville	60	682
Choung	Tuolumne Twp 5	71	524
Choy	Butte Ophir	56	804
Chury*	El Dorado Coloma	581	084
Han	Nevada Bridgeport	61	457
J*	Tuolumne Twp 5	71	524
Leon	El Dorado Placerville	58	832
Lon	El Dorado Placerville	58	839
Lone	Sacramento Natonia	63	283
Luey	San Francisco San Francisco 11	92 67	
Min			
Ong	Sacramento Ward 1	63	66
Poo	San Francisco San Francisco 4	681	189
Pur	Amador Twp 5	55	330
Sony	Calaveras Twp 5	57	190
Sung	Plumas Meadow Valley	62	909
Ung	Yuba Long Bar	72	764
Wa	Tuolumne Twp 5	71	524
Wuh	El Dorado Georgetown	58	701
YEA			
---	Amador Twp 5	55	349
---	Amador Twp 5	55	350
---	Amador Twp 5	55	351
---	Amador Twp 5	55	364

Name	County Locale	M653 Roll	Page
YEA			
---	Amador Twp 5	55	365
---	Amador Twp 3	55	410
---	Amador Twp 7	55	415
---	Amador Twp 6	55	433
---	Amador Twp 6	55	436
---	Amador Twp 1	55	495
---	Butte Ophir	56	779
---	Calaveras Twp 6	57	139
---	Calaveras Twp 4	57	334
---	Calaveras Twp 4	57	339
---	Fresno Twp 2	59	19
---	Mariposa Twp 1	60	662
---	Placer Secret R	62	624
---	Placer Virginia	62	679
---	Tuolumne Don Pedro	71	163
---	Tuolumne Twp 5	71	515
---	Tuolumne Twp 5	71	516
---	Tuolumne Don Pedro	71	535
Ah	Calaveras Twp 7	57	30
M	Sacramento Granite	63	240
Om	Amador Twp 7	55	415
On	Amador Twp 7	55	415
On	Amador Twp 7	55	418
Tuck	Tuolumne Twp 6	71	529
Wu	Tuolumne Twp 6	71	540
YEADON			
Joshia*	El Dorado Diamond	58	767
YEAH			
---*	Placer Dutch Fl	62	722
YEAKLE			
Wm	Sacramento Ward 1	63	39
YEALY			
Henry	Sonoma Armally	69	504
YEAM			
---*	Placer Auburn	62	576
YEAMAN			
Richd	Sacramento Cosumnes	63	394
YEAN			
---	Amador Twp 5	55	352
---	Placer Secret R	62	622
---	Placer Rattle Snake	62	627
---	Placer Illinois	62	704
---*	Placer Dutch Fl	62	722
YEAR			
---	Calaveras Twp 6	57	139
---	Nevada Nevada	61	301
Chow	Placer Dutch Fl	62	721
YEARGER			
Daniel	Calaveras Twp 9	57	370
J R	Calaveras Twp 9	57	361
YEARGOR			
J R	Calaveras Twp 9	57	361
YEARHART			
Fred	Sierra Downieville	66	976
YEARS			
Henry	San Francisco San Francisco 2	67	623
YEASENS			
David	Trinity Dead Wood	70	958
YEAST			
Jno	Butte Kimshaw	56	604
YEASY			
Edwin	Alameda Oakland	55	8
YEATES			
James H	Plumas Quincy	62	923
YEATON			
O C	Nevada Bloomfield	61	519
YEAU			
Nathaniel*	Yuba Parke Ba	72	782
YEAWA			
---	Tuolumne Don Pedro	71	540
YECCO			
John	Mariposa Coulterville	60	685
YECK			
---	Amador Twp 1	55	477
---	Calaveras Twp 7	57	39
---	Calaveras Twp 8	57	63
---	Calaveras Twp 8	57	84
---	El Dorado Coloma	581	084
---	El Dorado Mountain	581	185
---	El Dorado Mud Springs	58	978
---	Trinity Weaverville	701	072
---	Trinity Lewiston	70	956
---*	Yuba Foster B	72	827
No	Sacramento Granite	63	269
YECT			
---	Tuolumne Don Pedro	71	535
YEDERS			
Moore	Alameda Brooklyn	55	140
YEDT			
---	Tuolumne Twp 6	71	535
YEE SONG			
---	Sacramento Ward 1	63	71
YEE SUP			
---	Sacramento Ward 1	63	71
YEE			
---	Amador Twp 2	55	280

Name	County Locale	M653 Roll	Page
YEE			
---	Amador Twp 6	55	422
---	Amador Twp 6	55	423
---	Amador Twp 6	55	424
---	Amador Twp 1	55	477
---	Amador Twp 1	55	502
---	Amador Twp 1	55	503
---	Amador Twp 1	55	510
---	Butte Bidwell	56	714
---	Butte Bidwell	56	715
---	Butte Mountain	56	735
---	Butte Ophir	56	796
---	Butte Ophir	56	804
---	Calaveras Twp 5	57	148
---	Calaveras Twp 5	57	192
---	Calaveras Twp 5	57	194
---	Calaveras Twp 9	57	363
---	Calaveras Twp 7	57	40
---	Calaveras Twp 8	57	60
---	Calaveras Twp 8	57	63
---	Calaveras Twp 8	57	84
---	El Dorado Georgetown	58	705
---	Mariposa Twp 1	60	668
---	Mariposa Coulterville	60	681
---	Plumas Meadow Valley	62	913
---	Plumas Meadow Valley	62	914
---	Plumas Quincy	62	950
---	Sacramento Cosumnes	63	386
---	Sacramento Cosumnes	63	392
---	Sacramento Cosumnes	63	397
---	Sacramento Ward 3	63	492
---	San Francisco San Francisco 9	681	100
---	San Francisco San Francisco 4	681	191
---	Sierra Twp 5	66	945
---	Tuolumne Jacksonville	71	168
---	Tuolumne Jacksonville	71	515
---	Tuolumne Twp 6	71	535
---	Yolo Slate Ra	72	708
---	Yuba Slate Ro	72	708
---	Yuba Long Bar	72	766
---*	Sacramento Ward 1	63	67
---*	Tuolumne Big Oak	71	181
A	Klamath Klamath	59	229
Ah	Butte Mountain	56	735
Ah	Sacramento Cosumnes	63	386
Ah	Tuolumne Twp 4	71	160
Ah	Tuolumne Twp 4	71	168
Ang	Tuolumne Twp 4	71	181
Chan	San Francisco San Francisco 4	681	181
Chew La*	Yuba Foster B	72	830
Ching	Trinity Douglas	70	979
Ching	Yuba Long Bar	72	762
Fung	Yuba Long Bar	72	770
Goe	El Dorado Eldorado	58	939
Long	Sacramento Ward 1	63	71
Meoy	San Francisco San Francisco 4	681	195
Sony	Calaveras Twp 4	57	301
Sup	Sacramento Ward 1	63	71
Tin	Butte Cascade	56	702
Tye	Butte Bidwell	56	726
Uup	Yuba Long Bar	72	769
YEEK			
---	Calaveras Twp 8	57	66
YEEKMAN			
M	Sacramento Sutter	63	303
YEEN			
---	Amador Twp 7	55	412
---	Tuolumne Jacksonville	71	516
YEER			
---*	Amador Twp 6	55	433
YEEX			
---*	Calaveras Twp 5	57	192
YEF			
---	Sierra La Porte	66	767
YEGA			
Antonio	Amador Twp 1	55	483
YEGAN			
Patrick Y*	Solano Benecia	69	298
YEHOW			
---	Trinity Trininad Rvr	701	048
---	Trinity Trininad Rvr	701	050
YEI			
---	Butte Ophir	56	817
---	Calaveras Twp 5	57	202
YEIN			
---	Calaveras Twp 4	57	339
YEIS			
---	Calaveras Twp 5	57	139
YEISER			
D	Merced Twp 2	60	919
Frederick	Calaveras Twp 5	57	188
YEIX			
---	Calaveras Twp 5	57	192
YEIZER			
Dan	Calaveras Twp 9	57	389
YEK SAW			
---	Sacramento Ward 1	63	69

California 1860 Census Index

Name	County Locale	M653 Roll	Page
YEK			
---	San Francisco San Francisco 4	68	1176
---	San Francisco San Francisco 4	68	1186
---	Sierra Downieville	66	976
---	Tuolumne Chinese	71	524
Saw	Sacramento Ward 1	63	69
YEL			
---*	Yuba Marysville	72	916
YELBONDUG			
---	Tulara Visalia	71	114
YELE			
Stephen	Sierra Pine Grove	66	826
YELGER			
Joseph	Amador Twp 1	55	486
YELIX			
Jesse*	Calaveras Twp 6	57	167
Jessi	Calaveras Twp 6	57	167
YELL			
---	El Dorado Big Bar	58	736
Jno*	Mendocino Round Va	60	880
Zarrine	Sierra La Porte	66	768
YELLATT			
George	San Francisco San Francisco 5	67	515
YELLER			
John A*	San Francisco San Francisco 4	68	1112
YELLERSON			
Thomas	Contra Costa Twp 1	57	526
YELLIKIN			
G F	Calaveras Twp 9	57	410
YELLOR			
John A	San Francisco San Francisco 4	68	1112
YELLOW DOG			
---	Tulara Twp 1	71	114
YELLOWBEET			
---	Yuba Bear Rvr	72	1014
YELLOWBUT			
---	Yuba Bear Rvr	72	1014
---	Yuba Bear Rvr	72	1015
YELLOWS			
Charles	Solano Suisan	69	234
James	Santa Cruz Santa Cruz	66	604
YELMAN			
---	Mendocino Round Va	60	882
YELS			
Stephen*	Sierra Pine Grove	66	826
YELT			
Zarrion	Sierra La Porte	66	768
YEM			
---	El Dorado Mountain	58	1189
---	Shasta Shasta	66	678
---	Shasta Shasta	66	680
---	Sierra Downieville	66	981
---	Trinity Mouth Ca	70	1012
---	Trinity McGillev	70	1021
---	Trinity Weaverville	70	1052
---	Tuolumne Chinese	71	524
Ching	Plumas Quincy	62	948
Kin	El Dorado Georgetown	58	697
Lo	Calaveras Twp 8	57	74
Noo	Calaveras Twp 8	57	79
See	San Francisco San Francisco 11	67	159
YEMK			
Tack	Calaveras Twp 8	57	76
YEMY			
---	Amador Twp 6	55	434
YEN HOWE			
---	Siskiyou Scott Ri	69	66
YEN NY			
Die	Butte Ophir	56	818
YEN TIE			
---	Siskiyou Scott Ri	69	66
YEN			
---	Amador Twp 2	55	289
---	Amador Twp 2	55	290
---	Amador Twp 2	55	293
---	Amador Twp 2	55	323
---	Amador Twp 2	55	326
---	Amador Twp 2	55	328
---	Amador Twp 5	55	346
---	Amador Twp 5	55	353
---	Amador Twp 6	55	430
---	Butte Ophir	56	815
---	Calaveras Twp 6	57	134
---	Calaveras Twp 6	57	148
---	Calaveras Twp 5	57	212
---	Calaveras Twp 5	57	215
---	Calaveras Twp 5	57	219
---	Calaveras Twp 5	57	234
---	Calaveras Twp 5	57	237
---	Calaveras Twp 5	57	251
---	Calaveras Twp 10	57	271
---	Calaveras Twp 10	57	285
---	Calaveras Twp 10	57	295
---	Calaveras Twp 10	57	296
---	Calaveras Twp 4	57	303
YEN			
---	Calaveras Twp 4	57	327
---	Calaveras Twp 8	57	68
---	El Dorado Georgetown	58	691
---	El Dorado Georgetown	58	692
---	Mariposa Twp 1	60	651
---	Nevada Nevada	61	301
---	Placer Auburn	62	579
---	Placer Auburn	62	596
---	Placer Rattle Snake	62	633
---	Sacramento Granite	63	250
---	Sacramento Natonia	63	281
---	San Francisco San Francisco 4	68	1182
---	San Francisco San Francisco 4	68	1187
---	San Francisco San Francisco 4	68	1188
---	Sierra La Porte	66	774
---	Sierra La Porte	66	790
---	Sierra St Louis	66	815
---	Sierra Downieville	66	979
---	Sierra Downieville	66	996
---	Siskiyou Scott Ri	69	76
---	Siskiyou Klamath	69	89
---	Stanislaus Branch	70	714
---	Trinity Mouth Ca	70	1014
---	Trinity Mouth Ca	70	1015
---	Trinity Mouth Ca	70	1016
---	Trinity Raabs Ba	70	1020
---	Trinity McGillev	70	1021
---	Trinity Trinindad Rvr	70	1048
---	Trinity Weaverville	70	1051
---	Trinity Weaverville	70	1073
---	Trinity Lewiston	70	954
---	Trinity Lewiston	70	955
---	Trinity Lewiston	70	956
---	Trinity China Bar	70	959
---	Tuolumne Jacksonville	71	514
---	Tuolumne Green Springs	71	517
---	Tuolumne Twp 5	71	522
---	Tuolumne Chinese	71	524
---	Tuolumne Twp 6	71	528
---	Tuolumne Twp 6	71	529
---	Tuolumne Don Pedro	71	536
---	Yolo No E Twp	72	680
---	Yuba North Ea	72	680
---	Yuba Long Bar	72	757
---	Yuba Long Bar	72	761
---	Yuba Fosters	72	841
---*	Amador Twp 6	55	433
---*	Calaveras Twp 5	57	192
---*	Calaveras Twp 4	57	339
---*	Trinity E Weaver	70	1059
---*	Yuba Foster B	72	826
---*	Yuba Fosters	72	841
A	Sacramento Natonia	63	281
Ah	Siskiyou Klamath	69	89
Ar	Trinity Lewiston	70	956
Can	Mariposa Coulterville	60	682
Choy	Calaveras Twp 5	57	193
David	Calaveras Twp 4	57	316
Hong	Sacramento Granite	63	245
Kee	San Francisco San Francisco 4	68	1196
Ku	San Francisco San Francisco 4	68	1196
Ky	El Dorado Big Bar	58	736
La	Sacramento Ward 1	63	65
Lero	Tuolumne Twp 4	71	149
Lew	Sacramento Granite	63	269
Lon	San Francisco San Francisco 4	68	1184
Lon	Yuba Long Bar	72	761
Loo	Yuba Long Bar	72	761
Lou	San Francisco San Francisco 4	68	1184
Tie*	Siskiyou Scott Ri	69	66
Wah	Tuolumne Twp 6	71	531
YENARVINE			
Saml	Shasta Horsetown	66	692
YENAWIME			
Saml*	Shasta Horsetown	66	692
YENBOG			
---	Sierra Downieville	66	973
YENEN			
Paul	Alameda Brooklyn	55	115
YENG			
---	Calaveras Twp 5	57	202
---	Calaveras Twp 10	57	296
---	El Dorado Coloma	58	1110
---	Plumas Quincy	62	947
---	Trinity Trinindad Rvr	70	1047
---	Trinity Trinindad Rvr	70	1048
---	Trinity Trinindad Rvr	70	1050
---	Trinity Weaverville	70	1076
---	Trinity Lewiston	70	956
---	Trinity Eastman	70	960
---	Tuolumne Don Pedro	71	537
---*	Trinity Big Flat	70	1041
YENGLONG			
---	Trinity Trinindad Rvr	70	1047
YENK			
---	Trinity Trinindad Rvr	70	1050
YENKLE			
A	San Francisco San Francisco 5	67	500
YENLL			
James*	Sierra Poker Flats	66	842
YENN			
---	Sacramento Ward 4	63	610
---	San Francisco San Francisco 9	68	1087
YENNELLITCH			
---*	Tulara Twp 1	71	120
YENNG			
---	Trinity Weaverville	70	1079
YENNT			
John	Amador Twp 2	55	268
YENNY			
Die*	Butte Ophir	56	808
YENOH			
Wm	Tehama Lassen	70	877
YENR			
---	Calaveras Twp 8	57	65
YENSAN			
Martin	Siskiyou Scott Va	69	52
YENSAW			
Martin*	Siskiyou Scott Va	69	52
YENSEN			
Christen	Alameda Brooklyn	55	153
YENT			
---	Tuolumne Twp 6	71	537
YENTER			
M*	Butte Hamilton	56	524
YENTRAIN			
Ignatio*	Alameda Brooklyn	55	199
YENTRAM			
Ignatio*	Alameda Brooklyn	55	199
YENTZ			
---	Plumas Meadow Valley	62	910
YENY			
---	Amador Twp 2	55	314
---	Calaveras Twp 10	57	261
---	Calaveras Twp 4	57	320
YEO			
---	Amador Twp 1	55	502
---	Calaveras Twp 8	57	168
---	San Francisco San Francisco 4	68	1191
---	Tuolumne Twp 5	71	515
---*	Sierra Downieville	66	979
Ho	San Francisco San Francisco 11	67	145
Mo	San Francisco San Francisco 11	67	159
W H	Tuolumne Twp 2	71	298
YEOMAN			
Geo*	Sacramento Ward 3	63	427
YEOMANS			
A S	Siskiyou Scott Ri	69	70
Ruth*	Del Norte Crescent	58	625
YEON			
---	Placer Auburn	62	575
---	Placer Folsom	62	648
---	Tuolumne Twp 5	71	510
---	Tuolumne Twp 5	71	515
YEONG			
---	Amador Twp 1	55	499
---	Amador Twp 1	55	507
---	El Dorado Diamond	58	788
---	San Francisco San Francisco 4	68	1183
YEORISLE			
G*	San Francisco San Francisco 5	67	505
YEOST			
E K	Nevada Rough &	61	406
YEOW			
---	Tuolumne Chinese	71	510
YEOY			
Kuop	San Francisco San Francisco 5	67	1206
YEP			
---	Amador Twp 3	55	403
---	Amador Twp 6	55	423
---	Amador Twp 6	55	447
---	Calaveras Twp 7	57	39
---	Calaveras Twp 8	57	58
---	Placer Virginia	62	682
---	Sacramento Centre	63	181
---	Sacramento Cosummes	63	388
---	Sacramento Cosummes	63	395
---	Sierra La Porte	66	781
---	Trinity Price'S	70	1019
---	Trinity Trinindad Rvr	70	1050
---	Yuba Long Bar	72	757
---	Yuba Fosters	72	842
---*	Fresno Twp 2	59	19
---*	Yuba Fosters	72	842
C	Mariposa Coulterville	60	694
YEPE SING			
---*	Nevada Nevada	61	310
YEPP			
---	Yolo Slate Ra	72	715
---	Yuba Slate Ro	72	715

California 1860 Census Index

Name	County Locale	M653 RollPage	Name	County Locale	M653 RollPage	Name	County Locale	M653 RollPage
YEPP			**YET**			**YEW**		
M	Siskiyou Scott Ri	69 71	---	Mariposa Twp 1	60 626	---	Shasta Shasta	66 678
YER			---	Mariposa Twp 1	60 651	---	Sierra Twp 5	66 945
---	Amador Twp 5	55 350	---	Mariposa Twp 1	60 662	---	Sierra Downieville	66 979
---	Butte Cascade	56 699	---	Nevada Nevada	61 305	---	Sierra Downieville	66 980
---	Calaveras Twp 5	57 194	---	Placer Auburn	62 596	---	Sierra Downieville	66 982
---	Calaveras Twp 5	57 202	---	Placer Virginia	62 679	---	Trinity McGillev	701021
---	Calaveras Twp 5	57 233	---	Sacramento Cosummes	63 395	---	Tuolumne Don Pedro	71 533
---	Calaveras Twp 4	57 327	---	Sacramento Ward 4	63 609	---	Yolo No E Twp	72 677
---	Del Norte Crescent	58 631	---	Sacramento Ward 1	63 65	---	Yuba North Ea	72 677
---	San Francisco San Francisco 9	681096	---	San Francisco San Francisco 4	681173	---	Yuba Long Bar	72 762
---	Yuba Fosters	72 842	---	San Francisco San Francisco 4	681176	---*	Sierra Twp 5	66 945
Way	Mariposa Coulterville	60 694	---	San Francisco San Francisco 4	681179	---*	Tuolumne Twp 6	71 533
YERA			---	San Francisco San Francisco 4	681195	Ah	Sacramento Ward 1	63 152
Ramon*	Los Angeles Tejon	59 542	---	San Francisco San Francisco 4	681198	Lin*	Butte Ophir	56 817
YERDS			---	San Francisco San Francisco 11	92	Sin*	Butte Ophir	56 818
Antone	San Francisco San Francisco 9	68 943	---		67	Ting	Calaveras Twp 10	57 295
YERGENS			---	Sierra La Porte	66 785	Tuck	Tuolumne Knights	71 529
Henry	San Francisco San Francisco 1	68 928	---	Sierra St Louis	66 805	**YEWCAS**		
YERGESON			---	Sierra Whiskey	66 843	Hans	Alameda Brooklyn	55 167
Peter*	Plumas Quincy	62 978	---	Sierra Downieville	66 990	**YEWES**		
YERKES			---	Trinity Trininad Rvr	701044	Wm	Marin Cortemad	60 789
Isaac	San Francisco San Francisco 5	67 511	---	Trinity Trininad Rvr	701048	**YEWEY**		
YERKEY			---	Tulara Twp 1	71 113	---	Del Norte Happy Ca	58 663
David	Santa Cruz Soguel	66 597	---	Tuolumne Twp 6	71 535	**YEXETIS**		
YERLANG			---	Tuolumne Twp 6	71 537	---	Tulara Twp 1	71 119
L*	San Francisco San Francisco 5	67 504	---	Yuba Marysville	72 916	**YEY**		
YERMAN			Ah	Tuolumne Twp 4	71 159	Chan*	San Francisco San Francisco 4	681181
John*	Tulara Twp 1	71 88	Chang	Plumas Meadow Valley	62 909	**YEZ**		
YERMO			Choy	San Francisco San Francisco 4	681197	Moy	San Francisco San Francisco 4	681200
---	Tulara Keyesville	71 64	Chung	Plumas Quincy	621008	**YGARA**		
YERN WAY			Hon	San Francisco San Francisco 4	681173	Agapete	Monterey S Antoni	60 971
---*	Mariposa Coulterville	60 694	Hong	Plumas Quincy	62 948	Josefa	Monterey Alisal	601027
YERNALIO			Lah	Plumas Quincy	62 948	Juan	Monterey San Juan	60 996
Geo	Sonoma Vallejo	69 621	Lim	Del Norte Crescent	58 643	**YGENIA**		
YERNNSA			Lung	Plumas Quincy	621008	---	Monterey S Antoni	60 972
Juana*	Alameda Oakland	55 45	See	Plumas Meadow Valley	62 909	**YGLESIAS**		
YEROO			Sil	Plumas Meadow Valley	62 909	Benito	Los Angeles Santa Ana	59 450
Francis	Calaveras Twp 7	57 12	Sin	Plumas Meadow Valley	62 909	**YGNACIA**		
YERRELL			Som	El Dorado Coloma	581084	Maria	Los Angeles Los Angeles	59 400
John S	Siskiyou Yreka	69 179	**YETA**			Maria	Los Angeles San Gabriel	59 423
YERRES			---	Los Angeles San Jose	59 284	Maria	San Bernardino Santa Ba	64 219
C	Amador Twp 3	55 369	**YETER**			Maria	San Diego Temecula	64 798
YERRIMAN			Moses	El Dorado Georgetown	58 707	Maria	San Diego Temecula	64 799
---*	San Francisco San Francisco 7	681413	**YETMANA**			Maria	San Diego Agua Caliente	64 822
YERRY			Kakchanoly	Mendocino Big Rvr	60 855	Maria	San Diego Agua Caliente	64 823
Thos	Trinity Sturdiva	701007	**YETPAR**			Maria	San Diego Agua Caliente	64 836
YERU LA			Yar	Mariposa Twp 1	60 651	Maria	San Diego Agua Caliente	64 865
---	Sacramento Ward 1	63 65	**YETT**			Marie*	Monterey San Juan	601008
YERUNSA			---	Butte Ophir	56 819	Nicolas	San Diego Agua Caliente	64 822
Juana*	Alameda Oakland	55 45	Lin	Butte Cascade	56 700	**YGNACIO**		
YES			Sin	Butte Cascade	56 699	---	Los Angeles San Gabriel	59 420
---	Sierra La Porte	66 767	**YETTER**			---	Los Angeles San Juan	59 465
Ah	Calaveras Twp 7	57 34	Cal	Butte Ophir	56 778	---	Los Angeles San Juan	59 477
YESO			**YEU**			---	Monterey S Antoni	60 972
Antonio	Contra Costa Twp 1	57 502	---	Calaveras Twp 5	57 192	---	San Bernardino Santa Barbara	64 200
YESS			---	Calaveras Twp 5	57 234	---	San Diego Temecula	64 802
---*	Fresno Twp 2	59 19	---	Calaveras Twp 10	57 294	---	San Diego Agua Caliente	64 849
YESSEN			---	Sierra Downieville	66 981	---	San Diego Temecula	64 794
P F	San Francisco San Francisco 9	681051	---	Tuolumne Twp 5	71 514	Jose	San Diego Temecula	64 794
Paul*	Alameda Brooklyn	55 115	An	Del Norte Crescent	58 630	Maria	Monterey Alisal	601034
YESTER			David*	Calaveras Twp 4	57 316	**YGUACIA**		
C B	Amador Twp 3	55 373	**YEUN**			---	San Diego Agua Caliente	64 816
YESTES			---	San Francisco San Francisco 9	681087	Maria	San Diego S Luis R	64 782
I P	El Dorado Greenwood	58 709	**YEUNG**			Maria	San Diego Temecula	64 793
YET			---	Trinity Lewiston	70 964	Maria	San Diego Agua Caliente	64 817
---	Amador Twp 5	55 350	---	Trinity Rush Crk	70 965	Maria	San Diego Agua Caliente	64 819
---	Amador Twp 5	55 353	**YEUP**			**YGUACIO**		
---	Amador Twp 7	55 418	---	Placer Virginia	62 687	---	San Diego Temecula	64 800
---	Amador Twp 6	55 428	**YEUR**			---	San Diego Agua Caliente	64 816
---	Amador Twp 6	55 436	---	Amador Twp 2	55 314	**YGUERRA**		
---	Amador Twp 1	55 477	Ah	Calaveras Twp 7	57 31	Jesus	Monterey San Juan	60 997
---	Amador Twp 1	55 492	**YEURY**			**YHIM**		
---	Amador Twp 1	55 501	---	Amador Twp 5	55 364	---	El Dorado Big Bar	58 733
---	Butte Kimshaw	56 584	**YEUTER**			**YI**		
---	Calaveras Twp 6	57 159	M	Butte Hamilton	56 524	---	Calaveras Twp 5	57 176
---	Calaveras Twp 6	57 166	**YEVOLEY**			---	Calaveras Twp 5	57 234
---	Calaveras Twp 6	57 168	M	Nevada Eureka	61 366	---	Calaveras Twp 5	57 237
---	Calaveras Twp 5	57 219	**YEVST**			---	El Dorado Georgetown	58 678
---	Calaveras Twp 5	57 235	E K*	Nevada Rough &	61 406	---*	Calaveras Twp 6	57 176
---	Calaveras Twp 5	57 244	**YEW**			Fong	El Dorado Eldorado	58 948
---	Calaveras Twp 5	57 254	---	Calaveras Twp 6	57 167	Heny	Sacramento Granite	63 250
---	Calaveras Twp 10	57 259	---	Calaveras Twp 10	57 285	Hon	Calaveras Twp 5	57 255
---	Calaveras Twp 7	57 39	---	Calaveras Twp 10	57 286	Sehi	Sacramento Granite	63 269
---	Calaveras Twp 8	57 60	---	Calaveras Twp 10	57 296	Soul	Tuolumne Big Oak	71 150
---	El Dorado Salmon Falls	581045	---	Calaveras Twp 4	57 307	Yury	Sacramento Natonia	63 281
---	El Dorado Coloma	581086	---	Del Norte Crescent	58 630	**YIAN**		
---	El Dorado Kelsey	581144	---	Del Norte Crescent	58 633	---	Placer Secret R	62 622
---	El Dorado Georgetown	58 696	---	Del Norte Happy Ca	58 664	**YICK**		
---	El Dorado Diamond	58 768	---	Nevada Bridgeport	61 462	---	El Dorado Mountain	581185
---	El Dorado Placerville	58 825	---	Nevada Bridgeport	61 505	---	El Dorado Diamond	58 795
---	El Dorado Placerville	58 898	---	Nevada Bloomfield	61 528	---	Placer Forest H	62 771
---	El Dorado Placerville	58 903	---	Placer Virginia	62 682	---	Placer Iona Hills	62 883
---	El Dorado Mud Springs	58 955	---	Sacramento Mississipi	63 188	---	Placer Iona Hills	62 898
---	El Dorado Mud Springs	58 962	---	Sacramento Cosummes	63 392	---*	El Dorado Mountain	581185
---	El Dorado Mud Springs	58 987	---	San Francisco San Francisco 9	681088	Lee	Yuba Bear Rvr	721000
						See*	Yuba Bear Rvr	721000

California 1860 Census Index

Name	County Locale	M653 Roll/Page
YICKLEY		
A	Sutter Butte	70 785
YIE		
---	El Dorado Coloma	581121
YIEN		
---	Sacramento Ward 1	63 69
YIERCE		
Jacob	Tulara Visalia	71 28
YIESER		
Fred	San Joaquin Stockton	641036
YIEU		
---	Sacramento Ward 1	63 69
YIK		
Chock	San Francisco San Francisco 1	68 925
Fan	San Francisco San Francisco 1	68 925
Lit	San Francisco San Francisco 1	68 925
YILE		
Stephen*	Sierra Pine Grove	66 826
YILTON		
C A*	Nevada Bloomfield	61 520
YIM		
---	El Dorado Diamond	58 786
---	Placer Auburn	62 571
---	Placer Illinois	62 752
---	San Francisco San Francisco 4	681173
---	Sierra La Porte	66 780
YIME		
---	Sierra La Porte	66 782
YIMEN		
---	Sacramento Cosumnes	63 386
YIMG		
---	Nevada Nevada	61 299
---*	Butte Kimshaw	56 586
YIMK		
---	Butte Bidwell	56 724
YIMO		
---	Sierra La Porte	66 782
YIN		
---	Amador Twp 2	55 283
---	Amador Twp 5	55 335
---	Amador Twp 5	55 344
---	Amador Twp 5	55 345
---	Amador Twp 1	55 477
---	Amador Twp 1	55 496
---	Amador Twp 1	55 501
---	Calaveras Twp 6	57 136
---	Calaveras Twp 4	57 304
---	Calaveras Twp 8	57 60
---	Del Norte Crescent	58 643
---	Del Norte Happy Ca	58 664
---	Del Norte Happy Ca	58 668
---	El Dorado White Oaks	581021
---	El Dorado White Oaks	581023
---	El Dorado Salmon Falls	581054
---	El Dorado Salmon Falls	581065
---	El Dorado Coloma	581102
---	El Dorado Coloma	581114
---	El Dorado Casumnes	581162
---	El Dorado Georgetown	58 691
---	El Dorado Greenwood	58 728
---	El Dorado Greenwood	58 731
---	El Dorado Big Bar	58 734
---	El Dorado Diamond	58 785
---	El Dorado Diamond	58 790
---	El Dorado Diamond	58 805
---	El Dorado Diamond	58 806
---	El Dorado Eldorado	58 943
---	El Dorado Mud Springs	58 955
---	Mariposa Twp 1	60 673
---	Mariposa Coulterville	60 681
---	Nevada Bridgeport	61 463
---	Placer Rattle Snake	62 627
---	Placer Iona Hills	62 889
---	Sacramento Granite	63 269
---	Sacramento Ward 3	63 490
---	San Francisco San Francisco 4	681182
---	Shasta French G	66 712
---	Sierra Downieville	661007
---	Sierra Downieville	661009
---	Sierra Downieville	661024
---	Sierra Downieville	661025
---	Sierra Downieville	661026
---	Trinity Lewiston	70 966
---	Tuolumne Twp 5	71 517
---	Yuba Long Bar	72 758
---	Yuba Fosters	72 826
---*	Mariposa Twp 1	60 662
Chee	San Francisco San Francisco 4	681189
Chu	San Francisco San Francisco 4	681189
Cona	El Dorado Coloma	581084
Ferben	Butte Ophir	56 820
Gee	Sacramento Granite	63 269
Lim	El Dorado Big Bar	58 737
Sup	Sacramento Granite	63 269
Ti	Calaveras Twp 4	57 302
Wua	Butte Ophir	56 820
YIN		
Yup	Nevada Eureka	61 384
YINE		
John	Contra Costa Twp 2	57 556
Jsa J*	Contra Costa Twp 2	57 539
YINEY		
---	El Dorado Salmon Hills	581064
YING		
---	Amador No 6	55 429
---	Calaveras Twp 8	57 109
---	Calaveras Twp 5	57 208
---	Calaveras Twp 10	57 261
---	Calaveras Twp 10	57 270
---	Calaveras Twp 10	57 275
---	Calaveras Twp 4	57 320
---	Calaveras Twp 4	57 342
---	Calaveras Twp 8	57 66
---	Calaveras Twp 8	57 74
---	El Dorado White Oaks	581022
---	El Dorado White Oaks	581024
---	El Dorado Salmon Falls	581041
---	El Dorado Salmon Falls	581064
---	El Dorado Salmon Hills	581066
---	El Dorado Coloma	581090
---	El Dorado Coloma	581110
---	El Dorado Greenwood	58 727
---	El Dorado Greenwood	58 728
---	El Dorado Mud Springs	58 950
---	Napa Hot Springs	61 22
---	Nevada Grass Valley	61 233
---	Nevada Nevada	61 303
---	Sacramento Centre	63 181
---	Sacramento Granite	63 247
---	Sacramento Ward 3	63 493
---	San Francisco San Francisco 4	681190
---	Sierra Downieville	661024
---	Sierra La Porte	66 767
---	Sierra Twp 5	66 926
---	Sierra Twp 5	66 932
---	Sierra Twp 5	66 938
---	Yolo No E Twp	72 680
---	Yuba North Ea	72 680
---	Yuba Long Bar	72 757
---	Yuba Long Bar	72 758
---	Yuba Marysville	72 916
---*	Calaveras Twp 4	57 339
---*	Sierra Downieville	661024
Ah	Tuolumne Twp 4	71 168
Hoo	San Francisco San Francisco 1	68 926
Hoy	Yuba Long Bar	72 767
Lanerine	El Dorado Georgetown	58 680
YINGOIR		
Manuell	Calaveras Twp 5	57 194
YINK		
---	Butte Bidwell	56 724
---	Butte Bidwell	56 726
---	Sacramento Centre	63 181
Ah	Butte Bidwell	56 726
YINN		
---	Amador Twp 5	55 353
Chan	San Francisco San Francisco 4	681181
Henry	San Francisco San Francisco 5	67 475
YINNG		
Lo	Butte Oregon	56 625
YINSON		
John	Alameda Brooklyn	55 146
YINSTER		
Michael*	San Francisco San Francisco 3	67 15
YINY		
---	Calaveras Twp 10	57 270
---	Calaveras Twp 4	57 306
---	Calaveras Twp 4	57 320
---*	Amador Twp 6	55 429
YINYVIN		
Manuell	Calaveras Twp 5	57 194
YIO		
---	Sacramento Ward 3	63 493
YIOY		
Knop	San Francisco San Francisco 5	671206
YIP		
---	Calaveras Twp 5	57 251
---	Nevada Eureka	61 384
---	San Francisco San Francisco 4	681208
---*	Yuba Long Bar	72 767
Loo	San Francisco San Francisco 4	681211
Soo	San Francisco San Francisco 4	681211
YIR		
---	Calaveras Twp 5	57 202
YIRK		
Len	Tulara Visalia	71 87
YIRY		
---	Amador Twp 5	55 355
---	Amador Twp 6	55 447
YIS		
---	Calaveras Twp 5	57 136
---	Calaveras Twp 5	57 235
YIS		
---	Calaveras Twp 5	57 239
---	Calaveras Twp 5	57 244
---	Calaveras Twp 5	57 249
YISH		
Russel H*	Calaveras Twp 6	57 168
YIT		
---	Calaveras Twp 5	57 219
---	Calaveras Twp 5	57 239
---	Calaveras Twp 5	57 254
---	Calaveras Twp 4	57 322
---	El Dorado Coloma	581086
---	El Dorado Kelsey	581144
---	El Dorado Casumnes	581177
---	El Dorado Mountain	581188
---	El Dorado Diamond	58 796
---	Placer Illinois	62 746
YITEHNILLE		
William H*	Twp 1 Contra Costa	57 490
YITTEL		
Ernst*	San Francisco San Francisco 7	681396
YITUS		
---	Fresno Twp 2	59 93
YIU		
---	Calaveras Twp 10	57 267
YIULL		
James	Sierra Poker Flats	66 842
YIVEN		
Chan	San Francisco San Francisco 4	681181
YIW		
---	Calaveras Twp 5	57 235
---	Calaveras Twp 5	57 236
YLANIE		
---	Los Angeles Tejon	59 529
YLARCO		
---	San Diego Agua Caliente	64 830
YLARIO		
---	Los Angeles San Pedro	59 479
---	San Bernardino S Buenav	64 222
---	San Diego Temecula	64 805
---	San Diego Agua Caliente	64 841
---	San Diego Agua Caliente	64 864
YLBRICHT		
Charles	San Francisco San Francisco 3	67 48
Charles	San Francisco San Francisco 3	67 49
YLIMMSON		
R S	Butte Eureka	56 645
YMAN		
John*	San Francisco San Francisco 4	681164
YNCH		
Rebecca	Tuolumne Twp 6	71 540
YNDART		
J M	Monterey San Juan	60 986
YNEZ		
---	Mendocino Calpella	60 826
YNS		
---	Sierra Morristown	661056
YNUCT		
---*	Sacramento Granite	63 259
YNULS		
Phillippe	Alameda Brooklyn	55 104
YO		
---	Amador Twp 1	55 504
---	Calaveras Twp 5	57 230
---	Calaveras Twp 5	57 233
---	Calaveras Twp 5	57 244
---	Calaveras Twp 10	57 295
---	Mariposa Twp 1	60 651
---	Sacramento Centre	63 181
---	Sacramento Ward 1	63 50
---	Sacramento Ward 1	63 66
---	San Francisco San Francisco 9	681092
---	San Francisco San Francisco 9	681093
---	San Francisco San Francisco 4	681176
---	San Francisco San Francisco 7	681395
---	Sierra Downieville	661003
---	Sierra La Porte	66 782
---	Stanislaus Branch	70 714
---	Stanislaus Emory	70 743
---	Tuolumne Twp 6	71 535
Af*	Yuba Rose Bar	72 820
At	Yuba Rose Bar	72 820
Dan*	Mendocino Big Rvr	60 851
Kar	San Francisco San Francisco 10	67 356
Lin	Stanislaus Emory	70 744
Sap	Sacramento Granite	63 259
See*	Placer Iona Hills	62 897
Su	Placer Iona Hills	62 897
Tick	Butte Hamilton	56 530
YOA KIM		
---*	Plumas Quincy	62 969
YOA		
---	El Dorado Eldorado	58 939
---	Yuba Marysville	72 927

California 1860 Census Index

Name	County Locale	M653 RollPage
YOA		
Hee	Yuba Marysville	72 920
Sallig	Yuba Marysville	72 881
YOACHIM		
Archibald	Tulara Visalia	71 103
Frank	Mariposa Twp 3	60 592
YOAH		
Su?G*	Yuba Marysville	72 845
YOAKERM		
Isaac*	Alameda Brooklyn	55 95
YOAKIM		
Samuel	Santa Cruz Pajaro	66 560
YOAKUM		
Isaac	Alameda Brooklyn	55 95
YOALE		
Sung*	Yuba Marysville	72 845
YOBROUGH		
Achibald	Calaveras Twp 8	57 104
YOCAL		
---	Fresno Twp 2	59 109
YOCALE		
---*	Tulara Visalia	71 4
YOCCO		
Jhn*	Mariposa Coulterville	60 685
YOCHAM		
Andrew	Tuolumne Sonora	71 191
YOCK		
---	Amador Twp 1	55 507
---	Del Norte Crescent	58 643
YOCKAM		
Andrew	Tuolumne Twp 1	71 191
YOCKLY		
Lewis	Butte Bidwell	56 707
YOCOBIM		
---	Butte Chico	56 551
YOCOM		
G W B	Klamath Klamath	59 224
YOCOMB		
A H	Los Angeles Tejon	59 527
YOCSSETT		
Chas*	Sierra St Louis	66 814
YOCUM		
H F	Butte Chico	56 559
YOCUND		
R	Sutter Butte	70 785
YOD SING		
---	Butte Kimshaw	56 595
YODER		
Elisha	Sierra Downieville	661011
YODGES		
Daniel	Tulara Twp 2	71 3
YOE		
---	El Dorado Georgetown	58 708
---	Fresno Twp 1	59 27
---	Sierra Downieville	661003
---	Sierra Twp 5	66 945
---	Sierra Downieville	66 981
---	Trinity Weaverville	701079
J	Sierra Downieville	66 993
Sam	Fresno Twp 1	59 27
William*	Placer Michigan	62 820
YOEEO		
John*	Mariposa Coulterville	60 685
YOEK		
---	El Dorado Mud Springs	58 959
YOELL		
Geo M	Santa Clara San Jose	65 334
YOEN		
---	El Dorado Salmon Hills	581059
YOESSETT		
Chas*	Sierra St Louis	66 814
YOG		
---*	Nevada Washington	61 342
Rufus*	San Mateo Twp 3	65 91
YOGER		
Carl*	San Francisco San Francisco 7	681373
YOH		
---	Alameda Oakland	55 59
---	Calaveras Twp 10	57 284
---	El Dorado Big Bar	58 740
---	San Francisco San Francisco 8	681255
Kam*	Tuolumne Big Oak	71 182
YOHISSITY		
Patrick*	Calaveras Twp 5	57 195
YOHN		
A	Sacramento Granite	63 258
August	Alameda Brooklyn	55 148
YOHOSEL		
---	Del Norte Klamath	58 658
YOIR		
---	El Dorado Georgetown	58 680
YOIZEAR		
T	San Francisco San Francisco 6	67 449
YOJ		
---	El Dorado Diamond	58 796
---	El Dorado Placerville	58 840
YOK		
---	El Dorado Greenwood	58 731
---	San Francisco San Francisco 9	681092
---	San Francisco San Francisco 4	681177
---	San Francisco San Francisco 4	681187
---	San Francisco San Francisco 4	681188
---	San Francisco San Francisco 4	681194
---	San Francisco San Francisco 4	681195
---	Sierra Downieville	661009
---	Tuolumne Don Pedro	71 533
Kam	Tuolumne Twp 4	71 182
Set	San Francisco San Francisco 4	681211
Sing	San Francisco San Francisco 10	356
---		67
Synn	Stanislaus Branch	70 713
YOKE		
---	Amador Twp 4	55 246
---	Butte Bidwell	56 717
---	Calaveras Twp 5	57 246
---	El Dorado Salmon Hills	581054
---	El Dorado Salmon Hills	581058
---	El Dorado Salmon Hills	581062
---	El Dorado Salmon Hills	581063
---	El Dorado Coloma	581079
---	El Dorado Coloma	581106
---	El Dorado Coloma	581107
---	El Dorado Mud Springs	58 977
---	Mariposa Coulterville	60 681
---	Nevada Bridgeport	61 464
---	Nevada Bridgeport	61 506
---	Placer Virginia	62 665
---	San Francisco San Francisco 2	67 754
---	Shasta Horsetown	66 697
---	Trinity Mouth Ca	701015
---	Tuolumne Twp 5	71 509
---	Tuolumne Jacksonville	71 516
---*	Butte Ophir	56 809
Ah	Butte Oregon	56 638
Benj*	Sierra Downieville	661029
Come	San Francisco San Francisco 2	67 754
Geo	Trinity East For	701025
YOKEL		
---	Tulara Visalia	71 114
YOKES		
A	Amador Twp 1	55 470
YOKS		
---	Calaveras Twp 5	57 246
YOKUM		
Dennis	Tehama Antelope	70 895
YOLE		
---	El Dorado Mud Springs	58 958
P J	Sacramento Ward 4	63 527
YOLK		
---	El Dorado Coloma	581111
---	El Dorado Eldorado	58 940
YOLLAND		
Thos	San Joaquin Elkhorn	64 989
YOLLERS		
Fred*	El Dorado Mountain	581184
YOLMAN		
A	Sonoma Washington	69 667
YOLO		
Samuel	Sierra Twp 7	66 913
YOLOGE		
H*	San Francisco San Francisco 9	68 938
YOLTS		
Geo W*	San Joaquin Stockton	641013
YOM TO		
---*	Mariposa Coulterville	60 684
YOM		
---	El Dorado Salmon Falls	581057
---	El Dorado Diamond	58 788
---	Placer Virginia	62 665
---	Sierra Downieville	66 953
---	Sierra Downieville	66 981
---	Sierra Downieville	66 992
---	Sierra Downieville	66 993
---	Trinity Weaverville	701052
---*	Tulara Visalia	71 27
Chan	Yuba Long Bar	72 759
Chaw	Yuba Long Bar	72 759
Hing	Placer Virginia	62 684
Lup	Placer Virginia	62 672
Tow	Nevada Grass Valley	61 227
YOMAN		
Jose	Alameda Washington	55 173
YOMANS		
C*	San Francisco San Francisco 5	67 483
Ruth*	Del Norte Crescent	58 625
YOMARE		
Jose*	Alameda Brooklyn	55 173
YOME		
---	Placer Auburn	62 592
---	Tulara Twp 2	71 38
YOMEKA		
---	Tulara Twp 1	71 122
YOMG		
---	Sacramento Granite	63 247
---	Sierra Downieville	66 974
---*	Mariposa Coulterville	60 683
YOMO		
---	Sierra Downieville	661005
YON FONG		
William	Santa Cruz Santa Cruz	66 612
YON LA		
---	Sacramento Ward 1	63 65
YON LEE		
---	San Francisco San Francisco 4	681150
YON SURY		
---	Tuolumne Green Springs	71 521
YON TONG		
William	Santa Cruz Santa Cruz	66 612
YON		
---	Alameda Oakland	55 6
---	Amador Twp 5	55 335
---	Amador Twp 5	55 345
---	Amador Twp 5	55 346
---	Amador Twp 5	55 347
---	Amador Twp 5	55 349
---	Amador Twp 5	55 352
---	Amador Twp 5	55 353
---	Amador Twp 5	55 360
---	Amador Twp 5	55 364
---	Amador Twp 6	55 424
---	Amador Twp 6	55 430
---	Amador Twp 6	55 434
---	Amador Twp 6	55 446
---	Butte Bidwell	56 710
---	Butte Ophir	56 771
---	Butte Ophir	56 801
---	Butte Ophir	56 805
---	Calaveras Twp 8	57 107
---	Calaveras Twp 6	57 168
---	Calaveras Twp 5	57 203
---	Calaveras Twp 5	57 209
---	Calaveras Twp 5	57 233
---	Calaveras Twp 10	57 269
---	Calaveras Twp 10	57 291
---	Calaveras Twp 4	57 310
---	Calaveras Twp 4	57 322
---	Calaveras Twp 4	57 323
---	Calaveras Twp 4	57 326
---	Calaveras Twp 4	57 333
---	Calaveras Twp 9	57 348
---	Calaveras Twp 9	57 358
---	Calaveras Twp 8	57 56
---	Calaveras Twp 8	57 60
---	Calaveras Twp 8	57 68
---	Del Norte Crescent	58 630
---	El Dorado White Oaks	581011
---	El Dorado Salmon Falls	581052
---	El Dorado Salmon Hills	581060
---	El Dorado Coloma	581077
---	El Dorado Coloma	581078
---	El Dorado Coloma	581106
---	El Dorado Coloma	581107
---	El Dorado Coloma	581109
---	El Dorado Coloma	581121
---	El Dorado Coloma	581123
---	El Dorado Kelsey	581141
---	El Dorado Mountain	581190
---	El Dorado Georgetown	58 682
---	El Dorado Greenwood	58 720
---	El Dorado Greenwood	58 727
---	El Dorado Greenwood	58 732
---	El Dorado Diamond	58 788
---	El Dorado Diamond	58 789
---	El Dorado Diamond	58 795
---	El Dorado Diamond	58 800
---	El Dorado Diamond	58 805
---	El Dorado Diamond	58 806
---	El Dorado Placerville	58 829
---	El Dorado Placerville	58 830
---	El Dorado Placerville	58 886
---	El Dorado Placerville	58 898
---	El Dorado Eldorado	58 948
---	El Dorado Mud Springs	58 950
---	El Dorado Mud Springs	58 955
---	El Dorado Mud Springs	58 957
---	El Dorado Mud Springs	58 971
---	El Dorado Mud Springs	58 985
---	El Dorado Mud Springs	58 991
---	Klamath Liberty	59 232
---	Mariposa Twp 3	60 551
---	Mariposa Twp 3	60 578
---	Mariposa Twp 1	60 651
---	Mariposa Twp 1	60 673
---	Mariposa Coulterville	60 700
---	Nevada Nevada	61 301
---	Placer Secret R	62 622
---	Placer Rattle Snake	62 627
---	Placer Rattle Snake	62 629

California 1860 Census Index

Name	County Locale	M653 Roll	Page
YON			
---	Placer Rattle Snake	62	633
---	Placer Folsom	62	647
---	Placer Ophirville	62	653
---	Placer Ophirville	62	654
---	Placer Ophirville	62	655
---	Placer Virginia	62	665
---	Placer Illinois	62	754
---	Sacramento Cosumnes	63	387
---	Sacramento Ward 1	63	53
---	Sacramento Ward 1	63	59
---	Sacramento Ward 1	63	60
---	Sacramento Ward 1	63	70
---	San Francisco San Francisco 9	68	1092
---	San Francisco San Francisco 4	68	1174
---	San Francisco San Francisco 4	68	1175
---	San Francisco San Francisco 4	68	1176
---	San Francisco San Francisco 4	68	1177
---	San Francisco San Francisco 2	67	688
---	San Francisco San Francisco 2	67	798
---	Shasta Horsetown	66	703
---	Shasta Horsetown	66	704
---	Shasta French G	66	713
---	Sierra Downieville	66	1000
---	Sierra Downieville	66	1004
---	Sierra Downieville	66	1005
---	Sierra Downieville	66	1007
---	Sierra Downieville	66	1008
---	Sierra Downieville	66	1009
---	Sierra Downieville	66	1025
---	Sierra Downieville	66	1027
---	Sierra Morristown	66	1056
---	Sierra La Porte	66	782
---	Sierra La Porte	66	785
---	Sierra St Louis	66	812
---	Sierra St Louis	66	815
---	Sierra Twp 5	66	932
---	Sierra Twp 5	66	934
---	Sierra Twp 5	66	948
---	Sierra Cox'S Bar	66	949
---	Sierra Downieville	66	983
---	Sierra Downieville	66	995
---	Sierra Downieville	66	998
---	Stanislaus Branch	70	713
---	Stanislaus Emory	70	743
---	Trinity Mouth Ca	70	1016
---	Tuolumne Jamestown	71	433
---	Tuolumne Jamestown	71	434
---	Tuolumne Twp 3	71	457
---	Tuolumne Twp 1	71	477
---	Tuolumne Twp 5	71	526
---	Tuolumne Twp 6	71	535
---	Tuolumne Twp 6	71	536
---	Tuolumne Twp 6	71	538
---	Yuba Bear Rvr	72	1000
---	Yuba Long Bar	72	757
---	Yuba Fosters	72	826
---	Yuba Fosters	72	843
---	Yuba Marysville	72	916
---	Yuba Marysville	72	920
---	Yuba Marysville	72	925
---	Yuba Marysville	72	927
---	Yuba Linda	72	990
---*	Calaveras Twp 5	57	237
---*	Calaveras Twp 4	57	326
---*	Nevada Nevada	61	305
---*	Placer Auburn	62	563
---*	Sacramento Granite	63	243
---*	Sacramento Ward 1	63	53
---*	Sacramento Ward 1	63	60
---*	San Francisco San Francisco 9	68	1092
---*	Sierra Downieville	66	1024
---*	Yuba Foster B	72	826
---*	Yuba Linda	72	992
Ah	Butte Bidwell	56	710
Ar	Trinity Sturdiva	70	1007
Cam	Nevada Rough &	61	423
Cam*	Yuba Marysville	72	921
Ceum	Butte Ophir	56	819
Chew	Yuba Marysville	72	921
Chong	Plumas Quincy	62	948
Chow	Nevada Washington	61	341
Chow	Nevada Eureka	61	383
Choy	El Dorado Diamond	58	796
Chu	San Francisco San Francisco 4	68	1187
Cum*	Yuba Marysville	72	921
E	San Francisco San Francisco 2	67	645
Eoy	San Francisco San Francisco 1	68	891
F	El Dorado Placerville	58	899
Fat	Tuolumne Twp 5	71	522
Fe*	San Francisco San Francisco 4	68	1179
Fin	Nevada Rough &	61	397
Foo	Del Norte Crescent	58	643
Fouk	Del Norte Crescent	58	643
Gee	Sacramento Granite	63	269
Kum	Plumas Quincy	62	948

Name	County Locale	M653 Roll	Page
YON			
La	Sacramento Ward 1	63	65
Lee	San Francisco San Francisco 4	68	1150
Len	Butte Ophir	56	788
Lev	San Francisco San Francisco 4	68	1173
Linn	Butte Ophir	56	805
Liry	Amador Twp 3	55	387
Liu	Butte Ophir	56	803
Lon	Butte Ophir	56	820
Low	Sacramento Granite	63	259
Luy	Sacramento Natonia	63	283
Quey	Sacramento Ward 1	63	58
Ring	San Francisco San Francisco 4	68	1175
Roul	Butte Ophir	56	814
See	Nevada Rough &	61	397
See	San Francisco San Francisco 4	68	1175
Sin	El Dorado Mud Springs	58	953
Song*	Yuba Bear Rvr	72	1000
Ta	San Francisco San Francisco 1	68	925
Tin	Sierra Downieville	66	996
Ting	Nevada Grass Valley	61	233
Wa	Nevada Washington	61	340
Yok	Yuba Marysville	72	916
YONA			
---	Butte Ophir	56	805
---	Placer Virginia	62	665
YONAE			
---	Fresno Twp 1	59	27
Sam	Fresno Twp 3	59	31
YONB			
---	Sierra Downieville	66	1006
YONCKUM			
Henry*	San Joaquin Stockton	64	1018
YOND			
Charles	El Dorado Casumnes	58	1167
James	El Dorado Casumnes	58	1166
YONDER			
Jack	Nevada Little Y	61	535
YONE			
---	Amador Twp 1	55	507
---	El Dorado Mud Springs	58	985
---	Plumas Meadow Valley	62	914
---	Sierra Downieville	66	992
---	Tuolumne Montezuma	71	504
---	Tuolumne Chinese	71	524
---	Tuolumne Don Pedro	71	541
---*	Placer Auburn	62	575
YONG CHOY			
---	Sacramento Ward 1	63	58
YONG HEA			
---	Tuolumne Jacksonville	71	515
YONG PAN			
---	Tuolumne Green Springs	71	521
YONG			
---	Amador No 6	55	447
---	Amador Twp 1	55	490
---	Amador Twp 1	55	495
---	Amador Twp 1	55	497
---	Amador Twp 1	55	507
---	Calaveras Twp 5	57	148
---	Calaveras Twp 6	57	149
---	Calaveras Twp 6	57	151
---	Calaveras Twp 6	57	166
---	Calaveras Twp 5	57	202
---	Calaveras Twp 5	57	222
---	Calaveras Twp 5	57	233
---	Calaveras Twp 5	57	236
---	Calaveras Twp 5	57	252
---	Calaveras Twp 10	57	273
---	Calaveras Twp 10	57	276
---	Calaveras Twp 10	57	296
---	Calaveras Twp 4	57	302
---	Calaveras Twp 4	57	304
---	Calaveras Twp 7	57	31
---	Calaveras Twp 4	57	323
---	Calaveras Twp 4	57	327
---	Calaveras Twp 4	57	343
---	Calaveras Twp 9	57	358
---	Calaveras Twp 8	57	59
---	Calaveras Twp 8	57	60
---	Calaveras Twp 8	57	68
---	Calaveras Twp 8	57	84
---	El Dorado White Oaks	58	1010
---	El Dorado White Oaks	58	1032
---	El Dorado Salmon Falls	58	1057
---	El Dorado Salmon Falls	58	1065
---	El Dorado Coloma	58	1082
---	El Dorado Coloma	58	1102
---	El Dorado Coloma	58	1106
---	El Dorado Coloma	58	1120
---	El Dorado Diamond	58	796
---	El Dorado Diamond	58	802
---	El Dorado Diamond	58	812
---	El Dorado Placerville	58	832
---	El Dorado Placerville	58	899
---	El Dorado Placerville	58	917

Name	County Locale	M653 Roll	Page
YONG			
---	El Dorado Eldorado	58	944
---	El Dorado Mud Springs	58	958
---	El Dorado Mud Springs	58	961
---	El Dorado Mud Springs	58	972
---	El Dorado Mud Springs	58	976
---	Humbolt Bucksport	59	159
---	Mariposa Twp 1	60	639
---	Mariposa Twp 1	60	643
---	Mariposa Twp 1	60	648
---	Mariposa Twp 1	60	652
---	Mariposa Twp 1	60	655
---	Mariposa Twp 1	60	657
---	Mariposa Twp 1	60	662
---	Mariposa Twp 1	60	670
---	Mariposa Twp 1	60	673
---	Mariposa Coulterville	60	683
---	Nevada Bridgeport	61	463
---	Nevada Bridgeport	61	506
---	Nevada Bloomfield	61	520
---	Nevada Bloomfield	61	522
---	Placer Auburn	62	563
---	Placer Auburn	62	572
---	Placer Auburn	62	574
---	Placer Auburn	62	575
---	Placer Auburn	62	591
---	Placer Rattle Snake	62	598
---	Placer Rattle Snake	62	629
---	Placer Rattle Snake	62	633
---	Placer Folsom	62	649
---	Placer Ophirville	62	654
---	Placer Virginia	62	662
---	Placer Virginia	62	665
---	Placer Virginia	62	671
---	Placer Virginia	62	679
---	Placer Virginia	62	680
---	Placer Virginia	62	701
---	Placer Illinois	62	748
---	Placer Illinois	62	749
---	Plumas Quincy	62	947
---	Plumas Quincy	62	948
---	Plumas Quincy	62	949
---	Sacramento Granite	63	232
---	Sacramento Ward 3	63	489
---	San Francisco San Francisco 9	68	1092
---	San Francisco San Francisco 9	68	1094
---	San Francisco San Francisco 4	68	1196
---	San Francisco San Francisco 7	68	1417
---	San Francisco San Francisco 2	67	689
---	San Francisco San Francisco 2	67	754
---	Sierra Downieville	66	1000
---	Sierra Downieville	66	1005
---	Sierra Downieville	66	1025
---	Sierra Downieville	66	1030
---	Sierra La Porte	66	785
---	Sierra Poker Flats	66	840
---	Sierra St Louis	66	861
---	Sierra Twp 5	66	926
---	Sierra Twp 5	66	927
---	Sierra Twp 5	66	934
---	Sierra Twp 5	66	944
---	Sierra Twp 5	66	947
---	Sierra Downieville	66	974
---	Siskiyou Scott Ri	69	72
---	Tuolumne Twp 5	71	509
---	Tuolumne Twp 5	71	510
---	Tuolumne Twp 5	71	516
---	Tuolumne Twp 5	71	517
---	Tuolumne Twp 5	71	525
---	Tuolumne Twp 6	71	533
---	Tuolumne Twp 6	71	536
---	Tuolumne Twp 6	71	541
---	Yuba North Ea	72	682
---	Yuba Slate Ro	72	685
---	Yuba Slate Ro	72	688
---	Yuba Fosters	72	842
---*	Amador Twp 5	55	350
---*	El Dorado Georgetown	58	708
---*	Mariposa Twp 1	60	655
---*	Nevada Bridgeport	61	463
---*	Trinity Taylor'S	70	1035
---*	Yuba Fosters	72	843
Ah	Calaveras Twp 7	57	21
Andrew J	Calaveras Twp 4	57	345
Chick M*	Calaveras Twp 6	57	156
Chong	Mariposa Twp 1	60	626
Chow	Calaveras Twp 5	57	194
Clark M	Calaveras Twp 6	57	156
George	Sierra Pine Grove	66	823
Gir	Calaveras Twp 5	57	202
Hang	El Dorado Mud Springs	58	957
He	Placer Folsom	62	648
Hea	Tuolumne Twp 5	71	515
Hing	El Dorado Diamond	58	790
J*	Mariposa Twp 3	60	584
James	Tuolumne Twp 6	71	541

Name	County Locale	M653 Roll Page
YONG		
John	Placer Virginia	62 661
John	Sierra Pine Grove	66 834
John H	Sierra St Louis	66 814
Le	Placer Virginia	62 665
Pan	Tuolumne Twp 5	71 521
Peter	San Francisco San Francisco 2	67 717
R	Sierra Downieville	66 992
See	Plumas Quincy	62 948
Sigh	Butte Bidwell	56 731
Sin	Butte Ophir	56 801
Sum	Tuolumne Twp 6	71 529
Tim	El Dorado Diamond	58 790
Yin	San Francisco San Francisco 9	681094
YONGE		
Edward A	Alameda Oakland	55 71
YONGH		
---	San Francisco San Francisco 2	67 689
E	San Francisco San Francisco 2	67 770
YONGHA		
---	Fresno Twp 1	59 27
YONGMINA		
W	San Francisco San Francisco 9	681065
YONI		
---	Calaveras Twp 10	57 269
---	Stanislaus Emory	70 744
YONICK		
R B	Solano Montezuma	69 372
YONJ		
---	El Dorado Placerville	58 834
YONJG		
---	El Dorado Diamond	58 796
Eye	El Dorado Placerville	58 831
YONK		
---	Sierra Downieville	66 998
YONKE		
---	Mendocino Twp 1	60 892
YONKER		
Albert F	Yuba Marysville	72 897
Albert T	Yuba Marysville	72 897
August	San Francisco San Francisco 2	67 638
Chas R	Calaveras Twp 5	57 242
Thomas	El Dorado Diamond	58 766
YONKTAN		
---	Trinity Lewiston	70 955
YONLE		
W L	San Francisco San Francisco 7	681330
YONLEN		
Wm	Yolo No E Twp	72 670
YONLO		
W L	San Francisco San Francisco 7	681330
YONMAS		
Harriet*	Placer Auburn	62 560
YONN		
---	Placer Rattle Snake	62 602
---	Sierra St Louis	66 815
---	Sierra St Louis	66 816
---	Sierra Downieville	66 981
---	Sierra Downieville	66 984
---	Sierra Downieville	66 985
---	Sierra Downieville	66 990
---	Sierra Downieville	66 992
---	Sierra Downieville	66 999
Tow	Nevada Grass Valley	61 227
YONNG		
---	Calaveras Twp 6	57 181
---	Sacramento Ward 1	63 66
---	San Francisco San Francisco 2	67 754
---	Sierra Downieville	661000
---	Sierra Downieville	66 983
---	Sierra Downieville	66 984
---	Sierra Downieville	66 992
---	Sierra Downieville	66 993
---*	Siskiyou Callahan	69 12
Dill	Butte Ophir	56 787
Fell*	San Francisco San Francisco 1	68 926
Fong	Butte Ophir	56 787
Fonng	Butte Ophir	56 804
Foy	Butte Ophir	56 804
Le*	Calaveras Twp 4	57 337
Lewis*	Siskiyou Yreka	69 149
Long	San Francisco San Francisco 1	68 925
Tong	San Francisco San Francisco 1	68 925
YONNK		
---	Sierra Downieville	66 999
---*	Sierra Downieville	661024
YONNKER		
Joseph*	Del Norte Crescent	58 648
YONNO		
Sip	Placer Folsom	62 649
YONNT		
Geo C*	Napa Napa	61 83
YONNY		
---	Amador Twp 5	55 347
YONOCO		
---	Fresno Twp 1	59 27

Name	County Locale	M653 Roll Page
YONP		
---	Placer Illinois	62 752
YONRIE		
Frank*	Shasta Horsetown	66 699
YONRY		
---	Amador Twp 3	55 398
YONSMAH		
---	Fresno Twp 1	59 25
YONSON		
Albert	Alameda Brooklyn	55 148
Doming	Alameda Brooklyn	55 170
Domingo*	Alameda Washington	55 170
J*	Mariposa Twp 3	60 622
Phil*	Alameda Brooklyn	55 141
YONT		
---	Sierra Downieville	66 991
Jesse	El Dorado Mud Springs	58 983
John S*	Yuba Bear Rvr	72 999
John T*	Yuba Bear Rvr	72 999
N A	El Dorado Diamond	58 793
Soy	Yuba Fosters	72 841
YONTY		
Jno A	Sacramento Natonia	63 283
YONTZ		
J R*	San Francisco San Francisco 5	67 480
Jno A	Sacramento Natonia	63 283
John*	Santa Clara San Jose	65 390
YONUK		
---*	Sierra Downieville	661024
YONY		
---	Amador Twp 5	55 349
---	Amador Twp 5	55 350
---	Amador Twp 5	55 360
---	Amador Twp 6	55 429
---	Calaveras Twp 5	57 149
---	Calaveras Twp 5	57 202
---	Calaveras Twp 5	57 208
---	Calaveras Twp 5	57 222
---	Calaveras Twp 10	57 260
---	Calaveras Twp 10	57 275
---	Calaveras Twp 10	57 276
---	Calaveras Twp 10	57 296
---	Calaveras Twp 4	57 304
---	Calaveras Twp 4	57 305
Chow	Calaveras Twp 5	57 194
Clark M*	Calaveras Twp 6	57 156
No	Sacramento Granite	63 268
YOO		
---	Amador Twp 4	55 247
---	Calaveras Twp 8	57 63
---	Mariposa Twp 1	60 640
---	Sacramento Ward 1	63 65
---	San Francisco San Francisco 4	681189
---*	Yuba Linda	72 992
YOOH		
---	Yuba Marysville	72 895
YOOK		
---	Calaveras Twp 4	57 320
---	Yuba Marysville	72 874
---	Yuba Marysville	72 895
---	Yuba Linda	72 990
---*	San Francisco San Francisco 9	681092
Ah	Yuba Suida	72 990
YOON		
---	El Dorado Diamond	58 805
Castille	Tuolumne Columbia	71 366
Castillo	Tuolumne Twp 2	71 366
YOONG		
---	Tuolumne Chinese	71 525
YOOST		
Frank	Alameda Brooklyn	55 144
YOP		
---	Del Norte Crescent	58 651
---	Placer Illinois	62 746
---	Sacramento Cosumnes	63 388
---	Sacramento Ward 1	63 66
---	San Francisco San Francisco 9	681088
---	San Francisco San Francisco 9	681094
---	Sierra Downieville	661000
A	Sacramento Natonia	63 283
Gee	Sacramento Granite	63 245
Henry	Sacramento Natonia	63 281
Ho	Sacramento Granite	63 269
Leen	San Francisco San Francisco 9	681094
Leew*	San Francisco San Francisco 9	681094
Line	Sacramento Granite	63 258
YOPHY		
Fredrick*	Napa Hot Springs	61 25
YOPITZ		
---	Tulara Twp 2	71 37
YOPS		
---	Placer Illinois	62 751
YOR		
---	Calaveras Twp 4	57 337
---	Mariposa Twp 1	60 627
---	Sierra Twp 5	66 932

Name	County Locale	M653 Roll Page
YOR		
---	Sierra Downieville	66 973
Ah	Calaveras Twp 7	57 30
YORBA		
Andres	Los Angeles Santa Ana	59 446
Bernardo	Los Angeles Los Angeles	59 302
Bicente	Los Angeles Santa Ana	59 451
Catalina B	Los Angeles Los Angeles	59 296
Dolores	Los Angeles Santa Ana	59 447
Domingo	Los Angeles Santa Ana	59 457
Jesus	Los Angeles Santa Ana	59 448
Jose A	Los Angeles San Juan	59 470
Jose Ante	San Diego Agua Caliente	64 820
Jose De Pracia	San Diego	64 765
	San Diego	
Juan	Los Angeles San Juan	59 460
Miguel	Los Angeles San Juan	59 464
Ramon	Fresno Twp 1	59 33
Ramon	Los Angeles Santa Ana	59 441
Ranion	Los Angeles Santa Ana	59 441
Soledad	Los Angeles San Juan	59 470
Susana	Los Angeles San Juan	59 477
Teodocio	Los Angeles Santa Ana	59 454
Trinidad	Los Angeles Santa Ana	59 448
YORBOROUGH		
G	Sutter Yuba	70 769
YORDSELL		
D C	San Francisco San Francisco 9	681031
YORE		
---*	Sierra Downieville	661016
J W*	San Francisco San Francisco 9	681089
John P	San Francisco San Francisco 11	67 94
Patrick	Tuolumne Twp 2	71 297
Peter	Sierra Twp 5	66 917
YORENS		
M	San Francisco San Francisco 5	67 542
YORGOIR		
Manuell	Calaveras Twp 5	57 194
YORHAMS		
Jos F*	San Francisco San Francisco 9	681083
YORIK		
---	Mariposa Twp 1	60 627
YORK		
---	Amador Twp 2	55 293
---	Amador Twp 5	55 336
---	San Francisco San Francisco 9	681092
---	Sierra La Porte	66 785
---*	San Francisco San Francisco 9	681092
A M	Napa Hot Springs	61 3
Ann R	San Francisco San Francisco 8	681282
Charles*	Calaveras Twp 6	57 160
Chas	Sacramento Natonia	63 281
Eliza	Tuolumne Columbia	71 351
Francis	Tuolumne Jamestown	71 431
Jas L	Sacramento Ward 4	63 558
Jhn	Napa Hot Springs	61 8
Jno F	Sacramento Natonia	63 274
John	Alameda Oakland	55 66
John	Alameda Oakland	55 70
John	San Francisco San Francisco 2	67 596
John	Santa Clara Redwood	65 448
John	Shasta Shasta	66 735
John	Stanislaus Branch	70 702
John	Tuolumne Jamestown	71 432
L C	Nevada Grass Valley	61 182
Len*	Tulara Twp 1	71 87
Louis	Napa Yount	61 44
Lucinda J	Sonoma Armally	69 482
M J	Solano Vacaville	69 359
Mark	Sonoma Armally	69 482
Mary	Tuolumne Sonora	71 196
Meredith	Mendocino Little L	60 836
New*	Nevada Rough &	61 438
Newberry	Yolo Slate Ra	72 689
Newberry	Yuba Slate Ro	72 689
Peter S	Napa Hot Springs	61 9
S C	Tuolumne Twp 2	71 390
T J	Sierra Downieville	66 987
Thomas	Santa Cruz Pajaro	66 573
Thos F	Sacramento Natonia	63 274
W R	Nevada Bridgeport	61 444
William	Tuolumne Twp 5	71 495
Wm	Butte Chico	56 538
Wm	Santa Clara Redwood	65 447
YORLE		
Carl*	Sacramento Ward 1	63 150
YORN		
---	Amador Twp 5	55 360
YORNK		
J	Nevada Eureka	61 358
YORNNG		
Lewis*	Siskiyou Yreka	69 149
YORNY		
---	Amador Twp 6	55 430
YORO		
---	Calaveras Twp 5	57 193

California 1860 Census Index

Name	County Locale	M653 Roll Page
YOROW		
---	Sierra Downieville	66 991
YORRA		
Isabel	San Bernardino Santa Barbara	64 197
YORT		
Charles*	Calaveras Twp 6	57 160
YORTES		
W	Tehama Tehama	70 946
YORTRIES		
Danl*	Alameda Oakland	55 10
YORTUES		
Danl*	Alameda Oakland	55 10
YORUK		
J	Nevada Eureka	61 358
YORY		
---	Amador Twp 5	55 347
---	Amador Twp 6	55 447
---	Calaveras Twp 4	57 341
YORZTON		
John*	Mariposa Twp 1	60 663
YOS		
---	Calaveras Twp 4	57 337
YOSAWICK		
---	Tulara Twp 2	71 27
YOSE		
---	Tuolumne Twp 6	71 529
YOSSUP		
Matilda	Tulara Twp 2	71 28
YOST		
F	San Joaquin Stockton	641038
J H*	Sacramento Alabama	63 413
M	Yolo Cache Crk	72 665
Michael	Sacramento Ward 4	63 509
YOT		
---	Alameda Oakland	55 24
---	Calaveras Twp 5	57 218
---	Calaveras Twp 5	57 219
---	Calaveras Twp 5	57 242
---	Calaveras Twp 10	57 259
---	Calaveras Twp 10	57 271
---	Calaveras Twp 10	57 299
---	Calaveras Twp 9	57 349
---	Calaveras Twp 9	57 358
---	El Dorado Coloma	581111
---	El Dorado Eldorado	58 941
---	El Dorado Mud Springs	58 956
---	Nevada Nevada	61 310
---	Nevada Eureka	61 383
---	Nevada Bridgeport	61 458
---	Sacramento Cosumnes	63 398
---	San Francisco San Francisco 9	681088
---	San Francisco San Francisco 4	681187
---	San Francisco San Francisco 4	681194
Ah	Sacramento Cosumnes	63 401
Ah	Sacramento Ward 3	63 423
Chow	Nevada Eureka	61 383
Cow	San Francisco San Francisco 5	67 546
Kee	San Francisco San Francisco 4	681202
Ko	San Francisco San Francisco 4	681194
Ko	San Francisco San Francisco 4	681208
Ku	San Francisco San Francisco 4	681202
Ne	San Francisco San Francisco 4	681201
YOTO		
---	Mendocino Twp 1	60 889
---	Sierra Downieville	661000
---	Sierra Downieville	661005
YOTTMAN		
Wm	Tuolumne Jamestown	71 428
YOU CHOW		
---	Nevada Washington	61 341
YOU COW		
---	Trinity Trinindad Rvr	701046
YOU FAT		
---	Tuolumne Chinese	71 522
YOU WA		
---	Nevada Washington	61 340
YOU		
---	Alameda Oakland	55 23
---	Amador Twp 2	55 314
---	Amador Twp 2	55 315
---	Amador Twp 2	55 323
---	Amador Twp 2	55 328
---	Amador Twp 5	55 335
---	Amador Twp 5	55 338
---	Amador Twp 5	55 344
---	Amador Twp 7	55 418
---	Amador Twp 6	55 423
---	Amador Twp 6	55 427
---	Amador Twp 6	55 428
---	Amador Twp 6	55 434
---	Calaveras Twp 8	57 106
---	Calaveras Twp 6	57 167
---	Calaveras Twp 5	57 191
---	Calaveras Twp 5	57 202
---	Calaveras Twp 5	57 203
---	Calaveras Twp 5	57 215

Name	County Locale	M653 Roll Page
YOU		
---	Calaveras Twp 5	57 249
---	Calaveras Twp 5	57 251
---	Calaveras Twp 10	57 259
---	Calaveras Twp 10	57 267
---	Calaveras Twp 10	57 270
---	Calaveras Twp 10	57 291
---	Calaveras Twp 4	57 300
---	Calaveras Twp 4	57 300
---	Calaveras Twp 4	57 301
---	Calaveras Twp 4	57 303
---	Calaveras Twp 4	57 333
---	El Dorado White Oaks	581032
---	El Dorado Salmon Falls	581034
---	El Dorado Salmon Falls	581042
---	El Dorado Salmon Hills	581052
---	El Dorado Salmon Falls	581055
---	El Dorado Salmon Falls	581058
---	El Dorado Salmon Falls	581059
---	El Dorado Salmon Falls	581061
---	El Dorado Salmon Hills	581062
---	El Dorado Salmon Hills	581066
---	El Dorado Coloma	581075
---	El Dorado Coloma	581077
---	El Dorado Coloma	581078
---	El Dorado Coloma	581079
---	El Dorado Coloma	581084
---	El Dorado Coloma	581085
---	El Dorado Cold Spring	581101
---	El Dorado Coloma	581106
---	El Dorado Coloma	581109
---	El Dorado Coloma	581121
---	El Dorado Kelsey	581128
---	El Dorado Kelsey	581141
---	El Dorado Mountain	581188
---	El Dorado Mountain	581190
---	El Dorado Georgetown	58 682
---	El Dorado Georgetown	58 688
---	El Dorado Greenwood	58 731
---	El Dorado Diamond	58 775
---	El Dorado Diamond	58 783
---	El Dorado Placerville	58 900
---	El Dorado Placerville	58 902
---	El Dorado Placerville	58 929
---	El Dorado Mud Springs	58 956
---	Mariposa Twp 3	60 578
---	Mariposa Twp 1	60 627
---	Mariposa Twp 1	60 651
---	Mariposa Twp 1	60 655
---	Mariposa Twp 1	60 661
---	Mariposa Twp 1	60 662
---	Mariposa Twp 1	60 663
---	Mariposa Twp 1	60 673
---	Mariposa Coulterville	60 687
---	Mariposa Coulterville	60 692
---	Mariposa Coulterville	60 697
---	Mariposa Coulterville	60 700
---	Nevada Nevada	61 302
---	Nevada Nevada	61 305
---	Nevada Eureka	61 383
---	Nevada Bridgeport	61 460
---	Nevada Bridgeport	61 462
---	Nevada Bridgeport	61 463
---	Nevada Bridgeport	61 464
---	Nevada Bridgeport	61 466
---	Placer Auburn	62 572
---	Placer Auburn	62 575
---	Sacramento Granite	63 231
---	Sacramento Granite	63 233
---	Sacramento Granite	63 245
---	Sacramento Granite	63 259
---	Sacramento Granite	63 262
---	Sacramento Natonia	63 283
---	Sacramento Ward 3	63 491
---	Sacramento Ward 3	63 492
---	Sacramento Ward 3	63 493
---	Sacramento Ward 1	63 65
---	San Francisco San Francisco 4	681174
---	San Francisco San Francisco 4	681175
---	San Francisco San Francisco 4	681176
---	San Francisco San Francisco 4	681177
---	San Francisco San Francisco 4	681182
---	San Francisco San Francisco 4	681187
---	San Francisco San Francisco 4	681188
---	San Francisco San Francisco 4	681189
---	San Francisco San Francisco 4	681190
---	San Francisco San Francisco 4	681191
---	San Francisco San Francisco 4	681192
---	San Francisco San Francisco 4	681193
---	San Francisco San Francisco 4	681194
---	San Francisco San Francisco 4	681196
---	San Francisco San Francisco 4	681197
---	San Francisco San Francisco 4	681198
---	San Francisco San Francisco 4	681200
---	San Francisco San Francisco 4	681208
---	San Francisco San Francisco 4	681209

Name	County Locale	M653 Roll Page
YOU		
---	San Francisco San Francisco 4	681210
---	San Francisco San Francisco 4	681211
---	San Francisco San Francisco 4	681212
---	San Francisco San Francisco 1	68 925
---	Sierra Downieville	661004
---	Sierra Downieville	661005
---	Sierra Downieville	661008
---	Sierra Downieville	661009
---	Sierra La Porte	66 782
---	Sierra La Porte	66 785
---	Sierra Twp 5	66 932
---	Sierra Twp 5	66 934
---	Sierra Cox'S Bar	66 949
---	Siskiyou Yreka	69 194
---	Siskiyou Yreka	69 195
---	Stanislaus Emory	70 743
---	Trinity Weaverville	701076
---	Tuolumne Columbia	71 350
---	Tuolumne Twp 2	71 409
---	Tuolumne Twp 3	71 434
---	Tuolumne Twp 3	71 446
---	Tuolumne Twp 3	71 457
---	Tuolumne Sonora	71 477
---	Tuolumne Jacksonville	71 514
---	Tuolumne Chinese	71 526
---	Tuolumne Don Pedro	71 535
---	Tuolumne Don Pedro	71 538
---	Tuolumne Twp 6	71 540
---	Yuba Fosters	72 831
---*	Butte Ophir	56 771
---*	Calaveras Twp 5	57 237
---*	Calaveras Twp 5	57 247
---*	Nevada Nevada	61 305
---*	Nevada Bridgeport	61 460
---*	Nevada Red Dog	61 539
---*	Placer Auburn	62 563
---*	Sacramento Granite	63 243
---*	Sierra Downieville	661016
---*	Yuba Marysville	72 916
---*	Yuba Linda	72 992
A	Sacramento Granite	63 243
A	Sacramento Granite	63 250
A	Sacramento Granite	63 269
A	Sacramento Natonia	63 283
Ah	Calaveras Twp 7	57 15
Ah	Tuolumne Twp 2	71 350
Ah	Yuba Bear Rvr	721000
Ah	Yuba Suida	72 990
Ah	Yuba Suida	72 992
Ah	Yuba Suida	72 993
Ah*	Sacramento Granite	63 232
Aing	El Dorado Greenwood	58 730
Cam	Nevada Rough &	61 423
Can	Mariposa Coulterville	60 682
Chie	San Francisco San Francisco 4	681204
Cho	Tuolumne Twp 2	71 350
Choi	San Francisco San Francisco 4	681190
Choi	San Francisco San Francisco 4	681211
Chou	San Francisco San Francisco 4	681189
Chou	San Francisco San Francisco 4	681199
Chow	Calaveras Twp 5	57 193
Chow	Nevada Eureka	61 383
Chow	San Francisco San Francisco 4	681189
Chow	San Francisco San Francisco 4	681199
Choy	Calaveras Twp 5	57 193
Choy	San Francisco San Francisco 4	681211
Chu	San Francisco San Francisco 4	681187
Chu	San Francisco San Francisco 4	681204
Cive	Nevada Bridgeport	61 506
Cr*	San Francisco San Francisco 4	681202
Cwe*	Nevada Bridgeport	61 506
E	San Francisco San Francisco 1	68 872
F	El Dorado Placerville	58 902
Fe	San Francisco San Francisco 9	681093
Fe	San Francisco San Francisco 4	681179
Fin	Nevada Rough &	61 397
Fook	San Francisco San Francisco 4	681204
Gee	Mariposa Twp 3	60 578
Gee	Mariposa Twp 3	60 620
Gill*	Mariposa Twp 3	60 578
Go*	Mariposa Twp 3	60 620
Hon	San Francisco San Francisco 4	681204
Hou	San Francisco San Francisco 4	681204
J*	Nevada Bridgeport	61 460
John A	Yuba Fosters	72 838
Kei	Tuolumne Jacksonville	71 167
Ker	San Francisco San Francisco 5	671206
Kim	Butte Oro	56 680
Kon Ok	San Francisco San Francisco 4	681204
Ku	San Francisco San Francisco 5	671206
Ky	El Dorado Big Bar	58 738
Lan	San Francisco San Francisco 4	681204
Lawey	San Francisco San Francisco 4	681204
Lee	San Francisco San Francisco 4	681193

California 1860 Census Index

Name	County Locale	M653 Roll	Page
YOU			
Lem	Klamath Liberty	59	239
Leu	San Francisco San Francisco 4	681	173
Lon	El Dorado Greenwood	58	713
Looey	San Francisco San Francisco 4	681	204
Lou	Yuba Bear Rvr	72	1000
Lu	San Francisco San Francisco 4	681	193
Luy	Sacramento Granite	63	269
Man	San Francisco San Francisco 5	671	206
Mit	San Francisco San Francisco 4	681	185
Moy	San Francisco San Francisco 4	681	204
Nee	Tuolumne Big Oak	71	150
Or	San Francisco San Francisco 4	681	202
Pan	Tehama Red Bluff	70	932
Pow	San Francisco San Francisco 4	681	182
Qook	San Francisco San Francisco 4	681	204
Quok	San Francisco San Francisco 4	681	204
Ring	San Francisco San Francisco 4	681	175
See	San Francisco San Francisco 4	681	175
See	San Francisco San Francisco 4	681	192
Sill*	Mariposa Twp 3	60	578
Sing	El Dorado Placerville	58	931
Son*	Sacramento Granite	63	259
Su	San Francisco San Francisco 4	681	192
Sum	Placer Auburn	62	582
Sur	Sacramento Natonia	63	280
Ti	San Francisco San Francisco 4	681	193
Ting	Nevada Grass Valley	61	233
Tun	Sacramento Granite	63	233
Ya*	Sacramento Granite	63	259
Yook	Yuba Marysville	72	916
Yup	Nevada Eureka	61	384
Yut	Sacramento Granite	63	269
YOUA			
---	El Dorado Eldorado	58	941
YOUAT			
---	El Dorado Eldorado	58	948
YOUCOM			
Isaac	El Dorado Placerville	58	878
YOUCOME			
---*	Fresno Twp 3	59	31
YOUD			
James*	El Dorado Casumnes	581	166
YOUDEWNE			
---	Tulara Twp 1	71	120
YOUE			
---*	Placer Auburn	62	575
YOUG			
---	Calaveras Twp 6	57	126
---	Mariposa Twp 1	60	648
---	Mariposa Twp 1	60	662
---	Nevada Grass Valley	61	234
---	Sierra Downieville	661	005
---	Sierra Poker Flats	66	840
YOUGH			
---	Calaveras Twp 7	57	40
---	San Francisco San Francisco 2	67	689
YOUH			
---	Mariposa Twp 1	60	627
YOUK			
---	Placer Illinois	62	754
---	Sierra Downieville	66	998
Chin	Siskiyou Yreka	69	194
Hong	Placer Auburn	62	576
John	Shasta Shasta	66	735
S C	Tuolumne Shawsfla	71	390
YOUL			
---	Calaveras Twp 8	57	50
YOULE			
Adam	Sonoma Petaluma	69	567
YOULEN			
Wm	Yuba North Ea	72	670
YOULOUMINE			
---*	Tulara Visalia	71	35
YOULOUMNE			
---	Tulara Twp 2	71	35
YOULUME			
---	Tulara Twp 2	71	38
YOULUMNE			
---*	Tulara Twp 2	71	4
YOUM			
---	Placer Rattle Snake	62	603
---	Tuolumne Twp 1	71	477
YOUMAS			
Harriet*	Placer Auburn	62	560
YOUME			
---	Tulara Twp 2	71	39
YOUMILEAH			
---	Mendocino Round Va	60	883
YOUN CUA			
---*	Mariposa Twp 1	60	667
YOUN			
---	Calaveras Twp 10	57	274
---	Mariposa Twp 1	60	651
---	Sierra St Louis	66	816
---	Sierra Downieville	66	984
YOUN			
---	Sierra Downieville	66	999
---	Tuolumne Twp 3	71	457
Cha	Mariposa Twp 1	60	667
Cua	Mariposa Twp 1	60	667
John	Tehama Tehama	70	936
See*	Mariposa Twp 1	60	651
YOUNE			
---	Tuolumne Big Oak	71	147
Ah	Tuolumne Twp 4	71	147
YOUNG			
---	Amador Twp 2	55	323
---	Amador Twp 5	55	335
---	Amador Twp 5	55	342
---	Amador Twp 6	55	430
---	Amador Twp 5	55	434
---	Amador Twp 6	55	442
---	Butte Ophir	56	813
---	Butte Ophir	56	819
---	Calaveras Twp 6	57	171
---	Calaveras Twp 5	57	236
---	Calaveras Twp 5	57	237
---	El Dorado Salmon Hills	581	064
---	El Dorado Kelsey	581	134
---	El Dorado Diamond	58	783
---	El Dorado Diamond	58	787
---	El Dorado Diamond	58	790
---	El Dorado Diamond	58	797
---	El Dorado Diamond	58	798
---	El Dorado Diamond	58	806
---	El Dorado Eldorado	58	942
---	El Dorado Mud Springs	58	973
---	El Dorado Mud Springs	58	975
---	Fresno Twp 2	59	17
---	Fresno Twp 1	59	27
---	Klamath Liberty	59	238
---	Mariposa Twp 3	60	551
---	Mariposa Twp 1	60	652
---	Mariposa Twp 1	60	657
---	Mariposa Twp 1	60	659
---	Mariposa Twp 1	60	663
---	Mariposa Twp 1	60	666
---	Mariposa Coulterville	60	683
---	Mariposa Coulterville	60	694
---	Monterey Monterey	60	965
---	Nevada Bridgeport	61	459
---	Nevada Bridgeport	61	461
---	Placer Stewart	62	606
---	Plumas Meadow Valley	62	913
---	Sacramento Ward 1	63	66
---	San Joaquin Stockton	641	092
---	Sierra Downieville	661	000
---	Sierra Downieville	661	004
---	Sierra Downieville	661	008
---	Sierra Twp 7	66	889
---	Sierra Downieville	66	983
---	Sierra Downieville	66	984
---	Sierra Downieville	66	992
---	Sierra Downieville	66	993
---	Sierra Downieville	66	996
---	Siskiyou Callahan	69	12
---	Siskiyou Yreka	69	194
---	Stanislaus Branch	70	713
---	Stanislaus Branch	70	714
---	Stanislaus Branch	70	715
---	Tuolumne Big Oak	71	148
---	Tuolumne Jacksonville	71	168
---	Tuolumne Columbia	71	350
---	Tuolumne Twp 2	71	409
---	Tuolumne Jamestown	71	433
---	Tuolumne Twp 3	71	457
---	Tuolumne Twp 3	71	460
---	Tuolumne Twp 3	71	467
---	Tuolumne Columbia	71	474
---*	Mariposa Twp 3	60	612
---*	Mariposa Coulterville	60	683
---*	Placer Auburn	62	571
---*	Siskiyou Callahan	69	12
---*	Calaveras Twp 7	57	207
?Orel L	Amador Township	55	467
A	San Francisco San Francisco 2	67	711
A C	Sierra Twp 7	66	895
A H	Mariposa Twp 3	60	610
A J	San Francisco San Francisco 6	67	463
A L	Santa Clara Redwood	65	448
A O	Shasta Shasta	66	673
A W	Shasta Cottonwoood	66	724
Adam	Sierra Twp 5	66	942
Adorna	Yuba Foster B	72	829
Adorns	Yuba Fosters	72	829
Ah	Sacramento Franklin	63	334
Ah	Sacramento Cosummes	63	384
Ah	Sacramento Cosummes	63	396
Ah	Tuolumne Twp 4	71	148
Ah	Tuolumne Twp 4	71	168
Ah	Tuolumne Twp 2	71	350
YOUNG			
Albert	El Dorado Salmon Hills	581	062
Alex	Solano Suisan	69	240
Alexander	Butte Chico	56	550
Allert*	El Dorado Salmon Falls	581	062
Alphens	Tuolumne Montezuma	71	502
Alpheus	Tuolumne Twp 5	71	502
Amanda	Nevada Rough &	61	397
Amander*	Nevada Rough &	61	397
Amos	Plumas Quincy	62	920
Andrew	Contra Costa Twp 2	57	570
Andrew	Nevada Red Dog	61	554
Andrew	Trinity Mouth Ca	701	010
Andrew J	Calaveras Twp 4	57	345
Augustus	San Francisco San Francisco 4	681	154
B	Nevada Nevada	61	250
B F	El Dorado Grizzly	581	182
Benj	Nevada Nevada	61	328
Brigham	Los Angeles Los Angeles	59	349
Brigham	Tulara Twp 1	71	82
Bryant	Placer Virginia	62	670
C	El Dorado Kelsey	581	156
C	Nevada Eureka	61	349
C	Siskiyou Scott Ri	69	82
C	Tehama Red Bluff	70	919
C D	Sacramento San Joaquin	63	363
C E	Sacramento Ward 1	63	90
C L	Stanislaus Buena Village	70	722
C P	El Dorado Diamond	58	774
C W	Nevada Nevada	61	252
Cam	El Dorado Diamond	58	797
Charles	Placer Iona Hills	62	893
Charles	Siskiyou Yreka	69	190
Charley	Mariposa Twp 3	60	561
Chas	Butte Ophir	56	793
Chas	Sacramento Franklin	63	327
Chas	Trinity Trinity	701	022
Chas D	San Francisco San Francisco 2	67	696
Chs	Calaveras Twp 9	57	397
Chu	Siskiyou Yreka	69	195
Chung	Butte Ophir	56	806
Coniel	Yolo Merritt	72	582
Cope	Butte Bidwell	56	724
Corel L	Calaveras Twp 5	57	207
Coy	Yuba Long Bar	72	756
Cy	Yuba Long Bar	72	756
D	Siskiyou Scott Ri	69	81
Daniel	Tuolumne Twp 4	71	157
Daniel	Humbolt Eel Rvr	59	144
Daniel	Stanislaus Branch	70	712
David	Calaveras Twp 4	57	345
David	Santa Clara Redwood	65	459
Delilah	Shasta Cottonwoood	66	724
Denton	Trinity Trinity	70	971
Donald	Colusa Monroeville	57	454
Dorel L	Calaveras Twp 5	57	207
E G	Napa Napa	61	71
Edward	Colusa Muion	57	462
Edward	San Joaquin Elkhorn	64	976
Elijah	Santa Clara Santa Clara	65	501
Elisha	Sierra Twp 5	66	925
Ellen	Sacramento Ward 1	63	97
F L R*	Napa Clear Lake	61	134
F M	Sacramento Ward 4	63	510
F S R	Napa Clear Lake	61	134
Ferdinand	Tulara Visalia	71	105
Fou*	Plumas Quincy	621	009
Foung	Butte Ophir	56	812
Fred	Amador Twp 6	55	443
Frederick	Sierra Twp 7	66	885
Freeman	Colusa Monroeville	57	450
Fritz	Plumas Meadow Valley	62	933
Fung	Butte Ophir	56	806
Fung	Butte Ophir	56	813
Fung	Butte Ophir	56	818
Fung*	Butte Ophir	56	809
G	Nevada Eureka	61	363
G J*	Amador Twp 4	55	242
G W	Sacramento Ward 1	63	90
G W	San Francisco San Francisco 2	67	557
G W	Santa Clara Redwood	65	456
Geo	Butte Ophir	56	747
Geo	Butte Ophir	56	795
Geo	San Francisco San Francisco 10	67	199
Geo A	Nevada Nevada	61	298
Geo S	Sacramento Franklin	63	326
Geo W	San Francisco San Francisco 12	67	393
George	San Francisco San Francisco 7	681	333
George	Sierra Scales D	66	804
George	Sierra Twp 5	66	936
George	Sonoma Vallejo	69	621
George	Tulara Visalia	71	1
George E	Calaveras Twp 8	57	55
Gibson	Sonoma Santa Rosa	69	427

California 1860 Census Index

Name	County Locale	M653 Roll	Page
YOUNG			
Girch	Klamath Klamath	59	226
H	Tuolumne Big Oak	71	154
H A	Nevada Washington	61	331
H A	Nevada Washington	61	341
H A	Placer Forest H	62	794
Hannah	Los Angeles San Pedro	59	480
Harry	Butte Ophir	56	767
Harvey	Napa Napa	61	68
He	Siskiyou Yreka	69	195
Henry	El Dorado Mud Springs	58	983
Henry	Plumas Quincy	62	917
Henry	Plumas Quincy	62	992
Henry	Sonoma Vallejo	69	626
Henry D	San Francisco San Francisco 9	68	1053
Hiram	Sonoma Santa Rosa	69	412
Hiramy*	Shasta Cottonwoood	66	724
Hirany*	Shasta Cottonwoood	66	724
Hirum	Sonoma Santa Rosa	69	412
Ho	Siskiyou Yreka	69	195
I*	Shasta Shasta	66	681
I*	Nevada Bridgeport	61	491
Irving	San Francisco San Francisco 1	68	890
Isaac	Napa Clear Lake	61	123
Isaac D	Nevada Bridgeport	61	470
J	Nevada Eureka	61	349
J	Nevada Eureka	61	380
J	San Francisco San Francisco 5	67	523
J	Shasta Shasta	66	681
J	Sutter Nicolaus	70	835
J B	Merced Twp 1	60	910
J B	Sonoma Armally	69	508
J C	San Francisco San Francisco 6	67	471
J C	Sierra Twp 7	66	895
J D	Tuolumne Columbia	71	323
J R	San Francisco San Francisco 6	67	438
J S	Tehama Red Bluff	70	922
J W	Siskiyou Scott Va	69	20
J*	Nevada Bridgeport	61	491
J*	Sacramento Brighton	63	200
Jabez R	Calaveras Twp 5	57	210
Jaboz R	Calaveras Twp 5	57	210
Jacob	El Dorado White Oaks	58	1031
Jacob	Santa Clara Alviso	65	412
Jacob	Shasta Shasta	66	761
Jacob	Yuba Marysville	72	886
James	Los Angeles Azuza	59	272
James	Los Angeles Los Angeles	59	505
James	Plumas Quincy	62	973
James	San Francisco San Francisco 9	68	957
James	Sierra Twp 7	66	880
James	Sierra Twp 7	66	892
James	Sierra Downieville	66	989
James	Tehama Antelope	70	894
James	Trinity Mouth Ca	70	1012
James	Tulara Keyesville	71	54
James	Tuolumne Don Pedro	71	541
James	Yuba Bear Rvr	72	1001
James M*	Mendocino Ukiah	60	794
James R	Los Angeles Los Angeles	59	380
James S	Tuolumne Twp 1	71	216
James W	Mendocino Ukiah	60	794
Jas	Butte Ophir	56	764
Jas	Butte Ophir	56	768
Jas	San Francisco San Francisco 1	68	900
Jas	Sonoma Vallejo	69	621
Jas C	Butte Oro	56	680
Jas E	Placer Goods	62	699
Jas M	Butte Cascade	56	704
Jennie	Tulara Visalia	71	104
Jim	Calaveras Twp 4	57	345
Jno	Butte Hamilton	56	513
Jno	Butte Oregon	56	620
Jno	Butte Oregon	56	644
Jno	Nevada Eureka	61	356
Jno	Sacramento Ward 1	63	98
Jno G	Butte Kimshaw	56	575
Jobez R	Calaveras Twp 5	57	210
John	Calaveras Twp 7	57	22
John	Calaveras Twp 9	57	362
John	Contra Costa Twp 3	57	586
John	Mendocino Little L	60	833
John	Plumas Quincy	62	1007
John	Plumas Meadow Valley	62	931
John	Sacramento Ward 1	63	11
John	San Francisco San Francisco 8	68	1281
John	San Francisco San Francisco 7	68	1414
John	San Francisco San Francisco 11	67	150
John	Siskiyou Callahan	69	5
John	Sonoma Santa Rosa	69	412
John	Sonoma Mendocino	69	463
John	Sonoma Armally	69	482
John	Sonoma Bodega	69	539
John	Yuba Bear Rvr	72	1002
John	Yuba Rose Bar	72	818

Name	County Locale	M653 Roll	Page
YOUNG			
John	Yuba Marysville	72	969
Johnson	Contra Costa Twp 1	57	491
Jon G	Butte Kimshaw	56	575
Jonathan	Sonoma Petaluma	69	554
Jos	Butte Bidwell	56	712
Jos	Butte Bidwell	56	729
Joseph	Amador Twp 2	55	263
Joseph	Marin Bolinas	60	745
Joseph	Merced Monterey	60	940
Joseph	Monterey Monterey	60	940
Joseph	Siskiyou Callahan	69	15
Joseph	Yolo Slate Ra	72	691
Joseph	Yuba Slate Ro	72	691
Jow	Mariposa Twp 1	60	627
K B	San Francisco San Francisco 5	67	525
L	Sierra Twp 7	66	908
L D	Yuba New York	72	724
L E	Tehama Antelope	70	887
L G	Mariposa Twp 3	60	574
Larance	Yuba Marysville	72	871
Laura	Klamath Klamath	59	226
Le*	Calaveras Twp 4	57	337
Lee	Butte Ophir	56	820
Lewis	Siskiyou Yreka	69	149
Lin	Butte Ophir	56	807
Louis	Sacramento Ward 1	63	29
Lucinda	Siskiyou Yreka	69	168
Lud	El Dorado Diamond	58	784
M	Siskiyou Callahan	69	15
M	Sonoma Washington	69	673
M B	El Dorado Indian D	58	1157
M J	Sacramento Alabama	63	413
Margaret	Calaveras Twp 4	57	345
Marshall	Santa Clara Burnett	65	256
Martha	Sonoma Armally	69	505
Mary	San Francisco San Francisco 4	68	1142
Mary	San Francisco San Francisco 4	68	1149
Mary	San Francisco San Francisco 1	68	885
Mary A	Santa Clara Alviso	65	412
Mary Vincent Si	Solano Benecia	69	300
Michael	Plumas Quincy	62	987
Michiel	Nevada Red Dog	61	545
Milton	San Francisco San Francisco 11	67	148
Monis D*	San Francisco San Francisco 8	68	1308
Mories D*	San Francisco San Francisco 8	68	1308
	San Francisco		
Morris De	San Francisco San Francisco 8	68	1308
Murdoe	Sierra Eureka	66	1045
N	El Dorado Diamond	58	766
N	Siskiyou Klamath	69	90
N A	Trinity Weaverville	70	1072
N A	Yolo Slate Ra	72	699
N A	Yuba Slate Ro	72	699
N H	Sacramento Alabama	63	413
N M	Napa Clear Lake	61	135
Nahnm	San Francisco San Francisco 11	67	91
Nahum	San Francisco San Francisco 11	67	91
Nancy	Stanislaus Branch	70	711
Nathan	Tuolumne Twp 3	71	436
Nathaniel	Yuba Marysville	72	906
Newton	Tehama Moons	70	853
Nicholas	San Francisco San Francisco 6	67	406
O H P	Tuolumne Twp 3	71	452
Oliver	Yuba Marysville	72	878
P R	Nevada Bridgeport	61	455
P R	Sacramento Granite	63	223
Paul	Calaveras Twp 5	57	222
Pen	Fresno Twp 2	59	18
Penbrook*	Napa Clear Lake	61	123
Peter	Placer Secret R	62	611
Peter	San Diego Colorado	64	808
Peter	San Francisco San Francisco 2	67	717
Peter	San Joaquin O'Neal	64	1006
Peter	Sonoma Washington	69	673
Qui	Siskiyou Scott Ri	69	67
R	El Dorado Mud Springs	58	969
R	Sacramento Ward 1	63	2
R	San Francisco San Francisco 9	68	1061
R	San Francisco San Francisco 1	68	891
R	Trinity Honest B	70	1043
R J	Sacramento San Joaquin	63	362
R L*	Sacramento Brighton	63	204
R S*	Sacramento Brighton	63	204
R T	Butte Kimshaw	56	572
R T	Santa Clara Alviso	65	397
R T	Tuolumne Twp 2	71	382
R T	Tuolumne Shawsfla	71	384
R W	Trinity Weaverville	70	1070
Ran	Siskiyou Yreka	69	195
Reese	Butte Kimshaw	56	569
Reise	Butte Kimshaw	56	569
Robert	Monterey Monterey	60	965

Name	County Locale	M653 Roll	Page
YOUNG			
Robert	San Francisco San Francisco 2	67	605
Robert	San Joaquin Castoria	64	905
Robert	Siskiyou Yreka	69	129
Robert	Monterey Monterey	60	965
Robut	Tuolumne Big Oak	71	129
Rufus K	San Francisco San Francisco 5	67	484
S	Tehama Red Bluff	70	920
S	Tehama Red Bluff	70	925
S C	Santa Clara San Jose	65	374
S D	Colusa Monroeville	57	447
S H	Mariposa Twp 3	60	610
S*	Sacramento Brighton	63	200
Saey	Plumas Quincy	62	949
Sam	Klamath Klamath	59	226
Sam*	Yuba Long Bar	72	760
Saml	Sacramento Ward 3	63	445
Samuel	El Dorado Casumnes	58	1175
Samuel	Placer Iona Hills	62	874
Samuel	San Francisco San Francisco 9	68	1097
Sarah	Contra Costa Twp 2	57	571
Sarah	San Francisco San Francisco 2	67	692
Seth	Stanislaus Emory	70	740
Shepard	Tuolumne Springfield	71	373
Stephn	Placer Forest H	62	792
Su	Tuolumne Twp 2	71	346
T J*	Amador Twp 4	55	242
T W T	Merced Twp 2	60	924
Tho	Siskiyou Scott Ri	69	71
Thomas	El Dorado Casumnes	58	1160
Thomas	El Dorado Casumnes	58	1162
Thomas	Mendocino Big Rvr	60	844
Thomas	Placer Forest H	62	803
Thomas	San Joaquin Castoria	64	880
Thomas	Solano Suisan	69	236
Thomas W	Tuolumne Shawsfla	71	400
Thos	Amador Twp 2	55	268
Thos	Butte Ophir	56	793
Thos	San Francisco San Francisco 1	68	909
Thos	Trinity Indian C	70	989
Uhs*	Calaveras Twp 9	57	397
V S	Nevada Grass Valley	61	214
V S	Marin Point Re	60	731
W	San Francisco San Francisco 5	67	530
W	San Francisco San Francisco 1	68	929
W	Siskiyou Scott Ri	69	83
W	Butte Bidwell	56	718
W A	San Joaquin Stockton	64	1046
W D	Yolo Washington	72	564
W H	El Dorado White Oaks	58	1001
W L	El Dorado Placerville	58	883
W P	Marin Point Re	60	731
Wa	Shasta French G	66	720
Walter	San Mateo Twp 3	65	82
War	El Dorado Salmon Falls	58	1062
Wiliam	Plumas Quincy	62	963
Willet S	San Francisco San Francisco 10	67	337
William	Contra Costa Twp 1	57	492
William	Nevada Red Dog	61	542
William	San Joaquin Elkhorn	64	969
William	Shasta Cottonwoood	66	723
William E	Sierra Whiskey	66	847
Wm	Butte Bidwell	56	718
Wm	Butte Bidwell	56	727
Wm	Los Angeles Los Angeles	59	507
Wm	Napa Clear Lake	61	135
Wm	Sacramento Ward 4	63	498
Wm	San Francisco San Francisco 10	67	313
Wm	San Joaquin Stockton	64	1047
Wm	Santa Clara San Jose	65	356
Wm	Sonoma Bodega	69	536
Wm	Sonoma Petaluma	69	555
Wm	Stanislaus Branch	70	711
Wm H	Butte Bidwell	56	730
Wm H	Butte Ophir	56	768
Wm H	Colusa Colusi	57	419
Wm H	Sacramento Ward 3	63	443
Wm H	Sacramento Ward 1	63	46
Wm J	Humbolt Eureka	59	173
Wm J	Merced Twp 1	60	896
Wm M	Klamath Klamath	59	226
Wm P	Sierra Twp 5	66	939
Wm R	Placer Ophirville	62	654
Wm T	Klamath Klamath	59	226
Wm T	Sonoma Washington	69	667
Wy	Mariposa Twp 1	60	612
Yow	Mariposa Twp 1	60	627
Zow*	Mariposa Twp 1	60	627
YOUNGBLOOD			
David	Sacramento Ward 4	63	505
YOUNGBRUTE			
H W	San Francisco San Francisco 1	68	930
YOUNGE			
Ad	Alameda Brooklyn	55	107

Name	County Locale	M653 Roll	Page
YOUNGE			
Jno G	Alameda Brooklyn	55	185
John	Alameda Brooklyn	55	89
N*	Alameda Brooklyn	55	107
T H	El Dorado Diamond	58	774
Wm	Alameda Brooklyn	55	137
YOUNGER			
Alex J	San Francisco San Francisco 1	68	822
Caliman	Santa Clara San Jose	65	388
Fred	Santa Clara Santa Clara	65	489
Micheal	Amador Twp 5	55	365
R D	Amador Twp 3	55	391
Thomas	El Dorado Coloma	581	103
Wm	Yolo Slate Ra	72	714
Wm	Yuba Slate Ro	72	714
YOUNGLIF			
Jacob	El Dorado Placerville	58	911
YOUNGLIN			
Jason	Sonoma Petaluma	69	553
YOUNGLOVE			
E	Nevada Nevada	61	265
George	Yuba Bear Rvr	721	008
L	Nevada Nevada	61	263
YOUNGMAN			
George	Contra Costa Twp 1	57	504
YOUNGREN			
George	San Francisco San Francisco 3	67	51
YOUNGS			
James	Alameda Oakland	55	50
YOUNGSON			
George	San Francisco San Francisco 3	67	51
YOUNGWORTH			
C L	Tuolumne Twp 4	71	144
C T	Tuolumne Big Oak	71	144
YOUNK			
---	Sierra Downieville	661	014
---	Sierra Downieville	66	999
YOUNKER			
Joseph*	Del Norte Crescent	58	648
YOUNKIN			
Chas R	Calaveras Twp 5	57	242
YOUNNE			
---	Sierra Downieville	66	981
YOUNNO			
---	Sierra Downieville	66	981
YOUNS			
John*	Amador Twp 2	55	313
YOUNT			
A J	Solano Vacaville	69	361
David*	Napa Napa	61	83
Elizabeth	San Francisco San Francisco 8	681	249
Geo C*	Napa Napa	61	83
J	Shasta Shasta	66	758
John	Amador Twp 2	55	313
John	El Dorado Indian D	581	159
John*	Amador Twp 2	55	313
William	Tuolumne Twp 1	71	201
YOUNTE			
---	Sierra Downieville	661	014
YOUNTZ			
Christian	San Francisco San Francisco 7	681	381
YOUP			
---	Placer Illinois	62	751
Sing	Placer Auburn	62	578
YOUPE			
---	Placer Virginia	62	671
YOUR			
---	Amador Twp 5	55	336
---	Placer Folsom	62	649
---	Sierra Downieville	66	997
---	Sierra Downieville	66	999
---	Tuolumne Twp 3	71	433
---	Tuolumne Twp 3	71	442
---	Tuolumne Twp 3	71	446
---	Tuolumne Twp 1	71	476
---*	Tuolumne Don Pedro	71	540
YOURAN			
B	Nevada Grass Valley	61	151
YOURCE			
William	Amador Twp 3	55	408
YOURIE			
Frank	Shasta Horsetown	66	699
YOURJAN			
---	Sierra Downieville	661	005
YOURLY			
Robt	Amador Twp 3	55	369
YOURN			
---	Tuolumne Sonora	71	477
YOURY			
---	Amador Twp 5	55	351
YOUS			
---	Tuolumne Jamestown	71	446
YOUSE			
Samuel	Siskiyou Scott Va	69	44
YOUSELL			
Charles	Sierra Downieville	661	016

Name	County Locale	M653 Roll	Page
YOUSEN			
J*	Mariposa Twp 3	60	622
YOUSHINY			
---	Humbolt Eureka	59	173
YOUSON			
Phil*	Alameda Brooklyn	55	141
YOUST			
Herman	San Francisco San Francisco 10		348
		67	
YOUT			
---*	Sierra Downieville	66	991
John T	Yuba Bear Rvr	72	999
YOUTRAA			
---	Tulara Twp 1	71	122
YOUTZ			
John*	Santa Clara San Jose	65	390
YOUY			
---	Amador Twp 5	55	335
---	Calaveras Twp 5	57	208
---	Calaveras Twp 10	57	271
---	Calaveras Twp 4	57	302
---*	Amador Twp 5	55	350
YOV			
Tan	Yuba Foster B	72	827
YOVAHA			
Pedro*	Los Angeles Los Angeles	59	493
YOVANA			
Jose A*	Los Angeles Los Angeles	59	494
Pedro*	Los Angeles Los Angeles	59	493
YOVARRA			
Jose A*	Los Angeles Los Angeles	59	494
Pedro*	Los Angeles Los Angeles	59	493
YOVE			
To	Mariposa Coulterville	60	684
YOW CHIP			
---	Sacramento Ward 1	63	65
YOW COUNG			
Se*	Mariposa Twp 1	60	627
YOW TUCK			
---	Sacramento Ward 1	63	69
YOW			
---	Amador Twp 1	55	492
---	Calaveras Twp 8	57	109
---	Calaveras Twp 6	57	125
---	Calaveras Twp 6	57	126
---	Calaveras Twp 6	57	159
---	Calaveras Twp 6	57	167
---	Calaveras Twp 5	57	171
---	Calaveras Twp 5	57	181
---	Calaveras Twp 5	57	182
---	Calaveras Twp 5	57	193
---	Calaveras Twp 5	57	203
---	Calaveras Twp 5	57	209
---	Calaveras Twp 5	57	215
---	Calaveras Twp 5	57	219
---	Calaveras Twp 5	57	233
---	Calaveras Twp 5	57	235
---	Calaveras Twp 5	57	247
---	Calaveras Twp 5	57	251
---	Calaveras Twp 5	57	254
---	Calaveras Twp 5	57	256
---	Calaveras Twp 10	57	259
---	Calaveras Twp 10	57	267
---	Calaveras Twp 10	57	271
---	Calaveras Twp 10	57	273
---	Calaveras Twp 10	57	276
---	Calaveras Twp 10	57	284
---	Calaveras Twp 10	57	286
---	Calaveras Twp 10	57	291
---	Calaveras Twp 10	57	297
---	Calaveras Twp 4	57	299
---	Calaveras Twp 4	57	300
---	Calaveras Twp 4	57	301
---	Calaveras Twp 4	57	305
---	Calaveras Twp 4	57	327
---	Calaveras Twp 4	57	334
---	Calaveras Twp 4	57	343
---	Calaveras Twp 9	57	358
---	Calaveras Twp 8	57	68
---	Calaveras Twp 8	57	74
---	Calaveras Twp 8	57	92
---	Del Norte Happy Ca	58	663
---	Del Norte Happy Ca	58	664
---	El Dorado White Oaks	581	024
---	El Dorado Salmon Falls	581	059
---	El Dorado Salmon Falls	581	062
---	El Dorado Coloma	581	073
---	El Dorado Coloma	581	075
---	El Dorado Coloma	581	082
---	El Dorado Coloma	581	084
---	El Dorado Coloma	581	102
---	El Dorado Coloma	581	107
---	El Dorado Coloma	581	114
---	El Dorado Coloma	581	123
---	El Dorado Kelsey	581	144
---	El Dorado Casumnes	581	177

Name	County Locale	M653 Roll	Page
YOW			
---	El Dorado Mountain	581	189
---	El Dorado Placerville	58	829
---	El Dorado Placerville	58	830
---	El Dorado Placerville	58	831
---	El Dorado Placerville	58	834
---	El Dorado Placerville	58	923
---	El Dorado Mud Springs	58	961
---	El Dorado Mud Springs	58	985
---	Mariposa Twp 1	60	627
---	Mariposa Twp 1	60	637
---	Mariposa Twp 1	60	640
---	Mariposa Twp 1	60	651
---	Mariposa Twp 1	60	663
---	Nevada Bridgeport	61	462
---	Nevada Bridgeport	61	466
---	Placer Auburn	62	582
---	Placer Auburn	62	583
---	Placer Auburn	62	592
---	Placer Rattle Snake	62	598
---	Placer Rattle Snake	62	629
---	Placer Rattle Snake	62	636
---	Placer Folsom	62	648
---	Placer Virginia	62	665
---	Placer Virginia	62	675
---	Placer Virginia	62	684
---	Placer Virginia	62	687
---	Placer Illinois	62	751
---	Sacramento Ward 1	63	156
---	Sacramento Cosumnes	63	386
---	Sacramento Cosumnes	63	390
---	Sacramento Cosumnes	63	392
---	Sacramento Ward 3	63	491
---	Sacramento Ward 1	63	52
---	Sacramento Ward 1	63	55
---	Sacramento Ward 1	63	59
---	Sacramento Ward 4	63	613
---	Sacramento Ward 1	63	69
---	San Francisco San Francisco 9	681	088
---	San Francisco San Francisco 9	681	095
---	San Francisco San Francisco 4	681	174
---	San Francisco San Francisco 4	681	193
---	San Francisco San Francisco 4	681	194
---	San Francisco San Francisco 4	681	197
---	San Francisco San Francisco 4	681	199
---	San Francisco San Francisco 4	681	209
---	San Francisco San Francisco 4	681	210
---	San Joaquin Stockton	641	087
---	Sierra Downieville	661	004
---	Sierra Downieville	661	016
---	Sierra Downieville	661	024
---	Sierra Downieville	661	027
---	Sierra Downieville	661	032
---	Sierra Excelsior	661	034
---	Sierra Twp 7	66	894
---	Sierra Cox'S Bar	66	949
---	Sierra Downieville	66	980
---	Sierra Downieville	66	983
---	Sierra Downieville	66	984
---	Stanislaus Emory	70	744
---	Trinity Big Flat	701	042
---	Trinity Trinindad Rvr	701	046
---	Trinity Trinindad Rvr	701	047
---	Trinity E Weaver	701	057
---	Trinity Weaverville	701	072
---	Trinity Lewiston	70	955
---	Trinity Lewiston	70	956
---	Trinity Grass Valley	70	962
---	Tuolumne Jamestown	71	433
---	Tuolumne Jamestown	71	434
---	Tuolumne Twp 3	71	467
---	Tuolumne Twp 1	71	477
---	Tuolumne Twp 5	71	508
---	Tuolumne Green Springs	71	517
---	Tuolumne Twp 5	71	522
---	Tuolumne Twp 5	71	524
---	Tuolumne Twp 5	71	525
---	Tuolumne Don Pedro	71	540
---	Tuolumne Twp 6	71	541
---	Yuba Marysville	72	868
---	Yuba Marysville	72	895
---	Yuba Marysville	72	916
---	Yuba Linda	72	992
---*	Calaveras Twp 10	57	247
---*	Calaveras Twp 4	57	343
---*	Nevada Bridgeport	61	464
---*	Sacramento Ward 1	63	53
---*	Sacramento Ward 1	63	60
---*	San Francisco San Francisco 9	681	084
---*	Sierra Downieville	661	024
---*	Tuolumne Twp 6	71	533
---*	Tuolumne Don Pedro	71	540
---*	Yuba Foster B	72	831
---*	Yuba Marysville	72	916
Ah	Sacramento Cosumnes	63	388

California 1860 Census Index

Name	County Locale	M653 RollPage
YOW		
Ah	Tuolumne Twp 4	71 163
Ah	Yuba Suida	72 992
Ah*	Sacramento Granite	63 232
Cam	Nevada Rough &	61 423
Chip	Sacramento Ward 1	63 65
Com	Trinity Weaverville	701073
Go	Mariposa Twp 3	60 620
Ho Pung	Sacramento Ward 4	63 610
John A	Yuba Fosters	72 837
See	Nevada Rough &	61 397
Sing	Placer Folsom	62 649
Sing*	Mariposa Twp 1	60 627
Ti	San Francisco San Francisco 4	681193
To	Mariposa Coulterville	60 684
Tuck	Sacramento Ward 1	63 69
YOWCE		
---	Shasta Horsetown	66 709
YOWEE		
---*	Shasta Horsetown	66 709
YOWEL		
---*	Shasta Horsetown	66 709
YOWER		
---	Tuolumne Twp 1	71 477
YOWOW		
---	Tulara Twp 1	71 117
YOWRR		
---	Tuolumne Sonora	71 477
YOY		
---	Calaveras Twp 5	57 193
---	Mariposa Twp 1	60 627
---	Nevada Bloomfield	61 522
---	San Francisco San Francisco 4	681177
---	Sierra Downieville	661026
---*	Yuba Foster B	72 827
Ah	Calaveras Twp 7	57 36
Ban	Tuolumne Twp 4	71 169
C M	Butte Cascade	56 701
Kee	San Francisco San Francisco 4	681207
Ku	San Francisco San Francisco 4	681207
Sam	San Joaquin Elkhorn	64 969
YOZEAR		
T	San Francisco San Francisco 6	67 449
YPOLITO		
Jesus	Monterey Pajaro	601012
Teresa	Monterey Pajaro	601013
YR		
---	Calaveras Twp 6	57 164
YRAND		
Sarah J*	San Francisco San Francisco 1	68 807
YRASK		
Y S*	Siskiyou Scott Va	69 47
YREE		
---	Placer Rattle Snake	62 636
YREEND		
Sarah J	San Francisco San Francisco 1	68 807
YREIP		
---	Placer Rattle Snake	62 635
YRES		
Piere	Yuba Fosters	72 840
YRETAKEN		
---	Tulara Twp 1	71 122
YRI		
---	Calaveras Twp 6	57 148
YRON		
Isidro	Los Angeles Los Nieto	59 431
Manuel	Los Angeles Los Nieto	59 431
YRT		
---	El Dorado Big Bar	58 734
YRUE		
Jsa J*	Contra Costa Twp 2	57 539
YRY		
---	El Dorado Big Bar	58 734
YSABEL		
---	San Diego San Diego	64 774
---	San Diego Agua Caliente	64 821
---	San Diego Agua Caliente	64 823
---	San Diego Agua Caliente	64 841
---	San Diego Agua Caliente	64 863
YSAN		
Ah	Calaveras Twp 7	57 31
YSARRA		
Jose J	Marin Cortemad	60 782
YSIDORA		
---	San Diego Agua Caliente	64 829
YSIDRO		
---	San Diego San Diego	64 776
---	San Diego Temecula	64 800
---	San Diego Agua Caliente	64 824
YSLAS		
Manuel	Los Angeles Los Angeles	59 311
YSMAILA		
Maria	Los Angeles Los Angeles	59 294
YTURA		
Esteban*	Santa Clara Fremont	65 442
YU CAN		
---	Nevada Bridgeport	61 458
YU		
---	Alameda Oakland	55 23
---	Calaveras Twp 5	57 176
---	Calaveras Twp 5	57 193
---	Calaveras Twp 5	57 194
---	Calaveras Twp 5	57 230
---	Calaveras Twp 5	57 244
---	Calaveras Twp 5	57 249
---	Calaveras Twp 10	57 295
---	Calaveras Twp 8	57 74
---	Mariposa Twp 1	60 668
---	Nevada Nevada	61 299
---	Nevada Nevada	61 301
---	Placer Iona Hills	62 893
---	Plumas Meadow Valley	62 914
---	Sacramento Natonia	63 283
---	Sacramento Cosumnes	63 390
---	Sacramento Ward 3	63 491
---	Sacramento Ward 3	63 493
---	Sacramento Ward 1	63 55
---	Sacramento Ward 1	63 59
---	Sacramento Ward 1	63 67
---	San Francisco San Francisco 9	681096
---	San Francisco San Francisco 5	67 508
---	Sierra Downieville	66 979
---*	Sacramento Ward 1	63 67
---*	Yuba Fosters	72 842
Ah	Butte Cascade	56 699
Ah	Calaveras Twp 7	57 31
Gu	Sacramento Natonia	63 283
Hing	San Francisco San Francisco 11	67 160
Hong	San Francisco San Francisco 11	67 160
Leoy	San Francisco San Francisco 4	681195
Lich	Sacramento Natonia	63 283
Lin	Sacramento Natonia	63 283
Mong	San Francisco San Francisco 11	67 160
Nei	El Dorado Diamond	58 808
Nur	Sacramento Granite	63 269
See*	Sacramento Granite	63 268
Shing	San Francisco San Francisco 9	681086
Song	Calaveras Twp 4	57 301
Su	Sacramento Granite	63 269
Turn	San Francisco San Francisco 5	67 508
Wan	Yuba Marysville	72 916
Yee*	San Francisco San Francisco 5	67 507
Yu*	San Francisco San Francisco 5	67 507
Yung	El Dorado Georgetown	58 680
YUA		
---	Calaveras Twp 5	57 212
YUANG		
---	El Dorado Georgetown	58 691
San	Fresno Twp 2	59 19
YUBY		
F C	Yolo Cache Crk	72 621
YUCK		
---	Calaveras Twp 5	57 192
---	Nevada Washington	61 339
---	Sacramento Cosumnes	63 388
---	Sierra Downieville	66 993
---	Sierra Downieville	66 994
Fee	San Francisco San Francisco 1	68 925
Gum	Sierra Downieville	66 993
YUCKLY		
Lewis*	Butte Bidwell	56 707
YUCKS		
---	Calaveras Twp 5	57 192
YUE		
---	Plumas Meadow Valley	62 914
---	Sierra Downieville	66 980
---	Sierra Downieville	66 981
---	Sierra Downieville	66 998
YUEN		
Chan*	San Francisco San Francisco 4	681181
YUEY		
Yi	Sacramento Natonia	63 281
YUG		
---	Calaveras Twp 6	57 165
YUH		
---	Nevada Grass Valley	61 227
---	Sacramento Ward 1	63 54
---	Stanislaus Emory	70 743
Ah	Sacramento Ward 1	63 152
YUI		
---	Calaveras Twp 5	57 203
---	Calaveras Twp 5	57 249
---	Calaveras Twp 10	57 271
YUIG		
---*	Yuba Marysville	72 916
YUILL		
James*	Sierra Poker Flats	66 842
YUIN		
---	Sierra Twp 5	66 944
YUING		
---	Sierra Downieville	661008
YUK		
---	Amador Twp 4	55 246
---	Nevada Nevada	61 300
---	Sierra Downieville	661024
---	Yuba North Ea	72 681
---*	Nevada Washington	61 341
---*	Yuba Fosters	72 842
Kever	San Francisco San Francisco 5	67 508
Lee Don	Yuba Rose Bar	72 800
Wong	San Francisco San Francisco 5	67 508
YUKE		
---	El Dorado Georgetown	58 692
---	Tulara Twp 1	71 117
---	Yuba Long Bar	72 761
---*	Yuba Foster B	72 826
---*	Yuba Foster B	72 827
YUKEL		
---	Tulara Twp 1	71 114
YULE		
---*	Tulara Visalia	71 37
---*	Tulara Visalia	71 40
James*	Placer Michigan	62 815
Wm	Sacramento Ward 4	63 570
YULIE		
William	Siskiyou Yreka	69 178
YULLIM		
Alexander*	Calaveras Twp 10	57 262
Jeremiah*	Calaveras Twp 10	57 262
Thomas Jr*	Calaveras Twp 10	57 262
Thomas*	Calaveras Twp 10	57 262
YULLU		
Julius Y	San Francisco San Francisco 7	681395
YULUC		
---*	Butte Chico	56 550
YULUE		
---	Butte Chico	56 550
YUM		
---	Amador Twp 6	55 428
---	Butte Ophir	56 787
---	Butte Ophir	56 814
---	Calaveras Twp 5	57 244
---	Calaveras Twp 8	57 49
---	Calaveras Twp 8	57 92
---	Placer Illinois	62 742
---	Sierra La Porte	66 782
---	Tuolumne Big Oak	71 148
---	Tuolumne Twp 3	71 442
---	Tuolumne Twp 1	71 516
Ah	Tuolumne Twp 4	71 148
Chiong	San Francisco San Francisco 5	67 509
YUMA		
Jose	San Diego Agua Caliente	64 856
YUMG		
J	Nevada Eureka	61 380
YUMMAUNE		
---	Butte Chico	56 551
YUN		
---	Amador Twp 2	55 314
---	Amador Twp 6	55 447
---	Calaveras Twp 5	57 212
---	Calaveras Twp 5	57 244
---	Calaveras Twp 5	57 249
---	Calaveras Twp 5	57 252
---	Calaveras Twp 5	57 254
---	Calaveras Twp 10	57 260
---	Calaveras Twp 10	57 271
---	Calaveras Twp 10	57 273
---	Del Norte Crescent	58 651
---	El Dorado Greenwood	58 720
---	Mariposa Twp 3	60 598
---	Mariposa Twp 1	60 662
---	Nevada Grass Valley	61 227
---	Nevada Grass Valley	61 228
---	Nevada Grass Valley	61 232
---	Sacramento Natonia	63 283
---	San Francisco San Francisco 4	681173
---	Shasta Shasta	66 669
---	Shasta Horsetown	66 710
---	Shasta French G	66 720
---	Sierra Twp 5	66 944
---	Sierra Downieville	66 981
---	Stanislaus Branch	70 713
---	Stanislaus Emory	70 744
---	Tuolumne Twp 2	71 409
---*	Nevada Eureka	61 380
---*	Sacramento Cosumnes	63 396
---*	Tuolumne Garrote	71 174
Ah	Sacramento Cosumnes	63 392
Ah	Tuolumne Twp 4	71 174
An	Del Norte Crescent	58 631
So	San Francisco San Francisco 5	671207
Tiny	Calaveras Twp 10	57 295
Tom	Del Norte Crescent	58 659
YUNAHAH		
---*	Butte Chico	56 550

Name	County Locale	M653 Roll	Page
YUNCT			
---	Sacramento Granite	63	259
YUNE			
---	Calaveras Twp 6	57	170
---	Sierra Downieville	66	973
YUNG SARO			
---	San Francisco San Francisco 9	68	1099
YUNG			
---	Amador Twp 2	55	275
---	Amador Twp 2	55	323
---	Amador Twp 6	55	441
---	Butte Kimshaw	56	585
---	Butte Kimshaw	56	586
---	Calaveras Twp 6	57	136
---	Calaveras Twp 6	57	147
---	Calaveras Twp 6	57	165
---	Calaveras Twp 6	57	166
---	Calaveras Twp 6	57	176
---	Calaveras Twp 5	57	181
---	Calaveras Twp 5	57	222
---	Calaveras Twp 5	57	233
---	Calaveras Twp 5	57	244
---	Calaveras Twp 5	57	252
---	Calaveras Twp 5	57	256
---	Calaveras Twp 10	57	275
---	Calaveras Twp 10	57	284
---	Calaveras Twp 10	57	297
---	Calaveras Twp 4	57	305
---	Calaveras Twp 4	57	343
---	El Dorado Salmon Falls	58	1041
---	El Dorado Georgetown	58	692
---	Mendocino Big Rvr	60	851
---	Nevada Nevada	61	299
---	Nevada Bridgeport	61	439
---	Placer Secret R	62	624
---	Placer Virginia	62	665
---	Plumas Meadow Valley	62	913
---	Plumas Quincy	62	946
---	Sacramento Mississipi	63	188
---	Sacramento Granite	63	232
---	Sacramento Ward 3	63	491
---	Sacramento Ward 1	63	59
---	Sacramento Ward 1	63	60
---	Sacramento Ward 4	63	610
---	San Francisco San Francisco 4	68	1190
---	San Francisco San Francisco 4	68	1191
---	Shasta Horsetown	66	709
---	Stanislaus Emory	70	743
---	Tuolumne Jacksonville	71	168
---	Yuba Long Bar	72	756
---	Yuba Long Bar	72	758
---	Yuba Long Bar	72	766
---*	Butte Kimshaw	56	586
---*	Calaveras Twp 5	57	222
---*	Nevada Bridgeport	61	439
---*	Yuba Fosters	72	842
---*	Yuba Fosters	72	843
A	San Francisco San Francisco 5	67	513
Ah	Calaveras Twp 7	57	15
Ah	Sacramento Cosummes	63	394
Choy	Sacramento Ward 1	63	58
Chu	Sacramento Granite	63	259
Eh	El Dorado Greenwood	58	731
Foo	Plumas Quincy	62	948
Him	Plumas Quincy	62	1009
Ho	Sacramento Ward 3	63	492
Pung	Tuolumne Don Pedro	71	540
Saw	San Francisco San Francisco 9	68	1099
Sow	Calaveras Twp 10	57	295
Tan	Mariposa Twp 1	60	665
Tie	Nevada Bridgeport	61	458
YUNGER			
Wm	Monterey Alisal	60	1028
YUNI			
---	Calaveras Twp 5	57	170
YUNK			
---	San Francisco San Francisco 4	68	1189
---	Sierra Downieville	66	1024
---	Sierra Downieville	66	999
YUNKER			
John	Butte Wyandotte	56	659
YUNN			
Chan	San Francisco San Francisco 4	68	1181
G W	Butte Bidwell	56	712
YUNOWAWE			
---	Butte Chico	56	550
YUNT			
G W*	Yolo Slate Ra	72	706
G W*	Yuba Slate Ro	72	706
YUNY			
---	Calaveras Twp 6	57	122
---	Calaveras Twp 5	57	256
---	Calaveras Twp 10	57	283
---	Calaveras Twp 10	57	297
---	Yuba Long Bar	72	766
---*	Calaveras Twp 5	57	222

Name	County Locale	M653 Roll	Page
YUNY			
Sow	Calaveras Twp 10	57	295
YUNZ			
---	Sierra Downieville	66	1014
YUO			
---	Calaveras Twp 5	57	249
---	Calaveras Twp 5	57	251
---	Calaveras Twp 10	57	276
YUOK			
---	Calaveras Twp 4	57	320
YUONG			
---	Placer Virginia	62	681
---	Tuolumne Twp 5	71	517
YUP			
---	Amador Twp 5	55	365
---	Calaveras Twp 5	57	222
---	Nevada Grass Valley	61	229
---	Nevada Grass Valley	61	230
---	Nevada Grass Valley	61	231
---	Nevada Grass Valley	61	232
---	Nevada Grass Valley	61	233
---	Nevada Nevada	61	299
---	Nevada Nevada	61	301
---	Nevada Nevada	61	307
---	Nevada Nevada	61	308
---	Nevada Nevada	61	309
---	Nevada Nevada	61	310
---	Nevada Washington	61	339
---	Nevada Washington	61	340
---	Nevada Washington	61	341
---	Nevada Eureka	61	383
---	Nevada Eureka	61	384
---	Nevada Eureka	61	386
---	Placer Illinois	62	748
---	Sacramento Natonia	63	283
---	Stanislaus Emory	70	752
---*	Nevada Nevada	61	307
Chow	Nevada Eureka	61	386
Fon	Nevada Eureka	61	383
Lin	Sacramento Granite	63	269
Sam	Nevada Washington	61	339
Sam	Nevada Washington	61	340
Sam*	Nevada Washington	61	341
San	Sacramento Granite	63	268
San	Stanislaus Emory	70	744
See*	Placer Michigan	62	814
Ton	Nevada Eureka	61	383
Tot	Sacramento Granite	63	250
YUPE			
Sing	Nevada Nevada	61	310
YUPTIAL			
Wilson*	Mariposa Twp 1	60	638
YUR			
---	Mariposa Coulterville	60	692
---	Sacramento Granite	63	269
---	Sacramento Natonia	63	283
A	Sacramento Granite	63	269
YURAR			
Charlota	Sacramento Ward 1	63	17
YURBRO			
John	Tulara Twp 3	71	49
YURCKER			
John	Butte Wyandotte	56	659
YURDU			
Frank M	El Dorado Georgetown	58	699
YURK			
Henry	Colusa Muion	57	458
Thomas	Santa Cruz Pajaro	66	573
YURKIN			
C	El Dorado Kelsey	58	1139
YURMAIN			
Christain	San Francisco San Francisco 2	67	619
YURNMARINE			
---*	Butte Chico	56	551
YUROW			
---	Sierra Downieville	66	991
YURP			
Kim	El Dorado Greenwood	58	730
Sedim	El Dorado Greenwood	58	730
Sem	El Dorado Greenwood	58	730
YURPIN			
Dick	Tehama Lassen	70	878
Hamilton	Napa Yount	61	29
YURY			
---	Amador Twp 5	55	365
YUS			
---	Calaveras Twp 10	57	271
Piere	Yuba Fosters	72	840
YUSO			
---	Sierra Downieville	66	1005
YUT			
---	Calaveras Twp 5	57	215
---	Calaveras Twp 5	57	222
---	Calaveras Twp 10	57	271
---	Calaveras Twp 10	57	285
---	Mariposa Twp 1	60	668

Name	County Locale	M653 Roll	Page
YUT			
---	Mariposa Coulterville	60	680
---	Nevada Grass Valley	61	227
---	Nevada Grass Valley	61	228
---	Nevada Grass Valley	61	232
---	Nevada Nevada	61	301
---	Nevada Washington	61	341
---	Nevada Eureka	61	383
---	Placer Illinois	62	745
---	Sacramento Granite	63	231
---	Trinity Mouth Ca	70	1018
---*	Nevada Bridgeport	61	458
Chow	Nevada Eureka	61	383
J*	Nevada Bridgeport	61	458
Ko	San Francisco San Francisco 4	68	1194
Sam	Nevada Eureka	61	385
YUTT			
---	El Dorado Georgetown	58	692
---	Nevada Grass Valley	61	227
YUTTOO			
---	Tulara Twp 2	71	38
YUU			
---	Calaveras Twp 10	57	270
YUUAHAH			
---*	Butte Chico	56	550
YUW			
---	Calaveras Twp 5	57	256
---	Calaveras Twp 5	57	257
---	Calaveras Twp 10	57	259
---*	Calaveras Twp 5	57	251
YUWLS			
Phillippe*	Alameda Brooklyn	55	104
YVACHIM			
James W	Santa Cruz Pajaro	66	532
YVARRA			
Grabrial	Los Angeles Los Angeles	59	506
YVES			
Gullermo	San Francisco San Francisco 10	67	309
YWI			
---*	Mariposa Coulterville	60	692
YZARAGA			
Manuel	Monterey Monterey	60	935
YZASAGA			
Manuel*	Merced Monterey	60	935
Z			
---	Siskiyou Scott Ri	69	74
Z???G			
A*	Amador Twp 1	55	467
ZA			
---	Nevada Nevada	61	301
ZABALA			
Pedro	Merced Monterey	60	942
Pedro	Monterey Monterey	60	942
ZABIR			
A G*	Yolo Putah	72	549
ZABISCA			
Bolivar	Santa Cruz Pajaro	66	564
ZABRIKI			
John*	San Francisco San Francisco 3	67	27
ZABRISCA			
Bolivar	Santa Cruz Pajaro	66	564
ZABRISHIE			
Bolivar	Santa Cruz Pajaro	66	557
ZABRISKA			
C W	El Dorado Diamond	58	793
ZABRISKIE			
Bolivar	Santa Cruz Pajaro	66	557
E B	Yuba Long Bar	72	748
J C	Sacramento Ward 4	63	601
ZABROSKY			
T	San Francisco San Francisco 3	67	71
ZACH			
---	Yuba Fosters	72	843
Baptiste	Mendocino Anderson	60	866
John	Siskiyou Yreka	69	173
ZACHARIAS			
---	Santa Clara Fremont	65	423
ZACHARRIAH			
B*	Tuolumne Twp 2	71	344
ZACHEER			
Wm	Sacramento Granite	63	243
ZACHORIAS			
J H	Yuba Marysville	72	972
ZACK			
---	El Dorado Salmon Hills	58	1067
---	Mariposa Coulterville	60	688
ZACKA			
Maguil*	Napa Napa	61	84
ZACKANAZ			
Granvill*	Plumas Quincy	62	959
ZACKORIAS			
J H	Yuba Marysville	72	972
ZADDLE			
John	Shasta Shasta	66	681
Joseph	Shasta Shasta	66	681

California 1860 Census Index

Name	County Locale	M653 Roll	Page
ZADELLA			
John*	Shasta Shasta	66	681
ZADELLS			
John*	Shasta Shasta	66	681
ZAFF			
Harriet A*	Nevada Red Dog	61	538
ZAGE			
Carl	Butte Kimshaw	56	572
John	Trinity Steiner	70	999
ZAGER			
A	El Dorado Diamond	58	804
C	El Dorado Diamond	58	798
Guillermo	Santa Clara Almaden	65	273
Henry*	El Dorado Salmon Falls	58	1044
ZAGUE			
Juan*	San Bernardino San Salvador	64	641
ZAH TUNG			
---	Santa Clara San Jose	65	374
ZAHANIKAW			
Frank	Santa Clara San Jose	65	338
ZAHN			
Adam	San Francisco San Francisco 3	67	12
Henry	San Francisco San Francisco 2	67	606
ZAHREL			
Edward	Tuolumne Twp 2	71	284
ZAIS			
Gobbi	Sierra Downieville	66	1006
ZAIYNER			
Mossie*	San Francisco San Francisco 8	681	236
Mossu*	San Francisco San Francisco 8	681	236
ZALASUR			
Wicanor	Santa Clara San Jose	65	297
ZALLAMA			
A F	Calaveras Twp 8	57	72
ZALLAND			
John	Placer Illinois	62	703
ZAMATT			
Lafayette	Yuba Marysville	72	977
ZAMETI			
Angelo	Santa Cruz Watsonville	66	538
ZAMEY			
Theodore*	Plumas Quincy	62	971
ZAMIDAS			
Julian	Butte Kimshaw	56	573
ZAMNORDE			
Chas*	Butte Kimshaw	56	572
ZAMORA			
Luis	Santa Clara Gilroy	65	224
ZAMPATO			
---	Fresno Twp 2	59	68
ZAMY			
W*	Nevada Grass Valley	61	171
ZAN TIPO			
---	Fresno Twp 2	59	66
ZANANY			
O	San Mateo Twp 1	65	48
ZANDERS			
T P	San Joaquin Stockton	641	100
ZANDT			
J W Van	San Francisco San Francisco 3	67	61
ZANE			
Charles O*	Sierra Pine Grove	66	821
Samuel M	Calaveras Twp 7	57	16
Simeon	Humbolt Eel Rvr	59	152
Vincent*	San Francisco San Francisco 1	68	912
ZANER			
Anthony	San Francisco San Francisco 2	67	795
ZANES			
Jno	Butte Kimshaw	56	577
Mo	Butte Kimshaw	56	577
ZANETI			
Angelo	Santa Cruz Watsonville	66	538
ZANEZ			
Nolasco	Santa Clara Almaden	65	276
ZANG			
---	Mariposa Coulterville	60	694
Peter*	Plumas Quincy	621	007
ZANGE			
F	San Francisco San Francisco 2	67	795
ZANGER			
A	Butte Hamilton	56	517
ZANIN			
Louis	Sacramento Ward 1	63	15
ZANIX			
Pierre*	San Francisco San Francisco 11	133	67
ZANN			
George*	Tuolumne Twp 3	71	465
ZANNY			
Geo W	Santa Clara Fremont	65	418
W*	Nevada Grass Valley	61	171
ZANO			
Vincent	San Francisco San Francisco 1	68	912
ZANON			
---	Mendocino Calpella	60	825
ZANONI			
John	Plumas Meadow Valley	62	907

Name	County Locale	M653 Roll	Page
ZANSATH			
Lafayette	Yuba Marysville	72	977
ZANTMYRE			
J J*	Placer Auburn	62	564
ZANTS			
Eloric*	El Dorado Salmon Falls	581	035
Elorie	El Dorado Salmon Falls	581	035
ZANTYUFT			
Jacob	El Dorado White Oaks	581	030
ZAOARS			
Antonio*	Yuba Marysville	72	926
ZAPOSA			
Manuel	Contra Costa Twp 1	57	520
ZARA			
L	El Dorado Diamond	58	802
ZARAGO			
Frank	Tuolumne Twp 3	71	435
ZARALE			
Philipe	Sierra Downieville	66	970
ZARATE			
Philipe	Sierra Downieville	66	970
ZARBRO			
David C	Sonoma Mendocino	69	458
ZARDINER			
Edwin L*	Placer Secret R	62	611
ZARDON			
Louis	San Francisco San Francisco 3	67	80
ZARE			
Antonio	Contra Costa Twp 1	57	529
ZAREG			
Herman	San Francisco San Francisco 10	311 67	
ZARGUES			
Anton	Tuolumne Columbia	71	320
ZARKOSKY			
Nathan	Sierra La Porte	66	776
ZARNO			
Nicholas	Tuolumne Twp 1	71	269
ZARNS			
Nicholas	Tuolumne Twp 1	71	269
ZARO			
Martio	Tuolumne Twp 2	71	282
ZARRY			
Joseph	Mariposa Twp 3	60	570
ZARTMAN			
Wm	Sonoma Petaluma	69	595
ZARYNER			
Mossu*	San Francisco San Francisco 8	681	236
ZATES			
Chapman	Santa Clara San Jose	65	285
ZATITZ			
T	El Dorado White Oaks	581	029
ZAUFFIEGNOW			
Julius*	Santa Clara Fremont	65	428
ZAUG			
Peter*	Plumas Quincy	621	007
ZAUGH			
Ar	Trinity Mouth Ca	701	014
ZAUIX			
Pierre*	San Francisco San Francisco 11	133 67	
ZAVARO			
Antonio	Yuba Marysville	72	926
ZAVARS			
Antonio	Yuba Marysville	72	926
ZAVUT			
---*	Tulara Twp 1	71	119
ZAY			
---*	Mariposa Twp 3	60	552
ZAYER			
Jule	San Francisco San Francisco 4	681	155
ZAYNE			
John M	Plumas Quincy	62	968
ZCHMIDT			
Jno M*	Sacramento Ward 1	63	147
ZCHRDLICH			
Jno	Klamath Trinidad	59	220
ZE			
---	Yuba Slate Ro	72	684
ZEAGER			
N	Tehama Lassen	70	877
ZEAR			
F	Sutter Vernon	70	847
S	Trinity New Rvr	701	030
ZEARING			
David	Plumas Quincy	62	939
ZEBA			
Montimano	Calaveras Twp 7	57	31
ZEBAR			
Francis	Yuba New York	72	734
ZEBIANANSKI			
Wadslons	Sonoma Petaluma	69	578
ZEBORD			
Theo*	Alameda Brooklyn	55	155
ZEBRER			
David	Alameda Oakland	55	43

Name	County Locale	M653 Roll	Page
ZECHARIAH			
B	Tuolumne Columbia	71	344
R*	Tuolumne Twp 2	71	344
ZECK			
Joseph	Solano Vacaville	69	334
ZEDAKER			
Geo	Trinity Trinity	70	975
ZEDEIGER			
John	San Joaquin Stockton	641	032
ZEDIA			
Joseph	Sierra Downieville	661	013
ZEE HON			
---	Nevada Nevada	61	301
ZEE YUP			
---	Nevada Nevada	61	301
ZEE			
---	Amador Twp 2	55	310
---	Placer Virginia	62	701
---	San Francisco San Francisco 5	67	510
---	Tuolumne Twp 3	71	460
---	Yolo No E Twp	72	684
---	Yolo Slate Ra	72	712
---	Yuba Slate Ro	72	712
---	Yuba Marysville	72	925
Sin	Butte Cascade	56	700
ZEELE			
Frederick	San Francisco San Francisco 3	67	3
ZEEYENFUIS			
Geo*	Alameda Brooklyn	55	210
ZEFICRD			
S*	Siskiyou Scott Ri	69	77
ZEFIERD			
S*	Siskiyou Scott Ri	69	77
ZEH			
Geo C	Sacramento American	63	158
Godfrey	Sacramento Centre	63	173
John	El Dorado Georgetown	58	688
John*	San Joaquin Stockton	641	035
ZEHARA			
Jose	Santa Clara San Jose	65	330
ZEHENDULE			
George	Humbolt Union	59	191
ZEHR			
T	San Francisco San Francisco 1	68	832
ZEIDE			
Andrew	Siskiyou Yreka	69	152
ZEIGANSPECK			
Chris*	Del Norte Crescent	58	659
ZEIGANSPEEK			
Chris*	Del Norte Crescent	58	659
ZEIGLE			
Andrew*	Siskiyou Yreka	69	152
ZEIGLEMAN			
Ferdk	San Francisco San Francisco 3	67	71
Fredk	San Francisco San Francisco 3	67	71
ZEIGLER			
Amargio	San Francisco San Francisco 8	681	294
J	Trinity S Fork	701	032
Lewis	Calaveras Twp 4	57	329
ZEIGSELBER			
Charles P*	San Joaquin Stockton	641	015
ZEIGTER			
John	Santa Clara San Jose	65	392
ZEIKART			
Frederick*	Tuolumne Twp 2	71	281
ZEIKIEL			
---	Tulara Keyesville	71	68
---	Tulara Keyesville	71	71
ZEILE			
C R	San Francisco San Francisco 1	68	811
John*	San Francisco San Francisco 1	68	811
ZEILKEN			
Peter	Tuolumne Big Oak	71	125
Peter	Tuolumne Twp 4	71	127
ZEILKS			
Walter	Sonoma Petaluma	69	573
ZEINKER			
Lena	San Francisco San Francisco 8	681	288
ZEIR			
Mary	Sacramento Ward 1	63	131
ZEITSKA			
Antometto*	Sacramento Ward 1	63	23
Antonietto*	Sacramento Ward 1	63	23
Clotilda	Sacramento Ward 1	63	23
ZEKIN			
H M	Napa Clear Lake	61	125
ZELB			
Robt L*	Sacramento Ward 1	63	32
ZELCONS			
Batetisma	Tuolumne Columbia	71	302
ZELFE			
Delius	Sonoma Armally	69	479
Julius	Sonoma Armally	69	479
ZELGER			
A	El Dorado Diamond	58	798
ZELIAN			
Charles	Tuolumne Jamestown	71	448

Name	County Locale	M653 Roll Page
ZELICKSON		
H	San Francisco San Francisco 1	68 927
ZELK		
L	El Dorado Diamond	58 804
ZELL		
Robt L*	Sacramento Ward 1	63 32
Robt S	Sacramento Ward 1	63 32
ZELLA		
Frederick	Los Angeles Azuza	59 272
ZELLER		
Frank	Trinity Indian C	70 988
John	Tuolumne Twp 2	71 390
Michael	Santa Clara San Jose	65 287
ZELLING		
Julius C	San Francisco San Francisco 7	681354
ZELLOX		
Francois	San Francisco San Francisco 2	67 781
ZELNER		
Peter	San Francisco San Francisco 11	136 67
ZELORD		
Theo*	Alameda Brooklyn	55 155
ZELSA		
Auger	Mariposa Twp 1	60 666
ZELVEEGER		
John	Siskiyou Klamath	69 93
ZELVEEGOR		
John	Siskiyou Klamath	69 93
ZEM		
---	Placer Virginia	62 679
Wah	Sacramento Ward 1	63 50
ZEMAN		
Wm	San Francisco San Francisco 1	68 870
ZEMASTIES		
William	Monterey San Juan	60 989
ZEMASTRES		
William	Monterey San Juan	60 989
ZEMBER		
Chas	Sacramento Ward 3	63 457
ZEMERSHED		
Chas	Butte Chico	56 556
ZEMMITT		
A	San Francisco San Francisco 2	67 760
H	San Francisco San Francisco 2	67 760
ZEN		
---	Nevada Nevada	61 303
ZENABACK		
H*	San Francisco San Francisco 1	68 927
ZENCER		
Jacob*	San Francisco San Francisco 2	67 670
ZENCOS		
Jacob*	San Francisco San Francisco 2	67 670
ZENIKER		
Lena	San Francisco San Francisco 8	681288
ZENN		
---	Placer Dutch Fl	62 721
ZENOBITCH		
P*	Sacramento Ward 1	63 84
ZENOLRTCH		
P*	Sacramento Ward 1	63 84
ZENOTITCH		
P*	Sacramento Ward 1	63 84
ZENOTRTCH		
P*	Sacramento Ward 1	63 84
ZENOVICH		
M	Sacramento Ward 1	63 18
ZENOVICK		
M*	Sacramento Ward 1	63 18
ZENR WAH		
---	Sacramento Ward 1	63 50
ZENT		
Isaac	Sierra Gibsonville	66 851
Sampson	Yuba Parks Ba	72 781
ZEORISLE		
G*	San Francisco San Francisco 5	67 505
ZEORY		
A T	Yuba Long Bar	72 752
ZEOX		
John	Yuba Long Bar	72 755
ZEPA		
Felix	San Joaquin Stockton	641077
ZEPF		
Henry Ser	San Francisco San Francisco 10	317 67
ZEPHRIN		
Frazier	Sierra Poker Flats	66 839
ZEPHYR		
Lewis	San Francisco San Francisco 9	681097
ZEPP		
M*	Siskiyou Scott Ri	69 71
ZER		
John	Placer Dutch Fl	62 710
ZERAEYS		
John	Siskiyou Scott Ri	69 71
ZERASYS		
John	Siskiyou Scott Ri	69 71

Name	County Locale	M653 Roll Page
ZERE		
Lem	San Francisco San Francisco 2	67 795
ZERICK		
Geo*	Placer Virginia	62 683
Gus*	Placer Virginia	62 683
ZERNICE		
Peter	Tuolumne Jamestown	71 454
ZERNICO		
Peter	Tuolumne Twp 3	71 454
ZESHYR		
Lewis	San Francisco San Francisco 9	681097
ZESS		
Charles	Calaveras Twp 7	57 18
ZET		
Lang*	Yuba Bear Rvr	721000
ZETHERHOLM		
Olof	Plumas Quincy	62 955
ZEUABACK		
H*	San Francisco San Francisco 1	68 927
ZEVENGE		
Joseph*	Calaveras Twp 6	57 172
ZEYLER		
Wm	Sacramento Ward 1	63 27
ZEYON		
John P	Los Angeles Santa Ana	59 440
ZHE		
Frederick	San Francisco San Francisco 8	681270
ZI		
Fung	Placer Iona Hills	62 896
ZIBBLE		
John	Siskiyou Scott Ri	69 68
ZIBEL		
George	Los Angeles Tejon	59 525
ZIBIL		
George	Los Angeles Tejon	59 525
ZICGER		
Eliza*	Sacramento Ward 1	63 76
ZICKBERT		
B H	San Francisco San Francisco 1	68 927
ZIE		
---	Sacramento Ward 1	63 56
ZIEGENHART		
Louis	San Francisco San Francisco 2	67 627
ZIEGER		
Eliza	Sacramento Ward 1	63 76
ZIEGLE		
J A	Siskiyou Scott Va	69 47
ZIEGLER		
Teoder*	San Francisco San Francisco 1	68 825
ZIEGMOND		
C H	San Francisco San Francisco 3	67 85
ZIEL		
Gustave	San Francisco San Francisco 8	681278
ZIELE		
John*	San Francisco San Francisco 1	68 811
ZIER		
Mary	Sacramento Ward 4	63 589
Wm	Sacramento Ward 4	63 521
ZIGLER		
Chalrs	Mendocino Calpella	60 814
D	El Dorado Diamond	58 807
F	El Dorado Placerville	58 820
Frank	El Dorado Greenwood	58 722
G	El Dorado Diamond	58 803
J B	El Dorado Placerville	58 820
ZIGLEY		
Z	Tuolumne Twp 2	71 333
ZIHLER		
Charles	Mendocino Calpella	60 814
ZILBERTSON		
Alice	Placer Dutch Fl	62 723
ZILE		
John	San Francisco San Francisco 1	68 811
ZILHAM		
Joseph*	El Dorado Georgetown	58 674
ZILHART		
W H S	Sonoma Armally	69 493
ZILL		
A	Tehama Tehama	70 942
Bozil	Tuolumne Big Oak	71 145
ZIM		
William	Los Angeles Los Angeles	59 302
ZIMALT		
D	Yolo Cache	72 606
ZIMERMAN		
Bernard	Santa Cruz Pajaro	66 531
Rachel	Humbolt Mattole	59 121
ZIMMER		
Geo	Napa Napa	61 101
John	Amador Twp 4	55 235
ZIMMERE		
F*	San Francisco San Francisco 7	681425
ZIMMERL		
F	San Francisco San Francisco 7	681425
ZIMMERMAN		
C	Sacramento Ward 3	63 433

Name	County Locale	M653 Roll Page
ZIMMERMAN		
C A	Sacramento Ward 3	63 429
Charles F	Yuba Marysville	72 881
Chas	Sonoma Petaluma	69 560
Christ	Sacramento Ward 4	63 507
Conrad	Alameda Oakland	55 39
F	El Dorado White Oaks	581013
F	San Francisco San Francisco 3	67 72
George	Marin Tomales	60 725
Godlipp	Calaveras Twp 6	57 113
Henry	Tuolumne Sonora	71 199
J	Sutter Sutter	70 810
J P	San Francisco San Francisco 12	381 67
Jaseph*	Sierra Cold Can	66 836
John	Alameda Murray	55 222
Jos	Sacramento Ward 3	63 423
Joseph	Sierra Cold Can	66 836
Martin	Calaveras Twp 5	57 190
Nicholas	Calaveras Twp 4	57 303
Nicholos	Calaveras Twp 4	57 303
Simon	San Francisco San Francisco 2	67 793
W C	Butte Hamilton	56 525
Wm	Sonoma Petaluma	69 556
ZIMMERSHED		
C	Tehama Lassen	70 877
ZIMMERSON		
John*	Tuolumne Twp 1	71 480
ZIMWALL		
J L	Tehama Antelope	70 888
ZIN		
---	El Dorado Diamond	58 805
---	Mariposa Twp 1	60 662
---	Sierra Twp 5	66 948
---	Sonoma Sonoma	69 640
---*	Mariposa Twp 1	60 662
A	Sonoma Sonoma	69 640
ZINBER		
E E*	Mendocino Calpella	60 820
ZINCER		
Jacob*	San Francisco San Francisco 2	67 670
ZINCOS		
Jacob*	San Francisco San Francisco 2	67 670
ZINDA		
A T*	Yuba Rose Bar	72 791
ZING		
---	El Dorado Georgetown	58 690
---	San Francisco San Francisco 5	67 508
Chu	Placer Illinois	62 740
ZINK		
J	Sutter Nicolaus	70 831
Zacheriah	Sierra Port Win	66 791
ZINKER		
E E*	Mendocino Calpella	60 820
ZINKUGG		
William	Santa Cruz Santa Cruz	66 630
ZINN		
Henry	San Francisco San Francisco 5	67 475
John*	El Dorado Casumnes	581168
ZINNALT		
F F*	Butte Chico	56 536
N	Butte Chico	56 533
ZIO		
Baldas	San Mateo Twp 2	65 113
Santhos A	San Mateo Twp 2	65 113
ZIOVVENNI		
P	El Dorado Georgetown	58 701
ZIRGENBEIN		
John	Placer Goods	62 696
ZIVINGE		
Joseph*	Calaveras Twp 6	57 172
ZIVRKNN		
Thomas	San Francisco San Francisco 3	67 80
ZOACHIM		
Archibald	Tulara Visalia	71 103
ZOCCO		
John	Mariposa Coulterville	60 685
ZODIA		
Joseph	Sierra Downieville	661013
ZOEL		
William	Siskiyou Yreka	69 143
ZOERWOID		
Alexander	Los Angeles Santa Ana	59 443
ZOERWORD		
Alexander	Los Angeles Santa Ana	59 443
ZOGBAUM		
George	Contra Costa Twp 3	57 612
ZOLER		
Charles	San Francisco San Francisco 2	67 674
ZOLLERS		
Fred	El Dorado Mountain	581184
ZOLMAN		
Vassay	Sierra Pine Grove	66 823
ZOMERARM		
Curi	San Luis Obispo San Luis Obispo 65	26
ZONCHMEG		
---	Trinity Weaverville	701072

California 1860 Census Index

Name	County Locale	M653 Roll	Page
ZONE			
Edward	Sacramento Ward 4	63	547
ZONEN			
Masp*	San Francisco San Francisco 1	68	815
Max	San Francisco San Francisco 1	68	815
ZONG			
---	Mariposa Twp 3	60	587
---*	Mariposa Twp 1	60	655
Chin	Butte Bidwell	56	714
Chong*	Mariposa Twp 1	60	626
ZONKER			
Andrew*	San Mateo Twp 2	65	123
ZONLART			
Cassimere	Yolo Slate Ra	72	686
ZONNG			
C P	Yolo Merritt	72	577
ZONON			
---	Tulara Visalia	71	117
ZONSINS			
George*	Yuba Parks Ba	72	782
ZONSIUS			
George*	Yuba Parke Ba	72	782
ZONSON			
J*	Mariposa Twp 3	60	622
ZOO			
---	Amador Twp 2	55	311
---	Placer Virginia	62	679
ZOOANG			
Ah	Tehama Tehama	70	950
ZOODING			
Henry*	Placer Auburn	62	560
ZOOK			
Isaac	Shasta Horsetown	66	699
Jacob	Stanislaus Emory	70	746
Lisaac	Shasta Horsetown	66	699
M	Trinity Eastman	70	960
Saml	Trinity Minersville	70	969
ZOOVER			
J M	Marin Tomales	60	722
ZOPAINA			
---	Mendocino Calpella	60	824
ZOPHES			
Fedrick*	Napa Hot Springs	61	25
ZOPHY			
Fedrick*	Napa Hot Springs	61	25
ZORBA			
Ramond*	San Bernadino San Bernardino	64	639
Ramondo*	San Salvador San Bernardino	64	639
ZORING			
A*	Amador Twp 1	55	467
ZORN			
H	Shasta Shasta	66	662
ZORNINIA			
Joseph	Calaveras Twp 7	57	8
Peter	Calaveras Twp 7	57	8
ZORRG			
C P*	Yolo Merritt	72	577
ZOTO			
Andreas	Santa Cruz Santa Cruz	66	617
Jose M*	Santa Cruz Santa Cruz	66	617
ZOTT			
Peter	San Francisco San Francisco 2	67	699
ZOUNT			
David*	Napa Napa	61	83
Geo C*	Napa Napa	61	83
ZOURIGER			
Andrew	Santa Clara San Jose	65	281
ZOW			
Young*	Mariposa Twp 1	60	627
ZOY			
---	Nevada Nevada	61	302
ZRDNE			
John P	San Francisco San Francisco 7	68	1434
ZRISN			
---*	El Dorado Greenwood	58	732
ZRUMA			
D	Siskiyou Scott Va	69	50
ZSCHIESCHE			
Christian	San Francisco San Francisco 2	67	708
ZSIHUSCHE			
Christian	San Francisco San Francisco 2	67	708
ZSUMA			
D	Siskiyou Scott Va	69	50
ZTURA			
Esteban*	Santa Clara Fremont	65	442
ZU			
---	Yuba Marysville	72	925
ZUAGER			
Augustus	Plumas Meadow Valley	62	900
ZUAN			
Sabastian	Calaveras Twp 9	57	350
ZUANICK			
Peter	Tuolumne Twp 3	71	454
ZUARLES			
William*	San Francisco San Francisco 8	68	1248

Name	County Locale	M653 Roll	Page
ZUBER			
E E	Mendocino Calpella	60	820
William*	Calaveras Twp 6	57	153
ZUBIATE			
Luz	Santa Clara San Jose	65	368
ZUC			
---*	Stanislaus Branch	70	713
ZUCEN			
A*	Stanislaus Buena Village	70	721
ZUCK			
David	Santa Clara Gilroy	65	226
ZUCKER			
Thomas*	San Francisco San Francisco 3	67	80
ZUCKERMAN			
Jacob	Tuolumne Sonora	71	205
ZUDARVE			
---	Mendocino Calpella	60	823
ZUDARVO			
---	Mendocino Calpella	60	823
ZUE			
---*	Stanislaus Branch	70	713
ZUERILLACQU			
John	San Francisco San Francisco 7	68	1332
ZUEYBRUCK			
C F	San Francisco San Francisco 10	67	241
ZUG			
---	El Dorado Salmon Hills	58	1059
ZUGERFUSS			
T H	El Dorado Diamond	58	809
ZUGLE			
J G	Siskiyou Cottonwood	69	102
ZUGLER			
J	Trinity S Fork	70	1032
Teoder*	San Francisco San Francisco 1	68	825
ZUI			
---	Stanislaus Branch	70	715
ZUILSAE			
James*	El Dorado Georgetown	58	745
ZUIMTY			
C W	Trinity New Rvr	70	1031
ZUINLAND			
M	Trinity Taylor'S	70	1036
ZUINOGUE			
J*	Nevada Eureka	61	357
ZUK			
---	Shasta French G	66	712
ZUKIEL			
---	Tulara Twp 3	71	68
ZULE			
Frederick*	San Francisco San Francisco 3	67	3
ZULFER			
J	El Dorado Diamond	58	804
ZULI			
Frederick*	San Francisco San Francisco 3	67	3
ZULLIAN			
M R C	Butte Oregon	56	624
ZULO			
---	Mendocino Calpella	60	824
ZULUF			
John	Amador Twp 6	55	425
ZUMALH			
N*	Butte Chico	56	533
ZUMALK			
Peter	Butte Ophir	56	800
ZUMALT			
D	Yolo Cache Crk	72	606
J	El Dorado Placerville	58	848
J O	Yolo Putah	72	550
Joseph	Sacramento American	63	163
Marion	Butte Chico	56	536
N*	Butte Chico	56	533
T F*	Butte Chico	56	536
ZUMAWATT			
Wm	Butte Ophir	56	750
ZUMBERLICH			
N	Butte Ophir	56	789
ZUMBRO			
Isaac M	Los Angeles Los Angeles	59	357
ZUMDALL			
F	Shasta Shasta	66	658
ZUMFORDE			
John	Tuolumne Twp 2	71	369
ZUMNORDE			
Chas	Butte Kimshaw	56	572
ZUMOLT			
I O*	Yolo Putah	72	550
James	Solano Vacaville	69	361
Joseph	Solano Vacaville	69	364
Wilby	Solano Vacaville	69	364
ZUNA			
---	Sierra Downieville	66	979
ZUNEGA			
Agapito	Los Angeles San Pedro	59	486

Name	County Locale	M653 Roll	Page
ZUNEGA			
Munzeal	Sierra Gibsonville	66	856
ZUNEGER			
Munzeal*	Sierra Gibsonville	66	856
ZUNNALH			
N*	Butte Chico	56	533
ZUNRAWATT			
Wm*	Butte Ophir	56	750
ZUPTILL			
F W*	Mariposa Twp 1	60	635
ZURIELA			
---	Napa Clear Lake	61	118
ZURNBERLICH			
N*	Butte Ophir	56	789
ZURNBRO			
Isaac M	Los Angeles Los Angeles	59	357
ZUT			
---	Sacramento Ward 1	63	52
ZUY			
---	Stanislaus Branch	70	715
ZWEKER			
Thomas*	San Francisco San Francisco 3	67	80
ZWEYBRUCK			
C F	San Francisco San Francisco 10	67	241
ZWICKER			
Henry*	Sacramento Ward 1	63	33
John*	Sacramento Ward 1	63	33
ZWIEFEL			
Fred	Siskiyou Yreka	69	189
ZWIGG			
Herman	San Francisco San Francisco 10	67	311
ZWIKART			
Frederick	Tuolumne Twp 2	71	281
ZYCHOKE			
J	Sacramento Ward 1	63	13
ZYWICKER			
John*	Sacramento Ward 1	63	33
ZZENT			
Isaac	Sierra Gibsonville	66	851
ZZOPIN			
Antonio	San Mateo Twp 1	65	63